BARRON'S

PROFILES OF AMERICAN Colleges

34TH EDITION 2018

Compiled and Edited by
the College Division of
Barron's Educational Series

Opinions and details expressed in articles and profiles in this publication are those of the individual writers and the schools, and do not necessarily reflect those of the publisher.

All inquiries should be addressed to:
Barron's Educational Series, Inc.
250 Wireless Boulevard
Hauppauge, New York 11788
www.barronseduc.com

ISBN: 978-1-4380-1018-2

International Standard Serial No. 1065-5026

10%
POST-CONSUMER WASTE
Paper contains a minimum of 10% post-consumer waste (PCW). Paper used in this book was derived from certified, sustainable forestlands.

PRINTED IN THE UNITED STATES OF AMERICA
9 8 7 6 5 4 3 2 1

CONTENTS

PREFACE

Barron's *Profiles of American Colleges* is the most all-encompassing, easy-to-use guide available. All four-year institutions that offer bachelor's degrees are described if they are fully accredited or are recognized candidates for accreditation. The comprehensive, concise capsule and detailed essay on each school give an easy-to-absorb, complete picture of the colleges that interest the reader. The attractive graphic design provides added readability.

The capsule of each profile lists important information for quick reference: address and phone and fax numbers; enrollment; calendar; fall application deadline; size and salary level of the faculty; percentage of faculty members who hold doctorates; student/faculty ratio; tuition and fees; room-and-board costs; the number of students who applied to the freshman class, were accepted, and enrolled; the median SAT* and/or ACT scores; CEEB Code; and finally, the College Admissions Selector Rating for the school. The information in the essay portion of each profile ranges from available housing and the financial aid climate to admissions requirements and the success of graduates. There are twenty-one categories of information under eight main headings: Student Life, Faculty/Classrooms, Programs of Study, Activities, Services, Requirements, Admissions, and Financial Aid. The Admissions section also gives contact information and Internet addresses.

As a purchaser of the 34th edition of *Profiles of American Colleges*, you are eligible for a free six-month subscription to our *Profiles of American Colleges* on-line edition. The web site will simplify your college search and ease your college application process. To access, go to BarronsPAC.com and register today!

A Word of Thanks

To all the admissions officers, institutional research staff at the colleges, to participating high school advisers, to the students, parents, and other supporters of *Barron's Profiles of American Colleges*, over the last thirty-three editions, we offer our sincere thanks and appreciation.

Our appreciation to the editorial staff, including Bruce Morris, Lena Perfetto, and April Martinez; production department, including production director Chris Ciaschini, art director Bill Kuchler, designer Tara O'Hare, and graphic artist Lou Vasquez. Thanks and appreciation to Greg Hammond of Reliable Internet Solutions for database management and technical support.

CONTRIBUTORS

Steven R. Antonoff, Ph.D.
Educational Consultant
Antonoff Associates, Inc.
Denver, Colorado

Barbara J. Aronson
Career Center Coordinator
Miramonte High School
Orinda, California

Marguerite J. Dennis
Former Vice President for Enrollment and International Programs
Suffolk University
Boston, Massachusetts

Benjamin W. Griffith
Former Dean
University of West Georgia
Carrolton, Georgia

Sheldon Halpern
Former Dean
Enrollment Management
Caldwell College
Caldwell, New Jersey

Anthony F. Capraro, III, Ph.D.
President, Teach Inc.
College Counseling
Ocoee, Florida

James Wagner
Center for Academic Support and Advisement Center
Associate Professor of Education
Liberty University

*SAT is a registered trademark owned by the College Entrance Examination Board. No endorsement of this product is implied or given.

AN EXPLANATION OF THE BOOK

You have been thinking about going to college within the coming years, and have decided that it's time to get serious and take the necessary steps that will lead to your ultimate college decisions, right?

But how do you take these steps? How much will your college education cost? How can you and your parents afford it? What about the entrance exams? What kinds of scores are you going to need to be considered? How do you decide what to major in? Which colleges offer the skills and career preparation that you're going to need? Even if you get past these hurdles, what if you decide which colleges you want to attend, apply to them, and then get turned down? Is there anything you can do to prevent that from happening?

So where do you begin? In addition to hundreds of two-year schools, there are more than 1,650 accredited four-year colleges in the United States, and your options are almost unlimited. Barron's Profiles of American Colleges can help by pointing you in the right direction, and guiding you through the coming months of preparation and decision making.

Within the pages of this directory, you will find articles that will assist you in evaluating your own needs and interests, selecting the colleges you want to apply to, filling out the application, writing the essay, going through the interview process, finding the money, and surviving your freshman year.

The Index of College Majors lists which colleges offer the field that you're interested in. The section also offers advice on deciding your major, career opportunities and the skills you are going to need for the occupation you choose. More than 700 majors are listed, along with the in-state costs and the Admissions Selector Rating in easy-to-read columns.

Advice for international students is included, as well as a list of schools' in-state costs from least to most expensive. The Colleges at a Glance geographic chart provides students quick information about the schools on a state-by-state basis.

The College Admissions Selector Ratings give applicants an idea of the competition they will encounter when applying to a particular school. For your convenience, a key to abbreviations is also included, as well as an explanation of the actual college entries.

The heart of the book, of course, is the detailed descriptions of the colleges, including a special section of religious schools, for those students wishing to pursue a career in the clergy and related fields. The college Profiles are arranged in alphabetical order by state. Each chapter opens with a map that pinpoints the geographic location of the colleges mentioned. Barron's *Profiles of American Colleges* covers the United States, and describes colleges in Puerto Rico, and universities in Canada and abroad (along with advice for international students), for a total of approximately 1650 Profile entries.

This updated and revised edition of *Profiles of American Colleges* will prove to be a valuable resource as you embark on a tremendous learning and growth time of your life—your college education.

KEY TO ABBREVIATIONS

DEGREES

A.A.—Associate of Arts
A.A.S.—Associate of Applied Science
A.B. or **B.A.**—Bachelor of Arts
A.B.J.—Bachelor of Arts in Journalism
A.S.—Associate of Science

B.A.—Bachelor of Arts
B.A.A.—Bachelor of Applied Arts
B.A.A.S. or **B.Applied A.S.**—Bachelor of Applied Arts and Sciences
B.Ac. or **B.Acc.**—Bachelor of Accountancy
B.A.C.—Bachelor of Science in Air Commerce
B.A.C.V.I.—Bachelor of Arts in Computer and Video Imaging
B.A.E. or **B.A.Ed.**—Bachelor of Arts in Education
B.A.G.E.—Bachelor of Arts in General Education
B.Agri.—Bachelor of Agriculture
B.A.G.S.—Bachelor of Arts in General Studies
B.A.J.S.—Bachelor of Arts in Judaic Studies
B.A.M.—Bachelor of Arts in Music
B.Applied Sc.—Bachelor of Applied Science
B.A.R.—Bachelor of Religion
B.Arch.—Bachelor of Architecture
B.Arch.Hist.—Bachelor of Architectural History
B.Arch.Tech.—Bachelor of Architectural Technology
B.Ar.Sc.—Baccalaurium Artium et Scientiae (honors college degree) (Bachelor of Arts & Sciences)
B.Art.Ed.—Bachelor of Art Education
B.A.S.—Bachelor of Applied Science
B.A.S.—Bachelor of Arts and Sciences
B.A.Sec.Ed.—Bachelor of Arts in Secondary Ed.
B.A.S.W.—Bachelor of Arts in Social Work
B.A.T.—Bachelor of Arts in Teaching
B.B. or **B.Bus.**—Bachelor of Business
B.B.A.—Bachelor of Business Administration
B.B.E.—Bachelor of Business Education
B.C. or **B.Com.** or **B.Comm.**—Bachelor of Commerce
B.C.A.—Bachelor of Creative Arts
B.C.E.—Bachelor of Civil Engineering
B.C.E.—Bachelor of Computer Engineering
B.Ch. or **B.Chem.**—Bachelor of Chemistry
B.Ch.E.—Bachelor of Chemical Engineering
B.C.J.—Bachelor of Criminal Justice
B.C.M.—Bachelor of Christian Ministries
B.Church Mus.—Bachelor of Church Music
B.C.S.—Bachelor of College Studies
B.E.—Bachelor of English
B.E. or **B.Ed.**—Bachelor of Education
B.E.—Bachelor of Engineering
B.E.D.—Bachelor of Environmental Design
B.E.E.—Bachelor of Electrical Engineering
B.En. or **B.Eng.**—Bachelor of Engineering
B.E.S. or **B.Eng.Sc.**—Bachelor of Engineering Science
B.E.T.—Bachelor of Engineering Technology
B.F.A.—Bachelor of Fine Arts
B.G.S.—Bachelor of General Studies
B.G.S.—Bachelor of Geological Sciences
B.H.E.—Bachelor of Health Education
B.H.P.E.—Bachelor of Health and Physical Education
B.H.S.—Bachelor of Health Science
B.I.D.—Bachelor of Industrial Design
B.I.M.—Bachelor of Industrial Management
B.Ind.Tech.—Bachelor of Industrial Technology
B.Int.Arch.—Bachelor of Interior Architecture
B.Int.Design—Bachelor of Interior Design
B.I.S.—Bachelor of Industrial Safety
B.I.S.—Bachelor of Interdisciplinary Studies
B.J.—Bachelor of Journalism
B.J.S.—Bachelor of Judaic Studies
B.L.A. or **B.Lib.Arts**—Bachelor of Liberal Arts
B.L.A. or **B.Land.Arch.**—Bachelor in Landscape Architecture
B.L.I.—Bachelor of Literary Interpretation
B.L.S.—Bachelor of Liberal Studies
B.M. or **B.Mus.** or **Mus.Bac.**—Bachelor of Music
B.M.E.—Bachelor of Mechanical Engineering
B.M.E. or **B.M.Ed.** or **B.Mus.Ed.**—Bachelor of Music Education
B.Med.Lab.Sc.—Bachelor of Medical Laboratory Science
B.Min—Bachelor of Ministry
B.M.P. or **B.Mu.**—Bachelor of Music in Performance
B.Mus.A.—Bachelor of Applied Music
B.M.T.—Bachelor of Music Therapy
B.O.T.—Bachelor of Occupational Therapy
B.P.A.—Bachelor of Public Administration
B.P.E.—Bachelor of Physical Education
B.Perf.Arts—Bachelor of Performing Arts
B.Ph.—Bachelor of Philosophy
B.Pharm.—Bachelor of Pharmacy
B.Phys.Hlth.Ed.—Bachelor of Physical Health Education
B.P.S.—Bachelor of Professional Studies
B.P.T.—Bachelor of Physical Therapy
B.R.E.—Bachelor of Religious Education
B.R.T.—Bachelor of Respiratory Therapy
B.S. or **B.Sc.** or **S.B.**—Bachelor of Science
B.S.A. or **B.S.Ag.** or **B.S.Agr.**—Bachelor of Science in Agriculture
B.Sacred Mus.—Bachelor of Sacred Music
B.Sacred Theol.—Bachelor of Sacred Theology
B.S.A.E.—Bachelor of Science in Agricultural Engineering
B.S.A.E. or **B.S.Art Ed.**—Bachelor of Science in Art Education
B.S.Ag.E.—Bachelor of Science in Agricultural Engineering
B.S.A.S.—Bachelor of Science in Administrative Sciences
B.S.A.T.—Bachelor of Science in Athletic Training
B.S.B.—Bachelor of Science (Business)
B.S.B.A. or **B.S.Bus. Adm.**—Bachelor of Science in Business Administration
B.S.Bus.—Bachelor of Science in Business
B.S.Bus.Ed.—Bachelor of Science in Business Education
B.S.C.—Bachelor of Science in Commerce
B.S.C.E. or **B.S.C.I.E.**—Bachelor of Science in Civil Engineering
B.S.C.E.T.—B.S. in Computer Engineering Technology
B.S.Ch. or **B.S.Chem.** or **B.S. in Ch.**—Bachelor of Science in Chemistry
B.S.C.H.—Bachelor of Science in Community Health
B.S.Ch.E.—Bachelor of Science in Chemical Engineering
B.S.C.I.S.—Bachelor of Science in Computer Information Sciences
B.S.C.J.—Bachelor of Science in Criminal Justice
B.S.C.L.S.—Bachelor of Science in Clinical Laboratory Science
B.S.Comp.Eng.—Bachelor of Science in Computer Engineering
B.S.Comp.Sci. or **B.S.C.S.**—Bachelor of Science in Computer Science
B.S.Comp.Soft—Bachelor of Science in Computer Software
B.S.Comp.Tech.—Bachelor of Science in Computer Technology
B.Sc.P.T.—Bachelor of Science in Physical Therapy
B.S.C.S.T.—Bachelor of Science in Computer Science Technology
B.S.D.H.—Bachelor of Science in Dental Hygiene
B.S.Die—Bachelor of Science in Dietetics
B.S.E. or **B.S.Ed.** or **B.S.Educ.**—Bachelor of Science in Education
B.S.E. or **B.S in E.** or **B.S. in Eng.**—Bachelor of Science in Engineering
B.S.E.E.—Bachelor of Science in Electrical Engineering
B.S.E.E.T.—Bachelor of Science in Electrical Engineering Technology
B.S.E.H.—Bachelor of Science in Environmental Health
B.S.Elect.T.—Bachelor of Science in Electronics Technology
B.S.El.Ed. or **B.S. in Elem. Ed.**—Bachelor of Science in Elementary Education
B.S.E.P.H.—Bachelor of Science in Environmental and Public Health
B.S.E.S.—Bachelor of Science in Engineering Science
B.S.E.S.—Bachelor of Science in Environmental Studies
B.S.E.T.—Bachelor of Science in Engineering Technology

B.S.F.—Bachelor of Science in Forestry
B.S.F.R.—Bachelor of Science in Forestry Resources
B.S.F.W.—Bachelor of Science in Fisheries and Wildlife
B.S.G.—Bachelor of Science in Geology
B.S.G.—Bachelor of Science in Gerontology
B.S.G.E.—Bachelor of Science in Geological Engineering
B.S.G.S.—Bachelor of Science in General Studies
B.S.H.C.A.—Bachelor of Science in Health Care Administration
B.S.H.E.—Bachelor of Science in Home Economics
B.S.H.F.—Bachelor of Science in Health Fitness
B.S.H.M.S.—Bachelor of Science in Health Management Systems
B.S.H.S.—Bachelor of Science in Health Sciences
B.S.H.S.—Bachelor of Science in Human Services
B.S.I.A.—Bachelor of Science in Industrial Arts
B.S.I.E.—Bachelor of Science in Industrial Engineering
B.S.I.M.—Bachelor of Science in Industrial Management
B.S. in Biomed.Eng.—Bachelor of Science in Biomedical Engineering
B.S. in C.D.—Bachelor of Science in Communication Disorders
B.S.Ind.Ed.—Bachelor of Science in Industrial Education
B.S.Ind.Tech.—Bachelor of Science in Industrial Technology
B.S. in Sec.Ed.—Bachelor of Science in Secondary Education
B.S.I.S.—Bachelor of Science in Interdisciplinary Studies
B.S.I.T.—Bachelor of Science in Industrial Technology
B.S.J.—Bachelor of Science in Journalism
B.S.L.E.—Bachelor of Science in Law Enforcement
B.S.M.—Bachelor of Science in Management
B.S.M.—Bachelor of Science in Music
B.S.M.E.—Bachelor of Science in Mechanical Engineering
B.S.Med.Tech. or **B.S.M.T.**—Bachelor of Science in Medical Technology
B.S.Met.E.—Bachelor of Science in Metallurgical Engineering
B.S.M.R.A.—Bachelor of Science in Medical Records Administration
B.S.M.T.—Bachelor of Science in Medical Technology
B.S.M.T.—Bachelor of Science in Music Therapy
B.S.Mt.E.—Bachelor of Science in Materials Engineering
B.S.Mus.Ed.—Bachelor of Science in Music Education
B.S.N.—Bachelor of Science in Nursing
B.S.Nuc.T.—Bachelor of Science in Nuclear Technology
B.S.O.A.—Bachelor of Science in Office Administration
B.S.O.E.—Bachelor of Science in Occupational Education
B.S.O.T.—Bachelor of Science in Occupational Therapy
B.S.P. or **B.S.Pharm**—Bachelor of Science in Pharmacy
B.S.P.A.—Bachelor of Science in Public Administration
B.S.Pcs.—Bachelor of Science in Physics
B.S.P.E.—Bachelor of Science in Physical Education
B.S.P.T.—Bachelor of Science in Physical Therapy
B.S.Rad.Tech.—Bachelor of Science in Radiation Technology
B.S.R.C.—Bachelor of Science in Respiratory Care
B.S.R.S.—Bachelor of Science in Radiological Science
B.S.R.T.T.—Bachelor of Science in Radiation Therapy Technology
B.S.S.—Bachelor of Science in Surveying
B.S.S.—Bachelor of Special Studies
B.S.S.A.—Bachelor of Science in Systems Analysis
B.S.Soc. Work or **B.S.S.W.**—Bachelor of Science in Social Work
B.S.Sp.—Bachelor of Science in Speech
B.S.S.T.—Bachelor of Science in Surveying and Topography
B.S.T. or **B.S.Tech.**—Bachelor of Science in Technology
B.S.S.W.E.—Bachelor of Science in Software Engineering
B.S.V.T.E.—Bachelor of Science in Vocational Technical Education
B.S.W.—Bachelor of Social Work
B.T. or **B.Tech.**—Bachelor of Technology
B.Th.—Bachelor of Theology
B.T.S.—Bachelor of Technical Studies
B.U.S.—Bachelor of Urban Studies
B.V.M.—Bachelor of Veterinarian Medicine
B.Voc.Arts or **B.V.A.**—Bachelor of Vocational Arts
B.V.E.D. or **B.Voc.Ed.**—Bachelor of Vocational Education

D.D.S.—Doctor of Dental Surgery

Ed.D.—Doctor of Education
Ed.S.—Education Specialist

J.D.—Doctor of Jurisprudence

LL.B.—Bachelor of Laws

M.A.—Master of Arts
M.A.Ed.—Master of Arts in Education
M.A.T.—Master of Arts in Teaching
M.B.A.—Master of Business Administration
M.D.—Doctor of Medicine
M.F.A.—Master of Fine Arts
M.P.A.—Master of Public Administration
M.S.—Master of Science
Mus.B. or **Mus.Bac.**—Bachelor of Music

Ph.D.—Doctor of Philosophy

R.N.—Registered Nurse

S.B. or **B.S.** or **B.Sc.**—Bachelor of Science

OTHER ABBREVIATIONS

AAAHC—Accreditation Association for Ambulatory Health Care
AABC—Accrediting Association of Bible Colleges
AABI—Aviation Accreditation Board International
AACN—American Association of Colleges of Nursing
AACSB—American Assembly of Collegiate Schools of Business
AACT—American Association of Community Theatre
AACT—Advanced Application Certification Testing
AACTE—American Association of Colleges for Teacher Education
AAFCS—American Association of Family and Consumer Sciences
AAHE—American Association for Health Education
AAHE—American Association for Higher Education
AAHEP—Accreditation of Allied Health Programs
AAHPERD—American Alliance for Health, Physical Education, Recreation, and Dance
AAHPERD—American Association of Health, Physical Education, Recreation, and Dance
AALE—American Academy for Liberal Education
AALS—Association of American Law Schools
AAM—American Academy of Microbiology
AAMA—American Association for Medical Assistants
AAMA—American Alternative Medical Association
AAMC—Association of American Medical Colleges
AAMFT—American Association for Marriage and Family Therapy
AANA—American Association of Nurse Anesthetists
AAPAR—American Association for Physical Activity and Recreation
AATA—American Art Therapy Association, Inc.
AAVLD—American Association of Veterinary Laboratory Diagnosticians
ABA—American Bar Association
ABAI—American Board of Allergy & Immunology
ABE—Association of Building Engineers Association of Building Engineers
ABET—Accreditation Board for Engineering and Technology
ABFSE—American Board of Funeral Service Education
ABHE—Association for Biblical Higher Education
ABHES—Accrediting Bureau of Health Education Schools
ACA—American Chiropractic Association
ACAE—Accreditation Commission for Audiology Education
ACBSP—Accreditation Council for Business Schools and Programs
ACCE—American Council for Construction Education
ACCGC—Accrediting Council for Collegiate Graphic Communications

ACCME—Accreditation Council for Continuing Medical Education
ACCNE—American Catholic Church of New England
ACE HSA—Accrediting Commission on Education for Health Services Administration
ACEI—Association for Cultural Economics International
ACEJ—American Council on Education for Journalism
ACE JMC—American Council on Education in Journalism and Mass Communication
ACF—American Culinary Federation
ACFEF—American Culinary Federation's Education Foundation, Inc. Accrediting Commission
ACGME—Accreditation Council for Graduate Medical Education
ACICS—Accrediting Council for Independent Colleges and Schools
ACNM—American College of Nuclear Medicine
ACNM—American College of Nurse-Midwives
ACOT—American College of Technology
ACOT—Advanced Communications-Computer Officer Training
ACOTE—Accreditation Council for Occupational Therapy Education
ACPE—Association for Clinical Pastoral Education, Inc.
ACPE—Accreditation Council on Pharmaceutical Education
ACPHA—Accreditation Commission for Programs in Hospitality Administration
ACS—American Chemical Society
ACSCU—Accrediting Commission for Senior Colleges and Universities
ACSI—Association of Christian Schools International
ACT—American College Testing Program
ACTFL—American Council on the Teaching of Foreign Languages
ACU—Association of Commonwealth Universities
ADA—American Dietetic Association
ADA—American Dental Association
ADDA—American Design Drafting Association
AEE—Association for Experiential Education
AFIT—Accelerated Flight & Instrument Training
AFSA—Application for Federal Student Aid
AHEA—American Home Economics Association
AHIMA—American Health Information Management Association
AICE—Advanced International Certificate of Education
AIChe—American Institute of Chemical Engineers
ALA—American Library Association
ALIGU—American Language Institute of Georgetown University
AMA—American Medical Association
AMA- CAHEA—American Medical Association Committee on Allied Health Education and Accreditation
AMTA—American Music Therapy Association
AMTA—American Massage Therapy Association
AOA—American Osteopathic Association
AOA—American Optometric Association
AOBFP—American Osteopathic Board of Family Physicians
AOSA—American Optometric Student Association
AOSA—American Overseas Schools Archive
AOTA—American Occupational Therapy Association
AP—Advanced Placement
APA—American Podiatry Association
APA—American Psychological Association
APET—Asset Placement Evaluation Test
APIEL—Advance Placement International English Language Exam
APMA—American Podiatric Medical Association
APTA—American Physical Therapy Association
ARC-PA—Accreditation Review Commission on Education for the Physician Assistant, Inc.
ARC-PA—Accreditation Review Commission on Education for the Physician Assistant, Inc.
ASABE—American Society of Agricultural and Biological Engineers
ASC—Accredited Standards Committee
ASCP—Association of Collegiate Schools of Planning
ASCP—American Society of Concierge Physicians
ASCP—American Society of Cardiovascular Professionals
ASCP—American Society of Clinical Psychopharmacology
ASCP—American Society of Clinical Pathologists
ASHA—American Social Health Association
ASHA—American School Health Association
ASHA—American Speech-Language-Hearing Association
ASHA—American School Health Association
ASLA—American Society of Landscape Architects
ASLH—American Society for Legal History
ASLHA (ASHA)—American Speech-Language-Hearing Association
ASPT—American Society of Plant Taxonomists
ATEP—Athletic Training Education Program
ATMAE—Association of Technology, Management, and Applied Engineering
ATME—Association of Theatre Movement Educators
ATMNE—Association of Teachers of Mathematics in New England
ATS—Association of Theological Schools in the U.S. and Canada
ATSUSC—Association of Theological Schools in the United States and Canada
AUCC—Association of Universities and Colleges of Canada
AUPHA—Association of University Programs of Health Administration
AVMA—American Veterinary Medical Association
AWI—Agency for Workforce Innovation

BENHA—Board of Examiners of Nursing Home Administrators
BEOG—Basic Educational Opportunity Grant (now Pell Grant)

CAA—Council on Aviation Accreditation
CAADE—California Association for Alcohol/Drug Educators
CAAHEP—Commission on Accreditation of Allied Health Education Programs
CAAP—College Achievement Admission Program
CAAT—Center for Alternatives to Animal Testing
CAATE—Commission on Accreditation of Athletic Training Education
CACREP—Council for Accreditation of Counseling and Related Educational Programs
CADE—Commission on Accreditation for Dietetics Education
CAHEA—See AMA-CAHEA
CAHIIM—Commission on Accreditation for Health Informatics and Information Management Education
CAHME—Commission on Accreditation of Healthcare Management Education
CANAEP—Council on Accreditation of Nurse Anesthesia Educational Programs
CAPTE—Commission on Accreditation in Physical Therapy Education
CARC—Canadian Agri-Food Research Council
CARF—Commission on Accreditation of Rehabilitation Facilities
CAS—Certificate of Advanced Study
CCE—Council on Chiropractic Education
CCIE—California Colleges for International Education
CCNE—Commission on Collegiate Nursing Education
CCTC—California Commission on Teacher Credentialing
CDN—Canadian/Canada
CEA—Canadian Education Association
CEA—Colorado Education Association
CEC—Commission on Education and Communication
CEC—Community Education Council
CED—Council for Education of the Deaf
CEEB—College Entrance Examination Board
CELT—Comprehensive English Language Test
CEPH—Council on Education for Public Health
CHEA—Council for Higher Education Accreditation
CIDA—Council for Interior Design Accreditation
CLAST—College Level Academic Skills Test

CLEP—College-Level Examination Program
CNNE—Commission on Collegiate Nursing Education
CoA—Committee on Accreditation
CoA-NA—Council on Accreditation of Nurse Anesthesia Educational Programs
COA—Commission on Opticianry Accreditation
COAMFTE—Commission on Accreditation for Marriage and Family Therapy Education
CoARC—Committee on Accreditation for Respiratory Care
COAPRT—Council on Accreditation of Parks, Recreation, Tourism, and Related Professions
COC—Certificate of Completion
COCA—Comprehensive Outcomes of Cognitive Assessment
CODA—Commission on Dental Accreditation
COE—Council on Occupational Education
COLA—Commission on Office Laboratory Accreditation
COPRA—Commission on Peer Review and Accreditation
CORE—Central Operation of Resources for Educators
CORE—Council On Rehabilitation Education
CORE—Consortium for Oceanographic Research and Education
CORE—Center for Organ Recovery and Education
CPME—Council on Podiatric Medical Education
CRDA—Candidates Reply Date Agreement
CRE—Council on Rehabilitation Education
CSAB—Computing Science Accreditation Board
CSAC—Consensus Standards Advisory Committee (of NQF)
CSHSE—Council for Standards in Human Service Education
CSLE—Center for the Study of Law and Economics
CSS—College Scholarship Service
CSS/Profile—College Scholarship Service Financial Aid Profile
CSWE—Council on Social Work Education Office of Social Work Accreditation
CVTEA—Committee on Veterinary Technician Education and Activities
CWS—College Work-Study

DECA—Discovering the Educational Consequences of Advanced Technical Education (DECA), a National Science Foundation funded research grant
DECM—Department of Education of the Commonwealth of MA

EAC—Engineering Accreditation Commission
EESL—Examination of English as a Second Language
EHAC—National Environmental Health Science and Protection Accreditation Council
ELPT—English Language Proficiency Test (SAT subject)
ELS/ALA—English Language Services/American Language Academy
EMH—Educable Mentally Handicapped
EOP—Equal Opportunity Program
EPH—Epidemiology and Public Health
EPSB—Education Professional Standards Board
ESL—English as a Second Language
ETS—Educational Testing Service

FAFSA—Free Application for Federal Student Aid
FEF—Foundry Educational Foundation
FET—Full-time equivalent
FFS—Family Financial Statement
FIDER—Foundation for Interior Design Education Research
FISL—Federally Insured Student Loan
FTE—Full-Time Equivalent

GED—General Educational Development (high school equivalency examination)
GPA—Grade Point Average
GPSC—Georgia Professional Student Commission
GPSC—Graduate and Professional Student Council
GRE—Graduate Record Examination
GSLP—Guaranteed Student Loan Program
G-STEP—Georgia State Test for English Proficiency

HEPAC—Higher Education Program Alumni Council
HEOP—Higher Equal Opportunity Program
HLC—Higher Learning Commission
HPER—Health, Physical Education, and Recreation

IACBE—International Assembly for Collegiate Business Education
IAME—International Association for Management Education
IB—International Baccalaureate
IELTS—International English Language Testing System

JRC-AT—Joint Review Committee on Educational Programs in Athletic Training
JRCE—Joint Review Committee on Education
JRCDMS—Joint Review Committee on Education in Diagnostic Medical Sonography
JRCERT—Joint Review Committee on Education in Radiologic Technology
JRCNMT—Joint Review Committee on Educational Programs in Nuclear Medicine Technology

LAAB—Landscape Architectural Accreditation Board
LCME—Liaison Committee on Medical Education

MACTE—Montessori Accreditation Council for Teacher Education
MAPS—Multiple Assessment Program/Services
MBHE—Massachusetts Board of Higher Education
MDOE—Michigan Department of Education
MELAB—Michigan English Language Assessment Battery
MSACS—Middle States Association of Colleges and Schools
MSCHE—Middle States Commission on Higher Education
MUSIC—Multi User System for Interactive Computing

NAAB—National Architectural Accrediting Board
NAACLS—National Accrediting Agency for Clinical Laboratory Sciences
NAALS—National Assessment of Adult Literacy Survey
NACEP—Nurse Aide Competency Evaluation Program
NAEYC—National Association for the Education of Young Children
NAIT—National Association of Industrial Technology
NAMT—National Association for Music Therapy
NAPNES—National Association for Practical Nurse Education and Service
NASAD—National Association of Schools of Art and Design
NASD—National Association of Schools of Dance
NASDTEC—National Association of State Development Teacher Education
NASSM—North American Society for Sport Management
NASM—National Association of Schools of Music
NASO—National Adult School Organization
NASP—National Association of School Psychologists
NASPAA—National Association of Schools of Public Affairs and Administration
NASPE—National Association of Sport and Physical Education
NAST—National Association of Schools of Theatre
NATA—National Athletic Trainers' Association
NCA—North Central Association of Colleges and Schools, Higher Learning Commission
NCAA—National Collegiate Athletic Association
NCACE—National Council for Accreditation of Coaching Education
NCACS—North Central Association of Colleges and Schools
NCA-HLC—North Central Association of Colleges and Schools, The Higher Learning Commission
NCATE—National Council for Accreditation of Teacher Education
NCCAA—National Christian College Athletic Association
NCDPI—North Carolina Department of Public Instruction
NCIDQ—National Council for Interior Design Qualification
NCOPE—National Commission on Orthotic and Prosthetic Education
NCTE—National Council of Teachers of English

NCTM—National Council of Teachers of Mathematics
NDEA—National Defense Education Act
NEASC-CIHE—New England Association of Schools and Colleges, Commission on Institutions of Higher Education
NEASC-CTCI—New England Association of Schools and Colleges, Commission on Technical and Career Institutions
NEHA—National Environmental Health Association
NEHSPAC—National Environmental Health Science and Protection Council
NLN—National League for Nursing
NLNAC—National League for Nursing Accrediting Commission, Inc.
NMPED—New Mexico Public Education Department
NMSA—National Middle School Association
NRPA—National Recreation and Park Association
NSTA—National Science Teachers Association
NWCCU—Northwest Commission on Colleges and Universities
NYSED—New York State Education Department

OAKE—Organization of American Kodály Educators
OBN—Ohio Board of Nursing
ODE—Ohio Department of Education
ODPS—Ohio Department of Public Safety

PAB—Planning Accreditation Board
PAIR—PHEAA Aid Information Request
PCS—Parents' Confidential Statement
PDE—Pennsylvania Department of Education
PEP—Proficiency Examination Program
PHEAA—Pennsylvania Higher Education Assistance Agency
PSAT/NMSQT—Preliminary Scholastic Aptitude Test/ National Merit Scholarship Qualifying Test

ROTC—Reserve Officers Training Corps
RSE—Regents Scholarship Examination (New York State)

SAAC—Student Aid Application for California
SACU—Service for Admission to College and University (Canada)
SACS—Southern Association of Colleges and Schools, Commission on Colleges
SAF—Society of American Foresters
SAM—Single Application Method
SAR—Student Aid Report
SAT—Scholastic Assessment Testing (*formerly ATP–Admissions Testing Program*)
SATE—Security Awareness Training & Education
SBEC—State Board for Educator Certification (Texas)
SCAT—Scholastic College Aptitude Test
SCS—Students' Confidential Statement
SDBN—South Dakota Board of Nursing
SEOG—Supplementary Educational Opportunity Grant
SOA—Society of Actuaries

TAC—Technology Accreditation Commission
TAP—Tuition Assistance Program (New York State)
TDD/TTY—Telecommunications Device for the Deaf/ TeleTYpewriter
TEA—Texas Education Agency
TEAC—Teacher Education Accreditation Council
TOEFL—Test of English as a Foreign Language
TRACS—Transnational Association of Christian Colleges and Schools, Accreditation Commission

UAP—Undergraduate Assessment Program
UMC—United Methodist Church
UP—Undergraduate Program (area tests)

VFAF—Virginia Financial Assistance Form

WASC-ACCJC—Western Association of Schools and Colleges, Accrediting Commission for Community and Junior Colleges
WASC-ACSCU—Western Association of Schools and Colleges, Accrediting Commission for Senior Colleges and Universities
WPCT—Washington Pre-College Test

PART I

AN INTRODUCTION TO COLLEGE

You'll soon be on your way to college—but how much thought have you given it so far? Have you started thinking about the career that's in your future?

- Which college will help you make the most of your natural abilities and interests, and get you ready for life?
- Which courses should you take?

This section will help you find answers to these questions. It will also give you advice on:

- how to apply to schools
- how to increase your chances of acceptance
- how to finance your education

And just as important, this introductory section will give you valuable tips on how to get through that critical freshman year.

KNOWING YOURSELF

It's not just about statistics like median SAT scores, the endowment, the number of majors or student-professor ratios; a college should feel right to you, from the structure of the classrooms to the food that's served in the dining halls.

Arielle Shipper, Connecticut College, Class of 2010

You have in your hands a book that will give you answers to your questions about the qualities and features of more than 1650 colleges. But before you start reading the descriptions and getting the answers, you need to know what questions to ask about finding the college that is right for you. Although you need to ask questions about "getting in," i.e., exploring colleges in terms of ease of admission for you, most of your questions should focus on the more significant issue of "fitting in." Fitting in means finding a college where you will be comfortable; where you are compatible with your peers, and where the overall atmosphere encourages your growth as a student and as a person.

This article is designed to help you assess some values and attitudes that will help you determine where you will fit in. It will enable you to ask the right questions. Not all colleges are for everyone; careful thinking about your interests, ideals, and values will lead you to find the college that is right *for you*. Colleges are not "good" or "bad" in a generic sense; they are either good or bad matches for you.

The two assessments that follow will be helpful in thinking about yourself as a future college student; they should help you make the right college choice.

THE COLLEGE PLANNING VALUES ASSESSMENT

Students have different reasons for going to college. Eleven reasons or values are found to be most important to students as they think about college. Knowing about your values is the important first step in identifying the colleges where you will fit in and be happy.

To complete the assessment, read through the list of eleven values—A through K. Think about the outcomes you hope college will produce for you. Each student will rank them differently; hence, there are no "right" answers. Whereas several, or even most, of these values may be significant for you in one way or another, the goal is to decide which three are the most important. After you read each of the values, go back and circle the THREE most important ones on the basis of the following question:

What do you want college to do for you?

X A. To provide me with a place to learn and study.
— B. To provide me with opportunities to interact with teachers inside and outside the classroom.
— C. To provide me with lots of fun experiences.
— D. To prepare me to make a lot of money.
— E. To provide me with recognition for accomplishments.
— F. To get politically involved and/or to use much of my college years to help those who are disadvantaged.
X G. To help me prepare for a career.
X H. To enable me to be more independent.
— I. To provide opportunities for me to grow religiously or spiritually.
— J. To provide me with a variety of new experiences.
— K. To enable me to receive a degree from a prestigious school.

What do your college planning values say about you?

If ***A*** was among the top three priorities on your list, you will want to explore the academic character of the colleges you are considering. Although all colleges are, by definition, intellectual centers, some put more priority on challenging students and pushing them to their limits. Reading about the academic features of the colleges you are considering will be important. (In the college Profiles, pay attention to the *special* section to learn about these features.) Your high ranking of this value says that you will be able to take advantage of intellectual opportunities at college. You may want to select a college where your SAT scores are similar to or slightly above the ranges of other admitted students—at those colleges you will be able to shine academically. You may desire to take an active part in classroom discussions and will want a college where the student faculty ratio is low.

If ***B*** was among your top three priorities, you feel challenged and stimulated by academics and classroom learning. You will want to find a college where your mind will be stretched. You will want to choose a college where you can explore a range of new academic subjects. A liberal arts and sciences college may give you an enriching breadth of academic offerings. You will want to look for a college where academic clubs are popular and where you have a good chance of knowing professors and sharing ideas with them. Access to faculty is important to you and you will want to look at the student faculty ratio in colleges you consider. Also note the ratio of undergraduate students to graduate students. Primarily undergraduate institutions will be the colleges that may best be able to meet your needs, because you will be the focus of teachers' attention. Teachers at such colleges place their priority on teaching and are not distracted by the needs of graduate students or by pressure to balance teaching and student time with research and writing.

If ***C*** was circled, you derive satisfaction from social opportunities. You will want a college where the academic demands will not diminish your ability to socialize. You likely will want a good balance between the social and academic sides of campus life. You will want to explore the percentage of students who get involved in intramural sports, clubs, or fraternities and sororities. (This information is listed in each college profile.) Look at your college choices on the basis of school spirit and sporting events offered. The profiles list popular campus events—see if they sound exciting to you. Also look at the percentage of students who stay on campus over the weekend. You will also want a college where it is easy to make friends. Both small and larger colleges would be appropriate for you. Although a larger college would expose you to more students and a larger quantity of potential friends, studies show that students at smaller colleges become more involved in activities and build deep friendships more quickly. Look for supportiveness and camaraderie in the student body.

If ***D*** is circled, you will want to consider earning potential, advancement opportunities, and the future market for the careers you consider. You will want to consider this value in your career planning. Remember, however, that there is no sure road to riches! You not only must pick a career direction carefully, but must choose a college where the potential for academic success—good grades—is high. The name of a particular college is less important than good grades or contributions to campus life when securing a good job or being admitted to graduate school. Even if you find that a particular career has tremendous earning potential, those earnings may come to only those who are most successful in the profession. Look at average salaries, but also consider your interests, values, and personality before making your final career choice. Be sure to take advantage of hands-on learning opportunities. Perhaps, for example, there are internships that meet your needs. Also, finding good, career-focused summer jobs can be helpful.

If ***E*** is high on your list, you take pleasure in being known for your success in an area of interest. For instance, you might feel good about being recognized or known in school as a good student, a top athlete, or a leader in a club. No doubt this type of recognition contributes to your confidence. You might look for colleges where you will be able to acquire or continue to receive this recognition. Often, recognition is easier to achieve at smaller colleges where you would not be competing against large numbers of students hoping to achieve the same recognition. You will also want to choose colleges where it is easy to get involved and where the activities offered are appealing to you. You may want to consider the benefits of being a "big fish in a small pond."

If ***F*** is important, that value will no doubt guide your vocational or avocational pursuits. You may find yourself choosing a career in which this value can be fulfilled, or you may seek opportunities on a college campus where you can be of service to others. You will want to choose a college where community service is valued. Look at the *activities* section and note whether community service-related involvements are available. Colleges vary a great deal in terms of political awareness. At some colleges, students are attuned to national and international events, often express feelings about current issues and policies, and in general, show interest in political affairs. Students at other colleges show little or no interest in these matters and find other ways to interact with peers.

If ***G*** was circled, you may know what career you want to pursue or you may be concerned but uncertain about your career decision. If you have tentatively selected a career, you will want to choose a college where you can take courses leading to the attainment of a degree in your chosen field. Explore the *programs of study* section in the profiles to determine whether a college you are considering offers the course work you desire. You will want to make a note of the most popular majors and the strongest majors as they are listed. If you don't yet know what career would suit you, remember, that for most careers, a broad, solid liberal arts foundation is considered good preparation. You will want to look at opportunities for internships and take advantage of the career planning and placement office at your chosen college. Finding a career that will be fulfilling is one of the most important choices you will make in your life. Your selection of a college will be your first step toward achieving your career goal.

If ***H*** is circled, it suggests that personal autonomy is important to you. College is, in general, a time for independence, and students are often anxious to make their own decisions without parental involvement. If you feel you can handle lots of independence, you will want to look for colleges where there is some freedom in choosing courses and where students are given responsibility for their own lives. Colleges vary in terms of these factors. Note particularly the *required* section under *programs of study*, which tells you the courses that must be fulfilled by all students. Be certain that you will not be stifled by too many rules and regulations. You may also want to look for colleges where the personal development of students receives high priority. A priority on independence also suggests that you will be comfortable being away from home and on your own.

If ***I*** is one of your top three choices, you will want to look first at the religious affiliation of each of your college options. There are two ways to consider religious life on college campuses. First is the question of how religion affects the day-to-day life of the college. For example, are biblical references made in class? Are religious convocations mandatory? Second is the question of whether there is a religious heritage at the college. Many hundreds of colleges have historical relationships with a religious denomination, but this tie does not affect the rules or the general life of the students. (For example, the college may have a certain number of religion classes required to graduate, but these classes are typically broad-based and not doctrinal.) You may want a college that has a relationship with your particular religious group. Or you may desire a large number of students who belong to the same denomination as you do. The profiles will also give you the percentage of students who are members of the major religious denominations. As you explore colleges, you will also want to see if the college has a commitment to the values and ideals held by you or your family.

If ***J*** is appealing, you like newness and will likely be stimulated by new experiences and new activities. You are in for a treat at most colleges. New experiences are the "stuff" of which college life is made. You may see college-going as an adventure and will want to pick colleges where you can meet your need for stimulation and excitement. Because you value newness, you should not hesitate to attend college in a different part of the country or to experience an environment or a climate that is quite different from your high school. You will also want to look for evidence of diversity in the student body. As you read the descriptions, look for colleges with lots of new opportunities for growth and for personal expansion.

If ***K*** is appealing, be cautious. Students who are overly concerned about this value might find college planning traumatic, and even painful, because of the admission selectivity of "name brand" colleges. Even though it is perfectly acceptable for students to be attuned to the overall excellence of a college, academic quality and prestige are not the same thing. Some colleges are well-known because of, say, a fine football team or because of academic excellence in a subject like psychology or physics. Although it is appropriate to look for a strong faculty and a highly regarded college, you want a college that will give you the greatest chance of academic success. It is success in college, not just academic reputation or prestige, that will lead to admission into graduate school or a broad selection of jobs.

Now that you've read about your top three values, answer the following question on a separate sheet of paper: In your own words, what do your top three values say about what you are looking for in a college? Then, share that information with your college adviser as he or she assists you in finding colleges that are right for you.

SELF-KNOWLEDGE QUESTIONNAIRE

The following seven items—A–G—will help you in thinking about yourself as a college student and the ease with which you will likely proceed through the college selection process. Read each statement and determine whether it is true or not true of you. After each question, you will see numbers ranging from 1 to 5. Circle 1 if the statement is very true of you. Circle 5 if the statement is not true of you. Use 2, 3, or 4 to reflect varying levels of preference. Be realistic and honest.

A. My academic abilities for college (such as reading, writing, and note taking) are good.

Very true of me 1 2 3 4 5 Not true of me

Academic abilities such as reading speed and comprehension, writing, note taking, calculating, speaking, and listening are important for college students. You will be called upon to use such skills in your college classes. If you are confident about your academic skills, you can approach picking a college with the ease of knowing that you will be able to master the academic rigors of college life. If you circled 3, 4, or 5 you will want to work on these skills in your remaining days in high school. You will want to choose colleges where you can work to strengthen these skills. Some colleges provide a learning skills center in which you are able to get help if you are having difficulty writing a paper or understanding the content of a class. If you are less than confident, you might look to colleges where you will not be intimidated by the skills of the other students.

B. My study skills and time management are good.

Very true of me 1 2 3 4 5 Not true of me

Study skills and time management are two of the most important qualities for an efficient and productive college student. Successful college students are average or above in organizing themselves for studying, scheduling, and using study time productively, and differentiating important content of a lecture or a book from supplementary information. In addition, they complete assignments on time and don't get flustered if they have several papers or a couple of tests due on the same day. If you circled 3, 4, or 5, it is important to work on improving these skills during your remaining high school days. You might consider the following:

- Seek help from your parents, a teacher, a counselor, or a learning specialist in becoming more organized.
- Try keeping a calendar. Anticipate each step necessary in preparing for every test and every paper.
- Be responsible for your own appointments.
- Check to see if a study skills course is offered at a local community college or university. Or consider reading a book on study skills.

C. I am motivated to succeed in college.

Very true of me 1 2 3 4 5 Not true of me

Motivation is definitely the most important skill you bring to college. Those students who want to succeed do succeed! Studies show that it is motivation, not your SAT scores, that determines academic success in college. And motivation means knowing not only that you want to go to college, but that you also want to be a student. Some students want to go to college for the fun aspects, but forget that college is primarily an academic experience. So if you circled 1 or 2, great, you're off to a good start. If you circled 3, 4, or 5, it may be an appropriate time to consider your wants and needs in a college. What sort of college would help motivate you? Would a college with a balance between academics and social life be appealing? Would you be more motivated if you were near a large and interesting city? Would nice weather be a distraction rather than an energizer? Is a trade or technical school best for you? Have you considered taking some time off between high school and college? Considering such questions is important, and the time to do that exploration is now.

D. I am a good decision maker.

Very true of me 1 2 3 4 5 Not true of me

Decisions, decisions, decisions. The college selection process is full of decisions! What colleges will I initially consider? To which colleges will I apply for admission? What college will I eventually attend? You will be facing these decisions in the upcoming months. If you circled 1 or 2, you are on your way. If you circled 3, 4, or 5, think about an important decision you made recently. Why didn't it go well? If you can analyze your decision-making weakness in that situation, it may help to avoid any potential pitfalls in your college decision-making. The following suggestions will help you improve your ability to make the right college choice:

- Clearly articulate what you're looking for in a college. Write down those features that will make a college right for you.
- Involve lots of people and resources in your search for a college. Your parents, counselors, and friends can help you.
- List and compare pros and cons of alternative colleges. Every college has both.
- Evaluate each college on the basis of the criteria you set for yourself.

Remember, you're looking for a college where you will get in *and* fit in.

E. I'm a good information gatherer; for example, I am usually able to find books, articles, and so on to help me do a research paper for, say, a history class.

Very true of me 1 2 3 4 5 Not true of me

Finding a college requires you to be a good researcher. There is so much information about colleges to sort through and analyze. If you feel you can do good research, fine, you're on your way. If you circled 3, 4, or 5, the following ideas may be helpful:

- Start with this book and look for colleges that are consistent with what you want. Remember that your primary concern is where you will fit in. Use your college-going values and your responses in this questionnaire to guide your thinking about colleges that will match you.
- Work closely with your college counselor, and seek impressions from students and others with reliable and up-to-date information about colleges of interest. You will make a better decision with credible and extensive input.
- Look for differences in features that are important to you. Is ease of making friends important to you? What about balance between academics and social life? Do you want teachers to know you?

F. I feel I adapt to new situations easily.

Very true of me 1 2 3 4 5 Not true of me

Everyone goes through changes in life. Some move through transition periods with great ease, others find them more difficult. You may have experienced the changes that come after a change of schools (even from middle school to high school), the illness or death of a relative, or the divorce of your parents. If you circled 1 or 2, you are not likely to be intimidated by a college in another part of the country or a college very different from your high school. If you circled 3, 4, or 5, you may want to carefully look at colleges that are a bit closer to home or colleges where the same values, perceptions, and attitudes exist as were true in your high school. Almost everyone has fear and apprehension about leaving for college. But if that fear is significant, you will want to choose a college where you will feel comfortable. Visits to college campuses may be particularly significant in feeling good about potential choices.

G. It is easy for me to meet people and establish friendships.

Very true of me 1 2 3 4 5 Not true of me

Identifying and nurturing friendships is an important skill for college adjustment. If you circled 3, 4, or 5, you will want to look carefully at colleges where there are few cliques, where there is an atmosphere of sharing, and where students report that it is relatively easy to integrate into the campus environment. Your choice of a college is a quest for a good social fit. Your thorough review of the profiles and even visits to college campuses will be helpful in assuring your ability to fit in and be comfortable.

FINAL THOUGHTS

If you took time to carefully consider the issues raised in both the Values Assessment and the Self-Knowledge Questionnaire, you should have gained new insights and perspectives about yourself. You will want to share these results with your parents and with your guidance counselor. Elicit their help in getting more insight as to how they see you as a prospective college student. Finally, two suggestions:

- As you research colleges, consider what you have learned about yourself. You want a college that is a good match with your values and interests.
- Spend time on your college search. It will take many hours of organized planning and investigation. But the time spent will result in a better choice and a greater likelihood that you will spend four productive and exciting years in college.

Good luck. There are lots of colleges out there that want you. Let your knowledge of yourself and your objective analysis of potential college options guide you to college environments where you will be able to shine. Success in college is in your hands. Make the most of the opportunity.

Steven R. Antonoff, Ph.D., Certified Educational Planner
Educational Consultant
Antonoff Associates, Inc.
Denver, Colorado

FINDING THE RIGHT COLLEGE

Location is a key factor in looking at colleges. Those seeking adventures should look toward city schools where there are endless possibilities, and those looking for a quiet atmosphere should look for schools in rural locations.

Bryan Cosca, Boston University College of Engineering, Class of 2014

Start your college search positively. Start with the knowledge that there are many schools out there that want you. Start with the idea that there are many good college choices for every student. Too often these days, articles on college admission make students and their parents apprehensive. You can have choices. You can get financial aid. You can have a happy, successful college career.

When you begin to think about college, you are embarking on a major research project. You have many choices available to you in order to get the best possible education for which you are qualified. This article is intended to help you think of some of the important variables in your college search.

Let us help make the book work for you!

THE CURRENT ADMISSION SCENE

Today there are approximately 1,650 four-year colleges and universities accredited. Most existing institutions have grown larger, and many have expanded their programs, offering master's and doctoral degrees as well as bachelor's.

Total graduate and undergraduate students has also grown, from under 4 million in 1960 to more than 16 million today. Almost 40 percent are part-time students, including many working adults. Part-time enrollments are mostly concentrated in the two-year colleges, which enroll about a third of all students.

What does this all mean to you? There is good news and bad news. The good news is that most of the colleges you will read about in this book are colleges you can get into! In other words, the vast majority of colleges in the U.S. admit more than 70 percent of those who apply. Many hundreds admit all of those who apply. So, on one level, you shouldn't worry that you won't be able to get a college education. The bad news is for the student with extremely high grades who seeks admission to the 50 or so most competitive colleges in the country. These "brand name" colleges have many times more candidates than they admit. Even incredibly qualified students are sometimes denied admission.

The key to good college planning is, as mentioned above, research. Find out about what makes one college different from another. Find out what students say about their experiences. Rely on many sources of information—many people, many books, many web sites, and so on. There are lots of people and materials available to help you. This book is one of them. Let the information be your guide. But also let your instincts and your sense of what's best for you play a part. The higher education opportunities in the U.S. are unlimited. The opportunity to let education help pave the way to achieving your dreams is a worthy goal of your college search.

MAKING A SHORT LIST

You have probably already started a list of colleges you know about from friends or relatives who have attended them, from recommendations by counselors or teachers, or by their academic or social reputations. This list will grow as you read the Profiles, receive college mailings, and attend college fairs. If you are interested in preparing for a very specific career, such as engineering, agriculture, nursing, or architecture, you should add only institutions that offer that program. If you want to study business, teacher education, or the arts and sciences, almost every college can provide a suitable major. Either way, your list will soon include dozens of institutions. Most students apply to between four and seven colleges. To narrow your list, you should keep the following process in mind:

- As you explore, be attuned to the admission requirements. You will want to have colleges on your list that span the admission selectivity continuum—from "reach" colleges (those where your grades, test scores, etc., suggest less chance of admission) to "safety" schools (those where your credentials are a bit better than the average student admitted), eliminating colleges at which you clearly would not qualify for admission.
- You also will want to keep an eye on cost. You want to consider colleges that are generally in line with your family's ability to finance your education. Be very cautious as you do this. Literally millions of dollars are available each year for students. There is both "need-based" aid (aid based on your family's ability to pay) and "merit-based" aid (aid based on such things as grades, test scores, and leadership ability).
- Screen the list according to your preferences, such as size, academic competitiveness, religious focus, and location.
- Make quality judgments, using published information and campus visits, to decide which colleges can give you the best quality and value.

The following sections are organized around the factors most important in researching a college. Discussion of admission competitiveness and cost comes first. After that, a wide range of factors important to consider as you evaluate colleges is examined. These include size, housing, the faculty, academic programs, internships, accreditation, libraries and computer technology, and religious/racial considerations. The final two sections are a discussion of campus visits and, finally, a checklist of 25 important questions to ask about each of the colleges you are exploring.

In the end, you must allow yourself to be a good decision maker. You will have to make some quality judgments. It is not as difficult as you may think. You have to be willing to read the information in this book and the literature that the schools make available, to visit a few campuses, and to ask plenty of questions. Usually you can ask questions of the admissions office by regular mail, e-mail, or in person during a campus visit. Because colleges sincerely are interested in helping you make the right choice, they generally will welcome your questions and answer them politely and honestly. In addition, your high school counselor is a key person who can offer advice and guidance. Finally, there are many resources available, in printed form and on the web, to help you.

SELECTION FACTORS

Admissions Competitiveness

The first question most students ask about a college is, "How hard is it to get in?" It should certainly not be the last question. Admissions competitiveness is not the only, or even the most important, measurement of institutional quality. It makes sense to avoid wasting time, money, and useless disappointment applying to institutions for which you clearly are not qualified. Nevertheless, there are many colleges for which you are qualified, and you can make a good choice from among them. The most prestigious institutions are rarely affected by market conditions. Most of the better known private and public colleges and universities have raised their admission standards in recent years. But there remain hundreds of fine public and private colleges, with good local reputations, that will welcome your application.

Use the College Admissions Selector to compare your qualifications to the admissions competitiveness of the institutions of your list. Make sure you read the descriptions of standards very carefully. Even if you meet the stated qualifications for *Most Competitive* or *Highly Competitive* institutions, you cannot assume that you will be offered admission. These colleges receive applications from many more students than they can enroll and reject far more than they accept. When considering colleges rated *Very Competitive* or *Competitive*, remember that the median test scores identify the middle of the most recent freshman class; half of the admitted students had scores lower than the median, and half were above. Students of average ability are admissible to most of the colleges and universities rated as *Competitive* and to virtually all of those rated as *Less Competitive*.

Cost

The basic cost of the most expensive colleges and universities can exceed $40,000 a year. This is widely publicized and very frightening, especially to your parents. But you don't have to spend that much for a good education. Private colleges charge an average of nearly $30,000 a year for tuition and room and board. Public institutions generally cost an average of $14,000 a year for in-state residents. Because many states have been cutting budgets in recent years, tuition at public institutions is now rising faster than at private ones. If you can commute to school from home, you can save about $6000 to $12,000 in room and board, but should add the cost of transportation. The least expensive option is to attend a local community college for two years, at about $1500 a year, and then transfer to a four-year institution to complete your bachelor's degree. Depending on what you may qualify for in financial aid, and what your family is willing to sacrifice, you may have more choices than you think.

Size

Only one-fifth of American colleges and universities have enrollments of 5000 or more, but they account for more than half the ten million plus students who are pursuing bachelor's degrees. The rest are spread out among more than 1000 smaller schools. There are advantages and disadvantages that go with size.

At a college of 5000 or fewer students, you will get to know the campus quickly. You will not have to compete with many other students when registering for courses or for use of the library or other facilities. You can get to know your professors personally and become familiar with most of your fellow students. On the other hand, the school may not have as many majors and it may have less emphasis on spectator sports. Students at small schools are not able to be as "anonymous" as those at larger schools.

As colleges and universities enroll more students, they offer more courses and activities. Within a large campus community, you can probably find others who share your special interests and form a circle of good friends. But you may also find the facilities more crowded, classes closed out, and competition very stiff for athletic teams or musical groups.

Many of the largest institutions are universities offering medical, law, or other doctoral programs as well as bachelor's and master's degrees. Many colleges that do not offer these programs call themselves universities; and a few universities, Dartmouth among them, continue to call themselves colleges. Don't go by the name, but by the academic program. Universities emphasize research. University faculty need specialized laboratory equipment, computers, library material, and technical assistance for their research. Colleges tend to emphasize teaching.

Because research is very expensive, universities usually charge higher tuition than colleges, even to their undergraduate students. In effect, undergraduates at universities subsidize the high cost of graduate programs. Freshmen and sophomores usually receive some instruction from graduate student assistants and fellows, who are paid to be apprentice faculty members.

Of course, many larger private universities, and many public ones, have fine reputations. They have larger and more up-to-date libraries, laboratories, computers, and other special resources than colleges. They attract students from many states and countries and provide a rich social and cultural environment.

Housing

Deciding whether you will stay in a residence hall or at home is more than a matter of finances or how close to the college you live. You should be aware that students who live on campus, especially during the freshman year, are more likely to pass their courses and graduate than students who commute from home. Campus residents spend more time with faculty members, have more opportunity to use the library and laboratories, and are linked to other students who help one another with their studies. Residence hall life usually helps students mature faster as they participate in social and organizational activities.

If you commute to school, you can get maximum benefits from your college experience by spending time on campus between and after classes. If you need a part-time job, get employment in the college library, offices, or dining halls. Use the library to do homework in an environment that may be less distracting than home. If possible, have some dinners on campus, to make friends with other students and participate in evening social and cultural events. Get involved in campus activities, participating in athletics, working on the newspaper, attending a meeting, or rehearsing a play.

You will have a choice of food plans. Most meal plans include a certain number of meals per week. Other plans allow you to prepay a fixed dollar amount and purchase food by the item rather than by the meal. Choose a meal plan that fits your own eating habits. Most colleges today offer a tremendous variety of food and are accommodating to most diets and preferences.

Many students live off campus after their freshman or sophomore year, either by choice or because the school does not have room for them on campus. Schools try to provide listings of available off-campus rooms and apartments that meet good standards for safety and cleanliness. Many colleges also offer health care and food services to students who live off campus.

It is usually more expensive to live in an apartment than in a residence hall, especially if you plan to prepare your own meals. But that option is appealing to some students, particularly those in their junior or senior years.

The Faculty

The most important resources of any college or university are its professors. Admissions brochures usually point out the strengths of the faculty, but provide little detail. You should direct your questions about the faculty and other academic matters to the specific department or to the office that coordinates academic advising. Recruiting brochures also emphasize faculty research, because the prestige of professors depends largely on the books and articles they have published. Good researchers may or may not make good teachers. Ask how often the best researchers teach undergraduate courses, and whether they instruct small as well as large classes. For example, a Nobel prize chemist may lecture to 500 students at a time but never show up in the laboratories where graduate assistants actually teach individual students.

Also ask about class size, because this determines the amount of individual attention students get from professors. Student/faculty ratios, which usually range from 10 to 20 students per professor, don't really tell you much. Every school offers a mixture of large and small classes. Ask admission officers for the average size of a freshman class. You will want to look for such factors as those that follow:

- Science and technology courses should enroll only 25 to 30 students in each laboratory session, but may combine a number of laboratory classes for large weekly lectures.
- Skill development courses such as speech, foreign language, English composition, and fine and performing arts should have classes of 25 or fewer. Mathematics and computer science require considerable graded homework, and classes should be no larger than 35.

- Most other courses in humanities, social sciences, and professional areas are taught by classroom lectures and discussion. Classes should average 35 to 45 in introductory courses such as general psychology or American government. They should be smaller in advanced or specialized courses, such as Shakespeare or tax accounting.
- Many introductory courses, especially at universities, are taught in lecture classes of 100 or more. This is acceptable, if those courses also include small weekly discussion groups for individual instruction. Sometimes these discussion groups are taught by graduate student assistants rather than regular professors. Although graduate assistants lack teaching experience, they are very often highly capable. You should ask whether the teaching done by graduate assistants is closely supervised by regular faculty members.

Academic Programs

Even colleges and universities that boast fine and well qualified faculties can be short of professors in certain programs. Some schools depend on instruction by part-time faculty members or fill in with available teachers from other specializations. Many international students are enrolled in technical doctoral programs, so you may find yourself being taught mathematics or engineering by a teaching assistant who is not a native English speaker. If you are interested in these subjects, check to see whether full-time faculty members teach the majority of the courses.

Other programs may have sufficient faculty but too few student majors. Majors such as physics and philosophy, for example, often have many students in required introductory courses, but few taking the major. Because of small enrollments, these departments may not be able to offer their advanced and specialized courses on a regular basis.

Academic departments give strength to the program by bringing together faculty members who share a common area of study and make sure their students get the classes they need. Some programs, usually called interdisciplinary, are taught by groups of faculty members from several departments. These programs generally have the word *studies* in their titles; for example, Middle-Eastern Studies, Communication Studies, Women's Studies, or Ethnic Studies. If you are enrolled in one of these programs, be sure to ask about the student advising. (Sometimes, advising suffers if faculty members are primarily loyal to their own department.)

Internships

Internships are available at many colleges. They provide an opportunity to experience work in your major and learn from experienced people in your field. Many students have received job offers after participating in an internship program during the school year or during summer vacation. These internships can make a big difference as you enter the job market.

Accreditation

General standards of academic quality are established by associations of colleges and universities through a process called voluntary accreditation. The criteria include: standards for admission of students; faculty qualifications; content of courses; grading standards; professional success of alumni; adequacy of libraries, laboratories, computers, and other support facilities; administrative systems and policy decision making; and financial support.

Six regional associations (New England, Middle States, Southern, North Central, Northwest, and Western) evaluate and accredit colleges as total institutions. Bible colleges have their own accrediting association. Other organizations evaluate and accredit specific programs, primarily in technical fields, like engineering and architecture; or those that require licensing, such as teaching and health care.

Libraries and Computer Technology

Most people judge libraries by the size of the collection, the bigger the better. Collection size is important, but only in relation to the variety and level of programs offered. A small liberal arts college can support its baccalaureate programs with a collection of 200,000 to 400,000 volumes. A university with many professional schools and doctoral programs may require over 2 million. Many books and journals are available through various methods of information technology, computer storage, and the Internet.

The main stacks should be open to students, with the possible exception of rare books, bound journals, and other special items. Open stacks encourage browsing and save students from waiting on line while a library assistant fetches a few books at a time. Instead, assistants constantly should be picking up unused materials from reading desks or carts and putting them back on the shelves.

Good circulation policies encourage students to check materials out for short periods and to return them promptly. One week or less loans are appropriate for books regularly used in courses, and four week loans should be the maximum for other materials. A recall system should be available to get back borrowed material when it is needed. Journals, reference material, or books placed on reserve for assigned reading should be used within the library while it is open, and circulated overnight only at closing time.

Using a computer is integral to university study. Some institutions require students to have personal computers. Colleges often offer the best price for new computers. You may want to check out the options on campus before you purchase a computer elsewhere. Many residence hall rooms are wired for computers and direct connections are linked to the main campus system. More and more campuses have wireless capability.

Religious/Ethnic Considerations

For some students, the religious life of the campus is important as college choices are reviewed. Religious life can vary from being pervasive to being absent. Most colleges are independent of religious influence. Some are historically affiliated with a religious group, yet religious matters are not part of student life. Other schools exist, in part, to educate students in the doctrine and the practices of their own religious perspective. Information you find on these pages will give you answers to some of your initial questions about religious life at particular schools.

If connecting with and learning from members of your racial/ethnic heritage is important, you will find many colleges and universities from which to choose. Again, this guide provides information about the diversity of the campus and the composition of students who are white, African-American, Hispanic, Asian-American, Latino, and so forth.

GETTING THE MOST FROM YOUR CAMPUS VISIT

It is best not to eliminate any options without at least visiting a few campuses of different types to judge their feeling and style first hand.

To learn everything important about a college, you need more than the standard presentation and tour given to visiting students and parents. Plan your visit for a weekday during the school term. This will let you see how classes are taught and how students live. It also is the best time to meet faculty and staff members. If the college does not schedule group presentations or tours at the time you want, call the office of admissions to arrange for an individual tour and interview. (This is more likely at a small college.) At the same time, ask the admissions office to make appointments with people you want to meet.

To find out about a specific academic program, ask to meet the department chairperson or a professor. If you are interested in athletics, religion, or music, arrange to meet with the coach, the chaplain, or the conductor of the orchestra. Your parents will also want to talk to a financial aid counselor about scholarships, grants, and loans. The office of academic affairs can help with your questions about courses or the faculty. The office of student affairs is in charge of residence halls, health services, and extracurricular activities. Each of these areas has a dean or vice president and a number of assistants, so you should be able to get your questions answered even if you go in without an appointment.

Take advantage of a group presentation and tour if one is scheduled on the day of your visit. Much of what you learn may be familiar, but other students and parents will ask about some of the same things you want to know. Student tour guides are also good sources of information. They love to talk about their own courses, professors, and campus experiences.

Finally, explore the campus on your own. Check the condition of the buildings and the grounds. If they appear well maintained, the college probably has good overall management. If they look run down, the college may have financial problems that also make it scrimp on the book budget or laboratory supplies. Visit a service office, such as the registrar, career planning, or academic advising. Observe whether they treat students courteously and seem genuinely interested in helping them. Look at bulletin boards for signs of campus activities.

And, perhaps most importantly, talk to some of the students who are already enrolled at the college. They will usually speak frankly about weekend activities, whether they find it easy to talk to professors out of class, and how much drinking or drug abuse there is on campus. Most importantly, meeting other students will help you discover how friendly the campus is and whether the college will suit you socially and intellectually.

More than buildings and courses of study, a college is a community of people. Only during a campus visit can you experience the human environment in which you will live and work during four critical years.

25 CRITICAL QUESTIONS

The following questions form a checklist to evaluate each college or university you are considering. Use the profiles, material from the colleges, and your own inquiries and observations to get the answers.

1. Do I have a reasonable chance of being admitted?
2. Can my family manage the costs?
3. Is the overall size of the school right for my personality?
4. Is the location right? (Consider such specifics as region, distance from a major city, distance from home, and weather.)
5. Are class sizes right for my learning style and my need for involvement in class?
6. Will I be comfortable with the setting of the campus?
7. Are the housing and food services suitable?
8. Does the college offer the program I want to study? (Or, often more importantly, does the college offer people and classes that will help me decide what I want to study?)
9. Will the college push me academically, but not shove me?
10. Do the best professors teach undergraduate courses?
11. Can I change majors easily, if I need to?
12. Do students say the majority of classes are taught by fun, stimulating, interesting professors?
13. Is the library collection adequate and accessible?
14. Are computer facilities readily available and are campus networking opportunities up-to-date?
15. Is the connection to the Internet adequate?
16. Are there resources for career development?
17. Do the people in the financial aid, housing, and other service offices seem attentive and genuinely interested in helping students?
18. Are there opportunities for me to use my abilities on campus—for example, a musical or acting.
19. Does the campus seem well maintained and managed?
20. Will the college meet my religious and/or ethnic needs?

And, finally, the five most critical questions:

21. Is there a good chance I will be academically successful there?
22. Will I be happy as a student there?
23. Do I seem compatible with the student population? Do they seem to enjoy what I enjoy?
24. Does the student life seem in sync with my personality and my goals? Is the student life what I'm looking for in a college?
25. Does the college "feel" right for me?

Steven R. Antonoff
Sheldon Halpern
Barbara Aronson

SCORING HIGH ON ENTRANCE EXAMINATIONS

Take your entrance exams seriously. When the opportunity of a lifetime presents itself, you'd better be ready for everything life has to offer, or live with regrets forever.

2Lt Jocelyn Booker, United States Air Force Academy, Class of 2010

COLLEGE ENTRANCE EXAMINATIONS

By providing you with exactly the same information about each of the colleges in which you are interested, the book you are now reading, *Profiles of American Colleges*, will help you narrow down the list of colleges to which you will apply. Of course, your final decision will be influenced by many other factors, many of which are far more important: actual visits to the colleges; virtual visits on the Internet; viewings of videotapes; advice from guidance counselors, parents, teachers, and friends.

In much the same way, by providing college admissions officers with the same information about thousands of applicants, the results of college entrance exams can help them narrow down the list of students they are considering accepting. The results of these exams help admissions officers compare students with widely differing backgrounds. Students from different high schools in different states who earn the same grade in their biology classes, B+ say, have used different textbooks, have performed different labs, have taken different tests, and in general often exhibit great disparity in their level of mastery of the subject; indeed, even within the same school, a grade of B+ from one teacher might not represent the same level of accomplishment as a B+ from another teacher. However, a grade of 650 on the Biology SAT Subject Test, or a 4 on the Biology AP test means the same thing whether it was earned by a student from a rural community in Idaho, an inner-city school in New York, or a private prep school in Massachusetts. Because students all across the country take the same standardized test on the same day, colleges can give greater credence to the results of those tests than they can to the results of final exams from different schools.

KINDS OF COLLEGE ENTRANCE EXAMINATIONS

Although some students who go from high school to two-year community colleges do not take any college entrance tests, most do, and virtually all students who are applying to four-year colleges will take some of the following exams:

- PSAT/NMSQT or the Preliminary SAT/National Merit Scholarship Qualifying Test.
- SAT Reasoning Test.
- SAT Subject Tests.
- Advanced Placement (AP) Examinations.
- The ACT Assessment.

The PSAT/NMSQT

The PSAT/NMSQT measures verbal and mathematical reasoning necessary for success in college. It is a standardized test taken by students in high schools throughout the country in October of their junior year. The test consists of five sections: two 25-minute critical reading sections, two 25-minute math sections, and one 30-minute writing section.

This Preliminary SAT is also the qualifying test for the scholarship competition conducted by the National Merit Scholarship Corporation, an independent, nonprofit organization supported by grants from over 600 corporations, private foundations, colleges, and universities. All students whose scores are in the top 5% of students taking the exam that year receive National Merit Letters of Commendation. In addition, students whose scores are in the top 1% of those taking the exam that year become National Merit Semifinalists. Those who advance to finalist standing by meeting additional requirements compete for one-time National Merit $2000 Scholarships and renewable four-year Merit Scholarships, which may be worth as much as $2000 a year or more for four years.

In addition, this test is used by the National Achievement Scholarship Program for outstanding African-American students. Top-scoring African-American students in each of the regional selection units established for the competition continue in the competition for nonrenewable National Achievement $2000 Scholarships and for four-year Achievement Scholarships sponsored by more than 175 organizations.

Test-Taking Strategies for the PSAT/NMSQT

1. Know what to expect. Each critical reading section has sentence completion questions and reading comprehension questions. A few of the reading questions are based on short passages (often a single paragraph), whereas most are based on longer passages (typically four to seven paragraphs). The first math section has 20 multiple-choice questions; the second math section has 8 quantitative comparison questions and 10 questions for which no choices are provided and whose answers must be entered in a special grid. Calculators may be used on any question in the math sections. The writing skills section, which does *not* have an essay, has three types of multiple-choice questions that test your knowledge of standard written English (grammar and usage).

2. On average, wild guessing has no effect on your score. Educated guessing, on the other hand, can improve your score dramatically. On all multiple-choice questions, try to eliminate as many obviously incorrect answer choices as possible, and then guess from among the choices still remaining.

3. Expect easy questions at the beginning of each set of the same question type. Within each set (except for the reading comprehension questions), the questions progress from easy to difficult. In other words, the first sentence completion questions in a set will be easier than the last sentence completion questions in that set; the first grid-in questions will be easier than the last ones.

4. Take advantage of the easy questions to boost your score. Remember: each question is worth the same number of points. Whether it is easy or difficult, whether it takes you ten seconds or two minutes to answer, you get the same number of points for each question you answer correctly. Your job is to answer as many questions as you can without rushing so fast that you make careless errors. Take enough time to get those easy questions right!

You should be aware that there are eight primary changes coming to the PSAT/SAT. These begin with the PSAT offered in October 2015. The first SAT with the new changes is scheduled for March 2016. These changes affect the class of 2017 and beyond.

For detailed information on these changes, please refer to the SAT web sites below:

www.collegeboard.org/delivering-opportunity/sat/ redesign

www.collegeboard.org/delivering-opportunity/sat

The SAT

The SAT is a reasoning test consisting of three parts—critical reading, mathematical reasoning, and writing. It is designed to measure your ability to do college work. Part of the test deals with verbal skills with an emphasis on critical reading, including a double passage with different points of view. The critical reading sections measure the extent of your vocabulary, your ability to interpret and create ideas, and your ability to reason logically and draw conclusions correctly. The mathematics part measures your ability to reason with numbers and mathematical concepts. It tests your ability to handle general number concepts rather than specific achievement in mathematics. Calculators are permitted on each math section.

The writing part consists of a short essay and multiple-choice questions that test your knowledge of standard written English (grammar and usage).

The SAT is given on seven Saturdays during the year—once each in January, March, May, June, October, November, and December. Applicants may request, for religious reasons, to take the test on the Sunday following the regularly scheduled date.

You can register online at *www.collegeboard.org* or by mail by using the registration form available at your school.

On each part of the SAT—critical reading, math, and writing—you will receive a scaled score between 200 and 800. On each part the national mean is approximately 500.

Test-Taking Strategies for the SAT

1. Pace yourself properly. It is much better to slow down and avoid careless errors than it is to speed up in an effort to answer all the questions. You can earn an above-average score (over 1000) by correctly answering fewer than half of the questions on the test and omitting the rest. Even scores of 1300 can be achieved by omitting more than 20% of the questions.
2. Read carefully. Make sure you are answering the question asked, not a similar one you once encountered. Underline key words (e.g., NOT and EXCEPT) to make sure you do not answer the opposite of the question asked.
3. Learn the directions for each type of question before taking the test. During the test, do not waste even one second reading the directions or looking at the sample questions.
4. Always answer the easy questions first (the ones at the beginning of each section). Do not panic if you can't answer a question. Do not spend too much time on any one question. If you are truly stuck, make an educated guess if possible (see below), and move on. Remember that each question is worth the same one point, and the next few questions may be much easier for you.
5. On average, wild guessing does not affect your score—it is unlikely to help, but it is equally unlikely to hurt you. The choice is yours. However, educated guessing—when you can eliminate one or more of the answer choices—can significantly increase your score! In particular, don't omit critical reading questions if you have read the passage; you can always eliminate some of the choices. Most math questions contain at least one or two choices that are absurd (for example, negative choices when you know that the answer must be positive); eliminate them and guess.

SAT Subject Tests

These tests are one-hour multiple-choice question tests. You may take one, two, or three tests on any one test date. Some colleges do not require SAT Subject Tests. Of those that do, some colleges require specific subject tests, whereas others allow applicants to choose the ones they wish to present with the admission application. Those colleges that do require these tests may use them to determine acceptance or placement in college courses. The tests in foreign language are used not only for placement but also for possible exemption from a foreign language requirement. If the college of your choice does not require these tests but you would like to demonstrate proficiency in a particular field, take the test anyway and have your scores sent. Tests are given in literature, history, mathematics, sciences, and several foreign languages.

Advanced Placement (AP) Examinations

The College Board also conducts Advanced Placement tests, given to high school students who have completed advanced or honors courses and wish to get college credit. Many secondary schools offer college-level courses in calculus, statistics, art, psychology, European history, American history, Latin, Spanish, French, German, biology, chemistry, and physics. As a result of scores obtained on these tests, colleges grant credit or use the results for placement in advanced college courses.

The ACT Assessment

The registration form for the ACT includes a detailed questionnaire that takes about one hour to complete. As a result of the answers to those questions about your high school courses, personal interests, and career plans, plus the scores on your ACT, an ACT Assessment Student Report is produced. This is made available to you, your high school, and to any college or scholarship source that you request. Decisions regarding college acceptance and award of scholarships are the result. This information is kept confidential and is released only according to your written instructions. To obtain an ACT application form, log on to *www.actstudent.org*, and click on online registration. When you visit the website you will find answers to other questions you may have as well.

The ACT measures knowledge, understanding, and skills acquired in the educational process. The test is made up of four distinct sections: English, mathematics, reading, and science reasoning.

In addition, you may register to take an optional fifth section: a 30-minute writing test. Some colleges require their applicants to take the writing test, but most do not. Check with the colleges to which you will be applying to know whether you need to take the writing part of the ACT.

On the ACT, you should answer all questions, because your score is based on the number of questions you answer correctly. There is no penalty for wrong answers. For each of the four tests the total number of correct responses yields a raw score. A table is used to convert the raw scores to *scaled scores.* The highest possible scaled score for each test is 36. The average of the four scaled scores yields the *composite score.*

The ACT English Test is a 75-question, 45-minute test that measures punctuation, grammar, usage, and sentence structure. The test consists of five passages, each accompanied by multiple-choice test items.

Test-Taking Strategies for the ACT English Test

1. Pace yourself. You have 45 minutes to complete 75 questions.
2. Read the sentences immediately before and after the one containing an underlined portion.

The ACT Mathematics Test has 60 questions to answer in 60 minutes. The test emphasizes quantitative reasoning rather than memorized formulas. Five content areas are included in the mathematics test. About 14 questions deal with pre-algebra topics, such as operations with whole numbers, decimals, fractions, and integers and about 10 questions deal with elementary algebra. Usually 18 questions are based on intermediate algebra and coordinate geometry. About 14 questions are based on plane geometry and usually four items are based on right triangle trigonometry and basic trigonometric identities.

Test-Taking Strategies for the ACT Mathematics Test

1. Spend an average of one minute on each question, less on the easy questions, more on the difficult ones.
2. Be sure to answer each question even if you have to guess.
3. Make sure your answers are reasonable.

The ACT Reading Test is a 40-question, 35-minute test that measures reading comprehension. Three scores are reported for this test: a total score, a subscore based on the 20 items in the social studies and natural sciences sections, and a subscore on the 20 items in the prose fiction and humanities sections.

Test-Taking Strategies for the ACT Reading Test

1. Read each passage carefully. Underline important ideas in the passage.
2. Pace yourself. You have 40 questions to answer in 35 minutes.
3. Refer to the passage and in particular to your underlined sections when answering the questions.

The ACT Science Reasoning Test presents seven sets of scientific information in three different formats: data representations (graphs, tables, and other schematic forms); research summaries (description of experiments); and conflicting viewpoints. The 40 questions are to be answered in 35 minutes. The content of the test is drawn from biology, chemistry, physics, geology, astronomy, and meteorology. Background knowledge at the level of a high school general science course is all that is needed to answer these questions. The test emphasizes scientific reasoning skills rather than recall of scientific content, skill in mathematics, or reading ability.

Test-Taking Strategies for the ACT Science Reasoning Test

1. Read the scientific material before you begin answering a question. Read tables and text carefully, underlining important ideas.
2. Look for flaws in the experiments and devise ways of improving the experiments.
3. When you are asked to compare viewpoints, make notes in the margin of the printed material summarizing each viewpoint.

Beginning in the fall of 2015, students who took the ACT also received new readiness scores and indicators, which were designed to show performance and preparedness in areas important for success after high school. The addition of these new scores and indicators provide students, parents, and educators with a more detailed insight to better plan for future success.

For more information on these changes, please refer to the web site, *www.act.org*

A FINAL WORD

Don't take any examination without preparation, even though you will find descriptions of these tests that say they test skills developed over years of study both in and out of school. Don't walk in cold, even though you believe that you meet all the qualities colleges are looking for.

Although the College Board suggests no special preparation, it does distribute to applicants the booklet, "Taking the SAT Reasoning Test." It also makes available other publications containing former test questions along with advice on how to cope with the questions. Evidently, all candidates need some form of preparation.

The American College Testing Program furnishes the booklet, "Preparing for the ACT Assessment." This gives specific information about the test, test questions, and strategies for taking each of the four parts. It also describes what to expect on the test day and gives practice with typical questions.

Barron's Educational Series publishes books to help you prepare for these tests. They are available at all bookstores and in many libraries. You should be sure to use them before taking any of these tests.

Although no high school student takes all of the college-entrance exams described above, virtually all students planning to attend a four-year college take at least one of them—the SAT or ACT. Prepare conscientiously for each exam that you take and you will provide the colleges to which you are applying with valuable information about your abilities. Good luck!

Ira K. Wolf
President
PowerPrep, Inc.

Don't be afraid to be yourself in every aspect of the applications process. No admissions officer wants to see the proverbial "perfect" application; rather, they're looking for individuals with unique stories, interests and voices that will contribute to the college community.

Arielle Shipper, Connecticut College, Class of 2010

The college admission process—getting in—begins the minute you start making your first choices in course selection and in cocurricular activities in junior high school, middle school, and high school. These initial and ongoing decisions are crucial to your future well-being. They lay the groundwork for the curriculum you will follow throughout your high school career: they are not easily reversed. These are the decisions that will allow you to market yourself to the colleges of your choice.

STUDENTS TAKE NOTE!

There is a myth prevalent among college-bound students throughout the country that the best way to gain entrance to the selective colleges is to be well rounded. This term usually refers to students who have earned good grades in high school (B+ or better) and participated in a wide range of cocurricular activities.

However, most admission officers at the selective colleges prefer applications from candidates they term angular—students who have demonstrated solid academic achievement in and out of school *and* who have developed one or two particularly strong cocurricular skills, interests, and activities. These angular students are very different in character from the well-rounded students who are very good at everything, yet excel at little, if anything.

William Fitzsimmons, Dean of Admission at Harvard, says that Harvard is looking for a well-rounded class, which means Harvard is most interested in admitting angular students—students who have excelled at something. He cautions, though, that "...It is a mistake to denigrate or underestimate that persuasive power of high grades, rank, triple 800s on the SAT, 36 on the ACT, and equally impressive SAT Subject Test scores. The selective colleges take many of these academically high profile applicants. But the numbers game alone often won't get you in! It would be fairly simple for Harvard to enroll an entire freshman class with a superior academic profile and little depth of quality in areas that make up the personality of the class. We just would not do that!"

Dean Fitzsimmons is saying that the majority of the successful applicants to selective colleges must have some major commitment(s) combined with excellent academic qualities. A strong impact results from quality involvements rather than a proliferation of joinings and transient interests. Essentially, the angular applicant is a committed individual, while the well-rounded candidate is merely involved.

STUDENTS AND PARENTS TAKE AN EARLY, ACTIVE ROLE

Students and parents must make time to ensure an early, active role in the college admissions process. Each year, starting in the seventh grade, students and parents should take the time to sit down with the student's guidance counselor and talk meaningfully about the following:

- selection and level of courses, projecting through the senior year of high school;
- cocurricular activities available, such as drama, music, athletics, academic clubs, community activities, student government, and other special interest groups; and
- summer study, work, or recreation.

Why is this important to getting in? As sure as taxes and death, there is going to come a time in your senior year when you, the college-bound student, will be asked to choose colleges, complete the college application, write your college essay(s), and have an interview—either on the college campus, or in your hometown.

You must create the personal marketing, which will take place during the application process in your senior year, long before your senior year starts. By the time you reach that long-awaited dream of being a senior, you and you alone have created the person you must market to the colleges of your choice. You must understand that the person you have created is the only person you have to market. There is no Madison Avenue glitz involved in this marketing process! You don't create a pseudo marketing campaign that shows you jumping off a bridge with a bungee cord tied to your sneakers. Admission counselors can tell the difference between a real marketing effort and a pseudo marketing campaign.

THE APPLICATION FORM

Each college on-line application form differs from college to college, with the exception of those colleges that use the common application. When you start to work, be sure to note all deadlines, follow all directions, be complete, be neat, fill out the geographical data with accurate facts, and type it all (unless you print exceptionally well). Always review the entire application before you start to fill it out, and complete the entire application before you start the next one. Remember the application is *you* to the admissions committee member reading it. Even though "a book should not be judged by its cover," appearances do influence opinions.

It is best to work through a rough draft of the application before you actually work on the application copy to be submitted. Remember to make a copy of all parts of the finished application in the event that your submission gets lost and a replacement must be sent.

You are responsible for giving the Secondary School Report, found in each application, directly to your high school guidance counselor. Your counselor is responsible for sending official copies of grades, rank in class (if any), the school's profile, and a written recommendation regarding you. It also is your responsibility to call or fill out the appropriate forms for either the SAT and/or SAT Subject Tests or the ACT, to send the appropriate test information directly to each college to which you have applied, even if your scores are on your high school transcript. Your college file will not be considered complete, and will not be sent to the admission committee for a decision, without these official scores. Additionally, many colleges want recommendations from one or two teachers. Choose wisely and allow each teacher plenty of time. Request letters from teachers who know you best. If English is your interest, be sure to choose an English teacher. If you are fluent in Spanish and have future interest in Spanish at college, ask the Spanish teacher. Remember, though you have many interests and have participated in many activities—you are developing an admissions package as part of your marketing of yourself. Emphasize your strengths and show how they are integrated into your activities and achievements.

Cocurricular activities usually are athletic or nonathletic. If you have won athletic awards, note them. If you have had the starring role in the spring musical for the last two years, say so. If you are an editor on the school newspaper, specify this. Admissions people view your activities with special interest. They realize how very time consuming these activities can be and how they sometimes bring very few accolades. List these activities in the order of importance to you. If you do not believe that the application allows you the opportunity to show your depth of commitment to one or two cocurricular areas, you may add an addendum. Use the KISS (Keep It Short and Simple) method. This is an addendum, not an essay, letter, or dissertation. Be honest!

Some applications have mini essays. When space is provided, be sure you are concise, clear, and grammatically correct. Here, less is more. Your ability to organize your thoughts and present them concisely is being tested. You will receive your chance to impress each college with your prose in the long essay segment of the application. Some colleges have as many as four long essays, whereas some require none. In addition to the short and long essay questions, some colleges ask the student for a graded paper signed by the teacher.

Some colleges encourage you to support your application with additional materials. If you are given this option, consider what will strengthen your application: musical tapes, art and/or photography portfolios, published writings, an exceptional graded term paper, all the additional opportunities for the college to get to know you better and for you to increase your image as an angular candidate. Such additions help the admissions committee to get a better handle on who you are in relation to other applicants. Be sure your presentation is clear and as professional as possible. These additions are not going to be evaluated by the admissions committee. Your material will be directed to the appropriate department for evaluation and an evaluative note will be sent back to the admissions committee. It is this note that will become part of your admissions package, the same way an athletic coach evaluates potential student/athletes.

Proofread all parts of the application. Be sure you, the student, place your signature where it is required. If you are not sending your application on-line, then place everything, including the registration fee check, in a large manila envelope and give it to your college guidance counselor. After adding the completed Secondary School Report to the application, your guidance counselor will mail it. Your job is now finished and the waiting begins!

E-Mail, On-line Services through the College or the Internet

Applying online directly to the college(s) of your choice and communicating by e-mail has made the college application process less time consuming and easier than ever before. Certainly ecologically correct, by producing as close to a paperless process as possible, this method is still in cyberspace. Be sure you know what you are doing when you use any of these methods. It is seriously suggested that you take the time to call the college shortly after sending this type of application, to ensure that your application is on file. If you have an addendum or two, you may want to speak to an admission clerk to make sure each addendum has reached the office of admission in the format you desired. If it were my application and I chose any of these methods, I'd still send my musical tape, the slides for my art portfolio, and such, by certified or registered mail. Clarity is so important to the professionals who will be evaluating these addenda for your college admission process!

The Common Application

Almost all colleges in the United States have agreed that students may apply to their colleges by completing one common application. Some of the colleges using the common application also have their own application. Students applying to a college that allows an applicant a choice of using either the college's own application or the common application, obviously face a choice. The use of the common application substantially reduces the time spent composing different essay answers and neatly typing separate application forms. If you are one of those who must make a choice between the common application and the application of the college, you should understand that each college using the common application (either as its only application or as an alternative application) has the right to ask for a supplement. If you choose the common application, be very sure to read the pages surrounding the common application carefully. Each college has a paragraph in which they discuss their deadlines, requirements for admission, and specify if they require supplemental information. The supplemental information can range from an additional essay or two, to additional information about your cocurricular activities.

All the colleges participating in the common application have each member of their admission staff sign a statement that they will NOT discriminate in the admissions process among students who submit the common application versus students who submit the college's application. However, there are counselors who believe that when there is a choice, the applicant has a better chance of conveying information by using the college's application; there is a vast difference in format between the two applications, even if the college requires a supplement. Check with your guidance counselor if you are unsure regarding your choice of format. To access the common application online, go to:

www.commonapp.org

College Web Sites

Most colleges today have their own web site. Here you will find a wealth of information. Some colleges have even put their viewbook, course curriculum guide, a campus tour, as well as their application, on their site. Visit each college's web page—the addresses are in the Admissions Contact section of the college Profiles in this book. You'll be a much better informed consumer.

THE INTERVIEW

The interview is a contrived situation that few people enjoy, of which many people misunderstand the value, and about which everyone is apprehensive. However, no information from a college catalog, no friend's friend, no high school guidance counselor's comments, and no parental remembrances from bygone days can surpass the value of your college campus visit and interview. This first hand opportunity to assess your future alma mater will confirm or contradict other impressions and help you make a sound college acceptance.

Many colleges will recommend or request a personal interview. It is best to travel to the campus to meet with a member of the admissions staff if you can; however, if you can't, many colleges will arrange to have one of their representatives, usually an alumnus, interview you in your hometown.

Even though the thought of an interview might give you enough butterflies to lift you to the top of your high school's flagpole, here are some tips that might make it a little easier.

1. **Go prepared.** Read the college's catalog and this book's Profile ahead of time so you won't ask "How many books are in your library?" or "How many students do you have?" Ask intelligent questions that introduce a topic of conversation that you want the interviewer to know about you. The key is to distinguish yourself in a positive way from thousands of other applicants. Forge the final steps in the marketing process you have been building since your first choices in the college admission process back in junior high school. The interview is your chance to enhance those decisions.
2. **Nervousness** is absolutely and entirely normal. The best way to handle it is to admit it, out loud, to the interviewer. Richard Shaw, Dean of Undergraduate Admissions and Financial Aid at Stanford University, sometimes relates this true story to his apprehensive applicants. One extremely agitated young applicant sat opposite him for her interview with her legs crossed, wearing loafers on her feet. She swung her top leg back and forth to some inaudible rhythm. The loafer on her top foot flew off her foot, hit him in the

head, ricocheted to the desk lamp and broke it. She looked at him in terror, but when their glances met, they both dissolved in laughter. The moral of the story—the person on the other side of the desk is also a human being and wants to put you at ease. So admit to your anxiety, and don't swing your foot if you're wearing loafers! (And by the way, she was admitted.)

3. **Be yourself.** Nobody's perfect, and everyone knows nobody's perfect, so admit to a flaw or two before the interviewer goes hunting for them. The truly impressive candidate will convey a thorough knowledge of self.
4. **Interview the interviewer.** Don't passively sit there and allow the interviewer to ask all the questions and direct the conversation. Participate in this responsibility by assuming an active role. A thoughtful questioner will accomplish three important tasks in a successful interview:

   demonstrate interest, initiative, and maturity for taking partial responsibility for the content of the conversation;
   guide the conversation to areas where he/she feels most secure and accomplished; and
   obtain answers. Use your genuine feelings to react to the answers you hear. If you are delighted to learn of a certain program or activity, show it. If you are curious, ask more questions. If you are disappointed by something you learn, try to find a path to a positive answer. Then consider yourself lucky that you discovered this particular inadequacy in time.
5. **Parents** do belong in your college decision process as your advisers! Often it is they who spend the megabucks for your next four years. They can provide psychological support and a stabilizing influence for sensible, rational decisions. However, they do NOT belong in your interview session. In essence, the sage senior will find constructive ways to include parents in the decision-making process as catalysts, without letting them take over (as many are apt to do) the interview process. You may want your parents to meet and speak briefly to your interviewer prior to your interview and that is fine, but parents may not accompany you into the interview session! Arrange with your parents to meet somewhere out of the interview building after your interview is over. You do not want the interviewer inviting your parents back to the interview room. As intelligent as parents may be, they do not perceive the answers to questions the same way you do. The worst scenario I can imagine is the interviewer asking your parents some of the same questions that were asked you, and that is highly likely. Parents just answer questions differently than teenagers. At best, the scenario creates a long, long ride home, and when you get home you can't punish your parents by taking the car keys away from them, or grounding them for a week. At worst, the scenario has caused a blight in your admissions file. This is your time! Keep it that way!
6. **Practice makes perfect.** Begin your interviews at colleges that are low on your list of preferred choices, and leave your first-choice colleges until last. If you are shy, you will have a chance to practice vocalizing what your usually silent inner voice tells you. Others will have the opportunity to commit their inevitable first blunders where they won't count as much.
7. **Departing impressions.** There is a remarkable tendency for the student to base final college preferences on the quality of the interview only, or on the personal reaction to the interviewer as the personification of the entire institution. Do not do yourself the disservice of letting it influence an otherwise rational selection, one based on institutional programs, students, services, and environment. After the last good-bye and thank you has been smiled, and you exhale deeply on your way out the door, go ahead and congratulate yourself. If you used the interview properly, you will know whether or not you wish to attend that college and why.
8. **Send a thank-you note** to your interviewer. A short and simple handwritten or typed note will do—and if you forgot to mention something important about yourself at the interview, here's your chance.

WRITING THE COLLEGE ESSAY

Do the colleges read the essays you write on their applications? You bet your diploma they do. Here is your chance to strut your stuff, stand up, be counted, and stylize your way into the hearts of the decision makers.

Write it, edit it, review it. Rewrite it. Try to show why you are unique and how the college will benefit having you in its student body. This is not a routine homework assignment, but a college level essay that will be carefully examined for spelling, grammar, content, and style of a high school senior. As strenuous an effort as it may be, completing the essay gives the admissions committee a chance to know the real you, a three-dimensional human being with passions, preferences, strengths, weaknesses, imagination, energy, and ambition. Your ability to market yourself will help the deans and directors of admission remember your application from among the sea of thousands that flood their offices each year.

First, maximize your strengths—use your essays to say what you want to say. The answer to a specific question on the college's part still provides an opening for you to furnish background information about yourself, your interests, ambitions, and insights. For example, the essay that asks you to name your favorite book and the reason for your selection could be answered with the title of a Dr. Seuss book because you are considering a career as an elementary school teacher. If you are interested in business, read about a famous businessman you admire and then discuss your interest in business.

Whatever the essay questions are, autobiographical or otherwise, select the person or issue that puts you in the position to discuss the subject in which you are the most well versed. In essence, all of your essay responses are autobiographical in the sense that they will illustrate something important about yourself, your values, and the kind of person you are (or hope to become). If personal values are important to you, and they should be, then here is your opportunity to stress their importance.

Because many colleges will ask for more than one essay, make sure that the *sum* of the essays in any one college application covers your best points. Do not repeat your answers, even if the questions sound alike. Cover the most important academic and cocurricular activities (most important meaning the one in which you excelled and/or in which you spent the most quality time).

If you are fortunate to have a cooperative English teacher, you might request a critique of your first draft, but be sure to allow enough time for a careful evaluation and your revision.

Write the essays yourself—no substitutes or stand-ins. College admission professionals can discern mature adult prose from student prose.

PARTING WORDS

You may wish to ask yourself the following questions to help you decide which is your Paradise College. Most of this information is in the individual college Profiles in this book.

1. **Caliber of School Programs** Is the college known for its English department or chemistry department? What are its strengths?
2. **Selectivity of Admissions** Is the college Most Competitive, Highly Competitive, Very Competitive, Competitive, Less Competitive or Noncompetitive? Check the Selector Ratings.

3. **Chances of Admission** Be realistic. What are your chances of getting in? How far can you reach? Listen when you are given advice!
4. **Location of the School** Is the school near home, one hour away, 300 miles away, or across the United States?
5. **Rural, Suburban, Urban Campus** Is the school in the city or in a rural area?
6. **Size of the School** Can you spend four years at a small liberal arts college of 800 undergraduates? Do you need the larger atmosphere of a university? Do not equate size with social life!
7. **State College vs. Private College** Is the college a large state university with most of the student population from the state where it's located? Is it one of the public "Ivies"? Will you be a minority in the state school?
8. **Geographical Diversity** Is the college a regional one attracting students from the same state or region? Or is it a college, regardless of its size, which attracts students from all over the United States, or the world at large?
9. **Cost of College** What is the tuition? What are the living costs? What travel costs are there from home to campus? Are there hidden costs?
10. **Financial Aid** With a great percentage of undergraduates at many private colleges on financial aid of some type, where do you fit? What monies are available for the students at the schools of your choice? Is the college need blind in its admission program?
11. **Living Conditions** Is housing on campus guaranteed for all four years? Are the dorms coed? Are there single-sex dorms? Are alternatives in housing available?
12. **Socialization** Is it a grind school—all work, work, work? Is it fraternity- and sorority-oriented? What are the on-campus facilities for socialization?
13. **Safety on Campus** Are the dorms secure and locked? What's the safety system on the campus?
14. **Core Curriculum—Distribution Credits** Does the college require (for graduation) a specific number of credits in different academic disciplines? For example, does the student have to take six credits in philosophy before graduating? Is a self-designed curriculum possible?
15. **Sophomore Standing** Does the college accept AP credits? Does it offer advanced standing for an AP course, or just a credit toward graduation?
16. **Junior Year Abroad** Are there opportunities to study in Italy, Japan, or Australia, for example, while you are an undergraduate?
17. **Internships** Are there opportunities for hands-on experience while in college? Which departments have formal internship opportunities?
18. **Graduate School After College** What percentage of its graduates go on to graduate school immediately upon graduation, or within five years? What is the record of those who successfully get into the law, medical, or business school of their choice?
19. **Placement After Graduation** Is there an office for job placement after college? Is there an alumni network that helps in job placement?
20. **Weekend College** Do the students remain on campus on weekends, or is it a suitcase college?
21. **Minorities** What percentage of the students are minorities? Reflect on the racial, ethnic, and religious minority roles in the college you are considering. How would you feel being Jewish at a Roman Catholic college for example—or Catholic at a Jewish college?
22. **Sports Facilities** Is there a swimming pool? Are there horse stables? Is there an ice hockey rink on campus?
23. **Library Facilities** How many books are in the library? Is it computerized? Is the campus library tied into a larger network?
24. **Athletic Programs** Is the ice hockey team a varsity sport? Does the lacrosse team play Division I or III? Is basketball strong? Do they have a women's squash team?
25. **Honors Programs** Are honors programs available? What are they? Who is eligible?
26. **Student Body** Are the students politically active? Are they professional in orientation?
27. **Faculty** Are all classes taught by full professors? Or are TAs (teaching assistants) the norm?
28. **Computer Labs** Are computers required of incoming freshmen? What are the facilities on campus? Can you have your own PC in your room?
29. **Campus Visits** If possible, make a visit to the campus. Spend some time talking to students for a feel of the campus.
30. **Special Talents** Recognize your special talents and discover where they fit best. Often, a special talent becomes a scale-tipper in the admissions process.
31. **Special Family Circumstances** Talk with your parents about their expectations. Discuss your needs as well as their thoughts.
32. **Legacy** Does your family have a history at a specific school? Are you interested in continuing the tradition?
33. **Note Well—Final List** Be sure the final list is a realistic one. It should include "reaches," "targets," and "safeties." No matter which one admits you—it must fit!

Finding and applying to the best colleges for you is not supposed to be easy, but it can be fun. Parents, guidance counselors, and teachers are there to help you, so don't struggle alone. Keep your sense of humor and a smile on your face as you go about researching, exploring, and discovering your ideal college.

Last but not least is The Parent Credo: The right college is the one where your child will fit in scholastically and socially. Be realistic in your aspirations and support the child's choice!

Anthony F. Capraro, III, Ph.D.
President, Teach Inc.
College Counseling
Ocoee, Florida

FINDING THE MONEY

Sometimes getting more aid is a matter of simply applying for it.

Raymond A. Lutzky, Rensselaer Polytechnic Institute, Class of 2002

Postsecondary education is a major American industry. A greater proportion of students pursue postsecondary education in the United States than in any other industrialized country. Annually, more than 13 million students study at over 8000 institutions of higher learning. The diversity of our system of higher education is admired by educators and students throughout the world. There is no reason to believe that this system will change in the future. However, college costs and the resources available to parents and students to meet those costs have changed.

Unfortunately, many high school students and their parents believe either that there is no financial aid available or that they will not qualify for any type of financial assistance from any source. Neither assumption is correct. College costs have increased and will continue to increase. Federal allocations, for some financial aid programs, have decreased. But this decline has been met with generous increases in financial aid from state and school sources.

American students and their parents should realize that they must assume the primary role in planning to meet their future college costs and that the family financial planning process must begin much earlier than has been the case.

COLLEGE COSTS

- Nearly all parents believe college costs are too expensive.
- Currently, the average cost of education, including tuition and fees for one year at a public college would have been about $23,000 and for a private college and university, the cost could have exceeded $45,000.
- While college costs will increase each year, it is important to remember that currently a majority of all college students attend schools with tuition costs below $5,000.

STUDENT FINANCIAL AID

- As of 2015, the total amount of financial aid available from federal, state, and institutional sources to postsecondary students was approximately $170 billion.
- A majority of all students enrolled in higher education receive some type of financial assistance.
- Federal student aid remains the largest source of funding.
- Not long ago the majority of federal financial assistance was grants. Today, a greater amount of financial aid is from loan money.

TIMETABLE FOR APPLYING FOR FINANCIAL AID

Sophomore Year of High School

Most families wait until a child has been accepted into a college or university to begin planning on how the family will meet those college costs. However, a family's college financial planning should begin much earlier.

Students, as early as the sophomore year of high school, should begin a systematic search for colleges that offer courses of study that are of interest. There are many computer programs that can be helpful in this process. These programs can match a student's interest with colleges fitting the profile. Considering that half of all students who enter college either drop out or transfer to another school, this type of early selection analysis can be invaluable.

After selecting certain schools for further consideration, you should write to the school and request a viewbook, catalog, and financial aid brochure. After receiving this information, you and your family should compare the schools. Your comparison should include academic considerations as well as financial. Don't rule out a school because you think you can't afford it. Remember the financial aid programs at that school may be more generous than at a lower-priced school. If possible, visit the college and speak with both an admission and financial aid counselor. If it is not possible to visit all the schools, call the schools and obtain answers to your questions about admission, financial aid, and placement after graduation.

Junior Year of High School

The comparative analysis of colleges and universities that you began in your sophomore year should continue in your junior year. By the completion of your junior year, you and your parents should have some idea of what it will cost to attend and the financial aid policies of each of the schools you are considering.

Some colleges and universities offer prospective applicants an early estimate of their financial aid award. This estimate is based upon information supplied by the family and can provide assistance in planning a family's budget. Remember that for most families, financial aid from federal, state, and school sources will probably not meet the total cost of attendance.

Families should remember that college costs can be met over the course of the academic year. It is not necessary to have all of the money needed to attend school available at the beginning of the academic year. Student and family savings, as well as student employment throughout the year, can be used to meet college costs.

Senior Year of High School

January

By January of your senior year of high school you should know which colleges and universities you want to receive your financial aid application forms. Be certain that you have completed not only the federal financial aid application form, but also any necessary state or school forms. Read carefully all of the instructions. Application methods and deadline dates may differ from one college to another. Submit an application clean of erasures or notations in the margins, and sign all of the application forms.

February

You will receive a report from the service agency you selected containing information on your family's expected contribution and your eligibility for financial aid. You and your parents should discuss the results of the financial aid application with regard to family contribution, educational costs, and how those costs can be met.

March

Beginning in March, most colleges begin to make financial aid decisions. If your application is complete, your chances of receiving an award letter early are greater than if additional information is required.

The financial aid award letter you receive from your school serves as your official document indicating the amount of financial aid you will receive for the year. You must sign and return a copy of the award letter to your school if you agree to accept their offer of financial aid.

If your family's financial circumstances change and you need additional funding, you should make an appointment to speak with your school's financial aid director or counselor. College financial aid personnel are permitted to exercise professional judgment and make adjustments to a student's financial need. Your letter of appeal should state explicitly how much money you need and why you need it.

TIPS ON APPLYING FOR FINANCIAL AID

1. Families can no longer wait until a child is accepted into college before deciding how they will finance that education. Earlier college financial planning is necessary.
2. Families should assume a much more active role in locating the resources necessary to fund future college costs.
3. Families should assume that college costs will continue to increase.
4. Families should assume that in the future the federal government will not substantially increase financial aid allocations.
5. Families should obtain information on a wide range of colleges including the many excellent low-cost schools.
6. Families should seek information about all of the funding sources available at each school they are considering.
7. Families should seek the advice and expertise of financial experts for college financing strategies. College financial planning should specify the amount of money a family should invest or save each month in order to meet future college bills.
8. Families should investigate all of the legitimate ways of reducing their income and assets before filing for financial aid.
9. Families should know how financial aid is awarded and the financial aid policies and programs of each school they are considering.
10. Families should realize that although the job of financing a college education rests primarily with them, they probably will not be able to save the entire cost of their child's college education. They probably will be eligible to receive some type of financial aid from some source and they will have to borrow a portion of their child's college education costs.
11. Families should be advised that the federal government frequently changes the rules and regulations governing financial aid eligibility. Check with your high school guidance counselor or college financial aid administrator for the latest program qualifications.
12. Part-time employment during the school year and full-time employment during the summer should be a part of every family's financing plan.
13. Families should investigate all colleges and universities that offer three-year graduation options.
14. Not every student can afford to live on campus. Commuting to college is one way to reduce college costs
15. It is important to find out a school's policy on awarding financial aid on the basis of need and merit.
16. Check with the financial aid office on the availability of loan forgiveness programs.
17. Find out if the aid awarded in the first year will be awarded in subsequent years if the family income does not change.
18. Find out the statistics on graduating seniors: how many were employed or accepted to graduate schools at the time of graduation.
19. Plan for the future. What was the average debt of graduating students in each of the schools you applied to?
20. Going to college should be a family decision. All family members should be aware of the financial implications of attendance, not just for the first year, but for all four years.

Marguerite J. Dennis
Former Vice President for Enrollment
and International Programs
Suffolk University
Boston, Massachusetts

SURVIVING THE FRESHMAN YEAR

Explore the campus and make yourself aware of all it has to offer. Most colleges have what seems like an endless supply of resources for its students. By taking advantage of these resources sooner, rather than later, they will prepare you for the years to come.

Shannon Scott, James Madison University, Class of 2013

COLLEGE: IT'S DIFFERENT

In college you are likely to hear fellow students say, "I don't know what that prof *wants*, and she won't *tell* me." "I wrote about three papers in high school, and now they want one every week." Though these students may be exaggerating a bit, college *is* different, both in the quality and the amount of work expected. Sometimes in high school the basic concepts of a course are reduced to a set of facts on a study sheet, handed to students to be reviewed and learned for a test.

In college, it is the concepts and ideas that are most important. These can only be grasped through a real understanding of the facts as they interrelate and form larger patterns. Writing papers and answering essay questions on tests can demonstrate a genuine understanding of the concepts, and this is why they are so important to college instructors. Learning to deal with ideas in this way can be a long-term asset, developing your independence, intellectual interests, and self-awareness.

Don't be discouraged; you are not alone. Most of your fellow students are having equally difficult times adjusting to a new learning method. Persist, and you will improve, leading to a lifetime habit of critical thinking and problem solving that can benefit you in many important ways.

College is also different outside of classes. Now that you have the freedom to choose how to spend time and what types of relationships to make, you have a bewildering number of possibilities.

In high school, you competed against the entire population, and you did well enough to get accepted into college. But now the population has changed, and you are competing against the very best high school students, many of whom may have better academic profiles than you. Because of this reality, you need to be at your best from day one. Here are some tips to help you.

MAKING A GOOD IMPRESSION

Here you are, plopped down in a strange place, feeling a bit like Dorothy transported to Oz. Your first goal is to make a good impression, showing your best self to those who will be important in your life for the next four years and even longer.

Impressing Faculty Members Favorably

Faculty members come in all ranks, from the graduate assistant, who teaches part-time while pursuing a degree, to a lofty full professor, who teaches primarily graduate students. Though different in rank and seniority, they respond to their students in roughly the same ways. They are, after all, people, with families and relationships much like your own. To have a good working relationship with them, try the following suggestions:

- **Make up your own mind about your instructors.** Listening to other students talk about teachers can be confusing. If you listen long enough, you will hear arguments for and against each of them. Don't allow hearsay to affect your own personal opinion.
- **Get to know your instructors firsthand.** Set up a meeting, during regular office hours. Don't try to settle important issues in the few moments before and after class.
- **Approach a discussion of grades carefully.** If you honestly believe that you have been graded too low, schedule a conference. Do not attack your instructor's integrity or judgment. Instead, say that you had expected your work to result in a better grade and would like to know ways to improve. Be serious about overcoming faults.
- **Don't make excuses.** Instructors have heard them all and can rarely be fooled. Accept responsibility for your mistakes, and learn from them.
- **Pay attention in class.** Conversing and daydreaming can insult your instructor and inhibit the learning process.
- **Arrive ahead of time for class.** You will be more relaxed, and you can use these moments to review notes or talk with classmates. You also demonstrate to your instructor a commitment to the class.
- **Participate in class discussions.** Ask questions and give answers to the instructor's questions. Nothing pleases an instructor more than an intelligent question that proves you are interested and prepared.
- **Learn from criticism.** It is an instructor's job to correct your errors in thinking. Don't take in-class criticism personally.

Impressing Fellow Students Favorably

Relationships with other students can be complex, but there are some basic suggestions that may make life easier in the residence halls and classrooms:

- **Don't get into the habit of bragging.** Frequent references to your wealth, your outstanding friends, your social status, or your family's successes are offensive to others.
- **Don't pry.** When your fellow students share their feelings and problems, listen carefully and avoid any tendency to intrude or ask embarrassing questions.
- **Don't borrow.** Borrowing a book, a basketball, or a few bucks may seem like a small thing to you, but some people who have trouble saying no may resent your request.
- **Divide chores.** Do your part; agree on a fair division of work in a lab project or a household task.
- **Support others.** Respect your friends' study time and the "Do not disturb" signs on their doors. Helping them to reach their goals will help you as well.
- **Allow others to be upset.** Sometimes, turning someone's anger into a joke, minimizing their difficulties, or belittling their frustration is your worst response. Support them by letting them release their emotions.
- **Don't preach.** Share your opinions when asked for, but don't try to reform the world around you.
- **Tell the truth.** Your reputation is your most important asset. When you make an agreement, keep it.

MANAGING YOUR TIME

Everyone, no matter how prominent or how insignificant, has 168 hours a week to spend. In this one asset we are all equal. There are students on every college campus, however, who seem to accomplish all their goals and still find time for play and socializing. There are others who seem to be alternating between frantic dashes and dull idleness, accomplishing very little. To the first group, college is a happy, fulfilling experience; to the latter, it is maddeningly frustrating. The first group has gained control of time, the second is controlled by that elusive and precious commodity.

- **Know where your time goes.** Unfortunately, we cannot store up time as we do money, to be used when the need is greatest. We use it as it comes, and it is amazing how it sometimes comes slowly (as in the last five minutes of a Friday afternoon class) or quickly (as in the last hour before a final exam). The first step in controlling time is to determine exactly how you use it. For a while, at least, you should carefully record how much time you spend in class, going to and from class, studying, sleeping, eating, listening to music, watching television, and running errands. You need to know what happens to your 168 hours. Only then can you make sensible decisions about managing them.

- **Make a weekly schedule.** You can schedule your routine for the week, using the time plan forms available at most college bookstores or by making your own forms.
- **First schedule the inflexible blocks of time.** Your class periods, transportation time, sleeping, and eating will form relatively routine patterns throughout the week. Trying to shave minutes off these important activities is often a mistake.
- **Plan your study time.** It is preferable, though not always possible, to set your study hours at the same time every weekday. Try to make your study time *prime time,* when your body and mind are ready for a peak performance.
- **Plan time for fun.** No one should plan to spend four years of college as a working robot. Fun and recreation are important, but they can be enjoyed in short periods just as well as long. For example, jogging with friends for 30 minutes can clear the mind, tone up the muscles, and give you those all-important social contacts. Parties and group activities can be scheduled for weekends.
- **Be reasonable in your time allotments.** As you progress through your freshman year, you will learn more precisely how much time is required to write a paper or complete a book report. Until then, schedule some extra minutes for these tasks. You are being unfair to yourself by planning one hour for a job that requires two.
- **Allow flexibility.** The unexpected is to be expected. There will be interruptions to your routine and errands that must be run at certain times. Allow for these unforeseen circumstances.

LISTENING AND NOTE-TAKING IN CLASS

Listening

If you're interested in really improving your chances for success in college, you'll want to evaluate your listening skills to see if there are changes that you need to make. You'll also want to become familiar with note-taking strategies that can help you get more out of a lecture or PowerPoint presentation.

There is a difference between hearing and listening. Hearing just means that your ears are doing what they're designed to do; they're picking up sound waves. Listening requires that you pay attention and process information for later retrieval.

Here are some helpful tips for active listening.

1. Check the syllabus so that you'll be ready to discuss the topic for the day. Also, be sure to see if there's an assignment due in class so that you won't be caught off guard.
2. Reading the assignment before going to class really increases the chance of you being able to understand what is being presented. (Reading before class lays the foundation for the material that is given in class.)
3. Regular attendance at class is important, whether a professor requires it or not. Make class attendance a top priority and attend all classes.
4. Prepare mentally to pay attention to gain as much information as you can.
5. Sit in the "T-zone," or what is referred to in the military as "front and center."
6. Watch your posture. Don't slouch, but sit up straight and focus on what is being said or shown.
7. Do your best to stay healthy. Exercise, good nutrition, and adequate rest can all contribute to your being an active listener in class.

Being a more active listener can definitely lead to greater academic success.

Distractions can be a major problem in class, so here are some tips that may help you win the battle over distractions:

1. Don't sit with a friend.
2. Take careful notes. Taking notes helps you stay focused and can help all types of learners gain more information from a lecture.
3. Drinking water during class may help keep you from getting tired.
4. Avoid distractions during class such as the Internet, e-mail, or cell phones.
5. If you find yourself distracted by hunger, eat something before class or bring a "quiet" snack.
6. Plan ahead so that you arrive on time.

Note-taking

Effective note-taking will provide more material that will help you prepare adequately for tests and quizzes.

Tips for Effective Note-taking:

If you plan on handwriting your notes, consider the following:

1. Using a three ring binder with dividers for each subject is an effective way to take notes. Handouts don't get misplaced. They can easily be punched and added to notes taken in class. Notes can be removed and grouped together when studied.
2. Record the information from PowerPoints, drawings, charts, etc. when copies are not provided for the class.
3. Consider talking to professors and having them assess your note-taking in their classes.

The amount of material that you record should reflect the emphasis that was placed on the subject during the lecture.

You may want to take notes on your computer, but there are some things to consider:

1. The use of a computer in class is receiving mixed reviews from professors. Some welcome technology as a learning aid, while others reject it because it is a distraction.
2. If you want to take notes on your computer, you need to ask each professor.
3. Determine what note-taking or word processing software you're going to use. You may be able to use note-taking software, such as Notes PP or Microsoft OneNote. Most note-taking software allows you to easily format and customize your notes. If you choose word processing software, make sure you don't waste too much time formatting during the lecture. This could lead to missing valuable information given by your professor.
4. Power up your lap top prior to class. If possible, sit by a power outlet. This will ensure that your computer won't go dead during the middle of a lecture. Turn the brightness of your monitor down, so as not to draw attention to yourself. Make sure you have the mute function turned on.

5. Avoid distractions, such as instant messaging, e-mail, and the Internet.
6. Use the keyboard or a computer pen tablet. Keyboards allow you to type data, while you'll be able to draw and write notes with the help of a computer pen tablet. You may choose to stick with the keyboard method if you type faster than you write. For certain classes, such as engineering and science, you may find that the computer pen tablet provides you with greater note-taking flexibility.

You should be aware that some recent research indicates that taking notes on a computer is less effective than on paper, so choose wisely.

Note-taking Systems

There are several styles of taking notes:

Outline. This works best when the professor presents material in a very structured format. It's easy when main points and subpoints are clearly identified during a presentation. Outlining increases retention and memory recall, because you are determining how points relate to one another as you record them.

Block Style. This is very similar to outlines, but without the Roman numerals and letters. Main ideas are written flush with the left margin. Subpoints and bullets are indented to indicate their relationship to the main points.

Paragraphs. This works well when a main theme is presented with ideas and examples supporting it.

Visual (or Concept) Maps. They are made up of lines and circles. They help you to be able to see how each part fits together to form the whole picture. These maps work great for visual learners.

STUDYING EFFECTIVELY

Your most important activity in college is studying. Efficient study skills separate the inept student (who may spend just as many hours studying as an "A" student) from the excellent student, who thinks while studying and who uses common sense strategies to discover the important core of courses. The following suggested game plan for good study has worked in the past; it can work for you.

- **Make a commitment.** It is universally recommended that you spend two hours studying for every hour in class. At the beginning of your college career, be determined to do just that. It doesn't get easy until you make up your mind to do it.
- **Do the tough jobs first.** If certain courses are boring or particularly difficult, study them first. Don't read the interesting, enjoyable materials first, saving the toughies for the last sleepy twinges of your weary brain.
- **Study in short sessions.** Three two-hour sessions, separated from each other by a different activity, are much better than a long six-hour session.
- **Use your bits of time.** Use those minutes when you're waiting for a bus, a return call, laundry to wash, or a friend to arrive. Some of the best students I know carry 3 × 5 cards filled with definitions, formulas, or equations and learn during brief waiting periods. Most chief executives form the habit early of using bits of time wisely.

Digesting a Textbook

1. **Preview chapters.** Before you read a chapter in your textbook, preview it. Quickly examine the introductory paragraphs, headings, tables, illustrations, and other features of the chapter. The purpose is to discover the major topics. Then you can read with increased comprehension because you know where the author is leading.
2. **Underline the important points as you read.** Underlining should never be overdone; it can leave your textbook almost completely marked and less legible to read. Only the major ideas and concepts should be highlighted.
3. **Seven categories of information are commonly found in textbooks.** Be particularly alert when you see the following; get your marking pen ready.
   Definitions of terms.
   Types or *categories* of items.
   Methods of accomplishing certain tasks.
   Sequences of events or stages in a process.
   Reasons or *causes*.
   Results or *effects*.
   Contrasts or *comparisons* between items.
4. **Repeat information you need to learn.** When the object is to learn information, nothing is so effective as reciting the material, either silently or aloud.
5. **Don't read all material the same way.** Decide what you need to learn from the material and read accordingly. You read a work of fiction to learn the characters and the narrative; a poem, to learn an idea, an emotion, or a theme: a work of history, to learn the interrelationships of events. Do not read every sentence with the same speed and concentration; learn when to skim rapidly along. Remember, your study time is limited and the trick is to discriminate between the most important and the least important. No one can learn *everything* equally well.
6. **The five-minute golden secret.** As soon as possible after class is over—preferably at your desk in the classroom—skim through the chapter that has just been covered, marking the points primarily discussed. Copy what was written on the board. Now you know what the professor thinks is important!

TAKING TESTS SKILLFULLY

Try to predict the test questions. At some college libraries, copies of old examinations are made available to students. If you can legally find out your professor's previous test methods do so.

Ask your professor to describe the format of the upcoming test: multiple-choice? true-false? essay questions? problems? Adjust your study to the format described.

Listen for clues in the professor's lecture. Sometimes the questions posed in class have a way of reappearing on tests. If a statement is repeated several times or recurs in a subsequent lecture, note it as important.

As you review for the test, devise questions based on the material, and answer them. If you are part of a study group, have members ask questions of the others.

Common Sense Tactics

Arrive on the scene early; relax by breathing deeply. If the instructor gives instructions while distributing the test, listen very carefully.

- **Scan the whole test first.** Notice the point value for each section and budget your time accordingly.
- **Read the directions carefully** and then reread them. Don't lose points because you misread the directions.
- **Answer the short, easy questions first.** A bit of early success stimulates the mind and builds your confidence.
- **Leave space between answers.** You may think of a brilliant comment to add later.
- **Your first instinct is often the best** in answering true-false and multiple-choice questions. Look for qualifiers such as *never, all, often,* or *seldom* in true-false statements. Usually a qualifier that is absolute (*never, all,* or *none*) will indicate a false statement. Work fast on short-answer questions: they seldom count many points.

- **Open-book tests are no picnic.** Don't think that less study is required for an open-book test. They are often the most difficult of all examinations. If the material is unfamiliar, you won't have time to locate it and learn it during the test period.

Important Essay Strategies

- **Read the question carefully** and find out exactly what is asked for. If you are asked to contrast the French Revolution with the American Revolution and you spend your time describing each, without any contrasting references, your grade will be lowered.
- **Know the definitions of key words** used in essay questions:
  - **analyze:** discuss the component parts.
  - **compare:** examine for similarities.
  - **criticize:** give a judgment or evaluation.
  - **define:** state precise meaning of terms.
  - **describe:** give a detailed picture of qualities and characteristics.
  - **discuss:** give the pros and cons: debate them, and come to a conclusion.
  - **enumerate:** briefly mention a number of ideas, things, or events.
  - **evaluate:** give an opinion, with supporting evidence.
  - **illustrate:** give examples (illustrations) relating to a general statement.
  - **interpret:** usually means to state in other words, to explain, make clear.
  - **outline:** another way of asking for brief listings of principal ideas or characteristics. Normally the sentence or topic outline format is not required.
  - **prove:** give evidence and facts to support the premise stated in the test.
  - **summarize:** give an abbreviated account, with your conclusions.
- **Write a short outline** before you begin your essay. This organizes your thinking, making you less likely to leave out major topics.
- **Get to the point immediately.** Don't get bogged down in a lengthy introduction.
- **Read your essay over** before you hand it in. Words can be left out or misspelled. Remember that essay answers are graded somewhat subjectively, and papers that are correctly and neatly written make a better impression.
- **Learn from your test paper** when it is returned. Students who look at a test grade and discard the paper are throwing away a valuable tool. Analyze your mistakes honestly; look for clues for improvement in the professor's comments.

WRITING A TERM PAPER

Doing convincing library research and writing a term paper with correct footnotes and bibliography is a complicated procedure. Most first-year English composition courses include this process. Good students will work hard to master this skill because they know that research papers are integral parts of undergraduate and graduate courses.

Many students make the mistake of waiting until near the deadline to begin a term paper. At the busy end of the term, with final exams approaching, they embark on the uncertain time span of research and writing. Begin your term paper early, when the library staff is unhurried and ready to help and when you are under less pressure. It will pay dividends.

REGULATING YOUR RELATIONSHIPS

Find your special friends who believe in your definition of success. In a fast-paced environment like college, it is important to spend most of your time with people who share your ideas toward learning, where you can be yourself, without defensiveness. To find your kind of friends, first ask yourself: What is success? Is it a secure position and a comfortable home? A life of serving others? A position of power with a commodious executive suite? A challenging job that allows you to be creative? When you have answered honestly, you will have a set of long-range personal goals, and you can begin looking for kindred souls to walk with you on the road to success.

There will be, of course, some persons around you who are determined not to succeed, who for some reason program their lives for failure. Many college freshmen never receive a college degree; some may start college with no intention of passing courses. Their goal is to spend one hectic term as a party animal. If you intend to succeed at college, spending time among this type will be a considerable handicap. Consider making friends who will be around longer than the first year.

If possible, steer clear of highly emotional relationships during your first year of college. You don't have time for a broken heart, and relationships that begin with a rush often end that way.

MAINTAINING YOUR HEALTH

Poor health can threaten your success in the first year of college as nothing else can. No matter how busy you are, you must not forget your body and its needs: proper food, sufficient sleep, and healthy exercise. Many students, faced with the stress of college life, find themselves overmunching junk foods and gaining weight. Guard against this. Drugs and alcohol threaten the health and the success of many college students.

A FINAL WORD

So there it is. If you have read this far, you probably have a serious interest in succeeding in your first year of college. You probably have also realized that these suggestions, even if they sound a bit preachy, are practical and workable. They are based on many years of observing college students.

Benjamin W. Griffith
Former Dean,
University of West Georgia
Carrollton, Georgia

PART II

COLLEGE FACTS AND FINANCES

Now that you've read through Part I, you'll need specific information on the colleges that best match your needs and aptitudes. Here's where you'll find essential information in a nutshell.

Facts and figures on all schools are listed in chart form to help you make quick and easy comparisons. Thumbnail data include:

- campus environment
- degrees offered
- composition of the student body
- enrollment figures
- test scores of entering freshmen
- fall application deadlines

You'll also see at a glance how much it's going to cost you for tuition, room-and-board, and related expenses. In-state costs are broken down on a state-by-state basis, each range starting with colleges that don't charge tuition and going up the scale to the most expensive schools.

COLLEGES AT A GLANCE

The charts on these pages present some of the basic data that initially concerns many students. All of the four-year accredited schools in the United States are listed here alphabetically by state. The type of college environment (from urban to rural) is given, followed by degrees offered and whether the institution is public or private. Information about whether the student body is coed or primarily men or women, and whether fraternities or sororities are on campus follows. The undergraduate enrollment for the fall of 2016 is given as well as the median test scores for freshmen who took the ACT or the SAT. Finally, the fall admissions deadline is shown. "Open" usually indicates that admission applications will be accepted until a few weeks before classes begin.

NAME OF SCHOOL	TOWN	ENVIRONMENT U-Urban R-Rural SU-Suburban SM-Small Town	DEGREES AWARDED A-Associate B-Bachelor M-Master D-Doctorate	CONTROL Pri-Private, Pub-Public	FRATERNITIES AND SORORITIES F-Fraternities S-Sororities F, S-Both No-Neither	STUDENTS: C-Coed M-Men W-Women PM-Primarily Men PW-Primarily Women	UNDERGRADUATE ENROLLMENT FALL 2016	TEST SCORES: ACT Median	ACT Below 21	ACT 21-23	ACT 24-26	ACT 27-28	ACT Above 28	SAT CRITICAL READING Median	SAT CR Below 500	SAT CR 500-599	SAT CR 600-700	SAT CR Above 700	SAT MATHEMATICS Median	SAT M Below 500	SAT M 500-599	SAT M 600-700	SAT M Above 700	SAT WRITING Median	SAT W Below 500	SAT W 500-599	SAT W 600-700	SAT W Above 700	APPLICATION DEADLINE Month / Day
Alabama																													
Alabama A&M University	Normal	SU	A,B,M,D		F,S	C	4,415																						7/15
Alabama State University	Montgomery	SM	B,M,D	Pub	F,S	C	4,764	17	60	34	5			434	79	16	4	1	430	79	14	6							7/30
Amridge University	Montgomery	U	A,B,M,D	Pri	No	C	322																						Open
Auburn University	Auburn	SM	B,M,D		F,S	C	22,658	27			15	52	32	570	11	53	28	8	580	11	45	32	12	560	18	52	26	5	2/1
Auburn University at Montgomery	Montgomery	SU	B,M,D		F,S	C	4,273	21			74	26		483	78	11	11		471	67	33			430	88	13			8/1
Birmingham-Southern College	Birmingham	U	B	Pri	F,S	C	1,346	26			29	50	21	550	31	45	21	3	560	20	47	28	5		16	45	28	12	2/1
Concordia College - Alabama	Selma	SM	A,B	Pri	No	C	600																					12	2/1
Faulkner University	Montgomery	U	A,B,M,D	Pri	F,S	C	2,564	21		1	70	28	1	470	67	26	7		490	59	37	4		450	70	26	4		Open
Huntingdon College	Montgomery	SU	B	Pri	F,S	C	1,148	21		11	63	24	2	472	58	37	5		476	60	33	7							Open
Jacksonville State University	Jacksonville	SM	B,M,D	Pub	F,S	C	7,561																						Open
Judson College	Marion	SM	A,B	Pri	No	PW	347		60	18	6	8	8		17	16	50	17			50	50			17	33	50		Open
Miles College	Birmingham	U	B	Pri	F,S	C	1,634																						Open
Oakwood University	Huntsville	SU	A,B	Pri	No	C	2,000																						Open
Samford University	Birmingham	SU	B,M,D	Pri	F,S	C	3,341	26		1	26	54	19	570	16	45	31	8	550	22	44	27	5	560	18	48	28	5	7/1
Spring Hill College	Mobile	SU	B,M	Pri	F,S	C	1,395	24			43	49	8	553	20	49	29	2	547	22	60	16	2						7/15
Stillman College	Tuscaloosa	SM	B		F,S	C	1,580																						7/15
Talladega College	Talladega	SM	B		F,S	C	740																						Open
Troy University	Troy	R	A,B,M	Pub	F,S	C	14,064																						Open
Tuskegee University	Tuskegee	R	B,M,D	Pri	F,S	C	2,598	21	17	61	15	6	1	500	67	27	4		480	64	26	8							Open
University of Alabama	Tuscaloosa	SU	B,M,D	Pub	F,S	C	26,234																						3/1
University of Alabama at Birmingham	Birmingham	U	B,M,D	Pub	F,S	C	12,369	25			41	40	19																6/1
University of Alabama in Huntsville	Huntsville	SU	B,M,D	Pub	F,S	C	6,507				23	43	34		13	38	35	13		9	34	38	19						8/20
University of Mobile	Mobile	SU	A,B,M	Pri	No	C	1,466	22							67	24	9			64	33	3							8/1
University of Montevallo	Montevallo	SM	B,M	Pub	F,S	C	2,409	23																					8/1
University of North Alabama	Florence	U	B,M	Pub	F,S	C	6,313																						Open
University of South Alabama	Mobile	SU	B,M,D	Pub	F,S	C		24		6	53	35	5	512	42	37	19	2	502	42	40	18		507	52	34	13	1	7/15
University of West Alabama	Livingston	SM	A,B,M	Pub	F,S	C	1,978	20																					Open
Alaska																													
Alaska Pacific University	Anchorage	SU	A,B,M	Pri	No	C	545																						8/1
University of Alaska Anchorage	Anchorage	U	A,B,M	Pub	No	C		21						510	43	37	18	3	505	43	40	15	2	490	55	34	12	1	8/1
University of Alaska Fairbanks	Fairbanks	SM	A,B,M,D	Pub	F,S	C	3,597	24		7	42	41	10	560	23	45	27	5	550	26	41	25	7	530	32	43	22	3	6/15
University of Alaska Southeast	Juneau	SU	A,B,M	Pub	No	C	2,095																						8/1
Arizona																													
Arizona State University at the Downtown Phoenix Campus	Phoenix	U	B,M,D	Pub	No		9,238	23		6	45	42	7	540	30	46	22	2	530	32	45	21	3						2/1
Arizona State University at the Polytechnic Campus	Mesa	SU	B,M,D	Pub	No	C	3,869	25		3	35	46	16	550	26	45	19	9	580	17	38	35	10						2/1
Arizona State University at the Tempe Campus	Tempe	U	B,M,D	Pub	F,S	C	42,477	25		2	32	49	17	560	22	41	28	9	580	17	39	34	11						2/1
Arizona State University at the West Campus	Glendale	U	B,M,D	Pub	No	C	3,264	23		6	49	38	7	525	34	44	18	3	530	31	50	18	1						2/1
Embry-Riddle Aeronautical University - Prescott Campus	Prescott	R	B,M	Pri	F,S	C	2,377	27		2	23	47	28	570	21	38	33	8	600	15	30	45	10	535	31	43	21	4	7/1
Grand Canyon University	Phoenix	SU	B,M,D	Pri	No	C	27,680																						8/22
Northern Arizona University	Flagstaff	SM	B,M,D	Pub	F,S	C	26,506	23		11	48	36	5		39	42	17	2		38	44	16	2		47	40	12	1	Open
Prescott College	Prescott	SM	B,M,D	Pri	No	C	545	23	8	42		33	17	565	29	41	18	12	520	44	26	24	6	534	33	50	11	6	8/15
SAGU American Indian College	Phoenix	SM	A,B		No	C	130																						8/14
University of Arizona	Tucson	U	B,M,D		F,S	C	34,072	22		7	37	43	13	515	31	41	23	5	525	27	41	26	6	515	37	42	17	4	11/5
Arkansas																													
Arkansas Baptist College	Little Rock	SM	A,B	Pri	F,S	C	1,193																					4	11/5
Arkansas State University	State University	SM	A,B,M,D	Pub	F,S	C	9,592	24	20	30	26	14	11	420	64	36			500	44	36	20		450	80	20			8/18
Arkansas Tech University	Russellville	SM	A,B,M,D	Pub	F,S	C	11,053	22		17	47	32	4	465	67	33			500	47	47	7							Open
Harding University	Searcy	SM	B,M,D	Pri	No	C	4,419	25		4	34	43	19	550	23	43	25	9	550	32	38	26	4						6/1
Henderson State University	Arkadelphia	SM	A,B,M	Pub	F,S	C	3,052	22		15	50	30	5	460	58	21	18	1	510	48	30	18	1						8/18
Hendrix College	Conway	SU	B,M	Pri	No	C	1,322	28	1	12	18	18	51	603	10	35	34	21	606	7	36	43	14						11/15
John Brown University	Siloam Springs	SM	A,B,M	Pri	No	C	1,670	26		3	26	52	19	600	18	32	41	10	540	29	43	23	5	530	22	48	27	4	5/1
Lyon College	Batesville	SM	B	Pri	F,S	C	690	24		1	45	43	10	530	48	39	6	6	550	24	63	12		510	57	36	6		8/1
Ouachita Baptist University	Arkadelphia	SM	A,B	Pri	F,S	C	1,494	24		6	40	38	16	539	32	35	29	4	539	33	43	23	1						Open

Philander Smith College	Little Rock	U	B	Pri	F,S	C	732	18	81	9	8	1	1	450	67	29	5		439	62	38			437	76	24			7/15
Southern Arkansas University	Magnolia	SM	A,B,M	Pub	F,S	C	3,036																						Open
University of Arkansas at Fayetteville	Fayetteville	U	B,M,D	Pub	F,S	C	22,548	26			26	54	20	550	22	49	25	4	560	19	45	31	5						8/1
University of Arkansas at Little Rock	Little Rock	U	A,B,M,D	Pub	F,S	C	7,720	21	10	55			35	395	95	5			485	5	58	11							Open
University of Arkansas at Monticello	Monticello	SM	A,B,M	Pub	F,S	C	3,363		63	19	13	3	2																Open
University of Arkansas at Pine Bluff	Pine Bluff	SM	A,B,M,D	Pub	F,S	C	2,545																						8/1
University of Central Arkansas	Conway	SM	A,B,M,D	Pub	F,S	C	9,616					40	12																Open
University of the Ozarks	Clarksville	SM	B	Pri	No	C	660																						4/1
Williams Baptist College	Walnut Ridge	R	A,B	Pri	No	C	465	21																					Open

California

American Jewish University - College of Arts and Sciences Campus	Los Angeles	SU	B,M	Pri	No	C	110																						5/31
ArtCenter College of Design	Pasadena	SU	B,M	Pri	No	C	1,565																						Open
Ashford University	San Diego	SM	A,B,M	Pri	No	C	45,348																						Open
Azusa Pacific University	Azusa	SM	B,M,D	Pri	No	C	5,883	24		4	42	44	10	530	32	45	21	3	540	4	34	21	2						5/1
Biola University	La Mirada	SU	B,M,D	Pri	No	C		25						555	26	42	26	5	555	26	44	25	5	550	27	43	25	5	3/1
California Baptist University	Riverside	SU	A,B,M,D	Pri	No	C	6,937	22		16	52	29	3	480	54	32	13	1	480	55	32	12	1	470	57	35	7	1	Open
California College of the Arts	San Francisco	SM	B,M	Pri	F,S	C	1,533	24		7	44	40	9	534	36	38	23	3	550	35	25	28	12	526	39	33	24	4	Open
California Institute of Technology	Pasadena	SU	B,M,D	Pri	No	C		35					100	765			8	92	785				100	760			9	91	1/3
California Institute of the Arts	Valencia	SU	B,M,D	Pri	No	C	895																						1/5
California Lutheran University	Thousand Oaks	SU	B,M,D	Pri	No	C	2,892	25		1	37	52	9	545	25	51	22	2	553	22	48	27	3	541	26	51	23	1	1/1
California Polytechnic State University	San Luis Obispo	SU	B,M	Pub	F,S	C		29						610	6	36	44	14	645	1	27	46	25						11/30
California State Polytechnic University, Pomona	Pomona	SU	B,M,D	Pub	F,S	C	23,731	23		10	40	40	10	500	49	35	14	2	530	37	36	22	5						11/1
California State University, Maritime Academy	Vallejo	SU	B	Pub	No	C	868																						11/1
California State University, Bakersfield	Bakersfield	SM	B,M	Pub	F,S	C	7,118	19						450					450										Open
California State University, Chico	Chico	SM	B,M	Pub	F,S	C	12,498	21	1	16	54	27	2	495	42	38	10	1	500	40	39	11	1						11/30
California State University, Dominguez Hills	Carson	SU	B,M	Pub	F,S	C	12,632	17	2	55	36	6	1	420	86	13	1		430	83	15	2		420	87	11	1		11/30
California State University, East Bay	Hayward	SM	B,M,D	Pub	F,S	C	11,853																						12/15
California State University, Fresno	Fresno	U	B,M,D	Pub	F,S	C		19	2	43	42	12	1	445	74	21	4	1	455	71	24	5		450	78	19	3		11/30
California State University, Fullerton	Fullerton	SU	B,M,D	Pub	F,S	C	34,576	23		4	52	41	4	520	32	52	15	1	550	25	51	22	2						11/30
California State University, Long Beach	Long Beach	U	B,M,D	Pub	F,S	C	32,246	23	42	25	20	7	6	514	42	41	15	2	531	35	41	21	3						11/30
California State University, Los Angeles	Los Angeles	SM	B,M,D	Pub	F,S	C	19,574	17	79	12	6	2	1	430	79	17	3	1	440	70	23	6	1	430	80	17	2	1	6/15
California State University, Monterey Bay	Seaside	SU	B,M	Pub	F,S	C	6,234	21	25	50		24	1	485	55	37	8	1	485	54	37	8	1	485	59	35	6		3/15
California State University, Northridge	Northridge	U	B,M,D	Pub	F,S	C		19						455	71	23	6		460	67	26	7							3/15
California State University, Sacramento	Sacramento	SU	B,M,D	Pub	F,S	C	24,701																						11/30
California State University, San Bernardino	San Bernardino	SU	B,M	Pub	F,S	C	14,732																						Open
California State University, San Marcos	San Marcos	SU	B,M,D	Pub	F,S	C	9,482							470	60	32	7	1	490	52	37	10	1						11/30
California State University, Stanislaus	Turlock	SU	B,M	Pub	F,S	C	6,620																						8/18
Chapman University	Orange	SU	B,M,D	Pri	F,S	C	6,410	27			15	58	26	600	6	40	42	11	600	6	38	46	10	600	6	38	44	12	1/15
Claremont McKenna College	Claremont	SU	B,M	Pri	No	C	1,344	32				19	81	690			50	50	700		2	45	53	720		4	35	61	1/1
Cogswell Polytechnical College	San Jose	SU	B,M	Pri	No	C	288																						Open
Concordia University	Irvine	SU	A,B,M	Pri	No	C	1,738																						Open
Dominican University of California	San Rafael	SU	B,M	Pri	No	C	1,625																						Open
Fresno Pacific University	Fresno	SU	A,B,M	Pri	No	C	2,439																						Open
Golden Gate University	San Francisco	U	B,M,D		No	C	645																						Open
Harvey Mudd College	Claremont	SU	B	Pri	No	C	814	34				6	94	720		4	31	65	770			12	88	720		4	33	63	1/5
Holy Names University	Oakland	U	B,M	Pri	No	C	640																					63	1/5
Hope International University	Fullerton	U	A,B,M	Pri	No	C	914																						Open
Humboldt State University	Arcata	SM	B,M	Pub	F,S	C	6,830																						Open
Humphreys College	Stockton	SU	A,B,D	Pri	No	C	620																						Open
La Sierra University	Riverside	SU	B,M,D	Pri	No	C	1,680																						Open
Laguna College of Art and Design	Laguna Beach	SM	B,M	Pri	No	C	583																						Open
Loyola Marymount University	Los Angeles	SU	B,M,D	Pri	F,S	C	6,261	28			5	62	33	600	7	39	40	14	620	5	34	46	15	600	7	37	43	13	1/15
Menlo College	Atherton	SU	B	Pri	No	C	713	20	50	12	25	10	3	470	63	33	3	1	500	46	43	9	2	480	64	30	6	13	1/15
Mills College	Oakland	U	B,M,D	Pri	No	W	808	27	2	3	23	51	23	580	28	23	36	12	510	43	32	20	4	560	33	29	25	12	1/15
Mount St. Mary's University - Chalon Campus	Los Angeles	U	A,B,M,D	Pri	S	PW	2,288		67	21	10	2	1		70	26	4			72	25	3			65	30	5		2/15
National University	La Jolla	U	A,B,M	Pri	No	C	5,920																						Open
NewSchool of Architecture & Design	San Diego	U	B,M	Pri	No	C	414																						Open
Notre Dame de Namur University	Belmont	SU	B,M,D	Pri	No	C	1,147	20	54	29	12	2	3	470	60	31	8	1	470	63	28	9		480	59	37	4		Open
Occidental College	Los Angeles	U	B,M	Pri	F,S	C		30			2	51	46	645	2	22	56	20	645	1	23	53	24	648	1	21	55	23	1/15
Otis College of Art and Design	Los Angeles	U	B,M	Pri	No	C	1,158	19	46	31	8	8	7	510	46	34	17	3	500	36	38	20	6	480	48	35	15	2	Open
Pacific Union College	Angwin	R	A,B,M	Pri	No	C	1,375																						Open
Pepperdine University	Malibu	SU	B,M,D	Pri	F,S	C	3,488	29	6	8	19	21	46	604	6	39	42	13	623	5	28	46	21	610	5	34	43	18	1/5
Pitzer College	Claremont	SU	B	Pri	No	C	1,099	30						652		15	60	25	641		24	60	16						1/1
Point Loma Nazarene University	San Diego	SU	B,M	Pri	No	C	3,053	26		1	26	57	16	560	17	47	32	4	565	16	48	32	5	560	23	47	27	4	2/15
Pomona College	Claremont	SU	B	Pri	F	C	1,642	32			1	16	82	720		6	31	63	720		6	29	65	730		6	28	67	1/1
Saint Mary's College of California	Moraga	SU	B,M,D	Pri	No	C	3,035	24	13	33	27	14	11	552	23	49	23	5	558	23	46	29	4						2/1
San Diego Christian College	Santee	SU	A,B	Pri	No	C	752																						Open
San Diego State University	San Diego	U	B,M,D	Pub	F,S	C	29,853	25		3	28	56	13	548	25	46	25	3	566	19	44	33	4		30	46	22	2	11/30
San Francisco Art Institute	San Francisco	U	B,M	Pri	No	C	338	25			43	57		563	25	33	42		523	33	50	17		527	27	55	18		2/15
San Francisco Conservatory of Music	San Francisco	U	B,M	Pri	No	C	171																						12/1

NAME OF SCHOOL	TOWN	ENVIRONMENT U-Urban R-Rural SU-Suburban SM-Small Town	DEGREES AWARDED A-Associate B-Bachelor M-Master D-Doctorate	CONTROL Pri-Private, Pub-Public	FRATERNITIES AND SORORITIES F-Fraternities S-Sororities F, S-Both No-Neither	STUDENTS: C-Coed M-Men W-Women PM-Primarily Men PW-Primarily Women	UNDERGRADUATE ENROLLMENT FALL 2016	TEST SCORES ACT Median	ACT Below 21	ACT 21-23	ACT 24-26	ACT 27-28	ACT Above 28	SAT CRITICAL READING Median	CR Below 500	CR 500-599	CR 600-700	CR Above 700	SAT MATHEMATICS Median	M Below 500	M 500-599	M 600-700	M Above 700	SAT WRITING Median	W Below 500	W 500-599	W 600-700	W Above 700	APPLICATION DEADLINE Month / Day
San Francisco State University	San Francisco	U	B,M,D	Pub	F,S	C								490	54	35	10	1	505	46	40	13							11/30
San Jose State University	San Jose	U	B,M,D	Pub	F,S	C	26,432	23		12	48	34	5	502	46	40	13	2	522	52	34	12	2	497	37	38	20	4	11/30
Scripps College	Claremont	SU	B	Pri	No	W	1,030	30			2	35	63	700		4	42	55	665		12	58	29	700		4	43	53	1/1
Shepherd University	Los Angeles	U	A,B,M,D	Pri	No	C																							8/15
Simpson University	Redding	SU	A,B,M	Pri	No	C	1,019	21	44	26	13	11	4	500	35	41	22	2	500	36	50	14		490	42	43	15		Open
Sonoma State University	Rohnert Park	SU	B,M	Pub	F,S	C	8,606	21		16	52	30	2	490	51	38	10	1	495	52	39	8	1		56	37	6	1	11/30
Stanford University	Stanford	U	B,M,D	Pri	F,S	C	7,089		1		11		88			5	26	69			3	19	78			4	22	74	1/3
The Master's University	Santa Clarita	SU	B,M,D	Pri	No	C		25		5	43	39	13	560	25	39	28	8	520	40	38	19	3	550	37	34	24	5	1/3
Thomas Aquinas College	Santa Paula	R	B	Pri	No	C	389	28			4	67	30	660	3	19	41	37	600	3	49	37	11	620	3	31	51	14	Open
University of California at Berkeley	Berkeley	U	B,M,D	Pub	F,S	C		32			7	21	72	670	5	16	38	40	705	4	12	28	58	685	5	14	34	48	11/30
University of California at Davis	Davis	SU	B,M,D		F,S	C	28,414			1	18	48	33		20	39	31	10		11	23	36	29		16	33	38	13	11/30
University of California at Irvine	Irvine	SU	B,M,D	Pub	F,S	C	22,216							540	34	37	24	5	610	15	30	40	15	550	27	40	28	5	11/30
University of California at Los Angeles	Los Angeles	U	B,M,D	Pub	F,S	C	26,162	29	8	13	16	14	53	640	8	24	45	23	680	6	16	36	42	660	6	21	40	33	11/30
University of California at Riverside	Riverside	SU	B,M,D	Pub	F,S	C	19,799			3	43	43	11		40	42	16	2		32	39	23	6		39	43	16	2	11/30
University of California at Santa Barbara	Santa Barbara	SU	B,M,D	Pub	F,S	C	19,362	27	7	14	21	17	41	610	10	32	42	16	640	6	23	45	27	630	6	29	45	19	11/30
University of California San Diego	La Jolla	SU	B,M,D	Pub	F,S	C	26,590	30						648	7	32	44	16	689	3	15	33	49	660					11/30
University of California, Santa Cruz	Santa Cruz	SM	B,M,D	Pub	F,S	C	16,962	24	23	21	24	12	18	550	27	36	29	8	560	21	34	33	11	550	26	38	30	6	11/30
University of La Verne	La Verne	SU	A,B,M,D	Pri	F,S	C		22		3	58	34	5	520	39	48	12	1	520	37	45	17	1	510	44	44	11	1	2/1
University of Redlands	Redlands	SU	B,M	Pri	F,S	C	2,375																						1/15
University of San Diego	San Diego	U	B,M,D	Pri	F,S	C	5,711	28		1	9	57	33	600	11	35	45	9	610	6	34	51	9	600	9	36	45	9	12/15
University of San Francisco	San Francisco	U	B,M,D	Pri	F,S	C	6,745	26		1	27	59	13	570	18	47	30	5	560	15	45	33	7	560	19	46	30	5	1/15
University of Southern California	Los Angeles	U	B,M,D	Pri	F,S	C	18,794				4	21	75		2	14	48	36		2	10	32	57		2	9	38	50	1/15
University of the Pacific	Stockton	SU	B,M,D	Pri	F,S	C		25	4		30		66	570	21	38	31	10	605	15	29	34	22	570	23	37	29	11	2/15
Vanguard University of Southern California	Costa Mesa	SU	A,B,M	Pri	No	C	2,041																						3/2
Westmont College	Santa Barbara	SU	B	Pri	No	C	1,340																						8/15
Whittier College	Whittier	SU	B,M,D	Pri	F,S	C	1,368	22	36	27	23	8	6	526	38	42	17	3	532	36	41	21	2		40	42	16	2	2/1
Woodbury University	Burbank	SU	B,M	Pri	F,S	C	1,310																						Open
Colorado																													
Adams State University	Alamosa	SM	A,B,M	Pub	No	C	2,143	20	62	21	10	5	2	480	53	37	10		500	49	42	9		460	64	30	6		8/1
Colorado Christian University	Lakewood	SU	A,B,M	Pri	No	C	1,475																						8/1
Colorado College	Colorado Springs	U	B,M	Pri	F,S	C	2,101	30			2	33	65	670	3	19	38	40	660	1	13	54	32	660	4	12	56	28	1/15
Colorado Mesa University	Grand Junction	SM	A,B,M,D	Pub	F,S	C	9,266	20		25	50	22	3	480	55	33	10	2	490	56	32	11	1						Open
Colorado School of Mines	Golden	SM	B,M,D	Pub	F,S	C	4,383	30						635					680					605					Open
Colorado State University	Fort Collins	SU	B,M,D		F,S	C	23,768	25		1	34	51	14	570	19	43	32	6	570	18	43	33	6						2/1
Colorado State University-Pueblo	Pueblo	U	B,M	Pub	F,S	C	36,207	21																					8/1
Colorado Technical University	Colorado Springs	SU	A,B,M,D	Pri	No	C	1,200																						Open
Fort Lewis College	Durango	SM	B,M	Pub	No	C		22		11	56	30	4	505	43	46	10	2	518	44	38	16		465	60	31	8		8/1
Johnson & Wales University/Denver Campus	Denver	SU	A,B	Pri	S	C																							Open
Metropolitan State University of Denver	Denver	U	B	Pub	No	C	21,975																						Open
Naropa University	Boulder	U	B,M	Pri	No	C	381																						1/15
Regis University	Denver	SU	B,M,D	Pri	No	C	4,070			6	35	29	28		25	47	24	4		37	43	18	2		38	43	19		Open
Rocky Mountain College of Art and Design	Denver	SU	B,M	Pri	No	C	670																						Open
United States Air Force Academy	Colorado Springs	SU	B	Pub	No	C	4,470																						Open
University of Colorado Boulder	Boulder	SU	B,M,D	Pub	F,S	C	26,491	27			17	54	29	590	14	41	36	9	600	8	38	40	14						1/15
University of Colorado Colorado Springs	Colorado Springs	SU	B,M,D	Pub	F,S	C	10,187	23		6	47	40	6	531	33	43	21	3	533	33	44	21	2	502	46	44	9	1	5/1
University of Colorado Denver	Denver	U	B,M,D	Pub	No	C	10,493	23						555	26	42	27	5	540	26	47	25	2						7/22
University of Denver	Denver	U	B,M,D	Pri	F,S	C	5,629	28						595	10	37	44	9	610	5	37	46	12	565	19	45	31	4	1/15
University of Northern Colorado	Greeley	SU	B,M,D	Pub	F,S	C	16,795	22						525	38	47	12	3	530	37	40	20	3						8/1
Western State Colorado University	Gunnison	R	B,M	Pub	No	C		22		11	53	30	4						516	45	40	14	1						6/1
Connecticut																													
Albertus Magnus College	New Haven	SU	A,B,M	Pri	No	C	1,605							456	43	41	14	2	448	53	30	15	1	472	48	36	15	1	Open
Central Connecticut State University	New Britain	SU	B,M,D	Pub	F,S	C	9,538			7	62	27	4	500	46	44	9	1	510	43	44	12	1	500	49	42	9	1	12/1
Charter Oak State College	New Britain	SU	A,B	Pub	No	C	1,533																						Open
Connecticut College	New London	SM	B,M	Pri	No	C		30			1	47	52	655		15	57	30	655		16	56	27	654		19	56	26	1/1
Eastern Connecticut State University	Willimantic	SM	A,B,M	Pub	No	C	5,171	22		8	53	37	3	520	38	46	14	1	510	40	46	13	1	510	39	48	11	1	5/1
Fairfield University	Fairfield	SU	B,M,D	Pri	No	C	4,032	27			8	76	15	590	5	48	43	4	610	4	41	50	5	600	4	44	46	6	1/15
Goodwin College	East Hartford	SU	A,B	Pri	No	C	3,388																						Open

Mitchell College	New London	SU	A,B	Pri	No	C	858																						Open
Post University	Waterbury	U	A,B		No	C	1,275																						Open
Quinnipiac University	Hamden	SU	B,M,D	Pri	F,S	C	7,102	25		3	34	55	8	530	31	47	20	2	550	25	46	26	3						2/1
Sacred Heart University	Fairfield	SU	A,B,M,D	Pri	F,S	C	5,428	25			35	61	4	550	16	63	21	1	565	10	60	29	1	552	19	56	24	1	2/1
Southern Connecticut State University	New Haven	U	B,M,D	Pub	F,S	C	7,963	20		21	53	25	1	481	58	33	8	1	470	61	32	6	1	482	57	35	7	1	4/1
Trinity College	Hartford	U	B,M		F,S	C	2,223	28			4	61	35	610	7	30	49	15	650	2	30	51	17	630	5	29	53	13	1/1
United States Coast Guard Academy	New London	SU	B	Pub	No	C	898	28		1	7	60	33	610	5	35	50	10	650	10	17	59	24	605	7	39	45	9	2/1
University of Bridgeport	Bridgeport	SM	A,B,M,D	Pri	F,S	C	2,503	20						468	67	27	6		472	70	23	6	1	457	74	23	3		4/1
University of Connecticut	Storrs	R	A,B,M,D	Pub	F,S	C	18,395								8	39	43	10		4	25	49	22		9	36	44	11	12/1
University of Hartford	West Hartford	SU	A,B,M,D	Pri	F,S	C	5,284	22	38	28	20	6	8	521	46	39	14	1	530	44	37	17	2						Open
University of New Haven	West Haven	SU	A,B,M,D	Pri	F,S	C	4,936							520	41	42	15	2	530	38	44	16	2						Open
University of Saint Joseph	West Hartford	SU	B,M,D	Pri	No	PW	960																						Open
Wesleyan University	Middletown	SU	B,M,D	Pri	F,S	C	2,971	32			2	21	77	690	3	14	34	49	680		14	43	43	690	3	10	39	49	1/1
Western Connecticut State University	Danbury	SU	A,B,M,D	Pub	F,S	C	5,298							490	53	35	11	1	490	50	39	10	1	490	49	38	12	1	5/1
Yale University	New Haven	U	B,M,D	Pri	F,S	C		33						760		3	17	80	755		1	17	82	750		2	17	81	1/1

Delaware

Delaware State University	Dover	SU	B,M	Pub	F,S	C	3,719																						8/20
Goldey-Beacom College	Wilmington	SU	A,B,M	Pri	No	C	625																						8/20
University of Delaware	Newark	SM	A,B,M,D		F,S	C	17,575	27		1	15	64	20	600		41	39	14	610	6	33	48	13	600	8	41	43	8	1/15
Wesley College	Dover	SM	A,B,M		F,S	C	1,603							410	83	13	3	1	420	81	18	1		410	87	11	2		Open
Wilmington University	New Castle	U	A,B,M,D	Pri	No	C	9,034																						Open

District of Columbia

American University	Washington	SU	A,B,M,D	Pri	F,S	C	7,903	28			6	56	38	640	3	25	48	24	610	5	38	48	9	620	3	32	50	15	1/10
Gallaudet University	Washington	U	B,M,D	Pri	F,S	C	1,112	18																					Open
George Washington University	Washington	U	A,B,M,D	Pri	F,S	C	10,443																						Open
Georgetown University	Washington	U	B,M,D	Pri	No	C	7,552																						1/10
Howard University	Washington	U	B,M,D	Pri	F,S	C	6,883	24		3	43	47	7	563	22	46	28	4	561	24	45	26	5	555	26	46	25	3	2/15
The Catholic University of America	Washington	U	B,M,D	Pri	F,S	C	3,799																						2/15
Trinity Washington University	Washington	U	A,B,M	Pri	No	W	1,391																						7/31
University of the District of Columbia	Washington	SU	A,B,M	Pub	F,S	C	5,110																						Open

Florida

Adventist University of Health Sciences	Orlando	U	A,B,M	Pri	No	C	2,576	19	71	21	4	2	2	455	72	23	5		440	73	24	3							7/1
Barry University	Miami Shores	SU	B,M,D	Pri	F,S	C	5,150																						Open
Beacon College	Leesburg	SM	A,B	Pri	F,S	C	223																						Open
Bethune-Cookman University	Daytona Beach	SM	B,M	Pri	F,S	C	3,527		93	5	1	1			91	8	1			91	8	1			91	8	1		7/30
Carlos Albizu University	Miami	SM	B,M,D	Pri	No	C	431																						Open
Eckerd College	St. Petersburg	SU	B	Pri	No	C	1,844	25		1	32	50	17	550	24	45	25	6	540	26	50	21	3						4/1
Edward Waters College	Jacksonville	U	B	Pri	F,S	C	1,400																						4/1
Embry-Riddle Aeronautical University - Daytona Beach	Daytona Beach	U	A,B,M,D	Pri	F,S	C	5,447	25		5	30	47	18	550	27	43	26	4	580	18	39	35	8	530	36	44	18	2	7/1
Embry-Riddle Aeronautical University - Worldwide	Daytona Beach	SU	A,B,M,D	Pri	No	C	11,137																						Open
Flagler College	St. Augustine	SM	B,M	Pri	No	C	2,616	24			47	47	6	540	24	51	21	3	510	42	43	15	1	530	31	52	15	2	3/1
Florida Agricultural and Mechanical University	Tallahassee	U	A,B,M,D	Pub	F,S	C	7,810	23		18	61	19	2	515	61	27	11	2	503	63	28	9		494	68	23	8		5/15
Florida Atlantic University	Boca Raton	SU	A,B,M,D	Pub	F,S	C	24,823	23			59	37	3	525	30	53	15	3	535	27	53	18	2	520	32	54	13	1	5/1
Florida Gulf Coast University	Fort Myers	SU	A,B,M,D	Pub	F,S	C	12,861		5	70		23	2		43	46	10	1		41	46	12	1		52	40	7	1	5/1
Florida Institute of Technology	Melbourne	SU	B,M,D	Pri	F,S	C	3,629	25			22	56	22	556	20	49	27	4	604	4	44	42	10						Open
Florida International University	Miami	U	B,M,D	Pub	F,S	C	41,038	24			38	55	7	560	10	61	27	2	550	16	58	24	2	540	19	59	20	2	Open
Florida Memorial University	Miami, Gardens	U	B		No	C																							Open
Florida State University	Tallahassee	SU	A,B,M,D	Pub	F,S	C	32,706	28		1	19	69	11	623	2	44	46	8	618	3	42	48	6	615	3	45	45	6	1/25
Hodges University	Naples	SU	A,B,M	Pri	No	C	1,515																						Open
Jacksonville University	Jacksonville	SU	B,M	Pri	F,S	C	2,410	22						505					505										Open
Johnson & Wales University/North Miami Campus	North Miami	SM	A,B	Pri	F,S	C																							Open
Keiser University	West Palm Beach	SU	A,B,M	Pri	No	C	497								67	28	4	1		42	42	12	4		80	15	4	1	Open
Lynn University	Boca Raton	SU	B,M,D	Pri	F,S	C	2,095	20	1	24	56	18	1	470	70	22	7		460	69	25	5		470	71	19	5		Open
New College of Florida	Sarasota	SU	B	Pub	No	C	861	29			4	51	45	670	1	18	45	35	610	3	40	44	13	620	3	29	51	17	2/15
Nova Southeastern University	Fort Lauderdale	SU	A,B,M,D	Pri	F,S	C	4,641	25		1	39	40	20	550	26	45	25	4	550	27	39	29	5						8/1
Palm Beach Atlantic University	West Palm Beach	U	A,B,M,D	Pri	No	C		24		5	40	40	14	535	34	38	22	5	515	45	37	14	4	516	44	37	16	3	Open
Ringling College of Art and Design	Sarasota	U	B	Pri	No	C	1,341																					3	Open
Rollins College	Winter Park	SU	B,M	Pri	F,S	C	1,948								4	41	45	10		5	43	40	13		8	44	39	10	2/15
Saint Leo University	Saint Leo	R	A,B,M,D	Pri	F,S	C	2,264	22		3	59	31	7	490	52	35	13		500	46	43	10	1	470	64	28	7	1	Open
Southeastern University	Lakeland	SU	A,B,M,D	Pri	No	C	2,448	21	50	22	18	6	4	509	45	39	15	2	487	53	35	12	1	494	52	35	12	2	Open
St. Thomas University	Miami	SU	B,M	Pri	No	C	1,145	17	83	13	4			440	78	20	2		440	80	18	2		430	79	19	2		Open
Stetson University	DeLand	SM	B,M,D	Pri	F,S	C	3,089	26		1	26	55	19	590	14	49	29	8	570	20	46	28	5	560	23	52	23	3	Open
University of Central Florida	Orlando	SU	A,B,M,D	Pub	F,S	C	55,776	26		1	21	61	17	588	8	48	36	8	593	8	45	39	8	558	18	53	25	4	5/1
University of Florida	Gainesville	SU	A,B,M,D	Pub	F,S	C	34,464	29			6	47	46	631	4	28	49	19	644	4	22	50	24	628	5	28	50	17	11/1
University of Miami	Coral Gables	SU	B,M,D	Pri	F,S	C		30		1	2	39	58	640	4	21	53	22	660	2	18	49	30	635	4	26	53	18	4/1

NAME OF SCHOOL	TOWN	ENVIRONMENT U-Urban R-Rural SU-Suburban SM-Small Town	DEGREES AWARDED A-Associate B-Bachelor M-Master D-Doctorate	CONTROL Pri-Private, Pub-Public	FRATERNITIES AND SORORITIES F-Fraternities S-Sororities F, S-Both No-Neither	STUDENTS: C-Coed M-Men W-Women PM-Primarily Men PW-Primarily Women	UNDERGRADUATE ENROLLMENT FALL 2016	TEST SCORES: ACT Median	ACT Below 21	ACT 21-23	ACT 24-26	ACT 27-28	ACT Above 28	SAT CRITICAL READING Median	SAT CR Below 500	SAT CR 500-599	SAT CR 600-700	SAT CR Above 700	SAT MATHEMATICS Median	SAT M Below 500	SAT M 500-599	SAT M 600-700	SAT M Above 700	SAT WRITING Median	SAT W Below 500	SAT W 500-599	SAT W 600-700	SAT W Above 700	APPLICATION DEADLINE Month / Day
University of North Florida	Jacksonville	U	A,B,M,D	Pub	F,S	C	13,846	26				80	20	612	3	37	52	8	597	2	48	47	3		13	52	33	2	Open
University of South Florida/St. Petersburg	St. Petersburg	U	B,M	Pub	No	C	4,006	23						530					530					510					3/15
University of South Florida/Tampa	Tampa	U	A,B,M,D	Pub	F,S	C		26			17	64	19	575	9	52	33	6	585	9	48	35	7	555	16	56	26	3	3/15
University of Tampa	Tampa	U	B,M	Pri	F,S	C	7,363	20			38	53	9	540	26	56	16	1	550	22	57	19	2	520	31	53	15	1	Open
University of West Florida	Pensacola	SU	A,B,M,D	Pub	F,S	C	10,332		8	56	32	2	2		44	44	10	1		49	41	9	1		60	34	5	1	6/30
Warner University	Lake Wales	R	A,B,M	Pri	No	C	1,090																						Open
Webber International University	Babson Park	SM	A,B,M	Pri	No	C	655		70	20		1			68	29	3			63	32	4	1						8/1
Georgia																													
Agnes Scott College	Decatur	U	B	Pri	No	W	927	27			19	55	26	610	8	33	41	18	580	13	48	29	9		8	39	44	9	3/15
Albany State University	Albany	U	A,B,M	Pub	F,S	C	3,025																						6/1
Armstrong State University	Savannah	SU	A,B,M,D	Pub	F,S	C	6,397	21		10	66	23	1	506	50	38	11	2	488	58	36	6		475	64	30	5	1	7/1
Augusta University	Augusta	U	A,B,M,D	Pub	F,S	C	5,224																					1	7/1
Berry College	Mount Berry	SU	B,M	Pri	No	C	2,073	26			24	56	20	580	13	44	35	8	570	10	51	34	5	560	20	51	24	5	7/1
Brenau University - Women's College	Gainesville	SU	B,M	Pri	S	W	867		42	32	16	7	2		39	46	14	1		59	31	10							Open
Brewton-Parker College	Mt. Vernon	R	A,B	Pri	F,S	C	629			87		11	2		65	29	5	1		65	29	6			65	29	6		Open
Clark Atlanta University	Atlanta	U	B,M,D		F,S	C	3,093	19		25	63	12		450	76	22	2		440	79	19	2							Open
Clayton State University	Morrow	SU	A,B,M	Pub	F,S	C		20						500					458										Open
Columbus State University	Columbus	SU	A,B,M,D	Pub	F,S	C	6,789	20		12	67	19	2	490	50	36	13	1	480	54	36	9	1	470	59	31	9	1	6/30
Covenant College	Lookout Mountain	SU	B,M	Pri	No	C	1,066	26	7	18	25	21	28	610	10	38	35	17	570	17	45	32	6	590	19	35	37	9	5/1
Emory University	Atlanta	SU	A,B,M,D	Pri	F,S	C	7,836	31			2	32	66	660	1	19	47	33	700		10	36	54	690	1	10	44	45	1/1
Fort Valley State University	Fort Valley	R	A,B,M		F,S	C	3,421																						6/15
Georgia College & State University	Milledgeville	SM	B,M,D	Pub	F,S	C	6,047	24		1	38	55	5	570	16	51	30	4	560	17	50	31	2	540	24	52	21	3	Open
Georgia Institute of Technology	Atlanta	U	B,M,D	Pub	F,S	C	15,489	32			1	16	83	680	1	9	45	45	730	1	4	29	66	690	2	9	43	46	1/1
Georgia Southern University	Statesboro	SM	B,M,D	Pub	F,S	C	17,975	23	1	54	27	10	7	550	13	63	23	2	550	15	59	25	2	520	33	51	16	1	5/1
Georgia Southwestern State University	Americus	SM	B,M	Pub	F,S	C	2,558	21		10	67	21	2	490	56	36	7		470	63	31	6							7/21
Georgia State University	Atlanta	U	A,B,M,D	Pub	F,S	C	25,455								33	48	17	2		37	43	18	3						7/1
Kennesaw State University	Kennesaw	SU	B,M,D	Pub	F,S	C	32,166	23		1	56	38	5	540	22	54	22	2	540	21	54	22	3	520	36	49	14	1	5/5
LaGrange College	LaGrange	SM	B,M	Pri	F,S	C	902	22			70	28	1	500	47	37	12	3	490	55	37	9							Open
Mercer University	Macon	SU	B,M,D	Pri	F,S	C	2,538	26						580	9	47	35	9	590	7	48	37	8	560	19	46	29	6	4/1
Morehouse College	Atlanta	U	B	Pri	F	M	2,104	21		19	51	24	6	490	55	35	9	2	490	55	34	10	1	470	63	30	7		2/15
Oglethorpe University	Atlanta	SU	B	Pri	F,S	C	1,184	24	12	30	25	14	19	570	8	51	35	6	550	20	52	23	4	550	24	49	24	3	2/15
Paine College	Augusta	U	B	Pri	F,S	C	924		95	2	1	1	1		94	6				92	8				96	4			7/1
Piedmont College	Demorest	SM	B,M,D	Pri	No	C	1,295	22		11	58	27	2	496	55	35	9	1	487	57	32	10							8/1
Reinhardt University	Waleska	SM	A,B		No	C	1,120																						Open
Savannah College of Art and Design	Savannah	U	B,M	Pri	No	C	10,573	24		6	41	41	12	546	28	42	26	4	519	39	42	17	1	524	37	41	19	2	Open
Savannah State University	Savannah	SU	A,B,M	Pub	F,S	C	4,413																						7/15
Shorter University	Rome	SM	A,B,M	Pri	F,S	C	1,555	20		19	55	24	2	470	63	28	8	1	470	59	32	9		470	61	31	8		Open
South University	Savannah	U	A,B,M,D	Pri	No	C																							Open
Spelman College	Atlanta	U	B		S	W	2,318	23																					2/1
The Art Institute of Atlanta	Atlanta	SU	A,B	Pri	No	C	2,720																						Open
Thomas University	Thomasville	SM	A,B,M	Pri	No	C																							Open
Toccoa Falls College	Toccoa Falls	SM	A,B	Pri	No	C	874	19	69	18	9	3	1	505	44	36	20		500	49	41	9	1						8/1
University of Georgia	Athens	SM	B,M,D	Pub	F,S	C	27,951				7	51	42		6	32	47	15		4	31	49	16		5	36	46	13	1/15
University of North Georgia	Dahlonega	SM	A,B,M,D	Pub	F,S	C	17,704	23		7	50	39	3	530	33	47	18	2	530	30	47	21	2	500	45	41	12	1	2/15
University of West Georgia	Carrollton	R	B,M,D	Pub	F,S	C	11,155	20		16	69	14	1	470	66	27	6	1	460	71	24	5		450	73	24	3		6/1
Valdosta State University	Valdosta	SU	A,B	Pub	F,S	C	10,368	21						503	51	40	8		492	58	35	7		482	59	35	6		7/1
Wesleyan College	Macon	SU	B,M	Pri	No	W	592	22	36	27	25	7	7																8/1
Hawaii																													
Brigham Young University/Hawaii	Laie	R	B	Pri	No	C	2,397	23	26	22	24	16	12																2/15
Chaminade University of Honolulu	Honolulu	U	A,B,M	Pri	No	C	1,183	21		14	66	18	2	480	61	30	9		490	51	40	8	1						Open
Hawaii Pacific University	Honolulu	U	A,B,M	Pri	No	C	6,168	21	47	30	14	5	5	480	57	35	8	1	490	52	38	9	1	470	63	32	5		8/15
University of Hawaii at Hilo	Hilo	SM	B,M	Pub	No	C	2,850																						7/1
University of Hawaii at Manoa	Honolulu	SM	B,M,D	Pub	F,S	C		24		5	55	34	6	530	35	44	18	3	555	25	45	24	5	520	42	41	15	2	5/1
Idaho																													
Boise State University	Boise	U	A,B,M,D	Pub	F,S	C	20,209	23		8	49	37	6	510	43	40	15	2	510	41	40	16	2		51	38	10	1	5/15

Idaho State University	Pocatello	U	A,B,M,D	Pub	F,S	C	11,087	22		17	45	31	5	480	58	31	9	1	470	63	26	10	1	460	69	26	5		8/1
Lewis-Clark State College	Lewiston	U	A,B	Pub	No	C	3,495																						Open
Northwest Nazarene University	Nampa	SM	A,B,M,D	Pri	No	C		24		8	39	40	13	525	32	46	16	6	515	38	42	16	4	510	53	25	19	3	8/15
The College of Idaho	Caldwell	SM	B,M	Pri	F,S	C	1,039	23		2	53	37	8	510	40	42	16	2	505	41	40	16	3	490	51	35	13	1	7/15
University of Idaho	Moscow	SM	B,M,D	Pub	F,S	C	9,116	24		9	40	40	11	523	41	37	17	5	528	38	38	18	6	506	47	36	14	3	8/1
Illinois																													
Augustana College	Rock Island	SU	B	Pri	F,S	C	2,537	25		1	30	54	14	570					570					550					Open
Aurora University	Aurora	SU	B,M,D	Pri	F,S	C	3,796	22		7	68	24	1	481	24	13	7		481	24	13	7							Open
Benedictine University	Lisle	SU	A,B,M,D	Pri	No	C	2,940	23	30	27	26	9	8																Open
Blackburn College	Carlinville	R	B	Pri	No	C	596	20		21	57	19	2	440	100				390	100									8/1
Chicago State University	Chicago	U	B,M,D	Pub	F,S	C	4,618																						7/15
Columbia College Chicago	Chicago	U	B,M	Pri	No	C	7,809	23		13	45	34	8																7/15
Concordia University, Chicago	River Forest	SU	B,M,D	Pri	No	C	1,032		36	23	20	9	12																Open
DePaul University	Chicago	U	B,M,D	Pri	F,S	C	16,153	25	10	22	29	17	22	586	13	41	37	8	569	18	43	32	6						2/1
Dominican University	River Forest	SU	B,M,D	Pri	No	C	2,269	23		3	60	34	2	550	33	42	17	8	534	42	25	25	8	515	58	25	8	8	Open
Eastern Illinois University	Charleston	SM	B,M	Pub	F,S	C	5,957	21		15	58	23	4																8/15
Elmhurst College	Elmhurst	SU	B,M	Pri	F,S	C	2,856	23		5	52	37	7	490	56	22	19	4	510	44	37	19		460	63	26	11		8/15
Eureka College	Eureka	SM	B	Pri	F,S	C	700	23																					8/1
Greenville College	Greenville	SM	B,M	Pri	No	C	1,382	23	32	20	21	13	14	480	56	26	17	1	490	51	36	13		470	60	21	19		8/1
Illinois College	Jacksonville	SM	B	Pri	No	C	970																						Open
Illinois Institute of Technology	Chicago	U	B,M,D	Pri	F,S	C	3,046	28	11		53		37	580	13	44	32	11	690		8	44	48	580	12	40	41	7	Open
Illinois State University	Normal	U	B,M,D	Pub	F,S	C	18,427	24		1	54	37	4																4/1
Illinois Wesleyan University	Bloomington	SU	B	Pri	F,S	C		27			13	63	24																3/1
Judson University	Elgin	SU	B,M	Pri	No	C	1,195																						Open
Kendall College	Chicago	U	A,B	Pri	No	C	2,545																						Open
Knox College	Galesburg	SM	B	Pri	F,S	C	1,357	27			21	48	30	635	17	26	41	17	580	26	26	38	10	565	10	57	24	10	1/15
Lake Forest College	Lake Forest	SU	B,M	Pri	F,S	C	1,607																						2/15
Lewis University	Romeoville	SU	A,B,M,D	Pri	F,S	C	4,553	23		4	54	36	6	530	41	35	21	3	555	21	47	26	6						Open
Loyola University Chicago	Chicago	U	A,B,M,D	Pri	F,S	C	11,129	26			22	57	21	580	17	40	34	9	570	18	44	32	6	570	20	41	32	7	5/1
MacMurray College	Jacksonville	SM	A,B		F,S	C	701	21	50	28	15	4	3																Open
McKendree University	Lebanon	SU	B,M,D	Pri	F,S	C	2,342	24	27	34	27	4	7		56	44				41	54	5			79	15	5		Open
Millikin University	Decatur	SU	B,M,D	Pri	F,S	C	1,971	23		8	52	32	8	528	34	47	19		477	71	19	10		496	52	32	16		Open
Monmouth College	Monmouth	SM	B	Pri	F,S	C	1,198	23		5	55	33	7																Open
National Louis University	Chicago	SU	B,M,D	Pri	No	PW	2,084																						Open
North Central College	Naperville	SU	B,M	Pri	No	C	2,755	24	11	30	31	15	13																Open
North Park University	Chicago	U	B,M,D	Pri	No	C	2,224	22	41	25	16	9	9	530	33	49	17	1	500	40	43	14	3						4/1
Northeastern Illinois University	Chicago	U	B,M	Pub	F,S	C	8,412	19	72	19	7	2	1																7/1
Northern Illinois University	DeKalb	SM	B,M,D	Pub	F,S	C	18,277	22	37	30	21	7	5																8/1
Northwestern University	Evanston	SU	B,M,D	Pri	F,S	C	8,314				1	24	75			4	25	72			3	16	81						1/1
Olivet Nazarene University	Bourbonnais	SU	A,B,M,D	Pri	No	C	3,358	24		3	46	41	10																8/1
Principia College	Elsah	R	B	Pri	No	C	460	25		2	27	55	16	560	20	41	30	9	550	28	43	25	4	540	33	42	24	1	8/1
Quincy University	Quincy	SM	A,B,M	Pri	F,S	C	1,241	21	44	30	15	8	3	450	79	21			460	53	32	10	5						Open
Rockford University	Rockford	SU	B,M	Pri	No	C	869	22	43	26	24	3																	Open
Roosevelt University	Chicago	U	B,M,D		F,S	C	4,300																						Open
Saint Xavier University	Chicago	U	B,M		No	C	3,070																						5/1
School of the Art Institute of Chicago	Chicago	U	B,M		No	C	3,393	25											565					581					5/1
Shimer College	Chicago	U	B	Pri	No	C	77							690			34	67	570		67	34		560					8/1
Southern Illinois University Carbondale	Carbondale	SM	A,B,M,D	Pub	F,S	C		22		7	54	32	7	505	45	36	19		500	42	41	15	2						5/1
Southern Illinois University Edwardsville	Edwardsville	SU	B,M	Pub	F,S	C	11,341	23	31	30	22	9	8																5/1
Trinity Christian College	Palos Heights	SU	B,M	Pri	No	C	1,450	23	35	22	14	13	16	543	32	52	11	5	552	37	47	16							8/15
Trinity College of Nursing and Health Sciences	Rock Island	U	A,B	Pri	No	C																							8/15
Trinity International University	Deerfield	SU	B,M,D	Pri	No	C	1,265																						Open
University of Chicago	Chicago	U	B,M,D	Pri	F,S	C	5,941	34				4	96	760		1	15	84	765			13	87	740		1	20	79	1/1
University of Illinois at Chicago	Chicago	U	B,M,D	Pub	F,S	C	17,959	24		3	45	43	10	550	25	44	23	8	575	27	31	29	13	530	36	43	15	6	1/1
University of Illinois at Urbana-Champaign	Urbana	SM	B,M,D		F,S	C	32,695																						12/1
University of St. Francis	Joliet	SU	B,M,D	Pri	S	C	1,362	23		3	54	40	3		50	50				38	50	12			63	25	12		8/1
VanderCook College of Music	Chicago	U	B,M		F,S	C	90																						8/1
Western Illinois University	Macomb	R	B,M,D	Pub	F,S	C	8,543	21		18	60	18	4																5/15
Wheaton College	Wheaton	SU	B,M,D	Pri	No	C	2,456	30			7	42	51	660	4	23	42	32	640	6	24	47	23	630	5	26	48	21	1/10
Indiana																													
Anderson University	Anderson	SU	A,B,M,D	Pri	No	C	1,883	22		17	42	38	3	501	443	37	13	2	509	43	44	12	1						Open
Ball State University	Muncie	SU	A,B,M,D	Pub	F,S	C	17,011	22		3	59	33	5	546	37	46	15	2	538	38	48	13	1	527	46	44	9	1	8/10
Bethel College	Mishawaka	SU	A,B,M	Pri	No	C	1,388	23		8	49	39	4	500	48	40	9	3	520	44	34	20	2	490	54	37	9	1	Open
Butler University	Indianapolis	SU	A,B,M,D	Pri	F,S	C	4,551	27			15	59	26	580	12	49	33	5	580	12	46	36	6	560	17	52	29	3	2/1
Calumet College of St. Joseph	Whiting	SM	A,B,M		No	C	1,200																						Open
DePauw University	Greencastle	R	B	Pri	F,S	C	2,225	27						580	14	40	35	10	600	8	36	41	14	580	13	42	37	7	3/1
Earlham College	Richmond	SM	B,M	Pri	No	C	1,031	28			13	52	35	620	4	32	44	20	610	9	32	35	24	600	10	38	34	18	2/15

NAME OF SCHOOL	TOWN	ENVIRONMENT U-Urban R-Rural SU-Suburban SM-Small Town	DEGREES AWARDED A-Associate B-Bachelor M-Master D-Doctorate	CONTROL Pri-Private, Pub-Public	FRATERNITIES AND SORORITIES F-Fraternities S-Sororities F, S-Both No-Neither	STUDENTS: C-Coed M-Men W-Women PM-Primarily Men PW-Primarily Women	UNDERGRADUATE ENROLLMENT FALL 2016	TEST SCORES ACT Median	ACT Below 21	ACT 21-23	ACT 24-26	ACT 27-28	ACT Above 28	SAT CRITICAL READING Median	SAT CR Below 500	SAT CR 500-599	SAT CR 600-700	SAT CR Above 700	SAT MATHEMATICS Median	SAT M Below 500	SAT M 500-599	SAT M 600-700	SAT M Above 700	SAT WRITING Median	SAT W Below 500	SAT W 500-599	SAT W 600-700	SAT W Above 700	APPLICATION DEADLINE Month / Day
Franklin College	Franklin	SM	B,M	Pri	F,S	C	1,016	22		18	50	27	5	480	57	30	12	1	500	50	38	11	1	480	60	31	9		Open
Goshen College	Goshen	SM	B,M	Pri	No	C	800	25		8	27	44	21	510	48	23	23	7	500	49	29	16	7	490	55	19	20	7	8/1
Grace College and Seminary	Winona Lake	SM	A,B,M,D	Pri	No	C	1,934	24		6	34	50	10	519	40	41	17	2	512	40	39	19	2						3/1
Hanover College	Hanover	R	B	Pri	F,S	C	1,090	25		1	34	56	9	520	40	47	11	2	520	38	43	19		500	47	44	9		3/1
Huntington University	Huntington	SM	A,B,M,D	Pri	No	C	1,001	22		16	45	35	4	508	48	34	15	3	512	45	36	17	2	486	57	29	13	1	Open
Indiana Institute of Technology	Fort Wayne	U	A,B,M,D	Pri	F,S	C	5,697	20	53	27	16	2	2	447	69	27	4		468	59	32	8	1	430	81	18	1		8/15
Indiana State University	Terre Haute	U	B,M,D	Pub	F,S	C	11,257	19						460	69	26	5		455	69	26	6		435	80	18	3		8/15
Indiana University Bloomington	Bloomington	SM	A,B,M,D	Pub	F,S	C	39,184	27		1	17	51	31	573	16	45	30	8	598	11	40	35	15	565	19	47	28	6	2/1
Indiana University East	Richmond	SM	A,B,M	Pub	F,S	C	4,287	20		24	53	21	1	470	67	28	5	1	469	67	26	7		451	73	24	3		Open
Indiana University Kokomo	Kokomo	SM	A,B,M	Pub	F,S	C	3,977	21	1	19	64	16	1	468	64	31	5		465	67	28	5		446	77	19	4		Open
Indiana University Northwest	Gary	U	A,B,M	Pub	F,S	C	5,244	21		24	52	20	4	464	70	26	3	1	456	71	24	6		453	74	23	3		7/1
Indiana University South Bend	South Bend	SU	A,B,M	Pub	F,S	C	6,653	21		22	55	22	1	479	64	27	8	1	479	61	30	8	1	456	72	23	5		Open
Indiana University Southeast	New Albany	SU	A,B,M	Pub	F,S	C	5,486	20		27	54	18	1	475	62	29	8	1	464	68	26	5		459	69	27	3		8/12
Indiana University-Purdue University Fort Wayne	Fort Wayne	SU	A,B,M,D	Pub	F,S	C	11,453	22		18	52	24	6	490	57	33	9	1	490	55	34	9	2	470	66	29	5	1	8/1
Indiana University-Purdue University Indianapolis	Indianapolis	U	A,B,M,D	Pub	F,S	C	21,748	23		13	47	33	7	504	49	37	13	2	510	45	38	15	2	485	58	33	9	1	Open
Indiana Wesleyan University	Marion	SM	A,B,M,D	Pri	No	C		24		7	37	45	11	525	36	40	20	4	535	36	424	19	3	515	44	37	17	2	Open
Manchester University	North Manchester	SM	A,B	Pri	No	C	1,217																						Open
Marian University	Indianapolis	SU	A,B,M,D	Pri	No	C	2,147	22		10	49	34	7	530	46	39	12	3	520	40	46	13	1	520	59	33	7	1	8/1
Martin University	Indianapolis	U	B,M	Pri	No	C	615																						Open
Oakland City University	Oakland City	SM	A,B,M	Pri	No	C	2,100																						9/8
Purdue University/Northwest	Hammond	U	A,B,M,D	Pub	F,S	C	14,385	21		24	50	23	2	479	61	32	7		474	63	30	6	1	460	71	24	4		8/1
Purdue University/West Lafayette	West Lafayette	SU	A,B,M,D	Pub	F,S	C	30,043	29	8	16	23	13	41	570	16	44	32	9	680	7	27	37	28	570	16	43	33	7	8/1
Rose-Hulman Institute of Technology	Terre Haute	SU	B,M	Pri	F,S	C	2,202	30			4	41	55	620	3	35	50	13	680		11	55	35	600	8	40	44	9	2/1
Saint Mary-of-the-Woods College	St Mary of the Woods	R	A,B,M	Pri	No	PW	748	20	60	20	5		15	460	66	30	2	2	440	68	32			450	75	16	7		Open
Saint Mary's College	Notre Dame	SU	B,M,D	Pri	No	W	1,594	25		1	35	52	11	545	25	51	22	3	529	33	47	17	3	543	28	46	24	1	2/15
Taylor University	Upland	R	A,B,M	Pri	No	C	2,133	25		3	30	48	18	560	31	35	23	10	550	30	35	29	6	540	30	41	23	5	12/1
Trine University	Angola	SM	A,B,M,D	Pri	F,S	C	1,780	23		8	45	38	9	510	42	38	17	3	540	27	40	29	4						8/1
University of Evansville	Evansville	U	A,B,M,D	Pri	F,S	C	2,234	27		2	27	49	22	560	21	46	25	8	570	20	43	31	6	535	29	46	21	4	8/1
University of Indianapolis	Indianapolis	SU	A,B,M,D	Pri	No	C	4,125	23	2	7	55	31	7	505	50	38	11	1	513	44	40	14	1	492	56	35	8	1	Open
University of Notre Dame	Notre Dame	SU	B,M,D	Pri	No	C	8,530	34			1	9	90	710	1	7	30	62	730		4	28	68	700	1	9	38	52	1/1
University of Saint Francis	Fort Wayne	U	A,B,M	Pri	No	C	1,810	22		15	55	28	1	500	50	41	9		490	51	40	8	1	480	56	36	7	1	Open
University of Southern Indiana	Evansville	SU	A,B,M,D	Pub	F,S	C	7,956	22		13	55	29	3	490	51	40	8	1	500	50	39	11		470	63	32	5		8/15
Valparaiso University	Valparaiso	SM	A,B,M,D	Pri	F,S	C	3,299	26		1	26	52	21	540	24	51	19	7	550	28	43	24	5	520	35	48	14	3	Open
Wabash College	Crawfordsville	SM	B	Pri	F	M	843	25			35	47	18	546	26	48	23	3	580	14	44	37	5	510	39	38	21	2	1/15
Iowa																													
Allen College	Waterloo	SU	A,B,M,D	Pri	No	PW	360																						2/1
Briar Cliff University	Sioux City	SU	A,B,M	Pri	No	C	1,079	21	40	28	20	9	3																Open
Buena Vista University	Storm Lake	SM	B,M	Pri	No	C	795	22		12	49	34	5																Open
Central College	Pella	SM	B	Pri	F,S	C	1,248	23		4	47	39	10						530					540					8/15
Clarke University	Dubuque	SM	A,B,M,D	Pri	No	C	868	23		4	56	37	3	507	43	43	14		520	48	33	14	5						Open
Coe College	Cedar Rapids	U	B	Pri	F,S	C	1,409	25		1	37	46	16	580	13	48	23	16	570	16	42	29	13	545	40	25	30	5	Open
Cornell College	Mount Vernon	SM	B	Pri	F,S	C	974	26		1	27	53	19	560	30	26	30	15	580	25	41	26	8	540	39	36	20	5	3/1
Dordt College	Sioux Center	R	A,B,M		No	C	1,430	25	15	25	36	20	15		47	29	21	3		22	45	30	3		43	40	17		8/1
Drake University	Des Moines	U	B,M,D	Pri	F,S	C	3,267	27			13	58	29		18	33	38	10		10	40	32	18						3/1
Graceland University	Lamoni	SM	B,M,D	Pri	No	C	1,556			18	55	24	3		87	11	2			78	16	5	1						3/1
Grand View University	Des Moines	U	B,M	Pri	No	C	2,094	21	48	27	18	3	5		96	4				80	20				96	4			8/15
Grinnell College	Grinnell	SM	B	Pri	No	C	1,699	32						685		12	44	43	710		1	9	37						1/15
Iowa State University	Ames	U	B,M,D	Pub	F,S	C	30,671																						1/15
Iowa Wesleyan University	Mount Pleasant	SM	B	Pri	F,S	C	523	22		2	75	22	1																Open
Loras College	Dubuque	SM	A,B,M	Pri	F,S	C	1,463	23		3	57	36	4																Open
Luther College	Decorah	SM	B	Pri	F,S	C	2,169	26			28	51	21	500	47	32	13	8	550	27	39	13	21	490	55	26	11	8	Open
Maharishi University of Management	Fairfield	SM	B,M,D	Pri	No	C	220																						Open
Mercy College of Health Sciences	Des Moines	U	A,B	Pri	No	C	771	21		15	60	25																	6/15
Morningside College	Sioux City	SU	B,M	Pri	F,S	C	1,321	23		7	52	32	9																Open
Mount Mercy University	Cedar Rapids	U	B,M	Pri	No	C	1,543	22	2	10	66	21	3																8/14
Northwestern College of Iowa	Orange City	SM	B,M	Pri	No	C	1,099	24		4	39	40	17	500	47	35	7	11	540	33	35	24	8	580	56	33		11	Open
Simpson College	Indianola	SM	B,M	Pri	F,S	C	1,543	24		2	41	45	12																Open
St. Ambrose University	Davenport	U	B,M,D	Pri	No	C	2,398	23		2	59	35	4																Open
University of Dubuque	Dubuque	SU	A,B,M,D	Pri	F,S	C	1,185																						8/15

University of Iowa	Iowa City	SM	B,M,D	Pub	F,S	C	24,476	26		1	30	50	19	570	30	29	28	13	610	14	29	39	18						4/1
Upper Iowa University	Fayette	R	A,B,M		F,S	C	720																						Open
Wartburg College	Waverly	SM	B	Pri	No	C	1,482	24		5	43	42	10	490	43	36	14	7	500	36	43	14	7	480	36	43	21		5/1
William Penn University	Oskaloosa	R	A,B,M	Pub	F,S	C	1,835																						Open
Kansas																													
Baker University	Baldwin City	R	B	Pri	F,S	C	989	24		6	54	37	3																Open
Benedictine College	Atchison	SM	A,B,M	Pri	No	C	1,993	25																					Open
Bethany College	Lindsborg	SM	B	Pri	F,S	C	483		36	29	24	6	5		74	26				57	38	5							Open
Bethel College	North Newton	SU	B	Pri	No	C	460	22		2	68	28	2																Open
Emporia State University	Emporia	SM	B,M,D	Pub	F,S	C	3,702	22		12	54	29	5																Open
Fort Hays State University	Hays	SM	A,B,M	Pub	F,S	C	11,299	21																					Open
Friends University	Wichita	U	A,B,M	Pri	No	C	1,192			6	57	30	7																Open
Kansas State University	Manhattan	SU	A,B,M,D		F,S	C	19,859	25		3	37	44	16																Open
Kansas Wesleyan University	Salina	U	A,B,M	Pri	No	C	800																						Open
McPherson College	McPherson	SM	B,M	Pri	No	C	632																						8/1
MidAmerica Nazarene University	Olathe	SU	A,B,M	Pri	No	C	1,309		1	17	48	29	5																8/1
Newman University	Wichita	U	A,B,M	Pri	No	C	2,795	24						509	38	46		8	548	31	38	31		487	46	46		8	Open
Ottawa University	Ottawa	SM	B	Pri	No	C	585																						Open
Pittsburg State University	Pittsburg	SM	A,B,M,D	Pub	F,S	C		22		12	57	28	3																Open
Southwestern College	Winfield	SM	B,M,D	Pri	F	C	522	22	31	29	27	9	4	455	69	25	3	3	486	61	29	7	3	433	75	22	3		8/1
Sterling College	Sterling	R	B	Pri	No	C	642	21	37	31	20	5	7	460	73	23	4		470	65	31	4		460	77	15	8		Open
Tabor College	Hillsboro	SM	A,B,M	Pri	No	C	670	21																					8/1
University of Kansas	Lawrence	SU	B,M,D	Pub	F,S	C	19,262	26		1	39	41	19																Open
University of Saint Mary	Leavenworth	SM	A,B,M,D	Pri	No	C	837	22																					Open
Washburn University	Topeka	U	A,B,M,D	Pub	F,S	C	5,780	22		15	51	32	2																8/1
Wichita State University	Wichita	U	A,B,M,D	Pub	F,S	C	11,299	24						550	34	32	28	6	560	19	49	28	4						Open
Kentucky																													
Alice Lloyd College	Pippa Passes	R	B	Pri	No	C	612	20	48	35	13	3	1																Open
Asbury University	Wilmore	SM	A,B,M	Pri	No	C	1,532	24	17	27	26	11	19	568	21	41	33	5	558	24	40	32	4						Open
Bellarmine University	Louisville	SU	B,M,D	Pri	F,S	C	2,730	24	12	33	30	12	11	546	28	46	25	1	551	24	48	24	4						8/15
Berea College	Berea	SU	B	Pri	No	C	1,665	24			43	48	9	530	29	44	27		560	12	56	29	2	550	22	46	29	2	Open
Brescia University	Owensboro	U	A,B,M	Pri	No	C	801		20	45	17	15	3							53	47								Open
Campbellsville University	Campbellsville	SM	A,B,M	Pri	No	C	3,349	21		15	56	25	4		65	24	9	3		42	39	13	5		71	26	3		Open
Centre College	Danville	SM	B	Pri	F,S	C	1,430	29			7	50	43	590	14	41	32	13	630	8	28	40	24	600	9	40	39	12	1/15
Eastern Kentucky University	Richmond	SM	A,B,M,D	Pub	F,S	C	14,327																						8/1
Georgetown College	Georgetown	SU	B,M	Pri	F,S	C	984	23		4	50	39	7	494	57	29	14		511	43	46	11							8/1
Kentucky Christian University	Grayson	SM	B,M	Pri	No	C	570	19	62	22	10	3	2	450	73	20	7		460	53	40	7							8/1
Kentucky State University	Frankfort	SM	A,B,M		F,S	C	2,300	17																					Open
Kentucky Wesleyan College	Owensboro	SU	B	Pri	F,S	C	678	22	38	29	16	7	10	470	58	36	6		490	55	36	9		460	61	36	3		Open
Lindsey Wilson College	Columbia	SM	A,B,M,D	Pri	No	C	2,144	21	46	28	18	5	3	480	62	30	8		500	46	54			395	100				Open
Midway University	Midway	R	A,B,M		No	PW	1,169	20	62	21	10	3	4																Open
Morehead State University	Morehead	SM	A,B,M,D	Pub	F,S	C	9,754	23		8	52	35	5																Open
Murray State University	Murray	SM	A,B,M,D	Pub	F,S	C	8,886	24		1	43	46	10	540	38	31	27	4	525	35	51	12	2						8/15
Northern Kentucky University	Highland Heights	SU	A,B,M,D	Pub	F,S	C	11,651	23						505	47	38	12	4	505	46	36	14	3	480	55	34	7	4	8/18
Spalding University	Louisville	U	A,B,M,D	Pri	F,S	C	1,316	20		20	55	24	1						510	47	24	29							Open
Thomas More College	Crestview Hills	SU	A,B,M	Pri	F,S	C	1,502	22	28	35	24	5	8	480	55	36	9		490	51	31	13	5						8/1
Transylvania University	Lexington	U	B	Pri	F,S	C	966	27			14	58	28	560	17	48	31	3	560	34	24	14	28						2/1
Union College	Barbourville	SM	B,M	Pri	No	C	912	20		22	61	16	1						506										Open
University of Kentucky	Lexington	SU	B,M,D	Pub	F,S	C	20,767								23	46	22	9		20	41	28	10		24	47	23	6	2/15
University of Louisville	Louisville	U	A,B,M,D	Pub	F,S	C	15,827	25			36	43	20	540	24	44	24	8	550	24	42	26	8						Open
University of Pikeville	Pikeville	SM	A,B,M,D	Pri	No	C	1,658	20	1	28	56	13	2		92	8				64	24	12			83	17			8/15
University of the Cumberlands	Williamsburg	SM	A,B,M,D	Pri	No	C	3,082	22		8	57	27	8	482	64	33	3		478	64	28	5	3						8/31
Western Kentucky University	Bowling Green	SU	A,B,M,D	Pub	F,S	C	17,459	23		7	48	35	10	520	39	38	20	2	510	45	36	16	3						8/1
Louisiana																													
Centenary College of Louisiana	Shreveport	U	B,M	Pri	F,S	C	586	25						510	33	45	18	3	560	24	45	30							8/1
Dillard University	New Orleans	U	B	Pri	F,S	C	1,249																						8/1
Grambling State University	Grambling	SM	A,B,M,D	Pub	F,S	C	3,883			41	54	14			86	14				80	19	1			91	10			7/1
Louisiana College	Pineville	SM	A,B	Pri	F,S	C	1,056	22	38	29	16	9	8																Open
Louisiana State University and A&M College	Baton Rouge	U	B,M,D	Pub	F,S	C	24,923	26	5	27	31	17	21	559	22	51	24	4	577	15	44	35	6						4/15
Louisiana State University in Shreveport	Shreveport	U	B,M,D	Pub	F,S	C	2,819	22	30	32	24	6	5	500	40	60			530	17	83								4/15
Louisiana Tech University	Ruston	SM	A,B,M,D	Pub	F,S	C	10,800	24																					9/1
Loyola University New Orleans	New Orleans	SU	B,M,D	Pri	F,S	C	2,483	26			30	50	19	580	11	47	33	9	550	22	49	25	4						Open
McNeese State University	Lake Charles	SU	A,B,M	Pub	F,S	C	7,501	20	36	37	17	5	5						490										Open
Nicholls State University	Thibodaux	SM	A,B,M	Pub	F,S	C	5,515	21																					Open
Southeastern Louisiana University	Hammond	SM	A,B,M,D	Pub	F,S	C	13,586	22		4	64	30	2																8/1

NAME OF SCHOOL	TOWN	ENVIRONMENT U-Urban R-Rural SU-Suburban SM-Small Town	DEGREES AWARDED A-Associate B-Bachelor M-Master D-Doctorate	CONTROL Pri-Private, Pub-Public	FRATERNITIES AND SORORITIES F-Fraternities S-Sororities F, S-Both No-Neither	STUDENTS: C-Coed M-Men W-Women PM-Primarily Men PW-Primarily Women	UNDERGRADUATE ENROLLMENT FALL 2016	TEST SCORES: ACT Median	ACT Below 21	ACT 21-23	ACT 24-26	ACT 27-28	ACT Above 28	SAT CRITICAL READING Median	SAT CR Below 500	SAT CR 500-599	SAT CR 600-700	SAT CR Above 700	SAT MATHEMATICS Median	SAT M Below 500	SAT M 500-599	SAT M 600-700	SAT M Above 700	SAT WRITING Median	SAT W Below 500	SAT W 500-599	SAT W 600-700	SAT W Above 700	APPLICATION DEADLINE Month / Day
Southern University and A&M College	Baton Rouge	U	B,M,D	Pub	F,S	C	6,491	19					1																7/1
Southern University at New Orleans	New Orleans	SU	A,B,M	Pub	No	C	3,165																						7/1
Tulane University	New Orleans	U	A,B,M,D	Pri	F,S	C	8,339	31						670	2	12	56	30	670	1	12	58	29	680	1	6	53	39	1/15
University of Holy Cross	New Orleans	SU	A,B,M,D	Pri	No	C	773																					39	1/15
University of Louisiana at Lafayette	Lafayette	U	B,M,D	Pub	F,S	C	14,560																						Open
University of Louisiana at Monroe	Monroe	U	A,B,M,D	Pub	F,S	C	7,778	22		6	58	54	5	500	50	34	14	2	570	32	27	27	14						Open
University of New Orleans	New Orleans	U	B,M,D	Pub	F,S	C	8,653	21	37	35	18	6	4	550	35	31	30	4	550	32	34	29	5	540	35	40	22	3	7/25
Xavier University of Louisiana	New Orleans	U	B,M,D	Pri	F,S	C		24						509					494					476					7/1
Maine																													
Bates College	Lewiston	SM	B	Pri	No	C	1,780	30		1	9	36	54	630	5	28	45	22	640	5	27	42	26	630	6	24	47	23	1/1
Bowdoin College	Brunswick	SM	B	Pri	No	C	1,806	32			3	17	80	710	2	9	30	59	710	3	10	33	54	710	3	7	34	56	1/1
Colby College	Waterville	SM	B	Pri	No	C		31			2	36	62	675	1	13	53	34	690	1	7	48	44	680		11	43	45	1/1
College of the Atlantic	Bar Harbor	SM	B,M	Pri	No	C	337	28			6	63	31	650	6	24	49	21	550	15	58	27		600	3	42	46	9	2/1
Husson University	Bangor	SU	A,B,M,D	Pri	F,S	C	2,834	20		32	55	13		480	59	31	9	1	486	54	38	7	1	472	64	31	5		8/1
Maine College of Art	Portland	U	B,M	Pri	No	C	370																						Open
Maine Maritime Academy	Castine	SM	A,B,M	Pub	F	C	935																						5/1
Saint Joseph's College of Maine	Standish	R	A,B		No	C	930	21																					8/1
Thomas College	Waterville	R	A,B,M	Pri	F	C	1,339	18	50	40	10			445	70	26	3	1	453	66	27	7		435	77	19	4		Open
Unity College	Unity	SM	A,B,M	Pri	No	C	729																						2/15
University of Maine	Orono	SM	B,M,D		F,S	C	9,323	23		7	45	41	7	530	34	45	18	3	540	32	42	22	4	510	40	44	14	2	2/1
University of Maine at Augusta	Augusta	SM	A,B	Pub	No	C	4,990																						8/15
University of Maine at Farmington	Farmington	SM	B,M	Pub	No	C	1,782							510	42	39	17	2	490	51	36	11	2	500	50	39	10	1	Open
University of Maine at Fort Kent	Fort Kent	SM	A,B	Pub	F,S	C	1,904	20		38	50	12		450	72	28			440	79	18	3		440	76	24			Open
University of Maine at Machias	Machias	R	A,B	Pub	F,S	C	1,187	22	43	14	29	7	7																8/15
University of Maine at Presque Isle	Presque Isle	R	A,B	Pub	F,S	C		21																					Open
University of New England	Biddeford	SM	B,M,D	Pri	No	C	2,374	23		4	46	45	4	523	39	45	14	2	529	35	43	20	2	510	42	45	13		2/15
University of Southern Maine	Gorham	U	A,B,M,D	Pub	F,S	C	7,618	21	45	32	15	3	5	500	47	39	12	2	500	50	40	9	1	490	51	37	11	1	2/15
Maryland																													
Bowie State University	Bowie	SU	B,M,D	Pub	F,S	C	4,711							410	77	21	2		400	82	16	2		390					4/1
Capitol Technology University	Laurel	R	A,B,M	Pri	No	C	300																						Open
Coppin State University	Baltimore	U	B,M	Pub	F,S	C	3,242																						6/15
Frostburg State University	Frostburg	SM	B,M,D	Pub	F,S	C	4,884	20						488	59	33	6	1	492	58	34	8	1	469	66	27	6	1	Open
Goucher College	Baltimore	SU	B,M	Pri	No	C	1,473	25		5	35	46	14	580	24	34	32	10	570	22	45	23	10	560	27	37	30	6	2/1
Hood College	Frederick	SU	B,M,D	Pri	No	C	1,174	22		2	67	28	3	500	48	36	12	4	500	45	42	13		480	57	33	9	1	Open
Johns Hopkins University	Baltimore	SU	B,M,D	Pri	F,S	C	5,365	34			1	3	96	730	1	3	26	70	750	1	1	20	78	730	1	5	26	69	1/1
Loyola University Maryland	Baltimore	U	B,M,D	Pri	No	C	4,084	27					19	591	4	51	39	6	599	6	40	48	6						1/15
Maryland Institute College of Art	Baltimore	SM	B,M	Pri	No	C	1,680																						1/15
McDaniel College	Westminster	SU	B,M	Pri	F,S	C	1,559	24		2	43	42	13	545	31	43	19	7	546	27	45	23	5						2/1
Morgan State University	Baltimore	SU	B,M,D	Pub	F,S	C	6,119	17	1	54	41	4		440	80	18	2		440	79	17	4		420	84	15	1		11/15
Mount St. Mary's University	Emmitsburg	R	B,M	Pri	No	C	1,729	21	1	8	61	26	4	530	36	43	18	3	520	38	42	19	1	500	50	38	11	1	Open
Notre Dame of Maryland University	Baltimore	SU	B,M		No	PW	1,620																						Open
Salisbury University	Salisbury	R	B,M,D	Pub	F,S	C	7,861	23		4	57	35	4	570	6	60	31	3	580	6	55	37	2	560	9	62	27	2	1/15
St. John's College-Annapolis	Annapolis	SM	B,M	Pri	No	C	412	29			16	42	42	680	6	17	38	39	640	4	19	45	29		4	17	47	33	Open
St. Mary's College of Maryland	St. Marys City	R	B,M	Pub	No	C	1,643	26		3	23	50	24	580	20	36	34	10	550	27	41	25	6	540	28	45	23	4	2/15
Stevenson University	Stevenson	SU	B,M	Pri	S	C		22		12	53	32	3	510	44	42	13	1	510	43	40	16	1	500	49	40	11		Open
Towson University	Towson	SU	B,M,D	Pub	F,S	C	16,230																						Open
United States Naval Academy	Annapolis	SM	B	Pub	No	C	4,487							674	2	19	37	41	667		15	41	40						1/31
University of Maryland/Baltimore County	Baltimore	SU	B,M,D	Pub	F,S	C	11,274			1	19	53	26	540		46	36	10	570	3	35	46	16	530	10	44	38	8	2/1
University of Maryland/College Park	College Park	SU	B,M,D	Pub	F,S	C	28,472				7	35	58		5	22	49	24		4	15	43	38						1/20
University of Maryland/Eastern Shore	Princess Anne	SM	B,M,D	Pub	F,S	C																							6/30
University of Maryland/University College	Adelphi	U	B,M,D	Pub	No	C	28,119																						Open
Washington Adventist University	Takoma Park	SU	A,B,M	Pri	No	C	995	18	56	24	20			451	74	21	4	1	429	76	22	2							8/1
Washington College	Chestertown	SM	B,M	Pri	F,S	C	1,479							586	10	46	34	10	571	16	45	34	5						2/15
Massachusetts																													
American International College	Springfield	U	A,B,M,D	Pri	F,S	C	1,729	19	60	30	4	4	2	467	67	28	4	1	471	64	26	10	1	461	66	29	5		8/15

Amherst College	Amherst	SM	B	Pri	No	C	1,849	33				11	89	740		1	31	68	740		1	32	67	730		3	27	70	1/1
Anna Maria College	Paxton	R	B,M	Pri	No	C	1,128																						Open
Assumption College	Worcester	SU	B,M	Pri	No	C	1,976	25		3	31	53	13	550	24	48	26	2	560	17	55	26	2						2/15
Atlantic Union College	South Lancaster	SM	A,B,M	Pri	No	C	450																						8/1
Babson College	Babson Park	SU	B,M	Pri	F,S	C	1,800																						1/4
Bard College at Simon's Rock	Great Barrington	SM	A,B	Pri	No	C	362	28			14	57	14	692		4	41	52	656		22	48	30	661		11	26	19	Open
Bay Path University	Longmeadow	SU	A,B,M	Pri	No	W	1,893			19	48	26	7		55	33	11	1		63	32	5			60	34	5	1	Open
Becker College	Worcester	U	A,B	Pri	No	C	1,826	21						490	54	30	14	2	490	51	32	14	3	470	63	27	9	1	Open
Benjamin Franklin Institute of Technology	Boston	U	A,B	Pri	No	C	500																					1	Open
Bentley University	Waltham	SU	B,M,D	Pri	F,S	C	4,222	28			6	64	30	590	9	44	41	6	650	2	20	54	24	600	7	39	48	6	1/7
Berklee College of Music	Boston	U	B,M	Pri	No	C																							1/15
Boston Architectural College	Boston	U	B,M	Pri	No	C	329																						Open
Boston College	Chestnut Hill	SU	B,M,D	Pri	No	C	9,309	32			2	15	83	670	2	13	50	34	690	1	10	44	44	685	2	12	41	44	1/1
Boston University	Boston	U	B,M,D	Pri	F,S	C	17,944	30		1	8	18	73	650	1	16	60	23	660		14	56	29	660	1	13	59	27	1/3
Brandeis University	Waltham	SU	B,M,D	Pri	No	C	3,608	31			1	23	76	680	2	8	49	41	690	2	6	47	46	690	2	7	45	47	1/1
Bridgewater State University	Bridgewater	SU	B,M	Pub	F,S	C	8,307	21		14	58	26	2	490	53	38	9		500	49	41	10							2/15
Cambridge College	Cambridge	U	B,M,D	Pri	No	C	1,048																						Open
Clark University	Worcester	U	B,M,D	Pri	No	C	2,289	29			6	50	44	620	6	34	44	16	610	6	36	47	11	610	8	33	47	12	1/15
College of Art and Design at Lesley University	Boston	U	B,M	Pri	No	C	1,267		9	50	13	24	4		27	47	24	2		41	46	12	1		27	50	20	3	2/15
College of the Holy Cross	Worcester	SU	B	Pri	No	C	2,941	29			3	47	50	640	2	21	58	19	654	1	14	61	24	648	1	21	52	26	1/15
Curry College	Milton	SU	B,M	Pri	No	C	2,688	21		21	58	19	2	470	60	30	3		470	58	30	5		460	63	27	3		4/1
Eastern Nazarene College	Quincy	SU	A,B,M		No	C	640																						9/1
Elms College	Chicopee	SU	A,B,M		No	C	640																						Open
Emerson College	Boston	U	B,M,D	Pri	F,S	C	3,784	27		1	9	66	24	620	5	33	48	14	590	9	42	40	9	610	6	34	47	13	1/15
Emmanuel College	Boston	U	B,M	Pri	No	C		25			33	57	10	565	10	56	33	1	555	17	56	26		555	18	54	26	2	2/15
Endicott College	Beverly	SU	A,B,M,D	Pri	No	C	3,258	27						532	29	53	17	1	543	23	53	22	2	530	31	51	17	1	2/15
Fitchburg State University	Fitchburg	SU	B,M	Pub	F,S	C	4,165	21	41	37	11	7	4	490	48	40	11	1	450	40	46	14	1	480	51	39	9	1	3/1
Framingham State University	Framingham	SU	B,M	Pub	No	C	4,337	22	1	11	48	38	2	480	55	34	9	1	500	48	42	10		480	58	35	6	1	2/15
Franklin W. Olin College of Engineering	Needham	SU	B	Pri	No	C	378	34				2	98	730		4	22	74	770			12	88	720		4	37	59	1/1
Gordon College	Wenham	SU	B,M	Pri	No	C	1,657	26		3	30	45	22	557	29	38	25	8	551	30	38	26	6	549	31	38	28	3	2/1
Hampshire College	Amherst	R	B	Pri	No	C	1,396																						1/15
Harvard College/Harvard University	Cambridge	U	B,M,D		No	C	6,670																						1/1
Hellenic College/Holy Cross Greek Orthodox School of Theology	Brookline	U	B,M	Pri	No	C	91	22	20	60	20			550	30	35	30	5	450	55	35	5	5	460	45	35	20		8/1
Lasell College	Newton	SU	B,M	Pri	No	C	1,778	21		17	55	26	2	484	55	36	8	1	479	59	33	7	1	481	59	33	7	1	9/1
Lesley University	Cambridge	U	A,B,M,D	Pri	No	C		23		5	36	54	5	545	26	48	22	3	520	37	46	16		540	29	47	22	2	2/15
Massachusetts College of Art and Design	Boston	U	B,M	Pub	No	C	1,772							560	18	47	30	5	540	26	49	22	3	540	23	49	24	3	2/1
Massachusetts College of Liberal Arts	North Adams	R	B,M	Pub	F,S	C	1,444	23		7	53	35	5	520	42	36	21	2	500	47	41	11	1						Open
Massachusetts Institute of Technology	Cambridge	U	B,M,D	Pri	F,S	C	4,524	34				2	98	750		3	20	77	780			3	97	740		3	23	74	1/1
Massachusetts Maritime Academy	Buzzards Bay	SM	B,M	Pub	No	C	1,677	22		9	55	36		500	47	41	12		540	25	52	22	1	490	53	41	6		Open
MCPHS University	Boston	U	B,M,D	Pri	F	C	2,883	24	20	28	34	14	4	525	31	55	13	1	570	16	47	34	4	540	26	51	22	1	2/1
Merrimack College	North Andover	SU	A,B,M	Pri	F,S	C	2,319																						2/15
Montserrat College of Art	Beverly	SU	B	Pri	No	C	305																						Open
Mount Holyoke College	South Hadley	SM	B,M	Pri	No	W	2,126	30			2	34	64	670		15	48	37	660	3	16	43	38	670		11	51	38	1/15
Mount Ida College	Newton	SU	A,B	Pri	No	C	1,130																						8/15
New England Conservatory of Music	Boston	U	B,M,D	Pri	No	C	436																						12/1
Newbury College	Brookline	SU	A,B	Pri	No	C	751																						Open
Nichols College	Dudley	SU	A,B,M	Pri	No	C	1,332	20	70	13	8	7	2	450	73	24	3		470	64	27	9		450	72	26	2		Open
Northeastern University	Boston	U	B,M,D	Pri	F,S	C	17,107	31						690	2	9	46	44	700	1	5	36	57	680	1	9	50	40	1/1
Pine Manor College	Chestnut Hill	SU	A,B,M	Pri	No	W	458																						Open
Regis College	Weston	SU	A,B,M,D	Pri	No	C	1,235	23		24	33	38	5	480	64	32	4		485	56	36	8		470	65	31	4		6/1
Salem State University	Salem	U	B,M	Pub	No	C	7,298																						Open
Simmons College	Boston	U	B,M,D	Pri	No	PW	1,802	26			19	53	28	600	8	42	35	10	580	12	55	31	2	570	13	45	35	7	2/1
Smith College	Northampton	SM	B,M,D	Pri	No	W		31		1	5	29	65	685	1	9	42	47	670	1	21	42	36	685	1	12	44	43	1/15
Springfield College	Springfield	SU	B,M,D		No	C	2,200																						12/1
Stonehill College	Easton	SU	B	Pri	No	C		25						555	20	51	26	3	565	19	44	33	3	555	23	46	29	2	1/15
Suffolk University	Boston	U	A,B,M,D	Pri	F,S	C	5,290	23		10	46	39	5	508	45	40	13	2	512	41	44	14	1	502	45	43	11	1	3/1
The Boston Conservatory at Berklee	Boston	U	B,M	Pri	F,S	C	512	25						549					577									1	3/1
Tufts University	Medford	SU	B,M,D	Pri	F,S	C	5,508	32			1	10	89	680		4	32	64	710		2	25	73	690	1	2	31	66	1/1
University of Massachusetts Amherst	Amherst	SM	A,B,M,D		F,S	C		27			9	63	28	600	8	42	42	9	630	3	29	42	16						1/15
University of Massachusetts Boston	Boston	U	B,M,D	Pub	No	C	12,847			3	48	43	6	520	37	44	17	3	540	27	47	24	2						3/1
University of Massachusetts Dartmouth	North Dartmouth	SU	B,M,D	Pub	F,S	C	6,999	23		9	49	37	5	500	46	40	12	2	520	37	45	16	2	487	55	36	8	1	Open
University of Massachusetts Lowell	Lowell	U	A,B,M,D	Pub	F,S	C	13,639	26		1	23	59	17	571	14	51	29	6	601	5	42	43	9	546	24	51	22	2	Open
Wellesley College	Wellesley	SU	B	Pri	No	W	2,197	31			1	26	73	694		6	44	49	703		9	44	46	696		7	35	57	1/15
Wentworth Institute of Technology	Boston	U	A,B,M	Pri	No	C	4,324	23	1	2	43	48	7	520	33	48	18	2	580	12	48	35	6		43	42	13	1	2/15
Western New England University	Springfield	SU	A,B,M,D	Pri	No	C	2,724	24		2	37	51	10	530	30	50	18	2	560	19	49	29	3						Open
Westfield State University	Westfield	SU	B,M	Pub	No	C	5,610	21	2	15	60	23		490	44	45	10	1	500	40	48	11		480	50	43	6		3/1
Wheaton College	Norton	SU	B	Pri	No	C	1,651	27		1	16	57	26	580	14	48	29	9	580	11	48	35	7	580	16	44	34	6	1/1
Wheelock College	Boston	U	B,M	Pri	No	C	726			43	47	10			70	23	7			69	29	2			67	27	6		3/1
Williams College	Williamstown	SM	B,M	Pri	No	C	2,099	33			1	14	85	730		6	28	66	720		7	31	62	730	1	5	29	65	1/1
Worcester Polytechnic Institute	Worcester	SU	B,M,D	Pri	F,S	C	4,432	30			4	40	56	630	3	29	50	18	680		9	54	37	620	5	32	50	12	2/1
Worcester State University	Worcester	U	B,M	Pub	No	C	5,381	23		5	48	43	3	501	50	39	11	1	509	44	44	11	1						5/1

NAME OF SCHOOL	TOWN	ENVIRONMENT U-Urban R-Rural SU-Suburban SM-Small Town	DEGREES AWARDED A-Associate B-Bachelor M-Master D-Doctorate	CONTROL Pri-Private, Pub-Public	FRATERNITIES AND SORORITIES F-Fraternities S-Sororities F, S-Both No-Neither	STUDENTS: C-Coed M-Men W-Women PM-Primarily Men PW-Primarily Women	UNDERGRADUATE ENROLLMENT FALL 2016	TEST SCORES: ACT						SAT CRITICAL READING					SAT MATHEMATICS					SAT WRITING					APPLICATION DEADLINE Month / Day
								Median	Below 21	21-23	24-26	27-28	Above 28	Median	Below 500	500-599	600-700	Above 700	Median	Below 500	500-599	600-700	Above 700	Median	Below 500	500-599	600-700	Above 700	
Michigan																													
Adrian College	Adrian	SM	A,B,M	Pri	F,S	C	1,606	22	38	34	16	6	6	480	55	45			500	41	52	7							Open
Albion College	Albion	SM	B	Pri	F,S	C	1,418	23		6	46	40	7																Open
Alma College	Alma	SM	B	Pri	F,S	C	1,451	24		2	46	46	6	503	54	23	15	8	526	35	38	23	4	496	61	11	22	6	Open
Andrews University	Berrien Springs	R	A,B,M,D	Pri	F,S	C	1,964	23	34	26	21	11	8																Open
Aquinas College - Michigan	Grand Rapids	SU	A,B,M	Pri	No	C	1,654	24		2	45	47	7																Open
Baker College of Flint	Flint	U	A,B		No	C	4,400																						9/20
Calvin College	Grand Rapids	SU	B,M	Pri	No	C	3,807	27			19	54	27	620	7	34	42	17	600	9	38	39	14						8/15
Central Michigan University	Mount Pleasant	SM	B,M,D	Pub	F,S	C	22,239	23	29	34	22	9	6																Open
College for Creative Studies	Detroit	U	B	Pri	No	C	3,901	22																					8/1
Concordia University, Ann Arbor	Ann Arbor	SU	A,B,M	Pri	No	C	521	22	36	20	27	11	6	575	36	21	21	22	550	28	43	29		560	43	7	29	21	8/15
Davenport University	Grand Rapids	SU	A,B,M	Pri	No	C	8,882																						Open
Eastern Michigan University	Ypsilanti	SU	B,M,D	Pub	F,S	C	17,780	22		11	54	32	3	483	47	26	14	3	509	41	40	17	2	486	57	33	9	1	8/30
Ferris State University	Big Rapids	SM	A,B,M,D	Pub	F,S	C	12,870	22		15	53	27	5																8/1
Grace Bible College	Grand Rapids	SU	A,B,M	Pri	No	C	303	21		20	70	7	3	560	35	66			540	34	66			500	34	33	33		Open
Grand Rapids Theological Seminary/Cornerstone University	Grand Rapids	SU	A,B,M	Pri	No	C	2,152	23	27	30	26	9	8	544	31	34	31	3	529	34	46	17	3	504	20	23	6		8/15
Grand Valley State University	Allendale	SM	B,M,D	Pub	F,S	C	21,231	24	19	31	28	12	10																7/23
Hillsdale College	Hillsdale	SM	B,M,D	Pri	F,S	C	1,486	31			1	40	59	680	2	11	42	45	640	5	25	46	24	660		20	46	34	4/1
Hope College	Holland	U	B	Pri	F,S	C	3,404	26		1	24	54	21		13	36	42	9	600	7	323	44	15						Open
Kalamazoo College	Kalamazoo	SU	B	Pri	No	C	1,443	28		2	13	48	37	610	16	29	33	22	640	9	22	37	31	610	13	28	39	19	1/15
Kettering University	Flint	SU	B,M	Pri	F,S	C		27			10	66	35	590	4	50	33	13	640	4	30	39	26						Open
Lawrence Technological University	Southfield	SU	A,B,M,D	Pri	F,S	C	2,164	25		5	27	49	19	540	30	40	27	3	610	15	24	58	3	530	28	53	19		Open
Madonna University	Livonia	SU	A,B,M,D	Pri	No	C	2,629	21		23	53	23	1																Open
Marygrove College	Detroit	U	A,B,M	Pri	F,S	C	788	17																					8/28
Michigan State University	East Lansing	SU	B,M,D		F,S	C	39,090	26		2	22	57	19		41	35	18	6		37	41	18	3		38	43	15	4	7/25
Michigan Technological University	Houghton	SM	A,B,M,D	Pub	F,S	C	5,829	27			15	58	27	590	16	35	28	20	620	4	29	49	18	560	32	37	30	1	Open
Northern Michigan University	Marquette	U	A,B,M,D	Pub	F,S	C	7,082	23																					Open
Northwood University - Michigan	Midland	SU	A,B,M	Pri	F,S	C	1,819		48	27	16	6	3		76	17	3	3		55	34	10			64	29	7		8/1
Oakland University	Rochester	SU	B,M,D	Pub	F,S	C	17,161	22																					3/24
Olivet College	Olivet	SM	B,M	Pri	F,S	C	1,052	19	25	40	15	15	5																Open
Rochester College	Rochester Hills	SU	A,B,M	Pri	F,S	C	908	20	50	20	21	7	2																8/30
Saginaw Valley State University	University Center	SU	B,M,D	Pub	F,S	C	8,397	22		7	55	32	5																Open
Siena Heights University	Adrian	SM	A,B,M		F,S	C	2,402	21																					8/1
Spring Arbor University	Spring Arbor	SM	A,B,M	Pri	No	C	1,555																						8/1
University of Detroit Mercy	Detroit	U	B,M,D	Pri	F,S	C	2,646	25		2	45	45	9	526	39	32	29		543	32	32	29	7	517	50	21	21	7	8/1
University of Michigan/Ann Arbor	Ann Arbor	SU	B,M,D	Pub	F,S	C		31			3	26	71	680	2	13	47	39	715	1	8	31	60	685	2	10	41	46	2/1
University of Michigan/Dearborn	Dearborn	SU	B,M,D	Pub	F,S	C	7,141	25			39	48	13															46	2/1
University of Michigan-Flint	Flint	U	B,M,D	Pub	F,S	C	7,143	21	45	25	16	7	7	610	30	10	40	20	595	20	30	30	20	580	20	50		30	8/20
Wayne State University	Detroit	U	B,M,D	Pub	F,S	C	17,280	24		4	44	40	12																8/1
Western Michigan University	Kalamazoo	U	B,M,D	Pub	F,S	C	17,984	22		14	50	31	5																Open
Minnesota																													
Augsburg College	Minneapolis	U	B,M	Pri	No	C	3,124	22	38	27	23	8	4	505	50	25	21	4	565	21	33	38	8						8/15
Bemidji State University	Bemidji	SM	A,B,M	Pub	F,S	C	4,744																						Open
Bethel University	St. Paul	SU	A,B,M,D	Pri	No	C	3,421	25	17	23	26	14	21	590	20	31	30	19	580	20	39	28	14						Open
Carleton College	Northfield	SM	B	Pri	No	C	2,063				1	22	77		1	6	30	64			8	32	60			12	37	51	1/15
College of Saint Benedict	St. Joseph	SM	B	Pri	No	C	1,958			1	35	46	18		38	41	18	3		51	39	10			41	51	3	5	Open
College of St. Scholastica	Duluth	SU	B,M,D	Pri	No	C	2,841	24		6	46	41	6	520	47	42	11		490	58	32	11		490	58	42			Open
Concordia College - Moorhead	Moorhead	SU	B,M	Pri	No	C	2,531	25	13	22	29	16	20	570	23	33	35	10	550	33	29	23	15		31	37	23	10	Open
Concordia University Saint Paul	St. Paul	U	A,B,M,D	Pri	No	C	2,567	21		16	54	25	5																8/1
Gustavus Adolphus College	St. Peter	SM	B	Pri	F,S	C	2,455	27	2	13	31	20	34																11/1
Hamline University	St. Paul	U	B,M,D	Pri	F,S	C	2,242	24	20	24	21	11	19	550	36	32	22	10	540	27	51	19	3	540	31	36	31	3	Open
Macalester College	St. Paul	U	B	Pri	No	C	2,146	31			3	29	68	700	2	12	31	55	680	1	14	49	36	690	1	10	44	45	1/15
Metropolitan State University	St. Paul	U	B,M,D	Pub	No	C	6,974																						6/15
Minneapolis College of Art and Design	Minneapolis	U	B,M	Pri	No	C	740																						6/15
Minnesota State University, Mankato	Mankato	R	A,B,M,D	Pub	F,S	C	13,388	23	9	62	16	12	1																8/24
Minnesota State University, Moorhead	Moorhead	SU	A,B,M,D	Pub	F,S	C	7,012																						8/1
North Central University	Minneapolis	U	A,B	Pri	No	C	1,366	21																					6/1
Saint John's University	Collegeville	R	B,M	Pri	No	C	1,754			2	34	47	17		33	53	12	2		35	41	24			59	31	8	2	Open

Saint Mary's University of Minnesota	Winona	SM	B,M,D	Pri	F,S	C	1,590	23		8	51	36	5	501	48	43	5	5	497	48	33	14	5	485	59	29	6	6	5/1
Southwest Minnesota State University	Marshall	R	A,B,M	Pub	No	C	2,710																						8/1
St. Catherine University	St. Paul	U	A,B,M,D	Pri	No	W	3,559	24	1		48	44	7	560	27	39	17	17	525	27	56	17							Open
St. Cloud State University	St. Cloud	SU	A,B,M,D	Pub	F,S	C	14,525																						Open
St. Olaf College	Northfield	SM	B	Pri	No	C	3,040	29			11	47	42	630	13	25	33	29	630	10	26	37	27	610					1/15
University of Minnesota Crookston	Crookston	SM	B	Pub	F,S	C	2,764	22	41	29	19	9	2	480	53	27	13		520	20	53	7	7	490	57	43			8/15
University of Minnesota/Duluth	Duluth	U	B,M,D		F,S	C	8,929	24	15	33	33	11	8	510	40	34	23	3	540	28	46	21	5	530	36	41	21	2	8/1
University of Minnesota/Morris	Morris	SM	B	Pub	No	C	1,771	25		2	33	49	15	560	32	44	12	12	590	16	40	24	20	540	28	44	24	4	3/15
University of Minnesota/Twin Cities	Minneapolis	U	B,M,D	Pub	F,S	C	34,871	28			9	53	38	630	8	29	36	27	690	4	14	34	48	640	4	26	47	23	Open
University of Northwestern - St. Paul	St. Paul	SU	A,B,M	Pri	No	C	1,865																						8/1
University of St. Thomas	St. Paul	U	B,M,D	Pri	No	C	6,111	26			19	62	19	580	20	34	32	14	590	6	40	42	12						Open
Winona State University	Winona	U	A,B,M,D	Pub	F,S	C	7,656	23																					7/14

Mississippi

Alcorn State University	Lorman	R	A,B,M	Pub	F,S	C	3,010																						Open
Belhaven University	Jackson	U	A,B,M	Pri	No	C	2,641	21		3	65	28	4	540	32	35	33		515	40	46	14							8/12
Blue Mountain College	Blue Mountain	R	B,M	Pri	No	C	544	21		21	59	15	5	555	50		50		480	50	50			495	50	50			Open
Delta State University	Cleveland	SM	B,M,D	Pub	F,S	C	2,659	20		23	59	15	2	510	38	38	13	13	475	63		25	13						8/1
Jackson State University	Jackson	U	B,M,D	Pub	F,S	C	7,492	19		36	51	12																	9/10
Millsaps College	Jackson	U	B,M	Pri	F,S	C	744	26	9	23	27	18	23	540	25	39	28	8	560	17	47	33	3						9/10
Mississippi College	Clinton	SU	B,M,D	Pri	F,S	C	3,000	24						550					520										Open
Mississippi State University	Mississippi State	SM	B,M,D		F,S	C	18,090	24		5	41	39	15																8/1
Mississippi University for Women	Columbus	SM	A,B,M,D	Pub	F,S	C	3,200																						Open
Mississippi Valley State University	Itta Bena	SM	B,M	Pub	F,S	C	2,748	17	91	6	3																		8/10
Rust College	Holly Springs	SM	A,B		F,S	C	1,015																						8/10
Tougaloo College	Tougaloo	SU	A,B	Pri	F,S	C	940																						Open
University of Mississippi	university	SM	B,M,D	Pub	F,S	C	19,213	25		2	33	46	19	562	22	46	24	8	564	18	48	26	8						Open
University of Southern Mississippi	Hattiesburg	SU	B,M,D	Pub	F,S	C	13,658	22	41	24	19	7	9		35	43	18	4		42	40	18							6/30
William Carey University	Hattiesburg	SM	B,M		F,S	C	1,850																						6/30

Missouri

Avila University	Kansas City	SU	B,M	Pri	No	C	1,135																						8/25
Central Methodist University	Fayette	SM	A,B,M	Pri	F,S	C	1,173																						Open
College of the Ozarks	Point Lookout	SM	B	Pri	No	C	1,512	23		1	55	40	4	595	14	36	43	7	530	21	50	21	7	570	29	43	21	7	12/31
Columbia College - Missouri	Columbia	U	A,B,M	Pri	No	C	936	23		3	52	39	6	500	46	31	8	15	550	22	62	8	8						8/12
Cox College	Springfield	U	A,B,M		No	C	600																						8/12
Culver-Stockton College	Canton	SM	B,M	Pri	F,S	C	1,058	21		13	69	17	1		53	40	7			33	67								Open
Drury University	Springfield	U	A,B,M	Pri	F,S	C	1,370	25		1	39	46	14		17	39	22	22		13	52	30	5		43	26	22	9	8/22
Evangel University	Springfield	U	A,B,M	Pri	No	C	1,879																					9	8/22
Fontbonne University	St. Louis	SU	B,M	Pri	No	C	2,085																					9	8/22
Hannibal-LaGrange University	Hannibal	SM	A,B,M	Pri	No	C	1,711		20	43	27	4	6																8
Harris-Stowe State University	St. Louis	U	B	Pub	No	C	1,464		91	8	1																		Open
Kansas City Art Institute	Kansas City	U	B	Pri	No	C	660	24	28	22	21	14	15	580	13	50	34	3	440	34	66			560	38	53	9		8/1
Lincoln University	Jefferson City	SM	A,B,M	Pub	F,S	C	2,618	18	2	55	37	7																	Open
Lindenwood University	St. Charles	SU	B,M,D	Pri	F,S	C	5,905																						Open
Maryville University of Saint Louis	St. Louis	SU	B,M,D	Pri	No	C	2,967	26		6	31	53	10																8/19
Missouri Baptist University	St. Louis	SU	A,B,M,D	Pri	No	C	4,631	21																					Open
Missouri Southern State University	Joplin	SM	A,B,M	Pub	F,S	C	5,732	22		15	53	28	4																9/1
Missouri State University	Springfield	SU	B,M,D	Pub	F,S	C		24		2	47	43	8	540	33	31	33	3	552	27	41	25	7						7/20
Missouri University of Science and Technology	Rolla	SM	B,M,D		F,S	C	6,146	28	1	8	26	19	46	590	14	35	36	15	640	5	21	54	21						7/1
Missouri Valley College	Marshall	SM	A,B,M	Pri	F,S	C	1,430																						Open
Missouri Western State University	St. Joseph	SU	A,B	Pub	F,S	C	5,250																						Open
Northwest Missouri State University	Maryville	SM	A,B,M	Pub	F,S	C	5,628	22																					Open
Park University	Parkville	SU	A,B,M	Pri	No	C	1,674	21	50	29	9	5	7																Open
Research College of Nursing	Kansas City	U	B,M	Pri	F,S	C	330	23		33	37	17	13																6/30
Rockhurst University	Kansas City	U	B,M,D		F,S	C	2,325																						6/30
Saint Louis University	St. Louis	U	B,M,D	Pri	F,S	C	8,248	28			13	51	36		13	31	44	12		7	32	45	16						12/1
Southeast Missouri State University	Cape Girardeau	SM	A,B,M	Pub	F,S	C	10,693	23		5	58	32	5																7/1
Southwest Baptist University	Bolivar	SM	A,B,M,D	Pri	No	C	3,009																						Open
Stephens College	Columbia	U	B,M	Pri	S	PW	679		29		14	43																	8/1
Truman State University	Kirksville	SM	B,M	Pub	F,S	C	6,039	27			18	54	28	600	10	39	33	18	590	16	35	33	16						3/1
University of Central Missouri	Warrensburg	SM	A,B,M	Pub	F,S	C	9,739	22	40	29	16	6	4																8/19
University of Missouri/Columbia	Columbia	SU	B,M,D	Pub	F,S	C	26,996		6	23	31	18	23																5/1
University of Missouri-Kansas City	Kansas City	U	B,M,D	Pub	F,S	C	11,708	24		5	39	40	16						609	27	37	19	16	578	23	33	30	14	7/1
University of Missouri-St. Louis	St. Louis	U	B,M,D	Pub	F,S	C	13,923	24						520	67	33			560	36	45	18		560	38	38	15	38	8/25
Washington University in St. Louis	St. Louis	SU	A,B,M,D	Pri	F,S	C	7,540					7	93			1	27	72			2	18	80			2	26	72	1/15
Webster University	St. Louis	SU	B,M,D	Pri	S	C	2,622	24		7	39	44	10																8/1
Westminster College	Fulton	SM	B	Pri	F,S	C	933	24	17	28	22	17	18																Open
William Jewell College	Liberty	SU	B	Pri	F,S	C	1,030	26	9	22	25	18	26		24	30	39	7		21	34	39	11						8/15

NAME OF SCHOOL	TOWN	ENVIRONMENT U-Urban R-Rural SU-Suburban SM-Small Town	DEGREES AWARDED A-Associate B-Bachelor M-Master D-Doctorate	CONTROL Pri-Private, Pub-Public	FRATERNITIES AND SORORITIES F-Fraternities S-Sororities F, S-Both No-Neither	STUDENTS: C-Coed M-Men W-Women PM-Primarily Men PW-Primarily Women	UNDERGRADUATE ENROLLMENT FALL 2016	TEST SCORES: ACT Median	ACT Below 21	ACT 21-23	ACT 24-26	ACT 27-28	ACT Above 28	SAT CRITICAL READING Median	CR Below 500	CR 500-599	CR 600-700	CR Above 700	SAT MATHEMATICS Median	M Below 500	M 500-599	M 600-700	M Above 700	SAT WRITING Median	W Below 500	W 500-599	W 600-700	W Above 700	APPLICATION DEADLINE Month / Day
William Woods University	Fulton	SM	A,B,M,D	Pri	F,S	C	973	22		14	49	28	9	490	53	31	16		500	47	27	16							8/15
Montana																													
Carroll College	Helena	SM	A,B		No	C	1,469	25						565					555					545					6/1
Montana State University	Bozeman	SM	A,B,M,D	Pub	F,S	C	13,707	25						570	22	39	32	7	565	22	38	33	7	545	32	39	25	4	Open
Montana State University-Billings	Billings	U	A,B,M	Pub	No	C		21		18	57	24	1	480	55	31	11	3	500	52	31	14	3						Open
Montana State University-Northern	Havre	SM	A,B,M	Pub	No	C	1,440																						Open
Montana Tech of the University of Montana	Butte	SM	A,B,M	Pub	No	C	2,770	25			33	59	8	560	21	52	25	2	600	10	35	52	3	510	40	54	6		Open
Rocky Mountain College	Billings	SU	A,B,M	Pri	No	C	908	22		11	60	24	5	500	48	41	11		495	50	38	11	1	445	67	29	2	2	Open
University of Great Falls	Great Falls	U	A,B,M	Pri	No	C	577																						9/1
University of Montana	Missoula	U	A,B,M,D	Pub	F,S	C	11,692	23						550	26	44	25	5	542	26	50	20	3	530	35	45	18	2	3/1
University of Montana-Western	Dillon	SM	A,B	Pub	No	C	1,255	20	62	23	13	3		460	68	20	10	2	470	63	29	8							7/1
Nebraska																													
Bellevue University	Bellevue	SU	B,M	Pri	No	C	3,775																						Open
Chadron State College	Chadron	R	B,M	Pub	No	C	2,375	22																					Open
Clarkson College	Omaha	U	A,B,M	Pri	No	PW	770																						8/16
College of Saint Mary	Omaha	U	A,B,M,D	Pri	No	PW	770	23	26	35	23	10	6																Open
Concordia University Nebraska	Seward	SM	B,M	Pri	No	C	1,085																						Open
Creighton University	Omaha	U	A,B,M,D	Pri	F,S	C	4,203	27			17	56	27	580	16	42	34	8	590	8	45	37	10	560	18	49	27	6	2/15
Doane University	Crete	SM	B	Pri	F,S	C	1,047	23		3	52	40	5																Open
Hastings College	Hastings	R	B,M	Pri	F,S	C	1,104	24	37	23	20	10	10																8/1
Midland University	Fremont	U	B,M	Pri	F,S	C	1,200																						Open
Nebraska Methodist College	Omaha	SU	A,B,M,D	Pri	S	C	747		21	45	28	3	3																3/1
Nebraska Wesleyan University	Lincoln	SU	B,M	Pri	F,S	C	1,903	26																					8/15
Peru State College	Peru	R	B,M	Pub	No	C	1,485																						Open
Union College	Lincoln	SU	A,B,M	Pri	No	C	813	22																					Open
University of Nebraska - Kearney	Kearney	R	B,M	Pub	F,S	C	5,502	23	30	29	22	9	10		37	42	16	5		11	42	42	5						Open
University of Nebraska - Lincoln	Lincoln	U	B,M,D	Pub	F,S	C	20,182	25		3	35	43	19	560	25	37	25	13	580	23	33	30	14						5/1
University of Nebraska - Omaha	Omaha	SU	B,M,D	Pub	F,S	C	11,525																						8/1
Wayne State College	Wayne	R	B,M	Pub	F,S	C	2,991	21	45	26	15	8	6																Open
York College	York	SM	A,B,M	Pri	F,S	C	415																						Open
Nevada																													
Sierra Nevada College	Incline Village	R	B		No	C		23		21	42	34	3																8/22
University of Nevada, Las Vegas	Las Vegas	U	B,M,D	Pub	F,S	C	23,336	22						495	49	39	11	1	500	48	37	13	2	475	62	30	7	1	2/1
University of Nevada/Reno	Reno	U	B,M,D	Pub	F,S	C	18,191	24		7	47	39	7	540	29	46	22	3	550	27	44	26	3	520	39	43	16	1	2/1
New Hampshire																													
Colby-Sawyer College	New London	SM	A,B	Pri	No	C	1,375																					1	2/1
Daniel Webster College	Nashua	SU	A,B,M	Pri	No	C	725																						Open
Dartmouth College	Hanover	R	B,M,D	Pri	F,S	C	4,310	32						740	1	8	25	66	740		5	27	68	740		7	23	70	1/1
Franklin Pierce University	Rindge	R	A,B,M,D	Pri	No	C	1,687	21	9	72			19	480	58	36	6		480	54	37	7		470	63	32	5		Open
Granite State College	Concord	SM	A,B	Pub	No	C	1,518																						Open
Keene State College	Keene	SM	B,M	Pub	F,S	C	4,068			21	52	23	4	480	56	34	9	1	490	55	37	7	1	470	61	33	6		4/1
New England College	Henniker	SM	A,B,M,D	Pri	F,S	C	1,782			30	30	40			59	26	12			54	41	5			73	23	2		Open
Plymouth State University	Plymouth	SM	B,M	Pub	S	C	4,064	20	59	20	14	4	1	479	62	31	7		484	57	34	8	1		65	30	5		4/1
Rivier University	Nashua	SU	A,B,M		No	C	1,630																						Open
Saint Anselm College	Manchester	SU	B	Pri	No	C	1,930	25	4	3	23	64	8	560	17	50	29	4	570	13	56	28	4	570	17	58	22	3	2/1
Southern New Hampshire University	Manchester	SU	A,B,M,D	Pri	F,S	C	3,027	23		12	51	37																3	2/1
Thomas More College of Liberal Arts	Merrimack	SM	B	Pri	No	C	96																						Open
University of New Hampshire	Durham	SM	A,B,M,D		F,S	C	12,871	25		3	34	53	10	590	8	42	43	7	570	10	52	31	7						2/1
University of New Hampshire - Manchester	Manchester		A,B,M	Pub	No	C	842	21	40	40	40		20	520	41	46	11	2	517	41	44	15		494	50	41	9		2/1
New Jersey																													
Berkeley College/New Jersey	Woodland Park	SU	A,B	Pri	No	C	3,052																						Open

Bloomfield College	Bloomfield	SU	B,M	Pri	F,S	C	1,978	17		58	37	5		420	88	10	2		430	80	18	2							8/1
Caldwell University	Caldwell	SU	B,M,D	Pri	No	C	1,595	21	46	31	20	3		490	60	30	9	1	480	50	37	12	1	490	52	39	9	1	Open
Centenary College	Hackettstown	SU	A,B,M	Pri	F,S	C	1,993	21	29	43	7	7	14	465	67	25	7	1	463	65	30	5							Open
College of Saint Elizabeth	Morristown	SU	B,M,D	Pri	No	PW	805							425	83	15	2		420	85	12	2	1	433	83	13	3	1	8/15
Drew University/College of Liberal Arts	Madison	SU	B,M,D	Pri	No	C	1,521	26		1	23	60	16	590	15	37	36	12	560	15	54	27	4	570	17	45	31	7	2/1
Fairleigh Dickinson University/College at Florham	Madison	SU	B,M	Pri	F,S	C	2,480							520	36	51	13	1	530	31	49	18	1	520	36	50	13	1	2/1
Fairleigh Dickinson University/Metropolitan Campus	Teaneck	SU	A,B,M,D	Pri	F,S	C	6,044							510	42	46	11		530	30	52	16	2	500	43	49	8		3/15
Felician University	Lodi	SU	A,B,M,D	Pri	F,S	C	1,648	18		41	55	4		440	75	23	2		450	70	27	3		430	79	18	3		Open
Georgian Court University	Lakewood	SU	B,M	Pri	No	C	1,591	19		44	36	16	4	460	69	26	4	1	470	57	37	5	1	450	71	26	2	1	8/1
Kean University	Union	SU	B,M,D	Pub	F,S	C	11,812	21						480					500										4/30
Monmouth University	West Long Branch	SU	A,B,M,D	Pri	F,S	C	4,693	23		3	61	34	3	511	42	48	9	1	525	34	51	14	2	518	38	48	13	1	3/1
Montclair State University	Montclair	SU	B,M,D	Pub	F,S	C	16,653							480	58	34	8		490		39	9		480		36	7		3/1
New Jersey City University	Jersey City	U	B,M,D	Pub	F,S	C	6,229							440	77	18	3	1	460	65	29								4/1
New Jersey Institute of Technology	Newark	U	B,M,D	Pub	F,S	C								575	21	45	28	6	635		36	47	17	570	24	44	25	7	3/1
Princeton University	Princeton	SM	B,M,D	Pri	No	C	5,244	33			1	6	93	740		3	21	76	760		1	19	80	750		3	18	79	1/1
Ramapo College of New Jersey	Mahwah	SU	B,M	Pub	F,S	C	5,425							540	27	51	19	3	552	21	50	25	4	535	30	47	20	3	3/1
Rider University	Lawrenceville	SU	A,B,M	Pri	F,S	C	4,060	21		12	53	30	5	490	52	36	11	2	500	44	40	14	1	480	53	34	12	1	Open
Rowan University	Glassboro	SU	B,M,D	Pub	F,S	C	13,169							582	28	46	23	3	622	20	43	31	6	565	35	44	19	2	3/1
Rutgers University - Camden	Camden	U	B,M,D	Pub	No	C	5,021							500	47	41	11	1	520	41	41	16	2	490	51	40	8	1	Open
Rutgers University - New Brunswick	Piscataway	U	A,B,M,D	Pub	F,S	C	36,168							600	8	40	38	14	640	4	26	44	27	610	6	37	38	18	Open
Rutgers University - Newark	Newark	U	A,B,M,D	Pub	No	C	8,170							490	55	36	8	1	520	36	46	16	2	500	50	39	9	1	Open
Saint Peter's University	Jersey City	U	A,B,M,D	Pri	No	C	2,317																						Open
Seton Hall University	South Orange	SU	B,M,D	Pri	F,S	C	5,148	23	20	33	27	8	13	530	29	49	21	1	540	26	49	24	2	550	24	48	26	2	Open
Stevens Institute of Technology	Hoboken	U	B,M,D	Pri	F,S	C	2,976	31			1	33	66	635		27	57	16	698		4	47	49						12/15
Stockton University	Galloway	SU	B,M,D	Pub	F,S	C	6,790																						12/15
The College of New Jersey	Ewing	SU	B,M	Pub	F,S	C	6,536	27						595	8	44	40	8	620	4	32	49	15	605	9	36	43	12	1/15
Thomas Edison State University	Trenton	U	A,B,M,D	Pub	No	C	16,506																						Open
Westminster Choir College	Princeton	SU	B,M	Pri	No	C	355																						Open
William Paterson University of New Jersey	Wayne	SU	B,M,D	Pub	F,S	C	10,089							517	49	39	9	2	526	42	46	12							6/1

New Mexico

Eastern New Mexico University	Portales	SM	A,B,M	Pub	F,S	C	4,572	21	56	25	15	2	2	470	60	23	9		490	54	33	9	1						8/20
New Mexico Highlands University	Las Vegas	SM	A,B,M	Pub	No	C	2,275	18	48	44	7			425	76	19	5		430	80	15	5		410	81	19			Open
New Mexico Institute of Mining and Technology	Socorro	SM	A,B,M,D	Pub	No	C	1,569	27			26	50	24	630	12	24	46	18	620	9	30	47	14						8/1
New Mexico State University	Las Cruces	SM	A,B,M,D		F,S	C	12,784	21	49	24	17	6	4	460	60	30	9	1	480	55	34	11		450	65	28	7		Open
Santa Fe University of Art and Design	Santa Fe	SU	B	Pri	No	C	544																						Open
St. John's College, Santa Fe	Santa Fe	SU	B,M	Pri	No	C	330	28		14	19	14	52	695		11	37	52	592	15	41	37	7	642	4	22	52	19	2/15
University of New Mexico	Albuquerque	U	A,B,M,D	Pub	F,S	C	20,852						7																6/15
University of the Southwest	Hobbs	SM	B,M	Pri	No	C	425																						Open
Western New Mexico University	Silver City	SM	A,B,M	Pub	F,S	C	660																						8/1

New York

Adelphi University	Garden City	SU	A,B,M,D	Pri	F,S	C		22		9	55	34	2	550	21	53	22	3	565	20	45	27	8	560	20	47	27	6	Open
Albany College of Pharmacy and Health Sciences	Albany	U	B,M,D	Pri	F,S	C	902	24			39	44	19	540	20	52	27	2	580	5	53	39	3	535	30	47	20	3	2/1
Alfred State College	Alfred	R	A,B	Pub	F,S	C	3,600	23						520					540					490					Open
Alfred University	Alfred	R	B,M,D	Pri	No	C	1,960	24	16	28	30	15	11	530	27	51	19	3	550	20	49	27	4	510	43	40	15	2	8/1
Bard College	Annandale-on-Hudson	R	A,B,M,D	Pri	No	C	2,100							650					620										1/1
Barnard College/Columbia University	New York	U	B	Pri	No	W	2,548				2	34	64		2	12	41	46		2	16	47	35		3	8	38	51	1/1
Berkeley College/New York City Campus	New York	U	A,B	Pri	No	C	2,622																						Open
Berkeley College/White Plains Campus	White Plains	SU	A,B		No	C	640																						Open
Boricua College	New York	U	A,B	Pri	No	C	1,170																						Open
Canisius College	Buffalo	U	B,M	Pri	F,S	C	2,595	25		2	37	50	11	535	33	45	20	2	545	27	45	24	4						3/1
Cazenovia College	Cazenovia	SM	A,B	Pri	No	C	1,105																						Open
City University of New York/Baruch College	New York	U	B,M	Pub	No	C	14,857								14	43	35	8		3	25	51	22						2/1
City University of New York/Brooklyn College	Brooklyn	U	B,M	Pub	F,S	C	13,099								30	50	15	5		12	54	26	8						2/1
City University of New York/City College	New York	U	B,M,D	Pub	F,S	C								520	43	34	16	6	580	14	45	29	12	515					12/1
City University of New York/College of Staten Island	Staten Island	U	A,B,M,D	Pub	No	C	13,398							490	54	38	7	1	525	84	14	2		479	61	31	7	1	Open
City University of New York/College of Technology	Brooklyn	U	A,B	Pub	No	C	17,424							400	88	10	1		430	77	18	5		390	92	8			2/1
City University of New York/Hunter College	New York	U	B,M	Pub	F,S	C	16,638							574	12	54	26	8	598	3	50	37	10						Open
City University of New York/John Jay College of Criminal Justice	New York	U	B,M	Pub	No	C	13,305							460	71	25	4		480	59	34	7							Open
City University of New York/Lehman College	Bronx	U	B,M	Pub	No	C	9,577							470	67	26	5	2	490	51	38	9	2	460	69	24	5	2	8/15
City University of New York/Meger Evers College	Brooklyn	U	A,B	Pub	No	C	7,081							380	91	8	1		380	92	8			380	93	6	1		Open
City University of New York/Queens College	Queens	U	B,M	Pub	F,S	C	16,326							520	37	46	14	3	560	13	54	26	7	510	42	40	9	2	Open
City University of New York/York College	Jamaica	U	B,M	Pub	No	C	7,245							430	86	13	1		450	74	23	4		425	86	13	1		Open
Clarkson University	Potsdam	SM	B,M,D	Pri	F,S	C	3,268	26			18	58	24	570	17	45	33	5	610	6	34	47	13	540	30	47	20	3	1/15
Colgate University	Hamilton	R	B,M	Pri	F,S	C	2,915	31			2	19	79	670	2	16	47	34	690		10	51	39						1/15
College of Mount Saint Vincent	Riverdale	U	B,M,D	Pri	No	C	1,595	20						500					500										3/1
Columbia University/ School of General Studies	New York	U	B	Pri	F,S	C	2,005				4	23	73		1	12	33	54			10	39	51		3	13	27	57	6/1
Columbia University/City of New York	New York	U	B,M,D	Pri	F,S	C	6,084	33				10	90	740		3	21	76	750		2	20	78	750		2	24	74	1/1

NAME OF SCHOOL	TOWN	ENVIRONMENT U-Urban R-Rural SU-Suburban SM-Small Town	DEGREES AWARDED A-Associate B-Bachelor M-Master D-Doctorate	CONTROL Pri-Private, Pub-Public	FRATERNITIES AND SORORITIES F-Fraternities S-Sororities F, S-Both No-Neither	STUDENTS: C-Coed M-Men W-Women PM-Primarily Men PW-Primarily Women	UNDERGRADUATE ENROLLMENT FALL 2016	TEST SCORES: ACT Median	ACT Below 21	ACT 21-23	ACT 24-26	ACT 27-28	ACT Above 28	SAT CRITICAL READING Median	SAT CR Below 500	SAT CR 500-599	SAT CR 600-700	SAT CR Above 700	SAT MATHEMATICS Median	SAT M Below 500	SAT M 500-599	SAT M 600-700	SAT M Above 700	SAT WRITING Median	SAT W Below 500	SAT W 500-599	SAT W 600-700	SAT W Above 700	APPLICATION DEADLINE Month / Day
Concordia College - New York	Bronxville	SU	A,B,M	Pri	F,S	C	887	18						460					460					448					8/15
Cooper Union for the Advancement of Science and Art	New York	U	B,M	Pri	F	C	868	31				25	75	650	3	19	47	31	730	9	17	18	57						1/1
Cornell University	Ithaca	R	B,M,D		F,S	C	14,566				1	14	85			8	37	55			5	25	70						1/2
Daemen College	Amherst	SU	B,M,D	Pri	F,S	C	2,045																						Open
Dominican College	Orangeburg	SU	A,B,M,D	Pri	No	C	1,677	18	32	58	5	5		451	77	20	2	1	451	75	21	4		448	75	21	3	1	Open
D'Youville College	Buffalo	U	B,M,D	Pri	No	C	1,716	1010		4	51	44	2	500	37	50	12	1	520	48	44	7	1	470	60	34	5	1	Open
Eastman School of Music/University of Rochester	Rochester	U	B,M,D	Pri	F,S	C	548																						12/1
Elmira College	Elmira	SU	A,B,M	Pri	No	C	1,101	24		2	45	50	2	510	37	49	12	1	530	31	47	22		500					Open
Eugene Lang College/The New School for Liberal Arts	New York	U	B	Pri	No	C	1,437	24	11	18	26	20	25	560	11	32	43	14	555	20	51	27	2	570	11	37	44	8	1/6
Excelsior College	Albany	SU	A,B,M	Pri	No	C	37,219																						Open
Farmingdale State College	Farmingdale	SU	A,B,M	Pub	F,S	C	9,235	21		12	67	20	1	480	63	32	5		500	49	42	8							6/1
Fashion Institute of Technology/State University of New York	New York	U	A,B,M	Pub	No	C	10,710																						1/4
Five Towns College	Dix Hills	SU	A,B,M,D	Pri	No	C	749	21	40	45	15			450	67	26	5	2	430	68	24	7	1	430	75	21	3	1	1/4
Fordham University	Bronx	U	B,M,D	Pri	No	C	9,258	29			3	51	46	640	2	24	53	21	640	1	22	57	19	650	2	23	54	21	1/4
Hamilton College	Clinton	R	B	Pri	F,S	C	1,867	32				11	89	700		10	38	53	690		11	43	47	700	1	9	39	51	1/1
Hartwick College	Oneonta	SM	B	Pri	F,S	C	1,384	24						505	51	34	15		505	41	45	13	1	480	52	39	9		Open
Hilbert College	Hamburg	SU	A,B,M	Pri	No	C	810	21		15	69	16		465	69	27	4		490	53	44	3		440	84	14	2		Open
Hofstra University	Hempstead	SU	B,M,D	Pri	F,S	C	6,899	26			17	65	18	580	10	48	35	7	580	9	46	38	6						Open
Houghton College	Houghton	R	A,B,M	Pri	No	C		25		9	32	43	16	565	25	37	29	9	555	26	40	31	2	540	30	42	21	6	Open
Iona College	New Rochelle	SU	B,M	Pri	F,S	C	3,462	22	28	37	20	6	10	500	49	41	9	1	500	44	42	13	2						2/15
Ithaca College	Ithaca	SM	B,M,D	Pri	F	C	6,221	27			12	65	23	600	8	41	43	8	590	10	43	42	5	580	8	47	37	7	2/1
Juilliard School	New York	U	B,M,D	Pri	No	C	495																						12/1
Keuka College	Keuka Park	R	B,M	Pri	No	C	1,724	21		10	63	26		475	58	36	4		487	49	43	6	1		75	21	2	2	Open
Le Moyne College	Syracuse	SU	B,M	Pri	No	C	2,897	25		1	39	49	11	540	24	48	23	5	560	16	53	27	4						2/1
LIM College	New York	SM	A,B,M	Pri	No	C	1,357	20	58	29	13			483	61	34	5		474	67	28	5							Open
List College	New York	U	B		No	C	210																						Open
LIU Brooklyn	Brooklyn	U	A,B,M,D	Pri	F,S	C	4,305	21	1	14	57	22	6	460	61	26	12	1	480	58	26	14	2	460	63	27	9	1	Open
LIU Post	Brookville	SU	A,B,M,D	Pri	F,S	C	6,290	24		3	41	53	3	520	32	50	16	2	530	28	49	21	2	510	42	43	14	1	Open
Manhattan College	Riverdale	U	B,M	Pri	F,S	C	3,351	24	16	27	30	12	15	526	38	44	16	2	535	29	40	27	4	528	35	45	19	2	3/1
Manhattan School of Music	New York	U	B,M,D		F,S	C	430																					2	3/1
Manhattanville College	Purchase	SU	B,M,D	Pri	No	C	1,794	24						525	35	46	17	2	525	33	51	14	2	525	36	44	16	4	Open
Mannes School for Music	New York	U	B,M	Pri	No	C	210																						12/1
Marist College	Poughkeepsie	SU	B,M	Pri	F,S	C	5,616	27			12	66	22	580	9	47	37	7	600	7	41	46	6	590	9	44	38	9	2/1
Marymount Manhattan College	New York	U	A,B	Pri	S	C	1,945																						Open
Medaille College	Buffalo	U	A,B,M	Pri	No	C	1,843	21						460	80	17	2	1	460	72	22	6							Open
Mercy College	Dobbs Ferry	SU	A,B,M,D	Pri	No	C	8,016																						Open
Metropolitan College of New York	New York	U	A,B,M	Pri	No	C	697																						Open
Molloy College	Rockville Centre	SU	A,B,M,D	Pri	No	C	3,336	24	14	34	36	10	6	520	29	58	11	2	530	26	53	19	2	510	39	45	15	1	Open
Monroe College	Bronx		A,B,M	Pri	No	C	5,480																						8/15
Mount Saint Mary College	Newburgh	SU	B,M	Pri	No	C	2,128	22		8	65	26	1	493	57	36	7		493	50	40	10		483	55	40	5		8/15
Nazareth College	Rochester	SU	B,M,D	Pri	No	C	2,034	25	15	26	31	14	14	540	29	49	20	2	540	24	49	23	4	520	33	45	19	3	2/1
New York Institute of Technology	Old Westbury	SU	A,B,M,D	Pri	F,S	C	3,610			1	37	50	12		37	46	15	2		21	48	25	7						Open
New York University	New York	U	A,B,M,D	Pri	F,S	C	22,615	30		1	10	18	71	670	1	14	50	35	680	1	13	43	43	680	1	10	47	42	1/1
Niagara University	Niagara University	SU	A,B,M,D	Pri	F,S	C	3,176	23	27	29	26	13	5	510	10	48	11	1	530	32	51	17	1	500	49	40	10	1	8/1
Nyack College	Nyack	SU	A,B,M,D	Pri	No	C	1,540	19		47	36	18		455	70	24	6		445	69	22	8	1						Open
Pace University	New York	U	A,B,M,D	Pri	F,S	C	8,914	25		1	38	52	10	550	21	53	23	3	540	22	53	23	2						2/15
Parsons The New School for Design	New York	U	A,B,M	Pri	No	C	4,260		29	24	32	7	8		32	41	25	2		28	43	26	3		28	49	22	2	Open
Pratt Institute	Brooklyn	U	A,B,M	Pri	F,S	C	3,158	26		1	27	57	15	587	11	43	39	7	570	19	39	37	5	574	13	42	40	5	1/5
Rensselaer Polytechnic Institute	Troy	SU	B,M,D	Pri	F,S	C	5,781	30			3	41	56	660	1	19	48	32	720		3	33	64						1/15
Roberts Wesleyan College	Rochester	SU	A,B,M	Pri	No	C	1,336	24	23	22	18	22	15	553	38	46	12	4	548	40	37	21	2		55	35	8	2	2/1
Rochester Institute of Technology	Rochester	SU	A,B,M,D	Pri	F,S	C	14,224	29			7	50	43	600	7	39	42	12	635	2	27	51	20						1/15
Russell Sage College	Troy	U	B,M	Pri	No	W	823	22						500					500										1/15
Sarah Lawrence College	Bronxville	SU	B,M	Pri	No	C	1,330																						3/1
School of Visual Arts	New York	U	B,M	Pri	No	C	3,335																						2/1
Siena College	Loudonville	SU	B,M	Pri	No	C	3,186	25		4	34	50	13	530	32	44	21	3	550	24	45	26	6	520	39	44	15	2	2/15
Skidmore College	Saratoga Springs	SM	B	Pri	No	C	2,661	29			9	56	35	620	7	29	47	16	610	6	35	46	13	620	7	26	53	13	1/15
St. Bonaventure University	St. Bonaventure	SM	B,M	Pri	No	C	1,660	24		5	43	35	12	520	40	41	17	2	530	34	43	20	3	510	47	38	13	2	7/1
St. Francis College	Brooklyn	U	A,B,M	Pri	F,S	C	2,563			18	57	22	3	474	70	27	3		472	67	28	5			73	25	2		Open
St. John Fisher College	Rochester	SU	B,M,D	Pri	No	C	2,786	24		2	46	45	7	527	32	53	14	1	546	23	55	21	1	506	47	43	9	1	Open
St. John's University	Queens	SU	A,B,M,D	Pri	F,S	C	16,440	24		1	38	50	11	520	36	45	17	2	540	28	44	22	5						Open
St. Joseph's College, New York/Brooklyn Campus	Brooklyn	U	B,M	Pri	F,S	C	965	20		14	58	28		470	67	28	4	1	470	65	28	6	1	470	66	28	5	1	8/31

St. Joseph's College, New York/Long Island Campus	Patchogue	SU	B,M	Pri	F,S	C	3,075	23		6	48	43	3	520	37	50	12	1	530	32	48	18	2	500	47	44	8	1	Open
St. Lawrence University	Canton	SM	B,M	Pri	F,S	C	2,377	28			12	62	27	610	12	35	44	10	610	7	37	44	9	600	10	45	37	8	2/1
St. Thomas Aquinas College	Sparkill	SU	A,B,M		No	C	2,120																					8	2/1
State University of New York / Buffalo State College	Buffalo	U	B,M	Pub	F,S	C	9,822							480	57	36	7	1	490	51	41	8						8	2/1
State University of New York / Empire State College	Saratoga Springs		A,B,M	Pub	No	C	10,851																						6/1
State University of New York / SUNY College at Old Westbury	Old Westbury	SU	B,M	Pub	F,S	C	4,158							490	55	39	5	1		40	50	10			64	32	4		Open
State University of New York / SUNY Cortland	Cortland	SM	B,M	Pub	F,S	C		24						520	32	55	11	1	545	19	64	17							Open
State University of New York / SUNY Fredonia	Fredonia	SM	B,M	Pub	F,S	C	4,386	24		4	44	41	10	540	44	40	13	3	540	44	43	12	1						Open
State University of New York / SUNY Oneonta	Oneonta	R	B,M	Pub	F,S	C	5,863	24						538	23	62	14	1	563	14	59	25	2						Open
State University of New York / SUNY Plattsburgh	Plattsburgh	SU	B,M	Pub	F,S	C	5,639		19	42	25	10	4	525	33	51	14	2	535	25	53	21	1						8/1
State University of New York / SUNY Potsdam	Potsdam	R	B,M	Pub	F,S	C	3,416	27		2	44	37	17	610	24	46	26	4	600	25	48	23	4						Open
State University of New York / The College of Environmental Science and Forestry	Syracuse	U	A,B,M,D	Pub	F,S	C	1,753	25			19	64	17	575	9	43	41	7	590	4	43	45	8						2/1
State University of New York / University at Buffalo	Buffalo	SU	B,M,D	Pub	F,S	C	20,411	22			19	60	21	559	19	50	26	4	603	8	41	40	12						2/1
State University of New York /College of Agriculture and Tech at Cobleskill	Cobleskill	R	A,B	Pub	No	C	2,446	20	62	22	10	3	3	440					440	71	25	3							Open
State University of New York /Maritime College	Throgs Neck	SU	A,B,M	Pub	No	C	1,575	22	35	40	16	4	5	510	42	45	11	2	550	20	52	26	2						9/1
State University of New York at Binghamton	Binghamton	SU	B,M,D	Pub	F,S	C	13,632	29			3	50	48	650	4	17	58	21	670	1	12	57	30	620	3	17	58	22	Open
State University of New York at Geneseo	Geneseo	SM	B,M	Pub	F,S	C	5,431	27			12	65	23	610	6	37	42	15	610	5	32	53	10						1/1
State University of New York at New Paltz	New Paltz	SM	B,M	Pub	F,S	C	6,130																						4/1
State University of New York at Oswego	Oswego	SM	B,M	Pub	F,S	C	7,150	24	11	40	29	15	5	540	22	58	18	2	560	16	59	23	2						1/15
State University of New York at Purchase	Purchase	SU	B,M	Pub	No	C	3,830																						8/15
State University of New York Polytechnic Institute	Utica	SU	B,M,D	Pub	No	C	2,082							541	33	43	20	4	578	17	47	28	8						7/1
State University of New York SUNY Albany	Albany	SU	B,M,D	Pub	F,S	C	13,139															2							8/1
Stony Brook University/The State University of New York	Stony Brook	SU	B,M,D	Pub	F,S	C	17,026	29			3	57	41	620	3	30	50	18	670	2	14	50	34	620	5	35	45	16	1/15
Syracuse University	Syracuse	U	A,B,M,D	Pri	F,S	C	15,218			1	15	61	23		13	43	37	7		7	34	46	14		11	45	38	7	1/1
The College at Brockport - State University of New York	Brockport	SM	B,M	Pub	F,S	C	7,128	23		7	50	38	5	500	49	39	10	2	510	39	46	15	1						Open
The College of New Rochelle	New Rochelle	SU	B,M	Pri	No	PW	1,025																						8/31
The College of Saint Rose	Albany	U	B,M	Pri	No	C	2,602	24		7	44	38	11	520	38	43	17	2	510	42	42	14	2						2/1
Touro College	New York	U	A,B,M,D	Pri	No	C	6,036							555	40	28	20	12	540	46	26	19	8	535	50	29	16	5	2/1
Union College	Schenectady	SM	B	Pri	F,S	C	2,208								3	25	53	19		2	17	52	29		4	31	48	17	1/15
United States Merchant Marine Academy	Kings Point	SU	B,M	Pub	No	C	987			2	35	35	28	614	4	40	45	11	643		15	66	19						3/1
United States Military Academy at West Point	West Point	SM	B	Pub	No	C	4,389	28			9	49	42	629	3	29	49	19	654	1	23	49	27	616	7	38	41	14	2/28
University of Rochester	Rochester	SU	B,M,D	Pri	F,S	C	6,390																						1/5
Utica College	Utica	SU	B,M,D	Pri	F,S	C	3,550			9	57	32	3		52	39	8	1		42	45	11	1		62	32	5	1	Open
Vassar College	Poughkeepsie	SU	B,M	Pri	No	C	2,424	31				14	86	710		3	33	64	700		3	42	55	710		6	38	56	1/1
Vaughn College of Aeronautics and Technology	Flushing	U	A,B,M	Pri	No	C	1,799	22	16	67			17	498	54	37	8	1	547	25	48	24	3						Open
Wagner College	Staten Island	SU	B,M	Pri	F,S	C		25		6	34	51	9	565	15	49	31	5	565	12	43	38	7	565	20	43	31	6	2/15
Webb Institute	Glen Cove	SU	B	Pri	No	C	92	34						700					740										8/16
Wells College	Aurora	SM	B	Pri	No	C	572	24			54	41	5	510	49	37	12	2	500	56	35	7	2	480	59	32	9		3/1
Yeshiva University	New York	U	A,B		No	C	2,869	26						619	6	35	39	20	622	5	35	40	20	610	6	37	40	17	12/1

North Carolina

Appalachian State University	Boone	SM	B,M,D	Pub	F,S	C	15,712	26	3	14	47	19	17	572	11	55	30	4	581	6	52	38	4	548	22	55	21	2	3/15
Barton College	Wilson	SU	B	Pri	F,S	C	1,150	19	85	17	4	2		460	74	21	4	1	470	67	24	7	2						Open
Belmont Abbey College	Belmont	SU	B	Pri	F,S	C	1,706	23	27	33	28	4	7	510	54	29	13	3	510	42	39	17	2						8/1
Bennett College	Greensboro	U	B	Pri	S	W	766								90	10	1			92		8							Open
Cabarrus College of Health Sciences	Concord	SU	A,B	Pri	No	C	524																						Open
Catawba College	Salisbury	SM	B,M	Pri	No	C	1,297	20	51	25	18	4	2	480	53	36	11	1	500	48	41	10	1						Open
Davidson College	Davidson	SM	B	Pri	F,S	C	1,796	31			1	35	64	670	2	13	46	40	680		12	50	38	670	3	13	44	40	1/2
Duke University	Durham	SU	B,M,D	Pri	F,S	C	6,270																						1/2
East Carolina University	Greenville	U	B,M,D	Pub	F,S	C	21,298	22	18	55	19	6	3	510	49	43	7	1	540	32	55	12	1	490	57	37	6		3/15
Elizabeth City State University	Elizabeth City	SM	B,M	Pub	F,S	C	3,395								89	10	1			83	16	1			92	8			8/1
Elon University	Elon	SU	B,M,D	Pri	F,S	C	6,008	27			12	65	23	594	7	44	41	8	598	7	39	47	7	599	8	40	43	9	1/10
Fayetteville State University	Fayetteville	U	B,M,D	Pub	F,S	C	5,287																					9	1/10
Gardner-Webb University	Boiling Springs	SM	A,B,M,D	Pri	No	C	2,572		36	31	19	8	6		47	39	13	1		45	38	16	1						Open
Greensboro College	Greensboro	U	B,M	Pri	F,S	C	1,066								70	24	5	1		63	26	11							Open
Guilford College	Greensboro	SU	B	Pri	No	C	1,809	22		16	43	34	7	505	46	31	19	4	495	50	34	15	1	480	54	28	13	4	12/1
High Point University	High Point	SU	B,M,D	Pri	F,S	C	4,546	24		4	47	43	6	544	28	50	21	1	544	23	51	24	2	533	32	48	18	2	3/15
Johnson & Wales University/Charlotte Campus	Charlotte	U	A,B	Pri	No	C																							Open
Johnson C. Smith University	Charlotte	U	B,M	Pri	F,S	C	1,326	17	2	60	35	2		420	91	6	3		420	87	11	2							Open
Lees-McRae College	Banner Elk	R	B	Pri	No	C	940								59	34	6	1		53	35	12							Open
Lenoir-Rhyne University	Hickory	SU	B,M		F,S	C	1,564	21	74	6	17	2	1	480	57	33	10		500	46	39	14	1						Open
Livingstone College	Salisbury	SM	A,B	Pri	F,S	C	895	15																					6
Mars Hill University	Mars Hill	R	B		F,S	C	1,250																						Open
Meredith College	Raleigh	U	B,M	Pri	No	W	1,967	21	47	24	21	5	6	519	41	42	16	1	520	39	43	17	1						2/15
Methodist University	Fayetteville	SU	A,B,M	Pri	F,S	C	2,280	21	50	30	10	6	4	484	59	34	6	1	510	45	40	14	1	466	60	33	6	1	Open
Montreat College	Montreat	SM	A,B,M	Pri	No	C	735							475	20	73	7	1	466	16	76	7	1	445					Open
North Carolina A&T State University	Greensboro	U	B,M,D	Pub	F,S	C	9,203	18	44	49	6	2		450	76	21	2		460	71	26	3		440	81	17	1		Open
North Carolina Central University	Durham	U	B,M	Pub	F,S	C	5,300																						8/1
North Carolina State University	Raleigh	U	A,B,M,D		F,S	C	23,847	29		1	3	55	42	617	4	34	49	14	646	1	21	56	22	589	8	47	38	7	1/15

UNC - Charolotte
UNC- Greensboro
UNC- Wilmington
East Carolina
Belmont Abbey
Elon
High Point

NAME OF SCHOOL	TOWN	ENVIRONMENT U-Urban R-Rural SU-Suburban SM-Small Town	DEGREES AWARDED A-Associate B-Bachelor M-Master D-Doctorate	CONTROL Pri-Private, Pub-Public	FRATERNITIES AND SORORITIES F-Fraternities S-Sororities F, S-Both No-Neither	STUDENTS: C-Coed M-Men W-Women PM-Primarily Men PW-Primarily Women	UNDERGRADUATE ENROLLMENT FALL 2016	ACT Median	ACT Below 21	ACT 21-23	ACT 24-26	ACT 27-28	ACT Above 28	SAT Critical Reading Median	SAT Critical Reading Below 500	SAT Critical Reading 500-599	SAT Critical Reading 600-700	SAT Critical Reading Above 700	SAT Mathematics Median	SAT Mathematics Below 500	SAT Mathematics 500-599	SAT Mathematics 600-700	SAT Mathematics Above 700	SAT Writing Median	SAT Writing Below 500	SAT Writing 500-599	SAT Writing 600-700	SAT Writing Above 700	APPLICATION DEADLINE Month / Day
North Carolina Wesleyan College	Rocky Mount	SU	B	Pri	F,S	C	1,756																						Open
Pfeiffer University	Misenheimer	R	B,M	Pri	No	C	955	20	55	32	7	5		460	63	31	6		500	49	40	11		450	71	26	2	1	8/25
Queens University of Charlotte	Charlotte	SU	B,M	Pri	F,S	C	1,703	24	22	26	29	13	10	520	41	44	11	3	520	39	43	17	1	510	45	37	15	3	Open
Saint Augustine's University	Raleigh	U	B		F,S	C	1,360																					3	Open
Salem College	Winston-Salem	U	B,M	Pri	No	W	871	28																					Open
Shaw University	Raleigh	U	A,B,M	Pri	F,S	C	2,572																						7/30
St. Andrews University	Laurinburg	SM	B,M	Pri	No	C	460	19					2	460	67	27	4		480	66	29	5							Open
University of Mount Olive	Mount Olive	SM	A,B		No	C	3,116																						Open
University of North Carolina at Asheville	Asheville	U	B,M	Pub	F,S	C	3,806	26			31	54	14	580	16	41	34	8	558	20	48	29	3	544	29	47	21	4	2/15
University of North Carolina at Chapel Hill	Chapel Hill	SU	B,M,D	Pub	F,S	C	18,523	30			6	41	53	640	3	22	49	26	650	2	20	48	30	630	6	26	45	23	1/15
University of North Carolina at Charlotte	Charlotte	SU	B,M,D	Pub	F,S	C	22,216	23	17	43	26	8	6	530	26	57	16	1	560	17	57	23	3	520	35	52	12	1	7/1
University of North Carolina at Greensboro	Greensboro	U	B,M,D	Pub	F,S	C	16,281	23			59	37	4	530	35	42	14	2	490	55	35	9		490	53	38	8	1	3/1
University of North Carolina at Pembroke	Pembroke	SM	B,M	Pub	F,S	C	5,514	19		25	65	10	1	455	71	25	4		450	77	20	3	1	425	87	12	1		Open
University of North Carolina at Wilmington	Wilmington	SU	B,M,D	Pub	F,S	C	11,770	26	10	30	39	14	8	592	6	56	35	3	605	4	50	42	4	561	16	56	26	2	2/1
University of North Carolina School of the Arts	Winston-Salem	U	B,M	Pub	No	C	781																						3/1
Wake Forest University	Winston-Salem	SU	B,M,D	Pri	F,S	C		30			7	39	54	640	4	24	49	23	665	2	17	43	38	650		17	48	30	1/1
Warren Wilson College	Asheville	SU	B,M	Pri	No	C	650	26	8	21	32	17	22	580	15	39	35	11	540	32	46	20	2					30	1/1
Western Carolina University	Cullowhee	R	B,M,D	Pub	F,S	C	7,979	22	34	38	16	6	6	515	43	43	13	1	526	36	47	16	1	486	60	32	7	1	3/1
William Peace University	Raleigh	U	B	Pri	S	C	791	18	64	10	15	3	8	440	72	23	5		440	73	24	3							Open
Wingate University	Wingate	SM	B,M,D	Pri	F,S	C	2,084	22		6	57	31	6	510	41	45	13	1	520	37	45	17	1						Open
Winston-Salem State University	Winston-Salem	SU	B,M	Pub	F,S	C	5,458												440	78	12	1		420	79	7	1		Open

North Dakota

NAME OF SCHOOL	TOWN	ENVIRONMENT	DEGREES AWARDED	CONTROL	FRATERNITIES AND SORORITIES	STUDENTS	UNDERGRADUATE ENROLLMENT FALL 2016	ACT Median	ACT Below 21	ACT 21-23	ACT 24-26	ACT 27-28	ACT Above 28	SAT Critical Reading Median	SAT Critical Reading Below 500	SAT Critical Reading 500-599	SAT Critical Reading 600-700	SAT Critical Reading Above 700	SAT Mathematics Median	SAT Mathematics Below 500	SAT Mathematics 500-599	SAT Mathematics 600-700	SAT Mathematics Above 700	SAT Writing Median	SAT Writing Below 500	SAT Writing 500-599	SAT Writing 600-700	SAT Writing Above 700	APPLICATION DEADLINE Month / Day
Dickinson State University	Dickinson	R	A,B	Pub	No	C	1,140	20		19	67	14																	8/1
Mayville State University	Mayville	R	A,B	Pub	No	C	1,036	19	68	20	7	3	2																Open
Minot State University	Minot	SM	A,B,M	Pub	No	C	3,298																						Open
North Dakota State University	Fargo	U	B,M,D	Pub	F,S	C	12,010	24			45	44	8		26	36	32	6		23	26	36	15		34	38	26	2	Open
University of Jamestown	Jamestown	SM	B,M,D	Pri	No	C	955	22		6	61	28	4	498	55	28	13	2	495	57	28	11	2						Open
University of Mary	Bismarck	SU	B,M	Pri	No	C	2,060	23	27	33	27	8	5																8/15
University of North Dakota	Grand Forks	U	B,M,D	Pub	F,S	C	11,255	24		4	48	41	7																7/1
Valley City State University	Valley City	SM	B,M	Pub	F,S	C	1,295	21		17	57	19	3																Open

Ohio

NAME OF SCHOOL	TOWN	ENVIRONMENT	DEGREES AWARDED	CONTROL	FRATERNITIES AND SORORITIES	STUDENTS	UNDERGRADUATE ENROLLMENT FALL 2016	ACT Median	ACT Below 21	ACT 21-23	ACT 24-26	ACT 27-28	ACT Above 28	SAT Critical Reading Median	SAT Critical Reading Below 500	SAT Critical Reading 500-599	SAT Critical Reading 600-700	SAT Critical Reading Above 700	SAT Mathematics Median	SAT Mathematics Below 500	SAT Mathematics 500-599	SAT Mathematics 600-700	SAT Mathematics Above 700	SAT Writing Median	SAT Writing Below 500	SAT Writing 500-599	SAT Writing 600-700	SAT Writing Above 700	APPLICATION DEADLINE Month / Day
Art Academy of Cincinnati	Cincinnati	U	A,B,M	Pri	No	C	138	21	43	36	14		7	550	33	50	6	11	460	68	26	6		500	47	47		6	6/30
Ashland University	Ashland	SM	A,B,M,D	Pri	F,S	C	2,785																						Open
Baldwin Wallace University	Berea	SU	B,M	Pri	F,S	C	3,305	24		8	38	46	8	540	32	44	19	5	530	32	47	18	3	510	43	41	13	3	Open
Bluffton University	Bluffton	SM	B,M	Pri	No	C	865	22		17	57	24	2																8/15
Bowling Green State University	Bowling Green	SM	B,M,D	Pub	F,S	C	14,852	22		6	56	33	5	520	43	37	18	2	520	38	41	20	1	490	51	36	11	2	7/15
Capital University	Columbus	SU	B,M,D	Pri	F,S	C	2,718	25		3	35	47	15	537	29	43	24	4	548	34	35	27	4	537	37	48	15	2	7/15
Case Western Reserve University	Cleveland	U	B,M,D	Pri	F,S	C	5,152	32			1	20	79	670	1	21	42	36	740		4	27	69	670	1	14	51	34	1/15
Cedarville University	Cedarville	SM	B,M,D	Pri	No	C	3,388	26		1	25	55	20	600	11	35	40	14	590	16	38	36	10	570	21	41	32	6	Open
Central State University	Wilberforce	R	B,M	Pub	F,S	C	1,335																					6	Open
Cleveland Institute of Art	Cleveland	U	B	Pri	F,S	C	625	24		6	40	43	11	550	30	37	28	5	520	40	42	16	2	530	35	46	17	2	3/1
Cleveland Institute of Music	Cleveland	U	B,M,D	Pri	No	C	243																					2	3/1
Cleveland State University	Cleveland	U	B,M,D	Pub	F,S	C	12,433	22		14	50	32	4	510	45	37	14	3	510	42	41	14	3					2	3/1
Columbus College of Art and Design	Columbus	U	B,M	Pri	No	C	1,333	22	40	23	22	9	6	540	33	37	27	3	570	39	42	18	1	570	49	37	14		8/15
Defiance College	Defiance	SM	A,B,M	Pri	F,S	C	957	22	42	25	22	6	3	470	60	32	8		490	48	48	4		430	72	28			8/15
Denison University	Granville	SU	B	Pri	F,S	C	2,282	29			4	56	40	647	5	28	51	16	639	2	27	50	21						1/15
Franciscan University of Steubenville	Steubenville	SM	A,B,M	Pri	No	C	2,090	25			32	52	16	590	9	42	32	17	560	21	44	28	7	570	18	45	30	7	1/15
Franklin University	Columbus	U	A,B,M		No	C	7,055																						Open
Heidelberg University	Tiffin	SM	B,M	Pri	F,S	C	1,110	22	48	24	16	7	5	420	51	35	12	2	490	52	35	13		400	60	30	9	2	8/1
Hiram College	Hiram	R	B,M	Pri	F,S	C	1,090	22		13	51	31	6	485	55	34	8	3	465	63	26	8	3	450	69	26	6		Open
John Carroll University	University Heights	SU	B,M	Pri	F,S	C	3,028	25		1	36	51	12	544	25	53	19	3	549	22	49	28	3	532	31	51	15	3	2/1
Kent State University	Kent	SU	A,B,M,D	Pub	F,S	C	23,607	23		2	57	35	6	530	63	35	2		530	65	32	3		510	54	41	5		Open
Kenyon College	Gambier	R	B	Pri	F,S	C	1,708	31				28	72	674	2	14	39	45	658	1	20	50	29	674	2	13	41	44	1/15
Lake Erie College	Painesville	SM	B,M	Pri	F,S	C	955	20		21	64	14	1	450	73	22	4		470	69	24	7		410	81	17	2		8/7
Lourdes University	Sylvania	SU	A,B,M	Pri	No	C	2,118	20	63	25	10	3		422	79	21			438	80	13	7							Open
Malone University	Canton	SU	B,M	Pri	No	C	1,311	22		13	55	26	6	485	55	34	11		482	58	32	6	4						Open
Marietta College	Marietta	SM	A,B,M	Pri	F,S	C	1,487	24	23	27	23	13	15	539	33	40	25	2	555	27	36	34	3	517	40	42	17	1	4/15

Miami University	Oxford	SM	A,B,M,D	Pub	F,S	C	16,981	28			5	56	40	600	14	32	41	13	640	4	25	47	25						2/1
Mount St. Joseph University	Cincinnati	SU	A,B,M,D	Pri	No	C	1,795	22	40	29	22	6	3	475	62	30	7	1	468	61	30	9							2/1
Mount Vernon Nazarene University	Mount Vernon	SM	A,B,M	Pri	No	C	1,831	23		7	50	36	7	514	33	40	21	6	510	46	35	19							5/1
Muskingum University	New Concord	SM	B,M	Pri	F,S	C	1,741	22	40	28	19	6	6	491	50	43	5	2	513	45	36	14	5						5/1
Notre Dame College	South Euclid	SU	A,B,M	Pri	No	C	1,363																						Open
Oberlin College	Oberlin	SM	B,M	Pri	No	C	2,895	30			3	30	67	690	1	11	42	46	671	2	15	49	34	683	2	12	46	40	1/15
Ohio Dominican University	Columbus	U	A,B,M	Pri	No	C	2,005		33	33	22	7	4		53	28	14	5		35	42	23							Open
Ohio Northern University	Ada	SM	B,D		F,S	C	2,234	26						570					590					555					8/15
Ohio State University at Columbus	Columbus	U	A,B,M,D		F,S	C	45,831	29	2	5	14	21	58	630	5	30	51	14	650	4	19	56	21	610	7	34	47	12	2/1
Ohio State University at Lima	Lima	SU	A,B,M	Pub	No	C	999	22	29	32	25	8	6	540	25	58	17		545	17	58	24		450	58	17	25		Open
Ohio State University at Mansfield	Mansfield	SU	A,B,M	Pub	No	C	1,189	22	32	28	25	8	7	510	46	35	16	3	550	38	30	27	5	520	35	51	11	3	Open
Ohio State University at Marion	Marion	R	A,B,M	Pub	No	C	1,083	22	34	28	20	11	7	535	37	42	21		555	29	38	29	4	490	54	38	8		Open
Ohio State University at Newark	Newark	SU	A,B,M	Pub	No	C	2,448	22	33	29	24	9	5	510	42	45	12	1	520	37	47	16		490	50	39	11		6/1
Ohio University	Athens	SM	A,B,M,D	Pub	F,S	C	23,795	24		1	46	46	7	550	26	45	24	5	550	24	48	24	4	520	36	46	15	3	6/1
Ohio Wesleyan University	Delaware	SM	B	Pri	F,S	C	1,639	26	11	23	26	19	25	569	20	44	26	10	581	13	41	36	10						3/1
Otterbein University	Westerville	SU	B,M,D	Pri	F,S	C	2,343	23	31	29	24	9	7	530	35	41	22	2	531	33	43	22	2	527	36	39	20	4	8/15
The College of Wooster	Wooster	SU	B	Pri	F,S	C	2,003	27			20	49	30	593	13	36	31	20	612	9	30	42	19	589	13	35	39	13	8/15
The University of Akron	Akron	U	A,B,M,D	Pub	F,S	C	19,037	22		15	45	33	7	520	42	38	18	3	540	36	36	23	5						8/11
Tiffin University	Tiffin	SM	A,B,M	Pri	F,S	C	2,459	21		6	65	26	3	480	50	37	13		480	55	28	17							Open
Union Institute & University	Cincinnati	SM	B,M,D	Pri	No	C	1,129																						10/1
University of Cincinnati	Cincinnati	U	A,B,M,D	Pub	F,S	C	25,860	25			30	53	17	570	20	42	29	9	590	15	36	36	13	550	27	43	24	6	3/1
University of Dayton	Dayton	SU	B,M,D	Pri	F,S	C	8,330	26			21	56	23						570	17	43	34	6	555	23	48	25	4	2/1
University of Findlay	Findlay	SM	A,B,M,D	Pri	F,S	C	4,004	23	16	31	27	15	11	510	37	45	16	2	530	31	46	21	2	515	36	41	19	4	8/1
University of Mount Union	Alliance	SU	B,M,D	Pri	F,S	C	2,140	22		11	52	35	2	490	53	34	11	2	510	50	35	15		470					Open
University of Rio Grande & Rio Grande Community College	Rio Grande	R	A,B,M		F,S	C	1,855																						Open
University of Toledo	Toledo	U	A,B,M,D	Pub	F,S	C	16,877	22	41	25	19	8	6																Open
Urbana University	Urbana	SM	A,B,M	Pri	No	C	1,457																						Open
Ursuline College	Pepper Pike	SU	B,M,D	Pri	No	PW	953	20	56	26	15	2	2	456	68	21	11		459	74	21	5		441	74	21	5		Open
Walsh University	North Canton	SM	A,B,M,D	Pri	No	C	2,136	23		8	57	30	5	520					520										Open
Wilberforce University	Wilberforce	R	B,M		F,S	C	800																						Open
Wilmington College	Wilmington	SM	B,M	Pri	F,S	C	1,395	21	20	59	10	10	1	510	61	28	9	1	550	49	35	16							8/1
Wittenberg University	Springfield	SU	B,M	Pri	F,S	C	1,972	25		1	50	37	12	560	27	29	40	5	550	24	35	40			27	29	40	5	3/15
Wright State University	Dayton	SU	A,B,M,D	Pub	F,S	C	12,682	22	40	25	18	9	8	520	40	36	21	3	520	40	39	18	3	490	54	33	11	1	Open
Xavier University	Cincinnati	U	A,B,M,D	Pri	No	C	4,563	25			30	55	15	540	25	54	17	4	555	16	52	28	4		35	43	19	3	2/1
Youngstown State University	Youngstown	U	A,B,M,D	Pub	F,S	C	11,391	21		18	51	26	5	480	59	29	10	2	490	53	33	12	2	450	70	22	7	1	8/1

Oklahoma

Cameron University	Lawton	SU	A,B,M	Pub	F,S	C	4,446	20		27	55	17	1																Open
East Central University	Ada	SM	B,M	Pub	F,S	C	3,455	20		26	53	18	3		95	5			540	30	48	18	4	400					Open
Langston University	Langston	R	A,B,M	Pub	F,S	C	4,020																						Open
Northeastern State University	Tahlequah	SM	B,M,D	Pub	F,S	C	8,659	24																					Open
Northwestern Oklahoma State University	Alva	SM	B,M	Pub	F,S	C	1,809	19	68	22	8	1	1																Open
Oklahoma Baptist University	Shawnee	SM	A,B,M	Pri	F,S	C	1,904	23		8	52	33	7	540	47	31	16	6	530	45	41	8	7						8/1
Oklahoma Christian University	Oklahoma City	SU	B,M	Pri	F,S	C	1,974	25	6	4	35	41	18	540	42	25	26	7	560	37	36	18	9	520	49	33	14	4	9/1
Oklahoma City University	Oklahoma City	U	B,M,D	Pri	F,S	C	1,804	25		1	31	55	12	560	28	42	23	7	540	29	42	24	3	550	35	46	14	5	Open
Oklahoma Panhandle State University	Goodwell	R	A,B	Pub	F	C	1,387	22	25	35	28	11	1	525	16	67	17		520	33	50	17							Open
Oklahoma State University	Stillwater	SM	B,M,D		F,S	C	20,581	25						540	28	45	23	4	565	21	45	29	6						Open
Oklahoma Wesleyan University	Bartlesville	SU	A,B,M	Pri	No	C	1,059																						Open
Oral Roberts University	Tulsa	U	B,M,D	Pri	No	C	3,057	22		16	54	24	6	503	47	40	10	3	505	49	35	15	1						Open
Southeastern Oklahoma State University	Durant	R	B,M	Pub	F,S	C	3,463	21																					Open
Southern Nazarene University	Bethany	SU	A,B,M	Pri	No	C	1,653	23	36	26	18	8	12																Open
Southwestern Oklahoma State University	Weatherford	SM	A,B,M,D	Pub	F,S	C	4,546	21		19	52	24	5																Open
St. Gregory's University	Shawnee	SU	A,B,M	Pri	F,S	C	770																						Open
University of Central Oklahoma	Edmond	SU	A,B,M	Pub	F,S	C	15,067	21		11	61	25	3																Open
University of Oklahoma	Norman	SU	B,M,D	Pub	F,S	C	21,628	26			25	52	23	580	14	41	27	18	600	10	37	34	19						2/1
University of Science and Arts of Oklahoma	Chickasha	SM	B	Pub	F,S	C	845	24	18	29	28	16	9																9/1
University of Tulsa	Tulsa	U	B,M,D	Pri	F,S	C	3,406	30			10	37	53	620	14	25	33	28	620	11	27	37	25	590	22	32	30	16	Open

Oregon

Art Institute of Portland	Portland	U	A,B		No	C	1,327																						Open
Concordia University	Portland	U	A,B,M,D	Pri	No	C	1,257	20	40	35	16	9	2	500					500										Open
Corban University	Salem	SU	A,B,M,D	Pri	No	C	975	22		4	53	40	4	530	29	48	20	3	520	39	43	17	2	500	48	37	13	2	8/1
Eastern Oregon University	La Grande	R	B,M	Pub	No	C		21		25	58	17			61	31	7			65	27	7			77	19	4		9/1
George Fox University	Newberg	SM	B,M,D	Pri	No	C	2,496	23						540	30	42	22	6	545	29	42	22	6	528	38	41	19	3	2/1
Lewis & Clark College	Portland	SU	B,M,D	Pri	No	C	2,134	29			3	57	39	645	3	21	53	23	630	1	28	53	17	620	3	31	50	15	1/15
Linfield College	McMinnville	SM	B	Pri	F,S	C	1,632	24		9	40	41	9	520	39	37	21	3	520	39	44	15	2	510	43	40	15	2	2/1
Marylhurst University	Marylhurst	SU	B,M	Pri	No	C	817																						Open
Northwest Christian University	Eugene	U	A,B,M	Pri	No	C	705																						Open
Oregon Institute of Technology	Klamath Falls	SM	A,B,M	Pub	F,S	C	3,070																						6/1

NAME OF SCHOOL	TOWN	ENVIRONMENT U-Urban R-Rural SU-Suburban SM-Small Town	DEGREES AWARDED A-Associate B-Bachelor M-Master D-Doctorate	CONTROL Pri-Private, Pub-Public	FRATERNITIES AND SORORITIES F-Fraternities S-Sororities F, S-Both No-Neither	STUDENTS: C-Coed M-Men W-Women PM-Primarily Men PW-Primarily Women	UNDERGRADUATE ENROLLMENT FALL 2016	TEST SCORES: ACT						SAT CRITICAL READING					SAT MATHEMATICS					SAT WRITING					APPLICATION DEADLINE
								Median	Below 21	21-23	24-26	27-28	Above 28	Median	Below 500	500-599	600-700	Above 700	Median	Below 500	500-599	600-700	Above 700	Median	Below 500	500-599	600-700	Above 700	Month / Day
Oregon State University	Corvallis	SM	B,M,D		F,S	C	25,327	25		4	35	44	17	550	26	41	26	7	560	25	40	27	8	530	35	42	20	3	9/1
Pacific Northwest College of Art	Portland	U	B,M	Pri	No	C	446																						8/1
Pacific University	Forest Grove	SM	B,M,D	Pri	F,S	C		24		5	42	46	7	540	28	48	20	3	550	21	52	25	2						2/15
Portland State University	Portland	U	B,M,D	Pub	F,S	C	23,170	22	38	26	20	10	6	520	39	39	19	3	510	42	4	16	1		50	36	13	1	Open
Reed College	Portland	U	B,M	Pri	No	C		31			1	25	74	715		5	36	59	670	1	12	50	37	685	1	8	50	41	1/15
Southern Oregon University	Ashland	SM	B,M	Pub	No	C	5,444	23						525	39	38	19	3	505	47	40	12		490	52	38	9		Open
University of Oregon	Eugene	SU	B,M,D	Pub	F,S	C	20,047	25		5	34	50	12	550	26	41	28	6	550	27	42	27	4	540	30	43	23	4	1/15
University of Portland	Portland	U	B,M,D	Pri	No	C	3,741							590	10	43	32	15	600	8	35	47	9						2/1
Warner Pacific College	Portland	U	A,B	Pri	No	C	1,550								54	36	8	2		57	31	11	1						Open
Western Oregon University	Monmouth	R	A,B,M	Pub	No	C	4,875	20	56	32	7	4	1	480	57	33	9	1	490	55	36	8	1	450	72	23	4	1	Open
Willamette University	Salem	U	B,M,D	Pri	F,S	C		28			14	59	28	610	6	36	40	18	605	8	36	45	10	600	10	35	44	11	2/1
Pennsylvania																													
Albright College	Reading	SU	B,M	Pri	F,S	C	2,304							510	42	43	14	1	520	36	48	14	2						Open
Allegheny College	Meadville	SU	B	Pri	F,S	C	1,920	26		2	22	55	21	600	11	35	41	13	590	9	43	40	8	572	21	38	34	7	2/15
Alvernia University	Reading	SU	A,B,M,D	Pri	No	C		22		12	56	31	1	495	52	41	7		500	47	45	8		475	58	35	7		Open
Arcadia University	Glenside	SU	B,M,D	Pri	No	C	1,957	25																					Open
Bloomsburg University of Pennsylvania	Bloomsburg	SM	B,M,D	Pub	F,S	C	8,995	20		24	56	19	1	480	57	36	7		490	52	38	9	1	460	67	28	5		Open
Bryn Athyn College	Bryn Athyn	SU	A,B,M	Pri	No	C	267	22	11	56	11		22	510	44	27	25	4	510	44	35	18	3	470	56	26	12	6	Open
Bryn Mawr College	Bryn Mawr	SU	B,M,D	Pri	No	W	1,308	29	3	6	14	25	52	660	2	20	47	31	650	1	24	41	34	670	2	13	51	35	1/15
Bucknell University	Lewisburg	SM	B,M	Pri	F,S	C	3,571	30			1	40	59	640	3	23	55	20	660	1	16	55	29	650	3	21	55	21	1/15
Cabrini University	Radnor	SU	B,M,D	Pri	F,S	C	1,521	20	55	23	16	6		450	70	26	4		440	73	23	4		440	74	24	2		Open
Cairn University	Langhorne	SU	B,M	Pri	No	C	744	22		15	59	19	7	510	38	44	15	3	500	48	39	14	3	490	51	29	16	3	Open
California University of Pennsylvania	California	R	A,B,M	Pub	F,S	C		20	68	21	7	3	1																Open
Carlow University	Pittsburgh	U	B,M,D	Pri	No	PW		22						490	50	39	10	1	480	61	31	7							8/1
Carnegie Mellon University	Pittsburgh	U	B,M,D	Pri	F,S	C	6,673	33			1	13	86	700	1	6	41	52	770	1	3	17	79	720		6	32	62	8/1
Cedar Crest College	Allentown	SU	B,M	Pri	No	W	1,387	22						460	64	30	6		470	57	38	5		460	70	23	7		Open
Chatham University	Pittsburgh	U	B,M,D	Pri	No	C	1,002	24		3	42	48	7	550	32	36	27	5	530	33	49	17	1	520	38	44	15	3	8/1
Chestnut Hill College	Philadelphia	SU	A,B,M,D	Pri	No	C	1,373	20		34	55	9	2	470	59	31	9	1	470	63	31	7		460	64	28	7	1	Open
Cheyney University of Pennsylvania	Cheyney	SU	A,B,M	Pub	F,S	C	1,224								94	5	1			94	6				96	3	1		5/30
Clarion University of Pennsylvania	Clarion	SM	A,B,M,D	Pub	F,S	C	4,330	20		24	56	18	2	470	61	31	7	1	470	60	32	8		450	71	24	4	1	Open
Curtis Institute of Music	Philadelphia	U	B		No	C	130																						Open
Delaware Valley University	Doylestown	SU	A,B,M	Pri	F,S	C	2,000	22	38	25	25	13																	Open
DeSales University	Center Valley	SU	B,M,D	Pri	No	C	2,381								44	37	15	5		46	36	15	3		48	34	15	3	8/1
Dickinson College	Carlisle	SU	B	Pri	F,S	C	2,381	30			3	50	48	635	2	24	54	20	658	1	20	51	28	645	3	20	53	23	2/1
Drexel University	Philadelphia	U	B,M,D	Pri	F,S	C	15,499	27			20	55	25	580	11	43	37	10	620	6	35	44	15	580	17	45	30	8	1/15
Duquesne University	Pittsburgh	U	B,M,D	Pri	F,S	C	6,099	26			16	64	20	560	9	60	28	3	570	11	52	32	5	550	20	56	23	1	7/1
East Stroudsburg University	East Stroudsburg	SM	A,B,M,D	Pub	F,S	C	6,159	21		11	57	28	4	460	68	28	4		460	65	30	5		450	75	22	2	1	7/1
Eastern University	St. Davids	SU	A,B,M,D	Pri	No	C	2,402	22	29	32	18	14	7	524	39	43	14	4	516	46	34	17	3	513	47	32	20	1	Open
Edinboro University	Edinboro	SM	A,B,M	Pub	F,S	C	5,595	20					1	482	63	29	7	1	478	62	30	7	1	462					Open
Elizabethtown College	Elizabethtown	SM	B,M	Pri	No	C	1,737	24		6	39	39	16	550	24	47	23	5	550	28	42	25	5	540	32	46	19	3	Open
Elizabethtown College School of Continuing and Professional Studies	Elizabethtown	SM	A,B,M	Pri	No	C	346																						Open
Franklin and Marshall College	Lancaster	SU	B	Pri	F,S	C	2,255	29			2	52	46	627	4	32	42	22	673	1	13	52	34						1/15
Gannon University	Erie	U	A,B,M,D	Pri	F,S	C	3,098	23		9	44	42	5	500	44	42	12	2	520	37	46	16	1						Open
Geneva College	Beaver Falls	SM	A,B,M	Pri	No	C	1,458	25		9	34	41	16	530	32	43	21	4	540	36	34	24	6	500	47	34	15	3	Open
Gettysburg College	Gettysburg	SU	B	Pri	F,S	C	2,384									25	59	16			19	64	17						1/15
Grove City College	Grove City	SM	B	Pri	F,S	C	2,392	26		1	26	51	22	595	11	42	34	13	590	12	40	38	10						2/1
Gwynedd Mercy University	Gwynedd Valley	SU	A,B,M,D	Pri	No	C	2,035	20		34	49	17		490	67	31	2		490	63	30	7		450	69	29	2		2/1
Haverford College	Haverford	SU	B	Pri	No	C	1,268	33				12	88	710		6	34	60	710		7	32	61	710		3	38	59	1/15
Holy Family University	Philadelphia	SU	A,B,M,D	Pri	No	C	2,139							471	71	25	4		476	64	32	4		472					Open
Indiana University of Pennsylvania	Indiana	SM	A,B,M,D	Pub	F,S	C	10,618							480	60	33	7		470	61	33	6		450	70	25	5		Open
Juniata College	Huntingdon	SM	B,M	Pri	No	C	1,569				25	55	20	570	18	49	27	7	580	18	47	32	3		30	41	26	3	6/15
Keystone College	La Plume	R	A,B	Pri	No	C	1,641	17	86	6			8	445	80	19	1	1	440	79	18	4		445	82	16	1	1	6/15
King's College	Wilkes Barre	U	B,M	Pri	No	C	2,082	23		7	48	42	3	520	39	46	14	1	530	31	47	20	1	500	47	43	10		Open
Kutztown University of Pennsylvania	Kutztown	SM	B,M,D	Pub	F,S	C	7,718	21		20	62	16	2	493	58	32	9	1	492	56	35	8	1	469	67	28	5		Open
La Roche College	Pittsburgh	SU	A,B,M,D	Pri	No	C	1,406	19		34	51	15		460	70	23	6	1	460	70	25	4	1	440	73	24	3		Open
La Salle University	Philadelphia	U	A,B,M,D	Pri	F,S	C	3,652	22	1	4	54	33	8	520	37	46	15	2	510	42	42	14	3						4/1
Lafayette College	Easton	SU	B	Pri	F,S	C	2,550	29			4	44	52	626	4	29	51	17	662		17	52	31	637	4	22	52	22	1/15
Lebanon Valley College	Annville	SM	A,B,M,D	Pri	F,S	C		22		4	42	45	8	540	32	45	21	2	565	23	42	29	6	530	36	44	17	3	Open
Lehigh University	Bethlehem	SU	B,M,D	Pri	F,S	C	5,080	31			2	31	67	630	3	25	55	17	690	1	10	47	42						1/1

Lock Haven University of Pennsylvania	Lock Haven	R	A,B,M	Pub	F,S	C	4,521	20	54	22	12	4	8	471	66	27	6	1	478	61	31	8		456	74	21	4		Open
Lycoming College	Williamsport	SM	B	Pri	F,S	C	1,272	22		5	61	30	4	510	39	50	10	2	520	38	48	13	1	480	56	35	8		8/1
Mansfield University	Mansfield	R	A,B,M	Pub	F,S	C								480	61	30	8		480	60	32	7	1	450	72	25	4		8/1
Marywood University	Scranton	SU	B,M,D	Pri	S	C	1,931							515	39	49	12		523	34	53	12	1	508	43	47	10		Open
Mercyhurst University	Erie	SU	A,B,M,D	Pri	No	C	3,840	23	21	46	33			550					530					510					9/1
Messiah College	Mechanicsburg	SM	B,M,D	Pri	No	C	2,788	26		1	30	48	21	580	19	42	30	9	570	18	41	30	10	550	26	45	24	5	Open
Millersville University of Pennsylvania	Millersville	SM	A,B,M,D	Pub	F,S	C	6,980	22		14	52	30	4	510	43	43	12	2	510	42	43	13	2	490	56	37	7		Open
Misericordia University	Dallas	SU	B,M,D	Pri	No	C	2,195	24		4	42	48	6	520	35	50	14	1	530	29	50	18	1						Open
Moore College of Art and Design	Philadelphia	U	B	Pri	No	PW	437																						Open
Moravian College	Bethlehem	SU	B,M	Pri	F,S	C	1,770	19						553	21	52	23	4	561	20	49	26	5	545	29	47	20	4	3/1
Mount Aloysius College	Cresson	SM	A,B,M	Pri	No	C	1,611								49	49	2			45	52	2							8/3
Muhlenberg College	Allentown	SU	A,B	Pri	F,S	C	2,397	28			9	60	31	605	7	39	40	13	613	10	32	52	10	604	13	42	36	8	2/15
Neumann University	Aston	SU	A,B,M,D	Pri	No	C	2,278	18		41	47	12		440	78	19	3		440	79	18	4		440	80	17	1	1	Open
Peirce College	Philadelphia	U	A,B	Pri	No	C	1,962																						Open
Penn State Erie/The Behrend College	Erie	SU	A,B,M	Pub	F,S	C	4,015																						Open
Penn State University/Altoona	Altoona	SU	A,B,M		F,S	C	4,032																						Open
Pennsylvania College of Technology	Williamsport	SU	A,B	Pub	F	C	5,457																						7/1
Pennsylvania State University - University Park	University Park	SU	A,B,M,D	Pub	F,S	C	40,891	27			14	63	23	580	13	47	33	7	610	7	34	44	15						11/30
Philadelphia University	Philadelphia	SU	A,B,M,D	Pri	F,S	C		24		3	51	40	6	535	31	51	17		545	28	46	23	3	520	34	47	15	1	Open
Point Park University	Pittsburgh	U	A,B,M	Pri	No	C	3,226		34	22	25	20	6		45	39	14	2		57	34	8	1		52	35	12	2	Open
Robert Morris University	Moon Township	SU	B,M,D	Pri	F,S	C	4,384	22						517	42	44	12	2	535	36	44	17	3	494	56	35	8	1	5/1
Rosemont College	Rosemont	SU	B,M	Pri	No	C	529	23				17	83	460	67	26	5	2	430	74	18	6	2	440	74	21	3	2	8/1
Saint Francis University	Loretto	R	B,M	Pri	F,S	C	1,772																					2	8/1
Saint Joseph's University	Philadelphia	SU	A,B,M,D	Pri	F,S	C	5,377	26			29	55	16	560	15	49	32	4	570	11	51	34	4						2/1
Saint Vincent College	Latrobe	SU	B,M,D	Pri	No	C	1,646	23		9	47	37	7	520	37	41	17	5	520	38	41	19	2	500	50	34	14	2	5/1
Seton Hill University	Greensburg	SM	B,M	Pri	No	C	1,606			7	42	41	10		37	42	16	5		36	45	17	2		43	39	15	3	8/15
Shippensburg University of Pennsylvania	Shippensburg	R	B,M,D	Pub	F,S	C	5,912	21		18	57	24	1	480	56	35	8	1	490	51	40	9		460	67	27	6		Open
Slippery Rock University of Pennsylvania	Slippery Rock	SM	B,M,D	Pub	F,S	C	7,065																						Open
Susquehanna University	Selinsgrove	SM	B	Pri	F,S	C	2,196				33	61	6		21	47	27	5		20	51	26	3						2/15
Swarthmore College	Swarthmore	SU	B	Pri	F,S	C		32				22	78	730		4	33	62	720		3	34	62	720		4	29	67	1/1
Temple University	Philadelphia	U	A,B,M,D	Pub	F,S	C	28,243	24	16	27	28	12	17	558	22	48	25	5	571	17	46	30	7	553	24	46	25	5	3/1
The Lincoln University	Lincoln University	R	B,M	Pub	F,S	C	1,624	16	67	33				410	88	11	1		490	88	11	1			86	11	1		Open
Thiel College	Greenville	R	A,B	Pri	F,S	C	894	21						472					477										Open
University of Pennsylvania	Philadelphia	U	A,B,M,D	Pri	F,S	C	9,712									5	31	64			2	24	74			3	22	75	1/1
University of Pittsburgh	Pittsburgh	SU	B,M,D	Pub	F,S	C	19,123	29	6	3	21	22	53	630	2	28	50	20	650	1	20	53	26	620	3	34	47	16	Open
University of Pittsburgh at Bradford	Bradford	SM	A,B	Pub	F,S	C	1,476	21		16	59	23	2	520	35	49	14	2	520	34	49	14	3	460	72	25	3		Open
University of Pittsburgh at Greensburg	Greensburg	SU	B	Pub	No	C	1,795																						Open
University of Pittsburgh at Johnstown	Johnstown	SU	A,B	Pub	F,S	C	2,932	20	52	36	10	1	1	505	50	41	8	1	520	41	43	15	1	500	55	38	6	1	Open
University of Scranton	Scranton	U	A,B,M,D	Pri	No	C	4,041								15	56	25	4		12	51	31	5						3/1
University of the Arts	Philadelphia	U	B,M	Pri	No	C	2,079	22	48	11	27	7	7																Open
University of the Sciences	Philadelphia	U	B,M,D	Pri	F,S	C	2,438	25	3	34	31	16	16	557	15	61	21	3	603	6	43	40	11	567	16	52	26	6	Open
Ursinus College	Collegeville	SU	B	Pri	F,S	C	1,556	26		5	23	52	21	580	18	38	33	10	580	16	39	34	10	560	16	48	27	8	2/1
Villanova University	Villanova	SU	A,B,M,D	Pri	F,S	C	6,999	31			2	23	75	650	3	19	52	25	670	2	15	47	36	650	4	20	50	25	1/15
Washington & Jefferson College	Washington	SM	B,M	Pri	F,S	C	1,396	26		1	22	55	22	583	8	52	32	8	587	9	47	39	5						3/1
Waynesburg University	Waynesburg	SM	B,M,D	Pri	No	C	1,400	22						480					480					460					Open
West Chester University of Pennsylvania	West Chester	SU	B,M,D	Pub	F,S	C	14,398	24		5	50	41	4	540	34	51	13	2	540	30	52	17	1	530	39	48	12	1	Open
Westminster College	New Wilmington	R	B,M		F,S	C	1,469	24	73	13	8	2	3															1	Open
Widener University	Chester	SU	A,B,M,D	Pri	F,S	C	3,591			6	44	44	6	505	54	37	8	1	525	44	40	15	1						2/15
Wilkes University	Wilkes Barre	U	B,M,D	Pri	No	C	2,421							520	40	43	15	2	530	33	42	22	3	500	48	39	12	1	Open
Wilson College	Chambersburg	SM	A,B,M	Pri	No	C	607	21		33	33	42		480	59	36	4	1	470	60	30	9		460	70	25	3		8/1
York College of Pennsylvania	York	SU	A,B,M,D	Pri	F,S	C		23		5	57	36	3	520	37	48	13	1	535	30	49	19	1	500	50	39	11		Open

Puerto Rico

American University of Puerto Rico	Bayamon	U	A,B	Pri	No	C	1,211																						Open
Bayamon Central University	Bayamon	U	A,B,M		No	C	2,910																						Open
Caribbean University	Bayamon	U	A,B,M,D	Pri	No	C	3,602																						Open
Conservatory of Music of Puerto Rico	San Juan	U	B	Pub	No	C	255																						Open
Escuela de Artes Plasticas de Puerto Rico	San Juan	U	B	Pub	No	C	515																						Open
Inter-American University of Puerto Rico Ponce	Ponce	U	B		No	C	5,361																						Open
Inter-American University of Puerto Rico-Aguadilla Campus	Aguadilla	SU	A,B,M	Pri	No	C	4,357																						5/1
Inter-American University of Puerto Rico-Arecibo Campus	Arecibo	SU	A,B,M		F,S	C	4,135																						5/1
Inter-American University of Puerto Rico-Barranquitas	Barranquitas	SM	A,B		No	C	1,720																						5/1
Inter-American University of Puerto Rico-Bayamon	Bayamon	U	A,B,M	Pri	No	C	4,942																						5/1
Inter-American University of Puerto Rico-Fajardo Campus	Fajardo	U	A,B,M,D	Pri	No	C	2,171																						8/15
Inter-American University of Puerto Rico-Metropolitan Campus	San Juan	U	A,B,M,D	Pri	No	C	7,100																						8/15
Inter-American University of Puerto Rico-San Germán	San Germán	R	A,B,M,D		No	C	5,090																						8/15
Pontifical Catholic University of Puerto Rico	Ponce	U	A,B,M,D	Pri	F,S	C	8,020																						8/15
Universidad Adventista de las Antillas	Mayaguez	SM	A,B,M	Pri	F,S	C	760																						Open
Universidad del Turabo	Gurabo	SU	A,B,M		No																								Open
Universidad Metropolitana	Rio Piedras	U	A,B,M	Pri	No	C																							Open
Universidad Politecnica de Puerto Rico, Hato Rey campus	Hato Rey	U	A,B,M,D	Pri	F	C	3,357																						Open

NAME OF SCHOOL	TOWN	ENVIRONMENT U-Urban R-Rural SU-Suburban SM-Small Town	DEGREES AWARDED A-Associate B-Bachelor M-Master D-Doctorate	CONTROL Pri-Private, Pub-Public	FRATERNITIES AND SORORITIES F-Fraternities S-Sororities F, S-Both No-Neither	STUDENTS: C-Coed M-Men W-Women PM-Primarily Men PW-Primarily Women	UNDERGRADUATE ENROLLMENT FALL 2016	TEST SCORES: ACT						SAT CRITICAL READING					SAT MATHEMATICS					SAT WRITING					APPLICATION DEADLINE Month / Day
								Median	Below 21	21-23	24-26	27-28	Above 28	Median	Below 500	500-599	600-700	Above 700	Median	Below 500	500-599	600-700	Above 700	Median	Below 500	500-599	600-700	Above 700	
University of Puerto Rico, at Arecibo	Arecibo	U	A,B	Pub	No	C	4,146																						11/30
University of Puerto Rico, at Bayamon	Bayamon	SU	A,B	Pub	No	C	5,327																						11/30
University of Puerto Rico, at Cayey	Cayey	U	B	Pub	No	C	3,707																						11/30
University of Puerto Rico, at Humacao	Humacao	SU	A,B	Pub	S	C	4,542																						11/14
University of Puerto Rico, at Mayaguez	Mayaguez	U	A,B,M,D	Pub	F,S	C	11,095																						11/14
University of Puerto Rico-Rio Piedras campus	San Juan	U	B,M,D	Pub	F,S	C	17,860																						11/14
University of the Sacred Heart	Santurce	U	A,B,M	Pri	No	C	4,565																						11/14
Rhode Island																													
Brown University	Providence	U	B,M,D	Pri	F,S	C	6,580	33			1	16	83	740		5	24	71	750		4	23	73	740		6	21	73	1/1
Bryant University	Smithfield	SU	B,M	Pri	F,S	C	3,462	26		1	19	66	14	560	10	57	30	3	600	5	43	45	7	560	17	54	28	1	1/1
Johnson & Wales University/Providence Campus	Providence	SM	A,B,M,D	Pri	F,S	C																							Open
Providence College	Providence	SU	A,B,M	Pri	No	C	4,270	26		2	27	55	16	560	20	48	27	5	570	16	45	33	6	560	18	47	30	5	1/15
Rhode Island College	Providence	SU	B,M,D	Pub	F,S	C	7,271	18	71	13	12	1	4	460	63	31	5	1	460	68	27	5		450	69	26	5		3/15
Rhode Island School of Design	Providence	U	B,M	Pri	No	C	2,000				9			623					640					615					2/1
Roger Williams University	Bristol	SM	A,B,M	Pri	No	C	4,610	25						545	18	57	23	2	570	12	57	29	2	555	19	53	25	3	2/1
Salve Regina University	Newport	SU	A,B,M,D	Pri	No	C	2,124	24			40	56	4	550	17	59	22	2	540	18	60	21	1	550	20	57	22	1	2/1
University of Rhode Island	Kingston	SM	B,M,D		F,S	C	14,801	24		6	32	56	6	540	25	52	21	2	550	22	50	25	3	530	29	50	20	1	2/1
South Carolina																													
Allen University	Columbia	SM	A,B	Pri	F,S	C	350																					1	2/1
Benedict College	Columbia	U	B	Pri	F,S	C	2,641																						Open
Charleston Southern University	Charleston	SU	A,B,M		No	C	2,490																						8/15
Claflin University	Orangeburg	SU	B,M	Pri	F,S	C	1,883	18	77	17	8			436	78	18	4		440	72	19	8	2						Open
Clemson University	Clemson	SM	B,M,D	Pub	F,S	C	18,599	28			9	50	41	611	6	34	47	12	641	3	22	51	24						12/1
Coastal Carolina University	Conway	SU	B,M,D	Pub	F,S	C	9,747	22		1	65	31	3	500	50	40	9	1	510	42	47	10	1						8/1
Coker College	Hartsville	SM	B,M	Pri	No	C	1,178	19	60	23	16			460	66	24	10		480	58	31	10	1						Open
College of Charleston	Charleston	U	B,M	Pub	F,S	C	10,375	24		2	39	48	11	550	24	49	22	5	540	24	54	20	2						4/1
Columbia College	Columbia	U	B,M	Pri	No	PW	1,239							500	49	32	16	3	500	50	36	13	1						8/1
Converse College	Spartanburg	U	B,M	Pri	No	W	690	23	32	25	25	13	6	530	29	43	25	3	520	35	50	14	1						8/1
Erskine College	Due West	R	B,M,D	Pri	No	C	553							531	40	36	19	5	543	37	35	23	5						Open
Francis Marion University	Florence	R	B,M	Pub	F,S	C	3,714	20	69	15	12	3	1	476	65	26	8	1	476	64	28	7	1	446	74	24	2		8/15
Furman University	Greenville	SU	B,M	Pri	F,S	C	2,731	28		1	16	63	21	610	9	36	42	13	610	7	35	45	13	610	10	35	43	12	1/15
Lander University	Greenwood	SM	B,M	Pub	F,S	C	2,363	21	47	32	15	4	2	470	59	32	8		500	47	38	14	1						Open
Limestone College	Gaffney	SU	A,B,M	Pri	F,S	C	1,246	21			75	19	4	500	60	31	8		510	39	51	9							Open
Morris College	Sumter	SM	B	Pri	F,S	C	754																						4/30
Newberry College	Newberry	SM	B	Pri	F,S	C	795																						Open
North Greenville University	Tigerville	R	B,M,D	Pub	No	C	2,481	24		4	42	45	9	562	15	60	21	4	552	21	54	22	3	528	20	53	21	6	Open
South Carolina State University	Orangeburg	SM	B,M,D	Pub	F,S	C		17						405					410										7/31
Southern Wesleyan University	Central	SM	A,B,M	Pri	No	C	1,677	20						490	54	39	7		490	54	33	13		480	56	36	8		Open
The Citadel, The Military College of South Carolina	Charleston	SU	B,M	Pub	No	C	2,735	23	22	35	27	7	9	538	36	46	15	3	549	23	51	23	3						Open
University of South Carolina Aiken	Aiken	SU	B,M	Pub	F,S	C	3,239	21	38	27	20	10	5	480	57	33	10		480	55	34	11		460	68	27	5		8/1
University of South Carolina at Columbia	Columbia	U	A,B,M,D	Pub	F,S	C	23,363	27	3	17	29	22	29	590	10	45	36	10	610	5	37	48	11						12/1
University of South Carolina Upstate	Spartanburg	U	B,M	Pub	F,S	C	5,334	20	59	25	11	4	1	470	65	29	5	1	470	63	31	6		450	73	23	4		Open
Voorhees College	Denmark	SM	B	Pri	F,S	C	415																						Open
Winthrop University	Rock Hill	SM	B,M	Pub	F,S	C	5,091	23		7	53	35	5	521	37	40	19	2	509	44	38	13	1						5/1
Wofford College	Spartanburg	U	B	Pri	F,S	C	1,584	26	3	15	27	23	32	585	12	40	42	6	597	11	35	42	11		21	38	37	4	2/1
South Dakota																													
Augustana University	Sioux Falls	U	B,M	Pri	No	C	1,665	26			29	53	18																Open
Black Hills State University	Spearfish	SM	A,B,M	Pub	F,S	C	4,020	21																					Open
Dakota State University	Madison	R	A,B,M,D	Pub	No	C																							Open
Dakota Wesleyan University	Mitchell	SM	A,B,M	Pri	No	C	756	21					26																8/25
Mount Marty College	Yankton	SM	A,B,M	Pri	No	C	1,092		10	50	30	5	5																Open
Northern State University	Aberdeen	U	A,B,M	Pub	No	C	3,001	22	42	26	115	14	3		58	30	8	4		47	38	12	3						9/1
Oglala Lakota College	Kyle	R	A,B,M		No	C																							Open
Presentation College	Aberdeen	SM	A,B	Pri	No	C	630	21																					8/1
Sinte Gleska University	Rosebud	R	A,B,M	Pri	No	C	341																						Open

South Dakota School of Mines and Technology	Rapid City	SU	A,B,M,D	Pub	F,S	C	2,101	26	4	17	35	20	24	560	31	40	22	7	600	12	40	29	19	500	42	40	16	2	Open
South Dakota State University	Brookings	SM	A,B,M,D		F,S	C	11,007			7	47	40	6		60	23	14	3		30	46	21	3						Open
University of Sioux Falls	Sioux Falls	SU	A,B,M	Pri	No	C	1,185	23		5	50	40	5	510	55	40	5		490	40	50	10							Open
University of South Dakota	Vermillion	SM	A,B,M,D	Pub	F,S	C	7,633	23	24	31	26	11	8	509	46	34	18	2	527	39	32	25	4						Open

Tennessee

Aquinas College	Nashville	U	A,B,M	Pri	No	C	312	25			48	39	13	560	21	42	16	21	540	26	37	32	5						Open
Austin Peay State University	Clarksville	U	A,B,M	Pub	F,S	C	9,513	22		12	61	24	3																8/8
Belmont University	Nashville	U	B,M,D	Pri	F,S	C	5,983	26			29	54	17	580	13	47	34	6	570	18	46	31	5						8/1
Bethel University	McKenzie	SM	B,M	Pri	F,S	C	2,232		62	24	15	3	2																8/30
Bryan College	Dayton	SM	A,B,M	Pri	No	C	1,011																						Open
Carson-Newman University	Jefferson City	SM	A,B,M	Pri	F,S	C	1,646	23	35	30	20	7	8	455					520										8/1
Christian Brothers University	Memphis	U	B,M	Pri	F,S	C	1,351	25	4	42	28	11	15																8/1
Cumberland University	Lebanon	SM	A,B,M	Pri	F,S	C	623	21	44	33	10	11	2		65	30		5		50	50					88	12		Open
East Tennessee State University	Johnson City	SM	A,B,M,D	Pub	F,S	C	9,580																						Open
Fisk University	Nashville	U	B,M	Pri	F,S	C	868	20	60	21	14	3	1																Open
Freed-Hardeman University	Henderson	SM	A,B,M		No	C	1,479	23	30	27	21	10	12																Open
King University	Bristol	SM	A,B,M,D	Pri	No	C	2,467	23		9	51	35	5	500	55	36	9		500	53	33	14							Open
Lane College	Jackson	SM	B	Pri	F,S	C	1,500																						8/1
Lee University	Cleveland	SU	B,M	Pri	F,S	C	.	24						520	39	38	21	2	480	46	40	11	2						9/1
LeMoyne-Owen College	Memphis	U	A,B	Pri	F,S	C	785																						9/1
Lincoln Memorial University	Harrogate	R	A,B,M	Pri	F,S	C	1,654																						Open
Lipscomb University	Nashville	SU	A,B,M,D	Pri	F,S	C	2,986	25		1	34	48	17	570	22	36	35	8	570	27	35	31	8						Open
Maryville College	Maryville	SU	B	Pri	No	C	1,176	24	20	26	23	16	15	537	35	34	27	4	535	34	42	23	1	528	35	37	25	3	3/1
Memphis College of Art	Memphis	U	B,M	Pri	No	C	377	22	23	39	23	13	3																8/3
Middle Tennessee State University	Murfreesboro	U	B,M,D	Pub	F,S	C	22,299	22	32	35	20	7	5																7/1
Milligan College	Milligan College	SU	B,M,D	Pri	No	C	885	24						530					530					500					8/1
Rhodes College	Memphis	U	B,M	Pri	F,S	C	2,031	28		4	22	24	46	630	3	20	53	24	630	2	22	56	20	620					1/15
Sewanee: The University of the South	Sewanee	SM	B,M,D	Pri	F,S	C	1,731	29			5	59	36	630	4	24	56	16	620	5	33	46	16	610	5	35	44	16	2/1
Southern Adventist University	Collegedale	SM	A,B,M	Pri	No	C	2,477	22	34	27	21	10	8																Open
Tennessee State University	Nashville	U	A,B,M,D	Pub	F,S	C	7,007	18	77	17	5	1	1																8/1
Tennessee Technological University	Cookeville	SM	B,M,D	Pub	F,S	C	8,060	23							38	30	28	4		26	38	6	30		42	35	21	2	8/1
The University of Tennessee at Chattanooga	Chattanooga	U	B,M,D	Pub	F,S	C	10,084	23		1	55	38	6	510	40	40	18	2	510	38	43	17	2						5/1
The University of Tennessee at Knoxville	Knoxville	U	B,M,D	Pub	F,S	C	21,396	27						575	15	47	29	10	585	14	44	32	10						12/1
The University of Tennessee at Martin	Martin	R	B,M	Pub	F,S	C	6,279	23		1	59	36	4																8/1
Trevecca Nazarene University	Nashville	U	A,B,M,D	Pri	No	C	1,677	23	28	29	22	8	13	530	31	44	15	10	520	37	41	18	4						8/1
Tusculum College	Greeneville	SM	A,B,M	Pri	No	C	1,585	21		19	62	18	1	450	68	29	3		480	56	37	7							Open
Union University	Jackson	SU	A,B,M,D	Pri	F,S	C	2,829	25	16	21	22	12	29	590	13	23	30	23	590	13	35	36	10						8/15
University of Memphis	Memphis	U	B,M,D	Pub	F,S	C	16,088	23						515	38	45	12	6	515	37	44	13	4	500	52	31	13	4	7/1
Vanderbilt University	Nashville	U	B,M,D	Pri	F,S	C	6,871			1	2	7	91		1	3	16	80		1	3	14	82		2	3	26	69	1/1

Texas

Abilene Christian University	Abilene	SM	A,B,M,D	Pri	F,S	C	3,758	24		5	41	42	12	526	36	42	18	4	525	38	40	20	2	502	50	35	14	1	2/15
Angelo State University	San Angelo	U	B,M,D	Pub	F,S	C	8,094			30	36	32	2		63	28	9			59	32	8	1						8/14
Austin College	Sherman	R	B,M	Pri	F,S	C	1,288	26	13	20	55	12	20	601	14	30	42	14	604	8	34	41	17		15	40	34	11	3/1
Baylor University	Waco	SM	B,M,D	Pri	F,S	C	14,348	28			9	57	34	601	7	42	39	12	619	3	37	45	15	582	12	46	33	8	2/1
Concordia University Texas	Austin	U	A,B,M	Pri	No	C	1,030																						8/15
Dallas Baptist University	Dallas	SU	A,B,M,D	Pri	F,S	C	3,223	22		10	60	25	4	563	18	51	28	4	555	17	60	23	1						Open
East Texas Baptist University	Marshall	SM	B,M	Pri	F,S	C	1,233	21		15	66	19		490	61	27	11	1	510	41	45	13	1						8/17
Hardin-Simmons University	Abilene	U	B,M,D	Pri	F,S	C	2,030	22	39	25	24	6	6	510	43	35	20	2	520	38	44	17	1	510	43	45	11	1	Open
Houston Baptist University	Houston	U	B,M	Pri	F,S	C	2,447	22	40	30	16	8	6	530	37	38	22	3	540	35	41	22	2	520	39	40	17	4	Open
Howard Payne University	Brownwood	R	A,B	Pri	F,S	C		21		20	56	20	4		62	28	8	2		58	34	8							3/15
Huston-Tillotson University	Austin	U	A,B,M	Pri	F,S	C	972	16	56	35			7	405	88	9	3		415	84	14	1							7/1
Jarvis Christian College	Hawkins	R	A,B	Pri	F,S	C	863	15	7	73	20	1		360	96	3	1		360	93	6	1		350	100				8/1
Lamar University	Beaumont	U	A,B,M,D	Pub	F,S	C	8,430																						8/1
LeTourneau University	Longview	SM	A,B,M	Pri	No	C	2,253			5	33	43	20		21	41	29	10		16	41	33	11		34	40	22	3	Open
Lubbock Christian University	Lubbock	SU	A,B,M	Pri	F,S	C	1,471	22		10	48	38	4	560	53	27	15	11	506	57	27	11	5	453	66		33		8/15
McMurry University	Abilene	U	B	Pri	F,S	C	1,509	20	53	19	16	5	7	460	61	28	10	1	500	49	38	13							8/15
Midwestern State University	Wichita Falls	U	A,B,M	Pub	F,S	C		22		8	62	27	3	495	55	36	8		500	45	44	11		465	68	26	5	1	8/7
Our Lady of the Lake University	San Antonio	U	B,M,D		No	C	1,792	19	68	23	6	2																	Open
Paul Quinn College	Dallas	U	B	Pri	F,S	C	193																						Open
Prairie View A&M University	Prairie View	SM	B,M,D	Pub	F,S	C	6,757	17	57	36	4	4		410	85	13	1		420	82	16	2		417					6/1
Rice University	Houston	U	B,M,D	Pri	No	C	3,839	34			2	9	90	720	2	5	24	69	755	1	4	16	79	725	3	5	26	66	6/1
Sam Houston State University	Huntsville	SM	B,M,D	Pub	F,S	C	14,995		25	12	5	2	1		46	30	6	1		40	33	9	1						8/1
Schreiner University	Kerrville	R	A,B,M	Pri	F,S	C	1,182			14	59	23	4		53	38	7	2		47	41	11	1		64	31	4	1	8/1
Southern Methodist University	Dallas	U	B,M,D	Pri	F,S	C	6,487	30		1	3	44	53	650	3	18	53	25	670	1	14	50	35	640	4	23	51	22	1/15
Southwestern Adventist University	Keene	R	A,B,M	Pri	No	C	875																						8/15
Southwestern University	Georgetown	SU	B	Pri	F,S	C	1,489	26		1	30	49	21	590	13	40	35	12	580	13	48	31	7						2/1
St. Edward's University	Austin	U	B,M	Pri	No	C	4,056	25		1	34	57	8	560	19	49	27	5	540	21	56	20	3	540	31	47	20	2	5/1

NAME OF SCHOOL	TOWN	ENVIRONMENT U-Urban R-Rural SU-Suburban SM-Small Town	DEGREES AWARDED A-Associate B-Bachelor M-Master D-Doctorate	CONTROL Pri-Private, Pub-Public	FRATERNITIES AND SORORITIES F-Fraternities S-Sororities F, S-Both No-Neither	STUDENTS: C-Coed M-Men W-Women PM-Primarily Men PW-Primarily Women	UNDERGRADUATE ENROLLMENT FALL 2016	TEST SCORES: ACT Median	ACT Below 21	ACT 21-23	ACT 24-26	ACT 27-28	ACT Above 28	SAT CRITICAL READING Median	SAT CR Below 500	SAT CR 500-599	SAT CR 600-700	SAT CR Above 700	SAT MATHEMATICS Median	SAT Math Below 500	SAT Math 500-599	SAT Math 600-700	SAT Math Above 700	SAT WRITING Median	SAT Writing Below 500	SAT Writing 500-599	SAT Writing 600-700	SAT Writing Above 700	APPLICATION DEADLINE Month / Day
St. Mary's University	San Antonio	SU	B,M,D	Pri	F,S	C	2,391	22	25	42	21	6	6	510	43	42	12	2	530	31	51	17	1	490	52	38	9	1	Open
Stephen F. Austin State University	Nacogdoches	SM	B,M,D	Pub	F,S	C	11,269	20	52	26	16	4	2	470	62	29	8	1	490	55	35	10	1	460	67	28	5	1	Open
Sul Ross State University	Alpine	R	B,M	Pub	No	C	1,359		2	53	39	5	1		85	13	2			76	21	3			89	11			Open
Tarleton State University	Stephenville	SM	A,B,M,D	Pub	F,S	C	10,750	20		21	57	20	1	470	65	29	6		480	57	35	7		460	71	26	3		8/1
Texas A&M University	College Station	U	B,M,D		F,S	C	50,747	27		1	17	49	33	590	18	38	34	10	610	11	33	41	15	550	26	43	26	5	12/1
Texas A&M University at Commerce	Commerce	SM	B,M,D	Pub	F,S	C	5,185	21																					8/15
Texas A&M University at Galveston	Galveston	SU	B,M	Pub	No	C	1,565	23	20	30	40	7	3	520	30	55	14	1	540	30	55	14	1						Open
Texas A&M University at Kingsville	Kingsville	SM	B,M,D	Pub	F,S	C	5,580																						Open
Texas Christian University	Fort Worth	SU	B,M,D	Pri	F,S	C	8,891																						2/15
Texas Lutheran University	Seguin	SM	B,M	Pri	F,S	C	1,283	21		13	64	22	1	490	55	35	10		500	52	36	11		460	72	24	3		8/1
Texas Southern University	Houston	U	B,M,D	Pub	F,S	C	7,021	17	93	5	2			400	90	9	1		420	86	13	1		400	92	8			8/15
Texas State University	San Marcos	SU	B,M,D	Pub	F,S	C	34,244	23		3	56	36	5	510	44	42	12	2	510	41	46	12	1	480	56	36	7	1	5/1
Texas Tech University	Lubbock	U	B,M,D	Pub	F,S	C	29,963	24		1	39	54	9	540	21	54	22	3	560	14	54	28	4	520	37	48	14	1	8/1
Texas Wesleyan University	Fort Worth	U	B,M,D	Pri	F,S	C	1,909	21		3	77	18	2	501	50	42	7	1	504	46	48	6		463	74	22	4		Open
Texas Woman's University	Denton	U	B,M,D	Pub	F,S	PW	8,668																						7/15
Trinity University	San Antonio	U	B,M	Pri	F,S	C	2,294	29			2	51	47	640	3	29	48	21	630	1	30	52	18	610	6	35	45	14	2/1
University of Dallas	Irving	U	B,M,D	Pri	No	C	1,404	27	4	22	29	14	31	615	7	36	39	18	595	12	44	29	15	595	13	40	30	17	3/1
University of Houston	Houston	U	B,M,D	Pub	F,S	C	35,871	25		2	30	53	15	561	20	48	26	6	585	12	44	36	8						6/30
University of Houston-Downtown	Houston	U	B,M	Pub	F,S	C		19	1	32	63	4		440	80	18			465	70	27	3							8/1
University of Mary Hardin-Baylor	Belton	SM	B,M,D	Pri	No	C	3,278	24		5	50	38	7	520	44	43	11	2	525	40	46	13	1	475	61	32	6	1	Open
University of North Texas	Denton	SU	B,M,D	Pub	F,S	C	31,171	23		6	47	40	7	545	29	46	21	4	550	24	49	21	6	520	38	41	14	3	8/1
University of St. Thomas - Houston	Houston	U	B,M,D	Pri	No	C	1,814	23	12	30	30	7	22	530	27	46	20	7	560	23	43	29	6	526	33	50	13	4	5/1
University of Texas at Arlington	Arlington	U	B,M,D	Pub	F,S	C	25,736																						6/1
University of Texas at Austin	Austin	U	B,M,D	Pub	F,S	C	39,955	26	10	16	26	18	30																2/1
University of Texas at Dallas	Richardson	SU	B,M,D	Pub	F,S	C	17,351	28			13	47	39	610	9	35	38	18	650	3	24	44	29	580	16	39	32	13	7/1
University of Texas at El Paso	El Paso	U	B,M,D	Pub	F,S	C	15,806																						7/31
University of Texas at San Antonio	San Antonio	SU	B,M,D	Pub	F,S	C	24,342	22	38	29	21	7	5	500	49	36	13	2	530	35	45	18	2						7/1
University of the Incarnate Word	San Antonio	U	A,B,M,D	Pri	F,S	C	6,445	20		24	54	20	1	470	61	31	8		480	55	36	7	1	460	69	25	5		Open
Wayland Baptist University	Plainview	SM	A,B,M,D	Pri	F,S	C	3,821	19		32	54	12	2	440	71	23	5	1	470	63	28	8	1	420	81	17	1	1	Open
West Texas A&M University	Canyon	SM	B,M,D	Pub	F,S	C	6,908	21	49	28	15	5	2																Open
Wiley College	Marshall	SM	B		No		741																						9/3
Utah																													
Brigham Young University	Provo	SU	B,M,D	Pri	No	C	30,979				7	52	41		6	29	45	21		4	27	49	21		9	35	44	11	2/15
Southern Utah University	Cedar City	SM	A,B,M	Pub	F,S	C	6,953								39	43	16	2		44	42	11	3		50	36	12	2	5/1
The University of Utah	Salt Lake City	U	B,M,D	Pub	F,S	C	23,789	25		4	34	43	19	570	19	41	29	11	590	11	40	35	14	560	24	41	28	7	4/1
Utah State University	Logan	SM	A,B,M,D	Pub	F,S	C	24,838	24		10	40	36	14	550	27	41	26	6	550	27	43	24	6						4/1
Weber State University	Ogden	U	A,B,M	Pub	F,S	C	25,318	21		23	49	24	3																8/21
Westminster College	Salt Lake City	U	B,M	Pri	No	C	2,127	24		1	42	44	12	540	22	45	28	4	540	21	48	24	4						8/15
Vermont																													
Bennington College	Bennington	SM	B,M	Pri	No	C	688	29	5		23	23	50	690		13	46	41	610	2	38	48	13	660	2	21	51	27	1/3
Castleton University	Castleton	R	A,B,M	Pub	No	C	1,985								60	31	8	1		56	34	9	1		64	28	7	1	Open
Champlain College	Burlington	U	A,B,M	Pri	No	C	2,211	26	10	20	28	14	28	570	16	43	32	9	560	20	43	33	4	540	26	46	23	4	2/1
College of St Joseph	Rutland	SM	A,B,M	Pri	No	C	256	17	100					417	25	75			427	100				435	25	75			Open
Goddard College	Plainfield	R	B,M	Pri	No	C	209																						Open
Green Mountain College	Poultney	SM	B,M	Pri	No	C	573																						Open
Johnson State College	Johnson	SM	A,B,M	Pub	No	C	1,540	20						500					500										Open
Lyndon State College	Lyndonville	SM	A,B,M	Pub	No	C	1,430																						Open
Middlebury College	Middlebury	SM	B,M,D	Pri	No	C	2,532	31				24	76	684		11	38	50	692		10	40	50	693		9	37	54	Open
Norwich University	Northfield	R	A,B	Pri	No	C	1,903	22	40	28	20	7	5																Open
Saint Michael's College	Colchester	SU	B,M	Pri	No	C	1,997	26		2	18	65	15	590	8	36	45	10	580	4	41	43	11	580	6	36	44	14	2/1
Southern Vermont College	Bennington	SM	A,B	Pri	No	C	532	19	5	2	1	1		450	78	19	2	1	450	76	24	1			78	19	1		Open
Sterling College	Craftsbury Common	R	B	Pri	No	C	105	22						555					580					590					2/15
University of Vermont	Burlington	SU	B,M,D		F,S	C	11,159	27		1	14	58	27	600	7	37	44	12	600	6	38	46	10	600	7	41	43	9	1/15
Vermont Technical College	Randolph Center	R	A,B	Pub	No	C	1,356																						Open

Virginia

Averett University	Danville	SM	A,B,M	Pri	F,S	C	859	18		41	45	14		460	72	24	4		450	71	26	3		430	81	17	2		7/15
Bluefield College	Bluefield	SM	B	Pri	F,S	C	776	21	57	20	13	3	7																8/31
Bridgewater College	Bridgewater	SM	B	Pri	No	C	1,882	24		4	44	44	8	500	45	42	11	2	510	44	43	11	2	480	60	32	7	1	5/1
Christendom College	Front Royal	R	A,B,M		No	C	433	25	3	28	50	12	7	632	5	33	33	29	570	20	46	24	10	616	11	24	43	22	3/1
Christopher Newport University	Newport News	SU	B,M	Pub	F,S	C	4,930	26		1	25	61	13	583	10	47	37	6	575	11	51	34	4						2/1
College of William & Mary	Williamsburg	SM	B,M,D	Pub	F,S	C	6,248	31			3	32	64	680	1	12	41	46	680	1	15	42	42	670	3	15	45	37	1/1
Eastern Mennonite University	Harrisonburg	SM	A,B,M	Pri	No	C	1,221	22		6	16	9	4	505	41	26	13	1	503	43	25	11	2						Open
Emory and Henry College	Emory	R	B,M	Pri	F,S	C	1,211								53	34	11	2		43	42	14	1		55	35	9	1	4/15
Ferrum College	Ferrum	R	B	Pri	F,S	C	1,240																						Open
George Mason University	Fairfax	SU	B,M,D	Pub	F,S	C	19,702	25	4	30	37	15	14	560	15	52	28	6	570	12	49	34	5						1/15
Hampden-Sydney College	Hampden-Sydney	R	B	Pri	F	PM	1,027	25		4	40	41	15	558	25	45	21	10	563	22	46	27	5	515	38	44	17	1	3/1
Hampton University	Hampton	SU	A,B,M,D	Pri	F,S	C	3,836	20		21	57	21	1	500	47	45	7	1	490	51	41	7	1						3/1
Hollins University	Roanoke	SU	B,M	Pri	No	PW		26		1	31	54	14	575	13	44	32	11	525	30	46	23	1	555	27	46	21	3	2/1
James Madison University	Harrisonburg	SM	B,M,D	Pub	F,S	C	18,107							570	13	52	31	4	580	10	47	39	4	565	14	51	31	4	1/15
Liberty University	Lynchburg	SU	A,B,M,D		No	C	6,330																						Open
Longwood University	Farmville	SM	B,M	Pub	F,S	C	4,375	21						500	43	44	10	1	500	44	45	9							3/1
Lynchburg College	Lynchburg	SU	B,M,D	Pri	F,S	C	2,079	22		14	49	35	2	500	45	39	15	1	510	44	42	13	1						3/1
Mary Baldwin University	Staunton	SM	B,M,D	Pri	No	PW	1,310	22		18	44	35	3	500	48	34	14	4	460	61	30	7	2	470	57	26	16	1	4/15
Marymount University	Arlington	SU	B,M,D	Pri	No	C	2,323	20	4	19	57	20		490	54	38	7	1	470	59	31	10		470	60	35	5		Open
Norfolk State University	Norfolk	U	A,B,M,D	Pub	F,S	C	5,337	18	81	13	6																		5/31
Old Dominion University	Norfolk	U	B,M,D	Pub	F,S	C	19,793	21		20	48	27	5	510	45	40	13	2	500	47	36	15	2						2/1
Radford University	Radford	SM	B,M,D	Pub	F,S	C	8,453	20	1	27	53	17	2	480	61	31	7	1	470	64	30	5	1	450	71	25	3	1	2/1
Randolph College	Lynchburg	SU	B,M	Pri	No	C	665	22		9	59	28	4	515	42	40	16	2	500	46	41	11	2	495	44	32	14	2	2/15
Randolph-Macon College	Ashland	SU	B	Pri	F,S	C	1,446	24						546	28	45	23	4	538	30	49	19	3	516	43	42	13	3	3/1
Roanoke College	Salem	SU	B	Pri	F,S	C	1,992	24		5	36	48	10	550	26	44	24	5	540	30	46	23	2	520	37	44	16	2	3/15
Shenandoah University	Winchester	SM	B,M,D	Pri	No	C	2,099	22		17	48	29	6	490	52	31	14	3	480	53	36	10	1						Open
The University of Virginia's College at Wise	Wise	SM	B	Pub	F,S	C	1,892	20	58	24	11	4	3																8/15
University of Mary Washington	Fredericksburg	SU	B,M	Pub	No	C	4,515	25	7	24	34	18	17	570	10	42	37	10	560	14	47	34	4	560	12	45	37	6	2/1
University of Richmond	University of Richmond	SU	B,M,D	Pri	F,S	C	3,036	31			3	25	72	650	3	19	53	25	670	2	17	43	38	660	4	16	54	26	1/15
University of Virginia	Charlottesville	SU	B,M,D	Pub	F,S	C	16,331	31			3	27	69	670	2	14	46	38	680	2	13	41	44	670	3	16	43	38	1/1
Virginia Commonwealth University	Richmond	U	B,M,D	Pub	F,S	C	24,212	24		3	44	40	13	550	25	46	23	6	530	29	47	20	4	520	35	43	19	3	1/15
Virginia Military Institute	Lexington	SM	B	Pub	No	C	1,713	26						580	11	47	35	7	580	10	48	39	5	550	24	48	26	1	2/1
Virginia Polytechnic Institute and State University	Blacksburg	R	B,M,D	Pub	F,S	C								590	9	43	39	8	625	4	31	46	19	585	12	44	38	7	1/15
Virginia State University	Petersburg	SU	B,M		F,S	C	3,600																					7	1/15
Virginia Union University	Richmond	U	B,M,D		F,S	C	1,260																					7	1/15
Virginia Wesleyan College	Norfolk	SU	B	Pri	F,S	C	1,671	20	55	23	19	2	2																Open
Washington and Lee University	Lexington	SM	B,M,D	Pri	F,S	C	1,830	32				12	88	690		5	47	47	690		2	49	48	683		5	55	40	1/1

Washington

Central Washington University	Ellensburg	SM	B,M	Pub	No	C	11,047	21	1	20	52	24	3	530	33	47	18	2	523	34	52	12	2	466	66	28	5	1	4/1
City University of Seattle	Seattle	U	A,B,M,D	Pri	No	C	1,470																						Open
Cornish College of the Arts	Seattle	U	B	Pri	No	C	724																						8/15
Eastern Washington University	Cheney	SM	B,M	Pub	F,S	C	12,411	20						475	59	32	8	1	485	54	36	9	1	455	68	27	5		2/15
Gonzaga University	Spokane	U	B,M,D	Pri	No	C	5,160	27			11	64	25	590	6	46	38	10	600	5	39	45	10						2/1
Heritage University	Toppenish	R	A,B,M	Pri	No	C	834																						9/1
Northwest University	Kirkland	SU	A,B,M,D	Pri	No	C	1,057																						8/15
Pacific Lutheran University	Tacoma	SU	B,M,D	Pri	No	C	2,783	25		6	30	48	16	560	27	41	26	6	550	25	42	28	5	530	34	46	18	2	Open
Saint Martin's University	Lacey	SU	B,M	Pri	No	C	1,281	22		7	58	28	7	510	49	33	13	4	515	49	29	20	2	495	55	34	9	2	4/1
Seattle Pacific University	Seattle	U	B,M,D	Pri	No	C	3,202	25		2	29	54	15	560	18	44	32	6	560	21	44	29	6		23				3/1
Seattle University	Seattle	U	B,M,D	Pri	No	C	4,780	27			15	58	27	590	11	43	36	9	590	11	42	39	8	580	14	45	32	10	1/15
The Evergreen State College	Olympia	SM	B,M	Pub	No	C	3,787	23	1	12	37	40	10	545	32	35	27	6	495	49	37	13	1	509	41	43	14	2	2/1
University of Puget Sound	Tacoma	U	B,M,D	Pri	F,S	C	2,476	27		1	16	53	30	616	7	34	41	18	593	12	38	40	10	606	9	37	41	14	1/15
University of Washington	Seattle	U	B,M,D	Pub	F,S	C	28,570		9	16	27	20	28		16	36	36	12		9	32	44	16		17	42	34	8	1/15
Walla Walla University	College Place	SM	A,B,M	Pri	No	C	1,563																						Open
Washington State University	Pullman	SM	B,M,D		F,S	C	24,904			10	41	42	7		42	38	17	3		36	42	19	3		51	37	11	1	1/31
Western Washington University	Bellingham	SM	B,M	Pub	No	C	14,592	25		3	31	52	14	560	23	41	29	7	550	25	47	24	4	530	34	44	19	2	1/31
Whitman College	Walla Walla	SM	B	Pri	F,S	C	1,493	30			3	40	57	650	4	19	44	34	650	2	19	53	25	650	1	23	48	28	1/15
Whitworth University	Spokane	SU	B,M	Pri	No	C	2,308	26		6	28	46	20	570	25	34	30	11	560	23	44	28	5	560	29	37	27	7	3/1

West Virginia

Alderson Broaddus University	Philippi	SM	A,B,M	Pri	F,S	C	1,052	21	47	29	19	3	2	470	57	38	5		470	61	32	7		470	69	29	2		8/1
Bethany College	Bethany	R	B,M	Pri	F,S	C	710	19		35	49	16		450	71	24	5	1	470	61	32	6	1	440	81	17	2		8/20
Bluefield State College	Bluefield	SM	A,B	Pub	F,S	C	2,063	18	73	17	8	1	1		55	43	2			57	33	10							Open
Concord University	Athens	SM	A,B,M	Pub	F,S	C	2,142	21						486	58	32	10		482	58	34	7	1		68	23	8	1	Open
Davis & Elkins College	Elkins	SM	A,B	Pri	F	C	805	20		25	55	18	2	463	68	30	2		482	61	36	3							Open
Fairmont State University	Fairmont	SM	A,B,M	Pub	F,S	C		21		18	60	21	1																8/15
Glenville State College	Glenville	R	A,B	Pub	F,S	C	1,891	20	61	24	12	2	1	428	75	20	4	1	438	77	19	4							Open

NAME OF SCHOOL	TOWN	ENVIRONMENT U-Urban R-Rural SU-Suburban SM-Small Town	DEGREES AWARDED A-Associate B-Bachelor M-Master D-Doctorate	CONTROL Pri-Private, Pub-Public	FRATERNITIES AND SORORITIES F-Fraternities S-Sororities F, S-Both No-Neither	STUDENTS: C-Coed M-Men W-Women PM-Primarily Men PW-Primarily Women	UNDERGRADUATE ENROLLMENT FALL 2016	TEST SCORES: ACT Median	ACT Below 21	ACT 21-23	ACT 24-26	ACT 27-28	ACT Above 28	SAT CRITICAL READING Median	SAT CR Below 500	SAT CR 500-599	SAT CR 600-700	SAT CR Above 700	SAT MATHEMATICS Median	SAT Math Below 500	SAT Math 500-599	SAT Math 600-700	SAT Math Above 700	SAT WRITING Median	SAT Writing Below 500	SAT Writing 500-599	SAT Writing 600-700	SAT Writing Above 700	APPLICATION DEADLINE Month / Day
Marshall University	Huntington	U	A,B,M,D	Pub	F,S	C	9,762																						Open
Ohio Valley University	Vienna	SU	A,B	Pri	No	C	659	23	75	25	9	3	2																8/15
Salem International University	Salem	R	A,B,M	Pri	F,S	C	568	21	51	29	18	2																	Open
Shepherd University, West Virginia	Shepherdstown	SM	B,M,D	Pub	F,S	C	3,436	21	1	12	57	27	3	500	47	44	8	1	490	56	37	7							Open
University of Charleston	Charleston	SM	A,B,M,D	Pri	F,S	C	1,727	22		10	64	24	1	480	61	35	4		490	514	38	8	1						Open
West Liberty University	West Liberty	R	A,B	Pub	F,S	C	2,266																						Open
West Virginia State University	Institute	SU	A,B	Pub	F,S	C	3,449	19																					8/10
West Virginia University	Morgantown	SM	B,M,D	Pub	F,S	C	22,350	24		10	50	35	5																8/1
West Virginia University Institute of Technology	Montgomery	SM	B	Pub	F,S	C		21		27	51	21																	8/1
West Virginia Wesleyan College	Buckhannon	SM	B,M	Pri	F,S	C	1,327	23	18	19	16	6	4																8/1
Wheeling Jesuit University	Wheeling	SU	B,M,D	Pri	No	C	945	21		15	60	22	3	486	65	26	9		493	50	43	7		440	79	21			Open
Wisconsin																													
Alverno College	Milwaukee	U	A,B,M	Pri	S	W	1,558	19		36	50	13	1																Open
Beloit College	Beloit	SM	B	Pri	F,S	C	1,394	27		2	18	52	28	630	11	34	30	25	620	13	31	43	13						1/15
Cardinal Stritch University	Milwaukee	SU	A,B,M,D		No	C	3,130																						8/1
Carroll University	Waukesha	SU	B,M,D	Pri	F,S	C	3,015	24	17	31	29	13	10																Open
Carthage College	Kenosha	SU	B,M	Pri	F,S	C	2,265																						Open
Concordia University Wisconsin	Mequon	SU	A,B,M,D	Pri	No	C	4,338	22																					8/15
Edgewood College	Madison	SU	B,M,D	Pri	No	C	1,813	23		9	51	36	4																8/14
Lakeland University	Plymouth	R	B,M	Pri	F,S	C	840																						9/1
Lawrence University	Appleton	U	B	Pri	F,S	C	1,496		1	6	15	20	58		1	21	48	30		2	26	48	24		6	31	38	25	1/15
Marian University	Fond du Lac	SM	B,M,D	Pri	S	C	1,553	20		24	53	21	2																Open
Marquette University	Milwaukee	U	B,M,D	Pri	F,S	C	8,334	27	3	12	27	21	37	590	13	40	40	7	600	10	36	46	7	580	17	41	37	5	12/1
Milwaukee Institute of Art and Design	Milwaukee	U	B	Pri	No	C	628																					5	12/1
Milwaukee School of Engineering	Milwaukee	U	B,M	Pri	F,S	C	2,712	27			8	64	28	580	6	33	39	22	660		11	67	22						Open
Mount Mary University	Milwaukee	U	B,M,D	Pri	No	PW	816	19		31	57	11	1																Open
Northland College	Ashland	SM	B		No	C	739	24																					Open
Ripon College	Ripon	SM	B	Pri	F,S	C	793	24		3	50	34	13	506	65	14	21		514	36	50	14							8/1
Silver Lake College of the Holy Family	Manitowoc	R	B,M	Pri	No	C	357	17	2	59	28	9	2																Open
St. Norbert College	De Pere	SU	B,M	Pri	F,S	C	2,102	25		2	41	47	10																Open
University of Wisconsin-Eau Claire	Eau Claire	U	A,B,M,D	Pub	F,S	C	9,981	24		2	46	45	6		6	38	38	19		6	50	31	13						Open
University of Wisconsin-Green Bay	Green Bay	SU	A,B,M	Pub	F,S	C	6,758	23		5	56	36	2																8/26
University of Wisconsin-La Crosse	La Crosse	SM	A,B,M	Pub	F,S	C	9,699	24			36	57	7	560	8	58	33		580	8	42	33	17	570	17	42	33	8	Open
University of Wisconsin-Madison	Madison	U	B,M,D	Pub	F,S	C	31,710				4	55	41		4	34	49	13		2	9	34	55						2/1
University of Wisconsin-Milwaukee	Milwaukee	U	B,M,D	Pub	F,S	C	21,375	22		8	57	31	4																7/1
University of Wisconsin-Oshkosh	Oshkosh	U	A,B,M	Pub	F,S	C		22		6	62	30	2																7/1
University of Wisconsin-Parkside	Kenosha	SU	A,B,M	Pub	F,S	C	4,300	21		18	60	21	1																8/1
University of Wisconsin-Platteville	Platteville	SM	A,B,M	Pub	F,S	C	7,793	25		7	49	38	6	540	58	33		8	318	33	42	25							Open
University of Wisconsin-River Falls	River Falls	SU	B,M	Pub	F,S	C	6,390																						Open
University of Wisconsin-Stevens Point	Stevens Point	SM	A,B,M,D	Pub	F,S	C	9,118	23	27	37	23	8	5	546	23	55	14	9	536	32	41	23	5	528	46	32	23		Open
University of Wisconsin-Stout	Menomonie	R	B,M,D	Pub	F,S	C	8,194	22		9	59	29	3																Open
University of Wisconsin-Superior	Superior	U	A,B,M	Pub	No	C	2,362	21		12	64	20	2																8/1
University of Wisconsin-Whitewater	Whitewater	SM	A,B,M,D	Pub	F,S	C	10,584	23																					5/1
Viterbo University	La Crosse	SU	A,B,M	Pri	No	C	2,105	23	24	34	29	8	5																8/15
Wisconsin Lutheran College	Milwaukee	SU	B,M	Pri	No	C	740																						8/15
Wyoming																													
University of Wyoming	Laramie	SM	B,M,D		F,S	C	10,045	25		4	36	49	12	545	28	42	22	8	557	28	34	30	7						8/10

IN-STATE COST RANGES DIRECTORY

The breakdown of in-state tuition, room, and board costs for the 2016-2017 academic year is arranged from least expensive to most expensive. Within each range are lists of schools that don't charge for tuition or room and board, and those that do. Listings that say (no R & B) means complete information was not provided by the school at press time. For any late additions, please refer to the school profile on our website, *barronspac.com.*

Colleges without Tuition, Room, and Board

Berea College, KY
College of the Ozarks, MO
United States Air Force Academy, CO
United States Coast Guard Academy, CT
United States Merchant Marine Academy, NY
United States Military Academy at West Point, NY
United States Naval Academy, MD

Colleges with Room and Board Only

Curtis Institute of Music, PA
Metropolitan College of New York, NY
Ursuline College, OH

$4000-$5999

Augusta University, GA (no R & B)
Bluefield State College, WV
City University of New York/Brooklyn College, NY (no R & B)
City University of New York/Lehman College, NY

$6000-$7999

Colleges with Tuition, Room, and Board

Charter Oak State College, CT (no R & B)
City University of New York/College of Technology, NY
City University of New York/John Jay College of Criminal Justice, NY (no R & B)
City University of New York/Meger Evers College, NY (no R & B)
City University of New York/York College, NY (no R & B)
Indiana University East, IN (no R & B)
Indiana University Kokomo, IN (no R & B)
Indiana University Northwest, IN (no R & B)
Louisiana State University in Shreveport, LA (no R & B)
McNeese State University, LA (no R & B)
Metropolitan State University, MN (no R & B)
Ohio State University at Lima , OH (no R & B)
Ohio State University at Marion , OH
Ohio State University at Newark , OH
Oklahoma Panhandle State University, OK
Texas A&M University at Kingsville, TX
Thomas Edison State University, NJ (no R & B)
University of Houston-Downtown, TX (no R & B)
University of Maine at Augusta, ME

$8000-$9999

Colleges with Tuition, Room, and Board

Alice Lloyd College, KY
Florida Gulf Coast University, FL
Middle Tennessee State University, TN
North Carolina Central University, NC
Northeastern State University, OK
Oregon Institute of Technology, OR
Southern University at New Orleans, LA
State University of New York / Empire State College, NY (no R & B)
Union Institute & University, OH (no R & B)
University of Rio Grande & Rio Grande Community College, OH
West Virginia State University, WV
Wilmington University, DE (no R & B)

$10,000-$11,999

Colleges with Tuition, Room, and Board

Amridge University, AL (no R & B)
Ashford University , CA (no R & B)
Boricua College, NY (no R & B)
Brigham Young University/Hawaii, HI
Cabarrus College of Health Sciences, NC (no R & B)
Cameron University, OK
Escuela de Artes Plasticas de Puerto Rico, PR
Louisiana Tech University, LA
Mississippi State University, MS
Montana State University-Northern, MT
New Mexico Highlands University, NM
Nicholls State University, LA
Pontifical Catholic University of Puerto Rico, PR
Rust College, MS
Slippery Rock University of Pennsylvania, PA
Southeastern Oklahoma State University, OK
Southwestern Oklahoma State University, OK
St. Cloud State University, MN
Texas A&M University at Commerce, TX
University of Alaska Southeast, AK
University of Michigan/Dearborn, MI (no R & B)
University of Missouri-St. Louis, MO (no R & B)
University of Montana-Western, MT
University of Science and Arts of Oklahoma, OK
Weber State University, UT

$12,000-$13,999

Colleges with Tuition, Room, and Board

Baker College of Flint, MI
Bayamon Central University, PR
Brigham Young University, UT
California State University, San Bernardino, CA
Carlos Albizu University, FL (no R & B)
Conservatory of Music of Puerto Rico, PR
Dakota State University, SD
Delta State University, MS
Dickinson State University, ND
East Central University, OK
East Tennessee State University, TN
Fort Hays State University, KS
Georgia Southwestern State University, GA
Idaho State University, ID
Kentucky State University, KY
Lincoln University, MO
Minot State University, ND
Mississippi Valley State University, MS
Missouri Southern State University, MO
NewSchool of Architecture & Design, CA
North Carolina A&T State University, NC
Northeastern Illinois University, IL (no R & B)
Northwestern Oklahoma State University, OK
Ohio State University at Mansfield , OH
Pittsburg State University, KS
Sinte Gleska University, SD
Southern Utah University, UT
University of Puerto Rico, at Arecibo, PR
University of Arkansas at Monticello, AR
University of Arkansas at Pine Bluff, AR
University of Central Oklahoma, OK
University of Massachusetts Boston, MA
University of New Orleans, LA
University of Puerto Rico, at Bayamon, PR
University of Puerto Rico, at Cayey, PR
University of Puerto Rico, at Mayaguez, PR
University of Puerto Rico-Rio Piedras campus, PR
University of Southern Mississippi, MS
University of Wisconsin-Whitewater, WI
Utah State University, UT
Valley City State University, ND
Wayne State College, NE
West Texas A&M University, TX
Western Carolina University, NC

$14,000-$15,999

Colleges with Tuition, Room, and Board

Alabama State University, AL
Alcorn State University, MS
Angelo State University, TX
Appalachian State University, NC
Arkansas Tech University, AR
Auburn University at Montgomery, AL
Black Hills State University, SD
Blue Mountain College, MS
Boise State University, ID
California University of Pennsylvania, PA
Cambridge College, MA (no R & B)
Caribbean University, PR
Chadron State College, NE
Clemson University, SC
Columbus State University, GA
Concord University, WV
Concordia College - Alabama, AL
Eastern New Mexico University, NM
Edinboro University , PA
Elizabeth City State University, NC
Emporia State University, KS
Excelsior College, NY
Fairmont State University, WV
Florida Agricultural and Mechanical University, FL
George Mason University, VA
Grambling State University, LA
Harris-Stowe State University, MO
Henderson State University, AR
Indiana University South Bend, IN
Indiana University Southeast, IN
Jackson State University, MS
Jacksonville State University, AL
Langston University, OK
Lewis-Clark State College, ID
Minnesota State University, Mankato, MN
Minnesota State University, Moorhead, MN
Missouri State University, MO
Montana State University, MT
Montana Tech of the University of Montana, MT
National University, CA (no R & B)
New College of Florida, FL
New Mexico Institute of Mining and Technology, NM
New Mexico State University, NM
Northern State University , SD
Oglala Lakota College, SD
Peru State College, NE
Prairie View A&M University, TX
Purdue University/Northwest, IN
Savannah State University, GA
South Dakota State University, SD
Southeast Missouri State University, MO
Sul Ross State University, TX
Tarleton State University, TX
Tennessee State University, TN
Texas A&M University at Galveston, TX
Texas Woman's University, TX
The Lincoln University, PA
The University of Tennessee at Martin, TN
University of Central Arkansas, AR
University of Central Florida, FL
University of Idaho, ID
University of Louisiana at Lafayette, LA
University of Louisiana at Monroe, LA
University of Maine at Fort Kent, ME
University of Maine at Presque Isle, ME
University of Montana, MT
University of New Hampshire - Manchester, NH (no R & B)
University of New Mexico, NM
University of North Alabama, AL
University of North Carolina at Asheville, NC
University of North Carolina at Charlotte, NC
University of North Carolina at Greensboro, NC
University of North Carolina at Pembroke, NC
University of North Carolina at Wilmington, NC
University of North Dakota, ND
University of North Florida, FL
University of Puerto Rico, at Humacao, PR
University of South Florida/St. Petersburg, FL
University of Texas Rio Grande Valley, TX
University of West Alabama, AL
University of West Florida, FL
University of Wisconsin-Eau Claire, WI
University of Wisconsin-Green Bay, WI
University of Wisconsin-La Crosse, WI
University of Wisconsin-Oshkosh, WI
University of Wisconsin-Parkside, WI
University of Wisconsin-Platteville, WI
University of Wisconsin-River Falls, WI
University of Wisconsin-Stevens Point, WI
University of Wisconsin-Superior, WI
University of Wyoming, WY
Valdosta State University, GA
Washburn University, KS
West Liberty University, WV
Western Oregon University, OR

$16,000-$17,999

Colleges with Tuition, Room, and Board

Adams State University, CO
American University of Puerto Rico, PR
Arkansas State University, AR
Armstrong State University, GA
Austin Peay State University, TN
Bemidji State University, MN
California Polytechnic State University, CA
California State University, Fresno, CA
California State University, Los Angeles, CA
California State University, Northridge, CA
California State University, Stanislaus, CA
Central Washington University, WA
City University of New York/College of Staten Island, NY
Coppin State University, MD
East Carolina University, NC
Eastern Kentucky University, KY
Eastern Oregon University, OR
Embry-Riddle Aeronautical University - Worldwide, FL
Fayetteville State University, NC
Florida Atlantic University, FL
Florida State University, FL
Fort Valley State University, GA
Francis Marion University, SC
Frostburg State University, MD

Georgia Southern University, GA
Glenville State College, WV
Goddard College, VT
Grand Canyon University, AZ
Indiana University-Purdue University Fort Wayne, IN
Iowa State University, IA
Kansas State University, KS
Lane College, TN
LeMoyne-Owen College, TN
Livingstone College, NC
Marshall University, WV
Mercy College of Health Sciences, IA (no R & B)
Midwestern State University, TX
Mississippi University for Women, MS
Missouri Western State University, MO
Morehead State University, KY
Morgan State University, MD
Murray State University, KY
National Louis University, IL (no R & B)
North Dakota State University, ND
Northern Kentucky University, KY
Northwest Missouri State University, MO
Northwestern State University of Louisiana, LA
Oklahoma State University, OK
Peirce College, PA
Penn State Erie/The Behrend College, PA
Rhode Island College, RI
Salem State University, MA
Shawnee State University, OH
Shepherd University, West Virginia, WV
Southeastern Louisiana University, LA
Southern University and A&M College, LA
Southwest Minnesota State University, MN
State University of New York / SUNY College at Old Westbury, NY
State University of New York /Maritime College, NY
State University of New York at Purchase, NY
Tennessee Technological University, TN
Texas A&M University at Corpus Christi, TX
The Evergreen State College, WA
The University of Tennessee at Chattanooga, TN
The University of Utah, UT
Tougaloo College, MS
Towson University, MD
Troy University, AL
Truman State University, MO
Universidad Adventista de las Antillas, PR
Universidad del Turabo, PR
Universidad Metropolitana, PR
University of Alaska Anchorage, AK
University of Alaska Fairbanks, AK
University of Florida, FL
University of Maryland/Eastern Shore, MD
University of Michigan-Flint, MI
University of Mississippi, MS
University of Nebraska - Kearney, NE
University of Nebraska - Omaha, NE
University of Nevada, Las Vegas, NV
University of North Georgia, GA
University of Northern Iowa, IA
University of South Alabama, AL
University of South Carolina Aiken, SC
University of South Dakota, SD
University of South Florida/Tampa, FL
University of Southern Indiana, IN
University of the Sacred Heart, PR
University of West Georgia, GA
West Virginia University Institute of Technology, WV
Western Kentucky University, KY
Western New Mexico University, NM
Winona State University, MN
Wright State University, OH
Youngstown State University, OH

$18,000-$19,999

Colleges with Tuition, Room, and Board

Alabama A&M University, AL
Albany State University, GA
Alfred State College, NY
Allen University, SC
Ball State University, IN
Bloomsburg University of Pennsylvania, PA
Bowling Green State University, OH
California State University, Maritime Academy, CA
California State University, Bakersfield, CA
California State University, Dominguez Hills, CA
California State University, East Bay, CA
California State University, Long Beach, CA
Central State University, OH
Clayton State University, GA
Coastal Carolina University, SC
Colorado Mesa University, CO
Colorado State University-Pueblo, CO
Cox College, MO
Delaware State University, DE
East Stroudsburg University , PA
Eastern Michigan University, MI
Elizabethtown College School of Continuing and Professional Studies, PA (no R & B)
Fashion Institute of Technology/State University of New York, NY
Florida International University, FL
Fort Lewis College, CO
Granite State College, NH
Heritage University, WA (no R & B)
Hodges University, FL (no R & B)
Huston-Tillotson University, TX
Indiana University-Purdue University Indianapolis, IN
Inter-American University of Puerto Rico Ponce , PR
Inter-American University of Puerto Rico-Arecibo Campus, PR
Inter-American University of Puerto Rico-Barranquitas , PR
Inter-American University of Puerto Rico-Bayamon, PR
Inter-American University of Puerto Rico-Fajardo Campus, PR
James Madison University, VA
Kennesaw State University, GA
Kutztown University of Pennsylvania, PA
Lake Superior State University, MI
Lamar University, TX
Liberty University, VA
Lock Haven University of Pennsylvania, PA
Louisiana State University and A&M College, LA
Massachusetts Maritime Academy, MA
Mayville State University, ND
Miles College, AL
Missouri University of Science and Technology, MO
Morris College, SC
North Carolina State University , NC
Northern Michigan University, MI
Paine College, GA
Portland State University, OR
Radford University, VA
Saginaw Valley State University, MI
SAGU American Indian College , AZ
Sam Houston State University, TX
San Francisco State University, CA
South Dakota School of Mines and Technology, SD
Southern Oregon University, OR
State University of New York / SUNY Oneonta, NY
State University of New York / SUNY Plattsburgh, NY
State University of New York at New Paltz, NY
State University of New York Polytechnic Institute, NY
Stephen F. Austin State University, TX
Talladega College, AL
Texas Southern University, TX
Texas State University, TX
Texas Tech University, TX
The University of Virginia's College at Wise, VA
University of Alabama at Birmingham, AL
University of Alabama in Huntsville, AL
University of Arkansas at Fayetteville, AR
University of Arkansas at Little Rock, AR
University of Central Missouri, MO
University of Colorado Colorado Springs, CO
University of Hawaii at Hilo, HI
University of Iowa, IA
University of Louisville, KY
University of Maine at Farmington, ME
University of Memphis, TN
University of Minnesota Crookston, MN
University of Missouri/Columbia, MO
University of Missouri-Kansas City, MO
University of Montevallo, AL
University of Mount Olive , NC
University of Nebraska - Lincoln, NE
University of Nevada/Reno, NV
University of North Carolina School of the Arts, NC
University of North Texas, TX
University of Oklahoma, OK
University of South Carolina at Columbia, SC
University of South Carolina Upstate, SC
University of Southern Maine, ME
University of Texas at Arlington, TX
University of Toledo, OH
University of Wisconsin-Stout, WI
Virginia State University, VA
Voorhees College, SC
West Chester University of Pennsylvania, PA
West Virginia University, WV
Western State Colorado University, CO
Western Washington University, WA
Westfield State University, MA
Wilberforce University, OH
Wiley College, TX

$20,000-$21,999

Colleges with Tuition, Room, and Board

Arizona State University at the Polytechnic Campus, AZ
Arizona State University at the Tempe Campus, AZ
Arizona State University at the West Campus, AZ
Arkansas Baptist College, AR
Ashland University, OH
Bellevue University, NE
Boston Architectural College, MA (no R & B)
Bridgewater State University, MA
California State Polytechnic University, Pomona, CA
California State University, Chico, CA
California State University, Fullerton, CA
California State University, Sacramento, CA
Castleton University, VT
Central Connecticut State University, CT
Central Michigan University, MI
Cheyney University of Pennsylvania, PA
Chicago State University, IL
City University of New York/Baruch College, NY
City University of New York/City College, NY
Clarion University of Pennsylvania, PA
College of William & Mary, VA (no R & B)
Colorado Technical University, CO
Dillard University, LA
Eastern Illinois University, IL
Edward Waters College, FL
Farmingdale State College, NY
Ferris State University, MI
Fitchburg State University, MA
Framingham State University, MA
Georgia College & State University, GA
Humboldt State University, CA
Indiana University Bloomington, IN
Inter-American University of Puerto Rico-Aguadilla Campus, PR
Inter-American University of Puerto Rico-Metropolitan Campus, PR
Inter-American University of Puerto Rico-San Germán, PR
Jarvis Christian College, TX
Johnson State College, VT
Kent State University, OH
Louisiana College, LA
Lyndon State College, VT
Martin University, IN
Marylhurst University, OR (no R & B)
Massachusetts College of Liberal Arts, MA
New Jersey City University, NJ
Northern Arizona University, AZ
Northern Illinois University, IL
Oakland University, MI
Ohio State University at Columbus , OH
Old Dominion University, VA
Park University, MO
Philander Smith College, AR
Purdue University/West Lafayette, IN
Salem International University, WV
Salisbury University, MD
San Diego State University, CA
San Jose State University, CA
South Carolina State University, SC
Southern Arkansas University, AR
Southern Connecticut State University, CT
St. Gregory's University, OK
State University of New York / Buffalo State College, NY
State University of New York / SUNY Cortland, NY
State University of New York / SUNY Fredonia, NY
State University of New York / SUNY Potsdam, NY
State University of New York /College of Agriculture and Tech at Cobleskill, NY
State University of New York at Geneseo , NY
State University of New York at Oswego, NY
Stillman College, AL
Stony Brook University/The State University of New York, NY
Texas A&M University, TX
The College at Brockport - State University of New York, NY
The University of Akron, OH
Thomas University, GA
University of Cincinnati, OH
University of Georgia, GA
University of Holy Cross, LA
University of Houston, TX
University of Kansas, KS
University of Maine, ME
University of Maryland/Baltimore County, MD
University of Maryland/College Park, MD
University of Minnesota/Duluth, MN
University of Minnesota/Morris, MN
University of North Carolina at Chapel Hill, NC
University of Northern Colorado, CO
University of Texas at San Antonio, TX
University of the District of Columbia, DC
University of Wisconsin-Madison, WI
University of Wisconsin-Milwaukee, WI
Virginia Polytechnic Institute and State University, VA
Western Connecticut State University, CT
Western Illinois University, IL
Western Michigan University, MI
Wichita State University, KS
Worcester State University, MA

$22,000-$23,999

Colleges with Tuition, Room, and Board

Arizona State University at the Downtown Phoenix Campus, AZ
Auburn University, AL
Berkeley College/New York City Campus, NY (no R & B)
Bethune-Cookman University, FL
Brewton-Parker College, GA
Calumet College of St. Joseph, IN
Christopher Newport University, VA
Cleveland State University, OH
College of Charleston, SC
Colorado State University, CO
Eastern Connecticut State University, CT
Florida Memorial University, FL
Georgia Institute of Technology, GA
Grand Valley State University, MI
Illinois State University, IL
Indiana State University, IN
Indiana University of Pennsylvania, PA
Lee University, TN
Longwood University, VA (no R & B)
Maine Maritime Academy, ME
Mansfield University, PA
Michigan State University, MI
Millersville University of Pennsylvania, PA
Monroe College, NY
Montana State University-Billings, MT
Ohio University, OH
Oregon State University, OR
Plymouth State University, NH
Shippensburg University of Pennsylvania, PA
Southern Illinois University Carbondale, IL
Southern Illinois University Edwardsville, IL

State University of New York / The College of Environmental Science and Forestry, NY
State University of New York / University at Buffalo, NY
State University of New York at Binghamton, NY
State University of New York SUNY Albany , NY
The University of Tennessee at Knoxville, TN
Union College, NE
Universidad Politecnica de Puerto Rico, Hato Rey campus, PR
University of Arizona, AZ
University of Colorado Denver , CO
University of Hawaii at Manoa, HI
University of Maine at Machias, ME
University of Mary, ND
University of Minnesota/Twin Cities, MN
University of Oregon, OR
University of Pittsburgh at Bradford, PA
University of Pittsburgh at Greensburg, PA
University of Pittsburgh at Johnstown, PA
University of Texas at Dallas, TX
University of the Southwest, NM
University of Washington, WA
Vermont Technical College, VT
Virginia Commonwealth University, VA
Virginia Union University, VA
Washington State University, WA
Wayland Baptist University, TX
Wayne State University, MI
William Carey University, MS
William Paterson University of New Jersey, NJ
Winthrop University, SC

$24,000-$25,999

Colleges with Tuition, Room, and Board

Bethel University, TN (no R & B)
California State University, San Marcos, CA
City University of Seattle, WA
Davenport University, MI
Eastern Washington University, WA
Georgia State University, GA
Grace Bible College, MI
Grove City College, PA
Harding University, AR
Husson University, ME
Johnson C. Smith University, NC
Kean University, NJ
Keene State College, NH
Lindenwood University, MO
Massachusetts College of Art and Design, MA
Michigan Technological University, MI
Mississippi College, MS
Nebraska Methodist College , NE
Norfolk State University, VA
North Greenville University, SC
Paul Quinn College, TX
Penn State University/Altoona, PA
Presentation College, SD
Ramapo College of New Jersey, NJ
Rowan University, NJ
Shaw University, NC
St. Joseph's College, New York/Brooklyn Campus, NY (no R & B)
St. Joseph's College, New York/Long Island Campus, NY (no R & B)
Stockton University, NJ
Temple University, PA
University of Alabama , AL
University of Colorado Boulder, CO
University of Connecticut, CT
University of Delaware, DE
University of Illinois at Chicago, IL
University of Mary Washington, VA
University of Maryland/University College, MD
University of Massachusetts Dartmouth, MA
University of Michigan/Ann Arbor, MI
University of Rhode Island, RI
University of Virginia, VA
Williams Baptist College, AR
York College, NE

$26,000-$29,999

Colleges with Tuition, Room, and Board

Adventist University of Health Sciences, FL
Alaska Pacific University, AK
Alderson Broaddus University, WV
Andrews University, MI
Atlantic Union College, MA
Benedict College, SC
Benjamin Franklin Institute of Technology, MA
Bennett College , NC
Blackburn College, IL
Bowie State University, MD
Brescia University, KY
California State University, Monterey Bay, CA
City University of New York/Queens College, NY
Colorado School of Mines, CO
Columbia College - Missouri, MO
Concordia University Saint Paul, MN
Converse College, SC
Cumberland University, TN
Daniel Webster College, NH
Evangel University, MO
Faulkner University, AL
Flagler College, FL
Freed-Hardeman University, TN
Gallaudet University, DC
Goodwin College, CT
Greenville College, IL
Hannibal-LaGrange University, MO
Humphreys College, CA
Judson College, AL
Kentucky Christian University, KY
Keystone College, PA
Lincoln Memorial University, TN
Lourdes University, OH
Lubbock Christian University, TX
Madonna University, MI
Marygrove College, MI
Metropolitan State University of Denver, CO
Miami University, OH
Missouri Valley College, MO
Montclair State University, NJ
Mount Aloysius College, PA
New Jersey Institute of Technology, NJ
North Central University, MN
Norwich University, VT
Ohio Valley University, WV
Oklahoma Christian University, OK
Pennsylvania College of Technology, PA
Pennsylvania State University - University Park, PA
Reinhardt University, GA
Rochester College, MI
Rockhurst University, MO
Rocky Mountain College of Art and Design, CO
Rutgers University - Camden, NJ
Rutgers University - New Brunswick, NJ
Rutgers University - Newark, NJ
Saint Augustine's University, NC
Sonoma State University, CA
Southern Adventist University, TN
Southwest Baptist University, MO
Southwestern Adventist University, TX
St. Mary's College of Maryland, MD
Toccoa Falls College, GA
Touro College , NY
Tuskegee University, AL
University of California at Berkeley, CA
University of California at Davis, CA
University of California at Irvine, CA
University of California at Riverside, CA
University of California at Santa Barbara, CA
University of California, Santa Cruz, CA
University of Illinois at Urbana-Champaign, IL
University of Jamestown, ND
University of Massachusetts Amherst, MA
University of Massachusetts Lowell, MA
University of Mobile, AL
University of New Hampshire, NH
University of Pikeville, KY
University of Pittsburgh , PA
University of Texas at Austin, TX
University of Vermont, VT
Virginia Military Institute, VA
Warner University, FL
Wesleyan College, GA
William Penn University, IA
Winston-Salem State University, NC
York College of Pennsylvania, PA

$30,000 and over

Colleges with Tuition, Room, and Board

Abilene Christian University, TX
Adelphi University, NY
Adrian College, MI
Agnes Scott College, GA
Albany College of Pharmacy and Health Sciences, NY
Albertus Magnus College, CT
Albion College, MI
Albright College, PA
Alfred University, NY
Allegheny College, PA
Allen College, IA
Alma College, MI
Alvernia University, PA
Alverno College, WI
American International College, MA
American Jewish University - College of Arts and Sciences Campus, CA
American University, DC
Amherst College, MA
Anderson University, IN
Anna Maria College, MA
Aquinas College, TN
Aquinas College - Michigan, MI
Arcadia University, PA
Art Academy of Cincinnati, OH
Art Institute of Portland, OR
ArtCenter College of Design, CA
Asbury University, KY
Assumption College, MA
Augsburg College, MN
Augustana College, IL
Augustana University, SD
Aurora University, IL
Austin College, TX
Averett University, VA
Avila University, MO
Azusa Pacific University, CA
Babson College, MA
Baker University, KS
Baldwin Wallace University, OH
Bard College, NY
Bard College at Simon's Rock, MA
Barnard College/Columbia University, NY
Barry University, FL
Barton College, NC
Bates College, ME
Bay Path University, MA
Baylor University, TX
Beacon College, FL
Becker College, MA
Belhaven University, MS
Bellarmine University, KY
Belmont Abbey College, NC
Belmont University, TN
Beloit College, WI
Benedictine College, KS
Benedictine University, IL
Bennington College, VT
Bentley University, MA
Berkeley College/New Jersey, NJ
Berkeley College/White Plains Campus, NY
Berklee College of Music, MA
Berry College, GA
Bethany College, KS
Bethany College, WV
Bethel College, IN
Bethel College, KS
Bethel University, MN
Biola University, CA
Birmingham-Southern College, AL
Bloomfield College, NJ
Bluefield College, VA
Bluffton University, OH
Boston College, MA
Boston University, MA
Bowdoin College, ME
Bradley University, IL
Brandeis University, MA
Brenau University - Women's College, GA (no R & B)
Briar Cliff University, IA
Bridgewater College, VA
Brown University, RI
Bryan College, TN
Bryant University, RI
Bryn Athyn College , PA
Bryn Mawr College, PA
Bucknell University, PA
Buena Vista University, IA
Butler University, IN
Cabrini University, PA
Cairn University, PA
Caldwell University, NJ
California Baptist University, CA
California College of the Arts, CA
California Institute of Technology, CA
California Institute of the Arts, CA
California Lutheran University, CA
Calvin College, MI
Campbell University, NC
Campbellsville University, KY
Canisius College, NY
Capital University, OH
Capitol Technology University, MD
Cardinal Stritch University, WI
Carleton College, MN
Carlow University, PA
Carnegie Mellon University, PA
Carroll College, MT
Carroll University, WI
Carson-Newman University, TN
Carthage College, WI
Case Western Reserve University, OH
Catawba College, NC
Cazenovia College, NY
Cedar Crest College, PA
Cedarville University, OH
Centenary College, NJ
Centenary College of Louisiana, LA
Central College, IA
Central Methodist University, MO
Centre College, KY
Chaminade University of Honolulu, HI
Champlain College, VT
Chapman University, CA
Charleston Southern University, SC
Chatham University, PA
Chestnut Hill College, PA
Christendom College, VA
Christian Brothers University, TN
City University of New York/Hunter College, NY
Claflin University, SC
Claremont McKenna College, CA
Clark Atlanta University, GA
Clark University, MA
Clarke University, IA
Clarkson College, NE
Clarkson University, NY
Cleveland Institute of Art, OH
Cleveland Institute of Music, OH
Coe College, IA
Cogswell Polytechnical College, CA
Coker College, SC
Colby College, ME
Colby-Sawyer College, NH
Colgate University, NY
College for Creative Studies, MI
College of Art and Design at Lesley University, MA
College of Mount Saint Vincent, NY
College of Saint Benedict , MN
College of Saint Elizabeth, NJ
College of Saint Mary, NE
College of St Joseph, VT
College of St. Scholastica, MN
College of the Atlantic, ME
College of the Holy Cross, MA
Colorado Christian University, CO
Colorado College, CO
Columbia College , SC
Columbia College Chicago, IL
Columbia University/ School of General Studies, NY
Columbia University/City of New York, NY
Columbus College of Art and Design, OH
Concordia College - Moorhead, MN
Concordia College - New York, NY
Concordia University , CA
Concordia University , OR
Concordia University Nebraska, NE
Concordia University Texas, TX
Concordia University Wisconsin, WI
Concordia University, Ann Arbor, MI
Concordia University, Chicago, IL
Connecticut College, CT (no R & B)
Cooper Union for the Advancement of Science and Art, NY
Corban University, OR
Cornell College, IA
Cornell University, NY
Cornish College of the Arts, WA
Covenant College, GA
Creighton University, NE
Culver-Stockton College, MO
Curry College, MA
Daemen College, NY
Dakota Wesleyan University, SD
Dallas Baptist University, TX
Dartmouth College, NH
Davidson College, NC
Davis & Elkins College, WV
Defiance College, OH

Delaware Valley University, PA
Denison University, OH
DePaul University, IL
DePauw University, IN
DeSales University, PA
Dickinson College, PA
Doane University , NE
Dominican College, NY
Dominican University, IL
Dominican University of California, CA
Dordt College, IA
Drake University, IA
Drew University/College of Liberal Arts, NJ
Drexel University, PA
Drury University, MO
Duke University, NC
Duquesne University, PA
D'Youville College, NY
Earlham College, IN
East Texas Baptist University, TX
Eastern Mennonite University, VA
Eastern Nazarene College, MA
Eastern University, PA
Eastman School of Music/University of Rochester, NY
Eckerd College, FL
Edgewood College, WI
Elizabethtown College, PA
Elmhurst College, IL
Elmira College, NY
Elms College, MA
Elon University, NC
Embry-Riddle Aeronautical University - Daytona Beach, FL
Embry-Riddle Aeronautical University - Prescott Campus, AZ
Emerson College, MA
Emmanuel College, MA
Emory and Henry College, VA
Emory University, GA
Endicott College, MA
Erskine College, SC
Eugene Lang College/The New School for Liberal Arts, NY
Eureka College, IL
Fairfield University, CT
Fairleigh Dickinson University/College at Florham, NJ
Fairleigh Dickinson University/ Metropolitan Campus, NJ
Felician University, NJ
Ferrum College, VA
Fisk University, TN
Five Towns College, NY
Florida Institute of Technology, FL
Florida Southern College, FL
Fontbonne University, MO
Fordham University, NY
Franciscan University of Steubenville, OH
Franklin and Marshall College, PA
Franklin College, IN
Franklin Pierce University, NH
Franklin University, OH
Franklin W. Olin College of Engineering, MA
Fresno Pacific University, CA
Friends University, KS
Furman University, SC
Gannon University, PA
Gardner-Webb University, NC
Geneva College, PA
George Fox University, OR
George Washington University, DC
Georgetown College, KY
Georgetown University, DC
Georgian Court University, NJ
Gettysburg College, PA
Golden Gate University, CA
Goldey-Beacom College, DE
Gonzaga University, WA
Gordon College, MA
Goshen College, IN
Goucher College, MD
Grace College and Seminary, IN
Graceland University, IA
Grand Rapids Theological Seminary/ Cornerstone University, MI
Grand View University, IA
Green Mountain College, VT
Greensboro College, NC
Grinnell College, IA
Guilford College, NC
Gustavus Adolphus College, MN
Gwynedd Mercy University, PA
Hamilton College, NY
Hamline University, MN
Hampden-Sydney College, VA
Hampshire College, MA
Hampton University, VA
Hanover College, IN
Hardin-Simmons University, TX
Hartwick College, NY
Harvard College/Harvard University, MA
Harvey Mudd College, CA
Hastings College, NE
Haverford College, PA
Hawaii Pacific University, HI
Heidelberg University, OH
Hellenic College/Holy Cross Greek Orthodox School of Theology, MA
Hendrix College, AR
High Point University, NC
Hilbert College, NY
Hillsdale College, MI
Hiram College, OH
Hobart and William Smith Colleges, NY
Hofstra University, NY
Hollins University, VA
Holy Family University, PA
Holy Names University, CA
Hood College, MD
Hope College, MI
Hope International University, CA
Houghton College, NY
Houston Baptist University, TX
Howard Payne University, TX
Howard University, DC
Huntingdon College, AL
Huntington University, IN
Illinois College, IL
Illinois Institute of Technology, IL
Illinois Wesleyan University, IL
Immaculata University, PA
Indiana Institute of Technology, IN
Indiana Wesleyan University, IN
Iona College, NY
Iowa Wesleyan University, IA
Ithaca College, NY
Jacksonville University, FL
John Brown University, AR
John Carroll University, OH
Johns Hopkins University, MD
Johnson & Wales University/Charlotte Campus, NC
Johnson & Wales University/Denver Campus, CO
Johnson & Wales University/North Miami Campus, FL
Johnson & Wales University/Providence Campus, RI
Judson University, IL
Juilliard School, NY
Juniata College, PA
Kalamazoo College, MI
Kansas City Art Institute, MO
Kansas Wesleyan University, KS
Keiser University, FL
Kendall College, IL
Kentucky Wesleyan College, KY
Kenyon College, OH
Kettering University, MI
Keuka College, NY
King University, TN
King's College, PA
Knox College, IL
La Roche College, PA
La Salle University, PA
La Sierra University, CA
Lafayette College, PA
LaGrange College, GA
Laguna College of Art and Design, CA
Lake Erie College, OH
Lake Forest College, IL
Lakeland University, WI
Lander University, SC
Lasell College, MA
Lawrence Technological University, MI
Lawrence University, WI
Le Moyne College, NY
Lebanon Valley College, PA
Lees-McRae College, NC
Lehigh University, PA
Lenoir-Rhyne University, NC
Lesley University, MA
LeTourneau University, TX
Lewis & Clark College, OR
Lewis University, IL
LIM College, NY
Limestone College, SC
Lindsey Wilson College, KY
Linfield College, OR
Lipscomb University, TN
List College , NY
LIU Brooklyn, NY
LIU Post, NY
Loras College, IA
Loyola Marymount University, CA
Loyola University Chicago, IL
Loyola University Maryland, MD
Loyola University New Orleans, LA
Luther College, IA
Lycoming College, PA
Lynchburg College, VA
Lynn University, FL
Lyon College, AR
Macalester College, MN
MacMurray College, IL
Maharishi University of Management, IA
Maine College of Art, ME
Malone University, OH
Manchester University, IN
Manhattan College, NY
Manhattan School of Music, NY
Manhattanville College, NY
Mannes School for Music, NY
Marian University, IN
Marian University, WI
Marietta College, OH
Marist College, NY
Marlboro College, VT
Marquette University, WI
Mars Hill University, NC
Mary Baldwin University, VA
Maryland Institute College of Art, MD
Marymount Manhattan College, NY
Marymount University, VA
Maryville College, TN
Maryville University of Saint Louis, MO
Marywood University, PA
Massachusetts Institute of Technology, MA
McDaniel College, MD
McKendree University, IL
McMurry University, TX
McPherson College, KS
MCPHS University, MA
Medaille College, NY
Memphis College of Art, TN
Menlo College, CA
Mercer University, GA
Mercy College, NY
Mercyhurst University, PA
Meredith College, NC
Merrimack College, MA
Messiah College, PA
Methodist University, NC
MidAmerica Nazarene University, KS
Middlebury College, VT
Midland University, NE
Midway University, KY
Milligan College, TN
Millikin University, IL
Mills College, CA
Millsaps College, MS
Milwaukee Institute of Art and Design, WI
Milwaukee School of Engineering, WI
Minneapolis College of Art and Design, MN
Misericordia University, PA
Missouri Baptist University, MO
Mitchell College, CT
Molloy College, NY
Monmouth College, IL
Monmouth University, NJ
Montreat College, NC
Montserrat College of Art, MA
Moore College of Art and Design, PA
Moravian College, PA
Morehouse College, GA
Morningside College, IA
Mount Holyoke College, MA
Mount Ida College, MA
Mount Marty College, SD
Mount Mary University, WI
Mount Mercy University, IA
Mount Saint Mary College, NY
Mount St. Joseph University, OH
Mount St. Mary's University, MD
Mount St. Mary's University - Chalon Campus, CA
Mount Vernon Nazarene University, OH
Muhlenberg College, PA
Muskingum University, OH
Naropa University, CO
Nazareth College , NY
Nebraska Wesleyan University, NE
Neumann University, PA
New England College, NH
New England Conservatory of Music, MA
New York Institute of Technology, NY
New York University, NY
Newberry College, SC
Newbury College, MA
Newman University, KS
Niagara University, NY
Nichols College, MA
North Carolina Wesleyan College, NC
North Central College, IL
North Park University, IL
Northeastern University, MA
Northland College, WI
Northwest Christian University, OR
Northwest Nazarene University, ID
Northwest University, WA
Northwestern College of Iowa, IA
Northwestern University, IL
Northwood University - Michigan, MI
Notre Dame College, OH
Notre Dame de Namur University, CA
Notre Dame of Maryland University, MD
Nova Southeastern University, FL
Nyack College, NY
Oakland City University, IN
Oakwood University, AL
Oberlin College, OH
Occidental College, CA
Oglethorpe University, GA
Ohio Dominican University, OH
Ohio Northern University, OH
Ohio Wesleyan University, OH
Oklahoma Baptist University, OK
Oklahoma City University, OK
Oklahoma Wesleyan University, OK
Olivet College, MI
Olivet Nazarene University, IL
Oral Roberts University, OK
Otis College of Art and Design, CA (no R & B)
Ottawa University, KS
Otterbein University, OH
Ouachita Baptist University, AR
Our Lady of the Lake University, TX
Pace University, NY
Pacific Lutheran University, WA
Pacific Northwest College of Art, OR
Pacific Union College, CA
Pacific University, OR
Palm Beach Atlantic University, FL
Parsons The New School for Design, NY
Pepperdine University, CA
Pfeiffer University, NC
Philadelphia University, PA
Piedmont College, GA
Pine Manor College, MA
Pitzer College, CA
Point Loma Nazarene University, CA
Point Park University, PA
Pomona College, CA
Post University, CT
Pratt Institute, NY
Presbyterian College, SC
Prescott College, AZ
Princeton University, NJ
Principia College, IL
Providence College, RI
Queens University of Charlotte, NC
Quincy University, IL
Quinnipiac University, CT
Randolph College, VA
Randolph-Macon College, VA
Reed College, OR
Regis College, MA
Regis University, CO
Rensselaer Polytechnic Institute, NY
Research College of Nursing, MO
Rhode Island School of Design, RI
Rhodes College, TN
Rice University, TX
Rider University, NJ
Ringling College of Art and Design, FL
Ripon College, WI
Rivier University, NH
Roanoke College, VA
Robert Morris University, PA
Roberts Wesleyan College, NY
Rochester Institute of Technology, NY
Rockford University, IL
Rocky Mountain College, MT
Roger Williams University, RI
Rollins College, FL
Roosevelt University, IL
Rose-Hulman Institute of Technology, IN
Rosemont College, PA
Russell Sage College, NY
Sacred Heart University, CT
Saint Anselm College, NH
Saint Francis University, PA
Saint John's University, MN
Saint Joseph's College, IN
Saint Joseph's College of Maine, ME
Saint Joseph's University, PA
Saint Leo University, FL
Saint Louis University, MO
Saint Martin's University, WA
Saint Mary-of-the-Woods College, IN
Saint Mary's College, IN
Saint Mary's College of California, CA
Saint Mary's University of Minnesota, MN
Saint Michael's College, VT
Saint Peter's University, NJ
Saint Vincent College, PA

Saint Xavier University, IL
Salem College, NC
Salve Regina University, RI
Samford University, AL
San Diego Christian College, CA
San Francisco Art Institute, CA
San Francisco Conservatory of Music, CA
Santa Fe University of Art and Design, NM
Sarah Lawrence College, NY
Savannah College of Art and Design, GA
School of the Art Institute of Chicago, IL
School of Visual Arts, NY
Schreiner University, TX
Scripps College, CA
Seattle Pacific University, WA
Seattle University, WA
Seton Hall University, NJ
Seton Hill University, PA
Sewanee: The University of the South, TN
Shenandoah University, VA
Shimer College, IL
Shorter University, GA
Siena College, NY
Siena Heights University, MI
Sierra Nevada College, NV
Silver Lake College of the Holy Family, WI
Simmons College, MA
Simpson College, IA
Simpson University, CA
Skidmore College, NY
Smith College, MA
South University, GA
Southeastern University, FL
Southern Methodist University, TX
Southern Nazarene University, OK
Southern New Hampshire University, NH
Southern Vermont College, VT
Southern Wesleyan University, SC
Southwestern College, KS
Southwestern University, TX
Spalding University, KY
Spelman College, GA
Spring Arbor University, MI
Spring Hill College, AL
Springfield College, MA
St. Ambrose University, IA
St. Andrews University, NC
St. Bonaventure University, NY
St. Catherine University, MN
St. Edward's University, TX
St. Francis College, NY
St. John Fisher College, NY
St. John's College, Santa Fe, NM
St. John's College-Annapolis, MD
St. John's University, NY
St. Lawrence University, NY
St. Mary's University , TX
St. Norbert College, WI
St. Olaf College, MN
St. Thomas Aquinas College, NY
St. Thomas University, FL
Stanford University, CA
Stephens College, MO
Sterling College, KS
Sterling College, VT
Stetson University, FL
Stevens Institute of Technology, NJ
Stevenson University, MD
Stonehill College, MA
Suffolk University, MA
Susquehanna University, PA
Swarthmore College, PA
Syracuse University, NY
Tabor College, KS
Taylor University, IN
Tennessee Wesleyan University, TN
Texas Christian University, TX
Texas Lutheran University, TX
Texas Wesleyan University, TX
The Art Institute of Atlanta, GA
The Boston Conservatory at Berklee, MA
The Catholic University of America, DC
The Citadel, The Military College of South Carolina, SC
The College of Idaho, ID
The College of New Jersey, NJ
The College of New Rochelle, NY
The College of Saint Rose, NY
The College of Wooster, OH
The Master's University, CA
Thiel College, PA
Thomas Aquinas College, CA
Thomas College, ME
Thomas More College, KY
Thomas More College of Liberal Arts, NH
Tiffin University, OH
Transylvania University, KY
Trevecca Nazarene University, TN
Trine University, IN
Trinity Christian College, IL
Trinity College, CT
Trinity College of Nursing and Health Sciences, IL
Trinity International University, IL
Trinity University, TX
Trinity Washington University, DC
Tufts University, MA
Tulane University, LA
Tusculum College, TN
Union College, KY
Union College, NY
Union University, TN
Unity College, ME
University of Bridgeport, CT
University of California at Los Angeles, CA
University of California San Diego, CA
University of Charleston, WV
University of Chicago, IL
University of Dallas, TX
University of Dayton, OH
University of Denver, CO
University of Detroit Mercy, MI
University of Dubuque, IA
University of Evansville, IN
University of Findlay, OH
University of Great Falls, MT
University of Hartford, CT
University of Indianapolis, IN
University of Kentucky, KY
University of La Verne, CA
University of Mary Hardin-Baylor, TX
University of Miami, FL
University of Mount Union , OH
University of New England, ME
University of New Haven, CT
University of Northwestern - St. Paul, MN
University of Notre Dame, IN
University of Pennsylvania, PA
University of Portland, OR
University of Puget Sound, WA
University of Redlands, CA
University of Richmond, VA
University of Rochester, NY
University of Saint Francis, IN
University of Saint Joseph , CT
University of Saint Mary, KS
University of San Diego, CA
University of San Francisco, CA
University of Scranton, PA
University of Sioux Falls, SD
University of Southern California, CA
University of St. Francis, IL
University of St. Thomas, MN
University of St. Thomas - Houston, TX
University of Tampa, FL
University of Texas at El Paso, TX
University of the Arts, PA
University of the Cumberlands, KY
University of the Incarnate Word, TX
University of the Ozarks, AR
University of the Pacific, CA
University of the Sciences , PA
University of Tulsa, OK
Upper Iowa University, IA
Urbana University, OH
Ursinus College, PA
Utica College, NY
Valparaiso University, IN
Vanderbilt University, TN
VanderCook College of Music, IL
Vanguard University of Southern California, CA
Vassar College, NY
Vaughn College of Aeronautics and Technology, NY
Villanova University, PA
Virginia Wesleyan College, VA
Viterbo University, WI
Wabash College, IN
Wagner College, NY
Wake Forest University, NC
Walla Walla University, WA
Walsh University, OH
Warner Pacific College, OR
Warren Wilson College, NC
Wartburg College, IA
Washington & Jefferson College, PA
Washington Adventist University, MD
Washington and Lee University, VA
Washington College, MD
Washington University in St. Louis, MO
Waynesburg University, PA
Webb Institute, NY
Webber International University, FL
Webster University, MO
Wellesley College, MA
Wells College, NY
Wentworth Institute of Technology, MA
Wesley College, DE
Wesleyan University, CT
West Virginia Wesleyan College, WV
Western New England University, MA
Westminster Choir College, NJ
Westminster College, MO
Westminster College, PA
Westminster College, UT
Westmont College, CA
Wheaton College, IL
Wheaton College, MA
Wheeling Jesuit University, WV
Wheelock College, MA
Whitman College, WA
Whittier College, CA
Whitworth University, WA
Widener University, PA
Wilkes University, PA
Willamette University, OR
William Jewell College, MO
William Peace University, NC
William Woods University, MO
Williams College, MA
Wilmington College, OH
Wilson College, PA
Wingate University, NC
Wisconsin Lutheran College, WI
Wittenberg University, OH
Wofford College, SC
Woodbury University, CA
Worcester Polytechnic Institute, MA
Xavier University, OH
Xavier University of Louisiana, LA
Yale University, CT
Yeshiva University, NY

PART III

INDEX OF COLLEGE MAJORS

By now, you either have a clear idea about what your college major will be, or you are worrying about it. This section presents an overview of academic majors as well as information about some of the careers for which each major prepares you.

Majors are listed alphabetically in chart form. This lets you compare the various schools that offer the majors that interest you. You'll also be able to compare each school's Selector Rating and in-state costs.

After you've found a representative sampling of the schools that offer majors in the fields you may want to pursue, go on to the college Profiles that make up this book's main section.

DECIDING ON A COLLEGE MAJOR AND CAREER

What Is a College Major? A major is a field of study in which a student chooses an academic specialty to receive a college degree. A major consists of a concentration of specialized subject matter in a field of study. Most majors occupy about one-quarter to two-thirds of courses in that subject. Most college and university students must complete a required number of courses in their major to earn a Bachelor of Arts (B.A.) or a Bachelor of Science (B.S.) degree. The other twenty-five to fifty percent of courses are occupied by "general education" requirements for graduation, or electives that enhance and broaden a student's academic knowledge. Students' choice of major should be made carefully considering their interests and special talents.

What Is a College Minor? A minor in a field of study usually consists of a number of courses in a field of study other than the major. However, the required units of study are fewer than those required of the major. Many colleges today do not require a formal minor for graduation. The practical reason for a minor is to supplement and strengthen a major. For example, a computer science major may require specified courses in mathematics that, when totaled up, meet the definition of a minor, or perhaps a dual major.

Majors and Careers. Choosing a field of study is one of the most important decisions a student will make in the process of choosing a college major leading to an associate or bachelor's degree. A major with a structured course of study not only provides for intellectual growth, self-improvement, general knowledge, and a search for truth and understanding, but often provides the required technical training to enter and become successful in the world of work. Personal enlightenment is a noble goal, but most students no longer can afford the monetary expenses and the time to pursue courses that do not lead to a major that ties into career goals. Information on majors and careers is presented here to help students to make wise educational and career decisions. Informed educational and career decisions should include interests, academic abilities, and work values.

WHAT ARE SOME DIFFERENT APPROACHES TO CHOOSING A COLLEGE MAJOR?

JOB TRAINING: A student may want to go to college for one main reason: to acquire specific job skills to qualify for direct job entry. Job training course work is usually work-related and technical and it is evident that the skills learned in class can be directly applied to an occupation. For example, students who want to work as engineers in one of the many engineering specialties should pursue a two-year program course work as engineering technicians, or a four- to five-year engineering curriculum to become professional engineers.

Technical preparation: Technical preparation students generally enroll in associate degree programs that provide them with advanced skills through studies and experiences in applied academics, skills, and advanced technology. These students join the workforce after grade 14 or continue their formal preparation by working toward a baccalaureate degree in applied technology. Technical majors can be planned in agriculture, arts and communications, business, engineering and mechanics, health, human service, and natural science.

A general approach: Students may want to pursue a more general major that may not directly tie in to job entry, but will improve their general knowledge and prepare them as generalists with intellectual and problem-solving skills rather than technical training. This kind of major is often referred to as liberal arts, humanities, or general studies. Liberal arts majors can be planned in Social and Behavioral Sciences, The Arts, Communications, Humanities, and Ethnic Studies. A liberal arts major, leading to a baccalaureate degree, may not guarantee direct entry into an occupation associated with the major.

Special talent approach: Students may want to select a major because of a special talent and a strong interest in a certain field of study. Students with a strong interest in writing, drama, music, art, or an academic subject should select a major that helps to further the talent. College life will be more enjoyable if students select majors that will provide personal satisfaction. Designing a career plan that will allow a lifestyle compatible with the special talent will also provide personal satisfaction.

Double major approach: Students often decide to choose two majors in preparation for a career. A double major may be necessary in preparing for occupations in the science field where it is essential to be well-grounded in both the physical and biological sciences.

Independent approach: Students may have highly divergent interests that cut across two or more fields of study. Many colleges allow students to design a major to satisfy their goals. For example, students may have artistic talents and scientific interests. They might combine the two interests and design a scientific illustration major that meets faculty approval.

CONNECTING COLLEGE MAJOR PLANNING AND CAREER PLANNING

All students from the ninth grade through postsecondary school should be following a program of study that will prepare them for specific careers—studies that blend appropriate academics with appropriate skills and knowledge in a particular career area. All students in postsecondary studies should be preparing for life and work after completing their studies. This assertion eliminates a justification for a "general plan" of studies that in theory "leads anywhere," but in fact "leads nowhere." Students should either be in a postsecondary associate, technical, or baccalaureate educational plan that leads to a satisfying career.

The next section presents relevant educational and career information on 14 fields of study from which students may choose a major based on career plans. Each of the 14 fields of study has specific information on majors and careers that students should consider carefully when choosing a college major. Information about employment, growth, and earnings is taken from the Department of Labor figures for 2012, with growth projected to 2022.

1. AGRICULTURAL SCIENCES

Agriculture is a broad and diverse field of study that trains scientists for many rewarding and satisfying careers. These play an important part in maintaining the nation's food supply through ensuring agricultural productivity and the safety of the food supply. Agricultural scientists engage in research, development, and production of farm crops and animals, food sciences, plant sciences, and soil sciences. Others manage marketing or production operations in companies that produce food products or agricultural chemicals, supplies, and machinery. Other agricultural scientists are consultants to business firms, private clients, or governmental agencies.

Interests: Agricultural research, development, and production of farm crops and animals, and development of ways to improve their quantity and quality

Popular majors in this field of study: Agribusiness, Agricultural Education, Agronomy, Animal Science, Entomology, Farm and Ranch Management, Fisheries and Wildlife, Food Sciences, Forestry, Horticultural Science, and Soil Sciences

Employment information/outlook: More than 2,024,179 people worked in related occupations in this field of study in 2012. The 2012-2022 employment growth is expected to be 9%.

As of May 2012, the median annual wages of food scientists and technologists were $58,070; soil and plant scientists, $58,740; and animal scientists, $61,680. Incomes of farmers and ranchers vary greatly from year to year, because prices of farm products fluctuate with weather conditions and other factors that influence the quantity and quality of farm output and the demand for those products. In addition to farm business income, farmers often receive government subsidies or other payments that supplement their incomes and reduce some of the risk of farming. Many farmers—primarily operators of small farms—have recently been relying more and more on off-farm sources of income. Full-time, salaried agricultural managers had median weekly earnings of $1,332.80 in 2012. Farm income can vary substantially depending on a number of factors, including the type of crop or livestock being raised, price fluctuations for various agricultural products, and weather conditions that affect yield. In some cases, government subsidies may supplement a farmer's income. For a growing number of farmers and ranchers, particularly those working on farms for residential and lifestyle reasons, crop or livestock production is not their major occupation or source of income.

Agribusiness

Agribusiness majors will learn the business aspect of farms, firms, and industries that supply and service the farmer and other farm-related businesses. They will study merchandising, advertising, finance, marketing, and international trade.

Interests: Taking initiative, leadership, decision making, problem solving, analyzing data, global interdependence, working with people

Skills and abilities: Planning, organizing, making business decisions, leadership, teamwork, creative and critical thinking, working with people, written and verbal skills, adapting to change

Occupations related to this major: Agricultural Crop Farm Managers, Farm Products Purchasing Agents and Buyers, Farm and Ranch Managers, Fish Hatchery Managers, Farmers and Ranchers, Agricultural Statisticians, and Farm and Home Management advisers.

Agricultural Education

Agricultural Education majors will study those basic courses in agriculture that will prepare them to teach agricultural science in high schools, community colleges, or universities. They will also complete general preparation for a service-type career in agriculture, such as extension services. They will learn to supervise youth and adult groups and to direct programs in both agricultural and human resources.

Interests: Working with people, working with plants, working with animals

Skills and abilities: Communication, science (especially natural sciences and chemistry)

Occupations related to this major: Farm and Home Management Advisers, Park Naturalists, Farmers and Ranchers, Agricultural Science Teachers, and 4-H and Agricultural Extension Agents

Agronomy

Agronomy majors will learn about three basic natural elements—crops, soils, and climates—and their interdependence in producing food, feed, fiber, and fuel. Agronomists study theory and practices for improving crop production while conserving natural resources and maintaining environmental quality.

Interests: Nature and the outdoors, environmental quality (soil, water, and air), conservation of natural resources, biological and physical sciences, problem solving, plant growth and experimentation, weather, climate, geologic formations

Skills and qualities: Oral and written communication skills, group dynamics, leadership, organizational (interpersonal) skills, analytic reasoning, creative thinking

Occupations related to this major: Agricultural Climatologists, Agrochemical Technologists, Environmental Technicians, Food and Drug Inspectors, Farm or Ranch Managers, Plant Breeders, Agricultural Technicians, Soil and Water Conservationists, and Greenhouse Managers

Animal Science

Animal Science majors will learn how to manage livestock and poultry. They will study the role of animals in the economy, how animal products influence eating habits and are part of the global food supply, and how animals help serve people's recreation needs. They will carry out investigations and experiments in the areas of breeding, feeding, management, and disease control in farm and domestic animals.

Interests: Working with plants, working with animals, working with people

Skills and abilities: Speaking and writing effectively

Occupations related to this major: Animal Scientists, Soil and Plant Scientists, Park Naturalists, Biologists, Farm and Ranch Managers, and Soil Conservationists

Entomology

Entomology majors will study the biology, ecology, classification, distribution, physiology, economic importance, and management of insects and their relation to plant and animal life. They will learn to identify species of insects and allied forms, such as mites and spiders. They will study methods of controlling and eliminating agricultural, structural, and forest pests by developing new and improved pesticides and cultural and biological methods, including using natural enemies of pests. They will also study insect distribution and habitat, and methods to prevent importation and spread of injurious species.

Interests: Science, techniques of scientific research, the environment, the health and well-being of people

Skills and abilities: Curiosity, rational thinking, objective thinking, performing laboratory tasks carefully

Occupations related to this major: Entomologists, Environmental Scientists, Soil and Plant Scientists, Biologists, Clinical Laboratory Technologists, and Pest Control Workers

Farm and Ranch Management

Farm and Ranch Management majors will learn to guide and assist farmers and ranchers in maximizing the financial returns to their land by managing the day-to-day activities. Duties and responsibilities may vary widely. For example, the owner of a very large livestock farm may employ a farm manager to oversee a single activity, such as feeding livestock. When managing a small crop farm, on the other hand, a farm manager may assume responsibility for all functions, from selecting the crop to participating in planting and harvesting.

Interests: Directing and coordinating worker activities, decision making, problem solving, nature and the outdoors, conservation of natural resources, biological and physical science

Skills and abilities: Speaking, motivating people, creative and critical thinking, oral and written expression and comprehension, organizational skills, leadership

Occupations related to this major: Agricultural Crop Farm Managers, Farm and Ranch Managers, Foresters, Dairy Farm Managers, Poultry Farm Managers, and Farm and Home Management Advisers

Fisheries and Wildlife

Fisheries and Wildlife majors will learn about fish eggs, larvae, fish parasites, and diseases. They will learn to operate fish culture facilities, tag and mark fish, detect problems of water pollution, analyze, identify, collect, control, and preserve populations of fur and game animals.

Interests: Nature and the outdoors, science, research

Skills and abilities: Solving problems, communicating effectively, working with others

Occupations related to this major: Fish Culturists, Fish Hatchery Managers, Environmental Scientists, Zoo Workers, Fisheries and Wildlife Biologists, and Park Naturalists

Food Sciences

Food Science majors will learn to use biological, physical, and social sciences to transform raw materials into safe, nutritious, and economical foods. They will learn to apply scientific and engineering principles in research, development, and food production technology. They will also work to improve methods of processing, preserving, packaging, distributing, and preparing food.

Interests: Biological and physical science, public well-being, teamwork, observing details, solving complex problems

Skills and abilities: Good laboratory technique, oral and written expression and comprehension, mathematical reasoning

Occupations related to this major: Food Scientists, Food Science Technicians, Food Chemists, Food Plant Managers, Food Microbiologists, and Biological and Agricultural Technologists

Forestry

Forestry majors will learn to manage, protect, and develop forest lands and other resources for economic and recreational purposes; plan and supervise the cutting and harvesting of timber; carry out forestation and reforestation activities and manage parks and camps.

Interests: Nature and the outdoors, working with people, planning activities, investigative research, solving problems

Skills and abilities: Communicating effectively, working with quantitative and qualitative problems, presenting ideas to others

Occupations related to this major: Foresters, Soil Conservationists, Environmental Scientists, Biologists, Range Managers, Nursery and Greenhouse Managers, Agricultural Engineers, and Forest and Conservation Technicians

Horticultural Science

Horticultural Science majors will study problems of plant production, processing, and disease resistance. They will also study soil and climate to learn the conditions in which different types of plants thrive. They will be concerned with orchards, garden plants, flowers, ornamental plants, and nursery stock.

Interests: Science, working with plants, business, working with people, solving problems, improving the environment

Skills and abilities: Biological and physical sciences, written and oral communication, organization, creativity, quantitative thinking, computer competency, working with people

Occupations related to this major: Horticulturists, Foresters, Conservation Scientists, Landscape Architects, Plant Scientists, Farmers, and Farm Managers

Soil Sciences

Soil Science majors will study the physical, chemical, and geological characteristics and behaviors of soils. They will learn how to investigate soil both in the field and in the lab, and to classify soils in terms of their capability in producing crops, grasses, and trees. They also will learn how to make land appraisals.

Interests: Nature and the outdoors, conservation of natural resources, the environment, science

Skills and abilities: Quantitative reasoning, keen observation of natural phenomena, oral and written communication, applying scientific knowledge to complex systems

Occupations related to this major: Plant Scientists, Conservation Scientists, Botanists, Biochemists, Park Naturalists, and Farm and Range Managers

2. ARCHITECTURE AND DESIGN

Architects learn to plan, design, and supervise the construction of buildings, houses, factories, skyscrapers, schools, and other structures. They learn to make them attractive, usable, energy efficient, and economical. Architects must qualify for a state license after graduation. Most architects work for architectural firms. Others work directly for builders, real estate developers, or large construction projects, as well as governmental agencies responsible for housing and community planning, such as the Department of Defense, Interior, and Housing and Urban Development. Students interested in the field of architecture will do well in such courses as architectural theory design, computer graphics, computer science, general engineering urban planning, mathematics, physics, and economics.

Interests: Architects have an interest in planning, designing, and supervising the construction of buildings, houses, factories, skyscrapers, schools, and other structures.

Popular majors in this field of study: Architectural Engineering, Architecture, City and Regional Planning, Construction Science, Interior Design, Landscape Architecture, Marine Architecture, and Surveying

Employment information/outlook: More than 2,474,500 people worked in related occupations in this field of study in 2012. The 2012-2022 employment growth is expected to be 7.3%.

Median annual wages of wage-and-salary architects were $73,900 in May 2012. Those just starting their internships can expect to earn considerably less. Earnings of partners in established architectural firms may fluctuate because of changing business conditions. Some architects may have difficulty establishing their own practices and may go through a period when their expenses are greater than their incomes, requiring substantial financial resources. Many firms pay tuition and fees toward continuing education requirements for their employees. Median annual wages of urban and regional planners were $65,230 in May 2012. Earnings also vary by the worker's education and experience, type of work, complexity of the construction project, and geographic location. Wages of construction workers often are affected when poor weather prevents them from working. Traditionally, winter is the slack period for construction activity, especially in colder parts of the country, but there is a trend toward more year-round construction, even in colder areas. Construction trades are dependent on one another to complete specific parts of a project—especially on large projects—so work delays affecting one trade can delay or stop the work of another trade.

Architectural Engineering

Architectural Engineering majors will learn how different materials interact. They also will learn to calculate loads and stress and study the strength, durability, and safety-factor of materials. They will use artistic, applied physics, and material science skills in the design of buildings.

Interests: Mathematics, physical science, building things, applying mathematics and science to practical use, design, computers

Skills and abilities: Oral and written expression and comprehension, speech clarity, logical thinking, interpersonal skills, teamwork

Occupations related to this major: Architects, Civil Engineers, Marine Architects, Materials Engineers, and Architectural Drafters

Architecture

Architecture majors learn to plan, design, and supervise the construction of buildings, houses, factories, skyscrapers, schools, and other structures. They learn to make them attractive, usable, energy efficient, and economical. They must qualify for a license after graduation. They work in design studios that develop skills and foster creative expression. Architecture students also study the history of the building environment (rooms, buildings, landscapes, cities), the technology required to create it, and related graphic communication.

Interests: The formation of the physical environment; the history of buildings, cities, and landscapes; applied creative expression

Skills and abilities: Communicating by sketching and drafting; solving spatial problems; sensitivity to visual forms, proportions, and colors

Occupations related to this major: Architects, Naval Architects, Landscape Architects, Civil Engineers, Industrial Designers, Interior Designers, and Drafters

City and Regional Planning

City and Regional Planning majors learn to deal with land use and environmental issues created by population movements. They learn how to draw plans for new city environments including streets, sewers, water, and electricity. They also learn to zone areas for residential, commercial, or industrial use. Students commit themselves, through planning, to the future, and to social and environmental improvement.

Interests: Solving problems, working with people, helping groups, communities, and organizations improve people's lives

Skills and abilities: Working with numbers, listening, interpreting and communicating what was observed or heard

Occupations related to this major: Urban and Regional Planners, Architects, Landscape Architects, City Managers, Civil Engineers, and Environmental Engineers

Construction Science

Construction Science majors learn about all areas of construction technology. These areas include contracting, remodeling, cabinet making, building inspection, carpentry, and estimating the costs of building projects.

Interests: Starting and completing projects; leading people and making decisions; risk taking; activities that include practical, hands-on problems and solutions

Skills and abilities: Listening to and understanding information; reading and understanding information; managing one's own time and the time of others; communicating information and ideas in writing

Occupations related to this major: Architects, Property and Real Estate Managers, Real Estate Appraisers, Construction and Building Inspectors, and Industrial Engineers

Interior Design

Interior Design majors learn to arrange the interiors of buildings to fit the functional and aesthetic needs of their owners. They will design everything from lighting and furniture to home decorating accessories. Interior design majors study all aspects of the building environment: scale, proportion, arrangement, light, acoustics, temperature, textures, colors, and materials. They learn how to develop surroundings that are satisfying, creative, and appropriate to human needs.

Interests: Architecture, design (interior, industrial, graphic), building construction, interaction of colors, nature of materials, and textures

Skills and abilities: Design, organization, working with people, drawing, communicating ideas

Occupations related to this major: Interior Designers, Fashion, Furniture, Textile, and Floral Designers, Exhibition Designers, Architects, and Landscape Architects

Landscape Architecture

Landscape Architecture majors learn skills and techniques for planning, designing, and managing the land. They learn about weather, drainage, botany, and construction. They are frequently involved in mapping and consultation. They creatively apply information and principles drawn from both the arts and the sciences to reshape and conserve landscapes.

Interests: Visual arts, ecology, nature, environmental issues

Skills and abilities: Drawing and graphic expression, problem solving, written communication

Occupations related to this major: Landscape Architects, Architects, Surveyors, Civil Engineers, Urban and Regional Planners, Botanists, and Park Naturalists

Marine Architecture

Marine Architecture majors learn to design and oversee construction and repair of marine craft and floating structures, such as ships, barges, tugs, dredges, submarines, torpedoes, floats, and buoys. May confer with marine engineers.

Interests: Design techniques, engineering science and technology, building materials, construction and repair of structures

Skills and abilities: Problem solving, listening and understanding information and ideas, creativity, communicating information and ideas in writing, fluency of ideas

Occupations related to this major: Marine Architects, Aerospace Engineers, Civil Engineers, Materials Engineers, Engineering Technicians, and Drafters

Surveying

Surveying majors learn to make exact measurements and determine property boundaries. They learn to provide data relevant to the shape, contour, gravitation, location, elevation, or dimension of land, or land features on or near the earth's surface, for engineering, mapping, mining, land evaluation, construction, and other purposes.

Interests: Shapes and elevations of geomorphic and topographic features, geography, and methods for describing the features of land, sea, and air masses

Skills and abilities: Communicating effectively in writing; using mathematics to solve problems; understanding written information; using scientific methods to solve problems; motivating, developing, and directing people as they work

Occupations related to this major: Surveyors, Cartographers, Urban Planners, Civil Drafters, Agricultural Engineers, and Landscape Architects

3. THE ARTS

The Arts is a field of study that includes a wider range of subjects than found in other areas of concentration. If students major in one of the arts, they will learn to design products, articles, and materials; they will develop talents as actors; they will study the theory and practice of film production; they will develop talents to draw, paint, or design interpretations of objects, people, and nature, or they will develop talents dealing with the art of sound that express ideas and emotions either by song, dance, or by instrumental musical instruments. This field, in contrast to a liberal arts education, is often thought of as professional training. A major in this field gives information, methods, procedures, and techniques needed in a career. A professional program in this field will offer students good training to make a contribution in the world of art.

Interests: Developing talents to draw, paint, or design interpretations of objects, people, and nature; or developing the art of sound that expresses ideas and emotions either by speech, song, dance, or musical instruments.

Popular majors in this field of study: Art Education, Art History, Arts Management, Dance, Dramatic Arts, Film Arts, Fine Arts, Graphic Design, Music Business Management, Music Education, Music Performance, Music Therapy, Photography, Religious Music, and Studio Art

Employment information/outlook: More than 2,570,900 people worked in related occupations in this field of study in 2012. The 2012-2022 employment growth is expected to be 7.0%.

In May 2012, median annual wages of salaried art directors were $80,880; advertising, public relations and related services, $115,750; salaried craft artists, $44,380; multimedia artists and animators were $61,370; motion picture and video industries, $71,350; advertising and related services, $46,290. The hourly wages of actors were $20.26; hourly wages for performing arts companies were $15.87; and motion picture and video industry occupations came in at $34.31. The median annual wages in May 2012 for producers and directors were $71,350; radio and television broadcasting, $37,090; graphic designers, $44,150. Hourly wages of wage-and-salary musicians and singers were $23.50; performing arts companies, $18.33; and religious organizations, $14.69. The median annual wages for salaried music directors and composers were $47,350 in May 2012. Self-employed artist wages vary considerably. Most artists, including actors, musicians, and singers, were not available because of the variation in the number of hours they work, and the lack of guaranteed employment. The more successful performers may belong to one of the talent unions, such as SAG/AFTRA, American Guild of Musical Artists, or The American Federation of Musicians, which negotiates minimum contracts.

Art Education

Art Education majors learn to develop their artistic talents and gain the knowledge and skills needed to teach art at various education levels. They will explore the value of art both to the individual and to various cultures throughout history.

Interests: Visual arts, creating art, teaching

Skills and abilities: Working with others, solving problems creatively, manipulating materials creatively, responding to other people's art with sensitivity

Occupations related to this major: Art Teachers, Curriculum Specialists, Art Administrators, Manual Arts Therapists, Craft Demonstrators, Curators, Archivists, and Museum Research Workers

Art History

Art History majors study works of art—how they came about and what they mean. They will examine works of art as they appear now and also consider appearance and function in their original contexts. Through their visual analysis and extensive reading and writing, students explore the traditions of appearance and technique that guided the creation of art in different cultures.

Interests: Visual arts, past civilizations, the connections between different aspects of a civilization, artists, art technique

Skills and abilities: Observing carefully, information gathering, reading critically, written expression and comprehension

Occupations related to this major: High School Teachers, College Teachers, Curators, Archivists, Conservators, Museum Directors, and Museum Technicians

Arts Management

Arts Management majors learn to organize and manage art organizations and facilities. They receive instruction in business and financial management and labor relations, event promotion and management, public relations and arts advocacy, and arts law. They will learn to analyze and address the issues concerning the health of theaters, dance companies, museums, and other arts organizations.

Interests: Visual and performance arts, leadership, working with people

Skills and abilities: Oral and written communication, organizational ability, creative thinking, critical thinking

Occupations related to this major: Theater Managers, Symphony Orchestra Managers, Dance Company Managers, Curators, and Museum Technicians and Conservators

Dance

Dance majors learn to interpret an idea or a story through physical expression or rhythm and/or sound. Dance forms vary from ballet and modern interpretative dance to tap and chorus lines. Dance is a demanding discipline. Students learn to develop their bodies as articulate instruments for dance expression: to understand contributions that dance has made to the arts, and to create their own dances.

Interests: Dance, other arts, the physicality of movement

Skills and abilities: Sense of rhythm and musicality, physical stamina, dynamic strength, speed of limb movement, gross body coordination

Occupations related to this major: Dance Teachers, Actors and Performers, Choreographers, Dance Researchers, and Dance Therapists

Dramatic Arts

Dramatic Arts majors learn how to play a part to entertain, inform, or instruct an audience. They learn to be involved in interpreting plays or scripts, selecting plays or scripts, or planning and supervising performances. They gain breadth of knowledge about past and present culture, art, literature, politics, psychology, and philosophy.

Interests: Self-expression, communication of ideas and feelings, literature and language, art and music, human personality and motivation

Skills and abilities: Speech clarity, memorization, originality, oral and written expression and comprehension, emotional openness

Occupations related to this major: Actors, Directors, Designers, Playwrights, Stage Managers, Talent Directors, and Teachers

Film Arts

Film Arts majors study the theory and practice of film production and the techniques used in this medium of communication. They learn to do creative work, as well as learn the rapidly changing technology. They study cinema history, screenwriting, and the aesthetic and technical aspects of cinema production, including directing, cinematography, and editing. They also examine the economic, technical, social, cultural, and ideological aspects of film as a medium for communication and personal expression.

Interests: Film literature, psychology, theater, music, art history, biography, current events

Skills and abilities: Creativity, ability to express oneself verbally and visually, self-discipline, understanding of human psychology, organization, attention to detail, flexibility, working with people

Occupations related to this major: Directors—Stage, Motion Pictures, Television and Radio, Cinematographers, Technical Directors, Programming and Script Editors, Production Assistants

Fine Arts

Fine Arts majors learn to draw or design their interpretations of objects, people, and nature, using a wide variety of materials from watercolors and oils to stone and metal. They learn to create art to satisfy their own need for self-expression. They learn about the creation of art historically, in contemporary society, and through their own efforts in studio classes. They may display their work in museums, art galleries, corporate collections, and private homes.

Interests: Making things with the hands, other cultures, history, paintings, sculpture, film, self-expression

Skills and abilities: Oral and written expression and comprehension, fluency of ideas, originality, visual color discrimination, manual and finger dexterity

Occupations related to this major: Fine Artists, Graphic Artists, Sculptors, Painters, Illustrators, and Cartoonists and Animators

Graphic Design

Graphic Design majors study the principles of design to learn how to create attractive and effective advertisements, flyers, brochures, logos, magazines, or books. They learn how to create images through the use of silkscreen, computers, and printing presses. Students learn to communicate information visually using words and images. They also study how people perceive and interpret information.

Interests: Visual arts, creativity, critical thinking, working with people

Skills and abilities: Drawing, photography, originality, fluency of ideas, oral expression, visual color discrimination

Occupations related to this major: Graphic Designers, Painters, Illustrators, Cartoonists, Animators, Fashion Designers, and Interior Designers

Music Business Management

Music Business Management majors learn to organize and manage music operations, facilities, and personnel. They receive instruction in business and financial management, personnel management and labor relations, event promotion, and music products merchandising. They study the functional area of business as well as music performance, history, and theory.

Interests: Music, leadership, organizing people, business, solving problems, negotiating

Skills and abilities: Oral expression and comprehension, written expression and comprehension, leadership, organization, creative thinking

Occupations related to this major: Music Facilities Managers, Recording Studio Managers, Artists' Representatives, Orchestra Managers, Music Directors, and Concert Booking Agents

Music Education

Music Education majors learn to become music teachers in public and private schools. They learn the basics of music and the fundamentals of teaching to share music with people of all ages and abilities.

Interests: Listening to music, performing, working with young people, leadership

Skills and abilities: Musical ability, a sense of rhythm and pitch, oral and written expression and comprehension, speech clarity, discriminating listening

Occupations related to this major: Music Teachers, Music Therapists, Choir Directors, Conductors, Composers, Arrangers, and Music Librarians

Music Performance

Music Performance majors learn to develop a high level of performance skill and musical understanding. They reach a high level of technical proficiency and musical sensitivity as music performance majors. They become well-rounded musicians through the study of core music theory and history courses.

Interests: Communicating through music performance, the theoretical and historical aspects of musical structure and style, the relation of music to society

Skills and abilities: Natural aptitude for music, technical skill, strong background in piano

Occupations related to this major: Musicians, Singers, Music Directors, Music Composers, Music Teachers, and Positions with Orchestras and Ensembles

Music Therapy

Music Therapy majors learn to design music experiences and activities to the treatment of individuals and groups in all age categories who have psychological, emotional, physical, social, intellectual, or medical disorders.

Interests: Music, the arts, behavioral and life sciences, helping others

Skills and abilities: Competency in music performance and theory, oral and written expression and comprehension, working with people

Occupations related to this major: Music Therapists, Occupational Therapists, Physical Therapists, Musicians, Singers, and Music Directors

Photography

Photography majors learn the use of camera and film to portray people, places, and events. They become involved in everything from creating motion pictures and video/television to still, portrait, aerial, and commercial photography. They learn both the artistic and technical aspects of photography and a broad understanding of the social, political, and interpersonal aspects of society.

Interests: Expressing oneself in a visual medium, creating images from ideas, helping people see and understand subjects to which they might not otherwise have access

Skills and abilities: Visualization, far vision, fluency of ideas, arm-hand steadiness, control precision, color discrimination

Occupations related to this major: Commercial Photographers, Portrait Photographers, Graphic Designers, Photojournalists, Photo Editors, and Technical and Science Photographers

Religious Music

Religious Music majors develop their skills and interests as musicians and learn to use music in religious celebrations while focusing on the role and history of music in worship. They study the history, theory, composition, and performance of music for religious or sacred purposes.

Interests: Music, music history, the fine arts, the place of music in religious celebrations, matters of faith, working with people

Skills and abilities: Ability to listen carefully, hearing sensitivity, auditory attention, oral expression and comprehension, working with people

Occupations related to this major: Music Directors, Music Teachers, Music Conductors, Organists, Cantors, Musicians, and Singers

Studio Art

Studio Art majors learn to create works of art by exploring a variety of techniques and materials. They learn to focus on learning to master new media, discovering unique solutions to visual problems, exploring fresh ways to create satisfying images, and evaluating what is worth doing.

Interests: Visual arts, manipulating materials, observing visual phenomena in nature and works of art, communicating and experimenting with forms, colors, images, and symbols

Skills and abilities: Working independently, creativity, problem solving, oral and written expression and comprehension

Occupations related to this major: Fine Artists, Commercial Artists, Graphic Designers, Art Teachers, Exhibit Designers, and Set Designers

4. BIOLOGICAL AND LIFE SCIENCES

Biological and Life Sciences majors are concerned with the world of living things—people and microbes, wild and domestic animals, plants and insects, birds and fish. Some biological scientists conduct research. Still others apply biological knowledge to the solution of practical problems, such as the development of new drugs and vaccines or new strains of plants. Biological scientists, who may also be called life scientists, study the structure of living organisms, their life processes, and evolutionary development. They may be classified into groups characterized by the type of organism with which they work or the specific activity they perform. Examples of these groups are botanists who study plants, microbiologists who work with microorganisms, and zoologists who work with animals.

Interests: The world of living things—people and microbes, wild and domestic animals, plants and insects, birds and fish—or the evolutionary development of living organisms.

Popular majors in this field of study: Biochemistry, Biology, Biophysics, Biotechnology, Botany, Marine/Aquatic Biology, Microbiology, Molecular and Cell Biology, Science Education, Wildlife Management, and Zoology

Employment information/outlook: More than 103,100 people worked in related occupations in this field of study in 2012. The 2012-2022 employment growth is expected to be 13%.

In May 2012, median annual wages of biochemists and biophysicists were $81,480; microbiologists, $66,260. Median annual wages of zoologists and wildlife biologists were $57,710 in May 2012.

Biochemistry

Biochemistry majors learn how chemical substances enter into or are created in living things; how drugs, foods, hormones, serums, and other substances can influence organisms. They perform tests to identify, classify, and analyze various chemical reactions. They learn to use the physical and biological sciences to explore the nature of living organisms. They study the structure and behavior of complex molecules and how they interact to form cells, tissues, and entire organisms. They also gain a fundamental grasp of metabolism, energy flow, and the regulation of various life processes.

Interests: Nature, problem solving, investigative research

Skills and abilities: Using information from many areas of science, inductive and deductive reasoning, handling and interpreting data, written expression and comprehension

Occupations related to this major: Microbiologists, Biologists, Toxicologists, Plant Pathologists, Physiologists, Cytologists, and Food Scientists

Biology

Biology majors learn about the structure of living organisms, their life processes and evolutionary development, and the relation between these organisms and their environment. They may specialize in research centering on plants, animals, or human organisms. They study animals, plants, and microorganisms that constitute the living world at the levels of molecule, cell, organism, and population.

Interests: Quality of life, investigative laboratory work, fieldwork

Skills and abilities: Problem solving, deductive and inductive reasoning, information gathering, written expression and comprehension

Occupations related to this major: Biologists, Biochemists, Botanists, Microbiologists, Geneticists, and Zoologists

Biophysics

Biophysics majors learn to apply the laws of physics to biological systems. They study vision, hearing, nerve action, blood flow, and even the behavior of DNA. They also study the effects of radiation and radioactivity on biological systems, and the use of ultrasound scanners to construct images of body interiors. They use biology, physics, chemistry, and mathematics to explore the properties of biological molecules and groups of molecules. They study the inner workings of biological systems with precision to learn how proteins fold, how genes are switched on and off, how organisms respond to light, how cells move, and how the nervous system works.

Interests: Natural history, investigative problem solving

Skills and abilities: Curiosity, deductive and inductive reasoning, written expression and comprehension, information ordering, manual dexterity

Occupations related to this major: Biophysicists, Biologists, Botanists, Geneticists, Microbiologists, and Soil Scientists

Biotechnology

Biotechnology is an interdisciplinary field of study involving the molecular life sciences and engineering fields of study. Students learn techniques for using living matter to develop new products and services in agriculture (plant growth hormones, food additives), health care (vaccines, improved drugs and vitamins), the environment (detoxification of chemicals), and other areas.

Interests: Science, treating and preventing disease, investigative research, and problem solving

Skills and abilities: Creative thinking, oral and written expression and comprehension, deductive and inductive reasoning, problem sensitivity

Occupations related to this major: Biological Technologists, Agricultural Technologists, Environmental Scientists, Food Scientists, Animal Scientists, Botanists, and Microbiologists

Botany

Botany majors focus on all aspects of plant life including taxonomy, genetics, physiology, and plant anatomy. They learn about the economic value of plants in their application to agronomy, forestry, horticulture, and pharmacology. Students study all aspects of plant biology to become familiar with the cellular and molecular functioning of life.

Interests: Nature, investigative problem solving, analytic reasoning

Skills and abilities: Deductive and inductive reasoning, information ordering, written expression and comprehension

Occupations related to this major: Botanists, Agricultural Scientists, Soil Scientists, Ecologists, Microbiologists, Physiologists

Marine/Aquatic Biology

Marine/Aquatic Biology majors learn to research and study marine organisms and their environments. They receive instruction in freshwater and saltwater organisms, physiological and anatomical marine adaptations, ocean and freshwater ecologies, marine microbiology, marine mammalogy, ichthyology, marine botany, and biochemical products of marine life used by humans. They learn about the diversity of life in the ocean, how ocean species relate to each other as food and prey, and how different species depend on and use the physical and chemical structures of the ocean.

Interests: Life in the ocean, how organisms use the sea as a habitat

Skills and abilities: Quantitative thinking, deductive and inductive reasoning, information ordering, written expression and comprehension

Occupations related to this major: Marine Biologists, Aquatic Biologists, Biochemists, Botanists, Agricultural Scientists, and Zoologists

Microbiology

Microbiology majors concentrate on microorganisms, bacteria, yeasts, fungi, protozoa, and one-celled algae. They learn about the application of these organisms in the production of food products, antibiotics, and industrial chemicals. They learn to use the basic knowledge acquired from other biological sciences, chemistry/ biochemistry, and physics to study microscopic organisms such as bacteria, yeasts, molds, viruses, rickettsia, and protozoa.

Interests: Biological sciences, health and medicine, ecology, food production, investigative research

Skills and abilities: Working with detail, analytic thinking, deductive and inductive reasoning, information ordering

Occupations related to this major: Microbiologists, Botanists, Medical Scientists, Zoologists, Physiologists, and Geneticists

Molecular and Cell Biology

Molecular and Cell Biology majors study the nature of biological phenomena at the molecular level through the study of DNA proteins and other macromolecules relating to genetic information and cell function. They study what cells are, how they are put together, what makes them work, what makes them differ from each other, how they associate and interact, what goes wrong in disease states, and how they can intervene beneficially in these processes. They study how molecular biology underlies many aspects of genetic engineering, protein engineering, and other new approaches to improving upon nature.

Interests: Organisms and their development, how things work, the molecular basis of plant, animal, and human disease, disease prevention

Skills and abilities: Investigative research, laboratory skills, information gathering, deductive and inductive reasoning, oral and written expression and comprehension

Occupations related to this major: Molecular Biologists, Medical Doctors, Toxicologists, Botanists, Plant Pathologists, and Biologists

Science Education

Science Education majors prepare to teach science in grades 7 through 12. Students typically major in one science and take additional course work in two other sciences. They learn techniques for teaching science.

Interests: Working with young people, helping others, the learning process, solving practical problems, understanding complex processes, learning how things work

Skills and abilities: Oral and written expression and comprehension, speech clarity, fluency of ideas, deductive reasoning, working with numbers

Occupations related to this major: Biological Technicians, Health Specialties Teachers, Elementary School Teachers, Dietitians, Nutritionists, Pharmacists, Psychiatrists, Veterinarians, and Medical and Clinical Laboratory Technologists

Wildlife Management

Wildlife Management majors receive a solid background in basic biology. They study natural resources and wildlife management. They study conservation of animal populations and their habitats, paying special attention to species that are hunted regularly and species that are threatened or endangered. They learn to analyze characteristics of animals to identify and classify them; to conduct experimental studies with live animals in controlled or natural surroundings; to study animals in their natural habitats; and to study characteristics of animals such as origin, interrelationships, classification, life histories and diseases, development, genetics, and distribution.

Interests: Nature, conservation of natural resources, hunting, bird-watching

Skills and abilities: Using scientific rules and methods to solve problems, mathematics, deductive and inductive reasoning, problem sensitivity

Occupations related to this major: Wildlife Biologists, Environmental Scientists, Park Naturalists, and Research Wildlife Biologists

Zoology

Zoology majors study the identification, description, and classification of animals. They study life histories, habits, diseases, life processes, and distribution of animal species within the environment. They study living organisms in the animal kingdom, exploring their form and function, chemistry and structure, growth, reproduction, maintenance, and interactions with each other and their world. They study the transmission of characteristics from one generation to the next (genetics and evolution).

Interests: Natural history, wildlife, the outdoors, bird-watching, how things work, living things, fossils, working with animals

Skills and abilities: Deductive and inductive reasoning, synthesizing information, gathering and analyzing information, working with numbers

Occupations related to this major: Zoologists, Ecologists, Agricultural Scientists, Physiologists, Cytologists, Microbiologists, and Botanists

5. BUSINESS AND MANAGEMENT

Business and Management majors are found in every industry. Business executives, administrators, managers, and support staff are found in every organization. They direct and coordinate operations and activities of an organization. Business majors must be comfortable with numbers and the manipulation of data, enjoy working with a computer, and have good communication skills, both written and oral. Business majors deal with large amounts of information to make production, personnel, financial, and marketing decisions.

Interests: Business managers and support workers have an interest in directing and coordinating operations and activities of a business or organization; an interest in making production, personnel, financial, and market decisions of a business.

Popular majors in this field of study: Accounting, Business Administration, Business Education, Finance, Human Resource Management, Insurance and Risk Management, International Business Management, Labor Relations Management, Management, Management Information Systems, Management Science, Marketing, and Real Estate

Employment information/outlook: More than 10,228,200 people worked in related occupations in this field of study in 2012. The 2012-2022 employment growth is expected to be 13.8%.

In May 2012, median annual wages of wage and salary accountants and auditors were $63,550. Median annual wages, excluding annual bonuses and stock options, of wage and salary financial managers were $109,740. Annual salary rates for human resources workers vary according to occupation, level of experience, training, location, and firm size. Median annual wages in May 2012 were $80,220 for advertising and promotions managers, $134,250 for marketing managers, $129,870 for sales managers, and $108,260 for public relations managers. Median annual wages of salaried property, real estate, and community association managers were $52,610 in May 2012.

Accounting

Accounting majors learn to keep track of expenditures, income, profit and loss, prepare financial reports, and calculate taxes. They may specialize in auditing, taxes, or consulting. Many accountants seek Certified Public Accountant (CPA) certification after graduation. Students will learn to apply this knowledge in all areas of business, government, and nonprofit enterprises.

Interests: Working with numbers, competition, economics, computers, mathematics, entrepreneurship, social and political activism, moral and ethical responsibility

Skills and abilities: Mathematical reasoning, written and oral expression and comprehension, working with people, leadership

Occupations related to this major: Accountants, Auditors, Loan Officers, Loan Counselors, Credit Analysts, Tax Preparers, Budget Analysts, and Marketing Managers

Business Administration

Business Administration majors learn about a variety of managerial opportunities in finance, accounting, marketing, information management, operations and production, general management, retailing, and consulting. They learn the fundamental principles, concepts, and applications of accounting, finance, and management.

Interests: Leadership, organizing people, taking initiative, starting and running a business, working with numbers, solving problems, competing, taking risks, working with people

Skills and abilities: Oral and written expression and comprehension, speech clarity, inductive reasoning, creative and critical thinking

Occupations related to this major: Private Sector Executives, Administrative Services Managers, Human Resources Specialists, Production Managers, Labor Relations Specialists, and Financial Analysts

Business Education

Business Education majors learn to teach vocational business programs at various education levels. They develop instructional methods and training techniques including curriculum design principles, learning theory, group and individual teaching techniques, design of individual development plans, and test design principles.

Interests: Teaching young people, helping people develop their academic interests in business, and helping people develop career plans

Skills and abilities: Working with young people, speech clarity, oral and written expression and comprehension, teaching, learning, understanding human behavior

Occupations related to this major: Business Education Teacher, Education Administrators, Training and Development Managers, and Educational Program Directors

Finance

Finance majors study financial and accounting information, economic models, and analytic techniques that can be applied to financing problems. They learn to determine prices of assets such as stocks, bonds, and businesses, and to manage assets to maximize their economic value.

Interests: Business, the stock market, the economy, budgets

Skills and abilities: Logical thinking, organizational skills, oral and written expression and comprehension, problem sensitivity, mathematical reasoning, working with people, solving problems with computers

Occupations related to this major: Financial Managers, Financial Planners, Treasurers, Controllers, Chief Financial Officers, and Loan Officers and Counselors

Human Resource Management

Human Resource Management majors learn to deal with many personnel activities, including hiring competent workers and dismissing workers when necessary, keeping records, classifying jobs, evaluating and properly placing workers, analyzing and assisting in morale and discipline problems, and promoting and rewarding employees. They learn to deal with issues that affect men and women at work.

Interests: Solving problems, working with numbers, working with people of different ages and backgrounds, leadership

Skills and abilities: Logical and critical thinking, speech clarity, oral and written expression and comprehension, analyzing numerical data, teamwork

Occupations related to this major: Human Resource Specialists, Training and Development Managers, Labor Relations Managers, Employee Assistance Specialists, Employee Benefits Managers, and Career Planning and Placement Counselors

Insurance and Risk Management

Insurance and Risk Management majors learn to analyze and solve problems involving loss of personal and corporate assets. They study programs, integrate knowledge from finance, quantitative analysis, and management, and include study of the legal, social, and institutional environment in which losses may occur.

Interests: Working with numbers, solving problems, competing, leadership, taking initiative

Skills and abilities: Oral and written expression and comprehension, fluency of ideas, problem sensitivity, deductive and inductive reasoning, creative and critical thinking

Occupations related to this major: Insurance Adjusters, Insurance Appraisers, Risk Managers, Insurance Brokers, Insurance Sales Representatives, and Insurance Underwriters

International Business Management

International Business Management majors learn to determine and formulate policies, and provide the overall direction of international companies or private and public sector organizations with international business activities. They learn to conduct management guidelines set up by a board of directors or similar governing body. They learn basic business management techniques and practices and how business is conducted in other countries and between different countries.

Interests: Business operations, other cultures, different people and environments

Skills and abilities: Learning languages, organizing and managing people, oral and written expression and comprehension, deductive and inductive reasoning, fluency of ideas

Occupations related to this major: International Business Managers, International Purchasing Agents and Buyers, International Marketing Managers, International Advertising and Promotions Managers, Compliance Officers and Inspectors, and Investment Bankers

Labor Relations Management

Labor Relations Management majors learn to deal with various aspects of employer-employee relations. They learn to deal with wage and salary negotiations, benefits and welfare, affirmative action, grievances, abuses and demands, labor laws, union organization, and collective bargaining. Particular attention is given to government policies, labor unions, and human resources management.

Interests: The employment relationship, human behavior, problem solving

Skills and abilities: Working with people, oral and written expression and comprehension, problem sensitivity, inductive reasoning

Occupations related to this major: Labor Relations Managers, Human Resource Managers, Training and Development Managers, Employee Assistance Specialists, Employee Benefits Managers, and Union Organizers

Management

Management majors study courses designed for the generalist who wants a broad business background. They take courses in business areas, such as accounting, marketing, finance, and business law, and courses that prepare them to function as managers in any organization.

Interests: Working with people, listening, persuading, leading, starting new systems

Skills and abilities: Thinking analytically, problem sensitivity, oral and written expression and comprehension, speech clarity

Occupations related to this major: General and Operations Managers, Marketing Managers, Public Relations Managers, Corporate Communications Specialists, Human Resource Specialists, and Human Resources Recruiters

Management Information Systems

Management Information Systems majors unite studies in computer science and business knowledge. They learn to act as intermediaries between persons with information needs and the computer programmers who provide the solutions to the problems.

Interests: Computer languages, computer programming, problem solving, logic, taking initiative, organizing groups

Skills and abilities: Oral and written expression and comprehension, deductive and inductive reasoning, information ordering, fluency of ideas, creativity

Occupations related to this major: Management Information Systems Managers, Systems Analysts, Computer Support Specialists, Database Administrators, and Computer Programmers

Management Science

Management Science majors learn to plan, organize, direct, and control the functions and processes of a business firm or organization. They learn about management theory, human resources, management and behavior, accounting and other quantitative methods, purchasing and logistics organization and production, marketing and business decision making. They learn to use mathematics, computers, and statistical and economic analysis to solve managerial and business problems.

Interests: Mathematics, solving business and management problems, computer languages, computer programming

Skills and abilities: Quantitative thinking, computer programming, creativity, oral and written expression and comprehension, speech clarity

Occupations related to this major: Employee Training Specialists, Administrative Service Managers, Purchasing Managers, Association Managers, and Property Managers

Marketing

Marketing majors learn to increase sales of products or services by analyzing and compiling data, and researching and influencing the purchasing power of the public through inventory procedures. They study trend forecasting, product development, management, wholesale selling, and operations. They learn how to display and to buy and sell items through showrooms, department stores, and specialty shops. They learn to make decisions about product design and quality, pricing, advertising, selling, and distribution.

Interests: Running a business, economic issues, social issues, working on new products, problem solving, analyzing data, understanding how people buy, use, and sell products and services

Skills and abilities: Oral and written expression and comprehension, speech clarity, originality, fluency of ideas, mathematical reasoning, persuasion

Occupations related to this major: Marketing Managers, Sales Managers, Public Relations Representatives, Advertising and Promotions Managers, Market Research Analysts, and Advertising Account Executives

Real Estate

Real Estate majors learn to show real estate properties to clients, evaluate and list properties for sale, and advise and arrange financing. They study property management and insurance. They act as independent agents, brokers, or appraisers. They gain an understanding of and proficiency in the business and social principles that affect how real property—buildings and land—is developed, operated, and traded.

Interests: Business, people and social conditions, the economy, public affairs

Skills and abilities: Oral and written expression and comprehension, mathematical reasoning, working independently, critical and analytic thinking

Occupations related to this major: Property Managers, Real Estate Sales Agents, Real Estate Financial Analysts, Real Estate Brokers, Loan Processors, and Real Estate Appraisers

6. COMMUNICATIONS

Communications is the giving or exchanging of information. It is a way to share facts, experiences, or emotions with others. A message can be conveyed through a wide variety of means. These can include writing, speaking, drawing, or using face, hand, and body movements. People receive messages through each of the five senses: taste, touch, sight, smell, and hearing. Communications studies involve the understanding of the role of mass communication in society; broadcast satellites, cable television transmitters, computer networks, and other mass media technology provide a global communication system. The field of communications includes training for those occupations necessary for the system to work efficiently.

Interests: The ways and means of exchanging information; an interest in broadcast satellites, television transmitters, computer networks, and other mass media technology.

Popular majors in this field of study: Advertising, Communications, Creative Writing, Journalism, Public Relations, Radio/Television Broadcasting, and Speech

Employment information/outlook: More than 1,531,000 people worked in related occupations in this field of study in 2012. The 2012-2022 employment growth is expected to be 10.8%.

In 2012, nonsupervisory workers in advertising and public relations services earned an average of $747 a week—significantly higher than the $608 a week for all nonsupervisory workers in private industry.

Median annual wages for salaried writers and authors were $51,510 in May 2012. Median annual wages were $76,790 for those working in advertising, public relations, and related services and $51,510 for those working for newspaper, periodical, book and directory publishers. In May 2012, median annual wages for salaried editors were $53,880; those working for newspaper, periodical, book, and directory publishers were $52,000. Freelance writers earn income from their articles, books, and less commonly, television and movie scripts. While most work on an individual project basis for multiple publishers, many support themselves with income derived from other sources. Unless gotten from another job, freelancers generally have to provide for their own health insurance and pension. Weekly earnings of nonsupervisory workers in broadcasting averaged $852 in 2012, higher than the average of $608 for all private industry. Earnings of broadcast personnel typically are highest in large metropolitan areas.

Advertising

Advertising majors learn to plan and prepare advertisements for newspapers, magazines, radio, television, billboards, and brochures. They may specialize in writing copy, layout, or research. They use creative talents to market a product to prospective clients. They learn how advertising campaigns are produced, how advertising is coordinated with marketing, and how advertising strategies develop from research. They learn to write advertising copy for broadcasting and print, and to select media for advertising campaigns.

Interests: Writing, art and design, analysis, knowing something about lots of things, investigative research

Skills and abilities: Oral and written expression and comprehension, originality, fluency of ideas, analytic reasoning, public speaking, art and design

Occupations related to this major: Advertising and Promotions Managers, Advertising Agency Account Executives, Marketing Managers, Sales Managers, Fund-raising Directors, and Advertising Research Specialists

Communications

Communications majors study the role of mass communication in society. They study the nature, function, content, values, and effects of communication on public policy and opinion. They study the nature of language and how it is communicated. They study the history of political and religious oratory; explore the sociology of interpersonal relations, group dynamics, and messages; examine ways of thinking about human symbol systems (semiotics); and examine the ethics of communication.

Interests: Politics, presentations, advertising, television, film, analyzing oral and electronic messages

Skills and abilities: Oral and written expression and comprehension, critical listening, logical analysis, leadership

Occupations related to this major: Communications Managers, Public Relations Specialists, Television Producers and Directors, Press Secretaries, Reporters, and Speech Writers

Creative Writing

Creative Writing majors study the processes and techniques of original composition in various literary forms, such as short stories, novels, biographies, articles, plays, and scripts. They receive instruction in technical and editorial skills, criticism, and the marketing of finished manuscripts.

Interests: Reading, fiction and nonfiction prose, writing, factual information, English language, critical thinking, computers

Skills and abilities: Written and oral expression and comprehension, information ordering, deductive and inductive reasoning, fluency of ideas

Occupations related to this major: Radio and Television Announcers, Broadcast News Analysts, Reporters and Correspondents, Editors, Technical Writers, and Poets and Lyricists

Journalism

Journalism majors learn to write, edit, manage, and produce newspapers and magazines. They learn to interview people, review records, observe events, and conduct journalistic research. They study the liberal arts and sciences to acquire the depth and breadth of knowledge they need to understand the world better and communicate information about it to others. They learn special skills needed by reporters, editors, broadcasters, and photojournalists.

Interests: Human psychology and behavior, reading widely, photography, world events

Skills and abilities: Writing, oral and written expression and comprehension, speech clarity, learning quickly about a wide range of topics

Occupations related to this major: Reporters and Correspondents, Magazine Writers and Editors, Columnists, Critics, Commentators, Creative Writers, Radio and Television Reporters, and Photojournalists

Public Relations

Public Relations majors learn how to manage an organization's or an individual's communication and relationship with others. They develop skills to build trust between an organization and the public. They learn how to write news articles and press releases, give speeches, and create audiovisual presentations designed to build trust. They learn technical and managerial skills, such as writing and producing printed and visual materials, and study strategic planning and problem solving.

Interests: Solving problems, mediating between opposing groups, writing, public speaking, giving advice

Skills and abilities: Communicating clearly, oral and written expression and comprehension, speech clarity, fluency of ideas, creative and critical thinking

Occupations related to this major: Public Relations Specialists, Publicity Writers, Advertising and Promotions Managers, Corporate Video Producers, Staff Writers and Editors, Special Events Planners, and Reporters and Correspondents

Radio/Television Broadcasting

Radio/Television Broadcasting majors learn about the planning, preparation, and production of radio and television programs. They may specialize in announcing, programming, engineering, or sales. They study the relationship between the mass media and society and develop skills in such specialties as reporting, performance, production, sales, and management

Interests: Writing, speaking, editing words, pictures, or sound; operating a camera; sound recording

Skills and abilities: Interviewing people, oral and written expression and comprehension, speech clarity, persuasion, operating technical equipment

Occupations related to this major: Broadcast News Analysts, Reporters and Correspondents, Radio/Television Announcers, Radio/Television Producers, Station Managers, Radio/Television Writers

Speech

Speech majors learn about the human communication process. They learn the principles and practical application of speech communication, and the skills and techniques essential for effective interpersonal communication. They learn to develop listening skills.

Interests: Public speaking, human behavior

Skills and abilities: Working with people, oral and written expression and comprehension, speech clarity

Occupations related to this major: Speech Teachers, Speech Writers, Public Relations Specialists, Journalists, Writers, Editors, and Radio and Television Reporters

7. COMPUTER AND INFORMATION SCIENCES

Computer and Information Sciences field of study prepares students for a wide variety of occupations in most sectors of the economy. This field of study prepares a wide range of professionals who design computers and the software that runs them. Information technology occupations are comprised of computer-related occupations engaged in either managing, storing, transmitting, or generating the information organizations use to make decisions, as well as installing and repairing computer hardware and software used to perform such tasks. Computer science is distinguished by a high level of theoretical expertise and innovation applied to complex problems, as well as the creation or application of new technology. Computer scientists and technicians can be theorists, researchers, or inventors. They may work at an academic institution on theory, hardware, or language design. Others work in industry to apply theory, develop specialized languages, or design programming tools and knowledge-based systems.

Interests: Designing computers and the software that runs them; managing, storing, transmitting, or generating and repairing computer hardware and software used to perform such tasks

Popular majors in this field of study: Computer Software Engineering, Computer Science, Information Sciences and Systems, Computer Programming, Mathematics, Mathematics Education, and Statistics

Employment information/outlook: More than 1,549,700 people worked in related occupations in this field of study in 2012. The 2012-2022 employment growth is expected to be 16.8%.

In May 2012, median annual wages of wage-and-salary computer applications software engineers were $85,430; computer systems software engineers, $92,430; mathematicians, $95,150; and statisticians, $72,610.

Computer Software Engineering

Computer Software Engineering majors study applied mathematical and scientific principles to the design, development, and operational evaluation of computer hardware and software systems and related equipment and facilities. They learn to develop, create, and test applications software and/or operating systems level software. They learn to analyze specific problems in computer applications.

Interests: Computers and electronics, computer programming, problem solving, engineering technology, design

Skills and abilities: Using mathematics to solve problems, computer programming, critical thinking, oral and written expression and comprehension, speech clarity, problem sensitivity

Occupations related to this major: Computer Support Specialists, Mathematical Technicians, Computer Science Teachers, and Numerical Tool and Process Control Programmers

Computer Science

Computer Science majors learn to design new computers, computer languages, and related devices, and research new ways to use computers effectively. They become involved in aspects of artificial intelligence, from pattern recognition to problem solving. They learn how computers work and how to program computers to perform tasks and provide services. They study the physical hardware components of computer systems and software procedures for making computers work.

Interests: Mathematics, electronics, investigative research

Skills and abilities: Oral and written expression and comprehension, mathematical reasoning, problem solving, abstract reasoning, working with people

Occupations related to this major: Computer Scientists, Computer Engineers, Computer Science Teachers, Computer Programmers, Software and Hardware Developers

Information Sciences and Systems

Information Sciences and Systems majors receive broad exposure to computer and programming concepts. They learn to bring people and computers together to solve problems in businesses and other organizations. They learn to plan, direct, and coordinate activities in such fields as electronic data processing, information systems, systems analysis, and computer programming.

Interests: Solving problems, working with details, taking initiative, working with numbers, organizing information, working with people

Skills and abilities: Oral and written expression and comprehension, mathematical reasoning, deductive reasoning, critical and logical thinking, working with changing technology

Occupations related to this major: Computer Programmers, Information Systems Designers, Information Systems Analysts, Computer Security Specialists, Database Administrators

Computer Programming

Computer Programming majors learn to write step-by-step instructions in several computer languages and create video games and software packages. They learn how to write software to handle specific jobs. They learn to convert project specifications and statements of problems and procedures to detailed logical flowcharts for coding into computer language. They learn to develop and write computer programs to store, locate, and retrieve specific documents, data, and information. They learn how to maintain software that controls the operations of entire computer systems.

Interests: Mathematics, electronics, using computers, investigative research, problem solving

Skills and abilities: Programming, critical thinking, active listening, oral and written expression and comprehension, mathematical reasoning, fluency of ideas, problem sensitivity

Occupations related to this major: Computer Programmers, Computer and Information Systems Managers, Computer Support Specialists, Computer Systems Analysts, Numerical Tool and Process Control Programmers, and Computer Science Teachers

Mathematics

Mathematics majors learn to solve both theoretical and practical problems that can be explained in mathematical terms. They study all aspects of algebra, geometry, advanced mathematics, and computer languages. They develop the abilities to explore, conjecture, and reason logically as well as the ability to use various mathematical methods effectively to solve problems.

Interests: Problem solving, working with numbers, games requiring analytic reasoning, investigative research

Skills and abilities: Oral and written comprehension, number facility, mathematical reasoning, deductive reasoning, analytic skills

Occupations related to this major: Mathematicians, Statisticians, Mathematics Teachers, and Financial Analysts

Mathematics Education

Mathematics Education majors learn to teach mathematics at the high school or middle school level. They learn techniques to help students develop skills and knowledge in the field of mathematics; they also take professional education courses.

Interests: Problem solving, analytic reasoning, working with young students, working with computers, leadership, organizing people

Skills and abilities: Oral and written expression and comprehension, speech clarity, organizational skills, creativity, using computers

Occupations related to this major: Middle School Teachers, High School Teachers, Insurance Underwriters, Business Training Specialists, and Education Administrators

Statistics

Statistics majors learn the science of dealing with data. They learn to design efficient data collection systems and to analyze and interpret information derived from the data. They learn to use mathematical theory or apply statistical theory and methods to collect, organize, interpret, and summarize numerical data to provide usable information. They may specialize in fields such as biostatistics, agricultural statistics, business statistics, economic statistics, or other fields.

Interests: Mathematics, working with numbers, problem solving, quantitative problems

Skills and abilities: Mathematical reasoning, computer operations, critical thinking, deductive and inductive reasoning, written expression

Occupations related to this major: Statisticians, Actuaries, Mathematicians, Operations Research Analysts, and Cost Estimators

8. EDUCATION

Education is a people-oriented field of study providing teachers, librarians, and school counselors involved in helping others to learn, acquire information, or gain insight into it. There are many levels on which one can teach. These include preschool and day care facilities, elementary schools, secondary schools, colleges and universities, as well as public and private vocational education institutions, dance, music, and art studios, and many other places. Librarianship and counseling are smaller fields than teaching. Archivists and curators are more involved with things than people. They may also help people learn and gain information, but they do not usually work as closely with people as do teachers, librarians, and counselors. All of these professions usually require a bachelor's degree, although some require a master's or doctoral degree.

Interest: Helping others learn, acquire information; teaching, counseling, or librarianship

Popular majors in this field of study: Early Childhood Education, Elementary School Education, Library Science, Middle School Education, Parks and Recreation Management, Physical Education, Secondary School Education, Special Education, Technology Education, and Vocational and Educational Counseling

Employment information/outlook: More than 6,758,700 people worked in related occupations in this field of study in 2012. The 2012-2022 employment growth is expected to be 15%.

In May 2012, median annual wages of preschool teachers was $27,130; kindergarten, elementary, middle, and secondary school teachers ranged from $53,090 to $57,810 in that same period. In 2012, the majority of all elementary, middle, and secondary school teachers belonged to unions—mainly the American Federation of Teachers and the National Education Association—that bargain with school systems over salaries, hours, and other terms and conditions of employment. Median annual wages in May 2012 of special education teachers who worked primarily in preschools, kindergartens, and elementary schools was $55,060; middle school special education teachers, $87,760; and special education teachers who worked primarily in secondary schools, $51,260. Median annual wages of vocational education teachers in elementary and secondary schools in May 2012 were $56,270.

Early Childhood Education

Early Childhood Education majors learn to teach through art, music, play, poetry, and stories to p language, science, numbers, and social stud design programs to develop students' mental abilities, and emotional health. They learn a variety of app teaching methods and strategies.

Interests: Childhood development, working with children, communicating with children and their parents

Skills and abilities: Oral expression and comprehension, speech clarity, problem sensitivity, time sharing, creativity, music or artistic ability

Occupations related to this major: Preschool Teachers, Kindergarten Teachers, Elementary School Teachers, Early Childhood Education Program Directors, Child Care Administrators, and Family Service Coordinators

Elementary School Education

Elementary School Education majors learn to teach young students (kindergarten through grade 6) basic academic, social, and manipulative skills. They learn to instill good study and work habits and an appreciation for learning. They learn to prepare lesson plans, tests, records, and reports, and to conduct conferences with parents. They learn a variety of methods for understanding how and why children develop socially and intellectually, and get professional experience that includes research in teaching and learning.

Interests: Communication, creativity, problem solving, flexibility, ability to organize, energy, enthusiasm

Skills and abilities: Oral and written expression and comprehension, speech clarity, problem sensitivity

Occupations related to this major: Elementary School Teachers, Kindergarten Teachers, Middle School Teachers, Secondary School Teachers, Special Education Teachers, and School Counselors

Library Science

Library Science majors learn the science of acquiring and organizing collections of books, pamphlets, manuscripts, clippings, and reports, and assisting readers in their use. They learn how to analyze reader needs, prepare bibliographies, and organize films, tapes, and maps.

Interests: Reading, multimedia communication, working with people, computers

Skills and abilities: Reading comprehension, active listening, oral and written expression and comprehension, speech clarity, fluency of ideas, information ordering

Occupations related to this major: Librarians, Computer and Information Systems Managers, Elementary School Teachers, Secondary School Teachers, and School Administrators

Middle School Education

Middle School Education majors learn to develop a wide array of instructional skills, which include multimedia approaches, classroom management, advisory ability, effective communication, and alternatives to teacher-centered instruction. They learn to build on and extend basic academic skills developed in elementary school students, and introduce them to the world of more abstract thinking and knowledge that they will encounter in high school.

Interests: Helping or providing service to others, communicating with young people, teaching young people, working with ideas

Skills and abilities: Instructing others, active listening, social perceptiveness, oral and written expression and comprehension, speech clarity, problem sensitivity

Occupations related to this major: Middle School Teachers, High School Teachers, Vocational Education Teachers, School Counselors, and Librarians

Parks and Recreation Management

Parks and Recreation Management majors study how individuals and communities pursue leisure and recreation. They explore what recreation is, investigate what motivates people's recreational choices, and develop skills to manage a variety of leisure and recreation enterprises and organizations.

Interests: Working with people; scientific, historic, and natural features of parks, forests, and other attractions

Skills and abilities: Helping others, leadership, solving problems, oral and written expression, speech clarity, problem sensitivity

Occupations related to this major: Community Recreation Planners/Directors, Social Directors, Park Naturalists, Forest Rangers, Amusement and Recreation Establishment Managers, and Camp Directors

Physical Education

Physical Education majors learn to teach and supervise individual and team sports. They learn to demonstrate sports techniques, analyze physical capabilities and needs of students, and administer corrective exercises and physical conditioning. They learn to provide students with activities to maximize physical fitness.

Interests: Physical activity, sports, working with people, health-related issues, biological science

Skills and abilities: Physical stamina, leadership, oral expression, speech clarity, multilimb coordination

Occupations related to this major: Physical Education Teachers, Sports Coaches, Physical Training Instructors, Aerobic Dance Instructors, Athletic Trainers, Fitness Directors, and Athletic Administrators

Secondary School Education

Secondary School Education majors learn to teach one or more high school subjects using various teaching methods. They learn to develop and plan teaching materials and assignments. They learn to construct tests to evaluate learning. They gain depth of knowledge in the subject they intend to teach and develop teaching skills in subject matters such as science, mathematics, social studies, English, music, art, business, physical education, or other subjects.

Interests: Serving others, teaching young people and helping them develop their academic interests and career choices

Skills and abilities: Working with people, teaching, learning, understanding human behavior, oral and written expression and comprehension, speech clarity

Occupations related to this major: Secondary School Teachers, Middle School Teachers, Special Education Teachers, Vocational Education Teachers, and Vocational and Educational School Counselors

Special Education

Special Education majors prepare for a career working with disabled children and adults in a variety of settings. They learn to coordinate the services available to people with disabilities, and provide appropriate educational experiences for people with varying disabilities, including deafness, blindness, aphasia, and mobility impairments.

Interests: Helping others, working with people

Skills and abilities: Accepting differences in people, communicating effectively, teaching, oral and written expression and comprehension, speech clarity, problem sensitivity

Occupations related to this major: Special Education Teachers; Teachers of the Emotionally and Mentally Impaired; Teachers of the Physically, Visually, and Hearing Impaired; Rehabilitation Counselors

Technology Education

Technology Education majors are trained to teach the design, operation, and impact of technological systems to students. They learn technical skills to be used in advanced communication, applied higher mathematics, and science. This major prepares students to teach technical pathway programs found in middle schools, high schools, and colleges. Technical majors can be planned in agriculture, arts, communication, business, engineering, information science, mechanics, and other fields.

Interests: Helping people, design, technological systems, network technology, graphics and multimedia, system designs, programming, teaching

Skills and abilities: Working with people, oral and written expression and comprehension, analyzing and describing technological systems

Occupations related to this major: Agriculture Teachers, Art Teachers, Computer Science Teachers, Business Teachers, Engineering Technology Teachers, and Science Teachers

Vocational and Educational Counseling

Vocational and Educational Counseling majors learn to counsel individuals and provide group educational and vocational guidance services. They learn to promote and enhance student learning through three broad and interrelated areas of student development: academic development, career development, and personal/social development.

Interests: Working with, communicating with, and teaching people; providing service to others

Skills and abilities: Speaking, active listening, oral and written expression and comprehension, problem sensitivity, speech clarity, fluency of ideas

Occupations related to this major: Educational and Vocational School Counselors, Child, Family, and School Social Workers, Health Educators, and Probation Officers

9. ENGINEERING

Engineering field of study involves planning and designing various things. Engineers design machines, processes, systems, and structures. They apply physical laws and mathematical theories and principles to solve practical technical problems. Engineers work in research, development, design, manufacturing and construction, operations, management, technical sales, teaching, and consulting services.

Interests: Designing machines, processes, systems and structures; research, development, design, manufacturing and construction, operations, management, and technical consulting services

Popular majors in this field of study: Aerospace/Aeronautical Engineering, Agricultural Engineering, Chemical Engineering, Civil Engineering, Computer Engineering, Electrical Engineering, Industrial Engineering, Materials Engineering, Mechanical Engineering, and Petroleum Engineering

Employment information/outlook: More than 1,166,700 people worked in related occupations in this field of study in 2012. The 2012-2022 employment growth is expected to be 9.7%.

Earnings for engineers vary significantly by specialty, industry, and education. Variation in median earnings and in the earnings distributions for engineers in a number of specialties is especially significant. Median annual wages of aerospace engineers in May 2012 was $103,720; agricultural engineers, $74,000; chemical engineers, $94,350; civil engineers, $79,340; computer engineers, $100,920; electrical engineers, $89,630; industrial engineers, $78,860; materials engineers, $85,150; mechanical engineers, $80,580; and petroleum engineers, $130,280.

Aerospace/Aeronautical Engineering

Aerospace/Aeronautical Engineering majors learn to perform a variety of engineering work in designing, constructing, and testing aircraft, missiles, and spacecraft. They learn to conduct basic and applied research to evaluate adaptability of materials and equipment to aircraft design and manufacture. They learn to make improvements in testing equipment and techniques.

Interests: Model aircraft and rocketry, astronomy, piloting, space exploration, computers, problem solving, working with people

Skills and abilities: Leadership, computer technology, physical science, oral and written expression and comprehension, mathematical reasoning, deductive and inductive reasoning

Occupations related to this major: Aerospace/Aeronautical Engineers, Electronics Engineers, Nuclear Engineers, Ceramic Engineers, Chemical Engineers, and Civil Engineers

Agricultural Engineering

Agricultural Engineering majors learn to apply knowledge of engineering technology and biological science to agricultural problems concerned with power and machinery, electrification, structures, soil and water conservation, and processing of agricultural products.

Interests: Solving problems, improving the quality of life, computers, leadership

Skills and abilities: Problem solving, oral and written expression and comprehension, computer operation, deductive and inductive reasoning, number facility

Occupations related to this major: Soil Conservationists, Landscape Architects, Geoscientists, Foresters, Chemical Engineers, Industrial Engineers, and Mechanical Engineers

Chemical Engineering

Chemical Engineering majors learn to turn chemicals into products through research and development. They learn to devise economical and efficient production processes. They learn to work in a number of fields, such as cosmetics, fertilizers, paints, dyes, pesticides, oil refining, and pollution prevention.

Interests: Science, chemistry, mathematics

Skills and abilities: Applying knowledge of science and mathematics to real-world problems, written expression and comprehension, mathematical reasoning, originality, deductive reasoning

Occupations related to this major: Chemical Engineers, Nuclear Engineers, Civil Engineers, Petroleum Engineers, Agricultural Engineers, and Electrical Engineers

Civil Engineering

Civil Engineering majors learn to solve technical problems involved in providing buildings, bridges, airports, transportation systems, foundations, coastal facilities, environmental control systems, and water supply and purification systems. They become involved in the conception, planning, design, construction, operation, and maintenance of these important public facilities. Studies will include soil mechanics, hydraulics, and structural engineering.

Interests: Mathematics, physical sciences, computers, building things, public service, applying mathematics and science to practical uses

Skills and abilities: Mathematics, physical sciences, logical thinking, interpersonal skills, oral and written expression and comprehension, inductive and deductive reasoning

Occupations related to this major: Civil Engineers, Civil Engineering Technicians, Architectural Engineers, Nuclear Engineers, Electrical Engineers, and Industrial Engineers

Computer Engineering

Computer Engineering majors learn to design and develop computer and computer-related systems. These systems include software systems, hardware systems, and combined hardware/software systems. Students take courses in basic sciences, mathematics, and engineering science and design.

Interests: Mathematics, science, computing, investigative research

Skills and abilities: Mathematics, computer operations, oral and written expression and comprehension, inductive and deductive reasoning

Occupations related to this major: Computer Hardware Engineers, Computer Software Engineers, Electronics Engineers, and Computer Service Technicians

Electrical Engineering

Electrical Engineering majors learn to design, develop, test, or supervise the manufacturing and installation of electrical equipment components or systems for commercial, industrial, military, or scientific use. They learn to design and manufacture a broad array of electrical and electronic devices and systems to meet society's needs.

Interests: Computer languages, computer programming, electronic equipment

Skills and abilities: Mathematics, physical science, oral and written expression and comprehension, deductive reasoning

Occupations related to this major: Electrical Engineers, Electronics Engineers, Mechanical Engineers, Electricians, Nuclear Engineers, and Production Engineers

Industrial Engineering

Industrial Engineering majors learn to plan, design, and implement complex systems for industry that take into account the availability, capabilities, and needs of people, machines, and materials. They learn to plan the layout of factories for efficiency, and engage in time, motion, and incentive studies. They learn about safety studies, cost, and quality control measures, and long-range planning goals.

Interests: Problem solving, leadership

Skills and abilities: Working with people, critical thinking, written and oral expression and comprehension, fluency of ideas, mathematical reasoning

Occupations related to this major: Aerospace Engineers, Materials Engineers, Petroleum Engineers, Industrial Engineers, Mechanical Engineers, and Engineering Technicians

Materials Engineering

Materials Engineering majors learn to evaluate properties of materials used to manufacture products that must meet specialized design and performance criteria. They learn to develop machinery and processes to manufacture materials, such as polymers, plastics, and alloys.

Interests: Nature and the physical sciences, problem solving, computer operations, working with ideas

Skills and abilities: Creative and critical thinking, problem sensitivity, oral and written expression and comprehension, deductive and inductive reasoning

Occupations related to this major: Materials Engineers, Marine Architects, Mechanical Engineers, Electrical Drafters, and Electrical Engineering Technicians

Mechanical Engineering

Mechanical Engineering majors learn to plan and design tools, engines, machines, and other mechanically functioning equipment. They learn to oversee installation, operation, maintenance, and repair of such equipment as centralized heat, gas, water, and steam systems. They learn to create and build machines, devices, and systems that perform useful services.

Interests: Mechanical devices, computers, cars, solving problems, mathematics, physical science

Skills and abilities: Mathematics, critical thinking, complex problem solving, mathematical reasoning, deductive and inductive reasoning, oral and written comprehension

Occupations related to this major: Mechanical Engineers, Marine Architects, Materials Engineers, Petroleum Engineers, Engineering Technicians, and Mechanical Drafters

Petroleum Engineering

Petroleum Engineering majors learn about exploring and drilling for fossil fuel, both on land and under the sea, and how to maximize the recovery of oil and gas through engineering processes. They learn methods of searching for new sources of energy, for example, geothermal energy. They learn to devise methods to improve oil and gas well production and determine the need for new or modified tool designs.

Interests: Solving problems, working with others, using computers, outdoor activities

Skills and abilities: Mathematics, physics, oral and written expression and comprehension, inductive and deductive reasoning, problem sensitivity, fluency of ideas

Occupations related to this major: Petroleum Engineers, Aerospace Engineers, Marine Engineers, Materials Engineers, Mining and Geological Engineers, and Geologists

10. FAMILY AND CONSUMER SCIENCES

Family and Consumer Sciences majors concentrate on issues concerning feeding, clothing, and caring for children, managing resources, and providing housing for individuals and families. Family and Consumer Science majors provide information, gained through research, about families and individuals as consumers and decision makers. These majors provide information about child care, elder care, food, clothing, housing, finance, and other issues of resource management.

Interests: Issues concerning feeding, clothing, and caring for children, managing resources, and providing housing for individuals and families; an interest in families as consumers and decision makers.

Popular majors in this field of study: Day Care Administration, Family and Consumer Education, Fashion Merchandising, Food Science and Nutrition, Hotel and Motel Management, Housing and Human Development, Individual and Family Development, Leisure Studies, Textile Sciences, and Tourism

Employment information/outlook: More than 1,011,500 people worked in related occupations in this field of study in 2012. The 2012-2022 employment growth is expected to be 7.8%.

Pay depends on the educational attainment of the worker and the type of establishment. Although the pay generally is very low, more education usually means higher earnings. Median hourly wages of child care workers were $9.38 in May 2012. Hourly earnings of nonsupervisory workers in clothing, accessory, and general merchandise stores in 2012 were well below the average for all workers in private industry. This reality reflects both the high proportion of part-time and less experienced workers in these stores and the fact that even experienced workers receive relatively low pay compared with the pay of experienced workers in many other industries. Median annual wages of dietitians and nutritionists were $55,240 in May 2012. For that same period, lodging managers were $46,810; lodging managers in traveler accommodations, $53,780. Salaries of lodging managers vary greatly according to their responsibilities, location, and the segment of the hotel industry in which they work.

Day Care Administration

Day Care Administration majors learn to manage programs that provide education or social services to young children and their families. They gain knowledge of child development and develop skills in teaching young children, in supervising staff, and in business management.

Interests: Leadership, management, supervising people, administering programs, working with children

Skills and abilities: Organizational and managerial skills, program development, oral and written expression and comprehension, speech clarity

Occupations related to this major: Day Care Director, Preschool Director, Head Start Directors, Early Childhood Education Program Directors, and Child Care Workers

Family and Consumer Education

Family and Consumer Education majors learn to use community resources to meet the needs of the individual and the family in the management of time, energy, and money. They learn about parenting skills, communication skills, relationship skills, wellness, foods and nutrition, consumerism, clothing selection, and job skills. They prepare to become family and consumer teachers for preschool through adult education in subjects related to the family. They study various aspects of family life including human development, nutrition, and decision making, in addition to teaching strategies.

Interests: Family life, using current technology, working with people

Skills and abilities: Critical and analytical thinking, oral and written expression and comprehension, speech clarity

Occupations related to this major: Family and Consumer Science Teachers, Consumer Advocates, Education Consultants, Extension Agents, Financial Planners, Housing Administrators

Fashion Merchandising

Fashion Merchandising majors study how to manufacture fashions for consumers and effectively sell those fashions.

Interests: Current trends in apparel, arts, furnishings, travel and leisure, food business trends, fabrics, fashion and fashion designers

Skills and abilities: Motivating people, leadership, organizational ability, originality, fluency of ideas, color discrimination, oral comprehension

Occupations related to this major: Retail Buyers, Manufacturers' Representatives, Product Designer-Pattern Makers, and Fashion Designers

Food Science and Nutrition

Food Science and Nutrition majors study the nature of foods, the causes of their deterioration, and the principles of food processing. They will learn about the selection, preservation, processing, packaging, distribution, and use of safe, nutritious, and wholesome food.

Interests: Social, health, economic, and political issues involved in food production and availability; chemical reactions and what happens to food when it enters the human body; solving problems

Skills and abilities: Organizational abilities, critical thinking, oral and written expression and comprehension, speech clarity, mathematical reasoning

Occupations related to this major: Dietitians, Nutritionists, Nutrition Educators, and Food Scientists and Technicians

Hotel and Motel Management

Hotel Management majors learn the operation of a hotel. They learn the principles of managing lodging facilities efficiently and profitably. They learn about personnel management, services, supplies, business aspects, decision making, accounting, and public relations. They are introduced to the principles of managing these key components of the hospitality industry.

Interests: Working with people, problem solving, attention to detail, leadership

Skills and abilities: Organization ability, creativity, oral and written expression and comprehension, speech clarity, speech recognition

Occupations related to this major: Lodging Managers, Food Service Managers, Retail Store Managers, and Office Managers

Housing and Human Development

Housing and Human Development majors learn to analyze the use of investment in housing and its impact on families, the community, and the larger economy and society.

Interests: Working with people, serving others, real estate, home automation, the family, marketing, management, interior design, environmental design, finance

Skills and abilities: Computer skills, analytical skills, oral and written expression and comprehension, problem sensitivity

Occupations related to this major: Real Estate Managers, Property Managers, Consumer Affairs Specialists, Extension Agents, and Financial/Mortgage Specialists

Individual and Family Development

Individual and Family Development majors study interpersonal relationships and human development from infancy to old age. They study theories of development with an emphasis on techniques to improve quality of life for individuals and families.

Interests: Helping others, family and individual well-being, prevention and elimination of problems facing people in their daily lives

Skills and abilities: Working with people, critical thinking, oral and written expression and comprehension, curiosity about interpersonal and family dynamics, speech clarity

Occupations related to this major: Child Life Specialists, Day Care Teachers, Recreation Activities Directors, Drug and Alcohol Rehabilitation Counselors, and Crisis Center Directors

Leisure Studies

Leisure Studies majors learn to design, manage, and deliver leisure services to a variety of people in diverse settings. They learn about the impact of leisure services upon individual satisfaction and the quality of life.

Interests: Helping people, leadership, organizing individual and group activities

Skills and abilities: Working with people, oral and written expression and comprehension, speech clarity, problem sensitivity, fluency of ideas, memorization

Occupations related to this major: Amusement and Recreation Establishment Managers, Recreation Workers, Tour Guides and Escorts, Social and Community Service Managers, and Meeting and Convention Planners

Textile Sciences

Textile Sciences majors learn how to design fabrics for garments, upholstery, rugs, and other products. They study print, woven, and embroidery styles, and learn how to buy and sell certain fabrics and trims. They learn how to analyze fabric performance in the marketplace.

Interests: Fashion design, garment fashion, art, history of textiles, textile technology, design principles

Skills and abilities: Originality, visualization, visual color discrimination, fluency of ideas, oral expression and comprehension

Occupations related to this major: Textile Designers, Fashion Designers, Quality Control Analysts, Sales Representatives, and Wardrobe Planners

Tourism

Tourism majors study how to manage travel-related enterprises and conventions and tour services. They learn about travel agency management, travel industry operations and procedures, tourism marketing and promotion strategies, and travel industry law.

Interests: Travel, tourism planning, human resource management, travel industry operations, marketing

Skills and abilities: Oral and written expression and comprehension, mathematical reasoning, speech clarity, fluency of ideas

Occupations related to this major: Travel Agents, Travel Guides, Tour Guides and Escorts, Reservation and Transportation Ticket Agents, and Amusement and Recreation Establishment Managers

11. HEALTH SCIENCE

The **Health Science** field of study trains workers in a vast array of occupations. Occupational titles vary, and the training necessary to fill these occupations requires lengthy postgraduate education. Health practitioners diagnose, treat, and prevent illness and disease. While all health practitioners practice the art of healing, they differ in methods of treatment and areas of specialization. Training for this profession is more rigorous than training for most other professional occupations, but practice also offers unusual rewards. Incomes of health practitioners generally are higher than those of other professional workers with similar years of education. Furthermore, most health practitioners derive considerable satisfaction from knowing that their work contributes directly to the well-being of others. Workers in the industry must have the ability and perseverance to complete the years of study required. They should be emotionally stable, able to make decisions in emergencies, and have a strong desire to help the sick and injured. Sincerity and an ability to gain the confidence of patients are important qualities.

Interests: Diagnosing, treating, and preventing illness and disease; an interest in the well-being of others and a desire to help the sick and injured

Popular majors in this field of study: Athletic Training, Clinical Laboratory Science, Dental Hygiene, Health Services Management, Medical Record Administration, Nuclear Medical Technology, Nursing, Occupational Therapy, Pharmacy, and Physical Therapy

Employment information/outlook: More than 2,775,600 people worked in related occupations in this field of study in 2012. The 2012-2022 employment growth is expected to be 27%.

Most athletic trainers work in full-time positions, and typically receive benefits. The salary of an athletic trainer depends on experience and job responsibilities, and varies by job setting. In May 2012, median annual wages for athletic trainers were \$42,690; medical and clinical laboratory technologists, \$47,820; and dental hygienists, \$70,210; Earnings vary by geographic location, employment setting, and years of experience. Dental hygienists may be paid on an hourly, daily, salary, or commission basis. Median annual wages of wage and salary medical and health services managers were \$88,580; medical records and health information technicians, \$34,160. The median annual wage in May 2012 of nuclear medicine technologists was \$70,180; registered nurses, \$65,470; occupational therapists, \$75,400; salary pharmacists, \$116,670; physical therapists, \$79,860; and speech-language pathologists, \$69,870.

Athletic Training

Athletic Training majors learn to prevent, recognize, refer, and treat injuries and illnesses sustained by athletes. They learn about the administration of athletic training programs in public and private schools, colleges, universities, and with professional teams. They study exercise sciences and the medical aspects of sport. Together with clinical experience, this prepares students for national certification in the field.

Interests: Sports, helping others, health and medicine, physical fitness and exercise, anatomy, nutrition, first aid

Skills and abilities: Manual skills, science, problem solving, interpersonal communication, integrity, oral expression, speech clarity, physical strength

Occupations related to this major: Athletic Trainers, Sports Medicine Clinic Administrators, Exercise Physiologists, Physical and Corrective Therapists, and Occupational Therapists

Clinical Laboratory Science

Clinical Laboratory Science majors learn to perform medical tests to determine the presence and cause of disease. They study sophisticated instrumentation used to perform a variety of laboratory procedures. They study blood and other body fluids that aid in the diagnosis of disease and the maintenance of health.

Interests: Solving problems, working with complex machinery, computer science, laboratory work, helping others, medicine, biological science

Skills and abilities: Computer skills, analytic skills, oral and written expression and comprehension, arm-hand steadiness, visual color discrimination

Occupations related to this major: Laboratory Technologists and Technicians, Research Analysts, Coroners, Clinical Scientists, Environmental Health Officers, and Toxicologists

Dental Hygiene

Dental Hygiene majors learn to work under the supervision of a dentist to clean and polish teeth, massage gums, apply fluoride to prevent decay, and provide dental health education. They obtain the knowledge and clinical skills needed to provide preventive oral health care. They learn skills as an assistant to a dentist performing a number of duties.

Interests: Working with people, helping individuals maintain their health, science

Skills and abilities: Critical thinking, oral expression, arm-hand steadiness, manual dexterity, near vision

Occupations related to this major: Dental Hygienists, Dental Assistants, Dentists, and Medical Assistants

Health Services Management

Health Services Management majors prepare for entry-level positions managing a wide variety of health care organizations such as hospitals, nursing homes, insurance companies, and public agencies. They learn to direct the many activities of health care organizations and coordinate administrative duties with medical services. They learn about space needs, staffing, and supplies. They learn to supervise personnel, prepare budgets, and direct the policies of the organization.

Interests: Working with people, taking initiative, solving problems, working with data

Skills and abilities: Oral and written expression and comprehension, speech clarity, organizational skills, interpersonal skills, critical thinking

Occupations related to this major: Medical and Health Services Managers, Public Health Directors, Educational Program Directors, Nursing Directors, Social Welfare Administrators, and Health Insurance Underwriters

Medical Record Administration

Medical Record Administration majors learn to supervise and manage the preparation, storage, and use of medical records and related information systems. They study the legal and technical aspects of medical records, and the design and management of secure data systems. They learn to merge the study of business and medicine. Students prepare to direct medical record departments in varied health care settings by exploring the health care environment, health care organizations, clinical information systems, medical record department operations, and health care reimbursement systems.

Interests: Leadership, working with people, designing and implementing systems, problem solving, working with detail

Skills and abilities: Writing and speaking effectively, working in a changing environment, oral and written expression and comprehension, near vision, mathematical reasoning

Occupations related to this major: Medical Records Administrators and Directors, Quality Assurance Coordinators, Health Care Administrators, Medical Records Educators, and Research Coordinators

Nuclear Medicine Technology

Nuclear Medicine Technology majors learn how to administer radionuclides to patients and to monitor the characteristics and functions of tissues or organs in which they localize. They learn to operate the cameras that detect the radionuclides and maintain patient records. They learn to prepare and administer radioactive drugs to patients, operate radiation detection equipment, and perform the calculations or computer analysis needed to complete the patient's examination.

Interests: Biological sciences, new technologies, helping others, working in a medical setting, working with people

Skills and abilities: Biological and physical science, working with others, oral and written expression and comprehension, problem sensitivity

Occupations related to this major: Nuclear Medicine Technologists, Radiation Therapists, Radiologic Technologists, Electroneurodiagnostic Technologists, and Medical and Clinical Laboratory Technologists

Nursing

Nursing majors learn to administer nursing care to ill or injured persons. They learn to administer medication and treatments prescribed by medical doctors, observe and record symptoms and behaviors of patients, and promote good health. They learn how to rehabilitate, counsel, and educate patients, and how to work as part of a health care team in many settings. They study humanities, natural sciences, and nursing theory to serve individuals, families, groups, and communities.

Interests: Provide intimate helping services to people, ethical care, chemistry, physics, anatomy, biology

Skills and abilities: Clear thinking, oral and written expression and comprehension, problem sensitivity, speech clarity

Occupations related to this major: Registered Nurses, Doctors of Medicine, Nursing Instructors, Physical Therapists, Medical Assistants, Chiropractors, and Podiatrists

Occupational Therapy

Occupational Therapy majors learn to determine the educational, recreational, and vocational activities needed to hasten a patient's recovery from physical, psychological, social, or developmental problems. They learn to instruct patients in the use of artificial limbs or to regain the use of muscles. They learn to help patients function independently so that they may work, play, take care of themselves, and relate to others in a productive and satisfying manner.

Interests: Solving problems, anatomy, working with people, medicine, health, rehabilitation

Skills and abilities: Logical thinking, working with others, oral and written expression and comprehension, deductive reasoning

Occupations related to this major: Occupational Therapists, Respiratory Therapists, Physical Therapists, Speech-Language Pathologists and Audiologists, Recreational Therapists, and Exercise Physiologists

Pharmacy

Pharmacy majors study the science of drugs, including their chemical and physical properties and composition. They learn to understand the effects of drugs, to test those drugs for purity and strength. They learn to provide drug products and drug information in all areas of patient care. They learn to monitor drug therapy to ensure that the treatment is appropriate, safe, therapeutically effective, and cost-effective.

Interests: Chemistry, biology, mathematics, solving problems, helping others

Skills and abilities: Patience, tact, adapting to change, working carefully, oral and written expression and comprehension, information ordering, mathematical reasoning

Occupations related to this major: Pharmacists, Pharmacy Technicians, Physician Assistants, Opticians, Licensed Practical Nurses, and Dietitians and Nutritionists

Physical Therapy

Physical Therapy majors learn to assist and help persons with injuries, muscle, nerve, and joint problems, burns, and bone diseases. They learn to use exercise, massage, and heat and light to assist in healing. They prepare to take state licensure examinations in this field and qualify for service in the prevention of disabilities and the rehabilitation of the disabled. They learn to test, evaluate, and plan a treatment program for patients who are physically incapacitated as the result of accidents or disease, and for healthy individuals who wish to prevent injuries in work or recreational settings.

Interests: Biological and physical sciences, exercise and fitness, people, analytic reasoning

Skills and abilities: Interpersonal communication, problem solving, visual spatial perception, emotional sensitivity, oral and written expression, speech clarity, problem sensitivity, manual dexterity

Occupations related to this major: Physical Therapists, Occupational Therapists, Respiratory Therapists, Manual Arts Therapists, Corrective Therapists, and Speech-Language Pathologists and Audiologists

Speech Pathology/Audiology

Speech Pathology majors learn to treat people with speech, language, voice, hearing, and communication disorders. These disorders may be the result of hearing loss, brain injury or deterioration, cerebral palsy, stroke, cleft palate, mental retardation, or emotional problems. They receive training in the identification and treatment of human communication disorders. They learn about the normal processes of speech and language development, why problems may occur, and what can be done to minimize their impact.

Interests: Working with children, working with adults, identifying and solving behavioral problems, applying technology to human needs

Skills and abilities: Oral and written expression and comprehension, speech clarity, creativity, working cooperatively in groups

Occupations related to this major: Speech-Language Pathologists and Audiologists, Recreation Therapists, Corrective Therapists, Exercise Physiologists, Occupational Therapists, and Respiratory Therapists

12. HUMANITIES

Humanities students explore thought and expression through aesthetic, historical, philosophical, social, political, psychological, and symbolic contexts. Humanities studies serve as a liberal and broad training for professional careers. Students will enjoy courses in English, literature, history, classics, culture studies, history of art and music, philosophy, foreign language, social and natural sciences. Graduates with a bachelor's degree may qualify for management trainee positions in corporations, banks, and federal and state governmental agencies. Many students use humanities as an undergraduate degree for the teaching or law professions. Other students may become writers or communications specialists in humanistic endeavors.

Interests: Exploring thoughts and expressions through aesthetic, historical, philosophical, social, political, psychological and symbolic contests; literature, history, foreign language, social and natural sciences

Popular majors in this field of study: American Literature, Anthropology, Classics, Comparative Literature, English, English Education, Foreign Language, History, Linguistics, Philosophy, Religion, and Sociology

Employment information/outlook: More than 972,100 people worked in related occupations in this field of study in 2012. The 2012-2022 employment growth is expected to be 11%.

In May 2012, median annual wages for anthropologists and archaeologists were $57,420; historians, $52,480; sociologists, $74,960. Wages of anthropologists and archaeologists, geographers, and historians vary. The same applies to English and Foreign Language specialists and people in the clergy.

American Literature

American Literature majors study the historical development of the culture in which they live. They study the literature and literary development of the United States from the Colonial Era to the present. They learn about the forces—intellectual, economic, geographic, and social—that have shaped their own character. They study periods and genres, authors, literary criticism, and regional and oral traditions.

Interests: Sensitivity to language, the power of ideas, exploring the development of different regional and ethnic traditions that make up American culture

Skills and abilities: Assessing conflicting points of view, oral and written expression and comprehension, speech clarity

Occupations related to this major: English Teachers, Creative Writers, Art, Drama, and Music Teachers, Reporters and Correspondents, and Publicity Writers

Anthropology

Anthropology majors learn to make comparative studies of the distribution, origin, and evolution of man, cultures that man has created, and their social and physical characteristics. Studies include ancient as well as modern man.

Interests: Writing, archeology, sociology, social sciences, investigative research

Skills and abilities: Writing, science, critical thinking, oral and written expression and comprehension, inductive reasoning, fluency of ideas

Occupations related to this major: Anthropologists, Archeologists, Historians, Sociologists, Linguistic Scientists, and Genealogists

Classics

Classics majors immerse themselves in two cultures fundamental to the West—the cultures of ancient Greece and ancient Rome. Students explore the literature, history, art, philosophy, and architecture of those civilizations. Connecting with the past creates a sense of belonging to humanity and participating in human achievement and evokes reflections on the present. Students will explore their poetry, prose, and drama, and consider the relation of literature to other arts and to other fields of study.

Interests: Language, literature, exploring the past, acquiring a broad liberal education

Skills and abilities: Oral and written expression and comprehension, information ordering, skills of analysis and criticism

Occupations related to this major: Classicists, Anthropologists, Art History Teachers, English Teachers, Foreign Language Teachers, and Literature Teachers

Comparative Literature

Comparative Literature majors study the literature of different countries, cultures, and languages. They explore their poetry, prose, and drama, and consider the relation of literature to other arts and to other fields of study.

Interests: Literature, foreign languages, differences between cultures as expressed in their languages and works of art

Skills and abilities: Reading critically, speaking, active listening, oral and written expression and comprehension, speech recognition, information ordering

Occupations related to this major: English Teachers, Foreign Language Teachers, Postsecondary Teachers, Journalists, Lawyers, Reporters and Correspondents, and Writers

English

English majors study the linguistic and literary richness of the English language as well as some of the cultural history of the English-speaking world. They concentrate on specific areas such as creative writing, comparative or American literature, or semantics. They study important works of literature—drama, prose, and poetry—focusing on the point of view, organization, and language of the works. They develop critical and analytical reading skills, and practice language use and composition.

Interests: Reading, talking, writing about literature; music, theater, and film

Skills and abilities: Speaking, writing, oral and written expression and comprehension, speech clarity

Occupations related to this major: English Teachers, Teachers, Journalists, Publishers, Radio and Television Broadcasters, and Social Workers

English Education

English Education majors learn to teach students about English grammar and linguistics. They learn to instruct students in different types of literature such as poetry, short stories, plays, and novels. They learn how to teach students to research and prepare research papers. They learn how to teach public speaking, drama, and English as a second language

Interests: Nature and history of languages, reading, literature, journalism, creative writing, linguistic development of children and teenagers

Skills and abilities: Speaking, working with students, art, guiding discussions

Occupations related to this major: Elementary School Teachers, Secondary School Teachers, Postsecondary School Teachers, Linguistic Scientists, and Speech-Language Pathologists and Audiologists

Foreign Language

Foreign Language majors study foreign languages (French, German, Italian, Japanese, Russian, Spanish, etc.). They study the language, literature, and culture of the country where the language is spoken.

Interests: Literature, history, culture of a language

Skills and abilities: Fluency in speaking and writing, learning languages, oral and written expression and comprehension, speech clarity

Occupations related to this major: Foreign Language Teachers, Translators, Journalists, Foreign Travel Consultants, Diplomats, and Linguists

History

History majors study the social, economic, and political developments of societies. They learn to analyze historical happenings and, as reporters, writers, or teachers, report on their significance. Students expand their knowledge and understanding of the past. Working with written, oral, visual, and art factual evidence they examine the causes, contexts, and chronologies of historical events, thus cultivating a sense of continuity and change in human experiences.

Interests: Curiosity about when, where, and why historical happenings occurred; what it was like to have lived in different times and places

Skills and abilities: Reading carefully, writing clearly, speaking articulately, thinking analytically, oral and written expression and comprehension, expressing ideas with clarity and precision

Occupations related to this major: Historians, Archeologists, Anthropologists, Genealogists, Curators, Archivists, and Teachers

Linguistics

Linguistics majors study the common properties of the world's languages. They study the structure and development of a specific language or language group. They trace the origin and evolution of words through comparative analysis of ancient parent languages and modern language groups. They study word and structural characteristics, such as phonetics and phonology, morphology, syntax, and semantics.

Interests: Language, foreign languages, how people talk and express themselves

Skills and abilities: Learning foreign languages, problem solving, oral and written expression and comprehension, speech recognition

Occupations related to this major: Linguistic Scientists, English as a Second Language Teachers, English Teachers, Foreign Language Teachers, Interpreters, Translators, Public Relations Specialists, and Speech Pathologists

Philosophy

Philosophy majors learn the process of developing a philosophy. They gain insight into how the great minds of the past and present have attempted to answer the most serious questions of the universe. They participate in a tradition of thought as old as civilized life and as new as artificial intelligence and medical ethics. They examine issues of morality, reality, and knowledge. Philosophy is a foundation for teaching, religion, wisdom, and logical thinking.

Interests: Solitary meditation, argument with family and friends, reading, asking the "why" question, seeing the connections between different things

Skills and abilities: Writing, debating, thinking logically, mathematics, oral and written expression and comprehension, speech recognition, information ordering

Occupations related to this major: Philologists, Political Scientists, Anthropologists, Psychologists, Sociologists, and Historians

Religion

Religion majors study and compare the major world religions, as well as many of the lesser-known religions. They study the various branches, sects, and denominations of particular religions. They learn how religion plays an integral part in all societies. They learn to use a range of approaches when examining religion—historical, textual, psychological, philosophical, sociological, and anthropological.

Interests: Different cultures and societies, world religions, human problems and mysteries, such as birth, growth, love, death, grief

Skills and abilities: Reading carefully and critically, foreign languages, oral and written expression and comprehension, problem sensitivity, speech clarity

Occupations related to this major: Clergy, Directors of Religious Activities and Education, Therapists and Counselors, Psychologists, Social Workers, and Teachers

Sociology

Sociology majors study the origin, development, organization, and functions of human society. They trace the origin and growth of human organizations and the behavior and interaction within social groups. They analyze the influence of group activities on individual and group behavior.

Interests: Anthropology, geography, criminology, psychology, investigative research, politics

Skills and abilities: Reading critically, critical thinking, solving problems, oral and written expression and comprehension, deductive reasoning

Occupations related to this major: Sociologists, Anthropologists, Political Scientists, Counseling Psychologists, Historians, and Linguistic Scientists

13. PHYSICAL SCIENCES

Physical Sciences majors in this field of study investigate the structure and composition of the Earth and the universe. Everything in our physical environment, whether naturally occurring or of human design, is composed of chemicals. Chemists search for, and put to practical use, new knowledge about chemicals. Geological scientists play an important role in preserving and cleaning up the environment. Meteorologists forecast the weather. Physicists design and perform experiments with lasers, cyclotrons, telescopes, mass spectrometers, and other equipment. Physical science technicians use the principles and theories of science and mathematics to solve problems in research and development and to help invent and improve products and processes.

Interests: The structure and composition of the Earth and the universe; an interest in our physical environment, whether naturally occurring or of human design

Popular majors in this field of study: Astronomy, Atmospheric Sciences, Chemistry, Environmental Sciences, Geology, Geophysics, and Physics

Employment information/outlook: More than 978,300 people worked in related occupations in this field of study in 2012. The 2012-2022 employment growth is expected to be 10%.

In May 2012, median wages for physicists and astronomers were $106,360; chemists were $73,060; and environmental scientists, $63,570.

Astronomy

Astronomy majors study the sizes, shapes, motions, and all other physical properties of the sun, moon, stars, and planets. They may use knowledge of astronomy in space exploration and the development of space technology. Students seek to understand the entire universe—its constituent parts, such as the stars and planets, and the physical and mathematical laws that govern them.

Interests: Nature, the night sky, the expanding universe, physical science, astronomical science

Skills and abilities: Mathematics, science, computers, inductive and deductive reasoning, written comprehension

Occupations related to this major: Astronomers, Geophysicists, Physicists, Geologists, Chemists, and Atmospheric and Space Scientists

Atmospheric Sciences

Atmospheric Sciences majors learn to investigate atmospheric phenomena and interpret meteorological data gathered by surface and air stations, satellites, and radar to prepare reports and weather forecasts for public and other uses. They study the basic principles of atmospheric physics and dynamics and are concerned with understanding and forecasting weather.

Interests: Weather, environment, climate, science, mathematics, computer science, geography, serving the public

Skills and abilities: Analytic reasoning, mechanical reasoning, problem solving, oral and written expression and comprehension, speech clarity, inductive reasoning

Occupations related to this major: Atmospheric Scientists, Space Scientists, Climatologists, Geophysicists, Astronomers, and Meteorologists

Chemistry

Chemistry majors study the sciences of physical substances, atoms, molecules, elements, and compounds. They learn to perform chemical tests, develop new chemical products, and monitor the purity of air, food, and drugs. Because it is an experimental science, students learn to design and perform the experiments that allow a better understanding of the physical world.

Interests: Investigative research, problem solving, curiosity about how things work

Skills and abilities: Analytic and mathematical skills, oral and written expression and comprehension, deductive reasoning, mathematical reasoning

Occupations related to this major: Chemists, Chemical Engineers, Chemical Engineering Technicians, Agricultural Scientists, Biological Scientists, and Physicists

Environmental Sciences

Environmental Sciences majors study the biological and physical aspects of the environment. They learn about the conservation and/or improvement of natural resources, such as air, soil, water, land, fish, and wildlife, as well as methods of controlling environmental pollution. They conduct research or perform investigation for the purpose of identifying, abating, or eliminating sources of pollutants or hazards that affect either the environment or the health of the population.

Interests: Investigative research, solving problems, working with ideas

Skills and abilities: Working with others, oral and written expression and comprehension, problem sensitivity, mathematical reasoning, inductive reasoning

Occupations related to this major: Environmental Scientists, Materials Scientists, Geographers, Geologists, Atmospheric Scientists, and Space Scientists

Geology

Geology majors study the Earth's structure, composition, and history. They examine rocks, minerals, and fossils. They record data, prepare maps, conduct surveys, and advise suitability of sites. They develop skills that are useful for basic research and applied problem solving.

Interests: The outdoors, remote places, problem solving, collecting minerals or fossils

Skills and abilities: Reasoning ability, critical thinking, mathematics, oral and written expression and comprehension, number facility, inductive reasoning

Occupations related to this major: Geologists, Physicists, Geophysicists, Materials Scientists, Geological Data Technicians, and Geographers

Geophysics

Geophysics majors study aspects of the earth, including the atmosphere and hydrosphere. They investigate and measure seismic, gravitational, electrical, thermal, and magnetic forces affecting the Earth, and utilize principles of physics, mathematics, and chemistry. They study the Earth and its atmosphere by physical measurements. Students learn to use mathematics and physics, along with electrical engineering, computer science, geology, and other earth sciences to analyze measurements taken at the surface to infer properties and processes deep within the Earth's complex interior.

Interests: The outdoors, travel, taking measurements, computer languages, graphics, computer programming

Skills and abilities: Natural curiosity, mathematics, physical science, computers, oral and written comprehension, mathematical reasoning, deductive reasoning

Occupations related to this major: Geophysicists, Geologists, Astronomers, Physicists, Atmospheric Scientists, Space Scientists, and Chemists

Physics

Physics majors learn to explore and identify the basic principles of the structure and behavior of matter, the generation and transfer of energy, and the interaction of matter and energy. They learn to use these principles in theoretical areas such as the origin of the universe, or in practical areas to develop advanced materials, electronic devices, or medical equipment.

Interests: Investigative research, mathematics, problem solving, improving the quality of life

Skills and abilities: Computational skills, reasoning logically, solving problems, oral and written expression and comprehension, mathematical reasoning

Occupations related to this major: Physicists, Astronomers, Geologists, Atmospheric Scientists, Space Scientists, Geophysicists, and Environmental Scientists

14. SOCIAL AND BEHAVIORAL SCIENCES

Social and Behavioral Sciences majors learn about the social needs of people. Clinical psychologists help the mentally or emotionally disturbed adjust to life through behavior modification programs and other techniques. Social workers address the needs of individuals, families, groups, and communities. Their work may involve everything from helping an elderly person adjust to life in a nursing home, to organizing fund-raising for community social welfare activities. Other social scientists conduct basic and applied research in the social sciences. They use established methods to assemble a body of fact and theory that contributes to human knowledge. Social scientists investigate all aspects of human society—from anthropologists studying the origins of the human race, or historians studying an ancient civilization—to political scientists analyzing the results of presidential elections.

Interests: Social and emotional needs of people; an interest in all aspects of society—from the origins of the human race, or an ancient civilization, to political results of presidential elections

Popular majors in this field of study: Criminal Justice Studies, Economics, Geography, Gerontology, Political Sciences, Psychology, Public Administration, Social Studies Education, and Social Work

Employment information/outlook: More than 4,153,700 people worked in related occupations in this field of study in 2012. The 2012-2022 employment growth is expected to be 19%.

In May 2012, median annual wages of probation officers and correctional treatment specialists were $38,970; economists, $91,860; salary clinical, counseling, and school psychologists, $69,280; social and human service assistants, $28,850; political scientists, $102,000; sociologists, $74,960; child, family, and school social workers, $44,200. Public administration positions vary by occupation, size of the state or locality, and region of the country.

Criminal Justice Studies

Criminal Justice Studies majors learn about the dimensions and causes of crime and delinquency; the structure of the American criminal justice system; the operation of criminal courts; and the techniques and theories of law enforcement.

Interests: Serving others, court procedures, criminal law, private security, criminal justice

Skills and abilities: Working with others, making decisions, oral and written expression and comprehension, inductive reasoning, speech clarity, problem sensitivity

Occupations related to this major: Criminal Investigators, United States Marshals, Police Detectives, Sheriffs and Deputy Sheriffs, Correction Officers and Jailers, and Child Support and Missing Persons Investigators

Economics

Economics majors learn to plan, design, and conduct research into activities devoted to satisfying human wants. They learn to analyze the relationship between supply and demand. They study the problems of inflation, unemployment, tariffs, taxation, and foreign trade. They learn to analyze such issues as inflation, unemployment, monopoly, and economic growth. They study theory, policy, and trends and explore ways to deal with the economic problems of society and the individual.

Interests: Current issues such as taxes, poverty, health, inflation, the environment, human behavior

Skills and abilities: Solving problems, oral and written expression and comprehension, mathematical reasoning, logical reasoning

Occupations related to this major: Economists, Market Research Analysts, Urban and Regional Planners, Financial Managers, Financial Analysts, and Underwriters

Geography

Geography majors study the activities of people. Students study where people live, why they are located there, and how they earn a living. Students study the physical characteristics of the Earth, such as landforms, vegetation, climate, locale, and mineral and water resources. They study how people relate to and are shaped by their environment. They gain a broad perspective on the world's environments and its peoples while gaining a strong background in the physical and social sciences.

Interests: Analyzing and solving social and environmental problems, doing social and physical scientific research, the relationship between people and their environment

Skills and abilities: Oral and written expression and comprehension, spatial orientation, working individually and in groups, information gathering, working with computers

Occupations related to this major: Geographers, Geophysicists, Geologists, Atmospheric and Space Scientists, Environmental Scientists, and Materials Scientists

Gerontology

Gerontology majors learn about aging and older persons. They study physical, emotional, and intellectual changes in the elderly, cultural aspects of aging, and governmental policies and programs for the aging.

Interests: Helping people, human development, older people, family relations, improving the quality of life

Skills and abilities: Oral and written expression and comprehension, listening, objectivity, deductive reasoning, determining needs and interests, organizing and managing projects

Occupations related to this major: Gerontologists, Geriatric Nurses, Nursing Home Administrators, Social Welfare Administrators, and Occupational and Physical Therapists

Political Sciences

Political Sciences majors study government and the nature of politics. They analyze the operations of different forms of government, and attempt to find theoretical and practical solutions to political problems. Students learn about the origins, historical development, and social functions of government. They study how electoral, legislative, judicial, and administrative structures and processes vary from one country and one age to another; how and why governments change, fall, and engage in wars. They study the behavior of public officials and other citizens involved in politics.

Interests: Public policy issues such as health care and environmental protection; politicians and public figures, justice, good and bad government, law, criminal justice, the legal system

Skills and abilities: Reading critically, thinking analytically, oral and written expression and comprehension, understanding graphic material

Occupations related to this major: Political Scientists, Legislators, Sociologists, Historians, Anthropologists, and Political Science Teachers

Psychology

Psychology majors learn to collect and interpret scientific data relating to human behavior to understand people and explain their actions. They learn to interview patients, give diagnostic tests, and offer therapy to help people make behavioral adjustments. Students study human and animal behavior and explore the processes involved in normal and abnormal thoughts, feelings, and actions. They increase their understanding of behavior while learning psychological facts, methods, principles, and generalizations about individuals and groups.

Interests: Working with people, scientific method, human and animal behavior

Skills and abilities: Critical thinking, oral and written expression and comprehension, inductive reasoning

Occupations related to this major: Developmental Psychologists, Experimental Psychologists, Educational Psychologists, Social Psychologists, Clinical Psychologists, and Counseling Psychologists

Public Administration

Public Administration majors may study in five areas of specialization: personnel, management, public relations, finance, and planning. They learn to establish government policy, and develop laws, rules and regulations. These studies will prepare students to find positions managing public agencies. Students deal with the operations of all forms and levels of government. Students learn about the many skills and challenges associated with implementing public policy in government and in nonprofit organizations.

Interests: Public and community service, organizing people, leadership, working with people from different backgrounds

Skills and abilities: Leadership, organizational ability, problem solving, oral and written expression and comprehension, inductive reasoning

Occupations related to this major: Government Service Executives, City Managers, Management Analysts, Government Affairs Specialists, and Legislators

Social Studies Education

Social Studies Education majors learn to teach courses pertaining to human society and its characteristic elements. They learn to teach subjects such as psychology, economics, history, political science, and sociology. They learn to teach students in middle school and high school courses in history, citizenship, and other social sciences.

Interests: Serving people, working with people, history, social sciences

Skills and abilities: Speaking, organizing working with people, oral and written expression and comprehension, speech clarity

Occupations related to this major: Middle School Teachers, High School Teachers, Postsecondary School Teachers, Historians, Sociologists, and Psychologists

Social Work

Social Work majors study many types of social issues and needs. They learn to aid families with physical, mental, or social problems, such as poverty, unemployment, illness, broken homes, various disabilities, antisocial behavior, and inadequate housing. Students acquire the knowledge and skills to assist individuals, families, groups, and communities in preventing and alleviating the problems of a modern, rapidly changing society. They learn to help others and to modify harmful social conditions, promote social and economic well being, and increase opportunities for all people to live with dignity and freedom.

Interests: Helping those in need, particularly children, the poor, minorities, the aged, the disabled, and women, enabling others to develop unique, positive responses and solutions to their problems

Skills and abilities: Objectivity, ability to listen, analytic ability, oral and written expression and comprehension, problem sensitivity

Occupations related to this major: Social Workers, Medical and Psychiatric Social Workers, Community Organization Social Workers, Residential Counselors, Probation and Correctional Treatment Specialists, and Human Services Workers

LOCATING OCCUPATIONAL INFORMATION RELATED TO YOUR MAJOR

Students may find occupations in a Field of Study in which they have a work interest. They may wish to conduct research to find specific information about an occupation. Good sources for occupational information are public libraries, high school and college career resource centers, One-Stop Career Centers, America's InfoNet (*www.acinet.org*) and O*Net (*www.online.onetcenter.org*), the occupational information Network.

Recommended books for occupations and college entry research:

Occupational Outlook Handbook, 2014–2024 Edition,
U.S. Bureau of Labor Statistics, Postal Square Building
2 Massachusetts Avenue, NE, Washington, DC 20212-0001
www.bls.gov

A Guide to the College Admission Process,
National Association for College Admissions Counseling,
1050 North Highland Street, Suite 400, Arlington, VA 22201
www.nacacnet.org

Federal Student Aid Information Center,
An Office of the U.S. Department of Education, 400 Maryland Avenue, SW, Washington, DC 20202
www.fafsa.ed.gov

CHOOSING A COLLEGE

A student's choice of institution may depend on individual needs and talents. A person's career goals, career plans, and choice of college major are very important criteria in choosing a college. A student's choice may be limited by financial or other considerations. However, if at all possible, students should give high priority to their career plans and choice of a college major when choosing a college that best matches their career plans. Students' choice of their college major may influence their final college choice.

Some majors are rare and specialized. Special attention must be given to those majors that are fairly rare and specialized. Students will be limited in the number of colleges from which to choose. There are more than 1800 four-year colleges in the United States; only 78 offer aerospace engineering; 42 offer landscape architecture; 81 offer astronomy; 24 offer petroleum engineering; 8 offer statistics; 8 offer business statistics; 26 offer oceanography; 59 offer pharmacy; and 115 offer occupational therapy majors. This is a partial listing. A student who chooses a specialized major may find it necessary to travel a distance to find a college offering that major. School career centers and public libraries may carry listings of colleges that offer the major of the student's choice.

The most widely offered baccalaureate-level majors are found in four-year colleges. No college, not even the largest university, offers every major; some offer relatively few. Students will want to attend a college that offers several of the majors they are considering. Students can keep their choice of major open by selecting a university or college that offers a wide range of majors. The most common majors are found in the Art, Business, Computer and Information Science, Education, Engineering, Health, Humanities, and the Social and Behavioral Science fields of study.

MAKING THE FINAL DECISION

Making important decisions and setting long-range goals is never an easy task. Making a decision on what to study in college for four or more years, and how this will fit into students' lifestyles and career goals is very important and very personal. With the soaring costs of education and the increasing complexity of the job market, students cannot afford the luxury of trial and error in preparing for a career that requires college training; entering college without a career or major in mind can add time and expense to the entire journey. Good decision-making calls for awareness of one's needs and the matching of those needs with a wide variety of alternate choices. It is to this end that sufficient information has been explored for making a final decision.

In making a final decision, students must take a broad view of the fourteen Fields of Study. They should look carefully at all career and major options within the fourteen fields. Students should not limit themselves to a career or major that has been recommended to them by family or friends. The final decision should be the student's, along with the responsibility to reach their goals. In the final analysis, students will have to look at themselves. As Plato once said, "Know thyself, and to thine own self be true."

- **Assess work interests.** Identify work-related interests. Discover the type of work activities and occupations that match work interests. Identify and learn about the most relevant broad interest areas. Use interest results to explore the world of work.
- **Assess work values.** Pinpoint what is important in a job. Identify occupations that provide satisfaction based on the similarity among work values, conditions of work, and the characteristics of an occupation.
- **Assess work abilities.** Identify user ability strength, parts of work that the user likes to do, parts of work that the user finds important, and training needs of the user.

The more students know about their interests, work values, abilities, and career goals, the better their decisions will be. In the final analysis, good decision-making by students is based on knowing oneself and being flexible enough to sense whether they are on the right track, and to alter decisions when they are not in their best interest. No matter what major is chosen, students must keep in ming that intellectual flexibility is the skill that enables them to work productively when the knowledge they have mastered is challenged or replaced by new ideas.

We wish all students well in their college studies and in the career path that they have chosen.

Robert Kauk and Francis Ferry

Occupational information was gathered from *O*Net,* U.S. Department of Labor.

INDEX OF COLLEGE MAJORS

This section of *Profiles of American Colleges* will help you quickly determine which schools offer the major in which you are interested, the in-state tuition, room and board costs, and the Selector Rating. The colleges are listed alphabetically and the first column indicates the state where each is located. These data reflect the 2016-2017 academic year. You will be able to compare schools offering those majors that interest you the most and see what their in-state costs and Selector Ratings are, before reading the Profiles in the main section of the book (see page 253 for Selector Rating details). You may also discover some new schools or majors that interset you.

ACCOUNTING

School	ST	$IS	SR
Abilene Christian Univ	TX	41,800	C+
Adams State Univ	CO	17,703	LC
Adelphi Univ	NY	48,244	C
Adrian College	MI	42,400	C
Alabama A&M Univ	AL	18,796	C
Alabama State Univ	AL	14,142	NC
Albany State Univ	GA	19,462	C
Albertus Magnus College	CT	43,258	LC
Albion College	MI	52,650	C
Albright College	PA	46,660	C
Alcorn State Univ	MS	15,854	C
Alderson Broaddus Univ	WV	26,149	C
Alfred Univ	NY	42,296	C+
Alma College	MI	47,548	C
Alvernia Univ	PA	43,900	C
Alverno College	WI	33,294	LC
American International College	MA	46,300	LC
Anderson Univ	IN	38,200	C
Andrews Univ	MI	28,030	C+
Angelo State Univ	TX	15,263	NC
Appalachian State Univ	NC	14,416	VC
Aquinas College - Mich	MI	38,876	HC
Arcadia Univ	PA	33,570	C+
Arizona State Univ at the Tempe Campus	AZ	21,756	VC
Arizona State Univ at the West Campus	AZ	20,640	C
Arkansas Baptist College	AR	20,280	NC
Arkansas State Univ	AR	16,190	C
Arkansas Tech Univ	AR	15,484	C
Asbury Univ	KY	35,180	C+
Ashford Univ	CA	10,480	C
Ashland Univ	OH	21,440	C
Assumption College	MA	47,920	C+
Atlantic Union College	MA	27,228	C
Auburn Univ	AL	23,594	VC+
Auburn Univ at Montgomery	AL	15,290	C
Augsburg College	MN	43,929	C
Augusta Univ	GA	4,632	C
Augustana College	IL	49,658	VC
Augustana Univ	SD	38,424	VC
Aurora Univ	IL	33,970	C
Austin Peay State Univ	TN	16,397	C
Averett Univ	VA	40,970	LC
Avila Univ	MO	35,480	C
Azusa Pacific Univ	CA	43,972	C
Baker College of Flint	MI	13,880	NC
Baker Univ	KS	33,350	C+
Baldwin Wallace Univ	OH	41,106	C
Ball State Univ	IN	19,590	C
Barry Univ	FL	37,830	C
Barton College	NC	38,686	LC
Bay Path Univ	MA	45,349	C
Bayamon Central Univ	PR	12,490	
Baylor Univ	TX	53,760	HC
Belhaven Univ	MS	31,016	C
Bellarmine Univ	KY	51,220	C
Bellevue Univ	NE	20,300	NC
Belmont Abbey College	NC	48,156	C
Belmont Univ	TN	40,970	VC
Bemidji State Univ	MN	16,056	VC
Benedict College	SC	28,238	NC
Benedictine College	KS	36,200	VC
Benedictine Univ	IL	38,300	C
Bennett College	NC	27,302	NC
Bentley Univ	MA	60,890	HC
Berkeley College/New Jersey	NJ	38,082	LC
Berkeley College/New York City Campus	NY	23,350	LC
Berkeley College/White Plains Campus	NY	35,100	LC
Berry College	GA	45,286	C+
Bethany College	KS	46,100	NC
Bethany College	WV	36,300	NC
Bethel College	IN	35,860	C
Bethel Univ	MN	45,270	VC
Bethune-Cookman Univ	FL	22,970	C
Biola Univ	CA	46,402	C+
Birmingham-Southern College	AL	44,478	VC
Black Hills State Univ	SD	15,899	C
Blackburn College	IL	28,526	LC
Bloomfield College	NJ	39,100	LC
Bloomsburg Univ of Pennsylvania	PA	19,066	LC
Bluefield State College	WV	5,832	LC
Bluffton Univ	OH	40,950	C
Boise State Univ	ID	14,860	C
Boston College	MA	65,737	MC
Bowling Green State Univ	OH	19,747	C
Brenau Univ - Women's College	GA	37,876	LC
Brescia Univ	KY	29,890	VC+
Brewton-Parker College	GA	23,490	C
Briar Cliff Univ	IA	36,956	C
Bridgewater State Univ	MA	21,810	C
Brigham Young Univ	UT	12,748	HC
Brigham Young Univ/Hawaii	HI	11,290	C
Bryant Univ	RI	55,646	VC
Bucknell Univ	PA	64,616	MC
Buena Vista Univ	IA	41,514	C
Butler Univ	IN	51,352	VC
Cabrini Univ	PA	42,591	LC
Cairn Univ	PA	36,296	C
Caldwell Univ	NJ	42,165	NC
Calif Baptist Univ	CA	41,392	C
Calif Lutheran Univ	CA	52,853	C
Calif State Polytechnic Univ, Pomona	CA	21,541	C
Cal State, East Bay	CA	19,413	C
Cal State, Fresno	CA	16,902	LC
Cal State, Long Beach	CA	18,850	C
Cal State, Northridge	CA	16,859	LC
Cal State, Sacramento	CA	20,332	C
Cal State, San Bernardino	CA	12,000	C
Calif Univ of Pennsylvania	PA	14,217	LC
Calumet College of St. Joseph	IN	22,735	C
Calvin College	MI	41,570	VC+
Cameron Univ	OK	11,072	NC
Campbellsville Univ	KY	32,492	C
Canisius College	NY	47,537	C
Capital Univ	OH	42,982	C
Cardinal Stritch Univ	WI	36,462	C
Caribbean Univ	PR	15,471	
Carlow Univ	PA	38,549	LC
Carroll College	MT	39,972	C+
Carroll Univ	WI	38,100	C+
Carson-Newman Univ	TN	34,160	C
Carthage College	WI	48,835	C
Case Western Reserve Univ	OH	60,304	MC
Catawba College	NC	39,820	C
Cedar Crest College	PA	46,715	C
Cedarville Univ	OH	34,990	VC
Centenary College	NJ	43,602	C
Central College	IA	44,592	C
Central Conn State Univ	CT	21,203	C
Central Methodist Univ	MO	36,830	VC
Central Mich Univ	MI	20,330	C
Central State Univ	OH	18,564	C
Central Washington Univ	WA	16,803	C
Chaminade Univ of Honolulu	HI	36,000	C
Champlain College	VT	53,132	C+
Chapman Univ	CA	63,078	VC+
Chatham Univ	PA	46,517	C
Chestnut Hill College	PA	43,410	C
Cheyney Univ of Pennsylvania	PA	20,896	LC
Chicago State Univ	IL	20,144	C
Christian Brothers Univ	TN	31,670	VC
Christopher Newport Univ	VA	23,968	VC+
CUNY/Baruch College	NY	21,609	HC
CUNY/Brooklyn College	NY	5,884	C+
CUNY/College of Staten Island	NY	17,840	NC
CUNY/Hunter College	NY	31,098	VC
CUNY/Lehman College	NY	5,778	HC+
CUNY/Meger Evers College	NY	6,680	NC
CUNY/Queens College	NY	27,896	C
CUNY/York College	NY	6,747	LC
City Univ of Seattle	WA	24,340	NC
Claremont McKenna College	CA	67,185	MC
Clarion Univ of Pennsylvania	PA	21,608	LC
Clark Atlanta Univ	GA	31,019	LC
Clarke Univ	IA	38,940	C
Clayton State Univ	GA	19,735	C
Clemson Univ	SC		HC
Cleveland State Univ	OH	22,196	C
Coastal Carolina Univ	SC	19,766	C
Coe College	IA	51,570	VC
Colby-Sawyer College	NH	50,790	C
College of Charleston	SC	22,699	C
College of St. Benedict	MN	52,806	C
College of St Joseph	VT	32,400	LC
College of St. Scholastica	MN	44,640	C
College of the Holy Cross	MA	62,165	MC
College of the Ozarks	MO	7,230	C
College of William & Mary	VA		MC
Colo Christian Univ	CO	39,940	VC
Colo Mesa Univ	CO	18,955	LC
Colo State Univ	CO	22,162	VC
Colo State Univ-Pueblo	CO	18,234	C
Columbia College	SC	36,550	C
Columbia College - Missouri	MO	27,803	C
Columbus State Univ	GA	14,336	LC
Concord Univ	WV	14,954	C
Concordia College - Moorhead	MN	51,088	C+
Concordia College - New York	NY	39,035	LC
Concordia Univ Nebr	NE	36,280	VC
Concordia Univ St. Paul	MN	29,050	C
Concordia Univ Texas	TX	40,210	C
Concordia Univ Wisc	WI	35,910	C
Concordia Univ, Ann Arbor	MI	35,945	VC
Concordia Univ, Chicago	IL	39,694	C
Converse College	SC	26,495	C
Coppin State Univ	MD	17,041	VC
Corban Univ	OR	40,306	C
Creighton Univ	NE	48,206	VC+
Culver-Stockton College	MO	33,525	C
Cumberland Univ	TN	27,710	C
Curry College	MA	51,815	C
Daemen College	NY	38,045	C
Dakota Wesleyan Univ	SD	32,850	C
Dallas Baptist Univ	TX	33,713	C
Daniel Webster College	NH	26,984	C
Davenport Univ	MI	25,896	LC
Davis & Elkins College	WV	38,242	LC
Defiance College	OH	41,630	C
Delaware State Univ	DE	19,376	NC
Delaware Valley Univ	PA	49,796	C
Delta State Univ	MS	13,176	C
DePaul Univ	IL	47,623	VC
DeSales Univ	PA	43,970	C
Dickinson State Univ	ND	12,372	LC
Dillard Univ	LA	20,940	VC
Doane Univ	NE	39,184	VC
Dominican College	NY	31,270	LC
Dominican Univ	IL	41,222	C
Dordt College	IA	37,860	C+
Drake Univ	IA	45,056	HC
Drexel Univ	PA	65,432	VC+
Drury Univ	MO	33,791	VC
Duquesne Univ	PA	46,822	VC
D'Youville College	NY	36,780	C
East Carolina Univ	NC	16,937	C
East Central Univ	OK	13,056	C
East Tenn State Univ	TN	13,994	C
Eastern Conn State Univ	CT	23,059	C
Eastern Illinois Univ	IL	21,126	C
Eastern Kentucky Univ	KY	16,908	C
Eastern Mennonite Univ	VA	42,550	C
Eastern Mich Univ	MI	19,761	C
Eastern Nazarene College	MA	39,955	C
Eastern New Mexico Univ	NM	14,416	C
Eastern Oregon Univ	OR	17,715	C
Eastern Univ	PA	39,540	C
Eastern Washington Univ	WA	25,572	LC
Edgewood College	WI	35,950	C
Edward Waters College	FL	20,607	NC
Elizabeth City State Univ	NC	14,745	C
Elizabethtown College	PA	54,050	C
Elizabethtown College School of Continuing and Professional Studies	PA	18,900	C
Elmhurst College	IL	45,428	C
Elmira College	NY	53,900	C
Elms College	MA	45,646	VC
Elon Univ	NC	44,599	VC+
Emmanuel College	MA	52,110	C+
Emory Univ	GA	60,786	MC
Emporia State Univ	KS	14,570	C
Endicott College	MA	44,604	VC+
Eureka College	IL	30,220	C
Evangel Univ	MO	28,898	C
Excelsior College	NY	14,080	SP
Fairfield Univ	CT	59,860	VC+
Fairleigh Dickinson Univ/ College at Florham	NJ	52,062	C
Fairleigh Dickinson Univ/ Metropolitan Campus	NJ	40,254	C
Fairmont State Univ	WV	15,726	C
Faulkner Univ	AL	26,410	C
Fayetteville State Univ	NC	17,756	C
Felician Univ	NJ	45,370	LC
Ferris State Univ	MI	21,445	C
Ferrum College	VA	39,650	C
Fitchburg State Univ	MA	21,819	C
Flagler College	FL	27,620	C
Florida A&M Univ	FL	15,361	C
Florida Atlantic Univ	FL	17,339	C
Florida Gulf Coast Univ	FL	9,682	C
Florida Inst of Technology	FL	53,306	VC
Florida International Univ	FL	19,854	C+
Florida Memorial Univ	FL	22,270	LC
Florida State Univ	FL	16,771	HC
Fontbonne Univ	MO	33,717	C
Fordham Univ	NY	65,918	MC
Fort Hays State Univ	KS	12,131	C
Fort Lewis College	CO	18,980	C
Fort Valley State Univ	GA	17,988	VC
Framingham State Univ	MA	20,584	C
Francis Marion Univ	SC	16,464	LC
Franciscan Univ of Steubenville	OH	33,980	VC
Franklin College	IN	39,380	C
Franklin Pierce Univ	NH	46,750	C
Franklin Univ	OH	56,262	SP
Freed-Hardeman Univ	TN	29,450	C
Fresno Pacific Univ	CA	37,370	C
Friends Univ	KS	34,455	C
Frostburg State Univ	MD	17,280	LC
Furman Univ	SC	58,092	VC+
Gallaudet Univ	DC	29,118	LC
Gannon Univ	PA	42,032	C
Gardner-Webb Univ	NC	39,200	C+
Geneva College	PA	35,450	C
George Fox Univ	OR	42,938	C
George Mason Univ	VA	15,724	VC
George Washington Univ	DC	62,835	MC
Georgetown College	KY	41,440	C
Georgetown Univ	DC	65,926	MC
Georgia College & State Univ	GA	21,148	C+
Georgia Southern Univ	GA	16,596	C
Georgia Southwestern State Univ	GA	13,870	C
Georgia State Univ	GA	24,332	VC
Georgian Court Univ	NJ	42,426	LC
Glenville State College	WV	17,386	NC
Golden Gate Univ	CA	32,110	C
Goldey-Beacom College	DE	31,750	C
Gonzaga Univ	WA	50,888	HC
Gordon College	MA	46,472	C+
Goshen College	IN	42,500	C
Grace College and Seminary	IN	31,524	C
Graceland Univ	IA	35,290	C
Grambling State Univ	LA	15,701	C
Grand Canyon Univ	AZ	16,950	VC
Grand Rapids Theological Seminary/Cornerstone Univ	MI	33,338	C
Grand Valley State Univ	MI	22,250	C+
Grand View Univ	IA	32,302	C
Greensboro College	NC	42,400	LC
Greenville College	IL	27,012	C
Grove City College	PA	25,692	VC
Guilford College	NC	44,090	C
Gustavus Adolphus College	MN	52,433	HC
Gwynedd Mercy Univ	PA	43,780	LC
Hamline Univ	MN	45,678	VC
Hampton Univ	VA	34,926	LC
Hannibal-LaGrange Univ	MO	29,815	C
Harding Univ	AR	25,421	C
Hardin-Simmons Univ	TX	33,966	C
Harris-Stowe State Univ	MO	14,360	NC
Hartwick College	NY	51,270	C
Hastings College	NE	35,380	C+
Hawaii Pacific Univ	HI	33,420	C
Heidelberg Univ	OH	39,200	C
Henderson State Univ	AR	15,516	LC
Hendrix College	AR	54,020	VC+
Heritage Univ	WA	19,825	NC
Hilbert College	NY	30,850	C
Hillsdale College	MI	35,722	MC
Hiram College	OH	43,230	C
Hodges Univ	FL	19,080	LC
Hofstra Univ	NY	55,960	C+
Holy Family Univ	PA	43,326	LC
Hood College	MD	54,840	C
Hope College	MI	39,940	VC
Houghton College	NY	39,090	C
Houston Baptist Univ	TX	36,450	C
Howard Payne Univ	TX	34,320	C
Howard Univ	DC	37,616	C+
Humphreys College	CA	27,790	C
Huntingdon College	AL	34,900	C
Huntington Univ	IN	33,996	C
Husson Univ	ME	25,720	LC
Idaho State Univ	ID	13,619	NC
Illinois College	IL	40,850	VC
Illinois State Univ	IL	23,418	VC
Illinois Wesleyan Univ	IL	56,430	VC+
Indiana Inst of Technology	IN	34,240	LC
Indiana State Univ	IN	23,223	LC
Indiana Univ Bloomington	IN	20,429	VC
Indiana Univ Northwest	IN	7,072	C
Indiana Univ of Pennsylvania	PA	23,614	LC

ST = STATE $IS = IN-STATE COSTS   SR = SELECTOR RATING

School	ST	$IS	SR
Indiana Univ-Purdue Univ Fort Wayne	IN	17,553	C
Indiana Wesleyan Univ	IN	33,674	C
Inter-American Univ of PR Ponce	PR	19,549	
Inter-American Univ of PR-Aguadilla Campus	PR	21,657	
Inter-American Univ of PR-Arecibo Campus	PR	18,245	
Inter-American Univ of PR-Barranquitas	PR	18,336	
Inter-American Univ of PR-Bayamon	PR	18,785	
Inter-American Univ of PR-Fajardo Campus	PR	18,336	
Inter-American Univ of PR-Metropolitan Campus	PR	20,045	
Inter-American Univ of PR-San Germán	PR	20,042	
Iona College	NY	50,984	C
Iowa State Univ	IA	17,570	C
Iowa Wesleyan Univ	IA	39,200	C
Ithaca College	NY	56,766	VC
Jackson State Univ	MS	15,879	LC
Jacksonville State Univ	AL	14,628	LC
Jacksonville Univ	FL	46,230	C
James Madison Univ	VA	19,084	VC
John Brown Univ	AR	33,132	VC
John Carroll Univ	OH	49,740	C+
Johnson & Wales Univ/Charlotte Campus	NC	43,988	C
Johnson & Wales Univ/North Miami Campus	FL	42,707	C
Johnson & Wales Univ/Providence Campus	RI	42,248	C
Judson Univ	IL	37,700	C
Juniata College	PA	53,760	VC
Kansas State Univ	KS	17,780	VC
Kansas Wesleyan Univ	KS	36,600	C
Kean Univ	NJ	24,650	C
Keiser Univ	FL	35,010	LC
Kennesaw State Univ	GA	19,592	VC
Kent State Univ	OH	20,732	C
Kentucky Wesleyan College	KY	32,080	C
Keuka College	NY	39,762	C
Keystone College	PA	28,680	LC
King's College	PA	46,858	C
Kutztown Univ of Pennsylvania	PA	19,056	LC
La Roche College	PA	37,924	LC
La Salle Univ	PA	55,790	C
La Sierra Univ	CA	39,690	VC
LaGrange College	GA	39,930	C
Lake Erie College	OH	38,914	LC
Lakeland Univ	WI	35,130	C
Lamar Univ	TX	18,014	LC
Langston Univ	OK	14,314	C
Lasell College	MA	47,500	C
Le Moyne College	NY	46,000	C
Lebanon Valley College	PA	51,530	C
Lee Univ	TN	22,045	C
Lehigh Univ	PA	61,010	MC
LeMoyne-Owen College	TN	16,980	C
Lenoir-Rhyne Univ	NC	43,200	C
LeTourneau Univ	TX	38,250	VC
Lewis Univ	IL	40,370	C
Liberty Univ	VA	19,101	C
Limestone College	SC	32,100	C
Lincoln Memorial Univ	TN	28,070	C
Lincoln Univ	MO	13,602	NC
Lindenwood Univ	MO	25,132	C
Lindsey Wilson College	KY	32,882	C
Linfield College	OR	52,010	C
Lipscomb Univ	TN	41,296	VC
LIU Brooklyn	NY	49,682	C
LIU Post	NY	49,682	C
Loras College	IA	39,222	C
Louisiana State Univ and A&M College	LA	18,677	VC
Louisiana State Univ in Shreveport	LA	6,902	C
Louisiana Tech Univ	LA	11,422	VC
Lourdes Univ	OH	29,520	NC
Loyola Marymount Univ	CA	58,038	HC
Loyola Univ Chicago	IL	55,802	VC
Loyola Univ Maryland	MD	60,300	VC
Loyola Univ New Orleans	LA	51,708	VC+
Lubbock Christian Univ	TX	28,426	C
Luther College	IA	48,540	C+
Lycoming College	PA	48,580	C
Lynchburg College	VA	46,740	C
Lyndon State College	VT	20,714	C
Lyon College	AR	34,730	C+
MacMurray College	IL	33,620	C
Madonna Univ	MI	29,050	C
Malone Univ	OH	38,448	C
Manchester Univ	IN	40,422	C
Manhattan College	NY	51,750	C+
Manhattanville College	NY	51,440	C+
Marian Univ	IN	41,220	C
Marian Univ	WI	32,420	LC
Marietta College	OH	46,190	C
Marist College	NY	49,860	VC
Marquette Univ	WI	48,390	VC+
Mars Hill Univ	NC	42,688	C
Marshall Univ	WV	17,242	C
Martin Univ	IN	20,264	LC
Marymount Manhattan College	NY	46,280	VC
Maryville Univ of St. Louis	MO	38,046	VC+
Marywood Univ	PA	46,900	C
Mass College of Liberal Arts	MA	20,128	C
McKendree Univ	IL	37,940	C+
McMurry Univ	TX	34,259	LC
McNeese State Univ	LA	7,838	C
Menlo College	CA	51,380	LC
Mercer Univ	GA	45,348	VC
Mercy College	NY	31,776	C
Mercyhurst Univ	PA	47,420	C
Meredith College	NC	45,297	C
Merrimack College	MA	52,770	C
Messiah College	PA	43,100	C+
Methodist Univ	NC	43,600	C
Metropolitan State Univ	MN	7,566	C
Metropolitan State Univ of Denver	CO	29,889	LC
Miami Univ	OH	27,190	HC+
Mich State Univ	MI	23,898	VC+
Mich Tech Univ	MI	24,739	VC+
MidAmerica Nazarene Univ	KS	35,550	C
Middle Tenn State Univ	TN	8,650	C
Midland Univ	NE	37,468	
Midwestern State Univ	TX	17,572	C
Miles College	AL	18,646	NC
Millersville Univ of Pennsylvania	PA	23,782	C
Milligan College	TN	38,150	C
Millikin Univ	IL	42,158	C
Millsaps College	MS	50,080	C+
Minn State Univ, Mankato	MN	15,616	C
Minn State Univ, Moorhead	MN	15,941	C
Minot State Univ	ND	12,732	C
Misericordia Univ	PA	43,840	C
Miss College	MS	25,850	C
Miss State Univ	MS	11,454	C+
Miss Univ for Women	MS	17,065	C
Miss Valley State Univ	MS	13,233	LC
Missouri Baptist Univ	MO	35,594	C
Missouri Southern State Univ	MO	12,499	C
Missouri State Univ	MO	15,190	C+
Missouri Valley College	MO	28,150	C
Missouri Western State Univ	MO	16,741	
Molloy College	NY	40,440	C
Monmouth College	IL	42,260	C
Monmouth Univ	NJ	46,234	C
Monroe College	NY	23,660	C
Montclair State Univ	NJ	26,210	LC
Moravian College	PA	53,117	
Morehead State Univ	KY	17,422	C
Morgan State Univ	MD	17,190	LC
Mount Aloysius College	PA	29,976	C
Mount Marty College	SD	32,972	C
Mount Mary Univ	WI	34,650	LC
Mount Mercy Univ	IA	36,826	C
Mount St. Mary College	NY	42,061	C
Mount St. Joseph Univ	OH	33,880	C
Mount St. Mary's Univ	MD	51,610	C
Mount Vernon Nazarene Univ	OH	34,500	C
Muhlenberg College	PA	56,645	VC+
Murray State Univ	KY	16,998	C
Muskingum Univ	OH	35,966	C
National Univ	CA	14,730	LC
Nazareth College	NY	45,574	C
Nebr Wesleyan Univ	NE	38,140	C+
Neumann Univ	PA	40,678	LC
New Jersey City Univ	NJ	21,456	LC
New Mexico Highlands Univ	NM	11,904	NC
New Mexico State Univ	NM	14,050	C
New York Inst of Technology	NY	48,730	C
New York Univ	NY	65,860	MC
Newbury College	MA	46,950	C
Newman Univ	KS	35,390	C
Niagara Univ	NY	41,010	C
Nicholls State Univ	LA	10,534	C
Nichols College	MA	46,800	LC
Norfolk State Univ	VA	25,702	LC
N Car A&T State Univ	NC	13,365	LC
N Car Central Univ	NC	9,000	C
N Car State Univ	NC	19,515	HC+
N Car Wesleyan College	NC	39,200	C
North Central College	IL	48,712	VC
N Dak State Univ	ND	16,245	C
North Greenville Univ	SC	25,930	C+
North Park Univ	IL	35,860	C
Northeastern Illinois Univ	IL	12,529	LC
Northeastern State Univ	OK	8,615	VC
Northeastern Univ	MA	62,703	MC
Northern Arizona Univ	AZ	20,246	VC
Northern Illinois Univ	IL	20,176	C
Northern Kentucky Univ	KY	16,486	C
Northern Mich Univ	MI	19,604	C
Northern State Univ	SD	14,505	C
Northwest Christian Univ	OR	36,580	C
Northwest Missouri State Univ	MO	17,737	C
Northwest Nazarene Univ	ID	36,000	C
Northwestern College of Iowa	IA	38,400	C+
Northwestern Okla State Univ	OK	13,072	NC
Northwood Univ - Mich	MI	35,010	LC
Norwich Univ	VT	28,212	C
Notre Dame College	OH	37,150	VC
Notre Dame de Namur Univ	CA	46,526	LC
Notre Dame of Maryland Univ	MD	46,465	VC
Nova Southeastern Univ	FL	38,534	C+
Nyack College	NY	34,050	NC
Oakland City Univ	IN	33,360	NC
Oakland Univ	MI	20,763	C
Oakwood Univ	AL	43,758	C
Oglethorpe Univ	GA	44,200	C+
Ohio Dominican Univ	OH	41,340	C+
Ohio Northern Univ	OH	44,050	VC
Ohio State Univ at Columbus	OH	21,703	HC+
Ohio Univ	OH	22,924	C
Ohio Valley Univ	WV	29,480	C
Ohio Wesleyan Univ	OH	49,460	VC
Okla Baptist Univ	OK	32,320	C
Okla Christian Univ	OK	27,650	VC
Okla City Univ	OK	40,476	VC
Okla Panhandle State Univ	OK	6,152	NC
Okla State Univ	OK	17,180	VC
Okla Wesleyan Univ	OK	33,206	C
Old Dominion Univ	VA	20,910	C
Olivet College	MI	36,110	LC
Olivet Nazarene Univ	IL	41,840	C
Oral Roberts Univ	OK	34,316	C
Oregon State Univ	OR	22,519	VC
Ottawa Univ	KS	36,074	VC
Otterbein Univ	OH	41,630	C
Ouachita Baptist Univ	AR	32,320	C
Our Lady of the Lake Univ	TX	35,012	LC
Pace Univ	NY	58,248	C
Park Univ	MO	20,329	C
Paul Quinn College	TX	25,350	LC
Peirce College	PA	16,780	NC
Penn State Erie/The Behrend College	PA	16,256	C
Pennsylvania College of Technology	PA	27,333	NC
Pennsylvania State Univ - Univ Park	PA	29,760	HC
Pepperdine Univ	CA	74,460	HC+
Peru State College	NE	14,768	NC
Pfeiffer Univ	NC	39,695	LC
Philadelphia Univ	PA	50,370	C
Pittsburg State Univ	KS	13,880	NC
Plymouth State Univ	NH	23,180	LC
Point Loma Nazarene Univ	CA	43,450	C
Point Park Univ	PA	41,270	C
Pontifical Catholic Univ of PR	PR	10,534	
Portland State Univ	OR	19,443	C
Post Univ	CT	41,150	C
Prairie View A&M Univ	TX	15,205	LC
Providence College	RI	60,760	VC
Purdue Univ/Northwest	IN	15,038	C
Purdue Univ/West Lafayette	IN	20,032	MC
Queens Univ of Charlotte	NC	39,543	C
Quincy Univ	IL	36,998	C
Quinnipiac Univ	CT	59,110	C
Radford Univ	VA	19,027	LC
Ramapo College of New Jersey	NJ	25,338	C
Randolph-Macon College	VA	49,910	C
Regis Univ	CO	44,520	C
Rhode Island College	RI	17,694	LC
Rider Univ	NJ	54,050	C
Robert Morris Univ	PA	37,834	C
Roberts Wesleyan College	NY	38,306	C
Rochester College	MI	28,574	LC
Rochester Inst of Technology	NY	50,842	HC
Rockford Univ	IL	36,030	C
Rocky Mountain College	MT	34,270	C
Roger Williams Univ	RI	46,296	C+
Roosevelt Univ	IL	40,651	VC
Rosemont College	PA	30,980	C
Rowan Univ	NJ	24,491	VC+
Rutgers Univ - Camden	NJ	26,146	C
Rutgers Univ - New Brunswick	NJ	26,632	HC
Rutgers Univ - Newark	NJ	27,288	C
Sacred Heart Univ	CT	52,750	C
Saginaw Valley State Univ	MI	18,530	C
St. Anselm College	NH	52,560	C+
St. Augustine's Univ	NC	26,048	C
St. Francis Univ	PA	42,268	NC
St. John's Univ	MN	51,624	C
St. Joseph's Univ	PA	57,544	VC+
St. Leo Univ	FL	31,650	C
St. Louis Univ	MO	49,866	HC
St. Martin's Univ	WA	45,056	C
St. Mary-of-the-Woods College	IN	39,632	LC
St. Mary's College	IN	50,600	C
St. Mary's College of Calif	CA	57,420	C
St. Mary's Univ of Minn	MN	41,210	VC
St. Michael's College	VT	51,725	VC+
St. Peter's Univ	NJ	49,192	C
St. Vincent College	PA	44,626	C
St. Xavier Univ	IL	43,310	C
Salem College	NC	37,694	HC
Salem State Univ	MA	17,303	LC
Salisbury Univ	MD	20,714	VC
Salve Regina Univ	RI	51,470	C
Sam Houston State Univ	TX	18,792	C
Samford Univ	AL	39,232	VC
San Diego State Univ	CA	21,896	C+
San Francisco State Univ	CA	18,514	LC
San Jose State Univ	CA	21,540	C
Savannah State Univ	GA	15,631	C
Schreiner Univ	TX	34,626	LC
Seattle Pacific Univ	WA	47,439	C+
Seattle Univ	WA	50,811	VC+
Seton Hall Univ	NJ	55,514	C
Seton Hill Univ	PA	46,972	C
Shaw Univ	NC	24,638	C
Shepherd Univ, West Virginia	WV	17,224	C
Shippensburg Univ of Pennsylvania	PA	23,208	C
Shorter Univ	GA	31,130	LC
Siena College	NY	48,916	C+
Siena Heights Univ	MI	32,040	C
Silver Lake College of the Holy Family	WI	36,290	LC
Simpson College	IA	43,839	VC
Simpson Univ	CA	33,700	C
Slippery Rock Univ of Pennsylvania	PA	10,360	C
S Car State Univ	SC	20,805	LC
Southeast Missouri State Univ	MO	15,498	C
Southeastern Louisiana Univ	LA	16,237	C
Southeastern Okla State Univ	OK	11,875	C
Southeastern Univ	FL	31,765	C
Southern Adventist Univ	TN	27,600	C
Southern Arkansas Univ	AR	21,532	C
Southern Conn State Univ	CT	21,924	LC
Southern Illinois Univ Carbondale	IL	23,667	C
Southern Illinois Univ Edwardsville	IL	22,643	C
Southern Methodist Univ	TX	66,483	MC
Southern Nazarene Univ	OK	32,798	NC
Southern New Hampshire Univ	NH	43,198	C
Southern Oregon Univ	OR	19,117	C
Southern Univ and A&M College	LA	16,074	LC+
Southern Univ at New Orleans	LA	8,014	LC
Southwest Baptist Univ	MO	29,900	LC
Southwest Minn State Univ	MN	17,783	C
Southwestern College	KS	31,531	C
Southwestern Okla State Univ	OK	11,790	C
Spalding Univ	KY	31,938	SP
Spring Arbor Univ	MI	36,000	C
Spring Hill College	AL	48,488	C
St. Bonaventure Univ	NY	44,237	C
St. Catherine Univ	MN	45,630	VC
St. Cloud State Univ	MN	10,600	C
St. Edward's Univ	TX	53,100	VC
St. Francis College	NY	38,800	LC
St. John Fisher College	NY	43,620	C
St. John's Univ	NY	55,850	C
St. Joseph's College, New York/Brooklyn Campus	NY	25,114	LC
St. Joseph's College, New York/Long Island Campus	NY	25,124	C
St. Mary's Univ	TX	37,500	C
St. Norbert College	WI	44,525	VC
St. Thomas Aquinas College	NY	42,200	C
St. Thomas Univ	FL	36,360	LC
SUNY / Empire State College	NY	9,145	SP
SUNY / SUNY College at Old Westbury	NY	16,860	C
SUNY / SUNY Fredonia	NY	20,818	C
SUNY / SUNY Oneonta	NY	19,712	C+
SUNY / SUNY Plattsburgh	NY	18,814	C
SUNY / Univ at Buffalo	NY	23,122	C+
SUNY at Binghamton	NY	22,861	MC
SUNY at Geneseo	NY	20,440	VC+
SUNY at New Paltz	NY	19,200	C
SUNY at Oswego	NY	21,351	C
SUNY Polytechnic Inst	NY	19,473	VC
SUNY SUNY Albany	NY	22,165	C
Stephen F. Austin State Univ	TX	18,406	LC
Stephens College	MO	38,042	C
Stetson Univ	FL	53,544	VC
Stevenson Univ	MD	72,770	C
Stockton Univ	NJ	25,059	
Stonehill College	MA	55,030	C+
Suffolk Univ	MA	50,308	C
Sul Ross State Univ	TX	15,021	LC
Susquehanna Univ	PA	55,340	VC
Syracuse Univ	NY	60,239	VC
Tabor College	KS	35,870	C
Talladega College	AL	19,215	C
Tarleton State Univ	TX	15,248	LC
Taylor Univ	IN	40,317	C+
Temple Univ	PA	24,392	VC
Tenn State Univ	TN	14,423	C
Tenn Tech Univ	TN	17,050	C
Texas A&M Univ	TX	20,521	VC+
Texas A&M Univ at Commerce	TX	10,496	C
Texas A&M Univ at Corpus Christi	TX	16,851	LC
Texas A&M Univ at Kingsville	TX	7,500	LC
Texas Christian Univ	TX	54,670	HC
Texas Lutheran Univ	TX	38,620	C
Texas Southern Univ	TX	18,212	LC
Texas State Univ	TX	19,350	C
Texas Tech Univ	TX	18,736	C+
Texas Wesleyan Univ	TX	35,134	C
Texas Woman's Univ	TX	15,302	LC
The Catholic Univ of America	DC	56,356	VC
The College at Brockport - SUNY	NY	20,346	C
The College of Idaho	ID	36,415	C
The College of New Jersey	NJ	31,909	HC
The College of St. Rose	NY	43,048	C
The College of Wooster	OH	57,900	VC+
The Lincoln Univ	PA	15,154	NC

ST = STATE $IS = IN-STATE COSTS SR = SELECTOR RATING

School	ST	$IS	SR
The Master's Univ	CA	43,870	C+
The Univ of Akron	OH	21,477	C
The Univ of Tenn at Knoxville	TN	22,112	VC
The Univ of Tenn at Martin	TN	14,876	C
The Univ of Utah	UT	17,924	VC
The Univ of Virginia's College at Wise	VA	18,192	LC
Thiel College	PA	41,590	C
Thomas College	ME	35,268	LC
Thomas Edison State Univ	NJ	6,350	NC
Thomas More College	KY	36,720	C
Tiffin Univ	OH	31,380	C
Touro College	NY	28,950	VC
Towson Univ	MD	17,408	VC
Transylvania Univ	KY	45,690	VC+
Trevecca Nazarene Univ	TN	31,186	C
Trine Univ	IN	41,310	C
Trinity Christian College	IL	35,580	C
Trinity International Univ	IL	31,070	VC
Trinity Univ	TX	52,314	HC+
Troy Univ	AL	16,171	C
Truman State Univ	MO	16,014	HC
Tulane Univ	LA	63,396	HC+
Tuskegee Univ	AL	28,164	C
Union College	KY	32,310	C
Union College	NE	23,270	C
Union Univ	TN	33,970	VC
Universidad del Turabo	PR	17,828	
Universidad Metropolitana	PR	17,828	
Univ of PR, at Arecibo	PR	12,652	
Univ of Alabama	AL	24,320	C+
Univ of Alabama at Birmingham	AL	19,906	C
Univ of Alabama in Huntsville	AL	19,445	VC
Univ of Alaska Anchorage	AK	16,652	NC
Univ of Alaska Fairbanks	AK	16,179	C
Univ of Alaska Southeast	AK	11,493	C
Univ of Arizona	AZ	23,100	C
Univ of Arkansas at Fayetteville	AR	19,152	C+
Univ of Arkansas at Little Rock	AR	18,211	C
Univ of Arkansas at Monticello	AR	13,134	NC
Univ of Arkansas at Pine Bluff	AR	13,541	C
Univ of Bridgeport	CT	44,430	LC
Univ of Calif at Santa Barbara	CA	29,091	HC
Univ of Central Arkansas	AR	14,472	VC
Univ of Central Florida	FL	15,922	VC
Univ of Central Missouri	MO	18,982	C
Univ of Central Okla	OK	13,486	C
Univ of Charleston	WV	35,000	C
Univ of Cincinnati	OH	21,964	VC
Univ of Colo Boulder	CO	24,285	VC+
Univ of Conn	CT	25,538	HC
Univ of Dayton	OH	53,620	C
Univ of Delaware	DE	24,976	VC+
Univ of Denver	CO	58,443	VC+
Univ of Detroit Mercy	MI	48,816	C+
Univ of Dubuque	IA	37,824	C
Univ of Evansville	IN	44,186	VC+
Univ of Findlay	OH	60,139	C
Univ of Florida	FL	16,291	HC+
Univ of Georgia	GA	21,250	HC
Univ of Great Falls	MT	38,524	C
Univ of Hartford	CT	49,776	C
Univ of Hawaii at Manoa	HI	23,221	C
Univ of Holy Cross	LA	21,523	C
Univ of Houston	TX	21,483	VC
Univ of Houston-Downtown	TX	7,241	C
Univ of Idaho	ID	15,348	C
Univ of Illinois at Chicago	IL	25,006	VC
Univ of Illinois at Urbana-Champaign	IL	27,006	HC
Univ of Indianapolis	IN	36,480	C
Univ of Iowa	IA	18,683	VC+
Univ of Jamestown	ND	28,508	C
Univ of Kansas	KS	20,135	C+
Univ of Kentucky	KY	33,306	C
Univ of La Verne	CA	55,600	C
Univ of Louisiana at Lafayette	LA	14,516	C
Univ of Louisiana at Monroe	LA	15,970	C
Univ of Louisville	KY	19,824	C
Univ of Maine	ME	20,792	C
Univ of Maine at Augusta	ME	7,812	C
Univ of Maine at Machias	ME	22,960	C
Univ of Maine at Presque Isle	ME	14,870	C
Univ of Mary	ND	23,180	C
Univ of Mary Hardin-Baylor	TX	33,950	C+
Univ of Maryland/College Park	MD	21,938	HC
Univ of Maryland/Eastern Shore	MD	17,013	C
Univ of Maryland/Univ College	MD	25,966	LC
Univ of Mass Amherst	MA	26,199	VC+
Univ of Mass Dartmouth	MA	25,658	C
Univ of Memphis	TN	18,278	C
Univ of Miami	FL	63,494	MC
Univ of Mich/Dearborn	MI	11,757	VC
Univ of Mich-Flint	MI	17,607	C+
Univ of Minn Crookston	MN	19,739	C
Univ of Minn/Duluth	MN	20,292	C+
Univ of Minn/Twin Cities	MN	23,519	HC+
Univ of Missouri/Columbia	MO	18,201	MC
Univ of Missouri-Kansas City	MO	19,563	VC
Univ of Missouri-St. Louis	MO		C
Univ of Mobile	AL	28,935	C
Univ of Montana	MT	14,105	C
Univ of Montevallo	AL	19,502	C
Univ of Mount Olive	NC	18,426	C
Univ of Mount Union	OH	38,970	C
Univ of Nebr - Kearney	NE	16,546	LC
Univ of Nebr - Lincoln	NE	18,589	VC
Univ of Nebr - Omaha	NE	16,120	C
Univ of Nevada, Las Vegas	NV	17,553	C
Univ of Nevada/Reno	NV	18,010	C
Univ of New Haven	CT	52,190	C
Univ of New Orleans	LA	12,840	C
Univ of North Alabama	AL	15,398	C
Univ of N Car at Asheville	NC	15,723	VC+
Univ of N Car at Charlotte	NC	15,547	C
Univ of N Car at Greensboro	NC	14,690	C
Univ of N Car at Pembroke	NC	14,388	LC
Univ of N Car at Wilmington	NC	14,590	VC
Univ of N Dak	ND	15,373	C
Univ of North Florida	FL	15,996	VC
Univ of North Georgia	GA	17,316	C
Univ of North Texas	TX	19,198	C
Univ of Northwestern - St. Paul	MN	38,160	C
Univ of Notre Dame	IN	64,043	MC
Univ of Okla	OK	18,911	VC
Univ of Oregon	OR	22,972	C
Univ of Pennsylvania	PA	63,526	MC
Univ of Pittsburgh	PA	29,568	HC+
Univ of Pittsburgh at Bradford	PA	22,402	C
Univ of Pittsburgh at Greensburg	PA	23,132	C
Univ of Pittsburgh at Johnstown	PA	22,092	C
Univ of Portland	OR	52,152	VC
Univ of PR, at Bayamon	PR	13,145	
Univ of PR, at Cayey	PR		
Univ of PR, at Humacao	PR	14,000	
Univ of PR, at Mayaguez	PR	13,995	
Univ of PR-Rio Piedras campus	PR	13,327	
Univ of Redlands	CA	60,200	VC
Univ of Rhode Island	RI	24,906	C
Univ of Richmond	VA	60,880	MC
Univ of Rio Grande & Rio Grande Community College	OH	8,750	NC
Univ of St. Francis	IN	37,400	C
Univ of St. Joseph	CT	49,550	C
Univ of St. Mary	KS	34,690	C
Univ of San Diego	CA	58,442	VC+
Univ of San Francisco	CA	58,484	VC
Univ of Scranton	PA	54,962	VC
Univ of Sioux Falls	SD	34,330	C
Univ of South Alabama	AL	16,400	C
Univ of S Car at Columbia	SC	19,725	VC+
Univ of S Car Upstate	SC	18,200	LC
Univ of S Dak	SD	16,109	C
Univ of South Florida/St. Petersburg	FL	15,980	C
Univ of South Florida/Tampa	FL	16,110	VC+
Univ of Southern Calif	CA	66,631	C
Univ of Southern Indiana	IN	16,501	C
Univ of Southern Maine	ME	18,320	C
Univ of Southern Miss	MS	13,170	C
Univ of St. Francis	IL	39,924	C
Univ of St. Thomas - Houston	TX	40,020	VC
Univ of Tampa	FL	36,944	C
Univ of Texas at Arlington	TX	18,026	LC
Univ of Texas at Austin	TX	26,102	HC
Univ of Texas at Dallas	TX	22,830	VC+
Univ of Texas at El Paso	TX	34,452	NC
Univ of Texas at San Antonio	TX	20,157	C
Univ of the Cumberlands	KY	32,000	C
Univ of the District of Columbia	DC	21,044	LC
Univ of the Ozarks	AR	52,176	C
Univ of the Sacred Heart	PR	17,932	
Univ of the Southwest	NM	22,766	C
Univ of Toledo	OH	19,336	NC
Univ of Tulsa	OK	52,625	HC+
Univ of Washington	WA	23,149	VC
Univ of West Alabama	AL	15,516	NC
Univ of West Florida	FL	15,848	C
Univ of West Georgia	GA	16,360	LC
Univ of Wisc-Eau Claire	WI	15,797	VC
Univ of Wisc-Green Bay	WI	15,064	C
Univ of Wisc-La Crosse	WI	15,247	C+
Univ of Wisc-Madison	WI	20,934	MC
Univ of Wisc-Milwaukee	WI	21,496	C
Univ of Wisc-Oshkosh	WI	15,200	C
Univ of Wisc-Parkside	WI	15,193	C
Univ of Wisc-Platteville	WI	14,614	VC
Univ of Wisc-River Falls	WI	14,485	C
Univ of Wisc-Stevens Point	WI	14,043	C
Univ of Wisc-Superior	WI	14,446	C
Univ of Wisc-Whitewater	WI	13,976	C
Univ of Wyoming	WY	15,375	C+
Upper Iowa Univ	IA	34,990	NC
Ursuline College	OH	41,076	LC
Utah State Univ	UT	12,736	C
Utica College	NY	30,430	C
Valparaiso Univ	IN	48,370	C+
Vanguard Univ of Southern Calif	CA	40,740	VC
Villanova Univ	PA	62,523	MC
Virginia Commonwealth Univ	VA	23,049	C
Virginia Polytechnic Inst and State Univ	VA	21,276	HC
Virginia State Univ	VA	19,802	C+
Virginia Union Univ	VA	22,421	C
Viterbo Univ	WI	34,660	C
Voorhees College	SC	19,976	C
Wagner College	NY	55,480	C+
Wake Forest Univ	NC	64,056	MC
Walsh Univ	OH	39,010	C
Warner Univ	FL	28,216	C
Wartburg College	IA	47,840	C
Washburn Univ	KS	15,827	C
Washington & Jefferson College	PA	56,512	VC
Washington Adventist Univ	MD	31,440	LC
Washington and Lee Univ	VA	59,647	MC
Washington State Univ	WA	22,495	C
Washington Univ in St. Louis	MO	65,366	VC
Wayland Baptist Univ	TX	22,356	LC
Wayne State Univ	MI	22,016	C
Waynesburg Univ	PA	32,290	C
Webber International Univ	FL	31,904	C
Weber State Univ	UT	10,721	C
Webster Univ	MO	37,490	C
Wesley College	DE	37,026	LC
West Chester Univ of Pennsylvania	PA	18,456	C
West Liberty Univ	WV	15,512	C
West Texas A&M Univ	TX	13,478	C
West Virginia State Univ	WV	8,378	NC
West Virginia Univ	WV	18,210	C
West Virginia Univ Inst of Technology	WV	16,462	NC
West Virginia Wesleyan College	WV	36,858	C
Western Carolina Univ	NC	13,965	C
Western Conn State Univ	CT	21,254	LC
Western Illinois Univ	IL	20,825	C
Western Kentucky Univ	KY	16,850	C
Western Mich Univ	MI	21,054	C
Western New England Univ	MA	48,088	C
Western New Mexico Univ	NM	16,734	LC
Western State Colo Univ	CO	18,639	C
Western Washington Univ	WA	18,003	C+
Westminster College	MO	32,820	C
Westminster College	PA	39,180	C+
Westminster College	UT	41,078	C+
Wheeling Jesuit Univ	WV	37,106	LC
Whitworth Univ	WA	51,732	VC
Wichita State Univ	KS	21,643	C
Widener Univ	PA	56,486	C
Wilberforce Univ	OH	19,016	C
Wilkes Univ	PA	45,622	C
William Jewell College	MO	41,210	C+
William Paterson Univ of New Jersey	NJ	23,133	C
William Penn Univ	IA	26,000	C
William Woods Univ	MO	32,040	C
Wilmington College	OH	34,600	C
Wilmington Univ	DE	8,546	NC
Wilson College	PA	35,620	C
Wingate Univ	NC	39,950	C
Winona State Univ	MN	17,535	C
Winston-Salem State Univ	NC	26,166	LC
Wisc Lutheran College	WI	36,290	VC
Wittenberg Univ	OH	48,156	C+
Wofford College	SC	49,885	VC
Woodbury Univ	CA	46,958	C
Wright State Univ	OH	16,983	C
Xavier Univ	OH	47,880	C+
Xavier Univ of Louisiana	LA	31,689	C+
Yeshiva Univ	NY	47,250	VC+
York College	NE	24,300	C
York College of Pennsylvania	PA	29,240	C
Youngstown State Univ	OH	17,307	C

ACCOUNTING (FINANCE)

School	ST	$IS	SR
Bentley Univ	MA	60,890	HC
Bryant Univ	RI	55,646	VC
Clayton State Univ	GA	19,735	C
Delta State Univ	MS	13,176	C
East Central Univ	OK	13,056	C
Ferris State Univ	MI	21,445	C
High Point Univ	NC	45,977	C
Huntington Univ	IN	33,996	C
Murray State Univ	KY	16,998	C
Northern Mich Univ	MI	19,604	C
Regis Univ	CO	44,520	C
St. Ambrose Univ	IA	39,019	C
The Master's Univ	CA	43,870	C+
Univ of Dayton	OH	53,620	C
Univ of Georgia	GA	21,250	HC
Univ of Miss	MS	17,746	C+
Univ of Tulsa	OK	52,625	HC+
William Woods Univ	MO	32,040	C

ACCOUNTING (INFORMATION SYSTEMS)

School	ST	$IS	SR
Bentley Univ	MA	60,890	HC
Bryant Univ	RI	55,646	VC
Ferris State Univ	MI	21,445	C
Huntington Univ	IN	33,996	C
Murray State Univ	KY	16,998	C
Northern Mich Univ	MI	19,604	C
St. Edward's Univ	TX	53,100	VC
SUNY SUNY Albany	NY	22,165	C
Univ of Tulsa	OK	52,625	HC+

ACTING

School	ST	$IS	SR
Azusa Pacific Univ	CA	43,972	C
Baldwin Wallace Univ	OH	41,106	C
Ball State Univ	IN	19,590	C
Baylor Univ	TX	53,760	HC
Boston Univ	MA	65,110	MC
Carnegie Mellon Univ	PA	67,980	MC
Chapman Univ	CA	63,078	VC+
Columbia College Chicago	IL	43,168	C
Elon Univ	NC	44,599	VC+
Howard Univ	DC	37,616	C+
Huntington Univ	IN	33,996	C
Lipscomb Univ	TN	41,296	VC
Millikin Univ	IL	42,158	C
Oberlin College	OH	66,012	MC
Ohio Univ	OH	22,924	C
Okla City Univ	OK	40,476	VC
Old Dominion Univ	VA	20,910	C
Otterbein Univ	OH	41,630	C
Pace Univ	NY	58,248	C
Pennsylvania State Univ - Univ Park	PA	29,760	HC
Shenandoah Univ	VA	41,312	C
St. Edward's Univ	TX	53,100	VC
SUNY / SUNY Fredonia	NY	20,818	C
Syracuse Univ	NY	60,239	VC
Univ of Maryland/Baltimore County	MD	21,296	VC
Univ of Minn/Twin Cities	MN	23,519	HC+
Webster Univ	MO	37,490	C
Western Kentucky Univ	KY	16,850	C

ACTUARIAL MATHEMATICS

School	ST	$IS	SR
Albion College	MI	52,650	C
Asbury Univ	KY	35,180	C+
Bryant Univ	RI	55,646	VC
Cabrini Univ	PA	42,591	LC
Huntington Univ	IN	33,996	C
Lycoming College	PA	48,580	C
Millikin Univ	IL	42,158	C
St. Mary's College	IN	50,600	C
SUNY at Binghamton	NY	22,861	MC
Univ of Conn	CT	25,538	HC
Univ of Pittsburgh	PA	29,568	HC+
Univ of Texas at San Antonio	TX	20,157	C
West Chester Univ of Pennsylvania	PA	18,456	C
Wilson College	PA	35,620	C
Youngstown State Univ	OH	17,307	C

ACTUARIAL SCIENCE

School	ST	$IS	SR
Appalachian State Univ	NC	14,416	VC
Arizona State Univ at the Tempe Campus	AZ	21,756	VC
Ashland Univ	OH	21,440	C
Assumption College	MA	47,920	C+
Auburn Univ	AL	23,594	VC+
Aurora Univ	IL	33,970	C
Ball State Univ	IN	19,590	C
Bellarmine Univ	KY	51,220	C
Bentley Univ	MA	60,890	HC
Bethany College	WV	36,300	NC
Brigham Young Univ	UT	12,748	HC
Bryant Univ	RI	55,646	VC
Butler Univ	IN	51,352	VC
Calif Baptist Univ	CA	41,392	C
Calvin College	MI	41,570	VC+
Carroll Univ	WI	38,100	C+
Central College	IA	44,592	C
Central Mich Univ	MI	20,330	C
Central Washington Univ	WA	16,803	C
CUNY/Baruch College	NY	21,609	HC
CUNY/Queens College	NY	27,896	C
Dordt College	IA	37,860	C+
Drake Univ	IA	45,056	HC
Eastern Mich Univ	MI	19,761	C
Elizabethtown College	PA	54,050	C
Elmhurst College	IL	45,428	C
Ferris State Univ	MI	21,445	C
Florida A&M Univ	FL	15,361	C
Florida State Univ	FL	16,771	HC
Georgia State Univ	GA	24,332	VC
High Point Univ	NC	45,977	C
Hofstra Univ	NY	55,960	C+
Huntington Univ	IN	33,996	C
Indiana Univ Northwest	IN	7,072	C
Indiana Univ South Bend	IN	14,242	C
Indiana Univ-Purdue Univ Fort Wayne	IN	17,553	C
Le Moyne College	NY	46,000	C
Lebanon Valley College	PA	51,530	C
Maryville Univ of St. Louis	MO	38,046	VC+
Mich State Univ	MI	23,898	VC+
Millersville Univ of Pennsylvania	PA	23,782	C
Milwaukee School of Engineering	WI	45,153	HC
Mount Mercy Univ	IA	36,826	C
New York Univ	NY	65,860	MC
North Central College	IL	48,712	VC

ST = STATE $IS = IN-STATE COSTS SR = SELECTOR RATING

School	ST	$IS	SR
N Dak State Univ	ND	16,245	C
Northwestern College of Iowa	IA	38,400	C+
Ohio State Univ at Columbus	OH	21,703	HC+
Ohio Univ	OH	22,924	C
Olivet Nazarene Univ	IL	41,840	C
Otterbein Univ	OH	41,630	C
Purdue Univ/West Lafayette	IN	20,032	MC
Rider Univ	NJ	54,050	C
Roanoke College	VA	54,114	VC
Robert Morris Univ	PA	37,834	C
Rochester Inst of Technology	NY	50,842	HC
Roosevelt Univ	IL	40,651	VC
St. Joseph's Univ	PA	57,544	VC+
St. Mary's Univ of Minn	MN	41,210	VC
Seton Hill Univ	PA	46,972	C
Siena College	NY	48,916	C+
Silver Lake College of the Holy Family	WI	36,290	LC
Simpson College	IA	43,839	VC
Southeast Missouri State Univ	MO	15,498	C
Southern Illinois Univ Edwardsville	IL	22,643	C
St. John's Univ	NY	55,850	C
SUNY SUNY Albany	NY	22,165	C
Temple Univ	PA	24,392	VC
Thiel College	PA	41,590	C
Univ of Calif at Santa Barbara	CA	29,091	HC
Univ of Central Missouri	MO	18,982	C
Univ of Central Okla	OK	13,486	C
Univ of Illinois at Urbana-Champaign	IL	27,006	HC
Univ of Indianapolis	IN	36,480	C
Univ of Iowa	IA	18,683	VC+
Univ of Maine at Farmington	ME	18,187	C
Univ of Minn/Duluth	MN	20,292	C+
Univ of Nebr - Lincoln	NE	18,589	VC
Univ of Pennsylvania	PA	63,526	MC
Univ of Texas at Dallas	TX	22,830	VC+
Univ of Texas at San Antonio	TX	20,157	C
Univ of Wisc-Madison	WI	20,934	MC
Univ of Wisc-Milwaukee	WI	21,496	C
Valparaiso Univ	IN	48,370	C+
Western Kentucky Univ	KY	16,850	C
Western New England Univ	MA	48,088	C
Worcester Polytechnic Inst	MA	60,730	MC
Xavier Univ	OH	47,880	C+

ADDICTION STUDIES

School	ST	$IS	SR
Bethany College	KS	46,100	NC
Brescia Univ	KY	29,890	VC+
Elizabethtown College School of Continuing and Professional Studies	PA	18,900	C
Goddard College	VT	17,040	VC
Graceland Univ	IA	35,290	C
Grand Canyon Univ	AZ	16,950	VC
Indiana Wesleyan Univ	IN	33,674	C
Kansas Wesleyan Univ	KS	36,600	C
Keene State College	NH	24,003	LC
Lewis-Clark State College	ID	14,202	C
Metropolitan State Univ	MN	7,566	C
Minot State Univ	ND	12,732	C
Missouri Valley College	MO	28,150	C
Okla City Univ	OK	40,476	VC
Prescott College	AZ	33,284	C
Rhode Island College	RI	17,694	LC
Southern Univ at New Orleans	LA	8,014	LC
Texas Tech Univ	TX	18,736	C+
Univ of Central Arkansas	AR	14,472	VC
Univ of Central Okla	OK	13,486	C
Univ of Cincinnati	OH	21,964	VC
Univ of Detroit Mercy	MI	48,816	C+
Univ of Great Falls	MT	38,524	C
Univ of Mary	ND	23,180	C
Univ of S Dak	SD	16,109	C
Univ of St. Francis	IL	39,924	C
Viterbo Univ	WI	34,660	C

ADMINISTRATION OF JUSTICE

School	ST	$IS	SR
Catawba College	NC	39,820	C
Howard Univ	DC	37,616	C+
Texas Southern Univ	TX	18,212	LC
Tiffin Univ	OH	31,380	C
Univ of Hawaii at Hilo	HI	18,038	C
Univ of Louisville	KY	19,824	C
Univ of Pittsburgh	PA	29,568	HC+

ADVERTISING

School	ST	$IS	SR
Abilene Christian Univ	TX	41,800	C+
Adams State Univ	CO	17,703	LC
American International College	MA	46,300	LC
Appalachian State Univ	NC	14,416	VC
Art Inst of Portland	OR	132,329	SP
ArtCenter College of Design	CA	54,212	SP
Ball State Univ	IN	19,590	C
Barry Univ	FL	37,830	C
Bethany College	WV	36,300	NC
Biola Univ	CA	46,402	C+
Brigham Young Univ	UT	12,748	HC
Butler Univ	IN	51,352	VC
Cal State, East Bay	CA	19,413	C
Cal State, Fullerton	CA	21,902	C
Central Mich Univ	MI	20,330	C
Central State Univ	OH	18,564	C
Champlain College	VT	53,132	C+
Chapman Univ	CA	63,078	VC+
CUNY/Baruch College	NY	21,609	HC
College for Creative Studies	MI	48,875	SP
College of St. Scholastica	MN	44,640	C
Columbia College Chicago	IL	43,168	C
Columbus College of Art and Design	OH	37,732	C
Davenport Univ	MI	25,896	LC
Dordt College	IA	37,860	C+
Drake Univ	IA	45,056	HC
Drury Univ	MO	33,791	VC
Duquesne Univ	PA	46,822	VC
East Central Univ	OK	13,056	C
Eastern Mich Univ	MI	19,761	C
Eastern Nazarene College	MA	39,955	C
Emerson College	MA	54,736	HC
Fashion Inst of Technology/ SUNY	NY	18,521	SP
Ferris State Univ	MI	21,445	C
Florida State Univ	FL	16,771	HC
Fontbonne Univ	MO	33,717	C
Gannon Univ	PA	42,032	C
Grand Rapids Theological Seminary/Cornerstone Univ	MI	33,338	C
Grand Valley State Univ	MI	22,250	C+
Harding Univ	AR	25,421	C
Hawaii Pacific Univ	HI	33,420	C
Howard Univ	DC	37,616	C+
Iowa State Univ	IA	17,570	C
Johnson & Wales Univ/ Providence Campus	RI	42,248	C
Keiser Univ	FL	35,010	LC
Kent State Univ	OH	20,732	C
Lamar Univ	TX	18,014	LC
Lasell College	MA	47,500	C
Loyola Univ Chicago	IL	55,802	VC
Loyola Univ New Orleans	LA	51,708	VC+
Lynn Univ	FL	49,480	LC
Marietta College	OH	46,190	C
Marquette Univ	WI	48,390	VC+
Marshall Univ	WV	17,242	C
Marywood Univ	PA	46,900	C
Mercyhurst Univ	PA	47,420	C
Metropolitan State Univ	MN	7,566	C
Mich State Univ	MI	23,898	VC+
Midland Univ	NE	37,468	
Minneapolis College of Art and Design	MN	44,238	SP
Morningside College	IA	36,865	C
Murray State Univ	KY	16,998	C
New York Inst of Technology	NY	48,730	C
North Park Univ	IL	35,860	C
Northeastern State Univ	OK	8,615	VC
Northwest Missouri State Univ	MO	17,737	C
Northwood Univ - Mich	MI	35,010	LC
Okla Christian Univ	OK	27,650	VC
Okla City Univ	OK	40,476	VC
Otis College of Art and Design	CA	55,858	SP
Pace Univ	NY	58,248	C
Parsons The New School for Design	NY	56,610	SP
Pennsylvania State Univ - Univ Park	PA	29,760	HC
Pepperdine Univ	CA	74,460	HC+
Point Park Univ	PA	41,270	C
Portland State Univ	OR	19,443	C
Purdue Univ/Northwest	IN	15,038	C
Purdue Univ/West Lafayette	IN	20,032	MC
Quinnipiac Univ	CT	59,110	C
Rider Univ	NJ	54,050	C
Ringling College of Art and Design	FL	57,430	SP
Rochester Inst of Technology	NY	50,842	HC
Roosevelt Univ	IL	40,651	VC
Rowan Univ	NJ	24,491	VC+
Salem State Univ	MA	17,303	LC
San Diego State Univ	CA	21,896	C+
San Jose State Univ	CA	21,540	C
Savannah College of Art and Design	GA	49,595	C
School of Visual Arts	NY	47,500	SP
Southeast Missouri State Univ	MO	15,498	C
Southern Methodist Univ	TX	66,483	MC
Southern New Hampshire Univ	NH	43,198	C
Spring Arbor Univ	MI	36,000	C
St. Cloud State Univ	MN	10,600	C
St. John's Univ	NY	55,850	C
Suffolk Univ	MA	50,308	C
Syracuse Univ	NY	60,239	VC
Temple Univ	PA	24,392	VC
Texas A&M Univ at Commerce	TX	10,496	C
Texas State Univ	TX	19,350	C
Texas Tech Univ	TX	18,736	C+
The Art Inst of Atlanta	GA	34,334	SP
The Univ of Tenn at Knoxville	TN	22,112	VC
Union Univ	TN	33,970	VC
Univ of Alabama	AL	24,320	C+
Univ of Arkansas at Little Rock	AR	18,211	C
Univ of Central Florida	FL	15,922	VC
Univ of Central Okla	OK	13,486	C
Univ of Colo Boulder	CO	24,285	VC+
Univ of Florida	FL	16,291	HC+
Univ of Georgia	GA	21,250	HC
Univ of Idaho	ID	15,348	C
Univ of Illinois at Urbana-Champaign	IL	27,006	HC
Univ of Kentucky	KY	33,306	C
Univ of Louisiana at Lafayette	LA	14,516	C
Univ of Miami	FL	63,494	MC
Univ of Missouri/Columbia	MO	18,201	MC
Univ of Nebr - Kearney	NE	16,546	LC
Univ of Nebr - Lincoln	NE	18,589	VC
Univ of Okla	OK	18,911	VC
Univ of Oregon	OR	22,972	C
Univ of San Francisco	CA	58,484	VC
Univ of S Car at Columbia	SC	19,725	VC+
Univ of Southern Indiana	IN	16,501	C
Univ of Southern Miss	MS	13,170	C
Univ of Tampa	FL	36,944	C
Univ of Texas at Austin	TX	26,102	HC
Univ of the Sacred Heart	PR	17,932	
Washington State Univ	WA	22,495	C
Washington Univ in St. Louis	MO	65,366	VC
Waynesburg Univ	PA	32,290	C
Weber State Univ	UT	10,721	C
Webster Univ	MO	37,490	C
Wesleyan College	GA	29,694	C+
West Liberty Univ	WV	15,512	C
West Virginia Univ	WV	18,210	C
Western Kentucky Univ	KY	16,850	C
Western Mich Univ	MI	21,054	C
Western New England Univ	MA	48,088	C
Wilmington College	OH	34,600	C
Xavier Univ	OH	47,880	C+
Youngstown State Univ	OH	17,307	C

AERONAUTICAL ENGINEERING

School	ST	$IS	SR
Auburn Univ	AL	23,594	VC+
Calif Polytechnic State Univ	CA	17,979	HC+
Clarkson Univ	NY	60,392	HC
Daniel Webster College	NH	26,984	C
Florida Inst of Technology	FL	53,306	VC
Illinois Inst of Technology	IL	56,826	HC+
Iowa State Univ	IA	17,570	C
Mass Inst of Technology	MA	62,662	MC
Missouri Univ of Science and Technology	MO	18,655	HC
N Car State Univ	NC	19,515	HC+
Ohio State Univ at Columbus	OH	21,703	HC+
Princeton Univ	NJ	57,610	MC
Purdue Univ/West Lafayette	IN	20,032	MC
Rensselaer Polytechnic Inst	NY	63,436	MC
St. Louis Univ	MO	49,866	HC
San Jose State Univ	CA	21,540	C
Stanford Univ	CA	60,409	MC
Tuskegee Univ	AL	28,164	C
United States Air Force Academy	CO		C
Univ of Calif at Davis	CA	28,468	HC
Univ of Calif at Irvine	CA	26,484	VC
Univ of Calif at Los Angeles	CA	30,162	MC
Univ of Central Florida	FL	15,922	VC
Univ of Cincinnati	OH	21,964	VC
Univ of Colo Boulder	CO	24,285	VC+
Univ of Florida	FL	16,291	HC+
Univ of Illinois at Urbana-Champaign	IL	27,006	HC
Univ of Mich/Ann Arbor	MI	24,410	MC
Univ of Okla	OK	18,911	VC
Univ of Southern Calif	CA	66,631	C
Univ of Washington	WA	23,149	VC
West Virginia Univ	WV	18,210	C
Wichita State Univ	KS	21,643	C

AERONAUTICAL SCIENCE

School	ST	$IS	SR
Bridgewater State Univ	MA	21,810	C
Embry-Riddle Aeronautical Univ - Daytona Beach	FL	44,712	VC
Embry-Riddle Aeronautical Univ - Prescott Campus	AZ	44,054	VC
Farmingdale State College	NY	20,624	C
Florida Inst of Technology	FL	53,306	VC
Inter-American Univ of PR-Bayamon	PR	18,785	
Kent State Univ	OH	20,732	C
LeTourneau Univ	TX	38,250	VC
Rocky Mountain College	MT	34,270	C
Univ of Maryland/Eastern Shore	MD	17,013	C
Wilmington Univ	DE	8,546	NC

AERONAUTICAL TECHNOLOGY

School	ST	$IS	SR
Andrews Univ	MI	28,030	C+
Arizona State Univ at the Polytechnic Campus	AZ	21,360	VC
Central Washington Univ	WA	16,803	C
Indiana State Univ	IN	23,223	LC
Inter-American Univ of PR-Bayamon	PR	18,785	
Kansas State Univ	KS	17,780	VC
LeTourneau Univ	TX	38,250	VC
Purdue Univ/West Lafayette	IN	20,032	MC
St. Louis Univ	MO	49,866	HC
Tenn State Univ	TN	14,423	C
Univ of Alaska Anchorage	AK	16,652	NC

AEROSPACE ENGINEERING

School	ST	$IS	SR
Arizona State Univ at the Tempe Campus	AZ	21,756	VC
Calif State Polytechnic Univ, Pomona	CA	21,541	C
Cal State, Long Beach	CA	18,850	C
Case Western Reserve Univ	OH	60,304	MC
Embry-Riddle Aeronautical Univ - Daytona Beach	FL	44,712	VC
Embry-Riddle Aeronautical Univ - Prescott Campus	AZ	44,054	VC
Embry-Riddle Aeronautical Univ - Worldwide	FL	17,480	C
Georgia Inst of Technology	GA	23,360	MC
Kent State Univ	OH	20,732	C
New Mexico State Univ	NM	14,050	C
Pennsylvania State Univ - Univ Park	PA	29,760	HC
St. Louis Univ	MO	49,866	HC
San Diego State Univ	CA	21,896	C+
Syracuse Univ	NY	60,239	VC
Texas A&M Univ	TX	20,521	VC+
United States Naval Academy	MD		MC
Univ of Arizona	AZ	23,100	C
Univ of Calif San Diego	CA	30,150	MC
Univ of Kansas	KS	20,135	C+
Univ of Maryland/College Park	MD	21,938	HC
Univ of Minn/Twin Cities	MN	23,519	HC+
Univ of Notre Dame	IN	64,043	MC
Western Mich Univ	MI	21,054	C
Worcester Polytechnic Inst	MA	60,730	MC

AEROSPACE STUDIES

School	ST	$IS	SR
Averett Univ	VA	40,970	LC
Embry-Riddle Aeronautical Univ - Daytona Beach	FL	44,712	VC
Mass Inst of Technology	MA	62,662	MC
Miss State Univ	MS	11,454	C+
New Mexico State Univ	NM	14,050	C
Okla State Univ	OK	17,180	VC
Rochester Inst of Technology	NY	50,842	HC
St. Louis Univ	MO	49,866	HC
SUNY / Univ at Buffalo	NY	23,122	C+
The Univ of Tenn at Knoxville	TN	22,112	VC
United States Air Force Academy	CO		C
Univ of Alabama	AL	24,320	C+
Univ of Alaska Anchorage	AK	16,652	NC
Univ of Calif at Los Angeles	CA	30,162	MC
Univ of Calif San Diego	CA	30,150	MC
Univ of Central Florida	FL	15,922	VC
Univ of Miami	FL	63,494	MC
Univ of Mich/Ann Arbor	MI	24,410	MC
Univ of Southern Calif	CA	66,631	C
Univ of Texas at Austin	TX	26,102	HC
Univ of Virginia	VA	25,891	MC
Virginia Polytechnic Inst and State Univ	VA	21,276	HC
West Virginia Univ	WV	18,210	C
Western Kentucky Univ	KY	16,850	C

AFRICAN AMERICAN STUDIES

School	ST	$IS	SR
Amherst College	MA		HC+
Arizona State Univ at the Tempe Campus	AZ	21,756	VC
Bard College at Simon's Rock	MA	65,795	MC
Bates College	ME	64,500	MC
Berea College	KY	7,042	C
Brandeis Univ	MA	65,925	MC
Brown Univ	RI	64,566	MC
Cabrini Univ	PA	42,591	LC
Cal State, Fresno	CA	16,902	LC
Cal State, Fullerton	CA	21,902	C
Cal State, Los Angeles	CA	17,186	LC
Cal State, Northridge	CA	16,859	LC
Carleton College	MN	64,071	MC
Chicago State Univ	IL	20,144	C
CUNY/College of Staten Island	NY	17,840	NC
CUNY/Hunter College	NY	31,098	VC
CUNY/Lehman College	NY	5,778	HC+
CUNY/York College	NY	6,747	LC
Claflin Univ	SC	33,764	LC
Coe College	IA	51,570	VC
Colby College	ME	64,060	MC
College of Charleston	SC	22,699	C
Columbia Univ/ School of General Studies	NY	61,470	MC
Columbia Univ/City of New York	NY	62,958	MC
Dartmouth College	NH	66,174	MC
Denison Univ	OH	58,860	MC
DePauw Univ	IN	58,688	HC+
Duke Univ	NC	64,188	
Earlham College	IN	54,870	HC
East Carolina Univ	NC	16,937	C
Eastern Mich Univ	MI	19,761	C
Elon Univ	NC	44,599	VC+
Emory Univ	GA	60,786	MC
Fordham Univ	NY	65,918	MC
Georgia State Univ	GA	24,332	VC
Guilford College	NC	44,090	C
Hampshire College	MA	63,824	MC

ST = STATE $IS = IN-STATE COSTS   SR = SELECTOR RATING

School	ST	$IS	SR
Harvard College/Harvard Univ	MA	60,659	MC
Howard Univ	DC	37,616	C+
Indiana State Univ	IN	23,223	LC
Indiana Univ Bloomington	IN	20,429	VC
Indiana Univ Northwest	IN	7,072	C
Loyola Marymount Univ	CA	58,038	HC
Loyola Univ Chicago	IL	55,802	VC
Luther College	IA	48,540	C+
Martin Univ	IN	20,264	LC
Metropolitan State Univ of Denver	CO	29,889	LC
Miami Univ	OH	27,190	HC+
Middlebury College	VT	64,332	MC
Morehouse College	GA	40,064	C
Morgan State Univ	MD	17,190	LC
New York Univ	NY	65,860	MC
Northeastern Univ	MA	62,703	MC
Northwestern Univ	IL	66,344	MC
Oakland Univ	MI	20,763	C
Oberlin College	OH	66,012	MC
Ohio State Univ at Columbus	OH	21,703	HC+
Ohio Univ	OH	22,924	C
Ohio Wesleyan Univ	OH	49,460	VC
Old Dominion Univ	VA	20,910	C
Pennsylvania State Univ - Univ Park	PA	29,760	HC
Pitzer College	CA	66,192	MC
Purdue Univ/West Lafayette	IN	20,032	MC
Rhode Island College	RI	17,694	LC
Roosevelt Univ	IL	40,651	VC
Rutgers Univ - Camden	NJ	26,146	C
Rutgers Univ - New Brunswick	NJ	26,632	HC
Rutgers Univ - Newark	NJ	27,288	C
St. Augustine's Univ	NC	26,048	C
St. Louis Univ	MO	49,866	HC
St. Peter's Univ	NJ	49,192	C
San Diego State Univ	CA	21,896	C+
Scripps College	CA	66,664	MC
Seton Hall Univ	NJ	55,514	C
Simmons College	MA	53,090	VC
Smith College	MA	63,914	MC
Sonoma State Univ	CA	27,806	C
Southern Methodist Univ	TX	66,483	MC
Stanford Univ	CA	60,409	MC
SUNY / SUNY Cortland	NY	20,706	VC
SUNY / Univ at Buffalo	NY	23,122	C+
SUNY at Geneseo	NY	20,440	VC+
SUNY at New Paltz	NY	19,200	C
SUNY SUNY Albany	NY	22,165	C
Suffolk Univ	MA	50,308	C
Syracuse Univ	NY	60,239	VC
Temple Univ	PA	24,392	VC
The College at Brockport - SUNY	NY	20,346	C
The College of Wooster	OH	57,900	VC+
Univ of Alabama at Birmingham	AL	19,906	C
Univ of Arkansas at Fayetteville	AR	19,152	C+
Univ of Calif at Berkeley	CA	28,853	MC
Univ of Calif at Irvine	CA	26,484	VC
Univ of Calif at Los Angeles	CA	30,162	MC
Univ of Calif at Riverside	CA	29,227	C+
Univ of Calif at Santa Barbara	CA	29,091	HC
Univ of Central Arkansas	AR	14,472	VC
Univ of Chicago	IL	67,584	MC
Univ of Cincinnati	OH	21,964	VC
Univ of Georgia	GA	21,250	HC
Univ of Illinois at Chicago	IL	25,006	VC
Univ of Iowa	IA	18,683	VC+
Univ of Kansas	KS	20,135	C+
Univ of Maryland/Baltimore County	MD	21,296	VC
Univ of Maryland/College Park	MD	21,938	HC
Univ of Mass Amherst	MA	26,199	VC+
Univ of Mass Boston	MA	13,435	C
Univ of Memphis	TN	18,278	C
Univ of Mich/Ann Arbor	MI	24,410	MC
Univ of Mich/Dearborn	MI	11,757	VC
Univ of Minn/Twin Cities	MN	23,519	HC+
Univ of Miss	MS	17,746	C+
Univ of Nebr - Omaha	NE	16,120	C
Univ of N Car at Chapel Hill	NC	20,052	HC+
Univ of N Car at Greensboro	NC	14,690	C
Univ of Northern Colo	CO	20,851	C
Univ of Okla	OK	18,911	VC
Univ of Pennsylvania	PA	63,526	MC
Univ of Rochester	NY	65,032	MC
Univ of S Car at Columbia	SC	19,725	VC+
Univ of South Florida/Tampa	FL	16,110	VC+
Univ of Southern Calif	CA	66,631	C
Univ of Virginia	VA	25,891	MC
Univ of Washington	WA	23,149	VC
Univ of Wisc-Madison	WI	20,934	MC
Univ of Wisc-Milwaukee	WI	21,496	C
Vanderbilt Univ	TN	60,572	MC
Virginia Commonwealth Univ	VA	23,049	C
Washington Univ in St. Louis	MO	65,366	VC
Wellesley College	MA	63,916	MC
Wesleyan Univ	CT	65,516	MC
Western Kentucky Univ	KY	16,850	C
Wheaton College	MA	61,512	VC
William Paterson Univ of New Jersey	NJ	23,133	C
Wofford College	SC	49,885	VC
Wright State Univ	OH	16,983	C
Yale Univ	CT	64,650	MC

AFRICAN LANGUAGES

School	ST	$IS	SR
Cal State, Northridge	CA	16,859	LC
Duke Univ	NC	64,188	
Univ of Wisc-Madison	WI	20,934	MC

AFRICAN STUDIES

School	ST	$IS	SR
Agnes Scott College	GA	51,930	VC+
Bard College	NY	64,024	HC
Berea College	KY	7,042	C
Bowling Green State Univ	OH	19,747	C
Brown Univ	RI	64,566	MC
Cal State, Dominguez Hills	CA	19,022	LC
Cal State, Long Beach	CA	18,850	C
Carleton College	MN	64,071	MC
CUNY/Brooklyn College	NY	5,884	C+
CUNY/Queens College	NY	27,896	C
Claflin Univ	SC	33,764	LC
Claremont McKenna College	CA	67,185	MC
Clayton State Univ	GA	19,735	C
Colgate Univ	NY	65,030	MC
Conn College	CT	65,000	MC
Delaware State Univ	DE	19,376	NC
DePaul Univ	IL	47,623	VC
Dickinson College	PA	63,974	MC
Drew Univ/College of Liberal Arts	NJ	61,048	VC
Duke Univ	NC	64,188	
Eastern Mich Univ	MI	19,761	C
Emory Univ	GA	60,786	MC
Fordham Univ	NY	65,918	MC
Franklin and Marshall College	PA	63,170	HC
Hamilton College	NY	64,250	MC
Hampshire College	MA	63,824	MC
Hofstra Univ	NY	55,960	C+
Howard Univ	DC	37,616	C+
Johns Hopkins Univ	MD	65,386	MC
Kalamazoo College	MI	53,931	HC+
Kennesaw State Univ	GA	19,592	VC
Kent State Univ	OH	20,732	C
Lafayette College	PA	63,355	MC
Lehigh Univ	PA	61,010	MC
Linfield College	OR	52,010	C
Loyola Univ Chicago	IL	55,802	VC
Mercer Univ	GA	45,348	VC
New York Univ	NY	65,860	MC
North Park Univ	IL	35,860	C
Old Dominion Univ	VA	20,910	C
Ramapo College of New Jersey	NJ	25,338	C
Rowan Univ	NJ	24,491	VC+
San Francisco State Univ	CA	18,514	LC
Savannah State Univ	GA	15,631	C
Shaw Univ	NC	24,638	C
Smith College	MA	63,914	MC
St. Lawrence Univ	NY	64,390	VC
SUNY / SUNY Oneonta	NY	19,712	C+
Tenn State Univ	TN	14,423	C
The College at Brockport - SUNY	NY	20,346	C
Tulane Univ	LA	63,396	HC+
Univ of Arkansas at Fayetteville	AR	19,152	C+
Univ of Calif at Davis	CA	28,468	HC
Univ of Calif at Los Angeles	CA	30,162	MC
Univ of Calif San Diego	CA	30,150	MC
Univ of Kansas	KS	20,135	C+
Univ of Mich/Ann Arbor	MI	24,410	MC
Univ of Mich/Dearborn	MI	11,757	VC
Univ of Pennsylvania	PA	63,526	MC
Vassar College	NY	65,491	MC
Washington Univ in St. Louis	MO	65,366	VC
Wayne State Univ	MI	22,016	C
Wheaton College	MA	61,512	VC
Yale Univ	CT	64,650	MC

AFRICANA STUDIES

School	ST	$IS	SR
Augustana College	IL	49,658	VC
Bowdoin College	ME	63,500	MC
Brown Univ	RI	64,566	MC
College of William & Mary	VA		MC
Cornell Univ	NY	64,853	MC
Davidson College	NC	60,119	MC
Eastern Illinois Univ	IL	21,126	C
Indiana Univ-Purdue Univ Indianapolis	IN	18,635	C
Knox College	IL	52,615	VC+
Mount Holyoke College	MA	56,746	MC
New York Univ	NY	65,860	MC
Oberlin College	OH	66,012	MC
Pomona College	CA	64,957	MC
Southern Illinois Univ Carbondale	IL	23,667	C
SUNY at Binghamton	NY	22,861	MC
Stony Brook Univ/The SUNY	NY	21,881	MC
Tufts Univ	MA		MC
Univ of Arizona	AZ	23,100	C
Univ of Maryland/Baltimore County	MD	21,296	VC
Univ of Miami	FL	63,494	MC
Univ of New Mexico	NM	15,404	C
Univ of N Car at Charlotte	NC	15,547	C
Univ of Notre Dame	IN	64,043	MC
Univ of Pittsburgh	PA	29,568	HC+
Univ of Rhode Island	RI	24,906	C
Western Mich Univ	MI	21,054	C
Wheaton College	MA	61,512	VC

AGRICULTURAL BUSINESS MANAGEMENT

School	ST	$IS	SR
Abilene Christian Univ	TX	41,800	C+
Adams State Univ	CO	17,703	LC
Alabama A&M Univ	AL	18,796	C
Alcorn State Univ	MS	15,854	C
Angelo State Univ	TX	15,263	NC
Appalachian State Univ	NC	14,416	VC
Arizona State Univ at the Polytechnic Campus	AZ	21,360	VC
Arkansas State Univ	AR	16,190	C
Arkansas Tech Univ	AR	15,484	C
Auburn Univ	AL	23,594	VC+
Brigham Young Univ	UT	12,748	HC
Calif Polytechnic State Univ	CA	17,979	HC+
Calif State Polytechnic Univ, Pomona	CA	21,541	C
Cal State, Chico	CA	21,440	C
Cal State, Fresno	CA	16,902	LC
College of the Ozarks	MO	7,230	C
Colo State Univ	CO	22,162	VC
Delaware State Univ	DE	19,376	NC
Dickinson State Univ	ND	12,372	LC
Dordt College	IA	37,860	C+
Eastern New Mexico Univ	NM	14,416	C
Eastern Oregon Univ	OR	17,715	C
Fort Hays State Univ	KS	12,131	C
Hardin-Simmons Univ	TX	33,966	C
Huntington Univ	IN	33,996	C
Illinois State Univ	IL	23,418	VC
Iowa State Univ	IA	17,570	C
Kansas State Univ	KS	17,780	VC
Lincoln Univ	MO	13,602	NC
Louisiana State Univ and A&M College	LA	18,677	VC
Louisiana Tech Univ	LA	11,422	VC
Mich State Univ	MI	23,898	VC+
Middle Tenn State Univ	TN	8,650	C
Miss State Univ	MS	11,454	C+
Montana State Univ	MT	15,500	C+
Morningside College	IA	36,865	C
Murray State Univ	KY	16,998	C
New Mexico State Univ	NM	14,050	C
Nicholls State Univ	LA	10,534	C
N Car A&T State Univ	NC	13,365	LC
N Car State Univ	NC	19,515	HC+
N Dak State Univ	ND	16,245	C
Northwest Missouri State Univ	MO	17,737	C
Northwestern College of Iowa	IA	38,400	C+
Northwestern Okla State Univ	OK	13,072	NC
Ohio State Univ at Columbus	OH	21,703	HC+
Okla Panhandle State Univ	OK	6,152	NC
Okla State Univ	OK	17,180	VC
Oregon State Univ	OR	22,519	VC
Pennsylvania State Univ - Univ Park	PA	29,760	HC
Prairie View A&M Univ	TX	15,205	LC
Purdue Univ/West Lafayette	IN	20,032	MC
S Car State Univ	SC	20,805	LC
S Dak State Univ	SD	15,634	C
Southeast Missouri State Univ	MO	15,498	C
Southern Arkansas Univ	AR	21,532	C
Southwest Minn State Univ	MN	17,783	C
SUNY /College of Agriculture and Tech at Cobleskill	NY	20,527	LC
Stephen F. Austin State Univ	TX	18,406	LC
Sul Ross State Univ	TX	15,021	LC
Tarleton State Univ	TX	15,248	LC
Texas A&M Univ	TX	20,521	VC+
Texas A&M Univ at Kingsville	TX	7,500	LC
Texas State Univ	TX	19,350	C
Texas Tech Univ	TX	18,736	C+
The Univ of Tenn at Martin	TN	14,876	C
Truman State Univ	MO	16,014	HC
Univ of Arizona	AZ	23,100	C
Univ of Arkansas at Fayetteville	AR	19,152	C+
Univ of Calif at Davis	CA	28,468	HC
Univ of Central Missouri	MO	18,982	C
Univ of Delaware	DE	24,976	VC+
Univ of Florida	FL	16,291	HC+
Univ of Idaho	ID	15,348	C
Univ of Illinois at Urbana-Champaign	IL	27,006	HC
Univ of Louisiana at Monroe	LA	15,970	C
Univ of Maine at Machias	ME	22,960	C
Univ of Maryland/College Park	MD	21,938	HC
Univ of Minn Crookston	MN	19,739	C
Univ of Minn/Twin Cities	MN	23,519	HC+
Univ of Missouri/Columbia	MO	18,201	MC
Univ of Nebr - Lincoln	NE	18,589	VC
Univ of Wisc-Madison	WI	20,934	MC
Univ of Wisc-Platteville	WI	14,614	VC
Univ of Wisc-River Falls	WI	14,485	C
Univ of Wyoming	WY	15,375	C+
Urbana Univ	OH	30,820	C
Utah State Univ	UT	12,736	C
Washington State Univ	WA	22,495	C
West Texas A&M Univ	TX	13,478	C
Wilmington College	OH	34,600	C

AGRICULTURAL COMMUNICATIONS

School	ST	$IS	SR
Auburn Univ	AL	23,594	VC+
Calif Polytechnic State Univ	CA	17,979	HC+
Cal State, Fresno	CA	16,902	LC
Kansas State Univ	KS	17,780	VC
N Dak State Univ	ND	16,245	C
Okla State Univ	OK	17,180	VC
Purdue Univ/West Lafayette	IN	20,032	MC
S Dak State Univ	SD	15,634	C
Texas A&M Univ	TX	20,521	VC+
Texas Tech Univ	TX	18,736	C+
Univ of Arkansas at Fayetteville	AR	19,152	C+
Univ of Georgia	GA	21,250	HC
Univ of Idaho	ID	15,348	C
Univ of Illinois at Urbana-Champaign	IL	27,006	HC
Univ of Minn/Twin Cities	MN	23,519	HC+
Univ of Nebr - Lincoln	NE	18,589	VC
Univ of Wisc-Madison	WI	20,934	MC
Univ of Wyoming	WY	15,375	C+
Washington State Univ	WA	22,495	C

AGRICULTURAL ECONOMICS

School	ST	$IS	SR
Alabama A&M Univ	AL	18,796	C
Alcorn State Univ	MS	15,854	C
Auburn Univ	AL	23,594	VC+
Colo State Univ	CO	22,162	VC
Eastern Oregon Univ	OR	17,715	C
Fort Valley State Univ	GA	17,988	VC
Kansas State Univ	KS	17,780	VC
Langston Univ	OK	14,314	C
Miss State Univ	MS	11,454	C+
New Mexico State Univ	NM	14,050	C
N Car A&T State Univ	NC	13,365	LC
N Car State Univ	NC	19,515	HC+
N Dak State Univ	ND	16,245	C
Northwest Missouri State Univ	MO	17,737	C
Ohio State Univ at Columbus	OH	21,703	HC+
Okla State Univ	OK	17,180	VC
Prairie View A&M Univ	TX	15,205	LC
Purdue Univ/West Lafayette	IN	20,032	MC
S Dak State Univ	SD	15,634	C
Southern Illinois Univ Carbondale	IL	23,667	C
Southern Univ and A&M College	LA	16,074	LC+
Tarleton State Univ	TX	15,248	LC
Tenn Tech Univ	TN	17,050	C
Texas A&M Univ	TX	20,521	VC+
Texas A&M Univ at Commerce	TX	10,496	C
Texas Tech Univ	TX	18,736	C+
The Univ of Tenn at Knoxville	TN	22,112	VC
Tuskegee Univ	AL	28,164	C
Univ of Arizona	AZ	23,100	C
Univ of Calif at Davis	CA	28,468	HC
Univ of Conn	CT	25,538	HC
Univ of Delaware	DE	24,976	VC+
Univ of Idaho	ID	15,348	C
Univ of Illinois at Urbana-Champaign	IL	27,006	HC
Univ of Kentucky	KY	33,306	C
Univ of Maryland/College Park	MD	21,938	HC
Univ of Mass Amherst	MA	26,199	VC+
Univ of Missouri/Columbia	MO	18,201	MC
Univ of Nebr - Lincoln	NE	18,589	VC
Univ of Wisc-Madison	WI	20,934	MC
Utah State Univ	UT	12,736	C
Virginia Polytechnic Inst and State Univ	VA	21,276	HC
Washington State Univ	WA	22,495	C
West Texas A&M Univ	TX	13,478	C
West Virginia Univ	WV	18,210	C

AGRICULTURAL EDUCATION

School	ST	$IS	SR
Alabama A&M Univ	AL	18,796	C
Arkansas Tech Univ	AR	15,484	C
Calif Polytechnic State Univ	CA	17,979	HC+
Cal State, Fresno	CA	16,902	LC
Clemson Univ	SC		HC
College of the Ozarks	MO	7,230	C
Colo State Univ	CO	22,162	VC
Delaware State Univ	DE	19,376	NC
Dordt College	IA	37,860	C+
Eastern New Mexico Univ	NM	14,416	C
Fort Valley State Univ	GA	17,988	VC
Huntington Univ	IN	33,996	C
Iowa State Univ	IA	17,570	C
Kansas State Univ	KS	17,780	VC
Louisiana State Univ and A&M College	LA	18,677	VC
Mich State Univ	MI	23,898	VC+
Miss State Univ	MS	11,454	C+
Missouri State Univ	MO	15,190	C+
Montana State Univ	MT	15,500	C+
Morehead State Univ	KY	17,422	C
Murray State Univ	KY	16,998	C

School	ST	$IS	SR
New Mexico State Univ	NM	14,050	C
N Car A&T State Univ	NC	13,365	LC
N Car State Univ	NC	19,515	HC+
N Dak State Univ	ND	16,245	C
Northwest Missouri State Univ	MO	17,737	C
Ohio State Univ at Columbus	OH	21,703	HC+
Okla Panhandle State Univ	OK	6,152	NC
Okla State Univ	OK	17,180	VC
Pennsylvania State Univ - Univ Park	PA	29,760	HC
Prescott College	AZ	33,284	C
Purdue Univ/West Lafayette	IN	20,032	MC
S Dak State Univ	SD	15,634	C
Southern Arkansas Univ	AR	21,532	C
Southern Univ and A&M College	LA	16,074	LC+
SUNY at Oswego	NY	21,351	C
Stephen F. Austin State Univ	TX	18,406	LC
Tarleton State Univ	TX	15,248	LC
Tenn Tech Univ	TN	17,050	C
Texas A&M Univ	TX	20,521	VC+
Texas A&M Univ at Commerce	TX	10,496	C
Texas A&M Univ at Kingsville	TX	7,500	LC
Univ of Arizona	AZ	23,100	C
Univ of Arkansas at Fayetteville	AR	19,152	C+
Univ of Arkansas at Pine Bluff	AR	13,541	C
Univ of Central Missouri	MO	18,982	C
Univ of Conn	CT	25,538	HC
Univ of Florida	FL	16,291	HC+
Univ of Georgia	GA	21,250	HC
Univ of Idaho	ID	15,348	C
Univ of Illinois at Urbana-Champaign	IL	27,006	HC
Univ of Kentucky	KY	33,306	C
Univ of Louisiana at Lafayette	LA	14,516	C
Univ of Maryland/Eastern Shore	MD	17,013	C
Univ of Minn/Twin Cities	MN	23,519	HC+
Univ of Nebr - Lincoln	NE	18,589	VC
Univ of Wisc-Platteville	WI	14,614	VC
Univ of Wisc-River Falls	WI	14,485	C
Univ of Wyoming	WY	15,375	C+
Utah State Univ	UT	12,736	C
Virginia Polytechnic Inst and State Univ	VA	21,276	HC
Washington State Univ	WA	22,495	C
West Virginia Univ	WV	18,210	C
Western Illinois Univ	IL	20,825	C
Western Kentucky Univ	KY	16,850	C
Wilmington College	OH	34,600	C

AGRICULTURAL ENGINEERING

School	ST	$IS	SR
Auburn Univ	AL	23,594	VC+
Clemson Univ	SC		HC
Iowa State Univ	IA	17,570	C
Kansas State Univ	KS	17,780	VC
N Car State Univ	NC	19,515	HC+
N Dak State Univ	ND	16,245	C
Oregon State Univ	OR	22,519	VC
Purdue Univ/West Lafayette	IN	20,032	MC
S Dak State Univ	SD	15,634	C
Univ of Arizona	AZ	23,100	C
Univ of Calif at Davis	CA	28,468	HC
Univ of Florida	FL	16,291	HC+
Univ of Georgia	GA	21,250	HC
Univ of Illinois at Urbana-Champaign	IL	27,006	HC
Univ of Nebr - Lincoln	NE	18,589	VC
Univ of Wisc-River Falls	WI	14,485	C
Utah State Univ	UT	12,736	C
Virginia Polytechnic Inst and State Univ	VA	21,276	HC
Washington State Univ	WA	22,495	C

AGRICULTURAL ENGINEERING TECHNOLOGY

School	ST	$IS	SR
Fort Valley State Univ	GA	17,988	VC
Kansas State Univ	KS	17,780	VC
Kennesaw State Univ	GA	19,592	VC
Miss State Univ	MS	11,454	C+
Montana State Univ	MT	15,500	C+
Murray State Univ	KY	16,998	C
N Dak State Univ	ND	16,245	C
S Dak State Univ	SD	15,634	C
Univ of Central Missouri	MO	18,982	C
Univ of Minn Crookston	MN	19,739	C
Washington State Univ	WA	22,495	C
Western Kentucky Univ	KY	16,850	C

AGRICULTURAL MECHANICS

School	ST	$IS	SR
Calif Polytechnic State Univ	CA	17,979	HC+
Montana State Univ-Northern	MT	11,370	NC
Murray State Univ	KY	16,998	C
N Dak State Univ	ND	16,245	C
Northwest Missouri State Univ	MO	17,737	C
SUNY /College of Agriculture and Tech at Cobleskill	NY	20,527	LC
Stephen F. Austin State Univ	TX	18,406	LC
Tarleton State Univ	TX	15,248	LC
Univ of Idaho	ID	15,348	C
Univ of Illinois at Urbana-Champaign	IL	27,006	HC
Univ of Nebr - Lincoln	NE	18,589	VC
Washington State Univ	WA	22,495	C
Western Kentucky Univ	KY	16,850	C

AGRICULTURAL SCIENCES

School	ST	$IS	SR
Angelo State Univ	TX	15,263	NC
Calif Polytechnic State Univ	CA	17,979	HC+
Calif State Polytechnic Univ, Pomona	CA	21,541	C
College of the Ozarks	MO	7,230	C
Cornell Univ	NY	64,853	MC
Huntington Univ	IN	33,996	C
Morningside College	IA	36,865	C
Murray State Univ	KY	16,998	C
Northwest Missouri State Univ	MO	17,737	C
Pennsylvania State Univ - Univ Park	PA	29,760	HC
Texas A&M Univ	TX	20,521	VC+
Univ of Arkansas at Pine Bluff	AR	13,541	C
Univ of Idaho	ID	15,348	C
Univ of Maine at Machias	ME	22,960	C
Univ of Nevada/Reno	NV	18,010	C
Washington State Univ	WA	22,495	C
West Virginia Univ	WV	18,210	C

AGRICULTURE

School	ST	$IS	SR
Andrews Univ	MI	28,030	C+
Arkansas State Univ	AR	16,190	C
Auburn Univ	AL	23,594	VC+
Austin Peay State Univ	TN	16,397	C
Berea College	KY	7,042	C
Cal State, Chico	CA	21,440	C
Cal State, Stanislaus	CA	16,212	C
Cameron Univ	OK	11,072	NC
Clemson Univ	SC		HC
College of the Ozarks	MO	7,230	C
Dordt College	IA	37,860	C+
Eastern Kentucky Univ	KY	16,908	C
Eastern New Mexico Univ	NM	14,416	C
Ferrum College	VA	39,650	C
Fort Hays State Univ	KS	12,131	C
Green Mountain College	VT	45,228	LC
Hampshire College	MA	63,824	MC
Hardin-Simmons Univ	TX	33,966	C
Huntington Univ	IN	33,996	C
Illinois State Univ	IL	23,418	VC
Iowa State Univ	IA	17,570	C
Lincoln Univ	MO	13,602	NC
McNeese State Univ	LA	7,838	C
Mich State Univ	MI	23,898	VC+
Miss State Univ	MS	11,454	C+
Missouri State Univ	MO	15,190	C+
Morehead State Univ	KY	17,422	C
New Mexico State Univ	NM	14,050	C
N Car State Univ	NC	19,515	HC+
N Dak State Univ	ND	16,245	C
Northwest Missouri State Univ	MO	17,737	C
Northwestern Okla State Univ	OK	13,072	NC
Oregon State Univ	OR	22,519	VC
Pennsylvania State Univ - Univ Park	PA	29,760	HC
Prescott College	AZ	33,284	C
Purdue Univ/West Lafayette	IN	20,032	MC
Rutgers Univ - New Brunswick	NJ	26,632	HC
Sam Houston State Univ	TX	18,792	C
S Dak State Univ	SD	15,634	C
Southern Arkansas Univ	AR	21,532	C
Southern Illinois Univ Carbondale	IL	23,667	C
Southern Univ and A&M College	LA	16,074	LC+
Stephen F. Austin State Univ	TX	18,406	LC
Sterling College	VT	41,894	VC
Tarleton State Univ	TX	15,248	LC
Tenn State Univ	TN	14,423	C
Tenn Tech Univ	TN	17,050	C
Texas A&M Univ at Commerce	TX	10,496	C
Texas State Univ	TX	19,350	C
Texas Tech Univ	TX	18,736	C+
The Univ of Tenn at Knoxville	TN	22,112	VC
The Univ of Tenn at Martin	TN	14,876	C
Truman State Univ	MO	16,014	HC
Unity College	ME	37,670	C
Univ of Arkansas at Monticello	AR	13,134	NC
Univ of Arkansas at Pine Bluff	AR	13,541	C
Univ of Conn	CT	25,538	HC
Univ of Delaware	DE	24,976	VC+
Univ of Hawaii at Hilo	HI	18,038	C
Univ of Idaho	ID	15,348	C
Univ of Kentucky	KY	33,306	C
Univ of Maine	ME	20,792	C
Univ of Maryland/College Park	MD	21,938	HC
Univ of Maryland/Eastern Shore	MD	17,013	C
Univ of Missouri/Columbia	MO	18,201	MC
Univ of Nebr - Lincoln	NE	18,589	VC
Virginia State Univ	VA	19,802	C+
Washington State Univ	WA	22,495	C
West Texas A&M Univ	TX	13,478	C
West Virginia Univ	WV	18,210	C
Western Illinois Univ	IL	20,825	C
Western Kentucky Univ	KY	16,850	C
Xavier Univ	OH	47,880	C+

AGRONOMY

School	ST	$IS	SR
Alabama A&M Univ	AL	18,796	C
Auburn Univ	AL	23,594	VC+
Calif Polytechnic State Univ	CA	17,979	HC+
College of the Ozarks	MO	7,230	C
Colo State Univ	CO	22,162	VC
Delaware Valley Univ	PA	49,796	C
Iowa State Univ	IA	17,570	C
Kansas State Univ	KS	17,780	VC
Miss State Univ	MS	11,454	C+
Murray State Univ	KY	16,998	C
New Mexico State Univ	NM	14,050	C
N Car State Univ	NC	19,515	HC+
Northwest Missouri State Univ	MO	17,737	C
Okla Panhandle State Univ	OK	6,152	NC
Oregon State Univ	OR	22,519	VC
Prairie View A&M Univ	TX	15,205	LC
Purdue Univ/West Lafayette	IN	20,032	MC
S Dak State Univ	SD	15,634	C
Tarleton State Univ	TX	15,248	LC
Texas A&M Univ	TX	20,521	VC+
Truman State Univ	MO	16,014	HC
Univ of Conn	CT	25,538	HC
Univ of Florida	FL	16,291	HC+
Univ of Illinois at Urbana-Champaign	IL	27,006	HC
Univ of Minn Crookston	MN	19,739	C
Univ of Nebr - Lincoln	NE	18,589	VC
Univ of Wisc-Madison	WI	20,934	MC
Univ of Wisc-River Falls	WI	14,485	C
Washington State Univ	WA	22,495	C
West Virginia Univ	WV	18,210	C
Western Kentucky Univ	KY	16,850	C
Wilmington College	OH	34,600	C

AIR TRAFFIC CONTROL

School	ST	$IS	SR
Daniel Webster College	NH	26,984	C
Florida Memorial Univ	FL	22,270	LC
Lewis Univ	IL	40,370	C
Purdue Univ/West Lafayette	IN	20,032	MC
Thomas Edison State Univ	NJ	6,350	NC
Univ of Alaska Anchorage	AK	16,652	NC
Univ of N Dak	ND	15,373	C
Vaughn College of Aeronautics and Technology	NY	37,180	C

AIR TRAFFIC MANAGEMENT

School	ST	$IS	SR
Arizona State Univ at the Polytechnic Campus	AZ	21,360	VC
Daniel Webster College	NH	26,984	C
Embry-Riddle Aeronautical Univ - Daytona Beach	FL	44,712	VC
Embry-Riddle Aeronautical Univ - Prescott Campus	AZ	44,054	VC
Lewis Univ	IL	40,370	C

AIRCRAFT MECHANICS

School	ST	$IS	SR
Andrews Univ	MI	28,030	C+
Embry-Riddle Aeronautical Univ - Daytona Beach	FL	44,712	VC
Idaho State Univ	ID	13,619	NC
Lewis Univ	IL	40,370	C
Pennsylvania College of Technology	PA	27,333	NC
Vaughn College of Aeronautics and Technology	NY	37,180	C

AIRLINE PILOTING AND NAVIGATION

School	ST	$IS	SR
Averett Univ	VA	40,970	LC
Baylor Univ	TX	53,760	HC
Eastern Kentucky Univ	KY	16,908	C
Eastern Mich Univ	MI	19,761	C
Indiana State Univ	IN	23,223	LC
Kansas State Univ	KS	17,780	VC
Lewis Univ	IL	40,370	C
Louisiana Tech Univ	LA	11,422	VC
Metropolitan State Univ of Denver	CO	29,889	LC
Ohio Univ	OH	22,924	C
Pacific Union College	CA	36,009	VC
Purdue Univ/West Lafayette	IN	20,032	MC
St. Louis Univ	MO	49,866	HC
Univ of Alaska Anchorage	AK	16,652	NC
Univ of Illinois at Urbana-Champaign	IL	27,006	HC
Univ of Minn Crookston	MN	19,739	C
Vaughn College of Aeronautics and Technology	NY	37,180	C
Western Mich Univ	MI	21,054	C

ALLIED HEALTH

School	ST	$IS	SR
Adams State Univ	CO	17,703	LC
Albany State Univ	GA	19,462	C
Andrews Univ	MI	28,030	C+
Azusa Pacific Univ	CA	43,972	C
Bloomfield College	NJ	39,100	LC
Cedarville Univ	OH	34,990	VC
Clayton State Univ	GA	19,735	C
College of Mount St. Vincent	NY	45,620	C
College of the Ozarks	MO	7,230	C
East Tenn State Univ	TN	13,994	C
Eastern Mich Univ	MI	19,761	C
Fairleigh Dickinson Univ/ College at Florham	NJ	52,062	C
Fairleigh Dickinson Univ/ Metropolitan Campus	NJ	40,254	C
Felician Univ	NJ	45,370	LC
Ferris State Univ	MI	21,445	C
George Fox Univ	OR	42,938	C
Georgian Court Univ	NJ	42,426	LC
Hendrix College	AR	54,020	VC+
Howard Univ	DC	37,616	C+
Indiana Univ Bloomington	IN	20,429	VC
Ithaca College	NY	56,766	VC
Johnson State College	VT	20,752	C
Mars Hill Univ	NC	42,688	C
Marshall Univ	WV	17,242	C
Mass College of Liberal Arts	MA	20,128	C
MCPHS Univ	MA	45,470	SP
Merrimack College	MA	52,770	C
Millersville Univ of Pennsylvania	PA	23,782	C
Milligan College	TN	38,150	C
Millikin Univ	IL	42,158	C
Minn State Univ, Mankato	MN	15,616	C
Montclair State Univ	NJ	26,210	LC
Mount Aloysius College	PA	29,976	C
National Univ	CA	14,730	LC
Nebr Methodist College	NE	25,134	SP
Oakland Univ	MI	20,763	C
Oakwood Univ	AL	43,758	C
Okla Baptist Univ	OK	32,320	C
Ramapo College of New Jersey	NJ	25,338	C
Rochester Inst of Technology	NY	50,842	HC
Roosevelt Univ	IL	40,651	VC
Rutgers Univ - New Brunswick	NJ	26,632	HC
Rutgers Univ - Newark	NJ	27,288	C
St. Louis Univ	MO	49,866	HC
Silver Lake College of the Holy Family	WI	36,290	LC
Texas State Univ	TX	19,350	C
Tuskegee Univ	AL	28,164	C
Univ of Central Okla	OK	13,486	C
Univ of Florida	FL	16,291	HC+
Univ of Illinois at Chicago	IL	25,006	VC
Univ of Maine at Machias	ME	22,960	C
Univ of Maryland/Baltimore County	MD	21,296	VC
Univ of St. Francis	IL	39,924	C
Univ of Tampa	FL	36,944	C
Univ of Texas at El Paso	TX	34,452	NC
Univ of Tulsa	OK	52,625	HC+
Washington Univ in St. Louis	MO	65,366	VC
West Texas A&M Univ	TX	13,478	C
Western Kentucky Univ	KY	16,850	C
Youngstown State Univ	OH	17,307	C

AMERICAN INDIAN STUDIES

School	ST	$IS	SR
Arizona State Univ at the Tempe Campus	AZ	21,756	VC
Brown Univ	RI	64,566	MC
Fort Lewis College	CO	18,980	C
Minn State Univ, Mankato	MN	15,616	C
Northland College	WI	41,103	C+
San Diego State Univ	CA	21,896	C+
Sonoma State Univ	CA	27,806	C
Southern Oregon Univ	OR	19,117	C
Southwestern Okla State Univ	OK	11,790	C
Univ of Alaska Fairbanks	AK	16,179	C
Univ of Arizona	AZ	23,100	C
Univ of Calif at Los Angeles	CA	30,162	MC
Univ of Minn/Morris	MN	20,760	VC
Univ of Minn/Twin Cities	MN	23,519	HC+
Univ of N Car at Pembroke	NC	14,388	LC
Univ of N Dak	ND	15,373	C
Univ of Science and Arts of Okla	OK	11,140	VC
Univ of S Dak	SD	16,109	C
Univ of Wisc-Eau Claire	WI	15,797	VC
Univ of Wisc-Green Bay	WI	15,064	C
Univ of Wyoming	WY	15,375	C+
West Virginia Univ	WV	18,210	C

AMERICAN LITERATURE

School	ST	$IS	SR
American Univ	DC	59,379	HC+
Bennington College	VT	63,960	MC
Biola Univ	CA	46,402	C+
Brown Univ	RI	64,566	MC
Bryant Univ	RI	55,646	VC
Calvin College	MI	41,570	VC+
Eastern Mich Univ	MI	19,761	C
Florida State Univ	FL	16,771	HC

ST = STATE $IS = IN-STATE COSTS SR = SELECTOR RATING

School	ST	$IS	SR
Hofstra Univ	NY	55,960	C+
Mount Ida College	MA	46,820	C
New York Univ	NY	65,860	MC
Southern Illinois Univ Edwardsville	IL	22,643	C
Univ of Calif at Los Angeles	CA	30,162	MC
Washington Univ in St. Louis	MO	65,366	VC
Wellesley College	MA	63,916	MC

AMERICAN SIGN LANGUAGE

School	ST	$IS	SR
Augustana Univ	SD	38,424	VC
Bethel College	IN	35,860	C
Biola Univ	CA	46,402	C+
Bloomsburg Univ of Pennsylvania	PA	19,066	LC
Columbia College Chicago	IL	43,168	C
Framingham State Univ	MA	20,584	C
Gallaudet Univ	DC	29,118	LC
Gardner-Webb Univ	NC	39,200	C+
Goshen College	IN	42,500	C
Indiana Univ-Purdue Univ Indianapolis	IN	18,635	C
Kent State Univ	OH	20,732	C
Keuka College	NY	39,762	C
Lamar Univ	TX	18,014	LC
Maryville College	TN	44,410	C
Mount Aloysius College	PA	29,976	C
Northeastern Univ	MA	62,703	MC
Rochester Inst of Technology	NY	50,842	HC
St. Catherine Univ	MN	45,630	VC
Univ of Arkansas at Little Rock	AR	18,211	C
Univ of Houston	TX	21,483	VC
Univ of Louisville	KY	19,824	C
Univ of New Mexico	NM	15,404	C
Univ of North Florida	FL	15,996	VC
Univ of Northern Colo	CO	20,851	C
Univ of Rochester	NY	65,032	MC
Western Oregon Univ	OR	15,021	LC
William Woods Univ	MO	32,040	C
Wright State Univ	OH	16,983	C

AMERICAN STUDIES

School	ST	$IS	SR
Albright College	PA	46,660	C
American Univ	DC	59,379	HC+
Amherst College	MA		HC+
Arizona State Univ at the West Campus	AZ	20,640	C
Ashland Univ	OH	21,440	C
Augustana Univ	SD	38,424	VC
Austin College	TX	45,875	VC
Bard College	NY	64,024	HC
Barnard College/Columbia Univ	NY	62,741	MC
Bates College	ME	64,500	MC
Baylor Univ	TX	53,760	HC
Bennington College	VT	63,960	MC
Boston Univ	MA	65,110	MC
Bowling Green State Univ	OH	19,747	C
Brandeis Univ	MA	65,925	MC
Brigham Young Univ	UT	12,748	HC
Brown Univ	RI	64,566	MC
Bryant Univ	RI	55,646	VC
Cabrini Univ	PA	42,591	LC
Cal State, Fullerton	CA	21,902	C
Cal State, Long Beach	CA	18,850	C
Cal State, San Bernardino	CA	12,000	C
Carleton College	MN	64,071	MC
Case Western Reserve Univ	OH	60,304	MC
Christopher Newport Univ	VA	23,968	VC+
CUNY/Brooklyn College	NY	5,884	C+
CUNY/City College	NY	20,319	VC
CUNY/College of Staten Island	NY	17,840	NC
CUNY/Lehman College	NY	5,778	HC+
CUNY/Queens College	NY	27,896	C
Claflin Univ	SC	33,764	LC
Claremont McKenna College	CA	67,185	MC
Coe College	IA	51,570	VC
Colby College	ME	64,060	MC
College of St. Elizabeth	NJ	44,432	LC
College of William & Mary	VA		MC
Columbia College - Missouri	MO	27,803	C
Columbia Univ/City of New York	NY	62,958	MC
Conn College	CT	65,000	MC
Cornell Univ	NY	64,853	MC
Creighton Univ	NE	48,206	VC+
Cumberland Univ	TN	27,710	C
DePaul Univ	IL	47,623	VC
Dickinson College	PA	63,974	MC
Dominican Univ	IL	41,222	C
Drury Univ	MO	33,791	VC
Eckerd College	FL	52,874	C
Elmhurst College	IL	45,428	C
Elmira College	NY	53,900	C
Elms College	MA	45,646	VC
Elon Univ	NC	44,599	VC+
Emmanuel College	MA	52,110	C+
Emory Univ	GA	60,786	MC
Erskine College	SC	45,460	C
Fairfield Univ	CT	59,860	VC+
Florida State Univ	FL	16,771	HC
Fordham Univ	NY	65,918	MC
Franklin and Marshall College	PA	63,170	HC
Franklin Pierce Univ	NH	46,750	C
George Washington Univ	DC	62,835	MC
Georgetown College	KY	41,440	C
Georgetown Univ	DC	65,926	MC
Goucher College	MD	55,716	VC
Hamilton College	NY	64,250	MC
Hampshire College	MA	63,824	MC
Harding Univ	AR	25,421	C
Harvard College/Harvard Univ	MA	60,659	MC
Hendrix College	AR	54,020	VC+
Hillsdale College	MI	35,722	MC
Hofstra Univ	NY	55,960	C+
Illinois College	IL	40,850	VC
Illinois Wesleyan Univ	IL	56,430	VC+
Indiana Univ Bloomington	IN	20,429	VC
Keene State College	NH	24,003	LC
Kent State Univ	OH	20,732	C
Kenyon College	OH	63,330	MC
Knox College	IL	52,615	VC+
Lafayette College	PA	63,355	MC
Lake Forest College	IL	50,652	VC
Lebanon Valley College	PA	51,530	C
Lenoir-Rhyne Univ	NC	43,200	C
Lindsey Wilson College	KY	32,882	C
Lipscomb Univ	TN	41,296	VC
LIU Post	NY	49,682	C
Lycoming College	PA	48,580	C
Macalester College	MN	61,905	MC
Manhattanville College	NY	51,440	C+
Marist College	NY	49,860	VC
Mary Baldwin Univ	VA	39,865	C
Meredith College	NC	45,297	C
Miami Univ	OH	27,190	HC+
Mich State Univ	MI	23,898	VC+
Middlebury College	VT	64,332	MC
Miss College	MS	25,850	C
Montreat College	NC	31,298	LC
Mount Ida College	MA	46,820	C
Mount St. Mary's Univ - Chalon Campus	CA	43,897	VC+
Muhlenberg College	PA	56,645	VC+
Muskingum Univ	OH	35,966	C
Nazareth College	NY	45,574	C
New York Univ	NY	65,860	MC
Northwestern Univ	IL	66,344	MC
Oberlin College	OH	66,012	MC
Occidental College	CA	65,530	MC
Oglethorpe Univ	GA	44,200	C+
Okla State Univ	OK	17,180	VC
Oregon State Univ	OR	22,519	VC
Pace Univ	NY	58,248	C
Pitzer College	CA	66,192	MC
Pomona College	CA	64,957	MC
Providence College	RI	60,760	VC
Ramapo College of New Jersey	NJ	25,338	C
Reed College	OR	65,300	MC
Rider Univ	NJ	54,050	C
Roger Williams Univ	RI	46,296	C+
Roosevelt Univ	IL	40,651	VC
Rowan Univ	NJ	24,491	VC+
Rutgers Univ - New Brunswick	NJ	26,632	HC
Rutgers Univ - Newark	NJ	27,288	C
St. Louis Univ	MO	49,866	HC
St. Michael's College	VT	51,725	VC+
St. Peter's Univ	NJ	49,192	C
Salem College	NC	37,694	HC
Salve Regina Univ	RI	51,470	C
San Francisco State Univ	CA	18,514	LC
Scripps College	CA	66,664	MC
Sewanee: The Univ of the South	TN	54,500	MC
Siena College	NY	48,916	C+
Skidmore College	NY	64,214	HC
Smith College	MA	63,914	MC
Southern Nazarene Univ	OK	32,798	NC
St. John Fisher College	NY	43,620	C
St. Olaf College	MN	54,260	HC+
Stanford Univ	CA	60,409	MC
SUNY / SUNY College at Old Westbury	NY	16,860	C
SUNY / SUNY Fredonia	NY	20,818	C
SUNY / Univ at Buffalo	NY	23,122	C+
SUNY at Geneseo	NY	20,440	VC+
SUNY at Oswego	NY	21,351	C
Stetson Univ	FL	53,544	VC
Stonehill College	MA	55,030	C+
Stony Brook Univ/The SUNY	NY	21,881	MC
Suffolk Univ	MA	50,308	C
Temple Univ	PA	24,392	VC
Texas State Univ	TX	19,350	C
Trinity College	CT	63,920	HC+
Tufts Univ	MA		MC
Tulane Univ	LA	63,396	HC+
Union College	NY	64,320	MC
Univ of Alabama	AL	24,320	C+
Univ of Arkansas at Fayetteville	AR	19,152	C+
Univ of Calif at Berkeley	CA	28,853	MC
Univ of Calif at Davis	CA	28,468	HC
Univ of Calif, Santa Cruz	CA	28,731	C+
Univ of Dayton	OH	53,620	C
Univ of Florida	FL	16,291	HC+
Univ of Hawaii at Manoa	HI	23,221	C
Univ of Iowa	IA	18,683	VC+
Univ of Kansas	KS	20,135	C+
Univ of Mary Washington	VA	24,764	VC
Univ of Maryland/Baltimore County	MD	21,296	VC
Univ of Maryland/College Park	MD	21,938	HC
Univ of Mass Boston	MA	13,435	C
Univ of Mass Lowell	MA	26,380	C
Univ of Miami	FL	63,494	MC
Univ of Mich/Ann Arbor	MI	24,410	MC
Univ of Mich/Dearborn	MI	11,757	VC
Univ of Minn/Twin Cities	MN	23,519	HC+
Univ of Mount Union	OH	38,970	C
Univ of New Mexico	NM	15,404	C
Univ of N Car at Chapel Hill	NC	20,052	HC+
Univ of Notre Dame	IN	64,043	MC
Univ of Pennsylvania	PA	63,526	MC
Univ of Pittsburgh at Greensburg	PA	23,132	C
Univ of Pittsburgh at Johnstown	PA	22,092	C
Univ of Richmond	VA	60,880	MC
Univ of Rio Grande & Rio Grande Community College	OH	8,750	NC
Univ of Rochester	NY	65,032	MC
Univ of San Francisco	CA	58,484	VC
Univ of South Florida/Tampa	FL	16,110	VC+
Univ of Southern Calif	CA	66,631	C
Univ of Texas at Austin	TX	26,102	HC
Univ of Texas at Dallas	TX	22,830	VC+
Univ of Texas at San Antonio	TX	20,157	C
Univ of Wisc-Stevens Point	WI	14,043	C
Univ of Wyoming	WY	15,375	C+
Upper Iowa Univ	IA	34,990	NC
Ursinus College	PA	61,690	VC
Utah State Univ	UT	12,736	C
Valparaiso Univ	IN	48,370	C+
Vanderbilt Univ	TN	60,572	MC
Vassar College	NY	65,491	MC
Virginia Wesleyan College	VA	43,728	LC
Warner Pacific College	OR	33,790	C
Washington College	MD	54,666	VC
Washington State Univ	WA	22,495	C
Washington Univ in St. Louis	MO	65,366	VC
Webster Univ	MO	37,490	C
Wellesley College	MA	63,916	MC
Wesley College	DE	37,026	LC
Wesleyan College	GA	29,694	C+
Wesleyan Univ	CT	65,516	MC
West Chester Univ of Pennsylvania	PA	18,456	C
Western Conn State Univ	CT	21,254	LC
Western New England Univ	MA	48,088	C
Western Washington Univ	WA	18,003	C+
Wheaton College	MA	61,512	VC
Wheelock College	MA	49,225	C
Whitworth Univ	WA	51,732	VC
Willamette Univ	OR	61,817	VC+
Williams College	MA	63,290	MC
Yale Univ	CT	64,650	MC

ANATOMY

School	ST	$IS	SR
Andrews Univ	MI	28,030	C+
Duke Univ	NC	64,188	
Howard Univ	DC	37,616	C+
Marshall Univ	WV	17,242	C

ANIMAL FEED SCIENCE

School	ST	$IS	SR
Kansas State Univ	KS	17,780	VC

ANIMAL SCIENCE

School	ST	$IS	SR
Abilene Christian Univ	TX	41,800	C+
Alabama A&M Univ	AL	18,796	C
Andrews Univ	MI	28,030	C+
Angelo State Univ	TX	15,263	NC
Arkansas State Univ	AR	16,190	C
Auburn Univ	AL	23,594	VC+
Becker College	MA	57,628	C
Berry College	GA	45,286	C+
Bucknell Univ	PA	64,616	MC
Calif Polytechnic State Univ	CA	17,979	HC+
Calif State Polytechnic Univ, Pomona	CA	21,541	C
Cal State, Chico	CA	21,440	C
Cal State, Fresno	CA	16,902	LC
Clemson Univ	SC		HC
College of the Ozarks	MO	7,230	C
Colo State Univ	CO	22,162	VC
Cornell Univ	NY	64,853	MC
Delaware Valley Univ	PA	49,796	C
Dordt College	IA	37,860	C+
Eastern New Mexico Univ	NM	14,416	C
Florida A&M Univ	FL	15,361	C
Fort Valley State Univ	GA	17,988	VC
Hampshire College	MA	63,824	MC
Hardin-Simmons Univ	TX	33,966	C
Indiana Univ Bloomington	IN	20,429	VC
Iowa State Univ	IA	17,570	C
Kansas State Univ	KS	17,780	VC
Langston Univ	OK	14,314	C
Louisiana State Univ and A&M College	LA	18,677	VC
Louisiana Tech Univ	LA	11,422	VC
Lubbock Christian Univ	TX	28,426	C
Mich State Univ	MI	23,898	VC+
Middle Tenn State Univ	TN	8,650	C
Millersville Univ of Pennsylvania	PA	23,782	C
Miss State Univ	MS	11,454	C+
Missouri State Univ	MO	15,190	C+
Montana State Univ	MT	15,500	C+
New Mexico State Univ	NM	14,050	C
N Car A&T State Univ	NC	13,365	LC
N Car State Univ	NC	19,515	HC+
N Dak State Univ	ND	16,245	C
Northwest Missouri State Univ	MO	17,737	C
Ohio State Univ at Columbus	OH	21,703	HC+
Okla Panhandle State Univ	OK	6,152	NC
Okla State Univ	OK	17,180	VC
Oregon State Univ	OR	22,519	VC
Pennsylvania State Univ - Univ Park	PA	29,760	HC
Prairie View A&M Univ	TX	15,205	LC
Purdue Univ/West Lafayette	IN	20,032	MC
Rutgers Univ - New Brunswick	NJ	26,632	HC
Sam Houston State Univ	TX	18,792	C
S Dak State Univ	SD	15,634	C
Southeast Missouri State Univ	MO	15,498	C
Southern Illinois Univ Carbondale	IL	23,667	C
SUNY / The College of Environmental Science and Forestry	NY	23,853	VC
SUNY /College of Agriculture and Tech at Cobleskill	NY	20,527	LC
Stephen F. Austin State Univ	TX	18,406	LC
Sul Ross State Univ	TX	15,021	LC
Tarleton State Univ	TX	15,248	LC
Tenn Tech Univ	TN	17,050	C
Texas A&M Univ	TX	20,521	VC+
Texas A&M Univ at Commerce	TX	10,496	C
Texas A&M Univ at Kingsville	TX	7,500	LC
Texas State Univ	TX	19,350	C
Texas Tech Univ	TX	18,736	C+
The Univ of Tenn at Knoxville	TN	22,112	VC
The Univ of Tenn at Martin	TN	14,876	C
Truman State Univ	MO	16,014	HC
Tuskegee Univ	AL	28,164	C
Unity College	ME	37,670	C
Univ of Arizona	AZ	23,100	C
Univ of Arkansas at Fayetteville	AR	19,152	C+
Univ of Calif at Davis	CA	28,468	HC
Univ of Conn	CT	25,538	HC
Univ of Delaware	DE	24,976	VC+
Univ of Findlay	OH	60,139	C
Univ of Florida	FL	16,291	HC+
Univ of Georgia	GA	21,250	HC
Univ of Hawaii at Manoa	HI	23,221	C
Univ of Idaho	ID	15,348	C
Univ of Illinois at Urbana-Champaign	IL	27,006	HC
Univ of Kentucky	KY	33,306	C
Univ of Maine	ME	20,792	C
Univ of Maryland/College Park	MD	21,938	HC
Univ of Mass Amherst	MA	26,199	VC+
Univ of Minn Crookston	MN	19,739	C
Univ of Minn/Twin Cities	MN	23,519	HC+
Univ of Missouri/Columbia	MO	18,201	MC
Univ of Montana-Western	MT	11,220	LC
Univ of Nebr - Lincoln	NE	18,589	VC
Univ of New England	ME	48,420	MC
Univ of New Hampshire	NH	28,562	VC
Univ of PR, at Mayaguez	PR	13,995	
Univ of Vermont	VT	28,878	HC
Univ of Wisc-Madison	WI	20,934	MC
Univ of Wisc-Platteville	WI	14,614	VC
Univ of Wisc-River Falls	WI	14,485	C
Univ of Wyoming	WY	15,375	C+
Utah State Univ	UT	12,736	C
Utica College	NY	30,430	C
Virginia Polytechnic Inst and State Univ	VA	21,276	HC
Washington State Univ	WA	22,495	C
West Texas A&M Univ	TX	13,478	C
West Virginia Univ	WV	18,210	C
Western Illinois Univ	IL	20,825	C
Wilmington College	OH	34,600	C
Wilson College	PA	35,620	C

ANIMAL SCIENCE & TECHNOLOGY

School	ST	$IS	SR
Tarleton State Univ	TX	15,248	LC
Univ of Rhode Island	RI	24,906	C

ANIMATION

School	ST	$IS	SR
Art Inst of Portland	OR	132,329	SP
Ball State Univ	IN	19,590	C
Bennington College	VT	63,960	MC
Bloomfield College	NJ	39,100	LC
Brigham Young Univ	UT	12,748	HC
Buena Vista Univ	IA	41,514	C
Calif College of the Arts	CA	52,758	SP
Calif Inst of the Arts	CA	56,426	SP
Cleveland Inst of Art	OH	51,439	C+
Cogswell Polytechnical College	CA	30,531	C

School	ST	$IS	SR
College for Creative Studies	MI	48,875	SP
Colo Mesa Univ	CO	18,955	LC
Columbus College of Art and Design	OH	37,732	C
Daemen College	NY	38,045	C
DePaul Univ	IL	47,623	VC
Drexel Univ	PA	65,432	VC+
Eastern Mich Univ	MI	19,761	C
Fairleigh Dickinson Univ/ College at Florham	NJ	52,062	C
Huntington Univ	IN	33,996	C
Kansas City Art Inst	MO	44,308	C+
Laguna College of Art and Design	CA	41,422	LC
Lawrence Tech Univ	MI	39,770	VC
Loyola Marymount Univ	CA	58,038	HC
Maryland Inst College of Art	MD	56,795	SP
Mass College of Art and Design	MA	24,800	SP
Memphis College of Art	TN	39,750	C
Minneapolis College of Art and Design	MN	44,238	SP
Moore College of Art and Design	PA	50,135	SP
Moore College of Art and Design	PA	50,135	SP
New Mexico State Univ	NM	14,050	C
New York Univ	NY	65,860	MC
NewSchool of Architecture & Design	CA	12,341	SP
Ringling College of Art and Design	FL	57,430	SP
Rochester Inst of Technology	NY	50,842	HC
Rocky Mountain College of Art and Design	CO	27,052	SP
Santa Fe Univ of Art and Design	NM	39,980	SP
Savannah College of Art and Design	GA	49,595	C
School of Visual Arts	NY	47,500	SP
Southern Adventist Univ	TN	27,600	C
SUNY / SUNY Fredonia	NY	20,818	C
The Art Inst of Atlanta	GA	34,334	SP
Univ of Denver	CO	58,443	VC+
Univ of Idaho	ID	15,348	C
Univ of Northwestern - St. Paul	MN	38,160	C
Univ of St. Francis	IN	37,400	C
Webster Univ	MO	37,490	C
Woodbury Univ	CA	46,958	C

ANTHROPOLOGY

School	ST	$IS	SR
Adelphi Univ	NY	48,244	C
Agnes Scott College	GA	51,930	VC+
Albion College	MI	52,650	C
Alma College	MI	47,548	C
American Univ	DC	59,379	HC+
Amherst College	MA		HC+
Andrews Univ	MI	28,030	C+
Appalachian State Univ	NC	14,416	VC
Arizona State Univ at the Tempe Campus	AZ	21,756	VC
Ashford Univ	CA	10,480	C
Auburn Univ	AL	23,594	VC+
Augusta Univ	GA	4,632	C
Augustana College	IL	49,658	VC
Augustana Univ	SD	38,424	VC
Ball State Univ	IN	19,590	C
Bard College	NY	64,024	HC
Barnard College/Columbia Univ	NY	62,741	MC
Bates College	ME	64,500	MC
Baylor Univ	TX	53,760	HC
Beloit College	WI	55,206	HC
Bennington College	VT	63,960	MC
Berry College	GA	45,286	C+
Biola Univ	CA	46,402	C+
Bloomsburg Univ of Pennsylvania	PA	19,066	LC
Boise State Univ	ID	14,860	C
Boston Univ	MA	65,110	MC
Bowdoin College	ME	63,500	MC
Brandeis Univ	MA	65,925	MC
Bridgewater State Univ	MA	21,810	C
Brigham Young Univ	UT	12,748	HC
Brown Univ	RI	64,566	MC
Bryn Athyn College	PA	31,470	C
Bryn Mawr College	PA	59,890	MC
Bucknell Univ	PA	64,616	MC
Butler Univ	IN	51,352	VC
Calif Baptist Univ	CA	41,392	C
Calif Polytechnic State Univ	CA	17,979	HC+
Calif State Polytechnic Univ, Pomona	CA	21,541	C
Cal State, Bakersfield	CA	19,191	LC
Cal State, Chico	CA	21,440	C
Cal State, Dominguez Hills	CA	19,022	LC
Cal State, East Bay	CA	19,413	C
Cal State, Fresno	CA	16,902	LC
Cal State, Fullerton	CA	21,902	C
Cal State, Long Beach	CA	18,850	C
Cal State, Los Angeles	CA	17,186	LC
Cal State, Northridge	CA	16,859	LC
Cal State, Sacramento	CA	20,332	C
Cal State, San Bernardino	CA	12,000	C
Cal State, Stanislaus	CA	16,212	C
Canisius College	NY	47,537	C
Carleton College	MN	64,071	MC
Case Western Reserve Univ	OH	60,304	MC
Central College	IA	44,592	C
Central Conn State Univ	CT	21,203	C
Central Mich Univ	MI	20,330	C
Central Washington Univ	WA	16,803	C
Centre College	KY	49,250	HC
CUNY/Brooklyn College	NY	5,884	C+
CUNY/City College	NY	20,319	VC
CUNY/Hunter College	NY	31,098	VC
CUNY/Lehman College	NY	5,778	HC+
CUNY/Queens College	NY	27,896	C
CUNY/York College	NY	6,747	LC
Clarion Univ of Pennsylvania	PA	21,608	LC
Cleveland State Univ	OH	22,196	C
Colby College	ME	64,060	MC
Colgate Univ	NY	65,030	MC
College of Charleston	SC	22,699	C
College of the Holy Cross	MA	62,165	MC
College of William & Mary	VA		MC
Colo College	CO	62,560	MC
Colo State Univ	CO	22,162	VC
Columbia Univ/ School of General Studies	NY	61,470	MC
Columbia Univ/City of New York	NY	62,958	MC
Conn College	CT	65,000	MC
Cornell Univ	NY	64,853	MC
Dartmouth College	NH	66,174	MC
Davidson College	NC	60,119	MC
Denison Univ	OH	58,860	MC
DePaul Univ	IL	47,623	VC
DePauw Univ	IN	58,688	HC+
Dickinson College	PA	63,974	MC
Drew Univ/College of Liberal Arts	NJ	61,048	VC
Drexel Univ	PA	65,432	VC+
Duke Univ	NC	64,188	
Earlham College	IN	54,870	HC
East Carolina Univ	NC	16,937	C
Eastern Kentucky Univ	KY	16,908	C
Eastern Mich Univ	MI	19,761	C
Eastern New Mexico Univ	NM	14,416	C
Eastern Oregon Univ	OR	17,715	C
Eastern Washington Univ	WA	25,572	LC
Eckerd College	FL	52,874	C
Edinboro Univ	PA	15,940	LC
Elon Univ	NC	44,599	VC+
Emory Univ	GA	60,786	MC
Eugene Lang College/The New School for Liberal Arts	NY	55,650	C
Florida Atlantic Univ	FL	17,339	C
Florida Gulf Coast Univ	FL	9,682	C
Florida State Univ	FL	16,771	HC
Fordham Univ	NY	65,918	MC
Fort Lewis College	CO	18,980	C
Franciscan Univ of Steubenville	OH	33,980	VC
Franklin and Marshall College	PA	63,170	HC
Franklin Pierce Univ	NH	46,750	C
George Mason Univ	VA	15,724	VC
George Washington Univ	DC	62,835	MC
Georgetown Univ	DC	65,926	MC
Georgia Southern Univ	GA	16,596	C
Georgia State Univ	GA	24,332	VC
Gettysburg College	PA	63,000	HC
Goucher College	MD	55,716	VC
Grand Valley State Univ	MI	22,250	C+
Grinnell College	IA	60,738	MC
Guilford College	NC	44,090	C
Gustavus Adolphus College	MN	52,433	HC
Hamilton College	NY	64,250	MC
Hamline Univ	MN	45,678	VC
Hampshire College	MA	63,824	MC
Hanover College	IN	46,364	C+
Hartwick College	NY	51,270	C
Harvard College/Harvard Univ	MA	60,659	MC
Haverford College	PA	66,490	MC
Hawaii Pacific Univ	HI	33,420	C
Heidelberg Univ	OH	39,200	C
Hendrix College	AR	54,020	VC+
Hofstra Univ	NY	55,960	C+
Howard Univ	DC	37,616	C+
Humboldt State Univ	CA	20,514	C
Idaho State Univ	ID	13,619	NC
Illinois State Univ	IL	23,418	VC
Illinois Wesleyan Univ	IL	56,430	VC+
Indiana State Univ	IN	23,223	LC
Indiana Univ Bloomington	IN	20,429	VC
Indiana Univ Northwest	IN	7,072	C
Indiana Univ of Pennsylvania	PA	23,614	LC
Indiana Univ South Bend	IN	14,242	C
Indiana Univ-Purdue Univ Fort Wayne	IN	17,553	C
Indiana Univ-Purdue Univ Indianapolis	IN	18,635	C
Iowa State Univ	IA	17,570	C
Ithaca College	NY	56,766	VC
James Madison Univ	VA	19,084	VC
Johns Hopkins Univ	MD	65,386	MC
Johnson State College	VT	20,752	C
Judson Univ	IL	37,700	C
Juniata College	PA	53,760	VC
Kalamazoo College	MI	53,931	HC+
Kansas State Univ	KS	17,780	VC
Keene State College	NH	24,003	LC
Kennesaw State Univ	GA	19,592	VC
Kent State Univ	OH	20,732	C
Kenyon College	OH	63,330	MC
Knox College	IL	52,615	VC+
Kutztown Univ of Pennsylvania	PA	19,056	LC
Lafayette College	PA	63,355	MC
Lake Forest College	IL	50,652	VC
Lawrence Univ	WI	54,498	HC
Le Moyne College	NY	46,000	C
Lee Univ	TN	22,045	C
Lehigh Univ	PA	61,010	MC
Lewis & Clark College	OR	58,434	HC+
Linfield College	OR	52,010	C
Longwood Univ	VA	22,184	C
Louisiana State Univ and A&M College	LA	18,677	VC
Loyola Univ Chicago	IL	55,802	VC
Luther College	IA	48,540	C+
Lycoming College	PA	48,580	C
Lyon College	AR	34,730	C+
Macalester College	MN	61,905	MC
Marquette Univ	WI	48,390	VC+
Mass Inst of Technology	MA	62,662	MC
Mercer Univ	GA	45,348	VC
Mercyhurst Univ	PA	47,420	C
Metropolitan State Univ of Denver	CO	29,889	LC
Miami Univ	OH	27,190	HC+
Mich State Univ	MI	23,898	VC+
Mich Tech Univ	MI	24,739	VC+
Middle Tenn State Univ	TN	8,650	C
Middlebury College	VT	64,332	MC
Millersville Univ of Pennsylvania	PA	23,782	C
Mills College	CA	59,163	VC
Millsaps College	MS	50,080	C+
Minn State Univ, Mankato	MN	15,616	C
Minn State Univ, Moorhead	MN	15,941	C
Miss State Univ	MS	11,454	C+
Missouri State Univ	MO	15,190	C+
Missouri Valley College	MO	28,150	C
Monmouth College	IL	42,260	C
Monmouth Univ	NJ	46,234	C
Montana State Univ	MT	15,500	C+
Montclair State Univ	NJ	26,210	LC
Mount Holyoke College	MA	56,746	MC
Muhlenberg College	PA	56,645	VC+
National Louis Univ	IL	16,920	LC
Nazareth College	NY	45,574	C
New College of Florida	FL	15,848	MC
New Mexico Highlands Univ	NM	11,904	NC
New Mexico State Univ	NM	14,050	C
New York Univ	NY	65,860	MC
North Central College	IL	48,712	VC
N Dak State Univ	ND	16,245	C
North Park Univ	IL	35,860	C
Northeastern Illinois Univ	IL	12,529	LC
Northeastern Univ	MA	62,703	MC
Northern Arizona Univ	AZ	20,246	VC
Northern Illinois Univ	IL	20,176	C
Northern Kentucky Univ	KY	16,486	C
Northwestern Univ	IL	66,344	MC
Nova Southeastern Univ	FL	38,534	C+
Oakland Univ	MI	20,763	C
Oberlin College	OH	66,012	MC
Ohio State Univ at Columbus	OH	21,703	HC+
Ohio Univ	OH	22,924	C
Ohio Wesleyan Univ	OH	49,460	VC
Okla Baptist Univ	OK	32,320	C
Olivet College	MI	36,110	LC
Oregon State Univ	OR	22,519	VC
Pacific Lutheran Univ	WA	49,960	VC
Pennsylvania State Univ - Univ Park	PA	29,760	HC
Pitzer College	CA	66,192	MC
Plymouth State Univ	NH	23,180	LC
Pomona College	CA	64,957	MC
Portland State Univ	OR	19,443	C
Prescott College	AZ	33,284	C
Princeton Univ	NJ	57,610	MC
Purdue Univ/West Lafayette	IN	20,032	MC
Radford Univ	VA	19,027	LC
Reed College	OR	65,300	MC
Rhode Island College	RI	17,694	LC
Rhodes College	TN	51,900	HC
Rice Univ	TX	57,668	MC
Ripon College	WI	46,911	C+
Rochester Inst of Technology	NY	50,842	HC
Rockford Univ	IL	36,030	C
Roger Williams Univ	RI	46,296	C+
Rollins College	FL	58,670	HC
Rutgers Univ - New Brunswick	NJ	26,632	HC
Rutgers Univ - Newark	NJ	27,288	C
St. Louis Univ	MO	49,866	HC
St. Mary's College of Calif	CA	57,420	C
St. Michael's College	VT	51,725	VC+
St. Vincent College	PA	44,626	C
San Diego State Univ	CA	21,896	C+
San Francisco State Univ	CA	18,514	LC
San Jose State Univ	CA	21,540	C
Sarah Lawrence College	NY	63,388	HC
Scripps College	CA	66,664	MC
Seattle Univ	WA	50,811	VC+
Seton Hall Univ	NJ	55,514	C
Sewanee: The Univ of the South	TN	54,500	MC
Skidmore College	NY	64,214	HC
Slippery Rock Univ of Pennsylvania	PA	10,360	C
Smith College	MA	63,914	MC
Sonoma State Univ	CA	27,806	C
Southern Illinois Univ Carbondale	IL	23,667	C
Southern Illinois Univ Edwardsville	IL	22,643	C
Southern Methodist Univ	TX	66,483	MC
Southern Oregon Univ	OR	19,117	C
Southwestern Univ	TX	50,720	VC
Spelman College	GA	38,751	C
St. Cloud State Univ	MN	10,600	C
St. John Fisher College	NY	43,620	C
St. John's Univ	NY	55,850	C
St. Lawrence Univ	NY	64,390	VC
St. Mary's College of Maryland	MD	26,634	VC
Stanford Univ	CA	60,409	MC
SUNY / Buffalo State College	NY	20,842	C
SUNY / SUNY Cortland	NY	20,706	VC
SUNY / SUNY Oneonta	NY	19,712	C+
SUNY / SUNY Plattsburgh	NY	18,814	C
SUNY / SUNY Potsdam	NY	20,404	C+
SUNY / Univ at Buffalo	NY	23,122	C+
SUNY at Binghamton	NY	22,861	MC
SUNY at Geneseo	NY	20,440	VC+
SUNY at New Paltz	NY	19,200	C
SUNY at Oswego	NY	21,351	C
SUNY at Purchase	NY	17,900	C
SUNY SUNY Albany	NY	22,165	C
Stockton Univ	NJ	25,059	
Stony Brook Univ/The SUNY	NY	21,881	MC
Susquehanna Univ	PA	55,340	VC
Swarthmore College	PA	63,550	MC
Syracuse Univ	NY	60,239	VC
Temple Univ	PA	24,392	VC
Texas A&M Univ	TX	20,521	VC+
Texas A&M Univ at Commerce	TX	10,496	C
Texas A&M Univ at Kingsville	TX	7,500	LC
Texas Christian Univ	TX	54,670	HC
Texas State Univ	TX	19,350	C
Texas Tech Univ	TX	18,736	C+
The Catholic Univ of America	DC	56,356	VC
The College at Brockport - SUNY	NY	20,346	C
The College of Idaho	ID	36,415	C
The College of Wooster	OH	57,900	VC+
The Evergreen State College	WA	16,599	C
The Lincoln Univ	PA	15,154	NC
The Univ of Akron	OH	21,477	C
The Univ of Tenn at Knoxville	TN	22,112	VC
The Univ of Utah	UT	17,924	VC
Thomas Edison State Univ	NJ	6,350	NC
Towson Univ	MD	17,408	VC
Transylvania Univ	KY	45,690	VC+
Trinity College	CT	63,920	HC+
Trinity Univ	TX	52,314	HC+
Truman State Univ	MO	16,014	HC
Tufts Univ	MA		MC
Tulane Univ	LA	63,396	HC+
Union College	NY	64,320	MC
Univ of Alabama	AL	24,320	C+
Univ of Alabama at Birmingham	AL	19,906	C
Univ of Alaska Anchorage	AK	16,652	NC
Univ of Alaska Fairbanks	AK	16,179	C
Univ of Arizona	AZ	23,100	C
Univ of Arkansas at Fayetteville	AR	19,152	C+
Univ of Calif at Berkeley	CA	28,853	MC
Univ of Calif at Davis	CA	28,468	HC
Univ of Calif at Irvine	CA	26,484	VC
Univ of Calif at Los Angeles	CA	30,162	MC
Univ of Calif at Riverside	CA	29,227	C+
Univ of Calif at Santa Barbara	CA	29,091	HC
Univ of Calif San Diego	CA	30,150	MC
Univ of Calif, Santa Cruz	CA	28,731	C+
Univ of Central Arkansas	AR	14,472	VC
Univ of Central Florida	FL	15,922	VC
Univ of Chicago	IL	67,584	MC
Univ of Cincinnati	OH	21,964	VC
Univ of Colo Boulder	CO	24,285	VC+
Univ of Colo Colo Springs	CO	19,663	C
Univ of Colo Denver	CO	23,230	C
Univ of Conn	CT	25,538	HC
Univ of Delaware	DE	24,976	VC+
Univ of Denver	CO	58,443	VC+
Univ of Florida	FL	16,291	HC+
Univ of Georgia	GA	21,250	HC
Univ of Hawaii at Hilo	HI	18,038	C
Univ of Hawaii at Manoa	HI	23,221	C
Univ of Houston	TX	21,483	VC
Univ of Idaho	ID	15,348	C
Univ of Illinois at Chicago	IL	25,006	VC
Univ of Illinois at Urbana-Champaign	IL	27,006	HC
Univ of Indianapolis	IN	36,480	C
Univ of Iowa	IA	18,683	VC+
Univ of Kansas	KS	20,135	C+
Univ of Kentucky	KY	33,306	C
Univ of La Verne	CA	55,600	C
Univ of Louisiana at Lafayette	LA	14,516	C
Univ of Louisville	KY	19,824	C

ST = STATE $IS = IN-STATE COSTS SR = SELECTOR RATING

School	ST	$IS	SR
Univ of Maine	ME	20,792	C
Univ of Maine at Farmington	ME	18,187	C
Univ of Mary Washington	VA	24,764	VC
Univ of Maryland/Baltimore County	MD	21,296	VC
Univ of Maryland/College Park	MD	21,938	HC
Univ of Mass Amherst	MA	26,199	VC+
Univ of Mass Boston	MA	13,435	C
Univ of Mass Dartmouth	MA	25,658	C
Univ of Memphis	TN	18,278	C
Univ of Miami	FL	63,494	MC
Univ of Mich/Ann Arbor	MI	24,410	MC
Univ of Mich/Dearborn	MI	11,757	VC
Univ of Mich-Flint	MI	17,607	C+
Univ of Minn/Duluth	MN	20,292	C+
Univ of Minn/Morris	MN	20,760	VC
Univ of Minn/Twin Cities	MN	23,519	HC+
Univ of Miss	MS	17,746	C+
Univ of Missouri/Columbia	MO	18,201	MC
Univ of Missouri-St. Louis	MO		C
Univ of Montana	MT	14,105	C
Univ of Montana-Western	MT	11,220	LC
Univ of Nebr - Lincoln	NE	18,589	VC
Univ of Nevada, Las Vegas	NV	17,553	C
Univ of Nevada/Reno	NV	18,010	C
Univ of New Hampshire	NH	28,562	VC
Univ of New Mexico	NM	15,404	C
Univ of New Orleans	LA	12,840	C
Univ of N Car at Asheville	NC	15,723	VC+
Univ of N Car at Chapel Hill	NC	20,052	HC+
Univ of N Car at Charlotte	NC	15,547	C
Univ of N Car at Greensboro	NC	14,690	C
Univ of N Car at Wilmington	NC	14,590	VC
Univ of N Dak	ND	15,373	C
Univ of North Florida	FL	15,996	VC
Univ of North Texas	TX	19,198	C
Univ of Northern Colo	CO	20,851	C
Univ of Notre Dame	IN	64,043	MC
Univ of Okla	OK	18,911	VC
Univ of Oregon	OR	22,972	C
Univ of Pennsylvania	PA	63,526	MC
Univ of Pittsburgh	PA	29,568	HC+
Univ of Pittsburgh at Greensburg	PA	23,132	C
Univ of PR-Rio Piedras campus	PR	13,327	
Univ of Redlands	CA	60,200	VC
Univ of Rhode Island	RI	24,906	C
Univ of Richmond	VA	60,880	MC
Univ of Rochester	NY	65,032	MC
Univ of San Diego	CA	58,442	VC+
Univ of South Alabama	AL	16,400	C
Univ of S Car at Columbia	SC	19,725	VC+
Univ of S Dak	SD	16,109	C
Univ of South Florida/St. Petersburg	FL	15,980	C
Univ of South Florida/Tampa	FL	16,110	VC+
Univ of Southern Calif	CA	66,631	C
Univ of Southern Indiana	IN	16,501	C
Univ of Southern Maine	ME	18,320	C
Univ of Southern Miss	MS	13,170	C
Univ of Texas at Arlington	TX	18,026	LC
Univ of Texas at Austin	TX	26,102	HC
Univ of Texas at El Paso	TX	34,452	NC
Univ of Texas at San Antonio	TX	20,157	C
Univ of Toledo	OH	19,336	NC
Univ of Tulsa	OK	52,625	HC+
Univ of Vermont	VT	28,878	HC
Univ of Virginia	VA	25,891	MC
Univ of Washington	WA	23,149	VC
Univ of West Georgia	GA	16,360	LC
Univ of Wisc-Madison	WI	20,934	MC
Univ of Wisc-Milwaukee	WI	21,496	C
Univ of Wisc-Oshkosh	WI	15,200	C
Univ of Wyoming	WY	15,375	C+
Ursinus College	PA	61,690	VC
Vanderbilt Univ	TN	60,572	MC
Vanguard Univ of Southern Calif	CA	40,740	VC
Vassar College	NY	65,491	MC
Virginia Commonwealth Univ	VA	23,049	C
Wagner College	NY	55,480	C+
Wake Forest Univ	NC	64,056	MC
Warren Wilson College	NC	44,220	VC
Washburn Univ	KS	15,827	C
Washington and Lee Univ	VA	59,647	MC
Washington College	MD	54,666	VC
Washington State Univ	WA	22,495	C
Washington Univ in St. Louis	MO	65,366	VC
Wayne State Univ	MI	22,016	C
Weber State Univ	UT	10,721	C
Wellesley College	MA	63,916	MC
Wells College	NY	50,500	C
Wesleyan Univ	CT	65,516	MC
West Chester Univ of Pennsylvania	PA	18,456	C
West Virginia Univ	WV	18,210	C
Western Carolina Univ	NC	13,965	C
Western Conn State Univ	CT	21,254	LC
Western Illinois Univ	IL	20,825	C
Western Kentucky Univ	KY	16,850	C
Western Mich Univ	MI	21,054	C
Western Oregon Univ	OR	15,021	LC
Western State Colo Univ	CO	18,639	C
Western Washington Univ	WA	18,003	C+
Westminster College	MO	32,820	C
Wheaton College	IL	43,610	MC
Wheaton College	MA	61,512	VC
Whitman College	WA	59,772	MC
Wichita State Univ	KS	21,643	C
Widener Univ	PA	56,486	C
Willamette Univ	OR	61,817	VC+
William Paterson Univ of New Jersey	NJ	23,133	C
Williams College	MA	63,290	MC
Wright State Univ	OH	16,983	C
Yale Univ	CT	64,650	MC
Youngstown State Univ	OH	17,307	C

APPAREL AND ACCESSORIES MARKETING

School	ST	$IS	SR
Auburn Univ	AL	23,594	VC+
Baylor Univ	TX	53,760	HC
Calif State Polytechnic Univ, Pomona	CA	21,541	C
Cheyney Univ of Pennsylvania	PA	20,896	LC
Colo State Univ	CO	22,162	VC
Dominican Univ	IL	41,222	C
Eastern Mich Univ	MI	19,761	C
Fashion Inst of Technology/SUNY	NY	18,521	SP
Fontbonne Univ	MO	33,717	C
Indiana Univ Bloomington	IN	20,429	VC
Johnson & Wales Univ/Denver Campus	CO	42,707	C
Kansas State Univ	KS	17,780	VC
Kentucky State Univ	KY	13,364	LC
S Dak State Univ	SD	15,634	C
Univ of Arkansas at Fayetteville	AR	19,152	C+
Univ of Nebr - Lincoln	NE	18,589	VC
Univ of N Car at Greensboro	NC	14,690	C
Virginia Polytechnic Inst and State Univ	VA	21,276	HC
Western Mich Univ	MI	21,054	C
Youngstown State Univ	OH	17,307	C

APPAREL AND TEXTILES

School	ST	$IS	SR
Baylor Univ	TX	53,760	HC
Kennesaw State Univ	GA	19,592	VC
Mich State Univ	MI	23,898	VC+
Missouri State Univ	MO	15,190	C+
Northwest Missouri State Univ	MO	17,737	C
Univ of Nebr - Lincoln	NE	18,589	VC
Univ of Wisc-Madison	WI	20,934	MC
Washington State Univ	WA	22,495	C
Western Illinois Univ	IL	20,825	C

APPAREL DESIGN

School	ST	$IS	SR
Appalachian State Univ	NC	14,416	VC
Art Inst of Portland	OR	132,329	SP
Auburn Univ	AL	23,594	VC+
Baylor Univ	TX	53,760	HC
Bowling Green State Univ	OH	19,747	C
Central Mich Univ	MI	20,330	C
Colo State Univ	CO	22,162	VC
Dominican Univ	IL	41,222	C
Eastern Kentucky Univ	KY	16,908	C
Florida State Univ	FL	16,771	HC
Kansas State Univ	KS	17,780	VC
N Dak State Univ	ND	16,245	C
Oregon State Univ	OR	22,519	VC
Purdue Univ/West Lafayette	IN	20,032	MC
Rhode Island School of Design	RI	59,960	SP
San Francisco State Univ	CA	18,514	LC
Texas Tech Univ	TX	18,736	C+
Univ of Delaware	DE	24,976	VC+
Univ of Hawaii at Manoa	HI	23,221	C
Univ of Idaho	ID	15,348	C
Univ of Minn/Twin Cities	MN	23,519	HC+
Univ of Nebr - Lincoln	NE	18,589	VC
Univ of Wisc-Stout	WI	19,667	C
Western Mich Univ	MI	21,054	C
Western Washington Univ	WA	18,003	C+

APPLIED ART

School	ST	$IS	SR
Centenary College	NJ	43,602	C
Daemen College	NY	38,045	C
Edinboro Univ	PA	15,940	LC
Goddard College	VT	17,040	VC
Lamar Univ	TX	18,014	LC
Marshall Univ	WV	17,242	C
Memphis College of Art	TN	39,750	C
Oral Roberts Univ	OK	34,316	C
Oregon State Univ	OR	22,519	VC
Point Park Univ	PA	41,270	C
Roberts Wesleyan College	NY	38,306	C
Rochester Inst of Technology	NY	50,842	HC
Santa Fe Univ of Art and Design	NM	39,980	SP
Tabor College	KS	35,870	C
Texas State Univ	TX	19,350	C
Univ of Arkansas at Little Rock	AR	18,211	C
Univ of Idaho	ID	15,348	C
Univ of Maine at Presque Isle	ME	14,870	C
Univ of Maryland/Baltimore County	MD	21,296	VC
Univ of North Texas	TX	19,198	C
West Texas A&M Univ	TX	13,478	C

APPLIED AVIATION

School	ST	$IS	SR
Calif Baptist Univ	CA	41,392	C
Eastern Mich Univ	MI	19,761	C
Univ of Minn Crookston	MN	19,739	C

APPLIED CHEMISTRY

School	ST	$IS	SR
Bethany College	WV	36,300	NC
Bridgewater College	VA	44,510	C
Delaware State Univ	DE	19,376	NC

APPLIED COMMUNICATION

School	ST	$IS	SR
Bryant Univ	RI	55,646	VC
Johnson & Wales Univ/Denver Campus	CO	42,707	C
Kent State Univ	OH	20,732	C
Ohio Univ	OH	22,924	C
Okla Baptist Univ	OK	32,320	C
Univ of Rhode Island	RI	24,906	C

APPLIED COMPUTING

School	ST	$IS	SR
Bryant Univ	RI	55,646	VC
SUNY Polytechnic Inst	NY	19,473	VC
Univ of Central Arkansas	AR	14,472	VC

APPLIED ECONOMICS / MANAGEMENT

School	ST	$IS	SR
Auburn Univ at Montgomery	AL	15,290	C
Bentley Univ	MA	60,890	HC
Bethany College	WV	36,300	NC
Bryant Univ	RI	55,646	VC
Cornell Univ	NY	64,853	MC
Farmingdale State College	NY	20,624	C
Ithaca College	NY	56,766	VC
Univ of Minn/Twin Cities	MN	23,519	HC+
Univ of San Francisco	CA	58,484	VC

APPLIED GEOSCIENCE

School	ST	$IS	SR
Bryant Univ	RI	55,646	VC
Texas Christian Univ	TX	54,670	HC

APPLIED MANAGEMENT

School	ST	$IS	SR
Bryant Univ	RI	55,646	VC
Madonna Univ	MI	29,050	C
Missouri Baptist Univ	MO	35,594	C
Pennsylvania College of Technology	PA	27,333	NC

APPLIED MATHEMATICS

School	ST	$IS	SR
American Univ	DC	59,379	HC+
Andrews Univ	MI	28,030	C+
Arizona State Univ at the Polytechnic Campus	AZ	21,360	VC
Arizona State Univ at the Tempe Campus	AZ	21,756	VC
Arizona State Univ at the West Campus	AZ	20,640	C
Armstrong State Univ	GA	16,962	C
Asbury Univ	KY	35,180	C+
Auburn Univ	AL	23,594	VC+
Augustana College	IL	49,658	VC
Ball State Univ	IN	19,590	C
Baylor Univ	TX	53,760	HC
Belmont Univ	TN	40,970	VC
Berea College	KY	7,042	C
Bethany College	WV	36,300	NC
Biola Univ	CA	46,402	C+
Brown Univ	RI	64,566	MC
Bryant Univ	RI	55,646	VC
Bucknell Univ	PA	64,616	MC
Calif Inst of Technology	CA	58,761	MC
Cal State, Fullerton	CA	21,902	C
Cal State, Long Beach	CA	18,850	C
Case Western Reserve Univ	OH	60,304	MC
Christopher Newport Univ	VA	23,968	VC+
CUNY/College of Technology	NY	6,669	NC
Clarkson Univ	NY	60,392	HC
Colby College	ME	64,060	MC
Colo State Univ	CO	22,162	VC
Columbia Univ/ School of General Studies	NY	61,470	MC
Columbia Univ/City of New York	NY	62,958	MC
DePaul Univ	IL	47,623	VC
East Central Univ	OK	13,056	C
Eastern Mich Univ	MI	19,761	C
Elizabethtown College	PA	54,050	C
Elon Univ	NC	44,599	VC+
Endicott College	MA	44,604	VC+
Farmingdale State College	NY	20,624	C
Ferris State Univ	MI	21,445	C
Fitchburg State Univ	MA	21,819	C
Florida Inst of Technology	FL	53,306	VC
Florida State Univ	FL	16,771	HC
Franklin College	IN	39,380	C
Geneva College	PA	35,450	C
George Washington Univ	DC	62,835	MC
Georgia Inst of Technology	GA	23,360	MC
Hampden-Sydney College	VA	56,248	C+
Harvard College/Harvard Univ	MA	60,659	MC
Hawaii Pacific Univ	HI	33,420	C
Hillsdale College	MI	35,722	MC
Hofstra Univ	NY	55,960	C+
Illinois Inst of Technology	IL	56,826	HC+
Iona College	NY	50,984	C
Johns Hopkins Univ	MD	65,386	MC
Johnson C. Smith Univ	NC	25,336	LC
Kent State Univ	OH	20,732	C
Kentucky State Univ	KY	13,364	LC
Kettering Univ	MI	47,570	HC
Lasell College	MA	47,500	C
Le Moyne College	NY	46,000	C
Lehigh Univ	PA	61,010	MC
Lipscomb Univ	TN	41,296	VC
LIU Post	NY	49,682	C
Loyola Marymount Univ	CA	58,038	HC
Marist College	NY	49,860	VC
Marshall Univ	WV	17,242	C
Mary Baldwin Univ	VA	39,865	C
Metropolitan State Univ	MN	7,566	C
Millersville Univ of Pennsylvania	PA	23,782	C
Millsaps College	MS	50,080	C+
Missouri Univ of Science and Technology	MO	18,655	HC
Montclair State Univ	NJ	26,210	LC
Murray State Univ	KY	16,998	C
New College of Florida	FL	15,848	MC
New Jersey Inst of Technology	NJ	29,569	VC
North Central College	IL	48,712	VC
Northwestern Univ	IL	66,344	MC
Oberlin College	OH	66,012	MC
Ohio Univ	OH	22,924	C
Pacific Union College	CA	36,009	VC
Piedmont College	GA	32,512	C
Purdue Univ/West Lafayette	IN	20,032	MC
Rice Univ	TX	57,668	MC
Robert Morris Univ	PA	37,834	C
Rochester Inst of Technology	NY	50,842	HC
Rutgers Univ - Newark	NJ	27,288	C
Saginaw Valley State Univ	MI	18,530	C
St. Augustine's Univ	NC	26,048	C
St. Louis Univ	MO	49,866	HC
St. Mary's College	IN	50,600	C
San Diego State Univ	CA	21,896	C+
San Francisco State Univ	CA	18,514	LC
San Jose State Univ	CA	21,540	C
Seattle Univ	WA	50,811	VC+
Southern Illinois Univ Edwardsville	IL	22,643	C
SUNY / SUNY Fredonia	NY	20,818	C
SUNY at Oswego	NY	21,351	C
SUNY Polytechnic Inst	NY	19,473	VC
SUNY SUNY Albany	NY	22,165	C
Stevenson Univ	MD	72,770	C
Stony Brook Univ/The SUNY	NY	21,881	MC
Syracuse Univ	NY	60,239	VC
Temple Univ	PA	24,392	VC
Texas A&M Univ	TX	20,521	VC+
Texas State Univ	TX	19,350	C
The Master's Univ	CA	43,870	C+
The Univ of Akron	OH	21,477	C
The Univ of Tenn at Chattanooga	TN	16,744	C
The Univ of Utah	UT	17,924	VC
Tufts Univ	MA		MC
Univ of Arizona	AZ	23,100	C
Univ of Arkansas at Little Rock	AR	18,211	C
Univ of Calif at Berkeley	CA	28,853	MC
Univ of Calif at Los Angeles	CA	30,162	MC
Univ of Calif San Diego	CA	30,150	MC
Univ of Central Arkansas	AR	14,472	VC
Univ of Central Okla	OK	13,486	C
Univ of Chicago	IL	67,584	MC
Univ of Colo Boulder	CO	24,285	VC+
Univ of Houston-Downtown	TX	7,241	C
Univ of Idaho	ID	15,348	C
Univ of Mass Lowell	MA	26,380	C
Univ of Mich/Dearborn	MI	11,757	VC
Univ of Montana-Western	MT	11,220	LC
Univ of New England	ME	48,880	C
Univ of New Hampshire	NH	28,562	VC
Univ of New Haven	CT	52,190	C
Univ of N Car at Chapel Hill	NC	20,052	HC+
Univ of North Florida	FL	15,996	VC
Univ of Notre Dame	IN	64,043	MC
Univ of Pittsburgh	PA	29,568	HC+
Univ of Pittsburgh at Bradford	PA	22,402	C
Univ of Pittsburgh at Greensburg	PA	23,132	C
Univ of PR-Rio Piedras campus	PR	13,327	
Univ of Rochester	NY	65,032	MC
Univ of S Car Aiken	SC	16,712	C
Univ of Southern Calif	CA	66,631	C
Univ of St. Thomas - Houston	TX	40,020	VC
Univ of Texas at El Paso	TX	34,452	NC
Univ of the Pacific	CA	57,006	VC
Univ of Tulsa	OK	52,625	HC+
Univ of Wisc-Madison	WI	20,934	MC
Univ of Wisc-Milwaukee	WI	21,496	C
Univ of Wisc-Stout	WI	19,667	C

School	ST	$IS	SR
Washington State Univ	WA	22,495	C
Washington Univ in St. Louis	MO	65,366	VC
Weber State Univ	UT	10,721	C
Wentworth Inst of Technology	MA	47,112	C
West Virginia State Univ	WV	8,378	NC
West Virginia Univ	WV	18,210	C
Western Mich Univ	MI	21,054	C
Western Washington Univ	WA	18,003	C+
Wheaton College	IL	43,610	MC
Wofford College	SC	49,885	VC
Wright State Univ	OH	16,983	C
Yale Univ	CT	64,650	MC
Youngstown State Univ	OH	17,307	C

APPLIED METEOROLOGY

School	ST	$IS	SR
Embry-Riddle Aeronautical Univ - Prescott Campus	AZ	44,054	VC
Western Illinois Univ	IL	20,825	C

APPLIED MUSIC

School	ST	$IS	SR
Baldwin Wallace Univ	OH	41,106	C
Baylor Univ	TX	53,760	HC
Concordia College - New York	NY	39,035	LC
Dallas Baptist Univ	TX	33,713	C
Eastern Mich Univ	MI	19,761	C
Geneva College	PA	35,450	C
Grand Rapids Theological Seminary/Cornerstone Univ	MI	33,338	C
Indiana Wesleyan Univ	IN	33,674	C
Inter-American Univ of PR Ponce	PR	19,549	
Inter-American Univ of PR-Fajardo Campus	PR	18,336	
Judson College	AL	27,066	C
Kansas State Univ	KS	17,780	VC
Lenoir-Rhyne Univ	NC	43,200	C
Mannes School for Music	NY	44,500	SP
Meredith College	NC	45,297	C
Miss College	MS	25,850	C
Nebr Wesleyan Univ	NE	38,140	C+
New England Conservatory of Music	MA	58,655	SP
Newberry College	SC	34,550	C
Ouachita Baptist Univ	AR	32,320	C
Roberts Wesleyan College	NY	38,306	C
Seton Hall Univ	NJ	55,514	C
Trinity Christian College	IL	35,580	C
Univ of Delaware	DE	24,976	VC+
Univ of Houston	TX	21,483	VC
Univ of Idaho	ID	15,348	C
Univ of Illinois at Chicago	IL	25,006	VC
Univ of Nevada/Reno	NV	18,010	C
Univ of Texas at Austin	TX	26,102	HC
Wartburg College	IA	47,840	C
West Chester Univ of Pennsylvania	PA	18,456	C
Youngstown State Univ	OH	17,307	C

APPLIED NUTRITION

School	ST	$IS	SR
Johnson & Wales Univ/ Denver Campus	CO	42,707	C
Ohio Univ	OH	22,924	C
Rochester Inst of Technology	NY	50,842	HC

APPLIED PHYSICS

School	ST	$IS	SR
Angelo State Univ	TX	15,263	NC
Armstrong State Univ	GA	16,962	C
Ball State Univ	IN	19,590	C
Beloit College	WI	55,206	HC
Bethel Univ	MN	45,270	VC
Bridgewater College	VA	44,510	C
Cal State, San Bernardino	CA	12,000	C
Cal State, Stanislaus	CA	16,212	C
Carroll Univ	WI	38,100	C+
Christopher Newport Univ	VA	23,968	VC+
Columbia Univ/City of New York	NY	62,958	MC
East Carolina Univ	NC	16,937	C
Hofstra Univ	NY	55,960	C+
Houghton College	NY	39,090	C
Indiana Univ of Pennsylvania	PA	23,614	LC
Kettering Univ	MI	47,570	HC
Linfield College	OR	52,010	C
Marietta College	OH	46,190	C
Mich Tech Univ	MI	24,739	VC+
Murray State Univ	KY	16,998	C
New Jersey Inst of Technology	NJ	29,569	VC
Northeastern Univ	MA	62,703	MC
Ohio Univ	OH	22,924	C
Pacific Lutheran Univ	WA	49,960	VC
Piedmont College	GA	32,512	C
Providence College	RI	60,760	VC
Purdue Univ/West Lafayette	IN	20,032	MC
Rensselaer Polytechnic Inst	NY	63,436	MC
Rutgers Univ - Newark	NJ	27,288	C
Shippensburg Univ of Pennsylvania	PA	23,208	C
SUNY at Geneseo	NY	20,440	VC+
Stetson Univ	FL	53,544	VC
Tufts Univ	MA		MC
Univ of Alaska Fairbanks	AK	16,179	C
Univ of Calif San Diego	CA	30,150	MC
Univ of Iowa	IA	18,683	VC+
Univ of Maryland/Baltimore County	MD	21,296	VC
Univ of Minn/Duluth	MN	20,292	C+
Univ of Nevada, Las Vegas	NV	17,553	C
Western Washington Univ	WA	18,003	C+
Whitworth Univ	WA	51,732	VC
Worcester Polytechnic Inst	MA	60,730	MC
Xavier Univ	OH	47,880	C+
Yale Univ	CT	64,650	MC

APPLIED PHYSICS (PRE-MBA)

School	ST	$IS	SR
Murray State Univ	KY	16,998	C

APPLIED PHYSICS ANALYSIS

School	ST	$IS	SR
Creighton Univ	NE	48,206	VC+

APPLIED PSYCHOLOGY

School	ST	$IS	SR
Belhaven Univ	MS	31,016	C
Belmont Abbey College	NC	48,156	C
Biola Univ	CA	46,402	C+
Boston College	MA	65,737	MC
Bryant Univ	RI	55,646	VC
Christian Brothers Univ	TN	31,670	VC
College of St. Mary	NE	35,184	C
Coppin State Univ	MD	17,041	VC
Farmingdale State College	NY	20,624	C
Franklin Univ	OH	56,262	SP
Gwynedd Mercy Univ	PA	43,780	LC
Hodges Univ	FL	19,080	LC
Ithaca College	NY	56,766	VC
Loyola Univ Chicago	IL	55,802	VC
Mayville State Univ	ND	18,371	NC
New York Univ	NY	65,860	MC
Pace Univ	NY	58,248	C
Regis Univ	CO	44,520	C
Russell Sage College	NY	39,370	C
SUNY /College of Agriculture and Tech at Cobleskill	NY	20,527	LC
Univ of Illinois at Chicago	IL	25,006	VC
Univ of Mich-Flint	MI	17,607	C+
Univ of North Texas	TX	19,198	C
Univ of Pittsburgh	PA	29,568	HC+
Univ of St. Mary	KS	34,690	C
Wright State Univ	OH	16,983	C

APPLIED SCIENCE

School	ST	$IS	SR
Alcorn State Univ	MS	15,854	C
Arizona State Univ at the Downtown Phoenix Campus	AZ	23,680	VC
Arizona State Univ at the Polytechnic Campus	AZ	21,360	VC
Arizona State Univ at the West Campus	AZ	20,640	C
Black Hills State Univ	SD	15,899	C
Bluefield State College	WV	5,832	LC
Bryant Univ	RI	55,646	VC
Concordia College - Moorhead	MN	51,088	C+
Florida Gulf Coast Univ	FL	9,682	C
Georgian Court Univ	NJ	42,426	LC
Granite State College	NH	19,639	SP
Indiana Univ East	IN	7,072	C
Indiana Univ Kokomo	IN	7,073	C
Indiana Univ Northwest	IN	7,072	C
Indiana Univ South Bend	IN	14,242	C
Indiana Univ Southeast	IN	14,242	LC
Kent State Univ	OH	20,732	C
King Univ	TN	34,660	C
Lamar Univ	TX	18,014	LC
Lehigh Univ	PA	61,010	MC
Madonna Univ	MI	29,050	C
Messiah College	PA	43,100	C+
Missouri Southern State Univ	MO	12,499	C
Montana State Univ-Billings	MT	22,960	C
Northern Arizona Univ	AZ	20,246	VC
Saginaw Valley State Univ	MI	18,530	C
Southwest Minn State Univ	MN	17,783	C
Southwestern Univ	TX	50,720	VC
Tarleton State Univ	TX	15,248	LC
Texas Lutheran Univ	TX	38,620	C
Univ of Arizona	AZ	23,100	C
Univ of Arkansas at Little Rock	AR	18,211	C
Univ of Arkansas at Monticello	AR	13,134	NC
Univ of Central Florida	FL	15,922	VC
Univ of Maine at Augusta	ME	7,812	C
Univ of Mich-Flint	MI	17,607	C+
Univ of Montana	MT	14,105	C
Univ of Nebr - Lincoln	NE	18,589	VC
Univ of N Car at Chapel Hill	NC	20,052	HC+
Univ of Pennsylvania	PA	63,526	MC
Univ of San Francisco	CA	58,484	VC
Univ of Wisc-Stout	WI	19,667	C
Wheeling Jesuit Univ	WV	37,106	LC
Winona State Univ	MN	17,535	C

APPLIED SOCIAL SCIENCE

School	ST	$IS	SR
Bryant Univ	RI	55,646	VC
CUNY/Queens College	NY	27,896	C
East Carolina Univ	NC	16,937	C
Univ of New England	ME	48,880	C
Univ of Wisc-Stout	WI	19,667	C

APPLIED SPEECH COMMUNICATION

School	ST	$IS	SR
Bryant Univ	RI	55,646	VC
Ferris State Univ	MI	21,445	C

AQUACULTURE & FISHERY TECHNOLOGY

School	ST	$IS	SR
Univ of New England	ME	48,880	C
Univ of Rhode Island	RI	24,906	C

ARABIC

School	ST	$IS	SR
American Univ	DC	59,379	HC+
Bard College	NY	64,024	HC
Dartmouth College	NH	66,174	MC
DePaul Univ	IL	47,623	VC
Georgetown Univ	DC	65,926	MC
Mich State Univ	MI	23,898	VC+
Middlebury College	VT	64,332	MC
New York Univ	NY	65,860	MC
Ohio State Univ at Columbus	OH	21,703	HC+
SUNY at Binghamton	NY	22,861	MC
Thomas Edison State Univ	NJ	6,350	NC
Tufts Univ	MA		MC
United States Naval Academy	MD		MC
Univ of Calif at Los Angeles	CA	30,162	MC
Univ of Cincinnati	OH	21,964	VC
Univ of Georgia	GA	21,250	HC
Univ of Maryland/College Park	MD	21,938	HC
Univ of Mich/Ann Arbor	MI	24,410	MC
Univ of Miss	MS	17,746	C+
Univ of Notre Dame	IN	64,043	MC
Univ of Okla	OK	18,911	VC
Univ of Richmond	VA	60,880	MC
Univ of Texas at Austin	TX	26,102	HC
Washington Univ in St. Louis	MO	65,366	VC
Wellesley College	MA	63,916	MC
Western Kentucky Univ	KY	16,850	C
Western Washington Univ	WA	18,003	C+
Williams College	MA	63,290	MC

ARCHEOLOGY

School	ST	$IS	SR
Biola Univ	CA	46,402	C+
Boston Univ	MA	65,110	MC
Bowdoin College	ME	63,500	MC
Brigham Young Univ	UT	12,748	HC
Brown Univ	RI	64,566	MC
Bryn Mawr College	PA	59,890	MC
CUNY/Hunter College	NY	31,098	VC
College of Charleston	SC	22,699	C
Columbia Univ/ School of General Studies	NY	61,470	MC
Columbia Univ/City of New York	NY	62,958	MC
Cornell Univ	NY	64,853	MC
Dickinson College	PA	63,974	MC
George Washington Univ	DC	62,835	MC
Hamilton College	NY	64,250	MC
Haverford College	PA	66,490	MC
Hood College	MD	54,840	C
Johns Hopkins Univ	MD	65,386	MC
Lycoming College	PA	48,580	C
Mass Inst of Technology	MA	62,662	MC
Mercyhurst Univ	PA	47,420	C
Millersville Univ of Pennsylvania	PA	23,782	C
Murray State Univ	KY	16,998	C
Oberlin College	OH	66,012	MC
Pennsylvania State Univ - Univ Park	PA	29,760	HC
Prescott College	AZ	33,284	C
Princeton Univ	NJ	57,610	MC
Randolph-Macon College	VA	49,910	C
Stanford Univ	CA	60,409	MC
SUNY / SUNY Potsdam	NY	20,404	C+
Texas A&M Univ at Galveston	TX	15,920	C
The College of Wooster	OH	57,900	VC+
Tufts Univ	MA		MC
Univ of Cincinnati	OH	21,964	VC
Univ of Evansville	IN	44,186	VC+
Univ of Indianapolis	IN	36,480	C
Univ of Kansas	KS	20,135	C+
Univ of Mich/Ann Arbor	MI	24,410	MC
Univ of Missouri/Columbia	MO	18,201	MC
Univ of N Car at Chapel Hill	NC	20,052	HC+
Univ of Rochester	NY	65,032	MC
Univ of Texas at Austin	TX	26,102	HC
Univ of Tulsa	OK	52,625	HC+
Univ of Wisc-La Crosse	WI	15,247	C+
Washington and Lee Univ	VA	59,647	MC
Washington Univ in St. Louis	MO	65,366	VC
Wellesley College	MA	63,916	MC
Wesleyan Univ	CT	65,516	MC
Western Kentucky Univ	KY	16,850	C
Wheaton College	IL	43,610	MC
Yale Univ	CT	64,650	MC

ARCHITECTURAL ENGINEERING

School	ST	$IS	SR
Calif Polytechnic State Univ	CA	17,979	HC+
Dordt College	IA	37,860	C+
Drexel Univ	PA	65,432	VC+
Illinois Inst of Technology	IL	56,826	HC+
Kansas State Univ	KS	17,780	VC
Lawrence Tech Univ	MI	39,770	VC
Milwaukee School of Engineering	WI	45,153	HC
Missouri Univ of Science and Technology	MO	18,655	HC
N Car A&T State Univ	NC	13,365	LC
Northern Kentucky Univ	KY	16,486	C
Okla State Univ	OK	17,180	VC
Parsons The New School for Design	NY	56,610	SP
Pennsylvania State Univ - Univ Park	PA	29,760	HC
Princeton Univ	NJ	57,610	MC
Rice Univ	TX	57,668	MC
Stanford Univ	CA	60,409	MC
Tenn State Univ	TN	14,423	C
Univ of Cincinnati	OH	21,964	VC
Univ of Colo Boulder	CO	24,285	VC+
Univ of Detroit Mercy	MI	48,816	C+
Univ of Hartford	CT	49,776	C
Univ of Illinois at Urbana-Champaign	IL	27,006	HC
Univ of Kansas	KS	20,135	C+
Univ of Miami	FL	63,494	MC
Univ of Nebr - Lincoln	NE	18,589	VC
Univ of Nevada, Las Vegas	NV	17,553	C
Univ of Okla	OK	18,911	VC
Univ of Texas at Austin	TX	26,102	HC
Univ of Wyoming	WY	15,375	C+
Vermont Technical College	VT	23,838	C
Washington State Univ	WA	22,495	C
Worcester Polytechnic Inst	MA	60,730	MC

ARCHITECTURAL HISTORY

School	ST	$IS	SR
Boston Univ	MA	65,110	MC
Brown Univ	RI	64,566	MC
DePaul Univ	IL	47,623	VC
Miami Univ	OH	27,190	HC+
Middlebury College	VT	64,332	MC
Savannah College of Art and Design	GA	49,595	C
Univ of Virginia	VA	25,891	MC

ARCHITECTURAL STUDIES

School	ST	$IS	SR
Amherst College	MA		HC+
Arizona State Univ at the Tempe Campus	AZ	21,756	VC
Boston Univ	MA	65,110	MC
Bowling Green State Univ	OH	19,747	C
Brown Univ	RI	64,566	MC
Clayton State Univ	GA	19,735	C
College of the Holy Cross	MA	62,165	MC
Ithaca College	NY	56,766	VC
Kennesaw State Univ	GA	19,592	VC
Kent State Univ	OH	20,732	C
Lawrence Tech Univ	MI	39,770	VC
New York Univ	NY	65,860	MC
Southern Illinois Univ Carbondale	IL	23,667	C
The Univ of Utah	UT	17,924	VC
Univ of Arkansas at Fayetteville	AR	19,152	C+
Univ of Illinois at Chicago	IL	25,006	VC
Univ of Kansas	KS	20,135	C+
Univ of Nebr - Lincoln	NE	18,589	VC
Univ of Pittsburgh	PA	29,568	HC+
Univ of San Diego	CA	58,442	VC+
Washington State Univ	WA	22,495	C

ARCHITECTURAL TECHNOLOGY

School	ST	$IS	SR
Alfred State College	NY	19,895	C
CUNY/College of Technology	NY	6,669	NC
Fairmont State Univ	WV	15,726	C
Farmingdale State College	NY	20,624	C
Fitchburg State Univ	MA	21,819	C
Murray State Univ	KY	16,998	C
New York Inst of Technology	NY	48,730	C
Pennsylvania College of Technology	PA	27,333	NC
Univ of Cincinnati	OH	21,964	VC
Univ of Southern Miss	MS	13,170	C
Washington Univ in St. Louis	MO	65,366	VC

ARCHITECTURE

School	ST	$IS	SR
Andrews Univ	MI	28,030	C+
Appalachian State Univ	NC	14,416	VC
Auburn Univ	AL	23,594	VC+
Ball State Univ	IN	19,590	C
Barnard College/Columbia Univ	NY	62,741	MC
Bennington College	VT	63,960	MC
Boston Architectural College	MA	20,666	NC
Brown Univ	RI	64,566	MC
Calif Baptist Univ	CA	41,392	C
Calif College of the Arts	CA	52,758	SP
Calif Polytechnic State Univ	CA	17,979	HC+

ST = STATE $IS = IN-STATE COSTS SR = SELECTOR RATING

School	ST	$IS	SR
Calif State Polytechnic Univ, Pomona	CA	21,541	C
Carnegie Mellon Univ	PA	67,980	MC
CUNY/City College	NY	20,319	VC
Columbia Univ/ School of General Studies	NY	61,470	MC
Columbia Univ/City of New York	NY	62,958	MC
Conn College	CT	65,000	MC
Cooper Union for the Advancement of Science and Art	NY	58,210	MC
Cornell Univ	NY	64,853	MC
Drexel Univ	PA	65,432	VC+
Drury Univ	MO	33,791	VC
Fairmont State Univ	WV	15,726	C
Florida Atlantic Univ	FL	17,339	C
Florida International Univ	FL	19,854	C+
Fordham Univ	NY	65,918	MC
Georgia Inst of Technology	GA	23,360	MC
Hampshire College	MA	63,824	MC
Hampton Univ	VA	34,926	LC
Howard Univ	DC	37,616	C+
Illinois Inst of Technology	IL	56,826	HC+
Iowa State Univ	IA	17,570	C
Judson Univ	IL	37,700	C
Kansas State Univ	KS	17,780	VC
Kean Univ	NJ	24,650	C
Keene State College	NH	24,003	LC
Kent State Univ	OH	20,732	C
Lawrence Tech Univ	MI	39,770	VC
Lehigh Univ	PA	61,010	MC
Louisiana State Univ and A&M College	LA	18,677	VC
Louisiana Tech Univ	LA	11,422	VC
Marywood Univ	PA	46,900	C
Mass College of Art and Design	MA	24,800	SP
Mass Inst of Technology	MA	62,662	MC
Miami Univ	OH	27,190	HC+
Miss State Univ	MS	11,454	C+
Mount Holyoke College	MA	56,746	MC
New Jersey Inst of Technology	NJ	29,569	VC
New York Inst of Technology	NY	48,730	C
NewSchool of Architecture & Design	CA	12,341	SP
N Car State Univ	NC	19,515	HC+
N Dak State Univ	ND	16,245	C
Northeastern Univ	MA	62,703	MC
Norwich Univ	VT	28,212	C
Ohio State Univ at Columbus	OH	21,703	HC+
Okla State Univ	OK	17,180	VC
Otis College of Art and Design	CA	55,858	SP
Pennsylvania State Univ - Univ Park	PA	29,760	HC
Philadelphia Univ	PA	50,370	C
Portland State Univ	OR	19,443	C
Prairie View A&M Univ	TX	15,205	LC
Pratt Inst	NY	58,082	VC
Princeton Univ	NJ	57,610	MC
Rensselaer Polytechnic Inst	NY	63,436	MC
Rhode Island School of Design	RI	59,960	SP
Rice Univ	TX	57,668	MC
Roger Williams Univ	RI	46,296	C+
Savannah College of Art and Design	GA	49,595	C
Smith College	MA	63,914	MC
S Dak State Univ	SD	15,634	C
Southern Illinois Univ Carbondale	IL	23,667	C
Southern Univ and A&M College	LA	16,074	LC+
SUNY / Univ at Buffalo	NY	23,122	C+
Syracuse Univ	NY	60,239	VC
Temple Univ	PA	24,392	VC
Texas Tech Univ	TX	18,736	C+
The Catholic Univ of America	DC	56,356	VC
The College of Wooster	OH	57,900	VC+
The Univ of Tenn at Knoxville	TN	22,112	VC
Tufts Univ	MA		MC
Tulane Univ	LA	63,396	HC+
Tuskegee Univ	AL	28,164	C
Univ of Arizona	AZ	23,100	C
Univ of Arkansas at Fayetteville	AR	19,152	C+
Univ of Calif at Berkeley	CA	28,853	MC
Univ of Calif at Los Angeles	CA	30,162	MC
Univ of Central Florida	FL	15,922	VC
Univ of Colo Denver	CO	23,230	C
Univ of Detroit Mercy	MI	48,816	C+
Univ of Florida	FL	16,291	HC+
Univ of Houston	TX	21,483	VC
Univ of Idaho	ID	15,348	C
Univ of Illinois at Chicago	IL	25,006	VC
Univ of Illinois at Urbana-Champaign	IL	27,006	HC
Univ of Kansas	KS	20,135	C+
Univ of Maine at Augusta	ME	7,812	C
Univ of Maryland/College Park	MD	21,938	HC
Univ of Mass Amherst	MA	26,199	VC+
Univ of Memphis	TN	18,278	C
Univ of Miami	FL	63,494	MC
Univ of Mich/Ann Arbor	MI	24,410	MC
Univ of Minn/Twin Cities	MN	23,519	HC+
Univ of Nebr - Lincoln	NE	18,589	VC
Univ of New Mexico	NM	15,404	C
Univ of N Car at Charlotte	NC	15,547	C
Univ of Notre Dame	IN	64,043	MC
Univ of Okla	OK	18,911	VC
Univ of Oregon	OR	22,972	C
Univ of Pennsylvania	PA	63,526	MC
Univ of San Francisco	CA	58,484	VC
Univ of Southern Calif	CA	66,631	C
Univ of Texas at Arlington	TX	18,026	LC
Univ of Texas at Austin	TX	26,102	HC
Univ of Texas at San Antonio	TX	20,157	C
Univ of the District of Columbia	DC	21,044	LC
Univ of Virginia	VA	25,891	MC
Univ of Wisc-Milwaukee	WI	21,496	C
Virginia Polytechnic Inst and State Univ	VA	21,276	HC
Washington State Univ	WA	22,495	C
Washington Univ in St. Louis	MO	65,366	VC
Wellesley College	MA	63,916	MC
Wentworth Inst of Technology	MA	47,112	C
Woodbury Univ	CA	46,958	C
Yale Univ	CT	64,650	MC

ARCHITECTURE & SUSTAINABILITY

School	ST	$IS	SR
Ferris State Univ	MI	21,445	C

AREA STUDIES

School	ST	$IS	SR
American Univ	DC	59,379	HC+
Appalachian State Univ	NC	14,416	VC
Bard College	NY	64,024	HC
Baylor Univ	TX	53,760	HC
Calvin College	MI	41,570	VC+
CUNY/City College	NY	20,319	VC
Columbia Univ/City of New York	NY	62,958	MC
Duke Univ	NC	64,188	
Eastern Mich Univ	MI	19,761	C
Huntington Univ	IN	33,996	C
Ithaca College	NY	56,766	VC
Lake Forest College	IL	50,652	VC
Mercer Univ	GA	45,348	VC
New York Univ	NY	65,860	MC
Prescott College	AZ	33,284	C
Rutgers Univ - Newark	NJ	27,288	C
St. Ambrose Univ	IA	39,019	C
Stanford Univ	CA	60,409	MC
The College of Wooster	OH	57,900	VC+
Univ of Alaska Fairbanks	AK	16,179	C
Univ of Mich/Dearborn	MI	11,757	VC
Univ of Miss	MS	17,746	C+
Univ of Okla	OK	18,911	VC
Univ of Vermont	VT	28,878	HC
Univ of Virginia	VA	25,891	MC
Washington Univ in St. Louis	MO	65,366	VC
Webster Univ	MO	37,490	C
Wheaton College	MA	61,512	VC

ART

School	ST	$IS	SR
Abilene Christian Univ	TX	41,800	C+
Adams State Univ	CO	17,703	LC
Alabama A&M Univ	AL	18,796	C
Alabama State Univ	AL	14,142	NC
Albany State Univ	GA	19,462	C
Albion College	MI	52,650	C
Albright College	PA	46,660	C
Allegheny College	PA	55,420	VC
Alma College	MI	47,548	C
Alverno College	WI	33,294	LC
American Univ	DC	59,379	HC+
Andrews Univ	MI	28,030	C+
Angelo State Univ	TX	15,263	NC
Anna Maria College	MA	48,186	C
Appalachian State Univ	NC	14,416	VC
Aquinas College - Mich	MI	38,876	HC
Arizona State Univ at the Tempe Campus	AZ	21,756	VC
Arkansas State Univ	AR	16,190	C
Arkansas Tech Univ	AR	15,484	C
Armstrong State Univ	GA	16,962	C
Asbury Univ	KY	35,180	C+
Ashland Univ	OH	21,440	C
Atlantic Union College	MA	27,228	C
Auburn Univ	AL	23,594	VC+
Augsburg College	MN	43,929	C
Augusta Univ	GA	4,632	C
Augustana College	IL	49,658	VC
Augustana Univ	SD	38,424	VC
Aurora Univ	IL	33,970	C
Austin College	TX	45,875	VC
Austin Peay State Univ	TN	16,397	C
Averett Univ	VA	40,970	LC
Avila Univ	MO	35,480	C
Ball State Univ	IN	19,590	C
Barry Univ	FL	37,830	C
Baylor Univ	TX	53,760	HC
Belhaven Univ	MS	31,016	C
Beloit College	WI	55,206	HC
Benedictine College	KS	36,200	VC
Bennington College	VT	63,960	MC
Berea College	KY	7,042	C
Berry College	GA	45,286	C+
Bethany College	KS	46,100	NC
Bethel College	KS	35,370	C
Bethel Univ	MN	45,270	VC
Biola Univ	CA	46,402	C+
Birmingham-Southern College	AL	44,478	VC
Black Hills State Univ	SD	15,899	C
Blackburn College	IL	28,526	LC
Bluffton Univ	OH	40,950	C
Boise State Univ	ID	14,860	C
Bowling Green State Univ	OH	19,747	C
Brescia Univ	KY	29,890	VC+
Briar Cliff Univ	IA	36,956	C
Bridgewater College	VA	44,510	C
Bridgewater State Univ	MA	21,810	C
Brigham Young Univ	UT	12,748	HC
Brigham Young Univ/Hawaii	HI	11,290	C
Brown Univ	RI	64,566	MC
Bucknell Univ	PA	64,616	MC
Buena Vista Univ	IA	41,514	C
Butler Univ	IN	51,352	VC
Caldwell Univ	NJ	42,165	NC
Calif College of the Arts	CA	52,758	SP
Calif Lutheran Univ	CA	52,853	C
Cal State, Bakersfield	CA	19,191	LC
Cal State, Chico	CA	21,440	C
Cal State, Dominguez Hills	CA	19,022	LC
Cal State, East Bay	CA	19,413	C
Cal State, Fresno	CA	16,902	LC
Cal State, Fullerton	CA	21,902	C
Cal State, Long Beach	CA	18,850	C
Cal State, Northridge	CA	16,859	LC
Cal State, San Bernardino	CA	12,000	C
Cal State, Stanislaus	CA	16,212	C
Calif Univ of Pennsylvania	PA	14,217	LC
Calvin College	MI	41,570	VC+
Cameron Univ	OK	11,072	NC
Campbellsville Univ	KY	32,492	C
Capital Univ	OH	42,982	C
Cardinal Stritch Univ	WI	36,462	C
Carlow Univ	PA	38,549	LC
Carnegie Mellon Univ	PA	67,980	MC
Carroll Univ	WI	38,100	C+
Carthage College	WI	48,835	C
Castleton Univ	VT	20,186	C
Cedar Crest College	PA	46,715	C
Centenary College of Louisiana	LA	45,650	C+
Central College	IA	44,592	C
Central Conn State Univ	CT	21,203	C
Central Mich Univ	MI	20,330	C
Central Washington Univ	WA	16,803	C
Chadron State College	NE	14,819	NC
Chapman Univ	CA	63,078	VC+
Chestnut Hill College	PA	43,410	C
Chicago State Univ	IL	20,144	C
CUNY/Brooklyn College	NY	5,884	C+
CUNY/City College	NY	20,319	VC
CUNY/College of Staten Island	NY	17,840	NC
Claflin Univ	SC	33,764	LC
Clarion Univ of Pennsylvania	PA	21,608	LC
Clark Atlanta Univ	GA	31,019	LC
Cleveland State Univ	OH	22,196	C
Coe College	IA	51,570	VC
Coker College	SC	34,810	LC
Colby-Sawyer College	NH	50,790	C
College of St. Benedict	MN	52,806	C
College of St. Elizabeth	NJ	44,432	LC
College of St. Mary	NE	35,184	C
College of St. Scholastica	MN	44,640	C
College of the Ozarks	MO	7,230	C
College of William & Mary	VA		MC
Colo Christian Univ	CO	39,940	VC
Colo Mesa Univ	CO	18,955	LC
Colo State Univ	CO	22,162	VC
Colo State Univ-Pueblo	CO	18,234	C
Columbia College - Missouri	MO	27,803	C
Columbia College Chicago	IL	43,168	C
Columbus State Univ	GA	14,336	LC
Concordia College - Moorhead	MN	51,088	C+
Concordia Univ	CA	41,580	VC
Concordia Univ St. Paul	MN	29,050	C
Concordia Univ Wisc	WI	35,910	C
Concordia Univ, Ann Arbor	MI	35,945	VC
Concordia Univ, Chicago	IL	39,694	C
Conn College	CT	65,000	MC
Covenant College	GA	38,990	VC
Culver-Stockton College	MO	33,525	C
Daemen College	NY	38,045	C
Dakota Wesleyan Univ	SD	32,850	C
Dallas Baptist Univ	TX	33,713	C
Davidson College	NC	60,119	MC
Davis & Elkins College	WV	38,242	LC
Defiance College	OH	41,630	C
Delta State Univ	MS	13,176	C
DePaul Univ	IL	47,623	VC
Dillard Univ	LA	20,940	VC
Doane Univ	NE	39,184	VC
Dominican Univ of Calif	CA	57,050	C
Dordt College	IA	37,860	C+
Drew Univ/College of Liberal Arts	NJ	61,048	VC
Earlham College	IN	54,870	HC
East Carolina Univ	NC	16,937	C
East Central Univ	OK	13,056	C
East Tenn State Univ	TN	13,994	C
Eastern Illinois Univ	IL	21,126	C
Eastern Kentucky Univ	KY	16,908	C
Eastern Mennonite Univ	VA	42,550	C
Eastern Mich Univ	MI	19,761	C
Eastern New Mexico Univ	NM	14,416	C
Eastern Oregon Univ	OR	17,715	C
Eastern Washington Univ	WA	25,572	LC
Edgewood College	WI	35,950	C
Edinboro Univ	PA	15,940	LC
Elizabeth City State Univ	NC	14,745	C
Elmhurst College	IL	45,428	C
Elon Univ	NC	44,599	VC+
Emory and Henry College	VA	41,410	C
Emory Univ	GA	60,786	MC
Emporia State Univ	KS	14,570	C
Erskine College	SC	45,460	C
Evangel Univ	MO	28,898	C
Felician Univ	NJ	45,370	LC
Ferrum College	VA	39,650	C
Florida Atlantic Univ	FL	17,339	C
Florida Gulf Coast Univ	FL	9,682	C
Florida International Univ	FL	19,854	C+
Fontbonne Univ	MO	33,717	C
Fort Hays State Univ	KS	12,131	C
Fort Lewis College	CO	18,980	C
Freed-Hardeman Univ	TN	29,450	C
Friends Univ	KS	34,455	C
Furman Univ	SC	58,092	VC+
Gardner-Webb Univ	NC	39,200	C+
George Fox Univ	OR	42,938	C
Georgetown College	KY	41,440	C
Georgetown Univ	DC	65,926	MC
Georgia College & State Univ	GA	21,148	C+
Georgia Southern Univ	GA	16,596	C
Georgia Southwestern State Univ	GA	13,870	C
Georgia State Univ	GA	24,332	VC
Goddard College	VT	17,040	VC
Gonzaga Univ	WA	50,888	HC
Gordon College	MA	46,472	C+
Goshen College	IN	42,500	C
Goucher College	MD	55,716	VC
Grace College and Seminary	IN	31,524	C
Grand Valley State Univ	MI	22,250	C+
Green Mountain College	VT	45,228	LC
Greensboro College	NC	42,400	LC
Greenville College	IL	27,012	C
Guilford College	NC	44,090	C
Hamilton College	NY	64,250	MC
Hamline Univ	MN	45,678	VC
Hampton Univ	VA	34,926	LC
Hannibal-LaGrange Univ	MO	29,815	C
Hanover College	IN	46,364	C+
Harding Univ	AR	25,421	C
Hardin-Simmons Univ	TX	33,966	C
Hartwick College	NY	51,270	C
Hendrix College	AR	54,020	VC+
Heritage Univ	WA	19,825	NC
Hillsdale College	MI	35,722	MC
Hiram College	OH	43,230	C
Holy Family Univ	PA	43,326	LC
Hood College	MD	54,840	C
Hope College	MI	39,940	VC
Houghton College	NY	39,090	C
Houston Baptist Univ	TX	36,450	C
Howard Payne Univ	TX	34,320	C
Humboldt State Univ	CA	20,514	C
Huntingdon College	AL	34,900	C
Huntington Univ	IN	33,996	C
Idaho State Univ	ID	13,619	NC
Illinois State Univ	IL	23,418	VC
Illinois Wesleyan Univ	IL	56,430	VC+
Indiana Univ of Pennsylvania	PA	23,614	LC
Indiana Wesleyan Univ	IN	33,674	C
Ithaca College	NY	56,766	VC
Jackson State Univ	MS	15,879	LC
James Madison Univ	VA	19,084	VC
Johnson State College	VT	20,752	C
Judson College	AL	27,066	C
Kalamazoo College	MI	53,931	HC+
Kansas State Univ	KS	17,780	VC
Keene State College	NH	24,003	LC
Kennesaw State Univ	GA	19,592	VC
Kentucky State Univ	KY	13,364	LC
Kentucky Wesleyan College	KY	32,080	C
Kenyon College	OH	63,330	MC
La Sierra Univ	CA	39,690	VC
Lafayette College	PA	63,355	MC
LaGrange College	GA	39,930	C
Lake Forest College	IL	50,652	VC
Lakeland Univ	WI	35,130	C
Lebanon Valley College	PA	51,530	C
Lees-McRae College	NC	33,944	C
Lehigh Univ	PA	61,010	MC
LeMoyne-Owen College	TN	16,980	C
Lewis Univ	IL	40,370	C
Lindsey Wilson College	KY	32,882	C
Linfield College	OR	52,010	C
Lipscomb Univ	TN	41,296	VC
LIU Post	NY	49,682	C
Longwood Univ	VA	22,184	C
Lourdes Univ	OH	29,520	NC
Luther College	IA	48,540	C+
Lycoming College	PA	48,580	C
Lynchburg College	VA	46,740	C
Lyon College	AR	34,730	C+
Macalester College	MN	61,905	MC
MacMurray College	IL	33,620	C
Malone Univ	OH	38,448	C

ST = STATE **$IS** = IN-STATE COSTS **SR** = SELECTOR RATING

School	ST	$IS	SR
Manchester Univ	IN	40,422	C
Marian Univ	WI	32,420	LC
Marshall Univ	WV	17,242	C
Mary Baldwin Univ	VA	39,865	C
Marygrove College	MI	28,926	NC
Marylhurst Univ	OR	20,295	NC
Marymount Univ	VA	41,570	LC
Maryville College	TN	44,410	C
Mass College of Liberal Arts	MA	20,128	C
McKendree Univ	IL	37,940	C+
McMurry Univ	TX	34,259	LC
McNeese State Univ	LA	7,838	C
McPherson College	KS	34,909	C
Mercer Univ	GA	45,348	VC
Meredith College	NC	45,297	C
Methodist Univ	NC	43,600	C
Metropolitan State Univ of Denver	CO	29,889	LC
Miami Univ	OH	27,190	HC+
Millersville Univ of Pennsylvania	PA	23,782	C
Milligan College	TN	38,150	C
Millikin Univ	IL	42,158	C
Minn State Univ, Mankato	MN	15,616	C
Minot State Univ	ND	12,732	C
Miss College	MS	25,850	C
Miss State Univ	MS	11,454	C+
Miss Valley State Univ	MS	13,233	LC
Missouri Southern State Univ	MO	12,499	C
Missouri State Univ	MO	15,190	C+
Missouri Valley College	MO	28,150	C
Molloy College	NY	40,440	C
Monmouth College	IL	42,260	C
Monmouth Univ	NJ	46,234	C
Montana State Univ	MT	15,500	C+
Montana State Univ-Billings	MT	22,960	C
Montclair State Univ	NJ	26,210	LC
Morehouse College	GA	40,064	C
Morningside College	IA	36,865	C
Mount Mercy Univ	IA	36,826	C
Mount St. Joseph Univ	OH	33,880	C
Mount St. Mary's Univ - Chalon Campus	CA	43,897	VC+
Mount Vernon Nazarene Univ	OH	34,500	C
Muhlenberg College	PA	56,645	VC+
Muskingum Univ	OH	35,966	C
Nazareth College	NY	45,574	C
Nebr Wesleyan Univ	NE	38,140	C+
Neumann Univ	PA	40,678	LC
New College of Florida	FL	15,848	MC
New Mexico Highlands Univ	NM	11,904	NC
New Mexico State Univ	NM	14,050	C
Newberry College	SC	34,550	C
Newman Univ	KS	35,390	C
Nicholls State Univ	LA	10,534	C
N Car Central Univ	NC	9,000	C
North Central College	IL	48,712	VC
N Dak State Univ	ND	16,245	C
Northeastern Illinois Univ	IL	12,529	LC
Northeastern Univ	MA	62,703	MC
Northern Illinois Univ	IL	20,176	C
Northwest Missouri State Univ	MO	17,737	C
Northwest Nazarene Univ	ID	36,000	C
Northwestern Univ	IL	66,344	MC
Notre Dame College	OH	37,150	VC
Notre Dame de Namur Univ	CA	46,526	LC
Nova Southeastern Univ	FL	38,534	C+
Oberlin College	OH	66,012	MC
Oglethorpe Univ	GA	44,200	C+
Ohio Dominican Univ	OH	41,340	C+
Ohio State Univ at Columbus	OH	21,703	HC+
Ohio Univ	OH	22,924	C
Ohio Wesleyan Univ	OH	49,460	VC
Okla Baptist Univ	OK	32,320	C
Okla Christian Univ	OK	27,650	VC
Okla City Univ	OK	40,476	VC
Okla State Univ	OK	17,180	VC
Olivet Nazarene Univ	IL	41,840	C
Oregon State Univ	OR	22,519	VC
Ottawa Univ	KS	36,074	VC
Otterbein Univ	OH	41,630	C
Ouachita Baptist Univ	AR	32,320	C
Our Lady of the Lake Univ	TX	35,012	LC
Pace Univ	NY	58,248	C
Palm Beach Atlantic Univ	FL	39,720	C
Pennsylvania State Univ - Univ Park	PA	29,760	HC
Pepperdine Univ	CA	74,460	HC+
Pfeiffer Univ	NC	39,695	LC
Piedmont College	GA	32,512	C
Pine Manor College	MA	41,660	LC
Pittsburg State Univ	KS	13,880	NC
Pitzer College	CA	66,192	MC
Plymouth State Univ	NH	23,180	LC
Point Loma Nazarene Univ	CA	43,450	C
Prairie View A&M Univ	TX	15,205	LC
Prescott College	AZ	33,284	C
Queens Univ of Charlotte	NC	39,543	C
Radford Univ	VA	19,027	LC
Ramapo College of New Jersey	NJ	25,338	C
Randolph College	VA	45,660	VC
Reed College	OR	65,300	MC
Rhodes College	TN	51,900	HC
Ripon College	WI	46,911	C+
Roanoke College	VA	54,114	VC
Roberts Wesleyan College	NY	38,306	C
Rochester Inst of Technology	NY	50,842	HC
Rockford Univ	IL	36,030	C
Rocky Mountain College	MT	34,270	C
Rowan Univ	NJ	24,491	VC+
Rutgers Univ - Camden	NJ	26,146	C
Rutgers Univ - New Brunswick	NJ	26,632	HC
Rutgers Univ - Newark	NJ	27,288	C
Saginaw Valley State Univ	MI	18,530	C
St. John's Univ	MN	51,624	C
St. Joseph's Univ	PA	57,544	VC+
St. Mary-of-the-Woods College	IN	39,632	LC
St. Mary's College	IN	50,600	C
St. Mary's College of Calif	CA	57,420	C
St. Mary's Univ of Minn	MN	41,210	VC
St. Vincent College	PA	44,626	C
Salisbury Univ	MD	20,714	VC
Sam Houston State Univ	TX	18,792	C
Samford Univ	AL	39,232	VC
San Diego State Univ	CA	21,896	C+
San Francisco State Univ	CA	18,514	LC
Savannah College of Art and Design	GA	49,595	C
Schreiner Univ	TX	34,626	LC
Seattle Pacific Univ	WA	47,439	C+
Shepherd Univ, West Virginia	WV	17,224	C
Shippensburg Univ of Pennsylvania	PA	23,208	C
Shorter Univ	GA	31,130	LC
Silver Lake College of the Holy Family	WI	36,290	LC
Simpson College	IA	43,839	VC
Sinte Gleska Univ	SD	13,154	NC
Skidmore College	NY	64,214	HC
Sonoma State Univ	CA	27,806	C
S Dak State Univ	SD	15,634	C
Southeast Missouri State Univ	MO	15,498	C
Southeastern Louisiana Univ	LA	16,237	C
Southeastern Okla State Univ	OK	11,875	C
Southern Adventist Univ	TN	27,600	C
Southern Arkansas Univ	AR	21,532	C
Southern Illinois Univ Carbondale	IL	23,667	C
Southern Illinois Univ Edwardsville	IL	22,643	C
Southern Oregon Univ	OR	19,117	C
Southwest Baptist Univ	MO	29,900	LC
Southwest Minn State Univ	MN	17,783	C
Southwestern Okla State Univ	OK	11,790	C
Southwestern Univ	TX	50,720	VC
Spelman College	GA	38,751	C
Spring Arbor Univ	MI	36,000	C
St. Catherine Univ	MN	45,630	VC
St. Edward's Univ	TX	53,100	VC
St. Lawrence Univ	NY	64,390	VC
St. Mary's College of Maryland	MD	26,634	VC
St. Norbert College	WI	44,525	VC
Stanford Univ	CA	60,409	MC
SUNY / Buffalo State College	NY	20,842	C
SUNY / SUNY Cortland	NY	20,706	VC
SUNY / SUNY Oneonta	NY	19,712	C+
SUNY / SUNY Plattsburgh	NY	18,814	C
SUNY / SUNY Potsdam	NY	20,404	C+
SUNY at Binghamton	NY	22,861	MC
SUNY at Oswego	NY	21,351	C
Stephen F. Austin State Univ	TX	18,406	LC
Sterling College	KS	32,830	C
Stevenson Univ	MD	72,770	C
Stillman College	AL	20,738	C
Swarthmore College	PA	63,550	MC
Syracuse Univ	NY	60,239	VC
Tarleton State Univ	TX	15,248	LC
Taylor Univ	IN	40,317	C+
Temple Univ	PA	24,392	VC
Tenn State Univ	TN	14,423	C
Texas A&M Univ at Corpus Christi	TX	16,851	LC
Texas Lutheran Univ	TX	38,620	C
Texas Southern Univ	TX	18,212	LC
Texas State Univ	TX	19,350	C
Texas Tech Univ	TX	18,736	C+
Texas Woman's Univ	TX	15,302	LC
The Catholic Univ of America	DC	56,356	VC
The College of Idaho	ID	36,415	C
The College of New Jersey	NJ	31,909	HC
The Univ of Akron	OH	21,477	C
The Univ of Tenn at Chattanooga	TN	16,744	C
The Univ of Tenn at Knoxville	TN	22,112	VC
The Univ of Utah	UT	17,924	VC
The Univ of Virginia's College at Wise	VA	18,192	LC
Thiel College	PA	41,590	C
Thomas Edison State Univ	NJ	6,350	NC
Thomas More College	KY	36,720	C
Tougaloo College	MS	17,980	NC
Towson Univ	MD	17,408	VC
Transylvania Univ	KY	45,690	VC+
Trinity Christian College	IL	35,580	C
Trinity Univ	TX	52,314	HC+
Troy Univ	AL	16,171	C
Truman State Univ	MO	16,014	HC
Union Univ	TN	33,970	VC
Unity College	ME	37,670	C
Univ of Alabama at Birmingham	AL	19,906	C
Univ of Alabama in Huntsville	AL	19,445	VC
Univ of Alaska Anchorage	AK	16,652	NC
Univ of Alaska Fairbanks	AK	16,179	C
Univ of Alaska Southeast	AK	11,493	C
Univ of Arizona	AZ	23,100	C
Univ of Arkansas at Fayetteville	AR	19,152	C+
Univ of Arkansas at Little Rock	AR	18,211	C
Univ of Arkansas at Monticello	AR	13,134	NC
Univ of Arkansas at Pine Bluff	AR	13,541	C
Univ of Calif at Berkeley	CA	28,853	MC
Univ of Calif at Los Angeles	CA	30,162	MC
Univ of Calif at Riverside	CA	29,227	C+
Univ of Calif at Santa Barbara	CA	29,091	HC
Univ of Calif San Diego	CA	30,150	MC
Univ of Calif, Santa Cruz	CA	28,731	C+
Univ of Central Florida	FL	15,922	VC
Univ of Central Okla	OK	13,486	C
Univ of Charleston	WV	35,000	C
Univ of Conn	CT	25,538	HC
Univ of Dayton	OH	53,620	C
Univ of Delaware	DE	24,976	VC+
Univ of Denver	CO	58,443	VC+
Univ of Evansville	IN	44,186	VC+
Univ of Findlay	OH	60,139	C
Univ of Florida	FL	16,291	HC+
Univ of Georgia	GA	21,250	HC
Univ of Great Falls	MT	38,524	C
Univ of Hawaii at Hilo	HI	18,038	C
Univ of Hawaii at Manoa	HI	23,221	C
Univ of Houston	TX	21,483	VC
Univ of Idaho	ID	15,348	C
Univ of Indianapolis	IN	36,480	C
Univ of Iowa	IA	18,683	VC+
Univ of Kansas	KS	20,135	C+
Univ of La Verne	CA	55,600	C
Univ of Louisiana at Monroe	LA	15,970	C
Univ of Louisville	KY	19,824	C
Univ of Maine at Augusta	ME	7,812	C
Univ of Maine at Farmington	ME	18,187	C
Univ of Maine at Presque Isle	ME	14,870	C
Univ of Mary Hardin-Baylor	TX	33,950	C+
Univ of Maryland/Baltimore County	MD	21,296	VC
Univ of Mass Boston	MA	13,435	C
Univ of Memphis	TN	18,278	C
Univ of Miami	FL	63,494	MC
Univ of Mich/Ann Arbor	MI	24,410	MC
Univ of Mich-Flint	MI	17,607	C+
Univ of Minn/Duluth	MN	20,292	C+
Univ of Minn/Twin Cities	MN	23,519	HC+
Univ of Miss	MS	17,746	C+
Univ of Missouri/Columbia	MO	18,201	MC
Univ of Mobile	AL	28,935	C
Univ of Montana-Western	MT	11,220	LC
Univ of Montevallo	AL	19,502	C
Univ of Mount Olive	NC	18,426	C
Univ of Mount Union	OH	38,970	C
Univ of Nebr - Lincoln	NE	18,589	VC
Univ of Nebr - Omaha	NE	16,120	C
Univ of Nevada/Reno	NV	18,010	C
Univ of New Haven	CT	52,190	C
Univ of New Mexico	NM	15,404	C
Univ of New Orleans	LA	12,840	C
Univ of North Alabama	AL	15,398	C
Univ of N Car at Asheville	NC	15,723	VC+
Univ of N Car at Charlotte	NC	15,547	C
Univ of N Car at Greensboro	NC	14,690	C
Univ of N Car at Pembroke	NC	14,388	LC
Univ of N Car at Wilmington	NC	14,590	VC
Univ of North Florida	FL	15,996	VC
Univ of North Georgia	GA	17,316	C
Univ of North Texas	TX	19,198	C
Univ of Northern Colo	CO	20,851	C
Univ of Okla	OK	18,911	VC
Univ of Oregon	OR	22,972	C
Univ of Pikeville	KY	28,700	NC
Univ of Puget Sound	WA	56,456	VC+
Univ of Redlands	CA	60,200	VC
Univ of Rhode Island	RI	24,906	C
Univ of Rio Grande & Rio Grande Community College	OH	8,750	NC
Univ of St. Mary	KS	34,690	C
Univ of Science and Arts of Okla	OK	11,140	VC
Univ of S Dak	SD	16,109	C
Univ of Southern Indiana	IN	16,501	C
Univ of Tampa	FL	36,944	C
Univ of Texas at El Paso	TX	34,452	NC
Univ of Texas at San Antonio	TX	20,157	C
Univ of the Cumberlands	KY	32,000	C
Univ of the Incarnate Word	TX	39,162	LC
Univ of the Ozarks	AR	52,176	C
Univ of the Pacific	CA	57,006	VC
Univ of Tulsa	OK	52,625	HC+
Univ of Vermont	VT	28,878	HC
Univ of Virginia	VA	25,891	MC
Univ of West Georgia	GA	16,360	LC
Univ of Wisc-Eau Claire	WI	15,797	VC
Univ of Wisc-Green Bay	WI	15,064	C
Univ of Wisc-La Crosse	WI	15,247	C+
Univ of Wisc-Madison	WI	20,934	MC
Univ of Wisc-Milwaukee	WI	21,496	C
Univ of Wisc-Oshkosh	WI	15,200	C
Univ of Wisc-Platteville	WI	14,614	VC
Univ of Wisc-River Falls	WI	14,485	C
Univ of Wisc-Stevens Point	WI	14,043	C
Univ of Wisc-Stout	WI	19,667	C
Univ of Wisc-Superior	WI	14,446	C
Univ of Wyoming	WY	15,375	C+
Upper Iowa Univ	IA	34,990	NC
Ursinus College	PA	61,690	VC
Ursuline College	OH	41,076	LC
Valley City State Univ	ND	13,267	C
Valparaiso Univ	IN	48,370	C+
Vanderbilt Univ	TN	60,572	MC
Vassar College	NY	65,491	MC
Virginia Polytechnic Inst and State Univ	VA	21,276	HC
Virginia Wesleyan College	VA	43,728	LC
Viterbo Univ	WI	34,660	C
Wabash College	IN	50,650	VC
Wake Forest Univ	NC	64,056	MC
Walla Walla Univ	WA	30,417	NC
Warren Wilson College	NC	44,220	VC
Wartburg College	IA	47,840	C
Washburn Univ	KS	15,827	C
Washington College	MD	54,666	VC
Washington State Univ	WA	22,495	C
Wayland Baptist Univ	TX	22,356	LC
Wayne State College	NE	12,802	C
Wayne State Univ	MI	22,016	C
Waynesburg Univ	PA	32,290	C
Weber State Univ	UT	10,721	C
Webster Univ	MO	37,490	C
Wellesley College	MA	63,916	MC
West Chester Univ of Pennsylvania	PA	18,456	C
West Texas A&M Univ	TX	13,478	C
West Virginia Univ	WV	18,210	C
Western Carolina Univ	NC	13,965	C
Western Conn State Univ	CT	21,254	LC
Western Illinois Univ	IL	20,825	C
Western Mich Univ	MI	21,054	C
Western Oregon Univ	OR	15,021	LC
Western State Colo Univ	CO	18,639	C
Western Washington Univ	WA	18,003	C+
Westfield State Univ	MA	19,671	C
Westminster College	PA	39,180	C+
Westminster College	UT	41,078	C+
Westmont College	CA	56,410	HC
Wheaton College	IL	43,610	MC
Whitman College	WA	59,772	MC
Whittier College	CA	57,891	C
Whitworth Univ	WA	51,732	VC
Wichita State Univ	KS	21,643	C
Widener Univ	PA	56,486	C
William Carey Univ	MS	23,950	LC
William Jewell College	MO	41,210	C+
William Woods Univ	MO	32,040	C
Williams Baptist College	AR	24,720	C
Williams College	MA	63,290	MC
Wilmington College	OH	34,600	C
Wilson College	PA	35,620	C
Winston-Salem State Univ	NC	26,166	LC
Winthrop Univ	SC	23,082	C
Wisc Lutheran College	WI	36,290	VC
Wittenberg Univ	OH	48,156	C+
Wright State Univ	OH	16,983	C
Xavier Univ	OH	47,880	C+
Yale Univ	CT	64,650	MC
Youngstown State Univ	OH	17,307	C

ART AND DESIGN

School	ST	$IS	SR
Appalachian State Univ	NC	14,416	VC
Bryant Univ	RI	55,646	VC
Calif Polytechnic State Univ	CA	17,979	HC+
Calvin College	MI	41,570	VC+
Doane Univ	NE	39,184	VC
East Stroudsburg Univ	PA	18,334	C
Frostburg State Univ	MD	17,280	LC
Judson Univ	IL	37,700	C
Lewis Univ	IL	40,370	C
Missouri Southern State Univ	MO	12,499	C
Mount Ida College	MA	46,820	C
Northern Mich Univ	MI	19,604	C
Point Loma Nazarene Univ	CA	43,450	C
Rochester Inst of Technology	NY	50,842	HC
Seton Hill Univ	PA	46,972	C
Sterling College	KS	32,830	C
Taylor Univ	IN	40,317	C+
Tusculum College	TN	31,625	C
Univ of Maryland/Baltimore County	MD	21,296	VC
Univ of New England	ME	48,880	C
Univ of San Diego	CA	58,442	VC+
Univ of St. Francis	IL	39,924	C

ART EDUCATION

School	ST	$IS	SR
Adams State Univ	CO	17,703	LC
Adelphi Univ	NY	48,244	C
Alabama A&M Univ	AL	18,796	C
Alabama State Univ	AL	14,142	NC
Alfred Univ	NY	42,296	C+
Alverno College	WI	33,294	LC
Anderson Univ	IN	38,200	C
Andrews Univ	MI	28,030	C+

ST = STATE $IS = IN-STATE COSTS SR = SELECTOR RATING

School	ST	$IS	SR
Appalachian State Univ	NC	14,416	VC
Aquinas College - Mich	MI	38,876	HC
Arcadia Univ	PA	33,570	C+
Arkansas Tech Univ	AR	15,484	C
Armstrong State Univ	GA	16,962	C
Asbury Univ	KY	35,180	C+
Ashland Univ	OH	21,440	C
Augustana College	IL	49,658	VC
Averett Univ	VA	40,970	LC
Azusa Pacific Univ	CA	43,972	C
Baldwin Wallace Univ	OH	41,106	C
Barton College	NC	38,686	LC
Baylor Univ	TX	53,760	HC
Belmont Univ	TN	40,970	VC
Beloit College	WI	55,206	HC
Bemidji State Univ	MN	16,056	VC
Berry College	GA	45,286	C+
Bethany College	KS	46,100	NC
Bethany College	WV	36,300	NC
Bethel College	IN	35,860	C
Boise State Univ	ID	14,860	C
Boston Univ	MA	65,110	MC
Bowling Green State Univ	OH	19,747	C
Brenau Univ - Women's College	GA	37,876	LC
Brescia Univ	KY	29,890	VC+
Bridgewater State Univ	MA	21,810	C
Brigham Young Univ	UT	12,748	HC
Brigham Young Univ/Hawaii	HI	11,290	C
Buena Vista Univ	IA	41,514	C
Cal State, Chico	CA	21,440	C
Calvin College	MI	41,570	VC+
Capital Univ	OH	42,982	C
Carlow Univ	PA	38,549	LC
Carroll Univ	WI	38,100	C+
Carson-Newman Univ	TN	34,160	C
Case Western Reserve Univ	OH	60,304	MC
Central Conn State Univ	CT	21,203	C
Central State Univ	OH	18,564	C
Central Washington Univ	WA	16,803	C
Chicago State Univ	IL	20,144	C
CUNY/Brooklyn College	NY	5,884	C+
CUNY/City College	NY	20,319	VC
CUNY/Hunter College	NY	31,098	VC
CUNY/Lehman College	NY	5,778	HC+
CUNY/Queens College	NY	27,896	C
Claflin Univ	SC	33,764	LC
Clarke Univ	IA	38,940	C
Clayton State Univ	GA	19,735	C
Coker College	SC	34,810	LC
Colby-Sawyer College	NH	50,790	C
College for Creative Studies	MI	48,875	SP
College of the Ozarks	MO	7,230	C
Colo State Univ	CO	22,162	VC
Columbus State Univ	GA	14,336	LC
Concord Univ	WV	14,954	C
Concordia College - Moorhead	MN	51,088	C+
Concordia College - New York	NY	39,035	LC
Concordia Univ St. Paul	MN	29,050	C
Converse College	SC	26,495	C
Culver-Stockton College	MO	33,525	C
Daemen College	NY	38,045	C
Defiance College	OH	41,630	C
Delaware State Univ	DE	19,376	NC
DePaul Univ	IL	47,623	VC
Dickinson State Univ	ND	12,372	LC
Dordt College	IA	37,860	C+
East Carolina Univ	NC	16,937	C
East Central Univ	OK	13,056	C
Eastern Kentucky Univ	KY	16,908	C
Eastern Mich Univ	MI	19,761	C
Eastern Washington Univ	WA	25,572	LC
Edgewood College	WI	35,950	C
Edinboro Univ	PA	15,940	LC
Elizabethtown College	PA	54,050	C
Elmhurst College	IL	45,428	C
Elmira College	NY	53,900	C
Emporia State Univ	KS	14,570	C
Escuela de Artes Plasticas de PR	PR	11,236	
Fairmont State Univ	WV	15,726	C
Ferris State Univ	MI	21,445	C
Fisk Univ	TN	32,066	LC
Flagler College	FL	27,620	C
Florida A&M Univ	FL	15,361	C
Florida International Univ	FL	19,854	C+
Florida State Univ	FL	16,771	HC
Fort Hays State Univ	KS	12,131	C
Francis Marion Univ	SC	16,464	LC
Freed-Hardeman Univ	TN	29,450	C
Friends Univ	KS	34,455	C
Georgia State Univ	GA	24,332	VC
Goddard College	VT	17,040	VC
Goshen College	IN	42,500	C
Grace College and Seminary	IN	31,524	C
Grand Valley State Univ	MI	22,250	C+
Grand View Univ	IA	32,302	C
Green Mountain College	VT	45,228	LC
Greensboro College	NC	42,400	LC
Gustavus Adolphus College	MN	52,433	HC
Hardin-Simmons Univ	TX	33,966	C
Hastings College	NE	35,380	C+
Henderson State Univ	AR	15,516	LC
Heritage Univ	WA	19,825	NC
Hofstra Univ	NY	55,960	C+
Hope College	MI	39,940	VC
Houghton College	NY	39,090	C
Houston Baptist Univ	TX	36,450	C
Howard Univ	DC	37,616	C+
Huntington Univ	IN	33,996	C
Indiana State Univ	IN	23,223	LC
Indiana Univ of Pennsylvania	PA	23,614	LC
Indiana Univ South Bend	IN	14,242	C
Indiana Univ-Purdue Univ Fort Wayne	IN	17,553	C
Indiana Univ-Purdue Univ Indianapolis	IN	18,635	C
Indiana Wesleyan Univ	IN	33,674	C
Inter-American Univ of PR-San Germán	PR	20,042	
Ithaca College	NY	56,766	VC
Jacksonville Univ	FL	46,230	C
Johnson State College	VT	20,752	C
Kansas State Univ	KS	17,780	VC
Kansas Wesleyan Univ	KS	36,600	C
Kennesaw State Univ	GA	19,592	VC
Kent State Univ	OH	20,732	C
Kentucky State Univ	KY	13,364	LC
Kentucky Wesleyan College	KY	32,080	C
Keystone College	PA	28,680	LC
Kutztown Univ of Pennsylvania	PA	19,056	LC
Lamar Univ	TX	18,014	LC
Lincoln Univ	MO	13,602	NC
Lindsey Wilson College	KY	32,882	C
Lipscomb Univ	TN	41,296	VC
LIU Brooklyn	NY	49,682	C
LIU Post	NY	49,682	C
Longwood Univ	VA	22,184	C
Louisiana College	LA	21,886	C
Louisiana Tech Univ	LA	11,422	VC
Lubbock Christian Univ	TX	28,426	C
Madonna Univ	MI	29,050	C
Manchester Univ	IN	40,422	C
Marian Univ	WI	32,420	LC
Mars Hill Univ	NC	42,688	C
Marymount Univ	VA	41,570	LC
Maryville Univ of St. Louis	MO	38,046	VC+
Marywood Univ	PA	46,900	C
Mass College of Art and Design	MA	24,800	SP
McKendree Univ	IL	37,940	C+
McMurry Univ	TX	34,259	LC
Mercyhurst Univ	PA	47,420	C
Messiah College	PA	43,100	C+
Methodist Univ	NC	43,600	C
Miami Univ	OH	27,190	HC+
Mich State Univ	MI	23,898	VC+
Middle Tenn State Univ	TN	8,650	C
Midland Univ	NE	37,468	
Millersville Univ of Pennsylvania	PA	23,782	C
Millikin Univ	IL	42,158	C
Minn State Univ, Mankato	MN	15,616	C
Minn State Univ, Moorhead	MN	15,941	C
Miss College	MS	25,850	C
Miss Univ for Women	MS	17,065	C
Missouri Western State Univ	MO	16,741	
Monmouth Univ	NJ	46,234	C
Montana State Univ-Billings	MT	22,960	C
Montclair State Univ	NJ	26,210	LC
Montserrat College of Art	MA	38,150	SP
Moore College of Art and Design	PA	50,135	SP
Moravian College	PA	53,117	
Morningside College	IA	36,865	C
Mount Mary Univ	WI	34,650	LC
Mount St. Joseph Univ	OH	33,880	C
Murray State Univ	KY	16,998	C
Nazareth College	NY	45,574	C
New Jersey City Univ	NJ	21,456	LC
New York Univ	NY	65,860	MC
N Car A&T State Univ	NC	13,365	LC
North Central College	IL	48,712	VC
Northeastern State Univ	OK	8,615	VC
Northern Illinois Univ	IL	20,176	C
Northern Mich Univ	MI	19,604	C
Northern State Univ	SD	14,505	C
Northwest Missouri State Univ	MO	17,737	C
Northwest Nazarene Univ	ID	36,000	C
Northwestern College of Iowa	IA	38,400	C+
Notre Dame of Maryland Univ	MD	46,465	VC
Oakland City Univ	IN	33,360	NC
Ohio State Univ at Columbus	OH	21,703	HC+
Ohio Wesleyan Univ	OH	49,460	VC
Old Dominion Univ	VA	20,910	C
Olivet Nazarene Univ	IL	41,840	C
Oral Roberts Univ	OK	34,316	C
Ouachita Baptist Univ	AR	32,320	C
Our Lady of the Lake Univ	TX	35,012	LC
Palm Beach Atlantic Univ	FL	39,720	C
Pennsylvania State Univ - Univ Park	PA	29,760	HC
Peru State College	NE	14,768	NC
Piedmont College	GA	32,512	C
Plymouth State Univ	NH	23,180	LC
Point Loma Nazarene Univ	CA	43,450	C
Pontifical Catholic Univ of PR	PR	10,534	
Pratt Inst	NY	58,082	VC
Prescott College	AZ	33,284	C
Purdue Univ/West Lafayette	IN	20,032	MC
Rhode Island College	RI	17,694	LC
Rivier Univ	NH	40,410	VC
Rocky Mountain College	MT	34,270	C
Rocky Mountain College of Art and Design	CO	27,052	SP
Rosemont College	PA	30,980	C
Rowan Univ	NJ	24,491	VC+
Saginaw Valley State Univ	MI	18,530	C
St. Joseph's Univ	PA	57,544	VC+
St. Mary-of-the-Woods College	IN	39,632	LC
St. Michael's College	VT	51,725	VC+
St. Vincent College	PA	44,626	C
St. Xavier Univ	IL	43,310	C
Salem State Univ	MA	17,303	LC
School of the Art Inst of Chicago	IL	56,230	SP
Seton Hill Univ	PA	46,972	C
Shepherd Univ, West Virginia	WV	17,224	C
Shippensburg Univ of Pennsylvania	PA	23,208	C
Siena Heights Univ	MI	32,040	C
Silver Lake College of the Holy Family	WI	36,290	LC
S Car State Univ	SC	20,805	LC
S Dak State Univ	SD	15,634	C
Southeast Missouri State Univ	MO	15,498	C
Southeastern Okla State Univ	OK	11,875	C
Southern Arkansas Univ	AR	21,532	C
Southern Conn State Univ	CT	21,924	LC
Southern Illinois Univ Edwardsville	IL	22,643	C
Southern Univ and A&M College	LA	16,074	LC+
Southern Univ at New Orleans	LA	8,014	LC
Southwest Baptist Univ	MO	29,900	LC
Southwest Minn State Univ	MN	17,783	C
Southwestern Okla State Univ	OK	11,790	C
Spelman College	GA	38,751	C
St. Ambrose Univ	IA	39,019	C
St. Catherine Univ	MN	45,630	VC
St. Cloud State Univ	MN	10,600	C
St. Edward's Univ	TX	53,100	VC
St. Thomas Aquinas College	NY	42,200	C
SUNY / Buffalo State College	NY	20,842	C
SUNY at New Paltz	NY	19,200	C
Sul Ross State Univ	TX	15,021	LC
Syracuse Univ	NY	60,239	VC
Tarleton State Univ	TX	15,248	LC
Taylor Univ	IN	40,317	C+
Temple Univ	PA	24,392	VC
Tenn Tech Univ	TN	17,050	C
Texas Christian Univ	TX	54,670	HC
The Catholic Univ of America	DC	56,356	VC
The College of New Jersey	NJ	31,909	HC
The College of New Rochelle	NY	46,300	VC
The Univ of Akron	OH	21,477	C
The Univ of Tenn at Chattanooga	TN	16,744	C
The Univ of Utah	UT	17,924	VC
Thomas More College	KY	36,720	C
Tougaloo College	MS	17,980	NC
Towson Univ	MD	17,408	VC
Trinity Christian College	IL	35,580	C
Troy Univ	AL	16,171	C
Union College	NE	23,270	C
Univ of Arizona	AZ	23,100	C
Univ of Arkansas at Pine Bluff	AR	13,541	C
Univ of Central Arkansas	AR	14,472	VC
Univ of Central Florida	FL	15,922	VC
Univ of Central Missouri	MO	18,982	C
Univ of Central Okla	OK	13,486	C
Univ of Cincinnati	OH	21,964	VC
Univ of Dallas	TX	45,500	VC+
Univ of Dayton	OH	53,620	C
Univ of Evansville	IN	44,186	VC+
Univ of Findlay	OH	60,139	C
Univ of Florida	FL	16,291	HC+
Univ of Georgia	GA	21,250	HC
Univ of Idaho	ID	15,348	C
Univ of Illinois at Chicago	IL	25,006	VC
Univ of Illinois at Urbana-Champaign	IL	27,006	HC
Univ of Indianapolis	IN	36,480	C
Univ of Iowa	IA	18,683	VC+
Univ of Kansas	KS	20,135	C+
Univ of Kentucky	KY	33,306	C
Univ of Louisiana at Lafayette	LA	14,516	C
Univ of Louisville	KY	19,824	C
Univ of Maine	ME	20,792	C
Univ of Maine at Presque Isle	ME	14,870	C
Univ of Mary Hardin-Baylor	TX	33,950	C+
Univ of Maryland/Baltimore County	MD	21,296	VC
Univ of Maryland/College Park	MD	21,938	HC
Univ of Maryland/Eastern Shore	MD	17,013	C
Univ of Mass Dartmouth	MA	25,658	C
Univ of Minn/Duluth	MN	20,292	C+
Univ of Missouri/Columbia	MO	18,201	MC
Univ of Montana-Western	MT	11,220	LC
Univ of Montevallo	AL	19,502	C
Univ of Nebr - Kearney	NE	16,546	LC
Univ of New England	ME	48,880	C
Univ of New Mexico	NM	15,404	C
Univ of North Alabama	AL	15,398	C
Univ of N Car at Greensboro	NC	14,690	C
Univ of North Florida	FL	15,996	VC
Univ of North Georgia	GA	17,316	C
Univ of Northwestern - St. Paul	MN	38,160	C
Univ of Rio Grande & Rio Grande Community College	OH	8,750	NC
Univ of St. Francis	IN	37,400	C
Univ of San Francisco	CA	58,484	VC
Univ of Sioux Falls	SD	34,330	C
Univ of S Car at Columbia	SC	19,725	VC+
Univ of S Car Upstate	SC	18,200	LC
Univ of S Dak	SD	16,109	C
Univ of South Florida/Tampa	FL	16,110	VC+
Univ of Southern Indiana	IN	16,501	C
Univ of Southern Miss	MS	13,170	C
Univ of St. Francis	IL	39,924	C
Univ of the Cumberlands	KY	32,000	C
Univ of the Incarnate Word	TX	39,162	LC
Univ of Toledo	OH	19,336	NC
Univ of Vermont	VT	28,878	HC
Univ of West Florida	FL	15,848	C
Univ of Wisc-Green Bay	WI	15,064	C
Univ of Wisc-Madison	WI	20,934	MC
Univ of Wisc-Milwaukee	WI	21,496	C
Univ of Wisc-Oshkosh	WI	15,200	C
Univ of Wisc-Platteville	WI	14,614	VC
Univ of Wisc-River Falls	WI	14,485	C
Univ of Wisc-Stout	WI	19,667	C
Univ of Wisc-Superior	WI	14,446	C
Univ of Wisc-Whitewater	WI	13,976	C
Utah State Univ	UT	12,736	C
Valparaiso Univ	IN	48,370	C+
Virginia Commonwealth Univ	VA	23,049	C
Virginia Union Univ	VA	22,421	C
Virginia Wesleyan College	VA	43,728	LC
Viterbo Univ	WI	34,660	C
Wartburg College	IA	47,840	C
Washburn Univ	KS	15,827	C
Washington & Jefferson College	PA	56,512	VC
Washington Univ in St. Louis	MO	65,366	VC
Wayne State Univ	MI	22,016	C
Weber State Univ	UT	10,721	C
Webster Univ	MO	37,490	C
West Liberty Univ	WV	15,512	C
West Texas A&M Univ	TX	13,478	C
West Virginia State Univ	WV	8,378	NC
West Virginia Univ	WV	18,210	C
West Virginia Wesleyan College	WV	36,858	C
Western Carolina Univ	NC	13,965	C
Western Illinois Univ	IL	20,825	C
Western Kentucky Univ	KY	16,850	C
Western Mich Univ	MI	21,054	C
Western New Mexico Univ	NM	16,734	LC
Western State Colo Univ	CO	18,639	C
Western Washington Univ	WA	18,003	C+
Westmont College	CA	56,410	HC
Wichita State Univ	KS	21,643	C
Winona State Univ	MN	17,535	C
Wright State Univ	OH	16,983	C
Xavier Univ of Louisiana	LA	31,689	C+
Youngstown State Univ	OH	17,307	C

ART HISTORY

School	ST	$IS	SR
Amherst College	MA		HC+
Aquinas College - Mich	MI	38,876	HC
Assumption College	MA	47,920	C+
Austin College	TX	45,875	VC
Baylor Univ	TX	53,760	HC
Belmont Univ	TN	40,970	VC
Beloit College	WI	55,206	HC
Bloomsburg Univ of Pennsylvania	PA	19,066	LC
Bowdoin College	ME	63,500	MC
Bowling Green State Univ	OH	19,747	C
Brandeis Univ	MA	65,925	MC
Brown Univ	RI	64,566	MC
Cal State, Fullerton	CA	21,902	C
Cal State, Long Beach	CA	18,850	C
Canisius College	NY	47,537	C
Case Western Reserve Univ	OH	60,304	MC
Chapman Univ	CA	63,078	VC+
CUNY/Queens College	NY	27,896	C
Colby College	ME	64,060	MC
College of Charleston	SC	22,699	C
College of William & Mary	VA		MC
Columbia College Chicago	IL	43,168	C
Cornell Univ	NY	64,853	MC
Creighton Univ	NE	48,206	VC+
DePaul Univ	IL	47,623	VC
Dickinson College	PA	63,974	MC
Dominican Univ	IL	41,222	C
Dordt College	IA	37,860	C+
Drexel Univ	PA	65,432	VC+
Elon Univ	NC	44,599	VC+
Fairfield Univ	CT	59,860	VC+
Ferris State Univ	MI	21,445	C
Flagler College	FL	27,620	C
Fordham Univ	NY	65,918	MC
Franklin College	IN	39,380	C
Georgetown Univ	DC	65,926	MC
Goucher College	MD	55,716	VC
Hamline Univ	MN	45,678	VC
Hiram College	OH	43,230	C
Indiana Univ Bloomington	IN	20,429	VC

ST = STATE $IS = IN-STATE COSTS SR = SELECTOR RATING

School	ST	$IS	SR
Indiana Univ-Purdue Univ Indianapolis	IN	18,635	C
Ithaca College	NY	56,766	VC
John Carroll Univ	OH	49,740	C+
Kennesaw State Univ	GA	19,592	VC
Kenyon College	OH	63,330	MC
Lebanon Valley College	PA	51,530	C
Loyola Marymount Univ	CA	58,038	HC
Loyola Univ Chicago	IL	55,802	VC
Mills College	CA	59,163	VC
Missouri State Univ	MO	15,190	C+
Moore College of Art and Design	PA	50,135	SP
Mount St. Joseph Univ	OH	33,880	C
Murray State Univ	KY	16,998	C
Nazareth College	NY	45,574	C
New York Univ	NY	65,860	MC
Niagara Univ	NY	41,010	C
North Central College	IL	48,712	VC
Northeastern Illinois Univ	IL	12,529	LC
Oberlin College	OH	66,012	MC
Occidental College	CA	65,530	MC
Ohio Univ	OH	22,924	C
Ohio Wesleyan Univ	OH	49,460	VC
Pace Univ	NY	58,248	C
Pacific Lutheran Univ	WA	49,960	VC
Plymouth State Univ	NH	23,180	LC
Point Loma Nazarene Univ	CA	43,450	C
Providence College	RI	60,760	VC
Regis Univ	CO	44,520	C
St. Louis Univ	MO	49,866	HC
San Diego State Univ	CA	21,896	C+
San Jose State Univ	CA	21,540	C
Seattle Univ	WA	50,811	VC+
Seton Hall Univ	NJ	55,514	C
Sewanee: The Univ of the South	TN	54,500	MC
Southern Oregon Univ	OR	19,117	C
Southwestern Univ	TX	50,720	VC
St. Ambrose Univ	IA	39,019	C
St. Bonaventure Univ	NY	44,237	C
SUNY / SUNY Potsdam	NY	20,404	C+
SUNY at Binghamton	NY	22,861	MC
Stetson Univ	FL	53,544	VC
Stony Brook Univ/The SUNY	NY	21,881	MC
Syracuse Univ	NY	60,239	VC
Texas Christian Univ	TX	54,670	HC
The Catholic Univ of America	DC	56,356	VC
The Univ of Tenn at Knoxville	TN	22,112	VC
The Univ of Utah	UT	17,924	VC
Transylvania Univ	KY	45,690	VC+
Trinity Univ	TX	52,314	HC+
Tufts Univ	MA		MC
Univ of Arizona	AZ	23,100	C
Univ of Calif at Irvine	CA	26,484	VC
Univ of Calif at Riverside	CA	29,227	C+
Univ of Calif San Diego	CA	30,150	MC
Univ of Central Okla	OK	13,486	C
Univ of Cincinnati	OH	21,964	VC
Univ of Colo Boulder	CO	24,285	VC+
Univ of Denver	CO	58,443	VC+
Univ of Evansville	IN	44,186	VC+
Univ of Georgia	GA	21,250	HC
Univ of Illinois at Chicago	IL	25,006	VC
Univ of Kansas	KS	20,135	C+
Univ of Louisville	KY	19,824	C
Univ of Maine	ME	20,792	C
Univ of Maryland/Baltimore County	MD	21,296	VC
Univ of Miami	FL	63,494	MC
Univ of Nebr - Lincoln	NE	18,589	VC
Univ of Nevada/Reno	NV	18,010	C
Univ of New Hampshire	NH	28,562	VC
Univ of New Mexico	NM	15,404	C
Univ of Notre Dame	IN	64,043	MC
Univ of Rhode Island	RI	24,906	C
Univ of Richmond	VA	60,880	MC
Univ of St. Francis	IN	37,400	C
Univ of San Diego	CA	58,442	VC+
Univ of Tulsa	OK	52,625	HC+
Univ of Wisc-Milwaukee	WI	21,496	C
Univ of Wisc-Superior	WI	14,446	C
Ursinus College	PA	61,690	VC
Vanderbilt Univ	TN	60,572	MC
Vassar College	NY	65,491	MC
Wake Forest Univ	NC	64,056	MC
Walsh Univ	OH	39,010	C
Webster Univ	MO	37,490	C
Wellesley College	MA	63,916	MC
Western Kentucky Univ	KY	16,850	C
Western Mich Univ	MI	21,054	C
Wheaton College	MA	61,512	VC
Whitman College	WA	59,772	MC
Wofford College	SC	49,885	VC
Wright State Univ	OH	16,983	C
Yale Univ	CT	64,650	MC
Youngstown State Univ	OH	17,307	C

ART HISTORY AND APPRECIATION

School	ST	$IS	SR
Adams State Univ	CO	17,703	LC
Adelphi Univ	NY	48,244	C
Agnes Scott College	GA	51,930	VC+
Albertus Magnus College	CT	43,258	LC
Albion College	MI	52,650	C
Alfred Univ	NY	42,296	C+
Allegheny College	PA	55,420	VC
American Univ	DC	59,379	HC+
Aquinas College - Mich	MI	38,876	HC
Arcadia Univ	PA	33,570	C+
Art Academy of Cincinnati	OH	36,252	SP
Augsburg College	MN	43,929	C
Augustana College	IL	49,658	VC
Baker Univ	KS	33,350	C+
Bard College	NY	64,024	HC
Bard College at Simon's Rock	MA	65,795	MC
Barnard College/Columbia Univ	NY	62,741	MC
Baylor Univ	TX	53,760	HC
Berry College	GA	45,286	C+
Birmingham-Southern College	AL	44,478	VC
Boston College	MA	65,737	MC
Boston Univ	MA	65,110	MC
Bridgewater State Univ	MA	21,810	C
Brigham Young Univ	UT	12,748	HC
Brown Univ	RI	64,566	MC
Bryn Mawr College	PA	59,890	MC
Bucknell Univ	PA	64,616	MC
Calif State Polytechnic Univ, Pomona	CA	21,541	C
Cal State, San Bernardino	CA	12,000	C
Cal State, Stanislaus	CA	16,212	C
Carleton College	MN	64,071	MC
Carlow Univ	PA	38,549	LC
Centre College	KY	49,250	HC
Chatham Univ	PA	46,517	C
CUNY/Brooklyn College	NY	5,884	C+
CUNY/York College	NY	6,747	LC
Clark Univ	MA	51,600	HC+
Clarke Univ	IA	38,940	C
Coe College	IA	51,570	VC
Colgate Univ	NY	65,030	MC
College of the Holy Cross	MA	62,165	MC
Colo College	CO	62,560	MC
Colo State Univ	CO	22,162	VC
Columbia Univ/ School of General Studies	NY	61,470	MC
Columbia Univ/City of New York	NY	62,958	MC
Columbus State Univ	GA	14,336	LC
Conn College	CT	65,000	MC
Cornell College	IA	48,800	VC
Dartmouth College	NH	66,174	MC
Denison Univ	OH	58,860	MC
DePauw Univ	IN	58,688	HC+
Dominican Univ of Calif	CA	57,050	C
Drake Univ	IA	45,056	HC
Drew Univ/College of Liberal Arts	NJ	61,048	VC
Drury Univ	MO	33,791	VC
Duke Univ	NC	64,188	
Duquesne Univ	PA	46,822	VC
East Carolina Univ	NC	16,937	C
Eastern Mich Univ	MI	19,761	C
Eastern Washington Univ	WA	25,572	LC
Edinboro Univ	PA	15,940	LC
Elizabethtown College	PA	54,050	C
Emory Univ	GA	60,786	MC
Ferris State Univ	MI	21,445	C
Florida International Univ	FL	19,854	C+
Florida State Univ	FL	16,771	HC
Framingham State Univ	MA	20,584	C
Franklin and Marshall College	PA	63,170	HC
George Mason Univ	VA	15,724	VC
George Washington Univ	DC	62,835	MC
Georgia State Univ	GA	24,332	VC
Gettysburg College	PA	63,000	HC
Grand Valley State Univ	MI	22,250	C+
Grinnell College	IA	60,738	MC
Hamilton College	NY	64,250	MC
Hampshire College	MA	63,824	MC
Hanover College	IN	46,364	C+
Hartwick College	NY	51,270	C
Harvard College/Harvard Univ	MA	60,659	MC
Haverford College	PA	66,490	MC
Hofstra Univ	NY	55,960	C+
Hollins Univ	VA	49,635	VC
Hope College	MI	39,940	VC
Howard Univ	DC	37,616	C+
Indiana State Univ	IN	23,223	LC
Ithaca College	NY	56,766	VC
Jacksonville Univ	FL	46,230	C
James Madison Univ	VA	19,084	VC
John Carroll Univ	OH	49,740	C+
Johns Hopkins Univ	MD	65,386	MC
Juniata College	PA	53,760	VC
Kalamazoo College	MI	53,931	HC+
Kansas City Art Inst	MO	44,308	C+
Kean Univ	NJ	24,650	C
Kent State Univ	OH	20,732	C
Knox College	IL	52,615	VC+
Lawrence Univ	WI	54,498	HC
Lehigh Univ	PA	61,010	MC
Lewis & Clark College	OR	58,434	HC+
Lindenwood Univ	MO	25,132	C
LIU Post	NY	49,682	C
Lourdes Univ	OH	29,520	NC
Lycoming College	PA	48,580	C
Malone Univ	OH	38,448	C
Manhattanville College	NY	51,440	C+
Mansfield Univ	PA	23,376	LC
Mars Hill Univ	NC	42,688	C
Mary Baldwin Univ	VA	39,865	C
Maryland Inst College of Art	MD	56,795	SP
Maryville College	TN	44,410	C
Mass College of Art and Design	MA	24,800	SP
McDaniel College	MD	51,380	VC
Messiah College	PA	43,100	C+
Miami Univ	OH	27,190	HC+
Mich State Univ	MI	23,898	VC+
Millsaps College	MS	50,080	C+
Monmouth Univ	NJ	46,234	C
Montclair State Univ	NJ	26,210	LC
Moravian College	PA	53,117	
Mount Holyoke College	MA	56,746	MC
New College of Florida	FL	15,848	MC
New England College	NH	50,364	C
New York Univ	NY	65,860	MC
Northern Illinois Univ	IL	20,176	C
Northwestern Univ	IL	66,344	MC
Notre Dame of Maryland Univ	MD	46,465	VC
Oakland Univ	MI	20,763	C
Oglethorpe Univ	GA	44,200	C+
Old Dominion Univ	VA	20,910	C
Pace Univ	NY	58,248	C
Pepperdine Univ	CA	74,460	HC+
Point Loma Nazarene Univ	CA	43,450	C
Pomona College	CA	64,957	MC
Portland State Univ	OR	19,443	C
Pratt Inst	NY	58,082	VC
Purdue Univ/West Lafayette	IN	20,032	MC
Randolph-Macon College	VA	49,910	C
Rhode Island College	RI	17,694	LC
Rice Univ	TX	57,668	MC
Ripon College	WI	46,911	C+
Roanoke College	VA	54,114	VC
Rockford Univ	IL	36,030	C
Roger Williams Univ	RI	46,296	C+
Rollins College	FL	58,670	HC
Roosevelt Univ	IL	40,651	VC
Rutgers Univ - Camden	NJ	26,146	C
Rutgers Univ - New Brunswick	NJ	26,632	HC
St. Peter's Univ	NJ	49,192	C
St. Vincent College	PA	44,626	C
Salem College	NC	37,694	HC
Salve Regina Univ	RI	51,470	C
San Francisco Art Inst	CA	58,505	SP
Sarah Lawrence College	NY	63,388	HC
Savannah College of Art and Design	GA	49,595	C
School of the Art Inst of Chicago	IL	56,230	SP
Scripps College	CA	66,664	MC
Seton Hill Univ	PA	46,972	C
Siena Heights Univ	MI	32,040	C
Skidmore College	NY	64,214	HC
Smith College	MA	63,914	MC
Southern Conn State Univ	CT	21,924	LC
Southern Illinois Univ Edwardsville	IL	22,643	C
Southern Methodist Univ	TX	66,483	MC
St. Lawrence Univ	NY	64,390	VC
St. Mary's College of Maryland	MD	26,634	VC
St. Olaf College	MN	54,260	HC+
Stanford Univ	CA	60,409	MC
SUNY / Buffalo State College	NY	20,842	C
SUNY / Univ at Buffalo	NY	23,122	C+
SUNY at Geneseo	NY	20,440	VC+
SUNY at New Paltz	NY	19,200	C
SUNY at Purchase	NY	17,900	C
SUNY SUNY Albany	NY	22,165	C
Stephen F. Austin State Univ	TX	18,406	LC
Stonehill College	MA	55,030	C+
Suffolk Univ	MA	50,308	C
Susquehanna Univ	PA	55,340	VC
Swarthmore College	PA	63,550	MC
Syracuse Univ	NY	60,239	VC
Temple Univ	PA	24,392	VC
Texas State Univ	TX	19,350	C
The Catholic Univ of America	DC	56,356	VC
The College of New Jersey	NJ	31,909	HC
The College of New Rochelle	NY	46,300	VC
Trinity College	CT	63,920	HC+
Troy Univ	AL	16,171	C
Truman State Univ	MO	16,014	HC
Tulane Univ	LA	63,396	HC+
Univ of Alabama	AL	24,320	C+
Univ of Arkansas at Little Rock	AR	18,211	C
Univ of Calif at Berkeley	CA	28,853	MC
Univ of Calif at Davis	CA	28,468	HC
Univ of Calif at Los Angeles	CA	30,162	MC
Univ of Calif at Riverside	CA	29,227	C+
Univ of Calif at Santa Barbara	CA	29,091	HC
Univ of Calif San Diego	CA	30,150	MC
Univ of Calif, Santa Cruz	CA	28,731	C+
Univ of Chicago	IL	67,584	MC
Univ of Conn	CT	25,538	HC
Univ of Dallas	TX	45,500	VC+
Univ of Dayton	OH	53,620	C
Univ of Delaware	DE	24,976	VC+
Univ of Denver	CO	58,443	VC+
Univ of Florida	FL	16,291	HC+
Univ of Hartford	CT	49,776	C
Univ of Illinois at Chicago	IL	25,006	VC
Univ of Illinois at Urbana-Champaign	IL	27,006	HC
Univ of Iowa	IA	18,683	VC+
Univ of Kentucky	KY	33,306	C
Univ of La Verne	CA	55,600	C
Univ of Louisville	KY	19,824	C
Univ of Mary Washington	VA	24,764	VC
Univ of Maryland/Baltimore County	MD	21,296	VC
Univ of Maryland/College Park	MD	21,938	HC
Univ of Mass Amherst	MA	26,199	VC+
Univ of Mass Dartmouth	MA	25,658	C
Univ of Memphis	TN	18,278	C
Univ of Mich/Ann Arbor	MI	24,410	MC
Univ of Mich/Dearborn	MI	11,757	VC
Univ of Minn/Duluth	MN	20,292	C+
Univ of Minn/Morris	MN	20,760	VC
Univ of Minn/Twin Cities	MN	23,519	HC+
Univ of Miss	MS	17,746	C+
Univ of Missouri/Columbia	MO	18,201	MC
Univ of Missouri-Kansas City	MO	19,563	VC
Univ of Missouri-St. Louis	MO		C
Univ of Nebr - Lincoln	NE	18,589	VC
Univ of Nebr - Omaha	NE	16,120	C
Univ of Nevada, Las Vegas	NV	17,553	C
Univ of New Orleans	LA	12,840	C
Univ of N Car at Chapel Hill	NC	20,052	HC+
Univ of N Car at Charlotte	NC	15,547	C
Univ of N Car at Wilmington	NC	14,590	VC
Univ of North Texas	TX	19,198	C
Univ of Okla	OK	18,911	VC
Univ of Oregon	OR	22,972	C
Univ of Pennsylvania	PA	63,526	MC
Univ of Rochester	NY	65,032	MC
Univ of St. Joseph	CT	49,550	C
Univ of San Francisco	CA	58,484	VC
Univ of S Car at Columbia	SC	19,725	VC+
Univ of Southern Calif	CA	66,631	C
Univ of Texas at Arlington	TX	18,026	LC
Univ of Texas at Austin	TX	26,102	HC
Univ of Texas at San Antonio	TX	20,157	C
Univ of Toledo	OH	19,336	NC
Univ of Vermont	VT	28,878	HC
Univ of Washington	WA	23,149	VC
Univ of Wisc-Madison	WI	20,934	MC
Univ of Wisc-Milwaukee	WI	21,496	C
Univ of Wisc-Whitewater	WI	13,976	C
Villanova Univ	PA	62,523	MC
Virginia Commonwealth Univ	VA	23,049	C
Washburn Univ	KS	15,827	C
Washington and Lee Univ	VA	59,647	MC
Washington Univ in St. Louis	MO	65,366	VC
Wayne State Univ	MI	22,016	C
Webster Univ	MO	37,490	C
Wellesley College	MA	63,916	MC
Wesleyan College	GA	29,694	C+
Wesleyan Univ	CT	65,516	MC
Wichita State Univ	KS	21,643	C
Willamette Univ	OR	61,817	VC+
William Paterson Univ of New Jersey	NJ	23,133	C
Williams College	MA	63,290	MC
Winthrop Univ	SC	23,082	C
Wright State Univ	OH	16,983	C
Youngstown State Univ	OH	17,307	C

ART THERAPY

School	ST	$IS	SR
Albertus Magnus College	CT	43,258	LC
Alverno College	WI	33,294	LC
Andrews Univ	MI	28,030	C+
Anna Maria College	MA	48,186	C
Arcadia Univ	PA	33,570	C+
Bethany College	KS	46,100	NC
Buena Vista Univ	IA	41,514	C
Capital Univ	OH	42,982	C
Carlow Univ	PA	38,549	LC
Converse College	SC	26,495	C
DePaul Univ	IL	47,623	VC
Edgewood College	WI	35,950	C
Emmanuel College	MA	52,110	C+
Endicott College	MA	44,604	VC+
Lipscomb Univ	TN	41,296	VC
LIU Post	NY	49,682	C
Marygrove College	MI	28,926	NC
Marywood Univ	PA	46,900	C
Mercyhurst Univ	PA	47,420	C
Millikin Univ	IL	42,158	C
Mount Mary Univ	WI	34,650	LC
Naropa Univ	CO	42,826	NC
New York Univ	NY	65,860	MC
Prescott College	AZ	33,284	C
Russell Sage College	NY	39,370	C
Seton Hill Univ	PA	46,972	C
Springfield College	MA	45,995	C
The College of New Rochelle	NY	46,300	VC
Univ of Central Okla	OK	13,486	C
Univ of Indianapolis	IN	36,480	C
Univ of Montana-Western	MT	11,220	LC
Univ of St. Francis	IN	37,400	C
Univ of Wisc-Superior	WI	14,446	C

ART/ART STUDIES

School	ST	$IS	SR
Amherst College	MA		HC+
Belmont Univ	TN	40,970	VC

ST = STATE $IS = IN-STATE COSTS SR = SELECTOR RATING

School	ST	$IS	SR
Black Hills State Univ	SD	15,899	C
Calvin College	MI	41,570	VC+
Colgate Univ	NY	65,030	MC
Gallaudet Univ	DC	29,118	LC
Georgian Court Univ	NJ	42,426	LC
John Brown Univ	AR	33,132	VC
Lewis Univ	IL	40,370	C
Ohio Wesleyan Univ	OH	49,460	VC
Pennsylvania State Univ - Univ Park	PA	29,760	HC
St. Joseph's Univ	PA	57,544	VC+
Siena College	NY	48,916	C+
Syracuse Univ	NY	60,239	VC
Univ of Denver	CO	58,443	VC+
Univ of Hawaii at Hilo	HI	18,038	C
Univ of Illinois at Chicago	IL	25,006	VC
Univ of Maryland/Baltimore County	MD	21,296	VC
Wellesley College	MA	63,916	MC

ART/VISUAL CULTURE

School	ST	$IS	SR
Appalachian State Univ	NC	14,416	VC
Bates College	ME	64,500	MC
Bryant Univ	RI	55,646	VC
Calvin College	MI	41,570	VC+
Missouri Southern State Univ	MO	12,499	C
Oberlin College	OH	66,012	MC
Ringling College of Art and Design	FL	57,430	SP
Univ of Arizona	AZ	23,100	C
Univ of Maryland/Baltimore County	MD	21,296	VC

ARTS ADMINISTRATION/ MANAGEMENT

School	ST	$IS	SR
Adrian College	MI	42,400	C
Appalachian State Univ	NC	14,416	VC
Aquinas College - Mich	MI	38,876	HC
Baldwin Wallace Univ	OH	41,106	C
Belhaven Univ	MS	31,016	C
Bellarmine Univ	KY	51,220	C
Benedictine Univ	IL	38,300	C
Bennett College	NC	27,302	NC
Bethany College	KS	46,100	NC
Brenau Univ - Women's College	GA	37,876	LC
Buena Vista Univ	IA	41,514	C
Butler Univ	IN	51,352	VC
Chatham Univ	PA	46,517	C
College of Charleston	SC	22,699	C
Columbia College Chicago	IL	43,168	C
Concordia College - New York	NY	39,035	LC
Culver-Stockton College	MO	33,525	C
Daemen College	NY	38,045	C
Drury Univ	MO	33,791	VC
Eastern Mich Univ	MI	19,761	C
Elmhurst College	IL	45,428	C
Elon Univ	NC	44,599	VC+
Franklin Pierce Univ	NH	46,750	C
Indiana Univ Bloomington	IN	20,429	VC
King Univ	TN	34,660	C
LIU Post	NY	49,682	C
Mary Baldwin Univ	VA	39,865	C
Marywood Univ	PA	46,900	C
Mass College of Liberal Arts	MA	20,128	C
Messiah College	PA	43,100	C+
New York Univ	NY	65,860	MC
Nichols College	MA	46,800	LC
Nova Southeastern Univ	FL	38,534	C+
Piedmont College	GA	32,512	C
Point Park Univ	PA	41,270	C
Prescott College	AZ	33,284	C
Randolph-Macon College	VA	49,910	C
Ringling College of Art and Design	FL	57,430	SP
St. Vincent College	PA	44,626	C
Salem College	NC	37,694	HC
Seton Hill Univ	PA	46,972	C
Simmons College	MA	53,090	VC
Spring Hill College	AL	48,488	C
SUNY / SUNY Fredonia	NY	20,818	C
Tiffin Univ	OH	31,380	C
Univ of Findlay	OH	60,139	C
Univ of Kentucky	KY	33,306	C
Univ of Maryland/Baltimore County	MD	21,296	VC
Univ of Montana-Western	MT	11,220	LC
Univ of North Georgia	GA	17,316	C
Univ of San Francisco	CA	58,484	VC
Univ of Tulsa	OK	52,625	HC+
Univ of Wisc-Green Bay	WI	15,064	C
Univ of Wisc-Stevens Point	WI	14,043	C
Upper Iowa Univ	IA	34,990	NC
Viterbo Univ	WI	34,660	C
Wagner College	NY	55,480	C+
Wartburg College	IA	47,840	C
Waynesburg Univ	PA	32,290	C
Westminster College	UT	41,078	C+
Wright State Univ	OH	16,983	C

ARTS/SCIENCES PLANNED PROGRAM

School	ST	$IS	SR
Sinte Gleska Univ	SD	13,154	NC
Syracuse Univ	NY	60,239	VC
Texas Tech Univ	TX	18,736	C+
Univ of Okla	OK	18,911	VC

ASIAN STUDIES

School	ST	$IS	SR
Amherst College	MA		HC+
Arizona State Univ at the Tempe Campus	AZ	21,756	VC
Bates College	ME	64,500	MC
Boston Univ	MA	65,110	MC
Bowdoin College	ME	63,500	MC
Cal State, Chico	CA	21,440	C
Calvin College	MI	41,570	VC+
Case Western Reserve Univ	OH	60,304	MC
Colgate Univ	NY	65,030	MC
Cornell Univ	NY	64,853	MC
Elon Univ	NC	44,599	VC+
Indiana Univ Bloomington	IN	20,429	VC
Indiana Univ of Pennsylvania	PA	23,614	LC
Kenyon College	OH	63,330	MC
Loyola Marymount Univ	CA	58,038	HC
McDaniel College	MD	51,380	VC
Nazareth College	NY	45,574	C
New York Univ	NY	65,860	MC
Occidental College	CA	65,530	MC
Pace Univ	NY	58,248	C
Pennsylvania State Univ - Univ Park	PA	29,760	HC
St. Joseph's Univ	PA	57,544	VC+
Seattle Univ	WA	50,811	VC+
Univ of Arkansas at Fayetteville	AR	19,152	C+
Univ of Colo Boulder	CO	24,285	VC+
Univ of Georgia	GA	21,250	HC
Univ of Louisville	KY	19,824	C
Univ of Mass Boston	MA	13,435	C
Univ of Minn/Twin Cities	MN	23,519	HC+
Univ of San Francisco	CA	58,484	MC
Vanderbilt Univ	TN	60,572	MC
Washington State Univ	WA	22,495	C
Western Kentucky Univ	KY	16,850	C
Wheaton College	MA	61,512	VC

ASIAN/AMERICAN STUDIES

School	ST	$IS	SR
Arizona State Univ at the Tempe Campus	AZ	21,756	VC
Brigham Young Univ	UT	12,748	HC
Brown Univ	RI	64,566	MC
Cal State, Fullerton	CA	21,902	C
Cal State, Northridge	CA	16,859	LC
Columbia Univ/City of New York	NY	62,958	MC
Emory Univ	GA	60,786	MC
Indiana Univ Bloomington	IN	20,429	VC
New York Univ	NY	65,860	MC
Ohio Univ	OH	22,924	C
Pitzer College	CA	66,192	MC
Pomona College	CA	64,957	MC
Purdue Univ/West Lafayette	IN	20,032	MC
San Francisco State Univ	CA	18,514	LC
Scripps College	CA	66,664	MC
St. Olaf College	MN	54,260	HC+
Stanford Univ	CA	60,409	MC
SUNY at Binghamton	NY	22,861	MC
Stony Brook Univ/The SUNY	NY	21,881	MC
Univ of Calif at Berkeley	CA	28,853	MC
Univ of Calif at Irvine	CA	26,484	VC
Univ of Calif at Los Angeles	CA	30,162	MC
Univ of Calif at Riverside	CA	29,227	C+
Univ of Calif at Santa Barbara	CA	29,091	HC
Univ of Denver	CO	58,443	VC+
Univ of Northern Colo	CO	20,851	C
Univ of Southern Calif	CA	66,631	C
Univ of Washington	WA	23,149	VC
Univ of Wisc-Milwaukee	WI	21,496	C
Wellesley College	MA	63,916	MC

ASIAN/ORIENTAL STUDIES

School	ST	$IS	SR
Augustana College	IL	49,658	VC
Bard College	NY	64,024	HC
Bard College at Simon's Rock	MA	65,795	MC
Baylor Univ	TX	53,760	HC
Belmont Univ	TN	40,970	VC
Berea College	KY	7,042	C
Birmingham-Southern College	AL	44,478	VC
Bowling Green State Univ	OH	19,747	C
Brigham Young Univ	UT	12,748	HC
Cal State, Long Beach	CA	18,850	C
Calvin College	MI	41,570	VC+
Carleton College	MN	64,071	MC
Central Washington Univ	WA	16,803	C
CUNY/City College	NY	20,319	VC
Claremont McKenna College	CA	67,185	MC
Clark Univ	MA	51,600	HC+
Coe College	IA	51,570	VC
College of St. Benedict	MN	52,806	C
College of the Holy Cross	MA	62,165	MC
Colo College	CO	62,560	MC
Dartmouth College	NH	66,174	MC
Duke Univ	NC	64,188	
Eastern Mich Univ	MI	19,761	C
Emory Univ	GA	60,786	MC
Florida International Univ	FL	19,854	C+
Florida State Univ	FL	16,771	HC
Furman Univ	SC	58,092	VC+
Hamilton College	NY	64,250	MC
Hampshire College	MA	63,824	MC
Harvard College/Harvard Univ	MA	60,659	MC
John Carroll Univ	OH	49,740	C+
Kean Univ	NJ	24,650	C
Knox College	IL	52,615	VC+
Lafayette College	PA	63,355	MC
Lake Forest College	IL	50,652	VC
Lehigh Univ	PA	61,010	MC
Macalester College	MN	61,905	MC
Manhattanville College	NY	51,440	C+
Marietta College	OH	46,190	C
Mary Baldwin Univ	VA	39,865	C
Mount Holyoke College	MA	56,746	MC
New York Univ	NY	65,860	MC
Northeastern Univ	MA	62,703	MC
Old Dominion Univ	VA	20,910	C
Pitzer College	CA	66,192	MC
Pomona College	CA	64,957	MC
Purdue Univ/West Lafayette	IN	20,032	MC
Randolph-Macon College	VA	49,910	C
Rice Univ	TX	57,668	MC
Rollins College	FL	58,670	HC
Rutgers Univ - New Brunswick	NJ	26,632	HC
St. John's Univ	MN	51,624	C
San Diego State Univ	CA	21,896	C+
Sarah Lawrence College	NY	63,388	HC
Scripps College	CA	66,664	MC
Seton Hall Univ	NJ	55,514	C
Sewanee: The Univ of the South	TN	54,500	MC
Skidmore College	NY	64,214	HC
St. John's Univ	NY	55,850	C
St. Lawrence Univ	NY	64,390	VC
St. Mary's College of Maryland	MD	26,634	VC
SUNY / Univ at Buffalo	NY	23,122	C+
SUNY at New Paltz	NY	19,200	C
SUNY SUNY Albany	NY	22,165	C
Swarthmore College	PA	63,550	MC
Temple Univ	PA	24,392	VC
Texas State Univ	TX	19,350	C
The Univ of Utah	UT	17,924	VC
Tufts Univ	MA		MC
Tulane Univ	LA	63,396	HC+
Union College	NY	64,320	MC
Univ of Calif at Berkeley	CA	28,853	MC
Univ of Calif at Los Angeles	CA	30,162	MC
Univ of Calif at Riverside	CA	29,227	C+
Univ of Calif at Santa Barbara	CA	29,091	HC
Univ of Cincinnati	OH	21,964	VC
Univ of Florida	FL	16,291	HC+
Univ of Hawaii at Manoa	HI	23,221	C
Univ of Iowa	IA	18,683	VC+
Univ of Maryland/Univ College	MD	25,966	LC
Univ of Mich/Ann Arbor	MI	24,410	MC
Univ of New Mexico	NM	15,404	C
Univ of N Car at Chapel Hill	NC	20,052	HC+
Univ of Oregon	OR	22,972	C
Univ of Pennsylvania	PA	63,526	MC
Univ of Puget Sound	WA	56,456	VC+
Univ of Redlands	CA	60,200	VC
Univ of Texas at Austin	TX	26,102	HC
Univ of Vermont	VT	28,878	HC
Univ of Washington	WA	23,149	VC
Univ of Wisc-Madison	WI	20,934	MC
Vassar College	NY	65,491	MC
Washington Univ in St. Louis	MO	65,366	VC
Wayne State Univ	MI	22,016	C
Wellesley College	MA	63,916	MC
Whitman College	WA	59,772	MC
Willamette Univ	OR	61,817	VC+
Williams College	MA	63,290	MC

ASTRONOMY

School	ST	$IS	SR
Amherst College	MA		HC+
Ball State Univ	IN	19,590	C
Barnard College/Columbia Univ	NY	62,741	MC
Benedictine College	KS	36,200	VC
Bennington College	VT	63,960	MC
Boston Univ	MA	65,110	MC
Brigham Young Univ	UT	12,748	HC
Brown Univ	RI	64,566	MC
Bryn Mawr College	PA	59,890	MC
Case Western Reserve Univ	OH	60,304	MC
Colgate Univ	NY	65,030	MC
College of Charleston	SC	22,699	C
Columbia Univ/ School of General Studies	NY	61,470	MC
Columbia Univ/City of New York	NY	62,958	MC
Cornell Univ	NY	64,853	MC
Dartmouth College	NH	66,174	MC
Eastern Mich Univ	MI	19,761	C
Embry-Riddle Aeronautical Univ - Prescott Campus	AZ	44,054	VC
Florida Inst of Technology	FL	53,306	VC
Franklin and Marshall College	PA	63,170	HC
George Mason Univ	VA	15,724	VC
Harvard College/Harvard Univ	MA	60,659	MC
Haverford College	PA	66,490	MC
Indiana Univ Bloomington	IN	20,429	VC
Lehigh Univ	PA	61,010	MC
Lycoming College	PA	48,580	C
Montclair State Univ	NJ	26,210	LC
Mount Holyoke College	MA	56,746	MC
New Mexico State Univ	NM	14,050	C
Northern Arizona Univ	AZ	20,246	VC
Northwestern Univ	IL	66,344	MC
Oberlin College	OH	66,012	MC
Ohio State Univ at Columbus	OH	21,703	HC+
Pennsylvania State Univ - Univ Park	PA	29,760	HC
San Diego State Univ	CA	21,896	C+
San Francisco State Univ	CA	18,514	LC
Smith College	MA	63,914	MC
Stony Brook Univ/The SUNY	NY	21,881	MC
Swarthmore College	PA	63,550	MC
Union College	NY	64,320	MC
Univ of Arizona	AZ	23,100	C
Univ of Colo Boulder	CO	24,285	VC+
Univ of Delaware	DE	24,976	VC+
Univ of Florida	FL	16,291	HC+
Univ of Hawaii at Hilo	HI	18,038	C
Univ of Illinois at Urbana-Champaign	IL	27,006	HC
Univ of Iowa	IA	18,683	VC+
Univ of Kansas	KS	20,135	C+
Univ of Maryland/College Park	MD	21,938	HC
Univ of Mass Amherst	MA	26,199	VC+
Univ of Mich/Ann Arbor	MI	24,410	MC
Univ of Mount Union	OH	38,970	C
Univ of Nebr - Lincoln	NE	18,589	VC
Univ of Okla	OK	18,911	VC
Univ of Pittsburgh	PA	29,568	HC+
Univ of Rochester	NY	65,032	MC
Univ of Southern Calif	CA	66,631	C
Univ of Texas at Austin	TX	26,102	HC
Univ of Virginia	VA	25,891	MC
Univ of Washington	WA	23,149	VC
Univ of Wisc-Madison	WI	20,934	MC
Valparaiso Univ	IN	48,370	C+
Vassar College	NY	65,491	MC
Villanova Univ	PA	62,523	MC
Wayne State Univ	MI	22,016	C
Wellesley College	MA	63,916	MC
Wesleyan Univ	CT	65,516	MC
Western Kentucky Univ	KY	16,850	C
Wheaton College	MA	61,512	VC
Whitman College	WA	59,772	MC
Williams College	MA	63,290	MC
Wilmington College	OH	34,600	C
Yale Univ	CT	64,650	MC

ASTRONOMY AND PHYSICS

School	ST	$IS	SR
Albion College	MI	52,650	C
Boston Univ	MA	65,110	MC
Brown Univ	RI	64,566	MC
Dartmouth College	NH	66,174	MC
Embry-Riddle Aeronautical Univ - Daytona Beach	FL	44,712	VC
Oberlin College	OH	66,012	MC
Texas Christian Univ	TX	54,670	HC
Univ of Georgia	GA	21,250	HC
Univ of Mass Dartmouth	MA	25,658	C
Univ of Wyoming	WY	15,375	C+
Western Kentucky Univ	KY	16,850	C
Wheaton College	MA	61,512	VC
Youngstown State Univ	OH	17,307	C

ASTROPHYSICS

School	ST	$IS	SR
Agnes Scott College	GA	51,930	VC+
Boston Univ	MA	65,110	MC
Brown Univ	RI	64,566	MC
Calif Inst of Technology	CA	58,761	MC
Cal State, Northridge	CA	16,859	LC
Colgate Univ	NY	65,030	MC
College of Charleston	SC	22,699	C
Columbia Univ/City of New York	NY	62,958	MC
Dartmouth College	NH	66,174	MC
Florida Inst of Technology	FL	53,306	VC
Franklin and Marshall College	PA	63,170	HC
Haverford College	PA	66,490	MC
Indiana Univ Bloomington	IN	20,429	VC
Lehigh Univ	PA	61,010	MC
Lycoming College	PA	48,580	C
Mich State Univ	MI	23,898	VC+
Ohio State Univ at Columbus	OH	21,703	HC+
Ohio Univ	OH	22,924	C
Princeton Univ	NJ	57,610	MC
Rutgers Univ - New Brunswick	NJ	26,632	HC
San Francisco State Univ	CA	18,514	LC
Swarthmore College	PA	63,550	MC
Tufts Univ	MA		MC
Univ of Calif at Berkeley	CA	28,853	MC
Univ of Calif at Los Angeles	CA	30,162	MC
Univ of Cincinnati	OH	21,964	VC
Univ of Mich/Ann Arbor	MI	24,410	MC
Univ of Minn/Twin Cities	MN	23,519	HC+
Univ of New Mexico	NM	15,404	C
Univ of Okla	OK	18,911	VC
Villanova Univ	PA	62,523	MC
Wellesley College	MA	63,916	MC

School	ST	$IS	SR
Whitman College	WA	59,772	MC
Williams College	MA	63,290	MC

ATHLETIC TRAINING

School	ST	$IS	SR
Adams State Univ	CO	17,703	LC
Albion College	MI	52,650	C
Alderson Broaddus Univ	WV	26,149	C
Alfred Univ	NY	42,296	C+
Alma College	MI	47,548	C
Alvernia Univ	PA	43,900	C
Angelo State Univ	TX	15,263	NC
Appalachian State Univ	NC	14,416	VC
Aquinas College - Mich	MI	38,876	HC
Arkansas State Univ	AR	16,190	C
Ashland Univ	OH	21,440	C
Augustana Univ	SD	38,424	VC
Aurora Univ	IL	33,970	C
Averett Univ	VA	40,970	LC
Azusa Pacific Univ	CA	43,972	C
Baldwin Wallace Univ	OH	41,106	C
Barton College	NC	38,686	LC
Baylor Univ	TX	53,760	HC
Belhaven Univ	MS	31,016	C
Benedictine College	KS	36,200	VC
Bethany College	KS	46,100	NC
Bethel College	KS	35,370	C
Bethel Univ	MN	45,270	VC
Boston Univ	MA	65,110	MC
Bowling Green State Univ	OH	19,747	C
Bridgewater College	VA	44,510	C
Bridgewater State Univ	MA	21,810	C
Buena Vista Univ	IA	41,514	C
Cal State, Fullerton	CA	21,902	C
Calif Univ of Pennsylvania	PA	14,217	LC
Canisius College	NY	47,537	C
Capital Univ	OH	42,982	C
Carroll Univ	WI	38,100	C+
Castleton Univ	VT	20,186	C
Catawba College	NC	39,820	C
Cedarville Univ	OH	34,990	VC
Central College	IA	44,592	C
Central Conn State Univ	CT	21,203	C
Central Methodist Univ	MO	36,830	VC
Central Mich Univ	MI	20,330	C
Chapman Univ	CA	63,078	VC+
Clarion Univ of Pennsylvania	PA	21,608	LC
Clarke Univ	IA	38,940	C
Coe College	IA	51,570	VC
Colby-Sawyer College	NH	50,790	C
College of Charleston	SC	22,699	C
Colo Mesa Univ	CO	18,955	LC
Concordia Univ Wisc	WI	35,910	C
Culver-Stockton College	MO	33,525	C
Dakota Wesleyan Univ	SD	32,850	C
Defiance College	OH	41,630	C
Dominican College	NY	31,270	LC
Dordt College	IA	37,860	C+
Duquesne Univ	PA	46,822	VC
East Carolina Univ	NC	16,937	C
East Central Univ	OK	13,056	C
East Stroudsburg Univ	PA	18,334	C
East Texas Baptist Univ	TX	33,134	C
Eastern Illinois Univ	IL	21,126	C
Eastern Mich Univ	MI	19,761	C
Eastern Nazarene College	MA	39,955	C
Eastern Univ	PA	39,540	C
Emporia State Univ	KS	14,570	C
Endicott College	MA	44,604	VC+
Erskine College	SC	45,460	C
Eureka College	IL	30,220	C
Florida Gulf Coast Univ	FL	9,682	C
Florida State Univ	FL	16,771	HC
Fort Lewis College	CO	18,980	C
Franklin College	IN	39,380	C
Gardner-Webb Univ	NC	39,200	C+
George Fox Univ	OR	42,938	C
George Mason Univ	VA	15,724	VC
Georgetown College	KY	41,440	C
Georgia College & State Univ	GA	21,148	C+
Georgia Southern Univ	GA	16,596	C
Graceland Univ	IA	35,290	C
Grand Canyon Univ	AZ	16,950	VC
Grand Valley State Univ	MI	22,250	C+
Greensboro College	NC	42,400	LC
Hamline Univ	MN	45,678	VC
Harding Univ	AR	25,421	C
Hardin-Simmons Univ	TX	33,966	C
Heidelberg Univ	OH	39,200	C
Hofstra Univ	NY	55,960	C+
Hope College	MI	39,940	VC
Howard Payne Univ	TX	34,320	C
Indiana Univ Bloomington	IN	20,429	VC
Indiana Univ of Pennsylvania	PA	23,614	LC
Indiana Wesleyan Univ	IN	33,674	C
Ithaca College	NY	56,766	VC
James Madison Univ	VA	19,084	VC
Johnson State College	VT	20,752	C
Kansas State Univ	KS	17,780	VC
Kean Univ	NJ	24,650	C
Keene State College	NH	24,003	LC
Kent State Univ	OH	20,732	C
King Univ	TN	34,660	C
Lasell College	MA	47,500	C
Lee Univ	TN	22,045	C
Lees-McRae College	NC	33,944	C
Lenoir-Rhyne Univ	NC	43,200	C
Lewis Univ	IL	40,370	C
Liberty Univ	VA	19,101	C
Limestone College	SC	32,100	C
Lincoln Memorial Univ	TN	28,070	C
Lindenwood Univ	MO	25,132	C
Linfield College	OR	52,010	C
LIU Brooklyn	NY	49,682	C
Longwood Univ	VA	22,184	C
Loras College	IA	39,222	C
Louisiana College	LA	21,886	C
Louisiana State Univ and A&M College	LA	18,677	VC
Lubbock Christian Univ	TX	28,426	C
Luther College	IA	48,540	C+
Lynchburg College	VA	46,740	C
Marietta College	OH	46,190	C
Marist College	NY	49,860	VC
Marquette Univ	WI	48,390	VC+
Mars Hill Univ	NC	42,688	C
Marshall Univ	WV	17,242	C
Marywood Univ	PA	46,900	C
Mass College of Liberal Arts	MA	20,128	C
McKendree Univ	IL	37,940	C+
McMurry Univ	TX	34,259	LC
McNeese State Univ	LA	7,838	C
Mercyhurst Univ	PA	47,420	C
Messiah College	PA	43,100	C+
Methodist Univ	NC	43,600	C
Miami Univ	OH	27,190	HC+
MidAmerica Nazarene Univ	KS	35,550	C
Middle Tenn State Univ	TN	8,650	C
Millersville Univ of Pennsylvania	PA	23,782	C
Millikin Univ	IL	42,158	C
Minn State Univ, Moorhead	MN	15,941	C
Missouri State Univ	MO	15,190	C+
Montana State Univ-Billings	MT	22,960	C
Montclair State Univ	NJ	26,210	LC
Mount Marty College	SD	32,972	C
Mount St. Joseph Univ	OH	33,880	C
Murray State Univ	KY	16,998	C
Nebr Wesleyan Univ	NE	38,140	C+
Neumann Univ	PA	40,678	LC
New Mexico State Univ	NM	14,050	C
North Central College	IL	48,712	VC
N Dak State Univ	ND	16,245	C
North Park Univ	IL	35,860	C
Northern Kentucky Univ	KY	16,486	C
Northwestern College of Iowa	IA	38,400	C+
Nova Southeastern Univ	FL	38,534	C+
Ohio Northern Univ	OH	44,050	VC
Ohio State Univ at Columbus	OH	21,703	HC+
Ohio Univ	OH	22,924	C
Okla State Univ	OK	17,180	VC
Olivet College	MI	36,110	LC
Olivet Nazarene Univ	IL	41,840	C
Otterbein Univ	OH	41,630	C
Palm Beach Atlantic Univ	FL	39,720	C
Park Univ	MO	20,329	C
Pennsylvania State Univ - Univ Park	PA	29,760	HC
Piedmont College	GA	32,512	C
Plymouth State Univ	NH	23,180	LC
Point Loma Nazarene Univ	CA	43,450	C
Purdue Univ/West Lafayette	IN	20,032	MC
Quinnipiac Univ	CT	59,110	C
Radford Univ	VA	19,027	LC
Roanoke College	VA	54,114	VC
Rowan Univ	NJ	24,491	VC+
Sacred Heart Univ	CT	52,750	C
Saginaw Valley State Univ	MI	18,530	C
Salem International Univ	WV	21,090	LC
Salisbury Univ	MD	20,714	VC
Samford Univ	AL	39,232	VC
San Diego State Univ	CA	21,896	C+
Shaw Univ	NC	24,638	C
Simpson College	IA	43,839	VC
S Dak State Univ	SD	15,634	C
Southeast Missouri State Univ	MO	15,498	C
Southeastern Louisiana Univ	LA	16,237	C
Southern Nazarene Univ	OK	32,798	NC
Southwest Baptist Univ	MO	29,900	LC
Southwestern College	KS	31,531	C
St. Edward's Univ	TX	53,100	VC
SUNY / SUNY Cortland	NY	20,706	VC
Sterling College	KS	32,830	C
Stony Brook Univ/The SUNY	NY	21,881	MC
Tabor College	KS	35,870	C
Temple Univ	PA	24,392	VC
Texas Christian Univ	TX	54,670	HC
Texas Lutheran Univ	TX	38,620	C
Texas State Univ	TX	19,350	C
Texas Wesleyan Univ	TX	35,134	C
The College at Brockport - SUNY	NY	20,346	C
The Univ of Akron	OH	21,477	C
The Univ of Utah	UT	17,924	VC
Towson Univ	MD	17,408	VC
Trinity International Univ	IL	31,070	VC
Troy Univ	AL	16,171	C
Truman State Univ	MO	16,014	HC
Tusculum College	TN	31,625	C
Union College	KY	32,310	C
Univ of Alabama	AL	24,320	C+
Univ of Central Arkansas	AR	14,472	VC
Univ of Central Florida	FL	15,922	VC
Univ of Central Okla	OK	13,486	C
Univ of Charleston	WV	35,000	C
Univ of Cincinnati	OH	21,964	VC
Univ of Conn	CT	25,538	HC
Univ of Delaware	DE	24,976	VC+
Univ of Evansville	IN	44,186	VC+
Univ of Georgia	GA	21,250	HC
Univ of Illinois at Urbana-Champaign	IL	27,006	HC
Univ of Indianapolis	IN	36,480	C
Univ of Iowa	IA	18,683	VC+
Univ of Kansas	KS	20,135	C+
Univ of La Verne	CA	55,600	C
Univ of Maine	ME	20,792	C
Univ of Maine at Presque Isle	ME	14,870	C
Univ of Mary	ND	23,180	C
Univ of Miami	FL	63,494	MC
Univ of Mich/Ann Arbor	MI	24,410	MC
Univ of Minn/Duluth	MN	20,292	C+
Univ of Mobile	AL	28,935	C
Univ of Montana	MT	14,105	C
Univ of Montana-Western	MT	11,220	LC
Univ of Mount Union	OH	38,970	C
Univ of Nebr - Lincoln	NE	18,589	VC
Univ of New England	ME	48,880	C
Univ of New Hampshire	NH	28,562	VC
Univ of New Mexico	NM	15,404	C
Univ of N Car at Charlotte	NC	15,547	C
Univ of N Car at Pembroke	NC	14,388	LC
Univ of N Car at Wilmington	NC	14,590	VC
Univ of N Dak	ND	15,373	C
Univ of North Florida	FL	15,996	VC
Univ of Northern Colo	CO	20,851	C
Univ of Pittsburgh	PA	29,568	HC+
Univ of Pittsburgh at Bradford	PA	22,402	C
Univ of Tampa	FL	36,944	C
Univ of the Incarnate Word	TX	39,162	LC
Univ of Tulsa	OK	52,625	HC+
Univ of Vermont	VT	28,878	HC
Univ of West Alabama	AL	15,516	NC
Univ of Wisc-Eau Claire	WI	15,797	VC
Univ of Wisc-La Crosse	WI	15,247	C+
Univ of Wisc-Madison	WI	20,934	MC
Univ of Wisc-Milwaukee	WI	21,496	C
Univ of Wisc-Stevens Point	WI	14,043	C
Upper Iowa Univ	IA	34,990	NC
Vanguard Univ of Southern Calif	CA	40,740	VC
Virginia State Univ	VA	19,802	C+
Washburn Univ	KS	15,827	C
Washington State Univ	WA	22,495	C
Waynesburg Univ	PA	32,290	C
Weber State Univ	UT	10,721	C
West Chester Univ of Pennsylvania	PA	18,456	C
West Texas A&M Univ	TX	13,478	C
West Virginia Univ	WV	18,210	C
Western Kentucky Univ	KY	16,850	C
Western Mich Univ	MI	21,054	C
Westfield State Univ	MA	19,671	C
Wheeling Jesuit Univ	WV	37,106	LC
Whitworth Univ	WA	51,732	VC
William Woods Univ	MO	32,040	C
Wilmington College	OH	34,600	C
Wingate Univ	NC	39,950	C
Winona State Univ	MN	17,535	C
Winthrop Univ	SC	23,082	C
Wright State Univ	OH	16,983	C

ATMOSPHERIC SCIENCE

School	ST	$IS	SR
Cornell Univ	NY	64,853	MC
Northland College	WI	41,103	C+
Stony Brook Univ/The SUNY	NY	21,881	MC
Univ of Louisiana at Monroe	LA	15,970	C
Univ of Wisc-Milwaukee	WI	21,496	C

ATMOSPHERIC SCIENCES AND METEOROLOGY

School	ST	$IS	SR
CUNY/City College	NY	20,319	VC
East Carolina Univ	NC	16,937	C
Florida Inst of Technology	FL	53,306	VC
Florida State Univ	FL	16,771	HC
Howard Univ	DC	37,616	C+
Iowa State Univ	IA	17,570	C
Jackson State Univ	MS	15,879	LC
Lyndon State College	VT	20,714	C
Metropolitan State Univ of Denver	CO	29,889	LC
Millersville Univ of Pennsylvania	PA	23,782	C
N Car State Univ	NC	19,515	HC+
Northern Illinois Univ	IL	20,176	C
Northland College	WI	41,103	C+
Ohio State Univ at Columbus	OH	21,703	HC+
Ohio Univ	OH	22,924	C
Pennsylvania State Univ - Univ Park	PA	29,760	HC
Plymouth State Univ	NH	23,180	LC
Purdue Univ/West Lafayette	IN	20,032	MC
Rutgers Univ - New Brunswick	NJ	26,632	HC
St. Louis Univ	MO	49,866	HC
San Francisco State Univ	CA	18,514	LC
St. Cloud State Univ	MN	10,600	C
SUNY / SUNY Oneonta	NY	19,712	C+
SUNY /Maritime College	NY	16,020	C
SUNY at Oswego	NY	21,351	C
SUNY SUNY Albany	NY	22,165	C
The College at Brockport - SUNY	NY	20,346	C
The Univ of Utah	UT	17,924	VC
United States Air Force Academy	CO		C
Univ of Arizona	AZ	23,100	C
Univ of Calif at Davis	CA	28,468	HC
Univ of Calif at Los Angeles	CA	30,162	MC
Univ of Hawaii at Manoa	HI	23,221	C
Univ of Kansas	KS	20,135	C+
Univ of Louisville	KY	19,824	C
Univ of Maryland/College Park	MD	21,938	HC
Univ of Miami	FL	63,494	MC
Univ of Mich/Ann Arbor	MI	24,410	MC
Univ of Missouri/Columbia	MO	18,201	MC
Univ of Nebr - Lincoln	NE	18,589	VC
Univ of N Car at Asheville	NC	15,723	VC+
Univ of N Car at Charlotte	NC	15,547	C
Univ of N Dak	ND	15,373	C
Univ of Okla	OK	18,911	VC
Univ of South Alabama	AL	16,400	C
Univ of Washington	WA	23,149	VC
Univ of Wisc-Madison	WI	20,934	MC
Univ of Wisc-Milwaukee	WI	21,496	C
Valparaiso Univ	IN	48,370	C+
Western Conn State Univ	CT	21,254	LC
Western Kentucky Univ	KY	16,850	C

AUDIO TECHNOLOGY

School	ST	$IS	SR
American Univ	DC	59,379	HC+
Belmont Univ	TN	40,970	VC
Brigham Young Univ	UT	12,748	HC
Cogswell Polytechnical College	CA	30,531	C
Columbia College Chicago	IL	43,168	C
Five Towns College	NY	35,350	C
Grand Rapids Theological Seminary/Cornerstone Univ	MI	33,338	C
Ithaca College	NY	56,766	VC
Lawrence Tech Univ	MI	39,770	VC
Lebanon Valley College	PA	51,530	C
Mich Tech Univ	MI	24,739	VC+
Ohio Univ	OH	22,924	C
Purdue Univ/West Lafayette	IN	20,032	MC
Savannah College of Art and Design	GA	49,595	C
School of the Art Inst of Chicago	IL	56,230	SP
SUNY / SUNY Fredonia	NY	20,818	C
Texas State Univ	TX	19,350	C
Univ of Hartford	CT	49,776	C
Univ of Mich/Ann Arbor	MI	24,410	MC
Univ of New Haven	CT	52,190	C
Univ of Rochester	NY	65,032	MC
Webster Univ	MO	37,490	C
Wichita State Univ	KS	21,643	C

AUTOMOTIVE TECHNOLOGY

School	ST	$IS	SR
Benjamin Franklin Inst of Technology	MA	28,190	C
Colo State Univ-Pueblo	CO	18,234	C
Farmingdale State College	NY	20,624	C
Ferris State Univ	MI	21,445	C
Idaho State Univ	ID	13,619	NC
Lewis-Clark State College	ID	14,202	C
Minn State Univ, Mankato	MN	15,616	C
Montana State Univ-Northern	MT	11,370	NC
Pennsylvania College of Technology	PA	27,333	NC
Pittsburg State Univ	KS	13,880	NC
Southern Illinois Univ Carbondale	IL	23,667	C
The Univ of Akron	OH	21,477	C
Univ of Central Missouri	MO	18,982	C
Walla Walla Univ	WA	30,417	NC
Weber State Univ	UT	10,721	C

AVIAN SCIENCES

School	ST	$IS	SR
Bowling Green State Univ	OH	19,747	C
Eastern New Mexico Univ	NM	14,416	C
Ohio State Univ at Columbus	OH	21,703	HC+
Univ of Calif at Davis	CA	28,468	HC
Univ of Georgia	GA	21,250	HC

AVIATION ADMINISTRATION/ MANAGEMENT

School	ST	$IS	SR
Andrews Univ	MI	28,030	C+
Auburn Univ	AL	23,594	VC+
Averett Univ	VA	40,970	LC
Baker College of Flint	MI	13,880	NC
Calif Baptist Univ	CA	41,392	C
Central Washington Univ	WA	16,803	C
Daniel Webster College	NH	26,984	C
Delaware State Univ	DE	19,376	NC
Delta State Univ	MS	13,176	C
Eastern Mich Univ	MI	19,761	C
Farmingdale State College	NY	20,624	C
Florida Inst of Technology	FL	53,306	VC
Florida Memorial Univ	FL	22,270	LC
Geneva College	PA	35,450	C
Henderson State Univ	AR	15,516	LC

ST = STATE $IS = IN-STATE COSTS SR = SELECTOR RATING

School	ST	$IS	SR
Inter-American Univ of PR-Bayamon	PR	18,785	
Jacksonville Univ	FL	46,230	C
Lewis Univ	IL	40,370	C
Louisiana Tech Univ	LA	11,422	VC
Lynn Univ	FL	49,480	LC
Marywood Univ	PA	46,900	C
Metropolitan State Univ of Denver	CO	29,889	LC
Minn State Univ, Mankato	MN	15,616	C
Ohio Univ	OH	22,924	C
Park Univ	MO	20,329	C
Purdue Univ/West Lafayette	IN	20,032	MC
Quincy Univ	IL	36,998	C
Rocky Mountain College	MT	34,270	C
Salem International Univ	WV	21,090	LC
San Diego Christian College	CA	39,068	C
S Dak State Univ	SD	15,634	C
Southeastern Okla State Univ	OK	11,875	C
Southern Illinois Univ Carbondale	IL	23,667	C
Southern Nazarene Univ	OK	32,798	NC
St. Cloud State Univ	MN	10,600	C
Texas Southern Univ	TX	18,212	LC
Univ of Alaska Anchorage	AK	16,652	NC
Univ of Dubuque	IA	37,824	C
Univ of Illinois at Urbana-Champaign	IL	27,006	HC
Univ of Nebr - Kearney	NE	16,546	LC
Univ of Nebr - Omaha	NE	16,120	C
Univ of North Texas	TX	19,198	C
Univ of Okla	OK	18,911	VC
Univ of the District of Columbia	DC	21,044	LC
Vaughn College of Aeronautics and Technology	NY	37,180	C
Western Mich Univ	MI	21,054	C
Westminster College	UT	41,078	C+
Wilmington Univ	DE	8,546	NC

AVIATION BUSINESS ADMINISTRATION

School	ST	$IS	SR
Embry-Riddle Aeronautical Univ - Daytona Beach	FL	44,712	VC
Embry-Riddle Aeronautical Univ - Prescott Campus	AZ	44,054	VC
Embry-Riddle Aeronautical Univ - Worldwide	FL	17,480	C
Univ of Louisiana at Monroe	LA	15,970	C

AVIATION COMPUTER TECHNOLOGY

School	ST	$IS	SR
Andrews Univ	MI	28,030	C+
Florida Inst of Technology	FL	53,306	VC
Florida Memorial Univ	FL	22,270	LC
Inter-American Univ of PR-Bayamon	PR	18,785	
Metropolitan State Univ of Denver	CO	29,889	LC
Purdue Univ/West Lafayette	IN	20,032	MC
Southern Illinois Univ Carbondale	IL	23,667	C
Univ of Central Missouri	MO	18,982	C
Walla Walla Univ	WA	30,417	NC
Westminster College	UT	41,078	C+

AVIATION FLIGHT TECHNOLOGY

School	ST	$IS	SR
Calif Baptist Univ	CA	41,392	C
Delta State Univ	MS	13,176	C
Lewis Univ	IL	40,370	C
Thomas Edison State Univ	NJ	6,350	NC

AVIATION MAINTENANCE MANAGEMENT

School	ST	$IS	SR
Central Washington Univ	WA	16,803	C
Embry-Riddle Aeronautical Univ - Worldwide	FL	17,480	C
Lewis Univ	IL	40,370	C
S Dak State Univ	SD	15,634	C
Univ of N Dak	ND	15,373	C

AVIATION MAINTENANCE TECHNOLOGY

School	ST	$IS	SR
Embry-Riddle Aeronautical Univ - Daytona Beach	FL	44,712	VC
Lewis Univ	IL	40,370	C
Thomas Edison State Univ	NJ	6,350	NC
Univ of Alaska Anchorage	AK	16,652	NC
Western Mich Univ	MI	21,054	C

BACTERIOLOGY

School	ST	$IS	SR
Univ of Calif at Davis	CA	28,468	HC
Wilmington College	OH	34,600	C

BAKERY SCIENCE

School	ST	$IS	SR
Kansas State Univ	KS	17,780	VC

BALLET

School	ST	$IS	SR
Belhaven Univ	MS	31,016	C
Friends Univ	KS	34,455	C
Indiana Univ Bloomington	IN	20,429	VC
Texas Christian Univ	TX	54,670	HC
The Univ of Utah	UT	17,924	VC
Univ of N Car School of the Arts	NC	18,040	SP
Webster Univ	MO	37,490	C

BALLET MODERN DANCE

School	ST	$IS	SR
Texas Christian Univ	TX	54,670	HC
The Univ of Utah	UT	17,924	VC

BANKING AND FINANCE

School	ST	$IS	SR
Adams State Univ	CO	17,703	LC
Adelphi Univ	NY	48,244	C
Alabama A&M Univ	AL	18,796	C
Alabama State Univ	AL	14,142	NC
Alfred State College	NY	19,895	C
Anderson Univ	IN	38,200	C
Andrews Univ	MI	28,030	C+
Angelo State Univ	TX	15,263	NC
Appalachian State Univ	NC	14,416	VC
Arcadia Univ	PA	33,570	C+
Arkansas State Univ	AR	16,190	C
Ashland Univ	OH	21,440	C
Auburn Univ	AL	23,594	VC+
Augusta Univ	GA	4,632	C
Avila Univ	MO	35,480	C
Baylor Univ	TX	53,760	HC
Bellarmine Univ	KY	51,220	C
Benedictine Univ	IL	38,300	C
Bethel Univ	MN	45,270	VC
Boston College	MA	65,737	MC
Brescia Univ	KY	29,890	VC+
Bryant Univ	RI	55,646	VC
Buena Vista Univ	IA	41,514	C
Butler Univ	IN	51,352	VC
Cal State, Long Beach	CA	18,850	C
Cal State, Northridge	CA	16,859	LC
Cal State, Sacramento	CA	20,332	C
Cal State, San Bernardino	CA	12,000	C
Canisius College	NY	47,537	C
Caribbean Univ	PR	15,471	
Central State Univ	OH	18,564	C
Central Washington Univ	WA	16,803	C
Chicago State Univ	IL	20,144	C
CUNY/Brooklyn College	NY	5,884	C+
Clarion Univ of Pennsylvania	PA	21,608	LC
Clemson Univ	SC		HC
Coastal Carolina Univ	SC	19,766	C
College of William & Mary	VA		MC
Colo State Univ	CO	22,162	VC
Columbia College - Missouri	MO	27,803	C
Columbus State Univ	GA	14,336	LC
Concord Univ	WV	14,954	C
Concordia Univ St. Paul	MN	29,050	C
Concordia Univ Wisc	WI	35,910	C
Davenport Univ	MI	25,896	LC
Defiance College	OH	41,630	C
DePaul Univ	IL	47,623	VC
Dominican College	NY	31,270	LC
Dordt College	IA	37,860	C+
Drake Univ	IA	45,056	HC
Drury Univ	MO	33,791	VC
Duquesne Univ	PA	46,822	VC
East Carolina Univ	NC	16,937	C
East Central Univ	OK	13,056	C
Eastern Kentucky Univ	KY	16,908	C
Eastern Mich Univ	MI	19,761	C
Eastern Washington Univ	WA	25,572	LC
Emory Univ	GA	60,786	MC
Excelsior College	NY	14,080	SP
Fairleigh Dickinson Univ/ College at Florham	NJ	52,062	C
Fayetteville State Univ	NC	17,756	C
Florida A&M Univ	FL	15,361	C
Florida Atlantic Univ	FL	17,339	C
Florida Gulf Coast Univ	FL	9,682	C
Florida International Univ	FL	19,854	C+
Florida State Univ	FL	16,771	HC
Fort Hays State Univ	KS	12,131	C
Francis Marion Univ	SC	16,464	LC
Franklin Pierce Univ	NH	46,750	C
Franklin Univ	OH	56,262	SP
Freed-Hardeman Univ	TN	29,450	C
Friends Univ	KS	34,455	C
Gannon Univ	PA	42,032	C
George Mason Univ	VA	15,724	VC
George Washington Univ	DC	62,835	MC
Georgetown College	KY	41,440	C
Georgetown Univ	DC	65,926	MC
Georgia State Univ	GA	24,332	VC
Golden Gate Univ	CA	32,110	C
Goldey-Beacom College	DE	31,750	C
Gordon College	MA	46,472	C+
Grand Valley State Univ	MI	22,250	C+
Gwynedd Mercy Univ	PA	43,780	LC
Hampton Univ	VA	34,926	LC
Harding Univ	AR	25,421	C
Hardin-Simmons Univ	TX	33,966	C
Hawaii Pacific Univ	HI	33,420	C
Hofstra Univ	NY	55,960	C+
Houston Baptist Univ	TX	36,450	C
Howard Univ	DC	37,616	C+
Husson Univ	ME	25,720	LC
Idaho State Univ	ID	13,619	NC
Indiana State Univ	IN	23,223	LC
Indiana Univ-Purdue Univ Fort Wayne	IN	17,553	C
Indiana Wesleyan Univ	IN	33,674	C
Inter-American Univ of PR Ponce	PR	19,549	
Inter-American Univ of PR-Bayamon	PR	18,785	
Inter-American Univ of PR-Fajardo Campus	PR	18,336	
Inter-American Univ of PR-Metropolitan Campus	PR	20,045	
Inter-American Univ of PR-San Germán	PR	20,042	
Iowa State Univ	IA	17,570	C
Jacksonville State Univ	AL	14,628	LC
Jacksonville Univ	FL	46,230	C
James Madison Univ	VA	19,084	VC
John Carroll Univ	OH	49,740	C+
Juniata College	PA	53,760	VC
Kansas State Univ	KS	17,780	VC
King's College	PA	46,858	C
Kutztown Univ of Pennsylvania	PA	19,056	LC
La Roche College	PA	37,924	LC
La Salle Univ	PA	55,790	C
La Sierra Univ	CA	39,690	VC
Lasell College	MA	47,500	C
Le Moyne College	NY	46,000	C
Lindenwood Univ	MO	25,132	C
Linfield College	OR	52,010	C
Louisiana State Univ and A&M College	LA	18,677	VC
Louisiana State Univ in Shreveport	LA	6,902	C
Louisiana Tech Univ	LA	11,422	VC
Loyola Univ New Orleans	LA	51,708	VC+
Lubbock Christian Univ	TX	28,426	C
Manchester Univ	IN	40,422	C
Manhattan College	NY	51,750	C+
Manhattanville College	NY	51,440	C+
Marietta College	OH	46,190	C
Marshall Univ	WV	17,242	C
Marywood Univ	PA	46,900	C
McKendree Univ	IL	37,940	C+
McMurry Univ	TX	34,259	LC
Mercy College	NY	31,776	C
Mercyhurst Univ	PA	47,420	C
Metropolitan State Univ	MN	7,566	C
Metropolitan State Univ of Denver	CO	29,889	LC
Mich State Univ	MI	23,898	VC+
Middle Tenn State Univ	TN	8,650	C
Midwestern State Univ	TX	17,572	C
Minn State Univ, Mankato	MN	15,616	C
Minn State Univ, Moorhead	MN	15,941	C
Minot State Univ	ND	12,732	C
Miss State Univ	MS	11,454	C+
Monmouth Univ	NJ	46,234	C
Montclair State Univ	NJ	26,210	LC
Morehead State Univ	KY	17,422	C
Muhlenberg College	PA	56,645	VC+
National Univ	CA	14,730	LC
New Mexico Highlands Univ	NM	11,904	NC
New York Univ	NY	65,860	MC
Nicholls State Univ	LA	10,534	C
Norfolk State Univ	VA	25,702	LC
North Park Univ	IL	35,860	C
Northeastern Illinois Univ	IL	12,529	LC
Northeastern State Univ	OK	8,615	VC
Northern Illinois Univ	IL	20,176	C
Northern Mich Univ	MI	19,604	C
Northern State Univ	SD	14,505	C
Northwest Missouri State Univ	MO	17,737	C
Northwood Univ - Mich	MI	35,010	LC
Notre Dame of Maryland Univ	MD	46,465	VC
Oakland Univ	MI	20,763	C
Ohio Dominican Univ	OH	41,340	C+
Ohio State Univ at Columbus	OH	21,703	HC+
Ohio Univ	OH	22,924	C
Okla Baptist Univ	OK	32,320	C
Okla Christian Univ	OK	27,650	VC
Okla City Univ	OK	40,476	VC
Okla State Univ	OK	17,180	VC
Oral Roberts Univ	OK	34,316	C
Pace Univ	NY	58,248	C
Palm Beach Atlantic Univ	FL	39,720	C
Penn State Erie/The Behrend College	PA	16,256	C
Philadelphia Univ	PA	50,370	C
Pittsburg State Univ	KS	13,880	NC
Pontifical Catholic Univ of PR	PR	10,534	
Post Univ	CT	41,150	C
Prairie View A&M Univ	TX	15,205	LC
Purdue Univ/Northwest	IN	15,038	C
Purdue Univ/West Lafayette	IN	20,032	MC
Quincy Univ	IL	36,998	C
Quinnipiac Univ	CT	59,110	C
Radford Univ	VA	19,027	LC
Rhode Island College	RI	17,694	LC
Rider Univ	NJ	54,050	C
Robert Morris Univ	PA	37,834	C
Rochester Inst of Technology	NY	50,842	HC
Roger Williams Univ	RI	46,296	C+
Roosevelt Univ	IL	40,651	VC
Rutgers Univ - Camden	NJ	26,146	C
Rutgers Univ - New Brunswick	NJ	26,632	HC
Rutgers Univ - Newark	NJ	27,288	C
Saginaw Valley State Univ	MI	18,530	C
St. Anselm College	NH	52,560	C+
St. Vincent College	PA	44,626	C
St. Xavier Univ	IL	43,310	C
Salem State Univ	MA	17,303	LC
Sam Houston State Univ	TX	18,792	C
San Francisco State Univ	CA	18,514	LC
San Jose State Univ	CA	21,540	C
Siena College	NY	48,916	C+
Southeastern Univ	FL	31,765	C
Southern Adventist Univ	TN	27,600	C
Southern Conn State Univ	CT	21,924	LC
Southern Illinois Univ Carbondale	IL	23,667	C
Southern Nazarene Univ	OK	32,798	NC
Southern Univ and A&M College	LA	16,074	LC+
St. Bonaventure Univ	NY	44,237	C
St. Cloud State Univ	MN	10,600	C
St. Edward's Univ	TX	53,100	VC
St. Mary's Univ	TX	37,500	C
St. Thomas Aquinas College	NY	42,200	C
St. Thomas Univ	FL	36,360	LC
SUNY / SUNY College at Old Westbury	NY	16,860	C
SUNY at New Paltz	NY	19,200	C
SUNY Polytechnic Inst	NY	19,473	VC
Stephen F. Austin State Univ	TX	18,406	LC
Stetson Univ	FL	53,544	VC
Stockton Univ	NJ	25,059	
Stonehill College	MA	55,030	C+
Suffolk Univ	MA	50,308	C
Talladega College	AL	19,215	C
Tarleton State Univ	TX	15,248	LC
Taylor Univ	IN	40,317	C+
Temple Univ	PA	24,392	VC
Tenn Tech Univ	TN	17,050	C
Texas A&M Univ at Commerce	TX	10,496	C
Texas A&M Univ at Corpus Christi	TX	16,851	LC
Texas A&M Univ at Kingsville	TX	7,500	LC
Texas Southern Univ	TX	18,212	LC
Texas State Univ	TX	19,350	C
The Catholic Univ of America	DC	56,356	VC
The Univ of Akron	OH	21,477	C
Tiffin Univ	OH	31,380	C
Touro College	NY	28,950	VC
Trine Univ	IN	41,310	C
Troy Univ	AL	16,171	C
Tulane Univ	LA	63,396	HC+
Tuskegee Univ	AL	28,164	C
Union College	NE	23,270	C
Union Univ	TN	33,970	VC
Univ of PR, at Arecibo	PR	12,652	
Univ of Alabama at Birmingham	AL	19,906	C
Univ of Alabama in Huntsville	AL	19,445	VC
Univ of Alaska Anchorage	AK	16,652	NC
Univ of Arkansas at Fayetteville	AR	19,152	C+
Univ of Arkansas at Little Rock	AR	18,211	C
Univ of Bridgeport	CT	44,430	LC
Univ of Central Arkansas	AR	14,472	VC
Univ of Central Florida	FL	15,922	VC
Univ of Central Okla	OK	13,486	C
Univ of Cincinnati	OH	21,964	VC
Univ of Conn	CT	25,538	HC
Univ of Dayton	OH	53,620	C
Univ of Delaware	DE	24,976	VC+
Univ of Denver	CO	58,443	VC+
Univ of Findlay	OH	60,139	C
Univ of Florida	FL	16,291	HC+
Univ of Hartford	CT	49,776	C
Univ of Hawaii at Manoa	HI	23,221	C
Univ of Houston-Downtown	TX	7,241	C
Univ of Illinois at Chicago	IL	25,006	VC
Univ of Illinois at Urbana-Champaign	IL	27,006	HC
Univ of Indianapolis	IN	36,480	C
Univ of Iowa	IA	18,683	VC+
Univ of Kentucky	KY	33,306	C
Univ of Louisiana at Lafayette	LA	14,516	C
Univ of Louisville	KY	19,824	C
Univ of Mass Amherst	MA	26,199	VC+
Univ of Memphis	TN	18,278	C
Univ of Mich-Flint	MI	17,607	C+
Univ of Miss	MS	17,746	C+
Univ of Missouri/Columbia	MO	18,201	MC
Univ of Montana	MT	14,105	C
Univ of Montevallo	AL	19,502	C
Univ of Nebr - Kearney	NE	16,546	LC
Univ of Nebr - Lincoln	NE	18,589	VC
Univ of Nebr - Omaha	NE	16,120	C
Univ of Nevada, Las Vegas	NV	17,553	C
Univ of New Haven	CT	52,190	C
Univ of New Orleans	LA	12,840	C
Univ of North Alabama	AL	15,398	C
Univ of N Car at Charlotte	NC	15,547	C

ST = STATE $IS = IN-STATE COSTS SR = SELECTOR RATING

School	ST	$IS	SR
Univ of N Car at Greensboro	NC	14,690	C
Univ of N Car at Wilmington	NC	14,590	VC
Univ of N Dak	ND	15,373	C
Univ of North Florida	FL	15,996	VC
Univ of North Georgia	GA	17,316	C
Univ of North Texas	TX	19,198	C
Univ of Northwestern - St. Paul	MN	38,160	C
Univ of Pittsburgh at Johnstown	PA	22,092	C
Univ of Portland	OR	52,152	VC
Univ of PR, at Bayamon	PR	13,145	
Univ of PR, at Mayaguez	PR	13,995	
Univ of PR-Rio Piedras campus	PR	13,327	
Univ of Scranton	PA	54,962	VC
Univ of South Alabama	AL	16,400	C
Univ of S Car at Columbia	SC	19,725	VC+
Univ of S Dak	SD	16,109	C
Univ of South Florida/Tampa	FL	16,110	VC+
Univ of Southern Miss	MS	13,170	C
Univ of St. Francis	IL	39,924	C
Univ of St. Thomas - Houston	TX	40,020	VC
Univ of Tampa	FL	36,944	C
Univ of Texas at Arlington	TX	18,026	LC
Univ of Texas at Austin	TX	26,102	HC
Univ of Texas at Dallas	TX	22,830	VC+
Univ of Texas at El Paso	TX	34,452	NC
Univ of the District of Columbia	DC	21,044	LC
Univ of Toledo	OH	19,336	NC
Univ of Tulsa	OK	52,625	HC+
Univ of Washington	WA	23,149	VC
Univ of West Florida	FL	15,848	C
Univ of Wisc-Eau Claire	WI	15,797	VC
Univ of Wisc-La Crosse	WI	15,247	C+
Univ of Wisc-Madison	WI	20,934	MC
Univ of Wisc-Oshkosh	WI	15,200	C
Univ of Wisc-Whitewater	WI	13,976	C
Upper Iowa Univ	IA	34,990	NC
Utah State Univ	UT	12,736	C
Valparaiso Univ	IN	48,370	C+
Villanova Univ	PA	62,523	MC
Virginia Polytechnic Inst and State Univ	VA	21,276	HC
Virginia Union Univ	VA	22,421	C
Wake Forest Univ	NC	64,056	MC
Warner Univ	FL	28,216	C
Wartburg College	IA	47,840	C
Washburn Univ	KS	15,827	C
Washington Univ in St. Louis	MO	65,366	VC
Wayne State Univ	MI	22,016	C
Webber International Univ	FL	31,904	C
Weber State Univ	UT	10,721	C
West Chester Univ of Pennsylvania	PA	18,456	C
West Liberty Univ	WV	15,512	C
West Texas A&M Univ	TX	13,478	C
West Virginia State Univ	WV	8,378	NC
West Virginia Univ	WV	18,210	C
Western Carolina Univ	NC	13,965	C
Western Conn State Univ	CT	21,254	LC
Western Kentucky Univ	KY	16,850	C
Westminster College	PA	39,180	C+
Westminster College	UT	41,078	C+
Wichita State Univ	KS	21,643	C
Wilberforce Univ	OH	19,016	C
William Paterson Univ of New Jersey	NJ	23,133	C
Wilmington Univ	DE	8,546	NC
Winona State Univ	MN	17,535	C
Wofford College	SC	49,885	VC
Wright State Univ	OH	16,983	C
Xavier Univ	OH	47,880	C+
York College of Pennsylvania	PA	29,240	C
Youngstown State Univ	OH	17,307	C

BEHAVIORAL SCIENCE

School	ST	$IS	SR
Alvernia Univ	PA	43,900	C
Andrews Univ	MI	28,030	C+
Ashford Univ	CA	10,480	C
Bethel College	IN	35,860	C
Calif Baptist Univ	CA	41,392	C
Cal State, Dominguez Hills	CA	19,022	LC
Cal State, Monterey Bay	CA	26,871	LC
Capital Univ	OH	42,982	C
Chaminade Univ of Honolulu	HI	36,000	C
College of St. Scholastica	MN	44,640	C
Concordia College - New York	NY	39,035	LC
Concordia Univ	CA	41,580	VC
Concordia Univ Nebr	NE	36,280	VC
Concordia Univ Texas	TX	40,210	C
Corban Univ	OR	40,306	C
Dakota Wesleyan Univ	SD	32,850	C
Duquesne Univ	PA	46,822	VC
Elizabethtown College School of Continuing and Professional Studies	PA	18,900	C
Erskine College	SC	45,460	C
Fontbonne Univ	MO	33,717	C
George Fox Univ	OR	42,938	C
Grand Valley State Univ	MI	22,250	C+
Granite State College	NH	19,639	SP
Johns Hopkins Univ	MD	65,386	MC
Johnson State College	VT	20,752	C
Lakeland Univ	WI	35,130	C
Lehigh Univ	PA	61,010	MC
Mercy College	NY	31,776	C
Metropolitan State Univ of Denver	CO	29,889	LC
Missouri Baptist Univ	MO	35,594	C
Mount Aloysius College	PA	29,976	C
Mount Marty College	SD	32,972	C
Mount Mary Univ	WI	34,650	LC
National Univ	CA	14,730	LC
New York Inst of Technology	NY	48,730	C
North Central Univ	MN	26,400	C
Northwest Univ	WA	35,876	VC
Nova Southeastern Univ	FL	38,534	C+
Oglethorpe Univ	GA	44,200	C+
Okla City Univ	OK	40,476	VC
Okla Wesleyan Univ	OK	33,206	C
Our Lady of the Lake Univ	TX	35,012	LC
Point Park Univ	PA	41,270	C
Purdue Univ/Northwest	IN	15,038	C
Purdue Univ/West Lafayette	IN	20,032	MC
Rochester College	MI	28,574	LC
St. Louis Univ	MO	49,866	HC
Savannah State Univ	GA	15,631	C
Southern Adventist Univ	TN	27,600	C
Sterling College	KS	32,830	C
Tabor College	KS	35,870	C
The Univ of Utah	UT	17,924	VC
Trevecca Nazarene Univ	TN	31,186	C
United States Air Force Academy	CO		C
Univ of Calif at Davis	CA	28,468	HC
Univ of Holy Cross	LA	21,523	C
Univ of Kansas	KS	20,135	C+
Univ of La Verne	CA	55,600	C
Univ of Maine at Fort Kent	ME	15,165	LC
Univ of Maine at Machias	ME	22,960	C
Univ of Mary	ND	23,180	C
Univ of Mich/Ann Arbor	MI	24,410	MC
Univ of Rio Grande & Rio Grande Community College	OH	8,750	NC
Univ of St. Mary	KS	34,690	C
Univ of San Diego	CA	58,442	VC+
Univ of Wisc-Milwaukee	WI	21,496	C
Villanova Univ	PA	62,523	MC
Western Mich Univ	MI	21,054	C
Western Washington Univ	WA	18,003	C+
Widener Univ	PA	56,486	C
Wilmington Univ	DE	8,546	NC
York College of Pennsylvania	PA	29,240	C

BIBLICAL LANGUAGES

School	ST	$IS	SR
Asbury Univ	KY	35,180	C+
Baylor Univ	TX	53,760	HC
Belmont Univ	TN	40,970	VC
Concordia Univ	CA	41,580	VC
Concordia Univ Wisc	WI	35,910	C
Concordia Univ, Ann Arbor	MI	35,945	VC
Faulkner Univ	AL	26,410	C
Harding Univ	AR	25,421	C
Houston Baptist Univ	TX	36,450	C
Lipscomb Univ	TN	41,296	VC
Luther College	IA	48,540	C+
North Central Univ	MN	26,400	C
Okla Baptist Univ	OK	32,320	C
Ouachita Baptist Univ	AR	32,320	C
The Master's Univ	CA	43,870	C+
Union Univ	TN	33,970	VC
Walla Walla Univ	WA	30,417	NC

BIBLICAL STUDIES

School	ST	$IS	SR
Abilene Christian Univ	TX	41,800	C+
Amridge Univ	AL	10,860	LC
Asbury Univ	KY	35,180	C+
Azusa Pacific Univ	CA	43,972	C
Belhaven Univ	MS	31,016	C
Belmont Univ	TN	40,970	VC
Bethel College	IN	35,860	C
Bethel Univ	MN	45,270	VC
Biola Univ	CA	46,402	C+
Blue Mountain College	MS	15,949	VC
Bluffton Univ	OH	40,950	C
Cairn Univ	PA	36,296	C
Campbellsville Univ	KY	32,492	C
Canisius College	NY	47,537	C
Cedarville Univ	OH	34,990	VC
College of the Ozarks	MO	7,230	C
Colo Christian Univ	CO	39,940	VC
Corban Univ	OR	40,306	C
Covenant College	GA	38,990	VC
Dallas Baptist Univ	TX	33,713	C
East Texas Baptist Univ	TX	33,134	C
Eastern Mennonite Univ	VA	42,550	C
Eastern Univ	PA	39,540	C
Evangel Univ	MO	28,898	C
Faulkner Univ	AL	26,410	C
Freed-Hardeman Univ	TN	29,450	C
Geneva College	PA	35,450	C
George Fox Univ	OR	42,938	C
Gordon College	MA	46,472	C+
Goshen College	IN	42,500	C
Grace Bible College	MI	25,250	C
Grace College and Seminary	IN	31,524	C
Grand Rapids Theological Seminary/Cornerstone Univ	MI	33,338	C
Grove City College	PA	25,692	VC
Hannibal-LaGrange Univ	MO	29,815	C
Harding Univ	AR	25,421	C
Hardin-Simmons Univ	TX	33,966	C
Hope International Univ	CA	41,150	C
Houghton College	NY	39,090	C
Huntington Univ	IN	33,996	C
Indiana Wesleyan Univ	IN	33,674	C
John Brown Univ	AR	33,132	VC
Judson Univ	IL	37,700	C
Kentucky Christian Univ	KY	26,560	LC
King Univ	TN	34,660	C
Lee Univ	TN	22,045	C
LeTourneau Univ	TX	38,250	VC
Lipscomb Univ	TN	41,296	VC
List College	NY	37,870	C
Lubbock Christian Univ	TX	28,426	C
Malone Univ	OH	38,448	C
Messiah College	PA	43,100	C+
Milligan College	TN	38,150	C
Montreat College	NC	31,298	LC
Mount Vernon Nazarene Univ	OH	34,500	C
North Park Univ	IL	35,860	C
Northwest Nazarene Univ	ID	36,000	C
Northwest Univ	WA	35,876	VC
Nyack College	NY	34,050	NC
Ohio Valley Univ	WV	29,480	C
Okla Baptist Univ	OK	32,320	C
Okla Christian Univ	OK	27,650	VC
Olivet Nazarene Univ	IL	41,840	C
Oral Roberts Univ	OK	34,316	C
Ouachita Baptist Univ	AR	32,320	C
Palm Beach Atlantic Univ	FL	39,720	C
Point Loma Nazarene Univ	CA	43,450	C
Roberts Wesleyan College	NY	38,306	C
Rochester College	MI	28,574	LC
San Diego Christian College	CA	39,068	C
Simpson Univ	CA	33,700	C
Southeastern Univ	FL	31,765	C
Southwest Baptist Univ	MO	29,900	LC
Spring Arbor Univ	MI	36,000	C
Sterling College	KS	32,830	C
Tabor College	KS	35,870	C
Taylor Univ	IN	40,317	C+
The Master's Univ	CA	43,870	C+
Toccoa Falls College	GA	27,920	C
Trinity Bible College	ND		
Trinity Christian College	IL	35,580	C
Trinity International Univ	IL	31,070	VC
Union Univ	TN	33,970	VC
Univ of Evansville	IN	44,186	VC+
Univ of Mary Hardin-Baylor	TX	33,950	C+
Univ of Mich/Ann Arbor	MI	24,410	MC
Univ of Minn/Twin Cities	MN	23,519	HC+
Univ of Northwestern - St. Paul	MN	38,160	C
Vanguard Univ of Southern Calif	CA	40,740	VC
Warner Univ	FL	28,216	C
Waynesburg Univ	PA	32,290	C
Wheaton College	IL	43,610	MC
York College	NE	24,300	C

BILINGUAL EARLY CHILDHOOD EDUCATION

School	ST	$IS	SR
Texas Christian Univ	TX	54,670	HC

BILINGUAL/BICULTURAL EDUCATION

School	ST	$IS	SR
Aurora Univ	IL	33,970	C
Boston Univ	MA	65,110	MC
Cal State, San Bernardino	CA	12,000	C
Chicago State Univ	IL	20,144	C
CUNY/Brooklyn College	NY	5,884	C+
CUNY/City College	NY	20,319	VC
Eastern Mich Univ	MI	19,761	C
Elms College	MA	45,646	VC
Loyola Univ Chicago	IL	55,802	VC
Mount Mary Univ	WI	34,650	LC
New Mexico State Univ	NM	14,050	C
New York Univ	NY	65,860	MC
Northeastern Illinois Univ	IL	12,529	LC
St. Thomas Aquinas College	NY	42,200	C
SUNY / SUNY College at Old Westbury	NY	16,860	C
Univ of Central Okla	OK	13,486	C
Univ of Findlay	OH	60,139	C
Univ of Minn/Twin Cities	MN	23,519	HC+
Washington State Univ	WA	22,495	C
Western Illinois Univ	IL	20,825	C

BIOCHEMISTRY

School	ST	$IS	SR
Abilene Christian Univ	TX	41,800	C+
Adams State Univ	CO	17,703	LC
Adelphi Univ	NY	48,244	C
Agnes Scott College	GA	51,930	VC+
Albion College	MI	52,650	C
Albright College	PA	46,660	C
Allegheny College	PA	55,420	VC
Alma College	MI	47,548	C
Alvernia Univ	PA	43,900	C
American International College	MA	46,300	LC
American Univ	DC	59,379	HC+
Amherst College	MA		HC+
Andrews Univ	MI	28,030	C+
Angelo State Univ	TX	15,263	NC
Arizona State Univ at the Tempe Campus	AZ	21,756	VC
Armstrong State Univ	GA	16,962	C
Asbury Univ	KY	35,180	C+
Auburn Univ	AL	23,594	VC+
Augustana College	IL	49,658	VC
Augustana Univ	SD	38,424	VC
Austin College	TX	45,875	VC
Averett Univ	VA	40,970	LC
Avila Univ	MO	35,480	C
Azusa Pacific Univ	CA	43,972	C
Barnard College/Columbia Univ	NY	62,741	MC
Bates College	ME	64,500	MC
Bay Path Univ	MA	45,349	C
Baylor Univ	TX	53,760	HC
Bellarmine Univ	KY	51,220	C
Belmont Univ	TN	40,970	VC
Beloit College	WI	55,206	HC
Benedictine College	KS	36,200	VC
Benedictine Univ	IL	38,300	C
Berry College	GA	45,286	C+
Bethany College	WV	36,300	NC
Bethel College	IN	35,860	C
Bethel Univ	MN	45,270	VC
Biola Univ	CA	46,402	C+
Blackburn College	IL	28,526	LC
Bloomfield College	NJ	39,100	LC
Boston College	MA	65,737	MC
Boston Univ	MA	65,110	MC
Bowdoin College	ME	63,500	MC
Brandeis Univ	MA	65,925	MC
Brescia Univ	KY	29,890	VC+
Bridgewater College	VA	44,510	C
Brigham Young Univ	UT	12,748	HC
Brown Univ	RI	64,566	MC
Bryant Univ	RI	55,646	VC
Bucknell Univ	PA	64,616	MC
Buena Vista Univ	IA	41,514	C
Butler Univ	IN	51,352	VC
Calif Baptist Univ	CA	41,392	C
Calif Lutheran Univ	CA	52,853	C
Calif Polytechnic State Univ	CA	17,979	HC+
Cal State, Chico	CA	21,440	C
Cal State, Dominguez Hills	CA	19,022	LC
Cal State, Fullerton	CA	21,902	C
Cal State, Long Beach	CA	18,850	C
Cal State, Los Angeles	CA	17,186	LC
Cal State, Northridge	CA	16,859	LC
Cal State, San Bernardino	CA	12,000	C
Cal State, San Marcos	CA	24,184	LC
Calvin College	MI	41,570	VC+
Canisius College	NY	47,537	C
Capital Univ	OH	42,982	C
Carnegie Mellon Univ	PA	67,980	MC
Carroll College	MT	39,972	C+
Carroll Univ	WI	38,100	C+
Case Western Reserve Univ	OH	60,304	MC
Cedar Crest College	PA	46,715	C
Centenary College of Louisiana	LA	45,650	C+
Central College	IA	44,592	C
Central Conn State Univ	CT	21,203	C
Central Mich Univ	MI	20,330	C
Centre College	KY	49,250	HC
Chaminade Univ of Honolulu	HI	36,000	C
Chapman Univ	CA	63,078	VC+
Charleston Southern Univ	SC	32,400	C
Chatham Univ	PA	46,517	C
Chestnut Hill College	PA	43,410	C
Chicago State Univ	IL	20,144	C
Christian Brothers Univ	TN	31,670	VC
Christopher Newport Univ	VA	23,968	VC+
CUNY/College of Staten Island	NY	17,840	NC
Claflin Univ	SC	33,764	LC
Claremont McKenna College	CA	67,185	MC
Clark Univ	MA	51,600	HC+
Clarke Univ	IA	38,940	C
Clemson Univ	SC		HC
Coastal Carolina Univ	SC	19,766	C
Coe College	IA	51,570	VC
Colby College	ME	64,060	MC
Colgate Univ	NY	65,030	MC
College of Charleston	SC	22,699	C
College of Mount St. Vincent	NY	45,620	C
College of St. Benedict	MN	52,806	C
College of St. Elizabeth	NJ	44,432	LC
College of St. Scholastica	MN	44,640	C
Colo College	CO	62,560	MC
Colo State Univ	CO	22,162	VC
Colo State Univ-Pueblo	CO	18,234	C
Columbia Univ/City of New York	NY	62,958	MC
Conn College	CT	65,000	MC
Cornell College	IA	48,800	VC
Culver-Stockton College	MO	33,525	C
Curry College	MA	51,815	C
Daemen College	NY	38,045	C
Dartmouth College	NH	66,174	MC
Denison Univ	OH	58,860	MC
DePauw Univ	IN	58,688	HC+
DeSales Univ	PA	43,970	C
Dickinson College	PA	63,974	MC
Doane Univ	NE	39,184	VC
Dominican Univ	IL	41,222	C

ST = STATE $IS = IN-STATE COSTS SR = SELECTOR RATING

School	ST	$IS	SR
Drew Univ/College of Liberal Arts	NJ	61,048	VC
Duquesne Univ	PA	46,822	VC
Earlham College	IN	54,870	HC
East Carolina Univ	NC	16,937	C
East Stroudsburg Univ	PA	18,334	C
Eastern Conn State Univ	CT	23,059	C
Eastern Mennonite Univ	VA	42,550	C
Eastern Mich Univ	MI	19,761	C
Eastern New Mexico Univ	NM	14,416	C
Eastern Univ	PA	39,540	C
Eastern Washington Univ	WA	25,572	LC
Eckerd College	FL	52,874	C
Elizabethtown College	PA	54,050	C
Elmira College	NY	53,900	C
Elon Univ	NC	44,599	VC+
Emmanuel College	MA	52,110	C+
Emporia State Univ	KS	14,570	C
Fairfield Univ	CT	59,860	VC+
Fairleigh Dickinson Univ/College at Florham	NJ	52,062	C
Fairleigh Dickinson Univ/Metropolitan Campus	NJ	40,254	C
Faulkner Univ	AL	26,410	C
Ferris State Univ	MI	21,445	C
Florida Inst of Technology	FL	53,306	VC
Florida State Univ	FL	16,771	HC
Fort Lewis College	CO	18,980	C
Framingham State Univ	MA	20,584	C
Franklin and Marshall College	PA	63,170	HC
Freed-Hardeman Univ	TN	29,450	C
Georgetown College	KY	41,440	C
Georgetown Univ	DC	65,926	MC
Georgia Inst of Technology	GA	23,360	MC
Georgian Court Univ	NJ	42,426	LC
Gettysburg College	PA	63,000	HC
Gonzaga Univ	WA	50,888	HC
Goshen College	IN	42,500	C
Goucher College	MD	55,716	VC
Grand View Univ	IA	32,302	C
Grinnell College	IA	60,738	MC
Grove City College	PA	25,692	VC
Gustavus Adolphus College	MN	52,433	HC
Hamilton College	NY	64,250	MC
Hamline Univ	MN	45,678	VC
Hanover College	IN	46,364	C+
Harding Univ	AR	25,421	C
Hardin-Simmons Univ	TX	33,966	C
Hartwick College	NY	51,270	C
Harvard College/Harvard Univ	MA	60,659	MC
Hawaii Pacific Univ	HI	33,420	C
Heidelberg Univ	OH	39,200	C
Hendrix College	AR	54,020	VC+
High Point Univ	NC	45,977	C
Hillsdale College	MI	35,722	MC
Hiram College	OH	43,230	C
Hofstra Univ	NY	55,960	C+
Holy Family Univ	PA	43,326	LC
Hood College	MD	54,840	C
Hope College	MI	39,940	VC
Houghton College	NY	39,090	C
Howard Univ	DC	37,616	C+
Huntingdon College	AL	34,900	C
Idaho State Univ	ID	13,619	NC
Illinois College	IL	40,850	VC
Illinois Inst of Technology	IL	56,826	HC+
Illinois State Univ	IL	23,418	VC
Indiana Univ Bloomington	IN	20,429	VC
Indiana Univ East	IN	7,072	C
Indiana Univ Kokomo	IN	7,073	C
Indiana Univ Northwest	IN	7,072	C
Indiana Univ of Pennsylvania	PA	23,614	LC
Indiana Univ South Bend	IN	14,242	C
Indiana Univ-Purdue Univ Fort Wayne	IN	17,553	C
Iona College	NY	50,984	C
Iowa State Univ	IA	17,570	C
Ithaca College	NY	56,766	VC
John Brown Univ	AR	33,132	VC
John Carroll Univ	OH	49,740	C+
Juniata College	PA	53,760	VC
Kalamazoo College	MI	53,931	HC+
Kansas State Univ	KS	17,780	VC
Kennesaw State Univ	GA	19,592	VC
Kenyon College	OH	63,330	MC
Kettering Univ	MI	47,570	HC
Keuka College	NY	39,762	C
King Univ	TN	34,660	C
Knox College	IL	52,615	VC+
Kutztown Univ of Pennsylvania	PA	19,056	LC
La Roche College	PA	37,924	LC
La Salle Univ	PA	55,790	C
La Sierra Univ	CA	39,690	VC
Lafayette College	PA	63,355	MC
LaGrange College	GA	39,930	C
Lawrence Tech Univ	MI	39,770	VC
Lawrence Univ	WI	54,498	HC
Le Moyne College	NY	46,000	C
Lebanon Valley College	PA	51,530	C
Lee Univ	TN	22,045	C
Lehigh Univ	PA	61,010	MC
Lewis & Clark College	OR	58,434	HC+
Lewis Univ	IL	40,370	C
Linfield College	OR	52,010	C
Lipscomb Univ	TN	41,296	VC
LIU Brooklyn	NY	49,682	C
Loras College	IA	39,222	C
Louisiana State Univ and A&M College	LA	18,677	VC
Louisiana State Univ in Shreveport	LA	6,902	C
Loyola Marymount Univ	CA	58,038	HC
Loyola Univ Chicago	IL	55,802	VC
Lubbock Christian Univ	TX	28,426	C
Madonna Univ	MI	29,050	C
Malone Univ	OH	38,448	C
Manchester Univ	IN	40,422	C
Manhattan College	NY	51,750	C+
Manhattanville College	NY	51,440	C+
Marietta College	OH	46,190	C
Marist College	NY	49,860	VC
Marquette Univ	WI	48,390	VC+
Marshall Univ	WV	17,242	C
Marymount Univ	VA	41,570	LC
Maryville College	TN	44,410	C
Maryville Univ of St. Louis	MO	38,046	VC+
McMurry Univ	TX	34,259	LC
Mercer Univ	GA	45,348	VC
Mercyhurst Univ	PA	47,420	C
Merrimack College	MA	52,770	C
Messiah College	PA	43,100	C+
Miami Univ	OH	27,190	HC+
Mich State Univ	MI	23,898	VC+
Mich Tech Univ	MI	24,739	VC+
Middlebury College	VT	64,332	MC
Millersville Univ of Pennsylvania	PA	23,782	C
Millikin Univ	IL	42,158	C
Mills College	CA	59,163	VC
Millsaps College	MS	50,080	C+
Minn State Univ, Mankato	MN	15,616	C
Misericordia Univ	PA	43,840	C
Miss College	MS	25,850	C
Miss State Univ	MS	11,454	C+
Missouri Baptist Univ	MO	35,594	C
Missouri Southern State Univ	MO	12,499	C
Monmouth College	IL	42,260	C
Montclair State Univ	NJ	26,210	LC
Moravian College	PA	53,117	
Mount Holyoke College	MA	56,746	MC
Mount St. Joseph Univ	OH	33,880	C
Mount St. Mary's Univ	MD	51,610	C
Mount St. Mary's Univ - Chalon Campus	CA	43,897	VC+
Muhlenberg College	PA	56,645	VC+
Nazareth College	NY	45,574	C
Nebr Wesleyan Univ	NE	38,140	C+
New College of Florida	FL	15,848	MC
New Mexico State Univ	NM	14,050	C
New York Univ	NY	65,860	MC
Newman Univ	KS	35,390	C
Niagara Univ	NY	41,010	C
N Car State Univ	NC	19,515	HC+
North Central College	IL	48,712	VC
N Dak State Univ	ND	16,245	C
Northeastern Univ	MA	62,703	MC
Northern Mich Univ	MI	19,604	C
Northwest Nazarene Univ	ID	36,000	C
Northwestern College of Iowa	IA	38,400	C+
Norwich Univ	VT	28,212	C
Notre Dame de Namur Univ	CA	46,526	LC
Oakland Univ	MI	20,763	C
Oakwood Univ	AL	43,758	C
Oberlin College	OH	66,012	MC
Occidental College	CA	65,530	MC
Ohio Northern Univ	OH	44,050	VC
Ohio State Univ at Columbus	OH	21,703	HC+
Ohio Univ	OH	22,924	C
Ohio Valley Univ	WV	29,480	C
Ohio Wesleyan Univ	OH	49,460	VC
Okla Christian Univ	OK	27,650	VC
Okla City Univ	OK	40,476	VC
Okla State Univ	OK	17,180	VC
Old Dominion Univ	VA	20,910	C
Olivet College	MI	36,110	LC
Oregon State Univ	OR	22,519	VC
Otterbein Univ	OH	41,630	C
Pace Univ	NY	58,248	C
Pennsylvania State Univ - Univ Park	PA	29,760	HC
Philadelphia Univ	PA	50,370	C
Pittsburg State Univ	KS	13,880	NC
Pitzer College	CA	66,192	MC
Point Loma Nazarene Univ	CA	43,450	C
Portland State Univ	OR	19,443	C
Providence College	RI	60,760	VC
Purdue Univ/West Lafayette	IN	20,032	MC
Queens Univ of Charlotte	NC	39,543	C
Quinnipiac Univ	CT	59,110	C
Ramapo College of New Jersey	NJ	25,338	C
Reed College	OR	65,300	MC
Regis College	MA	51,920	C
Regis Univ	CO	44,520	C
Rensselaer Polytechnic Inst	NY	63,436	MC
Rhodes College	TN	51,900	HC
Rider Univ	NJ	54,050	C
Ripon College	WI	46,911	C+
Roanoke College	VA	54,114	VC
Roberts Wesleyan College	NY	38,306	C
Rochester Inst of Technology	NY	50,842	HC
Rockford Univ	IL	36,030	C
Rockhurst Univ	MO	29,220	C
Roger Williams Univ	RI	46,296	C+
Rollins College	FL	58,670	HC
Rose-Hulman Inst of Technology	IN	57,303	MC
Rosemont College	PA	30,980	C
Rowan Univ	NJ	24,491	VC+
Russell Sage College	NY	39,370	C
Rutgers Univ - Camden	NJ	26,146	C
Rutgers Univ - New Brunswick	NJ	26,632	HC
Saginaw Valley State Univ	MI	18,530	C
St. Anselm College	NH	52,560	C+
St. John's Univ	MN	51,624	C
St. Joseph's Univ	PA	57,544	VC+
St. Louis Univ	MO	49,866	HC
St. Mary's Univ of Minn	MN	41,210	VC
St. Michael's College	VT	51,725	VC+
St. Peter's Univ	NJ	49,192	C
St. Vincent College	PA	44,626	C
Samford Univ	AL	39,232	VC
San Francisco State Univ	CA	18,514	LC
San Jose State Univ	CA	21,540	C
Schreiner Univ	TX	34,626	LC
Seattle Pacific Univ	WA	47,439	C+
Seattle Univ	WA	50,811	VC+
Seton Hall Univ	NJ	55,514	C
Seton Hill Univ	PA	46,972	C
Sewanee: The Univ of the South	TN	54,500	MC
Siena College	NY	48,916	C+
Simmons College	MA	53,090	VC
Simpson College	IA	43,839	VC
Smith College	MA	63,914	MC
Sonoma State Univ	CA	27,806	C
S Dak State Univ	SD	15,634	C
Southern Conn State Univ	CT	21,924	LC
Southern Illinois Univ Edwardsville	IL	22,643	C
Southern Methodist Univ	TX	66,483	MC
Southern Nazarene Univ	OK	32,798	NC
Southwestern College	KS	31,531	C
Southwestern Univ	TX	50,720	VC
Spelman College	GA	38,751	C
Spring Arbor Univ	MI	36,000	C
Spring Hill College	AL	48,488	C
Springfield College	MA	45,995	C
St. Bonaventure Univ	NY	44,237	C
St. Catherine Univ	MN	45,630	VC
St. Edward's Univ	TX	53,100	VC
St. Lawrence Univ	NY	64,390	VC
St. Mary's College of Maryland	MD	26,634	VC
St. Mary's Univ	TX	37,500	C
SUNY / SUNY College at Old Westbury	NY	16,860	C
SUNY / SUNY Fredonia	NY	20,818	C
SUNY / SUNY Plattsburgh	NY	18,814	C
SUNY / SUNY Potsdam	NY	20,404	C+
SUNY / Univ at Buffalo	NY	23,122	C+
SUNY at Binghamton	NY	22,861	MC
SUNY at Geneseo	NY	20,440	VC+
SUNY at Oswego	NY	21,351	C
SUNY SUNY Albany	NY	22,165	C
Stetson Univ	FL	53,544	VC
Stevens Inst of Technology	NJ	62,338	MC
Stockton Univ	NJ	25,059	
Stonehill College	MA	55,030	C+
Stony Brook Univ/The SUNY	NY	21,881	MC
Suffolk Univ	MA	50,308	C
Susquehanna Univ	PA	55,340	VC
Swarthmore College	PA	63,550	MC
Syracuse Univ	NY	60,239	VC
Tabor College	KS	35,870	C
Taylor Univ	IN	40,317	C+
Temple Univ	PA	24,392	VC
Tenn Tech Univ	TN	17,050	C
Texas A&M Univ	TX	20,521	VC+
Texas Christian Univ	TX	54,670	HC
Texas Lutheran Univ	TX	38,620	C
Texas State Univ	TX	19,350	C
Texas Tech Univ	TX	18,736	C+
Texas Wesleyan Univ	TX	35,134	C
The Catholic Univ of America	DC	56,356	VC
The College at Brockport - SUNY	NY	20,346	C
The College of St. Rose	NY	43,048	C
The College of Wooster	OH	57,900	VC+
Transylvania Univ	KY	45,690	VC+
Trinity Christian College	IL	35,580	C
Trinity College	CT	63,920	HC+
Trinity Univ	TX	52,314	HC+
Trinity Washington Univ	DC	33,826	C+
Tufts Univ	MA		MC
Tulane Univ	LA	63,396	HC+
Union College	NY	64,320	MC
Univ of Arizona	AZ	23,100	C
Univ of Calif at Davis	CA	28,468	HC
Univ of Calif at Irvine	CA	26,484	VC
Univ of Calif at Los Angeles	CA	30,162	MC
Univ of Calif at Riverside	CA	29,227	C+
Univ of Calif at Santa Barbara	CA	29,091	HC
Univ of Calif San Diego	CA	30,150	MC
Univ of Calif, Santa Cruz	CA	28,731	C+
Univ of Chicago	IL	67,584	MC
Univ of Cincinnati	OH	21,964	VC
Univ of Colo Boulder	CO	24,285	VC+
Univ of Colo Colo Springs	CO	19,663	C
Univ of Dallas	TX	45,500	VC+
Univ of Dayton	OH	53,620	C
Univ of Delaware	DE	24,976	VC+
Univ of Denver	CO	58,443	VC+
Univ of Detroit Mercy	MI	48,816	C+
Univ of Evansville	IN	44,186	VC+
Univ of Georgia	GA	21,250	HC
Univ of Idaho	ID	15,348	C
Univ of Illinois at Chicago	IL	25,006	VC
Univ of Iowa	IA	18,683	VC+
Univ of Jamestown	ND	28,508	C
Univ of Kansas	KS	20,135	C+
Univ of Maine	ME	20,792	C
Univ of Maryland/Baltimore County	MD	21,296	VC
Univ of Maryland/College Park	MD	21,938	HC
Univ of Mass Amherst	MA	26,199	VC+
Univ of Mass Boston	MA	13,435	C
Univ of Mass Dartmouth	MA	25,658	C
Univ of Miami	FL	63,494	MC
Univ of Mich/Ann Arbor	MI	24,410	MC
Univ of Mich/Dearborn	MI	11,757	VC
Univ of Minn/Duluth	MN	20,292	C+
Univ of Minn/Twin Cities	MN	23,519	HC+
Univ of Missouri/Columbia	MO	18,201	MC
Univ of Missouri-St. Louis	MO		C
Univ of Montana	MT	14,105	C
Univ of Mount Union	OH	38,970	C
Univ of Nebr - Lincoln	NE	18,589	VC
Univ of Nevada/Reno	NV	18,010	C
Univ of New England	ME	48,880	C
Univ of New Hampshire	NH	28,562	VC
Univ of New Mexico	NM	15,404	C
Univ of N Car at Greensboro	NC	14,690	C
Univ of N Car at Wilmington	NC	14,590	VC
Univ of North Texas	TX	19,198	C
Univ of Northwestern - St. Paul	MN	38,160	C
Univ of Notre Dame	IN	64,043	MC
Univ of Okla	OK	18,911	VC
Univ of Oregon	OR	22,972	C
Univ of Pennsylvania	PA	63,526	MC
Univ of PR, at Mayaguez	PR	13,995	
Univ of Puget Sound	WA	56,456	VC+
Univ of Redlands	CA	60,200	VC
Univ of Richmond	VA	60,880	MC
Univ of Rochester	NY	65,032	MC
Univ of St. Joseph	CT	49,550	C
Univ of San Diego	CA	58,442	VC+
Univ of Scranton	PA	54,962	VC
Univ of Southern Indiana	IN	16,501	C
Univ of St. Thomas - Houston	TX	40,020	VC
Univ of Tampa	FL	36,944	C
Univ of Texas at Arlington	TX	18,026	LC
Univ of Texas at Austin	TX	26,102	HC
Univ of Texas at Dallas	TX	22,830	VC+
Univ of Texas at San Antonio	TX	20,157	C
Univ of the Pacific	CA	57,006	VC
Univ of the Sciences	PA	54,038	VC
Univ of Tulsa	OK	52,625	HC+
Univ of Vermont	VT	28,878	HC
Univ of Washington	WA	23,149	VC
Univ of Wisc-Eau Claire	WI	15,797	VC
Univ of Wisc-Madison	WI	20,934	MC
Univ of Wisc-Milwaukee	WI	21,496	C
Univ of Wisc-Stevens Point	WI	14,043	C
Ursinus College	PA	61,690	VC
Utah State Univ	UT	12,736	C
Utica College	NY	30,430	C
Valparaiso Univ	IN	48,370	C+
Vanderbilt Univ	TN	60,572	MC
Vanguard Univ of Southern Calif	CA	40,740	VC
Vassar College	NY	65,491	MC
Villanova Univ	PA	62,523	MC
Virginia Polytechnic Inst and State Univ	VA	21,276	HC
Viterbo Univ	WI	34,660	C
Wabash College	IN	50,650	VC
Walla Walla Univ	WA	30,417	NC
Walsh Univ	OH	39,010	C
Wartburg College	IA	47,840	C
Washburn Univ	KS	15,827	C
Washington & Jefferson College	PA	56,512	VC
Washington Adventist Univ	MD	31,440	LC
Washington and Lee Univ	VA	59,647	MC
Washington State Univ	WA	22,495	C
Washington Univ in St. Louis	MO	65,366	VC
Wayne State Univ	MI	22,016	C
Wellesley College	MA	63,916	MC
Wells College	NY	50,500	C
West Chester Univ of Pennsylvania	PA	18,456	C
West Virginia Wesleyan College	WV	36,858	C
Western Kentucky Univ	KY	16,850	C
Western Mich Univ	MI	21,054	C
Western Washington Univ	WA	18,003	C+
Westminster College	MO	32,820	C
Wheaton College	MA	61,512	VC
Whitman College	WA	59,772	MC
Whittier College	CA	57,891	C
Widener Univ	PA	56,486	C
Wilkes Univ	PA	45,622	C
William Jewell College	MO	41,210	C+
Wilmington College	OH	34,600	C
Wilson College	PA	35,620	C
Wisc Lutheran College	WI	36,290	VC

ST = STATE **$IS** = IN-STATE COSTS **SR** = SELECTOR RATING

School	ST	$IS	SR
Wittenberg Univ	OH	48,156	C+
Worcester Polytechnic Inst	MA	60,730	MC
Xavier Univ of Louisiana	LA	31,689	C+
Yale Univ	CT	64,650	MC
Youngstown State Univ	OH	17,307	C

BIOENGINEERING

School	ST	$IS	SR
Brown Univ	RI	64,566	MC
Calif Baptist Univ	CA	41,392	C
Cornell Univ	NY	64,853	MC
Dordt College	IA	37,860	C+
Endicott College	MA	44,604	VC+
Fairfield Univ	CT	59,860	VC+
Florida State Univ	FL	16,771	HC
Georgia Inst of Technology	GA	23,360	MC
Lehigh Univ	PA	61,010	MC
Louisiana State Univ and A&M College	LA	18,677	VC
Loyola Univ Chicago	IL	55,802	VC
Marquette Univ	WI	48,390	VC+
Mass Inst of Technology	MA	62,662	MC
Miami Univ	OH	27,190	HC+
Miss State Univ	MS	11,454	C+
Ohio Univ	OH	22,924	C
Okla State Univ	OK	17,180	VC
Oral Roberts Univ	OK	34,316	C
Oregon State Univ	OR	22,519	VC
Pennsylvania State Univ - Univ Park	PA	29,760	HC
Purdue Univ/West Lafayette	IN	20,032	MC
Rice Univ	TX	57,668	MC
Rochester Inst of Technology	NY	50,842	HC
St. Louis Univ	MO	49,866	HC
Stanford Univ	CA	60,409	MC
SUNY at Binghamton	NY	22,861	MC
Syracuse Univ	NY	60,239	VC
Texas A&M Univ	TX	20,521	VC+
Union College	NY	64,320	MC
Univ of Arkansas at Fayetteville	AR	19,152	C+
Univ of Calif at Berkeley	CA	28,853	MC
Univ of Calif at Davis	CA	28,468	HC
Univ of Calif at Los Angeles	CA	30,162	MC
Univ of Calif at Riverside	CA	29,227	C+
Univ of Calif San Diego	CA	30,150	MC
Univ of Cincinnati	OH	21,964	VC
Univ of Colo Boulder	CO	24,285	VC+
Univ of Colo Denver	CO	23,230	C
Univ of Delaware	DE	24,976	VC+
Univ of Denver	CO	58,443	VC+
Univ of Georgia	GA	21,250	HC
Univ of Hawaii at Manoa	HI	23,221	C
Univ of Idaho	ID	15,348	C
Univ of Illinois at Chicago	IL	25,006	VC
Univ of Illinois at Urbana-Champaign	IL	27,006	HC
Univ of Louisville	KY	19,824	C
Univ of Maine	ME	20,792	C
Univ of Maryland/College Park	MD	21,938	HC
Univ of Mass Dartmouth	MA	25,658	C
Univ of Mich/Dearborn	MI	11,757	VC
Univ of Minn/Twin Cities	MN	23,519	HC+
Univ of Nebr - Lincoln	NE	18,589	VC
Univ of New Hampshire	NH	28,562	VC
Univ of Pennsylvania	PA	63,526	MC
Univ of Pittsburgh	PA	29,568	HC+
Univ of Toledo	OH	19,336	NC
Univ of Wisc-Madison	WI	20,934	MC
Vanderbilt Univ	TN	60,572	MC
Virginia Commonwealth Univ	VA	23,049	C
Walla Walla Univ	WA	30,417	NC
Washington State Univ	WA	22,495	C
Washington Univ in St. Louis	MO	65,366	VC

BIOINFORMATICS

School	ST	$IS	SR
Baylor Univ	TX	53,760	HC
Brigham Young Univ	UT	12,748	HC
Canisius College	NY	47,537	C
CUNY/College of Technology	NY	6,669	NC
Claflin Univ	SC	33,764	LC
Gannon Univ	PA	42,032	C
Inter-American Univ of PR-Bayamon	PR	18,785	
King Univ	TN	34,660	C
Lewis Univ	IL	40,370	C
Loyola Univ Chicago	IL	55,802	VC
MCPHS Univ	MA	45,470	SP
Mich State Univ	MI	23,898	VC+
Mich Tech Univ	MI	24,739	VC+
Missouri Southern State Univ	MO	12,499	C
Niagara Univ	NY	41,010	C
Ramapo College of New Jersey	NJ	25,338	C
Rochester Inst of Technology	NY	50,842	HC
Rockhurst Univ	MO	29,220	C
Rowan Univ	NJ	24,491	VC+
St. Vincent College	PA	44,626	C
St. Bonaventure Univ	NY	44,237	C
St. Edward's Univ	TX	53,100	VC
SUNY / Univ at Buffalo	NY	23,122	C+
Stevens Inst of Technology	NJ	62,338	MC
Trinity Christian College	IL	35,580	C
Univ of Arizona	AZ	23,100	C
Univ of Arkansas at Little Rock	AR	18,211	C
Univ of Calif at Irvine	CA	26,484	VC
Univ of Calif San Diego	CA	30,150	MC
Univ of Calif, Santa Cruz	CA	28,731	C+
Univ of Denver	CO	58,443	VC+
Univ of Maryland/Baltimore County	MD	21,296	VC
Univ of Missouri-Kansas City	MO	19,563	VC
Univ of Nebr - Omaha	NE	16,120	C
Univ of Pittsburgh	PA	29,568	HC+
Univ of St. Thomas - Houston	TX	40,020	VC
Univ of the Sciences	PA	54,038	VC
Virginia Commonwealth Univ	VA	23,049	C
Walsh Univ	OH	39,010	C
Washington Univ in St. Louis	MO	65,366	VC
Wheaton College	MA	61,512	VC
Whitworth Univ	WA	51,732	VC
Worcester Polytechnic Inst	MA	60,730	MC

BIOLOGICAL SCIENCES

School	ST	$IS	SR
Arizona State Univ at the Tempe Campus	AZ	21,756	VC
Arkansas State Univ	AR	16,190	C
Brown Univ	RI	64,566	MC
Bryant Univ	RI	55,646	VC
Cabrini Univ	PA	42,591	LC
Huntington Univ	IN	33,996	C
Lewis Univ	IL	40,370	C
Miami Univ	OH	27,190	HC+
Mich State Univ	MI	23,898	VC+
North Greenville Univ	SC	25,930	C+
Nova Southeastern Univ	FL	38,534	C+
Ohio Wesleyan Univ	OH	49,460	VC
Pennsylvania State Univ - Univ Park	PA	29,760	HC
Southern Vermont College	VT	34,670	LC
The Master's Univ	CA	43,870	C+
Univ of Calif San Diego	CA	30,150	MC
Univ of Louisiana at Monroe	LA	15,970	C
Univ of Maine at Machias	ME	22,960	C
Univ of Maryland/Baltimore County	MD	21,296	VC
Univ of New Hampshire - Manchester	NH	14,490	C
Univ of Notre Dame	IN	64,043	MC
Univ of Rhode Island	RI	24,906	C
Wellesley College	MA	63,916	MC
West Virginia Wesleyan College	WV	36,858	C

BIOLOGY

School	ST	$IS	SR
Angelo State Univ	TX	15,263	NC
Arkansas Tech Univ	AR	15,484	C
Aurora Univ	IL	33,970	C
Averett Univ	VA	40,970	LC
Azusa Pacific Univ	CA	43,972	C
Black Hills State Univ	SD	15,899	C
Bloomfield College	NJ	39,100	LC
Bowling Green State Univ	OH	19,747	C
Brown Univ	RI	64,566	MC
Bryant Univ	RI	55,646	VC
Cabrini Univ	PA	42,591	LC
Calvin College	MI	41,570	VC+
CUNY/Queens College	NY	27,896	C
Clayton State Univ	GA	19,735	C
Colgate Univ	NY	65,030	MC
College of William & Mary	VA		MC
Creighton Univ	NE	48,206	VC+
Dallas Baptist Univ	TX	33,713	C
Davis & Elkins College	WV	38,242	LC
East Stroudsburg Univ	PA	18,334	C
East Texas Baptist Univ	TX	33,134	C
Edgewood College	WI	35,950	C
Elon Univ	NC	44,599	VC+
Ferris State Univ	MI	21,445	C
Franklin College	IN	39,380	C
Georgian Court Univ	NJ	42,426	LC
Huntington Univ	IN	33,996	C
Indiana Univ Bloomington	IN	20,429	VC
Indiana Univ East	IN	7,072	C
Indiana Univ Kokomo	IN	7,073	C
Indiana Univ Northwest	IN	7,072	C
Indiana Univ Southeast	IN	14,242	LC
Indiana Univ-Purdue Univ Indianapolis	IN	18,635	C
Iowa Wesleyan Univ	IA	39,200	C
Lebanon Valley College	PA	51,530	C
Lewis Univ	IL	40,370	C
Loras College	IA	39,222	C
MidAmerica Nazarene Univ	KS	35,550	C
Millersville Univ of Pennsylvania	PA	23,782	C
Montreat College	NC	31,298	LC
Mount Vernon Nazarene Univ	OH	34,500	C
New York Inst of Technology	NY	48,730	C
Niagara Univ	NY	41,010	C
Northwest Missouri State Univ	MO	17,737	C
Nova Southeastern Univ	FL	38,534	C+
Nyack College	NY	34,050	NC
Oberlin College	OH	66,012	MC
Ohio Valley Univ	WV	29,480	C
Ohio Wesleyan Univ	OH	49,460	VC
Okla Christian Univ	OK	27,650	VC
Okla City Univ	OK	40,476	VC
Otterbein Univ	OH	41,630	C
Providence College	RI	60,760	VC
Regis Univ	CO	44,520	C
Roberts Wesleyan College	NY	38,306	C
Rochester Inst of Technology	NY	50,842	HC
Rocky Mountain College	MT	34,270	C
St. Louis Univ	MO	49,866	HC
Seton Hill Univ	PA	46,972	C
Silver Lake College of the Holy Family	WI	36,290	LC
Southeast Missouri State Univ	MO	15,498	C
Southern Oregon Univ	OR	19,117	C
St. Ambrose Univ	IA	39,019	C
Syracuse Univ	NY	60,239	VC
Taylor Univ	IN	40,317	C+
Texas Tech Univ	TX	18,736	C+
Texas Wesleyan Univ	TX	35,134	C
The Master's Univ	CA	43,870	C+
Thomas Edison State Univ	NJ	6,350	NC
Tougaloo College	MS	17,980	NC
Trevecca Nazarene Univ	TN	31,186	C
Tufts Univ	MA		MC
Univ of Chicago	IL	67,584	MC
Univ of Denver	CO	58,443	VC+
Univ of Georgia	GA	21,250	HC
Univ of Maine at Machias	ME	22,960	C
Univ of Maryland/Baltimore County	MD	21,296	VC
Univ of Miami	FL	63,494	MC
Univ of Mich/Dearborn	MI	11,757	VC
Univ of Minn/Twin Cities	MN	23,519	HC+
Univ of Rhode Island	RI	24,906	C
Univ of St. Mary	KS	34,690	C
Univ of Tulsa	OK	52,625	HC+
Univ of Wisc-Superior	WI	14,446	C
Univ of Wyoming	WY	15,375	C+
Warren Wilson College	NC	44,220	VC
Washington State Univ	WA	22,495	C
Wayne State Univ	MI	22,016	C
Wellesley College	MA	63,916	MC
West Virginia Univ	WV	18,210	C
Western Illinois Univ	IL	20,825	C
Western Kentucky Univ	KY	16,850	C
Wheaton College	MA	61,512	VC
Whitman College	WA	59,772	MC
Wilson College	PA	35,620	C
Wingate Univ	NC	39,950	C

BIOLOGY (PRE-PHYSICIAN ASSISTANT)

School	ST	$IS	SR
Arizona State Univ at the West Campus	AZ	20,640	C
Bryant Univ	RI	55,646	VC
Cabrini Univ	PA	42,591	LC
East Central Univ	OK	13,056	C
Lewis Univ	IL	40,370	C
Murray State Univ	KY	16,998	C
Thomas Univ	GA	21,420	LC
Univ of St. Francis	IN	37,400	C
Wingate Univ	NC	39,950	C

BIOLOGY AND SOCIETY

School	ST	$IS	SR
Brown Univ	RI	64,566	MC
Cornell Univ	NY	64,853	MC
Univ of Minn/Twin Cities	MN	23,519	HC+

BIOLOGY ECOLOGY AND FIELD BIOLOGY

School	ST	$IS	SR
Beloit College	WI	55,206	HC
Brown Univ	RI	64,566	MC
Bryant Univ	RI	55,646	VC
College of the Ozarks	MO	7,230	C
Colo College	CO	62,560	MC
Franklin College	IN	39,380	C
Iowa Wesleyan Univ	IA	39,200	C
Northland College	WI	41,103	C+
Purdue Univ/Northwest	IN	15,038	C
St. Leo Univ	FL	31,650	C
Univ of Maine at Machias	ME	22,960	C
Univ of Maryland/Baltimore County	MD	21,296	VC
West Chester Univ of Pennsylvania	PA	18,456	C

BIOLOGY/ GEN SCIENCE SECONDARY EDUCATION

School	ST	$IS	SR
Abilene Christian Univ	TX	41,800	C+
Averett Univ	VA	40,970	LC
Ferris State Univ	MI	21,445	C
Grove City College	PA	25,692	VC
Gwynedd Mercy Univ	PA	43,780	LC
King Univ	TN	34,660	C
Lewis Univ	IL	40,370	C
Neumann Univ	PA	40,678	LC
St. Ambrose Univ	IA	39,019	C
St. Edward's Univ	TX	53,100	VC
Syracuse Univ	NY	60,239	VC
The Univ of Utah	UT	17,924	VC
West Chester Univ of Pennsylvania	PA	18,456	C
Western Mich Univ	MI	21,054	C
Wilson College	PA	35,620	C
Wingate Univ	NC	39,950	C

BIOLOGY/ADOLESCENCE EDUCATION

School	ST	$IS	SR
Arkansas State Univ	AR	16,190	C
Augustana College	IL	49,658	VC
Bethany College	WV	36,300	NC
Biola Univ	CA	46,402	C+
Black Hills State Univ	SD	15,899	C
Cabrini Univ	PA	42,591	LC
College of the Ozarks	MO	7,230	C
Duquesne Univ	PA	46,822	VC
Edgewood College	WI	35,950	C
Elizabethtown College	PA	54,050	C
Faulkner Univ	AL	26,410	C
Gannon Univ	PA	42,032	C
Hope College	MI	39,940	VC
Houghton College	NY	39,090	C
Huntingdon College	AL	34,900	C
Indiana Univ Bloomington	IN	20,429	VC
Indiana Univ Northwest	IN	7,072	C
Indiana Univ South Bend	IN	14,242	C
King Univ	TN	34,660	C
Lipscomb Univ	TN	41,296	VC
LIU Post	NY	49,682	C
Marist College	NY	49,860	VC
Messiah College	PA	43,100	C+
Millikin Univ	IL	42,158	C
Missouri Southern State Univ	MO	12,499	C
Murray State Univ	KY	16,998	C
Nazareth College	NY	45,574	C
Niagara Univ	NY	41,010	C
Northern Kentucky Univ	KY	16,486	C
Old Dominion Univ	VA	20,910	C
Pace Univ	NY	58,248	C
Roberts Wesleyan College	NY	38,306	C
Seattle Univ	WA	50,811	VC+
St. John's Univ	NY	55,850	C
SUNY / SUNY Fredonia	NY	20,818	C
SUNY / SUNY Plattsburgh	NY	18,814	C
SUNY at Oswego	NY	21,351	C
Temple Univ	PA	24,392	VC
Texas Wesleyan Univ	TX	35,134	C
The College of St. Rose	NY	43,048	C
Univ of Mary Hardin-Baylor	TX	33,950	C+

BIOLOGY/BIOLOGICAL SCIENCE

School	ST	$IS	SR
Abilene Christian Univ	TX	41,800	C+
Adams State Univ	CO	17,703	LC
Adelphi Univ	NY	48,244	C
Adrian College	MI	42,400	C
Agnes Scott College	GA	51,930	VC+
Alabama A&M Univ	AL	18,796	C
Alabama State Univ	AL	14,142	NC
Albany State Univ	GA	19,462	C
Albertus Magnus College	CT	43,258	LC
Albion College	MI	52,650	C
Albright College	PA	46,660	C
Alcorn State Univ	MS	15,854	C
Alderson Broaddus Univ	WV	26,149	C
Alfred Univ	NY	42,296	C+
Alice Lloyd College	KY	8,190	C
Allegheny College	PA	55,420	VC
Allen Univ	SC	19,300	NC
Alma College	MI	47,548	C
Alvernia Univ	PA	43,900	C
Alverno College	WI	33,294	LC
American International College	MA	46,300	LC
American Univ	DC	59,379	HC+
Amherst College	MA		HC+
Anderson Univ	IN	38,200	C
Andrews Univ	MI	28,030	C+
Angelo State Univ	TX	15,263	NC
Appalachian State Univ	NC	14,416	VC
Aquinas College - Mich	MI	38,876	HC
Arcadia Univ	PA	33,570	C+
Arkansas Tech Univ	AR	15,484	C
Armstrong State Univ	GA	16,962	C
Asbury Univ	KY	35,180	C+
Ashford Univ	CA	10,480	C
Ashland Univ	OH	21,440	C
Assumption College	MA	47,920	C+
Atlantic Union College	MA	27,228	C
Auburn Univ	AL	23,594	VC+
Auburn Univ at Montgomery	AL	15,290	C
Augsburg College	MN	43,929	C
Augusta Univ	GA	4,632	C
Augustana College	IL	49,658	VC
Augustana Univ	SD	38,424	VC
Aurora Univ	IL	33,970	C
Austin College	TX	45,875	VC
Austin Peay State Univ	TN	16,397	C
Averett Univ	VA	40,970	LC
Avila Univ	MO	35,480	C
Azusa Pacific Univ	CA	43,972	C
Baker Univ	KS	33,350	C+
Baldwin Wallace Univ	OH	41,106	C
Ball State Univ	IN	19,590	C
Bard College	NY	64,024	HC
Bard College at Simon's Rock	MA	65,795	MC
Barnard College/Columbia Univ	NY	62,741	MC
Barry Univ	FL	37,830	C
Barton College	NC	38,686	LC
Bates College	ME	64,500	MC
Bay Path Univ	MA	45,349	C
Bayamon Central Univ	PR	12,490	

ST = STATE $IS = IN-STATE COSTS SR = SELECTOR RATING

School	ST	$IS	SR
Baylor Univ	TX	53,760	HC
Becker College	MA	57,628	C
Belhaven Univ	MS	31,016	C
Bellarmine Univ	KY	51,220	C
Belmont Abbey College	NC	48,156	C
Belmont Univ	TN	40,970	VC
Beloit College	WI	55,206	HC
Bemidji State Univ	MN	16,056	VC
Benedict College	SC	28,238	NC
Benedictine College	KS	36,200	VC
Benedictine Univ	IL	38,300	C
Bennett College	NC	27,302	NC
Bennington College	VT	63,960	MC
Berea College	KY	7,042	C
Berry College	GA	45,286	C+
Bethany College	KS	46,100	NC
Bethany College	WV	36,300	NC
Bethel College	IN	35,860	C
Bethel College	KS	35,370	C
Bethel Univ	MN	45,270	VC
Bethel Univ	TN	24,738	C
Bethune-Cookman Univ	FL	22,970	C
Biola Univ	CA	46,402	C+
Birmingham-Southern College	AL	44,478	VC
Black Hills State Univ	SD	15,899	C
Blackburn College	IL	28,526	LC
Bloomfield College	NJ	39,100	LC
Bloomsburg Univ of Pennsylvania	PA	19,066	LC
Blue Mountain College	MS	15,949	VC
Bluefield College	VA	34,120	C+
Bluefield State College	WV	5,832	LC
Bluffton Univ	OH	40,950	C
Boise State Univ	ID	14,860	C
Boston College	MA	65,737	MC
Boston Univ	MA	65,110	MC
Bowdoin College	ME	63,500	MC
Bowie State Univ	MD	26,728	LC
Brandeis Univ	MA	65,925	MC
Brenau Univ - Women's College	GA	37,876	LC
Brescia Univ	KY	29,890	VC+
Brewton-Parker College	GA	23,490	C
Briar Cliff Univ	IA	36,956	C
Bridgewater College	VA	44,510	C
Bridgewater State Univ	MA	21,810	C
Brigham Young Univ	UT	12,748	HC
Brigham Young Univ/Hawaii	HI	11,290	C
Brown Univ	RI	64,566	MC
Bryan College	TN	31,440	C
Bryant Univ	RI	55,646	VC
Bryn Athyn College	PA	31,470	C
Bryn Mawr College	PA	59,890	MC
Bucknell Univ	PA	64,616	MC
Buena Vista Univ	IA	41,514	C
Butler Univ	IN	51,352	VC
Cabrini Univ	PA	42,591	LC
Caldwell Univ	NJ	42,165	NC
Calif Baptist Univ	CA	41,392	C
Calif Inst of Technology	CA	58,761	MC
Calif Lutheran Univ	CA	52,853	C
Calif Polytechnic State Univ	CA	17,979	HC+
Calif State Polytechnic Univ, Pomona	CA	21,541	C
Cal State, Bakersfield	CA	19,191	LC
Cal State, Chico	CA	21,440	C
Cal State, Dominguez Hills	CA	19,022	LC
Cal State, East Bay	CA	19,413	C
Cal State, Fresno	CA	16,902	LC
Cal State, Fullerton	CA	21,902	C
Cal State, Long Beach	CA	18,850	C
Cal State, Los Angeles	CA	17,186	LC
Cal State, Monterey Bay	CA	26,871	LC
Cal State, Northridge	CA	16,859	LC
Cal State, Sacramento	CA	20,332	C
Cal State, San Bernardino	CA	12,000	C
Cal State, San Marcos	CA	24,184	LC
Cal State, Stanislaus	CA	16,212	C
Calif Univ of Pennsylvania	PA	14,217	LC
Calvin College	MI	41,570	VC+
Cameron Univ	OK	11,072	NC
Campbellsville Univ	KY	32,492	C
Canisius College	NY	47,537	C
Capital Univ	OH	42,982	C
Cardinal Stritch Univ	WI	36,462	C
Caribbean Univ	PR	15,471	
Carleton College	MN	64,071	MC
Carlow Univ	PA	38,549	LC
Carnegie Mellon Univ	PA	67,980	MC
Carroll College	MT	39,972	C+
Carroll Univ	WI	38,100	C+
Carson-Newman Univ	TN	34,160	C
Carthage College	WI	48,835	C
Case Western Reserve Univ	OH	60,304	MC
Castleton Univ	VT	20,186	C
Catawba College	NC	39,820	C
Cedar Crest College	PA	46,715	C
Cedarville Univ	OH	34,990	VC
Centenary College	NJ	43,602	C
Centenary College of Louisiana	LA	45,650	C+
Central College	IA	44,592	C
Central Conn State Univ	CT	21,203	C
Central Methodist Univ	MO	36,830	VC
Central Mich Univ	MI	20,330	C
Central State Univ	OH	18,564	C
Central Washington Univ	WA	16,803	C
Centre College	KY	49,250	HC
Chadron State College	NE	14,819	NC
Chaminade Univ of Honolulu	HI	36,000	C
Chapman Univ	CA	63,078	VC+
Charleston Southern Univ	SC	32,400	C
Chatham Univ	PA	46,517	C
Chestnut Hill College	PA	43,410	C
Cheyney Univ of Pennsylvania	PA	20,896	LC
Chicago State Univ	IL	20,144	C
Christian Brothers Univ	TN	31,670	VC
Christopher Newport Univ	VA	23,968	VC+
CUNY/Brooklyn College	NY	5,884	C+
CUNY/City College	NY	20,319	VC
CUNY/College of Staten Island	NY	17,840	NC
CUNY/Hunter College	NY	31,098	VC
CUNY/Lehman College	NY	5,778	HC+
CUNY/Meger Evers College	NY	6,680	NC
CUNY/York College	NY	6,747	LC
Claflin Univ	SC	33,764	LC
Claremont McKenna College	CA	67,185	MC
Clarion Univ of Pennsylvania	PA	21,608	LC
Clark Atlanta Univ	GA	31,019	LC
Clark Univ	MA	51,600	HC+
Clarke Univ	IA	38,940	C
Clarkson Univ	NY	60,392	HC
Clemson Univ	SC		HC
Cleveland State Univ	OH	22,196	C
Coastal Carolina Univ	SC	19,766	C
Coe College	IA	51,570	VC
Coker College	SC	34,810	LC
Colby College	ME	64,060	MC
Colby-Sawyer College	NH	50,790	C
Colgate Univ	NY	65,030	MC
College of Charleston	SC	22,699	C
College of Mount St. Vincent	NY	45,620	C
College of St. Benedict	MN	52,806	C
College of St. Elizabeth	NJ	44,432	LC
College of St. Mary	NE	35,184	C
College of St. Scholastica	MN	44,640	C
College of the Holy Cross	MA	62,165	MC
College of the Ozarks	MO	7,230	C
Colo Christian Univ	CO	39,940	VC
Colo Mesa Univ	CO	18,955	LC
Colo State Univ	CO	22,162	VC
Colo State Univ-Pueblo	CO	18,234	C
Columbia College	SC	36,550	C
Columbia College - Missouri	MO	27,803	C
Columbia Univ/ School of General Studies	NY	61,470	MC
Columbia Univ/City of New York	NY	62,958	MC
Columbus State Univ	GA	14,336	LC
Concord Univ	WV	14,954	C
Concordia College - Moorhead	MN	51,088	C+
Concordia College - New York	NY	39,035	LC
Concordia Univ	CA	41,580	VC
Concordia Univ	OR	35,000	C
Concordia Univ Nebr	NE	36,280	VC
Concordia Univ St. Paul	MN	29,050	C
Concordia Univ Wisc	WI	35,910	C
Concordia Univ, Ann Arbor	MI	35,945	VC
Concordia Univ, Chicago	IL	39,694	C
Conn College	CT	65,000	MC
Converse College	SC	26,495	C
Coppin State Univ	MD	17,041	VC
Cornell College	IA	48,800	VC
Cornell Univ	NY	64,853	MC
Covenant College	GA	38,990	VC
Culver-Stockton College	MO	33,525	C
Cumberland Univ	TN	27,710	C
Curry College	MA	51,815	C
Daemen College	NY	38,045	C
Dakota State Univ	SD	13,811	C
Dakota Wesleyan Univ	SD	32,850	C
Dallas Baptist Univ	TX	33,713	C
Dartmouth College	NH	66,174	MC
Davidson College	NC	60,119	MC
Defiance College	OH	41,630	C
Delaware State Univ	DE	19,376	NC
Delaware Valley Univ	PA	49,796	C
Delta State Univ	MS	13,176	C
Denison Univ	OH	58,860	MC
DePaul Univ	IL	47,623	VC
DePauw Univ	IN	58,688	HC+
DeSales Univ	PA	43,970	C
Dickinson College	PA	63,974	MC
Dickinson State Univ	ND	12,372	LC
Dillard Univ	LA	20,940	VC
Doane Univ	NE	39,184	VC
Dominican College	NY	31,270	LC
Dominican Univ	IL	41,222	C
Dominican Univ of Calif	CA	57,050	C
Dordt College	IA	37,860	C+
Drake Univ	IA	45,056	HC
Drew Univ/College of Liberal Arts	NJ	61,048	VC
Drexel Univ	PA	65,432	VC+
Drury Univ	MO	33,791	VC
Duke Univ	NC	64,188	
Duquesne Univ	PA	46,822	VC
D'Youville College	NY	36,780	C
Earlham College	IN	54,870	HC
East Carolina Univ	NC	16,937	C
East Central Univ	OK	13,056	C
East Tenn State Univ	TN	13,994	C
East Texas Baptist Univ	TX	33,134	C
Eastern Conn State Univ	CT	23,059	C
Eastern Illinois Univ	IL	21,126	C
Eastern Kentucky Univ	KY	16,908	C
Eastern Mennonite Univ	VA	42,550	C
Eastern Mich Univ	MI	19,761	C
Eastern Nazarene College	MA	39,955	C
Eastern New Mexico Univ	NM	14,416	C
Eastern Oregon Univ	OR	17,715	C
Eastern Univ	PA	39,540	C
Eastern Washington Univ	WA	25,572	LC
Eckerd College	FL	52,874	C
Edinboro Univ	PA	15,940	LC
Edward Waters College	FL	20,607	NC
Elizabeth City State Univ	NC	14,745	C
Elizabethtown College	PA	54,050	C
Elmhurst College	IL	45,428	C
Elmira College	NY	53,900	C
Elms College	MA	45,646	VC
Emmanuel College	MA	52,110	C+
Emory and Henry College	VA	41,410	C
Emory Univ	GA	60,786	MC
Emporia State Univ	KS	14,570	C
Erskine College	SC	45,460	C
Eureka College	IL	30,220	C
Evangel Univ	MO	28,898	C
Excelsior College	NY	14,080	SP
Fairfield Univ	CT	59,860	VC+
Fairleigh Dickinson Univ/ College at Florham	NJ	52,062	C
Fairleigh Dickinson Univ/ Metropolitan Campus	NJ	40,254	C
Fairmont State Univ	WV	15,726	C
Farmingdale State College	NY	20,624	C
Faulkner Univ	AL	26,410	C
Fayetteville State Univ	NC	17,756	C
Felician Univ	NJ	45,370	LC
Ferris State Univ	MI	21,445	C
Ferrum College	VA	39,650	C
Fisk Univ	TN	32,066	LC
Fitchburg State Univ	MA	21,819	C
Florida A&M Univ	FL	15,361	C
Florida Atlantic Univ	FL	17,339	C
Florida Gulf Coast Univ	FL	9,682	C
Florida Inst of Technology	FL	53,306	VC
Florida International Univ	FL	19,854	C+
Florida Memorial Univ	FL	22,270	LC
Florida State Univ	FL	16,771	HC
Fontbonne Univ	MO	33,717	C
Fordham Univ	NY	65,918	MC
Fort Hays State Univ	KS	12,131	C
Fort Lewis College	CO	18,980	C
Fort Valley State Univ	GA	17,988	VC
Framingham State Univ	MA	20,584	C
Francis Marion Univ	SC	16,464	LC
Franciscan Univ of Steubenville	OH	33,980	VC
Franklin and Marshall College	PA	63,170	HC
Franklin College	IN	39,380	C
Franklin Pierce Univ	NH	46,750	C
Freed-Hardeman Univ	TN	29,450	C
Fresno Pacific Univ	CA	37,370	C
Friends Univ	KS	34,455	C
Frostburg State Univ	MD	17,280	LC
Furman Univ	SC	58,092	VC+
Gallaudet Univ	DC	29,118	LC
Gannon Univ	PA	42,032	C
Gardner-Webb Univ	NC	39,200	C+
Geneva College	PA	35,450	C
George Fox Univ	OR	42,938	C
George Mason Univ	VA	15,724	VC
George Washington Univ	DC	62,835	MC
Georgetown College	KY	41,440	C
Georgetown Univ	DC	65,926	MC
Georgia College & State Univ	GA	21,148	C+
Georgia Inst of Technology	GA	23,360	MC
Georgia Southern Univ	GA	16,596	C
Georgia Southwestern State Univ	GA	13,870	C
Georgia State Univ	GA	24,332	VC
Gettysburg College	PA	63,000	HC
Glenville State College	WV	17,386	NC
Gonzaga Univ	WA	50,888	HC
Gordon College	MA	46,472	C+
Goshen College	IN	42,500	C
Goucher College	MD	55,716	VC
Grace College and Seminary	IN	31,524	C
Graceland Univ	IA	35,290	C
Grambling State Univ	LA	15,701	C
Grand Canyon Univ	AZ	16,950	VC
Grand Rapids Theological Seminary/Cornerstone Univ	MI	33,338	C
Grand Valley State Univ	MI	22,250	C+
Grand View Univ	IA	32,302	C
Green Mountain College	VT	45,228	LC
Greensboro College	NC	42,400	LC
Greenville College	IL	27,012	C
Grinnell College	IA	60,738	MC
Grove City College	PA	25,692	VC
Guilford College	NC	44,090	C
Gustavus Adolphus College	MN	52,433	HC
Gwynedd Mercy Univ	PA	43,780	LC
Hamilton College	NY	64,250	MC
Hamline Univ	MN	45,678	VC
Hampden-Sydney College	VA	56,248	C+
Hampshire College	MA	63,824	MC
Hampton Univ	VA	34,926	LC
Hannibal-LaGrange Univ	MO	29,815	C
Hanover College	IN	46,364	C+
Harding Univ	AR	25,421	C
Hardin-Simmons Univ	TX	33,966	C
Harris-Stowe State Univ	MO	14,360	NC
Hartwick College	NY	51,270	C
Harvard College/Harvard Univ	MA	60,659	MC
Harvey Mudd College	CA	67,155	MC
Hastings College	NE	35,380	C+
Haverford College	PA	66,490	MC
Hawaii Pacific Univ	HI	33,420	C
Heidelberg Univ	OH	39,200	C
Henderson State Univ	AR	15,516	LC
Hendrix College	AR	54,020	VC+
High Point Univ	NC	45,977	C
Hillsdale College	MI	35,722	MC
Hiram College	OH	43,230	C
Hofstra Univ	NY	55,960	C+
Hollins Univ	VA	49,635	VC
Holy Family Univ	PA	43,326	LC
Holy Names Univ	CA	46,630	LC
Hood College	MD	54,840	C
Hope College	MI	39,940	VC
Houghton College	NY	39,090	C
Houston Baptist Univ	TX	36,450	C
Howard Payne Univ	TX	34,320	C
Howard Univ	DC	37,616	C+
Humboldt State Univ	CA	20,514	C
Huntingdon College	AL	34,900	C
Huntington Univ	IN	33,996	C
Husson Univ	ME	25,720	LC
Huston-Tillotson Univ	TX	18,124	LC
Idaho State Univ	ID	13,619	NC
Illinois College	IL	40,850	VC
Illinois Inst of Technology	IL	56,826	HC+
Illinois State Univ	IL	23,418	VC
Illinois Wesleyan Univ	IL	56,430	VC+
Indiana State Univ	IN	23,223	LC
Indiana Univ Kokomo	IN	7,073	C
Indiana Univ of Pennsylvania	PA	23,614	LC
Indiana Univ South Bend	IN	14,242	C
Indiana Univ-Purdue Univ Fort Wayne	IN	17,553	C
Indiana Wesleyan Univ	IN	33,674	C
Inter-American Univ of PR Ponce	PR	19,549	
Inter-American Univ of PR- Aguadilla Campus	PR	21,657	
Inter-American Univ of PR- Arecibo Campus	PR	18,245	
Inter-American Univ of PR- Bayamon	PR	18,785	
Inter-American Univ of PR- Fajardo Campus	PR	18,336	
Inter-American Univ of PR- Metropolitan Campus	PR	20,045	
Inter-American Univ of PR-San Germán	PR	20,042	
Iona College	NY	50,984	C
Iowa State Univ	IA	17,570	C
Iowa Wesleyan Univ	IA	39,200	C
Ithaca College	NY	56,766	VC
Jackson State Univ	MS	15,879	LC
Jacksonville State Univ	AL	14,628	LC
Jacksonville Univ	FL	46,230	C
James Madison Univ	VA	19,084	VC
Jarvis Christian College	TX	20,160	NC
John Brown Univ	AR	33,132	VC
John Carroll Univ	OH	49,740	C+
Johns Hopkins Univ	MD	65,386	MC
Johnson C. Smith Univ	NC	25,336	LC
Johnson State College	VT	20,752	C
Judson College	AL	27,066	C
Judson Univ	IL	37,700	C
Juniata College	PA	53,760	VC
Kalamazoo College	MI	53,931	HC+
Kansas State Univ	KS	17,780	VC
Kansas Wesleyan Univ	KS	36,600	C
Kean Univ	NJ	24,650	C
Keene State College	NH	24,003	LC
Kennesaw State Univ	GA	19,592	VC
Kent State Univ	OH	20,732	C
Kentucky State Univ	KY	13,364	LC
Kentucky Wesleyan College	KY	32,080	C
Kenyon College	OH	63,330	MC
Keuka College	NY	39,762	C
Keystone College	PA	28,680	LC
King Univ	TN	34,660	C
King's College	PA	46,858	C
Knox College	IL	52,615	VC+
Kutztown Univ of Pennsylvania	PA	19,056	LC
La Roche College	PA	37,924	LC
La Salle Univ	PA	55,790	C
La Sierra Univ	CA	39,690	VC
Lafayette College	PA	63,355	MC
LaGrange College	GA	39,930	C
Lake Erie College	OH	38,914	LC
Lake Forest College	IL	50,652	VC
Lakeland Univ	WI	35,130	C
Lamar Univ	TX	18,014	LC
Lander Univ	SC	43,994	C
Lane College	TN	16,550	C
Langston Univ	OK	14,314	C
Lawrence Univ	WI	54,498	HC
Le Moyne College	NY	46,000	C
Lebanon Valley College	PA	51,530	C
Lee Univ	TN	22,045	C
Lees-McRae College	NC	33,944	C

ST = STATE $IS = IN-STATE COSTS SR = SELECTOR RATING

School	ST	$IS	SR
Lehigh Univ	PA	61,010	MC
LeMoyne-Owen College	TN	16,980	C
Lenoir-Rhyne Univ	NC	43,200	C
LeTourneau Univ	TX	38,250	VC
Lewis & Clark College	OR	58,434	HC+
Lewis Univ	IL	40,370	C
Lewis-Clark State College	ID	14,202	C
Liberty Univ	VA	19,101	C
Limestone College	SC	32,100	C
Lincoln Memorial Univ	TN	28,070	C
Lincoln Univ	MO	13,602	NC
Lindenwood Univ	MO	25,132	C
Lindsey Wilson College	KY	32,882	C
Linfield College	OR	52,010	C
Lipscomb Univ	TN	41,296	VC
LIU Brooklyn	NY	49,682	C
LIU Post	NY	49,682	C
Livingstone College	NC	17,815	LC
Lock Haven Univ of Pennsylvania	PA	18,028	LC
Longwood Univ	VA	22,184	C
Louisiana College	LA	21,886	C
Louisiana State Univ and A&M College	LA	18,677	VC
Louisiana State Univ in Shreveport	LA	6,902	C
Louisiana Tech Univ	LA	11,422	VC
Lourdes Univ	OH	29,520	NC
Loyola Marymount Univ	CA	58,038	HC
Loyola Univ Chicago	IL	55,802	VC
Loyola Univ Maryland	MD	60,300	VC
Loyola Univ New Orleans	LA	51,708	VC+
Lubbock Christian Univ	TX	28,426	C
Luther College	IA	48,540	C+
Lycoming College	PA	48,580	C
Lynchburg College	VA	46,740	C
Lynn Univ	FL	49,480	LC
Lyon College	AR	34,730	C+
Macalester College	MN	61,905	MC
MacMurray College	IL	33,620	C
Madonna Univ	MI	29,050	C
Malone Univ	OH	38,448	C
Manchester Univ	IN	40,422	C
Manhattan College	NY	51,750	C+
Manhattanville College	NY	51,440	C+
Mansfield Univ	PA	23,376	LC
Marian Univ	IN	41,220	C
Marian Univ	WI	32,420	LC
Marietta College	OH	46,190	C
Marist College	NY	49,860	VC
Marquette Univ	WI	48,390	VC+
Mars Hill Univ	NC	42,688	C
Marshall Univ	WV	17,242	C
Martin Univ	IN	20,264	LC
Mary Baldwin Univ	VA	39,865	C
Marygrove College	MI	28,926	NC
Marymount Manhattan College	NY	46,280	VC
Marymount Univ	VA	41,570	LC
Maryville College	TN	44,410	C
Maryville Univ of St. Louis	MO	38,046	VC+
Marywood Univ	PA	46,900	C
Mass College of Liberal Arts	MA	20,128	C
Mass Inst of Technology	MA	62,662	MC
Mayville State Univ	ND	18,371	NC
McDaniel College	MD	51,380	VC
McKendree Univ	IL	37,940	C+
McMurry Univ	TX	34,259	LC
McNeese State Univ	LA	7,838	C
McPherson College	KS	34,909	C
Medaille College	NY	35,112	C
Mercer Univ	GA	45,348	VC
Mercy College	NY	31,776	C
Mercyhurst Univ	PA	47,420	C
Meredith College	NC	45,297	C
Merrimack College	MA	52,770	C
Messiah College	PA	43,100	C+
Methodist Univ	NC	43,600	C
Metropolitan State Univ	MN	7,566	C
Metropolitan State Univ of Denver	CO	29,889	LC
Mich State Univ	MI	23,898	VC+
Mich Tech Univ	MI	24,739	VC+
Middle Tenn State Univ	TN	8,650	C
Middlebury College	VT	64,332	MC
Midland Univ	NE	37,468	
Midway Univ	KY	31,640	LC
Midwestern State Univ	TX	17,572	C
Miles College	AL	18,646	NC
Millersville Univ of Pennsylvania	PA	23,782	C
Milligan College	TN	38,150	C
Millikin Univ	IL	42,158	C
Mills College	CA	59,163	VC
Millsaps College	MS	50,080	C+
Minn State Univ, Mankato	MN	15,616	C
Minn State Univ, Moorhead	MN	15,941	C
Minot State Univ	ND	12,732	C
Misericordia Univ	PA	43,840	C
Miss College	MS	25,850	C
Miss State Univ	MS	11,454	C+
Miss Univ for Women	MS	17,065	C
Miss Valley State Univ	MS	13,233	LC
Missouri Baptist Univ	MO	35,594	C
Missouri State Univ	MO	15,190	C+
Missouri Univ of Science and Technology	MO	18,655	HC
Missouri Valley College	MO	28,150	C
Missouri Western State Univ	MO	16,741	
Molloy College	NY	40,440	C
Monmouth College	IL	42,260	C
Monmouth Univ	NJ	46,234	C
Montana State Univ	MT	15,500	C+
Montana State Univ-Billings	MT	22,960	C
Montana State Univ-Northern	MT	11,370	NC
Montana Tech of the Univ of Montana	MT	15,447	C+
Montclair State Univ	NJ	26,210	LC
Moravian College	PA	53,117	
Morehead State Univ	KY	17,422	C
Morehouse College	GA	40,064	C
Morgan State Univ	MD	17,190	LC
Morningside College	IA	36,865	C
Morris College	SC	18,500	LC
Mount Aloysius College	PA	29,976	C
Mount Holyoke College	MA	56,746	MC
Mount Marty College	SD	32,972	C
Mount Mary Univ	WI	34,650	LC
Mount Mercy Univ	IA	36,826	C
Mount St. Mary College	NY	42,061	C
Mount St. Joseph Univ	OH	33,880	C
Mount St. Mary's Univ	MD	51,610	C
Mount St. Mary's Univ - Chalon Campus	CA	43,897	VC+
Muhlenberg College	PA	56,645	VC+
Murray State Univ	KY	16,998	C
Muskingum Univ	OH	35,966	C
National Louis Univ	IL	16,920	LC
Nazareth College	NY	45,574	C
Nebr Wesleyan Univ	NE	38,140	C+
Neumann Univ	PA	40,678	LC
New College of Florida	FL	15,848	MC
New England College	NH	50,364	C
New Jersey City Univ	NJ	21,456	LC
New Jersey Inst of Technology	NJ	29,569	VC
New Mexico Highlands Univ	NM	11,904	NC
New Mexico Inst of Mining and Technology	NM	14,833	HC
New Mexico State Univ	NM	14,050	C
New York Univ	NY	65,860	MC
Newberry College	SC	34,550	C
Newman Univ	KS	35,390	C
Niagara Univ	NY	41,010	C
Nicholls State Univ	LA	10,534	C
Norfolk State Univ	VA	25,702	LC
N Car A&T State Univ	NC	13,365	LC
N Car Central Univ	NC	9,000	C
N Car State Univ	NC	19,515	HC+
N Car Wesleyan College	NC	39,200	C
North Central College	IL	48,712	VC
N Dak State Univ	ND	16,245	C
North Park Univ	IL	35,860	C
Northeastern Illinois Univ	IL	12,529	LC
Northeastern State Univ	OK	8,615	VC
Northeastern Univ	MA	62,703	MC
Northern Arizona Univ	AZ	20,246	VC
Northern Illinois Univ	IL	20,176	C
Northern Kentucky Univ	KY	16,486	C
Northern Mich Univ	MI	19,604	C
Northern State Univ	SD	14,505	C
Northland College	WI	41,103	C+
Northwest Missouri State Univ	MO	17,737	C
Northwest Nazarene Univ	ID	36,000	C
Northwestern College of Iowa	IA	38,400	C+
Northwestern Okla State Univ	OK	13,072	NC
Northwestern Univ	IL	66,344	MC
Norwich Univ	VT	28,212	C
Notre Dame College	OH	37,150	VC
Notre Dame de Namur Univ	CA	46,526	LC
Notre Dame of Maryland Univ	MD	46,465	VC
Oakland City Univ	IN	33,360	NC
Oakland Univ	MI	20,763	C
Oakwood Univ	AL	43,758	C
Oberlin College	OH	66,012	MC
Occidental College	CA	65,530	MC
Oglethorpe Univ	GA	44,200	C+
Ohio Dominican Univ	OH	41,340	C+
Ohio Northern Univ	OH	44,050	VC
Ohio State Univ at Columbus	OH	21,703	HC+
Ohio State Univ at Lima	OH	7,140	C
Ohio Univ	OH	22,924	C
Ohio Wesleyan Univ	OH	49,460	VC
Okla Baptist Univ	OK	32,320	C
Okla Christian Univ	OK	27,650	VC
Okla Panhandle State Univ	OK	6,152	NC
Okla State Univ	OK	17,180	VC
Okla Wesleyan Univ	OK	33,206	C
Old Dominion Univ	VA	20,910	C
Olivet College	MI	36,110	LC
Olivet Nazarene Univ	IL	41,840	C
Oral Roberts Univ	OK	34,316	C
Oregon State Univ	OR	22,519	VC
Ottawa Univ	KS	36,074	VC
Ouachita Baptist Univ	AR	32,320	C
Our Lady of the Lake Univ	TX	35,012	LC
Pace Univ	NY	58,248	C
Pacific Lutheran Univ	WA	49,960	VC
Pacific Union College	CA	36,009	VC
Pacific Univ	OR	52,876	C
Paine College	GA	19,506	LC
Palm Beach Atlantic Univ	FL	39,720	C
Park Univ	MO	20,329	C
Penn State Erie/The Behrend College	PA	16,256	C
Penn State Univ/Altoona	PA	24,584	C
Pennsylvania State Univ - Univ Park	PA	29,760	HC
Pepperdine Univ	CA	74,460	HC+
Peru State College	NE	14,768	NC
Pfeiffer Univ	NC	39,695	LC
Philadelphia Univ	PA	50,370	C
Philander Smith College	AR	20,814	LC
Piedmont College	GA	32,512	C
Pine Manor College	MA	41,660	LC
Pittsburg State Univ	KS	13,880	NC
Pitzer College	CA	66,192	MC
Plymouth State Univ	NH	23,180	LC
Point Loma Nazarene Univ	CA	43,450	C
Point Park Univ	PA	41,270	C
Pomona College	CA	64,957	MC
Pontifical Catholic Univ of PR	PR	10,534	
Portland State Univ	OR	19,443	C
Prairie View A&M Univ	TX	15,205	LC
Prescott College	AZ	33,284	C
Presentation College	SD	25,454	NC
Principia College	IL	39,010	C+
Purdue Univ/Northwest	IN	15,038	C
Purdue Univ/West Lafayette	IN	20,032	MC
Queens Univ of Charlotte	NC	39,543	C
Quincy Univ	IL	36,998	C
Quinnipiac Univ	CT	59,110	C
Radford Univ	VA	19,027	LC
Ramapo College of New Jersey	NJ	25,338	C
Randolph College	VA	45,660	VC
Randolph-Macon College	VA	49,910	C
Reed College	OR	65,300	MC
Regis College	MA	51,920	C
Regis Univ	CO	44,520	C
Reinhardt Univ	GA	29,492	C
Rensselaer Polytechnic Inst	NY	63,436	MC
Rhode Island College	RI	17,694	LC
Rhodes College	TN	51,900	HC
Rice Univ	TX	57,668	MC
Rider Univ	NJ	54,050	C
Ripon College	WI	46,911	C+
Rivier Univ	NH	40,410	VC
Roanoke College	VA	54,114	VC
Robert Morris Univ	PA	37,834	C
Roberts Wesleyan College	NY	38,306	C
Rochester Inst of Technology	NY	50,842	HC
Rockford Univ	IL	36,030	C
Rockhurst Univ	MO	29,220	C
Roger Williams Univ	RI	46,296	C+
Rollins College	FL	58,670	HC
Roosevelt Univ	IL	40,651	VC
Rose-Hulman Inst of Technology	IN	57,303	MC
Rosemont College	PA	30,980	C
Rowan Univ	NJ	24,491	VC+
Russell Sage College	NY	39,370	C
Rust College	MS	10,600	C
Rutgers Univ - Camden	NJ	26,146	C
Rutgers Univ - New Brunswick	NJ	26,632	HC
Rutgers Univ - Newark	NJ	27,288	C
Sacred Heart Univ	CT	52,750	C
Saginaw Valley State Univ	MI	18,530	C
St. Anselm College	NH	52,560	C+
St. Augustine's Univ	NC	26,048	C
St. Francis Univ	PA	42,268	NC
St. John's Univ	MN	51,624	C
St. Joseph's College of Maine	ME	46,485	C
St. Joseph's Univ	PA	57,544	VC+
St. Leo Univ	FL	31,650	C
St. Louis Univ	MO	49,866	HC
St. Martin's Univ	WA	45,056	C
St. Mary-of-the-Woods College	IN	39,632	LC
St. Mary's College	IN	50,600	C
St. Mary's College of Calif	CA	57,420	C
St. Mary's Univ of Minn	MN	41,210	VC
St. Michael's College	VT	51,725	VC+
St. Peter's Univ	NJ	49,192	C
St. Vincent College	PA	44,626	C
St. Xavier Univ	IL	43,310	C
Salem College	NC	37,694	HC
Salem International Univ	WV	21,090	LC
Salem State Univ	MA	17,303	LC
Salisbury Univ	MD	20,714	VC
Salve Regina Univ	RI	51,470	C
Sam Houston State Univ	TX	18,792	C
Samford Univ	AL	39,232	VC
San Diego Christian College	CA	39,068	C
San Diego State Univ	CA	21,896	C+
San Francisco State Univ	CA	18,514	LC
San Jose State Univ	CA	21,540	C
Sarah Lawrence College	NY	63,388	HC
Savannah State Univ	GA	15,631	C
Schreiner Univ	TX	34,626	LC
Scripps College	CA	66,664	MC
Seattle Pacific Univ	WA	47,439	C+
Seattle Univ	WA	50,811	VC+
Seton Hall Univ	NJ	55,514	C
Seton Hill Univ	PA	46,972	C
Sewanee: The Univ of the South	TN	54,500	MC
Shaw Univ	NC	24,638	C
Shenandoah Univ	VA	41,312	C
Shepherd Univ, West Virginia	WV	17,224	C
Shippensburg Univ of Pennsylvania	PA	23,208	C
Shorter Univ	GA	31,130	LC
Siena College	NY	48,916	C+
Siena Heights Univ	MI	32,040	C
Silver Lake College of the Holy Family	WI	36,290	LC
Simmons College	MA	53,090	VC
Simpson College	IA	43,839	VC
Simpson Univ	CA	33,700	C
Skidmore College	NY	64,214	HC
Slippery Rock Univ of Pennsylvania	PA	10,360	C
Smith College	MA	63,914	MC
Sonoma State Univ	CA	27,806	C
S Car State Univ	SC	20,805	LC
S Dak State Univ	SD	15,634	C
Southeastern Louisiana Univ	LA	16,237	C
Southeastern Okla State Univ	OK	11,875	C
Southeastern Univ	FL	31,765	C
Southern Adventist Univ	TN	27,600	C
Southern Arkansas Univ	AR	21,532	C
Southern Conn State Univ	CT	21,924	LC
Southern Illinois Univ Carbondale	IL	23,667	C
Southern Illinois Univ Edwardsville	IL	22,643	C
Southern Methodist Univ	TX	66,483	MC
Southern Nazarene Univ	OK	32,798	NC
Southern Oregon Univ	OR	19,117	C
Southern Univ and A&M College	LA	16,074	LC+
Southern Univ at New Orleans	LA	8,014	LC
Southern Wesleyan Univ	SC	32,130	LC
Southwest Baptist Univ	MO	29,900	LC
Southwest Minn State Univ	MN	17,783	C
Southwestern Adventist Univ	TX	27,756	LC
Southwestern College	KS	31,531	C
Southwestern Okla State Univ	OK	11,790	C
Southwestern Univ	TX	50,720	VC
Spelman College	GA	38,751	C
Spring Arbor Univ	MI	36,000	C
Spring Hill College	AL	48,488	C
Springfield College	MA	45,995	C
St. Andrews Univ	NC	44,634	LC
St. Bonaventure Univ	NY	44,237	C
St. Catherine Univ	MN	45,630	VC
St. Cloud State Univ	MN	10,600	C
St. Edward's Univ	TX	53,100	VC
St. Francis College	NY	38,800	LC
St. John Fisher College	NY	43,620	C
St. John's College-Annapolis	MD	60,142	MC
St. John's Univ	NY	55,850	C
St. Joseph's College, New York/Brooklyn Campus	NY	25,114	LC
St. Joseph's College, New York/Long Island Campus	NY	25,124	C
St. Lawrence Univ	NY	64,390	VC
St. Mary's College of Maryland	MD	26,634	VC
St. Mary's Univ	TX	37,500	C
St. Norbert College	WI	44,525	VC
St. Olaf College	MN	54,260	HC+
St. Thomas Univ	FL	36,360	LC
Stanford Univ	CA	60,409	MC
SUNY / Buffalo State College	NY	20,842	C
SUNY / SUNY College at Old Westbury	NY	16,860	C
SUNY / SUNY Cortland	NY	20,706	VC
SUNY / SUNY Fredonia	NY	20,818	C
SUNY / SUNY Oneonta	NY	19,712	C+
SUNY / SUNY Plattsburgh	NY	18,814	C
SUNY / SUNY Potsdam	NY	20,404	C+
SUNY / The College of Environmental Science and Forestry	NY	23,853	VC
SUNY / Univ at Buffalo	NY	23,122	C+
SUNY at Binghamton	NY	22,861	MC
SUNY at Geneseo	NY	20,440	VC+
SUNY at New Paltz	NY	19,200	C
SUNY at Oswego	NY	21,351	C
SUNY at Purchase	NY	17,900	C
SUNY Polytechnic Inst	NY	19,473	VC
SUNY SUNY Albany	NY	22,165	C
Stephen F. Austin State Univ	TX	18,406	LC
Stephens College	MO	38,042	C
Sterling College	KS	32,830	C
Stetson Univ	FL	53,544	VC
Stevenson Univ	MD	72,770	C
Stillman College	AL	20,738	C
Stockton Univ	NJ	25,059	
Stonehill College	MA	55,030	C+
Stony Brook Univ/The SUNY	NY	21,881	MC
Suffolk Univ	MA	50,308	C
Sul Ross State Univ	TX	15,021	LC
Susquehanna Univ	PA	55,340	VC
Swarthmore College	PA	63,550	MC
Tabor College	KS	35,870	C
Talladega College	AL	19,215	C
Tarleton State Univ	TX	15,248	LC
Taylor Univ	IN	40,317	C+
Temple Univ	PA	24,392	VC
Tenn State Univ	TN	14,423	C
Tenn Tech Univ	TN	17,050	C
Texas A&M Univ	TX	20,521	VC+
Texas A&M Univ at Commerce	TX	10,496	C

ST = STATE $IS = IN-STATE COSTS SR = SELECTOR RATING

School	ST	$IS	SR
Texas A&M Univ at Corpus Christi	TX	16,851	LC
Texas A&M Univ at Galveston	TX	15,920	C
Texas A&M Univ at Kingsville	TX	7,500	LC
Texas Christian Univ	TX	54,670	HC
Texas Lutheran Univ	TX	38,620	C
Texas Southern Univ	TX	18,212	LC
Texas State Univ	TX	19,350	C
Texas Wesleyan Univ	TX	35,134	C
Texas Woman's Univ	TX	15,302	LC
The Catholic Univ of America	DC	56,356	VC
The Citadel, The Military College of S Car	SC	35,339	C
The College at Brockport - SUNY	NY	20,346	C
The College of Idaho	ID	36,415	C
The College of New Jersey	NJ	31,909	HC
The College of New Rochelle	NY	46,300	VC
The College of St. Rose	NY	43,048	C
The College of Wooster	OH	57,900	VC+
The Evergreen State College	WA	16,599	C
The Lincoln Univ	PA	15,154	NC
The Master's Univ	CA	43,870	C+
The Univ of Akron	OH	21,477	C
The Univ of Tenn at Chattanooga	TN	16,744	C
The Univ of Tenn at Knoxville	TN	22,112	VC
The Univ of Tenn at Martin	TN	14,876	C
The Univ of Utah	UT	17,924	VC
The Univ of Virginia's College at Wise	VA	18,192	LC
Thiel College	PA	41,590	C
Thomas More College	KY	36,720	C
Thomas Univ	GA	21,420	LC
Toccoa Falls College	GA	27,920	C
Tougaloo College	MS	17,980	NC
Touro College	NY	28,950	VC
Towson Univ	MD	17,408	VC
Transylvania Univ	KY	45,690	VC+
Trevecca Nazarene Univ	TN	31,186	C
Trine Univ	IN	41,310	C
Trinity Christian College	IL	35,580	C
Trinity College	CT	63,920	HC+
Trinity International Univ	IL	31,070	VC
Trinity Univ	TX	52,314	HC+
Trinity Washington Univ	DC	33,826	C+
Troy Univ	AL	16,171	C
Truman State Univ	MO	16,014	HC
Tufts Univ	MA		MC
Tusculum College	TN	31,625	C
Tuskegee Univ	AL	28,164	C
Union College	KY	32,310	C
Union College	NE	23,270	C
Union College	NY	64,320	MC
Union Univ	TN	33,970	VC
United States Air Force Academy	CO		C
Unity College	ME	37,670	C
Universidad Adventista de las Antillas	PR	16,606	
Universidad del Turabo	PR	17,828	
Univ of Alabama	AL	24,320	C+
Univ of Alabama at Birmingham	AL	19,906	C
Univ of Alabama in Huntsville	AL	19,445	VC
Univ of Alaska Anchorage	AK	16,652	NC
Univ of Alaska Fairbanks	AK	16,179	C
Univ of Alaska Southeast	AK	11,493	C
Univ of Arizona	AZ	23,100	C
Univ of Arkansas at Fayetteville	AR	19,152	C+
Univ of Arkansas at Little Rock	AR	18,211	C
Univ of Arkansas at Monticello	AR	13,134	NC
Univ of Arkansas at Pine Bluff	AR	13,541	C
Univ of Bridgeport	CT	44,430	LC
Univ of Calif at Berkeley	CA	28,853	MC
Univ of Calif at Davis	CA	28,468	HC
Univ of Calif at Irvine	CA	26,484	VC
Univ of Calif at Los Angeles	CA	30,162	MC
Univ of Calif at Riverside	CA	29,227	C+
Univ of Calif at Santa Barbara	CA	29,091	HC
Univ of Calif San Diego	CA	30,150	MC
Univ of Calif, Santa Cruz	CA	28,731	C+
Univ of Central Arkansas	AR	14,472	VC
Univ of Central Florida	FL	15,922	VC
Univ of Central Missouri	MO	18,982	C
Univ of Central Okla	OK	13,486	C
Univ of Charleston	WV	35,000	C
Univ of Chicago	IL	67,584	MC
Univ of Cincinnati	OH	21,964	VC
Univ of Colo Colo Springs	CO	19,663	C
Univ of Colo Denver	CO	23,230	C
Univ of Conn	CT	25,538	HC
Univ of Dallas	TX	45,500	VC+
Univ of Dayton	OH	53,620	C
Univ of Delaware	DE	24,976	VC+
Univ of Denver	CO	58,443	VC+
Univ of Detroit Mercy	MI	48,816	C+
Univ of Dubuque	IA	37,824	C
Univ of Evansville	IN	44,186	VC+
Univ of Findlay	OH	60,139	C
Univ of Georgia	GA	21,250	HC
Univ of Great Falls	MT	38,524	C
Univ of Hartford	CT	49,776	C
Univ of Hawaii at Hilo	HI	18,038	C
Univ of Hawaii at Manoa	HI	23,221	C
Univ of Holy Cross	LA	21,523	C
Univ of Houston	TX	21,483	VC
Univ of Houston-Downtown	TX	7,241	C
Univ of Idaho	ID	15,348	C
Univ of Illinois at Chicago	IL	25,006	VC
Univ of Illinois at Urbana-Champaign	IL	27,006	HC
Univ of Indianapolis	IN	36,480	C
Univ of Iowa	IA	18,683	VC+
Univ of Jamestown	ND	28,508	C
Univ of Kansas	KS	20,135	C+
Univ of Kentucky	KY	33,306	C
Univ of La Verne	CA	55,600	C
Univ of Louisville	KY	19,824	C
Univ of Maine	ME	20,792	C
Univ of Maine at Augusta	ME	7,812	C
Univ of Maine at Farmington	ME	18,187	C
Univ of Maine at Fort Kent	ME	15,165	LC
Univ of Maine at Machias	ME	22,960	C
Univ of Maine at Presque Isle	ME	14,870	C
Univ of Mary	ND	23,180	C
Univ of Mary Hardin-Baylor	TX	33,950	C+
Univ of Mary Washington	VA	24,764	VC
Univ of Maryland/Baltimore County	MD	21,296	VC
Univ of Maryland/College Park	MD	21,938	HC
Univ of Maryland/Eastern Shore	MD	17,013	C
Univ of Mass Amherst	MA	26,199	VC+
Univ of Mass Boston	MA	13,435	C
Univ of Mass Dartmouth	MA	25,658	C
Univ of Mass Lowell	MA	26,380	C
Univ of Memphis	TN	18,278	C
Univ of Mich/Ann Arbor	MI	24,410	MC
Univ of Mich/Dearborn	MI	11,757	VC
Univ of Mich-Flint	MI	17,607	C+
Univ of Minn Crookston	MN	19,739	C
Univ of Minn/Duluth	MN	20,292	C+
Univ of Minn/Morris	MN	20,760	VC
Univ of Minn/Twin Cities	MN	23,519	HC+
Univ of Miss	MS	17,746	C+
Univ of Missouri/Columbia	MO	18,201	MC
Univ of Missouri-Kansas City	MO	19,563	VC
Univ of Missouri-St. Louis	MO		C
Univ of Mobile	AL	28,935	C
Univ of Montana	MT	14,105	C
Univ of Montevallo	AL	19,502	C
Univ of Mount Olive	NC	18,426	C
Univ of Mount Union	OH	38,970	C
Univ of Nebr - Kearney	NE	16,546	LC
Univ of Nebr - Lincoln	NE	18,589	VC
Univ of Nebr - Omaha	NE	16,120	C
Univ of Nevada, Las Vegas	NV	17,553	C
Univ of Nevada/Reno	NV	18,010	C
Univ of New England	ME	48,880	C
Univ of New Hampshire	NH	28,562	VC
Univ of New Haven	CT	52,190	C
Univ of New Mexico	NM	15,404	C
Univ of New Orleans	LA	12,840	C
Univ of North Alabama	AL	15,398	C
Univ of N Car at Asheville	NC	15,723	VC+
Univ of N Car at Chapel Hill	NC	20,052	HC+
Univ of N Car at Charlotte	NC	15,547	C
Univ of N Car at Greensboro	NC	14,690	C
Univ of N Car at Pembroke	NC	14,388	LC
Univ of N Car at Wilmington	NC	14,590	VC
Univ of N Dak	ND	15,373	C
Univ of North Florida	FL	15,996	VC
Univ of North Georgia	GA	17,316	C
Univ of North Texas	TX	19,198	C
Univ of Northern Colo	CO	20,851	C
Univ of Northwestern - St. Paul	MN	38,160	C
Univ of Oregon	OR	22,972	C
Univ of Pennsylvania	PA	63,526	MC
Univ of Pikeville	KY	28,700	NC
Univ of Pittsburgh	PA	29,568	HC+
Univ of Pittsburgh at Bradford	PA	22,402	C
Univ of Pittsburgh at Greensburg	PA	23,132	C
Univ of Pittsburgh at Johnstown	PA	22,092	C
Univ of Portland	OR	52,152	VC
Univ of PR, at Cayey	PR		
Univ of PR, at Humacao	PR	14,000	
Univ of PR, at Mayaguez	PR	13,995	
Univ of PR-Rio Piedras campus	PR	13,327	
Univ of Puget Sound	WA	56,456	VC+
Univ of Redlands	CA	60,200	VC
Univ of Richmond	VA	60,880	MC
Univ of Rio Grande & Rio Grande Community College	OH	8,750	NC
Univ of Rochester	NY	65,032	MC
Univ of St. Francis	IN	37,400	C
Univ of St. Joseph	CT	49,550	C
Univ of St. Mary	KS	34,690	C
Univ of San Diego	CA	58,442	VC+
Univ of San Francisco	CA	58,484	VC
Univ of Science and Arts of Okla	OK	11,140	VC
Univ of Scranton	PA	54,962	VC
Univ of Sioux Falls	SD	34,330	C
Univ of South Alabama	AL	16,400	C
Univ of S Car Aiken	SC	16,712	C
Univ of S Car at Columbia	SC	19,725	VC+
Univ of S Car Upstate	SC	18,200	LC
Univ of S Dak	SD	16,109	C
Univ of South Florida/St. Petersburg	FL	15,980	C
Univ of South Florida/Tampa	FL	16,110	VC+
Univ of Southern Calif	CA	66,631	C
Univ of Southern Indiana	IN	16,501	C
Univ of Southern Maine	ME	18,320	C
Univ of Southern Miss	MS	13,170	C
Univ of St. Francis	IL	39,924	C
Univ of St. Thomas - Houston	TX	40,020	VC
Univ of Tampa	FL	36,944	C
Univ of Texas at Arlington	TX	18,026	LC
Univ of Texas at Austin	TX	26,102	HC
Univ of Texas at Dallas	TX	22,830	VC+
Univ of Texas at El Paso	TX	34,452	NC
Univ of Texas at San Antonio	TX	20,157	C
Univ of the Cumberlands	KY	32,000	C
Univ of the District of Columbia	DC	21,044	LC
Univ of the Incarnate Word	TX	39,162	LC
Univ of the Ozarks	AR	52,176	C
Univ of the Pacific	CA	57,006	VC
Univ of the Sacred Heart	PR	17,932	
Univ of the Sciences	PA	54,038	VC
Univ of the Southwest	NM	22,766	C
Univ of Toledo	OH	19,336	NC
Univ of Tulsa	OK	52,625	HC+
Univ of Vermont	VT	28,878	HC
Univ of Virginia	VA	25,891	MC
Univ of Washington	WA	23,149	VC
Univ of West Alabama	AL	15,516	NC
Univ of West Florida	FL	15,848	C
Univ of West Georgia	GA	16,360	LC
Univ of Wisc-Eau Claire	WI	15,797	VC
Univ of Wisc-Green Bay	WI	15,064	C
Univ of Wisc-La Crosse	WI	15,247	C+
Univ of Wisc-Madison	WI	20,934	MC
Univ of Wisc-Milwaukee	WI	21,496	C
Univ of Wisc-Oshkosh	WI	15,200	C
Univ of Wisc-Parkside	WI	15,193	C
Univ of Wisc-Platteville	WI	14,614	VC
Univ of Wisc-River Falls	WI	14,485	C
Univ of Wisc-Stevens Point	WI	14,043	C
Univ of Wisc-Superior	WI	14,446	C
Univ of Wisc-Whitewater	WI	13,976	C
Upper Iowa Univ	IA	34,990	NC
Ursinus College	PA	61,690	VC
Ursuline College	OH	41,076	LC
Utah State Univ	UT	12,736	C
Utica College	NY	30,430	C
Valley City State Univ	ND	13,267	C
Valparaiso Univ	IN	48,370	C+
Vanderbilt Univ	TN	60,572	MC
Vanguard Univ of Southern Calif	CA	40,740	VC
Vassar College	NY	65,491	MC
Villanova Univ	PA	62,523	MC
Virginia Commonwealth Univ	VA	23,049	C
Virginia Military Inst	VA	26,460	C+
Virginia Polytechnic Inst and State Univ	VA	21,276	HC
Virginia State Univ	VA	19,802	C+
Virginia Union Univ	VA	22,421	C
Virginia Wesleyan College	VA	43,728	LC
Viterbo Univ	WI	34,660	C
Voorhees College	SC	19,976	C
Wabash College	IN	50,650	VC
Wagner College	NY	55,480	C+
Wake Forest Univ	NC	64,056	MC
Walla Walla Univ	WA	30,417	NC
Walsh Univ	OH	39,010	C
Warner Pacific College	OR	33,790	C
Warner Univ	FL	28,216	C
Warren Wilson College	NC	44,220	VC
Wartburg College	IA	47,840	C
Washburn Univ	KS	15,827	C
Washington & Jefferson College	PA	56,512	VC
Washington Adventist Univ	MD	31,440	LC
Washington and Lee Univ	VA	59,647	MC
Washington College	MD	54,666	VC
Washington State Univ	WA	22,495	C
Washington Univ in St. Louis	MO	65,366	VC
Wayland Baptist Univ	TX	22,356	LC
Wayne State College	NE	12,802	C
Wayne State Univ	MI	22,016	C
Waynesburg Univ	PA	32,290	C
Weber State Univ	UT	10,721	C
Webster Univ	MO	37,490	C
Wellesley College	MA	63,916	MC
Wells College	NY	50,500	C
Wesley College	DE	37,026	LC
Wesleyan College	GA	29,694	C+
Wesleyan Univ	CT	65,516	MC
West Chester Univ of Pennsylvania	PA	18,456	C
West Liberty Univ	WV	15,512	C
West Texas A&M Univ	TX	13,478	C
West Virginia State Univ	WV	8,378	NC
West Virginia Univ	WV	18,210	C
West Virginia Univ Inst of Technology	WV	16,462	NC
West Virginia Wesleyan College	WV	36,858	C
Western Carolina Univ	NC	13,965	C
Western Conn State Univ	CT	21,254	LC
Western Kentucky Univ	KY	16,850	C
Western Mich Univ	MI	21,054	C
Western New England Univ	MA	48,088	C
Western New Mexico Univ	NM	16,734	LC
Western Oregon Univ	OR	15,021	LC
Western State Colo Univ	CO	18,639	C
Western Washington Univ	WA	18,003	C+
Westfield State Univ	MA	19,671	C
Westminster College	MO	32,820	C
Westminster College	PA	39,180	C+
Westminster College	UT	41,078	C+
Westmont College	CA	56,410	HC
Wheaton College	IL	43,610	MC
Wheaton College	MA	61,512	VC
Wheeling Jesuit Univ	WV	37,106	LC
Whittier College	CA	57,891	C
Whitworth Univ	WA	51,732	VC
Wichita State Univ	KS	21,643	C
Widener Univ	PA	56,486	C
Wilberforce Univ	OH	19,016	C
Wiley College	TX	18,504	C
Wilkes Univ	PA	45,622	C
Willamette Univ	OR	61,817	VC+
William Carey Univ	MS	23,950	LC
William Jewell College	MO	41,210	C+
William Paterson Univ of New Jersey	NJ	23,133	C
William Peace Univ	NC	37,430	LC
William Penn Univ	IA	26,000	C
William Woods Univ	MO	32,040	C
Williams Baptist College	AR	24,720	C
Williams College	MA	63,290	MC
Wilmington College	OH	34,600	C
Wilson College	PA	35,620	C
Wingate Univ	NC	39,950	C
Winona State Univ	MN	17,535	C
Winston-Salem State Univ	NC	26,166	LC
Winthrop Univ	SC	23,082	C
Wisc Lutheran College	WI	36,290	VC
Wittenberg Univ	OH	48,156	C+
Wofford College	SC	49,885	VC
Worcester Polytechnic Inst	MA	60,730	MC
Worcester State Univ	MA	20,977	C
Wright State Univ	OH	16,983	C
Xavier Univ	OH	47,880	C+
Xavier Univ of Louisiana	LA	31,689	C+
Yale Univ	CT	64,650	MC
Yeshiva Univ	NY	47,250	VC+
York College	NE	24,300	C
York College of Pennsylvania	PA	29,240	C
Youngstown State Univ	OH	17,307	C

BIOLOGY/GEN SCI/ENVIR SCI SECOND ED

School	ST	$IS	SR
Bay Path Univ	MA	45,349	C
MidAmerica Nazarene Univ	KS	35,550	C
Northern Mich Univ	MI	19,604	C
Wilson College	PA	35,620	C

BIOMATHEMATICS

School	ST	$IS	SR
Averett Univ	VA	40,970	LC
Brown Univ	RI	64,566	MC
Emmanuel College	MA	52,110	C+
Florida Inst of Technology	FL	53,306	VC
Rutgers Univ - New Brunswick	NJ	26,632	HC
Univ of Montana-Western	MT	11,220	LC
Univ of Scranton	PA	54,962	VC
Washington Univ in St. Louis	MO	65,366	VC

BIOMEDICAL ART

School	ST	$IS	SR
Cleveland Inst of Art	OH	51,439	C+
Rochester Inst of Technology	NY	50,842	HC

BIOMEDICAL ELECTRONICS

School	ST	$IS	SR
Thomas Edison State Univ	NJ	6,350	NC

BIOMEDICAL ENGINEERING

School	ST	$IS	SR
Arizona State Univ at the Tempe Campus	AZ	21,756	VC
Boston Univ	MA	65,110	MC
Brown Univ	RI	64,566	MC
Bucknell Univ	PA	64,616	MC
Butler Univ	IN	51,352	VC
Calif Baptist Univ	CA	41,392	C
Calif Polytechnic State Univ	CA	17,979	HC+
Case Western Reserve Univ	OH	60,304	MC
CUNY/City College	NY	20,319	VC
Colo State Univ	CO	22,162	VC
Columbia Univ/City of New York	NY	62,958	MC
Dartmouth College	NH	66,174	MC
Drexel Univ	PA	65,432	VC+
Duke Univ	NC	64,188	
Duquesne Univ	PA	46,822	VC
Elon Univ	NC	44,599	VC+

School	ST	$IS	SR
Florida Inst of Technology	FL	53,306	VC
Florida International Univ	FL	19,854	C+
Florida State Univ	FL	16,771	HC
Gannon Univ	PA	42,032	C
Georgia Inst of Technology	GA	23,360	MC
Harding Univ	AR	25,421	C
Hofstra Univ	NY	55,960	C+
Indiana Inst of Technology	IN	34,240	LC
Indiana Univ-Purdue Univ Indianapolis	IN	18,635	C
Jackson State Univ	MS	15,879	LC
Johns Hopkins Univ	MD	65,386	MC
Lawrence Tech Univ	MI	39,770	VC
Louisiana Tech Univ	LA	11,422	VC
Marquette Univ	WI	48,390	VC+
Mass Inst of Technology	MA	62,662	MC
Mich Tech Univ	MI	24,739	VC+
Milwaukee School of Engineering	WI	45,153	HC
New Jersey Inst of Technology	NJ	29,569	VC
New York Univ	NY	65,860	MC
N Dak State Univ	ND	16,245	C
Northwestern Univ	IL	66,344	MC
Ohio State Univ at Columbus	OH	21,703	HC+
Pennsylvania State Univ - Univ Park	PA	29,760	HC
Purdue Univ/West Lafayette	IN	20,032	MC
Rensselaer Polytechnic Inst	NY	63,436	MC
Rochester Inst of Technology	NY	50,842	HC
Rose-Hulman Inst of Technology	IN	57,303	MC
Rowan Univ	NJ	24,491	VC+
Rutgers Univ - New Brunswick	NJ	26,632	HC
St. Louis Univ	MO	49,866	HC
San Jose State Univ	CA	21,540	C
SUNY / Univ at Buffalo	NY	23,122	C+
SUNY at Binghamton	NY	22,861	MC
Stevens Inst of Technology	NJ	62,338	MC
Stony Brook Univ/The SUNY	NY	21,881	MC
Texas A&M Univ	TX	20,521	VC+
The Catholic Univ of America	DC	56,356	VC
The College of New Jersey	NJ	31,909	HC
The Univ of Akron	OH	21,477	C
The Univ of Tenn at Knoxville	TN	22,112	VC
The Univ of Utah	UT	17,924	VC
Tufts Univ	MA		MC
Tulane Univ	LA	63,396	HC+
Tuskegee Univ	AL	28,164	C
Universidad Politecnica de PR, Hato Rey campus	PR	23,514	
Univ of Alabama at Birmingham	AL	19,906	C
Univ of Arizona	AZ	23,100	C
Univ of Calif at Irvine	CA	26,484	VC
Univ of Calif at Los Angeles	CA	30,162	MC
Univ of Central Okla	OK	13,486	C
Univ of Cincinnati	OH	21,964	VC
Univ of Conn	CT	25,538	HC
Univ of Hartford	CT	49,776	C
Univ of Houston	TX	21,483	VC
Univ of Idaho	ID	15,348	C
Univ of Iowa	IA	18,683	VC+
Univ of Mass Lowell	MA	26,380	C
Univ of Memphis	TN	18,278	C
Univ of Miami	FL	63,494	MC
Univ of Mich/Ann Arbor	MI	24,410	MC
Univ of Mich/Dearborn	MI	11,757	VC
Univ of Minn/Twin Cities	MN	23,519	HC+
Univ of Missouri/Columbia	MO	18,201	MC
Univ of N Car at Chapel Hill	NC	20,052	HC+
Univ of Okla	OK	18,911	VC
Univ of Rhode Island	RI	24,906	C
Univ of Rochester	NY	65,032	MC
Univ of S Car at Columbia	SC	19,725	VC+
Univ of Southern Calif	CA	66,631	C
Univ of Texas at Austin	TX	26,102	HC
Univ of Texas at Dallas	TX	22,830	VC+
Univ of Texas at San Antonio	TX	20,157	C
Univ of Virginia	VA	25,891	MC
Univ of Wisc-Madison	WI	20,934	MC
Vanderbilt Univ	TN	60,572	MC
Virginia Commonwealth Univ	VA	23,049	C
Washington State Univ	WA	22,495	C
Washington Univ in St. Louis	MO	65,366	VC
Wayne State Univ	MI	22,016	C
Wentworth Inst of Technology	MA	47,112	C
Western New England Univ	MA	48,088	C
Widener Univ	PA	56,486	C
Worcester Polytechnic Inst	MA	60,730	MC
Wright State Univ	OH	16,983	C
Yale Univ	CT	64,650	MC

BIOMEDICAL EQUIPMENT TECHNOLOGY

School	ST	$IS	SR
Andrews Univ	MI	28,030	C+
Roberts Wesleyan College	NY	38,306	C

BIOMEDICAL SCIENCE

School	ST	$IS	SR
Adventist Univ of Health Sciences	FL	26,430	NC
Albany College of Pharmacy and Health Sciences	NY	42,681	SP
Andrews Univ	MI	28,030	C+
Auburn Univ	AL	23,594	VC+
Averett Univ	VA	40,970	LC
Bay Path Univ	MA	45,349	C
Boston Univ	MA	65,110	MC
Brown Univ	RI	64,566	MC
Buena Vista Univ	IA	41,514	C
Cal State, Northridge	CA	16,859	LC
Central Mich Univ	MI	20,330	C
Christian Brothers Univ	TN	31,670	VC
CUNY/City College	NY	20,319	VC
Colo State Univ	CO	22,162	VC
Grand Valley State Univ	MI	22,250	C+
Heritage Univ	WA	19,825	NC
Hiram College	OH	43,230	C
Hodges Univ	FL	19,080	LC
LIU Post	NY	49,682	C
Lynchburg College	VA	46,740	C
Madonna Univ	MI	29,050	C
Marquette Univ	WI	48,390	VC+
McMurry Univ	TX	34,259	LC
Murray State Univ	KY	16,998	C
New Mexico Inst of Mining and Technology	NM	14,833	HC
Northern Arizona Univ	AZ	20,246	VC
Ohio State Univ at Columbus	OH	21,703	HC+
Okla City Univ	OK	40,476	VC
Oral Roberts Univ	OK	34,316	C
Oregon State Univ	OR	22,519	VC
Pennsylvania State Univ - Univ Park	PA	29,760	HC
Quinnipiac Univ	CT	59,110	C
Rochester Inst of Technology	NY	50,842	HC
Rutgers Univ - New Brunswick	NJ	26,632	HC
St. Leo Univ	FL	31,650	C
St. Louis Univ	MO	49,866	HC
St. Peter's Univ	NJ	49,192	C
Silver Lake College of the Holy Family	WI	36,290	LC
Southeast Missouri State Univ	MO	15,498	C
Southern Oregon Univ	OR	19,117	C
Southwestern Okla State Univ	OK	11,790	C
SUNY / Univ at Buffalo	NY	23,122	C+
Susquehanna Univ	PA	55,340	VC
Tarleton State Univ	TX	15,248	LC
Texas A&M Univ	TX	20,521	VC+
Texas Wesleyan Univ	TX	35,134	C
Tufts Univ	MA		MC
Univ of Alabama at Birmingham	AL	19,906	C
Univ of Calif at Riverside	CA	29,227	C+
Univ of Central Florida	FL	15,922	VC
Univ of Illinois at Urbana-Champaign	IL	27,006	HC
Univ of New England	ME	48,880	C
Univ of New Hampshire	NH	28,562	VC
Univ of St. Mary	KS	34,690	C
Univ of South Alabama	AL	16,400	C
Univ of Vermont	VT	28,878	HC
Univ of Wisc-Milwaukee	WI	21,496	C
Washington State Univ	WA	22,495	C
Western Mich Univ	MI	21,054	C

BIOMETRICS AND BIOSTATISTICS

School	ST	$IS	SR
Cornell Univ	NY	64,853	MC
La Sierra Univ	CA	39,690	VC
Simmons College	MA	53,090	VC
Univ of Arizona	AZ	23,100	C
Univ of N Car at Chapel Hill	NC	20,052	HC+

BIOPHYSICS

School	ST	$IS	SR
Amherst College	MA		HC+
Andrews Univ	MI	28,030	C+
Arizona State Univ at the Tempe Campus	AZ	21,756	VC
Bellarmine Univ	KY	51,220	C
Brandeis Univ	MA	65,925	MC
Brigham Young Univ	UT	12,748	HC
Brown Univ	RI	64,566	MC
Cal State, Fresno	CA	16,902	LC
Centenary College of Louisiana	LA	45,650	C+
Claremont McKenna College	CA	67,185	MC
Columbia Univ/City of New York	NY	62,958	MC
Elon Univ	NC	44,599	VC+
Harvard College/Harvard Univ	MA	60,659	MC
Illinois Inst of Technology	IL	56,826	HC+
Iowa State Univ	IA	17,570	C
Johns Hopkins Univ	MD	65,386	MC
La Sierra Univ	CA	39,690	VC
Lipscomb Univ	TN	41,296	VC
Loyola Univ Chicago	IL	55,802	VC
Pacific Union College	CA	36,009	VC
Rensselaer Polytechnic Inst	NY	63,436	MC
St. Mary's Univ of Minn	MN	41,210	VC
Southern Nazarene Univ	OK	32,798	NC
St. Bonaventure Univ	NY	44,237	C
St. Lawrence Univ	NY	64,390	VC
SUNY / Univ at Buffalo	NY	23,122	C+
SUNY at Geneseo	NY	20,440	VC+
Syracuse Univ	NY	60,239	VC
Temple Univ	PA	24,392	VC
Tufts Univ	MA		MC
Univ of Calif at Los Angeles	CA	30,162	MC
Univ of Calif San Diego	CA	30,150	MC
Univ of Conn	CT	25,538	HC
Univ of Illinois at Chicago	IL	25,006	VC
Univ of Illinois at Urbana-Champaign	IL	27,006	HC
Univ of Mich/Ann Arbor	MI	24,410	MC
Univ of Pennsylvania	PA	63,526	MC
Univ of San Diego	CA	58,442	VC+
Univ of San Francisco	CA	58,484	VC
Univ of Scranton	PA	54,962	VC
Univ of Southern Calif	CA	66,631	C
Univ of Southern Indiana	IN	16,501	C
Walla Walla Univ	WA	30,417	NC
Washington & Jefferson College	PA	56,512	VC
Washington Univ in St. Louis	MO	65,366	VC
Wayne State Univ	MI	22,016	C
Western Kentucky Univ	KY	16,850	C
Whitman College	WA	59,772	MC
Whitworth Univ	WA	51,732	VC
Xavier Univ	OH	47,880	C+
Yale Univ	CT	64,650	MC

BIOPSYCHOLOGY

School	ST	$IS	SR
Averett Univ	VA	40,970	LC
Barnard College/Columbia Univ	NY	62,741	MC
Birmingham-Southern College	AL	44,478	VC
Grand Valley State Univ	MI	22,250	C+
McKendree Univ	IL	37,940	C+
Messiah College	PA	43,100	C+
Mills College	CA	59,163	VC
Monmouth College	IL	42,260	C
Nebr Wesleyan Univ	NE	38,140	C+
Oglethorpe Univ	GA	44,200	C+
Pace Univ	NY	58,248	C
Philadelphia Univ	PA	50,370	C
Rider Univ	NJ	54,050	C
Simmons College	MA	53,090	VC
Spring Hill College	AL	48,488	C
The Lincoln Univ	PA	15,154	NC
Tufts Univ	MA		MC
Univ of Calif at Santa Barbara	CA	29,091	HC
Viterbo Univ	WI	34,660	C
Washington Univ in St. Louis	MO	65,366	VC
Wellesley College	MA	63,916	MC
York College	NE	24,300	C

BIORESOURCE ENGINEERING

School	ST	$IS	SR
Calif Polytechnic State Univ	CA	17,979	HC+
Oregon State Univ	OR	22,519	VC
Rutgers Univ - New Brunswick	NJ	26,632	HC

BIOTECHNOLOGY

School	ST	$IS	SR
Alma College	MI	47,548	C
Arkansas State Univ	AR	16,190	C
Ashland Univ	OH	21,440	C
Bay Path Univ	MA	45,349	C
Brigham Young Univ	UT	12,748	HC
Calif State Polytechnic Univ, Pomona	CA	21,541	C
Cal State, San Marcos	CA	24,184	LC
CUNY/York College	NY	6,747	LC
Claflin Univ	SC	33,764	LC
Colo State Univ-Pueblo	CO	18,234	C
East Stroudsburg Univ	PA	18,334	C
Elizabethtown College	PA	54,050	C
Endicott College	MA	44,604	VC+
Ferris State Univ	MI	21,445	C
Fitchburg State Univ	MA	21,819	C
Florida Gulf Coast Univ	FL	9,682	C
Grand View Univ	IA	32,302	C
Indiana Univ Bloomington	IN	20,429	VC
Indiana Univ East	IN	7,072	C
Indiana Univ-Purdue Univ Indianapolis	IN	18,635	C
Inter-American Univ of PR-Bayamon	PR	18,785	
Jackson State Univ	MS	15,879	LC
James Madison Univ	VA	19,084	VC
Kennesaw State Univ	GA	19,592	VC
Kent State Univ	OH	20,732	C
Lawrence Tech Univ	MI	39,770	VC
Marshall Univ	WV	17,242	C
Marywood Univ	PA	46,900	C
Mich State Univ	MI	23,898	VC+
Millersville Univ of Pennsylvania	PA	23,782	C
Minn State Univ, Mankato	MN	15,616	C
Missouri Baptist Univ	MO	35,594	C
Montana State Univ	MT	15,500	C+
Mount Aloysius College	PA	29,976	C
New York Inst of Technology	NY	48,730	C
N Dak State Univ	ND	16,245	C
Ohio Univ	OH	22,924	C
Oregon State Univ	OR	22,519	VC
Pennsylvania State Univ - Univ Park	PA	29,760	HC
Plymouth State Univ	NH	23,180	LC
Point Park Univ	PA	41,270	C
Purdue Univ/Northwest	IN	15,038	C
Quinnipiac Univ	CT	59,110	C
Roberts Wesleyan College	NY	38,306	C
Rochester Inst of Technology	NY	50,842	HC
Rutgers Univ - New Brunswick	NJ	26,632	HC
S Dak State Univ	SD	15,634	C
Southeastern Okla State Univ	OK	11,875	C
Springfield College	MA	45,995	C
SUNY / The College of Environmental Science and Forestry	NY	23,853	VC
SUNY / Univ at Buffalo	NY	23,122	C+
SUNY /College of Agriculture and Tech at Cobleskill	NY	20,527	LC
Stevenson Univ	MD	72,770	C
Suffolk Univ	MA	50,308	C
Syracuse Univ	NY	60,239	VC
The Catholic Univ of America	DC	56,356	VC
Tufts Univ	MA		MC
Univ of Calif San Diego	CA	30,150	MC
Univ of Central Florida	FL	15,922	VC
Univ of Delaware	DE	24,976	VC+
Univ of Georgia	GA	21,250	HC
Univ of Houston-Downtown	TX	7,241	C
Univ of Illinois at Urbana-Champaign	IL	27,006	HC
Univ of Kansas	KS	20,135	C+
Univ of Maryland/Univ College	MD	25,966	LC
Univ of Missouri-Kansas City	MO	19,563	VC
Univ of Missouri-St. Louis	MO		C
Univ of Nebr - Omaha	NE	16,120	C
Univ of Nevada/Reno	NV	18,010	C
Univ of New Hampshire - Manchester	NH	14,490	C
Univ of New Haven	CT	52,190	C
Univ of N Car at Pembroke	NC	14,388	LC
Univ of PR, at Mayaguez	PR	13,995	
Univ of Wisc-River Falls	WI	14,485	C
Ursuline College	OH	41,076	LC
Washington State Univ	WA	22,495	C
West Texas A&M Univ	TX	13,478	C
William Paterson Univ of New Jersey	NJ	23,133	C
William Penn Univ	IA	26,000	C
Worcester State Univ	MA	20,977	C

BOTANY

School	ST	$IS	SR
Andrews Univ	MI	28,030	C+
Auburn Univ	AL	23,594	VC+
Bennington College	VT	63,960	MC
Brigham Young Univ	UT	12,748	HC
Calif State Polytechnic Univ, Pomona	CA	21,541	C
Cal State, Long Beach	CA	18,850	C
Colo State Univ	CO	22,162	VC
Conn College	CT	65,000	MC
Delaware State Univ	DE	19,376	NC
Eastern Washington Univ	WA	25,572	LC
Hampshire College	MA	63,824	MC
Humboldt State Univ	CA	20,514	C
Idaho State Univ	ID	13,619	NC
Kent State Univ	OH	20,732	C
Mars Hill Univ	NC	42,688	C
Miami Univ	OH	27,190	HC+
Mich State Univ	MI	23,898	VC+
Millersville Univ of Pennsylvania	PA	23,782	C
N Car State Univ	NC	19,515	HC+
N Dak State Univ	ND	16,245	C
Northern Mich Univ	MI	19,604	C
Northwest Missouri State Univ	MO	17,737	C
Ohio Univ	OH	22,924	C
Ohio Wesleyan Univ	OH	49,460	VC
Okla State Univ	OK	17,180	VC
Oregon State Univ	OR	22,519	VC
Rutgers Univ - New Brunswick	NJ	26,632	HC
Rutgers Univ - Newark	NJ	27,288	C
San Francisco State Univ	CA	18,514	LC
San Jose State Univ	CA	21,540	C
Southern Illinois Univ Carbondale	IL	23,667	C
SUNY / The College of Environmental Science and Forestry	NY	23,853	VC
Texas A&M Univ at Commerce	TX	10,496	C
Univ of Calif at Davis	CA	28,468	HC
Univ of Calif at Irvine	CA	26,484	VC
Univ of Florida	FL	16,291	HC+
Univ of Hawaii at Manoa	HI	23,221	C
Univ of Illinois at Urbana-Champaign	IL	27,006	HC
Univ of Kentucky	KY	33,306	C
Univ of Maine	ME	20,792	C
Univ of Mich/Ann Arbor	MI	24,410	MC
Univ of Minn/Twin Cities	MN	23,519	HC+
Univ of Montana	MT	14,105	C
Univ of Okla	OK	18,911	VC
Univ of Vermont	VT	28,878	HC
Univ of Washington	WA	23,149	VC
Univ of Wisc-Madison	WI	20,934	MC
Univ of Wyoming	WY	15,375	C+
Washington State Univ	WA	22,495	C

ST = STATE $IS = IN-STATE COSTS SR = SELECTOR RATING

School	ST	$IS	SR
Weber State Univ	UT	10,721	C
Western New Mexico Univ	NM	16,734	LC

BROADCASTING

School	ST	$IS	SR
Alabama State Univ	AL	14,142	NC
Ashland Univ	OH	21,440	C
Baldwin Wallace Univ	OH	41,106	C
Barry Univ	FL	37,830	C
Baylor Univ	TX	53,760	HC
Belhaven Univ	MS	31,016	C
Bemidji State Univ	MN	16,056	VC
Biola Univ	CA	46,402	C+
Bloomfield College	NJ	39,100	LC
Bluffton Univ	OH	40,950	C
Cedarville Univ	OH	34,990	VC
Central Methodist Univ	MO	36,830	VC
Central Mich Univ	MI	20,330	C
Central State Univ	OH	18,564	C
Central Washington Univ	WA	16,803	C
Champlain College	VT	53,132	C+
Chapman Univ	CA	63,078	VC+
Chicago State Univ	IL	20,144	C
CUNY/Brooklyn College	NY	5,884	C+
Colo State Univ-Pueblo	CO	18,234	C
Concord Univ	WV	14,954	C
Dallas Baptist Univ	TX	33,713	C
Dordt College	IA	37,860	C+
Drake Univ	IA	45,056	HC
Eastern Kentucky Univ	KY	16,908	C
Eastern Nazarene College	MA	39,955	C
Eastern Washington Univ	WA	25,572	LC
Emerson College	MA	54,736	HC
Evangel Univ	MO	28,898	C
Florida State Univ	FL	16,771	HC
Freed-Hardeman Univ	TN	29,450	C
Geneva College	PA	35,450	C
George Washington Univ	DC	62,835	MC
Gonzaga Univ	WA	50,888	HC
Goshen College	IN	42,500	C
Grand Valley State Univ	MI	22,250	C+
Grand View Univ	IA	32,302	C
Harding Univ	AR	25,421	C
Hardin-Simmons Univ	TX	33,966	C
Hastings College	NE	35,380	C+
Howard Univ	DC	37,616	C+
Huntington Univ	IN	33,996	C
Ithaca College	NY	56,766	VC
Lewis Univ	IL	40,370	C
Lincoln Memorial Univ	TN	28,070	C
LIU Post	NY	49,682	C
Madonna Univ	MI	29,050	C
Malone Univ	OH	38,448	C
Manhattan College	NY	51,750	C+
Marietta College	OH	46,190	C
Marquette Univ	WI	48,390	VC+
Marshall Univ	WV	17,242	C
Marywood Univ	PA	46,900	C
Mercy College	NY	31,776	C
Mercyhurst Univ	PA	47,420	C
Millersville Univ of Pennsylvania	PA	23,782	C
Minn State Univ, Moorhead	MN	15,941	C
Minot State Univ	ND	12,732	C
Missouri Baptist Univ	MO	35,594	C
Montclair State Univ	NJ	26,210	LC
North Central College	IL	48,712	VC
North Greenville Univ	SC	25,930	C+
Northern Mich Univ	MI	19,604	C
Northwest Missouri State Univ	MO	17,737	C
Northwestern Okla State Univ	OK	13,072	NC
Ohio Northern Univ	OH	44,050	VC
Ohio Univ	OH	22,924	C
Okla Baptist Univ	OK	32,320	C
Okla Christian Univ	OK	27,650	VC
Okla City Univ	OK	40,476	VC
Okla State Univ	OK	17,180	VC
Oral Roberts Univ	OK	34,316	C
Otterbein Univ	OH	41,630	C
Point Loma Nazarene Univ	CA	43,450	C
Point Park Univ	PA	41,270	C
Prairie View A&M Univ	TX	15,205	LC
Purdue Univ/Northwest	IN	15,038	C
Purdue Univ/West Lafayette	IN	20,032	MC
Roosevelt Univ	IL	40,651	VC
Rowan Univ	NJ	24,491	VC+
San Francisco State Univ	CA	18,514	LC
San Jose State Univ	CA	21,540	C
Savannah College of Art and Design	GA	49,595	C
Seton Hall Univ	NJ	55,514	C
Shaw Univ	NC	24,638	C
Southeastern Univ	FL	31,765	C
Southern Adventist Univ	TN	27,600	C
Southern Arkansas Univ	AR	21,532	C
Southern Illinois Univ Carbondale	IL	23,667	C
Southern Methodist Univ	TX	66,483	MC
Southwestern Adventist Univ	TX	27,756	LC
Spring Arbor Univ	MI	36,000	C
St. Cloud State Univ	MN	10,600	C
SUNY / Buffalo State College	NY	20,842	C
SUNY at Oswego	NY	21,351	C
Stephen F. Austin State Univ	TX	18,406	LC
Suffolk Univ	MA	50,308	C
Syracuse Univ	NY	60,239	VC
Temple Univ	PA	24,392	VC
Texas A&M Univ at Commerce	TX	10,496	C
Texas State Univ	TX	19,350	C
The Lincoln Univ	PA	15,154	NC
Troy Univ	AL	16,171	C
Union Univ	TN	33,970	VC
Univ of Central Florida	FL	15,922	VC
Univ of Central Missouri	MO	18,982	C
Univ of Central Okla	OK	13,486	C
Univ of Cincinnati	OH	21,964	VC
Univ of Findlay	OH	60,139	C
Univ of Idaho	ID	15,348	C
Univ of Illinois at Urbana-Champaign	IL	27,006	HC
Univ of Indianapolis	IN	36,480	C
Univ of La Verne	CA	55,600	C
Univ of Louisiana at Lafayette	LA	14,516	C
Univ of Missouri/Columbia	MO	18,201	MC
Univ of Nebr - Kearney	NE	16,546	LC
Univ of Nebr - Lincoln	NE	18,589	VC
Univ of Nebr - Omaha	NE	16,120	C
Univ of North Texas	TX	19,198	C
Univ of Northwestern - St. Paul	MN	38,160	C
Univ of Okla	OK	18,911	VC
Univ of S Car at Columbia	SC	19,725	VC+
Univ of Southern Calif	CA	66,631	C
Univ of Southern Indiana	IN	16,501	C
Univ of Texas at Arlington	TX	18,026	LC
Vanguard Univ of Southern Calif	CA	40,740	VC
Wartburg College	IA	47,840	C
Washington State Univ	WA	22,495	C
Waynesburg Univ	PA	32,290	C
West Liberty Univ	WV	15,512	C
West Texas A&M Univ	TX	13,478	C
West Virginia Univ	WV	18,210	C
Western Illinois Univ	IL	20,825	C
Western Kentucky Univ	KY	16,850	C
Westminster College	PA	39,180	C+
Winona State Univ	MN	17,535	C
York College of Pennsylvania	PA	29,240	C
Youngstown State Univ	OH	17,307	C

BUSINESS (DUAL MAJOR PROGRAM)

School	ST	$IS	SR
Bentley Univ	MA	60,890	HC
Calvin College	MI	41,570	VC+
CUNY/Brooklyn College	NY	5,884	C+
Clayton State Univ	GA	19,735	C
John Carroll Univ	OH	49,740	C+
Mercy College	NY	31,776	C
Neumann Univ	PA	40,678	LC
Southern Oregon Univ	OR	19,117	C
The Master's Univ	CA	43,870	C+
Univ of New Hampshire - Manchester	NH	14,490	C
Univ of Pittsburgh	PA	29,568	HC+
Univ of Tulsa	OK	52,625	HC+
Western Kentucky Univ	KY	16,850	C

BUSINESS ADMINISTRATION - INTERNATIONAL

School	ST	$IS	SR
Aquinas College - Mich	MI	38,876	HC
Ball State Univ	IN	19,590	C
Bloomfield College	NJ	39,100	LC
Bryant Univ	RI	55,646	VC
Cabrini Univ	PA	42,591	LC
CUNY/Queens College	NY	27,896	C
Clayton State Univ	GA	19,735	C
College of the Ozarks	MO	7,230	C
Dallas Baptist Univ	TX	33,713	C
Embry-Riddle Aeronautical Univ - Prescott Campus	AZ	44,054	VC
Franklin College	IN	39,380	C
Lewis Univ	IL	40,370	C
Lynn Univ	FL	49,480	LC
Lyon College	AR	34,730	C+
Millersville Univ of Pennsylvania	PA	23,782	C
Monmouth Univ	NJ	46,234	C
Neumann Univ	PA	40,678	LC
Okla Christian Univ	OK	27,650	VC
Point Loma Nazarene Univ	CA	43,450	C
Regis College	MA	51,920	C
Rochester Inst of Technology	NY	50,842	HC
St. Ambrose Univ	IA	39,019	C
The Master's Univ	CA	43,870	C+
Trevecca Nazarene Univ	TN	31,186	C
Univ of Nevada/Reno	NV	18,010	C
Univ of Rhode Island	RI	24,906	C
Univ of Tulsa	OK	52,625	HC+
West Chester Univ of Pennsylvania	PA	18,456	C
Western Kentucky Univ	KY	16,850	C

BUSINESS ADMINISTRATION AND MANAGEMENT

School	ST	$IS	SR
Adams State Univ	CO	17,703	LC
Adelphi Univ	NY	48,244	C
Adrian College	MI	42,400	C
Agnes Scott College	GA	51,930	VC+
Alabama A&M Univ	AL	18,796	C
Alabama State Univ	AL	14,142	NC
Alaska Pacific Univ	AK	26,680	VC
Albertus Magnus College	CT	43,258	LC
Albion College	MI	52,650	C
Albright College	PA	46,660	C
Alcorn State Univ	MS	15,854	C
Alderson Broaddus Univ	WV	26,149	C
Alfred Univ	NY	42,296	C+
Alice Lloyd College	KY	8,190	C
Allen Univ	SC	19,300	NC
Alma College	MI	47,548	C
Alvernia Univ	PA	43,900	C
Alverno College	WI	33,294	LC
American International College	MA	46,300	LC
American Jewish Univ - College of A&S Campus	CA	44,234	C
American Univ	DC	59,379	HC+
Amridge Univ	AL	10,860	LC
Anderson Univ	IN	38,200	C
Andrews Univ	MI	28,030	C+
Angelo State Univ	TX	15,263	NC
Anna Maria College	MA	48,186	C
Aquinas College	TN	30,800	C+
Aquinas College - Mich	MI	38,876	HC
Arcadia Univ	PA	33,570	C+
Arizona State Univ at the Polytechnic Campus	AZ	21,360	VC
Arizona State Univ at the Tempe Campus	AZ	21,756	VC
Arizona State Univ at the West Campus	AZ	20,640	C
Arkansas Baptist College	AR	20,280	NC
Arkansas State Univ	AR	16,190	C
Asbury Univ	KY	35,180	C+
Ashford Univ	CA	10,480	C
Ashland Univ	OH	21,440	C
Assumption College	MA	47,920	C+
Atlantic Union College	MA	27,228	C
Auburn Univ	AL	23,594	VC+
Auburn Univ at Montgomery	AL	15,290	C
Augsburg College	MN	43,929	C
Augusta Univ	GA	4,632	C
Augustana College	IL	49,658	VC
Augustana Univ	SD	38,424	VC
Aurora Univ	IL	33,970	C
Austin College	TX	45,875	VC
Austin Peay State Univ	TN	16,397	C
Averett Univ	VA	40,970	LC
Avila Univ	MO	35,480	C
Azusa Pacific Univ	CA	43,972	C
Babson College	MA	63,664	HC
Baker College of Flint	MI	13,880	NC
Baker Univ	KS	33,350	C+
Baldwin Wallace Univ	OH	41,106	C
Ball State Univ	IN	19,590	C
Barton College	NC	38,686	LC
Bay Path Univ	MA	45,349	C
Bayamon Central Univ	PR	12,490	
Baylor Univ	TX	53,760	HC
Becker College	MA	57,628	C
Belhaven Univ	MS	31,016	C
Bellarmine Univ	KY	51,220	C
Bellevue Univ	NE	20,300	NC
Belmont Abbey College	NC	48,156	C
Belmont Univ	TN	40,970	VC
Beloit College	WI	55,206	HC
Bemidji State Univ	MN	16,056	VC
Benedict College	SC	28,238	NC
Benedictine College	KS	36,200	VC
Benedictine Univ	IL	38,300	C
Bennett College	NC	27,302	NC
Bentley Univ	MA	60,890	HC
Berea College	KY	7,042	C
Berkeley College/New Jersey	NJ	38,082	LC
Berkeley College/New York City Campus	NY	23,350	LC
Berkeley College/White Plains Campus	NY	35,100	LC
Berry College	GA	45,286	C+
Bethany College	KS	46,100	NC
Bethany College	WV	36,300	NC
Bethel College	IN	35,860	C
Bethel College	KS	35,370	C
Bethel Univ	MN	45,270	VC
Bethel Univ	TN	24,738	C
Bethune-Cookman Univ	FL	22,970	C
Biola Univ	CA	46,402	C+
Birmingham-Southern College	AL	44,478	VC
Black Hills State Univ	SD	15,899	C
Blackburn College	IL	28,526	LC
Bloomfield College	NJ	39,100	LC
Bloomsburg Univ of Pennsylvania	PA	19,066	LC
Blue Mountain College	MS	15,949	VC
Bluefield College	VA	34,120	C+
Bluefield State College	WV	5,832	LC
Bluffton Univ	OH	40,950	C
Boise State Univ	ID	14,860	C
Boricua College	NY	10,100	C
Boston College	MA	65,737	MC
Boston Univ	MA	65,110	MC
Bowie State Univ	MD	26,728	LC
Bowling Green State Univ	OH	19,747	C
Brandeis Univ	MA	65,925	MC
Brenau Univ - Women's College	GA	37,876	LC
Brescia Univ	KY	29,890	VC+
Brewton-Parker College	GA	23,490	C
Briar Cliff Univ	IA	36,956	C
Bridgewater College	VA	44,510	C
Brigham Young Univ	UT	12,748	HC
Bryan College	TN	31,440	C
Bryant Univ	RI	55,646	VC
Bucknell Univ	PA	64,616	MC
Buena Vista Univ	IA	41,514	C
Cabrini Univ	PA	42,591	LC
Cairn Univ	PA	36,296	C
Caldwell Univ	NJ	42,165	NC
Calif Baptist Univ	CA	41,392	C
Calif Inst of Technology	CA	58,761	MC
Calif Lutheran Univ	CA	52,853	C
Calif Polytechnic State Univ	CA	17,979	HC+
Calif State Polytechnic Univ, Pomona	CA	21,541	C
Cal State, Maritime Academy	CA	19,450	LC
Cal State, Bakersfield	CA	19,191	LC
Cal State, Chico	CA	21,440	C
Cal State, Dominguez Hills	CA	19,022	LC
Cal State, East Bay	CA	19,413	C
Cal State, Fresno	CA	16,902	LC
Cal State, Fullerton	CA	21,902	C
Cal State, Long Beach	CA	18,850	C
Cal State, Los Angeles	CA	17,186	LC
Cal State, Monterey Bay	CA	26,871	LC
Cal State, Northridge	CA	16,859	LC
Cal State, Sacramento	CA	20,332	C
Cal State, San Bernardino	CA	12,000	C
Cal State, San Marcos	CA	24,184	LC
Cal State, Stanislaus	CA	16,212	C
Calif Univ of Pennsylvania	PA	14,217	LC
Calumet College of St. Joseph	IN	22,735	C
Calvin College	MI	41,570	VC+
Cameron Univ	OK	11,072	NC
Campbellsville Univ	KY	32,492	C
Canisius College	NY	47,537	C
Capital Univ	OH	42,982	C
Cardinal Stritch Univ	WI	36,462	C
Caribbean Univ	PR	15,471	
Carlos Albizu Univ	FL		LC
Carlow Univ	PA	38,549	LC
Carnegie Mellon Univ	PA	67,980	MC
Carroll College	MT	39,972	C+
Carroll Univ	WI	38,100	C+
Carson-Newman Univ	TN	34,160	C
Carthage College	WI	48,835	C
Case Western Reserve Univ	OH	60,304	MC
Castleton Univ	VT	20,186	C
Catawba College	NC	39,820	C
Cazenovia College	NY	46,470	C
Cedar Crest College	PA	46,715	C
Cedarville Univ	OH	34,990	VC
Centenary College	NJ	43,602	C
Centenary College of Louisiana	LA	45,650	C+
Central College	IA	44,592	C
Central Conn State Univ	CT	21,203	C
Central Methodist Univ	MO	36,830	VC
Central Mich Univ	MI	20,330	C
Central State Univ	OH	18,564	C
Central Washington Univ	WA	16,803	C
Chadron State College	NE	14,819	NC
Chaminade Univ of Honolulu	HI	36,000	C
Champlain College	VT	53,132	C+
Chapman Univ	CA	63,078	VC+
Charleston Southern Univ	SC	32,400	C
Charter Oak State College	CT	7,671	LC
Chatham Univ	PA	46,517	C
Chestnut Hill College	PA	43,410	C
Cheyney Univ of Pennsylvania	PA	20,896	LC
Chicago State Univ	IL	20,144	C
Christian Brothers Univ	TN	31,670	VC
Christopher Newport Univ	VA	23,968	VC+
CUNY/Brooklyn College	NY	5,884	C+
CUNY/City College	NY	20,319	VC
CUNY/College of Staten Island	NY	17,840	NC
CUNY/Lehman College	NY	5,778	HC+
CUNY/Meger Evers College	NY	6,680	NC
CUNY/York College	NY	6,747	LC
City Univ of Seattle	WA	24,340	NC
Claflin Univ	SC	33,764	LC
Clarion Univ of Pennsylvania	PA	21,608	LC
Clark Atlanta Univ	GA	31,019	LC
Clark Univ	MA	51,600	HC+
Clarke Univ	IA	38,940	C
Clarkson College	NE	31,868	C
Clayton State Univ	GA	19,735	C
Clemson Univ	SC		HC
Coastal Carolina Univ	SC	19,766	C
Coe College	IA	51,570	VC
Coker College	SC	34,810	LC
Colby-Sawyer College	NH	50,790	C
College of Charleston	SC	22,699	C
College of Mount St. Vincent	NY	45,620	C
College of St. Elizabeth	NJ	44,432	LC
College of St Joseph	VT	32,400	LC
College of St. Scholastica	MN	44,640	C
College of the Ozarks	MO	7,230	C
College of William & Mary	VA		MC
Colo Christian Univ	CO	39,940	VC
Colo Mesa Univ	CO	18,955	LC
Colo State Univ	CO	22,162	VC
Colo State Univ-Pueblo	CO	18,234	C
Colo Technical Univ	CO	21,455	NC
Columbia College	SC	36,550	C
Columbia College - Missouri	MO	27,803	C
Columbus State Univ	GA	14,336	LC

ST = STATE **$IS** = IN-STATE COSTS **SR** = SELECTOR RATING

School	ST	$IS	SR
Concord Univ	WV	14,954	C
Concordia College - Alabama	AL	15,720	NC
Concordia College - Moorhead	MN	51,088	C+
Concordia College - New York	NY	39,035	LC
Concordia Univ	CA	41,580	VC
Concordia Univ	OR	35,000	C
Concordia Univ Nebr	NE	36,280	VC
Concordia Univ St. Paul	MN	29,050	C
Concordia Univ Texas	TX	40,210	C
Concordia Univ Wisc	WI	35,910	C
Concordia Univ, Ann Arbor	MI	35,945	VC
Concordia Univ, Chicago	IL	39,694	C
Converse College	SC	26,495	C
Coppin State Univ	MD	17,041	VC
Corban Univ	OR	40,306	C
Covenant College	GA	38,990	VC
Culver-Stockton College	MO	33,525	C
Cumberland Univ	TN	27,710	C
Curry College	MA	51,815	C
Daemen College	NY	38,045	C
Dakota State Univ	SD	13,811	C
Dakota Wesleyan Univ	SD	32,850	C
Dallas Baptist Univ	TX	33,713	C
Daniel Webster College	NH	26,984	C
Davenport Univ	MI	25,896	LC
Davis & Elkins College	WV	38,242	LC
Defiance College	OH	41,630	C
Delaware State Univ	DE	19,376	NC
Delaware Valley Univ	PA	49,796	C
Delta State Univ	MS	13,176	C
DePaul Univ	IL	47,623	VC
DeSales Univ	PA	43,970	C
Dickinson State Univ	ND	12,372	LC
Dillard Univ	LA	20,940	VC
Doane Univ	NE	39,184	VC
Dominican College	NY	31,270	LC
Dominican Univ	IL	41,222	C
Dominican Univ of Calif	CA	57,050	C
Dordt College	IA	37,860	C+
Drake Univ	IA	45,056	HC
Drew Univ/College of Liberal Arts	NJ	61,048	VC
Drexel Univ	PA	65,432	VC+
Drury Univ	MO	33,791	VC
Duquesne Univ	PA	46,822	VC
D'Youville College	NY	36,780	C
Earlham College	IN	54,870	HC
East Carolina Univ	NC	16,937	C
East Central Univ	OK	13,056	C
East Texas Baptist Univ	TX	33,134	C
Eastern Conn State Univ	CT	23,059	C
Eastern Illinois Univ	IL	21,126	C
Eastern Kentucky Univ	KY	16,908	C
Eastern Mennonite Univ	VA	42,550	C
Eastern Mich Univ	MI	19,761	C
Eastern Nazarene College	MA	39,955	C
Eastern New Mexico Univ	NM	14,416	C
Eastern Oregon Univ	OR	17,715	C
Eastern Univ	PA	39,540	C
Eastern Washington Univ	WA	25,572	LC
Eckerd College	FL	52,874	C
Edgewood College	WI	35,950	C
Edinboro Univ	PA	15,940	LC
Edward Waters College	FL	20,607	NC
Elizabeth City State Univ	NC	14,745	C
Elizabethtown College	PA	54,050	C
Elizabethtown College School of Continuing and Professional Studies	PA	18,900	C
Elmhurst College	IL	45,428	C
Elmira College	NY	53,900	C
Elms College	MA	45,646	VC
Elon Univ	NC	44,599	VC+
Embry-Riddle Aeronautical Univ - Prescott Campus	AZ	44,054	VC
Emmanuel College	MA	52,110	C+
Emory and Henry College	VA	41,410	C
Emory Univ	GA	60,786	MC
Emporia State Univ	KS	14,570	C
Endicott College	MA	44,604	VC+
Erskine College	SC	45,460	C
Eureka College	IL	30,220	C
Excelsior College	NY	14,080	SP
Fairleigh Dickinson Univ/ College at Florham	NJ	52,062	C
Fairleigh Dickinson Univ/ Metropolitan Campus	NJ	40,254	C
Fairmont State Univ	WV	15,726	C
Farmingdale State College	NY	20,624	C
Faulkner Univ	AL	26,410	C
Fayetteville State Univ	NC	17,756	C
Felician Univ	NJ	45,370	LC
Ferris State Univ	MI	21,445	C
Ferrum College	VA	39,650	C
Fisk Univ	TN	32,066	LC
Fitchburg State Univ	MA	21,819	C
Flagler College	FL	27,620	C
Florida A&M Univ	FL	15,361	C
Florida Atlantic Univ	FL	17,339	C
Florida Inst of Technology	FL	53,306	VC
Florida International Univ	FL	19,854	C+
Florida Memorial Univ	FL	22,270	LC
Florida State Univ	FL	16,771	HC
Fontbonne Univ	MO	33,717	C
Fordham Univ	NY	65,918	MC
Fort Hays State Univ	KS	12,131	C
Fort Lewis College	CO	18,980	C
Fort Valley State Univ	GA	17,988	VC
Framingham State Univ	MA	20,584	C
Francis Marion Univ	SC	16,464	LC
Franciscan Univ of Steubenville	OH	33,980	VC
Franklin and Marshall College	PA	63,170	HC
Franklin College	IN	39,380	C
Franklin Pierce Univ	NH	46,750	C
Franklin Univ	OH	56,262	SP
Freed-Hardeman Univ	TN	29,450	C
Fresno Pacific Univ	CA	37,370	C
Friends Univ	KS	34,455	C
Frostburg State Univ	MD	17,280	LC
Furman Univ	SC	58,092	VC+
Gallaudet Univ	DC	29,118	LC
Gannon Univ	PA	42,032	C
Gardner-Webb Univ	NC	39,200	C+
Geneva College	PA	35,450	C
George Fox Univ	OR	42,938	C
George Mason Univ	VA	15,724	VC
George Washington Univ	DC	62,835	MC
Georgetown College	KY	41,440	C
Georgetown Univ	DC	65,926	MC
Georgia College & State Univ	GA	21,148	C+
Georgia Inst of Technology	GA	23,360	MC
Georgia Southwestern State Univ	GA	13,870	C
Georgia State Univ	GA	24,332	VC
Georgian Court Univ	NJ	42,426	LC
Gettysburg College	PA	63,000	HC
Glenville State College	WV	17,386	NC
Goldey-Beacom College	DE	31,750	C
Gonzaga Univ	WA	50,888	HC
Goodwin College	CT	28,370	LC
Gordon College	MA	46,472	C+
Goshen College	IN	42,500	C
Goucher College	MD	55,716	VC
Grace Bible College	MI	25,250	C
Grace College and Seminary	IN	31,524	C
Graceland Univ	IA	35,290	C
Grambling State Univ	LA	15,701	C
Grand Canyon Univ	AZ	16,950	VC
Grand Rapids Theological Seminary/Cornerstone Univ	MI	33,338	C
Grand Valley State Univ	MI	22,250	C+
Grand View Univ	IA	32,302	C
Green Mountain College	VT	45,228	LC
Greensboro College	NC	42,400	LC
Greenville College	IL	27,012	C
Grove City College	PA	25,692	VC
Guilford College	NC	44,090	C
Gustavus Adolphus College	MN	52,433	HC
Gwynedd Mercy Univ	PA	43,780	LC
Hamline Univ	MN	45,678	VC
Hampton Univ	VA	34,926	LC
Hannibal-LaGrange Univ	MO	29,815	C
Harding Univ	AR	25,421	C
Hardin-Simmons Univ	TX	33,966	C
Harris-Stowe State Univ	MO	14,360	NC
Hartwick College	NY	51,270	C
Hastings College	NE	35,380	C+
Hawaii Pacific Univ	HI	33,420	C
Heidelberg Univ	OH	39,200	C
Hellenic College/Holy Cross Greek Orthodox School of Theology	MA	39,906	C
Henderson State Univ	AR	15,516	LC
Heritage Univ	WA	19,825	NC
High Point Univ	NC	45,977	C
Hilbert College	NY	30,850	C
Hodges Univ	FL	19,080	LC
Hollins Univ	VA	49,635	VC
Holy Family Univ	PA	43,326	LC
Holy Names Univ	CA	46,630	LC
Hood College	MD	54,840	C
Hope College	MI	39,940	VC
Hope International Univ	CA	41,150	C
Houghton College	NY	39,090	C
Houston Baptist Univ	TX	36,450	C
Howard Payne Univ	TX	34,320	C
Howard Univ	DC	37,616	C+
Humboldt State Univ	CA	20,514	C
Humphreys College	CA	27,790	C
Huntingdon College	AL	34,900	C
Huntington Univ	IN	33,996	C
Husson Univ	ME	25,720	LC
Huston-Tillotson Univ	TX	18,124	LC
Idaho State Univ	ID	13,619	NC
Illinois College	IL	40,850	VC
Illinois State Univ	IL	23,418	VC
Illinois Wesleyan Univ	IL	56,430	VC+
Indiana Inst of Technology	IN	34,240	LC
Indiana State Univ	IN	23,223	LC
Indiana Univ Bloomington	IN	20,429	VC
Indiana Univ East	IN	7,072	C
Indiana Univ Kokomo	IN	7,073	C
Indiana Univ Northwest	IN	7,072	C
Indiana Univ South Bend	IN	14,242	C
Indiana Univ Southeast	IN	14,242	LC
Indiana Univ-Purdue Univ Fort Wayne	IN	17,553	C
Indiana Univ-Purdue Univ Indianapolis	IN	18,635	C
Indiana Wesleyan Univ	IN	33,674	C
Inter-American Univ of PR Ponce	PR	19,549	
Inter-American Univ of PR-Aguadilla Campus	PR	21,657	
Inter-American Univ of PR-Arecibo Campus	PR	18,245	
Inter-American Univ of PR-Barranquitas	PR	18,336	
Inter-American Univ of PR-Bayamon	PR	18,785	
Inter-American Univ of PR-Fajardo Campus	PR	18,336	
Inter-American Univ of PR-Metropolitan Campus	PR	20,045	
Inter-American Univ of PR-San Germán	PR	20,042	
Iona College	NY	50,984	C
Iowa State Univ	IA	17,570	C
Iowa Wesleyan Univ	IA	39,200	C
Ithaca College	NY	56,766	VC
Jackson State Univ	MS	15,879	LC
Jacksonville Univ	FL	46,230	C
James Madison Univ	VA	19,084	VC
Jarvis Christian College	TX	20,160	NC
John Brown Univ	AR	33,132	VC
John Carroll Univ	OH	49,740	C+
Johnson & Wales Univ/ Charlotte Campus	NC	43,988	C
Johnson & Wales Univ/ Denver Campus	CO	42,707	C
Johnson & Wales Univ/North Miami Campus	FL	42,707	C
Johnson & Wales Univ/ Providence Campus	RI	42,248	C
Johnson C. Smith Univ	NC	25,336	LC
Johnson State College	VT	20,752	C
Judson College	AL	27,066	C
Judson Univ	IL	37,700	C
Juniata College	PA	53,760	VC
Kansas State Univ	KS	17,780	VC
Keene State College	NH	24,003	LC
Keiser Univ	FL	35,010	LC
Kendall College	IL	32,610	C
Kennesaw State Univ	GA	19,592	VC
Kent State Univ	OH	20,732	C
Kentucky Christian Univ	KY	26,560	LC
Kentucky State Univ	KY	13,364	LC
Kentucky Wesleyan College	KY	32,080	C
Keuka College	NY	39,762	C
Keystone College	PA	28,680	LC
King Univ	TN	34,660	C
King's College	PA	46,858	C
Kutztown Univ of Pennsylvania	PA	19,056	LC
La Roche College	PA	37,924	LC
La Salle Univ	PA	55,790	C
La Sierra Univ	CA	39,690	VC
LaGrange College	GA	39,930	C
Lake Erie College	OH	38,914	LC
Lakeland Univ	WI	35,130	C
Lamar Univ	TX	18,014	LC
Lander Univ	SC	43,994	C
Lane College	TN	16,550	C
Langston Univ	OK	14,314	C
Lasell College	MA	47,500	C
Lawrence Tech Univ	MI	39,770	VC
Lebanon Valley College	PA	51,530	C
Lee Univ	TN	22,045	C
Lees-McRae College	NC	33,944	C
LeMoyne-Owen College	TN	16,980	C
Lenoir-Rhyne Univ	NC	43,200	C
LeTourneau Univ	TX	38,250	VC
Lewis Univ	IL	40,370	C
Lewis-Clark State College	ID	14,202	C
Liberty Univ	VA	19,101	C
LIM College	NY	41,575	LC
Limestone College	SC	32,100	C
Lincoln Memorial Univ	TN	28,070	C
Lincoln Univ	MO	13,602	NC
Lindenwood Univ	MO	25,132	C
Lindsey Wilson College	KY	32,882	C
Linfield College	OR	52,010	C
Lipscomb Univ	TN	41,296	VC
LIU Brooklyn	NY	49,682	C
LIU Post	NY	49,682	C
Livingstone College	NC	17,815	LC
Lock Haven Univ of Pennsylvania	PA	18,028	LC
Longwood Univ	VA	22,184	C
Loras College	IA	39,222	C
Louisiana College	LA	21,886	C
Louisiana State Univ and A&M College	LA	18,677	VC
Louisiana State Univ in Shreveport	LA	6,902	C
Louisiana Tech Univ	LA	11,422	VC
Lourdes Univ	OH	29,520	NC
Loyola Univ Chicago	IL	55,802	VC
Loyola Univ Maryland	MD	60,300	VC
Loyola Univ New Orleans	LA	51,708	VC+
Lubbock Christian Univ	TX	28,426	C
Lycoming College	PA	48,580	C
Lynchburg College	VA	46,740	C
Lyndon State College	VT	20,714	C
Lynn Univ	FL	49,480	LC
Lyon College	AR	34,730	C+
MacMurray College	IL	33,620	C
Madonna Univ	MI	29,050	C
Malone Univ	OH	38,448	C
Manchester Univ	IN	40,422	C
Manhattanville College	NY	51,440	C+
Mansfield Univ	PA	23,376	LC
Marian Univ	IN	41,220	C
Marian Univ	WI	32,420	LC
Marietta College	OH	46,190	C
Marist College	NY	49,860	VC
Marquette Univ	WI	48,390	VC+
Mars Hill Univ	NC	42,688	C
Martin Univ	IN	20,264	LC
Mary Baldwin Univ	VA	39,865	C
Marygrove College	MI	28,926	NC
Marylhurst Univ	OR	20,295	NC
Marymount Manhattan College	NY	46,280	VC
Marymount Univ	VA	41,570	LC
Maryville College	TN	44,410	C
Maryville Univ of St. Louis	MO	38,046	VC+
Marywood Univ	PA	46,900	C
Mass College of Liberal Arts	MA	20,128	C
Mayville State Univ	ND	18,371	NC
McDaniel College	MD	51,380	VC
McKendree Univ	IL	37,940	C+
McMurry Univ	TX	34,259	LC
McNeese State Univ	LA	7,838	C
McPherson College	KS	34,909	C
Medaille College	NY	35,112	C
Mercer Univ	GA	45,348	VC
Mercy College	NY	31,776	C
Mercyhurst Univ	PA	47,420	C
Meredith College	NC	45,297	C
Merrimack College	MA	52,770	C
Messiah College	PA	43,100	C+
Methodist Univ	NC	43,600	C
Metropolitan College of New York	NY		VC
Metropolitan State Univ	MN	7,566	C
Mich State Univ	MI	23,898	VC+
MidAmerica Nazarene Univ	KS	35,550	C
Middle Tenn State Univ	TN	8,650	C
Midland Univ	NE	37,468	
Midway Univ	KY	31,640	LC
Midwestern State Univ	TX	17,572	C
Miles College	AL	18,646	NC
Millersville Univ of Pennsylvania	PA	23,782	C
Milligan College	TN	38,150	C
Millikin Univ	IL	42,158	C
Millsaps College	MS	50,080	C+
Milwaukee School of Engineering	WI	45,153	HC
Minn State Univ, Mankato	MN	15,616	C
Minn State Univ, Moorhead	MN	15,941	C
Misericordia Univ	PA	43,840	C
Miss College	MS	25,850	C
Miss State Univ	MS	11,454	C+
Miss Univ for Women	MS	17,065	C
Miss Valley State Univ	MS	13,233	LC
Missouri Baptist Univ	MO	35,594	C
Missouri Southern State Univ	MO	12,499	C
Missouri State Univ	MO	15,190	C+
Missouri Univ of Science and Technology	MO	18,655	HC
Missouri Valley College	MO	28,150	C
Missouri Western State Univ	MO	16,741	
Mitchell College	CT	43,280	C
Molloy College	NY	40,440	C
Monmouth College	IL	42,260	C
Monmouth Univ	NJ	46,234	C
Monroe College	NY	23,660	C
Montana State Univ	MT	15,500	C+
Montana State Univ-Billings	MT	22,960	C
Montclair State Univ	NJ	26,210	LC
Montreat College	NC	31,298	LC
Moravian College	PA	53,117	
Morehouse College	GA	40,064	C
Morgan State Univ	MD	17,190	LC
Morningside College	IA	36,865	C
Morris College	SC	18,500	LC
Mount Aloysius College	PA	29,976	C
Mount Ida College	MA	46,820	C
Mount Marty College	SD	32,972	C
Mount Mary Univ	WI	34,650	LC
Mount Mercy Univ	IA	36,826	C
Mount St. Mary College	NY	42,061	C
Mount St. Joseph Univ	OH	33,880	C
Mount St. Mary's Univ	MD	51,610	C
Mount St. Mary's Univ - Chalon Campus	CA	43,897	VC+
Mount Vernon Nazarene Univ	OH	34,500	C
Muhlenberg College	PA	56,645	VC+
Murray State Univ	KY	16,998	C
Muskingum Univ	OH	35,966	C
National Louis Univ	IL	16,920	LC
Nazareth College	NY	45,574	C
Nebr Wesleyan Univ	NE	38,140	C+
New England College	NH	50,364	C
New Jersey City Univ	NJ	21,456	LC
New Mexico Highlands Univ	NM	11,904	NC
New Mexico Inst of Mining and Technology	NM	14,833	HC
New Mexico State Univ	NM	14,050	C
New York Inst of Technology	NY	48,730	C
New York Univ	NY	65,860	MC
Newberry College	SC	34,550	C
Newbury College	MA	46,950	C
Newman Univ	KS	35,390	C
Niagara Univ	NY	41,010	C
Nicholls State Univ	LA	10,534	C
Nichols College	MA	46,800	LC

ST = STATE **$IS** = IN-STATE COSTS **SR** = SELECTOR RATING

School	ST	$IS	SR
N Car A&T State Univ	NC	13,365	LC
N Car Central Univ	NC	9,000	C
N Car State Univ	NC	19,515	HC+
N Car Wesleyan College	NC	39,200	C
North Central College	IL	48,712	VC
N Dak State Univ	ND	16,245	C
North Park Univ	IL	35,860	C
Northeastern Illinois Univ	IL	12,529	LC
Northeastern State Univ	OK	8,615	VC
Northeastern Univ	MA	62,703	MC
Northern Arizona Univ	AZ	20,246	VC
Northern Illinois Univ	IL	20,176	C
Northern Kentucky Univ	KY	16,486	C
Northern Mich Univ	MI	19,604	C
Northern State Univ	SD	14,505	C
Northland College	WI	41,103	C+
Northwest Christian Univ	OR	36,580	C
Northwest Missouri State Univ	MO	17,737	C
Northwest Nazarene Univ	ID	36,000	C
Northwest Univ	WA	35,876	VC
Northwestern College of Iowa	IA	38,400	C+
Northwestern Okla State Univ	OK	13,072	NC
Northwood Univ - Mich	MI	35,010	LC
Norwich Univ	VT	28,212	C
Notre Dame de Namur Univ	CA	46,526	LC
Notre Dame of Maryland Univ	MD	46,465	VC
Nova Southeastern Univ	FL	38,534	C+
Nyack College	NY	34,050	NC
Oakland City Univ	IN	33,360	NC
Oakland Univ	MI	20,763	C
Oakwood Univ	AL	43,758	C
Oglala Lakota College	SD	15,050	NC
Oglethorpe Univ	GA	44,200	C+
Ohio Dominican Univ	OH	41,340	C+
Ohio Northern Univ	OH	44,050	VC
Ohio State Univ at Columbus	OH	21,703	HC+
Ohio State Univ at Lima	OH	7,140	C
Ohio State Univ at Mansfield	OH	13,160	C
Ohio State Univ at Marion	OH	7,140	C
Ohio State Univ at Newark	OH	7,140	C
Ohio Univ	OH	22,924	C
Ohio Valley Univ	WV	29,480	C
Ohio Wesleyan Univ	OH	49,460	VC
Okla Baptist Univ	OK	32,320	C
Okla Christian Univ	OK	27,650	VC
Okla City Univ	OK	40,476	VC
Okla Panhandle State Univ	OK	6,152	NC
Okla State Univ	OK	17,180	VC
Okla Wesleyan Univ	OK	33,206	C
Old Dominion Univ	VA	20,910	C
Olivet College	MI	36,110	LC
Olivet Nazarene Univ	IL	41,840	C
Oral Roberts Univ	OK	34,316	C
Oregon State Univ	OR	22,519	VC
Ottawa Univ	KS	36,074	VC
Otterbein Univ	OH	41,630	C
Ouachita Baptist Univ	AR	32,320	C
Our Lady of the Lake Univ	TX	35,012	LC
Pace Univ	NY	58,248	C
Pacific Lutheran Univ	WA	49,960	VC
Pacific Union College	CA	36,009	VC
Pacific Univ	OR	52,876	C
Paine College	GA	19,506	LC
Palm Beach Atlantic Univ	FL	39,720	C
Park Univ	MO	20,329	C
Paul Quinn College	TX	25,350	LC
Peirce College	PA	16,780	NC
Penn State Erie/The Behrend College	PA	16,256	C
Penn State Univ/Altoona	PA	24,584	C
Pennsylvania College of Technology	PA	27,333	NC
Pennsylvania State Univ - Univ Park	PA	29,760	HC
Pepperdine Univ	CA	74,460	HC+
Peru State College	NE	14,768	NC
Pfeiffer Univ	NC	39,695	LC
Philander Smith College	AR	20,814	LC
Piedmont College	GA	32,512	C
Pine Manor College	MA	41,660	LC
Pittsburg State Univ	KS	13,880	NC
Plymouth State Univ	NH	23,180	LC
Point Loma Nazarene Univ	CA	43,450	C
Point Park Univ	PA	41,270	C
Pontifical Catholic Univ of PR	PR	10,534	
Portland State Univ	OR	19,443	C
Post Univ	CT	41,150	C
Prairie View A&M Univ	TX	15,205	LC
Presentation College	SD	25,454	NC
Principia College	IL	39,010	C+
Providence College	RI	60,760	VC
Queens Univ of Charlotte	NC	39,543	C
Quincy Univ	IL	36,998	C
Quinnipiac Univ	CT	59,110	C
Radford Univ	VA	19,027	LC
Ramapo College of New Jersey	NJ	25,338	C
Randolph College	VA	45,660	VC
Randolph-Macon College	VA	49,910	C
Regis Univ	CO	44,520	C
Reinhardt Univ	GA	29,492	C
Rhode Island College	RI	17,694	LC
Rhodes College	TN	51,900	HC
Rider Univ	NJ	54,050	C
Ripon College	WI	46,911	C+
Rivier Univ	NH	40,410	VC
Roanoke College	VA	54,114	VC
Robert Morris Univ	PA	37,834	C
Roberts Wesleyan College	NY	38,306	C
Rochester Inst of Technology	NY	50,842	HC
Rockford Univ	IL	36,030	C
Rockhurst Univ	MO	29,220	C
Rocky Mountain College	MT	34,270	C
Roger Williams Univ	RI	46,296	C+
Roosevelt Univ	IL	40,651	VC
Rosemont College	PA	30,980	C
Rowan Univ	NJ	24,491	VC+
Rust College	MS	10,600	C
Rutgers Univ - New Brunswick	NJ	26,632	HC
Rutgers Univ - Newark	NJ	27,288	C
Sacred Heart Univ	CT	52,750	C
Saginaw Valley State Univ	MI	18,530	C
St. Anselm College	NH	52,560	C+
St. Augustine's Univ	NC	26,048	C
St. Joseph's College of Maine	ME	46,485	C
St. Joseph's Univ	PA	57,544	VC+
St. Louis Univ	MO	49,866	HC
St. Martin's Univ	WA	45,056	C
St. Mary-of-the-Woods College	IN	39,632	LC
St. Mary's College	IN	50,600	C
St. Mary's College of Calif	CA	57,420	C
St. Mary's Univ of Minn	MN	41,210	VC
St. Michael's College	VT	51,725	VC+
St. Peter's Univ	NJ	49,192	C
St. Vincent College	PA	44,626	C
St. Xavier Univ	IL	43,310	C
Salem College	NC	37,694	HC
Salem International Univ	WV	21,090	LC
Salem State Univ	MA	17,303	LC
Salisbury Univ	MD	20,714	VC
Salve Regina Univ	RI	51,470	C
Sam Houston State Univ	TX	18,792	C
San Diego Christian College	CA	39,068	C
San Diego State Univ	CA	21,896	C+
San Francisco State Univ	CA	18,514	LC
San Jose State Univ	CA	21,540	C
Savannah State Univ	GA	15,631	C
Schreiner Univ	TX	34,626	LC
Seattle Pacific Univ	WA	47,439	C+
Seattle Univ	WA	50,811	VC+
Seton Hall Univ	NJ	55,514	C
Seton Hill Univ	PA	46,972	C
Shaw Univ	NC	24,638	C
Shenandoah Univ	VA	41,312	C
Shepherd Univ, West Virginia	WV	17,224	C
Shippensburg Univ of Pennsylvania	PA	23,208	C
Shorter Univ	GA	31,130	LC
Siena College	NY	48,916	C+
Siena Heights Univ	MI	32,040	C
Sierra Nevada College	NV	43,482	C
Silver Lake College of the Holy Family	WI	36,290	LC
Simmons College	MA	53,090	VC
Simpson College	IA	43,839	VC
Simpson Univ	CA	33,700	C
Skidmore College	NY	64,214	HC
Slippery Rock Univ of Pennsylvania	PA	10,360	C
Sonoma State Univ	CA	27,806	C
S Car State Univ	SC	20,805	LC
South Univ	GA	36,070	LC
Southeast Missouri State Univ	MO	15,498	C
Southeastern Louisiana Univ	LA	16,237	C
Southeastern Okla State Univ	OK	11,875	C
Southeastern Univ	FL	31,765	C
Southern Adventist Univ	TN	27,600	C
Southern Arkansas Univ	AR	21,532	C
Southern Conn State Univ	CT	21,924	LC
Southern Illinois Univ Carbondale	IL	23,667	C
Southern Illinois Univ Edwardsville	IL	22,643	C
Southern Methodist Univ	TX	66,483	MC
Southern Nazarene Univ	OK	32,798	NC
Southern New Hampshire Univ	NH	43,198	C
Southern Oregon Univ	OR	19,117	C
Southern Univ and A&M College	LA	16,074	LC+
Southern Univ at New Orleans	LA	8,014	LC
Southern Vermont College	VT	34,670	LC
Southern Wesleyan Univ	SC	32,130	LC
Southwest Baptist Univ	MO	29,900	LC
Southwest Minn State Univ	MN	17,783	C
Southwestern Adventist Univ	TX	27,756	LC
Southwestern College	KS	31,531	C
Southwestern Okla State Univ	OK	11,790	C
Southwestern Univ	TX	50,720	VC
Spalding Univ	KY	31,938	SP
Spring Arbor Univ	MI	36,000	C
Spring Hill College	AL	48,488	C
Springfield College	MA	45,995	C
St. Andrews Univ	NC	44,634	LC
St. Catherine Univ	MN	45,630	VC
St. Cloud State Univ	MN	10,600	C
St. Edward's Univ	TX	53,100	VC
St. Francis College	NY	38,800	LC
St. John Fisher College	NY	43,620	C
St. John's Univ	NY	55,850	C
St. Joseph's College, New York/Brooklyn Campus	NY	25,114	LC
St. Joseph's College, New York/Long Island Campus	NY	25,124	C
St. Mary's Univ	TX	37,500	C
St. Norbert College	WI	44,525	VC
St. Thomas Aquinas College	NY	42,200	C
St. Thomas Univ	FL	36,360	LC
SUNY / Buffalo State College	NY	20,842	C
SUNY / Empire State College	NY	9,145	SP
SUNY / SUNY College at Old Westbury	NY	16,860	C
SUNY / SUNY Fredonia	NY	20,818	C
SUNY / SUNY Plattsburgh	NY	18,814	C
SUNY / SUNY Potsdam	NY	20,404	C+
SUNY / Univ at Buffalo	NY	23,122	C+
SUNY /College of Agriculture and Tech at Cobleskill	NY	20,527	LC
SUNY /Maritime College	NY	16,020	C
SUNY at Binghamton	NY	22,861	MC
SUNY at Geneseo	NY	20,440	VC+
SUNY at New Paltz	NY	19,200	C
SUNY at Oswego	NY	21,351	C
SUNY Polytechnic Inst	NY	19,473	VC
SUNY SUNY Albany	NY	22,165	C
Stephen F. Austin State Univ	TX	18,406	LC
Stephens College	MO	38,042	C
Sterling College	KS	32,830	C
Stetson Univ	FL	53,544	VC
Stevens Inst of Technology	NJ	62,338	MC
Stevenson Univ	MD	72,770	C
Stillman College	AL	20,738	C
Stockton Univ	NJ	25,059	
Stonehill College	MA	55,030	C+
Stony Brook Univ/The SUNY	NY	21,881	MC
Sul Ross State Univ	TX	15,021	LC
Susquehanna Univ	PA	55,340	VC
Tabor College	KS	35,870	C
Talladega College	AL	19,215	C
Tarleton State Univ	TX	15,248	LC
Taylor Univ	IN	40,317	C+
Temple Univ	PA	24,392	VC
Tenn State Univ	TN	14,423	C
Tenn Tech Univ	TN	17,050	C
Texas A&M Univ	TX	20,521	VC+
Texas A&M Univ at Commerce	TX	10,496	C
Texas A&M Univ at Corpus Christi	TX	16,851	LC
Texas A&M Univ at Kingsville	TX	7,500	LC
Texas Lutheran Univ	TX	38,620	C
Texas Southern Univ	TX	18,212	LC
Texas State Univ	TX	19,350	C
Texas Wesleyan Univ	TX	35,134	C
Texas Woman's Univ	TX	15,302	LC
The Catholic Univ of America	DC	56,356	VC
The Citadel, The Military College of S Car	SC	35,339	C
The College at Brockport - SUNY	NY	20,346	C
The College of Idaho	ID	36,415	C
The College of New Jersey	NJ	31,909	HC
The College of New Rochelle	NY	46,300	VC
The College of St. Rose	NY	43,048	C
The Master's Univ	CA	43,870	C+
The Univ of Akron	OH	21,477	C
The Univ of Tenn at Chattanooga	TN	16,744	C
The Univ of Tenn at Martin	TN	14,876	C
The Univ of Utah	UT	17,924	VC
The Univ of Virginia's College at Wise	VA	18,192	LC
Thiel College	PA	41,590	C
Thomas College	ME	35,268	LC
Thomas Edison State Univ	NJ	6,350	NC
Thomas More College	KY	36,720	C
Tiffin Univ	OH	31,380	C
Toccoa Falls College	GA	27,920	C
Touro College	NY	28,950	VC
Towson Univ	MD	17,408	VC
Transylvania Univ	KY	45,690	VC+
Trevecca Nazarene Univ	TN	31,186	C
Trine Univ	IN	41,310	C
Trinity Christian College	IL	35,580	C
Trinity International Univ	IL	31,070	VC
Trinity Univ	TX	52,314	HC+
Trinity Washington Univ	DC	33,826	C+
Troy Univ	AL	16,171	C
Truman State Univ	MO	16,014	HC
Tulane Univ	LA	63,396	HC+
Tuskegee Univ	AL	28,164	C
Union College	KY	32,310	C
Union College	NE	23,270	C
Union Inst & Univ	OH	8,912	SP
Union Univ	TN	33,970	VC
Universidad Adventista de las Antillas	PR	16,606	
Universidad del Turabo	PR	17,828	
Universidad Metropolitana	PR	17,828	
Universidad Politecnica de PR, Hato Rey campus	PR	23,514	
Univ of PR, at Arecibo	PR	12,652	
Univ of Alabama in Huntsville	AL	19,445	VC
Univ of Alaska Anchorage	AK	16,652	NC
Univ of Alaska Southeast	AK	11,493	C
Univ of Arizona	AZ	23,100	C
Univ of Arkansas at Fayetteville	AR	19,152	C+
Univ of Arkansas at Little Rock	AR	18,211	C
Univ of Arkansas at Monticello	AR	13,134	NC
Univ of Arkansas at Pine Bluff	AR	13,541	C
Univ of Bridgeport	CT	44,430	LC
Univ of Calif at Berkeley	CA	28,853	MC
Univ of Calif at Irvine	CA	26,484	VC
Univ of Calif at Riverside	CA	29,227	C+
Univ of Central Arkansas	AR	14,472	VC
Univ of Central Florida	FL	15,922	VC
Univ of Central Missouri	MO	18,982	C
Univ of Central Okla	OK	13,486	C
Univ of Charleston	WV	35,000	C
Univ of Cincinnati	OH	21,964	VC
Univ of Colo Boulder	CO	24,285	VC+
Univ of Colo Colo Springs	CO	19,663	C
Univ of Colo Denver	CO	23,230	C
Univ of Conn	CT	25,538	HC
Univ of Dallas	TX	45,500	VC+
Univ of Dayton	OH	53,620	C
Univ of Delaware	DE	24,976	VC+
Univ of Denver	CO	58,443	VC+
Univ of Detroit Mercy	MI	48,816	C+
Univ of Dubuque	IA	37,824	C
Univ of Evansville	IN	44,186	VC+
Univ of Findlay	OH	60,139	C
Univ of Florida	FL	16,291	HC+
Univ of Great Falls	MT	38,524	C
Univ of Hartford	CT	49,776	C
Univ of Hawaii at Hilo	HI	18,038	C
Univ of Hawaii at Manoa	HI	23,221	C
Univ of Holy Cross	LA	21,523	C
Univ of Houston-Downtown	TX	7,241	C
Univ of Idaho	ID	15,348	C
Univ of Illinois at Chicago	IL	25,006	VC
Univ of Indianapolis	IN	36,480	C
Univ of Iowa	IA	18,683	VC+
Univ of Jamestown	ND	28,508	C
Univ of Kansas	KS	20,135	C+
Univ of La Verne	CA	55,600	C
Univ of Louisiana at Lafayette	LA	14,516	C
Univ of Louisiana at Monroe	LA	15,970	C
Univ of Louisville	KY	19,824	C
Univ of Maine	ME	20,792	C
Univ of Maine at Augusta	ME	7,812	C
Univ of Maine at Farmington	ME	18,187	C
Univ of Maine at Fort Kent	ME	15,165	LC
Univ of Maine at Machias	ME	22,960	C
Univ of Maine at Presque Isle	ME	14,870	C
Univ of Mary	ND	23,180	C
Univ of Mary Hardin-Baylor	TX	33,950	C+
Univ of Mary Washington	VA	24,764	VC
Univ of Maryland/College Park	MD	21,938	HC
Univ of Maryland/Eastern Shore	MD	17,013	C
Univ of Maryland/Univ College	MD	25,966	LC
Univ of Mass Amherst	MA	26,199	VC+
Univ of Mass Dartmouth	MA	25,658	C
Univ of Mass Lowell	MA	26,380	C
Univ of Mich/Ann Arbor	MI	24,410	MC
Univ of Mich/Dearborn	MI	11,757	VC
Univ of Mich-Flint	MI	17,607	C+
Univ of Minn Crookston	MN	19,739	C
Univ of Minn/Duluth	MN	20,292	C+
Univ of Minn/Twin Cities	MN	23,519	HC+
Univ of Miss	MS	17,746	C+
Univ of Missouri/Columbia	MO	18,201	MC
Univ of Missouri-Kansas City	MO	19,563	VC
Univ of Missouri-St. Louis	MO		C
Univ of Mobile	AL	28,935	C
Univ of Montana	MT	14,105	C
Univ of Montevallo	AL	19,502	C
Univ of Mount Olive	NC	18,426	C
Univ of Mount Union	OH	38,970	C
Univ of Nebr - Kearney	NE	16,546	LC
Univ of Nebr - Lincoln	NE	18,589	VC
Univ of New England	ME	48,880	C
Univ of New Hampshire	NH	28,562	VC
Univ of New Haven	CT	52,190	C
Univ of New Mexico	NM	15,404	C
Univ of New Orleans	LA	12,840	C
Univ of N Car at Asheville	NC	15,723	VC+
Univ of N Car at Chapel Hill	NC	20,052	HC+
Univ of N Car at Charlotte	NC	15,547	C
Univ of N Car at Greensboro	NC	14,690	C
Univ of N Car at Pembroke	NC	14,388	LC
Univ of N Car at Wilmington	NC	14,590	VC
Univ of North Florida	FL	15,996	VC
Univ of North Georgia	GA	17,316	C
Univ of North Texas	TX	19,198	C
Univ of Northern Colo	CO	20,851	C
Univ of Northwestern - St. Paul	MN	38,160	C
Univ of Okla	OK	18,911	VC
Univ of Oregon	OR	22,972	C
Univ of Pennsylvania	PA	63,526	MC
Univ of Pikeville	KY	28,700	NC
Univ of Pittsburgh at Bradford	PA	22,402	C
Univ of Pittsburgh at Johnstown	PA	22,092	C
Univ of PR, at Bayamon	PR	13,145	
Univ of PR, at Cayey	PR		

ST = STATE **$IS** = IN-STATE COSTS **SR** = SELECTOR RATING

School	ST	$IS	SR
Univ of PR, at Humacao	PR	14,000	
Univ of PR, at Mayaguez	PR	13,995	
Univ of PR-Rio Piedras campus	PR	13,327	
Univ of Puget Sound	WA	56,456	VC+
Univ of Redlands	CA	60,200	VC
Univ of Rhode Island	RI	24,906	C
Univ of Richmond	VA	60,880	MC
Univ of Rio Grande & Rio Grande Community College	OH	8,750	NC
Univ of Rochester	NY	65,032	MC
Univ of St. Francis	IN	37,400	C
Univ of St. Mary	KS	34,690	C
Univ of San Diego	CA	58,442	VC+
Univ of San Francisco	CA	58,484	VC
Univ of Science and Arts of Okla	OK	11,140	VC
Univ of Scranton	PA	54,962	VC
Univ of Sioux Falls	SD	34,330	C
Univ of South Alabama	AL	16,400	C
Univ of S Car Aiken	SC	16,712	C
Univ of S Car at Columbia	SC	19,725	VC+
Univ of S Car Upstate	SC	18,200	LC
Univ of South Florida/St. Petersburg	FL	15,980	C
Univ of South Florida/Tampa	FL	16,110	VC+
Univ of Southern Calif	CA	66,631	C
Univ of Southern Indiana	IN	16,501	C
Univ of Southern Maine	ME	18,320	C
Univ of Southern Miss	MS	13,170	C
Univ of St. Francis	IL	39,924	C
Univ of St. Thomas - Houston	TX	40,020	VC
Univ of Tampa	FL	36,944	C
Univ of Texas at Arlington	TX	18,026	LC
Univ of Texas at Austin	TX	26,102	HC
Univ of Texas at Dallas	TX	22,830	VC+
Univ of Texas at San Antonio	TX	20,157	C
Univ of the Cumberlands	KY	32,000	C
Univ of the District of Columbia	DC	21,044	LC
Univ of the Incarnate Word	TX	39,162	LC
Univ of the Ozarks	AR	52,176	C
Univ of the Pacific	CA	57,006	VC
Univ of the Sacred Heart	PR	17,932	
Univ of the Southwest	NM	22,766	C
Univ of Toledo	OH	19,336	NC
Univ of Tulsa	OK	52,625	HC+
Univ of Vermont	VT	28,878	HC
Univ of Virginia	VA	25,891	MC
Univ of Washington	WA	23,149	VC
Univ of West Alabama	AL	15,516	NC
Univ of West Florida	FL	15,848	C
Univ of West Georgia	GA	16,360	LC
Univ of Wisc-Eau Claire	WI	15,797	VC
Univ of Wisc-Green Bay	WI	15,064	C
Univ of Wisc-La Crosse	WI	15,247	C+
Univ of Wisc-Milwaukee	WI	21,496	C
Univ of Wisc-Oshkosh	WI	15,200	C
Univ of Wisc-Parkside	WI	15,193	C
Univ of Wisc-Platteville	WI	14,614	VC
Univ of Wisc-River Falls	WI	14,485	C
Univ of Wisc-Stevens Point	WI	14,043	C
Univ of Wisc-Stout	WI	19,667	C
Univ of Wisc-Superior	WI	14,446	C
Univ of Wisc-Whitewater	WI	13,976	C
Univ of Wyoming	WY	15,375	C+
Upper Iowa Univ	IA	34,990	NC
Urbana Univ	OH	30,820	C
Ursuline College	OH	41,076	LC
Utah State Univ	UT	12,736	C
Utica College	NY	30,430	C
Valley City State Univ	ND	13,267	C
Valparaiso Univ	IN	48,370	C+
Vanguard Univ of Southern Calif	CA	40,740	VC
Vaughn College of Aeronautics and Technology	NY	37,180	C
Villanova Univ	PA	62,523	MC
Virginia Commonwealth Univ	VA	23,049	C
Virginia State Univ	VA	19,802	C+
Virginia Union Univ	VA	22,421	C
Virginia Wesleyan College	VA	43,728	LC
Voorhees College	SC	19,976	C
Wagner College	NY	55,480	C+
Wake Forest Univ	NC	64,056	MC
Walla Walla Univ	WA	30,417	NC
Walsh Univ	OH	39,010	C
Warner Pacific College	OR	33,790	C
Warner Univ	FL	28,216	C
Wartburg College	IA	47,840	C
Washburn Univ	KS	15,827	C
Washington & Jefferson College	PA	56,512	VC
Washington Adventist Univ	MD	31,440	LC
Washington and Lee Univ	VA	59,647	MC
Washington College	MD	54,666	VC
Washington State Univ	WA	22,495	C
Washington Univ in St. Louis	MO	65,366	VC
Wayland Baptist Univ	TX	22,356	LC
Wayne State College	NE	12,802	C
Wayne State Univ	MI	22,016	C
Webber International Univ	FL	31,904	C
Weber State Univ	UT	10,721	C
Webster Univ	MO	37,490	C
Wells College	NY	50,500	C
Wesley College	DE	37,026	LC
Wesleyan College	GA	29,694	C+
West Chester Univ of Pennsylvania	PA	18,456	C
West Liberty Univ	WV	15,512	C
West Texas A&M Univ	TX	13,478	C
West Virginia State Univ	WV	8,378	NC
West Virginia Univ	WV	18,210	C
West Virginia Univ Inst of Technology	WV	16,462	NC
West Virginia Wesleyan College	WV	36,858	C
Western Conn State Univ	CT	21,254	LC
Western Illinois Univ	IL	20,825	C
Western Kentucky Univ	KY	16,850	C
Western New England Univ	MA	48,088	C
Western New Mexico Univ	NM	16,734	LC
Western Oregon Univ	OR	15,021	LC
Western State Colo Univ	CO	18,639	C
Western Washington Univ	WA	18,003	C+
Westfield State Univ	MA	19,671	C
Westminster College	MO	32,820	C
Westminster College	PA	39,180	C+
Westminster College	UT	41,078	C+
Wheaton College	MA	61,512	VC
Wheeling Jesuit Univ	WV	37,106	LC
Whittier College	CA	57,891	C
Whitworth Univ	WA	51,732	VC
Wichita State Univ	KS	21,643	C
Widener Univ	PA	56,486	C
Wilberforce Univ	OH	19,016	C
Wiley College	TX	18,504	C
Wilkes Univ	PA	45,622	C
William Carey Univ	MS	23,950	LC
William Jewell College	MO	41,210	C+
William Paterson Univ of New Jersey	NJ	23,133	C
William Peace Univ	NC	37,430	LC
William Penn Univ	IA	26,000	C
William Woods Univ	MO	32,040	C
Williams Baptist College	AR	24,720	C
Wilmington College	OH	34,600	C
Wilmington Univ	DE	8,546	NC
Wilson College	PA	35,620	C
Winona State Univ	MN	17,535	C
Winston-Salem State Univ	NC	26,166	LC
Winthrop Univ	SC	23,082	C
Wisc Lutheran College	WI	36,290	VC
Wittenberg Univ	OH	48,156	C+
Woodbury Univ	CA	46,958	C
Worcester Polytechnic Inst	MA	60,730	MC
Worcester State Univ	MA	20,977	C
Xavier Univ	OH	47,880	C+
Xavier Univ of Louisiana	LA	31,689	C+
Yeshiva Univ	NY	47,250	VC+
York College	NE	24,300	C
York College of Pennsylvania	PA	29,240	C
Youngstown State Univ	OH	17,307	C

BUSINESS ADMINISTRATION MARKETING

School	ST	$IS	SR
Aquinas College - Mich	MI	38,876	HC
Bay Path Univ	MA	45,349	C
Black Hills State Univ	SD	15,899	C
Bloomfield College	NJ	39,100	LC
Bryant Univ	RI	55,646	VC
Cabrini Univ	PA	42,591	LC
Calif State Polytechnic Univ, Pomona	CA	21,541	C
Clayton State Univ	GA	19,735	C
College of the Ozarks	MO	7,230	C
Corban Univ	OR	40,306	C
East Central Univ	OK	13,056	C
East Texas Baptist Univ	TX	33,134	C
Franklin College	IN	39,380	C
Gwynedd Mercy Univ	PA	43,780	LC
Hood College	MD	54,840	C
Huntington Univ	IN	33,996	C
Iowa Wesleyan Univ	IA	39,200	C
King Univ	TN	34,660	C
Lewis Univ	IL	40,370	C
Millersville Univ of Pennsylvania	PA	23,782	C
Monmouth Univ	NJ	46,234	C
Niagara Univ	NY	41,010	C
Okla Christian Univ	OK	27,650	VC
Pennsylvania State Univ - Univ Park	PA	29,760	HC
Rochester Inst of Technology	NY	50,842	HC
St. Ambrose Univ	IA	39,019	C
Taylor Univ	IN	40,317	C+
The Master's Univ	CA	43,870	C+
Univ of Alaska Fairbanks	AK	16,179	C
Univ of Arkansas at Fayetteville	AR	19,152	C+
Univ of Maine	ME	20,792	C
Univ of Maine at Machias	ME	22,960	C
Urbana Univ	OH	30,820	C
West Chester Univ of Pennsylvania	PA	18,456	C
West Virginia Univ	WV	18,210	C
Western Illinois Univ	IL	20,825	C
Western Kentucky Univ	KY	16,850	C

BUSINESS ADMINISTRATION W/ LEGAL STUDIES

School	ST	$IS	SR
Bryant Univ	RI	55,646	VC
East Central Univ	OK	13,056	C
Ferris State Univ	MI	21,445	C
Ithaca College	NY	56,766	VC
Milligan College	TN	38,150	C
The Master's Univ	CA	43,870	C+

BUSINESS ADMINISTRATION, MGMT, OPERATIONS

School	ST	$IS	SR
American Univ of PR	PR	16,130	
Ball State Univ	IN	19,590	C
Black Hills State Univ	SD	15,899	C
Calif State Polytechnic Univ, Pomona	CA	21,541	C
Clayton State Univ	GA	19,735	C
College of the Ozarks	MO	7,230	C
Concordia College - New York	NY	39,035	LC
East Central Univ	OK	13,056	C
Excelsior College	NY	14,080	SP
Five Towns College	NY	35,350	C
Huntington Univ	IN	33,996	C
Lewis Univ	IL	40,370	C
Northwest Nazarene Univ	ID	36,000	C
Okla Christian Univ	OK	27,650	VC
Rochester Inst of Technology	NY	50,842	HC
St. Ambrose Univ	IA	39,019	C
The Master's Univ	CA	43,870	C+
Thomas Univ	GA	21,420	LC
Univ of Wisc-Madison	WI	20,934	MC
Western Kentucky Univ	KY	16,850	C

BUSINESS ADMINISTRATION/ AVIATION

School	ST	$IS	SR
Embry-Riddle Aeronautical Univ - Daytona Beach	FL	44,712	VC
Ferris State Univ	MI	21,445	C
Lewis Univ	IL	40,370	C

BUSINESS AND TECHNOLOGY

School	ST	$IS	SR
Bentley Univ	MA	60,890	HC
Framingham State Univ	MA	20,584	C
Regis Univ	CO	44,520	C
Univ of Miami	FL	63,494	MC

BUSINESS COMMUNICATIONS

School	ST	$IS	SR
Aquinas College - Mich	MI	38,876	HC
Augustana Univ	SD	38,424	VC
Bentley Univ	MA	60,890	HC
Biola Univ	CA	46,402	C+
Bryant Univ	RI	55,646	VC
Calvin College	MI	41,570	VC+
Canisius College	NY	47,537	C
Carlow Univ	PA	38,549	LC
Chestnut Hill College	PA	43,410	C
Duquesne Univ	PA	46,822	VC
George Fox Univ	OR	42,938	C
Ithaca College	NY	56,766	VC
Murray State Univ	KY	16,998	C
Nichols College	MA	46,800	LC
Olivet Nazarene Univ	IL	41,840	C
Point Loma Nazarene Univ	CA	43,450	C
Rockhurst Univ	MO	29,220	C
St. Leo Univ	FL	31,650	C
Southeast Missouri State Univ	MO	15,498	C
Southwestern College	KS	31,531	C
Stevenson Univ	MD	72,770	C
The Univ of Akron	OH	21,477	C
Univ of Indianapolis	IN	36,480	C
Univ of Mary	ND	23,180	C
Univ of Nebr - Omaha	NE	16,120	C
Walsh Univ	OH	39,010	C
Webber International Univ	FL	31,904	C
Western Kentucky Univ	KY	16,850	C
Westminster College	MO	32,820	C

BUSINESS DATA PROCESSING

School	ST	$IS	SR
Bryant Univ	RI	55,646	VC
Cal State, Fresno	CA	16,902	LC
Eastern Mich Univ	MI	19,761	C
Ferris State Univ	MI	21,445	C
Idaho State Univ	ID	13,619	NC
Mount Vernon Nazarene Univ	OH	34,500	C

BUSINESS ECONOMICS

School	ST	$IS	SR
Adams State Univ	CO	17,703	LC
Alabama State Univ	AL	14,142	NC
American International College	MA	46,300	LC
Andrews Univ	MI	28,030	C+
Aquinas College - Mich	MI	38,876	HC
Arkansas State Univ	AR	16,190	C
Armstrong State Univ	GA	16,962	C
Ashford Univ	CA	10,480	C
Ashland Univ	OH	21,440	C
Auburn Univ	AL	23,594	VC+
Ball State Univ	IN	19,590	C
Baylor Univ	TX	53,760	HC
Beloit College	WI	55,206	HC
Benedictine Univ	IL	38,300	C
Bentley Univ	MA	60,890	HC
Bethany College	KS	46,100	NC
Bethel College	IN	35,860	C
Biola Univ	CA	46,402	C+
Bloomfield College	NJ	39,100	LC
Bloomsburg Univ of Pennsylvania	PA	19,066	LC
Boston College	MA	65,737	MC
Brescia Univ	KY	29,890	VC+
Brown Univ	RI	64,566	MC
Bryant Univ	RI	55,646	VC
Buena Vista Univ	IA	41,514	C
Cal State, Fullerton	CA	21,902	C
Cal State, Long Beach	CA	18,850	C
Cal State, San Bernardino	CA	12,000	C
Campbellsville Univ	KY	32,492	C
Canisius College	NY	47,537	C
Carnegie Mellon Univ	PA	67,980	MC
Carroll Univ	WI	38,100	C+
Carson-Newman Univ	TN	34,160	C
Centenary College of Louisiana	LA	45,650	C+
Central Washington Univ	WA	16,803	C
Chatham Univ	PA	46,517	C
Clarion Univ of Pennsylvania	PA	21,608	LC
Clayton State Univ	GA	19,735	C
Cleveland State Univ	OH	22,196	C
College of the Ozarks	MO	7,230	C
Cornell College	IA	48,800	VC
DePaul Univ	IL	47,623	VC
Dominican College	NY	31,270	LC
Dordt College	IA	37,860	C+
Drexel Univ	PA	65,432	VC+
Duquesne Univ	PA	46,822	VC
Eastern Mich Univ	MI	19,761	C
Elizabethtown College	PA	54,050	C
Elmira College	NY	53,900	C
Emory Univ	GA	60,786	MC
Eureka College	IL	30,220	C
Fairleigh Dickinson Univ/ Metropolitan Campus	NJ	40,254	C
Fayetteville State Univ	NC	17,756	C
Florida A&M Univ	FL	15,361	C
Florida Atlantic Univ	FL	17,339	C
Fordham Univ	NY	65,918	MC
Fort Lewis College	CO	18,980	C
Francis Marion Univ	SC	16,464	LC
Friends Univ	KS	34,455	C
George Washington Univ	DC	62,835	MC
Georgetown College	KY	41,440	C
Georgia State Univ	GA	24,332	VC
Gonzaga Univ	WA	50,888	HC
Grambling State Univ	LA	15,701	C
Grand Valley State Univ	MI	22,250	C+
Grove City College	PA	25,692	VC
Gustavus Adolphus College	MN	52,433	HC
Hampden-Sydney College	VA	56,248	C+
Hawaii Pacific Univ	HI	33,420	C
Heidelberg Univ	OH	39,200	C
Hendrix College	AR	54,020	VC+
Hofstra Univ	NY	55,960	C+
Humboldt State Univ	CA	20,514	C
Indiana Univ-Purdue Univ Fort Wayne	IN	17,553	C
Inter-American Univ of PR-Bayamon	PR	18,785	
James Madison Univ	VA	19,084	VC
Johnson C. Smith Univ	NC	25,336	LC
Kalamazoo College	MI	53,931	HC+
Kansas Wesleyan Univ	KS	36,600	C
Kentucky Wesleyan College	KY	32,080	C
King Univ	TN	34,660	C
Kutztown Univ of Pennsylvania	PA	19,056	LC
Lafayette College	PA	63,355	MC
Lake Forest College	IL	50,652	VC
Lakeland Univ	WI	35,130	C
Lamar Univ	TX	18,014	LC
Lehigh Univ	PA	61,010	MC
Lewis Univ	IL	40,370	C
Limestone College	SC	32,100	C
Louisiana Tech Univ	LA	11,422	VC
Loyola Univ Chicago	IL	55,802	VC
Manhattan College	NY	51,750	C+
Marquette Univ	WI	48,390	VC+
Marshall Univ	WV	17,242	C
Merrimack College	MA	52,770	C
Miami Univ	OH	27,190	HC+
Midland Univ	NE	37,468	
Midwestern State Univ	TX	17,572	C
Mills College	CA	59,163	VC
Monmouth Univ	NJ	46,234	C
Montclair State Univ	NJ	26,210	LC
Moravian College	PA	53,117	
Morehead State Univ	KY	17,422	C
Mount Aloysius College	PA	29,976	C
New Mexico State Univ	NM	14,050	C
New York Univ	NY	65,860	MC
Niagara Univ	NY	41,010	C
N Car State Univ	NC	19,515	HC+
Northern Arizona Univ	AZ	20,246	VC
Northern State Univ	SD	14,505	C
Northwest Missouri State Univ	MO	17,737	C
Northwestern College of Iowa	IA	38,400	C+
Northwood Univ - Mich	MI	35,010	LC

ST = STATE $IS = IN-STATE COSTS SR = SELECTOR RATING

School	ST	$IS	SR
Norwich Univ	VT	28,212	C
Notre Dame College	OH	37,150	VC
Oakland Univ	MI	20,763	C
Ohio Northern Univ	OH	44,050	VC
Ohio Univ	OH	22,924	C
Ohio Wesleyan Univ	OH	49,460	VC
Pace Univ	NY	58,248	C
Park Univ	MO	20,329	C
Penn State Erie/The Behrend College	PA	16,256	C
Pittsburg State Univ	KS	13,880	NC
Pontifical Catholic Univ of PR	PR	10,534	
Providence College	RI	60,760	VC
Purdue Univ/Northwest	IN	15,038	C
Regis Univ	CO	44,520	C
Rider Univ	NJ	54,050	C
Rockhurst Univ	MO	29,220	C
Sacred Heart Univ	CT	52,750	C
Saginaw Valley State Univ	MI	18,530	C
St. Louis Univ	MO	49,866	HC
Salisbury Univ	MD	20,714	VC
Seattle Univ	WA	50,811	VC+
Seton Hall Univ	NJ	55,514	C
Seton Hill Univ	PA	46,972	C
Skidmore College	NY	64,214	HC
S Car State Univ	SC	20,805	LC
Southeast Missouri State Univ	MO	15,498	C
Southern Conn State Univ	CT	21,924	LC
Southern Illinois Univ Carbondale	IL	23,667	C
Southern Illinois Univ Edwardsville	IL	22,643	C
Southern Univ and A&M College	LA	16,074	LC+
St. Ambrose Univ	IA	39,019	C
St. Cloud State Univ	MN	10,600	C
SUNY / SUNY Fredonia	NY	20,818	C
SUNY / SUNY Oneonta	NY	19,712	C+
SUNY / SUNY Potsdam	NY	20,404	C+
Stetson Univ	FL	53,544	VC
Tenn State Univ	TN	14,423	C
Texas A&M Univ at Kingsville	TX	7,500	LC
Texas State Univ	TX	19,350	C
Texas Wesleyan Univ	TX	35,134	C
The College of Wooster	OH	57,900	VC+
The Univ of Tenn at Martin	TN	14,876	C
Thomas College	ME	35,268	LC
Troy Univ	AL	16,171	C
Tuskegee Univ	AL	28,164	C
Univ of Arizona	AZ	23,100	C
Univ of Arkansas at Fayetteville	AR	19,152	C+
Univ of Calif at Irvine	CA	26,484	VC
Univ of Calif at Los Angeles	CA	30,162	MC
Univ of Calif at Riverside	CA	29,227	C+
Univ of Calif, Santa Cruz	CA	28,731	C+
Univ of Central Arkansas	AR	14,472	VC
Univ of Central Florida	FL	15,922	VC
Univ of Dayton	OH	53,620	C
Univ of Denver	CO	58,443	VC+
Univ of Findlay	OH	60,139	C
Univ of Idaho	ID	15,348	C
Univ of Illinois at Chicago	IL	25,006	VC
Univ of Indianapolis	IN	36,480	C
Univ of Iowa	IA	18,683	VC+
Univ of Kentucky	KY	33,306	C
Univ of La Verne	CA	55,600	C
Univ of Louisville	KY	19,824	C
Univ of Maine	ME	20,792	C
Univ of Maine at Farmington	ME	18,187	C
Univ of Memphis	TN	18,278	C
Univ of Miss	MS	17,746	C+
Univ of Missouri/Columbia	MO	18,201	MC
Univ of Nebr - Kearney	NE	16,546	LC
Univ of Nebr - Lincoln	NE	18,589	VC
Univ of North Alabama	AL	15,398	C
Univ of N Car at Charlotte	NC	15,547	C
Univ of N Car at Greensboro	NC	14,690	C
Univ of N Car at Wilmington	NC	14,590	VC
Univ of N Dak	ND	15,373	C
Univ of North Florida	FL	15,996	VC
Univ of North Georgia	GA	17,316	C
Univ of Okla	OK	18,911	VC
Univ of Pittsburgh at Johnstown	PA	22,092	C
Univ of PR, at Mayaguez	PR	13,995	
Univ of PR-Rio Piedras campus	PR	13,327	
Univ of Rio Grande & Rio Grande Community College	OH	8,750	NC
Univ of San Diego	CA	58,442	VC+
Univ of San Francisco	CA	58,484	VC
Univ of Scranton	PA	54,962	VC
Univ of Sioux Falls	SD	34,330	C
Univ of South Alabama	AL	16,400	C
Univ of S Car at Columbia	SC	19,725	VC+
Univ of South Florida/Tampa	FL	16,110	VC+
Univ of Southern Miss	MS	13,170	C
Univ of Tampa	FL	36,944	C
Univ of Texas at Arlington	TX	18,026	LC
Univ of Texas at El Paso	TX	34,452	NC
Univ of Washington	WA	23,149	VC
Univ of West Florida	FL	15,848	C
Univ of West Georgia	GA	16,360	LC
Univ of Wisc-Whitewater	WI	13,976	C
Univ of Wyoming	WY	15,375	C+
Ursinus College	PA	61,690	VC
Utah State Univ	UT	12,736	C
Utica College	NY	30,430	C
Villanova Univ	PA	62,523	MC
Virginia Military Inst	VA	26,460	C+
Virginia Polytechnic Inst and State Univ	VA	21,276	HC
Washburn Univ	KS	15,827	C
Washington State Univ	WA	22,495	C
Washington Univ in St. Louis	MO	65,366	VC
Weber State Univ	UT	10,721	C
West Chester Univ of Pennsylvania	PA	18,456	C
West Liberty Univ	WV	15,512	C
West Texas A&M Univ	TX	13,478	C
Western Kentucky Univ	KY	16,850	C
Western Mich Univ	MI	21,054	C
Westmont College	CA	56,410	HC
Wheaton College	IL	43,610	MC
Widener Univ	PA	56,486	C
Wilberforce Univ	OH	19,016	C
William Jewell College	MO	41,210	C+
Wilson College	PA	35,620	C
Winona State Univ	MN	17,535	C
Wofford College	SC	49,885	VC
Wright State Univ	OH	16,983	C
Xavier Univ	OH	47,880	C+
Xavier Univ of Louisiana	LA	31,689	C+
Youngstown State Univ	OH	17,307	C

BUSINESS EDUCATION

School	ST	$IS	SR
Adams State Univ	CO	17,703	LC
Alabama State Univ	AL	14,142	NC
Alfred Univ	NY	42,296	C+
Appalachian State Univ	NC	14,416	VC
Arkansas State Univ	AR	16,190	C
Arkansas Tech Univ	AR	15,484	C
Auburn Univ	AL	23,594	VC+
Avila Univ	MO	35,480	C
Baylor Univ	TX	53,760	HC
Bethany College	KS	46,100	NC
Bethel Univ	MN	45,270	VC
Bethune-Cookman Univ	FL	22,970	C
Black Hills State Univ	SD	15,899	C
Bloomsburg Univ of Pennsylvania	PA	19,066	LC
Bowling Green State Univ	OH	19,747	C
Brigham Young Univ/Hawaii	HI	11,290	C
Buena Vista Univ	IA	41,514	C
Cal State, Northridge	CA	16,859	LC
Cal State, Sacramento	CA	20,332	C
Canisius College	NY	47,537	C
Caribbean Univ	PR	15,471	
Central Washington Univ	WA	16,803	C
Chicago State Univ	IL	20,144	C
CUNY/Lehman College	NY	5,778	HC+
Clark Atlanta Univ	GA	31,019	LC
College of the Ozarks	MO	7,230	C
Concord Univ	WV	14,954	C
Concordia College - Moorhead	MN	51,088	C+
Concordia Univ Nebr	NE	36,280	VC
Corban Univ	OR	40,306	C
Dakota State Univ	SD	13,811	C
Delaware State Univ	DE	19,376	NC
Dickinson State Univ	ND	12,372	LC
Dordt College	IA	37,860	C+
East Carolina Univ	NC	16,937	C
East Central Univ	OK	13,056	C
Eastern Kentucky Univ	KY	16,908	C
Eastern Mich Univ	MI	19,761	C
Eastern New Mexico Univ	NM	14,416	C
Edgewood College	WI	35,950	C
Elizabeth City State Univ	NC	14,745	C
Emporia State Univ	KS	14,570	C
Evangel Univ	MO	28,898	C
Fayetteville State Univ	NC	17,756	C
Ferris State Univ	MI	21,445	C
Florida A&M Univ	FL	15,361	C
Friends Univ	KS	34,455	C
Glenville State College	WV	17,386	NC
Goshen College	IN	42,500	C
Grace College and Seminary	IN	31,524	C
Gustavus Adolphus College	MN	52,433	HC
Gwynedd Mercy Univ	PA	43,780	LC
Hardin-Simmons Univ	TX	33,966	C
Hastings College	NE	35,380	C+
Henderson State Univ	AR	15,516	LC
Humboldt State Univ	CA	20,514	C
Illinois State Univ	IL	23,418	VC
Indiana State Univ	IN	23,223	LC
Indiana Univ of Pennsylvania	PA	23,614	LC
Jackson State Univ	MS	15,879	LC
Lakeland Univ	WI	35,130	C
Langston Univ	OK	14,314	C
Lee Univ	TN	22,045	C
LeTourneau Univ	TX	38,250	VC
Lincoln Memorial Univ	TN	28,070	C
Lincoln Univ	MO	13,602	NC
Lindenwood Univ	MO	25,132	C
Louisiana College	LA	21,886	C
McKendree Univ	IL	37,940	C+
McMurry Univ	TX	34,259	LC
Mercyhurst Univ	PA	47,420	C
Middle Tenn State Univ	TN	8,650	C
Midland Univ	NE	37,468	
Minot State Univ	ND	12,732	C
Miss College	MS	25,850	C
Miss State Univ	MS	11,454	C+
Missouri Baptist Univ	MO	35,594	C
Missouri Southern State Univ	MO	12,499	C
Missouri State Univ	MO	15,190	C+
Montana State Univ-Northern	MT	11,370	NC
Montclair State Univ	NJ	26,210	LC
Morehead State Univ	KY	17,422	C
Mount Vernon Nazarene Univ	OH	34,500	C
Nazareth College	NY	45,574	C
Niagara Univ	NY	41,010	C
Nicholls State Univ	LA	10,534	C
Norfolk State Univ	VA	25,702	LC
N Car A&T State Univ	NC	13,365	LC
Northern Kentucky Univ	KY	16,486	C
Northern Mich Univ	MI	19,604	C
Northern State Univ	SD	14,505	C
Northwest Missouri State Univ	MO	17,737	C
Northwestern College of Iowa	IA	38,400	C+
Northwestern Okla State Univ	OK	13,072	NC
Oakland City Univ	IN	33,360	NC
Oakwood Univ	AL	43,758	C
Oglala Lakota College	SD	15,050	NC
Ohio Univ	OH	22,924	C
Okla Panhandle State Univ	OK	6,152	NC
Okla Wesleyan Univ	OK	33,206	C
Oral Roberts Univ	OK	34,316	C
Ouachita Baptist Univ	AR	32,320	C
Philander Smith College	AR	20,814	LC
Pontifical Catholic Univ of PR	PR	10,534	
Rider Univ	NJ	54,050	C
Robert Morris Univ	PA	37,834	C
Rust College	MS	10,600	C
SAGU American Indian College	AZ	18,142	C
St. Augustine's Univ	NC	26,048	C
St. Vincent College	PA	44,626	C
Salem State Univ	MA	17,303	LC
S Car State Univ	SC	20,805	LC
Southeastern Okla State Univ	OK	11,875	C
Southern Arkansas Univ	AR	21,532	C
Southern New Hampshire Univ	NH	43,198	C
Southern Univ at New Orleans	LA	8,014	LC
Southwestern Adventist Univ	TX	27,756	LC
St. Ambrose Univ	IA	39,019	C
St. Mary's Univ	TX	37,500	C
SUNY / Buffalo State College	NY	20,842	C
SUNY / SUNY Oneonta	NY	19,712	C+
SUNY at Oswego	NY	21,351	C
Suffolk Univ	MA	50,308	C
Tarleton State Univ	TX	15,248	LC
Texas A&M Univ at Commerce	TX	10,496	C
Thomas College	ME	35,268	LC
Thomas More College	KY	36,720	C
Trevecca Nazarene Univ	TN	31,186	C
Union College	NE	23,270	C
Univ of Arkansas at Fayetteville	AR	19,152	C+
Univ of Arkansas at Pine Bluff	AR	13,541	C
Univ of Central Florida	FL	15,922	VC
Univ of Central Missouri	MO	18,982	C
Univ of Cincinnati	OH	21,964	VC
Univ of Kentucky	KY	33,306	C
Univ of Louisville	KY	19,824	C
Univ of Maine at Machias	ME	22,960	C
Univ of Maryland/Eastern Shore	MD	17,013	C
Univ of Minn/Twin Cities	MN	23,519	HC+
Univ of Montana-Western	MT	11,220	LC
Univ of Nebr - Kearney	NE	16,546	LC
Univ of Nebr - Lincoln	NE	18,589	VC
Univ of North Alabama	AL	15,398	C
Univ of N Dak	ND	15,373	C
Univ of Pittsburgh at Bradford	PA	22,402	C
Univ of Rio Grande & Rio Grande Community College	OH	8,750	NC
Univ of South Florida/Tampa	FL	16,110	VC+
Univ of Southern Miss	MS	13,170	C
Univ of St. Thomas - Houston	TX	40,020	VC
Univ of the Ozarks	AR	52,176	C
Univ of Toledo	OH	19,336	NC
Univ of Wisc-Whitewater	WI	13,976	C
Utah State Univ	UT	12,736	C
Valley City State Univ	ND	13,267	C
Vermont Technical College	VT	23,838	C
Virginia Polytechnic Inst and State Univ	VA	21,276	HC
Virginia State Univ	VA	19,802	C+
Virginia Union Univ	VA	22,421	C
Viterbo Univ	WI	34,660	C
Walla Walla Univ	WA	30,417	NC
Warner Univ	FL	28,216	C
Wayland Baptist Univ	TX	22,356	LC
Weber State Univ	UT	10,721	C
West Texas A&M Univ	TX	13,478	C
Western Kentucky Univ	KY	16,850	C
Western Mich Univ	MI	21,054	C
Western New Mexico Univ	NM	16,734	LC
Wiley College	TX	18,504	C
Winona State Univ	MN	17,535	C
Wright State Univ	OH	16,983	C

BUSINESS INFORMATION SYSTEMS

School	ST	$IS	SR
Ashford Univ	CA	10,480	C
Bentley Univ	MA	60,890	HC
Biola Univ	CA	46,402	C+
Bloomfield College	NJ	39,100	LC
Bryant Univ	RI	55,646	VC
CUNY/Brooklyn College	NY	5,884	C+
East Central Univ	OK	13,056	C
Eastern Conn State Univ	CT	23,059	C
Faulkner Univ	AL	26,410	C
Illinois State Univ	IL	23,418	VC
Kent State Univ	OH	20,732	C
Lehigh Univ	PA	61,010	MC
Lewis Univ	IL	40,370	C
Montana Tech of the Univ of Montana	MT	15,447	C+
Northern Kentucky Univ	KY	16,486	C
Okla Baptist Univ	OK	32,320	C
Point Loma Nazarene Univ	CA	43,450	C
Rochester Inst of Technology	NY	50,842	HC
Stetson Univ	FL	53,544	VC
Texas Christian Univ	TX	54,670	HC
The Master's Univ	CA	43,870	C+
Univ of Arkansas at Fayetteville	AR	19,152	C+
Univ of Illinois at Chicago	IL	25,006	VC
Univ of Kansas	KS	20,135	C+
Univ of Pittsburgh	PA	29,568	HC+

BUSINESS INSTITUTIONS

School	ST	$IS	SR
Univ of Rhode Island	RI	24,906	C

BUSINESS INTELLIGENCE AND ANALYTICS

School	ST	$IS	SR
Arkansas Tech Univ	AR	15,484	C
Bryant Univ	RI	55,646	VC
Clarkson Univ	NY	60,392	HC
College of St. Mary	NE	35,184	C
College of William & Mary	VA		MC
Cornell College	IA	48,800	VC
Creighton Univ	NE	48,206	VC+
Drexel Univ	PA	65,432	VC+
La Salle Univ	PA	55,790	C
Loyola Univ New Orleans	LA	51,708	VC+
Marian Univ	IN	41,220	C
Murray State Univ	KY	16,998	C
Old Dominion Univ	VA	20,910	C
St. Mary's Univ of Minn	MN	41,210	VC
Stetson Univ	FL	53,544	VC
Trinity Univ	TX	52,314	HC+
Valparaiso Univ	IN	48,370	C+
Western Mich Univ	MI	21,054	C
Xavier Univ	OH	47,880	C+

BUSINESS LAW

School	ST	$IS	SR
Adams State Univ	CO	17,703	LC
Bryant Univ	RI	55,646	VC
Cal State, Fresno	CA	16,902	LC
Hofstra Univ	NY	55,960	C+
Lamar Univ	TX	18,014	LC
New York Univ	NY	65,860	MC
Ohio Univ	OH	22,924	C
Peirce College	PA	16,780	NC
Roger Williams Univ	RI	46,296	C+
Warner Univ	FL	28,216	C
Washington State Univ	WA	22,495	C
West Virginia Univ	WV	18,210	C
Western Carolina Univ	NC	13,965	C
Western Mich Univ	MI	21,054	C

BUSINESS LEADERSHIP

School	ST	$IS	SR
Ashford Univ	CA	10,480	C
Bryant Univ	RI	55,646	VC
Miami Univ	OH	27,190	HC+

BUSINESS MANAGEMENT

School	ST	$IS	SR
Bentley Univ	MA	60,890	HC
Bryant Univ	RI	55,646	VC
Clayton State Univ	GA	19,735	C
College of St. Scholastica	MN	44,640	C
East Stroudsburg Univ	PA	18,334	C
Lewis Univ	IL	40,370	C
Rochester Inst of Technology	NY	50,842	HC
Thomas Univ	GA	21,420	LC
Wentworth Inst of Technology	MA	47,112	C
West Chester Univ of Pennsylvania	PA	18,456	C

BUSINESS STATISTICS

School	ST	$IS	SR
Baylor Univ	TX	53,760	HC
Bryant Univ	RI	55,646	VC
Univ of Denver	CO	58,443	VC+
Univ of PR-Rio Piedras campus	PR	13,327	

ST = STATE $IS = IN-STATE COSTS SR = SELECTOR RATING

School	ST	$IS	SR
Univ of Texas at San Antonio	TX	20,157	C
Washington State Univ	WA	22,495	C

BUSINESS SYSTEMS ANALYSIS

School	ST	$IS	SR
Baylor Univ	TX	53,760	HC
Bryant Univ	RI	55,646	VC
CUNY/Brooklyn College	NY	5,884	C+
Cornell College	IA	48,800	VC
Eastern Mich Univ	MI	19,761	C
Elizabethtown College	PA	54,050	C
Husson Univ	ME	25,720	LC
Johnson State College	VT	20,752	C
Louisiana Tech Univ	LA	11,422	VC
Montana Tech of the Univ of Montana	MT	15,447	C+
Oregon State Univ	OR	22,519	VC
Rochester Inst of Technology	NY	50,842	HC
Stevenson Univ	MD	72,770	C
Texas A&M Univ	TX	20,521	VC+
The Univ of Tenn at Knoxville	TN	22,112	VC
Univ of Findlay	OH	60,139	C
Univ of N Car at Wilmington	NC	14,590	VC

CANADIAN STUDIES

School	ST	$IS	SR
Duke Univ	NC	64,188	
St. Lawrence Univ	NY	64,390	VC
SUNY / SUNY Plattsburgh	NY	18,814	C
Univ of Washington	WA	23,149	VC
Western Washington Univ	WA	18,003	C+

CARDIAC SONOGRAPHY

School	ST	$IS	SR
Piedmont College	GA	32,512	C
St. Mary's Univ of Minn	MN	41,210	VC
Thomas Edison State Univ	NJ	6,350	NC
Weber State Univ	UT	10,721	C

CAREER, TECHNICAL EDUCATION & TRAINING

School	ST	$IS	SR
Temple Univ	PA	24,392	VC
Univ of Arkansas at Fayetteville	AR	19,152	C+
Univ of Idaho	ID	15,348	C
Univ of Wisc-Stout	WI	19,667	C
Wright State Univ	OH	16,983	C

CARIBBEAN STUDIES

School	ST	$IS	SR
CUNY/Brooklyn College	NY	5,884	C+
Emory Univ	GA	60,786	MC
Florida State Univ	FL	16,771	HC
Gettysburg College	PA	63,000	HC
Hofstra Univ	NY	55,960	C+
Pitzer College	CA	66,192	MC
SUNY at Binghamton	NY	22,861	MC
SUNY SUNY Albany	NY	22,165	C
Union College	NY	64,320	MC
Univ of Mich/Ann Arbor	MI	24,410	MC

CARTOGRAPHY

School	ST	$IS	SR
East Central Univ	OK	13,056	C
Salem State Univ	MA	17,303	LC
Texas State Univ	TX	19,350	C
Univ of Wisc-Madison	WI	20,934	MC

CELL & MOLECULAR BIOLOGY

School	ST	$IS	SR
Bryant Univ	RI	55,646	VC
Christopher Newport Univ	VA	23,968	VC+
Indiana Univ of Pennsylvania	PA	23,614	LC
King Univ	TN	34,660	C
MCPHS Univ	MA	45,470	SP
Texas Tech Univ	TX	18,736	C+
Univ of Georgia	GA	21,250	HC
Univ of Maryland/Baltimore County	MD	21,296	VC
Univ of Rhode Island	RI	24,906	C
West Chester Univ of Pennsylvania	PA	18,456	C

CELL BIOLOGY

School	ST	$IS	SR
Adams State Univ	CO	17,703	LC
Auburn Univ	AL	23,594	VC+
Augusta Univ	GA	4,632	C
Beloit College	WI	55,206	HC
Bryant Univ	RI	55,646	VC
Bucknell Univ	PA	64,616	MC
Cal State, Long Beach	CA	18,850	C
Canisius College	NY	47,537	C
Dallas Baptist Univ	TX	33,713	C
Florida State Univ	FL	16,771	HC
Grand Valley State Univ	MI	22,250	C+
Hope College	MI	39,940	VC
Huntingdon College	AL	34,900	C
John Carroll Univ	OH	49,740	C+
Johns Hopkins Univ	MD	65,386	MC
Johnson State College	VT	20,752	C
LIU Post	NY	49,682	C
Marshall Univ	WV	17,242	C
Missouri State Univ	MO	15,190	C+
Montana State Univ	MT	15,500	C+
New York Univ	NY	65,860	MC
Ohio Univ	OH	22,924	C
Okla City Univ	OK	40,476	VC
Okla State Univ	OK	17,180	VC
Purdue Univ/West Lafayette	IN	20,032	MC
Rutgers Univ - New Brunswick	NJ	26,632	HC
San Francisco State Univ	CA	18,514	LC
Seattle Univ	WA	50,811	VC+
SUNY at Binghamton	NY	22,861	MC
Tulane Univ	LA	63,396	HC+
Univ of Arizona	AZ	23,100	C
Univ of Calif at Irvine	CA	26,484	VC
Univ of Calif at Los Angeles	CA	30,162	MC
Univ of Calif at Riverside	CA	29,227	C+
Univ of Calif at Santa Barbara	CA	29,091	HC
Univ of Calif, Santa Cruz	CA	28,731	C+
Univ of Georgia	GA	21,250	HC
Univ of Illinois at Urbana-Champaign	IL	27,006	HC
Univ of Mich/Ann Arbor	MI	24,410	MC
Univ of Minn/Duluth	MN	20,292	C+
Univ of Minn/Twin Cities	MN	23,519	HC+
Univ of Montana-Western	MT	11,220	LC
Univ of Puget Sound	WA	56,456	VC+
Univ of Rochester	NY	65,032	MC
Washington & Jefferson College	PA	56,512	VC
Washington State Univ	WA	22,495	C
West Chester Univ of Pennsylvania	PA	18,456	C
Western Washington Univ	WA	18,003	C+

CELTIC STUDIES

School	ST	$IS	SR
Bard College	NY	64,024	HC
Univ of Calif at Berkeley	CA	28,853	MC

CERAMIC ART AND DESIGN

School	ST	$IS	SR
Adams State Univ	CO	17,703	LC
Alfred Univ	NY	42,296	C+
Andrews Univ	MI	28,030	C+
Aquinas College - Mich	MI	38,876	HC
Bennington College	VT	63,960	MC
Calif College of the Arts	CA	52,758	SP
Cal State, San Bernardino	CA	12,000	C
Cleveland Inst of Art	OH	51,439	C+
College for Creative Studies	MI	48,875	SP
Columbia College - Missouri	MO	27,803	C
Hofstra Univ	NY	55,960	C+
Howard Univ	DC	37,616	C+
Indiana Wesleyan Univ	IN	33,674	C
Kansas City Art Inst	MO	44,308	C+
Kutztown Univ of Pennsylvania	PA	19,056	LC
Marshall Univ	WV	17,242	C
Maryland Inst College of Art	MD	56,795	SP
Marywood Univ	PA	46,900	C
Mass College of Art and Design	MA	24,800	SP
Northland College	WI	41,103	C+
Ohio Northern Univ	OH	44,050	VC
Ohio Univ	OH	22,924	C
Rhode Island School of Design	RI	59,960	SP
Rochester Inst of Technology	NY	50,842	HC
School of the Art Inst of Chicago	IL	56,230	SP
Syracuse Univ	NY	60,239	VC
Temple Univ	PA	24,392	VC
The Catholic Univ of America	DC	56,356	VC
Univ of Dallas	TX	45,500	VC+
Univ of Hartford	CT	49,776	C
Univ of Iowa	IA	18,683	VC+
Univ of Kansas	KS	20,135	C+
Univ of Mass Dartmouth	MA	25,658	C
Univ of Miami	FL	63,494	MC
Univ of Mich/Ann Arbor	MI	24,410	MC
Univ of Oregon	OR	22,972	C
Washington Univ in St. Louis	MO	65,366	VC
Webster Univ	MO	37,490	C
Western Washington Univ	WA	18,003	C+

CERAMIC ENGINEERING

School	ST	$IS	SR
Alfred Univ	NY	42,296	C+
Clemson Univ	SC		HC
Missouri Univ of Science and Technology	MO	18,655	HC
Rutgers Univ - New Brunswick	NJ	26,632	HC
Univ of Illinois at Urbana-Champaign	IL	27,006	HC
Univ of Washington	WA	23,149	VC

CERAMIC SCIENCE

School	ST	$IS	SR
Maine College of Art	ME	43,794	SP

CHEMICAL BIOTECHNOLOGY

School	ST	$IS	SR
East Stroudsburg Univ	PA	18,334	C

CHEMICAL ENGINEERING

School	ST	$IS	SR
Arizona State Univ at the Tempe Campus	AZ	21,756	VC
Auburn Univ	AL	23,594	VC+
Brigham Young Univ	UT	12,748	HC
Brown Univ	RI	64,566	MC
Bucknell Univ	PA	64,616	MC
Calif Baptist Univ	CA	41,392	C
Calif Inst of Technology	CA	58,761	MC
Calif State Polytechnic Univ, Pomona	CA	21,541	C
Cal State, Long Beach	CA	18,850	C
Calvin College	MI	41,570	VC+
Carnegie Mellon Univ	PA	67,980	MC
Case Western Reserve Univ	OH	60,304	MC
Christian Brothers Univ	TN	31,670	VC
CUNY/City College	NY	20,319	VC
Clarkson Univ	NY	60,392	HC
Clemson Univ	SC		HC
Cleveland State Univ	OH	22,196	C
Colo School of Mines	CO	29,319	MC
Colo State Univ	CO	22,162	VC
Columbia Univ/City of New York	NY	62,958	MC
Cooper Union for the Advancement of Science and Art	NY	58,210	MC
Cornell Univ	NY	64,853	MC
Delaware State Univ	DE	19,376	NC
Dordt College	IA	37,860	C+
Drexel Univ	PA	65,432	VC+
Elon Univ	NC	44,599	VC+
Florida A&M Univ	FL	15,361	C
Florida Inst of Technology	FL	53,306	VC
Florida State Univ	FL	16,771	HC
Gannon Univ	PA	42,032	C
Geneva College	PA	35,450	C
Georgia Inst of Technology	GA	23,360	MC
Hampton Univ	VA	34,926	LC
Howard Univ	DC	37,616	C+
Illinois Inst of Technology	IL	56,826	HC+
Iowa State Univ	IA	17,570	C
Johns Hopkins Univ	MD	65,386	MC
Kansas State Univ	KS	17,780	VC
Lafayette College	PA	63,355	MC
Lamar Univ	TX	18,014	LC
Lehigh Univ	PA	61,010	MC
Louisiana State Univ and A&M College	LA	18,677	VC
Louisiana Tech Univ	LA	11,422	VC
Manhattan College	NY	51,750	C+
Mass Inst of Technology	MA	62,662	MC
Miami Univ	OH	27,190	HC+
Mich State Univ	MI	23,898	VC+
Mich Tech Univ	MI	24,739	VC+
Miss State Univ	MS	11,454	C+
Missouri Univ of Science and Technology	MO	18,655	HC
Montana State Univ	MT	15,500	C+
New Jersey Inst of Technology	NJ	29,569	VC
New Mexico Inst of Mining and Technology	NM	14,833	HC
New Mexico State Univ	NM	14,050	C
New York Univ	NY	65,860	MC
N Car A&T State Univ	NC	13,365	LC
N Car State Univ	NC	19,515	HC+
Northeastern Univ	MA	62,703	MC
Northwestern Univ	IL	66,344	MC
Ohio State Univ at Columbus	OH	21,703	HC+
Ohio Univ	OH	22,924	C
Okla State Univ	OK	17,180	VC
Oregon State Univ	OR	22,519	VC
Pennsylvania State Univ - Univ Park	PA	29,760	HC
Prairie View A&M Univ	TX	15,205	LC
Princeton Univ	NJ	57,610	MC
Purdue Univ/West Lafayette	IN	20,032	MC
Rensselaer Polytechnic Inst	NY	63,436	MC
Rice Univ	TX	57,668	MC
Rochester Inst of Technology	NY	50,842	HC
Rose-Hulman Inst of Technology	IN	57,303	MC
Rowan Univ	NJ	24,491	VC+
Rutgers Univ - New Brunswick	NJ	26,632	HC
San Jose State Univ	CA	21,540	C
S Dak School of Mines and Technology	SD	18,645	VC
Southwestern College	KS	31,531	C
Stanford Univ	CA	60,409	MC
SUNY / The College of Environmental Science and Forestry	NY	23,853	VC
SUNY / Univ at Buffalo	NY	23,122	C+
Stevens Inst of Technology	NJ	62,338	MC
Stony Brook Univ/The SUNY	NY	21,881	MC
Syracuse Univ	NY	60,239	VC
Tenn Tech Univ	TN	17,050	C
Texas A&M Univ	TX	20,521	VC+
Texas A&M Univ at Kingsville	TX	7,500	LC
Texas Tech Univ	TX	18,736	C+
The Univ of Akron	OH	21,477	C
The Univ of Tenn at Chattanooga	TN	16,744	C
The Univ of Tenn at Knoxville	TN	22,112	VC
The Univ of Utah	UT	17,924	VC
Trine Univ	IN	41,310	C
Tufts Univ	MA		MC
Tulane Univ	LA	63,396	HC+
Tuskegee Univ	AL	28,164	C
Universidad Politecnica de PR, Hato Rey campus	PR	23,514	
Univ of Alabama	AL	24,320	C+
Univ of Alabama in Huntsville	AL	19,445	VC
Univ of Arizona	AZ	23,100	C
Univ of Arkansas at Fayetteville	AR	19,152	C+
Univ of Calif at Berkeley	CA	28,853	MC
Univ of Calif at Davis	CA	28,468	HC
Univ of Calif at Irvine	CA	26,484	VC
Univ of Calif at Los Angeles	CA	30,162	MC
Univ of Calif at Riverside	CA	29,227	C+
Univ of Calif at Santa Barbara	CA	29,091	HC
Univ of Calif San Diego	CA	30,150	MC
Univ of Cincinnati	OH	21,964	VC
Univ of Colo Boulder	CO	24,285	VC+
Univ of Conn	CT	25,538	HC
Univ of Dayton	OH	53,620	C
Univ of Delaware	DE	24,976	VC+
Univ of Florida	FL	16,291	HC+
Univ of Houston	TX	21,483	VC
Univ of Idaho	ID	15,348	C
Univ of Illinois at Chicago	IL	25,006	VC
Univ of Illinois at Urbana-Champaign	IL	27,006	HC
Univ of Iowa	IA	18,683	VC+
Univ of Kansas	KS	20,135	C+
Univ of Kentucky	KY	33,306	C
Univ of Louisiana at Lafayette	LA	14,516	C
Univ of Louisville	KY	19,824	C
Univ of Maine	ME	20,792	C
Univ of Maryland/Baltimore County	MD	21,296	VC
Univ of Maryland/College Park	MD	21,938	HC
Univ of Mass Amherst	MA	26,199	VC+
Univ of Mass Lowell	MA	26,380	C
Univ of Mich/Ann Arbor	MI	24,410	MC
Univ of Minn/Duluth	MN	20,292	C+
Univ of Minn/Twin Cities	MN	23,519	HC+
Univ of Miss	MS	17,746	C+
Univ of Missouri/Columbia	MO	18,201	MC
Univ of Nebr - Lincoln	NE	18,589	VC
Univ of Nevada/Reno	NV	18,010	C
Univ of New Hampshire	NH	28,562	VC
Univ of New Haven	CT	52,190	C
Univ of New Mexico	NM	15,404	C
Univ of N Dak	ND	15,373	C
Univ of Notre Dame	IN	64,043	MC
Univ of Okla	OK	18,911	VC
Univ of Pennsylvania	PA	63,526	MC
Univ of Pittsburgh	PA	29,568	HC+
Univ of PR, at Mayaguez	PR	13,995	
Univ of Rhode Island	RI	24,906	C
Univ of Rochester	NY	65,032	MC
Univ of South Alabama	AL	16,400	C
Univ of S Car at Columbia	SC	19,725	VC+
Univ of South Florida/Tampa	FL	16,110	VC+
Univ of Southern Calif	CA	66,631	C
Univ of Texas at Austin	TX	26,102	HC
Univ of Toledo	OH	19,336	NC
Univ of Tulsa	OK	52,625	HC+
Univ of Virginia	VA	25,891	MC
Univ of Washington	WA	23,149	VC
Univ of Wisc-Madison	WI	20,934	MC
Univ of Wyoming	WY	15,375	C+
Vanderbilt Univ	TN	60,572	MC
Villanova Univ	PA	62,523	MC
Virginia Commonwealth Univ	VA	23,049	C
Virginia Polytechnic Inst and State Univ	VA	21,276	HC
Washington and Lee Univ	VA	59,647	MC
Washington State Univ	WA	22,495	C
Washington Univ in St. Louis	MO	65,366	VC
Wayne State Univ	MI	22,016	C
West Virginia Univ	WV	18,210	C
West Virginia Univ Inst of Technology	WV	16,462	NC
Western Kentucky Univ	KY	16,850	C
Western Mich Univ	MI	21,054	C
Widener Univ	PA	56,486	C
Worcester Polytechnic Inst	MA	60,730	MC
Yale Univ	CT	64,650	MC
Youngstown State Univ	OH	17,307	C

CHEMICAL ENGINEERING TECHNOLOGY

School	ST	$IS	SR
Purdue Univ/West Lafayette	IN	20,032	MC
Univ of PR, at Arecibo	PR	12,652	
Univ of Calif San Diego	CA	30,150	MC
Univ of Hartford	CT	49,776	C

CHEMICAL PHYSICS

School	ST	$IS	SR
Adams State Univ	CO	17,703	LC
Augustana Univ	SD	38,424	VC
Bowdoin College	ME	63,500	MC
Brown Univ	RI	64,566	MC
Centre College	KY	49,250	HC
Hamilton College	NY	64,250	MC

ST = STATE $IS = IN-STATE COSTS   SR = SELECTOR RATING

School	ST	$IS	SR
Hendrix College	AR	54,020	VC+
Lewis Univ	IL	40,370	C
Maryville College	TN	44,410	C
Mich State Univ	MI	23,898	VC+
Reed College	OR	65,300	MC
Saginaw Valley State Univ	MI	18,530	C
San Diego State Univ	CA	21,896	C+
Swarthmore College	PA	63,550	MC
The Catholic Univ of America	DC	56,356	VC

CHEMICAL TECHNOLOGY

School	ST	$IS	SR
Florida State Univ	FL	16,771	HC
Inter-American Univ of PR Ponce	PR	19,549	
Inter-American Univ of PR-Arecibo Campus	PR	18,245	
Inter-American Univ of PR-Bayamon	PR	18,785	
Inter-American Univ of PR-Fajardo Campus	PR	18,336	
Midwestern State Univ	TX	17,572	C
Univ of Cincinnati	OH	21,964	VC

CHEMISTRY

School	ST	$IS	SR
Abilene Christian Univ	TX	41,800	C+
Adams State Univ	CO	17,703	LC
Adelphi Univ	NY	48,244	C
Adrian College	MI	42,400	C
Agnes Scott College	GA	51,930	VC+
Alabama A&M Univ	AL	18,796	C
Alabama State Univ	AL	14,142	NC
Albany College of Pharmacy and Health Sciences	NY	42,681	SP
Albany State Univ	GA	19,462	C
Albion College	MI	52,650	C
Albright College	PA	46,660	C
Alcorn State Univ	MS	15,854	C
Alderson Broaddus Univ	WV	26,149	C
Alfred Univ	NY	42,296	C+
Allegheny College	PA	55,420	VC
Alma College	MI	47,548	C
Alvernia Univ	PA	43,900	C
Alverno College	WI	33,294	LC
American International College	MA	46,300	LC
American Univ	DC	59,379	HC+
Amherst College	MA		HC+
Anderson Univ	IN	38,200	C
Andrews Univ	MI	28,030	C+
Angelo State Univ	TX	15,263	NC
Appalachian State Univ	NC	14,416	VC
Aquinas College - Mich	MI	38,876	HC
Arcadia Univ	PA	33,570	C+
Arizona State Univ at the Tempe Campus	AZ	21,756	VC
Arkansas State Univ	AR	16,190	C
Arkansas Tech Univ	AR	15,484	C
Armstrong State Univ	GA	16,962	C
Asbury Univ	KY	35,180	C+
Ashland Univ	OH	21,440	C
Assumption College	MA	47,920	C+
Auburn Univ	AL	23,594	VC+
Auburn Univ at Montgomery	AL	15,290	C
Augsburg College	MN	43,929	C
Augusta Univ	GA	4,632	C
Augustana College	IL	49,658	VC
Augustana Univ	SD	38,424	VC
Austin College	TX	45,875	VC
Austin Peay State Univ	TN	16,397	C
Averett Univ	VA	40,970	LC
Avila Univ	MO	35,480	C
Azusa Pacific Univ	CA	43,972	C
Baker Univ	KS	33,350	C+
Baldwin Wallace Univ	OH	41,106	C
Ball State Univ	IN	19,590	C
Bard College	NY	64,024	HC
Bard College at Simon's Rock	MA	65,795	MC
Barnard College/Columbia Univ	NY	62,741	MC
Barry Univ	FL	37,830	C
Barton College	NC	38,686	LC
Bates College	ME	64,500	MC
Bayamon Central Univ	PR	12,490	
Baylor Univ	TX	53,760	HC
Belhaven Univ	MS	31,016	C
Bellarmine Univ	KY	51,220	C
Belmont Univ	TN	40,970	VC
Beloit College	WI	55,206	HC
Bemidji State Univ	MN	16,056	VC
Benedict College	SC	28,238	NC
Benedictine College	KS	36,200	VC
Benedictine Univ	IL	38,300	C
Bennett College	NC	27,302	NC
Bennington College	VT	63,960	MC
Berea College	KY	7,042	C
Berry College	GA	45,286	C+
Bethany College	KS	46,100	NC
Bethany College	WV	36,300	NC
Bethel College	IN	35,860	C
Bethel College	KS	35,370	C
Bethel Univ	MN	45,270	VC
Bethel Univ	TN	24,738	C
Bethune-Cookman Univ	FL	22,970	C
Biola Univ	CA	46,402	C+
Birmingham-Southern College	AL	44,478	VC
Black Hills State Univ	SD	15,899	C
Blackburn College	IL	28,526	LC
Bloomfield College	NJ	39,100	LC
Bloomsburg Univ of Pennsylvania	PA	19,066	LC
Bluefield College	VA	34,120	C+
Bluffton Univ	OH	40,950	C
Boise State Univ	ID	14,860	C
Boston College	MA	65,737	MC
Boston Univ	MA	65,110	MC
Bowdoin College	ME	63,500	MC
Bowling Green State Univ	OH	19,747	C
Brandeis Univ	MA	65,925	MC
Brescia Univ	KY	29,890	VC+
Briar Cliff Univ	IA	36,956	C
Bridgewater College	VA	44,510	C
Bridgewater State Univ	MA	21,810	C
Brigham Young Univ	UT	12,748	HC
Brown Univ	RI	64,566	MC
Bryn Mawr College	PA	59,890	MC
Bucknell Univ	PA	64,616	MC
Buena Vista Univ	IA	41,514	C
Butler Univ	IN	51,352	VC
Cabrini Univ	PA	42,591	LC
Caldwell Univ	NJ	42,165	NC
Calif Baptist Univ	CA	41,392	C
Calif Inst of Technology	CA	58,761	MC
Calif Lutheran Univ	CA	52,853	C
Calif Polytechnic State Univ	CA	17,979	HC+
Calif State Polytechnic Univ, Pomona	CA	21,541	C
Cal State, Bakersfield	CA	19,191	LC
Cal State, Chico	CA	21,440	C
Cal State, Dominguez Hills	CA	19,022	LC
Cal State, East Bay	CA	19,413	C
Cal State, Fresno	CA	16,902	LC
Cal State, Fullerton	CA	21,902	C
Cal State, Long Beach	CA	18,850	C
Cal State, Los Angeles	CA	17,186	LC
Cal State, Northridge	CA	16,859	LC
Cal State, Sacramento	CA	20,332	C
Cal State, San Bernardino	CA	12,000	C
Cal State, San Marcos	CA	24,184	LC
Cal State, Stanislaus	CA	16,212	C
Calif Univ of Pennsylvania	PA	14,217	LC
Calvin College	MI	41,570	VC+
Cameron Univ	OK	11,072	NC
Campbellsville Univ	KY	32,492	C
Canisius College	NY	47,537	C
Capital Univ	OH	42,982	C
Cardinal Stritch Univ	WI	36,462	C
Carleton College	MN	64,071	MC
Carlow Univ	PA	38,549	LC
Carnegie Mellon Univ	PA	67,980	MC
Carroll College	MT	39,972	C+
Carroll Univ	WI	38,100	C+
Carthage College	WI	48,835	C
Case Western Reserve Univ	OH	60,304	MC
Castleton Univ	VT	20,186	C
Catawba College	NC	39,820	C
Cedar Crest College	PA	46,715	C
Cedarville Univ	OH	34,990	VC
Centenary College of Louisiana	LA	45,650	C+
Central College	IA	44,592	C
Central Conn State Univ	CT	21,203	C
Central Methodist Univ	MO	36,830	VC
Central Mich Univ	MI	20,330	C
Central State Univ	OH	18,564	C
Central Washington Univ	WA	16,803	C
Centre College	KY	49,250	HC
Chadron State College	NE	14,819	NC
Chapman Univ	CA	63,078	VC+
Charleston Southern Univ	SC	32,400	C
Chatham Univ	PA	46,517	C
Chestnut Hill College	PA	43,410	C
Cheyney Univ of Pennsylvania	PA	20,896	LC
Chicago State Univ	IL	20,144	C
Christian Brothers Univ	TN	31,670	VC
Christopher Newport Univ	VA	23,968	VC+
CUNY/Brooklyn College	NY	5,884	C+
CUNY/City College	NY	20,319	VC
CUNY/College of Staten Island	NY	17,840	NC
CUNY/Hunter College	NY	31,098	VC
CUNY/Lehman College	NY	5,778	HC+
CUNY/Queens College	NY	27,896	C
CUNY/York College	NY	6,747	LC
Claflin Univ	SC	33,764	LC
Claremont McKenna College	CA	67,185	MC
Clarion Univ of Pennsylvania	PA	21,608	LC
Clark Atlanta Univ	GA	31,019	LC
Clark Univ	MA	51,600	HC+
Clarke Univ	IA	38,940	C
Clarkson Univ	NY	60,392	HC
Clayton State Univ	GA	19,735	C
Clemson Univ	SC		HC
Cleveland State Univ	OH	22,196	C
Coastal Carolina Univ	SC	19,766	C
Coe College	IA	51,570	VC
Coker College	SC	34,810	LC
Colby College	ME	64,060	MC
Colgate Univ	NY	65,030	MC
College of Charleston	SC	22,699	C
College of Mount St. Vincent	NY	45,620	C
College of St. Benedict	MN	52,806	C
College of St. Elizabeth	NJ	44,432	LC
College of St. Mary	NE	35,184	C
College of St. Scholastica	MN	44,640	C
College of the Holy Cross	MA	62,165	MC
College of the Ozarks	MO	7,230	C
College of William & Mary	VA		MC
Colo College	CO	62,560	MC
Colo Mesa Univ	CO	18,955	LC
Colo School of Mines	CO	29,319	MC
Colo State Univ	CO	22,162	VC
Colo State Univ-Pueblo	CO	18,234	C
Columbia College	SC	36,550	C
Columbia College - Missouri	MO	27,803	C
Columbia Univ/ School of General Studies	NY	61,470	MC
Columbia Univ/City of New York	NY	62,958	MC
Columbus State Univ	GA	14,336	LC
Concord Univ	WV	14,954	C
Concordia College - Moorhead	MN	51,088	C+
Concordia Univ	CA	41,580	VC
Concordia Univ	OR	35,000	C
Concordia Univ Nebr	NE	36,280	VC
Concordia Univ, Ann Arbor	MI	35,945	VC
Concordia Univ, Chicago	IL	39,694	C
Conn College	CT	65,000	MC
Converse College	SC	26,495	C
Coppin State Univ	MD	17,041	VC
Cornell College	IA	48,800	VC
Covenant College	GA	38,990	VC
Creighton Univ	NE	48,206	VC+
Dartmouth College	NH	66,174	MC
Davidson College	NC	60,119	MC
Davis & Elkins College	WV	38,242	LC
Delaware State Univ	DE	19,376	NC
Delaware Valley Univ	PA	49,796	C
Delta State Univ	MS	13,176	C
Denison Univ	OH	58,860	MC
DePaul Univ	IL	47,623	VC
DePauw Univ	IN	58,688	HC+
DeSales Univ	PA	43,970	C
Dickinson College	PA	63,974	MC
Dickinson State Univ	ND	12,372	LC
Dillard Univ	LA	20,940	VC
Doane Univ	NE	39,184	VC
Dominican Univ	IL	41,222	C
Dordt College	IA	37,860	C+
Drake Univ	IA	45,056	HC
Drew Univ/College of Liberal Arts	NJ	61,048	VC
Drexel Univ	PA	65,432	VC+
Drury Univ	MO	33,791	VC
Duke Univ	NC	64,188	
Duquesne Univ	PA	46,822	VC
Earlham College	IN	54,870	HC
East Carolina Univ	NC	16,937	C
East Central Univ	OK	13,056	C
East Stroudsburg Univ	PA	18,334	C
East Tenn State Univ	TN	13,994	C
East Texas Baptist Univ	TX	33,134	C
Eastern Illinois Univ	IL	21,126	C
Eastern Kentucky Univ	KY	16,908	C
Eastern Mennonite Univ	VA	42,550	C
Eastern Mich Univ	MI	19,761	C
Eastern Nazarene College	MA	39,955	C
Eastern New Mexico Univ	NM	14,416	C
Eastern Oregon Univ	OR	17,715	C
Eastern Univ	PA	39,540	C
Eastern Washington Univ	WA	25,572	LC
Eckerd College	FL	52,874	C
Edgewood College	WI	35,950	C
Edinboro Univ	PA	15,940	LC
Elizabeth City State Univ	NC	14,745	C
Elizabethtown College	PA	54,050	C
Elmhurst College	IL	45,428	C
Elmira College	NY	53,900	C
Elms College	MA	45,646	VC
Elon Univ	NC	44,599	VC+
Emmanuel College	MA	52,110	C+
Emory and Henry College	VA	41,410	C
Emory Univ	GA	60,786	MC
Emporia State Univ	KS	14,570	C
Erskine College	SC	45,460	C
Eureka College	IL	30,220	C
Evangel Univ	MO	28,898	C
Excelsior College	NY	14,080	SP
Fairfield Univ	CT	59,860	VC+
Fairleigh Dickinson Univ/ College at Florham	NJ	52,062	C
Fairleigh Dickinson Univ/ Metropolitan Campus	NJ	40,254	C
Fairmont State Univ	WV	15,726	C
Faulkner Univ	AL	26,410	C
Fayetteville State Univ	NC	17,756	C
Ferris State Univ	MI	21,445	C
Ferrum College	VA	39,650	C
Fisk Univ	TN	32,066	LC
Fitchburg State Univ	MA	21,819	C
Florida A&M Univ	FL	15,361	C
Florida Atlantic Univ	FL	17,339	C
Florida Gulf Coast Univ	FL	9,682	C
Florida Inst of Technology	FL	53,306	VC
Florida International Univ	FL	19,854	C+
Florida Memorial Univ	FL	22,270	LC
Florida State Univ	FL	16,771	HC
Fordham Univ	NY	65,918	MC
Fort Hays State Univ	KS	12,131	C
Fort Lewis College	CO	18,980	C
Fort Valley State Univ	GA	17,988	VC
Framingham State Univ	MA	20,584	C
Francis Marion Univ	SC	16,464	LC
Franciscan Univ of Steubenville	OH	33,980	VC
Franklin and Marshall College	PA	63,170	HC
Franklin College	IN	39,380	C
Freed-Hardeman Univ	TN	29,450	C
Fresno Pacific Univ	CA	37,370	C
Friends Univ	KS	34,455	C
Frostburg State Univ	MD	17,280	LC
Furman Univ	SC	58,092	VC+
Gallaudet Univ	DC	29,118	LC
Gannon Univ	PA	42,032	C
Gardner-Webb Univ	NC	39,200	C+
Geneva College	PA	35,450	C
George Fox Univ	OR	42,938	C
George Mason Univ	VA	15,724	VC
George Washington Univ	DC	62,835	MC
Georgetown College	KY	41,440	C
Georgetown Univ	DC	65,926	MC
Georgia College & State Univ	GA	21,148	C+
Georgia Inst of Technology	GA	23,360	MC
Georgia Southern Univ	GA	16,596	C
Georgia Southwestern State Univ	GA	13,870	C
Georgia State Univ	GA	24,332	VC
Georgian Court Univ	NJ	42,426	LC
Gettysburg College	PA	63,000	HC
Glenville State College	WV	17,386	NC
Gonzaga Univ	WA	50,888	HC
Gordon College	MA	46,472	C+
Goshen College	IN	42,500	C
Goucher College	MD	55,716	VC
Graceland Univ	IA	35,290	C
Grambling State Univ	LA	15,701	C
Grand Rapids Theological Seminary/Cornerstone Univ	MI	33,338	C
Grand Valley State Univ	MI	22,250	C+
Greensboro College	NC	42,400	LC
Greenville College	IL	27,012	C
Grinnell College	IA	60,738	MC
Grove City College	PA	25,692	VC
Guilford College	NC	44,090	C
Gustavus Adolphus College	MN	52,433	HC
Hamilton College	NY	64,250	MC
Hamline Univ	MN	45,678	VC
Hampden-Sydney College	VA	56,248	C+
Hampshire College	MA	63,824	MC
Hampton Univ	VA	34,926	LC
Hanover College	IN	46,364	C+
Harding Univ	AR	25,421	C
Hardin-Simmons Univ	TX	33,966	C
Hartwick College	NY	51,270	C
Harvard College/Harvard Univ	MA	60,659	MC
Harvey Mudd College	CA	67,155	MC
Hastings College	NE	35,380	C+
Haverford College	PA	66,490	MC
Hawaii Pacific Univ	HI	33,420	C
Heidelberg Univ	OH	39,200	C
Henderson State Univ	AR	15,516	LC
Hendrix College	AR	54,020	VC+
High Point Univ	NC	45,977	C
Hillsdale College	MI	35,722	MC
Hiram College	OH	43,230	C
Hofstra Univ	NY	55,960	C+
Hollins Univ	VA	49,635	VC
Hood College	MD	54,840	LC
Hope College	MI	39,940	VC
Houghton College	NY	39,090	C
Houston Baptist Univ	TX	36,450	C
Howard Payne Univ	TX	34,320	C
Howard Univ	DC	37,616	C+
Humboldt State Univ	CA	20,514	C
Huntingdon College	AL	34,900	C
Huntington Univ	IN	33,996	C
Husson Univ	ME	25,720	LC
Huston-Tillotson Univ	TX	18,124	LC
Idaho State Univ	ID	13,619	NC
Illinois College	IL	40,850	VC
Illinois Inst of Technology	IL	56,826	HC+
Illinois State Univ	IL	23,418	VC
Illinois Wesleyan Univ	IL	56,430	VC+
Indiana State Univ	IN	23,223	LC
Indiana Univ Bloomington	IN	20,429	VC
Indiana Univ Kokomo	IN	7,073	C
Indiana Univ Northwest	IN	7,072	C
Indiana Univ of Pennsylvania	PA	23,614	LC
Indiana Univ South Bend	IN	14,242	C
Indiana Univ Southeast	IN	14,242	LC
Indiana Univ-Purdue Univ Fort Wayne	IN	17,553	C
Indiana Univ-Purdue Univ Indianapolis	IN	18,635	C
Indiana Wesleyan Univ	IN	33,674	C
Inter-American Univ of PR Ponce	PR	19,549	
Inter-American Univ of PR-Arecibo Campus	PR	18,245	
Inter-American Univ of PR-Bayamon	PR	18,785	
Inter-American Univ of PR-Fajardo Campus	PR	18,336	
Inter-American Univ of PR-Metropolitan Campus	PR	20,045	
Inter-American Univ of PR-San Germán	PR	20,042	
Iona College	NY	50,984	C

ST = STATE $IS = IN-STATE COSTS SR = SELECTOR RATING

School	ST	$IS	SR
Iowa State Univ	IA	17,570	C
Iowa Wesleyan Univ	IA	39,200	C
Ithaca College	NY	56,766	VC
Jackson State Univ	MS	15,879	LC
Jacksonville State Univ	AL	14,628	LC
Jacksonville Univ	FL	46,230	C
James Madison Univ	VA	19,084	VC
Jarvis Christian College	TX	20,160	NC
John Brown Univ	AR	33,132	VC
John Carroll Univ	OH	49,740	C+
Johns Hopkins Univ	MD	65,386	MC
Johnson C. Smith Univ	NC	25,336	LC
Judson College	AL	27,066	C
Judson Univ	IL	37,700	C
Juniata College	PA	53,760	VC
Kalamazoo College	MI	53,931	HC+
Kansas State Univ	KS	17,780	VC
Kansas Wesleyan Univ	KS	36,600	C
Kean Univ	NJ	24,650	C
Keene State College	NH	24,003	LC
Kennesaw State Univ	GA	19,592	VC
Kent State Univ	OH	20,732	C
Kentucky State Univ	KY	13,364	LC
Kentucky Wesleyan College	KY	32,080	C
Kenyon College	OH	63,330	MC
Kettering Univ	MI	47,570	HC
King Univ	TN	34,660	C
King's College	PA	46,858	C
Knox College	IL	52,615	VC+
Kutztown Univ of Pennsylvania	PA	19,056	LC
La Roche College	PA	37,924	LC
La Salle Univ	PA	55,790	C
La Sierra Univ	CA	39,690	VC
Lafayette College	PA	63,355	MC
LaGrange College	GA	39,930	C
Lake Erie College	OH	38,914	LC
Lake Forest College	IL	50,652	VC
Lakeland Univ	WI	35,130	C
Lamar Univ	TX	18,014	LC
Lander Univ	SC	43,994	C
Lane College	TN	16,550	C
Langston Univ	OK	14,314	C
Lawrence Tech Univ	MI	39,770	VC
Lawrence Univ	WI	54,498	HC
Le Moyne College	NY	46,000	C
Lebanon Valley College	PA	51,530	C
Lee Univ	TN	22,045	C
Lehigh Univ	PA	61,010	MC
LeMoyne-Owen College	TN	16,980	C
Lenoir-Rhyne Univ	NC	43,200	C
LeTourneau Univ	TX	38,250	VC
Lewis & Clark College	OR	58,434	HC+
Lewis Univ	IL	40,370	C
Lewis-Clark State College	ID	14,202	C
Limestone College	SC	32,100	C
Lincoln Memorial Univ	TN	28,070	C
Lincoln Univ	MO	13,602	NC
Lindenwood Univ	MO	25,132	C
Linfield College	OR	52,010	C
Lipscomb Univ	TN	41,296	VC
LIU Brooklyn	NY	49,682	C
LIU Post	NY	49,682	C
Lock Haven Univ of Pennsylvania	PA	18,028	LC
Longwood Univ	VA	22,184	C
Loras College	IA	39,222	C
Louisiana College	LA	21,886	C
Louisiana State Univ and A&M College	LA	18,677	VC
Louisiana State Univ in Shreveport	LA	6,902	C
Louisiana Tech Univ	LA	11,422	VC
Loyola Marymount Univ	CA	58,038	HC
Loyola Univ Chicago	IL	55,802	VC
Loyola Univ Maryland	MD	60,300	VC
Loyola Univ New Orleans	LA	51,708	VC+
Lubbock Christian Univ	TX	28,426	C
Luther College	IA	48,540	C+
Lycoming College	PA	48,580	C
Lynchburg College	VA	46,740	C
Lyon College	AR	34,730	C+
Macalester College	MN	61,905	MC
MacMurray College	IL	33,620	C
Madonna Univ	MI	29,050	C
Malone Univ	OH	38,448	C
Manchester Univ	IN	40,422	C
Manhattan College	NY	51,750	C+
Manhattanville College	NY	51,440	C+
Mansfield Univ	PA	23,376	LC
Marian Univ	IN	41,220	C
Marian Univ	WI	32,420	LC
Marietta College	OH	46,190	C
Marist College	NY	49,860	VC
Marquette Univ	WI	48,390	VC+
Mars Hill Univ	NC	42,688	C
Marshall Univ	WV	17,242	C
Martin Univ	IN	20,264	LC
Mary Baldwin Univ	VA	39,865	C
Marygrove College	MI	28,926	NC
Maryville College	TN	44,410	C
Maryville Univ of St. Louis	MO	38,046	VC+
Mass College of Liberal Arts	MA	20,128	C
Mass Inst of Technology	MA	62,662	MC
Mayville State Univ	ND	18,371	NC
McDaniel College	MD	51,380	VC
McKendree Univ	IL	37,940	C+
McMurry Univ	TX	34,259	LC
McNeese State Univ	LA	7,838	C
McPherson College	KS	34,909	C
MCPHS Univ	MA	45,470	SP
Mercer Univ	GA	45,348	VC
Mercyhurst Univ	PA	47,420	C
Meredith College	NC	45,297	C
Merrimack College	MA	52,770	C
Messiah College	PA	43,100	C+
Methodist Univ	NC	43,600	C
Metropolitan State Univ of Denver	CO	29,889	LC
Miami Univ	OH	27,190	HC+
Mich State Univ	MI	23,898	VC+
Mich Tech Univ	MI	24,739	VC+
MidAmerica Nazarene Univ	KS	35,550	C
Middle Tenn State Univ	TN	8,650	C
Middlebury College	VT	64,332	MC
Midland Univ	NE	37,468	
Midway Univ	KY	31,640	LC
Midwestern State Univ	TX	17,572	C
Miles College	AL	18,646	NC
Millersville Univ of Pennsylvania	PA	23,782	C
Milligan College	TN	38,150	C
Millikin Univ	IL	42,158	C
Mills College	CA	59,163	VC
Millsaps College	MS	50,080	C+
Minn State Univ, Mankato	MN	15,616	C
Minn State Univ, Moorhead	MN	15,941	C
Minot State Univ	ND	12,732	C
Misericordia Univ	PA	43,840	C
Miss College	MS	25,850	C
Miss State Univ	MS	11,454	C+
Miss Univ for Women	MS	17,065	C
Miss Valley State Univ	MS	13,233	LC
Missouri Baptist Univ	MO	35,594	C
Missouri Southern State Univ	MO	12,499	C
Missouri State Univ	MO	15,190	C+
Missouri Univ of Science and Technology	MO	18,655	HC
Missouri Western State Univ	MO	16,741	
Monmouth College	IL	42,260	C
Monmouth Univ	NJ	46,234	C
Montana State Univ	MT	15,500	C+
Montana State Univ-Billings	MT	22,960	C
Montana State Univ-Northern	MT	11,370	NC
Montana Tech of the Univ of Montana	MT	15,447	C+
Montclair State Univ	NJ	26,210	LC
Moravian College	PA	53,117	
Morehead State Univ	KY	17,422	C
Morehouse College	GA	40,064	C
Morgan State Univ	MD	17,190	LC
Morningside College	IA	36,865	C
Mount Holyoke College	MA	56,746	MC
Mount Marty College	SD	32,972	C
Mount Mary Univ	WI	34,650	LC
Mount St. Mary College	NY	42,061	C
Mount St. Joseph Univ	OH	33,880	C
Mount St. Mary's Univ	MD	51,610	C
Mount St. Mary's Univ - Chalon Campus	CA	43,897	VC+
Mount Vernon Nazarene Univ	OH	34,500	C
Muhlenberg College	PA	56,645	VC+
Murray State Univ	KY	16,998	C
Muskingum Univ	OH	35,966	C
Nazareth College	NY	45,574	C
Nebr Wesleyan Univ	NE	38,140	C+
New College of Florida	FL	15,848	MC
New Jersey City Univ	NJ	21,456	LC
New Jersey Inst of Technology	NJ	29,569	VC
New Mexico Highlands Univ	NM	11,904	NC
New Mexico Inst of Mining and Technology	NM	14,833	HC
New Mexico State Univ	NM	14,050	C
New York Inst of Technology	NY	48,730	C
New York Univ	NY	65,860	MC
Newberry College	SC	34,550	C
Newman Univ	KS	35,390	C
Niagara Univ	NY	41,010	C
Nicholls State Univ	LA	10,534	C
Norfolk State Univ	VA	25,702	LC
N Car A&T State Univ	NC	13,365	LC
N Car Central Univ	NC	9,000	C
N Car State Univ	NC	19,515	HC+
N Car Wesleyan College	NC	39,200	C
North Central College	IL	48,712	VC
N Dak State Univ	ND	16,245	C
North Park Univ	IL	35,860	C
Northeastern Illinois Univ	IL	12,529	LC
Northeastern State Univ	OK	8,615	VC
Northeastern Univ	MA	62,703	MC
Northern Arizona Univ	AZ	20,246	VC
Northern Illinois Univ	IL	20,176	C
Northern Kentucky Univ	KY	16,486	C
Northern Mich Univ	MI	19,604	C
Northern State Univ	SD	14,505	C
Northland College	WI	41,103	C+
Northwest Missouri State Univ	MO	17,737	C
Northwest Nazarene Univ	ID	36,000	C
Northwestern College of Iowa	IA	38,400	C+
Northwestern Okla State Univ	OK	13,072	NC
Northwestern Univ	IL	66,344	MC
Norwich Univ	VT	28,212	C
Notre Dame College	OH	37,150	VC
Notre Dame of Maryland Univ	MD	46,465	VC
Nova Southeastern Univ	FL	38,534	C+
Oakland Univ	MI	20,763	C
Oakwood Univ	AL	43,758	C
Oberlin College	OH	66,012	MC
Occidental College	CA	65,530	MC
Oglethorpe Univ	GA	44,200	C+
Ohio Dominican Univ	OH	41,340	C+
Ohio Northern Univ	OH	44,050	VC
Ohio State Univ at Columbus	OH	21,703	HC+
Ohio Univ	OH	22,924	C
Ohio Wesleyan Univ	OH	49,460	VC
Okla Baptist Univ	OK	32,320	C
Okla Christian Univ	OK	27,650	VC
Okla City Univ	OK	40,476	VC
Okla Panhandle State Univ	OK	6,152	NC
Okla State Univ	OK	17,180	VC
Okla Wesleyan Univ	OK	33,206	C
Old Dominion Univ	VA	20,910	C
Olivet College	MI	36,110	LC
Olivet Nazarene Univ	IL	41,840	C
Oral Roberts Univ	OK	34,316	C
Oregon State Univ	OR	22,519	VC
Ottawa Univ	KS	36,074	VC
Otterbein Univ	OH	41,630	C
Ouachita Baptist Univ	AR	32,320	C
Our Lady of the Lake Univ	TX	35,012	LC
Pace Univ	NY	58,248	C
Pacific Lutheran Univ	WA	49,960	VC
Pacific Union College	CA	36,009	VC
Pacific Univ	OR	52,876	C
Paine College	GA	19,506	LC
Palm Beach Atlantic Univ	FL	39,720	C
Park Univ	MO	20,329	C
Penn State Erie/The Behrend College	PA	16,256	C
Pennsylvania State Univ - Univ Park	PA	29,760	HC
Pepperdine Univ	CA	74,460	HC+
Pfeiffer Univ	NC	39,695	LC
Philadelphia Univ	PA	50,370	C
Philander Smith College	AR	20,814	LC
Piedmont College	GA	32,512	C
Pittsburg State Univ	KS	13,880	NC
Pitzer College	CA	66,192	MC
Plymouth State Univ	NH	23,180	LC
Point Loma Nazarene Univ	CA	43,450	C
Pomona College	CA	64,957	MC
Pontifical Catholic Univ of PR	PR	10,534	
Portland State Univ	OR	19,443	C
Prairie View A&M Univ	TX	15,205	LC
Princeton Univ	NJ	57,610	MC
Principia College	IL	39,010	C+
Providence College	RI	60,760	VC
Purdue Univ/Northwest	IN	15,038	C
Purdue Univ/West Lafayette	IN	20,032	MC
Queens Univ of Charlotte	NC	39,543	C
Quincy Univ	IL	36,998	C
Quinnipiac Univ	CT	59,110	C
Radford Univ	VA	19,027	LC
Ramapo College of New Jersey	NJ	25,338	C
Randolph College	VA	45,660	VC
Randolph-Macon College	VA	49,910	C
Reed College	OR	65,300	MC
Regis College	MA	51,920	C
Regis Univ	CO	44,520	C
Rensselaer Polytechnic Inst	NY	63,436	MC
Rhode Island College	RI	17,694	LC
Rhodes College	TN	51,900	HC
Rice Univ	TX	57,668	MC
Rider Univ	NJ	54,050	C
Ripon College	WI	46,911	C+
Roanoke College	VA	54,114	VC
Roberts Wesleyan College	NY	38,306	C
Rochester Inst of Technology	NY	50,842	HC
Rockford Univ	IL	36,030	C
Rockhurst Univ	MO	29,220	C
Rocky Mountain College	MT	34,270	C
Roger Williams Univ	RI	46,296	C+
Rollins College	FL	58,670	HC
Roosevelt Univ	IL	40,651	VC
Rose-Hulman Inst of Technology	IN	57,303	MC
Rosemont College	PA	30,980	C
Rowan Univ	NJ	24,491	VC+
Russell Sage College	NY	39,370	C
Rust College	MS	10,600	C
Rutgers Univ - Camden	NJ	26,146	C
Rutgers Univ - New Brunswick	NJ	26,632	HC
Rutgers Univ - Newark	NJ	27,288	C
Sacred Heart Univ	CT	52,750	C
Saginaw Valley State Univ	MI	18,530	C
St. Anselm College	NH	52,560	C+
St. Augustine's Univ	NC	26,048	C
St. Francis Univ	PA	42,268	NC
St. John's Univ	MN	51,624	C
St. Joseph's College of Maine	ME	46,485	C
St. Joseph's Univ	PA	57,544	VC+
St. Louis Univ	MO	49,866	HC
St. Martin's Univ	WA	45,056	C
St. Mary's College	IN	50,600	C
St. Mary's College of Calif	CA	57,420	C
St. Mary's Univ of Minn	MN	41,210	VC
St. Michael's College	VT	51,725	VC+
St. Peter's Univ	NJ	49,192	C
St. Vincent College	PA	44,626	C
St. Xavier Univ	IL	43,310	C
Salem College	NC	37,694	HC
Salem State Univ	MA	17,303	LC
Salisbury Univ	MD	20,714	VC
Salve Regina Univ	RI	51,470	C
Sam Houston State Univ	TX	18,792	C
Samford Univ	AL	39,232	VC
San Diego State Univ	CA	21,896	C+
San Francisco State Univ	CA	18,514	LC
San Jose State Univ	CA	21,540	C
Sarah Lawrence College	NY	63,388	HC
Savannah State Univ	GA	15,631	C
Schreiner Univ	TX	34,626	LC
Scripps College	CA	66,664	MC
Seattle Pacific Univ	WA	47,439	C+
Seattle Univ	WA	50,811	VC+
Seton Hall Univ	NJ	55,514	C
Seton Hill Univ	PA	46,972	C
Sewanee: The Univ of the South	TN	54,500	MC
Shaw Univ	NC	24,638	C
Shenandoah Univ	VA	41,312	C
Shepherd Univ, West Virginia	WV	17,224	C
Shippensburg Univ of Pennsylvania	PA	23,208	C
Shorter Univ	GA	31,130	LC
Siena College	NY	48,916	C+
Siena Heights Univ	MI	32,040	C
Silver Lake College of the Holy Family	WI	36,290	LC
Simmons College	MA	53,090	VC
Simpson College	IA	43,839	VC
Skidmore College	NY	64,214	HC
Slippery Rock Univ of Pennsylvania	PA	10,360	C
Smith College	MA	63,914	MC
Sonoma State Univ	CA	27,806	C
S Car State Univ	SC	20,805	LC
S Dak School of Mines and Technology	SD	18,645	VC
S Dak State Univ	SD	15,634	C
Southeast Missouri State Univ	MO	15,498	C
Southeastern Louisiana Univ	LA	16,237	C
Southeastern Okla State Univ	OK	11,875	C
Southern Adventist Univ	TN	27,600	C
Southern Arkansas Univ	AR	21,532	C
Southern Conn State Univ	CT	21,924	LC
Southern Illinois Univ Carbondale	IL	23,667	C
Southern Illinois Univ Edwardsville	IL	22,643	C
Southern Methodist Univ	TX	66,483	MC
Southern Nazarene Univ	OK	32,798	NC
Southern Oregon Univ	OR	19,117	C
Southern Univ and A&M College	LA	16,074	LC+
Southern Univ at New Orleans	LA	8,014	LC
Southern Wesleyan Univ	SC	32,130	LC
Southwest Baptist Univ	MO	29,900	LC
Southwest Minn State Univ	MN	17,783	C
Southwestern Adventist Univ	TX	27,756	LC
Southwestern College	KS	31,531	C
Southwestern Okla State Univ	OK	11,790	C
Southwestern Univ	TX	50,720	VC
Spelman College	GA	38,751	C
Spring Arbor Univ	MI	36,000	C
Spring Hill College	AL	48,488	C
Springfield College	MA	45,995	C
St. Ambrose Univ	IA	39,019	C
St. Bonaventure Univ	NY	44,237	C
St. Catherine Univ	MN	45,630	VC
St. Cloud State Univ	MN	10,600	C
St. Edward's Univ	TX	53,100	VC
St. Francis College	NY	38,800	LC
St. John Fisher College	NY	43,620	C
St. John's College-Annapolis	MD	60,142	MC
St. John's Univ	NY	55,850	C
St. Joseph's College, New York/Brooklyn Campus	NY	25,114	LC
St. Joseph's College, New York/Long Island Campus	NY	25,124	C
St. Lawrence Univ	NY	64,390	VC
St. Mary's College of Maryland	MD	26,634	VC
St. Mary's Univ	TX	37,500	C
St. Norbert College	WI	44,525	VC
St. Olaf College	MN	54,260	HC+
Stanford Univ	CA	60,409	MC
SUNY / Buffalo State College	NY	20,842	C
SUNY / SUNY College at Old Westbury	NY	16,860	C
SUNY / SUNY Cortland	NY	20,706	VC
SUNY / SUNY Fredonia	NY	20,818	C
SUNY / SUNY Oneonta	NY	19,712	C+
SUNY / SUNY Plattsburgh	NY	18,814	C
SUNY / SUNY Potsdam	NY	20,404	C+
SUNY / The College of Environmental Science and Forestry	NY	23,853	VC
SUNY / Univ at Buffalo	NY	23,122	C+
SUNY at Binghamton	NY	22,861	MC
SUNY at Geneseo	NY	20,440	VC+
SUNY at New Paltz	NY	19,200	C
SUNY at Oswego	NY	21,351	C
SUNY at Purchase	NY	17,900	C
SUNY SUNY Albany	NY	22,165	C
Stephen F. Austin State Univ	TX	18,406	LC

ST = STATE $IS = IN-STATE COSTS   SR = SELECTOR RATING

School	ST	$IS	SR
Sterling College	KS	32,830	C
Stetson Univ	FL	53,544	VC
Stevens Inst of Technology	NJ	62,338	MC
Stevenson Univ	MD	72,770	C
Stockton Univ	NJ	25,059	
Stonehill College	MA	55,030	C+
Stony Brook Univ/The SUNY	NY	21,881	MC
Suffolk Univ	MA	50,308	C
Susquehanna Univ	PA	55,340	VC
Swarthmore College	PA	63,550	MC
Syracuse Univ	NY	60,239	VC
Tabor College	KS	35,870	C
Talladega College	AL	19,215	C
Tarleton State Univ	TX	15,248	LC
Taylor Univ	IN	40,317	C+
Temple Univ	PA	24,392	VC
Tenn State Univ	TN	14,423	C
Tenn Tech Univ	TN	17,050	C
Texas A&M Univ	TX	20,521	VC+
Texas A&M Univ at Commerce	TX	10,496	C
Texas A&M Univ at Corpus Christi	TX	16,851	LC
Texas A&M Univ at Kingsville	TX	7,500	LC
Texas Christian Univ	TX	54,670	HC
Texas Lutheran Univ	TX	38,620	C
Texas Southern Univ	TX	18,212	LC
Texas State Univ	TX	19,350	C
Texas Tech Univ	TX	18,736	C+
Texas Wesleyan Univ	TX	35,134	C
Texas Woman's Univ	TX	15,302	LC
The Catholic Univ of America	DC	56,356	VC
The Citadel, The Military College of S Car	SC	35,339	C
The College at Brockport - SUNY	NY	20,346	C
The College of Idaho	ID	36,415	C
The College of New Jersey	NJ	31,909	HC
The College of New Rochelle	NY	46,300	VC
The College of St. Rose	NY	43,048	C
The College of Wooster	OH	57,900	VC+
The Lincoln Univ	PA	15,154	NC
The Univ of Akron	OH	21,477	C
The Univ of Tenn at Chattanooga	TN	16,744	C
The Univ of Tenn at Knoxville	TN	22,112	VC
The Univ of Tenn at Martin	TN	14,876	C
The Univ of Utah	UT	17,924	VC
The Univ of Virginia's College at Wise	VA	18,192	LC
Thiel College	PA	41,590	C
Thomas More College	KY	36,720	C
Tougaloo College	MS	17,980	NC
Touro College	NY	28,950	VC
Towson Univ	MD	17,408	VC
Transylvania Univ	KY	45,690	VC+
Trevecca Nazarene Univ	TN	31,186	C
Trine Univ	IN	41,310	C
Trinity Christian College	IL	35,580	C
Trinity College	CT	63,920	HC+
Trinity International Univ	IL	31,070	VC
Trinity Univ	TX	52,314	HC+
Trinity Washington Univ	DC	33,826	C+
Troy Univ	AL	16,171	C
Truman State Univ	MO	16,014	HC
Tufts Univ	MA		MC
Tulane Univ	LA	63,396	HC+
Tusculum College	TN	31,625	C
Tuskegee Univ	AL	28,164	C
Union College	KY	32,310	C
Union College	NE	23,270	C
Union College	NY	64,320	MC
Union Univ	TN	33,970	VC
United States Air Force Academy	CO		C
United States Military Academy at West Point	NY		HC+
United States Naval Academy	MD		MC
Universidad del Turabo	PR	17,828	
Univ of Alabama	AL	24,320	C+
Univ of Alabama at Birmingham	AL	19,906	C
Univ of Alabama in Huntsville	AL	19,445	VC
Univ of Alaska Anchorage	AK	16,652	NC
Univ of Alaska Fairbanks	AK	16,179	C
Univ of Arizona	AZ	23,100	C
Univ of Arkansas at Fayetteville	AR	19,152	C+
Univ of Arkansas at Little Rock	AR	18,211	C
Univ of Arkansas at Monticello	AR	13,134	NC
Univ of Arkansas at Pine Bluff	AR	13,541	C
Univ of Calif at Berkeley	CA	28,853	MC
Univ of Calif at Davis	CA	28,468	HC
Univ of Calif at Irvine	CA	26,484	VC
Univ of Calif at Los Angeles	CA	30,162	MC
Univ of Calif at Riverside	CA	29,227	C+
Univ of Calif at Santa Barbara	CA	29,091	HC
Univ of Calif San Diego	CA	30,150	MC
Univ of Calif, Santa Cruz	CA	28,731	C+
Univ of Central Arkansas	AR	14,472	VC
Univ of Central Florida	FL	15,922	VC
Univ of Central Missouri	MO	18,982	C
Univ of Central Okla	OK	13,486	C
Univ of Charleston	WV	35,000	C
Univ of Chicago	IL	67,584	MC
Univ of Cincinnati	OH	21,964	VC
Univ of Colo Boulder	CO	24,285	VC+
Univ of Colo Colo Springs	CO	19,663	C
Univ of Colo Denver	CO	23,230	C
Univ of Conn	CT	25,538	HC
Univ of Dallas	TX	45,500	VC+
Univ of Dayton	OH	53,620	C
Univ of Delaware	DE	24,976	VC+
Univ of Denver	CO	58,443	VC+
Univ of Detroit Mercy	MI	48,816	C+
Univ of Evansville	IN	44,186	VC+
Univ of Findlay	OH	60,139	C
Univ of Florida	FL	16,291	HC+
Univ of Georgia	GA	21,250	HC
Univ of Hartford	CT	49,776	C
Univ of Hawaii at Hilo	HI	18,038	C
Univ of Hawaii at Manoa	HI	23,221	C
Univ of Houston	TX	21,483	VC
Univ of Houston-Downtown	TX	7,241	C
Univ of Idaho	ID	15,348	C
Univ of Illinois at Chicago	IL	25,006	VC
Univ of Illinois at Urbana-Champaign	IL	27,006	HC
Univ of Indianapolis	IN	36,480	C
Univ of Iowa	IA	18,683	VC+
Univ of Jamestown	ND	28,508	C
Univ of Kansas	KS	20,135	C+
Univ of Kentucky	KY	33,306	C
Univ of La Verne	CA	55,600	C
Univ of Louisiana at Lafayette	LA	14,516	C
Univ of Louisville	KY	19,824	C
Univ of Maine	ME	20,792	C
Univ of Mary Hardin-Baylor	TX	33,950	C+
Univ of Mary Washington	VA	24,764	VC
Univ of Maryland/Baltimore County	MD	21,296	VC
Univ of Maryland/College Park	MD	21,938	HC
Univ of Maryland/Eastern Shore	MD	17,013	C
Univ of Mass Amherst	MA	26,199	VC+
Univ of Mass Boston	MA	13,435	C
Univ of Mass Dartmouth	MA	25,658	C
Univ of Mass Lowell	MA	26,380	C
Univ of Memphis	TN	18,278	C
Univ of Miami	FL	63,494	MC
Univ of Mich/Ann Arbor	MI	24,410	MC
Univ of Mich/Dearborn	MI	11,757	VC
Univ of Mich-Flint	MI	17,607	C+
Univ of Minn/Duluth	MN	20,292	C+
Univ of Minn/Morris	MN	20,760	VC
Univ of Minn/Twin Cities	MN	23,519	HC+
Univ of Miss	MS	17,746	C+
Univ of Missouri/Columbia	MO	18,201	MC
Univ of Missouri-Kansas City	MO	19,563	VC
Univ of Missouri-St. Louis	MO		C
Univ of Montana	MT	14,105	C
Univ of Montevallo	AL	19,502	C
Univ of Mount Union	OH	38,970	C
Univ of Nebr - Kearney	NE	16,546	LC
Univ of Nebr - Lincoln	NE	18,589	VC
Univ of Nebr - Omaha	NE	16,120	C
Univ of Nevada, Las Vegas	NV	17,553	C
Univ of Nevada/Reno	NV	18,010	C
Univ of New England	ME	48,880	C
Univ of New Hampshire	NH	28,562	VC
Univ of New Haven	CT	52,190	C
Univ of New Mexico	NM	15,404	C
Univ of New Orleans	LA	12,840	C
Univ of North Alabama	AL	15,398	C
Univ of N Car at Asheville	NC	15,723	VC+
Univ of N Car at Chapel Hill	NC	20,052	HC+
Univ of N Car at Charlotte	NC	15,547	C
Univ of N Car at Greensboro	NC	14,690	C
Univ of N Car at Pembroke	NC	14,388	LC
Univ of N Car at Wilmington	NC	14,590	VC
Univ of N Dak	ND	15,373	C
Univ of North Florida	FL	15,996	VC
Univ of North Georgia	GA	17,316	C
Univ of North Texas	TX	19,198	C
Univ of Northern Colo	CO	20,851	C
Univ of Notre Dame	IN	64,043	MC
Univ of Okla	OK	18,911	VC
Univ of Oregon	OR	22,972	C
Univ of Pennsylvania	PA	63,526	MC
Univ of Pikeville	KY	28,700	NC
Univ of Pittsburgh	PA	29,568	HC+
Univ of Pittsburgh at Bradford	PA	22,402	C
Univ of Pittsburgh at Johnstown	PA	22,092	C
Univ of Portland	OR	52,152	VC
Univ of PR, at Cayey	PR		
Univ of PR, at Humacao	PR	14,000	
Univ of PR, at Mayaguez	PR	13,995	
Univ of PR-Rio Piedras campus	PR	13,327	
Univ of Puget Sound	WA	56,456	VC+
Univ of Redlands	CA	60,200	VC
Univ of Rhode Island	RI	24,906	C
Univ of Richmond	VA	60,880	MC
Univ of Rio Grande & Rio Grande Community College	OH	8,750	NC
Univ of Rochester	NY	65,032	MC
Univ of St. Francis	IN	37,400	C
Univ of St. Joseph	CT	49,550	C
Univ of St. Mary	KS	34,690	C
Univ of San Diego	CA	58,442	VC+
Univ of San Francisco	CA	58,484	VC
Univ of Science and Arts of Okla	OK	11,140	VC
Univ of Scranton	PA	54,962	VC
Univ of Sioux Falls	SD	34,330	C
Univ of South Alabama	AL	16,400	C
Univ of S Car Aiken	SC	16,712	C
Univ of S Car at Columbia	SC	19,725	VC+
Univ of S Car Upstate	SC	18,200	LC
Univ of S Dak	SD	16,109	C
Univ of South Florida/Tampa	FL	16,110	VC+
Univ of Southern Calif	CA	66,631	C
Univ of Southern Indiana	IN	16,501	C
Univ of Southern Maine	ME	18,320	C
Univ of Southern Miss	MS	13,170	C
Univ of St. Thomas - Houston	TX	40,020	VC
Univ of Tampa	FL	36,944	C
Univ of Texas at Arlington	TX	18,026	LC
Univ of Texas at Austin	TX	26,102	HC
Univ of Texas at Dallas	TX	22,830	VC+
Univ of Texas at El Paso	TX	34,452	NC
Univ of Texas at San Antonio	TX	20,157	C
Univ of the Cumberlands	KY	32,000	C
Univ of the District of Columbia	DC	21,044	LC
Univ of the Incarnate Word	TX	39,162	LC
Univ of the Ozarks	AR	52,176	C
Univ of the Pacific	CA	57,006	VC
Univ of the Sacred Heart	PR	17,932	
Univ of the Sciences	PA	54,038	VC
Univ of Toledo	OH	19,336	NC
Univ of Tulsa	OK	52,625	HC+
Univ of Vermont	VT	28,878	HC
Univ of Virginia	VA	25,891	MC
Univ of West Alabama	AL	15,516	NC
Univ of West Florida	FL	15,848	C
Univ of West Georgia	GA	16,360	LC
Univ of Wisc-Eau Claire	WI	15,797	VC
Univ of Wisc-Green Bay	WI	15,064	C
Univ of Wisc-La Crosse	WI	15,247	C+
Univ of Wisc-Madison	WI	20,934	MC
Univ of Wisc-Milwaukee	WI	21,496	C
Univ of Wisc-Oshkosh	WI	15,200	C
Univ of Wisc-Parkside	WI	15,193	C
Univ of Wisc-Platteville	WI	14,614	VC
Univ of Wisc-River Falls	WI	14,485	C
Univ of Wisc-Stevens Point	WI	14,043	C
Univ of Wisc-Superior	WI	14,446	C
Univ of Wisc-Whitewater	WI	13,976	C
Univ of Wyoming	WY	15,375	C+
Upper Iowa Univ	IA	34,990	NC
Ursinus College	PA	61,690	VC
Utah State Univ	UT	12,736	C
Utica College	NY	30,430	C
Valley City State Univ	ND	13,267	C
Valparaiso Univ	IN	48,370	C+
Vanderbilt Univ	TN	60,572	MC
Vanguard Univ of Southern Calif	CA	40,740	VC
Vassar College	NY	65,491	MC
Villanova Univ	PA	62,523	MC
Virginia Commonwealth Univ	VA	23,049	C
Virginia Military Inst	VA	26,460	C+
Virginia Polytechnic Inst and State Univ	VA	21,276	HC
Virginia State Univ	VA	19,802	C+
Virginia Union Univ	VA	22,421	C
Virginia Wesleyan College	VA	43,728	LC
Viterbo Univ	WI	34,660	C
Wabash College	IN	50,650	VC
Wagner College	NY	55,480	C+
Wake Forest Univ	NC	64,056	MC
Walla Walla Univ	WA	30,417	NC
Walsh Univ	OH	39,010	C
Warren Wilson College	NC	44,220	VC
Wartburg College	IA	47,840	C
Washburn Univ	KS	15,827	C
Washington & Jefferson College	PA	56,512	VC
Washington Adventist Univ	MD	31,440	LC
Washington and Lee Univ	VA	59,647	MC
Washington College	MD	54,666	VC
Washington State Univ	WA	22,495	C
Washington Univ in St. Louis	MO	65,366	VC
Wayland Baptist Univ	TX	22,356	LC
Wayne State College	NE	12,802	C
Wayne State Univ	MI	22,016	C
Waynesburg Univ	PA	32,290	C
Weber State Univ	UT	10,721	C
Wellesley College	MA	63,916	MC
Wells College	NY	50,500	C
Wesleyan College	GA	29,694	C+
Wesleyan Univ	CT	65,516	MC
West Chester Univ of Pennsylvania	PA	18,456	C
West Liberty Univ	WV	15,512	C
West Texas A&M Univ	TX	13,478	C
West Virginia State Univ	WV	8,378	NC
West Virginia Univ	WV	18,210	C
West Virginia Univ Inst of Technology	WV	16,462	NC
West Virginia Wesleyan College	WV	36,858	C
Western Carolina Univ	NC	13,965	C
Western Conn State Univ	CT	21,254	LC
Western Illinois Univ	IL	20,825	C
Western Kentucky Univ	KY	16,850	C
Western Mich Univ	MI	21,054	C
Western New England Univ	MA	48,088	C
Western New Mexico Univ	NM	16,734	LC
Western Oregon Univ	OR	15,021	LC
Western State Colo Univ	CO	18,639	C
Western Washington Univ	WA	18,003	C+
Westfield State Univ	MA	19,671	C
Westminster College	MO	32,820	C
Westminster College	PA	39,180	C+
Westminster College	UT	41,078	C+
Westmont College	CA	56,410	HC
Wheaton College	IL	43,610	MC
Wheaton College	MA	61,512	VC
Wheeling Jesuit Univ	WV	37,106	LC
Whitman College	WA	59,772	MC
Whittier College	CA	57,891	C
Whitworth Univ	WA	51,732	VC
Wichita State Univ	KS	21,643	C
Widener Univ	PA	56,486	C
Wilberforce Univ	OH	19,016	C
Wiley College	TX	18,504	C
Wilkes Univ	PA	45,622	C
Willamette Univ	OR	61,817	VC+
William Carey Univ	MS	23,950	LC
William Jewell College	MO	41,210	C+
William Paterson Univ of New Jersey	NJ	23,133	C
Williams College	MA	63,290	MC
Wilmington College	OH	34,600	C
Wilson College	PA	35,620	C
Wingate Univ	NC	39,950	C
Winona State Univ	MN	17,535	C
Winston-Salem State Univ	NC	26,166	LC
Winthrop Univ	SC	23,082	C
Wisc Lutheran College	WI	36,290	VC
Wittenberg Univ	OH	48,156	C+
Wofford College	SC	49,885	VC
Worcester Polytechnic Inst	MA	60,730	MC
Worcester State Univ	MA	20,977	C
Wright State Univ	OH	16,983	C
Xavier Univ	OH	47,880	C+
Xavier Univ of Louisiana	LA	31,689	C+
Yale Univ	CT	64,650	MC
Yeshiva Univ	NY	47,250	VC+
York College of Pennsylvania	PA	29,240	C
Youngstown State Univ	OH	17,307	C

CHEMISTRY (PRE-MBA)

School	ST	$IS	SR
Murray State Univ	KY	16,998	C
Univ of Great Falls	MT	38,524	C

CHEMISTRY / CHEMICAL BIOLOGY

School	ST	$IS	SR
Bethany College	WV	36,300	NC
Bryant Univ	RI	55,646	VC
Case Western Reserve Univ	OH	60,304	MC
Cornell Univ	NY	64,853	MC
Huntington Univ	IN	33,996	C
Indiana Univ Kokomo	IN	7,073	C
Murray State Univ	KY	16,998	C
West Chester Univ of Pennsylvania	PA	18,456	C

CHEMISTRY EDUCATION

School	ST	$IS	SR
Arkansas State Univ	AR	16,190	C
Ashland Univ	OH	21,440	C
Bethany College	WV	36,300	NC
Bloomfield College	NJ	39,100	LC
Boston Univ	MA	65,110	MC
Cedarville Univ	OH	34,990	VC
Edgewood College	WI	35,950	C
Ferris State Univ	MI	21,445	C
Georgia Southern Univ	GA	16,596	C
Hope College	MI	39,940	VC
Indiana Univ of Pennsylvania	PA	23,614	LC
Mayville State Univ	ND	18,371	NC
Monmouth Univ	NJ	46,234	C
Niagara Univ	NY	41,010	C
Oakwood Univ	AL	43,758	C
Silver Lake College of the Holy Family	WI	36,290	LC
St. Ambrose Univ	IA	39,019	C
Weber State Univ	UT	10,721	C
West Chester Univ of Pennsylvania	PA	18,456	C

CHEMISTRY SECONDARY EDUCATION

School	ST	$IS	SR
Grove City College	PA	25,692	VC
King Univ	TN	34,660	C
Lewis Univ	IL	40,370	C
Providence College	RI	60,760	VC
Syracuse Univ	NY	60,239	VC
West Chester Univ of Pennsylvania	PA	18,456	C
Western Mich Univ	MI	21,054	C
Wilson College	PA	35,620	C

ST = STATE $IS = IN-STATE COSTS SR = SELECTOR RATING

CHEMISTRY/ADOLESCENCE EDUCATION

School	ST	$IS	SR
Arkansas Tech Univ	AR	15,484	C
Augustana College	IL	49,658	VC
Bethany College	WV	36,300	NC
Black Hills State Univ	SD	15,899	C
College of the Ozarks	MO	7,230	C
Duquesne Univ	PA	46,822	VC
Elizabethtown College	PA	54,050	C
Houghton College	NY	39,090	C
Huntingdon College	AL	34,900	C
Indiana Univ Bloomington	IN	20,429	VC
Indiana Univ Northwest	IN	7,072	C
Indiana Univ South Bend	IN	14,242	C
King Univ	TN	34,660	C
Lipscomb Univ	TN	41,296	VC
LIU Post	NY	49,682	C
Marist College	NY	49,860	VC
Messiah College	PA	43,100	C+
Millikin Univ	IL	42,158	C
Minn State Univ, Mankato	MN	15,616	C
Murray State Univ	KY	16,998	C
Nazareth College	NY	45,574	C
Niagara Univ	NY	41,010	C
Northern Kentucky Univ	KY	16,486	C
Old Dominion Univ	VA	20,910	C
Roberts Wesleyan College	NY	38,306	C
St. Mary's Univ of Minn	MN	41,210	VC
Seattle Univ	WA	50,811	VC+
SUNY / SUNY Fredonia	NY	20,818	C
SUNY / SUNY Plattsburgh	NY	18,814	C
Temple Univ	PA	24,392	VC
Trevecca Nazarene Univ	TN	31,186	C
Univ of Mary Hardin-Baylor	TX	33,950	C+
Univ of Nebr - Lincoln	NE	18,589	VC

CHEMISTRY/FORENSIC CHEMISTRY

School	ST	$IS	SR
Lewis Univ	IL	40,370	C
Missouri Baptist Univ	MO	35,594	C
Okla Baptist Univ	OK	32,320	C
Univ of Rhode Island	RI	24,906	C
Univ of St. Francis	IN	37,400	C
West Chester Univ of Pennsylvania	PA	18,456	C
Western New England Univ	MA	48,088	C

CHEMISTRY/GEN SCIENCE SECOND EDUCATION

School	ST	$IS	SR
Grove City College	PA	25,692	VC
Huntingdon College	AL	34,900	C
Lewis Univ	IL	40,370	C
St. Edward's Univ	TX	53,100	VC
Syracuse Univ	NY	60,239	VC
West Chester Univ of Pennsylvania	PA	18,456	C
Wilson College	PA	35,620	C

CHILD CARE/CHILD AND FAMILY STUDIES

School	ST	$IS	SR
Abilene Christian Univ	TX	41,800	C+
Albright College	PA	46,660	C
Armstrong State Univ	GA	16,962	C
Ashland Univ	OH	21,440	C
Baylor Univ	TX	53,760	HC
Berea College	KY	7,042	C
Cal State, Fresno	CA	16,902	LC
Cal State, Fullerton	CA	21,902	C
Cal State, Long Beach	CA	18,850	C
Cameron Univ	OK	11,072	NC
Chestnut Hill College	PA	43,410	C
CUNY/Brooklyn College	NY	5,884	C+
College of the Ozarks	MO	7,230	C
Concordia Univ St. Paul	MN	29,050	C
Davis & Elkins College	WV	38,242	LC
East Carolina Univ	NC	16,937	C
East Central Univ	OK	13,056	C
Eastern Kentucky Univ	KY	16,908	C
Eastern Mich Univ	MI	19,761	C
Edgewood College	WI	35,950	C
Eureka College	IL	30,220	C
Florida State Univ	FL	16,771	HC
Fontbonne Univ	MO	33,717	C
Freed-Hardeman Univ	TN	29,450	C
Georgia Southern Univ	GA	16,596	C
Goodwin College	CT	28,370	LC
Harding Univ	AR	25,421	C
Indiana State Univ	IN	23,223	LC
Indiana Univ of Pennsylvania	PA	23,614	LC
Iowa State Univ	IA	17,570	C
Jackson State Univ	MS	15,879	LC
Kansas State Univ	KS	17,780	VC
La Roche College	PA	37,924	LC
Lasell College	MA	47,500	C
Limestone College	SC	32,100	C
Louisiana State Univ and A&M College	LA	18,677	VC
Mayville State Univ	ND	18,371	NC
Messiah College	PA	43,100	C+
Metropolitan College of New York	NY		VC
Mount Aloysius College	PA	29,976	C
New York Univ	NY	65,860	MC
N Car Central Univ	NC	9,000	C
N Dak State Univ	ND	16,245	C
Northern Illinois Univ	IL	20,176	C
Northwest Missouri State Univ	MO	17,737	C
Ohio Univ	OH	22,924	C
Okla Baptist Univ	OK	32,320	C
Okla Christian Univ	OK	27,650	VC
Okla State Univ	OK	17,180	VC
Park Univ	MO	20,329	C
Plymouth State Univ	NH	23,180	LC
Portland State Univ	OR	19,443	C
Rutgers Univ - Camden	NJ	26,146	C
Seton Hill Univ	PA	46,972	C
Silver Lake College of the Holy Family	WI	36,290	LC
St. Bonaventure Univ	NY	44,237	C
SUNY / Empire State College	NY	9,145	SP
SUNY / SUNY Oneonta	NY	19,712	C+
SUNY / SUNY Plattsburgh	NY	18,814	C
SUNY /College of Agriculture and Tech at Cobleskill	NY	20,527	LC
Syracuse Univ	NY	60,239	VC
Tenn Tech Univ	TN	17,050	C
Texas A&M Univ at Kingsville	TX	7,500	LC
Texas State Univ	TX	19,350	C
The Univ of Tenn at Knoxville	TN	22,112	VC
The Univ of Tenn at Martin	TN	14,876	C
Univ of Alaska Fairbanks	AK	16,179	C
Univ of Georgia	GA	21,250	HC
Univ of Idaho	ID	15,348	C
Univ of Maine	ME	20,792	C
Univ of Missouri/Columbia	MO	18,201	MC
Univ of Nebr - Lincoln	NE	18,589	VC
Univ of Nevada/Reno	NV	18,010	C
Univ of New Mexico	NM	15,404	C
Univ of N Car at Chapel Hill	NC	20,052	HC+
Univ of N Car at Charlotte	NC	15,547	C
Univ of N Car at Greensboro	NC	14,690	C
Univ of North Texas	TX	19,198	C
Univ of Texas at Austin	TX	26,102	HC
Univ of Texas at San Antonio	TX	20,157	C
Univ of the Incarnate Word	TX	39,162	LC
Univ of Vermont	VT	28,878	HC
Univ of Wisc-Stout	WI	19,667	C
Utah State Univ	UT	12,736	C
Weber State Univ	UT	10,721	C
West Virginia Univ	WV	18,210	C
Western Mich Univ	MI	21,054	C
Wheelock College	MA	49,225	C
Youngstown State Univ	OH	17,307	C

CHILD PSYCHOLOGY/DEVELOPMENT

School	ST	$IS	SR
Alcorn State Univ	MS	15,854	C
Angelo State Univ	TX	15,263	NC
Appalachian State Univ	NC	14,416	VC
Ashford Univ	CA	10,480	C
Bay Path Univ	MA	45,349	C
Bennington College	VT	63,960	MC
Bethel Univ	TN	24,738	C
Bluffton Univ	OH	40,950	C
Calif Polytechnic State Univ	CA	17,979	HC+
Cal State, Bakersfield	CA	19,191	LC
Cal State, Chico	CA	21,440	C
Cal State, Dominguez Hills	CA	19,022	LC
Cal State, Fresno	CA	16,902	LC
Cal State, Long Beach	CA	18,850	C
Cal State, Los Angeles	CA	17,186	LC
Cal State, Northridge	CA	16,859	LC
Cal State, San Bernardino	CA	12,000	C
Cal State, Stanislaus	CA	16,212	C
Central Mich Univ	MI	20,330	C
Colby-Sawyer College	NH	50,790	C
East Tenn State Univ	TN	13,994	C
East Texas Baptist Univ	TX	33,134	C
Eastern Nazarene College	MA	39,955	C
Florida Gulf Coast Univ	FL	9,682	C
Fort Valley State Univ	GA	17,988	VC
Hope International Univ	CA	41,150	C
Howard Univ	DC	37,616	C+
Humboldt State Univ	CA	20,514	C
Iowa State Univ	IA	17,570	C
Madonna Univ	MI	29,050	C
Marygrove College	MI	28,926	NC
Meredith College	NC	45,297	C
Metropolitan State Univ	MN	7,566	C
Mich State Univ	MI	23,898	VC+
Mills College	CA	59,163	VC
Missouri Baptist Univ	MO	35,594	C
Missouri State Univ	MO	15,190	C+
Mount Ida College	MA	46,820	C
Mount St. Mary's Univ - Chalon Campus	CA	43,897	VC+
Niagara Univ	NY	41,010	C
N Car A&T State Univ	NC	13,365	LC
N Car Central Univ	NC	9,000	C
Okla Baptist Univ	OK	32,320	C
Olivet Nazarene Univ	IL	41,840	C
Point Loma Nazarene Univ	CA	43,450	C
San Diego State Univ	CA	21,896	C+
Siena Heights Univ	MI	32,040	C
Southern New Hampshire Univ	NH	43,198	C
Spelman College	GA	38,751	C
St. Joseph's College, New York/Long Island Campus	NY	25,124	C
Stephen F. Austin State Univ	TX	18,406	LC
Texas Christian Univ	TX	54,670	HC
Texas Woman's Univ	TX	15,302	LC
The Univ of Akron	OH	21,477	C
Tougaloo College	MS	17,980	NC
Tufts Univ	MA		MC
Univ of Central Okla	OK	13,486	C
Univ of Illinois at Urbana-Champaign	IL	27,006	HC
Univ of La Verne	CA	55,600	C
Univ of Minn/Twin Cities	MN	23,519	HC+
Univ of N Car at Charlotte	NC	15,547	C
Univ of St. Joseph	CT	49,550	C
Univ of St. Mary	KS	34,690	C
Univ of Texas at Dallas	TX	22,830	VC+
Univ of Virginia	VA	25,891	MC
Utica College	NY	30,430	C
Vanderbilt Univ	TN	60,572	MC
Wellesley College	MA	63,916	MC
Western Mich Univ	MI	21,054	C
Western Washington Univ	WA	18,003	C+
Whittier College	CA	57,891	C

CHILDHOOD EDUCATION

School	ST	$IS	SR
Bethel College	IN	35,860	C
Bloomfield College	NJ	39,100	LC
Canisius College	NY	47,537	C
CUNY/Brooklyn College	NY	5,884	C+
Clayton State Univ	GA	19,735	C
Dordt College	IA	37,860	C+
Hofstra Univ	NY	55,960	C+
Houghton College	NY	39,090	C
Iona College	NY	50,984	C
Kennesaw State Univ	GA	19,592	VC
Marshall Univ	WV	17,242	C
Mass College of Liberal Arts	MA	20,128	C
Missouri Southern State Univ	MO	12,499	C
Mount Aloysius College	PA	29,976	C
New York Univ	NY	65,860	MC
Niagara Univ	NY	41,010	C
Point Park Univ	PA	41,270	C
Silver Lake College of the Holy Family	WI	36,290	LC
St. Ambrose Univ	IA	39,019	C
SUNY at Oswego	NY	21,351	C
Taylor Univ	IN	40,317	C+
Univ of Arkansas at Fayetteville	AR	19,152	C+
Univ of Georgia	GA	21,250	HC
Univ of Maryland/Baltimore County	MD	21,296	VC
Univ of Nebr - Lincoln	NE	18,589	VC
Univ of N Car at Pembroke	NC	14,388	LC
Univ of Texas at San Antonio	TX	20,157	C
Wellesley College	MA	63,916	MC
West Chester Univ of Pennsylvania	PA	18,456	C
Western Kentucky Univ	KY	16,850	C
Wilson College	PA	35,620	C
Wright State Univ	OH	16,983	C
Youngstown State Univ	OH	17,307	C

CHINA ASIA-PACIFIC STUDIES

School	ST	$IS	SR
Cornell Univ	NY	64,853	MC
Hofstra Univ	NY	55,960	C+
Wellesley College	MA	63,916	MC

CHINESE

School	ST	$IS	SR
American Univ	DC	59,379	HC+
Ball State Univ	IN	19,590	C
Bard College	NY	64,024	HC
Bates College	ME	64,500	MC
Beloit College	WI	55,206	HC
Bennington College	VT	63,960	MC
Boston Univ	MA	65,110	MC
Brigham Young Univ	UT	12,748	HC
Bryant Univ	RI	55,646	VC
Cal State, Long Beach	CA	18,850	C
Calvin College	MI	41,570	VC+
Central Washington Univ	WA	16,803	C
CUNY/Hunter College	NY	31,098	VC
CUNY/Queens College	NY	27,896	C
Colgate Univ	NY	65,030	MC
College of the Holy Cross	MA	62,165	MC
College of William & Mary	VA		MC
Concordia College - Moorhead	MN	51,088	C+
Conn College	CT	65,000	MC
Dartmouth College	NH	66,174	MC
Davidson College	NC	60,119	MC
DePaul Univ	IL	47,623	VC
Drew Univ/College of Liberal Arts	NJ	61,048	VC
Emory Univ	GA	60,786	MC
George Washington Univ	DC	62,835	MC
Georgetown Univ	DC	65,926	MC
Grand Valley State Univ	MI	22,250	C+
Grinnell College	IA	60,738	MC
Hamilton College	NY	64,250	MC
Harvard College/Harvard Univ	MA	60,659	MC
Hofstra Univ	NY	55,960	C+
Lawrence Univ	WI	54,498	HC
Lehigh Univ	PA	61,010	MC
Macalester College	MN	61,905	MC
Mich State Univ	MI	23,898	VC+
Middlebury College	VT	64,332	MC
Nazareth College	NY	45,574	C
New College of Florida	FL	15,848	MC
North Central College	IL	48,712	VC
Oakland Univ	MI	20,763	C
Occidental College	CA	65,530	MC
Ohio State Univ at Columbus	OH	21,703	HC+
Pomona College	CA	64,957	MC
Portland State Univ	OR	19,443	C
Reed College	OR	65,300	MC
Rutgers Univ - New Brunswick	NJ	26,632	HC
San Francisco State Univ	CA	18,514	LC
San Jose State Univ	CA	21,540	C
Scripps College	CA	66,664	MC
Stanford Univ	CA	60,409	MC
SUNY SUNY Albany	NY	22,165	C
Swarthmore College	PA	63,550	MC
The Univ of Utah	UT	17,924	VC
Thomas Edison State Univ	NJ	6,350	NC
Trinity Univ	TX	52,314	HC+
Tufts Univ	MA		MC
United States Naval Academy	MD		MC
Univ of Calif at Berkeley	CA	28,853	MC
Univ of Calif at Davis	CA	28,468	HC
Univ of Calif at Los Angeles	CA	30,162	MC
Univ of Calif at Riverside	CA	29,227	C+
Univ of Calif at Santa Barbara	CA	29,091	HC
Univ of Calif San Diego	CA	30,150	MC
Univ of Colo Boulder	CO	24,285	VC+
Univ of Hawaii at Manoa	HI	23,221	C
Univ of Houston	TX	21,483	VC
Univ of Iowa	IA	18,683	VC+
Univ of Maryland/College Park	MD	21,938	HC
Univ of Mass Amherst	MA	26,199	VC+
Univ of Minn/Twin Cities	MN	23,519	HC+
Univ of Miss	MS	17,746	C+
Univ of N Dak	ND	15,373	C
Univ of Notre Dame	IN	64,043	MC
Univ of Okla	OK	18,911	VC
Univ of Oregon	OR	22,972	C
Univ of Pittsburgh	PA	29,568	HC+
Univ of Puget Sound	WA	56,456	VC+
Univ of Rhode Island	RI	24,906	C
Univ of Vermont	VT	28,878	HC
Univ of Wisc-Madison	WI	20,934	MC
Vassar College	NY	65,491	MC
Wake Forest Univ	NC	64,056	MC
Washington State Univ	WA	22,495	C
Washington Univ in St. Louis	MO	65,366	VC
Wellesley College	MA	63,916	MC
Western Kentucky Univ	KY	16,850	C
Whittier College	CA	57,891	C
Wofford College	SC	49,885	VC
Yale Univ	CT	64,650	MC

CHINESE STUDIES

School	ST	$IS	SR
Beloit College	WI	55,206	HC
Bryant Univ	RI	55,646	VC
Carnegie Mellon Univ	PA	67,980	MC
Eugene Lang College/The New School for Liberal Arts	NY	55,650	C
Hofstra Univ	NY	55,960	C+
Messiah College	PA	43,100	C+
Pacific Lutheran Univ	WA	49,960	VC
Pennsylvania State Univ - Univ Park	PA	29,760	HC
SUNY at Binghamton	NY	22,861	MC
Swarthmore College	PA	63,550	MC
Trinity Univ	TX	52,314	HC+
Univ of Calif at Irvine	CA	26,484	VC
Univ of Georgia	GA	21,250	HC
Univ of Richmond	VA	60,880	MC
Univ of Tulsa	OK	52,625	HC+
Washington State Univ	WA	22,495	C
Wellesley College	MA	63,916	MC
Wisc Lutheran College	WI	36,290	VC

CHIROPRACTIC

School	ST	$IS	SR
Colo State Univ-Pueblo	CO	18,234	C
Mount Aloysius College	PA	29,976	C
Walla Walla Univ	WA	30,417	NC

CHORAL MUSIC

School	ST	$IS	SR
Baylor Univ	TX	53,760	HC
Concordia Univ St. Paul	MN	29,050	C
Dallas Baptist Univ	TX	33,713	C
Faulkner Univ	AL	26,410	C
Mannes School for Music	NY	44,500	SP
Missouri Southern State Univ	MO	12,499	C
Mount Aloysius College	PA	29,976	C
Ohio Univ	OH	22,924	C
Toccoa Falls College	GA	27,920	C
Univ of Kansas	KS	20,135	C+
Univ of North Texas	TX	19,198	C
Webster Univ	MO	37,490	C

CHRISTIAN EDUCATION

School	ST	$IS	SR
Anderson Univ	IN	38,200	C

ST = STATE $IS = IN-STATE COSTS SR = SELECTOR RATING

School	ST	$IS	SR
Asbury Univ	KY	35,180	C+
Bethany College	KS	46,100	NC
Biola Univ	CA	46,402	C+
Cedarville Univ	OH	34,990	VC
Columbia College	SC	36,550	C
Concordia Univ	CA	41,580	VC
Concordia Univ Nebr	NE	36,280	VC
Concordia Univ St. Paul	MN	29,050	C
Corban Univ	OR	40,306	C
Dallas Baptist Univ	TX	33,713	C
Defiance College	OH	41,630	C
Erskine College	SC	45,460	C
Hannibal-LaGrange Univ	MO	29,815	C
Harding Univ	AR	25,421	C
Houghton College	NY	39,090	C
Lenoir-Rhyne Univ	NC	43,200	C
Malone Univ	OH	38,448	C
Muskingum Univ	OH	35,966	C
Northwest Nazarene Univ	ID	36,000	C
Northwestern College of Iowa	IA	38,400	C+
Olivet Nazarene Univ	IL	41,840	C
Pfeiffer Univ	NC	39,695	LC
Southern Nazarene Univ	OK	32,798	NC
Spring Arbor Univ	MI	36,000	C
Taylor Univ	IN	40,317	C+
The Master's Univ	CA	43,870	C+
West Virginia Wesleyan College	WV	36,858	C
Westminster College	PA	39,180	C+
Wheaton College	IL	43,610	MC

CHRISTIAN STUDIES

School	ST	$IS	SR
Alderson Broaddus Univ	WV	26,149	C
Aquinas College - Mich	MI	38,876	HC
Belmont Univ	TN	40,970	VC
Bethel College	IN	35,860	C
Blue Mountain College	MS	15,949	VC
Bluefield College	VA	34,120	C+
Brewton-Parker College	GA	23,490	C
Bryan College	TN	31,440	C
Calif Baptist Univ	CA	41,392	C
Campbellsville Univ	KY	32,492	C
College of the Ozarks	MO	7,230	C
Dallas Baptist Univ	TX	33,713	C
Eastern Nazarene College	MA	39,955	C
Friends Univ	KS	34,455	C
Grand Canyon Univ	AZ	16,950	VC
Grand Rapids Theological Seminary/Cornerstone Univ	MI	33,338	C
Hillsdale College	MI	35,722	MC
Houghton College	NY	39,090	C
Houston Baptist Univ	TX	36,450	C
Howard Payne Univ	TX	34,320	C
Huntingdon College	AL	34,900	C
Iowa Wesleyan Univ	IA	39,200	C
John Brown Univ	AR	33,132	VC
Mercer Univ	GA	45,348	VC
Miss College	MS	25,850	C
Missouri Baptist Univ	MO	35,594	C
North Greenville Univ	SC	25,930	C+
Okla Baptist Univ	OK	32,320	C
Ouachita Baptist Univ	AR	32,320	C
Point Loma Nazarene Univ	CA	43,450	C
Roanoke College	VA	54,114	VC
Roberts Wesleyan College	NY	38,306	C
Seattle Pacific Univ	WA	47,439	C+
Shorter Univ	GA	31,130	LC
Sterling College	KS	32,830	C
Stonehill College	MA	55,030	C+
Tabor College	KS	35,870	C
Taylor Univ	IN	40,317	C+
The Master's Univ	CA	43,870	C+
Toccoa Falls College	GA	27,920	C
Trinity International Univ	IL	31,070	VC
Union Univ	TN	33,970	VC
Univ of Mary Hardin-Baylor	TX	33,950	C+
Vanguard Univ of Southern Calif	CA	40,740	VC
Wayland Baptist Univ	TX	22,356	LC

CHURCH MUSIC

School	ST	$IS	SR
Averett Univ	VA	40,970	LC
Belmont Univ	TN	40,970	VC
Blue Mountain College	MS	15,949	VC
Concordia Univ St. Paul	MN	29,050	C
Dallas Baptist Univ	TX	33,713	C
Dordt College	IA	37,860	C+
Hope International Univ	CA	41,150	C
Madonna Univ	MI	29,050	C
Montreat College	NC	31,298	LC
Mount Vernon Nazarene Univ	OH	34,500	C
Nyack College	NY	34,050	NC
Okla Baptist Univ	OK	32,320	C
Okla City Univ	OK	40,476	VC
Ouachita Baptist Univ	AR	32,320	C
Shenandoah Univ	VA	41,312	C
Texas Christian Univ	TX	54,670	HC
The Master's Univ	CA	43,870	C+
Univ of Mary Hardin-Baylor	TX	33,950	C+
Univ of the Cumberlands	KY	32,000	C
Wingate Univ	NC	39,950	C

CITY/COMMUNITY/REGIONAL PLANNING

School	ST	$IS	SR
Alabama A&M Univ	AL	18,796	C
Ball State Univ	IN	19,590	C
Brigham Young Univ	UT	12,748	HC
Calif Polytechnic State Univ	CA	17,979	HC+
East Carolina Univ	NC	16,937	C
Eastern Mich Univ	MI	19,761	C
Indiana Univ of Pennsylvania	PA	23,614	LC
Iowa State Univ	IA	17,570	C
Mich State Univ	MI	23,898	VC+
New Mexico State Univ	NM	14,050	C
Ohio State Univ at Columbus	OH	21,703	HC+
Plymouth State Univ	NH	23,180	LC
Temple Univ	PA	24,392	VC
Texas State Univ	TX	19,350	C
Univ of Cincinnati	OH	21,964	VC
Univ of Illinois at Urbana-Champaign	IL	27,006	HC
Univ of New Hampshire	NH	28,562	VC
Univ of Virginia	VA	25,891	MC
Univ of Wisc-Green Bay	WI	15,064	C
Western Kentucky Univ	KY	16,850	C
Western Mich Univ	MI	21,054	C
Westfield State Univ	MA	19,671	C

CIVIL AND ENVIRONMENTAL ENGINEERING

School	ST	$IS	SR
Angelo State Univ	TX	15,263	NC
Univ of Nevada/Reno	NV	18,010	C

CIVIL ENGINEERING

School	ST	$IS	SR
Alabama A&M Univ	AL	18,796	C
Angelo State Univ	TX	15,263	NC
Arizona State Univ at the Tempe Campus	AZ	21,756	VC
Auburn Univ	AL	23,594	VC+
Boise State Univ	ID	14,860	C
Brigham Young Univ	UT	12,748	HC
Bucknell Univ	PA	64,616	MC
Calif Baptist Univ	CA	41,392	C
Calif Polytechnic State Univ	CA	17,979	HC+
Calif State Polytechnic Univ, Pomona	CA	21,541	C
Cal State, Chico	CA	21,440	C
Cal State, Fresno	CA	16,902	LC
Cal State, Fullerton	CA	21,902	C
Cal State, Long Beach	CA	18,850	C
Cal State, Los Angeles	CA	17,186	LC
Cal State, Northridge	CA	16,859	LC
Cal State, Sacramento	CA	20,332	C
Calvin College	MI	41,570	VC+
Caribbean Univ	PR	15,471	
Carnegie Mellon Univ	PA	67,980	MC
Carroll College	MT	39,972	C+
Case Western Reserve Univ	OH	60,304	MC
Central Conn State Univ	CT	21,203	C
Christian Brothers Univ	TN	31,670	VC
CUNY/City College	NY	20,319	VC
Clarkson Univ	NY	60,392	HC
Clemson Univ	SC		HC
Cleveland State Univ	OH	22,196	C
Colo Mesa Univ	CO	18,955	LC
Colo State Univ	CO	22,162	VC
Columbia Univ/City of New York	NY	62,958	MC
Cooper Union for the Advancement of Science and Art	NY	58,210	MC
Cornell Univ	NY	64,853	MC
Delaware State Univ	DE	19,376	NC
Dordt College	IA	37,860	C+
Drexel Univ	PA	65,432	VC+
Duke Univ	NC	64,188	
Embry-Riddle Aeronautical Univ - Daytona Beach	FL	44,712	VC
Florida A&M Univ	FL	15,361	C
Florida Atlantic Univ	FL	17,339	C
Florida Gulf Coast Univ	FL	9,682	C
Florida Inst of Technology	FL	53,306	VC
Florida International Univ	FL	19,854	C+
Florida State Univ	FL	16,771	HC
George Mason Univ	VA	15,724	VC
George Washington Univ	DC	62,835	MC
Georgia Inst of Technology	GA	23,360	MC
Georgia Southern Univ	GA	16,596	C
Gonzaga Univ	WA	50,888	HC
Hofstra Univ	NY	55,960	C+
Howard Univ	DC	37,616	C+
Idaho State Univ	ID	13,619	NC
Illinois Inst of Technology	IL	56,826	HC+
Indiana Univ-Purdue Univ Fort Wayne	IN	17,553	C
Iowa State Univ	IA	17,570	C
Jackson State Univ	MS	15,879	LC
Johns Hopkins Univ	MD	65,386	MC
Kansas State Univ	KS	17,780	VC
Kennesaw State Univ	GA	19,592	VC
King's College	PA	46,858	C
Lafayette College	PA	63,355	MC
Lamar Univ	TX	18,014	LC
Lawrence Tech Univ	MI	39,770	VC
Lehigh Univ	PA	61,010	MC
Lipscomb Univ	TN	41,296	VC
Louisiana State Univ and A&M College	LA	18,677	VC
Louisiana Tech Univ	LA	11,422	VC
Loyola Marymount Univ	CA	58,038	HC
Manhattan College	NY	51,750	C+
Marquette Univ	WI	48,390	VC+
Marshall Univ	WV	17,242	C
Mass Inst of Technology	MA	62,662	MC
Merrimack College	MA	52,770	C
Mich State Univ	MI	23,898	VC+
Mich Tech Univ	MI	24,739	VC+
Minn State Univ, Mankato	MN	15,616	C
Miss State Univ	MS	11,454	C+
Missouri Univ of Science and Technology	MO	18,655	HC
Montana State Univ	MT	15,500	C+
Morgan State Univ	MD	17,190	LC
New Jersey Inst of Technology	NJ	29,569	VC
New Mexico Inst of Mining and Technology	NM	14,833	HC
New Mexico State Univ	NM	14,050	C
New York Univ	NY	65,860	MC
N Car A&T State Univ	NC	13,365	LC
N Car State Univ	NC	19,515	HC+
N Dak State Univ	ND	16,245	C
Northeastern Univ	MA	62,703	MC
Northern Arizona Univ	AZ	20,246	VC
Northwestern Univ	IL	66,344	MC
Norwich Univ	VT	28,212	C
Ohio Northern Univ	OH	44,050	VC
Ohio State Univ at Columbus	OH	21,703	HC+
Ohio Univ	OH	22,924	C
Okla State Univ	OK	17,180	VC
Old Dominion Univ	VA	20,910	C
Oregon Inst of Technology	OR	8,910	C
Oregon State Univ	OR	22,519	VC
Pennsylvania State Univ - Univ Park	PA	29,760	HC
Point Park Univ	PA	41,270	C
Portland State Univ	OR	19,443	C
Prairie View A&M Univ	TX	15,205	LC
Princeton Univ	NJ	57,610	MC
Purdue Univ/Northwest	IN	15,038	C
Purdue Univ/West Lafayette	IN	20,032	MC
Quinnipiac Univ	CT	59,110	C
Rensselaer Polytechnic Inst	NY	63,436	MC
Rice Univ	TX	57,668	MC
Rose-Hulman Inst of Technology	IN	57,303	MC
Rowan Univ	NJ	24,491	VC+
Rutgers Univ - New Brunswick	NJ	26,632	HC
St. Louis Univ	MO	49,866	HC
St. Martin's Univ	WA	45,056	C
San Diego State Univ	CA	21,896	C+
San Francisco State Univ	CA	18,514	LC
San Jose State Univ	CA	21,540	C
Savannah State Univ	GA	15,631	C
Seattle Univ	WA	50,811	VC+
S Dak School of Mines and Technology	SD	18,645	VC
S Dak State Univ	SD	15,634	C
Southern Illinois Univ Carbondale	IL	23,667	C
Southern Illinois Univ Edwardsville	IL	22,643	C
Southern Methodist Univ	TX	66,483	MC
Southern Univ and A&M College	LA	16,074	LC+
Stanford Univ	CA	60,409	MC
SUNY / Univ at Buffalo	NY	23,122	C+
SUNY Polytechnic Inst	NY	19,473	VC
Stevens Inst of Technology	NJ	62,338	MC
Stony Brook Univ/The SUNY	NY	21,881	MC
Syracuse Univ	NY	60,239	VC
Tarleton State Univ	TX	15,248	LC
Temple Univ	PA	24,392	VC
Tenn State Univ	TN	14,423	C
Tenn Tech Univ	TN	17,050	C
Texas A&M Univ	TX	20,521	VC+
Texas A&M Univ at Galveston	TX	15,920	C
Texas A&M Univ at Kingsville	TX	7,500	LC
Texas Tech Univ	TX	18,736	C+
The Catholic Univ of America	DC	56,356	VC
The Citadel, The Military College of S Car	SC	35,339	C
The College of New Jersey	NJ	31,909	HC
The Univ of Akron	OH	21,477	C
The Univ of Tenn at Chattanooga	TN	16,744	C
The Univ of Tenn at Knoxville	TN	22,112	VC
The Univ of Utah	UT	17,924	VC
Trine Univ	IN	41,310	C
Tufts Univ	MA		MC
United States Air Force Academy	CO		C
United States Coast Guard Academy	CT	942	MC
United States Military Academy at West Point	NY		HC+
Universidad Politecnica de PR, Hato Rey campus	PR	23,514	
Univ of Alabama	AL	24,320	C+
Univ of Alabama at Birmingham	AL	19,906	C
Univ of Alabama in Huntsville	AL	19,445	VC
Univ of Alaska Anchorage	AK	16,652	NC
Univ of Alaska Fairbanks	AK	16,179	C
Univ of Arizona	AZ	23,100	C
Univ of Arkansas at Fayetteville	AR	19,152	C+
Univ of Calif at Berkeley	CA	28,853	MC
Univ of Calif at Davis	CA	28,468	HC
Univ of Calif at Irvine	CA	26,484	VC
Univ of Calif at Los Angeles	CA	30,162	MC
Univ of Central Florida	FL	15,922	VC
Univ of Cincinnati	OH	21,964	VC
Univ of Colo Boulder	CO	24,285	VC+
Univ of Colo Denver	CO	23,230	C
Univ of Conn	CT	25,538	HC
Univ of Dayton	OH	53,620	C
Univ of Delaware	DE	24,976	VC+
Univ of Detroit Mercy	MI	48,816	C+
Univ of Evansville	IN	44,186	VC+
Univ of Florida	FL	16,291	HC+
Univ of Georgia	GA	21,250	HC
Univ of Hartford	CT	49,776	C
Univ of Hawaii at Manoa	HI	23,221	C
Univ of Houston	TX	21,483	VC
Univ of Idaho	ID	15,348	C
Univ of Illinois at Chicago	IL	25,006	VC
Univ of Illinois at Urbana-Champaign	IL	27,006	HC
Univ of Iowa	IA	18,683	VC+
Univ of Kansas	KS	20,135	C+
Univ of Kentucky	KY	33,306	C
Univ of Louisiana at Lafayette	LA	14,516	C
Univ of Louisville	KY	19,824	C
Univ of Maine	ME	20,792	C
Univ of Maryland/College Park	MD	21,938	HC
Univ of Mass Amherst	MA	26,199	VC+
Univ of Mass Dartmouth	MA	25,658	C
Univ of Mass Lowell	MA	26,380	C
Univ of Memphis	TN	18,278	C
Univ of Miami	FL	63,494	MC
Univ of Mich/Ann Arbor	MI	24,410	MC
Univ of Minn/Duluth	MN	20,292	C+
Univ of Minn/Twin Cities	MN	23,519	HC+
Univ of Miss	MS	17,746	C+
Univ of Missouri/Columbia	MO	18,201	MC
Univ of Missouri-Kansas City	MO	19,563	VC
Univ of Missouri-St. Louis	MO		C
Univ of Mount Union	OH	38,970	C
Univ of Nebr - Lincoln	NE	18,589	VC
Univ of Nevada, Las Vegas	NV	17,553	C
Univ of Nevada/Reno	NV	18,010	C
Univ of New Hampshire	NH	28,562	VC
Univ of New Haven	CT	52,190	C
Univ of New Mexico	NM	15,404	C
Univ of New Orleans	LA	12,840	C
Univ of N Car at Charlotte	NC	15,547	C
Univ of N Dak	ND	15,373	C
Univ of North Florida	FL	15,996	VC
Univ of Notre Dame	IN	64,043	MC
Univ of Okla	OK	18,911	VC
Univ of Pennsylvania	PA	63,526	MC
Univ of Pittsburgh	PA	29,568	HC+
Univ of Portland	OR	52,152	VC
Univ of PR, at Mayaguez	PR	13,995	
Univ of Rhode Island	RI	24,906	C
Univ of South Alabama	AL	16,400	C
Univ of S Car at Columbia	SC	19,725	VC+
Univ of South Florida/Tampa	FL	16,110	VC+
Univ of Southern Calif	CA	66,631	C
Univ of Texas at Arlington	TX	18,026	LC
Univ of Texas at Austin	TX	26,102	HC
Univ of Texas at El Paso	TX	34,452	NC
Univ of Texas at San Antonio	TX	20,157	C
Univ of the District of Columbia	DC	21,044	LC
Univ of the Pacific	CA	57,006	VC
Univ of Toledo	OH	19,336	NC
Univ of Vermont	VT	28,878	HC
Univ of Virginia	VA	25,891	MC
Univ of Washington	WA	23,149	VC
Univ of Wisc-Madison	WI	20,934	MC
Univ of Wisc-Milwaukee	WI	21,496	C
Univ of Wisc-Platteville	WI	14,614	VC
Univ of Wyoming	WY	15,375	C+
Utah State Univ	UT	12,736	C
Valparaiso Univ	IN	48,370	C+
Vanderbilt Univ	TN	60,572	MC
Villanova Univ	PA	62,523	MC
Virginia Military Inst	VA	26,460	C+
Virginia Polytechnic Inst and State Univ	VA	21,276	HC
Washington State Univ	WA	22,495	C
Washington Univ in St. Louis	MO	65,366	VC
Wayne State Univ	MI	22,016	C
Wentworth Inst of Technology	MA	47,112	C
West Virginia Univ	WV	18,210	C
West Virginia Univ Inst of Technology	WV	16,462	NC
Western Kentucky Univ	KY	16,850	C
Western Mich Univ	MI	21,054	C
Western New England Univ	MA	48,088	C
Widener Univ	PA	56,486	C
Worcester Polytechnic Inst	MA	60,730	MC
Youngstown State Univ	OH	17,307	C

ST = STATE $IS = IN-STATE COSTS SR = SELECTOR RATING

CIVIL ENGINEERING TECHNOLOGY

School	ST	$IS	SR
Alabama A&M Univ	AL	18,796	C
Arkansas State Univ	AR	16,190	C
Cal State, Fresno	CA	16,902	LC
Central Conn State Univ	CT	21,203	C
Colo State Univ-Pueblo	CO	18,234	C
Fairleigh Dickinson Univ/ Metropolitan Campus	NJ	40,254	C
Fairmont State Univ	WV	15,726	C
Idaho State Univ	ID	13,619	NC
Kennesaw State Univ	GA	19,592	VC
Lincoln Univ	MO	13,602	NC
Metropolitan State Univ of Denver	CO	29,889	LC
Montana State Univ-Northern	MT	11,370	NC
Murray State Univ	KY	16,998	C
Old Dominion Univ	VA	20,910	C
Pennsylvania College of Technology	PA	27,333	NC
Point Park Univ	PA	41,270	C
Rochester Inst of Technology	NY	50,842	HC
St. Louis Univ	MO	49,866	HC
S Car State Univ	SC	20,805	LC
Southern Univ and A&M College	LA	16,074	LC+
SUNY Polytechnic Inst	NY	19,473	VC
Texas Southern Univ	TX	18,212	LC
Univ of N Car at Charlotte	NC	15,547	C
Univ of Pittsburgh at Johnstown	PA	22,092	C
Univ of Southern Indiana	IN	16,501	C
Western Kentucky Univ	KY	16,850	C
Youngstown State Univ	OH	17,307	C

CLASSICAL AND NEAR EASTERN CIVILIZATION

School	ST	$IS	SR
Brown Univ	RI	64,566	MC
Calvin College	MI	41,570	VC+
Creighton Univ	NE	48,206	VC+
Indiana Univ Bloomington	IN	20,429	VC

CLASSICAL LANGUAGES

School	ST	$IS	SR
Agnes Scott College	GA	51,930	VC+
Asbury Univ	KY	35,180	C+
Austin College	TX	45,875	VC
Ball State Univ	IN	19,590	C
Bard College	NY	64,024	HC
Beloit College	WI	55,206	HC
Boston Univ	MA	65,110	MC
Brigham Young Univ	UT	12,748	HC
Bryn Mawr College	PA	59,890	MC
Canisius College	NY	47,537	C
Carroll College	MT	39,972	C+
Concordia College - Moorhead	MN	51,088	C+
Creighton Univ	NE	48,206	VC+
Dartmouth College	NH	66,174	MC
DePauw Univ	IN	58,688	HC+
Dickinson College	PA	63,974	MC
Duke Univ	NC	64,188	
Duquesne Univ	PA	46,822	VC
Eastern Mich Univ	MI	19,761	C
Fordham Univ	NY	65,918	MC
Hollins Univ	VA	49,635	VC
Hope College	MI	39,940	VC
John Carroll Univ	OH	49,740	C+
Luther College	IA	48,540	C+
Marquette Univ	WI	48,390	VC+
Miami Univ	OH	27,190	HC+
New York Univ	NY	65,860	MC
Pacific Lutheran Univ	WA	49,960	VC
Pennsylvania State Univ - Univ Park	PA	29,760	HC
St. Louis Univ	MO	49,866	HC
St. Mary's College of Calif	CA	57,420	C
St. Peter's Univ	NJ	49,192	C
Scripps College	CA	66,664	MC
Sewanee: The Univ of the South	TN	54,500	MC
St. Bonaventure Univ	NY	44,237	C
Univ of Calif at Berkeley	CA	28,853	MC
Univ of Calif at Riverside	CA	29,227	C+
Univ of Calif, Santa Cruz	CA	28,731	C+
Univ of Georgia	GA	21,250	HC
Univ of Kansas	KS	20,135	C+
Univ of Mass Boston	MA	13,435	C
Univ of Mich/Ann Arbor	MI	24,410	MC
Univ of Minn/Twin Cities	MN	23,519	HC+
Univ of Nebr - Lincoln	NE	18,589	VC
Univ of N Car at Greensboro	NC	14,690	C
Univ of N Dak	ND	15,373	C
Vanderbilt Univ	TN	60,572	MC
Washington Univ in St. Louis	MO	65,366	VC
Wellesley College	MA	63,916	MC
Wheaton College	IL	43,610	MC
Wright State Univ	OH	16,983	C
Yeshiva Univ	NY	47,250	VC+

CLASSICAL STUDIES

School	ST	$IS	SR
Colgate Univ	NY	65,030	MC
Hollins Univ	VA	49,635	VC
Univ of Georgia	GA	21,250	HC
Univ of Minn/Twin Cities	MN	23,519	HC+
Univ of Notre Dame	IN	64,043	MC
Univ of Rhode Island	RI	24,906	C
Wellesley College	MA	63,916	MC
Wheaton College	MA	61,512	VC

CLASSICAL/ANCIENT CIVILIZATION

School	ST	$IS	SR
Agnes Scott College	GA	51,930	VC+
Bard College	NY	64,024	HC
Barnard College/Columbia Univ	NY	62,741	MC
Bates College	ME	64,500	MC
Beloit College	WI	55,206	HC
Boston College	MA	65,737	MC
Boston Univ	MA	65,110	MC
Bowdoin College	ME	63,500	MC
Brigham Young Univ	UT	12,748	HC
Brown Univ	RI	64,566	MC
Carleton College	MN	64,071	MC
Centre College	KY	49,250	HC
Christendom College	VA	32,600	VC
Clark Univ	MA	51,600	HC+
Cleveland State Univ	OH	22,196	C
Colby College	ME	64,060	MC
College of William & Mary	VA		MC
Columbia Univ/ School of General Studies	NY	61,470	MC
Columbia Univ/City of New York	NY	62,958	MC
Cornell College	IA	48,800	VC
Dartmouth College	NH	66,174	MC
Denison Univ	OH	58,860	MC
DePauw Univ	IN	58,688	HC+
Dickinson College	PA	63,974	MC
Duke Univ	NC	64,188	
Duquesne Univ	PA	46,822	VC
Earlham College	IN	54,870	HC
Eckerd College	FL	52,874	C
Emory Univ	GA	60,786	MC
Florida State Univ	FL	16,771	HC
Fordham Univ	NY	65,918	MC
Gonzaga Univ	WA	50,888	HC
Hawaii Pacific Univ	HI	33,420	C
Howard Univ	DC	37,616	C+
Indiana Univ Bloomington	IN	20,429	VC
Kalamazoo College	MI	53,931	HC+
Lehigh Univ	PA	61,010	MC
Loyola Marymount Univ	CA	58,038	HC
Loyola Univ Chicago	IL	55,802	VC
Loyola Univ Maryland	MD	60,300	VC
Loyola Univ New Orleans	LA	51,708	VC+
Mich State Univ	MI	23,898	VC+
Mount Holyoke College	MA	56,746	MC
New York Univ	NY	65,860	MC
North Central College	IL	48,712	VC
Ohio Univ	OH	22,924	C
Rhodes College	TN	51,900	HC
Rice Univ	TX	57,668	MC
Rollins College	FL	58,670	HC
Rutgers Univ - Newark	NJ	27,288	C
St. Peter's Univ	NJ	49,192	C
Scripps College	CA	66,664	MC
Smith College	MA	63,914	MC
St. Olaf College	MN	54,260	HC+
SUNY at Binghamton	NY	22,861	MC
Swarthmore College	PA	63,550	MC
Syracuse Univ	NY	60,239	VC
Trinity College	CT	63,920	HC+
Univ of Arkansas at Fayetteville	AR	19,152	C+
Univ of Calif at Berkeley	CA	28,853	MC
Univ of Calif at Davis	CA	28,468	HC
Univ of Calif at Irvine	CA	26,484	VC
Univ of Calif at Los Angeles	CA	30,162	MC
Univ of Calif at Riverside	CA	29,227	C+
Univ of Chicago	IL	67,584	MC
Univ of Cincinnati	OH	21,964	VC
Univ of Evansville	IN	44,186	VC+
Univ of Florida	FL	16,291	HC+
Univ of Illinois at Chicago	IL	25,006	VC
Univ of Iowa	IA	18,683	VC+
Univ of Kansas	KS	20,135	C+
Univ of Maryland/Baltimore County	MD	21,296	VC
Univ of Mich/Ann Arbor	MI	24,410	MC
Univ of Miss	MS	17,746	C+
Univ of Nebr - Lincoln	NE	18,589	VC
Univ of Oregon	OR	22,972	C
Univ of Richmond	VA	60,880	MC
Univ of Southern Calif	CA	66,631	C
Univ of Texas at Arlington	TX	18,026	LC
Univ of Texas at Austin	TX	26,102	HC
Vassar College	NY	65,491	MC
Wellesley College	MA	63,916	MC
Wesleyan Univ	CT	65,516	MC
Wheaton College	MA	61,512	VC
Willamette Univ	OR	61,817	VC+
Yale Univ	CT	64,650	MC

CLASSICS

School	ST	$IS	SR
Alabama A&M Univ	AL	18,796	C
Amherst College	MA		HC+
Assumption College	MA	47,920	C+
Augustana College	IL	49,658	VC
Augustana Univ	SD	38,424	VC
Austin College	TX	45,875	VC
Ball State Univ	IN	19,590	C
Barnard College/Columbia Univ	NY	62,741	MC
Baylor Univ	TX	53,760	HC
Beloit College	WI	55,206	HC
Boston College	MA	65,737	MC
Boston Univ	MA	65,110	MC
Bowdoin College	ME	63,500	MC
Bowling Green State Univ	OH	19,747	C
Brandeis Univ	MA	65,925	MC
Brigham Young Univ	UT	12,748	HC
Brown Univ	RI	64,566	MC
Bryn Mawr College	PA	59,890	MC
Bucknell Univ	PA	64,616	MC
Cal State, Long Beach	CA	18,850	C
Carleton College	MN	64,071	MC
Case Western Reserve Univ	OH	60,304	MC
CUNY/Brooklyn College	NY	5,884	C+
CUNY/Hunter College	NY	31,098	VC
CUNY/Queens College	NY	27,896	C
Claremont McKenna College	CA	67,185	MC
Colby College	ME	64,060	MC
Colgate Univ	NY	65,030	MC
College of Charleston	SC	22,699	C
College of St. Benedict	MN	52,806	C
College of the Holy Cross	MA	62,165	MC
Colo College	CO	62,560	MC
Columbia Univ/ School of General Studies	NY	61,470	MC
Columbia Univ/City of New York	NY	62,958	MC
Concordia College - Moorhead	MN	51,088	C+
Conn College	CT	65,000	MC
Cornell Univ	NY	64,853	MC
Dartmouth College	NH	66,174	MC
Davidson College	NC	60,119	MC
Drew Univ/College of Liberal Arts	NJ	61,048	VC
Elmira College	NY	53,900	C
Emory Univ	GA	60,786	MC
Florida State Univ	FL	16,771	HC
Fordham Univ	NY	65,918	MC
Franciscan Univ of Steubenville	OH	33,980	VC
Franklin and Marshall College	PA	63,170	HC
Furman Univ	SC	58,092	VC+
George Washington Univ	DC	62,835	MC
Georgetown Univ	DC	65,926	MC
Georgia State Univ	GA	24,332	VC
Gettysburg College	PA	63,000	HC
Gonzaga Univ	WA	50,888	HC
Grand Valley State Univ	MI	22,250	C+
Grinnell College	IA	60,738	MC
Gustavus Adolphus College	MN	52,433	HC
Hamilton College	NY	64,250	MC
Hampden-Sydney College	VA	56,248	C+
Hanover College	IN	46,364	C+
Harvard College/Harvard Univ	MA	60,659	MC
Haverford College	PA	66,490	MC
Hellenic College/Holy Cross Greek Orthodox School of Theology	MA	39,906	C
Hillsdale College	MI	35,722	MC
Hofstra Univ	NY	55,960	C+
Illinois Wesleyan Univ	IL	56,430	VC+
John Carroll Univ	OH	49,740	C+
Johns Hopkins Univ	MD	65,386	MC
Kent State Univ	OH	20,732	C
Kenyon College	OH	63,330	MC
Knox College	IL	52,615	VC+
Lawrence Univ	WI	54,498	HC
Lehigh Univ	PA	61,010	MC
Lewis & Clark College	OR	58,434	HC+
Macalester College	MN	61,905	MC
Marquette Univ	WI	48,390	VC+
Marshall Univ	WV	17,242	C
Miami Univ	OH	27,190	HC+
Middlebury College	VT	64,332	MC
Millsaps College	MS	50,080	C+
Monmouth College	IL	42,260	C
Montclair State Univ	NJ	26,210	LC
Moravian College	PA	53,117	
Mount Holyoke College	MA	56,746	MC
New College of Florida	FL	15,848	MC
New York Univ	NY	65,860	MC
Northwestern Univ	IL	66,344	MC
Notre Dame of Maryland Univ	MD	46,465	VC
Oberlin College	OH	66,012	MC
Ohio State Univ at Columbus	OH	21,703	HC+
Ohio Univ	OH	22,924	C
Ohio Wesleyan Univ	OH	49,460	VC
Pacific Lutheran Univ	WA	49,960	VC
Pitzer College	CA	66,192	MC
Pomona College	CA	64,957	MC
Princeton Univ	NJ	57,610	MC
Providence College	RI	60,760	VC
Purdue Univ/West Lafayette	IN	20,032	MC
Randolph College	VA	45,660	VC
Randolph-Macon College	VA	49,910	C
Reed College	OR	65,300	MC
Rice Univ	TX	57,668	MC
Rockford Univ	IL	36,030	C
Rutgers Univ - New Brunswick	NJ	26,632	HC
St. Anselm College	NH	52,560	C+
St. John's Univ	MN	51,624	C
St. Louis Univ	MO	49,866	HC
Samford Univ	AL	39,232	VC
San Diego State Univ	CA	21,896	C+
San Francisco State Univ	CA	18,514	LC
Sarah Lawrence College	NY	63,388	HC
Seattle Pacific Univ	WA	47,439	C+
Seton Hall Univ	NJ	55,514	C
Siena College	NY	48,916	C+
Skidmore College	NY	64,214	HC
Smith College	MA	63,914	MC
Southwestern Univ	TX	50,720	VC
St. Catherine Univ	MN	45,630	VC
St. Olaf College	MN	54,260	HC+
Stanford Univ	CA	60,409	MC
SUNY / Univ at Buffalo	NY	23,122	C+
SUNY at Binghamton	NY	22,861	MC
Swarthmore College	PA	63,550	MC
Syracuse Univ	NY	60,239	VC
Temple Univ	PA	24,392	VC
Texas Tech Univ	TX	18,736	C+
The Catholic Univ of America	DC	56,356	VC
The College of New Rochelle	NY	46,300	VC
The Univ of Akron	OH	21,477	C
The Univ of Tenn at Knoxville	TN	22,112	VC
The Univ of Utah	UT	17,924	VC
Transylvania Univ	KY	45,690	VC+
Trinity College	CT	63,920	HC+
Trinity Univ	TX	52,314	HC+
Truman State Univ	MO	16,014	HC
Tufts Univ	MA		MC
Tulane Univ	LA	63,396	HC+
Union College	NY	64,320	MC
Univ of Alabama	AL	24,320	C+
Univ of Arizona	AZ	23,100	C
Univ of Calif at Irvine	CA	26,484	VC
Univ of Calif at Los Angeles	CA	30,162	MC
Univ of Calif at Santa Barbara	CA	29,091	HC
Univ of Calif San Diego	CA	30,150	MC
Univ of Chicago	IL	67,584	MC
Univ of Colo Boulder	CO	24,285	VC+
Univ of Conn	CT	25,538	HC
Univ of Dallas	TX	45,500	VC+
Univ of Hawaii at Manoa	HI	23,221	C
Univ of Illinois at Urbana-Champaign	IL	27,006	HC
Univ of Iowa	IA	18,683	VC+
Univ of Mary Washington	VA	24,764	VC
Univ of Maryland/College Park	MD	21,938	HC
Univ of Mass Amherst	MA	26,199	VC+
Univ of Mass Boston	MA	13,435	C
Univ of Miami	FL	63,494	MC
Univ of Mich/Ann Arbor	MI	24,410	MC
Univ of Missouri/Columbia	MO	18,201	MC
Univ of Montana	MT	14,105	C
Univ of Nebr - Lincoln	NE	18,589	VC
Univ of New Hampshire	NH	28,562	VC
Univ of New Mexico	NM	15,404	C
Univ of N Car at Asheville	NC	15,723	VC+
Univ of N Car at Chapel Hill	NC	20,052	HC+
Univ of Okla	OK	18,911	VC
Univ of Oregon	OR	22,972	C
Univ of Pennsylvania	PA	63,526	MC
Univ of Pittsburgh	PA	29,568	HC+
Univ of Puget Sound	WA	56,456	VC+
Univ of Rochester	NY	65,032	MC
Univ of S Car at Columbia	SC	19,725	VC+
Univ of South Florida/Tampa	FL	16,110	VC+
Univ of Southern Calif	CA	66,631	C
Univ of Texas at Austin	TX	26,102	HC
Univ of Texas at San Antonio	TX	20,157	C
Univ of Vermont	VT	28,878	HC
Univ of Virginia	VA	25,891	MC
Univ of Washington	WA	23,149	VC
Univ of Wisc-Madison	WI	20,934	MC
Univ of Wisc-Milwaukee	WI	21,496	C
Valparaiso Univ	IN	48,370	C+
Vanderbilt Univ	TN	60,572	MC
Villanova Univ	PA	62,523	MC
Virginia Wesleyan College	VA	43,728	LC
Wabash College	IN	50,650	VC
Wake Forest Univ	NC	64,056	MC
Washington and Lee Univ	VA	59,647	MC
Washington Univ in St. Louis	MO	65,366	VC
Wayne State Univ	MI	22,016	C
Wellesley College	MA	63,916	MC
Wesleyan Univ	CT	65,516	MC
Western Kentucky Univ	KY	16,850	C
Western Washington Univ	WA	18,003	C+
Wheaton College	MA	61,512	VC
Whitman College	WA	59,772	MC
Williams College	MA	63,290	MC
Xavier Univ	OH	47,880	C+
Yale Univ	CT	64,650	MC

CLINICAL LABORATORY SCIENCE

School	ST	$IS	SR
Albany College of Pharmacy and Health Sciences	NY	42,681	SP
Arkansas State Univ	AR	16,190	C
Bloomfield College	NJ	39,100	LC

School	ST	$IS	SR
Bryant Univ	RI	55,646	VC
Eastern Illinois Univ	IL	21,126	C
Eastern Mennonite Univ	VA	42,550	C
Indiana Univ Kokomo	IN	7,073	C
Indiana Univ of Pennsylvania	PA	23,614	LC
Indiana Univ South Bend	IN	14,242	C
Indiana Univ Southeast	IN	14,242	LC
Indiana Univ-Purdue Univ Indianapolis	IN	18,635	C
Loyola Univ Chicago	IL	55,802	VC
Marian Univ	IN	41,220	C
Monmouth Univ	NJ	46,234	C
Neumann Univ	PA	40,678	LC
St. Louis Univ	MO	49,866	HC
Stony Brook Univ/The SUNY	NY	21,881	MC
Thomas Edison State Univ	NJ	6,350	NC
Univ of Evansville	IN	44,186	VC+
Univ of Mary Hardin-Baylor	TX	33,950	C+
Univ of Mass Lowell	MA	26,380	C
Univ of St. Francis	IN	37,400	C
Western Illinois Univ	IL	20,825	C

CLINICAL PSYCHOLOGY

School	ST	$IS	SR
Averett Univ	VA	40,970	LC
Eastern Nazarene College	MA	39,955	C
Faulkner Univ	AL	26,410	C
Goddard College	VT	17,040	VC
Kutztown Univ of Pennsylvania	PA	19,056	LC
Marywood Univ	PA	46,900	C
Seattle Pacific Univ	WA	47,439	C+
The Lincoln Univ	PA	15,154	NC
Univ of Louisville	KY	19,824	C
Univ of New Haven	CT	52,190	C
Western Kentucky Univ	KY	16,850	C

CLINICAL SCIENCE

School	ST	$IS	SR
Bellarmine Univ	KY	51,220	C
Benedictine Univ	IL	38,300	C
Bethune-Cookman Univ	FL	22,970	C
Brigham Young Univ	UT	12,748	HC
Cal State, Bakersfield	CA	19,191	LC
Cal State, Dominguez Hills	CA	19,022	LC
Canisius College	NY	47,537	C
Carroll College	MT	39,972	C+
Concordia College - Moorhead	MN	51,088	C+
DePaul Univ	IL	47,623	VC
Fairleigh Dickinson Univ/ College at Florham	NJ	52,062	C
Fairleigh Dickinson Univ/ Metropolitan Campus	NJ	40,254	C
Florida Gulf Coast Univ	FL	9,682	C
George Washington Univ	DC	62,835	MC
Georgian Court Univ	NJ	42,426	LC
Grand Valley State Univ	MI	22,250	C+
Gwynedd Mercy Univ	PA	43,780	LC
Howard Univ	DC	37,616	C+
Ithaca College	NY	56,766	VC
LIU Brooklyn	NY	49,682	C
LIU Post	NY	49,682	C
Loyola Univ Chicago	IL	55,802	VC
Marquette Univ	WI	48,390	VC+
Mary Baldwin Univ	VA	39,865	C
Maryville Univ of St. Louis	MO	38,046	VC+
McNeese State Univ	LA	7,838	C
Mich State Univ	MI	23,898	VC+
Minn State Univ, Mankato	MN	15,616	C
Missouri State Univ	MO	15,190	C+
New Mexico State Univ	NM	14,050	C
N Dak State Univ	ND	16,245	C
Northern Illinois Univ	IL	20,176	C
Northern Mich Univ	MI	19,604	C
Purdue Univ/West Lafayette	IN	20,032	MC
Quincy Univ	IL	36,998	C
Ramapo College of New Jersey	NJ	25,338	C
Rockhurst Univ	MO	29,220	C
Rutgers Univ - Newark	NJ	27,288	C
St. Louis Univ	MO	49,866	HC
San Francisco State Univ	CA	18,514	LC
S Dak State Univ	SD	15,634	C
St. John's Univ	NY	55,850	C
Texas A&M Univ at Corpus Christi	TX	16,851	LC
Texas State Univ	TX	19,350	C
The College of Idaho	ID	36,415	C
The Univ of Tenn at Knoxville	TN	22,112	VC
Truman State Univ	MO	16,014	HC
Univ of Jamestown	ND	28,508	C
Univ of Mass Dartmouth	MA	25,658	C
Univ of Nevada, Las Vegas	NV	17,553	C
Univ of N Car at Chapel Hill	NC	20,052	HC+
Univ of N Car at Wilmington	NC	14,590	VC
Univ of N Dak	ND	15,373	C
Univ of St. Mary	KS	34,690	C
Univ of Texas at El Paso	TX	34,452	NC
Univ of Wisc-Stevens Point	WI	14,043	C
Virginia Commonwealth Univ	VA	23,049	C
Walsh Univ	OH	39,010	C
Washburn Univ	KS	15,827	C
Wayne State Univ	MI	22,016	C
Weber State Univ	UT	10,721	C
West Liberty Univ	WV	15,512	C
Wright State Univ	OH	16,983	C
Youngstown State Univ	OH	17,307	C

CLOTHING AND TEXTILES MANAGEMENT/PRODUCTION/ SERVICES

School	ST	$IS	SR
Cheyney Univ of Pennsylvania	PA	20,896	LC
College of the Ozarks	MO	7,230	C
East Carolina Univ	NC	16,937	C
Eastern Mich Univ	MI	19,761	C
Florida State Univ	FL	16,771	HC
Johnson & Wales Univ/ Charlotte Campus	NC	43,988	C
Johnson & Wales Univ/North Miami Campus	FL	42,707	C
Johnson & Wales Univ/ Providence Campus	RI	42,248	C
N Car A&T State Univ	NC	13,365	LC
N Car State Univ	NC	19,515	HC+
San Francisco State Univ	CA	18,514	LC
Southern Illinois Univ Carbondale	IL	23,667	C
Univ of Alabama	AL	24,320	C+
Washington State Univ	WA	22,495	C
Western Mich Univ	MI	21,054	C

COASTAL ENVIORNMENTAL STUDIES

School	ST	$IS	SR
Brown Univ	RI	64,566	MC

COGNITIVE SCIENCE

School	ST	$IS	SR
Ashford Univ	CA	10,480	C
Beloit College	WI	55,206	HC
Brown Univ	RI	64,566	MC
Cal State, Stanislaus	CA	16,212	C
Canisius College	NY	47,537	C
Case Western Reserve Univ	OH	60,304	MC
Central Mich Univ	MI	20,330	C
Dartmouth College	NH	66,174	MC
Fitchburg State Univ	MA	21,819	C
George Fox Univ	OR	42,938	C
Hampshire College	MA	63,824	MC
Indiana Univ Bloomington	IN	20,429	VC
Johns Hopkins Univ	MD	65,386	MC
Lawrence Univ	WI	54,498	HC
Lehigh Univ	PA	61,010	MC
Mass Inst of Technology	MA	62,662	MC
Minn State Univ, Mankato	MN	15,616	C
Northwestern Univ	IL	66,344	MC
Occidental College	CA	65,530	MC
Pomona College	CA	64,957	MC
Rice Univ	TX	57,668	MC
Smith College	MA	63,914	MC
SUNY at Oswego	NY	21,351	C
Tufts Univ	MA		MC
Tulane Univ	LA	63,396	HC+
Univ of Calif at Berkeley	CA	28,853	MC
Univ of Calif at Los Angeles	CA	30,162	MC
Univ of Calif San Diego	CA	30,150	MC
Univ of Denver	CO	58,443	VC+
Univ of Evansville	IN	44,186	VC+
Univ of Georgia	GA	21,250	HC
Univ of Mich/Ann Arbor	MI	24,410	MC
Univ of Mount Union	OH	38,970	C
Univ of Pennsylvania	PA	63,526	MC
Univ of Richmond	VA	60,880	MC
Univ of Rochester	NY	65,032	MC
Univ of Texas at Dallas	TX	22,830	VC+
Univ of Wisc-Stout	WI	19,667	C
Vanderbilt Univ	TN	60,572	MC
Vassar College	NY	65,491	MC
Villanova Univ	PA	62,523	MC
Wellesley College	MA	63,916	MC
Wright State Univ	OH	16,983	C
Yale Univ	CT	64,650	MC

COLLABORATIVE DESIGN

School	ST	$IS	SR
Ferris State Univ	MI	21,445	C

COLLABORATIVE EDUCATION

School	ST	$IS	SR
Birmingham-Southern College	AL	44,478	VC
Goddard College	VT	17,040	VC
Huntingdon College	AL	34,900	C
Rowan Univ	NJ	24,491	VC+
Troy Univ	AL	16,171	C

COLLABORATIVE PIANO

School	ST	$IS	SR
Shenandoah Univ	VA	41,312	C

COMBINED SCIENCE

School	ST	$IS	SR
Calif Baptist Univ	CA	41,392	C
Indiana Univ Kokomo	IN	7,073	C
Texas Christian Univ	TX	54,670	HC
Univ of Montana	MT	14,105	C

COMMERCIAL ART

School	ST	$IS	SR
Ashland Univ	OH	21,440	C
Brenau Univ - Women's College	GA	37,876	LC
Calif Univ of Pennsylvania	PA	14,217	LC
Cazenovia College	NY	46,470	C
Fort Valley State Univ	GA	17,988	VC
Graceland Univ	IA	35,290	C
LIU Brooklyn	NY	49,682	C
LIU Post	NY	49,682	C
Millikin Univ	IL	42,158	C
Oral Roberts Univ	OK	34,316	C
Southwest Baptist Univ	MO	29,900	LC
St. Norbert College	WI	44,525	VC
St. Thomas Aquinas College	NY	42,200	C
Univ of Central Missouri	MO	18,982	C
Univ of Indianapolis	IN	36,480	C
Univ of North Texas	TX	19,198	C
Univ of S Car Upstate	SC	18,200	LC
Washington Univ in St. Louis	MO	65,366	VC

COMMUNICATION ARTS - SPEECH

School	ST	$IS	SR
Black Hills State Univ	SD	15,899	C
Bryant Univ	RI	55,646	VC
CUNY/Queens College	NY	27,896	C
College of the Ozarks	MO	7,230	C
East Central Univ	OK	13,056	C
Indiana Univ Kokomo	IN	7,073	C
LIU Brooklyn	NY	49,682	C
Millersville Univ of Pennsylvania	PA	23,782	C
San Diego State Univ	CA	21,896	C+
St. Joseph's College, New York/Brooklyn Campus	NY	25,114	LC
St. Joseph's College, New York/Long Island Campus	NY	25,124	C
SUNY / SUNY Potsdam	NY	20,404	C+
Washington State Univ	WA	22,495	C

COMMUNICATION DESIGN

School	ST	$IS	SR
Bryant Univ	RI	55,646	VC
Cal State, Chico	CA	21,440	C
CUNY/College of Technology	NY	6,669	NC
Dallas Baptist Univ	TX	33,713	C
Elon Univ	NC	44,599	VC+
Rochester Inst of Technology	NY	50,842	HC
Syracuse Univ	NY	60,239	VC
Texas State Univ	TX	19,350	C

COMMUNICATION RHETORIC/ COMMUNICATION

School	ST	$IS	SR
Bryant Univ	RI	55,646	VC
Cedarville Univ	OH	34,990	VC
Huntingdon College	AL	34,900	C
Lewis Univ	IL	40,370	C
Marshall Univ	WV	17,242	C
Mercer Univ	GA	45,348	VC
Nazareth College	NY	45,574	C
Nyack College	NY	34,050	NC
Spalding Univ	KY	31,938	SP
Syracuse Univ	NY	60,239	VC
Univ of Nebr - Lincoln	NE	18,589	VC
Univ of Pittsburgh	PA	29,568	HC+
Univ of Richmond	VA	60,880	MC
Washington & Jefferson College	PA	56,512	VC
Waynesburg Univ	PA	32,290	C
Whitman College	WA	59,772	MC
Wingate Univ	NC	39,950	C
Xavier Univ	OH	47,880	C+

COMMUNICATION SCIENCE

School	ST	$IS	SR
Bryant Univ	RI	55,646	VC
Elmhurst College	IL	45,428	C
Howard Univ	DC	37,616	C+
Idaho State Univ	ID	13,619	NC
LIU Brooklyn	NY	49,682	C
Missouri State Univ	MO	15,190	C+
Pennsylvania State Univ - Univ Park	PA	29,760	HC
Samford Univ	AL	39,232	VC
Univ of Cincinnati	OH	21,964	VC
Univ of Georgia	GA	21,250	HC
Univ of Miss	MS	17,746	C+
Univ of Oregon	OR	22,972	C
Univ of Pittsburgh	PA	29,568	HC+
Univ of Wisc-Madison	WI	20,934	MC
Wayne State Univ	MI	22,016	C

COMMUNICATION SCIENCES & DISORDERS

School	ST	$IS	SR
Abilene Christian Univ	TX	41,800	C+
Arkansas State Univ	AR	16,190	C
Armstrong State Univ	GA	16,962	C
Augustana College	IL	49,658	VC
Baldwin Wallace Univ	OH	41,106	C
Calif Baptist Univ	CA	41,392	C
Cal State, Chico	CA	21,440	C
Eastern Illinois Univ	IL	21,126	C
Elmhurst College	IL	45,428	C
Fontbonne Univ	MO	33,717	C
Jackson State Univ	MS	15,879	LC
Marywood Univ	PA	46,900	C
Mercy College	NY	31,776	C
Minn State Univ, Mankato	MN	15,616	C
Mount Vernon Nazarene Univ	OH	34,500	C
Nazareth College	NY	45,574	C
Ohio Univ	OH	22,924	C
Pace Univ	NY	58,248	C
St. Louis Univ	MO	49,866	HC
St. Mary's College	IN	50,600	C
Southeastern Louisiana Univ	LA	16,237	C
Southern Illinois Univ Carbondale	IL	23,667	C
SUNY / SUNY Plattsburgh	NY	18,814	C
Syracuse Univ	NY	60,239	VC
Texas State Univ	TX	19,350	C
The College of St. Rose	NY	43,048	C
Univ of Central Arkansas	AR	14,472	VC
Univ of Montana	MT	14,105	C
Univ of Tulsa	OK	52,625	HC+
Univ of Vermont	VT	28,878	HC
Univ of Wisc-Eau Claire	WI	15,797	VC
Univ of Wisc-Milwaukee	WI	21,496	C
Wayne State Univ	MI	22,016	C
West Chester Univ of Pennsylvania	PA	18,456	C
Western Illinois Univ	IL	20,825	C
Western Kentucky Univ	KY	16,850	C

COMMUNICATION STUDIES

School	ST	$IS	SR
Albion College	MI	52,650	C
American Univ	DC	59,379	HC+
Arizona State Univ at the West Campus	AZ	20,640	C
Ashford Univ	CA	10,480	C
Augustana College	IL	49,658	VC
Averett Univ	VA	40,970	LC
Baldwin Wallace Univ	OH	41,106	C
Black Hills State Univ	SD	15,899	C
Bloomsburg Univ of Pennsylvania	PA	19,066	LC
Bryant Univ	RI	55,646	VC
Calif Baptist Univ	CA	41,392	C
Calif Polytechnic State Univ	CA	17,979	HC+
Cal State, Northridge	CA	16,859	LC
Chapman Univ	CA	63,078	VC+
Creighton Univ	NE	48,206	VC+
East Stroudsburg Univ	PA	18,334	C
Eastern Illinois Univ	IL	21,126	C
Edgewood College	WI	35,950	C
Fordham Univ	NY	65,918	MC
Grove City College	PA	25,692	VC
Illinois State Univ	IL	23,418	VC
Indiana Univ Bloomington	IN	20,429	VC
Indiana Univ East	IN	7,072	C
Indiana Univ South Bend	IN	14,242	C
Indiana Univ-Purdue Univ Indianapolis	IN	18,635	C
Kent State Univ	OH	20,732	C
Lewis Univ	IL	40,370	C
Loras College	IA	39,222	C
Loyola Marymount Univ	CA	58,038	HC
Madonna Univ	MI	29,050	C
Millersville Univ of Pennsylvania	PA	23,782	C
Minn State Univ, Mankato	MN	15,616	C
Mount Vernon Nazarene Univ	OH	34,500	C
Niagara Univ	NY	41,010	C
Nova Southeastern Univ	FL	38,534	C+
Okla Baptist Univ	OK	32,320	C
Pace Univ	NY	58,248	C
San Jose State Univ	CA	21,540	C
Southeast Missouri State Univ	MO	15,498	C
St. Joseph's College, New York/Brooklyn Campus	NY	25,114	LC
SUNY / SUNY Fredonia	NY	20,818	C
Texas State Univ	TX	19,350	C
Texas Tech Univ	TX	18,736	C+
The Master's Univ	CA	43,870	C+
Tiffin Univ	OH	31,380	C
Trevecca Nazarene Univ	TN	31,186	C
Univ of Denver	CO	58,443	VC+
Univ of Georgia	GA	21,250	HC
Univ of Kansas	KS	20,135	C+
Univ of Miami	FL	63,494	MC
Univ of N Car at Pembroke	NC	14,388	LC
Univ of North Georgia	GA	17,316	C
Univ of Rhode Island	RI	24,906	C
Univ of San Francisco	CA	58,484	VC
Univ of S Dak	SD	16,109	C
West Chester Univ of Pennsylvania	PA	18,456	C
West Virginia Wesleyan College	WV	36,858	C
Western Kentucky Univ	KY	16,850	C
Western Mich Univ	MI	21,054	C
Wingate Univ	NC	39,950	C
Winona State Univ	MN	17,535	C

COMMUNICATIONS

School	ST	$IS	SR
Abilene Christian Univ	TX	41,800	C+
Adams State Univ	CO	17,703	LC
Adelphi Univ	NY	48,244	C
Adrian College	MI	42,400	C
Alabama State Univ	AL	14,142	NC
Albertus Magnus College	CT	43,258	LC
Albright College	PA	46,660	C

School	ST	$IS	SR
Alcorn State Univ	MS	15,854	C
Alderson Broaddus Univ	WV	26,149	C
Alfred Univ	NY	42,296	C+
Allegheny College	PA	55,420	VC
Alma College	MI	47,548	C
Alvernia Univ	PA	43,900	C
Alverno College	WI	33,294	LC
American International College	MA	46,300	LC
American Univ	DC	59,379	HC+
Anderson Univ	IN	38,200	C
Andrews Univ	MI	28,030	C+
Angelo State Univ	TX	15,263	NC
Appalachian State Univ	NC	14,416	VC
Aquinas College - Mich	MI	38,876	HC
Arcadia Univ	PA	33,570	C+
Arizona State Univ at the Downtown Phoenix Campus	AZ	23,680	VC
Arizona State Univ at the Polytechnic Campus	AZ	21,360	VC
Arizona State Univ at the Tempe Campus	AZ	21,756	VC
Arizona State Univ at the West Campus	AZ	20,640	C
Arkansas State Univ	AR	16,190	C
Arkansas Tech Univ	AR	15,484	C
Asbury Univ	KY	35,180	C+
Ashland Univ	OH	21,440	C
Auburn Univ	AL	23,594	VC+
Auburn Univ at Montgomery	AL	15,290	C
Augsburg College	MN	43,929	C
Augusta Univ	GA	4,632	C
Augustana Univ	SD	38,424	VC
Aurora Univ	IL	33,970	C
Austin College	TX	45,875	VC
Austin Peay State Univ	TN	16,397	C
Avila Univ	MO	35,480	C
Azusa Pacific Univ	CA	43,972	C
Baker Univ	KS	33,350	C+
Barry Univ	FL	37,830	C
Barton College	NC	38,686	LC
Bay Path Univ	MA	45,349	C
Baylor Univ	TX	53,760	HC
Becker College	MA	57,628	C
Belhaven Univ	MS	31,016	C
Bellarmine Univ	KY	51,220	C
Bellevue Univ	NE	20,300	NC
Belmont Univ	TN	40,970	VC
Bemidji State Univ	MN	16,056	VC
Benedictine Univ	IL	38,300	C
Bennett College	NC	27,302	NC
Berea College	KY	7,042	C
Berry College	GA	45,286	C+
Bethany College	KS	46,100	NC
Bethany College	WV	36,300	NC
Bethel College	IN	35,860	C
Bethel College	KS	35,370	C
Bethel Univ	MN	45,270	VC
Bethune-Cookman Univ	FL	22,970	C
Biola Univ	CA	46,402	C+
Black Hills State Univ	SD	15,899	C
Blackburn College	IL	28,526	LC
Bloomfield College	NJ	39,100	LC
Bloomsburg Univ of Pennsylvania	PA	19,066	LC
Bluefield College	VA	34,120	C+
Bluffton Univ	OH	40,950	C
Boise State Univ	ID	14,860	C
Boston College	MA	65,737	MC
Boston Univ	MA	65,110	MC
Bowling Green State Univ	OH	19,747	C
Brenau Univ - Women's College	GA	37,876	LC
Brewton-Parker College	GA	23,490	C
Briar Cliff Univ	IA	36,956	C
Bridgewater College	VA	44,510	C
Brigham Young Univ	UT	12,748	HC
Bryan College	TN	31,440	C
Bryant Univ	RI	55,646	VC
Buena Vista Univ	IA	41,514	C
Butler Univ	IN	51,352	VC
Cabrini Univ	PA	42,591	LC
Caldwell Univ	NJ	42,165	NC
Calif Baptist Univ	CA	41,392	C
Calif Lutheran Univ	CA	52,853	C
Calif State Polytechnic Univ, Pomona	CA	21,541	C
Cal State, Bakersfield	CA	19,191	LC
Cal State, Chico	CA	21,440	C
Cal State, Dominguez Hills	CA	19,022	LC
Cal State, East Bay	CA	19,413	C
Cal State, Fresno	CA	16,902	LC
Cal State, Fullerton	CA	21,902	C
Cal State, Long Beach	CA	18,850	C
Cal State, Sacramento	CA	20,332	C
Cal State, San Bernardino	CA	12,000	C
Cal State, San Marcos	CA	24,184	LC
Cal State, Stanislaus	CA	16,212	C
Calvin College	MI	41,570	VC+
Cameron Univ	OK	11,072	NC
Campbellsville Univ	KY	32,492	C
Canisius College	NY	47,537	C
Capital Univ	OH	42,982	C
Cardinal Stritch Univ	WI	36,462	C
Carlow Univ	PA	38,549	LC
Carnegie Mellon Univ	PA	67,980	MC
Carroll College	MT	39,972	C+
Carroll Univ	WI	38,100	C+
Carson-Newman Univ	TN	34,160	C
Castleton Univ	VT	20,186	C
Catawba College	NC	39,820	C
Cazenovia College	NY	46,470	C
Cedar Crest College	PA	46,715	C
Centenary College	NJ	43,602	C
Centenary College of Louisiana	LA	45,650	C+
Central College	IA	44,592	C
Central Methodist Univ	MO	36,830	VC
Central Mich Univ	MI	20,330	C
Central Washington Univ	WA	16,803	C
Chaminade Univ of Honolulu	HI	36,000	C
Champlain College	VT	53,132	C+
Chatham Univ	PA	46,517	C
Chestnut Hill College	PA	43,410	C
Cheyney Univ of Pennsylvania	PA	20,896	LC
Christopher Newport Univ	VA	23,968	VC+
CUNY/Baruch College	NY	21,609	HC
CUNY/Brooklyn College	NY	5,884	C+
CUNY/City College	NY	20,319	VC
CUNY/College of Staten Island	NY	17,840	NC
CUNY/Lehman College	NY	5,778	HC+
Claflin Univ	SC	33,764	LC
Clarion Univ of Pennsylvania	PA	21,608	LC
Clark Atlanta Univ	GA	31,019	LC
Clark Univ	MA	51,600	HC+
Clarke Univ	IA	38,940	C
Clarkson Univ	NY	60,392	HC
Clemson Univ	SC		HC
Cleveland State Univ	OH	22,196	C
Coastal Carolina Univ	SC	19,766	C
Coe College	IA	51,570	VC
Coker College	SC	34,810	LC
Colby-Sawyer College	NH	50,790	C
College of Charleston	SC	22,699	C
College of Mount St. Vincent	NY	45,620	C
College of St. Benedict	MN	52,806	C
College of St. Elizabeth	NJ	44,432	LC
College of St. Scholastica	MN	44,640	C
College of the Ozarks	MO	7,230	C
Colo Christian Univ	CO	39,940	VC
Colo Mesa Univ	CO	18,955	LC
Colo State Univ	CO	22,162	VC
Colo State Univ-Pueblo	CO	18,234	C
Columbia College	SC	36,550	C
Columbia College - Missouri	MO	27,803	C
Columbus State Univ	GA	14,336	LC
Concord Univ	WV	14,954	C
Concordia College - Moorhead	MN	51,088	C+
Concordia Univ	CA	41,580	VC
Concordia Univ Nebr	NE	36,280	VC
Concordia Univ St. Paul	MN	29,050	C
Concordia Univ Texas	TX	40,210	C
Concordia Univ Wisc	WI	35,910	C
Concordia Univ, Ann Arbor	MI	35,945	VC
Concordia Univ, Chicago	IL	39,694	C
Corban Univ	OR	40,306	C
Cornell Univ	NY	64,853	MC
Culver-Stockton College	MO	33,525	C
Curry College	MA	51,815	C
Dakota Wesleyan Univ	SD	32,850	C
Dallas Baptist Univ	TX	33,713	C
Defiance College	OH	41,630	C
Denison Univ	OH	58,860	MC
DePaul Univ	IL	47,623	VC
DePauw Univ	IN	58,688	HC+
DeSales Univ	PA	43,970	C
Dickinson State Univ	ND	12,372	LC
Dillard Univ	LA	20,940	VC
Dominican Univ	IL	41,222	C
Dominican Univ of Calif	CA	57,050	C
Dordt College	IA	37,860	C+
Drake Univ	IA	45,056	HC
Drexel Univ	PA	65,432	VC+
Drury Univ	MO	33,791	VC
Duquesne Univ	PA	46,822	VC
East Carolina Univ	NC	16,937	C
East Central Univ	OK	13,056	C
East Tenn State Univ	TN	13,994	C
East Texas Baptist Univ	TX	33,134	C
Eastern Conn State Univ	CT	23,059	C
Eastern Mennonite Univ	VA	42,550	C
Eastern Mich Univ	MI	19,761	C
Eastern Nazarene College	MA	39,955	C
Eastern New Mexico Univ	NM	14,416	C
Eastern Univ	PA	39,540	C
Eastern Washington Univ	WA	25,572	LC
Eckerd College	FL	52,874	C
Edinboro Univ	PA	15,940	LC
Edward Waters College	FL	20,607	NC
Elizabethtown College	PA	54,050	C
Elizabethtown College School of Continuing and Professional Studies	PA	18,900	C
Elmhurst College	IL	45,428	C
Elon Univ	NC	44,599	VC+
Embry-Riddle Aeronautical Univ - Daytona Beach	FL	44,712	VC
Embry-Riddle Aeronautical Univ - Worldwide	FL	17,480	C
Emerson College	MA	54,736	HC
Emmanuel College	MA	52,110	C+
Emory and Henry College	VA	41,410	C
Emporia State Univ	KS	14,570	C
Endicott College	MA	44,604	VC+
Eureka College	IL	30,220	C
Evangel Univ	MO	28,898	C
Excelsior College	NY	14,080	SP
Fairfield Univ	CT	59,860	VC+
Fairleigh Dickinson Univ/College at Florham	NJ	52,062	C
Fairleigh Dickinson Univ/Metropolitan Campus	NJ	40,254	C
Fairmont State Univ	WV	15,726	C
Felician Univ	NJ	45,370	LC
Ferris State Univ	MI	21,445	C
Fitchburg State Univ	MA	21,819	C
Five Towns College	NY	35,350	C
Flagler College	FL	27,620	C
Florida Atlantic Univ	FL	17,339	C
Florida Gulf Coast Univ	FL	9,682	C
Florida Inst of Technology	FL	53,306	VC
Florida State Univ	FL	16,771	HC
Fontbonne Univ	MO	33,717	C
Fort Hays State Univ	KS	12,131	C
Fort Valley State Univ	GA	17,988	VC
Framingham State Univ	MA	20,584	C
Francis Marion Univ	SC	16,464	LC
Franciscan Univ of Steubenville	OH	33,980	VC
Franklin Pierce Univ	NH	46,750	C
Freed-Hardeman Univ	TN	29,450	C
Friends Univ	KS	34,455	C
Frostburg State Univ	MD	17,280	LC
Furman Univ	SC	58,092	VC+
Gallaudet Univ	DC	29,118	LC
Gannon Univ	PA	42,032	C
Gardner-Webb Univ	NC	39,200	C+
Geneva College	PA	35,450	C
George Fox Univ	OR	42,938	C
George Mason Univ	VA	15,724	VC
George Washington Univ	DC	62,835	MC
Georgetown College	KY	41,440	C
Georgia Southern Univ	GA	16,596	C
Gonzaga Univ	WA	50,888	HC
Gordon College	MA	46,472	C+
Goshen College	IN	42,500	C
Goucher College	MD	55,716	VC
Grace College and Seminary	IN	31,524	C
Graceland Univ	IA	35,290	C
Grambling State Univ	LA	15,701	C
Grand Canyon Univ	AZ	16,950	VC
Grand Rapids Theological Seminary/Cornerstone Univ	MI	33,338	C
Grand Valley State Univ	MI	22,250	C+
Grand View Univ	IA	32,302	C
Green Mountain College	VT	45,228	LC
Greenville College	IL	27,012	C
Gustavus Adolphus College	MN	52,433	HC
Gwynedd Mercy Univ	PA	43,780	LC
Hamline Univ	MN	45,678	VC
Hampshire College	MA	63,824	MC
Hampton Univ	VA	34,926	LC
Hannibal-LaGrange Univ	MO	29,815	C
Hanover College	IN	46,364	C+
Harding Univ	AR	25,421	C
Hardin-Simmons Univ	TX	33,966	C
Hastings College	NE	35,380	C+
Hawaii Pacific Univ	HI	33,420	C
Heidelberg Univ	OH	39,200	C
Henderson State Univ	AR	15,516	LC
High Point Univ	NC	45,977	C
Hiram College	OH	43,230	C
Hollins Univ	VA	49,635	VC
Holy Family Univ	PA	43,326	LC
Holy Names Univ	CA	46,630	LC
Hood College	MD	54,840	C
Hope College	MI	39,940	VC
Houghton College	NY	39,090	C
Houston Baptist Univ	TX	36,450	C
Howard Payne Univ	TX	34,320	C
Howard Univ	DC	37,616	C+
Humboldt State Univ	CA	20,514	C
Huntington Univ	IN	33,996	C
Idaho State Univ	ID	13,619	NC
Illinois College	IL	40,850	VC
Indiana Inst of Technology	IN	34,240	LC
Indiana State Univ	IN	23,223	LC
Indiana Univ Kokomo	IN	7,073	C
Indiana Univ Northwest	IN	7,072	C
Indiana Univ Southeast	IN	14,242	LC
Indiana Univ-Purdue Univ Fort Wayne	IN	17,553	C
Indiana Wesleyan Univ	IN	33,674	C
Iona College	NY	50,984	C
Iowa State Univ	IA	17,570	C
Ithaca College	NY	56,766	VC
Jackson State Univ	MS	15,879	LC
Jacksonville State Univ	AL	14,628	LC
Jacksonville Univ	FL	46,230	C
James Madison Univ	VA	19,084	VC
John Brown Univ	AR	33,132	VC
John Carroll Univ	OH	49,740	C+
Johnson & Wales Univ/Denver Campus	CO	42,707	C
Johnson C. Smith Univ	NC	25,336	LC
Judson Univ	IL	37,700	C
Juniata College	PA	53,760	VC
Kansas State Univ	KS	17,780	VC
Kansas Wesleyan Univ	KS	36,600	C
Kean Univ	NJ	24,650	C
Keene State College	NH	24,003	LC
Kennesaw State Univ	GA	19,592	VC
Kentucky Wesleyan College	KY	32,080	C
Keuka College	NY	39,762	C
Keystone College	PA	28,680	LC
King Univ	TN	34,660	C
King's College	PA	46,858	C
La Roche College	PA	37,924	LC
La Salle Univ	PA	55,790	C
La Sierra Univ	CA	39,690	VC
Lake Erie College	OH	38,914	LC
Lake Forest College	IL	50,652	VC
Lamar Univ	TX	18,014	LC
Lander Univ	SC	43,994	C
Lane College	TN	16,550	C
Lasell College	MA	47,500	C
Lawrence Tech Univ	MI	39,770	VC
Le Moyne College	NY	46,000	C
Lee Univ	TN	22,045	C
Lees-McRae College	NC	33,944	C
Lenoir-Rhyne Univ	NC	43,200	C
Lewis & Clark College	OR	58,434	HC+
Lewis Univ	IL	40,370	C
Lewis-Clark State College	ID	14,202	C
Liberty Univ	VA	19,101	C
Limestone College	SC	32,100	C
Lincoln Memorial Univ	TN	28,070	C
Lindenwood Univ	MO	25,132	C
Lindsey Wilson College	KY	32,882	C
Linfield College	OR	52,010	C
Lipscomb Univ	TN	41,296	VC
Lock Haven Univ of Pennsylvania	PA	18,028	LC
Longwood Univ	VA	22,184	C
Louisiana College	LA	21,886	C
Louisiana State Univ and A&M College	LA	18,677	VC
Louisiana State Univ in Shreveport	LA	6,902	C
Loyola Univ Chicago	IL	55,802	VC
Loyola Univ Maryland	MD	60,300	VC
Loyola Univ New Orleans	LA	51,708	VC+
Lubbock Christian Univ	TX	28,426	C
Luther College	IA	48,540	C+
Lycoming College	PA	48,580	C
Lynchburg College	VA	46,740	C
Lyndon State College	VT	20,714	C
Malone Univ	OH	38,448	C
Manchester Univ	IN	40,422	C
Manhattan College	NY	51,750	C+
Manhattanville College	NY	51,440	C+
Mansfield Univ	PA	23,376	LC
Marian Univ	IN	41,220	C
Marian Univ	WI	32,420	LC
Marietta College	OH	46,190	C
Marist College	NY	49,860	VC
Marquette Univ	WI	48,390	VC+
Mars Hill Univ	NC	42,688	C
Marshall Univ	WV	17,242	C
Martin Univ	IN	20,264	LC
Marylhurst Univ	OR	20,295	NC
Marymount Manhattan College	NY	46,280	VC
Marymount Univ	VA	41,570	LC
Maryville Univ of St. Louis	MO	38,046	VC+
Marywood Univ	PA	46,900	C
Mass College of Liberal Arts	MA	20,128	C
Mayville State Univ	ND	18,371	NC
McDaniel College	MD	51,380	VC
McNeese State Univ	LA	7,838	C
McPherson College	KS	34,909	C
Medaille College	NY	35,112	C
Mercer Univ	GA	45,348	VC
Mercy College	NY	31,776	C
Mercyhurst Univ	PA	47,420	C
Meredith College	NC	45,297	C
Merrimack College	MA	52,770	C
Messiah College	PA	43,100	C+
Methodist Univ	NC	43,600	C
Metropolitan State Univ	MN	7,566	C
Metropolitan State Univ of Denver	CO	29,889	LC
Miami Univ	OH	27,190	HC+
Mich State Univ	MI	23,898	VC+
Mich Tech Univ	MI	24,739	VC+
MidAmerica Nazarene Univ	KS	35,550	C
Middle Tenn State Univ	TN	8,650	C
Midland Univ	NE	37,468	
Midwestern State Univ	TX	17,572	C
Miles College	AL	18,646	NC
Milligan College	TN	38,150	C
Millikin Univ	IL	42,158	C
Millsaps College	MS	50,080	C+
Minn State Univ, Mankato	MN	15,616	C
Minn State Univ, Moorhead	MN	15,941	C
Minot State Univ	ND	12,732	C
Misericordia Univ	PA	43,840	C
Miss College	MS	25,850	C
Miss State Univ	MS	11,454	C+
Miss Univ for Women	MS	17,065	C
Miss Valley State Univ	MS	13,233	LC
Missouri Baptist Univ	MO	35,594	C
Missouri Southern State Univ	MO	12,499	C
Missouri State Univ	MO	15,190	C+
Missouri Valley College	MO	28,150	C
Missouri Western State Univ	MO	16,741	
Mitchell College	CT	43,280	C
Molloy College	NY	40,440	C
Monmouth College	IL	42,260	C
Monmouth Univ	NJ	46,234	C
Montana State Univ-Billings	MT	22,960	C

ST = STATE **$IS** = IN-STATE COSTS **SR** = SELECTOR RATING

School	ST	$IS	SR
Montana State Univ-Northern	MT	11,370	NC
Montana Tech of the Univ of Montana	MT	15,447	C+
Montclair State Univ	NJ	26,210	LC
Montreat College	NC	31,298	LC
Morehead State Univ	KY	17,422	C
Morningside College	IA	36,865	C
Morris College	SC	18,500	LC
Mount Ida College	MA	46,820	C
Mount Mary Univ	WI	34,650	LC
Mount Mercy Univ	IA	36,826	C
Mount St. Joseph Univ	OH	33,880	C
Mount St. Mary's Univ	MD	51,610	C
Mount Vernon Nazarene Univ	OH	34,500	C
Muhlenberg College	PA	56,645	VC+
Muskingum Univ	OH	35,966	C
Nebr Wesleyan Univ	NE	38,140	C+
New England College	NH	50,364	C
New Jersey Inst of Technology	NJ	29,569	VC
New Mexico Highlands Univ	NM	11,904	NC
New Mexico State Univ	NM	14,050	C
New York Inst of Technology	NY	48,730	C
New York Univ	NY	65,860	MC
Newberry College	SC	34,550	C
Newbury College	MA	46,950	C
Newman Univ	KS	35,390	C
Niagara Univ	NY	41,010	C
Nicholls State Univ	LA	10,534	C
Norfolk State Univ	VA	25,702	LC
N Car A&T State Univ	NC	13,365	LC
N Car State Univ	NC	19,515	HC+
North Central College	IL	48,712	VC
North Central Univ	MN	26,400	C
N Dak State Univ	ND	16,245	C
North Park Univ	IL	35,860	C
Northeastern Illinois Univ	IL	12,529	LC
Northeastern State Univ	OK	8,615	VC
Northeastern Univ	MA	62,703	MC
Northern Arizona Univ	AZ	20,246	VC
Northern Illinois Univ	IL	20,176	C
Northern Kentucky Univ	KY	16,486	C
Northern Mich Univ	MI	19,604	C
Northwest Christian Univ	OR	36,580	C
Northwest Missouri State Univ	MO	17,737	C
Northwest Nazarene Univ	ID	36,000	C
Northwest Univ	WA	35,876	VC
Northwestern Okla State Univ	OK	13,072	NC
Northwestern Univ	IL	66,344	MC
Norwich Univ	VT	28,212	C
Notre Dame College	OH	37,150	VC
Notre Dame de Namur Univ	CA	46,526	LC
Notre Dame of Maryland Univ	MD	46,465	VC
Nyack College	NY	34,050	NC
Oakland Univ	MI	20,763	C
Oakwood Univ	AL	43,758	C
Oglethorpe Univ	GA	44,200	C+
Ohio Dominican Univ	OH	41,340	C+
Ohio Northern Univ	OH	44,050	VC
Ohio State Univ at Columbus	OH	21,703	HC+
Ohio Univ	OH	22,924	C
Ohio Wesleyan Univ	OH	49,460	VC
Okla Baptist Univ	OK	32,320	C
Okla Christian Univ	OK	27,650	VC
Okla City Univ	OK	40,476	VC
Okla Wesleyan Univ	OK	33,206	C
Old Dominion Univ	VA	20,910	C
Olivet College	MI	36,110	LC
Olivet Nazarene Univ	IL	41,840	C
Oral Roberts Univ	OK	34,316	C
Ottawa Univ	KS	36,074	VC
Otterbein Univ	OH	41,630	C
Ouachita Baptist Univ	AR	32,320	C
Our Lady of the Lake Univ	TX	35,012	LC
Pace Univ	NY	58,248	C
Pacific Lutheran Univ	WA	49,960	VC
Pacific Union College	CA	36,009	VC
Paine College	GA	19,506	LC
Palm Beach Atlantic Univ	FL	39,720	C
Park Univ	MO	20,329	C
Paul Quinn College	TX	25,350	LC
Penn State Erie/The Behrend College	PA	16,256	C
Penn State Univ/Altoona	PA	24,584	C
Pepperdine Univ	CA	74,460	HC+
Pfeiffer Univ	NC	39,695	LC
Piedmont College	GA	32,512	C
Pine Manor College	MA	41,660	LC
Pittsburg State Univ	KS	13,880	NC
Plymouth State Univ	NH	23,180	LC
Point Loma Nazarene Univ	CA	43,450	C
Point Park Univ	PA	41,270	C
Pontifical Catholic Univ of PR	PR	10,534	
Prairie View A&M Univ	TX	15,205	LC
Pratt Inst	NY	58,082	VC
Prescott College	AZ	33,284	C
Presentation College	SD	25,454	NC
Principia College	IL	39,010	C+
Purdue Univ/Northwest	IN	15,038	C
Purdue Univ/West Lafayette	IN	20,032	MC
Queens Univ of Charlotte	NC	39,543	C
Quincy Univ	IL	36,998	C
Quinnipiac Univ	CT	59,110	C
Radford Univ	VA	19,027	LC
Ramapo College of New Jersey	NJ	25,338	C
Randolph College	VA	45,660	VC
Randolph-Macon College	VA	49,910	C
Regis College	MA	51,920	C
Regis Univ	CO	44,520	C
Reinhardt Univ	GA	29,492	C
Rensselaer Polytechnic Inst	NY	63,436	MC
Rhode Island College	RI	17,694	LC
Rider Univ	NJ	54,050	C
Ripon College	WI	46,911	C+
Rivier Univ	NH	40,410	VC
Roanoke College	VA	54,114	VC
Robert Morris Univ	PA	37,834	C
Roberts Wesleyan College	NY	38,306	C
Rochester College	MI	28,574	LC
Rochester Inst of Technology	NY	50,842	HC
Rockhurst Univ	MO	29,220	C
Rocky Mountain College	MT	34,270	C
Roger Williams Univ	RI	46,296	C+
Rollins College	FL	58,670	HC
Roosevelt Univ	IL	40,651	VC
Rosemont College	PA	30,980	C
Rowan Univ	NJ	24,491	VC+
Rust College	MS	10,600	C
Rutgers Univ - New Brunswick	NJ	26,632	HC
Sacred Heart Univ	CT	52,750	C
Saginaw Valley State Univ	MI	18,530	C
St. Augustine's Univ	NC	26,048	C
St. Francis Univ	PA	42,268	NC
St. John's Univ	MN	51,624	C
St. Joseph's College of Maine	ME	46,485	C
St. Joseph's Univ	PA	57,544	VC+
St. Louis Univ	MO	49,866	HC
St. Martin's Univ	WA	45,056	C
St. Mary's College	IN	50,600	C
St. Mary's College of Calif	CA	57,420	C
St. Peter's Univ	NJ	49,192	C
St. Vincent College	PA	44,626	C
St. Xavier Univ	IL	43,310	C
Salem College	NC	37,694	HC
Salem International Univ	WV	21,090	LC
Salem State Univ	MA	17,303	LC
Salisbury Univ	MD	20,714	VC
Salve Regina Univ	RI	51,470	C
Samford Univ	AL	39,232	VC
San Diego Christian College	CA	39,068	C
San Diego State Univ	CA	21,896	C+
San Francisco State Univ	CA	18,514	LC
Savannah College of Art and Design	GA	49,595	C
Savannah State Univ	GA	15,631	C
Scripps College	CA	66,664	MC
Seattle Pacific Univ	WA	47,439	C+
Seattle Univ	WA	50,811	VC+
Seton Hall Univ	NJ	55,514	C
Seton Hill Univ	PA	46,972	C
Shepherd Univ, West Virginia	WV	17,224	C
Shippensburg Univ of Pennsylvania	PA	23,208	C
Shorter Univ	GA	31,130	LC
Siena Heights Univ	MI	32,040	C
Simmons College	MA	53,090	VC
Simpson College	IA	43,839	VC
Simpson Univ	CA	33,700	C
Slippery Rock Univ of Pennsylvania	PA	10,360	C
Sonoma State Univ	CA	27,806	C
S Dak State Univ	SD	15,634	C
Southeastern Louisiana Univ	LA	16,237	C
Southeastern Okla State Univ	OK	11,875	C
Southeastern Univ	FL	31,765	C
Southern Adventist Univ	TN	27,600	C
Southern Arkansas Univ	AR	21,532	C
Southern Conn State Univ	CT	21,924	LC
Southern Illinois Univ Edwardsville	IL	22,643	C
Southern Methodist Univ	TX	66,483	MC
Southern Nazarene Univ	OK	32,798	NC
Southern New Hampshire Univ	NH	43,198	C
Southern Oregon Univ	OR	19,117	C
Southern Univ and A&M College	LA	16,074	LC+
Southern Vermont College	VT	34,670	LC
Southern Wesleyan Univ	SC	32,130	LC
Southwest Baptist Univ	MO	29,900	LC
Southwest Minn State Univ	MN	17,783	C
Southwestern Adventist Univ	TX	27,756	LC
Southwestern College	KS	31,531	C
Southwestern Okla State Univ	OK	11,790	C
Southwestern Univ	TX	50,720	VC
Spring Arbor Univ	MI	36,000	C
Spring Hill College	AL	48,488	C
St. Bonaventure Univ	NY	44,237	C
St. Catherine Univ	MN	45,630	VC
St. Cloud State Univ	MN	10,600	C
St. Edward's Univ	TX	53,100	VC
St. Francis College	NY	38,800	LC
St. John Fisher College	NY	43,620	C
St. John's Univ	NY	55,850	C
St. Lawrence Univ	NY	64,390	VC
St. Mary's Univ	TX	37,500	C
St. Norbert College	WI	44,525	VC
St. Thomas Aquinas College	NY	42,200	C
St. Thomas Univ	FL	36,360	LC
Stanford Univ	CA	60,409	MC
SUNY / Buffalo State College	NY	20,842	C
SUNY / SUNY College at Old Westbury	NY	16,860	C
SUNY / SUNY Cortland	NY	20,706	VC
SUNY / SUNY Fredonia	NY	20,818	C
SUNY / SUNY Oneonta	NY	19,712	C+
SUNY / SUNY Plattsburgh	NY	18,814	C
SUNY / SUNY Potsdam	NY	20,404	C+
SUNY / Univ at Buffalo	NY	23,122	C+
SUNY /College of Agriculture and Tech at Cobleskill	NY	20,527	LC
SUNY at Geneseo	NY	20,440	VC+
SUNY at New Paltz	NY	19,200	C
SUNY at Oswego	NY	21,351	C
SUNY SUNY Albany	NY	22,165	C
Stephen F. Austin State Univ	TX	18,406	LC
Sterling College	KS	32,830	C
Stetson Univ	FL	53,544	VC
Stockton Univ	NJ	25,059	
Stonehill College	MA	55,030	C+
Suffolk Univ	MA	50,308	C
Sul Ross State Univ	TX	15,021	LC
Susquehanna Univ	PA	55,340	VC
Tabor College	KS	35,870	C
Tarleton State Univ	TX	15,248	LC
Taylor Univ	IN	40,317	C+
Temple Univ	PA	24,392	VC
Texas A&M Univ	TX	20,521	VC+
Texas A&M Univ at Corpus Christi	TX	16,851	LC
Texas A&M Univ at Kingsville	TX	7,500	LC
Texas Christian Univ	TX	54,670	HC
Texas Lutheran Univ	TX	38,620	C
Texas Southern Univ	TX	18,212	LC
Texas State Univ	TX	19,350	C
Texas Woman's Univ	TX	15,302	LC
The Catholic Univ of America	DC	56,356	VC
The College at Brockport - SUNY	NY	20,346	C
The College of New Jersey	NJ	31,909	HC
The College of New Rochelle	NY	46,300	VC
The College of St. Rose	NY	43,048	C
The College of Wooster	OH	57,900	VC+
The Master's Univ	CA	43,870	C+
The Univ of Tenn at Chattanooga	TN	16,744	C
The Univ of Tenn at Knoxville	TN	22,112	VC
The Univ of Tenn at Martin	TN	14,876	C
The Univ of Utah	UT	17,924	VC
The Univ of Virginia's College at Wise	VA	18,192	LC
Thiel College	PA	41,590	C
Thomas College	ME	35,268	LC
Thomas Edison State Univ	NJ	6,350	NC
Thomas More College	KY	36,720	C
Tiffin Univ	OH	31,380	C
Toccoa Falls College	GA	27,920	C
Tougaloo College	MS	17,980	NC
Towson Univ	MD	17,408	VC
Trine Univ	IN	41,310	C
Trinity Christian College	IL	35,580	C
Trinity International Univ	IL	31,070	VC
Trinity Univ	TX	52,314	HC+
Trinity Washington Univ	DC	33,826	C+
Troy Univ	AL	16,171	C
Truman State Univ	MO	16,014	HC
Tulane Univ	LA	63,396	HC+
Union College	KY	32,310	C
Union College	NE	23,270	C
Union Inst & Univ	OH	8,912	SP
Union Univ	TN	33,970	VC
Univ of Alabama	AL	24,320	C+
Univ of Alabama at Birmingham	AL	19,906	C
Univ of Alabama in Huntsville	AL	19,445	VC
Univ of Alaska Anchorage	AK	16,652	NC
Univ of Alaska Fairbanks	AK	16,179	C
Univ of Alaska Southeast	AK	11,493	C
Univ of Arizona	AZ	23,100	C
Univ of Arkansas at Fayetteville	AR	19,152	C+
Univ of Bridgeport	CT	44,430	LC
Univ of Calif at Berkeley	CA	28,853	MC
Univ of Calif at Davis	CA	28,468	HC
Univ of Calif at Los Angeles	CA	30,162	MC
Univ of Calif at Santa Barbara	CA	29,091	HC
Univ of Calif San Diego	CA	30,150	MC
Univ of Central Arkansas	AR	14,472	VC
Univ of Central Florida	FL	15,922	VC
Univ of Central Missouri	MO	18,982	C
Univ of Central Okla	OK	13,486	C
Univ of Charleston	WV	35,000	C
Univ of Cincinnati	OH	21,964	VC
Univ of Colo Boulder	CO	24,285	VC+
Univ of Colo Colo Springs	CO	19,663	C
Univ of Colo Denver	CO	23,230	C
Univ of Conn	CT	25,538	HC
Univ of Dayton	OH	53,620	C
Univ of Delaware	DE	24,976	VC+
Univ of Detroit Mercy	MI	48,816	C+
Univ of Evansville	IN	44,186	VC+
Univ of Findlay	OH	60,139	C
Univ of Hartford	CT	49,776	C
Univ of Hawaii at Hilo	HI	18,038	C
Univ of Hawaii at Manoa	HI	23,221	C
Univ of Houston	TX	21,483	VC
Univ of Houston-Downtown	TX	7,241	C
Univ of Illinois at Chicago	IL	25,006	VC
Univ of Illinois at Urbana-Champaign	IL	27,006	HC
Univ of Indianapolis	IN	36,480	C
Univ of Iowa	IA	18,683	VC+
Univ of Jamestown	ND	28,508	C
Univ of Kentucky	KY	33,306	C
Univ of La Verne	CA	55,600	C
Univ of Louisiana at Lafayette	LA	14,516	C
Univ of Louisiana at Monroe	LA	15,970	C
Univ of Louisville	KY	19,824	C
Univ of Maine	ME	20,792	C
Univ of Mary	ND	23,180	C
Univ of Mary Hardin-Baylor	TX	33,950	C+
Univ of Maryland/Baltimore County	MD	21,296	VC
Univ of Maryland/College Park	MD	21,938	HC
Univ of Maryland/Univ College	MD	25,966	LC
Univ of Mass Amherst	MA	26,199	VC+
Univ of Mass Boston	MA	13,435	C
Univ of Memphis	TN	18,278	C
Univ of Miami	FL	63,494	MC
Univ of Mich/Ann Arbor	MI	24,410	MC
Univ of Mich/Dearborn	MI	11,757	VC
Univ of Mich-Flint	MI	17,607	C+
Univ of Minn Crookston	MN	19,739	C
Univ of Minn/Duluth	MN	20,292	C+
Univ of Minn/Morris	MN	20,760	VC
Univ of Missouri/Columbia	MO	18,201	MC
Univ of Missouri-Kansas City	MO	19,563	VC
Univ of Missouri-St. Louis	MO		C
Univ of Mobile	AL	28,935	C
Univ of Montana	MT	14,105	C
Univ of Montana-Western	MT	11,220	LC
Univ of Montevallo	AL	19,502	C
Univ of Mount Olive	NC	18,426	C
Univ of Mount Union	OH	38,970	C
Univ of Nebr - Kearney	NE	16,546	LC
Univ of Nebr - Lincoln	NE	18,589	VC
Univ of Nebr - Omaha	NE	16,120	C
Univ of Nevada, Las Vegas	NV	17,553	C
Univ of Nevada/Reno	NV	18,010	C
Univ of New England	ME	48,880	C
Univ of New Hampshire	NH	28,562	VC
Univ of New Hampshire - Manchester	NH	14,490	C
Univ of New Haven	CT	52,190	C
Univ of New Mexico	NM	15,404	C
Univ of New Orleans	LA	12,840	C
Univ of North Alabama	AL	15,398	C
Univ of N Car at Asheville	NC	15,723	VC+
Univ of N Car at Chapel Hill	NC	20,052	HC+
Univ of N Car at Charlotte	NC	15,547	C
Univ of N Car at Greensboro	NC	14,690	C
Univ of N Car at Wilmington	NC	14,590	VC
Univ of N Dak	ND	15,373	C
Univ of North Florida	FL	15,996	VC
Univ of North Texas	TX	19,198	C
Univ of Northern Colo	CO	20,851	C
Univ of Northwestern - St. Paul	MN	38,160	C
Univ of Okla	OK	18,911	VC
Univ of Oregon	OR	22,972	C
Univ of Pennsylvania	PA	63,526	MC
Univ of Pikeville	KY	28,700	NC
Univ of Pittsburgh at Bradford	PA	22,402	C
Univ of Pittsburgh at Greensburg	PA	23,132	C
Univ of Pittsburgh at Johnstown	PA	22,092	C
Univ of Portland	OR	52,152	VC
Univ of Puget Sound	WA	56,456	VC+
Univ of Rio Grande & Rio Grande Community College	OH	8,750	NC
Univ of St. Francis	IN	37,400	C
Univ of San Diego	CA	58,442	VC+
Univ of San Francisco	CA	58,484	VC
Univ of Science and Arts of Okla	OK	11,140	VC
Univ of Scranton	PA	54,962	VC
Univ of Sioux Falls	SD	34,330	C
Univ of South Alabama	AL	16,400	C
Univ of S Car Aiken	SC	16,712	C
Univ of S Car at Columbia	SC	19,725	VC+
Univ of S Car Upstate	SC	18,200	LC
Univ of South Florida/St. Petersburg	FL	15,980	C
Univ of South Florida/Tampa	FL	16,110	VC+
Univ of Southern Calif	CA	66,631	C
Univ of Southern Indiana	IN	16,501	C
Univ of Southern Maine	ME	18,320	C
Univ of Southern Miss	MS	13,170	C
Univ of St. Francis	IL	39,924	C
Univ of St. Thomas - Houston	TX	40,020	VC
Univ of Tampa	FL	36,944	C
Univ of Texas at Arlington	TX	18,026	LC
Univ of Texas at El Paso	TX	34,452	NC
Univ of Texas at San Antonio	TX	20,157	C
Univ of the Arts	PA	56,579	SP
Univ of the Cumberlands	KY	32,000	C
Univ of the Incarnate Word	TX	39,162	LC

ST = STATE **$IS** = IN-STATE COSTS **SR** = SELECTOR RATING

School	ST	$IS	SR
Univ of the Ozarks	AR	52,176	C
Univ of the Pacific	CA	57,006	VC
Univ of the Sacred Heart	PR	17,932	
Univ of Toledo	OH	19,336	NC
Univ of Tulsa	OK	52,625	HC+
Univ of Vermont	VT	28,878	HC
Univ of Washington	WA	23,149	VC
Univ of West Florida	FL	15,848	C
Univ of Wisc-Eau Claire	WI	15,797	VC
Univ of Wisc-Green Bay	WI	15,064	C
Univ of Wisc-La Crosse	WI	15,247	C+
Univ of Wisc-Madison	WI	20,934	MC
Univ of Wisc-Milwaukee	WI	21,496	C
Univ of Wisc-Parkside	WI	15,193	C
Univ of Wisc-River Falls	WI	14,485	C
Univ of Wisc-Stevens Point	WI	14,043	C
Univ of Wisc-Stout	WI	19,667	C
Univ of Wisc-Superior	WI	14,446	C
Univ of Wisc-Whitewater	WI	13,976	C
Univ of Wyoming	WY	15,375	C+
Upper Iowa Univ	IA	34,990	NC
Urbana Univ	OH	30,820	C
Ursinus College	PA	61,690	VC
Utica College	NY	30,430	C
Valparaiso Univ	IN	48,370	C+
Vanderbilt Univ	TN	60,572	MC
Vanguard Univ of Southern Calif	CA	40,740	VC
Villanova Univ	PA	62,523	MC
Virginia Commonwealth Univ	VA	23,049	C
Virginia Polytechnic Inst and State Univ	VA	21,276	HC
Virginia Wesleyan College	VA	43,728	LC
Viterbo Univ	WI	34,660	C
Voorhees College	SC	19,976	C
Wake Forest Univ	NC	64,056	MC
Walla Walla Univ	WA	30,417	NC
Walsh Univ	OH	39,010	C
Warner Univ	FL	28,216	C
Wartburg College	IA	47,840	C
Washburn Univ	KS	15,827	C
Washington Adventist Univ	MD	31,440	LC
Washington State Univ	WA	22,495	C
Washington Univ in St. Louis	MO	65,366	VC
Wayland Baptist Univ	TX	22,356	LC
Wayne State College	NE	12,802	C
Wayne State Univ	MI	22,016	C
Weber State Univ	UT	10,721	C
Webster Univ	MO	37,490	C
Wesleyan College	GA	29,694	C+
West Chester Univ of Pennsylvania	PA	18,456	C
West Liberty Univ	WV	15,512	C
West Virginia State Univ	WV	8,378	NC
West Virginia Univ	WV	18,210	C
Western Carolina Univ	NC	13,965	C
Western Conn State Univ	CT	21,254	LC
Western Illinois Univ	IL	20,825	C
Western Kentucky Univ	KY	16,850	C
Western Mich Univ	MI	21,054	C
Western New England Univ	MA	48,088	C
Western State Colo Univ	CO	18,639	C
Western Washington Univ	WA	18,003	C+
Westfield State Univ	MA	19,671	C
Westminster College	PA	39,180	C+
Westminster College	UT	41,078	C+
Westmont College	CA	56,410	HC
Wheaton College	IL	43,610	MC
Wheeling Jesuit Univ	WV	37,106	LC
Wheelock College	MA	49,225	C
Whitworth Univ	WA	51,732	VC
Wichita State Univ	KS	21,643	C
Widener Univ	PA	56,486	C
Wilberforce Univ	OH	19,016	C
Wiley College	TX	18,504	C
Wilkes Univ	PA	45,622	C
William Carey Univ	MS	23,950	LC
William Jewell College	MO	41,210	C+
William Paterson Univ of New Jersey	NJ	23,133	C
William Peace Univ	NC	37,430	LC
William Penn Univ	IA	26,000	C
William Woods Univ	MO	32,040	C
Wilmington College	OH	34,600	C
Wilson College	PA	35,620	C
Winston-Salem State Univ	NC	26,166	LC
Winthrop Univ	SC	23,082	C
Wisc Lutheran College	WI	36,290	VC
Wittenberg Univ	OH	48,156	C+
Woodbury Univ	CA	46,958	C
Worcester State Univ	MA	20,977	C
Wright State Univ	OH	16,983	C
Xavier Univ of Louisiana	LA	31,689	C+
Yeshiva Univ	NY	47,250	VC+
York College	NE	24,300	C
York College of Pennsylvania	PA	29,240	C
Youngstown State Univ	OH	17,307	C

COMMUNICATIONS TECHNOLOGY

School	ST	$IS	SR
Alverno College	WI	33,294	LC
Calif College of the Arts	CA	52,758	SP
Cal State, Monterey Bay	CA	26,871	LC
Champlain College	VT	53,132	C+
Chestnut Hill College	PA	43,410	C
College of the Ozarks	MO	7,230	C
Dakota State Univ	SD	13,811	C
Eastern Mich Univ	MI	19,761	C
George Mason Univ	VA	15,724	VC
Grand Canyon Univ	AZ	16,950	VC
Indiana Univ of Pennsylvania	PA	23,614	LC
Inter-American Univ of PR-Bayamon	PR	18,785	
James Madison Univ	VA	19,084	VC
Lebanon Valley College	PA	51,530	C
Lewis Univ	IL	40,370	C
Lubbock Christian Univ	TX	28,426	C
Montana Tech of the Univ of Montana	MT	15,447	C+
Montclair State Univ	NJ	26,210	LC
New York Univ	NY	65,860	MC
Northwestern Univ	IL	66,344	MC
Ohio Univ	OH	22,924	C
Rochester Inst of Technology	NY	50,842	HC
Salve Regina Univ	RI	51,470	C
SUNY Polytechnic Inst	NY	19,473	VC
Taylor Univ	IN	40,317	C+
The College of Wooster	OH	57,900	VC+
Univ of New Haven	CT	52,190	C
Univ of S Dak	SD	16,109	C
Western Kentucky Univ	KY	16,850	C
Wilmington Univ	DE	8,546	NC

COMMUNICATIVE DISORDERS

School	ST	$IS	SR
Calif Baptist Univ	CA	41,392	C
East Stroudsburg Univ	PA	18,334	C
Jackson State Univ	MS	15,879	LC
San Diego State Univ	CA	21,896	C+
Univ of Georgia	GA	21,250	HC
Univ of Kansas	KS	20,135	C+
Univ of Rhode Island	RI	24,906	C
Western Kentucky Univ	KY	16,850	C

COMMUNITY HEALTH WORK

School	ST	$IS	SR
Arizona State Univ at the Downtown Phoenix Campus	AZ	23,680	VC
Arizona State Univ at the West Campus	AZ	20,640	C
Ashford Univ	CA	10,480	C
Bethel Univ	MN	45,270	VC
Brown Univ	RI	64,566	MC
Central Mich Univ	MI	20,330	C
Central Washington Univ	WA	16,803	C
CUNY/York College	NY	6,747	LC
Concordia Univ St. Paul	MN	29,050	C
Delaware State Univ	DE	19,376	NC
Elmira College	NY	53,900	C
Florida Gulf Coast Univ	FL	9,682	C
Florida State Univ	FL	16,771	HC
George Mason Univ	VA	15,724	VC
Georgia College & State Univ	GA	21,148	C+
Hofstra Univ	NY	55,960	C+
Howard Univ	DC	37,616	C+
Indiana Univ Bloomington	IN	20,429	VC
Ithaca College	NY	56,766	VC
Johnson C. Smith Univ	NC	25,336	LC
Kent State Univ	OH	20,732	C
Liberty Univ	VA	19,101	C
Longwood Univ	VA	22,184	C
Louisiana State Univ in Shreveport	LA	6,902	C
Malone Univ	OH	38,448	C
Minn State Univ, Mankato	MN	15,616	C
Minn State Univ, Moorhead	MN	15,941	C
Montclair State Univ	NJ	26,210	LC
Morris College	SC	18,500	LC
Murray State Univ	KY	16,998	C
New Mexico State Univ	NM	14,050	C
Northern Illinois Univ	IL	20,176	C
Ohio Univ	OH	22,924	C
Prescott College	AZ	33,284	C
Rhode Island College	RI	17,694	LC
Salisbury Univ	MD	20,714	VC
Slippery Rock Univ of Pennsylvania	PA	10,360	C
Southern Illinois Univ Edwardsville	IL	22,643	C
SUNY / SUNY College at Old Westbury	NY	16,860	C
SUNY / SUNY Potsdam	NY	20,404	C+
Texas A&M Univ	TX	20,521	VC+
Tufts Univ	MA		MC
Tulane Univ	LA	63,396	HC+
Univ of Calif at Davis	CA	28,468	HC
Univ of Central Okla	OK	13,486	C
Univ of Illinois at Urbana-Champaign	IL	27,006	HC
Univ of Kansas	KS	20,135	C+
Univ of Maine at Farmington	ME	18,187	C
Univ of Maryland/College Park	MD	21,938	HC
Univ of Mass Lowell	MA	26,380	C
Univ of Nebr - Omaha	NE	16,120	C
Univ of Scranton	PA	54,962	VC
Univ of Wisc-La Crosse	WI	15,247	C+
Univ of Wisc-Superior	WI	14,446	C
Western Mich Univ	MI	21,054	C
Whitworth Univ	WA	51,732	VC
William Paterson Univ of New Jersey	NJ	23,133	C
Winona State Univ	MN	17,535	C
Wright State Univ	OH	16,983	C

COMMUNITY PSYCHOLOGY

School	ST	$IS	SR
Mount Aloysius College	PA	29,976	C
Okla Baptist Univ	OK	32,320	C
Univ of Mich-Flint	MI	17,607	C+
Univ of New Haven	CT	52,190	C

COMMUNITY SERVICES

School	ST	$IS	SR
Alverno College	WI	33,294	LC
Aquinas College - Mich	MI	38,876	HC
Bemidji State Univ	MN	16,056	VC
Bryant Univ	RI	55,646	VC
Central Mich Univ	MI	20,330	C
DePaul Univ	IL	47,623	VC
Emory and Henry College	VA	41,410	C
Guilford College	NC	44,090	C
Humphreys College	CA	27,790	C
Martin Univ	IN	20,264	LC
Metropolitan College of New York	NY		VC
Midland Univ	NE	37,468	
New Mexico State Univ	NM	14,050	C
Northern State Univ	SD	14,505	C
Ohio State Univ at Columbus	OH	21,703	HC+
Ohio Univ	OH	22,924	C
Portland State Univ	OR	19,443	C
Prescott College	AZ	33,284	C
Providence College	RI	60,760	VC
Queens Univ of Charlotte	NC	39,543	C
Roger Williams Univ	RI	46,296	C+
Southern Arkansas Univ	AR	21,532	C
SUNY / Empire State College	NY	9,145	SP
Univ of Calif, Santa Cruz	CA	28,731	C+
Univ of Mass Boston	MA	13,435	C
Univ of Toledo	OH	19,336	NC

COMPARATIVE LITERATURE

School	ST	$IS	SR
Barnard College/Columbia Univ	NY	62,741	MC
Beloit College	WI	55,206	HC
Bennington College	VT	63,960	MC
Brandeis Univ	MA	65,925	MC
Brigham Young Univ	UT	12,748	HC
Brown Univ	RI	64,566	MC
Bryant Univ	RI	55,646	VC
Bryn Mawr College	PA	59,890	MC
Cal State, Fullerton	CA	21,902	C
Cal State, Long Beach	CA	18,850	C
Case Western Reserve Univ	OH	60,304	MC
CUNY/Brooklyn College	NY	5,884	C+
CUNY/City College	NY	20,319	VC
CUNY/Hunter College	NY	31,098	VC
CUNY/Lehman College	NY	5,778	HC+
CUNY/Queens College	NY	27,896	C
Clark Univ	MA	51,600	HC+
Colo College	CO	62,560	MC
Columbia Univ/ School of General Studies	NY	61,470	MC
Columbia Univ/City of New York	NY	62,958	MC
Cornell Univ	NY	64,853	MC
Dartmouth College	NH	66,174	MC
Eckerd College	FL	52,874	C
Emory Univ	GA	60,786	MC
Fordham Univ	NY	65,918	MC
Georgetown Univ	DC	65,926	MC
Goddard College	VT	17,040	VC
Hamilton College	NY	64,250	MC
Hampshire College	MA	63,824	MC
Haverford College	PA	66,490	MC
Hillsdale College	MI	35,722	MC
Hofstra Univ	NY	55,960	C+
Indiana Univ Bloomington	IN	20,429	VC
Lycoming College	PA	48,580	C
Middlebury College	VT	64,332	MC
New York Univ	NY	65,860	MC
Northland College	WI	41,103	C+
Northwestern Univ	IL	66,344	MC
Oberlin College	OH	66,012	MC
Pennsylvania State Univ - Univ Park	PA	29,760	HC
Princeton Univ	NJ	57,610	MC
Purdue Univ/West Lafayette	IN	20,032	MC
Rutgers Univ - New Brunswick	NJ	26,632	HC
San Diego State Univ	CA	21,896	C+
San Francisco State Univ	CA	18,514	LC
Smith College	MA	63,914	MC
Stanford Univ	CA	60,409	MC
SUNY at Binghamton	NY	22,861	MC
SUNY at Geneseo	NY	20,440	VC+
Stony Brook Univ/The SUNY	NY	21,881	MC
Swarthmore College	PA	63,550	MC
The College of Wooster	OH	57,900	VC+
The Univ of Utah	UT	17,924	VC
Trinity College	CT	63,920	HC+
Univ of Calif at Berkeley	CA	28,853	MC
Univ of Calif at Davis	CA	28,468	HC
Univ of Calif at Irvine	CA	26,484	VC
Univ of Calif at Riverside	CA	29,227	C+
Univ of Calif at Santa Barbara	CA	29,091	HC
Univ of Chicago	IL	67,584	MC
Univ of Cincinnati	OH	21,964	VC
Univ of Delaware	DE	24,976	VC+
Univ of Georgia	GA	21,250	HC
Univ of Illinois at Urbana-Champaign	IL	27,006	HC
Univ of Iowa	IA	18,683	VC+
Univ of La Verne	CA	55,600	C
Univ of Mass Amherst	MA	26,199	VC+
Univ of Mich/Ann Arbor	MI	24,410	MC
Univ of New Mexico	NM	15,404	C
Univ of N Car at Chapel Hill	NC	20,052	HC+
Univ of Oregon	OR	22,972	C
Univ of Pennsylvania	PA	63,526	MC
Univ of PR-Rio Piedras campus	PR	13,327	
Univ of Rochester	NY	65,032	MC
Univ of San Francisco	CA	58,484	VC
Univ of S Car at Columbia	SC	19,725	VC+
Univ of Southern Calif	CA	66,631	C
Univ of Virginia	VA	25,891	MC
Univ of Washington	WA	23,149	VC
Univ of Wisc-Madison	WI	20,934	MC
Univ of Wisc-Milwaukee	WI	21,496	C
Washington Univ in St. Louis	MO	65,366	VC
Wellesley College	MA	63,916	MC
Willamette Univ	OR	61,817	VC+

COMPLEMENTARY/ ALTERNATIVE HEALTH

School	ST	$IS	SR
Ashford Univ	CA	10,480	C

COMPOSITION

School	ST	$IS	SR
Arizona State Univ at the Tempe Campus	AZ	21,756	VC
Lynn Univ	FL	49,480	LC
Mich State Univ	MI	23,898	VC+
Oberlin College	OH	66,012	MC
Samford Univ	AL	39,232	VC
Shenandoah Univ	VA	41,312	C
Vanderbilt Univ	TN	60,572	MC

COMPUTATIONAL SCIENCES

School	ST	$IS	SR
American Univ	DC	59,379	HC+
Arizona State Univ at the Tempe Campus	AZ	21,756	VC
Biola Univ	CA	46,402	C+
Brown Univ	RI	64,566	MC
Bryant Univ	RI	55,646	VC
Canisius College	NY	47,537	C
Carroll Univ	WI	38,100	C+
Champlain College	VT	53,132	C+
DePaul Univ	IL	47,623	VC
Fairfield Univ	CT	59,860	VC+
George Mason Univ	VA	15,724	VC
Hood College	MD	54,840	C
Huntington Univ	IN	33,996	C
Indiana Univ Bloomington	IN	20,429	VC
Marquette Univ	WI	48,390	VC+
Mercer Univ	GA	45,348	VC
Mich State Univ	MI	23,898	VC+
Mount Aloysius College	PA	29,976	C
New College of Florida	FL	15,848	MC
New York Univ	NY	65,860	MC
Park Univ	MO	20,329	C
Purdue Univ/West Lafayette	IN	20,032	MC
SUNY / Univ at Buffalo	NY	23,122	C+
Stevens Inst of Technology	NJ	62,338	MC
Stockton Univ	NJ	25,059	
The College at Brockport - SUNY	NY	20,346	C
Univ of Illinois at Urbana-Champaign	IL	27,006	HC
Univ of Wisc-Superior	WI	14,446	C
Western Kentucky Univ	KY	16,850	C

COMPUTER EDUCATION

School	ST	$IS	SR
Abilene Christian Univ	TX	41,800	C+
Appalachian State Univ	NC	14,416	VC
Arkansas Tech Univ	AR	15,484	C
Baylor Univ	TX	53,760	HC
Clayton State Univ	GA	19,735	C
Concordia Univ, Chicago	IL	39,694	C
Dakota State Univ	SD	13,811	C
Eastern Mich Univ	MI	19,761	C
Eastern Washington Univ	WA	25,572	LC
Edgewood College	WI	35,950	C
Hardin-Simmons Univ	TX	33,966	C
Indiana Univ-Purdue Univ Fort Wayne	IN	17,553	C
Missouri Southern State Univ	MO	12,499	C
Missouri State Univ	MO	15,190	C+
Northern Mich Univ	MI	19,604	C
Union College	NE	23,270	C
Univ of Illinois at Urbana-Champaign	IL	27,006	HC
Univ of Montana-Western	MT	11,220	LC
Univ of Nebr - Lincoln	NE	18,589	VC

COMPUTER ENGINEERING

School	ST	$IS	SR
Auburn Univ	AL	23,594	VC+
Baylor Univ	TX	53,760	HC
Bellarmine Univ	KY	51,220	C
Benedict College	SC	28,238	NC
Bethune-Cookman Univ	FL	22,970	C
Boston Univ	MA	65,110	MC
Brigham Young Univ	UT	12,748	HC

ST = STATE $IS = IN-STATE COSTS SR = SELECTOR RATING

School	ST	$IS	SR
Brown Univ	RI	64,566	MC
Bucknell Univ	PA	64,616	MC
Calif Inst of Technology	CA	58,761	MC
Calif Polytechnic State Univ	CA	17,979	HC+
Calif State Polytechnic Univ, Pomona	CA	21,541	C
Cal State, Chico	CA	21,440	C
Cal State, Fresno	CA	16,902	LC
Cal State, Fullerton	CA	21,902	C
Cal State, Long Beach	CA	18,850	C
Cal State, Sacramento	CA	20,332	C
Calvin College	MI	41,570	VC+
Capitol Technology Univ	MD	31,410	C
Carnegie Mellon Univ	PA	67,980	MC
Case Western Reserve Univ	OH	60,304	MC
Cedarville Univ	OH	34,990	VC
Christopher Newport Univ	VA	23,968	VC+
CUNY/City College	NY	20,319	VC
CUNY/College of Technology	NY	6,669	NC
Claflin Univ	SC	33,764	LC
Clarkson Univ	NY	60,392	HC
Clemson Univ	SC		HC
Cogswell Polytechnical College	CA	30,531	C
Colo State Univ	CO	22,162	VC
Colo Technical Univ	CO	21,455	NC
Columbia Univ/City of New York	NY	62,958	MC
Dordt College	IA	37,860	C+
Drexel Univ	PA	65,432	VC+
Eastern Mich Univ	MI	19,761	C
Eastern Nazarene College	MA	39,955	C
Elizabethtown College	PA	54,050	C
Elon Univ	NC	44,599	VC+
Embry-Riddle Aeronautical Univ - Daytona Beach	FL	44,712	VC
Embry-Riddle Aeronautical Univ - Prescott Campus	AZ	44,054	VC
Fairfield Univ	CT	59,860	VC+
Florida Atlantic Univ	FL	17,339	C
Florida Inst of Technology	FL	53,306	VC
Florida International Univ	FL	19,854	C+
Florida State Univ	FL	16,771	HC
Gannon Univ	PA	42,032	C
George Mason Univ	VA	15,724	VC
George Washington Univ	DC	62,835	MC
Georgia Inst of Technology	GA	23,360	MC
Gonzaga Univ	WA	50,888	HC
Harding Univ	AR	25,421	C
Hofstra Univ	NY	55,960	C+
Howard Univ	DC	37,616	C+
Illinois Inst of Technology	IL	56,826	HC+
Indiana Inst of Technology	IN	34,240	LC
Indiana Univ-Purdue Univ Fort Wayne	IN	17,553	C
Indiana Univ-Purdue Univ Indianapolis	IN	18,635	C
Iowa State Univ	IA	17,570	C
Jackson State Univ	MS	15,879	LC
Johns Hopkins Univ	MD	65,386	MC
Johnson C. Smith Univ	NC	25,336	LC
Kansas State Univ	KS	17,780	VC
Kettering Univ	MI	47,570	HC
Lawrence Tech Univ	MI	39,770	VC
Lehigh Univ	PA	61,010	MC
LeTourneau Univ	TX	38,250	VC
Lewis Univ	IL	40,370	C
Lipscomb Univ	TN	41,296	VC
Louisiana State Univ and A&M College	LA	18,677	VC
Marquette Univ	WI	48,390	VC+
Miami Univ	OH	27,190	HC+
Mich State Univ	MI	23,898	VC+
Mich Tech Univ	MI	24,739	VC+
Milwaukee School of Engineering	WI	45,153	HC
Minn State Univ, Mankato	MN	15,616	C
Miss State Univ	MS	11,454	C+
Missouri Univ of Science and Technology	MO	18,655	HC
Montana State Univ	MT	15,500	C+
Montana Tech of the Univ of Montana	MT	15,447	C+
New Jersey Inst of Technology	NJ	29,569	VC
New York Univ	NY	65,860	MC
N Car State Univ	NC	19,515	HC+
N Dak State Univ	ND	16,245	C
Northeastern Univ	MA	62,703	MC
Northwestern Univ	IL	66,344	MC
Norwich Univ	VT	28,212	C
Nova Southeastern Univ	FL	38,534	C+
Oakland Univ	MI	20,763	C
Ohio Northern Univ	OH	44,050	VC
Ohio State Univ at Columbus	OH	21,703	HC+
Ohio Univ	OH	22,924	C
Okla Christian Univ	OK	27,650	VC
Okla State Univ	OK	17,180	VC
Old Dominion Univ	VA	20,910	C
Olivet Nazarene Univ	IL	41,840	C
Oral Roberts Univ	OK	34,316	C
Oregon State Univ	OR	22,519	VC
Penn State Erie/The Behrend College	PA	16,256	C
Pennsylvania College of Technology	PA	27,333	NC
Pennsylvania State Univ - Univ Park	PA	29,760	HC
Portland State Univ	OR	19,443	C
Prairie View A&M Univ	TX	15,205	LC
Purdue Univ/Northwest	IN	15,038	C
Purdue Univ/West Lafayette	IN	20,032	MC
Rensselaer Polytechnic Inst	NY	63,436	MC
Rochester Inst of Technology	NY	50,842	HC
Rose-Hulman Inst of Technology	IN	57,303	MC
St. Louis Univ	MO	49,866	HC
San Diego State Univ	CA	21,896	C+
San Francisco State Univ	CA	18,514	LC
San Jose State Univ	CA	21,540	C
Seattle Univ	WA	50,811	VC+
Shepherd Univ, West Virginia	WV	17,224	C
Shippensburg Univ of Pennsylvania	PA	23,208	C
S Dak School of Mines and Technology	SD	18,645	VC
Southern Illinois Univ Carbondale	IL	23,667	C
Southern Illinois Univ Edwardsville	IL	22,643	C
Southern Methodist Univ	TX	66,483	MC
St. Mary's Univ	TX	37,500	C
SUNY / Univ at Buffalo	NY	23,122	C+
SUNY at Binghamton	NY	22,861	MC
SUNY at New Paltz	NY	19,200	C
SUNY SUNY Albany	NY	22,165	C
Stevens Inst of Technology	NJ	62,338	MC
Stony Brook Univ/The SUNY	NY	21,881	MC
Suffolk Univ	MA	50,308	C
Syracuse Univ	NY	60,239	VC
Taylor Univ	IN	40,317	C+
Texas A&M Univ	TX	20,521	VC+
Texas Tech Univ	TX	18,736	C+
The Catholic Univ of America	DC	56,356	VC
The College of New Jersey	NJ	31,909	HC
The Univ of Akron	OH	21,477	C
The Univ of Tenn at Knoxville	TN	22,112	VC
The Univ of Utah	UT	17,924	VC
Trine Univ	IN	41,310	C
Tufts Univ	MA		MC
Union College	NY	64,320	MC
United States Air Force Academy	CO		C
United States Naval Academy	MD		MC
Universidad Politecnica de PR, Hato Rey campus	PR	23,514	
Univ of Alabama in Huntsville	AL	19,445	VC
Univ of Alaska Fairbanks	AK	16,179	C
Univ of Arkansas at Fayetteville	AR	19,152	C+
Univ of Bridgeport	CT	44,430	LC
Univ of Calif at Berkeley	CA	28,853	MC
Univ of Calif at Davis	CA	28,468	HC
Univ of Calif at Irvine	CA	26,484	VC
Univ of Calif at Los Angeles	CA	30,162	MC
Univ of Calif at Santa Barbara	CA	29,091	HC
Univ of Calif San Diego	CA	30,150	MC
Univ of Calif, Santa Cruz	CA	28,731	C+
Univ of Central Florida	FL	15,922	VC
Univ of Cincinnati	OH	21,964	VC
Univ of Colo Boulder	CO	24,285	VC+
Univ of Colo Colo Springs	CO	19,663	C
Univ of Conn	CT	25,538	HC
Univ of Dayton	OH	53,620	C
Univ of Delaware	DE	24,976	VC+
Univ of Denver	CO	58,443	VC+
Univ of Evansville	IN	44,186	VC+
Univ of Florida	FL	16,291	HC+
Univ of Georgia	GA	21,250	HC
Univ of Hartford	CT	49,776	C
Univ of Houston	TX	21,483	VC
Univ of Idaho	ID	15,348	C
Univ of Illinois at Chicago	IL	25,006	VC
Univ of Illinois at Urbana-Champaign	IL	27,006	HC
Univ of Kansas	KS	20,135	C+
Univ of La Verne	CA	55,600	C
Univ of Louisiana at Lafayette	LA	14,516	C
Univ of Louisville	KY	19,824	C
Univ of Maine	ME	20,792	C
Univ of Maryland/Baltimore County	MD	21,296	VC
Univ of Maryland/College Park	MD	21,938	HC
Univ of Mass Amherst	MA	26,199	VC+
Univ of Mass Dartmouth	MA	25,658	C
Univ of Mass Lowell	MA	26,380	C
Univ of Memphis	TN	18,278	C
Univ of Miami	FL	63,494	MC
Univ of Mich/Ann Arbor	MI	24,410	MC
Univ of Mich/Dearborn	MI	11,757	VC
Univ of Minn/Duluth	MN	20,292	C+
Univ of Missouri/Columbia	MO	18,201	MC
Univ of Nebr - Lincoln	NE	18,589	VC
Univ of Nevada, Las Vegas	NV	17,553	C
Univ of New Hampshire	NH	28,562	VC
Univ of New Haven	CT	52,190	C
Univ of New Mexico	NM	15,404	C
Univ of N Car at Charlotte	NC	15,547	C
Univ of North Texas	TX	19,198	C
Univ of Notre Dame	IN	64,043	MC
Univ of Okla	OK	18,911	VC
Univ of Pennsylvania	PA	63,526	MC
Univ of Pittsburgh	PA	29,568	HC+
Univ of Pittsburgh at Johnstown	PA	22,092	C
Univ of PR, at Mayaguez	PR	13,995	
Univ of Rhode Island	RI	24,906	C
Univ of Scranton	PA	54,962	VC
Univ of South Alabama	AL	16,400	C
Univ of S Car at Columbia	SC	19,725	VC+
Univ of South Florida/Tampa	FL	16,110	VC+
Univ of Southern Calif	CA	66,631	C
Univ of Texas at Arlington	TX	18,026	LC
Univ of Texas at Dallas	TX	22,830	VC+
Univ of Texas at San Antonio	TX	20,157	C
Univ of the Pacific	CA	57,006	VC
Univ of Toledo	OH	19,336	NC
Univ of Tulsa	OK	52,625	HC+
Univ of Virginia	VA	25,891	MC
Univ of Washington	WA	23,149	VC
Univ of West Florida	FL	15,848	C
Univ of Wisc-Madison	WI	20,934	MC
Univ of Wisc-Milwaukee	WI	21,496	C
Univ of Wisc-Stout	WI	19,667	C
Univ of Wyoming	WY	15,375	C+
Valparaiso Univ	IN	48,370	C+
Vanderbilt Univ	TN	60,572	MC
Vermont Technical College	VT	23,838	C
Villanova Univ	PA	62,523	MC
Virginia Commonwealth Univ	VA	23,049	C
Virginia Polytechnic Inst and State Univ	VA	21,276	HC
Washington State Univ	WA	22,495	C
Washington Univ in St. Louis	MO	65,366	VC
Weber State Univ	UT	10,721	C
Wentworth Inst of Technology	MA	47,112	C
West Virginia Univ	WV	18,210	C
Western Mich Univ	MI	21,054	C
Western New England Univ	MA	48,088	C
Wichita State Univ	KS	21,643	C
Wright State Univ	OH	16,983	C
York College of Pennsylvania	PA	29,240	C

COMPUTER ENGINEERING TECHNOLOGY

School	ST	$IS	SR
Calif Baptist Univ	CA	41,392	C
Cal State, Fresno	CA	16,902	LC
Cal State, Long Beach	CA	18,850	C
Central Conn State Univ	CT	21,203	C
Drexel Univ	PA	65,432	VC+
Farmingdale State College	NY	20,624	C
Howard Univ	DC	37,616	C+
Indiana Univ-Purdue Univ Indianapolis	IN	18,635	C
Kennesaw State Univ	GA	19,592	VC
Loyola Univ Chicago	IL	55,802	VC
Minn State Univ, Mankato	MN	15,616	C
Missouri Southern State Univ	MO	12,499	C
New York Univ	NY	65,860	MC
Northern Kentucky Univ	KY	16,486	C
Nova Southeastern Univ	FL	38,534	C+
Rochester Inst of Technology	NY	50,842	HC
Taylor Univ	IN	40,317	C+
Univ of Cincinnati	OH	21,964	VC
Univ of S Car Upstate	SC	18,200	LC

COMPUTER GAME DESIGN/ DEVELOPMENT

School	ST	$IS	SR
Abilene Christian Univ	TX	41,800	C+
Arkansas Tech Univ	AR	15,484	C
Becker College	MA	57,628	C
Bloomfield College	NJ	39,100	LC
Champlain College	VT	53,132	C+
Columbia College Chicago	IL	43,168	C
Dakota State Univ	SD	13,811	C
Daniel Webster College	NH	26,984	C
DePaul Univ	IL	47,623	VC
DeSales Univ	PA	43,970	C
Drexel Univ	PA	65,432	VC+
Elmhurst College	IL	45,428	C
Indiana Inst of Technology	IN	34,240	LC
Kennesaw State Univ	GA	19,592	VC
Marist College	NY	49,860	VC
Marshall Univ	WV	17,242	C
Okla Christian Univ	OK	27,650	VC
Rochester Inst of Technology	NY	50,842	HC
Univ of Calif, Santa Cruz	CA	28,731	C+
Univ of Colo Colo Springs	CO	19,663	C
Univ of Denver	CO	58,443	VC+
Univ of St. Francis	IN	37,400	C
Univ of Tulsa	OK	52,625	HC+

COMPUTER GRAPHICS

School	ST	$IS	SR
Andrews Univ	MI	28,030	C+
Ashford Univ	CA	10,480	C
Bloomfield College	NJ	39,100	LC
Brown Univ	RI	64,566	MC
Cal State, Chico	CA	21,440	C
Cogswell Polytechnical College	CA	30,531	C
Columbia College Chicago	IL	43,168	C
Dakota State Univ	SD	13,811	C
DePaul Univ	IL	47,623	VC
Eastern Mich Univ	MI	19,761	C
Escuela de Artes Plasticas de PR	PR	11,236	
Fashion Inst of Technology/ SUNY	NY	18,521	SP
Indiana Univ-Purdue Univ Fort Wayne	IN	17,553	C
Indiana Univ-Purdue Univ Indianapolis	IN	18,635	C
Indiana Wesleyan Univ	IN	33,674	C
Jacksonville Univ	FL	46,230	C
La Salle Univ	PA	55,790	C
Lawrence Tech Univ	MI	39,770	VC
Millikin Univ	IL	42,158	C
Monmouth Univ	NJ	46,234	C
New York Inst of Technology	NY	48,730	C
Northwest Nazarene Univ	ID	36,000	C
Pennsylvania College of Technology	PA	27,333	NC
Pratt Inst	NY	58,082	VC
Purdue Univ/Northwest	IN	15,038	C
Purdue Univ/West Lafayette	IN	20,032	MC
Rochester Inst of Technology	NY	50,842	HC
Savannah College of Art and Design	GA	49,595	C
School of Visual Arts	NY	47,500	SP
Springfield College	MA	45,995	C
Syracuse Univ	NY	60,239	VC
Taylor Univ	IN	40,317	C+
The Art Inst of Atlanta	GA	34,334	SP
Univ of Dubuque	IA	37,824	C
Univ of Mary Hardin-Baylor	TX	33,950	C+
Univ of Miami	FL	63,494	MC
Univ of Tampa	FL	36,944	C

COMPUTER INFORMATION SYSTEMS

School	ST	$IS	SR
Arizona State Univ at the Polytechnic Campus	AZ	21,360	VC
Arizona State Univ at the Tempe Campus	AZ	21,756	VC
Averett Univ	VA	40,970	LC
Bentley Univ	MA	60,890	HC
Bloomfield College	NJ	39,100	LC
Bryant Univ	RI	55,646	VC
Cabrini Univ	PA	42,591	LC
Calif State Polytechnic Univ, Pomona	CA	21,541	C
Cal State, Chico	CA	21,440	C
Clarke Univ	IA	38,940	C
College of Charleston	SC	22,699	C
Delta State Univ	MS	13,176	C
Faulkner Univ	AL	26,410	C
Ferris State Univ	MI	21,445	C
Grove City College	PA	25,692	VC
Husson Univ	ME	25,720	LC
Indiana Univ Northwest	IN	7,072	C
Keene State College	NH	24,003	LC
Lewis Univ	IL	40,370	C
Livingstone College	NC	17,815	LC
Loyola Univ New Orleans	LA	51,708	VC+
Mayville State Univ	ND	18,371	NC
McKendree Univ	IL	37,940	C+
Mich Tech Univ	MI	24,739	VC+
Milligan College	TN	38,150	C
Missouri Southern State Univ	MO	12,499	C
Molloy College	NY	40,440	C
Murray State Univ	KY	16,998	C
Neumann Univ	PA	40,678	LC
Niagara Univ	NY	41,010	C
Northern Arizona Univ	AZ	20,246	VC
Northwest Nazarene Univ	ID	36,000	C
Nova Southeastern Univ	FL	38,534	C+
Okla Baptist Univ	OK	32,320	C
Pennsylvania State Univ - Univ Park	PA	29,760	HC
Rochester Inst of Technology	NY	50,842	HC
St. Leo Univ	FL	31,650	C
St. Louis Univ	MO	49,866	HC
Siena Heights Univ	MI	32,040	C
Silver Lake College of the Holy Family	WI	36,290	LC
Southeast Missouri State Univ	MO	15,498	C
Southern Oregon Univ	OR	19,117	C
St. Joseph's College, New York/Brooklyn Campus	NY	25,114	LC
St. Joseph's College, New York/Long Island Campus	NY	25,124	C
St. Thomas Aquinas College	NY	42,200	C
SUNY / SUNY Fredonia	NY	20,818	C
Tarleton State Univ	TX	15,248	LC
Texas State Univ	TX	19,350	C
The Master's Univ	CA	43,870	C+
Thomas Edison State Univ	NJ	6,350	NC
Univ of Indianapolis	IN	36,480	C
Univ of Louisiana at Monroe	LA	15,970	C
Univ of St. Francis	IN	37,400	C
Univ of San Francisco	CA	58,484	VC
Wentworth Inst of Technology	MA	47,112	C
Western Mich Univ	MI	21,054	C
Western New England Univ	MA	48,088	C

COMPUTER INFORMATION TECHNOLOGY

School	ST	$IS	SR
Biola Univ	CA	46,402	C+
Bryant Univ	RI	55,646	VC
Champlain College	VT	53,132	C+

ST = STATE $IS = IN-STATE COSTS SR = SELECTOR RATING

School	ST	$IS	SR
CUNY/John Jay College of Criminal Justice	NY	6,359	NC
City Univ of Seattle	WA	24,340	NC
Clayton State Univ	GA	19,735	C
Ferris State Univ	MI	21,445	C
Georgia Southwestern State Univ	GA	13,870	C
Indiana Univ-Purdue Univ Indianapolis	IN	18,635	C
Lewis Univ	IL	40,370	C
Limestone College	SC	32,100	C
Mills College	CA	59,163	VC
Minn State Univ, Mankato	MN	15,616	C
New York Inst of Technology	NY	48,730	C
Niagara Univ	NY	41,010	C
Northern Arizona Univ	AZ	20,246	VC
Northern Kentucky Univ	KY	16,486	C
Ohio Valley Univ	WV	29,480	C
Point Loma Nazarene Univ	CA	43,450	C
Rochester Inst of Technology	NY	50,842	HC
St. Louis Univ	MO	49,866	HC
St. Edward's Univ	TX	53,100	VC
St. Joseph's College, New York/Brooklyn Campus	NY	25,114	LC
St. Joseph's College, New York/Long Island Campus	NY	25,124	C
Texas Christian Univ	TX	54,670	HC
Thomas College	ME	35,268	LC
Trevecca Nazarene Univ	TN	31,186	C
Univ of Cincinnati	OH	21,964	VC
Univ of New Hampshire - Manchester	NH	14,490	C
Washington & Jefferson College	PA	56,512	VC

COMPUTER MANAGEMENT

School	ST	$IS	SR
Bryant Univ	RI	55,646	VC
Caldwell Univ	NJ	42,165	NC
Chestnut Hill College	PA	43,410	C
Colo Christian Univ	CO	39,940	VC
Emory and Henry College	VA	41,410	C
Johnson & Wales Univ/ Providence Campus	RI	42,248	C
Mayville State Univ	ND	18,371	NC
Metropolitan State Univ of Denver	CO	29,889	LC
New Jersey Inst of Technology	NJ	29,569	VC
Northwest Missouri State Univ	MO	17,737	C
Northwest Univ	WA	35,876	VC
Northwood Univ - Mich	MI	35,010	LC
Peirce College	PA	16,780	NC
Peru State College	NE	14,768	NC
Rochester College	MI	28,574	LC
Southern Adventist Univ	TN	27,600	C
Southern Illinois Univ Edwardsville	IL	22,643	C
Univ of Illinois at Urbana-Champaign	IL	27,006	HC
Univ of Mount Olive	NC	18,426	C
Univ of New Haven	CT	52,190	C
Webster Univ	MO	37,490	C

COMPUTER MATHEMATICS

School	ST	$IS	SR
Bethany College	WV	36,300	NC
Biola Univ	CA	46,402	C+
Bowdoin College	ME	63,500	MC
Brown Univ	RI	64,566	MC
Calif Inst of Technology	CA	58,761	MC
Ithaca College	NY	56,766	VC
Keene State College	NH	24,003	LC
LeTourneau Univ	TX	38,250	VC
Lewis & Clark College	OR	58,434	HC+
New York Univ	NY	65,860	MC
Oakwood Univ	AL	43,758	C
Rochester Inst of Technology	NY	50,842	HC
Salem International Univ	WV	21,090	LC
Southern Oregon Univ	OR	19,117	C
Univ of Illinois at Chicago	IL	25,006	VC
Univ of Illinois at Urbana-Champaign	IL	27,006	HC
Univ of New Haven	CT	52,190	C
Univ of S Car Aiken	SC	16,712	C
Wheaton College	MA	61,512	VC
Whitman College	WA	59,772	MC

COMPUTER NETWORKS & SYSTEMS

School	ST	$IS	SR
Bloomfield College	NJ	39,100	LC
Ferris State Univ	MI	21,445	C
Frostburg State Univ	MD	17,280	LC
Keene State College	NH	24,003	LC
Lewis Univ	IL	40,370	C
Mount Vernon Nazarene Univ	OH	34,500	C
Regis Univ	CO	44,520	C
Rochester Inst of Technology	NY	50,842	HC
Silver Lake College of the Holy Family	WI	36,290	LC
St. Ambrose Univ	IA	39,019	C
Univ of Alaska Anchorage	AK	16,652	NC
Univ of Georgia	GA	21,250	HC
Weber State Univ	UT	10,721	C
Wentworth Inst of Technology	MA	47,112	C

COMPUTER PROGRAMMING

School	ST	$IS	SR
Baker College of Flint	MI	13,880	NC
Bloomfield College	NJ	39,100	LC
Calvin College	MI	41,570	VC+
Caribbean Univ	PR	15,471	
Carnegie Mellon Univ	PA	67,980	MC
Central Washington Univ	WA	16,803	C
City Univ of Seattle	WA	24,340	NC
Cogswell Polytechnical College	CA	30,531	C
Concord Univ	WV	14,954	C
Concordia Univ, Chicago	IL	39,694	C
Curry College	MA	51,815	C
Dakota State Univ	SD	13,811	C
DePaul Univ	IL	47,623	VC
Dickinson State Univ	ND	12,372	LC
Dordt College	IA	37,860	C+
Eastern Kentucky Univ	KY	16,908	C
Eastern Mich Univ	MI	19,761	C
Farmingdale State College	NY	20,624	C
Franklin College	IN	39,380	C
Freed-Hardeman Univ	TN	29,450	C
Hannibal-LaGrange Univ	MO	29,815	C
Hawaii Pacific Univ	HI	33,420	C
Idaho State Univ	ID	13,619	NC
Indiana Univ-Purdue Univ Fort Wayne	IN	17,553	C
Ithaca College	NY	56,766	VC
Lamar Univ	TX	18,014	LC
Le Moyne College	NY	46,000	C
Limestone College	SC	32,100	C
Mayville State Univ	ND	18,371	NC
Midland Univ	NE	37,468	
Missouri Western State Univ	MO	16,741	
Monmouth College	IL	42,260	C
Montana Tech of the Univ of Montana	MT	15,447	C+
Northeastern Univ	MA	62,703	MC
Northern Mich Univ	MI	19,604	C
Peirce College	PA	16,780	NC
Pennsylvania College of Technology	PA	27,333	NC
Peru State College	NE	14,768	NC
Pontifical Catholic Univ of PR	PR	10,534	
Purdue Univ/Northwest	IN	15,038	C
St. Louis Univ	MO	49,866	HC
Salem State Univ	MA	17,303	LC
Southern Oregon Univ	OR	19,117	C
St. Thomas Univ	FL	36,360	LC
Stephen F. Austin State Univ	TX	18,406	LC
Suffolk Univ	MA	50,308	C
Tarleton State Univ	TX	15,248	LC
Universidad del Turabo	PR	17,828	
Univ of Arkansas at Little Rock	AR	18,211	C
Univ of Illinois at Urbana-Champaign	IL	27,006	HC
Univ of Nebr - Kearney	NE	16,546	LC
Univ of New Haven	CT	52,190	C
Univ of St. Francis	IL	39,924	C
Univ of Wisc-River Falls	WI	14,485	C
Univ of Wisc-Whitewater	WI	13,976	C
Washington Univ in St. Louis	MO	65,366	VC
Weber State Univ	UT	10,721	C
West Virginia Univ Inst of Technology	WV	16,462	NC
Youngstown State Univ	OH	17,307	C

COMPUTER SCIENCE

School	ST	$IS	SR
Abilene Christian Univ	TX	41,800	C+
Adams State Univ	CO	17,703	LC
Adelphi Univ	NY	48,244	C
Agnes Scott College	GA	51,930	VC+
Alabama A&M Univ	AL	18,796	C
Albany State Univ	GA	19,462	C
Albright College	PA	46,660	C
Alcorn State Univ	MS	15,854	C
Alderson Broaddus Univ	WV	26,149	C
Allegheny College	PA	55,420	VC
Alma College	MI	47,548	C
American Univ	DC	59,379	HC+
American Univ of PR	PR	16,130	
Amherst College	MA		HC+
Anderson Univ	IN	38,200	C
Andrews Univ	MI	28,030	C+
Angelo State Univ	TX	15,263	NC
Anna Maria College	MA	48,186	C
Appalachian State Univ	NC	14,416	VC
Arcadia Univ	PA	33,570	C+
Arizona State Univ at the Tempe Campus	AZ	21,756	VC
Arkansas Baptist College	AR	20,280	NC
Arkansas State Univ	AR	16,190	C
Arkansas Tech Univ	AR	15,484	C
Armstrong State Univ	GA	16,962	C
Ashford Univ	CA	10,480	C
Ashland Univ	OH	21,440	C
Assumption College	MA	47,920	C+
Atlantic Union College	MA	27,228	C
Auburn Univ	AL	23,594	VC+
Auburn Univ at Montgomery	AL	15,290	C
Augsburg College	MN	43,929	C
Augusta Univ	GA	4,632	C
Augustana College	IL	49,658	VC
Augustana Univ	SD	38,424	VC
Aurora Univ	IL	33,970	C
Austin College	TX	45,875	VC
Austin Peay State Univ	TN	16,397	C
Averett Univ	VA	40,970	LC
Avila Univ	MO	35,480	C
Azusa Pacific Univ	CA	43,972	C
Baker Univ	KS	33,350	C+
Baldwin Wallace Univ	OH	41,106	C
Ball State Univ	IN	19,590	C
Bard College	NY	64,024	HC
Bard College at Simon's Rock	MA	65,795	MC
Barnard College/Columbia Univ	NY	62,741	MC
Barry Univ	FL	37,830	C
Bayamon Central Univ	PR	12,490	
Baylor Univ	TX	53,760	HC
Belhaven Univ	MS	31,016	C
Bellarmine Univ	KY	51,220	C
Belmont Univ	TN	40,970	VC
Beloit College	WI	55,206	HC
Bemidji State Univ	MN	16,056	VC
Benedict College	SC	28,238	NC
Benedictine College	KS	36,200	VC
Benedictine Univ	IL	38,300	C
Bennett College	NC	27,302	NC
Bennington College	VT	63,960	MC
Berea College	KY	7,042	C
Bethany College	WV	36,300	NC
Bethel Univ	MN	45,270	VC
Bethune-Cookman Univ	FL	22,970	C
Biola Univ	CA	46,402	C+
Blackburn College	IL	28,526	LC
Bloomfield College	NJ	39,100	LC
Bloomsburg Univ of Pennsylvania	PA	19,066	LC
Bluefield State College	WV	5,832	LC
Bluffton Univ	OH	40,950	C
Boise State Univ	ID	14,860	C
Boston College	MA	65,737	MC
Boston Univ	MA	65,110	MC
Bowdoin College	ME	63,500	MC
Bowie State Univ	MD	26,728	LC
Bowling Green State Univ	OH	19,747	C
Brandeis Univ	MA	65,925	MC
Brescia Univ	KY	29,890	VC+
Briar Cliff Univ	IA	36,956	C
Bridgewater College	VA	44,510	C
Bridgewater State Univ	MA	21,810	C
Brigham Young Univ	UT	12,748	HC
Brigham Young Univ/Hawaii	HI	11,290	C
Brown Univ	RI	64,566	MC
Bryan College	TN	31,440	C
Bryant Univ	RI	55,646	VC
Bryn Mawr College	PA	59,890	MC
Bucknell Univ	PA	64,616	MC
Buena Vista Univ	IA	41,514	C
Butler Univ	IN	51,352	VC
Caldwell Univ	NJ	42,165	NC
Calif Baptist Univ	CA	41,392	C
Calif Inst of Technology	CA	58,761	MC
Calif Lutheran Univ	CA	52,853	C
Calif Polytechnic State Univ	CA	17,979	HC+
Calif State Polytechnic Univ, Pomona	CA	21,541	C
Cal State, Bakersfield	CA	19,191	LC
Cal State, Chico	CA	21,440	C
Cal State, Dominguez Hills	CA	19,022	LC
Cal State, East Bay	CA	19,413	C
Cal State, Fresno	CA	16,902	LC
Cal State, Fullerton	CA	21,902	C
Cal State, Long Beach	CA	18,850	C
Cal State, Los Angeles	CA	17,186	LC
Cal State, Monterey Bay	CA	26,871	LC
Cal State, Northridge	CA	16,859	LC
Cal State, Sacramento	CA	20,332	C
Cal State, San Bernardino	CA	12,000	C
Cal State, San Marcos	CA	24,184	LC
Cal State, Stanislaus	CA	16,212	C
Calvin College	MI	41,570	VC+
Cameron Univ	OK	11,072	NC
Campbellsville Univ	KY	32,492	C
Canisius College	NY	47,537	C
Capital Univ	OH	42,982	C
Cardinal Stritch Univ	WI	36,462	C
Caribbean Univ	PR	15,471	
Carleton College	MN	64,071	MC
Carnegie Mellon Univ	PA	67,980	MC
Carroll College	MT	39,972	C+
Carroll Univ	WI	38,100	C+
Case Western Reserve Univ	OH	60,304	MC
Castleton Univ	VT	20,186	C
Catawba College	NC	39,820	C
Cedar Crest College	PA	46,715	C
Cedarville Univ	OH	34,990	VC
Central College	IA	44,592	C
Central Conn State Univ	CT	21,203	C
Central Methodist Univ	MO	36,830	VC
Central Mich Univ	MI	20,330	C
Central State Univ	OH	18,564	C
Central Washington Univ	WA	16,803	C
Centre College	KY	49,250	HC
Chaminade Univ of Honolulu	HI	36,000	C
Champlain College	VT	53,132	C+
Chapman Univ	CA	63,078	VC+
Charleston Southern Univ	SC	32,400	C
Chestnut Hill College	PA	43,410	C
Cheyney Univ of Pennsylvania	PA	20,896	LC
Chicago State Univ	IL	20,144	C
Christian Brothers Univ	TN	31,670	VC
Christopher Newport Univ	VA	23,968	VC+
CUNY/Brooklyn College	NY	5,884	C+
CUNY/City College	NY	20,319	VC
CUNY/College of Staten Island	NY	17,840	NC
CUNY/Hunter College	NY	31,098	VC
CUNY/Lehman College	NY	5,778	HC+
CUNY/Meger Evers College	NY	6,680	NC
CUNY/Queens College	NY	27,896	C
Claflin Univ	SC	33,764	LC
Clarion Univ of Pennsylvania	PA	21,608	LC
Clark Atlanta Univ	GA	31,019	LC
Clark Univ	MA	51,600	HC+
Clarke Univ	IA	38,940	C
Clarkson Univ	NY	60,392	HC
Clemson Univ	SC		HC
Cleveland State Univ	OH	22,196	C
Coastal Carolina Univ	SC	19,766	C
Coe College	IA	51,570	VC
Coker College	SC	34,810	LC
Colby College	ME	64,060	MC
Colgate Univ	NY	65,030	MC
College of Charleston	SC	22,699	C
College of Mount St. Vincent	NY	45,620	C
College of St. Benedict	MN	52,806	C
College of St. Elizabeth	NJ	44,432	LC
College of St. Scholastica	MN	44,640	C
College of the Holy Cross	MA	62,165	MC
College of the Ozarks	MO	7,230	C
College of William & Mary	VA		MC
Colo College	CO	62,560	MC
Colo Mesa Univ	CO	18,955	LC
Colo State Univ	CO	22,162	VC
Colo Technical Univ	CO	21,455	NC
Columbia College - Missouri	MO	27,803	C
Columbia Univ/ School of General Studies	NY	61,470	MC
Columbia Univ/City of New York	NY	62,958	MC
Columbus State Univ	GA	14,336	LC
Concord Univ	WV	14,954	C
Concordia Univ Nebr	NE	36,280	VC
Concordia Univ St. Paul	MN	29,050	C
Concordia Univ Texas	TX	40,210	C
Concordia Univ, Ann Arbor	MI	35,945	VC
Concordia Univ, Chicago	IL	39,694	C
Converse College	SC	26,495	C
Coppin State Univ	MD	17,041	VC
Cornell College	IA	48,800	VC
Cornell Univ	NY	64,853	MC
Covenant College	GA	38,990	VC
Dakota State Univ	SD	13,811	C
Dallas Baptist Univ	TX	33,713	C
Daniel Webster College	NH	26,984	C
Dartmouth College	NH	66,174	MC
Davis & Elkins College	WV	38,242	LC
Delaware State Univ	DE	19,376	NC
Delaware Valley Univ	PA	49,796	C
Denison Univ	OH	58,860	MC
DePaul Univ	IL	47,623	VC
DePauw Univ	IN	58,688	HC+
DeSales Univ	PA	43,970	C
Dickinson College	PA	63,974	MC
Dickinson State Univ	ND	12,372	LC
Dillard Univ	LA	20,940	VC
Doane Univ	NE	39,184	VC
Dominican College	NY	31,270	LC
Dominican Univ	IL	41,222	C
Dordt College	IA	37,860	C+
Drake Univ	IA	45,056	HC
Drew Univ/College of Liberal Arts	NJ	61,048	VC
Drexel Univ	PA	65,432	VC+
Drury Univ	MO	33,791	VC
Duke Univ	NC	64,188	
Duquesne Univ	PA	46,822	VC
Earlham College	IN	54,870	HC
East Carolina Univ	NC	16,937	C
East Central Univ	OK	13,056	C
East Stroudsburg Univ	PA	18,334	C
East Tenn State Univ	TN	13,994	C
Eastern Conn State Univ	CT	23,059	C
Eastern Illinois Univ	IL	21,126	C
Eastern Kentucky Univ	KY	16,908	C
Eastern Mennonite Univ	VA	42,550	C
Eastern Mich Univ	MI	19,761	C
Eastern Nazarene College	MA	39,955	C
Eastern New Mexico Univ	NM	14,416	C
Eastern Oregon Univ	OR	17,715	C
Eastern Washington Univ	WA	25,572	LC
Eckerd College	FL	52,874	C
Edinboro Univ	PA	15,940	LC
Edward Waters College	FL	20,607	NC
Elizabeth City State Univ	NC	14,745	C
Elizabethtown College	PA	54,050	C
Elmhurst College	IL	45,428	C
Elms College	MA	45,646	VC
Elon Univ	NC	44,599	VC+
Embry-Riddle Aeronautical Univ - Daytona Beach	FL	44,712	VC
Emory and Henry College	VA	41,410	C
Emory Univ	GA	60,786	MC
Emporia State Univ	KS	14,570	C
Endicott College	MA	44,604	VC+
Eureka College	IL	30,220	C
Evangel Univ	MO	28,898	C
Fairleigh Dickinson Univ/ College at Florham	NJ	52,062	C

ST = STATE $IS = IN-STATE COSTS SR = SELECTOR RATING

School	ST	$IS	SR
Fairleigh Dickinson Univ/ Metropolitan Campus	NJ	40,254	C
Fairmont State Univ	WV	15,726	C
Faulkner Univ	AL	26,410	C
Fayetteville State Univ	NC	17,756	C
Fisk Univ	TN	32,066	LC
Fitchburg State Univ	MA	21,819	C
Florida A&M Univ	FL	15,361	C
Florida Atlantic Univ	FL	17,339	C
Florida Gulf Coast Univ	FL	9,682	C
Florida Inst of Technology	FL	53,306	VC
Florida International Univ	FL	19,854	C+
Florida Memorial Univ	FL	22,270	LC
Florida State Univ	FL	16,771	HC
Fontbonne Univ	MO	33,717	C
Fordham Univ	NY	65,918	MC
Fort Hays State Univ	KS	12,131	C
Fort Valley State Univ	GA	17,988	VC
Framingham State Univ	MA	20,584	C
Francis Marion Univ	SC	16,464	LC
Franciscan Univ of Steubenville	OH	33,980	VC
Franklin College	IN	39,380	C
Franklin Univ	OH	56,262	SP
Freed-Hardeman Univ	TN	29,450	C
Friends Univ	KS	34,455	C
Frostburg State Univ	MD	17,280	LC
Furman Univ	SC	58,092	VC+
Gannon Univ	PA	42,032	C
Gardner-Webb Univ	NC	39,200	C+
Geneva College	PA	35,450	C
George Fox Univ	OR	42,938	C
George Mason Univ	VA	15,724	VC
George Washington Univ	DC	62,835	MC
Georgetown Univ	DC	65,926	MC
Georgia College & State Univ	GA	21,148	C+
Georgia Inst of Technology	GA	23,360	MC
Georgia Southern Univ	GA	16,596	C
Georgia Southwestern State Univ	GA	13,870	C
Georgia State Univ	GA	24,332	VC
Gettysburg College	PA	63,000	HC
Gonzaga Univ	WA	50,888	HC
Gordon College	MA	46,472	C+
Goshen College	IN	42,500	C
Goucher College	MD	55,716	VC
Graceland Univ	IA	35,290	C
Grambling State Univ	LA	15,701	C
Grand Valley State Univ	MI	22,250	C+
Grand View Univ	IA	32,302	C
Greenville College	IL	27,012	C
Grinnell College	IA	60,738	MC
Grove City College	PA	25,692	VC
Gustavus Adolphus College	MN	52,433	HC
Gwynedd Mercy Univ	PA	43,780	LC
Hamilton College	NY	64,250	MC
Hampden-Sydney College	VA	56,248	C+
Hampshire College	MA	63,824	MC
Hampton Univ	VA	34,926	LC
Hanover College	IN	46,364	C+
Harding Univ	AR	25,421	C
Hardin-Simmons Univ	TX	33,966	C
Hartwick College	NY	51,270	C
Harvard College/Harvard Univ	MA	60,659	MC
Harvey Mudd College	CA	67,155	MC
Hastings College	NE	35,380	C+
Haverford College	PA	66,490	MC
Hawaii Pacific Univ	HI	33,420	C
Heidelberg Univ	OH	39,200	C
Henderson State Univ	AR	15,516	LC
Hendrix College	AR	54,020	VC+
Heritage Univ	WA	19,825	NC
High Point Univ	NC	45,977	C
Hiram College	OH	43,230	C
Hofstra Univ	NY	55,960	C+
Holy Names Univ	CA	46,630	LC
Hood College	MD	54,840	C
Hope College	MI	39,940	VC
Houghton College	NY	39,090	C
Howard Payne Univ	TX	34,320	C
Howard Univ	DC	37,616	C+
Huntington Univ	IN	33,996	C
Huston-Tillotson Univ	TX	18,124	LC
Idaho State Univ	ID	13,619	NC
Illinois College	IL	40,850	VC
Illinois Inst of Technology	IL	56,826	HC+
Illinois State Univ	IL	23,418	VC
Illinois Wesleyan Univ	IL	56,430	VC+
Indiana Inst of Technology	IN	34,240	LC
Indiana State Univ	IN	23,223	LC
Indiana Univ Bloomington	IN	20,429	VC
Indiana Univ of Pennsylvania	PA	23,614	LC
Indiana Univ South Bend	IN	14,242	C
Indiana Univ Southeast	IN	14,242	LC
Indiana Univ-Purdue Univ Fort Wayne	IN	17,553	C
Indiana Univ-Purdue Univ Indianapolis	IN	18,635	C
Indiana Wesleyan Univ	IN	33,674	C
Inter-American Univ of PR Ponce	PR	19,549	
Inter-American Univ of PR-Aguadilla Campus	PR	21,657	
Inter-American Univ of PR-Arecibo Campus	PR	18,245	
Inter-American Univ of PR-Bayamon	PR	18,785	
Inter-American Univ of PR-Fajardo Campus	PR	18,336	
Inter-American Univ of PR-Metropolitan Campus	PR	20,045	
Inter-American Univ of PR-San Germán	PR	20,042	
Iona College	NY	50,984	C
Iowa State Univ	IA	17,570	C
Ithaca College	NY	56,766	VC
Jackson State Univ	MS	15,879	LC
Jacksonville State Univ	AL	14,628	LC
Jacksonville Univ	FL	46,230	C
James Madison Univ	VA	19,084	VC
John Carroll Univ	OH	49,740	C+
Johns Hopkins Univ	MD	65,386	MC
Johnson & Wales Univ/ Providence Campus	RI	42,248	C
Johnson C. Smith Univ	NC	25,336	LC
Judson Univ	IL	37,700	C
Juniata College	PA	53,760	VC
Kalamazoo College	MI	53,931	HC+
Kansas State Univ	KS	17,780	VC
Kansas Wesleyan Univ	KS	36,600	C
Kean Univ	NJ	24,650	C
Keene State College	NH	24,003	LC
Kennesaw State Univ	GA	19,592	VC
Kent State Univ	OH	20,732	C
Kentucky State Univ	KY	13,364	LC
Kentucky Wesleyan College	KY	32,080	C
Kettering Univ	MI	47,570	HC
King's College	PA	46,858	C
Knox College	IL	52,615	VC+
Kutztown Univ of Pennsylvania	PA	19,056	LC
La Roche College	PA	37,924	LC
La Salle Univ	PA	55,790	C
La Sierra Univ	CA	39,690	VC
Lafayette College	PA	63,355	MC
LaGrange College	GA	39,930	C
Lake Forest College	IL	50,652	VC
Lakeland Univ	WI	35,130	C
Lamar Univ	TX	18,014	LC
Lander Univ	SC	43,994	C
Lane College	TN	16,550	C
Langston Univ	OK	14,314	C
Lawrence Tech Univ	MI	39,770	VC
Lawrence Univ	WI	54,498	HC
Le Moyne College	NY	46,000	C
Lebanon Valley College	PA	51,530	C
Lehigh Univ	PA	61,010	MC
LeMoyne-Owen College	TN	16,980	C
Lenoir-Rhyne Univ	NC	43,200	C
LeTourneau Univ	TX	38,250	VC
Lewis & Clark College	OR	58,434	HC+
Lewis Univ	IL	40,370	C
Lewis-Clark State College	ID	14,202	C
Liberty Univ	VA	19,101	C
Limestone College	SC	32,100	C
Lincoln Univ	MO	13,602	NC
Lindenwood Univ	MO	25,132	C
Linfield College	OR	52,010	C
Lipscomb Univ	TN	41,296	VC
LIU Brooklyn	NY	49,682	C
LIU Post	NY	49,682	C
Lock Haven Univ of Pennsylvania	PA	18,028	LC
Longwood Univ	VA	22,184	C
Loras College	IA	39,222	C
Louisiana State Univ and A&M College	LA	18,677	VC
Louisiana State Univ in Shreveport	LA	6,902	C
Louisiana Tech Univ	LA	11,422	VC
Loyola Marymount Univ	CA	58,038	HC
Loyola Univ Chicago	IL	55,802	VC
Loyola Univ Maryland	MD	60,300	VC
Luther College	IA	48,540	C+
Lynchburg College	VA	46,740	C
Macalester College	MN	61,905	MC
MacMurray College	IL	33,620	C
Madonna Univ	MI	29,050	C
Maharishi Univ of Management	IA	34,930	VC
Malone Univ	OH	38,448	C
Manchester Univ	IN	40,422	C
Manhattan College	NY	51,750	C+
Manhattanville College	NY	51,440	C+
Mansfield Univ	PA	23,376	LC
Marietta College	OH	46,190	C
Marist College	NY	49,860	VC
Marquette Univ	WI	48,390	VC+
Mars Hill Univ	NC	42,688	C
Marshall Univ	WV	17,242	C
Marygrove College	MI	28,926	NC
Maryville College	TN	44,410	C
Mass College of Liberal Arts	MA	20,128	C
Mass Inst of Technology	MA	62,662	MC
McDaniel College	MD	51,380	VC
McKendree Univ	IL	37,940	C+
McMurry Univ	TX	34,259	LC
McNeese State Univ	LA	7,838	C
Mercer Univ	GA	45,348	VC
Mercy College	NY	31,776	C
Meredith College	NC	45,297	C
Merrimack College	MA	52,770	C
Messiah College	PA	43,100	C+
Methodist Univ	NC	43,600	C
Metropolitan State Univ	MN	7,566	C
Metropolitan State Univ of Denver	CO	29,889	LC
Miami Univ	OH	27,190	HC+
Mich State Univ	MI	23,898	VC+
Mich Tech Univ	MI	24,739	VC+
Middle Tenn State Univ	TN	8,650	C
Middlebury College	VT	64,332	MC
Midland Univ	NE	37,468	
Midwestern State Univ	TX	17,572	C
Miles College	AL	18,646	NC
Millersville Univ of Pennsylvania	PA	23,782	C
Milligan College	TN	38,150	C
Mills College	CA	59,163	VC
Minn State Univ, Moorhead	MN	15,941	C
Minot State Univ	ND	12,732	C
Misericordia Univ	PA	43,840	C
Miss College	MS	25,850	C
Miss State Univ	MS	11,454	C+
Miss Valley State Univ	MS	13,233	LC
Missouri Southern State Univ	MO	12,499	C
Missouri State Univ	MO	15,190	C+
Missouri Univ of Science and Technology	MO	18,655	HC
Missouri Western State Univ	MO	16,741	
Molloy College	NY	40,440	C
Monmouth College	IL	42,260	C
Monmouth Univ	NJ	46,234	C
Montana State Univ	MT	15,500	C+
Montana Tech of the Univ of Montana	MT	15,447	C+
Montclair State Univ	NJ	26,210	LC
Moravian College	PA	53,117	
Morehead State Univ	KY	17,422	C
Morehouse College	GA	40,064	C
Morgan State Univ	MD	17,190	LC
Morningside College	IA	36,865	C
Mount Holyoke College	MA	56,746	MC
Mount Marty College	SD	32,972	C
Mount Mercy Univ	IA	36,826	C
Mount St. Mary's Univ	MD	51,610	C
Mount Vernon Nazarene Univ	OH	34,500	C
Muhlenberg College	PA	56,645	VC+
Murray State Univ	KY	16,998	C
Muskingum Univ	OH	35,966	C
National Univ	CA	14,730	LC
Nebr Wesleyan Univ	NE	38,140	C+
New England College	NH	50,364	C
New Jersey City Univ	NJ	21,456	LC
New Jersey Inst of Technology	NJ	29,569	VC
New Mexico Highlands Univ	NM	11,904	NC
New Mexico Inst of Mining and Technology	NM	14,833	HC
New Mexico State Univ	NM	14,050	C
New York Inst of Technology	NY	48,730	C
New York Univ	NY	65,860	MC
Newberry College	SC	34,550	C
Newbury College	MA	46,950	C
Niagara Univ	NY	41,010	C
Nicholls State Univ	LA	10,534	C
Norfolk State Univ	VA	25,702	LC
N Car A&T State Univ	NC	13,365	LC
N Car Central Univ	NC	9,000	C
N Car State Univ	NC	19,515	HC+
North Central College	IL	48,712	VC
N Dak State Univ	ND	16,245	C
Northeastern Illinois Univ	IL	12,529	LC
Northeastern State Univ	OK	8,615	VC
Northeastern Univ	MA	62,703	MC
Northern Arizona Univ	AZ	20,246	VC
Northern Illinois Univ	IL	20,176	C
Northern Kentucky Univ	KY	16,486	C
Northern Mich Univ	MI	19,604	C
Northwest Christian Univ	OR	36,580	C
Northwest Missouri State Univ	MO	17,737	C
Northwest Nazarene Univ	ID	36,000	C
Northwestern College of Iowa	IA	38,400	C+
Northwestern Okla State Univ	OK	13,072	NC
Northwestern Univ	IL	66,344	MC
Norwich Univ	VT	28,212	C
Notre Dame de Namur Univ	CA	46,526	LC
Notre Dame of Maryland Univ	MD	46,465	VC
Nova Southeastern Univ	FL	38,534	C+
Nyack College	NY	34,050	NC
Oakland Univ	MI	20,763	C
Oakwood Univ	AL	43,758	C
Oberlin College	OH	66,012	MC
Ohio Dominican Univ	OH	41,340	C+
Ohio Northern Univ	OH	44,050	VC
Ohio State Univ at Columbus	OH	21,703	HC+
Ohio Univ	OH	22,924	C
Ohio Wesleyan Univ	OH	49,460	VC
Okla Baptist Univ	OK	32,320	C
Okla Christian Univ	OK	27,650	VC
Okla State Univ	OK	17,180	VC
Old Dominion Univ	VA	20,910	C
Olivet College	MI	36,110	LC
Olivet Nazarene Univ	IL	41,840	C
Oral Roberts Univ	OK	34,316	C
Oregon State Univ	OR	22,519	VC
Otterbein Univ	OH	41,630	C
Ouachita Baptist Univ	AR	32,320	C
Pace Univ	NY	58,248	C
Pacific Lutheran Univ	WA	49,960	VC
Pacific Union College	CA	36,009	VC
Pacific Univ	OR	52,876	C
Palm Beach Atlantic Univ	FL	39,720	C
Park Univ	MO	20,329	C
Penn State Erie/The Behrend College	PA	16,256	C
Pennsylvania College of Technology	PA	27,333	NC
Pepperdine Univ	CA	74,460	HC+
Peru State College	NE	14,768	NC
Philander Smith College	AR	20,814	LC
Plymouth State Univ	NH	23,180	LC
Point Loma Nazarene Univ	CA	43,450	C
Point Park Univ	PA	41,270	C
Pomona College	CA	64,957	MC
Portland State Univ	OR	19,443	C
Prairie View A&M Univ	TX	15,205	LC
Princeton Univ	NJ	57,610	MC
Principia College	IL	39,010	C+
Providence College	RI	60,760	VC
Purdue Univ/Northwest	IN	15,038	C
Purdue Univ/West Lafayette	IN	20,032	MC
Quincy Univ	IL	36,998	C
Quinnipiac Univ	CT	59,110	C
Radford Univ	VA	19,027	LC
Ramapo College of New Jersey	NJ	25,338	C
Randolph-Macon College	VA	49,910	C
Regis Univ	CO	44,520	C
Rensselaer Polytechnic Inst	NY	63,436	MC
Rhode Island College	RI	17,694	LC
Rhodes College	TN	51,900	HC
Rice Univ	TX	57,668	MC
Rivier Univ	NH	40,410	VC
Roanoke College	VA	54,114	VC
Rochester Inst of Technology	NY	50,842	HC
Rockford Univ	IL	36,030	C
Rockhurst Univ	MO	29,220	C
Rocky Mountain College	MT	34,270	C
Roger Williams Univ	RI	46,296	C+
Rollins College	FL	58,670	HC
Roosevelt Univ	IL	40,651	VC
Rose-Hulman Inst of Technology	IN	57,303	MC
Rowan Univ	NJ	24,491	VC+
Rust College	MS	10,600	C
Rutgers Univ - Camden	NJ	26,146	C
Rutgers Univ - New Brunswick	NJ	26,632	HC
Rutgers Univ - Newark	NJ	27,288	C
Sacred Heart Univ	CT	52,750	C
Saginaw Valley State Univ	MI	18,530	C
St. Anselm College	NH	52,560	C+
St. Augustine's Univ	NC	26,048	C
St. Francis Univ	PA	42,268	NC
St. John's Univ	MN	51,624	C
St. Joseph's Univ	PA	57,544	VC+
St. Louis Univ	MO	49,866	HC
St. Martin's Univ	WA	45,056	C
St. Mary-of-the-Woods College	IN	39,632	LC
St. Mary's College of Calif	CA	57,420	C
St. Mary's Univ of Minn	MN	41,210	VC
St. Michael's College	VT	51,725	VC+
St. Peter's Univ	NJ	49,192	C
St. Vincent College	PA	44,626	C
St. Xavier Univ	IL	43,310	C
Salisbury Univ	MD	20,714	VC
Sam Houston State Univ	TX	18,792	C
Samford Univ	AL	39,232	VC
San Diego State Univ	CA	21,896	C+
San Francisco State Univ	CA	18,514	LC
San Jose State Univ	CA	21,540	C
Savannah State Univ	GA	15,631	C
Scripps College	CA	66,664	MC
Seattle Pacific Univ	WA	47,439	C+
Seattle Univ	WA	50,811	VC+
Seton Hall Univ	NJ	55,514	C
Seton Hill Univ	PA	46,972	C
Sewanee: The Univ of the South	TN	54,500	MC
Shaw Univ	NC	24,638	C
Shepherd Univ, West Virginia	WV	17,224	C
Shippensburg Univ of Pennsylvania	PA	23,208	C
Siena College	NY	48,916	C+
Silver Lake College of the Holy Family	WI	36,290	LC
Simmons College	MA	53,090	VC
Simpson College	IA	43,839	VC
Skidmore College	NY	64,214	HC
Slippery Rock Univ of Pennsylvania	PA	10,360	C
Smith College	MA	63,914	MC
Sonoma State Univ	CA	27,806	C
S Car State Univ	SC	20,805	LC
S Dak School of Mines and Technology	SD	18,645	VC
S Dak State Univ	SD	15,634	C
Southeast Missouri State Univ	MO	15,498	C
Southeastern Louisiana Univ	LA	16,237	C
Southeastern Okla State Univ	OK	11,875	C
Southern Adventist Univ	TN	27,600	C
Southern Arkansas Univ	AR	21,532	C
Southern Conn State Univ	CT	21,924	LC
Southern Illinois Univ Carbondale	IL	23,667	C
Southern Illinois Univ Edwardsville	IL	22,643	C

ST = STATE **$IS** = IN-STATE COSTS **SR** = SELECTOR RATING

School	ST	$IS	SR
Southern Methodist Univ	TX	66,483	MC
Southern Nazarene Univ	OK	32,798	NC
Southern New Hampshire Univ	NH	43,198	C
Southern Oregon Univ	OR	19,117	C
Southern Univ and A&M College	LA	16,074	LC+
Southern Univ at New Orleans	LA	8,014	LC
Southern Wesleyan Univ	SC	32,130	LC
Southwest Baptist Univ	MO	29,900	LC
Southwest Minn State Univ	MN	17,783	C
Southwestern Adventist Univ	TX	27,756	LC
Southwestern College	KS	31,531	C
Southwestern Okla State Univ	OK	11,790	C
Southwestern Univ	TX	50,720	VC
Spelman College	GA	38,751	C
Spring Arbor Univ	MI	36,000	C
Spring Hill College	AL	48,488	C
St. Ambrose Univ	IA	39,019	C
St. Bonaventure Univ	NY	44,237	C
St. Cloud State Univ	MN	10,600	C
St. Edward's Univ	TX	53,100	VC
St. John Fisher College	NY	43,620	C
St. John's Univ	NY	55,850	C
St. Joseph's College, New York/Long Island Campus	NY	25,124	C
St. Lawrence Univ	NY	64,390	VC
St. Mary's College of Maryland	MD	26,634	VC
St. Mary's Univ	TX	37,500	C
St. Norbert College	WI	44,525	VC
St. Olaf College	MN	54,260	HC+
St. Thomas Univ	FL	36,360	LC
Stanford Univ	CA	60,409	MC
SUNY / Empire State College	NY	9,145	SP
SUNY / SUNY College at Old Westbury	NY	16,860	C
SUNY / SUNY Fredonia	NY	20,818	C
SUNY / SUNY Oneonta	NY	19,712	C+
SUNY / SUNY Plattsburgh	NY	18,814	C
SUNY / SUNY Potsdam	NY	20,404	C+
SUNY / Univ at Buffalo	NY	23,122	C+
SUNY at Binghamton	NY	22,861	MC
SUNY at New Paltz	NY	19,200	C
SUNY at Oswego	NY	21,351	C
SUNY Polytechnic Inst	NY	19,473	VC
SUNY SUNY Albany	NY	22,165	C
Stephen F. Austin State Univ	TX	18,406	LC
Stetson Univ	FL	53,544	VC
Stevens Inst of Technology	NJ	62,338	MC
Stillman College	AL	20,738	C
Stockton Univ	NJ	25,059	
Stonehill College	MA	55,030	C+
Stony Brook Univ/The SUNY	NY	21,881	MC
Suffolk Univ	MA	50,308	C
Sul Ross State Univ	TX	15,021	LC
Susquehanna Univ	PA	55,340	VC
Swarthmore College	PA	63,550	MC
Syracuse Univ	NY	60,239	VC
Talladega College	AL	19,215	C
Tarleton State Univ	TX	15,248	LC
Taylor Univ	IN	40,317	C+
Temple Univ	PA	24,392	VC
Tenn State Univ	TN	14,423	C
Tenn Tech Univ	TN	17,050	C
Texas A&M Univ	TX	20,521	VC+
Texas A&M Univ at Commerce	TX	10,496	C
Texas A&M Univ at Corpus Christi	TX	16,851	LC
Texas A&M Univ at Kingsville	TX	7,500	LC
Texas Christian Univ	TX	54,670	HC
Texas Lutheran Univ	TX	38,620	C
Texas Southern Univ	TX	18,212	LC
Texas State Univ	TX	19,350	C
Texas Tech Univ	TX	18,736	C+
Texas Wesleyan Univ	TX	35,134	C
Texas Woman's Univ	TX	15,302	LC
The Catholic Univ of America	DC	56,356	VC
The Citadel, The Military College of S Car	SC	35,339	C
The College at Brockport - SUNY	NY	20,346	C
The College of New Jersey	NJ	31,909	HC
The College of St. Rose	NY	43,048	C
The College of Wooster	OH	57,900	VC+
The Lincoln Univ	PA	15,154	NC
The Univ of Akron	OH	21,477	C
The Univ of Tenn at Chattanooga	TN	16,744	C
The Univ of Tenn at Knoxville	TN	22,112	VC
The Univ of Tenn at Martin	TN	14,876	C
The Univ of Utah	UT	17,924	VC
Thiel College	PA	41,590	C
Thomas College	ME	35,268	LC
Thomas Edison State Univ	NJ	6,350	NC
Thomas More College	KY	36,720	C
Tougaloo College	MS	17,980	NC
Touro College	NY	28,950	VC
Towson Univ	MD	17,408	VC
Transylvania Univ	KY	45,690	VC+
Trine Univ	IN	41,310	C
Trinity Christian College	IL	35,580	C
Trinity College	CT	63,920	HC+
Trinity Univ	TX	52,314	HC+
Troy Univ	AL	16,171	C
Truman State Univ	MO	16,014	HC
Tufts Univ	MA		MC
Tusculum College	TN	31,625	C
Tuskegee Univ	AL	28,164	C
Union College	NE	23,270	C
Union College	NY	64,320	MC
Union Inst & Univ	OH	8,912	SP
Union Univ	TN	33,970	VC
United States Air Force Academy	CO		C
United States Military Academy at West Point	NY		HC+
United States Naval Academy	MD		MC
Universidad Adventista de las Antillas	PR	16,606	
Universidad Politecnica de PR, Hato Rey campus	PR	23,514	
Univ of PR, at Arecibo	PR	12,652	
Univ of Alabama	AL	24,320	C+
Univ of Alabama at Birmingham	AL	19,906	C
Univ of Alabama in Huntsville	AL	19,445	VC
Univ of Alaska Anchorage	AK	16,652	NC
Univ of Alaska Fairbanks	AK	16,179	C
Univ of Arizona	AZ	23,100	C
Univ of Arkansas at Fayetteville	AR	19,152	C+
Univ of Arkansas at Little Rock	AR	18,211	C
Univ of Arkansas at Pine Bluff	AR	13,541	C
Univ of Bridgeport	CT	44,430	LC
Univ of Calif at Berkeley	CA	28,853	MC
Univ of Calif at Davis	CA	28,468	HC
Univ of Calif at Irvine	CA	26,484	VC
Univ of Calif at Los Angeles	CA	30,162	MC
Univ of Calif at Riverside	CA	29,227	C+
Univ of Calif at Santa Barbara	CA	29,091	HC
Univ of Calif San Diego	CA	30,150	MC
Univ of Calif, Santa Cruz	CA	28,731	C+
Univ of Central Arkansas	AR	14,472	VC
Univ of Central Florida	FL	15,922	VC
Univ of Central Missouri	MO	18,982	C
Univ of Central Okla	OK	13,486	C
Univ of Chicago	IL	67,584	MC
Univ of Cincinnati	OH	21,964	VC
Univ of Colo Boulder	CO	24,285	VC+
Univ of Colo Colo Springs	CO	19,663	C
Univ of Colo Denver	CO	23,230	C
Univ of Conn	CT	25,538	HC
Univ of Dallas	TX	45,500	VC+
Univ of Dayton	OH	53,620	C
Univ of Delaware	DE	24,976	VC+
Univ of Denver	CO	58,443	VC+
Univ of Detroit Mercy	MI	48,816	C+
Univ of Dubuque	IA	37,824	C
Univ of Evansville	IN	44,186	VC+
Univ of Findlay	OH	60,139	C
Univ of Florida	FL	16,291	HC+
Univ of Georgia	GA	21,250	HC
Univ of Great Falls	MT	38,524	C
Univ of Hartford	CT	49,776	C
Univ of Hawaii at Hilo	HI	18,038	C
Univ of Hawaii at Manoa	HI	23,221	C
Univ of Houston-Downtown	TX	7,241	C
Univ of Idaho	ID	15,348	C
Univ of Illinois at Chicago	IL	25,006	VC
Univ of Indianapolis	IN	36,480	C
Univ of Iowa	IA	18,683	VC+
Univ of Jamestown	ND	28,508	C
Univ of Kansas	KS	20,135	C+
Univ of Kentucky	KY	33,306	C
Univ of La Verne	CA	55,600	C
Univ of Louisiana at Lafayette	LA	14,516	C
Univ of Louisiana at Monroe	LA	15,970	C
Univ of Louisville	KY	19,824	C
Univ of Maine	ME	20,792	C
Univ of Maine at Farmington	ME	18,187	C
Univ of Maine at Fort Kent	ME	15,165	LC
Univ of Mary Hardin-Baylor	TX	33,950	C+
Univ of Mary Washington	VA	24,764	VC
Univ of Maryland/Baltimore County	MD	21,296	VC
Univ of Maryland/College Park	MD	21,938	HC
Univ of Maryland/Eastern Shore	MD	17,013	C
Univ of Maryland/Univ College	MD	25,966	LC
Univ of Mass Amherst	MA	26,199	VC+
Univ of Mass Boston	MA	13,435	C
Univ of Mass Dartmouth	MA	25,658	C
Univ of Mass Lowell	MA	26,380	C
Univ of Memphis	TN	18,278	C
Univ of Miami	FL	63,494	MC
Univ of Mich/Ann Arbor	MI	24,410	MC
Univ of Mich/Dearborn	MI	11,757	VC
Univ of Mich-Flint	MI	17,607	C+
Univ of Minn/Duluth	MN	20,292	C+
Univ of Minn/Morris	MN	20,760	VC
Univ of Minn/Twin Cities	MN	23,519	HC+
Univ of Miss	MS	17,746	C+
Univ of Missouri/Columbia	MO	18,201	MC
Univ of Missouri-Kansas City	MO	19,563	VC
Univ of Missouri-St. Louis	MO		C
Univ of Montana	MT	14,105	C
Univ of Mount Union	OH	38,970	C
Univ of Nebr - Kearney	NE	16,546	LC
Univ of Nebr - Lincoln	NE	18,589	VC
Univ of Nebr - Omaha	NE	16,120	C
Univ of Nevada, Las Vegas	NV	17,553	C
Univ of Nevada/Reno	NV	18,010	C
Univ of New Hampshire	NH	28,562	VC
Univ of New Hampshire - Manchester	NH	14,490	C
Univ of New Haven	CT	52,190	C
Univ of New Mexico	NM	15,404	C
Univ of New Orleans	LA	12,840	C
Univ of North Alabama	AL	15,398	C
Univ of N Car at Asheville	NC	15,723	VC+
Univ of N Car at Chapel Hill	NC	20,052	HC+
Univ of N Car at Charlotte	NC	15,547	C
Univ of N Car at Greensboro	NC	14,690	C
Univ of N Car at Pembroke	NC	14,388	LC
Univ of N Car at Wilmington	NC	14,590	VC
Univ of N Dak	ND	15,373	C
Univ of North Florida	FL	15,996	VC
Univ of North Georgia	GA	17,316	C
Univ of North Texas	TX	19,198	C
Univ of Notre Dame	IN	64,043	MC
Univ of Okla	OK	18,911	VC
Univ of Oregon	OR	22,972	C
Univ of Pennsylvania	PA	63,526	MC
Univ of Pikeville	KY	28,700	NC
Univ of Pittsburgh	PA	29,568	HC+
Univ of Pittsburgh at Johnstown	PA	22,092	C
Univ of Portland	OR	52,152	VC
Univ of PR, at Bayamon	PR	13,145	
Univ of PR, at Mayaguez	PR	13,995	
Univ of PR-Rio Piedras campus	PR	13,327	
Univ of Puget Sound	WA	56,456	VC+
Univ of Redlands	CA	60,200	VC
Univ of Rhode Island	RI	24,906	C
Univ of Richmond	VA	60,880	MC
Univ of Rio Grande & Rio Grande Community College	OH	8,750	NC
Univ of Rochester	NY	65,032	MC
Univ of San Diego	CA	58,442	VC+
Univ of San Francisco	CA	58,484	VC
Univ of Scranton	PA	54,962	VC
Univ of Sioux Falls	SD	34,330	C
Univ of South Alabama	AL	16,400	C
Univ of S Car at Columbia	SC	19,725	VC+
Univ of S Car Upstate	SC	18,200	LC
Univ of S Dak	SD	16,109	C
Univ of Southern Calif	CA	66,631	C
Univ of Southern Indiana	IN	16,501	C
Univ of Southern Maine	ME	18,320	C
Univ of Southern Miss	MS	13,170	C
Univ of St. Francis	IL	39,924	C
Univ of St. Thomas - Houston	TX	40,020	VC
Univ of Texas at Arlington	TX	18,026	LC
Univ of Texas at Austin	TX	26,102	HC
Univ of Texas at Dallas	TX	22,830	VC+
Univ of Texas at El Paso	TX	34,452	NC
Univ of Texas at San Antonio	TX	20,157	C
Univ of the District of Columbia	DC	21,044	LC
Univ of the Pacific	CA	57,006	VC
Univ of the Sacred Heart	PR	17,932	
Univ of the Sciences	PA	54,038	VC
Univ of Toledo	OH	19,336	NC
Univ of Tulsa	OK	52,625	HC+
Univ of Vermont	VT	28,878	HC
Univ of Virginia	VA	25,891	MC
Univ of Washington	WA	23,149	VC
Univ of West Alabama	AL	15,516	NC
Univ of West Florida	FL	15,848	C
Univ of West Georgia	GA	16,360	LC
Univ of Wisc-Eau Claire	WI	15,797	VC
Univ of Wisc-Green Bay	WI	15,064	C
Univ of Wisc-La Crosse	WI	15,247	C+
Univ of Wisc-Madison	WI	20,934	MC
Univ of Wisc-Milwaukee	WI	21,496	C
Univ of Wisc-Oshkosh	WI	15,200	C
Univ of Wisc-Parkside	WI	15,193	C
Univ of Wisc-Platteville	WI	14,614	VC
Univ of Wisc-Superior	WI	14,446	C
Univ of Wyoming	WY	15,375	C+
Ursinus College	PA	61,690	VC
Utah State Univ	UT	12,736	C
Utica College	NY	30,430	C
Valparaiso Univ	IN	48,370	C+
Vanderbilt Univ	TN	60,572	MC
Vassar College	NY	65,491	MC
Villanova Univ	PA	62,523	MC
Virginia Commonwealth Univ	VA	23,049	C
Virginia Military Inst	VA	26,460	C+
Virginia Polytechnic Inst and State Univ	VA	21,276	HC
Virginia Wesleyan College	VA	43,728	LC
Voorhees College	SC	19,976	C
Wagner College	NY	55,480	C+
Wake Forest Univ	NC	64,056	MC
Walla Walla Univ	WA	30,417	NC
Walsh Univ	OH	39,010	C
Wartburg College	IA	47,840	C
Washburn Univ	KS	15,827	C
Washington Adventist Univ	MD	31,440	LC
Washington and Lee Univ	VA	59,647	MC
Washington College	MD	54,666	VC
Washington State Univ	WA	22,495	C
Washington Univ in St. Louis	MO	65,366	VC
Wayland Baptist Univ	TX	22,356	LC
Wayne State College	NE	12,802	C
Wayne State Univ	MI	22,016	C
Waynesburg Univ	PA	32,290	C
Weber State Univ	UT	10,721	C
Webster Univ	MO	37,490	C
Wellesley College	MA	63,916	MC
Wells College	NY	50,500	C
Wentworth Inst of Technology	MA	47,112	C
Wesleyan Univ	CT	65,516	MC
West Chester Univ of Pennsylvania	PA	18,456	C
West Texas A&M Univ	TX	13,478	C
West Virginia Univ	WV	18,210	C
West Virginia Univ Inst of Technology	WV	16,462	NC
West Virginia Wesleyan College	WV	36,858	C
Western Carolina Univ	NC	13,965	C
Western Conn State Univ	CT	21,254	LC
Western Illinois Univ	IL	20,825	C
Western Kentucky Univ	KY	16,850	C
Western Mich Univ	MI	21,054	C
Western New England Univ	MA	48,088	C
Western New Mexico Univ	NM	16,734	LC
Western Oregon Univ	OR	15,021	LC
Western State Colo Univ	CO	18,639	C
Western Washington Univ	WA	18,003	C+
Westfield State Univ	MA	19,671	C
Westminster College	MO	32,820	C
Westminster College	PA	39,180	C+
Westminster College	UT	41,078	C+
Westmont College	CA	56,410	HC
Wheaton College	IL	43,610	MC
Wheaton College	MA	61,512	VC
Wheeling Jesuit Univ	WV	37,106	LC
Whitworth Univ	WA	51,732	VC
Wichita State Univ	KS	21,643	C
Widener Univ	PA	56,486	C
Wilberforce Univ	OH	19,016	C
Wiley College	TX	18,504	C
Wilkes Univ	PA	45,622	C
Willamette Univ	OR	61,817	VC+
William Paterson Univ of New Jersey	NJ	23,133	C
William Penn Univ	IA	26,000	C
William Woods Univ	MO	32,040	C
Williams Baptist College	AR	24,720	C
Williams College	MA	63,290	MC
Wilmington College	OH	34,600	C
Winona State Univ	MN	17,535	C
Winston-Salem State Univ	NC	26,166	LC
Winthrop Univ	SC	23,082	C
Wisc Lutheran College	WI	36,290	VC
Wittenberg Univ	OH	48,156	C+
Wofford College	SC	49,885	VC
Worcester Polytechnic Inst	MA	60,730	MC
Worcester State Univ	MA	20,977	C
Wright State Univ	OH	16,983	C
Xavier Univ	OH	47,880	C+
Xavier Univ of Louisiana	LA	31,689	C+
Yale Univ	CT	64,650	MC
Yeshiva Univ	NY	47,250	VC+
York College of Pennsylvania	PA	29,240	C
Youngstown State Univ	OH	17,307	C

COMPUTER SCIENCE & INFORMATICS

School	ST	$IS	SR
Bryant Univ	RI	55,646	VC
Creighton Univ	NE	48,206	VC+
Lewis Univ	IL	40,370	C
Luther College	IA	48,540	C+
Rochester Inst of Technology	NY	50,842	HC

COMPUTER SECURITY

School	ST	$IS	SR
East Stroudsburg Univ	PA	18,334	C
Lewis Univ	IL	40,370	C
Rochester Inst of Technology	NY	50,842	HC
St. Leo Univ	FL	31,650	C
St. Ambrose Univ	IA	39,019	C
Univ of St. Francis	IN	37,400	C
Univ of Tampa	FL	36,944	C

COMPUTER SECURITY AND INFORMATION ASSURANCE

School	ST	$IS	SR
Baldwin Wallace Univ	OH	41,106	C
Bloomfield College	NJ	39,100	LC
Champlain College	VT	53,132	C+
Charter Oak State College	CT	7,671	LC
Dakota State Univ	SD	13,811	C
DePaul Univ	IL	47,623	VC
Drexel Univ	PA	65,432	VC+
Eastern Mich Univ	MI	19,761	C
Felician Univ	NJ	45,370	LC
Florida Atlantic Univ	FL	17,339	C
Fontbonne Univ	MO	33,717	C
Frostburg State Univ	MD	17,280	LC
Hilbert College	NY	30,850	C
Kennesaw State Univ	GA	19,592	VC
Lewis Univ	IL	40,370	C
Limestone College	SC	32,100	C

ST = STATE $IS = IN-STATE COSTS SR = SELECTOR RATING

School	ST	$IS	SR
Loyola Univ Chicago	IL	55,802	VC
Marshall Univ	WV	17,242	C
Marymount Univ	VA	41,570	LC
Metropolitan State Univ	MN	7,566	C
Minn State Univ, Mankato	MN	15,616	C
Minn State Univ, Moorhead	MN	15,941	C
Mount Aloysius College	PA	29,976	C
Norwich Univ	VT	28,212	C
Pace Univ	NY	58,248	C
Pennsylvania College of Technology	PA	27,333	NC
Rochester Inst of Technology	NY	50,842	HC
Roger Williams Univ	RI	46,296	C+
St. John's Univ	NY	55,850	C
SUNY SUNY Albany	NY	22,165	C
Stevens Inst of Technology	NJ	62,338	MC
Stevenson Univ	MD	72,770	C
The Univ of Akron	OH	21,477	C
Thomas College	ME	35,268	LC
Univ of Maryland/Univ College	MD	25,966	LC
Univ of Texas at San Antonio	TX	20,157	C
Utica College	NY	30,430	C
Webber International Univ	FL	31,904	C
Weber State Univ	UT	10,721	C

COMPUTER TECHNOLOGY

School	ST	$IS	SR
Alcorn State Univ	MS	15,854	C
Alfred State College	NY	19,895	C
Alverno College	WI	33,294	LC
Andrews Univ	MI	28,030	C+
Appalachian State Univ	NC	14,416	VC
Bellarmine Univ	KY	51,220	C
Biola Univ	CA	46,402	C+
Bowie State Univ	MD	26,728	LC
Bryant Univ	RI	55,646	VC
Cal State, Dominguez Hills	CA	19,022	LC
Calif Univ of Pennsylvania	PA	14,217	LC
Central Mich Univ	MI	20,330	C
Chestnut Hill College	PA	43,410	C
Colo State Univ	CO	22,162	VC
Daniel Webster College	NH	26,984	C
DePaul Univ	IL	47,623	VC
Duquesne Univ	PA	46,822	VC
Eastern Mich Univ	MI	19,761	C
Eastern Washington Univ	WA	25,572	LC
Excelsior College	NY	14,080	SP
Guilford College	NC	44,090	C
Hodges Univ	FL	19,080	LC
Idaho State Univ	ID	13,619	NC
Indiana State Univ	IN	23,223	LC
Inter-American Univ of PR-Bayamon	PR	18,785	
LeTourneau Univ	TX	38,250	VC
Lewis Univ	IL	40,370	C
Limestone College	SC	32,100	C
Martin Univ	IN	20,264	LC
Methodist Univ	NC	43,600	C
New Jersey Inst of Technology	NJ	29,569	VC
New Mexico State Univ	NM	14,050	C
Norfolk State Univ	VA	25,702	LC
Oregon Inst of Technology	OR	8,910	C
Peirce College	PA	16,780	NC
Purdue Univ/Northwest	IN	15,038	C
Purdue Univ/West Lafayette	IN	20,032	MC
Rochester Inst of Technology	NY	50,842	HC
Rockhurst Univ	MO	29,220	C
St. Louis Univ	MO	49,866	HC
Shepherd Univ, West Virginia	WV	17,224	C
Southern Wesleyan Univ	SC	32,130	LC
SUNY Polytechnic Inst	NY	19,473	VC
Tulane Univ	LA	63,396	HC+
Union College	KY	32,310	C
Univ of Arkansas at Little Rock	AR	18,211	C
Univ of Dayton	OH	53,620	C
Univ of Illinois at Urbana-Champaign	IL	27,006	HC
Univ of Maryland/Univ College	MD	25,966	LC
Univ of Memphis	TN	18,278	C
Univ of Minn Crookston	MN	19,739	C
Univ of Rio Grande & Rio Grande Community College	OH	8,750	NC
Univ of Southern Miss	MS	13,170	C
Univ of St. Francis	IL	39,924	C
Univ of Wisc-Stevens Point	WI	14,043	C
Valparaiso Univ	IN	48,370	C+
Wayne State Univ	MI	22,016	C
Youngstown State Univ	OH	17,307	C

CONDUCTING

School	ST	$IS	SR
Oberlin College	OH	66,012	MC
Okla Baptist Univ	OK	32,320	C

CONGREGATIONAL AND YOUTH MINISTRIES

School	ST	$IS	SR
Eastern Mennonite Univ	VA	42,550	C
Okla Baptist Univ	OK	32,320	C

CONSERVATION AND REGULATION

School	ST	$IS	SR
Bryant Univ	RI	55,646	VC
College of the Ozarks	MO	7,230	C
Florida Inst of Technology	FL	53,306	VC
Lipscomb Univ	TN	41,296	VC
Marist College	NY	49,860	VC
Missouri Southern State Univ	MO	12,499	C
Mount Mercy Univ	IA	36,826	C
Muskingum Univ	OH	35,966	C
N Car State Univ	NC	19,515	HC+
Northwest Missouri State Univ	MO	17,737	C
Northwestern Okla State Univ	OK	13,072	NC
Southeastern Okla State Univ	OK	11,875	C
St. Lawrence Univ	NY	64,390	VC
Texas Tech Univ	TX	18,736	C+
Unity College	ME	37,670	C
Univ of Arkansas at Pine Bluff	AR	13,541	C
Univ of Calif at Berkeley	CA	28,853	MC
Univ of Central Missouri	MO	18,982	C
Univ of Montana	MT	14,105	C
Univ of Wisc-River Falls	WI	14,485	C
Upper Iowa Univ	IA	34,990	NC

CONSTRUCTION

School	ST	$IS	SR
Cal State, Northridge	CA	16,859	LC
Daniel Webster College	NH	26,984	C
Thomas Edison State Univ	NJ	6,350	NC
Univ of Alaska Anchorage	AK	16,652	NC

CONSTRUCTION ENGINEERING

School	ST	$IS	SR
Arizona State Univ at the Tempe Campus	AZ	21,756	VC
Calif State Polytechnic Univ, Pomona	CA	21,541	C
Daniel Webster College	NH	26,984	C
Fairleigh Dickinson Univ/Metropolitan Campus	NJ	40,254	C
Florida Inst of Technology	FL	53,306	VC
Florida International Univ	FL	19,854	C+
Indiana Univ-Purdue Univ Indianapolis	IN	18,635	C
Iowa State Univ	IA	17,570	C
Kennesaw State Univ	GA	19,592	VC
Louisiana Tech Univ	LA	11,422	VC
Marquette Univ	WI	48,390	VC+
Montana State Univ	MT	15,500	C+
National Univ	CA	14,730	LC
N Dak State Univ	ND	16,245	C
Purdue Univ/West Lafayette	IN	20,032	MC
Rensselaer Polytechnic Inst	NY	63,436	MC
San Diego State Univ	CA	21,896	C+
Texas Tech Univ	TX	18,736	C+
The Catholic Univ of America	DC	56,356	VC
Univ of Arkansas at Little Rock	AR	18,211	C
Univ of Central Florida	FL	15,922	VC
Univ of Florida	FL	16,291	HC+
Univ of Nebr - Lincoln	NE	18,589	VC
Univ of New Mexico	NM	15,404	C
Univ of North Florida	FL	15,996	VC
Univ of North Texas	TX	19,198	C
Univ of Southern Calif	CA	66,631	C
Univ of the District of Columbia	DC	21,044	LC
Univ of Washington	WA	23,149	VC
Virginia Polytechnic Inst and State Univ	VA	21,276	HC
Western Mich Univ	MI	21,054	C

CONSTRUCTION MANAGEMENT

School	ST	$IS	SR
Alfred State College	NY	19,895	C
Appalachian State Univ	NC	14,416	VC
Arizona State Univ at the Tempe Campus	AZ	21,756	VC
Auburn Univ	AL	23,594	VC+
Boise State Univ	ID	14,860	C
Bowling Green State Univ	OH	19,747	C
Brigham Young Univ	UT	12,748	HC
Calif Baptist Univ	CA	41,392	C
Calif Polytechnic State Univ	CA	17,979	HC+
Cal State, Chico	CA	21,440	C
Cal State, Fresno	CA	16,902	LC
Central Conn State Univ	CT	21,203	C
Central Washington Univ	WA	16,803	C
Clemson Univ	SC		HC
Colo Mesa Univ	CO	18,955	LC
Colo State Univ	CO	22,162	VC
Dordt College	IA	37,860	C+
Drexel Univ	PA	65,432	VC+
East Carolina Univ	NC	16,937	C
Eastern Mich Univ	MI	19,761	C
Ferris State Univ	MI	21,445	C
Florida Inst of Technology	FL	53,306	VC
Georgia Southern Univ	GA	16,596	C
Illinois State Univ	IL	23,418	VC
John Brown Univ	AR	33,132	VC
Kansas State Univ	KS	17,780	VC
Lawrence Tech Univ	MI	39,770	VC
Louisiana State Univ and A&M College	LA	18,677	VC
Mich State Univ	MI	23,898	VC+
Mich Tech Univ	MI	24,739	VC+
Milwaukee School of Engineering	WI	45,153	HC
Minn State Univ, Mankato	MN	15,616	C
Minn State Univ, Moorhead	MN	15,941	C
Missouri State Univ	MO	15,190	C+
National Univ	CA	14,730	LC
New York Inst of Technology	NY	48,730	C
New York Univ	NY	65,860	MC
NewSchool of Architecture & Design	CA	12,341	SP
N Car State Univ	NC	19,515	HC+
N Dak State Univ	ND	16,245	C
Northern Arizona Univ	AZ	20,246	VC
Northern Kentucky Univ	KY	16,486	C
Northern Mich Univ	MI	19,604	C
Ohio State Univ at Columbus	OH	21,703	HC+
Okla State Univ	OK	17,180	VC
Oregon State Univ	OR	22,519	VC
Pennsylvania College of Technology	PA	27,333	NC
Pittsburg State Univ	KS	13,880	NC
Pratt Inst	NY	58,082	VC
Purdue Univ/West Lafayette	IN	20,032	MC
Roger Williams Univ	RI	46,296	C+
S Dak State Univ	SD	15,634	C
Southern Illinois Univ Edwardsville	IL	22,643	C
SUNY / The College of Environmental Science and Forestry	NY	23,853	VC
Temple Univ	PA	24,392	VC
Texas State Univ	TX	19,350	C
The Univ of Tenn at Chattanooga	TN	16,744	C
Tuskegee Univ	AL	28,164	C
Univ of Arkansas at Little Rock	AR	18,211	C
Univ of Central Missouri	MO	18,982	C
Univ of Cincinnati	OH	21,964	VC
Univ of Denver	CO	58,443	VC+
Univ of Houston	TX	21,483	VC
Univ of Louisiana at Monroe	LA	15,970	C
Univ of Nebr - Kearney	NE	16,546	LC
Univ of Nebr - Lincoln	NE	18,589	VC
Univ of Nevada, Las Vegas	NV	17,553	C
Univ of New Mexico	NM	15,404	C
Univ of N Car at Charlotte	NC	15,547	C
Univ of North Florida	FL	15,996	VC
Univ of Okla	OK	18,911	VC
Univ of Texas at San Antonio	TX	20,157	C
Utica College	NY	30,430	C
Virginia Polytechnic Inst and State Univ	VA	21,276	HC
Washington State Univ	WA	22,495	C
Wayne State Univ	MI	22,016	C
Weber State Univ	UT	10,721	C
Wentworth Inst of Technology	MA	47,112	C
Western Carolina Univ	NC	13,965	C
Western Illinois Univ	IL	20,825	C
Western Kentucky Univ	KY	16,850	C

CONSTRUCTION MGMT/ COMMERCIAL/INDUSTRIAL

School	ST	$IS	SR
Ferris State Univ	MI	21,445	C
Tarleton State Univ	TX	15,248	LC
Western Kentucky Univ	KY	16,850	C

CONSTRUCTION TECHNOLOGY

School	ST	$IS	SR
Appalachian State Univ	NC	14,416	VC
Black Hills State Univ	SD	15,899	C
Eastern Kentucky Univ	KY	16,908	C
Farmingdale State College	NY	20,624	C
Fitchburg State Univ	MA	21,819	C
Florida International Univ	FL	19,854	C+
Idaho State Univ	ID	13,619	NC
Indiana State Univ	IN	23,223	LC
Millersville Univ of Pennsylvania	PA	23,782	C
Montana State Univ-Northern	MT	11,370	NC
Murray State Univ	KY	16,998	C
Norfolk State Univ	VA	25,702	LC
Northern Kentucky Univ	KY	16,486	C
Okla State Univ	OK	17,180	VC
Pennsylvania College of Technology	PA	27,333	NC
Pittsburg State Univ	KS	13,880	NC
Purdue Univ/Northwest	IN	15,038	C
Purdue Univ/West Lafayette	IN	20,032	MC
Texas State Univ	TX	19,350	C
The Univ of Akron	OH	21,477	C
Univ of Arkansas at Little Rock	AR	18,211	C
Univ of Maine	ME	20,792	C
Univ of Maryland/Eastern Shore	MD	17,013	C
Univ of Mass Amherst	MA	26,199	VC+
Univ of Southern Miss	MS	13,170	C
Univ of Wisc-Stout	WI	19,667	C

CONSUMER SERVICES

School	ST	$IS	SR
San Francisco State Univ	CA	18,514	LC
S Dak State Univ	SD	15,634	C
Texas Woman's Univ	TX	15,302	LC
The Univ of Utah	UT	17,924	VC
Univ of Georgia	GA	21,250	HC

CONTEMPORARY CHRISTIAN MUSIC

School	ST	$IS	SR
Greenville College	IL	27,012	C

CORE STUDIES

School	ST	$IS	SR
Shenandoah Univ	VA	41,312	C

CORRECTIONS

School	ST	$IS	SR
Adams State Univ	CO	17,703	LC
College of the Ozarks	MO	7,230	C
Eastern Kentucky Univ	KY	16,908	C
Hardin-Simmons Univ	TX	33,966	C
Jackson State Univ	MS	15,879	LC
Minn State Univ, Mankato	MN	15,616	C
Stephen F. Austin State Univ	TX	18,406	LC
Texas State Univ	TX	19,350	C
Tiffin Univ	OH	31,380	C
Univ of New Haven	CT	52,190	C
Washburn Univ	KS	15,827	C
Western Oregon Univ	OR	15,021	LC

COSTUME DESIGN

School	ST	$IS	SR
Webster Univ	MO	37,490	C

COUNSELING/PSYCHOLOGY

School	ST	$IS	SR
Adams State Univ	CO	17,703	LC
Anna Maria College	MA	48,186	C
Averett Univ	VA	40,970	LC
Biola Univ	CA	46,402	C+
Blackburn College	IL	28,526	LC
Cal State, Fresno	CA	16,902	LC
City Univ of Seattle	WA	24,340	NC
Corban Univ	OR	40,306	C
Dallas Baptist Univ	TX	33,713	C
East Central Univ	OK	13,056	C
East Texas Baptist Univ	TX	33,134	C
Eastern Mich Univ	MI	19,761	C
Eastern New Mexico Univ	NM	14,416	C
Edinboro Univ	PA	15,940	LC
Emmanuel College	MA	52,110	C+
Faulkner Univ	AL	26,410	C
Florida Gulf Coast Univ	FL	9,682	C
Friends Univ	KS	34,455	C
Geneva College	PA	35,450	C
Goddard College	VT	17,040	VC
Grace College and Seminary	IN	31,524	C
Houghton College	NY	39,090	C
Howard Univ	DC	37,616	C+
Huntington Univ	IN	33,996	C
Husson Univ	ME	25,720	LC
Johnson & Wales Univ/ Denver Campus	CO	42,707	C
Kentucky Christian Univ	KY	26,560	LC
Kutztown Univ of Pennsylvania	PA	19,056	LC
Lewis Univ	IL	40,370	C
Martin Univ	IN	20,264	LC
Missouri State Univ	MO	15,190	C+
Mount St. Mary's Univ - Chalon Campus	CA	43,897	VC+
New York Univ	NY	65,860	MC
Newman Univ	KS	35,390	C
Northwest Univ	WA	35,876	VC
Okla Baptist Univ	OK	32,320	C
Pittsburg State Univ	KS	13,880	NC
Prescott College	AZ	33,284	C
Rochester College	MI	28,574	LC
Samford Univ	AL	39,232	VC
Southwestern Okla State Univ	OK	11,790	C
SUNY / Empire State College	NY	9,145	SP
Tarleton State Univ	TX	15,248	LC
Toccoa Falls College	GA	27,920	C
Univ of Arizona	AZ	23,100	C
Univ of Great Falls	MT	38,524	C
Univ of Idaho	ID	15,348	C
Univ of Missouri/Columbia	MO	18,201	MC
Univ of New Haven	CT	52,190	C
Univ of N Car at Pembroke	NC	14,388	LC
Univ of North Florida	FL	15,996	VC
Univ of St. Francis	IL	39,924	C
Washington Adventist Univ	MD	31,440	LC
Wayne State College	NE	12,802	C
Williams Baptist College	AR	24,720	C
Xavier Univ	OH	47,880	C+

COURT REPORTING

School	ST	$IS	SR
Humphreys College	CA	27,790	C

CRAFTS

School	ST	$IS	SR
Indiana Univ-Purdue Univ Fort Wayne	IN	17,553	C
Kent State Univ	OH	20,732	C

ST = STATE $IS = IN-STATE COSTS SR = SELECTOR RATING

School	ST	$IS	SR
Kutztown Univ of Pennsylvania	PA	19,056	LC
Malone Univ	OH	38,448	C
Rochester Inst of Technology	NY	50,842	HC
Univ of Illinois at Urbana-Champaign	IL	27,006	HC
Virginia Commonwealth Univ	VA	23,049	C

CREATIVE WRITING

School	ST	$IS	SR
Adams State Univ	CO	17,703	LC
Agnes Scott College	GA	51,930	VC+
Albion College	MI	52,650	C
Alderson Broaddus Univ	WV	26,149	C
American Univ	DC	59,379	HC+
Andrews Univ	MI	28,030	C+
Arkansas Tech Univ	AR	15,484	C
Asbury Univ	KY	35,180	C+
Ashland Univ	OH	21,440	C
Augustana College	IL	49,658	VC
Baldwin Wallace Univ	OH	41,106	C
Bard College	NY	64,024	HC
Bard College at Simon's Rock	MA	65,795	MC
Baylor Univ	TX	53,760	HC
Belhaven Univ	MS	31,016	C
Beloit College	WI	55,206	HC
Benedictine Univ	IL	38,300	C
Bennington College	VT	63,960	MC
Berry College	GA	45,286	C+
Bethany College	WV	36,300	NC
Blackburn College	IL	28,526	LC
Bloomfield College	NJ	39,100	LC
Bluffton Univ	OH	40,950	C
Bowling Green State Univ	OH	19,747	C
Brandeis Univ	MA	65,925	MC
Brown Univ	RI	64,566	MC
Bryan College	TN	31,440	C
Calif Baptist Univ	CA	41,392	C
Calif College of the Arts	CA	52,758	SP
Cal State, Long Beach	CA	18,850	C
Calvin College	MI	41,570	VC+
Canisius College	NY	47,537	C
Capital Univ	OH	42,982	C
Cardinal Stritch Univ	WI	36,462	C
Carlow Univ	PA	38,549	LC
Carnegie Mellon Univ	PA	67,980	MC
Carroll College	MT	39,972	C+
Chapman Univ	CA	63,078	VC+
Chatham Univ	PA	46,517	C
CUNY/Brooklyn College	NY	5,884	C+
CUNY/Hunter College	NY	31,098	VC
Coe College	IA	51,570	VC
Colby College	ME	64,060	MC
Colby-Sawyer College	NH	50,790	C
Colo College	CO	62,560	MC
Colo State Univ	CO	22,162	VC
Columbia College Chicago	IL	43,168	C
Concordia Univ St. Paul	MN	29,050	C
Corban Univ	OR	40,306	C
DePaul Univ	IL	47,623	VC
Dominican Univ of Calif	CA	57,050	C
Eastern Mich Univ	MI	19,761	C
Eastern Washington Univ	WA	25,572	LC
Eckerd College	FL	52,874	C
Elon Univ	NC	44,599	VC+
Emerson College	MA	54,736	HC
Emory and Henry College	VA	41,410	C
Emory Univ	GA	60,786	MC
Fairleigh Dickinson Univ/ College at Florham	NJ	52,062	C
Florida State Univ	FL	16,771	HC
Franklin College	IN	39,380	C
Geneva College	PA	35,450	C
George Fox Univ	OR	42,938	C
Georgetown College	KY	41,440	C
Goddard College	VT	17,040	VC
Goshen College	IN	42,500	C
Grand Valley State Univ	MI	22,250	C+
Green Mountain College	VT	45,228	LC
Hamilton College	NY	64,250	MC
Hamline Univ	MN	45,678	VC
Hampshire College	MA	63,824	MC
Harvard College/Harvard Univ	MA	60,659	MC
Hiram College	OH	43,230	C
Hofstra Univ	NY	55,960	C+
Hope College	MI	39,940	VC
Huntington Univ	IN	33,996	C
Indiana Wesleyan Univ	IN	33,674	C
Iowa State Univ	IA	17,570	C
Ithaca College	NY	56,766	VC
Johns Hopkins Univ	MD	65,386	MC
Johnson State College	VT	20,752	C
Kansas City Art Inst	MO	44,308	C+
Knox College	IL	52,615	VC+
La Roche College	PA	37,924	LC
Lakeland Univ	WI	35,130	C
Le Moyne College	NY	46,000	C
Lesley Univ	MA	41,550	C
Lewis Univ	IL	40,370	C
Lindenwood Univ	MO	25,132	C
Linfield College	OR	52,010	C
Loras College	IA	39,222	C
Loyola Univ Maryland	MD	60,300	VC
Loyola Univ New Orleans	LA	51,708	VC+
Lycoming College	PA	48,580	C
Malone Univ	OH	38,448	C
Marshall Univ	WV	17,242	C
Maryville College	TN	44,410	C
Mass Inst of Technology	MA	62,662	MC
Mercer Univ	GA	45,348	VC
Methodist Univ	NC	43,600	C
Mills College	CA	59,163	VC
Millsaps College	MS	50,080	C+
Montclair State Univ	NJ	26,210	LC
Murray State Univ	KY	16,998	C
New England College	NH	50,364	C
New York Univ	NY	65,860	MC
Northland College	WI	41,103	C+
Oberlin College	OH	66,012	MC
Ohio Northern Univ	OH	44,050	VC
Ohio Univ	OH	22,924	C
Ohio Wesleyan Univ	OH	49,460	VC
Okla Baptist Univ	OK	32,320	C
Okla Christian Univ	OK	27,650	VC
Old Dominion Univ	VA	20,910	C
Pacific Univ	OR	52,876	C
Pepperdine Univ	CA	74,460	HC+
Pfeiffer Univ	NC	39,695	LC
Pratt Inst	NY	58,082	VC
Prescott College	AZ	33,284	C
Providence College	RI	60,760	VC
Purdue Univ/West Lafayette	IN	20,032	MC
Queens Univ of Charlotte	NC	39,543	C
Ringling College of Art and Design	FL	57,430	SP
Roanoke College	VA	54,114	VC
Rocky Mountain College	MT	34,270	C
Roger Williams Univ	RI	46,296	C+
Rosemont College	PA	30,980	C
Rutgers Univ - Newark	NJ	27,288	C
Saginaw Valley State Univ	MI	18,530	C
St. Mary-of-the-Woods College	IN	39,632	LC
St. Mary's College	IN	50,600	C
San Francisco State Univ	CA	18,514	LC
Santa Fe Univ of Art and Design	NM	39,980	SP
Sarah Lawrence College	NY	63,388	HC
School of the Art Inst of Chicago	IL	56,230	SP
Seattle Pacific Univ	WA	47,439	C+
Seattle Univ	WA	50,811	VC+
Seton Hall Univ	NJ	55,514	C
Seton Hill Univ	PA	46,972	C
Smith College	MA	63,914	MC
Southern Methodist Univ	TX	66,483	MC
Southern New Hampshire Univ	NH	43,198	C
Southern Vermont College	VT	34,670	LC
Southwest Minn State Univ	MN	17,783	C
Spalding Univ	KY	31,938	SP
St. Andrews Univ	NC	44,634	LC
St. Lawrence Univ	NY	64,390	VC
SUNY / SUNY Potsdam	NY	20,404	C+
SUNY at Binghamton	NY	22,861	MC
SUNY at Oswego	NY	21,351	C
SUNY at Purchase	NY	17,900	C
Stephens College	MO	38,042	C
Sterling College	KS	32,830	C
Suffolk Univ	MA	50,308	C
The College of Idaho	ID	36,415	C
Truman State Univ	MO	16,014	HC
Univ of Arizona	AZ	23,100	C
Univ of Calif at Irvine	CA	26,484	VC
Univ of Calif at Riverside	CA	29,227	C+
Univ of Central Arkansas	AR	14,472	VC
Univ of Central Okla	OK	13,486	C
Univ of Cincinnati	OH	21,964	VC
Univ of Evansville	IN	44,186	VC+
Univ of Florida	FL	16,291	HC+
Univ of Idaho	ID	15,348	C
Univ of Maine at Farmington	ME	18,187	C
Univ of Maine at Machias	ME	22,960	C
Univ of Mich/Ann Arbor	MI	24,410	MC
Univ of Missouri/Columbia	MO	18,201	MC
Univ of Montana-Western	MT	11,220	LC
Univ of Mount Union	OH	38,970	C
Univ of Nebr - Omaha	NE	16,120	C
Univ of New Haven	CT	52,190	C
Univ of N Car at Wilmington	NC	14,590	VC
Univ of Oregon	OR	22,972	C
Univ of Pittsburgh	PA	29,568	HC+
Univ of Pittsburgh at Greensburg	PA	23,132	C
Univ of Pittsburgh at Johnstown	PA	22,092	C
Univ of Redlands	CA	60,200	VC
Univ of Southern Calif	CA	66,631	C
Univ of Tampa	FL	36,944	C
Univ of Texas at Austin	TX	26,102	HC
Univ of Tulsa	OK	52,625	HC+
Univ of Wisc-Green Bay	WI	15,064	C
Valparaiso Univ	IN	48,370	C+
Warren Wilson College	NC	44,220	VC
Wartburg College	IA	47,840	C
Washington Univ in St. Louis	MO	65,366	VC
Waynesburg Univ	PA	32,290	C
Weber State Univ	UT	10,721	C
Webster Univ	MO	37,490	C
Wellesley College	MA	63,916	MC
Wells College	NY	50,500	C
West Virginia Univ	WV	18,210	C
Western Mich Univ	MI	21,054	C
Western New England Univ	MA	48,088	C
Western Washington Univ	WA	18,003	C+
Wheaton College	MA	61,512	VC
Wichita State Univ	KS	21,643	C
Widener Univ	PA	56,486	C
Wilson College	PA	35,620	C
Wofford College	SC	49,885	VC
Wright State Univ	OH	16,983	C
York College of Pennsylvania	PA	29,240	C

CRIMINAL JUSTICE

School	ST	$IS	SR
Abilene Christian Univ	TX	41,800	C+
Adelphi Univ	NY	48,244	C
Adrian College	MI	42,400	C
Alabama State Univ	AL	14,142	NC
Albany State Univ	GA	19,462	C
Albright College	PA	46,660	C
Alcorn State Univ	MS	15,854	C
Alfred Univ	NY	42,296	C+
Alvernia Univ	PA	43,900	C
American International College	MA	46,300	LC
American Univ	DC	59,379	HC+
Anderson Univ	IN	38,200	C
Angelo State Univ	TX	15,263	NC
Anna Maria College	MA	48,186	C
Appalachian State Univ	NC	14,416	VC
Arcadia Univ	PA	33,570	C+
Arizona State Univ at the Downtown Phoenix Campus	AZ	23,680	VC
Armstrong State Univ	GA	16,962	C
Asbury Univ	KY	35,180	C+
Ashford Univ	CA	10,480	C
Ashland Univ	OH	21,440	C
Auburn Univ at Montgomery	AL	15,290	C
Augusta Univ	GA	4,632	C
Aurora Univ	IL	33,970	C
Austin Peay State Univ	TN	16,397	C
Averett Univ	VA	40,970	LC
Azusa Pacific Univ	CA	43,972	C
Baldwin Wallace Univ	OH	41,106	C
Ball State Univ	IN	19,590	C
Barton College	NC	38,686	LC
Bay Path Univ	MA	45,349	C
Becker College	MA	57,628	C
Bellarmine Univ	KY	51,220	C
Bellevue Univ	NE	20,300	NC
Belmont Abbey College	NC	48,156	C
Bemidji State Univ	MN	16,056	VC
Benedict College	SC	28,238	NC
Bethany College	KS	46,100	NC
Bethel College	IN	35,860	C
Bethune-Cookman Univ	FL	22,970	C
Blackburn College	IL	28,526	LC
Bloomfield College	NJ	39,100	LC
Bloomsburg Univ of Pennsylvania	PA	19,066	LC
Blue Mountain College	MS	15,949	VC
Bluefield College	VA	34,120	C+
Bluefield State College	WV	5,832	LC
Bluffton Univ	OH	40,950	C
Boise State Univ	ID	14,860	C
Boston Univ	MA	65,110	MC
Bowie State Univ	MD	26,728	LC
Bowling Green State Univ	OH	19,747	C
Briar Cliff Univ	IA	36,956	C
Bridgewater State Univ	MA	21,810	C
Buena Vista Univ	IA	41,514	C
Butler Univ	IN	51,352	VC
Caldwell Univ	NJ	42,165	NC
Calif Baptist Univ	CA	41,392	C
Calif Lutheran Univ	CA	52,853	C
Cal State, Bakersfield	CA	19,191	LC
Cal State, Chico	CA	21,440	C
Cal State, Dominguez Hills	CA	19,022	LC
Cal State, East Bay	CA	19,413	C
Cal State, Fullerton	CA	21,902	C
Cal State, Long Beach	CA	18,850	C
Cal State, Los Angeles	CA	17,186	LC
Cal State, Sacramento	CA	20,332	C
Cal State, San Bernardino	CA	12,000	C
Cal State, Stanislaus	CA	16,212	C
Calif Univ of Pennsylvania	PA	14,217	LC
Calumet College of St. Joseph	IN	22,735	C
Cameron Univ	OK	11,072	NC
Campbellsville Univ	KY	32,492	C
Canisius College	NY	47,537	C
Capital Univ	OH	42,982	C
Caribbean Univ	PR	15,471	
Carroll Univ	WI	38,100	C+
Carthage College	WI	48,835	C
Castleton Univ	VT	20,186	C
Cedar Crest College	PA	46,715	C
Cedarville Univ	OH	34,990	VC
Centenary College	NJ	43,602	C
Central Methodist Univ	MO	36,830	VC
Central Mich Univ	MI	20,330	C
Central Washington Univ	WA	16,803	C
Chadron State College	NE	14,819	NC
Chaminade Univ of Honolulu	HI	36,000	C
Champlain College	VT	53,132	C+
Charleston Southern Univ	SC	32,400	C
Chestnut Hill College	PA	43,410	C
Cheyney Univ of Pennsylvania	PA	20,896	LC
Chicago State Univ	IL	20,144	C
CUNY/John Jay College of Criminal Justice	NY	6,359	NC
City Univ of Seattle	WA	24,340	NC
Claflin Univ	SC	33,764	LC
Clayton State Univ	GA	19,735	C
College of St Joseph	VT	32,400	LC
College of the Ozarks	MO	7,230	C
Colo Mesa Univ	CO	18,955	LC
Colo Technical Univ	CO	21,455	NC
Columbia College - Missouri	MO	27,803	C
Columbus State Univ	GA	14,336	LC
Concordia Univ St. Paul	MN	29,050	C
Concordia Univ Wisc	WI	35,910	C
Concordia Univ, Ann Arbor	MI	35,945	VC
Coppin State Univ	MD	17,041	VC
Corban Univ	OR	40,306	C
Culver-Stockton College	MO	33,525	C
Cumberland Univ	TN	27,710	C
Curry College	MA	51,815	C
Dakota Wesleyan Univ	SD	32,850	C
Dallas Baptist Univ	TX	33,713	C
Defiance College	OH	41,630	C
Delaware Valley Univ	PA	49,796	C
Delta State Univ	MS	13,176	C
DeSales Univ	PA	43,970	C
Dominican College	NY	31,270	LC
Dominican Univ	IL	41,222	C
Dordt College	IA	37,860	C+
Drexel Univ	PA	65,432	VC+
Drury Univ	MO	33,791	VC
East Carolina Univ	NC	16,937	C
East Central Univ	OK	13,056	C
East Stroudsburg Univ	PA	18,334	C
East Tenn State Univ	TN	13,994	C
East Texas Baptist Univ	TX	33,134	C
Eastern Mich Univ	MI	19,761	C
Eastern New Mexico Univ	NM	14,416	C
Eastern Univ	PA	39,540	C
Eastern Washington Univ	WA	25,572	LC
Edgewood College	WI	35,950	C
Edinboro Univ	PA	15,940	LC
Edward Waters College	FL	20,607	NC
Elizabeth City State Univ	NC	14,745	C
Elizabethtown College	PA	54,050	C
Elizabethtown College School of Continuing and Professional Studies	PA	18,900	C
Elmhurst College	IL	45,428	C
Elmira College	NY	53,900	C
Elon Univ	NC	44,599	VC+
Emporia State Univ	KS	14,570	C
Endicott College	MA	44,604	VC+
Evangel Univ	MO	28,898	C
Excelsior College	NY	14,080	SP
Fairleigh Dickinson Univ/ Metropolitan Campus	NJ	40,254	C
Fairmont State Univ	WV	15,726	C
Farmingdale State College	NY	20,624	C
Faulkner Univ	AL	26,410	C
Fayetteville State Univ	NC	17,756	C
Felician Univ	NJ	45,370	LC
Ferris State Univ	MI	21,445	C
Ferrum College	VA	39,650	C
Fitchburg State Univ	MA	21,819	C
Florida A&M Univ	FL	15,361	C
Florida Atlantic Univ	FL	17,339	C
Florida Gulf Coast Univ	FL	9,682	C
Florida International Univ	FL	19,854	C+
Florida Memorial Univ	FL	22,270	LC
Fort Hays State Univ	KS	12,131	C
Fort Valley State Univ	GA	17,988	VC
Franklin Pierce Univ	NH	46,750	C
Freed-Hardeman Univ	TN	29,450	C
Friends Univ	KS	34,455	C
Frostburg State Univ	MD	17,280	LC
Gannon Univ	PA	42,032	C
George Mason Univ	VA	15,724	VC
George Washington Univ	DC	62,835	MC
Georgia College & State Univ	GA	21,148	C+
Georgia Southwestern State Univ	GA	13,870	C
Georgia State Univ	GA	24,332	VC
Georgian Court Univ	NJ	42,426	LC
Glenville State College	WV	17,386	NC
Gonzaga Univ	WA	50,888	HC
Grace Bible College	MI	25,250	C
Grace College and Seminary	IN	31,524	C
Graceland Univ	IA	35,290	C
Grambling State Univ	LA	15,701	C
Grand Valley State Univ	MI	22,250	C+
Grand View Univ	IA	32,302	C
Granite State College	NH	19,639	SP
Greenville College	IL	27,012	C
Guilford College	NC	44,090	C
Gwynedd Mercy Univ	PA	43,780	LC
Hamline Univ	MN	45,678	VC
Hannibal-LaGrange Univ	MO	29,815	C
Harding Univ	AR	25,421	C
Hardin-Simmons Univ	TX	33,966	C
Harris-Stowe State Univ	MO	14,360	NC
Hawaii Pacific Univ	HI	33,420	C
Heidelberg Univ	OH	39,200	C
Henderson State Univ	AR	15,516	LC
Heritage Univ	WA	19,825	NC
High Point Univ	NC	45,977	C
Hilbert College	NY	30,850	C
Hodges Univ	FL	19,080	LC
Holy Family Univ	PA	43,326	LC
Hope International Univ	CA	41,150	C
Howard Univ	DC	37,616	C+
Huntingdon College	AL	34,900	C
Huntington Univ	IN	33,996	C
Husson Univ	ME	25,720	LC

ST = STATE $IS = IN-STATE COSTS   SR = SELECTOR RATING

School	ST	$IS	SR
Huston-Tillotson Univ	TX	18,124	LC
Illinois State Univ	IL	23,418	VC
Indiana Inst of Technology	IN	34,240	LC
Indiana Univ Bloomington	IN	20,429	VC
Indiana Univ East	IN	7,072	C
Indiana Univ Kokomo	IN	7,073	C
Indiana Univ Northwest	IN	7,072	C
Indiana Univ South Bend	IN	14,242	C
Indiana Univ Southeast	IN	14,242	LC
Indiana Univ-Purdue Univ Fort Wayne	IN	17,553	C
Indiana Univ-Purdue Univ Indianapolis	IN	18,635	C
Indiana Wesleyan Univ	IN	33,674	C
Inter-American Univ of PR Ponce	PR	19,549	
Inter-American Univ of PR-Aguadilla Campus	PR	21,657	
Inter-American Univ of PR-Arecibo Campus	PR	18,245	
Inter-American Univ of PR-Barranquitas	PR	18,336	
Inter-American Univ of PR-Fajardo Campus	PR	18,336	
Inter-American Univ of PR-Metropolitan Campus	PR	20,045	
Iona College	NY	50,984	C
Iowa Wesleyan Univ	IA	39,200	C
Jackson State Univ	MS	15,879	LC
Jacksonville State Univ	AL	14,628	LC
James Madison Univ	VA	19,084	VC
Jarvis Christian College	TX	20,160	NC
John Carroll Univ	OH	49,740	C+
Johnson & Wales Univ/Denver Campus	CO	42,707	C
Johnson & Wales Univ/North Miami Campus	FL	42,707	C
Johnson & Wales Univ/Providence Campus	RI	42,248	C
Johnson C. Smith Univ	NC	25,336	LC
Judson College	AL	27,066	C
Kansas Wesleyan Univ	KS	36,600	C
Kean Univ	NJ	24,650	C
Keene State College	NH	24,003	LC
Kennesaw State Univ	GA	19,592	VC
Kentucky State Univ	KY	13,364	LC
Kentucky Wesleyan College	KY	32,080	C
Keuka College	NY	39,762	C
Keystone College	PA	28,680	LC
King Univ	TN	34,660	C
King's College	PA	46,858	C
Kutztown Univ of Pennsylvania	PA	19,056	LC
La Roche College	PA	37,924	LC
La Salle Univ	PA	55,790	C
Lake Erie College	OH	38,914	LC
Lakeland Univ	WI	35,130	C
Lamar Univ	TX	18,014	LC
Lane College	TN	16,550	C
Langston Univ	OK	14,314	C
Lasell College	MA	47,500	C
Lebanon Valley College	PA	51,530	C
Lees-McRae College	NC	33,944	C
LeMoyne-Owen College	TN	16,980	C
Lewis Univ	IL	40,370	C
Lewis-Clark State College	ID	14,202	C
Limestone College	SC	32,100	C
Lincoln Univ	MO	13,602	NC
Lindenwood Univ	MO	25,132	C
Lindsey Wilson College	KY	32,882	C
LIU Post	NY	49,682	C
Livingstone College	NC	17,815	LC
Lock Haven Univ of Pennsylvania	PA	18,028	LC
Longwood Univ	VA	22,184	C
Loras College	IA	39,222	C
Louisiana College	LA	21,886	C
Lourdes Univ	OH	29,520	NC
Loyola Univ Chicago	IL	55,802	VC
Loyola Univ New Orleans	LA	51,708	VC+
Lubbock Christian Univ	TX	28,426	C
Lycoming College	PA	48,580	C
Lynn Univ	FL	49,480	LC
MacMurray College	IL	33,620	C
Madonna Univ	MI	29,050	C
Malone Univ	OH	38,448	C
Mansfield Univ	PA	23,376	LC
Marian Univ	WI	32,420	LC
Marist College	NY	49,860	VC
Marshall Univ	WV	17,242	C
Martin Univ	IN	20,264	LC
Mary Baldwin Univ	VA	39,865	C
Marygrove College	MI	28,926	NC
Marymount Univ	VA	41,570	LC
Marywood Univ	PA	46,900	C
McKendree Univ	IL	37,940	C+
McNeese State Univ	LA	7,838	C
Medaille College	NY	35,112	C
Mercer Univ	GA	45,348	VC
Mercy College	NY	31,776	C
Mercyhurst Univ	PA	47,420	C
Messiah College	PA	43,100	C+
Methodist Univ	NC	43,600	C
Metropolitan State Univ	MN	7,566	C
Metropolitan State Univ of Denver	CO	29,889	LC
Miami Univ	OH	27,190	HC+
Mich State Univ	MI	23,898	VC+
MidAmerica Nazarene Univ	KS	35,550	C
Middle Tenn State Univ	TN	8,650	C
Midwestern State Univ	TX	17,572	C
Miles College	AL	18,646	NC
Minn State Univ, Mankato	MN	15,616	C
Minn State Univ, Moorhead	MN	15,941	C
Minot State Univ	ND	12,732	C
Miss College	MS	25,850	C
Miss Valley State Univ	MS	13,233	LC
Missouri Baptist Univ	MO	35,594	C
Missouri Southern State Univ	MO	12,499	C
Missouri Valley College	MO	28,150	C
Missouri Western State Univ	MO	16,741	
Mitchell College	CT	43,280	C
Molloy College	NY	40,440	C
Monmouth Univ	NJ	46,234	C
Monroe College	NY	23,660	C
Montana State Univ-Billings	MT	22,960	C
Montclair State Univ	NJ	26,210	LC
Moravian College	PA	53,117	
Morris College	SC	18,500	LC
Mount Aloysius College	PA	29,976	C
Mount Ida College	MA	46,820	C
Mount Marty College	SD	32,972	C
Mount Mercy Univ	IA	36,826	C
Mount St. Mary's Univ	MD	51,610	C
Mount Vernon Nazarene Univ	OH	34,500	C
Murray State Univ	KY	16,998	C
Muskingum Univ	OH	35,966	C
National Univ	CA	14,730	LC
Neumann Univ	PA	40,678	LC
New England College	NH	50,364	C
New Jersey City Univ	NJ	21,456	LC
New Mexico State Univ	NM	14,050	C
New York Inst of Technology	NY	48,730	C
Newbury College	MA	46,950	C
Newman Univ	KS	35,390	C
Niagara Univ	NY	41,010	C
Nichols College	MA	46,800	LC
N Car Central Univ	NC	9,000	C
N Car State Univ	NC	19,515	HC+
N Car Wesleyan College	NC	39,200	C
N Dak State Univ	ND	16,245	C
North Park Univ	IL	35,860	C
Northeastern State Univ	OK	8,615	VC
Northeastern Univ	MA	62,703	MC
Northern Arizona Univ	AZ	20,246	VC
Northern Kentucky Univ	KY	16,486	C
Northern Mich Univ	MI	19,604	C
Northern State Univ	SD	14,505	C
Northwest Nazarene Univ	ID	36,000	C
Northwestern College of Iowa	IA	38,400	C+
Northwestern Okla State Univ	OK	13,072	NC
Norwich Univ	VT	28,212	C
Nova Southeastern Univ	FL	38,534	C+
Nyack College	NY	34,050	NC
Ohio Dominican Univ	OH	41,340	C+
Ohio Northern Univ	OH	44,050	VC
Ohio State Univ at Columbus	OH	21,703	HC+
Ohio Univ	OH	22,924	C
Ohio Valley Univ	WV	29,480	C
Okla Baptist Univ	OK	32,320	C
Old Dominion Univ	VA	20,910	C
Olivet College	MI	36,110	LC
Olivet Nazarene Univ	IL	41,840	C
Pace Univ	NY	58,248	C
Park Univ	MO	20,329	C
Penn State Univ/Altoona	PA	24,584	C
Pennsylvania State Univ - Univ Park	PA	29,760	HC
Pfeiffer Univ	NC	39,695	LC
Piedmont College	GA	32,512	C
Pittsburg State Univ	KS	13,880	NC
Plymouth State Univ	NH	23,180	LC
Point Loma Nazarene Univ	CA	43,450	C
Point Park Univ	PA	41,270	C
Post Univ	CT	41,150	C
Prairie View A&M Univ	TX	15,205	LC
Purdue Univ/Northwest	IN	15,038	C
Purdue Univ/West Lafayette	IN	20,032	MC
Quincy Univ	IL	36,998	C
Quinnipiac Univ	CT	59,110	C
Radford Univ	VA	19,027	LC
Regis College	MA	51,920	C
Rhode Island College	RI	17,694	LC
Roanoke College	VA	54,114	VC
Roberts Wesleyan College	NY	38,306	C
Rochester Inst of Technology	NY	50,842	HC
Roger Williams Univ	RI	46,296	C+
Rowan Univ	NJ	24,491	VC+
Russell Sage College	NY	39,370	C
Rutgers Univ - Camden	NJ	26,146	C
Rutgers Univ - New Brunswick	NJ	26,632	HC
Rutgers Univ - Newark	NJ	27,288	C
Sacred Heart Univ	CT	52,750	C
Saginaw Valley State Univ	MI	18,530	C
St. Anselm College	NH	52,560	C+
St. Augustine's Univ	NC	26,048	C
St. Francis Univ	PA	42,268	NC
St. Joseph's College of Maine	ME	46,485	C
St. Joseph's Univ	PA	57,544	VC+
St. Leo Univ	FL	31,650	C
St. Louis Univ	MO	49,866	HC
St. Martin's Univ	WA	45,056	C
St. Mary's Univ of Minn	MN	41,210	VC
St. Peter's Univ	NJ	49,192	C
St. Xavier Univ	IL	43,310	C
Salem International Univ	WV	21,090	LC
Salem State Univ	MA	17,303	LC
Salve Regina Univ	RI	51,470	C
Sam Houston State Univ	TX	18,792	C
Samford Univ	AL	39,232	VC
San Diego State Univ	CA	21,896	C+
San Francisco State Univ	CA	18,514	LC
San Jose State Univ	CA	21,540	C
Savannah State Univ	GA	15,631	C
Seattle Univ	WA	50,811	VC+
Seton Hall Univ	NJ	55,514	C
Seton Hill Univ	PA	46,972	C
Shaw Univ	NC	24,638	C
Shenandoah Univ	VA	41,312	C
Shippensburg Univ of Pennsylvania	PA	23,208	C
Shorter Univ	GA	31,130	LC
Siena Heights Univ	MI	32,040	C
Simpson College	IA	43,839	VC
Sonoma State Univ	CA	27,806	C
S Car State Univ	SC	20,805	LC
South Univ	GA	36,070	LC
Southeast Missouri State Univ	MO	15,498	C
Southeastern Louisiana Univ	LA	16,237	C
Southeastern Okla State Univ	OK	11,875	C
Southeastern Univ	FL	31,765	C
Southern Illinois Univ Carbondale	IL	23,667	C
Southern Illinois Univ Edwardsville	IL	22,643	C
Southern Oregon Univ	OR	19,117	C
Southern Univ and A&M College	LA	16,074	LC+
Southern Univ at New Orleans	LA	8,014	LC
Southern Vermont College	VT	34,670	LC
Southern Wesleyan Univ	SC	32,130	LC
Southwest Baptist Univ	MO	29,900	LC
Southwestern Okla State Univ	OK	11,790	C
St. Ambrose Univ	IA	39,019	C
St. Ambrose Univ	IA	39,019	C
St. Cloud State Univ	MN	10,600	C
St. Edward's Univ	TX	53,100	VC
St. Francis College	NY	38,800	LC
St. John's Univ	NY	55,850	C
St. Joseph's College, New York/Brooklyn Campus	NY	25,114	LC
St. Joseph's College, New York/Long Island Campus	NY	25,124	C
St. Mary's Univ	TX	37,500	C
St. Thomas Aquinas College	NY	42,200	C
St. Thomas Univ	FL	36,360	LC
SUNY / Buffalo State College	NY	20,842	C
SUNY / Empire State College	NY	9,145	SP
SUNY / SUNY Oneonta	NY	19,712	C+
SUNY / SUNY Plattsburgh	NY	18,814	C
SUNY / SUNY Potsdam	NY	20,404	C+
SUNY at Oswego	NY	21,351	C
SUNY SUNY Albany	NY	22,165	C
Stephen F. Austin State Univ	TX	18,406	LC
Sterling College	KS	32,830	C
Stockton Univ	NJ	25,059	
Suffolk Univ	MA	50,308	C
Sul Ross State Univ	TX	15,021	LC
Tabor College	KS	35,870	C
Tarleton State Univ	TX	15,248	LC
Temple Univ	PA	24,392	VC
Tenn State Univ	TN	14,423	C
Texas A&M Univ at Commerce	TX	10,496	C
Texas A&M Univ at Corpus Christi	TX	16,851	LC
Texas Christian Univ	TX	54,670	HC
Texas Southern Univ	TX	18,212	LC
Texas State Univ	TX	19,350	C
Texas Wesleyan Univ	TX	35,134	C
Texas Woman's Univ	TX	15,302	LC
The Citadel, The Military College of S Car	SC	35,339	C
The College at Brockport - SUNY	NY	20,346	C
The College of New Jersey	NJ	31,909	HC
The College of St. Rose	NY	43,048	C
The Lincoln Univ	PA	15,154	NC
The Univ of Akron	OH	21,477	C
The Univ of Tenn at Chattanooga	TN	16,744	C
The Univ of Tenn at Martin	TN	14,876	C
The Univ of Virginia's College at Wise	VA	18,192	LC
Thiel College	PA	41,590	C
Thomas College	ME	35,268	LC
Thomas Edison State Univ	NJ	6,350	NC
Thomas More College	KY	36,720	C
Thomas Univ	GA	21,420	LC
Tiffin Univ	OH	31,380	C
Trevecca Nazarene Univ	TN	31,186	C
Trine Univ	IN	41,310	C
Trinity Christian College	IL	35,580	C
Trinity International Univ	IL	31,070	VC
Trinity Washington Univ	DC	33,826	C+
Troy Univ	AL	16,171	C
Truman State Univ	MO	16,014	HC
Tusculum College	TN	31,625	C
Union College	KY	32,310	C
Union Inst & Univ	OH	8,912	SP
Univ of Alabama	AL	24,320	C+
Univ of Alabama at Birmingham	AL	19,906	C
Univ of Arizona	AZ	23,100	C
Univ of Arkansas at Fayetteville	AR	19,152	C+
Univ of Arkansas at Little Rock	AR	18,211	C
Univ of Arkansas at Monticello	AR	13,134	NC
Univ of Arkansas at Pine Bluff	AR	13,541	C
Univ of Bridgeport	CT	44,430	LC
Univ of Central Florida	FL	15,922	VC
Univ of Central Missouri	MO	18,982	C
Univ of Central Okla	OK	13,486	C
Univ of Cincinnati	OH	21,964	VC
Univ of Colo Colo Springs	CO	19,663	C
Univ of Colo Denver	CO	23,230	C
Univ of Dayton	OH	53,620	C
Univ of Delaware	DE	24,976	VC+
Univ of Detroit Mercy	MI	48,816	C+
Univ of Evansville	IN	44,186	VC+
Univ of Findlay	OH	60,139	C
Univ of Georgia	GA	21,250	HC
Univ of Great Falls	MT	38,524	C
Univ of Hartford	CT	49,776	C
Univ of Hawaii at Hilo	HI	18,038	C
Univ of Houston-Downtown	TX	7,241	C
Univ of Illinois at Chicago	IL	25,006	VC
Univ of Indianapolis	IN	36,480	C
Univ of Jamestown	ND	28,508	C
Univ of Louisiana at Lafayette	LA	14,516	C
Univ of Louisiana at Monroe	LA	15,970	C
Univ of Louisville	KY	19,824	C
Univ of Maine at Fort Kent	ME	15,165	LC
Univ of Maine at Machias	ME	22,960	C
Univ of Maine at Presque Isle	ME	14,870	C
Univ of Mary	ND	23,180	C
Univ of Mary Hardin-Baylor	TX	33,950	C+
Univ of Maryland/College Park	MD	21,938	HC
Univ of Maryland/Eastern Shore	MD	17,013	C
Univ of Maryland/Univ College	MD	25,966	LC
Univ of Mass Boston	MA	13,435	C
Univ of Mass Dartmouth	MA	25,658	C
Univ of Mass Lowell	MA	26,380	C
Univ of Memphis	TN	18,278	C
Univ of Mich/Dearborn	MI	11,757	VC
Univ of Mich-Flint	MI	17,607	C+
Univ of Minn Crookston	MN	19,739	C
Univ of Miss	MS	17,746	C+
Univ of Missouri-Kansas City	MO	19,563	VC
Univ of Missouri-St. Louis	MO		C
Univ of Montana-Western	MT	11,220	LC
Univ of Mount Olive	NC	18,426	C
Univ of Mount Union	OH	38,970	C
Univ of Nebr - Kearney	NE	16,546	LC
Univ of Nebr - Omaha	NE	16,120	C
Univ of Nevada, Las Vegas	NV	17,553	C
Univ of Nevada/Reno	NV	18,010	C
Univ of New Haven	CT	52,190	C
Univ of North Alabama	AL	15,398	C
Univ of N Car at Charlotte	NC	15,547	C
Univ of N Car at Pembroke	NC	14,388	LC
Univ of N Car at Wilmington	NC	14,590	VC
Univ of N Dak	ND	15,373	C
Univ of North Florida	FL	15,996	VC
Univ of North Georgia	GA	17,316	C
Univ of North Texas	TX	19,198	C
Univ of Northern Colo	CO	20,851	C
Univ of Northwestern - St. Paul	MN	38,160	C
Univ of Okla	OK	18,911	VC
Univ of Pikeville	KY	28,700	NC
Univ of Pittsburgh at Bradford	PA	22,402	C
Univ of Pittsburgh at Johnstown	PA	22,092	C
Univ of Rhode Island	RI	24,906	C
Univ of St. Francis	IN	37,400	C
Univ of St. Joseph	CT	49,550	C
Univ of Scranton	PA	54,962	VC
Univ of South Alabama	AL	16,400	C
Univ of S Car at Columbia	SC	19,725	VC+
Univ of S Car Upstate	SC	18,200	LC
Univ of S Dak	SD	16,109	C
Univ of Southern Indiana	IN	16,501	C
Univ of Southern Miss	MS	13,170	C
Univ of St. Francis	IL	39,924	C
Univ of Texas at Arlington	TX	18,026	LC
Univ of Texas at El Paso	TX	34,452	NC
Univ of Texas at San Antonio	TX	20,157	C
Univ of the Cumberlands	KY	32,000	C
Univ of the District of Columbia	DC	21,044	LC
Univ of the Sacred Heart	PR	17,932	
Univ of the Southwest	NM	22,766	C
Univ of Toledo	OH	19,336	NC
Univ of West Florida	FL	15,848	C
Univ of Wisc-Eau Claire	WI	15,797	VC
Univ of Wisc-Milwaukee	WI	21,496	C
Univ of Wisc-Oshkosh	WI	15,200	C
Univ of Wisc-Platteville	WI	14,614	VC
Univ of Wisc-Superior	WI	14,446	C
Univ of Wyoming	WY	15,375	C+
Urbana Univ	OH	30,820	C
Utica College	NY	30,430	C
Villanova Univ	PA	62,523	MC

ST = STATE $IS = IN-STATE COSTS   SR = SELECTOR RATING

School	ST	$IS	SR
Virginia Commonwealth Univ	VA	23,049	C
Virginia Wesleyan College	VA	43,728	LC
Viterbo Univ	WI	34,660	C
Voorhees College	SC	19,976	C
Walsh Univ	OH	39,010	C
Washburn Univ	KS	15,827	C
Washington State Univ	WA	22,495	C
Wayland Baptist Univ	TX	22,356	LC
Wayne State College	NE	12,802	C
Wayne State Univ	MI	22,016	C
Waynesburg Univ	PA	32,290	C
Weber State Univ	UT	10,721	C
West Chester Univ of Pennsylvania	PA	18,456	C
West Liberty Univ	WV	15,512	C
West Texas A&M Univ	TX	13,478	C
West Virginia State Univ	WV	8,378	NC
West Virginia Wesleyan College	WV	36,858	C
Western Carolina Univ	NC	13,965	C
Western Conn State Univ	CT	21,254	LC
Western Mich Univ	MI	21,054	C
Western New England Univ	MA	48,088	C
Westfield State Univ	MA	19,671	C
Westminster College	PA	39,180	C+
Westminster College	UT	41,078	C+
Wheeling Jesuit Univ	WV	37,106	LC
Wichita State Univ	KS	21,643	C
Widener Univ	PA	56,486	C
Wilmington College	OH	34,600	C
Wilmington Univ	DE	8,546	NC
Wingate Univ	NC	39,950	C
Winona State Univ	MN	17,535	C
Worcester State Univ	MA	20,977	C
Wright State Univ	OH	16,983	C
Xavier Univ	OH	47,880	C+
York College of Pennsylvania	PA	29,240	C
Youngstown State Univ	OH	17,307	C

CRIMINOLOGY

School	ST	$IS	SR
Adams State Univ	CO	17,703	LC
Alabama A&M Univ	AL	18,796	C
Albertus Magnus College	CT	43,258	LC
Alderson Broaddus Univ	WV	26,149	C
Arizona State Univ at the Downtown Phoenix Campus	AZ	23,680	VC
Arkansas State Univ	AR	16,190	C
Assumption College	MA	47,920	C+
Auburn Univ	AL	23,594	VC+
Barry Univ	FL	37,830	C
Cabrini Univ	PA	42,591	LC
Cal State, Fresno	CA	16,902	LC
Cal State, Long Beach	CA	18,850	C
Cal State, Northridge	CA	16,859	LC
Cal State, San Marcos	CA	24,184	LC
Cazenovia College	NY	46,470	C
Central Conn State Univ	CT	21,203	C
Chatham Univ	PA	46,517	C
CUNY/John Jay College of Criminal Justice	NY	6,359	NC
Cleveland State Univ	OH	22,196	C
Coker College	SC	34,810	LC
College of the Ozarks	MO	7,230	C
Colo State Univ-Pueblo	CO	18,234	C
Davis & Elkins College	WV	38,242	LC
Drexel Univ	PA	65,432	VC+
Drury Univ	MO	33,791	VC
Eastern Conn State Univ	CT	23,059	C
Faulkner Univ	AL	26,410	C
Flagler College	FL	27,620	C
Florida Gulf Coast Univ	FL	9,682	C
Florida State Univ	FL	16,771	HC
Framingham State Univ	MA	20,584	C
Hilbert College	NY	30,850	C
Hofstra Univ	NY	55,960	C+
Indiana Inst of Technology	IN	34,240	LC
Indiana State Univ	IN	23,223	LC
Indiana Univ of Pennsylvania	PA	23,614	LC
Indiana Univ Southeast	IN	14,242	LC
John Carroll Univ	OH	49,740	C+
Johnson & Wales Univ/ Denver Campus	CO	42,707	C
Kent State Univ	OH	20,732	C
Le Moyne College	NY	46,000	C
Longwood Univ	VA	22,184	C
Loyola Univ Chicago	IL	55,802	VC
Lycoming College	PA	48,580	C
Lynchburg College	VA	46,740	C
Marquette Univ	WI	48,390	VC+
Maryville Univ of St. Louis	MO	38,046	VC+
Millersville Univ of Pennsylvania	PA	23,782	C
Missouri State Univ	MO	15,190	C+
Mount Aloysius College	PA	29,976	C
Mount St. Joseph Univ	OH	33,880	C
Niagara Univ	NY	41,010	C
Northern Arizona Univ	AZ	20,246	VC
Northwest Missouri State Univ	MO	17,737	C
Ohio State Univ at Columbus	OH	21,703	HC+
Ohio Univ	OH	22,924	C
Pontifical Catholic Univ of PR	PR	10,534	
Regis Univ	CO	44,520	C
St. Mary-of-the-Woods College	IN	39,632	LC
Southern Oregon Univ	OR	19,117	C
St. Edward's Univ	TX	53,100	VC
St. John Fisher College	NY	43,620	C
SUNY / SUNY College at Old Westbury	NY	16,860	C
Stonehill College	MA	55,030	C+
The Univ of Akron	OH	21,477	C
Universidad del Turabo	PR	17,828	
Univ of Calif at Irvine	CA	26,484	VC
Univ of Central Arkansas	AR	14,472	VC
Univ of Denver	CO	58,443	VC+
Univ of Florida	FL	16,291	HC+
Univ of Illinois at Chicago	IL	25,006	VC
Univ of La Verne	CA	55,600	C
Univ of Maryland/College Park	MD	21,938	HC
Univ of Memphis	TN	18,278	C
Univ of Miami	FL	63,494	MC
Univ of Minn/Duluth	MN	20,292	C+
Univ of New Haven	CT	52,190	C
Univ of New Mexico	NM	15,404	C
Univ of Rhode Island	RI	24,906	C
Univ of St. Mary	KS	34,690	C
Univ of South Florida/St. Petersburg	FL	15,980	C
Univ of South Florida/Tampa	FL	16,110	VC+
Univ of Tampa	FL	36,944	C
Univ of Texas at Dallas	TX	22,830	VC+
Univ of West Georgia	GA	16,360	LC
Upper Iowa Univ	IA	34,990	NC
Valparaiso Univ	IN	48,370	C+
Virginia Union Univ	VA	22,421	C
Washington State Univ	WA	22,495	C
Webster Univ	MO	37,490	C
West Virginia Univ	WV	18,210	C
Western Kentucky Univ	KY	16,850	C
Wilkes Univ	PA	45,622	C
William Penn Univ	IA	26,000	C

CROSSCULTURAL STUDIES

School	ST	$IS	SR
Alfred Univ	NY	42,296	C+
Andrews Univ	MI	28,030	C+
Bard College at Simon's Rock	MA	65,795	MC
Biola Univ	CA	46,402	C+
Chatham Univ	PA	46,517	C
Columbia College Chicago	IL	43,168	C
Corban Univ	OR	40,306	C
Goddard College	VT	17,040	VC
Hampshire College	MA	63,824	MC
Hope International Univ	CA	41,150	C
Houghton College	NY	39,090	C
Kentucky Christian Univ	KY	26,560	LC
Lee Univ	TN	22,045	C
Linfield College	OR	52,010	C
Malone Univ	OH	38,448	C
National Louis Univ	IL	16,920	LC
Nyack College	NY	34,050	NC
Okla Baptist Univ	OK	32,320	C
Olivet Nazarene Univ	IL	41,840	C
Palm Beach Atlantic Univ	FL	39,720	C
Rollins College	FL	58,670	HC
Simpson Univ	CA	33,700	C
Stanford Univ	CA	60,409	MC
Toccoa Falls College	GA	27,920	C
Towson Univ	MD	17,408	VC
Univ of Northwestern - St. Paul	MN	38,160	C
Villanova Univ	PA	62,523	MC
Washington State Univ	WA	22,495	C
Western Kentucky Univ	KY	16,850	C
Whitworth Univ	WA	51,732	VC
Wofford College	SC	49,885	VC

CULINARY ARTS

School	ST	$IS	SR
Atlantic Union College	MA	27,228	C
College of the Ozarks	MO	7,230	C
Drexel Univ	PA	65,432	VC+
Idaho State Univ	ID	13,619	NC
Kendall College	IL	32,610	C
Kennesaw State Univ	GA	19,592	VC
Livingstone College	NC	17,815	LC
Miss Univ for Women	MS	17,065	C
Pennsylvania College of Technology	PA	27,333	NC
Southern New Hampshire Univ	NH	43,198	C
SUNY /College of Agriculture and Tech at Cobleskill	NY	20,527	LC
The Art Inst of Atlanta	GA	34,334	SP
Univ of Alaska Anchorage	AK	16,652	NC
Univ of Nebr - Lincoln	NE	18,589	VC

CULTURAL ANTHROPOLOGY

School	ST	$IS	SR
Creighton Univ	NE	48,206	VC+
Univ of Maryland/Baltimore County	MD	21,296	VC
Webster Univ	MO	37,490	C
Western Kentucky Univ	KY	16,850	C

CULTURAL STUDIES/CRITICAL THEORY & ANALYSIS

School	ST	$IS	SR
Arkansas Tech Univ	AR	15,484	C
Bard College at Simon's Rock	MA	65,795	MC
Bethany College	WV	36,300	NC
Bryant Univ	RI	55,646	VC
Chatham Univ	PA	46,517	C
Columbia College Chicago	IL	43,168	C
Dallas Baptist Univ	TX	33,713	C
Goddard College	VT	17,040	VC
Indiana Univ Bloomington	IN	20,429	VC
MidAmerica Nazarene Univ	KS	35,550	C
Northwest Nazarene Univ	ID	36,000	C
Occidental College	CA	65,530	MC
Univ of Maryland/Baltimore County	MD	21,296	VC

CUSTOMER SERVICE

School	ST	$IS	SR
Ohio Univ	OH	22,924	C

CYBER INTELLIGENCE/ SECURITY STUDIES

School	ST	$IS	SR
Armstrong State Univ	GA	16,962	C
Bay Path Univ	MA	45,349	C
Bloomsburg Univ of Pennsylvania	PA	19,066	LC
Champlain College	VT	53,132	C+
Embry-Riddle Aeronautical Univ - Daytona Beach	FL	44,712	VC
Embry-Riddle Aeronautical Univ - Prescott Campus	AZ	44,054	VC
Excelsior College	NY	14,080	SP
Hilbert College	NY	30,850	C
Lewis Univ	IL	40,370	C
Maryville Univ of St. Louis	MO	38,046	VC+
Montreat College	NC	31,298	LC
Northern Mich Univ	MI	19,604	C
Southeast Missouri State Univ	MO	15,498	C
St. Bonaventure Univ	NY	44,237	C
Thomas Edison State Univ	NJ	6,350	NC
Tiffin Univ	OH	31,380	C
Trine Univ	IN	41,310	G
Univ of Maine at Fort Kent	ME	15,165	LC
Univ of Maryland/Baltimore County	MD	21,296	VC
Univ of South Alabama	AL	16,400	C
Utica College	NY	30,430	C

CYBER OPERATIONS

School	ST	$IS	SR
Embry-Riddle Aeronautical Univ - Prescott Campus	AZ	44,054	VC
United States Naval Academy	MD		MC
Univ of Maryland/Baltimore County	MD	21,296	VC
Univ of New Haven	CT	52,190	C

CYBERNETICS

School	ST	$IS	SR
Univ of Maryland/Baltimore County	MD	21,296	VC

CYTOTECHNOLOGY

School	ST	$IS	SR
Barry Univ	FL	37,830	C
Bloomfield College	NJ	39,100	LC
Edgewood College	WI	35,950	C
Indiana Univ Kokomo	IN	7,073	C
Indiana Univ-Purdue Univ Indianapolis	IN	18,635	C
Marian Univ	WI	32,420	LC
Marshall Univ	WV	17,242	C
Mass College of Liberal Arts	MA	20,128	C
Old Dominion Univ	VA	20,910	C
St. Louis Univ	MO	49,866	HC
St. Mary's Univ of Minn	MN	41,210	VC
SUNY / SUNY Plattsburgh	NY	18,814	C
The College of St. Rose	NY	43,048	C
Thiel College	PA	41,590	C
Univ of Conn	CT	25,538	HC
Univ of Mass Dartmouth	MA	25,658	C
Univ of Miss	MS	17,746	C+
Univ of N Dak	ND	15,373	C
Univ of North Texas	TX	19,198	C
Winona State Univ	MN	17,535	C

DAIRY SCIENCE

School	ST	$IS	SR
Calif Polytechnic State Univ	CA	17,979	HC+
Cal State, Fresno	CA	16,902	LC
Delaware Valley Univ	PA	49,796	C
Iowa State Univ	IA	17,570	C
S Dak State Univ	SD	15,634	C
Univ of Florida	FL	16,291	HC+
Univ of Georgia	GA	21,250	HC
Univ of Idaho	ID	15,348	C
Univ of New Hampshire	NH	28,562	VC
Univ of Wisc-Madison	WI	20,934	MC
Univ of Wisc-Platteville	WI	14,614	VC
Utah State Univ	UT	12,736	C
Virginia Polytechnic Inst and State Univ	VA	21,276	HC
Western Kentucky Univ	KY	16,850	C

DANCE

School	ST	$IS	SR
Adelphi Univ	NY	48,244	C
Agnes Scott College	GA	51,930	VC+
Alma College	MI	47,548	C
Amherst College	MA		HC+
Appalachian State Univ	NC	14,416	VC
Arizona State Univ at the Tempe Campus	AZ	21,756	VC
Ball State Univ	IN	19,590	C
Bard College	NY	64,024	HC
Bard College at Simon's Rock	MA	65,795	MC
Barnard College/Columbia Univ	NY	62,741	MC
Belhaven Univ	MS	31,016	C
Beloit College	WI	55,206	HC
Bennington College	VT	63,960	MC
Bowling Green State Univ	OH	19,747	C
Brenau Univ - Women's College	GA	37,876	LC
Brigham Young Univ	UT	12,748	HC
Bryn Athyn College	PA	31,470	C
Butler Univ	IN	51,352	VC
Calif Inst of the Arts	CA	56,426	SP
Cal State, Fullerton	CA	21,902	C
Cal State, Long Beach	CA	18,850	C
Cal State, Northridge	CA	16,859	LC
Cal State, San Bernardino	CA	12,000	C
Case Western Reserve Univ	OH	60,304	MC
Cedar Crest College	PA	46,715	C
Centenary College of Louisiana	LA	45,650	C+
Chapman Univ	CA	63,078	VC+
CUNY/Hunter College	NY	31,098	VC
CUNY/Lehman College	NY	5,778	HC+
Coker College	SC	34,810	LC
College of Charleston	SC	22,699	C
Colo College	CO	62,560	MC
Colo Mesa Univ	CO	18,955	LC
Colo State Univ	CO	22,162	VC
Columbia College	SC	36,550	C
Columbia College Chicago	IL	43,168	C
Columbia Univ/ School of General Studies	NY	61,470	MC
Columbia Univ/City of New York	NY	62,958	MC
Conn College	CT	65,000	MC
Cornish College of the Arts	WA	47,750	SP
Davis & Elkins College	WV	38,242	LC
Denison Univ	OH	58,860	MC
DeSales Univ	PA	43,970	C
Dickinson College	PA	63,974	MC
Dominican Univ of Calif	CA	57,050	C
Drexel Univ	PA	65,432	VC+
East Carolina Univ	NC	16,937	C
Eastern Mich Univ	MI	19,761	C
Eastern Univ	PA	39,540	C
Eastern Washington Univ	WA	25,572	LC
Elon Univ	NC	44,599	VC+
Emory Univ	GA	60,786	MC
Eugene Lang College/The New School for Liberal Arts	NY	55,650	C
Florida State Univ	FL	16,771	HC
Fordham Univ	NY	65,918	MC
Franklin Pierce Univ	NH	46,750	C
George Mason Univ	VA	15,724	VC
George Washington Univ	DC	62,835	MC
Georgian Court Univ	NJ	42,426	LC
Goucher College	MD	55,716	VC
Grand Valley State Univ	MI	22,250	C+
Gustavus Adolphus College	MN	52,433	HC
Hamilton College	NY	64,250	MC
Hampshire College	MA	63,824	MC
Hofstra Univ	NY	55,960	C+
Hollins Univ	VA	49,635	VC
Hope College	MI	39,940	VC
Howard Univ	DC	37,616	C+
Indiana Univ Bloomington	IN	20,429	VC
Jacksonville Univ	FL	46,230	C
James Madison Univ	VA	19,084	VC
Juilliard School	NY	57,162	SP
Keene State College	NH	24,003	LC
Kennesaw State Univ	GA	19,592	VC
Kent State Univ	OH	20,732	C
Kenyon College	OH	63,330	MC
La Roche College	PA	37,924	LC
Lindenwood Univ	MO	25,132	C
LIU Brooklyn	NY	49,682	C
LIU Post	NY	49,682	C
Loyola Marymount Univ	CA	58,038	HC
Loyola Univ Chicago	IL	55,802	VC
Luther College	IA	48,540	C+
Manhattanville College	NY	51,440	C+
Marygrove College	MI	28,926	NC
Marymount Manhattan College	NY	46,280	VC
Mercyhurst Univ	PA	47,420	C
Meredith College	NC	45,297	C
Messiah College	PA	43,100	C+
Middlebury College	VT	64,332	MC
Mills College	CA	59,163	VC
Minn State Univ, Mankato	MN	15,616	C
Montclair State Univ	NJ	26,210	LC
Mount Holyoke College	MA	56,746	MC
Muhlenberg College	PA	56,645	VC+
New Mexico State Univ	NM	14,050	C
New York Univ	NY	65,860	MC
Northeastern Illinois Univ	IL	12,529	LC
Northwestern Univ	IL	66,344	MC
Nova Southeastern Univ	FL	38,534	C+
Oakland Univ	MI	20,763	C
Oberlin College	OH	66,012	MC
Ohio State Univ at Columbus	OH	21,703	HC+
Ohio Univ	OH	22,924	C
Ohio Wesleyan Univ	OH	49,460	VC

ST = STATE $IS = IN-STATE COSTS SR = SELECTOR RATING

School	ST	$IS	SR
Okla City Univ	OK	40,476	VC
Old Dominion Univ	VA	20,910	C
Oral Roberts Univ	OK	34,316	C
Otterbein Univ	OH	41,630	C
Pace Univ	NY	58,248	C
Palm Beach Atlantic Univ	FL	39,720	C
Pitzer College	CA	66,192	MC
Point Park Univ	PA	41,270	C
Pomona College	CA	64,957	MC
Prescott College	AZ	33,284	C
Radford Univ	VA	19,027	LC
Randolph College	VA	45,660	VC
Rhode Island College	RI	17,694	LC
Rider Univ	NJ	54,050	C
Roger Williams Univ	RI	46,296	C+
Rutgers Univ - New Brunswick	NJ	26,632	HC
Sam Houston State Univ	TX	18,792	C
San Diego State Univ	CA	21,896	C+
San Francisco State Univ	CA	18,514	LC
San Jose State Univ	CA	21,540	C
Santa Fe Univ of Art and Design	NM	39,980	SP
Sarah Lawrence College	NY	63,388	HC
Scripps College	CA	66,664	MC
Seton Hill Univ	PA	46,972	C
Shenandoah Univ	VA	41,312	C
Skidmore College	NY	64,214	HC
Slippery Rock Univ of Pennsylvania	PA	10,360	C
Smith College	MA	63,914	MC
Southeast Missouri State Univ	MO	15,498	C
Southern Illinois Univ Edwardsville	IL	22,643	C
Southern Methodist Univ	TX	66,483	MC
St. Olaf College	MN	54,260	HC+
SUNY / SUNY Fredonia	NY	20,818	C
SUNY / SUNY Potsdam	NY	20,404	C+
SUNY / Univ at Buffalo	NY	23,122	C+
SUNY at Binghamton	NY	22,861	MC
SUNY at Purchase	NY	17,900	C
Stephen F. Austin State Univ	TX	18,406	LC
Stephens College	MO	38,042	C
Stockton Univ	NJ	25,059	
Swarthmore College	PA	63,550	MC
Temple Univ	PA	24,392	VC
Texas State Univ	TX	19,350	C
Texas Tech Univ	TX	18,736	C+
Texas Woman's Univ	TX	15,302	LC
The Boston Conservatory at Berklee	MA	61,042	C+
The College at Brockport - SUNY	NY	20,346	C
The College of Wooster	OH	57,900	VC+
The Univ of Akron	OH	21,477	C
Towson Univ	MD	17,408	VC
Trinity College	CT	63,920	HC+
Tulane Univ	LA	63,396	HC+
Univ of Alabama	AL	24,320	C+
Univ of Arizona	AZ	23,100	C
Univ of Arkansas at Little Rock	AR	18,211	C
Univ of Calif at Berkeley	CA	28,853	MC
Univ of Calif at Irvine	CA	26,484	VC
Univ of Calif at Riverside	CA	29,227	C+
Univ of Calif at Santa Barbara	CA	29,091	HC
Univ of Calif San Diego	CA	30,150	MC
Univ of Central Okla	OK	13,486	C
Univ of Cincinnati	OH	21,964	VC
Univ of Colo Boulder	CO	24,285	VC+
Univ of Florida	FL	16,291	HC+
Univ of Georgia	GA	21,250	HC
Univ of Hartford	CT	49,776	C
Univ of Hawaii at Manoa	HI	23,221	C
Univ of Houston	TX	21,483	VC
Univ of Idaho	ID	15,348	C
Univ of Illinois at Urbana-Champaign	IL	27,006	HC
Univ of Iowa	IA	18,683	VC+
Univ of Kansas	KS	20,135	C+
Univ of Louisiana at Lafayette	LA	14,516	C
Univ of Maryland/Baltimore County	MD	21,296	VC
Univ of Maryland/College Park	MD	21,938	HC
Univ of Mass Amherst	MA	26,199	VC+
Univ of Mich/Ann Arbor	MI	24,410	MC
Univ of Minn/Twin Cities	MN	23,519	HC+
Univ of Missouri-Kansas City	MO	19,563	VC
Univ of Missouri-St. Louis	MO		C
Univ of Nebr - Lincoln	NE	18,589	VC
Univ of Nevada, Las Vegas	NV	17,553	C
Univ of New Mexico	NM	15,404	C
Univ of N Car at Charlotte	NC	15,547	C
Univ of N Car at Greensboro	NC	14,690	C
Univ of N Car School of the Arts	NC	18,040	SP
Univ of North Texas	TX	19,198	C
Univ of Okla	OK	18,911	VC
Univ of Oregon	OR	22,972	C
Univ of Richmond	VA	60,880	MC
Univ of St. Francis	IN	37,400	C
Univ of S Car at Columbia	SC	19,725	VC+
Univ of South Florida/Tampa	FL	16,110	VC+
Univ of Southern Miss	MS	13,170	C
Univ of Tampa	FL	36,944	C
Univ of Texas at Austin	TX	26,102	HC
Univ of the Arts	PA	56,579	SP
Univ of Washington	WA	23,149	VC
Univ of Wisc-Madison	WI	20,934	MC
Univ of Wisc-Milwaukee	WI	21,496	C
Univ of Wisc-Stevens Point	WI	14,043	C
Univ of Wyoming	WY	15,375	C+
Ursinus College	PA	61,690	VC
Utah State Univ	UT	12,736	C
Virginia Commonwealth Univ	VA	23,049	C
Washington Univ in St. Louis	MO	65,366	VC
Wayne State Univ	MI	22,016	C
Weber State Univ	UT	10,721	C
Webster Univ	MO	37,490	C
Wells College	NY	50,500	C
Wesleyan Univ	CT	65,516	MC
West Chester Univ of Pennsylvania	PA	18,456	C
West Texas A&M Univ	TX	13,478	C
West Virginia Univ	WV	18,210	C
Western Kentucky Univ	KY	16,850	C
Western Mich Univ	MI	21,054	C
Western Oregon Univ	OR	15,021	LC
Western Washington Univ	WA	18,003	C+
Wichita State Univ	KS	21,643	C
Winthrop Univ	SC	23,082	C
Wittenberg Univ	OH	48,156	C+
Wright State Univ	OH	16,983	C
Youngstown State Univ	OH	17,307	C

DANCE EDUCATION

School	ST	$IS	SR
Brenau Univ - Women's College	GA	37,876	LC
Bridgewater State Univ	MA	21,810	C
Brigham Young Univ	UT	12,748	HC
Central Conn State Univ	CT	21,203	C
Columbia College	SC	36,550	C
East Carolina Univ	NC	16,937	C
Grand Canyon Univ	AZ	16,950	VC
Hofstra Univ	NY	55,960	C+
Hope College	MI	39,940	VC
Jacksonville Univ	FL	46,230	C
Marywood Univ	PA	46,900	C
Minn State Univ, Mankato	MN	15,616	C
New York Univ	NY	65,860	MC
Ohio State Univ at Columbus	OH	21,703	HC+
Old Dominion Univ	VA	20,910	C
Point Park Univ	PA	41,270	C
Stephen F. Austin State Univ	TX	18,406	LC
Towson Univ	MD	17,408	VC
Univ of Central Okla	OK	13,486	C
Univ of N Car at Greensboro	NC	14,690	C
Univ of the Arts	PA	56,579	SP

DATA PROCESSING

School	ST	$IS	SR
Ball State Univ	IN	19,590	C
Calvin College	MI	41,570	VC+
College of Charleston	SC	22,699	C
Husson Univ	ME	25,720	LC
Northwest Missouri State Univ	MO	17,737	C

DENTAL EDUCATION

School	ST	$IS	SR
Seton Hill Univ	PA	46,972	C
Thomas Edison State Univ	NJ	6,350	NC
Wichita State Univ	KS	21,643	C

DENTAL HYGIENE

School	ST	$IS	SR
Allen College	IA	32,367	NC
Augusta Univ	GA	4,632	C
Clayton State Univ	GA	19,735	C
Creighton Univ	NE	48,206	VC+
East Central Univ	OK	13,056	C
East Tenn State Univ	TN	13,994	C
Eastern Washington Univ	WA	25,572	LC
Farmingdale State College	NY	20,624	C
Ferris State Univ	MI	21,445	C
Howard Univ	DC	37,616	C+
Idaho State Univ	ID	13,619	NC
Indiana Univ Kokomo	IN	7,073	C
Indiana Univ Northwest	IN	7,072	C
Indiana Univ South Bend	IN	14,242	C
Indiana Univ-Purdue Univ Indianapolis	IN	18,635	C
Lewis Univ	IL	40,370	C
MCPHS Univ	MA	45,470	SP
Metropolitan State Univ	MN	7,566	C
Midwestern State Univ	TX	17,572	C
Minn State Univ, Mankato	MN	15,616	C
Missouri Southern State Univ	MO	12,499	C
New York Univ	NY	65,860	MC
Northern Arizona Univ	AZ	20,246	VC
Ohio State Univ at Columbus	OH	21,703	HC+
Ohio State Univ at Lima	OH	7,140	C
Old Dominion Univ	VA	20,910	C
Oregon Inst of Technology	OR	8,910	C
Pennsylvania College of Technology	PA	27,333	NC
Rhode Island College	RI	17,694	LC
Southern Illinois Univ Carbondale	IL	23,667	C
Tenn State Univ	TN	14,423	C
Texas A&M Univ	TX	20,521	VC+
Texas Woman's Univ	TX	15,302	LC
The Univ of Tenn at Knoxville	TN	22,112	VC
Thomas Edison State Univ	NJ	6,350	NC
Univ of Alaska Anchorage	AK	16,652	NC
Univ of Bridgeport	CT	44,430	LC
Univ of Detroit Mercy	MI	48,816	C+
Univ of Hawaii at Manoa	HI	23,221	C
Univ of Louisiana at Monroe	LA	15,970	C
Univ of Louisville	KY	19,824	C
Univ of Maine at Augusta	ME	7,812	C
Univ of Mich/Ann Arbor	MI	24,410	MC
Univ of Minn/Twin Cities	MN	23,519	HC+
Univ of Miss	MS	17,746	C+
Univ of Missouri-Kansas City	MO	19,563	VC
Univ of New England	ME	48,880	C
Univ of New Haven	CT	52,190	C
Univ of New Mexico	NM	15,404	C
Univ of N Car at Chapel Hill	NC	20,052	HC+
Univ of Pittsburgh	PA	29,568	HC+
Univ of S Dak	SD	16,109	C
Univ of Southern Calif	CA	66,631	C
Univ of Southern Indiana	IN	16,501	C
Univ of Washington	WA	23,149	VC
Univ of Wyoming	WY	15,375	C+
Virginia Commonwealth Univ	VA	23,049	C
Walla Walla Univ	WA	30,417	NC
Weber State Univ	UT	10,721	C
West Liberty Univ	WV	15,512	C
West Virginia Univ	WV	18,210	C
Western Kentucky Univ	KY	16,850	C
Youngstown State Univ	OH	17,307	C

DENTAL LABORATORY TECHNOLOGY

School	ST	$IS	SR
Minot State Univ	ND	12,732	C
Southwest Minn State Univ	MN	17,783	C
Univ of Southern Indiana	IN	16,501	C

DESIGN

School	ST	$IS	SR
Adams State Univ	CO	17,703	LC
Adelphi Univ	NY	48,244	C
Andrews Univ	MI	28,030	C+
Arizona State Univ at the Tempe Campus	AZ	21,756	VC
ArtCenter College of Design	CA	54,212	SP
Auburn Univ	AL	23,594	VC+
Becker College	MA	57,628	C
Belmont Univ	TN	40,970	VC
Bennington College	VT	63,960	MC
Boston Architectural College	MA	20,666	NC
Bowling Green State Univ	OH	19,747	C
Cal State, Long Beach	CA	18,850	C
Carnegie Mellon Univ	PA	67,980	MC
Central Mich Univ	MI	20,330	C
CUNY/Queens College	NY	27,896	C
Clemson Univ	SC		HC
College of Art and Design at Lesley Univ	MA	39,730	SP
Concordia Univ St. Paul	MN	29,050	C
Cornish College of the Arts	WA	47,750	SP
Drexel Univ	PA	65,432	VC+
Drury Univ	MO	33,791	VC
East Carolina Univ	NC	16,937	C
Eastern Mich Univ	MI	19,761	C
Evangel Univ	MO	28,898	C
Fashion Inst of Technology/ SUNY	NY	18,521	SP
Grand Valley State Univ	MI	22,250	C+
Harding Univ	AR	25,421	C
Hofstra Univ	NY	55,960	C+
Howard Univ	DC	37,616	C+
Iowa State Univ	IA	17,570	C
Kansas City Art Inst	MO	44,308	C+
Lamar Univ	TX	18,014	LC
Lees-McRae College	NC	33,944	C
Lehigh Univ	PA	61,010	MC
Loyola Univ New Orleans	LA	51,708	VC+
Memphis College of Art	TN	39,750	C
Minneapolis College of Art and Design	MN	44,238	SP
Missouri State Univ	MO	15,190	C+
National Univ	CA	14,730	LC
New York Univ	NY	65,860	MC
N Car State Univ	NC	19,515	HC+
Northern Mich Univ	MI	19,604	C
Ohio Univ	OH	22,924	C
Okla Christian Univ	OK	27,650	VC
Okla State Univ	OK	17,180	VC
Olivet College	MI	36,110	LC
Otis College of Art and Design	CA	55,858	SP
Parsons The New School for Design	NY	56,610	SP
Pennsylvania State Univ - Univ Park	PA	29,760	HC
Radford Univ	VA	19,027	LC
Rochester Inst of Technology	NY	50,842	HC
Saginaw Valley State Univ	MI	18,530	C
Salem State Univ	MA	17,303	LC
San Francisco State Univ	CA	18,514	LC
San Jose State Univ	CA	21,540	C
Savannah College of Art and Design	GA	49,595	C
School of the Art Inst of Chicago	IL	56,230	SP
Southern Illinois Univ Carbondale	IL	23,667	C
SUNY / Buffalo State College	NY	20,842	C
The Univ of Utah	UT	17,924	VC
Troy Univ	AL	16,171	C
Tusculum College	TN	31,625	C
Univ of Calif at Davis	CA	28,468	HC
Univ of Cincinnati	OH	21,964	VC
Univ of Hartford	CT	49,776	C
Univ of Idaho	ID	15,348	C
Univ of Kansas	KS	20,135	C+
Univ of Maryland/Baltimore County	MD	21,296	VC
Univ of Mich/Ann Arbor	MI	24,410	MC
Univ of Missouri/Columbia	MO	18,201	MC
Univ of New Haven	CT	52,190	C
Univ of North Texas	TX	19,198	C
Univ of Notre Dame	IN	64,043	MC
Univ of Oregon	OR	22,972	C
Univ of Pennsylvania	PA	63,526	MC
Univ of San Francisco	CA	58,484	VC
Univ of Southern Miss	MS	13,170	C
Univ of Texas at Austin	TX	26,102	HC
Univ of Wisc-Green Bay	WI	15,064	C
Washington Univ in St. Louis	MO	65,366	VC
Wayne State Univ	MI	22,016	C
Western Kentucky Univ	KY	16,850	C
Western Washington Univ	WA	18,003	C+
Xavier Univ	OH	47,880	C+
Youngstown State Univ	OH	17,307	C

DESIGN AND ENVIRONMENTAL ANALYSIS

School	ST	$IS	SR
Bryant Univ	RI	55,646	VC
Cornell Univ	NY	64,853	MC

DEVELOPMENT ECONOMICS

School	ST	$IS	SR
Calvin College	MI	41,570	VC+
Taylor Univ	IN	40,317	C+

DEVELOPMENTAL PSYCHOLOGY

School	ST	$IS	SR
Boston College	MA	65,737	MC
Brown Univ	RI	64,566	MC
Cal State, Stanislaus	CA	16,212	C
Emmanuel College	MA	52,110	C+
Fitchburg State Univ	MA	21,819	C
Metropolitan State Univ	MN	7,566	C
New York Univ	NY	65,860	MC
St. Leo Univ	FL	31,650	C
Silver Lake College of the Holy Family	WI	36,290	LC
Univ of Detroit Mercy	MI	48,816	C+

DEVELOPMENTAL SOCIOLOGY

School	ST	$IS	SR
Cornell Univ	NY	64,853	MC

DIAGNOSTIC MEDICAL SONOGRAPHY

School	ST	$IS	SR
Carroll Univ	WI	38,100	C+
Lewis Univ	IL	40,370	C
Nova Southeastern Univ	FL	38,534	C+
Thomas Edison State Univ	NJ	6,350	NC
Univ of Charleston	WV	35,000	C

DIETETICS

School	ST	$IS	SR
Andrews Univ	MI	28,030	C+
Arkansas State Univ	AR	16,190	C
Ball State Univ	IN	19,590	C
Baylor Univ	TX	53,760	HC
Bowling Green State Univ	OH	19,747	C
Brigham Young Univ	UT	12,748	HC
Cal State, Chico	CA	21,440	C
Cal State, Los Angeles	CA	17,186	LC
Case Western Reserve Univ	OH	60,304	MC
Central Mich Univ	MI	20,330	C
CUNY/Lehman College	NY	5,778	HC+
College of the Ozarks	MO	7,230	C
Dominican Univ	IL	41,222	C
D'Youville College	NY	36,780	C
East Carolina Univ	NC	16,937	C
Eastern Kentucky Univ	KY	16,908	C
Eastern Mich Univ	MI	19,761	C
Florida International Univ	FL	19,854	C+
Florida State Univ	FL	16,771	HC
Fontbonne Univ	MO	33,717	C
Harding Univ	AR	25,421	C
Idaho State Univ	ID	13,619	NC
Indiana State Univ	IN	23,223	LC
Indiana Univ Bloomington	IN	20,429	VC
Iowa State Univ	IA	17,570	C
James Madison Univ	VA	19,084	VC
Kansas State Univ	KS	17,780	VC
Lipscomb Univ	TN	41,296	VC
Louisiana Tech Univ	LA	11,422	VC
Madonna Univ	MI	29,050	C
Marshall Univ	WV	17,242	C
Marywood Univ	PA	46,900	C
Messiah College	PA	43,100	C+
Mich State Univ	MI	23,898	VC+
Minn State Univ, Mankato	MN	15,616	C
Missouri State Univ	MO	15,190	C+

ST = STATE $IS = IN-STATE COSTS SR = SELECTOR RATING

School	ST	$IS	SR
Montclair State Univ	NJ	26,210	LC
Mount Mary Univ	WI	34,650	LC
Nicholls State Univ	LA	10,534	C
N Dak State Univ	ND	16,245	C
Northern Illinois Univ	IL	20,176	C
Northwest Missouri State Univ	MO	17,737	C
Oakwood Univ	AL	43,758	C
Olivet Nazarene Univ	IL	41,840	C
Ouachita Baptist Univ	AR	32,320	C
Point Loma Nazarene Univ	CA	43,450	C
Prairie View A&M Univ	TX	15,205	LC
Purdue Univ/West Lafayette	IN	20,032	MC
Rochester Inst of Technology	NY	50,842	HC
San Francisco State Univ	CA	18,514	LC
Seton Hill Univ	PA	46,972	C
Simmons College	MA	53,090	VC
Southern Illinois Univ Carbondale	IL	23,667	C
St. Catherine Univ	MN	45,630	VC
SUNY / Buffalo State College	NY	20,842	C
SUNY / SUNY Oneonta	NY	19,712	C+
Stephen F. Austin State Univ	TX	18,406	LC
Tarleton State Univ	TX	15,248	LC
Texas Christian Univ	TX	54,670	HC
Texas Southern Univ	TX	18,212	LC
Texas Woman's Univ	TX	15,302	LC
The Univ of Akron	OH	21,477	C
Thomas Edison State Univ	NJ	6,350	NC
Tuskegee Univ	AL	28,164	C
Univ of Arkansas at Fayetteville	AR	19,152	C+
Univ of Calif at Davis	CA	28,468	HC
Univ of Central Arkansas	AR	14,472	VC
Univ of Central Missouri	MO	18,982	C
Univ of Cincinnati	OH	21,964	VC
Univ of Conn	CT	25,538	HC
Univ of Dayton	OH	53,620	C
Univ of Delaware	DE	24,976	VC+
Univ of Georgia	GA	21,250	HC
Univ of Illinois at Urbana-Champaign	IL	27,006	HC
Univ of Louisiana at Lafayette	LA	14,516	C
Univ of Miss	MS	17,746	C+
Univ of Nebr - Lincoln	NE	18,589	VC
Univ of New Haven	CT	52,190	C
Univ of N Dak	ND	15,373	C
Univ of North Florida	FL	15,996	VC
Univ of Northern Colo	CO	20,851	C
Univ of Texas at Austin	TX	26,102	HC
Univ of Vermont	VT	28,878	HC
Univ of Wisc-Green Bay	WI	15,064	C
Univ of Wisc-Stevens Point	WI	14,043	C
Univ of Wisc-Stout	WI	19,667	C
Virginia Polytechnic Inst and State Univ	VA	21,276	HC
Viterbo Univ	WI	34,660	C
Wayne State Univ	MI	22,016	C
West Chester Univ of Pennsylvania	PA	18,456	C
Western Carolina Univ	NC	13,965	C
Western Illinois Univ	IL	20,825	C
Western Mich Univ	MI	21,054	C
Youngstown State Univ	OH	17,307	C

DIGITAL ANIMATION & GAME DESIGN

School	ST	$IS	SR
Bloomfield College	NJ	39,100	LC
Ferris State Univ	MI	21,445	C
Rochester Inst of Technology	NY	50,842	HC

DIGITAL ARTS/TECHNOLOGY

School	ST	$IS	SR
Art Academy of Cincinnati	OH	36,252	SP
Baldwin Wallace Univ	OH	41,106	C
Bennington College	VT	63,960	MC
Bowling Green State Univ	OH	19,747	C
Calif Baptist Univ	CA	41,392	C
Calif College of the Arts	CA	52,758	SP
Cal State, Dominguez Hills	CA	19,022	LC
Calvin College	MI	41,570	VC+
Chapman Univ	CA	63,078	VC+
Claflin Univ	SC	33,764	LC
Clarkson Univ	NY	60,392	HC
Cogswell Polytechnical College	CA	30,531	C
College for Creative Studies	MI	48,875	SP
Dakota State Univ	SD	13,811	C
Delta State Univ	MS	13,176	C
DePaul Univ	IL	47,623	VC
Dominican Univ	IL	41,222	C
Drexel Univ	PA	65,432	VC+
Elon Univ	NC	44,599	VC+
Grand Canyon Univ	AZ	16,950	VC
Greenville College	IL	27,012	C
Hamline Univ	MN	45,678	VC
Huntingdon College	AL	34,900	C
Illinois State Univ	IL	23,418	VC
John Brown Univ	AR	33,132	VC
Kansas City Art Inst	MO	44,308	C+
King Univ	TN	34,660	C
Lake Erie College	OH	38,914	LC
LIU Post	NY	49,682	C
Lubbock Christian Univ	TX	28,426	C
Lynn Univ	FL	49,480	LC
Memphis College of Art	TN	39,750	C
Mercy College	NY	31,776	C
Messiah College	PA	43,100	C+
Minneapolis College of Art and Design	MN	44,238	SP
Moore College of Art and Design	PA	50,135	SP
Moore College of Art and Design	PA	50,135	SP
New York Univ	NY	65,860	MC
NewSchool of Architecture & Design	CA	12,341	SP
Northeastern Univ	MA	62,703	MC
Ohio Univ	OH	22,924	C
Olivet Nazarene Univ	IL	41,840	C
Otis College of Art and Design	CA	55,858	SP
Parsons The New School for Design	NY	56,610	SP
Philadelphia Univ	PA	50,370	C
Point Park Univ	PA	41,270	C
Quinnipiac Univ	CT	59,110	C
Roberts Wesleyan College	NY	38,306	C
San Francisco Art Inst	CA	58,505	SP
Santa Fe Univ of Art and Design	NM	39,980	SP
Savannah College of Art and Design	GA	49,595	C
School of the Art Inst of Chicago	IL	56,230	SP
Seattle Univ	WA	50,811	VC+
Southern New Hampshire Univ	NH	43,198	C
Southern Oregon Univ	OR	19,117	C
Southwestern College	KS	31,531	C
Stetson Univ	FL	53,544	VC
Stevens Inst of Technology	NJ	62,338	MC
The College of New Jersey	NJ	31,909	HC
Trinity Christian College	IL	35,580	C
Tulane Univ	LA	63,396	HC+
Univ of Central Florida	FL	15,922	VC
Univ of Denver	CO	58,443	VC+
Univ of Idaho	ID	15,348	C
Univ of Illinois at Chicago	IL	25,006	VC
Univ of Maryland/Univ College	MD	25,966	LC
Univ of Oregon	OR	22,972	C
Univ of Pennsylvania	PA	63,526	MC
Univ of Tampa	FL	36,944	C
Viterbo Univ	WI	34,660	C
Walla Walla Univ	WA	30,417	NC
Washington State Univ	WA	22,495	C
Youngstown State Univ	OH	17,307	C

DIGITAL COMMUNICATIONS

School	ST	$IS	SR
Albright College	PA	46,660	C
Bennington College	VT	63,960	MC
Bethany College	WV	36,300	NC
Cabrini Univ	PA	42,591	LC
Calvin College	MI	41,570	VC+
Canisius College	NY	47,537	C
Endicott College	MA	44,604	VC+
Georgia Inst of Technology	GA	23,360	MC
Georgian Court Univ	NJ	42,426	LC
Henderson State Univ	AR	15,516	LC
Hilbert College	NY	30,850	C
Huntington Univ	IN	33,996	C
Indiana Inst of Technology	IN	34,240	LC
Juniata College	PA	53,760	VC
Kansas City Art Inst	MO	44,308	C+
Lebanon Valley College	PA	51,530	C
Loyola Univ Chicago	IL	55,802	VC
Lycoming College	PA	48,580	C
Marywood Univ	PA	46,900	C
Mass Inst of Technology	MA	62,662	MC
Muskingum Univ	OH	35,966	C
New York Univ	NY	65,860	MC
Ohio Univ	OH	22,924	C
Olivet Nazarene Univ	IL	41,840	C
Oregon State Univ	OR	22,519	VC
Queens Univ of Charlotte	NC	39,543	C
Spring Hill College	AL	48,488	C
St. Bonaventure Univ	NY	44,237	C
St. Edward's Univ	TX	53,100	VC
St. John Fisher College	NY	43,620	C
Trevecca Nazarene Univ	TN	31,186	C
Trinity International Univ	IL	31,070	VC
Univ of Cincinnati	OH	21,964	VC
Univ of Idaho	ID	15,348	C
Univ of Indianapolis	IN	36,480	C
Univ of Oregon	OR	22,972	C
Univ of Rochester	NY	65,032	MC
Valparaiso Univ	IN	48,370	C+
Vanguard Univ of Southern Calif	CA	40,740	VC
Washington State Univ	WA	22,495	C
Webster Univ	MO	37,490	C
William Penn Univ	IA	26,000	C

DIGITAL MEDIA

School	ST	$IS	SR
Ball State Univ	IN	19,590	C
Bethany College	WV	36,300	NC
Bloomfield College	NJ	39,100	LC
Buena Vista Univ	IA	41,514	C
Calif Baptist Univ	CA	41,392	C
Cedarville Univ	OH	34,990	VC
Eastern Conn State Univ	CT	23,059	C
Eastern Mennonite Univ	VA	42,550	C
Ferris State Univ	MI	21,445	C
Fordham Univ	NY	65,918	MC
Georgia Inst of Technology	GA	23,360	MC
Huntington Univ	IN	33,996	C
Iowa Wesleyan Univ	IA	39,200	C
King Univ	TN	34,660	C
Manhattanville College	NY	51,440	C+
Marist College	NY	49,860	VC
Millikin Univ	IL	42,158	C
Neumann Univ	PA	40,678	LC
Ohio Univ	OH	22,924	C
Okla Baptist Univ	OK	32,320	C
Rochester Inst of Technology	NY	50,842	HC
Southern Oregon Univ	OR	19,117	C
Tarleton State Univ	TX	15,248	LC
Taylor Univ	IN	40,317	C+
Texas State Univ	TX	19,350	C
Trinity International Univ	IL	31,070	VC
Univ of Detroit Mercy	MI	48,816	C+
Univ of Indianapolis	IN	36,480	C
Walsh Univ	OH	39,010	C
Xavier Univ	OH	47,880	C+
Youngstown State Univ	OH	17,307	C

DIGITAL MEDIA SOFTWARE ENGINEERING

School	ST	$IS	SR
Ferris State Univ	MI	21,445	C

DIGITAL MEDIA TECHNOLOGIES

School	ST	$IS	SR
Central Conn State Univ	CT	21,203	C
Chestnut Hill College	PA	43,410	C
East Stroudsburg Univ	PA	18,334	C
Fordham Univ	NY	65,918	MC

DISABILITIES STUDIES

School	ST	$IS	SR
Aurora Univ	IL	33,970	C
Indiana Univ of Pennsylvania	PA	23,614	LC
West Liberty Univ	WV	15,512	C

DRAFTING AND DESIGN

School	ST	$IS	SR
Pennsylvania College of Technology	PA	27,333	NC

DRAFTING AND DESIGN TECHNOLOGY

School	ST	$IS	SR
Alabama A&M Univ	AL	18,796	C
Baker College of Flint	MI	13,880	NC
Montana State Univ-Northern	MT	11,370	NC
Norfolk State Univ	VA	25,702	LC
School of the Art Inst of Chicago	IL	56,230	SP
Texas Southern Univ	TX	18,212	LC
Trine Univ	IN	41,310	C
Univ of Central Missouri	MO	18,982	C
Univ of Rio Grande & Rio Grande Community College	OH	8,750	NC
Western Mich Univ	MI	21,054	C

DRAMA EDUCATION

School	ST	$IS	SR
Appalachian State Univ	NC	14,416	VC
Augustana Univ	SD	38,424	VC
Averett Univ	VA	40,970	LC
Baylor Univ	TX	53,760	HC
Bennington College	VT	63,960	MC
Bridgewater State Univ	MA	21,810	C
Brigham Young Univ	UT	12,748	HC
Columbus State Univ	GA	14,336	LC
Culver-Stockton College	MO	33,525	C
East Carolina Univ	NC	16,937	C
East Texas Baptist Univ	TX	33,134	C
Eastern Mich Univ	MI	19,761	C
Fontbonne Univ	MO	33,717	C
Friends Univ	KS	34,455	C
Greensboro College	NC	42,400	LC
Hardin-Simmons Univ	TX	33,966	C
Lees-McRae College	NC	33,944	C
Lipscomb Univ	TN	41,296	VC
Mars Hill Univ	NC	42,688	C
Minot State Univ	ND	12,732	C
Old Dominion Univ	VA	20,910	C
Oral Roberts Univ	OK	34,316	C
Point Park Univ	PA	41,270	C
Saginaw Valley State Univ	MI	18,530	C
St. Louis Univ	MO	49,866	HC
Southwestern College	KS	31,531	C
St. Edward's Univ	TX	53,100	VC
The Catholic Univ of America	DC	56,356	VC
Trevecca Nazarene Univ	TN	31,186	C
Univ of Evansville	IN	44,186	VC+
Univ of Indianapolis	IN	36,480	C
Univ of Maryland/College Park	MD	21,938	HC
Univ of Montana-Western	MT	11,220	LC
Univ of Nebr - Lincoln	NE	18,589	VC
Univ of New Mexico	NM	15,404	C
Univ of N Car at Greensboro	NC	14,690	C
West Texas A&M Univ	TX	13,478	C
York College	NE	24,300	C

DRAMATIC ARTS

School	ST	$IS	SR
Abilene Christian Univ	TX	41,800	C+
Adams State Univ	CO	17,703	LC
Adelphi Univ	NY	48,244	C
Adrian College	MI	42,400	C
Agnes Scott College	GA	51,930	VC+
Alabama A&M Univ	AL	18,796	C
Alabama State Univ	AL	14,142	NC
Albany State Univ	GA	19,462	C
Albertus Magnus College	CT	43,258	LC
Albright College	PA	46,660	C
Alfred Univ	NY	42,296	C+
Allegheny College	PA	55,420	VC
American Univ	DC	59,379	HC+
Anderson Univ	IN	38,200	C
Appalachian State Univ	NC	14,416	VC
Arcadia Univ	PA	33,570	C+
Asbury Univ	KY	35,180	C+
Ashland Univ	OH	21,440	C
Auburn Univ	AL	23,594	VC+
Augsburg College	MN	43,929	C
Augustana Univ	SD	38,424	VC
Avila Univ	MO	35,480	C
Bard College	NY	64,024	HC
Bard College at Simon's Rock	MA	65,795	MC
Barnard College/Columbia Univ	NY	62,741	MC
Barry Univ	FL	37,830	C
Barton College	NC	38,686	LC
Baylor Univ	TX	53,760	HC
Belhaven Univ	MS	31,016	C
Beloit College	WI	55,206	HC
Benedictine College	KS	36,200	VC
Bennington College	VT	63,960	MC
Berea College	KY	7,042	C
Bethel College	IN	35,860	C
Bethel Univ	MN	45,270	VC
Bethune-Cookman Univ	FL	22,970	C
Biola Univ	CA	46,402	C+
Boise State Univ	ID	14,860	C
Boston College	MA	65,737	MC
Boston Univ	MA	65,110	MC
Brenau Univ - Women's College	GA	37,876	LC
Brewton-Parker College	GA	23,490	C
Briar Cliff Univ	IA	36,956	C
Brigham Young Univ	UT	12,748	HC
Bucknell Univ	PA	64,616	MC
Butler Univ	IN	51,352	VC
Calif Inst of the Arts	CA	56,426	SP
Cal State, Bakersfield	CA	19,191	LC
Cal State, Dominguez Hills	CA	19,022	LC
Cal State, East Bay	CA	19,413	C
Cal State, Fresno	CA	16,902	LC
Cal State, Fullerton	CA	21,902	C
Cal State, Long Beach	CA	18,850	C
Cal State, Los Angeles	CA	17,186	LC
Cal State, Northridge	CA	16,859	LC
Cal State, Sacramento	CA	20,332	C
Cal State, San Bernardino	CA	12,000	C
Cal State, Stanislaus	CA	16,212	C
Calif Univ of Pennsylvania	PA	14,217	LC
Capital Univ	OH	42,982	C
Cardinal Stritch Univ	WI	36,462	C
Carnegie Mellon Univ	PA	67,980	MC
Carroll College	MT	39,972	C+
Carroll Univ	WI	38,100	C+
Case Western Reserve Univ	OH	60,304	MC
Cedar Crest College	PA	46,715	C
Centenary College	NJ	43,602	C
Centenary College of Louisiana	LA	45,650	C+
Central College	IA	44,592	C
Central Methodist Univ	MO	36,830	VC
Central Mich Univ	MI	20,330	C
Central Washington Univ	WA	16,803	C
Centre College	KY	49,250	HC
Chadron State College	NE	14,819	NC
Chapman Univ	CA	63,078	VC+
Charleston Southern Univ	SC	32,400	C
Cheyney Univ of Pennsylvania	PA	20,896	LC
CUNY/City College	NY	20,319	VC
CUNY/College of Staten Island	NY	17,840	NC
CUNY/Hunter College	NY	31,098	VC
CUNY/York College	NY	6,747	LC
Clarion Univ of Pennsylvania	PA	21,608	LC
Clark Univ	MA	51,600	HC+
Clarke Univ	IA	38,940	C
Cleveland State Univ	OH	22,196	C
Coastal Carolina Univ	SC	19,766	C
Coker College	SC	34,810	LC
Colgate Univ	NY	65,030	MC
College of the Ozarks	MO	7,230	C
Colo College	CO	62,560	MC
Colo State Univ	CO	22,162	VC
Columbia College Chicago	IL	43,168	C
Columbia Univ/ School of General Studies	NY	61,470	MC
Columbia Univ/City of New York	NY	62,958	MC
Columbus State Univ	GA	14,336	LC
Concordia College - Moorhead	MN	51,088	C+
Concordia Univ	CA	41,580	VC
Concordia Univ Nebr	NE	36,280	VC

ST = STATE $IS = IN-STATE COSTS SR = SELECTOR RATING

School	ST	$IS	SR
Concordia Univ St. Paul	MN	29,050	C
Concordia Univ, Ann Arbor	MI	35,945	VC
Conn College	CT	65,000	MC
Cornish College of the Arts	WA	47,750	SP
Covenant College	GA	38,990	VC
Culver-Stockton College	MO	33,525	C
Dakota Wesleyan Univ	SD	32,850	C
Davidson College	NC	60,119	MC
Denison Univ	OH	58,860	MC
DePaul Univ	IL	47,623	VC
DeSales Univ	PA	43,970	C
Doane Univ	NE	39,184	VC
Dominican Univ	IL	41,222	C
Dordt College	IA	37,860	C+
Drake Univ	IA	45,056	HC
Drury Univ	MO	33,791	VC
Duke Univ	NC	64,188	
Duquesne Univ	PA	46,822	VC
Earlham College	IN	54,870	HC
East Carolina Univ	NC	16,937	C
East Central Univ	OK	13,056	C
Eastern Kentucky Univ	KY	16,908	C
Eastern Mich Univ	MI	19,761	C
Eastern Nazarene College	MA	39,955	C
Eastern New Mexico Univ	NM	14,416	C
Eastern Oregon Univ	OR	17,715	C
Eastern Washington Univ	WA	25,572	LC
Eckerd College	FL	52,874	C
Edinboro Univ	PA	15,940	LC
Elizabethtown College	PA	54,050	C
Elmira College	NY	53,900	C
Elon Univ	NC	44,599	VC+
Emerson College	MA	54,736	HC
Emory and Henry College	VA	41,410	C
Emory Univ	GA	60,786	MC
Emporia State Univ	KS	14,570	C
Eugene Lang College/The New School for Liberal Arts	NY	55,650	C
Eureka College	IL	30,220	C
Evangel Univ	MO	28,898	C
Fairleigh Dickinson Univ/ College at Florham	NJ	52,062	C
Fayetteville State Univ	NC	17,756	C
Ferrum College	VA	39,650	C
Fisk Univ	TN	32,066	LC
Fitchburg State Univ	MA	21,819	C
Five Towns College	NY	35,350	C
Flagler College	FL	27,620	C
Florida A&M Univ	FL	15,361	C
Florida Atlantic Univ	FL	17,339	C
Florida International Univ	FL	19,854	C+
Florida State Univ	FL	16,771	HC
Fontbonne Univ	MO	33,717	C
Fordham Univ	NY	65,918	MC
Fort Lewis College	CO	18,980	C
Francis Marion Univ	SC	16,464	LC
Franciscan Univ of Steubenville	OH	33,980	VC
Franklin and Marshall College	PA	63,170	HC
Franklin Pierce Univ	NH	46,750	C
Freed-Hardeman Univ	TN	29,450	C
Furman Univ	SC	58,092	VC+
Gannon Univ	PA	42,032	C
George Fox Univ	OR	42,938	C
George Mason Univ	VA	15,724	VC
George Washington Univ	DC	62,835	MC
Georgetown College	KY	41,440	C
Georgia Southwestern State Univ	GA	13,870	C
Gettysburg College	PA	63,000	HC
Goddard College	VT	17,040	VC
Gonzaga Univ	WA	50,888	HC
Gordon College	MA	46,472	C+
Goshen College	IN	42,500	C
Graceland Univ	IA	35,290	C
Grand Valley State Univ	MI	22,250	C+
Greensboro College	NC	42,400	LC
Greenville College	IL	27,012	C
Guilford College	NC	44,090	C
Gustavus Adolphus College	MN	52,433	HC
Hamilton College	NY	64,250	MC
Hamline Univ	MN	45,678	VC
Hampshire College	MA	63,824	MC
Hampton Univ	VA	34,926	LC
Hannibal-LaGrange Univ	MO	29,815	C
Hanover College	IN	46,364	C+
Harding Univ	AR	25,421	C
Hardin-Simmons Univ	TX	33,966	C
Hartwick College	NY	51,270	C
Hastings College	NE	35,380	C+
Heidelberg Univ	OH	39,200	C
Henderson State Univ	AR	15,516	LC
Hendrix College	AR	54,020	VC+
Hofstra Univ	NY	55,960	C+
Hope College	MI	39,940	VC
Howard Payne Univ	TX	34,320	C
Howard Univ	DC	37,616	C+
Humboldt State Univ	CA	20,514	C
Huntington Univ	IN	33,996	C
Idaho State Univ	ID	13,619	NC
Illinois College	IL	40,850	VC
Illinois State Univ	IL	23,418	VC
Indiana State Univ	IN	23,223	LC
Indiana Univ-Purdue Univ Fort Wayne	IN	17,553	C
Ithaca College	NY	56,766	VC
Jacksonville State Univ	AL	14,628	LC
Jacksonville Univ	FL	46,230	C
James Madison Univ	VA	19,084	VC
Judson Univ	IL	37,700	C
Juilliard School	NY	57,162	SP
Juniata College	PA	53,760	VC
Kalamazoo College	MI	53,931	HC+
Kansas State Univ	KS	17,780	VC
Kansas Wesleyan Univ	KS	36,600	C
Kenyon College	OH	63,330	MC
King's College	PA	46,858	C
Knox College	IL	52,615	VC+
Kutztown Univ of Pennsylvania	PA	19,056	LC
Lakeland Univ	WI	35,130	C
Lamar Univ	TX	18,014	LC
Lander Univ	SC	43,994	C
Langston Univ	OK	14,314	C
Lawrence Univ	WI	54,498	HC
Le Moyne College	NY	46,000	C
Lee Univ	TN	22,045	C
Lees-McRae College	NC	33,944	C
Lenoir-Rhyne Univ	NC	43,200	C
Lewis & Clark College	OR	58,434	HC+
Lindenwood Univ	MO	25,132	C
Linfield College	OR	52,010	C
LIU Post	NY	49,682	C
Louisiana College	LA	21,886	C
Louisiana State Univ and A&M College	LA	18,677	VC
Loyola Univ New Orleans	LA	51,708	VC+
Lycoming College	PA	48,580	C
Lynn Univ	FL	49,480	LC
Lyon College	AR	34,730	C+
Macalester College	MN	61,905	MC
MacMurray College	IL	33,620	C
Maharishi Univ of Management	IA	34,930	VC
Manhattanville College	NY	51,440	C+
Marietta College	OH	46,190	C
Marquette Univ	WI	48,390	VC+
Mars Hill Univ	NC	42,688	C
Marymount Manhattan College	NY	46,280	VC
Maryville College	TN	44,410	C
Marywood Univ	PA	46,900	C
McDaniel College	MD	51,380	VC
McKendree Univ	IL	37,940	C+
McMurry Univ	TX	34,259	LC
McPherson College	KS	34,909	C
Mercer Univ	GA	45,348	VC
Meredith College	NC	45,297	C
Messiah College	PA	43,100	C+
Methodist Univ	NC	43,600	C
Metropolitan State Univ	MN	7,566	C
Miami Univ	OH	27,190	HC+
Mich State Univ	MI	23,898	VC+
Middlebury College	VT	64,332	MC
Midwestern State Univ	TX	17,572	C
Millikin Univ	IL	42,158	C
Minn State Univ, Mankato	MN	15,616	C
Minn State Univ, Moorhead	MN	15,941	C
Missouri Valley College	MO	28,150	C
Monmouth College	IL	42,260	C
Montana State Univ-Billings	MT	22,960	C
Montana State Univ-Northern	MT	11,370	NC
Montclair State Univ	NJ	26,210	LC
Moravian College	PA	53,117	
Morehead State Univ	KY	17,422	C
Morehouse College	GA	40,064	C
Morgan State Univ	MD	17,190	LC
Morningside College	IA	36,865	C
Mount Holyoke College	MA	56,746	MC
Mount Vernon Nazarene Univ	OH	34,500	C
Muhlenberg College	PA	56,645	VC+
Muskingum Univ	OH	35,966	C
Nebr Wesleyan Univ	NE	38,140	C+
New England College	NH	50,364	C
New Mexico State Univ	NM	14,050	C
New York Univ	NY	65,860	MC
Newberry College	SC	34,550	C
Niagara Univ	NY	41,010	C
N Car A&T State Univ	NC	13,365	LC
N Car Central Univ	NC	9,000	C
N Car Wesleyan College	NC	39,200	C
N Dak State Univ	ND	16,245	C
Northeastern Univ	MA	62,703	MC
Northern Illinois Univ	IL	20,176	C
Northern Kentucky Univ	KY	16,486	C
Northwest Missouri State Univ	MO	17,737	C
Northwestern College of Iowa	IA	38,400	C+
Northwestern Okla State Univ	OK	13,072	NC
Northwestern Univ	IL	66,344	MC
Notre Dame de Namur Univ	CA	46,526	LC
Nova Southeastern Univ	FL	38,534	C+
Oakland Univ	MI	20,763	C
Oberlin College	OH	66,012	MC
Ohio Northern Univ	OH	44,050	VC
Ohio Univ	OH	22,924	C
Ohio Wesleyan Univ	OH	49,460	VC
Okla Baptist Univ	OK	32,320	C
Okla State Univ	OK	17,180	VC
Old Dominion Univ	VA	20,910	C
Olivet Nazarene Univ	IL	41,840	C
Oral Roberts Univ	OK	34,316	C
Ottawa Univ	KS	36,074	VC
Otterbein Univ	OH	41,630	C
Ouachita Baptist Univ	AR	32,320	C
Our Lady of the Lake Univ	TX	35,012	LC
Pacific Univ	OR	52,876	C
Park Univ	MO	20,329	C
Pepperdine Univ	CA	74,460	HC+
Piedmont College	GA	32,512	C
Pitzer College	CA	66,192	MC
Point Park Univ	PA	41,270	C
Portland State Univ	OR	19,443	C
Prairie View A&M Univ	TX	15,205	LC
Prescott College	AZ	33,284	C
Principia College	IL	39,010	C+
Purdue Univ/West Lafayette	IN	20,032	MC
Queens Univ of Charlotte	NC	39,543	C
Quinnipiac Univ	CT	59,110	C
Ramapo College of New Jersey	NJ	25,338	C
Randolph College	VA	45,660	VC
Randolph-Macon College	VA	49,910	C
Reed College	OR	65,300	MC
Rhode Island College	RI	17,694	LC
Rider Univ	NJ	54,050	C
Ripon College	WI	46,911	C+
Rockford Univ	IL	36,030	C
Roger Williams Univ	RI	46,296	C+
Rollins College	FL	58,670	HC
Roosevelt Univ	IL	40,651	VC
Rowan Univ	NJ	24,491	VC+
Rutgers Univ - Camden	NJ	26,146	C
Rutgers Univ - New Brunswick	NJ	26,632	HC
Rutgers Univ - Newark	NJ	27,288	C
Saginaw Valley State Univ	MI	18,530	C
St. Louis Univ	MO	49,866	HC
St. Michael's College	VT	51,725	VC+
Salem State Univ	MA	17,303	LC
Salve Regina Univ	RI	51,470	C
Sam Houston State Univ	TX	18,792	C
San Francisco State Univ	CA	18,514	LC
San Jose State Univ	CA	21,540	C
Santa Fe Univ of Art and Design	NM	39,980	SP
Sarah Lawrence College	NY	63,388	HC
Schreiner Univ	TX	34,626	LC
Scripps College	CA	66,664	MC
Seton Hill Univ	PA	46,972	C
Shenandoah Univ	VA	41,312	C
Shorter Univ	GA	31,130	LC
Simpson College	IA	43,839	VC
Skidmore College	NY	64,214	HC
Smith College	MA	63,914	MC
S Car State Univ	SC	20,805	LC
S Dak State Univ	SD	15,634	C
Southeastern Okla State Univ	OK	11,875	C
Southeastern Univ	FL	31,765	C
Southern Conn State Univ	CT	21,924	LC
Southern Illinois Univ Carbondale	IL	23,667	C
Southern Illinois Univ Edwardsville	IL	22,643	C
Southern Methodist Univ	TX	66,483	MC
Southern Oregon Univ	OR	19,117	C
Southern Univ and A&M College	LA	16,074	LC+
Southwest Minn State Univ	MN	17,783	C
Southwestern College	KS	31,531	C
Southwestern Univ	TX	50,720	VC
Spelman College	GA	38,751	C
St. Bonaventure Univ	NY	44,237	C
St. Catherine Univ	MN	45,630	VC
St. Cloud State Univ	MN	10,600	C
St. Lawrence Univ	NY	64,390	VC
St. Mary's College of Maryland	MD	26,634	VC
Stanford Univ	CA	60,409	MC
SUNY / Buffalo State College	NY	20,842	C
SUNY / SUNY Fredonia	NY	20,818	C
SUNY / SUNY Oneonta	NY	19,712	C+
SUNY at Binghamton	NY	22,861	MC
SUNY at New Paltz	NY	19,200	C
SUNY at Oswego	NY	21,351	C
SUNY at Purchase	NY	17,900	C
Stephen F. Austin State Univ	TX	18,406	LC
Stephens College	MO	38,042	C
Sterling College	KS	32,830	C
Stetson Univ	FL	53,544	VC
Stevenson Univ	MD	72,770	C
Stockton Univ	NJ	25,059	
Suffolk Univ	MA	50,308	C
Sul Ross State Univ	TX	15,021	LC
Swarthmore College	PA	63,550	MC
Syracuse Univ	NY	60,239	VC
Tarleton State Univ	TX	15,248	LC
Taylor Univ	IN	40,317	C+
Tenn State Univ	TN	14,423	C
Texas A&M Univ at Commerce	TX	10,496	C
Texas A&M Univ at Corpus Christi	TX	16,851	LC
Texas A&M Univ at Kingsville	TX	7,500	LC
Texas Lutheran Univ	TX	38,620	C
Texas Southern Univ	TX	18,212	LC
Texas State Univ	TX	19,350	C
Texas Wesleyan Univ	TX	35,134	C
Texas Woman's Univ	TX	15,302	LC
The Catholic Univ of America	DC	56,356	VC
The College of Wooster	OH	57,900	VC+
The Univ of Tenn at Chattanooga	TN	16,744	C
The Univ of Virginia's College at Wise	VA	18,192	LC
Thomas More College	KY	36,720	C
Transylvania Univ	KY	45,690	VC+
Trevecca Nazarene Univ	TN	31,186	C
Trinity College	CT	63,920	HC+
Trinity Univ	TX	52,314	HC+
Troy Univ	AL	16,171	C
Truman State Univ	MO	16,014	HC
Tufts Univ	MA		MC
Tulane Univ	LA	63,396	HC+
Union College	KY	32,310	C
Union Univ	TN	33,970	VC
Univ of Alabama at Birmingham	AL	19,906	C
Univ of Alaska Anchorage	AK	16,652	NC
Univ of Arkansas at Fayetteville	AR	19,152	C+
Univ of Arkansas at Little Rock	AR	18,211	C
Univ of Calif at Berkeley	CA	28,853	MC
Univ of Calif at Davis	CA	28,468	HC
Univ of Calif at Irvine	CA	26,484	VC
Univ of Calif at Los Angeles	CA	30,162	MC
Univ of Calif at Riverside	CA	29,227	C+
Univ of Calif at Santa Barbara	CA	29,091	HC
Univ of Calif San Diego	CA	30,150	MC
Univ of Calif, Santa Cruz	CA	28,731	C+
Univ of Central Florida	FL	15,922	VC
Univ of Cincinnati	OH	21,964	VC
Univ of Conn	CT	25,538	HC
Univ of Dallas	TX	45,500	VC+
Univ of Dayton	OH	53,620	C
Univ of Denver	CO	58,443	VC+
Univ of Detroit Mercy	MI	48,816	C+
Univ of Evansville	IN	44,186	VC+
Univ of Findlay	OH	60,139	C
Univ of Hartford	CT	49,776	C
Univ of Hawaii at Manoa	HI	23,221	C
Univ of Idaho	ID	15,348	C
Univ of Illinois at Chicago	IL	25,006	VC
Univ of Illinois at Urbana-Champaign	IL	27,006	HC
Univ of Indianapolis	IN	36,480	C
Univ of Iowa	IA	18,683	VC+
Univ of Kansas	KS	20,135	C+
Univ of Kentucky	KY	33,306	C
Univ of La Verne	CA	55,600	C
Univ of Louisiana at Lafayette	LA	14,516	C
Univ of Louisville	KY	19,824	C
Univ of Maine	ME	20,792	C
Univ of Mary Washington	VA	24,764	VC
Univ of Maryland/Baltimore County	MD	21,296	VC
Univ of Maryland/College Park	MD	21,938	HC
Univ of Mass Amherst	MA	26,199	VC+
Univ of Mass Boston	MA	13,435	C
Univ of Memphis	TN	18,278	C
Univ of Mich/Ann Arbor	MI	24,410	MC
Univ of Mich-Flint	MI	17,607	C+
Univ of Minn/Duluth	MN	20,292	C+
Univ of Minn/Morris	MN	20,760	VC
Univ of Missouri/Columbia	MO	18,201	MC
Univ of Missouri-Kansas City	MO	19,563	VC
Univ of Missouri-St. Louis	MO		C
Univ of Montana	MT	14,105	C
Univ of Montana-Western	MT	11,220	LC
Univ of Montevallo	AL	19,502	C
Univ of Mount Union	OH	38,970	C
Univ of Nebr - Kearney	NE	16,546	LC
Univ of Nebr - Lincoln	NE	18,589	VC
Univ of Nebr - Omaha	NE	16,120	C
Univ of Nevada, Las Vegas	NV	17,553	C
Univ of Nevada/Reno	NV	18,010	C
Univ of New Orleans	LA	12,840	C
Univ of North Alabama	AL	15,398	C
Univ of N Car at Asheville	NC	15,723	VC+
Univ of N Car at Chapel Hill	NC	20,052	HC+
Univ of N Car at Greensboro	NC	14,690	C
Univ of N Car at Pembroke	NC	14,388	LC
Univ of N Car at Wilmington	NC	14,590	VC
Univ of N Car School of the Arts	NC	18,040	SP
Univ of North Texas	TX	19,198	C
Univ of Northwestern - St. Paul	MN	38,160	C
Univ of Okla	OK	18,911	VC
Univ of Oregon	OR	22,972	C
Univ of Pennsylvania	PA	63,526	MC
Univ of Pittsburgh at Johnstown	PA	22,092	C
Univ of Portland	OR	52,152	VC
Univ of PR-Rio Piedras campus	PR	13,327	
Univ of Puget Sound	WA	56,456	VC+
Univ of Redlands	CA	60,200	VC
Univ of St. Mary	KS	34,690	C
Univ of Science and Arts of Okla	OK	11,140	VC
Univ of South Alabama	AL	16,400	C
Univ of S Car at Columbia	SC	19,725	VC+
Univ of S Dak	SD	16,109	C
Univ of South Florida/Tampa	FL	16,110	VC+
Univ of Southern Calif	CA	66,631	C

ST = STATE **$IS** = IN-STATE COSTS **SR** = SELECTOR RATING

School	ST	$IS	SR
Univ of Southern Maine	ME	18,320	C
Univ of Southern Miss	MS	13,170	C
Univ of St. Thomas - Houston	TX	40,020	VC
Univ of Tampa	FL	36,944	C
Univ of Texas at Arlington	TX	18,026	LC
Univ of Texas at Austin	TX	26,102	HC
Univ of Texas at El Paso	TX	34,452	NC
Univ of the Cumberlands	KY	32,000	C
Univ of the District of Columbia	DC	21,044	LC
Univ of the Incarnate Word	TX	39,162	LC
Univ of the Ozarks	AR	52,176	C
Univ of the Pacific	CA	57,006	VC
Univ of Toledo	OH	19,336	NC
Univ of Vermont	VT	28,878	HC
Univ of Virginia	VA	25,891	MC
Univ of Washington	WA	23,149	VC
Univ of Wisc-Green Bay	WI	15,064	C
Univ of Wisc-La Crosse	WI	15,247	C+
Univ of Wisc-Madison	WI	20,934	MC
Univ of Wisc-Milwaukee	WI	21,496	C
Univ of Wisc-Parkside	WI	15,193	C
Univ of Wisc-Stevens Point	WI	14,043	C
Univ of Wisc-Superior	WI	14,446	C
Univ of Wisc-Whitewater	WI	13,976	C
Ursinus College	PA	61,690	VC
Utah State Univ	UT	12,736	C
Valparaiso Univ	IN	48,370	C+
Vanguard Univ of Southern Calif	CA	40,740	VC
Vassar College	NY	65,491	MC
Virginia Commonwealth Univ	VA	23,049	C
Virginia Polytechnic Inst and State Univ	VA	21,276	HC
Virginia Wesleyan College	VA	43,728	LC
Viterbo Univ	WI	34,660	C
Wabash College	IN	50,650	VC
Wagner College	NY	55,480	C+
Wartburg College	IA	47,840	C
Washburn Univ	KS	15,827	C
Washington and Lee Univ	VA	59,647	MC
Washington College	MD	54,666	VC
Washington Univ in St. Louis	MO	65,366	VC
Wayland Baptist Univ	TX	22,356	LC
Wayne State College	NE	12,802	C
Wayne State Univ	MI	22,016	C
Weber State Univ	UT	10,721	C
Webster Univ	MO	37,490	C
Wellesley College	MA	63,916	MC
Wells College	NY	50,500	C
Wesleyan College	GA	29,694	C+
Wesleyan Univ	CT	65,516	MC
West Chester Univ of Pennsylvania	PA	18,456	C
West Texas A&M Univ	TX	13,478	C
West Virginia Univ	WV	18,210	C
West Virginia Wesleyan College	WV	36,858	C
Western Carolina Univ	NC	13,965	C
Western Conn State Univ	CT	21,254	LC
Western Kentucky Univ	KY	16,850	C
Western Oregon Univ	OR	15,021	LC
Western State Colo Univ	CO	18,639	C
Western Washington Univ	WA	18,003	C+
Westminster College	PA	39,180	C+
Westminster College	UT	41,078	C+
Westmont College	CA	56,410	HC
Wheaton College	MA	61,512	VC
Whittier College	CA	57,891	C
Whitworth Univ	WA	51,732	VC
Wilkes Univ	PA	45,622	C
Willamette Univ	OR	61,817	VC+
William Carey Univ	MS	23,950	LC
William Jewell College	MO	41,210	C+
William Paterson Univ of New Jersey	NJ	23,133	C
William Woods Univ	MO	32,040	C
Williams College	MA	63,290	MC
Wilmington College	OH	34,600	C
Winona State Univ	MN	17,535	C
Wittenberg Univ	OH	48,156	C+
Wofford College	SC	49,885	VC
Wright State Univ	OH	16,983	C
Yale Univ	CT	64,650	MC
York College of Pennsylvania	PA	29,240	C
Youngstown State Univ	OH	17,307	C

DRAWING

School	ST	$IS	SR
Adams State Univ	CO	17,703	LC
Aquinas College - Mich	MI	38,876	HC
Art Academy of Cincinnati	OH	36,252	SP
Bard College at Simon's Rock	MA	65,795	MC
Bennington College	VT	63,960	MC
Biola Univ	CA	46,402	C+
Calif College of the Arts	CA	52,758	SP
Cleveland Inst of Art	OH	51,439	C+
Colo State Univ	CO	22,162	VC
Ferris State Univ	MI	21,445	C
Indiana Univ-Purdue Univ Fort Wayne	IN	17,553	C
Kutztown Univ of Pennsylvania	PA	19,056	LC
Laguna College of Art and Design	CA	41,422	LC
Lewis Univ	IL	40,370	C
Maryland Inst College of Art	MD	56,795	SP
Memphis College of Art	TN	39,750	C
Milwaukee Inst of Art and Design	WI	44,960	SP
Minneapolis College of Art and Design	MN	44,238	SP
Old Dominion Univ	VA	20,910	C
Olivet Nazarene Univ	IL	41,840	C
Pacific Northwest College of Art	OR	38,494	SP
School of the Art Inst of Chicago	IL	56,230	SP
SUNY / SUNY Fredonia	NY	20,818	C
SUNY at Binghamton	NY	22,861	MC
Univ of Hartford	CT	49,776	C
Univ of Iowa	IA	18,683	VC+
Univ of Mich/Ann Arbor	MI	24,410	MC
Univ of San Francisco	CA	58,484	VC
Washington Univ in St. Louis	MO	65,366	VC

DRAWING WITH PRINTMAKING FOCUS

School	ST	$IS	SR
Ferris State Univ	MI	21,445	C
Univ of Mass Dartmouth	MA	25,658	C

DUTCH

School	ST	$IS	SR
Calvin College	MI	41,570	VC+
Dordt College	IA	37,860	C+
Univ of Calif at Berkeley	CA	28,853	MC

EARLY CHILDHOOD EDUCATION

School	ST	$IS	SR
Alabama A&M Univ	AL	18,796	C
Alabama State Univ	AL	14,142	NC
Albany State Univ	GA	19,462	C
Alfred Univ	NY	42,296	C+
Alma College	MI	47,548	C
American International College	MA	46,300	LC
Angelo State Univ	TX	15,263	NC
Anna Maria College	MA	48,186	C
Aquinas College - Mich	MI	38,876	HC
Arcadia Univ	PA	33,570	C+
Arizona State Univ at the Tempe Campus	AZ	21,756	VC
Arkansas State Univ	AR	16,190	C
Arkansas Tech Univ	AR	15,484	C
Armstrong State Univ	GA	16,962	C
Ashford Univ	CA	10,480	C
Ashland Univ	OH	21,440	C
Atlantic Union College	MA	27,228	C
Auburn Univ	AL	23,594	VC+
Averett Univ	VA	40,970	LC
Baldwin Wallace Univ	OH	41,106	C
Ball State Univ	IN	19,590	C
Barry Univ	FL	37,830	C
Bay Path Univ	MA	45,349	C
Becker College	MA	57,628	C
Belmont Univ	TN	40,970	VC
Bemidji State Univ	MN	16,056	VC
Benedict College	SC	28,238	NC
Bennington College	VT	63,960	MC
Berry College	GA	45,286	C+
Bethel College	IN	35,860	C
Bethel Univ	MN	45,270	VC
Biola Univ	CA	46,402	C+
Black Hills State Univ	SD	15,899	C
Bloomfield College	NJ	39,100	LC
Bloomsburg Univ of Pennsylvania	PA	19,066	LC
Bluefield State College	WV	5,832	LC
Bluffton Univ	OH	40,950	C
Boston College	MA	65,737	MC
Boston Univ	MA	65,110	MC
Bowie State Univ	MD	26,728	LC
Bowling Green State Univ	OH	19,747	C
Brenau Univ - Women's College	GA	37,876	LC
Brescia Univ	KY	29,890	VC+
Brewton-Parker College	GA	23,490	C
Bridgewater State Univ	MA	21,810	C
Brigham Young Univ	UT	12,748	HC
Bucknell Univ	PA	64,616	MC
Cal State, Sacramento	CA	20,332	C
Calif Univ of Pennsylvania	PA	14,217	LC
Calvin College	MI	41,570	VC+
Cameron Univ	OK	11,072	NC
Campbellsville Univ	KY	32,492	C
Canisius College	NY	47,537	C
Cardinal Stritch Univ	WI	36,462	C
Carlow Univ	PA	38,549	LC
Carroll Univ	WI	38,100	C+
Carson-Newman Univ	TN	34,160	C
Cazenovia College	NY	46,470	C
Cedar Crest College	PA	46,715	C
Cedarville Univ	OH	34,990	VC
Central Methodist Univ	MO	36,830	VC
Central Washington Univ	WA	16,803	C
Chadron State College	NE	14,819	NC
Chaminade Univ of Honolulu	HI	36,000	C
Champlain College	VT	53,132	C+
Charleston Southern Univ	SC	32,400	C
Chatham Univ	PA	46,517	C
Chestnut Hill College	PA	43,410	C
Cheyney Univ of Pennsylvania	PA	20,896	LC
Chicago State Univ	IL	20,144	C
Christian Brothers Univ	TN	31,670	VC
CUNY/Brooklyn College	NY	5,884	C+
CUNY/City College	NY	20,319	VC
CUNY/Hunter College	NY	31,098	VC
CUNY/Lehman College	NY	5,778	HC+
CUNY/Queens College	NY	27,896	C
Claflin Univ	SC	33,764	LC
Clarion Univ of Pennsylvania	PA	21,608	LC
Clark Atlanta Univ	GA	31,019	LC
Clemson Univ	SC		HC
Cleveland State Univ	OH	22,196	C
Coastal Carolina Univ	SC	19,766	C
Coker College	SC	34,810	LC
Colby-Sawyer College	NH	50,790	C
College of Charleston	SC	22,699	C
College of St. Mary	NE	35,184	C
College of the Ozarks	MO	7,230	C
Colo State Univ	CO	22,162	VC
Columbia College	SC	36,550	C
Columbia College Chicago	IL	43,168	C
Columbus State Univ	GA	14,336	LC
Concord Univ	WV	14,954	C
Concordia College - Alabama	AL	15,720	NC
Concordia College - New York	NY	39,035	LC
Concordia Univ	CA	41,580	VC
Concordia Univ	OR	35,000	C
Concordia Univ Nebr	NE	36,280	VC
Concordia Univ St. Paul	MN	29,050	C
Concordia Univ Wisc	WI	35,910	C
Concordia Univ, Ann Arbor	MI	35,945	VC
Concordia Univ, Chicago	IL	39,694	C
Converse College	SC	26,495	C
Corban Univ	OR	40,306	C
Curry College	MA	51,815	C
Daemen College	NY	38,045	C
Dallas Baptist Univ	TX	33,713	C
Defiance College	OH	41,630	C
Delaware State Univ	DE	19,376	NC
DePaul Univ	IL	47,623	VC
DeSales Univ	PA	43,970	C
Dickinson State Univ	ND	12,372	LC
Dominican Univ	IL	41,222	C
Dordt College	IA	37,860	C+
Duquesne Univ	PA	46,822	VC
East Carolina Univ	NC	16,937	C
East Central Univ	OK	13,056	C
East Stroudsburg Univ	PA	18,334	C
East Texas Baptist Univ	TX	33,134	C
Eastern Conn State Univ	CT	23,059	C
Eastern Illinois Univ	IL	21,126	C
Eastern Mennonite Univ	VA	42,550	C
Eastern Mich Univ	MI	19,761	C
Eastern New Mexico Univ	NM	14,416	C
Eastern Univ	PA	39,540	C
Edgewood College	WI	35,950	C
Edinboro Univ	PA	15,940	LC
Edward Waters College	FL	20,607	NC
Elizabethtown College	PA	54,050	C
Elmhurst College	IL	45,428	C
Elmira College	NY	53,900	C
Elms College	MA	45,646	VC
Elon Univ	NC	44,599	VC+
Erskine College	SC	45,460	C
Evangel Univ	MO	28,898	C
Fairmont State Univ	WV	15,726	C
Faulkner Univ	AL	26,410	C
Fayetteville State Univ	NC	17,756	C
Felician Univ	NJ	45,370	LC
Ferris State Univ	MI	21,445	C
Fitchburg State Univ	MA	21,819	C
Florida A&M Univ	FL	15,361	C
Florida Gulf Coast Univ	FL	9,682	C
Florida International Univ	FL	19,854	C+
Florida State Univ	FL	16,771	HC
Fontbonne Univ	MO	33,717	C
Fort Valley State Univ	GA	17,988	VC
Framingham State Univ	MA	20,584	C
Francis Marion Univ	SC	16,464	LC
Freed-Hardeman Univ	TN	29,450	C
Frostburg State Univ	MD	17,280	LC
Gallaudet Univ	DC	29,118	LC
Gannon Univ	PA	42,032	C
Geneva College	PA	35,450	C
Georgia College & State Univ	GA	21,148	C+
Georgia Southern Univ	GA	16,596	C
Georgia Southwestern State Univ	GA	13,870	C
Georgia State Univ	GA	24,332	VC
Glenville State College	WV	17,386	NC
Goddard College	VT	17,040	VC
Gordon College	MA	46,472	C+
Goshen College	IN	42,500	C
Grambling State Univ	LA	15,701	C
Granite State College	NH	19,639	SP
Greensboro College	NC	42,400	LC
Greenville College	IL	27,012	C
Grove City College	PA	25,692	VC
Hannibal-LaGrange Univ	MO	29,815	C
Harding Univ	AR	25,421	C
Hardin-Simmons Univ	TX	33,966	C
Harris-Stowe State Univ	MO	14,360	NC
Hendrix College	AR	54,020	VC+
Heritage Univ	WA	19,825	NC
Holy Family Univ	PA	43,326	LC
Hood College	MD	54,840	C
Houghton College	NY	39,090	C
Houston Baptist Univ	TX	36,450	C
Howard Univ	DC	37,616	C+
Humphreys College	CA	27,790	C
Idaho State Univ	ID	13,619	NC
Illinois State Univ	IL	23,418	VC
Indiana State Univ	IN	23,223	LC
Indiana Univ Bloomington	IN	20,429	VC
Indiana Univ of Pennsylvania	PA	23,614	LC
Indiana Univ-Purdue Univ Fort Wayne	IN	17,553	C
Inter-American Univ of PR Ponce	PR	19,549	
Inter-American Univ of PR-Aguadilla Campus	PR	21,657	
Inter-American Univ of PR-Barranquitas	PR	18,336	
Inter-American Univ of PR-Fajardo Campus	PR	18,336	
Inter-American Univ of PR-Metropolitan Campus	PR	20,045	
Inter-American Univ of PR-San Germán	PR	20,042	
Iona College	NY	50,984	C
Iowa State Univ	IA	17,570	C
Iowa Wesleyan Univ	IA	39,200	C
Jacksonville State Univ	AL	14,628	LC
John Brown Univ	AR	33,132	VC
John Carroll Univ	OH	49,740	C+
Judson Univ	IL	37,700	C
Juniata College	PA	53,760	VC
Kansas State Univ	KS	17,780	VC
Kean Univ	NJ	24,650	C
Keene State College	NH	24,003	LC
Kendall College	IL	32,610	C
Kennesaw State Univ	GA	19,592	VC
Kent State Univ	OH	20,732	C
Kentucky State Univ	KY	13,364	LC
Keystone College	PA	28,680	LC
King's College	PA	46,858	C
Kutztown Univ of Pennsylvania	PA	19,056	LC
LaGrange College	GA	39,930	C
Lake Erie College	OH	38,914	LC
Lakeland Univ	WI	35,130	C
Lamar Univ	TX	18,014	LC
Lander Univ	SC	43,994	C
Lasell College	MA	47,500	C
Lebanon Valley College	PA	51,530	C
LeMoyne-Owen College	TN	16,980	C
Lenoir-Rhyne Univ	NC	43,200	C
Lesley Univ	MA	41,550	C
Lewis Univ	IL	40,370	C
Lewis-Clark State College	ID	14,202	C
Limestone College	SC	32,100	C
Lincoln Memorial Univ	TN	28,070	C
Lindenwood Univ	MO	25,132	C
Lipscomb Univ	TN	41,296	VC
LIU Brooklyn	NY	49,682	C
LIU Post	NY	49,682	C
Livingstone College	NC	17,815	LC
Lock Haven Univ of Pennsylvania	PA	18,028	LC
Louisiana State Univ and A&M College	LA	18,677	VC
Louisiana Tech Univ	LA	11,422	VC
Loyola Univ Chicago	IL	55,802	VC
Lubbock Christian Univ	TX	28,426	C
Lyndon State College	VT	20,714	C
Lynn Univ	FL	49,480	LC
Lyon College	AR	34,730	C+
Madonna Univ	MI	29,050	C
Malone Univ	OH	38,448	C
Manhattan College	NY	51,750	C+
Mansfield Univ	PA	23,376	LC
Marian Univ	WI	32,420	LC
Marietta College	OH	46,190	C
Marshall Univ	WV	17,242	C
Martin Univ	IN	20,264	LC
Marygrove College	MI	28,926	NC
Maryville Univ of St. Louis	MO	38,046	VC+
Marywood Univ	PA	46,900	C
Mayville State Univ	ND	18,371	NC
McNeese State Univ	LA	7,838	C
Medaille College	NY	35,112	C
Mercer Univ	GA	45,348	VC
Mercyhurst Univ	PA	47,420	C
Messiah College	PA	43,100	C+
Metropolitan College of New York	NY		VC
Metropolitan State Univ	MN	7,566	C
Miami Univ	OH	27,190	HC+
Middle Tenn State Univ	TN	8,650	C
Midland Univ	NE	37,468	
Miles College	AL	18,646	NC
Millersville Univ of Pennsylvania	PA	23,782	C
Milligan College	TN	38,150	C
Millikin Univ	IL	42,158	C
Minn State Univ, Mankato	MN	15,616	C
Minn State Univ, Moorhead	MN	15,941	C
Misericordia Univ	PA	43,840	C
Miss Valley State Univ	MS	13,233	LC
Missouri Baptist Univ	MO	35,594	C
Missouri Southern State Univ	MO	12,499	C
Missouri State Univ	MO	15,190	C+
Missouri Western State Univ	MO	16,741	
Mitchell College	CT	43,280	C
Molloy College	NY	40,440	C
Monmouth Univ	NJ	46,234	C
Montana State Univ-Billings	MT	22,960	C

ST = STATE $IS = IN-STATE COSTS SR = SELECTOR RATING

School	ST	$IS	SR
Montclair State Univ	NJ	26,210	LC
Morehouse College	GA	40,064	C
Morris College	SC	18,500	LC
Mount Aloysius College	PA	29,976	C
Mount Ida College	MA	46,820	C
Mount Mary Univ	WI	34,650	LC
Mount Mercy Univ	IA	36,826	C
Mount St. Joseph Univ	OH	33,880	C
Mount Vernon Nazarene Univ	OH	34,500	C
Murray State Univ	KY	16,998	C
Muskingum Univ	OH	35,966	C
Naropa Univ	CO	42,826	NC
National Louis Univ	IL	16,920	LC
New Jersey City Univ	NJ	21,456	LC
New Mexico Highlands Univ	NM	11,904	NC
New Mexico State Univ	NM	14,050	C
New York Univ	NY	65,860	MC
Newberry College	SC	34,550	C
Newman Univ	KS	35,390	C
Niagara Univ	NY	41,010	C
Norfolk State Univ	VA	25,702	LC
N Car A&T State Univ	NC	13,365	LC
North Park Univ	IL	35,860	C
Northeastern Illinois Univ	IL	12,529	LC
Northeastern State Univ	OK	8,615	VC
Northern Arizona Univ	AZ	20,246	VC
Northern Illinois Univ	IL	20,176	C
Northern Kentucky Univ	KY	16,486	C
Northern State Univ	SD	14,505	C
Northwest Missouri State Univ	MO	17,737	C
Northwestern College of Iowa	IA	38,400	C+
Northwestern Okla State Univ	OK	13,072	NC
Notre Dame College	OH	37,150	VC
Notre Dame of Maryland Univ	MD	46,465	VC
Nova Southeastern Univ	FL	38,534	C+
Nyack College	NY	34,050	NC
Oglala Lakota College	SD	15,050	NC
Ohio Dominican Univ	OH	41,340	C+
Ohio Northern Univ	OH	44,050	VC
Ohio Univ	OH	22,924	C
Ohio Wesleyan Univ	OH	49,460	VC
Okla Baptist Univ	OK	32,320	C
Okla Christian Univ	OK	27,650	VC
Okla City Univ	OK	40,476	VC
Olivet Nazarene Univ	IL	41,840	C
Oral Roberts Univ	OK	34,316	C
Otterbein Univ	OH	41,630	C
Ouachita Baptist Univ	AR	32,320	C
Our Lady of the Lake Univ	TX	35,012	LC
Pacific Union College	CA	36,009	VC
Paine College	GA	19,506	LC
Park Univ	MO	20,329	C
Pennsylvania State Univ - Univ Park	PA	29,760	HC
Philander Smith College	AR	20,814	LC
Piedmont College	GA	32,512	C
Pittsburg State Univ	KS	13,880	NC
Point Park Univ	PA	41,270	C
Prescott College	AZ	33,284	C
Purdue Univ/Northwest	IN	15,038	C
Purdue Univ/West Lafayette	IN	20,032	MC
Rhode Island College	RI	17,694	LC
Rider Univ	NJ	54,050	C
Ripon College	WI	46,911	C+
Rivier Univ	NH	40,410	VC
Roberts Wesleyan College	NY	38,306	C
Roosevelt Univ	IL	40,651	VC
Rowan Univ	NJ	24,491	VC+
St. Joseph's Univ	PA	57,544	VC+
St. Mary-of-the-Woods College	IN	39,632	LC
St. Vincent College	PA	44,626	C
St. Xavier Univ	IL	43,310	C
Salisbury Univ	MD	20,714	VC
Salve Regina Univ	RI	51,470	C
Samford Univ	AL	39,232	VC
San Jose State Univ	CA	21,540	C
Schreiner Univ	TX	34,626	LC
Seton Hill Univ	PA	46,972	C
Shippensburg Univ of Pennsylvania	PA	23,208	C
Shorter Univ	GA	31,130	LC
Silver Lake College of the Holy Family	WI	36,290	LC
Sinte Gleska Univ	SD	13,154	NC
Slippery Rock Univ of Pennsylvania	PA	10,360	C
Smith College	MA	63,914	MC
S Car State Univ	SC	20,805	LC
S Dak State Univ	SD	15,634	C
Southeast Missouri State Univ	MO	15,498	C
Southeastern Louisiana Univ	LA	16,237	C
Southeastern Okla State Univ	OK	11,875	C
Southern Conn State Univ	CT	21,924	LC
Southern Illinois Univ Carbondale	IL	23,667	C
Southern Illinois Univ Edwardsville	IL	22,643	C
Southern Nazarene Univ	OK	32,798	NC
Southern New Hampshire Univ	NH	43,198	C
Southern Oregon Univ	OR	19,117	C
Southern Univ and A&M College	LA	16,074	LC+
Southern Univ at New Orleans	LA	8,014	LC
Southern Wesleyan Univ	SC	32,130	LC
Southwest Baptist Univ	MO	29,900	LC
Southwest Minn State Univ	MN	17,783	C
Southwestern College	KS	31,531	C
Southwestern Okla State Univ	OK	11,790	C
Spring Hill College	AL	48,488	C
Springfield College	MA	45,995	C
St. Ambrose Univ	IA	39,019	C
St. Ambrose Univ	IA	39,019	C
St. Catherine Univ	MN	45,630	VC
St. Cloud State Univ	MN	10,600	C
St. Joseph's College, New York/Brooklyn Campus	NY	25,114	LC
SUNY / SUNY College at Old Westbury	NY	16,860	C
SUNY / SUNY Fredonia	NY	20,818	C
SUNY / SUNY Potsdam	NY	20,404	C+
SUNY at Geneseo	NY	20,440	VC+
SUNY at New Paltz	NY	19,200	C
Stephens College	MO	38,042	C
Stevenson Univ	MD	72,770	C
Susquehanna Univ	PA	55,340	VC
Syracuse Univ	NY	60,239	VC
Taylor Univ	IN	40,317	C+
Temple Univ	PA	24,392	VC
Tenn State Univ	TN	14,423	C
Texas A&M Univ at Commerce	TX	10,496	C
Texas Christian Univ	TX	54,670	HC
Texas Tech Univ	TX	18,736	C+
The Catholic Univ of America	DC	56,356	VC
The College of New Jersey	NJ	31,909	HC
The College of St. Rose	NY	43,048	C
The Lincoln Univ	PA	15,154	NC
The Univ of Akron	OH	21,477	C
The Univ of Tenn at Chattanooga	TN	16,744	C
Thomas College	ME	35,268	LC
Thomas Univ	GA	21,420	LC
Toccoa Falls College	GA	27,920	C
Towson Univ	MD	17,408	VC
Trevecca Nazarene Univ	TN	31,186	C
Trinity Washington Univ	DC	33,826	C+
Troy Univ	AL	16,171	C
Tulane Univ	LA	63,396	HC+
Tusculum College	TN	31,625	C
Tuskegee Univ	AL	28,164	C
Univ of Alabama	AL	24,320	C+
Univ of Alabama at Birmingham	AL	19,906	C
Univ of Arizona	AZ	23,100	C
Univ of Arkansas at Fayetteville	AR	19,152	C+
Univ of Arkansas at Little Rock	AR	18,211	C
Univ of Arkansas at Monticello	AR	13,134	NC
Univ of Arkansas at Pine Bluff	AR	13,541	C
Univ of Central Arkansas	AR	14,472	VC
Univ of Central Florida	FL	15,922	VC
Univ of Central Missouri	MO	18,982	C
Univ of Central Okla	OK	13,486	C
Univ of Cincinnati	OH	21,964	VC
Univ of Dayton	OH	53,620	C
Univ of Delaware	DE	24,976	VC+
Univ of Georgia	GA	21,250	HC
Univ of Hartford	CT	49,776	C
Univ of Illinois at Chicago	IL	25,006	VC
Univ of Illinois at Urbana-Champaign	IL	27,006	HC
Univ of Kansas	KS	20,135	C+
Univ of Kentucky	KY	33,306	C
Univ of Louisville	KY	19,824	C
Univ of Maine at Farmington	ME	18,187	C
Univ of Mary	ND	23,180	C
Univ of Mary Hardin-Baylor	TX	33,950	C+
Univ of Maryland/College Park	MD	21,938	HC
Univ of Mass Boston	MA	13,435	C
Univ of Mich/Dearborn	MI	11,757	VC
Univ of Mich-Flint	MI	17,607	C+
Univ of Minn Crookston	MN	19,739	C
Univ of Minn/Twin Cities	MN	23,519	HC+
Univ of Missouri/Columbia	MO	18,201	MC
Univ of Missouri-Kansas City	MO	19,563	VC
Univ of Missouri-St. Louis	MO		C
Univ of Mobile	AL	28,935	C
Univ of Montana-Western	MT	11,220	LC
Univ of Mount Union	OH	38,970	C
Univ of Nebr - Kearney	NE	16,546	LC
Univ of Nebr - Lincoln	NE	18,589	VC
Univ of Nevada/Reno	NV	18,010	C
Univ of New Mexico	NM	15,404	C
Univ of New Orleans	LA	12,840	C
Univ of North Alabama	AL	15,398	C
Univ of N Car at Greensboro	NC	14,690	C
Univ of N Car at Pembroke	NC	14,388	LC
Univ of N Car at Wilmington	NC	14,590	VC
Univ of N Dak	ND	15,373	C
Univ of North Georgia	GA	17,316	C
Univ of Northwestern - St. Paul	MN	38,160	C
Univ of Okla	OK	18,911	VC
Univ of PR, at Bayamon	PR	13,145	
Univ of Rio Grande & Rio Grande Community College	OH	8,750	NC
Univ of Science and Arts of Okla	OK	11,140	VC
Univ of Scranton	PA	54,962	VC
Univ of Sioux Falls	SD	34,330	C
Univ of South Alabama	AL	16,400	C
Univ of S Car Aiken	SC	16,712	C
Univ of S Car at Columbia	SC	19,725	VC+
Univ of S Car Upstate	SC	18,200	LC
Univ of Southern Indiana	IN	16,501	C
Univ of Southern Miss	MS	13,170	C
Univ of Texas at San Antonio	TX	20,157	C
Univ of the District of Columbia	DC	21,044	LC
Univ of the Ozarks	AR	52,176	C
Univ of Toledo	OH	19,336	NC
Univ of Vermont	VT	28,878	HC
Univ of West Alabama	AL	15,516	NC
Univ of West Florida	FL	15,848	C
Univ of West Georgia	GA	16,360	LC
Univ of Wisc-Stevens Point	WI	14,043	C
Univ of Wisc-Stout	WI	19,667	C
Univ of Wisc-Whitewater	WI	13,976	C
Urbana Univ	OH	30,820	C
Ursuline College	OH	41,076	LC
Utah State Univ	UT	12,736	C
Vanderbilt Univ	TN	60,572	MC
Virginia Union Univ	VA	22,421	C
Walsh Univ	OH	39,010	C
Washburn Univ	KS	15,827	C
Washington State Univ	WA	22,495	C
Wayland Baptist Univ	TX	22,356	LC
Waynesburg Univ	PA	32,290	C
Weber State Univ	UT	10,721	C
Webster Univ	MO	37,490	C
Wellesley College	MA	63,916	MC
Wells College	NY	50,500	C
Wesleyan College	GA	29,694	C+
West Chester Univ of Pennsylvania	PA	18,456	C
West Liberty Univ	WV	15,512	C
West Virginia State Univ	WV	8,378	NC
Western Carolina Univ	NC	13,965	C
Western Kentucky Univ	KY	16,850	C
Western Mich Univ	MI	21,054	C
Western Washington Univ	WA	18,003	C+
Westfield State Univ	MA	19,671	C
Westminster College	UT	41,078	C+
Wheaton College	MA	61,512	VC
Wheelock College	MA	49,225	C
Widener Univ	PA	56,486	C
William Woods Univ	MO	32,040	C
Wilmington College	OH	34,600	C
Wilmington Univ	DE	8,546	NC
Wilson College	PA	35,620	C
Winona State Univ	MN	17,535	C
Winthrop Univ	SC	23,082	C
Worcester State Univ	MA	20,977	C
Wright State Univ	OH	16,983	C
Xavier Univ	OH	47,880	C+
Youngstown State Univ	OH	17,307	C

EARLY CHILDHOOD STUDIES

School	ST	$IS	SR
Becker College	MA	57,628	C
Biola Univ	CA	46,402	C+
Bluffton Univ	OH	40,950	C
Boise State Univ	ID	14,860	C
Calif Baptist Univ	CA	41,392	C
Central Mich Univ	MI	20,330	C
Grace Bible College	MI	25,250	C
Idaho State Univ	ID	13,619	NC
Langston Univ	OK	14,314	C
Mayville State Univ	ND	18,371	NC
Metropolitan State Univ	MN	7,566	C
Mills College	CA	59,163	VC
Missouri Southern State Univ	MO	12,499	C
Mount Mary Univ	WI	34,650	LC
National Univ	CA	14,730	LC
New York Univ	NY	65,860	MC
Niagara Univ	NY	41,010	C
Northern Illinois Univ	IL	20,176	C
Plymouth State Univ	NH	23,180	LC
Point Park Univ	PA	41,270	C
Purdue Univ/Northwest	IN	15,038	C
Rochester College	MI	28,574	LC
S Dak State Univ	SD	15,634	C
St. Ambrose Univ	IA	39,019	C
St. Ambrose Univ	IA	39,019	C
SUNY / Empire State College	NY	9,145	SP
SUNY / SUNY Fredonia	NY	20,818	C
Univ of Dayton	OH	53,620	C
Univ of Maryland/College Park	MD	21,938	HC
Univ of Minn/Duluth	MN	20,292	C+
Univ of Missouri/Columbia	MO	18,201	MC
Univ of Nebr - Lincoln	NE	18,589	VC
Univ of N Dak	ND	15,373	C
Wayne State College	NE	12,802	C
Weber State Univ	UT	10,721	C
West Chester Univ of Pennsylvania	PA	18,456	C
Youngstown State Univ	OH	17,307	C

EARTH & SPACE SCIENCE

School	ST	$IS	SR
Arizona State Univ at the Tempe Campus	AZ	21,756	VC
Brown Univ	RI	64,566	MC
East Stroudsburg Univ	PA	18,334	C
Stony Brook Univ/The SUNY	NY	21,881	MC
West Chester Univ of Pennsylvania	PA	18,456	C

EARTH SCIENCE

School	ST	$IS	SR
Adams State Univ	CO	17,703	LC
Adrian College	MI	42,400	C
Alaska Pacific Univ	AK	26,680	VC
Albion College	MI	52,650	C
Arizona State Univ at the Tempe Campus	AZ	21,756	VC
Baylor Univ	TX	53,760	HC
Bemidji State Univ	MN	16,056	VC
Boston Univ	MA	65,110	MC
Bowdoin College	ME	63,500	MC
Bowling Green State Univ	OH	19,747	C
Bridgewater State Univ	MA	21,810	C
Bryant Univ	RI	55,646	VC
Calif Polytechnic State Univ	CA	17,979	HC+
Cal State, Long Beach	CA	18,850	C
Cal State, Monterey Bay	CA	26,871	LC
Cal State, Northridge	CA	16,859	LC
Calvin College	MI	41,570	VC+
Central Conn State Univ	CT	21,203	C
Central Mich Univ	MI	20,330	C
Central Washington Univ	WA	16,803	C
CUNY/Brooklyn College	NY	5,884	C+
CUNY/City College	NY	20,319	VC
Columbia Univ/City of New York	NY	62,958	MC
Columbus State Univ	GA	14,336	LC
Dartmouth College	NH	66,174	MC
DePauw Univ	IN	58,688	HC+
Dickinson College	PA	63,974	MC
Dickinson State Univ	ND	12,372	LC
Eastern Mich Univ	MI	19,761	C
Edinboro Univ	PA	15,940	LC
Emporia State Univ	KS	14,570	C
Fitchburg State Univ	MA	21,819	C
Frostburg State Univ	MD	17,280	LC
George Mason Univ	VA	15,724	VC
Georgia Inst of Technology	GA	23,360	MC
Grand Valley State Univ	MI	22,250	C+
Indiana Univ of Pennsylvania	PA	23,614	LC
Indiana Univ-Purdue Univ Fort Wayne	IN	17,553	C
Iowa State Univ	IA	17,570	C
Jackson State Univ	MS	15,879	LC
Johns Hopkins Univ	MD	65,386	MC
Kean Univ	NJ	24,650	C
Keene State College	NH	24,003	LC
Kent State Univ	OH	20,732	C
Lehigh Univ	PA	61,010	MC
Lock Haven Univ of Pennsylvania	PA	18,028	LC
Mass Inst of Technology	MA	62,662	MC
Mercer Univ	GA	45,348	VC
Mercyhurst Univ	PA	47,420	C
Miami Univ	OH	27,190	HC+
Mich State Univ	MI	23,898	VC+
Millersville Univ of Pennsylvania	PA	23,782	C
Minn State Univ, Mankato	MN	15,616	C
Minn State Univ, Moorhead	MN	15,941	C
Minot State Univ	ND	12,732	C
Montana State Univ	MT	15,500	C+
Morehead State Univ	KY	17,422	C
Murray State Univ	KY	16,998	C
Muskingum Univ	OH	35,966	C
National Univ	CA	14,730	LC
New Mexico Inst of Mining and Technology	NM	14,833	HC
New York Univ	NY	65,860	MC
N Car State Univ	NC	19,515	HC+
N Dak State Univ	ND	16,245	C
Northeastern Illinois Univ	IL	12,529	LC
Northeastern Univ	MA	62,703	MC
Northern Mich Univ	MI	19,604	C
Northland College	WI	41,103	C+
Northwest Missouri State Univ	MO	17,737	C
Ohio State Univ at Columbus	OH	21,703	HC+
Ohio Univ	OH	22,924	C
Ohio Wesleyan Univ	OH	49,460	VC
Old Dominion Univ	VA	20,910	C
Oregon State Univ	OR	22,519	VC
Otterbein Univ	OH	41,630	C
Point Park Univ	PA	41,270	C
Prescott College	AZ	33,284	C
Purdue Univ/West Lafayette	IN	20,032	MC
Rice Univ	TX	57,668	MC
St. Louis Univ	MO	49,866	HC
Salem State Univ	MA	17,303	LC
Salisbury Univ	MD	20,714	VC
San Francisco State Univ	CA	18,514	LC
Shippensburg Univ of Pennsylvania	PA	23,208	C
Slippery Rock Univ of Pennsylvania	PA	10,360	C
Southern Conn State Univ	CT	21,924	LC

ST = STATE $IS = IN-STATE COSTS SR = SELECTOR RATING

School	ST	$IS	SR
Southern Illinois Univ Edwardsville	IL	22,643	C
St. Cloud State Univ	MN	10,600	C
St. Mary's Univ	TX	37,500	C
Stanford Univ	CA	60,409	MC
SUNY / Buffalo State College	NY	20,842	C
SUNY / SUNY Fredonia	NY	20,818	C
SUNY / SUNY Oneonta	NY	19,712	C+
SUNY at Oswego	NY	21,351	C
SUNY SUNY Albany	NY	22,165	C
Susquehanna Univ	PA	55,340	VC
Syracuse Univ	NY	60,239	VC
Tarleton State Univ	TX	15,248	LC
Texas A&M Univ at Commerce	TX	10,496	C
Texas A&M Univ at Galveston	TX	15,920	C
The College at Brockport - SUNY	NY	20,346	C
The Univ of Utah	UT	17,924	VC
Towson Univ	MD	17,408	VC
Tulane Univ	LA	63,396	HC+
Univ of Alabama in Huntsville	AL	19,445	VC
Univ of Alaska Fairbanks	AK	16,179	C
Univ of Arkansas at Fayetteville	AR	19,152	C+
Univ of Calif at Berkeley	CA	28,853	MC
Univ of Calif at Irvine	CA	26,484	VC
Univ of Calif at Los Angeles	CA	30,162	MC
Univ of Calif at Santa Barbara	CA	29,091	HC
Univ of Calif San Diego	CA	30,150	MC
Univ of Calif, Santa Cruz	CA	28,731	C+
Univ of Central Missouri	MO	18,982	C
Univ of Florida	FL	16,291	HC+
Univ of Illinois at Chicago	IL	25,006	VC
Univ of Indianapolis	IN	36,480	C
Univ of Maine	ME	20,792	C
Univ of Mass Amherst	MA	26,199	VC+
Univ of Mass Boston	MA	13,435	C
Univ of Mass Lowell	MA	26,380	C
Univ of Memphis	TN	18,278	C
Univ of Mich/Ann Arbor	MI	24,410	MC
Univ of Nevada, Las Vegas	NV	17,553	C
Univ of New Hampshire	NH	28,562	VC
Univ of New Mexico	NM	15,404	C
Univ of New Orleans	LA	12,840	C
Univ of N Car at Charlotte	NC	15,547	C
Univ of Northern Colo	CO	20,851	C
Univ of S Dak	SD	16,109	C
Univ of Texas at El Paso	TX	34,452	NC
Univ of Wisc-Green Bay	WI	15,064	C
Univ of Wyoming	WY	15,375	C+
Utah State Univ	UT	12,736	C
Vanderbilt Univ	TN	60,572	MC
Vassar College	NY	65,491	MC
Virginia Wesleyan College	VA	43,728	LC
Washington State Univ	WA	22,495	C
Washington Univ in St. Louis	MO	65,366	VC
Weber State Univ	UT	10,721	C
Wesleyan Univ	CT	65,516	MC
West Chester Univ of Pennsylvania	PA	18,456	C
Western Conn State Univ	CT	21,254	LC
Western Mich Univ	MI	21,054	C
Western Oregon Univ	OR	15,021	LC
Western Washington Univ	WA	18,003	C+
Wilkes Univ	PA	45,622	C
Winona State Univ	MN	17,535	C

EARTH SCIENCE / ADOLESCENCE EDUCATION

School	ST	$IS	SR
Augustana College	IL	49,658	VC
Elizabethtown College	PA	54,050	C
Indiana Univ Bloomington	IN	20,429	VC
LIU Post	NY	49,682	C
Murray State Univ	KY	16,998	C
Old Dominion Univ	VA	20,910	C
Pace Univ	NY	58,248	C
SUNY / SUNY Potsdam	NY	20,404	C+
SUNY at Oswego	NY	21,351	C
Syracuse Univ	NY	60,239	VC
Temple Univ	PA	24,392	VC
Univ of Nebr - Lincoln	NE	18,589	VC
Univ of New Hampshire	NH	28,562	VC
Weber State Univ	UT	10,721	C
Wichita State Univ	KS	21,643	C
Winona State Univ	MN	17,535	C

EAST ASIAN LANGUAGES AND LITERATURE

School	ST	$IS	SR
Austin College	TX	45,875	VC
Beloit College	WI	55,206	HC
Indiana Univ Bloomington	IN	20,429	VC
Miami Univ	OH	27,190	HC+
Mich State Univ	MI	23,898	VC+
Rutgers Univ - New Brunswick	NJ	26,632	HC
Smith College	MA	63,914	MC
Univ of Chicago	IL	67,584	MC
Univ of Florida	FL	16,291	HC+
Univ of Illinois at Urbana-Champaign	IL	27,006	HC
Univ of Kansas	KS	20,135	C+
Univ of Puget Sound	WA	56,456	VC+
Univ of Southern Calif	CA	66,631	C
Washington Univ in St. Louis	MO	65,366	VC
Wellesley College	MA	63,916	MC
Yale Univ	CT	64,650	MC

EAST ASIAN STUDIES

School	ST	$IS	SR
Appalachian State Univ	NC	14,416	VC
Augsburg College	MN	43,929	C
Barnard College/Columbia Univ	NY	62,741	MC
Bates College	ME	64,500	MC
Brandeis Univ	MA	65,925	MC
Brown Univ	RI	64,566	MC
Bryn Mawr College	PA	59,890	MC
Bucknell Univ	PA	64,616	MC
CUNY/Queens College	NY	27,896	C
Colby College	ME	64,060	MC
Columbia Univ/ School of General Studies	NY	61,470	MC
Columbia Univ/City of New York	NY	62,958	MC
Conn College	CT	65,000	MC
Dallas Baptist Univ	TX	33,713	C
Davidson College	NC	60,119	MC
Denison Univ	OH	58,860	MC
DePaul Univ	IL	47,623	VC
DePauw Univ	IN	58,688	HC+
Dickinson College	PA	63,974	MC
Eckerd College	FL	52,874	C
Emory and Henry College	VA	41,410	C
George Washington Univ	DC	62,835	MC
Hamline Univ	MN	45,678	VC
Haverford College	PA	66,490	MC
Indiana Univ Bloomington	IN	20,429	VC
John Carroll Univ	OH	49,740	C+
Johns Hopkins Univ	MD	65,386	MC
Kalamazoo College	MI	53,931	HC+
Lawrence Univ	WI	54,498	HC
Lewis & Clark College	OR	58,434	HC+
Middlebury College	VT	64,332	MC
Minn State Univ, Moorhead	MN	15,941	C
Mount Holyoke College	MA	56,746	MC
New York Univ	NY	65,860	MC
North Central College	IL	48,712	VC
Oakland Univ	MI	20,763	C
Oberlin College	OH	66,012	MC
Occidental College	CA	65,530	MC
Ohio Wesleyan Univ	OH	49,460	VC
Princeton Univ	NJ	57,610	MC
Simmons College	MA	53,090	VC
Stanford Univ	CA	60,409	MC
SUNY at Binghamton	NY	22,861	MC
SUNY SUNY Albany	NY	22,165	C
Univ of Arizona	AZ	23,100	C
Univ of Calif at Davis	CA	28,468	HC
Univ of Calif at Irvine	CA	26,484	VC
Univ of Calif at Los Angeles	CA	30,162	MC
Univ of Delaware	DE	24,976	VC+
Univ of Illinois at Urbana-Champaign	IL	27,006	HC
Univ of Minn/Twin Cities	MN	23,519	HC+
Univ of Rochester	NY	65,032	MC
Univ of Southern Calif	CA	66,631	C
Ursinus College	PA	61,690	VC
Valparaiso Univ	IN	48,370	C+
Vanderbilt Univ	TN	60,572	MC
Washington and Lee Univ	VA	59,647	MC
Washington Univ in St. Louis	MO	65,366	VC
Wesleyan Univ	CT	65,516	MC
Western Washington Univ	WA	18,003	C+
Wittenberg Univ	OH	48,156	C+
Yale Univ	CT	64,650	MC

EASTERN EUROPEAN STUDIES

School	ST	$IS	SR
Bowdoin College	ME	63,500	MC
Florida State Univ	FL	16,771	HC
Indiana Univ Bloomington	IN	20,429	VC
Oberlin College	OH	66,012	MC
Ohio Univ	OH	22,924	C
Rutgers Univ - Newark	NJ	27,288	C
Univ of Mich/Ann Arbor	MI	24,410	MC
Univ of Texas at Austin	TX	26,102	HC
Washington Univ in St. Louis	MO	65,366	VC
Yale Univ	CT	64,650	MC

ECOGASTRONOMY

School	ST	$IS	SR
Univ of New Hampshire	NH	28,562	VC

ECOLOGY

School	ST	$IS	SR
Adams State Univ	CO	17,703	LC
Angelo State Univ	TX	15,263	NC
Appalachian State Univ	NC	14,416	VC
Augusta Univ	GA	4,632	C
Beloit College	WI	55,206	HC
Bennington College	VT	63,960	MC
Boston Univ	MA	65,110	MC
Brown Univ	RI	64,566	MC
Bryant Univ	RI	55,646	VC
Cal State, Long Beach	CA	18,850	C
Castleton Univ	VT	20,186	C
Colo State Univ	CO	22,162	VC
Defiance College	OH	41,630	C
Florida Inst of Technology	FL	53,306	VC
Florida State Univ	FL	16,771	HC
Goshen College	IN	42,500	C
Hampshire College	MA	63,824	MC
Idaho State Univ	ID	13,619	NC
Kutztown Univ of Pennsylvania	PA	19,056	LC
Le Moyne College	NY	46,000	C
Marshall Univ	WV	17,242	C
Mich Tech Univ	MI	24,739	VC+
Missouri Southern State Univ	MO	12,499	C
Montana State Univ-Northern	MT	11,370	NC
New Mexico State Univ	NM	14,050	C
Northern Mich Univ	MI	19,604	C
Northwest Missouri State Univ	MO	17,737	C
Northwestern Univ	IL	66,344	MC
Ohio State Univ at Columbus	OH	21,703	HC+
Ohio Univ	OH	22,924	C
Oregon State Univ	OR	22,519	VC
Prescott College	AZ	33,284	C
Princeton Univ	NJ	57,610	MC
Purdue Univ/Northwest	IN	15,038	C
Purdue Univ/West Lafayette	IN	20,032	MC
Rutgers Univ - New Brunswick	NJ	26,632	HC
San Diego State Univ	CA	21,896	C+
San Francisco State Univ	CA	18,514	LC
Sewanee: The Univ of the South	TN	54,500	MC
S Dak State Univ	SD	15,634	C
Southern Illinois Univ Edwardsville	IL	22,643	C
SUNY / SUNY Plattsburgh	NY	18,814	C
SUNY / The College of Environmental Science and Forestry	NY	23,853	VC
Sterling College	VT	41,894	VC
Susquehanna Univ	PA	55,340	VC
Texas A&M Univ	TX	20,521	VC+
Tulane Univ	LA	63,396	HC+
Unity College	ME	37,670	C
Univ of Arizona	AZ	23,100	C
Univ of Calif at Davis	CA	28,468	HC
Univ of Calif at Irvine	CA	26,484	VC
Univ of Calif at Los Angeles	CA	30,162	MC
Univ of Calif at Santa Barbara	CA	29,091	HC
Univ of Calif San Diego	CA	30,150	MC
Univ of Calif, Santa Cruz	CA	28,731	C+
Univ of Colo Boulder	CO	24,285	VC+
Univ of Denver	CO	58,443	VC+
Univ of Georgia	GA	21,250	HC
Univ of Mich/Ann Arbor	MI	24,410	MC
Univ of Mich-Flint	MI	17,607	C+
Univ of Minn/Twin Cities	MN	23,519	HC+
Univ of Montana	MT	14,105	C
Univ of Pittsburgh	PA	29,568	HC+
Univ of Rochester	NY	65,032	MC
Univ of Wyoming	WY	15,375	C+
Vanderbilt Univ	TN	60,572	MC
Washington Univ in St. Louis	MO	65,366	VC
West Liberty Univ	WV	15,512	C
Western Washington Univ	WA	18,003	C+

ECONOMICS

School	ST	$IS	SR
Adams State Univ	CO	17,703	LC
Adelphi Univ	NY	48,244	C
Adrian College	MI	42,400	C
Agnes Scott College	GA	51,930	VC+
Alabama A&M Univ	AL	18,796	C
Albion College	MI	52,650	C
Albright College	PA	46,660	C
Alcorn State Univ	MS	15,854	C
Allegheny College	PA	55,420	VC
Alma College	MI	47,548	C
American International College	MA	46,300	LC
American Univ	DC	59,379	HC+
Amherst College	MA		HC+
Anderson Univ	IN	38,200	C
Andrews Univ	MI	28,030	C+
Appalachian State Univ	NC	14,416	VC
Aquinas College - Mich	MI	38,876	HC
Arizona State Univ at the Tempe Campus	AZ	21,756	VC
Arkansas State Univ	AR	16,190	C
Arkansas Tech Univ	AR	15,484	C
Armstrong State Univ	GA	16,962	C
Ashland Univ	OH	21,440	C
Assumption College	MA	47,920	C+
Auburn Univ	AL	23,594	VC+
Auburn Univ at Montgomery	AL	15,290	C
Augsburg College	MN	43,929	C
Augustana College	IL	49,658	VC
Augustana Univ	SD	38,424	VC
Austin College	TX	45,875	VC
Baker Univ	KS	33,350	C+
Baldwin Wallace Univ	OH	41,106	C
Ball State Univ	IN	19,590	C
Bard College	NY	64,024	HC
Barnard College/Columbia Univ	NY	62,741	MC
Barry Univ	FL	37,830	C
Barton College	NC	38,686	LC
Bates College	ME	64,500	MC
Baylor Univ	TX	53,760	HC
Bellarmine Univ	KY	51,220	C
Belmont Univ	TN	40,970	VC
Beloit College	WI	55,206	HC
Bemidji State Univ	MN	16,056	VC
Benedict College	SC	28,238	NC
Benedictine College	KS	36,200	VC
Benedictine Univ	IL	38,300	C
Bentley Univ	MA	60,890	HC
Berea College	KY	7,042	C
Berry College	GA	45,286	C+
Bethany College	WV	36,300	NC
Bethel College	IN	35,860	C
Bethel Univ	MN	45,270	VC
Biola Univ	CA	46,402	C+
Birmingham-Southern College	AL	44,478	VC
Black Hills State Univ	SD	15,899	C
Bloomsburg Univ of Pennsylvania	PA	19,066	LC
Bluffton Univ	OH	40,950	C
Boise State Univ	ID	14,860	C
Boston College	MA	65,737	MC
Boston Univ	MA	65,110	MC
Bowdoin College	ME	63,500	MC
Bowling Green State Univ	OH	19,747	C
Brandeis Univ	MA	65,925	MC
Bridgewater College	VA	44,510	C
Bridgewater State Univ	MA	21,810	C
Brigham Young Univ	UT	12,748	HC
Brown Univ	RI	64,566	MC
Bryant Univ	RI	55,646	VC
Bryn Mawr College	PA	59,890	MC
Bucknell Univ	PA	64,616	MC
Butler Univ	IN	51,352	VC
Cabrini Univ	PA	42,591	LC
Calif Inst of Technology	CA	58,761	MC
Calif Lutheran Univ	CA	52,853	C
Calif Polytechnic State Univ	CA	17,979	HC+
Calif State Polytechnic Univ, Pomona	CA	21,541	C
Cal State, Bakersfield	CA	19,191	LC
Cal State, Chico	CA	21,440	C
Cal State, East Bay	CA	19,413	C
Cal State, Fresno	CA	16,902	LC
Cal State, Fullerton	CA	21,902	C
Cal State, Long Beach	CA	18,850	C
Cal State, Los Angeles	CA	17,186	LC
Cal State, Northridge	CA	16,859	LC
Cal State, Sacramento	CA	20,332	C
Cal State, San Bernardino	CA	12,000	C
Cal State, San Marcos	CA	24,184	LC
Cal State, Stanislaus	CA	16,212	C
Calvin College	MI	41,570	VC+
Campbellsville Univ	KY	32,492	C
Capital Univ	OH	42,982	C
Carleton College	MN	64,071	MC
Carnegie Mellon Univ	PA	67,980	MC
Carroll Univ	WI	38,100	C+
Carson-Newman Univ	TN	34,160	C
Carthage College	WI	48,835	C
Case Western Reserve Univ	OH	60,304	MC
Castleton Univ	VT	20,186	C
Catawba College	NC	39,820	C
Cedarville Univ	OH	34,990	VC
Centenary College of Louisiana	LA	45,650	C+
Central College	IA	44,592	C
Central Conn State Univ	CT	21,203	C
Central Mich Univ	MI	20,330	C
Central State Univ	OH	18,564	C
Central Washington Univ	WA	16,803	C
Centre College	KY	49,250	HC
Chapman Univ	CA	63,078	VC+
Charleston Southern Univ	SC	32,400	C
Chatham Univ	PA	46,517	C
Cheyney Univ of Pennsylvania	PA	20,896	LC
Chicago State Univ	IL	20,144	C
Christopher Newport Univ	VA	23,968	VC+
CUNY/Baruch College	NY	21,609	HC
CUNY/Brooklyn College	NY	5,884	C+
CUNY/City College	NY	20,319	VC
CUNY/College of Staten Island	NY	17,840	NC
CUNY/Hunter College	NY	31,098	VC
CUNY/John Jay College of Criminal Justice	NY	6,359	NC
CUNY/Lehman College	NY	5,778	HC+
CUNY/Queens College	NY	27,896	C
CUNY/York College	NY	6,747	LC
Claremont McKenna College	CA	67,185	MC
Clarion Univ of Pennsylvania	PA	21,608	LC
Clark Atlanta Univ	GA	31,019	LC
Clark Univ	MA	51,600	HC+
Clayton State Univ	GA	19,735	C
Clemson Univ	SC		HC
Cleveland State Univ	OH	22,196	C
Coastal Carolina Univ	SC	19,766	C
Coe College	IA	51,570	VC
Colby College	ME	64,060	MC
Colgate Univ	NY	65,030	MC
College of Charleston	SC	22,699	C
College of Mount St. Vincent	NY	45,620	C
College of St. Benedict	MN	52,806	C
College of St. Elizabeth	NJ	44,432	LC
College of St. Scholastica	MN	44,640	C
College of the Holy Cross	MA	62,165	MC
College of William & Mary	VA		MC
Colo College	CO	62,560	MC
Colo School of Mines	CO	29,319	MC
Colo State Univ	CO	22,162	VC

ST = STATE $IS = IN-STATE COSTS SR = SELECTOR RATING

School	ST	$IS	SR
Colo State Univ-Pueblo	CO	18,234	C
Columbia Univ/ School of General Studies	NY	61,470	MC
Columbia Univ/City of New York	NY	62,958	MC
Conn College	CT	65,000	MC
Converse College	SC	26,495	C
Cornell College	IA	48,800	VC
Cornell Univ	NY	64,853	MC
Covenant College	GA	38,990	VC
Creighton Univ	NE	48,206	VC+
Dartmouth College	NH	66,174	MC
Davidson College	NC	60,119	MC
Davis & Elkins College	WV	38,242	LC
Delaware State Univ	DE	19,376	NC
Denison Univ	OH	58,860	MC
DePaul Univ	IL	47,623	VC
DePauw Univ	IN	58,688	HC+
Dickinson College	PA	63,974	MC
Dillard Univ	LA	20,940	VC
Doane Univ	NE	39,184	VC
Dominican Univ	IL	41,222	C
Dordt College	IA	37,860	C+
Drake Univ	IA	45,056	HC
Drew Univ/College of Liberal Arts	NJ	61,048	VC
Drexel Univ	PA	65,432	VC+
Drury Univ	MO	33,791	VC
Duke Univ	NC	64,188	
Duquesne Univ	PA	46,822	VC
Earlham College	IN	54,870	HC
East Carolina Univ	NC	16,937	C
East Stroudsburg Univ	PA	18,334	C
East Tenn State Univ	TN	13,994	C
Eastern Conn State Univ	CT	23,059	C
Eastern Illinois Univ	IL	21,126	C
Eastern Kentucky Univ	KY	16,908	C
Eastern Mennonite Univ	VA	42,550	C
Eastern Mich Univ	MI	19,761	C
Eastern Washington Univ	WA	25,572	LC
Eckerd College	FL	52,874	C
Edgewood College	WI	35,950	C
Edinboro Univ	PA	15,940	LC
Elizabethtown College	PA	54,050	C
Elmhurst College	IL	45,428	C
Elon Univ	NC	44,599	VC+
Emory and Henry College	VA	41,410	C
Emory Univ	GA	60,786	MC
Emporia State Univ	KS	14,570	C
Eugene Lang College/The New School for Liberal Arts	NY	55,650	C
Excelsior College	NY	14,080	SP
Fairfield Univ	CT	59,860	VC+
Fairleigh Dickinson Univ/ College at Florham	NJ	52,062	C
Fairleigh Dickinson Univ/ Metropolitan Campus	NJ	40,254	C
Fayetteville State Univ	NC	17,756	C
Fisk Univ	TN	32,066	LC
Fitchburg State Univ	MA	21,819	C
Flagler College	FL	27,620	C
Florida A&M Univ	FL	15,361	C
Florida Atlantic Univ	FL	17,339	C
Florida Gulf Coast Univ	FL	9,682	C
Florida International Univ	FL	19,854	C+
Florida State Univ	FL	16,771	HC
Fordham Univ	NY	65,918	MC
Fort Hays State Univ	KS	12,131	C
Fort Lewis College	CO	18,980	C
Fort Valley State Univ	GA	17,988	VC
Framingham State Univ	MA	20,584	C
Francis Marion Univ	SC	16,464	LC
Franciscan Univ of Steubenville	OH	33,980	VC
Franklin and Marshall College	PA	63,170	HC
Franklin College	IN	39,380	C
Frostburg State Univ	MD	17,280	LC
Furman Univ	SC	58,092	VC+
Gallaudet Univ	DC	29,118	LC
George Fox Univ	OR	42,938	C
George Mason Univ	VA	15,724	VC
George Washington Univ	DC	62,835	MC
Georgetown College	KY	41,440	C
Georgetown Univ	DC	65,926	MC
Georgia College & State Univ	GA	21,148	C+
Georgia Inst of Technology	GA	23,360	MC
Georgia Southern Univ	GA	16,596	C
Georgia State Univ	GA	24,332	VC
Gettysburg College	PA	63,000	HC
Goldey-Beacom College	DE	31,750	C
Gonzaga Univ	WA	50,888	HC
Gordon College	MA	46,472	C+
Goshen College	IN	42,500	C
Goucher College	MD	55,716	VC
Graceland Univ	IA	35,290	C
Grambling State Univ	LA	15,701	C
Grand Valley State Univ	MI	22,250	C+
Grinnell College	IA	60,738	MC
Grove City College	PA	25,692	VC
Guilford College	NC	44,090	C
Gustavus Adolphus College	MN	52,433	HC
Hamilton College	NY	64,250	MC
Hamline Univ	MN	45,678	VC
Hampden-Sydney College	VA	56,248	C+
Hampshire College	MA	63,824	MC
Hampton Univ	VA	34,926	LC
Hanover College	IN	46,364	C+
Harding Univ	AR	25,421	C
Hardin-Simmons Univ	TX	33,966	C
Hartwick College	NY	51,270	C
Harvard College/Harvard Univ	MA	60,659	MC
Hastings College	NE	35,380	C+
Haverford College	PA	66,490	MC
Hawaii Pacific Univ	HI	33,420	C
Heidelberg Univ	OH	39,200	C
Hendrix College	AR	54,020	VC+
Hillsdale College	MI	35,722	MC
Hiram College	OH	43,230	C
Hofstra Univ	NY	55,960	C+
Hollins Univ	VA	49,635	VC
Hood College	MD	54,840	C
Hope College	MI	39,940	VC
Houston Baptist Univ	TX	36,450	C
Howard Univ	DC	37,616	C+
Huntington Univ	IN	33,996	C
Idaho State Univ	ID	13,619	NC
Illinois College	IL	40,850	VC
Illinois State Univ	IL	23,418	VC
Illinois Wesleyan Univ	IL	56,430	VC+
Indiana State Univ	IN	23,223	LC
Indiana Univ Bloomington	IN	20,429	VC
Indiana Univ Northwest	IN	7,072	C
Indiana Univ of Pennsylvania	PA	23,614	LC
Indiana Univ South Bend	IN	14,242	C
Indiana Univ Southeast	IN	14,242	LC
Indiana Univ-Purdue Univ Fort Wayne	IN	17,553	C
Indiana Univ-Purdue Univ Indianapolis	IN	18,635	C
Indiana Wesleyan Univ	IN	33,674	C
Inter-American Univ of PR-San Germán	PR	20,042	
Iona College	NY	50,984	C
Iowa State Univ	IA	17,570	C
Ithaca College	NY	56,766	VC
Jackson State Univ	MS	15,879	LC
Jacksonville State Univ	AL	14,628	LC
Jacksonville Univ	FL	46,230	C
James Madison Univ	VA	19,084	VC
John Carroll Univ	OH	49,740	C+
Johns Hopkins Univ	MD	65,386	MC
Johnson C. Smith Univ	NC	25,336	LC
Juniata College	PA	53,760	VC
Kalamazoo College	MI	53,931	HC+
Kansas State Univ	KS	17,780	VC
Kean Univ	NJ	24,650	C
Keene State College	NH	24,003	LC
Kennesaw State Univ	GA	19,592	VC
Kent State Univ	OH	20,732	C
Kenyon College	OH	63,330	MC
King's College	PA	46,858	C
Knox College	IL	52,615	VC+
La Salle Univ	PA	55,790	C
Lafayette College	PA	63,355	MC
Lake Forest College	IL	50,652	VC
Lakeland Univ	WI	35,130	C
Lamar Univ	TX	18,014	LC
Langston Univ	OK	14,314	C
Lawrence Univ	WI	54,498	HC
Le Moyne College	NY	46,000	C
Lebanon Valley College	PA	51,530	C
Lehigh Univ	PA	61,010	MC
Lenoir-Rhyne Univ	NC	43,200	C
Lewis & Clark College	OR	58,434	HC+
Lewis Univ	IL	40,370	C
Limestone College	SC	32,100	C
Linfield College	OR	52,010	C
Lipscomb Univ	TN	41,296	VC
LIU Brooklyn	NY	49,682	C
LIU Post	NY	49,682	C
Lock Haven Univ of Pennsylvania	PA	18,028	LC
Longwood Univ	VA	22,184	C
Loras College	IA	39,222	C
Louisiana College	LA	21,886	C
Louisiana State Univ and A&M College	LA	18,677	VC
Loyola Marymount Univ	CA	58,038	HC
Loyola Univ Chicago	IL	55,802	VC
Loyola Univ Maryland	MD	60,300	VC
Loyola Univ New Orleans	LA	51,708	VC+
Lubbock Christian Univ	TX	28,426	C
Luther College	IA	48,540	C+
Lycoming College	PA	48,580	C
Lynchburg College	VA	46,740	C
Lyon College	AR	34,730	C+
Macalester College	MN	61,905	MC
Manchester Univ	IN	40,422	C
Manhattan College	NY	51,750	C+
Manhattanville College	NY	51,440	C+
Marietta College	OH	46,190	C
Marist College	NY	49,860	VC
Marquette Univ	WI	48,390	VC+
Marshall Univ	WV	17,242	C
Mary Baldwin Univ	VA	39,865	C
Marymount Univ	VA	41,570	LC
Maryville College	TN	44,410	C
Mass Inst of Technology	MA	62,662	MC
McDaniel College	MD	51,380	VC
McKendree Univ	IL	37,940	C+
Mercer Univ	GA	45,348	VC
Meredith College	NC	45,297	C
Merrimack College	MA	52,770	C
Messiah College	PA	43,100	C+
Methodist Univ	NC	43,600	C
Metropolitan State Univ	MN	7,566	C
Metropolitan State Univ of Denver	CO	29,889	LC
Miami Univ	OH	27,190	HC+
Mich State Univ	MI	23,898	VC+
Mich Tech Univ	MI	24,739	VC+
Middle Tenn State Univ	TN	8,650	C
Middlebury College	VT	64,332	MC
Midland Univ	NE	37,468	
Midwestern State Univ	TX	17,572	C
Millersville Univ of Pennsylvania	PA	23,782	C
Mills College	CA	59,163	VC
Millsaps College	MS	50,080	C+
Minn State Univ, Mankato	MN	15,616	C
Minn State Univ, Moorhead	MN	15,941	C
Minot State Univ	ND	12,732	C
Miss State Univ	MS	11,454	C+
Missouri Southern State Univ	MO	12,499	C
Missouri State Univ	MO	15,190	C+
Missouri Univ of Science and Technology	MO	18,655	HC
Missouri Valley College	MO	28,150	C
Missouri Western State Univ	MO	16,741	
Monmouth College	IL	42,260	C
Montana State Univ	MT	15,500	C+
Montclair State Univ	NJ	26,210	LC
Moravian College	PA	53,117	
Morehouse College	GA	40,064	C
Morgan State Univ	MD	17,190	LC
Mount Holyoke College	MA	56,746	MC
Mount St. Mary's Univ	MD	51,610	C
Muhlenberg College	PA	56,645	VC+
Murray State Univ	KY	16,998	C
Muskingum Univ	OH	35,966	C
Nazareth College	NY	45,574	C
Nebr Wesleyan Univ	NE	38,140	C+
New College of Florida	FL	15,848	MC
New Jersey City Univ	NJ	21,456	LC
New Mexico State Univ	NM	14,050	C
New York Univ	NY	65,860	MC
Niagara Univ	NY	41,010	C
Nichols College	MA	46,800	LC
N Car A&T State Univ	NC	13,365	LC
N Car State Univ	NC	19,515	HC+
North Central College	IL	48,712	VC
N Dak State Univ	ND	16,245	C
North Park Univ	IL	35,860	C
Northeastern Illinois Univ	IL	12,529	LC
Northeastern Univ	MA	62,703	MC
Northern Illinois Univ	IL	20,176	C
Northern Kentucky Univ	KY	16,486	C
Northern Mich Univ	MI	19,604	C
Northern State Univ	SD	14,505	C
Northwest Missouri State Univ	MO	17,737	C
Northwestern College of Iowa	IA	38,400	C+
Northwestern Okla State Univ	OK	13,072	NC
Northwestern Univ	IL	66,344	MC
Notre Dame College	OH	37,150	VC
Notre Dame of Maryland Univ	MD	46,465	VC
Oakland Univ	MI	20,763	C
Oberlin College	OH	66,012	MC
Occidental College	CA	65,530	MC
Oglethorpe Univ	GA	44,200	C+
Ohio Dominican Univ	OH	41,340	C+
Ohio State Univ at Columbus	OH	21,703	HC+
Ohio Univ	OH	22,924	C
Ohio Wesleyan Univ	OH	49,460	VC
Okla City Univ	OK	40,476	VC
Okla State Univ	OK	17,180	VC
Old Dominion Univ	VA	20,910	C
Olivet College	MI	36,110	LC
Olivet Nazarene Univ	IL	41,840	C
Oregon State Univ	OR	22,519	VC
Otterbein Univ	OH	41,630	C
Pace Univ	NY	58,248	C
Pacific Lutheran Univ	WA	49,960	VC
Pacific Univ	OR	52,876	C
Park Univ	MO	20,329	C
Penn State Erie/The Behrend College	PA	16,256	C
Pennsylvania State Univ - Univ Park	PA	29,760	HC
Pepperdine Univ	CA	74,460	HC+
Pitzer College	CA	66,192	MC
Plymouth State Univ	NH	23,180	LC
Point Loma Nazarene Univ	CA	43,450	C
Pomona College	CA	64,957	MC
Portland State Univ	OR	19,443	C
Prescott College	AZ	33,284	C
Princeton Univ	NJ	57,610	MC
Principia College	IL	39,010	C+
Providence College	RI	60,760	VC
Purdue Univ/West Lafayette	IN	20,032	MC
Quinnipiac Univ	CT	59,110	C
Radford Univ	VA	19,027	LC
Ramapo College of New Jersey	NJ	25,338	C
Randolph College	VA	45,660	VC
Randolph-Macon College	VA	49,910	C
Reed College	OR	65,300	MC
Regis Univ	CO	44,520	C
Rensselaer Polytechnic Inst	NY	63,436	MC
Rhode Island College	RI	17,694	LC
Rhodes College	TN	51,900	HC
Rice Univ	TX	57,668	MC
Rider Univ	NJ	54,050	C
Ripon College	WI	46,911	C+
Roanoke College	VA	54,114	VC
Robert Morris Univ	PA	37,834	C
Rochester Inst of Technology	NY	50,842	HC
Rockford Univ	IL	36,030	C
Rockhurst Univ	MO	29,220	C
Roger Williams Univ	RI	46,296	C+
Rollins College	FL	58,670	HC
Roosevelt Univ	IL	40,651	VC
Rose-Hulman Inst of Technology	IN	57,303	MC
Rosemont College	PA	30,980	C
Rowan Univ	NJ	24,491	VC+
Rutgers Univ - Camden	NJ	26,146	C
Rutgers Univ - New Brunswick	NJ	26,632	HC
Rutgers Univ - Newark	NJ	27,288	C
Saginaw Valley State Univ	MI	18,530	C
St. Anselm College	NH	52,560	C+
St. Francis Univ	PA	42,268	NC
St. John's Univ	MN	51,624	C
St. Joseph's Univ	PA	57,544	VC+
St. Leo Univ	FL	31,650	C
St. Mary's College	IN	50,600	C
St. Mary's College of Calif	CA	57,420	C
St. Michael's College	VT	51,725	VC+
St. Peter's Univ	NJ	49,192	C
St. Vincent College	PA	44,626	C
Salem College	NC	37,694	HC
Salem State Univ	MA	17,303	LC
Salisbury Univ	MD	20,714	VC
Salve Regina Univ	RI	51,470	C
Sam Houston State Univ	TX	18,792	C
Samford Univ	AL	39,232	VC
San Diego State Univ	CA	21,896	C+
San Francisco State Univ	CA	18,514	LC
San Jose State Univ	CA	21,540	C
Sarah Lawrence College	NY	63,388	HC
Scripps College	CA	66,664	MC
Seattle Pacific Univ	WA	47,439	C+
Seattle Univ	WA	50,811	VC+
Seton Hall Univ	NJ	55,514	C
Seton Hill Univ	PA	46,972	C
Sewanee: The Univ of the South	TN	54,500	MC
Shenandoah Univ	VA	41,312	C
Shepherd Univ, West Virginia	WV	17,224	C
Shippensburg Univ of Pennsylvania	PA	23,208	C
Shorter Univ	GA	31,130	LC
Siena College	NY	48,916	C+
Simmons College	MA	53,090	VC
Simpson College	IA	43,839	VC
Skidmore College	NY	64,214	HC
Slippery Rock Univ of Pennsylvania	PA	10,360	C
Smith College	MA	63,914	MC
Sonoma State Univ	CA	27,806	C
S Dak State Univ	SD	15,634	C
Southeast Missouri State Univ	MO	15,498	C
Southeastern Okla State Univ	OK	11,875	C
Southern Conn State Univ	CT	21,924	LC
Southern Illinois Univ Carbondale	IL	23,667	C
Southern Illinois Univ Edwardsville	IL	22,643	C
Southern Methodist Univ	TX	66,483	MC
Southern Oregon Univ	OR	19,117	C
Southern Univ at New Orleans	LA	8,014	LC
Southwest Baptist Univ	MO	29,900	LC
Southwestern Univ	TX	50,720	VC
Spelman College	GA	38,751	C
Spring Hill College	AL	48,488	C
St. Ambrose Univ	IA	39,019	C
St. Ambrose Univ	IA	39,019	C
St. Catherine Univ	MN	45,630	VC
St. Cloud State Univ	MN	10,600	C
St. Edward's Univ	TX	53,100	VC
St. Francis College	NY	38,800	LC
St. John Fisher College	NY	43,620	C
St. John's College-Annapolis	MD	60,142	MC
St. John's Univ	NY	55,850	C
St. Lawrence Univ	NY	64,390	VC
St. Mary's College of Maryland	MD	26,634	VC
St. Mary's Univ	TX	37,500	C
St. Norbert College	WI	44,525	VC
St. Olaf College	MN	54,260	HC+
Stanford Univ	CA	60,409	MC
SUNY / Buffalo State College	NY	20,842	C
SUNY / Empire State College	NY	9,145	SP
SUNY / SUNY Cortland	NY	20,706	VC
SUNY / SUNY Fredonia	NY	20,818	C
SUNY / SUNY Oneonta	NY	19,712	C+
SUNY / SUNY Plattsburgh	NY	18,814	C
SUNY / SUNY Potsdam	NY	20,404	C+
SUNY / Univ at Buffalo	NY	23,122	C+
SUNY at Binghamton	NY	22,861	MC
SUNY at Geneseo	NY	20,440	VC+
SUNY at New Paltz	NY	19,200	C
SUNY at Oswego	NY	21,351	C
SUNY at Purchase	NY	17,900	C
SUNY SUNY Albany	NY	22,165	C
Stephen F. Austin State Univ	TX	18,406	LC
Stetson Univ	FL	53,544	VC
Stockton Univ	NJ	25,059	
Stonehill College	MA	55,030	C+

ST = STATE **$IS** = IN-STATE COSTS **SR** = SELECTOR RATING

School	ST	$IS	SR
Stony Brook Univ/The SUNY	NY	21,881	MC
Suffolk Univ	MA	50,308	C
Susquehanna Univ	PA	55,340	VC
Swarthmore College	PA	63,550	MC
Syracuse Univ	NY	60,239	VC
Talladega College	AL	19,215	C
Tarleton State Univ	TX	15,248	LC
Taylor Univ	IN	40,317	C+
Temple Univ	PA	24,392	VC
Tenn Tech Univ	TN	17,050	C
Texas A&M Univ	TX	20,521	VC+
Texas A&M Univ at Commerce	TX	10,496	C
Texas Christian Univ	TX	54,670	HC
Texas Lutheran Univ	TX	38,620	C
Texas Southern Univ	TX	18,212	LC
Texas State Univ	TX	19,350	C
Texas Tech Univ	TX	18,736	C+
The Catholic Univ of America	DC	56,356	VC
The College of New Jersey	NJ	31,909	HC
The College of New Rochelle	NY	46,300	VC
The College of Wooster	OH	57,900	VC+
The Univ of Akron	OH	21,477	C
The Univ of Tenn at Chattanooga	TN	16,744	C
The Univ of Tenn at Knoxville	TN	22,112	VC
The Univ of Tenn at Martin	TN	14,876	C
The Univ of Utah	UT	17,924	VC
The Univ of Virginia's College at Wise	VA	18,192	LC
Thomas Edison State Univ	NJ	6,350	NC
Thomas More College	KY	36,720	C
Tiffin Univ	OH	31,380	C
Tougaloo College	MS	17,980	NC
Touro College	NY	28,950	VC
Towson Univ	MD	17,408	VC
Transylvania Univ	KY	45,690	VC+
Trinity College	CT	63,920	HC+
Trinity Univ	TX	52,314	HC+
Trinity Washington Univ	DC	33,826	C+
Truman State Univ	MO	16,014	HC
Tufts Univ	MA		MC
Tulane Univ	LA	63,396	HC+
Tuskegee Univ	AL	28,164	C
Union College	NY	64,320	MC
Union Univ	TN	33,970	VC
United States Air Force Academy	CO		C
United States Military Academy at West Point	NY		HC+
United States Naval Academy	MD		MC
Universidad del Turabo	PR	17,828	
Univ of Alabama	AL	24,320	C+
Univ of Alabama at Birmingham	AL	19,906	C
Univ of Alaska Anchorage	AK	16,652	NC
Univ of Alaska Fairbanks	AK	16,179	C
Univ of Arizona	AZ	23,100	C
Univ of Arkansas at Fayetteville	AR	19,152	C+
Univ of Arkansas at Little Rock	AR	18,211	C
Univ of Calif at Berkeley	CA	28,853	MC
Univ of Calif at Davis	CA	28,468	HC
Univ of Calif at Irvine	CA	26,484	VC
Univ of Calif at Los Angeles	CA	30,162	MC
Univ of Calif at Riverside	CA	29,227	C+
Univ of Calif at Santa Barbara	CA	29,091	HC
Univ of Calif San Diego	CA	30,150	MC
Univ of Calif, Santa Cruz	CA	28,731	C+
Univ of Central Arkansas	AR	14,472	VC
Univ of Central Florida	FL	15,922	VC
Univ of Central Missouri	MO	18,982	C
Univ of Central Okla	OK	13,486	C
Univ of Chicago	IL	67,584	MC
Univ of Cincinnati	OH	21,964	VC
Univ of Colo Boulder	CO	24,285	VC+
Univ of Colo Colo Springs	CO	19,663	C
Univ of Colo Denver	CO	23,230	C
Univ of Conn	CT	25,538	HC
Univ of Dallas	TX	45,500	VC+
Univ of Dayton	OH	53,620	C
Univ of Delaware	DE	24,976	VC+
Univ of Denver	CO	58,443	VC+
Univ of Detroit Mercy	MI	48,816	C+
Univ of Evansville	IN	44,186	VC+
Univ of Findlay	OH	60,139	C
Univ of Florida	FL	16,291	HC+
Univ of Georgia	GA	21,250	HC
Univ of Hartford	CT	49,776	C
Univ of Hawaii at Hilo	HI	18,038	C
Univ of Hawaii at Manoa	HI	23,221	C
Univ of Idaho	ID	15,348	C
Univ of Illinois at Chicago	IL	25,006	VC
Univ of Illinois at Urbana-Champaign	IL	27,006	HC
Univ of Indianapolis	IN	36,480	C
Univ of Iowa	IA	18,683	VC+
Univ of Kansas	KS	20,135	C+
Univ of Kentucky	KY	33,306	C
Univ of Louisiana at Lafayette	LA	14,516	C
Univ of Maine	ME	20,792	C
Univ of Mary Hardin-Baylor	TX	33,950	C+
Univ of Mary Washington	VA	24,764	VC
Univ of Maryland/Baltimore County	MD	21,296	VC

School	ST	$IS	SR
Univ of Maryland/College Park	MD	21,938	HC
Univ of Mass Amherst	MA	26,199	VC+
Univ of Mass Boston	MA	13,435	C
Univ of Mass Dartmouth	MA	25,658	C
Univ of Mass Lowell	MA	26,380	C
Univ of Memphis	TN	18,278	C
Univ of Miami	FL	63,494	MC
Univ of Mich/Ann Arbor	MI	24,410	MC
Univ of Mich/Dearborn	MI	11,757	VC
Univ of Mich-Flint	MI	17,607	C+
Univ of Minn/Duluth	MN	20,292	C+
Univ of Minn/Morris	MN	20,760	VC
Univ of Minn/Twin Cities	MN	23,519	HC+
Univ of Miss	MS	17,746	C+
Univ of Missouri/Columbia	MO	18,201	MC
Univ of Missouri-Kansas City	MO	19,563	VC
Univ of Missouri-St. Louis	MO		C
Univ of Montana	MT	14,105	C
Univ of Mount Union	OH	38,970	C
Univ of Nebr - Kearney	NE	16,546	LC
Univ of Nebr - Lincoln	NE	18,589	VC
Univ of Nebr - Omaha	NE	16,120	C
Univ of Nevada, Las Vegas	NV	17,553	C
Univ of Nevada/Reno	NV	18,010	C
Univ of New Hampshire	NH	28,562	VC
Univ of New Haven	CT	52,190	C
Univ of New Mexico	NM	15,404	C
Univ of New Orleans	LA	12,840	C
Univ of N Car at Asheville	NC	15,723	VC+
Univ of N Car at Chapel Hill	NC	20,052	HC+
Univ of N Car at Charlotte	NC	15,547	C
Univ of N Car at Greensboro	NC	14,690	C
Univ of N Car at Wilmington	NC	14,590	VC
Univ of N Dak	ND	15,373	C
Univ of North Florida	FL	15,996	VC
Univ of North Texas	TX	19,198	C
Univ of Northern Colo	CO	20,851	C
Univ of Notre Dame	IN	64,043	MC
Univ of Okla	OK	18,911	VC
Univ of Oregon	OR	22,972	C
Univ of Pennsylvania	PA	63,526	MC
Univ of Pittsburgh	PA	29,568	HC+
Univ of Pittsburgh at Bradford	PA	22,402	C
Univ of Pittsburgh at Johnstown	PA	22,092	C
Univ of Portland	OR	52,152	VC
Univ of PR, at Cayey	PR		
Univ of PR, at Mayaguez	PR	13,995	
Univ of PR-Rio Piedras campus	PR	13,327	
Univ of Puget Sound	WA	56,456	VC+
Univ of Redlands	CA	60,200	VC
Univ of Rhode Island	RI	24,906	C
Univ of Richmond	VA	60,880	MC
Univ of Rio Grande & Rio Grande Community College	OH	8,750	NC
Univ of Rochester	NY	65,032	MC
Univ of San Diego	CA	58,442	VC+
Univ of San Francisco	CA	58,484	VC
Univ of Science and Arts of Okla	OK	11,140	VC
Univ of Scranton	PA	54,962	VC
Univ of S Car at Columbia	SC	19,725	VC+
Univ of S Car Upstate	SC	18,200	LC
Univ of S Dak	SD	16,109	C
Univ of South Florida/St. Petersburg	FL	15,980	C
Univ of South Florida/Tampa	FL	16,110	VC+
Univ of Southern Calif	CA	66,631	C
Univ of Southern Indiana	IN	16,501	C
Univ of Southern Maine	ME	18,320	C
Univ of Southern Miss	MS	13,170	C
Univ of St. Thomas - Houston	TX	40,020	VC
Univ of Tampa	FL	36,944	C
Univ of Texas at Arlington	TX	18,026	LC
Univ of Texas at Austin	TX	26,102	HC
Univ of Texas at Dallas	TX	22,830	VC+
Univ of Texas at El Paso	TX	34,452	NC
Univ of Texas at San Antonio	TX	20,157	C
Univ of the District of Columbia	DC	21,044	LC
Univ of the Ozarks	AR	52,176	C
Univ of the Pacific	CA	57,006	VC
Univ of Toledo	OH	19,336	NC
Univ of Tulsa	OK	52,625	HC+
Univ of Vermont	VT	28,878	HC
Univ of Virginia	VA	25,891	MC
Univ of Washington	WA	23,149	VC
Univ of West Georgia	GA	16,360	LC
Univ of Wisc-Eau Claire	WI	15,797	VC
Univ of Wisc-Green Bay	WI	15,064	C
Univ of Wisc-La Crosse	WI	15,247	C+
Univ of Wisc-Madison	WI	20,934	MC
Univ of Wisc-Milwaukee	WI	21,496	C
Univ of Wisc-Oshkosh	WI	15,200	C
Univ of Wisc-Parkside	WI	15,193	C
Univ of Wisc-Platteville	WI	14,614	VC
Univ of Wisc-River Falls	WI	14,485	C
Univ of Wisc-Stevens Point	WI	14,043	C
Univ of Wisc-Superior	WI	14,446	C
Univ of Wisc-Whitewater	WI	13,976	C
Univ of Wyoming	WY	15,375	C+
Ursinus College	PA	61,690	VC
Utah State Univ	UT	12,736	C
Utica College	NY	30,430	C

School	ST	$IS	SR
Valparaiso Univ	IN	48,370	C+
Vanderbilt Univ	TN	60,572	MC
Vassar College	NY	65,491	MC
Villanova Univ	PA	62,523	MC
Virginia Commonwealth Univ	VA	23,049	C
Virginia Polytechnic Inst and State Univ	VA	21,276	HC
Virginia State Univ	VA	19,802	C+
Wabash College	IN	50,650	VC
Wake Forest Univ	NC	64,056	MC
Wartburg College	IA	47,840	C
Washburn Univ	KS	15,827	C
Washington & Jefferson College	PA	56,512	VC
Washington and Lee Univ	VA	59,647	MC
Washington College	MD	54,666	VC
Washington State Univ	WA	22,495	C
Washington Univ in St. Louis	MO	65,366	VC
Wayland Baptist Univ	TX	22,356	LC
Wayne State Univ	MI	22,016	C
Weber State Univ	UT	10,721	C
Webster Univ	MO	37,490	C
Wellesley College	MA	63,916	MC
Wells College	NY	50,500	C
Wesleyan College	GA	29,694	C+
Wesleyan Univ	CT	65,516	MC
West Chester Univ of Pennsylvania	PA	18,456	C
West Liberty Univ	WV	15,512	C
West Texas A&M Univ	TX	13,478	C
West Virginia State Univ	WV	8,378	NC
West Virginia Univ	WV	18,210	C
West Virginia Wesleyan College	WV	36,858	C
Western Conn State Univ	CT	21,254	LC
Western Illinois Univ	IL	20,825	C
Western Kentucky Univ	KY	16,850	C
Western Mich Univ	MI	21,054	C
Western New England Univ	MA	48,088	C
Western Oregon Univ	OR	15,021	LC
Western State Colo Univ	CO	18,639	C
Western Washington Univ	WA	18,003	C+
Westfield State Univ	MA	19,671	C
Westminster College	MO	32,820	C
Westminster College	PA	39,180	C+
Westminster College	UT	41,078	C+
Wheaton College	IL	43,610	MC
Wheaton College	MA	61,512	VC
Whitman College	WA	59,772	MC
Whittier College	CA	57,891	C
Whitworth Univ	WA	51,732	VC
Wichita State Univ	KS	21,643	C
Widener Univ	PA	56,486	C
Wilberforce Univ	OH	19,016	C
Willamette Univ	OR	61,817	VC+
William Paterson Univ of New Jersey	NJ	23,133	C
Williams College	MA	63,290	MC
Wilmington College	OH	34,600	C
Wilson College	PA	35,620	C
Winona State Univ	MN	17,535	C
Winston-Salem State Univ	NC	26,166	LC
Winthrop Univ	SC	23,082	C
Wittenberg Univ	OH	48,156	C+
Wofford College	SC	49,885	VC
Worcester Polytechnic Inst	MA	60,730	MC
Worcester State Univ	MA	20,977	C
Wright State Univ	OH	16,983	C
Xavier Univ	OH	47,880	C+
Yale Univ	CT	64,650	MC
Yeshiva Univ	NY	47,250	VC+
York College of Pennsylvania	PA	29,240	C
Youngstown State Univ	OH	17,307	C

ECONOMICS – STATISTICS

School	ST	$IS	SR
Augsburg College	MN	43,929	C
Ball State Univ	IN	19,590	C
Biola Univ	CA	46,402	C+
Boise State Univ	ID	14,860	C
Brown Univ	RI	64,566	MC
Bryant Univ	RI	55,646	VC
Southern Methodist Univ	TX	66,483	MC
St. Ambrose Univ	IA	39,019	C
St. Ambrose Univ	IA	39,019	C
Univ of Alabama in Huntsville	AL	19,445	VC
Univ of Calif at Irvine	CA	26,484	VC
Univ of Calif San Diego	CA	30,150	MC
Univ of Pittsburgh	PA	29,568	HC+
Wichita State Univ	KS	21,643	C

EDUCATION

School	ST	$IS	SR
Adams State Univ	CO	17,703	LC
Albertus Magnus College	CT	43,258	LC
American Univ of PR	PR	16,130	
Appalachian State Univ	NC	14,416	VC
Aquinas College - Mich	MI	38,876	HC
Arizona State Univ at the Tempe Campus	AZ	21,756	VC
Arkansas Tech Univ	AR	15,484	C
Ashford Univ	CA	10,480	C
Assumption College	MA	47,920	C+
Auburn Univ	AL	23,594	VC+
Augsburg College	MN	43,929	C
Averett Univ	VA	40,970	LC
Belmont Abbey College	NC	48,156	C
Beloit College	WI	55,206	HC
Bennington College	VT	63,960	MC
Berea College	KY	7,042	C
Bethany College	WV	36,300	NC
Bethel College	IN	35,860	C
Bethel Univ	MN	45,270	VC
Bethune-Cookman Univ	FL	22,970	C
Birmingham-Southern College	AL	44,478	VC
Bloomfield College	NJ	39,100	LC
Boise State Univ	ID	14,860	C
Boston Univ	MA	65,110	MC
Bowdoin College	ME	63,500	MC
Bowling Green State Univ	OH	19,747	C
Brandeis Univ	MA	65,925	MC
Brown Univ	RI	64,566	MC
Bryn Athyn College	PA	31,470	C
Bucknell Univ	PA	64,616	MC
Cabrini Univ	PA	42,591	LC
Cairn Univ	PA	36,296	C
Calif Polytechnic State Univ	CA	17,979	HC+
Cal State, Monterey Bay	CA	26,871	LC
Calif Univ of Pennsylvania	PA	14,217	LC
Calvin College	MI	41,570	VC+
Canisius College	NY	47,537	C
Carroll Univ	WI	38,100	C+
Case Western Reserve Univ	OH	60,304	MC
Castleton Univ	VT	20,186	C
Catawba College	NC	39,820	C
Cedar Crest College	PA	46,715	C
Central Mich Univ	MI	20,330	C
Chapman Univ	CA	63,078	VC+
Chatham Univ	PA	46,517	C
Clayton State Univ	GA	19,735	C
Coker College	SC	34,810	LC
Colgate Univ	NY	65,030	MC
College of St. Elizabeth	NJ	44,432	LC
College of St. Mary	NE	35,184	C
College of St. Scholastica	MN	44,640	C
Colo College	CO	62,560	MC
Colo Mesa Univ	CO	18,955	LC
Colo State Univ	CO	22,162	VC
Columbia College - Missouri	MO	27,803	C
Columbia Univ/City of New York	NY	62,958	MC
Concordia College - New York	NY	39,035	LC
Corban Univ	OR	40,306	C
Culver-Stockton College	MO	33,525	C
Curry College	MA	51,815	C
Dallas Baptist Univ	TX	33,713	C
Davis & Elkins College	WV	38,242	LC
Denison Univ	OH	58,860	MC
DePaul Univ	IL	47,623	VC
Dominican Univ	IL	41,222	C
Dordt College	IA	37,860	C+
Drexel Univ	PA	65,432	VC+
Duquesne Univ	PA	46,822	VC
East Texas Baptist Univ	TX	33,134	C
Eastern Mich Univ	MI	19,761	C
Eastern Nazarene College	MA	39,955	C
Eastern Oregon Univ	OR	17,715	C
Elizabethtown College	PA	54,050	C
Elon Univ	NC	44,599	VC+
Endicott College	MA	44,604	VC+
Eugene Lang College/The New School for Liberal Arts	NY	55,650	C
Eureka College	IL	30,220	C
Faulkner Univ	AL	26,410	C
Felician Univ	NJ	45,370	LC
Fitchburg State Univ	MA	21,819	C
Florida International Univ	FL	19,854	C+
Fontbonne Univ	MO	33,717	C
Franklin Pierce Univ	NH	46,750	C
Friends Univ	KS	34,455	C
Furman Univ	SC	58,092	VC+
Gallaudet Univ	DC	29,118	LC
Geneva College	PA	35,450	C
Georgian Court Univ	NJ	42,426	LC
Goddard College	VT	17,040	VC
Goucher College	MD	55,716	VC
Grand Canyon Univ	AZ	16,950	VC
Grand Rapids Theological Seminary/Cornerstone Univ	MI	33,338	C
Guilford College	NC	44,090	C
Hamline Univ	MN	45,678	VC
Hampshire College	MA	63,824	MC
Hardin-Simmons Univ	TX	33,966	C
Harris-Stowe State Univ	MO	14,360	NC
Henderson State Univ	AR	15,516	LC
Heritage Univ	WA	19,825	NC
Hiram College	OH	43,230	C
Hope International Univ	CA	41,150	C
Howard Univ	DC	37,616	C+
Huntington Univ	IN	33,996	C
Huston-Tillotson Univ	TX	18,124	LC
Illinois Wesleyan Univ	IL	56,430	VC+
Indiana Univ Southeast	IN	14,242	LC
Ithaca College	NY	56,766	VC
John Carroll Univ	OH	49,740	C+
Johnson State College	VT	20,752	C
Judson Univ	IL	37,700	C
Keene State College	NH	24,003	LC
Kent State Univ	OH	20,732	C
LaGrange College	GA	39,930	C
Lake Forest College	IL	50,652	VC
Lees-McRae College	NC	33,944	C

ST = STATE $IS = IN-STATE COSTS SR = SELECTOR RATING

School	ST	$IS	SR
LeMoyne-Owen College	TN	16,980	C
Lewis Univ	IL	40,370	C
Lewis-Clark State College	ID	14,202	C
Lipscomb Univ	TN	41,296	VC
Lourdes Univ	OH	29,520	NC
Lynchburg College	VA	46,740	C
Macalester College	MN	61,905	MC
Maharishi Univ of Management	IA	34,930	VC
Manhattan College	NY	51,750	C+
Manhattanville College	NY	51,440	C+
Marian Univ	IN	41,220	C
Marquette Univ	WI	48,390	VC+
Marshall Univ	WV	17,242	C
Martin Univ	IN	20,264	LC
Mary Baldwin Univ	VA	39,865	C
Mass College of Liberal Arts	MA	20,128	C
Mayville State Univ	ND	18,371	NC
Mercer Univ	GA	45,348	VC
Mich State Univ	MI	23,898	VC+
Midway Univ	KY	31,640	LC
Millikin Univ	IL	42,158	C
Millsaps College	MS	50,080	C+
Minn State Univ, Mankato	MN	15,616	C
Miss State Univ	MS	11,454	C+
Monmouth Univ	NJ	46,234	C
Montana State Univ-Billings	MT	22,960	C
Morningside College	IA	36,865	C
Mount Aloysius College	PA	29,976	C
Mount St. Mary College	NY	42,061	C
New England College	NH	50,364	C
New York Univ	NY	65,860	MC
Niagara Univ	NY	41,010	C
N Car State Univ	NC	19,515	HC+
North Greenville Univ	SC	25,930	C+
Northland College	WI	41,103	C+
Northwest Christian Univ	OR	36,580	C
Northwest Univ	WA	35,876	VC
Northwestern Univ	IL	66,344	MC
Nova Southeastern Univ	FL	38,534	C+
Oakwood Univ	AL	43,758	C
Ohio State Univ at Columbus	OH	21,703	HC+
Ohio State Univ at Lima	OH	7,140	C
Ohio State Univ at Marion	OH	7,140	C
Ohio Wesleyan Univ	OH	49,460	VC
Okla Baptist Univ	OK	32,320	C
Okla City Univ	OK	40,476	VC
Okla State Univ	OK	17,180	VC
Oregon State Univ	OR	22,519	VC
Piedmont College	GA	32,512	C
Pittsburg State Univ	KS	13,880	NC
Point Loma Nazarene Univ	CA	43,450	C
Point Park Univ	PA	41,270	C
Prescott College	AZ	33,284	C
Purdue Univ/West Lafayette	IN	20,032	MC
Quincy Univ	IL	36,998	C
Radford Univ	VA	19,027	LC
Randolph College	VA	45,660	VC
Regis Univ	CO	44,520	C
Rocky Mountain College	MT	34,270	C
Roger Williams Univ	RI	46,296	C+
Rosemont College	PA	30,980	C
Rowan Univ	NJ	24,491	VC+
St. Anselm College	NH	52,560	C+
St. Louis Univ	MO	49,866	HC
Salem State Univ	MA	17,303	LC
San Diego Christian College	CA	39,068	C
Schreiner Univ	TX	34,626	LC
Seattle Pacific Univ	WA	47,439	C+
Silver Lake College of the Holy Family	WI	36,290	LC
Simmons College	MA	53,090	VC
Smith College	MA	63,914	MC
S Car State Univ	SC	20,805	LC
S Dak State Univ	SD	15,634	C
Southern Nazarene Univ	OK	32,798	NC
Southern New Hampshire Univ	NH	43,198	C
Southern Oregon Univ	OR	19,117	C
Southwestern Univ	TX	50,720	VC
Spalding Univ	KY	31,938	SP
St. Ambrose Univ	IA	39,019	C
St. Ambrose Univ	IA	39,019	C
St. Bonaventure Univ	NY	44,237	C
St. Francis College	NY	38,800	LC
St. John's Univ	NY	55,850	C
St. Joseph's College, New York/Long Island Campus	NY	25,124	C
SUNY / Empire State College	NY	9,145	SP
SUNY / SUNY Fredonia	NY	20,818	C
Stockton Univ	NJ	25,059	
Stonehill College	MA	55,030	C+
Swarthmore College	PA	63,550	MC
Taylor Univ	IN	40,317	C+
Texas A&M Univ at Corpus Christi	TX	16,851	LC
Texas Lutheran Univ	TX	38,620	C
Texas State Univ	TX	19,350	C
Texas Wesleyan Univ	TX	35,134	C
The Catholic Univ of America	DC	56,356	VC
The College of Idaho	ID	36,415	C
The Univ of Akron	OH	21,477	C
The Univ of Tenn at Chattanooga	TN	16,744	C
The Univ of Tenn at Knoxville	TN	22,112	VC
Towson Univ	MD	17,408	VC
Transylvania Univ	KY	45,690	VC+
Trevecca Nazarene Univ	TN	31,186	C
Trinity Christian College	IL	35,580	C
Trinity College	CT	63,920	HC+
Trinity Washington Univ	DC	33,826	C+
Tufts Univ	MA		MC
Tusculum College	TN	31,625	C
Union College	KY	32,310	C
Union Inst & Univ	OH	8,912	SP
Union Univ	TN	33,970	VC
Unity College	ME	37,670	C
Univ of Arizona	AZ	23,100	C
Univ of Central Arkansas	AR	14,472	VC
Univ of Colo Colo Springs	CO	19,663	C
Univ of Colo Denver	CO	23,230	C
Univ of Conn	CT	25,538	HC
Univ of Dallas	TX	45,500	VC+
Univ of Delaware	DE	24,976	VC+
Univ of Dubuque	IA	37,824	C
Univ of Idaho	ID	15,348	C
Univ of Illinois at Urbana-Champaign	IL	27,006	HC
Univ of La Verne	CA	55,600	C
Univ of Louisiana at Monroe	LA	15,970	C
Univ of Maryland/College Park	MD	21,938	HC
Univ of Mass Amherst	MA	26,199	VC+
Univ of Mich/Dearborn	MI	11,757	VC
Univ of Mich-Flint	MI	17,607	C+
Univ of Minn/Morris	MN	20,760	VC
Univ of Missouri/Columbia	MO	18,201	MC
Univ of Missouri-St. Louis	MO		C
Univ of Montana-Western	MT	11,220	LC
Univ of Nebr - Lincoln	NE	18,589	VC
Univ of New England	ME	48,880	C
Univ of Northern Colo	CO	20,851	C
Univ of Oregon	OR	22,972	C
Univ of PR-Rio Piedras campus	PR	13,327	
Univ of St. Mary	KS	34,690	C
Univ of South Alabama	AL	16,400	C
Univ of S Dak	SD	16,109	C
Univ of South Florida/St. Petersburg	FL	15,980	C
Univ of South Florida/Tampa	FL	16,110	VC+
Univ of St. Thomas - Houston	TX	40,020	VC
Univ of Texas at San Antonio	TX	20,157	C
Univ of the Pacific	CA	57,006	VC
Univ of Tulsa	OK	52,625	HC+
Univ of Vermont	VT	28,878	HC
Univ of Wisc-Green Bay	WI	15,064	C
Univ of Wisc-Milwaukee	WI	21,496	C
Univ of Wisc-Parkside	WI	15,193	C
Univ of Wisc-Platteville	WI	14,614	VC
Univ of Wisc-Stevens Point	WI	14,043	C
Utica College	NY	30,430	C
Vanderbilt Univ	TN	60,572	MC
Vanguard Univ of Southern Calif	CA	40,740	VC
Vassar College	NY	65,491	MC
Wake Forest Univ	NC	64,056	MC
Washburn Univ	KS	15,827	C
Washington & Jefferson College	PA	56,512	VC
Washington State Univ	WA	22,495	C
Washington Univ in St. Louis	MO	65,366	VC
Weber State Univ	UT	10,721	C
Webster Univ	MO	37,490	C
Western Mich Univ	MI	21,054	C
Western Oregon Univ	OR	15,021	LC
William Peace Univ	NC	37,430	LC
Wilmington College	OH	34,600	C
Wittenberg Univ	OH	48,156	C+
Wright State Univ	OH	16,983	C
Xavier Univ	OH	47,880	C+
York College	NE	24,300	C
York College of Pennsylvania	PA	29,240	C
Youngstown State Univ	OH	17,307	C

EDUCATION ADMINISTRATION

School	ST	$IS	SR
Ashford Univ	CA	10,480	C
Ashland Univ	OH	21,440	C
Auburn Univ	AL	23,594	VC+
Cairn Univ	PA	36,296	C
Canisius College	NY	47,537	C
Columbia College - Missouri	MO	27,803	C
DePaul Univ	IL	47,623	VC
Howard Univ	DC	37,616	C+
Lewis Univ	IL	40,370	C
Missouri State Univ	MO	15,190	C+
Nova Southeastern Univ	FL	38,534	C+
Radford Univ	VA	19,027	LC
San Jose State Univ	CA	21,540	C
Southwestern Okla State Univ	OK	11,790	C
St. Ambrose Univ	IA	39,019	C
St. Ambrose Univ	IA	39,019	C
The Univ of Tenn at Martin	TN	14,876	C
Univ of Arkansas at Little Rock	AR	18,211	C
Univ of Missouri/Columbia	MO	18,201	MC
West Virginia Univ	WV	18,210	C
Western Washington Univ	WA	18,003	C+
Wingate Univ	NC	39,950	C

EDUCATION OF THE DEAF AND HEARING IMPAIRED

School	ST	$IS	SR
Barton College	NC	38,686	LC
Boston Univ	MA	65,110	MC
Bowling Green State Univ	OH	19,747	C
Cal State, Northridge	CA	16,859	LC
Canisius College	NY	47,537	C
Eastern Kentucky Univ	KY	16,908	C
Eastern Mich Univ	MI	19,761	C
Elmira College	NY	53,900	C
Flagler College	FL	27,620	C
Fontbonne Univ	MO	33,717	C
Ithaca College	NY	56,766	VC
MacMurray College	IL	33,620	C
Marywood Univ	PA	46,900	C
Minot State Univ	ND	12,732	C
Pace Univ	NY	58,248	C
Rochester Inst of Technology	NY	50,842	HC
San Jose State Univ	CA	21,540	C
Southern Univ at New Orleans	LA	8,014	LC
Stephen F. Austin State Univ	TX	18,406	LC
The College of New Jersey	NJ	31,909	HC
Towson Univ	MD	17,408	VC
Univ of Arkansas at Little Rock	AR	18,211	C
Univ of Montevallo	AL	19,502	C
Univ of N Car at Greensboro	NC	14,690	C
Univ of Science and Arts of Okla	OK	11,140	VC
Univ of Tulsa	OK	52,625	HC+

EDUCATION OF THE EMOTIONALLY HANDICAPPED

School	ST	$IS	SR
CUNY/City College	NY	20,319	VC
Concordia Univ St. Paul	MN	29,050	C
East Carolina Univ	NC	16,937	C
Eastern Mich Univ	MI	19,761	C
Florida State Univ	FL	16,771	HC
Manhattan College	NY	51,750	C+
Prescott College	AZ	33,284	C
Univ of South Florida/Tampa	FL	16,110	VC+
Walsh Univ	OH	39,010	C
Western Mich Univ	MI	21,054	C

EDUCATION OF THE EXCEPTIONAL CHILD

School	ST	$IS	SR
Ashland Univ	OH	21,440	C
Bethel Univ	TN	24,738	C
Bethune-Cookman Univ	FL	22,970	C
Canisius College	NY	47,537	C
Edgewood College	WI	35,950	C
Flagler College	FL	27,620	C
Florida Atlantic Univ	FL	17,339	C
Houghton College	NY	39,090	C
Jacksonville Univ	FL	46,230	C
Mayville State Univ	ND	18,371	NC
Minot State Univ	ND	12,732	C
Niagara Univ	NY	41,010	C
Northwest Nazarene Univ	ID	36,000	C
Nova Southeastern Univ	FL	38,534	C+
Prescott College	AZ	33,284	C
St. Augustine's Univ	NC	26,048	C
Southeast Missouri State Univ	MO	15,498	C
Southeastern Univ	FL	31,765	C
The Univ of Tenn at Chattanooga	TN	16,744	C
Univ of Central Arkansas	AR	14,472	VC
Univ of Central Florida	FL	15,922	VC
Univ of Great Falls	MT	38,524	C
Univ of Wisc-Stevens Point	WI	14,043	C
Walsh Univ	OH	39,010	C
Warner Univ	FL	28,216	C
Western Kentucky Univ	KY	16,850	C

EDUCATION OF THE MENTALLY HANDICAPPED

School	ST	$IS	SR
Brescia Univ	KY	29,890	VC+
CUNY/City College	NY	20,319	VC
East Carolina Univ	NC	16,937	C
Eastern Mich Univ	MI	19,761	C
Florida State Univ	FL	16,771	HC
Kutztown Univ of Pennsylvania	PA	19,056	LC
Minot State Univ	ND	12,732	C
Northwest Missouri State Univ	MO	17,737	C
Prescott College	AZ	33,284	C
Southeastern Okla State Univ	OK	11,875	C
Univ of Rio Grande & Rio Grande Community College	OH	8,750	NC
Univ of South Florida/Tampa	FL	16,110	VC+
Urbana Univ	OH	30,820	C
Walsh Univ	OH	39,010	C
Western Mich Univ	MI	21,054	C

EDUCATION OF THE MULTIPLY HANDICAPPED

School	ST	$IS	SR
Aquinas College - Mich	MI	38,876	HC
Bowling Green State Univ	OH	19,747	C
Eastern Mich Univ	MI	19,761	C
Univ of Illinois at Urbana-Champaign	IL	27,006	HC

EDUCATION OF THE PHYSICALLY HANDICAPPED

School	ST	$IS	SR
Aquinas College - Mich	MI	38,876	HC
Eastern Mich Univ	MI	19,761	C
Kutztown Univ of Pennsylvania	PA	19,056	LC
Walsh Univ	OH	39,010	C

EDUCATION OF THE VISUALLY HANDICAPPED

School	ST	$IS	SR
Eastern Mich Univ	MI	19,761	C
Florida State Univ	FL	16,771	HC
Kutztown Univ of Pennsylvania	PA	19,056	LC
Stephen F. Austin State Univ	TX	18,406	LC

EDUCATION SERVICES

School	ST	$IS	SR
SUNY / SUNY Cortland	NY	20,706	VC
Univ of Findlay	OH	60,139	C

EDUCATIONAL MEDIA

School	ST	$IS	SR
Eastern Mich Univ	MI	19,761	C
Pennsylvania State Univ - Univ Park	PA	29,760	HC

EDUCATIONAL STATISTICS AND RESEARCH

School	ST	$IS	SR
Emory Univ	GA	60,786	MC

EDUCATIONAL STUDIES

School	ST	$IS	SR
Alma College	MI	47,548	C
Arizona State Univ at the Polytechnic Campus	AZ	21,360	VC
Arizona State Univ at the Tempe Campus	AZ	21,756	VC
Arizona State Univ at the West Campus	AZ	20,640	C
Ashford Univ	CA	10,480	C
Avila Univ	MO	35,480	C
Bay Path Univ	MA	45,349	C
Blackburn College	IL	28,526	LC
Cabrini Univ	PA	42,591	LC
Dickinson College	PA	63,974	MC
Edgewood College	WI	35,950	C
Gwynedd Mercy Univ	PA	43,780	LC
John Brown Univ	AR	33,132	VC
Marian Univ	IN	41,220	C
Neumann Univ	PA	40,678	LC
St. Martin's Univ	WA	45,056	C
Syracuse Univ	NY	60,239	VC
Tabor College	KS	35,870	C
Texas Christian Univ	TX	54,670	HC
Univ of Arkansas at Fayetteville	AR	19,152	C+
Univ of St. Francis	IN	37,400	C
Univ of South Alabama	AL	16,400	C
Wheelock College	MA	49,225	C

ELECTRICAL AND COMPUTER ENGINEERING

School	ST	$IS	SR
Bowling Green State Univ	OH	19,747	C
Calif Baptist Univ	CA	41,392	C
Calif State Polytechnic Univ, Pomona	CA	21,541	C
Christopher Newport Univ	VA	23,968	VC+
Cornell Univ	NY	64,853	MC
Daniel Webster College	NH	26,984	C
Embry-Riddle Aeronautical Univ - Daytona Beach	FL	44,712	VC
Franklin W. Olin College of Engineering	MA	63,130	MC
Grove City College	PA	25,692	VC
New York Inst of Technology	NY	48,730	C
New York Univ	NY	65,860	MC
Ohio Univ	OH	22,924	C
Okla Christian Univ	OK	27,650	VC
SUNY at Oswego	NY	21,351	C
Univ of Denver	CO	58,443	VC+
Univ of Idaho	ID	15,348	C
Univ of Kansas	KS	20,135	C+
Univ of Mass Boston	MA	13,435	C
Univ of New Hampshire - Manchester	NH	14,490	C
Univ of Rhode Island	RI	24,906	C
Wayne State Univ	MI	22,016	C
Western Mich Univ	MI	21,054	C

ELECTRICAL ENGINEERING

School	ST	$IS	SR
Brown Univ	RI	64,566	MC
Embry-Riddle Aeronautical Univ - Daytona Beach	FL	44,712	VC
Northern Arizona Univ	AZ	20,246	VC
Syracuse Univ	NY	60,239	VC
Washington State Univ	WA	22,495	C

ELECTRICAL TECHNOLOGY

School	ST	$IS	SR
St. Louis Univ	MO	49,866	HC
Thomas Edison State Univ	NJ	6,350	NC

ELECTRICAL/ELECTRONICS ENGINEERING

School	ST	$IS	SR
Alabama A&M Univ	AL	18,796	C
Andrews Univ	MI	28,030	C+
Arizona State Univ at the Tempe Campus	AZ	21,756	VC
Arkansas State Univ	AR	16,190	C
Arkansas Tech Univ	AR	15,484	C
Auburn Univ	AL	23,594	VC+
Baylor Univ	TX	53,760	HC
Benedict College	SC	28,238	NC
Bloomsburg Univ of Pennsylvania	PA	19,066	LC
Boise State Univ	ID	14,860	C
Boston Univ	MA	65,110	MC
Brigham Young Univ	UT	12,748	HC
Bucknell Univ	PA	64,616	MC
Calif Baptist Univ	CA	41,392	C
Calif Inst of Technology	CA	58,761	MC
Calif Polytechnic State Univ	CA	17,979	HC+
Calif State Polytechnic Univ, Pomona	CA	21,541	C
Cal State, Chico	CA	21,440	C
Cal State, Fresno	CA	16,902	LC
Cal State, Fullerton	CA	21,902	C
Cal State, Long Beach	CA	18,850	C
Cal State, Los Angeles	CA	17,186	LC
Cal State, Sacramento	CA	20,332	C
Calvin College	MI	41,570	VC+
Capitol Technology Univ	MD	31,410	C
Carnegie Mellon Univ	PA	67,980	MC
Case Western Reserve Univ	OH	60,304	MC
Cedarville Univ	OH	34,990	VC
Central Mich Univ	MI	20,330	C
Central Washington Univ	WA	16,803	C
Christian Brothers Univ	TN	31,670	VC
CUNY/City College	NY	20,319	VC
Clarkson Univ	NY	60,392	HC
Clemson Univ	SC		HC
Cleveland State Univ	OH	22,196	C
Colo State Univ	CO	22,162	VC
Colo Technical Univ	CO	21,455	NC
Columbia Univ/City of New York	NY	62,958	MC
Cooper Union for the Advancement of Science and Art	NY	58,210	MC
Delaware State Univ	DE	19,376	NC
Dordt College	IA	37,860	C+
Drexel Univ	PA	65,432	VC+
Duke Univ	NC	64,188	
Elizabethtown College	PA	54,050	C
Embry-Riddle Aeronautical Univ - Prescott Campus	AZ	44,054	VC
Fairfield Univ	CT	59,860	VC+
Fairleigh Dickinson Univ/ Metropolitan Campus	NJ	40,254	C
Florida A&M Univ	FL	15,361	C
Florida Atlantic Univ	FL	17,339	C
Florida Inst of Technology	FL	53,306	VC
Florida International Univ	FL	19,854	C+
Florida State Univ	FL	16,771	HC
Gannon Univ	PA	42,032	C
George Mason Univ	VA	15,724	VC
George Washington Univ	DC	62,835	MC
Georgia Inst of Technology	GA	23,360	MC
Georgia Southern Univ	GA	16,596	C
Gonzaga Univ	WA	50,888	HC
Hampton Univ	VA	34,926	LC
Harding Univ	AR	25,421	C
Hofstra Univ	NY	55,960	C+
Howard Univ	DC	37,616	C+
Idaho State Univ	ID	13,619	NC
Illinois Inst of Technology	IL	56,826	HC+
Indiana Inst of Technology	IN	34,240	LC
Indiana Univ-Purdue Univ Fort Wayne	IN	17,553	C
Indiana Univ-Purdue Univ Indianapolis	IN	18,635	C
Inter-American Univ of PR-Bayamon	PR	18,785	
Iowa State Univ	IA	17,570	C
Jackson State Univ	MS	15,879	LC
Jacksonville Univ	FL	46,230	C
John Brown Univ	AR	33,132	VC
Johns Hopkins Univ	MD	65,386	MC
Johnson & Wales Univ/North Miami Campus	FL	42,707	C
Johnson & Wales Univ/ Providence Campus	RI	42,248	C
Kansas State Univ	KS	17,780	VC
Kennesaw State Univ	GA	19,592	VC
Kettering Univ	MI	47,570	HC
Lafayette College	PA	63,355	MC
Lamar Univ	TX	18,014	LC
Lawrence Tech Univ	MI	39,770	VC
Lehigh Univ	PA	61,010	MC
LeTourneau Univ	TX	38,250	VC
Lipscomb Univ	TN	41,296	VC
Louisiana State Univ and A&M College	LA	18,677	VC
Loyola Marymount Univ	CA	58,038	HC
Manhattan College	NY	51,750	C+
Marquette Univ	WI	48,390	VC+
Mass Inst of Technology	MA	62,662	MC
Merrimack College	MA	52,770	C
Miami Univ	OH	27,190	HC+
Mich State Univ	MI	23,898	VC+
Mich Tech Univ	MI	24,739	VC+
Milwaukee School of Engineering	WI	45,153	HC
Minn State Univ, Mankato	MN	15,616	C
Miss State Univ	MS	11,454	C+
Missouri Univ of Science and Technology	MO	18,655	HC
Montana State Univ	MT	15,500	C+
Morgan State Univ	MD	17,190	LC
New Jersey Inst of Technology	NJ	29,569	VC
New Mexico Inst of Mining and Technology	NM	14,833	HC
New Mexico State Univ	NM	14,050	C
New York Univ	NY	65,860	MC
N Car A&T State Univ	NC	13,365	LC
N Car State Univ	NC	19,515	HC+
N Dak State Univ	ND	16,245	C
Northeastern Univ	MA	62,703	MC
Northern Illinois Univ	IL	20,176	C
Northwestern Univ	IL	66,344	MC
Norwich Univ	VT	28,212	C
Oakland Univ	MI	20,763	C
Ohio Northern Univ	OH	44,050	VC
Ohio State Univ at Columbus	OH	21,703	HC+
Ohio Univ	OH	22,924	C
Okla Christian Univ	OK	27,650	VC
Okla State Univ	OK	17,180	VC
Old Dominion Univ	VA	20,910	C
Oral Roberts Univ	OK	34,316	C
Oregon State Univ	OR	22,519	VC
Pennsylvania State Univ - Univ Park	PA	29,760	HC
Point Park Univ	PA	41,270	C
Portland State Univ	OR	19,443	C
Prairie View A&M Univ	TX	15,205	LC
Princeton Univ	NJ	57,610	MC
Purdue Univ/Northwest	IN	15,038	C
Purdue Univ/West Lafayette	IN	20,032	MC
Rensselaer Polytechnic Inst	NY	63,436	MC
Rice Univ	TX	57,668	MC
Rochester Inst of Technology	NY	50,842	HC
Rose-Hulman Inst of Technology	IN	57,303	MC
Rutgers Univ - New Brunswick	NJ	26,632	HC
Saginaw Valley State Univ	MI	18,530	C
St. Louis Univ	MO	49,866	HC
San Diego State Univ	CA	21,896	C+
San Francisco State Univ	CA	18,514	LC
San Jose State Univ	CA	21,540	C
Seattle Pacific Univ	WA	47,439	C+
Seattle Univ	WA	50,811	VC+
Shippensburg Univ of Pennsylvania	PA	23,208	C
S Dak School of Mines and Technology	SD	18,645	VC
S Dak State Univ	SD	15,634	C
Southern Illinois Univ Carbondale	IL	23,667	C
Southern Illinois Univ Edwardsville	IL	22,643	C
Southern Methodist Univ	TX	66,483	MC
Southern Univ and A&M College	LA	16,074	LC+
St. Cloud State Univ	MN	10,600	C
St. Mary's Univ	TX	37,500	C
Stanford Univ	CA	60,409	MC
SUNY / Univ at Buffalo	NY	23,122	C+
SUNY /Maritime College	NY	16,020	C
SUNY at Binghamton	NY	22,861	MC
SUNY at New Paltz	NY	19,200	C
SUNY Polytechnic Inst	NY	19,473	VC
Stevens Inst of Technology	NJ	62,338	MC
Stony Brook Univ/The SUNY	NY	21,881	MC
Suffolk Univ	MA	50,308	C
Tarleton State Univ	TX	15,248	LC
Temple Univ	PA	24,392	VC
Tenn State Univ	TN	14,423	C
Tenn Tech Univ	TN	17,050	C
Texas A&M Univ	TX	20,521	VC+
Texas A&M Univ at Kingsville	TX	7,500	LC
Texas Christian Univ	TX	54,670	HC
Texas State Univ	TX	19,350	C
Texas Tech Univ	TX	18,736	C+
The Catholic Univ of America	DC	56,356	VC
The Citadel, The Military College of S Car	SC	35,339	C
The College of New Jersey	NJ	31,909	HC
The Univ of Akron	OH	21,477	C
The Univ of Tenn at Chattanooga	TN	16,744	C
The Univ of Tenn at Knoxville	TN	22,112	VC
The Univ of Utah	UT	17,924	VC
Trine Univ	IN	41,310	C
Tufts Univ	MA		MC
Tuskegee Univ	AL	28,164	C
Union College	NY	64,320	MC
United States Air Force Academy	CO		C
United States Coast Guard Academy	CT	942	MC
United States Military Academy at West Point	NY		HC+
United States Naval Academy	MD		MC
Universidad Politecnica de PR, Hato Rey campus	PR	23,514	
Univ of Alabama	AL	24,320	C+
Univ of Alabama at Birmingham	AL	19,906	C
Univ of Alabama in Huntsville	AL	19,445	VC
Univ of Alaska Anchorage	AK	16,652	NC
Univ of Alaska Fairbanks	AK	16,179	C
Univ of Arizona	AZ	23,100	C
Univ of Arkansas at Fayetteville	AR	19,152	C+
Univ of Calif at Berkeley	CA	28,853	MC
Univ of Calif at Davis	CA	28,468	HC
Univ of Calif at Irvine	CA	26,484	VC
Univ of Calif at Los Angeles	CA	30,162	MC
Univ of Calif at Riverside	CA	29,227	C+
Univ of Calif at Santa Barbara	CA	29,091	HC
Univ of Calif San Diego	CA	30,150	MC
Univ of Calif, Santa Cruz	CA	28,731	C+
Univ of Central Florida	FL	15,922	VC
Univ of Central Missouri	MO	18,982	C
Univ of Central Okla	OK	13,486	C
Univ of Cincinnati	OH	21,964	VC
Univ of Colo Boulder	CO	24,285	VC+
Univ of Colo Colo Springs	CO	19,663	C
Univ of Colo Denver	CO	23,230	C
Univ of Conn	CT	25,538	HC
Univ of Dayton	OH	53,620	C
Univ of Delaware	DE	24,976	VC+
Univ of Denver	CO	58,443	VC+
Univ of Detroit Mercy	MI	48,816	C+
Univ of Evansville	IN	44,186	VC+
Univ of Florida	FL	16,291	HC+
Univ of Georgia	GA	21,250	HC
Univ of Hartford	CT	49,776	C
Univ of Hawaii at Manoa	HI	23,221	C
Univ of Houston	TX	21,483	VC
Univ of Idaho	ID	15,348	C
Univ of Illinois at Chicago	IL	25,006	VC
Univ of Illinois at Urbana-Champaign	IL	27,006	HC
Univ of Indianapolis	IN	36,480	C
Univ of Iowa	IA	18,683	VC+
Univ of Kansas	KS	20,135	C+
Univ of Kentucky	KY	33,306	C
Univ of Louisiana at Lafayette	LA	14,516	C
Univ of Louisville	KY	19,824	C
Univ of Maine	ME	20,792	C
Univ of Maryland/College Park	MD	21,938	HC
Univ of Mass Amherst	MA	26,199	VC+
Univ of Mass Dartmouth	MA	25,658	C
Univ of Mass Lowell	MA	26,380	C
Univ of Memphis	TN	18,278	C
Univ of Miami	FL	63,494	MC
Univ of Mich/Ann Arbor	MI	24,410	MC
Univ of Minn/Duluth	MN	20,292	C+
Univ of Minn/Twin Cities	MN	23,519	HC+
Univ of Miss	MS	17,746	C+
Univ of Missouri/Columbia	MO	18,201	MC
Univ of Missouri-Kansas City	MO	19,563	VC
Univ of Missouri-St. Louis	MO		C
Univ of Nebr - Lincoln	NE	18,589	VC
Univ of Nevada, Las Vegas	NV	17,553	C
Univ of Nevada/Reno	NV	18,010	C
Univ of New Hampshire	NH	28,562	VC
Univ of New Haven	CT	52,190	C
Univ of New Mexico	NM	15,404	C
Univ of New Orleans	LA	12,840	C
Univ of N Car at Charlotte	NC	15,547	C
Univ of N Dak	ND	15,373	C
Univ of North Florida	FL	15,996	VC
Univ of North Texas	TX	19,198	C
Univ of Notre Dame	IN	64,043	MC
Univ of Okla	OK	18,911	VC
Univ of Pennsylvania	PA	63,526	MC
Univ of Pittsburgh	PA	29,568	HC+
Univ of Portland	OR	52,152	VC
Univ of PR, at Mayaguez	PR	13,995	
Univ of Rochester	NY	65,032	MC
Univ of San Diego	CA	58,442	VC+
Univ of Scranton	PA	54,962	VC
Univ of South Alabama	AL	16,400	C
Univ of S Car at Columbia	SC	19,725	VC+
Univ of South Florida/Tampa	FL	16,110	VC+
Univ of Southern Calif	CA	66,631	C
Univ of Southern Maine	ME	18,320	C
Univ of Texas at Arlington	TX	18,026	LC
Univ of Texas at Austin	TX	26,102	HC
Univ of Texas at Dallas	TX	22,830	VC+
Univ of Texas at El Paso	TX	34,452	NC
Univ of Texas at San Antonio	TX	20,157	C
Univ of the District of Columbia	DC	21,044	LC
Univ of the Pacific	CA	57,006	VC
Univ of Toledo	OH	19,336	NC
Univ of Tulsa	OK	52,625	HC+
Univ of Vermont	VT	28,878	HC
Univ of Virginia	VA	25,891	MC
Univ of Washington	WA	23,149	VC
Univ of West Florida	FL	15,848	C
Univ of Wisc-Madison	WI	20,934	MC
Univ of Wisc-Milwaukee	WI	21,496	C
Univ of Wisc-Platteville	WI	14,614	VC
Univ of Wyoming	WY	15,375	C+
Utah State Univ	UT	12,736	C
Valparaiso Univ	IN	48,370	C+
Vanderbilt Univ	TN	60,572	MC
Villanova Univ	PA	62,523	MC
Virginia Commonwealth Univ	VA	23,049	C
Virginia Military Inst	VA	26,460	C+
Virginia Polytechnic Inst and State Univ	VA	21,276	HC
Washington State Univ	WA	22,495	C
Washington Univ in St. Louis	MO	65,366	VC
Wayne State Univ	MI	22,016	C
Weber State Univ	UT	10,721	C
Wentworth Inst of Technology	MA	47,112	C
West Virginia Univ	WV	18,210	C
West Virginia Univ Inst of Technology	WV	16,462	NC
Western Carolina Univ	NC	13,965	C
Western Kentucky Univ	KY	16,850	C
Western New England Univ	MA	48,088	C
Western Washington Univ	WA	18,003	C+
Wichita State Univ	KS	21,643	C
Widener Univ	PA	56,486	C
Wilkes Univ	PA	45,622	C
Worcester Polytechnic Inst	MA	60,730	MC
Wright State Univ	OH	16,983	C
Yale Univ	CT	64,650	MC
York College of Pennsylvania	PA	29,240	C
Youngstown State Univ	OH	17,307	C

ELECTRICAL/ELECTRONICS ENGINEERING TECHNOLOGY

School	ST	$IS	SR
Alabama A&M Univ	AL	18,796	C
Alfred State College	NY	19,895	C
Appalachian State Univ	NC	14,416	VC
Arizona State Univ at the Polytechnic Campus	AZ	21,360	VC
Baker College of Flint	MI	13,880	NC
Bowling Green State Univ	OH	19,747	C
Brigham Young Univ	UT	12,748	HC
Calif Univ of Pennsylvania	PA	14,217	LC
Central Conn State Univ	CT	21,203	C
Cleveland State Univ	OH	22,196	C
Colo State Univ-Pueblo	CO	18,234	C
Colo Technical Univ	CO	21,455	NC
East Carolina Univ	NC	16,937	C
Eastern Mich Univ	MI	19,761	C
Eastern New Mexico Univ	NM	14,416	C
Excelsior College	NY	14,080	SP
Fairleigh Dickinson Univ/ Metropolitan Campus	NJ	40,254	C
Fairmont State Univ	WV	15,726	C
Farmingdale State College	NY	20,624	C
Ferris State Univ	MI	21,445	C
Fitchburg State Univ	MA	21,819	C
Fort Valley State Univ	GA	17,988	VC
Indiana State Univ	IN	23,223	LC
Indiana Univ-Purdue Univ Fort Wayne	IN	17,553	C
Indiana Univ-Purdue Univ Indianapolis	IN	18,635	C
Inter-American Univ of PR Ponce	PR	19,549	
Inter-American Univ of PR-Aguadilla Campus	PR	21,657	
Inter-American Univ of PR-Bayamon	PR	18,785	
Inter-American Univ of PR-Fajardo Campus	PR	18,336	
Kansas State Univ	KS	17,780	VC
Kennesaw State Univ	GA	19,592	VC
Louisiana Tech Univ	LA	11,422	VC
Metropolitan State Univ of Denver	CO	29,889	LC
Mich Tech Univ	MI	24,739	VC+
Minn State Univ, Mankato	MN	15,616	C
Montana State Univ-Northern	MT	11,370	NC
Murray State Univ	KY	16,998	C
New York Inst of Technology	NY	48,730	C
Norfolk State Univ	VA	25,702	LC
Northern Kentucky Univ	KY	16,486	C
Northern Mich Univ	MI	19,604	C
Okla State Univ	OK	17,180	VC
Old Dominion Univ	VA	20,910	C
Oregon Inst of Technology	OR	8,910	C
Pennsylvania College of Technology	PA	27,333	NC
Pittsburg State Univ	KS	13,880	NC
Point Park Univ	PA	41,270	C
Purdue Univ/Northwest	IN	15,038	C
Purdue Univ/West Lafayette	IN	20,032	MC
Rochester Inst of Technology	NY	50,842	HC
Roosevelt Univ	IL	40,651	VC
St. Louis Univ	MO	49,866	HC
Savannah State Univ	GA	15,631	C
S Car State Univ	SC	20,805	LC
S Dak State Univ	SD	15,634	C
Southern Illinois Univ Carbondale	IL	23,667	C
SUNY / Buffalo State College	NY	20,842	C
SUNY Polytechnic Inst	NY	19,473	VC
Texas A&M Univ at Galveston	TX	15,920	C

ST = STATE $IS = IN-STATE COSTS SR = SELECTOR RATING

School	ST	$IS	SR
Texas Southern Univ	TX	18,212	LC
The Univ of Akron	OH	21,477	C
Thomas Edison State Univ	NJ	6,350	NC
Tuskegee Univ	AL	28,164	C
Univ of Arkansas at Little Rock	AR	18,211	C
Univ of Central Missouri	MO	18,982	C
Univ of Cincinnati	OH	21,964	VC
Univ of Dallas	TX	45,500	VC+
Univ of Dayton	OH	53,620	C
Univ of Hartford	CT	49,776	C
Univ of Maine	ME	20,792	C
Univ of Mass Lowell	MA	26,380	C
Univ of Memphis	TN	18,278	C
Univ of Mich/Dearborn	MI	11,757	VC
Univ of N Car at Charlotte	NC	15,547	C
Univ of North Texas	TX	19,198	C
Univ of Pittsburgh at Johnstown	PA	22,092	C
Univ of PR, at Bayamon	PR	13,145	
Univ of Rio Grande & Rio Grande Community College	OH	8,750	NC
Univ of Southern Indiana	IN	16,501	C
Univ of Southern Miss	MS	13,170	C
Univ of Wisc-Green Bay	WI	15,064	C
Vaughn College of Aeronautics and Technology	NY	37,180	C
Virginia Commonwealth Univ	VA	23,049	C
Wayne State Univ	MI	22,016	C
Weber State Univ	UT	10,721	C
West Virginia Univ Inst of Technology	WV	16,462	NC
Western Carolina Univ	NC	13,965	C
Western Washington Univ	WA	18,003	C+
Youngstown State Univ	OH	17,307	C

ELECTROMECHANICAL TECHNOLOGY

School	ST	$IS	SR
Idaho State Univ	ID	13,619	NC
Penn State Univ/Altoona	PA	24,584	C
Texas A&M Univ at Galveston	TX	15,920	C
Univ of the District of Columbia	DC	21,044	LC
Univ of Toledo	OH	19,336	NC
Vermont Technical College	VT	23,838	C
Wayne State Univ	MI	22,016	C
Wentworth Inst of Technology	MA	47,112	C
Western Kentucky Univ	KY	16,850	C

ELECTRONIC BUSINESS

School	ST	$IS	SR
Davenport Univ	MI	25,896	LC
Florida Inst of Technology	FL	53,306	VC
La Sierra Univ	CA	39,690	VC
Limestone College	SC	32,100	C
Old Dominion Univ	VA	20,910	C
San Francisco State Univ	CA	18,514	LC
Southern Univ and A&M College	LA	16,074	LC+
Thiel College	PA	41,590	C
Trevecca Nazarene Univ	TN	31,186	C
Univ of La Verne	CA	55,600	C
Univ of North Texas	TX	19,198	C
Univ of Scranton	PA	54,962	VC
Univ of Southern Indiana	IN	16,501	C
Washington State Univ	WA	22,495	C
Winthrop Univ	SC	23,082	C

ELEMENTARY EDUCATION

School	ST	$IS	SR
Adams State Univ	CO	17,703	LC
Adrian College	MI	42,400	C
Alabama A&M Univ	AL	18,796	C
Alabama State Univ	AL	14,142	NC
Alaska Pacific Univ	AK	26,680	VC
Albright College	PA	46,660	C
Alcorn State Univ	MS	15,854	C
Alderson Broaddus Univ	WV	26,149	C
Alice Lloyd College	KY	8,190	C
Alma College	MI	47,548	C
Alvernia Univ	PA	43,900	C
Alverno College	WI	33,294	LC
American International College	MA	46,300	LC
American Univ	DC	59,379	HC+
Anderson Univ	IN	38,200	C
Andrews Univ	MI	28,030	C+
Anna Maria College	MA	48,186	C
Appalachian State Univ	NC	14,416	VC
Aquinas College	TN	30,800	C+
Aquinas College - Mich	MI	38,876	HC
Arcadia Univ	PA	33,570	C+
Arizona State Univ at the Polytechnic Campus	AZ	21,360	VC
Arizona State Univ at the Tempe Campus	AZ	21,756	VC
Arizona State Univ at the West Campus	AZ	20,640	C
Arkansas Baptist College	AR	20,280	NC
Arkansas State Univ	AR	16,190	C
Arkansas Tech Univ	AR	15,484	C
Asbury Univ	KY	35,180	C+
Ashford Univ	CA	10,480	C
Ashland Univ	OH	21,440	C
Atlantic Union College	MA	27,228	C
Auburn Univ	AL	23,594	VC+
Auburn Univ at Montgomery	AL	15,290	C
Augsburg College	MN	43,929	C
Augusta Univ	GA	4,632	C
Augustana College	IL	49,658	VC
Augustana Univ	SD	38,424	VC
Aurora Univ	IL	33,970	C
Avila Univ	MO	35,480	C
Baker Univ	KS	33,350	C+
Ball State Univ	IN	19,590	C
Barton College	NC	38,686	LC
Bay Path Univ	MA	45,349	C
Bayamon Central Univ	PR	12,490	
Baylor Univ	TX	53,760	HC
Becker College	MA	57,628	C
Belhaven Univ	MS	31,016	C
Bellarmine Univ	KY	51,220	C
Belmont Abbey College	NC	48,156	C
Belmont Univ	TN	40,970	VC
Bemidji State Univ	MN	16,056	VC
Benedict College	SC	28,238	NC
Benedictine College	KS	36,200	VC
Benedictine Univ	IL	38,300	C
Bennett College	NC	27,302	NC
Bennington College	VT	63,960	MC
Berea College	KY	7,042	C
Bethany College	KS	46,100	NC
Bethany College	WV	36,300	NC
Bethel College	IN	35,860	C
Bethel College	KS	35,370	C
Bethel Univ	MN	45,270	VC
Bethune-Cookman Univ	FL	22,970	C
Black Hills State Univ	SD	15,899	C
Blackburn College	IL	28,526	LC
Bloomfield College	NJ	39,100	LC
Blue Mountain College	MS	15,949	VC
Bluefield State College	WV	5,832	LC
Boise State Univ	ID	14,860	C
Boricua College	NY	10,100	C
Boston College	MA	65,737	MC
Boston Univ	MA	65,110	MC
Bowie State Univ	MD	26,728	LC
Bowling Green State Univ	OH	19,747	C
Brescia Univ	KY	29,890	VC+
Briar Cliff Univ	IA	36,956	C
Bridgewater State Univ	MA	21,810	C
Brigham Young Univ	UT	12,748	HC
Brigham Young Univ/Hawaii	HI	11,290	C
Bryan College	TN	31,440	C
Buena Vista Univ	IA	41,514	C
Butler Univ	IN	51,352	VC
Cabrini Univ	PA	42,591	LC
Caldwell Univ	NJ	42,165	NC
Cal State, Long Beach	CA	18,850	C
Calif Univ of Pennsylvania	PA	14,217	LC
Calumet College of St. Joseph	IN	22,735	C
Calvin College	MI	41,570	VC+
Cameron Univ	OK	11,072	NC
Campbellsville Univ	KY	32,492	C
Canisius College	NY	47,537	C
Capital Univ	OH	42,982	C
Cardinal Stritch Univ	WI	36,462	C
Caribbean Univ	PR	15,471	
Carlos Albizu Univ	FL		LC
Carlow Univ	PA	38,549	LC
Carroll College	MT	39,972	C+
Carroll Univ	WI	38,100	C+
Carson-Newman Univ	TN	34,160	C
Carthage College	WI	48,835	C
Catawba College	NC	39,820	C
Cazenovia College	NY	46,470	C
Cedar Crest College	PA	46,715	C
Centenary College	NJ	43,602	C
Central College	IA	44,592	C
Central Conn State Univ	CT	21,203	C
Central Methodist Univ	MO	36,830	VC
Central Mich Univ	MI	20,330	C
Central State Univ	OH	18,564	C
Central Washington Univ	WA	16,803	C
Chadron State College	NE	14,819	NC
Chaminade Univ of Honolulu	HI	36,000	C
Champlain College	VT	53,132	C+
Charleston Southern Univ	SC	32,400	C
Chatham Univ	PA	46,517	C
Chestnut Hill College	PA	43,410	C
Cheyney Univ of Pennsylvania	PA	20,896	LC
Chicago State Univ	IL	20,144	C
CUNY/Brooklyn College	NY	5,884	C+
CUNY/City College	NY	20,319	VC
CUNY/Hunter College	NY	31,098	VC
CUNY/Lehman College	NY	5,778	HC+
CUNY/Meger Evers College	NY	6,680	NC
CUNY/Queens College	NY	27,896	C
City Univ of Seattle	WA	24,340	NC
Claflin Univ	SC	33,764	LC
Clarion Univ of Pennsylvania	PA	21,608	LC
Clarke Univ	IA	38,940	C
Clemson Univ	SC		HC
Cleveland State Univ	OH	22,196	C
Coastal Carolina Univ	SC	19,766	C
Coe College	IA	51,570	VC
Coker College	SC	34,810	LC
College of Charleston	SC	22,699	C
College of St. Benedict	MN	52,806	C
College of St. Elizabeth	NJ	44,432	LC
College of St. Mary	NE	35,184	C
College of St Joseph	VT	32,400	LC
College of the Ozarks	MO	7,230	C
Colo Christian Univ	CO	39,940	VC
Columbia College	SC	36,550	C
Columbia College - Missouri	MO	27,803	C
Concord Univ	WV	14,954	C
Concordia College - Alabama	AL	15,720	NC
Concordia College - Moorhead	MN	51,088	C+
Concordia College - New York	NY	39,035	LC
Concordia Univ	OR	35,000	C
Concordia Univ Nebr	NE	36,280	VC
Concordia Univ St. Paul	MN	29,050	C
Concordia Univ Texas	TX	40,210	C
Concordia Univ Wisc	WI	35,910	C
Concordia Univ, Ann Arbor	MI	35,945	VC
Concordia Univ, Chicago	IL	39,694	C
Converse College	SC	26,495	C
Coppin State Univ	MD	17,041	VC
Corban Univ	OR	40,306	C
Cornell College	IA	48,800	VC
Covenant College	GA	38,990	VC
Creighton Univ	NE	48,206	VC+
Culver-Stockton College	MO	33,525	C
Cumberland Univ	TN	27,710	C
Curry College	MA	51,815	C
Daemen College	NY	38,045	C
Dakota State Univ	SD	13,811	C
Dakota Wesleyan Univ	SD	32,850	C
Dallas Baptist Univ	TX	33,713	C
Davis & Elkins College	WV	38,242	LC
Defiance College	OH	41,630	C
Delaware State Univ	DE	19,376	NC
Delta State Univ	MS	13,176	C
DePaul Univ	IL	47,623	VC
DePauw Univ	IN	58,688	HC+
DeSales Univ	PA	43,970	C
Dickinson State Univ	ND	12,372	LC
Doane Univ	NE	39,184	VC
Dominican College	NY	31,270	LC
Dominican Univ	IL	41,222	C
Dordt College	IA	37,860	C
Drake Univ	IA	45,056	HC
Drexel Univ	PA	65,432	VC+
Drury Univ	MO	33,791	VC
East Carolina Univ	NC	16,937	C
East Central Univ	OK	13,056	C
East Texas Baptist Univ	TX	33,134	C
Eastern Conn State Univ	CT	23,059	C
Eastern Illinois Univ	IL	21,126	C
Eastern Kentucky Univ	KY	16,908	C
Eastern Mennonite Univ	VA	42,550	C
Eastern Mich Univ	MI	19,761	C
Eastern Nazarene College	MA	39,955	C
Eastern New Mexico Univ	NM	14,416	C
Eastern Washington Univ	WA	25,572	LC
Edgewood College	WI	35,950	C
Edinboro Univ	PA	15,940	LC
Edward Waters College	FL	20,607	NC
Elizabeth City State Univ	NC	14,745	C
Elizabethtown College	PA	54,050	C
Elmhurst College	IL	45,428	C
Elms College	MA	45,646	VC
Elon Univ	NC	44,599	VC+
Emmanuel College	MA	52,110	C+
Emporia State Univ	KS	14,570	C
Erskine College	SC	45,460	C
Eureka College	IL	30,220	C
Evangel Univ	MO	28,898	C
Fairmont State Univ	WV	15,726	C
Faulkner Univ	AL	26,410	C
Fayetteville State Univ	NC	17,756	C
Felician Univ	NJ	45,370	LC
Ferris State Univ	MI	21,445	C
Fitchburg State Univ	MA	21,819	C
Five Towns College	NY	35,350	C
Flagler College	FL	27,620	C
Florida A&M Univ	FL	15,361	C
Florida Atlantic Univ	FL	17,339	C
Florida Gulf Coast Univ	FL	9,682	C
Florida International Univ	FL	19,854	C+
Florida Memorial Univ	FL	22,270	LC
Florida State Univ	FL	16,771	HC
Fontbonne Univ	MO	33,717	C
Fort Hays State Univ	KS	12,131	C
Framingham State Univ	MA	20,584	C
Francis Marion Univ	SC	16,464	LC
Franciscan Univ of Steubenville	OH	33,980	VC
Franklin College	IN	39,380	C
Franklin Pierce Univ	NH	46,750	C
Freed-Hardeman Univ	TN	29,450	C
Friends Univ	KS	34,455	C
Frostburg State Univ	MD	17,280	LC
Furman Univ	SC	58,092	VC+
Gallaudet Univ	DC	29,118	LC
Gardner-Webb Univ	NC	39,200	C+
Geneva College	PA	35,450	C
George Fox Univ	OR	42,938	C
Georgetown College	KY	41,440	C
Gettysburg College	PA	63,000	HC
Glenville State College	WV	17,386	NC
Goddard College	VT	17,040	VC
Gordon College	MA	46,472	C+
Goshen College	IN	42,500	C
Grace Bible College	MI	25,250	C
Grace College and Seminary	IN	31,524	C
Graceland Univ	IA	35,290	C
Grambling State Univ	LA	15,701	C
Grand Canyon Univ	AZ	16,950	VC
Grand Rapids Theological Seminary/Cornerstone Univ	MI	33,338	C
Grand Valley State Univ	MI	22,250	C+
Grand View Univ	IA	32,302	C
Green Mountain College	VT	45,228	LC
Greensboro College	NC	42,400	LC
Greenville College	IL	27,012	C
Gustavus Adolphus College	MN	52,433	HC
Gwynedd Mercy Univ	PA	43,780	LC
Hamline Univ	MN	45,678	VC
Hannibal-LaGrange Univ	MO	29,815	C
Hanover College	IN	46,364	C+
Harding Univ	AR	25,421	C
Hardin-Simmons Univ	TX	33,966	C
Harris-Stowe State Univ	MO	14,360	NC
Hastings College	NE	35,380	C+
Hawaii Pacific Univ	HI	33,420	C
Heidelberg Univ	OH	39,200	C
Hellenic College/Holy Cross Greek Orthodox School of Theology	MA	39,906	C
Henderson State Univ	AR	15,516	LC
Heritage Univ	WA	19,825	NC
High Point Univ	NC	45,977	C
Hofstra Univ	NY	55,960	C+
Holy Family Univ	PA	43,326	LC
Hood College	MD	54,840	C
Hope College	MI	39,940	VC
Hope International Univ	CA	41,150	C
Houghton College	NY	39,090	C
Houston Baptist Univ	TX	36,450	C
Howard Payne Univ	TX	34,320	C
Howard Univ	DC	37,616	C+
Humboldt State Univ	CA	20,514	C
Huntingdon College	AL	34,900	C
Huntington Univ	IN	33,996	C
Husson Univ	ME	25,720	LC
Huston-Tillotson Univ	TX	18,124	LC
Idaho State Univ	ID	13,619	NC
Illinois College	IL	40,850	VC
Illinois State Univ	IL	23,418	VC
Indiana Inst of Technology	IN	34,240	LC
Indiana State Univ	IN	23,223	LC
Indiana Univ Bloomington	IN	20,429	VC
Indiana Univ East	IN	7,072	C
Indiana Univ Kokomo	IN	7,073	C
Indiana Univ Northwest	IN	7,072	C
Indiana Univ South Bend	IN	14,242	C
Indiana Univ Southeast	IN	14,242	LC
Indiana Univ-Purdue Univ Fort Wayne	IN	17,553	C
Indiana Univ-Purdue Univ Indianapolis	IN	18,635	C
Indiana Wesleyan Univ	IN	33,674	C
Inter-American Univ of PR Ponce	PR	19,549	
Inter-American Univ of PR-Aguadilla Campus	PR	21,657	
Inter-American Univ of PR-Arecibo Campus	PR	18,245	
Inter-American Univ of PR-Barranquitas	PR	18,336	
Inter-American Univ of PR-Fajardo Campus	PR	18,336	
Inter-American Univ of PR-Metropolitan Campus	PR	20,045	
Inter-American Univ of PR-San Germán	PR	20,042	
Iowa State Univ	IA	17,570	C
Iowa Wesleyan Univ	IA	39,200	C
Jackson State Univ	MS	15,879	LC
Jacksonville State Univ	AL	14,628	LC
Jacksonville Univ	FL	46,230	C
Jarvis Christian College	TX	20,160	NC
John Brown Univ	AR	33,132	VC
Johnson State College	VT	20,752	C
Judson College	AL	27,066	C
Judson Univ	IL	37,700	C
Juniata College	PA	53,760	VC
Kansas State Univ	KS	17,780	VC
Kean Univ	NJ	24,650	C
Keene State College	NH	24,003	LC
Kentucky Christian Univ	KY	26,560	LC
Kentucky State Univ	KY	13,364	LC
Kentucky Wesleyan College	KY	32,080	C
Keuka College	NY	39,762	C
Keystone College	PA	28,680	LC
King Univ	TN	34,660	C
King's College	PA	46,858	C
Knox College	IL	52,615	VC+
Kutztown Univ of Pennsylvania	PA	19,056	LC
La Roche College	PA	37,924	LC
La Salle Univ	PA	55,790	C
La Sierra Univ	CA	39,690	VC
Lakeland Univ	WI	35,130	C
Lamar Univ	TX	18,014	LC
Lander Univ	SC	43,994	C
Langston Univ	OK	14,314	C
Lasell College	MA	47,500	C
Le Moyne College	NY	46,000	C
Lebanon Valley College	PA	51,530	C
Lee Univ	TN	22,045	C
Lees-McRae College	NC	33,944	C
Lenoir-Rhyne Univ	NC	43,200	C
Lesley Univ	MA	41,550	C

School	ST	$IS	SR
LeTourneau Univ	TX	38,250	VC
Lewis Univ	IL	40,370	C
Lewis-Clark State College	ID	14,202	C
Liberty Univ	VA	19,101	C
Limestone College	SC	32,100	C
Lincoln Memorial Univ	TN	28,070	C
Lincoln Univ	MO	13,602	NC
Lindenwood Univ	MO	25,132	C
Lindsey Wilson College	KY	32,882	C
Linfield College	OR	52,010	C
Lipscomb Univ	TN	41,296	VC
LIU Brooklyn	NY	49,682	C
LIU Post	NY	49,682	C
Livingstone College	NC	17,815	LC
Lock Haven Univ of Pennsylvania	PA	18,028	LC
Longwood Univ	VA	22,184	C
Loras College	IA	39,222	C
Louisiana College	LA	21,886	C
Louisiana State Univ and A&M College	LA	18,677	VC
Louisiana State Univ in Shreveport	LA	6,902	C
Louisiana Tech Univ	LA	11,422	VC
Loyola Univ Chicago	IL	55,802	VC
Loyola Univ Maryland	MD	60,300	VC
Lubbock Christian Univ	TX	28,426	C
Luther College	IA	48,540	C+
Lynchburg College	VA	46,740	C
Lyndon State College	VT	20,714	C
Lynn Univ	FL	49,480	LC
MacMurray College	IL	33,620	C
Manchester Univ	IN	40,422	C
Manhattan College	NY	51,750	C+
Mansfield Univ	PA	23,376	LC
Marian Univ	IN	41,220	C
Marian Univ	WI	32,420	LC
Mars Hill Univ	NC	42,688	C
Marshall Univ	WV	17,242	C
Marymount Manhattan College	NY	46,280	VC
Maryville College	TN	44,410	C
Maryville Univ of St. Louis	MO	38,046	VC+
Marywood Univ	PA	46,900	C
Mayville State Univ	ND	18,371	NC
McKendree Univ	IL	37,940	C+
McMurry Univ	TX	34,259	LC
McNeese State Univ	LA	7,838	C
McPherson College	KS	34,909	C
Medaille College	NY	35,112	C
Mercer Univ	GA	45,348	VC
Mercy College	NY	31,776	C
Mercyhurst Univ	PA	47,420	C
Merrimack College	MA	52,770	C
Messiah College	PA	43,100	C+
Methodist Univ	NC	43,600	C
Miami Univ	OH	27,190	HC+
MidAmerica Nazarene Univ	KS	35,550	C
Midland Univ	NE	37,468	
Miles College	AL	18,646	NC
Millersville Univ of Pennsylvania	PA	23,782	C
Millikin Univ	IL	42,158	C
Minn State Univ, Mankato	MN	15,616	C
Minn State Univ, Moorhead	MN	15,941	C
Minot State Univ	ND	12,732	C
Miss College	MS	25,850	C
Miss State Univ	MS	11,454	C+
Miss Univ for Women	MS	17,065	C
Miss Valley State Univ	MS	13,233	LC
Missouri Baptist Univ	MO	35,594	C
Missouri Southern State Univ	MO	12,499	C
Missouri State Univ	MO	15,190	C+
Missouri Valley College	MO	28,150	C
Missouri Western State Univ	MO	16,741	
Monmouth College	IL	42,260	C
Monmouth Univ	NJ	46,234	C
Montana State Univ	MT	15,500	C+
Montana State Univ-Billings	MT	22,960	C
Montana State Univ-Northern	MT	11,370	NC
Montreat College	NC	31,298	LC
Moravian College	PA	53,117	
Morehead State Univ	KY	17,422	C
Morgan State Univ	MD	17,190	LC
Morningside College	IA	36,865	C
Morris College	SC	18,500	LC
Mount Aloysius College	PA	29,976	C
Mount Marty College	SD	32,972	C
Mount Mercy Univ	IA	36,826	C
Mount St. Joseph Univ	OH	33,880	C
Mount St. Mary's Univ	MD	51,610	C
Mount St. Mary's Univ - Chalon Campus	CA	43,897	VC+
Murray State Univ	KY	16,998	C
Muskingum Univ	OH	35,966	C
National Louis Univ	IL	16,920	LC
Nazareth College	NY	45,574	C
Nebr Wesleyan Univ	NE	38,140	C+
New England College	NH	50,364	C
New Jersey City Univ	NJ	21,456	LC
New Mexico Highlands Univ	NM	11,904	NC
New Mexico State Univ	NM	14,050	C
New York Univ	NY	65,860	MC
Newberry College	SC	34,550	C
Newman Univ	KS	35,390	C
Niagara Univ	NY	41,010	C
Nicholls State Univ	LA	10,534	C
N Car Central Univ	NC	9,000	C
N Car Wesleyan College	NC	39,200	C
North Central College	IL	48,712	VC
North Central Univ	MN	26,400	C
N Dak State Univ	ND	16,245	C
North Park Univ	IL	35,860	C
Northeastern Illinois Univ	IL	12,529	LC
Northeastern State Univ	OK	8,615	VC
Northern Arizona Univ	AZ	20,246	VC
Northern Illinois Univ	IL	20,176	C
Northern Kentucky Univ	KY	16,486	C
Northern Mich Univ	MI	19,604	C
Northern State Univ	SD	14,505	C
Northland College	WI	41,103	C+
Northwest Christian Univ	OR	36,580	C
Northwest Missouri State Univ	MO	17,737	C
Northwest Nazarene Univ	ID	36,000	C
Northwest Univ	WA	35,876	VC
Northwestern College of Iowa	IA	38,400	C+
Northwestern Okla State Univ	OK	13,072	NC
Notre Dame College	OH	37,150	VC
Notre Dame of Maryland Univ	MD	46,465	VC
Nova Southeastern Univ	FL	38,534	C+
Nyack College	NY	34,050	NC
Oakland City Univ	IN	33,360	NC
Oakland Univ	MI	20,763	C
Oakwood Univ	AL	43,758	C
Oglala Lakota College	SD	15,050	NC
Ohio State Univ at Mansfield	OH	13,160	C
Ohio State Univ at Marion	OH	7,140	C
Ohio State Univ at Newark	OH	7,140	C
Ohio Valley Univ	WV	29,480	C
Ohio Wesleyan Univ	OH	49,460	VC
Okla Baptist Univ	OK	32,320	C
Okla Christian Univ	OK	27,650	VC
Okla City Univ	OK	40,476	VC
Okla State Univ	OK	17,180	VC
Okla Wesleyan Univ	OK	33,206	C
Old Dominion Univ	VA	20,910	C
Olivet College	MI	36,110	LC
Olivet Nazarene Univ	IL	41,840	C
Oral Roberts Univ	OK	34,316	C
Ottawa Univ	KS	36,074	VC
Otterbein Univ	OH	41,630	C
Ouachita Baptist Univ	AR	32,320	C
Pace Univ	NY	58,248	C
Pacific Lutheran Univ	WA	49,960	VC
Palm Beach Atlantic Univ	FL	39,720	C
Park Univ	MO	20,329	C
Penn State Univ/Altoona	PA	24,584	C
Pennsylvania State Univ - Univ Park	PA	29,760	HC
Pepperdine Univ	CA	74,460	HC+
Peru State College	NE	14,768	NC
Pfeiffer Univ	NC	39,695	LC
Pittsburg State Univ	KS	13,880	NC
Plymouth State Univ	NH	23,180	LC
Point Park Univ	PA	41,270	C
Pontifical Catholic Univ of PR	PR	10,534	
Prescott College	AZ	33,284	C
Principia College	IL	39,010	C+
Providence College	RI	60,760	VC
Purdue Univ/Northwest	IN	15,038	C
Purdue Univ/West Lafayette	IN	20,032	MC
Queens Univ of Charlotte	NC	39,543	C
Quincy Univ	IL	36,998	C
Quinnipiac Univ	CT	59,110	C
Rhode Island College	RI	17,694	LC
Rider Univ	NJ	54,050	C
Ripon College	WI	46,911	C+
Rivier Univ	NH	40,410	VC
Robert Morris Univ	PA	37,834	C
Roberts Wesleyan College	NY	38,306	C
Rockford Univ	IL	36,030	C
Rockhurst Univ	MO	29,220	C
Rocky Mountain College	MT	34,270	C
Roger Williams Univ	RI	46,296	C+
Rollins College	FL	58,670	HC
Roosevelt Univ	IL	40,651	VC
Rowan Univ	NJ	24,491	VC+
Russell Sage College	NY	39,370	C
Rust College	MS	10,600	C
Saginaw Valley State Univ	MI	18,530	C
SAGU American Indian College	AZ	18,142	C
St. Augustine's Univ	NC	26,048	C
St. Francis Univ	PA	42,268	NC
St. John's Univ	MN	51,624	C
St. Joseph's College of Maine	ME	46,485	C
St. Joseph's Univ	PA	57,544	VC+
St. Leo Univ	FL	31,650	C
St. Louis Univ	MO	49,866	HC
St. Martin's Univ	WA	45,056	C
St. Mary-of-the-Woods College	IN	39,632	LC
St. Mary's College	IN	50,600	C
St. Mary's Univ of Minn	MN	41,210	VC
St. Michael's College	VT	51,725	VC+
St. Peter's Univ	NJ	49,192	C
St. Xavier Univ	IL	43,310	C
Salem International Univ	WV	21,090	LC
Salisbury Univ	MD	20,714	VC
Salve Regina Univ	RI	51,470	C
Samford Univ	AL	39,232	VC
San Francisco State Univ	CA	18,514	LC
Schreiner Univ	TX	34,626	LC
Seattle Pacific Univ	WA	47,439	C+
Seton Hall Univ	NJ	55,514	C
Seton Hill Univ	PA	46,972	C
Shaw Univ	NC	24,638	C
Shepherd Univ, West Virginia	WV	17,224	C
Shippensburg Univ of Pennsylvania	PA	23,208	C
Siena Heights Univ	MI	32,040	C
Silver Lake College of the Holy Family	WI	36,290	LC
Simmons College	MA	53,090	VC
Simpson College	IA	43,839	VC
Simpson Univ	CA	33,700	C
Sinte Gleska Univ	SD	13,154	NC
Skidmore College	NY	64,214	HC
Slippery Rock Univ of Pennsylvania	PA	10,360	C
Smith College	MA	63,914	MC
S Car State Univ	SC	20,805	LC
Southeast Missouri State Univ	MO	15,498	C
Southeastern Louisiana Univ	LA	16,237	C
Southeastern Okla State Univ	OK	11,875	C
Southeastern Univ	FL	31,765	C
Southern Adventist Univ	TN	27,600	C
Southern Arkansas Univ	AR	21,532	C
Southern Conn State Univ	CT	21,924	LC
Southern Illinois Univ Carbondale	IL	23,667	C
Southern Illinois Univ Edwardsville	IL	22,643	C
Southern Nazarene Univ	OK	32,798	NC
Southern New Hampshire Univ	NH	43,198	C
Southern Oregon Univ	OR	19,117	C
Southern Univ and A&M College	LA	16,074	LC+
Southern Univ at New Orleans	LA	8,014	LC
Southern Wesleyan Univ	SC	32,130	LC
Southwest Baptist Univ	MO	29,900	LC
Southwest Minn State Univ	MN	17,783	C
Southwestern Adventist Univ	TX	27,756	LC
Southwestern College	KS	31,531	C
Southwestern Okla State Univ	OK	11,790	C
Spalding Univ	KY	31,938	SP
Spring Hill College	AL	48,488	C
Springfield College	MA	45,995	C
St. Ambrose Univ	IA	39,019	C
St. Ambrose Univ	IA	39,019	C
St. Andrews Univ	NC	44,634	LC
St. Bonaventure Univ	NY	44,237	C
St. Catherine Univ	MN	45,630	VC
St. Cloud State Univ	MN	10,600	C
St. Francis College	NY	38,800	LC
St. John Fisher College	NY	43,620	C
St. John's Univ	NY	55,850	C
St. Joseph's College, New York/Brooklyn Campus	NY	25,114	LC
St. Mary's Univ	TX	37,500	C
St. Norbert College	WI	44,525	VC
St. Thomas Aquinas College	NY	42,200	C
St. Thomas Univ	FL	36,360	LC
SUNY / Buffalo State College	NY	20,842	C
SUNY / SUNY College at Old Westbury	NY	16,860	C
SUNY / SUNY Fredonia	NY	20,818	C
SUNY / SUNY Oneonta	NY	19,712	C+
SUNY at Geneseo	NY	20,440	VC+
SUNY at New Paltz	NY	19,200	C
SUNY at Oswego	NY	21,351	C
Stephens College	MO	38,042	C
Sterling College	KS	32,830	C
Stetson Univ	FL	53,544	VC
Stevenson Univ	MD	72,770	C
Stillman College	AL	20,738	C
Sul Ross State Univ	TX	15,021	LC
Syracuse Univ	NY	60,239	VC
Tabor College	KS	35,870	C
Taylor Univ	IN	40,317	C+
Temple Univ	PA	24,392	VC
Texas A&M Univ	TX	20,521	VC+
Texas A&M Univ at Commerce	TX	10,496	C
Texas A&M Univ at Kingsville	TX	7,500	LC
Texas Wesleyan Univ	TX	35,134	C
The Catholic Univ of America	DC	56,356	VC
The College of Idaho	ID	36,415	C
The College of New Jersey	NJ	31,909	HC
The Master's Univ	CA	43,870	C+
The Univ of Tenn at Martin	TN	14,876	C
The Univ of Utah	UT	17,924	VC
Thomas College	ME	35,268	LC
Thomas More College	KY	36,720	C
Tougaloo College	MS	17,980	NC
Touro College	NY	28,950	VC
Towson Univ	MD	17,408	VC
Transylvania Univ	KY	45,690	VC+
Trine Univ	IN	41,310	C
Trinity Bible College	ND		
Trinity Christian College	IL	35,580	C
Trinity International Univ	IL	31,070	VC
Trinity Washington Univ	DC	33,826	C+
Troy Univ	AL	16,171	C
Tusculum College	TN	31,625	C
Tuskegee Univ	AL	28,164	C
Union College	KY	32,310	C
Union College	NE	23,270	C
Union Univ	TN	33,970	VC
Universidad Adventista de las Antillas	PR	16,606	
Universidad del Turabo	PR	17,828	
Universidad Metropolitana	PR	17,828	
Univ of PR, at Arecibo	PR	12,652	
Univ of Alabama	AL	24,320	C+
Univ of Alabama at Birmingham	AL	19,906	C
Univ of Alabama in Huntsville	AL	19,445	VC
Univ of Alaska Anchorage	AK	16,652	NC
Univ of Alaska Fairbanks	AK	16,179	C
Univ of Alaska Southeast	AK	11,493	C
Univ of Arizona	AZ	23,100	C
Univ of Arkansas at Fayetteville	AR	19,152	C+
Univ of Arkansas at Little Rock	AR	18,211	C
Univ of Central Arkansas	AR	14,472	VC
Univ of Central Florida	FL	15,922	VC
Univ of Central Missouri	MO	18,982	C
Univ of Central Okla	OK	13,486	C
Univ of Charleston	WV	35,000	C
Univ of Cincinnati	OH	21,964	VC
Univ of Conn	CT	25,538	HC
Univ of Dallas	TX	45,500	VC+
Univ of Dayton	OH	53,620	C
Univ of Delaware	DE	24,976	VC+
Univ of Detroit Mercy	MI	48,816	C+
Univ of Evansville	IN	44,186	VC+
Univ of Findlay	OH	60,139	C
Univ of Florida	FL	16,291	HC+
Univ of Great Falls	MT	38,524	C
Univ of Hartford	CT	49,776	C
Univ of Hawaii at Manoa	HI	23,221	C
Univ of Holy Cross	LA	21,523	C
Univ of Idaho	ID	15,348	C
Univ of Illinois at Chicago	IL	25,006	VC
Univ of Illinois at Urbana-Champaign	IL	27,006	HC
Univ of Indianapolis	IN	36,480	C
Univ of Iowa	IA	18,683	VC+
Univ of Jamestown	ND	28,508	C
Univ of Kansas	KS	20,135	C+
Univ of Kentucky	KY	33,306	C
Univ of Louisiana at Lafayette	LA	14,516	C
Univ of Louisiana at Monroe	LA	15,970	C
Univ of Louisville	KY	19,824	C
Univ of Maine	ME	20,792	C
Univ of Maine at Farmington	ME	18,187	C
Univ of Maine at Fort Kent	ME	15,165	LC
Univ of Maine at Machias	ME	22,960	C
Univ of Maine at Presque Isle	ME	14,870	C
Univ of Mary	ND	23,180	C
Univ of Mary Hardin-Baylor	TX	33,950	C+
Univ of Maryland/College Park	MD	21,938	HC
Univ of Maryland/Eastern Shore	MD	17,013	C
Univ of Miami	FL	63,494	MC
Univ of Mich/Ann Arbor	MI	24,410	MC
Univ of Mich/Dearborn	MI	11,757	VC
Univ of Mich-Flint	MI	17,607	C+
Univ of Minn Crookston	MN	19,739	C
Univ of Minn/Duluth	MN	20,292	C+
Univ of Minn/Morris	MN	20,760	VC
Univ of Minn/Twin Cities	MN	23,519	HC+
Univ of Miss	MS	17,746	C+
Univ of Missouri/Columbia	MO	18,201	MC
Univ of Missouri-Kansas City	MO	19,563	VC
Univ of Missouri-St. Louis	MO		C
Univ of Mobile	AL	28,935	C
Univ of Montana	MT	14,105	C
Univ of Montana-Western	MT	11,220	LC
Univ of Montevallo	AL	19,502	C
Univ of Mount Union	OH	38,970	C
Univ of Nebr - Kearney	NE	16,546	LC
Univ of Nebr - Lincoln	NE	18,589	VC
Univ of Nebr - Omaha	NE	16,120	C
Univ of Nevada, Las Vegas	NV	17,553	C
Univ of Nevada/Reno	NV	18,010	C
Univ of New England	ME	48,880	C
Univ of New Mexico	NM	15,404	C
Univ of New Orleans	LA	12,840	C
Univ of North Alabama	AL	15,398	C
Univ of N Car at Chapel Hill	NC	20,052	HC+
Univ of N Car at Charlotte	NC	15,547	C
Univ of N Car at Greensboro	NC	14,690	C
Univ of N Car at Pembroke	NC	14,388	LC
Univ of N Car at Wilmington	NC	14,590	VC
Univ of N Dak	ND	15,373	C
Univ of North Florida	FL	15,996	VC
Univ of North Georgia	GA	17,316	C
Univ of Northwestern - St. Paul	MN	38,160	C
Univ of Okla	OK	18,911	VC
Univ of Pennsylvania	PA	63,526	MC
Univ of Pikeville	KY	28,700	NC
Univ of Pittsburgh at Bradford	PA	22,402	C
Univ of Pittsburgh at Johnstown	PA	22,092	C
Univ of Portland	OR	52,152	VC
Univ of PR, at Bayamon	PR	13,145	
Univ of PR, at Cayey	PR		
Univ of PR, at Humacao	PR	14,000	
Univ of PR-Rio Piedras campus	PR	13,327	

ST = STATE $IS = IN-STATE COSTS SR = SELECTOR RATING

School	ST	$IS	SR
Univ of Rhode Island	RI	24,906	C
Univ of Rio Grande & Rio Grande Community College	OH	8,750	NC
Univ of St. Francis	IN	37,400	C
Univ of St. Mary	KS	34,690	C
Univ of Science and Arts of Okla	OK	11,140	VC
Univ of Scranton	PA	54,962	VC
Univ of Sioux Falls	SD	34,330	C
Univ of South Alabama	AL	16,400	C
Univ of S Car Aiken	SC	16,712	C
Univ of S Car at Columbia	SC	19,725	VC+
Univ of S Car Upstate	SC	18,200	LC
Univ of S Dak	SD	16,109	C
Univ of South Florida/Tampa	FL	16,110	VC+
Univ of Southern Indiana	IN	16,501	C
Univ of Southern Miss	MS	13,170	C
Univ of St. Francis	IL	39,924	C
Univ of Tampa	FL	36,944	C
Univ of the Cumberlands	KY	32,000	C
Univ of the District of Columbia	DC	21,044	LC
Univ of the Incarnate Word	TX	39,162	LC
Univ of the Sacred Heart	PR	17,932	
Univ of the Southwest	NM	22,766	C
Univ of Toledo	OH	19,336	NC
Univ of Tulsa	OK	52,625	HC+
Univ of Vermont	VT	28,878	HC
Univ of West Alabama	AL	15,516	NC
Univ of West Florida	FL	15,848	C
Univ of Wisc-Eau Claire	WI	15,797	VC
Univ of Wisc-Green Bay	WI	15,064	C
Univ of Wisc-La Crosse	WI	15,247	C+
Univ of Wisc-Madison	WI	20,934	MC
Univ of Wisc-Oshkosh	WI	15,200	C
Univ of Wisc-Platteville	WI	14,614	VC
Univ of Wisc-River Falls	WI	14,485	C
Univ of Wisc-Stevens Point	WI	14,043	C
Univ of Wisc-Superior	WI	14,446	C
Univ of Wisc-Whitewater	WI	13,976	C
Univ of Wyoming	WY	15,375	C+
Upper Iowa Univ	IA	34,990	NC
Urbana Univ	OH	30,820	C
Ursuline College	OH	41,076	LC
Utah State Univ	UT	12,736	C
Valley City State Univ	ND	13,267	C
Valparaiso Univ	IN	48,370	C+
Vanderbilt Univ	TN	60,572	MC
Vanguard Univ of Southern Calif	CA	40,740	VC
Virginia Union Univ	VA	22,421	C
Virginia Wesleyan College	VA	43,728	LC
Viterbo Univ	WI	34,660	C
Wagner College	NY	55,480	C+
Walla Walla Univ	WA	30,417	NC
Walsh Univ	OH	39,010	C
Warner Univ	FL	28,216	C
Wartburg College	IA	47,840	C
Washburn Univ	KS	15,827	C
Washington Adventist Univ	MD	31,440	LC
Washington State Univ	WA	22,495	C
Washington Univ in St. Louis	MO	65,366	VC
Wayne State College	NE	12,802	C
Wayne State Univ	MI	22,016	C
Waynesburg Univ	PA	32,290	C
Weber State Univ	UT	10,721	C
Webster Univ	MO	37,490	C
Wellesley College	MA	63,916	MC
Wells College	NY	50,500	C
Wesley College	DE	37,026	LC
West Chester Univ of Pennsylvania	PA	18,456	C
West Liberty Univ	WV	15,512	C
West Virginia State Univ	WV	8,378	NC
West Virginia Wesleyan College	WV	36,858	C
Western Carolina Univ	NC	13,965	C
Western Conn State Univ	CT	21,254	LC
Western Illinois Univ	IL	20,825	C
Western Kentucky Univ	KY	16,850	C
Western Mich Univ	MI	21,054	C
Western New England Univ	MA	48,088	C
Western New Mexico Univ	NM	16,734	LC
Western State Colo Univ	CO	18,639	C
Western Washington Univ	WA	18,003	C+
Westfield State Univ	MA	19,671	C
Westminster College	MO	32,820	C
Westminster College	PA	39,180	C+
Westminster College	UT	41,078	C+
Wheaton College	IL	43,610	MC
Wheeling Jesuit Univ	WV	37,106	LC
Wheelock College	MA	49,225	C
Whitworth Univ	WA	51,732	VC
Wichita State Univ	KS	21,643	C
Widener Univ	PA	56,486	C
Wiley College	TX	18,504	C
Wilkes Univ	PA	45,622	C
William Carey Univ	MS	23,950	LC
William Jewell College	MO	41,210	C+
William Penn Univ	IA	26,000	C
William Woods Univ	MO	32,040	C
Williams Baptist College	AR	24,720	C
Wilmington College	OH	34,600	C
Wilmington Univ	DE	8,546	NC
Wilson College	PA	35,620	C
Wingate Univ	NC	39,950	C
Winona State Univ	MN	17,535	C
Winston-Salem State Univ	NC	26,166	LC
Winthrop Univ	SC	23,082	C
Wisc Lutheran College	WI	36,290	VC
Wittenberg Univ	OH	48,156	C+
Worcester State Univ	MA	20,977	C
Wright State Univ	OH	16,983	C
Xavier Univ of Louisiana	LA	31,689	C+
York College	NE	24,300	C
York College of Pennsylvania	PA	29,240	C

ELEMENTARY PARTICLE PHYSICS

School	ST	$IS	SR
The Catholic Univ of America	DC	56,356	VC

EMERGENCY MEDICAL SERVICES

School	ST	$IS	SR
Anna Maria College	MA	48,186	C
Creighton Univ	NE	48,206	VC+
Univ of South Alabama	AL	16,400	C

EMERGENCY MEDICAL TECHNOLOGIES

School	ST	$IS	SR
Central Washington Univ	WA	16,803	C
George Washington Univ	DC	62,835	MC
Idaho State Univ	ID	13,619	NC
Pennsylvania College of Technology	PA	27,333	NC
Springfield College	MA	45,995	C
Univ of Maryland/Baltimore County	MD	21,296	VC
Univ of New Mexico	NM	15,404	C
Univ of Pittsburgh	PA	29,568	HC+
Western Carolina Univ	NC	13,965	C

EMERGENCY/DISASTER SCIENCE

School	ST	$IS	SR
Arkansas State Univ	AR	16,190	C
Arkansas Tech Univ	AR	15,484	C
Embry-Riddle Aeronautical Univ - Worldwide	FL	17,480	C
N Dak State Univ	ND	16,245	C
Northwest Missouri State Univ	MO	17,737	C
St. Louis Univ	MO	49,866	HC
Southeast Missouri State Univ	MO	15,498	C
The Univ of Akron	OH	21,477	C
Univ of Florida	FL	16,291	HC+
Univ of Maryland/Univ College	MD	25,966	LC
Univ of North Texas	TX	19,198	C
West Texas A&M Univ	TX	13,478	C
Western Carolina Univ	NC	13,965	C
Western Illinois Univ	IL	20,825	C

ENERGY MANAGEMENT TECHNOLOGY

School	ST	$IS	SR
CUNY/Hunter College	NY	31,098	VC
Fitchburg State Univ	MA	21,819	C
Idaho State Univ	ID	13,619	NC
Illinois State Univ	IL	23,418	VC
Ohio Univ	OH	22,924	C
Univ of Tulsa	OK	52,625	HC+
Univ of Wyoming	WY	15,375	C+

ENERGY SCIENCE

School	ST	$IS	SR
Indiana Univ-Purdue Univ Indianapolis	IN	18,635	C
Miami Univ	OH	27,190	HC+
Syracuse Univ	NY	60,239	VC
Texas Tech Univ	TX	18,736	C+

ENERGY SYSTEMS TECHNOLOGY

School	ST	$IS	SR
Thomas Edison State Univ	NJ	6,350	NC
Univ of Illinois at Chicago	IL	25,006	VC
Univ of Wyoming	WY	15,375	C+

ENERGY UTILITY TECHNOLOGY

School	ST	$IS	SR
Thomas Edison State Univ	NJ	6,350	NC

ENGINEERING

School	ST	$IS	SR
Abilene Christian Univ	TX	41,800	C+
Agnes Scott College	GA	51,930	VC+
Alabama State Univ	AL	14,142	NC
Albion College	MI	52,650	C
Andrews Univ	MI	28,030	C+
Arcadia Univ	PA	33,570	C+
Arizona State Univ at the Polytechnic Campus	AZ	21,360	VC
Arkansas State Univ	AR	16,190	C
Baldwin Wallace Univ	OH	41,106	C
Baylor Univ	TX	53,760	HC
Benedictine College	KS	36,200	VC
Biola Univ	CA	46,402	C+
Birmingham-Southern College	AL	44,478	VC
Boston Univ	MA	65,110	MC
Brown Univ	RI	64,566	MC
Bucknell Univ	PA	64,616	MC
Butler Univ	IN	51,352	VC
Calif Baptist Univ	CA	41,392	C
Cal State, East Bay	CA	19,413	C
Cal State, Los Angeles	CA	17,186	LC
Cal State, Northridge	CA	16,859	LC
Calvin College	MI	41,570	VC+
Carnegie Mellon Univ	PA	67,980	MC
Case Western Reserve Univ	OH	60,304	MC
Central College	IA	44,592	C
Colo School of Mines	CO	29,319	MC
Colo State Univ	CO	22,162	VC
Cooper Union for the Advancement of Science and Art	NY	58,210	MC
Dominican Univ	IL	41,222	C
Dordt College	IA	37,860	C+
Drexel Univ	PA	65,432	VC+
East Carolina Univ	NC	16,937	C
Eastern Illinois Univ	IL	21,126	C
Eastern Washington Univ	WA	25,572	LC
Elizabethtown College	PA	54,050	C
Elon Univ	NC	44,599	VC+
Florida Atlantic Univ	FL	17,339	C
Franklin W. Olin College of Engineering	MA	63,130	MC
Frostburg State Univ	MD	17,280	LC
Geneva College	PA	35,450	C
George Washington Univ	DC	62,835	MC
Grand Valley State Univ	MI	22,250	C+
Harvard College/Harvard Univ	MA	60,659	MC
Harvey Mudd College	CA	67,155	MC
Hope College	MI	39,940	VC
Indiana Inst of Technology	IN	34,240	LC
Indiana Univ-Purdue Univ Fort Wayne	IN	17,553	C
Iowa State Univ	IA	17,570	C
James Madison Univ	VA	19,084	VC
John Brown Univ	AR	33,132	VC
Johns Hopkins Univ	MD	65,386	MC
Johnson C. Smith Univ	NC	25,336	LC
Kalamazoo College	MI	53,931	HC+
Lafayette College	PA	63,355	MC
Lamar Univ	TX	18,014	LC
Lawrence Tech Univ	MI	39,770	VC
LeTourneau Univ	TX	38,250	VC
Lindenwood Univ	MO	25,132	C
Loyola Univ Maryland	MD	60,300	VC
Lubbock Christian Univ	TX	28,426	C
Maine Maritime Academy	ME	22,536	C
Manchester Univ	IN	40,422	C
Marquette Univ	WI	48,390	VC+
Marshall Univ	WV	17,242	C
Maryville College	TN	44,410	C
Maryville Univ of St. Louis	MO	38,046	VC+
Mass Inst of Technology	MA	62,662	MC
Mass Maritime Academy	MA	19,982	C
McNeese State Univ	LA	7,838	C
Mercer Univ	GA	45,348	VC
Messiah College	PA	43,100	C+
Miami Univ	OH	27,190	HC+
Mich State Univ	MI	23,898	VC+
Mich Tech Univ	MI	24,739	VC+
Millersville Univ of Pennsylvania	PA	23,782	C
Milligan College	TN	38,150	C
Milwaukee School of Engineering	WI	45,153	HC
Montana Tech of the Univ of Montana	MT	15,447	C+
Mount Vernon Nazarene Univ	OH	34,500	C
Muskingum Univ	OH	35,966	C
New Mexico Highlands Univ	NM	11,904	NC
New York Univ	NY	65,860	MC
N Car State Univ	NC	19,515	HC+
Northwest Nazarene Univ	ID	36,000	C
Northwestern Univ	IL	66,344	MC
Olivet Nazarene Univ	IL	41,840	C
Oral Roberts Univ	OK	34,316	C
Penn State Erie/The Behrend College	PA	16,256	C
Pennsylvania State Univ - Univ Park	PA	29,760	HC
Pepperdine Univ	CA	74,460	HC+
Philadelphia Univ	PA	50,370	C
Providence College	RI	60,760	VC
Purdue Univ/Northwest	IN	15,038	C
Quinnipiac Univ	CT	59,110	C
Rensselaer Polytechnic Inst	NY	63,436	MC
Robert Morris Univ	PA	37,834	C
Rochester Inst of Technology	NY	50,842	HC
Roger Williams Univ	RI	46,296	C+
Rowan Univ	NJ	24,491	VC+
St. Anselm College	NH	52,560	C+
St. Louis Univ	MO	49,866	HC
St. Vincent College	PA	44,626	C
San Diego State Univ	CA	21,896	C+
San Jose State Univ	CA	21,540	C
Seattle Pacific Univ	WA	47,439	C+
Seton Hill Univ	PA	46,972	C
Smith College	MA	63,914	MC
S Dak State Univ	SD	15,634	C
Spelman College	GA	38,751	C
Spring Hill College	AL	48,488	C
St. Ambrose Univ	IA	39,019	C
St. Ambrose Univ	IA	39,019	C
St. Mary's Univ	TX	37,500	C
Stanford Univ	CA	60,409	MC
SUNY /Maritime College	NY	16,020	C
SUNY at Binghamton	NY	22,861	MC
Swarthmore College	PA	63,550	MC
Tarleton State Univ	TX	15,248	LC
Temple Univ	PA	24,392	VC
Tenn Tech Univ	TN	17,050	C
Texas Christian Univ	TX	54,670	HC
The Catholic Univ of America	DC	56,356	VC
The Univ of Akron	OH	21,477	C
The Univ of Tenn at Chattanooga	TN	16,744	C
The Univ of Tenn at Martin	TN	14,876	C
The Univ of Utah	UT	17,924	VC
Trinity College	CT	63,920	HC+
Tufts Univ	MA		MC
United States Air Force Academy	CO		C
United States Naval Academy	MD		MC
Univ of Arizona	AZ	23,100	C
Univ of Calif at Irvine	CA	26,484	VC
Univ of Calif San Diego	CA	30,150	MC
Univ of Central Missouri	MO	18,982	C
Univ of Central Okla	OK	13,486	C
Univ of Cincinnati	OH	21,964	VC
Univ of Delaware	DE	24,976	VC+
Univ of Detroit Mercy	MI	48,816	C+
Univ of Hartford	CT	49,776	C
Univ of Idaho	ID	15,348	C
Univ of Illinois at Chicago	IL	25,006	VC
Univ of Illinois at Urbana-Champaign	IL	27,006	HC
Univ of Iowa	IA	18,683	VC+
Univ of Louisville	KY	19,824	C
Univ of Maryland/College Park	MD	21,938	HC
Univ of Mass Boston	MA	13,435	C
Univ of Mich/Ann Arbor	MI	24,410	MC
Univ of Mich/Dearborn	MI	11,757	VC
Univ of Mich-Flint	MI	17,607	C+
Univ of Miss	MS	17,746	C+
Univ of Missouri/Columbia	MO	18,201	MC
Univ of New Haven	CT	52,190	C
Univ of N Car at Asheville	NC	15,723	VC+
Univ of Pittsburgh at Bradford	PA	22,402	C
Univ of Portland	OR	52,152	VC
Univ of PR, at Mayaguez	PR	13,995	
Univ of South Florida/Tampa	FL	16,110	VC+
Univ of Southern Indiana	IN	16,501	C
Univ of Texas at San Antonio	TX	20,157	C
Univ of Toledo	OH	19,336	NC
Univ of Vermont	VT	28,878	HC
Univ of Washington	WA	23,149	VC
Univ of Wisc-Milwaukee	WI	21,496	C
Utah State Univ	UT	12,736	C
Walla Walla Univ	WA	30,417	NC
Washington Univ in St. Louis	MO	65,366	VC
Waynesburg Univ	PA	32,290	C
Wentworth Inst of Technology	MA	47,112	C
West Virginia Univ	WV	18,210	C
West Virginia Wesleyan College	WV	36,858	C
Western Illinois Univ	IL	20,825	C
Wheaton College	IL	43,610	MC
Wheeling Jesuit Univ	WV	37,106	LC
Whitworth Univ	WA	51,732	VC
Widener Univ	PA	56,486	C
Yale Univ	CT	64,650	MC
York College of Pennsylvania	PA	29,240	C
Youngstown State Univ	OH	17,307	C

ENGINEERING AND APPLIED SCIENCE

School	ST	$IS	SR
Benedictine Univ	IL	38,300	C
Bethel Univ	MN	45,270	VC
Calif Inst of Technology	CA	58,761	MC
Cal State, Fullerton	CA	21,902	C
CUNY/College of Staten Island	NY	17,840	NC
Colo State Univ	CO	22,162	VC
George Fox Univ	OR	42,938	C
Hofstra Univ	NY	55,960	C+
New Jersey Inst of Technology	NJ	29,569	VC
Pacific Lutheran Univ	WA	49,960	VC
Rutgers Univ - New Brunswick	NJ	26,632	HC
Seattle Pacific Univ	WA	47,439	C+
The College of New Jersey	NJ	31,909	HC
Trinity Univ	TX	52,314	HC+
Tufts Univ	MA		MC
United States Air Force Academy	CO		C
Univ of Calif at Berkeley	CA	28,853	MC
Univ of Calif at Riverside	CA	29,227	C+
Univ of Florida	FL	16,291	HC+
Univ of Mary	ND	23,180	C
Univ of Rochester	NY	65,032	MC
Univ of Virginia	VA	25,891	MC
Vanderbilt Univ	TN	60,572	MC
Wartburg College	IA	47,840	C
Wilkes Univ	PA	45,622	C
Yale Univ	CT	64,650	MC

ST = STATE $IS = IN-STATE COSTS SR = SELECTOR RATING

ENGINEERING CHEMISTRY

School	ST	$IS	SR
Ithaca College	NY	56,766	VC
New York Univ	NY	65,860	MC
Oakland Univ	MI	20,763	C
Stony Brook Univ/The SUNY	NY	21,881	MC

ENGINEERING GRAPHICS & DESIGN

School	ST	$IS	SR
Murray State Univ	KY	16,998	C
Western Mich Univ	MI	21,054	C

ENGINEERING MANAGEMENT

School	ST	$IS	SR
Arizona State Univ at the Tempe Campus	AZ	21,756	VC
Bethel College	IN	35,860	C
Christian Brothers Univ	TN	31,670	VC
Clarkson Univ	NY	60,392	HC
Columbia Univ/City of New York	NY	62,958	MC
Embry-Riddle Aeronautical Univ - Worldwide	FL	17,480	C
Gonzaga Univ	WA	50,888	HC
Illinois Inst of Technology	IL	56,826	HC+
Kansas State Univ	KS	17,780	VC
Miami Univ	OH	27,190	HC+
Missouri Univ of Science and Technology	MO	18,655	HC
New York Inst of Technology	NY	48,730	C
N Dak State Univ	ND	16,245	C
Oral Roberts Univ	OK	34,316	C
Park Univ	MO	20,329	C
Point Park Univ	PA	41,270	C
Purdue Univ/West Lafayette	IN	20,032	MC
St. Louis Univ	MO	49,866	HC
Stevens Inst of Technology	NJ	62,338	MC
Texas A&M Univ at Kingsville	TX	7,500	LC
The Univ of Tenn at Chattanooga	TN	16,744	C
Trine Univ	IN	41,310	C
United States Military Academy at West Point	NY		HC+
Univ of Arizona	AZ	23,100	C
Univ of Louisville	KY	19,824	C
Univ of N Car at Asheville	NC	15,723	VC+
Univ of the Incarnate Word	TX	39,162	LC
Univ of the Pacific	CA	57,006	VC
Univ of Vermont	VT	28,878	HC
Western Mich Univ	MI	21,054	C
Wilkes Univ	PA	45,622	C
York College of Pennsylvania	PA	29,240	C

ENGINEERING MECHANICS

School	ST	$IS	SR
Columbia Univ/City of New York	NY	62,958	MC
Johns Hopkins Univ	MD	65,386	MC
Lehigh Univ	PA	61,010	MC
Mich State Univ	MI	23,898	VC+
Missouri Univ of Science and Technology	MO	18,655	HC
New York Univ	NY	65,860	MC
Purdue Univ/Northwest	IN	15,038	C
United States Air Force Academy	CO		C
Univ of Arkansas at Little Rock	AR	18,211	C
Univ of Calif at Riverside	CA	29,227	C+
Univ of Cincinnati	OH	21,964	VC
Univ of Illinois at Urbana-Champaign	IL	27,006	HC
Univ of Wisc-Madison	WI	20,934	MC
Virginia Polytechnic Inst and State Univ	VA	21,276	HC
Washington Univ in St. Louis	MO	65,366	VC

ENGINEERING PHYSICS

School	ST	$IS	SR
Albion College	MI	52,650	C
Arkansas Tech Univ	AR	15,484	C
Augustana College	IL	49,658	VC
Augustana Univ	SD	38,424	VC
Belmont Univ	TN	40,970	VC
Bethel College	IN	35,860	C
Brown Univ	RI	64,566	MC
Case Western Reserve Univ	OH	60,304	MC
Christian Brothers Univ	TN	31,670	VC
Colo State Univ	CO	22,162	VC
Cornell Univ	NY	64,853	MC
Dartmouth College	NH	66,174	MC
Doane Univ	NE	39,184	VC
Eastern Mich Univ	MI	19,761	C
Eastern Nazarene College	MA	39,955	C
Edinboro Univ	PA	15,940	LC
Elon Univ	NC	44,599	VC+
Embry-Riddle Aeronautical Univ - Daytona Beach	FL	44,712	VC
Fordham Univ	NY	65,918	MC
Henderson State Univ	AR	15,516	LC
Ithaca College	NY	56,766	VC
Jacksonville Univ	FL	46,230	C
John Carroll Univ	OH	49,740	C+
Juniata College	PA	53,760	VC
Kettering Univ	MI	47,570	HC
Lehigh Univ	PA	61,010	MC
Loras College	IA	39,222	C
Loyola Marymount Univ	CA	58,038	HC
Miami Univ	OH	27,190	HC+
Miss College	MS	25,850	C
Morehouse College	GA	40,064	C
Morgan State Univ	MD	17,190	LC
Murray State Univ	KY	16,998	C
New Mexico State Univ	NM	14,050	C
New York Univ	NY	65,860	MC
N Car A&T State Univ	NC	13,365	LC
Northwest Nazarene Univ	ID	36,000	C
Oakland Univ	MI	20,763	C
Ohio State Univ at Columbus	OH	21,703	HC+
Ohio Univ	OH	22,924	C
Point Loma Nazarene Univ	CA	43,450	C
Purdue Univ/Northwest	IN	15,038	C
Ramapo College of New Jersey	NJ	25,338	C
Randolph College	VA	45,660	VC
Randolph-Macon College	VA	49,910	C
Rensselaer Polytechnic Inst	NY	63,436	MC
Rose-Hulman Inst of Technology	IN	57,303	MC
St. Louis Univ	MO	49,866	HC
St. Mary's Univ of Minn	MN	41,210	VC
Samford Univ	AL	39,232	VC
S Dak State Univ	SD	15,634	C
Southeast Missouri State Univ	MO	15,498	C
Southwestern College	KS	31,531	C
Southwestern Okla State Univ	OK	11,790	C
St. Bonaventure Univ	NY	44,237	C
Stanford Univ	CA	60,409	MC
SUNY / Univ at Buffalo	NY	23,122	C+
Stevens Inst of Technology	NJ	62,338	MC
Syracuse Univ	NY	60,239	VC
Tarleton State Univ	TX	15,248	LC
Taylor Univ	IN	40,317	C+
Tufts Univ	MA		MC
Tulane Univ	LA	63,396	HC+
United States Military Academy at West Point	NY		HC+
Univ of Calif at Berkeley	CA	28,853	MC
Univ of Calif San Diego	CA	30,150	MC
Univ of Central Okla	OK	13,486	C
Univ of Colo Boulder	CO	24,285	VC+
Univ of Illinois at Chicago	IL	25,006	VC
Univ of Illinois at Urbana-Champaign	IL	27,006	HC
Univ of Kansas	KS	20,135	C+
Univ of Maine	ME	20,792	C
Univ of Mass Boston	MA	13,435	C
Univ of Mich/Ann Arbor	MI	24,410	MC
Univ of Nebr - Omaha	NE	16,120	C
Univ of Nevada/Reno	NV	18,010	C
Univ of New Hampshire	NH	28,562	VC
Univ of North Texas	TX	19,198	C
Univ of Okla	OK	18,911	VC
Univ of Pittsburgh	PA	29,568	HC+
Univ of San Francisco	CA	58,484	VC
Univ of the Pacific	CA	57,006	VC
Univ of Tulsa	OK	52,625	HC+
Univ of Wisc-Madison	WI	20,934	MC
Univ of Wisc-Platteville	WI	14,614	VC
Washington and Lee Univ	VA	59,647	MC
West Chester Univ of Pennsylvania	PA	18,456	C
West Virginia Wesleyan College	WV	36,858	C
Westmont College	CA	56,410	HC
Whitworth Univ	WA	51,732	VC
Wright State Univ	OH	16,983	C
Xavier Univ	OH	47,880	C+

ENGINEERING SCIENCE

School	ST	$IS	SR
Calif Polytechnic State Univ	CA	17,979	HC+
Cornell College	IA	48,800	VC
Dartmouth College	NH	66,174	MC
Embry-Riddle Aeronautical Univ - Worldwide	FL	17,480	C
Loyola Univ Chicago	IL	55,802	VC
Morehouse College	GA	40,064	C
Pennsylvania State Univ - Univ Park	PA	29,760	HC
Stony Brook Univ/The SUNY	NY	21,881	MC
Univ of Mary Hardin-Baylor	TX	33,950	C+
Univ of Miami	FL	63,494	MC
Univ of Pittsburgh	PA	29,568	HC+

ENGINEERING TECHNOLOGY

School	ST	$IS	SR
Appalachian State Univ	NC	14,416	VC
Austin Peay State Univ	TN	16,397	C
Bluefield State College	WV	5,832	LC
Bowling Green State Univ	OH	19,747	C
Calif State Polytechnic Univ, Pomona	CA	21,541	C
Cal State, Maritime Academy	CA	19,450	LC
Cal State, Long Beach	CA	18,850	C
Cal State, Sacramento	CA	20,332	C
Calif Univ of Pennsylvania	PA	14,217	LC
Capitol Technology Univ	MD	31,410	C
Central Mich Univ	MI	20,330	C
Central Washington Univ	WA	16,803	C
Colo Mesa Univ	CO	18,955	LC
Drexel Univ	PA	65,432	VC+
East Tenn State Univ	TN	13,994	C
Eastern Mich Univ	MI	19,761	C
Eastern Washington Univ	WA	25,572	LC
Embry-Riddle Aeronautical Univ - Worldwide	FL	17,480	C
Fairmont State Univ	WV	15,726	C
Ferris State Univ	MI	21,445	C
Florida A&M Univ	FL	15,361	C
Grambling State Univ	LA	15,701	C
Grand Canyon Univ	AZ	16,950	VC
Indiana Univ-Purdue Univ Fort Wayne	IN	17,553	C
Indiana Univ-Purdue Univ Indianapolis	IN	18,635	C
Iowa State Univ	IA	17,570	C
Kansas State Univ	KS	17,780	VC
Kent State Univ	OH	20,732	C
Lawrence Tech Univ	MI	39,770	VC
LeTourneau Univ	TX	38,250	VC
Maine Maritime Academy	ME	22,536	C
McNeese State Univ	LA	7,838	C
Middle Tenn State Univ	TN	8,650	C
Midwestern State Univ	TX	17,572	C
Minn State Univ, Mankato	MN	15,616	C
Missouri Western State Univ	MO	16,741	
Montana State Univ-Northern	MT	11,370	NC
New Jersey Inst of Technology	NJ	29,569	VC
New Mexico State Univ	NM	14,050	C
Ohio Univ	OH	22,924	C
Old Dominion Univ	VA	20,910	C
Oregon Inst of Technology	OR	8,910	C
Penn State Erie/The Behrend College	PA	16,256	C
Pennsylvania College of Technology	PA	27,333	NC
Point Park Univ	PA	41,270	C
Prairie View A&M Univ	TX	15,205	LC
Purdue Univ/Northwest	IN	15,038	C
Rochester Inst of Technology	NY	50,842	HC
Saginaw Valley State Univ	MI	18,530	C
S Car State Univ	SC	20,805	LC
S Dak State Univ	SD	15,634	C
Southeast Missouri State Univ	MO	15,498	C
Southeastern Louisiana Univ	LA	16,237	C
Southern Illinois Univ Carbondale	IL	23,667	C
Southern Univ and A&M College	LA	16,074	LC+
Southwestern Okla State Univ	OK	11,790	C
St. Cloud State Univ	MN	10,600	C
Temple Univ	PA	24,392	VC
Texas A&M Univ	TX	20,521	VC+
Texas A&M Univ at Commerce	TX	10,496	C
Texas A&M Univ at Corpus Christi	TX	16,851	LC
Texas Southern Univ	TX	18,212	LC
Texas State Univ	TX	19,350	C
Univ of Arkansas at Little Rock	AR	18,211	C
Univ of Central Missouri	MO	18,982	C
Univ of Cincinnati	OH	21,964	VC
Univ of Dayton	OH	53,620	C
Univ of Delaware	DE	24,976	VC+
Univ of Hartford	CT	49,776	C
Univ of Houston-Downtown	TX	7,241	C
Univ of Maryland/Eastern Shore	MD	17,013	C
Univ of Memphis	TN	18,278	C
Univ of N Car at Charlotte	NC	15,547	C
Univ of North Texas	TX	19,198	C
Univ of S Car Upstate	SC	18,200	LC
Univ of Southern Miss	MS	13,170	C
Univ of Toledo	OH	19,336	NC
Univ of Wisc-Green Bay	WI	15,064	C
Univ of Wisc-Stout	WI	19,667	C
Virginia State Univ	VA	19,802	C+
West Texas A&M Univ	TX	13,478	C
West Virginia Univ Inst of Technology	WV	16,462	NC
Western Carolina Univ	NC	13,965	C
Western Illinois Univ	IL	20,825	C
Western Washington Univ	WA	18,003	C+

ENGINEERING/MECHANICAL EMP/ENERGY SYS FOCUS

School	ST	$IS	SR
Malone Univ	OH	38,448	C
Mass Maritime Academy	MA	19,982	C
Oregon State Univ	OR	22,519	VC
Texas Christian Univ	TX	54,670	HC

ENGLISH

School	ST	$IS	SR
Abilene Christian Univ	TX	41,800	C+
Adams State Univ	CO	17,703	LC
Adelphi Univ	NY	48,244	C
Adrian College	MI	42,400	C
Alabama A&M Univ	AL	18,796	C
Alabama State Univ	AL	14,142	NC
Albany State Univ	GA	19,462	C
Albertus Magnus College	CT	43,258	LC
Albion College	MI	52,650	C
Albright College	PA	46,660	C
Alcorn State Univ	MS	15,854	C
Alfred Univ	NY	42,296	C+
Alice Lloyd College	KY	8,190	C
Allegheny College	PA	55,420	VC
Allen Univ	SC	19,300	NC
Alma College	MI	47,548	C
Alvernia Univ	PA	43,900	C
Alverno College	WI	33,294	LC
American International College	MA	46,300	LC
Amherst College	MA		HC+
Anderson Univ	IN	38,200	C
Andrews Univ	MI	28,030	C+
Angelo State Univ	TX	15,263	NC
Anna Maria College	MA	48,186	C
Appalachian State Univ	NC	14,416	VC
Aquinas College	TN	30,800	C+
Aquinas College - Mich	MI	38,876	HC
Arcadia Univ	PA	33,570	C+
Arizona State Univ at the Polytechnic Campus	AZ	21,360	VC
Arizona State Univ at the Tempe Campus	AZ	21,756	VC
Arizona State Univ at the West Campus	AZ	20,640	C
Arkansas State Univ	AR	16,190	C
Arkansas Tech Univ	AR	15,484	C
Armstrong State Univ	GA	16,962	C
Asbury Univ	KY	35,180	C+
Ashford Univ	CA	10,480	C
Ashland Univ	OH	21,440	C
Assumption College	MA	47,920	C+
Atlantic Union College	MA	27,228	C
Auburn Univ	AL	23,594	VC+
Auburn Univ at Montgomery	AL	15,290	C
Augsburg College	MN	43,929	C
Augusta Univ	GA	4,632	C
Augustana College	IL	49,658	VC
Augustana Univ	SD	38,424	VC
Aurora Univ	IL	33,970	C
Austin College	TX	45,875	VC
Austin Peay State Univ	TN	16,397	C
Averett Univ	VA	40,970	LC
Avila Univ	MO	35,480	C
Azusa Pacific Univ	CA	43,972	C
Baker Univ	KS	33,350	C+
Baldwin Wallace Univ	OH	41,106	C
Ball State Univ	IN	19,590	C
Barnard College/Columbia Univ	NY	62,741	MC
Barry Univ	FL	37,830	C
Barton College	NC	38,686	LC
Bates College	ME	64,500	MC
Baylor Univ	TX	53,760	HC
Belhaven Univ	MS	31,016	C
Bellarmine Univ	KY	51,220	C
Bellevue Univ	NE	20,300	NC
Belmont Abbey College	NC	48,156	C
Belmont Univ	TN	40,970	VC
Beloit College	WI	55,206	HC
Bemidji State Univ	MN	16,056	VC
Benedict College	SC	28,238	NC
Benedictine College	KS	36,200	VC
Bennett College	NC	27,302	NC
Bennington College	VT	63,960	MC
Bentley Univ	MA	60,890	HC
Berea College	KY	7,042	C
Berry College	GA	45,286	C+
Bethany College	KS	46,100	NC
Bethany College	WV	36,300	NC
Bethel College	KS	35,370	C
Bethel Univ	MN	45,270	VC
Bethel Univ	TN	24,738	C
Bethune-Cookman Univ	FL	22,970	C
Biola Univ	CA	46,402	C+
Birmingham-Southern College	AL	44,478	VC
Black Hills State Univ	SD	15,899	C
Bloomfield College	NJ	39,100	LC
Bloomsburg Univ of Pennsylvania	PA	19,066	LC
Blue Mountain College	MS	15,949	VC
Bluefield College	VA	34,120	C+
Bluffton Univ	OH	40,950	C
Boise State Univ	ID	14,860	C
Boston College	MA	65,737	MC
Boston Univ	MA	65,110	MC
Bowdoin College	ME	63,500	MC
Bowie State Univ	MD	26,728	LC
Bowling Green State Univ	OH	19,747	C
Brandeis Univ	MA	65,925	MC
Brenau Univ - Women's College	GA	37,876	LC
Brescia Univ	KY	29,890	VC+
Brewton-Parker College	GA	23,490	C
Briar Cliff Univ	IA	36,956	C
Bridgewater College	VA	44,510	C
Bridgewater State Univ	MA	21,810	C
Brigham Young Univ	UT	12,748	HC
Brigham Young Univ/Hawaii	HI	11,290	C
Brown Univ	RI	64,566	MC
Bryan College	TN	31,440	C
Bryant Univ	RI	55,646	VC
Bryn Athyn College	PA	31,470	C
Bryn Mawr College	PA	59,890	MC
Bucknell Univ	PA	64,616	MC
Buena Vista Univ	IA	41,514	C
Butler Univ	IN	51,352	VC
Cabrini Univ	PA	42,591	LC
Cairn Univ	PA	36,296	C
Caldwell Univ	NJ	42,165	NC
Calif Baptist Univ	CA	41,392	C
Calif College of the Arts	CA	52,758	SP
Calif Lutheran Univ	CA	52,853	C
Calif Polytechnic State Univ	CA	17,979	HC+

ST = STATE $IS = IN-STATE COSTS SR = SELECTOR RATING

School	ST	$IS	SR
Calif State Polytechnic Univ, Pomona	CA	21,541	C
Cal State, Bakersfield	CA	19,191	LC
Cal State, Chico	CA	21,440	C
Cal State, Dominguez Hills	CA	19,022	LC
Cal State, East Bay	CA	19,413	C
Cal State, Fresno	CA	16,902	LC
Cal State, Fullerton	CA	21,902	C
Cal State, Long Beach	CA	18,850	C
Cal State, Los Angeles	CA	17,186	LC
Cal State, Northridge	CA	16,859	LC
Cal State, Sacramento	CA	20,332	C
Cal State, San Bernardino	CA	12,000	C
Cal State, Stanislaus	CA	16,212	C
Calif Univ of Pennsylvania	PA	14,217	LC
Calumet College of St. Joseph	IN	22,735	C
Calvin College	MI	41,570	VC+
Cameron Univ	OK	11,072	NC
Campbellsville Univ	KY	32,492	C
Canisius College	NY	47,537	C
Capital Univ	OH	42,982	C
Cardinal Stritch Univ	WI	36,462	C
Carleton College	MN	64,071	MC
Carlow Univ	PA	38,549	LC
Carnegie Mellon Univ	PA	67,980	MC
Carroll College	MT	39,972	C+
Carroll Univ	WI	38,100	C+
Carson-Newman Univ	TN	34,160	C
Carthage College	WI	48,835	C
Case Western Reserve Univ	OH	60,304	MC
Castleton Univ	VT	20,186	C
Catawba College	NC	39,820	C
Cazenovia College	NY	46,470	C
Cedar Crest College	PA	46,715	C
Cedarville Univ	OH	34,990	VC
Centenary College	NJ	43,602	C
Centenary College of Louisiana	LA	45,650	C+
Central College	IA	44,592	C
Central Conn State Univ	CT	21,203	C
Central Methodist Univ	MO	36,830	VC
Central Mich Univ	MI	20,330	C
Central State Univ	OH	18,564	C
Central Washington Univ	WA	16,803	C
Centre College	KY	49,250	HC
Chadron State College	NE	14,819	NC
Chaminade Univ of Honolulu	HI	36,000	C
Chapman Univ	CA	63,078	VC+
Charleston Southern Univ	SC	32,400	C
Chatham Univ	PA	46,517	C
Cheyney Univ of Pennsylvania	PA	20,896	LC
Chicago State Univ	IL	20,144	C
Christendom College	VA	32,600	VC
Christian Brothers Univ	TN	31,670	VC
Christopher Newport Univ	VA	23,968	VC+
CUNY/Baruch College	NY	21,609	HC
CUNY/Brooklyn College	NY	5,884	C+
CUNY/City College	NY	20,319	VC
CUNY/College of Staten Island	NY	17,840	NC
CUNY/Hunter College	NY	31,098	VC
CUNY/John Jay College of Criminal Justice	NY	6,359	NC
CUNY/Lehman College	NY	5,778	HC+
CUNY/Meger Evers College	NY	6,680	NC
CUNY/Queens College	NY	27,896	C
CUNY/York College	NY	6,747	LC
Claflin Univ	SC	33,764	LC
Clarion Univ of Pennsylvania	PA	21,608	LC
Clark Atlanta Univ	GA	31,019	LC
Clark Univ	MA	51,600	HC+
Clarke Univ	IA	38,940	C
Clemson Univ	SC		HC
Cleveland State Univ	OH	22,196	C
Coastal Carolina Univ	SC	19,766	C
Coe College	IA	51,570	VC
Coker College	SC	34,810	LC
Colby College	ME	64,060	MC
Colby-Sawyer College	NH	50,790	C
Colgate Univ	NY	65,030	MC
College of Charleston	SC	22,699	C
College of Mount St. Vincent	NY	45,620	C
College of St. Benedict	MN	52,806	C
College of St. Elizabeth	NJ	44,432	LC
College of St. Mary	NE	35,184	C
College of St Joseph	VT	32,400	LC
College of St. Scholastica	MN	44,640	C
College of the Holy Cross	MA	62,165	MC
College of the Ozarks	MO	7,230	C
College of William & Mary	VA		MC
Colo Christian Univ	CO	39,940	VC
Colo College	CO	62,560	MC
Colo Mesa Univ	CO	18,955	LC
Colo State Univ	CO	22,162	VC
Colo State Univ-Pueblo	CO	18,234	C
Columbia College	SC	36,550	C
Columbia College - Missouri	MO	27,803	C
Columbia Univ/City of New York	NY	62,958	MC
Columbus State Univ	GA	14,336	LC
Concord Univ	WV	14,954	C
Concordia College - Moorhead	MN	51,088	C+
Concordia College - New York	NY	39,035	LC
Concordia Univ	CA	41,580	VC
Concordia Univ	OR	35,000	C
Concordia Univ Nebr	NE	36,280	VC
Concordia Univ St. Paul	MN	29,050	C
Concordia Univ Texas	TX	40,210	C
Concordia Univ Wisc	WI	35,910	C
Concordia Univ, Ann Arbor	MI	35,945	VC
Concordia Univ, Chicago	IL	39,694	C
Conn College	CT	65,000	MC
Converse College	SC	26,495	C
Coppin State Univ	MD	17,041	VC
Corban Univ	OR	40,306	C
Cornell College	IA	48,800	VC
Cornell Univ	NY	64,853	MC
Covenant College	GA	38,990	VC
Creighton Univ	NE	48,206	VC+
Culver-Stockton College	MO	33,525	C
Cumberland Univ	TN	27,710	C
Curry College	MA	51,815	C
Daemen College	NY	38,045	C
Dakota State Univ	SD	13,811	C
Dakota Wesleyan Univ	SD	32,850	C
Dallas Baptist Univ	TX	33,713	C
Dartmouth College	NH	66,174	MC
Davidson College	NC	60,119	MC
Davis & Elkins College	WV	38,242	LC
Delaware State Univ	DE	19,376	NC
Delaware Valley Univ	PA	49,796	C
Delta State Univ	MS	13,176	C
Denison Univ	OH	58,860	MC
DePaul Univ	IL	47,623	VC
DePauw Univ	IN	58,688	HC+
DeSales Univ	PA	43,970	C
Dickinson College	PA	63,974	MC
Dickinson State Univ	ND	12,372	LC
Dillard Univ	LA	20,940	VC
Doane Univ	NE	39,184	VC
Dominican College	NY	31,270	LC
Dominican Univ	IL	41,222	C
Dordt College	IA	37,860	C+
Drake Univ	IA	45,056	HC
Drew Univ/College of Liberal Arts	NJ	61,048	VC
Drexel Univ	PA	65,432	VC+
Drury Univ	MO	33,791	VC
Duke Univ	NC	64,188	
Duquesne Univ	PA	46,822	VC
D'Youville College	NY	36,780	C
Earlham College	IN	54,870	HC
East Carolina Univ	NC	16,937	C
East Central Univ	OK	13,056	C
East Stroudsburg Univ	PA	18,334	C
East Tenn State Univ	TN	13,994	C
East Texas Baptist Univ	TX	33,134	C
Eastern Conn State Univ	CT	23,059	C
Eastern Illinois Univ	IL	21,126	C
Eastern Kentucky Univ	KY	16,908	C
Eastern Mennonite Univ	VA	42,550	C
Eastern Mich Univ	MI	19,761	C
Eastern Nazarene College	MA	39,955	C
Eastern New Mexico Univ	NM	14,416	C
Eastern Oregon Univ	OR	17,715	C
Eastern Univ	PA	39,540	C
Eastern Washington Univ	WA	25,572	LC
Edgewood College	WI	35,950	C
Edinboro Univ	PA	15,940	LC
Edward Waters College	FL	20,607	NC
Elizabeth City State Univ	NC	14,745	C
Elizabethtown College	PA	54,050	C
Elmhurst College	IL	45,428	C
Elms College	MA	45,646	VC
Elon Univ	NC	44,599	VC+
Emmanuel College	MA	52,110	C+
Emory Univ	GA	60,786	MC
Emporia State Univ	KS	14,570	C
Endicott College	MA	44,604	VC+
Erskine College	SC	45,460	C
Eureka College	IL	30,220	C
Evangel Univ	MO	28,898	C
Fairfield Univ	CT	59,860	VC+
Fairmont State Univ	WV	15,726	C
Faulkner Univ	AL	26,410	C
Fayetteville State Univ	NC	17,756	C
Felician Univ	NJ	45,370	LC
Ferris State Univ	MI	21,445	C
Ferrum College	VA	39,650	C
Fisk Univ	TN	32,066	LC
Fitchburg State Univ	MA	21,819	C
Flagler College	FL	27,620	C
Florida A&M Univ	FL	15,361	C
Florida Atlantic Univ	FL	17,339	C
Florida Gulf Coast Univ	FL	9,682	C
Florida International Univ	FL	19,854	C+
Florida Memorial Univ	FL	22,270	LC
Florida State Univ	FL	16,771	HC
Fontbonne Univ	MO	33,717	C
Fordham Univ	NY	65,918	MC
Fort Hays State Univ	KS	12,131	C
Fort Lewis College	CO	18,980	C
Fort Valley State Univ	GA	17,988	VC
Framingham State Univ	MA	20,584	C
Francis Marion Univ	SC	16,464	LC
Franciscan Univ of Steubenville	OH	33,980	VC
Franklin and Marshall College	PA	63,170	HC
Franklin College	IN	39,380	C
Franklin Pierce Univ	NH	46,750	C
Freed-Hardeman Univ	TN	29,450	C
Fresno Pacific Univ	CA	37,370	C
Friends Univ	KS	34,455	C
Frostburg State Univ	MD	17,280	LC
Furman Univ	SC	58,092	VC+
Gallaudet Univ	DC	29,118	LC
Gannon Univ	PA	42,032	C
Gardner-Webb Univ	NC	39,200	C+
Geneva College	PA	35,450	C
George Mason Univ	VA	15,724	VC
George Washington Univ	DC	62,835	MC
Georgetown College	KY	41,440	C
Georgetown Univ	DC	65,926	MC
Georgia College & State Univ	GA	21,148	C+
Georgia Southern Univ	GA	16,596	C
Georgia Southwestern State Univ	GA	13,870	C
Georgia State Univ	GA	24,332	VC
Georgian Court Univ	NJ	42,426	LC
Gettysburg College	PA	63,000	HC
Glenville State College	WV	17,386	NC
Goddard College	VT	17,040	VC
Gonzaga Univ	WA	50,888	HC
Gordon College	MA	46,472	C+
Goshen College	IN	42,500	C
Goucher College	MD	55,716	VC
Grace College and Seminary	IN	31,524	C
Graceland Univ	IA	35,290	C
Grambling State Univ	LA	15,701	C
Grand Canyon Univ	AZ	16,950	VC
Grand Rapids Theological Seminary/Cornerstone Univ	MI	33,338	C
Grand Valley State Univ	MI	22,250	C+
Grand View Univ	IA	32,302	C
Green Mountain College	VT	45,228	LC
Greensboro College	NC	42,400	LC
Greenville College	IL	27,012	C
Grinnell College	IA	60,738	MC
Grove City College	PA	25,692	VC
Guilford College	NC	44,090	C
Gustavus Adolphus College	MN	52,433	HC
Gwynedd Mercy Univ	PA	43,780	LC
Hamilton College	NY	64,250	MC
Hamline Univ	MN	45,678	VC
Hampden-Sydney College	VA	56,248	C+
Hampton Univ	VA	34,926	LC
Hannibal-LaGrange Univ	MO	29,815	C
Hanover College	IN	46,364	C+
Harding Univ	AR	25,421	C
Hardin-Simmons Univ	TX	33,966	C
Hartwick College	NY	51,270	C
Harvard College/Harvard Univ	MA	60,659	MC
Hastings College	NE	35,380	C+
Haverford College	PA	66,490	MC
Hawaii Pacific Univ	HI	33,420	C
Heidelberg Univ	OH	39,200	C
Henderson State Univ	AR	15,516	LC
Hendrix College	AR	54,020	VC+
Heritage Univ	WA	19,825	NC
Hilbert College	NY	30,850	C
Hillsdale College	MI	35,722	MC
Hiram College	OH	43,230	C
Hollins Univ	VA	49,635	VC
Holy Family Univ	PA	43,326	LC
Holy Names Univ	CA	46,630	LC
Hood College	MD	54,840	C
Hope College	MI	39,940	VC
Houghton College	NY	39,090	C
Houston Baptist Univ	TX	36,450	C
Howard Payne Univ	TX	34,320	C
Howard Univ	DC	37,616	C+
Humboldt State Univ	CA	20,514	C
Huntingdon College	AL	34,900	C
Huntington Univ	IN	33,996	C
Husson Univ	ME	25,720	LC
Huston-Tillotson Univ	TX	18,124	LC
Idaho State Univ	ID	13,619	NC
Illinois College	IL	40,850	VC
Illinois State Univ	IL	23,418	VC
Illinois Wesleyan Univ	IL	56,430	VC+
Indiana State Univ	IN	23,223	LC
Indiana Univ Bloomington	IN	20,429	VC
Indiana Univ East	IN	7,072	C
Indiana Univ Kokomo	IN	7,073	C
Indiana Univ Northwest	IN	7,072	C
Indiana Univ of Pennsylvania	PA	23,614	LC
Indiana Univ South Bend	IN	14,242	C
Indiana Univ Southeast	IN	14,242	LC
Indiana Univ-Purdue Univ Fort Wayne	IN	17,553	C
Indiana Univ-Purdue Univ Indianapolis	IN	18,635	C
Indiana Wesleyan Univ	IN	33,674	C
Inter-American Univ of PR-San Germán	PR	20,042	
Iona College	NY	50,984	C
Iowa State Univ	IA	17,570	C
Ithaca College	NY	56,766	VC
Jackson State Univ	MS	15,879	LC
Jacksonville State Univ	AL	14,628	LC
Jacksonville Univ	FL	46,230	C
James Madison Univ	VA	19,084	VC
Jarvis Christian College	TX	20,160	NC
John Brown Univ	AR	33,132	VC
John Carroll Univ	OH	49,740	C+
Johns Hopkins Univ	MD	65,386	MC
Johnson & Wales Univ/Denver Campus	CO	42,707	C
Johnson C. Smith Univ	NC	25,336	LC
Johnson State College	VT	20,752	C
Judson College	AL	27,066	C
Judson Univ	IL	37,700	C
Juniata College	PA	53,760	VC
Kalamazoo College	MI	53,931	HC+
Kansas State Univ	KS	17,780	VC
Kansas Wesleyan Univ	KS	36,600	C
Kean Univ	NJ	24,650	C
Keene State College	NH	24,003	LC
Kennesaw State Univ	GA	19,592	VC
Kent State Univ	OH	20,732	C
Kentucky State Univ	KY	13,364	LC
Kentucky Wesleyan College	KY	32,080	C
Kenyon College	OH	63,330	MC
Keuka College	NY	39,762	C
King Univ	TN	34,660	C
King's College	PA	46,858	C
Kutztown Univ of Pennsylvania	PA	19,056	LC
La Roche College	PA	37,924	LC
La Salle Univ	PA	55,790	C
La Sierra Univ	CA	39,690	VC
Lafayette College	PA	63,355	MC
LaGrange College	GA	39,930	C
Lake Erie College	OH	38,914	LC
Lake Forest College	IL	50,652	VC
Lakeland Univ	WI	35,130	C
Lamar Univ	TX	18,014	LC
Lander Univ	SC	43,994	C
Lane College	TN	16,550	C
Langston Univ	OK	14,314	C
Lasell College	MA	47,500	C
Lawrence Tech Univ	MI	39,770	VC
Lawrence Univ	WI	54,498	HC
Le Moyne College	NY	46,000	C
Lebanon Valley College	PA	51,530	C
Lee Univ	TN	22,045	C
Lees-McRae College	NC	33,944	C
Lehigh Univ	PA	61,010	MC
LeMoyne-Owen College	TN	16,980	C
Lenoir-Rhyne Univ	NC	43,200	C
LeTourneau Univ	TX	38,250	VC
Lewis & Clark College	OR	58,434	HC+
Lewis Univ	IL	40,370	C
Lewis-Clark State College	ID	14,202	C
Liberty Univ	VA	19,101	C
Limestone College	SC	32,100	C
Lincoln Memorial Univ	TN	28,070	C
Lincoln Univ	MO	13,602	NC
Lindenwood Univ	MO	25,132	C
Lindsey Wilson College	KY	32,882	C
Linfield College	OR	52,010	C
Lipscomb Univ	TN	41,296	VC
LIU Brooklyn	NY	49,682	C
LIU Post	NY	49,682	C
Livingstone College	NC	17,815	LC
Lock Haven Univ of Pennsylvania	PA	18,028	LC
Longwood Univ	VA	22,184	C
Louisiana College	LA	21,886	C
Louisiana State Univ and A&M College	LA	18,677	VC
Louisiana State Univ in Shreveport	LA	6,902	C
Louisiana Tech Univ	LA	11,422	VC
Lourdes Univ	OH	29,520	NC
Loyola Marymount Univ	CA	58,038	HC
Loyola Univ Chicago	IL	55,802	VC
Loyola Univ Maryland	MD	60,300	VC
Luther College	IA	48,540	C+
Lycoming College	PA	48,580	C
Lynchburg College	VA	46,740	C
Lyndon State College	VT	20,714	C
Lyon College	AR	34,730	C+
Macalester College	MN	61,905	MC
MacMurray College	IL	33,620	C
Madonna Univ	MI	29,050	C
Malone Univ	OH	38,448	C
Manchester Univ	IN	40,422	C
Manhattan College	NY	51,750	C+
Manhattanville College	NY	51,440	C+
Mansfield Univ	PA	23,376	LC
Marian Univ	IN	41,220	C
Marian Univ	WI	32,420	LC
Marietta College	OH	46,190	C
Marist College	NY	49,860	VC
Marquette Univ	WI	48,390	VC+
Mars Hill Univ	NC	42,688	C
Marshall Univ	WV	17,242	C
Mary Baldwin Univ	VA	39,865	C
Marygrove College	MI	28,926	NC
Marymount Manhattan College	NY	46,280	VC
Marymount Univ	VA	41,570	LC
Maryville College	TN	44,410	C
Maryville Univ of St. Louis	MO	38,046	VC+
Marywood Univ	PA	46,900	C
Mass College of Liberal Arts	MA	20,128	C
Mayville State Univ	ND	18,371	NC
McDaniel College	MD	51,380	VC
McKendree Univ	IL	37,940	C+
McMurry Univ	TX	34,259	LC
McNeese State Univ	LA	7,838	C
McPherson College	KS	34,909	C
Medaille College	NY	35,112	C
Mercy College	NY	31,776	C
Mercyhurst Univ	PA	47,420	C
Meredith College	NC	45,297	C
Merrimack College	MA	52,770	C
Messiah College	PA	43,100	C+
Methodist Univ	NC	43,600	C

ST = STATE $IS = IN-STATE COSTS SR = SELECTOR RATING

School	ST	$IS	SR
Metropolitan State Univ	MN	7,566	C
Metropolitan State Univ of Denver	CO	29,889	LC
Miami Univ	OH	27,190	HC+
Mich State Univ	MI	23,898	VC+
Mich Tech Univ	MI	24,739	VC+
MidAmerica Nazarene Univ	KS	35,550	C
Middle Tenn State Univ	TN	8,650	C
Middlebury College	VT	64,332	MC
Midland Univ	NE	37,468	
Midway Univ	KY	31,640	LC
Midwestern State Univ	TX	17,572	C
Miles College	AL	18,646	NC
Millersville Univ of Pennsylvania	PA	23,782	C
Milligan College	TN	38,150	C
Millikin Univ	IL	42,158	C
Mills College	CA	59,163	VC
Millsaps College	MS	50,080	C+
Minn State Univ, Mankato	MN	15,616	C
Minn State Univ, Moorhead	MN	15,941	C
Minot State Univ	ND	12,732	C
Misericordia Univ	PA	43,840	C
Miss College	MS	25,850	C
Miss State Univ	MS	11,454	C+
Miss Univ for Women	MS	17,065	C
Miss Valley State Univ	MS	13,233	LC
Missouri Baptist Univ	MO	35,594	C
Missouri Southern State Univ	MO	12,499	C
Missouri State Univ	MO	15,190	C+
Missouri Univ of Science and Technology	MO	18,655	HC
Missouri Valley College	MO	28,150	C
Missouri Western State Univ	MO	16,741	
Molloy College	NY	40,440	C
Monmouth College	IL	42,260	C
Monmouth Univ	NJ	46,234	C
Montana State Univ	MT	15,500	C+
Montana State Univ-Billings	MT	22,960	C
Montana State Univ-Northern	MT	11,370	NC
Montclair State Univ	NJ	26,210	LC
Montreat College	NC	31,298	LC
Moravian College	PA	53,117	
Morehead State Univ	KY	17,422	C
Morehouse College	GA	40,064	C
Morgan State Univ	MD	17,190	LC
Morningside College	IA	36,865	C
Morris College	SC	18,500	LC
Mount Aloysius College	PA	29,976	C
Mount Holyoke College	MA	56,746	MC
Mount Ida College	MA	46,820	C
Mount Marty College	SD	32,972	C
Mount Mary Univ	WI	34,650	LC
Mount Mercy Univ	IA	36,826	C
Mount St. Mary College	NY	42,061	C
Mount St. Joseph Univ	OH	33,880	C
Mount St. Mary's Univ	MD	51,610	C
Mount St. Mary's Univ - Chalon Campus	CA	43,897	VC+
Mount Vernon Nazarene Univ	OH	34,500	C
Muhlenberg College	PA	56,645	VC+
Muskingum Univ	OH	35,966	C
Naropa Univ	CO	42,826	NC
National Louis Univ	IL	16,920	LC
National Univ	CA	14,730	LC
Nazareth College	NY	45,574	C
Nebr Wesleyan Univ	NE	38,140	C+
Neumann Univ	PA	40,678	LC
New College of Florida	FL	15,848	MC
New Jersey City Univ	NJ	21,456	LC
New Mexico Highlands Univ	NM	11,904	NC
New Mexico State Univ	NM	14,050	C
New York Inst of Technology	NY	48,730	C
New York Univ	NY	65,860	MC
Newberry College	SC	34,550	C
Newman Univ	KS	35,390	C
Niagara Univ	NY	41,010	C
Nicholls State Univ	LA	10,534	C
Nichols College	MA	46,800	LC
Norfolk State Univ	VA	25,702	LC
N Car A&T State Univ	NC	13,365	LC
N Car Central Univ	NC	9,000	C
N Car State Univ	NC	19,515	HC+
N Car Wesleyan College	NC	39,200	C
North Central College	IL	48,712	VC
N Dak State Univ	ND	16,245	C
North Park Univ	IL	35,860	C
Northeastern Illinois Univ	IL	12,529	LC
Northeastern State Univ	OK	8,615	VC
Northeastern Univ	MA	62,703	MC
Northern Arizona Univ	AZ	20,246	VC
Northern Illinois Univ	IL	20,176	C
Northern Kentucky Univ	KY	16,486	C
Northern Mich Univ	MI	19,604	C
Northern State Univ	SD	14,505	C
Northland College	WI	41,103	C+
Northwest Missouri State Univ	MO	17,737	C
Northwest Nazarene Univ	ID	36,000	C
Northwest Univ	WA	35,876	VC
Northwestern Okla State Univ	OK	13,072	NC
Northwestern Univ	IL	66,344	MC
Norwich Univ	VT	28,212	C
Notre Dame College	OH	37,150	VC
Notre Dame de Namur Univ	CA	46,526	LC
Notre Dame of Maryland Univ	MD	46,465	VC
Nyack College	NY	34,050	NC
Oakland City Univ	IN	33,360	NC
Oakland Univ	MI	20,763	C
Oakwood Univ	AL	43,758	C
Oberlin College	OH	66,012	MC
Occidental College	CA	65,530	MC
Oglethorpe Univ	GA	44,200	C+
Ohio Dominican Univ	OH	41,340	C+
Ohio Northern Univ	OH	44,050	VC
Ohio State Univ at Columbus	OH	21,703	HC+
Ohio State Univ at Lima	OH	7,140	C
Ohio State Univ at Mansfield	OH	13,160	C
Ohio State Univ at Marion	OH	7,140	C
Ohio State Univ at Newark	OH	7,140	C
Ohio Univ	OH	22,924	C
Ohio Valley Univ	WV	29,480	C
Ohio Wesleyan Univ	OH	49,460	VC
Okla Baptist Univ	OK	32,320	C
Okla Christian Univ	OK	27,650	VC
Okla City Univ	OK	40,476	VC
Okla Panhandle State Univ	OK	6,152	NC
Okla State Univ	OK	17,180	VC
Okla Wesleyan Univ	OK	33,206	C
Old Dominion Univ	VA	20,910	C
Olivet College	MI	36,110	LC
Olivet Nazarene Univ	IL	41,840	C
Oral Roberts Univ	OK	34,316	C
Oregon State Univ	OR	22,519	VC
Ottawa Univ	KS	36,074	VC
Otterbein Univ	OH	41,630	C
Ouachita Baptist Univ	AR	32,320	C
Our Lady of the Lake Univ	TX	35,012	LC
Pace Univ	NY	58,248	C
Pacific Lutheran Univ	WA	49,960	VC
Pacific Union College	CA	36,009	VC
Paine College	GA	19,506	LC
Palm Beach Atlantic Univ	FL	39,720	C
Park Univ	MO	20,329	C
Paul Quinn College	TX	25,350	LC
Penn State Erie/The Behrend College	PA	16,256	C
Penn State Univ/Altoona	PA	24,584	C
Pepperdine Univ	CA	74,460	HC+
Peru State College	NE	14,768	NC
Philander Smith College	AR	20,814	LC
Piedmont College	GA	32,512	C
Pine Manor College	MA	41,660	LC
Pittsburg State Univ	KS	13,880	NC
Pitzer College	CA	66,192	MC
Plymouth State Univ	NH	23,180	LC
Point Park Univ	PA	41,270	C
Pomona College	CA	64,957	MC
Pontifical Catholic Univ of PR	PR	10,534	
Portland State Univ	OR	19,443	C
Post Univ	CT	41,150	C
Prairie View A&M Univ	TX	15,205	LC
Prescott College	AZ	33,284	C
Princeton Univ	NJ	57,610	MC
Principia College	IL	39,010	C+
Providence College	RI	60,760	VC
Purdue Univ/Northwest	IN	15,038	C
Purdue Univ/West Lafayette	IN	20,032	MC
Quincy Univ	IL	36,998	C
Quinnipiac Univ	CT	59,110	C
Radford Univ	VA	19,027	LC
Randolph College	VA	45,660	VC
Randolph-Macon College	VA	49,910	C
Regis College	MA	51,920	C
Regis Univ	CO	44,520	C
Rhode Island College	RI	17,694	LC
Rhodes College	TN	51,900	HC
Rice Univ	TX	57,668	MC
Rider Univ	NJ	54,050	C
Ripon College	WI	46,911	C+
Rivier Univ	NH	40,410	VC
Robert Morris Univ	PA	37,834	C
Roberts Wesleyan College	NY	38,306	C
Rochester College	MI	28,574	LC
Rockford Univ	IL	36,030	C
Rockhurst Univ	MO	29,220	C
Roger Williams Univ	RI	46,296	C+
Rollins College	FL	58,670	HC
Roosevelt Univ	IL	40,651	VC
Rosemont College	PA	30,980	C
Rowan Univ	NJ	24,491	VC+
Russell Sage College	NY	39,370	C
Rust College	MS	10,600	C
Rutgers Univ - Camden	NJ	26,146	C
Rutgers Univ - New Brunswick	NJ	26,632	HC
Rutgers Univ - Newark	NJ	27,288	C
Sacred Heart Univ	CT	52,750	C
Saginaw Valley State Univ	MI	18,530	C
St. Anselm College	NH	52,560	C+
St. Augustine's Univ	NC	26,048	C
St. Francis Univ	PA	42,268	NC
St. John's Univ	MN	51,624	C
St. Joseph's College of Maine	ME	46,485	C
St. Joseph's Univ	PA	57,544	VC+
St. Leo Univ	FL	31,650	C
St. Louis Univ	MO	49,866	HC
St. Martin's Univ	WA	45,056	C
St. Mary-of-the-Woods College	IN	39,632	LC
St. Mary's College of Calif	CA	57,420	C
St. Michael's College	VT	51,725	VC+
St. Peter's Univ	NJ	49,192	C
St. Vincent College	PA	44,626	C
St. Xavier Univ	IL	43,310	C
Salem College	NC	37,694	HC
Salem State Univ	MA	17,303	LC
Salisbury Univ	MD	20,714	VC
Salve Regina Univ	RI	51,470	C
Sam Houston State Univ	TX	18,792	C
Samford Univ	AL	39,232	VC
San Diego Christian College	CA	39,068	C
San Diego State Univ	CA	21,896	C+
San Francisco State Univ	CA	18,514	LC
San Jose State Univ	CA	21,540	C
Sarah Lawrence College	NY	63,388	HC
Savannah State Univ	GA	15,631	C
Schreiner Univ	TX	34,626	LC
Scripps College	CA	66,664	MC
Seattle Pacific Univ	WA	47,439	C+
Seattle Univ	WA	50,811	VC+
Seton Hall Univ	NJ	55,514	C
Seton Hill Univ	PA	46,972	C
Sewanee: The Univ of the South	TN	54,500	MC
Shaw Univ	NC	24,638	C
Shenandoah Univ	VA	41,312	C
Shepherd Univ, West Virginia	WV	17,224	C
Shippensburg Univ of Pennsylvania	PA	23,208	C
Shorter Univ	GA	31,130	LC
Siena College	NY	48,916	C+
Siena Heights Univ	MI	32,040	C
Silver Lake College of the Holy Family	WI	36,290	LC
Simmons College	MA	53,090	VC
Simpson College	IA	43,839	VC
Simpson Univ	CA	33,700	C
Skidmore College	NY	64,214	HC
Slippery Rock Univ of Pennsylvania	PA	10,360	C
Smith College	MA	63,914	MC
Sonoma State Univ	CA	27,806	C
S Car State Univ	SC	20,805	LC
S Dak State Univ	SD	15,634	C
Southeast Missouri State Univ	MO	15,498	C
Southeastern Louisiana Univ	LA	16,237	C
Southeastern Okla State Univ	OK	11,875	C
Southeastern Univ	FL	31,765	C
Southern Adventist Univ	TN	27,600	C
Southern Arkansas Univ	AR	21,532	C
Southern Conn State Univ	CT	21,924	LC
Southern Illinois Univ Carbondale	IL	23,667	C
Southern Illinois Univ Edwardsville	IL	22,643	C
Southern Methodist Univ	TX	66,483	MC
Southern Nazarene Univ	OK	32,798	NC
Southern New Hampshire Univ	NH	43,198	C
Southern Oregon Univ	OR	19,117	C
Southern Univ and A&M College	LA	16,074	LC+
Southern Univ at New Orleans	LA	8,014	LC
Southern Vermont College	VT	34,670	LC
Southern Wesleyan Univ	SC	32,130	LC
Southwest Baptist Univ	MO	29,900	LC
Southwestern Adventist Univ	TX	27,756	LC
Southwestern College	KS	31,531	C
Southwestern Okla State Univ	OK	11,790	C
Southwestern Univ	TX	50,720	VC
Spelman College	GA	38,751	C
Spring Arbor Univ	MI	36,000	C
Spring Hill College	AL	48,488	C
Springfield College	MA	45,995	C
St. Ambrose Univ	IA	39,019	C
St. Ambrose Univ	IA	39,019	C
St. Bonaventure Univ	NY	44,237	C
St. Catherine Univ	MN	45,630	VC
St. Cloud State Univ	MN	10,600	C
St. Francis College	NY	38,800	LC
St. John Fisher College	NY	43,620	C
St. John's Univ	NY	55,850	C
St. Joseph's College, New York/Brooklyn Campus	NY	25,114	LC
St. Joseph's College, New York/Long Island Campus	NY	25,124	C
St. Lawrence Univ	NY	64,390	VC
St. Mary's College of Maryland	MD	26,634	VC
St. Mary's Univ	TX	37,500	C
St. Norbert College	WI	44,525	VC
St. Olaf College	MN	54,260	HC+
St. Thomas Aquinas College	NY	42,200	C
St. Thomas Univ	FL	36,360	LC
Stanford Univ	CA	60,409	MC
SUNY / Buffalo State College	NY	20,842	C
SUNY / SUNY Cortland	NY	20,706	VC
SUNY / SUNY Fredonia	NY	20,818	C
SUNY / SUNY Oneonta	NY	19,712	C+
SUNY / SUNY Plattsburgh	NY	18,814	C
SUNY / SUNY Potsdam	NY	20,404	C+
SUNY / Univ at Buffalo	NY	23,122	C+
SUNY at Binghamton	NY	22,861	MC
SUNY at Geneseo	NY	20,440	VC+
SUNY at New Paltz	NY	19,200	C
SUNY at Oswego	NY	21,351	C
SUNY SUNY Albany	NY	22,165	C
Stephen F. Austin State Univ	TX	18,406	LC
Stephens College	MO	38,042	C
Sterling College	KS	32,830	C
Stetson Univ	FL	53,544	VC
Stillman College	AL	20,738	C
Stonehill College	MA	55,030	C+
Stony Brook Univ/The SUNY	NY	21,881	MC
Suffolk Univ	MA	50,308	C
Sul Ross State Univ	TX	15,021	LC
Susquehanna Univ	PA	55,340	VC
Syracuse Univ	NY	60,239	VC
Tabor College	KS	35,870	C
Talladega College	AL	19,215	C
Tarleton State Univ	TX	15,248	LC
Taylor Univ	IN	40,317	C+
Temple Univ	PA	24,392	VC
Tenn State Univ	TN	14,423	C
Tenn Tech Univ	TN	17,050	C
Texas A&M Univ	TX	20,521	VC+
Texas A&M Univ at Commerce	TX	10,496	C
Texas A&M Univ at Corpus Christi	TX	16,851	LC
Texas A&M Univ at Kingsville	TX	7,500	LC
Texas Christian Univ	TX	54,670	HC
Texas Lutheran Univ	TX	38,620	C
Texas Southern Univ	TX	18,212	LC
Texas State Univ	TX	19,350	C
Texas Tech Univ	TX	18,736	C+
Texas Wesleyan Univ	TX	35,134	C
Texas Woman's Univ	TX	15,302	LC
The Catholic Univ of America	DC	56,356	VC
The Citadel, The Military College of S Car	SC	35,339	C
The College at Brockport - SUNY	NY	20,346	C
The College of New Jersey	NJ	31,909	HC
The College of New Rochelle	NY	46,300	VC
The College of St. Rose	NY	43,048	C
The College of Wooster	OH	57,900	VC+
The Master's Univ	CA	43,870	C+
The Univ of Akron	OH	21,477	C
The Univ of Tenn at Chattanooga	TN	16,744	C
The Univ of Tenn at Knoxville	TN	22,112	VC
The Univ of Tenn at Martin	TN	14,876	C
The Univ of Utah	UT	17,924	VC
The Univ of Virginia's College at Wise	VA	18,192	LC
Thiel College	PA	41,590	C
Thomas College	ME	35,268	LC
Thomas Edison State Univ	NJ	6,350	NC
Thomas More College	KY	36,720	C
Tiffin Univ	OH	31,380	C
Toccoa Falls College	GA	27,920	C
Tougaloo College	MS	17,980	NC
Touro College	NY	28,950	VC
Towson Univ	MD	17,408	VC
Transylvania Univ	KY	45,690	VC+
Trevecca Nazarene Univ	TN	31,186	C
Trinity Christian College	IL	35,580	C
Trinity College	CT	63,920	HC+
Trinity International Univ	IL	31,070	VC
Trinity Univ	TX	52,314	HC+
Trinity Washington Univ	DC	33,826	C+
Troy Univ	AL	16,171	C
Truman State Univ	MO	16,014	HC
Tufts Univ	MA		MC
Tulane Univ	LA	63,396	HC+
Tusculum College	TN	31,625	C
Tuskegee Univ	AL	28,164	C
Union College	KY	32,310	C
Union College	NE	23,270	C
Union College	NY	64,320	MC
Union Univ	TN	33,970	VC
United States Air Force Academy	CO		C
United States Military Academy at West Point	NY		HC+
United States Naval Academy	MD		MC
Universidad del Turabo	PR	17,828	
Univ of Alabama	AL	24,320	C+
Univ of Alabama at Birmingham	AL	19,906	C
Univ of Alabama in Huntsville	AL	19,445	VC
Univ of Alaska Anchorage	AK	16,652	NC
Univ of Alaska Fairbanks	AK	16,179	C
Univ of Arizona	AZ	23,100	C
Univ of Arkansas at Fayetteville	AR	19,152	C+
Univ of Arkansas at Little Rock	AR	18,211	C
Univ of Arkansas at Monticello	AR	13,134	NC
Univ of Arkansas at Pine Bluff	AR	13,541	C
Univ of Bridgeport	CT	44,430	LC
Univ of Calif at Berkeley	CA	28,853	MC
Univ of Calif at Davis	CA	28,468	HC
Univ of Calif at Irvine	CA	26,484	VC
Univ of Calif at Los Angeles	CA	30,162	MC
Univ of Calif at Riverside	CA	29,227	C+
Univ of Calif at Santa Barbara	CA	29,091	HC
Univ of Central Arkansas	AR	14,472	VC
Univ of Central Florida	FL	15,922	VC
Univ of Central Missouri	MO	18,982	C

ST = STATE $IS = IN-STATE COSTS SR = SELECTOR RATING

School	ST	$IS	SR
Univ of Central Okla	OK	13,486	C
Univ of Chicago	IL	67,584	MC
Univ of Cincinnati	OH	21,964	VC
Univ of Colo Boulder	CO	24,285	VC+
Univ of Colo Colo Springs	CO	19,663	C
Univ of Colo Denver	CO	23,230	C
Univ of Conn	CT	25,538	HC
Univ of Dallas	TX	45,500	VC+
Univ of Dayton	OH	53,620	C
Univ of Delaware	DE	24,976	VC+
Univ of Denver	CO	58,443	VC+
Univ of Detroit Mercy	MI	48,816	C+
Univ of Dubuque	IA	37,824	C
Univ of Findlay	OH	60,139	C
Univ of Florida	FL	16,291	HC+
Univ of Georgia	GA	21,250	HC
Univ of Great Falls	MT	38,524	C
Univ of Hartford	CT	49,776	C
Univ of Hawaii at Hilo	HI	18,038	C
Univ of Hawaii at Manoa	HI	23,221	C
Univ of Holy Cross	LA	21,523	C
Univ of Houston	TX	21,483	VC
Univ of Houston-Downtown	TX	7,241	C
Univ of Idaho	ID	15,348	C
Univ of Illinois at Chicago	IL	25,006	VC
Univ of Illinois at Urbana-Champaign	IL	27,006	HC
Univ of Indianapolis	IN	36,480	C
Univ of Iowa	IA	18,683	VC+
Univ of Jamestown	ND	28,508	C
Univ of Kansas	KS	20,135	C+
Univ of Kentucky	KY	33,306	C
Univ of La Verne	CA	55,600	C
Univ of Louisiana at Lafayette	LA	14,516	C
Univ of Louisiana at Monroe	LA	15,970	C
Univ of Louisville	KY	19,824	C
Univ of Maine	ME	20,792	C
Univ of Maine at Augusta	ME	7,812	C
Univ of Maine at Farmington	ME	18,187	C
Univ of Maine at Fort Kent	ME	15,165	LC
Univ of Maine at Machias	ME	22,960	C
Univ of Maine at Presque Isle	ME	14,870	C
Univ of Mary	ND	23,180	C
Univ of Mary Hardin-Baylor	TX	33,950	C+
Univ of Mary Washington	VA	24,764	VC
Univ of Maryland/Baltimore County	MD	21,296	VC
Univ of Maryland/College Park	MD	21,938	HC
Univ of Maryland/Eastern Shore	MD	17,013	C
Univ of Maryland/Univ College	MD	25,966	LC
Univ of Mass Amherst	MA	26,199	VC+
Univ of Mass Boston	MA	13,435	C
Univ of Mass Lowell	MA	26,380	C
Univ of Memphis	TN	18,278	C
Univ of Miami	FL	63,494	MC
Univ of Mich/Ann Arbor	MI	24,410	MC
Univ of Mich/Dearborn	MI	11,757	VC
Univ of Mich-Flint	MI	17,607	C+
Univ of Minn/Duluth	MN	20,292	C+
Univ of Minn/Morris	MN	20,760	VC
Univ of Minn/Twin Cities	MN	23,519	HC+
Univ of Miss	MS	17,746	C+
Univ of Missouri/Columbia	MO	18,201	MC
Univ of Missouri-Kansas City	MO	19,563	VC
Univ of Missouri-St. Louis	MO		C
Univ of Mobile	AL	28,935	C
Univ of Montana	MT	14,105	C
Univ of Montana-Western	MT	11,220	LC
Univ of Montevallo	AL	19,502	C
Univ of Mount Olive	NC	18,426	C
Univ of Mount Union	OH	38,970	C
Univ of Nebr - Kearney	NE	16,546	LC
Univ of Nebr - Lincoln	NE	18,589	VC
Univ of Nebr - Omaha	NE	16,120	C
Univ of Nevada, Las Vegas	NV	17,553	C
Univ of Nevada/Reno	NV	18,010	C
Univ of New England	ME	48,880	C
Univ of New Hampshire	NH	28,562	VC
Univ of New Hampshire - Manchester	NH	14,490	C
Univ of New Haven	CT	52,190	C
Univ of New Mexico	NM	15,404	C
Univ of New Orleans	LA	12,840	C
Univ of North Alabama	AL	15,398	C
Univ of N Car at Asheville	NC	15,723	VC+
Univ of N Car at Chapel Hill	NC	20,052	HC+
Univ of N Car at Charlotte	NC	15,547	C
Univ of N Car at Greensboro	NC	14,690	C
Univ of N Car at Pembroke	NC	14,388	LC
Univ of N Car at Wilmington	NC	14,590	VC
Univ of N Dak	ND	15,373	C
Univ of North Florida	FL	15,996	VC
Univ of North Georgia	GA	17,316	C
Univ of North Texas	TX	19,198	C
Univ of Northern Colo	CO	20,851	C
Univ of Northwestern - St. Paul	MN	38,160	C
Univ of Notre Dame	IN	64,043	MC
Univ of Okla	OK	18,911	VC
Univ of Oregon	OR	22,972	C
Univ of Pennsylvania	PA	63,526	MC
Univ of Pikeville	KY	28,700	NC
Univ of Pittsburgh at Bradford	PA	22,402	C
Univ of Pittsburgh at Johnstown	PA	22,092	C
Univ of Portland	OR	52,152	VC
Univ of PR, at Cayey	PR		
Univ of PR, at Humacao	PR	14,000	
Univ of PR, at Mayaguez	PR	13,995	
Univ of PR-Rio Piedras campus	PR	13,327	
Univ of Puget Sound	WA	56,456	VC+
Univ of Redlands	CA	60,200	VC
Univ of Rhode Island	RI	24,906	C
Univ of Richmond	VA	60,880	MC
Univ of Rio Grande & Rio Grande Community College	OH	8,750	NC
Univ of Rochester	NY	65,032	MC
Univ of St. Francis	IN	37,400	C
Univ of St. Joseph	CT	49,550	C
Univ of St. Mary	KS	34,690	C
Univ of San Diego	CA	58,442	VC+
Univ of San Francisco	CA	58,484	VC
Univ of Science and Arts of Okla	OK	11,140	VC
Univ of Scranton	PA	54,962	VC
Univ of Sioux Falls	SD	34,330	C
Univ of South Alabama	AL	16,400	C
Univ of S Car Aiken	SC	16,712	C
Univ of S Car at Columbia	SC	19,725	VC+
Univ of S Car Upstate	SC	18,200	LC
Univ of S Dak	SD	16,109	C
Univ of South Florida/St. Petersburg	FL	15,980	C
Univ of Southern Calif	CA	66,631	C
Univ of Southern Indiana	IN	16,501	C
Univ of Southern Maine	ME	18,320	C
Univ of Southern Miss	MS	13,170	C
Univ of St. Francis	IL	39,924	C
Univ of St. Thomas - Houston	TX	40,020	VC
Univ of Tampa	FL	36,944	C
Univ of Texas at Arlington	TX	18,026	LC
Univ of Texas at Austin	TX	26,102	HC
Univ of Texas at El Paso	TX	34,452	NC
Univ of Texas at San Antonio	TX	20,157	C
Univ of the Cumberlands	KY	32,000	C
Univ of the District of Columbia	DC	21,044	LC
Univ of the Incarnate Word	TX	39,162	LC
Univ of the Ozarks	AR	52,176	C
Univ of the Pacific	CA	57,006	VC
Univ of the Southwest	NM	22,766	C
Univ of Toledo	OH	19,336	NC
Univ of Tulsa	OK	52,625	HC+
Univ of Vermont	VT	28,878	HC
Univ of Virginia	VA	25,891	MC
Univ of Washington	WA	23,149	VC
Univ of West Alabama	AL	15,516	NC
Univ of West Florida	FL	15,848	C
Univ of West Georgia	GA	16,360	LC
Univ of Wisc-Eau Claire	WI	15,797	VC
Univ of Wisc-Green Bay	WI	15,064	C
Univ of Wisc-La Crosse	WI	15,247	C+
Univ of Wisc-Madison	WI	20,934	MC
Univ of Wisc-Milwaukee	WI	21,496	C
Univ of Wisc-Oshkosh	WI	15,200	C
Univ of Wisc-Parkside	WI	15,193	C
Univ of Wisc-Platteville	WI	14,614	VC
Univ of Wisc-River Falls	WI	14,485	C
Univ of Wisc-Stevens Point	WI	14,043	C
Univ of Wisc-Superior	WI	14,446	C
Univ of Wisc-Whitewater	WI	13,976	C
Univ of Wyoming	WY	15,375	C+
Upper Iowa Univ	IA	34,990	NC
Urbana Univ	OH	30,820	C
Ursinus College	PA	61,690	VC
Ursuline College	OH	41,076	LC
Utah State Univ	UT	12,736	C
Utica College	NY	30,430	C
Valley City State Univ	ND	13,267	C
Valparaiso Univ	IN	48,370	C+
Vanderbilt Univ	TN	60,572	MC
Vanguard Univ of Southern Calif	CA	40,740	VC
Vassar College	NY	65,491	MC
Villanova Univ	PA	62,523	MC
Virginia Commonwealth Univ	VA	23,049	C
Virginia Military Inst	VA	26,460	C+
Virginia Polytechnic Inst and State Univ	VA	21,276	HC
Virginia Union Univ	VA	22,421	C
Virginia Wesleyan College	VA	43,728	LC
Viterbo Univ	WI	34,660	C
Voorhees College	SC	19,976	C
Wabash College	IN	50,650	VC
Wagner College	NY	55,480	C+
Wake Forest Univ	NC	64,056	MC
Walla Walla Univ	WA	30,417	NC
Walsh Univ	OH	39,010	C
Warner Pacific College	OR	33,790	C
Warner Univ	FL	28,216	C
Warren Wilson College	NC	44,220	VC
Wartburg College	IA	47,840	C
Washburn Univ	KS	15,827	C
Washington & Jefferson College	PA	56,512	VC
Washington Adventist Univ	MD	31,440	LC
Washington and Lee Univ	VA	59,647	MC
Washington College	MD	54,666	VC
Washington State Univ	WA	22,495	C
Washington Univ in St. Louis	MO	65,366	VC
Wayland Baptist Univ	TX	22,356	LC
Wayne State College	NE	12,802	C
Wayne State Univ	MI	22,016	C
Waynesburg Univ	PA	32,290	C
Weber State Univ	UT	10,721	C
Webster Univ	MO	37,490	C
Wellesley College	MA	63,916	MC
Wells College	NY	50,500	C
Wesley College	DE	37,026	LC
Wesleyan College	GA	29,694	C+
Wesleyan Univ	CT	65,516	MC
West Chester Univ of Pennsylvania	PA	18,456	C
West Liberty Univ	WV	15,512	C
West Texas A&M Univ	TX	13,478	C
West Virginia State Univ	WV	8,378	NC
West Virginia Univ	WV	18,210	C
West Virginia Wesleyan College	WV	36,858	C
Western Carolina Univ	NC	13,965	C
Western Conn State Univ	CT	21,254	LC
Western Illinois Univ	IL	20,825	C
Western Kentucky Univ	KY	16,850	C
Western Mich Univ	MI	21,054	C
Western New England Univ	MA	48,088	C
Western New Mexico Univ	NM	16,734	LC
Western Oregon Univ	OR	15,021	LC
Western State Colo Univ	CO	18,639	C
Western Washington Univ	WA	18,003	C+
Westfield State Univ	MA	19,671	C
Westminster College	MO	32,820	C
Westminster College	PA	39,180	C+
Westminster College	UT	41,078	C+
Westmont College	CA	56,410	HC
Wheaton College	IL	43,610	MC
Wheaton College	MA	61,512	VC
Wheeling Jesuit Univ	WV	37,106	LC
Whitman College	WA	59,772	MC
Whittier College	CA	57,891	C
Whitworth Univ	WA	51,732	VC
Wichita State Univ	KS	21,643	C
Widener Univ	PA	56,486	C
Wiley College	TX	18,504	C
Wilkes Univ	PA	45,622	C
Willamette Univ	OR	61,817	VC+
William Carey Univ	MS	23,950	LC
William Jewell College	MO	41,210	C+
William Paterson Univ of New Jersey	NJ	23,133	C
William Peace Univ	NC	37,430	LC
William Penn Univ	IA	26,000	C
William Woods Univ	MO	32,040	C
Williams Baptist College	AR	24,720	C
Williams College	MA	63,290	MC
Wilmington College	OH	34,600	C
Wilson College	PA	35,620	C
Wingate Univ	NC	39,950	C
Winona State Univ	MN	17,535	C
Winston-Salem State Univ	NC	26,166	LC
Winthrop Univ	SC	23,082	C
Wisc Lutheran College	WI	36,290	VC
Wittenberg Univ	OH	48,156	C+
Wofford College	SC	49,885	VC
Worcester State Univ	MA	20,977	C
Wright State Univ	OH	16,983	C
Xavier Univ	OH	47,880	C+
Xavier Univ of Louisiana	LA	31,689	C+
Yale Univ	CT	64,650	MC
Yeshiva Univ	NY	47,250	VC+
York College	NE	24,300	C
York College of Pennsylvania	PA	29,240	C
Youngstown State Univ	OH	17,307	C

ENGLISH AND PROFESSIONAL COMMUNICATION

School	ST	$IS	SR
Black Hills State Univ	SD	15,899	C
Bloomfield College	NJ	39,100	LC
Farmingdale State College	NY	20,624	C
Johnson & Wales Univ/Denver Campus	CO	42,707	C
Okla Baptist Univ	OK	32,320	C
Taylor Univ	IN	40,317	C+

ENGLISH AS A SECOND/FOREIGN LANGUAGE

School	ST	$IS	SR
Bloomfield College	NJ	39,100	LC
Doane Univ	NE	39,184	VC
Dordt College	IA	37,860	C+
Holy Names Univ	CA	46,630	LC
Houghton College	NY	39,090	C
Huntington Univ	IN	33,996	C
La Sierra Univ	CA	39,690	VC
Lenoir-Rhyne Univ	NC	43,200	C
Lewis Univ	IL	40,370	C
Liberty Univ	VA	19,101	C
Maryville College	TN	44,410	C
Millersville Univ of Pennsylvania	PA	23,782	C
Minn State Univ, Mankato	MN	15,616	C
Salem International Univ	WV	21,090	LC
Salisbury Univ	MD	20,714	VC
Southern New Hampshire Univ	NH	43,198	C
St. Ambrose Univ	IA	39,019	C
St. Ambrose Univ	IA	39,019	C
SUNY at Oswego	NY	21,351	C
Taylor Univ	IN	40,317	C+
Union Univ	TN	33,970	VC
Univ of Arizona	AZ	23,100	C
Univ of Central Okla	OK	13,486	C
Univ of Findlay	OH	60,139	C
Univ of Hawaii at Manoa	HI	23,221	C
Univ of Northwestern - St. Paul	MN	38,160	C
Univ of Southern Indiana	IN	16,501	C
Univ of Wisc-Green Bay	WI	15,064	C
Western Kentucky Univ	KY	16,850	C

ENGLISH COMM SECONDARY EDUCATION

School	ST	$IS	SR
Grove City College	PA	25,692	VC
Ithaca College	NY	56,766	VC
Western Mich Univ	MI	21,054	C
Wilson College	PA	35,620	C

ENGLISH EDUCATION

School	ST	$IS	SR
Abilene Christian Univ	TX	41,800	C+
Adams State Univ	CO	17,703	LC
Alabama State Univ	AL	14,142	NC
Albion College	MI	52,650	C
Andrews Univ	MI	28,030	C+
Appalachian State Univ	NC	14,416	VC
Aquinas College - Mich	MI	38,876	HC
Arkansas State Univ	AR	16,190	C
Armstrong State Univ	GA	16,962	C
Asbury Univ	KY	35,180	C+
Ashford Univ	CA	10,480	C
Ashland Univ	OH	21,440	C
Auburn Univ	AL	23,594	VC+
Augustana College	IL	49,658	VC
Averett Univ	VA	40,970	LC
Bayamon Central Univ	PR	12,490	
Baylor Univ	TX	53,760	HC
Bennett College	NC	27,302	NC
Bethany College	KS	46,100	NC
Bethany College	WV	36,300	NC
Bethel Univ	MN	45,270	VC
Bethune-Cookman Univ	FL	22,970	C
Black Hills State Univ	SD	15,899	C
Blackburn College	IL	28,526	LC
Bloomfield College	NJ	39,100	LC
Blue Mountain College	MS	15,949	VC
Boise State Univ	ID	14,860	C
Boston Univ	MA	65,110	MC
Brigham Young Univ	UT	12,748	HC
Brigham Young Univ/Hawaii	HI	11,290	C
Calvin College	MI	41,570	VC+
Cameron Univ	OK	11,072	NC
Canisius College	NY	47,537	C
Carthage College	WI	48,835	C
Cedarville Univ	OH	34,990	VC
Central Washington Univ	WA	16,803	C
CUNY/Brooklyn College	NY	5,884	C+
CUNY/City College	NY	20,319	VC
Claflin Univ	SC	33,764	LC
Coker College	SC	34,810	LC
Colby-Sawyer College	NH	50,790	C
College of the Ozarks	MO	7,230	C
Colo State Univ	CO	22,162	VC
Concordia Univ St. Paul	MN	29,050	C
Covenant College	GA	38,990	VC
Daemen College	NY	38,045	C
Dakota State Univ	SD	13,811	C
Dallas Baptist Univ	TX	33,713	C
Delaware State Univ	DE	19,376	NC
Delta State Univ	MS	13,176	C
Dordt College	IA	37,860	C+
Duquesne Univ	PA	46,822	VC
East Carolina Univ	NC	16,937	C
East Central Univ	OK	13,056	C
East Texas Baptist Univ	TX	33,134	C
Eastern Mich Univ	MI	19,761	C
Edgewood College	WI	35,950	C
Elizabethtown College	PA	54,050	C
Emory and Henry College	VA	41,410	C
Faulkner Univ	AL	26,410	C
Ferris State Univ	MI	21,445	C
Flagler College	FL	27,620	C
Florida Atlantic Univ	FL	17,339	C
Florida State Univ	FL	16,771	HC
Fontbonne Univ	MO	33,717	C
Franklin College	IN	39,380	C
Fresno Pacific Univ	CA	37,370	C
Friends Univ	KS	34,455	C
Gannon Univ	PA	42,032	C
Georgetown College	KY	41,440	C
Glenville State College	WV	17,386	NC
Goddard College	VT	17,040	VC
Goshen College	IN	42,500	C
Grace College and Seminary	IN	31,524	C
Grambling State Univ	LA	15,701	C
Grand Rapids Theological Seminary/Cornerstone Univ	MI	33,338	C
Green Mountain College	VT	45,228	LC
Greensboro College	NC	42,400	LC
Greenville College	IL	27,012	C
Hardin-Simmons Univ	TX	33,966	C
Hofstra Univ	NY	55,960	C+
Hood College	MD	54,840	C
Hope College	MI	39,940	VC
Houghton College	NY	39,090	C

ST = STATE $IS = IN-STATE COSTS SR = SELECTOR RATING

School	ST	$IS	SR
Humboldt State Univ	CA	20,514	C
Huntingdon College	AL	34,900	C
Huntington Univ	IN	33,996	C
Husson Univ	ME	25,720	LC
Indiana Univ Bloomington	IN	20,429	VC
Indiana Univ Northwest	IN	7,072	C
Indiana Univ of Pennsylvania	PA	23,614	LC
Indiana Univ South Bend	IN	14,242	C
Indiana Univ-Purdue Univ Fort Wayne	IN	17,553	C
Indiana Univ-Purdue Univ Indianapolis	IN	18,635	C
Indiana Wesleyan Univ	IN	33,674	C
Ithaca College	NY	56,766	VC
John Brown Univ	AR	33,132	VC
Johnson State College	VT	20,752	C
Judson College	AL	27,066	C
Juniata College	PA	53,760	VC
Kennesaw State Univ	GA	19,592	VC
Kentucky Christian Univ	KY	26,560	LC
Kutztown Univ of Pennsylvania	PA	19,056	LC
Le Moyne College	NY	46,000	C
Lenoir-Rhyne Univ	NC	43,200	C
Limestone College	SC	32,100	C
Lincoln Univ	MO	13,602	NC
Lipscomb Univ	TN	41,296	VC
LIU Brooklyn	NY	49,682	C
LIU Post	NY	49,682	C
Louisiana College	LA	21,886	C
Lyndon State College	VT	20,714	C
Marian Univ	WI	32,420	LC
Marist College	NY	49,860	VC
Marshall Univ	WV	17,242	C
Marymount Univ	VA	41,570	LC
Marywood Univ	PA	46,900	C
Mayville State Univ	ND	18,371	NC
McMurry Univ	TX	34,259	LC
Messiah College	PA	43,100	C+
Miami Univ	OH	27,190	HC+
MidAmerica Nazarene Univ	KS	35,550	C
Millersville Univ of Pennsylvania	PA	23,782	C
Millikin Univ	IL	42,158	C
Minn State Univ, Moorhead	MN	15,941	C
Minot State Univ	ND	12,732	C
Miss Valley State Univ	MS	13,233	LC
Missouri Southern State Univ	MO	12,499	C
Monmouth Univ	NJ	46,234	C
Morningside College	IA	36,865	C
Morris College	SC	18,500	LC
Mount Aloysius College	PA	29,976	C
Mount Mary Univ	WI	34,650	LC
Mount Vernon Nazarene Univ	OH	34,500	C
Murray State Univ	KY	16,998	C
Nazareth College	NY	45,574	C
Nebr Wesleyan Univ	NE	38,140	C+
New York Univ	NY	65,860	MC
Niagara Univ	NY	41,010	C
N Car A&T State Univ	NC	13,365	LC
Northeastern Illinois Univ	IL	12,529	LC
Northern Kentucky Univ	KY	16,486	C
Northwest Missouri State Univ	MO	17,737	C
Northwest Nazarene Univ	ID	36,000	C
Northwestern Okla State Univ	OK	13,072	NC
Nova Southeastern Univ	FL	38,534	C+
Nyack College	NY	34,050	NC
Oakwood Univ	AL	43,758	C
Ohio Valley Univ	WV	29,480	C
Okla Baptist Univ	OK	32,320	C
Okla Christian Univ	OK	27,650	VC
Okla Wesleyan Univ	OK	33,206	C
Old Dominion Univ	VA	20,910	C
Olivet Nazarene Univ	IL	41,840	C
Oral Roberts Univ	OK	34,316	C
Palm Beach Atlantic Univ	FL	39,720	C
Pfeiffer Univ	NC	39,695	LC
Piedmont College	GA	32,512	C
Pittsburg State Univ	KS	13,880	NC
Purdue Univ/Northwest	IN	15,038	C
Purdue Univ/West Lafayette	IN	20,032	MC
Rider Univ	NJ	54,050	C
Rivier Univ	NH	40,410	VC
Roberts Wesleyan College	NY	38,306	C
Rocky Mountain College	MT	34,270	C
Rust College	MS	10,600	C
Saginaw Valley State Univ	MI	18,530	C
St. Augustine's Univ	NC	26,048	C
St. Louis Univ	MO	49,866	HC
St. Mary's Univ of Minn	MN	41,210	VC
Samford Univ	AL	39,232	VC
Schreiner Univ	TX	34,626	LC
Seton Hill Univ	PA	46,972	C
Shaw Univ	NC	24,638	C
Shepherd Univ, West Virginia	WV	17,224	C
Shippensburg Univ of Pennsylvania	PA	23,208	C
Shorter Univ	GA	31,130	LC
Simpson Univ	CA	33,700	C
Southeast Missouri State Univ	MO	15,498	C
Southeastern Louisiana Univ	LA	16,237	C
Southern Nazarene Univ	OK	32,798	NC
Southern New Hampshire Univ	NH	43,198	C
Southern Oregon Univ	OR	19,117	C
Southern Univ and A&M College	LA	16,074	LC+
Southern Univ at New Orleans	LA	8,014	LC
Southern Wesleyan Univ	SC	32,130	LC
Southwestern Okla State Univ	OK	11,790	C
St. Edward's Univ	TX	53,100	VC
St. John Fisher College	NY	43,620	C
SUNY / SUNY Fredonia	NY	20,818	C
SUNY / SUNY Oneonta	NY	19,712	C+
SUNY / SUNY Plattsburgh	NY	18,814	C
SUNY / SUNY Potsdam	NY	20,404	C+
SUNY at New Paltz	NY	19,200	C
SUNY at Oswego	NY	21,351	C
Suffolk Univ	MA	50,308	C
Syracuse Univ	NY	60,239	VC
Taylor Univ	IN	40,317	C+
Texas Southern Univ	TX	18,212	LC
The Catholic Univ of America	DC	56,356	VC
The College of New Jersey	NJ	31,909	HC
The College of St. Rose	NY	43,048	C
The Lincoln Univ	PA	15,154	NC
The Univ of Tenn at Chattanooga	TN	16,744	C
The Univ of Utah	UT	17,924	VC
Tiffin Univ	OH	31,380	C
Tougaloo College	MS	17,980	NC
Trevecca Nazarene Univ	TN	31,186	C
Trine Univ	IN	41,310	C
Troy Univ	AL	16,171	C
Union College	NE	23,270	C
Universidad del Turabo	PR	17,828	
Univ of Arkansas at Pine Bluff	AR	13,541	C
Univ of Central Florida	FL	15,922	VC
Univ of Central Missouri	MO	18,982	C
Univ of Central Okla	OK	13,486	C
Univ of Charleston	WV	35,000	C
Univ of Conn	CT	25,538	HC
Univ of Delaware	DE	24,976	VC+
Univ of Evansville	IN	44,186	VC+
Univ of Georgia	GA	21,250	HC
Univ of Illinois at Chicago	IL	25,006	VC
Univ of Illinois at Urbana-Champaign	IL	27,006	HC
Univ of Indianapolis	IN	36,480	C
Univ of Louisiana at Lafayette	LA	14,516	C
Univ of Maine at Machias	ME	22,960	C
Univ of Mary	ND	23,180	C
Univ of Mary Hardin-Baylor	TX	33,950	C+
Univ of Minn/Twin Cities	MN	23,519	HC+
Univ of Miss	MS	17,746	C+
Univ of Missouri/Columbia	MO	18,201	MC
Univ of Montana-Western	MT	11,220	LC
Univ of Nebr - Lincoln	NE	18,589	VC
Univ of New Hampshire - Manchester	NH	14,490	C
Univ of New Orleans	LA	12,840	C
Univ of N Car at Charlotte	NC	15,547	C
Univ of N Car at Greensboro	NC	14,690	C
Univ of North Florida	FL	15,996	VC
Univ of Northwestern - St. Paul	MN	38,160	C
Univ of Pittsburgh at Bradford	PA	22,402	C
Univ of Pittsburgh at Johnstown	PA	22,092	C
Univ of Rio Grande & Rio Grande Community College	OH	8,750	NC
Univ of S Car Upstate	SC	18,200	LC
Univ of South Florida/Tampa	FL	16,110	VC+
Univ of Southern Indiana	IN	16,501	C
Univ of the Cumberlands	KY	32,000	C
Univ of Vermont	VT	28,878	HC
Univ of Wisc-Green Bay	WI	15,064	C
Univ of Wisc-Superior	WI	14,446	C
Urbana Univ	OH	30,820	C
Valparaiso Univ	IN	48,370	C+
Viterbo Univ	WI	34,660	C
Warner Univ	FL	28,216	C
Wartburg College	IA	47,840	C
Washington Adventist Univ	MD	31,440	LC
Washington State Univ	WA	22,495	C
Wayne State Univ	MI	22,016	C
Weber State Univ	UT	10,721	C
West Chester Univ of Pennsylvania	PA	18,456	C
West Texas A&M Univ	TX	13,478	C
Western Carolina Univ	NC	13,965	C
Westmont College	CA	56,410	HC
Whitworth Univ	WA	51,732	VC
Wiley College	TX	18,504	C
Wilmington College	OH	34,600	C
Wilson College	PA	35,620	C
Wingate Univ	NC	39,950	C
Xavier Univ of Louisiana	LA	31,689	C+
York College	NE	24,300	C
York College of Pennsylvania	PA	29,240	C
Youngstown State Univ	OH	17,307	C

ENGLISH LITERATURE

School	ST	$IS	SR
Agnes Scott College	GA	51,930	VC+
Aquinas College - Mich	MI	38,876	HC
Bard College	NY	64,024	HC
Beloit College	WI	55,206	HC
Bennington College	VT	63,960	MC
Bethany College	WV	36,300	NC
Bethel Univ	MN	45,270	VC
Blackburn College	IL	28,526	LC
Boise State Univ	ID	14,860	C
Bowling Green State Univ	OH	19,747	C
Brown Univ	RI	64,566	MC
Bryant Univ	RI	55,646	VC
Calvin College	MI	41,570	VC+
Carroll College	MT	39,972	C+
Chatham Univ	PA	46,517	C
Chestnut Hill College	PA	43,410	C
CUNY/Hunter College	NY	31,098	VC
Columbia Univ/ School of General Studies	NY	61,470	MC
Concordia College - New York	NY	39,035	LC
Cornell College	IA	48,800	VC
DePauw Univ	IN	58,688	HC+
Dominican Univ of Calif	CA	57,050	C
East Texas Baptist Univ	TX	33,134	C
Eastern Mich Univ	MI	19,761	C
Edinboro Univ	PA	15,940	LC
Elizabethtown College	PA	54,050	C
Elmira College	NY	53,900	C
Emmanuel College	MA	52,110	C+
Emory and Henry College	VA	41,410	C
Excelsior College	NY	14,080	SP
Fairleigh Dickinson Univ/ Metropolitan Campus	NJ	40,254	C
Fontbonne Univ	MO	33,717	C
Fordham Univ	NY	65,918	MC
Hamilton College	NY	64,250	MC
High Point Univ	NC	45,977	C
Hofstra Univ	NY	55,960	C+
Hope International Univ	CA	41,150	C
Houghton College	NY	39,090	C
Huntington Univ	IN	33,996	C
Indiana Univ-Purdue Univ Fort Wayne	IN	17,553	C
Ithaca College	NY	56,766	VC
Johnson & Wales Univ/ Denver Campus	CO	42,707	C
King Univ	TN	34,660	C
Knox College	IL	52,615	VC+
Lewis Univ	IL	40,370	C
Loras College	IA	39,222	C
Loyola Univ New Orleans	LA	51,708	VC+
Marshall Univ	WV	17,242	C
Marylhurst Univ	OR	20,295	NC
Mass College of Liberal Arts	MA	20,128	C
Mercer Univ	GA	45,348	VC
Millersville Univ of Pennsylvania	PA	23,782	C
Mills College	CA	59,163	VC
Missouri Southern State Univ	MO	12,499	C
Murray State Univ	KY	16,998	C
New York Univ	NY	65,860	MC
North Central College	IL	48,712	VC
Northeastern Illinois Univ	IL	12,529	LC
Oral Roberts Univ	OK	34,316	C
Otterbein Univ	OH	41,630	C
Pace Univ	NY	58,248	C
Pennsylvania State Univ - Univ Park	PA	29,760	HC
Pfeiffer Univ	NC	39,695	LC
Purdue Univ/Northwest	IN	15,038	C
Queens Univ of Charlotte	NC	39,543	C
Reed College	OR	65,300	MC
Rider Univ	NJ	54,050	C
St. Leo Univ	FL	31,650	C
St. Louis Univ	MO	49,866	HC
St. Mary's College	IN	50,600	C
Santa Fe Univ of Art and Design	NM	39,980	SP
Southern Illinois Univ Carbondale	IL	23,667	C
Southern New Hampshire Univ	NH	43,198	C
St. Edward's Univ	TX	53,100	VC
St. Thomas Aquinas College	NY	42,200	C
SUNY / SUNY Plattsburgh	NY	18,814	C
SUNY / SUNY Potsdam	NY	20,404	C+
SUNY at Binghamton	NY	22,861	MC
Stevenson Univ	MD	72,770	C
Swarthmore College	PA	63,550	MC
Taylor Univ	IN	40,317	C+
The Catholic Univ of America	DC	56,356	VC
The Lincoln Univ	PA	15,154	NC
Union Univ	TN	33,970	VC
Univ of Calif San Diego	CA	30,150	MC
Univ of Illinois at Chicago	IL	25,006	VC
Univ of Illinois at Urbana-Champaign	IL	27,006	HC
Univ of Maryland/College Park	MD	21,938	HC
Univ of Mass Dartmouth	MA	25,658	C
Univ of Mich/Ann Arbor	MI	24,410	MC
Univ of Missouri/Columbia	MO	18,201	MC
Univ of Montana-Western	MT	11,220	LC
Univ of North Florida	FL	15,996	VC
Univ of Pittsburgh	PA	29,568	HC+
Univ of Pittsburgh at Greensburg	PA	23,132	C
Univ of Redlands	CA	60,200	VC
Univ of Rochester	NY	65,032	MC
Univ of South Florida/Tampa	FL	16,110	VC+
Univ of Southern Calif	CA	66,631	C
Virginia State Univ	VA	19,802	C+
Warren Wilson College	NC	44,220	VC
Washington Univ in St. Louis	MO	65,366	VC
Wellesley College	MA	63,916	MC
Wesleyan Univ	CT	65,516	MC
West Chester Univ of Pennsylvania	PA	18,456	C
Winthrop Univ	SC	23,082	C
York College of Pennsylvania	PA	29,240	C
Youngstown State Univ	OH	17,307	C

ENGLISH SECONDARY EDUCATION

School	ST	$IS	SR
Abilene Christian Univ	TX	41,800	C+
Bethel College	IN	35,860	C
Calvin College	MI	41,570	VC+
Grove City College	PA	25,692	VC
Ithaca College	NY	56,766	VC
King Univ	TN	34,660	C
Lewis Univ	IL	40,370	C
Neumann Univ	PA	40,678	LC
North Greenville Univ	SC	25,930	C+
Okla Baptist Univ	OK	32,320	C
Providence College	RI	60,760	VC
St. Leo Univ	FL	31,650	C
St. Ambrose Univ	IA	39,019	C
St. Ambrose Univ	IA	39,019	C
West Chester Univ of Pennsylvania	PA	18,456	C
Western Kentucky Univ	KY	16,850	C
Western Mich Univ	MI	21,054	C
Wilson College	PA	35,620	C

ENGLISH WRITING

School	ST	$IS	SR
Aquinas College - Mich	MI	38,876	HC
Augustana College	IL	49,658	VC
Bethel College	IN	35,860	C
Bloomfield College	NJ	39,100	LC
Boise State Univ	ID	14,860	C
Cabrini Univ	PA	42,591	LC
Calvin College	MI	41,570	VC+
Carroll College	MT	39,972	C+
Concordia Univ St. Paul	MN	29,050	C
Cornell College	IA	48,800	VC
East Texas Baptist Univ	TX	33,134	C
Elizabethtown College	PA	54,050	C
Fontbonne Univ	MO	33,717	C
Fordham Univ	NY	65,918	MC
Goddard College	VT	17,040	VC
Goshen College	IN	42,500	C
Grand Rapids Theological Seminary/Cornerstone Univ	MI	33,338	C
High Point Univ	NC	45,977	C
Houghton College	NY	39,090	C
Ithaca College	NY	56,766	VC
Johnson & Wales Univ/ Denver Campus	CO	42,707	C
King Univ	TN	34,660	C
Lewis Univ	IL	40,370	C
Limestone College	SC	32,100	C
Marylhurst Univ	OR	20,295	NC
Mass College of Liberal Arts	MA	20,128	C
Millersville Univ of Pennsylvania	PA	23,782	C
Mills College	CA	59,163	VC
Missouri Southern State Univ	MO	12,499	C
North Central College	IL	48,712	VC
Okla Christian Univ	OK	27,650	VC
Purdue Univ/Northwest	IN	15,038	C
St. Leo Univ	FL	31,650	C
St. Louis Univ	MO	49,866	HC
St. Mary's College	IN	50,600	C
San Diego State Univ	CA	21,896	C+
Seton Hill Univ	PA	46,972	C
Southern Oregon Univ	OR	19,117	C
Spring Hill College	AL	48,488	C
St. Ambrose Univ	IA	39,019	C
St. Ambrose Univ	IA	39,019	C
St. Edward's Univ	TX	53,100	VC
SUNY / SUNY Plattsburgh	NY	18,814	C
SUNY / SUNY Potsdam	NY	20,404	C+
SUNY at Oswego	NY	21,351	C
Taylor Univ	IN	40,317	C+
Univ of Colo Denver	CO	23,230	C
Univ of Idaho	ID	15,348	C
Univ of Mass Dartmouth	MA	25,658	C
Valparaiso Univ	IN	48,370	C+
Warren Wilson College	NC	44,220	VC
Wellesley College	MA	63,916	MC
West Chester Univ of Pennsylvania	PA	18,456	C
Wilson College	PA	35,620	C

ENTOMOLOGY

School	ST	$IS	SR
Cornell Univ	NY	64,853	MC
Iowa State Univ	IA	17,570	C
Mich State Univ	MI	23,898	VC+
Ohio State Univ at Columbus	OH	21,703	HC+
Okla State Univ	OK	17,180	VC
Purdue Univ/West Lafayette	IN	20,032	MC
SUNY / The College of Environmental Science and Forestry	NY	23,853	VC
Texas A&M Univ	TX	20,521	VC+
Univ of Arizona	AZ	23,100	C

ST = STATE $IS = IN-STATE COSTS SR = SELECTOR RATING

School	ST	$IS	SR
Univ of Calif at Davis	CA	28,468	HC
Univ of Calif at Riverside	CA	29,227	C+
Univ of Delaware	DE	24,976	VC+
Univ of Florida	FL	16,291	HC+
Univ of Georgia	GA	21,250	HC
Univ of Illinois at Urbana-Champaign	IL	27,006	HC
Univ of Nebr - Lincoln	NE	18,589	VC
Univ of Wisc-Madison	WI	20,934	MC
Washington State Univ	WA	22,495	C

ENTREPRENEURIAL STUDIES

School	ST	$IS	SR
American International College	MA	46,300	LC
Ashford Univ	CA	10,480	C
Ashland Univ	OH	21,440	C
Auburn Univ at Montgomery	AL	15,290	C
Baldwin Wallace Univ	OH	41,106	C
Baylor Univ	TX	53,760	HC
Belmont Univ	TN	40,970	VC
Black Hills State Univ	SD	15,899	C
Brown Univ	RI	64,566	MC
Bryant Univ	RI	55,646	VC
Calif Baptist Univ	CA	41,392	C
Cal State, Fullerton	CA	21,902	C
Canisius College	NY	47,537	C
Central Mich Univ	MI	20,330	C
Clarkson Univ	NY	60,392	HC
Cogswell Polytechnical College	CA	30,531	C
College of William & Mary	VA		MC
Columbia College - Missouri	MO	27,803	C
Dallas Baptist Univ	TX	33,713	C
Davenport Univ	MI	25,896	LC
Drexel Univ	PA	65,432	VC+
Duquesne Univ	PA	46,822	VC
East Central Univ	OK	13,056	C
Eastern Mich Univ	MI	19,761	C
Eastern Univ	PA	39,540	C
Elon Univ	NC	44,599	VC+
Endicott College	MA	44,604	VC+
Fairleigh Dickinson Univ/College at Florham	NJ	52,062	C
Fairleigh Dickinson Univ/Metropolitan Campus	NJ	40,254	C
Florida State Univ	FL	16,771	HC
Gannon Univ	PA	42,032	C
Grand Canyon Univ	AZ	16,950	VC
Grove City College	PA	25,692	VC
Hawaii Pacific Univ	HI	33,420	C
High Point Univ	NC	45,977	C
Hofstra Univ	NY	55,960	C+
Houston Baptist Univ	TX	36,450	C
Huntington Univ	IN	33,996	C
Indiana Univ Bloomington	IN	20,429	VC
Jackson State Univ	MS	15,879	LC
John Carroll Univ	OH	49,740	C+
Johnson & Wales Univ/Charlotte Campus	NC	43,988	C
Johnson & Wales Univ/Denver Campus	CO	42,707	C
Johnson & Wales Univ/North Miami Campus	FL	42,707	C
Johnson & Wales Univ/Providence Campus	RI	42,248	C
Juniata College	PA	53,760	VC
Kansas State Univ	KS	17,780	VC
Kent State Univ	OH	20,732	C
Lake Erie College	OH	38,914	LC
Lasell College	MA	47,500	C
Lipscomb Univ	TN	41,296	VC
LIU Brooklyn	NY	49,682	C
Loyola Marymount Univ	CA	58,038	HC
Loyola Univ Chicago	IL	55,802	VC
Lynn Univ	FL	49,480	LC
Marquette Univ	WI	48,390	VC+
Menlo College	CA	51,380	LC
Mercy College	NY	31,776	C
Middle Tenn State Univ	TN	8,650	C
Millikin Univ	IL	42,158	C
Missouri State Univ	MO	15,190	C+
Mount Aloysius College	PA	29,976	C
Murray State Univ	KY	16,998	C
New York Inst of Technology	NY	48,730	C
Northern Kentucky Univ	KY	16,486	C
Northern Mich Univ	MI	19,604	C
Ohio Univ	OH	22,924	C
Okla State Univ	OK	17,180	VC
Pace Univ	NY	58,248	C
Paul Quinn College	TX	25,350	LC
Peirce College	PA	16,780	NC
Pennsylvania State Univ - Univ Park	PA	29,760	HC
Purdue Univ/West Lafayette	IN	20,032	MC
Quinnipiac Univ	CT	59,110	C
Rowan Univ	NJ	24,491	VC+
St. Joseph's Univ	PA	57,544	VC+
St. Louis Univ	MO	49,866	HC
St. Mary's Univ of Minn	MN	41,210	VC
Samford Univ	AL	39,232	VC
San Francisco State Univ	CA	18,514	LC
Seton Hill Univ	PA	46,972	C
Shenandoah Univ	VA	41,312	C
Shippensburg Univ of Pennsylvania	PA	23,208	C
S Dak State Univ	SD	15,634	C
Southeast Missouri State Univ	MO	15,498	C
Southern Adventist Univ	TN	27,600	C
Southern Illinois Univ Edwardsville	IL	22,643	C
Southern Vermont College	VT	34,670	LC
Southwestern Okla State Univ	OK	11,790	C
St. Edward's Univ	TX	53,100	VC
SUNY / SUNY Plattsburgh	NY	18,814	C
SUNY at Binghamton	NY	22,861	MC
Suffolk Univ	MA	50,308	C
Syracuse Univ	NY	60,239	VC
Temple Univ	PA	24,392	VC
Texas Christian Univ	TX	54,670	HC
The Univ of Utah	UT	17,924	VC
Thomas Edison State Univ	NJ	6,350	NC
Tulane Univ	LA	63,396	HC+
Univ of Alaska Anchorage	AK	16,652	NC
Univ of Arizona	AZ	23,100	C
Univ of Dayton	OH	53,620	C
Univ of Hartford	CT	49,776	C
Univ of Illinois at Chicago	IL	25,006	VC
Univ of Illinois at Urbana-Champaign	IL	27,006	HC
Univ of Indianapolis	IN	36,480	C
Univ of Kansas	KS	20,135	C+
Univ of Louisville	KY	19,824	C
Univ of Maine at Machias	ME	22,960	C
Univ of Maryland/Baltimore County	MD	21,296	VC
Univ of Miami	FL	63,494	MC
Univ of Nebr - Lincoln	NE	18,589	VC
Univ of N Car at Greensboro	NC	14,690	C
Univ of N Car at Pembroke	NC	14,388	LC
Univ of North Texas	TX	19,198	C
Univ of Pennsylvania	PA	63,526	MC
Univ of Portland	OR	52,152	VC
Univ of Rhode Island	RI	24,906	C
Univ of San Francisco	CA	58,484	VC
Univ of South Florida/St. Petersburg	FL	15,980	C
Univ of St. Francis	IL	39,924	C
Univ of Tampa	FL	36,944	C
Univ of Wisc-Milwaukee	WI	21,496	C
Virginia Polytechnic Inst and State Univ	VA	21,276	HC
Washburn Univ	KS	15,827	C
Washington State Univ	WA	22,495	C
Washington Univ in St. Louis	MO	65,366	VC
Waynesburg Univ	PA	32,290	C
West Virginia Univ	WV	18,210	C
Western Carolina Univ	NC	13,965	C
Western Kentucky Univ	KY	16,850	C
Western Mich Univ	MI	21,054	C
Western New England Univ	MA	48,088	C
Wichita State Univ	KS	21,643	C
Wilkes Univ	PA	45,622	C
Xavier Univ	OH	47,880	C+
York College of Pennsylvania	PA	29,240	C

ENVIRONMENT & NATNL RESOURCE ECONOMICS

School	ST	$IS	SR
Arizona State Univ at the Polytechnic Campus	AZ	21,360	VC
Bryant Univ	RI	55,646	VC
Northland College	WI	41,103	C+
Oregon State Univ	OR	22,519	VC
Univ of Arizona	AZ	23,100	C
Univ of Maine at Machias	ME	22,960	C
Univ of New Hampshire	NH	28,562	VC
Univ of Rhode Island	RI	24,906	C
Western Kentucky Univ	KY	16,850	C

ENVIRONMENTAL BIOLOGY

School	ST	$IS	SR
Aquinas College - Mich	MI	38,876	HC
Belmont Univ	TN	40,970	VC
Beloit College	WI	55,206	HC
Bennington College	VT	63,960	MC
Blackburn College	IL	28,526	LC
Boston Univ	MA	65,110	MC
Brown Univ	RI	64,566	MC
Bryant Univ	RI	55,646	VC
Calif State Polytechnic Univ, Pomona	CA	21,541	C
Cal State, Northridge	CA	16,859	LC
Cedar Crest College	PA	46,715	C
Christopher Newport Univ	VA	23,968	VC+
Colby College	ME	64,060	MC
Colgate Univ	NY	65,030	MC
Columbia Univ/City of New York	NY	62,958	MC
Faulkner Univ	AL	26,410	C
Fitchburg State Univ	MA	21,819	C
Georgetown Univ	DC	65,926	MC
Greenville College	IL	27,012	C
Hanover College	IN	46,364	C+
Heidelberg Univ	OH	39,200	C
Houghton College	NY	39,090	C
Kent State Univ	OH	20,732	C
Lock Haven Univ of Pennsylvania	PA	18,028	LC
Mercer Univ	GA	45,348	VC
Mich State Univ	MI	23,898	VC+
Millersville Univ of Pennsylvania	PA	23,782	C
Missouri Univ of Science and Technology	MO	18,655	HC
Montclair State Univ	NJ	26,210	LC
Mount Aloysius College	PA	29,976	C
Norfolk State Univ	VA	25,702	LC
Northland College	WI	41,103	C+
Ohio Univ	OH	22,924	C
Plymouth State Univ	NH	23,180	LC
Prescott College	AZ	33,284	C
St. Mary's Univ of Minn	MN	41,210	VC
Salve Regina Univ	RI	51,470	C
Sewanee: The Univ of the South	TN	54,500	MC
Silver Lake College of the Holy Family	WI	36,290	LC
S Dak State Univ	SD	15,634	C
Southeast Missouri State Univ	MO	15,498	C
Southwestern Okla State Univ	OK	11,790	C
SUNY / The College of Environmental Science and Forestry	NY	23,853	VC
Texas A&M Univ at Galveston	TX	15,920	C
Tulane Univ	LA	63,396	HC+
Univ of Calif at Davis	CA	28,468	HC
Univ of Calif San Diego	CA	30,150	MC
Univ of Dayton	OH	53,620	C
Univ of La Verne	CA	55,600	C
Univ of Mount Union	OH	38,970	C
Univ of North Alabama	AL	15,398	C
Washington Univ in St. Louis	MO	65,366	VC
West Chester Univ of Pennsylvania	PA	18,456	C
Wilmington College	OH	34,600	C
Wingate Univ	NC	39,950	C

ENVIRONMENTAL CHEMISTRY

School	ST	$IS	SR
Ashland Univ	OH	21,440	C
Lawrence Tech Univ	MI	39,770	VC
Marshall Univ	WV	17,242	C
Millersville Univ of Pennsylvania	PA	23,782	C
Northland College	WI	41,103	C+
Ohio Univ	OH	22,924	C
Southeast Missouri State Univ	MO	15,498	C
St. Edward's Univ	TX	53,100	VC
SUNY at Binghamton	NY	22,861	MC
Univ of Calif San Diego	CA	30,150	MC
Univ of Denver	CO	58,443	VC+
Univ of Georgia	GA	21,250	HC

ENVIRONMENTAL DESIGN

School	ST	$IS	SR
Arizona State Univ at the Tempe Campus	AZ	21,756	VC
ArtCenter College of Design	CA	54,212	SP
Ball State Univ	IN	19,590	C
Brigham Young Univ	UT	12,748	HC
Bryant Univ	RI	55,646	VC
Green Mountain College	VT	45,228	LC
Hampshire College	MA	63,824	MC
Harvard College/Harvard Univ	MA	60,659	MC
Maryland Inst College of Art	MD	56,795	SP
Marywood Univ	PA	46,900	C
Montana State Univ	MT	15,500	C+
N Car State Univ	NC	19,515	HC+
N Dak State Univ	ND	16,245	C
Olivet Nazarene Univ	IL	41,840	C
Prescott College	AZ	33,284	C
Rutgers Univ - New Brunswick	NJ	26,632	HC
SUNY / The College of Environmental Science and Forestry	NY	23,853	VC
SUNY / Univ at Buffalo	NY	23,122	C+
SUNY at Binghamton	NY	22,861	MC
Stony Brook Univ/The SUNY	NY	21,881	MC
Syracuse Univ	NY	60,239	VC
Texas A&M Univ	TX	20,521	VC+
Univ of Calif at Davis	CA	28,468	HC
Univ of Colo Boulder	CO	24,285	VC+
Univ of Houston	TX	21,483	VC
Univ of Mass Amherst	MA	26,199	VC+
Univ of Minn/Twin Cities	MN	23,519	HC+
Univ of New Mexico	NM	15,404	C
Univ of Okla	OK	18,911	VC
Univ of PR-Rio Piedras campus	PR	13,327	

ENVIRONMENTAL DESIGN, POLICY AND PLANNING

School	ST	$IS	SR
St. Edward's Univ	TX	53,100	VC

ENVIRONMENTAL EARTH RESOURCES

School	ST	$IS	SR
Bryant Univ	RI	55,646	VC
SUNY at Binghamton	NY	22,861	MC
Univ of Notre Dame	IN	64,043	MC

ENVIRONMENTAL EDUCATION

School	ST	$IS	SR
Catawba College	NC	39,820	C
East Stroudsburg Univ	PA	18,334	C
Goshen College	IN	42,500	C
Johnson State College	VT	20,752	C
Northland College	WI	41,103	C+
Ohio State Univ at Columbus	OH	21,703	HC+
Prescott College	AZ	33,284	C
Seattle Univ	WA	50,811	VC+
Southern Oregon Univ	OR	19,117	C
SUNY / The College of Environmental Science and Forestry	NY	23,853	VC
Univ of Montana-Western	MT	11,220	LC
Univ of Nebr - Lincoln	NE	18,589	VC
Univ of Pittsburgh at Bradford	PA	22,402	C
Virginia Polytechnic Inst and State Univ	VA	21,276	HC
West Virginia Univ	WV	18,210	C

ENVIRONMENTAL ENGINEERING

School	ST	$IS	SR
Alabama A&M Univ	AL	18,796	C
Brown Univ	RI	64,566	MC
Bucknell Univ	PA	64,616	MC
Calif Polytechnic State Univ	CA	17,979	HC+
CUNY/City College	NY	20,319	VC
Clarkson Univ	NY	60,392	HC
Colo State Univ	CO	22,162	VC
Cornell Univ	NY	64,853	MC
Drexel Univ	PA	65,432	VC+
Elon Univ	NC	44,599	VC+
Florida Gulf Coast Univ	FL	9,682	C
Florida International Univ	FL	19,854	C+
Florida State Univ	FL	16,771	HC
Gannon Univ	PA	42,032	C
Georgia Inst of Technology	GA	23,360	MC
Humboldt State Univ	CA	20,514	C
Johns Hopkins Univ	MD	65,386	MC
Lehigh Univ	PA	61,010	MC
Louisiana State Univ and A&M College	LA	18,677	VC
Loyola Univ Chicago	IL	55,802	VC
Manhattan College	NY	51,750	C+
Marquette Univ	WI	48,390	VC+
Mass Inst of Technology	MA	62,662	MC
Mich Tech Univ	MI	24,739	VC+
Missouri Univ of Science and Technology	MO	18,655	HC
Montana Tech of the Univ of Montana	MT	15,447	C+
New Jersey Inst of Technology	NJ	29,569	VC
New Mexico Inst of Mining and Technology	NM	14,833	HC
New Mexico State Univ	NM	14,050	C
N Car State Univ	NC	19,515	HC+
Northern Arizona Univ	AZ	20,246	VC
Northwestern Univ	IL	66,344	MC
Ohio State Univ at Columbus	OH	21,703	HC+
Ohio Univ	OH	22,924	C
Oregon State Univ	OR	22,519	VC
Rensselaer Polytechnic Inst	NY	63,436	MC
Rice Univ	TX	57,668	MC
San Diego State Univ	CA	21,896	C+
Seattle Univ	WA	50,811	VC+
S Dak School of Mines and Technology	SD	18,645	VC
S Dak State Univ	SD	15,634	C
Southern Methodist Univ	TX	66,483	MC
Stanford Univ	CA	60,409	MC
SUNY / The College of Environmental Science and Forestry	NY	23,853	VC
SUNY / Univ at Buffalo	NY	23,122	C+
Stevens Inst of Technology	NJ	62,338	MC
Suffolk Univ	MA	50,308	C
Syracuse Univ	NY	60,239	VC
Tarleton State Univ	TX	15,248	LC
Taylor Univ	IN	40,317	C+
Tenn Tech Univ	TN	17,050	C
Texas Tech Univ	TX	18,736	C+
The Catholic Univ of America	DC	56,356	VC
The Univ of Tenn at Chattanooga	TN	16,744	C
Tufts Univ	MA		MC
United States Air Force Academy	CO		C
United States Military Academy at West Point	NY		HC+
Universidad Politecnica de PR, Hato Rey campus	PR	23,514	
Univ of Arizona	AZ	23,100	C
Univ of Calif at Berkeley	CA	28,853	MC
Univ of Calif at Irvine	CA	26,484	VC
Univ of Calif at Riverside	CA	29,227	C+
Univ of Calif San Diego	CA	30,150	MC
Univ of Central Florida	FL	15,922	VC
Univ of Colo Boulder	CO	24,285	VC+
Univ of Conn	CT	25,538	HC
Univ of Delaware	DE	24,976	VC+
Univ of Florida	FL	16,291	HC+
Univ of Georgia	GA	21,250	HC
Univ of Idaho	ID	15,348	C
Univ of Miami	FL	63,494	MC
Univ of Mich/Ann Arbor	MI	24,410	MC
Univ of New Hampshire	NH	28,562	VC
Univ of Notre Dame	IN	64,043	MC
Univ of Okla	OK	18,911	VC
Univ of Southern Calif	CA	66,631	C
Univ of Vermont	VT	28,878	HC
Univ of Wisc-Platteville	WI	14,614	VC
Wilkes Univ	PA	45,622	C
Worcester Polytechnic Inst	MA	60,730	MC
Yale Univ	CT	64,650	MC

ST = STATE **$IS** = IN-STATE COSTS **SR** = SELECTOR RATING

ENVIRONMENTAL ENGINEERING TECHNOLOGY

School	ST	$IS	SR
East Carolina Univ	NC	16,937	C
Indiana Inst of Technology	IN	34,240	LC
Inter-American Univ of PR-Bayamon	PR	18,785	
Kennesaw State Univ	GA	19,592	VC
Loyola Univ Chicago	IL	55,802	VC
Mich State Univ	MI	23,898	VC+
Murray State Univ	KY	16,998	C
Rochester Inst of Technology	NY	50,842	HC
Texas Southern Univ	TX	18,212	LC
Univ of Calif San Diego	CA	30,150	MC
Univ of Wisc-Green Bay	WI	15,064	C

ENVIRONMENTAL GEOLOGY

School	ST	$IS	SR
Allegheny College	PA	55,420	VC
Beloit College	WI	55,206	HC
Brown Univ	RI	64,566	MC
Calvin College	MI	41,570	VC+
Case Western Reserve Univ	OH	60,304	MC
Colgate Univ	NY	65,030	MC
Hanover College	IN	46,364	C+
Juniata College	PA	53,760	VC
Kutztown Univ of Pennsylvania	PA	19,056	LC
Millersville Univ of Pennsylvania	PA	23,782	C
Murray State Univ	KY	16,998	C
Northland College	WI	41,103	C+
Ohio Univ	OH	22,924	C
Prescott College	AZ	33,284	C
Southern Methodist Univ	TX	66,483	MC
SUNY / Univ at Buffalo	NY	23,122	C+
SUNY at Binghamton	NY	22,861	MC
SUNY at New Paltz	NY	19,200	C
SUNY at Oswego	NY	21,351	C
The Univ of Akron	OH	21,477	C
The Univ of Utah	UT	17,924	VC
Univ of Calif at Irvine	CA	26,484	VC
Univ of Dayton	OH	53,620	C
Univ of Illinois at Chicago	IL	25,006	VC
Univ of Mich/Ann Arbor	MI	24,410	MC
Univ of Notre Dame	IN	64,043	MC
Univ of Wyoming	WY	15,375	C+

ENVIRONMENTAL HEALTH SCIENCE

School	ST	$IS	SR
Benedict College	SC	28,238	NC
Boise State Univ	ID	14,860	C
Calif Inst of Technology	CA	58,761	MC
Cal State, Sacramento	CA	20,332	C
Cal State, San Bernardino	CA	12,000	C
CUNY/York College	NY	6,747	LC
Clarkson Univ	NY	60,392	HC
Colo State Univ	CO	22,162	VC
Colo State Univ-Pueblo	CO	18,234	C
Delaware State Univ	DE	19,376	NC
Drury Univ	MO	33,791	VC
East Carolina Univ	NC	16,937	C
East Central Univ	OK	13,056	C
East Tenn State Univ	TN	13,994	C
Eastern Kentucky Univ	KY	16,908	C
Illinois State Univ	IL	23,418	VC
Indiana State Univ	IN	23,223	LC
Indiana Univ Bloomington	IN	20,429	VC
Iowa Wesleyan Univ	IA	39,200	C
Miss Valley State Univ	MS	13,233	LC
Missouri Southern State Univ	MO	12,499	C
New Mexico State Univ	NM	14,050	C
New York Univ	NY	65,860	MC
Ohio Univ	OH	22,924	C
Old Dominion Univ	VA	20,910	C
Pennsylvania State Univ - Univ Park	PA	29,760	HC
Point Park Univ	PA	41,270	C
Purdue Univ/Northwest	IN	15,038	C
Purdue Univ/West Lafayette	IN	20,032	MC
Springfield College	MA	45,995	C
Texas Southern Univ	TX	18,212	LC
Univ of Arizona	AZ	23,100	C
Univ of Arkansas at Little Rock	AR	18,211	C
Univ of Calif at Davis	CA	28,468	HC
Univ of Georgia	GA	21,250	HC
Univ of Mass Lowell	MA	26,380	C
Univ of Mich-Flint	MI	17,607	C+
Univ of N Car at Chapel Hill	NC	20,052	HC+
Univ of Southern Maine	ME	18,320	C
Univ of Washington	WA	23,149	VC
West Chester Univ of Pennsylvania	PA	18,456	C
Western Carolina Univ	NC	13,965	C
Western Kentucky Univ	KY	16,850	C
Wright State Univ	OH	16,983	C

ENVIRONMENTAL HORTICULTURE

School	ST	$IS	SR
Univ of New Hampshire	NH	28,562	VC

ENVIRONMENTAL HORTICULTURE & TURF MANAGEMENT

School	ST	$IS	SR
Univ of Rhode Island	RI	24,906	C
Univ of Wisc-Platteville	WI	14,614	VC

ENVIRONMENTAL SCIENCE

School	ST	$IS	SR
Abilene Christian Univ	TX	41,800	C+
Adrian College	MI	42,400	C
Alaska Pacific Univ	AK	26,680	VC
Albion College	MI	52,650	C
Albright College	PA	46,660	C
Alderson Broaddus Univ	WV	26,149	C
Allegheny College	PA	55,420	VC
Alverno College	WI	33,294	LC
American Univ	DC	59,379	HC+
Andrews Univ	MI	28,030	C+
Anna Maria College	MA	48,186	C
Appalachian State Univ	NC	14,416	VC
Aquinas College - Mich	MI	38,876	HC
Arcadia Univ	PA	33,570	C+
Arizona State Univ at the West Campus	AZ	20,640	C
Arkansas Tech Univ	AR	15,484	C
Ashland Univ	OH	21,440	C
Assumption College	MA	47,920	C+
Auburn Univ	AL	23,594	VC+
Auburn Univ at Montgomery	AL	15,290	C
Ball State Univ	IN	19,590	C
Barnard College/Columbia Univ	NY	62,741	MC
Barton College	NC	38,686	LC
Baylor Univ	TX	53,760	HC
Benedictine Univ	IL	38,300	C
Bennington College	VT	63,960	MC
Berry College	GA	45,286	C+
Bethany College	WV	36,300	NC
Bethel Univ	MN	45,270	VC
Biola Univ	CA	46,402	C+
Boston College	MA	65,737	MC
Bowling Green State Univ	OH	19,747	C
Briar Cliff Univ	IA	36,956	C
Bridgewater College	VA	44,510	C
Brown Univ	RI	64,566	MC
Bryant Univ	RI	55,646	VC
Bucknell Univ	PA	64,616	MC
Buena Vista Univ	IA	41,514	C
Cabrini Univ	PA	42,591	LC
Calif Baptist Univ	CA	41,392	C
Calif Polytechnic State Univ	CA	17,979	HC+
Cal State, Chico	CA	21,440	C
Cal State, East Bay	CA	19,413	C
Cal State, Long Beach	CA	18,850	C
Calif Univ of Pennsylvania	PA	14,217	LC
Calvin College	MI	41,570	VC+
Canisius College	NY	47,537	C
Capital Univ	OH	42,982	C
Carroll College	MT	39,972	C+
Carroll Univ	WI	38,100	C+
Case Western Reserve Univ	OH	60,304	MC
Castleton Univ	VT	20,186	C
Catawba College	NC	39,820	C
Cedarville Univ	OH	34,990	VC
Centenary College of Louisiana	LA	45,650	C+
Central College	IA	44,592	C
Central Methodist Univ	MO	36,830	VC
Central Mich Univ	MI	20,330	C
Chapman Univ	CA	63,078	VC+
Charleston Southern Univ	SC	32,400	C
Chatham Univ	PA	46,517	C
Chestnut Hill College	PA	43,410	C
CUNY/City College	NY	20,319	VC
CUNY/Hunter College	NY	31,098	VC
CUNY/Meger Evers College	NY	6,680	NC
Claflin Univ	SC	33,764	LC
Claremont McKenna College	CA	67,185	MC
Clarion Univ of Pennsylvania	PA	21,608	LC
Clark Univ	MA	51,600	HC+
Clarke Univ	IA	38,940	C
Clarkson Univ	NY	60,392	HC
Cleveland State Univ	OH	22,196	C
Coe College	IA	51,570	VC
Colby-Sawyer College	NH	50,790	C
Colgate Univ	NY	65,030	MC
Colo College	CO	62,560	MC
Colo Mesa Univ	CO	18,955	LC
Columbia Univ/ School of General Studies	NY	61,470	MC
Columbia Univ/City of New York	NY	62,958	MC
Concordia College - Moorhead	MN	51,088	C+
Concordia College - New York	NY	39,035	LC
Concordia Univ	OR	35,000	C
Concordia Univ Texas	TX	40,210	C
Conn College	CT	65,000	MC
Cornell College	IA	48,800	VC
Creighton Univ	NE	48,206	VC+
Dallas Baptist Univ	TX	33,713	C
Davis & Elkins College	WV	38,242	LC
Defiance College	OH	41,630	C
Delaware Valley Univ	PA	49,796	C
Delta State Univ	MS	13,176	C
DePaul Univ	IL	47,623	VC
DePauw Univ	IN	58,688	HC+
Dickinson College	PA	63,974	MC
Doane Univ	NE	39,184	VC
Dominican Univ	IL	41,222	C
Dordt College	IA	37,860	C+
Drake Univ	IA	45,056	HC
Drexel Univ	PA	65,432	VC+
Drury Univ	MO	33,791	VC
Duke Univ	NC	64,188	
Duquesne Univ	PA	46,822	VC
Earlham College	IN	54,870	HC
Eastern Conn State Univ	CT	23,059	C
Eastern Kentucky Univ	KY	16,908	C
Eastern Mennonite Univ	VA	42,550	C
Eastern Nazarene College	MA	39,955	C
Eastern New Mexico Univ	NM	14,416	C
Eastern Univ	PA	39,540	C
Edinboro Univ	PA	15,940	LC
Elizabethtown College	PA	54,050	C
Elmhurst College	IL	45,428	C
Elon Univ	NC	44,599	VC+
Emory and Henry College	VA	41,410	C
Endicott College	MA	44,604	VC+
Ferrum College	VA	39,650	C
Flagler College	FL	27,620	C
Florida Inst of Technology	FL	53,306	VC
Florida International Univ	FL	19,854	C+
Florida State Univ	FL	16,771	HC
Fordham Univ	NY	65,918	MC
Framingham State Univ	MA	20,584	C
Franklin and Marshall College	PA	63,170	HC
Franklin Pierce Univ	NH	46,750	C
Fresno Pacific Univ	CA	37,370	C
Friends Univ	KS	34,455	C
Frostburg State Univ	MD	17,280	LC
Furman Univ	SC	58,092	VC+
Gannon Univ	PA	42,032	C
George Washington Univ	DC	62,835	MC
Georgetown College	KY	41,440	C
Georgia College & State Univ	GA	21,148	C+
Gettysburg College	PA	63,000	HC
Glenville State College	WV	17,386	NC
Goshen College	IN	42,500	C
Hampshire College	MA	63,824	MC
Hanover College	IN	46,364	C+
Hardin-Simmons Univ	TX	33,966	C
Hartwick College	NY	51,270	C
Harvard College/Harvard Univ	MA	60,659	MC
Hawaii Pacific Univ	HI	33,420	C
Heritage Univ	WA	19,825	NC
Hiram College	OH	43,230	C
Hollins Univ	VA	49,635	VC
Hood College	MD	54,840	C
Houghton College	NY	39,090	C
Howard Univ	DC	37,616	C+
Humboldt State Univ	CA	20,514	C
Husson Univ	ME	25,720	LC
Idaho State Univ	ID	13,619	NC
Illinois College	IL	40,850	VC
Indiana Univ Bloomington	IN	20,429	VC
Indiana Univ-Purdue Univ Indianapolis	IN	18,635	C
Iona College	NY	50,984	C
Iowa State Univ	IA	17,570	C
Ithaca College	NY	56,766	VC
Jacksonville Univ	FL	46,230	C
John Carroll Univ	OH	49,740	C+
Johns Hopkins Univ	MD	65,386	MC
Johnson State College	VT	20,752	C
Juniata College	PA	53,760	VC
Kalamazoo College	MI	53,931	HC+
Kennesaw State Univ	GA	19,592	VC
Keuka College	NY	39,762	C
Keystone College	PA	28,680	LC
Kutztown Univ of Pennsylvania	PA	19,056	LC
La Salle Univ	PA	55,790	C
Lake Erie College	OH	38,914	LC
Lake Forest College	IL	50,652	VC
Lander Univ	SC	43,994	C
Le Moyne College	NY	46,000	C
Lehigh Univ	PA	61,010	MC
Lewis Univ	IL	40,370	C
Lincoln Memorial Univ	TN	28,070	C
Lincoln Univ	MO	13,602	NC
Lipscomb Univ	TN	41,296	VC
Louisiana State Univ and A&M College	LA	18,677	VC
Louisiana Tech Univ	LA	11,422	VC
Lourdes Univ	OH	29,520	NC
Loyola Marymount Univ	CA	58,038	HC
Loyola Univ Chicago	IL	55,802	VC
Loyola Univ New Orleans	LA	51,708	VC+
Lynchburg College	VA	46,740	C
Madonna Univ	MI	29,050	C
Marietta College	OH	46,190	C
Marist College	NY	49,860	VC
Marshall Univ	WV	17,242	C
Martin Univ	IN	20,264	LC
Marygrove College	MI	28,926	NC
Maryville Univ of St. Louis	MO	38,046	VC+
Marywood Univ	PA	46,900	C
Mass Maritime Academy	MA	19,982	C
McDaniel College	MD	51,380	VC
Mercyhurst Univ	PA	47,420	C
Merrimack College	MA	52,770	C
Messiah College	PA	43,100	C+
Metropolitan State Univ of Denver	CO	29,889	LC
Miami Univ	OH	27,190	HC+
Mich Tech Univ	MI	24,739	VC+
Middle Tenn State Univ	TN	8,650	C
Midway Univ	KY	31,640	LC
Midwestern State Univ	TX	17,572	C
Miles College	AL	18,646	NC
Mills College	CA	59,163	VC
Minn State Univ, Mankato	MN	15,616	C
Monmouth College	IL	42,260	C
Montana State Univ	MT	15,500	C+
Montana State Univ-Billings	MT	22,960	C
Montana State Univ-Northern	MT	11,370	NC
Montreat College	NC	31,298	LC
Moravian College	PA	53,117	
Mount Aloysius College	PA	29,976	C
Mount Marty College	SD	32,972	C
Mount St. Mary's Univ	MD	51,610	C
Muhlenberg College	PA	56,645	VC+
Muskingum Univ	OH	35,966	C
National Univ	CA	14,730	LC
Nazareth College	NY	45,574	C
New England College	NH	50,364	C
New Jersey Inst of Technology	NJ	29,569	VC
New Mexico Highlands Univ	NM	11,904	NC
New Mexico Inst of Mining and Technology	NM	14,833	HC
New Mexico State Univ	NM	14,050	C
N Car Central Univ	NC	9,000	C
N Car State Univ	NC	19,515	HC+
N Car Wesleyan College	NC	39,200	C
North Park Univ	IL	35,860	C
Northeastern Univ	MA	62,703	MC
Northern Arizona Univ	AZ	20,246	VC
Northern Kentucky Univ	KY	16,486	C
Northern State Univ	SD	14,505	C
Northland College	WI	41,103	C+
Northwest Univ	WA	35,876	VC
Northwestern Univ	IL	66,344	MC
Norwich Univ	VT	28,212	C
Notre Dame College	OH	37,150	VC
Nova Southeastern Univ	FL	38,534	C+
Oakland Univ	MI	20,763	C
Ohio State Univ at Columbus	OH	21,703	HC+
Ohio Wesleyan Univ	OH	49,460	VC
Okla State Univ	OK	17,180	VC
Olivet College	MI	36,110	LC
Olivet Nazarene Univ	IL	41,840	C
Oregon Inst of Technology	OR	8,910	C
Oregon State Univ	OR	22,519	VC
Otterbein Univ	OH	41,630	C
Pace Univ	NY	58,248	C
Pacific Lutheran Univ	WA	49,960	VC
Pfeiffer Univ	NC	39,695	LC
Philadelphia Univ	PA	50,370	C
Piedmont College	GA	32,512	C
Pitzer College	CA	66,192	MC
Point Loma Nazarene Univ	CA	43,450	C
Point Park Univ	PA	41,270	C
Portland State Univ	OR	19,443	C
Prescott College	AZ	33,284	C
Principia College	IL	39,010	C+
Purdue Univ/Northwest	IN	15,038	C
Purdue Univ/West Lafayette	IN	20,032	MC
Queens Univ of Charlotte	NC	39,543	C
Ramapo College of New Jersey	NJ	25,338	C
Randolph College	VA	45,660	VC
Regis Univ	CO	44,520	C
Rhodes College	TN	51,900	HC
Rider Univ	NJ	54,050	C
Ripon College	WI	46,911	C+
Robert Morris Univ	PA	37,834	C
Rochester Inst of Technology	NY	50,842	HC
Rocky Mountain College	MT	34,270	C
Roger Williams Univ	RI	46,296	C+
Rollins College	FL	58,670	HC
Roosevelt Univ	IL	40,651	VC
Rosemont College	PA	30,980	C
Russell Sage College	NY	39,370	C
Rutgers Univ - New Brunswick	NJ	26,632	HC
Rutgers Univ - Newark	NJ	27,288	C
St. Anselm College	NH	52,560	C+
St. Joseph's College of Maine	ME	46,485	C
St. Joseph's Univ	PA	57,544	VC+
St. Louis Univ	MO	49,866	HC
St. Mary's College of Calif	CA	57,420	C
St. Vincent College	PA	44,626	C
Salem International Univ	WV	21,090	LC
Sam Houston State Univ	TX	18,792	C
Samford Univ	AL	39,232	VC
San Diego State Univ	CA	21,896	C+
Savannah State Univ	GA	15,631	C
Scripps College	CA	66,664	MC
Seattle Univ	WA	50,811	VC+
Shaw Univ	NC	24,638	C
Shenandoah Univ	VA	41,312	C
Shippensburg Univ of Pennsylvania	PA	23,208	C
Siena College	NY	48,916	C+
Sierra Nevada College	NV	43,482	C
Simpson College	IA	43,839	VC
Smith College	MA	63,914	MC
Sonoma State Univ	CA	27,806	C
Southeast Missouri State Univ	MO	15,498	C

ST = STATE $IS = IN-STATE COSTS SR = SELECTOR RATING

School	ST	$IS	SR
Southern Methodist Univ	TX	66,483	MC
Southern Oregon Univ	OR	19,117	C
Southwest Minn State Univ	MN	17,783	C
St. Bonaventure Univ	NY	44,237	C
St. Edward's Univ	TX	53,100	VC
St. Lawrence Univ	NY	64,390	VC
St. Mary's Univ	TX	37,500	C
St. Norbert College	WI	44,525	VC
SUNY / SUNY Cortland	NY	20,706	VC
SUNY / SUNY Fredonia	NY	20,818	C
SUNY / SUNY Oneonta	NY	19,712	C+
SUNY / SUNY Plattsburgh	NY	18,814	C
SUNY / The College of Environmental Science and Forestry	NY	23,853	VC
SUNY /College of Agriculture and Tech at Cobleskill	NY	20,527	LC
SUNY /Maritime College	NY	16,020	C
SUNY at Binghamton	NY	22,861	MC
SUNY at Purchase	NY	17,900	C
Stephen F. Austin State Univ	TX	18,406	LC
Stetson Univ	FL	53,544	VC
Stockton Univ	NJ	25,059	
Stony Brook Univ/The SUNY	NY	21,881	MC
Suffolk Univ	MA	50,308	C
Susquehanna Univ	PA	55,340	VC
Tarleton State Univ	TX	15,248	LC
Taylor Univ	IN	40,317	C+
Temple Univ	PA	24,392	VC
Texas A&M Univ	TX	20,521	VC+
Texas A&M Univ at Corpus Christi	TX	16,851	LC
Texas A&M Univ at Galveston	TX	15,920	C
Texas Christian Univ	TX	54,670	HC
Texas State Univ	TX	19,350	C
The Catholic Univ of America	DC	56,356	VC
The College at Brockport - SUNY	NY	20,346	C
The Lincoln Univ	PA	15,154	NC
The Univ of Tenn at Chattanooga	TN	16,744	C
The Univ of Tenn at Knoxville	TN	22,112	VC
The Univ of Virginia's College at Wise	VA	18,192	LC
Thiel College	PA	41,590	C
Thomas Edison State Univ	NJ	6,350	NC
Thomas More College	KY	36,720	C
Towson Univ	MD	17,408	VC
Trine Univ	IN	41,310	C
Trinity College	CT	63,920	HC+
Troy Univ	AL	16,171	C
Tufts Univ	MA		MC
Tulane Univ	LA	63,396	HC+
Tusculum College	TN	31,625	C
Union College	NY	64,320	MC
United States Military Academy at West Point	NY		HC+
Unity College	ME	37,670	C
Univ of Alabama	AL	24,320	C+
Univ of Alaska Southeast	AK	11,493	C
Univ of Arizona	AZ	23,100	C
Univ of Arkansas at Fayetteville	AR	19,152	C+
Univ of Calif at Berkeley	CA	28,853	MC
Univ of Calif at Davis	CA	28,468	HC
Univ of Calif at Irvine	CA	26,484	VC
Univ of Calif at Los Angeles	CA	30,162	MC
Univ of Calif at Riverside	CA	29,227	C+
Univ of Calif at Santa Barbara	CA	29,091	HC
Univ of Calif San Diego	CA	30,150	MC
Univ of Central Arkansas	AR	14,472	VC
Univ of Chicago	IL	67,584	MC
Univ of Colo Boulder	CO	24,285	VC+
Univ of Conn	CT	25,538	HC
Univ of Delaware	DE	24,976	VC+
Univ of Denver	CO	58,443	VC+
Univ of Dubuque	IA	37,824	C
Univ of Evansville	IN	44,186	VC+
Univ of Findlay	OH	60,139	C
Univ of Georgia	GA	21,250	HC
Univ of Hawaii at Hilo	HI	18,038	C
Univ of Hawaii at Manoa	HI	23,221	C
Univ of Houston	TX	21,483	VC
Univ of Idaho	ID	15,348	C
Univ of Indianapolis	IN	36,480	C
Univ of Iowa	IA	18,683	VC+
Univ of La Verne	CA	55,600	C
Univ of Maine	ME	20,792	C
Univ of Maine at Farmington	ME	18,187	C
Univ of Maine at Fort Kent	ME	15,165	LC
Univ of Maine at Machias	ME	22,960	C
Univ of Maine at Presque Isle	ME	14,870	C
Univ of Mary Washington	VA	24,764	VC
Univ of Maryland/Baltimore County	MD	21,296	VC
Univ of Maryland/College Park	MD	21,938	HC
Univ of Maryland/Eastern Shore	MD	17,013	C
Univ of Maryland/Univ College	MD	25,966	LC
Univ of Mass Amherst	MA	26,199	VC+
Univ of Mass Boston	MA	13,435	C
Univ of Mass Lowell	MA	26,380	C
Univ of Miami	FL	63,494	MC
Univ of Mich/Dearborn	MI	11,757	VC
Univ of Minn Crookston	MN	19,739	C
Univ of Minn/Duluth	MN	20,292	C+
Univ of Minn/Morris	MN	20,760	VC
Univ of Missouri-Kansas City	MO	19,563	VC
Univ of Montana-Western	MT	11,220	LC
Univ of Montevallo	AL	19,502	C
Univ of Mount Olive	NC	18,426	C
Univ of Mount Union	OH	38,970	C
Univ of Nebr - Lincoln	NE	18,589	VC
Univ of Nevada, Las Vegas	NV	17,553	C
Univ of Nevada/Reno	NV	18,010	C
Univ of New England	ME	48,880	C
Univ of New Hampshire	NH	28,562	VC
Univ of New Haven	CT	52,190	C
Univ of New Mexico	NM	15,404	C
Univ of New Orleans	LA	12,840	C
Univ of N Car at Asheville	NC	15,723	VC+
Univ of N Car at Chapel Hill	NC	20,052	HC+
Univ of N Car at Pembroke	NC	14,388	LC
Univ of N Car at Wilmington	NC	14,590	VC
Univ of Notre Dame	IN	64,043	MC
Univ of Okla	OK	18,911	VC
Univ of Oregon	OR	22,972	C
Univ of Pittsburgh	PA	29,568	HC+
Univ of Portland	OR	52,152	VC
Univ of Redlands	CA	60,200	VC
Univ of Rhode Island	RI	24,906	C
Univ of Rio Grande & Rio Grande Community College	OH	8,750	NC
Univ of Rochester	NY	65,032	MC
Univ of St. Francis	IN	37,400	C
Univ of San Francisco	CA	58,484	VC
Univ of Scranton	PA	54,962	VC
Univ of S Car at Columbia	SC	19,725	VC+
Univ of South Florida/St. Petersburg	FL	15,980	C
Univ of South Florida/Tampa	FL	16,110	VC+
Univ of Southern Calif	CA	66,631	C
Univ of Southern Indiana	IN	16,501	C
Univ of Southern Maine	ME	18,320	C
Univ of St. Francis	IL	39,924	C
Univ of St. Thomas - Houston	TX	40,020	VC
Univ of Tampa	FL	36,944	C
Univ of Texas at San Antonio	TX	20,157	C
Univ of the District of Columbia	DC	21,044	LC
Univ of the Incarnate Word	TX	39,162	LC
Univ of the Ozarks	AR	52,176	C
Univ of the Pacific	CA	57,006	VC
Univ of the Sciences	PA	54,038	VC
Univ of Toledo	OH	19,336	NC
Univ of Vermont	VT	28,878	HC
Univ of Virginia	VA	25,891	MC
Univ of West Alabama	AL	15,516	NC
Univ of Wisc-Green Bay	WI	15,064	C
Univ of Wisc-Madison	WI	20,934	MC
Univ of Wisc-Milwaukee	WI	21,496	C
Ursinus College	PA	61,690	VC
Utah State Univ	UT	12,736	C
Valparaiso Univ	IN	48,370	C+
Villanova Univ	PA	62,523	MC
Virginia Polytechnic Inst and State Univ	VA	21,276	HC
Walla Walla Univ	WA	30,417	NC
Walsh Univ	OH	39,010	C
Washington & Jefferson College	PA	56,512	VC
Washington and Lee Univ	VA	59,647	MC
Washington College	MD	54,666	VC
Washington State Univ	WA	22,495	C
Washington Univ in St. Louis	MO	65,366	VC
Wayland Baptist Univ	TX	22,356	LC
Wayne State Univ	MI	22,016	C
Waynesburg Univ	PA	32,290	C
Weber State Univ	UT	10,721	C
Wells College	NY	50,500	C
Wesley College	DE	37,026	LC
Wesleyan College	GA	29,694	C+
West Texas A&M Univ	TX	13,478	C
West Virginia Univ	WV	18,210	C
West Virginia Wesleyan College	WV	36,858	C
Western Conn State Univ	CT	21,254	LC
Western Washington Univ	WA	18,003	C+
Westfield State Univ	MA	19,671	C
Westminster College	MO	32,820	C
Wheaton College	IL	43,610	MC
Wheaton College	MA	61,512	VC
Whitman College	WA	59,772	MC
Whittier College	CA	57,891	C
Widener Univ	PA	56,486	C
Willamette Univ	OR	61,817	VC+
William Paterson Univ of New Jersey	NJ	23,133	C
William Penn Univ	IA	26,000	C
Wilson College	PA	35,620	C
Winthrop Univ	SC	23,082	C
Wisc Lutheran College	WI	36,290	VC
Wittenberg Univ	OH	48,156	C+
Worcester State Univ	MA	20,977	C
Wright State Univ	OH	16,983	C
Xavier Univ	OH	47,880	C+

ENVIRONMENTAL STUDIES

School	ST	$IS	SR
Adelphi Univ	NY	48,244	C
Adrian College	MI	42,400	C
Alaska Pacific Univ	AK	26,680	VC
Albion College	MI	52,650	C
Alfred Univ	NY	42,296	C+
Allegheny College	PA	55,420	VC
Alma College	MI	47,548	C
American Univ	DC	59,379	HC+
Amherst College	MA		HC+
Appalachian State Univ	NC	14,416	VC
Aquinas College - Mich	MI	38,876	HC
Arizona State Univ at the Tempe Campus	AZ	21,756	VC
Ashford Univ	CA	10,480	C
Augsburg College	MN	43,929	C
Augustana College	IL	49,658	VC
Averett Univ	VA	40,970	LC
Bard College	NY	64,024	HC
Bard College at Simon's Rock	MA	65,795	MC
Bates College	ME	64,500	MC
Beloit College	WI	55,206	HC
Bemidji State Univ	MN	16,056	VC
Bennington College	VT	63,960	MC
Bentley Univ	MA	60,890	HC
Berea College	KY	7,042	C
Bethel Univ	MN	45,270	VC
Birmingham-Southern College	AL	44,478	VC
Blackburn College	IL	28,526	LC
Boise State Univ	ID	14,860	C
Boston Univ	MA	65,110	MC
Bowdoin College	ME	63,500	MC
Bowling Green State Univ	OH	19,747	C
Brandeis Univ	MA	65,925	MC
Brenau Univ - Women's College	GA	37,876	LC
Brigham Young Univ	UT	12,748	HC
Brown Univ	RI	64,566	MC
Bryant Univ	RI	55,646	VC
Calif Lutheran Univ	CA	52,853	C
Cal State, East Bay	CA	19,413	C
Cal State, San Bernardino	CA	12,000	C
Calvin College	MI	41,570	VC+
Canisius College	NY	47,537	C
Carleton College	MN	64,071	MC
Catawba College	NC	39,820	C
Cazenovia College	NY	46,470	C
Central Mich Univ	MI	20,330	C
Centre College	KY	49,250	HC
Chaminade Univ of Honolulu	HI	36,000	C
Champlain College	VT	53,132	C+
Chatham Univ	PA	46,517	C
Christopher Newport Univ	VA	23,968	VC+
CUNY/Brooklyn College	NY	5,884	C+
CUNY/Queens College	NY	27,896	C
Claremont McKenna College	CA	67,185	MC
Clarke Univ	IA	38,940	C
Coe College	IA	51,570	VC
Colby College	ME	64,060	MC
Colby-Sawyer College	NH	50,790	C
College of St. Benedict	MN	52,806	C
College of the Holy Cross	MA	62,165	MC
Columbia College - Missouri	MO	27,803	C
Concordia College - New York	NY	39,035	LC
Daemen College	NY	38,045	C
Dartmouth College	NH	66,174	MC
Davidson College	NC	60,119	MC
Denison Univ	OH	58,860	MC
Dickinson College	PA	63,974	MC
Doane Univ	NE	39,184	VC
Dominican Univ of Calif	CA	57,050	C
Drew Univ/College of Liberal Arts	NJ	61,048	VC
Drexel Univ	PA	65,432	VC+
Drury Univ	MO	33,791	VC
Earlham College	IN	54,870	HC
Eckerd College	FL	52,874	C
Edgewood College	WI	35,950	C
Elon Univ	NC	44,599	VC+
Emmanuel College	MA	52,110	C+
Emory Univ	GA	60,786	MC
Eugene Lang College/The New School for Liberal Arts	NY	55,650	C
Fairfield Univ	CT	59,860	VC+
Florida Gulf Coast Univ	FL	9,682	C
Florida Inst of Technology	FL	53,306	VC
Florida State Univ	FL	16,771	HC
Fort Lewis College	CO	18,980	C
Franklin and Marshall College	PA	63,170	HC
George Mason Univ	VA	15,724	VC
Goddard College	VT	17,040	VC
Gonzaga Univ	WA	50,888	HC
Goodwin College	CT	28,370	LC
Goshen College	IN	42,500	C
Goucher College	MD	55,716	VC
Green Mountain College	VT	45,228	LC
Guilford College	NC	44,090	C
Gustavus Adolphus College	MN	52,433	HC
Hamilton College	NY	64,250	MC
Hamline Univ	MN	45,678	VC
Hawaii Pacific Univ	HI	33,420	C
Hendrix College	AR	54,020	VC+
Hofstra Univ	NY	55,960	C+
Hollins Univ	VA	49,635	VC
Illinois Wesleyan Univ	IL	56,430	VC+
Indiana Univ Bloomington	IN	20,429	VC
Ithaca College	NY	56,766	VC
Juniata College	PA	53,760	VC
Keene State College	NH	24,003	LC
King's College	PA	46,858	C
Knox College	IL	52,615	VC+
Lasell College	MA	47,500	C
Lawrence Univ	WI	54,498	HC
Lehigh Univ	PA	61,010	MC
Lenoir-Rhyne Univ	NC	43,200	C
Lewis & Clark College	OR	58,434	HC+
Linfield College	OR	52,010	C
Louisiana State Univ and A&M College	LA	18,677	VC
Loyola Univ New Orleans	LA	51,708	VC+
Luther College	IA	48,540	C+
Lynchburg College	VA	46,740	C
Lynn Univ	FL	49,480	LC
Lyon College	AR	34,730	C+
Macalester College	MN	61,905	MC
Manchester Univ	IN	40,422	C
Manhattanville College	NY	51,440	C+
Marietta College	OH	46,190	C
Maryville College	TN	44,410	C
Mass College of Liberal Arts	MA	20,128	C
McKendree Univ	IL	37,940	C+
Mercer Univ	GA	45,348	VC
Meredith College	NC	45,297	C
Mich State Univ	MI	23,898	VC+
Middlebury College	VT	64,332	MC
Millersville Univ of Pennsylvania	PA	23,782	C
Millikin Univ	IL	42,158	C
Mills College	CA	59,163	VC
Missouri State Univ	MO	15,190	C+
Mitchell College	CT	43,280	C
Molloy College	NY	40,440	C
Moravian College	PA	53,117	
Mount Holyoke College	MA	56,746	MC
Naropa Univ	CO	42,826	NC
New College of Florida	FL	15,848	MC
New York Univ	NY	65,860	MC
Niagara Univ	NY	41,010	C
Northeastern Illinois Univ	IL	12,529	LC
Northeastern Univ	MA	62,703	MC
Northern Arizona Univ	AZ	20,246	VC
Northern Mich Univ	MI	19,604	C
Northland College	WI	41,103	C+
Oberlin College	OH	66,012	MC
Ohio Dominican Univ	OH	41,340	C+
Ohio Northern Univ	OH	44,050	VC
Okla City Univ	OK	40,476	VC
Pace Univ	NY	58,248	C
Penn State Univ/Altoona	PA	24,584	C
Pennsylvania State Univ - Univ Park	PA	29,760	HC
Piedmont College	GA	32,512	C
Plymouth State Univ	NH	23,180	LC
Point Park Univ	PA	41,270	C
Pomona College	CA	64,957	MC
Prescott College	AZ	33,284	C
Queens Univ of Charlotte	NC	39,543	C
Ramapo College of New Jersey	NJ	25,338	C
Randolph College	VA	45,660	VC
Randolph-Macon College	VA	49,910	C
Reed College	OR	65,300	MC
Regis Univ	CO	44,520	C
Rhodes College	TN	51,900	HC
Roanoke College	VA	54,114	VC
Rocky Mountain College	MT	34,270	C
Rowan Univ	NJ	24,491	VC+
St. John's Univ	MN	51,624	C
St. Louis Univ	MO	49,866	HC
St. Mary's College of Calif	CA	57,420	C
St. Michael's College	VT	51,725	VC+
Salisbury Univ	MD	20,714	VC
San Diego State Univ	CA	21,896	C+
San Francisco State Univ	CA	18,514	LC
San Jose State Univ	CA	21,540	C
Scripps College	CA	66,664	MC
Seattle Univ	WA	50,811	VC+
Seton Hall Univ	NJ	55,514	C
Sewanee: The Univ of the South	TN	54,500	MC
Shepherd Univ, West Virginia	WV	17,224	C
Siena College	NY	48,916	C+
Silver Lake College of the Holy Family	WI	36,290	LC
Simmons College	MA	53,090	VC
Skidmore College	NY	64,214	HC
Southeastern Okla State Univ	OK	11,875	C
Southern Methodist Univ	TX	66,483	MC
Southern Nazarene Univ	OK	32,798	NC
Southern New Hampshire Univ	NH	43,198	C
Southern Oregon Univ	OR	19,117	C
Southwestern Univ	TX	50,720	VC
St. Bonaventure Univ	NY	44,237	C
St. John's Univ	NY	55,850	C
St. Lawrence Univ	NY	64,390	VC
St. Mary's College of Maryland	MD	26,634	VC
St. Olaf College	MN	54,260	HC+
SUNY / SUNY Fredonia	NY	20,818	C
SUNY / SUNY Potsdam	NY	20,404	C+
SUNY / The College of Environmental Science and Forestry	NY	23,853	VC
SUNY / Univ at Buffalo	NY	23,122	C+
SUNY at Binghamton	NY	22,861	MC

School	ST	$IS	SR
SUNY SUNY Albany	NY	22,165	C
Stonehill College	MA	55,030	C+
Stony Brook Univ/The SUNY	NY	21,881	MC
Suffolk Univ	MA	50,308	C
Taylor Univ	IN	40,317	C+
Temple Univ	PA	24,392	VC
Texas A&M Univ at Galveston	TX	15,920	C
Texas Tech Univ	TX	18,736	C+
The College of Idaho	ID	36,415	C
The College of New Rochelle	NY	46,300	VC
The Univ of Utah	UT	17,924	VC
Thomas Edison State Univ	NJ	6,350	NC
Trinity Univ	TX	52,314	HC+
Union College	NY	64,320	MC
United States Military Academy at West Point	NY		HC+
Unity College	ME	37,670	C
Univ of Arizona	AZ	23,100	C
Univ of Calif at Irvine	CA	26,484	VC
Univ of Calif at Los Angeles	CA	30,162	MC
Univ of Calif San Diego	CA	30,150	MC
Univ of Calif, Santa Cruz	CA	28,731	C+
Univ of Cincinnati	OH	21,964	VC
Univ of Evansville	IN	44,186	VC+
Univ of Hawaii at Hilo	HI	18,038	C
Univ of Illinois at Chicago	IL	25,006	VC
Univ of Kansas	KS	20,135	C+
Univ of Maine at Farmington	ME	18,187	C
Univ of Maine at Machias	ME	22,960	C
Univ of Maryland/Baltimore County	MD	21,296	VC
Univ of Mass Lowell	MA	26,380	C
Univ of Mich/Ann Arbor	MI	24,410	MC
Univ of Mich/Dearborn	MI	11,757	VC
Univ of Minn/Duluth	MN	20,292	C+
Univ of Minn/Morris	MN	20,760	VC
Univ of Montana	MT	14,105	C
Univ of Montana-Western	MT	11,220	LC
Univ of Nebr - Lincoln	NE	18,589	VC
Univ of Nebr - Omaha	NE	16,120	C
Univ of New England	ME	48,880	C
Univ of New Hampshire	NH	28,562	VC
Univ of N Car at Chapel Hill	NC	20,052	HC+
Univ of N Dak	ND	15,373	C
Univ of Okla	OK	18,911	VC
Univ of Oregon	OR	22,972	C
Univ of Pennsylvania	PA	63,526	MC
Univ of Pittsburgh	PA	29,568	HC+
Univ of Pittsburgh at Bradford	PA	22,402	C
Univ of Pittsburgh at Johnstown	PA	22,092	C
Univ of Redlands	CA	60,200	VC
Univ of Rhode Island	RI	24,906	C
Univ of Richmond	VA	60,880	MC
Univ of Rochester	NY	65,032	MC
Univ of San Diego	CA	58,442	VC+
Univ of San Francisco	CA	58,484	VC
Univ of Southern Calif	CA	66,631	C
Univ of St. Thomas - Houston	TX	40,020	VC
Univ of Tulsa	OK	52,625	HC+
Univ of Vermont	VT	28,878	HC
Univ of Wisc-Green Bay	WI	15,064	C
Univ of Wisc-Madison	WI	20,934	MC
Univ of Wyoming	WY	15,375	C+
Vanderbilt Univ	TN	60,572	MC
Vassar College	NY	65,491	MC
Villanova Univ	PA	62,523	MC
Virginia Commonwealth Univ	VA	23,049	C
Virginia Wesleyan College	VA	43,728	LC
Viterbo Univ	WI	34,660	C
Warren Wilson College	NC	44,220	VC
Washington & Jefferson College	PA	56,512	VC
Washington College	MD	54,666	VC
Washington Univ in St. Louis	MO	65,366	VC
Wayland Baptist Univ	TX	22,356	LC
Webster Univ	MO	37,490	C
Wellesley College	MA	63,916	MC
Wesleyan Univ	CT	65,516	MC
West Virginia Wesleyan College	WV	36,858	C
Western Kentucky Univ	KY	16,850	C
Western Mich Univ	MI	21,054	C
Western State Colo Univ	CO	18,639	C
Western Washington Univ	WA	18,003	C+
Westminster College	UT	41,078	C+
Wheeling Jesuit Univ	WV	37,106	LC
Wheelock College	MA	49,225	C
Whitman College	WA	59,772	MC
Wilson College	PA	35,620	C
Winthrop Univ	SC	23,082	C
Wisc Lutheran College	WI	36,290	VC
Wofford College	SC	49,885	VC
Worcester Polytechnic Inst	MA	60,730	MC
Yale Univ	CT	64,650	MC
Youngstown State Univ	OH	17,307	C

EQUESTRIAN STUDIES

School	ST	$IS	SR
Averett Univ	VA	40,970	LC
Rocky Mountain College	MT	34,270	C

EQUINE SCIENCE

School	ST	$IS	SR
Asbury Univ	KY	35,180	C+
Auburn Univ	AL	23,594	VC+
Averett Univ	VA	40,970	LC
Bethany College	WV	36,300	NC
Centenary College	NJ	43,602	C
Colo State Univ	CO	22,162	VC
Delaware Valley Univ	PA	49,796	C
Houghton College	NY	39,090	C
Johnson & Wales Univ/Providence Campus	RI	42,248	C
Judson College	AL	27,066	C
Lake Erie College	OH	38,914	LC
Midway Univ	KY	31,640	LC
Mount Ida College	MA	46,820	C
Murray State Univ	KY	16,998	C
N Dak State Univ	ND	16,245	C
Okla Panhandle State Univ	OK	6,152	NC
Otterbein Univ	OH	41,630	C
Rocky Mountain College	MT	34,270	C
St. Mary-of-the-Woods College	IN	39,632	LC
Salem International Univ	WV	21,090	LC
Savannah College of Art and Design	GA	49,595	C
Stephens College	MO	38,042	C
Truman State Univ	MO	16,014	HC
Univ of Findlay	OH	60,139	C
Univ of Louisville	KY	19,824	C
Univ of Minn Crookston	MN	19,739	C
Univ of Montana-Western	MT	11,220	LC
William Woods Univ	MO	32,040	C
Wilmington College	OH	34,600	C
Wilson College	PA	35,620	C

EQUINE STUDIES

School	ST	$IS	SR
Univ of New Hampshire	NH	28,562	VC

ESKIMO

School	ST	$IS	SR
Univ of Alaska Fairbanks	AK	16,179	C

ETHICS, POLITICS, AND SOCIAL POLICY

School	ST	$IS	SR
American Jewish Univ - College of A&S Campus	CA	44,234	C
Central Mich Univ	MI	20,330	C
Drake Univ	IA	45,056	HC
Goddard College	VT	17,040	VC
Millikin Univ	IL	42,158	C
Northwestern Univ	IL	66,344	MC
Pine Manor College	MA	41,660	LC
Prescott College	AZ	33,284	C
Smith College	MA	63,914	MC
Syracuse Univ	NY	60,239	VC
Unity College	ME	37,670	C
Univ of Dayton	OH	53,620	C
Univ of Mass Boston	MA	13,435	C
Univ of Northern Colo	CO	20,851	C
Univ of Southern Calif	CA	66,631	C
Yale Univ	CT	64,650	MC

ETHNIC STUDIES

School	ST	$IS	SR
Albion College	MI	52,650	C
Arizona State Univ at the West Campus	AZ	20,640	C
Bowling Green State Univ	OH	19,747	C
Brown Univ	RI	64,566	MC
Calif Polytechnic State Univ	CA	17,979	HC+
Cal State, East Bay	CA	19,413	C
Cal State, Fullerton	CA	21,902	C
Cal State, San Bernardino	CA	12,000	C
Cal State, Stanislaus	CA	16,212	C
CUNY/City College	NY	20,319	VC
Colo State Univ	CO	22,162	VC
Cornell College	IA	48,800	VC
Edgewood College	WI	35,950	C
Kalamazoo College	MI	53,931	HC+
Kansas State Univ	KS	17,780	VC
Messiah College	PA	43,100	C+
Metropolitan State Univ	MN	7,566	C
Mills College	CA	59,163	VC
Minn State Univ, Mankato	MN	15,616	C
Moravian College	PA	53,117	
New York Univ	NY	65,860	MC
Oregon State Univ	OR	22,519	VC
Sonoma State Univ	CA	27,806	C
St. Catherine Univ	MN	45,630	VC
St. Olaf College	MN	54,260	HC+
SUNY at Purchase	NY	17,900	C
The Univ of Utah	UT	17,924	VC
Univ of Calif at Berkeley	CA	28,853	MC
Univ of Calif at Riverside	CA	29,227	C+
Univ of Calif San Diego	CA	30,150	MC
Univ of Colo Boulder	CO	24,285	VC+
Univ of Colo Colo Springs	CO	19,663	C
Univ of Colo Denver	CO	23,230	C
Univ of Hawaii at Manoa	HI	23,221	C
Univ of Illinois at Chicago	IL	25,006	VC
Univ of Nebr - Lincoln	NE	18,589	VC
Univ of North Florida	FL	15,996	VC
Univ of Oregon	OR	22,972	C
Univ of San Diego	CA	58,442	VC+
Univ of Texas at Austin	TX	26,102	HC
Univ of Vermont	VT	28,878	HC
Univ of Washington	WA	23,149	VC
Univ of Wisc-Milwaukee	WI	21,496	C
Washington State Univ	WA	22,495	C
Washington Univ in St. Louis	MO	65,366	VC
Westfield State Univ	MA	19,671	C
Whitman College	WA	59,772	MC
Wichita State Univ	KS	21,643	C
Yale Univ	CT	64,650	MC

EUROPEAN STUDIES

School	ST	$IS	SR
Amherst College	MA		HC+
Barnard College/Columbia Univ	NY	62,741	MC
Bates College	ME	64,500	MC
Bennington College	VT	63,960	MC
Boston Univ	MA	65,110	MC
Brandeis Univ	MA	65,925	MC
Cal State, Fullerton	CA	21,902	C
Canisius College	NY	47,537	C
Central Mich Univ	MI	20,330	C
Dallas Baptist Univ	TX	33,713	C
Emory and Henry College	VA	41,410	C
George Washington Univ	DC	62,835	MC
Georgetown College	KY	41,440	C
Harvard College/Harvard Univ	MA	60,659	MC
Hillsdale College	MI	35,722	MC
John Carroll Univ	OH	49,740	C+
Lipscomb Univ	TN	41,296	VC
Loyola Marymount Univ	CA	58,038	HC
Middlebury College	VT	64,332	MC
Millsaps College	MS	50,080	C+
New York Univ	NY	65,860	MC
Northwestern Univ	IL	66,344	MC
Ohio Univ	OH	22,924	C
Pitzer College	CA	66,192	MC
St. Joseph's Univ	PA	57,544	VC+
San Diego State Univ	CA	21,896	C+
Scripps College	CA	66,664	MC
Seattle Pacific Univ	WA	47,439	C+
Smith College	MA	63,914	MC
Stony Brook Univ/The SUNY	NY	21,881	MC
Suffolk Univ	MA	50,308	C
Texas State Univ	TX	19,350	C
Univ of Arkansas at Fayetteville	AR	19,152	C+
Univ of Calif at Irvine	CA	26,484	VC
Univ of Calif at Los Angeles	CA	30,162	MC
Univ of Delaware	DE	24,976	VC+
Univ of Kansas	KS	20,135	C+
Univ of Mich/Ann Arbor	MI	24,410	MC
Univ of Minn/Morris	MN	20,760	VC
Univ of New Hampshire	NH	28,562	VC
Univ of New Mexico	NM	15,404	C
Univ of N Car at Chapel Hill	NC	20,052	HC+
Univ of S Car at Columbia	SC	19,725	VC+
Univ of Vermont	VT	28,878	HC
Vanderbilt Univ	TN	60,572	MC
Washington Univ in St. Louis	MO	65,366	VC
Webster Univ	MO	37,490	C
Westmont College	CA	56,410	HC

EVOLUTIONARY BIOLOGY

School	ST	$IS	SR
Angelo State Univ	TX	15,263	NC
Bennington College	VT	63,960	MC
Case Western Reserve Univ	OH	60,304	MC
Florida State Univ	FL	16,771	HC
Marshall Univ	WV	17,242	C
Ohio State Univ at Columbus	OH	21,703	HC+
Princeton Univ	NJ	57,610	MC
Rutgers Univ - New Brunswick	NJ	26,632	HC
SUNY at Binghamton	NY	22,861	MC
Tulane Univ	LA	63,396	HC+
Univ of Calif at Santa Barbara	CA	29,091	HC
Univ of Calif, Santa Cruz	CA	28,731	C+
Univ of Colo Boulder	CO	24,285	VC+
Univ of Conn	CT	25,538	HC
Univ of Mich/Ann Arbor	MI	24,410	MC
Univ of Minn/Twin Cities	MN	23,519	HC+
Yale Univ	CT	64,650	MC

EXERCISE SCIENCE

School	ST	$IS	SR
Adams State Univ	CO	17,703	LC
Adrian College	MI	42,400	C
Albion College	MI	52,650	C
Alma College	MI	47,548	C
Angelo State Univ	TX	15,263	NC
Appalachian State Univ	NC	14,416	VC
Arizona State Univ at the Downtown Phoenix Campus	AZ	23,680	VC
Arkansas State Univ	AR	16,190	C
Asbury Univ	KY	35,180	C+
Augustana Univ	SD	38,424	VC
Aurora Univ	IL	33,970	C
Baker Univ	KS	33,350	C+
Baldwin Wallace Univ	OH	41,106	C
Barton College	NC	38,686	LC
Becker College	MA	57,628	C
Belhaven Univ	MS	31,016	C
Bellarmine Univ	KY	51,220	C
Belmont Univ	TN	40,970	VC
Berry College	GA	45,286	C+
Bethel College	IN	35,860	C
Bethel Univ	MN	45,270	VC
Black Hills State Univ	SD	15,899	C
Bloomsburg Univ of Pennsylvania	PA	19,066	LC
Blue Mountain College	MS	15,949	VC
Bluefield College	VA	34,120	C+
Bowling Green State Univ	OH	19,747	C
Bridgewater College	VA	44,510	C
Brigham Young Univ	UT	12,748	HC
Bryan College	TN	31,440	C
Buena Vista Univ	IA	41,514	C
Cabrini Univ	PA	42,591	LC
Calif Baptist Univ	CA	41,392	C
Calif Lutheran Univ	CA	52,853	C
Cal State, Fullerton	CA	21,902	C
Cal State, Northridge	CA	16,859	LC
Cal State, San Bernardino	CA	12,000	C
Calvin College	MI	41,570	VC+
Campbellsville Univ	KY	32,492	C
Canisius College	NY	47,537	C
Capital Univ	OH	42,982	C
Carroll Univ	WI	38,100	C+
Castleton Univ	VT	20,186	C
Cedarville Univ	OH	34,990	VC
Central College	IA	44,592	C
Central Conn State Univ	CT	21,203	C
Central Washington Univ	WA	16,803	C
Chatham Univ	PA	46,517	C
CUNY/York College	NY	6,747	LC
Clayton State Univ	GA	19,735	C
Cleveland State Univ	OH	22,196	C
Coastal Carolina Univ	SC	19,766	C
Colby-Sawyer College	NH	50,790	C
College of Charleston	SC	22,699	C
College of St. Scholastica	MN	44,640	C
Colo Mesa Univ	CO	18,955	LC
Colo State Univ	CO	22,162	VC
Colo State Univ-Pueblo	CO	18,234	C
Columbus State Univ	GA	14,336	LC
Concordia College - Moorhead	MN	51,088	C+
Concordia Univ	CA	41,580	VC
Concordia Univ Nebr	NE	36,280	VC
Corban Univ	OR	40,306	C
Creighton Univ	NE	48,206	VC+
Davis & Elkins College	WV	38,242	LC
DeSales Univ	PA	43,970	C
Dordt College	IA	37,860	C+
Drury Univ	MO	33,791	VC
D'Youville College	NY	36,780	C
East Carolina Univ	NC	16,937	C
East Central Univ	OK	13,056	C
East Stroudsburg Univ	PA	18,334	C
East Texas Baptist Univ	TX	33,134	C
Eastern Mich Univ	MI	19,761	C
Eastern Univ	PA	39,540	C
Elmhurst College	IL	45,428	C
Elon Univ	NC	44,599	VC+
Endicott College	MA	44,604	VC+
Fitchburg State Univ	MA	21,819	C
Florida Gulf Coast Univ	FL	9,682	C
Florida International Univ	FL	19,854	C+
Fort Lewis College	CO	18,980	C
Franklin College	IN	39,380	C
Frostburg State Univ	MD	17,280	LC
Furman Univ	SC	58,092	VC+
George Fox Univ	OR	42,938	C
Georgetown College	KY	41,440	C
Georgia College & State Univ	GA	21,148	C+
Georgia Southern Univ	GA	16,596	C
Georgia Southwestern State Univ	GA	13,870	C
Georgia State Univ	GA	24,332	VC
Gonzaga Univ	WA	50,888	HC
Grand Canyon Univ	AZ	16,950	VC
Grand Rapids Theological Seminary/Cornerstone Univ	MI	33,338	C
Grand Valley State Univ	MI	22,250	C+
Greensboro College	NC	42,400	LC
Grove City College	PA	25,692	VC
Guilford College	NC	44,090	C
Hamline Univ	MN	45,678	VC
Hannibal-LaGrange Univ	MO	29,815	C
Harding Univ	AR	25,421	C
Hardin-Simmons Univ	TX	33,966	C
Hendrix College	AR	54,020	VC+
High Point Univ	NC	45,977	C
Hillsdale College	MI	35,722	MC
Hiram College	OH	43,230	C
Hofstra Univ	NY	55,960	C+
Hope College	MI	39,940	VC
Howard Payne Univ	TX	34,320	C
Huntingdon College	AL	34,900	C
Huntington Univ	IN	33,996	C
Illinois College	IL	40,850	VC
Illinois State Univ	IL	23,418	VC
Indiana Univ Bloomington	IN	20,429	VC
Ithaca College	NY	56,766	VC
John Brown Univ	AR	33,132	VC
John Carroll Univ	OH	49,740	C+
Kansas State Univ	KS	17,780	VC
Kennesaw State Univ	GA	19,592	VC
Kent State Univ	OH	20,732	C
King's College	PA	46,858	C
La Roche College	PA	37,924	LC
La Sierra Univ	CA	39,690	VC
LaGrange College	GA	39,930	C
Lander Univ	SC	43,994	C
Lenoir-Rhyne Univ	NC	43,200	C

School	ST	$IS	SR
Lewis Univ	IL	40,370	C
Liberty Univ	VA	19,101	C
Linfield College	OR	52,010	C
Lipscomb Univ	TN	41,296	VC
Loras College	IA	39,222	C
Louisiana College	LA	21,886	C
Loyola Univ Chicago	IL	55,802	VC
Lubbock Christian Univ	TX	28,426	C
Lynchburg College	VA	46,740	C
Malone Univ	OH	38,448	C
Marian Univ	IN	41,220	C
Marquette Univ	WI	48,390	VC+
Marshall Univ	WV	17,242	C
McMurry Univ	TX	34,259	LC
Mercy College	NY	31,776	C
Meredith College	NC	45,297	C
Mich Tech Univ	MI	24,739	VC+
Milligan College	TN	38,150	C
Minn State Univ, Mankato	MN	15,616	C
Minn State Univ, Moorhead	MN	15,941	C
Missouri Baptist Univ	MO	35,594	C
Missouri State Univ	MO	15,190	C+
Missouri Valley College	MO	28,150	C
Monmouth College	IL	42,260	C
Montana State Univ-Billings	MT	22,960	C
Montreat College	NC	31,298	LC
Mount Vernon Nazarene Univ	OH	34,500	C
Murray State Univ	KY	16,998	C
Nebr Wesleyan Univ	NE	38,140	C+
Norfolk State Univ	VA	25,702	LC
N Car Wesleyan College	NC	39,200	C
North Central College	IL	48,712	VC
North Park Univ	IL	35,860	C
Northern Arizona Univ	AZ	20,246	VC
Northern Kentucky Univ	KY	16,486	C
Northern Mich Univ	MI	19,604	C
Northwest Christian Univ	OR	36,580	C
Nova Southeastern Univ	FL	38,534	C+
Ohio Dominican Univ	OH	41,340	C+
Ohio State Univ at Columbus	OH	21,703	HC+
Ohio Univ	OH	22,924	C
Okla City Univ	OK	40,476	VC
Olivet Nazarene Univ	IL	41,840	C
Palm Beach Atlantic Univ	FL	39,720	C
Pennsylvania College of Technology	PA	27,333	NC
Pfeiffer Univ	NC	39,695	LC
Piedmont College	GA	32,512	C
Point Loma Nazarene Univ	CA	43,450	C
Purdue Univ/West Lafayette	IN	20,032	MC
Queens Univ of Charlotte	NC	39,543	C
Quincy Univ	IL	36,998	C
Radford Univ	VA	19,027	LC
Rice Univ	TX	57,668	MC
Ripon College	WI	46,911	C+
Roanoke College	VA	54,114	VC
Rochester Inst of Technology	NY	50,842	HC
Rocky Mountain College	MT	34,270	C
Rutgers Univ - New Brunswick	NJ	26,632	HC
Sacred Heart Univ	CT	52,750	C
Saginaw Valley State Univ	MI	18,530	C
St. Louis Univ	MO	49,866	HC
Samford Univ	AL	39,232	VC
San Diego State Univ	CA	21,896	C+
San Francisco State Univ	CA	18,514	LC
Schreiner Univ	TX	34,626	LC
Seattle Pacific Univ	WA	47,439	C+
Seattle Univ	WA	50,811	VC+
Shenandoah Univ	VA	41,312	C
Shippensburg Univ of Pennsylvania	PA	23,208	C
Simmons College	MA	53,090	VC
Simpson College	IA	43,839	VC
Skidmore College	NY	64,214	HC
Smith College	MA	63,914	MC
S Dak State Univ	SD	15,634	C
Southern Illinois Univ Edwardsville	IL	22,643	C
Southern Nazarene Univ	OK	32,798	NC
Southwestern Adventist Univ	TX	27,756	LC
Southwestern Okla State Univ	OK	11,790	C
Southwestern Univ	TX	50,720	VC
Spring Arbor Univ	MI	36,000	C
St. Ambrose Univ	IA	39,019	C
St. Ambrose Univ	IA	39,019	C
St. Catherine Univ	MN	45,630	VC
St. Olaf College	MN	54,260	HC+
SUNY / SUNY Potsdam	NY	20,404	C+
SUNY / Univ at Buffalo	NY	23,122	C+
Sterling College	KS	32,830	C
Taylor Univ	IN	40,317	C+
Texas State Univ	TX	19,350	C
Texas Wesleyan Univ	TX	35,134	C
The College at Brockport - SUNY	NY	20,346	C
The College of Idaho	ID	36,415	C
The College of New Jersey	NJ	31,909	HC
The Univ of Akron	OH	21,477	C
The Univ of Utah	UT	17,924	VC
Thomas Edison State Univ	NJ	6,350	NC
Tiffin Univ	OH	31,380	C
Towson Univ	MD	17,408	VC
Transylvania Univ	KY	45,690	VC+
Trevecca Nazarene Univ	TN	31,186	C
Trinity Washington Univ	DC	33,826	C+
Truman State Univ	MO	16,014	HC
Union College	KY	32,310	C
Univ of Arkansas at Fayetteville	AR	19,152	C+
Univ of Arkansas at Monticello	AR	13,134	NC
Univ of Central Arkansas	AR	14,472	VC
Univ of Central Florida	FL	15,922	VC
Univ of Central Okla	OK	13,486	C
Univ of Conn	CT	25,538	HC
Univ of Dayton	OH	53,620	C
Univ of Evansville	IN	44,186	VC+
Univ of Florida	FL	16,291	HC+
Univ of Georgia	GA	21,250	HC
Univ of Hawaii at Manoa	HI	23,221	C
Univ of Idaho	ID	15,348	C
Univ of Illinois at Chicago	IL	25,006	VC
Univ of Illinois at Urbana-Champaign	IL	27,006	HC
Univ of Indianapolis	IN	36,480	C
Univ of Jamestown	ND	28,508	C
Univ of Kansas	KS	20,135	C+
Univ of Louisiana at Monroe	LA	15,970	C
Univ of Maine at Machias	ME	22,960	C
Univ of Mary	ND	23,180	C
Univ of Mary Hardin-Baylor	TX	33,950	C+
Univ of Mass Amherst	MA	26,199	VC+
Univ of Mass Boston	MA	13,435	C
Univ of Mass Lowell	MA	26,380	C
Univ of Miami	FL	63,494	MC
Univ of Mich/Ann Arbor	MI	24,410	MC
Univ of Miss	MS	17,746	C+
Univ of Mount Union	OH	38,970	C
Univ of Nebr - Lincoln	NE	18,589	VC
Univ of Nevada, Las Vegas	NV	17,553	C
Univ of New England	ME	48,880	C
Univ of New Mexico	NM	15,404	C
Univ of N Car at Chapel Hill	NC	20,052	HC+
Univ of N Car at Charlotte	NC	15,547	C
Univ of N Car at Greensboro	NC	14,690	C
Univ of N Car at Pembroke	NC	14,388	LC
Univ of Northern Colo	CO	20,851	C
Univ of Northwestern - St. Paul	MN	38,160	C
Univ of Okla	OK	18,911	VC
Univ of Puget Sound	WA	56,456	VC+
Univ of St. Francis	IN	37,400	C
Univ of San Francisco	CA	58,484	VC
Univ of Scranton	PA	54,962	VC
Univ of S Car Aiken	SC	16,712	C
Univ of S Car at Columbia	SC	19,725	VC+
Univ of S Dak	SD	16,109	C
Univ of Southern Calif	CA	66,631	C
Univ of Southern Indiana	IN	16,501	C
Univ of Tampa	FL	36,944	C
Univ of the Cumberlands	KY	32,000	C
Univ of Tulsa	OK	52,625	HC+
Univ of Vermont	VT	28,878	HC
Univ of Wisc-Green Bay	WI	15,064	C
Univ of Wisc-La Crosse	WI	15,247	C+
Univ of Wisc-Milwaukee	WI	21,496	C
Univ of Wisc-Superior	WI	14,446	C
Urbana Univ	OH	30,820	C
Ursinus College	PA	61,690	VC
Valparaiso Univ	IN	48,370	C+
Vanguard Univ of Southern Calif	CA	40,740	VC
Wake Forest Univ	NC	64,056	MC
Walsh Univ	OH	39,010	C
Warner Univ	FL	28,216	C
Washington Adventist Univ	MD	31,440	LC
Washington State Univ	WA	22,495	C
Wayne State College	NE	12,802	C
Wayne State Univ	MI	22,016	C
Waynesburg Univ	PA	32,290	C
Webster Univ	MO	37,490	C
Wesley College	DE	37,026	LC
West Chester Univ of Pennsylvania	PA	18,456	C
West Texas A&M Univ	TX	13,478	C
West Virginia Wesleyan College	WV	36,858	C
Western Illinois Univ	IL	20,825	C
Western Kentucky Univ	KY	16,850	C
Western Mich Univ	MI	21,054	C
Westmont College	CA	56,410	HC
Willamette Univ	OR	61,817	VC+
Wilson College	PA	35,620	C
Wingate Univ	NC	39,950	C
Winona State Univ	MN	17,535	C
Winthrop Univ	SC	23,082	C
Wisc Lutheran College	WI	36,290	VC
Wittenberg Univ	OH	48,156	C+
Wright State Univ	OH	16,983	C
Youngstown State Univ	OH	17,307	C

EXPERIMENTAL PSYCHOLOGY

School	ST	$IS	SR
Blackburn College	IL	28,526	LC
Prescott College	AZ	33,284	C
St. Leo Univ	FL	31,650	C
Univ of S Car at Columbia	SC	19,725	VC+

FACILITIES MANAGEMENT

School	ST	$IS	SR
Farmingdale State College	NY	20,624	C
Ferris State Univ	MI	21,445	C

FAMILY AND COMMUNITY SERVICES

School	ST	$IS	SR
Central Washington Univ	WA	16,803	C
East Carolina Univ	NC	16,937	C
John Brown Univ	AR	33,132	VC
Kansas State Univ	KS	17,780	VC
Mich State Univ	MI	23,898	VC+
Montclair State Univ	NJ	26,210	LC
Ohio Univ	OH	22,924	C
Prairie View A&M Univ	TX	15,205	LC
Purdue Univ/West Lafayette	IN	20,032	MC
Trinity International Univ	IL	31,070	VC
Union Univ	TN	33,970	VC
Univ of Delaware	DE	24,976	VC+
Univ of Oregon	OR	22,972	C
Western Kentucky Univ	KY	16,850	C

FAMILY STUDIES/SOC SERV/ MARRIAGE FAMILY

School	ST	$IS	SR
College of the Ozarks	MO	7,230	C
Okla Baptist Univ	OK	32,320	C

FAMILY/CONSUMER RESOURCE MANAGEMENT

School	ST	$IS	SR
Cal State, Northridge	CA	16,859	LC
East Central Univ	OK	13,056	C
Indiana Univ of Pennsylvania	PA	23,614	LC
Iowa State Univ	IA	17,570	C
Mich State Univ	MI	23,898	VC+
Ohio State Univ at Columbus	OH	21,703	HC+
Ohio State Univ at Lima	OH	7,140	C
Ohio Univ	OH	22,924	C
Seattle Pacific Univ	WA	47,439	C+
Seton Hill Univ	PA	46,972	C
S Dak State Univ	SD	15,634	C
Southeastern Louisiana Univ	LA	16,237	C
Univ of Hawaii at Manoa	HI	23,221	C
Univ of Missouri/Columbia	MO	18,201	MC
West Virginia Univ	WV	18,210	C

FAMILY/CONSUMER STUDIES

School	ST	$IS	SR
Alabama A&M Univ	AL	18,796	C
Alderson Broaddus Univ	WV	26,149	C
Anderson Univ	IN	38,200	C
Andrews Univ	MI	28,030	C+
Appalachian State Univ	NC	14,416	VC
Ashford Univ	CA	10,480	C
Ball State Univ	IN	19,590	C
Baylor Univ	TX	53,760	HC
Bluffton Univ	OH	40,950	C
Bowling Green State Univ	OH	19,747	C
Bridgewater College	VA	44,510	C
Brigham Young Univ	UT	12,748	HC
Cal State, Fresno	CA	16,902	LC
Cal State, Long Beach	CA	18,850	C
Cal State, Northridge	CA	16,859	LC
Central Mich Univ	MI	20,330	C
Central Washington Univ	WA	16,803	C
CUNY/Queens College	NY	27,896	C
College of the Ozarks	MO	7,230	C
Colo State Univ	CO	22,162	VC
Concordia Univ, Ann Arbor	MI	35,945	VC
Delta State Univ	MS	13,176	C
East Central Univ	OK	13,056	C
Eastern Illinois Univ	IL	21,126	C
Florida State Univ	FL	16,771	HC
Fontbonne Univ	MO	33,717	C
Freed-Hardeman Univ	TN	29,450	C
George Fox Univ	OR	42,938	C
Grand Rapids Theological Seminary/Cornerstone Univ	MI	33,338	C
Hampshire College	MA	63,824	MC
Henderson State Univ	AR	15,516	LC
Idaho State Univ	ID	13,619	NC
Illinois State Univ	IL	23,418	VC
Iowa State Univ	IA	17,570	C
Kansas State Univ	KS	17,780	VC
Lamar Univ	TX	18,014	LC
Liberty Univ	VA	19,101	C
Lipscomb Univ	TN	41,296	VC
Lubbock Christian Univ	TX	28,426	C
Madonna Univ	MI	29,050	C
Marywood Univ	PA	46,900	C
Mercyhurst Univ	PA	47,420	C
Meredith College	NC	45,297	C
Messiah College	PA	43,100	C+
Miami Univ	OH	27,190	HC+
Mich State Univ	MI	23,898	VC+
Middle Tenn State Univ	TN	8,650	C
Minn State Univ, Mankato	MN	15,616	C
Miss College	MS	25,850	C
Missouri State Univ	MO	15,190	C+
New Mexico State Univ	NM	14,050	C
Nicholls State Univ	LA	10,534	C
Oakwood Univ	AL	43,758	C
Ohio State Univ at Columbus	OH	21,703	HC+
Ohio Univ	OH	22,924	C
Olivet Nazarene Univ	IL	41,840	C
Pittsburg State Univ	KS	13,880	NC
Purdue Univ/West Lafayette	IN	20,032	MC
San Francisco State Univ	CA	18,514	LC
Seattle Pacific Univ	WA	47,439	C+
Seton Hill Univ	PA	46,972	C
Shepherd Univ, West Virginia	WV	17,224	C
Silver Lake College of the Holy Family	WI	36,290	LC
S Car State Univ	SC	20,805	LC
S Dak State Univ	SD	15,634	C
Southern Univ and A&M College	LA	16,074	LC+
St. Catherine Univ	MN	45,630	VC
SUNY at Oswego	NY	21,351	C
Stephen F. Austin State Univ	TX	18,406	LC
Tarleton State Univ	TX	15,248	LC
Tenn State Univ	TN	14,423	C
Texas State Univ	TX	19,350	C
Texas Tech Univ	TX	18,736	C+
Texas Woman's Univ	TX	15,302	LC
The Master's Univ	CA	43,870	C+
The Univ of Akron	OH	21,477	C
The Univ of Utah	UT	17,924	VC
Towson Univ	MD	17,408	VC
Univ of Arizona	AZ	23,100	C
Univ of Arkansas at Pine Bluff	AR	13,541	C
Univ of Central Arkansas	AR	14,472	VC
Univ of Central Okla	OK	13,486	C
Univ of Georgia	GA	21,250	HC
Univ of Idaho	ID	15,348	C
Univ of Illinois at Urbana-Champaign	IL	27,006	HC
Univ of Maryland/College Park	MD	21,938	HC
Univ of Montevallo	AL	19,502	C
Univ of Nebr - Kearney	NE	16,546	LC
Univ of Nebr - Lincoln	NE	18,589	VC
Univ of New Hampshire	NH	28,562	VC
Univ of New Mexico	NM	15,404	C
Univ of PR-Rio Piedras campus	PR	13,327	
Univ of St. Joseph	CT	49,550	C
Univ of Wisc-Madison	WI	20,934	MC
Univ of Wisc-Stevens Point	WI	14,043	C
Univ of Wisc-Stout	WI	19,667	C
Univ of Wyoming	WY	15,375	C+
Urbana Univ	OH	30,820	C
Washington State Univ	WA	22,495	C
Wayne State College	NE	12,802	C
Weber State Univ	UT	10,721	C
Western Kentucky Univ	KY	16,850	C
Western Mich Univ	MI	21,054	C
Youngstown State Univ	OH	17,307	C

FAMILY/JUVENILE JUSTICE

School	ST	$IS	SR
East Central Univ	OK	13,056	C
Georgetown College	KY	41,440	C
The Univ of Akron	OH	21,477	C
Univ of New Haven	CT	52,190	C
William Woods Univ	MO	32,040	C

FASHION DESIGN AND TECHNOLOGY

School	ST	$IS	SR
Baylor Univ	TX	53,760	HC
Bennington College	VT	63,960	MC
Calif College of the Arts	CA	52,758	SP
Cazenovia College	NY	46,470	C
Centenary College	NJ	43,602	C
Columbus College of Art and Design	OH	37,732	C
Dominican Univ	IL	41,222	C
Drexel Univ	PA	65,432	VC+
Fashion Inst of Technology/ SUNY	NY	18,521	SP
Florida State Univ	FL	16,771	HC
Framingham State Univ	MA	20,584	C
Howard Univ	DC	37,616	C+
Illinois State Univ	IL	23,418	VC
Indiana Univ Bloomington	IN	20,429	VC
Iowa State Univ	IA	17,570	C
Kent State Univ	OH	20,732	C
Lasell College	MA	47,500	C
Lindenwood Univ	MO	25,132	C
Marist College	NY	49,860	VC
Marymount Univ	VA	41,570	LC
Mass College of Art and Design	MA	24,800	SP
Missouri State Univ	MO	15,190	C+
Moore College of Art and Design	PA	50,135	SP
Mount Ida College	MA	46,820	C
Mount Mary Univ	WI	34,650	LC
Otis College of Art and Design	CA	55,858	SP
Parsons The New School for Design	NY	56,610	SP
Philadelphia Univ	PA	50,370	C
Pratt Inst	NY	58,082	VC
Purdue Univ/West Lafayette	IN	20,032	MC
Savannah College of Art and Design	GA	49,595	C
School of the Art Inst of Chicago	IL	56,230	SP
St. Catherine Univ	MN	45,630	VC
Stephens College	MO	38,042	C
Stevenson Univ	MD	72,770	C
Syracuse Univ	NY	60,239	VC
Texas Woman's Univ	TX	15,302	LC
Univ of Cincinnati	OH	21,964	VC
Univ of Delaware	DE	24,976	VC+

ST = STATE $IS = IN-STATE COSTS SR = SELECTOR RATING

School	ST	$IS	SR
Univ of North Texas	TX	19,198	C
Univ of the Incarnate Word	TX	39,162	LC
Ursuline College	OH	41,076	LC
Virginia Commonwealth Univ	VA	23,049	C
Washington Univ in St. Louis	MO	65,366	VC
Western Mich Univ	MI	21,054	C
Woodbury Univ	CA	46,958	C

FASHION MERCHANDISING

School	ST	$IS	SR
Albright College	PA	46,660	C
Ashland Univ	OH	21,440	C
Auburn Univ	AL	23,594	VC+
Baylor Univ	TX	53,760	HC
Brenau Univ - Women's College	GA	37,876	LC
Canisius College	NY	47,537	C
Central Washington Univ	WA	16,803	C
Delaware State Univ	DE	19,376	NC
Dominican Univ	IL	41,222	C
Drexel Univ	PA	65,432	VC+
East Central Univ	OK	13,056	C
Eastern Mich Univ	MI	19,761	C
Fashion Inst of Technology/ SUNY	NY	18,521	SP
Florida State Univ	FL	16,771	HC
Fontbonne Univ	MO	33,717	C
Framingham State Univ	MA	20,584	C
Harding Univ	AR	25,421	C
Howard Univ	DC	37,616	C+
Indiana Inst of Technology	IN	34,240	LC
Indiana Univ of Pennsylvania	PA	23,614	LC
Iowa State Univ	IA	17,570	C
Johnson & Wales Univ/ Providence Campus	RI	42,248	C
Kent State Univ	OH	20,732	C
Lasell College	MA	47,500	C
LIM College	NY	41,575	LC
Lipscomb Univ	TN	41,296	VC
Marist College	NY	49,860	VC
Mars Hill Univ	NC	42,688	C
Marymount Univ	VA	41,570	LC
Mercyhurst Univ	PA	47,420	C
Meredith College	NC	45,297	C
Missouri State Univ	MO	15,190	C+
Mount Ida College	MA	46,820	C
Mount Mary Univ	WI	34,650	LC
New Mexico State Univ	NM	14,050	C
Newbury College	MA	46,950	C
Northwood Univ - Mich	MI	35,010	LC
Ohio State Univ at Columbus	OH	21,703	HC+
Ohio Univ	OH	22,924	C
Old Dominion Univ	VA	20,910	C
Olivet Nazarene Univ	IL	41,840	C
Philadelphia Univ	PA	50,370	C
Purdue Univ/West Lafayette	IN	20,032	MC
Savannah College of Art and Design	GA	49,595	C
Southeast Missouri State Univ	MO	15,498	C
Southern Illinois Univ Carbondale	IL	23,667	C
Southern New Hampshire Univ	NH	43,198	C
St. Catherine Univ	MN	45,630	VC
SUNY / SUNY Oneonta	NY	19,712	C+
Stephen F. Austin State Univ	TX	18,406	LC
Stephens College	MO	38,042	C
Stevenson Univ	MD	72,770	C
Tarleton State Univ	TX	15,248	LC
Texas A&M Univ at Kingsville	TX	7,500	LC
Texas Christian Univ	TX	54,670	HC
Texas State Univ	TX	19,350	C
Texas Woman's Univ	TX	15,302	LC
The Univ of Akron	OH	21,477	C
Univ of Bridgeport	CT	44,430	LC
Univ of Central Okla	OK	13,486	C
Univ of Georgia	GA	21,250	HC
Univ of Louisiana at Lafayette	LA	14,516	C
Univ of Nebr - Lincoln	NE	18,589	VC
Univ of the Incarnate Word	TX	39,162	LC
Ursuline College	OH	41,076	LC
Utah State Univ	UT	12,736	C
West Virginia Univ	WV	18,210	C
Western Mich Univ	MI	21,054	C
Western Washington Univ	WA	18,003	C+
Woodbury Univ	CA	46,958	C
Youngstown State Univ	OH	17,307	C

FASHION STUDIES

School	ST	$IS	SR
Columbia College Chicago	IL	43,168	C
Ferris State Univ	MI	21,445	C
Lynn Univ	FL	49,480	LC
Marist College	NY	49,860	VC

FEMINIST, GENDER, SEXUALITY STUDIES

School	ST	$IS	SR
Brown Univ	RI	64,566	MC
Bryant Univ	RI	55,646	VC
Cornell Univ	NY	64,853	MC
Northland College	WI	41,103	C+
St. Ambrose Univ	IA	39,019	C
St. Ambrose Univ	IA	39,019	C
Tufts Univ	MA		MC
Wellesley College	MA	63,916	MC

FIBER SCIENCE AND APPAREL DESIGN

School	ST	$IS	SR
Cornell Univ	NY	64,853	MC

FIBER/TEXTILES/WEAVING

School	ST	$IS	SR
Adams State Univ	CO	17,703	LC
Colo State Univ	CO	22,162	VC
Fashion Inst of Technology/ SUNY	NY	18,521	SP
Florida State Univ	FL	16,771	HC
Kansas City Art Inst	MO	44,308	C+
Kutztown Univ of Pennsylvania	PA	19,056	LC
Maryland Inst College of Art	MD	56,795	SP
Mass College of Art and Design	MA	24,800	SP
Savannah College of Art and Design	GA	49,595	C
School of the Art Inst of Chicago	IL	56,230	SP
Temple Univ	PA	24,392	VC
Univ of Kansas	KS	20,135	C+
Univ of Mass Dartmouth	MA	25,658	C
Univ of Mich/Ann Arbor	MI	24,410	MC
Univ of Oregon	OR	22,972	C

FILM AND MEDIA STUDIES

School	ST	$IS	SR
Ball State Univ	IN	19,590	C
Birmingham-Southern College	AL	44,478	VC
Boston Univ	MA	65,110	MC
Calvin College	MI	41,570	VC+
Central Conn State Univ	CT	21,203	C
CUNY/Queens College	NY	27,896	C
Clayton State Univ	GA	19,735	C
Flagler College	FL	27,620	C
Lynn Univ	FL	49,480	LC
Marist College	NY	49,860	VC
Pennsylvania State Univ - Univ Park	PA	29,760	HC
Tufts Univ	MA		MC
Univ of Georgia	GA	21,250	HC
Univ of Kansas	KS	20,135	C+
Wellesley College	MA	63,916	MC
Wells College	NY	50,500	C
Western Kentucky Univ	KY	16,850	C
Wheaton College	MA	61,512	VC
Whitman College	WA	59,772	MC

FILM ARTS

School	ST	$IS	SR
American Univ	DC	59,379	HC+
Arizona State Univ at the Tempe Campus	AZ	21,756	VC
ArtCenter College of Design	CA	54,212	SP
Bard College	NY	64,024	HC
Barnard College/Columbia Univ	NY	62,741	MC
Bennington College	VT	63,960	MC
Berklee College of Music	MA	60,930	SP
Biola Univ	CA	46,402	C+
Boston College	MA	65,737	MC
Boston Univ	MA	65,110	MC
Bowling Green State Univ	OH	19,747	C
Brandeis Univ	MA	65,925	MC
Calif Baptist Univ	CA	41,392	C
Calif College of the Arts	CA	52,758	SP
Cal State, Long Beach	CA	18,850	C
Cal State, Northridge	CA	16,859	LC
Calvin College	MI	41,570	VC+
Champlain College	VT	53,132	C+
Chapman Univ	CA	63,078	VC+
CUNY/Brooklyn College	NY	5,884	C+
CUNY/City College	NY	20,319	VC
CUNY/College of Staten Island	NY	17,840	NC
CUNY/Hunter College	NY	31,098	VC
Claremont McKenna College	CA	67,185	MC
Clark Univ	MA	51,600	HC+
Clayton State Univ	GA	19,735	C
Coe College	IA	51,570	VC
Colo College	CO	62,560	MC
Columbia College Chicago	IL	43,168	C
Columbia Univ/ School of General Studies	NY	61,470	MC
Columbia Univ/City of New York	NY	62,958	MC
Columbus College of Art and Design	OH	37,732	C
Concordia Univ	CA	41,580	VC
Conn College	CT	65,000	MC
Cornish College of the Arts	WA	47,750	SP
Dartmouth College	NH	66,174	MC
Denison Univ	OH	58,860	MC
DeSales Univ	PA	43,970	C
Dominican Univ	IL	41,222	C
Drexel Univ	PA	65,432	VC+
Eastern Mich Univ	MI	19,761	C
Elon Univ	NC	44,599	VC+
Emerson College	MA	54,736	HC
Emory Univ	GA	60,786	MC
Fairleigh Dickinson Univ/ College at Florham	NJ	52,062	C
Florida State Univ	FL	16,771	HC
George Fox Univ	OR	42,938	C
George Mason Univ	VA	15,724	VC
Georgia State Univ	GA	24,332	VC
Grand Valley State Univ	MI	22,250	C+
Hamilton College	NY	64,250	MC
Hampshire College	MA	63,824	MC
Hofstra Univ	NY	55,960	C+
Hollins Univ	VA	49,635	VC
Howard Univ	DC	37,616	C+
Huntington Univ	IN	33,996	C
Ithaca College	NY	56,766	VC
Kansas City Art Inst	MO	44,308	C+
Keene State College	NH	24,003	LC
Kenyon College	OH	63,330	MC
LIU Post	NY	49,682	C
Mass College of Art and Design	MA	24,800	SP
Memphis College of Art	TN	39,750	C
Messiah College	PA	43,100	C+
Miami Univ	OH	27,190	HC+
Mich State Univ	MI	23,898	VC+
Middlebury College	VT	64,332	MC
Minneapolis College of Art and Design	MN	44,238	SP
Minn State Univ, Moorhead	MN	15,941	C
Montclair State Univ	NJ	26,210	LC
Mount Holyoke College	MA	56,746	MC
Mount St. Mary's Univ - Chalon Campus	CA	43,897	VC+
Muhlenberg College	PA	56,645	VC+
New Mexico State Univ	NM	14,050	C
New York Univ	NY	65,860	MC
Northeastern Univ	MA	62,703	MC
Oakland Univ	MI	20,763	C
Oberlin College	OH	66,012	MC
Ohio Univ	OH	22,924	C
Okla City Univ	OK	40,476	VC
Old Dominion Univ	VA	20,910	C
Oral Roberts Univ	OK	34,316	C
Pace Univ	NY	58,248	C
Palm Beach Atlantic Univ	FL	39,720	C
Pepperdine Univ	CA	74,460	HC+
Pitzer College	CA	66,192	MC
Point Park Univ	PA	41,270	C
Pratt Inst	NY	58,082	VC
Purdue Univ/West Lafayette	IN	20,032	MC
Rhode Island College	RI	17,694	LC
Rhode Island School of Design	RI	59,960	SP
Ringling College of Art and Design	FL	57,430	SP
Rochester Inst of Technology	NY	50,842	HC
San Francisco Art Inst	CA	58,505	SP
San Francisco State Univ	CA	18,514	LC
San Jose State Univ	CA	21,540	C
Santa Fe Univ of Art and Design	NM	39,980	SP
Sarah Lawrence College	NY	63,388	HC
Savannah College of Art and Design	GA	49,595	C
School of the Art Inst of Chicago	IL	56,230	SP
School of Visual Arts	NY	47,500	SP
Seattle Univ	WA	50,811	VC+
Smith College	MA	63,914	MC
Southern Adventist Univ	TN	27,600	C
Southern Illinois Univ Carbondale	IL	23,667	C
Southern Methodist Univ	TX	66,483	MC
Spring Arbor Univ	MI	36,000	C
St. Mary's College of Maryland	MD	26,634	VC
Stanford Univ	CA	60,409	MC
SUNY / SUNY Cortland	NY	20,706	VC
SUNY / Univ at Buffalo	NY	23,122	C+
SUNY at Binghamton	NY	22,861	MC
SUNY at Oswego	NY	21,351	C
SUNY at Purchase	NY	17,900	C
Stephens College	MO	38,042	C
Stevenson Univ	MD	72,770	C
Suffolk Univ	MA	50,308	C
Swarthmore College	PA	63,550	MC
Syracuse Univ	NY	60,239	VC
Taylor Univ	IN	40,317	C+
Temple Univ	PA	24,392	VC
The Univ of Utah	UT	17,924	VC
Tulane Univ	LA	63,396	HC+
Univ of Alaska Fairbanks	AK	16,179	C
Univ of Arizona	AZ	23,100	C
Univ of Calif at Berkeley	CA	28,853	MC
Univ of Calif at Irvine	CA	26,484	VC
Univ of Calif at Los Angeles	CA	30,162	MC
Univ of Calif at Riverside	CA	29,227	C+
Univ of Calif at Santa Barbara	CA	29,091	HC
Univ of Calif, Santa Cruz	CA	28,731	C+
Univ of Central Florida	FL	15,922	VC
Univ of Chicago	IL	67,584	MC
Univ of Colo Boulder	CO	24,285	VC+
Univ of Denver	CO	58,443	VC+
Univ of Georgia	GA	21,250	HC
Univ of Hartford	CT	49,776	C
Univ of Illinois at Chicago	IL	25,006	VC
Univ of Illinois at Urbana-Champaign	IL	27,006	HC
Univ of Iowa	IA	18,683	VC+
Univ of Maryland/College Park	MD	21,938	HC
Univ of Miami	FL	63,494	MC
Univ of Mich/Ann Arbor	MI	24,410	MC
Univ of Minn/Twin Cities	MN	23,519	HC+
Univ of Nebr - Lincoln	NE	18,589	VC
Univ of Nevada, Las Vegas	NV	17,553	C
Univ of N Car at Wilmington	NC	14,590	VC
Univ of N Car School of the Arts	NC	18,040	SP
Univ of Okla	OK	18,911	VC
Univ of Oregon	OR	22,972	C
Univ of Pittsburgh	PA	29,568	HC+
Univ of Richmond	VA	60,880	MC
Univ of Rochester	NY	65,032	MC
Univ of Southern Calif	CA	66,631	C
Univ of Tampa	FL	36,944	C
Univ of Texas at Austin	TX	26,102	HC
Univ of the Arts	PA	56,579	SP
Univ of Toledo	OH	19,336	NC
Univ of Tulsa	OK	52,625	HC+
Univ of Vermont	VT	28,878	HC
Univ of Wisc-Milwaukee	WI	21,496	C
Vassar College	NY	65,491	MC
Virginia Commonwealth Univ	VA	23,049	C
Washington Univ in St. Louis	MO	65,366	VC
Wayne State Univ	MI	22,016	C
Webster Univ	MO	37,490	C
Wellesley College	MA	63,916	MC
Wesleyan Univ	CT	65,516	MC
Western Kentucky Univ	KY	16,850	C
Wheaton College	MA	61,512	VC
Wright State Univ	OH	16,983	C
Yale Univ	CT	64,650	MC

FILM, TELEVISION AND DIGITAL MEDIA

School	ST	$IS	SR
Amherst College	MA		HC+
Asbury Univ	KY	35,180	C+
Baldwin Wallace Univ	OH	41,106	C
Calvin College	MI	41,570	VC+
Chapman Univ	CA	63,078	VC+
Chatham Univ	PA	46,517	C
CUNY/Queens College	NY	27,896	C
Clayton State Univ	GA	19,735	C
Cleveland State Univ	OH	22,196	C
Dallas Baptist Univ	TX	33,713	C
Dordt College	IA	37,860	C+
Fairfield Univ	CT	59,860	VC+
Five Towns College	NY	35,350	C
Fordham Univ	NY	65,918	MC
Goshen College	IN	42,500	C
Kalamazoo College	MI	53,931	HC+
Kansas City Art Inst	MO	44,308	C+
Loyola Marymount Univ	CA	58,038	HC
Loyola Univ New Orleans	LA	51,708	VC+
Mercy College	NY	31,776	C
Messiah College	PA	43,100	C+
Millersville Univ of Pennsylvania	PA	23,782	C
Morehouse College	GA	40,064	C
New York Inst of Technology	NY	48,730	C
Northern Arizona Univ	AZ	20,246	VC
Rochester Inst of Technology	NY	50,842	HC
Southern Oregon Univ	OR	19,117	C
St. John's Univ	NY	55,850	C
SUNY / SUNY Fredonia	NY	20,818	C
Taylor Univ	IN	40,317	C+
Texas Christian Univ	TX	54,670	HC
The Master's Univ	CA	43,870	C+
The Univ of Utah	UT	17,924	VC
Univ of Arizona	AZ	23,100	C
Univ of Georgia	GA	21,250	HC
Univ of Illinois at Chicago	IL	25,006	VC
Univ of Kansas	KS	20,135	C+
Univ of Nebr - Lincoln	NE	18,589	VC
Univ of New Mexico	NM	15,404	C
Univ of Notre Dame	IN	64,043	MC
Univ of Pikeville	KY	28,700	NC
Univ of Rhode Island	RI	24,906	C
Wayne State Univ	MI	22,016	C
Western Mich Univ	MI	21,054	C
Youngstown State Univ	OH	17,307	C

FINANCE

School	ST	$IS	SR
Abilene Christian Univ	TX	41,800	C+
Albion College	MI	52,650	C
Alma College	MI	47,548	C
Aquinas College	TN	30,800	C+
Arizona State Univ at the Tempe Campus	AZ	21,756	VC
Arkansas Tech Univ	AR	15,484	C
Ashford Univ	CA	10,480	C
Auburn Univ at Montgomery	AL	15,290	C
Aurora Univ	IL	33,970	C
Austin Peay State Univ	TN	16,397	C
Baldwin Wallace Univ	OH	41,106	C
Ball State Univ	IN	19,590	C
Belmont Univ	TN	40,970	VC
Bentley Univ	MA	60,890	HC
Berry College	GA	45,286	C+
Bethany College	KS	46,100	NC
Bethany College	WV	36,300	NC
Bloomfield College	NJ	39,100	LC
Boise State Univ	ID	14,860	C
Bridgewater State Univ	MA	21,810	C
Bryant Univ	RI	55,646	VC
Cabrini Univ	PA	42,591	LC
Cal State, Fullerton	CA	21,902	C

ST = STATE $IS = IN-STATE COSTS SR = SELECTOR RATING

School	ST	$IS	SR
Cal State, Long Beach	CA	18,850	C
Calvin College	MI	41,570	VC+
Canisius College	NY	47,537	C
Carroll College	MT	39,972	C+
Carroll Univ	WI	38,100	C+
Case Western Reserve Univ	OH	60,304	MC
Cedarville Univ	OH	34,990	VC
Central Conn State Univ	CT	21,203	C
Centre College	KY	49,250	HC
Champlain College	VT	53,132	C+
Christopher Newport Univ	VA	23,968	VC+
CUNY/Queens College	NY	27,896	C
Clarkson Univ	NY	60,392	HC
Clayton State Univ	GA	19,735	C
Cleveland State Univ	OH	22,196	C
College of Charleston	SC	22,699	C
College of St. Scholastica	MN	44,640	C
Columbia College - Missouri	MO	27,803	C
Concordia Univ, Ann Arbor	MI	35,945	VC
Creighton Univ	NE	48,206	VC+
Culver-Stockton College	MO	33,525	C
Dallas Baptist Univ	TX	33,713	C
Davis & Elkins College	WV	38,242	LC
DePaul Univ	IL	47,623	VC
DeSales Univ	PA	43,970	C
Dominican Univ	IL	41,222	C
Eastern Conn State Univ	CT	23,059	C
Eastern Illinois Univ	IL	21,126	C
Elmhurst College	IL	45,428	C
Elon Univ	NC	44,599	VC+
Endicott College	MA	44,604	VC+
Fairfield Univ	CT	59,860	VC+
Ferris State Univ	MI	21,445	C
Fordham Univ	NY	65,918	MC
Framingham State Univ	MA	20,584	C
Georgetown Univ	DC	65,926	MC
Georgia Southern Univ	GA	16,596	C
Gordon College	MA	46,472	C+
Grove City College	PA	25,692	VC
Hardin-Simmons Univ	TX	33,966	C
Hawaii Pacific Univ	HI	33,420	C
Hawaii Pacific Univ	HI	33,420	C
Hawaii Pacific Univ	HI	33,420	C
Hillsdale College	MI	35,722	MC
Holy Family Univ	PA	43,326	LC
Illinois State Univ	IL	23,418	VC
Indiana Univ Bloomington	IN	20,429	VC
Indiana Univ of Pennsylvania	PA	23,614	LC
Iona College	NY	50,984	C
Jackson State Univ	MS	15,879	LC
John Carroll Univ	OH	49,740	C+
Kean Univ	NJ	24,650	C
Keiser Univ	FL	35,010	LC
Kennesaw State Univ	GA	19,592	VC
Kent State Univ	OH	20,732	C
Lake Erie College	OH	38,914	LC
Lake Forest College	IL	50,652	VC
Lehigh Univ	PA	61,010	MC
Lewis Univ	IL	40,370	C
Limestone College	SC	32,100	C
Lipscomb Univ	TN	41,296	VC
LIU Brooklyn	NY	49,682	C
Loras College	IA	39,222	C
Lourdes Univ	OH	29,520	NC
Loyola Marymount Univ	CA	58,038	HC
Loyola Univ Chicago	IL	55,802	VC
Lubbock Christian Univ	TX	28,426	C
Malone Univ	OH	38,448	C
Manhattanville College	NY	51,440	C+
Marian Univ	IN	41,220	C
Marquette Univ	WI	48,390	VC+
Marshall Univ	WV	17,242	C
Menlo College	CA	51,380	LC
Mercer Univ	GA	45,348	VC
Miami Univ	OH	27,190	HC+
Mich State Univ	MI	23,898	VC+
Mich Tech Univ	MI	24,739	VC+
Millersville Univ of Pennsylvania	PA	23,782	C
Minn State Univ, Mankato	MN	15,616	C
Missouri Southern State Univ	MO	12,499	C
Missouri State Univ	MO	15,190	C+
Molloy College	NY	40,440	C
Mount Mercy Univ	IA	36,826	C
Mount Vernon Nazarene Univ	OH	34,500	C
Murray State Univ	KY	16,998	C
Nazareth College	NY	45,574	C
Neumann Univ	PA	40,678	LC
New Mexico State Univ	NM	14,050	C
New York Inst of Technology	NY	48,730	C
New York Univ	NY	65,860	MC
Niagara Univ	NY	41,010	C
North Central College	IL	48,712	VC
N Dak State Univ	ND	16,245	C
Northern Arizona Univ	AZ	20,246	VC
Northern Kentucky Univ	KY	16,486	C
Northern Mich Univ	MI	19,604	C
Northwest Missouri State Univ	MO	17,737	C
Nova Southeastern Univ	FL	38,534	C+
Ohio Univ	OH	22,924	C
Okla Christian Univ	OK	27,650	VC
Old Dominion Univ	VA	20,910	C
Oregon State Univ	OR	22,519	VC
Our Lady of the Lake Univ	TX	35,012	LC
Pace Univ	NY	58,248	C
Pennsylvania State Univ - Univ Park	PA	29,760	HC
Point Loma Nazarene Univ	CA	43,450	C
Point Park Univ	PA	41,270	C
Providence College	RI	60,760	VC
Purdue Univ/Northwest	IN	15,038	C
Queens Univ of Charlotte	NC	39,543	C
Quinnipiac Univ	CT	59,110	C
Regis Univ	CO	44,520	C
Rochester Inst of Technology	NY	50,842	HC
Rutgers Univ - New Brunswick	NJ	26,632	HC
Rutgers Univ - Newark	NJ	27,288	C
Saginaw Valley State Univ	MI	18,530	C
St. Joseph's Univ	PA	57,544	VC+
St. Louis Univ	MO	49,866	HC
St. Mary's Univ of Minn	MN	41,210	VC
Salisbury Univ	MD	20,714	VC
Salve Regina Univ	RI	51,470	C
Samford Univ	AL	39,232	VC
San Diego State Univ	CA	21,896	C+
Seattle Univ	WA	50,811	VC+
Seton Hall Univ	NJ	55,514	C
Shippensburg Univ of Pennsylvania	PA	23,208	C
Simmons College	MA	53,090	VC
Southeast Missouri State Univ	MO	15,498	C
Southeastern Louisiana Univ	LA	16,237	C
Southern Methodist Univ	TX	66,483	MC
Southern Univ and A&M College	LA	16,074	LC+
Southwestern Okla State Univ	OK	11,790	C
St. Ambrose Univ	IA	39,019	C
St. Ambrose Univ	IA	39,019	C
St. John's Univ	NY	55,850	C
SUNY / SUNY Fredonia	NY	20,818	C
SUNY / SUNY Plattsburgh	NY	18,814	C
SUNY at Binghamton	NY	22,861	MC
SUNY at Oswego	NY	21,351	C
Stephen F. Austin State Univ	TX	18,406	LC
Susquehanna Univ	PA	55,340	VC
Syracuse Univ	NY	60,239	VC
Tarleton State Univ	TX	15,248	LC
Taylor Univ	IN	40,317	C+
Temple Univ	PA	24,392	VC
Texas A&M Univ	TX	20,521	VC+
Texas Christian Univ	TX	54,670	HC
Texas State Univ	TX	19,350	C
Texas Tech Univ	TX	18,736	C+
The Catholic Univ of America	DC	56,356	VC
The College at Brockport - SUNY	NY	20,346	C
The Lincoln Univ	PA	15,154	NC
The Univ of Tenn at Knoxville	TN	22,112	VC
The Univ of Utah	UT	17,924	VC
Thomas College	ME	35,268	LC
Thomas Edison State Univ	NJ	6,350	NC
Tiffin Univ	OH	31,380	C
Trinity Univ	TX	52,314	HC+
Tulane Univ	LA	63,396	HC+
Univ of Arizona	AZ	23,100	C
Univ of Arkansas at Fayetteville	AR	19,152	C+
Univ of Central Arkansas	AR	14,472	VC
Univ of Central Okla	OK	13,486	C
Univ of Charleston	WV	35,000	C
Univ of Cincinnati	OH	21,964	VC
Univ of Colo Boulder	CO	24,285	VC+
Univ of Denver	CO	58,443	VC+
Univ of Detroit Mercy	MI	48,816	C+
Univ of Evansville	IN	44,186	VC+
Univ of Georgia	GA	21,250	HC
Univ of Idaho	ID	15,348	C
Univ of Illinois at Chicago	IL	25,006	VC
Univ of Kansas	KS	20,135	C+
Univ of Louisiana at Monroe	LA	15,970	C
Univ of Maine	ME	20,792	C
Univ of Mary Hardin-Baylor	TX	33,950	C+
Univ of Maryland/College Park	MD	21,938	HC
Univ of Mass Dartmouth	MA	25,658	C
Univ of Miami	FL	63,494	MC
Univ of Miss	MS	17,746	C+
Univ of Missouri-St. Louis	MO		C
Univ of Nebr - Lincoln	NE	18,589	VC
Univ of Nevada/Reno	NV	18,010	C
Univ of N Car at Charlotte	NC	15,547	C
Univ of N Car at Greensboro	NC	14,690	C
Univ of North Florida	FL	15,996	VC
Univ of North Georgia	GA	17,316	C
Univ of Notre Dame	IN	64,043	MC
Univ of Okla	OK	18,911	VC
Univ of Pittsburgh	PA	29,568	HC+
Univ of Rhode Island	RI	24,906	C
Univ of St. Francis	IN	37,400	C
Univ of San Diego	CA	58,442	VC+
Univ of San Francisco	CA	58,484	VC
Univ of S Dak	SD	16,109	C
Univ of South Florida/St. Petersburg	FL	15,980	C
Univ of Southern Indiana	IN	16,501	C
Univ of St. Thomas - Houston	TX	40,020	VC
Univ of Texas at San Antonio	TX	20,157	C
Univ of West Georgia	GA	16,360	LC
Univ of Wisc-Green Bay	WI	15,064	C
Univ of Wisc-Milwaukee	WI	21,496	C
Univ of Wisc-Superior	WI	14,446	C
Univ of Wyoming	WY	15,375	C+
Valparaiso Univ	IN	48,370	C+
Villanova Univ	PA	62,523	MC
Wabash College	IN	50,650	VC
Walla Walla Univ	WA	30,417	NC
Walsh Univ	OH	39,010	C
Washburn Univ	KS	15,827	C
Washington State Univ	WA	22,495	C
Washington Univ in St. Louis	MO	65,366	VC
Waynesburg Univ	PA	32,290	C
Weber State Univ	UT	10,721	C
Webster Univ	MO	37,490	C
West Virginia Univ	WV	18,210	C
Western Illinois Univ	IL	20,825	C
Western Mich Univ	MI	21,054	C
Western New England Univ	MA	48,088	C
Wichita State Univ	KS	21,643	C
Widener Univ	PA	56,486	C
Wingate Univ	NC	39,950	C
Wittenberg Univ	OH	48,156	C+
Wofford College	SC	49,885	VC

FINANCE (FINANCIAL PLANNING)

School	ST	$IS	SR
Bryant Univ	RI	55,646	VC
Murray State Univ	KY	16,998	C
Southern Methodist Univ	TX	66,483	MC
SUNY Polytechnic Inst	NY	19,473	VC
Univ of Georgia	GA	21,250	HC

FINANCE ENTERPRISE SYSTEMS

School	ST	$IS	SR
Univ of Tampa	FL	36,944	C

FINANCIAL INSTITUTIONS MANAGEMENT

School	ST	$IS	SR
Bryant Univ	RI	55,646	VC
Thomas Edison State Univ	NJ	6,350	NC

FINANCIAL SERVICES

School	ST	$IS	SR
Bethel College	IN	35,860	C
Bryant Univ	RI	55,646	VC
Missouri Southern State Univ	MO	12,499	C
Old Dominion Univ	VA	20,910	C
San Diego State Univ	CA	21,896	C+
SUNY /College of Agriculture and Tech at Cobleskill	NY	20,527	LC
Univ of Texas at Arlington	TX	18,026	LC

FINE ARTS

School	ST	$IS	SR
Abilene Christian Univ	TX	41,800	C+
Adelphi Univ	NY	48,244	C
Alabama State Univ	AL	14,142	NC
Albany State Univ	GA	19,462	C
Albertus Magnus College	CT	43,258	LC
Alfred Univ	NY	42,296	C+
American Univ	DC	59,379	HC+
Amherst College	MA		HC+
Anderson Univ	IN	38,200	C
Aquinas College - Mich	MI	38,876	HC
Arcadia Univ	PA	33,570	C+
Arkansas Tech Univ	AR	15,484	C
Art Academy of Cincinnati	OH	36,252	SP
ArtCenter College of Design	CA	54,212	SP
Ashland Univ	OH	21,440	C
Auburn Univ	AL	23,594	VC+
Auburn Univ at Montgomery	AL	15,290	C
Azusa Pacific Univ	CA	43,972	C
Bellarmine Univ	KY	51,220	C
Bellevue Univ	NE	20,300	NC
Bemidji State Univ	MN	16,056	VC
Benedictine Univ	IL	38,300	C
Bennington College	VT	63,960	MC
Bethany College	WV	36,300	NC
Biola Univ	CA	46,402	C+
Blue Mountain College	MS	15,949	VC
Bluefield College	VA	34,120	C+
Boise State Univ	ID	14,860	C
Bowie State Univ	MD	26,728	LC
Bowling Green State Univ	OH	19,747	C
Brenau Univ - Women's College	GA	37,876	LC
Bridgewater State Univ	MA	21,810	C
Brigham Young Univ	UT	12,748	HC
Brigham Young Univ/Hawaii	HI	11,290	C
Bryn Athyn College	PA	31,470	C
Bryn Mawr College	PA	59,890	MC
Bucknell Univ	PA	64,616	MC
Caldwell Univ	NJ	42,165	NC
Calif Inst of the Arts	CA	56,426	SP
Cal State, Chico	CA	21,440	C
Cal State, Fullerton	CA	21,902	C
Cal State, Stanislaus	CA	16,212	C
Calvin College	MI	41,570	VC+
Canisius College	NY	47,537	C
Cardinal Stritch Univ	WI	36,462	C
Carnegie Mellon Univ	PA	67,980	MC
Carson-Newman Univ	TN	34,160	C
Carthage College	WI	48,835	C
Cedar Crest College	PA	46,715	C
Central Washington Univ	WA	16,803	C
Centre College	KY	49,250	HC
Champlain College	VT	53,132	C+
Charleston Southern Univ	SC	32,400	C
Christopher Newport Univ	VA	23,968	VC+
CUNY/City College	NY	20,319	VC
CUNY/Hunter College	NY	31,098	VC
CUNY/Lehman College	NY	5,778	HC+
Clark Univ	MA	51,600	HC+
Clemson Univ	SC		HC
Coastal Carolina Univ	SC	19,766	C
College for Creative Studies	MI	48,875	SP
College of Art and Design at Lesley Univ	MA	39,730	SP
College of St. Elizabeth	NJ	44,432	LC
Colo State Univ	CO	22,162	VC
Columbia College - Missouri	MO	27,803	C
Columbus College of Art and Design	OH	37,732	C
Concordia Univ Nebr	NE	36,280	VC
Converse College	SC	26,495	C
Cooper Union for the Advancement of Science and Art	NY	58,210	MC
Cornell Univ	NY	64,853	MC
Cornish College of the Arts	WA	47,750	SP
Culver-Stockton College	MO	33,525	C
Cumberland Univ	TN	27,710	C
Daemen College	NY	38,045	C
Dallas Baptist Univ	TX	33,713	C
Denison Univ	OH	58,860	MC
DePaul Univ	IL	47,623	VC
Dickinson State Univ	ND	12,372	LC
Dominican Univ	IL	41,222	C
Dordt College	IA	37,860	C+
Drury Univ	MO	33,791	VC
East Stroudsburg Univ	PA	18,334	C
East Tenn State Univ	TN	13,994	C
Eastern Mich Univ	MI	19,761	C
Edinboro Univ	PA	15,940	LC
Elizabethtown College	PA	54,050	C
Elmira College	NY	53,900	C
Elms College	MA	45,646	VC
Elon Univ	NC	44,599	VC+
Emory Univ	GA	60,786	MC
Endicott College	MA	44,604	VC+
Eureka College	IL	30,220	C
Fairleigh Dickinson Univ/ College at Florham	NJ	52,062	C
Fairleigh Dickinson Univ/ Metropolitan Campus	NJ	40,254	C
Felician Univ	NJ	45,370	LC
Ferris State Univ	MI	21,445	C
Fisk Univ	TN	32,066	LC
Flagler College	FL	27,620	C
Florida A&M Univ	FL	15,361	C
Florida Atlantic Univ	FL	17,339	C
Florida International Univ	FL	19,854	C+
Florida Memorial Univ	FL	22,270	LC
Fontbonne Univ	MO	33,717	C
Fordham Univ	NY	65,918	MC
Fort Hays State Univ	KS	12,131	C
Franklin and Marshall College	PA	63,170	HC
Franklin Pierce Univ	NH	46,750	C
Freed-Hardeman Univ	TN	29,450	C
Friends Univ	KS	34,455	C
George Washington Univ	DC	62,835	MC
Georgetown Univ	DC	65,926	MC
Georgia Southwestern State Univ	GA	13,870	C
Georgia State Univ	GA	24,332	VC
Goddard College	VT	17,040	VC
Grand Rapids Theological Seminary/Cornerstone Univ	MI	33,338	C
Grand Valley State Univ	MI	22,250	C+
Green Mountain College	VT	45,228	LC
Gustavus Adolphus College	MN	52,433	HC
Hamline Univ	MN	45,678	VC
Hampden-Sydney College	VA	56,248	C+
Hampshire College	MA	63,824	MC
Harding Univ	AR	25,421	C
Harvard College/Harvard Univ	MA	60,659	MC
Hastings College	NE	35,380	C+
Haverford College	PA	66,490	MC
Hofstra Univ	NY	55,960	C+
Hope College	MI	39,940	VC
Humboldt State Univ	CA	20,514	C
Huntington Univ	IN	33,996	C
Illinois College	IL	40,850	VC
Indiana State Univ	IN	23,223	LC
Indiana Univ Bloomington	IN	20,429	VC
Indiana Univ East	IN	7,072	C
Indiana Univ Kokomo	IN	7,073	C
Indiana Univ Northwest	IN	7,072	C
Indiana Univ of Pennsylvania	PA	23,614	LC
Indiana Univ South Bend	IN	14,242	C
Indiana Univ Southeast	IN	14,242	LC
Indiana Univ-Purdue Univ Fort Wayne	IN	17,553	C
Indiana Univ-Purdue Univ Indianapolis	IN	18,635	C
Inter-American Univ of PR-San Germán	PR	20,042	
Iowa State Univ	IA	17,570	C
Iowa Wesleyan Univ	IA	39,200	C
Ithaca College	NY	56,766	VC
James Madison Univ	VA	19,084	VC
Johnson State College	VT	20,752	C
Judson Univ	IL	37,700	C
Kansas City Art Inst	MO	44,308	C+
Kean Univ	NJ	24,650	C

ST = STATE **$IS** = IN-STATE COSTS **SR** = SELECTOR RATING

School	ST	$IS	SR
Kentucky State Univ	KY	13,364	LC
Kentucky Wesleyan College	KY	32,080	C
Kutztown Univ of Pennsylvania	PA	19,056	LC
La Salle Univ	PA	55,790	C
La Sierra Univ	CA	39,690	VC
Lake Erie College	OH	38,914	LC
Lamar Univ	TX	18,014	LC
Lewis & Clark College	OR	58,434	HC+
Lincoln Memorial Univ	TN	28,070	C
Lincoln Univ	MO	13,602	NC
LIU Brooklyn	NY	49,682	C
LIU Post	NY	49,682	C
Lock Haven Univ of Pennsylvania	PA	18,028	LC
Louisiana State Univ in Shreveport	LA	6,902	C
Louisiana Tech Univ	LA	11,422	VC
Loyola Univ Chicago	IL	55,802	VC
Loyola Univ Maryland	MD	60,300	VC
Loyola Univ New Orleans	LA	51,708	VC+
Madonna Univ	MI	29,050	C
Maharishi Univ of Management	IA	34,930	VC
Marist College	NY	49,860	VC
Martin Univ	IN	20,264	LC
Maryland Inst College of Art	MD	56,795	SP
Marylhurst Univ	OR	20,295	NC
Marymount Manhattan College	NY	46,280	VC
Mass College of Art and Design	MA	24,800	SP
Mass College of Liberal Arts	MA	20,128	C
McDaniel College	MD	51,380	VC
Memphis College of Art	TN	39,750	C
Mercy College	NY	31,776	C
Meredith College	NC	45,297	C
Metropolitan State Univ of Denver	CO	29,889	LC
Midland Univ	NE	37,468	
Midwestern State Univ	TX	17,572	C
Milligan College	TN	38,150	C
Milwaukee Inst of Art and Design	WI	44,960	SP
Minn State Univ, Moorhead	MN	15,941	C
Miss Univ for Women	MS	17,065	C
Miss Valley State Univ	MS	13,233	LC
Missouri Southern State Univ	MO	12,499	C
Missouri Western State Univ	MO	16,741	
Montana State Univ	MT	15,500	C+
Montana State Univ-Northern	MT	11,370	NC
Montclair State Univ	NJ	26,210	LC
Montserrat College of Art	MA	38,150	SP
Moore College of Art and Design	PA	50,135	SP
Morgan State Univ	MD	17,190	LC
Mount Mary Univ	WI	34,650	LC
Mount St. Joseph Univ	OH	33,880	C
Mount St. Mary's Univ	MD	51,610	C
National Louis Univ	IL	16,920	LC
Nazareth College	NY	45,574	C
New England College	NH	50,364	C
New Jersey City Univ	NJ	21,456	LC
New Mexico State Univ	NM	14,050	C
New York Univ	NY	65,860	MC
Norfolk State Univ	VA	25,702	LC
Northeastern State Univ	OK	8,615	VC
Northern Kentucky Univ	KY	16,486	C
Northern Mich Univ	MI	19,604	C
Northern State Univ	SD	14,505	C
Northland College	WI	41,103	C+
Northwest Missouri State Univ	MO	17,737	C
Northwestern Univ	IL	66,344	MC
Notre Dame de Namur Univ	CA	46,526	LC
Nova Southeastern Univ	FL	38,534	C+
Oakland City Univ	IN	33,360	NC
Oberlin College	OH	66,012	MC
Ohio Northern Univ	OH	44,050	VC
Ohio State Univ at Columbus	OH	21,703	HC+
Ohio Wesleyan Univ	OH	49,460	VC
Okla Baptist Univ	OK	32,320	C
Okla Panhandle State Univ	OK	6,152	NC
Old Dominion Univ	VA	20,910	C
Olivet College	MI	36,110	LC
Our Lady of the Lake Univ	TX	35,012	LC
Pace Univ	NY	58,248	C
Pacific Northwest College of Art	OR	38,494	SP
Pacific Union College	CA	36,009	VC
Park Univ	MO	20,329	C
Parsons The New School for Design	NY	56,610	SP
Piedmont College	GA	32,512	C
Pomona College	CA	64,957	MC
Pontifical Catholic Univ of PR	PR	10,534	
Portland State Univ	OR	19,443	C
Pratt Inst	NY	58,082	VC
Prescott College	AZ	33,284	C
Principia College	IL	39,010	C+
Purdue Univ/West Lafayette	IN	20,032	MC
Radford Univ	VA	19,027	LC
Rider Univ	NJ	54,050	C
Ringling College of Art and Design	FL	57,430	SP
Rochester Inst of Technology	NY	50,842	HC
Rocky Mountain College of Art and Design	CO	27,052	SP
Rosemont College	PA	30,980	C
Rowan Univ	NJ	24,491	VC+
Saginaw Valley State Univ	MI	18,530	C
St. Anselm College	NH	52,560	C+
St. Augustine's Univ	NC	26,048	C
St. Mary's College	IN	50,600	C
St. Michael's College	VT	51,725	VC+
St. Peter's Univ	NJ	49,192	C
St. Vincent College	PA	44,626	C
Salem State Univ	MA	17,303	LC
Salisbury Univ	MD	20,714	VC
San Jose State Univ	CA	21,540	C
Santa Fe Univ of Art and Design	NM	39,980	SP
Sarah Lawrence College	NY	63,388	HC
School of Visual Arts	NY	47,500	SP
Seattle Pacific Univ	WA	47,439	C+
Seattle Univ	WA	50,811	VC+
Seton Hall Univ	NJ	55,514	C
Seton Hill Univ	PA	46,972	C
Sewanee: The Univ of the South	TN	54,500	MC
Siena Heights Univ	MI	32,040	C
Sierra Nevada College	NV	43,482	C
Silver Lake College of the Holy Family	WI	36,290	LC
Slippery Rock Univ of Pennsylvania	PA	10,360	C
Sonoma State Univ	CA	27,806	C
S Car State Univ	SC	20,805	LC
Southeastern Okla State Univ	OK	11,875	C
Southern Adventist Univ	TN	27,600	C
Southern Conn State Univ	CT	21,924	LC
Southern Illinois Univ Carbondale	IL	23,667	C
Southern Oregon Univ	OR	19,117	C
Southern Univ and A&M College	LA	16,074	LC+
Southern Univ at New Orleans	LA	8,014	LC
Spelman College	GA	38,751	C
Springfield College	MA	45,995	C
St. Catherine Univ	MN	45,630	VC
St. Cloud State Univ	MN	10,600	C
St. John's Univ	NY	55,850	C
St. Lawrence Univ	NY	64,390	VC
St. Thomas Aquinas College	NY	42,200	C
Stanford Univ	CA	60,409	MC
SUNY / Buffalo State College	NY	20,842	C
SUNY / SUNY Fredonia	NY	20,818	C
SUNY / SUNY Oneonta	NY	19,712	C+
SUNY / SUNY Potsdam	NY	20,404	C+
SUNY / Univ at Buffalo	NY	23,122	C+
SUNY SUNY Albany	NY	22,165	C
Stockton Univ	NJ	25,059	
Stonehill College	MA	55,030	C+
Suffolk Univ	MA	50,308	C
Sul Ross State Univ	TX	15,021	LC
Syracuse Univ	NY	60,239	VC
Tarleton State Univ	TX	15,248	LC
Taylor Univ	IN	40,317	C+
Tenn Tech Univ	TN	17,050	C
Texas A&M Univ at Commerce	TX	10,496	C
Texas A&M Univ at Kingsville	TX	7,500	LC
Texas Woman's Univ	TX	15,302	LC
The College of New Jersey	NJ	31,909	HC
The College of Wooster	OH	57,900	VC+
The Univ of Tenn at Chattanooga	TN	16,744	C
The Univ of Tenn at Martin	TN	14,876	C
Trinity College	CT	63,920	HC+
Truman State Univ	MO	16,014	HC
Tusculum College	TN	31,625	C
Union College	KY	32,310	C
Union College	NY	64,320	MC
Univ of Alaska Anchorage	AK	16,652	NC
Univ of Arizona	AZ	23,100	C
Univ of Calif at Davis	CA	28,468	HC
Univ of Central Florida	FL	15,922	VC
Univ of Cincinnati	OH	21,964	VC
Univ of Colo Boulder	CO	24,285	VC+
Univ of Colo Denver	CO	23,230	C
Univ of Dayton	OH	53,620	C
Univ of Delaware	DE	24,976	VC+
Univ of Great Falls	MT	38,524	C
Univ of Houston-Downtown	TX	7,241	C
Univ of Idaho	ID	15,348	C
Univ of Illinois at Chicago	IL	25,006	VC
Univ of Illinois at Urbana-Champaign	IL	27,006	HC
Univ of Iowa	IA	18,683	VC+
Univ of Jamestown	ND	28,508	C
Univ of Kansas	KS	20,135	C+
Univ of Louisiana at Lafayette	LA	14,516	C
Univ of Maine at Machias	ME	22,960	C
Univ of Maryland/Baltimore County	MD	21,296	VC
Univ of Mass Lowell	MA	26,380	C
Univ of Miami	FL	63,494	MC
Univ of Montana	MT	14,105	C
Univ of Mount Olive	NC	18,426	C
Univ of Nebr - Kearney	NE	16,546	LC
Univ of Nebr - Lincoln	NE	18,589	VC
Univ of Nebr - Omaha	NE	16,120	C
Univ of Nevada, Las Vegas	NV	17,553	C
Univ of New Hampshire	NH	28,562	VC
Univ of New Haven	CT	52,190	C
Univ of New Orleans	LA	12,840	C
Univ of N Car at Asheville	NC	15,723	VC+
Univ of N Car at Charlotte	NC	15,547	C
Univ of N Car at Greensboro	NC	14,690	C
Univ of North Florida	FL	15,996	VC
Univ of North Georgia	GA	17,316	C
Univ of Northern Colo	CO	20,851	C
Univ of Oregon	OR	22,972	C
Univ of Pennsylvania	PA	63,526	MC
Univ of PR, at Mayaguez	PR	13,995	
Univ of PR-Rio Piedras campus	PR	13,327	
Univ of Rio Grande & Rio Grande Community College	OH	8,750	NC
Univ of San Francisco	CA	58,484	VC
Univ of Science and Arts of Okla	OK	11,140	VC
Univ of Sioux Falls	SD	34,330	C
Univ of South Alabama	AL	16,400	C
Univ of S Car Aiken	SC	16,712	C
Univ of S Car at Columbia	SC	19,725	VC+
Univ of Southern Calif	CA	66,631	C
Univ of Southern Maine	ME	18,320	C
Univ of Southern Miss	MS	13,170	C
Univ of Texas at Dallas	TX	22,830	VC+
Univ of the District of Columbia	DC	21,044	LC
Univ of the Southwest	NM	22,766	C
Univ of Toledo	OH	19,336	NC
Univ of Wisc-Green Bay	WI	15,064	C
Univ of Wisc-La Crosse	WI	15,247	C+
Univ of Wisc-Oshkosh	WI	15,200	C
Univ of Wisc-Parkside	WI	15,193	C
Univ of Wisc-River Falls	WI	14,485	C
Univ of Wisc-Stevens Point	WI	14,043	C
Univ of Wisc-Stout	WI	19,667	C
Univ of Wisc-Superior	WI	14,446	C
Upper Iowa Univ	IA	34,990	NC
Utah State Univ	UT	12,736	C
Wagner College	NY	55,480	C+
Washington College	MD	54,666	VC
Washington State Univ	WA	22,495	C
Washington Univ in St. Louis	MO	65,366	VC
Wayne State Univ	MI	22,016	C
Weber State Univ	UT	10,721	C
West Liberty Univ	WV	15,512	C
West Virginia State Univ	WV	8,378	NC
Western Kentucky Univ	KY	16,850	C
Western New Mexico Univ	NM	16,734	LC
Western State Colo Univ	CO	18,639	C
Western Washington Univ	WA	18,003	C+
Westminster College	PA	39,180	C+
Westminster College	UT	41,078	C+
Wheaton College	MA	61,512	VC
Widener Univ	PA	56,486	C
Wilberforce Univ	OH	19,016	C
William Paterson Univ of New Jersey	NJ	23,133	C
William Penn Univ	IA	26,000	C
Williams College	MA	63,290	MC
Wilson College	PA	35,620	C
Winona State Univ	MN	17,535	C
Winthrop Univ	SC	23,082	C
Wittenberg Univ	OH	48,156	C+
Wright State Univ	OH	16,983	C
Xavier Univ	OH	47,880	C+
Xavier Univ of Louisiana	LA	31,689	C+
York College of Pennsylvania	PA	29,240	C

FINE/STUDIO ARTS, GENERAL

School	ST	$IS	SR
East Central Univ	OK	13,056	C
Georgetown College	KY	41,440	C
Kean Univ	NJ	24,650	C
Loyola Univ New Orleans	LA	51,708	VC+
Missouri Southern State Univ	MO	12,499	C
Rochester Inst of Technology	NY	50,842	HC
St. Louis Univ	MO	49,866	HC
Southern Methodist Univ	TX	66,483	MC
Univ of Maine at Machias	ME	22,960	C
Univ of New Haven	CT	52,190	C
Wellesley College	MA	63,916	MC
Wheaton College	MA	61,512	VC

FIRE CONTROL AND SAFETY TECHNOLOGY

School	ST	$IS	SR
Cogswell Polytechnical College	CA	30,531	C
Okla State Univ	OK	17,180	VC
Univ of New Haven	CT	52,190	C
Univ of N Car at Charlotte	NC	15,547	C

FIRE PROTECTION

School	ST	$IS	SR
Cal State, Los Angeles	CA	17,186	LC
Cogswell Polytechnical College	CA	30,531	C
Eastern Kentucky Univ	KY	16,908	C
Park Univ	MO	20,329	C
Southern Illinois Univ Carbondale	IL	23,667	C
Univ of New Haven	CT	52,190	C
Western Illinois Univ	IL	20,825	C
Western Oregon Univ	OR	15,021	LC

FIRE PROTECTION ENGINEERING

School	ST	$IS	SR
Univ of Houston-Downtown	TX	7,241	C
Univ of Maryland/College Park	MD	21,938	HC
Univ of New Haven	CT	52,190	C

FIRE PROTECTION SCIENCE

School	ST	$IS	SR
Southwestern Okla State Univ	OK	11,790	C

FIRE SCIENCE

School	ST	$IS	SR
Anna Maria College	MA	48,186	C
CUNY/John Jay College of Criminal Justice	NY	6,359	NC
Lewis Univ	IL	40,370	C
Madonna Univ	MI	29,050	C
Univ of Idaho	ID	15,348	C
Univ of Maryland/Univ College	MD	25,966	LC
Univ of New Haven	CT	52,190	C
Univ of the District of Columbia	DC	21,044	LC

FIRE SERVICES ADMINISTRATION

School	ST	$IS	SR
Bowling Green State Univ	OH	19,747	C
CUNY/John Jay College of Criminal Justice	NY	6,359	NC
Colo State Univ	CO	22,162	VC
Columbia College - Missouri	MO	27,803	C
Holy Family Univ	PA	43,326	LC
Idaho State Univ	ID	13,619	NC
Lewis Univ	IL	40,370	C
Park Univ	MO	20,329	C
SUNY / Empire State College	NY	9,145	SP
Univ of New Haven	CT	52,190	C

FISH AND GAME MANAGEMENT

School	ST	$IS	SR
Delaware State Univ	DE	19,376	NC
Frostburg State Univ	MD	17,280	LC
Kansas State Univ	KS	17,780	VC
Northland College	WI	41,103	C+
S Dak State Univ	SD	15,634	C
Stephen F. Austin State Univ	TX	18,406	LC
Tenn Tech Univ	TN	17,050	C
Univ of Idaho	ID	15,348	C
Univ of Maine at Machias	ME	22,960	C
Univ of Montana-Western	MT	11,220	LC
Univ of Nebr - Lincoln	NE	18,589	VC
Univ of Wyoming	WY	15,375	C+
West Virginia Univ	WV	18,210	C

FISHING AND FISHERIES

School	ST	$IS	SR
Arkansas Tech Univ	AR	15,484	C
Auburn Univ	AL	23,594	VC+
Colo State Univ	CO	22,162	VC
Humboldt State Univ	CA	20,514	C
Mich State Univ	MI	23,898	VC+
Miss State Univ	MS	11,454	C+
N Car State Univ	NC	19,515	HC+
Northern Mich Univ	MI	19,604	C
Ohio State Univ at Columbus	OH	21,703	HC+
Oregon State Univ	OR	22,519	VC
Purdue Univ/West Lafayette	IN	20,032	MC
SUNY / The College of Environmental Science and Forestry	NY	23,853	VC
SUNY /College of Agriculture and Tech at Cobleskill	NY	20,527	LC
Texas A&M Univ at Galveston	TX	15,920	C
Univ of Alaska Fairbanks	AK	16,179	C
Univ of Arkansas at Pine Bluff	AR	13,541	C
Univ of Georgia	GA	21,250	HC
Univ of Idaho	ID	15,348	C
Univ of Maine at Machias	ME	22,960	C
Univ of Minn/Twin Cities	MN	23,519	HC+
Univ of Missouri/Columbia	MO	18,201	MC
Univ of N Dak	ND	15,373	C
Univ of Vermont	VT	28,878	HC
Univ of Washington	WA	23,149	VC
Univ of Wisc-Stevens Point	WI	14,043	C
West Virginia Univ	WV	18,210	C

FOLKLORE AND MYTHOLOGY

School	ST	$IS	SR
Goddard College	VT	17,040	VC
Harvard College/Harvard Univ	MA	60,659	MC
Indiana Univ Bloomington	IN	20,429	VC
Univ of Oregon	OR	22,972	C
Univ of Pennsylvania	PA	63,526	MC

FOOD PRODUCTION/ MANAGEMENT/SERVICES

School	ST	$IS	SR
Arizona State Univ at the Polytechnic Campus	AZ	21,360	VC
Belmont Univ	TN	40,970	VC
Central Mich Univ	MI	20,330	C

ST = STATE $IS = IN-STATE COSTS SR = SELECTOR RATING

School	ST	$IS	SR
Delaware Valley Univ	PA	49,796	C
Dominican Univ	IL	41,222	C
Johnson & Wales Univ/ Charlotte Campus	NC	43,988	C
Johnson & Wales Univ/ Denver Campus	CO	42,707	C
Johnson & Wales Univ/North Miami Campus	FL	42,707	C
Johnson & Wales Univ/ Providence Campus	RI	42,248	C
Lipscomb Univ	TN	41,296	VC
Loyola Univ New Orleans	LA	51,708	VC+
Metropolitan State Univ	MN	7,566	C
Mich State Univ	MI	23,898	VC+
Miss Univ for Women	MS	17,065	C
Montclair State Univ	NJ	26,210	LC
Mount Marty College	SD	32,972	C
Murray State Univ	KY	16,998	C
Newbury College	MA	46,950	C
Nicholls State Univ	LA	10,534	C
Purdue Univ/West Lafayette	IN	20,032	MC
Rochester Inst of Technology	NY	50,842	HC
Seton Hill Univ	PA	46,972	C
Simmons College	MA	53,090	VC
S Dak State Univ	SD	15,634	C
Texas A&M Univ at Kingsville	TX	7,500	LC
Texas Christian Univ	TX	54,670	HC
Univ of Central Florida	FL	15,922	VC
Univ of Delaware	DE	24,976	VC+
Univ of Georgia	GA	21,250	HC
Univ of Illinois at Urbana-Champaign	IL	27,006	HC
Univ of Nebr - Lincoln	NE	18,589	VC
Univ of Nevada, Las Vegas	NV	17,553	C
Univ of Wisc-Stout	WI	19,667	C
Western Mich Univ	MI	21,054	C

FOOD SCIENCE

School	ST	$IS	SR
Alabama A&M Univ	AL	18,796	C
Ashland Univ	OH	21,440	C
Auburn Univ	AL	23,594	VC+
Bluffton Univ	OH	40,950	C
Brigham Young Univ	UT	12,748	HC
Calif Polytechnic State Univ	CA	17,979	HC+
Calif State Polytechnic Univ, Pomona	CA	21,541	C
Cal State, Fresno	CA	16,902	LC
Cal State, San Bernardino	CA	12,000	C
Central Washington Univ	WA	16,803	C
Clarke Univ	IA	38,940	C
Clemson Univ	SC		HC
College of the Ozarks	MO	7,230	C
Colo State Univ	CO	22,162	VC
Cornell Univ	NY	64,853	MC
Delaware State Univ	DE	19,376	NC
Delaware Valley Univ	PA	49,796	C
Dominican Univ	IL	41,222	C
Florida State Univ	FL	16,771	HC
Framingham State Univ	MA	20,584	C
Indiana State Univ	IN	23,223	LC
Iowa State Univ	IA	17,570	C
Kansas State Univ	KS	17,780	VC
Madonna Univ	MI	29,050	C
Mich State Univ	MI	23,898	VC+
Miss State Univ	MS	11,454	C+
N Car State Univ	NC	19,515	HC+
N Dak State Univ	ND	16,245	C
Northwest Missouri State Univ	MO	17,737	C
Okla State Univ	OK	17,180	VC
Oregon State Univ	OR	22,519	VC
Pennsylvania State Univ - Univ Park	PA	29,760	HC
Purdue Univ/West Lafayette	IN	20,032	MC
Rutgers Univ - New Brunswick	NJ	26,632	HC
San Jose State Univ	CA	21,540	C
Seattle Pacific Univ	WA	47,439	C+
Simmons College	MA	53,090	VC
S Car State Univ	SC	20,805	LC
S Dak State Univ	SD	15,634	C
Syracuse Univ	NY	60,239	VC
Texas A&M Univ at Kingsville	TX	7,500	LC
Texas Tech Univ	TX	18,736	C+
The Univ of Tenn at Knoxville	TN	22,112	VC
Tuskegee Univ	AL	28,164	C
Univ of Alabama	AL	24,320	C+
Univ of Arkansas at Fayetteville	AR	19,152	C+
Univ of Calif at Davis	CA	28,468	HC
Univ of Delaware	DE	24,976	VC+
Univ of Florida	FL	16,291	HC+
Univ of Georgia	GA	21,250	HC
Univ of Hawaii at Manoa	HI	23,221	C
Univ of Idaho	ID	15,348	C
Univ of Illinois at Urbana-Champaign	IL	27,006	HC
Univ of Kentucky	KY	33,306	C
Univ of Maine	ME	20,792	C
Univ of Mass Amherst	MA	26,199	VC+
Univ of Minn/Twin Cities	MN	23,519	HC+
Univ of Missouri/Columbia	MO	18,201	MC
Univ of Nebr - Lincoln	NE	18,589	VC
Univ of the District of Columbia	DC	21,044	LC

School	ST	$IS	SR
Univ of Vermont	VT	28,878	HC
Univ of Washington	WA	23,149	VC
Univ of Wisc-Madison	WI	20,934	MC
Univ of Wisc-River Falls	WI	14,485	C
Utah State Univ	UT	12,736	C
Virginia Polytechnic Inst and State Univ	VA	21,276	HC
Washington State Univ	WA	22,495	C
Wayne State Univ	MI	22,016	C
Youngstown State Univ	OH	17,307	C

FOOD SERVICES TECHNOLOGY

School	ST	$IS	SR
Brigham Young Univ	UT	12,748	HC
Delaware Valley Univ	PA	49,796	C
Inter-American Univ of PR-Bayamon	PR	18,785	
Johnson & Wales Univ/ Charlotte Campus	NC	43,988	C
Johnson & Wales Univ/North Miami Campus	FL	42,707	C
Johnson & Wales Univ/ Providence Campus	RI	42,248	C
Minn State Univ, Mankato	MN	15,616	C
Purdue Univ/West Lafayette	IN	20,032	MC
St. Catherine Univ	MN	45,630	VC
Univ of Central Florida	FL	15,922	VC
Univ of Wisc-Stout	WI	19,667	C

FOOD TECHNOLOGY FOR COMPANION ANIMALS

School	ST	$IS	SR
Texas A&M Univ	TX	20,521	VC+
Univ of Nebr - Lincoln	NE	18,589	VC

FOREIGN LANGUAGE

School	ST	$IS	SR
Arkansas State Univ	AR	16,190	C
Austin Peay State Univ	TN	16,397	C
Bentley Univ	MA	60,890	HC
Bloomsburg Univ of Pennsylvania	PA	19,066	LC
Bowling Green State Univ	OH	19,747	C
Bryant Univ	RI	55,646	VC
Colo State Univ	CO	22,162	VC
Eastern Illinois Univ	IL	21,126	C
Gannon Univ	PA	42,032	C
New Mexico State Univ	NM	14,050	C
Niagara Univ	NY	41,010	C
Oakwood Univ	AL	43,758	C
Providence College	RI	60,760	VC
Southern Illinois Univ Carbondale	IL	23,667	C
Southern Oregon Univ	OR	19,117	C
St. Joseph's College, New York/Brooklyn Campus	NY	25,114	LC
Thomas Edison State Univ	NJ	6,350	NC
United States Military Academy at West Point	NY		HC+
Univ of Alabama at Birmingham	AL	19,906	C
Univ of Alaska Fairbanks	AK	16,179	C
Univ of Louisiana at Monroe	LA	15,970	C
Univ of Maryland/College Park	MD	21,938	HC
West Virginia Univ	WV	18,210	C
Western Illinois Univ	IL	20,825	C

FOREIGN LANGUAGES EDUCATION

School	ST	$IS	SR
Abilene Christian Univ	TX	41,800	C+
Adams State Univ	CO	17,703	LC
Alabama State Univ	AL	14,142	NC
American International College	MA	46,300	LC
American Univ	DC	59,379	HC+
Anderson Univ	IN	38,200	C
Appalachian State Univ	NC	14,416	VC
Arkansas State Univ	AR	16,190	C
Arkansas Tech Univ	AR	15,484	C
Asbury Univ	KY	35,180	C+
Ashland Univ	OH	21,440	C
Auburn Univ	AL	23,594	VC+
Augusta Univ	GA	4,632	C
Baylor Univ	TX	53,760	HC
Bemidji State Univ	MN	16,056	VC
Bennington College	VT	63,960	MC
Bethel Univ	MN	45,270	VC
Boston Univ	MA	65,110	MC
Bowling Green State Univ	OH	19,747	C
Canisius College	NY	47,537	C
Carroll College	MT	39,972	C+
Carson-Newman Univ	TN	34,160	C
Carthage College	WI	48,835	C
Central Mich Univ	MI	20,330	C
Central Washington Univ	WA	16,803	C
CUNY/Brooklyn College	NY	5,884	C+
CUNY/City College	NY	20,319	VC
CUNY/Hunter College	NY	31,098	VC
CUNY/Lehman College	NY	5,778	HC+
Clarion Univ of Pennsylvania	PA	21,608	LC
College of Charleston	SC	22,699	C
Colo State Univ	CO	22,162	VC
Columbus State Univ	GA	14,336	LC
Concordia College - Moorhead	MN	51,088	C+
Converse College	SC	26,495	C
Cornell College	IA	48,800	VC
Daemen College	NY	38,045	C
DePaul Univ	IL	47,623	VC
DePauw Univ	IN	58,688	HC+
Dordt College	IA	37,860	C+
Duquesne Univ	PA	46,822	VC
East Carolina Univ	NC	16,937	C
East Tenn State Univ	TN	13,994	C
East Texas Baptist Univ	TX	33,134	C
Eastern Kentucky Univ	KY	16,908	C
Eastern Mich Univ	MI	19,761	C
Eastern Washington Univ	WA	25,572	LC
Edinboro Univ	PA	15,940	LC
Elmira College	NY	53,900	C
Elms College	MA	45,646	VC
Elon Univ	NC	44,599	VC+
Emporia State Univ	KS	14,570	C
Erskine College	SC	45,460	C
Eugene Lang College/The New School for Liberal Arts	NY	55,650	C
Evangel Univ	MO	28,898	C
Fairmont State Univ	WV	15,726	C
Florida Atlantic Univ	FL	17,339	C
Florida State Univ	FL	16,771	HC
Friends Univ	KS	34,455	C
Gardner-Webb Univ	NC	39,200	C+
Georgetown College	KY	41,440	C
Georgia Inst of Technology	GA	23,360	MC
Gettysburg College	PA	63,000	HC
Goshen College	IN	42,500	C
Grace College and Seminary	IN	31,524	C
Grand Valley State Univ	MI	22,250	C+
Greensboro College	NC	42,400	LC
Gustavus Adolphus College	MN	52,433	HC
Hamline Univ	MN	45,678	VC
Harding Univ	AR	25,421	C
Hardin-Simmons Univ	TX	33,966	C
Hastings College	NE	35,380	C+
Heidelberg Univ	OH	39,200	C
Hofstra Univ	NY	55,960	C+
Holy Family Univ	PA	43,326	LC
Hood College	MD	54,840	C
Hope College	MI	39,940	VC
Houghton College	NY	39,090	C
Illinois College	IL	40,850	VC
Indiana State Univ	IN	23,223	LC
Indiana Univ-Purdue Univ Fort Wayne	IN	17,553	C
Ithaca College	NY	56,766	VC
Juniata College	PA	53,760	VC
King's College	PA	46,858	C
Kutztown Univ of Pennsylvania	PA	19,056	LC
La Salle Univ	PA	55,790	C
Lamar Univ	TX	18,014	LC
Le Moyne College	NY	46,000	C
Lenoir-Rhyne Univ	NC	43,200	C
Lipscomb Univ	TN	41,296	VC
LIU Post	NY	49,682	C
Lock Haven Univ of Pennsylvania	PA	18,028	LC
Louisiana Tech Univ	LA	11,422	VC
Manhattan College	NY	51,750	C+
Marshall Univ	WV	17,242	C
Marywood Univ	PA	46,900	C
Messiah College	PA	43,100	C+
Miami Univ	OH	27,190	HC+
Millikin Univ	IL	42,158	C
Minn State Univ, Mankato	MN	15,616	C
Minn State Univ, Moorhead	MN	15,941	C
Minot State Univ	ND	12,732	C
Missouri Western State Univ	MO	16,741	
Monmouth Univ	NJ	46,234	C
Murray State Univ	KY	16,998	C
Muskingum Univ	OH	35,966	C
Nazareth College	NY	45,574	C
New York Univ	NY	65,860	MC
Niagara Univ	NY	41,010	C
N Car State Univ	NC	19,515	HC+
Northern State Univ	SD	14,505	C
Northwestern College of Iowa	IA	38,400	C+
Notre Dame of Maryland Univ	MD	46,465	VC
Ohio Wesleyan Univ	OH	49,460	VC
Old Dominion Univ	VA	20,910	C
Oral Roberts Univ	OK	34,316	C
Ouachita Baptist Univ	AR	32,320	C
Pennsylvania State Univ - Univ Park	PA	29,760	HC
Prescott College	AZ	33,284	C
Providence College	RI	60,760	VC
Purdue Univ/Northwest	IN	15,038	C
Purdue Univ/West Lafayette	IN	20,032	MC
Radford Univ	VA	19,027	LC
Rhode Island College	RI	17,694	LC
Rider Univ	NJ	54,050	C
Rockhurst Univ	MO	29,220	C
Rosemont College	PA	30,980	C
Rowan Univ	NJ	24,491	VC+
Saginaw Valley State Univ	MI	18,530	C
St. Michael's College	VT	51,725	VC+
St. Xavier Univ	IL	43,310	C
Seton Hill Univ	PA	46,972	C
Shippensburg Univ of Pennsylvania	PA	23,208	C
Slippery Rock Univ of Pennsylvania	PA	10,360	C
Southeast Missouri State Univ	MO	15,498	C
Southern Conn State Univ	CT	21,924	LC
Southern Univ at New Orleans	LA	8,014	LC
Southwest Minn State Univ	MN	17,783	C
St. Ambrose Univ	IA	39,019	C
St. Ambrose Univ	IA	39,019	C
St. Cloud State Univ	MN	10,600	C
St. Edward's Univ	TX	53,100	VC
St. John Fisher College	NY	43,620	C
St. Thomas Aquinas College	NY	42,200	C
SUNY / Buffalo State College	NY	20,842	C
SUNY / SUNY College at Old Westbury	NY	16,860	C
SUNY / SUNY Cortland	NY	20,706	VC
SUNY / SUNY Fredonia	NY	20,818	C
SUNY / SUNY Oneonta	NY	19,712	C+
SUNY at New Paltz	NY	19,200	C
SUNY at Oswego	NY	21,351	C
Taylor Univ	IN	40,317	C+
Texas Southern Univ	TX	18,212	LC
Texas Wesleyan Univ	TX	35,134	C
Universidad del Turabo	PR	17,828	
Univ of Central Arkansas	AR	14,472	VC
Univ of Central Florida	FL	15,922	VC
Univ of Central Missouri	MO	18,982	C
Univ of Central Okla	OK	13,486	C
Univ of Cincinnati	OH	21,964	VC
Univ of Conn	CT	25,538	HC
Univ of Delaware	DE	24,976	VC+
Univ of Evansville	IN	44,186	VC+
Univ of Findlay	OH	60,139	C
Univ of Idaho	ID	15,348	C
Univ of Illinois at Urbana-Champaign	IL	27,006	HC
Univ of Indianapolis	IN	36,480	C
Univ of Iowa	IA	18,683	VC+
Univ of Kentucky	KY	33,306	C
Univ of Louisiana at Lafayette	LA	14,516	C
Univ of Louisville	KY	19,824	C
Univ of Mary Hardin-Baylor	TX	33,950	C+
Univ of Mich-Flint	MI	17,607	C+
Univ of Minn/Duluth	MN	20,292	C+
Univ of Nebr - Kearney	NE	16,546	LC
Univ of Nebr - Lincoln	NE	18,589	VC
Univ of New Orleans	LA	12,840	C
Univ of North Alabama	AL	15,398	C
Univ of N Car at Charlotte	NC	15,547	C
Univ of N Car at Greensboro	NC	14,690	C
Univ of North Georgia	GA	17,316	G
Univ of Okla	OK	18,911	VC
Univ of PR, at Mayaguez	PR	13,995	
Univ of South Florida/Tampa	FL	16,110	VC+
Univ of Southern Miss	MS	13,170	C
Univ of Toledo	OH	19,336	NC
Univ of Vermont	VT	28,878	HC
Univ of West Georgia	GA	16,360	LC
Univ of Wisc-Green Bay	WI	15,064	C
Univ of Wisc-River Falls	WI	14,485	C
Univ of Wisc-Whitewater	WI	13,976	C
Utah State Univ	UT	12,736	C
Utica College	NY	30,430	C
Valparaiso Univ	IN	48,370	C+
Virginia Commonwealth Univ	VA	23,049	C
Virginia Polytechnic Inst and State Univ	VA	21,276	HC
Wartburg College	IA	47,840	C
Washington State Univ	WA	22,495	C
Washington Univ in St. Louis	MO	65,366	VC
Weber State Univ	UT	10,721	C
Webster Univ	MO	37,490	C
West Texas A&M Univ	TX	13,478	C
Western Carolina Univ	NC	13,965	C
Western Mich Univ	MI	21,054	C
Western State Colo Univ	CO	18,639	C
Western Washington Univ	WA	18,003	C+
Whitworth Univ	WA	51,732	VC
Wilson College	PA	35,620	C
Winona State Univ	MN	17,535	C
Wittenberg Univ	OH	48,156	C+
Wright State Univ	OH	16,983	C

FORENSIC PSYCHOLOGY

School	ST	$IS	SR
Bay Path Univ	MA	45,349	C
Corban Univ	OR	40,306	C
Embry-Riddle Aeronautical Univ - Prescott Campus	AZ	44,054	VC
Faulkner Univ	AL	26,410	C
St. Ambrose Univ	IA	39,019	C
St. Ambrose Univ	IA	39,019	C
The College of St. Rose	NY	43,048	C
Tiffin Univ	OH	31,380	C
Univ of Central Okla	OK	13,486	C

FORENSIC SCIENCE

School	ST	$IS	SR
Alvernia Univ	PA	43,900	C
Arizona State Univ at the West Campus	AZ	20,640	C
Bay Path Univ	MA	45,349	C
Bethany College	KS	46,100	NC
Bethany College	WV	36,300	NC
Bryant Univ	RI	55,646	VC
Embry-Riddle Aeronautical Univ - Prescott Campus	AZ	44,054	VC
Hilbert College	NY	30,850	C
Indiana Univ-Purdue Univ Indianapolis	IN	18,635	C

ST = STATE $IS = IN-STATE COSTS SR = SELECTOR RATING

School	ST	$IS	SR
King Univ	TN	34,660	C
Lewis Univ	IL	40,370	C
Lynn Univ	FL	49,480	LC
Madonna Univ	MI	29,050	C
Missouri Southern State Univ	MO	12,499	C
Murray State Univ	KY	16,998	C
Northern Mich Univ	MI	19,604	C
Okla Baptist Univ	OK	32,320	C
Okla Christian Univ	OK	27,650	VC
Pace Univ	NY	58,248	C
Pennsylvania State Univ - Univ Park	PA	29,760	HC
Piedmont College	GA	32,512	C
Point Park Univ	PA	41,270	C
Purdue Univ/Northwest	IN	15,038	C
Roberts Wesleyan College	NY	38,306	C
St. Louis Univ	MO	49,866	HC
San Jose State Univ	CA	21,540	C
Southeast Missouri State Univ	MO	15,498	C
Syracuse Univ	NY	60,239	VC
The College of St. Rose	NY	43,048	C
Tiffin Univ	OH	31,380	C
Univ of Central Florida	FL	15,922	VC
Univ of Central Okla	OK	13,486	C
Univ of Illinois at Chicago	IL	25,006	VC
Univ of Nebr - Lincoln	NE	18,589	VC
Waynesburg Univ	PA	32,290	C
West Virginia Univ	WV	18,210	C
Western Illinois Univ	IL	20,825	C

FORENSIC STUDIES

School	ST	$IS	SR
Albany State Univ	GA	19,462	C
Ashland Univ	OH	21,440	C
Bay Path Univ	MA	45,349	C
Baylor Univ	TX	53,760	HC
Becker College	MA	57,628	C
Bryant Univ	RI	55,646	VC
Cal State, Fresno	CA	16,902	LC
Carlow Univ	PA	38,549	LC
Cedarville Univ	OH	34,990	VC
Chaminade Univ of Honolulu	HI	36,000	C
Champlain College	VT	53,132	C+
Chatham Univ	PA	46,517	C
Chestnut Hill College	PA	43,410	C
CUNY/John Jay College of Criminal Justice	NY	6,359	NC
Columbia College - Missouri	MO	27,803	C
Defiance College	OH	41,630	C
Eastern Kentucky Univ	KY	16,908	C
Eastern New Mexico Univ	NM	14,416	C
Edinboro Univ	PA	15,940	LC
Embry-Riddle Aeronautical Univ - Prescott Campus	AZ	44,054	VC
Emmanuel College	MA	52,110	C+
Fairmont State Univ	WV	15,726	C
Florida Gulf Coast Univ	FL	9,682	C
Florida Inst of Technology	FL	53,306	VC
Friends Univ	KS	34,455	C
Gannon Univ	PA	42,032	C
Grand Canyon Univ	AZ	16,950	VC
Guilford College	NC	44,090	C
Hamline Univ	MN	45,678	VC
Heidelberg Univ	OH	39,200	C
Hilbert College	NY	30,850	C
Hofstra Univ	NY	55,960	C+
Husson Univ	ME	25,720	LC
Inter-American Univ of PR-Aguadilla Campus	PR	21,657	
Inter-American Univ of PR-Bayamon	PR	18,785	
Keystone College	PA	28,680	LC
Lewis Univ	IL	40,370	C
LIU Post	NY	49,682	C
Loyola Univ Chicago	IL	55,802	VC
Loyola Univ New Orleans	LA	51,708	VC+
Marshall Univ	WV	17,242	C
Marygrove College	MI	28,926	NC
Maryville Univ of St. Louis	MO	38,046	VC+
Mercyhurst Univ	PA	47,420	C
Missouri Southern State Univ	MO	12,499	C
Newman Univ	KS	35,390	C
Northern Kentucky Univ	KY	16,486	C
Ohio Univ	OH	22,924	C
Pace Univ	NY	58,248	C
Russell Sage College	NY	39,370	C
St. Anselm College	NH	52,560	C+
St. Louis Univ	MO	49,866	HC
Seattle Univ	WA	50,811	VC+
Seton Hill Univ	PA	46,972	C
Simpson College	IA	43,839	VC
Southern Illinois Univ Edwardsville	IL	22,643	C
Southern Univ at New Orleans	LA	8,014	LC
Southern Wesleyan Univ	SC	32,130	LC
St. Andrews Univ	NC	44,634	LC
St. Edward's Univ	TX	53,100	VC
Texas A&M Univ	TX	20,521	VC+
Thomas More College	KY	36,720	C
Tiffin Univ	OH	31,380	C
Trine Univ	IN	41,310	C
Univ of Central Florida	FL	15,922	VC
Univ of Central Okla	OK	13,486	C
Univ of Findlay	OH	60,139	C
Univ of Illinois at Chicago	IL	25,006	VC
Univ of Miss	MS	17,746	C+
Univ of New Haven	CT	52,190	C
Univ of N Dak	ND	15,373	C
Univ of Scranton	PA	54,962	VC
Univ of Tampa	FL	36,944	C
Univ of Wisc-Milwaukee	WI	21,496	C
Univ of Wisc-Platteville	WI	14,614	VC
Virginia Commonwealth Univ	VA	23,049	C
Washburn Univ	KS	15,827	C
West Chester Univ of Pennsylvania	PA	18,456	C
West Virginia Univ	WV	18,210	C
Western Carolina Univ	NC	13,965	C
Western New England Univ	MA	48,088	C
Youngstown State Univ	OH	17,307	C

FOREST ENGINEERING

School	ST	$IS	SR
Auburn Univ	AL	23,594	VC+
Oregon State Univ	OR	22,519	VC
SUNY / The College of Environmental Science and Forestry	NY	23,853	VC
Univ of Maine	ME	20,792	C
Univ of Washington	WA	23,149	VC

FORESTRY AND RELATED SCIENCES

School	ST	$IS	SR
Alabama A&M Univ	AL	18,796	C
Albion College	MI	52,650	C
Beloit College	WI	55,206	HC
Calif Polytechnic State Univ	CA	17,979	HC+
Clemson Univ	SC		HC
Colo State Univ	CO	22,162	VC
Davis & Elkins College	WV	38,242	LC
Eastern Oregon Univ	OR	17,715	C
Elizabethtown College	PA	54,050	C
Glenville State College	WV	17,386	NC
Humboldt State Univ	CA	20,514	C
Iowa State Univ	IA	17,570	C
Louisiana State Univ and A&M College	LA	18,677	VC
Louisiana Tech Univ	LA	11,422	VC
Mich State Univ	MI	23,898	VC+
Mich Tech Univ	MI	24,739	VC+
N Car State Univ	NC	19,515	HC+
Northern Arizona Univ	AZ	20,246	VC
Northland College	WI	41,103	C+
Northwest Missouri State Univ	MO	17,737	C
Ohio State Univ at Columbus	OH	21,703	HC+
Oregon State Univ	OR	22,519	VC
Pennsylvania State Univ - Univ Park	PA	29,760	HC
Prescott College	AZ	33,284	C
Purdue Univ/West Lafayette	IN	20,032	MC
Sewanee: The Univ of the South	TN	54,500	MC
S Dak State Univ	SD	15,634	C
Southern Illinois Univ Carbondale	IL	23,667	C
Southern Univ and A&M College	LA	16,074	LC+
SUNY / The College of Environmental Science and Forestry	NY	23,853	VC
Stephen F. Austin State Univ	TX	18,406	LC
The Univ of Tenn at Knoxville	TN	22,112	VC
Univ of Arkansas at Monticello	AR	13,134	NC
Univ of Calif at Berkeley	CA	28,853	MC
Univ of Florida	FL	16,291	HC+
Univ of Georgia	GA	21,250	HC
Univ of Idaho	ID	15,348	C
Univ of Illinois at Urbana-Champaign	IL	27,006	HC
Univ of Kentucky	KY	33,306	C
Univ of Maine	ME	20,792	C
Univ of Maine at Fort Kent	ME	15,165	LC
Univ of Minn/Twin Cities	MN	23,519	HC+
Univ of Missouri/Columbia	MO	18,201	MC
Univ of Montana	MT	14,105	C
Univ of New Hampshire	NH	28,562	VC
Univ of Vermont	VT	28,878	HC
Univ of Wisc-Madison	WI	20,934	MC
Univ of Wisc-Stevens Point	WI	14,043	C
Utah State Univ	UT	12,736	C
Virginia Polytechnic Inst and State Univ	VA	21,276	HC
Washington State Univ	WA	22,495	C
West Virginia Univ	WV	18,210	C
Western New Mexico Univ	NM	16,734	LC
Whitman College	WA	59,772	MC

FORESTRY PRODUCTION AND PROCESSING

School	ST	$IS	SR
Auburn Univ	AL	23,594	VC+
Clemson Univ	SC		HC
Miss State Univ	MS	11,454	C+
Stephen F. Austin State Univ	TX	18,406	LC
Univ of Idaho	ID	15,348	C
Univ of Minn/Twin Cities	MN	23,519	HC+
Univ of Washington	WA	23,149	VC

FRENCH

School	ST	$IS	SR
Adelphi Univ	NY	48,244	C
Adrian College	MI	42,400	C
Agnes Scott College	GA	51,930	VC+
Alabama A&M Univ	AL	18,796	C
Alabama State Univ	AL	14,142	NC
Albany State Univ	GA	19,462	C
Albion College	MI	52,650	C
Albright College	PA	46,660	C
Allegheny College	PA	55,420	VC
Alma College	MI	47,548	C
American Univ	DC	59,379	HC+
Amherst College	MA		HC+
Anderson Univ	IN	38,200	C
Andrews Univ	MI	28,030	C+
Appalachian State Univ	NC	14,416	VC
Aquinas College - Mich	MI	38,876	HC
Arizona State Univ at the Tempe Campus	AZ	21,756	VC
Armstrong State Univ	GA	16,962	C
Asbury Univ	KY	35,180	C+
Ashland Univ	OH	21,440	C
Assumption College	MA	47,920	C+
Auburn Univ	AL	23,594	VC+
Augsburg College	MN	43,929	C
Augustana College	IL	49,658	VC
Augustana Univ	SD	38,424	VC
Austin College	TX	45,875	VC
Baker Univ	KS	33,350	C+
Baldwin Wallace Univ	OH	41,106	C
Ball State Univ	IN	19,590	C
Bard College	NY	64,024	HC
Barnard College/Columbia Univ	NY	62,741	MC
Barry Univ	FL	37,830	C
Baylor Univ	TX	53,760	HC
Belmont Univ	TN	40,970	VC
Beloit College	WI	55,206	HC
Benedictine College	KS	36,200	VC
Bennington College	VT	63,960	MC
Berea College	KY	7,042	C
Berry College	GA	45,286	C+
Bethel Univ	MN	45,270	VC
Boise State Univ	ID	14,860	C
Boston College	MA	65,737	MC
Boston Univ	MA	65,110	MC
Bowdoin College	ME	63,500	MC
Bowling Green State Univ	OH	19,747	C
Brandeis Univ	MA	65,925	MC
Bridgewater College	VA	44,510	C
Brigham Young Univ	UT	12,748	HC
Bryant Univ	RI	55,646	VC
Bryn Mawr College	PA	59,890	MC
Bucknell Univ	PA	64,616	MC
Butler Univ	IN	51,352	VC
Cabrini Univ	PA	42,591	LC
Caldwell Univ	NJ	42,165	NC
Calif Lutheran Univ	CA	52,853	C
Cal State, Fresno	CA	16,902	LC
Cal State, Fullerton	CA	21,902	C
Cal State, Long Beach	CA	18,850	C
Cal State, Los Angeles	CA	17,186	LC
Cal State, Northridge	CA	16,859	LC
Cal State, Sacramento	CA	20,332	C
Cal State, San Bernardino	CA	12,000	C
Cal State, Stanislaus	CA	16,212	C
Calif Univ of Pennsylvania	PA	14,217	LC
Calvin College	MI	41,570	VC+
Canisius College	NY	47,537	C
Capital Univ	OH	42,982	C
Cardinal Stritch Univ	WI	36,462	C
Carleton College	MN	64,071	MC
Carnegie Mellon Univ	PA	67,980	MC
Carroll College	MT	39,972	C+
Carson-Newman Univ	TN	34,160	C
Carthage College	WI	48,835	C
Case Western Reserve Univ	OH	60,304	MC
Centenary College of Louisiana	LA	45,650	C+
Central College	IA	44,592	C
Central Conn State Univ	CT	21,203	C
Central Mich Univ	MI	20,330	C
Central Washington Univ	WA	16,803	C
Centre College	KY	49,250	HC
Chapman Univ	CA	63,078	VC+
Chestnut Hill College	PA	43,410	C
Christopher Newport Univ	VA	23,968	VC+
CUNY/Brooklyn College	NY	5,884	C+
CUNY/City College	NY	20,319	VC
CUNY/Hunter College	NY	31,098	VC
CUNY/Lehman College	NY	5,778	HC+
CUNY/Queens College	NY	27,896	C
CUNY/York College	NY	6,747	LC
Claremont McKenna College	CA	67,185	MC
Clark Univ	MA	51,600	HC+
Clemson Univ	SC		HC
Cleveland State Univ	OH	22,196	C
Coe College	IA	51,570	VC
Colgate Univ	NY	65,030	MC
College of Mount St. Vincent	NY	45,620	C
College of St. Benedict	MN	52,806	C
College of the Holy Cross	MA	62,165	MC
College of William & Mary	VA		MC
Colo State Univ	CO	22,162	VC
Columbia College	SC	36,550	C
Columbia Univ/ School of General Studies	NY	61,470	MC
Columbia Univ/City of New York	NY	62,958	MC
Concordia College - Moorhead	MN	51,088	C+
Conn College	CT	65,000	MC
Converse College	SC	26,495	C
Cornell College	IA	48,800	VC
Cornell Univ	NY	64,853	MC
Covenant College	GA	38,990	VC
Daemen College	NY	38,045	C
Dartmouth College	NH	66,174	MC
Davidson College	NC	60,119	MC
Delaware State Univ	DE	19,376	NC
Denison Univ	OH	58,860	MC
DePaul Univ	IL	47,623	VC
DePauw Univ	IN	58,688	HC+
Dickinson College	PA	63,974	MC
Doane Univ	NE	39,184	VC
Dominican Univ	IL	41,222	C
Drew Univ/College of Liberal Arts	NJ	61,048	VC
Drury Univ	MO	33,791	VC
Earlham College	IN	54,870	HC
East Carolina Univ	NC	16,937	C
Eastern Kentucky Univ	KY	16,908	C
Eastern Mich Univ	MI	19,761	C
Eastern Nazarene College	MA	39,955	C
Eastern Washington Univ	WA	25,572	LC
Eckerd College	FL	52,874	C
Edgewood College	WI	35,950	C
Elizabethtown College	PA	54,050	C
Elmhurst College	IL	45,428	C
Elon Univ	NC	44,599	VC+
Emory Univ	GA	60,786	MC
Fairfield Univ	CT	59,860	VC+
Fisk Univ	TN	32,066	LC
Florida Atlantic Univ	FL	17,339	C
Florida International Univ	FL	19,854	C+
Florida State Univ	FL	16,771	HC
Fordham Univ	NY	65,918	MC
Fort Hays State Univ	KS	12,131	C
Franciscan Univ of Steubenville	OH	33,980	VC
Franklin and Marshall College	PA	63,170	HC
Franklin College	IN	39,380	C
Furman Univ	SC	58,092	VC+
Gardner-Webb Univ	NC	39,200	C+
George Mason Univ	VA	15,724	VC
George Washington Univ	DC	62,835	MC
Georgetown College	KY	41,440	C
Georgetown Univ	DC	65,926	MC
Georgia State Univ	GA	24,332	VC
Gettysburg College	PA	63,000	HC
Gonzaga Univ	WA	50,888	HC
Gordon College	MA	46,472	C+
Goucher College	MD	55,716	VC
Grace College and Seminary	IN	31,524	C
Grand Valley State Univ	MI	22,250	C+
Greensboro College	NC	42,400	LC
Grinnell College	IA	60,738	MC
Grove City College	PA	25,692	VC
Guilford College	NC	44,090	C
Gustavus Adolphus College	MN	52,433	HC
Hamilton College	NY	64,250	MC
Hamline Univ	MN	45,678	VC
Hampden-Sydney College	VA	56,248	C+
Hanover College	IN	46,364	C+
Harding Univ	AR	25,421	C
Hartwick College	NY	51,270	C
Harvard College/Harvard Univ	MA	60,659	MC
Haverford College	PA	66,490	MC
Hendrix College	AR	54,020	VC+
High Point Univ	NC	45,977	C
Hillsdale College	MI	35,722	MC
Hiram College	OH	43,230	C
Hofstra Univ	NY	55,960	C+
Hollins Univ	VA	49,635	VC
Hood College	MD	54,840	C
Hope College	MI	39,940	VC
Houston Baptist Univ	TX	36,450	C
Howard Univ	DC	37,616	C+
Humboldt State Univ	CA	20,514	C
Idaho State Univ	ID	13,619	NC
Illinois College	IL	40,850	VC
Illinois State Univ	IL	23,418	VC
Illinois Wesleyan Univ	IL	56,430	VC+
Indiana State Univ	IN	23,223	LC
Indiana Univ Bloomington	IN	20,429	VC
Indiana Univ Northwest	IN	7,072	C
Indiana Univ South Bend	IN	14,242	C
Indiana Univ Southeast	IN	14,242	LC
Indiana Univ-Purdue Univ Fort Wayne	IN	17,553	C
Indiana Univ-Purdue Univ Indianapolis	IN	18,635	C
Iona College	NY	50,984	C
Iowa State Univ	IA	17,570	C
Ithaca College	NY	56,766	VC
Jacksonville Univ	FL	46,230	C
John Carroll Univ	OH	49,740	C+
Johns Hopkins Univ	MD	65,386	MC
Johnson C. Smith Univ	NC	25,336	LC
Juniata College	PA	53,760	VC
Kalamazoo College	MI	53,931	HC+
Keene State College	NH	24,003	LC
Kenyon College	OH	63,330	MC
King Univ	TN	34,660	C
King's College	PA	46,858	C
Knox College	IL	52,615	VC+
Kutztown Univ of Pennsylvania	PA	19,056	LC

ST = STATE $IS = IN-STATE COSTS SR = SELECTOR RATING

School	ST	$IS	SR
Lafayette College	PA	63,355	MC
Lake Forest College	IL	50,652	VC
Lamar Univ	TX	18,014	LC
Lane College	TN	16,550	C
Lawrence Univ	WI	54,498	HC
Le Moyne College	NY	46,000	C
Lebanon Valley College	PA	51,530	C
Lee Univ	TN	22,045	C
Lehigh Univ	PA	61,010	MC
Lenoir-Rhyne Univ	NC	43,200	C
Lindenwood Univ	MO	25,132	C
Linfield College	OR	52,010	C
Lipscomb Univ	TN	41,296	VC
LIU Brooklyn	NY	49,682	C
LIU Post	NY	49,682	C
Lock Haven Univ of Pennsylvania	PA	18,028	LC
Louisiana College	LA	21,886	C
Louisiana State Univ and A&M College	LA	18,677	VC
Louisiana Tech Univ	LA	11,422	VC
Loyola Marymount Univ	CA	58,038	HC
Loyola Univ Chicago	IL	55,802	VC
Loyola Univ Maryland	MD	60,300	VC
Loyola Univ New Orleans	LA	51,708	VC+
Luther College	IA	48,540	C+
Lycoming College	PA	48,580	C
Lynchburg College	VA	46,740	C
Macalester College	MN	61,905	MC
Manchester Univ	IN	40,422	C
Manhattan College	NY	51,750	C+
Manhattanville College	NY	51,440	C+
Marist College	NY	49,860	VC
Marquette Univ	WI	48,390	VC+
Marshall Univ	WV	17,242	C
Marywood Univ	PA	46,900	C
McDaniel College	MD	51,380	VC
Mercer Univ	GA	45,348	VC
Meredith College	NC	45,297	C
Methodist Univ	NC	43,600	C
Miami Univ	OH	27,190	HC+
Mich State Univ	MI	23,898	VC+
Middle Tenn State Univ	TN	8,650	C
Middlebury College	VT	64,332	MC
Millersville Univ of Pennsylvania	PA	23,782	C
Mills College	CA	59,163	VC
Minn State Univ, Mankato	MN	15,616	C
Minot State Univ	ND	12,732	C
Miss College	MS	25,850	C
Missouri Southern State Univ	MO	12,499	C
Missouri State Univ	MO	15,190	C+
Missouri Western State Univ	MO	16,741	
Monmouth College	IL	42,260	C
Montana State Univ-Northern	MT	11,370	NC
Montclair State Univ	NJ	26,210	LC
Moravian College	PA	53,117	
Morehouse College	GA	40,064	C
Mount Holyoke College	MA	56,746	MC
Mount St. Mary's Univ	MD	51,610	C
Mount St. Mary's Univ - Chalon Campus	CA	43,897	VC+
Muhlenberg College	PA	56,645	VC+
Murray State Univ	KY	16,998	C
Muskingum Univ	OH	35,966	C
Nazareth College	NY	45,574	C
Nebr Wesleyan Univ	NE	38,140	C+
New College of Florida	FL	15,848	MC
New York Univ	NY	65,860	MC
Newberry College	SC	34,550	C
Niagara Univ	NY	41,010	C
Nicholls State Univ	LA	10,534	C
N Car A&T State Univ	NC	13,365	LC
N Car Central Univ	NC	9,000	C
N Car State Univ	NC	19,515	HC+
North Central College	IL	48,712	VC
N Dak State Univ	ND	16,245	C
North Park Univ	IL	35,860	C
Northeastern Illinois Univ	IL	12,529	LC
Northern Illinois Univ	IL	20,176	C
Northern Kentucky Univ	KY	16,486	C
Northern Mich Univ	MI	19,604	C
Northern State Univ	SD	14,505	C
Northwestern Univ	IL	66,344	MC
Oakland Univ	MI	20,763	C
Oakwood Univ	AL	43,758	C
Oberlin College	OH	66,012	MC
Occidental College	CA	65,530	MC
Oglethorpe Univ	GA	44,200	C+
Ohio Northern Univ	OH	44,050	VC
Ohio State Univ at Columbus	OH	21,703	HC+
Ohio Univ	OH	22,924	C
Ohio Wesleyan Univ	OH	49,460	VC
Okla City Univ	OK	40,476	VC
Okla State Univ	OK	17,180	VC
Old Dominion Univ	VA	20,910	C
Oral Roberts Univ	OK	34,316	C
Oregon State Univ	OR	22,519	VC
Otterbein Univ	OH	41,630	C
Pacific Lutheran Univ	WA	49,960	VC
Pacific Union College	CA	36,009	VC
Pennsylvania State Univ - Univ Park	PA	29,760	HC
Pepperdine Univ	CA	74,460	HC+
Pitzer College	CA	66,192	MC
Plymouth State Univ	NH	23,180	LC
Point Loma Nazarene Univ	CA	43,450	C
Pomona College	CA	64,957	MC
Portland State Univ	OR	19,443	C
Princeton Univ	NJ	57,610	MC
Principia College	IL	39,010	C+
Providence College	RI	60,760	VC
Purdue Univ/Northwest	IN	15,038	C
Purdue Univ/West Lafayette	IN	20,032	MC
Queens Univ of Charlotte	NC	39,543	C
Randolph College	VA	45,660	VC
Randolph-Macon College	VA	49,910	C
Regis Univ	CO	44,520	C
Rhode Island College	RI	17,694	LC
Rhodes College	TN	51,900	HC
Rider Univ	NJ	54,050	C
Roanoke College	VA	54,114	VC
Rockford Univ	IL	36,030	C
Rockhurst Univ	MO	29,220	C
Rollins College	FL	58,670	HC
Roosevelt Univ	IL	40,651	VC
Rosemont College	PA	30,980	C
Rutgers Univ - Camden	NJ	26,146	C
Rutgers Univ - New Brunswick	NJ	26,632	HC
Rutgers Univ - Newark	NJ	27,288	C
Saginaw Valley State Univ	MI	18,530	C
St. Anselm College	NH	52,560	C+
St. Augustine's Univ	NC	26,048	C
St. Francis Univ	PA	42,268	NC
St. John's Univ	MN	51,624	C
St. Joseph's Univ	PA	57,544	VC+
St. Louis Univ	MO	49,866	HC
St. Mary's College of Calif	CA	57,420	C
St. Michael's College	VT	51,725	VC+
St. Vincent College	PA	44,626	C
St. Xavier Univ	IL	43,310	C
Salem College	NC	37,694	HC
Salisbury Univ	MD	20,714	VC
Salve Regina Univ	RI	51,470	C
Sam Houston State Univ	TX	18,792	C
Samford Univ	AL	39,232	VC
San Diego State Univ	CA	21,896	C+
San Francisco State Univ	CA	18,514	LC
San Jose State Univ	CA	21,540	C
Sarah Lawrence College	NY	63,388	HC
Seattle Pacific Univ	WA	47,439	C+
Seattle Univ	WA	50,811	VC+
Seton Hall Univ	NJ	55,514	C
Sewanee: The Univ of the South	TN	54,500	MC
Shippensburg Univ of Pennsylvania	PA	23,208	C
Shorter Univ	GA	31,130	LC
Siena College	NY	48,916	C+
Simmons College	MA	53,090	VC
Simpson College	IA	43,839	VC
Skidmore College	NY	64,214	HC
Slippery Rock Univ of Pennsylvania	PA	10,360	C
Smith College	MA	63,914	MC
Sonoma State Univ	CA	27,806	C
S Car State Univ	SC	20,805	LC
Southern Conn State Univ	CT	21,924	LC
Southern Illinois Univ Edwardsville	IL	22,643	C
Southern Methodist Univ	TX	66,483	MC
Southern Univ and A&M College	LA	16,074	LC+
Southwestern Univ	TX	50,720	VC
Spelman College	GA	38,751	C
St. Ambrose Univ	IA	39,019	C
St. Ambrose Univ	IA	39,019	C
St. Bonaventure Univ	NY	44,237	C
St. Catherine Univ	MN	45,630	VC
St. Edward's Univ	TX	53,100	VC
St. John Fisher College	NY	43,620	C
St. John's Univ	NY	55,850	C
St. Lawrence Univ	NY	64,390	VC
St. Mary's Univ	TX	37,500	C
St. Norbert College	WI	44,525	VC
St. Olaf College	MN	54,260	HC+
Stanford Univ	CA	60,409	MC
SUNY / Buffalo State College	NY	20,842	C
SUNY / SUNY Fredonia	NY	20,818	C
SUNY / SUNY Oneonta	NY	19,712	C+
SUNY / SUNY Plattsburgh	NY	18,814	C
SUNY / SUNY Potsdam	NY	20,404	C+
SUNY / Univ at Buffalo	NY	23,122	C+
SUNY at Binghamton	NY	22,861	MC
SUNY at Geneseo	NY	20,440	VC+
SUNY at New Paltz	NY	19,200	C
SUNY at Oswego	NY	21,351	C
Stephen F. Austin State Univ	TX	18,406	LC
Stetson Univ	FL	53,544	VC
Stonehill College	MA	55,030	C+
Suffolk Univ	MA	50,308	C
Susquehanna Univ	PA	55,340	VC
Swarthmore College	PA	63,550	MC
Temple Univ	PA	24,392	VC
Tenn Tech Univ	TN	17,050	C
Texas A&M Univ	TX	20,521	VC+
Texas A&M Univ at Commerce	TX	10,496	C
Texas Christian Univ	TX	54,670	HC
Texas State Univ	TX	19,350	C
Texas Tech Univ	TX	18,736	C+
The Catholic Univ of America	DC	56,356	VC
The Citadel, The Military College of S Car	SC	35,339	C
The College at Brockport - SUNY	NY	20,346	C
The College of New Rochelle	NY	46,300	VC
The College of Wooster	OH	57,900	VC+
The Lincoln Univ	PA	15,154	NC
The Univ of Akron	OH	21,477	C
The Univ of Tenn at Chattanooga	TN	16,744	C
The Univ of Tenn at Knoxville	TN	22,112	VC
The Univ of Tenn at Martin	TN	14,876	C
The Univ of Utah	UT	17,924	VC
The Univ of Virginia's College at Wise	VA	18,192	LC
Thomas Edison State Univ	NJ	6,350	NC
Towson Univ	MD	17,408	VC
Transylvania Univ	KY	45,690	VC+
Trinity College	CT	63,920	HC+
Trinity Univ	TX	52,314	HC+
Truman State Univ	MO	16,014	HC
Tufts Univ	MA		MC
Tulane Univ	LA	63,396	HC+
Union College	NE	23,270	C
Union Univ	TN	33,970	VC
Univ of Alabama	AL	24,320	C+
Univ of Arizona	AZ	23,100	C
Univ of Arkansas at Fayetteville	AR	19,152	C+
Univ of Arkansas at Little Rock	AR	18,211	C
Univ of Calif at Berkeley	CA	28,853	MC
Univ of Calif at Davis	CA	28,468	HC
Univ of Calif at Irvine	CA	26,484	VC
Univ of Calif at Los Angeles	CA	30,162	MC
Univ of Calif at Riverside	CA	29,227	C+
Univ of Calif at Santa Barbara	CA	29,091	HC
Univ of Central Arkansas	AR	14,472	VC
Univ of Central Florida	FL	15,922	VC
Univ of Central Missouri	MO	18,982	C
Univ of Central Okla	OK	13,486	C
Univ of Cincinnati	OH	21,964	VC
Univ of Colo Boulder	CO	24,285	VC+
Univ of Colo Denver	CO	23,230	C
Univ of Conn	CT	25,538	HC
Univ of Dallas	TX	45,500	VC+
Univ of Dayton	OH	53,620	C
Univ of Denver	CO	58,443	VC+
Univ of Evansville	IN	44,186	VC+
Univ of Florida	FL	16,291	HC+
Univ of Georgia	GA	21,250	HC
Univ of Hawaii at Manoa	HI	23,221	C
Univ of Houston	TX	21,483	VC
Univ of Idaho	ID	15,348	C
Univ of Illinois at Chicago	IL	25,006	VC
Univ of Illinois at Urbana-Champaign	IL	27,006	HC
Univ of Indianapolis	IN	36,480	C
Univ of Iowa	IA	18,683	VC+
Univ of Jamestown	ND	28,508	C
Univ of Kansas	KS	20,135	C+
Univ of Kentucky	KY	33,306	C
Univ of La Verne	CA	55,600	C
Univ of Louisiana at Lafayette	LA	14,516	C
Univ of Louisville	KY	19,824	C
Univ of Maine	ME	20,792	C
Univ of Maine at Fort Kent	ME	15,165	LC
Univ of Mary Washington	VA	24,764	VC
Univ of Maryland/Baltimore County	MD	21,296	VC
Univ of Maryland/College Park	MD	21,938	HC
Univ of Mass Boston	MA	13,435	C
Univ of Mass Dartmouth	MA	25,658	C
Univ of Miami	FL	63,494	MC
Univ of Mich/Ann Arbor	MI	24,410	MC
Univ of Mich/Dearborn	MI	11,757	VC
Univ of Mich-Flint	MI	17,607	C+
Univ of Minn/Morris	MN	20,760	VC
Univ of Minn/Twin Cities	MN	23,519	HC+
Univ of Miss	MS	17,746	C+
Univ of Missouri/Columbia	MO	18,201	MC
Univ of Missouri-Kansas City	MO	19,563	VC
Univ of Missouri-St. Louis	MO		C
Univ of Montana	MT	14,105	C
Univ of Montevallo	AL	19,502	C
Univ of Mount Union	OH	38,970	C
Univ of Nebr - Kearney	NE	16,546	LC
Univ of Nebr - Lincoln	NE	18,589	VC
Univ of Nebr - Omaha	NE	16,120	C
Univ of Nevada, Las Vegas	NV	17,553	C
Univ of Nevada/Reno	NV	18,010	C
Univ of New Hampshire	NH	28,562	VC
Univ of New Mexico	NM	15,404	C
Univ of New Orleans	LA	12,840	C
Univ of North Alabama	AL	15,398	C
Univ of N Car at Asheville	NC	15,723	VC+
Univ of N Car at Charlotte	NC	15,547	C
Univ of N Car at Greensboro	NC	14,690	C
Univ of N Car at Wilmington	NC	14,590	VC
Univ of N Dak	ND	15,373	C
Univ of North Georgia	GA	17,316	C
Univ of North Texas	TX	19,198	C
Univ of Northern Colo	CO	20,851	C
Univ of Notre Dame	IN	64,043	MC
Univ of Okla	OK	18,911	VC
Univ of Oregon	OR	22,972	C
Univ of Pennsylvania	PA	63,526	MC
Univ of Pittsburgh	PA	29,568	HC+
Univ of PR, at Mayaguez	PR	13,995	
Univ of Puget Sound	WA	56,456	VC+
Univ of Redlands	CA	60,200	VC
Univ of Rhode Island	RI	24,906	C
Univ of Richmond	VA	60,880	MC
Univ of Rochester	NY	65,032	MC
Univ of San Diego	CA	58,442	VC+
Univ of San Francisco	CA	58,484	VC
Univ of Scranton	PA	54,962	VC
Univ of S Car at Columbia	SC	19,725	VC+
Univ of South Florida/Tampa	FL	16,110	VC+
Univ of Southern Calif	CA	66,631	C
Univ of Southern Indiana	IN	16,501	C
Univ of Southern Maine	ME	18,320	C
Univ of St. Thomas - Houston	TX	40,020	VC
Univ of Texas at Arlington	TX	18,026	LC
Univ of Texas at Austin	TX	26,102	HC
Univ of Texas at El Paso	TX	34,452	NC
Univ of the District of Columbia	DC	21,044	LC
Univ of the Pacific	CA	57,006	VC
Univ of Toledo	OH	19,336	NC
Univ of Tulsa	OK	52,625	HC+
Univ of Vermont	VT	28,878	HC
Univ of Virginia	VA	25,891	MC
Univ of Washington	WA	23,149	VC
Univ of Wisc-Eau Claire	WI	15,797	VC
Univ of Wisc-Green Bay	WI	15,064	C
Univ of Wisc-La Crosse	WI	15,247	C+
Univ of Wisc-Madison	WI	20,934	MC
Univ of Wisc-Milwaukee	WI	21,496	C
Univ of Wisc-Oshkosh	WI	15,200	C
Univ of Wisc-Parkside	WI	15,193	C
Univ of Wisc-Stevens Point	WI	14,043	C
Univ of Wisc-Whitewater	WI	13,976	C
Univ of Wyoming	WY	15,375	C+
Ursinus College	PA	61,690	VC
Utah State Univ	UT	12,736	C
Valparaiso Univ	IN	48,370	C+
Vanderbilt Univ	TN	60,572	MC
Vassar College	NY	65,491	MC
Villanova Univ	PA	62,523	MC
Virginia Polytechnic Inst and State Univ	VA	21,276	HC
Virginia Wesleyan College	VA	43,728	LC
Wabash College	IN	50,650	VC
Wake Forest Univ	NC	64,056	MC
Walla Walla Univ	WA	30,417	NC
Walsh Univ	OH	39,010	C
Wartburg College	IA	47,840	C
Washburn Univ	KS	15,827	C
Washington & Jefferson College	PA	56,512	VC
Washington and Lee Univ	VA	59,647	MC
Washington College	MD	54,666	VC
Washington State Univ	WA	22,495	C
Washington Univ in St. Louis	MO	65,366	VC
Weber State Univ	UT	10,721	C
Webster Univ	MO	37,490	C
Wellesley College	MA	63,916	MC
Wesleyan College	GA	29,694	C+
West Chester Univ of Pennsylvania	PA	18,456	C
Western Carolina Univ	NC	13,965	C
Western Kentucky Univ	KY	16,850	C
Western Mich Univ	MI	21,054	C
Western Washington Univ	WA	18,003	C+
Westminster College	MO	32,820	C
Westminster College	PA	39,180	C+
Westmont College	CA	56,410	HC
Wheaton College	IL	43,610	MC
Wheeling Jesuit Univ	WV	37,106	LC
Whitman College	WA	59,772	MC
Whittier College	CA	57,891	C
Whitworth Univ	WA	51,732	VC
Wichita State Univ	KS	21,643	C
Widener Univ	PA	56,486	C
Willamette Univ	OR	61,817	VC+
William Jewell College	MO	41,210	C+
Williams College	MA	63,290	MC
Wilson College	PA	35,620	C
Winthrop Univ	SC	23,082	C
Wittenberg Univ	OH	48,156	C+
Wofford College	SC	49,885	VC
Wright State Univ	OH	16,983	C
Xavier Univ	OH	47,880	C+
Xavier Univ of Louisiana	LA	31,689	C+
Yale Univ	CT	64,650	MC
Yeshiva Univ	NY	47,250	VC+

FRENCH AND FRANCOPHONE STUDIES

School	ST	$IS	SR
Bates College	ME	64,500	MC
Brown Univ	RI	64,566	MC
Bryant Univ	RI	55,646	VC
Cal State, Long Beach	CA	18,850	C
Creighton Univ	NE	48,206	VC+
Kent State Univ	OH	20,732	C
Linfield College	OR	52,010	C
Rhode Island College	RI	17,694	LC
Syracuse Univ	NY	60,239	VC
Univ of Illinois at Chicago	IL	25,006	VC
Wellesley College	MA	63,916	MC

ST = STATE $IS = IN-STATE COSTS SR = SELECTOR RATING

FRENCH LANGUAGE AND LITERATURE

School	ST	$IS	SR
Brown Univ	RI	64,566	MC
Messiah College	PA	43,100	C+
Stony Brook Univ/The SUNY	NY	21,881	MC

FRENCH STUDIES

School	ST	$IS	SR
American Univ	DC	59,379	HC+
Appalachian State Univ	NC	14,416	VC
Aquinas College - Mich	MI	38,876	HC
Bard College	NY	64,024	HC
Bard College at Simon's Rock	MA	65,795	MC
Boston Univ	MA	65,110	MC
Brown Univ	RI	64,566	MC
Bryant Univ	RI	55,646	VC
Cal State, Chico	CA	21,440	C
Cal State, Fresno	CA	16,902	LC
Cal State, Northridge	CA	16,859	LC
Case Western Reserve Univ	OH	60,304	MC
Coe College	IA	51,570	VC
Colby College	ME	64,060	MC
College of Charleston	SC	22,699	C
Colo College	CO	62,560	MC
Columbia Univ/ School of General Studies	NY	61,470	MC
Dartmouth College	NH	66,174	MC
Duke Univ	NC	64,188	
Emory Univ	GA	60,786	MC
Fairleigh Dickinson Univ/ College at Florham	NJ	52,062	C
Fordham Univ	NY	65,918	MC
Lake Erie College	OH	38,914	LC
Lebanon Valley College	PA	51,530	C
Lewis & Clark College	OR	58,434	HC+
Mills College	CA	59,163	VC
New College of Florida	FL	15,848	MC
New York Univ	NY	65,860	MC
North Park Univ	IL	35,860	C
Northeastern Illinois Univ	IL	12,529	LC
Ohio State Univ at Columbus	OH	21,703	HC+
Otterbein Univ	OH	41,630	C
Purdue Univ/West Lafayette	IN	20,032	MC
Reed College	OR	65,300	MC
Rice Univ	TX	57,668	MC
St. Joseph's Univ	PA	57,544	VC+
St. Louis Univ	MO	49,866	HC
Scripps College	CA	66,664	MC
Sewanee: The Univ of the South	TN	54,500	MC
Skidmore College	NY	64,214	HC
Smith College	MA	63,914	MC
S Dak State Univ	SD	15,634	C
SUNY / SUNY Plattsburgh	NY	18,814	C
SUNY / SUNY Potsdam	NY	20,404	C+
SUNY at Oswego	NY	21,351	C
Stony Brook Univ/The SUNY	NY	21,881	MC
The Catholic Univ of America	DC	56,356	VC
Union College	NY	64,320	MC
Univ of Calif at Los Angeles	CA	30,162	MC
Univ of Calif San Diego	CA	30,150	MC
Univ of Illinois at Chicago	IL	25,006	VC
Univ of Mass Amherst	MA	26,199	VC+
Univ of New Hampshire	NH	28,562	VC
Univ of North Florida	FL	15,996	VC
Univ of Portland	OR	52,152	VC
Univ of S Dak	SD	16,109	C
Univ of Wisc-Green Bay	WI	15,064	C
Wartburg College	IA	47,840	C
Wellesley College	MA	63,916	MC
Wesleyan Univ	CT	65,516	MC
West Chester Univ of Pennsylvania	PA	18,456	C
Wheaton College	MA	61,512	VC

FRENCH STUDIES K-12 EDUCATION

School	ST	$IS	SR
Augustana College	IL	49,658	VC
Colo State Univ	CO	22,162	VC
Edgewood College	WI	35,950	C
Grove City College	PA	25,692	VC
Indiana Univ South Bend	IN	14,242	C
The Univ of Utah	UT	17,924	VC

FUNERAL HOME SERVICES

School	ST	$IS	SR
Gannon Univ	PA	42,032	C
Mount Ida College	MA	46,820	C
Point Park Univ	PA	41,270	C
Southern Illinois Univ Carbondale	IL	23,667	C
Univ of Central Okla	OK	13,486	C
Wayne State Univ	MI	22,016	C

FURNITURE DESIGN

School	ST	$IS	SR
Calif College of the Arts	CA	52,758	SP
Cal State, Fresno	CA	16,902	LC
Ferris State Univ	MI	21,445	C
Minneapolis College of Art and Design	MN	44,238	SP
N Car State Univ	NC	19,515	HC+
Northern Mich Univ	MI	19,604	C
Rhode Island School of Design	RI	59,960	SP
Rochester Inst of Technology	NY	50,842	HC
Savannah College of Art and Design	GA	49,595	C

GAME ART

School	ST	$IS	SR
Champlain College	VT	53,132	C+
Ringling College of Art and Design	FL	57,430	SP

GAME DESIGN AND DEVELOPMENT

School	ST	$IS	SR
Arkansas Tech Univ	AR	15,484	C
Bloomfield College	NJ	39,100	LC
Champlain College	VT	53,132	C+
Cleveland Inst of Art	OH	51,439	C+
Columbia College Chicago	IL	43,168	C
Hofstra Univ	NY	55,960	C+
Indiana Univ Bloomington	IN	20,429	VC
Lawrence Tech Univ	MI	39,770	VC
Marist College	NY	49,860	VC
Maryville Univ of St. Louis	MO	38,046	VC+
Okla Christian Univ	OK	27,650	VC
Rocky Mountain College of Art and Design	CO	27,052	SP
St. Edward's Univ	TX	53,100	VC
Univ of Tulsa	OK	52,625	HC+
Univ of Wisc-Stout	WI	19,667	C
William Peace Univ	NC	37,430	LC
Worcester Polytechnic Inst	MA	60,730	MC

GAME PROGRAMMING

School	ST	$IS	SR
Bloomfield College	NJ	39,100	LC
Champlain College	VT	53,132	C+
Columbia College Chicago	IL	43,168	C
Kansas City Art Inst	MO	44,308	C+
Loyola Univ New Orleans	LA	51,708	VC+
New England College	NH	50,364	C
Univ of Tulsa	OK	52,625	HC+

GENDER STUDIES

School	ST	$IS	SR
Albion College	MI	52,650	C
American Univ	DC	59,379	HC+
Bard College	NY	64,024	HC
Bard College at Simon's Rock	MA	65,795	MC
Beloit College	WI	55,206	HC
Bowdoin College	ME	63,500	MC
Brown Univ	RI	64,566	MC
Bryant Univ	RI	55,646	VC
Butler Univ	IN	51,352	VC
Cabrini Univ	PA	42,591	LC
Calif State Polytechnic Univ, Pomona	CA	21,541	C
Cal State, Chico	CA	21,440	C
CUNY/John Jay College of Criminal Justice	NY	6,359	NC
Coe College	IA	51,570	VC
College of St. Benedict	MN	52,806	C
College of William & Mary	VA		MC
Colo College	CO	62,560	MC
Conn College	CT	65,000	MC
Cornell College	IA	48,800	VC
Davidson College	NC	60,119	MC
DePauw Univ	IN	58,688	HC+
Dominican Univ	IL	41,222	C
Eastern Mich Univ	MI	19,761	C
Eugene Lang College/The New School for Liberal Arts	NY	55,650	C
Fort Lewis College	CO	18,980	C
Gettysburg College	PA	63,000	HC
Grinnell College	IA	60,738	MC
Guilford College	NC	44,090	C
Hanover College	IN	46,364	C+
Hollins Univ	VA	49,635	VC
Indiana Univ Bloomington	IN	20,429	VC
John Carroll Univ	OH	49,740	C+
Lawrence Univ	WI	54,498	HC
McNeese State Univ	LA	7,838	C
Mercer Univ	GA	45,348	VC
Missouri Baptist Univ	MO	35,594	C
Mount Holyoke College	MA	56,746	MC
New College of Florida	FL	15,848	MC
New York Univ	NY	65,860	MC
Northeastern Illinois Univ	IL	12,529	LC
Northern Mich Univ	MI	19,604	C
Northwestern Univ	IL	66,344	MC
Oberlin College	OH	66,012	MC
Ohio Univ	OH	22,924	C
Prescott College	AZ	33,284	C
St. John's Univ	MN	51,624	C
St. Michael's College	VT	51,725	VC+
San Diego State Univ	CA	21,896	C+
Seton Hill Univ	PA	46,972	C
Skidmore College	NY	64,214	HC
Sonoma State Univ	CA	27,806	C
Southern Oregon Univ	OR	19,117	C
St. Ambrose Univ	IA	39,019	C
St. Ambrose Univ	IA	39,019	C
SUNY / SUNY Plattsburgh	NY	18,814	C
Stonehill College	MA	55,030	C+
Swarthmore College	PA	63,550	MC
The Univ of Utah	UT	17,924	VC
Tulane Univ	LA	63,396	HC+
Univ of Arizona	AZ	23,100	C
Univ of Calif San Diego	CA	30,150	MC
Univ of Chicago	IL	67,584	MC
Univ of Illinois at Chicago	IL	25,006	VC
Univ of Iowa	IA	18,683	VC+
Univ of Kansas	KS	20,135	C+
Univ of Maryland/Baltimore County	MD	21,296	VC
Univ of Mass Amherst	MA	26,199	VC+
Univ of Miami	FL	63,494	MC
Univ of Notre Dame	IN	64,043	MC
Univ of Pennsylvania	PA	63,526	MC
Univ of Rhode Island	RI	24,906	C
Univ of Vermont	VT	28,878	HC
Univ of Wisc-Green Bay	WI	15,064	C
Univ of Wisc-Madison	WI	20,934	MC
Villanova Univ	PA	62,523	MC
Wellesley College	MA	63,916	MC
Wesleyan Univ	CT	65,516	MC
West Virginia Univ	WV	18,210	C
West Virginia Wesleyan College	WV	36,858	C
Western Mich Univ	MI	21,054	C
Westminster College	UT	41,078	C+
Whitman College	WA	59,772	MC
Widener Univ	PA	56,486	C
Wofford College	SC	49,885	VC
Xavier Univ	OH	47,880	C+

GENERAL STUDIES

School	ST	$IS	SR
Aquinas College - Mich	MI	38,876	HC
Arizona State Univ at the Downtown Phoenix Campus	AZ	23,680	VC
Arizona State Univ at the Tempe Campus	AZ	21,756	VC
Arkansas State Univ	AR	16,190	C
Austin Peay State Univ	TN	16,397	C
Black Hills State Univ	SD	15,899	C
Bryant Univ	RI	55,646	VC
East Central Univ	OK	13,056	C
East Texas Baptist Univ	TX	33,134	C
Eastern Illinois Univ	IL	21,126	C
Fontbonne Univ	MO	33,717	C
Houghton College	NY	39,090	C
Indiana Univ Bloomington	IN	20,429	VC
Indiana Univ East	IN	7,072	C
Indiana Univ Kokomo	IN	7,073	C
Indiana Univ Northwest	IN	7,072	C
Indiana Univ South Bend	IN	14,242	C
Indiana Univ Southeast	IN	14,242	LC
Indiana Univ-Purdue Univ Indianapolis	IN	18,635	C
Kent State Univ	OH	20,732	C
King Univ	TN	34,660	C
Millersville Univ of Pennsylvania	PA	23,782	C
Minn State Univ, Mankato	MN	15,616	C
Mount St. Joseph Univ	OH	33,880	C
New York Univ	NY	65,860	MC
Nova Southeastern Univ	FL	38,534	C+
Rowan Univ	NJ	24,491	VC+
St. Louis Univ	MO	49,866	HC
Southeast Missouri State Univ	MO	15,498	C
Tabor College	KS	35,870	C
Texas Christian Univ	TX	54,670	HC
Texas Tech Univ	TX	18,736	C+
Univ of Arizona	AZ	23,100	C
Univ of Central Okla	OK	13,486	C
Univ of Dayton	OH	53,620	C
Univ of Idaho	ID	15,348	C
Univ of Maine at Machias	ME	22,960	C
Univ of Nevada/Reno	NV	18,010	C
West Virginia Univ	WV	18,210	C
Western Kentucky Univ	KY	16,850	C
Western Mich Univ	MI	21,054	C
Wichita State Univ	KS	21,643	C
Youngstown State Univ	OH	17,307	C

GENETICS

School	ST	$IS	SR
Cal State, Northridge	CA	16,859	LC
Cedar Crest College	PA	46,715	C
Dartmouth College	NH	66,174	MC
Florida State Univ	FL	16,771	HC
Howard Univ	DC	37,616	C+
Iowa State Univ	IA	17,570	C
New Mexico State Univ	NM	14,050	C
Northern Mich Univ	MI	19,604	C
Northwestern College of Iowa	IA	38,400	C+
Ohio Wesleyan Univ	OH	49,460	VC
Purdue Univ/West Lafayette	IN	20,032	MC
Rutgers Univ - New Brunswick	NJ	26,632	HC
Southern Illinois Univ Edwardsville	IL	22,643	C
SUNY / SUNY Fredonia	NY	20,818	C
Texas A&M Univ	TX	20,521	VC+
Univ of Arizona	AZ	23,100	C
Univ of Calif at Davis	CA	28,468	HC
Univ of Calif at Irvine	CA	26,484	VC
Univ of Calif at Riverside	CA	29,227	C+
Univ of Conn	CT	25,538	HC
Univ of Georgia	GA	21,250	HC
Univ of Minn/Twin Cities	MN	23,519	HC+
Univ of New Hampshire	NH	28,562	VC
Univ of Vermont	VT	28,878	HC
Univ of Wisc-Madison	WI	20,934	MC
Washington State Univ	WA	22,495	C
West Virginia Univ	WV	18,210	C
Western Kentucky Univ	KY	16,850	C

GEOCHEMISTRY

School	ST	$IS	SR
Bridgewater State Univ	MA	21,810	C
Brown Univ	RI	64,566	MC
Calif Inst of Technology	CA	58,761	MC
Columbia Univ/City of New York	NY	62,958	MC
Grand Valley State Univ	MI	22,250	C+
SUNY / SUNY Cortland	NY	20,706	VC
SUNY / SUNY Fredonia	NY	20,818	C
SUNY at Geneseo	NY	20,440	VC+
SUNY at Oswego	NY	21,351	C
Washington Univ in St. Louis	MO	65,366	VC
Western Mich Univ	MI	21,054	C

GEODETIC SCIENCE

School	ST	$IS	SR
Univ of Arkansas at Monticello	AR	13,134	NC

GEOENVIRONMENTAL STUDIES

School	ST	$IS	SR
Bryant Univ	RI	55,646	VC
Northeastern Illinois Univ	IL	12,529	LC
Shippensburg Univ of Pennsylvania	PA	23,208	C
Univ of Illinois at Chicago	IL	25,006	VC
Univ of N Car at Pembroke	NC	14,388	LC
West Chester Univ of Pennsylvania	PA	18,456	C

GEOGRAPHY

School	ST	$IS	SR
Adams State Univ	CO	17,703	LC
Appalachian State Univ	NC	14,416	VC
Aquinas College - Mich	MI	38,876	HC
Arizona State Univ at the Tempe Campus	AZ	21,756	VC
Auburn Univ	AL	23,594	VC+
Augustana College	IL	49,658	VC
Ball State Univ	IN	19,590	C
Bard College at Simon's Rock	MA	65,795	MC
Bellevue Univ	NE	20,300	NC
Bemidji State Univ	MN	16,056	VC
Bloomsburg Univ of Pennsylvania	PA	19,066	LC
Boston Univ	MA	65,110	MC
Bowling Green State Univ	OH	19,747	C
Bridgewater State Univ	MA	21,810	C
Brigham Young Univ	UT	12,748	HC
Bucknell Univ	PA	64,616	MC
Calif State Polytechnic Univ, Pomona	CA	21,541	C
Cal State, Chico	CA	21,440	C
Cal State, Dominguez Hills	CA	19,022	LC
Cal State, East Bay	CA	19,413	C
Cal State, Fresno	CA	16,902	LC
Cal State, Fullerton	CA	21,902	C
Cal State, Long Beach	CA	18,850	C
Cal State, Los Angeles	CA	17,186	LC
Cal State, Northridge	CA	16,859	LC
Cal State, Sacramento	CA	20,332	C
Cal State, San Bernardino	CA	12,000	C
Cal State, Stanislaus	CA	16,212	C
Calif Univ of Pennsylvania	PA	14,217	LC
Calvin College	MI	41,570	VC+
Carthage College	WI	48,835	C
Central Conn State Univ	CT	21,203	C
Central Mich Univ	MI	20,330	C
Central Washington Univ	WA	16,803	C
Charleston Southern Univ	SC	32,400	C
Cheyney Univ of Pennsylvania	PA	20,896	LC
Chicago State Univ	IL	20,144	C
CUNY/Hunter College	NY	31,098	VC
CUNY/Lehman College	NY	5,778	HC+
Clark Univ	MA	51,600	HC+
Colgate Univ	NY	65,030	MC
Concord Univ	WV	14,954	C
Concordia Univ Nebr	NE	36,280	VC
Concordia Univ, Chicago	IL	39,694	C
Dartmouth College	NH	66,174	MC
DePaul Univ	IL	47,623	VC
DePauw Univ	IN	58,688	HC+
Dickinson State Univ	ND	12,372	LC
East Carolina Univ	NC	16,937	C
East Central Univ	OK	13,056	C
East Tenn State Univ	TN	13,994	C
Eastern Illinois Univ	IL	21,126	C
Eastern Kentucky Univ	KY	16,908	C
Eastern Mich Univ	MI	19,761	C
Eastern Washington Univ	WA	25,572	LC
Edinboro Univ	PA	15,940	LC
Elmhurst College	IL	45,428	C
Elon Univ	NC	44,599	VC+
Emory and Henry College	VA	41,410	C
Excelsior College	NY	14,080	SP
Fayetteville State Univ	NC	17,756	C
Fitchburg State Univ	MA	21,819	C
Florida Atlantic Univ	FL	17,339	C
Florida International Univ	FL	19,854	C+
Florida State Univ	FL	16,771	HC
Framingham State Univ	MA	20,584	C

ST = STATE $IS = IN-STATE COSTS SR = SELECTOR RATING

School	ST	$IS	SR
Frostburg State Univ	MD	17,280	LC
George Mason Univ	VA	15,724	VC
George Washington Univ	DC	62,835	MC
Georgia College & State Univ	GA	21,148	C+
Georgia Southern Univ	GA	16,596	C
Georgia State Univ	GA	24,332	VC
Grand Valley State Univ	MI	22,250	C+
Gustavus Adolphus College	MN	52,433	HC
Hampshire College	MA	63,824	MC
Hofstra Univ	NY	55,960	C+
Howard Univ	DC	37,616	C+
Humboldt State Univ	CA	20,514	C
Illinois State Univ	IL	23,418	VC
Indiana State Univ	IN	23,223	LC
Indiana Univ Bloomington	IN	20,429	VC
Indiana Univ of Pennsylvania	PA	23,614	LC
Indiana Univ-Purdue Univ Indianapolis	IN	18,635	C
Jacksonville State Univ	AL	14,628	LC
Jacksonville Univ	FL	46,230	C
James Madison Univ	VA	19,084	VC
Kansas State Univ	KS	17,780	VC
Keene State College	NH	24,003	LC
Kennesaw State Univ	GA	19,592	VC
Kent State Univ	OH	20,732	C
Kutztown Univ of Pennsylvania	PA	19,056	LC
LIU Post	NY	49,682	C
Lock Haven Univ of Pennsylvania	PA	18,028	LC
Louisiana State Univ and A&M College	LA	18,677	VC
Louisiana Tech Univ	LA	11,422	VC
Macalester College	MN	61,905	MC
Marshall Univ	WV	17,242	C
Mayville State Univ	ND	18,371	NC
Miami Univ	OH	27,190	HC+
Mich State Univ	MI	23,898	VC+
Middle Tenn State Univ	TN	8,650	C
Middlebury College	VT	64,332	MC
Millersville Univ of Pennsylvania	PA	23,782	C
Minn State Univ, Mankato	MN	15,616	C
Missouri State Univ	MO	15,190	C+
Montclair State Univ	NJ	26,210	LC
Mount Holyoke College	MA	56,746	MC
New Jersey City Univ	NJ	21,456	LC
New Mexico State Univ	NM	14,050	C
N Car Central Univ	NC	9,000	C
Northeastern Illinois Univ	IL	12,529	LC
Northeastern State Univ	OK	8,615	VC
Northern Arizona Univ	AZ	20,246	VC
Northern Illinois Univ	IL	20,176	C
Northern Kentucky Univ	KY	16,486	C
Northern Mich Univ	MI	19,604	C
Northwest Missouri State Univ	MO	17,737	C
Northwestern Univ	IL	66,344	MC
Ohio State Univ at Columbus	OH	21,703	HC+
Ohio Univ	OH	22,924	C
Ohio Wesleyan Univ	OH	49,460	VC
Okla State Univ	OK	17,180	VC
Old Dominion Univ	VA	20,910	C
Olivet Nazarene Univ	IL	41,840	C
Park Univ	MO	20,329	C
Pittsburg State Univ	KS	13,880	NC
Plymouth State Univ	NH	23,180	LC
Portland State Univ	OR	19,443	C
Prairie View A&M Univ	TX	15,205	LC
Prescott College	AZ	33,284	C
Rhode Island College	RI	17,694	LC
Rowan Univ	NJ	24,491	VC+
Rutgers Univ - New Brunswick	NJ	26,632	HC
Saginaw Valley State Univ	MI	18,530	C
Salem State Univ	MA	17,303	LC
Salisbury Univ	MD	20,714	VC
Sam Houston State Univ	TX	18,792	C
Samford Univ	AL	39,232	VC
San Diego State Univ	CA	21,896	C+
San Francisco State Univ	CA	18,514	LC
San Jose State Univ	CA	21,540	C
Shippensburg Univ of Pennsylvania	PA	23,208	C
Slippery Rock Univ of Pennsylvania	PA	10,360	C
Sonoma State Univ	CA	27,806	C
S Dak State Univ	SD	15,634	C
Southern Conn State Univ	CT	21,924	LC
Southern Illinois Univ Carbondale	IL	23,667	C
Southern Illinois Univ Edwardsville	IL	22,643	C
Southern Oregon Univ	OR	19,117	C
St. Cloud State Univ	MN	10,600	C
SUNY / Buffalo State College	NY	20,842	C
SUNY / SUNY Cortland	NY	20,706	VC
SUNY / SUNY Oneonta	NY	19,712	C+
SUNY / SUNY Plattsburgh	NY	18,814	C
SUNY / Univ at Buffalo	NY	23,122	C+
SUNY at Binghamton	NY	22,861	HC
SUNY at Geneseo	NY	20,440	VC+
SUNY at New Paltz	NY	19,200	C
SUNY SUNY Albany	NY	22,165	C
Stephen F. Austin State Univ	TX	18,406	LC
Stetson Univ	FL	53,544	VC
Syracuse Univ	NY	60,239	VC
Taylor Univ	IN	40,317	C+
Temple Univ	PA	24,392	VC
Texas A&M Univ	TX	20,521	VC+
Texas A&M Univ at Commerce	TX	10,496	C
Texas A&M Univ at Corpus Christi	TX	16,851	LC
Texas A&M Univ at Galveston	TX	15,920	C
Texas A&M Univ at Kingsville	TX	7,500	LC
Texas Christian Univ	TX	54,670	HC
Texas State Univ	TX	19,350	C
Texas Tech Univ	TX	18,736	C+
The Evergreen State College	WA	16,599	C
The Univ of Akron	OH	21,477	C
The Univ of Tenn at Knoxville	TN	22,112	VC
The Univ of Tenn at Martin	TN	14,876	C
The Univ of Utah	UT	17,924	VC
Towson Univ	MD	17,408	VC
United States Air Force Academy	CO		C
United States Military Academy at West Point	NY		HC+
Univ of Alabama	AL	24,320	C+
Univ of Alaska Fairbanks	AK	16,179	C
Univ of Arizona	AZ	23,100	C
Univ of Arkansas at Fayetteville	AR	19,152	C+
Univ of Calif at Berkeley	CA	28,853	MC
Univ of Calif at Davis	CA	28,468	HC
Univ of Calif at Los Angeles	CA	30,162	MC
Univ of Calif at Santa Barbara	CA	29,091	HC
Univ of Central Arkansas	AR	14,472	VC
Univ of Central Missouri	MO	18,982	C
Univ of Central Okla	OK	13,486	C
Univ of Chicago	IL	67,584	MC
Univ of Cincinnati	OH	21,964	VC
Univ of Colo Boulder	CO	24,285	VC+
Univ of Colo Colo Springs	CO	19,663	C
Univ of Colo Denver	CO	23,230	C
Univ of Conn	CT	25,538	HC
Univ of Delaware	DE	24,976	VC+
Univ of Denver	CO	58,443	VC+
Univ of Florida	FL	16,291	HC+
Univ of Georgia	GA	21,250	HC
Univ of Hawaii at Hilo	HI	18,038	C
Univ of Hawaii at Manoa	HI	23,221	C
Univ of Idaho	ID	15,348	C
Univ of Illinois at Urbana-Champaign	IL	27,006	HC
Univ of Iowa	IA	18,683	VC+
Univ of Kansas	KS	20,135	C+
Univ of Kentucky	KY	33,306	C
Univ of Louisville	KY	19,824	C
Univ of Maine at Farmington	ME	18,187	C
Univ of Mary Washington	VA	24,764	VC
Univ of Maryland/Baltimore County	MD	21,296	VC
Univ of Maryland/College Park	MD	21,938	HC
Univ of Mass Amherst	MA	26,199	VC+
Univ of Mass Boston	MA	13,435	C
Univ of Memphis	TN	18,278	C
Univ of Miami	FL	63,494	MC
Univ of Mich-Flint	MI	17,607	C+
Univ of Minn/Duluth	MN	20,292	C+
Univ of Minn/Twin Cities	MN	23,519	HC+
Univ of Missouri/Columbia	MO	18,201	MC
Univ of Missouri-Kansas City	MO	19,563	VC
Univ of Montana	MT	14,105	C
Univ of Nebr - Kearney	NE	16,546	LC
Univ of Nebr - Lincoln	NE	18,589	VC
Univ of Nebr - Omaha	NE	16,120	C
Univ of Nevada/Reno	NV	18,010	C
Univ of New Hampshire	NH	28,562	VC
Univ of New Mexico	NM	15,404	C
Univ of New Orleans	LA	12,840	C
Univ of North Alabama	AL	15,398	C
Univ of N Car at Chapel Hill	NC	20,052	HC+
Univ of N Car at Charlotte	NC	15,547	C
Univ of N Car at Greensboro	NC	14,690	C
Univ of N Car at Wilmington	NC	14,590	VC
Univ of N Dak	ND	15,373	C
Univ of North Texas	TX	19,198	C
Univ of Northern Colo	CO	20,851	C
Univ of Okla	OK	18,911	VC
Univ of Oregon	OR	22,972	C
Univ of Pittsburgh at Johnstown	PA	22,092	C
Univ of PR-Rio Piedras campus	PR	13,327	
Univ of Richmond	VA	60,880	MC
Univ of South Alabama	AL	16,400	C
Univ of S Car at Columbia	SC	19,725	VC+
Univ of South Florida/Tampa	FL	16,110	VC+
Univ of Southern Calif	CA	66,631	C
Univ of Southern Maine	ME	18,320	C
Univ of Southern Miss	MS	13,170	C
Univ of Texas at Austin	TX	26,102	HC
Univ of Texas at Dallas	TX	22,830	VC+
Univ of Texas at San Antonio	TX	20,157	C
Univ of the District of Columbia	DC	21,044	LC
Univ of Toledo	OH	19,336	NC
Univ of Vermont	VT	28,878	HC
Univ of Washington	WA	23,149	VC
Univ of West Georgia	GA	16,360	LC
Univ of Wisc-Eau Claire	WI	15,797	VC
Univ of Wisc-La Crosse	WI	15,247	C+
Univ of Wisc-Madison	WI	20,934	MC
Univ of Wisc-Milwaukee	WI	21,496	C
Univ of Wisc-Oshkosh	WI	15,200	C
Univ of Wisc-Parkside	WI	15,193	C
Univ of Wisc-Platteville	WI	14,614	VC
Univ of Wisc-River Falls	WI	14,485	C
Univ of Wisc-Stevens Point	WI	14,043	C
Univ of Wisc-Whitewater	WI	13,976	C
Univ of Wyoming	WY	15,375	C+
Utah State Univ	UT	12,736	C
Valparaiso Univ	IN	48,370	C+
Vassar College	NY	65,491	MC
Villanova Univ	PA	62,523	MC
Virginia Polytechnic Inst and State Univ	VA	21,276	HC
Wayne State College	NE	12,802	C
Weber State Univ	UT	10,721	C
West Chester Univ of Pennsylvania	PA	18,456	C
West Texas A&M Univ	TX	13,478	C
West Virginia Univ	WV	18,210	C
Western Carolina Univ	NC	13,965	C
Western Illinois Univ	IL	20,825	C
Western Kentucky Univ	KY	16,850	C
Western Mich Univ	MI	21,054	C
Western Oregon Univ	OR	15,021	LC
Western Washington Univ	WA	18,003	C+
William Paterson Univ of New Jersey	NJ	23,133	C
Worcester State Univ	MA	20,977	C
Wright State Univ	OH	16,983	C
Youngstown State Univ	OH	17,307	C

GEOGRAPHY INFORMATION SCIENCE

School	ST	$IS	SR
Appalachian State Univ	NC	14,416	VC
Arizona State Univ at the Tempe Campus	AZ	21,756	VC
Auburn Univ at Montgomery	AL	15,290	C
Elmhurst College	IL	45,428	C
Elon Univ	NC	44,599	VC+
Murray State Univ	KY	16,998	C
Northeastern Illinois Univ	IL	12,529	LC
Ohio Univ	OH	22,924	C
Old Dominion Univ	VA	20,910	C
Pennsylvania State Univ - Univ Park	PA	29,760	HC
SUNY / Univ at Buffalo	NY	23,122	C+
Univ of Central Arkansas	AR	14,472	VC
Univ of Okla	OK	18,911	VC

GEOLOGICAL ENGINEERING

School	ST	$IS	SR
Colo School of Mines	CO	29,319	MC
Mich Tech Univ	MI	24,739	VC+
Missouri Univ of Science and Technology	MO	18,655	HC
Montana Tech of the Univ of Montana	MT	15,447	C+
Olivet Nazarene Univ	IL	41,840	C
Pennsylvania State Univ - Univ Park	PA	29,760	HC
Rutgers Univ - Newark	NJ	27,288	C
S Dak School of Mines and Technology	SD	18,645	VC
Texas A&M Univ	TX	20,521	VC+
The Univ of Akron	OH	21,477	C
The Univ of Utah	UT	17,924	VC
Univ of Alaska Fairbanks	AK	16,179	C
Univ of Calif at Los Angeles	CA	30,162	MC
Univ of Idaho	ID	15,348	C
Univ of Illinois at Urbana-Champaign	IL	27,006	HC
Univ of Mich/Ann Arbor	MI	24,410	MC
Univ of Minn/Twin Cities	MN	23,519	HC+
Univ of Miss	MS	17,746	C+
Univ of Nevada/Reno	NV	18,010	C
Univ of N Dak	ND	15,373	C
Univ of Okla	OK	18,911	VC
Univ of Rochester	NY	65,032	MC
Univ of Wisc-Madison	WI	20,934	MC

GEOLOGY

School	ST	$IS	SR
Adams State Univ	CO	17,703	LC
Albion College	MI	52,650	C
Alfred Univ	NY	42,296	C+
Allegheny College	PA	55,420	VC
Amherst College	MA		HC+
Appalachian State Univ	NC	14,416	VC
Arkansas Tech Univ	AR	15,484	C
Ashland Univ	OH	21,440	C
Auburn Univ	AL	23,594	VC+
Augustana College	IL	49,658	VC
Ball State Univ	IN	19,590	C
Bates College	ME	64,500	MC
Baylor Univ	TX	53,760	HC
Beloit College	WI	55,206	HC
Bemidji State Univ	MN	16,056	VC
Boise State Univ	ID	14,860	C
Boston College	MA	65,737	MC
Bowling Green State Univ	OH	19,747	C
Brigham Young Univ	UT	12,748	HC
Brown Univ	RI	64,566	MC
Bryn Mawr College	PA	59,890	MC
Bucknell Univ	PA	64,616	MC
Calif Inst of Technology	CA	58,761	MC
Calif Lutheran Univ	CA	52,853	C
Calif State Polytechnic Univ, Pomona	CA	21,541	C
Cal State, Bakersfield	CA	19,191	LC
Cal State, Chico	CA	21,440	C
Cal State, Dominguez Hills	CA	19,022	LC
Cal State, East Bay	CA	19,413	C
Cal State, Fresno	CA	16,902	LC
Cal State, Fullerton	CA	21,902	C
Cal State, Long Beach	CA	18,850	C
Cal State, Los Angeles	CA	17,186	LC
Cal State, Northridge	CA	16,859	LC
Cal State, Sacramento	CA	20,332	C
Cal State, San Bernardino	CA	12,000	C
Cal State, Stanislaus	CA	16,212	C
Calif Univ of Pennsylvania	PA	14,217	LC
Calvin College	MI	41,570	VC+
Carleton College	MN	64,071	MC
Case Western Reserve Univ	OH	60,304	MC
Castleton Univ	VT	20,186	C
Cedarville Univ	OH	34,990	VC
Centenary College of Louisiana	LA	45,650	C+
Central Mich Univ	MI	20,330	C
Central Washington Univ	WA	16,803	C
Charleston Southern Univ	SC	32,400	C
CUNY/Brooklyn College	NY	5,884	C+
CUNY/City College	NY	20,319	VC
CUNY/Lehman College	NY	5,778	HC+
CUNY/Queens College	NY	27,896	C
CUNY/York College	NY	6,747	LC
Clarion Univ of Pennsylvania	PA	21,608	LC
Clemson Univ	SC		HC
Cleveland State Univ	OH	22,196	C
Colby College	ME	64,060	MC
Colgate Univ	NY	65,030	MC
College of Charleston	SC	22,699	C
College of William & Mary	VA		MC
Colo College	CO	62,560	MC
Colo Mesa Univ	CO	18,955	LC
Colo State Univ	CO	22,162	VC
Columbia Univ/City of New York	NY	62,958	MC
Cornell College	IA	48,800	VC
Denison Univ	OH	58,860	MC
DePauw Univ	IN	58,688	HC+
Duke Univ	NC	64,188	
Earlham College	IN	54,870	HC
East Carolina Univ	NC	16,937	C
Eastern Illinois Univ	IL	21,126	C
Eastern Kentucky Univ	KY	16,908	C
Eastern Mich Univ	MI	19,761	C
Eastern New Mexico Univ	NM	14,416	C
Eastern Washington Univ	WA	25,572	LC
Edinboro Univ	PA	15,940	LC
Elizabeth City State Univ	NC	14,745	C
Excelsior College	NY	14,080	SP
Florida Atlantic Univ	FL	17,339	C
Florida International Univ	FL	19,854	C+
Florida State Univ	FL	16,771	HC
Fort Hays State Univ	KS	12,131	C
Fort Lewis College	CO	18,980	C
Franklin and Marshall College	PA	63,170	HC
George Mason Univ	VA	15,724	VC
George Washington Univ	DC	62,835	MC
Georgia Southern Univ	GA	16,596	C
Georgia Southwestern State Univ	GA	13,870	C
Georgia State Univ	GA	24,332	VC
Grand Valley State Univ	MI	22,250	C+
Guilford College	NC	44,090	C
Gustavus Adolphus College	MN	52,433	HC
Hampshire College	MA	63,824	MC
Hanover College	IN	46,364	C+
Hardin-Simmons Univ	TX	33,966	C
Hartwick College	NY	51,270	C
Harvard College/Harvard Univ	MA	60,659	MC
Haverford College	PA	66,490	MC
Hofstra Univ	NY	55,960	C+
Hope College	MI	39,940	VC
Humboldt State Univ	CA	20,514	C
Idaho State Univ	ID	13,619	NC
Illinois State Univ	IL	23,418	VC
Indiana State Univ	IN	23,223	LC
Indiana Univ Bloomington	IN	20,429	VC
Indiana Univ Northwest	IN	7,072	C
Indiana Univ of Pennsylvania	PA	23,614	LC
Indiana Univ-Purdue Univ Fort Wayne	IN	17,553	C
Indiana Univ-Purdue Univ Indianapolis	IN	18,635	C
Iowa State Univ	IA	17,570	C
James Madison Univ	VA	19,084	VC
Juniata College	PA	53,760	VC
Kansas State Univ	KS	17,780	VC
Keene State College	NH	24,003	LC
Kent State Univ	OH	20,732	C
Kutztown Univ of Pennsylvania	PA	19,056	LC
Lafayette College	PA	63,355	MC
Lamar Univ	TX	18,014	LC
Lawrence Univ	WI	54,498	HC
LIU Post	NY	49,682	C
Lock Haven Univ of Pennsylvania	PA	18,028	LC

ST = STATE $IS = IN-STATE COSTS SR = SELECTOR RATING

School	ST	$IS	SR
Louisiana State Univ and A&M College	LA	18,677	VC
Louisiana Tech Univ	LA	11,422	VC
Macalester College	MN	61,905	MC
Marietta College	OH	46,190	C
Marshall Univ	WV	17,242	C
Mercyhurst Univ	PA	47,420	C
Miami Univ	OH	27,190	HC+
Mich State Univ	MI	23,898	VC+
Mich Tech Univ	MI	24,739	VC+
Middlebury College	VT	64,332	MC
Midwestern State Univ	TX	17,572	C
Millersville Univ of Pennsylvania	PA	23,782	C
Millsaps College	MS	50,080	C+
Minot State Univ	ND	12,732	C
Missouri State Univ	MO	15,190	C+
Missouri Univ of Science and Technology	MO	18,655	HC
Morehead State Univ	KY	17,422	C
Mount Holyoke College	MA	56,746	MC
Muskingum Univ	OH	35,966	C
New Jersey City Univ	NJ	21,456	LC
New Mexico State Univ	NM	14,050	C
N Car State Univ	NC	19,515	HC+
N Dak State Univ	ND	16,245	C
Northern Arizona Univ	AZ	20,246	VC
Northern Illinois Univ	IL	20,176	C
Northern Kentucky Univ	KY	16,486	C
Northland College	WI	41,103	C+
Northwest Missouri State Univ	MO	17,737	C
Northwestern Univ	IL	66,344	MC
Norwich Univ	VT	28,212	C
Oberlin College	OH	66,012	MC
Occidental College	CA	65,530	MC
Ohio State Univ at Columbus	OH	21,703	HC+
Ohio Univ	OH	22,924	C
Ohio Wesleyan Univ	OH	49,460	VC
Okla State Univ	OK	17,180	VC
Old Dominion Univ	VA	20,910	C
Pennsylvania State Univ - Univ Park	PA	29,760	HC
Pomona College	CA	64,957	MC
Portland State Univ	OR	19,443	C
Prescott College	AZ	33,284	C
Purdue Univ/West Lafayette	IN	20,032	MC
Radford Univ	VA	19,027	LC
Rensselaer Polytechnic Inst	NY	63,436	MC
Rice Univ	TX	57,668	MC
Rocky Mountain College	MT	34,270	C
Rutgers Univ - New Brunswick	NJ	26,632	HC
Rutgers Univ - Newark	NJ	27,288	C
St. Louis Univ	MO	49,866	HC
Salem State Univ	MA	17,303	LC
Sam Houston State Univ	TX	18,792	C
San Diego State Univ	CA	21,896	C+
San Francisco State Univ	CA	18,514	LC
San Jose State Univ	CA	21,540	C
Scripps College	CA	66,664	MC
Sewanee: The Univ of the South	TN	54,500	MC
Skidmore College	NY	64,214	HC
Slippery Rock Univ of Pennsylvania	PA	10,360	C
Smith College	MA	63,914	MC
Sonoma State Univ	CA	27,806	C
S Dak School of Mines and Technology	SD	18,645	VC
Southern Illinois Univ Carbondale	IL	23,667	C
Southern Methodist Univ	TX	66,483	MC
St. Cloud State Univ	MN	10,600	C
St. Lawrence Univ	NY	64,390	VC
St. Norbert College	WI	44,525	VC
Stanford Univ	CA	60,409	MC
SUNY / Buffalo State College	NY	20,842	C
SUNY / SUNY Cortland	NY	20,706	VC
SUNY / SUNY Fredonia	NY	20,818	C
SUNY / SUNY Oneonta	NY	19,712	C+
SUNY / SUNY Plattsburgh	NY	18,814	C
SUNY / SUNY Potsdam	NY	20,404	C+
SUNY / Univ at Buffalo	NY	23,122	C+
SUNY at Binghamton	NY	22,861	MC
SUNY at Geneseo	NY	20,440	VC+
SUNY at New Paltz	NY	19,200	C
SUNY at Oswego	NY	21,351	C
Stephen F. Austin State Univ	TX	18,406	LC
Stockton Univ	NJ	25,059	
Stony Brook Univ/The SUNY	NY	21,881	MC
Sul Ross State Univ	TX	15,021	LC
Tarleton State Univ	TX	15,248	LC
Temple Univ	PA	24,392	VC
Tenn Tech Univ	TN	17,050	C
Texas A&M Univ	TX	20,521	VC+
Texas A&M Univ at Commerce	TX	10,496	C
Texas A&M Univ at Corpus Christi	TX	16,851	LC
Texas A&M Univ at Kingsville	TX	7,500	LC
Texas Christian Univ	TX	54,670	HC
The College at Brockport - SUNY	NY	20,346	C
The College of Wooster	OH	57,900	VC+
The Univ of Akron	OH	21,477	C
The Univ of Tenn at Chattanooga	TN	16,744	C
The Univ of Tenn at Knoxville	TN	22,112	VC
The Univ of Tenn at Martin	TN	14,876	C
The Univ of Utah	UT	17,924	VC
Towson Univ	MD	17,408	VC
Tufts Univ	MA		MC
Tulane Univ	LA	63,396	HC+
Union College	NY	64,320	MC
Univ of Alabama	AL	24,320	C+
Univ of Arizona	AZ	23,100	C
Univ of Arkansas at Fayetteville	AR	19,152	C+
Univ of Arkansas at Little Rock	AR	18,211	C
Univ of Calif at Davis	CA	28,468	HC
Univ of Calif at Irvine	CA	26,484	VC
Univ of Calif at Los Angeles	CA	30,162	MC
Univ of Calif at Riverside	CA	29,227	C+
Univ of Calif at Santa Barbara	CA	29,091	HC
Univ of Calif, Santa Cruz	CA	28,731	C+
Univ of Central Missouri	MO	18,982	C
Univ of Cincinnati	OH	21,964	VC
Univ of Colo Boulder	CO	24,285	VC+
Univ of Conn	CT	25,538	HC
Univ of Dayton	OH	53,620	C
Univ of Delaware	DE	24,976	VC+
Univ of Florida	FL	16,291	HC+
Univ of Georgia	GA	21,250	HC
Univ of Hawaii at Hilo	HI	18,038	C
Univ of Hawaii at Manoa	HI	23,221	C
Univ of Houston	TX	21,483	VC
Univ of Idaho	ID	15,348	C
Univ of Illinois at Urbana-Champaign	IL	27,006	HC
Univ of Iowa	IA	18,683	VC+
Univ of Kansas	KS	20,135	C+
Univ of Kentucky	KY	33,306	C
Univ of Louisiana at Lafayette	LA	14,516	C
Univ of Maine at Farmington	ME	18,187	C
Univ of Maryland/College Park	MD	21,938	HC
Univ of Mass Amherst	MA	26,199	VC+
Univ of Miami	FL	63,494	MC
Univ of Mich/Ann Arbor	MI	24,410	MC
Univ of Mich/Dearborn	MI	11,757	VC
Univ of Minn/Duluth	MN	20,292	C+
Univ of Minn/Morris	MN	20,760	VC
Univ of Minn/Twin Cities	MN	23,519	HC+
Univ of Miss	MS	17,746	C+
Univ of Missouri/Columbia	MO	18,201	MC
Univ of Missouri-Kansas City	MO	19,563	VC
Univ of Montana	MT	14,105	C
Univ of Montana-Western	MT	11,220	LC
Univ of Mount Union	OH	38,970	C
Univ of Nebr - Lincoln	NE	18,589	VC
Univ of Nebr - Omaha	NE	16,120	C
Univ of Nevada, Las Vegas	NV	17,553	C
Univ of Nevada/Reno	NV	18,010	C
Univ of New Hampshire	NH	28,562	VC
Univ of New Orleans	LA	12,840	C
Univ of North Alabama	AL	15,398	C
Univ of N Car at Chapel Hill	NC	20,052	HC+
Univ of N Car at Charlotte	NC	15,547	C
Univ of N Car at Wilmington	NC	14,590	VC
Univ of N Dak	ND	15,373	C
Univ of Northern Colo	CO	20,851	C
Univ of Okla	OK	18,911	VC
Univ of Oregon	OR	22,972	C
Univ of Pennsylvania	PA	63,526	MC
Univ of Pittsburgh	PA	29,568	HC+
Univ of Pittsburgh at Johnstown	PA	22,092	C
Univ of PR, at Mayaguez	PR	13,995	
Univ of Puget Sound	WA	56,456	VC+
Univ of Rochester	NY	65,032	MC
Univ of South Alabama	AL	16,400	C
Univ of S Car at Columbia	SC	19,725	VC+
Univ of South Florida/Tampa	FL	16,110	VC+
Univ of Southern Calif	CA	66,631	C
Univ of Southern Indiana	IN	16,501	C
Univ of Southern Maine	ME	18,320	C
Univ of Southern Miss	MS	13,170	C
Univ of Texas at Arlington	TX	18,026	LC
Univ of Texas at Austin	TX	26,102	HC
Univ of Texas at El Paso	TX	34,452	NC
Univ of Texas at San Antonio	TX	20,157	C
Univ of the Pacific	CA	57,006	VC
Univ of Toledo	OH	19,336	NC
Univ of Tulsa	OK	52,625	HC+
Univ of Vermont	VT	28,878	HC
Univ of Washington	WA	23,149	VC
Univ of West Georgia	GA	16,360	LC
Univ of Wisc-Eau Claire	WI	15,797	VC
Univ of Wisc-Madison	WI	20,934	MC
Univ of Wisc-Milwaukee	WI	21,496	C
Univ of Wisc-Oshkosh	WI	15,200	C
Univ of Wisc-Parkside	WI	15,193	C
Univ of Wisc-River Falls	WI	14,485	C
Univ of Wyoming	WY	15,375	C+
Utah State Univ	UT	12,736	C
Valparaiso Univ	IN	48,370	C+
Vassar College	NY	65,491	MC
Virginia Polytechnic Inst and State Univ	VA	21,276	HC
Washington and Lee Univ	VA	59,647	MC
Washington State Univ	WA	22,495	C
Washington Univ in St. Louis	MO	65,366	VC
Wayland Baptist Univ	TX	22,356	LC
Wayne State Univ	MI	22,016	C
Weber State Univ	UT	10,721	C
Wellesley College	MA	63,916	MC
West Chester Univ of Pennsylvania	PA	18,456	C
West Texas A&M Univ	TX	13,478	C
West Virginia Univ	WV	18,210	C
Western Carolina Univ	NC	13,965	C
Western Illinois Univ	IL	20,825	C
Western Kentucky Univ	KY	16,850	C
Western Mich Univ	MI	21,054	C
Western State Colo Univ	CO	18,639	C
Western Washington Univ	WA	18,003	C+
Wheaton College	IL	43,610	MC
Whitman College	WA	59,772	MC
Wichita State Univ	KS	21,643	C
Williams College	MA	63,290	MC
Wilmington College	OH	34,600	C
Winona State Univ	MN	17,535	C
Wittenberg Univ	OH	48,156	C+
Wright State Univ	OH	16,983	C
Yale Univ	CT	64,650	MC
Youngstown State Univ	OH	17,307	C

GEOLOGY & GEOLOGY OCEANOGRAPHY

School	ST	$IS	SR
Univ of Rhode Island	RI	24,906	C
Wittenberg Univ	OH	48,156	C+

GEOPHYSICAL ENGINEERING

School	ST	$IS	SR
Colo School of Mines	CO	29,319	MC
Montana Tech of the Univ of Montana	MT	15,447	C+
New Jersey Inst of Technology	NJ	29,569	VC
Univ of Mich/Ann Arbor	MI	24,410	MC
Univ of Okla	OK	18,911	VC
Univ of Texas at Austin	TX	26,102	HC

GEOPHYSICS AND SEISMOLOGY

School	ST	$IS	SR
Baylor Univ	TX	53,760	HC
Boise State Univ	ID	14,860	C
Boston College	MA	65,737	MC
Boston Univ	MA	65,110	MC
Calif Inst of Technology	CA	58,761	MC
Colgate Univ	NY	65,030	MC
Columbia Univ/City of New York	NY	62,958	MC
Harvard College/Harvard Univ	MA	60,659	MC
Mich State Univ	MI	23,898	VC+
Mich Tech Univ	MI	24,739	VC+
Missouri Univ of Science and Technology	MO	18,655	HC
Rice Univ	TX	57,668	MC
Southern Methodist Univ	TX	66,483	MC
Stanford Univ	CA	60,409	MC
SUNY / SUNY Cortland	NY	20,706	VC
SUNY at Geneseo	NY	20,440	VC+
Texas A&M Univ	TX	20,521	VC+
The Univ of Akron	OH	21,477	C
The Univ of Utah	UT	17,924	VC
Univ of Calif at Los Angeles	CA	30,162	MC
Univ of Calif at Riverside	CA	29,227	C+
Univ of Calif at Santa Barbara	CA	29,091	HC
Univ of Hawaii at Manoa	HI	23,221	C
Univ of Minn/Twin Cities	MN	23,519	HC+
Univ of Nevada/Reno	NV	18,010	C
Univ of New Orleans	LA	12,840	C
Univ of S Car at Columbia	SC	19,725	VC+
Univ of Texas at Austin	TX	26,102	HC
Univ of Texas at El Paso	TX	34,452	NC
Univ of the Pacific	CA	57,006	VC
Univ of Tulsa	OK	52,625	HC+
Univ of Wisc-Madison	WI	20,934	MC
Washington Univ in St. Louis	MO	65,366	VC
Western Mich Univ	MI	21,054	C
Wright State Univ	OH	16,983	C

GEOSCIENCE

School	ST	$IS	SR
Angelo State Univ	TX	15,263	NC
Austin Peay State Univ	TN	16,397	C
Bloomsburg Univ of Pennsylvania	PA	19,066	LC
Boise State Univ	ID	14,860	C
Brown Univ	RI	64,566	MC
Cedarville Univ	OH	34,990	VC
Colby College	ME	64,060	MC
Columbia Univ/ School of General Studies	NY	61,470	MC
Drexel Univ	PA	65,432	VC+
Eckerd College	FL	52,874	C
Hamilton College	NY	64,250	MC
Idaho State Univ	ID	13,619	NC
Indiana Univ Southeast	IN	14,242	LC
Lewis-Clark State College	ID	14,202	C
Mansfield Univ	PA	23,376	LC
Mich State Univ	MI	23,898	VC+
Minn State Univ, Moorhead	MN	15,941	C
Miss State Univ	MS	11,454	C+
Montclair State Univ	NJ	26,210	LC
Northern Illinois Univ	IL	20,176	C
Ohio Univ	OH	22,924	C
Olivet Nazarene Univ	IL	41,840	C
Pacific Lutheran Univ	WA	49,960	VC
Princeton Univ	NJ	57,610	MC
Radford Univ	VA	19,027	LC
Rider Univ	NJ	54,050	C
Rutgers Univ - Newark	NJ	27,288	C
S Dak State Univ	SD	15,634	C
Stanford Univ	CA	60,409	MC
SUNY / SUNY Fredonia	NY	20,818	C
Tarleton State Univ	TX	15,248	LC
Texas A&M Univ at Galveston	TX	15,920	C
Texas Tech Univ	TX	18,736	C+
The Univ of Utah	UT	17,924	VC
Towson Univ	MD	17,408	VC
Trinity Univ	TX	52,314	HC+
Univ of Alaska Fairbanks	AK	16,179	C
Univ of Arizona	AZ	23,100	C
Univ of Calif at Riverside	CA	29,227	C+
Univ of Chicago	IL	67,584	MC
Univ of Miami	FL	63,494	MC
Univ of Mich/Ann Arbor	MI	24,410	MC
Univ of Montana	MT	14,105	C
Univ of Montana-Western	MT	11,220	LC
Univ of Southern Maine	ME	18,320	C
Univ of Texas at Dallas	TX	22,830	VC+
Univ of Tulsa	OK	52,625	HC+
Univ of Wisc-Eau Claire	WI	15,797	VC
Univ of Wisc-Green Bay	WI	15,064	C
Univ of Wisc-Stevens Point	WI	14,043	C
Utica College	NY	30,430	C
West Chester Univ of Pennsylvania	PA	18,456	C
West Virginia Univ	WV	18,210	C

GERMAN

School	ST	$IS	SR
Adrian College	MI	42,400	C
Agnes Scott College	GA	51,930	VC+
Alabama A&M Univ	AL	18,796	C
Albion College	MI	52,650	C
Allegheny College	PA	55,420	VC
Alma College	MI	47,548	C
American Univ	DC	59,379	HC+
Amherst College	MA		HC+
Aquinas College - Mich	MI	38,876	HC
Arizona State Univ at the Tempe Campus	AZ	21,756	VC
Auburn Univ	AL	23,594	VC+
Augsburg College	MN	43,929	C
Augustana College	IL	49,658	VC
Augustana Univ	SD	38,424	VC
Austin College	TX	45,875	VC
Baker Univ	KS	33,350	C+
Baldwin Wallace Univ	OH	41,106	C
Ball State Univ	IN	19,590	C
Barnard College/Columbia Univ	NY	62,741	MC
Bates College	ME	64,500	MC
Baylor Univ	TX	53,760	HC
Belmont Univ	TN	40,970	VC
Beloit College	WI	55,206	HC
Bemidji State Univ	MN	16,056	VC
Berea College	KY	7,042	C
Berry College	GA	45,286	C+
Boise State Univ	ID	14,860	C
Bowdoin College	ME	63,500	MC
Bowling Green State Univ	OH	19,747	C
Brandeis Univ	MA	65,925	MC
Brigham Young Univ	UT	12,748	HC
Bryn Mawr College	PA	59,890	MC
Bucknell Univ	PA	64,616	MC
Butler Univ	IN	51,352	VC
Calif Lutheran Univ	CA	52,853	C
Cal State, Chico	CA	21,440	C
Cal State, Fresno	CA	16,902	LC
Cal State, Long Beach	CA	18,850	C
Cal State, Northridge	CA	16,859	LC
Cal State, Sacramento	CA	20,332	C
Calvin College	MI	41,570	VC+
Canisius College	NY	47,537	C
Carleton College	MN	64,071	MC
Carnegie Mellon Univ	PA	67,980	MC
Carthage College	WI	48,835	C
Case Western Reserve Univ	OH	60,304	MC
Centenary College of Louisiana	LA	45,650	C+
Central College	IA	44,592	C
Central Conn State Univ	CT	21,203	C
Central Mich Univ	MI	20,330	C
Central Washington Univ	WA	16,803	C
Centre College	KY	49,250	HC
Christopher Newport Univ	VA	23,968	VC+
CUNY/Hunter College	NY	31,098	VC
CUNY/Lehman College	NY	5,778	HC+
CUNY/Queens College	NY	27,896	C
Clemson Univ	SC		HC
Coe College	IA	51,570	VC
Colgate Univ	NY	65,030	MC
College of Charleston	SC	22,699	C
College of St. Benedict	MN	52,806	C
College of the Holy Cross	MA	62,165	MC
College of William & Mary	VA		MC
Colo State Univ	CO	22,162	VC
Columbia Univ/ School of General Studies	NY	61,470	MC
Columbia Univ/City of New York	NY	62,958	MC

ST = STATE $IS = IN-STATE COSTS SR = SELECTOR RATING

School	ST	$IS	SR
Concordia College - Moorhead	MN	51,088	C+
Conn College	CT	65,000	MC
Cornell College	IA	48,800	VC
Cornell Univ	NY	64,853	MC
Davidson College	NC	60,119	MC
Denison Univ	OH	58,860	MC
DePaul Univ	IL	47,623	VC
DePauw Univ	IN	58,688	HC+
Dickinson College	PA	63,974	MC
Doane Univ	NE	39,184	VC
Dordt College	IA	37,860	C+
Drew Univ/College of Liberal Arts	NJ	61,048	VC
Drury Univ	MO	33,791	VC
Earlham College	IN	54,870	HC
East Carolina Univ	NC	16,937	C
Eastern Mich Univ	MI	19,761	C
Eastern Washington Univ	WA	25,572	LC
Elizabethtown College	PA	54,050	C
Elmhurst College	IL	45,428	C
Fairfield Univ	CT	59,860	VC+
Florida Atlantic Univ	FL	17,339	C
Florida State Univ	FL	16,771	HC
Fordham Univ	NY	65,918	MC
Fort Hays State Univ	KS	12,131	C
Franciscan Univ of Steubenville	OH	33,980	VC
Franklin and Marshall College	PA	63,170	HC
Furman Univ	SC	58,092	VC+
George Washington Univ	DC	62,835	MC
Georgetown Univ	DC	65,926	MC
Georgia State Univ	GA	24,332	VC
Gettysburg College	PA	63,000	HC
Gordon College	MA	46,472	C+
Grace College and Seminary	IN	31,524	C
Graceland Univ	IA	35,290	C
Grand Valley State Univ	MI	22,250	C+
Grinnell College	IA	60,738	MC
Guilford College	NC	44,090	C
Hamline Univ	MN	45,678	VC
Hampden-Sydney College	VA	56,248	C+
Hartwick College	NY	51,270	C
Harvard College/Harvard Univ	MA	60,659	MC
Hastings College	NE	35,380	C+
Haverford College	PA	66,490	MC
Heidelberg Univ	OH	39,200	C
Hendrix College	AR	54,020	VC+
Hillsdale College	MI	35,722	MC
Hofstra Univ	NY	55,960	C+
Hood College	MD	54,840	C
Hope College	MI	39,940	VC
Humboldt State Univ	CA	20,514	C
Idaho State Univ	ID	13,619	NC
Illinois College	IL	40,850	VC
Illinois State Univ	IL	23,418	VC
Illinois Wesleyan Univ	IL	56,430	VC+
Indiana State Univ	IN	23,223	LC
Indiana Univ South Bend	IN	14,242	C
Indiana Univ Southeast	IN	14,242	LC
Indiana Univ-Purdue Univ Fort Wayne	IN	17,553	C
Indiana Univ-Purdue Univ Indianapolis	IN	18,635	C
Iowa State Univ	IA	17,570	C
Ithaca College	NY	56,766	VC
John Carroll Univ	OH	49,740	C+
Johns Hopkins Univ	MD	65,386	MC
Juniata College	PA	53,760	VC
Kalamazoo College	MI	53,931	HC+
Kenyon College	OH	63,330	MC
Knox College	IL	52,615	VC+
Kutztown Univ of Pennsylvania	PA	19,056	LC
Lafayette College	PA	63,355	MC
Lakeland Univ	WI	35,130	C
Lawrence Univ	WI	54,498	HC
Lebanon Valley College	PA	51,530	C
Lehigh Univ	PA	61,010	MC
Lenoir-Rhyne Univ	NC	43,200	C
Linfield College	OR	52,010	C
Lipscomb Univ	TN	41,296	VC
Lock Haven Univ of Pennsylvania	PA	18,028	LC
Loyola Univ Maryland	MD	60,300	VC
Luther College	IA	48,540	C+
Lycoming College	PA	48,580	C
Manchester Univ	IN	40,422	C
Marquette Univ	WI	48,390	VC+
Marshall Univ	WV	17,242	C
McDaniel College	MD	51,380	VC
Mercer Univ	GA	45,348	VC
Miami Univ	OH	27,190	HC+
Mich State Univ	MI	23,898	VC+
Middle Tenn State Univ	TN	8,650	C
Middlebury College	VT	64,332	MC
Millersville Univ of Pennsylvania	PA	23,782	C
Minn State Univ, Mankato	MN	15,616	C
Minot State Univ	ND	12,732	C
Missouri State Univ	MO	15,190	C+
Moravian College	PA	53,117	
Mount St. Mary's Univ	MD	51,610	C
Muhlenberg College	PA	56,645	VC+
Murray State Univ	KY	16,998	C
Muskingum Univ	OH	35,966	C
Nazareth College	NY	45,574	C
Nebr Wesleyan Univ	NE	38,140	C+
New York Univ	NY	65,860	MC
Newberry College	SC	34,550	C
North Central College	IL	48,712	VC
Northern Illinois Univ	IL	20,176	C
Northern Kentucky Univ	KY	16,486	C
Northern State Univ	SD	14,505	C
Northwestern Univ	IL	66,344	MC
Oakland Univ	MI	20,763	C
Oberlin College	OH	66,012	MC
Ohio State Univ at Columbus	OH	21,703	HC+
Ohio Univ	OH	22,924	C
Ohio Wesleyan Univ	OH	49,460	VC
Okla State Univ	OK	17,180	VC
Old Dominion Univ	VA	20,910	C
Oral Roberts Univ	OK	34,316	C
Oregon State Univ	OR	22,519	VC
Pacific Lutheran Univ	WA	49,960	VC
Pepperdine Univ	CA	74,460	HC+
Portland State Univ	OR	19,443	C
Princeton Univ	NJ	57,610	MC
Providence College	RI	60,760	VC
Purdue Univ/Northwest	IN	15,038	C
Purdue Univ/West Lafayette	IN	20,032	MC
Randolph-Macon College	VA	49,910	C
Rhodes College	TN	51,900	HC
Rider Univ	NJ	54,050	C
Rockford Univ	IL	36,030	C
Rosemont College	PA	30,980	C
Rutgers Univ - Camden	NJ	26,146	C
Rutgers Univ - New Brunswick	NJ	26,632	HC
Rutgers Univ - Newark	NJ	27,288	C
St. John's Univ	MN	51,624	C
St. Joseph's Univ	PA	57,544	VC+
Salem College	NC	37,694	HC
Sam Houston State Univ	TX	18,792	C
Samford Univ	AL	39,232	VC
San Diego State Univ	CA	21,896	C+
San Francisco State Univ	CA	18,514	LC
San Jose State Univ	CA	21,540	C
Sarah Lawrence College	NY	63,388	HC
Seattle Pacific Univ	WA	47,[illegible]39	C+
Sewanee: The Univ of the South	TN	54,500	MC
Simpson College	IA	43,839	VC
Skidmore College	NY	64,214	HC
Slippery Rock Univ of Pennsylvania	PA	10,360	C
S Dak State Univ	SD	15,634	C
Southeast Missouri State Univ	MO	15,498	C
Southern Conn State Univ	CT	21,924	LC
Southern Illinois Univ Edwardsville	IL	22,643	C
Southern Methodist Univ	TX	66,483	MC
Southwestern Univ	TX	50,720	VC
St. Lawrence Univ	NY	64,390	VC
St. Mary's Univ	TX	37,500	C
St. Norbert College	WI	44,525	VC
St. Olaf College	MN	54,260	HC+
SUNY / Univ at Buffalo	NY	23,122	C+
SUNY at Binghamton	NY	22,861	MC
SUNY at New Paltz	NY	19,200	C
SUNY at Oswego	NY	21,351	C
Stetson Univ	FL	53,544	VC
Susquehanna Univ	PA	55,340	VC
Swarthmore College	PA	63,550	MC
Temple Univ	PA	24,392	VC
Tenn Tech Univ	TN	17,050	C
Texas A&M Univ	TX	20,521	VC+
Texas A&M Univ at Commerce	TX	10,496	C
Texas Christian Univ	TX	54,670	HC
Texas State Univ	TX	19,350	C
Texas Tech Univ	TX	18,736	C+
The Catholic Univ of America	DC	56,356	VC
The Citadel, The Military College of S Car	SC	35,339	C
The College of Wooster	OH	57,900	VC+
The Univ of Tenn at Knoxville	TN	22,112	VC
The Univ of Utah	UT	17,924	VC
Thomas Edison State Univ	NJ	6,350	NC
Towson Univ	MD	17,408	VC
Trinity College	CT	63,920	HC+
Trinity Univ	TX	52,314	HC+
Truman State Univ	MO	16,014	HC
Tufts Univ	MA		MC
Tulane Univ	LA	63,396	HC+
Union College	NE	23,270	C
Univ of Alabama	AL	24,320	C+
Univ of Arkansas at Fayetteville	AR	19,152	C+
Univ of Calif at Berkeley	CA	28,853	MC
Univ of Calif at Davis	CA	28,468	HC
Univ of Calif at Los Angeles	CA	30,162	MC
Univ of Calif at Riverside	CA	29,227	C+
Univ of Calif at Santa Barbara	CA	29,091	HC
Univ of Central Missouri	MO	18,982	C
Univ of Central Okla	OK	13,486	C
Univ of Chicago	IL	67,584	MC
Univ of Cincinnati	OH	21,964	VC
Univ of Conn	CT	25,538	HC
Univ of Dallas	TX	45,500	VC+
Univ of Dayton	OH	53,620	C
Univ of Denver	CO	58,443	VC+
Univ of Evansville	IN	44,186	VC+
Univ of Florida	FL	16,291	HC+
Univ of Georgia	GA	21,250	HC
Univ of Hawaii at Manoa	HI	23,221	C
Univ of Illinois at Chicago	IL	25,006	VC
Univ of Indianapolis	IN	36,480	C
Univ of Iowa	IA	18,683	VC+
Univ of Jamestown	ND	28,508	C
Univ of Kansas	KS	20,135	C+
Univ of Kentucky	KY	33,306	C
Univ of La Verne	CA	55,600	C
Univ of Mary Washington	VA	24,764	VC
Univ of Maryland/Baltimore County	MD	21,296	VC
Univ of Miami	FL	63,494	MC
Univ of Mich/Ann Arbor	MI	24,410	MC
Univ of Minn/Morris	MN	20,760	VC
Univ of Minn/Twin Cities	MN	23,519	HC+
Univ of Miss	MS	17,746	C+
Univ of Missouri/Columbia	MO	18,201	MC
Univ of Missouri-Kansas City	MO	19,563	VC
Univ of Missouri-St. Louis	MO		C
Univ of Montana	MT	14,105	C
Univ of Montevallo	AL	19,502	C
Univ of Mount Union	OH	38,970	C
Univ of Nebr - Kearney	NE	16,546	LC
Univ of Nebr - Lincoln	NE	18,589	VC
Univ of Nebr - Omaha	NE	16,120	C
Univ of Nevada, Las Vegas	NV	17,553	C
Univ of New Hampshire	NH	28,562	VC
Univ of New Mexico	NM	15,404	C
Univ of North Alabama	AL	15,398	C
Univ of N Car at Asheville	NC	15,723	VC+
Univ of N Car at Chapel Hill	NC	20,052	HC+
Univ of N Car at Charlotte	NC	15,547	C
Univ of N Car at Greensboro	NC	14,690	C
Univ of N Car at Wilmington	NC	14,590	VC
Univ of N Dak	ND	15,373	C
Univ of North Texas	TX	19,198	C
Univ of Northern Colo	CO	20,851	C
Univ of Notre Dame	IN	64,043	MC
Univ of Okla	OK	18,911	VC
Univ of Oregon	OR	22,972	C
Univ of Pennsylvania	PA	63,526	MC
Univ of Puget Sound	WA	56,456	VC+
Univ of Redlands	CA	60,200	VC
Univ of Rhode Island	RI	24,906	C
Univ of Rochester	NY	65,032	MC
Univ of Scranton	PA	54,962	VC
Univ of S Car at Columbia	SC	19,725	VC+
Univ of S Dak	SD	16,109	C
Univ of South Florida/Tampa	FL	16,110	VC+
Univ of Southern Indiana	IN	16,501	C
Univ of Texas at Arlington	TX	18,026	LC
Univ of Texas at Austin	TX	26,102	HC
Univ of Texas at El Paso	TX	34,452	NC
Univ of the Pacific	CA	57,006	VC
Univ of Toledo	OH	19,336	NC
Univ of Tulsa	OK	52,625	HC+
Univ of Vermont	VT	28,878	HC
Univ of Virginia	VA	25,891	MC
Univ of Wisc-Eau Claire	WI	15,797	VC
Univ of Wisc-Green Bay	WI	15,064	C
Univ of Wisc-Madison	WI	20,934	MC
Univ of Wisc-Oshkosh	WI	15,200	C
Univ of Wisc-Platteville	WI	14,614	VC
Univ of Wisc-Stevens Point	WI	14,043	C
Univ of Wisc-Whitewater	WI	13,976	C
Univ of Wyoming	WY	15,375	C+
Ursinus College	PA	61,690	VC
Utah State Univ	UT	12,736	C
Valparaiso Univ	IN	48,370	C+
Vanderbilt Univ	TN	60,572	MC
Vassar College	NY	65,491	MC
Virginia Polytechnic Inst and State Univ	VA	21,276	HC
Virginia Wesleyan College	VA	43,728	LC
Wabash College	IN	50,650	VC
Wake Forest Univ	NC	64,056	MC
Walla Walla Univ	WA	30,417	NC
Wartburg College	IA	47,840	C
Washburn Univ	KS	15,827	C
Washington & Jefferson College	PA	56,512	VC
Washington and Lee Univ	VA	59,647	MC
Washington College	MD	54,666	VC
Washington State Univ	WA	22,495	C
Washington Univ in St. Louis	MO	65,366	VC
Wayne State Univ	MI	22,016	C
Weber State Univ	UT	10,721	C
Webster Univ	MO	37,490	C
Wellesley College	MA	63,916	MC
West Chester Univ of Pennsylvania	PA	18,456	C
Western Carolina Univ	NC	13,965	C
Western Kentucky Univ	KY	16,850	C
Western Mich Univ	MI	21,054	C
Western Washington Univ	WA	18,003	C+
Westminster College	PA	39,180	C+
Wheaton College	IL	43,610	MC
Wheaton College	MA	61,512	VC
Willamette Univ	OR	61,817	VC+
Williams College	MA	63,290	MC
Winthrop Univ	SC	23,082	C
Wisc Lutheran College	WI	36,290	VC
Wittenberg Univ	OH	48,156	C+
Wofford College	SC	49,885	VC
Wright State Univ	OH	16,983	C
Xavier Univ	OH	47,880	C+

GERMAN AREA STUDIES

School	ST	$IS	SR
American Univ	DC	59,379	HC+
Appalachian State Univ	NC	14,416	VC
Bard College	NY	64,024	HC
Bard College at Simon's Rock	MA	65,795	MC
Boston College	MA	65,737	MC
Brown Univ	RI	64,566	MC
Cal State, Northridge	CA	16,859	LC
Case Western Reserve Univ	OH	60,304	MC
Chestnut Hill College	PA	43,410	C
Coe College	IA	51,570	VC
Columbia Univ/ School of General Studies	NY	61,470	MC
Cornell Univ	NY	64,853	MC
Dartmouth College	NH	66,174	MC
Emory Univ	GA	60,786	MC
Fordham Univ	NY	65,918	MC
Hamilton College	NY	64,250	MC
Ithaca College	NY	56,766	VC
Lake Erie College	OH	38,914	LC
Lewis & Clark College	OR	58,434	HC+
Linfield College	OR	52,010	C
Macalester College	MN	61,905	MC
Moravian College	PA	53,117	
Mount Holyoke College	MA	56,746	MC
Muhlenberg College	PA	56,645	VC+
New College of Florida	FL	15,848	MC
Pomona College	CA	64,957	MC
Rice Univ	TX	57,668	MC
St. Anselm College	NH	52,560	C+
Scripps College	CA	66,664	MC
Stanford Univ	CA	60,409	MC
Suffolk Univ	MA	50,308	C
Swarthmore College	PA	63,550	MC
Tufts Univ	MA		MC
Union College	NY	64,320	MC
Univ of Arizona	AZ	23,100	C
Univ of Calif at Irvine	CA	26,484	VC
Univ of Calif, Santa Cruz	CA	28,731	C+
Univ of Illinois at Chicago	IL	25,006	VC
Univ of Minn/Duluth	MN	20,292	C+
Univ of N Car at Wilmington	NC	14,590	VC
Univ of Portland	OR	52,152	VC
Univ of Wisc-La Crosse	WI	15,247	C+
Wartburg College	IA	47,840	C
Wellesley College	MA	63,916	MC
Wesleyan Univ	CT	65,516	MC
Whitman College	WA	59,772	MC
Yale Univ	CT	64,650	MC

GERMAN STUDIES

School	ST	$IS	SR
Brown Univ	RI	64,566	MC
Cal State, Northridge	CA	16,859	LC
Creighton Univ	NE	48,206	VC+
Elon Univ	NC	44,599	VC+
Indiana Univ Bloomington	IN	20,429	VC
Ohio Wesleyan Univ	OH	49,460	VC
Syracuse Univ	NY	60,239	VC
Univ of Arizona	AZ	23,100	C
Univ of Colo Boulder	CO	24,285	VC+
Univ of Pittsburgh	PA	29,568	HC+
Univ of Richmond	VA	60,880	MC
Wellesley College	MA	63,916	MC
West Chester Univ of Pennsylvania	PA	18,456	C
Wheaton College	MA	61,512	VC

GERMANIC LANGUAGES AND LITERATURE

School	ST	$IS	SR
Bard College	NY	64,024	HC
Bennington College	VT	63,960	MC
Boston Univ	MA	65,110	MC
Brown Univ	RI	64,566	MC
Colby College	ME	64,060	MC
Colo College	CO	62,560	MC
Columbia Univ/City of New York	NY	62,958	MC
Duke Univ	NC	64,188	
Ithaca College	NY	56,766	VC
Johns Hopkins Univ	MD	65,386	MC
Kent State Univ	OH	20,732	C
Messiah College	PA	43,100	C+
New College of Florida	FL	15,848	MC
New York Univ	NY	65,860	MC
Oberlin College	OH	66,012	MC
Ohio State Univ at Columbus	OH	21,703	HC+
Pennsylvania State Univ - Univ Park	PA	29,760	HC
Reed College	OR	65,300	MC
St. Louis Univ	MO	49,866	HC
Scripps College	CA	66,664	MC
Smith College	MA	63,914	MC
SUNY at Binghamton	NY	22,861	MC
Stony Brook Univ/The SUNY	NY	21,881	MC
Transylvania Univ	KY	45,690	VC+
Univ of Calif at Riverside	CA	29,227	C+
Univ of Calif at Santa Barbara	CA	29,091	HC
Univ of Calif San Diego	CA	30,150	MC
Univ of Georgia	GA	21,250	HC
Univ of Illinois at Chicago	IL	25,006	VC
Univ of Illinois at Urbana-Champaign	IL	27,006	HC
Univ of Kansas	KS	20,135	C+

ST = STATE $IS = IN-STATE COSTS SR = SELECTOR RATING

School	ST	$IS	SR
Univ of Maryland/College Park	MD	21,938	HC
Univ of Mass Amherst	MA	26,199	VC+
Univ of Mich/Ann Arbor	MI	24,410	MC
Univ of Missouri-St. Louis	MO		C
Univ of Pittsburgh	PA	29,568	HC+
Univ of Washington	WA	23,149	VC
Univ of Wisc-Green Bay	WI	15,064	C
Univ of Wisc-Milwaukee	WI	21,496	C
Vassar College	NY	65,491	MC
Washington and Lee Univ	VA	59,647	MC
Washington Univ in St. Louis	MO	65,366	VC
West Chester Univ of Pennsylvania	PA	18,456	C
Wheaton College	MA	61,512	VC
Yale Univ	CT	64,650	MC

GERONTOLOGY

School	ST	$IS	SR
Alfred Univ	NY	42,296	C+
Ashford Univ	CA	10,480	C
Barton College	NC	38,686	LC
Bethune-Cookman Univ	FL	22,970	C
Bloomfield College	NJ	39,100	LC
Bowling Green State Univ	OH	19,747	C
Cal State, Fresno	CA	16,902	LC
Cal State, San Bernardino	CA	12,000	C
Calif Univ of Pennsylvania	PA	14,217	LC
Canisius College	NY	47,537	C
Case Western Reserve Univ	OH	60,304	MC
Central Washington Univ	WA	16,803	C
Chestnut Hill College	PA	43,410	C
CUNY/York College	NY	6,747	LC
Eastern Mich Univ	MI	19,761	C
Gwynedd Mercy Univ	PA	43,780	LC
Ithaca College	NY	56,766	VC
Langston Univ	OK	14,314	C
Madonna Univ	MI	29,050	C
Marywood Univ	PA	46,900	C
McKendree Univ	IL	37,940	C+
Metropolitan College of New York	NY		VC
Miami Univ	OH	27,190	HC+
Minn State Univ, Moorhead	MN	15,941	C
Missouri State Univ	MO	15,190	C+
Montclair State Univ	NJ	26,210	LC
Mount St. Mary's Univ - Chalon Campus	CA	43,897	VC+
Northeastern Illinois Univ	IL	12,529	LC
Pontifical Catholic Univ of PR	PR	10,534	
Quinnipiac Univ	CT	59,110	C
San Diego State Univ	CA	21,896	C+
Shaw Univ	NC	24,638	C
Southeastern Okla State Univ	OK	11,875	C
Southern Illinois Univ Edwardsville	IL	22,643	C
Springfield College	MA	45,995	C
St. Bonaventure Univ	NY	44,237	C
SUNY / SUNY Oneonta	NY	19,712	C+
Towson Univ	MD	17,408	VC
Univ of Arkansas at Pine Bluff	AR	13,541	C
Univ of Central Arkansas	AR	14,472	VC
Univ of Central Okla	OK	13,486	C
Univ of Maryland/Univ College	MD	25,966	LC
Univ of Mass Boston	MA	13,435	C
Univ of Northern Colo	CO	20,851	C
Univ of South Florida/Tampa	FL	16,110	VC+
Univ of Southern Calif	CA	66,631	C
Utica College	NY	30,430	C
Weber State Univ	UT	10,721	C
Wichita State Univ	KS	21,643	C
Youngstown State Univ	OH	17,307	C

GLASS

School	ST	$IS	SR
Alfred Univ	NY	42,296	C+
Calif College of the Arts	CA	52,758	SP
Cleveland Inst of Art	OH	51,439	C+
College for Creative Studies	MI	48,875	SP
Mass College of Art and Design	MA	24,800	SP
Rhode Island School of Design	RI	59,960	SP
Rochester Inst of Technology	NY	50,842	HC
Temple Univ	PA	24,392	VC

GLOBAL & PUBLIC HEALTH SCIENCES

School	ST	$IS	SR
Cornell Univ	NY	64,853	MC
Frostburg State Univ	MD	17,280	LC
MCPHS Univ	MA	45,470	SP
Univ of Calif San Diego	CA	30,150	MC

GLOBAL STUDIES

School	ST	$IS	SR
Abilene Christian Univ	TX	41,800	C+
Appalachian State Univ	NC	14,416	VC
Aquinas College - Mich	MI	38,876	HC
Bard College at Simon's Rock	MA	65,795	MC
Bentley Univ	MA	60,890	HC
Bridgewater College	VA	44,510	C
Bryant Univ	RI	55,646	VC
Castleton Univ	VT	20,186	C
Colby College	ME	64,060	MC
College of St. Scholastica	MN	44,640	C
Embry-Riddle Aeronautical Univ - Daytona Beach	FL	44,712	VC
Framingham State Univ	MA	20,584	C
Hofstra Univ	NY	55,960	C+
Hood College	MD	54,840	C
Lehigh Univ	PA	61,010	MC
Lewis Univ	IL	40,370	C
McKendree Univ	IL	37,940	C+
Millersville Univ of Pennsylvania	PA	23,782	C
Missouri State Univ	MO	15,190	C+
New York Univ	NY	65,860	MC
Ohio Univ	OH	22,924	C
Okla Baptist Univ	OK	32,320	C
Otterbein Univ	OH	41,630	C
Pacific Lutheran Univ	WA	49,960	VC
Providence College	RI	60,760	VC
St. Leo Univ	FL	31,650	C
St. Mary's College	IN	50,600	C
St. Mary's Univ of Minn	MN	41,210	VC
Samford Univ	AL	39,232	VC
Shepherd Univ, West Virginia	WV	17,224	C
Southeast Missouri State Univ	MO	15,498	C
St. Edward's Univ	TX	53,100	VC
SUNY / Univ at Buffalo	NY	23,122	C+
Texas Tech Univ	TX	18,736	C+
Tulane Univ	LA	63,396	HC+
Univ of Calif at Irvine	CA	26,484	VC
Univ of Central Florida	FL	15,922	VC
Univ of Kansas	KS	20,135	C+
Univ of New Haven	CT	52,190	C
Univ of Vermont	VT	28,878	HC
Univ of West Georgia	GA	16,360	LC
Valparaiso Univ	IN	48,370	C+
Warren Wilson College	NC	44,220	VC
Washington State Univ	WA	22,495	C
Wayne State Univ	MI	22,016	C
Wilson College	PA	35,620	C
Winona State Univ	MN	17,535	C

GLOBAL/GENERAL MANAGEMENT

School	ST	$IS	SR
Bryant Univ	RI	55,646	VC
Farmingdale State College	NY	20,624	C
Hamline Univ	MN	45,678	VC
Thomas Edison State Univ	NJ	6,350	NC
Univ of North Florida	FL	15,996	VC
Univ of Pittsburgh	PA	29,568	HC+
Univ of South Florida/St. Petersburg	FL	15,980	C

GOLF ENTERPRISE MANAGEMENT

School	ST	$IS	SR
Univ of Nebr - Lincoln	NE	18,589	VC
Univ of Wisc-Stout	WI	19,667	C

GOVERNMENT

School	ST	$IS	SR
American Univ	DC	59,379	HC+
Bryant Univ	RI	55,646	VC
Claremont McKenna College	CA	67,185	MC
Cornell Univ	NY	64,853	MC
Dartmouth College	NH	66,174	MC
Gallaudet Univ	DC	29,118	LC
Mills College	CA	59,163	VC
Wellesley College	MA	63,916	MC
West Chester Univ of Pennsylvania	PA	18,456	C

GRAPHIC AND PRINTING PRODUCTION

School	ST	$IS	SR
Brenau Univ - Women's College	GA	37,876	LC
CUNY/College of Technology	NY	6,669	NC
Pittsburg State Univ	KS	13,880	NC
Rochester Inst of Technology	NY	50,842	HC
Univ of Wisc-Stout	WI	19,667	C
Western Mich Univ	MI	21,054	C
Youngstown State Univ	OH	17,307	C

GRAPHIC ARTS TECHNOLOGY

School	ST	$IS	SR
Andrews Univ	MI	28,030	C+
Appalachian State Univ	NC	14,416	VC
Arizona State Univ at the Polytechnic Campus	AZ	21,360	VC
Ball State Univ	IN	19,590	C
Carroll Univ	WI	38,100	C+
Central State Univ	OH	18,564	C
Clemson Univ	SC		HC
College of the Ozarks	MO	7,230	C
Colo Mesa Univ	CO	18,955	LC
Colo Technical Univ	CO	21,455	NC
Emmanuel College	MA	52,110	C+
Florida State Univ	FL	16,771	HC
Idaho State Univ	ID	13,619	NC
Minn State Univ, Moorhead	MN	15,941	C
New York Univ	NY	65,860	MC
North Central College	IL	48,712	VC
Pacific Union College	CA	36,009	VC
Pennsylvania College of Technology	PA	27,333	NC
Pittsburg State Univ	KS	13,880	NC
Rochester Inst of Technology	NY	50,842	HC
Univ of Central Missouri	MO	18,982	C
Univ of Jamestown	ND	28,508	C
Univ of Wisc-Stout	WI	19,667	C

GRAPHIC COMMUNICATIONS

School	ST	$IS	SR
Bethany College	WV	36,300	NC
Calif Polytechnic State Univ	CA	17,979	HC+
Georgia Southern Univ	GA	16,596	C
Illinois State Univ	IL	23,418	VC
Millersville Univ of Pennsylvania	PA	23,782	C
Walla Walla Univ	WA	30,417	NC
Western Illinois Univ	IL	20,825	C

GRAPHIC COMMUNICATIONS MANAGEMENT

School	ST	$IS	SR
Black Hills State Univ	SD	15,899	C
Carroll Univ	WI	38,100	C+
Ferris State Univ	MI	21,445	C
Univ of Wisc-Stout	WI	19,667	C

GRAPHIC DESIGN

School	ST	$IS	SR
Abilene Christian Univ	TX	41,800	C+
Adams State Univ	CO	17,703	LC
Alabama A&M Univ	AL	18,796	C
American Univ	DC	59,379	HC+
Anderson Univ	IN	38,200	C
Andrews Univ	MI	28,030	C+
Anna Maria College	MA	48,186	C
Appalachian State Univ	NC	14,416	VC
Arcadia Univ	PA	33,570	C+
Arizona State Univ at the Tempe Campus	AZ	21,756	VC
Arkansas State Univ	AR	16,190	C
Art Academy of Cincinnati	OH	36,252	SP
Art Inst of Portland	OR	132,329	SP
ArtCenter College of Design	CA	54,212	SP
Assumption College	MA	47,920	C+
Auburn Univ	AL	23,594	VC+
Augustana College	IL	49,658	VC
Azusa Pacific Univ	CA	43,972	C
Barton College	NC	38,686	LC
Becker College	MA	57,628	C
Bethel College	IN	35,860	C
Bethel College	KS	35,370	C
Biola Univ	CA	46,402	C+
Black Hills State Univ	SD	15,899	C
Blackburn College	IL	28,526	LC
Bloomfield College	NJ	39,100	LC
Boston Univ	MA	65,110	MC
Bowling Green State Univ	OH	19,747	C
Brescia Univ	KY	29,890	VC+
Briar Cliff Univ	IA	36,956	C
Brigham Young Univ	UT	12,748	HC
Buena Vista Univ	IA	41,514	C
Cabrini Univ	PA	42,591	LC
Calif Baptist Univ	CA	41,392	C
Calif College of the Arts	CA	52,758	SP
Calif State Polytechnic Univ, Pomona	CA	21,541	C
Cal State, Chico	CA	21,440	C
Cal State, Fresno	CA	16,902	LC
Cal State, Los Angeles	CA	17,186	LC
Cal State, San Bernardino	CA	12,000	C
Calif Univ of Pennsylvania	PA	14,217	LC
Calvin College	MI	41,570	VC+
Carthage College	WI	48,835	C
Cedarville Univ	OH	34,990	VC
Central Conn State Univ	CT	21,203	C
Central Mich Univ	MI	20,330	C
Champlain College	VT	53,132	C+
Chapman Univ	CA	63,078	VC+
CUNY/Queens College	NY	27,896	C
Clarke Univ	IA	38,940	C
Cleveland Inst of Art	OH	51,439	C+
Coastal Carolina Univ	SC	19,766	C
Coker College	SC	34,810	LC
Colby-Sawyer College	NH	50,790	C
College for Creative Studies	MI	48,875	SP
Colo State Univ	CO	22,162	VC
Columbia College - Missouri	MO	27,803	C
Columbia College Chicago	IL	43,168	C
Columbus College of Art and Design	OH	37,732	C
Concordia Univ St. Paul	MN	29,050	C
Concordia Univ Wisc	WI	35,910	C
Cooper Union for the Advancement of Science and Art	NY	58,210	MC
Culver-Stockton College	MO	33,525	C
Curry College	MA	51,815	C
Daemen College	NY	38,045	C
Dallas Baptist Univ	TX	33,713	C
Defiance College	OH	41,630	C
DePaul Univ	IL	47,623	VC
Dominican Univ	IL	41,222	C
Dominican Univ of Calif	CA	57,050	C
Dordt College	IA	37,860	C+
Drake Univ	IA	45,056	HC
Drexel Univ	PA	65,432	VC+
Eastern Mich Univ	MI	19,761	C
Eastern Washington Univ	WA	25,572	LC
Edgewood College	WI	35,950	C
Edinboro Univ	PA	15,940	LC
Elmhurst College	IL	45,428	C
Endicott College	MA	44,604	VC+
Fairmont State Univ	WV	15,726	C
Fashion Inst of Technology/SUNY	NY	18,521	SP
Felician Univ	NJ	45,370	LC
Ferris State Univ	MI	21,445	C
Fitchburg State Univ	MA	21,819	C
Flagler College	FL	27,620	C
Florida Atlantic Univ	FL	17,339	C
Fordham Univ	NY	65,918	MC
Franklin Pierce Univ	NH	46,750	C
Grace College and Seminary	IN	31,524	C
Graceland Univ	IA	35,290	C
Grand Rapids Theological Seminary/Cornerstone Univ	MI	33,338	C
Grand View Univ	IA	32,302	C
Harding Univ	AR	25,421	C
Hardin-Simmons Univ	TX	33,966	C
High Point Univ	NC	45,977	C
Howard Univ	DC	37,616	C+
Huntington Univ	IN	33,996	C
Indiana Univ-Purdue Univ Fort Wayne	IN	17,553	C
Iowa State Univ	IA	17,570	C
John Brown Univ	AR	33,132	VC
Kutztown Univ of Pennsylvania	PA	19,056	LC
La Roche College	PA	37,924	LC
La Sierra Univ	CA	39,690	VC
Laguna College of Art and Design	CA	41,422	LC
Lasell College	MA	47,500	C
Lenoir-Rhyne Univ	NC	43,200	C
Lewis Univ	IL	40,370	C
Limestone College	SC	32,100	C
Lipscomb Univ	TN	41,296	VC
Louisiana College	LA	21,886	C
Loyola Univ New Orleans	LA	51,708	VC+
Lyndon State College	VT	20,714	C
Madonna Univ	MI	29,050	C
Maine College of Art	ME	43,794	SP
Malone Univ	OH	38,448	C
Mansfield Univ	PA	23,376	LC
Marietta College	OH	46,190	C
Marshall Univ	WV	17,242	C
Maryland Inst College of Art	MD	56,795	SP
Maryville Univ of St. Louis	MO	38,046	VC+
Marywood Univ	PA	46,900	C
Mass College of Art and Design	MA	24,800	SP
Memphis College of Art	TN	39,750	C
Mercyhurst Univ	PA	47,420	C
Miami Univ	OH	27,190	HC+
Mich State Univ	MI	23,898	VC+
MidAmerica Nazarene Univ	KS	35,550	C
Middle Tenn State Univ	TN	8,650	C
Millersville Univ of Pennsylvania	PA	23,782	C
Milwaukee Inst of Art and Design	WI	44,960	SP
Minneapolis College of Art and Design	MN	44,238	SP
Miss College	MS	25,850	C
Missouri Southern State Univ	MO	12,499	C
Missouri Western State Univ	MO	16,741	
Monmouth Univ	NJ	46,234	C
Montclair State Univ	NJ	26,210	LC
Montserrat College of Art	MA	38,150	SP
Moore College of Art and Design	PA	50,135	SP
Moravian College	PA	53,117	
Morningside College	IA	36,865	C
Mount Ida College	MA	46,820	C
Mount Mary Univ	WI	34,650	LC
Mount Mercy Univ	IA	36,826	C
Mount St. Joseph Univ	OH	33,880	C
Mount Vernon Nazarene Univ	OH	34,500	C
New Mexico Highlands Univ	NM	11,904	NC
New York Inst of Technology	NY	48,730	C
New York Univ	NY	65,860	MC
Newbury College	MA	46,950	C
Norfolk State Univ	VA	25,702	LC
N Car State Univ	NC	19,515	HC+
Northeastern Univ	MA	62,703	MC
Northland College	WI	41,103	C+
Northwest Nazarene Univ	ID	36,000	C
Northwestern College of Iowa	IA	38,400	C+
Notre Dame College	OH	37,150	VC
Notre Dame de Namur Univ	CA	46,526	LC
Notre Dame of Maryland Univ	MD	46,465	VC
Ohio Dominican Univ	OH	41,340	C+
Ohio Northern Univ	OH	44,050	VC
Ohio Univ	OH	22,924	C
Okla Baptist Univ	OK	32,320	C
Old Dominion Univ	VA	20,910	C
Oregon State Univ	OR	22,519	VC
Otis College of Art and Design	CA	55,858	SP
Ouachita Baptist Univ	AR	32,320	C
Pacific Northwest College of Art	OR	38,494	SP
Pacific Union College	CA	36,009	VC
Palm Beach Atlantic Univ	FL	39,720	C
Park Univ	MO	20,329	C
Parsons The New School for Design	NY	56,610	SP

School	ST	$IS	SR
Pennsylvania College of Technology	PA	27,333	NC
Pennsylvania State Univ - Univ Park	PA	29,760	HC
Philadelphia Univ	PA	50,370	C
Plymouth State Univ	NH	23,180	LC
Point Loma Nazarene Univ	CA	43,450	C
Purdue Univ/West Lafayette	IN	20,032	MC
Queens Univ of Charlotte	NC	39,543	C
Quincy Univ	IL	36,998	C
Rhode Island School of Design	RI	59,960	SP
Ringling College of Art and Design	FL	57,430	SP
Rivier Univ	NH	40,410	VC
Roberts Wesleyan College	NY	38,306	C
Rochester Inst of Technology	NY	50,842	HC
Rocky Mountain College of Art and Design	CO	27,052	SP
Roger Williams Univ	RI	46,296	C+
St. Mary's Univ of Minn	MN	41,210	VC
St. Peter's Univ	NJ	49,192	C
Sam Houston State Univ	TX	18,792	C
Samford Univ	AL	39,232	VC
San Diego State Univ	CA	21,896	C+
Santa Fe Univ of Art and Design	NM	39,980	SP
Savannah College of Art and Design	GA	49,595	C
School of Visual Arts	NY	47,500	SP
Schreiner Univ	TX	34,626	LC
Seton Hall Univ	NJ	55,514	C
Seton Hill Univ	PA	46,972	C
Siena Heights Univ	MI	32,040	C
Silver Lake College of the Holy Family	WI	36,290	LC
Simpson College	IA	43,839	VC
S Dak State Univ	SD	15,634	C
South Univ	GA	36,070	LC
Southern Adventist Univ	TN	27,600	C
Southern Nazarene Univ	OK	32,798	NC
Southern New Hampshire Univ	NH	43,198	C
Southern Oregon Univ	OR	19,117	C
Southwestern Okla State Univ	OK	11,790	C
Spring Hill College	AL	48,488	C
St. Ambrose Univ	IA	39,019	C
St. Ambrose Univ	IA	39,019	C
St. Edward's Univ	TX	53,100	VC
St. John's Univ	NY	55,850	C
St. Norbert College	WI	44,525	VC
SUNY / SUNY Fredonia	NY	20,818	C
SUNY / SUNY Potsdam	NY	20,404	C+
SUNY /College of Agriculture and Tech at Cobleskill	NY	20,527	LC
SUNY at New Paltz	NY	19,200	C
SUNY at Oswego	NY	21,351	C
Stephens College	MO	38,042	C
Suffolk Univ	MA	50,308	C
Susquehanna Univ	PA	55,340	VC
Syracuse Univ	NY	60,239	VC
Tabor College	KS	35,870	C
Temple Univ	PA	24,392	VC
Texas Christian Univ	TX	54,670	HC
The Art Inst of Atlanta	GA	34,334	SP
The College of New Jersey	NJ	31,909	HC
The College of St. Rose	NY	43,048	C
The Univ of Tenn at Knoxville	TN	22,112	VC
Trinity International Univ	IL	31,070	VC
Union College	NE	23,270	C
Union Univ	TN	33,970	VC
Univ of Arkansas at Fayetteville	AR	19,152	C+
Univ of Bridgeport	CT	44,430	LC
Univ of Central Okla	OK	13,486	C
Univ of Cincinnati	OH	21,964	VC
Univ of Dayton	OH	53,620	C
Univ of Evansville	IN	44,186	VC+
Univ of Findlay	OH	60,139	C
Univ of Florida	FL	16,291	HC+
Univ of Illinois at Chicago	IL	25,006	VC
Univ of Illinois at Urbana-Champaign	IL	27,006	HC
Univ of Iowa	IA	18,683	VC+
Univ of Kansas	KS	20,135	C+
Univ of Mass Dartmouth	MA	25,658	C
Univ of Miami	FL	63,494	MC
Univ of Mich/Ann Arbor	MI	24,410	MC
Univ of Minn/Duluth	MN	20,292	C+
Univ of New Haven	CT	52,190	C
Univ of N Dak	ND	15,373	C
Univ of Northern Colo	CO	20,851	C
Univ of Northwestern - St. Paul	MN	38,160	C
Univ of St. Francis	IN	37,400	C
Univ of San Francisco	CA	58,484	VC
Univ of S Car Upstate	SC	18,200	LC
Univ of South Florida/St. Petersburg	FL	15,980	C
Univ of Tampa	FL	36,944	C
Univ of the Arts	PA	56,579	SP
Univ of the Pacific	CA	57,006	VC
Univ of Washington	WA	23,149	VC
Upper Iowa Univ	IA	34,990	NC
Ursuline College	OH	41,076	LC
Virginia Commonwealth Univ	VA	23,049	C
Viterbo Univ	WI	34,660	C
Walla Walla Univ	WA	30,417	NC
Walsh Univ	OH	39,010	C
Wartburg College	IA	47,840	C
Washington Univ in St. Louis	MO	65,366	VC
Wayland Baptist Univ	TX	22,356	LC
Wayne State College	NE	12,802	C
Waynesburg Univ	PA	32,290	C
Weber State Univ	UT	10,721	C
Webster Univ	MO	37,490	C
West Liberty Univ	WV	15,512	C
West Texas A&M Univ	TX	13,478	C
Western Mich Univ	MI	21,054	C
Wichita State Univ	KS	21,643	C
William Woods Univ	MO	32,040	C
Wilson College	PA	35,620	C
Winona State Univ	MN	17,535	C
Woodbury Univ	CA	46,958	C
York College of Pennsylvania	PA	29,240	C
Youngstown State Univ	OH	17,307	C

GRAPHIC DESIGN & MEDIA

School	ST	$IS	SR
Baldwin Wallace Univ	OH	41,106	C
Bloomfield College	NJ	39,100	LC
Bluffton Univ	OH	40,950	C
Champlain College	VT	53,132	C+
Creighton Univ	NE	48,206	VC+
Lewis Univ	IL	40,370	C
Marymount Univ	VA	41,570	LC
Murray State Univ	KY	16,998	C
Point Loma Nazarene Univ	CA	43,450	C
Rochester Inst of Technology	NY	50,842	HC
Southern Oregon Univ	OR	19,117	C
Trinity International Univ	IL	31,070	VC
Univ of Illinois at Chicago	IL	25,006	VC
Western Kentucky Univ	KY	16,850	C
Wilson College	PA	35,620	C

GREAT PLAINS STUDIES

School	ST	$IS	SR
Univ of Nebr - Lincoln	NE	18,589	VC

GREEK

School	ST	$IS	SR
Ball State Univ	IN	19,590	C
Barnard College/Columbia Univ	NY	62,741	MC
Brigham Young Univ	UT	12,748	HC
Bryn Mawr College	PA	59,890	MC
Carleton College	MN	64,071	MC
CUNY/Hunter College	NY	31,098	VC
CUNY/Lehman College	NY	5,778	HC+
CUNY/Queens College	NY	27,896	C
Colgate Univ	NY	65,030	MC
Columbia Univ/City of New York	NY	62,958	MC
Concordia Univ, Ann Arbor	MI	35,945	VC
DePauw Univ	IN	58,688	HC+
Dickinson College	PA	63,974	MC
Emory Univ	GA	60,786	MC
Florida State Univ	FL	16,771	HC
Franklin and Marshall College	PA	63,170	HC
Furman Univ	SC	58,092	VC+
Gettysburg College	PA	63,000	HC
Hampden-Sydney College	VA	56,248	C+
Harvard College/Harvard Univ	MA	60,659	MC
Haverford College	PA	66,490	MC
Hillsdale College	MI	35,722	MC
John Carroll Univ	OH	49,740	C+
Loyola Univ Chicago	IL	55,802	VC
Monmouth College	IL	42,260	C
Mount Holyoke College	MA	56,746	MC
New York Univ	NY	65,860	MC
Northeastern Illinois Univ	IL	12,529	LC
Ohio State Univ at Columbus	OH	21,703	HC+
Ohio Univ	OH	22,924	C
Randolph-Macon College	VA	49,910	C
Samford Univ	AL	39,232	VC
Sarah Lawrence College	NY	63,388	HC
Sewanee: The Univ of the South	TN	54,500	MC
Smith College	MA	63,914	MC
Southwestern Univ	TX	50,720	VC
St. Olaf College	MN	54,260	HC+
Swarthmore College	PA	63,550	MC
The Univ of Tenn at Chattanooga	TN	16,744	C
Trinity Univ	TX	52,314	HC+
Tufts Univ	MA		MC
Union Univ	TN	33,970	VC
Univ of Calif at Berkeley	CA	28,853	MC
Univ of Calif at Davis	CA	28,468	HC
Univ of Calif at Los Angeles	CA	30,162	MC
Univ of Georgia	GA	21,250	HC
Univ of Iowa	IA	18,683	VC+
Univ of Mich/Ann Arbor	MI	24,410	MC
Univ of Minn/Twin Cities	MN	23,519	HC+
Univ of Notre Dame	IN	64,043	MC
Univ of Oregon	OR	22,972	C
Univ of Richmond	VA	60,880	MC
Univ of Scranton	PA	54,962	VC
Univ of Texas at Austin	TX	26,102	HC
Univ of Vermont	VT	28,878	HC
Wabash College	IN	50,650	VC
Wake Forest Univ	NC	64,056	MC
Wellesley College	MA	63,916	MC
Wheaton College	MA	61,512	VC
Wright State Univ	OH	16,983	C

GREEK (CLASSICAL)

School	ST	$IS	SR
Baylor Univ	TX	53,760	HC
Boston Univ	MA	65,110	MC
Butler Univ	IN	51,352	VC
Duquesne Univ	PA	46,822	VC
Indiana Univ Bloomington	IN	20,429	VC
Kenyon College	OH	63,330	MC
Knox College	IL	52,615	VC+
Loyola Univ Chicago	IL	55,802	VC
Loyola Univ New Orleans	LA	51,708	VC+
New York Univ	NY	65,860	MC
Ohio Univ	OH	22,924	C
The Catholic Univ of America	DC	56,356	VC
The College of Wooster	OH	57,900	VC+
Washington Univ in St. Louis	MO	65,366	VC
Wellesley College	MA	63,916	MC
Wheaton College	MA	61,512	VC
Whitman College	WA	59,772	MC

GREEK (MODERN)

School	ST	$IS	SR
New York Univ	NY	65,860	MC
Tulane Univ	LA	63,396	HC+
Univ of Mich/Ann Arbor	MI	24,410	MC

GUIDANCE EDUCATION

School	ST	$IS	SR
Calif Univ of Pennsylvania	PA	14,217	LC
Eastern Washington Univ	WA	25,572	LC
Prescott College	AZ	33,284	C
S Car State Univ	SC	20,805	LC
St. Cloud State Univ	MN	10,600	C
Texas A&M Univ at Commerce	TX	10,496	C
Univ of Central Arkansas	AR	14,472	VC
Univ of Cincinnati	OH	21,964	VC
Univ of Southern Miss	MS	13,170	C
Westminster College	PA	39,180	C+

GUITAR

School	ST	$IS	SR
Boston Univ	MA	65,110	MC
Central Washington Univ	WA	16,803	C
Illinois Wesleyan Univ	IL	56,430	VC+
Indiana Univ Bloomington	IN	20,429	VC
Loyola Univ New Orleans	LA	51,708	VC+
Mannes School for Music	NY	44,500	SP
Okla City Univ	OK	40,476	VC
Roosevelt Univ	IL	40,651	VC
San Francisco Conservatory of Music	CA	57,310	SP
Stetson Univ	FL	53,544	VC
The Boston Conservatory at Berklee	MA	61,042	C+
Wright State Univ	OH	16,983	C

HABILITATION OF THE DEAF

School	ST	$IS	SR
Texas Christian Univ	TX	54,670	HC

HAWAIIAN

School	ST	$IS	SR
Univ of Hawaii at Hilo	HI	18,038	C
Univ of Hawaii at Manoa	HI	23,221	C

HAWAIIAN STUDIES

School	ST	$IS	SR
Brigham Young Univ/Hawaii	HI	11,290	C
Univ of Hawaii at Hilo	HI	18,038	C
Univ of Hawaii at Manoa	HI	23,221	C

HEALTH

School	ST	$IS	SR
Albertus Magnus College	CT	43,258	LC
Aquinas College - Mich	MI	38,876	HC
Averett Univ	VA	40,970	LC
Bentley Univ	MA	60,890	HC
Cal State, Monterey Bay	CA	26,871	LC
Cal State, Northridge	CA	16,859	LC
Central Mich Univ	MI	20,330	C
Chicago State Univ	IL	20,144	C
Coastal Carolina Univ	SC	19,766	C
College of the Ozarks	MO	7,230	C
Concordia College - Moorhead	MN	51,088	C+
Concordia College - New York	NY	39,035	LC
Concordia Univ Nebr	NE	36,280	VC
Coppin State Univ	MD	17,041	VC
DePauw Univ	IN	58,688	HC+
Eastern Illinois Univ	IL	21,126	C
Eastern Oregon Univ	OR	17,715	C
George Fox Univ	OR	42,938	C
Georgetown Univ	DC	65,926	MC
Goddard College	VT	17,040	VC
Graceland Univ	IA	35,290	C
Harding Univ	AR	25,421	C
Hodges Univ	FL	19,080	LC
Husson Univ	ME	25,720	LC
Idaho State Univ	ID	13,619	NC
Indiana Wesleyan Univ	IN	33,674	C
Ithaca College	NY	56,766	VC
Johnson & Wales Univ/ Denver Campus	CO	42,707	C
Kentucky Wesleyan College	KY	32,080	C
Lebanon Valley College	PA	51,530	C
LeTourneau Univ	TX	38,250	VC
Luther College	IA	48,540	C+
McKendree Univ	IL	37,940	C+
Missouri Southern State Univ	MO	12,499	C
Molloy College	NY	40,440	C
Montana State Univ	MT	15,500	C+
Nebr Wesleyan Univ	NE	38,140	C+
New Mexico Highlands Univ	NM	11,904	NC
New York Inst of Technology	NY	48,730	C
Northeastern Illinois Univ	IL	12,529	LC
Ohio Northern Univ	OH	44,050	VC
Ohio Valley Univ	WV	29,480	C
Olivet College	MI	36,110	LC
Prairie View A&M Univ	TX	15,205	LC
Regis College	MA	51,920	C
Rowan Univ	NJ	24,491	VC+
Rust College	MS	10,600	C
St. Louis Univ	MO	49,866	HC
Sam Houston State Univ	TX	18,792	C
Southeast Missouri State Univ	MO	15,498	C
Southeastern Louisiana Univ	LA	16,237	C
Southern Oregon Univ	OR	19,117	C
Southwestern Adventist Univ	TX	27,756	LC
SUNY / Buffalo State College	NY	20,842	C
SUNY / SUNY College at Old Westbury	NY	16,860	C
SUNY Polytechnic Inst	NY	19,473	VC
Texas A&M Univ	TX	20,521	VC+
Texas Christian Univ	TX	54,670	HC
Texas Southern Univ	TX	18,212	LC
The College of Idaho	ID	36,415	C
The Evergreen State College	WA	16,599	C
Union College	KY	32,310	C
Union Inst & Univ	OH	8,912	SP
Univ of Delaware	DE	24,976	VC+
Univ of Houston	TX	21,483	VC
Univ of Louisville	KY	19,824	C
Univ of Mich/Dearborn	MI	11,757	VC
Univ of Minn Crookston	MN	19,739	C
Univ of Missouri-Kansas City	MO	19,563	VC
Univ of Mount Union	OH	38,970	C
Univ of New Mexico	NM	15,404	C
Univ of New Orleans	LA	12,840	C
Univ of North Texas	TX	19,198	C
Univ of Pennsylvania	PA	63,526	MC
Univ of Rochester	NY	65,032	MC
Univ of St. Mary	KS	34,690	C
Univ of Texas at San Antonio	TX	20,157	C
Univ of the Cumberlands	KY	32,000	C
Univ of Wisc-Stout	WI	19,667	C
Univ of Wisc-Superior	WI	14,446	C
Upper Iowa Univ	IA	34,990	NC
Voorhees College	SC	19,976	C
Walla Walla Univ	WA	30,417	NC
West Chester Univ of Pennsylvania	PA	18,456	C
Wichita State Univ	KS	21,643	C

HEALTH ADMINISTRATION AND POLICY

School	ST	$IS	SR
Columbia College - Missouri	MO	27,803	C
Creighton Univ	NE	48,206	VC+
Eastern Washington Univ	WA	25,572	LC
Indiana Univ Bloomington	IN	20,429	VC
Johnson & Wales Univ/ Denver Campus	CO	42,707	C
Old Dominion Univ	VA	20,910	C
Providence College	RI	60,760	VC
St. Louis Univ	MO	49,866	HC
Salve Regina Univ	RI	51,470	C
The Univ of Utah	UT	17,924	VC
Univ of Miami	FL	63,494	MC
Univ of New Hampshire	NH	28,562	VC
Univ of St. Francis	IL	39,924	C
Western Illinois Univ	IL	20,825	C
Xavier Univ	OH	47,880	C+

HEALTH AND EDUCATION SCIENCE

School	ST	$IS	SR
Aquinas College - Mich	MI	38,876	HC
Minot State Univ	ND	12,732	C

HEALTH AND PHYSICAL ACTIVITY

School	ST	$IS	SR
Aquinas College - Mich	MI	38,876	HC
Hanover College	IN	46,364	C+
Henderson State Univ	AR	15,516	LC
Millikin Univ	IL	42,158	C
Texas State Univ	TX	19,350	C
Univ of Wisc-Superior	WI	14,446	C
Washington State Univ	WA	22,495	C

HEALTH AND PHYSICAL EDUCATION

School	ST	$IS	SR
Aquinas College - Mich	MI	38,876	HC
Baldwin Wallace Univ	OH	41,106	C
Bethel College	KS	35,370	C
Bridgewater College	VA	44,510	C
Delta State Univ	MS	13,176	C

School	ST	$IS	SR
Eastern Mennonite Univ	VA	42,550	C
Georgia Southern Univ	GA	16,596	C
Georgia Southwestern State Univ	GA	13,870	C
Marian Univ	IN	41,220	C
Morehouse College	GA	40,064	C
Murray State Univ	KY	16,998	C
Oakwood Univ	AL	43,758	C
Okla Baptist Univ	OK	32,320	C
Rocky Mountain College	MT	34,270	C
Southwestern Okla State Univ	OK	11,790	C
Syracuse Univ	NY	60,239	VC
Univ of Arkansas at Pine Bluff	AR	13,541	C
Univ of Great Falls	MT	38,524	C
Univ of Pittsburgh	PA	29,568	HC+
West Chester Univ of Pennsylvania	PA	18,456	C
Wilson College	PA	35,620	C

HEALTH CARE ADMINISTRATION

School	ST	$IS	SR
Adams State Univ	CO	17,703	LC
Alaska Pacific Univ	AK	26,680	VC
Alma College	MI	47,548	C
Appalachian State Univ	NC	14,416	VC
Arcadia Univ	PA	33,570	C+
Ashford Univ	CA	10,480	C
Auburn Univ	AL	23,594	VC+
Baker College of Flint	MI	13,880	NC
Baldwin Wallace Univ	OH	41,106	C
Benedictine Univ	IL	38,300	C
Berkeley College/New Jersey	NJ	38,082	LC
Cabarrus College of Health Sciences	NC	11,948	SP
Calif Baptist Univ	CA	41,392	C
Cal State, Chico	CA	21,440	C
Cal State, Long Beach	CA	18,850	C
Cal State, Northridge	CA	16,859	LC
Cal State, San Bernardino	CA	12,000	C
Calumet College of St. Joseph	IN	22,735	C
Carlow Univ	PA	38,549	LC
Carroll College	MT	39,972	C+
Carroll Univ	WI	38,100	C+
Central Mich Univ	MI	20,330	C
Charter Oak State College	CT	7,671	LC
Chestnut Hill College	PA	43,410	C
Chicago State Univ	IL	20,144	C
CUNY/College of Technology	NY	6,669	NC
CUNY/Lehman College	NY	5,778	HC+
Clayton State Univ	GA	19,735	C
Coastal Carolina Univ	SC	19,766	C
College of St. Scholastica	MN	44,640	C
Columbia College - Missouri	MO	27,803	C
Concordia Univ	OR	35,000	C
Dallas Baptist Univ	TX	33,713	C
Daniel Webster College	NH	26,984	C
Delta State Univ	MS	13,176	C
Dominican College	NY	31,270	LC
Duquesne Univ	PA	46,822	VC
D'Youville College	NY	36,780	C
East Carolina Univ	NC	16,937	C
Eastern Kentucky Univ	KY	16,908	C
Eastern Mich Univ	MI	19,761	C
Eastern Washington Univ	WA	25,572	LC
Emporia State Univ	KS	14,570	C
Ferris State Univ	MI	21,445	C
Florida Atlantic Univ	FL	17,339	C
Florida International Univ	FL	19,854	C+
Franklin Pierce Univ	NH	46,750	C
Franklin Univ	OH	56,262	SP
Gardner-Webb Univ	NC	39,200	C+
George Fox Univ	OR	42,938	C
Gwynedd Mercy Univ	PA	43,780	LC
Harding Univ	AR	25,421	C
Harris-Stowe State Univ	MO	14,360	NC
Hastings College	NE	35,380	C+
Hodges Univ	FL	19,080	LC
Howard Univ	DC	37,616	C+
Husson Univ	ME	25,720	LC
Idaho State Univ	ID	13,619	NC
Illinois State Univ	IL	23,418	VC
Indiana Univ Bloomington	IN	20,429	VC
Indiana Univ South Bend	IN	14,242	C
Indiana Univ-Purdue Univ Fort Wayne	IN	17,553	C
Indiana Univ-Purdue Univ Indianapolis	IN	18,635	C
Jackson State Univ	MS	15,879	LC
James Madison Univ	VA	19,084	VC
Johnson & Wales Univ/ Denver Campus	CO	42,707	C
King Univ	TN	34,660	C
Langston Univ	OK	14,314	C
Lebanon Valley College	PA	51,530	C
Lee Univ	TN	22,045	C
Lewis Univ	IL	40,370	C
Limestone College	SC	32,100	C
LIU Post	NY	49,682	C
Lourdes Univ	OH	29,520	NC
Mary Baldwin Univ	VA	39,865	C
Marywood Univ	PA	46,900	C
Mercy College of Health Sciences	IA	16,920	C
Metropolitan State Univ of Denver	CO	29,889	LC
Midwestern State Univ	TX	17,572	C
Minn State Univ, Moorhead	MN	15,941	C
Misericordia Univ	PA	43,840	C
Missouri Baptist Univ	MO	35,594	C
Missouri State Univ	MO	15,190	C+
Monroe College	NY	23,660	C
Montana State Univ-Billings	MT	22,960	C
Mount Aloysius College	PA	29,976	C
Mount Marty College	SD	32,972	C
Mount Mercy Univ	IA	36,826	C
Mount St. Mary's Univ - Chalon Campus	CA	43,897	VC+
National Louis Univ	IL	16,920	LC
Nebr Methodist College	NE	25,134	SP
New England College	NH	50,364	C
New York Univ	NY	65,860	MC
Newbury College	MA	46,950	C
Norfolk State Univ	VA	25,702	LC
Northwest Christian Univ	OR	36,580	C
Ohio Univ	OH	22,924	C
Okla City Univ	OK	40,476	VC
Our Lady of the Lake Univ	TX	35,012	LC
Park Univ	MO	20,329	C
Pennsylvania College of Technology	PA	27,333	NC
Pennsylvania State Univ - Univ Park	PA	29,760	HC
Point Park Univ	PA	41,270	C
Presentation College	SD	25,454	NC
Regis Univ	CO	44,520	C
Rhode Island College	RI	17,694	LC
Robert Morris Univ	PA	37,834	C
Roger Williams Univ	RI	46,296	C+
St. Joseph's Univ	PA	57,544	VC+
St. Leo Univ	FL	31,650	C
St. Louis Univ	MO	49,866	HC
St. Mary-of-the-Woods College	IN	39,632	LC
St. Peter's Univ	NJ	49,192	C
Samford Univ	AL	39,232	VC
Shenandoah Univ	VA	41,312	C
Shippensburg Univ of Pennsylvania	PA	23,208	C
Simpson Univ	CA	33,700	C
South Univ	GA	36,070	LC
Southeast Missouri State Univ	MO	15,498	C
Southern Adventist Univ	TN	27,600	C
Southern Illinois Univ Carbondale	IL	23,667	C
Southern Univ at New Orleans	LA	8,014	LC
Southern Vermont College	VT	34,670	LC
Southwestern Okla State Univ	OK	11,790	C
Spring Hill College	AL	48,488	C
Springfield College	MA	45,995	C
St. Catherine Univ	MN	45,630	VC
St. Francis College	NY	38,800	LC
St. Joseph's College, New York/Brooklyn Campus	NY	25,114	LC
St. Joseph's College, New York/Long Island Campus	NY	25,124	C
SUNY / Empire State College	NY	9,145	SP
SUNY / SUNY Fredonia	NY	20,818	C
SUNY Polytechnic Inst	NY	19,473	VC
Stonehill College	MA	55,030	C+
Tenn State Univ	TN	14,423	C
Texas Southern Univ	TX	18,212	LC
Texas State Univ	TX	19,350	C
Thomas More College	KY	36,720	C
Tiffin Univ	OH	31,380	C
Towson Univ	MD	17,408	VC
Univ of Central Arkansas	AR	14,472	VC
Univ of Central Florida	FL	15,922	VC
Univ of Conn	CT	25,538	HC
Univ of Detroit Mercy	MI	48,816	C+
Univ of Evansville	IN	44,186	VC+
Univ of Findlay	OH	60,139	C
Univ of Illinois at Urbana-Champaign	IL	27,006	HC
Univ of La Verne	CA	55,600	C
Univ of Maine at Fort Kent	ME	15,165	LC
Univ of Miami	FL	63,494	MC
Univ of Mich-Flint	MI	17,607	C+
Univ of Minn Crookston	MN	19,739	C
Univ of Nebr - Omaha	NE	16,120	C
Univ of Nevada, Las Vegas	NV	17,553	C
Univ of N Car at Chapel Hill	NC	20,052	HC+
Univ of North Florida	FL	15,996	VC
Univ of Pennsylvania	PA	63,526	MC
Univ of St. Mary	KS	34,690	C
Univ of Scranton	PA	54,962	VC
Univ of S Dak	SD	16,109	C
Univ of Southern Indiana	IN	16,501	C
Univ of St. Francis	IL	39,924	C
Univ of Virginia	VA	25,891	MC
Univ of Washington	WA	23,149	VC
Univ of Wisc-Eau Claire	WI	15,797	VC
Univ of Wisc-Milwaukee	WI	21,496	C
Upper Iowa Univ	IA	34,990	NC
Ursuline College	OH	41,076	LC
Valparaiso Univ	IN	48,370	C+
Viterbo Univ	WI	34,660	C
Washburn Univ	KS	15,827	C
Washington Adventist Univ	MD	31,440	LC
Washington Univ in St. Louis	MO	65,366	VC
Wayland Baptist Univ	TX	22,356	LC
Weber State Univ	UT	10,721	C
West Virginia Univ Inst of Technology	WV	16,462	NC
Western Carolina Univ	NC	13,965	C
Western Kentucky Univ	KY	16,850	C
Wheeling Jesuit Univ	WV	37,106	LC
Wichita State Univ	KS	21,643	C
Wilberforce Univ	OH	19,016	C
Winona State Univ	MN	17,535	C
Xavier Univ	OH	47,880	C+

HEALTH COMMUNICATION

School	ST	$IS	SR
Johnson & Wales Univ/ Denver Campus	CO	42,707	C
Juniata College	PA	53,760	VC
N Dak State Univ	ND	16,245	C
San Diego State Univ	CA	21,896	C+
Southeast Missouri State Univ	MO	15,498	C

HEALTH EDUCATION

School	ST	$IS	SR
Albany State Univ	GA	19,462	C
American Univ	DC	59,379	HC+
Anderson Univ	IN	38,200	C
Anna Maria College	MA	48,186	C
Appalachian State Univ	NC	14,416	VC
Aquinas College - Mich	MI	38,876	HC
Arizona State Univ at the Downtown Phoenix Campus	AZ	23,680	VC
Arkansas State Univ	AR	16,190	C
Arkansas Tech Univ	AR	15,484	C
Armstrong State Univ	GA	16,962	C
Ashford Univ	CA	10,480	C
Ashland Univ	OH	21,440	C
Auburn Univ	AL	23,594	VC+
Augsburg College	MN	43,929	C
Augusta Univ	GA	4,632	C
Augustana Univ	SD	38,424	VC
Austin Peay State Univ	TN	16,397	C
Averett Univ	VA	40,970	LC
Ball State Univ	IN	19,590	C
Baylor Univ	TX	53,760	HC
Bemidji State Univ	MN	16,056	VC
Bethany College	KS	46,100	NC
Bethel Univ	MN	45,270	VC
Briar Cliff Univ	IA	36,956	C
Bridgewater State Univ	MA	21,810	C
Calif Baptist Univ	CA	41,392	C
Cal State, Sacramento	CA	20,332	C
Cal State, San Bernardino	CA	12,000	C
Cal State, Stanislaus	CA	16,212	C
Campbellsville Univ	KY	32,492	C
Carson-Newman Univ	TN	34,160	C
Castleton Univ	VT	20,186	C
Central State Univ	OH	18,564	C
Central Washington Univ	WA	16,803	C
Chadron State College	NE	14,819	NC
CUNY/Hunter College	NY	31,098	VC
CUNY/Lehman College	NY	5,778	HC+
Cleveland State Univ	OH	22,196	C
College of Mount St. Vincent	NY	45,620	C
Columbus State Univ	GA	14,336	LC
Concordia College - Moorhead	MN	51,088	C+
Concordia Univ, Ann Arbor	MI	35,945	VC
Curry College	MA	51,815	C
Dakota State Univ	SD	13,811	C
Defiance College	OH	41,630	C
Delaware State Univ	DE	19,376	NC
DePaul Univ	IL	47,623	VC
East Carolina Univ	NC	16,937	C
East Stroudsburg Univ	PA	18,334	C
Eastern Kentucky Univ	KY	16,908	C
Eastern Mich Univ	MI	19,761	C
Eastern Washington Univ	WA	25,572	LC
Edinboro Univ	PA	15,940	LC
Elon Univ	NC	44,599	VC+
Emporia State Univ	KS	14,570	C
Fairmont State Univ	WV	15,726	C
Fayetteville State Univ	NC	17,756	C
Florida State Univ	FL	16,771	HC
Freed-Hardeman Univ	TN	29,450	C
Friends Univ	KS	34,455	C
Gardner-Webb Univ	NC	39,200	C+
Georgia Southern Univ	GA	16,596	C
Glenville State College	WV	17,386	NC
Goddard College	VT	17,040	VC
Goshen College	IN	42,500	C
Gustavus Adolphus College	MN	52,433	HC
Hofstra Univ	NY	55,960	C+
Houghton College	NY	39,090	C
Howard Univ	DC	37,616	C+
Idaho State Univ	ID	13,619	NC
Illinois State Univ	IL	23,418	VC
Indiana State Univ	IN	23,223	LC
Indiana Univ Bloomington	IN	20,429	VC
Indiana Univ of Pennsylvania	PA	23,614	LC
Inter-American Univ of PR-San Germán	PR	20,042	
Iowa State Univ	IA	17,570	C
Ithaca College	NY	56,766	VC
Jackson State Univ	MS	15,879	LC
Jacksonville State Univ	AL	14,628	LC
Johnson C. Smith Univ	NC	25,336	LC
Kennesaw State Univ	GA	19,592	VC
Kent State Univ	OH	20,732	C
Lamar Univ	TX	18,014	LC
Lee Univ	TN	22,045	C
Lenoir-Rhyne Univ	NC	43,200	C
Lincoln Memorial Univ	TN	28,070	C
Linfield College	OR	52,010	C
Lipscomb Univ	TN	41,296	VC
LIU Post	NY	49,682	C
Louisiana College	LA	21,886	C
Manchester Univ	IN	40,422	C
Manhattan College	NY	51,750	C+
Mayville State Univ	ND	18,371	NC
McNeese State Univ	LA	7,838	C
MidAmerica Nazarene Univ	KS	35,550	C
Middle Tenn State Univ	TN	8,650	C
Minn State Univ, Mankato	MN	15,616	C
Minn State Univ, Moorhead	MN	15,941	C
Missouri Baptist Univ	MO	35,594	C
Monmouth Univ	NJ	46,234	C
Montana State Univ-Billings	MT	22,960	C
Montclair State Univ	NJ	26,210	LC
Morehead State Univ	KY	17,422	C
Morgan State Univ	MD	17,190	LC
New Jersey City Univ	NJ	21,456	LC
N Car Central Univ	NC	9,000	C
N Dak State Univ	ND	16,245	C
Northeastern Illinois Univ	IL	12,529	LC
Northeastern State Univ	OK	8,615	VC
Northern Illinois Univ	IL	20,176	C
Northern Mich Univ	MI	19,604	C
Northern State Univ	SD	14,505	C
Ohio Northern Univ	OH	44,050	VC
Ohio Valley Univ	WV	29,480	C
Okla State Univ	OK	17,180	VC
Oral Roberts Univ	OK	34,316	C
Otterbein Univ	OH	41,630	C
Pfeiffer Univ	NC	39,695	LC
Plymouth State Univ	NH	23,180	LC
Portland State Univ	OR	19,443	C
Purdue Univ/West Lafayette	IN	20,032	MC
Rhode Island College	RI	17,694	LC
St. Mary's College of Calif	CA	57,420	C
Shepherd Univ, West Virginia	WV	17,224	C
Slippery Rock Univ of Pennsylvania	PA	10,360	C
S Car State Univ	SC	20,805	LC
S Dak State Univ	SD	15,634	C
Southeastern Louisiana Univ	LA	16,237	C
Southern Arkansas Univ	AR	21,532	C
Southern Conn State Univ	CT	21,924	LC
Southern Illinois Univ Carbondale	IL	23,667	C
Southern Illinois Univ Edwardsville	IL	22,643	C
Southern Methodist Univ	TX	66,483	MC
Southwest Baptist Univ	MO	29,900	LC
Southwest Minn State Univ	MN	17,783	C
Springfield College	MA	45,995	C
St. Cloud State Univ	MN	10,600	C
SUNY / SUNY Cortland	NY	20,706	VC
Tabor College	KS	35,870	C
Taylor Univ	IN	40,317	C+
Tenn State Univ	TN	14,423	C
Texas A&M Univ at Commerce	TX	10,496	C
Texas A&M Univ at Kingsville	TX	7,500	LC
Texas State Univ	TX	19,350	C
The Citadel, The Military College of S Car	SC	35,339	C
The College of New Jersey	NJ	31,909	HC
The Lincoln Univ	PA	15,154	NC
The Univ of Utah	UT	17,924	VC
Troy Univ	AL	16,171	C
Tulane Univ	LA	63,396	HC+
Univ of Alabama at Birmingham	AL	19,906	C
Univ of Arkansas at Little Rock	AR	18,211	C
Univ of Arkansas at Monticello	AR	13,134	NC
Univ of Cincinnati	OH	21,964	VC
Univ of Florida	FL	16,291	HC+
Univ of Georgia	GA	21,250	HC
Univ of Illinois at Chicago	IL	25,006	VC
Univ of Iowa	IA	18,683	VC+
Univ of Kansas	KS	20,135	C+
Univ of Kentucky	KY	33,306	C
Univ of Louisiana at Lafayette	LA	14,516	C
Univ of Maine at Farmington	ME	18,187	C
Univ of Maine at Presque Isle	ME	14,870	C
Univ of Maryland/Eastern Shore	MD	17,013	C
Univ of Minn/Duluth	MN	20,292	C+
Univ of Montana-Western	MT	11,220	LC
Univ of Nebr - Kearney	NE	16,546	LC
Univ of Nevada, Las Vegas	NV	17,553	C
Univ of New Mexico	NM	15,404	C
Univ of N Car at Pembroke	NC	14,388	LC
Univ of North Georgia	GA	17,316	C
Univ of Pittsburgh at Bradford	PA	22,402	C
Univ of Rio Grande & Rio Grande Community College	OH	8,750	NC
Univ of South Alabama	AL	16,400	C
Univ of Southern Miss	MS	13,170	C
Univ of the Cumberlands	KY	32,000	C
Univ of the District of Columbia	DC	21,044	LC
Univ of Toledo	OH	19,336	NC
Univ of West Florida	FL	15,848	C
Univ of Wisc-La Crosse	WI	15,247	C+
Univ of Wisc-Stevens Point	WI	14,043	C
Univ of Wisc-Superior	WI	14,446	C
Utah State Univ	UT	12,736	C

ST = STATE $IS = IN-STATE COSTS SR = SELECTOR RATING

School	ST	$IS	SR
Valley City State Univ	ND	13,267	C
Virginia Commonwealth Univ	VA	23,049	C
Wayne State College	NE	12,802	C
Wayne State Univ	MI	22,016	C
Weber State Univ	UT	10,721	C
West Chester Univ of Pennsylvania	PA	18,456	C
West Liberty Univ	WV	15,512	C
Western Mich Univ	MI	21,054	C
Western Oregon Univ	OR	15,021	LC
Western Washington Univ	WA	18,003	C+
William Paterson Univ of New Jersey	NJ	23,133	C
William Penn Univ	IA	26,000	C
Wilmington College	OH	34,600	C
Winona State Univ	MN	17,535	C
Worcester State Univ	MA	20,977	C
Youngstown State Univ	OH	17,307	C

HEALTH INFORMATION MANAGEMENT

School	ST	$IS	SR
Arizona State Univ at the Polytechnic Campus	AZ	21,360	VC
Arkansas Tech Univ	AR	15,484	C
Armstrong State Univ	GA	16,962	C
Ashford Univ	CA	10,480	C
Augusta Univ	GA	4,632	C
Bluffton Univ	OH	40,950	C
Champlain College	VT	53,132	C+
Charter Oak State College	CT	7,671	LC
Coppin State Univ	MD	17,041	VC
Dakota State Univ	SD	13,811	C
Duquesne Univ	PA	46,822	VC
Ferris State Univ	MI	21,445	C
Gannon Univ	PA	42,032	C
Georgian Court Univ	NJ	42,426	LC
Idaho State Univ	ID	13,619	NC
Illinois State Univ	IL	23,418	VC
Indiana Inst of Technology	IN	34,240	LC
Indiana Univ Kokomo	IN	7,073	C
Indiana Univ Northwest	IN	7,072	C
Indiana Univ Southeast	IN	14,242	LC
Indiana Univ-Purdue Univ Indianapolis	IN	18,635	C
John Carroll Univ	OH	49,740	C+
Kean Univ	NJ	24,650	C
King Univ	TN	34,660	C
Loyola Univ Chicago	IL	55,802	VC
Marymount Univ	VA	41,570	LC
Montana Tech of the Univ of Montana	MT	15,447	C+
Mount St. Joseph Univ	OH	33,880	C
Murray State Univ	KY	16,998	C
Ohio State Univ at Columbus	OH	21,703	HC+
Ohio State Univ at Lima	OH	7,140	C
Regis Univ	CO	44,520	C
Rutgers Univ - New Brunswick	NJ	26,632	HC
St. Louis Univ	MO	49,866	HC
Simmons College	MA	53,090	VC
Southern Illinois Univ Carbondale	IL	23,667	C
Southern Illinois Univ Edwardsville	IL	22,643	C
Southern Univ at New Orleans	LA	8,014	LC
Southwestern Okla State Univ	OK	11,790	C
St. John's Univ	NY	55,850	C
Temple Univ	PA	24,392	VC
Texas State Univ	TX	19,350	C
The Univ of Tenn at Knoxville	TN	22,112	VC
Thomas Edison State Univ	NJ	6,350	NC
Univ of Central Florida	FL	15,922	VC
Univ of Cincinnati	OH	21,964	VC
Univ of Illinois at Chicago	IL	25,006	VC
Univ of Kansas	KS	20,135	C+
Univ of Maine at Farmington	ME	18,187	C
Univ of Maine at Fort Kent	ME	15,165	LC
Univ of Miss	MS	17,746	C+
Univ of Pittsburgh	PA	29,568	HC+
Univ of South Alabama	AL	16,400	C
Univ of S Car Upstate	SC	18,200	LC
Univ of Southern Indiana	IN	16,501	C
Univ of Wisc-Green Bay	WI	15,064	C
Weber State Univ	UT	10,721	C
Western Mich Univ	MI	21,054	C
Xavier Univ	OH	47,880	C+

HEALTH PROMOTION

School	ST	$IS	SR
American Univ	DC	59,379	HC+
Arkansas State Univ	AR	16,190	C
Ashford Univ	CA	10,480	C
Baldwin Wallace Univ	OH	41,106	C
Goddard College	VT	17,040	VC
Johnson & Wales Univ/ Denver Campus	CO	42,707	C
Keene State College	NH	24,003	LC
Lubbock Christian Univ	TX	28,426	C
Lynchburg College	VA	46,740	C
Missouri Southern State Univ	MO	12,499	C
Missouri State Univ	MO	15,190	C+
Nebr Methodist College	NE	25,134	SP
North Greenville Univ	SC	25,930	C+
Nova Southeastern Univ	FL	38,534	C+
Samford Univ	AL	39,232	VC
Univ of Georgia	GA	21,250	HC
Univ of Montana	MT	14,105	C
Univ of N Car at Asheville	NC	15,723	VC+
Univ of Wisc-Superior	WI	14,446	C
Weber State Univ	UT	10,721	C
Western Conn State Univ	CT	21,254	LC

HEALTH SCIENCE

School	ST	$IS	SR
Adventist Univ of Health Sciences	FL	26,430	NC
Albany College of Pharmacy and Health Sciences	NY	42,681	SP
Alcorn State Univ	MS	15,854	C
Alderson Broaddus Univ	WV	26,149	C
Alma College	MI	47,548	C
Alvernia Univ	PA	43,900	C
Appalachian State Univ	NC	14,416	VC
Arizona State Univ at the Downtown Phoenix Campus	AZ	23,680	VC
Arizona State Univ at the West Campus	AZ	20,640	C
Armstrong State Univ	GA	16,962	C
Asbury Univ	KY	35,180	C+
Ashford Univ	CA	10,480	C
Aurora Univ	IL	33,970	C
Ball State Univ	IN	19,590	C
Baylor Univ	TX	53,760	HC
Benedictine Univ	IL	38,300	C
Bloomsburg Univ of Pennsylvania	PA	19,066	LC
Boise State Univ	ID	14,860	C
Boston Univ	MA	65,110	MC
Bowling Green State Univ	OH	19,747	C
Brandeis Univ	MA	65,925	MC
Brigham Young Univ	UT	12,748	HC
Butler Univ	IN	51,352	VC
Calif Baptist Univ	CA	41,392	C
Cal State, Chico	CA	21,440	C
Cal State, Dominguez Hills	CA	19,022	LC
Cal State, East Bay	CA	19,413	C
Cal State, Fresno	CA	16,902	LC
Cal State, Fullerton	CA	21,902	C
Cal State, Long Beach	CA	18,850	C
Cal State, Los Angeles	CA	17,186	LC
Cal State, Northridge	CA	16,859	LC
Cal State, San Bernardino	CA	12,000	C
Carroll College	MT	39,972	C+
Castleton Univ	VT	20,186	C
Chapman Univ	CA	63,078	VC+
Chicago State Univ	IL	20,144	C
CUNY/Brooklyn College	NY	5,884	C+
Cleveland State Univ	OH	22,196	C
College of St Joseph	VT	32,400	LC
College of St. Scholastica	MN	44,640	C
College of William & Mary	VA		MC
Colo State Univ	CO	22,162	VC
Columbus State Univ	GA	14,336	LC
Corban Univ	OR	40,306	C
Culver-Stockton College	MO	33,525	C
Daemen College	NY	38,045	C
DePaul Univ	IL	47,623	VC
Dordt College	IA	37,860	C+
Drexel Univ	PA	65,432	VC+
Drury Univ	MO	33,791	VC
Duquesne Univ	PA	46,822	VC
East Tenn State Univ	TN	13,994	C
East Texas Baptist Univ	TX	33,134	C
Eastern Conn State Univ	CT	23,059	C
Elms College	MA	45,646	VC
Emporia State Univ	KS	14,570	C
Excelsior College	NY	14,080	SP
Ferrum College	VA	39,650	C
Fitchburg State Univ	MA	21,819	C
Florida Atlantic Univ	FL	17,339	C
Florida Gulf Coast Univ	FL	9,682	C
Franklin Pierce Univ	NH	46,750	C
Friends Univ	KS	34,455	C
Furman Univ	SC	58,092	VC+
Gannon Univ	PA	42,032	C
George Mason Univ	VA	15,724	VC
Gettysburg College	PA	63,000	HC
Goddard College	VT	17,040	VC
Goodwin College	CT	28,370	LC
Grand Canyon Univ	AZ	16,950	VC
Grand Valley State Univ	MI	22,250	C+
Grove City College	PA	25,692	VC
Guilford College	NC	44,090	C
Hampshire College	MA	63,824	MC
Harding Univ	AR	25,421	C
Hardin-Simmons Univ	TX	33,966	C
Henderson State Univ	AR	15,516	LC
Hofstra Univ	NY	55,960	C+
Howard Univ	DC	37,616	C+
Idaho State Univ	ID	13,619	NC
Indiana Univ Bloomington	IN	20,429	VC
Indiana Univ East	IN	7,072	C
Indiana Univ Kokomo	IN	7,073	C
Indiana Univ Northwest	IN	7,072	C
Indiana Univ South Bend	IN	14,242	C
Indiana Univ-Purdue Univ Indianapolis	IN	18,635	C
Ithaca College	NY	56,766	VC
James Madison Univ	VA	19,084	VC
Johnson & Wales Univ/ Denver Campus	CO	42,707	C
Johnson State College	VT	20,752	C
Kalamazoo College	MI	53,931	HC+
Keene State College	NH	24,003	LC
Kent State Univ	OH	20,732	C
La Roche College	PA	37,924	LC
La Sierra Univ	CA	39,690	VC
Lee Univ	TN	22,045	C
LIU Brooklyn	NY	49,682	C
LIU Post	NY	49,682	C
Lock Haven Univ of Pennsylvania	PA	18,028	LC
Loyola Marymount Univ	CA	58,038	HC
Madonna Univ	MI	29,050	C
Marietta College	OH	46,190	C
Marshall Univ	WV	17,242	C
Marymount Univ	VA	41,570	LC
Maryville Univ of St. Louis	MO	38,046	VC+
Marywood Univ	PA	46,900	C
MCPHS Univ	MA	45,470	SP
Mercy College	NY	31,776	C
Mercy College of Health Sciences	IA	16,920	C
Middle Tenn State Univ	TN	8,650	C
Midwestern State Univ	TX	17,572	C
Minn State Univ, Mankato	MN	15,616	C
Missouri Baptist Univ	MO	35,594	C
Missouri Southern State Univ	MO	12,499	C
Mount St. Mary's Univ	MD	51,610	C
Nazareth College	NY	45,574	C
New England College	NH	50,364	C
New York Inst of Technology	NY	48,730	C
Newman Univ	KS	35,390	C
Nicholls State Univ	LA	10,534	C
Norfolk State Univ	VA	25,702	LC
Northeastern Univ	MA	62,703	MC
Northern Arizona Univ	AZ	20,246	VC
Northern Illinois Univ	IL	20,176	C
Northern Kentucky Univ	KY	16,486	C
Oakland Univ	MI	20,763	C
Ohio State Univ at Columbus	OH	21,703	HC+
Old Dominion Univ	VA	20,910	C
Oral Roberts Univ	OK	34,316	C
Oregon Inst of Technology	OR	8,910	C
Pace Univ	NY	58,248	C
Pennsylvania College of Technology	PA	27,333	NC
Point Loma Nazarene Univ	CA	43,450	C
Purdue Univ/Northwest	IN	15,038	C
Purdue Univ/West Lafayette	IN	20,032	MC
Quinnipiac Univ	CT	59,110	C
Randolph College	VA	45,660	VC
Regis Univ	CO	44,520	C
Sacred Heart Univ	CT	52,750	C
Saginaw Valley State Univ	MI	18,530	C
St. Joseph's Univ	PA	57,544	VC+
St. Mary's College of Calif	CA	57,420	C
Samford Univ	AL	39,232	VC
San Diego State Univ	CA	21,896	C+
San Francisco State Univ	CA	18,514	LC
San Jose State Univ	CA	21,540	C
South Univ	GA	36,070	LC
Southeast Missouri State Univ	MO	15,498	C
Southern Adventist Univ	TN	27,600	C
Southwestern Okla State Univ	OK	11,790	C
Spalding Univ	KY	31,938	SP
St. Francis College	NY	38,800	LC
SUNY / SUNY Cortland	NY	20,706	VC
Stephen F. Austin State Univ	TX	18,406	LC
Sterling College	KS	32,830	C
Stetson Univ	FL	53,544	VC
Stony Brook Univ/The SUNY	NY	21,881	MC
Syracuse Univ	NY	60,239	VC
Taylor Univ	IN	40,317	C+
Texas A&M Univ at Corpus Christi	TX	16,851	LC
Texas Woman's Univ	TX	15,302	LC
The College at Brockport - SUNY	NY	20,346	C
The Lincoln Univ	PA	15,154	NC
The Univ of Tenn at Martin	TN	14,876	C
Towson Univ	MD	17,408	VC
Truman State Univ	MO	16,014	HC
Universidad Adventista de las Antillas	PR	16,606	
Univ of Alabama at Birmingham	AL	19,906	C
Univ of Arkansas at Fayetteville	AR	19,152	C+
Univ of Arkansas at Little Rock	AR	18,211	C
Univ of Calif, Santa Cruz	CA	28,731	C+
Univ of Central Arkansas	AR	14,472	VC
Univ of Central Florida	FL	15,922	VC
Univ of Colo Colo Springs	CO	19,663	C
Univ of Delaware	DE	24,976	VC+
Univ of Findlay	OH	60,139	C
Univ of Florida	FL	16,291	HC+
Univ of Hartford	CT	49,776	C
Univ of Holy Cross	LA	21,523	C
Univ of Louisiana at Monroe	LA	15,970	C
Univ of Maryland/Baltimore County	MD	21,296	VC
Univ of Memphis	TN	18,278	C
Univ of Miami	FL	63,494	MC
Univ of Mich-Flint	MI	17,607	C+
Univ of Minn Crookston	MN	19,739	C
Univ of Miss	MS	17,746	C+
Univ of Missouri-Kansas City	MO	19,563	VC
Univ of Nebr - Lincoln	NE	18,589	VC
Univ of North Florida	FL	15,996	VC
Univ of Richmond	VA	60,880	MC
Univ of S Dak	SD	16,109	C
Univ of South Florida/St. Petersburg	FL	15,980	C
Univ of Southern Maine	ME	18,320	C
Univ of Texas at El Paso	TX	34,452	NC
Univ of the Sciences	PA	54,038	VC
Univ of Vermont	VT	28,878	HC
Univ of Wisc-Stevens Point	WI	14,043	C
Valparaiso Univ	IN	48,370	C+
Washington Univ in St. Louis	MO	65,366	VC
Wayne State Univ	MI	22,016	C
West Chester Univ of Pennsylvania	PA	18,456	C
Western Conn State Univ	CT	21,254	LC
Western New England Univ	MA	48,088	C
Wheaton College	IL	43,610	MC
Whitworth Univ	WA	51,732	VC
William Paterson Univ of New Jersey	NJ	23,133	C
Yeshiva Univ	NY	47,250	VC+

HEALTH SERVICES ADMINISTRATION

School	ST	$IS	SR
Armstrong State Univ	GA	16,962	C
Drexel Univ	PA	65,432	VC+
Marian Univ	IN	41,220	C
Univ of Detroit Mercy	MI	48,816	C+
Univ of Rhode Island	RI	24,906	C
Univ of St. Francis	IN	37,400	C
Univ of San Francisco	CA	58,484	VC
Weber State Univ	UT	10,721	C

HEALTH SERVICES TECHNOLOGY

School	ST	$IS	SR
Concordia College - New York	NY	39,035	LC
John Carroll Univ	OH	49,740	C+
Thomas Edison State Univ	NJ	6,350	NC
Univ of Pittsburgh	PA	29,568	HC+
Weber State Univ	UT	10,721	C
Wichita State Univ	KS	21,643	C

HEALTHCARE MARKETING

School	ST	$IS	SR
Ferris State Univ	MI	21,445	C
MCPHS Univ	MA	45,470	SP

HEALTHY LIFESTYLE MANAGEMENT

School	ST	$IS	SR
Creighton Univ	NE	48,206	VC+
Samford Univ	AL	39,232	VC

HEAVY EQUIP SERVICE ENGINEERING

School	ST	$IS	SR
Ferris State Univ	MI	21,445	C

HEBREW

School	ST	$IS	SR
American Univ	DC	59,379	HC+
Bard College	NY	64,024	HC
CUNY/Hunter College	NY	31,098	VC
CUNY/Lehman College	NY	5,778	HC+
CUNY/Queens College	NY	27,896	C
Harvard College/Harvard Univ	MA	60,659	MC
Hofstra Univ	NY	55,960	C+
New York Univ	NY	65,860	MC
Ohio State Univ at Columbus	OH	21,703	HC+
SUNY at Binghamton	NY	22,861	MC
The Univ of Utah	UT	17,924	VC
Thomas Edison State Univ	NJ	6,350	NC
Touro College	NY	28,950	VC
Univ of Calif at Los Angeles	CA	30,162	MC
Univ of Cincinnati	OH	21,964	VC
Univ of Illinois at Urbana-Champaign	IL	27,006	HC
Univ of Mich/Ann Arbor	MI	24,410	MC
Univ of Minn/Twin Cities	MN	23,519	HC+
Univ of Rhode Island	RI	24,906	C
Univ of Texas at Austin	TX	26,102	HC
Washington Univ in St. Louis	MO	65,366	VC
Wellesley College	MA	63,916	MC
Yeshiva Univ	NY	47,250	VC+

HISPANIC AMERICAN STUDIES

School	ST	$IS	SR
Boston College	MA	65,737	MC
Boston Univ	MA	65,110	MC
Brown Univ	RI	64,566	MC
Cal State, Long Beach	CA	18,850	C
Carnegie Mellon Univ	PA	67,980	MC
CUNY/Brooklyn College	NY	5,884	C+
CUNY/Hunter College	NY	31,098	VC
Claremont McKenna College	CA	67,185	MC
College of St. Benedict	MN	52,806	C
Colo College	CO	62,560	MC
Columbia Univ/ School of General Studies	NY	61,470	MC
Columbia Univ/City of New York	NY	62,958	MC
Conn College	CT	65,000	MC
Dartmouth College	NH	66,174	MC
East Carolina Univ	NC	16,937	C

School	ST	$IS	SR
Hamilton College	NY	64,250	MC
Lewis & Clark College	OR	58,434	HC+
Loyola Marymount Univ	CA	58,038	HC
Mills College	CA	59,163	VC
Mount St. Mary College	NY	42,061	C
Northeastern Illinois Univ	IL	12,529	LC
Pacific Lutheran Univ	WA	49,960	VC
Pepperdine Univ	CA	74,460	HC+
Pomona College	CA	64,957	MC
Rice Univ	TX	57,668	MC
Rutgers Univ - New Brunswick	NJ	26,632	HC
St. John's Univ	MN	51,624	C
Scripps College	CA	66,664	MC
St. Olaf College	MN	54,260	HC+
Stanford Univ	CA	60,409	MC
SUNY / SUNY Oneonta	NY	19,712	C+
SUNY SUNY Albany	NY	22,165	C
The Univ of Tenn at Knoxville	TN	22,112	VC
Univ of Calif at Berkeley	CA	28,853	MC
Univ of Calif at Irvine	CA	26,484	VC
Univ of Mass Boston	MA	13,435	C
Univ of Mich/Ann Arbor	MI	24,410	MC
Univ of Mich/Dearborn	MI	11,757	VC
Univ of Pennsylvania	PA	63,526	MC
Univ of PR, at Cayey	PR		
Vassar College	NY	65,491	MC
Wabash College	IN	50,650	VC
Wellesley College	MA	63,916	MC
Wesleyan Univ	CT	65,516	MC
Western New Mexico Univ	NM	16,734	LC
Wheaton College	MA	61,512	VC

HISTORIC PRESERVATION

School	ST	$IS	SR
College of Charleston	SC	22,699	C
Eastern Mich Univ	MI	19,761	C
Roger Williams Univ	RI	46,296	C+
Salve Regina Univ	RI	51,470	C
Savannah College of Art and Design	GA	49,595	C
Southeast Missouri State Univ	MO	15,498	C
Univ of Delaware	DE	24,976	VC+
Univ of Mary Washington	VA	24,764	VC
Univ of Mich/Ann Arbor	MI	24,410	MC
Ursuline College	OH	41,076	LC

HISTORY

School	ST	$IS	SR
Abilene Christian Univ	TX	41,800	C+
Adams State Univ	CO	17,703	LC
Adelphi Univ	NY	48,244	C
Adrian College	MI	42,400	C
Agnes Scott College	GA	51,930	VC+
Alabama A&M Univ	AL	18,796	C
Alabama State Univ	AL	14,142	NC
Albany State Univ	GA	19,462	C
Albertus Magnus College	CT	43,258	LC
Albion College	MI	52,650	C
Albright College	PA	46,660	C
Alcorn State Univ	MS	15,854	C
Alderson Broaddus Univ	WV	26,149	C
Alfred Univ	NY	42,296	C+
Alice Lloyd College	KY	8,190	C
Allegheny College	PA	55,420	VC
Allen Univ	SC	19,300	NC
Alma College	MI	47,548	C
Alvernia Univ	PA	43,900	C
Alverno College	WI	33,294	LC
American International College	MA	46,300	LC
American Univ	DC	59,379	HC+
Amherst College	MA		HC+
Anderson Univ	IN	38,200	C
Andrews Univ	MI	28,030	C+
Angelo State Univ	TX	15,263	NC
Anna Maria College	MA	48,186	C
Appalachian State Univ	NC	14,416	VC
Aquinas College	TN	30,800	C+
Aquinas College - Mich	MI	38,876	HC
Arcadia Univ	PA	33,570	C+
Arizona State Univ at the Polytechnic Campus	AZ	21,360	VC
Arizona State Univ at the Tempe Campus	AZ	21,756	VC
Arizona State Univ at the West Campus	AZ	20,640	C
Arkansas State Univ	AR	16,190	C
Arkansas Tech Univ	AR	15,484	C
Armstrong State Univ	GA	16,962	C
Asbury Univ	KY	35,180	C+
Ashford Univ	CA	10,480	C
Ashland Univ	OH	21,440	C
Assumption College	MA	47,920	C+
Atlantic Union College	MA	27,228	C
Auburn Univ	AL	23,594	VC+
Auburn Univ at Montgomery	AL	15,290	C
Augsburg College	MN	43,929	C
Augusta Univ	GA	4,632	C
Augustana College	IL	49,658	VC
Augustana Univ	SD	38,424	VC
Aurora Univ	IL	33,970	C
Austin College	TX	45,875	VC
Austin Peay State Univ	TN	16,397	C
Averett Univ	VA	40,970	LC
Avila Univ	MO	35,480	C
Azusa Pacific Univ	CA	43,972	C
Baker Univ	KS	33,350	C+
Baldwin Wallace Univ	OH	41,106	C
Ball State Univ	IN	19,590	C
Bard College	NY	64,024	HC
Bard College at Simon's Rock	MA	65,795	MC
Barnard College/Columbia Univ	NY	62,741	MC
Barry Univ	FL	37,830	C
Barton College	NC	38,686	LC
Bates College	ME	64,500	MC
Baylor Univ	TX	53,760	HC
Belhaven Univ	MS	31,016	C
Bellarmine Univ	KY	51,220	C
Bellevue Univ	NE	20,300	NC
Belmont Abbey College	NC	48,156	C
Belmont Univ	TN	40,970	VC
Beloit College	WI	55,206	HC
Bemidji State Univ	MN	16,056	VC
Benedict College	SC	28,238	NC
Benedictine College	KS	36,200	VC
Benedictine Univ	IL	38,300	C
Bennington College	VT	63,960	MC
Bentley Univ	MA	60,890	HC
Berea College	KY	7,042	C
Berry College	GA	45,286	C+
Bethany College	KS	46,100	NC
Bethany College	WV	36,300	NC
Bethel College	IN	35,860	C
Bethel College	KS	35,370	C
Bethel Univ	MN	45,270	VC
Bethel Univ	TN	24,738	C
Bethune-Cookman Univ	FL	22,970	C
Biola Univ	CA	46,402	C+
Birmingham-Southern College	AL	44,478	VC
Black Hills State Univ	SD	15,899	C
Blackburn College	IL	28,526	LC
Bloomfield College	NJ	39,100	LC
Bloomsburg Univ of Pennsylvania	PA	19,066	LC
Blue Mountain College	MS	15,949	VC
Bluefield College	VA	34,120	C+
Bluffton Univ	OH	40,950	C
Boise State Univ	ID	14,860	C
Boston College	MA	65,737	MC
Boston Univ	MA	65,110	MC
Bowdoin College	ME	63,500	MC
Bowie State Univ	MD	26,728	LC
Bowling Green State Univ	OH	19,747	C
Brandeis Univ	MA	65,925	MC
Brenau Univ - Women's College	GA	37,876	LC
Brescia Univ	KY	29,890	VC+
Brewton-Parker College	GA	23,490	C
Briar Cliff Univ	IA	36,956	C
Bridgewater College	VA	44,510	C
Brigham Young Univ	UT	12,748	HC
Brigham Young Univ/Hawaii	HI	11,290	C
Brown Univ	RI	64,566	MC
Bryan College	TN	31,440	C
Bryant Univ	RI	55,646	VC
Bryn Athyn College	PA	31,470	C
Bryn Mawr College	PA	59,890	MC
Bucknell Univ	PA	64,616	MC
Buena Vista Univ	IA	41,514	C
Butler Univ	IN	51,352	VC
Cairn Univ	PA	36,296	C
Caldwell Univ	NJ	42,165	NC
Calif Baptist Univ	CA	41,392	C
Calif Inst of Technology	CA	58,761	MC
Calif Lutheran Univ	CA	52,853	C
Calif Polytechnic State Univ	CA	17,979	HC+
Calif State Polytechnic Univ, Pomona	CA	21,541	C
Cal State, Bakersfield	CA	19,191	LC
Cal State, Chico	CA	21,440	C
Cal State, Dominguez Hills	CA	19,022	LC
Cal State, East Bay	CA	19,413	C
Cal State, Fresno	CA	16,902	LC
Cal State, Fullerton	CA	21,902	C
Cal State, Long Beach	CA	18,850	C
Cal State, Los Angeles	CA	17,186	LC
Cal State, Northridge	CA	16,859	LC
Cal State, Sacramento	CA	20,332	C
Cal State, San Bernardino	CA	12,000	C
Cal State, San Marcos	CA	24,184	LC
Cal State, Stanislaus	CA	16,212	C
Calif Univ of Pennsylvania	PA	14,217	LC
Calvin College	MI	41,570	VC+
Cameron Univ	OK	11,072	NC
Campbellsville Univ	KY	32,492	C
Canisius College	NY	47,537	C
Capital Univ	OH	42,982	C
Cardinal Stritch Univ	WI	36,462	C
Carleton College	MN	64,071	MC
Carlow Univ	PA	38,549	LC
Carnegie Mellon Univ	PA	67,980	MC
Carroll College	MT	39,972	C+
Carroll Univ	WI	38,100	C+
Carson-Newman Univ	TN	34,160	C
Carthage College	WI	48,835	C
Case Western Reserve Univ	OH	60,304	MC
Castleton Univ	VT	20,186	C
Catawba College	NC	39,820	C
Cedar Crest College	PA	46,715	C
Cedarville Univ	OH	34,990	VC
Centenary College	NJ	43,602	C
Centenary College of Louisiana	LA	45,650	C+
Central College	IA	44,592	C
Central Conn State Univ	CT	21,203	C
Central Methodist Univ	MO	36,830	VC
Central Mich Univ	MI	20,330	C
Central State Univ	OH	18,564	C
Central Washington Univ	WA	16,803	C
Centre College	KY	49,250	HC
Chadron State College	NE	14,819	NC
Chaminade Univ of Honolulu	HI	36,000	C
Chapman Univ	CA	63,078	VC+
Charleston Southern Univ	SC	32,400	C
Chatham Univ	PA	46,517	C
Chestnut Hill College	PA	43,410	C
Chicago State Univ	IL	20,144	C
Christendom College	VA	32,600	VC
Christian Brothers Univ	TN	31,670	VC
Christopher Newport Univ	VA	23,968	VC+
CUNY/Baruch College	NY	21,609	HC
CUNY/Brooklyn College	NY	5,884	C+
CUNY/City College	NY	20,319	VC
CUNY/College of Staten Island	NY	17,840	NC
CUNY/Hunter College	NY	31,098	VC
CUNY/Lehman College	NY	5,778	HC+
CUNY/Queens College	NY	27,896	C
CUNY/York College	NY	6,747	LC
Claflin Univ	SC	33,764	LC
Claremont McKenna College	CA	67,185	MC
Clarion Univ of Pennsylvania	PA	21,608	LC
Clark Atlanta Univ	GA	31,019	LC
Clark Univ	MA	51,600	HC+
Clarke Univ	IA	38,940	C
Clarkson Univ	NY	60,392	HC
Clayton State Univ	GA	19,735	C
Clemson Univ	SC		HC
Cleveland State Univ	OH	22,196	C
Coastal Carolina Univ	SC	19,766	C
Coe College	IA	51,570	VC
Coker College	SC	34,810	LC
Colby College	ME	64,060	MC
Colby-Sawyer College	NH	50,790	C
Colgate Univ	NY	65,030	MC
College of Charleston	SC	22,699	C
College of Mount St. Vincent	NY	45,620	C
College of St. Benedict	MN	52,806	C
College of St. Elizabeth	NJ	44,432	LC
College of St Joseph	VT	32,400	LC
College of St. Scholastica	MN	44,640	C
College of the Holy Cross	MA	62,165	MC
College of the Ozarks	MO	7,230	C
College of William & Mary	VA		MC
Colo Christian Univ	CO	39,940	VC
Colo College	CO	62,560	MC
Colo Mesa Univ	CO	18,955	LC
Colo State Univ	CO	22,162	VC
Colo State Univ-Pueblo	CO	18,234	C
Columbia College	SC	36,550	C
Columbia College - Missouri	MO	27,803	C
Columbia Univ/ School of General Studies	NY	61,470	MC
Columbia Univ/City of New York	NY	62,958	MC
Columbus State Univ	GA	14,336	LC
Concord Univ	WV	14,954	C
Concordia College - Moorhead	MN	51,088	C+
Concordia College - New York	NY	39,035	LC
Concordia Univ	CA	41,580	VC
Concordia Univ Nebr	NE	36,280	VC
Concordia Univ St. Paul	MN	29,050	C
Concordia Univ Texas	TX	40,210	C
Concordia Univ Wisc	WI	35,910	C
Concordia Univ, Ann Arbor	MI	35,945	VC
Concordia Univ, Chicago	IL	39,694	C
Conn College	CT	65,000	MC
Converse College	SC	26,495	C
Coppin State Univ	MD	17,041	VC
Corban Univ	OR	40,306	C
Cornell College	IA	48,800	VC
Cornell Univ	NY	64,853	MC
Covenant College	GA	38,990	VC
Creighton Univ	NE	48,206	VC+
Culver-Stockton College	MO	33,525	C
Cumberland Univ	TN	27,710	C
Curry College	MA	51,815	C
Daemen College	NY	38,045	C
Dakota Wesleyan Univ	SD	32,850	C
Dallas Baptist Univ	TX	33,713	C
Dartmouth College	NH	66,174	MC
Davidson College	NC	60,119	MC
Davis & Elkins College	WV	38,242	LC
Defiance College	OH	41,630	C
Delaware State Univ	DE	19,376	NC
Delta State Univ	MS	13,176	C
Denison Univ	OH	58,860	MC
DePaul Univ	IL	47,623	VC
DePauw Univ	IN	58,688	HC+
DeSales Univ	PA	43,970	C
Dickinson College	PA	63,974	MC
Dickinson State Univ	ND	12,372	LC
Dillard Univ	LA	20,940	VC
Doane Univ	NE	39,184	VC
Dominican College	NY	31,270	LC
Dominican Univ	IL	41,222	C
Dominican Univ of Calif	CA	57,050	C
Dordt College	IA	37,860	C+
Drake Univ	IA	45,056	HC
Drew Univ/College of Liberal Arts	NJ	61,048	VC
Drexel Univ	PA	65,432	VC+
Drury Univ	MO	33,791	VC
Duke Univ	NC	64,188	
Duquesne Univ	PA	46,822	VC
D'Youville College	NY	36,780	C
Earlham College	IN	54,870	HC
East Carolina Univ	NC	16,937	C
East Central Univ	OK	13,056	C
East Stroudsburg Univ	PA	18,334	C
East Tenn State Univ	TN	13,994	C
East Texas Baptist Univ	TX	33,134	C
Eastern Conn State Univ	CT	23,059	C
Eastern Illinois Univ	IL	21,126	C
Eastern Kentucky Univ	KY	16,908	C
Eastern Mennonite Univ	VA	42,550	C
Eastern Mich Univ	MI	19,761	C
Eastern Nazarene College	MA	39,955	C
Eastern New Mexico Univ	NM	14,416	C
Eastern Oregon Univ	OR	17,715	C
Eastern Univ	PA	39,540	C
Eastern Washington Univ	WA	25,572	LC
Eckerd College	FL	52,874	C
Edgewood College	WI	35,950	C
Edinboro Univ	PA	15,940	LC
Edward Waters College	FL	20,607	NC
Elizabeth City State Univ	NC	14,745	C
Elizabethtown College	PA	54,050	C
Elmhurst College	IL	45,428	C
Elmira College	NY	53,900	C
Elon Univ	NC	44,599	VC+
Emmanuel College	MA	52,110	C+
Emory and Henry College	VA	41,410	C
Emory Univ	GA	60,786	MC
Emporia State Univ	KS	14,570	C
Endicott College	MA	44,604	VC+
Erskine College	SC	45,460	C
Eugene Lang College/The New School for Liberal Arts	NY	55,650	C
Eureka College	IL	30,220	C
Evangel Univ	MO	28,898	C
Excelsior College	NY	14,080	SP
Fairfield Univ	CT	59,860	VC+
Fairleigh Dickinson Univ/ College at Florham	NJ	52,062	C
Fairleigh Dickinson Univ/ Metropolitan Campus	NJ	40,254	C
Fairmont State Univ	WV	15,726	C
Faulkner Univ	AL	26,410	C
Fayetteville State Univ	NC	17,756	C
Felician Univ	NJ	45,370	LC
Ferris State Univ	MI	21,445	C
Ferrum College	VA	39,650	C
Fisk Univ	TN	32,066	LC
Fitchburg State Univ	MA	21,819	C
Flagler College	FL	27,620	C
Florida A&M Univ	FL	15,361	C
Florida Atlantic Univ	FL	17,339	C
Florida Gulf Coast Univ	FL	9,682	C
Florida International Univ	FL	19,854	C+
Florida State Univ	FL	16,771	HC
Fontbonne Univ	MO	33,717	C
Fordham Univ	NY	65,918	MC
Fort Hays State Univ	KS	12,131	C
Fort Lewis College	CO	18,980	C
Framingham State Univ	MA	20,584	C
Francis Marion Univ	SC	16,464	LC
Franciscan Univ of Steubenville	OH	33,980	VC
Franklin and Marshall College	PA	63,170	HC
Franklin College	IN	39,380	C
Franklin Pierce Univ	NH	46,750	C
Freed-Hardeman Univ	TN	29,450	C
Fresno Pacific Univ	CA	37,370	C
Friends Univ	KS	34,455	C
Frostburg State Univ	MD	17,280	LC
Furman Univ	SC	58,092	VC+
Gallaudet Univ	DC	29,118	LC
Gannon Univ	PA	42,032	C
Gardner-Webb Univ	NC	39,200	C+
Geneva College	PA	35,450	C
George Fox Univ	OR	42,938	C
George Mason Univ	VA	15,724	VC
George Washington Univ	DC	62,835	MC
Georgetown College	KY	41,440	C
Georgetown Univ	DC	65,926	MC
Georgia College & State Univ	GA	21,148	C+
Georgia Southern Univ	GA	16,596	C
Georgia Southwestern State Univ	GA	13,870	C
Georgia State Univ	GA	24,332	VC
Georgian Court Univ	NJ	42,426	LC
Gettysburg College	PA	63,000	HC
Glenville State College	WV	17,386	NC
Goddard College	VT	17,040	VC
Gonzaga Univ	WA	50,888	HC
Gordon College	MA	46,472	C+
Goshen College	IN	42,500	C
Goucher College	MD	55,716	VC
Graceland Univ	IA	35,290	C
Grambling State Univ	LA	15,701	C
Grand Canyon Univ	AZ	16,950	VC
Grand Rapids Theological Seminary/Cornerstone Univ	MI	33,338	C
Grand Valley State Univ	MI	22,250	C+
Green Mountain College	VT	45,228	LC
Greensboro College	NC	42,400	LC

ST = STATE $IS = IN-STATE COSTS SR = SELECTOR RATING

School	ST	$IS	SR
Greenville College	IL	27,012	C
Grinnell College	IA	60,738	MC
Grove City College	PA	25,692	VC
Guilford College	NC	44,090	C
Gustavus Adolphus College	MN	52,433	HC
Gwynedd Mercy Univ	PA	43,780	LC
Hamilton College	NY	64,250	MC
Hamline Univ	MN	45,678	VC
Hampden-Sydney College	VA	56,248	C+
Hampshire College	MA	63,824	MC
Hampton Univ	VA	34,926	LC
Hannibal-LaGrange Univ	MO	29,815	C
Hanover College	IN	46,364	C+
Harding Univ	AR	25,421	C
Hardin-Simmons Univ	TX	33,966	C
Hartwick College	NY	51,270	C
Harvard College/Harvard Univ	MA	60,659	MC
Hastings College	NE	35,380	C+
Haverford College	PA	66,490	MC
Hawaii Pacific Univ	HI	33,420	C
Heidelberg Univ	OH	39,200	C
Hellenic College/Holy Cross Greek Orthodox School of Theology	MA	39,906	C
Henderson State Univ	AR	15,516	LC
Hendrix College	AR	54,020	VC+
High Point Univ	NC	45,977	C
Hillsdale College	MI	35,722	MC
Hiram College	OH	43,230	C
Hofstra Univ	NY	55,960	C+
Hollins Univ	VA	49,635	VC
Holy Family Univ	PA	43,326	LC
Holy Names Univ	CA	46,630	LC
Hood College	MD	54,840	C
Hope College	MI	39,940	VC
Houghton College	NY	39,090	C
Houston Baptist Univ	TX	36,450	C
Howard Payne Univ	TX	34,320	C
Howard Univ	DC	37,616	C+
Humboldt State Univ	CA	20,514	C
Huntingdon College	AL	34,900	C
Huntington Univ	IN	33,996	C
Huston-Tillotson Univ	TX	18,124	LC
Idaho State Univ	ID	13,619	NC
Illinois College	IL	40,850	VC
Illinois State Univ	IL	23,418	VC
Illinois Wesleyan Univ	IL	56,430	VC+
Indiana State Univ	IN	23,223	LC
Indiana Univ Bloomington	IN	20,429	VC
Indiana Univ East	IN	7,072	C
Indiana Univ Northwest	IN	7,072	C
Indiana Univ of Pennsylvania	PA	23,614	LC
Indiana Univ South Bend	IN	14,242	C
Indiana Univ Southeast	IN	14,242	LC
Indiana Univ-Purdue Univ Fort Wayne	IN	17,553	C
Indiana Univ-Purdue Univ Indianapolis	IN	18,635	C
Indiana Wesleyan Univ	IN	33,674	C
Inter-American Univ of PR Ponce	PR	19,549	
Inter-American Univ of PR-Fajardo Campus	PR	18,336	
Inter-American Univ of PR-Metropolitan Campus	PR	20,045	
Inter-American Univ of PR-San Germán	PR	20,042	
Iona College	NY	50,984	C
Iowa State Univ	IA	17,570	C
Ithaca College	NY	56,766	VC
Jackson State Univ	MS	15,879	LC
Jacksonville State Univ	AL	14,628	LC
Jacksonville Univ	FL	46,230	C
James Madison Univ	VA	19,084	VC
Jarvis Christian College	TX	20,160	NC
John Brown Univ	AR	33,132	VC
John Carroll Univ	OH	49,740	C+
Johns Hopkins Univ	MD	65,386	MC
Johnson C. Smith Univ	NC	25,336	LC
Johnson State College	VT	20,752	C
Judson College	AL	27,066	C
Judson Univ	IL	37,700	C
Juniata College	PA	53,760	VC
Kalamazoo College	MI	53,931	HC+
Kansas State Univ	KS	17,780	VC
Kansas Wesleyan Univ	KS	36,600	C
Kean Univ	NJ	24,650	C
Keene State College	NH	24,003	LC
Kennesaw State Univ	GA	19,592	VC
Kent State Univ	OH	20,732	C
Kentucky Christian Univ	KY	26,560	LC
Kentucky State Univ	KY	13,364	LC
Kentucky Wesleyan College	KY	32,080	C
Kenyon College	OH	63,330	MC
King Univ	TN	34,660	C
King's College	PA	46,858	C
Knox College	IL	52,615	VC+
Kutztown Univ of Pennsylvania	PA	19,056	LC
La Roche College	PA	37,924	LC
La Salle Univ	PA	55,790	C
La Sierra Univ	CA	39,690	VC
Lafayette College	PA	63,355	MC
LaGrange College	GA	39,930	C
Lake Erie College	OH	38,914	LC
Lake Forest College	IL	50,652	VC
Lakeland Univ	WI	35,130	C
Lamar Univ	TX	18,014	LC
Lander Univ	SC	43,994	C
Lane College	TN	16,550	C
Langston Univ	OK	14,314	C
Lasell College	MA	47,500	C
Lawrence Univ	WI	54,498	HC
Le Moyne College	NY	46,000	C
Lebanon Valley College	PA	51,530	C
Lee Univ	TN	22,045	C
Lees-McRae College	NC	33,944	C
Lehigh Univ	PA	61,010	MC
LeMoyne-Owen College	TN	16,980	C
Lenoir-Rhyne Univ	NC	43,200	C
LeTourneau Univ	TX	38,250	VC
Lewis & Clark College	OR	58,434	HC+
Lewis Univ	IL	40,370	C
Lewis-Clark State College	ID	14,202	C
Liberty Univ	VA	19,101	C
Limestone College	SC	32,100	C
Lincoln Memorial Univ	TN	28,070	C
Lindenwood Univ	MO	25,132	C
Lindsey Wilson College	KY	32,882	C
Linfield College	OR	52,010	C
Lipscomb Univ	TN	41,296	VC
LIU Brooklyn	NY	49,682	C
LIU Post	NY	49,682	C
Livingstone College	NC	17,815	LC
Lock Haven Univ of Pennsylvania	PA	18,028	LC
Longwood Univ	VA	22,184	C
Loras College	IA	39,222	C
Louisiana College	LA	21,886	C
Louisiana State Univ and A&M College	LA	18,677	VC
Louisiana State Univ in Shreveport	LA	6,902	C
Louisiana Tech Univ	LA	11,422	VC
Lourdes Univ	OH	29,520	NC
Loyola Marymount Univ	CA	58,038	HC
Loyola Univ Chicago	IL	55,802	VC
Loyola Univ Maryland	MD	60,300	VC
Loyola Univ New Orleans	LA	51,708	VC+
Lubbock Christian Univ	TX	28,426	C
Luther College	IA	48,540	C+
Lycoming College	PA	48,580	C
Lynchburg College	VA	46,740	C
Lyon College	AR	34,730	C+
Macalester College	MN	61,905	MC
MacMurray College	IL	33,620	C
Madonna Univ	MI	29,050	C
Malone Univ	OH	38,448	C
Manchester Univ	IN	40,422	C
Manhattan College	NY	51,750	C+
Manhattanville College	NY	51,440	C+
Mansfield Univ	PA	23,376	LC
Marian Univ	IN	41,220	C
Marian Univ	WI	32,420	LC
Marietta College	OH	46,190	C
Marist College	NY	49,860	VC
Marquette Univ	WI	48,390	VC+
Mars Hill Univ	NC	42,688	C
Marshall Univ	WV	17,242	C
Martin Univ	IN	20,264	LC
Mary Baldwin Univ	VA	39,865	C
Marygrove College	MI	28,926	NC
Marymount Manhattan College	NY	46,280	VC
Marymount Univ	VA	41,570	LC
Maryville College	TN	44,410	C
Maryville Univ of St. Louis	MO	38,046	VC+
Marywood Univ	PA	46,900	C
Mass College of Liberal Arts	MA	20,128	C
Mass Inst of Technology	MA	62,662	MC
Mayville State Univ	ND	18,371	NC
McDaniel College	MD	51,380	VC
McKendree Univ	IL	37,940	C+
McMurry Univ	TX	34,259	LC
McNeese State Univ	LA	7,838	C
McPherson College	KS	34,909	C
Mercer Univ	GA	45,348	VC
Mercy College	NY	31,776	C
Mercyhurst Univ	PA	47,420	C
Meredith College	NC	45,297	C
Merrimack College	MA	52,770	C
Messiah College	PA	43,100	C+
Methodist Univ	NC	43,600	C
Metropolitan State Univ	MN	7,566	C
Metropolitan State Univ of Denver	CO	29,889	LC
Miami Univ	OH	27,190	HC+
Mich State Univ	MI	23,898	VC+
Mich Tech Univ	MI	24,739	VC+
MidAmerica Nazarene Univ	KS	35,550	C
Middle Tenn State Univ	TN	8,650	C
Middlebury College	VT	64,332	MC
Midland Univ	NE	37,468	
Midwestern State Univ	TX	17,572	C
Miles College	AL	18,646	NC
Millersville Univ of Pennsylvania	PA	23,782	C
Milligan College	TN	38,150	C
Millikin Univ	IL	42,158	C
Mills College	CA	59,163	VC
Millsaps College	MS	50,080	C+
Minn State Univ, Mankato	MN	15,616	C
Minn State Univ, Moorhead	MN	15,941	C
Minot State Univ	ND	12,732	C
Misericordia Univ	PA	43,840	C
Miss College	MS	25,850	C
Miss State Univ	MS	11,454	C+
Miss Univ for Women	MS	17,065	C
Miss Valley State Univ	MS	13,233	LC
Missouri Baptist Univ	MO	35,594	C
Missouri Southern State Univ	MO	12,499	C
Missouri State Univ	MO	15,190	C+
Missouri Univ of Science and Technology	MO	18,655	HC
Missouri Valley College	MO	28,150	C
Missouri Western State Univ	MO	16,741	
Molloy College	NY	40,440	C
Monmouth College	IL	42,260	C
Monmouth Univ	NJ	46,234	C
Montana State Univ	MT	15,500	C+
Montana State Univ-Billings	MT	22,960	C
Montana State Univ-Northern	MT	11,370	NC
Montclair State Univ	NJ	26,210	LC
Montreat College	NC	31,298	LC
Moravian College	PA	53,117	
Morehead State Univ	KY	17,422	C
Morehouse College	GA	40,064	C
Morgan State Univ	MD	17,190	LC
Morningside College	IA	36,865	C
Morris College	SC	18,500	LC
Mount Aloysius College	PA	29,976	C
Mount Holyoke College	MA	56,746	MC
Mount Marty College	SD	32,972	C
Mount Mary Univ	WI	34,650	LC
Mount Mercy Univ	IA	36,826	C
Mount St. Mary College	NY	42,061	C
Mount St. Joseph Univ	OH	33,880	C
Mount St. Mary's Univ	MD	51,610	C
Mount St. Mary's Univ - Chalon Campus	CA	43,897	VC+
Mount Vernon Nazarene Univ	OH	34,500	C
Muhlenberg College	PA	56,645	VC+
Murray State Univ	KY	16,998	C
Muskingum Univ	OH	35,966	C
National Univ	CA	14,730	LC
Nazareth College	NY	45,574	C
Nebr Wesleyan Univ	NE	38,140	C+
New College of Florida	FL	15,848	MC
New Jersey City Univ	NJ	21,456	LC
New Jersey Inst of Technology	NJ	29,569	VC
New Mexico Highlands Univ	NM	11,904	NC
New Mexico State Univ	NM	14,050	C
New York Univ	NY	65,860	MC
Newberry College	SC	34,550	C
Newman Univ	KS	35,390	C
Niagara Univ	NY	41,010	C
Nicholls State Univ	LA	10,534	C
Nichols College	MA	46,800	LC
Norfolk State Univ	VA	25,702	LC
N Car A&T State Univ	NC	13,365	LC
N Car Central Univ	NC	9,000	C
N Car State Univ	NC	19,515	HC+
N Car Wesleyan College	NC	39,200	C
North Central College	IL	48,712	VC
N Dak State Univ	ND	16,245	C
North Park Univ	IL	35,860	C
Northeastern Illinois Univ	IL	12,529	LC
Northeastern State Univ	OK	8,615	VC
Northeastern Univ	MA	62,703	MC
Northern Arizona Univ	AZ	20,246	VC
Northern Illinois Univ	IL	20,176	C
Northern Kentucky Univ	KY	16,486	C
Northern Mich Univ	MI	19,604	C
Northern State Univ	SD	14,505	C
Northland College	WI	41,103	C+
Northwest Missouri State Univ	MO	17,737	C
Northwest Nazarene Univ	ID	36,000	C
Northwest Univ	WA	35,876	VC
Northwestern College of Iowa	IA	38,400	C+
Northwestern Okla State Univ	OK	13,072	NC
Northwestern Univ	IL	66,344	MC
Norwich Univ	VT	28,212	C
Notre Dame College	OH	37,150	VC
Notre Dame de Namur Univ	CA	46,526	LC
Notre Dame of Maryland Univ	MD	46,465	VC
Nyack College	NY	34,050	NC
Oakland Univ	MI	20,763	C
Oakwood Univ	AL	43,758	C
Oberlin College	OH	66,012	MC
Occidental College	CA	65,530	MC
Oglala Lakota College	SD	15,050	NC
Oglethorpe Univ	GA	44,200	C+
Ohio Dominican Univ	OH	41,340	C+
Ohio Northern Univ	OH	44,050	VC
Ohio State Univ at Columbus	OH	21,703	HC+
Ohio State Univ at Lima	OH	7,140	C
Ohio State Univ at Mansfield	OH	13,160	C
Ohio State Univ at Marion	OH	7,140	C
Ohio State Univ at Newark	OH	7,140	C
Ohio Univ	OH	22,924	C
Ohio Valley Univ	WV	29,480	C
Ohio Wesleyan Univ	OH	49,460	VC
Okla Baptist Univ	OK	32,320	C
Okla Christian Univ	OK	27,650	VC
Okla City Univ	OK	40,476	VC
Okla Panhandle State Univ	OK	6,152	NC
Okla State Univ	OK	17,180	VC
Okla Wesleyan Univ	OK	33,206	C
Old Dominion Univ	VA	20,910	C
Olivet College	MI	36,110	LC
Olivet Nazarene Univ	IL	41,840	C
Oral Roberts Univ	OK	34,316	C
Oregon State Univ	OR	22,519	VC
Ottawa Univ	KS	36,074	VC
Otterbein Univ	OH	41,630	C
Ouachita Baptist Univ	AR	32,320	C
Our Lady of the Lake Univ	TX	35,012	LC
Pace Univ	NY	58,248	C
Pacific Lutheran Univ	WA	49,960	VC
Pacific Union College	CA	36,009	VC
Pacific Univ	OR	52,876	C
Paine College	GA	19,506	LC
Palm Beach Atlantic Univ	FL	39,720	C
Park Univ	MO	20,329	C
Penn State Erie/The Behrend College	PA	16,256	C
Penn State Univ/Altoona	PA	24,584	C
Pennsylvania State Univ - Univ Park	PA	29,760	HC
Pepperdine Univ	CA	74,460	HC+
Peru State College	NE	14,768	NC
Pfeiffer Univ	NC	39,695	LC
Piedmont College	GA	32,512	C
Pine Manor College	MA	41,660	LC
Pittsburg State Univ	KS	13,880	NC
Pitzer College	CA	66,192	MC
Plymouth State Univ	NH	23,180	LC
Point Loma Nazarene Univ	CA	43,450	C
Point Park Univ	PA	41,270	C
Pomona College	CA	64,957	MC
Pontifical Catholic Univ of PR	PR	10,534	
Portland State Univ	OR	19,443	C
Post Univ	CT	41,150	C
Prairie View A&M Univ	TX	15,205	LC
Prescott College	AZ	33,284	C
Princeton Univ	NJ	57,610	MC
Principia College	IL	39,010	C+
Providence College	RI	60,760	VC
Purdue Univ/Northwest	IN	15,038	C
Purdue Univ/West Lafayette	IN	20,032	MC
Queens Univ of Charlotte	NC	39,543	C
Quincy Univ	IL	36,998	C
Quinnipiac Univ	CT	59,110	C
Radford Univ	VA	19,027	LC
Ramapo College of New Jersey	NJ	25,338	C
Randolph College	VA	45,660	VC
Randolph-Macon College	VA	49,910	C
Reed College	OR	65,300	MC
Regis College	MA	51,920	C
Regis Univ	CO	44,520	C
Rhode Island College	RI	17,694	LC
Rhodes College	TN	51,900	HC
Rice Univ	TX	57,668	MC
Rider Univ	NJ	54,050	C
Ripon College	WI	46,911	C+
Rivier Univ	NH	40,410	VC
Roanoke College	VA	54,114	VC
Robert Morris Univ	PA	37,834	C
Roberts Wesleyan College	NY	38,306	C
Rochester College	MI	28,574	LC
Rockford Univ	IL	36,030	C
Rockhurst Univ	MO	29,220	C
Rocky Mountain College	MT	34,270	C
Roger Williams Univ	RI	46,296	C+
Rollins College	FL	58,670	HC
Roosevelt Univ	IL	40,651	VC
Rosemont College	PA	30,980	C
Rowan Univ	NJ	24,491	VC+
Russell Sage College	NY	39,370	C
Rutgers Univ - Camden	NJ	26,146	C
Rutgers Univ - New Brunswick	NJ	26,632	HC
Rutgers Univ - Newark	NJ	27,288	C
Sacred Heart Univ	CT	52,750	C
Saginaw Valley State Univ	MI	18,530	C
St. Anselm College	NH	52,560	C+
St. Augustine's Univ	NC	26,048	C
St. Francis Univ	PA	42,268	NC
St. John's Univ	MN	51,624	C
St. Joseph's College of Maine	ME	46,485	C
St. Joseph's Univ	PA	57,544	VC+
St. Leo Univ	FL	31,650	C
St. Louis Univ	MO	49,866	HC
St. Martin's Univ	WA	45,056	C
St. Mary's College	IN	50,600	C
St. Mary's College of Calif	CA	57,420	C
St. Mary's Univ of Minn	MN	41,210	VC
St. Michael's College	VT	51,725	VC+
St. Peter's Univ	NJ	49,192	C
St. Vincent College	PA	44,626	C
St. Xavier Univ	IL	43,310	C
Salem College	NC	37,694	HC
Salem State Univ	MA	17,303	LC
Salisbury Univ	MD	20,714	VC
Salve Regina Univ	RI	51,470	C
Sam Houston State Univ	TX	18,792	C
Samford Univ	AL	39,232	VC
San Diego Christian College	CA	39,068	C
San Diego State Univ	CA	21,896	C+
San Francisco State Univ	CA	18,514	LC
San Jose State Univ	CA	21,540	C
Sarah Lawrence College	NY	63,388	HC
Savannah State Univ	GA	15,631	C
Schreiner Univ	TX	34,626	LC
Scripps College	CA	66,664	MC
Seattle Pacific Univ	WA	47,439	C+
Seattle Univ	WA	50,811	VC+

ST = STATE $IS = IN-STATE COSTS SR = SELECTOR RATING

School	ST	$IS	SR
Seton Hall Univ	NJ	55,514	C
Seton Hill Univ	PA	46,972	C
Sewanee: The Univ of the South	TN	54,500	MC
Shenandoah Univ	VA	41,312	C
Shepherd Univ, West Virginia	WV	17,224	C
Shippensburg Univ of Pennsylvania	PA	23,208	C
Shorter Univ	GA	31,130	LC
Siena College	NY	48,916	C+
Siena Heights Univ	MI	32,040	C
Silver Lake College of the Holy Family	WI	36,290	LC
Simmons College	MA	53,090	VC
Simpson College	IA	43,839	VC
Simpson Univ	CA	33,700	C
Skidmore College	NY	64,214	HC
Slippery Rock Univ of Pennsylvania	PA	10,360	C
Smith College	MA	63,914	MC
Sonoma State Univ	CA	27,806	C
S Car State Univ	SC	20,805	LC
S Dak State Univ	SD	15,634	C
Southeast Missouri State Univ	MO	15,498	C
Southeastern Louisiana Univ	LA	16,237	C
Southeastern Okla State Univ	OK	11,875	C
Southeastern Univ	FL	31,765	C
Southern Adventist Univ	TN	27,600	C
Southern Arkansas Univ	AR	21,532	C
Southern Conn State Univ	CT	21,924	LC
Southern Illinois Univ Carbondale	IL	23,667	C
Southern Illinois Univ Edwardsville	IL	22,643	C
Southern Methodist Univ	TX	66,483	MC
Southern Nazarene Univ	OK	32,798	NC
Southern New Hampshire Univ	NH	43,198	C
Southern Oregon Univ	OR	19,117	C
Southern Univ and A&M College	LA	16,074	LC+
Southern Univ at New Orleans	LA	8,014	LC
Southern Vermont College	VT	34,670	LC
Southern Wesleyan Univ	SC	32,130	LC
Southwest Baptist Univ	MO	29,900	LC
Southwest Minn State Univ	MN	17,783	C
Southwestern Adventist Univ	TX	27,756	LC
Southwestern College	KS	31,531	C
Southwestern Okla State Univ	OK	11,790	C
Southwestern Univ	TX	50,720	VC
Spelman College	GA	38,751	C
Spring Arbor Univ	MI	36,000	C
Spring Hill College	AL	48,488	C
Springfield College	MA	45,995	C
St. Ambrose Univ	IA	39,019	C
St. Ambrose Univ	IA	39,019	C
St. Bonaventure Univ	NY	44,237	C
St. Catherine Univ	MN	45,630	VC
St. Cloud State Univ	MN	10,600	C
St. Edward's Univ	TX	53,100	VC
St. Francis College	NY	38,800	LC
St. John Fisher College	NY	43,620	C
St. John's College-Annapolis	MD	60,142	MC
St. John's Univ	NY	55,850	C
St. Joseph's College, New York/Brooklyn Campus	NY	25,114	LC
St. Joseph's College, New York/Long Island Campus	NY	25,124	C
St. Lawrence Univ	NY	64,390	VC
St. Mary's College of Maryland	MD	26,634	VC
St. Mary's Univ	TX	37,500	C
St. Norbert College	WI	44,525	VC
St. Olaf College	MN	54,260	HC+
St. Thomas Aquinas College	NY	42,200	C
St. Thomas Univ	FL	36,360	LC
Stanford Univ	CA	60,409	MC
SUNY / Buffalo State College	NY	20,842	C
SUNY / Empire State College	NY	9,145	SP
SUNY / SUNY College at Old Westbury	NY	16,860	C
SUNY / SUNY Cortland	NY	20,706	VC
SUNY / SUNY Fredonia	NY	20,818	C
SUNY / SUNY Oneonta	NY	19,712	C+
SUNY / SUNY Plattsburgh	NY	18,814	C
SUNY / SUNY Potsdam	NY	20,404	C+
SUNY / Univ at Buffalo	NY	23,122	C+
SUNY at Binghamton	NY	22,861	MC
SUNY at Geneseo	NY	20,440	VC+
SUNY at New Paltz	NY	19,200	C
SUNY at Oswego	NY	21,351	C
SUNY at Purchase	NY	17,900	C
SUNY SUNY Albany	NY	22,165	C
Stephen F. Austin State Univ	TX	18,406	LC
Sterling College	KS	32,830	C
Stetson Univ	FL	53,544	VC
Stevens Inst of Technology	NJ	62,338	MC
Stevenson Univ	MD	72,770	C
Stillman College	AL	20,738	C
Stockton Univ	NJ	25,059	
Stonehill College	MA	55,030	C+
Stony Brook Univ/The SUNY	NY	21,881	MC
Suffolk Univ	MA	50,308	C
Sul Ross State Univ	TX	15,021	LC
Susquehanna Univ	PA	55,340	VC
Swarthmore College	PA	63,550	MC
Syracuse Univ	NY	60,239	VC
Tabor College	KS	35,870	C
Talladega College	AL	19,215	C
Tarleton State Univ	TX	15,248	LC
Taylor Univ	IN	40,317	C+
Temple Univ	PA	24,392	VC
Tenn State Univ	TN	14,423	C
Tenn Tech Univ	TN	17,050	C
Texas A&M Univ	TX	20,521	VC+
Texas A&M Univ at Commerce	TX	10,496	C
Texas A&M Univ at Corpus Christi	TX	16,851	LC
Texas A&M Univ at Kingsville	TX	7,500	LC
Texas Christian Univ	TX	54,670	HC
Texas Lutheran Univ	TX	38,620	C
Texas Southern Univ	TX	18,212	LC
Texas State Univ	TX	19,350	C
Texas Tech Univ	TX	18,736	C+
Texas Wesleyan Univ	TX	35,134	C
Texas Woman's Univ	TX	15,302	LC
The Catholic Univ of America	DC	56,356	VC
The Citadel, The Military College of S Car	SC	35,339	C
The College at Brockport - SUNY	NY	20,346	C
The College of Idaho	ID	36,415	C
The College of New Jersey	NJ	31,909	HC
The College of New Rochelle	NY	46,300	VC
The College of St. Rose	NY	43,048	C
The College of Wooster	OH	57,900	VC+
The Evergreen State College	WA	16,599	C
The Lincoln Univ	PA	15,154	NC
The Master's Univ	CA	43,870	C+
The Univ of Akron	OH	21,477	C
The Univ of Tenn at Chattanooga	TN	16,744	C
The Univ of Tenn at Knoxville	TN	22,112	VC
The Univ of Tenn at Martin	TN	14,876	C
The Univ of Utah	UT	17,924	VC
The Univ of Virginia's College at Wise	VA	18,192	LC
Thiel College	PA	41,590	C
Thomas Edison State Univ	NJ	6,350	NC
Thomas More College	KY	36,720	C
Tiffin Univ	OH	31,380	C
Toccoa Falls College	GA	27,920	C
Tougaloo College	MS	17,980	NC
Touro College	NY	28,950	VC
Towson Univ	MD	17,408	VC
Transylvania Univ	KY	45,690	VC+
Trevecca Nazarene Univ	TN	31,186	C
Trinity Christian College	IL	35,580	C
Trinity College	CT	63,920	HC+
Trinity International Univ	IL	31,070	VC
Trinity Univ	TX	52,314	HC+
Trinity Washington Univ	DC	33,826	C+
Troy Univ	AL	16,171	C
Truman State Univ	MO	16,014	HC
Tufts Univ	MA		MC
Tulane Univ	LA	63,396	HC+
Tusculum College	TN	31,625	C
Tuskegee Univ	AL	28,164	C
Union College	KY	32,310	C
Union College	NE	23,270	C
Union College	NY	64,320	MC
Union Univ	TN	33,970	VC
United States Air Force Academy	CO		C
United States Military Academy at West Point	NY		HC+
United States Naval Academy	MD		MC
Universidad Adventista de las Antillas	PR	16,606	
Universidad del Turabo	PR	17,828	
Univ of Alabama	AL	24,320	C+
Univ of Alabama at Birmingham	AL	19,906	C
Univ of Alabama in Huntsville	AL	19,445	VC
Univ of Alaska Anchorage	AK	16,652	NC
Univ of Alaska Fairbanks	AK	16,179	C
Univ of Arizona	AZ	23,100	C
Univ of Arkansas at Fayetteville	AR	19,152	C+
Univ of Arkansas at Little Rock	AR	18,211	C
Univ of Arkansas at Monticello	AR	13,134	NC
Univ of Arkansas at Pine Bluff	AR	13,541	C
Univ of Calif at Berkeley	CA	28,853	MC
Univ of Calif at Davis	CA	28,468	HC
Univ of Calif at Irvine	CA	26,484	VC
Univ of Calif at Los Angeles	CA	30,162	MC
Univ of Calif at Riverside	CA	29,227	C+
Univ of Calif at Santa Barbara	CA	29,091	HC
Univ of Calif San Diego	CA	30,150	MC
Univ of Calif, Santa Cruz	CA	28,731	C+
Univ of Central Arkansas	AR	14,472	VC
Univ of Central Florida	FL	15,922	VC
Univ of Central Missouri	MO	18,982	C
Univ of Central Okla	OK	13,486	C
Univ of Charleston	WV	35,000	C
Univ of Chicago	IL	67,584	MC
Univ of Cincinnati	OH	21,964	VC
Univ of Colo Boulder	CO	24,285	VC+
Univ of Colo Colo Springs	CO	19,663	C
Univ of Colo Denver	CO	23,230	C
Univ of Conn	CT	25,538	HC
Univ of Dallas	TX	45,500	VC+
Univ of Dayton	OH	53,620	C
Univ of Delaware	DE	24,976	VC+
Univ of Denver	CO	58,443	VC+
Univ of Detroit Mercy	MI	48,816	C+
Univ of Evansville	IN	44,186	VC+
Univ of Findlay	OH	60,139	C
Univ of Florida	FL	16,291	HC+
Univ of Georgia	GA	21,250	HC
Univ of Great Falls	MT	38,524	C
Univ of Hartford	CT	49,776	C
Univ of Hawaii at Hilo	HI	18,038	C
Univ of Hawaii at Manoa	HI	23,221	C
Univ of Holy Cross	LA	21,523	C
Univ of Houston-Downtown	TX	7,241	C
Univ of Idaho	ID	15,348	C
Univ of Illinois at Chicago	IL	25,006	VC
Univ of Illinois at Urbana-Champaign	IL	27,006	HC
Univ of Indianapolis	IN	36,480	C
Univ of Iowa	IA	18,683	VC+
Univ of Jamestown	ND	28,508	C
Univ of Kansas	KS	20,135	C+
Univ of Kentucky	KY	33,306	C
Univ of La Verne	CA	55,600	C
Univ of Louisiana at Lafayette	LA	14,516	C
Univ of Louisiana at Monroe	LA	15,970	C
Univ of Louisville	KY	19,824	C
Univ of Maine	ME	20,792	C
Univ of Maine at Farmington	ME	18,187	C
Univ of Mary Hardin-Baylor	TX	33,950	C+
Univ of Mary Washington	VA	24,764	VC
Univ of Maryland/Baltimore County	MD	21,296	VC
Univ of Maryland/College Park	MD	21,938	HC
Univ of Maryland/Eastern Shore	MD	17,013	C
Univ of Maryland/Univ College	MD	25,966	LC
Univ of Mass Amherst	MA	26,199	VC+
Univ of Mass Boston	MA	13,435	C
Univ of Mass Dartmouth	MA	25,658	C
Univ of Mass Lowell	MA	26,380	C
Univ of Memphis	TN	18,278	C
Univ of Miami	FL	63,494	MC
Univ of Mich/Ann Arbor	MI	24,410	MC
Univ of Mich/Dearborn	MI	11,757	VC
Univ of Mich-Flint	MI	17,607	C+
Univ of Minn/Duluth	MN	20,292	C+
Univ of Minn/Morris	MN	20,760	VC
Univ of Minn/Twin Cities	MN	23,519	HC+
Univ of Miss	MS	17,746	C+
Univ of Missouri/Columbia	MO	18,201	MC
Univ of Missouri-Kansas City	MO	19,563	VC
Univ of Missouri-St. Louis	MO		C
Univ of Mobile	AL	28,935	C
Univ of Montana	MT	14,105	C
Univ of Montana-Western	MT	11,220	LC
Univ of Montevallo	AL	19,502	C
Univ of Mount Olive	NC	18,426	C
Univ of Mount Union	OH	38,970	C
Univ of Nebr - Kearney	NE	16,546	LC
Univ of Nebr - Lincoln	NE	18,589	VC
Univ of Nebr - Omaha	NE	16,120	C
Univ of Nevada, Las Vegas	NV	17,553	C
Univ of Nevada/Reno	NV	18,010	C
Univ of New England	ME	48,880	C
Univ of New Hampshire	NH	28,562	VC
Univ of New Hampshire - Manchester	NH	14,490	C
Univ of New Haven	CT	52,190	C
Univ of New Mexico	NM	15,404	C
Univ of New Orleans	LA	12,840	C
Univ of North Alabama	AL	15,398	C
Univ of N Car at Asheville	NC	15,723	VC+
Univ of N Car at Chapel Hill	NC	20,052	HC+
Univ of N Car at Charlotte	NC	15,547	C
Univ of N Car at Greensboro	NC	14,690	C
Univ of N Car at Pembroke	NC	14,388	LC
Univ of N Car at Wilmington	NC	14,590	VC
Univ of N Dak	ND	15,373	C
Univ of North Florida	FL	15,996	VC
Univ of North Georgia	GA	17,316	C
Univ of North Texas	TX	19,198	C
Univ of Northern Colo	CO	20,851	C
Univ of Northwestern - St. Paul	MN	38,160	C
Univ of Notre Dame	IN	64,043	MC
Univ of Okla	OK	18,911	VC
Univ of Oregon	OR	22,972	C
Univ of Pennsylvania	PA	63,526	MC
Univ of Pikeville	KY	28,700	NC
Univ of Pittsburgh	PA	29,568	HC+
Univ of Pittsburgh at Bradford	PA	22,402	C
Univ of Pittsburgh at Johnstown	PA	22,092	C
Univ of Portland	OR	52,152	VC
Univ of PR, at Cayey	PR		
Univ of PR, at Mayaguez	PR	13,995	
Univ of PR-Rio Piedras campus	PR	13,327	
Univ of Puget Sound	WA	56,456	VC+
Univ of Redlands	CA	60,200	VC
Univ of Rhode Island	RI	24,906	C
Univ of Richmond	VA	60,880	MC
Univ of Rio Grande & Rio Grande Community College	OH	8,750	NC
Univ of Rochester	NY	65,032	MC
Univ of St. Francis	IN	37,400	C
Univ of St. Joseph	CT	49,550	C
Univ of St. Mary	KS	34,690	C
Univ of San Diego	CA	58,442	VC+
Univ of San Francisco	CA	58,484	VC
Univ of Science and Arts of Okla	OK	11,140	VC
Univ of Scranton	PA	54,962	VC
Univ of Sioux Falls	SD	34,330	C
Univ of South Alabama	AL	16,400	C
Univ of S Car Aiken	SC	16,712	C
Univ of S Car at Columbia	SC	19,725	VC+
Univ of S Car Upstate	SC	18,200	LC
Univ of S Dak	SD	16,109	C
Univ of South Florida/St. Petersburg	FL	15,980	C
Univ of South Florida/Tampa	FL	16,110	VC+
Univ of Southern Calif	CA	66,631	C
Univ of Southern Indiana	IN	16,501	C
Univ of Southern Maine	ME	18,320	C
Univ of Southern Miss	MS	13,170	C
Univ of St. Francis	IL	39,924	C
Univ of St. Thomas - Houston	TX	40,020	VC
Univ of Tampa	FL	36,944	C
Univ of Texas at Arlington	TX	18,026	LC
Univ of Texas at Austin	TX	26,102	HC
Univ of Texas at Dallas	TX	22,830	VC+
Univ of Texas at El Paso	TX	34,452	NC
Univ of Texas at San Antonio	TX	20,157	C
Univ of the Cumberlands	KY	32,000	C
Univ of the District of Columbia	DC	21,044	LC
Univ of the Incarnate Word	TX	39,162	LC
Univ of the Ozarks	AR	52,176	C
Univ of the Pacific	CA	57,006	VC
Univ of the Southwest	NM	22,766	C
Univ of Toledo	OH	19,336	NC
Univ of Tulsa	OK	52,625	HC+
Univ of Vermont	VT	28,878	HC
Univ of Virginia	VA	25,891	MC
Univ of Washington	WA	23,149	VC
Univ of West Alabama	AL	15,516	NC
Univ of West Florida	FL	15,848	C
Univ of West Georgia	GA	16,360	LC
Univ of Wisc-Eau Claire	WI	15,797	VC
Univ of Wisc-Green Bay	WI	15,064	C
Univ of Wisc-La Crosse	WI	15,247	C+
Univ of Wisc-Madison	WI	20,934	MC
Univ of Wisc-Milwaukee	WI	21,496	C
Univ of Wisc-Oshkosh	WI	15,200	C
Univ of Wisc-Parkside	WI	15,193	C
Univ of Wisc-Platteville	WI	14,614	VC
Univ of Wisc-River Falls	WI	14,485	C
Univ of Wisc-Stevens Point	WI	14,043	C
Univ of Wisc-Superior	WI	14,446	C
Univ of Wisc-Whitewater	WI	13,976	C
Univ of Wyoming	WY	15,375	C+
Urbana Univ	OH	30,820	C
Ursinus College	PA	61,690	VC
Ursuline College	OH	41,076	LC
Utah State Univ	UT	12,736	C
Utica College	NY	30,430	C
Valley City State Univ	ND	13,267	C
Valparaiso Univ	IN	48,370	C+
Vanderbilt Univ	TN	60,572	MC
Vanguard Univ of Southern Calif	CA	40,740	VC
Vassar College	NY	65,491	MC
Villanova Univ	PA	62,523	MC
Virginia Commonwealth Univ	VA	23,049	C
Virginia Military Inst	VA	26,460	C+
Virginia Polytechnic Inst and State Univ	VA	21,276	HC
Virginia State Univ	VA	19,802	C+
Virginia Union Univ	VA	22,421	C
Virginia Wesleyan College	VA	43,728	LC
Viterbo Univ	WI	34,660	C
Wabash College	IN	50,650	VC
Wagner College	NY	55,480	C+
Wake Forest Univ	NC	64,056	MC
Walla Walla Univ	WA	30,417	NC
Walsh Univ	OH	39,010	C
Warner Pacific College	OR	33,790	C
Warner Univ	FL	28,216	C
Warren Wilson College	NC	44,220	VC
Wartburg College	IA	47,840	C
Washburn Univ	KS	15,827	C
Washington & Jefferson College	PA	56,512	VC
Washington Adventist Univ	MD	31,440	LC
Washington and Lee Univ	VA	59,647	MC
Washington College	MD	54,666	VC
Washington State Univ	WA	22,495	C
Washington Univ in St. Louis	MO	65,366	VC
Wayland Baptist Univ	TX	22,356	LC
Wayne State College	NE	12,802	C
Wayne State Univ	MI	22,016	C
Waynesburg Univ	PA	32,290	C
Weber State Univ	UT	10,721	C
Webster Univ	MO	37,490	C
Wellesley College	MA	63,916	MC
Wells College	NY	50,500	C

ST = STATE **$IS** = IN-STATE COSTS **SR** = SELECTOR RATING

School	ST	$IS	SR
Wesley College	DE	37,026	LC
Wesleyan College	GA	29,694	C+
Wesleyan Univ	CT	65,516	MC
West Chester Univ of Pennsylvania	PA	18,456	C
West Liberty Univ	WV	15,512	C
West Texas A&M Univ	TX	13,478	C
West Virginia State Univ	WV	8,378	NC
West Virginia Univ	WV	18,210	C
West Virginia Univ Inst of Technology	WV	16,462	NC
West Virginia Wesleyan College	WV	36,858	C
Western Carolina Univ	NC	13,965	C
Western Conn State Univ	CT	21,254	LC
Western Illinois Univ	IL	20,825	C
Western Kentucky Univ	KY	16,850	C
Western Mich Univ	MI	21,054	C
Western New England Univ	MA	48,088	C
Western New Mexico Univ	NM	16,734	LC
Western Oregon Univ	OR	15,021	LC
Western State Colo Univ	CO	18,639	C
Western Washington Univ	WA	18,003	C+
Westfield State Univ	MA	19,671	C
Westminster College	MO	32,820	C
Westminster College	PA	39,180	C+
Westminster College	UT	41,078	C+
Westmont College	CA	56,410	HC
Wheaton College	IL	43,610	MC
Wheaton College	MA	61,512	VC
Wheeling Jesuit Univ	WV	37,106	LC
Whitman College	WA	59,772	MC
Whittier College	CA	57,891	C
Whitworth Univ	WA	51,732	VC
Wichita State Univ	KS	21,643	C
Widener Univ	PA	56,486	C
Wiley College	TX	18,504	C
Wilkes Univ	PA	45,622	C
Willamette Univ	OR	61,817	VC+
William Carey Univ	MS	23,950	LC
William Jewell College	MO	41,210	C+
William Paterson Univ of New Jersey	NJ	23,133	C
William Penn Univ	IA	26,000	C
William Woods Univ	MO	32,040	C
Williams Baptist College	AR	24,720	C
Williams College	MA	63,290	MC
Wilmington College	OH	34,600	C
Wilson College	PA	35,620	C
Wingate Univ	NC	39,950	C
Winona State Univ	MN	17,535	C
Winston-Salem State Univ	NC	26,166	LC
Winthrop Univ	SC	23,082	C
Wisc Lutheran College	WI	36,290	VC
Wittenberg Univ	OH	48,156	C+
Wofford College	SC	49,885	VC
Woodbury Univ	CA	46,958	C
Worcester State Univ	MA	20,977	C
Wright State Univ	OH	16,983	C
Xavier Univ	OH	47,880	C+
Xavier Univ of Louisiana	LA	31,689	C+
Yale Univ	CT	64,650	MC
Yeshiva Univ	NY	47,250	VC+
York College	NE	24,300	C
York College of Pennsylvania	PA	29,240	C
Youngstown State Univ	OH	17,307	C

HISTORY AND POLITICAL SCIENCE

School	ST	$IS	SR
Black Hills State Univ	SD	15,899	C
Bridgewater College	VA	44,510	C
Bryant Univ	RI	55,646	VC
Corban Univ	OR	40,306	C
Indiana Univ Kokomo	IN	7,073	C
Mount St. Mary College	NY	42,061	C
North Greenville Univ	SC	25,930	C+
Okla Christian Univ	OK	27,650	VC
Univ of N Car at Asheville	NC	15,723	VC+
Western Illinois Univ	IL	20,825	C

HISTORY EDUCATION

School	ST	$IS	SR
Augustana College	IL	49,658	VC
Bloomfield College	NJ	39,100	LC
East Texas Baptist Univ	TX	33,134	C
Elon Univ	NC	44,599	VC+
Ferris State Univ	MI	21,445	C
Georgetown College	KY	41,440	C
Hope College	MI	39,940	VC
Huntingdon College	AL	34,900	C
King Univ	TN	34,660	C
Marist College	NY	49,860	VC
Mount Ida College	MA	46,820	C
Mount Mary Univ	WI	34,650	LC
Murray State Univ	KY	16,998	C
Nyack College	NY	34,050	NC
Shorter Univ	GA	31,130	LC
Southwestern Okla State Univ	OK	11,790	C
The Univ of Utah	UT	17,924	VC
Weber State Univ	UT	10,721	C

HISTORY OF ARCHITECTURE / URBAN DEVELOPMENT

School	ST	$IS	SR
Brown Univ	RI	64,566	MC
Univ of Illinois at Chicago	IL	25,006	VC

HISTORY OF PHILOSOPHY

School	ST	$IS	SR
Colo College	CO	62,560	MC
Univ of Pittsburgh	PA	29,568	HC+

HISTORY OF SCIENCE

School	ST	$IS	SR
Calif Inst of Technology	CA	58,761	MC
Case Western Reserve Univ	OH	60,304	MC
Georgia Inst of Technology	GA	23,360	MC
Johns Hopkins Univ	MD	65,386	MC
Univ of Jamestown	ND	28,508	C
Univ of Okla	OK	18,911	VC
Univ of Pennsylvania	PA	63,526	MC
Univ of Wisc-Madison	WI	20,934	MC
Yale Univ	CT	64,650	MC

HOME ECONOMICS

School	ST	$IS	SR
Ball State Univ	IN	19,590	C
Cal State, Fresno	CA	16,902	LC
CUNY/Queens College	NY	27,896	C
College of the Ozarks	MO	7,230	C
Florida State Univ	FL	16,771	HC
Harding Univ	AR	25,421	C
Illinois State Univ	IL	23,418	VC
Indiana State Univ	IN	23,223	LC
Langston Univ	OK	14,314	C
Montclair State Univ	NJ	26,210	LC
Morgan State Univ	MD	17,190	LC
Oakwood Univ	AL	43,758	C
SUNY / SUNY Oneonta	NY	19,712	C+
SUNY / SUNY Plattsburgh	NY	18,814	C
Tarleton State Univ	TX	15,248	LC
Texas A&M Univ at Kingsville	TX	7,500	LC
The Master's Univ	CA	43,870	C+
Univ of Florida	FL	16,291	HC+
Univ of Maryland/Eastern Shore	MD	17,013	C
Univ of PR-Rio Piedras campus	PR	13,327	
Utah State Univ	UT	12,736	C
Virginia State Univ	VA	19,802	C+

HOME ECONOMICS EDUCATION

School	ST	$IS	SR
Alabama A&M Univ	AL	18,796	C
Ashland Univ	OH	21,440	C
Auburn Univ	AL	23,594	VC+
Ball State Univ	IN	19,590	C
Baylor Univ	TX	53,760	HC
Bluffton Univ	OH	40,950	C
Brigham Young Univ	UT	12,748	HC
Cal State, Northridge	CA	16,859	LC
Carson-Newman Univ	TN	34,160	C
Central Washington Univ	WA	16,803	C
Cheyney Univ of Pennsylvania	PA	20,896	LC
Concordia Univ Nebr	NE	36,280	VC
Delaware State Univ	DE	19,376	NC
East Carolina Univ	NC	16,937	C
Eastern Kentucky Univ	KY	16,908	C
Eastern New Mexico Univ	NM	14,416	C
Florida State Univ	FL	16,771	HC
Fort Valley State Univ	GA	17,988	VC
Indiana State Univ	IN	23,223	LC
Jacksonville State Univ	AL	14,628	LC
Langston Univ	OK	14,314	C
Mercyhurst Univ	PA	47,420	C
Montclair State Univ	NJ	26,210	LC
Murray State Univ	KY	16,998	C
New Mexico State Univ	NM	14,050	C
N Car A&T State Univ	NC	13,365	LC
N Dak State Univ	ND	16,245	C
Oakwood Univ	AL	43,758	C
Pittsburg State Univ	KS	13,880	NC
Pontifical Catholic Univ of PR	PR	10,534	
San Francisco State Univ	CA	18,514	LC
Seattle Pacific Univ	WA	47,439	C+
Seton Hill Univ	PA	46,972	C
Shepherd Univ, West Virginia	WV	17,224	C
S Car State Univ	SC	20,805	LC
S Dak State Univ	SD	15,634	C
St. Catherine Univ	MN	45,630	VC
SUNY / SUNY Oneonta	NY	19,712	C+
Tarleton State Univ	TX	15,248	LC
Tenn Tech Univ	TN	17,050	C
The Univ of Akron	OH	21,477	C
Univ of Arkansas at Pine Bluff	AR	13,541	C
Univ of Louisiana at Lafayette	LA	14,516	C
Univ of Maryland/Eastern Shore	MD	17,013	C
Univ of Minn/Twin Cities	MN	23,519	HC+
Univ of Montevallo	AL	19,502	C
Univ of Nebr - Lincoln	NE	18,589	VC
Univ of North Alabama	AL	15,398	C
Univ of Southern Miss	MS	13,170	C
Univ of Wisc-Stout	WI	19,667	C
Utah State Univ	UT	12,736	C
Wayne State College	NE	12,802	C
Western Kentucky Univ	KY	16,850	C

HOME FURNISHINGS AND EQUIPMENT MANAGEMENT/ PRODUCTION/SERVICES

School	ST	$IS	SR
Auburn Univ	AL	23,594	VC+
Fashion Inst of Technology/ SUNY	NY	18,521	SP
Univ of Georgia	GA	21,250	HC
Univ of North Texas	TX	19,198	C

HOMELAND SECURITY

School	ST	$IS	SR
American Univ of PR	PR	16,130	
Angelo State Univ	TX	15,263	NC
Cal State, Sacramento	CA	20,332	C
Daniel Webster College	NH	26,984	C
Embry-Riddle Aeronautical Univ - Daytona Beach	FL	44,712	VC
Excelsior College	NY	14,080	SP
Marian Univ	WI	32,420	LC
Mitchell College	CT	43,280	C
Monmouth Univ	NJ	46,234	C
St. Leo Univ	FL	31,650	C
Savannah State Univ	GA	15,631	C
SUNY SUNY Albany	NY	22,165	C
Tiffin Univ	OH	31,380	C
Univ of New Hampshire - Manchester	NH	14,490	C
Virginia Commonwealth Univ	VA	23,049	C
Westminster College	UT	41,078	C+

HOMELAND SECURITY/ EMERGENCY PREPAREDNESS

School	ST	$IS	SR
Ashford Univ	CA	10,480	C
Auburn Univ at Montgomery	AL	15,290	C
La Roche College	PA	37,924	LC
Mass Maritime Academy	MA	19,982	C
Pennsylvania State Univ - Univ Park	PA	29,760	HC
St. Louis Univ	MO	49,866	HC
SUNY SUNY Albany	NY	22,165	C
Thomas Edison State Univ	NJ	6,350	NC
Tulane Univ	LA	63,396	HC+
Univ of Alaska Fairbanks	AK	16,179	C

HORTICULTURE

School	ST	$IS	SR
Alabama A&M Univ	AL	18,796	C
Andrews Univ	MI	28,030	C+
Auburn Univ	AL	23,594	VC+
Clemson Univ	SC		HC
College of the Ozarks	MO	7,230	C
Colo State Univ	CO	22,162	VC
Delaware Valley Univ	PA	49,796	C
Eastern Kentucky Univ	KY	16,908	C
Farmingdale State College	NY	20,624	C
Ferrum College	VA	39,650	C
Florida A&M Univ	FL	15,361	C
Fort Valley State Univ	GA	17,988	VC
Iowa State Univ	IA	17,570	C
Kansas State Univ	KS	17,780	VC
Mich State Univ	MI	23,898	VC+
Miss State Univ	MS	11,454	C+
Montana State Univ	MT	15,500	C+
Murray State Univ	KY	16,998	C
New Mexico State Univ	NM	14,050	C
N Car State Univ	NC	19,515	HC+
N Dak State Univ	ND	16,245	C
Northwest Missouri State Univ	MO	17,737	C
Okla State Univ	OK	17,180	VC
Oregon State Univ	OR	22,519	VC
Purdue Univ/West Lafayette	IN	20,032	MC
Sam Houston State Univ	TX	18,792	C
S Dak State Univ	SD	15,634	C
Southeast Missouri State Univ	MO	15,498	C
Southern Illinois Univ Carbondale	IL	23,667	C
Stephen F. Austin State Univ	TX	18,406	LC
Tarleton State Univ	TX	15,248	LC
Temple Univ	PA	24,392	VC
Texas A&M Univ	TX	20,521	VC+
Truman State Univ	MO	16,014	HC
Tuskegee Univ	AL	28,164	C
Univ of Arkansas at Fayetteville	AR	19,152	C+
Univ of Cincinnati	OH	21,964	VC
Univ of Conn	CT	25,538	HC
Univ of Florida	FL	16,291	HC+
Univ of Georgia	GA	21,250	HC
Univ of Idaho	ID	15,348	C
Univ of Illinois at Urbana-Champaign	IL	27,006	HC
Univ of Maine	ME	20,792	C
Univ of Minn Crookston	MN	19,739	C
Univ of Nebr - Lincoln	NE	18,589	VC
Univ of PR, at Mayaguez	PR	13,995	
Univ of Wisc-Madison	WI	20,934	MC
Univ of Wisc-Platteville	WI	14,614	VC
Univ of Wisc-River Falls	WI	14,485	C
Virginia Polytechnic Inst and State Univ	VA	21,276	HC
Washington State Univ	WA	22,495	C
West Virginia Univ	WV	18,210	C
Western Kentucky Univ	KY	16,850	C

HOSPICE CARE

School	ST	$IS	SR
Madonna Univ	MI	29,050	C

HOSPITAL ADMINISTRATION

School	ST	$IS	SR
Missouri State Univ	MO	15,190	C+
Thomas Edison State Univ	NJ	6,350	NC
Univ of Minn/Duluth	MN	20,292	C+
Univ of Wisc-Milwaukee	WI	21,496	C

HOSPITALITY MANAGEMENT SERVICES

School	ST	$IS	SR
Appalachian State Univ	NC	14,416	VC
Arkansas Tech Univ	AR	15,484	C
Ashford Univ	CA	10,480	C
Boston Univ	MA	65,110	MC
Brigham Young Univ/Hawaii	HI	11,290	C
Central Conn State Univ	CT	21,203	C
Central Mich Univ	MI	20,330	C
CUNY/College of Technology	NY	6,669	NC
College of Charleston	SC	22,699	C
Colo Mesa Univ	CO	18,955	LC
Colo State Univ	CO	22,162	VC
Concordia Univ, Ann Arbor	MI	35,945	VC
Dallas Baptist Univ	TX	33,713	C
Davis & Elkins College	WV	38,242	LC
DePaul Univ	IL	47,623	VC
East Carolina Univ	NC	16,937	C
Eastern Mich Univ	MI	19,761	C
Endicott College	MA	44,604	VC+
Ferris State Univ	MI	21,445	C
Florida Atlantic Univ	FL	17,339	C
Florida International Univ	FL	19,854	C+
Georgia State Univ	GA	24,332	VC
Harris-Stowe State Univ	MO	14,360	NC
Husson Univ	ME	25,720	LC
Indiana Univ of Pennsylvania	PA	23,614	LC
Indiana Univ-Purdue Univ Fort Wayne	IN	17,553	C
James Madison Univ	VA	19,084	VC
Johnson & Wales Univ/ Charlotte Campus	NC	43,988	C
Johnson & Wales Univ/ Denver Campus	CO	42,707	C
Johnson & Wales Univ/North Miami Campus	FL	42,707	C
Johnson & Wales Univ/ Providence Campus	RI	42,248	C
Johnson State College	VT	20,752	C
Kendall College	IL	32,610	C
Kent State Univ	OH	20,732	C
Lakeland Univ	WI	35,130	C
Lasell College	MA	47,500	C
Livingstone College	NC	17,815	LC
Madonna Univ	MI	29,050	C
Marywood Univ	PA	46,900	C
Metropolitan State Univ	MN	7,566	C
Metropolitan State Univ of Denver	CO	29,889	LC
Mich State Univ	MI	23,898	VC+
Mitchell College	CT	43,280	C
Monroe College	NY	23,660	C
Montclair State Univ	NJ	26,210	LC
Morgan State Univ	MD	17,190	LC
Mount Ida College	MA	46,820	C
New York Inst of Technology	NY	48,730	C
Norfolk State Univ	VA	25,702	LC
N Dak State Univ	ND	16,245	C
Ohio State Univ at Columbus	OH	21,703	HC+
Oregon State Univ	OR	22,519	VC
Pace Univ	NY	58,248	C
Pennsylvania State Univ - Univ Park	PA	29,760	HC
Purdue Univ/West Lafayette	IN	20,032	MC
Robert Morris Univ	PA	37,834	C
Rochester Inst of Technology	NY	50,842	HC
Rutgers Univ - Camden	NJ	26,146	C
St. Leo Univ	FL	31,650	C
San Diego State Univ	CA	21,896	C+
San Francisco State Univ	CA	18,514	LC
Southeast Missouri State Univ	MO	15,498	C
Southern Illinois Univ Carbondale	IL	23,667	C
Southern New Hampshire Univ	NH	43,198	C
Southern Oregon Univ	OR	19,117	C
St. John's Univ	NY	55,850	C
St. Joseph's College, New York/Brooklyn Campus	NY	25,114	LC
St. Joseph's College, New York/Long Island Campus	NY	25,124	C
St. Thomas Univ	FL	36,360	LC
SUNY / Buffalo State College	NY	20,842	C
Stephen F. Austin State Univ	TX	18,406	LC
Thomas Edison State Univ	NJ	6,350	NC
Tougaloo College	MS	17,980	NC
Tuskegee Univ	AL	28,164	C
Univ of Arkansas at Fayetteville	AR	19,152	C+
Univ of Central Florida	FL	15,922	VC
Univ of Denver	CO	58,443	VC+
Univ of Findlay	OH	60,139	C
Univ of Illinois at Urbana-Champaign	IL	27,006	HC
Univ of Mass Amherst	MA	26,199	VC+
Univ of Memphis	TN	18,278	C

School	ST	$IS	SR
Univ of Miss	MS	17,746	C+
Univ of Nebr - Lincoln	NE	18,589	VC
Univ of New Hampshire	NH	28,562	VC
Univ of New Haven	CT	52,190	C
Univ of N Car at Greensboro	NC	14,690	C
Univ of North Texas	TX	19,198	C
Univ of Pittsburgh at Bradford	PA	22,402	C
Univ of San Francisco	CA	58,484	VC
Univ of South Alabama	AL	16,400	C
Univ of Wisc-Stout	WI	19,667	C
Washington State Univ	WA	22,495	C
Webber International Univ	FL	31,904	C
Western Carolina Univ	NC	13,965	C
Western Illinois Univ	IL	20,825	C
Western Kentucky Univ	KY	16,850	C
Widener Univ	PA	56,486	C
Youngstown State Univ	OH	17,307	C

HOTEL AND RESTAURANT ADMINISTRATION

School	ST	$IS	SR
Cornell Univ	NY	64,853	MC
Ferris State Univ	MI	21,445	C
N Dak State Univ	ND	16,245	C
Rochester Inst of Technology	NY	50,842	HC
Southern Oregon Univ	OR	19,117	C
Washington State Univ	WA	22,495	C
Western Kentucky Univ	KY	16,850	C

HOTEL, RESTURANT/TOURISM MANAGEMENT

School	ST	$IS	SR
Boston Univ	MA	65,110	MC
East Stroudsburg Univ	PA	18,334	C

HOTEL/MOTEL AND RESTAURANT MANAGEMENT

School	ST	$IS	SR
Ashland Univ	OH	21,440	C
Auburn Univ	AL	23,594	VC+
Bethune-Cookman Univ	FL	22,970	C
Boston Univ	MA	65,110	MC
Calif State Polytechnic Univ, Pomona	CA	21,541	C
Cheyney Univ of Pennsylvania	PA	20,896	LC
College of the Ozarks	MO	7,230	C
Colo State Univ	CO	22,162	VC
Concord Univ	WV	14,954	C
Delaware State Univ	DE	19,376	NC
Drexel Univ	PA	65,432	VC+
Eastern Mich Univ	MI	19,761	C
Endicott College	MA	44,604	VC+
Fairleigh Dickinson Univ/ College at Florham	NJ	52,062	C
Fairleigh Dickinson Univ/ Metropolitan Campus	NJ	40,254	C
Ferris State Univ	MI	21,445	C
Florida State Univ	FL	16,771	HC
Grambling State Univ	LA	15,701	C
Grand Valley State Univ	MI	22,250	C+
Inter-American Univ of PR- Aguadilla Campus	PR	21,657	
Iowa State Univ	IA	17,570	C
Johnson & Wales Univ/ Charlotte Campus	NC	43,988	C
Johnson & Wales Univ/ Denver Campus	CO	42,707	C
Johnson & Wales Univ/North Miami Campus	FL	42,707	C
Johnson & Wales Univ/ Providence Campus	RI	42,248	C
Kansas State Univ	KS	17,780	VC
Keiser Univ	FL	35,010	LC
Kendall College	IL	32,610	C
Mercyhurst Univ	PA	47,420	C
New Mexico State Univ	NM	14,050	C
New York Univ	NY	65,860	MC
Newbury College	MA	46,950	C
Niagara Univ	NY	41,010	C
N Car Wesleyan College	NC	39,200	C
N Dak State Univ	ND	16,245	C
Northern Arizona Univ	AZ	20,246	VC
Northwood Univ - Mich	MI	35,010	LC
Ohio Univ	OH	22,924	C
Okla State Univ	OK	17,180	VC
Purdue Univ/Northwest	IN	15,038	C
Rochester Inst of Technology	NY	50,842	HC
Roosevelt Univ	IL	40,651	VC
San Francisco State Univ	CA	18,514	LC
S Dak State Univ	SD	15,634	C
Southwest Minn State Univ	MN	17,783	C
SUNY / SUNY Plattsburgh	NY	18,814	C
Tenn State Univ	TN	14,423	C
Texas Tech Univ	TX	18,736	C+
The Univ of Tenn at Knoxville	TN	22,112	VC
Tougaloo College	MS	17,980	NC
Univ of Alaska Anchorage	AK	16,652	NC
Univ of Central Missouri	MO	18,982	C
Univ of Delaware	DE	24,976	VC+
Univ of Houston	TX	21,483	VC
Univ of Kentucky	KY	33,306	C
Univ of Louisiana at Lafayette	LA	14,516	C
Univ of Maryland/Eastern Shore	MD	17,013	C
Univ of Missouri/Columbia	MO	18,201	MC
Univ of Nevada, Las Vegas	NV	17,553	C
Univ of New Haven	CT	52,190	C
Univ of New Orleans	LA	12,840	C
Univ of San Francisco	CA	58,484	VC
Univ of S Car at Columbia	SC	19,725	VC+
Univ of Southern Miss	MS	13,170	C
Univ of Wisc-Stout	WI	19,667	C
Virginia Polytechnic Inst and State Univ	VA	21,276	HC
Virginia State Univ	VA	19,802	C+
Washington State Univ	WA	22,495	C
Wiley College	TX	18,504	C
Youngstown State Univ	OH	17,307	C

HUMAN BIOLOGY

School	ST	$IS	SR
Brown Univ	RI	64,566	MC
Indiana Univ Bloomington	IN	20,429	VC
King Univ	TN	34,660	C
Mich State Univ	MI	23,898	VC+
Ohio Univ	OH	22,924	C
Univ of Calif San Diego	CA	30,150	MC
Univ of Kansas	KS	20,135	C+

HUMAN BIOLOGY, HEALTH, AND SOCIETY

School	ST	$IS	SR
Brown Univ	RI	64,566	MC
Cornell Univ	NY	64,853	MC
Indiana Univ Bloomington	IN	20,429	VC

HUMAN DEVELOPMENT

School	ST	$IS	SR
Alabama A&M Univ	AL	18,796	C
Amridge Univ	AL	10,860	LC
Andrews Univ	MI	28,030	C+
Anna Maria College	MA	48,186	C
Arizona State Univ at the Tempe Campus	AZ	21,756	VC
Auburn Univ	AL	23,594	VC+
Boston College	MA	65,737	MC
Bowling Green State Univ	OH	19,747	C
Brigham Young Univ	UT	12,748	HC
Brown Univ	RI	64,566	MC
Cal State, East Bay	CA	19,413	C
Cal State, Long Beach	CA	18,850	C
Cal State, San Bernardino	CA	12,000	C
Cal State, San Marcos	CA	24,184	LC
Colo State Univ	CO	22,162	VC
Conn College	CT	65,000	MC
Cornell Univ	NY	64,853	MC
Earlham College	IN	54,870	HC
East Tenn State Univ	TN	13,994	C
Eckerd College	FL	52,874	C
Goddard College	VT	17,040	VC
Hellenic College/Holy Cross Greek Orthodox School of Theology	MA	39,906	C
Hope International Univ	CA	41,150	C
Howard Univ	DC	37,616	C+
Kalamazoo College	MI	53,931	HC+
Kent State Univ	OH	20,732	C
Lee Univ	TN	22,045	C
Marylhurst Univ	OR	20,295	NC
Minn State Univ, Mankato	MN	15,616	C
Mitchell College	CT	43,280	C
Montana State Univ	MT	15,500	C+
National Louis Univ	IL	16,920	LC
N Dak State Univ	ND	16,245	C
Northwestern Univ	IL	66,344	MC
Nova Southeastern Univ	FL	38,534	C+
Oakwood Univ	AL	43,758	C
Ohio State Univ at Columbus	OH	21,703	HC+
Ohio Univ	OH	22,924	C
Okla State Univ	OK	17,180	VC
Oregon State Univ	OR	22,519	VC
Penn State Univ/Altoona	PA	24,584	C
Prescott College	AZ	33,284	C
Radford Univ	VA	19,027	LC
Rivier Univ	NH	40,410	VC
Samford Univ	AL	39,232	VC
San Diego Christian College	CA	39,068	C
Sonoma State Univ	CA	27,806	C
S Dak State Univ	SD	15,634	C
Southern Nazarene Univ	OK	32,798	NC
SUNY / Empire State College	NY	9,145	SP
SUNY / SUNY Plattsburgh	NY	18,814	C
SUNY at Binghamton	NY	22,861	MC
SUNY at Oswego	NY	21,351	C
Suffolk Univ	MA	50,308	C
Tarleton State Univ	TX	15,248	LC
Univ of Alabama	AL	24,320	C+
Univ of Arizona	AZ	23,100	C
Univ of Arkansas at Fayetteville	AR	19,152	C+
Univ of Bridgeport	CT	44,430	LC
Univ of Calif at Davis	CA	28,468	HC
Univ of Calif San Diego	CA	30,150	MC
Univ of Chicago	IL	67,584	MC
Univ of Conn	CT	25,538	HC
Univ of Delaware	DE	24,976	VC+
Univ of Illinois at Urbana-Champaign	IL	27,006	HC
Univ of Memphis	TN	18,278	C
Univ of Miami	FL	63,494	MC
Univ of Missouri/Columbia	MO	18,201	MC
Univ of Nebr - Kearney	NE	16,546	LC
Univ of New Mexico	NM	15,404	C
Univ of N Car at Greensboro	NC	14,690	C
Univ of Pittsburgh at Bradford	PA	22,402	C
Univ of Vermont	VT	28,878	HC
Univ of Wisc-Green Bay	WI	15,064	C
Univ of Wisc-Madison	WI	20,934	MC
Univ of Wisc-Stout	WI	19,667	C
Utah State Univ	UT	12,736	C
Vanderbilt Univ	TN	60,572	MC
Virginia Polytechnic Inst and State Univ	VA	21,276	HC
Warner Pacific College	OR	33,790	C
Washington State Univ	WA	22,495	C

HUMAN DEVELOPMENT & FAMILY STUDIES

School	ST	$IS	SR
Indiana Univ Bloomington	IN	20,429	VC
Mich State Univ	MI	23,898	VC+
Pennsylvania State Univ - Univ Park	PA	29,760	HC
Texas Tech Univ	TX	18,736	C+
Univ of Georgia	GA	21,250	HC
Univ of New Hampshire	NH	28,562	VC
Univ of Rhode Island	RI	24,906	C
Univ of Vermont	VT	28,878	HC
Washington State Univ	WA	22,495	C
Western Kentucky Univ	KY	16,850	C

HUMAN ECOLOGY

School	ST	$IS	SR
College of the Atlantic	ME	53,289	HC+
Goddard College	VT	17,040	VC
Kansas State Univ	KS	17,780	VC
Montclair State Univ	NJ	26,210	LC
Ohio State Univ at Columbus	OH	21,703	HC+
Prescott College	AZ	33,284	C
Tenn Tech Univ	TN	17,050	C
Univ of Calif at Davis	CA	28,468	HC
Univ of Texas at Austin	TX	26,102	HC
Virginia Wesleyan College	VA	43,728	LC

HUMAN EVOLUTIONARY BIOLOGY

School	ST	$IS	SR
Stony Brook Univ/The SUNY	NY	21,881	MC

HUMAN PERFORMANCE

School	ST	$IS	SR
Elon Univ	NC	44,599	VC+
Univ of Tampa	FL	36,944	C

HUMAN RELATIONS

School	ST	$IS	SR
High Point Univ	NC	45,977	C
Univ of Okla	OK	18,911	VC

HUMAN RESOURCES

School	ST	$IS	SR
Adelphi Univ	NY	48,244	C
Alderson Broaddus Univ	WV	26,149	C
Alvernia Univ	PA	43,900	C
American International College	MA	46,300	LC
Amridge Univ	AL	10,860	LC
Aquinas College - Mich	MI	38,876	HC
Baldwin Wallace Univ	OH	41,106	C
Ball State Univ	IN	19,590	C
Barton College	NC	38,686	LC
Baylor Univ	TX	53,760	HC
Black Hills State Univ	SD	15,899	C
Blackburn College	IL	28,526	LC
Bluffton Univ	OH	40,950	C
Boston College	MA	65,737	MC
Brescia Univ	KY	29,890	VC+
Briar Cliff Univ	IA	36,956	C
Bryant Univ	RI	55,646	VC
Cal State, San Bernardino	CA	12,000	C
Calvin College	MI	41,570	VC+
Carlow Univ	PA	38,549	LC
Central Mich Univ	MI	20,330	C
Chestnut Hill College	PA	43,410	C
Colo Christian Univ	CO	39,940	VC
Columbia College - Missouri	MO	27,803	C
Concordia Univ, Ann Arbor	MI	35,945	VC
Davenport Univ	MI	25,896	LC
Defiance College	OH	41,630	C
DePaul Univ	IL	47,623	VC
DeSales Univ	PA	43,970	C
Dominican College	NY	31,270	LC
Elizabethtown College School of Continuing and Professional Studies	PA	18,900	C
Excelsior College	NY	14,080	SP
Faulkner Univ	AL	26,410	C
Ferris State Univ	MI	21,445	C
Florida Atlantic Univ	FL	17,339	C
Franklin Univ	OH	56,262	SP
Friends Univ	KS	34,455	C
George Washington Univ	DC	62,835	MC
Golden Gate Univ	CA	32,110	C
Goldey-Beacom College	DE	31,750	C
Gwynedd Mercy Univ	PA	43,780	LC
Hawaii Pacific Univ	HI	33,420	C
Holy Names Univ	CA	46,630	LC
Idaho State Univ	ID	13,619	NC
Indiana Univ of Pennsylvania	PA	23,614	LC
Inter-American Univ of PR- Aguadilla Campus	PR	21,657	
Inter-American Univ of PR- Bayamon	PR	18,785	
John Carroll Univ	OH	49,740	C+
Juniata College	PA	53,760	VC
Kentucky Wesleyan College	KY	32,080	C
Lake Erie College	OH	38,914	LC
Le Moyne College	NY	46,000	C
Lewis Univ	IL	40,370	C
Limestone College	SC	32,100	C
Lindenwood Univ	MO	25,132	C
Louisiana State Univ and A&M College	LA	18,677	VC
Lourdes Univ	OH	29,520	NC
Loyola Univ Chicago	IL	55,802	VC
Lynchburg College	VA	46,740	C
Marietta College	OH	46,190	C
Marquette Univ	WI	48,390	VC+
Menlo College	CA	51,380	LC
Metropolitan State Univ	MN	7,566	C
Mich State Univ	MI	23,898	VC+
Midway Univ	KY	31,640	LC
Mount Aloysius College	PA	29,976	C
Mount Mercy Univ	IA	36,826	C
Neumann Univ	PA	40,678	LC
New York Univ	NY	65,860	MC
Niagara Univ	NY	41,010	C
Nichols College	MA	46,800	LC
North Central College	IL	48,712	VC
Northeastern Illinois Univ	IL	12,529	LC
Northern Kentucky Univ	KY	16,486	C
Notre Dame College	OH	37,150	VC
Oakland Univ	MI	20,763	C
Ohio State Univ at Columbus	OH	21,703	HC+
Okla Wesleyan Univ	OK	33,206	C
Our Lady of the Lake Univ	TX	35,012	LC
Pace Univ	NY	58,248	C
Park Univ	MO	20,329	C
Peirce College	PA	16,780	NC
Pennsylvania College of Technology	PA	27,333	NC
Point Park Univ	PA	41,270	C
Purdue Univ/Northwest	IN	15,038	C
Purdue Univ/West Lafayette	IN	20,032	MC
Rider Univ	NJ	54,050	C
Rowan Univ	NJ	24,491	VC+
Rutgers Univ - New Brunswick	NJ	26,632	HC
St. Joseph's Univ	PA	57,544	VC+
St. Mary-of-the-Woods College	IN	39,632	LC
Seton Hill Univ	PA	46,972	C
Silver Lake College of the Holy Family	WI	36,290	LC
Simpson Univ	CA	33,700	C
Southern Illinois Univ Edwardsville	IL	22,643	C
Spalding Univ	KY	31,938	SP
St. Mary's Univ	TX	37,500	C
SUNY / Empire State College	NY	9,145	SP
SUNY at Oswego	NY	21,351	C
Tarleton State Univ	TX	15,248	LC
Texas A&M Univ	TX	20,521	VC+
The Univ of Tenn at Knoxville	TN	22,112	VC
Thomas College	ME	35,268	LC
Trinity International Univ	IL	31,070	VC
Univ of Arkansas at Fayetteville	AR	19,152	C+
Univ of Central Missouri	MO	18,982	C
Univ of Central Okla	OK	13,486	C
Univ of Findlay	OH	60,139	C
Univ of Florida	FL	16,291	HC+
Univ of Hawaii at Manoa	HI	23,221	C
Univ of Idaho	ID	15,348	C
Univ of Illinois at Urbana-Champaign	IL	27,006	HC
Univ of Maryland/Univ College	MD	25,966	LC
Univ of Mich-Flint	MI	17,607	C+
Univ of Mount Olive	NC	18,426	C
Univ of Mount Union	OH	38,970	C
Univ of Nebr - Lincoln	NE	18,589	VC
Univ of Nevada, Las Vegas	NV	17,553	C
Univ of N Dak	ND	15,373	C
Univ of North Texas	TX	19,198	C
Univ of Okla	OK	18,911	VC
Univ of Pennsylvania	PA	63,526	MC
Univ of Pittsburgh	PA	29,568	HC+
Univ of PR, at Humacao	PR	14,000	
Univ of Scranton	PA	54,962	VC
Univ of S Dak	SD	16,109	C
Univ of Texas at San Antonio	TX	20,157	C
Univ of the Incarnate Word	TX	39,162	LC
Univ of Wisc-Green Bay	WI	15,064	C
Univ of Wisc-Madison	WI	20,934	MC
Univ of Wisc-Milwaukee	WI	21,496	C
Univ of Wisc-Oshkosh	WI	15,200	C
Ursuline College	OH	41,076	LC
Valley City State Univ	ND	13,267	C
Washington State Univ	WA	22,495	C
Washington Univ in St. Louis	MO	65,366	VC
Weber State Univ	UT	10,721	C
Western Washington Univ	WA	18,003	C+
Wichita State Univ	KS	21,643	C
Xavier Univ	OH	47,880	C+
York College	NE	24,300	C
Youngstown State Univ	OH	17,307	C

ST = STATE $IS = IN-STATE COSTS SR = SELECTOR RATING

HUMAN RESOURCES/ ORGANIZATIONAL MGMT

School	ST	$IS	SR
Albertus Magnus College	CT	43,258	LC
Ashford Univ	CA	10,480	C
Bay Path Univ	MA	45,349	C
Black Hills State Univ	SD	15,899	C
Bloomfield College	NJ	39,100	LC
Bryant Univ	RI	55,646	VC
Calif State Polytechnic Univ, Pomona	CA	21,541	C
Dallas Baptist Univ	TX	33,713	C
Georgia Southwestern State Univ	GA	13,870	C
Indiana Univ Bloomington	IN	20,429	VC
Lipscomb Univ	TN	41,296	VC
LIU Brooklyn	NY	49,682	C
Mercy College	NY	31,776	C
Mich State Univ	MI	23,898	VC+
Missouri Southern State Univ	MO	12,499	C
Murray State Univ	KY	16,998	C
New York Inst of Technology	NY	48,730	C
Purdue Univ/Northwest	IN	15,038	C
San Diego State Univ	CA	21,896	C+
Silver Lake College of the Holy Family	WI	36,290	LC
Southeast Missouri State Univ	MO	15,498	C
Tarleton State Univ	TX	15,248	LC
Thomas Edison State Univ	NJ	6,350	NC
Univ of Miami	FL	63,494	MC
Univ of San Francisco	CA	58,484	VC
Western Illinois Univ	IL	20,825	C
Western Mich Univ	MI	21,054	C
Winona State Univ	MN	17,535	C

HUMAN SERVICES

School	ST	$IS	SR
Alaska Pacific Univ	AK	26,680	VC
Albertus Magnus College	CT	43,258	LC
Aquinas College - Mich	MI	38,876	HC
Arkansas Baptist College	AR	20,280	NC
Assumption College	MA	47,920	C+
Beacon College	FL	46,862	C
Bethel College	IN	35,860	C
Bethel Univ	TN	24,738	C
Black Hills State Univ	SD	15,899	C
Bloomfield College	NJ	39,100	LC
Boricua College	NY	10,100	C
Brewton-Parker College	GA	23,490	C
Cal State, Dominguez Hills	CA	19,022	LC
Cal State, Fullerton	CA	21,902	C
Cal State, Monterey Bay	CA	26,871	LC
Cal State, San Bernardino	CA	12,000	C
Calumet College of St. Joseph	IN	22,735	C
Cambridge College	MA	15,734	NC
Cazenovia College	NY	46,470	C
Chestnut Hill College	PA	43,410	C
CUNY/College of Technology	NY	6,669	NC
College of St Joseph	VT	32,400	LC
Columbia College - Missouri	MO	27,803	C
Dakota Wesleyan Univ	SD	32,850	C
Drury Univ	MO	33,791	VC
East Central Univ	OK	13,056	C
Eastern New Mexico Univ	NM	14,416	C
Elizabethtown College School of Continuing and Professional Studies	PA	18,900	C
Elmira College	NY	53,900	C
Elon Univ	NC	44,599	VC+
Fitchburg State Univ	MA	21,819	C
Fontbonne Univ	MO	33,717	C
Friends Univ	KS	34,455	C
Geneva College	PA	35,450	C
George Washington Univ	DC	62,835	MC
Goodwin College	CT	28,370	LC
Grace Bible College	MI	25,250	C
Graceland Univ	IA	35,290	C
Grand View Univ	IA	32,302	C
Gwynedd Mercy Univ	PA	43,780	LC
Hastings College	NE	35,380	C+
Hawaii Pacific Univ	HI	33,420	C
Henderson State Univ	AR	15,516	LC
Hilbert College	NY	30,850	C
Holy Names Univ	CA	46,630	LC
Hope International Univ	CA	41,150	C
Indiana Inst of Technology	IN	34,240	LC
Indiana Univ-Purdue Univ Fort Wayne	IN	17,553	C
Kennesaw State Univ	GA	19,592	VC
Lasell College	MA	47,500	C
Le Moyne College	NY	46,000	C
Lenoir-Rhyne Univ	NC	43,200	C
Lesley Univ	MA	41,550	C
Lindenwood Univ	MO	25,132	C
Lindsey Wilson College	KY	32,882	C
Loyola Univ Chicago	IL	55,802	VC
Lyndon State College	VT	20,714	C
Metropolitan College of New York	NY		VC
Metropolitan State Univ	MN	7,566	C
Metropolitan State Univ of Denver	CO	29,889	LC
Millikin Univ	IL	42,158	C
Missouri Baptist Univ	MO	35,594	C
Missouri Valley College	MO	28,150	C
Montana State Univ-Billings	MT	22,960	C
Montreat College	NC	31,298	LC
Mount St. Mary College	NY	42,061	C
Mount St. Mary's Univ	MD	51,610	C
National Louis Univ	IL	16,920	LC
N Car Central Univ	NC	9,000	C
Northern State Univ	SD	14,505	C
Northwest Christian Univ	OR	36,580	C
Notre Dame de Namur Univ	CA	46,526	LC
Nova Southeastern Univ	FL	38,534	C+
Oglala Lakota College	SD	15,050	NC
Old Dominion Univ	VA	20,910	C
Ottawa Univ	KS	36,074	VC
Park Univ	MO	20,329	C
Pfeiffer Univ	NC	39,695	LC
Prescott College	AZ	33,284	C
Queens Univ of Charlotte	NC	39,543	C
Quincy Univ	IL	36,998	C
St. Mary-of-the-Woods College	IN	39,632	LC
St. Mary's Univ of Minn	MN	41,210	VC
Salem International Univ	WV	21,090	LC
Seton Hill Univ	PA	46,972	C
Siena Heights Univ	MI	32,040	C
Sinte Gleska Univ	SD	13,154	NC
S Car State Univ	SC	20,805	LC
Southern Oregon Univ	OR	19,117	C
Southern Wesleyan Univ	SC	32,130	LC
Southwest Baptist Univ	MO	29,900	LC
Springfield College	MA	45,995	C
St. John's Univ	NY	55,850	C
St. Joseph's College, New York/Brooklyn Campus	NY	25,114	LC
St. Joseph's College, New York/Long Island Campus	NY	25,124	C
St. Thomas Univ	FL	36,360	LC
SUNY / SUNY Cortland	NY	20,706	VC
Stevenson Univ	MD	72,770	C
Suffolk Univ	MA	50,308	C
Texas Southern Univ	TX	18,212	LC
The Lincoln Univ	PA	15,154	NC
Thomas Edison State Univ	NJ	6,350	NC
Touro College	NY	28,950	VC
Trinity International Univ	IL	31,070	VC
Trinity Washington Univ	DC	33,826	C+
Troy Univ	AL	16,171	C
Univ of Alaska Anchorage	AK	16,652	NC
Univ of Bridgeport	CT	44,430	LC
Univ of Delaware	DE	24,976	VC+
Univ of Maine at Machias	ME	22,960	C
Univ of Mass Boston	MA	13,435	C
Univ of Mount Olive	NC	18,426	C
Univ of New Mexico	NM	15,404	C
Univ of North Georgia	GA	17,316	C
Univ of North Texas	TX	19,198	C
Univ of Northern Colo	CO	20,851	C
Univ of Scranton	PA	54,962	VC
Univ of Wisc-Oshkosh	WI	15,200	C
Upper Iowa Univ	IA	34,990	NC
Washburn Univ	KS	15,827	C
Wayland Baptist Univ	TX	22,356	LC
Waynesburg Univ	PA	32,290	C
Western New Mexico Univ	NM	16,734	LC
Western Washington Univ	WA	18,003	C+
William Penn Univ	IA	26,000	C
Wingate Univ	NC	39,950	C
Wisc Lutheran College	WI	36,290	VC
York College	NE	24,300	C

HUMAN STUDIES

School	ST	$IS	SR
St. Edward's Univ	TX	53,100	VC
Texas Tech Univ	TX	18,736	C+
Univ of Rhode Island	RI	24,906	C

HUMANITIES

School	ST	$IS	SR
Albertus Magnus College	CT	43,258	LC
Anna Maria College	MA	48,186	C
Belhaven Univ	MS	31,016	C
Bennington College	VT	63,960	MC
Biola Univ	CA	46,402	C+
Bloomfield College	NJ	39,100	LC
Bluefield State College	WV	5,832	LC
Brigham Young Univ	UT	12,748	HC
Bryant Univ	RI	55,646	VC
Bucknell Univ	PA	64,616	MC
Cal State, Chico	CA	21,440	C
Cal State, Fresno	CA	16,902	LC
Cal State, Monterey Bay	CA	26,871	LC
Cal State, Northridge	CA	16,859	LC
Cal State, San Bernardino	CA	12,000	C
Chaminade Univ of Honolulu	HI	36,000	C
Charleston Southern Univ	SC	32,400	C
Clarkson Univ	NY	60,392	HC
Colby-Sawyer College	NH	50,790	C
Colgate Univ	NY	65,030	MC
College of St. Benedict	MN	52,806	C
College of St. Mary	NE	35,184	C
College of St. Scholastica	MN	44,640	C
Concordia College - Moorhead	MN	51,088	C+
Concordia Univ	CA	41,580	VC
Concordia Univ	OR	35,000	C
Concordia Univ Wisc	WI	35,910	C
Concordia Univ, Ann Arbor	MI	35,945	VC
Corban Univ	OR	40,306	C
Defiance College	OH	41,630	C
DePaul Univ	IL	47,623	VC
Dominican College	NY	31,270	LC
Dominican Univ of Calif	CA	57,050	C
Duquesne Univ	PA	46,822	VC
Eastern Washington Univ	WA	25,572	LC
Eckerd College	FL	52,874	C
Edinboro Univ	PA	15,940	LC
Fairleigh Dickinson Univ/College at Florham	NJ	52,062	C
Fairleigh Dickinson Univ/Metropolitan Campus	NJ	40,254	C
Faulkner Univ	AL	26,410	C
Felician Univ	NJ	45,370	LC
Florida Inst of Technology	FL	53,306	VC
Florida State Univ	FL	16,771	HC
Fort Lewis College	CO	18,980	C
George Washington Univ	DC	62,835	MC
Georgian Court Univ	NJ	42,426	LC
Grand Rapids Theological Seminary/Cornerstone Univ	MI	33,338	C
Hampden-Sydney College	VA	56,248	C+
Hampshire College	MA	63,824	MC
Harding Univ	AR	25,421	C
Harvard College/Harvard Univ	MA	60,659	MC
Hawaii Pacific Univ	HI	33,420	C
Heritage Univ	WA	19,825	NC
Holy Family Univ	PA	43,326	LC
Holy Names Univ	CA	46,630	LC
Houghton College	NY	39,090	C
Illinois Inst of Technology	IL	56,826	HC+
Indiana Univ East	IN	7,072	C
Indiana Univ Kokomo	IN	7,073	C
Jacksonville Univ	FL	46,230	C
John Carroll Univ	OH	49,740	C+
Johns Hopkins Univ	MD	65,386	MC
Johnson State College	VT	20,752	C
Juniata College	PA	53,760	VC
Kansas State Univ	KS	17,780	VC
Kentucky Christian Univ	KY	26,560	LC
Lasell College	MA	47,500	C
Lawrence Tech Univ	MI	39,770	VC
Lee Univ	TN	22,045	C
Lees-McRae College	NC	33,944	C
LeMoyne-Owen College	TN	16,980	C
Lesley Univ	MA	41,550	C
LIU Brooklyn	NY	49,682	C
LIU Post	NY	49,682	C
Loyola Marymount Univ	CA	58,038	HC
Loyola Univ New Orleans	LA	51,708	VC+
Lubbock Christian Univ	TX	28,426	C
Macalester College	MN	61,905	MC
Marshall Univ	WV	17,242	C
Martin Univ	IN	20,264	LC
Mass Inst of Technology	MA	62,662	MC
Mich State Univ	MI	23,898	VC+
Midwestern State Univ	TX	17,572	C
Milligan College	TN	38,150	C
Minn State Univ, Mankato	MN	15,616	C
Montana State Univ-Northern	MT	11,370	NC
Montclair State Univ	NJ	26,210	LC
Mount Aloysius College	PA	29,976	C
New College of Florida	FL	15,848	MC
New York Univ	NY	65,860	MC
N Dak State Univ	ND	16,245	C
Northern Arizona Univ	AZ	20,246	VC
Northland College	WI	41,103	C+
Northwest Christian Univ	OR	36,580	C
Northwest Missouri State Univ	MO	17,737	C
Notre Dame de Namur Univ	CA	46,526	LC
Oberlin College	OH	66,012	MC
Ohio Valley Univ	WV	29,480	C
Okla City Univ	OK	40,476	VC
Pacific Univ	OR	52,876	C
Paul Quinn College	TX	25,350	LC
Pepperdine Univ	CA	74,460	HC+
Plymouth State Univ	NH	23,180	LC
Prescott College	AZ	33,284	C
Providence College	RI	60,760	VC
Quincy Univ	IL	36,998	C
Roberts Wesleyan College	NY	38,306	C
Rockford Univ	IL	36,030	C
Roger Williams Univ	RI	46,296	C+
Rollins College	FL	58,670	HC
Rosemont College	PA	30,980	C
Rutgers Univ - New Brunswick	NJ	26,632	HC
St. John's Univ	MN	51,624	C
St. Mary-of-the-Woods College	IN	39,632	LC
St. Mary's College	IN	50,600	C
St. Peter's Univ	NJ	49,192	C
San Diego State Univ	CA	21,896	C+
San Francisco State Univ	CA	18,514	LC
Schreiner Univ	TX	34,626	LC
Scripps College	CA	66,664	MC
Seattle Univ	WA	50,811	VC+
Shimer College	IL	42,130	VC+
Siena Heights Univ	MI	32,040	C
Sierra Nevada College	NV	43,482	C
Southern Methodist Univ	TX	66,483	MC
Spring Hill College	AL	48,488	C
St. Andrews Univ	NC	44,634	LC
St. Norbert College	WI	44,525	VC
SUNY / Buffalo State College	NY	20,842	C
SUNY / SUNY College at Old Westbury	NY	16,860	C
SUNY /Maritime College	NY	16,020	C
Suffolk Univ	MA	50,308	C
Taylor Univ	IN	40,317	C+
The Univ of Tenn at Chattanooga	TN	16,744	C
Thomas Edison State Univ	NJ	6,350	NC
Thomas More College	KY	36,720	C
Thomas Univ	GA	21,420	LC
Tougaloo College	MS	17,980	NC
Trinity International Univ	IL	31,070	VC
Tulane Univ	LA	63,396	HC+
Union College	NY	64,320	MC
United States Air Force Academy	CO		C
United States Military Academy at West Point	NY		HC+
Universidad del Turabo	PR	17,828	
Universidad Metropolitana	PR	17,828	
Univ of Calif at Irvine	CA	26,484	VC
Univ of Central Florida	FL	15,922	VC
Univ of Central Okla	OK	13,486	C
Univ of Chicago	IL	67,584	MC
Univ of Colo Boulder	CO	24,285	VC+
Univ of Houston-Downtown	TX	7,241	C
Univ of Illinois at Chicago	IL	25,006	VC
Univ of Illinois at Urbana-Champaign	IL	27,006	HC
Univ of Kansas	KS	20,135	C+
Univ of Louisville	KY	19,824	C
Univ of Maryland/Univ College	MD	25,966	LC
Univ of Mich/Ann Arbor	MI	24,410	MC
Univ of Mich/Dearborn	MI	11,757	VC
Univ of Minn/Twin Cities	MN	23,519	HC+
Univ of Mobile	AL	28,935	C
Univ of New Hampshire	NH	28,562	VC
Univ of New Hampshire - Manchester	NH	14,490	C
Univ of Okla	OK	18,911	VC
Univ of Oregon	OR	22,972	C
Univ of Pittsburgh	PA	29,568	HC+
Univ of Pittsburgh at Greensburg	PA	23,132	C
Univ of Pittsburgh at Johnstown	PA	22,092	C
Univ of PR, at Cayey	PR		
Univ of Rio Grande & Rio Grande Community College	OH	8,750	NC
Univ of San Diego	CA	58,442	VC+
Univ of Sioux Falls	SD	34,330	C
Univ of South Florida/Tampa	FL	16,110	VC+
Univ of Texas at Austin	TX	26,102	HC
Univ of Texas at Dallas	TX	22,830	VC+
Univ of Texas at San Antonio	TX	20,157	C
Univ of the Southwest	NM	22,766	C
Univ of Toledo	OH	19,336	NC
Univ of Wisc-Green Bay	WI	15,064	C
Univ of Wisc-Parkside	WI	15,193	C
Univ of Wyoming	WY	15,375	C+
Ursuline College	OH	41,076	LC
Valparaiso Univ	IN	48,370	C+
Villanova Univ	PA	62,523	MC
Virginia Wesleyan College	VA	43,728	LC
Walla Walla Univ	WA	30,417	NC
Washington College	MD	54,666	VC
Washington State Univ	WA	22,495	C
Washington Univ in St. Louis	MO	65,366	VC
Wesleyan College	GA	29,694	C+
Western New Mexico Univ	NM	16,734	LC
Western Oregon Univ	OR	15,021	LC
Wheelock College	MA	49,225	C
Widener Univ	PA	56,486	C
Willamette Univ	OR	61,817	VC+
Wofford College	SC	49,885	VC
Worcester Polytechnic Inst	MA	60,730	MC
Wright State Univ	OH	16,983	C
Xavier Univ	OH	47,880	C+
Yale Univ	CT	64,650	MC
York College of Pennsylvania	PA	29,240	C

HUMANITIES AND SOCIAL SCIENCE

School	ST	$IS	SR
Alabama A&M Univ	AL	18,796	C
Bennington College	VT	63,960	MC
Bloomfield College	NJ	39,100	LC
Bryant Univ	RI	55,646	VC
Canisius College	NY	47,537	C
CUNY/John Jay College of Criminal Justice	NY	6,359	NC
Franciscan Univ of Steubenville	OH	33,980	VC
Goddard College	VT	17,040	VC
Lock Haven Univ of Pennsylvania	PA	18,028	LC
Mount Aloysius College	PA	29,976	C
New York Univ	NY	65,860	MC
Prescott College	AZ	33,284	C
San Francisco State Univ	CA	18,514	LC
Spalding Univ	KY	31,938	SP
SUNY / Empire State College	NY	9,145	SP
Sterling College	VT	41,894	VC
Texas A&M Univ at Galveston	TX	15,920	C
Univ of Calif at Riverside	CA	29,227	C+
Univ of the Sciences	PA	54,038	VC
Washington State Univ	WA	22,495	C

HVACR ENG TECH & ENERGY MANAGEMENT

School	ST	$IS	SR
Ferris State Univ	MI	21,445	C

HVACR ENGINEERING TECHNOLOGY

School	ST	$IS	SR
Ferris State Univ	MI	21,445	C

HYDROGEOLOGY

School	ST	$IS	SR
Eastern Mich Univ	MI	19,761	C
Rensselaer Polytechnic Inst	NY	63,436	MC
Western Mich Univ	MI	21,054	C

HYDROLOGY

School	ST	$IS	SR
Texas A&M Univ at Galveston	TX	15,920	C
Univ of Arizona	AZ	23,100	C
Univ of Calif at Davis	CA	28,468	HC
Univ of Calif at Santa Barbara	CA	29,091	HC
Univ of Nevada/Reno	NV	18,010	C

IBERIAN STUDIES

School	ST	$IS	SR
Bryant Univ	RI	55,646	VC
New York Univ	NY	65,860	MC
Southern Methodist Univ	TX	66,483	MC
Stanford Univ	CA	60,409	MC
Univ of PR, at Arecibo	PR	12,652	

ILLUSTRATION

School	ST	$IS	SR
Arcadia Univ	PA	33,570	C+
Art Academy of Cincinnati	OH	36,252	SP
ArtCenter College of Design	CA	54,212	SP
Bennington College	VT	63,960	MC
Brigham Young Univ	UT	12,748	HC
Calif College of the Arts	CA	52,758	SP
Cleveland Inst of Art	OH	51,439	C+
College for Creative Studies	MI	48,875	SP
College of Art and Design at Lesley Univ	MA	39,730	SP
Columbia College Chicago	IL	43,168	C
Columbus College of Art and Design	OH	37,732	C
Embry-Riddle Aeronautical Univ - Prescott Campus	AZ	44,054	VC
Fashion Inst of Technology/ SUNY	NY	18,521	SP
Ferris State Univ	MI	21,445	C
Indiana Wesleyan Univ	IN	33,674	C
John Brown Univ	AR	33,132	VC
Kansas City Art Inst	MO	44,308	C+
Kutztown Univ of Pennsylvania	PA	19,056	LC
Laguna College of Art and Design	CA	41,422	LC
Lawrence Tech Univ	MI	39,770	VC
Lewis Univ	IL	40,370	C
Maryland Inst College of Art	MD	56,795	SP
Marywood Univ	PA	46,900	C
Mass College of Art and Design	MA	24,800	SP
Memphis College of Art	TN	39,750	C
Milwaukee Inst of Art and Design	WI	44,960	SP
Minneapolis College of Art and Design	MN	44,238	SP
Montserrat College of Art	MA	38,150	SP
Moore College of Art and Design	PA	50,135	SP
Ohio Univ	OH	22,924	C
Olivet College	MI	36,110	LC
Otis College of Art and Design	CA	55,858	SP
Pacific Northwest College of Art	OR	38,494	SP
Parsons The New School for Design	NY	56,610	SP
Rhode Island School of Design	RI	59,960	SP
Ringling College of Art and Design	FL	57,430	SP
Rivier Univ	NH	40,410	VC
Rochester Inst of Technology	NY	50,842	HC
Rocky Mountain College of Art and Design	CO	27,052	SP
Savannah College of Art and Design	GA	49,595	C
School of Visual Arts	NY	47,500	SP
St. John's Univ	NY	55,850	C
SUNY / SUNY Fredonia	NY	20,818	C
Syracuse Univ	NY	60,239	VC
Univ of Bridgeport	CT	44,430	LC
Univ of Findlay	OH	60,139	C
Univ of Hartford	CT	49,776	C
Univ of Kansas	KS	20,135	C+
Univ of Mass Dartmouth	MA	25,658	C
Univ of Mich/Ann Arbor	MI	24,410	MC
Univ of Montana-Western	MT	11,220	LC
Univ of San Francisco	CA	58,484	VC
Univ of the Arts	PA	56,579	SP
Washington Univ in St. Louis	MO	65,366	VC
Western Conn State Univ	CT	21,254	LC

IMAGING SCIENCES

School	ST	$IS	SR
Thomas Edison State Univ	NJ	6,350	NC

INDUSTRIAL ADMINISTRATION/ MANAGEMENT

School	ST	$IS	SR
Central Mich Univ	MI	20,330	C
Clarion Univ of Pennsylvania	PA	21,608	LC
Clemson Univ	SC		HC
Colo State Univ-Pueblo	CO	18,234	C
Gardner-Webb Univ	NC	39,200	C+
Grove City College	PA	25,692	VC
Illinois Inst of Technology	IL	56,826	HC+
Inter-American Univ of PR-Bayamon	PR	18,785	
Lawrence Tech Univ	MI	39,770	VC
LeTourneau Univ	TX	38,250	VC
Mercer Univ	GA	45,348	VC
Metropolitan State Univ of Denver	CO	29,889	LC
Okla State Univ	OK	17,180	VC
Oregon Inst of Technology	OR	8,910	C
Purdue Univ/West Lafayette	IN	20,032	MC
Saginaw Valley State Univ	MI	18,530	C
St. Augustine's Univ	NC	26,048	C
San Francisco State Univ	CA	18,514	LC
S Dak State Univ	SD	15,634	C
St. Bonaventure Univ	NY	44,237	C
Trine Univ	IN	41,310	C
Universidad Politecnica de PR, Hato Rey campus	PR	23,514	
Univ of Alabama	AL	24,320	C+
Univ of Alabama at Birmingham	AL	19,906	C
Univ of Arkansas at Little Rock	AR	18,211	C
Univ of Cincinnati	OH	21,964	VC
Univ of Illinois at Urbana-Champaign	IL	27,006	HC
Univ of Iowa	IA	18,683	VC+
Univ of Minn Crookston	MN	19,739	C
Univ of Nebr - Kearney	NE	16,546	LC
Univ of N Car at Asheville	NC	15,723	VC+
Univ of N Car at Charlotte	NC	15,547	C
Univ of Southern Indiana	IN	16,501	C
Univ of Wisc-Parkside	WI	15,193	C
Univ of Wisc-Stout	WI	19,667	C
Washington State Univ	WA	22,495	C
Wentworth Inst of Technology	MA	47,112	C
West Virginia Univ Inst of Technology	WV	16,462	NC
William Penn Univ	IA	26,000	C

INDUSTRIAL AND LABOR RELATIONS

School	ST	$IS	SR
Bryant Univ	RI	55,646	VC
Cornell Univ	NY	64,853	MC
Eastern Conn State Univ	CT	23,059	C
New York Univ	NY	65,860	MC

INDUSTRIAL AND ORGANIZATIONAL PSYCHOLOGY

School	ST	$IS	SR
Albertus Magnus College	CT	43,258	LC
Arizona State Univ at the Polytechnic Campus	AZ	21,360	VC
Baldwin Wallace Univ	OH	41,106	C
Cedar Crest College	PA	46,715	C
CUNY/Baruch College	NY	21,609	HC
Coe College	IA	51,570	VC
Fitchburg State Univ	MA	21,819	C
Goddard College	VT	17,040	VC
Holy Family Univ	PA	43,326	LC
Ithaca College	NY	56,766	VC
Johnson & Wales Univ/ Denver Campus	CO	42,707	C
Kutztown Univ of Pennsylvania	PA	19,056	LC
Marywood Univ	PA	46,900	C
Northwest Missouri State Univ	MO	17,737	C
Ohio State Univ at Columbus	OH	21,703	HC+
Oregon Inst of Technology	OR	8,910	C
Texas Wesleyan Univ	TX	35,134	C
Univ of PR, at Arecibo	PR	12,652	
Washington Univ in St. Louis	MO	65,366	VC

INDUSTRIAL ARTS EDUCATION

School	ST	$IS	SR
Alabama A&M Univ	AL	18,796	C
Auburn Univ	AL	23,594	VC+
Ball State Univ	IN	19,590	C
Bemidji State Univ	MN	16,056	VC
Cal State, Los Angeles	CA	17,186	LC
Central Washington Univ	WA	16,803	C
Chicago State Univ	IL	20,144	C
Clemson Univ	SC		HC
Concordia Univ Nebr	NE	36,280	VC
Eastern Kentucky Univ	KY	16,908	C
Eastern Mich Univ	MI	19,761	C
Elizabeth City State Univ	NC	14,745	C
Fitchburg State Univ	MA	21,819	C
Florida A&M Univ	FL	15,361	C
Humboldt State Univ	CA	20,514	C
Indiana State Univ	IN	23,223	LC
Iowa State Univ	IA	17,570	C
Langston Univ	OK	14,314	C
Montana State Univ-Northern	MT	11,370	NC
Murray State Univ	KY	16,998	C
N Car A&T State Univ	NC	13,365	LC
N Car State Univ	NC	19,515	HC+
Northeastern State Univ	OK	8,615	VC
Northern Kentucky Univ	KY	16,486	C
Northern Mich Univ	MI	19,604	C
San Francisco State Univ	CA	18,514	LC
S Car State Univ	SC	20,805	LC
Southeast Missouri State Univ	MO	15,498	C
St. Cloud State Univ	MN	10,600	C
SUNY / Buffalo State College	NY	20,842	C
Tarleton State Univ	TX	15,248	LC
Texas A&M Univ at Commerce	TX	10,496	C
Univ of Arkansas at Pine Bluff	AR	13,541	C
Univ of Central Missouri	MO	18,982	C
Univ of Cincinnati	OH	21,964	VC
Univ of Louisiana at Lafayette	LA	14,516	C
Univ of Maryland/Eastern Shore	MD	17,013	C
Univ of Minn/Twin Cities	MN	23,519	HC+
Univ of Montana-Western	MT	11,220	LC
Univ of Southern Miss	MS	13,170	C
Utah State Univ	UT	12,736	C
Wayne State College	NE	12,802	C

INDUSTRIAL DESIGN

School	ST	$IS	SR
Appalachian State Univ	NC	14,416	VC
Arizona State Univ at the Tempe Campus	AZ	21,756	VC
ArtCenter College of Design	CA	54,212	SP
Auburn Univ	AL	23,594	VC+
Brigham Young Univ	UT	12,748	HC
Calif College of the Arts	CA	52,758	SP
Cedarville Univ	OH	34,990	VC
Cleveland Inst of Art	OH	51,439	C+
College for Creative Studies	MI	48,875	SP
Columbus College of Art and Design	OH	37,732	C
Escuela de Artes Plasticas de PR	PR	11,236	
Ferris State Univ	MI	21,445	C
Georgia Inst of Technology	GA	23,360	MC
Kean Univ	NJ	24,650	C
Lawrence Tech Univ	MI	39,770	VC
Mass College of Art and Design	MA	24,800	SP
Metropolitan State Univ of Denver	CO	29,889	LC
Milwaukee Inst of Art and Design	WI	44,960	SP
NewSchool of Architecture & Design	CA	12,341	SP
N Car State Univ	NC	19,515	HC+
Ohio State Univ at Columbus	OH	21,703	HC+
Otis College of Art and Design	CA	55,858	SP
Parsons The New School for Design	NY	56,610	SP
Philadelphia Univ	PA	50,370	C
Pratt Inst	NY	58,082	VC
Purdue Univ/West Lafayette	IN	20,032	MC
Rhode Island School of Design	RI	59,960	SP
Rochester Inst of Technology	NY	50,842	HC
Savannah College of Art and Design	GA	49,595	C
Syracuse Univ	NY	60,239	VC
Univ of Bridgeport	CT	44,430	LC
Univ of Houston	TX	21,483	VC
Univ of Illinois at Chicago	IL	25,006	VC
Univ of Illinois at Urbana-Champaign	IL	27,006	HC
Univ of Kansas	KS	20,135	C+
Univ of Mich/Ann Arbor	MI	24,410	MC
Univ of the Arts	PA	56,579	SP
Virginia Polytechnic Inst and State Univ	VA	21,276	HC
Wentworth Inst of Technology	MA	47,112	C

INDUSTRIAL ENGINEERING

School	ST	$IS	SR
Alabama A&M Univ	AL	18,796	C
Arizona State Univ at the Tempe Campus	AZ	21,756	VC
Auburn Univ	AL	23,594	VC+
Calif Baptist Univ	CA	41,392	C
Calif Polytechnic State Univ	CA	17,979	HC+
Calif State Polytechnic Univ, Pomona	CA	21,541	C
Cal State, East Bay	CA	19,413	C
Cal State, Fresno	CA	16,902	LC
Clemson Univ	SC		HC
Colo State Univ-Pueblo	CO	18,234	C
Elizabethtown College	PA	54,050	C
Florida A&M Univ	FL	15,361	C
Florida State Univ	FL	16,771	HC
Francis Marion Univ	SC	16,464	LC
George Mason Univ	VA	15,724	VC
Georgia Inst of Technology	GA	23,360	MC
Hofstra Univ	NY	55,960	C+
Indiana Inst of Technology	IN	34,240	LC
Inter-American Univ of PR-Bayamon	PR	18,785	
Kansas State Univ	KS	17,780	VC
Kettering Univ	MI	47,570	HC
Lamar Univ	TX	18,014	LC
Lawrence Tech Univ	MI	39,770	VC
Lehigh Univ	PA	61,010	MC
Louisiana State Univ and A&M College	LA	18,677	VC
Louisiana Tech Univ	LA	11,422	VC
Milwaukee School of Engineering	WI	45,153	HC
Miss State Univ	MS	11,454	C+
Montana State Univ	MT	15,500	C+
New Jersey Inst of Technology	NJ	29,569	VC
New Mexico State Univ	NM	14,050	C
N Car A&T State Univ	NC	13,365	LC
N Car State Univ	NC	19,515	HC+
N Dak State Univ	ND	16,245	C
Northeastern Univ	MA	62,703	MC
Northern Illinois Univ	IL	20,176	C
Northwestern Univ	IL	66,344	MC
Oakland Univ	MI	20,763	C
Ohio State Univ at Columbus	OH	21,703	HC+
Ohio Univ	OH	22,924	C
Okla State Univ	OK	17,180	VC
Oregon State Univ	OR	22,519	VC
Pennsylvania State Univ - Univ Park	PA	29,760	HC
Philadelphia Univ	PA	50,370	C
Purdue Univ/West Lafayette	IN	20,032	MC
Quinnipiac Univ	CT	59,110	C
Rensselaer Polytechnic Inst	NY	63,436	MC
Rochester Inst of Technology	NY	50,842	HC
Rutgers Univ - New Brunswick	NJ	26,632	HC
St. Augustine's Univ	NC	26,048	C
San Jose State Univ	CA	21,540	C
S Dak School of Mines and Technology	SD	18,645	VC
Southern Illinois Univ Edwardsville	IL	22,643	C
St. Ambrose Univ	IA	39,019	C
St. Ambrose Univ	IA	39,019	C
St. Mary's Univ	TX	37,500	C
Stanford Univ	CA	60,409	MC
SUNY / Univ at Buffalo	NY	23,122	C+
SUNY at Binghamton	NY	22,861	MC
Tenn Tech Univ	TN	17,050	C
Texas State Univ	TX	19,350	C
Texas Tech Univ	TX	18,736	C+
The Univ of Tenn at Chattanooga	TN	16,744	C
The Univ of Tenn at Knoxville	TN	22,112	VC
Universidad Politecnica de PR, Hato Rey campus	PR	23,514	
Univ of Alabama	AL	24,320	C+
Univ of Alabama in Huntsville	AL	19,445	VC
Univ of Arizona	AZ	23,100	C
Univ of Arkansas at Fayetteville	AR	19,152	C+
Univ of Calif at Berkeley	CA	28,853	MC
Univ of Central Florida	FL	15,922	VC
Univ of Houston	TX	21,483	VC
Univ of Illinois at Urbana-Champaign	IL	27,006	HC
Univ of Iowa	IA	18,683	VC+
Univ of Louisiana at Lafayette	LA	14,516	C
Univ of Louisville	KY	19,824	C
Univ of Mass Amherst	MA	26,199	VC+
Univ of Miami	FL	63,494	MC
Univ of Mich/Ann Arbor	MI	24,410	MC
Univ of Minn/Duluth	MN	20,292	C+
Univ of Minn/Twin Cities	MN	23,519	HC+
Univ of Missouri/Columbia	MO	18,201	MC
Univ of Okla	OK	18,911	VC
Univ of Pittsburgh	PA	29,568	HC+
Univ of PR, at Mayaguez	PR	13,995	
Univ of San Diego	CA	58,442	VC+
Univ of South Florida/Tampa	FL	16,110	VC+
Univ of Southern Calif	CA	66,631	C
Univ of Toledo	OH	19,336	NC
Univ of Wisc-Madison	WI	20,934	MC
Univ of Wisc-Milwaukee	WI	21,496	C
Univ of Wisc-Platteville	WI	14,614	VC
Utah State Univ	UT	12,736	C
Virginia Polytechnic Inst and State Univ	VA	21,276	HC
Wayne State Univ	MI	22,016	C
Western Mich Univ	MI	21,054	C
Western New England Univ	MA	48,088	C
Wichita State Univ	KS	21,643	C
Worcester Polytechnic Inst	MA	60,730	MC
Wright State Univ	OH	16,983	C
Youngstown State Univ	OH	17,307	C

INDUSTRIAL ENGINEERING TECHNOLOGY

School	ST	$IS	SR
Alabama A&M Univ	AL	18,796	C
Appalachian State Univ	NC	14,416	VC
Ball State Univ	IN	19,590	C
Bemidji State Univ	MN	16,056	VC
Berea College	KY	7,042	C

ST = STATE **$IS** = IN-STATE COSTS **SR** = SELECTOR RATING

School	ST	$IS	SR
Cal State, Fresno	CA	16,902	LC
Cal State, Los Angeles	CA	17,186	LC
Calif Univ of Pennsylvania	PA	14,217	LC
Caribbean Univ	PR	15,471	
Central Conn State Univ	CT	21,203	C
Central Washington Univ	WA	16,803	C
Chadron State College	NE	14,819	NC
Columbia Univ/City of New York	NY	62,958	MC
East Carolina Univ	NC	16,937	C
Eastern Illinois Univ	IL	21,126	C
Elizabeth City State Univ	NC	14,745	C
Farmingdale State College	NY	20,624	C
Fitchburg State Univ	MA	21,819	C
Grand Valley State Univ	MI	22,250	C+
Humboldt State Univ	CA	20,514	C
Illinois State Univ	IL	23,418	VC
Indiana State Univ	IN	23,223	LC
Indiana Univ-Purdue Univ Fort Wayne	IN	17,553	C
Iowa State Univ	IA	17,570	C
Jackson State Univ	MS	15,879	LC
Kennesaw State Univ	GA	19,592	VC
Lamar Univ	TX	18,014	LC
Langston Univ	OK	14,314	C
Metropolitan State Univ of Denver	CO	29,889	LC
Middle Tenn State Univ	TN	8,650	C
Millersville Univ of Pennsylvania	PA	23,782	C
Minn State Univ, Moorhead	MN	15,941	C
Miss State Univ	MS	11,454	C+
Miss Valley State Univ	MS	13,233	LC
Morehead State Univ	KY	17,422	C
Morgan State Univ	MD	17,190	LC
Northern Mich Univ	MI	19,604	C
Okla Panhandle State Univ	OK	6,152	NC
Prairie View A&M Univ	TX	15,205	LC
Purdue Univ/Northwest	IN	15,038	C
Purdue Univ/West Lafayette	IN	20,032	MC
Roger Williams Univ	RI	46,296	C+
San Francisco State Univ	CA	18,514	LC
S Car State Univ	SC	20,805	LC
Southeastern Louisiana Univ	LA	16,237	C
Southern Illinois Univ Carbondale	IL	23,667	C
SUNY / Buffalo State College	NY	20,842	C
Tarleton State Univ	TX	15,248	LC
Tenn Tech Univ	TN	17,050	C
Texas A&M Univ	TX	20,521	VC+
Texas A&M Univ at Kingsville	TX	7,500	LC
Texas Southern Univ	TX	18,212	LC
Texas State Univ	TX	19,350	C
Univ of Arkansas at Pine Bluff	AR	13,541	C
Univ of Central Missouri	MO	18,982	C
Univ of Cincinnati	OH	21,964	VC
Univ of Dayton	OH	53,620	C
Univ of Florida	FL	16,291	HC+
Univ of Illinois at Chicago	IL	25,006	VC
Univ of Mich/Dearborn	MI	11,757	VC
Univ of N Dak	ND	15,373	C
Univ of Rio Grande & Rio Grande Community College	OH	8,750	NC
Univ of Southern Maine	ME	18,320	C
Univ of Texas at Arlington	TX	18,026	LC
Univ of Texas at El Paso	TX	34,452	NC
Univ of West Alabama	AL	15,516	NC
Univ of Wisc-Platteville	WI	14,614	VC
Univ of Wisc-Stout	WI	19,667	C
Utah State Univ	UT	12,736	C
Washington State Univ	WA	22,495	C
West Virginia Univ Inst of Technology	WV	16,462	NC
Western Kentucky Univ	KY	16,850	C
Western Washington Univ	WA	18,003	C+
William Penn Univ	IA	26,000	C

INDUSTRIAL HYGIENE

School	ST	$IS	SR
Ohio Univ	OH	22,924	C
St. Augustine's Univ	NC	26,048	C
South Univ	GA	36,070	LC
Univ of Central Okla	OK	13,486	C
Univ of North Alabama	AL	15,398	C

INDUSTRIAL PSYCHOLOGY/ SAFETY

School	ST	$IS	SR
Embry-Riddle Aeronautical Univ - Prescott Campus	AZ	44,054	VC
Faulkner Univ	AL	26,410	C

INDUSTRIAL TECHNOLOGY

School	ST	$IS	SR
Black Hills State Univ	SD	15,899	C
Calif Polytechnic State Univ	CA	17,979	HC+
Ferris State Univ	MI	21,445	C
Missouri Southern State Univ	MO	12,499	C
Southwestern Okla State Univ	OK	11,790	C
Univ of Mass Lowell	MA	26,380	C
Western Kentucky Univ	KY	16,850	C

INDUSTRIAL/ORGANIZATIONAL PSYCHOLOGY

School	ST	$IS	SR
Embry-Riddle Aeronautical Univ - Worldwide	FL	17,480	C
Univ of Detroit Mercy	MI	48,816	C+

INDUSTRY & SYSTEMS ENGINEERING

School	ST	$IS	SR
Univ of Rhode Island	RI	24,906	C

INFORM, SCIENCE, SYSTMS & TECH

School	ST	$IS	SR
Armstrong State Univ	GA	16,962	C
Bryant Univ	RI	55,646	VC
Cornell Univ	NY	64,853	MC
Syracuse Univ	NY	60,239	VC
Univ of Mass Lowell	MA	26,380	C
Univ of Wisc-Milwaukee	WI	21,496	C

INFORMATICS AND COMPUTER SCIENCE

School	ST	$IS	SR
Arizona State Univ at the Tempe Campus	AZ	21,756	VC
Bloomfield College	NJ	39,100	LC
Bryant Univ	RI	55,646	VC
Faulkner Univ	AL	26,410	C
Indiana Univ Bloomington	IN	20,429	VC
Indiana Univ East	IN	7,072	C
Indiana Univ Kokomo	IN	7,073	C
Indiana Univ Northwest	IN	7,072	C
Indiana Univ South Bend	IN	14,242	C
Indiana Univ Southeast	IN	14,242	LC
Indiana Univ-Purdue Univ Indianapolis	IN	18,635	C
Silver Lake College of the Holy Family	WI	36,290	LC
SUNY / Univ at Buffalo	NY	23,122	C+

INFORMATION & COMMUNICATION TECHNOLOGY

School	ST	$IS	SR
Abilene Christian Univ	TX	41,800	C+
Aquinas College - Mich	MI	38,876	HC
Arizona State Univ at the Polytechnic Campus	AZ	21,360	VC
Bentley Univ	MA	60,890	HC
Bluffton Univ	OH	40,950	C
Bryant Univ	RI	55,646	VC
Cal State, Northridge	CA	16,859	LC
Coastal Carolina Univ	SC	19,766	C
Dominican Univ	IL	41,222	C
Goshen College	IN	42,500	C
Guilford College	NC	44,090	C
Marywood Univ	PA	46,900	C
Univ of Scranton	PA	54,962	VC
Univ of Tampa	FL	36,944	C
Univ of Wisc-Stout	WI	19,667	C

INFORMATION SCIENCE

School	ST	$IS	SR
Bloomfield College	NJ	39,100	LC
Bryant Univ	RI	55,646	VC
Christopher Newport Univ	VA	23,968	VC+
Columbus State Univ	GA	14,336	LC
Cornell Univ	NY	64,853	MC
Georgia Southern Univ	GA	16,596	C
Niagara Univ	NY	41,010	C
Pennsylvania State Univ - Univ Park	PA	29,760	HC
Rochester Inst of Technology	NY	50,842	HC
Univ of Colo Boulder	CO	24,285	VC+
Univ of South Alabama	AL	16,400	C

INFORMATION SCIENCES AND SYSTEMS

School	ST	$IS	SR
Abilene Christian Univ	TX	41,800	C+
Alabama State Univ	AL	14,142	NC
Albany State Univ	GA	19,462	C
Albright College	PA	46,660	C
Alfred State College	NY	19,895	C
Andrews Univ	MI	28,030	C+
Aquinas College - Mich	MI	38,876	HC
Arkansas Tech Univ	AR	15,484	C
Atlantic Union College	MA	27,228	C
Auburn Univ at Montgomery	AL	15,290	C
Augusta Univ	GA	4,632	C
Augustana Univ	SD	38,424	VC
Averett Univ	VA	40,970	LC
Avila Univ	MO	35,480	C
Azusa Pacific Univ	CA	43,972	C
Barton College	NC	38,686	LC
Baylor Univ	TX	53,760	HC
Beacon College	FL	46,862	C
Belhaven Univ	MS	31,016	C
Bellevue Univ	NE	20,300	NC
Bethune-Cookman Univ	FL	22,970	C
Biola Univ	CA	46,402	C+
Bloomfield College	NJ	39,100	LC
Boise State Univ	ID	14,860	C
Boston College	MA	65,737	MC
Brewton-Parker College	GA	23,490	C
Briar Cliff Univ	IA	36,956	C
Brigham Young Univ	UT	12,748	HC
Brigham Young Univ/Hawaii	HI	11,290	C
Bryant Univ	RI	55,646	VC
Cabrini Univ	PA	42,591	LC
Caldwell Univ	NJ	42,165	NC
Calif Lutheran Univ	CA	52,853	C
Cal State, Fullerton	CA	21,902	C
Cal State, Los Angeles	CA	17,186	LC
Cal State, Stanislaus	CA	16,212	C
Calif Univ of Pennsylvania	PA	14,217	LC
Calumet College of St. Joseph	IN	22,735	C
Calvin College	MI	41,570	VC+
Campbellsville Univ	KY	32,492	C
Canisius College	NY	47,537	C
Carlow Univ	PA	38,549	LC
Carnegie Mellon Univ	PA	67,980	MC
Catawba College	NC	39,820	C
Cedar Crest College	PA	46,715	C
Central Mich Univ	MI	20,330	C
Central Washington Univ	WA	16,803	C
Champlain College	VT	53,132	C+
Chapman Univ	CA	63,078	VC+
Chestnut Hill College	PA	43,410	C
Chicago State Univ	IL	20,144	C
CUNY/Baruch College	NY	21,609	HC
CUNY/Brooklyn College	NY	5,884	C+
CUNY/College of Technology	NY	6,669	NC
CUNY/York College	NY	6,747	LC
Clarion Univ of Pennsylvania	PA	21,608	LC
Clarkson Univ	NY	60,392	HC
Clayton State Univ	GA	19,735	C
Clemson Univ	SC		HC
Cleveland State Univ	OH	22,196	C
Coastal Carolina Univ	SC	19,766	C
College of the Ozarks	MO	7,230	C
Colo State Univ	CO	22,162	VC
Colo State Univ-Pueblo	CO	18,234	C
Colo Technical Univ	CO	21,455	NC
Columbia College	SC	36,550	C
Columbia College - Missouri	MO	27,803	C
Concord Univ	WV	14,954	C
Concordia Univ St. Paul	MN	29,050	C
Curry College	MA	51,815	C
Dakota State Univ	SD	13,811	C
Daniel Webster College	NH	26,984	C
Davenport Univ	MI	25,896	LC
Defiance College	OH	41,630	C
DePaul Univ	IL	47,623	VC
Doane Univ	NE	39,184	VC
Dominican College	NY	31,270	LC
Dordt College	IA	37,860	C+
Drake Univ	IA	45,056	HC
Drexel Univ	PA	65,432	VC+
D'Youville College	NY	36,780	C
East Carolina Univ	NC	16,937	C
East Tenn State Univ	TN	13,994	C
Eastern Mich Univ	MI	19,761	C
Eastern New Mexico Univ	NM	14,416	C
Eastern Washington Univ	WA	25,572	LC
Edgewood College	WI	35,950	C
Edinboro Univ	PA	15,940	LC
Elizabethtown College	PA	54,050	C
Elmhurst College	IL	45,428	C
Elon Univ	NC	44,599	VC+
Emporia State Univ	KS	14,570	C
Excelsior College	NY	14,080	SP
Fairfield Univ	CT	59,860	VC+
Fairleigh Dickinson Univ/ Metropolitan Campus	NJ	40,254	C
Farmingdale State College	NY	20,624	C
Faulkner Univ	AL	26,410	C
Felician Univ	NJ	45,370	LC
Ferrum College	VA	39,650	C
Florida Atlantic Univ	FL	17,339	C
Florida Inst of Technology	FL	53,306	VC
Florida State Univ	FL	16,771	HC
Fontbonne Univ	MO	33,717	C
Fordham Univ	NY	65,918	MC
Fort Hays State Univ	KS	12,131	C
Fort Valley State Univ	GA	17,988	VC
Francis Marion Univ	SC	16,464	LC
Franciscan Univ of Steubenville	OH	33,980	VC
Freed-Hardeman Univ	TN	29,450	C
Friends Univ	KS	34,455	C
Frostburg State Univ	MD	17,280	LC
Furman Univ	SC	58,092	VC+
Gannon Univ	PA	42,032	C
Gardner-Webb Univ	NC	39,200	C+
George Fox Univ	OR	42,938	C
George Mason Univ	VA	15,724	VC
George Washington Univ	DC	62,835	MC
Glenville State College	WV	17,386	NC
Goldey-Beacom College	DE	31,750	C
Goshen College	IN	42,500	C
Graceland Univ	IA	35,290	C
Grambling State Univ	LA	15,701	C
Grand Valley State Univ	MI	22,250	C+
Guilford College	NC	44,090	C
Gwynedd Mercy Univ	PA	43,780	LC
Hampton Univ	VA	34,926	LC
Hannibal-LaGrange Univ	MO	29,815	C
Harding Univ	AR	25,421	C
Hartwick College	NY	51,270	C
Haverford College	PA	66,490	MC
Heidelberg Univ	OH	39,200	C
Henderson State Univ	AR	15,516	LC
Hodges Univ	FL	19,080	LC
Hofstra Univ	NY	55,960	C+
Holy Family Univ	PA	43,326	LC
Houston Baptist Univ	TX	36,450	C
Humboldt State Univ	CA	20,514	C
Huntington Univ	IN	33,996	C
Idaho State Univ	ID	13,619	NC
Illinois College	IL	40,850	VC
Illinois Inst of Technology	IL	56,826	HC+
Illinois State Univ	IL	23,418	VC
Indiana Inst of Technology	IN	34,240	LC
Indiana Univ Kokomo	IN	7,073	C
Indiana Univ-Purdue Univ Fort Wayne	IN	17,553	C
Indiana Wesleyan Univ	IN	33,674	C
Inter-American Univ of PR-Aguadilla Campus	PR	21,657	
Iona College	NY	50,984	C
Jacksonville Univ	FL	46,230	C
James Madison Univ	VA	19,084	VC
Johnson & Wales Univ/ Providence Campus	RI	42,248	C
Juniata College	PA	53,760	VC
Kansas State Univ	KS	17,780	VC
Kennesaw State Univ	GA	19,592	VC
Keystone College	PA	28,680	LC
King's College	PA	46,858	C
Kutztown Univ of Pennsylvania	PA	19,056	LC
La Salle Univ	PA	55,790	C
La Sierra Univ	CA	39,690	VC
Lamar Univ	TX	18,014	LC
Lawrence Tech Univ	MI	39,770	VC
Le Moyne College	NY	46,000	C
Lee Univ	TN	22,045	C
Lewis Univ	IL	40,370	C
Limestone College	SC	32,100	C
Lincoln Memorial Univ	TN	28,070	C
Lincoln Univ	MO	13,602	NC
LIU Brooklyn	NY	49,682	C
LIU Post	NY	49,682	C
Lock Haven Univ of Pennsylvania	PA	18,028	LC
Louisiana State Univ and A&M College	LA	18,677	VC
Loyola Univ Chicago	IL	55,802	VC
Lubbock Christian Univ	TX	28,426	C
Manhattan College	NY	51,750	C+
Mansfield Univ	PA	23,376	LC
Marian Univ	WI	32,420	LC
Marietta College	OH	46,190	C
Marist College	NY	49,860	VC
Marshall Univ	WV	17,242	C
Marymount Manhattan College	NY	46,280	VC
Maryville Univ of St. Louis	MO	38,046	VC+
Marywood Univ	PA	46,900	C
McKendree Univ	IL	37,940	C+
Mercer Univ	GA	45,348	VC
Mercy College	NY	31,776	C
Meredith College	NC	45,297	C
Metropolitan State Univ	MN	7,566	C
Metropolitan State Univ of Denver	CO	29,889	LC
Miami Univ	OH	27,190	HC+
Mich State Univ	MI	23,898	VC+
Middle Tenn State Univ	TN	8,650	C
Midwestern State Univ	TX	17,572	C
Milligan College	TN	38,150	C
Millikin Univ	IL	42,158	C
Minn State Univ, Mankato	MN	15,616	C
Misericordia Univ	PA	43,840	C
Miss State Univ	MS	11,454	C+
Missouri Baptist Univ	MO	35,594	C
Missouri Univ of Science and Technology	MO	18,655	HC
Missouri Valley College	MO	28,150	C
Missouri Western State Univ	MO	16,741	
Monroe College	NY	23,660	C
Montana State Univ-Billings	MT	22,960	C
Montclair State Univ	NJ	26,210	LC
Morgan State Univ	MD	17,190	LC
Mount Aloysius College	PA	29,976	C
Mount St. Mary's Univ	MD	51,610	C
National Louis Univ	IL	16,920	LC
National Univ	CA	14,730	LC
Nebr Wesleyan Univ	NE	38,140	C+
New Jersey Inst of Technology	NJ	29,569	VC
New Mexico Inst of Mining and Technology	NM	14,833	HC
New Mexico State Univ	NM	14,050	C
New York Univ	NY	65,860	MC
Newman Univ	KS	35,390	C
Niagara Univ	NY	41,010	C
Nicholls State Univ	LA	10,534	C
N Car Wesleyan College	NC	39,200	C
Northeastern State Univ	OK	8,615	VC
Northeastern Univ	MA	62,703	MC
Northern Illinois Univ	IL	20,176	C
Northern Kentucky Univ	KY	16,486	C
Northern Mich Univ	MI	19,604	C
Northland College	WI	41,103	C+
Northwest Missouri State Univ	MO	17,737	C
Northwestern College of Iowa	IA	38,400	C+
Northwestern Univ	IL	66,344	MC
Norwich Univ	VT	28,212	C
Notre Dame College	OH	37,150	VC

ST = STATE $IS = IN-STATE COSTS SR = SELECTOR RATING

School	ST	$IS	SR
Notre Dame de Namur Univ	CA	46,526	LC
Notre Dame of Maryland Univ	MD	46,465	VC
Oakland Univ	MI	20,763	C
Oakwood Univ	AL	43,758	C
Ohio State Univ at Columbus	OH	21,703	HC+
Okla Baptist Univ	OK	32,320	C
Okla Christian Univ	OK	27,650	VC
Okla Panhandle State Univ	OK	6,152	NC
Old Dominion Univ	VA	20,910	C
Olivet Nazarene Univ	IL	41,840	C
Ottawa Univ	KS	36,074	VC
Our Lady of the Lake Univ	TX	35,012	LC
Pace Univ	NY	58,248	C
Park Univ	MO	20,329	C
Peirce College	PA	16,780	NC
Pennsylvania College of Technology	PA	27,333	NC
Pfeiffer Univ	NC	39,695	LC
Pittsburg State Univ	KS	13,880	NC
Plymouth State Univ	NH	23,180	LC
Point Park Univ	PA	41,270	C
Portland State Univ	OR	19,443	C
Purdue Univ/Northwest	IN	15,038	C
Purdue Univ/West Lafayette	IN	20,032	MC
Quincy Univ	IL	36,998	C
Radford Univ	VA	19,027	LC
Ramapo College of New Jersey	NJ	25,338	C
Rhode Island College	RI	17,694	LC
Rider Univ	NJ	54,050	LC
Robert Morris Univ	PA	37,834	C
Rochester Inst of Technology	NY	50,842	HC
Roosevelt Univ	IL	40,651	VC
Rutgers Univ - New Brunswick	NJ	26,632	HC
Rutgers Univ - Newark	NJ	27,288	C
Sacred Heart Univ	CT	52,750	C
Saginaw Valley State Univ	MI	18,530	C
St. Augustine's Univ	NC	26,048	C
St. Joseph's Univ	PA	57,544	VC+
St. Leo Univ	FL	31,650	C
St. Michael's College	VT	51,725	VC+
Salem International Univ	WV	21,090	LC
Salisbury Univ	MD	20,714	VC
San Diego State Univ	CA	21,896	C+
San Francisco State Univ	CA	18,514	LC
Seattle Pacific Univ	WA	47,439	C+
Shepherd Univ, West Virginia	WV	17,224	C
Siena Heights Univ	MI	32,040	C
Simpson College	IA	43,839	VC
Slippery Rock Univ of Pennsylvania	PA	10,360	C
Southeastern Okla State Univ	OK	11,875	C
Southern Adventist Univ	TN	27,600	C
Southern Illinois Univ Carbondale	IL	23,667	C
Southern New Hampshire Univ	NH	43,198	C
Southwest Baptist Univ	MO	29,900	LC
Southwestern Adventist Univ	TX	27,756	LC
Springfield College	MA	45,995	C
St. Catherine Univ	MN	45,630	VC
St. Edward's Univ	TX	53,100	VC
St. Francis College	NY	38,800	LC
SUNY / Buffalo State College	NY	20,842	C
SUNY / Empire State College	NY	9,145	SP
SUNY / SUNY College at Old Westbury	NY	16,860	C
SUNY /College of Agriculture and Tech at Cobleskill	NY	20,527	LC
SUNY at Binghamton	NY	22,861	MC
SUNY at Oswego	NY	21,351	C
SUNY SUNY Albany	NY	22,165	C
Stephen F. Austin State Univ	TX	18,406	LC
Stevens Inst of Technology	NJ	62,338	MC
Stevenson Univ	MD	72,770	C
Stockton Univ	NJ	25,059	
Stony Brook Univ/The SUNY	NY	21,881	MC
Suffolk Univ	MA	50,308	C
Syracuse Univ	NY	60,239	VC
Tarleton State Univ	TX	15,248	LC
Temple Univ	PA	24,392	VC
Texas Lutheran Univ	TX	38,620	C
The Master's Univ	CA	43,870	C+
The Univ of Tenn at Martin	TN	14,876	C
The Univ of Utah	UT	17,924	VC
The Univ of Virginia's College at Wise	VA	18,192	LC
Thomas College	ME	35,268	LC
Tiffin Univ	OH	31,380	C
Towson Univ	MD	17,408	VC
Trevecca Nazarene Univ	TN	31,186	C
Trine Univ	IN	41,310	C
Trinity Christian College	IL	35,580	C
Troy Univ	AL	16,171	C
Tulane Univ	LA	63,396	HC+
Tusculum College	TN	31,625	C
United States Naval Academy	MD		MC
Univ of Alabama at Birmingham	AL	19,906	C
Univ of Alabama in Huntsville	AL	19,445	VC
Univ of Arizona	AZ	23,100	C
Univ of Arkansas at Little Rock	AR	18,211	C
Univ of Arkansas at Monticello	AR	13,134	NC
Univ of Calif at Irvine	CA	26,484	VC
Univ of Calif at Riverside	CA	29,227	C+
Univ of Calif San Diego	CA	30,150	MC
Univ of Calif, Santa Cruz	CA	28,731	C+
Univ of Central Arkansas	AR	14,472	VC
Univ of Central Florida	FL	15,922	VC
Univ of Central Missouri	MO	18,982	C
Univ of Cincinnati	OH	21,964	VC
Univ of Dayton	OH	53,620	C
Univ of Delaware	DE	24,976	VC+
Univ of Denver	CO	58,443	VC+
Univ of Detroit Mercy	MI	48,816	C+
Univ of Florida	FL	16,291	HC+
Univ of Hartford	CT	49,776	C
Univ of Hawaii at Manoa	HI	23,221	C
Univ of Houston-Downtown	TX	7,241	C
Univ of Idaho	ID	15,348	C
Univ of Illinois at Chicago	IL	25,006	VC
Univ of Iowa	IA	18,683	VC+
Univ of Jamestown	ND	28,508	C
Univ of Kansas	KS	20,135	C+
Univ of Louisville	KY	19,824	C
Univ of Maine at Augusta	ME	7,812	C
Univ of Mary	ND	23,180	C
Univ of Mary Hardin-Baylor	TX	33,950	C+
Univ of Maryland/Baltimore County	MD	21,296	VC
Univ of Maryland/College Park	MD	21,938	HC
Univ of Maryland/Univ College	MD	25,966	LC
Univ of Mass Boston	MA	13,435	C
Univ of Mass Lowell	MA	26,380	C
Univ of Minn Crookston	MN	19,739	C
Univ of Minn/Duluth	MN	20,292	C+
Univ of Missouri-St. Louis	MO		C
Univ of Mobile	AL	28,935	C
Univ of Mount Olive	NC	18,426	C
Univ of Mount Union	OH	38,970	C
Univ of Nebr - Kearney	NE	16,546	LC
Univ of Nebr - Omaha	NE	16,120	C
Univ of Nevada/Reno	NV	18,010	C
Univ of North Alabama	AL	15,398	C
Univ of N Car at Chapel Hill	NC	20,052	HC+
Univ of N Dak	ND	15,373	C
Univ of North Florida	FL	15,996	VC
Univ of North Texas	TX	19,198	C
Univ of Northern Colo	CO	20,851	C
Univ of Okla	OK	18,911	VC
Univ of Pennsylvania	PA	63,526	MC
Univ of Pittsburgh	PA	29,568	HC+
Univ of PR, at Bayamon	PR	13,145	
Univ of PR, at Mayaguez	PR	13,995	
Univ of PR-Rio Piedras campus	PR	13,327	
Univ of Redlands	CA	60,200	VC
Univ of St. Mary	KS	34,690	C
Univ of San Francisco	CA	58,484	VC
Univ of Scranton	PA	54,962	VC
Univ of S Car Upstate	SC	18,200	LC
Univ of South Florida/St. Petersburg	FL	15,980	C
Univ of Southern Miss	MS	13,170	C
Univ of St. Francis	IL	39,924	C
Univ of Texas at Arlington	TX	18,026	LC
Univ of Texas at Dallas	TX	22,830	VC+
Univ of Texas at San Antonio	TX	20,157	C
Univ of the Cumberlands	KY	32,000	C
Univ of the Incarnate Word	TX	39,162	LC
Univ of the Pacific	CA	57,006	VC
Univ of Toledo	OH	19,336	NC
Univ of Tulsa	OK	52,625	HC+
Univ of Vermont	VT	28,878	HC
Univ of Washington	WA	23,149	VC
Univ of Wisc-Eau Claire	WI	15,797	VC
Univ of Wisc-Green Bay	WI	15,064	C
Univ of Wisc-La Crosse	WI	15,247	C+
Univ of Wisc-Madison	WI	20,934	MC
Univ of Wisc-Milwaukee	WI	21,496	C
Univ of Wisc-Stevens Point	WI	14,043	C
Utah State Univ	UT	12,736	C
Valley City State Univ	ND	13,267	C
Vermont Technical College	VT	23,838	C
Villanova Univ	PA	62,523	MC
Virginia Commonwealth Univ	VA	23,049	C
Walla Walla Univ	WA	30,417	NC
Warner Univ	FL	28,216	C
Wartburg College	IA	47,840	C
Washington Adventist Univ	MD	31,440	LC
Washington Univ in St. Louis	MO	65,366	VC
Wayne State Univ	MI	22,016	C
Waynesburg Univ	PA	32,290	C
Webber International Univ	FL	31,904	C
Weber State Univ	UT	10,721	C
Webster Univ	MO	37,490	C
Wentworth Inst of Technology	MA	47,112	C
Wesleyan College	GA	29,694	C+
West Liberty Univ	WV	15,512	C
West Texas A&M Univ	TX	13,478	C
Western Illinois Univ	IL	20,825	C
Western New England Univ	MA	48,088	C
Western Oregon Univ	OR	15,021	LC
Westfield State Univ	MA	19,671	C
Westminster College	UT	41,078	C+
Widener Univ	PA	56,486	C
Wilberforce Univ	OH	19,016	C
Wilkes Univ	PA	45,622	C
William Woods Univ	MO	32,040	C
Wilmington College	OH	34,600	C
Woodbury Univ	CA	46,958	C
Xavier Univ	OH	47,880	C+
Youngstown State Univ	OH	17,307	C

INFORMATION TECHNOLOGY

School	ST	$IS	SR
Arkansas State Univ	AR	16,190	C
Bloomfield College	NJ	39,100	LC
Bryant Univ	RI	55,646	VC
Cabrini Univ	PA	42,591	LC
Calif Baptist Univ	CA	41,392	C
Calvin College	MI	41,570	VC+
Cameron Univ	OK	11,072	NC
Carroll Univ	WI	38,100	C+
Cedarville Univ	OH	34,990	VC
Champlain College	VT	53,132	C+
Dakota State Univ	SD	13,811	C
DePaul Univ	IL	47,623	VC
Elizabethtown College School of Continuing and Professional Studies	PA	18,900	C
Elmhurst College	IL	45,428	C
Embry-Riddle Aeronautical Univ - Worldwide	FL	17,480	C
Faulkner Univ	AL	26,410	C
Gallaudet Univ	DC	29,118	LC
Harris-Stowe State Univ	MO	14,360	NC
Juniata College	PA	53,760	VC
Kean Univ	NJ	24,650	C
King Univ	TN	34,660	C
La Roche College	PA	37,924	LC
Lake Erie College	OH	38,914	LC
Lawrence Tech Univ	MI	39,770	VC
LeMoyne-Owen College	TN	16,980	C
Lewis Univ	IL	40,370	C
Marquette Univ	WI	48,390	VC+
Marshall Univ	WV	17,242	C
Marymount Univ	VA	41,570	LC
Missouri State Univ	MO	15,190	C+
Mount St. Mary College	NY	42,061	C
Mount Vernon Nazarene Univ	OH	34,500	C
Nazareth College	NY	45,574	C
New York Univ	NY	65,860	MC
Nova Southeastern Univ	FL	38,534	C+
Okla Baptist Univ	OK	32,320	C
Pace Univ	NY	58,248	C
Regis Univ	CO	44,520	C
Rochester Inst of Technology	NY	50,842	HC
St. Louis Univ	MO	49,866	HC
Silver Lake College of the Holy Family	WI	36,290	LC
Simmons College	MA	53,090	VC
Southeast Missouri State Univ	MO	15,498	C
Southeastern Louisiana Univ	LA	16,237	C
Southern Illinois Univ Carbondale	IL	23,667	C
St. John's Univ	NY	55,850	C
SUNY SUNY Albany	NY	22,165	C
Stephen F. Austin State Univ	TX	18,406	LC
Tarleton State Univ	TX	15,248	LC
Texas Tech Univ	TX	18,736	C+
The College of St. Rose	NY	43,048	C
The Lincoln Univ	PA	15,154	NC
Thomas Edison State Univ	NJ	6,350	NC
Univ of Arizona	AZ	23,100	C
Univ of Central Florida	FL	15,922	VC
Univ of Cincinnati	OH	21,964	VC
Univ of Kansas	KS	20,135	C+
Univ of Mass Boston	MA	13,435	C
Univ of Mass Lowell	MA	26,380	C
Univ of Missouri-Kansas City	MO	19,563	VC
Univ of Nebr - Lincoln	NE	18,589	VC
Univ of New Hampshire	NH	28,562	VC
Univ of N Car at Greensboro	NC	14,690	C
Univ of Notre Dame	IN	64,043	MC
Univ of South Alabama	AL	16,400	C
Univ of Wisc-Milwaukee	WI	21,496	C
Webster Univ	MO	37,490	C
Youngstown State Univ	OH	17,307	C

INSTITUTIONAL MANAGEMENT

School	ST	$IS	SR
Bryant Univ	RI	55,646	VC
Calumet College of St. Joseph	IN	22,735	C
CUNY/College of Technology	NY	6,669	NC
Goshen College	IN	42,500	C
San Francisco State Univ	CA	18,514	LC
SUNY / SUNY Fredonia	NY	20,818	C
Univ of La Verne	CA	55,600	C
Warner Univ	FL	28,216	C

INSTRUCTIONAL DESIGN

School	ST	$IS	SR
Ashford Univ	CA	10,480	C
Southwestern Okla State Univ	OK	11,790	C

INSTRUMENTAL MUSIC EDUCATION

School	ST	$IS	SR
Arkansas State Univ	AR	16,190	C
Concordia Univ St. Paul	MN	29,050	C
King Univ	TN	34,660	C
Marian Univ	IN	41,220	C
Missouri Southern State Univ	MO	12,499	C
Murray State Univ	KY	16,998	C
N Dak State Univ	ND	16,245	C
Ohio Univ	OH	22,924	C
Okla Baptist Univ	OK	32,320	C
Okla City Univ	OK	40,476	VC
Okla City Univ	OK	40,476	VC
Ouachita Baptist Univ	AR	32,320	C
Texas Christian Univ	TX	54,670	HC
Weber State Univ	UT	10,721	C
Webster Univ	MO	37,490	C
Western Mich Univ	MI	21,054	C

INSTRUMENTAL PERFORMANCE

School	ST	$IS	SR
Baldwin Wallace Univ	OH	41,106	C
Bowling Green State Univ	OH	19,747	C
Houghton College	NY	39,090	C
LIU Post	NY	49,682	C
Madonna Univ	MI	29,050	C
Marian Univ	IN	41,220	C
New York Univ	NY	65,860	MC
Okla Baptist Univ	OK	32,320	C
Okla Christian Univ	OK	27,650	VC
Okla City Univ	OK	40,476	VC
Ouachita Baptist Univ	AR	32,320	C
Southeast Missouri State Univ	MO	15,498	C
Texas Christian Univ	TX	54,670	HC
The Master's Univ	CA	43,870	C+
Univ of Miami	FL	63,494	MC
Weber State Univ	UT	10,721	C
Webster Univ	MO	37,490	C
Western Mich Univ	MI	21,054	C
Wingate Univ	NC	39,950	C
Wright State Univ	OH	16,983	C

INSURANCE

School	ST	$IS	SR
Baylor Univ	TX	53,760	HC
Bryant Univ	RI	55,646	VC
Cal State, Sacramento	CA	20,332	C
Idaho State Univ	ID	13,619	NC
Illinois State Univ	IL	23,418	VC
Indiana State Univ	IN	23,223	LC
Inter-American Univ of PR Ponce	PR	19,549	
Inter-American Univ of PR-Fajardo Campus	PR	18,336	
Martin Univ	IN	20,264	LC
Miss State Univ	MS	11,454	C+
Old Dominion Univ	VA	20,910	C
Olivet College	MI	36,110	LC
Roosevelt Univ	IL	40,651	VC
Troy Univ	AL	16,171	C
Univ of Central Okla	OK	13,486	C
Univ of Cincinnati	OH	21,964	VC
Univ of Florida	FL	16,291	HC+
Univ of Hartford	CT	49,776	C
Univ of Illinois at Urbana-Champaign	IL	27,006	HC
Univ of Louisiana at Monroe	LA	15,970	C
Univ of Miss	MS	17,746	C+
Univ of North Texas	TX	19,198	C
Univ of S Car at Columbia	SC	19,725	VC+
Washington State Univ	WA	22,495	C

INSURANCE AND RISK MANAGEMENT

School	ST	$IS	SR
Appalachian State Univ	NC	14,416	VC
Bryant Univ	RI	55,646	VC
Excelsior College	NY	14,080	SP
Ferris State Univ	MI	21,445	C
Florida State Univ	FL	16,771	HC
Gannon Univ	PA	42,032	C
Georgia State Univ	GA	24,332	VC
Illinois Wesleyan Univ	IL	56,430	VC+
Mercyhurst Univ	PA	47,420	C
Ohio State Univ at Columbus	OH	21,703	HC+
Roosevelt Univ	IL	40,651	VC
St. Joseph's Univ	PA	57,544	VC+
Southern Methodist Univ	TX	66,483	MC
St. John's Univ	NY	55,850	C
SUNY at Oswego	NY	21,351	C
Univ of Central Arkansas	AR	14,472	VC
Univ of Conn	CT	25,538	HC
Univ of Georgia	GA	21,250	HC
Univ of Houston-Downtown	TX	7,241	C
Univ of Nebr - Lincoln	NE	18,589	VC
Univ of Pennsylvania	PA	63,526	MC
Univ of St. Francis	IN	37,400	C
Univ of Wisc-Madison	WI	20,934	MC
Utica College	NY	30,430	C

INTEGRATED ART AND DESIGN

School	ST	$IS	SR
East Stroudsburg Univ	PA	18,334	C

INTEGRATIVE STUDIES

School	ST	$IS	SR
Christopher Newport Univ	VA	23,968	VC+
Ferris State Univ	MI	21,445	C
Kennesaw State Univ	GA	19,592	VC
Murray State Univ	KY	16,998	C
St. Ambrose Univ	IA	39,019	C
St. Ambrose Univ	IA	39,019	C

INTERDISCIPLINARY ART

School	ST	$IS	SR
Tufts Univ	MA		MC

ST = STATE $IS = IN-STATE COSTS SR = SELECTOR RATING

INTERDISCIPLINARY STUDIES

School	ST	$IS	SR
Adams State Univ	CO	17,703	LC
Alderson Broaddus Univ	WV	26,149	C
Alfred Univ	NY	42,296	C+
American Univ	DC	59,379	HC+
Amherst College	MA		HC+
Andrews Univ	MI	28,030	C+
Angelo State Univ	TX	15,263	NC
Appalachian State Univ	NC	14,416	VC
Aquinas College	TN	30,800	C+
Aquinas College - Mich	MI	38,876	HC
Arizona State Univ at the Downtown Phoenix Campus	AZ	23,680	VC
Arizona State Univ at the Polytechnic Campus	AZ	21,360	VC
Arizona State Univ at the Tempe Campus	AZ	21,756	VC
Arizona State Univ at the West Campus	AZ	20,640	C
Arkansas State Univ	AR	16,190	C
Augustana Univ	SD	38,424	VC
Austin College	TX	45,875	VC
Austin Peay State Univ	TN	16,397	C
Averett Univ	VA	40,970	LC
Baldwin Wallace Univ	OH	41,106	C
Bard College	NY	64,024	HC
Bates College	ME	64,500	MC
Baylor Univ	TX	53,760	HC
Belhaven Univ	MS	31,016	C
Bellarmine Univ	KY	51,220	C
Beloit College	WI	55,206	HC
Bennett College	NC	27,302	NC
Bennington College	VT	63,960	MC
Bentley Univ	MA	60,890	HC
Berry College	GA	45,286	C+
Bethany College	WV	36,300	NC
Bethel College	IN	35,860	C
Birmingham-Southern College	AL	44,478	VC
Blackburn College	IL	28,526	LC
Bloomfield College	NJ	39,100	LC
Bluefield College	VA	34,120	C+
Boise State Univ	ID	14,860	C
Boston Univ	MA	65,110	MC
Bowdoin College	ME	63,500	MC
Bowie State Univ	MD	26,728	LC
Bowling Green State Univ	OH	19,747	C
Brandeis Univ	MA	65,925	MC
Brigham Young Univ/Hawaii	HI	11,290	C
Bryn Athyn College	PA	31,470	C
Bucknell Univ	PA	64,616	MC
Buena Vista Univ	IA	41,514	C
Calif Baptist Univ	CA	41,392	C
Calif Lutheran Univ	CA	52,853	C
Calif Polytechnic State Univ	CA	17,979	HC+
Cal State, Dominguez Hills	CA	19,022	LC
Cal State, Long Beach	CA	18,850	C
Cal State, Los Angeles	CA	17,186	LC
Cal State, Stanislaus	CA	16,212	C
Calvin College	MI	41,570	VC+
Cambridge College	MA	15,734	NC
Cameron Univ	OK	11,072	NC
Centenary College	NJ	43,602	C
Centenary College of Louisiana	LA	45,650	C+
Central Methodist Univ	MO	36,830	VC
Central Mich Univ	MI	20,330	C
Chatham Univ	PA	46,517	C
Christopher Newport Univ	VA	23,968	VC+
CUNY/Brooklyn College	NY	5,884	C+
Claremont McKenna College	CA	67,185	MC
Clarkson Univ	NY	60,392	HC
Clayton State Univ	GA	19,735	C
Coastal Carolina Univ	SC	19,766	C
Coe College	IA	51,570	VC
College of the Ozarks	MO	7,230	C
College of William & Mary	VA		MC
Colo College	CO	62,560	MC
Colo State Univ	CO	22,162	VC
Columbia College - Missouri	MO	27,803	C
Concordia College - New York	NY	39,035	LC
Coppin State Univ	MD	17,041	VC
Corban Univ	OR	40,306	C
Covenant College	GA	38,990	VC
Dallas Baptist Univ	TX	33,713	C
Davidson College	NC	60,119	MC
Davis & Elkins College	WV	38,242	LC
Delta State Univ	MS	13,176	C
DePauw Univ	IN	58,688	HC+
D'Youville College	NY	36,780	C
East Stroudsburg Univ	PA	18,334	C
East Tenn State Univ	TN	13,994	C
East Texas Baptist Univ	TX	33,134	C
Eastern Mich Univ	MI	19,761	C
Embry-Riddle Aeronautical Univ - Daytona Beach	FL	44,712	VC
Embry-Riddle Aeronautical Univ - Prescott Campus	AZ	44,054	VC
Embry-Riddle Aeronautical Univ - Worldwide	FL	17,480	C
Emerson College	MA	54,736	HC
Emmanuel College	MA	52,110	C+
Emory and Henry College	VA	41,410	C
Emory Univ	GA	60,786	MC
Eugene Lang College/The New School for Liberal Arts	NY	55,650	C
Fairleigh Dickinson Univ/ Metropolitan Campus	NJ	40,254	C
Fitchburg State Univ	MA	21,819	C
Florida Atlantic Univ	FL	17,339	C
Florida Inst of Technology	FL	53,306	VC
Fort Lewis College	CO	18,980	C
Framingham State Univ	MA	20,584	C
Franklin and Marshall College	PA	63,170	HC
Franklin Pierce Univ	NH	46,750	C
Gannon Univ	PA	42,032	C
Geneva College	PA	35,450	C
George Mason Univ	VA	15,724	VC
George Washington Univ	DC	62,835	MC
Georgetown College	KY	41,440	C
Georgetown Univ	DC	65,926	MC
Georgia State Univ	GA	24,332	VC
Goddard College	VT	17,040	VC
Gonzaga Univ	WA	50,888	HC
Goshen College	IN	42,500	C
Goucher College	MD	55,716	VC
Grace Bible College	MI	25,250	C
Grand Canyon Univ	AZ	16,950	VC
Grand Rapids Theological Seminary/Cornerstone Univ	MI	33,338	C
Guilford College	NC	44,090	C
Hamilton College	NY	64,250	MC
Haverford College	PA	66,490	MC
Hendrix College	AR	54,020	VC+
Heritage Univ	WA	19,825	NC
Hodges Univ	FL	19,080	LC
Hollins Univ	VA	49,635	VC
Houghton College	NY	39,090	C
Howard Univ	DC	37,616	C+
Huston-Tillotson Univ	TX	18,124	LC
Illinois State Univ	IL	23,418	VC
Illinois Wesleyan Univ	IL	56,430	VC+
Indiana State Univ	IN	23,223	LC
Indiana Univ-Purdue Univ Indianapolis	IN	18,635	C
Ithaca College	NY	56,766	VC
John Brown Univ	AR	33,132	VC
Johns Hopkins Univ	MD	65,386	MC
Judson College	AL	27,066	C
Kalamazoo College	MI	53,931	HC+
King Univ	TN	34,660	C
Lafayette College	PA	63,355	MC
LaGrange College	GA	39,930	C
Lake Erie College	OH	38,914	LC
Lander Univ	SC	43,994	C
Lane College	TN	16,550	C
Lasell College	MA	47,500	C
Lee Univ	TN	22,045	C
Lehigh Univ	PA	61,010	MC
LeMoyne-Owen College	TN	16,980	C
LeTourneau Univ	TX	38,250	VC
Lewis & Clark College	OR	58,434	HC+
Lewis-Clark State College	ID	14,202	C
Liberty Univ	VA	19,101	C
Lipscomb Univ	TN	41,296	VC
LIU Brooklyn	NY	49,682	C
LIU Post	NY	49,682	C
Louisiana State Univ and A&M College	LA	18,677	VC
Lourdes Univ	OH	29,520	NC
Loyola Marymount Univ	CA	58,038	HC
Lyndon State College	VT	20,714	C
Madonna Univ	MI	29,050	C
Manchester Univ	IN	40,422	C
Marian Univ	WI	32,420	LC
Marietta College	OH	46,190	C
Marquette Univ	WI	48,390	VC+
Marylhurst Univ	OR	20,295	NC
Mass College of Liberal Arts	MA	20,128	C
Mass Inst of Technology	MA	62,662	MC
McMurry Univ	TX	34,259	LC
Mercy College	NY	31,776	C
Messiah College	PA	43,100	C+
Miami Univ	OH	27,190	HC+
Mich State Univ	MI	23,898	VC+
MidAmerica Nazarene Univ	KS	35,550	C
Middle Tenn State Univ	TN	8,650	C
Midwestern State Univ	TX	17,572	C
Millersville Univ of Pennsylvania	PA	23,782	C
Millikin Univ	IL	42,158	C
Miss State Univ	MS	11,454	C+
Molloy College	NY	40,440	C
Montana State Univ-Northern	MT	11,370	NC
Mount St. Mary College	NY	42,061	C
Mount St. Mary's Univ	MD	51,610	C
Naropa Univ	CO	42,826	NC
National Univ	CA	14,730	LC
New York Inst of Technology	NY	48,730	C
Newman Univ	KS	35,390	C
Norfolk State Univ	VA	25,702	LC
N Car State Univ	NC	19,515	HC+
Northeastern Illinois Univ	IL	12,529	LC
Northeastern Univ	MA	62,703	MC
Northern Arizona Univ	AZ	20,246	VC
Northwest Christian Univ	OR	36,580	C
Northwest Univ	WA	35,876	VC
Notre Dame of Maryland Univ	MD	46,465	VC
Nyack College	NY	34,050	NC
Ohio Dominican Univ	OH	41,340	C+
Ohio Valley Univ	WV	29,480	C
Okla Baptist Univ	OK	32,320	C
Okla Christian Univ	OK	27,650	VC
Old Dominion Univ	VA	20,910	C
Palm Beach Atlantic Univ	FL	39,720	C
Piedmont College	GA	32,512	C
Plymouth State Univ	NH	23,180	LC
Prairie View A&M Univ	TX	15,205	LC
Radford Univ	VA	19,027	LC
Rensselaer Polytechnic Inst	NY	63,436	MC
Rhodes College	TN	51,900	HC
Roberts Wesleyan College	NY	38,306	C
Rochester College	MI	28,574	LC
Russell Sage College	NY	39,370	C
Rutgers Univ - Camden	NJ	26,146	C
Rutgers Univ - Newark	NJ	27,288	C
Saginaw Valley State Univ	MI	18,530	C
St. Martin's Univ	WA	45,056	C
St. Peter's Univ	NJ	49,192	C
San Diego Christian College	CA	39,068	C
San Diego State Univ	CA	21,896	C+
San Francisco State Univ	CA	18,514	LC
Shippensburg Univ of Pennsylvania	PA	23,208	C
Simmons College	MA	53,090	VC
Simpson College	IA	43,839	VC
Sonoma State Univ	CA	27,806	C
S Dak School of Mines and Technology	SD	18,645	VC
Southeast Missouri State Univ	MO	15,498	C
Southeastern Univ	FL	31,765	C
Southern Oregon Univ	OR	19,117	C
Southwest Baptist Univ	MO	29,900	LC
Southwest Minn State Univ	MN	17,783	C
Southwestern College	KS	31,531	C
Southwestern Okla State Univ	OK	11,790	C
Spring Hill College	AL	48,488	C
St. Andrews Univ	NC	44,634	LC
St. Edward's Univ	TX	53,100	VC
St. John Fisher College	NY	43,620	C
St. Lawrence Univ	NY	64,390	VC
St. Olaf College	MN	54,260	HC+
SUNY / Empire State College	NY	9,145	SP
SUNY / SUNY Fredonia	NY	20,818	C
SUNY / SUNY Plattsburgh	NY	18,814	C
SUNY / SUNY Potsdam	NY	20,404	C+
SUNY at Binghamton	NY	22,861	MC
SUNY Polytechnic Inst	NY	19,473	VC
SUNY SUNY Albany	NY	22;165	C
Stephen F. Austin State Univ	TX	18,406	LC
Sterling College	KS	32,830	C
Stevenson Univ	MD	72,770	C
Stonehill College	MA	55,030	C+
Stony Brook Univ/The SUNY	NY	21,881	MC
Tarleton State Univ	TX	15,248	LC
Taylor Univ	IN	40,317	C+
Tenn State Univ	TN	14,423	C
Texas Southern Univ	TX	18,212	LC
Texas State Univ	TX	19,350	C
Texas Wesleyan Univ	TX	35,134	C
Texas Woman's Univ	TX	15,302	LC
The College of St. Rose	NY	43,048	C
The College of Wooster	OH	57,900	VC+
The Univ of Akron	OH	21,477	C
The Univ of Tenn at Knoxville	TN	22,112	VC
Thomas Univ	GA	21,420	LC
Touro College	NY	28,950	VC
Towson Univ	MD	17,408	VC
Trinity College	CT	63,920	HC+
Truman State Univ	MO	16,014	HC
Tufts Univ	MA		MC
Union College	NY	64,320	MC
Univ of Alabama	AL	24,320	C+
Univ of Alaska Anchorage	AK	16,652	NC
Univ of Arizona	AZ	23,100	C
Univ of Bridgeport	CT	44,430	LC
Univ of Calif at Berkeley	CA	28,853	MC
Univ of Calif at Irvine	CA	26,484	VC
Univ of Calif at Riverside	CA	29,227	C+
Univ of Calif at Santa Barbara	CA	29,091	HC
Univ of Central Florida	FL	15,922	VC
Univ of Chicago	IL	67,584	MC
Univ of Colo Denver	CO	23,230	C
Univ of Delaware	DE	24,976	VC+
Univ of Denver	CO	58,443	VC+
Univ of Evansville	IN	44,186	VC+
Univ of Florida	FL	16,291	HC+
Univ of Georgia	GA	21,250	HC
Univ of Hartford	CT	49,776	C
Univ of Hawaii at Manoa	HI	23,221	C
Univ of Houston	TX	21,483	VC
Univ of Houston-Downtown	TX	7,241	C
Univ of Idaho	ID	15,348	C
Univ of Maine	ME	20,792	C
Univ of Maine at Augusta	ME	7,812	C
Univ of Maine at Farmington	ME	18,187	C
Univ of Maine at Machias	ME	22,960	C
Univ of Maryland/Baltimore County	MD	21,296	VC
Univ of Maryland/College Park	MD	21,938	HC
Univ of Mass Amherst	MA	26,199	VC+
Univ of Mass Dartmouth	MA	25,658	C
Univ of Memphis	TN	18,278	C
Univ of Miami	FL	63,494	MC
Univ of Mich/Ann Arbor	MI	24,410	MC
Univ of Minn/Duluth	MN	20,292	C+
Univ of Minn/Morris	MN	20,760	VC
Univ of Missouri-St. Louis	MO		C
Univ of Nebr - Lincoln	NE	18,589	VC
Univ of Nebr - Omaha	NE	16,120	C
Univ of Nevada, Las Vegas	NV	17,553	C
Univ of New Mexico	NM	15,404	C
Univ of N Car at Chapel Hill	NC	20,052	HC+
Univ of N Car at Pembroke	NC	14,388	LC
Univ of N Dak	ND	15,373	C
Univ of North Florida	FL	15,996	VC
Univ of North Texas	TX	19,198	C
Univ of Northern Colo	CO	20,851	C
Univ of Northwestern - St. Paul	MN	38,160	C
Univ of Pikeville	KY	28,700	NC
Univ of Pittsburgh	PA	29,568	HC+
Univ of Pittsburgh at Bradford	PA	22,402	C
Univ of Portland	OR	52,152	VC
Univ of PR-Rio Piedras campus	PR	13,327	
Univ of Redlands	CA	60,200	VC
Univ of Richmond	VA	60,880	MC
Univ of Rochester	NY	65,032	MC
Univ of St. Mary	KS	34,690	C
Univ of South Alabama	AL	16,400	C
Univ of S Car Aiken	SC	16,712	C
Univ of S Car at Columbia	SC	19,725	VC+
Univ of S Car Upstate	SC	18,200	LC
Univ of Texas at Arlington	TX	18,026	LC
Univ of Texas at Dallas	TX	22,830	VC+
Univ of Texas at El Paso	TX	34,452	NC
Univ of Texas at San Antonio	TX	20,157	C
Univ of the Sciences	PA	54,038	VC
Univ of Virginia	VA	25,891	MC
Univ of Wisc-Green Bay	WI	15,064	C
Univ of Wisc-Milwaukee	WI	21,496	C
Univ of Wisc-Superior	WI	14,446	C
Univ of Wyoming	WY	15,375	C+
Valparaiso Univ	IN	48,370	C+
Vanderbilt Univ	TN	60,572	MC
Villanova Univ	PA	62,523	MC
Virginia Commonwealth Univ	VA	23,049	C
Virginia Polytechnic Inst and State Univ	VA	21,276	HC
Virginia State Univ	VA	19,802	C+
Virginia Wesleyan College	VA	43,728	LC
Warren Wilson College	NC	44,220	VC
Washburn Univ	KS	15,827	C
Washington & Jefferson College	PA	56,512	VC
Washington and Lee Univ	VA	59,647	MC
Washington College	MD	54,666	VC
Washington State Univ	WA	22,495	C
Washington Univ in St. Louis	MO	65,366	VC
Wayland Baptist Univ	TX	22,356	LC
Wayne State College	NE	12,802	C
Weber State Univ	UT	10,721	C
Webster Univ	MO	37,490	C
Wesleyan College	GA	29,694	C+
West Liberty Univ	WV	15,512	C
West Texas A&M Univ	TX	13,478	C
West Virginia Univ	WV	18,210	C
Western Illinois Univ	IL	20,825	C
Western Mich Univ	MI	21,054	C
Western Oregon Univ	OR	15,021	LC
Western Washington Univ	WA	18,003	C+
Wheaton College	IL	43,610	MC
William Woods Univ	MO	32,040	C
Wisc Lutheran College	WI	36,290	VC
Woodbury Univ	CA	46,958	C
Worcester Polytechnic Inst	MA	60,730	MC

INTERIOR ARCHITECTURE

School	ST	$IS	SR
Chatham Univ	PA	46,517	C
Cleveland Inst of Art	OH	51,439	C+
Lawrence Tech Univ	MI	39,770	VC
Univ of San Francisco	CA	58,484	VC

INTERIOR DESIGN

School	ST	$IS	SR
Abilene Christian Univ	TX	41,800	C+
Adrian College	MI	42,400	C
Appalachian State Univ	NC	14,416	VC
Arcadia Univ	PA	33,570	C+
Arizona State Univ at the Tempe Campus	AZ	21,756	VC
Art Inst of Portland	OR	132,329	SP
Auburn Univ	AL	23,594	VC+
Baker College of Flint	MI	13,880	NC
Bay Path Univ	MA	45,349	C
Baylor Univ	TX	53,760	HC
Boston Architectural College	MA	20,666	NC
Bowling Green State Univ	OH	19,747	C
Brenau Univ - Women's College	GA	37,876	LC
Calif College of the Arts	CA	52,758	SP
Cal State, Fresno	CA	16,902	LC
Cazenovia College	NY	46,470	C
Central Mich Univ	MI	20,330	C
Chaminade Univ of Honolulu	HI	36,000	C
Chatham Univ	PA	46,517	C
College for Creative Studies	MI	48,875	SP
Colo State Univ	CO	22,162	VC

ST = STATE $IS = IN-STATE COSTS SR = SELECTOR RATING

School	ST	$IS	SR
Columbus College of Art and Design	OH	37,732	C
Concordia Univ Wisc	WI	35,910	C
Converse College	SC	26,495	C
Drexel Univ	PA	65,432	VC+
East Carolina Univ	NC	16,937	C
Eastern Kentucky Univ	KY	16,908	C
Eastern Mich Univ	MI	19,761	C
Endicott College	MA	44,604	VC+
Fashion Inst of Technology/SUNY	NY	18,521	SP
Florida International Univ	FL	19,854	C+
Florida State Univ	FL	16,771	HC
Harding Univ	AR	25,421	C
High Point Univ	NC	45,977	C
Howard Univ	DC	37,616	C+
Indiana State Univ	IN	23,223	LC
Indiana Univ Bloomington	IN	20,429	VC
Indiana Univ of Pennsylvania	PA	23,614	LC
Indiana Univ-Purdue Univ Fort Wayne	IN	17,553	C
Indiana Univ-Purdue Univ Indianapolis	IN	18,635	C
Indiana Wesleyan Univ	IN	33,674	C
Iowa State Univ	IA	17,570	C
Kansas State Univ	KS	17,780	VC
Kean Univ	NJ	24,650	C
Kent State Univ	OH	20,732	C
La Roche College	PA	37,924	LC
Lawrence Tech Univ	MI	39,770	VC
Louisiana State Univ and A&M College	LA	18,677	VC
Marist College	NY	49,860	VC
Marymount Univ	VA	41,570	LC
Maryville Univ of St. Louis	MO	38,046	VC+
Marywood Univ	PA	46,900	C
Mercyhurst Univ	PA	47,420	C
Meredith College	NC	45,297	C
Miami Univ	OH	27,190	HC+
Mich State Univ	MI	23,898	VC+
Middle Tenn State Univ	TN	8,650	C
Milwaukee Inst of Art and Design	WI	44,960	SP
Miss College	MS	25,850	C
Missouri State Univ	MO	15,190	C+
Moore College of Art and Design	PA	50,135	SP
Mount Ida College	MA	46,820	C
Mount Mary Univ	WI	34,650	LC
Murray State Univ	KY	16,998	C
New York Inst of Technology	NY	48,730	C
Newbury College	MA	46,950	C
N Dak State Univ	ND	16,245	C
Northern Arizona Univ	AZ	20,246	VC
Ohio State Univ at Columbus	OH	21,703	HC+
Ohio Univ	OH	22,924	C
Okla Christian Univ	OK	27,650	VC
Oregon State Univ	OR	22,519	VC
Park Univ	MO	20,329	C
Parsons The New School for Design	NY	56,610	SP
Philadelphia Univ	PA	50,370	C
Pratt Inst	NY	58,082	VC
Purdue Univ/West Lafayette	IN	20,032	MC
Queens Univ of Charlotte	NC	39,543	C
Rhode Island School of Design	RI	59,960	SP
Ringling College of Art and Design	FL	57,430	SP
Rochester Inst of Technology	NY	50,842	HC
Rocky Mountain College of Art and Design	CO	27,052	SP
Salem College	NC	37,694	HC
Samford Univ	AL	39,232	VC
San Diego State Univ	CA	21,896	C+
San Francisco State Univ	CA	18,514	LC
San Jose State Univ	CA	21,540	C
Savannah College of Art and Design	GA	49,595	C
School of the Art Inst of Chicago	IL	56,230	SP
School of Visual Arts	NY	47,500	SP
Seattle Pacific Univ	WA	47,439	C+
S Dak State Univ	SD	15,634	C
Southeast Missouri State Univ	MO	15,498	C
Southern Illinois Univ Carbondale	IL	23,667	C
Stephen F. Austin State Univ	TX	18,406	LC
Stephens College	MO	38,042	C
Suffolk Univ	MA	50,308	C
Texas A&M Univ at Kingsville	TX	7,500	LC
Texas Christian Univ	TX	54,670	HC
Texas State Univ	TX	19,350	C
Texas Tech Univ	TX	18,736	C+
The Art Inst of Atlanta	GA	34,334	SP
The Univ of Akron	OH	21,477	C
The Univ of Tenn at Chattanooga	TN	16,744	C
The Univ of Tenn at Knoxville	TN	22,112	VC
Univ of Alabama	AL	24,320	C+
Univ of Arkansas at Fayetteville	AR	19,152	C+
Univ of Bridgeport	CT	44,430	LC
Univ of Central Arkansas	AR	14,472	VC
Univ of Central Missouri	MO	18,982	C
Univ of Central Okla	OK	13,486	C
Univ of Charleston	WV	35,000	C
Univ of Cincinnati	OH	21,964	VC
Univ of Florida	FL	16,291	HC+
Univ of Idaho	ID	15,348	C
Univ of Kansas	KS	20,135	C+
Univ of Louisiana at Lafayette	LA	14,516	C
Univ of Minn/Twin Cities	MN	23,519	HC+
Univ of Nebr - Kearney	NE	16,546	LC
Univ of Nebr - Lincoln	NE	18,589	VC
Univ of Nevada, Las Vegas	NV	17,553	C
Univ of New Haven	CT	52,190	C
Univ of North Alabama	AL	15,398	C
Univ of N Car at Greensboro	NC	14,690	C
Univ of North Texas	TX	19,198	C
Univ of Okla	OK	18,911	VC
Univ of San Francisco	CA	58,484	VC
Univ of Texas at Arlington	TX	18,026	LC
Univ of Texas at Austin	TX	26,102	HC
Univ of Texas at San Antonio	TX	20,157	C
Univ of the Incarnate Word	TX	39,162	LC
Univ of Wisc-Madison	WI	20,934	MC
Univ of Wisc-Stevens Point	WI	14,043	C
Utah State Univ	UT	12,736	C
Virginia Commonwealth Univ	VA	23,049	C
Virginia Polytechnic Inst and State Univ	VA	21,276	HC
Washington State Univ	WA	22,495	C
Weber State Univ	UT	10,721	C
Wentworth Inst of Technology	MA	47,112	C
West Virginia Univ	WV	18,210	C
Western Carolina Univ	NC	13,965	C
Western Mich Univ	MI	21,054	C
Winthrop Univ	SC	23,082	C
Woodbury Univ	CA	46,958	C

INTERMEDIA/MULTIMEDIA

School	ST	$IS	SR
Bard College at Simon's Rock	MA	65,795	MC
Beloit College	WI	55,206	HC
Bloomfield College	NJ	39,100	LC
Bryant Univ	RI	55,646	VC
Goddard College	VT	17,040	VC
Lewis Univ	IL	40,370	C
Lynn Univ	FL	49,480	LC

INTERNATIONAL ACCOUNTING

School	ST	$IS	SR
Bryant Univ	RI	55,646	VC
Texas Christian Univ	TX	54,670	HC

INTERNATIONAL AGRICULTURE

School	ST	$IS	SR
Iowa State Univ	IA	17,570	C
Tarleton State Univ	TX	15,248	LC
Univ of Calif at Davis	CA	28,468	HC
Utah State Univ	UT	12,736	C

INTERNATIONAL AGRICULTURE / RURAL DEVELOPMENT

School	ST	$IS	SR
Cornell Univ	NY	64,853	MC

INTERNATIONAL BUSINESS

School	ST	$IS	SR
Arkansas State Univ	AR	16,190	C
Ashford Univ	CA	10,480	C
Azusa Pacific Univ	CA	43,972	C
Baldwin Wallace Univ	OH	41,106	C
Bethany College	WV	36,300	NC
Bloomfield College	NJ	39,100	LC
Bryant Univ	RI	55,646	VC
Cal State, Long Beach	CA	18,850	C
Cedarville Univ	OH	34,990	VC
Creighton Univ	NE	48,206	VC+
Dallas Baptist Univ	TX	33,713	C
Drexel Univ	PA	65,432	VC+
Grove City College	PA	25,692	VC
Illinois State Univ	IL	23,418	VC
John Brown Univ	AR	33,132	VC
Lewis Univ	IL	40,370	C
Messiah College	PA	43,100	C+
Millersville Univ of Pennsylvania	PA	23,782	C
Minn State Univ, Mankato	MN	15,616	C
Missouri Southern State Univ	MO	12,499	C
Murray State Univ	KY	16,998	C
Niagara Univ	NY	41,010	C
Northwest Missouri State Univ	MO	17,737	C
Ohio Wesleyan Univ	OH	49,460	VC
Okla Baptist Univ	OK	32,320	C
Rochester Inst of Technology	NY	50,842	HC
St. Louis Univ	MO	49,866	HC
St. Mary's Univ of Minn	MN	41,210	VC
St. Ambrose Univ	IA	39,019	C
St. Ambrose Univ	IA	39,019	C
Tarleton State Univ	TX	15,248	LC
Taylor Univ	IN	40,317	C+
Texas Tech Univ	TX	18,736	C+
Thomas Edison State Univ	NJ	6,350	NC
Univ of Cincinnati	OH	21,964	VC
Univ of Evansville	IN	44,186	VC+
Univ of Georgia	GA	21,250	HC
Univ of Mary Hardin-Baylor	TX	33,950	C+
Univ of Okla	OK	18,911	VC
Univ of San Francisco	CA	58,484	VC
Univ of Wisc-Eau Claire	WI	15,797	VC
Univ of Wisc-Milwaukee	WI	21,496	C
Washington State Univ	WA	22,495	C
West Chester Univ of Pennsylvania	PA	18,456	C
West Virginia Wesleyan College	WV	36,858	C
Western New England Univ	MA	48,088	C

INTERNATIONAL BUSINESS INFORMATION SYSTEMS

School	ST	$IS	SR
Bryant Univ	RI	55,646	VC
Concordia College - New York	NY	39,035	LC
Holy Family Univ	PA	43,326	LC
Missouri Southern State Univ	MO	12,499	C
North Greenville Univ	SC	25,930	C+
Texas Christian Univ	TX	54,670	HC
Univ of Texas at Arlington	TX	18,026	LC

INTERNATIONAL BUSINESS MANAGEMENT

School	ST	$IS	SR
Adams State Univ	CO	17,703	LC
Adrian College	MI	42,400	C
Alma College	MI	47,548	C
Alverno College	WI	33,294	LC
American International College	MA	46,300	LC
American Univ	DC	59,379	HC+
Angelo State Univ	TX	15,263	NC
Appalachian State Univ	NC	14,416	VC
Aquinas College - Mich	MI	38,876	HC
Arcadia Univ	PA	33,570	C+
Assumption College	MA	47,920	C+
Auburn Univ	AL	23,594	VC+
Augsburg College	MN	43,929	C
Augustana College	IL	49,658	VC
Avila Univ	MO	35,480	C
Baker Univ	KS	33,350	C+
Barry Univ	FL	37,830	C
Baylor Univ	TX	53,760	HC
Belmont Univ	TN	40,970	VC
Benedictine Univ	IL	38,300	C
Berkeley College/New Jersey	NJ	38,082	LC
Berkeley College/New York City Campus	NY	23,350	LC
Berkeley College/White Plains Campus	NY	35,100	LC
Berry College	GA	45,286	C+
Bethune-Cookman Univ	FL	22,970	C
Biola Univ	CA	46,402	C+
Bloomfield College	NJ	39,100	LC
Boise State Univ	ID	14,860	C
Brigham Young Univ/Hawaii	HI	11,290	C
Bryant Univ	RI	55,646	VC
Butler Univ	IN	51,352	VC
Caldwell Univ	NJ	42,165	NC
Calif State Polytechnic Univ, Pomona	CA	21,541	C
Cal State, Fullerton	CA	21,902	C
Cal State, Long Beach	CA	18,850	C
Cal State, Sacramento	CA	20,332	C
Cal State, San Bernardino	CA	12,000	C
Canisius College	NY	47,537	C
Cardinal Stritch Univ	WI	36,462	C
Catawba College	NC	39,820	C
Central Mich Univ	MI	20,330	C
Central Washington Univ	WA	16,803	C
Champlain College	VT	53,132	C+
Chatham Univ	PA	46,517	C
Clarion Univ of Pennsylvania	PA	21,608	LC
College of Charleston	SC	22,699	C
College of the Ozarks	MO	7,230	C
Columbia College - Missouri	MO	27,803	C
Concordia College - Moorhead	MN	51,088	C+
Davenport Univ	MI	25,896	LC
Dickinson College	PA	63,974	MC
Dominican College	NY	31,270	LC
Dominican Univ	IL	41,222	C
Dominican Univ of Calif	CA	57,050	C
Drake Univ	IA	45,056	HC
Duquesne Univ	PA	46,822	VC
Eastern Mennonite Univ	VA	42,550	C
Eastern Mich Univ	MI	19,761	C
Eckerd College	FL	52,874	C
Elizabethtown College	PA	54,050	C
Elmhurst College	IL	45,428	C
Elms College	MA	45,646	VC
Elon Univ	NC	44,599	VC+
Endicott College	MA	44,604	VC+
Excelsior College	NY	14,080	SP
Fairfield Univ	CT	59,860	VC+
Felician Univ	NJ	45,370	LC
Fitchburg State Univ	MA	21,819	C
Florida Atlantic Univ	FL	17,339	C
Florida Inst of Technology	FL	53,306	VC
Florida International Univ	FL	19,854	C+
Florida State Univ	FL	16,771	HC
Fordham Univ	NY	65,918	MC
Franciscan Univ of Steubenville	OH	33,980	VC
Friends Univ	KS	34,455	C
Gannon Univ	PA	42,032	C
Gardner-Webb Univ	NC	39,200	C+
George Washington Univ	DC	62,835	MC
Georgetown College	KY	41,440	C
Georgetown Univ	DC	65,926	MC
Golden Gate Univ	CA	32,110	C
Goldey-Beacom College	DE	31,750	C
Graceland Univ	IA	35,290	C
Grand Rapids Theological Seminary/Cornerstone Univ	MI	33,338	C
Grand Valley State Univ	MI	22,250	C+
Guilford College	NC	44,090	C
Gustavus Adolphus College	MN	52,433	HC
Hamline Univ	MN	45,678	VC
Harding Univ	AR	25,421	C
Hawaii Pacific Univ	HI	33,420	C
High Point Univ	NC	45,977	C
Hilbert College	NY	30,850	C
Hillsdale College	MI	35,722	MC
Hofstra Univ	NY	55,960	C+
Howard Univ	DC	37,616	C+
Illinois Wesleyan Univ	IL	56,430	VC+
Indiana Univ of Pennsylvania	PA	23,614	LC
Iona College	NY	50,984	C
Iowa State Univ	IA	17,570	C
Jacksonville Univ	FL	46,230	C
James Madison Univ	VA	19,084	VC
John Carroll Univ	OH	49,740	C+
Johnson & Wales Univ/Providence Campus	RI	42,248	C
Judson Univ	IL	37,700	C
Juniata College	PA	53,760	VC
Kean Univ	NJ	24,650	C
Keiser Univ	FL	35,010	LC
Kennesaw State Univ	GA	19,592	VC
King's College	PA	46,858	C
Kutztown Univ of Pennsylvania	PA	19,056	LC
La Roche College	PA	37,924	LC
La Sierra Univ	CA	39,690	VC
Lake Erie College	OH	38,914	LC
Lakeland Univ	WI	35,130	C
Lasell College	MA	47,500	C
Lawrence Tech Univ	MI	39,770	VC
Lenoir-Rhyne Univ	NC	43,200	C
Lewis Univ	IL	40,370	C
Linfield College	OR	52,010	C
Lipscomb Univ	TN	41,296	VC
Loyola Univ Chicago	IL	55,802	VC
Loyola Univ New Orleans	LA	51,708	VC+
Madonna Univ	MI	29,050	C
Maine Maritime Academy	ME	22,536	C
Manhattan College	NY	51,750	C+
Marietta College	OH	46,190	C
Marquette Univ	WI	48,390	VC+
Marshall Univ	WV	17,242	C
Maryville Univ of St. Louis	MO	38,046	VC+
Marywood Univ	PA	46,900	C
Mass Maritime Academy	MA	19,982	C
Menlo College	CA	51,380	LC
Mercer Univ	GA	45,348	VC
Meredith College	NC	45,297	C
Merrimack College	MA	52,770	C
Messiah College	PA	43,100	C+
Metropolitan State Univ	MN	7,566	C
MidAmerica Nazarene Univ	KS	35,550	C
Millikin Univ	IL	42,158	C
Milwaukee School of Engineering	WI	45,153	HC
Minn State Univ, Mankato	MN	15,616	C
Minn State Univ, Moorhead	MN	15,941	C
Minot State Univ	ND	12,732	C
Monmouth College	IL	42,260	C
Monmouth Univ	NJ	46,234	C
Montclair State Univ	NJ	26,210	LC
Moravian College	PA	53,117	
Mount Vernon Nazarene Univ	OH	34,500	C
Muskingum Univ	OH	35,966	C
Nazareth College	NY	45,574	C
Nebr Wesleyan Univ	NE	38,140	C+
New Mexico State Univ	NM	14,050	C
New York Inst of Technology	NY	48,730	C
New York Univ	NY	65,860	MC
Newbury College	MA	46,950	C
Nichols College	MA	46,800	LC
North Central College	IL	48,712	VC
North Park Univ	IL	35,860	C
Northeastern Univ	MA	62,703	MC
Northern State Univ	SD	14,505	C
Northwest Missouri State Univ	MO	17,737	C
Northwood Univ - Mich	MI	35,010	LC
Notre Dame de Namur Univ	CA	46,526	LC
Notre Dame of Maryland Univ	MD	46,465	VC
Ohio Dominican Univ	OH	41,340	C+
Ohio Northern Univ	OH	44,050	VC
Ohio State Univ at Columbus	OH	21,703	HC+
Ohio Univ	OH	22,924	C
Ohio Wesleyan Univ	OH	49,460	VC
Okla Christian Univ	OK	27,650	VC
Okla State Univ	OK	17,180	VC
Old Dominion Univ	VA	20,910	C
Olivet College	MI	36,110	LC
Olivet Nazarene Univ	IL	41,840	C
Oral Roberts Univ	OK	34,316	C
Pace Univ	NY	58,248	C
Palm Beach Atlantic Univ	FL	39,720	C
Pepperdine Univ	CA	74,460	HC+
Pfeiffer Univ	NC	39,695	LC
Philadelphia Univ	PA	50,370	C

ST = STATE $IS = IN-STATE COSTS SR = SELECTOR RATING

School	ST	$IS	SR
Pittsburg State Univ	KS	13,880	NC
Quinnipiac Univ	CT	59,110	C
Ramapo College of New Jersey	NJ	25,338	C
Regis Univ	CO	44,520	C
Rider Univ	NJ	54,050	C
Roberts Wesleyan College	NY	38,306	C
Rochester Inst of Technology	NY	50,842	HC
Roger Williams Univ	RI	46,296	C+
Rollins College	FL	58,670	HC
Saginaw Valley State Univ	MI	18,530	C
St. Augustine's Univ	NC	26,048	C
St. Joseph's Univ	PA	57,544	VC+
St. Peter's Univ	NJ	49,192	C
St. Vincent College	PA	44,626	C
St. Xavier Univ	IL	43,310	C
Salem College	NC	37,694	HC
Salisbury Univ	MD	20,714	VC
Salve Regina Univ	RI	51,470	C
San Diego State Univ	CA	21,896	C+
San Francisco State Univ	CA	18,514	LC
San Jose State Univ	CA	21,540	C
Seattle Univ	WA	50,811	VC+
Seton Hill Univ	PA	46,972	C
Simpson College	IA	43,839	VC
Slippery Rock Univ of Pennsylvania	PA	10,360	C
Southeast Missouri State Univ	MO	15,498	C
Southern Adventist Univ	TN	27,600	C
Southern Illinois Univ Edwardsville	IL	22,643	C
Southern New Hampshire Univ	NH	43,198	C
Southwest Baptist Univ	MO	29,900	LC
Spring Hill College	AL	48,488	C
St. Catherine Univ	MN	45,630	VC
St. Cloud State Univ	MN	10,600	C
St. Edward's Univ	TX	53,100	VC
St. John's Univ	NY	55,850	C
St. Mary's Univ	TX	37,500	C
St. Norbert College	WI	44,525	VC
St. Thomas Univ	FL	36,360	LC
SUNY / SUNY Plattsburgh	NY	18,814	C
SUNY at New Paltz	NY	19,200	C
Stephen F. Austin State Univ	TX	18,406	LC
Stetson Univ	FL	53,544	VC
Stonehill College	MA	55,030	C+
Suffolk Univ	MA	50,308	C
Taylor Univ	IN	40,317	C+
Temple Univ	PA	24,392	VC
Texas A&M Univ at Galveston	TX	15,920	C
The College at Brockport - SUNY	NY	20,346	C
The Univ of Akron	OH	21,477	C
Thiel College	PA	41,590	C
Trinity International Univ	IL	31,070	VC
Truman State Univ	MO	16,014	HC
Union College	KY	32,310	C
Univ of Arkansas at Fayetteville	AR	19,152	C+
Univ of Bridgeport	CT	44,430	LC
Univ of Dayton	OH	53,620	C
Univ of Denver	CO	58,443	VC+
Univ of Findlay	OH	60,139	C
Univ of Hawaii at Manoa	HI	23,221	C
Univ of Houston-Downtown	TX	7,241	C
Univ of Indianapolis	IN	36,480	C
Univ of La Verne	CA	55,600	C
Univ of Maryland/College Park	MD	21,938	HC
Univ of Memphis	TN	18,278	C
Univ of Missouri-St. Louis	MO		C
Univ of Montana	MT	14,105	C
Univ of Mount Union	OH	38,970	C
Univ of Nebr - Lincoln	NE	18,589	VC
Univ of Nevada, Las Vegas	NV	17,553	C
Univ of N Car at Charlotte	NC	15,547	C
Univ of N Car at Greensboro	NC	14,690	C
Univ of North Florida	FL	15,996	VC
Univ of Northwestern - St. Paul	MN	38,160	C
Univ of Pittsburgh	PA	29,568	HC+
Univ of Portland	OR	52,152	VC
Univ of PR, at Humacao	PR	14,000	
Univ of Rio Grande & Rio Grande Community College	OH	8,750	NC
Univ of San Diego	CA	58,442	VC+
Univ of Scranton	PA	54,962	VC
Univ of Southern Calif	CA	66,631	C
Univ of Southern Miss	MS	13,170	C
Univ of St. Francis	IL	39,924	C
Univ of St. Thomas - Houston	TX	40,020	VC
Univ of Tampa	FL	36,944	C
Univ of Texas at Dallas	TX	22,830	VC+
Univ of Tulsa	OK	52,625	HC+
Univ of Washington	WA	23,149	VC
Univ of Wisc-La Crosse	WI	15,247	C+
Univ of Wisc-Madison	WI	20,934	MC
Univ of Wisc-Superior	WI	14,446	C
Utah State Univ	UT	12,736	C
Vanguard Univ of Southern Calif	CA	40,740	VC
Villanova Univ	PA	62,523	MC
Walsh Univ	OH	39,010	C
Wartburg College	IA	47,840	C
Washburn Univ	KS	15,827	C
Washington & Jefferson College	PA	56,512	VC
Washington State Univ	WA	22,495	C
Washington Univ in St. Louis	MO	65,366	VC
Waynesburg Univ	PA	32,290	C
Wesleyan College	GA	29,694	C+
Western Carolina Univ	NC	13,965	C
Western New Mexico Univ	NM	16,734	LC
Western Washington Univ	WA	18,003	C+
Westminster College	MO	32,820	C
Westminster College	PA	39,180	C+
Westminster College	UT	41,078	C+
Whitworth Univ	WA	51,732	VC
Wichita State Univ	KS	21,643	C
Widener Univ	PA	56,486	C
William Jewell College	MO	41,210	C+
Xavier Univ	OH	47,880	C+

INTERNATIONAL ECONOMICS

School	ST	$IS	SR
Austin College	TX	45,875	VC
Belmont Univ	TN	40,970	VC
Beloit College	WI	55,206	HC
Bethany College	WV	36,300	NC
Bryant Univ	RI	55,646	VC
Carthage College	WI	48,835	C
Colo College	CO	62,560	MC
Elon Univ	NC	44,599	VC+
Fitchburg State Univ	MA	21,819	C
Georgia Inst of Technology	GA	23,360	MC
Grand Rapids Theological Seminary/Cornerstone Univ	MI	33,338	C
La Salle Univ	PA	55,790	C
Lafayette College	PA	63,355	MC
Louisiana State Univ and A&M College	LA	18,677	VC
Mary Baldwin Univ	VA	39,865	C
Middlebury College	VT	64,332	MC
Midwestern State Univ	TX	17,572	C
Pontifical Catholic Univ of PR	PR	10,534	
St. Louis Univ	MO	49,866	HC
Seattle Univ	WA	50,811	VC+
Southwestern Adventist Univ	TX	27,756	LC
St. Catherine Univ	MN	45,630	VC
St. Lawrence Univ	NY	64,390	VC
Suffolk Univ	MA	50,308	C
Texas Christian Univ	TX	54,670	HC
Texas Tech Univ	TX	18,736	C+
The Catholic Univ of America	DC	56,356	VC
The College of Idaho	ID	36,415	C
Univ of Bridgeport	CT	44,430	LC
Univ of Calif, Santa Cruz	CA	28,731	C+
Univ of Notre Dame	IN	64,043	MC
Univ of Puget Sound	WA	56,456	VC+
Univ of San Francisco	CA	58,484	VC
Univ of Vermont	VT	28,878	HC
Univ of West Georgia	GA	16,360	LC
Valparaiso Univ	IN	48,370	C+
Washington Univ in St. Louis	MO	65,366	VC
Weber State Univ	UT	10,721	C
Western Washington Univ	WA	18,003	C+

INTERNATIONAL ENTREPRENEURIAL MANAGEMENT

School	ST	$IS	SR
Bryant Univ	RI	55,646	VC
Texas Christian Univ	TX	54,670	HC

INTERNATIONAL FINANCE

School	ST	$IS	SR
Bryant Univ	RI	55,646	VC
Bucknell Univ	PA	64,616	MC
Texas Christian Univ	TX	54,670	HC
Univ of Miami	FL	63,494	MC

INTERNATIONAL MARKETING

School	ST	$IS	SR
Bryant Univ	RI	55,646	VC
Pace Univ	NY	58,248	C
Texas Christian Univ	TX	54,670	HC
Univ of Miami	FL	63,494	MC

INTERNATIONAL POLITICAL SCIENCE

School	ST	$IS	SR
Bryant Univ	RI	55,646	VC
Carnegie Mellon Univ	PA	67,980	MC
La Salle Univ	PA	55,790	C
Reed College	OR	65,300	MC
Texas Christian Univ	TX	54,670	HC
Univ of Georgia	GA	21,250	HC
Univ of North Georgia	GA	17,316	C

INTERNATIONAL PUBLIC SERVICE

School	ST	$IS	SR
Baylor Univ	TX	53,760	HC
Union College	NE	23,270	C
Univ of Texas at Dallas	TX	22,830	VC+
Valparaiso Univ	IN	48,370	C+

INTERNATIONAL REAL ESTATE FINANCE

School	ST	$IS	SR
Texas Christian Univ	TX	54,670	HC

INTERNATIONAL RELATIONS

School	ST	$IS	SR
Agnes Scott College	GA	51,930	VC+
Alverno College	WI	33,294	LC
American International College	MA	46,300	LC
Aquinas College - Mich	MI	38,876	HC
Augsburg College	MN	43,929	C
Beloit College	WI	55,206	HC
Bennington College	VT	63,960	MC
Bethany College	WV	36,300	NC
Bethel Univ	MN	45,270	VC
Boston Univ	MA	65,110	MC
Brigham Young Univ	UT	12,748	HC
Brown Univ	RI	64,566	MC
Bryant Univ	RI	55,646	VC
Bucknell Univ	PA	64,616	MC
Cal State, Chico	CA	21,440	C
Cal State, Sacramento	CA	20,332	C
Calvin College	MI	41,570	VC+
Canisius College	NY	47,537	C
Capital Univ	OH	42,982	C
Carleton College	MN	64,071	MC
Carroll College	MT	39,972	C+
Centre College	KY	49,250	HC
Chaminade Univ of Honolulu	HI	36,000	C
Chatham Univ	PA	46,517	C
CUNY/Hunter College	NY	31,098	VC
CUNY/Lehman College	NY	5,778	HC+
Claremont McKenna College	CA	67,185	MC
Clark Univ	MA	51,600	HC+
Cleveland State Univ	OH	22,196	C
Colgate Univ	NY	65,030	MC
College of William & Mary	VA		MC
Conn College	CT	65,000	MC
Cornell College	IA	48,800	VC
Creighton Univ	NE	48,206	VC+
Dominican Univ	IL	41,222	C
Drake Univ	IA	45,056	HC
Drew Univ/College of Liberal Arts	NJ	61,048	VC
Duquesne Univ	PA	46,822	VC
Eastern Mich Univ	MI	19,761	C
Eastern Washington Univ	WA	25,572	LC
Eckerd College	FL	52,874	C
Edgewood College	WI	35,950	C
Florida International Univ	FL	19,854	C+
Florida State Univ	FL	16,771	HC
George Mason Univ	VA	15,724	VC
George Washington Univ	DC	62,835	MC
Georgetown Univ	DC	65,926	MC
Georgia Inst of Technology	GA	23,360	MC
Gettysburg College	PA	63,000	HC
Goucher College	MD	55,716	VC
Grand Valley State Univ	MI	22,250	C+
Hamilton College	NY	64,250	MC
Hampshire College	MA	63,824	MC
Hawaii Pacific Univ	HI	33,420	C
Hendrix College	AR	54,020	VC+
High Point Univ	NC	45,977	C
Illinois College	IL	40,850	VC
Iowa State Univ	IA	17,570	C
Kent State Univ	OH	20,732	C
King Univ	TN	34,660	C
Knox College	IL	52,615	VC+
Lafayette College	PA	63,355	MC
Lake Forest College	IL	50,652	VC
Le Moyne College	NY	46,000	C
Lehigh Univ	PA	61,010	MC
Lewis & Clark College	OR	58,434	HC+
Linfield College	OR	52,010	C
Loras College	IA	39,222	C
Loyola Marymount Univ	CA	58,038	HC
Lynchburg College	VA	46,740	C
Marquette Univ	WI	48,390	VC+
Marshall Univ	WV	17,242	C
Mary Baldwin Univ	VA	39,865	C
Maryville College	TN	44,410	C
McKendree Univ	IL	37,940	C+
Miami Univ	OH	27,190	HC+
Mich State Univ	MI	23,898	VC+
Middle Tenn State Univ	TN	8,650	C
Mills College	CA	59,163	VC
Minn State Univ, Mankato	MN	15,616	C
Morningside College	IA	36,865	C
Mount Holyoke College	MA	56,746	MC
Muskingum Univ	OH	35,966	C
New York Univ	NY	65,860	MC
North Park Univ	IL	35,860	C
Northern Arizona Univ	AZ	20,246	VC
Notre Dame of Maryland Univ	MD	46,465	VC
Nova Southeastern Univ	FL	38,534	C+
Oakland Univ	MI	20,763	C
Occidental College	CA	65,530	MC
Ohio Wesleyan Univ	OH	49,460	VC
Okla Baptist Univ	OK	32,320	C
Oral Roberts Univ	OK	34,316	C
Pennsylvania State Univ - Univ Park	PA	29,760	HC
Pitzer College	CA	66,192	MC
Pomona College	CA	64,957	MC
Prescott College	AZ	33,284	C
Princeton Univ	NJ	57,610	MC
Principia College	IL	39,010	C+
Regis College	MA	51,920	C
Roanoke College	VA	54,114	VC
Rockhurst Univ	MO	29,220	C
Roger Williams Univ	RI	46,296	C+
Rollins College	FL	58,670	HC
St. Joseph's Univ	PA	57,544	VC+
St. Louis Univ	MO	49,866	HC
St. Michael's College	VT	51,725	VC+
Salem College	NC	37,694	HC
Samford Univ	AL	39,232	VC
San Francisco State Univ	CA	18,514	LC
Seton Hall Univ	NJ	55,514	C
Shaw Univ	NC	24,638	C
Simmons College	MA	53,090	VC
Simpson College	IA	43,839	VC
Skidmore College	NY	64,214	HC
Smith College	MA	63,914	MC
Southern Methodist Univ	TX	66,483	MC
Southwestern Adventist Univ	TX	27,756	LC
St. Catherine Univ	MN	45,630	VC
St. Cloud State Univ	MN	10,600	C
St. Edward's Univ	TX	53,100	VC
St. Mary's Univ	TX	37,500	C
St. Norbert College	WI	44,525	VC
St. Thomas Univ	FL	36,360	LC
Stanford Univ	CA	60,409	MC
SUNY at Geneseo	NY	20,440	VC+
SUNY at New Paltz	NY	19,200	C
Suffolk Univ	MA	50,308	C
Syracuse Univ	NY	60,239	VC
Taylor Univ	IN	40,317	C+
Texas State Univ	TX	19,350	C
The College of Wooster	OH	57,900	VC+
Trinity Univ	TX	52,314	HC+
Tufts Univ	MA		MC
Univ of Arkansas at Fayetteville	AR	19,152	C+
Univ of Calif at Davis	CA	28,468	HC
Univ of Colo Boulder	CO	24,285	VC+
Univ of Delaware	DE	24,976	VC+
Univ of Idaho	ID	15,348	C
Univ of Indianapolis	IN	36,480	C
Univ of Mary Washington	VA	24,764	VC
Univ of Minn/Twin Cities	MN	23,519	HC+
Univ of Nevada/Reno	NV	18,010	C
Univ of Northern Colo	CO	20,851	C
Univ of Pennsylvania	PA	63,526	MC
Univ of Redlands	CA	60,200	VC
Univ of Rochester	NY	65,032	MC
Univ of San Diego	CA	58,442	VC+
Univ of South Florida/Tampa	FL	16,110	VC+
Univ of Southern Calif	CA	66,631	C
Univ of the Pacific	CA	57,006	VC
Univ of Toledo	OH	19,336	NC
Univ of Virginia	VA	25,891	MC
Univ of Washington	WA	23,149	VC
Univ of Wisc-Madison	WI	20,934	MC
Ursinus College	PA	61,690	VC
Utah State Univ	UT	12,736	C
Valparaiso Univ	IN	48,370	C+
Virginia Wesleyan College	VA	43,728	LC
Walsh Univ	OH	39,010	C
Wartburg College	IA	47,840	C
Washington Univ in St. Louis	MO	65,366	VC
Webster Univ	MO	37,490	C
Wellesley College	MA	63,916	MC
Wesleyan College	GA	29,694	C+
West Chester Univ of Pennsylvania	PA	18,456	C
Westminster College	PA	39,180	C+
Wheaton College	IL	43,610	MC
Wheaton College	MA	61,512	VC
Widener Univ	PA	56,486	C
William Jewell College	MO	41,210	C+
Wilson College	PA	35,620	C
Wittenberg Univ	OH	48,156	C+
Wright State Univ	OH	16,983	C

INTERNATIONAL SECURITY/ CONFLICT RESOLUTION MGMT

School	ST	$IS	SR
Baldwin Wallace Univ	OH	41,106	C
San Diego State Univ	CA	21,896	C+

INTERNATIONAL STUDIES

School	ST	$IS	SR
Adrian College	MI	42,400	C
Albion College	MI	52,650	C
Allegheny College	PA	55,420	VC
American Univ	DC	59,379	HC+
Aquinas College - Mich	MI	38,876	HC
Arcadia Univ	PA	33,570	C+
Arkansas Tech Univ	AR	15,484	C
Ashland Univ	OH	21,440	C
Assumption College	MA	47,920	C+
Auburn Univ at Montgomery	AL	15,290	C
Augustana Univ	SD	38,424	VC
Austin College	TX	45,875	VC
Azusa Pacific Univ	CA	43,972	C
Baker Univ	KS	33,350	C+
Baldwin Wallace Univ	OH	41,106	C
Ball State Univ	IN	19,590	C
Bard College	NY	64,024	HC
Barnard College/Columbia Univ	NY	62,741	MC

ST = STATE　$IS = IN-STATE COSTS　SR = SELECTOR RATING

School	ST	$IS	SR
Barry Univ	FL	37,830	C
Belhaven Univ	MS	31,016	C
Bellarmine Univ	KY	51,220	C
Benedictine Univ	IL	38,300	C
Bennington College	VT	63,960	MC
Berry College	GA	45,286	C+
Bethel College	IN	35,860	C
Bethune-Cookman Univ	FL	22,970	C
Bowling Green State Univ	OH	19,747	C
Brandeis Univ	MA	65,925	MC
Brenau Univ - Women's College	GA	37,876	LC
Brigham Young Univ/Hawaii	HI	11,290	C
Brown Univ	RI	64,566	MC
Bryant Univ	RI	55,646	VC
Bryn Mawr College	PA	59,890	MC
Butler Univ	IN	51,352	VC
Calif Baptist Univ	CA	41,392	C
Calif Lutheran Univ	CA	52,853	C
Cal State, East Bay	CA	19,413	C
Cal State, Long Beach	CA	18,850	C
Cal State, Monterey Bay	CA	26,871	LC
Calvin College	MI	41,570	VC+
Case Western Reserve Univ	OH	60,304	MC
Cedarville Univ	OH	34,990	VC
Centenary College	NJ	43,602	C
Central College	IA	44,592	C
Central Conn State Univ	CT	21,203	C
Chatham Univ	PA	46,517	C
Chestnut Hill College	PA	43,410	C
CUNY/City College	NY	20,319	VC
CUNY/College of Staten Island	NY	17,840	NC
Clark Univ	MA	51,600	HC+
College of Charleston	SC	22,699	C
College of St. Elizabeth	NJ	44,432	LC
College of the Holy Cross	MA	62,165	MC
Colo State Univ	CO	22,162	VC
Concordia College - Moorhead	MN	51,088	C+
Concordia College - New York	NY	39,035	LC
Concordia Univ	CA	41,580	VC
Coppin State Univ	MD	17,041	VC
Culver-Stockton College	MO	33,525	C
Defiance College	OH	41,630	C
Denison Univ	OH	58,860	MC
DePaul Univ	IL	47,623	VC
Dickinson College	PA	63,974	MC
Doane Univ	NE	39,184	VC
Dominican Univ of Calif	CA	57,050	C
Drexel Univ	PA	65,432	VC+
Drury Univ	MO	33,791	VC
D'Youville College	NY	36,780	C
Earlham College	IN	54,870	HC
East Texas Baptist Univ	TX	33,134	C
Elmira College	NY	53,900	C
Elms College	MA	45,646	VC
Elon Univ	NC	44,599	VC+
Emmanuel College	MA	52,110	C+
Emory and Henry College	VA	41,410	C
Emory Univ	GA	60,786	MC
Endicott College	MA	44,604	VC+
Evangel Univ	MO	28,898	C
Fairfield Univ	CT	59,860	VC+
Fairleigh Dickinson Univ/ Metropolitan Campus	NJ	40,254	C
Ferrum College	VA	39,650	C
Flagler College	FL	27,620	C
Fordham Univ	NY	65,918	MC
Francis Marion Univ	SC	16,464	LC
Frostburg State Univ	MD	17,280	LC
Gallaudet Univ	DC	29,118	LC
Gannon Univ	PA	42,032	C
George Fox Univ	OR	42,938	C
Georgia Inst of Technology	GA	23,360	MC
Georgia Southern Univ	GA	16,596	C
Gonzaga Univ	WA	50,888	HC
Gordon College	MA	46,472	C+
Graceland Univ	IA	35,290	C
Grand Canyon Univ	AZ	16,950	VC
Greenville College	IL	27,012	C
Guilford College	NC	44,090	C
Hampshire College	MA	63,824	MC
Hanover College	IN	46,364	C+
Harding Univ	AR	25,421	C
Hawaii Pacific Univ	HI	33,420	C
Heidelberg Univ	OH	39,200	C
Hollins Univ	VA	49,635	VC
Hood College	MD	54,840	C
Hope College	MI	39,940	VC
Houghton College	NY	39,090	C
Idaho State Univ	ID	13,619	NC
Illinois Wesleyan Univ	IL	56,430	VC+
Indiana Univ Bloomington	IN	20,429	VC
Indiana Univ East	IN	7,072	C
Indiana Univ of Pennsylvania	PA	23,614	LC
Indiana Univ Southeast	IN	14,242	LC
Indiana Univ-Purdue Univ Indianapolis	IN	18,635	C
Iona College	NY	50,984	C
Jacksonville Univ	FL	46,230	C
James Madison Univ	VA	19,084	VC
Johns Hopkins Univ	MD	65,386	MC
Juniata College	PA	53,760	VC
Kalamazoo College	MI	53,931	HC+
Kennesaw State Univ	GA	19,592	VC
Kenyon College	OH	63,330	MC
Knox College	IL	52,615	VC+
La Roche College	PA	37,924	LC
Lawrence Univ	WI	54,498	HC
Le Moyne College	NY	46,000	C
Liberty Univ	VA	19,101	C
Lindenwood Univ	MO	25,132	C
Lipscomb Univ	TN	41,296	VC
LIU Post	NY	49,682	C
Lock Haven Univ of Pennsylvania	PA	18,028	LC
Louisiana State Univ and A&M College	LA	18,677	VC
Loyola Univ Chicago	IL	55,802	VC
Luther College	IA	48,540	C+
Lycoming College	PA	48,580	C
Macalester College	MN	61,905	MC
Malone Univ	OH	38,448	C
Manhattanville College	NY	51,440	C+
Mars Hill Univ	NC	42,688	C
Marymount Manhattan College	NY	46,280	VC
Maryville Univ of St. Louis	MO	38,046	VC+
McKendree Univ	IL	37,940	C+
Meredith College	NC	45,297	C
Methodist Univ	NC	43,600	C
Miami Univ	OH	27,190	HC+
Millersville Univ of Pennsylvania	PA	23,782	C
Minn State Univ, Moorhead	MN	15,941	C
Monmouth College	IL	42,260	C
Morehouse College	GA	40,064	C
Mount Mary Univ	WI	34,650	LC
Mount Mercy Univ	IA	36,826	C
Mount St. Mary's Univ	MD	51,610	C
Muhlenberg College	PA	56,645	VC+
Murray State Univ	KY	16,998	C
National Univ	CA	14,730	LC
Nazareth College	NY	45,574	C
Nebr Wesleyan Univ	NE	38,140	C+
New College of Florida	FL	15,848	MC
Niagara Univ	NY	41,010	C
N Dak State Univ	ND	16,245	C
Northern Mich Univ	MI	19,604	C
Northwest Christian Univ	OR	36,580	C
Northwest Nazarene Univ	ID	36,000	C
Northwestern Univ	IL	66,344	MC
Norwich Univ	VT	28,212	C
Oakwood Univ	AL	43,758	C
Oberlin College	OH	66,012	MC
Oglethorpe Univ	GA	44,200	C+
Ohio Northern Univ	OH	44,050	VC
Ohio State Univ at Columbus	OH	21,703	HC+
Ohio Univ	OH	22,924	C
Old Dominion Univ	VA	20,910	C
Oral Roberts Univ	OK	34,316	C
Oregon State Univ	OR	22,519	VC
Otterbein Univ	OH	41,630	C
Pepperdine Univ	CA	74,460	HC+
Pittsburg State Univ	KS	13,880	NC
Point Loma Nazarene Univ	CA	43,450	C
Point Park Univ	PA	41,270	C
Portland State Univ	OR	19,443	C
Prescott College	AZ	33,284	C
Ramapo College of New Jersey	NJ	25,338	C
Randolph College	VA	45,660	VC
Randolph-Macon College	VA	49,910	C
Rhodes College	TN	51,900	HC
Ripon College	WI	46,911	C+
Rockford Univ	IL	36,030	C
Roosevelt Univ	IL	40,651	VC
Russell Sage College	NY	39,370	C
Saginaw Valley State Univ	MI	18,530	C
St. Francis Univ	PA	42,268	NC
St. Mary's College	IN	50,600	C
St. Mary's College of Calif	CA	57,420	C
St. Peter's Univ	NJ	49,192	C
Salisbury Univ	MD	20,714	VC
Salve Regina Univ	RI	51,470	C
San Diego State Univ	CA	21,896	C+
Seattle Univ	WA	50,811	VC+
Seton Hill Univ	PA	46,972	C
Sewanee: The Univ of the South	TN	54,500	MC
Shaw Univ	NC	24,638	C
Shippensburg Univ of Pennsylvania	PA	23,208	C
Sonoma State Univ	CA	27,806	C
Southern Adventist Univ	TN	27,600	C
Southern Methodist Univ	TX	66,483	MC
Southern Nazarene Univ	OK	32,798	NC
Southern Oregon Univ	OR	19,117	C
Southwestern Univ	TX	50,720	VC
Spring Hill College	AL	48,488	C
St. Ambrose Univ	IA	39,019	C
St. Ambrose Univ	IA	39,019	C
St. Bonaventure Univ	NY	44,237	C
St. Francis College	NY	38,800	LC
St. John Fisher College	NY	43,620	C
St. Lawrence Univ	NY	64,390	VC
St. Mary's Univ	TX	37,500	C
SUNY / SUNY Cortland	NY	20,706	VC
SUNY / SUNY Oneonta	NY	19,712	C+
SUNY at Binghamton	NY	22,861	MC
SUNY at Oswego	NY	21,351	C
Stetson Univ	FL	53,544	VC
Stonehill College	MA	55,030	C+
Susquehanna Univ	PA	55,340	VC
Tabor College	KS	35,870	C
Taylor Univ	IN	40,317	C+
Texas A&M Univ	TX	20,521	VC+
Texas Lutheran Univ	TX	38,620	C
Texas State Univ	TX	19,350	C
The College at Brockport - SUNY	NY	20,346	C
The College of New Jersey	NJ	31,909	HC
The College of New Rochelle	NY	46,300	VC
The Univ of Tenn at Martin	TN	14,876	C
The Univ of Utah	UT	17,924	VC
The Univ of Virginia's College at Wise	VA	18,192	LC
Thomas College	ME	35,268	LC
Thomas Edison State Univ	NJ	6,350	NC
Thomas More College	KY	36,720	C
Towson Univ	MD	17,408	VC
Trinity College	CT	63,920	HC+
Trinity Washington Univ	DC	33,826	C+
Union College	NE	23,270	C
United States Air Force Academy	CO		C
United States Military Academy at West Point	NY		HC+
Univ of Alabama	AL	24,320	C+
Univ of Alabama at Birmingham	AL	19,906	C
Univ of Arkansas at Little Rock	AR	18,211	C
Univ of Bridgeport	CT	44,430	LC
Univ of Calif at Irvine	CA	26,484	VC
Univ of Calif at Los Angeles	CA	30,162	MC
Univ of Calif at Santa Barbara	CA	29,091	HC
Univ of Calif San Diego	CA	30,150	MC
Univ of Central Florida	FL	15,922	VC
Univ of Chicago	IL	67,584	MC
Univ of Cincinnati	OH	21,964	VC
Univ of Colo Denver	CO	23,230	C
Univ of Dayton	OH	53,620	C
Univ of Denver	CO	58,443	VC+
Univ of Evansville	IN	44,186	VC+
Univ of Findlay	OH	60,139	C
Univ of Hartford	CT	49,776	C
Univ of Idaho	ID	15,348	C
Univ of Illinois at Urbana-Champaign	IL	27,006	HC
Univ of Iowa	IA	18,683	VC+
Univ of Kansas	KS	20,135	C+
Univ of La Verne	CA	55,600	C
Univ of Maine	ME	20,792	C
Univ of Maine at Farmington	ME	18,187	C
Univ of Maine at Presque Isle	ME	14,870	C
Univ of Memphis	TN	18,278	C
Univ of Miami	FL	63,494	MC
Univ of Mich/Ann Arbor	MI	24,410	MC
Univ of Mich/Dearborn	MI	11,757	VC
Univ of Minn/Duluth	MN	20,292	C+
Univ of Miss	MS	17,746	C+
Univ of Missouri/Columbia	MO	18,201	MC
Univ of Mount Union	OH	38,970	C
Univ of Nebr - Kearney	NE	16,546	LC
Univ of Nebr - Omaha	NE	16,120	C
Univ of New Hampshire	NH	28,562	VC
Univ of New Mexico	NM	15,404	C
Univ of New Orleans	LA	12,840	C
Univ of N Car at Chapel Hill	NC	20,052	HC+
Univ of N Car at Charlotte	NC	15,547	C
Univ of N Dak	ND	15,373	C
Univ of North Texas	TX	19,198	C
Univ of Okla	OK	18,911	VC
Univ of Oregon	OR	22,972	C
Univ of Pennsylvania	PA	63,526	MC
Univ of Pittsburgh	PA	29,568	HC+
Univ of Richmond	VA	60,880	MC
Univ of St. Joseph	CT	49,550	C
Univ of St. Mary	KS	34,690	C
Univ of San Francisco	CA	58,484	VC
Univ of Scranton	PA	54,962	VC
Univ of South Alabama	AL	16,400	C
Univ of S Dak	SD	16,109	C
Univ of Southern Indiana	IN	16,501	C
Univ of Southern Miss	MS	13,170	C
Univ of St. Thomas - Houston	TX	40,020	VC
Univ of Tampa	FL	36,944	C
Univ of the Pacific	CA	57,006	VC
Univ of Wisc-Madison	WI	20,934	MC
Univ of Wisc-Milwaukee	WI	21,496	C
Univ of Wisc-Oshkosh	WI	15,200	C
Univ of Wisc-Parkside	WI	15,193	C
Univ of Wisc-Platteville	WI	14,614	VC
Univ of Wisc-Stevens Point	WI	14,043	C
Univ of Wisc-Superior	WI	14,446	C
Univ of Wisc-Whitewater	WI	13,976	C
Univ of Wyoming	WY	15,375	C+
Vassar College	NY	65,491	MC
Virginia Commonwealth Univ	VA	23,049	C
Virginia Military Inst	VA	26,460	C+
Virginia Polytechnic Inst and State Univ	VA	21,276	HC
Washington & Jefferson College	PA	56,512	VC
Washington College	MD	54,666	VC
Washington Univ in St. Louis	MO	65,366	VC
Wells College	NY	50,500	C
Wesley College	DE	37,026	LC
West Virginia Univ	WV	18,210	C
West Virginia Wesleyan College	WV	36,858	C
Western Mich Univ	MI	21,054	C
Western New England Univ	MA	48,088	C
Western Oregon Univ	OR	15,021	LC
Western Washington Univ	WA	18,003	C+
Westminster College	MO	32,820	C
Wheeling Jesuit Univ	WV	37,106	LC
Whitman College	WA	59,772	MC
Whittier College	CA	57,891	C
Whitworth Univ	WA	51,732	VC
Wilkes Univ	PA	45,622	C
Willamette Univ	OR	61,817	VC+
William Woods Univ	MO	32,040	C
Wilson College	PA	35,620	C
Worcester Polytechnic Inst	MA	60,730	MC
Xavier Univ	OH	47,880	C+
Yale Univ	CT	64,650	MC

INTERNATIONAL SUPPLY AND VALUE CHAIN MANAGEMENT

School	ST	$IS	SR
Bryant Univ	RI	55,646	VC
Texas Christian Univ	TX	54,670	HC

INTERPRETER FOR THE DEAF

School	ST	$IS	SR
Bethel College	IN	35,860	C
Columbia College Chicago	IL	43,168	C
Gallaudet Univ	DC	29,118	LC
Gardner-Webb Univ	NC	39,200	C+
Idaho State Univ	ID	13,619	NC
MacMurray College	IL	33,620	C
Madonna Univ	MI	29,050	C
Maryville College	TN	44,410	C
Mount Aloysius College	PA	29,976	C
Quincy Univ	IL	36,998	C
Rochester Inst of Technology	NY	50,842	HC
St. Catherine Univ	MN	45,630	VC
Univ of Arkansas at Little Rock	AR	18,211	C
Virginia Polytechnic Inst and State Univ	VA	21,276	HC
Western Oregon Univ	OR	15,021	LC
William Woods Univ	MO	32,040	C

INVESTMENTS AND SECURITIES

School	ST	$IS	SR
Bryant Univ	RI	55,646	VC
CUNY/Baruch College	NY	21,609	HC
Lynn Univ	FL	49,480	LC
St. Joseph's Univ	PA	57,544	VC+
Univ of Nebr - Lincoln	NE	18,589	VC
Univ of N Dak	ND	15,373	C
Univ of North Texas	TX	19,198	C
Westminster College	UT	41,078	C+

ISLAMIC STUDIES

School	ST	$IS	SR
Brandeis Univ	MA	65,925	MC
DePaul Univ	IL	47,623	VC
Gettysburg College	PA	63,000	HC
New York Univ	NY	65,860	MC
Ohio State Univ at Columbus	OH	21,703	HC+
Univ of Calif at Santa Barbara	CA	29,091	HC
Univ of Mich/Ann Arbor	MI	24,410	MC
Univ of Texas at Austin	TX	26,102	HC
Washington Univ in St. Louis	MO	65,366	VC

ITALIAN

School	ST	$IS	SR
American Univ	DC	59,379	HC+
Arizona State Univ at the Tempe Campus	AZ	21,756	VC
Bard College	NY	64,024	HC
Barnard College/Columbia Univ	NY	62,741	MC
Bennington College	VT	63,960	MC
Boston College	MA	65,737	MC
Brigham Young Univ	UT	12,748	HC
Brown Univ	RI	64,566	MC
Bryn Mawr College	PA	59,890	MC
Central Conn State Univ	CT	21,203	C
CUNY/Brooklyn College	NY	5,884	C+
CUNY/Hunter College	NY	31,098	VC
CUNY/Lehman College	NY	5,778	HC+
CUNY/Queens College	NY	27,896	C
College of the Holy Cross	MA	62,165	MC
Columbia Univ/ School of General Studies	NY	61,470	MC
Cornell Univ	NY	64,853	MC
Dartmouth College	NH	66,174	MC
DePaul Univ	IL	47,623	VC
Dominican Univ	IL	41,222	C
Emory Univ	GA	60,786	MC
Fairfield Univ	CT	59,860	VC+
Florida Atlantic Univ	FL	17,339	C
Florida International Univ	FL	19,854	C+
Florida State Univ	FL	16,771	HC
Fordham Univ	NY	65,918	MC
Georgetown Univ	DC	65,926	MC
Harvard College/Harvard Univ	MA	60,659	MC
Haverford College	PA	66,490	MC
Hofstra Univ	NY	55,960	C+
Indiana Univ Bloomington	IN	20,429	VC
Iona College	NY	50,984	C
Johns Hopkins Univ	MD	65,386	MC
LIU Post	NY	49,682	C

ST = STATE $IS = IN-STATE COSTS SR = SELECTOR RATING

School	ST	$IS	SR
Loyola Univ Chicago	IL	55,802	VC
Marist College	NY	49,860	VC
Middlebury College	VT	64,332	MC
Montclair State Univ	NJ	26,210	LC
Mount Holyoke College	MA	56,746	MC
Nazareth College	NY	45,574	C
New York Univ	NY	65,860	MC
Northeastern Illinois Univ	IL	12,529	LC
Northwestern Univ	IL	66,344	MC
Ohio State Univ at Columbus	OH	21,703	HC+
Pepperdine Univ	CA	74,460	HC+
Princeton Univ	NJ	57,610	MC
Providence College	RI	60,760	VC
Rutgers Univ - New Brunswick	NJ	26,632	HC
Rutgers Univ - Newark	NJ	27,288	C
St. Joseph's Univ	PA	57,544	VC+
St. Louis Univ	MO	49,866	HC
San Francisco State Univ	CA	18,514	LC
Sarah Lawrence College	NY	63,388	HC
Scripps College	CA	66,664	MC
Seton Hall Univ	NJ	55,514	C
Smith College	MA	63,914	MC
Southern Conn State Univ	CT	21,924	LC
St. John's Univ	NY	55,850	C
Stanford Univ	CA	60,409	MC
SUNY / Univ at Buffalo	NY	23,122	C+
SUNY at Binghamton	NY	22,861	MC
Susquehanna Univ	PA	55,340	VC
Temple Univ	PA	24,392	VC
The Catholic Univ of America	DC	56,356	VC
The Univ of Tenn at Knoxville	TN	22,112	VC
Thomas Edison State Univ	NJ	6,350	NC
Trinity College	CT	63,920	HC+
Tufts Univ	MA		MC
Tulane Univ	LA	63,396	HC+
Univ of Arizona	AZ	23,100	C
Univ of Calif at Berkeley	CA	28,853	MC
Univ of Calif at Davis	CA	28,468	HC
Univ of Calif at Los Angeles	CA	30,162	MC
Univ of Calif San Diego	CA	30,150	MC
Univ of Colo Boulder	CO	24,285	VC+
Univ of Delaware	DE	24,976	VC+
Univ of Denver	CO	58,443	VC+
Univ of Georgia	GA	21,250	HC
Univ of Illinois at Chicago	IL	25,006	VC
Univ of Illinois at Urbana-Champaign	IL	27,006	HC
Univ of Iowa	IA	18,683	VC+
Univ of Kentucky	KY	33,306	C
Univ of Mass Boston	MA	13,435	C
Univ of Mich/Ann Arbor	MI	24,410	MC
Univ of Minn/Twin Cities	MN	23,519	HC+
Univ of Notre Dame	IN	64,043	MC
Univ of Okla	OK	18,911	VC
Univ of Oregon	OR	22,972	C
Univ of Pittsburgh	PA	29,568	HC+
Univ of Rhode Island	RI	24,906	C
Univ of South Florida/Tampa	FL	16,110	VC+
Univ of Southern Calif	CA	66,631	C
Univ of Texas at Austin	TX	26,102	HC
Univ of Virginia	VA	25,891	MC
Univ of Washington	WA	23,149	VC
Univ of Wisc-Madison	WI	20,934	MC
Vassar College	NY	65,491	MC
Villanova Univ	PA	62,523	MC
Washington Univ in St. Louis	MO	65,366	VC
Wellesley College	MA	63,916	MC
Yale Univ	CT	64,650	MC
Youngstown State Univ	OH	17,307	C

ITALIAN STUDIES

School	ST	$IS	SR
Assumption College	MA	47,920	C+
Bard College	NY	64,024	HC
Boston Univ	MA	65,110	MC
Brown Univ	RI	64,566	MC
CUNY/College of Staten Island	NY	17,840	NC
Colo College	CO	62,560	MC
Columbia Univ/ School of General Studies	NY	61,470	MC
Columbia Univ/City of New York	NY	62,958	MC
Conn College	CT	65,000	MC
Dartmouth College	NH	66,174	MC
Dickinson College	PA	63,974	MC
Duke Univ	NC	64,188	
Elon Univ	NC	44,599	VC+
Emory Univ	GA	60,786	MC
Fordham Univ	NY	65,918	MC
Gonzaga Univ	WA	50,888	HC
Ithaca College	NY	56,766	VC
Lake Erie College	OH	38,914	LC
Miami Univ	OH	27,190	HC+
New York Univ	NY	65,860	MC
Pennsylvania State Univ - Univ Park	PA	29,760	HC
Purdue Univ/West Lafayette	IN	20,032	MC
Rosemont College	PA	30,980	C
Scripps College	CA	66,664	MC
Southern Methodist Univ	TX	66,483	MC
Stony Brook Univ/The SUNY	NY	21,881	MC
Syracuse Univ	NY	60,239	VC
Univ of Calif at Los Angeles	CA	30,162	MC
Univ of Calif at Santa Barbara	CA	29,091	HC
Univ of Calif San Diego	CA	30,150	MC
Univ of Calif, Santa Cruz	CA	28,731	C+
Univ of Conn	CT	25,538	HC
Univ of Houston	TX	21,483	VC
Univ of Illinois at Chicago	IL	25,006	VC
Univ of Maryland/College Park	MD	21,938	HC
Univ of Mass Amherst	MA	26,199	VC+
Univ of New Hampshire	NH	28,562	VC
Univ of Pennsylvania	PA	63,526	MC
Univ of Richmond	VA	60,880	MC
Univ of San Diego	CA	58,442	VC+
Univ of Vermont	VT	28,878	HC
Univ of Wisc-Milwaukee	WI	21,496	C
Vanderbilt Univ	TN	60,572	MC
Wellesley College	MA	63,916	MC
Wesleyan Univ	CT	65,516	MC
Wheaton College	MA	61,512	VC
Youngstown State Univ	OH	17,307	C

JAPANESE

School	ST	$IS	SR
American Univ	DC	59,379	HC+
Ball State Univ	IN	19,590	C
Bard College	NY	64,024	HC
Bates College	ME	64,500	MC
Bennington College	VT	63,960	MC
Brigham Young Univ	UT	12,748	HC
Cal State, Fullerton	CA	21,902	C
Cal State, Long Beach	CA	18,850	C
Cal State, Los Angeles	CA	17,186	LC
Calvin College	MI	41,570	VC+
Central Washington Univ	WA	16,803	C
Colgate Univ	NY	65,030	MC
Conn College	CT	65,000	MC
Eastern Mich Univ	MI	19,761	C
Elizabethtown College	PA	54,050	C
Emory Univ	GA	60,786	MC
George Washington Univ	DC	62,835	MC
Georgetown Univ	DC	65,926	MC
Harvard College/Harvard Univ	MA	60,659	MC
Hofstra Univ	NY	55,960	C+
Lawrence Univ	WI	54,498	HC
Linfield College	OR	52,010	C
Macalester College	MN	61,905	MC
Marshall Univ	WV	17,242	C
Middlebury College	VT	64,332	MC
Murray State Univ	KY	16,998	C
North Central College	IL	48,712	VC
Northern Kentucky Univ	KY	16,486	C
Oakland Univ	MI	20,763	C
Occidental College	CA	65,530	MC
Ohio State Univ at Columbus	OH	21,703	HC+
Pacific Univ	OR	52,876	C
Pomona College	CA	64,957	MC
Portland State Univ	OR	19,443	C
Purdue Univ/West Lafayette	IN	20,032	MC
San Diego State Univ	CA	21,896	C+
San Francisco State Univ	CA	18,514	LC
San Jose State Univ	CA	21,540	C
Scripps College	CA	66,664	MC
Stanford Univ	CA	60,409	MC
The Univ of Utah	UT	17,924	VC
Thomas Edison State Univ	NJ	6,350	NC
Tufts Univ	MA		MC
Univ of Calif at Berkeley	CA	28,853	MC
Univ of Calif at Davis	CA	28,468	HC
Univ of Calif at Irvine	CA	26,484	VC
Univ of Calif at Los Angeles	CA	30,162	MC
Univ of Calif at Riverside	CA	29,227	C+
Univ of Calif at Santa Barbara	CA	29,091	HC
Univ of Calif San Diego	CA	30,150	MC
Univ of Colo Boulder	CO	24,285	VC+
Univ of Findlay	OH	60,139	C
Univ of Georgia	GA	21,250	HC
Univ of Hawaii at Hilo	HI	18,038	C
Univ of Hawaii at Manoa	HI	23,221	C
Univ of Iowa	IA	18,683	VC+
Univ of Maryland/College Park	MD	21,938	HC
Univ of Mass Amherst	MA	26,199	VC+
Univ of Minn/Twin Cities	MN	23,519	HC+
Univ of Missouri-St. Louis	MO		C
Univ of Montana	MT	14,105	C
Univ of Mount Union	OH	38,970	C
Univ of Notre Dame	IN	64,043	MC
Univ of Oregon	OR	22,972	C
Univ of Pittsburgh	PA	29,568	HC+
Univ of Puget Sound	WA	56,456	VC+
Univ of Rochester	NY	65,032	MC
Univ of the Pacific	CA	57,006	VC
Univ of Vermont	VT	28,878	HC
Univ of Washington	WA	23,149	VC
Univ of Wisc-Madison	WI	20,934	MC
Vassar College	NY	65,491	MC
Wake Forest Univ	NC	64,056	MC
Washington State Univ	WA	22,495	C
Washington Univ in St. Louis	MO	65,366	VC
Wellesley College	MA	63,916	MC
Western Mich Univ	MI	21,054	C
Western Washington Univ	WA	18,003	C+
Yale Univ	CT	64,650	MC

JAPANESE STUDIES

School	ST	$IS	SR
Adrian College	MI	42,400	C
Aquinas College - Mich	MI	38,876	HC
Boston Univ	MA	65,110	MC
Carnegie Mellon Univ	PA	67,980	MC
Case Western Reserve Univ	OH	60,304	MC
Earlham College	IN	54,870	HC
Gettysburg College	PA	63,000	HC
Hofstra Univ	NY	55,960	C+
Hope College	MI	39,940	VC
Linfield College	OR	52,010	C
New York Univ	NY	65,860	MC
Pennsylvania State Univ - Univ Park	PA	29,760	HC
Purdue Univ/West Lafayette	IN	20,032	MC
Salem International Univ	WV	21,090	LC
Smith College	MA	63,914	MC
SUNY at Binghamton	NY	22,861	MC
Swarthmore College	PA	63,550	MC
Univ of Alaska Fairbanks	AK	16,179	C
Univ of Calif San Diego	CA	30,150	MC
Univ of Hawaii at Hilo	HI	18,038	C
Univ of N Car at Charlotte	NC	15,547	C
Wellesley College	MA	63,916	MC
Willamette Univ	OR	61,817	VC+
William Jewell College	MO	41,210	C+

JAZZ

School	ST	$IS	SR
Alabama A&M Univ	AL	18,796	C
Aquinas College - Mich	MI	38,876	HC
Bennington College	VT	63,960	MC
Berklee College of Music	MA	60,930	SP
Bowling Green State Univ	OH	19,747	C
Brigham Young Univ	UT	12,748	HC
Butler Univ	IN	51,352	VC
Cal State, Fresno	CA	16,902	LC
DePaul Univ	IL	47,623	VC
Eastman School of Music/ Univ of Rochester	NY	65,644	SP
Elmhurst College	IL	45,428	C
Five Towns College	NY	35,350	C
Florida Atlantic Univ	FL	17,339	C
Florida State Univ	FL	16,771	HC
Hofstra Univ	NY	55,960	C+
Howard Univ	DC	37,616	C+
Indiana Univ Bloomington	IN	20,429	VC
Ithaca College	NY	56,766	VC
Johnson State College	VT	20,752	C
Limestone College	SC	32,100	C
LIU Brooklyn	NY	49,682	C
Loyola Univ New Orleans	LA	51,708	VC+
Manhattan School of Music	NY	57,200	SP
Marshall Univ	WV	17,242	C
Mich State Univ	MI	23,898	VC+
New England Conservatory of Music	MA	58,655	SP
N Car Central Univ	NC	9,000	C
North Central College	IL	48,712	VC
Northwestern Univ	IL	66,344	MC
Ohio State Univ at Columbus	OH	21,703	HC+
Roosevelt Univ	IL	40,651	VC
Rowan Univ	NJ	24,491	VC+
San Jose State Univ	CA	21,540	C
Shenandoah Univ	VA	41,312	C
Temple Univ	PA	24,392	VC
Texas State Univ	TX	19,350	C
Tulane Univ	LA	63,396	HC+
Univ of Cincinnati	OH	21,964	VC
Univ of Denver	CO	58,443	VC+
Univ of Hartford	CT	49,776	C
Univ of Illinois at Chicago	IL	25,006	VC
Univ of Iowa	IA	18,683	VC+
Univ of Maine at Augusta	ME	7,812	C
Univ of Miami	FL	63,494	MC
Univ of Mich/Ann Arbor	MI	24,410	MC
Univ of Minn/Duluth	MN	20,292	C+
Univ of N Car at Asheville	NC	15,723	VC+
Univ of N Car at Greensboro	NC	14,690	C
Univ of North Florida	FL	15,996	VC
Univ of North Texas	TX	19,198	C
Univ of Oregon	OR	22,972	C
Univ of Rochester	NY	65,032	MC
Univ of Southern Calif	CA	66,631	C
Univ of Washington	WA	23,149	VC
Webster Univ	MO	37,490	C
West Chester Univ of Pennsylvania	PA	18,456	C
Western Mich Univ	MI	21,054	C
Whitman College	WA	59,772	MC
Youngstown State Univ	OH	17,307	C

JOURNALISM

School	ST	$IS	SR
Abilene Christian Univ	TX	41,800	C+
Adrian College	MI	42,400	C
Alabama A&M Univ	AL	18,796	C
American Jewish Univ - College of A&S Campus	CA	44,234	C
American Univ	DC	59,379	HC+
Andrews Univ	MI	28,030	C+
Appalachian State Univ	NC	14,416	VC
Aquinas College - Mich	MI	38,876	HC
Arkansas State Univ	AR	16,190	C
Arkansas Tech Univ	AR	15,484	C
Asbury Univ	KY	35,180	C+
Ashford Univ	CA	10,480	C
Ashland Univ	OH	21,440	C
Auburn Univ	AL	23,594	VC+
Augustana Univ	SD	38,424	VC
Averett Univ	VA	40,970	LC
Azusa Pacific Univ	CA	43,972	C
Ball State Univ	IN	19,590	C
Bayamon Central Univ	PR	12,490	
Baylor Univ	TX	53,760	HC
Belmont Univ	TN	40,970	VC
Bemidji State Univ	MN	16,056	VC
Benedict College	SC	28,238	NC
Benedictine College	KS	36,200	VC
Bennington College	VT	63,960	MC
Bethel Univ	MN	45,270	VC
Biola Univ	CA	46,402	C+
Bloomfield College	NJ	39,100	LC
Bloomsburg Univ of Pennsylvania	PA	19,066	LC
Boston Univ	MA	65,110	MC
Bowling Green State Univ	OH	19,747	C
Briar Cliff Univ	IA	36,956	C
Butler Univ	IN	51,352	VC
Calif Baptist Univ	CA	41,392	C
Calif Polytechnic State Univ	CA	17,979	HC+
Cal State, Chico	CA	21,440	C
Cal State, Fresno	CA	16,902	LC
Cal State, Fullerton	CA	21,902	C
Cal State, Long Beach	CA	18,850	C
Cal State, Northridge	CA	16,859	LC
Cal State, Sacramento	CA	20,332	C
Cameron Univ	OK	11,072	NC
Canisius College	NY	47,537	C
Carnegie Mellon Univ	PA	67,980	MC
Cedarville Univ	OH	34,990	VC
Central Conn State Univ	CT	21,203	C
Central Mich Univ	MI	20,330	C
Central State Univ	OH	18,564	C
Central Washington Univ	WA	16,803	C
CUNY/Baruch College	NY	21,609	HC
CUNY/Brooklyn College	NY	5,884	C+
College of St. Scholastica	MN	44,640	C
College of the Ozarks	MO	7,230	C
Colo State Univ	CO	22,162	VC
Colo State Univ-Pueblo	CO	18,234	C
Columbia College Chicago	IL	43,168	C
Concordia College - Moorhead	MN	51,088	C+
Concordia Univ, Ann Arbor	MI	35,945	VC
Corban Univ	OR	40,306	C
Creighton Univ	NE	48,206	VC+
Delaware State Univ	DE	19,376	NC
DePaul Univ	IL	47,623	VC
Dickinson State Univ	ND	12,372	LC
Doane Univ	NE	39,184	VC
Dominican Univ	IL	41,222	C
Dordt College	IA	37,860	C+
Drake Univ	IA	45,056	HC
Duquesne Univ	PA	46,822	VC
Eastern Illinois Univ	IL	21,126	C
Eastern Kentucky Univ	KY	16,908	C
Eastern Mich Univ	MI	19,761	C
Eastern Nazarene College	MA	39,955	C
Eastern Washington Univ	WA	25,572	LC
Edinboro Univ	PA	15,940	LC
Elon Univ	NC	44,599	VC+
Emerson College	MA	54,736	HC
Emory and Henry College	VA	41,410	C
Emory Univ	GA	60,786	MC
Evangel Univ	MO	28,898	C
Felician Univ	NJ	45,370	LC
Flagler College	FL	27,620	C
Florida A&M Univ	FL	15,361	C
Florida Atlantic Univ	FL	17,339	C
Fordham Univ	NY	65,918	MC
Franklin College	IN	39,380	C
Freed-Hardeman Univ	TN	29,450	C
Gannon Univ	PA	42,032	C
George Washington Univ	DC	62,835	MC
Georgia College & State Univ	GA	21,148	C+
Georgia Southern Univ	GA	16,596	C
Georgia State Univ	GA	24,332	VC
Gonzaga Univ	WA	50,888	HC
Goshen College	IN	42,500	C
Grace College and Seminary	IN	31,524	C
Grand Valley State Univ	MI	22,250	C+
Grand View Univ	IA	32,302	C
Hampshire College	MA	63,824	MC
Harding Univ	AR	25,421	C
Hawaii Pacific Univ	HI	33,420	C
Hofstra Univ	NY	55,960	C+
Howard Univ	DC	37,616	C+
Humboldt State Univ	CA	20,514	C
Huntington Univ	IN	33,996	C
Illinois State Univ	IL	23,418	VC
Indiana State Univ	IN	23,223	LC
Indiana Univ Bloomington	IN	20,429	VC
Indiana Univ of Pennsylvania	PA	23,614	LC
Indiana Univ Southeast	IN	14,242	LC
Indiana Univ-Purdue Univ Indianapolis	IN	18,635	C
Iowa State Univ	IA	17,570	C
Ithaca College	NY	56,766	VC
Johnson State College	VT	20,752	C
Kansas State Univ	KS	17,780	VC
Keene State College	NH	24,003	LC
Kent State Univ	OH	20,732	C
Lasell College	MA	47,500	C
Lehigh Univ	PA	61,010	MC
Lenoir-Rhyne Univ	NC	43,200	C
Lewis Univ	IL	40,370	C
Lincoln Univ	MO	13,602	NC
Linfield College	OR	52,010	C
Lipscomb Univ	TN	41,296	VC

ST = STATE $IS = IN-STATE COSTS SR = SELECTOR RATING

School	ST	$IS	SR
LIU Brooklyn	NY	49,682	C
LIU Post	NY	49,682	C
Lock Haven Univ of Pennsylvania	PA	18,028	LC
Louisiana College	LA	21,886	C
Louisiana State Univ and A&M College	LA	18,677	VC
Louisiana Tech Univ	LA	11,422	VC
Loyola Univ Chicago	IL	55,802	VC
Loyola Univ New Orleans	LA	51,708	VC+
Lyndon State College	VT	20,714	C
Lynn Univ	FL	49,480	LC
Madonna Univ	MI	29,050	C
Manhattan College	NY	51,750	C+
Marietta College	OH	46,190	C
Marquette Univ	WI	48,390	VC+
Marshall Univ	WV	17,242	C
Mercer Univ	GA	45,348	VC
Mercy College	NY	31,776	C
Mercyhurst Univ	PA	47,420	C
Messiah College	PA	43,100	C+
Metropolitan State Univ of Denver	CO	29,889	LC
Miami Univ	OH	27,190	HC+
Mich State Univ	MI	23,898	VC+
Midland Univ	NE	37,468	
Millersville Univ of Pennsylvania	PA	23,782	C
Millikin Univ	IL	42,158	C
Minn State Univ, Mankato	MN	15,616	C
Minn State Univ, Moorhead	MN	15,941	C
Missouri Baptist Univ	MO	35,594	C
Missouri State Univ	MO	15,190	C+
Mount Ida College	MA	46,820	C
Mount Marty College	SD	32,972	C
Mount Mercy Univ	IA	36,826	C
Mount Vernon Nazarene Univ	OH	34,500	C
Murray State Univ	KY	16,998	C
Muskingum Univ	OH	35,966	C
Neumann Univ	PA	40,678	LC
New Mexico State Univ	NM	14,050	C
New York Inst of Technology	NY	48,730	C
New York Univ	NY	65,860	MC
Nicholls State Univ	LA	10,534	C
Norfolk State Univ	VA	25,702	LC
North Central College	IL	48,712	VC
Northeastern State Univ	OK	8,615	VC
Northeastern Univ	MA	62,703	MC
Northern Arizona Univ	AZ	20,246	VC
Northern Illinois Univ	IL	20,176	C
Northern Kentucky Univ	KY	16,486	C
Northwest Missouri State Univ	MO	17,737	C
Northwest Univ	WA	35,876	VC
Northwestern College of Iowa	IA	38,400	C+
Northwestern Univ	IL	66,344	MC
Oakland Univ	MI	20,763	C
Ohio Northern Univ	OH	44,050	VC
Ohio State Univ at Columbus	OH	21,703	HC+
Ohio Univ	OH	22,924	C
Ohio Wesleyan Univ	OH	49,460	VC
Okla Baptist Univ	OK	32,320	C
Okla Christian Univ	OK	27,650	VC
Okla State Univ	OK	17,180	VC
Old Dominion Univ	VA	20,910	C
Olivet College	MI	36,110	LC
Olivet Nazarene Univ	IL	41,840	C
Otterbein Univ	OH	41,630	C
Pacific Union College	CA	36,009	VC
Palm Beach Atlantic Univ	FL	39,720	C
Pennsylvania State Univ - Univ Park	PA	29,760	HC
Pepperdine Univ	CA	74,460	HC+
Point Loma Nazarene Univ	CA	43,450	C
Point Park Univ	PA	41,270	C
Prairie View A&M Univ	TX	15,205	LC
Prescott College	AZ	33,284	C
Purdue Univ/Northwest	IN	15,038	C
Purdue Univ/West Lafayette	IN	20,032	MC
Quinnipiac Univ	CT	59,110	C
Rider Univ	NJ	54,050	C
Rochester Inst of Technology	NY	50,842	HC
Roger Williams Univ	RI	46,296	C+
Roosevelt Univ	IL	40,651	VC
Rowan Univ	NJ	24,491	VC+
Rust College	MS	10,600	C
Rutgers Univ - New Brunswick	NJ	26,632	HC
Rutgers Univ - Newark	NJ	27,288	C
St. Mary-of-the-Woods College	IN	39,632	LC
St. Mary's Univ of Minn	MN	41,210	VC
St. Michael's College	VT	51,725	VC+
Sam Houston State Univ	TX	18,792	C
Samford Univ	AL	39,232	VC
San Diego State Univ	CA	21,896	C+
San Francisco State Univ	CA	18,514	LC
San Jose State Univ	CA	21,540	C
Seattle Univ	WA	50,811	VC+
Seton Hall Univ	NJ	55,514	C
Seton Hill Univ	PA	46,972	C
Shippensburg Univ of Pennsylvania	PA	23,208	C
Simpson College	IA	43,839	VC
S Dak State Univ	SD	15,634	C
Southeast Missouri State Univ	MO	15,498	C
Southeastern Univ	FL	31,765	C
Southern Adventist Univ	TN	27,600	C
Southern Arkansas Univ	AR	21,532	C
Southern Conn State Univ	CT	21,924	LC
Southern Illinois Univ Carbondale	IL	23,667	C
Southern Illinois Univ Edwardsville	IL	22,643	C
Southern Methodist Univ	TX	66,483	MC
Southern Nazarene Univ	OK	32,798	NC
Southern Univ at New Orleans	LA	8,014	LC
Southwest Baptist Univ	MO	29,900	LC
Southwestern Adventist Univ	TX	27,756	LC
Spring Hill College	AL	48,488	C
St. Bonaventure Univ	NY	44,237	C
St. Cloud State Univ	MN	10,600	C
St. John's Univ	NY	55,850	C
St. Joseph's College, New York/Brooklyn Campus	NY	25,114	LC
St. Joseph's College, New York/Long Island Campus	NY	25,124	C
SUNY / Buffalo State College	NY	20,842	C
SUNY / SUNY Fredonia	NY	20,818	C
SUNY / SUNY Plattsburgh	NY	18,814	C
SUNY at New Paltz	NY	19,200	C
SUNY at Oswego	NY	21,351	C
SUNY at Purchase	NY	17,900	C
Stephen F. Austin State Univ	TX	18,406	LC
Stony Brook Univ/The SUNY	NY	21,881	MC
Suffolk Univ	MA	50,308	C
Taylor Univ	IN	40,317	C+
Temple Univ	PA	24,392	VC
Tenn Tech Univ	TN	17,050	C
Texas A&M Univ at Commerce	TX	10,496	C
Texas Christian Univ	TX	54,670	HC
Texas State Univ	TX	19,350	C
Texas Tech Univ	TX	18,736	C+
Texas Wesleyan Univ	TX	35,134	C
The College at Brockport - SUNY	NY	20,346	C
The Lincoln Univ	PA	15,154	NC
The Univ of Tenn at Knoxville	TN	22,112	VC
Tougaloo College	MS	17,980	NC
Trevecca Nazarene Univ	TN	31,186	C
Troy Univ	AL	16,171	C
Truman State Univ	MO	16,014	HC
Tulane Univ	LA	63,396	HC+
Union College	NE	23,270	C
Union Univ	TN	33,970	VC
Univ of Alabama	AL	24,320	C+
Univ of Alaska Anchorage	AK	16,652	NC
Univ of Alaska Fairbanks	AK	16,179	C
Univ of Arizona	AZ	23,100	C
Univ of Arkansas at Fayetteville	AR	19,152	C+
Univ of Arkansas at Little Rock	AR	18,211	C
Univ of Arkansas at Pine Bluff	AR	13,541	C
Univ of Bridgeport	CT	44,430	LC
Univ of Calif at Irvine	CA	26,484	VC
Univ of Central Arkansas	AR	14,472	VC
Univ of Central Florida	FL	15,922	VC
Univ of Central Missouri	MO	18,982	C
Univ of Central Okla	OK	13,486	C
Univ of Cincinnati	OH	21,964	VC
Univ of Colo Boulder	CO	24,285	VC+
Univ of Conn	CT	25,538	HC
Univ of Delaware	DE	24,976	VC+
Univ of Denver	CO	58,443	VC+
Univ of Florida	FL	16,291	HC+
Univ of Georgia	GA	21,250	HC
Univ of Hawaii at Manoa	HI	23,221	C
Univ of Idaho	ID	15,348	C
Univ of Illinois at Urbana-Champaign	IL	27,006	HC
Univ of Indianapolis	IN	36,480	C
Univ of Iowa	IA	18,683	VC+
Univ of Kansas	KS	20,135	C+
Univ of Kentucky	KY	33,306	C
Univ of La Verne	CA	55,600	C
Univ of Maine	ME	20,792	C
Univ of Mary Hardin-Baylor	TX	33,950	C+
Univ of Maryland/College Park	MD	21,938	HC
Univ of Mass Amherst	MA	26,199	VC+
Univ of Memphis	TN	18,278	C
Univ of Miami	FL	63,494	MC
Univ of Miss	MS	17,746	C+
Univ of Missouri/Columbia	MO	18,201	MC
Univ of Montana	MT	14,105	C
Univ of Montevallo	AL	19,502	C
Univ of Nebr - Kearney	NE	16,546	LC
Univ of Nebr - Lincoln	NE	18,589	VC
Univ of Nebr - Omaha	NE	16,120	C
Univ of Nevada/Reno	NV	18,010	C
Univ of New Mexico	NM	15,404	C
Univ of North Alabama	AL	15,398	C
Univ of N Car at Chapel Hill	NC	20,052	HC+
Univ of North Texas	TX	19,198	C
Univ of Northern Colo	CO	20,851	C
Univ of Northwestern - St. Paul	MN	38,160	C
Univ of Okla	OK	18,911	VC
Univ of Oregon	OR	22,972	C
Univ of Pittsburgh at Johnstown	PA	22,092	C
Univ of PR-Rio Piedras campus	PR	13,327	
Univ of Rhode Island	RI	24,906	C
Univ of Richmond	VA	60,880	MC
Univ of S Car at Columbia	SC	19,725	VC+
Univ of S Dak	SD	16,109	C
Univ of Southern Calif	CA	66,631	C
Univ of Southern Indiana	IN	16,501	C
Univ of Southern Miss	MS	13,170	C
Univ of St. Francis	IL	39,924	C
Univ of Tampa	FL	36,944	C
Univ of Texas at Arlington	TX	18,026	LC
Univ of Texas at Austin	TX	26,102	HC
Univ of Texas at El Paso	TX	34,452	NC
Univ of the Cumberlands	KY	32,000	C
Univ of West Georgia	GA	16,360	LC
Univ of Wisc-Eau Claire	WI	15,797	VC
Univ of Wisc-Madison	WI	20,934	MC
Univ of Wisc-Oshkosh	WI	15,200	C
Univ of Wisc-River Falls	WI	14,485	C
Univ of Wisc-Whitewater	WI	13,976	C
Univ of Wyoming	WY	15,375	C+
Utah State Univ	UT	12,736	C
Utica College	NY	30,430	C
Virginia Union Univ	VA	22,421	C
Virginia Wesleyan College	VA	43,728	LC
Wartburg College	IA	47,840	C
Washington Adventist Univ	MD	31,440	LC
Washington and Lee Univ	VA	59,647	MC
Washington State Univ	WA	22,495	C
Washington Univ in St. Louis	MO	65,366	VC
Wayne State Univ	MI	22,016	C
Weber State Univ	UT	10,721	C
Webster Univ	MO	37,490	C
West Virginia Univ	WV	18,210	C
Western Illinois Univ	IL	20,825	C
Western Kentucky Univ	KY	16,850	C
Western Mich Univ	MI	21,054	C
Western Washington Univ	WA	18,003	C+
Whitworth Univ	WA	51,732	VC
William Penn Univ	IA	26,000	C
William Woods Univ	MO	32,040	C
Wilmington College	OH	34,600	C
Wingate Univ	NC	39,950	C
Winona State Univ	MN	17,535	C
Youngstown State Univ	OH	17,307	C

JOURNALISM - MAGAZINE JOURNALISM

School	ST	$IS	SR
Ohio Univ	OH	22,924	C
Syracuse Univ	NY	60,239	VC
Washington State Univ	WA	22,495	C

JOURNALISM - NEWS & INFORMATION

School	ST	$IS	SR
Bloomfield College	NJ	39,100	LC
Calif Baptist Univ	CA	41,392	C
Keene State College	NH	24,003	LC
N Dak State Univ	ND	16,245	C
Ohio Univ	OH	22,924	C
Okla Baptist Univ	OK	32,320	C
Syracuse Univ	NY	60,239	VC
Univ of Findlay	OH	60,139	C
Washington State Univ	WA	22,495	C

JOURNALISM - NEWSWRITING / EDIT

School	ST	$IS	SR
Ohio Univ	OH	22,924	C
Washington State Univ	WA	22,495	C

JOURNALISM & TECHNICAL COMMUNICATIONS

School	ST	$IS	SR
Arizona State Univ at the Downtown Phoenix Campus	AZ	23,680	VC
Fairfield Univ	CT	59,860	VC+
Ferris State Univ	MI	21,445	C
Pennsylvania State Univ - Univ Park	PA	29,760	HC
Syracuse Univ	NY	60,239	VC

JOURNALISM EDUCATION

School	ST	$IS	SR
Abilene Christian Univ	TX	41,800	C+
Baylor Univ	TX	53,760	HC
Cal State, Northridge	CA	16,859	LC
Carlow Univ	PA	38,549	LC
Grace College and Seminary	IN	31,524	C
Indiana Univ Bloomington	IN	20,429	VC
Stephen F. Austin State Univ	TX	18,406	LC
Univ of Nebr - Lincoln	NE	18,589	VC
Univ of S Dak	SD	16,109	C
Univ of Wisc-Milwaukee	WI	21,496	C
Wartburg College	IA	47,840	C
Webster Univ	MO	37,490	C

JUDAIC STUDIES

School	ST	$IS	SR
American Jewish Univ - College of A&S Campus	CA	44,234	C
American Univ	DC	59,379	HC+
Bard College	NY	64,024	HC
Bennington College	VT	63,960	MC
Brandeis Univ	MA	65,925	MC
Brown Univ	RI	64,566	MC
CUNY/Brooklyn College	NY	5,884	C+
CUNY/Hunter College	NY	31,098	VC
College of Charleston	SC	22,699	C
DePaul Univ	IL	47,623	VC
Dickinson College	PA	63,974	MC
Elon Univ	NC	44,599	VC+
Emory Univ	GA	60,786	MC
Florida Atlantic Univ	FL	17,339	C
George Washington Univ	DC	62,835	MC
Gettysburg College	PA	63,000	HC
Hampshire College	MA	63,824	MC
Hofstra Univ	NY	55,960	C+
Indiana Univ Bloomington	IN	20,429	VC
List College	NY	37,870	C
New York Univ	NY	65,860	MC
Northeastern Univ	MA	62,703	MC
Oberlin College	OH	66,012	MC
Ohio State Univ at Columbus	OH	21,703	HC+
Pennsylvania State Univ - Univ Park	PA	29,760	HC
Purdue Univ/West Lafayette	IN	20,032	MC
Rutgers Univ - New Brunswick	NJ	26,632	HC
San Francisco State Univ	CA	18,514	LC
Scripps College	CA	66,664	MC
Smith College	MA	63,914	MC
Stanford Univ	CA	60,409	MC
SUNY at Binghamton	NY	22,861	MC
Touro College	NY	28,950	VC
Trinity College	CT	63,920	HC+
Tufts Univ	MA		MC
Tulane Univ	LA	63,396	HC+
Univ of Arizona	AZ	23,100	C
Univ of Calif at Los Angeles	CA	30,162	MC
Univ of Calif San Diego	CA	30,150	MC
Univ of Chicago	IL	67,584	MC
Univ of Cincinnati	OH	21,964	VC
Univ of Colo Boulder	CO	24,285	VC+
Univ of Denver	CO	58,443	VC+
Univ of Florida	FL	16,291	HC+
Univ of Hartford	CT	49,776	C
Univ of Kansas	KS	20,135	C+
Univ of Maryland/College Park	MD	21,938	HC
Univ of Mass Amherst	MA	26,199	VC+
Univ of Miami	FL	63,494	MC
Univ of Mich/Ann Arbor	MI	24,410	MC
Univ of Missouri-Kansas City	MO	19,563	VC
Univ of Okla	OK	18,911	VC
Univ of Oregon	OR	22,972	C
Univ of Pennsylvania	PA	63,526	MC
Univ of Southern Calif	CA	66,631	C
Univ of Texas at Austin	TX	26,102	HC
Univ of Washington	WA	23,149	VC
Univ of Wisc-Madison	WI	20,934	MC
Univ of Wisc-Milwaukee	WI	21,496	C
Vanderbilt Univ	TN	60,572	MC
Vassar College	NY	65,491	MC
Washington Univ in St. Louis	MO	65,366	VC
Wellesley College	MA	63,916	MC
Yale Univ	CT	64,650	MC

JUSTICE AND SOCIETY

School	ST	$IS	SR
Concordia Univ, Ann Arbor	MI	35,945	VC
Creighton Univ	NE	48,206	VC+
Elon Univ	NC	44,599	VC+
Georgetown College	KY	41,440	C
Goddard College	VT	17,040	VC
Miami Univ	OH	27,190	HC+
Missouri Southern State Univ	MO	12,499	C
Moravian College	PA	53,117	
Mount Mary Univ	WI	34,650	LC
Northeastern Illinois Univ	IL	12,529	LC
Univ of Alaska Fairbanks	AK	16,179	C
Univ of New Hampshire	NH	28,562	VC

KEYBOARD - PIANO CONCENTRATION

School	ST	$IS	SR
Aquinas College - Mich	MI	38,876	HC
Baldwin Wallace Univ	OH	41,106	C
Cedarville Univ	OH	34,990	VC
Chapman Univ	CA	63,078	VC+
Dallas Baptist Univ	TX	33,713	C
East Central Univ	OK	13,056	C
Murray State Univ	KY	16,998	C
Ouachita Baptist Univ	AR	32,320	C
Texas Christian Univ	TX	54,670	HC
Univ of Cincinnati	OH	21,964	VC
West Chester Univ of Pennsylvania	PA	18,456	C
Western Mich Univ	MI	21,054	C
Youngstown State Univ	OH	17,307	C

KINESIOLOGY

School	ST	$IS	SR
Abilene Christian Univ	TX	41,800	C+
Aquinas College - Mich	MI	38,876	HC
Arizona State Univ at the Downtown Phoenix Campus	AZ	23,680	VC
Auburn Univ at Montgomery	AL	15,290	C
Augusta Univ	GA	4,632	C
Calif Baptist Univ	CA	41,392	C
Calif Polytechnic State Univ	CA	17,979	HC+

ST = STATE $IS = IN-STATE COSTS SR = SELECTOR RATING

School	ST	$IS	SR
Cal State, Fullerton	CA	21,902	C
Cal State, Long Beach	CA	18,850	C
Calvin College	MI	41,570	VC+
Chapman Univ	CA	63,078	VC+
College of William & Mary	VA		MC
Colo Mesa Univ	CO	18,955	LC
Corban Univ	OR	40,306	C
East Central Univ	OK	13,056	C
East Texas Baptist Univ	TX	33,134	C
Eastern Illinois Univ	IL	21,126	C
Gannon Univ	PA	42,032	C
Hanover College	IN	46,364	C+
Indiana Univ Bloomington	IN	20,429	VC
Indiana Univ-Purdue Univ Indianapolis	IN	18,635	C
LIU Brooklyn	NY	49,682	C
MidAmerica Nazarene Univ	KS	35,550	C
New Mexico State Univ	NM	14,050	C
Nova Southeastern Univ	FL	38,534	C+
Ohio Wesleyan Univ	OH	49,460	VC
Okla Baptist Univ	OK	32,320	C
Oregon State Univ	OR	22,519	VC
Our Lady of the Lake Univ	TX	35,012	LC
Pacific Lutheran Univ	WA	49,960	VC
Pennsylvania State Univ - Univ Park	PA	29,760	HC
St. Louis Univ	MO	49,866	HC
San Diego State Univ	CA	21,896	C+
Shenandoah Univ	VA	41,312	C
Southeastern Louisiana Univ	LA	16,237	C
Southern Illinois Univ Carbondale	IL	23,667	C
St. Ambrose Univ	IA	39,019	C
St. Ambrose Univ	IA	39,019	C
Tarleton State Univ	TX	15,248	LC
Taylor Univ	IN	40,317	C+
Texas Tech Univ	TX	18,736	C+
The College at Brockport - SUNY	NY	20,346	C
The Master's Univ	CA	43,870	C+
United States Military Academy at West Point	NY		HC+
Univ of Alabama at Birmingham	AL	19,906	C
Univ of Central Arkansas	AR	14,472	VC
Univ of Louisiana at Monroe	LA	15,970	C
Univ of Maine	ME	20,792	C
Univ of Nevada/Reno	NV	18,010	C
Univ of New Hampshire	NH	28,562	VC
Univ of Rhode Island	RI	24,906	C
Univ of Wisc-Madison	WI	20,934	MC
Univ of Wyoming	WY	15,375	C+
Washburn Univ	KS	15,827	C
Wayne State Univ	MI	22,016	C
West Virginia Univ	WV	18,210	C

KNOWLEDGE MANAGEMENT

School	ST	$IS	SR
Syracuse Univ	NY	60,239	VC

KOREAN

School	ST	$IS	SR
American Univ	DC	59,379	HC+
Brigham Young Univ	UT	12,748	HC
Northeastern Illinois Univ	IL	12,529	LC
Ohio State Univ at Columbus	OH	21,703	HC+
SUNY at Binghamton	NY	22,861	MC
Thomas Edison State Univ	NJ	6,350	NC
Univ of Calif at Irvine	CA	26,484	VC
Univ of Calif at Los Angeles	CA	30,162	MC
Univ of Hawaii at Manoa	HI	23,221	C
Wellesley College	MA	63,916	MC

LABOR STUDIES

School	ST	$IS	SR
Bryant Univ	RI	55,646	VC
Cal State, Dominguez Hills	CA	19,022	LC
CUNY/Queens College	NY	27,896	C
Cleveland State Univ	OH	22,196	C
Eastern Mich Univ	MI	19,761	C
Hofstra Univ	NY	55,960	C+
Howard Univ	DC	37,616	C+
Indiana Univ Bloomington	IN	20,429	VC
Indiana Univ Kokomo	IN	7,073	C
Indiana Univ Northwest	IN	7,072	C
Indiana Univ South Bend	IN	14,242	C
Indiana Univ-Purdue Univ Fort Wayne	IN	17,553	C
Indiana Univ-Purdue Univ Indianapolis	IN	18,635	C
Manhattan College	NY	51,750	C+
Northern Kentucky Univ	KY	16,486	C
Pennsylvania State Univ - Univ Park	PA	29,760	HC
Rutgers Univ - New Brunswick	NJ	26,632	HC
San Francisco State Univ	CA	18,514	LC
SUNY / Empire State College	NY	9,145	SP
SUNY / SUNY College at Old Westbury	NY	16,860	C
The Univ of Akron	OH	21,477	C
Thomas Edison State Univ	NJ	6,350	NC
Univ of Illinois at Urbana-Champaign	IL	27,006	HC
Univ of Mass Boston	MA	13,435	C
Univ of PR-Rio Piedras campus	PR	13,327	
Wayne State Univ	MI	22,016	C

LAND USE MANAGEMENT AND RECLAMATION

School	ST	$IS	SR
Cal State, Bakersfield	CA	19,191	LC
Eastern Mich Univ	MI	19,761	C
Humboldt State Univ	CA	20,514	C
Metropolitan State Univ of Denver	CO	29,889	LC
Montana State Univ	MT	15,500	C+
Prescott College	AZ	33,284	C
Texas A&M Univ at Galveston	TX	15,920	C
Texas State Univ	TX	19,350	C
Unity College	ME	37,670	C
Univ of Louisiana at Lafayette	LA	14,516	C
Univ of Wisc-Platteville	WI	14,614	VC
Univ of Wisc-River Falls	WI	14,485	C

LANDSCAPE ARCHITECTURE

School	ST	$IS	SR
Arizona State Univ at the Tempe Campus	AZ	21,756	VC
Calif Polytechnic State Univ	CA	17,979	HC+
Cornell Univ	NY	64,853	MC
Mich State Univ	MI	23,898	VC+
Pennsylvania State Univ - Univ Park	PA	29,760	HC
Texas A&M Univ	TX	20,521	VC+
Texas Tech Univ	TX	18,736	C+
Univ of Arkansas at Fayetteville	AR	19,152	C+
Univ of Georgia	GA	21,250	HC
Univ of Nebr - Lincoln	NE	18,589	VC
Univ of Rhode Island	RI	24,906	C

LANDSCAPE ARCHITECTURE/DESIGN

School	ST	$IS	SR
Andrews Univ	MI	28,030	C+
Auburn Univ	AL	23,594	VC+
Ball State Univ	IN	19,590	C
Boston Architectural College	MA	20,666	NC
Brigham Young Univ	UT	12,748	HC
Calif State Polytechnic Univ, Pomona	CA	21,541	C
CUNY/City College	NY	20,319	VC
Clemson Univ	SC		HC
Colo State Univ	CO	22,162	VC
Florida International Univ	FL	19,854	C+
Iowa State Univ	IA	17,570	C
Kansas State Univ	KS	17,780	VC
Louisiana State Univ and A&M College	LA	18,677	VC
Mich State Univ	MI	23,898	VC+
Miss State Univ	MS	11,454	C+
N Car A&T State Univ	NC	13,365	LC
N Car State Univ	NC	19,515	HC+
N Dak State Univ	ND	16,245	C
Northeastern Univ	MA	62,703	MC
Ohio State Univ at Columbus	OH	21,703	HC+
Okla State Univ	OK	17,180	VC
Pennsylvania State Univ - Univ Park	PA	29,760	HC
Philadelphia Univ	PA	50,370	C
Purdue Univ/West Lafayette	IN	20,032	MC
S Dak State Univ	SD	15,634	C
SUNY / The College of Environmental Science and Forestry	NY	23,853	VC
SUNY /College of Agriculture and Tech at Cobleskill	NY	20,527	LC
Temple Univ	PA	24,392	VC
Texas A&M Univ	TX	20,521	VC+
Univ of Arizona	AZ	23,100	C
Univ of Arkansas at Fayetteville	AR	19,152	C+
Univ of Calif at Berkeley	CA	28,853	MC
Univ of Calif at Davis	CA	28,468	HC
Univ of Conn	CT	25,538	HC
Univ of Delaware	DE	24,976	VC+
Univ of Florida	FL	16,291	HC+
Univ of Idaho	ID	15,348	C
Univ of Illinois at Urbana-Champaign	IL	27,006	HC
Univ of Kentucky	KY	33,306	C
Univ of Maryland/College Park	MD	21,938	HC
Univ of Mass Amherst	MA	26,199	VC+
Univ of Minn/Twin Cities	MN	23,519	HC+
Univ of Nebr - Lincoln	NE	18,589	VC
Univ of Nevada, Las Vegas	NV	17,553	C
Univ of Oregon	OR	22,972	C
Univ of Texas at Arlington	TX	18,026	LC
Univ of Texas at Austin	TX	26,102	HC
Univ of Washington	WA	23,149	VC
Univ of Wisc-Madison	WI	20,934	MC
Utah State Univ	UT	12,736	C
Virginia Polytechnic Inst and State Univ	VA	21,276	HC
Washington State Univ	WA	22,495	C
West Virginia Univ	WV	18,210	C

LANGUAGE ARTS

School	ST	$IS	SR
Aquinas College - Mich	MI	38,876	HC
Calvin College	MI	41,570	VC+
Catawba College	NC	39,820	C
Central Mich Univ	MI	20,330	C
Central Washington Univ	WA	16,803	C
College of St. Mary	NE	35,184	C
Concordia Univ, Ann Arbor	MI	35,945	VC
Eastern Mich Univ	MI	19,761	C
Hope College	MI	39,940	VC
Kent State Univ	OH	20,732	C
Lake Erie College	OH	38,914	LC
LeMoyne-Owen College	TN	16,980	C
Madonna Univ	MI	29,050	C
Malone Univ	OH	38,448	C
Marygrove College	MI	28,926	NC
Miles College	AL	18,646	NC
Missouri Southern State Univ	MO	12,499	C
Mount Vernon Nazarene Univ	OH	34,500	C
Nebr Wesleyan Univ	NE	38,140	C+
Northern Mich Univ	MI	19,604	C
Ohio Northern Univ	OH	44,050	VC
Ohio Univ	OH	22,924	C
Seattle Pacific Univ	WA	47,439	C+
Spring Arbor Univ	MI	36,000	C
Univ of Calif, Santa Cruz	CA	28,731	C+
Univ of Mich/Dearborn	MI	11,757	VC
Univ of Nebr - Lincoln	NE	18,589	VC
Univ of Okla	OK	18,911	VC
Western Kentucky Univ	KY	16,850	C
Wright State Univ	OH	16,983	C

LANGUAGES

School	ST	$IS	SR
Adelphi Univ	NY	48,244	C
Appalachian State Univ	NC	14,416	VC
Arkansas Tech Univ	AR	15,484	C
Assumption College	MA	47,920	C+
Auburn Univ	AL	23,594	VC+
Augsburg College	MN	43,929	C
Austin Peay State Univ	TN	16,397	C
Baylor Univ	TX	53,760	HC
Bellarmine Univ	KY	51,220	C
Bemidji State Univ	MN	16,056	VC
Bennington College	VT	63,960	MC
Bryant Univ	RI	55,646	VC
Cal State, Northridge	CA	16,859	LC
Cameron Univ	OK	11,072	NC
Carnegie Mellon Univ	PA	67,980	MC
Carroll Univ	WI	38,100	C+
Carson-Newman Univ	TN	34,160	C
Carthage College	WI	48,835	C
CUNY/Hunter College	NY	31,098	VC
CUNY/Lehman College	NY	5,778	HC+
Clark Atlanta Univ	GA	31,019	LC
Clark Univ	MA	51,600	HC+
College of St. Scholastica	MN	44,640	C
Colo State Univ	CO	22,162	VC
Columbia College	SC	36,550	C
Converse College	SC	26,495	C
Denison Univ	OH	58,860	MC
Dordt College	IA	37,860	C+
Earlham College	IN	54,870	HC
Elmira College	NY	53,900	C
Excelsior College	NY	14,080	SP
Frostburg State Univ	MD	17,280	LC
Geneva College	PA	35,450	C
Gordon College	MA	46,472	C+
Grand Valley State Univ	MI	22,250	C+
Hamilton College	NY	64,250	MC
Hartwick College	NY	51,270	C
Ithaca College	NY	56,766	VC
Jackson State Univ	MS	15,879	LC
Kent State Univ	OH	20,732	C
Lewis & Clark College	OR	58,434	HC+
Louisiana College	LA	21,886	C
Loyola Univ New Orleans	LA	51,708	VC+
McNeese State Univ	LA	7,838	C
Mercyhurst Univ	PA	47,420	C
Miss College	MS	25,850	C
Miss State Univ	MS	11,454	C+
New York Univ	NY	65,860	MC
Newberry College	SC	34,550	C
Northeastern Univ	MA	62,703	MC
Occidental College	CA	65,530	MC
Pomona College	CA	64,957	MC
Portland State Univ	OR	19,443	C
Principia College	IL	39,010	C+
Roger Williams Univ	RI	46,296	C+
Roosevelt Univ	IL	40,651	VC
Samford Univ	AL	39,232	VC
San Francisco State Univ	CA	18,514	LC
Scripps College	CA	66,664	MC
Southern Illinois Univ Edwardsville	IL	22,643	C
Southern Methodist Univ	TX	66,483	MC
Southern Oregon Univ	OR	19,117	C
St. Cloud State Univ	MN	10,600	C
St. John's College-Annapolis	MD	60,142	MC
St. Lawrence Univ	NY	64,390	VC
St. Mary's College of Maryland	MD	26,634	VC
Stockton Univ	NJ	25,059	
Tenn State Univ	TN	14,423	C
Texas A&M Univ at Commerce	TX	10,496	C
Texas Tech Univ	TX	18,736	C+
The Evergreen State College	WA	16,599	C
Univ of Alabama in Huntsville	AL	19,445	VC
Univ of Alaska Anchorage	AK	16,652	NC
Univ of Calif at Riverside	CA	29,227	C+
Univ of Central Florida	FL	15,922	VC
Univ of Delaware	DE	24,976	VC+
Univ of Denver	CO	58,443	VC+
Univ of Hartford	CT	49,776	C
Univ of Memphis	TN	18,278	C
Univ of Minn/Twin Cities	MN	23,519	HC+
Univ of New Mexico	NM	15,404	C
Univ of Okla	OK	18,911	VC
Univ of PR-Rio Piedras campus	PR	13,327	
Univ of South Alabama	AL	16,400	C
Univ of Southern Miss	MS	13,170	C
Univ of Texas at El Paso	TX	34,452	NC
Virginia Commonwealth Univ	VA	23,049	C
Virginia Wesleyan College	VA	43,728	LC
Washington Univ in St. Louis	MO	65,366	VC
Wilson College	PA	35,620	C
Xavier Univ of Louisiana	LA	31,689	C+

LASER ELECTRO-OPTICS TECHNOLOGY

School	ST	$IS	SR
Idaho State Univ	ID	13,619	NC
Oregon Inst of Technology	OR	8,910	C

LATIN

School	ST	$IS	SR
Austin College	TX	45,875	VC
Ball State Univ	IN	19,590	C
Barnard College/Columbia Univ	NY	62,741	MC
Baylor Univ	TX	53,760	HC
Boston Univ	MA	65,110	MC
Bowling Green State Univ	OH	19,747	C
Brigham Young Univ	UT	12,748	HC
Bryn Mawr College	PA	59,890	MC
Butler Univ	IN	51,352	VC
Carleton College	MN	64,071	MC
Centenary College of Louisiana	LA	45,650	C+
CUNY/Hunter College	NY	31,098	VC
CUNY/Lehman College	NY	5,778	HC+
CUNY/Queens College	NY	27,896	C
Colgate Univ	NY	65,030	MC
Columbia Univ/City of New York	NY	62,958	MC
Concordia College - Moorhead	MN	51,088	C+
Denison Univ	OH	58,860	MC
DePauw Univ	IN	58,688	HC+
Dickinson College	PA	63,974	MC
Duquesne Univ	PA	46,822	VC
Emory Univ	GA	60,786	MC
Florida State Univ	FL	16,771	HC
Fordham Univ	NY	65,918	MC
Franklin and Marshall College	PA	63,170	HC
Furman Univ	SC	58,092	VC+
Gettysburg College	PA	63,000	HC
Hampden-Sydney College	VA	56,248	C+
Harvard College/Harvard Univ	MA	60,659	MC
Haverford College	PA	66,490	MC
Hillsdale College	MI	35,722	MC
Hofstra Univ	NY	55,960	C+
Hope College	MI	39,940	VC
John Carroll Univ	OH	49,740	C+
Johns Hopkins Univ	MD	65,386	MC
Kenyon College	OH	63,330	MC
Knox College	IL	52,615	VC+
Loyola Univ Chicago	IL	55,802	VC
Loyola Univ Maryland	MD	60,300	VC
Mercer Univ	GA	45,348	VC
Mich State Univ	MI	23,898	VC+
Missouri State Univ	MO	15,190	C+
Monmouth College	IL	42,260	C
Montclair State Univ	NJ	26,210	LC
Mount Holyoke College	MA	56,746	MC
New York Univ	NY	65,860	MC
Ohio Univ	OH	22,924	C
Purdue Univ/West Lafayette	IN	20,032	MC
Purdue Univ/West Lafayette	IN	20,032	MC
Randolph-Macon College	VA	49,910	C
Rockford Univ	IL	36,030	C
Rutgers Univ - New Brunswick	NJ	26,632	HC
St. Joseph's Univ	PA	57,544	VC+
Samford Univ	AL	39,232	VC
Sarah Lawrence College	NY	63,388	HC
Seattle Pacific Univ	WA	47,439	C+
Sewanee: The Univ of the South	TN	54,500	MC
Smith College	MA	63,914	MC
Southwestern Univ	TX	50,720	VC
St. Catherine Univ	MN	45,630	VC
St. Olaf College	MN	54,260	HC+
SUNY at Binghamton	NY	22,861	MC
Swarthmore College	PA	63,550	MC
The Catholic Univ of America	DC	56,356	VC
The College of Wooster	OH	57,900	VC+
The Univ of Tenn at Chattanooga	TN	16,744	C
Trinity Univ	TX	52,314	HC+
Tufts Univ	MA		MC
Univ of Calif at Berkeley	CA	28,853	MC
Univ of Calif at Davis	CA	28,468	HC
Univ of Calif at Los Angeles	CA	30,162	MC
Univ of Georgia	GA	21,250	HC

School	ST	$IS	SR
Univ of Iowa	IA	18,683	VC+
Univ of Mich/Ann Arbor	MI	24,410	MC
Univ of Minn/Twin Cities	MN	23,519	HC+
Univ of Nebr - Lincoln	NE	18,589	VC
Univ of Oregon	OR	22,972	C
Univ of Richmond	VA	60,880	MC
Univ of Scranton	PA	54,962	VC
Univ of Texas at Austin	TX	26,102	HC
Univ of Vermont	VT	28,878	HC
Univ of Wisc-Madison	WI	20,934	MC
Wabash College	IN	50,650	VC
Wake Forest Univ	NC	64,056	MC
Washington Univ in St. Louis	MO	65,366	VC
Wellesley College	MA	63,916	MC
West Chester Univ of Pennsylvania	PA	18,456	C
Western Mich Univ	MI	21,054	C
Westminster College	PA	39,180	C+
Wheaton College	MA	61,512	VC
Whitman College	WA	59,772	MC
Wichita State Univ	KS	21,643	C
Wright State Univ	OH	16,983	C

LATIN AMERICAN STUDIES

School	ST	$IS	SR
Adelphi Univ	NY	48,244	C
Albright College	PA	46,660	C
American Univ	DC	59,379	HC+
Appalachian State Univ	NC	14,416	VC
Arizona State Univ at the West Campus	AZ	20,640	C
Assumption College	MA	47,920	C+
Austin College	TX	45,875	VC
Bard College	NY	64,024	HC
Bates College	ME	64,500	MC
Baylor Univ	TX	53,760	HC
Bennington College	VT	63,960	MC
Boston Univ	MA	65,110	MC
Bowdoin College	ME	63,500	MC
Brandeis Univ	MA	65,925	MC
Brigham Young Univ	UT	12,748	HC
Brown Univ	RI	64,566	MC
Bucknell Univ	PA	64,616	MC
Cal State, Chico	CA	21,440	C
Cal State, East Bay	CA	19,413	C
Cal State, Fresno	CA	16,902	LC
Cal State, Fullerton	CA	21,902	C
Cal State, Los Angeles	CA	17,186	LC
Canisius College	NY	47,537	C
Carleton College	MN	64,071	MC
CUNY/Brooklyn College	NY	5,884	C+
CUNY/City College	NY	20,319	VC
CUNY/Hunter College	NY	31,098	VC
CUNY/Queens College	NY	27,896	C
Colby College	ME	64,060	MC
Colgate Univ	NY	65,030	MC
College of Charleston	SC	22,699	C
College of the Holy Cross	MA	62,165	MC
College of William & Mary	VA		MC
Columbia Univ/ School of General Studies	NY	61,470	MC
Columbia Univ/City of New York	NY	62,958	MC
Conn College	CT	65,000	MC
Cornell College	IA	48,800	VC
Dartmouth College	NH	66,174	MC
Davidson College	NC	60,119	MC
Denison Univ	OH	58,860	MC
DePaul Univ	IL	47,623	VC
Dickinson College	PA	63,974	MC
Earlham College	IN	54,870	HC
Eastern Mich Univ	MI	19,761	C
Elon Univ	NC	44,599	VC+
Emory Univ	GA	60,786	MC
Flagler College	FL	27,620	C
Florida State Univ	FL	16,771	HC
Fordham Univ	NY	65,918	MC
George Mason Univ	VA	15,724	VC
George Washington Univ	DC	62,835	MC
Gettysburg College	PA	63,000	HC
Hamline Univ	MN	45,678	VC
Hampshire College	MA	63,824	MC
Hofstra Univ	NY	55,960	C+
Hood College	MD	54,840	C
Johns Hopkins Univ	MD	65,386	MC
Knox College	IL	52,615	VC+
Lake Forest College	IL	50,652	VC
Linfield College	OR	52,010	C
Lock Haven Univ of Pennsylvania	PA	18,028	LC
Loyola Univ New Orleans	LA	51,708	VC+
Macalester College	MN	61,905	MC
Miami Univ	OH	27,190	HC+
Middlebury College	VT	64,332	MC
Millsaps College	MS	50,080	C+
Mount Holyoke College	MA	56,746	MC
New College of Florida	FL	15,848	MC
New York Univ	NY	65,860	MC
Oakland Univ	MI	20,763	C
Oberlin College	OH	66,012	MC
Occidental College	CA	65,530	MC
Ohio Univ	OH	22,924	C
Pace Univ	NY	58,248	C
Pennsylvania State Univ - Univ Park	PA	29,760	HC
Pitzer College	CA	66,192	MC
Pomona College	CA	64,957	MC
Prescott College	AZ	33,284	C
Rhode Island College	RI	17,694	LC
Rhodes College	TN	51,900	HC
Rollins College	FL	58,670	HC
Rutgers Univ - New Brunswick	NJ	26,632	HC
St. Louis Univ	MO	49,866	HC
St. Peter's Univ	NJ	49,192	C
Samford Univ	AL	39,232	VC
San Diego State Univ	CA	21,896	C+
Scripps College	CA	66,664	MC
Seattle Pacific Univ	WA	47,439	C+
Seton Hall Univ	NJ	55,514	C
Smith College	MA	63,914	MC
Sonoma State Univ	CA	27,806	C
Southern Methodist Univ	TX	66,483	MC
Southern Nazarene Univ	OK	32,798	NC
Southwestern Univ	TX	50,720	VC
St. Mary's Univ	TX	37,500	C
Stanford Univ	CA	60,409	MC
SUNY / SUNY Plattsburgh	NY	18,814	C
SUNY at Binghamton	NY	22,861	MC
SUNY at New Paltz	NY	19,200	C
SUNY SUNY Albany	NY	22,165	C
Stephen F. Austin State Univ	TX	18,406	LC
Syracuse Univ	NY	60,239	VC
Temple Univ	PA	24,392	VC
Texas Tech Univ	TX	18,736	C+
The College of Wooster	OH	57,900	VC+
The Univ of Utah	UT	17,924	VC
Tufts Univ	MA		MC
Tulane Univ	LA	63,396	HC+
Union College	KY	32,310	C
Univ of Arizona	AZ	23,100	C
Univ of Arkansas at Fayetteville	AR	19,152	C+
Univ of Calif at Berkeley	CA	28,853	MC
Univ of Calif at Los Angeles	CA	30,162	MC
Univ of Calif at Riverside	CA	29,227	C+
Univ of Calif at Santa Barbara	CA	29,091	HC
Univ of Calif San Diego	CA	30,150	MC
Univ of Calif, Santa Cruz	CA	28,731	C+
Univ of Central Florida	FL	15,922	VC
Univ of Chicago	IL	67,584	MC
Univ of Cincinnati	OH	21,964	VC
Univ of Conn	CT	25,538	HC
Univ of Delaware	DE	24,976	VC+
Univ of Georgia	GA	21,250	HC
Univ of Idaho	ID	15,348	C
Univ of Illinois at Chicago	IL	25,006	VC
Univ of Illinois at Urbana-Champaign	IL	27,006	HC
Univ of Kansas	KS	20,135	C+
Univ of Kentucky	KY	33,306	C
Univ of Miami	FL	63,494	MC
Univ of Mich/Ann Arbor	MI	24,410	MC
Univ of Minn/Morris	MN	20,760	VC
Univ of Nebr - Lincoln	NE	18,589	VC
Univ of Nebr - Omaha	NE	16,120	C
Univ of New Mexico	NM	15,404	C
Univ of N Car at Chapel Hill	NC	20,052	HC+
Univ of N Car at Charlotte	NC	15,547	C
Univ of Oregon	OR	22,972	C
Univ of Pennsylvania	PA	63,526	MC
Univ of Rhode Island	RI	24,906	C
Univ of Rochester	NY	65,032	MC
Univ of San Francisco	CA	58,484	VC
Univ of S Car at Columbia	SC	19,725	VC+
Univ of Southern Calif	CA	66,631	C
Univ of Texas at Austin	TX	26,102	HC
Univ of Texas at El Paso	TX	34,452	NC
Univ of Vermont	VT	28,878	HC
Univ of Wisc-Eau Claire	WI	15,797	VC
Univ of Wisc-Madison	WI	20,934	MC
Univ of Wisc-Milwaukee	WI	21,496	C
Vanderbilt Univ	TN	60,572	MC
Vassar College	NY	65,491	MC
Villanova Univ	PA	62,523	MC
Washington Univ in St. Louis	MO	65,366	VC
Wellesley College	MA	63,916	MC
Wesleyan Univ	CT	65,516	MC
Willamette Univ	OR	61,817	VC+
Wofford College	SC	49,885	VC
Yale Univ	CT	64,650	MC

LAW

School	ST	$IS	SR
Amherst College	MA		HC+
Bryant Univ	RI	55,646	VC
Central Mich Univ	MI	20,330	C
CUNY/John Jay College of Criminal Justice	NY	6,359	NC
Dickinson College	PA	63,974	MC
Faulkner Univ	AL	26,410	C
Florida Gulf Coast Univ	FL	9,682	C
Grand Valley State Univ	MI	22,250	C+
Hampshire College	MA	63,824	MC
Hood College	MD	54,840	C
Howard Univ	DC	37,616	C+
Indiana Inst of Technology	IN	34,240	LC
Indiana Univ-Purdue Univ Indianapolis	IN	18,635	C
Lasell College	MA	47,500	C
Minn State Univ, Moorhead	MN	15,941	C
Montclair State Univ	NJ	26,210	LC
Mount Aloysius College	PA	29,976	C
Mount Ida College	MA	46,820	C
New York Univ	NY	65,860	MC
Nichols College	MA	46,800	LC
Oberlin College	OH	66,012	MC
Park Univ	MO	20,329	C
Ramapo College of New Jersey	NJ	25,338	C
Regis College	MA	51,920	C
Scripps College	CA	66,664	MC
South Univ	GA	36,070	LC
The College of St. Rose	NY	43,048	C
Towson Univ	MD	17,408	VC
United States Air Force Academy	CO		C
Univ of Arizona	AZ	23,100	C
Univ of Arkansas at Little Rock	AR	18,211	C
Univ of Calif at Berkeley	CA	28,853	MC
Univ of Calif, Santa Cruz	CA	28,731	C+
Univ of Chicago	IL	67,584	MC
Univ of Hartford	CT	49,776	C
Univ of Mass Amherst	MA	26,199	VC+
Univ of Pennsylvania	PA	63,526	MC
Univ of Wisc-Superior	WI	14,446	C
Ursuline College	OH	41,076	LC
Wellesley College	MA	63,916	MC
West Virginia Univ	WV	18,210	C
Western New England Univ	MA	48,088	C
Wilson College	PA	35,620	C

LAW ENFORCEMENT AND CORRECTIONS

School	ST	$IS	SR
Adams State Univ	CO	17,703	LC
Amridge Univ	AL	10,860	LC
Ashford Univ	CA	10,480	C
Calumet College of St. Joseph	IN	22,735	C
College of the Ozarks	MO	7,230	C
East Central Univ	OK	13,056	C
Faulkner Univ	AL	26,410	C
Frostburg State Univ	MD	17,280	LC
Idaho State Univ	ID	13,619	NC
Indiana Inst of Technology	IN	34,240	LC
Indiana Wesleyan Univ	IN	33,674	C
Johnson & Wales Univ/ Denver Campus	CO	42,707	C
Lewis Univ	IL	40,370	C
Metropolitan State Univ	MN	7,566	C
Minn State Univ, Mankato	MN	15,616	C
Missouri Southern State Univ	MO	12,499	C
Mount Aloysius College	PA	29,976	C
Point Park Univ	PA	41,270	C
Portland State Univ	OR	19,443	C
Sam Houston State Univ	TX	18,792	C
Southwest Minn State Univ	MN	17,783	C
Southwestern Okla State Univ	OK	11,790	C
Stephen F. Austin State Univ	TX	18,406	LC
Tarleton State Univ	TX	15,248	LC
Texas State Univ	TX	19,350	C
The Univ of Virginia's College at Wise	VA	18,192	LC
Thomas Univ	GA	21,420	LC
Tiffin Univ	OH	31,380	C
Unity College	ME	37,670	C
Univ of Great Falls	MT	38,524	C
Univ of Illinois at Chicago	IL	25,006	VC
Univ of Maine at Augusta	ME	7,812	C
Univ of New Haven	CT	52,190	C
Univ of San Francisco	CA	58,484	VC
Washburn Univ	KS	15,827	C
Weber State Univ	UT	10,721	C
Western Conn State Univ	CT	21,254	LC
Western Illinois Univ	IL	20,825	C
Western New Mexico Univ	NM	16,734	LC
Western Oregon Univ	OR	15,021	LC
Youngstown State Univ	OH	17,307	C

LEADERSHIP

School	ST	$IS	SR
Averett Univ	VA	40,970	LC
Bryant Univ	RI	55,646	VC
Calif Baptist Univ	CA	41,392	C
Creighton Univ	NE	48,206	VC+
Elon Univ	NC	44,599	VC+
Purdue Univ/Northwest	IN	15,038	C
St. Ambrose Univ	IA	39,019	C
St. Ambrose Univ	IA	39,019	C

LEARNER DESIGNED AREA OF STUDY

School	ST	$IS	SR
Bloomfield College	NJ	39,100	LC
Bowling Green State Univ	OH	19,747	C
Goddard College	VT	17,040	VC
King Univ	TN	34,660	C
Thomas Edison State Univ	NJ	6,350	NC
Univ of Illinois at Chicago	IL	25,006	VC
Western Mich Univ	MI	21,054	C

LEGAL STUDIES

School	ST	$IS	SR
Auburn Univ at Montgomery	AL	15,290	C
Bay Path Univ	MA	45,349	C
Blackburn College	IL	28,526	LC
Bryant Univ	RI	55,646	VC
Champlain College	VT	53,132	C+
Culver-Stockton College	MO	33,525	C
Dominican Univ	IL	41,222	C
Drexel Univ	PA	65,432	VC+
East Central Univ	OK	13,056	C
Elizabethtown College	PA	54,050	C
Faulkner Univ	AL	26,410	C
Harding Univ	AR	25,421	C
Hardin-Simmons Univ	TX	33,966	C
Hodges Univ	FL	19,080	LC
Howard Univ	DC	37,616	C+
Illinois State Univ	IL	23,418	VC
Indiana Univ Bloomington	IN	20,429	VC
Ithaca College	NY	56,766	VC
Lipscomb Univ	TN	41,296	VC
Manhattanville College	NY	51,440	C+
Mercy College	NY	31,776	C
Monmouth Univ	NJ	46,234	C
Nazareth College	NY	45,574	C
Newbury College	MA	46,950	C
Nova Southeastern Univ	FL	38,534	C+
Paul Quinn College	TX	25,350	LC
Point Park Univ	PA	41,270	C
Roger Williams Univ	RI	46,296	C+
St. Louis Univ	MO	49,866	HC
St. John Fisher College	NY	43,620	C
St. John's Univ	NY	55,850	C
Stephen F. Austin State Univ	TX	18,406	LC
Syracuse Univ	NY	60,239	VC
Temple Univ	PA	24,392	VC
Tulane Univ	LA	63,396	HC+
United States Military Academy at West Point	NY		HC+
Univ of Central Florida	FL	15,922	VC
Univ of Central Okla	OK	13,486	C
Univ of Detroit Mercy	MI	48,816	C+
Univ of Miami	FL	63,494	MC
Univ of New Haven	CT	52,190	C
Univ of Pittsburgh	PA	29,568	HC+
Univ of Wisc-Madison	WI	20,934	MC
Webster Univ	MO	37,490	C
Wesley College	DE	37,026	LC

LIBERAL ARTS, SCIENCES, GENERAL STUDIES, HUMANITIES

School	ST	$IS	SR
American Univ of PR	PR	16,130	
Aquinas College - Mich	MI	38,876	HC
Azusa Pacific Univ	CA	43,972	C
Bloomfield College	NJ	39,100	LC
Bryant Univ	RI	55,646	VC
Elmira College	NY	53,900	C
Excelsior College	NY	14,080	SP
Johnson & Wales Univ/ Denver Campus	CO	42,707	C
Lewis Univ	IL	40,370	C
LIU Post	NY	49,682	C
Milligan College	TN	38,150	C
Montana State Univ-Billings	MT	22,960	C
Murray State Univ	KY	16,998	C
Pennsylvania State Univ - Univ Park	PA	29,760	HC
St. John's College-Annapolis	MD	60,142	MC
St. Thomas Aquinas College	NY	42,200	C
Taylor Univ	IN	40,317	C+
The Master's Univ	CA	43,870	C+
Thomas Edison State Univ	NJ	6,350	NC
Univ of Maine at Machias	ME	22,960	C
Washington College	MD	54,666	VC
Washington State Univ	WA	22,495	C
Wellesley College	MA	63,916	MC
West Chester Univ of Pennsylvania	PA	18,456	C
Western Illinois Univ	IL	20,825	C
Western New England Univ	MA	48,088	C
Wilson College	PA	35,620	C

LIBERAL ARTS/ENGINEERING STUDIES

School	ST	$IS	SR
Calif Polytechnic State Univ	CA	17,979	HC+
Wellesley College	MA	63,916	MC
Worcester Polytechnic Inst	MA	60,730	MC

LIBERAL ARTS/GENERAL STUDIES

School	ST	$IS	SR
Abilene Christian Univ	TX	41,800	C+
Adams State Univ	CO	17,703	LC
Alaska Pacific Univ	AK	26,680	VC
Albertus Magnus College	CT	43,258	LC
Alvernia Univ	PA	43,900	C
American International College	MA	46,300	LC
American Jewish Univ - College of A&S Campus	CA	44,234	C
Amridge Univ	AL	10,860	LC
Angelo State Univ	TX	15,263	NC
Anna Maria College	MA	48,186	C
Aquinas College	TN	30,800	C+
Aquinas College - Mich	MI	38,876	HC
Arcadia Univ	PA	33,570	C+
Arizona State Univ at the Polytechnic Campus	AZ	21,360	VC
Armstrong State Univ	GA	16,962	C
Ashford Univ	CA	10,480	C
Atlantic Union College	MA	27,228	C
Auburn Univ at Montgomery	AL	15,290	C
Aurora Univ	IL	33,970	C
Austin Peay State Univ	TN	16,397	C
Averett Univ	VA	40,970	LC
Azusa Pacific Univ	CA	43,972	C
Ball State Univ	IN	19,590	C
Barry Univ	FL	37,830	C

ST = STATE $IS = IN-STATE COSTS SR = SELECTOR RATING

School	ST	$IS	SR
Bay Path Univ	MA	45,349	C
Beacon College	FL	46,862	C
Becker College	MA	57,628	C
Bellarmine Univ	KY	51,220	C
Belmont Abbey College	NC	48,156	C
Belmont Univ	TN	40,970	VC
Benedictine College	KS	36,200	VC
Bennington College	VT	63,960	MC
Bentley Univ	MA	60,890	HC
Bethel College	IN	35,860	C
Bethune-Cookman Univ	FL	22,970	C
Biola Univ	CA	46,402	C+
Bloomfield College	NJ	39,100	LC
Blue Mountain College	MS	15,949	VC
Boricua College	NY	10,100	C
Bowling Green State Univ	OH	19,747	C
Brenau Univ - Women's College	GA	37,876	LC
Brescia Univ	KY	29,890	VC+
Brewton-Parker College	GA	23,490	C
Bridgewater College	VA	44,510	C
Bryan College	TN	31,440	C
Bryant Univ	RI	55,646	VC
Cabrini Univ	PA	42,591	LC
Cairn Univ	PA	36,296	C
Calif Baptist Univ	CA	41,392	C
Calif Lutheran Univ	CA	52,853	C
Calif Polytechnic State Univ	CA	17,979	HC+
Calif State Polytechnic Univ, Pomona	CA	21,541	C
Cal State, Bakersfield	CA	19,191	LC
Cal State, Chico	CA	21,440	C
Cal State, Dominguez Hills	CA	19,022	LC
Cal State, East Bay	CA	19,413	C
Cal State, Fresno	CA	16,902	LC
Cal State, Fullerton	CA	21,902	C
Cal State, Los Angeles	CA	17,186	LC
Cal State, Monterey Bay	CA	26,871	LC
Cal State, Northridge	CA	16,859	LC
Cal State, San Bernardino	CA	12,000	C
Cal State, San Marcos	CA	24,184	LC
Cal State, Stanislaus	CA	16,212	C
Calif Univ of Pennsylvania	PA	14,217	LC
Calumet College of St. Joseph	IN	22,735	C
Canisius College	NY	47,537	C
Carlow Univ	PA	38,549	LC
Castleton Univ	VT	20,186	C
Cazenovia College	NY	46,470	C
Cedarville Univ	OH	34,990	VC
Centenary College of Louisiana	LA	45,650	C+
Central Washington Univ	WA	16,803	C
Chaminade Univ of Honolulu	HI	36,000	C
Champlain College	VT	53,132	C+
Charter Oak State College	CT	7,671	LC
Chestnut Hill College	PA	43,410	C
Cheyney Univ of Pennsylvania	PA	20,896	LC
Christian Brothers Univ	TN	31,670	VC
CUNY/Meger Evers College	NY	6,680	NC
CUNY/York College	NY	6,747	LC
City Univ of Seattle	WA	24,340	NC
Clarion Univ of Pennsylvania	PA	21,608	LC
Clarke Univ	IA	38,940	C
Cleveland State Univ	OH	22,196	C
College of Mount St. Vincent	NY	45,620	C
College of St. Benedict	MN	52,806	C
College of St. Mary	NE	35,184	C
College of St Joseph	VT	32,400	LC
Colo Christian Univ	CO	39,940	VC
Colo College	CO	62,560	MC
Colo Mesa Univ	CO	18,955	LC
Colo State Univ	CO	22,162	VC
Columbia College - Missouri	MO	27,803	C
Columbus State Univ	GA	14,336	LC
Concordia Univ	CA	41,580	VC
Concordia Univ Texas	TX	40,210	C
Coppin State Univ	MD	17,041	VC
Curry College	MA	51,815	C
Dallas Baptist Univ	TX	33,713	C
DeSales Univ	PA	43,970	C
Dominican Univ of Calif	CA	57,050	C
Duquesne Univ	PA	46,822	VC
East Carolina Univ	NC	16,937	C
East Central Univ	OK	13,056	C
East Tenn State Univ	TN	13,994	C
Eastern Conn State Univ	CT	23,059	C
Eastern Mennonite Univ	VA	42,550	C
Eastern Oregon Univ	OR	17,715	C
Edinboro Univ	PA	15,940	LC
Elmhurst College	IL	45,428	C
Emmanuel College	MA	52,110	C+
Emporia State Univ	KS	14,570	C
Endicott College	MA	44,604	VC+
Eureka College	IL	30,220	C
Excelsior College	NY	14,080	SP
Fairfield Univ	CT	59,860	VC+
Fairleigh Dickinson Univ/ College at Florham	NJ	52,062	C
Fairleigh Dickinson Univ/ Metropolitan Campus	NJ	40,254	C
Faulkner Univ	AL	26,410	C
Felician Univ	NJ	45,370	LC
Ferrum College	VA	39,650	C
Flagler College	FL	27,620	C
Florida Atlantic Univ	FL	17,339	C
Florida Gulf Coast Univ	FL	9,682	C
Florida International Univ	FL	19,854	C+
Fontbonne Univ	MO	33,717	C
Fort Hays State Univ	KS	12,131	C
Francis Marion Univ	SC	16,464	LC
Friends Univ	KS	34,455	C
Frostburg State Univ	MD	17,280	LC
Gallaudet Univ	DC	29,118	LC
George Washington Univ	DC	62,835	MC
Georgetown College	KY	41,440	C
Georgia College & State Univ	GA	21,148	C+
Glenville State College	WV	17,386	NC
Goddard College	VT	17,040	VC
Graceland Univ	IA	35,290	C
Grand Rapids Theological Seminary/Cornerstone Univ	MI	33,338	C
Grand Valley State Univ	MI	22,250	C+
Granite State College	NH	19,639	SP
Green Mountain College	VT	45,228	LC
Greenville College	IL	27,012	C
Hannibal-LaGrange Univ	MO	29,815	C
Harding Univ	AR	25,421	C
Harris-Stowe State Univ	MO	14,360	NC
Haverford College	PA	66,490	MC
Hilbert College	NY	30,850	C
Hofstra Univ	NY	55,960	C+
Holy Names Univ	CA	46,630	LC
Hope International Univ	CA	41,150	C
Houghton College	NY	39,090	C
Houston Baptist Univ	TX	36,450	C
Howard Payne Univ	TX	34,320	C
Humboldt State Univ	CA	20,514	C
Idaho State Univ	ID	13,619	NC
Indiana State Univ	IN	23,223	LC
Indiana Univ Bloomington	IN	20,429	VC
Indiana Univ-Purdue Univ Fort Wayne	IN	17,553	C
Indiana Wesleyan Univ	IN	33,674	C
Iona College	NY	50,984	C
Iowa State Univ	IA	17,570	C
Ithaca College	NY	56,766	VC
James Madison Univ	VA	19,084	VC
John Carroll Univ	OH	49,740	C+
Johnson & Wales Univ/ Denver Campus	CO	42,707	C
Johnson C. Smith Univ	NC	25,336	LC
Johnson State College	VT	20,752	C
Kentucky Christian Univ	KY	26,560	LC
Kentucky State Univ	KY	13,364	LC
Kutztown Univ of Pennsylvania	PA	19,056	LC
La Roche College	PA	37,924	LC
La Sierra Univ	CA	39,690	VC
Lasell College	MA	47,500	C
Lewis Univ	IL	40,370	C
Lewis-Clark State College	ID	14,202	C
Liberty Univ	VA	19,101	C
Limestone College	SC	32,100	C
Lincoln Univ	MO	13,602	NC
Lindenwood Univ	MO	25,132	C
Lindsey Wilson College	KY	32,882	C
Lipscomb Univ	TN	41,296	VC
LIU Brooklyn	NY	49,682	C
Lock Haven Univ of Pennsylvania	PA	18,028	LC
Longwood Univ	VA	22,184	C
Louisiana State Univ and A&M College	LA	18,677	VC
Louisiana State Univ in Shreveport	LA	6,902	C
Louisiana Tech Univ	LA	11,422	VC
Loyola Marymount Univ	CA	58,038	HC
Loyola Univ New Orleans	LA	51,708	VC+
Lynchburg College	VA	46,740	C
Lynn Univ	FL	49,480	LC
MacMurray College	IL	33,620	C
Madonna Univ	MI	29,050	C
Malone Univ	OH	38,448	C
Mansfield Univ	PA	23,376	LC
Marist College	NY	49,860	VC
Marymount Manhattan College	NY	46,280	VC
Marymount Univ	VA	41,570	LC
Maryville Univ of St. Louis	MO	38,046	VC+
Mass College of Liberal Arts	MA	20,128	C
Mayville State Univ	ND	18,371	NC
McNeese State Univ	LA	7,838	C
Medaille College	NY	35,112	C
Mercy College	NY	31,776	C
Metropolitan State Univ	MN	7,566	C
Mich Tech Univ	MI	24,739	VC+
Middlebury College	VT	64,332	MC
Midway Univ	KY	31,640	LC
Minot State Univ	ND	12,732	C
Misericordia Univ	PA	43,840	C
Miss State Univ	MS	11,454	C+
Missouri Baptist Univ	MO	35,594	C
Missouri Valley College	MO	28,150	C
Mitchell College	CT	43,280	C
Montana State Univ	MT	15,500	C+
Montana State Univ-Billings	MT	22,960	C
Montana Tech of the Univ of Montana	MT	15,447	C+
Montreat College	NC	31,298	LC
Morehead State Univ	KY	17,422	C
Morris College	SC	18,500	LC
Mount Aloysius College	PA	29,976	C
Mount Ida College	MA	46,820	C
Mount Mary Univ	WI	34,650	LC
Mount St. Joseph Univ	OH	33,880	C
Mount St. Mary's Univ - Chalon Campus	CA	43,897	VC+
National Univ	CA	14,730	LC
Neumann Univ	PA	40,678	LC
New Mexico Inst of Mining and Technology	NM	14,833	HC
Newman Univ	KS	35,390	C
Niagara Univ	NY	41,010	C
Northern Arizona Univ	AZ	20,246	VC
Northern Illinois Univ	IL	20,176	C
Northern Kentucky Univ	KY	16,486	C
Northwest Nazarene Univ	ID	36,000	C
Northwest Univ	WA	35,876	VC
Norwich Univ	VT	28,212	C
Notre Dame de Namur Univ	CA	46,526	LC
Notre Dame of Maryland Univ	MD	46,465	VC
Oakland Univ	MI	20,763	C
Ohio Dominican Univ	OH	41,340	C+
Okla Christian Univ	OK	27,650	VC
Okla City Univ	OK	40,476	VC
Okla State Univ	OK	17,180	VC
Okla Wesleyan Univ	OK	33,206	C
Oral Roberts Univ	OK	34,316	C
Oregon State Univ	OR	22,519	VC
Otterbein Univ	OH	41,630	C
Our Lady of the Lake Univ	TX	35,012	LC
Palm Beach Atlantic Univ	FL	39,720	C
Park Univ	MO	20,329	C
Paul Quinn College	TX	25,350	LC
Penn State Univ/Altoona	PA	24,584	C
Pepperdine Univ	CA	74,460	HC+
Pittsburg State Univ	KS	13,880	NC
Point Park Univ	PA	41,270	C
Pontifical Catholic Univ of PR	PR	10,534	
Portland State Univ	OR	19,443	C
Post Univ	CT	41,150	C
Prescott College	AZ	33,284	C
Providence College	RI	60,760	VC
Purdue Univ/Northwest	IN	15,038	C
Purdue Univ/West Lafayette	IN	20,032	MC
Quinnipiac Univ	CT	59,110	C
Radford Univ	VA	19,027	LC
Ramapo College of New Jersey	NJ	25,338	C
Regis College	MA	51,920	C
Regis Univ	CO	44,520	C
Reinhardt Univ	GA	29,492	C
Rider Univ	NJ	54,050	C
Rivier Univ	NH	40,410	VC
Roberts Wesleyan College	NY	38,306	C
Roosevelt Univ	IL	40,651	VC
Rosemont College	PA	30,980	C
Rowan Univ	NJ	24,491	VC+
Rutgers Univ - Camden	NJ	26,146	C
Sacred Heart Univ	CT	52,750	C
St. Anselm College	NH	52,560	C+
St. John's Univ	MN	51,624	C
St. Joseph's Univ	PA	57,544	VC+
St. Mary's College of Calif	CA	57,420	C
St. Vincent College	PA	44,626	C
Salem International Univ	WV	21,090	LC
Salisbury Univ	MD	20,714	VC
Salve Regina Univ	RI	51,470	C
Samford Univ	AL	39,232	VC
San Diego Christian College	CA	39,068	C
San Diego State Univ	CA	21,896	C+
San Francisco State Univ	CA	18,514	LC
Sarah Lawrence College	NY	63,388	HC
Schreiner Univ	TX	34,626	LC
Seattle Pacific Univ	WA	47,439	C+
Seattle Univ	WA	50,811	VC+
Seton Hall Univ	NJ	55,514	C
Seton Hill Univ	PA	46,972	C
Shaw Univ	NC	24,638	C
Shimer College	IL	42,130	VC+
Siena Heights Univ	MI	32,040	C
Simpson Univ	CA	33,700	C
Skidmore College	NY	64,214	HC
Sonoma State Univ	CA	27,806	C
S Dak State Univ	SD	15,634	C
Southeastern Louisiana Univ	LA	16,237	C
Southern Illinois Univ Carbondale	IL	23,667	C
Southern Illinois Univ Edwardsville	IL	22,643	C
Southern Methodist Univ	TX	66,483	MC
Southern New Hampshire Univ	NH	43,198	C
Southern Oregon Univ	OR	19,117	C
Southern Vermont College	VT	34,670	LC
Southwestern College	KS	31,531	C
Spalding Univ	KY	31,938	SP
Spring Hill College	AL	48,488	C
St. Edward's Univ	TX	53,100	VC
St. Francis College	NY	38,800	LC
St. John's College, Santa Fe	NM	60,109	HC+
St. John's College-Annapolis	MD	60,142	MC
St. John's Univ	NY	55,850	C
St. Joseph's College, New York/Brooklyn Campus	NY	25,114	LC
St. Joseph's College, New York/Long Island Campus	NY	25,124	C
St. Thomas Univ	FL	36,360	LC
SUNY / Empire State College	NY	9,145	SP
SUNY / SUNY Fredonia	NY	20,818	C
SUNY at New Paltz	NY	19,200	C
SUNY at Purchase	NY	17,900	C
SUNY Polytechnic Inst	NY	19,473	VC
Stephens College	MO	38,042	C
Stockton Univ	NJ	25,059	
Stony Brook Univ/The SUNY	NY	21,881	MC
Susquehanna Univ	PA	55,340	VC
Syracuse Univ	NY	60,239	VC
Tabor College	KS	35,870	C
Tarleton State Univ	TX	15,248	LC
Taylor Univ	IN	40,317	C+
Texas A&M Univ at Galveston	TX	15,920	C
Texas Southern Univ	TX	18,212	LC
Texas State Univ	TX	19,350	C
Texas Tech Univ	TX	18,736	C+
The Catholic Univ of America	DC	56,356	VC
The College at Brockport - SUNY	NY	20,346	C
The Evergreen State College	WA	16,599	C
The Master's Univ	CA	43,870	C+
The Univ of Virginia's College at Wise	VA	18,192	LC
Thomas Aquinas College	CA	32,450	HC
Thomas Edison State Univ	NJ	6,350	NC
Thomas More College	KY	36,720	C
Thomas More College of Liberal Arts	NH	30,100	C
Thomas Univ	GA	21,420	LC
Touro College	NY	28,950	VC
Trinity International Univ	IL	31,070	VC
Tulane Univ	LA	63,396	HC+
Union College	NY	64,320	MC
Union Inst & Univ	OH	8,912	SP
Univ of Alaska Anchorage	AK	16,652	NC
Univ of Alaska Southeast	AK	11,493	C
Univ of Arkansas at Little Rock	AR	18,211	C
Univ of Arkansas at Monticello	AR	13,134	NC
Univ of Arkansas at Pine Bluff	AR	13,541	C
Univ of Calif at Riverside	CA	29,227	C+
Univ of Central Florida	FL	15,922	VC
Univ of Central Okla	OK	13,486	C
Univ of Charleston	WV	35,000	C
Univ of Cincinnati	OH	21,964	VC
Univ of Dayton	OH	53,620	C
Univ of Delaware	DE	24,976	VC+
Univ of Detroit Mercy	MI	48,816	C+
Univ of Evansville	IN	44,186	VC+
Univ of Hawaii at Hilo	HI	18,038	C
Univ of Holy Cross	LA	21,523	C
Univ of Houston	TX	21,483	VC
Univ of Illinois at Urbana-Champaign	IL	27,006	HC
Univ of Iowa	IA	18,683	VC+
Univ of Kansas	KS	20,135	C+
Univ of La Verne	CA	55,600	C
Univ of Louisville	KY	19,824	C
Univ of Maine at Augusta	ME	7,812	C
Univ of Maine at Farmington	ME	18,187	C
Univ of Maine at Fort Kent	ME	15,165	LC
Univ of Maine at Machias	ME	22,960	C
Univ of Maine at Presque Isle	ME	14,870	C
Univ of Mary	ND	23,180	C
Univ of Mary Washington	VA	24,764	VC
Univ of Maryland/Eastern Shore	MD	17,013	C
Univ of Maryland/Univ College	MD	25,966	LC
Univ of Mass Amherst	MA	26,199	VC+
Univ of Mass Dartmouth	MA	25,658	C
Univ of Mass Lowell	MA	26,380	C
Univ of Memphis	TN	18,278	C
Univ of Miami	FL	63,494	MC
Univ of Mich/Ann Arbor	MI	24,410	MC
Univ of Mich/Dearborn	MI	11,757	VC
Univ of Minn/Morris	MN	20,760	VC
Univ of Miss	MS	17,746	C+
Univ of Missouri/Columbia	MO	18,201	MC
Univ of Missouri-Kansas City	MO	19,563	VC
Univ of Missouri-St. Louis	MO		C
Univ of Mobile	AL	28,935	C
Univ of Montana	MT	14,105	C
Univ of Montana-Western	MT	11,220	LC
Univ of Mount Olive	NC	18,426	C
Univ of Nebr - Lincoln	NE	18,589	VC
Univ of Nebr - Omaha	NE	16,120	C
Univ of New England	ME	48,880	C
Univ of New Haven	CT	52,190	C
Univ of New Mexico	NM	15,404	C
Univ of North Alabama	AL	15,398	C
Univ of N Car at Asheville	NC	15,723	VC+
Univ of N Car at Charlotte	NC	15,547	C
Univ of N Car at Greensboro	NC	14,690	C
Univ of North Texas	TX	19,198	C
Univ of Notre Dame	IN	64,043	MC
Univ of Okla	OK	18,911	VC
Univ of Pittsburgh	PA	29,568	HC+
Univ of Pittsburgh at Bradford	PA	22,402	C
Univ of PR-Rio Piedras campus	PR	13,327	
Univ of Redlands	CA	60,200	VC
Univ of St. Francis	IN	37,400	C
Univ of St. Mary	KS	34,690	C
Univ of San Diego	CA	58,442	VC+
Univ of San Francisco	CA	58,484	VC
Univ of S Car Upstate	SC	18,200	LC

ST = STATE **$IS** = IN-STATE COSTS **SR** = SELECTOR RATING

School	ST	$IS	SR
Univ of S Dak	SD	16,109	C
Univ of South Florida/Tampa	FL	16,110	VC+
Univ of St. Francis	IL	39,924	C
Univ of St. Thomas - Houston	TX	40,020	VC
Univ of Tampa	FL	36,944	C
Univ of Texas at Austin	TX	26,102	HC
Univ of the Ozarks	AR	52,176	C
Univ of the Pacific	CA	57,006	VC
Univ of Washington	WA	23,149	VC
Univ of Wisc-Eau Claire	WI	15,797	VC
Univ of Wisc-Green Bay	WI	15,064	C
Univ of Wisc-Milwaukee	WI	21,496	C
Univ of Wisc-Oshkosh	WI	15,200	C
Univ of Wisc-Platteville	WI	14,614	VC
Univ of Wisc-Stevens Point	WI	14,043	C
Urbana Univ	OH	30,820	C
Utah State Univ	UT	12,736	C
Utica College	NY	30,430	C
Vanguard Univ of Southern Calif	CA	40,740	VC
Villanova Univ	PA	62,523	MC
Virginia Wesleyan College	VA	43,728	LC
Viterbo Univ	WI	34,660	C
Walsh Univ	OH	39,010	C
Warner Pacific College	OR	33,790	C
Washburn Univ	KS	15,827	C
Washington Adventist Univ	MD	31,440	LC
Washington State Univ	WA	22,495	C
Weber State Univ	UT	10,721	C
Wellesley College	MA	63,916	MC
Wesley College	DE	37,026	LC
West Chester Univ of Pennsylvania	PA	18,456	C
West Texas A&M Univ	TX	13,478	C
West Virginia Univ	WV	18,210	C
Western Carolina Univ	NC	13,965	C
Western Conn State Univ	CT	21,254	LC
Western Kentucky Univ	KY	16,850	C
Western New England Univ	MA	48,088	C
Western Washington Univ	WA	18,003	C+
Westfield State Univ	MA	19,671	C
Westmont College	CA	56,410	HC
Wheeling Jesuit Univ	WV	37,106	LC
Wichita State Univ	KS	21,643	C
Wilberforce Univ	OH	19,016	C
Wiley College	TX	18,504	C
Wilkes Univ	PA	45,622	C
William Carey Univ	MS	23,950	LC
William Peace Univ	NC	37,430	LC
Wilmington College	OH	34,600	C
Wilson College	PA	35,620	C
Wingate Univ	NC	39,950	C
Worcester State Univ	MA	20,977	C
Wright State Univ	OH	16,983	C
Xavier Univ	OH	47,880	C+
York College	NE	24,300	C

LIBRARY SCIENCE

School	ST	$IS	SR
Ashford Univ	CA	10,480	C
Clarion Univ of Pennsylvania	PA	21,608	LC
Kutztown Univ of Pennsylvania	PA	19,056	LC
Northwestern Okla State Univ	OK	13,072	NC
Southern Conn State Univ	CT	21,924	LC
Univ of Arizona	AZ	23,100	C
Univ of Central Arkansas	AR	14,472	VC
Univ of Maine at Augusta	ME	7,812	C
Univ of Nebr - Omaha	NE	16,120	C
West Virginia Univ	WV	18,210	C

LIFE SCIENCE

School	ST	$IS	SR
Arkansas Tech Univ	AR	15,484	C
Atlantic Union College	MA	27,228	C
Baylor Univ	TX	53,760	HC
Biola Univ	CA	46,402	C+
Bowling Green State Univ	OH	19,747	C
Indiana Univ East	IN	7,072	C
Kansas State Univ	KS	17,780	VC
Malone Univ	OH	38,448	C
McMurry Univ	TX	34,259	LC
Minn State Univ, Mankato	MN	15,616	C
Missouri Southern State Univ	MO	12,499	C
Missouri Univ of Science and Technology	MO	18,655	HC
Mount Vernon Nazarene Univ	OH	34,500	C
National Univ	CA	14,730	LC
New York Inst of Technology	NY	48,730	C
Niagara Univ	NY	41,010	C
Northwest Univ	WA	35,876	VC
Ohio Univ	OH	22,924	C
Otterbein Univ	OH	41,630	C
Suffolk Univ	MA	50,308	C
United States Military Academy at West Point	NY		HC+
Wayland Baptist Univ	TX	22,356	LC
Wayne State College	NE	12,802	C
Western Washington Univ	WA	18,003	C+
Wright State Univ	OH	16,983	C
Xavier Univ	OH	47,880	C+

LIFE SCIENCE SECONDARY SCHOOL EDUCATION

School	ST	$IS	SR
Cedarville Univ	OH	34,990	VC
Franklin College	IN	39,380	C
Kent State Univ	OH	20,732	C
Minn State Univ, Mankato	MN	15,616	C
St. Mary's Univ of Minn	MN	41,210	VC
Univ of Nebr - Lincoln	NE	18,589	VC

LINGUISTICS

School	ST	$IS	SR
Alabama A&M Univ	AL	18,796	C
Ashford Univ	CA	10,480	C
Bard College at Simon's Rock	MA	65,795	MC
Barnard College/Columbia Univ	NY	62,741	MC
Boston College	MA	65,737	MC
Boston Univ	MA	65,110	MC
Brandeis Univ	MA	65,925	MC
Brigham Young Univ	UT	12,748	HC
Brown Univ	RI	64,566	MC
Bryn Mawr College	PA	59,890	MC
Bucknell Univ	PA	64,616	MC
Cal State, Fresno	CA	16,902	LC
Cal State, Fullerton	CA	21,902	C
Cal State, Monterey Bay	CA	26,871	LC
Cal State, Northridge	CA	16,859	LC
Calvin College	MI	41,570	VC+
Carleton College	MN	64,071	MC
Carnegie Mellon Univ	PA	67,980	MC
Cedarville Univ	OH	34,990	VC
Central College	IA	44,592	C
CUNY/Brooklyn College	NY	5,884	C+
CUNY/Lehman College	NY	5,778	HC+
CUNY/Queens College	NY	27,896	C
Cleveland State Univ	OH	22,196	C
College of William & Mary	VA		MC
Columbia Univ/City of New York	NY	62,958	MC
Corban Univ	OR	40,306	C
Cornell Univ	NY	64,853	MC
Dartmouth College	NH	66,174	MC
DePauw Univ	IN	58,688	HC+
Duke Univ	NC	64,188	
Earlham College	IN	54,870	HC
Eastern Mich Univ	MI	19,761	C
Emory Univ	GA	60,786	MC
Florida Atlantic Univ	FL	17,339	G
Florida State Univ	FL	16,771	HC
Georgetown Univ	DC	65,926	MC
Georgia Southern Univ	GA	16,596	C
Gordon College	MA	46,472	C+
Hampshire College	MA	63,824	MC
Harvard College/Harvard Univ	MA	60,659	MC
Haverford College	PA	66,490	MC
Hofstra Univ	NY	55,960	C+
Indiana Univ Bloomington	IN	20,429	VC
Iowa State Univ	IA	17,570	C
Lawrence Univ	WI	54,498	HC
Macalester College	MN	61,905	MC
Mass Inst of Technology	MA	62,662	MC
Miami Univ	OH	27,190	HC+
Mich State Univ	MI	23,898	VC+
Millersville Univ of Pennsylvania	PA	23,782	C
Montclair State Univ	NJ	26,210	LC
New York Univ	NY	65,860	MC
Northeastern Illinois Univ	IL	12,529	LC
Northeastern Univ	MA	62,703	MC
Northwestern Univ	IL	66,344	MC
Oakland Univ	MI	20,763	C
Ohio State Univ at Columbus	OH	21,703	HC+
Ohio Univ	OH	22,924	C
Old Dominion Univ	VA	20,910	C
Pitzer College	CA	66,192	MC
Pomona College	CA	64,957	MC
Purdue Univ/West Lafayette	IN	20,032	MC
Reed College	OR	65,300	MC
Rice Univ	TX	57,668	MC
Rutgers Univ - New Brunswick	NJ	26,632	HC
San Diego State Univ	CA	21,896	C+
Seattle Pacific Univ	WA	47,439	C+
Southern Illinois Univ Carbondale	IL	23,667	C
Stanford Univ	CA	60,409	MC
SUNY / Univ at Buffalo	NY	23,122	C+
SUNY at Binghamton	NY	22,861	MC
SUNY at Oswego	NY	21,351	C
SUNY SUNY Albany	NY	22,165	C
Stony Brook Univ/The SUNY	NY	21,881	MC
Swarthmore College	PA	63,550	MC
Syracuse Univ	NY	60,239	VC
Temple Univ	PA	24,392	VC
The Univ of Utah	UT	17,924	VC
Truman State Univ	MO	16,014	HC
Tulane Univ	LA	63,396	HC+
Univ of Alaska Fairbanks	AK	16,179	C
Univ of Arizona	AZ	23,100	C
Univ of Calif at Berkeley	CA	28,853	MC
Univ of Calif at Davis	CA	28,468	HC
Univ of Calif at Los Angeles	CA	30,162	MC
Univ of Calif at Riverside	CA	29,227	C+
Univ of Calif at Santa Barbara	CA	29,091	HC
Univ of Calif San Diego	CA	30,150	MC
Univ of Calif, Santa Cruz	CA	28,731	C+
Univ of Chicago	IL	67,584	MC
Univ of Cincinnati	OH	21,964	VC
Univ of Colo Boulder	CO	24,285	VC+
Univ of Conn	CT	25,538	HC
Univ of Florida	FL	16,291	HC+
Univ of Georgia	GA	21,250	HC
Univ of Hawaii at Hilo	HI	18,038	C
Univ of Hawaii at Manoa	HI	23,221	C
Univ of Illinois at Urbana-Champaign	IL	27,006	HC
Univ of Iowa	IA	18,683	VC+
Univ of Kansas	KS	20,135	C+
Univ of Kentucky	KY	33,306	C
Univ of Louisville	KY	19,824	C
Univ of Maryland/Baltimore County	MD	21,296	VC
Univ of Maryland/College Park	MD	21,938	HC
Univ of Mass Amherst	MA	26,199	VC+
Univ of Mich/Ann Arbor	MI	24,410	MC
Univ of Minn/Twin Cities	MN	23,519	HC+
Univ of Miss	MS	17,746	C+
Univ of Missouri/Columbia	MO	18,201	MC
Univ of Montana	MT	14,105	C
Univ of New Hampshire	NH	28,562	VC
Univ of New Mexico	NM	15,404	C
Univ of N Car at Chapel Hill	NC	20,052	HC+
Univ of Okla	OK	18,911	VC
Univ of Oregon	OR	22,972	C
Univ of Pennsylvania	PA	63,526	MC
Univ of Pittsburgh	PA	29,568	HC+
Univ of Rochester	NY	65,032	MC
Univ of Southern Calif	CA	66,631	C
Univ of Texas at Arlington	TX	18,026	LC
Univ of Texas at Austin	TX	26,102	HC
Univ of Texas at El Paso	TX	34,452	NC
Univ of Toledo	OH	19,336	NC
Univ of Vermont	VT	28,878	HC
Univ of Wisc-Madison	WI	20,934	MC
Univ of Wisc-Milwaukee	WI	21,496	C
Washington State Univ	WA	22,495	C
Washington Univ in St. Louis	MO	65,366	VC
Wayne State Univ	MI	22,016	C
Wellesley College	MA	63,916	MC
Western Washington Univ	WA	18,003	C+
Yale Univ	CT	64,650	MC

LITERATURE

School	ST	$IS	SR
Adrian College	MI	42,400	C
American Jewish Univ - College of A&S Campus	CA	44,234	C
American Univ	DC	59,379	HC+
Andrews Univ	MI	28,030	C+
Aquinas College - Mich	MI	38,876	HC
Ball State Univ	IN	19,590	C
Bard College	NY	64,024	HC
Bard College at Simon's Rock	MA	65,795	MC
Baylor Univ	TX	53,760	HC
Beloit College	WI	55,206	HC
Benedictine Univ	IL	38,300	C
Bennington College	VT	63,960	MC
Brigham Young Univ	UT	12,748	HC
Bryant Univ	RI	55,646	VC
Calif College of the Arts	CA	52,758	SP
Cal State, San Marcos	CA	24,184	LC
Calvin College	MI	41,570	VC+
Castleton Univ	VT	20,186	C
Claremont McKenna College	CA	67,185	MC
Coe College	IA	51,570	VC
College of the Holy Cross	MA	62,165	MC
Columbia Univ/ School of General Studies	NY	61,470	MC
Concordia College - New York	NY	39,035	LC
DePauw Univ	IN	58,688	HC+
Dordt College	IA	37,860	C+
Duke Univ	NC	64,188	
Eastern Mich Univ	MI	19,761	C
Eastern Nazarene College	MA	39,955	C
Eastern Washington Univ	WA	25,572	LC
Eckerd College	FL	52,874	C
Elon Univ	NC	44,599	VC+
Emory and Henry College	VA	41,410	C
Eugene Lang College/The New School for Liberal Arts	NY	55,650	C
Fairleigh Dickinson Univ/ College at Florham	NJ	52,062	C
Faulkner Univ	AL	26,410	C
Fitchburg State Univ	MA	21,819	C
George Fox Univ	OR	42,938	C
George Washington Univ	DC	62,835	MC
Goddard College	VT	17,040	VC
Gonzaga Univ	WA	50,888	HC
Graceland Univ	IA	35,290	C
Grand Rapids Theological Seminary/Cornerstone Univ	MI	33,338	C
Hampshire College	MA	63,824	MC
Harvard College/Harvard Univ	MA	60,659	MC
Hellenic College/Holy Cross Greek Orthodox School of Theology	MA	39,906	C
John Carroll Univ	OH	49,740	C+
Kutztown Univ of Pennsylvania	PA	19,056	LC
Le Moyne College	NY	46,000	C
Linfield College	OR	52,010	C
Lubbock Christian Univ	TX	28,426	C
Lycoming College	PA	48,580	C
Maharishi Univ of Management	IA	34,930	VC
Marshall Univ	WV	17,242	C
Mass Inst of Technology	MA	62,662	MC
Missouri Southern State Univ	MO	12,499	C
Nazareth College	NY	45,574	C
New College of Florida	FL	15,848	MC
New York Univ	NY	65,860	MC
Northwestern College of Iowa	IA	38,400	C+
Ohio Northern Univ	OH	44,050	VC
Ohio Univ	OH	22,924	C
Old Dominion Univ	VA	20,910	C
Oral Roberts Univ	OK	34,316	C
Pacific Univ	OR	52,876	C
Point Loma Nazarene Univ	CA	43,450	C
Pomona College	CA	64,957	MC
Prescott College	AZ	33,284	C
Ramapo College of New Jersey	NJ	25,338	C
Reed College	OR	65,300	MC
Roanoke College	VA	54,114	VC
Rocky Mountain College	MT	34,270	C
Roosevelt Univ	IL	40,651	VC
St. Mary-of-the-Woods College	IN	39,632	LC
St. Mary's Univ of Minn	MN	41,210	VC
San Jose State Univ	CA	21,540	C
Sarah Lawrence College	NY	63,388	HC
Seattle Pacific Univ	WA	47,439	C+
Southwest Minn State Univ	MN	17,783	C
St. John's College-Annapolis	MD	60,142	MC
SUNY / SUNY Potsdam	NY	20,404	C+
SUNY at Binghamton	NY	22,861	MC
SUNY at Purchase	NY	17,900	C
Stevens Inst of Technology	NJ	62,338	MC
Stockton Univ	NJ	25,059	
Swarthmore College	PA	63,550	MC
Texas Tech Univ	TX	18,736	C+
The College of Idaho	ID	36,415	C
Touro College	NY	28,950	VC
Union College	NE	23,270	C
United States Military Academy at West Point	NY		HC+
Univ of Alaska Southeast	AK	11,493	C
Univ of Bridgeport	CT	44,430	LC
Univ of Calif at Santa Barbara	CA	29,091	HC
Univ of Calif San Diego	CA	30,150	MC
Univ of Calif, Santa Cruz	CA	28,731	C+
Univ of Evansville	IN	44,186	VC+
Univ of Mich/Ann Arbor	MI	24,410	MC
Univ of New Haven	CT	52,190	C
Univ of N Car at Asheville	NC	15,723	VC+
Univ of Okla	OK	18,911	VC
Univ of Texas at Dallas	TX	22,830	VC+
Washington Univ in St. Louis	MO	65,366	VC
Waynesburg Univ	PA	32,290	C
Wellesley College	MA	63,916	MC
Wells College	NY	50,500	C
West Chester Univ of Pennsylvania	PA	18,456	C
Western Kentucky Univ	KY	16,850	C
Wheaton College	MA	61,512	VC
Wilberforce Univ	OH	19,016	C
Williams College	MA	63,290	MC
Wright State Univ	OH	16,983	C
Yale Univ	CT	64,650	MC
Youngstown State Univ	OH	17,307	C

LOGISTICS

School	ST	$IS	SR
Bryant Univ	RI	55,646	VC
Central Mich Univ	MI	20,330	C
Embry-Riddle Aeronautical Univ - Worldwide	FL	17,480	C
Georgia Southern Univ	GA	16,596	C
Inter-American Univ of PR-Bayamon	PR	18,785	
John Carroll Univ	OH	49,740	C+
Missouri Southern State Univ	MO	12,499	C
Missouri State Univ	MO	15,190	C+
Ohio State Univ at Columbus	OH	21,703	HC+
The Univ of Tenn at Knoxville	TN	22,112	VC
Univ of Alaska Anchorage	AK	16,652	NC
Univ of Illinois at Urbana-Champaign	IL	27,006	HC
Univ of Maryland/College Park	MD	21,938	HC
Univ of Memphis	TN	18,278	C
Univ of Missouri-St. Louis	MO		C
Univ of North Texas	TX	19,198	C
Univ of Pennsylvania	PA	63,526	MC
Univ of St. Francis	IL	39,924	C

LUSO-BRAZILIAN STUDIES

School	ST	$IS	SR
Brown Univ	RI	64,566	MC
New York Univ	NY	65,860	MC
Smith College	MA	63,914	MC

MANAGEMENT

School	ST	$IS	SR
Arizona State Univ at the Polytechnic Campus	AZ	21,360	VC

ST = STATE $IS = IN-STATE COSTS SR = SELECTOR RATING

School	ST	$IS	SR
Arizona State Univ at the Tempe Campus	AZ	21,756	VC
Arizona State Univ at the West Campus	AZ	20,640	C
Arkansas Tech Univ	AR	15,484	C
Bryant Univ	RI	55,646	VC
Central Conn State Univ	CT	21,203	C
Chatham Univ	PA	46,517	C
Christopher Newport Univ	VA	23,968	VC+
Clayton State Univ	GA	19,735	C
Creighton Univ	NE	48,206	VC+
Davis & Elkins College	WV	38,242	LC
East Central Univ	OK	13,056	C
Elon Univ	NC	44,599	VC+
Embry-Riddle Aeronautical Univ - Worldwide	FL	17,480	C
Framingham State Univ	MA	20,584	C
Franciscan Univ of Steubenville	OH	33,980	VC
Hiram College,	OH	43,230	C
Hofstra Univ	NY	55,960	C+
Indiana Univ Bloomington	IN	20,429	VC
John Brown Univ	AR	33,132	VC
Kent State Univ	OH	20,732	C
Lewis Univ	IL	40,370	C
Loyola Marymount Univ	CA	58,038	HC
Mich State Univ	MI	23,898	VC+
Mount Vernon Nazarene Univ	OH	34,500	C
Okla Baptist Univ	OK	32,320	C
Providence College	RI	60,760	VC
Purdue Univ/Northwest	IN	15,038	C
Rochester Inst of Technology	NY	50,842	HC
Southeast Missouri State Univ	MO	15,498	C
Southeastern Louisiana Univ	LA	16,237	C
Southwestern Okla State Univ	OK	11,790	C
St. Ambrose Univ	IA	39,019	C
St. Ambrose Univ	IA	39,019	C
Syracuse Univ	NY	60,239	VC
Texas Tech Univ	TX	18,736	C+
Univ of Georgia	GA	21,250	HC
Univ of Mass Dartmouth	MA	25,658	C
Univ of North Georgia	GA	17,316	C
Univ of Notre Dame	IN	64,043	MC
Univ of St. Francis	IN	37,400	C
Univ of Tampa	FL	36,944	C
Villanova Univ	PA	62,523	MC
Washington State Univ	WA	22,495	C
Wingate Univ	NC	39,950	C
Wittenberg Univ	OH	48,156	C+

MANAGEMENT & STRATEGIC LEADERSHIP

School	ST	$IS	SR
Bryant Univ	RI	55,646	VC
Carroll Univ	WI	38,100	C+
Embry-Riddle Aeronautical Univ - Worldwide	FL	17,480	C
Indiana Univ of Pennsylvania	PA	23,614	LC
Iowa Wesleyan Univ	IA	39,200	C
Lehigh Univ	PA	61,010	MC
Ohio Univ	OH	22,924	C
San Diego State Univ	CA	21,896	C+
Tarleton State Univ	TX	15,248	LC
Univ of Louisiana at Monroe	LA	15,970	C
Western Mich Univ	MI	21,054	C

MANAGEMENT ENGINEERING

School	ST	$IS	SR
Appalachian State Univ	NC	14,416	VC
Claremont McKenna College	CA	67,185	MC
Mich Tech Univ	MI	24,739	VC+
Pitzer College	CA	66,192	MC
Stanford Univ	CA	60,409	MC
Univ of PR, at Bayamon	PR	13,145	
Western Kentucky Univ	KY	16,850	C
Worcester Polytechnic Inst	MA	60,730	MC

MANAGEMENT INFORMATION SYSTEMS

School	ST	$IS	SR
Adams State Univ	CO	17,703	LC
Adelphi Univ	NY	48,244	C
Albertus Magnus College	CT	43,258	LC
Alverno College	WI	33,294	LC
Amridge Univ	AL	10,860	LC
Andrews Univ	MI	28,030	C+
Angelo State Univ	TX	15,263	NC
Aquinas College - Mich	MI	38,876	HC
Ashland Univ	OH	21,440	C
Augsburg College	MN	43,929	C
Augusta Univ	GA	4,632	C
Aurora Univ	IL	33,970	C
Barry Univ	FL	37,830	C
Baylor Univ	TX	53,760	HC
Benedictine Univ	IL	38,300	C
Biola Univ	CA	46,402	C+
Bloomfield College	NJ	39,100	LC
Bowling Green State Univ	OH	19,747	C
Brewton-Parker College	GA	23,490	C
Bridgewater College	VA	44,510	C
Brigham Young Univ	UT	12,748	HC
Bryant Univ	RI	55,646	VC
Butler Univ	IN	51,352	VC
Cal State, Long Beach	CA	18,850	C
Cal State, Northridge	CA	16,859	LC
Cal State, Sacramento	CA	20,332	C
Cal State, San Bernardino	CA	12,000	C
Calvin College	MI	41,570	VC+
Canisius College	NY	47,537	C
Central Conn State Univ	CT	21,203	C
Central Mich Univ	MI	20,330	C
Chatham Univ	PA	46,517	C
CUNY/Meger Evers College	NY	6,680	NC
Cleveland State Univ	OH	22,196	C
Colo Christian Univ	CO	39,940	VC
Colo Mesa Univ	CO	18,955	LC
Colo State Univ	CO	22,162	VC
Colo Technical Univ	CO	21,455	NC
Columbus State Univ	GA	14,336	LC
Dallas Baptist Univ	TX	33,713	C
Daniel Webster College	NH	26,984	C
DePaul Univ	IL	47,623	VC
DeSales Univ	PA	43,970	C
Dordt College	IA	37,860	C+
Drexel Univ	PA	65,432	VC+
Drury Univ	MO	33,791	VC
Duquesne Univ	PA	46,822	VC
East Carolina Univ	NC	16,937	C
Eastern Illinois Univ	IL	21,126	C
Eastern Mich Univ	MI	19,761	C
Embry-Riddle Aeronautical Univ - Worldwide	FL	17,480	C
Eureka College	IL	30,220	C
Excelsior College	NY	14,080	SP
Faulkner Univ	AL	26,410	C
Fayetteville State Univ	NC	17,756	C
Florida Atlantic Univ	FL	17,339	C
Florida Inst of Technology	FL	53,306	VC
Florida International Univ	FL	19,854	C+
Fort Hays State Univ	KS	12,131	C
Friends Univ	KS	34,455	C
George Fox Univ	OR	42,938	C
Georgetown College	KY	41,440	C
Georgia College & State Univ	GA	21,148	C+
Georgia State Univ	GA	24,332	VC
Goldey-Beacom College	DE	31,750	C
Grace College and Seminary	IN	31,524	C
Grand View Univ	IA	32,302	C
Greenville College	IL	27,012	C
Hawaii Pacific Univ	HI	33,420	C
Hawaii Pacific Univ	HI	33,420	C
Hawaii Pacific Univ	HI	33,420	C
Hofstra Univ	NY	55,960	C+
Humphreys College	CA	27,790	C
Idaho State Univ	ID	13,619	NC
Indiana State Univ	IN	23,223	LC
Indiana Univ of Pennsylvania	PA	23,614	LC
Inter-American Univ of PR Ponce	PR	19,549	
Inter-American Univ of PR-Aguadilla Campus	PR	21,657	
Inter-American Univ of PR-Bayamon	PR	18,785	
Inter-American Univ of PR-Fajardo Campus	PR	18,336	
Inter-American Univ of PR-Metropolitan Campus	PR	20,045	
John Carroll Univ	OH	49,740	C+
Johnson & Wales Univ/Providence Campus	RI	42,248	C
Kansas State Univ	KS	17,780	VC
La Salle Univ	PA	55,790	C
Le Moyne College	NY	46,000	C
Lenoir-Rhyne Univ	NC	43,200	C
LeTourneau Univ	TX	38,250	VC
Lewis Univ	IL	40,370	C
Liberty Univ	VA	19,101	C
Lindenwood Univ	MO	25,132	C
Lipscomb Univ	TN	41,296	VC
Loras College	IA	39,222	C
Loyola Marymount Univ	CA	58,038	HC
Loyola Univ Chicago	IL	55,802	VC
MacMurray College	IL	33,620	C
Madonna Univ	MI	29,050	C
Marietta College	OH	46,190	C
Marquette Univ	WI	48,390	VC+
Marshall Univ	WV	17,242	C
McMurry Univ	TX	34,259	LC
Menlo College	CA	51,380	LC
Mercyhurst Univ	PA	47,420	C
Metropolitan State Univ	MN	7,566	C
Miami Univ	OH	27,190	HC+
Mich Tech Univ	MI	24,739	VC+
Midland Univ	NE	37,468	
Milwaukee School of Engineering	WI	45,153	HC
Minot State Univ	ND	12,732	C
Missouri Southern State Univ	MO	12,499	C
Missouri Univ of Science and Technology	MO	18,655	HC
Montclair State Univ	NJ	26,210	LC
Morehead State Univ	KY	17,422	C
Morningside College	IA	36,865	C
Mount Aloysius College	PA	29,976	C
Mount Mercy Univ	IA	36,826	C
Mount Vernon Nazarene Univ	OH	34,500	C
New Mexico Highlands Univ	NM	11,904	NC
New Mexico State Univ	NM	14,050	C
New York Univ	NY	65,860	MC
Newman Univ	KS	35,390	C
Nichols College	MA	46,800	LC
N Dak State Univ	ND	16,245	C
Northeastern Univ	MA	62,703	MC
Northwest Christian Univ	OR	36,580	C
Northwood Univ - Mich	MI	35,010	LC
Oakland Univ	MI	20,763	C
Ohio Dominican Univ	OH	41,340	C+
Ohio State Univ at Columbus	OH	21,703	HC+
Ohio Univ	OH	22,924	C
Okla State Univ	OK	17,180	VC
Old Dominion Univ	VA	20,910	C
Oral Roberts Univ	OK	34,316	C
Oregon Inst of Technology	OR	8,910	C
Ottawa Univ	KS	36,074	VC
Our Lady of the Lake Univ	TX	35,012	LC
Park Univ	MO	20,329	C
Peirce College	PA	16,780	NC
Penn State Erie/The Behrend College	PA	16,256	C
Pennsylvania College of Technology	PA	27,333	NC
Pennsylvania State Univ - Univ Park	PA	29,760	HC
Philadelphia Univ	PA	50,370	C
Rensselaer Polytechnic Inst	NY	63,436	MC
Rivier Univ	NH	40,410	VC
Rochester Inst of Technology	NY	50,842	HC
Rockford Univ	IL	36,030	C
Rutgers Univ - New Brunswick	NJ	26,632	HC
St. Francis Univ	PA	42,268	NC
St. Joseph's Univ	PA	57,544	VC+
St. Leo Univ	FL	31,650	C
St. Louis Univ	MO	49,866	HC
St. Mary's College	IN	50,600	C
Savannah State Univ	GA	15,631	C
Schreiner Univ	TX	34,626	LC
Seton Hall Univ	NJ	55,514	C
Seton Hill Univ	PA	46,972	C
Shippensburg Univ of Pennsylvania	PA	23,208	C
Shorter Univ	GA	31,130	LC
Simmons College	MA	53,090	VC
Simpson College	IA	43,839	VC
Southeastern Univ	FL	31,765	C
Southern Illinois Univ Edwardsville	IL	22,643	C
Southern Nazarene Univ	OK	32,798	NC
Spring Arbor Univ	MI	36,000	C
St. Bonaventure Univ	NY	44,237	C
St. Catherine Univ	MN	45,630	VC
SUNY / Empire State College	NY	9,145	SP
SUNY / SUNY College at Old Westbury	NY	16,860	C
SUNY / SUNY Plattsburgh	NY	18,814	C
SUNY at Binghamton	NY	22,861	MC
Stephen F. Austin State Univ	TX	18,406	LC
Temple Univ	PA	24,392	VC
Texas A&M Univ	TX	20,521	VC+
Texas A&M Univ at Corpus Christi	TX	16,851	LC
Texas Tech Univ	TX	18,736	C+
The Univ of Utah	UT	17,924	VC
Thiel College	PA	41,590	C
Thomas College	ME	35,268	LC
Trine Univ	IN	41,310	C
Univ of Alabama	AL	24,320	C+
Univ of Alaska Anchorage	AK	16,652	NC
Univ of Arizona	AZ	23,100	C
Univ of Arkansas at Monticello	AR	13,134	NC
Univ of Bridgeport	CT	44,430	LC
Univ of Central Okla	OK	13,486	C
Univ of Conn	CT	25,538	HC
Univ of Dayton	OH	53,620	C
Univ of Delaware	DE	24,976	VC+
Univ of Georgia	GA	21,250	HC
Univ of Hartford	CT	49,776	C
Univ of Hawaii at Manoa	HI	23,221	C
Univ of Houston	TX	21,483	VC
Univ of Idaho	ID	15,348	C
Univ of Illinois at Urbana-Champaign	IL	27,006	HC
Univ of Indianapolis	IN	36,480	C
Univ of Jamestown	ND	28,508	C
Univ of Kansas	KS	20,135	C+
Univ of Mary	ND	23,180	C
Univ of Maryland/College Park	MD	21,938	HC
Univ of Maryland/Univ College	MD	25,966	LC
Univ of Mass Dartmouth	MA	25,658	C
Univ of Memphis	TN	18,278	C
Univ of Mich/Dearborn	MI	11,757	VC
Univ of Minn/Duluth	MN	20,292	C+
Univ of Miss	MS	17,746	C+
Univ of Missouri-St. Louis	MO		C
Univ of Montana	MT	14,105	C
Univ of Montana-Western	MT	11,220	LC
Univ of Nebr - Omaha	NE	16,120	C
Univ of Nevada, Las Vegas	NV	17,553	C
Univ of N Car at Charlotte	NC	15,547	C
Univ of North Texas	TX	19,198	C
Univ of Northwestern - St. Paul	MN	38,160	C
Univ of Okla	OK	18,911	VC
Univ of Pennsylvania	PA	63,526	MC
Univ of Rhode Island	RI	24,906	C
Univ of San Francisco	CA	58,484	VC
Univ of South Florida/Tampa	FL	16,110	VC+
Univ of Southern Indiana	IN	16,501	C
Univ of Tampa	FL	36,944	C
Univ of Texas at Austin	TX	26,102	HC
Univ of Texas at El Paso	TX	34,452	NC
Univ of the Sacred Heart	PR	17,932	
Univ of Tulsa	OK	52,625	HC+
Univ of West Georgia	GA	16,360	LC
Univ of Wisc-Milwaukee	WI	21,496	C
Univ of Wisc-Oshkosh	WI	15,200	C
Upper Iowa Univ	IA	34,990	NC
Ursuline College	OH	41,076	LC
Utah State Univ	UT	12,736	C
Villanova Univ	PA	62,523	MC
Virginia State Univ	VA	19,802	C+
Viterbo Univ	WI	34,660	C
Washington State Univ	WA	22,495	C
Wayland Baptist Univ	TX	22,356	LC
Wayne State Univ	MI	22,016	C
Weber State Univ	UT	10,721	C
West Virginia Univ	WV	18,210	C
Western Conn State Univ	CT	21,254	LC
Western Kentucky Univ	KY	16,850	C
Western Mich Univ	MI	21,054	C
Western New Mexico Univ	NM	16,734	LC
Western Washington Univ	WA	18,003	C+
Westminster College	MO	32,820	C
Widener Univ	PA	56,486	C
Winona State Univ	MN	17,535	C
Winston-Salem State Univ	NC	26,166	LC
Worcester Polytechnic Inst	MA	60,730	MC
Wright State Univ	OH	16,983	C
York College of Pennsylvania	PA	29,240	C
Youngstown State Univ	OH	17,307	C

MANAGEMENT SCIENCE

School	ST	$IS	SR
Abilene Christian Univ	TX	41,800	C+
Alabama A&M Univ	AL	18,796	C
Anderson Univ	IN	38,200	C
Aurora Univ	IL	33,970	C
Avila Univ	MO	35,480	C
Barry Univ	FL	37,830	C
Belmont Univ	TN	40,970	VC
Bethany College	WV	36,300	NC
Bethel Univ	TN	24,738	C
Biola Univ	CA	46,402	C+
Boston College	MA	65,737	MC
Bridgewater State Univ	MA	21,810	C
Brigham Young Univ	UT	12,748	HC
Bryant Univ	RI	55,646	VC
Caldwell Univ	NJ	42,165	NC
Cal State, Fullerton	CA	21,902	C
Cal State, Monterey Bay	CA	26,871	LC
Cal State, San Bernardino	CA	12,000	C
Calif Univ of Pennsylvania	PA	14,217	LC
Cambridge College	MA	15,734	NC
Canisius College	NY	47,537	C
Cazenovia College	NY	46,470	C
Central Mich Univ	MI	20,330	C
Chaminade Univ of Honolulu	HI	36,000	C
Champlain College	VT	53,132	C+
Chicago State Univ	IL	20,144	C
CUNY/Baruch College	NY	21,609	HC
CUNY/Lehman College	NY	5,778	HC+
Claflin Univ	SC	33,764	LC
Clemson Univ	SC		HC
Cleveland State Univ	OH	22,196	C
College of St. Benedict	MN	52,806	C
Colo Christian Univ	CO	39,940	VC
Colo Technical Univ	CO	21,455	NC
Concordia Univ Wisc	WI	35,910	C
Coppin State Univ	MD	17,041	VC
Cumberland Univ	TN	27,710	C
Davenport Univ	MI	25,896	LC
Defiance College	OH	41,630	C
Delta State Univ	MS	13,176	C
DePaul Univ	IL	47,623	VC
Drake Univ	IA	45,056	HC
Duquesne Univ	PA	46,822	VC
East Tenn State Univ	TN	13,994	C
Eastern Mich Univ	MI	19,761	C
Eastern Washington Univ	WA	25,572	LC
Eckerd College	FL	52,874	C
Elmhurst College	IL	45,428	C
Evangel Univ	MO	28,898	C
Fairfield Univ	CT	59,860	VC+
Faulkner Univ	AL	26,410	C
Fitchburg State Univ	MA	21,819	C
Florida State Univ	FL	16,771	HC
Franklin Pierce Univ	NH	46,750	C
Franklin Univ	OH	56,262	SP
Gannon Univ	PA	42,032	C
George Fox Univ	OR	42,938	C
Georgia Southern Univ	GA	16,596	C
Goodwin College	CT	28,370	LC
Grand Canyon Univ	AZ	16,950	VC
Grand Valley State Univ	MI	22,250	C+
Granite State College	NH	19,639	SP
Gwynedd Mercy Univ	PA	43,780	LC
Hardin-Simmons Univ	TX	33,966	C
Hawaii Pacific Univ	HI	33,420	C
Heidelberg Univ	OH	39,200	C
Idaho State Univ	ID	13,619	NC
Indiana Univ-Purdue Univ Fort Wayne	IN	17,553	C
Indiana Wesleyan Univ	IN	33,674	C
Iona College	NY	50,984	C
Iowa State Univ	IA	17,570	C
Kean Univ	NJ	24,650	C
Kennesaw State Univ	GA	19,592	VC
Langston Univ	OK	14,314	C
Lesley Univ	MA	41,550	C

School	ST	$IS	SR
Lewis Univ	IL	40,370	C
Limestone College	SC	32,100	C
Loras College	IA	39,222	C
Louisiana State Univ and A&M College	LA	18,677	VC
Louisiana State Univ in Shreveport	LA	6,902	C
Louisiana Tech Univ	LA	11,422	VC
Loyola Univ New Orleans	LA	51,708	VC+
Luther College	IA	48,540	C+
Lynchburg College	VA	46,740	C
Madonna Univ	MI	29,050	C
Maharishi Univ of Management	IA	34,930	VC
Marian Univ	IN	41,220	C
Marian Univ	WI	32,420	LC
Marylhurst Univ	OR	20,295	NC
Mass Inst of Technology	MA	62,662	MC
Metropolitan State Univ of Denver	CO	29,889	LC
Miami Univ	OH	27,190	HC+
Mich Tech Univ	MI	24,739	VC+
Midwestern State Univ	TX	17,572	C
Millikin Univ	IL	42,158	C
Milwaukee School of Engineering	WI	45,153	HC
Minn State Univ, Mankato	MN	15,616	C
Minn State Univ, Moorhead	MN	15,941	C
Minot State Univ	ND	12,732	C
Missouri Baptist Univ	MO	35,594	C
Missouri State Univ	MO	15,190	C+
Morehead State Univ	KY	17,422	C
Mount Aloysius College	PA	29,976	C
Murray State Univ	KY	16,998	C
National Louis Univ	IL	16,920	LC
National Univ	CA	14,730	LC
New Jersey Inst of Technology	NJ	29,569	VC
New York Univ	NY	65,860	MC
N Dak State Univ	ND	16,245	C
Northeastern Illinois Univ	IL	12,529	LC
Northern Arizona Univ	AZ	20,246	VC
Notre Dame College	OH	37,150	VC
Ohio Northern Univ	OH	44,050	VC
Ohio Univ	OH	22,924	C
Okla City Univ	OK	40,476	VC
Oral Roberts Univ	OK	34,316	C
Oregon State Univ	OR	22,519	VC
Palm Beach Atlantic Univ	FL	39,720	C
Pepperdine Univ	CA	74,460	HC+
Philadelphia Univ	PA	50,370	C
Point Park Univ	PA	41,270	C
Portland State Univ	OR	19,443	C
Post Univ	CT	41,150	C
Prescott College	AZ	33,284	C
Quinnipiac Univ	CT	59,110	C
Rensselaer Polytechnic Inst	NY	63,436	MC
Rice Univ	TX	57,668	MC
Rider Univ	NJ	54,050	C
Rivier Univ	NH	40,410	VC
Rochester Inst of Technology	NY	50,842	HC
Roger Williams Univ	RI	46,296	C+
Roosevelt Univ	IL	40,651	VC
Rutgers Univ - Camden	NJ	26,146	C
Rutgers Univ - New Brunswick	NJ	26,632	HC
Rutgers Univ - Newark	NJ	27,288	C
St. Francis Univ	PA	42,268	NC
St. John's Univ	MN	51,624	C
St. Leo Univ	FL	31,650	C
Salisbury Univ	MD	20,714	VC
Salve Regina Univ	RI	51,470	C
Samford Univ	AL	39,232	VC
San Francisco State Univ	CA	18,514	LC
Southern Illinois Univ Carbondale	IL	23,667	C
Southern Methodist Univ	TX	66,483	MC
Southern Nazarene Univ	OK	32,798	NC
Southwestern Adventist Univ	TX	27,756	LC
St. Bonaventure Univ	NY	44,237	C
St. Francis College	NY	38,800	LC
St. John's Univ	NY	55,850	C
SUNY / Empire State College	NY	9,145	SP
SUNY / SUNY Cortland	NY	20,706	VC
SUNY at Binghamton	NY	22,861	MC
SUNY at Oswego	NY	21,351	C
Stephen F. Austin State Univ	TX	18,406	LC
Stockton Univ	NJ	25,059	
Suffolk Univ	MA	50,308	C
Tarleton State Univ	TX	15,248	LC
Tenn Tech Univ	TN	17,050	C
Texas A&M Univ	TX	20,521	VC+
Texas A&M Univ at Kingsville	TX	7,500	LC
Texas State Univ	TX	19,350	C
The Catholic Univ of America	DC	56,356	VC
The Lincoln Univ	PA	15,154	NC
The Univ of Akron	OH	21,477	C
The Univ of Tenn at Knoxville	TN	22,112	VC
The Univ of Tenn at Martin	TN	14,876	C
The Univ of Utah	UT	17,924	VC
Thomas College	ME	35,268	LC
Touro College	NY	28,950	VC
Trevecca Nazarene Univ	TN	31,186	C
Trine Univ	IN	41,310	C
Troy Univ	AL	16,171	C
Tulane Univ	LA	63,396	HC+
Tusculum College	TN	31,625	C
Tuskegee Univ	AL	28,164	C
Union College	NE	23,270	C
Union Univ	TN	33,970	VC
United States Air Force Academy	CO		C
United States Coast Guard Academy	CT	942	MC
United States Military Academy at West Point	NY		HC+
Universidad del Turabo	PR	17,828	
Universidad Metropolitana	PR	17,828	
Univ of Arizona	AZ	23,100	C
Univ of Arkansas at Little Rock	AR	18,211	C
Univ of Bridgeport	CT	44,430	LC
Univ of Calif at Berkeley	CA	28,853	MC
Univ of Calif at Riverside	CA	29,227	C+
Univ of Calif San Diego	CA	30,150	MC
Univ of Central Florida	FL	15,922	VC
Univ of Central Missouri	MO	18,982	C
Univ of Cincinnati	OH	21,964	VC
Univ of Colo Boulder	CO	24,285	VC+
Univ of Delaware	DE	24,976	VC+
Univ of Florida	FL	16,291	HC+
Univ of Great Falls	MT	38,524	C
Univ of Hartford	CT	49,776	C
Univ of Hawaii at Manoa	HI	23,221	C
Univ of Illinois at Chicago	IL	25,006	VC
Univ of Illinois at Urbana-Champaign	IL	27,006	HC
Univ of Iowa	IA	18,683	VC+
Univ of Louisiana at Lafayette	LA	14,516	C
Univ of Louisville	KY	19,824	C
Univ of Maryland/Univ College	MD	25,966	LC
Univ of Mass Boston	MA	13,435	C
Univ of Memphis	TN	18,278	C
Univ of Miami	FL	63,494	MC
Univ of Mich/Dearborn	MI	11,757	VC
Univ of Minn/Morris	MN	20,760	VC
Univ of Minn/Twin Cities	MN	23,519	HC+
Univ of Miss	MS	17,746	C+
Univ of Montevallo	AL	19,502	C
Univ of Nebr - Lincoln	NE	18,589	VC
Univ of Nebr - Omaha	NE	16,120	C
Univ of Nevada, Las Vegas	NV	17,553	C
Univ of Nevada/Reno	NV	18,010	C
Univ of N Car at Chapel Hill	NC	20,052	HC+
Univ of North Texas	TX	19,198	C
Univ of Northern Colo	CO	20,851	C
Univ of Pittsburgh at Greensburg	PA	23,132	C
Univ of PR, at Cayey	PR		
Univ of PR-Rio Piedras campus	PR	13,327	
Univ of St. Joseph	CT	49,550	C
Univ of S Car at Columbia	SC	19,725	VC+
Univ of S Dak	SD	16,109	C
Univ of South Florida/St. Petersburg	FL	15,980	C
Univ of South Florida/Tampa	FL	16,110	VC+
Univ of St. Francis	IL	39,924	C
Univ of Texas at Arlington	TX	18,026	LC
Univ of Texas at Austin	TX	26,102	HC
Univ of Texas at El Paso	TX	34,452	NC
Univ of Texas at San Antonio	TX	20,157	C
Univ of Tulsa	OK	52,625	HC+
Univ of Wisc-Stout	WI	19,667	C
Univ of Wyoming	WY	15,375	C+
Upper Iowa Univ	IA	34,990	NC
Valparaiso Univ	IN	48,370	C+
Virginia Polytechnic Inst and State Univ	VA	21,276	HC
Viterbo Univ	WI	34,660	C
Waynesburg Univ	PA	32,290	C
Webber International Univ	FL	31,904	C
Webster Univ	MO	37,490	C
West Liberty Univ	WV	15,512	C
West Texas A&M Univ	TX	13,478	C
Western Carolina Univ	NC	13,965	C
Western Kentucky Univ	KY	16,850	C
Western New England Univ	MA	48,088	C
Western Washington Univ	WA	18,003	C+
Wichita State Univ	KS	21,643	C
Wilberforce Univ	OH	19,016	C
Wilmington College	OH	34,600	C
Wright State Univ	OH	16,983	C
Xavier Univ	OH	47,880	C+

MANUFACTURING ENGINEERING

School	ST	$IS	SR
Arizona State Univ at the Polytechnic Campus	AZ	21,360	VC
Boston Univ	MA	65,110	MC
Brigham Young Univ	UT	12,748	HC
Calif Polytechnic State Univ	CA	17,979	HC+
Calif State Polytechnic Univ, Pomona	CA	21,541	C
Central State Univ	OH	18,564	C
Eastern Mich Univ	MI	19,761	C
Ferris State Univ	MI	21,445	C
Hofstra Univ	NY	55,960	C+
Kansas State Univ	KS	17,780	VC
Miami Univ	OH	27,190	HC+
Mich State Univ	MI	23,898	VC+
Midwestern State Univ	TX	17,572	C
Minn State Univ, Mankato	MN	15,616	C
Missouri Univ of Science and Technology	MO	18,655	HC
New Jersey Inst of Technology	NJ	29,569	VC
N Dak State Univ	ND	16,245	C
Northern Kentucky Univ	KY	16,486	C
Northwestern Univ	IL	66,344	MC
Oregon State Univ	OR	22,519	VC
Pennsylvania College of Technology	PA	27,333	NC
Purdue Univ/West Lafayette	IN	20,032	MC
Robert Morris Univ	PA	37,834	C
Rochester Inst of Technology	NY	50,842	HC
Southern Illinois Univ Edwardsville	IL	22,643	C
St. Cloud State Univ	MN	10,600	C
Tarleton State Univ	TX	15,248	LC
Tenn Tech Univ	TN	17,050	C
Texas State Univ	TX	19,350	C
Univ of Arkansas at Little Rock	AR	18,211	C
Univ of Calif at Berkeley	CA	28,853	MC
Univ of Conn	CT	25,538	HC
Univ of Memphis	TN	18,278	C
Univ of Mich/Dearborn	MI	11,757	VC
Univ of North Texas	TX	19,198	C
Univ of Wisc-Stout	WI	19,667	C
Washington State Univ	WA	22,495	C
Weber State Univ	UT	10,721	C
Western Mich Univ	MI	21,054	C
Wichita State Univ	KS	21,643	C

MANUFACTURING TECHNOLOGY

School	ST	$IS	SR
Alabama State Univ	AL	14,142	NC
Alfred State College	NY	19,895	C
Arizona State Univ at the Polytechnic Campus	AZ	21,360	VC
Arkansas State Univ	AR	16,190	C
Black Hills State Univ	SD	15,899	C
Brigham Young Univ	UT	12,748	HC
Cal State, Northridge	CA	16,859	LC
Central Conn State Univ	CT	21,203	C
Central Mich Univ	MI	20,330	C
Eastern Kentucky Univ	KY	16,908	C
Eastern Mich Univ	MI	19,761	C
Edinboro Univ	PA	15,940	LC
Farmingdale State College	NY	20,624	C
Fitchburg State Univ	MA	21,819	C
Idaho State Univ	ID	13,619	NC
Illinois Inst of Technology	IL	56,826	HC+
Indiana State Univ	IN	23,223	LC
Millersville Univ of Pennsylvania	PA	23,782	C
Minn State Univ, Mankato	MN	15,616	C
Missouri Southern State Univ	MO	12,499	C
Montana State Univ-Northern	MT	11,370	NC
Murray State Univ	KY	16,998	C
Nicholls State Univ	LA	10,534	C
Northern Kentucky Univ	KY	16,486	C
Northern Mich Univ	MI	19,604	C
Oregon Inst of Technology	OR	8,910	C
Pittsburg State Univ	KS	13,880	NC
Purdue Univ/West Lafayette	IN	20,032	MC
Rochester Inst of Technology	NY	50,842	HC
S Dak State Univ	SD	15,634	C
Southern Arkansas Univ	AR	21,532	C
Tarleton State Univ	TX	15,248	LC
Texas A&M Univ	TX	20,521	VC+
Texas State Univ	TX	19,350	C
Univ of Central Missouri	MO	18,982	C
Univ of Dayton	OH	53,620	C
Univ of Rio Grande & Rio Grande Community College	OH	8,750	NC
Univ of Southern Indiana	IN	16,501	C
Washington State Univ	WA	22,495	C
Wayne State Univ	MI	22,016	C
Weber State Univ	UT	10,721	C
Western Carolina Univ	NC	13,965	C
Western Kentucky Univ	KY	16,850	C
Western Mich Univ	MI	21,054	C
Western Washington Univ	WA	18,003	C+

MARINE AFFAIRS

School	ST	$IS	SR
Univ of Miami	FL	63,494	MC
Univ of New England	ME	48,880	C
Univ of Rhode Island	RI	24,906	C

MARINE BIOLOGY

School	ST	$IS	SR
Alaska Pacific Univ	AK	26,680	VC
Auburn Univ	AL	23,594	VC+
Barry Univ	FL	37,830	C
Brown Univ	RI	64,566	MC
Cal State, Long Beach	CA	18,850	C
Carroll Univ	WI	38,100	C+
Central Methodist Univ	MO	36,830	VC
College of Charleston	SC	22,699	C
Eastern Nazarene College	MA	39,955	C
Fairleigh Dickinson Univ/Metropolitan Campus	NJ	40,254	C
Florida Atlantic Univ	FL	17,339	C
Florida Inst of Technology	FL	53,306	VC
Florida International Univ	FL	19,854	C+
Florida State Univ	FL	16,771	HC
Hampshire College	MA	63,824	MC
Hawaii Pacific Univ	HI	33,420	C
Hawaii Pacific Univ	HI	33,420	C
Hawaii Pacific Univ	HI	33,420	C
Millersville Univ of Pennsylvania	PA	23,782	C
Missouri Southern State Univ	MO	12,499	C
Monmouth Univ	NJ	46,234	C
Murray State Univ	KY	16,998	C
New College of Florida	FL	15,848	MC
Northeastern Univ	MA	62,703	MC
Northwest Missouri State Univ	MO	17,737	C
Nova Southeastern Univ	FL	38,534	C+
Ohio Univ	OH	22,924	C
Old Dominion Univ	VA	20,910	C
Prescott College	AZ	33,284	C
Roger Williams Univ	RI	46,296	C+
Rollins College	FL	58,670	HC
San Francisco State Univ	CA	18,514	LC
Savannah State Univ	GA	15,631	C
Seattle Univ	WA	50,811	VC+
Southeast Missouri State Univ	MO	15,498	C
Southwestern College	KS	31,531	C
Spring Hill College	AL	48,488	C
Stetson Univ	FL	53,544	VC
Texas A&M Univ	TX	20,521	VC+
Texas A&M Univ at Galveston	TX	15,920	C
Texas State Univ	TX	19,350	C
Troy Univ	AL	16,171	C
Unity College	ME	37,670	C
Univ of Alaska Southeast	AK	11,493	C
Univ of Calif at Los Angeles	CA	30,162	MC
Univ of Calif at Santa Barbara	CA	29,091	HC
Univ of Calif San Diego	CA	30,150	MC
Univ of Calif, Santa Cruz	CA	28,731	C+
Univ of Hawaii at Manoa	HI	23,221	C
Univ of Maine at Machias	ME	22,960	C
Univ of Mass Dartmouth	MA	25,658	C
Univ of Miami	FL	63,494	MC
Univ of New Hampshire	NH	28,562	VC
Univ of New Haven	CT	52,190	C
Univ of N Car at Wilmington	NC	14,590	VC
Univ of Oregon	OR	22,972	C
Univ of PR, at Humacao	PR	14,000	
Univ of Rhode Island	RI	24,906	C
Univ of West Alabama	AL	15,516	NC
Univ of West Florida	FL	15,848	C
Waynesburg Univ	PA	32,290	C
Western Washington Univ	WA	18,003	C+
Wisc Lutheran College	WI	36,290	VC

MARINE ENGINEERING

School	ST	$IS	SR
Cal State, Maritime Academy	CA	19,450	LC
Maine Maritime Academy	ME	22,536	C
Mass Maritime Academy	MA	19,982	C
SUNY /Maritime College	NY	16,020	C
Texas A&M Univ	TX	20,521	VC+
Texas A&M Univ at Galveston	TX	15,920	C
United States Merchant Marine Academy	NY		HC
United States Naval Academy	MD		MC
Univ of New Orleans	LA	12,840	C

MARINE ENGINEERING SYSTEMS

School	ST	$IS	SR
Texas A&M Univ	TX	20,521	VC+
United States Merchant Marine Academy	NY		HC

MARINE ENGINEERING/ SHIPYARD MANAGEMENT

School	ST	$IS	SR
United States Merchant Marine Academy	NY		HC

MARINE SCIENCE

School	ST	$IS	SR
Boston Univ	MA	65,110	MC
Coastal Carolina Univ	SC	19,766	C
East Stroudsburg Univ	PA	18,334	C
Eckerd College	FL	52,874	C
Florida Gulf Coast Univ	FL	9,682	C
Hawaii Pacific Univ	HI	33,420	C
Jacksonville Univ	FL	46,230	C
Kutztown Univ of Pennsylvania	PA	19,056	LC
Montclair State Univ	NJ	26,210	LC
Nova Southeastern Univ	FL	38,534	C+
Prescott College	AZ	33,284	C
Rider Univ	NJ	54,050	C
Rutgers Univ - New Brunswick	NJ	26,632	HC
Samford Univ	AL	39,232	VC
San Jose State Univ	CA	21,540	C
SUNY /Maritime College	NY	16,020	C
Stockton Univ	NJ	25,059	
Stony Brook Univ/The SUNY	NY	21,881	MC
Suffolk Univ	MA	50,308	C
Texas A&M Univ	TX	20,521	VC+
Texas A&M Univ at Galveston	TX	15,920	C

ST = STATE $IS = IN-STATE COSTS SR = SELECTOR RATING

School	ST	$IS	SR
United States Coast Guard Academy	CT	942	MC
Univ of Alabama	AL	24,320	C+
Univ of Calif San Diego	CA	30,150	MC
Univ of Conn	CT	25,538	HC
Univ of Hawaii at Hilo	HI	18,038	C
Univ of Maine	ME	20,792	C
Univ of Maine at Machias	ME	22,960	C
Univ of Miami	FL	63,494	MC
Univ of Mobile	AL	28,935	C
Univ of New England	ME	48,880	C
Univ of N Car at Wilmington	NC	14,590	VC
Univ of San Diego	CA	58,442	VC+
Univ of S Car at Columbia	SC	19,725	VC+
Univ of Tampa	FL	36,944	C
West Chester Univ of Pennsylvania	PA	18,456	C
Western Washington Univ	WA	18,003	C+

MARINE TRANSPORTATION

School	ST	$IS	SR
Mass Maritime Academy	MA	19,982	C
Texas A&M Univ	TX	20,521	VC+
United States Merchant Marine Academy	NY		HC

MARINE VERTEBRATE BIOLOGY

School	ST	$IS	SR
Stony Brook Univ/The SUNY	NY	21,881	MC

MARITIME LOGISTICS & SECURITY

School	ST	$IS	SR
United States Merchant Marine Academy	NY		HC

MARITIME SCIENCE

School	ST	$IS	SR
Cal State, Maritime Academy	CA	19,450	LC
Maine Maritime Academy	ME	22,536	C
SUNY /Maritime College	NY	16,020	C
Texas A&M Univ	TX	20,521	VC+
Texas A&M Univ at Galveston	TX	15,920	C

MARKETING

School	ST	$IS	SR
Albertus Magnus College	CT	43,258	LC
Alma College	MI	47,548	C
Arkansas State Univ	AR	16,190	C
Arkansas Tech Univ	AR	15,484	C
Ashford Univ	CA	10,480	C
Aurora Univ	IL	33,970	C
Austin Peay State Univ	TN	16,397	C
Baldwin Wallace Univ	OH	41,106	C
Ball State Univ	IN	19,590	C
Bentley Univ	MA	60,890	HC
Bloomfield College	NJ	39,100	LC
Bowling Green State Univ	OH	19,747	C
Bryant Univ	RI	55,646	VC
Bucknell Univ	PA	64,616	MC
Cabrini Univ	PA	42,591	LC
Champlain College	VT	53,132	C+
Chatham Univ	PA	46,517	C
Christopher Newport Univ	VA	23,968	VC+
Clayton State Univ	GA	19,735	C
College of Charleston	SC	22,699	C
Columbia College Chicago	IL	43,168	C
Creighton Univ	NE	48,206	VC+
Dallas Baptist Univ	TX	33,713	C
Davis & Elkins College	WV	38,242	LC
Defiance College	OH	41,630	C
East Central Univ	OK	13,056	C
Eastern Illinois Univ	IL	21,126	C
Elon Univ	NC	44,599	VC+
Fairfield Univ	CT	59,860	VC+
Ferris State Univ	MI	21,445	C
Framingham State Univ	MA	20,584	C
Georgia Southwestern State Univ	GA	13,870	C
High Point Univ	NC	45,977	C
Hofstra Univ	NY	55,960	C+
Hood College	MD	54,840	C
Illinois State Univ	IL	23,418	VC
Indiana Univ Bloomington	IN	20,429	VC
Kent State Univ	OH	20,732	C
Lehigh Univ	PA	61,010	MC
Lewis Univ	IL	40,370	C
Limestone College	SC	32,100	C
LIU Brooklyn	NY	49,682	C
Loras College	IA	39,222	C
Loyola Marymount Univ	CA	58,038	HC
Lubbock Christian Univ	TX	28,426	C
Madonna Univ	MI	29,050	C
Manhattanville College	NY	51,440	C+
Marian Univ	IN	41,220	C
McNeese State Univ	LA	7,838	C
Mich State Univ	MI	23,898	VC+
Mich Tech Univ	MI	24,739	VC+
Minn State Univ, Mankato	MN	15,616	C
Missouri Southern State Univ	MO	12,499	C
Molloy College	NY	40,440	C
Mount Vernon Nazarene Univ	OH	34,500	C
Murray State Univ	KY	16,998	C
Neumann Univ	PA	40,678	LC
New Mexico State Univ	NM	14,050	C
N Dak State Univ	ND	16,245	C
North Greenville Univ	SC	25,930	C+
Nova Southeastern Univ	FL	38,534	C+
Okla Baptist Univ	OK	32,320	C
Okla City Univ	OK	40,476	VC
Oregon State Univ	OR	22,519	VC
Point Loma Nazarene Univ	CA	43,450	C
Providence College	RI	60,760	VC
Roberts Wesleyan College	NY	38,306	C
Rochester Inst of Technology	NY	50,842	HC
Rutgers Univ - New Brunswick	NJ	26,632	HC
Rutgers Univ - Newark	NJ	27,288	C
St. Anselm College	NH	52,560	C+
St. Louis Univ	MO	49,866	HC
St. Mary's Univ of Minn	MN	41,210	VC
Salisbury Univ	MD	20,714	VC
Southeast Missouri State Univ	MO	15,498	C
Southeastern Louisiana Univ	LA	16,237	C
Southern Oregon Univ	OR	19,117	C
Spalding Univ	KY	31,938	SP
St. Ambrose Univ	IA	39,019	C
St. Ambrose Univ	IA	39,019	C
St. John's Univ	NY	55,850	C
Stephen F. Austin State Univ	TX	18,406	LC
Susquehanna Univ	PA	55,340	VC
Syracuse Univ	NY	60,239	VC
Taylor Univ	IN	40,317	C+
Texas Christian Univ	TX	54,670	HC
Texas Tech Univ	TX	18,736	C+
Thomas Edison State Univ	NJ	6,350	NC
Tiffin Univ	OH	31,380	C
Trevecca Nazarene Univ	TN	31,186	C
Univ of Arizona	AZ	23,100	C
Univ of Evansville	IN	44,186	VC+
Univ of Georgia	GA	21,250	HC
Univ of Louisiana at Monroe	LA	15,970	C
Univ of Maryland/College Park	MD	21,938	HC
Univ of Miami	FL	63,494	MC
Univ of Nevada/Reno	NV	18,010	C
Univ of N Car at Charlotte	NC	15,547	C
Univ of Notre Dame	IN	64,043	MC
Univ of Okla	OK	18,911	VC
Univ of Rhode Island	RI	24,906	C
Univ of Rochester	NY	65,032	MC
Univ of St. Francis	IN	37,400	C
Univ of San Francisco	CA	58,484	VC
Univ of St. Thomas - Houston	TX	40,020	VC
Univ of Wisc-Eau Claire	WI	15,797	VC
Univ of Wisc-Parkside	WI	15,193	C
Univ of Wyoming	WY	15,375	C+
Washington State Univ	WA	22,495	C
West Virginia Univ	WV	18,210	C
Western Illinois Univ	IL	20,825	C
Western Kentucky Univ	KY	16,850	C
Western New England Univ	MA	48,088	C
Wingate Univ	NC	39,950	C
Winona State Univ	MN	17,535	C
Wittenberg Univ	OH	48,156	C+

MARKETING AND DISTRIBUTION

School	ST	$IS	SR
Alvernia Univ	PA	43,900	C
Aquinas College - Mich	MI	38,876	HC
Becker College	MA	57,628	C
Bryant Univ	RI	55,646	VC
Caldwell Univ	NJ	42,165	NC
Central Mich Univ	MI	20,330	C
Clayton State Univ	GA	19,735	C
Florida Gulf Coast Univ	FL	9,682	C
Fort Lewis College	CO	18,980	C
Franklin Univ	OH	56,262	SP
Georgia College & State Univ	GA	21,148	C+
Gwynedd Mercy Univ	PA	43,780	LC
Indiana State Univ	IN	23,223	LC
Inter-American Univ of PR-Arecibo Campus	PR	18,245	
Johnson & Wales Univ/Charlotte Campus	NC	43,988	C
Johnson & Wales Univ/Providence Campus	RI	42,248	C
Lake Erie College	OH	38,914	LC
Limestone College	SC	32,100	C
Malone Univ	OH	38,448	C
Metropolitan State Univ	MN	7,566	C
Nazareth College	NY	45,574	C
New Mexico Highlands Univ	NM	11,904	NC
Northern Kentucky Univ	KY	16,486	C
Ohio State Univ at Columbus	OH	21,703	HC+
Salve Regina Univ	RI	51,470	C
Simmons College	MA	53,090	VC
Southern Illinois Univ Edwardsville	IL	22,643	C
Southwest Baptist Univ	MO	29,900	LC
SUNY / Empire State College	NY	9,145	SP
Tarleton State Univ	TX	15,248	LC
Texas A&M Univ	TX	20,521	VC+
The Catholic Univ of America	DC	56,356	VC
Union College	NE	23,270	C
Univ of Arizona	AZ	23,100	C
Univ of Houston	TX	21,483	VC
Univ of Illinois at Urbana-Champaign	IL	27,006	HC
Univ of South Florida/St. Petersburg	FL	15,980	C
Univ of West Georgia	GA	16,360	LC
West Virginia Univ	WV	18,210	C
Western Carolina Univ	NC	13,965	C
Western Kentucky Univ	KY	16,850	C
Wilkes Univ	PA	45,622	C
Wilmington College	OH	34,600	C

MARKETING AND DISTRIBUTION EDUCATION

School	ST	$IS	SR
Central Washington Univ	WA	16,803	C
Dakota State Univ	SD	13,811	C
East Carolina Univ	NC	16,937	C
Eastern Washington Univ	WA	25,572	LC
Fayetteville State Univ	NC	17,756	C
Johnson & Wales Univ/Providence Campus	RI	42,248	C
Murray State Univ	KY	16,998	C
N Car State Univ	NC	19,515	HC+
Rider Univ	NJ	54,050	C
The Univ of Tenn at Knoxville	TN	22,112	VC
Univ of Nebr - Lincoln	NE	18,589	VC
Univ of Wisc-Stout	WI	19,667	C
Western Kentucky Univ	KY	16,850	C

MARKETING MANAGEMENT

School	ST	$IS	SR
Adrian College	MI	42,400	C
Alverno College	WI	33,294	LC
Aquinas College	TN	30,800	C+
Aquinas College - Mich	MI	38,876	HC
Assumption College	MA	47,920	C+
Auburn Univ at Montgomery	AL	15,290	C
Averett Univ	VA	40,970	LC
Baker College of Flint	MI	13,880	NC
Benedictine Univ	IL	38,300	C
Berry College	GA	45,286	C+
Bethany College	KS	46,100	NC
Biola Univ	CA	46,402	C+
Brigham Young Univ	UT	12,748	HC
Bryant Univ	RI	55,646	VC
Calvin College	MI	41,570	VC+
Campbellsville Univ	KY	32,492	C
Canisius College	NY	47,537	C
Carthage College	WI	48,835	C
Case Western Reserve Univ	OH	60,304	MC
Catawba College	NC	39,820	C
Central Conn State Univ	CT	21,203	C
Central Mich Univ	MI	20,330	C
Champlain College	VT	53,132	C+
Chatham Univ	PA	46,517	C
CUNY/Baruch College	NY	21,609	HC
College of St. Scholastica	MN	44,640	C
College of the Ozarks	MO	7,230	C
College of William & Mary	VA		MC
Columbia College Chicago	IL	43,168	C
Concordia Univ St. Paul	MN	29,050	C
Culver-Stockton College	MO	33,525	C
Cumberland Univ	TN	27,710	C
Daniel Webster College	NH	26,984	C
Davenport Univ	MI	25,896	LC
DePaul Univ	IL	47,623	VC
Dominican Univ	IL	41,222	C
Dordt College	IA	37,860	C+
Drake Univ	IA	45,056	HC
Drury Univ	MO	33,791	VC
East Carolina Univ	NC	16,937	C
Eastern Mich Univ	MI	19,761	C
Elizabethtown College	PA	54,050	C
Elon Univ	NC	44,599	VC+
Emerson College	MA	54,736	HC
Endicott College	MA	44,604	VC+
Felician Univ	NJ	45,370	LC
Fitchburg State Univ	MA	21,819	C
Florida Inst of Technology	FL	53,306	VC
Fontbonne Univ	MO	33,717	C
Fordham Univ	NY	65,918	MC
Franciscan Univ of Steubenville	OH	33,980	VC
George Washington Univ	DC	62,835	MC
Georgia Southern Univ	GA	16,596	C
Goldey-Beacom College	DE	31,750	C
Goshen College	IN	42,500	C
Grove City College	PA	25,692	VC
Hardin-Simmons Univ	TX	33,966	C
Hawaii Pacific Univ	HI	33,420	C
Huntington Univ	IN	33,996	C
Indiana Univ of Pennsylvania	PA	23,614	LC
Iona College	NY	50,984	C
John Brown Univ	AR	33,132	VC
Johnson & Wales Univ/Charlotte Campus	NC	43,988	C
Johnson & Wales Univ/North Miami Campus	FL	42,707	C
Johnson & Wales Univ/Providence Campus	RI	42,248	C
Kean Univ	NJ	24,650	C
Keiser Univ	FL	35,010	LC
Kent State Univ	OH	20,732	C
La Roche College	PA	37,924	LC
La Sierra Univ	CA	39,690	VC
Lakeland Univ	WI	35,130	C
Le Moyne College	NY	46,000	C
LeTourneau Univ	TX	38,250	VC
Lewis Univ	IL	40,370	C
LIM College	NY	41,575	LC
Linfield College	OR	52,010	C
Lipscomb Univ	TN	41,296	VC
Lourdes Univ	OH	29,520	NC
Mary Baldwin Univ	VA	39,865	C
Maryville Univ of St. Louis	MO	38,046	VC+
Menlo College	CA	51,380	LC
Mercer Univ	GA	45,348	VC
Metropolitan State Univ	MN	7,566	C
Mich State Univ	MI	23,898	VC+
Missouri Baptist Univ	MO	35,594	C
Missouri Southern State Univ	MO	12,499	C
Monmouth Univ	NJ	46,234	C
Montclair State Univ	NJ	26,210	LC
Morehead State Univ	KY	17,422	C
Mount Aloysius College	PA	29,976	C
New York Inst of Technology	NY	48,730	C
New York Univ	NY	65,860	MC
Newbury College	MA	46,950	C
Northern Arizona Univ	AZ	20,246	VC
Northwood Univ - Mich	MI	35,010	LC
Ohio Univ	OH	22,924	C
Okla Christian Univ	OK	27,650	VC
Old Dominion Univ	VA	20,910	C
Olivet College	MI	36,110	LC
Our Lady of the Lake Univ	TX	35,012	LC
Palm Beach Atlantic Univ	FL	39,720	C
Park Univ	MO	20,329	C
Peirce College	PA	16,780	NC
Penn State Erie/The Behrend College	PA	16,256	C
Pennsylvania College of Technology	PA	27,333	NC
Pennsylvania State Univ - Univ Park	PA	29,760	HC
Pepperdine Univ	CA	74,460	HC+
Plymouth State Univ	NH	23,180	LC
Purdue Univ/West Lafayette	IN	20,032	MC
Quinnipiac Univ	CT	59,110	C
Rhode Island College	RI	17,694	LC
Rochester College	MI	28,574	LC
Rochester Inst of Technology	NY	50,842	HC
Sacred Heart Univ	CT	52,750	C
Saginaw Valley State Univ	MI	18,530	C
St. Joseph's Univ	PA	57,544	VC+
St. Leo Univ	FL	31,650	C
St. Louis Univ	MO	49,866	HC
Samford Univ	AL	39,232	VC
Seattle Univ	WA	50,811	VC+
Seton Hall Univ	NJ	55,514	C
Shippensburg Univ of Pennsylvania	PA	23,208	C
Siena College	NY	48,916	C+
Simpson College	IA	43,839	VC
Southern New Hampshire Univ	NH	43,198	C
Spring Hill College	AL	48,488	C
St. Edward's Univ	TX	53,100	VC
St. John Fisher College	NY	43,620	C
St. Joseph's College, New York/Brooklyn Campus	NY	25,114	LC
St. Joseph's College, New York/Long Island Campus	NY	25,124	C
SUNY at Binghamton	NY	22,861	MC
Stephen F. Austin State Univ	TX	18,406	LC
Stevenson Univ	MD	72,770	C
Texas Wesleyan Univ	TX	35,134	C
The College at Brockport - SUNY	NY	20,346	C
The Univ of Utah	UT	17,924	VC
Thomas College	ME	35,268	LC
Tiffin Univ	OH	31,380	C
Troy Univ	AL	16,171	C
Tulane Univ	LA	63,396	HC+
Union College	KY	32,310	C
Union Univ	TN	33,970	VC
Univ of Arkansas at Fayetteville	AR	19,152	C+
Univ of Colo Boulder	CO	24,285	VC+
Univ of Idaho	ID	15,348	C
Univ of Illinois at Urbana-Champaign	IL	27,006	HC
Univ of Iowa	IA	18,683	VC+
Univ of Maryland/Univ College	MD	25,966	LC
Univ of Mass Amherst	MA	26,199	VC+
Univ of Memphis	TN	18,278	C
Univ of Miami	FL	63,494	MC
Univ of Mich/Dearborn	MI	11,757	VC
Univ of Minn Crookston	MN	19,739	C
Univ of Missouri-St. Louis	MO		C
Univ of Nebr - Lincoln	NE	18,589	VC
Univ of N Dak	ND	15,373	C
Univ of North Florida	FL	15,996	VC
Univ of Northwestern - St. Paul	MN	38,160	C
Univ of PR-Rio Piedras campus	PR	13,327	
Univ of Rio Grande & Rio Grande Community College	OH	8,750	NC
Univ of San Diego	CA	58,442	VC+
Univ of S Car Upstate	SC	18,200	LC
Univ of Texas at Austin	TX	26,102	HC
Univ of Texas at Dallas	TX	22,830	VC+
Univ of Texas at San Antonio	TX	20,157	C
Univ of the Sciences	PA	54,038	VC
Univ of Wisc-Milwaukee	WI	21,496	C
Ursuline College	OH	41,076	LC
Virginia Polytechnic Inst and State Univ	VA	21,276	HC
Virginia State Univ	VA	19,802	C+

ST = STATE **$IS** = IN-STATE COSTS **SR** = SELECTOR RATING

School	ST	$IS	SR
Walsh Univ	OH	39,010	C
Warner Univ	FL	28,216	C
Washington State Univ	WA	22,495	C
Washington Univ in St. Louis	MO	65,366	VC
Webber International Univ	FL	31,904	C
Weber State Univ	UT	10,721	C
Webster Univ	MO	37,490	C
West Chester Univ of Pennsylvania	PA	18,456	C
Western Conn State Univ	CT	21,254	LC
Whitworth Univ	WA	51,732	VC
Wilmington College	OH	34,600	C
Youngstown State Univ	OH	17,307	C

MARKETING/RETAILING/ MERCHANDISING

School	ST	$IS	SR
Abilene Christian Univ	TX	41,800	C+
Adams State Univ	CO	17,703	LC
Alabama A&M Univ	AL	18,796	C
Alabama State Univ	AL	14,142	NC
Albany State Univ	GA	19,462	C
Alderson Broaddus Univ	WV	26,149	C
Alfred Univ	NY	42,296	C+
American International College	MA	46,300	LC
Anderson Univ	IN	38,200	C
Andrews Univ	MI	28,030	C+
Angelo State Univ	TX	15,263	NC
Appalachian State Univ	NC	14,416	VC
Arcadia Univ	PA	33,570	C+
Arizona State Univ at the Tempe Campus	AZ	21,756	VC
Ashland Univ	OH	21,440	C
Auburn Univ	AL	23,594	VC+
Auburn Univ at Montgomery	AL	15,290	C
Augsburg College	MN	43,929	C
Augusta Univ	GA	4,632	C
Avila Univ	MO	35,480	C
Azusa Pacific Univ	CA	43,972	C
Barry Univ	FL	37,830	C
Bay Path Univ	MA	45,349	C
Bayamon Central Univ	PR	12,490	
Baylor Univ	TX	53,760	HC
Belmont Univ	TN	40,970	VC
Benedictine Univ	IL	38,300	C
Berkeley College/New Jersey	NJ	38,082	LC
Berkeley College/New York City Campus	NY	23,350	LC
Berkeley College/White Plains Campus	NY	35,100	LC
Blackburn College	IL	28,526	LC
Bluffton Univ	OH	40,950	C
Boise State Univ	ID	14,860	C
Boston College	MA	65,737	MC
Brenau Univ - Women's College	GA	37,876	LC
Bryant Univ	RI	55,646	VC
Buena Vista Univ	IA	41,514	C
Butler Univ	IN	51,352	VC
Calif Baptist Univ	CA	41,392	C
Cal State, Fullerton	CA	21,902	C
Cal State, Long Beach	CA	18,850	C
Cal State, Northridge	CA	16,859	LC
Cal State, Sacramento	CA	20,332	C
Canisius College	NY	47,537	C
Caribbean Univ	PR	15,471	
Carnegie Mellon Univ	PA	67,980	MC
Cedar Crest College	PA	46,715	C
Cedarville Univ	OH	34,990	VC
Central Mich Univ	MI	20,330	C
Central State Univ	OH	18,564	C
Central Washington Univ	WA	16,803	C
Chestnut Hill College	PA	43,410	C
Chicago State Univ	IL	20,144	C
CUNY/Baruch College	NY	21,609	HC
CUNY/York College	NY	6,747	LC
City Univ of Seattle	WA	24,340	NC
Claflin Univ	SC	33,764	LC
Clarion Univ of Pennsylvania	PA	21,608	LC
Clemson Univ	SC		HC
Cleveland State Univ	OH	22,196	C
Coastal Carolina Univ	SC	19,766	C
Colo State Univ	CO	22,162	VC
Columbia College - Missouri	MO	27,803	C
Columbus State Univ	GA	14,336	LC
Concord Univ	WV	14,954	C
Concordia Univ Wisc	WI	35,910	C
Defiance College	OH	41,630	C
Delaware State Univ	DE	19,376	NC
Delaware Valley Univ	PA	49,796	C
Delta State Univ	MS	13,176	C
DeSales Univ	PA	43,970	C
Dominican College	NY	31,270	LC
Drexel Univ	PA	65,432	VC+
Duquesne Univ	PA	46,822	VC
East Carolina Univ	NC	16,937	C
East Tenn State Univ	TN	13,994	C
Eastern Kentucky Univ	KY	16,908	C
Eastern Mich Univ	MI	19,761	C
Eastern New Mexico Univ	NM	14,416	C
Eastern Univ	PA	39,540	C
Eastern Washington Univ	WA	25,572	LC
Elizabethtown College School of Continuing and Professional Studies	PA	18,900	C
Elmhurst College	IL	45,428	C
Elms College	MA	45,646	VC
Emory Univ	GA	60,786	MC
Emporia State Univ	KS	14,570	C
Evangel Univ	MO	28,898	C
Excelsior College	NY	14,080	SP
Fairleigh Dickinson Univ/ College at Florham	NJ	52,062	C
Fairleigh Dickinson Univ/ Metropolitan Campus	NJ	40,254	C
Fairmont State Univ	WV	15,726	C
Fashion Inst of Technology/ SUNY	NY	18,521	SP
Ferris State Univ	MI	21,445	C
Florida Atlantic Univ	FL	17,339	C
Florida International Univ	FL	19,854	C+
Florida State Univ	FL	16,771	HC
Fontbonne Univ	MO	33,717	C
Fort Hays State Univ	KS	12,131	C
Fort Valley State Univ	GA	17,988	VC
Francis Marion Univ	SC	16,464	LC
Franklin Pierce Univ	NH	46,750	C
Gannon Univ	PA	42,032	C
George Mason Univ	VA	15,724	VC
Georgetown College	KY	41,440	C
Georgetown Univ	DC	65,926	MC
Georgia State Univ	GA	24,332	VC
Glenville State College	WV	17,386	NC
Grambling State Univ	LA	15,701	C
Grand Canyon Univ	AZ	16,950	VC
Grand Rapids Theological Seminary/Cornerstone Univ	MI	33,338	C
Grand Valley State Univ	MI	22,250	C+
Greenville College	IL	27,012	C
Hampton Univ	VA	34,926	LC
Harding Univ	AR	25,421	C
Hillsdale College	MI	35,722	MC
Holy Family Univ	PA	43,326	LC
Howard Univ	DC	37,616	C+
Husson Univ	ME	25,720	LC
Huston-Tillotson Univ	TX	18,124	LC
Idaho State Univ	ID	13,619	NC
Indiana State Univ	IN	23,223	LC
Indiana Univ-Purdue Univ Fort Wayne	IN	17,553	C
Indiana Wesleyan Univ	IN	33,674	C
Inter-American Univ of PR Ponce	PR	19,549	
Inter-American Univ of PR- Aguadilla Campus	PR	21,657	
Inter-American Univ of PR- Bayamon	PR	18,785	
Inter-American Univ of PR- Fajardo Campus	PR	18,336	
Inter-American Univ of PR- Metropolitan Campus	PR	20,045	
Inter-American Univ of PR-San Germán	PR	20,042	
Iowa State Univ	IA	17,570	C
Jackson State Univ	MS	15,879	LC
Jacksonville State Univ	AL	14,628	LC
Jacksonville Univ	FL	46,230	C
James Madison Univ	VA	19,084	VC
John Carroll Univ	OH	49,740	C+
Johnson & Wales Univ/ Charlotte Campus	NC	43,988	C
Johnson & Wales Univ/ Denver Campus	CO	42,707	C
Johnson & Wales Univ/North Miami Campus	FL	42,707	C
Johnson & Wales Univ/ Providence Campus	RI	42,248	C
Juniata College	PA	53,760	VC
Kansas State Univ	KS	17,780	VC
Kennesaw State Univ	GA	19,592	VC
Keuka College	NY	39,762	C
King's College	PA	46,858	C
Kutztown Univ of Pennsylvania	PA	19,056	LC
La Salle Univ	PA	55,790	C
Lamar Univ	TX	18,014	LC
Lasell College	MA	47,500	C
LeTourneau Univ	TX	38,250	VC
Lincoln Univ	MO	13,602	NC
Lindenwood Univ	MO	25,132	C
Lipscomb Univ	TN	41,296	VC
LIU Post	NY	49,682	C
Louisiana State Univ and A&M College	LA	18,677	VC
Louisiana State Univ in Shreveport	LA	6,902	C
Louisiana Tech Univ	LA	11,422	VC
Loyola Univ Chicago	IL	55,802	VC
Loyola Univ New Orleans	LA	51,708	VC+
Lynchburg College	VA	46,740	C
Lynn Univ	FL	49,480	LC
MacMurray College	IL	33,620	C
Manhattan College	NY	51,750	C+
Marian Univ	WI	32,420	LC
Marietta College	OH	46,190	C
Marquette Univ	WI	48,390	VC+
Marshall Univ	WV	17,242	C
Martin Univ	IN	20,264	LC
Marywood Univ	PA	46,900	C
McKendree Univ	IL	37,940	C+
McMurry Univ	TX	34,259	LC
Mercyhurst Univ	PA	47,420	C
Merrimack College	MA	52,770	C
Messiah College	PA	43,100	C+
Methodist Univ	NC	43,600	C
Metropolitan State Univ of Denver	CO	29,889	LC
Miami Univ	OH	27,190	HC+
Mich State Univ	MI	23,898	VC+
MidAmerica Nazarene Univ	KS	35,550	C
Middle Tenn State Univ	TN	8,650	C
Midland Univ	NE	37,468	
Midwestern State Univ	TX	17,572	C
Millikin Univ	IL	42,158	C
Minn State Univ, Moorhead	MN	15,941	C
Minot State Univ	ND	12,732	C
Miss College	MS	25,850	C
Miss State Univ	MS	11,454	C+
Missouri State Univ	MO	15,190	C+
Missouri Western State Univ	MO	16,741	
Morgan State Univ	MD	17,190	LC
Mount Ida College	MA	46,820	C
Mount Mary Univ	WI	34,650	LC
Mount Mercy Univ	IA	36,826	C
New Mexico Highlands Univ	NM	11,904	NC
New Mexico State Univ	NM	14,050	C
New York Univ	NY	65,860	MC
Niagara Univ	NY	41,010	C
Nicholls State Univ	LA	10,534	C
Nichols College	MA	46,800	LC
North Central College	IL	48,712	VC
North Park Univ	IL	35,860	C
Northeastern Illinois Univ	IL	12,529	LC
Northeastern State Univ	OK	8,615	VC
Northern Illinois Univ	IL	20,176	C
Northern Mich Univ	MI	19,604	C
Northern State Univ	SD	14,505	C
Northwest Missouri State Univ	MO	17,737	C
Notre Dame College	OH	37,150	VC
Notre Dame de Namur Univ	CA	46,526	LC
Notre Dame of Maryland Univ	MD	46,465	VC
Oakland Univ	MI	20,763	C
Okla Christian Univ	OK	27,650	VC
Okla State Univ	OK	17,180	VC
Olivet Nazarene Univ	IL	41,840	C
Oral Roberts Univ	OK	34,316	C
Oregon State Univ	OR	22,519	VC
Pace Univ	NY	58,248	C
Parsons The New School for Design	NY	56,610	SP
Peru State College	NE	14,768	NC
Philadelphia Univ	PA	50,370	C
Pontifical Catholic Univ of PR	PR	10,534	
Portland State Univ	OR	19,443	C
Post Univ	CT	41,150	C
Prairie View A&M Univ	TX	15,205	LC
Purdue Univ/Northwest	IN	15,038	C
Purdue Univ/West Lafayette	IN	20,032	MC
Quincy Univ	IL	36,998	C
Quinnipiac Univ	CT	59,110	C
Radford Univ	VA	19,027	LC
Regis Univ	CO	44,520	C
Rider Univ	NJ	54,050	C
Robert Morris Univ	PA	37,834	C
Roger Williams Univ	RI	46,296	C+
Roosevelt Univ	IL	40,651	VC
Rowan Univ	NJ	24,491	VC+
Rutgers Univ - Camden	NJ	26,146	C
Rutgers Univ - New Brunswick	NJ	26,632	HC
Rutgers Univ - Newark	NJ	27,288	C
St. Joseph's Univ	PA	57,544	VC+
St. Mary-of-the-Woods College	IN	39,632	LC
St. Peter's Univ	NJ	49,192	C
St. Vincent College	PA	44,626	C
St. Xavier Univ	IL	43,310	C
Salem State Univ	MA	17,303	LC
Sam Houston State Univ	TX	18,792	C
San Diego State Univ	CA	21,896	C+
San Francisco State Univ	CA	18,514	LC
San Jose State Univ	CA	21,540	C
Savannah State Univ	GA	15,631	C
Seton Hill Univ	PA	46,972	C
Slippery Rock Univ of Pennsylvania	PA	10,360	C
S Car State Univ	SC	20,805	LC
Southeastern Univ	FL	31,765	C
Southern Adventist Univ	TN	27,600	C
Southern Conn State Univ	CT	21,924	LC
Southern Illinois Univ Carbondale	IL	23,667	C
Southern Methodist Univ	TX	66,483	MC
Southern Nazarene Univ	OK	32,798	NC
Southern New Hampshire Univ	NH	43,198	C
Southern Oregon Univ	OR	19,117	C
Southern Univ and A&M College	LA	16,074	LC+
Southwest Minn State Univ	MN	17,783	C
Southwestern Okla State Univ	OK	11,790	C
St. Bonaventure Univ	NY	44,237	C
St. Catherine Univ	MN	45,630	VC
St. Cloud State Univ	MN	10,600	C
St. Mary's Univ	TX	37,500	C
St. Thomas Aquinas College	NY	42,200	C
St. Thomas Univ	FL	36,360	LC
SUNY / SUNY College at Old Westbury	NY	16,860	C
SUNY / SUNY Plattsburgh	NY	18,814	C
SUNY at New Paltz	NY	19,200	C
SUNY at Oswego	NY	21,351	C
Stephen F. Austin State Univ	TX	18,406	LC
Stetson Univ	FL	53,544	VC
Stonehill College	MA	55,030	C+
Suffolk Univ	MA	50,308	C
Tarleton State Univ	TX	15,248	LC
Temple Univ	PA	24,392	VC
Tenn Tech Univ	TN	17,050	C
Texas A&M Univ at Commerce	TX	10,496	C
Texas A&M Univ at Corpus Christi	TX	16,851	LC
Texas A&M Univ at Kingsville	TX	7,500	LC
Texas Southern Univ	TX	18,212	LC
Texas State Univ	TX	19,350	C
Texas Wesleyan Univ	TX	35,134	C
Texas Woman's Univ	TX	15,302	LC
The Univ of Akron	OH	21,477	C
The Univ of Tenn at Martin	TN	14,876	C
The Univ of Utah	UT	17,924	VC
Touro College	NY	28,950	VC
Trevecca Nazarene Univ	TN	31,186	C
Trine Univ	IN	41,310	C
Trinity International Univ	IL	31,070	VC
Troy Univ	AL	16,171	C
Tuskegee Univ	AL	28,164	C
Union Univ	TN	33,970	VC
Universidad del Turabo	PR	17,828	
Univ of PR, at Arecibo	PR	12,652	
Univ of Alabama at Birmingham	AL	19,906	C
Univ of Alabama in Huntsville	AL	19,445	VC
Univ of Alaska Anchorage	AK	16,652	NC
Univ of Arkansas at Fayetteville	AR	19,152	C+
Univ of Arkansas at Little Rock	AR	18,211	C
Univ of Bridgeport	CT	44,430	LC
Univ of Central Arkansas	AR	14,472	VC
Univ of Central Florida	FL	15,922	VC
Univ of Central Missouri	MO	18,982	C
Univ of Central Okla	OK	13,486	C
Univ of Cincinnati	OH	21,964	VC
Univ of Conn	CT	25,538	HC
Univ of Dayton	OH	53,620	C
Univ of Delaware	DE	24,976	VC+
Univ of Denver	CO	58,443	VC+
Univ of Findlay	OH	60,139	C
Univ of Florida	FL	16,291	HC+
Univ of Hartford	CT	49,776	C
Univ of Hawaii at Manoa	HI	23,221	C
Univ of Houston-Downtown	TX	7,241	C
Univ of Idaho	ID	15,348	C
Univ of Illinois at Chicago	IL	25,006	VC
Univ of Illinois at Urbana-Champaign	IL	27,006	HC
Univ of Indianapolis	IN	36,480	C
Univ of Kansas	KS	20,135	C+
Univ of Kentucky	KY	33,306	C
Univ of Louisiana at Lafayette	LA	14,516	C
Univ of Louisville	KY	19,824	C
Univ of Maine at Machias	ME	22,960	C
Univ of Mary Hardin-Baylor	TX	33,950	C+
Univ of Mass Dartmouth	MA	25,658	C
Univ of Mich-Flint	MI	17,607	C+
Univ of Minn/Twin Cities	MN	23,519	HC+
Univ of Miss	MS	17,746	C+
Univ of Missouri/Columbia	MO	18,201	MC
Univ of Montana	MT	14,105	C
Univ of Montevallo	AL	19,502	C
Univ of Nebr - Kearney	NE	16,546	LC
Univ of Nebr - Lincoln	NE	18,589	VC
Univ of Nebr - Omaha	NE	16,120	C
Univ of Nevada, Las Vegas	NV	17,553	C
Univ of Nevada/Reno	NV	18,010	C
Univ of New Haven	CT	52,190	C
Univ of New Orleans	LA	12,840	C
Univ of North Alabama	AL	15,398	C
Univ of N Car at Charlotte	NC	15,547	C
Univ of N Car at Greensboro	NC	14,690	C
Univ of N Car at Wilmington	NC	14,590	VC
Univ of North Georgia	GA	17,316	C
Univ of North Texas	TX	19,198	C
Univ of Northern Colo	CO	20,851	C
Univ of Pennsylvania	PA	63,526	MC
Univ of Pittsburgh	PA	29,568	HC+
Univ of Portland	OR	52,152	VC
Univ of PR, at Bayamon	PR	13,145	
Univ of PR, at Mayaguez	PR	13,995	
Univ of Scranton	PA	54,962	VC
Univ of Sioux Falls	SD	34,330	C
Univ of South Alabama	AL	16,400	C
Univ of S Car at Columbia	SC	19,725	VC+
Univ of South Florida/Tampa	FL	16,110	VC+
Univ of Southern Indiana	IN	16,501	C
Univ of Southern Miss	MS	13,170	C
Univ of St. Francis	IL	39,924	C
Univ of St. Thomas - Houston	TX	40,020	VC
Univ of Tampa	FL	36,944	C
Univ of Texas at Arlington	TX	18,026	LC
Univ of Texas at El Paso	TX	34,452	NC
Univ of the District of Columbia	DC	21,044	LC
Univ of the Ozarks	AR	52,176	C
Univ of the Sacred Heart	PR	17,932	
Univ of Toledo	OH	19,336	NC

ST = STATE $IS = IN-STATE COSTS SR = SELECTOR RATING

School	ST	$IS	SR
Univ of Tulsa	OK	52,625	HC+
Univ of Washington	WA	23,149	VC
Univ of West Florida	FL	15,848	C
Univ of Wisc-La Crosse	WI	15,247	C+
Univ of Wisc-Madison	WI	20,934	MC
Univ of Wisc-Oshkosh	WI	15,200	C
Univ of Wisc-Stout	WI	19,667	C
Univ of Wisc-Whitewater	WI	13,976	C
Upper Iowa Univ	IA	34,990	NC
Utah State Univ	UT	12,736	C
Valparaiso Univ	IN	48,370	C+
Vanguard Univ of Southern Calif	CA	40,740	VC
Villanova Univ	PA	62,523	MC
Virginia Commonwealth Univ	VA	23,049	C
Viterbo Univ	WI	34,660	C
Wartburg College	IA	47,840	C
Washburn Univ	KS	15,827	C
Washington Univ in St. Louis	MO	65,366	VC
Wayne State Univ	MI	22,016	C
Waynesburg Univ	PA	32,290	C
West Liberty Univ	WV	15,512	C
West Texas A&M Univ	TX	13,478	C
West Virginia State Univ	WV	8,378	NC
West Virginia Wesleyan College	WV	36,858	C
Western Mich Univ	MI	21,054	C
Western New Mexico Univ	NM	16,734	LC
Western Washington Univ	WA	18,003	C+
Westminster College	PA	39,180	C+
Westminster College	UT	41,078	C+
Wichita State Univ	KS	21,643	C
Wilberforce Univ	OH	19,016	C
Woodbury Univ	CA	46,958	C
Wright State Univ	OH	16,983	C
Xavier Univ	OH	47,880	C+
Yeshiva Univ	NY	47,250	VC+
York College of Pennsylvania	PA	29,240	C
Youngstown State Univ	OH	17,307	C

MATERIALS ENGINEERING

School	ST	$IS	SR
Alfred Univ	NY	42,296	C+
Auburn Univ	AL	23,594	VC+
Brown Univ	RI	64,566	MC
Calif Polytechnic State Univ	CA	17,979	HC+
Carnegie Mellon Univ	PA	67,980	MC
Drexel Univ	PA	65,432	VC+
Florida State Univ	FL	16,771	HC
Georgia Inst of Technology	GA	23,360	MC
Iowa State Univ	IA	17,570	C
Johns Hopkins Univ	MD	65,386	MC
Mass Inst of Technology	MA	62,662	MC
Mich State Univ	MI	23,898	VC+
Mich Tech Univ	MI	24,739	VC+
Missouri Univ of Science and Technology	MO	18,655	HC
New Mexico Inst of Mining and Technology	NM	14,833	HC
Northwestern Univ	IL	66,344	MC
Ohio State Univ at Columbus	OH	21,703	HC+
Ohio Univ	OH	22,924	C
Rensselaer Polytechnic Inst	NY	63,436	MC
San Jose State Univ	CA	21,540	C
SUNY SUNY Albany	NY	22,165	C
The Univ of Tenn at Knoxville	TN	22,112	VC
The Univ of Utah	UT	17,924	VC
Univ of Alabama at Birmingham	AL	19,906	C
Univ of Arizona	AZ	23,100	C
Univ of Calif at Berkeley	CA	28,853	MC
Univ of Calif at Davis	CA	28,468	HC
Univ of Calif at Irvine	CA	26,484	VC
Univ of Calif at Los Angeles	CA	30,162	MC
Univ of Calif at Riverside	CA	29,227	C+
Univ of Cincinnati	OH	21,964	VC
Univ of Conn	CT	25,538	HC
Univ of Florida	FL	16,291	HC+
Univ of Idaho	ID	15,348	C
Univ of Illinois at Chicago	IL	25,006	VC
Univ of Illinois at Urbana-Champaign	IL	27,006	HC
Univ of Kentucky	KY	33,306	C
Univ of Maryland/College Park	MD	21,938	HC
Univ of Mich/Ann Arbor	MI	24,410	MC
Univ of Minn/Twin Cities	MN	23,519	HC+
Univ of Pennsylvania	PA	63,526	MC
Univ of Pittsburgh	PA	29,568	HC+
Univ of Wisc-Madison	WI	20,934	MC
Univ of Wisc-Milwaukee	WI	21,496	C
Virginia Polytechnic Inst and State Univ	VA	21,276	HC
Washington State Univ	WA	22,495	C
Winona State Univ	MN	17,535	C
Wright State Univ	OH	16,983	C

MATERIALS SCIENCE

School	ST	$IS	SR
Arizona State Univ at the Tempe Campus	AZ	21,756	VC
Boise State Univ	ID	14,860	C
Brown Univ	RI	64,566	MC
Calif Inst of Technology	CA	58,761	MC
Case Western Reserve Univ	OH	60,304	MC
Columbia Univ/City of New York	NY	62,958	MC
Duke Univ	NC	64,188	
Georgia Inst of Technology	GA	23,360	MC
Illinois Inst of Technology	IL	56,826	HC+
Johns Hopkins Univ	MD	65,386	MC
Mass Inst of Technology	MA	62,662	MC
Missouri State Univ	MO	15,190	C+
N Car State Univ	NC	19,515	HC+
Northwestern Univ	IL	66,344	MC
Ohio State Univ at Columbus	OH	21,703	HC+
Pennsylvania State Univ - Univ Park	PA	29,760	HC
Purdue Univ/Northwest	IN	15,038	C
Purdue Univ/West Lafayette	IN	20,032	MC
Rochester Inst of Technology	NY	50,842	HC
Stanford Univ	CA	60,409	MC
SUNY SUNY Albany	NY	22,165	C
The Univ of Utah	UT	17,924	VC
Univ of Arizona	AZ	23,100	C
Univ of Calif at Berkeley	CA	28,853	MC
Univ of Calif at Los Angeles	CA	30,162	MC
Univ of Denver	CO	58,443	VC+
Univ of Illinois at Urbana-Champaign	IL	27,006	HC
Univ of Mich/Ann Arbor	MI	24,410	MC
Univ of Minn/Twin Cities	MN	23,519	HC+
Univ of Pittsburgh	PA	29,568	HC+
Univ of the Ozarks	AR	52,176	C
Univ of Washington	WA	23,149	VC
Univ of Wisc-Eau Claire	WI	15,797	VC
Univ of Wisc-Madison	WI	20,934	MC
Washington State Univ	WA	22,495	C

MATERIALS SCIENCE AND ENGINEERING

School	ST	$IS	SR
Brown Univ	RI	64,566	MC
Cornell Univ	NY	64,853	MC
Drexel Univ	PA	65,432	VC+
Georgia Inst of Technology	GA	23,360	MC
Lehigh Univ	PA	61,010	MC
Mich State Univ	MI	23,898	VC+
Rutgers Univ - New Brunswick	NJ	26,632	HC
Univ of Wisc-Eau Claire	WI	15,797	VC
Washington State Univ	WA	22,495	C

MATHEMATICAL PROGRAMMING

School	ST	$IS	SR
Univ of Tampa	FL	36,944	C

MATHEMATICS

School	ST	$IS	SR
Abilene Christian Univ	TX	41,800	C+
Adams State Univ	CO	17,703	LC
Adelphi Univ	NY	48,244	C
Adrian College	MI	42,400	C
Agnes Scott College	GA	51,930	VC+
Alabama A&M Univ	AL	18,796	C
Alabama State Univ	AL	14,142	NC
Albany State Univ	GA	19,462	C
Albertus Magnus College	CT	43,258	LC
Albion College	MI	52,650	C
Albright College	PA	46,660	C
Alcorn State Univ	MS	15,854	C
Alderson Broaddus Univ	WV	26,149	C
Alfred Univ	NY	42,296	C+
Allegheny College	PA	55,420	VC
Allen Univ	SC	19,300	NC
Alma College	MI	47,548	C
Alvernia Univ	PA	43,900	C
Alverno College	WI	33,294	LC
American International College	MA	46,300	LC
American Univ	DC	59,379	HC+
Amherst College	MA		HC+
Anderson Univ	IN	38,200	C
Andrews Univ	MI	28,030	C+
Angelo State Univ	TX	15,263	NC
Appalachian State Univ	NC	14,416	VC
Aquinas College	TN	30,800	C+
Aquinas College - Mich	MI	38,876	HC
Arcadia Univ	PA	33,570	C+
Arizona State Univ at the Tempe Campus	AZ	21,756	VC
Arkansas State Univ	AR	16,190	C
Arkansas Tech Univ	AR	15,484	C
Armstrong State Univ	GA	16,962	C
Asbury Univ	KY	35,180	C+
Ashland Univ	OH	21,440	C
Assumption College	MA	47,920	C+
Atlantic Union College	MA	27,228	C
Auburn Univ	AL	23,594	VC+
Auburn Univ at Montgomery	AL	15,290	C
Augsburg College	MN	43,929	C
Augusta Univ	GA	4,632	C
Augustana College	IL	49,658	VC
Augustana Univ	SD	38,424	VC
Aurora Univ	IL	33,970	C
Austin College	TX	45,875	VC
Austin Peay State Univ	TN	16,397	C
Averett Univ	VA	40,970	LC
Avila Univ	MO	35,480	C
Azusa Pacific Univ	CA	43,972	C
Baker Univ	KS	33,350	C+
Baldwin Wallace Univ	OH	41,106	C
Ball State Univ	IN	19,590	C
Bard College	NY	64,024	HC
Bard College at Simon's Rock	MA	65,795	MC
Barnard College/Columbia Univ	NY	62,741	MC
Barry Univ	FL	37,830	C
Barton College	NC	38,686	LC
Bates College	ME	64,500	MC
Baylor Univ	TX	53,760	HC
Belhaven Univ	MS	31,016	C
Bellarmine Univ	KY	51,220	C
Belmont Abbey College	NC	48,156	C
Belmont Univ	TN	40,970	VC
Beloit College	WI	55,206	HC
Bemidji State Univ	MN	16,056	VC
Benedict College	SC	28,238	NC
Benedictine College	KS	36,200	VC
Benedictine Univ	IL	38,300	C
Bennett College	NC	27,302	NC
Bennington College	VT	63,960	MC
Bentley Univ	MA	60,890	HC
Berea College	KY	7,042	C
Berry College	GA	45,286	C+
Bethany College	KS	46,100	NC
Bethany College	WV	36,300	NC
Bethel College	IN	35,860	C
Bethel College	KS	35,370	C
Bethel Univ	MN	45,270	VC
Bethel Univ	TN	24,738	C
Bethune-Cookman Univ	FL	22,970	C
Biola Univ	CA	46,402	C+
Birmingham-Southern College	AL	44,478	VC
Black Hills State Univ	SD	15,899	C
Blackburn College	IL	28,526	LC
Bloomfield College	NJ	39,100	LC
Bloomsburg Univ of Pennsylvania	PA	19,066	LC
Blue Mountain College	MS	15,949	VC
Bluefield College	VA	34,120	C+
Bluffton Univ	OH	40,950	C
Boise State Univ	ID	14,860	C
Boston College	MA	65,737	MC
Boston Univ	MA	65,110	MC
Bowdoin College	ME	63,500	MC
Bowie State Univ	MD	26,728	LC
Bowling Green State Univ	OH	19,747	C
Brandeis Univ	MA	65,925	MC
Brescia Univ	KY	29,890	VC+
Briar Cliff Univ	IA	36,956	C
Bridgewater College	VA	44,510	C
Bridgewater State Univ	MA	21,810	C
Brigham Young Univ	UT	12,748	HC
Brigham Young Univ/Hawaii	HI	11,290	C
Brown Univ	RI	64,566	MC
Bryan College	TN	31,440	C
Bryant Univ	RI	55,646	VC
Bryn Mawr College	PA	59,890	MC
Bucknell Univ	PA	64,616	MC
Buena Vista Univ	IA	41,514	C
Butler Univ	IN	51,352	VC
Cabrini Univ	PA	42,591	LC
Caldwell Univ	NJ	42,165	NC
Calif Baptist Univ	CA	41,392	C
Calif Inst of Technology	CA	58,761	MC
Calif Lutheran Univ	CA	52,853	C
Calif Polytechnic State Univ	CA	17,979	HC+
Calif State Polytechnic Univ, Pomona	CA	21,541	C
Cal State, Bakersfield	CA	19,191	LC
Cal State, Chico	CA	21,440	C
Cal State, Dominguez Hills	CA	19,022	LC
Cal State, East Bay	CA	19,413	C
Cal State, Fresno	CA	16,902	LC
Cal State, Fullerton	CA	21,902	C
Cal State, Long Beach	CA	18,850	C
Cal State, Los Angeles	CA	17,186	LC
Cal State, Monterey Bay	CA	26,871	LC
Cal State, Northridge	CA	16,859	LC
Cal State, Sacramento	CA	20,332	C
Cal State, San Bernardino	CA	12,000	C
Cal State, San Marcos	CA	24,184	LC
Cal State, Stanislaus	CA	16,212	C
Calif Univ of Pennsylvania	PA	14,217	LC
Calvin College	MI	41,570	VC+
Cameron Univ	OK	11,072	NC
Campbellsville Univ	KY	32,492	C
Canisius College	NY	47,537	C
Capital Univ	OH	42,982	C
Cardinal Stritch Univ	WI	36,462	C
Caribbean Univ	PR	15,471	
Carleton College	MN	64,071	MC
Carlow Univ	PA	38,549	LC
Carnegie Mellon Univ	PA	67,980	MC
Carroll College	MT	39,972	C+
Carroll Univ	WI	38,100	C+
Carthage College	WI	48,835	C
Case Western Reserve Univ	OH	60,304	MC
Castleton Univ	VT	20,186	C
Catawba College	NC	39,820	C
Cedar Crest College	PA	46,715	C
Cedarville Univ	OH	34,990	VC
Centenary College	NJ	43,602	C
Centenary College of Louisiana	LA	45,650	C+
Central College	IA	44,592	C
Central Conn State Univ	CT	21,203	C
Central Methodist Univ	MO	36,830	VC
Central Mich Univ	MI	20,330	C
Central State Univ	OH	18,564	C
Central Washington Univ	WA	16,803	C
Centre College	KY	49,250	HC
Chadron State College	NE	14,819	NC
Chapman Univ	CA	63,078	VC+
Charleston Southern Univ	SC	32,400	C
Chatham Univ	PA	46,517	C
Chestnut Hill College	PA	43,410	C
Cheyney Univ of Pennsylvania	PA	20,896	LC
Chicago State Univ	IL	20,144	C
Christian Brothers Univ	TN	31,670	VC
Christopher Newport Univ	VA	23,968	VC+
CUNY/Baruch College	NY	21,609	HC
CUNY/Brooklyn College	NY	5,884	C+
CUNY/City College	NY	20,319	VC
CUNY/College of Staten Island	NY	17,840	NC
CUNY/Hunter College	NY	31,098	VC
CUNY/Lehman College	NY	5,778	HC+
CUNY/Meger Evers College	NY	6,680	NC
CUNY/Queens College	NY	27,896	C
CUNY/York College	NY	6,747	LC
Claflin Univ	SC	33,764	LC
Claremont McKenna College	CA	67,185	MC
Clarion Univ of Pennsylvania	PA	21,608	LC
Clark Atlanta Univ	GA	31,019	LC
Clark Univ	MA	51,600	HC+
Clarke Univ	IA	38,940	C
Clarkson Univ	NY	60,392	HC
Clayton State Univ	GA	19,735	C
Clemson Univ	SC		HC
Cleveland State Univ	OH	22,196	C
Coastal Carolina Univ	SC	19,766	C
Coe College	IA	51,570	VC
Coker College	SC	34,810	LC
Colby College	ME	64,060	MC
Colgate Univ	NY	65,030	MC
College of Charleston	SC	22,699	C
College of Mount St. Vincent	NY	45,620	C
College of St. Benedict	MN	52,806	C
College of St. Elizabeth	NJ	44,432	LC
College of St. Mary	NE	35,184	C
College of St. Scholastica	MN	44,640	C
College of the Holy Cross	MA	62,165	MC
College of the Ozarks	MO	7,230	C
College of William & Mary	VA		MC
Colo College	CO	62,560	MC
Colo Mesa Univ	CO	18,955	LC
Colo School of Mines	CO	29,319	MC
Colo State Univ	CO	22,162	VC
Colo State Univ-Pueblo	CO	18,234	C
Columbia College	SC	36,550	C
Columbia College - Missouri	MO	27,803	C
Columbia Univ/ School of General Studies	NY	61,470	MC
Columbia Univ/City of New York	NY	62,958	MC
Columbus State Univ	GA	14,336	LC
Concord Univ	WV	14,954	C
Concordia College - Moorhead	MN	51,088	C+
Concordia College - New York	NY	39,035	LC
Concordia Univ	CA	41,580	VC
Concordia Univ Nebr	NE	36,280	VC
Concordia Univ St. Paul	MN	29,050	C
Concordia Univ Wisc	WI	35,910	C
Concordia Univ, Ann Arbor	MI	35,945	VC
Concordia Univ, Chicago	IL	39,694	C
Conn College	CT	65,000	MC
Converse College	SC	26,495	C
Coppin State Univ	MD	17,041	VC
Corban Univ	OR	40,306	C
Cornell College	IA	48,800	VC
Cornell Univ	NY	64,853	MC
Covenant College	GA	38,990	VC
Creighton Univ	NE	48,206	VC+
Culver-Stockton College	MO	33,525	C
Cumberland Univ	TN	27,710	C
Daemen College	NY	38,045	C
Dakota State Univ	SD	13,811	C
Dakota Wesleyan Univ	SD	32,850	C
Dallas Baptist Univ	TX	33,713	C
Dartmouth College	NH	66,174	MC
Davidson College	NC	60,119	MC
Davis & Elkins College	WV	38,242	LC
Defiance College	OH	41,630	C
Delaware State Univ	DE	19,376	NC
Delta State Univ	MS	13,176	C
Denison Univ	OH	58,860	MC
DePaul Univ	IL	47,623	VC
DePauw Univ	IN	58,688	HC+
DeSales Univ	PA	43,970	C
Dickinson College	PA	63,974	MC
Dickinson State Univ	ND	12,372	LC
Doane Univ	NE	39,184	VC
Dominican College	NY	31,270	LC
Dominican Univ	IL	41,222	C
Dordt College	IA	37,860	C+
Drake Univ	IA	45,056	HC
Drew Univ/College of Liberal Arts	NJ	61,048	VC
Drexel Univ	PA	65,432	VC+
Drury Univ	MO	33,791	VC
Duke Univ	NC	64,188	
Duquesne Univ	PA	46,822	VC
D'Youville College	NY	36,780	C
Earlham College	IN	54,870	HC
East Carolina Univ	NC	16,937	C
East Central Univ	OK	13,056	C

ST = STATE $IS = IN-STATE COSTS SR = SELECTOR RATING

School	ST	$IS	SR
East Stroudsburg Univ	PA	18,334	C
East Tenn State Univ	TN	13,994	C
East Texas Baptist Univ	TX	33,134	C
Eastern Conn State Univ	CT	23,059	C
Eastern Illinois Univ	IL	21,126	C
Eastern Kentucky Univ	KY	16,908	C
Eastern Mennonite Univ	VA	42,550	C
Eastern Mich Univ	MI	19,761	C
Eastern Nazarene College	MA	39,955	C
Eastern New Mexico Univ	NM	14,416	C
Eastern Oregon Univ	OR	17,715	C
Eastern Univ	PA	39,540	C
Eastern Washington Univ	WA	25,572	LC
Eckerd College	FL	52,874	C
Edgewood College	WI	35,950	C
Edinboro Univ	PA	15,940	LC
Edward Waters College	FL	20,607	NC
Elizabeth City State Univ	NC	14,745	C
Elizabethtown College	PA	54,050	C
Elmhurst College	IL	45,428	C
Elmira College	NY	53,900	C
Elms College	MA	45,646	VC
Elon Univ	NC	44,599	VC+
Emmanuel College	MA	52,110	C+
Emory and Henry College	VA	41,410	C
Emory Univ	GA	60,786	MC
Emporia State Univ	KS	14,570	C
Endicott College	MA	44,604	VC+
Erskine College	SC	45,460	C
Eureka College	IL	30,220	C
Evangel Univ	MO	28,898	C
Excelsior College	NY	14,080	SP
Fairfield Univ	CT	59,860	VC+
Fairleigh Dickinson Univ/ College at Florham	NJ	52,062	C
Fairleigh Dickinson Univ/ Metropolitan Campus	NJ	40,254	C
Fairmont State Univ	WV	15,726	C
Faulkner Univ	AL	26,410	C
Fayetteville State Univ	NC	17,756	C
Felician Univ	NJ	45,370	LC
Ferrum College	VA	39,650	C
Fisk Univ	TN	32,066	LC
Fitchburg State Univ	MA	21,819	C
Florida A&M Univ	FL	15,361	C
Florida Atlantic Univ	FL	17,339	C
Florida Gulf Coast Univ	FL	9,682	C
Florida Inst of Technology	FL	53,306	VC
Florida International Univ	FL	19,854	C+
Florida Memorial Univ	FL	22,270	LC
Florida State Univ	FL	16,771	HC
Fontbonne Univ	MO	33,717	C
Fordham Univ	NY	65,918	MC
Fort Hays State Univ	KS	12,131	C
Fort Lewis College	CO	18,980	C
Fort Valley State Univ	GA	17,988	VC
Framingham State Univ	MA	20,584	C
Francis Marion Univ	SC	16,464	LC
Franciscan Univ of Steubenville	OH	33,980	VC
Franklin and Marshall College	PA	63,170	HC
Franklin College	IN	39,380	C
Franklin Pierce Univ	NH	46,750	C
Freed-Hardeman Univ	TN	29,450	C
Fresno Pacific Univ	CA	37,370	C
Friends Univ	KS	34,455	C
Frostburg State Univ	MD	17,280	LC
Furman Univ	SC	58,092	VC+
Gallaudet Univ	DC	29,118	LC
Gannon Univ	PA	42,032	C
Gardner-Webb Univ	NC	39,200	C+
George Fox Univ	OR	42,938	C
George Mason Univ	VA	15,724	VC
George Washington Univ	DC	62,835	MC
Georgetown College	KY	41,440	C
Georgetown Univ	DC	65,926	MC
Georgia College & State Univ	GA	21,148	C+
Georgia Inst of Technology	GA	23,360	MC
Georgia Southwestern State Univ	GA	13,870	C
Georgia State Univ	GA	24,332	VC
Georgian Court Univ	NJ	42,426	LC
Gettysburg College	PA	63,000	HC
Gonzaga Univ	WA	50,888	HC
Gordon College	MA	46,472	C+
Goshen College	IN	42,500	C
Goucher College	MD	55,716	VC
Grace College and Seminary	IN	31,524	C
Graceland Univ	IA	35,290	C
Grambling State Univ	LA	15,701	C
Grand Valley State Univ	MI	22,250	C+
Grand View Univ	IA	32,302	C
Greensboro College	NC	42,400	LC
Greenville College	IL	27,012	C
Grinnell College	IA	60,738	MC
Grove City College	PA	25,692	VC
Guilford College	NC	44,090	C
Gustavus Adolphus College	MN	52,433	HC
Gwynedd Mercy Univ	PA	43,780	LC
Hamilton College	NY	64,250	MC
Hamline Univ	MN	45,678	VC
Hampden-Sydney College	VA	56,248	C+
Hampshire College	MA	63,824	MC
Hampton Univ	VA	34,926	LC
Hannibal-LaGrange Univ	MO	29,815	C
Hanover College	IN	46,364	C+
Harding Univ	AR	25,421	C
Hardin-Simmons Univ	TX	33,966	C
Harris-Stowe State Univ	MO	14,360	NC
Hartwick College	NY	51,270	C
Harvard College/Harvard Univ	MA	60,659	MC
Harvey Mudd College	CA	67,155	MC
Hastings College	NE	35,380	C+
Haverford College	PA	66,490	MC
Hawaii Pacific Univ	HI	33,420	C
Heidelberg Univ	OH	39,200	C
Henderson State Univ	AR	15,516	LC
Hendrix College	AR	54,020	VC+
Heritage Univ	WA	19,825	NC
High Point Univ	NC	45,977	C
Hillsdale College	MI	35,722	MC
Hiram College	OH	43,230	C
Hofstra Univ	NY	55,960	C+
Hollins Univ	VA	49,635	VC
Holy Family Univ	PA	43,326	LC
Hood College	MD	54,840	C
Hope College	MI	39,940	VC
Houghton College	NY	39,090	C
Houston Baptist Univ	TX	36,450	C
Howard Payne Univ	TX	34,320	C
Howard Univ	DC	37,616	C+
Humboldt State Univ	CA	20,514	C
Huntingdon College	AL	34,900	C
Huntington Univ	IN	33,996	C
Huston-Tillotson Univ	TX	18,124	LC
Idaho State Univ	ID	13,619	NC
Illinois College	IL	40,850	VC
Illinois State Univ	IL	23,418	VC
Indiana State Univ	IN	23,223	LC
Indiana Univ Bloomington	IN	20,429	VC
Indiana Univ East	IN	7,072	C
Indiana Univ Kokomo	IN	7,073	C
Indiana Univ Northwest	IN	7,072	C
Indiana Univ of Pennsylvania	PA	23,614	LC
Indiana Univ South Bend	IN	14,242	C
Indiana Univ Southeast	IN	14,242	LC
Indiana Univ-Purdue Univ Fort Wayne	IN	17,553	C
Indiana Univ-Purdue Univ Indianapolis	IN	18,635	C
Indiana Wesleyan Univ	IN	33,674	C
Inter-American Univ of PR Ponce	PR	19,549	
Inter-American Univ of PR-Bayamon	PR	18,785	
Inter-American Univ of PR-Fajardo Campus	PR	18,336	
Inter-American Univ of PR-Metropolitan Campus	PR	20,045	
Inter-American Univ of PR-San Germán	PR	20,042	
Iona College	NY	50,984	C
Iowa State Univ	IA	17,570	C
Ithaca College	NY	56,766	VC
Jackson State Univ	MS	15,879	LC
Jacksonville State Univ	AL	14,628	LC
Jacksonville Univ	FL	46,230	C
James Madison Univ	VA	19,084	VC
Jarvis Christian College	TX	20,160	NC
John Brown Univ	AR	33,132	VC
John Carroll Univ	OH	49,740	C+
Johns Hopkins Univ	MD	65,386	MC
Johnson C. Smith Univ	NC	25,336	LC
Johnson State College	VT	20,752	C
Judson College	AL	27,066	C
Judson Univ	IL	37,700	C
Juniata College	PA	53,760	VC
Kalamazoo College	MI	53,931	HC+
Kansas State Univ	KS	17,780	VC
Kansas Wesleyan Univ	KS	36,600	C
Kean Univ	NJ	24,650	C
Keene State College	NH	24,003	LC
Kennesaw State Univ	GA	19,592	VC
Kent State Univ	OH	20,732	C
Kentucky State Univ	KY	13,364	LC
Kenyon College	OH	63,330	MC
Keuka College	NY	39,762	C
King Univ	TN	34,660	C
King's College	PA	46,858	C
Knox College	IL	52,615	VC+
Kutztown Univ of Pennsylvania	PA	19,056	LC
La Roche College	PA	37,924	LC
La Salle Univ	PA	55,790	C
La Sierra Univ	CA	39,690	VC
Lafayette College	PA	63,355	MC
LaGrange College	GA	39,930	C
Lake Erie College	OH	38,914	LC
Lake Forest College	IL	50,652	VC
Lakeland Univ	WI	35,130	C
Lamar Univ	TX	18,014	LC
Lander Univ	SC	43,994	C
Lane College	TN	16,550	C
Langston Univ	OK	14,314	C
Lawrence Tech Univ	MI	39,770	VC
Lawrence Univ	WI	54,498	HC
Le Moyne College	NY	46,000	C
Lebanon Valley College	PA	51,530	C
Lee Univ	TN	22,045	C
Lees-McRae College	NC	33,944	C
Lehigh Univ	PA	61,010	MC
LeMoyne-Owen College	TN	16,980	C
Lenoir-Rhyne Univ	NC	43,200	C
LeTourneau Univ	TX	38,250	VC
Lewis & Clark College	OR	58,434	HC+
Lewis Univ	IL	40,370	C
Lewis-Clark State College	ID	14,202	C
Liberty Univ	VA	19,101	C
Limestone College	SC	32,100	C
Lincoln Memorial Univ	TN	28,070	C
Lincoln Univ	MO	13,602	NC
Lindenwood Univ	MO	25,132	C
Lindsey Wilson College	KY	32,882	C
Linfield College	OR	52,010	C
Lipscomb Univ	TN	41,296	VC
LIU Brooklyn	NY	49,682	C
LIU Post	NY	49,682	C
Livingstone College	NC	17,815	LC
Lock Haven Univ of Pennsylvania	PA	18,028	LC
Longwood Univ	VA	22,184	C
Loras College	IA	39,222	C
Louisiana College	LA	21,886	C
Louisiana State Univ and A&M College	LA	18,677	VC
Louisiana State Univ in Shreveport	LA	6,902	C
Louisiana Tech Univ	LA	11,422	VC
Loyola Marymount Univ	CA	58,038	HC
Loyola Univ Chicago	IL	55,802	VC
Loyola Univ Maryland	MD	60,300	VC
Loyola Univ New Orleans	LA	51,708	VC+
Lubbock Christian Univ	TX	28,426	C
Luther College	IA	48,540	C+
Lycoming College	PA	48,580	C
Lynchburg College	VA	46,740	C
Lyndon State College	VT	20,714	C
Lyon College	AR	34,730	C+
Macalester College	MN	61,905	MC
MacMurray College	IL	33,620	C
Madonna Univ	MI	29,050	C
Maharishi Univ of Management	IA	34,930	VC
Malone Univ	OH	38,448	C
Manchester Univ	IN	40,422	C
Manhattan College	NY	51,750	C+
Manhattanville College	NY	51,440	C+
Mansfield Univ	PA	23,376	LC
Marian Univ	IN	41,220	C
Marian Univ	WI	32,420	LC
Marietta College	OH	46,190	C
Marist College	NY	49,860	VC
Marquette Univ	WI	48,390	VC+
Mars Hill Univ	NC	42,688	C
Marshall Univ	WV	17,242	C
Martin Univ	IN	20,264	LC
Mary Baldwin Univ	VA	39,865	C
Marygrove College	MI	28,926	NC
Marymount Univ	VA	41,570	LC
Maryville College	TN	44,410	C
Maryville Univ of St. Louis	MO	38,046	VC+
Marywood Univ	PA	46,900	C
Mass College of Liberal Arts	MA	20,128	C
Mass Inst of Technology	MA	62,662	MC
Mayville State Univ	ND	18,371	NC
McDaniel College	MD	51,380	VC
McKendree Univ	IL	37,940	C+
McMurry Univ	TX	34,259	LC
McNeese State Univ	LA	7,838	C
McPherson College	KS	34,909	C
Mercer Univ	GA	45,348	VC
Mercy College	NY	31,776	C
Mercyhurst Univ	PA	47,420	C
Meredith College	NC	45,297	C
Merrimack College	MA	52,770	C
Messiah College	PA	43,100	C+
Methodist Univ	NC	43,600	C
Metropolitan State Univ of Denver	CO	29,889	LC
Miami Univ	OH	27,190	HC+
Mich State Univ	MI	23,898	VC+
Mich Tech Univ	MI	24,739	VC+
MidAmerica Nazarene Univ	KS	35,550	C
Middle Tenn State Univ	TN	8,650	C
Middlebury College	VT	64,332	MC
Midland Univ	NE	37,468	
Midway Univ	KY	31,640	LC
Midwestern State Univ	TX	17,572	C
Miles College	AL	18,646	NC
Millersville Univ of Pennsylvania	PA	23,782	C
Milligan College	TN	38,150	C
Millikin Univ	IL	42,158	C
Mills College	CA	59,163	VC
Millsaps College	MS	50,080	C+
Minn State Univ, Mankato	MN	15,616	C
Minn State Univ, Moorhead	MN	15,941	C
Minot State Univ	ND	12,732	C
Misericordia Univ	PA	43,840	C
Miss College	MS	25,850	C
Miss State Univ	MS	11,454	C+
Miss Univ for Women	MS	17,065	C
Miss Valley State Univ	MS	13,233	LC
Missouri Baptist Univ	MO	35,594	C
Missouri Southern State Univ	MO	12,499	C
Missouri State Univ	MO	15,190	C+
Missouri Univ of Science and Technology	MO	18,655	HC
Missouri Valley College	MO	28,150	C
Missouri Western State Univ	MO	16,741	
Molloy College	NY	40,440	C
Monmouth College	IL	42,260	C
Monmouth Univ	NJ	46,234	C
Montana State Univ	MT	15,500	C+
Montana State Univ-Billings	MT	22,960	C
Montana Tech of the Univ of Montana	MT	15,447	C+
Montclair State Univ	NJ	26,210	LC
Moravian College	PA	53,117	
Morehead State Univ	KY	17,422	C
Morehouse College	GA	40,064	C
Morgan State Univ	MD	17,190	LC
Morningside College	IA	36,865	C
Morris College	SC	18,500	LC
Mount Holyoke College	MA	56,746	MC
Mount Marty College	SD	32,972	C
Mount Mary Univ	WI	34,650	LC
Mount Mercy Univ	IA	36,826	C
Mount St. Mary College	NY	42,061	C
Mount St. Joseph Univ	OH	33,880	C
Mount St. Mary's Univ	MD	51,610	C
Mount St. Mary's Univ - Chalon Campus	CA	43,897	VC+
Mount Vernon Nazarene Univ	OH	34,500	C
Muhlenberg College	PA	56,645	VC+
Murray State Univ	KY	16,998	C
Muskingum Univ	OH	35,966	C
National Louis Univ	IL	16,920	LC
National Univ	CA	14,730	LC
Nazareth College	NY	45,574	C
Nebr Wesleyan Univ	NE	38,140	C+
New College of Florida	FL	15,848	MC
New Jersey City Univ	NJ	21,456	LC
New Jersey Inst of Technology	NJ	29,569	VC
New Mexico Highlands Univ	NM	11,904	NC
New Mexico Inst of Mining and Technology	NM	14,833	HC
New Mexico State Univ	NM	14,050	C
New York Univ	NY	65,860	MC
Newberry College	SC	34,550	C
Newman Univ	KS	35,390	C
Niagara Univ	NY	41,010	C
Nicholls State Univ	LA	10,534	C
Nichols College	MA	46,800	LC
Norfolk State Univ	VA	25,702	LC
N Car A&T State Univ	NC	13,365	LC
N Car Central Univ	NC	9,000	C
N Car State Univ	NC	19,515	HC+
N Car Wesleyan College	NC	39,200	C
North Central College	IL	48,712	VC
N Dak State Univ	ND	16,245	C
North Greenville Univ	SC	25,930	C+
North Park Univ	IL	35,860	C
Northeastern Illinois Univ	IL	12,529	LC
Northeastern State Univ	OK	8,615	VC
Northeastern Univ	MA	62,703	MC
Northern Arizona Univ	AZ	20,246	VC
Northern Illinois Univ	IL	20,176	C
Northern Kentucky Univ	KY	16,486	C
Northern Mich Univ	MI	19,604	C
Northern State Univ	SD	14,505	C
Northland College	WI	41,103	C+
Northwest Missouri State Univ	MO	17,737	C
Northwest Nazarene Univ	ID	36,000	C
Northwestern College of Iowa	IA	38,400	C+
Northwestern Okla State Univ	OK	13,072	NC
Northwestern Univ	IL	66,344	MC
Norwich Univ	VT	28,212	C
Notre Dame College	OH	37,150	VC
Notre Dame of Maryland Univ	MD	46,465	VC
Nova Southeastern Univ	FL	38,534	C+
Nyack College	NY	34,050	NC
Oakland City Univ	IN	33,360	NC
Oakland Univ	MI	20,763	C
Oakwood Univ	AL	43,758	C
Oberlin College	OH	66,012	MC
Occidental College	CA	65,530	MC
Oglala Lakota College	SD	15,050	NC
Oglethorpe Univ	GA	44,200	C+
Ohio Dominican Univ	OH	41,340	C+
Ohio Northern Univ	OH	44,050	VC
Ohio State Univ at Columbus	OH	21,703	HC+
Ohio Univ	OH	22,924	C
Ohio Valley Univ	WV	29,480	C
Ohio Wesleyan Univ	OH	49,460	VC
Okla Baptist Univ	OK	32,320	C
Okla Christian Univ	OK	27,650	VC
Okla City Univ	OK	40,476	VC
Okla Panhandle State Univ	OK	6,152	NC
Okla State Univ	OK	17,180	VC
Okla Wesleyan Univ	OK	33,206	C
Old Dominion Univ	VA	20,910	C
Olivet College	MI	36,110	LC
Olivet Nazarene Univ	IL	41,840	C
Oral Roberts Univ	OK	34,316	C
Oregon State Univ	OR	22,519	VC
Ottawa Univ	KS	36,074	VC
Otterbein Univ	OH	41,630	C
Ouachita Baptist Univ	AR	32,320	C
Our Lady of the Lake Univ	TX	35,012	LC
Pace Univ	NY	58,248	C
Pacific Lutheran Univ	WA	49,960	VC
Pacific Union College	CA	36,009	VC
Pacific Univ	OR	52,876	C
Paine College	GA	19,506	LC
Palm Beach Atlantic Univ	FL	39,720	C
Park Univ	MO	20,329	C
Penn State Erie/The Behrend College	PA	16,256	C

ST = STATE $IS = IN-STATE COSTS SR = SELECTOR RATING

School	ST	$IS	SR
Penn State Univ/Altoona	PA	24,584	C
Pennsylvania State Univ - Univ Park	PA	29,760	HC
Pepperdine Univ	CA	74,460	HC+
Peru State College	NE	14,768	NC
Pfeiffer Univ	NC	39,695	LC
Philander Smith College	AR	20,814	LC
Piedmont College	GA	32,512	C
Pittsburg State Univ	KS	13,880	NC
Pitzer College	CA	66,192	MC
Plymouth State Univ	NH	23,180	LC
Point Loma Nazarene Univ	CA	43,450	C
Pomona College	CA	64,957	MC
Pontifical Catholic Univ of PR	PR	10,534	
Portland State Univ	OR	19,443	C
Prairie View A&M Univ	TX	15,205	LC
Prescott College	AZ	33,284	C
Princeton Univ	NJ	57,610	MC
Principia College	IL	39,010	C+
Providence College	RI	60,760	VC
Purdue Univ/Northwest	IN	15,038	C
Purdue Univ/West Lafayette	IN	20,032	MC
Queens Univ of Charlotte	NC	39,543	C
Quincy Univ	IL	36,998	C
Quinnipiac Univ	CT	59,110	C
Radford Univ	VA	19,027	LC
Ramapo College of New Jersey	NJ	25,338	C
Randolph College	VA	45,660	VC
Randolph-Macon College	VA	49,910	C
Reed College	OR	65,300	MC
Regis Univ	CO	44,520	C
Rensselaer Polytechnic Inst	NY	63,436	MC
Rhode Island College	RI	17,694	LC
Rhodes College	TN	51,900	HC
Rice Univ	TX	57,668	MC
Rider Univ	NJ	54,050	C
Ripon College	WI	46,911	C+
Rivier Univ	NH	40,410	VC
Roanoke College	VA	54,114	VC
Roberts Wesleyan College	NY	38,306	C
Rochester Inst of Technology	NY	50,842	HC
Rockford Univ	IL	36,030	C
Rockhurst Univ	MO	29,220	C
Rocky Mountain College	MT	34,270	C
Roger Williams Univ	RI	46,296	C+
Rollins College	FL	58,670	HC
Roosevelt Univ	IL	40,651	VC
Rose-Hulman Inst of Technology	IN	57,303	MC
Rosemont College	PA	30,980	C
Rowan Univ	NJ	24,491	VC+
Russell Sage College	NY	39,370	C
Rust College	MS	10,600	C
Rutgers Univ - Camden	NJ	26,146	C
Rutgers Univ - New Brunswick	NJ	26,632	HC
Rutgers Univ - Newark	NJ	27,288	C
Sacred Heart Univ	CT	52,750	C
Saginaw Valley State Univ	MI	18,530	C
St. Anselm College	NH	52,560	C+
St. Augustine's Univ	NC	26,048	C
St. Francis Univ	PA	42,268	NC
St. John's Univ	MN	51,624	C
St. Joseph's College of Maine	ME	46,485	C
St. Joseph's Univ	PA	57,544	VC+
St. Leo Univ	FL	31,650	C
St. Louis Univ	MO	49,866	HC
St. Martin's Univ	WA	45,056	C
St. Mary-of-the-Woods College	IN	39,632	LC
St. Mary's College	IN	50,600	C
St. Mary's College of Calif	CA	57,420	C
St. Mary's Univ of Minn	MN	41,210	VC
St. Michael's College	VT	51,725	VC+
St. Peter's Univ	NJ	49,192	C
St. Vincent College	PA	44,626	C
St. Xavier Univ	IL	43,310	C
Salem College	NC	37,694	HC
Salem State Univ	MA	17,303	LC
Salisbury Univ	MD	20,714	VC
Salve Regina Univ	RI	51,470	C
Sam Houston State Univ	TX	18,792	C
Samford Univ	AL	39,232	VC
San Diego Christian College	CA	39,068	C
San Diego State Univ	CA	21,896	C+
San Francisco State Univ	CA	18,514	LC
San Jose State Univ	CA	21,540	C
Sarah Lawrence College	NY	63,388	HC
Savannah State Univ	GA	15,631	C
Schreiner Univ	TX	34,626	LC
Scripps College	CA	66,664	MC
Seattle Pacific Univ	WA	47,439	C+
Seattle Univ	WA	50,811	VC+
Seton Hall Univ	NJ	55,514	C
Seton Hill Univ	PA	46,972	C
Sewanee: The Univ of the South	TN	54,500	MC
Shaw Univ	NC	24,638	C
Shenandoah Univ	VA	41,312	C
Shepherd Univ, West Virginia	WV	17,224	C
Shippensburg Univ of Pennsylvania	PA	23,208	C
Shorter Univ	GA	31,130	LC
Siena College	NY	48,916	C+
Siena Heights Univ	MI	32,040	C
Silver Lake College of the Holy Family	WI	36,290	LC
Simmons College	MA	53,090	VC
Simpson College	IA	43,839	VC
Simpson Univ	CA	33,700	C
Skidmore College	NY	64,214	HC
Slippery Rock Univ of Pennsylvania	PA	10,360	C
Smith College	MA	63,914	MC
Sonoma State Univ	CA	27,806	C
S Car State Univ	SC	20,805	LC
S Dak School of Mines and Technology	SD	18,645	VC
S Dak State Univ	SD	15,634	C
Southeast Missouri State Univ	MO	15,498	C
Southeastern Louisiana Univ	LA	16,237	C
Southeastern Okla State Univ	OK	11,875	C
Southeastern Univ	FL	31,765	C
Southern Adventist Univ	TN	27,600	C
Southern Arkansas Univ	AR	21,532	C
Southern Conn State Univ	CT	21,924	LC
Southern Illinois Univ Carbondale	IL	23,667	C
Southern Illinois Univ Edwardsville	IL	22,643	C
Southern Methodist Univ	TX	66,483	MC
Southern Nazarene Univ	OK	32,798	NC
Southern Oregon Univ	OR	19,117	C
Southern Univ and A&M College	LA	16,074	LC+
Southern Univ at New Orleans	LA	8,014	LC
Southern Wesleyan Univ	SC	32,130	LC
Southwest Baptist Univ	MO	29,900	LC
Southwest Minn State Univ	MN	17,783	C
Southwestern Adventist Univ	TX	27,756	LC
Southwestern College	KS	31,531	C
Southwestern Okla State Univ	OK	11,790	C
Southwestern Univ	TX	50,720	VC
Spelman College	GA	38,751	C
Spring Arbor Univ	MI	36,000	C
Spring Hill College	AL	48,488	C
Springfield College	MA	45,995	C
St. Ambrose Univ	IA	39,019	C
St. Ambrose Univ	IA	39,019	C
St. Bonaventure Univ	NY	44,237	C
St. Catherine Univ	MN	45,630	VC
St. Cloud State Univ	MN	10,600	C
St. Edward's Univ	TX	53,100	VC
St. Francis College	NY	38,800	LC
St. John Fisher College	NY	43,620	C
St. John's College, Santa Fe	NM	60,109	HC+
St. John's College-Annapolis	MD	60,142	MC
St. John's Univ	NY	55,850	C
St. Joseph's College, New York/Brooklyn Campus	NY	25,114	LC
St. Joseph's College, New York/Long Island Campus	NY	25,124	C
St. Lawrence Univ	NY	64,390	VC
St. Mary's College of Maryland	MD	26,634	VC
St. Mary's Univ	TX	37,500	C
St. Norbert College	WI	44,525	VC
St. Olaf College	MN	54,260	HC+
St. Thomas Aquinas College	NY	42,200	C
Stanford Univ	CA	60,409	MC
SUNY / Buffalo State College	NY	20,842	C
SUNY / Empire State College	NY	9,145	SP
SUNY / SUNY College at Old Westbury	NY	16,860	C
SUNY / SUNY Cortland	NY	20,706	VC
SUNY / SUNY Fredonia	NY	20,818	C
SUNY / SUNY Oneonta	NY	19,712	C+
SUNY / SUNY Plattsburgh	NY	18,814	C
SUNY / SUNY Potsdam	NY	20,404	C+
SUNY / Univ at Buffalo	NY	23,122	C+
SUNY at Binghamton	NY	22,861	MC
SUNY at Geneseo	NY	20,440	VC+
SUNY at New Paltz	NY	19,200	C
SUNY at Oswego	NY	21,351	C
SUNY at Purchase	NY	17,900	C
SUNY SUNY Albany	NY	22,165	C
Stephen F. Austin State Univ	TX	18,406	LC
Sterling College	KS	32,830	C
Stetson Univ	FL	53,544	VC
Stevens Inst of Technology	NJ	62,338	MC
Stevenson Univ	MD	72,770	C
Stillman College	AL	20,738	C
Stockton Univ	NJ	25,059	
Stonehill College	MA	55,030	C+
Stony Brook Univ/The SUNY	NY	21,881	MC
Suffolk Univ	MA	50,308	C
Sul Ross State Univ	TX	15,021	LC
Susquehanna Univ	PA	55,340	VC
Swarthmore College	PA	63,550	MC
Syracuse Univ	NY	60,239	VC
Tabor College	KS	35,870	C
Talladega College	AL	19,215	C
Tarleton State Univ	TX	15,248	LC
Taylor Univ	IN	40,317	C+
Temple Univ	PA	24,392	VC
Tenn State Univ	TN	14,423	C
Tenn Tech Univ	TN	17,050	C
Texas A&M Univ	TX	20,521	VC+
Texas A&M Univ at Commerce	TX	10,496	C
Texas A&M Univ at Corpus Christi	TX	16,851	LC
Texas A&M Univ at Kingsville	TX	7,500	LC
Texas Christian Univ	TX	54,670	HC
Texas Lutheran Univ	TX	38,620	C
Texas Southern Univ	TX	18,212	LC
Texas State Univ	TX	19,350	C
Texas Tech Univ	TX	18,736	C+
Texas Woman's Univ	TX	15,302	LC
The Catholic Univ of America	DC	56,356	VC
The Citadel, The Military College of S Car	SC	35,339	C
The College at Brockport - SUNY	NY	20,346	C
The College of Idaho	ID	36,415	C
The College of New Jersey	NJ	31,909	HC
The College of New Rochelle	NY	46,300	VC
The College of St. Rose	NY	43,048	C
The College of Wooster	OH	57,900	VC+
The Evergreen State College	WA	16,599	C
The Lincoln Univ	PA	15,154	NC
The Master's Univ	CA	43,870	C+
The Univ of Akron	OH	21,477	C
The Univ of Tenn at Chattanooga	TN	16,744	C
The Univ of Tenn at Knoxville	TN	22,112	VC
The Univ of Tenn at Martin	TN	14,876	C
The Univ of Utah	UT	17,924	VC
The Univ of Virginia's College at Wise	VA	18,192	LC
Thiel College	PA	41,590	C
Thomas Edison State Univ	NJ	6,350	NC
Thomas More College	KY	36,720	C
Tougaloo College	MS	17,980	NC
Touro College	NY	28,950	VC
Towson Univ	MD	17,408	VC
Transylvania Univ	KY	45,690	VC+
Trevecca Nazarene Univ	TN	31,186	C
Trine Univ	IN	41,310	C
Trinity Christian College	IL	35,580	C
Trinity College	CT	63,920	HC+
Trinity International Univ	IL	31,070	VC
Trinity Univ	TX	52,314	HC+
Trinity Washington Univ	DC	33,826	C+
Troy Univ	AL	16,171	C
Truman State Univ	MO	16,014	HC
Tufts Univ	MA		MC
Tulane Univ	LA	63,396	HC+
Tusculum College	TN	31,625	C
Tuskegee Univ	AL	28,164	C
Union College	KY	32,310	C
Union College	NE	23,270	C
Union College	NY	64,320	MC
Union Univ	TN	33,970	VC
United States Air Force Academy	CO		C
United States Military Academy at West Point	NY		HC+
United States Naval Academy	MD		MC
Universidad del Turabo	PR	17,828	
Univ of Alabama	AL	24,320	C+
Univ of Alabama at Birmingham	AL	19,906	C
Univ of Alabama in Huntsville	AL	19,445	VC
Univ of Alaska Anchorage	AK	16,652	NC
Univ of Alaska Fairbanks	AK	16,179	C
Univ of Alaska Southeast	AK	11,493	C
Univ of Arizona	AZ	23,100	C
Univ of Arkansas at Fayetteville	AR	19,152	C+
Univ of Arkansas at Little Rock	AR	18,211	C
Univ of Arkansas at Monticello	AR	13,134	NC
Univ of Arkansas at Pine Bluff	AR	13,541	C
Univ of Bridgeport	CT	44,430	LC
Univ of Calif at Berkeley	CA	28,853	MC
Univ of Calif at Davis	CA	28,468	HC
Univ of Calif at Irvine	CA	26,484	VC
Univ of Calif at Los Angeles	CA	30,162	MC
Univ of Calif at Riverside	CA	29,227	C+
Univ of Calif at Santa Barbara	CA	29,091	HC
Univ of Calif San Diego	CA	30,150	MC
Univ of Calif, Santa Cruz	CA	28,731	C+
Univ of Central Arkansas	AR	14,472	VC
Univ of Central Florida	FL	15,922	VC
Univ of Central Missouri	MO	18,982	C
Univ of Central Okla	OK	13,486	C
Univ of Chicago	IL	67,584	MC
Univ of Cincinnati	OH	21,964	VC
Univ of Colo Boulder	CO	24,285	VC+
Univ of Colo Colo Springs	CO	19,663	C
Univ of Colo Denver	CO	23,230	C
Univ of Conn	CT	25,538	HC
Univ of Dallas	TX	45,500	VC+
Univ of Dayton	OH	53,620	C
Univ of Delaware	DE	24,976	VC+
Univ of Denver	CO	58,443	VC+
Univ of Detroit Mercy	MI	48,816	C+
Univ of Evansville	IN	44,186	VC+
Univ of Findlay	OH	60,139	C
Univ of Florida	FL	16,291	HC+
Univ of Georgia	GA	21,250	HC
Univ of Great Falls	MT	38,524	C
Univ of Hartford	CT	49,776	C
Univ of Hawaii at Hilo	HI	18,038	C
Univ of Hawaii at Manoa	HI	23,221	C
Univ of Houston	TX	21,483	VC
Univ of Houston-Downtown	TX	7,241	C
Univ of Idaho	ID	15,348	C
Univ of Illinois at Chicago	IL	25,006	VC
Univ of Illinois at Urbana-Champaign	IL	27,006	HC
Univ of Indianapolis	IN	36,480	C
Univ of Iowa	IA	18,683	VC+
Univ of Jamestown	ND	28,508	C
Univ of Kansas	KS	20,135	C+
Univ of Kentucky	KY	33,306	C
Univ of La Verne	CA	55,600	C
Univ of Louisiana at Lafayette	LA	14,516	C
Univ of Louisiana at Monroe	LA	15,970	C
Univ of Louisville	KY	19,824	C
Univ of Maine	ME	20,792	C
Univ of Maine at Farmington	ME	18,187	C
Univ of Mary	ND	23,180	C
Univ of Mary Hardin-Baylor	TX	33,950	C+
Univ of Mary Washington	VA	24,764	VC
Univ of Maryland/Baltimore County	MD	21,296	VC
Univ of Maryland/College Park	MD	21,938	HC
Univ of Maryland/Eastern Shore	MD	17,013	C
Univ of Mass Amherst	MA	26,199	VC+
Univ of Mass Boston	MA	13,435	C
Univ of Mass Dartmouth	MA	25,658	C
Univ of Mass Lowell	MA	26,380	C
Univ of Memphis	TN	18,278	C
Univ of Miami	FL	63,494	MC
Univ of Mich/Ann Arbor	MI	24,410	MC
Univ of Mich/Dearborn	MI	11,757	VC
Univ of Mich-Flint	MI	17,607	C+
Univ of Minn/Duluth	MN	20,292	C+
Univ of Minn/Morris	MN	20,760	VC
Univ of Minn/Twin Cities	MN	23,519	HC+
Univ of Miss	MS	17,746	C+
Univ of Missouri/Columbia	MO	18,201	MC
Univ of Missouri-Kansas City	MO	19,563	VC
Univ of Missouri-St. Louis	MO		C
Univ of Mobile	AL	28,935	C
Univ of Montana	MT	14,105	C
Univ of Montana-Western	MT	11,220	LC
Univ of Montevallo	AL	19,502	C
Univ of Mount Olive	NC	18,426	C
Univ of Mount Union	OH	38,970	C
Univ of Nebr - Kearney	NE	16,546	LC
Univ of Nebr - Lincoln	NE	18,589	VC
Univ of Nebr - Omaha	NE	16,120	C
Univ of Nevada, Las Vegas	NV	17,553	C
Univ of Nevada/Reno	NV	18,010	C
Univ of New Hampshire	NH	28,562	VC
Univ of New Haven	CT	52,190	C
Univ of New Mexico	NM	15,404	C
Univ of New Orleans	LA	12,840	C
Univ of North Alabama	AL	15,398	C
Univ of N Car at Asheville	NC	15,723	VC+
Univ of N Car at Chapel Hill	NC	20,052	HC+
Univ of N Car at Charlotte	NC	15,547	C
Univ of N Car at Greensboro	NC	14,690	C
Univ of N Car at Pembroke	NC	14,388	LC
Univ of N Car at Wilmington	NC	14,590	VC
Univ of N Dak	ND	15,373	C
Univ of North Florida	FL	15,996	VC
Univ of North Georgia	GA	17,316	C
Univ of North Texas	TX	19,198	C
Univ of Northern Colo	CO	20,851	C
Univ of Northwestern - St. Paul	MN	38,160	C
Univ of Notre Dame	IN	64,043	MC
Univ of Okla	OK	18,911	VC
Univ of Oregon	OR	22,972	C
Univ of Pennsylvania	PA	63,526	MC
Univ of Pikeville	KY	28,700	NC
Univ of Pittsburgh	PA	29,568	HC+
Univ of Pittsburgh at Bradford	PA	22,402	C
Univ of Pittsburgh at Johnstown	PA	22,092	C
Univ of Portland	OR	52,152	VC
Univ of PR, at Cayey	PR		
Univ of PR, at Humacao	PR	14,000	
Univ of PR, at Mayaguez	PR	13,995	
Univ of Puget Sound	WA	56,456	VC+
Univ of Redlands	CA	60,200	VC
Univ of Richmond	VA	60,880	MC
Univ of Rio Grande & Rio Grande Community College	OH	8,750	NC
Univ of Rochester	NY	65,032	MC
Univ of St. Francis	IN	37,400	C
Univ of St. Joseph	CT	49,550	C
Univ of St. Mary	KS	34,690	C
Univ of San Diego	CA	58,442	VC+
Univ of San Francisco	CA	58,484	VC
Univ of Science and Arts of Okla	OK	11,140	VC
Univ of Scranton	PA	54,962	VC
Univ of Sioux Falls	SD	34,330	C
Univ of South Alabama	AL	16,400	C
Univ of S Car at Columbia	SC	19,725	VC+
Univ of S Car Upstate	SC	18,200	LC
Univ of S Dak	SD	16,109	C
Univ of South Florida/Tampa	FL	16,110	VC+
Univ of Southern Calif	CA	66,631	C
Univ of Southern Indiana	IN	16,501	C
Univ of Southern Maine	ME	18,320	C
Univ of Southern Miss	MS	13,170	C

School	ST	$IS	SR
Univ of St. Francis	IL	39,924	C
Univ of St. Thomas - Houston	TX	40,020	VC
Univ of Tampa	FL	36,944	C
Univ of Texas at Arlington	TX	18,026	LC
Univ of Texas at Austin	TX	26,102	HC
Univ of Texas at Dallas	TX	22,830	VC+
Univ of Texas at El Paso	TX	34,452	NC
Univ of Texas at San Antonio	TX	20,157	C
Univ of the Cumberlands	KY	32,000	C
Univ of the District of Columbia	DC	21,044	LC
Univ of the Incarnate Word	TX	39,162	LC
Univ of the Ozarks	AR	52,176	C
Univ of the Pacific	CA	57,006	VC
Univ of the Sacred Heart	PR	17,932	
Univ of the Southwest	NM	22,766	C
Univ of Toledo	OH	19,336	NC
Univ of Tulsa	OK	52,625	HC+
Univ of Vermont	VT	28,878	HC
Univ of Virginia	VA	25,891	MC
Univ of Washington	WA	23,149	VC
Univ of West Alabama	AL	15,516	NC
Univ of West Florida	FL	15,848	C
Univ of West Georgia	GA	16,360	LC
Univ of Wisc-Eau Claire	WI	15,797	VC
Univ of Wisc-Green Bay	WI	15,064	C
Univ of Wisc-La Crosse	WI	15,247	C+
Univ of Wisc-Madison	WI	20,934	MC
Univ of Wisc-Milwaukee	WI	21,496	C
Univ of Wisc-Oshkosh	WI	15,200	C
Univ of Wisc-Parkside	WI	15,193	C
Univ of Wisc-Platteville	WI	14,614	VC
Univ of Wisc-River Falls	WI	14,485	C
Univ of Wisc-Stevens Point	WI	14,043	C
Univ of Wisc-Superior	WI	14,446	C
Univ of Wisc-Whitewater	WI	13,976	C
Univ of Wyoming	WY	15,375	C+
Upper Iowa Univ	IA	34,990	NC
Urbana Univ	OH	30,820	C
Ursinus College	PA	61,690	VC
Ursuline College	OH	41,076	LC
Utah State Univ	UT	12,736	C
Utica College	NY	30,430	C
Valley City State Univ	ND	13,267	C
Valparaiso Univ	IN	48,370	C+
Vanderbilt Univ	TN	60,572	MC
Vanguard Univ of Southern Calif	CA	40,740	VC
Vassar College	NY	65,491	MC
Villanova Univ	PA	62,523	MC
Virginia Commonwealth Univ	VA	23,049	C
Virginia Military Inst	VA	26,460	C+
Virginia Polytechnic Inst and State Univ	VA	21,276	HC
Virginia State Univ	VA	19,802	C+
Virginia Union Univ	VA	22,421	C
Virginia Wesleyan College	VA	43,728	LC
Viterbo Univ	WI	34,660	C
Voorhees College	SC	19,976	C
Wabash College	IN	50,650	VC
Wagner College	NY	55,480	C+
Wake Forest Univ	NC	64,056	MC
Walla Walla Univ	WA	30,417	NC
Walsh Univ	OH	39,010	C
Warren Wilson College	NC	44,220	VC
Wartburg College	IA	47,840	C
Washburn Univ	KS	15,827	C
Washington & Jefferson College	PA	56,512	VC
Washington Adventist Univ	MD	31,440	LC
Washington and Lee Univ	VA	59,647	MC
Washington College	MD	54,666	VC
Washington State Univ	WA	22,495	C
Washington Univ in St. Louis	MO	65,366	VC
Wayland Baptist Univ	TX	22,356	LC
Wayne State College	NE	12,802	C
Wayne State Univ	MI	22,016	C
Waynesburg Univ	PA	32,290	C
Weber State Univ	UT	10,721	C
Webster Univ	MO	37,490	C
Wellesley College	MA	63,916	MC
Wells College	NY	50,500	C
Wesley College	DE	37,026	LC
Wesleyan College	GA	29,694	C+
Wesleyan Univ	CT	65,516	MC
West Chester Univ of Pennsylvania	PA	18,456	C
West Liberty Univ	WV	15,512	C
West Texas A&M Univ	TX	13,478	C
West Virginia State Univ	WV	8,378	NC
West Virginia Univ	WV	18,210	C
West Virginia Wesleyan College	WV	36,858	C
Western Carolina Univ	NC	13,965	C
Western Conn State Univ	CT	21,254	LC
Western Illinois Univ	IL	20,825	C
Western Kentucky Univ	KY	16,850	C
Western Mich Univ	MI	21,054	C
Western New England Univ	MA	48,088	C
Western New Mexico Univ	NM	16,734	LC
Western Oregon Univ	OR	15,021	LC
Western State Colo Univ	CO	18,639	C
Western Washington Univ	WA	18,003	C+
Westfield State Univ	MA	19,671	C
Westminster College	MO	32,820	C
Westminster College	PA	39,180	C+
Westminster College	UT	41,078	C+
Westmont College	CA	56,410	HC
Wheaton College	IL	43,610	MC
Wheaton College	MA	61,512	VC
Wheeling Jesuit Univ	WV	37,106	LC
Wheelock College	MA	49,225	C
Whitman College	WA	59,772	MC
Whittier College	CA	57,891	C
Whitworth Univ	WA	51,732	VC
Wichita State Univ	KS	21,643	C
Widener Univ	PA	56,486	C
Wilberforce Univ	OH	19,016	C
Wiley College	TX	18,504	C
Wilkes Univ	PA	45,622	C
Willamette Univ	OR	61,817	VC+
William Carey Univ	MS	23,950	LC
William Jewell College	MO	41,210	C+
William Paterson Univ of New Jersey	NJ	23,133	C
William Woods Univ	MO	32,040	C
Williams College	MA	63,290	MC
Wilmington College	OH	34,600	C
Wilson College	PA	35,620	C
Wingate Univ	NC	39,950	C
Winona State Univ	MN	17,535	C
Winston-Salem State Univ	NC	26,166	LC
Winthrop Univ	SC	23,082	C
Wisc Lutheran College	WI	36,290	VC
Wittenberg Univ	OH	48,156	C+
Wofford College	SC	49,885	VC
Worcester Polytechnic Inst	MA	60,730	MC
Worcester State Univ	MA	20,977	C
Wright State Univ	OH	16,983	C
Xavier Univ	OH	47,880	C+
Xavier Univ of Louisiana	LA	31,689	C+
Yale Univ	CT	64,650	MC
Yeshiva Univ	NY	47,250	VC+
York College of Pennsylvania	PA	29,240	C
Youngstown State Univ	OH	17,307	C

MATHEMATICS - ACTUARIAL CONCENTRATION

School	ST	$IS	SR
Bethany College	WV	36,300	NC
Bryant Univ	RI	55,646	VC
East Central Univ	OK	13,056	C
Indiana Univ of Pennsylvania	PA	23,614	LC
Kent State Univ	OH	20,732	C
Murray State Univ	KY	16,998	C
Pacific Lutheran Univ	WA	49,960	VC
Rochester Inst of Technology	NY	50,842	HC
Seattle Univ	WA	50,811	VC+
Silver Lake College of the Holy Family	WI	36,290	LC
Texas Christian Univ	TX	54,670	HC
West Chester Univ of Pennsylvania	PA	18,456	C

MATHEMATICS – ECONOMICS

School	ST	$IS	SR
Baldwin Wallace Univ	OH	41,106	C
Bethany College	WV	36,300	NC
Bowdoin College	ME	63,500	MC
Brown Univ	RI	64,566	MC
Bryant Univ	RI	55,646	VC
Calvin College	MI	41,570	VC+
Fordham Univ	NY	65,918	MC
Gettysburg College	PA	63,000	HC
High Point Univ	NC	45,977	C
Hofstra Univ	NY	55,960	C+
Ithaca College	NY	56,766	VC
New York Univ	NY	65,860	MC
Reed College	OR	65,300	MC
Southern Oregon Univ	OR	19,117	C
SUNY / Univ at Buffalo	NY	23,122	C+
Temple Univ	PA	24,392	VC
Univ of Dayton	OH	53,620	C
Univ of Pittsburgh	PA	29,568	HC+
Wake Forest Univ	NC	64,056	MC
Wayne State Univ	MI	22,016	C
Wheaton College	MA	61,512	VC
Whitman College	WA	59,772	MC
Whitworth Univ	WA	51,732	VC
Yale Univ	CT	64,650	MC

MATHEMATICS – PHILOSOPHY

School	ST	$IS	SR
Boston Univ	MA	65,110	MC
Yale Univ	CT	64,650	MC

MATHEMATICS EDUCATION

School	ST	$IS	SR
Abilene Christian Univ	TX	41,800	C+
Adams State Univ	CO	17,703	LC
Alfred Univ	NY	42,296	C+
Andrews Univ	MI	28,030	C+
Appalachian State Univ	NC	14,416	VC
Aquinas College - Mich	MI	38,876	HC
Arkansas State Univ	AR	16,190	C
Armstrong State Univ	GA	16,962	C
Asbury Univ	KY	35,180	C+
Auburn Univ	AL	23,594	VC+
Augustana College	IL	49,658	VC
Averett Univ	VA	40,970	LC
Baker Univ	KS	33,350	C+
Baylor Univ	TX	53,760	HC
Bennett College	NC	27,302	NC
Bennington College	VT	63,960	MC
Berry College	GA	45,286	C+
Bethany College	KS	46,100	NC
Bethany College	WV	36,300	NC
Bethel College	IN	35,860	C
Bethel Univ	MN	45,270	VC
Biola Univ	CA	46,402	C+
Black Hills State Univ	SD	15,899	C
Blackburn College	IL	28,526	LC
Bloomfield College	NJ	39,100	LC
Bloomsburg Univ of Pennsylvania	PA	19,066	LC
Blue Mountain College	MS	15,949	VC
Boston Univ	MA	65,110	MC
Bowdoin College	ME	63,500	MC
Bowling Green State Univ	OH	19,747	C
Brigham Young Univ	UT	12,748	HC
Brigham Young Univ/Hawaii	HI	11,290	C
Calif Baptist Univ	CA	41,392	C
Cal State, Long Beach	CA	18,850	C
Calvin College	MI	41,570	VC+
Cameron Univ	OK	11,072	NC
Canisius College	NY	47,537	C
Carthage College	WI	48,835	C
Catawba College	NC	39,820	C
Cedarville Univ	OH	34,990	VC
Central Washington Univ	WA	16,803	C
CUNY/Brooklyn College	NY	5,884	C+
CUNY/City College	NY	20,319	VC
CUNY/College of Technology	NY	6,669	NC
Claflin Univ	SC	33,764	LC
Coker College	SC	34,810	LC
College of the Ozarks	MO	7,230	C
Colo State Univ	CO	22,162	VC
Concordia College - Moorhead	MN	51,088	C+
Concordia College - New York	NY	39,035	LC
Concordia Univ St. Paul	MN	29,050	C
Corban Univ	OR	40,306	C
Covenant College	GA	38,990	VC
Daemen College	NY	38,045	C
Dakota State Univ	SD	13,811	C
Davis & Elkins College	WV	38,242	LC
Defiance College	OH	41,630	C
Delaware State Univ	DE	19,376	NC
Delta State Univ	MS	13,176	C
Dominican College	NY	31,270	LC
Dordt College	IA	37,860	C+
Drake Univ	IA	45,056	HC
Duquesne Univ	PA	46,822	VC
East Carolina Univ	NC	16,937	C
East Central Univ	OK	13,056	C
East Texas Baptist Univ	TX	33,134	C
Eastern Mich Univ	MI	19,761	C
Eastern Washington Univ	WA	25,572	LC
Edgewood College	WI	35,950	C
Edinboro Univ	PA	15,940	LC
Elizabethtown College	PA	54,050	C
Elmhurst College	IL	45,428	C
Elon Univ	NC	44,599	VC+
Emory and Henry College	VA	41,410	C
Faulkner Univ	AL	26,410	C
Ferris State Univ	MI	21,445	C
Florida Gulf Coast Univ	FL	9,682	C
Florida Inst of Technology	FL	53,306	VC
Florida State Univ	FL	16,771	HC
Fontbonne Univ	MO	33,717	C
Fort Valley State Univ	GA	17,988	VC
Franklin College	IN	39,380	C
Fresno Pacific Univ	CA	37,370	C
Gannon Univ	PA	42,032	C
Geneva College	PA	35,450	C
Georgetown College	KY	41,440	C
Georgia Southern Univ	GA	16,596	C
Glenville State College	WV	17,386	NC
Goshen College	IN	42,500	C
Grace College and Seminary	IN	31,524	C
Grambling State Univ	LA	15,701	C
Greensboro College	NC	42,400	LC
Greenville College	IL	27,012	C
Grove City College	PA	25,692	VC
Gwynedd Mercy Univ	PA	43,780	LC
Hardin-Simmons Univ	TX	33,966	C
Hofstra Univ	NY	55,960	C+
Hood College	MD	54,840	C
Houghton College	NY	39,090	C
Houston Baptist Univ	TX	36,450	C
Humboldt State Univ	CA	20,514	C
Huntingdon College	AL	34,900	C
Huntington Univ	IN	33,996	C
Indiana Univ Bloomington	IN	20,429	VC
Indiana Univ Northwest	IN	7,072	C
Indiana Univ South Bend	IN	14,242	C
Indiana Univ Southeast	IN	14,242	LC
Indiana Univ-Purdue Univ Fort Wayne	IN	17,553	C
Indiana Wesleyan Univ	IN	33,674	C
Ithaca College	NY	56,766	VC
Jackson State Univ	MS	15,879	LC
John Carroll Univ	OH	49,740	C+
Johnson State College	VT	20,752	C
Judson College	AL	27,066	C
Judson Univ	IL	37,700	C
Juniata College	PA	53,760	VC
Keene State College	NH	24,003	LC
Kennesaw State Univ	GA	19,592	VC
Kent State Univ	OH	20,732	C
Kentucky State Univ	KY	13,364	LC
Keystone College	PA	28,680	LC
King Univ	TN	34,660	C
Kutztown Univ of Pennsylvania	PA	19,056	LC
Langston Univ	OK	14,314	C
Le Moyne College	NY	46,000	C
Lee Univ	TN	22,045	C
Lewis Univ	IL	40,370	C
Limestone College	SC	32,100	C
Lincoln Univ	MO	13,602	NC
Lipscomb Univ	TN	41,296	VC
LIU Post	NY	49,682	C
Louisiana College	LA	21,886	C
Loyola Univ Chicago	IL	55,802	VC
Marian Univ	WI	32,420	LC
Marist College	NY	49,860	VC
Mars Hill Univ	NC	42,688	C
Marymount Univ	VA	41,570	LC
Marywood Univ	PA	46,900	C
Mass College of Liberal Arts	MA	20,128	C
Mayville State Univ	ND	18,371	NC
Mercyhurst Univ	PA	47,420	C
Messiah College	PA	43,100	C+
Miami Univ	OH	27,190	HC+
MidAmerica Nazarene Univ	KS	35,550	C
Miles College	AL	18,646	NC
Millersville Univ of Pennsylvania	PA	23,782	C
Milligan College	TN	38,150	C
Millikin Univ	IL	42,158	C
Minn State Univ, Mankato	MN	15,616	C
Minn State Univ, Moorhead	MN	15,941	C
Minot State Univ	ND	12,732	C
Miss Valley State Univ	MS	13,233	LC
Missouri Southern State Univ	MO	12,499	C
Monmouth Univ	NJ	46,234	C
Montana State Univ-Billings	MT	22,960	C
Morningside College	IA	36,865	C
Morris College	SC	18,500	LC
Mount Mary Univ	WI	34,650	LC
Mount Vernon Nazarene Univ	OH	34,500	C
Murray State Univ	KY	16,998	C
Nazareth College	NY	45,574	C
New York Univ	NY	65,860	MC
Niagara Univ	NY	41,010	C
N Car A&T State Univ	NC	13,365	LC
N Car State Univ	NC	19,515	HC+
North Greenville Univ	SC	25,930	C+
Northern Kentucky Univ	KY	16,486	C
Northwest Missouri State Univ	MO	17,737	C
Northwest Nazarene Univ	ID	36,000	C
Northwestern Okla State Univ	OK	13,072	NC
Northwestern Univ	IL	66,344	MC
Nyack College	NY	34,050	NC
Oakwood Univ	AL	43,758	C
Ohio Univ	OH	22,924	C
Ohio Valley Univ	WV	29,480	C
Okla Christian Univ	OK	27,650	VC
Okla Wesleyan Univ	OK	33,206	C
Old Dominion Univ	VA	20,910	C
Olivet Nazarene Univ	IL	41,840	C
Oral Roberts Univ	OK	34,316	C
Ouachita Baptist Univ	AR	32,320	C
Pacific Lutheran Univ	WA	49,960	VC
Palm Beach Atlantic Univ	FL	39,720	C
Pepperdine Univ	CA	74,460	HC+
Piedmont College	GA	32,512	C
Pittsburg State Univ	KS	13,880	NC
Pontifical Catholic Univ of PR	PR	10,534	
Providence College	RI	60,760	VC
Purdue Univ/Northwest	IN	15,038	C
Purdue Univ/West Lafayette	IN	20,032	MC
Radford Univ	VA	19,027	LC
Regis College	MA	51,920	C
Rider Univ	NJ	54,050	C
Rivier Univ	NH	40,410	VC
Roberts Wesleyan College	NY	38,306	C
Rocky Mountain College	MT	34,270	C
Rust College	MS	10,600	C
Saginaw Valley State Univ	MI	18,530	C
St. Augustine's Univ	NC	26,048	C
St. Louis Univ	MO	49,866	HC
St. Mary-of-the-Woods College	IN	39,632	LC
St. Mary's Univ of Minn	MN	41,210	VC
Schreiner Univ	TX	34,626	LC
Seattle Pacific Univ	WA	47,439	C+
Seattle Univ	WA	50,811	VC+
Seton Hill Univ	PA	46,972	C
Shaw Univ	NC	24,638	C
Shepherd Univ, West Virginia	WV	17,224	C
Shippensburg Univ of Pennsylvania	PA	23,208	C
Shorter Univ	GA	31,130	LC
Silver Lake College of the Holy Family	WI	36,290	LC
Simpson Univ	CA	33,700	C
Southeast Missouri State Univ	MO	15,498	C
Southeastern Okla State Univ	OK	11,875	C
Southern Illinois Univ Edwardsville	IL	22,643	C
Southern Nazarene Univ	OK	32,798	NC
Southern Univ and A&M College	LA	16,074	LC+
Southern Univ at New Orleans	LA	8,014	LC
Southern Wesleyan Univ	SC	32,130	LC

ST = STATE $IS = IN-STATE COSTS SR = SELECTOR RATING

School	ST	$IS	SR
Southwest Baptist Univ	MO	29,900	LC
Southwest Minn State Univ	MN	17,783	C
Southwestern College	KS	31,531	C
Southwestern Okla State Univ	OK	11,790	C
St. Ambrose Univ	IA	39,019	C
St. Ambrose Univ	IA	39,019	C
St. Edward's Univ	TX	53,100	VC
St. John Fisher College	NY	43,620	C
SUNY / SUNY College at Old Westbury	NY	16,860	C
SUNY / SUNY Fredonia	NY	20,818	C
SUNY / SUNY Oneonta	NY	19,712	C+
SUNY / SUNY Plattsburgh	NY	18,814	C
SUNY / SUNY Potsdam	NY	20,404	C+
SUNY at New Paltz	NY	19,200	C
SUNY at Oswego	NY	21,351	C
Suffolk Univ	MA	50,308	C
Syracuse Univ	NY	60,239	VC
Taylor Univ	IN	40,317	C+
Temple Univ	PA	24,392	VC
Texas Southern Univ	TX	18,212	LC
Texas Wesleyan Univ	TX	35,134	C
The Catholic Univ of America	DC	56,356	VC
The College of New Jersey	NJ	31,909	HC
The College of St. Rose	NY	43,048	C
The Univ of Utah	UT	17,924	VC
Tougaloo College	MS	17,980	NC
Trevecca Nazarene Univ	TN	31,186	C
Trine Univ	IN	41,310	C
Troy Univ	AL	16,171	C
Union College	NE	23,270	C
Universidad del Turabo	PR	17,828	
Univ of Arkansas at Pine Bluff	AR	13,541	C
Univ of Calif at Los Angeles	CA	30,162	MC
Univ of Calif at Riverside	CA	29,227	C+
Univ of Calif San Diego	CA	30,150	MC
Univ of Central Florida	FL	15,922	VC
Univ of Central Missouri	MO	18,982	C
Univ of Central Okla	OK	13,486	C
Univ of Conn	CT	25,538	HC
Univ of Delaware	DE	24,976	VC+
Univ of Evansville	IN	44,186	VC+
Univ of Georgia	GA	21,250	HC
Univ of Great Falls	MT	38,524	C
Univ of Idaho	ID	15,348	C
Univ of Illinois at Chicago	IL	25,006	VC
Univ of Illinois at Urbana-Champaign	IL	27,006	HC
Univ of Indianapolis	IN	36,480	C
Univ of Iowa	IA	18,683	VC+
Univ of Kentucky	KY	33,306	C
Univ of Louisiana at Lafayette	LA	14,516	C
Univ of Mary	ND	23,180	C
Univ of Mary Hardin-Baylor	TX	33,950	C+
Univ of Maryland/Eastern Shore	MD	17,013	C
Univ of Mich/Dearborn	MI	11,757	VC
Univ of Minn/Duluth	MN	20,292	C+
Univ of Minn/Twin Cities	MN	23,519	HC+
Univ of Miss	MS	17,746	C+
Univ of Missouri/Columbia	MO	18,201	MC
Univ of Montana-Western	MT	11,220	LC
Univ of Nebr - Lincoln	NE	18,589	VC
Univ of New Hampshire	NH	28,562	VC
Univ of New Haven	CT	52,190	C
Univ of New Orleans	LA	12,840	C
Univ of N Car at Charlotte	NC	15,547	C
Univ of N Car at Greensboro	NC	14,690	C
Univ of North Florida	FL	15,996	VC
Univ of North Georgia	GA	17,316	C
Univ of Northwestern - St. Paul	MN	38,160	C
Univ of Okla	OK	18,911	VC
Univ of Pittsburgh at Bradford	PA	22,402	C
Univ of Pittsburgh at Johnstown	PA	22,092	C
Univ of Rio Grande & Rio Grande Community College	OH	8,750	NC
Univ of S Car Upstate	SC	18,200	LC
Univ of South Florida/Tampa	FL	16,110	VC+
Univ of Southern Indiana	IN	16,501	C
Univ of the Cumberlands	KY	32,000	C
Univ of Vermont	VT	28,878	HC
Univ of Wisc-Green Bay	WI	15,064	C
Univ of Wisc-Superior	WI	14,446	C
Utah State Univ	UT	12,736	C
Valparaiso Univ	IN	48,370	C+
Viterbo Univ	WI	34,660	C
Wartburg College	IA	47,840	C
Washington Adventist Univ	MD	31,440	LC
Washington Univ in St. Louis	MO	65,366	VC
Wayne State Univ	MI	22,016	C
Weber State Univ	UT	10,721	C
Webster Univ	MO	37,490	C
West Chester Univ of Pennsylvania	PA	18,456	C
West Texas A&M Univ	TX	13,478	C
Western Carolina Univ	NC	13,965	C
Westmont College	CA	56,410	HC
Whitworth Univ	WA	51,732	VC
Widener Univ	PA	56,486	C
Wiley College	TX	18,504	C
Wilmington College	OH	34,600	C
Wilson College	PA	35,620	C
Wingate Univ	NC	39,950	C
Winona State Univ	MN	17,535	C
Wright State Univ	OH	16,983	C
Xavier Univ of Louisiana	LA	31,689	C+
York College of Pennsylvania	PA	29,240	C
Youngstown State Univ	OH	17,307	C

MATHEMATICS/ COMPUTATIONAL

School	ST	$IS	SR
Abilene Christian Univ	TX	41,800	C+
Aquinas College - Mich	MI	38,876	HC
Brown Univ	RI	64,566	MC
Bryant Univ	RI	55,646	VC
Christopher Newport Univ	VA	23,968	VC+
Embry-Riddle Aeronautical Univ - Daytona Beach	FL	44,712	VC
Lawrence Tech Univ	MI	39,770	VC
Loyola Univ Chicago	IL	55,802	VC
Loyola Univ New Orleans	LA	51,708	VC+
Missouri Southern State Univ	MO	12,499	C
St. Mary's College	IN	50,600	C
Shepherd Univ, West Virginia	WV	17,224	C
Southwestern Univ	TX	50,720	VC
Stanford Univ	CA	60,409	MC
Temple Univ	PA	24,392	VC
Univ of Illinois at Chicago	IL	25,006	VC
West Chester Univ of Pennsylvania	PA	18,456	C

MATHEMATICS/THEORETICAL

School	ST	$IS	SR
Aquinas College - Mich	MI	38,876	HC
Biola Univ	CA	46,402	C+
Brown Univ	RI	64,566	MC
Seattle Univ	WA	50,811	VC+

MECHANICAL DESIGN TECHNOLOGY

School	ST	$IS	SR
Pennsylvania College of Technology	PA	27,333	NC
Southeast Missouri State Univ	MO	15,498	C
Western Washington Univ	WA	18,003	C+

MECHANICAL ENGINEERING

School	ST	$IS	SR
Alabama A&M Univ	AL	18,796	C
Alfred Univ	NY	42,296	C+
Arizona State Univ at the Tempe Campus	AZ	21,756	VC
Arkansas State Univ	AR	16,190	C
Arkansas Tech Univ	AR	15,484	C
Auburn Univ	AL	23,594	VC+
Baylor Univ	TX	53,760	HC
Boise State Univ	ID	14,860	C
Boston Univ	MA	65,110	MC
Brigham Young Univ	UT	12,748	HC
Brown Univ	RI	64,566	MC
Bucknell Univ	PA	64,616	MC
Calif Baptist Univ	CA	41,392	C
Calif Inst of Technology	CA	58,761	MC
Calif Polytechnic State Univ	CA	17,979	HC+
Calif State Polytechnic Univ, Pomona	CA	21,541	C
Cal State, Maritime Academy	CA	19,450	LC
Cal State, Chico	CA	21,440	C
Cal State, Fresno	CA	16,902	LC
Cal State, Fullerton	CA	21,902	C
Cal State, Long Beach	CA	18,850	C
Cal State, Los Angeles	CA	17,186	LC
Cal State, Northridge	CA	16,859	LC
Cal State, Sacramento	CA	20,332	C
Calvin College	MI	41,570	VC+
Carnegie Mellon Univ	PA	67,980	MC
Case Western Reserve Univ	OH	60,304	MC
Cedarville Univ	OH	34,990	VC
Central Conn State Univ	CT	21,203	C
Central Mich Univ	MI	20,330	C
Central Washington Univ	WA	16,803	C
Christian Brothers Univ	TN	31,670	VC
CUNY/City College	NY	20,319	VC
Clarkson Univ	NY	60,392	HC
Clemson Univ	SC		HC
Cleveland State Univ	OH	22,196	C
Colo State Univ	CO	22,162	VC
Columbia Univ/City of New York	NY	62,958	MC
Cooper Union for the Advancement of Science and Art	NY	58,210	MC
Cornell Univ	NY	64,853	MC
Daniel Webster College	NH	26,984	C
Delaware State Univ	DE	19,376	NC
Dordt College	IA	37,860	C+
Drexel Univ	PA	65,432	VC+
Duke Univ	NC	64,188	
Elizabethtown College	PA	54,050	C
Embry-Riddle Aeronautical Univ - Daytona Beach	FL	44,712	VC
Embry-Riddle Aeronautical Univ - Prescott Campus	AZ	44,054	VC
Fairfield Univ	CT	59,860	VC+
Florida A&M Univ	FL	15,361	C
Florida Atlantic Univ	FL	17,339	C
Florida Inst of Technology	FL	53,306	VC
Florida International Univ	FL	19,854	C+
Florida State Univ	FL	16,771	HC
Franklin W. Olin College of Engineering	MA	63,130	MC
Gannon Univ	PA	42,032	C
George Washington Univ	DC	62,835	MC
Georgia Inst of Technology	GA	23,360	MC
Georgia Southern Univ	GA	16,596	C
Gonzaga Univ	WA	50,888	HC
Grove City College	PA	25,692	VC
Harding Univ	AR	25,421	C
Hofstra Univ	NY	55,960	C+
Howard Univ	DC	37,616	C+
Idaho State Univ	ID	13,619	NC
Illinois Inst of Technology	IL	56,826	HC+
Indiana Inst of Technology	IN	34,240	LC
Indiana Univ-Purdue Univ Fort Wayne	IN	17,553	C
Indiana Univ-Purdue Univ Indianapolis	IN	18,635	C
Inter-American Univ of PR-Bayamon	PR	18,785	
Iowa State Univ	IA	17,570	C
Jacksonville Univ	FL	46,230	C
Johns Hopkins Univ	MD	65,386	MC
Kansas State Univ	KS	17,780	VC
Kennesaw State Univ	GA	19,592	VC
Kettering Univ	MI	47,570	HC
King's College	PA	46,858	C
Lafayette College	PA	63,355	MC
Lamar Univ	TX	18,014	LC
Lawrence Tech Univ	MI	39,770	VC
Lehigh Univ	PA	61,010	MC
LeTourneau Univ	TX	38,250	VC
Lipscomb Univ	TN	41,296	VC
Louisiana State Univ and A&M College	LA	18,677	VC
Louisiana Tech Univ	LA	11,422	VC
Loyola Marymount Univ	CA	58,038	HC
Manhattan College	NY	51,750	C+
Marquette Univ	WI	48,390	VC+
Mass Inst of Technology	MA	62,662	MC
Miami Univ	OH	27,190	HC+
Mich State Univ	MI	23,898	VC+
Mich Tech Univ	MI	24,739	VC+
Milwaukee School of Engineering	WI	45,153	HC
Minn State Univ, Mankato	MN	15,616	C
Miss State Univ	MS	11,454	C+
Missouri Univ of Science and Technology	MO	18,655	HC
Montana State Univ	MT	15,500	C+
New Jersey Inst of Technology	NJ	29,569	VC
New Mexico Inst of Mining and Technology	NM	14,833	HC
New Mexico State Univ	NM	14,050	C
New York Inst of Technology	NY	48,730	C
New York Univ	NY	65,860	MC
N Car A&T State Univ	NC	13,365	LC
N Car State Univ	NC	19,515	HC+
N Dak State Univ	ND	16,245	C
Northeastern Univ	MA	62,703	MC
Northern Arizona Univ	AZ	20,246	VC
Northern Illinois Univ	IL	20,176	C
Northwestern Univ	IL	66,344	MC
Norwich Univ	VT	28,212	C
Oakland Univ	MI	20,763	C
Ohio Northern Univ	OH	44,050	VC
Ohio State Univ at Columbus	OH	21,703	HC+
Ohio Univ	OH	22,924	C
Okla Christian Univ	OK	27,650	VC
Okla State Univ	OK	17,180	VC
Old Dominion Univ	VA	20,910	C
Oral Roberts Univ	OK	34,316	C
Oregon State Univ	OR	22,519	VC
Pennsylvania College of Technology	PA	27,333	NC
Pennsylvania State Univ - Univ Park	PA	29,760	HC
Point Park Univ	PA	41,270	C
Prairie View A&M Univ	TX	15,205	LC
Princeton Univ	NJ	57,610	MC
Purdue Univ/Northwest	IN	15,038	C
Purdue Univ/West Lafayette	IN	20,032	MC
Quinnipiac Univ	CT	59,110	C
Rensselaer Polytechnic Inst	NY	63,436	MC
Rice Univ	TX	57,668	MC
Rochester Inst of Technology	NY	50,842	HC
Rose-Hulman Inst of Technology	IN	57,303	MC
Rowan Univ	NJ	24,491	VC+
Rutgers Univ - New Brunswick	NJ	26,632	HC
Saginaw Valley State Univ	MI	18,530	C
St. Louis Univ	MO	49,866	HC
St. Martin's Univ	WA	45,056	C
San Diego State Univ	CA	21,896	C+
San Francisco State Univ	CA	18,514	LC
San Jose State Univ	CA	21,540	C
Seattle Univ	WA	50,811	VC+
S Dak School of Mines and Technology	SD	18,645	VC
S Dak State Univ	SD	15,634	C
Southern Illinois Univ Carbondale	IL	23,667	C
Southern Illinois Univ Edwardsville	IL	22,643	C
Southern Methodist Univ	TX	66,483	MC
Southern Univ and A&M College	LA	16,074	LC+
St. Ambrose Univ	IA	39,019	C
St. Ambrose Univ	IA	39,019	C
St. Mary's Univ	TX	37,500	C
Stanford Univ	CA	60,409	MC
SUNY / Univ at Buffalo	NY	23,122	C+
SUNY at Binghamton	NY	22,861	MC
SUNY Polytechnic Inst	NY	19,473	VC
Stevens Inst of Technology	NJ	62,338	MC
Stony Brook Univ/The SUNY	NY	21,881	MC
Syracuse Univ	NY	60,239	VC
Temple Univ	PA	24,392	VC
Tenn State Univ	TN	14,423	C
Tenn Tech Univ	TN	17,050	C
Texas A&M Univ	TX	20,521	VC+
Texas A&M Univ at Kingsville	TX	7,500	LC
Texas Christian Univ	TX	54,670	HC
Texas Tech Univ	TX	18,736	C+
The Catholic Univ of America	DC	56,356	VC
The College of New Jersey	NJ	31,909	HC
The Univ of Akron	OH	21,477	C
The Univ of Tenn at Chattanooga	TN	16,744	C
The Univ of Tenn at Knoxville	TN	22,112	VC
The Univ of Utah	UT	17,924	VC
Trine Univ	IN	41,310	C
Tufts Univ	MA		MC
Tuskegee Univ	AL	28,164	C
Union College	NY	64,320	MC
United States Air Force Academy	CO		C
United States Coast Guard Academy	CT	942	MC
United States Military Academy at West Point	NY		HC+
United States Naval Academy	MD		MC
Universidad Politecnica de PR, Hato Rey campus	PR	23,514	
Univ of Alabama	AL	24,320	C+
Univ of Alabama at Birmingham	AL	19,906	C
Univ of Alabama in Huntsville	AL	19,445	VC
Univ of Alaska Fairbanks	AK	16,179	C
Univ of Arizona	AZ	23,100	C
Univ of Arkansas at Fayetteville	AR	19,152	C+
Univ of Calif at Berkeley	CA	28,853	MC
Univ of Calif at Davis	CA	28,468	HC
Univ of Calif at Irvine	CA	26,484	VC
Univ of Calif at Los Angeles	CA	30,162	MC
Univ of Calif at Riverside	CA	29,227	C+
Univ of Calif at Santa Barbara	CA	29,091	HC
Univ of Calif San Diego	CA	30,150	MC
Univ of Central Florida	FL	15,922	VC
Univ of Cincinnati	OH	21,964	VC
Univ of Colo Boulder	CO	24,285	VC+
Univ of Colo Colo Springs	CO	19,663	C
Univ of Colo Denver	CO	23,230	C
Univ of Conn	CT	25,538	HC
Univ of Dayton	OH	53,620	C
Univ of Delaware	DE	24,976	VC+
Univ of Denver	CO	58,443	VC+
Univ of Detroit Mercy	MI	48,816	C+
Univ of Evansville	IN	44,186	VC+
Univ of Florida	FL	16,291	HC+
Univ of Georgia	GA	21,250	HC
Univ of Hartford	CT	49,776	C
Univ of Hawaii at Manoa	HI	23,221	C
Univ of Houston	TX	21,483	VC
Univ of Idaho	ID	15,348	C
Univ of Illinois at Chicago	IL	25,006	VC
Univ of Illinois at Urbana-Champaign	IL	27,006	HC
Univ of Indianapolis	IN	36,480	C
Univ of Iowa	IA	18,683	VC+
Univ of Kansas	KS	20,135	C+
Univ of Kentucky	KY	33,306	C
Univ of Louisiana at Lafayette	LA	14,516	C
Univ of Louisville	KY	19,824	C
Univ of Maine	ME	20,792	C
Univ of Maryland/Baltimore County	MD	21,296	VC
Univ of Maryland/College Park	MD	21,938	HC
Univ of Mass Amherst	MA	26,199	VC+
Univ of Mass Dartmouth	MA	25,658	C
Univ of Mass Lowell	MA	26,380	C
Univ of Memphis	TN	18,278	C
Univ of Miami	FL	63,494	MC
Univ of Mich/Ann Arbor	MI	24,410	MC
Univ of Mich/Dearborn	MI	11,757	VC
Univ of Minn/Duluth	MN	20,292	C+
Univ of Minn/Twin Cities	MN	23,519	HC+
Univ of Miss	MS	17,746	C+
Univ of Missouri/Columbia	MO	18,201	MC
Univ of Missouri-Kansas City	MO	19,563	VC
Univ of Missouri-St. Louis	MO		C
Univ of Mount Union	OH	38,970	C
Univ of Nebr - Lincoln	NE	18,589	VC
Univ of Nevada, Las Vegas	NV	17,553	C
Univ of Nevada/Reno	NV	18,010	C
Univ of New Hampshire	NH	28,562	VC
Univ of New Haven	CT	52,190	C
Univ of New Mexico	NM	15,404	C
Univ of New Orleans	LA	12,840	C

ST = STATE $IS = IN-STATE COSTS SR = SELECTOR RATING

School	ST	$IS	SR
Univ of N Car at Charlotte	NC	15,547	C
Univ of N Dak	ND	15,373	C
Univ of North Florida	FL	15,996	VC
Univ of North Texas	TX	19,198	C
Univ of Notre Dame	IN	64,043	MC
Univ of Okla	OK	18,911	VC
Univ of Pittsburgh	PA	29,568	HC+
Univ of Portland	OR	52,152	VC
Univ of PR, at Mayaguez	PR	13,995	
Univ of Rhode Island	RI	24,906	C
Univ of Rochester	NY	65,032	MC
Univ of San Diego	CA	58,442	VC+
Univ of South Alabama	AL	16,400	C
Univ of S Car at Columbia	SC	19,725	VC+
Univ of South Florida/Tampa	FL	16,110	VC+
Univ of Southern Calif	CA	66,631	C
Univ of Texas at Arlington	TX	18,026	LC
Univ of Texas at Austin	TX	26,102	HC
Univ of Texas at Dallas	TX	22,830	VC+
Univ of Texas at El Paso	TX	34,452	NC
Univ of Texas at San Antonio	TX	20,157	C
Univ of the District of Columbia	DC	21,044	LC
Univ of the Pacific	CA	57,006	VC
Univ of Toledo	OH	19,336	NC
Univ of Tulsa	OK	52,625	HC+
Univ of Vermont	VT	28,878	HC
Univ of Virginia	VA	25,891	MC
Univ of Wisc-Madison	WI	20,934	MC
Univ of Wisc-Milwaukee	WI	21,496	C
Univ of Wisc-Platteville	WI	14,614	VC
Univ of Wyoming	WY	15,375	C+
Utah State Univ	UT	12,736	C
Valparaiso Univ	IN	48,370	C+
Vanderbilt Univ	TN	60,572	MC
Villanova Univ	PA	62,523	MC
Virginia Commonwealth Univ	VA	23,049	C
Virginia Military Inst	VA	26,460	C+
Virginia Polytechnic Inst and State Univ	VA	21,276	HC
Washington State Univ	WA	22,495	C
Washington Univ in St. Louis	MO	65,366	VC
Wayne State Univ	MI	22,016	C
West Texas A&M Univ	TX	13,478	C
West Virginia Univ	WV	18,210	C
West Virginia Univ Inst of Technology	WV	16,462	NC
Western Kentucky Univ	KY	16,850	C
Western Mich Univ	MI	21,054	C
Western New England Univ	MA	48,088	C
Wichita State Univ	KS	21,643	C
Widener Univ	PA	56,486	C
Wilkes Univ	PA	45,622	C
Worcester Polytechnic Inst	MA	60,730	MC
Wright State Univ	OH	16,983	C
Yale Univ	CT	64,650	MC
York College of Pennsylvania	PA	29,240	C
Youngstown State Univ	OH	17,307	C

MECHANICAL ENGINEERING TECHNOLOGY

School	ST	$IS	SR
Alabama A&M Univ	AL	18,796	C
Alfred State College	NY	19,895	C
Arizona State Univ at the Polytechnic Campus	AZ	21,360	VC
Central Conn State Univ	CT	21,203	C
Central Mich Univ	MI	20,330	C
CUNY/College of Technology	NY	6,669	NC
Cleveland State Univ	OH	22,196	C
Colo State Univ-Pueblo	CO	18,234	C
Eastern Mich Univ	MI	19,761	C
Eastern Washington Univ	WA	25,572	LC
Fairleigh Dickinson Univ/ Metropolitan Campus	NJ	40,254	C
Fairmont State Univ	WV	15,726	C
Farmingdale State College	NY	20,624	C
Ferris State Univ	MI	21,445	C
Indiana State Univ	IN	23,223	LC
Indiana Univ-Purdue Univ Fort Wayne	IN	17,553	C
Indiana Univ-Purdue Univ Indianapolis	IN	18,635	C
Kennesaw State Univ	GA	19,592	VC
Metropolitan State Univ of Denver	CO	29,889	LC
Mich Tech Univ	MI	24,739	VC+
Montana State Univ	MT	15,500	C+
Northern Kentucky Univ	KY	16,486	C
Okla State Univ	OK	17,180	VC
Old Dominion Univ	VA	20,910	C
Oregon Inst of Technology	OR	8,910	C
Penn State Erie/The Behrend College	PA	16,256	C
Pennsylvania College of Technology	PA	27,333	NC
Pittsburg State Univ	KS	13,880	NC
Point Park Univ	PA	41,270	C
Purdue Univ/Northwest	IN	15,038	C
Purdue Univ/West Lafayette	IN	20,032	MC
Rochester Inst of Technology	NY	50,842	HC
S Car State Univ	SC	20,805	LC
Southern Univ and A&M College	LA	16,074	LC+
SUNY / Buffalo State College	NY	20,842	C
SUNY Polytechnic Inst	NY	19,473	VC
Tarleton State Univ	TX	15,248	LC
Texas A&M Univ at Corpus Christi	TX	16,851	LC
Texas A&M Univ at Galveston	TX	15,920	C
The Univ of Akron	OH	21,477	C
Univ of Arkansas at Little Rock	AR	18,211	C
Univ of Cincinnati	OH	21,964	VC
Univ of Dayton	OH	53,620	C
Univ of Hartford	CT	49,776	C
Univ of Houston	TX	21,483	VC
Univ of Maine	ME	20,792	C
Univ of Mass Lowell	MA	26,380	C
Univ of New Hampshire - Manchester	NH	14,490	C
Univ of N Car at Charlotte	NC	15,547	C
Univ of North Texas	TX	19,198	C
Univ of Pittsburgh at Johnstown	PA	22,092	C
Univ of Southern Indiana	IN	16,501	C
Univ of Southern Miss	MS	13,170	C
Univ of Wisc-Green Bay	WI	15,064	C
Vaughn College of Aeronautics and Technology	NY	37,180	C
Wayne State Univ	MI	22,016	C
Weber State Univ	UT	10,721	C
Western Washington Univ	WA	18,003	C+
Youngstown State Univ	OH	17,307	C

MECHATRONICS ENGINEERING

School	ST	$IS	SR
Cal State, Chico	CA	21,440	C
Central Conn State Univ	CT	21,203	C
Purdue Univ/Northwest	IN	15,038	C
Univ of Denver	CO	58,443	VC+
Vaughn College of Aeronautics and Technology	NY	37,180	C
Worcester Polytechnic Inst	MA	60,730	MC

MEDIA ARTS

School	ST	$IS	SR
Alverno College	WI	33,294	LC
Anna Maria College	MA	48,186	C
Art Inst of Portland	OR	132,329	SP
Ashland Univ	OH	21,440	C
Baker Univ	KS	33,350	C+
Bentley Univ	MA	60,890	HC
Briar Cliff Univ	IA	36,956	C
Brigham Young Univ	UT	12,748	HC
Brown Univ	RI	64,566	MC
Butler Univ	IN	51,352	VC
Cal State, Fresno	CA	16,902	LC
Cal State, Los Angeles	CA	17,186	LC
Calumet College of St. Joseph	IN	22,735	C
Calvin College	MI	41,570	VC+
Canisius College	NY	47,537	C
Carleton College	MN	64,071	MC
Carlow Univ	PA	38,549	LC
Champlain College	VT	53,132	C+
Chatham Univ	PA	46,517	C
CUNY/Hunter College	NY	31,098	VC
Claremont McKenna College	CA	67,185	MC
College of the Ozarks	MO	7,230	C
Corban Univ	OR	40,306	C
Denison Univ	OH	58,860	MC
DePaul Univ	IL	47,623	VC
DeSales Univ	PA	43,970	C
Drexel Univ	PA	65,432	VC+
Drury Univ	MO	33,791	VC
Eastern Mich Univ	MI	19,761	C
Edinboro Univ	PA	15,940	LC
Elon Univ	NC	44,599	VC+
Emerson College	MA	54,736	HC
Florida Atlantic Univ	FL	17,339	C
Goddard College	VT	17,040	VC
Grand Rapids Theological Seminary/Cornerstone Univ	MI	33,338	C
Greenville College	IL	27,012	C
Hampshire College	MA	63,824	MC
Harding Univ	AR	25,421	C
Hofstra Univ	NY	55,960	C+
Houghton College	NY	39,090	C
Howard Univ	DC	37,616	C+
Huntington Univ	IN	33,996	C
Illinois State Univ	IL	23,418	VC
Indiana Univ Bloomington	IN	20,429	VC
Indiana Univ Kokomo	IN	7,073	C
Indiana Univ-Purdue Univ Indianapolis	IN	18,635	C
Ithaca College	NY	56,766	VC
James Madison Univ	VA	19,084	VC
Johns Hopkins Univ	MD	65,386	MC
Judson Univ	IL	37,700	C
Lake Erie College	OH	38,914	LC
Lasell College	MA	47,500	C
Lawrence Tech Univ	MI	39,770	VC
Lindsey Wilson College	KY	32,882	C
LIU Brooklyn	NY	49,682	C
Loyola Univ Chicago	IL	55,802	VC
Macalester College	MN	61,905	MC
Maine College of Art	ME	43,794	SP
Marquette Univ	WI	48,390	VC+
Maryland Inst College of Art	MD	56,795	SP
Marylhurst Univ	OR	20,295	NC
Mass College of Art and Design	MA	24,800	SP
Mass Inst of Technology	MA	62,662	MC
Mercer Univ	GA	45,348	VC
Mercy College	NY	31,776	C
Miami Univ	OH	27,190	HC+
Mills College	CA	59,163	VC
Montana State Univ	MT	15,500	C+
Mount Ida College	MA	46,820	C
Mount St. Mary College	NY	42,061	C
New Jersey City Univ	NJ	21,456	LC
New York Univ	NY	65,860	MC
NewSchool of Architecture & Design	CA	12,341	SP
Northeastern Illinois Univ	IL	12,529	LC
Ohio Univ	OH	22,924	C
Olivet Nazarene Univ	IL	41,840	C
Pepperdine Univ	CA	74,460	HC+
Pitzer College	CA	66,192	MC
Point Loma Nazarene Univ	CA	43,450	C
Point Park Univ	PA	41,270	C
Pomona College	CA	64,957	MC
Radford Univ	VA	19,027	LC
Rensselaer Polytechnic Inst	NY	63,436	MC
Robert Morris Univ	PA	37,834	C
Rochester Inst of Technology	NY	50,842	HC
Rocky Mountain College of Art and Design	CO	27,052	SP
Roger Williams Univ	RI	46,296	C+
Rollins College	FL	58,670	HC
Roosevelt Univ	IL	40,651	VC
Sacred Heart Univ	CT	52,750	C
Salve Regina Univ	RI	51,470	C
San Francisco Art Inst	CA	58,505	SP
Savannah College of Art and Design	GA	49,595	C
Southern Illinois Univ Edwardsville	IL	22,643	C
Southern Methodist Univ	TX	66,483	MC
Spalding Univ	KY	31,938	SP
St. Catherine Univ	MN	45,630	VC
SUNY / SUNY College at Old Westbury	NY	16,860	C
SUNY / SUNY Fredonia	NY	20,818	C
SUNY / Univ at Buffalo	NY	23,122	C+
Sterling College	KS	32,830	C
Suffolk Univ	MA	50,308	C
Swarthmore College	PA	63,550	MC
Taylor Univ	IN	40,317	C+
Temple Univ	PA	24,392	VC
The Univ of Akron	OH	21,477	C
Thiel College	PA	41,590	C
Towson Univ	MD	17,408	VC
Trinity International Univ	IL	31,070	VC
Tulane Univ	LA	63,396	HC+
Univ of Calif at Irvine	CA	26,484	VC
Univ of Chicago	IL	67,584	MC
Univ of Denver	CO	58,443	VC+
Univ of Hartford	CT	49,776	C
Univ of Illinois at Urbana-Champaign	IL	27,006	HC
Univ of Maine	ME	20,792	C
Univ of Maine at Farmington	ME	18,187	C
Univ of Missouri-St. Louis	MO		C
Univ of Montana	MT	14,105	C
Univ of Mount Union	OH	38,970	C
Univ of New Mexico	NM	15,404	C
Univ of N Car at Greensboro	NC	14,690	C
Univ of Pittsburgh	PA	29,568	HC+
Univ of Rochester	NY	65,032	MC
Univ of San Francisco	CA	58,484	VC
Univ of S Car at Columbia	SC	19,725	VC+
Univ of Texas at Dallas	TX	22,830	VC+
Univ of the District of Columbia	DC	21,044	LC
Univ of Wisc-Platteville	WI	14,614	VC
Vanderbilt Univ	TN	60,572	MC
Vassar College	NY	65,491	MC
Virginia Commonwealth Univ	VA	23,049	C
Washburn Univ	KS	15,827	C
Wayne State Univ	MI	22,016	C
Weber State Univ	UT	10,721	C
Webster Univ	MO	37,490	C
Wellesley College	MA	63,916	MC
Wesley College	DE	37,026	LC
Western Conn State Univ	CT	21,254	LC
Widener Univ	PA	56,486	C
Wilkes Univ	PA	45,622	C
Wilmington Univ	DE	8,546	NC
Wisc Lutheran College	WI	36,290	VC
Xavier Univ	OH	47,880	C+
Youngstown State Univ	OH	17,307	C

MEDIA MANAGEMENT

School	ST	$IS	SR
Elon Univ	NC	44,599	VC+
Lewis Univ	IL	40,370	C
Minn State Univ, Mankato	MN	15,616	C
Ohio Univ	OH	22,924	C
Pace Univ	NY	58,248	C
San Diego State Univ	CA	21,896	C+
Texas Tech Univ	TX	18,736	C+
Univ of Miami	FL	63,494	MC
Univ of S Dak	SD	16,109	C

MEDICAL ANTHROPOLOGY

School	ST	$IS	SR
Creighton Univ	NE	48,206	VC+

MEDICAL IMAGING

School	ST	$IS	SR
Georgian Court Univ	NJ	42,426	LC
Indiana Univ Kokomo	IN	7,073	C
Indiana Univ Northwest	IN	7,072	C
Indiana Univ South Bend	IN	14,242	C
Indiana Univ-Purdue Univ Indianapolis	IN	18,635	C
MCPHS Univ	MA	45,470	SP
Rochester Inst of Technology	NY	50,842	HC
Thomas Edison State Univ	NJ	6,350	NC

MEDICAL LABORATORY SCIENCE

School	ST	$IS	SR
Allen College	IA	32,367	NC
Armstrong State Univ	GA	16,962	C
Auburn Univ at Montgomery	AL	15,290	C
Augusta Univ	GA	4,632	C
Augustana Univ	SD	38,424	VC
Austin Peay State Univ	TN	16,397	C
Bloomfield College	NJ	39,100	LC
Eastern Mich Univ	MI	19,761	C
Ferris State Univ	MI	21,445	C
Heritage Univ	WA	19,825	NC
Idaho State Univ	ID	13,619	NC
Lewis Univ	IL	40,370	C
Marquette Univ	WI	48,390	VC+
Mich Tech Univ	MI	24,739	VC+
Minn State Univ, Mankato	MN	15,616	C
Monmouth Univ	NJ	46,234	C
Oakland Univ	MI	20,763	C
Ohio State Univ at Columbus	OH	21,703	HC+
Rhode Island College	RI	17,694	LC
Saginaw Valley State Univ	MI	18,530	C
St. Louis Univ	MO	49,866	HC
St. Mary's Univ of Minn	MN	41,210	VC
S Dak State Univ	SD	15,634	C
Southeast Missouri State Univ	MO	15,498	C
St. Edward's Univ	TX	53,100	VC
Tarleton State Univ	TX	15,248	LC
The Univ of Utah	UT	17,924	VC
Univ of Iowa	IA	18,683	VC+
Univ of Louisiana at Monroe	LA	15,970	C
Univ of Mass Dartmouth	MA	25,658	C
Univ of Miss	MS	17,746	C+
Univ of New England	ME	48,880	C
Univ of N Dak	ND	15,373	C
Univ of Rhode Island	RI	24,906	C
Univ of Vermont	VT	28,878	HC
Weber State Univ	UT	10,721	C
Western Carolina Univ	NC	13,965	C
York College of Pennsylvania	PA	29,240	C

MEDICAL LABORATORY TECHNOLOGY

School	ST	$IS	SR
Alabama A&M Univ	AL	18,796	C
American International College	MA	46,300	LC
Anderson Univ	IN	38,200	C
Andrews Univ	MI	28,030	C+
Angelo State Univ	TX	15,263	NC
Arkansas Tech Univ	AR	15,484	C
Auburn Univ	AL	23,594	VC+
Avila Univ	MO	35,480	C
Baylor Univ	TX	53,760	HC
Bemidji State Univ	MN	16,056	VC
Blackburn College	IL	28,526	LC
Bloomsburg Univ of Pennsylvania	PA	19,066	LC
Brescia Univ	KY	29,890	VC+
Caldwell Univ	NJ	42,165	NC
Cal State, Northridge	CA	16,859	LC
Cal State, Sacramento	CA	20,332	C
Calif Univ of Pennsylvania	PA	14,217	LC
Campbellsville Univ	KY	32,492	C
Canisius College	NY	47,537	C
Cheyney Univ of Pennsylvania	PA	20,896	LC
CUNY/Hunter College	NY	31,098	VC
CUNY/York College	NY	6,747	LC
Clemson Univ	SC		HC
Coker College	SC	34,810	LC
College of St. Mary	NE	35,184	C
Columbia College	SC	36,550	C
Concord Univ	WV	14,954	C
Concordia Univ Nebr	NE	36,280	VC
Defiance College	OH	41,630	C
Dordt College	IA	37,860	C+
East Stroudsburg Univ	PA	18,334	C
Eastern Mennonite Univ	VA	42,550	C
Eastern Mich Univ	MI	19,761	C
Eastern New Mexico Univ	NM	14,416	C
Eastern Washington Univ	WA	25,572	LC
Edinboro Univ	PA	15,940	LC
Elms College	MA	45,646	VC
Eureka College	IL	30,220	C
Evangel Univ	MO	28,898	C
Fairleigh Dickinson Univ/ College at Florham	NJ	52,062	C
Fairleigh Dickinson Univ/ Metropolitan Campus	NJ	40,254	C
Fayetteville State Univ	NC	17,756	C
Florida Atlantic Univ	FL	17,339	C
George Washington Univ	DC	62,835	MC
Graceland Univ	IA	35,290	C

ST = STATE $IS = IN-STATE COSTS SR = SELECTOR RATING

School	ST	$IS	SR
Grand Valley State Univ	MI	22,250	C+
Gwynedd Mercy Univ	PA	43,780	LC
Holy Family Univ	PA	43,326	LC
Illinois College	IL	40,850	VC
Illinois State Univ	IL	23,418	VC
Indiana State Univ	IN	23,223	LC
Indiana Wesleyan Univ	IN	33,674	C
Inter-American Univ of PR-San Germán	PR	20,042	
Judson Univ	IL	37,700	C
Kent State Univ	OH	20,732	C
Keuka College	NY	39,762	C
King's College	PA	46,858	C
Kutztown Univ of Pennsylvania	PA	19,056	LC
Lamar Univ	TX	18,014	LC
Langston Univ	OK	14,314	C
Lebanon Valley College	PA	51,530	C
Lee Univ	TN	22,045	C
Lenoir-Rhyne Univ	NC	43,200	C
Lincoln Memorial Univ	TN	28,070	C
LIU Post	NY	49,682	C
Lock Haven Univ of Pennsylvania	PA	18,028	LC
Louisiana College	LA	21,886	C
Louisiana Tech Univ	LA	11,422	VC
Malone Univ	OH	38,448	C
Manchester Univ	IN	40,422	C
Marshall Univ	WV	17,242	C
Mayville State Univ	ND	18,371	NC
McKendree Univ	IL	37,940	C+
Mercy College	NY	31,776	C
Mercyhurst Univ	PA	47,420	C
Mich State Univ	MI	23,898	VC+
Midwestern State Univ	TX	17,572	C
Minn State Univ, Moorhead	MN	15,941	C
Misericordia Univ	PA	43,840	C
Missouri Western State Univ	MO	16,741	
Monmouth Univ	NJ	46,234	C
Morgan State Univ	MD	17,190	LC
Mount Aloysius College	PA	29,976	C
Mount Mercy Univ	IA	36,826	C
National Louis Univ	IL	16,920	LC
N Car State Univ	NC	19,515	HC+
North Park Univ	IL	35,860	C
Northeastern State Univ	OK	8,615	VC
Northern Mich Univ	MI	19,604	C
Northern State Univ	SD	14,505	C
Northwestern College of Iowa	IA	38,400	C+
Northwestern Okla State Univ	OK	13,072	NC
Norwich Univ	VT	28,212	C
Okla Christian Univ	OK	27,650	VC
Oral Roberts Univ	OK	34,316	C
Pontifical Catholic Univ of PR	PR	10,534	
Purdue Univ/Northwest	IN	15,038	C
Purdue Univ/West Lafayette	IN	20,032	MC
Rutgers Univ - Camden	NJ	26,146	C
Rutgers Univ - New Brunswick	NJ	26,632	HC
Rutgers Univ - Newark	NJ	27,288	C
St. Augustine's Univ	NC	26,048	C
St. Francis Univ	PA	42,268	NC
St. Louis Univ	MO	49,866	HC
St. Peter's Univ	NJ	49,192	C
Salem College	NC	37,694	HC
Salem State Univ	MA	17,303	LC
Salisbury Univ	MD	20,714	VC
Seton Hill Univ	PA	46,972	C
Shorter Univ	GA	31,130	LC
Slippery Rock Univ of Pennsylvania	PA	10,360	C
Southeastern Okla State Univ	OK	11,875	C
Southern Arkansas Univ	AR	21,532	C
Southern Wesleyan Univ	SC	32,130	LC
Southwestern Okla State Univ	OK	11,790	C
St. Francis College	NY	38,800	LC
St. Thomas Aquinas College	NY	42,200	C
SUNY / SUNY Fredonia	NY	20,818	C
SUNY / SUNY Plattsburgh	NY	18,814	C
Stevenson Univ	MD	72,770	C
Suffolk Univ	MA	50,308	C
Tarleton State Univ	TX	15,248	LC
Texas A&M Univ at Kingsville	TX	7,500	LC
The Catholic Univ of America	DC	56,356	VC
The Univ of Tenn at Chattanooga	TN	16,744	C
The Univ of Utah	UT	17,924	VC
The Univ of Virginia's College at Wise	VA	18,192	LC
Thiel College	PA	41,590	C
Thomas More College	KY	36,720	C
Towson Univ	MD	17,408	VC
Union College	NE	23,270	C
Union Univ	TN	33,970	VC
Univ of Alaska Anchorage	AK	16,652	NC
Univ of Central Florida	FL	15,922	VC
Univ of Central Missouri	MO	18,982	C
Univ of Cincinnati	OH	21,964	VC
Univ of Conn	CT	25,538	HC
Univ of Delaware	DE	24,976	VC+
Univ of Hawaii at Manoa	HI	23,221	C
Univ of Indianapolis	IN	36,480	C
Univ of Iowa	IA	18,683	VC+
Univ of Kansas	KS	20,135	C+
Univ of Louisville	KY	19,824	C
Univ of Maine	ME	20,792	C
Univ of Mich-Flint	MI	17,607	C+
Univ of Minn/Twin Cities	MN	23,519	HC+
Univ of New Mexico	NM	15,404	C
Univ of North Texas	TX	19,198	C
Univ of Pittsburgh at Johnstown	PA	22,092	C
Univ of Scranton	PA	54,962	VC
Univ of Sioux Falls	SD	34,330	C
Univ of Southern Miss	MS	13,170	C
Univ of Texas at El Paso	TX	34,452	NC
Univ of Washington	WA	23,149	VC
Univ of West Florida	FL	15,848	C
Univ of Wisc-La Crosse	WI	15,247	C+
Univ of Wisc-Oshkosh	WI	15,200	C
Univ of Wyoming	WY	15,375	C+
Utah State Univ	UT	12,736	C
Wartburg College	IA	47,840	C
Wesley College	DE	37,026	LC
Western New Mexico Univ	NM	16,734	LC
Wichita State Univ	KS	21,643	C
William Carey Univ	MS	23,950	LC
William Jewell College	MO	41,210	C+
Winthrop Univ	SC	23,082	C
Wright State Univ	OH	16,983	C

MEDICAL PHYSICS

School	ST	$IS	SR
Belmont Univ	TN	40,970	VC
Oakland Univ	MI	20,763	C
Oregon State Univ	OR	22,519	VC
Univ of Arizona	AZ	23,100	C

MEDICAL RECORDS ADMINISTRATION/SERVICES

School	ST	$IS	SR
Dakota State Univ	SD	13,811	C
Davenport Univ	MI	25,896	LC
East Carolina Univ	NC	16,937	C
Ferris State Univ	MI	21,445	C
Louisiana Tech Univ	LA	11,422	VC
Norfolk State Univ	VA	25,702	LC
Pennsylvania College of Technology	PA	27,333	NC
St. Louis Univ	MO	49,866	HC
Southwestern Okla State Univ	OK	11,790	C
St. Catherine Univ	MN	45,630	VC
Tenn State Univ	TN	14,423	C
Texas State Univ	TX	19,350	C
Univ of Alabama at Birmingham	AL	19,906	C
Western Carolina Univ	NC	13,965	C

MEDICAL SCIENCE

School	ST	$IS	SR
Bay Path Univ	MA	45,349	C
Bloomfield College	NJ	39,100	LC
Boston Univ	MA	65,110	MC
Bryant Univ	RI	55,646	VC
Edgewood College	WI	35,950	C
Southern Illinois Univ Edwardsville	IL	22,643	C
The Univ of Utah	UT	17,924	VC
Univ of Arizona	AZ	23,100	C
Univ of Arkansas at Fayetteville	AR	19,152	C+
Univ of Chicago	IL	67,584	MC
Univ of Colo Denver	CO	23,230	C
Univ of Louisville	KY	19,824	C
Univ of Wisc-Milwaukee	WI	21,496	C

MEDICAL TECHNOLOGY

School	ST	$IS	SR
Armstrong State Univ	GA	16,962	C
Augusta Univ	GA	4,632	C
Averett Univ	VA	40,970	LC
Ball State Univ	IN	19,590	C
Barry Univ	FL	37,830	C
Bellarmine Univ	KY	51,220	C
Belmont Univ	TN	40,970	VC
Bloomfield College	NJ	39,100	LC
Blue Mountain College	MS	15,949	VC
Brescia Univ	KY	29,890	VC+
Briar Cliff Univ	IA	36,956	C
CUNY/College of Staten Island	NY	17,840	NC
Clarion Univ of Pennsylvania	PA	21,608	LC
Cleveland State Univ	OH	22,196	C
College of the Ozarks	MO	7,230	C
Colo State Univ-Pueblo	CO	18,234	C
East Carolina Univ	NC	16,937	C
East Central Univ	OK	13,056	C
Farmingdale State College	NY	20,624	C
Gannon Univ	PA	42,032	C
Gardner-Webb Univ	NC	39,200	C+
George Mason Univ	VA	15,724	VC
Harding Univ	AR	25,421	C
Hartwick College	NY	51,270	C
Henderson State Univ	AR	15,516	LC
Houghton College	NY	39,090	C
Idaho State Univ	ID	13,619	NC
Indiana Univ Kokomo	IN	7,073	C
Indiana Univ-Purdue Univ Fort Wayne	IN	17,553	C
Inter-American Univ of PR Ponce	PR	19,549	
Inter-American Univ of PR-Fajardo Campus	PR	18,336	
Inter-American Univ of PR-Metropolitan Campus	PR	20,045	
Kansas State Univ	KS	17,780	VC
Kean Univ	NJ	24,650	C
Kutztown Univ of Pennsylvania	PA	19,056	LC
Lincoln Univ	MO	13,602	NC
Lindenwood Univ	MO	25,132	C
Lipscomb Univ	TN	41,296	VC
Lubbock Christian Univ	TX	28,426	C
Marist College	NY	49,860	VC
Marywood Univ	PA	46,900	C
Millersville Univ of Pennsylvania	PA	23,782	C
Miss State Univ	MS	11,454	C+
Missouri Southern State Univ	MO	12,499	C
Morehead State Univ	KY	17,422	C
Morningside College	IA	36,865	C
Mount Aloysius College	PA	29,976	C
Mount Marty College	SD	32,972	C
Norfolk State Univ	VA	25,702	LC
Northern Kentucky Univ	KY	16,486	C
Oakwood Univ	AL	43,758	C
Ohio Northern Univ	OH	44,050	VC
Ohio State Univ at Columbus	OH	21,703	HC+
Old Dominion Univ	VA	20,910	C
Pittsburg State Univ	KS	13,880	NC
Prairie View A&M Univ	TX	15,205	LC
Roosevelt Univ	IL	40,651	VC
Rutgers Univ - New Brunswick	NJ	26,632	HC
Saginaw Valley State Univ	MI	18,530	C
St. Mary-of-the-Woods College	IN	39,632	LC
Sam Houston State Univ	TX	18,792	C
Seattle Univ	WA	50,811	VC+
Southern Adventist Univ	TN	27,600	C
Southern Illinois Univ Edwardsville	IL	22,643	C
Southwest Baptist Univ	MO	29,900	LC
Southwest Minn State Univ	MN	17,783	C
Southwestern Adventist Univ	TX	27,756	LC
St. Joseph's College, New York/Brooklyn Campus	NY	25,114	LC
St. Joseph's College, New York/Long Island Campus	NY	25,124	C
SUNY / SUNY Plattsburgh	NY	18,814	C
SUNY / Univ at Buffalo	NY	23,122	C+
Tenn State Univ	TN	14,423	C
Texas Southern Univ	TX	18,212	LC
Texas Woman's Univ	TX	15,302	LC
The Catholic Univ of America	DC	56,356	VC
The College at Brockport - SUNY	NY	20,346	C
The College of St. Rose	NY	43,048	C
The Univ of Tenn at Knoxville	TN	22,112	VC
Tusculum College	TN	31,625	C
Univ of Alabama at Birmingham	AL	19,906	C
Univ of Bridgeport	CT	44,430	LC
Univ of Central Arkansas	AR	14,472	VC
Univ of Hawaii at Manoa	HI	23,221	C
Univ of Mass Boston	MA	13,435	C
Univ of Miss	MS	17,746	C+
Univ of Montana	MT	14,105	C
Univ of Mount Union	OH	38,970	C
Univ of New Orleans	LA	12,840	C
Univ of N Car at Charlotte	NC	15,547	C
Univ of Rio Grande & Rio Grande Community College	OH	8,750	NC
Univ of S Dak	SD	16,109	C
Univ of South Florida/Tampa	FL	16,110	VC+
Univ of St. Francis	IL	39,924	C
Univ of Texas at Arlington	TX	18,026	LC
Univ of Texas at Austin	TX	26,102	HC
Univ of the Sacred Heart	PR	17,932	
Univ of the Sciences	PA	54,038	VC
West Chester Univ of Pennsylvania	PA	18,456	C
West Texas A&M Univ	TX	13,478	C
Western Kentucky Univ	KY	16,850	C
Wilkes Univ	PA	45,622	C
Winston-Salem State Univ	NC	26,166	LC

MEDICINE, HEALTH & SOCIETY

School	ST	$IS	SR
Vanderbilt Univ	TN	60,572	MC

MEDIEVAL STUDIES

School	ST	$IS	SR
Bard College	NY	64,024	HC
Barnard College/Columbia Univ	NY	62,741	MC
Bates College	ME	64,500	MC
Brown Univ	RI	64,566	MC
College of William & Mary	VA		MC
Columbia Univ/City of New York	NY	62,958	MC
Dickinson College	PA	63,974	MC
Duke Univ	NC	64,188	
Emory Univ	GA	60,786	MC
Fordham Univ	NY	65,918	MC
Hanover College	IN	46,364	C+
Mount Holyoke College	MA	56,746	MC
New College of Florida	FL	15,848	MC
New York Univ	NY	65,860	MC
Ohio State Univ at Columbus	OH	21,703	HC+
Pennsylvania State Univ - Univ Park	PA	29,760	HC
Pomona College	CA	64,957	MC
Purdue Univ/West Lafayette	IN	20,032	MC
Rice Univ	TX	57,668	MC
Rutgers Univ - New Brunswick	NJ	26,632	HC
Rutgers Univ - Newark	NJ	27,288	C
Sewanee: The Univ of the South	TN	54,500	MC
Smith College	MA	63,914	MC
Southern Methodist Univ	TX	66,483	MC
St. Olaf College	MN	54,260	HC+
SUNY at Binghamton	NY	22,861	MC
SUNY SUNY Albany	NY	22,165	C
Swarthmore College	PA	63,550	MC
The Catholic Univ of America	DC	56,356	VC
Tulane Univ	LA	63,396	HC+
Univ of Calif at Davis	CA	28,468	HC
Univ of Calif at Santa Barbara	CA	29,091	HC
Univ of Chicago	IL	67,584	MC
Univ of Mich/Ann Arbor	MI	24,410	MC
Univ of Nebr - Lincoln	NE	18,589	VC
Univ of Notre Dame	IN	64,043	MC
Univ of Oregon	OR	22,972	C
Vassar College	NY	65,491	MC
Washington and Lee Univ	VA	59,647	MC
Wellesley College	MA	63,916	MC
Wesleyan Univ	CT	65,516	MC

MEETING / SPECIAL EVENT MGMT

School	ST	$IS	SR
College of the Ozarks	MO	7,230	C
Johnson & Wales Univ/ Denver Campus	CO	42,707	C

MEETING/SPECIAL EVENT MANAGEMENT

School	ST	$IS	SR
College of the Ozarks	MO	7,230	C
Johnson & Wales Univ/ Denver Campus	CO	42,707	C

MENTAL HEALTH/HUMAN SERVICES

School	ST	$IS	SR
Bloomfield College	NJ	39,100	LC
Calif Univ of Pennsylvania	PA	14,217	LC
Indiana Univ-Purdue Univ Indianapolis	IN	18,635	C
Inter-American Univ of PR-Aguadilla Campus	PR	21,657	
Metropolitan College of New York	NY		VC
Morgan State Univ	MD	17,190	LC
Northern Kentucky Univ	KY	16,486	C
Pennsylvania College of Technology	PA	27,333	NC
Prescott College	AZ	33,284	C
Sinte Gleska Univ	SD	13,154	NC
Southern Oregon Univ	OR	19,117	C
Univ of Maine at Augusta	ME	7,812	C
Univ of Maine at Machias	ME	22,960	C
Univ of North Florida	FL	15,996	VC
Univ of the Sciences	PA	54,038	VC

METAL/JEWELRY

School	ST	$IS	SR
Adams State Univ	CO	17,703	LC
Calif College of the Arts	CA	52,758	SP
Cleveland Inst of Art	OH	51,439	C+
College for Creative Studies	MI	48,875	SP
Colo State Univ	CO	22,162	VC
Ferris State Univ	MI	21,445	C
Hofstra Univ	NY	55,960	C+
Maine College of Art	ME	43,794	SP
Mass College of Art and Design	MA	24,800	SP
Memphis College of Art	TN	39,750	C
Rhode Island School of Design	RI	59,960	SP
Rochester Inst of Technology	NY	50,842	HC
Savannah College of Art and Design	GA	49,595	C
SUNY at New Paltz	NY	19,200	C
Syracuse Univ	NY	60,239	VC
Temple Univ	PA	24,392	VC
Univ of Iowa	IA	18,683	VC+
Univ of Kansas	KS	20,135	C+
Univ of Mass Dartmouth	MA	25,658	C
Univ of Mich/Ann Arbor	MI	24,410	MC
Univ of Oregon	OR	22,972	C

METALLURGICAL ENGINEERING

School	ST	$IS	SR
Colo School of Mines	CO	29,319	MC
Columbia Univ/City of New York	NY	62,958	MC
Illinois Inst of Technology	IL	56,826	HC+
Missouri Univ of Science and Technology	MO	18,655	HC
Montana Tech of the Univ of Montana	MT	15,447	C+

ST = STATE $IS = IN-STATE COSTS SR = SELECTOR RATING

School	ST	$IS	SR
S Dak School of Mines and Technology	SD	18,645	VC
The Univ of Utah	UT	17,924	VC
Univ of Alabama	AL	24,320	C+
Univ of Cincinnati	OH	21,964	VC
Univ of Illinois at Urbana-Champaign	IL	27,006	HC
Univ of Minn/Twin Cities	MN	23,519	HC+
Univ of Nevada/Reno	NV	18,010	C
Univ of Texas at El Paso	TX	34,452	NC

MEXICAN-AMERICAN/CHICANO STUDIES

School	ST	$IS	SR
Cal State, Dominguez Hills	CA	19,022	LC
Cal State, Fresno	CA	16,902	LC
Cal State, Fullerton	CA	21,902	C
Cal State, Los Angeles	CA	17,186	LC
Cal State, Northridge	CA	16,859	LC
Concordia Univ Texas	TX	40,210	C
Metropolitan State Univ of Denver	CO	29,889	LC
Our Lady of the Lake Univ	TX	35,012	LC
Pitzer College	CA	66,192	MC
Pomona College	CA	64,957	MC
San Diego State Univ	CA	21,896	C+
San Jose State Univ	CA	21,540	C
Scripps College	CA	66,664	MC
Sonoma State Univ	CA	27,806	C
Southern Methodist Univ	TX	66,483	MC
Univ of Arizona	AZ	23,100	C
Univ of Calif at Davis	CA	28,468	HC
Univ of Calif at Los Angeles	CA	30,162	MC
Univ of Calif at Riverside	CA	29,227	C+
Univ of Calif at Santa Barbara	CA	29,091	HC
Univ of Mich/Ann Arbor	MI	24,410	MC
Univ of Minn/Twin Cities	MN	23,519	HC+
Univ of New Mexico	NM	15,404	C
Univ of Northern Colo	CO	20,851	C
Univ of Texas at El Paso	TX	34,452	NC
Univ of Texas at San Antonio	TX	20,157	C

MICROBIOLOGY

School	ST	$IS	SR
Albany College of Pharmacy and Health Sciences	NY	42,681	SP
Arizona State Univ at the Tempe Campus	AZ	21,756	VC
Auburn Univ	AL	23,594	VC+
Brigham Young Univ	UT	12,748	HC
Bryant Univ	RI	55,646	VC
Calif Polytechnic State Univ	CA	17,979	HC+
Calif State Polytechnic Univ, Pomona	CA	21,541	C
Cal State, Chico	CA	21,440	C
Cal State, Long Beach	CA	18,850	C
Cal State, Los Angeles	CA	17,186	LC
Cal State, Northridge	CA	16,859	LC
Cal State, Sacramento	CA	20,332	C
Clemson Univ	SC		HC
Colo State Univ	CO	22,162	VC
Eastern Kentucky Univ	KY	16,908	C
Eastern Washington Univ	WA	25,572	LC
Howard Univ	DC	37,616	C+
Idaho State Univ	ID	13,619	NC
Indiana Univ Bloomington	IN	20,429	VC
Inter-American Univ of PR-Aguadilla Campus	PR	21,657	
Inter-American Univ of PR-Arecibo Campus	PR	18,245	
Iowa State Univ	IA	17,570	C
Kansas State Univ	KS	17,780	VC
Kutztown Univ of Pennsylvania	PA	19,056	LC
Louisiana State Univ and A&M College	LA	18,677	VC
Miami Univ	OH	27,190	HC+
Mich State Univ	MI	23,898	VC+
Mills College	CA	59,163	VC
Miss State Univ	MS	11,454	C+
Miss Univ for Women	MS	17,065	C
Missouri Southern State Univ	MO	12,499	C
Montana State Univ	MT	15,500	C+
New Mexico State Univ	NM	14,050	C
New York Univ	NY	65,860	MC
N Car State Univ	NC	19,515	HC+
N Dak State Univ	ND	16,245	C
Northern Arizona Univ	AZ	20,246	VC
Northern Mich Univ	MI	19,604	C
Ohio State Univ at Columbus	OH	21,703	HC+
Ohio Univ	OH	22,924	C
Ohio Wesleyan Univ	OH	49,460	VC
Okla State Univ	OK	17,180	VC
Oregon State Univ	OR	22,519	VC
Pennsylvania State Univ - Univ Park	PA	29,760	HC
Purdue Univ/Northwest	IN	15,038	C
Purdue Univ/West Lafayette	IN	20,032	MC
Quinnipiac Univ	CT	59,110	C
Rutgers Univ - New Brunswick	NJ	26,632	HC
San Diego State Univ	CA	21,896	C+
San Francisco State Univ	CA	18,514	LC
San Jose State Univ	CA	21,540	C
S Dak State Univ	SD	15,634	C
Southern Illinois Univ Carbondale	IL	23,667	C
Southwestern Okla State Univ	OK	11,790	C
SUNY / The College of Environmental Science and Forestry	NY	23,853	VC
Texas A&M Univ	TX	20,521	VC+
Texas State Univ	TX	19,350	C
Texas Tech Univ	TX	18,736	C+
Univ of PR, at Arecibo	PR	12,652	
Univ of Alabama	AL	24,320	C+
Univ of Arizona	AZ	23,100	C
Univ of Calif at Berkeley	CA	28,853	MC
Univ of Calif at Davis	CA	28,468	HC
Univ of Calif at Irvine	CA	26,484	VC
Univ of Calif at Los Angeles	CA	30,162	MC
Univ of Calif at Riverside	CA	29,227	C+
Univ of Calif at Santa Barbara	CA	29,091	HC
Univ of Calif San Diego	CA	30,150	MC
Univ of Florida	FL	16,291	HC+
Univ of Georgia	GA	21,250	HC
Univ of Great Falls	MT	38,524	C
Univ of Hawaii at Manoa	HI	23,221	C
Univ of Houston-Downtown	TX	7,241	C
Univ of Idaho	ID	15,348	C
Univ of Illinois at Urbana-Champaign	IL	27,006	HC
Univ of Iowa	IA	18,683	VC+
Univ of Kansas	KS	20,135	C+
Univ of Maine	ME	20,792	C
Univ of Maryland/College Park	MD	21,938	HC
Univ of Mass Amherst	MA	26,199	VC+
Univ of Memphis	TN	18,278	C
Univ of Miami	FL	63,494	MC
Univ of Mich/Ann Arbor	MI	24,410	MC
Univ of Mich/Dearborn	MI	11,757	VC
Univ of Minn/Twin Cities	MN	23,519	HC+
Univ of Missouri/Columbia	MO	18,201	MC
Univ of Montana	MT	14,105	C
Univ of Nebr - Lincoln	NE	18,589	VC
Univ of New Hampshire	NH	28,562	VC
Univ of Okla	OK	18,911	VC
Univ of Pittsburgh	PA	29,568	HC+
Univ of PR, at Humacao	PR	14,000	
Univ of PR, at Mayaguez	PR	13,995	
Univ of Rhode Island	RI	24,906	C
Univ of Rochester	NY	65,032	MC
Univ of South Florida/Tampa	FL	16,110	VC+
Univ of Texas at Arlington	TX	18,026	LC
Univ of Texas at Austin	TX	26,102	HC
Univ of Texas at El Paso	TX	34,452	NC
Univ of the Sciences	PA	54,038	VC
Univ of Vermont	VT	28,878	HC
Univ of Washington	WA	23,149	VC
Univ of Wisc-La Crosse	WI	15,247	C+
Univ of Wisc-Madison	WI	20,934	MC
Univ of Wisc-Milwaukee	WI	21,496	C
Univ of Wisc-Oshkosh	WI	15,200	C
Univ of Wyoming	WY	15,375	C+
Utah State Univ	UT	12,736	C
Wagner College	NY	55,480	C+
Washington State Univ	WA	22,495	C
Weber State Univ	UT	10,721	C
West Chester Univ of Pennsylvania	PA	18,456	C
West Liberty Univ	WV	15,512	C

MIDDLE EASTERN STUDIES

School	ST	$IS	SR
Appalachian State Univ	NC	14,416	VC
Bard College	NY	64,024	HC
Barnard College/Columbia Univ	NY	62,741	MC
Baylor Univ	TX	53,760	HC
Boston Univ	MA	65,110	MC
Brandeis Univ	MA	65,925	MC
Brigham Young Univ	UT	12,748	HC
Brown Univ	RI	64,566	MC
CUNY/Queens College	NY	27,896	C
Claremont McKenna College	CA	67,185	MC
Colgate Univ	NY	65,030	MC
Columbia Univ/ School of General Studies	NY	61,470	MC
Columbia Univ/City of New York	NY	62,958	MC
Dartmouth College	NH	66,174	MC
Dickinson College	PA	63,974	MC
Eastern Mich Univ	MI	19,761	C
Elon Univ	NC	44,599	VC+
Emory and Henry College	VA	41,410	C
Emory Univ	GA	60,786	MC
Fordham Univ	NY	65,918	MC
George Washington Univ	DC	62,835	MC
Gettysburg College	PA	63,000	HC
Hampshire College	MA	63,824	MC
Harvard College/Harvard Univ	MA	60,659	MC
Hood College	MD	54,840	C
McDaniel College	MD	51,380	VC
Middlebury College	VT	64,332	MC
Mount Holyoke College	MA	56,746	MC
New York Univ	NY	65,860	MC
Pomona College	CA	64,957	MC
Rutgers Univ - New Brunswick	NJ	26,632	HC
Smith College	MA	63,914	MC
Syracuse Univ	NY	60,239	VC
Texas State Univ	TX	19,350	C
The College of Wooster	OH	57,900	VC+
The Univ of Utah	UT	17,924	VC
Tufts Univ	MA		MC
Univ of Arizona	AZ	23,100	C
Univ of Arkansas at Fayetteville	AR	19,152	C+
Univ of Calif at Berkeley	CA	28,853	MC
Univ of Calif at Los Angeles	CA	30,162	MC
Univ of Calif at Riverside	CA	29,227	C+
Univ of Calif at Santa Barbara	CA	29,091	HC
Univ of Conn	CT	25,538	HC
Univ of Mass Amherst	MA	26,199	VC+
Univ of Mich/Ann Arbor	MI	24,410	MC
Univ of Minn/Twin Cities	MN	23,519	HC+
Univ of Pennsylvania	PA	63,526	MC
Univ of Texas at Austin	TX	26,102	HC
Washington Univ in St. Louis	MO	65,366	VC
Wellesley College	MA	63,916	MC
Western Kentucky Univ	KY	16,850	C
Yale Univ	CT	64,650	MC

MIDDLE SCHOOL EDUCATION

School	ST	$IS	SR
Abilene Christian Univ	TX	41,800	C+
Alabama A&M Univ	AL	18,796	C
Albany State Univ	GA	19,462	C
Alice Lloyd College	KY	8,190	C
Alvernia Univ	PA	43,900	C
Alverno College	WI	33,294	LC
American International College	MA	46,300	LC
Appalachian State Univ	NC	14,416	VC
Arkansas State Univ	AR	16,190	C
Arkansas Tech Univ	AR	15,484	C
Armstrong State Univ	GA	16,962	C
Asbury Univ	KY	35,180	C+
Auburn Univ	AL	23,594	VC+
Augusta Univ	GA	4,632	C
Augustana Univ	SD	38,424	VC
Avila Univ	MO	35,480	C
Baldwin Wallace Univ	OH	41,106	C
Barton College	NC	38,686	LC
Bellarmine Univ	KY	51,220	C
Belmont Univ	TN	40,970	VC
Bemidji State Univ	MN	16,056	VC
Bennett College	NC	27,302	NC
Bennington College	VT	63,960	MC
Berry College	GA	45,286	C+
Bethany College	KS	46,100	NC
Bethany College	WV	36,300	NC
Bethel Univ	MN	45,270	VC
Bloomsburg Univ of Pennsylvania	PA	19,066	LC
Bluefield College	VA	34,120	C+
Bluefield State College	WV	5,832	LC
Bluffton Univ	OH	40,950	C
Bowling Green State Univ	OH	19,747	C
Brenau Univ - Women's College	GA	37,876	LC
Butler Univ	IN	51,352	VC
Cabrini Univ	PA	42,591	LC
Campbellsville Univ	KY	32,492	C
Canisius College	NY	47,537	C
Capital Univ	OH	42,982	C
Cardinal Stritch Univ	WI	36,462	C
Caribbean Univ	PR	15,471	
Carlow Univ	PA	38,549	LC
Carson-Newman Univ	TN	34,160	C
Carthage College	WI	48,835	C
Catawba College	NC	39,820	C
Cedarville Univ	OH	34,990	VC
Central Methodist Univ	MO	36,830	VC
Central Washington Univ	WA	16,803	C
Champlain College	VT	53,132	C+
CUNY/Hunter College	NY	31,098	VC
City Univ of Seattle	WA	24,340	NC
Claflin Univ	SC	33,764	LC
Clark Atlanta Univ	GA	31,019	LC
Clayton State Univ	GA	19,735	C
Coastal Carolina Univ	SC	19,766	C
College of Charleston	SC	22,699	C
Columbia College - Missouri	MO	27,803	C
Columbus State Univ	GA	14,336	LC
Concord Univ	WV	14,954	C
Concordia Univ Nebr	NE	36,280	VC
Concordia Univ St. Paul	MN	29,050	C
Concordia Univ, Chicago	IL	39,694	C
Cumberland Univ	TN	27,710	C
Dallas Baptist Univ	TX	33,713	C
Dickinson State Univ	ND	12,372	LC
Dordt College	IA	37,860	C+
Duquesne Univ	PA	46,822	VC
East Carolina Univ	NC	16,937	C
East Stroudsburg Univ	PA	18,334	C
Eastern Illinois Univ	IL	21,126	C
Eastern Kentucky Univ	KY	16,908	C
Eastern Mich Univ	MI	19,761	C
Eastern Univ	PA	39,540	C
Eastern Washington Univ	WA	25,572	LC
Edinboro Univ	PA	15,940	LC
Elizabeth City State Univ	NC	14,745	C
Elms College	MA	45,646	VC
Elon Univ	NC	44,599	VC+
Fairmont State Univ	WV	15,726	C
Fayetteville State Univ	NC	17,756	C
Fitchburg State Univ	MA	21,819	C
Florida Inst of Technology	FL	53,306	VC
Fontbonne Univ	MO	33,717	C
Fort Valley State Univ	GA	17,988	VC
Francis Marion Univ	SC	16,464	LC
Freed-Hardeman Univ	TN	29,450	C
Frostburg State Univ	MD	17,280	LC
Gannon Univ	PA	42,032	C
Gardner-Webb Univ	NC	39,200	C+
Georgetown College	KY	41,440	C
Georgia College & State Univ	GA	21,148	C+
Georgia Southern Univ	GA	16,596	C
Georgia Southwestern State Univ	GA	13,870	C
Glenville State College	WV	17,386	NC
Goddard College	VT	17,040	VC
Gordon College	MA	46,472	C+
Goshen College	IN	42,500	C
Grand Rapids Theological Seminary/Cornerstone Univ	MI	33,338	C
Grand Valley State Univ	MI	22,250	C+
Greensboro College	NC	42,400	LC
Grove City College	PA	25,692	VC
Gustavus Adolphus College	MN	52,433	HC
Hardin-Simmons Univ	TX	33,966	C
Harris-Stowe State Univ	MO	14,360	NC
Heidelberg Univ	OH	39,200	C
Henderson State Univ	AR	15,516	LC
High Point Univ	NC	45,977	C
Humboldt State Univ	CA	20,514	C
Illinois State Univ	IL	23,418	VC
Indiana State Univ	IN	23,223	LC
Indiana Univ-Purdue Univ Fort Wayne	IN	17,553	C
Ithaca College	NY	56,766	VC
John Carroll Univ	OH	49,740	C+
Johnson State College	VT	20,752	C
Kean Univ	NJ	24,650	C
Kennesaw State Univ	GA	19,592	VC
Kent State Univ	OH	20,732	C
Kentucky Christian Univ	KY	26,560	LC
Kentucky Wesleyan College	KY	32,080	C
King's College	PA	46,858	C
Lake Erie College	OH	38,914	LC
Lee Univ	TN	22,045	C
Lenoir-Rhyne Univ	NC	43,200	C
Lesley Univ	MA	41,550	C
Lincoln Memorial Univ	TN	28,070	C
Lipscomb Univ	TN	41,296	VC
LIU Brooklyn	NY	49,682	C
Lubbock Christian Univ	TX	28,426	C
Malone Univ	OH	38,448	C
Manchester Univ	IN	40,422	C
Manhattan College	NY	51,750	C+
Marian Univ	WI	32,420	LC
Mars Hill Univ	NC	42,688	C
Marshall Univ	WV	17,242	C
Maryville Univ of St. Louis	MO	38,046	VC+
Mass College of Liberal Arts	MA	20,128	C
McKendree Univ	IL	37,940	C+
McMurry Univ	TX	34,259	LC
Medaille College	NY	35,112	C
Methodist Univ	NC	43,600	C
Miami Univ	OH	27,190	HC+
Midland Univ	NE	37,468	
Millersville Univ of Pennsylvania	PA	23,782	C
Minn State Univ, Mankato	MN	15,616	C
Misericordia Univ	PA	43,840	C
Missouri Baptist Univ	MO	35,594	C
Missouri Southern State Univ	MO	12,499	C
Missouri State Univ	MO	15,190	C+
Montana State Univ-Billings	MT	22,960	C
Montclair State Univ	NJ	26,210	LC
Morehead State Univ	KY	17,422	C
Mount Aloysius College	PA	29,976	C
Mount Mary Univ	WI	34,650	LC
Mount Mercy Univ	IA	36,826	C
Mount St. Joseph Univ	OH	33,880	C
Mount Vernon Nazarene Univ	OH	34,500	C
Murray State Univ	KY	16,998	C
Nazareth College	NY	45,574	C
Nebr Wesleyan Univ	NE	38,140	C+
Niagara Univ	NY	41,010	C
N Car Central Univ	NC	9,000	C
N Car State Univ	NC	19,515	HC+
N Car Wesleyan College	NC	39,200	C
Northern Kentucky Univ	KY	16,486	C
Northern State Univ	SD	14,505	C
Northland College	WI	41,103	C+
Northwest Missouri State Univ	MO	17,737	C
Northwest Univ	WA	35,876	VC
Northwestern College of Iowa	IA	38,400	C+
Notre Dame College	OH	37,150	VC
Nova Southeastern Univ	FL	38,534	C+
Oakland City Univ	IN	33,360	NC
Ohio Dominican Univ	OH	41,340	C+
Ohio Northern Univ	OH	44,050	VC
Ohio State Univ at Columbus	OH	21,703	HC+
Ohio Wesleyan Univ	OH	49,460	VC
Okla Christian Univ	OK	27,650	VC
Okla Wesleyan Univ	OK	33,206	C
Otterbein Univ	OH	41,630	C
Ouachita Baptist Univ	AR	32,320	C
Paine College	GA	19,506	LC
Philander Smith College	AR	20,814	LC
Piedmont College	GA	32,512	C
Prescott College	AZ	33,284	C
Ripon College	WI	46,911	C+
St. Leo Univ	FL	31,650	C
St. Louis Univ	MO	49,866	HC

ST = STATE $IS = IN-STATE COSTS SR = SELECTOR RATING

School	ST	$IS	SR
St. Vincent College	PA	44,626	C
St. Xavier Univ	IL	43,310	C
Schreiner Univ	TX	34,626	LC
Shippensburg Univ of Pennsylvania	PA	23,208	C
Shorter Univ	GA	31,130	LC
Southeast Missouri State Univ	MO	15,498	C
Southeastern Louisiana Univ	LA	16,237	C
Southeastern Univ	FL	31,765	C
Southern Arkansas Univ	AR	21,532	C
Southern Univ and A&M College	LA	16,074	LC+
Southwest Baptist Univ	MO	29,900	LC
Spalding Univ	KY	31,938	SP
Springfield College	MA	45,995	C
St. Francis College	NY	38,800	LC
St. John Fisher College	NY	43,620	C
SUNY / SUNY College at Old Westbury	NY	16,860	C
SUNY / SUNY Cortland	NY	20,706	VC
SUNY / SUNY Fredonia	NY	20,818	C
SUNY at New Paltz	NY	19,200	C
Stevenson Univ	MD	72,770	C
Texas Christian Univ	TX	54,670	HC
The Univ of Akron	OH	21,477	C
Thomas More College	KY	36,720	C
Thomas Univ	GA	21,420	LC
Tiffin Univ	OH	31,380	C
Toccoa Falls College	GA	27,920	C
Transylvania Univ	KY	45,690	VC+
Tusculum College	TN	31,625	C
Union College	KY	32,310	C
Union Univ	TN	33,970	VC
Univ of Arizona	AZ	23,100	C
Univ of Arkansas at Fayetteville	AR	19,152	C+
Univ of Arkansas at Monticello	AR	13,134	NC
Univ of Arkansas at Pine Bluff	AR	13,541	C
Univ of Central Arkansas	AR	14,472	VC
Univ of Central Missouri	MO	18,982	C
Univ of Cincinnati	OH	21,964	VC
Univ of Dayton	OH	53,620	C
Univ of Detroit Mercy	MI	48,816	C+
Univ of Findlay	OH	60,139	C
Univ of Georgia	GA	21,250	HC
Univ of Great Falls	MT	38,524	C
Univ of Indianapolis	IN	36,480	C
Univ of Iowa	IA	18,683	VC+
Univ of Kansas	KS	20,135	C+
Univ of Kentucky	KY	33,306	C
Univ of Louisville	KY	19,824	C
Univ of Mary Hardin-Baylor	TX	33,950	C+
Univ of Maryland/College Park	MD	21,938	HC
Univ of Minn/Duluth	MN	20,292	C+
Univ of Missouri/Columbia	MO	18,201	MC
Univ of Missouri-Kansas City	MO	19,563	VC
Univ of Montana-Western	MT	11,220	LC
Univ of Mount Olive	NC	18,426	C
Univ of Mount Union	OH	38,970	C
Univ of Nebr - Kearney	NE	16,546	LC
Univ of N Car at Chapel Hill	NC	20,052	HC+
Univ of N Car at Charlotte	NC	15,547	C
Univ of N Car at Greensboro	NC	14,690	C
Univ of N Car at Wilmington	NC	14,590	VC
Univ of N Dak	ND	15,373	C
Univ of North Florida	FL	15,996	VC
Univ of North Georgia	GA	17,316	C
Univ of Pikeville	KY	28,700	NC
Univ of Sioux Falls	SD	34,330	C
Univ of S Car Aiken	SC	16,712	C
Univ of S Car at Columbia	SC	19,725	VC+
Univ of S Car Upstate	SC	18,200	LC
Univ of Southern Indiana	IN	16,501	C
Univ of Southern Miss	MS	13,170	C
Univ of the Cumberlands	KY	32,000	C
Univ of the Ozarks	AR	52,176	C
Univ of Vermont	VT	28,878	HC
Univ of West Alabama	AL	15,516	NC
Univ of West Florida	FL	15,848	C
Univ of Wisc-Green Bay	WI	15,064	C
Univ of Wisc-Platteville	WI	14,614	VC
Univ of Wisc-Whitewater	WI	13,976	C
Urbana Univ	OH	30,820	C
Ursuline College	OH	41,076	LC
Wagner College	NY	55,480	C+
Walsh Univ	OH	39,010	C
Washington Univ in St. Louis	MO	65,366	VC
Wayne State College	NE	12,802	C
Waynesburg Univ	PA	32,290	C
Webster Univ	MO	37,490	C
Wesleyan College	GA	29,694	C+
West Chester Univ of Pennsylvania	PA	18,456	C
West Liberty Univ	WV	15,512	C
Western Carolina Univ	NC	13,965	C
Western Kentucky Univ	KY	16,850	C
Western Mich Univ	MI	21,054	C
Westminster College	MO	32,820	C
Wilkes Univ	PA	45,622	C
William Woods Univ	MO	32,040	C
Wilmington College	OH	34,600	C
Wilson College	PA	35,620	C
Wingate Univ	NC	39,950	C
Winthrop Univ	SC	23,082	C
Wittenberg Univ	OH	48,156	C+
Wright State Univ	OH	16,983	C
Xavier Univ	OH	47,880	C+
Xavier Univ of Louisiana	LA	31,689	C+
York College	NE	24,300	C
Youngstown State Univ	OH	17,307	C

MILITARY SCIENCE

School	ST	$IS	SR
Ashford Univ	CA	10,480	C
Columbia College - Missouri	MO	27,803	C
Eastern Mich Univ	MI	19,761	C
Eastern Washington Univ	WA	25,572	LC
Florida Inst of Technology	FL	53,306	VC
Hawaii Pacific Univ	HI	33,420	C
Minn State Univ, Mankato	MN	15,616	C
Norfolk State Univ	VA	25,702	LC
Norwich Univ	VT	28,212	C
Rochester Inst of Technology	NY	50,842	HC
S Car State Univ	SC	20,805	LC
United States Air Force Academy	CO		C
United States Military Academy at West Point	NY		HC+
West Virginia Univ	WV	18,210	C

MILITARY TECHNOLOGY LEADERSHIP

School	ST	$IS	SR
Thomas Edison State Univ	NJ	6,350	NC

MILLING SCIENCE

School	ST	$IS	SR
Kansas State Univ	KS	17,780	VC

MINING AND MINERAL ENGINEERING

School	ST	$IS	SR
Colo School of Mines	CO	29,319	MC
Columbia Univ/City of New York	NY	62,958	MC
Missouri Univ of Science and Technology	MO	18,655	HC
Montana Tech of the Univ of Montana	MT	15,447	C+
New Mexico Inst of Mining and Technology	NM	14,833	HC
Pennsylvania State Univ - Univ Park	PA	29,760	HC
S Dak School of Mines and Technology	SD	18,645	VC
Southern Illinois Univ Carbondale	IL	23,667	C
The Univ of Utah	UT	17,924	VC
Univ of Alaska Fairbanks	AK	16,179	C
Univ of Arizona	AZ	23,100	C
Univ of Kentucky	KY	33,306	C
Univ of Nevada/Reno	NV	18,010	C
Univ of Southern Indiana	IN	16,501	C
Virginia Polytechnic Inst and State Univ	VA	21,276	HC
West Virginia Univ	WV	18,210	C

MINISTRIES

School	ST	$IS	SR
Abilene Christian Univ	TX	41,800	C+
Amridge Univ	AL	10,860	LC
Asbury Univ	KY	35,180	C+
Atlantic Union College	MA	27,228	C
Azusa Pacific Univ	CA	43,972	C
Belmont Univ	TN	40,970	VC
Bethel College	IN	35,860	C
Biola Univ	CA	46,402	C+
Bluffton Univ	OH	40,950	C
College of the Ozarks	MO	7,230	C
Concordia Univ Wisc	WI	35,910	C
Corban Univ	OR	40,306	C
Dallas Baptist Univ	TX	33,713	C
Dominican Univ	IL	41,222	C
Dordt College	IA	37,860	C+
East Texas Baptist Univ	TX	33,134	C
Eastern Mennonite Univ	VA	42,550	C
Eastern Nazarene College	MA	39,955	C
Faulkner Univ	AL	26,410	C
Freed-Hardeman Univ	TN	29,450	C
Fresno Pacific Univ	CA	37,370	C
Geneva College	PA	35,450	C
George Fox Univ	OR	42,938	C
Greenville College	IL	27,012	C
Harding Univ	AR	25,421	C
Hardin-Simmons Univ	TX	33,966	C
Hope International Univ	CA	41,150	C
Houghton College	NY	39,090	C
Huntington Univ	IN	33,996	C
Indiana Wesleyan Univ	IN	33,674	C
John Brown Univ	AR	33,132	VC
Kentucky Christian Univ	KY	26,560	LC
Lee Univ	TN	22,045	C
Lindenwood Univ	MO	25,132	C
Lindsey Wilson College	KY	32,882	C
Lubbock Christian Univ	TX	28,426	C
Malone Univ	OH	38,448	C
Messiah College	PA	43,100	C+
MidAmerica Nazarene Univ	KS	35,550	C
Missouri Baptist Univ	MO	35,594	C
Mount Vernon Nazarene Univ	OH	34,500	C
North Central Univ	MN	26,400	C
Northwest Christian Univ	OR	36,580	C
Northwest Nazarene Univ	ID	36,000	C
Northwest Univ	WA	35,876	VC
Notre Dame College	OH	37,150	VC
Oakwood Univ	AL	43,758	C
Okla Christian Univ	OK	27,650	VC
Olivet Nazarene Univ	IL	41,840	C
Oral Roberts Univ	OK	34,316	C
Ouachita Baptist Univ	AR	32,320	C
Palm Beach Atlantic Univ	FL	39,720	C
Point Loma Nazarene Univ	CA	43,450	C
Rochester College	MI	28,574	LC
SAGU American Indian College	AZ	18,142	C
Simpson Univ	CA	33,700	C
Southeastern Univ	FL	31,765	C
Southwest Baptist Univ	MO	29,900	LC
Tabor College	KS	35,870	C
Taylor Univ	IN	40,317	C+
Toccoa Falls College	GA	27,920	C
Trinity Bible College	ND		
Trinity Christian College	IL	35,580	C
Union College	KY	32,310	C
Union Univ	TN	33,970	VC
Univ of Mary	ND	23,180	C
Univ of Mary Hardin-Baylor	TX	33,950	C+
Univ of Mount Olive	NC	18,426	C
Univ of Northwestern - St. Paul	MN	38,160	C
Univ of St. Francis	IN	37,400	C
Valparaiso Univ	IN	48,370	C+
Vanguard Univ of Southern Calif	CA	40,740	VC
Warner Pacific College	OR	33,790	C
Waynesburg Univ	PA	32,290	C

MISSIONS

School	ST	$IS	SR
Asbury Univ	KY	35,180	C+
Bethel College	IN	35,860	C
Biola Univ	CA	46,402	C+
Cedarville Univ	OH	34,990	VC
Dordt College	IA	37,860	C+
East Texas Baptist Univ	TX	33,134	C
Eastern Univ	PA	39,540	C
Evangel Univ	MO	28,898	C
Faulkner Univ	AL	26,410	C
Fresno Pacific Univ	CA	37,370	C
Grace Bible College	MI	25,250	C
Hannibal-LaGrange Univ	MO	29,815	C
Harding Univ	AR	25,421	C
Hardin-Simmons Univ	TX	33,966	C
Lipscomb Univ	TN	41,296	VC
Lubbock Christian Univ	TX	28,426	C
Mount Vernon Nazarene Univ	OH	34,500	C
Northwest Univ	WA	35,876	VC
Okla Christian Univ	OK	27,650	VC
Olivet Nazarene Univ	IL	41,840	C
Simpson Univ	CA	33,700	C
Southern Nazarene Univ	OK	32,798	NC
Southwest Baptist Univ	MO	29,900	LC
Spring Arbor Univ	MI	36,000	C
The Master's Univ	CA	43,870	C+
Trinity Bible College	ND		
Union Univ	TN	33,970	VC
Univ of the Cumberlands	KY	32,000	C
Vanguard Univ of Southern Calif	CA	40,740	VC

MODERN DANCE

School	ST	$IS	SR
Texas Christian Univ	TX	54,670	HC
The Univ of Utah	UT	17,924	VC

MODERN JEWISH STUDIES

School	ST	$IS	SR
Cal State, Northridge	CA	16,859	LC
CUNY/Queens College	NY	27,896	C
San Diego State Univ	CA	21,896	C+
Syracuse Univ	NY	60,239	VC

MODERN LANGUAGE

School	ST	$IS	SR
Anna Maria College	MA	48,186	C
Aquinas College - Mich	MI	38,876	HC
Augustana Univ	SD	38,424	VC
Averett Univ	VA	40,970	LC
Beloit College	WI	55,206	HC
Bethune-Cookman Univ	FL	22,970	C
Bryant Univ	RI	55,646	VC
Calif Polytechnic State Univ	CA	17,979	HC+
Canisius College	NY	47,537	C
Clemson Univ	SC		HC
College of Mount St. Vincent	NY	45,620	C
Converse College	SC	26,495	C
Duquesne Univ	PA	46,822	VC
Elizabethtown College	PA	54,050	C
Emory and Henry College	VA	41,410	C
Emporia State Univ	KS	14,570	C
Fort Hays State Univ	KS	12,131	C
Framingham State Univ	MA	20,584	C
Francis Marion Univ	SC	16,464	LC
Graceland Univ	IA	35,290	C
Ithaca College	NY	56,766	VC
James Madison Univ	VA	19,084	VC
John Carroll Univ	OH	49,740	C+
Kansas State Univ	KS	17,780	VC
Kennesaw State Univ	GA	19,592	VC
Kenyon College	OH	63,330	MC
Knox College	IL	52,615	VC+
Lamar Univ	TX	18,014	LC
Longwood Univ	VA	22,184	C
Loyola Marymount Univ	CA	58,038	HC
Merrimack College	MA	52,770	C
Metropolitan State Univ of Denver	CO	29,889	LC
Mills College	CA	59,163	VC
Miss College	MS	25,850	C
Monmouth Univ	NJ	46,234	C
Montana State Univ	MT	15,500	C+
Moravian College	PA	53,117	
Northern Arizona Univ	AZ	20,246	VC
Notre Dame of Maryland Univ	MD	46,465	VC
Ohio Univ	OH	22,924	C
Okla Baptist Univ	OK	32,320	C
Pace Univ	NY	58,248	C
St. Francis Univ	PA	42,268	NC
St. Peter's Univ	NJ	49,192	C
Seton Hall Univ	NJ	55,514	C
St. Bonaventure Univ	NY	44,237	C
St. Lawrence Univ	NY	64,390	VC
Syracuse Univ	NY	60,239	VC
Texas A&M Univ	TX	20,521	VC+
Trinity College	CT	63,920	HC+
Union College	NY	64,320	MC
Univ of Arkansas at Monticello	AR	13,134	NC
Univ of Idaho	ID	15,348	C
Univ of Louisiana at Monroe	LA	15,970	C
Univ of Maine	ME	20,792	C
Univ of Maryland/Baltimore County	MD	21,296	VC
Univ of Mass Lowell	MA	26,380	C
Univ of North Georgia	GA	17,316	C
Univ of Texas at San Antonio	TX	20,157	C
Univ of Wisc-River Falls	WI	14,485	C
Warren Wilson College	NC	44,220	VC
Wayne State College	NE	12,802	C
Westmont College	CA	56,410	HC
Widener Univ	PA	56,486	C
Winthrop Univ	SC	23,082	C
Wright State Univ	OH	16,983	C
Xavier Univ	OH	47,880	C+

MOLECULAR BIOLOGY

School	ST	$IS	SR
Adams State Univ	CO	17,703	LC
Alverno College	WI	33,294	LC
Andrews Univ	MI	28,030	C+
Appalachian State Univ	NC	14,416	VC
Arizona State Univ at the Tempe Campus	AZ	21,756	VC
Assumption College	MA	47,920	C+
Auburn Univ	AL	23,594	VC+
Bellarmine Univ	KY	51,220	C
Benedictine Univ	IL	38,300	C
Bethel Univ	MN	45,270	VC
Brigham Young Univ	UT	12,748	HC
Brown Univ	RI	64,566	MC
Bryant Univ	RI	55,646	VC
Cedarville Univ	OH	34,990	VC
Centre College	KY	49,250	HC
Chestnut Hill College	PA	43,410	C
Claremont McKenna College	CA	67,185	MC
Clarion Univ of Pennsylvania	PA	21,608	LC
Clarkson Univ	NY	60,392	HC
Coe College	IA	51,570	VC
Coker College	SC	34,810	LC
Colgate Univ	NY	65,030	MC
Colo College	CO	62,560	MC
Florida Inst of Technology	FL	53,306	VC
Florida State Univ	FL	16,771	HC
Goshen College	IN	42,500	C
Grove City College	PA	25,692	VC
Hardin-Simmons Univ	TX	33,966	C
Houston Baptist Univ	TX	36,450	C
Illinois Inst of Technology	IL	56,826	HC+
Illinois State Univ	IL	23,418	VC
John Carroll Univ	OH	49,740	C+
Johns Hopkins Univ	MD	65,386	MC
Kenyon College	OH	63,330	MC
Kutztown Univ of Pennsylvania	PA	19,056	LC
Lawrence Tech Univ	MI	39,770	VC
Lehigh Univ	PA	61,010	MC
Lipscomb Univ	TN	41,296	VC
Marquette Univ	WI	48,390	VC+
Marshall Univ	WV	17,242	C
Messiah College	PA	43,100	C+
Middlebury College	VT	64,332	MC
Millikin Univ	IL	42,158	C
Mills College	CA	59,163	VC
Milwaukee School of Engineering	WI	45,153	HC
Montclair State Univ	NJ	26,210	LC
Murray State Univ	KY	16,998	C
Muskingum Univ	OH	35,966	C
Nebr Wesleyan Univ	NE	38,140	C+
New Mexico State Univ	NM	14,050	C
Northwestern Univ	IL	66,344	MC
Ohio Northern Univ	OH	44,050	VC
Ohio State Univ at Columbus	OH	21,703	HC+
Ohio Univ	OH	22,924	C
Okla State Univ	OK	17,180	VC
Oregon State Univ	OR	22,519	VC
Otterbein Univ	OH	41,630	C
Pomona College	CA	64,957	MC

ST = STATE $IS = IN-STATE COSTS   SR = SELECTOR RATING

School	ST	$IS	SR
Princeton Univ	NJ	57,610	MC
Purdue Univ/West Lafayette	IN	20,032	MC
Rhodes College	TN	51,900	HC
Rutgers Univ - New Brunswick	NJ	26,632	HC
Salem International Univ	WV	21,090	LC
Scripps College	CA	66,664	MC
SUNY / The College of Environmental Science and Forestry	NY	23,853	VC
SUNY at Binghamton	NY	22,861	MC
SUNY SUNY Albany	NY	22,165	C
Stetson Univ	FL	53,544	VC
Texas A&M Univ	TX	20,521	VC+
The Lincoln Univ	PA	15,154	NC
Towson Univ	MD	17,408	VC
Tulane Univ	LA	63,396	HC+
Univ of Arizona	AZ	23,100	C
Univ of Calif at Berkeley	CA	28,853	MC
Univ of Calif at Los Angeles	CA	30,162	MC
Univ of Calif at Santa Barbara	CA	29,091	HC
Univ of Calif San Diego	CA	30,150	MC
Univ of Calif, Santa Cruz	CA	28,731	C+
Univ of Colo Boulder	CO	24,285	VC+
Univ of Conn	CT	25,538	HC
Univ of Denver	CO	58,443	VC+
Univ of Great Falls	MT	38,524	C
Univ of Idaho	ID	15,348	C
Univ of Illinois at Urbana-Champaign	IL	27,006	HC
Univ of Kansas	KS	20,135	C+
Univ of Maine	ME	20,792	C
Univ of Mich/Ann Arbor	MI	24,410	MC
Univ of Minn/Duluth	MN	20,292	C+
Univ of New Hampshire	NH	28,562	VC
Univ of Pittsburgh	PA	29,568	HC+
Univ of Puget Sound	WA	56,456	VC+
Univ of Richmond	VA	60,880	MC
Univ of Rochester	NY	65,032	MC
Univ of Texas at Austin	TX	26,102	HC
Univ of Texas at Dallas	TX	22,830	VC+
Univ of Vermont	VT	28,878	HC
Univ of Wisc-Madison	WI	20,934	MC
Univ of Wisc-Milwaukee	WI	21,496	C
Univ of Wyoming	WY	15,375	C+
Vanderbilt Univ	TN	60,572	MC
Washburn Univ	KS	15,827	C
Wells College	NY	50,500	C
Wesleyan Univ	CT	65,516	MC
West Chester Univ of Pennsylvania	PA	18,456	C
Western Washington Univ	WA	18,003	C+
Westminster College	PA	39,180	C+
Whitman College	WA	59,772	MC
Yale Univ	CT	64,650	MC

MOLECULAR DIAGNOSTICS

School	ST	$IS	SR
Ferris State Univ	MI	21,445	C

MOVEMENT SCIENCE

School	ST	$IS	SR
Texas Christian Univ	TX	54,670	HC
Univ of Idaho	ID	15,348	C
Winona State Univ	MN	17,535	C

MULTIDISCIPLINARY STUDIES

School	ST	$IS	SR
Embry-Riddle Aeronautical Univ - Daytona Beach	FL	44,712	VC
Stony Brook Univ/The SUNY	NY	21,881	MC
Wheaton College	MA	61,512	VC

MULTIMEDIA

School	ST	$IS	SR
Abilene Christian Univ	TX	41,800	C+
American Univ	DC	59,379	HC+
Arkansas State Univ	AR	16,190	C
Art Inst of Portland	OR	132,329	SP
Augustana College	IL	49,658	VC
Belmont Univ	TN	40,970	VC
Bennington College	VT	63,960	MC
Bethel Univ	MN	45,270	VC
Bloomfield College	NJ	39,100	LC
Calif Lutheran Univ	CA	52,853	C
Champlain College	VT	53,132	C+
CUNY/Brooklyn College	NY	5,884	C+
CUNY/City College	NY	20,319	VC
Columbia College Chicago	IL	43,168	C
Dakota Wesleyan Univ	SD	32,850	C
Duquesne Univ	PA	46,822	VC
Florida Atlantic Univ	FL	17,339	C
Franklin College	IN	39,380	C
George Fox Univ	OR	42,938	C
George Washington Univ	DC	62,835	MC
Georgia Southern Univ	GA	16,596	C
Hawaii Pacific Univ	HI	33,420	C
Howard Payne Univ	TX	34,320	C
Keene State College	NH	24,003	LC
La Salle Univ	PA	55,790	C
Lasell College	MA	47,500	C
Lewis Univ	IL	40,370	C
Louisiana College	LA	21,886	C
Lyndon State College	VT	20,714	C
McMurry Univ	TX	34,259	LC
Minot State Univ	ND	12,732	C
National Univ	CA	14,730	LC
Northeastern Univ	MA	62,703	MC
Ohio Univ	OH	22,924	C
Rider Univ	NJ	54,050	C
St. Leo Univ	FL	31,650	C
San Diego State Univ	CA	21,896	C+
Simpson College	IA	43,839	VC
The Art Inst of Atlanta	GA	34,334	SP
The College of New Jersey	NJ	31,909	HC
Univ of Mary Hardin-Baylor	TX	33,950	C+
Univ of N Car at Asheville	NC	15,723	VC+
Univ of the Arts	PA	56,579	SP
Washington State Univ	WA	22,495	C
Waynesburg Univ	PA	32,290	C
Western Washington Univ	WA	18,003	C+
Wilmington Univ	DE	8,546	NC

MUSEUM STUDIES

School	ST	$IS	SR
Baylor Univ	TX	53,760	HC
Juniata College	PA	53,760	VC
Middlebury College	VT	64,332	MC
Niagara Univ	NY	41,010	C
Rochester Inst of Technology	NY	50,842	HC
Tusculum College	TN	31,625	C
Univ of Central Okla	OK	13,486	C
Univ of Illinois at Chicago	IL	25,006	VC
Univ of St. Francis	IN	37,400	C
Walsh Univ	OH	39,010	C

MUSIC

School	ST	$IS	SR
Abilene Christian Univ	TX	41,800	C+
Adams State Univ	CO	17,703	LC
Adelphi Univ	NY	48,244	C
Adrian College	MI	42,400	C
Agnes Scott College	GA	51,930	VC+
Alabama State Univ	AL	14,142	NC
Albany State Univ	GA	19,462	C
Albion College	MI	52,650	C
Alcorn State Univ	MS	15,854	C
Alderson Broaddus Univ	WV	26,149	C
Allegheny College	PA	55,420	VC
Allen Univ	SC	19,300	NC
Alma College	MI	47,548	C
Alverno College	WI	33,294	LC
American Univ	DC	59,379	HC+
Amherst College	MA		HC+
Andrews Univ	MI	28,030	C+
Angelo State Univ	TX	15,263	NC
Anna Maria College	MA	48,186	C
Aquinas College - Mich	MI	38,876	HC
Arizona State Univ at the Tempe Campus	AZ	21,756	VC
Arkansas State Univ	AR	16,190	C
Arkansas Tech Univ	AR	15,484	C
Armstrong State Univ	GA	16,962	C
Asbury Univ	KY	35,180	C+
Ashland Univ	OH	21,440	C
Assumption College	MA	47,920	C+
Atlantic Union College	MA	27,228	C
Augsburg College	MN	43,929	C
Augusta Univ	GA	4,632	C
Augustana College	IL	49,658	VC
Augustana Univ	SD	38,424	VC
Aurora Univ	IL	33,970	C
Austin College	TX	45,875	VC
Austin Peay State Univ	TN	16,397	C
Averett Univ	VA	40,970	LC
Avila Univ	MO	35,480	C
Azusa Pacific Univ	CA	43,972	C
Baker Univ	KS	33,350	C+
Baldwin Wallace Univ	OH	41,106	C
Ball State Univ	IN	19,590	C
Bard College	NY	64,024	HC
Bard College at Simon's Rock	MA	65,795	MC
Barnard College/Columbia Univ	NY	62,741	MC
Bates College	ME	64,500	MC
Baylor Univ	TX	53,760	HC
Belhaven Univ	MS	31,016	C
Bellarmine Univ	KY	51,220	C
Belmont Univ	TN	40,970	VC
Beloit College	WI	55,206	HC
Bemidji State Univ	MN	16,056	VC
Benedict College	SC	28,238	NC
Benedictine College	KS	36,200	VC
Benedictine Univ	IL	38,300	C
Bennett College	NC	27,302	NC
Bennington College	VT	63,960	MC
Berea College	KY	7,042	C
Berklee College of Music	MA	60,930	SP
Berry College	GA	45,286	C+
Bethany College	KS	46,100	NC
Bethany College	WV	36,300	NC
Bethel College	IN	35,860	C
Bethel College	KS	35,370	C
Bethel Univ	MN	45,270	VC
Bethel Univ	TN	24,738	C
Bethune-Cookman Univ	FL	22,970	C
Biola Univ	CA	46,402	C+
Birmingham-Southern College	AL	44,478	VC
Black Hills State Univ	SD	15,899	C
Bloomsburg Univ of Pennsylvania	PA	19,066	LC
Blue Mountain College	MS	15,949	VC
Bluefield College	VA	34,120	C+
Bluffton Univ	OH	40,950	C
Boise State Univ	ID	14,860	C
Boston College	MA	65,737	MC
Boston Univ	MA	65,110	MC
Bowdoin College	ME	63,500	MC
Bowling Green State Univ	OH	19,747	C
Brandeis Univ	MA	65,925	MC
Briar Cliff Univ	IA	36,956	C
Bridgewater College	VA	44,510	C
Bridgewater State Univ	MA	21,810	C
Brigham Young Univ	UT	12,748	HC
Brigham Young Univ/Hawaii	HI	11,290	C
Brown Univ	RI	64,566	MC
Bryan College	TN	31,440	C
Bryn Mawr College	PA	59,890	MC
Bucknell Univ	PA	64,616	MC
Buena Vista Univ	IA	41,514	C
Butler Univ	IN	51,352	VC
Cairn Univ	PA	36,296	C
Caldwell Univ	NJ	42,165	NC
Calif Baptist Univ	CA	41,392	C
Calif Lutheran Univ	CA	52,853	C
Calif Polytechnic State Univ	CA	17,979	HC+
Calif State Polytechnic Univ, Pomona	CA	21,541	C
Cal State, Bakersfield	CA	19,191	LC
Cal State, Chico	CA	21,440	C
Cal State, Dominguez Hills	CA	19,022	LC
Cal State, East Bay	CA	19,413	C
Cal State, Fresno	CA	16,902	LC
Cal State, Fullerton	CA	21,902	C
Cal State, Long Beach	CA	18,850	C
Cal State, Los Angeles	CA	17,186	LC
Cal State, Monterey Bay	CA	26,871	LC
Cal State, Northridge	CA	16,859	LC
Cal State, Sacramento	CA	20,332	C
Cal State, San Bernardino	CA	12,000	C
Cal State, Stanislaus	CA	16,212	C
Calvin College	MI	41,570	VC+
Cameron Univ	OK	11,072	NC
Campbellsville Univ	KY	32,492	C
Canisius College	NY	47,537	C
Capital Univ	OH	42,982	C
Cardinal Stritch Univ	WI	36,462	C
Carleton College	MN	64,071	MC
Carnegie Mellon Univ	PA	67,980	MC
Carroll Univ	WI	38,100	C+
Carson-Newman Univ	TN	34,160	C
Carthage College	WI	48,835	C
Case Western Reserve Univ	OH	60,304	MC
Castleton Univ	VT	20,186	C
Catawba College	NC	39,820	C
Cedar Crest College	PA	46,715	C
Cedarville Univ	OH	34,990	VC
Centenary College of Louisiana	LA	45,650	C+
Central College	IA	44,592	C
Central Conn State Univ	CT	21,203	C
Central Methodist Univ	MO	36,830	VC
Central Mich Univ	MI	20,330	C
Central State Univ	OH	18,564	C
Central Washington Univ	WA	16,803	C
Centre College	KY	49,250	HC
Chadron State College	NE	14,819	NC
Chapman Univ	CA	63,078	VC+
Charleston Southern Univ	SC	32,400	C
Chatham Univ	PA	46,517	C
Chestnut Hill College	PA	43,410	C
Cheyney Univ of Pennsylvania	PA	20,896	LC
Chicago State Univ	IL	20,144	C
Christopher Newport Univ	VA	23,968	VC+
CUNY/Baruch College	NY	21,609	HC
CUNY/Brooklyn College	NY	5,884	C+
CUNY/City College	NY	20,319	VC
CUNY/College of Staten Island	NY	17,840	NC
CUNY/Hunter College	NY	31,098	VC
CUNY/Lehman College	NY	5,778	HC+
CUNY/Queens College	NY	27,896	C
CUNY/York College	NY	6,747	LC
Claflin Univ	SC	33,764	LC
Clark Atlanta Univ	GA	31,019	LC
Clark Univ	MA	51,600	HC+
Clayton State Univ	GA	19,735	C
Cleveland State Univ	OH	22,196	C
Coastal Carolina Univ	SC	19,766	C
Coe College	IA	51,570	VC
Coker College	SC	34,810	LC
Colby College	ME	64,060	MC
Colgate Univ	NY	65,030	MC
College of Charleston	SC	22,699	C
College of St. Benedict	MN	52,806	C
College of St. Elizabeth	NJ	44,432	LC
College of St. Scholastica	MN	44,640	C
College of the Holy Cross	MA	62,165	MC
College of the Ozarks	MO	7,230	C
College of William & Mary	VA		MC
Colo Christian Univ	CO	39,940	VC
Colo College	CO	62,560	MC
Colo Mesa Univ	CO	18,955	LC
Colo State Univ	CO	22,162	VC
Columbia College	SC	36,550	C
Columbia College Chicago	IL	43,168	C
Columbia Univ/ School of General Studies	NY	61,470	MC
Columbia Univ/City of New York	NY	62,958	MC
Columbus State Univ	GA	14,336	LC
Concordia College - Moorhead	MN	51,088	C+
Concordia College - New York	NY	39,035	LC
Concordia Univ	CA	41,580	VC
Concordia Univ Nebr	NE	36,280	VC
Concordia Univ St. Paul	MN	29,050	C
Concordia Univ Texas	TX	40,210	C
Concordia Univ Wisc	WI	35,910	C
Concordia Univ, Ann Arbor	MI	35,945	VC
Concordia Univ, Chicago	IL	39,694	C
Conn College	CT	65,000	MC
Conservatory of Music of PR	PR	13,925	
Converse College	SC	26,495	C
Corban Univ	OR	40,306	C
Cornell College	IA	48,800	VC
Cornell Univ	NY	64,853	MC
Cornish College of the Arts	WA	47,750	SP
Covenant College	GA	38,990	VC
Creighton Univ	NE	48,206	VC+
Culver-Stockton College	MO	33,525	C
Cumberland Univ	TN	27,710	C
Curtis Inst of Music	PA	20,944	SP
Dakota Wesleyan Univ	SD	32,850	C
Dallas Baptist Univ	TX	33,713	C
Dartmouth College	NH	66,174	MC
Davidson College	NC	60,119	MC
Delaware State Univ	DE	19,376	NC
Delta State Univ	MS	13,176	C
Denison Univ	OH	58,860	MC
DePaul Univ	IL	47,623	VC
DePauw Univ	IN	58,688	HC+
Dickinson College	PA	63,974	MC
Dickinson State Univ	ND	12,372	LC
Dillard Univ	LA	20,940	VC
Doane Univ	NE	39,184	VC
Dominican Univ	IL	41,222	C
Dominican Univ of Calif	CA	57,050	C
Dordt College	IA	37,860	C+
Drake Univ	IA	45,056	HC
Drew Univ/College of Liberal Arts	NJ	61,048	VC
Drury Univ	MO	33,791	VC
Duke Univ	NC	64,188	
Earlham College	IN	54,870	HC
East Central Univ	OK	13,056	C
East Tenn State Univ	TN	13,994	C
East Texas Baptist Univ	TX	33,134	C
Eastern Conn State Univ	CT	23,059	C
Eastern Illinois Univ	IL	21,126	C
Eastern Kentucky Univ	KY	16,908	C
Eastern Mennonite Univ	VA	42,550	C
Eastern Mich Univ	MI	19,761	C
Eastern Nazarene College	MA	39,955	C
Eastern New Mexico Univ	NM	14,416	C
Eastern Oregon Univ	OR	17,715	C
Eastern Univ	PA	39,540	C
Eastern Washington Univ	WA	25,572	LC
Eastman School of Music/ Univ of Rochester	NY	65,644	SP
Eckerd College	FL	52,874	C
Edgewood College	WI	35,950	C
Edinboro Univ	PA	15,940	LC
Elizabeth City State Univ	NC	14,745	C
Elizabethtown College	PA	54,050	C
Elmhurst College	IL	45,428	C
Elmira College	NY	53,900	C
Elon Univ	NC	44,599	VC+
Emory Univ	GA	60,786	MC
Emporia State Univ	KS	14,570	C
Erskine College	SC	45,460	C
Eugene Lang College/The New School for Liberal Arts	NY	55,650	C
Eureka College	IL	30,220	C
Evangel Univ	MO	28,898	C
Excelsior College	NY	14,080	SP
Fairfield Univ	CT	59,860	VC+
Faulkner Univ	AL	26,410	C
Felician Univ	NJ	45,370	LC
Fisk Univ	TN	32,066	LC
Florida A&M Univ	FL	15,361	C
Florida Atlantic Univ	FL	17,339	C
Florida Gulf Coast Univ	FL	9,682	C
Florida International Univ	FL	19,854	C+
Florida Memorial Univ	FL	22,270	LC
Florida State Univ	FL	16,771	HC
Fordham Univ	NY	65,918	MC
Fort Hays State Univ	KS	12,131	C
Fort Lewis College	CO	18,980	C
Francis Marion Univ	SC	16,464	LC
Franklin and Marshall College	PA	63,170	HC
Franklin College	IN	39,380	C
Franklin Pierce Univ	NH	46,750	C
Fresno Pacific Univ	CA	37,370	C
Friends Univ	KS	34,455	C
Frostburg State Univ	MD	17,280	LC
Furman Univ	SC	58,092	VC+
Gardner-Webb Univ	NC	39,200	C+
Geneva College	PA	35,450	C
George Fox Univ	OR	42,938	C
George Mason Univ	VA	15,724	VC
George Washington Univ	DC	62,835	MC
Georgetown College	KY	41,440	C
Georgia College & State Univ	GA	21,148	C+
Georgia Southern Univ	GA	16,596	C
Georgia Southwestern State Univ	GA	13,870	C

ST = STATE $IS = IN-STATE COSTS SR = SELECTOR RATING

School	ST	$IS	SR
Georgia State Univ	GA	24,332	VC
Gettysburg College	PA	63,000	HC
Gonzaga Univ	WA	50,888	HC
Gordon College	MA	46,472	C+
Goshen College	IN	42,500	C
Goucher College	MD	55,716	VC
Grace Bible College	MI	25,250	C
Grace College and Seminary	IN	31,524	C
Graceland Univ	IA	35,290	C
Grambling State Univ	LA	15,701	C
Grand Canyon Univ	AZ	16,950	VC
Grand Rapids Theological Seminary/Cornerstone Univ	MI	33,338	C
Grand Valley State Univ	MI	22,250	C+
Grand View Univ	IA	32,302	C
Greensboro College	NC	42,400	LC
Greenville College	IL	27,012	C
Grinnell College	IA	60,738	MC
Grove City College	PA	25,692	VC
Guilford College	NC	44,090	C
Gustavus Adolphus College	MN	52,433	HC
Hamilton College	NY	64,250	MC
Hamline Univ	MN	45,678	VC
Hampshire College	MA	63,824	MC
Hampton Univ	VA	34,926	LC
Hannibal-LaGrange Univ	MO	29,815	C
Hanover College	IN	46,364	C+
Harding Univ	AR	25,421	C
Hardin-Simmons Univ	TX	33,966	C
Hartwick College	NY	51,270	C
Harvard College/Harvard Univ	MA	60,659	MC
Hastings College	NE	35,380	C+
Haverford College	PA	66,490	MC
Heidelberg Univ	OH	39,200	C
Henderson State Univ	AR	15,516	LC
Hendrix College	AR	54,020	VC+
High Point Univ	NC	45,977	C
Hillsdale College	MI	35,722	MC
Hiram College	OH	43,230	C
Hofstra Univ	NY	55,960	C+
Hollins Univ	VA	49,635	VC
Holy Names Univ	CA	46,630	LC
Hood College	MD	54,840	C
Hope College	MI	39,940	VC
Houghton College	NY	39,090	C
Houston Baptist Univ	TX	36,450	C
Howard Payne Univ	TX	34,320	C
Howard Univ	DC	37,616	C+
Humboldt State Univ	CA	20,514	C
Huntingdon College	AL	34,900	C
Huston-Tillotson Univ	TX	18,124	LC
Idaho State Univ	ID	13,619	NC
Illinois College	IL	40,850	VC
Illinois State Univ	IL	23,418	VC
Illinois Wesleyan Univ	IL	56,430	VC+
Indiana State Univ	IN	23,223	LC
Indiana Univ Bloomington	IN	20,429	VC
Indiana Univ of Pennsylvania	PA	23,614	LC
Indiana Univ South Bend	IN	14,242	LC
Indiana Univ Southeast	IN	14,242	LC
Indiana Univ-Purdue Univ Fort Wayne	IN	17,553	C
Indiana Wesleyan Univ	IN	33,674	C
Inter-American Univ of PR-San Germán	PR	20,042	
Iowa State Univ	IA	17,570	C
Iowa Wesleyan Univ	IA	39,200	C
Ithaca College	NY	56,766	VC
Jacksonville State Univ	AL	14,628	LC
Jacksonville Univ	FL	46,230	C
James Madison Univ	VA	19,084	VC
John Brown Univ	AR	33,132	VC
Johnson State College	VT	20,752	C
Judson Univ	IL	37,700	C
Juilliard School	NY	57,162	SP
Kalamazoo College	MI	53,931	HC+
Kansas State Univ	KS	17,780	VC
Kansas Wesleyan Univ	KS	36,600	C
Kean Univ	NJ	24,650	C
Keene State College	NH	24,003	LC
Kennesaw State Univ	GA	19,592	VC
Kent State Univ	OH	20,732	C
Kentucky Christian Univ	KY	26,560	LC
Kentucky Wesleyan College	KY	32,080	C
Kenyon College	OH	63,330	MC
King Univ	TN	34,660	C
Knox College	IL	52,615	VC+
Kutztown Univ of Pennsylvania	PA	19,056	LC
La Salle Univ	PA	55,790	C
La Sierra Univ	CA	39,690	VC
Lafayette College	PA	63,355	MC
LaGrange College	GA	39,930	C
Lake Forest College	IL	50,652	VC
Lakeland Univ	WI	35,130	C
Lamar Univ	TX	18,014	LC
Lander Univ	SC	43,994	C
Lane College	TN	16,550	C
Langston Univ	OK	14,314	C
Lebanon Valley College	PA	51,530	C
Lee Univ	TN	22,045	C
Lehigh Univ	PA	61,010	MC
LeMoyne-Owen College	TN	16,980	C
Lenoir-Rhyne Univ	NC	43,200	C
Lewis & Clark College	OR	58,434	HC+
Lewis Univ	IL	40,370	C
Liberty Univ	VA	19,101	C
Limestone College	SC	32,100	C
Lindenwood Univ	MO	25,132	C
Linfield College	OR	52,010	C
Lipscomb Univ	TN	41,296	VC
LIU Brooklyn	NY	49,682	C
LIU Post	NY	49,682	C
Livingstone College	NC	17,815	LC
Lock Haven Univ of Pennsylvania	PA	18,028	LC
Longwood Univ	VA	22,184	C
Loras College	IA	39,222	C
Louisiana College	LA	21,886	C
Louisiana State Univ and A&M College	LA	18,677	VC
Louisiana Tech Univ	LA	11,422	VC
Loyola Marymount Univ	CA	58,038	HC
Loyola Univ Chicago	IL	55,802	VC
Loyola Univ New Orleans	LA	51,708	VC+
Lubbock Christian Univ	TX	28,426	C
Luther College	IA	48,540	C+
Lycoming College	PA	48,580	C
Lynchburg College	VA	46,740	C
Lyon College	AR	34,730	C+
Macalester College	MN	61,905	MC
MacMurray College	IL	33,620	C
Madonna Univ	MI	29,050	C
Malone Univ	OH	38,448	C
Manchester Univ	IN	40,422	C
Manhattan School of Music	NY	57,200	SP
Manhattanville College	NY	51,440	C+
Mannes School for Music	NY	44,500	SP
Mansfield Univ	PA	23,376	LC
Marian Univ	IN	41,220	C
Marian Univ	WI	32,420	LC
Marietta College	OH	46,190	C
Mars Hill Univ	NC	42,688	C
Marshall Univ	WV	17,242	C
Martin Univ	IN	20,264	LC
Marygrove College	MI	28,926	NC
Marylhurst Univ	OR	20,295	NC
Maryville College	TN	44,410	C
Mass Inst of Technology	MA	62,662	MC
Mayville State Univ	ND	18,371	NC
McDaniel College	MD	51,380	VC
McKendree Univ	IL	37,940	C+
McMurry Univ	TX	34,259	LC
McNeese State Univ	LA	7,838	C
McPherson College	KS	34,909	C
Mercer Univ	GA	45,348	VC
Mercy College	NY	31,776	C
Mercyhurst Univ	PA	47,420	C
Meredith College	NC	45,297	C
Messiah College	PA	43,100	C+
Methodist Univ	NC	43,600	C
Miami Univ	OH	27,190	HC+
Mich State Univ	MI	23,898	VC+
MidAmerica Nazarene Univ	KS	35,550	C
Middle Tenn State Univ	TN	8,650	C
Middlebury College	VT	64,332	MC
Midland Univ	NE	37,468	
Midwestern State Univ	TX	17,572	C
Millersville Univ of Pennsylvania	PA	23,782	C
Milligan College	TN	38,150	C
Millikin Univ	IL	42,158	C
Mills College	CA	59,163	VC
Millsaps College	MS	50,080	C+
Minn State Univ, Mankato	MN	15,616	C
Minn State Univ, Moorhead	MN	15,941	C
Minot State Univ	ND	12,732	C
Miss College	MS	25,850	C
Miss Univ for Women	MS	17,065	C
Missouri Baptist Univ	MO	35,594	C
Missouri Southern State Univ	MO	12,499	C
Missouri State Univ	MO	15,190	C+
Missouri Western State Univ	MO	16,741	
Molloy College	NY	40,440	C
Monmouth College	IL	42,260	C
Monmouth Univ	NJ	46,234	C
Montana State Univ	MT	15,500	C+
Montana State Univ-Billings	MT	22,960	C
Montana State Univ-Northern	MT	11,370	NC
Montclair State Univ	NJ	26,210	LC
Moravian College	PA	53,117	
Morehead State Univ	KY	17,422	C
Morehouse College	GA	40,064	C
Morgan State Univ	MD	17,190	LC
Morningside College	IA	36,865	C
Mount Holyoke College	MA	56,746	MC
Mount Marty College	SD	32,972	C
Mount Mercy Univ	IA	36,826	C
Mount St. Joseph Univ	OH	33,880	C
Mount St. Mary's Univ - Chalon Campus	CA	43,897	VC+
Mount Vernon Nazarene Univ	OH	34,500	C
Muhlenberg College	PA	56,645	VC+
Murray State Univ	KY	16,998	C
Muskingum Univ	OH	35,966	C
Naropa Univ	CO	42,826	NC
Nazareth College	NY	45,574	C
Nebr Wesleyan Univ	NE	38,140	C+
New College of Florida	FL	15,848	MC
New England Conservatory of Music	MA	58,655	SP
New Jersey City Univ	NJ	21,456	LC
New Mexico Highlands Univ	NM	11,904	NC
New Mexico State Univ	NM	14,050	C
New York Univ	NY	65,860	MC
Newberry College	SC	34,550	C
Nicholls State Univ	LA	10,534	C
N Car A&T State Univ	NC	13,365	LC
N Car Central Univ	NC	9,000	C
North Central College	IL	48,712	VC
N Dak State Univ	ND	16,245	C
North Park Univ	IL	35,860	C
Northeastern Illinois Univ	IL	12,529	LC
Northeastern State Univ	OK	8,615	VC
Northeastern Univ	MA	62,703	MC
Northern Arizona Univ	AZ	20,246	VC
Northern Illinois Univ	IL	20,176	C
Northern Kentucky Univ	KY	16,486	C
Northern Mich Univ	MI	19,604	C
Northern State Univ	SD	14,505	C
Northwest Christian Univ	OR	36,580	C
Northwest Missouri State Univ	MO	17,737	C
Northwest Nazarene Univ	ID	36,000	C
Northwest Univ	WA	35,876	VC
Northwestern College of Iowa	IA	38,400	C+
Northwestern Okla State Univ	OK	13,072	NC
Northwestern Univ	IL	66,344	MC
Notre Dame de Namur Univ	CA	46,526	LC
Notre Dame of Maryland Univ	MD	46,465	VC
Nova Southeastern Univ	FL	38,534	C+
Nyack College	NY	34,050	NC
Oakland City Univ	IN	33,360	NC
Oakland Univ	MI	20,763	C
Oakwood Univ	AL	43,758	C
Oberlin College	OH	66,012	MC
Occidental College	CA	65,530	MC
Ohio Northern Univ	OH	44,050	VC
Ohio State Univ at Columbus	OH	21,703	HC+
Ohio Univ	OH	22,924	C
Ohio Wesleyan Univ	OH	49,460	VC
Okla Baptist Univ	OK	32,320	C
Okla Christian Univ	OK	27,650	VC
Okla City Univ	OK	40,476	VC
Okla Panhandle State Univ	OK	6,152	NC
Okla State Univ	OK	17,180	VC
Okla Wesleyan Univ	OK	33,206	C
Old Dominion Univ	VA	20,910	C
Olivet Nazarene Univ	IL	41,840	C
Oral Roberts Univ	OK	34,316	C
Oregon State Univ	OR	22,519	VC
Ottawa Univ	KS	36,074	VC
Otterbein Univ	OH	41,630	C
Ouachita Baptist Univ	AR	32,320	C
Our Lady of the Lake Univ	TX	35,012	LC
Pacific Lutheran Univ	WA	49,960	VC
Pacific Union College	CA	36,009	VC
Pacific Univ	OR	52,876	C
Palm Beach Atlantic Univ	FL	39,720	C
Park Univ	MO	20,329	C
Pennsylvania State Univ - Univ Park	PA	29,760	HC
Pepperdine Univ	CA	74,460	HC+
Peru State College	NE	14,768	NC
Philander Smith College	AR	20,814	LC
Piedmont College	GA	32,512	C
Pittsburg State Univ	KS	13,880	NC
Pitzer College	CA	66,192	MC
Plymouth State Univ	NH	23,180	LC
Point Loma Nazarene Univ	CA	43,450	C
Pomona College	CA	64,957	MC
Portland State Univ	OR	19,443	C
Prairie View A&M Univ	TX	15,205	LC
Prescott College	AZ	33,284	C
Princeton Univ	NJ	57,610	MC
Principia College	IL	39,010	C+
Providence College	RI	60,760	VC
Queens Univ of Charlotte	NC	39,543	C
Quincy Univ	IL	36,998	C
Radford Univ	VA	19,027	LC
Ramapo College of New Jersey	NJ	25,338	C
Randolph College	VA	45,660	VC
Randolph-Macon College	VA	49,910	C
Reed College	OR	65,300	MC
Regis Univ	CO	44,520	C
Rhode Island College	RI	17,694	LC
Rhodes College	TN	51,900	HC
Rice Univ	TX	57,668	MC
Rider Univ	NJ	54,050	C
Ripon College	WI	46,911	C+
Roanoke College	VA	54,114	VC
Roberts Wesleyan College	NY	38,306	C
Rochester College	MI	28,574	LC
Rockford Univ	IL	36,030	C
Roger Williams Univ	RI	46,296	C+
Rollins College	FL	58,670	HC
Roosevelt Univ	IL	40,651	VC
Rowan Univ	NJ	24,491	VC+
Rust College	MS	10,600	C
Rutgers Univ - Camden	NJ	26,146	C
Rutgers Univ - New Brunswick	NJ	26,632	HC
Rutgers Univ - Newark	NJ	27,288	C
Saginaw Valley State Univ	MI	18,530	C
St. Augustine's Univ	NC	26,048	C
St. John's Univ	MN	51,624	C
St. Joseph's Univ	PA	57,544	VC+
St. Louis Univ	MO	49,866	HC
St. Martin's Univ	WA	45,056	C
St. Mary-of-the-Woods College	IN	39,632	LC
St. Mary's College	IN	50,600	C
St. Mary's Univ of Minn	MN	41,210	VC
St. Michael's College	VT	51,725	VC+
St. Vincent College	PA	44,626	C
St. Xavier Univ	IL	43,310	C
Salem College	NC	37,694	HC
Salisbury Univ	MD	20,714	VC
Salve Regina Univ	RI	51,470	C
Sam Houston State Univ	TX	18,792	C
Samford Univ	AL	39,232	VC
San Diego Christian College	CA	39,068	C
San Diego State Univ	CA	21,896	C+
San Francisco Conservatory of Music	CA	57,310	SP
San Francisco State Univ	CA	18,514	LC
San Jose State Univ	CA	21,540	C
Santa Fe Univ of Art and Design	NM	39,980	SP
Sarah Lawrence College	NY	63,388	HC
Schreiner Univ	TX	34,626	LC
Scripps College	CA	66,664	MC
Seattle Pacific Univ	WA	47,439	C+
Seattle Univ	WA	50,811	VC+
Seton Hall Univ	NJ	55,514	C
Seton Hill Univ	PA	46,972	C
Sewanee: The Univ of the South	TN	54,500	MC
Shenandoah Univ	VA	41,312	C
Shepherd Univ, West Virginia	WV	17,224	C
Shorter Univ	GA	31,130	LC
Siena Heights Univ	MI	32,040	C
Sierra Nevada College	NV	43,482	C
Silver Lake College of the Holy Family	WI	36,290	LC
Simmons College	MA	53,090	VC
Simpson College	IA	43,839	VC
Simpson Univ	CA	33,700	C
Skidmore College	NY	64,214	HC
Slippery Rock Univ of Pennsylvania	PA	10,360	C
Smith College	MA	63,914	MC
Sonoma State Univ	CA	27,806	C
S Dak State Univ	SD	15,634	C
Southeast Missouri State Univ	MO	15,498	C
Southeastern Louisiana Univ	LA	16,237	C
Southeastern Okla State Univ	OK	11,875	C
Southeastern Univ	FL	31,765	C
Southern Adventist Univ	TN	27,600	C
Southern Illinois Univ Carbondale	IL	23,667	C
Southern Illinois Univ Edwardsville	IL	22,643	C
Southern Nazarene Univ	OK	32,798	NC
Southern Oregon Univ	OR	19,117	C
Southern Univ and A&M College	LA	16,074	LC+
Southern Wesleyan Univ	SC	32,130	LC
Southwest Baptist Univ	MO	29,900	LC
Southwest Minn State Univ	MN	17,783	C
Southwestern Adventist Univ	TX	27,756	LC
Southwestern College	KS	31,531	C
Southwestern Okla State Univ	OK	11,790	C
Southwestern Univ	TX	50,720	VC
Spelman College	GA	38,751	C
Spring Arbor Univ	MI	36,000	C
St. Ambrose Univ	IA	39,019	C
St. Ambrose Univ	IA	39,019	C
St. Bonaventure Univ	NY	44,237	C
St. Catherine Univ	MN	45,630	VC
St. Cloud State Univ	MN	10,600	C
St. John's College-Annapolis	MD	60,142	MC
St. Lawrence Univ	NY	64,390	VC
St. Mary's College of Maryland	MD	26,634	VC
St. Mary's Univ	TX	37,500	C
St. Norbert College	WI	44,525	VC
St. Olaf College	MN	54,260	HC+
Stanford Univ	CA	60,409	MC
SUNY / Buffalo State College	NY	20,842	C
SUNY / SUNY Fredonia	NY	20,818	C
SUNY / SUNY Oneonta	NY	19,712	C+
SUNY / SUNY Plattsburgh	NY	18,814	C
SUNY / SUNY Potsdam	NY	20,404	C+
SUNY / Univ at Buffalo	NY	23,122	C+
SUNY at Binghamton	NY	22,861	MC
SUNY at Geneseo	NY	20,440	VC+
SUNY at New Paltz	NY	19,200	C
SUNY at Oswego	NY	21,351	C
SUNY at Purchase	NY	17,900	C
SUNY SUNY Albany	NY	22,165	C
Stephen F. Austin State Univ	TX	18,406	LC
Sterling College	KS	32,830	C
Stetson Univ	FL	53,544	VC
Stillman College	AL	20,738	C
Stockton Univ	NJ	25,059	
Stonehill College	MA	55,030	C+
Stony Brook Univ/The SUNY	NY	21,881	MC
Susquehanna Univ	PA	55,340	VC
Swarthmore College	PA	63,550	MC
Syracuse Univ	NY	60,239	VC
Tabor College	KS	35,870	C
Tarleton State Univ	TX	15,248	LC
Taylor Univ	IN	40,317	C+
Temple Univ	PA	24,392	VC
Tenn State Univ	TN	14,423	C
Texas A&M Univ	TX	20,521	VC+

ST = STATE $IS = IN-STATE COSTS SR = SELECTOR RATING

School	ST	$IS	SR
Texas A&M Univ at Commerce	TX	10,496	C
Texas A&M Univ at Corpus Christi	TX	16,851	LC
Texas A&M Univ at Kingsville	TX	7,500	LC
Texas Christian Univ	TX	54,670	HC
Texas Lutheran Univ	TX	38,620	C
Texas Southern Univ	TX	18,212	LC
Texas State Univ	TX	19,350	C
Texas Tech Univ	TX	18,736	C+
Texas Wesleyan Univ	TX	35,134	C
Texas Woman's Univ	TX	15,302	LC
The Boston Conservatory at Berklee	MA	61,042	C+
The Catholic Univ of America	DC	56,356	VC
The College of Idaho	ID	36,415	C
The College of New Jersey	NJ	31,909	HC
The College of St. Rose	NY	43,048	C
The College of Wooster	OH	57,900	VC+
The Lincoln Univ	PA	15,154	NC
The Master's Univ	CA	43,870	C+
The Univ of Akron	OH	21,477	C
The Univ of Tenn at Chattanooga	TN	16,744	C
The Univ of Tenn at Knoxville	TN	22,112	VC
The Univ of Tenn at Martin	TN	14,876	C
The Univ of Utah	UT	17,924	VC
Thomas Edison State Univ	NJ	6,350	NC
Toccoa Falls College	GA	27,920	C
Tougaloo College	MS	17,980	NC
Towson Univ	MD	17,408	VC
Transylvania Univ	KY	45,690	VC+
Trevecca Nazarene Univ	TN	31,186	C
Trinity Christian College	IL	35,580	C
Trinity College	CT	63,920	HC+
Trinity International Univ	IL	31,070	VC
Trinity Univ	TX	52,314	HC+
Truman State Univ	MO	16,014	HC
Tufts Univ	MA		MC
Tulane Univ	LA	63,396	HC+
Union College	NE	23,270	C
Union Univ	TN	33,970	VC
Universidad Adventista de las Antillas	PR	16,606	
Univ of Alabama	AL	24,320	C+
Univ of Alabama at Birmingham	AL	19,906	C
Univ of Alabama in Huntsville	AL	19,445	VC
Univ of Alaska Anchorage	AK	16,652	NC
Univ of Alaska Fairbanks	AK	16,179	C
Univ of Arizona	AZ	23,100	C
Univ of Arkansas at Fayetteville	AR	19,152	C+
Univ of Arkansas at Little Rock	AR	18,211	C
Univ of Arkansas at Monticello	AR	13,134	NC
Univ of Arkansas at Pine Bluff	AR	13,541	C
Univ of Bridgeport	CT	44,430	LC
Univ of Calif at Berkeley	CA	28,853	MC
Univ of Calif at Davis	CA	28,468	HC
Univ of Calif at Irvine	CA	26,484	VC
Univ of Calif at Los Angeles	CA	30,162	MC
Univ of Calif at Riverside	CA	29,227	C+
Univ of Calif at Santa Barbara	CA	29,091	HC
Univ of Calif San Diego	CA	30,150	MC
Univ of Calif, Santa Cruz	CA	28,731	C+
Univ of Central Arkansas	AR	14,472	VC
Univ of Central Florida	FL	15,922	VC
Univ of Central Missouri	MO	18,982	C
Univ of Central Okla	OK	13,486	C
Univ of Chicago	IL	67,584	MC
Univ of Cincinnati	OH	21,964	VC
Univ of Colo Boulder	CO	24,285	VC+
Univ of Colo Denver	CO	23,230	C
Univ of Conn	CT	25,538	HC
Univ of Dayton	OH	53,620	C
Univ of Delaware	DE	24,976	VC+
Univ of Denver	CO	58,443	VC+
Univ of Evansville	IN	44,186	VC+
Univ of Florida	FL	16,291	HC+
Univ of Georgia	GA	21,250	HC
Univ of Hartford	CT	49,776	C
Univ of Hawaii at Hilo	HI	18,038	C
Univ of Hawaii at Manoa	HI	23,221	C
Univ of Idaho	ID	15,348	C
Univ of Illinois at Chicago	IL	25,006	VC
Univ of Illinois at Urbana-Champaign	IL	27,006	HC
Univ of Indianapolis	IN	36,480	C
Univ of Iowa	IA	18,683	VC+
Univ of Jamestown	ND	28,508	C
Univ of Kansas	KS	20,135	C+
Univ of Kentucky	KY	33,306	C
Univ of La Verne	CA	55,600	C
Univ of Louisiana at Lafayette	LA	14,516	C
Univ of Louisiana at Monroe	LA	15,970	C
Univ of Louisville	KY	19,824	C
Univ of Maine	ME	20,792	C
Univ of Mary	ND	23,180	C
Univ of Mary Hardin-Baylor	TX	33,950	C+
Univ of Mary Washington	VA	24,764	VC
Univ of Maryland/Baltimore County	MD	21,296	VC
Univ of Maryland/College Park	MD	21,938	HC
Univ of Mass Amherst	MA	26,199	VC+
Univ of Mass Boston	MA	13,435	C
Univ of Mass Dartmouth	MA	25,658	C
Univ of Mass Lowell	MA	26,380	C
Univ of Memphis	TN	18,278	C
Univ of Miami	FL	63,494	MC
Univ of Mich/Ann Arbor	MI	24,410	MC
Univ of Mich-Flint	MI	17,607	C+
Univ of Minn/Duluth	MN	20,292	C+
Univ of Minn/Morris	MN	20,760	VC
Univ of Minn/Twin Cities	MN	23,519	HC+
Univ of Miss	MS	17,746	C+
Univ of Missouri/Columbia	MO	18,201	MC
Univ of Missouri-Kansas City	MO	19,563	VC
Univ of Missouri-St. Louis	MO		C
Univ of Mobile	AL	28,935	C
Univ of Montana	MT	14,105	C
Univ of Montana-Western	MT	11,220	LC
Univ of Montevallo	AL	19,502	C
Univ of Mount Olive	NC	18,426	C
Univ of Mount Union	OH	38,970	C
Univ of Nebr - Kearney	NE	16,546	LC
Univ of Nebr - Lincoln	NE	18,589	VC
Univ of Nebr - Omaha	NE	16,120	C
Univ of Nevada, Las Vegas	NV	17,553	C
Univ of Nevada/Reno	NV	18,010	C
Univ of New Hampshire	NH	28,562	VC
Univ of New Haven	CT	52,190	C
Univ of New Mexico	NM	15,404	C
Univ of New Orleans	LA	12,840	C
Univ of North Alabama	AL	15,398	C
Univ of N Car at Asheville	NC	15,723	VC+
Univ of N Car at Chapel Hill	NC	20,052	HC+
Univ of N Car at Charlotte	NC	15,547	C
Univ of N Car at Greensboro	NC	14,690	C
Univ of N Car at Pembroke	NC	14,388	LC
Univ of N Car at Wilmington	NC	14,590	VC
Univ of N Car School of the Arts	NC	18,040	SP
Univ of N Dak	ND	15,373	C
Univ of North Florida	FL	15,996	VC
Univ of North Georgia	GA	17,316	C
Univ of North Texas	TX	19,198	C
Univ of Northern Colo	CO	20,851	C
Univ of Northwestern - St. Paul	MN	38,160	C
Univ of Notre Dame	IN	64,043	MC
Univ of Okla	OK	18,911	VC
Univ of Oregon	OR	22,972	C
Univ of Pennsylvania	PA	63,526	MC
Univ of Pittsburgh	PA	29,568	HC+
Univ of Portland	OR	52,152	VC
Univ of PR-Rio Piedras campus	PR	13,327	
Univ of Puget Sound	WA	56,456	VC+
Univ of Redlands	CA	60,200	VC
Univ of Rhode Island	RI	24,906	C
Univ of Richmond	VA	60,880	MC
Univ of Rio Grande & Rio Grande Community College	OH	8,750	NC
Univ of Rochester	NY	65,032	MC
Univ of St. Mary	KS	34,690	C
Univ of San Diego	CA	58,442	VC+
Univ of Science and Arts of Okla	OK	11,140	VC
Univ of Sioux Falls	SD	34,330	C
Univ of South Alabama	AL	16,400	C
Univ of S Car at Columbia	SC	19,725	VC+
Univ of S Dak	SD	16,109	C
Univ of South Florida/Tampa	FL	16,110	VC+
Univ of Southern Calif	CA	66,631	C
Univ of Southern Maine	ME	18,320	C
Univ of Southern Miss	MS	13,170	C
Univ of St. Francis	IL	39,924	C
Univ of St. Thomas - Houston	TX	40,020	VC
Univ of Tampa	FL	36,944	C
Univ of Texas at Arlington	TX	18,026	LC
Univ of Texas at Austin	TX	26,102	HC
Univ of Texas at El Paso	TX	34,452	NC
Univ of Texas at San Antonio	TX	20,157	C
Univ of the Cumberlands	KY	32,000	C
Univ of the District of Columbia	DC	21,044	LC
Univ of the Incarnate Word	TX	39,162	LC
Univ of the Ozarks	AR	52,176	C
Univ of the Pacific	CA	57,006	VC
Univ of Toledo	OH	19,336	NC
Univ of Tulsa	OK	52,625	HC+
Univ of Vermont	VT	28,878	HC
Univ of Virginia	VA	25,891	MC
Univ of West Florida	FL	15,848	C
Univ of Wisc-Eau Claire	WI	15,797	VC
Univ of Wisc-Green Bay	WI	15,064	C
Univ of Wisc-La Crosse	WI	15,247	C+
Univ of Wisc-Madison	WI	20,934	MC
Univ of Wisc-Milwaukee	WI	21,496	C
Univ of Wisc-Oshkosh	WI	15,200	C
Univ of Wisc-Parkside	WI	15,193	C
Univ of Wisc-Platteville	WI	14,614	VC
Univ of Wisc-River Falls	WI	14,485	C
Univ of Wisc-Stevens Point	WI	14,043	C
Univ of Wisc-Superior	WI	14,446	C
Univ of Wisc-Whitewater	WI	13,976	C
Univ of Wyoming	WY	15,375	C+
Ursinus College	PA	61,690	VC
Utah State Univ	UT	12,736	C
Valley City State Univ	ND	13,267	C
Valparaiso Univ	IN	48,370	C+
Vanguard Univ of Southern Calif	CA	40,740	VC
Vassar College	NY	65,491	MC
Virginia Commonwealth Univ	VA	23,049	C
Virginia Polytechnic Inst and State Univ	VA	21,276	HC
Virginia Union Univ	VA	22,421	C
Virginia Wesleyan College	VA	43,728	LC
Wabash College	IN	50,650	VC
Wagner College	NY	55,480	C+
Wake Forest Univ	NC	64,056	MC
Walla Walla Univ	WA	30,417	NC
Walsh Univ	OH	39,010	C
Warner Pacific College	OR	33,790	C
Wartburg College	IA	47,840	C
Washburn Univ	KS	15,827	C
Washington & Jefferson College	PA	56,512	VC
Washington Adventist Univ	MD	31,440	LC
Washington and Lee Univ	VA	59,647	MC
Washington College	MD	54,666	VC
Washington State Univ	WA	22,495	C
Washington Univ in St. Louis	MO	65,366	VC
Wayland Baptist Univ	TX	22,356	LC
Wayne State College	NE	12,802	C
Wayne State Univ	MI	22,016	C
Weber State Univ	UT	10,721	C
Webster Univ	MO	37,490	C
Wellesley College	MA	63,916	MC
Wesley College	DE	37,026	LC
Wesleyan College	GA	29,694	C+
Wesleyan Univ	CT	65,516	MC
West Chester Univ of Pennsylvania	PA	18,456	C
West Liberty Univ	WV	15,512	C
West Texas A&M Univ	TX	13,478	C
West Virginia Univ	WV	18,210	C
West Virginia Wesleyan College	WV	36,858	C
Western Carolina Univ	NC	13,965	C
Western Conn State Univ	CT	21,254	LC
Western Illinois Univ	IL	20,825	C
Western Kentucky Univ	KY	16,850	C
Western Mich Univ	MI	21,054	C
Western New Mexico Univ	NM	16,734	LC
Western Oregon Univ	OR	15,021	LC
Western State Colo Univ	CO	18,639	C
Western Washington Univ	WA	18,003	C+
Westfield State Univ	MA	19,671	C
Westminster Choir College	NJ	53,730	SP
Westminster College	PA	39,180	C+
Westminster College	UT	41,078	C+
Westmont College	CA	56,410	HC
Wheaton College	IL	43,610	MC
Wheaton College	MA	61,512	VC
Whitman College	WA	59,772	MC
Whittier College	CA	57,891	C
Whitworth Univ	WA	51,732	VC
Wichita State Univ	KS	21,643	C
Wilberforce Univ	OH	19,016	C
Wiley College	TX	18,504	C
Willamette Univ	OR	61,817	VC+
William Carey Univ	MS	23,950	LC
William Jewell College	MO	41,210	C+
William Paterson Univ of New Jersey	NJ	23,133	C
Williams Baptist College	AR	24,720	C
Williams College	MA	63,290	MC
Wilmington College	OH	34,600	C
Wingate Univ	NC	39,950	C
Winona State Univ	MN	17,535	C
Winthrop Univ	SC	23,082	C
Wisc Lutheran College	WI	36,290	VC
Wittenberg Univ	OH	48,156	C+
Wright State Univ	OH	16,983	C
Xavier Univ	OH	47,880	C+
Xavier Univ of Louisiana	LA	31,689	C+
Yale Univ	CT	64,650	MC
Yeshiva Univ	NY	47,250	VC+
York College of Pennsylvania	PA	29,240	C
Youngstown State Univ	OH	17,307	C

MUSIC BUSINESS MANAGEMENT

School	ST	$IS	SR
Albright College	PA	46,660	C
Anderson Univ	IN	38,200	C
Appalachian State Univ	NC	14,416	VC
Aquinas College - Mich	MI	38,876	HC
Belmont Univ	TN	40,970	VC
Berklee College of Music	MA	60,930	SP
Berry College	GA	45,286	C+
Bethel Univ	TN	24,738	C
Central Washington Univ	WA	16,803	C
College of the Ozarks	MO	7,230	C
Columbia College Chicago	IL	43,168	C
Concordia Univ St. Paul	MN	29,050	C
Dallas Baptist Univ	TX	33,713	C
Delta State Univ	MS	13,176	C
DePaul Univ	IL	47,623	VC
DePauw Univ	IN	58,688	HC+
Dillard Univ	LA	20,940	VC
Drake Univ	IA	45,056	HC
Duquesne Univ	PA	46,822	VC
Elmhurst College	IL	45,428	C
Five Towns College	NY	35,350	C
Geneva College	PA	35,450	C
Georgia State Univ	GA	24,332	VC
Greenville College	IL	27,012	C
Grove City College	PA	25,692	VC
Hardin-Simmons Univ	TX	33,966	C
Hofstra Univ	NY	55,960	C+
Howard Univ	DC	37,616	C+
Huntington Univ	IN	33,996	C
Johnson C. Smith Univ	NC	25,336	LC
Johnson State College	VT	20,752	C
Kentucky Christian Univ	KY	26,560	LC
Kentucky Wesleyan College	KY	32,080	C
Lebanon Valley College	PA	51,530	C
Lee Univ	TN	22,045	C
Lewis Univ	IL	40,370	C
Loyola Univ New Orleans	LA	51,708	VC+
Lubbock Christian Univ	TX	28,426	C
Madonna Univ	MI	29,050	C
Mansfield Univ	PA	23,376	LC
Marywood Univ	PA	46,900	C
McKendree Univ	IL	37,940	C+
Messiah College	PA	43,100	C+
Middle Tenn State Univ	TN	8,650	C
Millikin Univ	IL	42,158	C
Minn State Univ, Mankato	MN	15,616	C
Monmouth Univ	NJ	46,234	C
Montreat College	NC	31,298	LC
Murray State Univ	KY	16,998	C
Nazareth College	NY	45,574	C
New York Univ	NY	65,860	MC
Northwest Univ	WA	35,876	VC
Oakwood Univ	AL	43,758	C
Ohio Northern Univ	OH	44,050	VC
Old Dominion Univ	VA	20,910	C
Peru State College	NE	14,768	NC
St. Augustine's Univ	NC	26,048	C
S Car State Univ	SC	20,805	LC
Southern Illinois Univ Edwardsville	IL	22,643	C
Southern Nazarene Univ	OK	32,798	NC
Southern Oregon Univ	OR	19,117	C
SUNY / SUNY Oneonta	NY	19,712	C+
SUNY / SUNY Potsdam	NY	20,404	C+
Tiffin Univ	OH	31,380	C
Trevecca Nazarene Univ	TN	31,186	C
Univ of Evansville	IN	44,186	VC+
Univ of Hartford	CT	49,776	C
Univ of Mass Lowell	MA	26,380	C
Univ of Memphis	TN	18,278	C
Univ of Miami	FL	63,494	MC
Univ of New Haven	CT	52,190	C
Univ of the Incarnate Word	TX	39,162	LC
Univ of the Pacific	CA	57,006	VC
Wichita State Univ	KS	21,643	C
Winston-Salem State Univ	NC	26,166	LC

MUSIC COMPOSITION

School	ST	$IS	SR
Baldwin Wallace Univ	OH	41,106	C
Biola Univ	CA	46,402	C+
Boston Univ	MA	65,110	MC
Brown Univ	RI	64,566	MC
Cairn Univ	PA	36,296	C
Calif Baptist Univ	CA	41,392	C
Carnegie Mellon Univ	PA	67,980	MC
Cedarville Univ	OH	34,990	VC
Cleveland Inst of Music	OH	63,038	SP
Johns Hopkins Univ	MD	65,386	MC
Keene State College	NH	24,003	LC
Lipscomb Univ	TN	41,296	VC
Loyola Univ New Orleans	LA	51,708	VC+
Murray State Univ	KY	16,998	C
New York Univ	NY	65,860	MC
Northern Kentucky Univ	KY	16,486	C
Oberlin College	OH	66,012	MC
Ohio Univ	OH	22,924	C
Ohio Wesleyan Univ	OH	49,460	VC
Okla City Univ	OK	40,476	VC
Ouachita Baptist Univ	AR	32,320	C
Point Loma Nazarene Univ	CA	43,450	C
San Francisco Conservatory of Music	CA	57,310	SP
Southern Oregon Univ	OR	19,117	C
SUNY / SUNY Potsdam	NY	20,404	C+
Stetson Univ	FL	53,544	VC
Syracuse Univ	NY	60,239	VC
Temple Univ	PA	24,392	VC
The Master's Univ	CA	43,870	C+
Tulane Univ	LA	63,396	HC+
Univ of Georgia	GA	21,250	HC
Univ of Kansas	KS	20,135	C+
Univ of Miami	FL	63,494	MC
Univ of West Georgia	GA	16,360	LC
Washington State Univ	WA	22,495	C
Western Mich Univ	MI	21,054	C
Whitman College	WA	59,772	MC
Wichita State Univ	KS	21,643	C
Youngstown State Univ	OH	17,307	C

MUSIC EDUCATION

School	ST	$IS	SR
Abilene Christian Univ	TX	41,800	C+
Adams State Univ	CO	17,703	LC
Alabama A&M Univ	AL	18,796	C
Alabama State Univ	AL	14,142	NC
Albany State Univ	GA	19,462	C

ST = STATE $IS = IN-STATE COSTS SR = SELECTOR RATING

School	ST	$IS	SR
Albion College	MI	52,650	C
Alderson Broaddus Univ	WV	26,149	C
Anderson Univ	IN	38,200	C
Andrews Univ	MI	28,030	C+
Anna Maria College	MA	48,186	C
Appalachian State Univ	NC	14,416	VC
Aquinas College - Mich	MI	38,876	HC
Arcadia Univ	PA	33,570	C+
Arizona State Univ at the Tempe Campus	AZ	21,756	VC
Arkansas Tech Univ	AR	15,484	C
Armstrong State Univ	GA	16,962	C
Asbury Univ	KY	35,180	C+
Ashland Univ	OH	21,440	C
Atlantic Union College	MA	27,228	C
Auburn Univ	AL	23,594	VC+
Augsburg College	MN	43,929	C
Augusta Univ	GA	4,632	C
Augustana College	IL	49,658	VC
Augustana Univ	SD	38,424	VC
Azusa Pacific Univ	CA	43,972	C
Baker Univ	KS	33,350	C+
Baldwin Wallace Univ	OH	41,106	C
Baylor Univ	TX	53,760	HC
Benedictine College	KS	36,200	VC
Bennett College	NC	27,302	NC
Berklee College of Music	MA	60,930	SP
Berry College	GA	45,286	C+
Bethany College	KS	46,100	NC
Bethel College	IN	35,860	C
Bethel Univ	MN	45,270	VC
Bethel Univ	TN	24,738	C
Bethune-Cookman Univ	FL	22,970	C
Biola Univ	CA	46,402	C+
Bloomsburg Univ of Pennsylvania	PA	19,066	LC
Blue Mountain College	MS	15,949	VC
Bluffton Univ	OH	40,950	C
Boise State Univ	ID	14,860	C
Boston Univ	MA	65,110	MC
Bowling Green State Univ	OH	19,747	C
Brenau Univ - Women's College	GA	37,876	LC
Bridgewater State Univ	MA	21,810	C
Brigham Young Univ	UT	12,748	HC
Bucknell Univ	PA	64,616	MC
Buena Vista Univ	IA	41,514	C
Butler Univ	IN	51,352	VC
Cairn Univ	PA	36,296	C
Calif Baptist Univ	CA	41,392	C
Cal State, Fresno	CA	16,902	LC
Cal State, Fullerton	CA	21,902	C
Cal State, San Bernardino	CA	12,000	C
Calvin College	MI	41,570	VC+
Cameron Univ	OK	11,072	NC
Campbellsville Univ	KY	32,492	C
Carnegie Mellon Univ	PA	67,980	MC
Carroll Univ	WI	38,100	C+
Carson-Newman Univ	TN	34,160	C
Carthage College	WI	48,835	C
Case Western Reserve Univ	OH	60,304	MC
Castleton Univ	VT	20,186	C
Catawba College	NC	39,820	C
Cedarville Univ	OH	34,990	VC
Central College	IA	44,592	C
Central Conn State Univ	CT	21,203	C
Central Methodist Univ	MO	36,830	VC
Central Mich Univ	MI	20,330	C
Central State Univ	OH	18,564	C
Central Washington Univ	WA	16,803	C
Chapman Univ	CA	63,078	VC+
Charleston Southern Univ	SC	32,400	C
Chestnut Hill College	PA	43,410	C
Chicago State Univ	IL	20,144	C
CUNY/Brooklyn College	NY	5,884	C+
CUNY/Hunter College	NY	31,098	VC
CUNY/Queens College	NY	27,896	C
Claflin Univ	SC	33,764	LC
Clarke Univ	IA	38,940	C
Coe College	IA	51,570	VC
Coker College	SC	34,810	LC
College of the Ozarks	MO	7,230	C
Colo Christian Univ	CO	39,940	VC
Colo Mesa Univ	CO	18,955	LC
Colo State Univ	CO	22,162	VC
Colo State Univ-Pueblo	CO	18,234	C
Columbia College	SC	36,550	C
Columbus State Univ	GA	14,336	LC
Concord Univ	WV	14,954	C
Concordia College - Moorhead	MN	51,088	C+
Concordia College - New York	NY	39,035	LC
Concordia Univ Nebr	NE	36,280	VC
Concordia Univ St. Paul	MN	29,050	C
Concordia Univ, Chicago	IL	39,694	C
Conservatory of Music of PR	PR	13,925	
Converse College	SC	26,495	C
Corban Univ	OR	40,306	C
Cornell College	IA	48,800	VC
Culver-Stockton College	MO	33,525	C
Cumberland Univ	TN	27,710	C
Delaware State Univ	DE	19,376	NC
Delta State Univ	MS	13,176	C
DePaul Univ	IL	47,623	VC
DePauw Univ	IN	58,688	HC+
Dickinson State Univ	ND	12,372	LC
Dordt College	IA	37,860	C+
Drake Univ	IA	45,056	HC
Drury Univ	MO	33,791	VC
Duquesne Univ	PA	46,822	VC
East Carolina Univ	NC	16,937	C
East Central Univ	OK	13,056	C
East Texas Baptist Univ	TX	33,134	C
Eastern Kentucky Univ	KY	16,908	C
Eastern Mich Univ	MI	19,761	C
Eastern Nazarene College	MA	39,955	C
Eastern New Mexico Univ	NM	14,416	C
Eastern Washington Univ	WA	25,572	LC
Eastman School of Music/Univ of Rochester	NY	65,644	SP
Edgewood College	WI	35,950	C
Edinboro Univ	PA	15,940	LC
Elizabethtown College	PA	54,050	C
Elmhurst College	IL	45,428	C
Elon Univ	NC	44,599	VC+
Emporia State Univ	KS	14,570	C
Eureka College	IL	30,220	C
Evangel Univ	MO	28,898	C
Fairmont State Univ	WV	15,726	C
Faulkner Univ	AL	26,410	C
Fayetteville State Univ	NC	17,756	C
Fisk Univ	TN	32,066	LC
Five Towns College	NY	35,350	C
Florida A&M Univ	FL	15,361	C
Florida Gulf Coast Univ	FL	9,682	C
Florida State Univ	FL	16,771	HC
Fort Hays State Univ	KS	12,131	C
Freed-Hardeman Univ	TN	29,450	C
Fresno Pacific Univ	CA	37,370	C
Friends Univ	KS	34,455	C
Furman Univ	SC	58,092	VC+
Gardner-Webb Univ	NC	39,200	C+
Geneva College	PA	35,450	C
George Fox Univ	OR	42,938	C
Georgia College & State Univ	GA	21,148	C+
Gettysburg College	PA	63,000	HC
Glenville State College	WV	17,386	NC
Gonzaga Univ	WA	50,888	HC
Gordon College	MA	46,472	C+
Goshen College	IN	42,500	C
Grace College and Seminary	IN	31,524	C
Graceland Univ	IA	35,290	C
Grand Canyon Univ	AZ	16,950	VC
Grand Rapids Theological Seminary/Cornerstone Univ	MI	33,338	C
Grand Valley State Univ	MI	22,250	C+
Grand View Univ	IA	32,302	C
Greensboro College	NC	42,400	LC
Greenville College	IL	27,012	C
Grove City College	PA	25,692	VC
Gustavus Adolphus College	MN	52,433	HC
Hamline Univ	MN	45,678	VC
Harding Univ	AR	25,421	C
Hardin-Simmons Univ	TX	33,966	C
Hartwick College	NY	51,270	C
Hastings College	NE	35,380	C+
Heidelberg Univ	OH	39,200	C
Henderson State Univ	AR	15,516	LC
Hofstra Univ	NY	55,960	C+
Hope College	MI	39,940	VC
Houghton College	NY	39,090	C
Houston Baptist Univ	TX	36,450	C
Howard Univ	DC	37,616	C+
Humboldt State Univ	CA	20,514	C
Huntingdon College	AL	34,900	C
Huntington Univ	IN	33,996	C
Idaho State Univ	ID	13,619	NC
Illinois State Univ	IL	23,418	VC
Illinois Wesleyan Univ	IL	56,430	VC+
Indiana State Univ	IN	23,223	LC
Indiana Univ Bloomington	IN	20,429	VC
Indiana Univ of Pennsylvania	PA	23,614	LC
Indiana Univ South Bend	IN	14,242	C
Indiana Univ-Purdue Univ Fort Wayne	IN	17,553	C
Indiana Wesleyan Univ	IN	33,674	C
Inter-American Univ of PR Ponce	PR	19,549	
Inter-American Univ of PR-Fajardo Campus	PR	18,336	
Inter-American Univ of PR-San Germán	PR	20,042	
Iowa State Univ	IA	17,570	C
Iowa Wesleyan Univ	IA	39,200	C
Ithaca College	NY	56,766	VC
Jackson State Univ	MS	15,879	LC
Jacksonville State Univ	AL	14,628	LC
Jacksonville Univ	FL	46,230	C
John Brown Univ	AR	33,132	VC
Johns Hopkins Univ	MD	65,386	MC
Johnson State College	VT	20,752	C
Judson College	AL	27,066	C
Judson Univ	IL	37,700	C
Kansas State Univ	KS	17,780	VC
Kansas Wesleyan Univ	KS	36,600	C
Kean Univ	NJ	24,650	C
Keene State College	NH	24,003	LC
Kennesaw State Univ	GA	19,592	VC
Kent State Univ	OH	20,732	C
Kentucky Christian Univ	KY	26,560	LC
Kentucky State Univ	KY	13,364	LC
Kentucky Wesleyan College	KY	32,080	C
King Univ	TN	34,660	C
La Sierra Univ	CA	39,690	VC
Lake Forest College	IL	50,652	VC
Lakeland Univ	WI	35,130	C
Lamar Univ	TX	18,014	LC
Lander Univ	SC	43,994	C
Lawrence Univ	WI	54,498	HC
Lebanon Valley College	PA	51,530	C
Lee Univ	TN	22,045	C
Lenoir-Rhyne Univ	NC	43,200	C
Limestone College	SC	32,100	C
Lindenwood Univ	MO	25,132	C
Lindsey Wilson College	KY	32,882	C
Linfield College	OR	52,010	C
Lipscomb Univ	TN	41,296	VC
LIU Brooklyn	NY	49,682	C
LIU Post	NY	49,682	C
Livingstone College	NC	17,815	LC
Longwood Univ	VA	22,184	C
Loras College	IA	39,222	C
Louisiana College	LA	21,886	C
Louisiana State Univ and A&M College	LA	18,677	VC
Louisiana Tech Univ	LA	11,422	VC
Loyola Univ New Orleans	LA	51,708	VC+
Lubbock Christian Univ	TX	28,426	C
Lynchburg College	VA	46,740	C
MacMurray College	IL	33,620	C
Madonna Univ	MI	29,050	C
Malone Univ	OH	38,448	C
Mansfield Univ	PA	23,376	LC
Marian Univ	WI	32,420	LC
Marietta College	OH	46,190	C
Mars Hill Univ	NC	42,688	C
Marshall Univ	WV	17,242	C
Maryville College	TN	44,410	C
Marywood Univ	PA	46,900	C
McKendree Univ	IL	37,940	C+
Mercer Univ	GA	45,348	VC
Mercyhurst Univ	PA	47,420	C
Meredith College	NC	45,297	C
Messiah College	PA	43,100	C+
Methodist Univ	NC	43,600	C
Metropolitan State Univ of Denver	CO	29,889	LC
Miami Univ	OH	27,190	HC+
Mich State Univ	MI	23,898	VC+
MidAmerica Nazarene Univ	KS	35,550	C
Midland Univ	NE	37,468	
Midwestern State Univ	TX	17,572	C
Millersville Univ of Pennsylvania	PA	23,782	C
Milligan College	TN	38,150	C
Millikin Univ	IL	42,158	C
Minn State Univ, Mankato	MN	15,616	C
Minn State Univ, Moorhead	MN	15,941	C
Minot State Univ	ND	12,732	C
Miss College	MS	25,850	C
Miss State Univ	MS	11,454	C+
Miss Univ for Women	MS	17,065	C
Miss Valley State Univ	MS	13,233	LC
Missouri Baptist Univ	MO	35,594	C
Missouri Western State Univ	MO	16,741	
Molloy College	NY	40,440	C
Monmouth Univ	NJ	46,234	C
Montana State Univ	MT	15,500	C+
Montana State Univ-Billings	MT	22,960	C
Montclair State Univ	NJ	26,210	LC
Moravian College	PA	53,117	
Morningside College	IA	36,865	C
Mount Vernon Nazarene Univ	OH	34,500	C
Muskingum Univ	OH	35,966	C
Nazareth College	NY	45,574	C
Nebr Wesleyan Univ	NE	38,140	C+
New Jersey City Univ	NJ	21,456	LC
New Mexico State Univ	NM	14,050	C
New York Univ	NY	65,860	MC
Newberry College	SC	34,550	C
Nicholls State Univ	LA	10,534	C
Norfolk State Univ	VA	25,702	LC
N Car A&T State Univ	NC	13,365	LC
North Central College	IL	48,712	VC
N Dak State Univ	ND	16,245	C
North Greenville Univ	SC	25,930	C+
Northeastern Illinois Univ	IL	12,529	LC
Northeastern State Univ	OK	8,615	VC
Northern Arizona Univ	AZ	20,246	VC
Northern Illinois Univ	IL	20,176	C
Northern Kentucky Univ	KY	16,486	C
Northern Mich Univ	MI	19,604	C
Northern State Univ	SD	14,505	C
Northwest Missouri State Univ	MO	17,737	C
Northwest Nazarene Univ	ID	36,000	C
Northwestern College of Iowa	IA	38,400	C+
Northwestern Okla State Univ	OK	13,072	NC
Northwestern Univ	IL	66,344	MC
Notre Dame of Maryland Univ	MD	46,465	VC
Nyack College	NY	34,050	NC
Oakland City Univ	IN	33,360	NC
Oakland Univ	MI	20,763	C
Oakwood Univ	AL	43,758	C
Oberlin College	OH	66,012	MC
Ohio Northern Univ	OH	44,050	VC
Ohio State Univ at Columbus	OH	21,703	HC+
Ohio Univ	OH	22,924	C
Ohio Wesleyan Univ	OH	49,460	VC
Okla Baptist Univ	OK	32,320	C
Okla Christian Univ	OK	27,650	VC
Okla City Univ	OK	40,476	VC
Okla State Univ	OK	17,180	VC
Okla Wesleyan Univ	OK	33,206	C
Old Dominion Univ	VA	20,910	C
Olivet Nazarene Univ	IL	41,840	C
Oral Roberts Univ	OK	34,316	C
Otterbein Univ	OH	41,630	C
Ouachita Baptist Univ	AR	32,320	C
Pacific Lutheran Univ	WA	49,960	VC
Palm Beach Atlantic Univ	FL	39,720	C
Pennsylvania State Univ - Univ Park	PA	29,760	HC
Peru State College	NE	14,768	NC
Piedmont College	GA	32,512	C
Pittsburg State Univ	KS	13,880	NC
Plymouth State Univ	NH	23,180	LC
Point Loma Nazarene Univ	CA	43,450	C
Pontifical Catholic Univ of PR	PR	10,534	
Prescott College	AZ	33,284	C
Providence College	RI	60,760	VC
Quincy Univ	IL	36,998	C
Rhode Island College	RI	17,694	LC
Rider Univ	NJ	54,050	C
Roberts Wesleyan College	NY	38,306	C
Rocky Mountain College	MT	34,270	C
Roosevelt Univ	IL	40,651	VC
Rowan Univ	NJ	24,491	VC+
Saginaw Valley State Univ	MI	18,530	C
St. Augustine's Univ	NC	26,048	C
St. Mary's Univ of Minn	MN	41,210	VC
St. Xavier Univ	IL	43,310	C
Samford Univ	AL	39,232	VC
San Diego State Univ	CA	21,896	C+
San Jose State Univ	CA	21,540	C
Schreiner Univ	TX	34,626	LC
Seattle Pacific Univ	WA	47,439	C+
Seton Hill Univ	PA	46,972	C
Shenandoah Univ	VA	41,312	C
Shepherd Univ, West Virginia	WV	17,224	C
Shorter Univ	GA	31,130	LC
Siena Heights Univ	MI	32,040	C
Silver Lake College of the Holy Family	WI	36,290	LC
Simpson College	IA	43,839	VC
Simpson Univ	CA	33,700	C
Slippery Rock Univ of Pennsylvania	PA	10,360	C
S Car State Univ	SC	20,805	LC
S Dak State Univ	SD	15,634	C
Southeast Missouri State Univ	MO	15,498	C
Southeastern Okla State Univ	OK	11,875	C
Southeastern Univ	FL	31,765	C
Southern Adventist Univ	TN	27,600	C
Southern Arkansas Univ	AR	21,532	C
Southern Illinois Univ Edwardsville	IL	22,643	C
Southern Methodist Univ	TX	66,483	MC
Southern Nazarene Univ	OK	32,798	NC
Southern Univ and A&M College	LA	16,074	LC+
Southern Univ at New Orleans	LA	8,014	LC
Southern Wesleyan Univ	SC	32,130	LC
Southwest Baptist Univ	MO	29,900	LC
Southwest Minn State Univ	MN	17,783	C
Southwestern College	KS	31,531	C
Southwestern Okla State Univ	OK	11,790	C
Spring Arbor Univ	MI	36,000	C
St. Ambrose Univ	IA	39,019	C
St. Ambrose Univ	IA	39,019	C
St. Catherine Univ	MN	45,630	VC
St. Cloud State Univ	MN	10,600	C
St. Norbert College	WI	44,525	VC
St. Olaf College	MN	54,260	HC+
SUNY / SUNY Fredonia	NY	20,818	C
SUNY / SUNY Potsdam	NY	20,404	C+
Sterling College	KS	32,830	C
Stetson Univ	FL	53,544	VC
Susquehanna Univ	PA	55,340	VC
Syracuse Univ	NY	60,239	VC
Tabor College	KS	35,870	C
Talladega College	AL	19,215	C
Taylor Univ	IN	40,317	C+
Temple Univ	PA	24,392	VC
Tenn Tech Univ	TN	17,050	C
Texas A&M Univ at Commerce	TX	10,496	C
Texas A&M Univ at Kingsville	TX	7,500	LC
The Boston Conservatory at Berklee	MA	61,042	C+
The Catholic Univ of America	DC	56,356	VC
The College of New Jersey	NJ	31,909	HC
The College of St. Rose	NY	43,048	C
The Master's Univ	CA	43,870	C+
The Univ of Akron	OH	21,477	C
The Univ of Tenn at Chattanooga	TN	16,744	C
Toccoa Falls College	GA	27,920	C
Tougaloo College	MS	17,980	NC
Towson Univ	MD	17,408	VC
Trevecca Nazarene Univ	TN	31,186	C
Trinity Christian College	IL	35,580	C
Trinity International Univ	IL	31,070	VC
Troy Univ	AL	16,171	C
Union College	NE	23,270	C
Union Univ	TN	33,970	VC

ST = STATE **$IS** = IN-STATE COSTS **SR** = SELECTOR RATING

School	ST	$IS	SR
Universidad Adventista de las Antillas	PR	16,606	
Univ of Alabama	AL	24,320	C+
Univ of Alaska Anchorage	AK	16,652	NC
Univ of Alaska Fairbanks	AK	16,179	C
Univ of Arizona	AZ	23,100	C
Univ of Arkansas at Fayetteville	AR	19,152	C+
Univ of Arkansas at Monticello	AR	13,134	NC
Univ of Arkansas at Pine Bluff	AR	13,541	C
Univ of Central Arkansas	AR	14,472	VC
Univ of Central Florida	FL	15,922	VC
Univ of Central Missouri	MO	18,982	C
Univ of Central Okla	OK	13,486	C
Univ of Cincinnati	OH	21,964	VC
Univ of Colo Boulder	CO	24,285	VC+
Univ of Conn	CT	25,538	HC
Univ of Dayton	OH	53,620	C
Univ of Delaware	DE	24,976	VC+
Univ of Evansville	IN	44,186	VC+
Univ of Florida	FL	16,291	HC+
Univ of Georgia	GA	21,250	HC
Univ of Hartford	CT	49,776	C
Univ of Idaho	ID	15,348	C
Univ of Illinois at Urbana-Champaign	IL	27,006	HC
Univ of Indianapolis	IN	36,480	C
Univ of Iowa	IA	18,683	VC+
Univ of Kansas	KS	20,135	C+
Univ of Kentucky	KY	33,306	C
Univ of Louisiana at Lafayette	LA	14,516	C
Univ of Louisville	KY	19,824	C
Univ of Maine	ME	20,792	C
Univ of Mary	ND	23,180	C
Univ of Mary Hardin-Baylor	TX	33,950	C+
Univ of Maryland/College Park	MD	21,938	HC
Univ of Maryland/Eastern Shore	MD	17,013	C
Univ of Miami	FL	63,494	MC
Univ of Mich/Ann Arbor	MI	24,410	MC
Univ of Mich-Flint	MI	17,607	C+
Univ of Minn/Duluth	MN	20,292	C+
Univ of Minn/Twin Cities	MN	23,519	HC+
Univ of Missouri/Columbia	MO	18,201	MC
Univ of Missouri-Kansas City	MO	19,563	VC
Univ of Missouri-St. Louis	MO		C
Univ of Montana	MT	14,105	C
Univ of Montana-Western	MT	11,220	LC
Univ of Montevallo	AL	19,502	C
Univ of Mount Union	OH	38,970	C
Univ of Nebr - Kearney	NE	16,546	LC
Univ of Nebr - Lincoln	NE	18,589	VC
Univ of Nevada/Reno	NV	18,010	C
Univ of New Mexico	NM	15,404	C
Univ of New Orleans	LA	12,840	C
Univ of North Alabama	AL	15,398	C
Univ of N Car at Greensboro	NC	14,690	C
Univ of N Car at Wilmington	NC	14,590	VC
Univ of N Dak	ND	15,373	C
Univ of North Florida	FL	15,996	VC
Univ of North Georgia	GA	17,316	C
Univ of Northern Colo	CO	20,851	C
Univ of Northwestern - St. Paul	MN	38,160	C
Univ of Okla	OK	18,911	VC
Univ of Oregon	OR	22,972	C
Univ of Puget Sound	WA	56,456	VC+
Univ of Redlands	CA	60,200	VC
Univ of Rio Grande & Rio Grande Community College	OH	8,750	NC
Univ of Rochester	NY	65,032	MC
Univ of Sioux Falls	SD	34,330	C
Univ of S Car Aiken	SC	16,712	C
Univ of S Car at Columbia	SC	19,725	VC+
Univ of S Dak	SD	16,109	C
Univ of South Florida/Tampa	FL	16,110	VC+
Univ of Southern Maine	ME	18,320	C
Univ of Southern Miss	MS	13,170	C
Univ of St. Francis	IL	39,924	C
Univ of St. Thomas - Houston	TX	40,020	VC
Univ of Tampa	FL	36,944	C
Univ of the Cumberlands	KY	32,000	C
Univ of the Incarnate Word	TX	39,162	LC
Univ of the Pacific	CA	57,006	VC
Univ of Toledo	OH	19,336	NC
Univ of Tulsa	OK	52,625	HC+
Univ of Vermont	VT	28,878	HC
Univ of Washington	WA	23,149	VC
Univ of West Florida	FL	15,848	C
Univ of West Georgia	GA	16,360	LC
Univ of Wisc-Green Bay	WI	15,064	C
Univ of Wisc-Madison	WI	20,934	MC
Univ of Wisc-Milwaukee	WI	21,496	C
Univ of Wisc-Oshkosh	WI	15,200	C
Univ of Wisc-Platteville	WI	14,614	VC
Univ of Wisc-River Falls	WI	14,485	C
Univ of Wisc-Stevens Point	WI	14,043	C
Univ of Wisc-Superior	WI	14,446	C
Univ of Wisc-Whitewater	WI	13,976	C
Univ of Wyoming	WY	15,375	C+
Utah State Univ	UT	12,736	C
Valparaiso Univ	IN	48,370	C+
Vanderbilt Univ	TN	60,572	MC
VanderCook College of Music	IL	31,440	NC
Virginia Union Univ	VA	22,421	C
Viterbo Univ	WI	34,660	C
Walla Walla Univ	WA	30,417	NC
Warner Pacific College	OR	33,790	C
Warner Univ	FL	28,216	C
Wartburg College	IA	47,840	C
Washburn Univ	KS	15,827	C
Washington Adventist Univ	MD	31,440	LC
Washington State Univ	WA	22,495	C
Wayland Baptist Univ	TX	22,356	LC
Wayne State College	NE	12,802	C
Weber State Univ	UT	10,721	C
Webster Univ	MO	37,490	C
West Chester Univ of Pennsylvania	PA	18,456	C
West Liberty Univ	WV	15,512	C
West Texas A&M Univ	TX	13,478	C
West Virginia Wesleyan College	WV	36,858	C
Western Carolina Univ	NC	13,965	C
Western Conn State Univ	CT	21,254	LC
Western Mich Univ	MI	21,054	C
Western State Colo Univ	CO	18,639	C
Western Washington Univ	WA	18,003	C+
Westminster Choir College	NJ	53,730	SP
Westminster College	PA	39,180	C+
Westmont College	CA	56,410	HC
Wheaton College	IL	43,610	MC
Whitworth Univ	WA	51,732	VC
Wichita State Univ	KS	21,643	C
Wiley College	TX	18,504	C
Willamette Univ	OR	61,817	VC+
William Carey Univ	MS	23,950	LC
William Jewell College	MO	41,210	C+
William Paterson Univ of New Jersey	NJ	23,133	C
Wingate Univ	NC	39,950	C
Winona State Univ	MN	17,535	C
Winston-Salem State Univ	NC	26,166	LC
Winthrop Univ	SC	23,082	C
Wittenberg Univ	OH	48,156	C+
Wright State Univ	OH	16,983	C
Xavier Univ	OH	47,880	C+
Xavier Univ of Louisiana	LA	31,689	C+
York College	NE	24,300	C
York College of Pennsylvania	PA	29,240	C
Youngstown State Univ	OH	17,307	C

MUSIC HISTORY AND APPRECIATION

School	ST	$IS	SR
Aquinas College - Mich	MI	38,876	HC
Baldwin Wallace Univ	OH	41,106	C
Baylor Univ	TX	53,760	HC
Boston Univ	MA	65,110	MC
Bowling Green State Univ	OH	19,747	C
Bucknell Univ	PA	64,616	MC
Cal State, San Bernardino	CA	12,000	C
Calvin College	MI	41,570	VC+
Central Mich Univ	MI	20,330	C
Florida State Univ	FL	16,771	HC
Hardin-Simmons Univ	TX	33,966	C
Hofstra Univ	NY	55,960	C+
Howard Univ	DC	37,616	C+
Johnson State College	VT	20,752	C
McKendree Univ	IL	37,940	C+
Nazareth College	NY	45,574	C
New England Conservatory of Music	MA	58,655	SP
Oberlin College	OH	66,012	MC
Ohio State Univ at Columbus	OH	21,703	HC+
Ohio Univ	OH	22,924	C
Rice Univ	TX	57,668	MC
Roosevelt Univ	IL	40,651	VC
Southern Illinois Univ Edwardsville	IL	22,643	C
Suffolk Univ	MA	50,308	C
Syracuse Univ	NY	60,239	VC
Temple Univ	PA	24,392	VC
The Catholic Univ of America	DC	56,356	VC
The Univ of Akron	OH	21,477	C
Univ of Calif at Los Angeles	CA	30,162	MC
Univ of Calif San Diego	CA	30,150	MC
Univ of Cincinnati	OH	21,964	VC
Univ of Hartford	CT	49,776	C
Univ of Idaho	ID	15,348	C
Univ of Illinois at Urbana-Champaign	IL	27,006	HC
Univ of Kansas	KS	20,135	C+
Univ of Mich/Ann Arbor	MI	24,410	MC
Univ of Mich/Dearborn	MI	11,757	VC
Univ of North Texas	TX	19,198	C
Univ of the Pacific	CA	57,006	VC
Univ of Washington	WA	23,149	VC
West Chester Univ of Pennsylvania	PA	18,456	C
Western Washington Univ	WA	18,003	C+
Whitman College	WA	59,772	MC
Wichita State Univ	KS	21,643	C
Wright State Univ	OH	16,983	C
Youngstown State Univ	OH	17,307	C

MUSIC INDUSTRY

School	ST	$IS	SR
Cal State, Chico	CA	21,440	C
Delaware State Univ	DE	19,376	NC
Drexel Univ	PA	65,432	VC+
Edgewood College	WI	35,950	C
Ferris State Univ	MI	21,445	C
Loyola Univ New Orleans	LA	51,708	VC+
Mercy College	NY	31,776	C
Minn State Univ, Mankato	MN	15,616	C
Missouri Southern State Univ	MO	12,499	C
Monmouth Univ	NJ	46,234	C
St. Mary's Univ of Minn	MN	41,210	VC
Syracuse Univ	NY	60,239	VC
The College of St. Rose	NY	43,048	C

MUSIC MINISTRY

School	ST	$IS	SR
College of the Ozarks	MO	7,230	C
Hope International Univ	CA	41,150	C
Lipscomb Univ	TN	41,296	VC
Marian Univ	IN	41,220	C
Messiah College	PA	43,100	C+
Point Loma Nazarene Univ	CA	43,450	C
Samford Univ	AL	39,232	VC
The Master's Univ	CA	43,870	C+

MUSIC PERFORMANCE

School	ST	$IS	SR
Adams State Univ	CO	17,703	LC
Adrian College	MI	42,400	C
Albion College	MI	52,650	C
Anderson Univ	IN	38,200	C
Andrews Univ	MI	28,030	C+
Anna Maria College	MA	48,186	C
Appalachian State Univ	NC	14,416	VC
Aquinas College - Mich	MI	38,876	HC
Arizona State Univ at the Tempe Campus	AZ	21,756	VC
Armstrong State Univ	GA	16,962	C
Augusta Univ	GA	4,632	C
Augustana College	IL	49,658	VC
Averett Univ	VA	40,970	LC
Baldwin Wallace Univ	OH	41,106	C
Barry Univ	FL	37,830	C
Baylor Univ	TX	53,760	HC
Belmont Univ	TN	40,970	VC
Bennington College	VT	63,960	MC
Berklee College of Music	MA	60,930	SP
Bethel College	IN	35,860	C
Bethel Univ	MN	45,270	VC
Biola Univ	CA	46,402	C+
Blackburn College	IL	28,526	LC
Boston Univ	MA	65,110	MC
Bowling Green State Univ	OH	19,747	C
Brenau Univ - Women's College	GA	37,876	LC
Brigham Young Univ	UT	12,748	HC
Bucknell Univ	PA	64,616	MC
Butler Univ	IN	51,352	VC
Cairn Univ	PA	36,296	C
Calif Baptist Univ	CA	41,392	C
Calif Inst of the Arts	CA	56,426	SP
Calif Lutheran Univ	CA	52,853	C
Cal State, Fresno	CA	16,902	LC
Cal State, Fullerton	CA	21,902	C
Cal State, Los Angeles	CA	17,186	LC
Cal State, San Bernardino	CA	12,000	C
Cal State, Stanislaus	CA	16,212	C
Calvin College	MI	41,570	VC+
Campbellsville Univ	KY	32,492	C
Canisius College	NY	47,537	C
Carnegie Mellon Univ	PA	67,980	MC
Cedarville Univ	OH	34,990	VC
Centenary College of Louisiana	LA	45,650	C+
Central Mich Univ	MI	20,330	C
Chapman Univ	CA	63,078	VC+
CUNY/Brooklyn College	NY	5,884	C+
CUNY/Queens College	NY	27,896	C
Clayton State Univ	GA	19,735	C
Cleveland Inst of Music	OH	63,038	SP
Colo State Univ	CO	22,162	VC
Colo State Univ-Pueblo	CO	18,234	C
Columbia College	SC	36,550	C
Columbus State Univ	GA	14,336	LC
Concordia College - Moorhead	MN	51,088	C+
Corban Univ	OR	40,306	C
Covenant College	GA	38,990	VC
Dallas Baptist Univ	TX	33,713	C
DePaul Univ	IL	47,623	VC
DePauw Univ	IN	58,688	HC+
Dillard Univ	LA	20,940	VC
Dordt College	IA	37,860	C+
Drake Univ	IA	45,056	HC
Duquesne Univ	PA	46,822	VC
East Carolina Univ	NC	16,937	C
East Texas Baptist Univ	TX	33,134	C
Eastern Mich Univ	MI	19,761	C
Eastern Nazarene College	MA	39,955	C
Eastern Washington Univ	WA	25,572	LC
Eastman School of Music/Univ of Rochester	NY	65,644	SP
Elmhurst College	IL	45,428	C
Elon Univ	NC	44,599	VC+
Emory and Henry College	VA	41,410	C
Evangel Univ	MO	28,898	C
Five Towns College	NY	35,350	C
Florida State Univ	FL	16,771	HC
Fort Hays State Univ	KS	12,131	C
Friends Univ	KS	34,455	C
Furman Univ	SC	58,092	VC+
George Washington Univ	DC	62,835	MC
Gordon College	MA	46,472	C+
Grand Canyon Univ	AZ	16,950	VC
Grand Rapids Theological Seminary/Cornerstone Univ	MI	33,338	C
Grove City College	PA	25,692	VC
Hamline Univ	MN	45,678	VC
Hannibal-LaGrange Univ	MO	29,815	C
Hardin-Simmons Univ	TX	33,966	C
Hofstra Univ	NY	55,960	C+
Hope College	MI	39,940	VC
Houghton College	NY	39,090	C
Houston Baptist Univ	TX	36,450	C
Huntington Univ	IN	33,996	C
Idaho State Univ	ID	13,619	NC
Illinois State Univ	IL	23,418	VC
Illinois Wesleyan Univ	IL	56,430	VC+
Indiana Univ Bloomington	IN	20,429	VC
Indiana Univ of Pennsylvania	PA	23,614	LC
Indiana Univ-Purdue Univ Fort Wayne	IN	17,553	C
Inter-American Univ of PR-Metropolitan Campus	PR	20,045	
Ithaca College	NY	56,766	VC
Jacksonville Univ	FL	46,230	C
Johnson State College	VT	20,752	C
Kean Univ	NJ	24,650	C
Keene State College	NH	24,003	LC
Kennesaw State Univ	GA	19,592	VC
Kentucky Christian Univ	KY	26,560	LC
Kentucky State Univ	KY	13,364	LC
La Sierra Univ	CA	39,690	VC
Lawrence Univ	WI	54,498	HC
Lee Univ	TN	22,045	C
Lenoir-Rhyne Univ	NC	43,200	C
Lewis Univ	IL	40,370	C
Lipscomb Univ	TN	41,296	VC
LIU Brooklyn	NY	49,682	C
LIU Post	NY	49,682	C
Louisiana Tech Univ	LA	11,422	VC
Loyola Univ New Orleans	LA	51,708	VC+
Manhattan School of Music	NY	57,200	SP
Mannes School for Music	NY	44,500	SP
Mansfield Univ	PA	23,376	LC
Mars Hill Univ	NC	42,688	C
Marshall Univ	WV	17,242	C
Maryville College	TN	44,410	C
Marywood Univ	PA	46,900	C
McKendree Univ	IL	37,940	C+
Meredith College	NC	45,297	C
Messiah College	PA	43,100	C+
Methodist Univ	NC	43,600	C
Metropolitan State Univ of Denver	CO	29,889	LC
Miami Univ	OH	27,190	HC+
Mich State Univ	MI	23,898	VC+
Millikin Univ	IL	42,158	C
Missouri Baptist Univ	MO	35,594	C
Montana State Univ-Billings	MT	22,960	C
Montclair State Univ	NJ	26,210	LC
Murray State Univ	KY	16,998	C
Nazareth College	NY	45,574	C
New England Conservatory of Music	MA	58,655	SP
New Mexico State Univ	NM	14,050	C
New York Univ	NY	65,860	MC
Newberry College	SC	34,550	C
North Greenville Univ	SC	25,930	C+
Northern Arizona Univ	AZ	20,246	VC
Northern Kentucky Univ	KY	16,486	C
Northwestern Univ	IL	66,344	MC
Nyack College	NY	34,050	NC
Oakwood Univ	AL	43,758	C
Oberlin College	OH	66,012	MC
Ohio Northern Univ	OH	44,050	VC
Ohio State Univ at Columbus	OH	21,703	HC+
Ohio Univ	OH	22,924	C
Ohio Wesleyan Univ	OH	49,460	VC
Old Dominion Univ	VA	20,910	C
Olivet Nazarene Univ	IL	41,840	C
Oral Roberts Univ	OK	34,316	C
Otterbein Univ	OH	41,630	C
Pacific Lutheran Univ	WA	49,960	VC
Palm Beach Atlantic Univ	FL	39,720	C
Pennsylvania State Univ - Univ Park	PA	29,760	HC
Point Loma Nazarene Univ	CA	43,450	C
Regis Univ	CO	44,520	C
Rhode Island College	RI	17,694	LC
Rice Univ	TX	57,668	MC
Roberts Wesleyan College	NY	38,306	C
Rockford Univ	IL	36,030	C
Rocky Mountain College	MT	34,270	C
Rollins College	FL	58,670	HC
Roosevelt Univ	IL	40,651	VC
St. Mary's Univ of Minn	MN	41,210	VC
St. Vincent College	PA	44,626	C
Sam Houston State Univ	TX	18,792	C
Samford Univ	AL	39,232	VC
San Diego State Univ	CA	21,896	C+
San Francisco Conservatory of Music	CA	57,310	SP
Santa Fe Univ of Art and Design	NM	39,980	SP
Shenandoah Univ	VA	41,312	C
Silver Lake College of the Holy Family	WI	36,290	LC
Simpson College	IA	43,839	VC

ST = STATE $IS = IN-STATE COSTS SR = SELECTOR RATING

School	ST	$IS	SR
Southern Illinois Univ Edwardsville	IL	22,643	C
Southern Methodist Univ	TX	66,483	MC
Southern Nazarene Univ	OK	32,798	NC
Southern Oregon Univ	OR	19,117	C
Southwestern College	KS	31,531	C
St. Olaf College	MN	54,260	HC+
SUNY / SUNY Fredonia	NY	20,818	C
SUNY / SUNY Potsdam	NY	20,404	C+
SUNY / Univ at Buffalo	NY	23,122	C+
SUNY at Binghamton	NY	22,861	MC
Stetson Univ	FL	53,544	VC
Susquehanna Univ	PA	55,340	VC
Talladega College	AL	19,215	C
Taylor Univ	IN	40,317	C+
Temple Univ	PA	24,392	VC
Texas State Univ	TX	19,350	C
The Boston Conservatory at Berklee	MA	61,042	C+
The Catholic Univ of America	DC	56,356	VC
The Univ of Akron	OH	21,477	C
Toccoa Falls College	GA	27,920	C
Tougaloo College	MS	17,980	NC
Trinity Christian College	IL	35,580	C
Truman State Univ	MO	16,014	HC
Union College	NE	23,270	C
Union Univ	TN	33,970	VC
Univ of Alaska Anchorage	AK	16,652	NC
Univ of Alaska Fairbanks	AK	16,179	C
Univ of Calif at Irvine	CA	26,484	VC
Univ of Calif at Santa Barbara	CA	29,091	HC
Univ of Central Florida	FL	15,922	VC
Univ of Cincinnati	OH	21,964	VC
Univ of Colo Boulder	CO	24,285	VC+
Univ of Dayton	OH	53,620	C
Univ of Denver	CO	58,443	VC+
Univ of Evansville	IN	44,186	VC+
Univ of Georgia	GA	21,250	HC
Univ of Hartford	CT	49,776	C
Univ of Idaho	ID	15,348	C
Univ of Illinois at Chicago	IL	25,006	VC
Univ of Illinois at Urbana-Champaign	IL	27,006	HC
Univ of Indianapolis	IN	36,480	C
Univ of Kansas	KS	20,135	C+
Univ of Kentucky	KY	33,306	C
Univ of Maine	ME	20,792	C
Univ of Mary Hardin-Baylor	TX	33,950	C+
Univ of Maryland/College Park	MD	21,938	HC
Univ of Mass Amherst	MA	26,199	VC+
Univ of Mass Lowell	MA	26,380	C
Univ of Miami	FL	63,494	MC
Univ of Mich/Ann Arbor	MI	24,410	MC
Univ of Minn/Duluth	MN	20,292	C+
Univ of Missouri-Kansas City	MO	19,563	VC
Univ of Mobile	AL	28,935	C
Univ of Montana	MT	14,105	C
Univ of Montevallo	AL	19,502	C
Univ of Mount Union	OH	38,970	C
Univ of New Haven	CT	52,190	C
Univ of N Car at Chapel Hill	NC	20,052	HC+
Univ of N Car at Charlotte	NC	15,547	C
Univ of N Car at Greensboro	NC	14,690	C
Univ of N Car at Wilmington	NC	14,590	VC
Univ of N Dak	ND	15,373	C
Univ of North Florida	FL	15,996	VC
Univ of North Texas	TX	19,198	C
Univ of Northwestern - St. Paul	MN	38,160	C
Univ of Okla	OK	18,911	VC
Univ of Oregon	OR	22,972	C
Univ of Puget Sound	WA	56,456	VC+
Univ of Rochester	NY	65,032	MC
Univ of S Car Upstate	SC	18,200	C
Univ of S Dak	SD	16,109	C
Univ of Southern Calif	CA	66,631	C
Univ of Southern Maine	ME	18,320	C
Univ of St. Francis	IL	39,924	C
Univ of Tampa	FL	36,944	C
Univ of the Arts	PA	56,579	SP
Univ of the Pacific	CA	57,006	VC
Univ of Tulsa	OK	52,625	HC+
Univ of Washington	WA	23,149	VC
Univ of West Georgia	GA	16,360	LC
Univ of Wisc-Madison	WI	20,934	MC
Univ of Wisc-Superior	WI	14,446	C
Univ of Wyoming	WY	15,375	C+
Valparaiso Univ	IN	48,370	C+
Vanderbilt Univ	TN	60,572	MC
Virginia State Univ	VA	19,802	C+
Viterbo Univ	WI	34,660	C
Walla Walla Univ	WA	30,417	NC
Wartburg College	IA	47,840	C
Washburn Univ	KS	15,827	C
Washington Adventist Univ	MD	31,440	LC
Washington State Univ	WA	22,495	C
Weber State Univ	UT	10,721	C
Webster Univ	MO	37,490	C
West Chester Univ of Pennsylvania	PA	18,456	C
Western Conn State Univ	CT	21,254	LC
Western Mich Univ	MI	21,054	C
Westminster College	PA	39,180	C+
Whitman College	WA	59,772	MC
Wiley College	TX	18,504	C
Willamette Univ	OR	61,817	VC+
William Carey Univ	MS	23,950	LC
Winona State Univ	MN	17,535	C
Winthrop Univ	SC	23,082	C
Xavier Univ of Louisiana	LA	31,689	C+
York College	NE	24,300	C
Youngstown State Univ	OH	17,307	C

MUSIC PRODUCTION/ RECORDING TECHNOLOGY

School	ST	$IS	SR
Buena Vista Univ	IA	41,514	C
Calif Lutheran Univ	CA	52,853	C
Cleveland Inst of Music	OH	63,038	SP
Edgewood College	WI	35,950	C
Indiana Univ Bloomington	IN	20,429	VC
Loyola Marymount Univ	CA	58,038	HC
Shenandoah Univ	VA	41,312	C
Syracuse Univ	NY	60,239	VC
The Master's Univ	CA	43,870	C+
Trinity Christian College	IL	35,580	C
Univ of Denver	CO	58,443	VC+

MUSIC TECHNOLOGY

School	ST	$IS	SR
Bellarmine Univ	KY	51,220	C
Berklee College of Music	MA	60,930	SP
Bethany College	WV	36,300	NC
Bloomfield College	NJ	39,100	LC
Brigham Young Univ	UT	12,748	HC
Cal State, San Bernardino	CA	12,000	C
Cogswell Polytechnical College	CA	30,531	C
Conn College	CT	65,000	MC
Culver-Stockton College	MO	33,525	C
Duquesne Univ	PA	46,822	VC
Elon Univ	NC	44,599	VC+
Indiana Univ-Purdue Univ Indianapolis	IN	18,635	C
Keene State College	NH	24,003	LC
Malone Univ	OH	38,448	C
Mercy College	NY	31,776	C
Millersville Univ of Pennsylvania	PA	23,782	C
Minn State Univ, Moorhead	MN	15,941	C
Missouri Baptist Univ	MO	35,594	C
New York Univ	NY	65,860	MC
Northeastern Univ	MA	62,703	MC
Northwestern Univ	IL	66,344	MC
Santa Fe Univ of Art and Design	NM	39,980	SP
Shenandoah Univ	VA	41,312	C
Stetson Univ	FL	53,544	VC
Stevens Inst of Technology	NJ	62,338	MC
Transylvania Univ	KY	45,690	VC+
Univ of Calif San Diego	CA	30,150	MC
Univ of Hartford	CT	49,776	C
Univ of Miami	FL	63,494	MC
Univ of Mich/Ann Arbor	MI	24,410	MC
Univ of New Haven	CT	52,190	C
Univ of N Car at Asheville	NC	15,723	VC+
Univ of St. Francis	IN	37,400	C
York College of Pennsylvania	PA	29,240	C

MUSIC THEATRE ACCOMPANYING

School	ST	$IS	SR
College of the Ozarks	MO	7,230	C
Shenandoah Univ	VA	41,312	C

MUSIC THEORY AND COMPOSITION

School	ST	$IS	SR
Adams State Univ	CO	17,703	LC
Aquinas College - Mich	MI	38,876	HC
Baldwin Wallace Univ	OH	41,106	C
Baylor Univ	TX	53,760	HC
Belmont Univ	TN	40,970	VC
Bennington College	VT	63,960	MC
Berklee College of Music	MA	60,930	SP
Biola Univ	CA	46,402	C+
Boston Univ	MA	65,110	MC
Bowling Green State Univ	OH	19,747	C
Brigham Young Univ	UT	12,748	HC
Bucknell Univ	PA	64,616	MC
Butler Univ	IN	51,352	VC
Calif Inst of the Arts	CA	56,426	SP
Calvin College	MI	41,570	VC+
Central Mich Univ	MI	20,330	C
Central Washington Univ	WA	16,803	C
Chapman Univ	CA	63,078	VC+
CUNY/Brooklyn College	NY	5,884	C+
Clayton State Univ	GA	19,735	C
College of the Ozarks	MO	7,230	C
Colo State Univ	CO	22,162	VC
Colo State Univ-Pueblo	CO	18,234	C
Concordia College - Moorhead	MN	51,088	C+
Dallas Baptist Univ	TX	33,713	C
DePaul Univ	IL	47,623	VC
DePauw Univ	IN	58,688	HC+
Dordt College	IA	37,860	C+
East Carolina Univ	NC	16,937	C
Eastman School of Music/ Univ of Rochester	NY	65,644	SP
Elmhurst College	IL	45,428	C
Emory and Henry College	VA	41,410	C
Five Towns College	NY	35,350	C
Florida State Univ	FL	16,771	HC
Fordham Univ	NY	65,918	MC
Fort Hays State Univ	KS	12,131	C
Furman Univ	SC	58,092	VC+
Hardin-Simmons Univ	TX	33,966	C
Hofstra Univ	NY	55,960	C+
Houghton College	NY	39,090	C
Houston Baptist Univ	TX	36,450	C
Huntington Univ	IN	33,996	C
Illinois Wesleyan Univ	IL	56,430	VC+
Indiana Wesleyan Univ	IN	33,674	C
Ithaca College	NY	56,766	VC
Jacksonville Univ	FL	46,230	C
Lawrence Univ	WI	54,498	HC
Lehigh Univ	PA	61,010	MC
Loyola Univ New Orleans	LA	51,708	VC+
Manhattan School of Music	NY	57,200	SP
Mannes School for Music	NY	44,500	SP
Marshall Univ	WV	17,242	C
Mich State Univ	MI	23,898	VC+
Miss College	MS	25,850	C
Montclair State Univ	NJ	26,210	LC
Nazareth College	NY	45,574	C
New England Conservatory of Music	MA	58,655	SP
New York Univ	NY	65,860	MC
Newberry College	SC	34,550	C
North Park Univ	IL	35,860	C
Northwestern Univ	IL	66,344	MC
Nyack College	NY	34,050	NC
Oberlin College	OH	66,012	MC
Ohio Northern Univ	OH	44,050	VC
Ohio State Univ at Columbus	OH	21,703	HC+
Ohio Univ	OH	22,924	C
Old Dominion Univ	VA	20,910	C
Olivet Nazarene Univ	IL	41,840	C
Oral Roberts Univ	OK	34,316	C
Pacific Lutheran Univ	WA	49,960	VC
Palm Beach Atlantic Univ	FL	39,720	C
Rice Univ	TX	57,668	MC
Roosevelt Univ	IL	40,651	VC
Sam Houston State Univ	TX	18,792	C
Samford Univ	AL	39,232	VC
Santa Fe Univ of Art and Design	NM	39,980	SP
Seton Hill Univ	PA	46,972	C
Shenandoah Univ	VA	41,312	C
Southern Illinois Univ Edwardsville	IL	22,643	C
Southern Methodist Univ	TX	66,483	MC
St. Olaf College	MN	54,260	HC+
SUNY / SUNY Fredonia	NY	20,818	C
Stetson Univ	FL	53,544	VC
Taylor Univ	IN	40,317	C+
Temple Univ	PA	24,392	VC
Texas Christian Univ	TX	54,670	HC
The Boston Conservatory at Berklee	MA	61,042	C+
The Catholic Univ of America	DC	56,356	VC
The College of Idaho	ID	36,415	C
The College of Wooster	OH	57,900	VC+
The Master's Univ	CA	43,870	C+
The Univ of Akron	OH	21,477	C
Union Univ	TN	33,970	VC
Univ of Calif at Santa Barbara	CA	29,091	HC
Univ of Cincinnati	OH	21,964	VC
Univ of Dayton	OH	53,620	C
Univ of Delaware	DE	24,976	VC+
Univ of Georgia	GA	21,250	HC
Univ of Hartford	CT	49,776	C
Univ of Idaho	ID	15,348	C
Univ of Illinois at Urbana-Champaign	IL	27,006	HC
Univ of Kansas	KS	20,135	C+
Univ of Maryland/College Park	MD	21,938	HC
Univ of Mich/Ann Arbor	MI	24,410	MC
Univ of Missouri-Kansas City	MO	19,563	VC
Univ of N Car at Greensboro	NC	14,690	C
Univ of North Texas	TX	19,198	C
Univ of Northwestern - St. Paul	MN	38,160	C
Univ of Oregon	OR	22,972	C
Univ of Rochester	NY	65,032	MC
Univ of Texas at Austin	TX	26,102	HC
Univ of the Arts	PA	56,579	SP
Univ of the Pacific	CA	57,006	VC
Valparaiso Univ	IN	48,370	C+
Vanderbilt Univ	TN	60,572	MC
Wartburg College	IA	47,840	C
Washington State Univ	WA	22,495	C
Washington Univ in St. Louis	MO	65,366	VC
Webster Univ	MO	37,490	C
West Chester Univ of Pennsylvania	PA	18,456	C
West Texas A&M Univ	TX	13,478	C
Western Mich Univ	MI	21,054	C
Westminster Choir College	NJ	53,730	SP
Westminster College	PA	39,180	C+
Whitman College	WA	59,772	MC
Willamette Univ	OR	61,817	VC+
Wright State Univ	OH	16,983	C
Youngstown State Univ	OH	17,307	C

MUSIC THERAPY

School	ST	$IS	SR
Alverno College	WI	33,294	LC
Anna Maria College	MA	48,186	C
Appalachian State Univ	NC	14,416	VC
Arizona State Univ at the Tempe Campus	AZ	21,756	VC
Augsburg College	MN	43,929	C
Baldwin Wallace Univ	OH	41,106	C
Berklee College of Music	MA	60,930	SP
Carroll Univ	WI	38,100	C+
Charleston Southern Univ	SC	32,400	C
Colo State Univ	CO	22,162	VC
Drury Univ	MO	33,791	VC
Duquesne Univ	PA	46,822	VC
East Carolina Univ	NC	16,937	C
Eastern Mich Univ	MI	19,761	C
Elizabethtown College	PA	54,050	C
Florida State Univ	FL	16,771	HC
Georgia College & State Univ	GA	21,148	C+
Howard Univ	DC	37,616	C+
Indiana Univ-Purdue Univ Fort Wayne	IN	17,553	C
Louisiana College	LA	21,886	C
Loyola Univ New Orleans	LA	51,708	VC+
Lubbock Christian Univ	TX	28,426	C
Marylhurst Univ	OR	20,295	NC
Maryville Univ of St. Louis	MO	38,046	VC+
Marywood Univ	PA	46,900	C
Mich State Univ	MI	23,898	VC+
Molloy College	NY	40,440	C
Montclair State Univ	NJ	26,210	LC
Nazareth College	NY	45,574	C
New York Univ	NY	65,860	MC
Ohio Univ	OH	22,924	C
Queens Univ of Charlotte	NC	39,543	C
St. Mary-of-the-Woods College	IN	39,632	LC
Sam Houston State Univ	TX	18,792	C
Seton Hill Univ	PA	46,972	C
Shenandoah Univ	VA	41,312	C
Southern Methodist Univ	TX	66,483	MC
Southwestern Okla State Univ	OK	11,790	C
SUNY / SUNY Fredonia	NY	20,818	C
SUNY at New Paltz	NY	19,200	C
Taylor Univ	IN	40,317	C+
Temple Univ	PA	24,392	VC
Texas Woman's Univ	TX	15,302	LC
Univ of Alabama	AL	24,320	C+
Univ of Dayton	OH	53,620	C
Univ of Evansville	IN	44,186	VC+
Univ of Georgia	GA	21,250	HC
Univ of Iowa	IA	18,683	VC+
Univ of Kansas	KS	20,135	C+
Univ of Louisville	KY	19,824	C
Univ of Miami	FL	63,494	MC
Univ of Minn/Twin Cities	MN	23,519	HC+
Univ of Missouri-Kansas City	MO	19,563	VC
Univ of N Dak	ND	15,373	C
Univ of the Incarnate Word	TX	39,162	LC
Univ of the Pacific	CA	57,006	VC
Univ of Wisc-Oshkosh	WI	15,200	C
Utah State Univ	UT	12,736	C
Wartburg College	IA	47,840	C
West Texas A&M Univ	TX	13,478	C
Western Mich Univ	MI	21,054	C
William Carey Univ	MS	23,950	LC

MUSICAL THEATER

School	ST	$IS	SR
Adrian College	MI	42,400	C
American Univ	DC	59,379	HC+
Aquinas College - Mich	MI	38,876	HC
Arizona State Univ at the Tempe Campus	AZ	21,756	VC
Ashland Univ	OH	21,440	C
Aurora Univ	IL	33,970	C
Baldwin Wallace Univ	OH	41,106	C
Belmont Univ	TN	40,970	VC
Birmingham-Southern College	AL	44,478	VC
Blackburn College	IL	28,526	LC
Brenau Univ - Women's College	GA	37,876	LC
Brigham Young Univ	UT	12,748	HC
Cal State, Chico	CA	21,440	C
Catawba College	NC	39,820	C
Central Mich Univ	MI	20,330	C
Clarke Univ	IA	38,940	C
Clayton State Univ	GA	19,735	C
Coastal Carolina Univ	SC	19,766	C
Coker College	SC	34,810	LC
College of the Ozarks	MO	7,230	C
Creighton Univ	NE	48,206	VC+
Culver-Stockton College	MO	33,525	C
Elon Univ	NC	44,599	VC+
Emerson College	MA	54,736	HC
Faulkner Univ	AL	26,410	C
Florida State Univ	FL	16,771	HC
Friends Univ	KS	34,455	C
Grand Rapids Theological Seminary/Cornerstone Univ	MI	33,338	C
Howard Univ	DC	37,616	C+
Illinois Wesleyan Univ	IL	56,430	VC+
Indiana Univ Bloomington	IN	20,429	VC
Ithaca College	NY	56,766	VC
Kutztown Univ of Pennsylvania	PA	19,056	LC
Lees-McRae College	NC	33,944	C
Limestone College	SC	32,100	C
Lipscomb Univ	TN	41,296	VC
Mars Hill Univ	NC	42,688	C

School	ST	$IS	SR
Marywood Univ	PA	46,900	C
Mercyhurst Univ	PA	47,420	C
Meredith College	NC	45,297	C
Messiah College	PA	43,100	C+
Millikin Univ	IL	42,158	C
Missouri Baptist Univ	MO	35,594	C
Missouri State Univ	MO	15,190	C+
Montclair State Univ	NJ	26,210	LC
Nazareth College	NY	45,574	C
Neumann Univ	PA	40,678	LC
Otterbein Univ	OH	41,630	C
Ouachita Baptist Univ	AR	32,320	C
Pace Univ	NY	58,248	C
Palm Beach Atlantic Univ	FL	39,720	C
Piedmont College	GA	32,512	C
Providence College	RI	60,760	VC
Roosevelt Univ	IL	40,651	VC
Russell Sage College	NY	39,370	C
Sam Houston State Univ	TX	18,792	C
Samford Univ	AL	39,232	VC
Santa Fe Univ of Art and Design	NM	39,980	SP
Seton Hill Univ	PA	46,972	C
Shenandoah Univ	VA	41,312	C
Shorter Univ	GA	31,130	LC
Southern Illinois Univ Carbondale	IL	23,667	C
Southern Illinois Univ Edwardsville	IL	22,643	C
St. Catherine Univ	MN	45,630	VC
SUNY / SUNY Cortland	NY	20,706	VC
SUNY / SUNY Fredonia	NY	20,818	C
SUNY / Univ at Buffalo	NY	23,122	C+
SUNY at Geneseo	NY	20,440	VC+
SUNY at Oswego	NY	21,351	C
Syracuse Univ	NY	60,239	VC
Taylor Univ	IN	40,317	C+
Texas Christian Univ	TX	54,670	HC
Texas State Univ	TX	19,350	C
The Boston Conservatory at Berklee	MA	61,042	C+
The Catholic Univ of America	DC	56,356	VC
The Univ of Akron	OH	21,477	C
Univ of Alabama at Birmingham	AL	19,906	C
Univ of Arizona	AZ	23,100	C
Univ of Calif at Irvine	CA	26,484	VC
Univ of Hartford	CT	49,776	C
Univ of Indianapolis	IN	36,480	C
Univ of Miami	FL	63,494	MC
Univ of Mich/Ann Arbor	MI	24,410	MC
Univ of N Dak	ND	15,373	C
Univ of North Texas	TX	19,198	C
Univ of Northern Colo	CO	20,851	C
Univ of Okla	OK	18,911	VC
Univ of Tampa	FL	36,944	C
Univ of the Arts	PA	56,579	SP
Univ of Tulsa	OK	52,625	HC+
Weber State Univ	UT	10,721	C
Webster Univ	MO	37,490	C
West Chester Univ of Pennsylvania	PA	18,456	C
West Texas A&M Univ	TX	13,478	C
Western Illinois Univ	IL	20,825	C
Western Mich Univ	MI	21,054	C
Westminster Choir College	NJ	53,730	SP
Wilkes Univ	PA	45,622	C
William Peace Univ	NC	37,430	LC
Wright State Univ	OH	16,983	C
Youngstown State Univ	OH	17,307	C

MUSICOLOGY/ ETHNOMUSICOLOGY

School	ST	$IS	SR
Brown Univ	RI	64,566	MC
Cal State, San Bernardino	CA	12,000	C
Univ of Calif at Los Angeles	CA	30,162	MC
Univ of Kansas	KS	20,135	C+

NANOSCALE ENGINEERING

School	ST	$IS	SR
SUNY Polytechnic Inst	NY	19,473	VC

NANOSCALE SCIENCE

School	ST	$IS	SR
SUNY Polytechnic Inst	NY	19,473	VC

NATIVE AMERICAN STUDIES

School	ST	$IS	SR
Black Hills State Univ	SD	15,899	C
Brown Univ	RI	64,566	MC
Colgate Univ	NY	65,030	MC
College of St. Scholastica	MN	44,640	C
Dartmouth College	NH	66,174	MC
East Central Univ	OK	13,056	C
Heritage Univ	WA	19,825	NC
Humboldt State Univ	CA	20,514	C
Montana State Univ-Northern	MT	11,370	NC
Northern Arizona Univ	AZ	20,246	VC
Northland College	WI	41,103	C+
Southern Oregon Univ	OR	19,117	C
Stanford Univ	CA	60,409	MC
Univ of Calif at Berkeley	CA	28,853	MC
Univ of Calif at Davis	CA	28,488	HC
Univ of Calif at Riverside	CA	29,227	C+
Univ of Minn/Duluth	MN	20,292	C+
Univ of Montana	MT	14,105	C
Univ of New Mexico	NM	15,404	C
Univ of Okla	OK	18,911	VC

NATURAL RESOURCE MANAGEMENT

School	ST	$IS	SR
Alaska Pacific Univ	AK	26,680	VC
Angelo State Univ	TX	15,263	NC
Ball State Univ	IN	19,590	C
Bryant Univ	RI	55,646	VC
Calif Polytechnic State Univ	CA	17,979	HC+
Cal State, Sacramento	CA	20,332	C
Central Mich Univ	MI	20,330	C
Colo State Univ	CO	22,162	VC
Delaware State Univ	DE	19,376	NC
DePauw Univ	IN	58,688	HC+
Drury Univ	MO	33,791	VC
Glenville State College	WV	17,386	NC
Grand Valley State Univ	MI	22,250	C+
Green Mountain College	VT	45,228	LC
Humboldt State Univ	CA	20,514	C
Johnson State College	VT	20,752	C
Keystone College	PA	28,680	LC
Louisiana State Univ and A&M College	LA	18,677	VC
Lubbock Christian Univ	TX	28,426	C
Marshall Univ	WV	17,242	C
McNeese State Univ	LA	7,838	C
Mich State Univ	MI	23,898	VC+
Mich Tech Univ	MI	24,739	VC+
Montana State Univ	MT	15,500	C+
New Mexico Highlands Univ	NM	11,904	NC
New Mexico State Univ	NM	14,050	C
N Car State Univ	NC	19,515	HC+
N Dak State Univ	ND	16,245	C
Northland College	WI	41,103	C+
Ohio State Univ at Columbus	OH	21,703	HC+
Okla State Univ	OK	17,180	VC
Oregon State Univ	OR	22,519	VC
Pennsylvania State Univ - Univ Park	PA	29,760	HC
Purdue Univ/West Lafayette	IN	20,032	MC
Rutgers Univ - New Brunswick	NJ	26,632	HC
San Francisco State Univ	CA	18,514	LC
S Dak State Univ	SD	15,634	C
Southern Oregon Univ	OR	19,117	C
SUNY / The College of Environmental Science and Forestry	NY	23,853	VC
Sul Ross State Univ	TX	15,021	LC
Texas A&M Univ at Galveston	TX	15,920	C
Texas Tech Univ	TX	18,736	C+
The Univ of Tenn at Martin	TN	14,876	C
Unity College	ME	37,670	C
Univ of Alaska Fairbanks	AK	16,179	C
Univ of Arizona	AZ	23,100	C
Univ of Conn	CT	25,538	HC
Univ of Delaware	DE	24,976	VC+
Univ of Florida	FL	16,291	HC+
Univ of Hawaii at Manoa	HI	23,221	C
Univ of Idaho	ID	15,348	C
Univ of Illinois at Urbana-Champaign	IL	27,006	HC
Univ of Maryland/College Park	MD	21,938	HC
Univ of Mass Amherst	MA	26,199	VC+
Univ of Minn Crookston	MN	19,739	C
Univ of Minn/Twin Cities	MN	23,519	HC+
Univ of Montana-Western	MT	11,220	LC
Univ of Nebr - Lincoln	NE	18,589	VC
Univ of Nevada/Reno	NV	18,010	C
Univ of Northern Colo	CO	20,851	C
Univ of PR-Rio Piedras campus	PR	13,327	
Univ of Wisc-Stevens Point	WI	14,043	C
Utah State Univ	UT	12,736	C
Washington State Univ	WA	22,495	C
Washington Univ in St. Louis	MO	65,366	VC
West Virginia Univ	WV	18,210	C
Western Carolina Univ	NC	13,965	C

NATURAL RESOURCE/ ENVIRONMENTAL ECONOMICS

School	ST	$IS	SR
Bryant Univ	RI	55,646	VC
Rutgers Univ - New Brunswick	NJ	26,632	HC
Univ of Georgia	GA	21,250	HC
Univ of Nebr - Lincoln	NE	18,589	VC

NATURAL RESOURCES

School	ST	$IS	SR
Austin College	TX	45,875	VC
Bryant Univ	RI	55,646	VC
Colo State Univ	CO	22,162	VC
Pennsylvania State Univ - Univ Park	PA	29,760	HC
Sewanee: The Univ of the South	TN	54,500	MC
The Univ of Tenn at Knoxville	TN	22,112	VC
Univ of Maine at Machias	ME	22,960	C
Univ of Vermont	VT	28,878	HC

NATURAL SCIENCES

School	ST	$IS	SR
Alderson Broaddus Univ	WV	26,149	C
Ashford Univ	CA	10,480	C
Benedictine College	KS	36,200	VC
Bethel College	KS	35,370	C
Biola Univ	CA	46,402	C+
Cal State, Chico	CA	21,440	C
Cal State, Fresno	CA	16,902	LC
Cal State, Los Angeles	CA	17,186	LC
Calvin College	MI	41,570	VC+
Carthage College	WI	48,835	C
Case Western Reserve Univ	OH	60,304	MC
Castleton Univ	VT	20,186	C
Central College	IA	44,592	C
Charleston Southern Univ	SC	32,400	C
Christian Brothers Univ	TN	31,670	VC
Clarion Univ of Pennsylvania	PA	21,608	LC
Colby-Sawyer College	NH	50,790	C
Colgate Univ	NY	65,030	MC
College of St. Benedict	MN	52,806	C
College of St. Mary	NE	35,184	C
College of St. Scholastica	MN	44,640	C
Colo State Univ	CO	22,162	VC
Concordia Univ Nebr	NE	36,280	VC
Concordia Univ, Chicago	IL	39,694	C
Daemen College	NY	38,045	C
Dallas Baptist Univ	TX	33,713	C
Doane Univ	NE	39,184	VC
Dominican Univ	IL	41,222	C
Edgewood College	WI	35,950	C
Edinboro Univ	PA	15,940	LC
Elms College	MA	45,646	VC
Erskine College	SC	45,460	C
Felician Univ	NJ	45,370	LC
Fordham Univ	NY	65,918	MC
Fresno Pacific Univ	CA	37,370	C
Georgian Court Univ	NJ	42,426	LC
Gwynedd Mercy Univ	PA	43,780	LC
Indiana Univ of Pennsylvania	PA	23,614	LC
John Carroll Univ	OH	49,740	C+
Johns Hopkins Univ	MD	65,386	MC
Keystone College	PA	28,680	LC
LeMoyne-Owen College	TN	16,980	C
Lesley Univ	MA	41,550	C
Lewis-Clark State College	ID	14,202	C
Lyndon State College	VT	20,714	C
Madonna Univ	MI	29,050	C
Mercer Univ	GA	45,348	VC
Mich State Univ	MI	23,898	VC+
Missouri State Univ	MO	15,190	C+
Missouri Western State Univ	MO	16,741	
Muhlenberg College	PA	56,645	VC+
New College of Florida	FL	15,848	MC
Oakwood Univ	AL	43,758	C
Oglala Lakota College	SD	15,050	NC
Okla Baptist Univ	OK	32,320	C
Our Lady of the Lake Univ	TX	35,012	LC
Pacific Union College	CA	36,009	VC
Park Univ	MO	20,329	C
Pepperdine Univ	CA	74,460	HC+
Prescott College	AZ	33,284	C
St. Anselm College	NH	52,560	C+
St. John's Univ	MN	51,624	C
St. Peter's Univ	NJ	49,192	C
San Jose State Univ	CA	21,540	C
Shimer College	IL	42,130	VC+
Shorter Univ	GA	31,130	LC
Siena Heights Univ	MI	32,040	C
Southwestern Okla State Univ	OK	11,790	C
Spalding Univ	KY	31,938	SP
Spelman College	GA	38,751	C
St. Mary's College of Maryland	MD	26,634	VC
St. Norbert College	WI	44,525	VC
SUNY at Geneseo	NY	20,440	VC+
Taylor Univ	IN	40,317	C+
Texas A&M Univ at Galveston	TX	15,920	C
The Evergreen State College	WA	16,599	C
The Master's Univ	CA	43,870	C+
The Univ of Akron	OH	21,477	C
Thomas Edison State Univ	NJ	6,350	NC
Unity College	ME	37,670	C
Universidad del Turabo	PR	17,828	
Universidad Metropolitana	PR	17,828	
Univ of Alabama at Birmingham	AL	19,906	C
Univ of Alaska Anchorage	AK	16,652	NC
Univ of Arizona	AZ	23,100	C
Univ of Hawaii at Hilo	HI	18,038	C
Univ of La Verne	CA	55,600	C
Univ of New Haven	CT	52,190	C
Univ of N Dak	ND	15,373	C
Univ of Pittsburgh	PA	29,568	HC+
Univ of Pittsburgh at Greensburg	PA	23,132	C
Univ of PR, at Cayey	PR		
Univ of Puget Sound	WA	56,456	VC+
Univ of Science and Arts of Okla	OK	11,140	VC
Univ of Sioux Falls	SD	34,330	C
Univ of Wisc-Stevens Point	WI	14,043	C
Virginia Wesleyan College	VA	43,728	LC
Viterbo Univ	WI	34,660	C
Washington and Lee Univ	VA	59,647	MC
Western Oregon Univ	OR	15,021	LC
Worcester State Univ	MA	20,977	C
Xavier Univ	OH	47,880	C+
York College	NE	24,300	C

NATURAL SCIENCES/ MATHEMATICS

School	ST	$IS	SR
Indiana Univ East	IN	7,072	C
Thomas Edison State Univ	NJ	6,350	NC

NAVAL ARCHITECTURE AND MARINE ENGINEERING

School	ST	$IS	SR
SUNY /Maritime College	NY	16,020	C
Stevens Inst of Technology	NJ	62,338	MC
Texas A&M Univ at Galveston	TX	15,920	C
United States Coast Guard Academy	CT	942	MC
United States Naval Academy	MD		MC
Univ of Mich/Ann Arbor	MI	24,410	MC
Univ of New Orleans	LA	12,840	C
Univ of Wisc-Madison	WI	20,934	MC
Webb Inst	NY	61,800	MC

NEAR EASTERN STUDIES

School	ST	$IS	SR
Brandeis Univ	MA	65,925	MC
Brigham Young Univ	UT	12,748	HC
Cornell Univ	NY	64,853	MC
Indiana Univ Bloomington	IN	20,429	VC
Johns Hopkins Univ	MD	65,386	MC
Oberlin College	OH	66,012	MC
Princeton Univ	NJ	57,610	MC
The College of Wooster	OH	57,900	VC+
Univ of Calif at Berkeley	CA	28,853	MC
Univ of Calif at Los Angeles	CA	30,162	MC
Univ of Chicago	IL	67,584	MC
Univ of Mich/Ann Arbor	MI	24,410	MC
Univ of Mount Union	OH	38,970	C
Univ of Pennsylvania	PA	63,526	MC
Univ of Washington	WA	23,149	VC
Univ of Wisc-Milwaukee	WI	21,496	C
Washington Univ in St. Louis	MO	65,366	VC
Wayne State Univ	MI	22,016	C
Yale Univ	CT	64,650	MC

NETWORK & COMPUTER SECURITY

School	ST	$IS	SR
Hofstra Univ	NY	55,960	C+
SUNY Polytechnic Inst	NY	19,473	VC

NEUROSCIENCES

School	ST	$IS	SR
Agnes Scott College	GA	51,930	VC+
Alabama A&M Univ	AL	18,796	C
Allegheny College	PA	55,420	VC
Alma College	MI	47,548	C
American Univ	DC	59,379	HC+
Amherst College	MA		HC+
Augustana College	IL	49,658	VC
Baldwin Wallace Univ	OH	41,106	C
Bates College	ME	64,500	MC
Bay Path Univ	MA	45,349	C
Baylor Univ	TX	53,760	HC
Belmont Univ	TN	40,970	VC
Boston Univ	MA	65,110	MC
Bowdoin College	ME	63,500	MC
Bowling Green State Univ	OH	19,747	C
Brandeis Univ	MA	65,925	MC
Brigham Young Univ	UT	12,748	HC
Brown Univ	RI	64,566	MC
Bucknell Univ	PA	64,616	MC
Canisius College	NY	47,537	C
Carnegie Mellon Univ	PA	67,980	MC
Cedar Crest College	PA	46,715	C
Centenary College of Louisiana	LA	45,650	C+
Central Mich Univ	MI	20,330	C
Christopher Newport Univ	VA	23,968	VC+
CUNY/Queens College	NY	27,896	C
Claremont McKenna College	CA	67,185	MC
Coe College	IA	51,570	VC
Colby College	ME	64,060	MC
Colgate Univ	NY	65,030	MC
College of William & Mary	VA		MC
Colo College	CO	62,560	MC
Colo State Univ	CO	22,162	VC
Columbia Univ/City of New York	NY	62,958	MC
Conn College	CT	65,000	MC
Creighton Univ	NE	48,206	VC+
Dartmouth College	NH	66,174	MC
Delaware State Univ	DE	19,376	NC
Dickinson College	PA	63,974	MC
Dominican Univ	IL	41,222	C
Drake Univ	IA	45,056	HC
Drew Univ/College of Liberal Arts	NJ	61,048	VC
Earlham College	IN	54,870	HC
Elon Univ	NC	44,599	VC+
Emmanuel College	MA	52,110	C+
Emory Univ	GA	60,786	MC
Fitchburg State Univ	MA	21,819	C
Fordham Univ	NY	65,918	MC
Franklin and Marshall College	PA	63,170	HC

ST = STATE $IS = IN-STATE COSTS SR = SELECTOR RATING

School	ST	$IS	SR
Furman Univ	SC	58,092	VC+
George Mason Univ	VA	15,724	VC
Hamilton College	NY	64,250	MC
High Point Univ	NC	45,977	C
Hiram College	OH	43,230	C
Hofstra Univ	NY	55,960	C+
Indiana Univ Bloomington	IN	20,429	VC
Indiana Univ Southeast	IN	14,242	LC
Indiana Univ-Purdue Univ Indianapolis	IN	18,635	C
Johns Hopkins Univ	MD	65,386	MC
Kalamazoo College	MI	53,931	HC+
Kenyon College	OH	63,330	MC
King Univ	TN	34,660	C
King's College	PA	46,858	C
Knox College	IL	52,615	VC+
Lafayette College	PA	63,355	MC
Lake Forest College	IL	50,652	VC
Loras College	IA	39,222	C
Luther College	IA	48,540	C+
Macalester College	MN	61,905	MC
Mass Inst of Technology	MA	62,662	MC
Miami Univ	OH	27,190	HC+
Mich State Univ	MI	23,898	VC+
Middlebury College	VT	64,332	MC
Millsaps College	MS	50,080	C+
Montana State Univ	MT	15,500	C+
Moravian College	PA	53,117	
Morehead State Univ	KY	17,422	C
Mount Holyoke College	MA	56,746	MC
Mount St. Joseph Univ	OH	33,880	C
Muhlenberg College	PA	56,645	VC+
Muskingum Univ	OH	35,966	C
New College of Florida	FL	15,848	MC
New York Univ	NY	65,860	MC
Northeastern Univ	MA	62,703	MC
Northwestern Univ	IL	66,344	MC
Nova Southeastern Univ	FL	38,534	C+
Oberlin College	OH	66,012	MC
Ohio State Univ at Columbus	OH	21,703	HC+
Ohio Univ	OH	22,924	C
Ohio Wesleyan Univ	OH	49,460	VC
Pitzer College	CA	66,192	MC
Pomona College	CA	64,957	MC
Quinnipiac Univ	CT	59,110	C
Randolph-Macon College	VA	49,910	C
Regis Univ	CO	44,520	C
Rhodes College	TN	51,900	HC
St. Louis Univ	MO	49,866	HC
St. Michael's College	VT	51,725	VC+
Scripps College	CA	66,664	MC
Simpson College	IA	43,839	VC
Skidmore College	NY	64,214	HC
Smith College	MA	63,914	MC
St. Lawrence Univ	NY	64,390	VC
SUNY at Binghamton	NY	22,861	MC
SUNY at Geneseo	NY	20,440	VC+
Stonehill College	MA	55,030	C+
Swarthmore College	PA	63,550	MC
Syracuse Univ	NY	60,239	VC
Texas Christian Univ	TX	54,670	HC
Thiel College	PA	41,590	C
Transylvania Univ	KY	45,690	VC+
Trinity College	CT	63,920	HC+
Trinity Univ	TX	52,314	HC+
Tulane Univ	LA	63,396	HC+
Union College	NY	64,320	MC
Univ of Alabama at Birmingham	AL	19,906	C
Univ of Arizona	AZ	23,100	C
Univ of Calif at Irvine	CA	26,484	VC
Univ of Calif at Los Angeles	CA	30,162	MC
Univ of Calif at Riverside	CA	29,227	C+
Univ of Calif, Santa Cruz	CA	28,731	C+
Univ of Cincinnati	OH	21,964	VC
Univ of Colo Boulder	CO	24,285	VC+
Univ of Evansville	IN	44,186	VC+
Univ of Illinois at Chicago	IL	25,006	VC
Univ of Miami	FL	63,494	MC
Univ of Mich/Ann Arbor	MI	24,410	MC
Univ of Nevada/Reno	NV	18,010	C
Univ of New England	ME	48,880	C
Univ of New Hampshire	NH	28,562	VC
Univ of Notre Dame	IN	64,043	MC
Univ of Pittsburgh	PA	29,568	HC+
Univ of Rochester	NY	65,032	MC
Univ of Scranton	PA	54,962	VC
Univ of Southern Calif	CA	66,631	C
Univ of Texas at Dallas	TX	22,830	VC+
Univ of Vermont	VT	28,878	HC
Univ of Washington	WA	23,149	VC
Ursinus College	PA	61,690	VC
Utica College	NY	30,430	C
Vanderbilt Univ	TN	60,572	MC
Vassar College	NY	65,491	MC
Washington & Jefferson College	PA	56,512	VC
Washington and Lee Univ	VA	59,647	MC
Washington State Univ	WA	22,495	C
Washington Univ in St. Louis	MO	65,366	VC
Wellesley College	MA	63,916	MC
Wesleyan Univ	CT	65,516	MC
Western New England Univ	MA	48,088	C
Westminster College	UT	41,078	C+
Wheaton College	MA	61,512	VC
Wilkes Univ	PA	45,622	C

NEW MEDIA PRODUCTION

School	ST	$IS	SR
Univ of Tampa	FL	36,944	C

NONPROFIT/PUBLIC ORGANIZATION MANAGEMENT

School	ST	$IS	SR
Aquinas College - Mich	MI	38,876	HC
Arizona State Univ at the Downtown Phoenix Campus	AZ	23,680	VC
Bryant Univ	RI	55,646	VC
Duquesne Univ	PA	46,822	VC
High Point Univ	NC	45,977	C
Huntington Univ	IN	33,996	C
Juniata College	PA	53,760	VC
Mount Aloysius College	PA	29,976	C
Murray State Univ	KY	16,998	C
Prescott College	AZ	33,284	C
Rockhurst Univ	MO	29,220	C
Southern Adventist Univ	TN	27,600	C
Univ of S Car Upstate	SC	18,200	LC
Univ of Southern Indiana	IN	16,501	C
Univ of Wisc-Madison	WI	20,934	MC
Western Kentucky Univ	KY	16,850	C
Wright State Univ	OH	16,983	C

NORWEGIAN

School	ST	$IS	SR
Pacific Lutheran Univ	WA	49,960	VC
St. Olaf College	MN	54,260	HC+
Univ of N Dak	ND	15,373	C

NUCLEAR ENERGY ENGINEERING TECHNOLOGY

School	ST	$IS	SR
Thomas Edison State Univ	NJ	6,350	NC

NUCLEAR ENGINEERING

School	ST	$IS	SR
Excelsior College	NY	14,080	SP
Georgia Inst of Technology	GA	23,360	MC
Idaho State Univ	ID	13,619	NC
Mass Inst of Technology	MA	62,662	MC
Missouri Univ of Science and Technology	MO	18,655	HC
N Car State Univ	NC	19,515	HC+
Oregon State Univ	OR	22,519	VC
Pennsylvania State Univ - Univ Park	PA	29,760	HC
Purdue Univ/West Lafayette	IN	20,032	MC
Rensselaer Polytechnic Inst	NY	63,436	MC
Texas A&M Univ	TX	20,521	VC+
The Univ of Tenn at Chattanooga	TN	16,744	C
The Univ of Tenn at Knoxville	TN	22,112	VC
United States Military Academy at West Point	NY		HC+
United States Naval Academy	MD		MC
Univ of Calif at Berkeley	CA	28,853	MC
Univ of Cincinnati	OH	21,964	VC
Univ of Florida	FL	16,291	HC+
Univ of Illinois at Urbana-Champaign	IL	27,006	HC
Univ of Mich/Ann Arbor	MI	24,410	MC
Univ of New Mexico	NM	15,404	C
Univ of Wisc-Madison	WI	20,934	MC

NUCLEAR ENGINEERING TECHNOLOGY

School	ST	$IS	SR
Thomas Edison State Univ	NJ	6,350	NC
Univ of Florida	FL	16,291	HC+
Univ of North Texas	TX	19,198	C

NUCLEAR MEDICAL TECHNOLOGY

School	ST	$IS	SR
Adventist Univ of Health Sciences	FL	26,430	NC
Allen College	IA	32,367	NC
Augusta Univ	GA	4,632	C
Barry Univ	FL	37,830	C
Benedictine Univ	IL	38,300	C
Cedar Crest College	PA	46,715	C
Edinboro Univ	PA	15,940	LC
Ferris State Univ	MI	21,445	C
George Washington Univ	DC	62,835	MC
Indiana Univ of Pennsylvania	PA	23,614	LC
Mount Aloysius College	PA	29,976	C
North Central College	IL	48,712	VC
Old Dominion Univ	VA	20,910	C
Pennsylvania State Univ - Univ Park	PA	29,760	HC
Rhode Island College	RI	17,694	LC
Robert Morris Univ	PA	37,834	C
Roosevelt Univ	IL	40,651	VC
St. Louis Univ	MO	49,866	HC
SUNY / Univ at Buffalo	NY	23,122	C+
Univ of Alabama at Birmingham	AL	19,906	C
Univ of Central Arkansas	AR	14,472	VC
Univ of Cincinnati	OH	21,964	VC
Univ of Findlay	OH	60,139	C
Univ of Iowa	IA	18,683	VC+
Univ of Nevada, Las Vegas	NV	17,553	C
Univ of St. Francis	IL	39,924	C
Univ of the Incarnate Word	TX	39,162	LC
Univ of Vermont	VT	28,878	HC
Univ of Wisc-La Crosse	WI	15,247	C+
York College of Pennsylvania	PA	29,240	C

NUCLEAR MEDICINE

School	ST	$IS	SR
Thomas Edison State Univ	NJ	6,350	NC
Weber State Univ	UT	10,721	C

NUCLEAR MEDICINE TECHNOLOGY

School	ST	$IS	SR
Indiana Univ-Purdue Univ Indianapolis	IN	18,635	C
Lewis Univ	IL	40,370	C
MCPHS Univ	MA	45,470	SP
Millersville Univ of Pennsylvania	PA	23,782	C
Molloy College	NY	40,440	C
St. Mary's Univ of Minn	MN	41,210	VC
Thomas Edison State Univ	NJ	6,350	NC

NUCLEAR TECHNOLOGY

School	ST	$IS	SR
Excelsior College	NY	14,080	SP
Peru State College	NE	14,768	NC

NURSING

School	ST	$IS	SR
Abilene Christian Univ	TX	41,800	C+
Adams State Univ	CO	17,703	LC
Adelphi Univ	NY	48,244	C
Adventist Univ of Health Sciences	FL	26,430	NC
Agnes Scott College	GA	51,930	VC+
Alabama A&M Univ	AL	18,796	C
Albany State Univ	GA	19,462	C
Alcorn State Univ	MS	15,854	C
Alderson Broaddus Univ	WV	26,149	C
Allen College	IA	32,367	NC
Alma College	MI	47,548	C
Alvernia Univ	PA	43,900	C
Alverno College	WI	33,294	LC
American International College	MA	46,300	LC
Anderson Univ	IN	38,200	C
Andrews Univ	MI	28,030	C+
Angelo State Univ	TX	15,263	NC
Anna Maria College	MA	48,186	C
Appalachian State Univ	NC	14,416	VC
Aquinas College	TN	30,800	C+
Arizona State Univ at the Downtown Phoenix Campus	AZ	23,680	VC
Arkansas State Univ	AR	16,190	C
Arkansas Tech Univ	AR	15,484	C
Armstrong State Univ	GA	16,962	C
Ashland Univ	OH	21,440	C
Atlantic Union College	MA	27,228	C
Auburn Univ	AL	23,594	VC+
Auburn Univ at Montgomery	AL	15,290	C
Augusta Univ	GA	4,632	C
Augustana Univ	SD	38,424	VC
Aurora Univ	IL	33,970	C
Austin Peay State Univ	TN	16,397	C
Averett Univ	VA	40,970	LC
Avila Univ	MO	35,480	C
Azusa Pacific Univ	CA	43,972	C
Baker Univ	KS	33,350	C+
Baldwin Wallace Univ	OH	41,106	C
Ball State Univ	IN	19,590	C
Barry Univ	FL	37,830	C
Barton College	NC	38,686	LC
Bayamon Central Univ	PR	12,490	
Baylor Univ	TX	53,760	HC
Becker College	MA	57,628	C
Belhaven Univ	MS	31,016	C
Bellarmine Univ	KY	51,220	C
Belmont Univ	TN	40,970	VC
Bemidji State Univ	MN	16,056	VC
Benedictine College	KS	36,200	VC
Benedictine Univ	IL	38,300	C
Berea College	KY	7,042	C
Berry College	GA	45,286	C+
Bethel College	IN	35,860	C
Bethel College	KS	35,370	C
Bethel Univ	MN	45,270	VC
Bethel Univ	TN	24,738	C
Bethune-Cookman Univ	FL	22,970	C
Biola Univ	CA	46,402	C+
Birmingham-Southern College	AL	44,478	VC
Bloomfield College	NJ	39,100	LC
Bloomsburg Univ of Pennsylvania	PA	19,066	LC
Bluefield State College	WV	5,832	LC
Bluffton Univ	OH	40,950	C
Boise State Univ	ID	14,860	C
Boston College	MA	65,737	MC
Bowie State Univ	MD	26,728	LC
Bowling Green State Univ	OH	19,747	C
Brenau Univ - Women's College	GA	37,876	LC
Briar Cliff Univ	IA	36,956	C
Brigham Young Univ	UT	12,748	HC
Bryn Athyn College	PA	31,470	C
Cabarrus College of Health Sciences	NC	11,948	SP
Caldwell Univ	NJ	42,165	NC
Calif Baptist Univ	CA	41,392	C
Cal State, Bakersfield	CA	19,191	LC
Cal State, Chico	CA	21,440	C
Cal State, Dominguez Hills	CA	19,022	LC
Cal State, East Bay	CA	19,413	C
Cal State, Fresno	CA	16,902	LC
Cal State, Fullerton	CA	21,902	C
Cal State, Long Beach	CA	18,850	C
Cal State, Los Angeles	CA	17,186	LC
Cal State, Northridge	CA	16,859	LC
Cal State, Sacramento	CA	20,332	C
Cal State, San Bernardino	CA	12,000	C
Cal State, San Marcos	CA	24,184	LC
Cal State, Stanislaus	CA	16,212	C
Calif Univ of Pennsylvania	PA	14,217	LC
Calvin College	MI	41,570	VC+
Campbellsville Univ	KY	32,492	C
Capital Univ	OH	42,982	C
Cardinal Stritch Univ	WI	36,462	C
Caribbean Univ	PR	15,471	
Carlow Univ	PA	38,549	LC
Carroll College	MT	39,972	C+
Carroll Univ	WI	38,100	C+
Carson-Newman Univ	TN	34,160	C
Carthage College	WI	48,835	C
Case Western Reserve Univ	OH	60,304	MC
Castleton Univ	VT	20,186	C
Cedar Crest College	PA	46,715	C
Cedarville Univ	OH	34,990	VC
Central Conn State Univ	CT	21,203	C
Central Methodist Univ	MO	36,830	VC
Chaminade Univ of Honolulu	HI	36,000	C
Charleston Southern Univ	SC	32,400	C
Chatham Univ	PA	46,517	C
Chicago State Univ	IL	20,144	C
CUNY/College of Staten Island	NY	17,840	NC
CUNY/College of Technology	NY	6,669	NC
CUNY/Hunter College	NY	31,098	VC
CUNY/Lehman College	NY	5,778	HC+
CUNY/Meger Evers College	NY	6,680	NC
CUNY/York College	NY	6,747	LC
Clarion Univ of Pennsylvania	PA	21,608	LC
Clarke Univ	IA	38,940	C
Clarkson College	NE	31,868	C
Clayton State Univ	GA	19,735	C
Clemson Univ	SC		HC
Cleveland State Univ	OH	22,196	C
Coastal Carolina Univ	SC	19,766	C
Coe College	IA	51,570	VC
Colby-Sawyer College	NH	50,790	C
College of Mount St. Vincent	NY	45,620	C
College of St. Benedict	MN	52,806	C
College of St. Elizabeth	NJ	44,432	LC
College of St. Mary	NE	35,184	C
College of St. Scholastica	MN	44,640	C
College of the Ozarks	MO	7,230	C
Colo Mesa Univ	CO	18,955	LC
Colo State Univ-Pueblo	CO	18,234	C
Columbia College - Missouri	MO	27,803	C
Columbus State Univ	GA	14,336	LC
Concordia College - Moorhead	MN	51,088	C+
Concordia College - New York	NY	39,035	LC
Concordia Univ	OR	35,000	C
Concordia Univ St. Paul	MN	29,050	C
Concordia Univ Wisc	WI	35,910	C
Coppin State Univ	MD	17,041	VC
Cox College	MO	19,260	NC
Creighton Univ	NE	48,206	VC+
Culver-Stockton College	MO	33,525	C
Cumberland Univ	TN	27,710	C
Curry College	MA	51,815	C
Daemen College	NY	38,045	C
Dakota Wesleyan Univ	SD	32,850	C
Davenport Univ	MI	25,896	LC
Davis & Elkins College	WV	38,242	LC
Defiance College	OH	41,630	C
Delaware State Univ	DE	19,376	NC
Delta State Univ	MS	13,176	C
DePaul Univ	IL	47,623	VC
DeSales Univ	PA	43,970	C
Dickinson State Univ	ND	12,372	LC
Dillard Univ	LA	20,940	VC
Dominican College	NY	31,270	LC
Dominican Univ	IL	41,222	C
Dominican Univ of Calif	CA	57,050	C
Dordt College	IA	37,860	C+
Drexel Univ	PA	65,432	VC+
Duquesne Univ	PA	46,822	VC
D'Youville College	NY	36,780	C
East Carolina Univ	NC	16,937	C
East Central Univ	OK	13,056	C
East Stroudsburg Univ	PA	18,334	C
East Tenn State Univ	TN	13,994	C
East Texas Baptist Univ	TX	33,134	C
Eastern Illinois Univ	IL	21,126	C
Eastern Kentucky Univ	KY	16,908	C
Eastern Mennonite Univ	VA	42,550	C
Eastern Mich Univ	MI	19,761	C
Eastern New Mexico Univ	NM	14,416	C
Eastern Oregon Univ	OR	17,715	C
Eastern Univ	PA	39,540	C

ST = STATE $IS = IN-STATE COSTS SR = SELECTOR RATING

School	ST	$IS	SR
Eastern Washington Univ	WA	25,572	LC
Edgewood College	WI	35,950	C
Edinboro Univ	PA	15,940	LC
Elmhurst College	IL	45,428	C
Elmira College	NY	53,900	C
Elms College	MA	45,646	VC
Emmanuel College	MA	52,110	C+
Emory Univ	GA	60,786	MC
Emporia State Univ	KS	14,570	C
Endicott College	MA	44,604	VC+
Excelsior College	NY	14,080	SP
Fairfield Univ	CT	59,860	VC+
Fairleigh Dickinson Univ/ College at Florham	NJ	52,062	C
Fairleigh Dickinson Univ/ Metropolitan Campus	NJ	40,254	C
Fairmont State Univ	WV	15,726	C
Farmingdale State College	NY	20,624	C
Fayetteville State Univ	NC	17,756	C
Felician Univ	NJ	45,370	LC
Ferris State Univ	MI	21,445	C
Fitchburg State Univ	MA	21,819	C
Florida A&M Univ	FL	15,361	C
Florida Atlantic Univ	FL	17,339	C
Florida Gulf Coast Univ	FL	9,682	C
Florida State Univ	FL	16,771	HC
Fort Hays State Univ	KS	12,131	C
Framingham State Univ	MA	20,584	C
Francis Marion Univ	SC	16,464	LC
Franciscan Univ of Steubenville	OH	33,980	VC
Franklin Pierce Univ	NH	46,750	C
Frostburg State Univ	MD	17,280	LC
Gannon Univ	PA	42,032	C
Gardner-Webb Univ	NC	39,200	C+
George Fox Univ	OR	42,938	C
George Mason Univ	VA	15,724	VC
Georgetown Univ	DC	65,926	MC
Georgia College & State Univ	GA	21,148	C+
Georgia Southwestern State Univ	GA	13,870	C
Georgia State Univ	GA	24,332	VC
Georgian Court Univ	NJ	42,426	LC
Glenville State College	WV	17,386	NC
Gonzaga Univ	WA	50,888	HC
Goodwin College	CT	28,370	LC
Goshen College	IN	42,500	C
Graceland Univ	IA	35,290	C
Grambling State Univ	LA	15,701	C
Grand Canyon Univ	AZ	16,950	VC
Grand Valley State Univ	MI	22,250	C+
Grand View Univ	IA	32,302	C
Gustavus Adolphus College	MN	52,433	HC
Gwynedd Mercy Univ	PA	43,780	LC
Hampton Univ	VA	34,926	LC
Hannibal-LaGrange Univ	MO	29,815	C
Harding Univ	AR	25,421	C
Hardin-Simmons Univ	TX	33,966	C
Hartwick College	NY	51,270	C
Hawaii Pacific Univ	HI	33,420	C
Henderson State Univ	AR	15,516	LC
Heritage Univ	WA	19,825	NC
Hiram College	OH	43,230	C
Holy Family Univ	PA	43,326	LC
Holy Names Univ	CA	46,630	LC
Hood College	MD	54,840	C
Hope College	MI	39,940	VC
Houston Baptist Univ	TX	36,450	C
Howard Univ	DC	37,616	C+
Humboldt State Univ	CA	20,514	C
Huntington Univ	IN	33,996	C
Husson Univ	ME	25,720	LC
Idaho State Univ	ID	13,619	NC
Illinois State Univ	IL	23,418	VC
Illinois Wesleyan Univ	IL	56,430	VC+
Indiana State Univ	IN	23,223	LC
Indiana Univ Bloomington	IN	20,429	VC
Indiana Univ East	IN	7,072	C
Indiana Univ Kokomo	IN	7,073	C
Indiana Univ Northwest	IN	7,072	C
Indiana Univ of Pennsylvania	PA	23,614	LC
Indiana Univ South Bend	IN	14,242	C
Indiana Univ Southeast	IN	14,242	LC
Indiana Univ-Purdue Univ Fort Wayne	IN	17,553	C
Indiana Univ-Purdue Univ Indianapolis	IN	18,635	C
Indiana Wesleyan Univ	IN	33,674	C
Inter-American Univ of PR Ponce	PR	19,549	
Inter-American Univ of PR-Aguadilla Campus	PR	21,657	
Inter-American Univ of PR-Arecibo Campus	PR	18,245	
Inter-American Univ of PR-Fajardo Campus	PR	18,336	
Inter-American Univ of PR-Metropolitan Campus	PR	20,045	
Inter-American Univ of PR-San Germán	PR	20,042	
Iowa Wesleyan Univ	IA	39,200	C
Jacksonville State Univ	AL	14,628	LC
Jacksonville Univ	FL	46,230	C
James Madison Univ	VA	19,084	VC
John Brown Univ	AR	33,132	VC
Johnson C. Smith Univ	NC	25,336	LC
Judson College	AL	27,066	C
Judson Univ	IL	37,700	C
Kansas Wesleyan Univ	KS	36,600	C
Kean Univ	NJ	24,650	C
Keene State College	NH	24,003	LC
Kennesaw State Univ	GA	19,592	VC
Kent State Univ	OH	20,732	C
Kentucky Christian Univ	KY	26,560	LC
Kentucky State Univ	KY	13,364	LC
Keuka College	NY	39,762	C
King Univ	TN	34,660	C
Kutztown Univ of Pennsylvania	PA	19,056	LC
La Roche College	PA	37,924	LC
La Salle Univ	PA	55,790	C
LaGrange College	GA	39,930	C
Lamar Univ	TX	18,014	LC
Lander Univ	SC	43,994	C
Langston Univ	OK	14,314	C
Le Moyne College	NY	46,000	C
Lenoir-Rhyne Univ	NC	43,200	C
LeTourneau Univ	TX	38,250	VC
Lewis Univ	IL	40,370	C
Lewis-Clark State College	ID	14,202	C
Liberty Univ	VA	19,101	C
Lincoln Memorial Univ	TN	28,070	C
Lincoln Univ	MO	13,602	NC
Lindsey Wilson College	KY	32,882	C
Linfield College	OR	52,010	C
Lipscomb Univ	TN	41,296	VC
LIU Brooklyn	NY	49,682	C
LIU Post	NY	49,682	C
Longwood Univ	VA	22,184	C
Louisiana College	LA	21,886	C
Lourdes Univ	OH	29,520	NC
Loyola Univ Chicago	IL	55,802	VC
Loyola Univ New Orleans	LA	51,708	VC+
Lubbock Christian Univ	TX	28,426	C
Luther College	IA	48,540	C+
Lynchburg College	VA	46,740	C
MacMurray College	IL	33,620	C
Madonna Univ	MI	29,050	C
Malone Univ	OH	38,448	C
Mansfield Univ	PA	23,376	LC
Marian Univ	IN	41,220	C
Marian Univ	WI	32,420	LC
Marquette Univ	WI	48,390	VC+
Marshall Univ	WV	17,242	C
Mary Baldwin Univ	VA	39,865	C
Marymount Univ	VA	41,570	LC
Maryville College	TN	44,410	C
Maryville Univ of St. Louis	MO	38,046	VC+
Marywood Univ	PA	46,900	C
Mayville State Univ	ND	18,371	NC
McKendree Univ	IL	37,940	C+
McMurry Univ	TX	34,259	LC
McNeese State Univ	LA	7,838	C
MCPHS Univ	MA	45,470	SP
Mercy College	NY	31,776	C
Mercy College of Health Sciences	IA	16,920	C
Messiah College	PA	43,100	C+
Methodist Univ	NC	43,600	C
Metropolitan State Univ	MN	7,566	C
Metropolitan State Univ of Denver	CO	29,889	LC
Miami Univ	OH	27,190	HC+
Mich State Univ	MI	23,898	VC+
MidAmerica Nazarene Univ	KS	35,550	C
Middle Tenn State Univ	TN	8,650	C
Midland Univ	NE	37,468	
Midway Univ	KY	31,640	LC
Midwestern State Univ	TX	17,572	C
Millersville Univ of Pennsylvania	PA	23,782	C
Milligan College	TN	38,150	C
Millikin Univ	IL	42,158	C
Mills College	CA	59,163	VC
Milwaukee School of Engineering	WI	45,153	HC
Minn State Univ, Mankato	MN	15,616	C
Minn State Univ, Moorhead	MN	15,941	C
Minot State Univ	ND	12,732	C
Misericordia Univ	PA	43,840	C
Miss College	MS	25,850	C
Miss Univ for Women	MS	17,065	C
Missouri State Univ	MO	15,190	C+
Missouri Western State Univ	MO	16,741	
Molloy College	NY	40,440	C
Monmouth Univ	NJ	46,234	C
Montana State Univ	MT	15,500	C+
Montana State Univ-Northern	MT	11,370	NC
Montana Tech of the Univ of Montana	MT	15,447	C+
Moravian College	PA	53,117	
Morehead State Univ	KY	17,422	C
Morningside College	IA	36,865	C
Mount Aloysius College	PA	29,976	C
Mount Marty College	SD	32,972	C
Mount Mercy Univ	IA	36,826	C
Mount St. Mary College	NY	42,061	C
Mount St. Joseph Univ	OH	33,880	C
Mount St. Mary's Univ - Chalon Campus	CA	43,897	VC+
Mount Vernon Nazarene Univ	OH	34,500	C
Murray State Univ	KY	16,998	C
Muskingum Univ	OH	35,966	C
National Univ	CA	14,730	LC
Nazareth College	NY	45,574	C
Nebr Methodist College	NE	25,134	SP
Nebr Wesleyan Univ	NE	38,140	C+
Neumann Univ	PA	40,678	LC
New Jersey City Univ	NJ	21,456	LC
New Mexico State Univ	NM	14,050	C
New York Inst of Technology	NY	48,730	C
New York Univ	NY	65,860	MC
Newman Univ	KS	35,390	C
Niagara Univ	NY	41,010	C
Nicholls State Univ	LA	10,534	C
Norfolk State Univ	VA	25,702	LC
N Car A&T State Univ	NC	13,365	LC
N Car Central Univ	NC	9,000	C
N Dak State Univ	ND	16,245	C
North Park Univ	IL	35,860	C
Northeastern State Univ	OK	8,615	VC
Northeastern Univ	MA	62,703	MC
Northern Arizona Univ	AZ	20,246	VC
Northern Illinois Univ	IL	20,176	C
Northern Kentucky Univ	KY	16,486	C
Northern Mich Univ	MI	19,604	C
Northwest Nazarene Univ	ID	36,000	C
Northwest Univ	WA	35,876	VC
Northwestern College of Iowa	IA	38,400	C+
Northwestern Okla State Univ	OK	13,072	NC
Norwich Univ	VT	28,212	C
Notre Dame College	OH	37,150	VC
Notre Dame de Namur Univ	CA	46,526	LC
Notre Dame of Maryland Univ	MD	46,465	VC
Nova Southeastern Univ	FL	38,534	C+
Nyack College	NY	34,050	NC
Oakland Univ	MI	20,763	C
Oakwood Univ	AL	43,758	C
Ohio State Univ at Columbus	OH	21,703	HC+
Ohio State Univ at Lima	OH	7,140	C
Ohio State Univ at Mansfield	OH	13,160	C
Ohio State Univ at Marion	OH	7,140	C
Ohio State Univ at Newark	OH	7,140	C
Ohio Univ	OH	22,924	C
Okla Baptist Univ	OK	32,320	C
Okla Christian Univ	OK	27,650	VC
Okla City Univ	OK	40,476	VC
Okla Panhandle State Univ	OK	6,152	NC
Old Dominion Univ	VA	20,910	C
Olivet Nazarene Univ	IL	41,840	C
Oral Roberts Univ	OK	34,316	C
Otterbein Univ	OH	41,630	C
Pace Univ	NY	58,248	C
Pacific Lutheran Univ	WA	49,960	VC
Pacific Union College	CA	36,009	VC
Palm Beach Atlantic Univ	FL	39,720	C
Penn State Univ/Altoona	PA	24,584	C
Pennsylvania College of Technology	PA	27,333	NC
Pennsylvania State Univ - Univ Park	PA	29,760	HC
Pfeiffer Univ	NC	39,695	LC
Piedmont College	GA	32,512	C
Pittsburg State Univ	KS	13,880	NC
Plymouth State Univ	NH	23,180	LC
Point Loma Nazarene Univ	CA	43,450	C
Pontifical Catholic Univ of PR	PR	10,534	
Prairie View A&M Univ	TX	15,205	LC
Presentation College	SD	25,454	NC
Purdue Univ/Northwest	IN	15,038	C
Purdue Univ/West Lafayette	IN	20,032	MC
Queens Univ of Charlotte	NC	39,543	C
Quincy Univ	IL	36,998	C
Quinnipiac Univ	CT	59,110	C
Radford Univ	VA	19,027	LC
Ramapo College of New Jersey	NJ	25,338	C
Regis College	MA	51,920	C
Regis Univ	CO	44,520	C
Research College of Nursing	MO	38,790	SP
Rhode Island College	RI	17,694	LC
Rivier Univ	NH	40,410	VC
Robert Morris Univ	PA	37,834	C
Roberts Wesleyan College	NY	38,306	C
Rockford Univ	IL	36,030	C
Rockhurst Univ	MO	29,220	C
Rowan Univ	NJ	24,491	VC+
Russell Sage College	NY	39,370	C
Rutgers Univ - Camden	NJ	26,146	C
Rutgers Univ - New Brunswick	NJ	26,632	HC
Rutgers Univ - Newark	NJ	27,288	C
Saginaw Valley State Univ	MI	18,530	C
St. Anselm College	NH	52,560	C+
St. Francis Univ	PA	42,268	NC
St. John's Univ	MN	51,624	C
St. Joseph's College of Maine	ME	46,485	C
St. Louis Univ	MO	49,866	HC
St. Martin's Univ	WA	45,056	C
St. Mary-of-the-Woods College	IN	39,632	LC
St. Mary's College	IN	50,600	C
St. Peter's Univ	NJ	49,192	C
St. Xavier Univ	IL	43,310	C
Salem State Univ	MA	17,303	LC
Salisbury Univ	MD	20,714	VC
Salve Regina Univ	RI	51,470	C
Samford Univ	AL	39,232	VC
San Diego State Univ	CA	21,896	C+
San Francisco State Univ	CA	18,514	LC
San Jose State Univ	CA	21,540	C
Schreiner Univ	TX	34,626	LC
Seattle Pacific Univ	WA	47,439	C+
Seattle Univ	WA	50,811	VC+
Seton Hall Univ	NJ	55,514	C
Shenandoah Univ	VA	41,312	C
Shepherd Univ, West Virginia	WV	17,224	C
Shorter Univ	GA	31,130	LC
Siena College	NY	48,916	C+
Silver Lake College of the Holy Family	WI	36,290	LC
Simmons College	MA	53,090	VC
Simpson Univ	CA	33,700	C
Sinte Gleska Univ	SD	13,154	NC
Slippery Rock Univ of Pennsylvania	PA	10,360	C
Sonoma State Univ	CA	27,806	C
S Car State Univ	SC	20,805	LC
S Dak State Univ	SD	15,634	C
South Univ	GA	36,070	LC
Southeast Missouri State Univ	MO	15,498	C
Southeastern Louisiana Univ	LA	16,237	C
Southern Adventist Univ	TN	27,600	C
Southern Conn State Univ	CT	21,924	LC
Southern Illinois Univ Edwardsville	IL	22,643	C
Southern Nazarene Univ	OK	32,798	NC
Southern Oregon Univ	OR	19,117	C
Southern Univ and A&M College	LA	16,074	LC+
Southern Vermont College	VT	34,670	LC
Southwest Baptist Univ	MO	29,900	LC
Southwestern Adventist Univ	TX	27,756	LC
Southwestern Okla State Univ	OK	11,790	C
Spalding Univ	KY	31,938	SP
Spring Arbor Univ	MI	36,000	C
Spring Hill College	AL	48,488	C
St. Ambrose Univ	IA	39,019	C
St. Ambrose Univ	IA	39,019	C
St. Catherine Univ	MN	45,630	VC
St. Francis College	NY	38,800	LC
St. John Fisher College	NY	43,620	C
St. Joseph's College, New York/Brooklyn Campus	NY	25,114	LC
St. Joseph's College, New York/Long Island Campus	NY	25,124	C
St. Olaf College	MN	54,260	HC+
SUNY / Empire State College	NY	9,145	SP
SUNY / SUNY Plattsburgh	NY	18,814	C
SUNY / Univ at Buffalo	NY	23,122	C+
SUNY at Binghamton	NY	22,861	MC
SUNY at New Paltz	NY	19,200	C
SUNY Polytechnic Inst	NY	19,473	VC
Stephen F. Austin State Univ	TX	18,406	LC
Stevenson Univ	MD	72,770	C
Stockton Univ	NJ	25,059	
Stony Brook Univ/The SUNY	NY	21,881	MC
Tabor College	KS	35,870	C
Tarleton State Univ	TX	15,248	LC
Temple Univ	PA	24,392	VC
Tenn State Univ	TN	14,423	C
Tenn Tech Univ	TN	17,050	C
Texas A&M Univ	TX	20,521	VC+
Texas A&M Univ at Corpus Christi	TX	16,851	LC
Texas A&M Univ at Kingsville	TX	7,500	LC
Texas Christian Univ	TX	54,670	HC
Texas Lutheran Univ	TX	38,620	C
Texas State Univ	TX	19,350	C
Texas Woman's Univ	TX	15,302	LC
The Catholic Univ of America	DC	56,356	VC
The College at Brockport - SUNY	NY	20,346	C
The College of Idaho	ID	36,415	C
The College of New Jersey	NJ	31,909	HC
The College of New Rochelle	NY	46,300	VC
The Univ of Akron	OH	21,477	C
The Univ of Tenn at Chattanooga	TN	16,744	C
The Univ of Tenn at Knoxville	TN	22,112	VC
The Univ of Tenn at Martin	TN	14,876	C
The Univ of Utah	UT	17,924	VC
The Univ of Virginia's College at Wise	VA	18,192	LC
Thomas Edison State Univ	NJ	6,350	NC
Thomas More College	KY	36,720	C
Thomas Univ	GA	21,420	LC
Touro College	NY	28,950	VC
Towson Univ	MD	17,408	VC
Trevecca Nazarene Univ	TN	31,186	C
Trinity Christian College	IL	35,580	C
Trinity College of Nursing and Health Sciences	IL	53,138	SP
Trinity Washington Univ	DC	33,826	C+
Troy Univ	AL	16,171	C
Truman State Univ	MO	16,014	HC
Tusculum College	TN	31,625	C
Tuskegee Univ	AL	28,164	C
Union College	KY	32,310	C
Union College	NE	23,270	C
Union Univ	TN	33,970	VC
Universidad Adventista de las Antillas	PR	16,606	
Universidad Metropolitana	PR	17,828	
Univ of PR, at Arecibo	PR	12,652	
Univ of Alabama	AL	24,320	C+
Univ of Alabama at Birmingham	AL	19,906	C

ST = STATE **$IS** = IN-STATE COSTS **SR** = SELECTOR RATING

School	ST	$IS	SR
Univ of Alabama in Huntsville	AL	19,445	VC
Univ of Alaska Anchorage	AK	16,652	NC
Univ of Arizona	AZ	23,100	C
Univ of Arkansas at Fayetteville	AR	19,152	C+
Univ of Arkansas at Little Rock	AR	18,211	C
Univ of Arkansas at Monticello	AR	13,134	NC
Univ of Arkansas at Pine Bluff	AR	13,541	C
Univ of Calif at Irvine	CA	26,484	VC
Univ of Calif at Los Angeles	CA	30,162	MC
Univ of Central Arkansas	AR	14,472	VC
Univ of Central Florida	FL	15,922	VC
Univ of Central Missouri	MO	18,982	C
Univ of Central Okla	OK	13,486	C
Univ of Charleston	WV	35,000	C
Univ of Cincinnati	OH	21,964	VC
Univ of Colo Colo Springs	CO	19,663	C
Univ of Colo Denver	CO	23,230	C
Univ of Conn	CT	25,538	HC
Univ of Dallas	TX	45,500	VC+
Univ of Delaware	DE	24,976	VC+
Univ of Detroit Mercy	MI	48,816	C+
Univ of Dubuque	IA	37,824	C
Univ of Evansville	IN	44,186	VC+
Univ of Findlay	OH	60,139	C
Univ of Florida	FL	16,291	HC+
Univ of Hartford	CT	49,776	C
Univ of Hawaii at Hilo	HI	18,038	C
Univ of Hawaii at Manoa	HI	23,221	C
Univ of Holy Cross	LA	21,523	C
Univ of Illinois at Chicago	IL	25,006	VC
Univ of Indianapolis	IN	36,480	C
Univ of Iowa	IA	18,683	VC+
Univ of Jamestown	ND	28,508	C
Univ of Kansas	KS	20,135	C+
Univ of Kentucky	KY	33,306	C
Univ of Louisiana at Lafayette	LA	14,516	C
Univ of Louisiana at Monroe	LA	15,970	C
Univ of Louisville	KY	19,824	C
Univ of Maine	ME	20,792	C
Univ of Maine at Augusta	ME	7,812	C
Univ of Maine at Fort Kent	ME	15,165	LC
Univ of Mary	ND	23,180	C
Univ of Mary Hardin-Baylor	TX	33,950	C+
Univ of Mass Amherst	MA	26,199	VC+
Univ of Mass Boston	MA	13,435	C
Univ of Mass Dartmouth	MA	25,658	C
Univ of Mass Lowell	MA	26,380	C
Univ of Memphis	TN	18,278	C
Univ of Miami	FL	63,494	MC
Univ of Mich/Ann Arbor	MI	24,410	MC
Univ of Mich-Flint	MI	17,607	C+
Univ of Minn/Twin Cities	MN	23,519	HC+
Univ of Miss	MS	17,746	C+
Univ of Missouri/Columbia	MO	18,201	MC
Univ of Missouri-Kansas City	MO	19,563	VC
Univ of Missouri-St. Louis	MO		C
Univ of Mobile	AL	28,935	C
Univ of Nebr - Kearney	NE	16,546	LC
Univ of Nevada, Las Vegas	NV	17,553	C
Univ of Nevada/Reno	NV	18,010	C
Univ of New England	ME	48,880	C
Univ of New Hampshire	NH	28,562	VC
Univ of New Mexico	NM	15,404	C
Univ of North Alabama	AL	15,398	C
Univ of N Car at Chapel Hill	NC	20,052	HC+
Univ of N Car at Charlotte	NC	15,547	C
Univ of N Car at Greensboro	NC	14,690	C
Univ of N Car at Pembroke	NC	14,388	LC
Univ of N Car at Wilmington	NC	14,590	VC
Univ of N Dak	ND	15,373	C
Univ of North Florida	FL	15,996	VC
Univ of North Georgia	GA	17,316	C
Univ of Northern Colo	CO	20,851	C
Univ of Pennsylvania	PA	63,526	MC
Univ of Pikeville	KY	28,700	NC
Univ of Pittsburgh	PA	29,568	HC+
Univ of Pittsburgh at Bradford	PA	22,402	C
Univ of Pittsburgh at Johnstown	PA	22,092	C
Univ of Portland	OR	52,152	VC
Univ of PR, at Humacao	PR	14,000	
Univ of PR, at Mayaguez	PR	13,995	
Univ of Rhode Island	RI	24,906	C
Univ of Rio Grande & Rio Grande Community College	OH	8,750	NC
Univ of Rochester	NY	65,032	MC
Univ of St. Francis	IN	37,400	C
Univ of St. Joseph	CT	49,550	C
Univ of St. Mary	KS	34,690	C
Univ of San Francisco	CA	58,484	VC
Univ of Scranton	PA	54,962	VC
Univ of Sioux Falls	SD	34,330	C
Univ of South Alabama	AL	16,400	C
Univ of S Car Aiken	SC	16,712	C
Univ of S Car at Columbia	SC	19,725	VC+
Univ of S Car Upstate	SC	18,200	LC
Univ of S Dak	SD	16,109	C
Univ of South Florida/Tampa	FL	16,110	VC+
Univ of Southern Indiana	IN	16,501	C
Univ of Southern Maine	ME	18,320	C
Univ of Southern Miss	MS	13,170	C
Univ of St. Francis	IL	39,924	C
Univ of St. Thomas - Houston	TX	40,020	VC
Univ of Tampa	FL	36,944	C
Univ of Texas at Arlington	TX	18,026	LC
Univ of Texas at Austin	TX	26,102	HC
Univ of Texas at El Paso	TX	34,452	NC
Univ of the Cumberlands	KY	32,000	C
Univ of the District of Columbia	DC	21,044	LC
Univ of the Incarnate Word	TX	39,162	LC
Univ of the Sacred Heart	PR	17,932	
Univ of Toledo	OH	19,336	NC
Univ of Tulsa	OK	52,625	HC+
Univ of Vermont	VT	28,878	HC
Univ of Virginia	VA	25,891	MC
Univ of Washington	WA	23,149	VC
Univ of West Florida	FL	15,848	C
Univ of West Georgia	GA	16,360	LC
Univ of Wisc-Eau Claire	WI	15,797	VC
Univ of Wisc-Green Bay	WI	15,064	C
Univ of Wisc-Madison	WI	20,934	MC
Univ of Wisc-Milwaukee	WI	21,496	C
Univ of Wisc-Oshkosh	WI	15,200	C
Univ of Wyoming	WY	15,375	C+
Urbana Univ	OH	30,820	C
Ursuline College	OH	41,076	LC
Utica College	NY	30,430	C
Valparaiso Univ	IN	48,370	C+
Vanguard Univ of Southern Calif	CA	40,740	VC
Villanova Univ	PA	62,523	MC
Virginia Commonwealth Univ	VA	23,049	C
Viterbo Univ	WI	34,660	C
Wagner College	NY	55,480	C+
Walla Walla Univ	WA	30,417	NC
Walsh Univ	OH	39,010	C
Washburn Univ	KS	15,827	C
Washington Adventist Univ	MD	31,440	LC
Washington State Univ	WA	22,495	C
Wayland Baptist Univ	TX	22,356	LC
Wayne State Univ	MI	22,016	C
Waynesburg Univ	PA	32,290	C
Weber State Univ	UT	10,721	C
Webster Univ	MO	37,490	C
Wesley College	DE	37,026	LC
West Chester Univ of Pennsylvania	PA	18,456	C
West Liberty Univ	WV	15,512	C
West Texas A&M Univ	TX	13,478	C
West Virginia Univ	WV	18,210	C
West Virginia Univ Inst of Technology	WV	16,462	NC
West Virginia Wesleyan College	WV	36,858	C
Western Carolina Univ	NC	13,965	C
Western Conn State Univ	CT	21,254	LC
Western Illinois Univ	IL	20,825	C
Western Kentucky Univ	KY	16,850	C
Western Mich Univ	MI	21,054	C
Western Washington Univ	WA	18,003	C+
Westfield State Univ	MA	19,671	C
Westminster College	MO	32,820	C
Westminster College	UT	41,078	C+
Wheaton College	IL	43,610	MC
Wheeling Jesuit Univ	WV	37,106	LC
Whitworth Univ	WA	51,732	VC
Wichita State Univ	KS	21,643	C
Widener Univ	PA	56,486	C
Wilkes Univ	PA	45,622	C
William Carey Univ	MS	23,950	LC
William Jewell College	MO	41,210	C+
William Paterson Univ of New Jersey	NJ	23,133	C
Wilmington Univ	DE	8,546	NC
Wilson College	PA	35,620	C
Wingate Univ	NC	39,950	C
Winona State Univ	MN	17,535	C
Winston-Salem State Univ	NC	26,166	LC
Wisc Lutheran College	WI	36,290	VC
Worcester State Univ	MA	20,977	C
Wright State Univ	OH	16,983	C
Xavier Univ	OH	47,880	C+
York College of Pennsylvania	PA	29,240	C
Youngstown State Univ	OH	17,307	C

NURSING EDUCATION

School	ST	$IS	SR
Allen College	IA	32,367	NC
Cal State, Northridge	CA	16,859	LC
Georgia Southern Univ	GA	16,596	C
Indiana Wesleyan Univ	IN	33,674	C
New York Univ	NY	65,860	MC
Seattle Pacific Univ	WA	47,439	C+
Southern Univ and A&M College	LA	16,074	LC+
Univ of Alaska Anchorage	AK	16,652	NC
Univ of St. Thomas - Houston	TX	40,020	VC
Walla Walla Univ	WA	30,417	NC
Western Washington Univ	WA	18,003	C+

NURSING HOME ADMINISTRATION

School	ST	$IS	SR
Mount Aloysius College	PA	29,976	C
New York Univ	NY	65,860	MC
Ohio Univ	OH	22,924	C
Youngstown State Univ	OH	17,307	C

NUTRITION

School	ST	$IS	SR
Abilene Christian Univ	TX	41,800	C+
Alabama A&M Univ	AL	18,796	C
Alcorn State Univ	MS	15,854	C
Andrews Univ	MI	28,030	C+
Appalachian State Univ	NC	14,416	VC
Arizona State Univ at the Downtown Phoenix Campus	AZ	23,680	VC
Auburn Univ	AL	23,594	VC+
Baylor Univ	TX	53,760	HC
Benedictine Univ	IL	38,300	C
Boston Univ	MA	65,110	MC
Bowling Green State Univ	OH	19,747	C
Brigham Young Univ	UT	12,748	HC
Calif Polytechnic State Univ	CA	17,979	HC+
Case Western Reserve Univ	OH	60,304	MC
Cedar Crest College	PA	46,715	C
CUNY/Hunter College	NY	31,098	VC
College of St. Benedict	MN	52,806	C
College of St. Elizabeth	NJ	44,432	LC
Colo State Univ	CO	22,162	VC
Concordia College - Moorhead	MN	51,088	C+
Dominican Univ	IL	41,222	C
Drexel Univ	PA	65,432	VC+
East Carolina Univ	NC	16,937	C
Eastern Mich Univ	MI	19,761	C
Florida State Univ	FL	16,771	HC
Fort Valley State Univ	GA	17,988	VC
Framingham State Univ	MA	20,584	C
Gannon Univ	PA	42,032	C
Georgia Southern Univ	GA	16,596	C
Georgia State Univ	GA	24,332	VC
Goddard College	VT	17,040	VC
Hampshire College	MA	63,824	MC
Howard Univ	DC	37,616	C+
Indiana Univ of Pennsylvania	PA	23,614	LC
Iowa State Univ	IA	17,570	C
Johnson & Wales Univ/ Denver Campus	CO	42,707	C
Kansas State Univ	KS	17,780	VC
Keene State College	NH	24,003	LC
Kent State Univ	OH	20,732	C
La Salle Univ	PA	55,790	C
Langston Univ	OK	14,314	C
LIU Post	NY	49,682	C
Louisiana State Univ and A&M College	LA	18,677	VC
Madonna Univ	MI	29,050	C
Marshall Univ	WV	17,242	C
Meredith College	NC	45,297	C
Miami Univ	OH	27,190	HC+
Mich State Univ	MI	23,898	VC+
Middle Tenn State Univ	TN	8,650	C
Montclair State Univ	NJ	26,210	LC
Murray State Univ	KY	16,998	C
New Mexico State Univ	NM	14,050	C
New York Univ	NY	65,860	MC
N Car Central Univ	NC	9,000	C
N Dak State Univ	ND	16,245	C
Northern Illinois Univ	IL	20,176	C
Ohio State Univ at Columbus	OH	21,703	HC+
Ohio Univ	OH	22,924	C
Ohio Wesleyan Univ	OH	49,460	VC
Okla State Univ	OK	17,180	VC
Oregon State Univ	OR	22,519	VC
Pennsylvania State Univ - Univ Park	PA	29,760	HC
Pepperdine Univ	CA	74,460	HC+
Point Loma Nazarene Univ	CA	43,450	C
Purdue Univ/West Lafayette	IN	20,032	MC
Rochester Inst of Technology	NY	50,842	HC
Russell Sage College	NY	39,370	C
Rutgers Univ - New Brunswick	NJ	26,632	HC
St. John's Univ	MN	51,624	C
Samford Univ	AL	39,232	VC
San Diego State Univ	CA	21,896	C+
S Car State Univ	SC	20,805	LC
S Dak State Univ	SD	15,634	C
St. Catherine Univ	MN	45,630	VC
SUNY / SUNY Plattsburgh	NY	18,814	C
Stephen F. Austin State Univ	TX	18,406	LC
Syracuse Univ	NY	60,239	VC
Texas A&M Univ	TX	20,521	VC+
Texas Christian Univ	TX	54,670	HC
Texas Southern Univ	TX	18,212	LC
Texas State Univ	TX	19,350	C
Texas Tech Univ	TX	18,736	C+
The Univ of Tenn at Knoxville	TN	22,112	VC
The Univ of Tenn at Martin	TN	14,876	C
Univ of Arizona	AZ	23,100	C
Univ of Arkansas at Fayetteville	AR	19,152	C+
Univ of Calif at Berkeley	CA	28,853	MC
Univ of Calif at Davis	CA	28,468	HC
Univ of Central Okla	OK	13,486	C
Univ of Conn	CT	25,538	HC
Univ of Dayton	OH	53,620	C
Univ of Delaware	DE	24,976	VC+
Univ of Georgia	GA	21,250	HC
Univ of Illinois at Chicago	IL	25,006	VC
Univ of Illinois at Urbana-Champaign	IL	27,006	HC
Univ of Maine	ME	20,792	C
Univ of Maryland/College Park	MD	21,938	HC
Univ of Mass Amherst	MA	26,199	VC+
Univ of Minn/Twin Cities	MN	23,519	HC+
Univ of Missouri/Columbia	MO	18,201	MC
Univ of Nebr - Lincoln	NE	18,589	VC
Univ of Nevada/Reno	NV	18,010	C
Univ of New England	ME	48,880	C
Univ of New Hampshire	NH	28,562	VC
Univ of New Haven	CT	52,190	C
Univ of New Mexico	NM	15,404	C
Univ of N Car at Chapel Hill	NC	20,052	HC+
Univ of N Car at Greensboro	NC	14,690	C
Univ of North Florida	FL	15,996	VC
Univ of Northern Colo	CO	20,851	C
Univ of PR-Rio Piedras campus	PR	13,327	
Univ of St. Francis	IN	37,400	C
Univ of St. Joseph	CT	49,550	C
Univ of Southern Indiana	IN	16,501	C
Univ of Texas at Austin	TX	26,102	HC
Univ of the Incarnate Word	TX	39,162	LC
Univ of Vermont	VT	28,878	HC
Univ of Wisc-Madison	WI	20,934	MC
Univ of Wisc-Milwaukee	WI	21,496	C
Univ of Wisc-Stevens Point	WI	14,043	C
Virginia Polytechnic Inst and State Univ	VA	21,276	HC
Wayne State Univ	MI	22,016	C
West Chester Univ of Pennsylvania	PA	18,456	C
West Virginia Univ	WV	18,210	C
West Virginia Wesleyan College	WV	36,858	C
Western Illinois Univ	IL	20,825	C
Winthrop Univ	SC	23,082	C
Youngstown State Univ	OH	17,307	C

NUTRITION AND DIETETICS

School	ST	$IS	SR
Calif State Polytechnic Univ, Pomona	CA	21,541	C
CUNY/Queens College	NY	27,896	C
Mansfield Univ	PA	23,376	LC
Murray State Univ	KY	16,998	C
Radford Univ	VA	19,027	LC
Rochester Inst of Technology	NY	50,842	HC
St. Louis Univ	MO	49,866	HC
Samford Univ	AL	39,232	VC
Texas Tech Univ	TX	18,736	C+
Thomas Edison State Univ	NJ	6,350	NC
Univ of Nevada/Reno	NV	18,010	C
Univ of Rhode Island	RI	24,906	C

NUTRITION AND WELLNESS

School	ST	$IS	SR
Gannon Univ	PA	42,032	C
Piedmont College	GA	32,512	C
Rochester Inst of Technology	NY	50,842	HC
Samford Univ	AL	39,232	VC

NUTRITION EDUCATION

School	ST	$IS	SR
Ohio Univ	OH	22,924	C
St. Louis Univ	MO	49,866	HC
Univ of Cincinnati	OH	21,964	VC
Univ of Illinois at Chicago	IL	25,006	VC

NUTRITIONAL SCIENCES

School	ST	$IS	SR
Bridgewater College	VA	44,510	C
Calif Baptist Univ	CA	41,392	C
Cal State, Long Beach	CA	18,850	C
CUNY/Queens College	NY	27,896	C
Cornell Univ	NY	64,853	MC
Fontbonne Univ	MO	33,717	C
Madonna Univ	MI	29,050	C
McNeese State Univ	LA	7,838	C
Piedmont College	GA	32,512	C
Rochester Inst of Technology	NY	50,842	HC
St. Louis Univ	MO	49,866	HC
San Jose State Univ	CA	21,540	C
Syracuse Univ	NY	60,239	VC
Univ of Arizona	AZ	23,100	C
Univ of Georgia	GA	21,250	HC
Univ of Illinois at Chicago	IL	25,006	VC
Univ of Mass Lowell	MA	26,380	C
Univ of Nevada/Reno	NV	18,010	C
Univ of Wisc-Milwaukee	WI	21,496	C

OCCUPATIONAL HYGIENE & SAFETY

School	ST	$IS	SR
Ohio Univ	OH	22,924	C
Southeastern Louisiana Univ	LA	16,237	C

OCCUPATIONAL SAFETY AND HEALTH

School	ST	$IS	SR
Embry-Riddle Aeronautical Univ - Worldwide	FL	17,480	C
Fairmont State Univ	WV	15,726	C
Grand Valley State Univ	MI	22,250	C+
Howard Payne Univ	TX	34,320	C
Keene State College	NH	24,003	LC
Madonna Univ	MI	29,050	C
Marshall Univ	WV	17,242	C

School	ST	$IS	SR
Millersville Univ of Pennsylvania	PA	23,782	C
Montana Tech of the Univ of Montana	MT	15,447	C+
Murray State Univ	KY	16,998	C
N Car A&T State Univ	NC	13,365	LC
Oakland Univ	MI	20,763	C
Purdue Univ/West Lafayette	IN	20,032	MC
Southeastern Louisiana Univ	LA	16,237	C
Southeastern Okla State Univ	OK	11,875	C
Southwest Baptist Univ	MO	29,900	LC
Univ of Central Missouri	MO	18,982	C
Univ of Findlay	OH	60,139	C
Univ of N Dak	ND	15,373	C
Univ of Wisc-Milwaukee	WI	21,496	C
Western Kentucky Univ	KY	16,850	C

OCCUPATIONAL THERAPY

School	ST	$IS	SR
Allen College	IA	32,367	NC
American International College	MA	46,300	LC
Baker College of Flint	MI	13,880	NC
Barry Univ	FL	37,830	C
Bethany College	WV	36,300	NC
Boston Univ	MA	65,110	MC
Brenau Univ - Women's College	GA	37,876	LC
Cal State, Dominguez Hills	CA	19,022	LC
Calvin College	MI	41,570	VC+
Carroll Univ	WI	38,100	C+
CUNY/York College	NY	6,747	LC
Cleveland State Univ	OH	22,196	C
College of St. Benedict	MN	52,806	C
Colo State Univ-Pueblo	CO	18,234	C
Concordia Univ Wisc	WI	35,910	C
Dominican College	NY	31,270	LC
Dominican Univ of Calif	CA	57,050	C
Duquesne Univ	PA	46,822	VC
East Carolina Univ	NC	16,937	C
Eastern Kentucky Univ	KY	16,908	C
Eastern Mich Univ	MI	19,761	C
Elizabethtown College	PA	54,050	C
Florida A&M Univ	FL	15,361	C
Florida Gulf Coast Univ	FL	9,682	C
Gannon Univ	PA	42,032	C
Gwynedd Mercy Univ	PA	43,780	LC
Howard Univ	DC	37,616	C+
Husson Univ	ME	25,720	LC
Ithaca College	NY	56,766	VC
Keuka College	NY	39,762	C
Lamar Univ	TX	18,014	LC
Lenoir-Rhyne Univ	NC	43,200	C
LIU Brooklyn	NY	49,682	C
Maryville Univ of St. Louis	MO	38,046	VC+
McKendree Univ	IL	37,940	C+
Misericordia Univ	PA	43,840	C
Mount Aloysius College	PA	29,976	C
Mount Mary Univ	WI	34,650	LC
New York Univ	NY	65,860	MC
Ohio State Univ at Columbus	OH	21,703	HC+
Pennsylvania College of Technology	PA	27,333	NC
Quinnipiac Univ	CT	59,110	C
Russell Sage College	NY	39,370	C
St. Francis Univ	PA	42,268	NC
St. John's Univ	MN	51,624	C
St. Louis Univ	MO	49,866	HC
St. Vincent College	PA	44,626	C
San Jose State Univ	CA	21,540	C
Southwestern Okla State Univ	OK	11,790	C
Spalding Univ	KY	31,938	SP
St. Ambrose Univ	IA	39,019	C
St. Ambrose Univ	IA	39,019	C
St. Catherine Univ	MN	45,630	VC
SUNY / Univ at Buffalo	NY	23,122	C+
Tenn State Univ	TN	14,423	C
Touro College	NY	28,950	VC
Towson Univ	MD	17,408	VC
Tuskegee Univ	AL	28,164	C
Univ of Central Arkansas	AR	14,472	VC
Univ of Findlay	OH	60,139	C
Univ of Florida	FL	16,291	HC+
Univ of Illinois at Chicago	IL	25,006	VC
Univ of Kansas	KS	20,135	C+
Univ of Louisiana at Monroe	LA	15,970	C
Univ of Mary	ND	23,180	C
Univ of Minn/Twin Cities	MN	23,519	HC+
Univ of Missouri/Columbia	MO	18,201	MC
Univ of New England	ME	48,880	C
Univ of New Hampshire	NH	28,562	VC
Univ of Scranton	PA	54,962	VC
Univ of Southern Calif	CA	66,631	C
Univ of Southern Indiana	IN	16,501	C
Univ of the Sciences	PA	54,038	VC
Univ of Wisc-La Crosse	WI	15,247	C+
Univ of Wisc-Milwaukee	WI	21,496	C
Utica College	NY	30,430	C
Walla Walla Univ	WA	30,417	NC
Wartburg College	IA	47,840	C
West Virginia Univ	WV	18,210	C
Western Mich Univ	MI	21,054	C
Worcester State Univ	MA	20,977	C

OCEAN ENGINEERING

School	ST	$IS	SR
Florida Atlantic Univ	FL	17,339	C
Florida Inst of Technology	FL	53,306	VC
Mass Inst of Technology	MA	62,662	MC
Texas A&M Univ	TX	20,521	VC+
Texas A&M Univ at Galveston	TX	15,920	C
United States Naval Academy	MD		MC
Univ of New Hampshire	NH	28,562	VC
Univ of Rhode Island	RI	24,906	C
Univ of Washington	WA	23,149	VC
Virginia Polytechnic Inst and State Univ	VA	21,276	HC

OCEANOGRAPHY

School	ST	$IS	SR
Bowdoin College	ME	63,500	MC
Central Mich Univ	MI	20,330	C
Florida Inst of Technology	FL	53,306	VC
Hawaii Pacific Univ	HI	33,420	C
Humboldt State Univ	CA	20,514	C
Maine Maritime Academy	ME	22,536	C
Millersville Univ of Pennsylvania	PA	23,782	C
Old Dominion Univ	VA	20,910	C
Prescott College	AZ	33,284	C
Texas A&M Univ at Galveston	TX	15,920	C
United States Naval Academy	MD		MC
Univ of Mich/Ann Arbor	MI	24,410	MC
Univ of New England	ME	48,880	C
Univ of Washington	WA	23,149	VC
Whitman College	WA	59,772	MC

OFFICE SUPERVISION AND MANAGEMENT

School	ST	$IS	SR
Adams State Univ	CO	17,703	LC
Alabama A&M Univ	AL	18,796	C
Albany State Univ	GA	19,462	C
Baker College of Flint	MI	13,880	NC
Campbellsville Univ	KY	32,492	C
Central Conn State Univ	CT	21,203	C
Concord Univ	WV	14,954	C
Eastern Mich Univ	MI	19,761	C
Fayetteville State Univ	NC	17,756	C
Fort Hays State Univ	KS	12,131	C
Fort Valley State Univ	GA	17,988	VC
Georgia State Univ	GA	24,332	VC
Inter-American Univ of PR-Bayamon	PR	18,785	
Johnson & Wales Univ/Providence Campus	RI	42,248	C
Middle Tenn State Univ	TN	8,650	C
Miss Valley State Univ	MS	13,233	LC
Northwestern Okla State Univ	OK	13,072	NC
Rider Univ	NJ	54,050	C
S Car State Univ	SC	20,805	LC
Southwestern Adventist Univ	TX	27,756	LC
Sul Ross State Univ	TX	15,021	LC
Tarleton State Univ	TX	15,248	LC
Universidad Adventista de las Antillas	PR	16,606	
Univ of S Car at Columbia	SC	19,725	VC+
Univ of the Cumberlands	KY	32,000	C
Univ of the District of Columbia	DC	21,044	LC
Univ of Wisc-Whitewater	WI	13,976	C
Valley City State Univ	ND	13,267	C
Washington State Univ	WA	22,495	C
Wiley College	TX	18,504	C

OPERA

School	ST	$IS	SR
The Boston Conservatory at Berklee	MA	61,042	C+

OPERATIONS MANAGEMENT

School	ST	$IS	SR
Ashford Univ	CA	10,480	C
Ball State Univ	IN	19,590	C
Ferris State Univ	MI	21,445	C
George Mason Univ	VA	15,724	VC
Le Moyne College	NY	46,000	C
Marquette Univ	WI	48,390	VC+
Metropolitan State Univ	MN	7,566	C
Minn State Univ, Moorhead	MN	15,941	C
New York Univ	NY	65,860	MC
Oakland Univ	MI	20,763	C
Ohio State Univ at Columbus	OH	21,703	HC+
SUNY at Oswego	NY	21,351	C
The Univ of Utah	UT	17,924	VC
Thomas Edison State Univ	NJ	6,350	NC
Univ of Arizona	AZ	23,100	C
Univ of Cincinnati	OH	21,964	VC
Univ of Dayton	OH	53,620	C
Univ of Delaware	DE	24,976	VC+
Univ of Idaho	ID	15,348	C
Univ of Maryland/College Park	MD	21,938	HC
Univ of Mass Amherst	MA	26,199	VC+
Univ of Mass Dartmouth	MA	25,658	C
Univ of Missouri-St. Louis	MO		C
Univ of N Dak	ND	15,373	C
Univ of North Texas	TX	19,198	C
Univ of Pennsylvania	PA	63,526	MC
Univ of Portland	OR	52,152	VC
Univ of Scranton	PA	54,962	VC
Univ of Wisc-Madison	WI	20,934	MC
Univ of Wisc-Milwaukee	WI	21,496	C
Washington State Univ	WA	22,495	C
Western Washington Univ	WA	18,003	C+

OPERATIONS RESEARCH

School	ST	$IS	SR
Boston College	MA	65,737	MC
Bryant Univ	RI	55,646	VC
Canisius College	NY	47,537	C
CUNY/Baruch College	NY	21,609	HC
Columbia Univ/City of New York	NY	62,958	MC
LIU Brooklyn	NY	49,682	C
New York Univ	NY	65,860	MC
Princeton Univ	NJ	57,610	MC
United States Air Force Academy	CO		C
United States Coast Guard Academy	CT	942	MC
United States Military Academy at West Point	NY		HC+
United States Naval Academy	MD		MC
Univ of Calif at Berkeley	CA	28,853	MC
Univ of Dayton	OH	53,620	C
Univ of Illinois at Urbana-Champaign	IL	27,006	HC

OPERATIONS RESEARCH AND ENGINEERING

School	ST	$IS	SR
Cornell Univ	NY	64,853	MC

OPHTHALMIC TECHNOLOGY

School	ST	$IS	SR
Old Dominion Univ	VA	20,910	C

OPTICAL ENGINEERING

School	ST	$IS	SR
Rose-Hulman Inst of Technology	IN	57,303	MC
Univ of Alabama in Huntsville	AL	19,445	VC
Univ of Arizona	AZ	23,100	C
Univ of Rochester	NY	65,032	MC

OPTICS

School	ST	$IS	SR
Capitol Technology Univ	MD	31,410	C
Saginaw Valley State Univ	MI	18,530	C
Univ of Arizona	AZ	23,100	C
Univ of Central Florida	FL	15,922	VC
Univ of Rochester	NY	65,032	MC

OPTOMETRY

School	ST	$IS	SR
Baylor Univ	TX	53,760	HC
Indiana Univ Bloomington	IN	20,429	VC
Oral Roberts Univ	OK	34,316	C
Univ of Calif at Berkeley	CA	28,853	MC
Walla Walla Univ	WA	30,417	NC

ORGAN PERFORMANCE

School	ST	$IS	SR
Boston Univ	MA	65,110	MC
Houghton College	NY	39,090	C
Indiana Univ Bloomington	IN	20,429	VC
Samford Univ	AL	39,232	VC
Texas Christian Univ	TX	54,670	HC
The Master's Univ	CA	43,870	C+
Wright State Univ	OH	16,983	C

ORGANIZATIONAL BEHAVIOR

School	ST	$IS	SR
Assumption College	MA	47,920	C+
Benedictine Univ	IL	38,300	C
Bryant Univ	RI	55,646	VC
Coe College	IA	51,570	VC
College of St. Scholastica	MN	44,640	C
DePaul Univ	IL	47,623	VC
Franklin Univ	OH	56,262	SP
Hannibal-LaGrange Univ	MO	29,815	C
Huntington Univ	IN	33,996	C
Ithaca College	NY	56,766	VC
Johnson & Wales Univ/Denver Campus	CO	42,707	C
La Salle Univ	PA	55,790	C
Methodist Univ	NC	43,600	C
National Univ	CA	14,730	LC
New York Univ	NY	65,860	MC
Northwestern Univ	IL	66,344	MC
Oral Roberts Univ	OK	34,316	C
Pitzer College	CA	66,192	MC
Robert Morris Univ	PA	37,834	C
Rollins College	FL	58,670	HC
St. Louis Univ	MO	49,866	HC
The Lincoln Univ	PA	15,154	NC
United States Military Academy at West Point	NY		HC+
Univ of Calif at Davis	CA	28,468	HC
Univ of Central Missouri	MO	18,982	C
Univ of Cincinnati	OH	21,964	VC
Univ of Illinois at Urbana-Champaign	IL	27,006	HC
Univ of Mich/Ann Arbor	MI	24,410	MC
Univ of Minn Crookston	MN	19,739	C
Univ of North Texas	TX	19,198	C
Univ of Okla	OK	18,911	VC
Univ of San Francisco	CA	58,484	VC
Univ of Tulsa	OK	52,625	HC+
Woodbury Univ	CA	46,958	C

ORGANIZATIONAL LEADERSHIP AND MANAGEMENT

School	ST	$IS	SR
Adams State Univ	CO	17,703	LC
Alderson Broaddus Univ	WV	26,149	C
Arizona State Univ at the Polytechnic Campus	AZ	21,360	VC
Ashford Univ	CA	10,480	C
Auburn Univ at Montgomery	AL	15,290	C
Aurora Univ	IL	33,970	C
Baldwin Wallace Univ	OH	41,106	C
Blackburn College	IL	28,526	LC
Bluffton Univ	OH	40,950	C
Brown Univ	RI	64,566	MC
Bryant Univ	RI	55,646	VC
Calif Baptist Univ	CA	41,392	C
Cameron Univ	OK	11,072	NC
Carroll Univ	WI	38,100	C+
Claflin Univ	SC	33,764	LC
College of St Joseph	VT	32,400	LC
Concordia Univ St. Paul	MN	29,050	C
Defiance College	OH	41,630	C
Drexel Univ	PA	65,432	VC+
Drury Univ	MO	33,791	VC
Eastern Illinois Univ	IL	21,126	C
Eastern Univ	PA	39,540	C
Edgewood College	WI	35,950	C
George Fox Univ	OR	42,938	C
Greenville College	IL	27,012	C
Hilbert College	NY	30,850	C
Indiana Univ-Purdue Univ Fort Wayne	IN	17,553	C
Indiana Univ-Purdue Univ Indianapolis	IN	18,635	C
Keystone College	PA	28,680	LC
Le Moyne College	NY	46,000	C
Lewis Univ	IL	40,370	C
Loyola Univ Chicago	IL	55,802	VC
Lubbock Christian Univ	TX	28,426	C
Marquette Univ	WI	48,390	VC+
Maryville Univ of St. Louis	MO	38,046	VC+
McNeese State Univ	LA	7,838	C
MidAmerica Nazarene Univ	KS	35,550	C
Millikin Univ	IL	42,158	C
Missouri Baptist Univ	MO	35,594	C
Mount Aloysius College	PA	29,976	C
Mount St. Joseph Univ	OH	33,880	C
National Univ	CA	14,730	LC
Northern Kentucky Univ	KY	16,486	C
Nyack College	NY	34,050	NC
Ohio Valley Univ	WV	29,480	C
Palm Beach Atlantic Univ	FL	39,720	C
Point Loma Nazarene Univ	CA	43,450	C
Point Park Univ	PA	41,270	C
Prescott College	AZ	33,284	C
Purdue Univ/Northwest	IN	15,038	C
Purdue Univ/West Lafayette	IN	20,032	MC
St. Joseph's Univ	PA	57,544	VC+
St. Louis Univ	MO	49,866	HC
Samford Univ	AL	39,232	VC
Seattle Univ	WA	50,811	VC+
Simpson Univ	CA	33,700	C
Southwestern Okla State Univ	OK	11,790	C
Spring Hill College	AL	48,488	C
St. Ambrose Univ	IA	39,019	C
St. Ambrose Univ	IA	39,019	C
St. Joseph's College, New York/Brooklyn Campus	NY	25,114	LC
St. Joseph's College, New York/Long Island Campus	NY	25,124	C
Thomas Edison State Univ	NJ	6,350	NC
Tiffin Univ	OH	31,380	C
Union College	KY	32,310	C
Univ of Charleston	WV	35,000	C
Univ of Delaware	DE	24,976	VC+
Univ of Louisiana at Monroe	LA	15,970	C
Univ of Minn/Duluth	MN	20,292	C+
Univ of Nebr - Lincoln	NE	18,589	VC
Univ of North Texas	TX	19,198	C
Univ of St. Francis	IL	39,924	C
Univ of Wisc-Eau Claire	WI	15,797	VC
Univ of Wyoming	WY	15,375	C+
Viterbo Univ	WI	34,660	C
Voorhees College	SC	19,976	C
Washington Adventist Univ	MD	31,440	LC
Wayne State Univ	MI	22,016	C
West Liberty Univ	WV	15,512	C
Wheeling Jesuit Univ	WV	37,106	LC
Wright State Univ	OH	16,983	C

OUTDOOR LEADERSHIP/ EDUCATION

School	ST	$IS	SR
Black Hills State Univ	SD	15,899	C
Messiah College	PA	43,100	C+
Montana State Univ-Billings	MT	22,960	C
Montreat College	NC	31,298	LC
North Greenville Univ	SC	25,930	C+
West Liberty Univ	WV	15,512	C

OUTDOOR MINISTRY & ADVENTURE LEADERSHIP

School	ST	$IS	SR
Eastern Mennonite Univ	VA	42,550	C

ST = STATE $IS = IN-STATE COSTS SR = SELECTOR RATING

PACIFIC AREA STUDIES

School	ST	$IS	SR
Brigham Young Univ/Hawaii	HI	11,290	C
Hawaii Pacific Univ	HI	33,420	C
New York Univ	NY	65,860	MC
Univ of Hawaii at Manoa	HI	23,221	C

PACKAGING

School	ST	$IS	SR
Mich State Univ	MI	23,898	VC+
Univ of Wisc-Stout	WI	19,667	C

PAINTING

School	ST	$IS	SR
Adams State Univ	CO	17,703	LC
Andrews Univ	MI	28,030	C+
Aquinas College - Mich	MI	38,876	HC
Art Academy of Cincinnati	OH	36,252	SP
Barton College	NC	38,686	LC
Bennington College	VT	63,960	MC
Biola Univ	CA	46,402	C+
Boston Univ	MA	65,110	MC
Calif College of the Arts	CA	52,758	SP
Cal State, San Bernardino	CA	12,000	C
Cleveland Inst of Art	OH	51,439	C+
College for Creative Studies	MI	48,875	SP
Colo State Univ	CO	22,162	VC
Columbia College - Missouri	MO	27,803	C
Dominican Univ	IL	41,222	C
Escuela de Artes Plasticas de PR	PR	11,236	
Ferris State Univ	MI	21,445	C
Harding Univ	AR	25,421	C
Hofstra Univ	NY	55,960	C+
Howard Univ	DC	37,616	C+
Indiana Univ-Purdue Univ Fort Wayne	IN	17,553	C
Indiana Wesleyan Univ	IN	33,674	C
Kansas City Art Inst	MO	44,308	C+
Kutztown Univ of Pennsylvania	PA	19,056	LC
Laguna College of Art and Design	CA	41,422	LC
Lewis Univ	IL	40,370	C
Maine College of Art	ME	43,794	SP
Marshall Univ	WV	17,242	C
Maryland Inst College of Art	MD	56,795	SP
Marywood Univ	PA	46,900	C
Mass College of Art and Design	MA	24,800	SP
Memphis College of Art	TN	39,750	C
Milwaukee Inst of Art and Design	WI	44,960	SP
Minneapolis College of Art and Design	MN	44,238	SP
Montserrat College of Art	MA	38,150	SP
Moore College of Art and Design	PA	50,135	SP
Oberlin College	OH	66,012	MC
Ohio Univ	OH	22,924	C
Otis College of Art and Design	CA	55,858	SP
Pacific Northwest College of Art	OR	38,494	SP
Rhode Island School of Design	RI	59,960	SP
San Francisco Art Inst	CA	58,505	SP
Santa Fe Univ of Art and Design	NM	39,980	SP
Savannah College of Art and Design	GA	49,595	C
School of the Art Inst of Chicago	IL	56,230	SP
St. Ambrose Univ	IA	39,019	C
St. Ambrose Univ	IA	39,019	C
SUNY / Buffalo State College	NY	20,842	C
SUNY / SUNY Fredonia	NY	20,818	C
SUNY at Binghamton	NY	22,861	MC
SUNY at New Paltz	NY	19,200	C
Syracuse Univ	NY	60,239	VC
Temple Univ	PA	24,392	VC
The Catholic Univ of America	DC	56,356	VC
Univ of Dallas	TX	45,500	VC+
Univ of Hartford	CT	49,776	C
Univ of Illinois at Chicago	IL	25,006	VC
Univ of Illinois at Urbana-Champaign	IL	27,006	HC
Univ of Iowa	IA	18,683	VC+
Univ of Kansas	KS	20,135	C+
Univ of Mass Dartmouth	MA	25,658	C
Univ of Miami	FL	63,494	MC
Univ of Mich/Ann Arbor	MI	24,410	MC
Univ of Oregon	OR	22,972	C
Univ of San Francisco	CA	58,484	VC
Univ of the Arts	PA	56,579	SP
Univ of Washington	WA	23,149	VC
Virginia Commonwealth Univ	VA	23,049	C
Washington Univ in St. Louis	MO	65,366	VC
Webster Univ	MO	37,490	C
Western Washington Univ	WA	18,003	C+
Youngstown State Univ	OH	17,307	C

PAPER AND PULP SCIENCE

School	ST	$IS	SR
N Car State Univ	NC	19,515	HC+
SUNY / The College of Environmental Science and Forestry	NY	23,853	VC
Univ of Maine	ME	20,792	C
Univ of Washington	WA	23,149	VC
Univ of Wisc-Stevens Point	WI	14,043	C

PAPER ENGINEERING

School	ST	$IS	SR
SUNY / The College of Environmental Science and Forestry	NY	23,853	VC
Western Mich Univ	MI	21,054	C

PARALEGAL STUDIES

School	ST	$IS	SR
Anna Maria College	MA	48,186	C
Avila Univ	MO	35,480	C
Bay Path Univ	MA	45,349	C
Cal State, San Bernardino	CA	12,000	C
Calumet College of St. Joseph	IN	22,735	C
Central Washington Univ	WA	16,803	C
CUNY/College of Technology	NY	6,669	NC
College of St. Mary	NE	35,184	C
Concordia Univ Wisc	WI	35,910	C
Daemen College	NY	38,045	C
Davenport Univ	MI	25,896	LC
Defiance College	OH	41,630	C
Eastern Kentucky Univ	KY	16,908	C
Eastern Mich Univ	MI	19,761	C
Elms College	MA	45,646	VC
Hamline Univ	MN	45,678	VC
Hilbert College	NY	30,850	C
Hodges Univ	FL	19,080	LC
Humphreys College	CA	27,790	C
Husson Univ	ME	25,720	LC
Idaho State Univ	ID	13,619	NC
Johnson & Wales Univ/North Miami Campus	FL	42,707	C
Johnson & Wales Univ/ Providence Campus	RI	42,248	C
Kent State Univ	OH	20,732	C
Kutztown Univ of Pennsylvania	PA	19,056	LC
Lake Erie College	OH	38,914	LC
Lewis Univ	IL	40,370	C
Lock Haven Univ of Pennsylvania	PA	18,028	LC
Loyola Univ Chicago	IL	55,802	VC
Madonna Univ	MI	29,050	C
Maryville Univ of St. Louis	MO	38,046	VC+
Mercy College	NY	31,776	C
Minn State Univ, Moorhead	MN	15,941	C
Miss College	MS	25,850	C
Miss Univ for Women	MS	17,065	C
Montclair State Univ	NJ	26,210	LC
Morehead State Univ	KY	17,422	C
Mount Aloysius College	PA	29,976	C
Mount St. Joseph Univ	OH	33,880	C
Nebr Wesleyan Univ	NE	38,140	C+
Nova Southeastern Univ	FL	38,534	C+
Peirce College	PA	16,780	NC
Pennsylvania College of Technology	PA	27,333	NC
Point Park Univ	PA	41,270	C
Quinnipiac Univ	CT	59,110	C
Roger Williams Univ	RI	46,296	C+
St. Mary-of-the-Woods College	IN	39,632	LC
Samford Univ	AL	39,232	VC
Southern Illinois Univ Carbondale	IL	23,667	C
Stephen F. Austin State Univ	TX	18,406	LC
Stevenson Univ	MD	72,770	C
Suffolk Univ	MA	50,308	C
Texas Wesleyan Univ	TX	35,134	C
The Univ of Tenn at Chattanooga	TN	16,744	C
Tiffin Univ	OH	31,380	C
Tulane Univ	LA	63,396	HC+
Univ of Alaska Anchorage	AK	16,652	NC
Univ of Detroit Mercy	MI	48,816	C+
Univ of Great Falls	MT	38,524	C
Univ of La Verne	CA	55,600	C
Univ of Louisville	KY	19,824	C
Univ of Maryland/Univ College	MD	25,966	LC
Univ of Mass Boston	MA	13,435	C
Univ of Miss	MS	17,746	C+
Univ of North Georgia	GA	17,316	C
Washburn Univ	KS	15,827	C
Western Kentucky Univ	KY	16,850	C
William Woods Univ	MO	32,040	C
Winona State Univ	MN	17,535	C

PARKS AND RECREATION MANAGEMENT

School	ST	$IS	SR
Alabama State Univ	AL	14,142	NC
Arizona State Univ at the Downtown Phoenix Campus	AZ	23,680	VC
Arkansas Tech Univ	AR	15,484	C
Aurora Univ	IL	33,970	C
Belmont Abbey College	NC	48,156	C
Bemidji State Univ	MN	16,056	VC
Cal State, Sacramento	CA	20,332	C
Calif Univ of Pennsylvania	PA	14,217	LC
Central Mich Univ	MI	20,330	C
Central Washington Univ	WA	16,803	C
Cheyney Univ of Pennsylvania	PA	20,896	LC
Clemson Univ	SC		HC
Concord Univ	WV	14,954	C
Davenport Univ	MI	25,896	LC
Delaware State Univ	DE	19,376	NC
East Carolina Univ	NC	16,937	C
Eastern Washington Univ	WA	25,572	LC
Evangel Univ	MO	28,898	C
Florida International Univ	FL	19,854	C+
George Mason Univ	VA	15,724	VC
Houghton College	NY	39,090	C
Humboldt State Univ	CA	20,514	C
Huntington Univ	IN	33,996	C
Illinois State Univ	IL	23,418	VC
Indiana Inst of Technology	IN	34,240	LC
Indiana State Univ	IN	23,223	LC
Johnson & Wales Univ/ Charlotte Campus	NC	43,988	C
Johnson & Wales Univ/North Miami Campus	FL	42,707	C
Johnson & Wales Univ/ Providence Campus	RI	42,248	C
Kansas State Univ	KS	17,780	VC
Kent State Univ	OH	20,732	C
Marshall Univ	WV	17,242	C
Mich State Univ	MI	23,898	VC+
Midland Univ	NE	37,468	
Minn State Univ, Mankato	MN	15,616	C
Missouri Western State Univ	MO	16,741	
Montclair State Univ	NJ	26,210	LC
N Car State Univ	NC	19,515	HC+
Northern Arizona Univ	AZ	20,246	VC
Northern Mich Univ	MI	19,604	C
Northland College	WI	41,103	C+
Ohio Univ	OH	22,924	C
Oregon State Univ	OR	22,519	VC
Pennsylvania State Univ - Univ Park	PA	29,760	HC
Prescott College	AZ	33,284	C
Slippery Rock Univ of Pennsylvania	PA	10,360	C
S Dak State Univ	SD	15,634	C
Southwest Baptist Univ	MO	29,900	LC
Southwestern Okla State Univ	OK	11,790	C
Springfield College	MA	45,995	C
St. Thomas Aquinas College	NY	42,200	C
Stephen F. Austin State Univ	TX	18,406	LC
The Univ of Utah	UT	17,924	VC
Unity College	ME	37,670	C
Univ of Arkansas at Pine Bluff	AR	13,541	C
Univ of Idaho	ID	15,348	C
Univ of Illinois at Urbana-Champaign	IL	27,006	HC
Univ of Iowa	IA	18,683	VC+
Univ of Maine	ME	20,792	C
Univ of Maine at Machias	ME	22,960	C
Univ of Miss	MS	17,746	C+
Univ of Missouri/Columbia	MO	18,201	MC
Univ of Nebr - Lincoln	NE	18,589	VC
Univ of N Car at Greensboro	NC	14,690	C
Univ of N Car at Wilmington	NC	14,590	VC
Univ of Southern Miss	MS	13,170	C
Univ of Vermont	VT	28,878	HC
Univ of Wisc-La Crosse	WI	15,247	C+
Utah State Univ	UT	12,736	C
Virginia Polytechnic Inst and State Univ	VA	21,276	HC
Virginia Wesleyan College	VA	43,728	LC
West Virginia Univ	WV	18,210	C
Western Carolina Univ	NC	13,965	C
Western Illinois Univ	IL	20,825	C
Western Washington Univ	WA	18,003	C+
Wingate Univ	NC	39,950	C
York College of Pennsylvania	PA	29,240	C

PASTORAL STUDIES

School	ST	$IS	SR
Andrews Univ	MI	28,030	C+
Bethel College	IN	35,860	C
Brescia Univ	KY	29,890	VC+
Concordia Univ Wisc	WI	35,910	C
Corban Univ	OR	40,306	C
East Texas Baptist Univ	TX	33,134	C
Grace Bible College	MI	25,250	C
Greenville College	IL	27,012	C
Hope International Univ	CA	41,150	C
Houghton College	NY	39,090	C
Kentucky Christian Univ	KY	26,560	LC
Loyola Univ Chicago	IL	55,802	VC
Madonna Univ	MI	29,050	C
Marian Univ	IN	41,220	C
Morris College	SC	18,500	LC
Mount Vernon Nazarene Univ	OH	34,500	C
Newman Univ	KS	35,390	C
North Central Univ	MN	26,400	C
Northwest Univ	WA	35,876	VC
Nyack College	NY	34,050	NC
Okla Baptist Univ	OK	32,320	C
Okla Wesleyan Univ	OK	33,206	C
Olivet Nazarene Univ	IL	41,840	C
St. Mary's Univ of Minn	MN	41,210	VC
Simpson Univ	CA	33,700	C
Southeastern Univ	FL	31,765	C
Southwest Baptist Univ	MO	29,900	LC
St. Ambrose Univ	IA	39,019	C
St. Ambrose Univ	IA	39,019	C
The Master's Univ	CA	43,870	C+
Toccoa Falls College	GA	27,920	C
Trevecca Nazarene Univ	TN	31,186	C
Union College	NE	23,270	C
Union Univ	TN	33,970	VC
Universidad Adventista de las Antillas	PR	16,606	
Univ of Dallas	TX	45,500	VC+
Univ of Mary	ND	23,180	C
Univ of Northwestern - St. Paul	MN	38,160	C
Univ of St. Mary	KS	34,690	C
Vanguard Univ of Southern Calif	CA	40,740	VC
Warner Univ	FL	28,216	C

PEACE STUDIES

School	ST	$IS	SR
Berea College	KY	7,042	C
Cal State, Dominguez Hills	CA	19,022	LC
Chapman Univ	CA	63,078	VC+
Colgate Univ	NY	65,030	MC
College of St. Benedict	MN	52,806	C
College of St. Scholastica	MN	44,640	C
DePaul Univ	IL	47,623	VC
DePauw Univ	IN	58,688	HC+
Earlham College	IN	54,870	HC
Eastern Mennonite Univ	VA	42,550	C
Elon Univ	NC	44,599	VC+
Goshen College	IN	42,500	C
Goucher College	MD	55,716	VC
Guilford College	NC	44,090	C
Hamline Univ	MN	45,678	VC
Hampshire College	MA	63,824	MC
John Carroll Univ	OH	49,740	C+
Juniata College	PA	53,760	VC
Le Moyne College	NY	46,000	C
Manchester Univ	IN	40,422	C
Manhattan College	NY	51,750	C+
Marquette Univ	WI	48,390	VC+
Messiah College	PA	43,100	C+
Moravian College	PA	53,117	
Naropa Univ	CO	42,826	NC
Nazareth College	NY	45,574	C
Norwich Univ	VT	28,212	C
Ohio Dominican Univ	OH	41,340	C+
Prescott College	AZ	33,284	C
Regis Univ	CO	44,520	C
St. John's Univ	MN	51,624	C
Salisbury Univ	MD	20,714	VC
Swarthmore College	PA	63,550	MC
The Univ of Utah	UT	17,924	VC
Tufts Univ	MA		MC
Univ of Calif at Berkeley	CA	28,853	MC
Univ of Hawaii at Manoa	HI	23,221	C
Univ of Mass Lowell	MA	26,380	C
Univ of N Car at Chapel Hill	NC	20,052	HC+
Univ of Wisc-Milwaukee	WI	21,496	C
Wartburg College	IA	47,840	C
Wellesley College	MA	63,916	MC
Whitworth Univ	WA	51,732	VC

PERCUSSION

School	ST	$IS	SR
Boston Univ	MA	65,110	MC
Central Washington Univ	WA	16,803	C
Eastern Mich Univ	MI	19,761	C
Indiana Univ Bloomington	IN	20,429	VC
Indiana Univ-Purdue Univ Fort Wayne	IN	17,553	C
Marshall Univ	WV	17,242	C
Northwestern Univ	IL	66,344	MC
Roosevelt Univ	IL	40,651	VC
San Francisco Conservatory of Music	CA	57,310	SP
Syracuse Univ	NY	60,239	VC
Univ of Iowa	IA	18,683	VC+
Univ of Kansas	KS	20,135	C+
Wright State Univ	OH	16,983	C
Youngstown State Univ	OH	17,307	C

PERFORMING AND MEDIA ARTS

School	ST	$IS	SR
Cornell Univ	NY	64,853	MC

PERFORMING ARTS

School	ST	$IS	SR
Adelphi Univ	NY	48,244	C
American Univ	DC	59,379	HC+
Appalachian State Univ	NC	14,416	VC
Aquinas College - Mich	MI	38,876	HC
Arizona State Univ at the Tempe Campus	AZ	21,756	VC
Baylor Univ	TX	53,760	HC
Bennington College	VT	63,960	MC
Biola Univ	CA	46,402	C+
Blackburn College	IL	28,526	LC
Boston Univ	MA	65,110	MC
Bowling Green State Univ	OH	19,747	C
Brigham Young Univ	UT	12,748	HC
Brown Univ	RI	64,566	MC
Butler Univ	IN	51,352	VC
Calif Baptist Univ	CA	41,392	C
Carroll College	MT	39,972	C+
Carthage College	WI	48,835	C
CUNY/City College	NY	20,319	VC
Colby-Sawyer College	NH	50,790	C

School	ST	$IS	SR
College of the Ozarks	MO	7,230	C
Colo State Univ	CO	22,162	VC
Columbia College	SC	36,550	C
DePaul Univ	IL	47,623	VC
DeSales Univ	PA	43,970	C
Dominican Univ	IL	41,222	C
Eastern Kentucky Univ	KY	16,908	C
Eastern Mich Univ	MI	19,761	C
Elizabethtown College	PA	54,050	C
Emerson College	MA	54,736	HC
Ferrum College	VA	39,650	C
Fontbonne Univ	MO	33,717	C
Fordham Univ	NY	65,918	MC
Friends Univ	KS	34,455	C
Georgetown College	KY	41,440	C
Hampshire College	MA	63,824	MC
Huntington Univ	IN	33,996	C
Illinois Wesleyan Univ	IL	56,430	VC+
Ithaca College	NY	56,766	VC
Johnson C. Smith Univ	NC	25,336	LC
Johnson State College	VT	20,752	C
Kean Univ	NJ	24,650	C
Lees-McRae College	NC	33,944	C
Lindenwood Univ	MO	25,132	C
Lynn Univ	FL	49,480	LC
Mars Hill Univ	NC	42,688	C
Mary Baldwin Univ	VA	39,865	C
Mass College of Liberal Arts	MA	20,128	C
Millikin Univ	IL	42,158	C
Missouri State Univ	MO	15,190	C+
New York Univ	NY	65,860	MC
N Dak State Univ	ND	16,245	C
Northwestern Univ	IL	66,344	MC
Oakland Univ	MI	20,763	C
Oberlin College	OH	66,012	MC
Ohio Univ	OH	22,924	C
Old Dominion Univ	VA	20,910	C
Piedmont College	GA	32,512	C
Plymouth State Univ	NH	23,180	LC
Point Park Univ	PA	41,270	C
Prescott College	AZ	33,284	C
Roosevelt Univ	IL	40,651	VC
St. Mary's College of Calif	CA	57,420	C
Santa Fe Univ of Art and Design	NM	39,980	SP
Savannah College of Art and Design	GA	49,595	C
Seton Hill Univ	PA	46,972	C
Shenandoah Univ	VA	41,312	C
Southern Methodist Univ	TX	66,483	MC
Southwest Baptist Univ	MO	29,900	LC
SUNY at Geneseo	NY	20,440	VC+
Suffolk Univ	MA	50,308	C
Tarleton State Univ	TX	15,248	LC
Temple Univ	PA	24,392	VC
Texas A&M Univ	TX	20,521	VC+
The Univ of Tenn at Martin	TN	14,876	C
Univ of Arizona	AZ	23,100	C
Univ of Florida	FL	16,291	HC+
Univ of Hartford	CT	49,776	C
Univ of Iowa	IA	18,683	VC+
Univ of Mary Hardin-Baylor	TX	33,950	C+
Univ of Mich/Ann Arbor	MI	24,410	MC
Univ of Missouri-Kansas City	MO	19,563	VC
Univ of N Car School of the Arts	NC	18,040	SP
Univ of North Texas	TX	19,198	C
Univ of San Francisco	CA	58,484	VC
Univ of Southern Indiana	IN	16,501	C
Univ of Tampa	FL	36,944	C
Washington Univ in St. Louis	MO	65,366	VC
West Chester Univ of Pennsylvania	PA	18,456	C
West Texas A&M Univ	TX	13,478	C
Western Kentucky Univ	KY	16,850	C
Western Mich Univ	MI	21,054	C
Wheelock College	MA	49,225	C
Youngstown State Univ	OH	17,307	C

PERSONAL FINANCIAL PLANNING

School	ST	$IS	SR
Bryant Univ	RI	55,646	VC
Kansas State Univ	KS	17,780	VC
Lubbock Christian Univ	TX	28,426	C
Texas Tech Univ	TX	18,736	C+
Univ of Wisc-Madison	WI	20,934	MC
Western Mich Univ	MI	21,054	C

PERSONNEL MANAGEMENT

School	ST	$IS	SR
Arcadia Univ	PA	33,570	C+
Auburn Univ	AL	23,594	VC+
Auburn Univ at Montgomery	AL	15,290	C
Baylor Univ	TX	53,760	HC
Bellevue Univ	NE	20,300	NC
Bloomfield College	NJ	39,100	LC
Cal State, Long Beach	CA	18,850	C
CUNY/Baruch College	NY	21,609	HC
Dickinson State Univ	ND	12,372	LC
Eastern Mich Univ	MI	19,761	C
Eastern Washington Univ	WA	25,572	LC
Florida State Univ	FL	16,771	HC
Grand Valley State Univ	MI	22,250	C+
Hawaii Pacific Univ	HI	33,420	C
King's College	PA	46,858	C
Lamar Univ	TX	18,014	LC
Limestone College	SC	32,100	C
Louisiana Tech Univ	LA	11,422	VC
Mich State Univ	MI	23,898	VC+
Nicholls State Univ	LA	10,534	C
Northern State Univ	SD	14,505	C
Oakland Univ	MI	20,763	C
Our Lady of the Lake Univ	TX	35,012	LC
Portland State Univ	OR	19,443	C
Roosevelt Univ	IL	40,651	VC
Rowan Univ	NJ	24,491	VC+
San Francisco State Univ	CA	18,514	LC
Seton Hill Univ	PA	46,972	C
Silver Lake College of the Holy Family	WI	36,290	LC
St. Cloud State Univ	MN	10,600	C
Tarleton State Univ	TX	15,248	LC
Troy Univ	AL	16,171	C
Univ of Illinois at Urbana-Champaign	IL	27,006	HC
Univ of Louisiana at Lafayette	LA	14,516	C
Univ of Nebr - Kearney	NE	16,546	LC
Univ of PR-Rio Piedras campus	PR	13,327	
Univ of Southern Miss	MS	13,170	C
Univ of the Sacred Heart	PR	17,932	
Univ of Washington	WA	23,149	VC
Univ of Wisc-Whitewater	WI	13,976	C
Utah State Univ	UT	12,736	C
Weber State Univ	UT	10,721	C
Wilmington Univ	DE	8,546	NC

PETROLEUM SYSTEMS / GEOLOGY

School	ST	$IS	SR
Rocky Mountain College	MT	34,270	C

PETROLEUM/NATURAL GAS ENGINEERING

School	ST	$IS	SR
Colo School of Mines	CO	29,319	MC
Louisiana State Univ and A&M College	LA	18,677	VC
Marietta College	OH	46,190	C
Missouri Univ of Science and Technology	MO	18,655	HC
Montana Tech of the Univ of Montana	MT	15,447	C+
New Mexico Inst of Mining and Technology	NM	14,833	HC
Nicholls State Univ	LA	10,534	C
Pennsylvania State Univ - Univ Park	PA	29,760	HC
Stanford Univ	CA	60,409	MC
Texas A&M Univ	TX	20,521	VC+
Texas A&M Univ at Kingsville	TX	7,500	LC
Texas Tech Univ	TX	18,736	C+
Univ of Alaska Fairbanks	AK	16,179	C
Univ of Houston	TX	21,483	VC
Univ of Kansas	KS	20,135	C+
Univ of Louisiana at Lafayette	LA	14,516	C
Univ of N Dak	ND	15,373	C
Univ of Okla	OK	18,911	VC
Univ of Southern Calif	CA	66,631	C
Univ of Texas at Austin	TX	26,102	HC
Univ of Tulsa	OK	52,625	HC+
Univ of Wyoming	WY	15,375	C+
West Virginia Univ	WV	18,210	C
West Virginia Wesleyan College	WV	36,858	C

PHARMACEUTICAL CHEMISTRY

School	ST	$IS	SR
Lehigh Univ	PA	61,010	MC
Mich Tech Univ	MI	24,739	VC+
Univ of Dayton	OH	53,620	C
Univ of Mich/Ann Arbor	MI	24,410	MC
Univ of the Sciences	PA	54,038	VC

PHARMACEUTICAL SCIENCE

School	ST	$IS	SR
Albany College of Pharmacy and Health Sciences	NY	42,681	SP
Belmont Univ	TN	40,970	VC
Cedarville Univ	OH	34,990	VC
CUNY/York College	NY	6,747	LC
Cleveland State Univ	OH	22,196	C
DeSales Univ	PA	43,970	C
Duquesne Univ	PA	46,822	VC
Howard Univ	DC	37,616	C+
MCPHS Univ	MA	45,470	SP
Northeastern Univ	MA	62,703	MC
Ohio State Univ at Columbus	OH	21,703	HC+
Purdue Univ/West Lafayette	IN	20,032	MC
S Dak State Univ	SD	15,634	C
SUNY / Univ at Buffalo	NY	23,122	C+
Univ of Arizona	AZ	23,100	C
Univ of Calif at Irvine	CA	26,484	VC
Univ of Dayton	OH	53,620	C
Univ of Georgia	GA	21,250	HC
Univ of Houston	TX	21,483	VC
Univ of Louisiana at Monroe	LA	15,970	C
Univ of Mich/Ann Arbor	MI	24,410	MC
Univ of Miss	MS	17,746	C+
Univ of Pittsburgh	PA	29,568	HC+
Univ of Rhode Island	RI	24,906	C
Univ of the Sciences	PA	54,038	VC
West Chester Univ of Pennsylvania	PA	18,456	C

PHARMACOLOGY

School	ST	$IS	SR
Howard Univ	DC	37,616	C+
MCPHS Univ	MA	45,470	SP
New York Univ	NY	65,860	MC
SUNY / Univ at Buffalo	NY	23,122	C+
Stony Brook Univ/The SUNY	NY	21,881	MC
Univ of Arizona	AZ	23,100	C
Univ of Illinois at Chicago	IL	25,006	VC
Univ of Montana	MT	14,105	C
Univ of the Sciences	PA	54,038	VC
Univ of Wisc-Madison	WI	20,934	MC

PHARMACY

School	ST	$IS	SR
Butler Univ	IN	51,352	VC
Chapman Univ	CA	63,078	VC+
Drake Univ	IA	45,056	HC
Duquesne Univ	PA	46,822	VC
Florida A&M Univ	FL	15,361	C
Howard Univ	DC	37,616	C+
Husson Univ	ME	25,720	LC
Johnson C. Smith Univ	NC	25,336	LC
Lamar Univ	TX	18,014	LC
LIU Brooklyn	NY	49,682	C
MCPHS Univ	MA	45,470	SP
N Dak State Univ	ND	16,245	C
Northeastern Univ	MA	62,703	MC
Ohio Northern Univ	OH	44,050	VC
Regis Univ	CO	44,520	C
Roberts Wesleyan College	NY	38,306	C
Rutgers Univ - New Brunswick	NJ	26,632	HC
Samford Univ	AL	39,232	VC
Seton Hill Univ	PA	46,972	C
S Dak State Univ	SD	15,634	C
Southwestern Okla State Univ	OK	11,790	C
St. John's Univ	NY	55,850	C
SUNY / Univ at Buffalo	NY	23,122	C+
The College of Idaho	ID	36,415	C
Univ of Arizona	AZ	23,100	C
Univ of Calif at Santa Barbara	CA	29,091	HC
Univ of Conn	CT	25,538	HC
Univ of Illinois at Chicago	IL	25,006	VC
Univ of Iowa	IA	18,683	VC+
Univ of Kansas	KS	20,135	C+
Univ of Louisiana at Monroe	LA	15,970	C
Univ of Mich/Ann Arbor	MI	24,410	MC
Univ of Minn/Twin Cities	MN	23,519	HC+
Univ of Texas at Austin	TX	26,102	HC
Univ of the Sciences	PA	54,038	VC
Univ of Toledo	OH	19,336	NC
Walla Walla Univ	WA	30,417	NC
Washington Univ in St. Louis	MO	65,366	VC
West Virginia Univ	WV	18,210	C
Wingate Univ	NC	39,950	C

PHILOSOPHY

School	ST	$IS	SR
Adelphi Univ	NY	48,244	C
Adrian College	MI	42,400	C
Agnes Scott College	GA	51,930	VC+
Albertus Magnus College	CT	43,258	LC
Albion College	MI	52,650	C
Albright College	PA	46,660	C
Alfred Univ	NY	42,296	C+
Allegheny College	PA	55,420	VC
Alma College	MI	47,548	C
Alvernia Univ	PA	43,900	C
Alverno College	WI	33,294	LC
American International College	MA	46,300	LC
American Univ	DC	59,379	HC+
Amherst College	MA		HC+
Anderson Univ	IN	38,200	C
Angelo State Univ	TX	15,263	NC
Appalachian State Univ	NC	14,416	VC
Aquinas College	TN	30,800	C+
Aquinas College - Mich	MI	38,876	HC
Arcadia Univ	PA	33,570	C+
Arizona State Univ at the Tempe Campus	AZ	21,756	VC
Arkansas State Univ	AR	16,190	C
Asbury Univ	KY	35,180	C+
Ashland Univ	OH	21,440	C
Assumption College	MA	47,920	C+
Auburn Univ	AL	23,594	VC+
Augsburg College	MN	43,929	C
Augustana College	IL	49,658	VC
Augustana Univ	SD	38,424	VC
Aurora Univ	IL	33,970	C
Austin College	TX	45,875	VC
Azusa Pacific Univ	CA	43,972	C
Baker Univ	KS	33,350	C+
Baldwin Wallace Univ	OH	41,106	C
Ball State Univ	IN	19,590	C
Bard College	NY	64,024	HC
Bard College at Simon's Rock	MA	65,795	MC
Barnard College/Columbia Univ	NY	62,741	MC
Barry Univ	FL	37,830	C
Bates College	ME	64,500	MC
Bayamon Central Univ	PR	12,490	
Baylor Univ	TX	53,760	HC
Belhaven Univ	MS	31,016	C
Bellarmine Univ	KY	51,220	C
Bellevue Univ	NE	20,300	NC
Belmont Abbey College	NC	48,156	C
Belmont Univ	TN	40,970	VC
Beloit College	WI	55,206	HC
Bemidji State Univ	MN	16,056	VC
Benedict College	SC	28,238	NC
Benedictine College	KS	36,200	VC
Benedictine Univ	IL	38,300	C
Bennington College	VT	63,960	MC
Bentley Univ	MA	60,890	HC
Berea College	KY	7,042	C
Berry College	GA	45,286	C+
Bethel College	IN	35,860	C
Bethel Univ	MN	45,270	VC
Biola Univ	CA	46,402	C+
Birmingham-Southern College	AL	44,478	VC
Bloomfield College	NJ	39,100	LC
Bloomsburg Univ of Pennsylvania	PA	19,066	LC
Boise State Univ	ID	14,860	C
Boston College	MA	65,737	MC
Boston Univ	MA	65,110	MC
Bowdoin College	ME	63,500	MC
Bowling Green State Univ	OH	19,747	C
Brandeis Univ	MA	65,925	MC
Bridgewater State Univ	MA	21,810	C
Brigham Young Univ	UT	12,748	HC
Brown Univ	RI	64,566	MC
Bryn Athyn College	PA	31,470	C
Bryn Mawr College	PA	59,890	MC
Bucknell Univ	PA	64,616	MC
Butler Univ	IN	51,352	VC
Cabrini Univ	PA	42,591	LC
Calif Baptist Univ	CA	41,392	C
Calif Inst of Technology	CA	58,761	MC
Calif Lutheran Univ	CA	52,853	C
Calif Polytechnic State Univ	CA	17,979	HC+
Calif State Polytechnic Univ, Pomona	CA	21,541	C
Cal State, Bakersfield	CA	19,191	LC
Cal State, Chico	CA	21,440	C
Cal State, Dominguez Hills	CA	19,022	LC
Cal State, East Bay	CA	19,413	C
Cal State, Fresno	CA	16,902	LC
Cal State, Fullerton	CA	21,902	C
Cal State, Long Beach	CA	18,850	C
Cal State, Los Angeles	CA	17,186	LC
Cal State, Northridge	CA	16,859	LC
Cal State, Sacramento	CA	20,332	C
Cal State, San Bernardino	CA	12,000	C
Cal State, Stanislaus	CA	16,212	C
Calif Univ of Pennsylvania	PA	14,217	LC
Calvin College	MI	41,570	VC+
Canisius College	NY	47,537	C
Capital Univ	OH	42,982	C
Caribbean Univ	PR	15,471	
Carleton College	MN	64,071	MC
Carlow Univ	PA	38,549	LC
Carnegie Mellon Univ	PA	67,980	MC
Carroll College	MT	39,972	C+
Carson-Newman Univ	TN	34,160	C
Carthage College	WI	48,835	C
Case Western Reserve Univ	OH	60,304	MC
Castleton Univ	VT	20,186	C
Catawba College	NC	39,820	C
Centenary College of Louisiana	LA	45,650	C+
Central College	IA	44,592	C
Central Conn State Univ	CT	21,203	C
Central Methodist Univ	MO	36,830	VC
Central Mich Univ	MI	20,330	C
Central Washington Univ	WA	16,803	C
Centre College	KY	49,250	HC
Chapman Univ	CA	63,078	VC+
Christendom College	VA	32,600	VC
Christopher Newport Univ	VA	23,968	VC+
CUNY/Baruch College	NY	21,609	HC
CUNY/Brooklyn College	NY	5,884	C+
CUNY/City College	NY	20,319	VC
CUNY/College of Staten Island	NY	17,840	NC
CUNY/Hunter College	NY	31,098	VC
CUNY/John Jay College of Criminal Justice	NY	6,359	NC
CUNY/Lehman College	NY	5,778	HC+
CUNY/Queens College	NY	27,896	C
CUNY/York College	NY	6,747	LC
Claremont McKenna College	CA	67,185	MC
Clarion Univ of Pennsylvania	PA	21,608	LC
Clark Atlanta Univ	GA	31,019	LC
Clark Univ	MA	51,600	HC+
Clarke Univ	IA	38,940	C
Clemson Univ	SC		HC
Cleveland State Univ	OH	22,196	C
Coastal Carolina Univ	SC	19,766	C
Coe College	IA	51,570	VC
Colby College	ME	64,060	MC
Colby-Sawyer College	NH	50,790	C
Colgate Univ	NY	65,030	MC
College of Charleston	SC	22,699	C
College of Mount St. Vincent	NY	45,620	C
College of St. Benedict	MN	52,806	C
College of St. Elizabeth	NJ	44,432	LC
College of St. Scholastica	MN	44,640	C
College of the Holy Cross	MA	62,165	MC
College of the Ozarks	MO	7,230	C
College of William & Mary	VA		MC
Colo College	CO	62,560	MC
Colo State Univ	CO	22,162	VC

ST = STATE $IS = IN-STATE COSTS SR = SELECTOR RATING

School	ST	$IS	SR
Columbia College - Missouri	MO	27,803	C
Columbia Univ/ School of General Studies	NY	61,470	MC
Columbia Univ/City of New York	NY	62,958	MC
Concordia College - Moorhead	MN	51,088	C+
Concordia Univ, Ann Arbor	MI	35,945	VC
Conn College	CT	65,000	MC
Cornell College	IA	48,800	VC
Cornell Univ	NY	64,853	MC
Covenant College	GA	38,990	VC
Creighton Univ	NE	48,206	VC+
Curry College	MA	51,815	C
Dallas Baptist Univ	TX	33,713	C
Dartmouth College	NH	66,174	MC
Davidson College	NC	60,119	MC
Denison Univ	OH	58,860	MC
DePaul Univ	IL	47,623	VC
DePauw Univ	IN	58,688	HC+
DeSales Univ	PA	43,970	C
Dickinson College	PA	63,974	MC
Doane Univ	NE	39,184	VC
Dominican Univ	IL	41,222	C
Dordt College	IA	37,860	C+
Drake Univ	IA	45,056	HC
Drew Univ/College of Liberal Arts	NJ	61,048	VC
Drexel Univ	PA	65,432	VC+
Drury Univ	MO	33,791	VC
Duke Univ	NC	64,188	
Duquesne Univ	PA	46,822	VC
D'Youville College	NY	36,780	C
Earlham College	IN	54,870	HC
East Carolina Univ	NC	16,937	C
East Stroudsburg Univ	PA	18,334	C
East Tenn State Univ	TN	13,994	C
Eastern Conn State Univ	CT	23,059	C
Eastern Illinois Univ	IL	21,126	C
Eastern Kentucky Univ	KY	16,908	C
Eastern Mennonite Univ	VA	42,550	C
Eastern Mich Univ	MI	19,761	C
Eastern Univ	PA	39,540	C
Eastern Washington Univ	WA	25,572	LC
Eckerd College	FL	52,874	C
Edinboro Univ	PA	15,940	LC
Edward Waters College	FL	20,607	NC
Elizabethtown College	PA	54,050	C
Elmhurst College	IL	45,428	C
Elon Univ	NC	44,599	VC+
Emmanuel College	MA	52,110	C+
Emory and Henry College	VA	41,410	C
Emory Univ	GA	60,786	MC
Erskine College	SC	45,460	C
Eugene Lang College/The New School for Liberal Arts	NY	55,650	C
Eureka College	IL	30,220	C
Excelsior College	NY	14,080	SP
Fairfield Univ	CT	59,860	VC+
Fairleigh Dickinson Univ/ College at Florham	NJ	52,062	C
Fairleigh Dickinson Univ/ Metropolitan Campus	NJ	40,254	C
Faulkner Univ	AL	26,410	C
Felician Univ	NJ	45,370	LC
Ferrum College	VA	39,650	C
Fisk Univ	TN	32,066	LC
Florida Atlantic Univ	FL	17,339	C
Florida Gulf Coast Univ	FL	9,682	C
Florida International Univ	FL	19,854	C+
Florida Memorial Univ	FL	22,270	LC
Florida State Univ	FL	16,771	HC
Fordham Univ	NY	65,918	MC
Fort Hays State Univ	KS	12,131	C
Fort Lewis College	CO	18,980	C
Franciscan Univ of Steubenville	OH	33,980	VC
Franklin and Marshall College	PA	63,170	HC
Franklin College	IN	39,380	C
Fresno Pacific Univ	CA	37,370	C
Frostburg State Univ	MD	17,280	LC
Furman Univ	SC	58,092	VC+
Gallaudet Univ	DC	29,118	LC
Gannon Univ	PA	42,032	C
Geneva College	PA	35,450	C
George Fox Univ	OR	42,938	C
George Mason Univ	VA	15,724	VC
George Washington Univ	DC	62,835	MC
Georgetown College	KY	41,440	C
Georgetown Univ	DC	65,926	MC
Georgia College & State Univ	GA	21,148	C+
Georgia Southern Univ	GA	16,596	C
Georgia State Univ	GA	24,332	VC
Gettysburg College	PA	63,000	HC
Gonzaga Univ	WA	50,888	HC
Gordon College	MA	46,472	C+
Goucher College	MD	55,716	VC
Graceland Univ	IA	35,290	C
Grand Rapids Theological Seminary/Cornerstone Univ	MI	33,338	C
Grand Valley State Univ	MI	22,250	C+
Green Mountain College	VT	45,228	LC
Greenville College	IL	27,012	C
Grinnell College	IA	60,738	MC
Grove City College	PA	25,692	VC
Guilford College	NC	44,090	C
Gustavus Adolphus College	MN	52,433	HC
Hamilton College	NY	64,250	MC
Hamline Univ	MN	45,678	VC
Hampden-Sydney College	VA	56,248	C+
Hampshire College	MA	63,824	MC
Hanover College	IN	46,364	C+
Hardin-Simmons Univ	TX	33,966	C
Hartwick College	NY	51,270	C
Harvard College/Harvard Univ	MA	60,659	MC
Hastings College	NE	35,380	C+
Haverford College	PA	66,490	MC
Heidelberg Univ	OH	39,200	C
Hendrix College	AR	54,020	VC+
High Point Univ	NC	45,977	C
Hillsdale College	MI	35,722	MC
Hiram College	OH	43,230	C
Hofstra Univ	NY	55,960	C+
Hollins Univ	VA	49,635	VC
Holy Names Univ	CA	46,630	LC
Hood College	MD	54,840	C
Hope College	MI	39,940	VC
Houghton College	NY	39,090	C
Howard Univ	DC	37,616	C+
Humboldt State Univ	CA	20,514	C
Huntington Univ	IN	33,996	C
Idaho State Univ	ID	13,619	NC
Illinois College	IL	40,850	VC
Illinois State Univ	IL	23,418	VC
Illinois Wesleyan Univ	IL	56,430	VC+
Indiana State Univ	IN	23,223	LC
Indiana Univ Bloomington	IN	20,429	VC
Indiana Univ Northwest	IN	7,072	C
Indiana Univ of Pennsylvania	PA	23,614	LC
Indiana Univ South Bend	IN	14,242	C
Indiana Univ Southeast	IN	14,242	LC
Indiana Univ-Purdue Univ Fort Wayne	IN	17,553	C
Indiana Univ-Purdue Univ Indianapolis	IN	18,635	C
Iona College	NY	50,984	C
Iowa State Univ	IA	17,570	C
Ithaca College	NY	56,766	VC
Jacksonville Univ	FL	46,230	C
James Madison Univ	VA	19,084	VC
John Brown Univ	AR	33,132	VC
John Carroll Univ	OH	49,740	C+
Johns Hopkins Univ	MD	65,386	MC
Juniata College	PA	53,760	VC
Kalamazoo College	MI	53,931	HC+
Kansas State Univ	KS	17,780	VC
Kennesaw State Univ	GA	19,592	VC
Kent State Univ	OH	20,732	C
Kenyon College	OH	63,330	MC
King Univ	TN	34,660	C
King's College	PA	46,858	C
Knox College	IL	52,615	VC+
Kutztown Univ of Pennsylvania	PA	19,056	LC
La Salle Univ	PA	55,790	C
Lafayette College	PA	63,355	MC
Lake Forest College	IL	50,652	VC
Lakeland Univ	WI	35,130	C
Lawrence Univ	WI	54,498	HC
Le Moyne College	NY	46,000	C
Lebanon Valley College	PA	51,530	C
Lehigh Univ	PA	61,010	MC
Lenoir-Rhyne Univ	NC	43,200	C
Lewis & Clark College	OR	58,434	HC+
Lewis Univ	IL	40,370	C
Linfield College	OR	52,010	C
Lipscomb Univ	TN	41,296	VC
LIU Brooklyn	NY	49,682	C
LIU Post	NY	49,682	C
Lock Haven Univ of Pennsylvania	PA	18,028	LC
Loras College	IA	39,222	C
Louisiana College	LA	21,886	C
Louisiana State Univ and A&M College	LA	18,677	VC
Loyola Marymount Univ	CA	58,038	HC
Loyola Univ Chicago	IL	55,802	VC
Loyola Univ Maryland	MD	60,300	VC
Loyola Univ New Orleans	LA	51,708	VC+
Luther College	IA	48,540	C+
Lycoming College	PA	48,580	C
Lynchburg College	VA	46,740	C
Macalester College	MN	61,905	MC
MacMurray College	IL	33,620	C
Malone Univ	OH	38,448	C
Manchester Univ	IN	40,422	C
Manhattan College	NY	51,750	C+
Manhattanville College	NY	51,440	C+
Mansfield Univ	PA	23,376	LC
Marian Univ	IN	41,220	C
Marist College	NY	49,860	VC
Marquette Univ	WI	48,390	VC+
Marshall Univ	WV	17,242	C
Mary Baldwin Univ	VA	39,865	C
Marymount Univ	VA	41,570	LC
Marywood Univ	PA	46,900	C
Mass College of Liberal Arts	MA	20,128	C
Mass Inst of Technology	MA	62,662	MC
McDaniel College	MD	51,380	VC
McKendree Univ	IL	37,940	C+
McPherson College	KS	34,909	C
Mercer Univ	GA	45,348	VC
Mercyhurst Univ	PA	47,420	C
Merrimack College	MA	52,770	C
Messiah College	PA	43,100	C+
Metropolitan State Univ	MN	7,566	C
Metropolitan State Univ of Denver	CO	29,889	LC
Miami Univ	OH	27,190	HC+
Mich State Univ	MI	23,898	VC+
Middle Tenn State Univ	TN	8,650	C
Middlebury College	VT	64,332	MC
Millersville Univ of Pennsylvania	PA	23,782	C
Millikin Univ	IL	42,158	C
Mills College	CA	59,163	VC
Millsaps College	MS	50,080	C+
Minn State Univ, Mankato	MN	15,616	C
Minn State Univ, Moorhead	MN	15,941	C
Misericordia Univ	PA	43,840	C
Miss State Univ	MS	11,454	C+
Missouri State Univ	MO	15,190	C+
Missouri Univ of Science and Technology	MO	18,655	HC
Missouri Valley College	MO	28,150	C
Molloy College	NY	40,440	C
Monmouth College	IL	42,260	C
Montana State Univ	MT	15,500	C+
Montclair State Univ	NJ	26,210	LC
Moravian College	PA	53,117	
Morehead State Univ	KY	17,422	C
Morehouse College	GA	40,064	C
Morgan State Univ	MD	17,190	LC
Morningside College	IA	36,865	C
Mount Holyoke College	MA	56,746	MC
Mount Mary Univ	WI	34,650	LC
Mount Mercy Univ	IA	36,826	C
Mount St. Mary's Univ	MD	51,610	C
Mount St. Mary's Univ - Chalon Campus	CA	43,897	VC+
Mount Vernon Nazarene Univ	OH	34,500	C
Muhlenberg College	PA	56,645	VC+
Murray State Univ	KY	16,998	C
Muskingum Univ	OH	35,966	C
Nazareth College	NY	45,574	C
Nebr Wesleyan Univ	NE	38,140	C+
New College of Florida	FL	15,848	MC
New England College	NH	50,364	C
New Jersey City Univ	NJ	21,456	LC
New Mexico State Univ	NM	14,050	C
New York Univ	NY	65,860	MC
Newberry College	SC	34,550	C
Newman Univ	KS	35,390	C
Niagara Univ	NY	41,010	C
N Car State Univ	NC	19,515	HC+
North Central College	IL	48,712	VC
North Park Univ	IL	35,860	C
Northeastern Illinois Univ	IL	12,529	LC
Northeastern Univ	MA	62,703	MC
Northern Arizona Univ	AZ	20,246	VC
Northern Illinois Univ	IL	20,176	C
Northern Kentucky Univ	KY	16,486	C
Northern Mich Univ	MI	19,604	C
Northwest Missouri State Univ	MO	17,737	C
Northwest Univ	WA	35,876	VC
Northwestern College of Iowa	IA	38,400	C+
Northwestern Univ	IL	66,344	MC
Notre Dame de Namur Univ	CA	46,526	LC
Nova Southeastern Univ	FL	38,534	C+
Nyack College	NY	34,050	NC
Oakland Univ	MI	20,763	C
Oberlin College	OH	66,012	MC
Occidental College	CA	65,530	MC
Oglethorpe Univ	GA	44,200	C+
Ohio Dominican Univ	OH	41,340	C+
Ohio Northern Univ	OH	44,050	VC
Ohio State Univ at Columbus	OH	21,703	HC+
Ohio Univ	OH	22,924	C
Ohio Wesleyan Univ	OH	49,460	VC
Okla Baptist Univ	OK	32,320	C
Okla City Univ	OK	40,476	VC
Okla State Univ	OK	17,180	VC
Old Dominion Univ	VA	20,910	C
Olivet Nazarene Univ	IL	41,840	C
Oral Roberts Univ	OK	34,316	C
Oregon State Univ	OR	22,519	VC
Otterbein Univ	OH	41,630	C
Ouachita Baptist Univ	AR	32,320	C
Our Lady of the Lake Univ	TX	35,012	LC
Pacific Lutheran Univ	WA	49,960	VC
Pacific Univ	OR	52,876	C
Palm Beach Atlantic Univ	FL	39,720	C
Pennsylvania State Univ - Univ Park	PA	29,760	HC
Pepperdine Univ	CA	74,460	HC+
Piedmont College	GA	32,512	C
Pitzer College	CA	66,192	MC
Plymouth State Univ	NH	23,180	LC
Point Loma Nazarene Univ	CA	43,450	C
Pomona College	CA	64,957	MC
Pontifical Catholic Univ of PR	PR	10,534	
Portland State Univ	OR	19,443	C
Princeton Univ	NJ	57,610	MC
Principia College	IL	39,010	C+
Providence College	RI	60,760	VC
Purdue Univ/Northwest	IN	15,038	C
Purdue Univ/West Lafayette	IN	20,032	MC
Queens Univ of Charlotte	NC	39,543	C
Quinnipiac Univ	CT	59,110	C
Randolph College	VA	45,660	VC
Randolph-Macon College	VA	49,910	C
Reed College	OR	65,300	MC
Regis Univ	CO	44,520	C
Rensselaer Polytechnic Inst	NY	63,436	MC
Rhode Island College	RI	17,694	LC
Rhodes College	TN	51,900	HC
Rice Univ	TX	57,668	MC
Rider Univ	NJ	54,050	C
Ripon College	WI	46,911	C+
Roanoke College	VA	54,114	VC
Roberts Wesleyan College	NY	38,306	C
Rochester Inst of Technology	NY	50,842	HC
Rockford Univ	IL	36,030	C
Rockhurst Univ	MO	29,220	C
Roger Williams Univ	RI	46,296	C+
Rollins College	FL	58,670	HC
Roosevelt Univ	IL	40,651	VC
Rosemont College	PA	30,980	C
Rutgers Univ - Camden	NJ	26,146	C
Rutgers Univ - New Brunswick	NJ	26,632	HC
Rutgers Univ - Newark	NJ	27,288	C
St. Anselm College	NH	52,560	C+
St. Francis Univ	PA	42,268	NC
St. John's Univ	MN	51,624	C
St. Joseph's College of Maine	ME	46,485	C
St. Joseph's Univ	PA	57,544	VC+
St. Louis Univ	MO	49,866	HC
St. Mary's College	IN	50,600	C
St. Mary's College of Calif	CA	57,420	C
St. Mary's Univ of Minn	MN	41,210	VC
St. Michael's College	VT	51,725	VC+
St. Peter's Univ	NJ	49,192	C
St. Vincent College	PA	44,626	C
St. Xavier Univ	IL	43,310	C
Salem College	NC	37,694	HC
Salisbury Univ	MD	20,714	VC
Salve Regina Univ	RI	51,470	C
Sam Houston State Univ	TX	18,792	C
Samford Univ	AL	39,232	VC
San Diego State Univ	CA	21,896	C+
San Francisco State Univ	CA	18,514	LC
San Jose State Univ	CA	21,540	C
Sarah Lawrence College	NY	63,388	HC
Schreiner Univ	TX	34,626	LC
Scripps College	CA	66,664	MC
Seattle Pacific Univ	WA	47,439	C+
Seattle Univ	WA	50,811	VC+
Seton Hall Univ	NJ	55,514	C
Seton Hill Univ	PA	46,972	C
Sewanee: The Univ of the South	TN	54,500	MC
Siena College	NY	48,916	C+
Siena Heights Univ	MI	32,040	C
Silver Lake College of the Holy Family	WI	36,290	LC
Simmons College	MA	53,090	VC
Simpson College	IA	43,839	VC
Skidmore College	NY	64,214	HC
Slippery Rock Univ of Pennsylvania	PA	10,360	C
Smith College	MA	63,914	MC
Sonoma State Univ	CA	27,806	C
Southeast Missouri State Univ	MO	15,498	C
Southern Conn State Univ	CT	21,924	LC
Southern Illinois Univ Carbondale	IL	23,667	C
Southern Illinois Univ Edwardsville	IL	22,643	C
Southern Methodist Univ	TX	66,483	MC
Southern Nazarene Univ	OK	32,798	NC
Southern Oregon Univ	OR	19,117	C
Southwestern Univ	TX	50,720	VC
Spelman College	GA	38,751	C
Spring Arbor Univ	MI	36,000	C
Spring Hill College	AL	48,488	C
St. Ambrose Univ	IA	39,019	C
St. Ambrose Univ	IA	39,019	C
St. Bonaventure Univ	NY	44,237	C
St. Catherine Univ	MN	45,630	VC
St. Cloud State Univ	MN	10,600	C
St. Edward's Univ	TX	53,100	VC
St. Francis College	NY	38,800	LC
St. John Fisher College	NY	43,620	C
St. John's College, Santa Fe	NM	60,109	HC+
St. John's College-Annapolis	MD	60,142	MC
St. John's Univ	NY	55,850	C
St. Lawrence Univ	NY	64,390	VC
St. Mary's College of Maryland	MD	26,634	VC
St. Mary's Univ	TX	37,500	C
St. Norbert College	WI	44,525	VC
St. Olaf College	MN	54,260	HC+
St. Thomas Aquinas College	NY	42,200	C
Stanford Univ	CA	60,409	MC
SUNY / Buffalo State College	NY	20,842	C
SUNY / SUNY College at Old Westbury	NY	16,860	C
SUNY / SUNY Cortland	NY	20,706	VC
SUNY / SUNY Fredonia	NY	20,818	C
SUNY / SUNY Oneonta	NY	19,712	C+
SUNY / SUNY Plattsburgh	NY	18,814	C
SUNY / SUNY Potsdam	NY	20,404	C+
SUNY / Univ at Buffalo	NY	23,122	C+
SUNY at Binghamton	NY	22,861	MC
SUNY at Geneseo	NY	20,440	VC+
SUNY at New Paltz	NY	19,200	C
SUNY at Oswego	NY	21,351	C
SUNY at Purchase	NY	17,900	C

ST = STATE $IS = IN-STATE COSTS SR = SELECTOR RATING

School	ST	$IS	SR
SUNY SUNY Albany	NY	22,165	C
Stephen F. Austin State Univ	TX	18,406	LC
Stetson Univ	FL	53,544	VC
Stevens Inst of Technology	NJ	62,338	MC
Stockton Univ	NJ	25,059	
Stonehill College	MA	55,030	C+
Stony Brook Univ/The SUNY	NY	21,881	MC
Suffolk Univ	MA	50,308	C
Susquehanna Univ	PA	55,340	VC
Swarthmore College	PA	63,550	MC
Syracuse Univ	NY	60,239	VC
Taylor Univ	IN	40,317	C+
Temple Univ	PA	24,392	VC
Texas A&M Univ	TX	20,521	VC+
Texas Christian Univ	TX	54,670	HC
Texas Lutheran Univ	TX	38,620	C
Texas State Univ	TX	19,350	C
Texas Tech Univ	TX	18,736	C+
The Catholic Univ of America	DC	56,356	VC
The College at Brockport - SUNY	NY	20,346	C
The College of Idaho	ID	36,415	C
The College of New Jersey	NJ	31,909	HC
The College of New Rochelle	NY	46,300	VC
The College of Wooster	OH	57,900	VC+
The Lincoln Univ	PA	15,154	NC
The Univ of Akron	OH	21,477	C
The Univ of Tenn at Chattanooga	TN	16,744	C
The Univ of Tenn at Knoxville	TN	22,112	VC
The Univ of Tenn at Martin	TN	14,876	C
The Univ of Utah	UT	17,924	VC
Thiel College	PA	41,590	C
Thomas Edison State Univ	NJ	6,350	NC
Thomas More College	KY	36,720	C
Toccoa Falls College	GA	27,920	C
Touro College	NY	28,950	VC
Towson Univ	MD	17,408	VC
Transylvania Univ	KY	45,690	VC+
Trinity Christian College	IL	35,580	C
Trinity College	CT	63,920	HC+
Trinity International Univ	IL	31,070	VC
Trinity Univ	TX	52,314	HC+
Truman State Univ	MO	16,014	HC
Tufts Univ	MA		MC
Tulane Univ	LA	63,396	HC+
Union College	NY	64,320	MC
Union Univ	TN	33,970	VC
United States Military Academy at West Point	NY		HC+
Univ of Alabama	AL	24,320	C+
Univ of Alabama at Birmingham	AL	19,906	C
Univ of Alabama in Huntsville	AL	19,445	VC
Univ of Alaska Anchorage	AK	16,652	NC
Univ of Arizona	AZ	23,100	C
Univ of Arkansas at Fayetteville	AR	19,152	C+
Univ of Arkansas at Little Rock	AR	18,211	C
Univ of Calif at Davis	CA	28,468	HC
Univ of Calif at Irvine	CA	26,484	VC
Univ of Calif at Los Angeles	CA	30,162	MC
Univ of Calif at Riverside	CA	29,227	C+
Univ of Calif at Santa Barbara	CA	29,091	HC
Univ of Calif San Diego	CA	30,150	MC
Univ of Calif, Santa Cruz	CA	28,731	C+
Univ of Central Arkansas	AR	14,472	VC
Univ of Central Florida	FL	15,922	VC
Univ of Central Okla	OK	13,486	C
Univ of Chicago	IL	67,584	MC
Univ of Cincinnati	OH	21,964	VC
Univ of Colo Boulder	CO	24,285	VC+
Univ of Colo Colo Springs	CO	19,663	C
Univ of Colo Denver	CO	23,230	C
Univ of Conn	CT	25,538	HC
Univ of Dallas	TX	45,500	VC+
Univ of Dayton	OH	53,620	C
Univ of Delaware	DE	24,976	VC+
Univ of Denver	CO	58,443	VC+
Univ of Detroit Mercy	MI	48,816	C+
Univ of Dubuque	IA	37,824	C
Univ of Evansville	IN	44,186	VC+
Univ of Findlay	OH	60,139	C
Univ of Florida	FL	16,291	HC+
Univ of Georgia	GA	21,250	HC
Univ of Hartford	CT	49,776	C
Univ of Hawaii at Hilo	HI	18,038	C
Univ of Hawaii at Manoa	HI	23,221	C
Univ of Houston	TX	21,483	VC
Univ of Houston-Downtown	TX	7,241	C
Univ of Idaho	ID	15,348	C
Univ of Illinois at Chicago	IL	25,006	VC
Univ of Illinois at Urbana-Champaign	IL	27,006	HC
Univ of Indianapolis	IN	36,480	C
Univ of Iowa	IA	18,683	VC+
Univ of Kansas	KS	20,135	C+
Univ of Kentucky	KY	33,306	C
Univ of La Verne	CA	55,600	C
Univ of Louisiana at Lafayette	LA	14,516	C
Univ of Louisville	KY	19,824	C
Univ of Maine	ME	20,792	C
Univ of Mary Washington	VA	24,764	VC
Univ of Maryland/Baltimore County	MD	21,296	VC
Univ of Maryland/College Park	MD	21,938	HC
Univ of Mass Amherst	MA	26,199	VC+
Univ of Mass Boston	MA	13,435	C
Univ of Mass Dartmouth	MA	25,658	C
Univ of Mass Lowell	MA	26,380	C
Univ of Memphis	TN	18,278	C
Univ of Miami	FL	63,494	MC
Univ of Mich/Ann Arbor	MI	24,410	MC
Univ of Mich/Dearborn	MI	11,757	VC
Univ of Mich-Flint	MI	17,607	C+
Univ of Minn/Duluth	MN	20,292	C+
Univ of Minn/Morris	MN	20,760	VC
Univ of Minn/Twin Cities	MN	23,519	HC+
Univ of Miss	MS	17,746	C+
Univ of Missouri/Columbia	MO	18,201	MC
Univ of Missouri-Kansas City	MO	19,563	VC
Univ of Missouri-St. Louis	MO		C
Univ of Montana	MT	14,105	C
Univ of Mount Union	OH	38,970	C
Univ of Nebr - Lincoln	NE	18,589	VC
Univ of Nebr - Omaha	NE	16,120	C
Univ of Nevada, Las Vegas	NV	17,553	C
Univ of Nevada/Reno	NV	18,010	C
Univ of New Hampshire	NH	28,562	VC
Univ of New Mexico	NM	15,404	C
Univ of New Orleans	LA	12,840	C
Univ of N Car at Asheville	NC	15,723	VC+
Univ of N Car at Chapel Hill	NC	20,052	HC+
Univ of N Car at Charlotte	NC	15,547	C
Univ of N Car at Greensboro	NC	14,690	C
Univ of N Dak	ND	15,373	C
Univ of North Florida	FL	15,996	VC
Univ of North Texas	TX	19,198	C
Univ of Northern Colo	CO	20,851	C
Univ of Notre Dame	IN	64,043	MC
Univ of Okla	OK	18,911	VC
Univ of Oregon	OR	22,972	C
Univ of Pennsylvania	PA	63,526	MC
Univ of Pittsburgh	PA	29,568	HC+
Univ of Portland	OR	52,152	VC
Univ of PR, at Mayaguez	PR	13,995	
Univ of PR-Rio Piedras campus	PR	13,327	
Univ of Puget Sound	WA	56,456	VC+
Univ of Redlands	CA	60,200	VC
Univ of Rhode Island	RI	24,906	C
Univ of Richmond	VA	60,880	MC
Univ of Rochester	NY	65,032	MC
Univ of St. Francis	IN	37,400	C
Univ of St. Joseph	CT	49,550	C
Univ of San Diego	CA	58,442	VC+
Univ of San Francisco	CA	58,484	VC
Univ of Scranton	PA	54,962	VC
Univ of Sioux Falls	SD	34,330	C
Univ of South Alabama	AL	16,400	C
Univ of S Car at Columbia	SC	19,725	VC+
Univ of S Dak	SD	16,109	C
Univ of South Florida/Tampa	FL	16,110	VC+
Univ of Southern Calif	CA	66,631	C
Univ of Southern Indiana	IN	16,501	C
Univ of Southern Maine	ME	18,320	C
Univ of Southern Miss	MS	13,170	C
Univ of St. Thomas - Houston	TX	40,020	VC
Univ of Tampa	FL	36,944	C
Univ of Texas at Arlington	TX	18,026	LC
Univ of Texas at Austin	TX	26,102	HC
Univ of Texas at El Paso	TX	34,452	NC
Univ of Texas at San Antonio	TX	20,157	C
Univ of the District of Columbia	DC	21,044	LC
Univ of the Incarnate Word	TX	39,162	LC
Univ of the Pacific	CA	57,006	VC
Univ of Toledo	OH	19,336	NC
Univ of Tulsa	OK	52,625	HC+
Univ of Vermont	VT	28,878	HC
Univ of Virginia	VA	25,891	MC
Univ of Washington	WA	23,149	VC
Univ of West Florida	FL	15,848	C
Univ of West Georgia	GA	16,360	LC
Univ of Wisc-Eau Claire	WI	15,797	VC
Univ of Wisc-Green Bay	WI	15,064	C
Univ of Wisc-La Crosse	WI	15,247	C+
Univ of Wisc-Madison	WI	20,934	MC
Univ of Wisc-Milwaukee	WI	21,496	C
Univ of Wisc-Oshkosh	WI	15,200	C
Univ of Wisc-Parkside	WI	15,193	C
Univ of Wisc-Platteville	WI	14,614	VC
Univ of Wisc-Stevens Point	WI	14,043	C
Univ of Wyoming	WY	15,375	C+
Ursinus College	PA	61,690	VC
Ursuline College	OH	41,076	LC
Utah State Univ	UT	12,736	C
Utica College	NY	30,430	C
Valparaiso Univ	IN	48,370	C+
Vanderbilt Univ	TN	60,572	MC
Vassar College	NY	65,491	MC
Villanova Univ	PA	62,523	MC
Virginia Commonwealth Univ	VA	23,049	C
Virginia Polytechnic Inst and State Univ	VA	21,276	HC
Virginia Wesleyan College	VA	43,728	LC
Viterbo Univ	WI	34,660	C
Wabash College	IN	50,650	VC
Wagner College	NY	55,480	C+
Wake Forest Univ	NC	64,056	MC
Walsh Univ	OH	39,010	C
Warren Wilson College	NC	44,220	VC
Wartburg College	IA	47,840	C
Washburn Univ	KS	15,827	C
Washington & Jefferson College	PA	56,512	VC
Washington and Lee Univ	VA	59,647	MC
Washington College	MD	54,666	VC
Washington State Univ	WA	22,495	C
Washington Univ in St. Louis	MO	65,366	VC
Wayland Baptist Univ	TX	22,356	LC
Wayne State Univ	MI	22,016	C
Weber State Univ	UT	10,721	C
Webster Univ	MO	37,490	C
Wellesley College	MA	63,916	MC
Wells College	NY	50,500	C
Wesleyan College	GA	29,694	C+
Wesleyan Univ	CT	65,516	MC
West Chester Univ of Pennsylvania	PA	18,456	C
West Virginia Univ	WV	18,210	C
West Virginia Wesleyan College	WV	36,858	C
Western Carolina Univ	NC	13,965	C
Western Kentucky Univ	KY	16,850	C
Western Mich Univ	MI	21,054	C
Western New England Univ	MA	48,088	C
Western Oregon Univ	OR	15,021	LC
Western Washington Univ	WA	18,003	C+
Westminster College	MO	32,820	C
Westminster College	PA	39,180	C+
Westminster College	UT	41,078	C+
Westmont College	CA	56,410	HC
Wheaton College	IL	43,610	MC
Wheaton College	MA	61,512	VC
Wheeling Jesuit Univ	WV	37,106	LC
Whitman College	WA	59,772	MC
Whittier College	CA	57,891	C
Whitworth Univ	WA	51,732	VC
Wichita State Univ	KS	21,643	C
Wiley College	TX	18,504	C
Wilkes Univ	PA	45,622	C
Willamette Univ	OR	61,817	VC+
William Jewell College	MO	41,210	C+
William Paterson Univ of New Jersey	NJ	23,133	C
Williams College	MA	63,290	MC
Wilmington College	OH	34,600	C
Wilson College	PA	35,620	C
Winthrop Univ	SC	23,082	C
Wisc Lutheran College	WI	36,290	VC
Wittenberg Univ	OH	48,156	C+
Wofford College	SC	49,885	VC
Wright State Univ	OH	16,983	C
Xavier Univ	OH	47,880	C+
Xavier Univ of Louisiana	LA	31,689	C+
Yale Univ	CT	64,650	MC
Yeshiva Univ	NY	47,250	VC+
York College of Pennsylvania	PA	29,240	C
Youngstown State Univ	OH	17,307	C

PHILOSOPHY (AESTHETICS/MEDIA WRITING)

School	ST	$IS	SR
Murray State Univ	KY	16,998	C

PHILOSOPHY (HISTORY/CONTEMPORARY THOUGHT)

School	ST	$IS	SR
Bryant Univ	RI	55,646	VC
Murray State Univ	KY	16,998	C

PHILOSOPHY (POLITICAL THOUGHT)

School	ST	$IS	SR
Bryant Univ	RI	55,646	VC
Claremont McKenna College	CA	67,185	MC
Murray State Univ	KY	16,998	C
Syracuse Univ	NY	60,239	VC

PHILOSOPHY AND RELIGION

School	ST	$IS	SR
Arizona State Univ at the West Campus	AZ	20,640	C
Augustana Univ	SD	38,424	VC
Austin Peay State Univ	TN	16,397	C
Beloit College	WI	55,206	HC
Bethel College	IN	35,860	C
Biola Univ	CA	46,402	C+
Boston Univ	MA	65,110	MC
Bridgewater College	VA	44,510	C
Cal State, Fresno	CA	16,902	LC
Christian Brothers Univ	TN	31,670	VC
Claflin Univ	SC	33,764	LC
Colgate Univ	NY	65,030	MC
Covenant College	GA	38,990	VC
Dakota Wesleyan Univ	SD	32,850	C
Davis & Elkins College	WV	38,242	LC
Dordt College	IA	37,860	C+
Elmira College	NY	53,900	C
Flagler College	FL	27,620	C
Friends Univ	KS	34,455	C
Hendrix College	AR	54,020	VC+
Hillsdale College	MI	35,722	MC
Ithaca College	NY	56,766	VC
Juniata College	PA	53,760	VC
Kutztown Univ of Pennsylvania	PA	19,056	LC
Marymount Manhattan College	NY	46,280	VC
Mass College of Liberal Arts	MA	20,128	C
Murray State Univ	KY	16,998	C
New York Univ	NY	65,860	MC
N Dak State Univ	ND	16,245	C
Northeastern Univ	MA	62,703	MC
Northwest Nazarene Univ	ID	36,000	C
Nova Southeastern Univ	FL	38,534	C+
Nyack College	NY	34,050	NC
Okla Baptist Univ	OK	32,320	C
Okla City Univ	OK	40,476	VC
Ouachita Baptist Univ	AR	32,320	C
Pace Univ	NY	58,248	C
Paine College	GA	19,506	LC
Philander Smith College	AR	20,814	LC
Prescott College	AZ	33,284	C
Radford Univ	VA	19,027	LC
Rocky Mountain College	MT	34,270	C
Rowan Univ	NJ	24,491	VC+
Samford Univ	AL	39,232	VC
S Dak State Univ	SD	15,634	C
Southwestern College	KS	31,531	C
Spring Arbor Univ	MI	36,000	C
St. Joseph's College, New York/Brooklyn Campus	NY	25,114	LC
St. Joseph's College, New York/Long Island Campus	NY	25,124	C
Taylor Univ	IN	40,317	C+
Univ of Maine at Farmington	ME	18,187	C
Univ of N Car at Pembroke	NC	14,388	LC
Univ of N Car at Wilmington	NC	14,590	VC
Univ of Notre Dame	IN	64,043	MC
Univ of Texas at San Antonio	TX	20,157	C
Urbana Univ	OH	30,820	C
Virginia Commonwealth Univ	VA	23,049	C
Washington Adventist Univ	MD	31,440	LC
Wesley College	DE	37,026	LC
West Chester Univ of Pennsylvania	PA	18,456	C
Wheaton College	MA	61,512	VC
Wilson College	PA	35,620	C
Winthrop Univ	SC	23,082	C
Youngstown State Univ	OH	17,307	C

PHOTOGRAPHY

School	ST	$IS	SR
Adams State Univ	CO	17,703	LC
Andrews Univ	MI	28,030	C+
Appalachian State Univ	NC	14,416	VC
Aquinas College - Mich	MI	38,876	HC
Arcadia Univ	PA	33,570	C+
Art Academy of Cincinnati	OH	36,252	SP
ArtCenter College of Design	CA	54,212	SP
Bard College	NY	64,024	HC
Barry Univ	FL	37,830	C
Bellevue Univ	NE	20,300	NC
Bennington College	VT	63,960	MC
Biola Univ	CA	46,402	C+
Brigham Young Univ	UT	12,748	HC
Calif Baptist Univ	CA	41,392	C
Calif College of the Arts	CA	52,758	SP
Calif Inst of the Arts	CA	56,426	SP
Cal State, San Bernardino	CA	12,000	C
Carroll Univ	WI	38,100	C+
Central Mich Univ	MI	20,330	C
Cleveland Inst of Art	OH	51,439	C+
Coker College	SC	34,810	LC
College for Creative Studies	MI	48,875	SP
College of Art and Design at Lesley Univ	MA	39,730	SP
Colo State Univ	CO	22,162	VC
Columbia College - Missouri	MO	27,803	C
Columbia College Chicago	IL	43,168	C
Columbus College of Art and Design	OH	37,732	C
Dominican Univ	IL	41,222	C
Drexel Univ	PA	65,432	VC+
Eastern Mennonite Univ	VA	42,550	C
Endicott College	MA	44,604	VC+
Ferris State Univ	MI	21,445	C
Fitchburg State Univ	MA	21,819	C
Goddard College	VT	17,040	VC
Grand Valley State Univ	MI	22,250	C+
Hampshire College	MA	63,824	MC
Hofstra Univ	NY	55,960	C+
Howard Univ	DC	37,616	C+
Indiana Univ-Purdue Univ Fort Wayne	IN	17,553	C
Indiana Wesleyan Univ	IN	33,674	C
Ithaca College	NY	56,766	VC
John Brown Univ	AR	33,132	VC
Kansas City Art Inst	MO	44,308	C+
Kent State Univ	OH	20,732	C
King Univ	TN	34,660	C
Kutztown Univ of Pennsylvania	PA	19,056	LC
LIU Post	NY	49,682	C
Maine College of Art	ME	43,794	SP
Marshall Univ	WV	17,242	C
Maryland Inst College of Art	MD	56,795	SP
Marywood Univ	PA	46,900	C
Mass College of Art and Design	MA	24,800	SP
Memphis College of Art	TN	39,750	C
Milligan College	TN	38,150	C

ST = STATE **$IS** = IN-STATE COSTS **SR** = SELECTOR RATING

School	ST	$IS	SR
Milwaukee Inst of Art and Design	WI	44,960	SP
Minneapolis College of Art and Design	MN	44,238	SP
Montserrat College of Art	MA	38,150	SP
Moore College of Art and Design	PA	50,135	SP
Moore College of Art and Design	PA	50,135	SP
Morningside College	IA	36,865	C
New Jersey City Univ	NJ	21,456	LC
New York Univ	NY	65,860	MC
Northern Arizona Univ	AZ	20,246	VC
Notre Dame of Maryland Univ	MD	46,465	VC
Oberlin College	OH	66,012	MC
Ohio Univ	OH	22,924	C
Okla Christian Univ	OK	27,650	VC
Okla City Univ	OK	40,476	VC
Otis College of Art and Design	CA	55,858	SP
Pacific Northwest College of Art	OR	38,494	SP
Pacific Union College	CA	36,009	VC
Parsons The New School for Design	NY	56,610	SP
Point Park Univ	PA	41,270	C
Pratt Inst	NY	58,082	VC
Prescott College	AZ	33,284	C
Purdue Univ/West Lafayette	IN	20,032	MC
Rhode Island School of Design	RI	59,960	SP
Ringling College of Art and Design	FL	57,430	SP
Rochester Inst of Technology	NY	50,842	HC
Rocky Mountain College of Art and Design	CO	27,052	SP
Salem State Univ	MA	17,303	LC
Sam Houston State Univ	TX	18,792	C
San Francisco Art Inst	CA	58,505	SP
Santa Fe Univ of Art and Design	NM	39,980	SP
Savannah College of Art and Design	GA	49,595	C
School of the Art Inst of Chicago	IL	56,230	SP
School of Visual Arts	NY	47,500	SP
Seattle Univ	WA	50,811	VC+
Southern Illinois Univ Carbondale	IL	23,667	C
St. Edward's Univ	TX	53,100	VC
St. John's Univ	NY	55,850	C
SUNY / Buffalo State College	NY	20,842	C
SUNY / SUNY Fredonia	NY	20,818	C
SUNY at New Paltz	NY	19,200	C
Syracuse Univ	NY	60,239	VC
Temple Univ	PA	24,392	VC
Texas A&M Univ at Commerce	TX	10,496	C
Texas Christian Univ	TX	54,670	HC
Texas State Univ	TX	19,350	C
The Art Inst of Atlanta	GA	34,334	SP
Thomas Edison State Univ	NJ	6,350	NC
Univ of Central Florida	FL	15,922	VC
Univ of Central Missouri	MO	18,982	C
Univ of Central Okla	OK	13,486	C
Univ of Dayton	OH	53,620	C
Univ of Florida	FL	16,291	HC+
Univ of Hartford	CT	49,776	C
Univ of Illinois at Chicago	IL	25,006	VC
Univ of Illinois at Urbana-Champaign	IL	27,006	HC
Univ of Iowa	IA	18,683	VC+
Univ of La Verne	CA	55,600	C
Univ of Mass Dartmouth	MA	25,658	C
Univ of Miami	FL	63,494	MC
Univ of Mich/Ann Arbor	MI	24,410	MC
Univ of Oregon	OR	22,972	C
Univ of San Francisco	CA	58,484	VC
Univ of the Arts	PA	56,579	SP
Univ of Washington	WA	23,149	VC
Virginia Commonwealth Univ	VA	23,049	C
Washington Univ in St. Louis	MO	65,366	VC
Weber State Univ	UT	10,721	C
Webster Univ	MO	37,490	C
Western Washington Univ	WA	18,003	C+
Youngstown State Univ	OH	17,307	C

PHYSICAL CHEMISTRY

School	ST	$IS	SR
Aquinas College - Mich	MI	38,876	HC
Centre College	KY	49,250	HC
Union Univ	TN	33,970	VC
Univ of Calif San Diego	CA	30,150	MC

PHYSICAL ED TEACHER EDUCATION

School	ST	$IS	SR
Averett Univ	VA	40,970	LC
East Stroudsburg Univ	PA	18,334	C
Frostburg State Univ	MD	17,280	LC
Iowa Wesleyan Univ	IA	39,200	C
Tabor College	KS	35,870	C
Univ of Kansas	KS	20,135	C+
Washburn Univ	KS	15,827	C
William Woods Univ	MO	32,040	C

PHYSICAL EDUCATION

School	ST	$IS	SR
Adams State Univ	CO	17,703	LC
Adelphi Univ	NY	48,244	C
Adrian College	MI	42,400	C
Alabama A&M Univ	AL	18,796	C
Albany State Univ	GA	19,462	C
Alderson Broaddus Univ	WV	26,149	C
Alice Lloyd College	KY	8,190	C
Anderson Univ	IN	38,200	C
Appalachian State Univ	NC	14,416	VC
Aquinas College - Mich	MI	38,876	HC
Arkansas State Univ	AR	16,190	C
Arkansas Tech Univ	AR	15,484	C
Armstrong State Univ	GA	16,962	C
Asbury Univ	KY	35,180	C+
Ashford Univ	CA	10,480	C
Ashland Univ	OH	21,440	C
Auburn Univ	AL	23,594	VC+
Augsburg College	MN	43,929	C
Augustana Univ	SD	38,424	VC
Aurora Univ	IL	33,970	C
Averett Univ	VA	40,970	LC
Azusa Pacific Univ	CA	43,972	C
Baker Univ	KS	33,350	C+
Baldwin Wallace Univ	OH	41,106	C
Ball State Univ	IN	19,590	C
Barry Univ	FL	37,830	C
Barton College	NC	38,686	LC
Baylor Univ	TX	53,760	HC
Bellevue Univ	NE	20,300	NC
Belmont Univ	TN	40,970	VC
Benedictine College	KS	36,200	VC
Berea College	KY	7,042	C
Bethany College	KS	46,100	NC
Bethany College	WV	36,300	NC
Bethel College	IN	35,860	C
Bethel Univ	MN	45,270	VC
Bethel Univ	TN	24,738	C
Bethune-Cookman Univ	FL	22,970	C
Biola Univ	CA	46,402	C+
Black Hills State Univ	SD	15,899	C
Blackburn College	IL	28,526	LC
Blue Mountain College	MS	15,949	VC
Bluffton Univ	OH	40,950	C
Boise State Univ	ID	14,860	C
Boston Univ	MA	65,110	MC
Bowling Green State Univ	OH	19,747	C
Brewton-Parker College	GA	23,490	C
Bridgewater State Univ	MA	21,810	C
Bryan College	TN	31,440	C
Cal State, Dominguez Hills	CA	19,022	LC
Cal State, Los Angeles	CA	17,186	LC
Cal State, Northridge	CA	16,859	LC
Cal State, Stanislaus	CA	16,212	C
Calvin College	MI	41,570	VC+
Campbellsville Univ	KY	32,492	C
Canisius College	NY	47,537	C
Capital Univ	OH	42,982	C
Carroll College	MT	39,972	C+
Carroll Univ	WI	38,100	C+
Carthage College	WI	48,835	C
Castleton Univ	VT	20,186	C
Catawba College	NC	39,820	C
Cedarville Univ	OH	34,990	VC
Central Conn State Univ	CT	21,203	C
Central Methodist Univ	MO	36,830	VC
Central Mich Univ	MI	20,330	C
Central State Univ	OH	18,564	C
Central Washington Univ	WA	16,803	C
Charleston Southern Univ	SC	32,400	C
Chicago State Univ	IL	20,144	C
CUNY/Brooklyn College	NY	5,884	C+
CUNY/Queens College	NY	27,896	C
CUNY/York College	NY	6,747	LC
Clark Atlanta Univ	GA	31,019	LC
Cleveland State Univ	OH	22,196	C
Coastal Carolina Univ	SC	19,766	C
Coe College	IA	51,570	VC
Coker College	SC	34,810	LC
College of Charleston	SC	22,699	C
College of Mount St. Vincent	NY	45,620	C
College of the Ozarks	MO	7,230	C
Concordia College - Moorhead	MN	51,088	C+
Concordia Univ Nebr	NE	36,280	VC
Concordia Univ St. Paul	MN	29,050	C
Concordia Univ Wisc	WI	35,910	C
Concordia Univ, Ann Arbor	MI	35,945	VC
Concordia Univ, Chicago	IL	39,694	C
Corban Univ	OR	40,306	C
Culver-Stockton College	MO	33,525	C
Cumberland Univ	TN	27,710	C
Dakota Wesleyan Univ	SD	32,850	C
Dallas Baptist Univ	TX	33,713	C
Davis & Elkins College	WV	38,242	LC
Defiance College	OH	41,630	C
Delaware State Univ	DE	19,376	NC
Denison Univ	OH	58,860	MC
DePaul Univ	IL	47,623	VC
Doane Univ	NE	39,184	VC
Dordt College	IA	37,860	C+
Drury Univ	MO	33,791	VC
East Carolina Univ	NC	16,937	C
East Central Univ	OK	13,056	C
East Tenn State Univ	TN	13,994	C
East Texas Baptist Univ	TX	33,134	C
Eastern Conn State Univ	CT	23,059	C
Eastern Kentucky Univ	KY	16,908	C
Eastern Mennonite Univ	VA	42,550	C
Eastern Mich Univ	MI	19,761	C
Eastern New Mexico Univ	NM	14,416	C
Eastern Oregon Univ	OR	17,715	C
Eastern Washington Univ	WA	25,572	LC
Edinboro Univ	PA	15,940	LC
Edward Waters College	FL	20,607	NC
Elizabeth City State Univ	NC	14,745	C
Elmhurst College	IL	45,428	C
Elon Univ	NC	44,599	VC+
Emory and Henry College	VA	41,410	C
Emporia State Univ	KS	14,570	C
Endicott College	MA	44,604	VC+
Erskine College	SC	45,460	C
Eureka College	IL	30,220	C
Evangel Univ	MO	28,898	C
Faulkner Univ	AL	26,410	C
Ferrum College	VA	39,650	C
Florida Atlantic Univ	FL	17,339	C
Florida International Univ	FL	19,854	C+
Florida Memorial Univ	FL	22,270	LC
Florida State Univ	FL	16,771	HC
Fort Hays State Univ	KS	12,131	C
Fort Valley State Univ	GA	17,988	VC
Franklin College	IN	39,380	C
Freed-Hardeman Univ	TN	29,450	C
Fresno Pacific Univ	CA	37,370	C
Frostburg State Univ	MD	17,280	LC
Gallaudet Univ	DC	29,118	LC
Gardner-Webb Univ	NC	39,200	C+
George Mason Univ	VA	15,724	VC
Georgia State Univ	GA	24,332	VC
Glenville State College	WV	17,386	NC
Gonzaga Univ	WA	50,888	HC
Goshen College	IN	42,500	C
Grace College and Seminary	IN	31,524	C
Graceland Univ	IA	35,290	C
Grambling State Univ	LA	15,701	C
Grand Canyon Univ	AZ	16,950	VC
Grand Rapids Theological Seminary/Cornerstone Univ	MI	33,338	C
Grand View Univ	IA	32,302	C
Greensboro College	NC	42,400	LC
Greenville College	IL	27,012	C
Hampton Univ	VA	34,926	LC
Hardin-Simmons Univ	TX	33,966	C
Heidelberg Univ	OH	39,200	C
Henderson State Univ	AR	15,516	LC
High Point Univ	NC	45,977	C
Hillsdale College	MI	35,722	MC
Hofstra Univ	NY	55,960	C+
Houghton College	NY	39,090	C
Houston Baptist Univ	TX	36,450	C
Howard Univ	DC	37,616	C+
Humboldt State Univ	CA	20,514	C
Huntingdon College	AL	34,900	C
Huntington Univ	IN	33,996	C
Husson Univ	ME	25,720	LC
Huston-Tillotson Univ	TX	18,124	LC
Idaho State Univ	ID	13,619	NC
Indiana Inst of Technology	IN	34,240	LC
Indiana State Univ	IN	23,223	LC
Indiana Univ of Pennsylvania	PA	23,614	LC
Indiana Wesleyan Univ	IN	33,674	C
Inter-American Univ of PR-Aguadilla Campus	PR	21,657	
Iowa State Univ	IA	17,570	C
Iowa Wesleyan Univ	IA	39,200	C
Ithaca College	NY	56,766	VC
Jacksonville Univ	FL	46,230	C
John Carroll Univ	OH	49,740	C+
Johnson C. Smith Univ	NC	25,336	LC
Johnson State College	VT	20,752	C
Judson Univ	IL	37,700	C
Kalamazoo College	MI	53,931	HC+
Kansas Wesleyan Univ	KS	36,600	C
Kean Univ	NJ	24,650	C
Keene State College	NH	24,003	LC
Kennesaw State Univ	GA	19,592	VC
Kent State Univ	OH	20,732	C
Kentucky State Univ	KY	13,364	LC
Kentucky Wesleyan College	KY	32,080	C
King Univ	TN	34,660	C
La Sierra Univ	CA	39,690	VC
Lander Univ	SC	43,994	C
Lane College	TN	16,550	C
Langston Univ	OK	14,314	C
Lee Univ	TN	22,045	C
LeTourneau Univ	TX	38,250	VC
Liberty Univ	VA	19,101	C
Limestone College	SC	32,100	C
Lincoln Univ	MO	13,602	NC
Lindenwood Univ	MO	25,132	C
Linfield College	OR	52,010	C
Lipscomb Univ	TN	41,296	VC
LIU Brooklyn	NY	49,682	C
LIU Post	NY	49,682	C
Lock Haven Univ of Pennsylvania	PA	18,028	LC
Longwood Univ	VA	22,184	C
Louisiana Tech Univ	LA	11,422	VC
Lubbock Christian Univ	TX	28,426	C
Luther College	IA	48,540	C+
Lyndon State College	VT	20,714	C
MacMurray College	IL	33,620	C
Madonna Univ	MI	29,050	C
Manhattan College	NY	51,750	C+
Mars Hill Univ	NC	42,688	C
Marshall Univ	WV	17,242	C
Maryville College	TN	44,410	C
Marywood Univ	PA	46,900	C
Mayville State Univ	ND	18,371	NC
McDaniel College	MD	51,380	VC
McKendree Univ	IL	37,940	C+
McMurry Univ	TX	34,259	LC
McPherson College	KS	34,909	C
Messiah College	PA	43,100	C+
Methodist Univ	NC	43,600	C
Metropolitan State Univ of Denver	CO	29,889	LC
Mich State Univ	MI	23,898	VC+
MidAmerica Nazarene Univ	KS	35,550	C
Middle Tenn State Univ	TN	8,650	C
Midwestern State Univ	TX	17,572	C
Millikin Univ	IL	42,158	C
Minn State Univ, Mankato	MN	15,616	C
Minn State Univ, Moorhead	MN	15,941	C
Minot State Univ	ND	12,732	C
Miss State Univ	MS	11,454	C+
Miss Valley State Univ	MS	13,233	LC
Missouri Baptist Univ	MO	35,594	C
Missouri Southern State Univ	MO	12,499	C
Missouri State Univ	MO	15,190	C+
Missouri Valley College	MO	28,150	C
Monmouth College	IL	42,260	C
Monmouth Univ	NJ	46,234	C
Montana State Univ-Billings	MT	22,960	C
Montana State Univ-Northern	MT	11,370	NC
Montclair State Univ	NJ	26,210	LC
Morehead State Univ	KY	17,422	C
Morehouse College	GA	40,064	C
Morgan State Univ	MD	17,190	LC
Mount Marty College	SD	32,972	C
Mount Vernon Nazarene Univ	OH	34,500	C
Muskingum Univ	OH	35,966	C
Nebr Wesleyan Univ	NE	38,140	C+
New England College	NH	50,364	C
New Mexico State Univ	NM	14,050	C
Newberry College	SC	34,550	C
N Car A&T State Univ	NC	13,365	LC
N Car Central Univ	NC	9,000	C
N Dak State Univ	ND	16,245	C
Northeastern Illinois Univ	IL	12,529	LC
Northern Illinois Univ	IL	20,176	C
Northern Kentucky Univ	KY	16,486	C
Northern Mich Univ	MI	19,604	C
Northern State Univ	SD	14,505	C
Northwest Missouri State Univ	MO	17,737	C
Northwest Nazarene Univ	ID	36,000	C
Northwest Univ	WA	35,876	VC
Northwestern College of Iowa	IA	38,400	C+
Northwestern Okla State Univ	OK	13,072	NC
Norwich Univ	VT	28,212	C
Nova Southeastern Univ	FL	38,534	C+
Oakwood Univ	AL	43,758	C
Ohio Northern Univ	OH	44,050	VC
Ohio State Univ at Columbus	OH	21,703	HC+
Ohio Univ	OH	22,924	C
Ohio Wesleyan Univ	OH	49,460	VC
Okla Baptist Univ	OK	32,320	C
Okla Christian Univ	OK	27,650	VC
Okla Panhandle State Univ	OK	6,152	NC
Okla State Univ	OK	17,180	VC
Okla Wesleyan Univ	OK	33,206	C
Old Dominion Univ	VA	20,910	C
Olivet College	MI	36,110	LC
Olivet Nazarene Univ	IL	41,840	C
Oral Roberts Univ	OK	34,316	C
Ottawa Univ	KS	36,074	VC
Otterbein Univ	OH	41,630	C
Pacific Lutheran Univ	WA	49,960	VC
Pacific Union College	CA	36,009	VC
Palm Beach Atlantic Univ	FL	39,720	C
Pepperdine Univ	CA	74,460	HC+
Peru State College	NE	14,768	NC
Pfeiffer Univ	NC	39,695	LC
Philander Smith College	AR	20,814	LC
Pittsburg State Univ	KS	13,880	NC
Plymouth State Univ	NH	23,180	LC
Pontifical Catholic Univ of PR	PR	10,534	
Prairie View A&M Univ	TX	15,205	LC
Prescott College	AZ	33,284	C
Quincy Univ	IL	36,998	C
Radford Univ	VA	19,027	LC
Randolph College	VA	45,660	VC
Rhode Island College	RI	17,694	LC
Roanoke College	VA	54,114	VC
Roberts Wesleyan College	NY	38,306	C
Rockford Univ	IL	36,030	C
Saginaw Valley State Univ	MI	18,530	C
St. Augustine's Univ	NC	26,048	C
St. Joseph's College of Maine	ME	46,485	C
St. Mary's College of Calif	CA	57,420	C
Salisbury Univ	MD	20,714	VC
Sam Houston State Univ	TX	18,792	C
San Francisco State Univ	CA	18,514	LC
Schreiner Univ	TX	34,626	LC
Seattle Pacific Univ	WA	47,439	C+
Shaw Univ	NC	24,638	C
Shepherd Univ, West Virginia	WV	17,224	C
Simpson College	IA	43,839	VC

ST = STATE $IS = IN-STATE COSTS SR = SELECTOR RATING

School	ST	$IS	SR
S Car State Univ	SC	20,805	LC
S Dak State Univ	SD	15,634	C
Southeastern Louisiana Univ	LA	16,237	C
Southeastern Okla State Univ	OK	11,875	C
Southern Adventist Univ	TN	27,600	C
Southern Conn State Univ	CT	21,924	LC
Southern Illinois Univ Carbondale	IL	23,667	C
Southern Illinois Univ Edwardsville	IL	22,643	C
Southern Nazarene Univ	OK	32,798	NC
Southern Oregon Univ	OR	19,117	C
Southern Univ at New Orleans	LA	8,014	LC
Southern Wesleyan Univ	SC	32,130	LC
Southwest Baptist Univ	MO	29,900	LC
Southwest Minn State Univ	MN	17,783	C
Southwestern Adventist Univ	TX	27,756	LC
Southwestern College	KS	31,531	C
Springfield College	MA	45,995	C
St. Andrews Univ	NC	44,634	LC
St. Bonaventure Univ	NY	44,237	C
St. Catherine Univ	MN	45,630	VC
St. Edward's Univ	TX	53,100	VC
St. Francis College	NY	38,800	LC
SUNY / SUNY Cortland	NY	20,706	VC
Stillman College	AL	20,738	C
Syracuse Univ	NY	60,239	VC
Tabor College	KS	35,870	C
Tarleton State Univ	TX	15,248	LC
Taylor Univ	IN	40,317	C+
Temple Univ	PA	24,392	VC
Tenn Tech Univ	TN	17,050	C
Texas A&M Univ	TX	20,521	VC+
Texas A&M Univ at Kingsville	TX	7,500	LC
Texas Christian Univ	TX	54,670	HC
Texas Lutheran Univ	TX	38,620	C
Texas Southern Univ	TX	18,212	LC
Texas State Univ	TX	19,350	C
Texas Wesleyan Univ	TX	35,134	C
The Citadel, The Military College of S Car	SC	35,339	C
The College at Brockport - SUNY	NY	20,346	C
The College of Idaho	ID	36,415	C
The College of New Jersey	NJ	31,909	HC
The Master's Univ	CA	43,870	C+
The Univ of Akron	OH	21,477	C
Tougaloo College	MS	17,980	NC
Towson Univ	MD	17,408	VC
Trevecca Nazarene Univ	TN	31,186	C
Trine Univ	IN	41,310	C
Trinity International Univ	IL	31,070	VC
Troy Univ	AL	16,171	C
Truman State Univ	MO	16,014	HC
Tusculum College	TN	31,625	C
Tuskegee Univ	AL	28,164	C
Union College	KY	32,310	C
Union College	NE	23,270	C
Union Univ	TN	33,970	VC
Universidad del Turabo	PR	17,828	
Univ of PR, at Arecibo	PR	12,652	
Univ of Alabama	AL	24,320	C+
Univ of Alaska Anchorage	AK	16,652	NC
Univ of Arkansas at Monticello	AR	13,134	NC
Univ of Arkansas at Pine Bluff	AR	13,541	C
Univ of Calif at Davis	CA	28,468	HC
Univ of Central Arkansas	AR	14,472	VC
Univ of Central Missouri	MO	18,982	C
Univ of Central Okla	OK	13,486	C
Univ of Charleston	WV	35,000	C
Univ of Delaware	DE	24,976	VC+
Univ of Dubuque	IA	37,824	C
Univ of Findlay	OH	60,139	C
Univ of Great Falls	MT	38,524	C
Univ of Hawaii at Manoa	HI	23,221	C
Univ of Idaho	ID	15,348	C
Univ of Illinois at Chicago	IL	25,006	VC
Univ of Illinois at Urbana-Champaign	IL	27,006	HC
Univ of Indianapolis	IN	36,480	C
Univ of Jamestown	ND	28,508	C
Univ of Kentucky	KY	33,306	C
Univ of Louisville	KY	19,824	C
Univ of Maine	ME	20,792	C
Univ of Maine at Machias	ME	22,960	C
Univ of Maine at Presque Isle	ME	14,870	C
Univ of Mary	ND	23,180	C
Univ of Mary Hardin-Baylor	TX	33,950	C+
Univ of Maryland/College Park	MD	21,938	HC
Univ of Maryland/Eastern Shore	MD	17,013	C
Univ of Memphis	TN	18,278	C
Univ of Mich/Ann Arbor	MI	24,410	MC
Univ of Minn/Duluth	MN	20,292	C+
Univ of Minn/Twin Cities	MN	23,519	HC+
Univ of Missouri-St. Louis	MO		C
Univ of Mobile	AL	28,935	C
Univ of Montana-Western	MT	11,220	LC
Univ of Montevallo	AL	19,502	C
Univ of Mount Union	OH	38,970	C
Univ of Nebr - Kearney	NE	16,546	LC
Univ of Nebr - Omaha	NE	16,120	C
Univ of Nevada, Las Vegas	NV	17,553	C
Univ of New Hampshire	NH	28,562	VC
Univ of New Mexico	NM	15,404	C
Univ of New Orleans	LA	12,840	C
Univ of North Alabama	AL	15,398	C
Univ of N Car at Greensboro	NC	14,690	C
Univ of N Car at Wilmington	NC	14,590	VC
Univ of N Dak	ND	15,373	C
Univ of North Florida	FL	15,996	VC
Univ of North Georgia	GA	17,316	C
Univ of Northern Colo	CO	20,851	C
Univ of Northwestern - St. Paul	MN	38,160	C
Univ of Rio Grande & Rio Grande Community College	OH	8,750	NC
Univ of Science and Arts of Okla	OK	11,140	VC
Univ of South Alabama	AL	16,400	C
Univ of S Car at Columbia	SC	19,725	VC+
Univ of S Car Upstate	SC	18,200	LC
Univ of S Dak	SD	16,109	C
Univ of South Florida/Tampa	FL	16,110	VC+
Univ of Southern Indiana	IN	16,501	C
Univ of Tampa	FL	36,944	C
Univ of Texas at Arlington	TX	18,026	LC
Univ of the Cumberlands	KY	32,000	C
Univ of the District of Columbia	DC	21,044	LC
Univ of the Incarnate Word	TX	39,162	LC
Univ of the Ozarks	AR	52,176	C
Univ of the Pacific	CA	57,006	VC
Univ of the Sacred Heart	PR	17,932	
Univ of Toledo	OH	19,336	NC
Univ of Vermont	VT	28,878	HC
Univ of West Alabama	AL	15,516	NC
Univ of West Georgia	GA	16,360	LC
Univ of Wisc-Eau Claire	WI	15,797	VC
Univ of Wisc-La Crosse	WI	15,247	C+
Univ of Wisc-Madison	WI	20,934	MC
Univ of Wisc-Oshkosh	WI	15,200	C
Univ of Wisc-Platteville	WI	14,614	VC
Univ of Wisc-River Falls	WI	14,485	C
Univ of Wisc-Stevens Point	WI	14,043	C
Univ of Wisc-Superior	WI	14,446	C
Univ of Wisc-Whitewater	WI	13,976	C
Univ of Wyoming	WY	15,375	C+
Upper Iowa Univ	IA	34,990	NC
Utah State Univ	UT	12,736	C
Valley City State Univ	ND	13,267	C
Valparaiso Univ	IN	48,370	C+
Vanguard Univ of Southern Calif	CA	40,740	VC
Virginia State Univ	VA	19,802	C+
Walla Walla Univ	WA	30,417	NC
Walsh Univ	OH	39,010	C
Warner Pacific College	OR	33,790	C
Warner Univ	FL	28,216	C
Wartburg College	IA	47,840	C
Washburn Univ	KS	15,827	C
Washington Adventist Univ	MD	31,440	LC
Washington State Univ	WA	22,495	C
Wayland Baptist Univ	TX	22,356	LC
Wayne State Univ	MI	22,016	C
Weber State Univ	UT	10,721	C
Wesley College	DE	37,026	LC
West Chester Univ of Pennsylvania	PA	18,456	C
West Liberty Univ	WV	15,512	C
West Texas A&M Univ	TX	13,478	C
West Virginia Univ	WV	18,210	C
West Virginia Wesleyan College	WV	36,858	C
Western Carolina Univ	NC	13,965	C
Western Illinois Univ	IL	20,825	C
Western Kentucky Univ	KY	16,850	C
Western Mich Univ	MI	21,054	C
Western New Mexico Univ	NM	16,734	LC
Western Washington Univ	WA	18,003	C+
Westminster College	MO	32,820	C
Wichita State Univ	KS	21,643	C
Wiley College	TX	18,504	C
William Carey Univ	MS	23,950	LC
William Paterson Univ of New Jersey	NJ	23,133	C
William Penn Univ	IA	26,000	C
William Woods Univ	MO	32,040	C
Williams Baptist College	AR	24,720	C
Wilmington College	OH	34,600	C
Wilson College	PA	35,620	C
Winona State Univ	MN	17,535	C
Winston-Salem State Univ	NC	26,166	LC
Winthrop Univ	SC	23,082	C
Wright State Univ	OH	16,983	C
Youngstown State Univ	OH	17,307	C

PHYSICAL EDUCATION / EXERCISE SCIENCE

School	ST	$IS	SR
CUNY/Queens College	NY	27,896	C
College of the Ozarks	MO	7,230	C
Indiana Univ Bloomington	IN	20,429	VC
Keene State College	NH	24,003	LC
Salisbury Univ	MD	20,714	VC
Southeast Missouri State Univ	MO	15,498	C
Tabor College	KS	35,870	C
Univ of Montana	MT	14,105	C
Univ of Virginia	VA	25,891	MC
Walla Walla Univ	WA	30,417	NC
Western Kentucky Univ	KY	16,850	C

PHYSICAL FITNESS/MOVEMENT

School	ST	$IS	SR
Ashland Univ	OH	21,440	C
Auburn Univ	AL	23,594	VC+
Augustana Univ	SD	38,424	VC
Baylor Univ	TX	53,760	HC
Brigham Young Univ/Hawaii	HI	11,290	C
Buena Vista Univ	IA	41,514	C
Calif State Polytechnic Univ, Pomona	CA	21,541	C
Cal State, East Bay	CA	19,413	C
Cal State, Fresno	CA	16,902	LC
Cal State, Monterey Bay	CA	26,871	LC
Cal State, San Marcos	CA	24,184	LC
Capital Univ	OH	42,982	C
Colo Mesa Univ	CO	18,955	LC
Concordia Univ Nebr	NE	36,280	VC
Concordia Univ St. Paul	MN	29,050	C
Concordia Univ, Chicago	IL	39,694	C
Dallas Baptist Univ	TX	33,713	C
Defiance College	OH	41,630	C
DePauw Univ	IN	58,688	HC+
East Carolina Univ	NC	16,937	C
East Texas Baptist Univ	TX	33,134	C
Eastern Nazarene College	MA	39,955	C
Eureka College	IL	30,220	C
George Washington Univ	DC	62,835	MC
Grand Canyon Univ	AZ	16,950	VC
Hope College	MI	39,940	VC
Houston Baptist Univ	TX	36,450	C
Humboldt State Univ	CA	20,514	C
Ithaca College	NY	56,766	VC
James Madison Univ	VA	19,084	VC
Johnson State College	VT	20,752	C
Kansas State Univ	KS	17,780	VC
Lakeland Univ	WI	35,130	C
Lasell College	MA	47,500	C
Lewis-Clark State College	ID	14,202	C
Limestone College	SC	32,100	C
Louisiana State Univ and A&M College	LA	18,677	VC
Lubbock Christian Univ	TX	28,426	C
Lynchburg College	VA	46,740	C
Marshall Univ	WV	17,242	C
Marywood Univ	PA	46,900	C
Metropolitan State Univ of Denver	CO	29,889	LC
Miami Univ	OH	27,190	HC+
Minot State Univ	ND	12,732	C
Miss Univ for Women	MS	17,065	C
New England College	NH	50,364	C
New Mexico Highlands Univ	NM	11,904	NC
New Mexico State Univ	NM	14,050	C
N Dak State Univ	ND	16,245	C
Northern Illinois Univ	IL	20,176	C
Northern Mich Univ	MI	19,604	C
Northern State Univ	SD	14,505	C
Northwestern College of Iowa	IA	38,400	C+
Notre Dame de Namur Univ	CA	46,526	LC
Oakwood Univ	AL	43,758	C
Occidental College	CA	65,530	MC
Ohio State Univ at Columbus	OH	21,703	HC+
Purdue Univ/West Lafayette	IN	20,032	MC
St. Augustine's Univ	NC	26,048	C
Sam Houston State Univ	TX	18,792	C
San Diego Christian College	CA	39,068	C
Seattle Pacific Univ	WA	47,439	C+
Sonoma State Univ	CA	27,806	C
Southern Methodist Univ	TX	66,483	MC
Southern Nazarene Univ	OK	32,798	NC
Spring Arbor Univ	MI	36,000	C
Springfield College	MA	45,995	C
St. Edward's Univ	TX	53,100	VC
Stephen F. Austin State Univ	TX	18,406	LC
Sul Ross State Univ	TX	15,021	LC
Tarleton State Univ	TX	15,248	LC
Temple Univ	PA	24,392	VC
Texas Southern Univ	TX	18,212	LC
Texas Woman's Univ	TX	15,302	LC
Truman State Univ	MO	16,014	HC
Union College	NE	23,270	C
Univ of Central Okla	OK	13,486	C
Univ of Florida	FL	16,291	HC+
Univ of Illinois at Chicago	IL	25,006	VC
Univ of La Verne	CA	55,600	C
Univ of Mass Boston	MA	13,435	C
Univ of Mich/Ann Arbor	MI	24,410	MC
Univ of Nevada, Las Vegas	NV	17,553	C
Univ of New Hampshire	NH	28,562	VC
Univ of N Car at Charlotte	NC	15,547	C
Univ of North Texas	TX	19,198	C
Univ of Northern Colo	CO	20,851	C
Univ of Rio Grande & Rio Grande Community College	OH	8,750	NC
Univ of Texas at Austin	TX	26,102	HC
Univ of Texas at El Paso	TX	34,452	NC
Univ of Toledo	OH	19,336	NC
Upper Iowa Univ	IA	34,990	NC
Virginia Polytechnic Inst and State Univ	VA	21,276	HC
West Liberty Univ	WV	15,512	C
Western State Colo Univ	CO	18,639	C
Westfield State Univ	MA	19,671	C
Whittier College	CA	57,891	C
Winona State Univ	MN	17,535	C

PHYSICAL SCIENCE SECONDARY SCHOOL EDUCATION

School	ST	$IS	SR
Aquinas College - Mich	MI	38,876	HC
Cedarville Univ	OH	34,990	VC
Dordt College	IA	37,860	C+
Duquesne Univ	PA	46,822	VC
Keene State College	NH	24,003	LC
Kent State Univ	OH	20,732	C
Murray State Univ	KY	16,998	C
St. Louis Univ	MO	49,866	HC
Southern Illinois Univ Carbondale	IL	23,667	C
St. Edward's Univ	TX	53,100	VC
Univ of Maine at Machias	ME	22,960	C
Univ of Nebr - Lincoln	NE	18,589	VC
Weber State Univ	UT	10,721	C
Youngstown State Univ	OH	17,307	C

PHYSICAL SCIENCES

School	ST	$IS	SR
Arkansas Tech Univ	AR	15,484	C
Asbury Univ	KY	35,180	C+
Auburn Univ at Montgomery	AL	15,290	C
Bennington College	VT	63,960	MC
Bethany College	WV	36,300	NC
Bethel College	IN	35,860	C
Biola Univ	CA	46,402	C+
Black Hills State Univ	SD	15,899	C
Bluffton Univ	OH	40,950	C
Brescia Univ	KY	29,890	VC+
Cal State, East Bay	CA	19,413	C
Cal State, Sacramento	CA	20,332	C
Cal State, Stanislaus	CA	16,212	C
Calif Univ of Pennsylvania	PA	14,217	LC
Central Conn State Univ	CT	21,203	C
Central Mich Univ	MI	20,330	C
Colgate Univ	NY	65,030	MC
Colo Mesa Univ	CO	18,955	LC
Colo State Univ	CO	22,162	VC
Concordia Univ Nebr	NE	36,280	VC
Concordia Univ, Ann Arbor	MI	35,945	VC
Concordia Univ, Chicago	IL	39,694	C
Dakota State Univ	SD	13,811	C
DePaul Univ	IL	47,623	VC
Dordt College	IA	37,860	C+
Emporia State Univ	KS	14,570	C
Eureka College	IL	30,220	C
Fort Hays State Univ	KS	12,131	C
Freed-Hardeman Univ	TN	29,450	C
Harvard College/Harvard Univ	MA	60,659	MC
Indiana Univ Kokomo	IN	7,073	C
Indiana Univ-Purdue Univ Fort Wayne	IN	17,553	C
Kansas State Univ	KS	17,780	VC
Le Moyne College	NY	46,000	C
Mayville State Univ	ND	18,371	NC
Mich State Univ	MI	23,898	VC+
Minot State Univ	ND	12,732	C
Miss Univ for Women	MS	17,065	C
Muhlenberg College	PA	56,645	VC+
Okla Panhandle State Univ	OK	6,152	NC
Olivet Nazarene Univ	IL	41,840	C
Peru State College	NE	14,768	NC
Ripon College	WI	46,911	C+
Rowan Univ	NJ	24,491	VC+
St. Michael's College	VT	51,725	VC+
San Diego State Univ	CA	21,896	C+
St. John's Univ	NY	55,850	C
Trine Univ	IN	41,310	C
Union Univ	TN	33,970	VC
Univ of Arkansas at Monticello	AR	13,134	NC
Univ of Calif at Berkeley	CA	28,853	MC
Univ of Calif at Riverside	CA	29,227	C+
Univ of Dayton	OH	53,620	C
Univ of Great Falls	MT	38,524	C
Univ of Maryland/College Park	MD	21,938	HC
Univ of Mich-Flint	MI	17,607	C+
Univ of Pittsburgh at Bradford	PA	22,402	C
Univ of Rio Grande & Rio Grande Community College	OH	8,750	NC
Univ of South Florida/Tampa	FL	16,110	VC+
Univ of Southern Calif	CA	66,631	C
Univ of Wisc-Eau Claire	WI	15,797	VC
Univ of Wisc-Platteville	WI	14,614	VC
Washington State Univ	WA	22,495	C
Washington Univ in St. Louis	MO	65,366	VC
Wayland Baptist Univ	TX	22,356	LC
Wesleyan College	GA	29,694	C+
Youngstown State Univ	OH	17,307	C

PHYSICAL THERAPY

School	ST	$IS	SR
American International College	MA	46,300	LC
Biola Univ	CA	46,402	C+
Boston Univ	MA	65,110	MC
Cal State, Northridge	CA	16,859	LC
Cal State, Sacramento	CA	20,332	C
Carroll Univ	WI	38,100	C+
Carson-Newman Univ	TN	34,160	C
Chatham Univ	PA	46,517	C
CUNY/Hunter College	NY	31,098	VC

ST = STATE $IS = IN-STATE COSTS SR = SELECTOR RATING

School	ST	$IS	SR
Clarke Univ	IA	38,940	C
Cleveland State Univ	OH	22,196	C
Coe College	IA	51,570	VC
College of St. Scholastica	MN	44,640	C
DeSales Univ	PA	43,970	C
Duquesne Univ	PA	46,822	VC
Fairleigh Dickinson Univ/ Metropolitan Campus	NJ	40,254	C
Florida A&M Univ	FL	15,361	C
Gannon Univ	PA	42,032	C
Gordon College	MA	46,472	C+
Grand Valley State Univ	MI	22,250	C+
Gustavus Adolphus College	MN	52,433	HC
Howard Univ	DC	37,616	C+
Husson Univ	ME	25,720	LC
Ithaca College	NY	56,766	VC
Lamar Univ	TX	18,014	LC
Langston Univ	OK	14,314	C
Lebanon Valley College	PA	51,530	C
Maryville Univ of St. Louis	MO	38,046	VC+
MCPHS Univ	MA	45,470	SP
Misericordia Univ	PA	43,840	C
Missouri State Univ	MO	15,190	C+
Mount Aloysius College	PA	29,976	C
New York Univ	NY	65,860	MC
North Park Univ	IL	35,860	C
Northeastern Univ	MA	62,703	MC
Notre Dame College	OH	37,150	VC
Ohio State Univ at Columbus	OH	21,703	HC+
Okla Baptist Univ	OK	32,320	C
Purdue Univ/Northwest	IN	15,038	C
Quinnipiac Univ	CT	59,110	C
Regis Univ	CO	44,520	C
Russell Sage College	NY	39,370	C
St. Francis Univ	PA	42,268	NC
St. Vincent College	PA	44,626	C
Simmons College	MA	53,090	VC
St. Ambrose Univ	IA	39,019	C
St. Ambrose Univ	IA	39,019	C
Stockton Univ	NJ	25,059	
Tarleton State Univ	TX	15,248	LC
Tenn State Univ	TN	14,423	C
The Univ of Akron	OH	21,477	C
Touro College	NY	28,950	VC
Trine Univ	IN	41,310	C
Trinity International Univ	IL	31,070	VC
Truman State Univ	MO	16,014	HC
Univ of Alaska Anchorage	AK	16,652	NC
Univ of Central Arkansas	AR	14,472	VC
Univ of Conn	CT	25,538	HC
Univ of Florida	FL	16,291	HC+
Univ of Hartford	CT	49,776	C
Univ of Illinois at Chicago	IL	25,006	VC
Univ of Kentucky	KY	33,306	C
Univ of Mary	ND	23,180	C
Univ of Maryland/Eastern Shore	MD	17,013	C
Univ of Mich-Flint	MI	17,607	C+
Univ of Minn/Twin Cities	MN	23,519	HC+
Univ of Missouri/Columbia	MO	18,201	MC
Univ of N Car at Wilmington	NC	14,590	VC
Univ of N Dak	ND	15,373	C
Univ of North Florida	FL	15,996	VC
Univ of the Sciences	PA	54,038	VC
Univ of Toledo	OH	19,336	NC
Utica College	NY	30,430	C
Vanguard Univ of Southern Calif	CA	40,740	VC
Virginia Polytechnic Inst and State Univ	VA	21,276	HC
Walla Walla Univ	WA	30,417	NC
Walsh Univ	OH	39,010	C
West Virginia Univ	WV	18,210	C
Wingate Univ	NC	39,950	C
Winston-Salem State Univ	NC	26,166	LC

PHYSICAL THERAPY ASSISTANT

School	ST	$IS	SR
Calif Univ of Pennsylvania	PA	14,217	LC
Idaho State Univ	ID	13,619	NC
Mount Aloysius College	PA	29,976	C
Nebr Methodist College	NE	25,134	SP
Southwestern Okla State Univ	OK	11,790	C
Walla Walla Univ	WA	30,417	NC

PHYSICIAN'S ASSISTANT

School	ST	$IS	SR
Carroll Univ	WI	38,100	C+
CUNY/City College	NY	20,319	VC
Colo State Univ-Pueblo	CO	18,234	C
Daemen College	NY	38,045	C
DeSales Univ	PA	43,970	C
Duquesne Univ	PA	46,822	VC
D'Youville College	NY	36,780	C
Gannon Univ	PA	42,032	C
Gardner-Webb Univ	NC	39,200	C+
George Washington Univ	DC	62,835	MC
Grand Valley State Univ	MI	22,250	C+
Hofstra Univ	NY	55,960	C+
Howard Univ	DC	37,616	C+
King's College	PA	46,858	C
LIU Brooklyn	NY	49,682	C
Marietta College	OH	46,190	C
Mars Hill Univ	NC	42,688	C
Marywood Univ	PA	46,900	C
MCPHS Univ	MA	45,470	SP
Methodist Univ	NC	43,600	C
Missouri State Univ	MO	15,190	C+
Mount Aloysius College	PA	29,976	C
Northern Mich Univ	MI	19,604	C
Pennsylvania College of Technology	PA	27,333	NC
Philadelphia Univ	PA	50,370	C
Quinnipiac Univ	CT	59,110	C
Rochester Inst of Technology	NY	50,842	HC
St. Francis Univ	PA	42,268	NC
St. Vincent College	PA	44,626	C
Seton Hill Univ	PA	46,972	C
South Univ	GA	36,070	LC
St. Ambrose Univ	IA	39,019	C
St. Ambrose Univ	IA	39,019	C
St. Francis College	NY	38,800	LC
St. John's Univ	NY	55,850	C
Union College	NE	23,270	C
Univ of Findlay	OH	60,139	C
Univ of Kentucky	KY	33,306	C
Univ of the Sciences	PA	54,038	VC
Univ of Wisc-La Crosse	WI	15,247	C+
Wagner College	NY	55,480	C+
Walla Walla Univ	WA	30,417	NC
Wichita State Univ	KS	21,643	C
Wingate Univ	NC	39,950	C

PHYSICS

School	ST	$IS	SR
Abilene Christian Univ	TX	41,800	C+
Adams State Univ	CO	17,703	LC
Adelphi Univ	NY	48,244	C
Adrian College	MI	42,400	C
Agnes Scott College	GA	51,930	VC+
Alabama A&M Univ	AL	18,796	C
Alabama State Univ	AL	14,142	NC
Albion College	MI	52,650	C
Albright College	PA	46,660	C
Alfred Univ	NY	42,296	C+
Allegheny College	PA	55,420	VC
Alma College	MI	47,548	C
American Univ	DC	59,379	HC+
Amherst College	MA		HC+
Anderson Univ	IN	38,200	C
Andrews Univ	MI	28,030	C+
Angelo State Univ	TX	15,263	NC
Appalachian State Univ	NC	14,416	VC
Arizona State Univ at the Tempe Campus	AZ	21,756	VC
Arkansas State Univ	AR	16,190	C
Arkansas Tech Univ	AR	15,484	C
Ashland Univ	OH	21,440	C
Auburn Univ	AL	23,594	VC+
Augsburg College	MN	43,929	C
Augusta Univ	GA	4,632	C
Augustana College	IL	49,658	VC
Augustana Univ	SD	38,424	VC
Austin College	TX	45,875	VC
Austin Peay State Univ	TN	16,397	C
Azusa Pacific Univ	CA	43,972	C
Baker Univ	KS	33,350	C+
Baldwin Wallace Univ	OH	41,106	C
Ball State Univ	IN	19,590	C
Bard College	NY	64,024	HC
Bard College at Simon's Rock	MA	65,795	MC
Barnard College/Columbia Univ	NY	62,741	MC
Bates College	ME	64,500	MC
Baylor Univ	TX	53,760	HC
Bellarmine Univ	KY	51,220	C
Belmont Univ	TN	40,970	VC
Beloit College	WI	55,206	HC
Bemidji State Univ	MN	16,056	VC
Benedict College	SC	28,238	NC
Benedictine College	KS	36,200	VC
Benedictine Univ	IL	38,300	C
Bennington College	VT	63,960	MC
Berea College	KY	7,042	C
Berry College	GA	45,286	C+
Bethel Univ	MN	45,270	VC
Biola Univ	CA	46,402	C+
Birmingham-Southern College	AL	44,478	VC
Bloomsburg Univ of Pennsylvania	PA	19,066	LC
Bluffton Univ	OH	40,950	C
Boise State Univ	ID	14,860	C
Boston College	MA	65,737	MC
Boston Univ	MA	65,110	MC
Bowdoin College	ME	63,500	MC
Bowling Green State Univ	OH	19,747	C
Brandeis Univ	MA	65,925	MC
Bridgewater College	VA	44,510	C
Bridgewater State Univ	MA	21,810	C
Brigham Young Univ	UT	12,748	HC
Brown Univ	RI	64,566	MC
Bryn Mawr College	PA	59,890	MC
Bucknell Univ	PA	64,616	MC
Buena Vista Univ	IA	41,514	C
Butler Univ	IN	51,352	VC
Calif Inst of Technology	CA	58,761	MC
Calif Lutheran Univ	CA	52,853	C
Calif Polytechnic State Univ	CA	17,979	HC+
Calif State Polytechnic Univ, Pomona	CA	21,541	C
Cal State, Bakersfield	CA	19,191	LC
Cal State, Chico	CA	21,440	C
Cal State, Dominguez Hills	CA	19,022	LC
Cal State, East Bay	CA	19,413	C
Cal State, Fresno	CA	16,902	LC
Cal State, Fullerton	CA	21,902	C
Cal State, Long Beach	CA	18,850	C
Cal State, Los Angeles	CA	17,186	LC
Cal State, Northridge	CA	16,859	LC
Cal State, Sacramento	CA	20,332	C
Cal State, San Bernardino	CA	12,000	C
Cal State, Stanislaus	CA	16,212	C
Calif Univ of Pennsylvania	PA	14,217	LC
Calvin College	MI	41,570	VC+
Cameron Univ	OK	11,072	NC
Canisius College	NY	47,537	C
Carleton College	MN	64,071	MC
Carnegie Mellon Univ	PA	67,980	MC
Carthage College	WI	48,835	C
Case Western Reserve Univ	OH	60,304	MC
Cedarville Univ	OH	34,990	VC
Centenary College of Louisiana	LA	45,650	C+
Central College	IA	44,592	C
Central Conn State Univ	CT	21,203	C
Central Methodist Univ	MO	36,830	VC
Central Mich Univ	MI	20,330	C
Central Washington Univ	WA	16,803	C
Centre College	KY	49,250	HC
Chadron State College	NE	14,819	NC
Chapman Univ	CA	63,078	VC+
Chatham Univ	PA	46,517	C
Chicago State Univ	IL	20,144	C
Christian Brothers Univ	TN	31,670	VC
CUNY/Brooklyn College	NY	5,884	C+
CUNY/City College	NY	20,319	VC
CUNY/College of Staten Island	NY	17,840	NC
CUNY/Hunter College	NY	31,098	VC
CUNY/Lehman College	NY	5,778	HC+
CUNY/Queens College	NY	27,896	C
CUNY/York College	NY	6,747	LC
Claremont McKenna College	CA	67,185	MC
Clarion Univ of Pennsylvania	PA	21,608	LC
Clark Atlanta Univ	GA	31,019	LC
Clark Univ	MA	51,600	HC+
Clarkson Univ	NY	60,392	HC
Clemson Univ	SC		HC
Cleveland State Univ	OH	22,196	C
Coastal Carolina Univ	SC	19,766	C
Coe College	IA	51,570	VC
Colby College	ME	64,060	MC
Colgate Univ	NY	65,030	MC
College of Charleston	SC	22,699	C
College of Mount St. Vincent	NY	45,620	C
College of St. Benedict	MN	52,806	C
College of the Holy Cross	MA	62,165	MC
College of William & Mary	VA		MC
Colo College	CO	62,560	MC
Colo Mesa Univ	CO	18,955	LC
Colo School of Mines	CO	29,319	MC
Colo State Univ	CO	22,162	VC
Colo State Univ-Pueblo	CO	18,234	C
Columbia Univ/ School of General Studies	NY	61,470	MC
Columbia Univ/City of New York	NY	62,958	MC
Concordia College - Moorhead	MN	51,088	C+
Concordia Univ, Ann Arbor	MI	35,945	VC
Conn College	CT	65,000	MC
Cornell College	IA	48,800	VC
Cornell Univ	NY	64,853	MC
Covenant College	GA	38,990	VC
Creighton Univ	NE	48,206	VC+
Dartmouth College	NH	66,174	MC
Davidson College	NC	60,119	MC
Delaware State Univ	DE	19,376	NC
Denison Univ	OH	58,860	MC
DePaul Univ	IL	47,623	VC
DePauw Univ	IN	58,688	HC+
Dickinson College	PA	63,974	MC
Dillard Univ	LA	20,940	VC
Doane Univ	NE	39,184	VC
Dordt College	IA	37,860	C+
Drake Univ	IA	45,056	HC
Drew Univ/College of Liberal Arts	NJ	61,048	VC
Drexel Univ	PA	65,432	VC+
Drury Univ	MO	33,791	VC
Duke Univ	NC	64,188	
Duquesne Univ	PA	46,822	VC
Earlham College	IN	54,870	HC
East Carolina Univ	NC	16,937	C
East Central Univ	OK	13,056	C
East Stroudsburg Univ	PA	18,334	C
East Tenn State Univ	TN	13,994	C
Eastern Illinois Univ	IL	21,126	C
Eastern Mich Univ	MI	19,761	C
Eastern Nazarene College	MA	39,955	C
Eastern Oregon Univ	OR	17,715	C
Eastern Washington Univ	WA	25,572	LC
Eckerd College	FL	52,874	C
Edgewood College	WI	35,950	C
Edinboro Univ	PA	15,940	LC
Elizabeth City State Univ	NC	14,745	C
Elizabethtown College	PA	54,050	C
Elmhurst College	IL	45,428	C
Elon Univ	NC	44,599	VC+
Emory and Henry College	VA	41,410	C
Emory Univ	GA	60,786	MC
Emporia State Univ	KS	14,570	C
Erskine College	SC	45,460	C
Excelsior College	NY	14,080	SP
Fairfield Univ	CT	59,860	VC+
Fisk Univ	TN	32,066	LC
Florida A&M Univ	FL	15,361	C
Florida Atlantic Univ	FL	17,339	C
Florida Inst of Technology	FL	53,306	VC
Florida International Univ	FL	19,854	C+
Florida State Univ	FL	16,771	HC
Fordham Univ	NY	65,918	MC
Fort Hays State Univ	KS	12,131	C
Fort Lewis College	CO	18,980	C
Francis Marion Univ	SC	16,464	LC
Franklin and Marshall College	PA	63,170	HC
Frostburg State Univ	MD	17,280	LC
Furman Univ	SC	58,092	VC+
Geneva College	PA	35,450	C
George Mason Univ	VA	15,724	VC
George Washington Univ	DC	62,835	MC
Georgetown College	KY	41,440	C
Georgetown Univ	DC	65,926	MC
Georgia College & State Univ	GA	21,148	C+
Georgia Inst of Technology	GA	23,360	MC
Georgia Southern Univ	GA	16,596	C
Georgia State Univ	GA	24,332	VC
Gettysburg College	PA	63,000	HC
Gonzaga Univ	WA	50,888	HC
Gordon College	MA	46,472	C+
Goshen College	IN	42,500	C
Goucher College	MD	55,716	VC
Grambling State Univ	LA	15,701	C
Grand Valley State Univ	MI	22,250	C+
Greenville College	IL	27,012	C
Grinnell College	IA	60,738	MC
Grove City College	PA	25,692	VC
Guilford College	NC	44,090	C
Gustavus Adolphus College	MN	52,433	HC
Hamilton College	NY	64,250	MC
Hamline Univ	MN	45,678	VC
Hampden-Sydney College	VA	56,248	C+
Hampshire College	MA	63,824	MC
Hampton Univ	VA	34,926	LC
Hanover College	IN	46,364	C+
Harding Univ	AR	25,421	C
Hardin-Simmons Univ	TX	33,966	C
Hartwick College	NY	51,270	C
Harvard College/Harvard Univ	MA	60,659	MC
Harvey Mudd College	CA	67,155	MC
Hastings College	NE	35,380	C+
Haverford College	PA	66,490	MC
Heidelberg Univ	OH	39,200	C
Henderson State Univ	AR	15,516	LC
Hendrix College	AR	54,020	VC+
High Point Univ	NC	45,977	C
Hillsdale College	MI	35,722	MC
Hiram College	OH	43,230	C
Hofstra Univ	NY	55,960	C+
Hope College	MI	39,940	VC
Houghton College	NY	39,090	C
Houston Baptist Univ	TX	36,450	C
Howard Univ	DC	37,616	C+
Humboldt State Univ	CA	20,514	C
Huntington Univ	IN	33,996	C
Idaho State Univ	ID	13,619	NC
Illinois College	IL	40,850	VC
Illinois Inst of Technology	IL	56,826	HC+
Illinois State Univ	IL	23,418	VC
Illinois Wesleyan Univ	IL	56,430	VC+
Indiana State Univ	IN	23,223	LC
Indiana Univ Bloomington	IN	20,429	VC
Indiana Univ of Pennsylvania	PA	23,614	LC
Indiana Univ South Bend	IN	14,242	C
Indiana Univ Southeast	IN	14,242	LC
Indiana Univ-Purdue Univ Fort Wayne	IN	17,553	C
Indiana Univ-Purdue Univ Indianapolis	IN	18,635	C
Iona College	NY	50,984	C
Iowa State Univ	IA	17,570	C
Ithaca College	NY	56,766	VC
Jackson State Univ	MS	15,879	LC
Jacksonville State Univ	AL	14,628	LC
Jacksonville Univ	FL	46,230	C
James Madison Univ	VA	19,084	VC
John Carroll Univ	OH	49,740	C+
Johns Hopkins Univ	MD	65,386	MC
Johnson C. Smith Univ	NC	25,336	LC
Juniata College	PA	53,760	VC
Kalamazoo College	MI	53,931	HC+
Kansas State Univ	KS	17,780	VC
Kansas Wesleyan Univ	KS	36,600	C
Keene State College	NH	24,003	LC
Kennesaw State Univ	GA	19,592	VC
Kent State Univ	OH	20,732	C
Kentucky Wesleyan College	KY	32,080	C
Kenyon College	OH	63,330	MC
King Univ	TN	34,660	C
King's College	PA	46,858	C
Knox College	IL	52,615	VC+
Kutztown Univ of Pennsylvania	PA	19,056	LC
La Sierra Univ	CA	39,690	VC
Lafayette College	PA	63,355	MC
Lake Forest College	IL	50,652	VC
Lamar Univ	TX	18,014	LC
Lane College	TN	16,550	C
Lawrence Tech Univ	MI	39,770	VC
Lawrence Univ	WI	54,498	HC
Le Moyne College	NY	46,000	C
Lebanon Valley College	PA	51,530	C

ST = STATE   **$IS** = IN-STATE COSTS   **SR** = SELECTOR RATING

School	ST	$IS	SR
Lehigh Univ	PA	61,010	MC
Lenoir-Rhyne Univ	NC	43,200	C
Lewis & Clark College	OR	58,434	HC+
Lewis Univ	IL	40,370	C
Lincoln Univ	MO	13,602	NC
Linfield College	OR	52,010	C
Lipscomb Univ	TN	41,296	VC
LIU Post	NY	49,682	C
Lock Haven Univ of Pennsylvania	PA	18,028	LC
Longwood Univ	VA	22,184	C
Louisiana State Univ and A&M College	LA	18,677	VC
Louisiana State Univ in Shreveport	LA	6,902	C
Louisiana Tech Univ	LA	11,422	VC
Loyola Marymount Univ	CA	58,038	HC
Loyola Univ Chicago	IL	55,802	VC
Loyola Univ Maryland	MD	60,300	VC
Loyola Univ New Orleans	LA	51,708	VC+
Luther College	IA	48,540	C+
Lycoming College	PA	48,580	C
Lynchburg College	VA	46,740	C
Macalester College	MN	61,905	MC
MacMurray College	IL	33,620	C
Madonna Univ	MI	29,050	C
Manchester Univ	IN	40,422	C
Manhattan College	NY	51,750	C+
Marietta College	OH	46,190	C
Marquette Univ	WI	48,390	VC+
Marshall Univ	WV	17,242	C
Mary Baldwin Univ	VA	39,865	C
Mass College of Liberal Arts	MA	20,128	C
Mass Inst of Technology	MA	62,662	MC
McDaniel College	MD	51,380	VC
McMurry Univ	TX	34,259	LC
Mercer Univ	GA	45,348	VC
Merrimack College	MA	52,770	C
Messiah College	PA	43,100	C+
Metropolitan State Univ of Denver	CO	29,889	LC
Miami Univ	OH	27,190	HC+
Mich State Univ	MI	23,898	VC+
Mich Tech Univ	MI	24,739	VC+
MidAmerica Nazarene Univ	KS	35,550	C
Middle Tenn State Univ	TN	8,650	C
Middlebury College	VT	64,332	MC
Millersville Univ of Pennsylvania	PA	23,782	C
Millikin Univ	IL	42,158	C
Millsaps College	MS	50,080	C+
Minn State Univ, Mankato	MN	15,616	C
Minn State Univ, Moorhead	MN	15,941	C
Minot State Univ	ND	12,732	C
Miss College	MS	25,850	C
Miss State Univ	MS	11,454	C+
Missouri Southern State Univ	MO	12,499	C
Missouri Univ of Science and Technology	MO	18,655	HC
Monmouth College	IL	42,260	C
Montana State Univ	MT	15,500	C+
Montclair State Univ	NJ	26,210	LC
Moravian College	PA	53,117	
Morehead State Univ	KY	17,422	C
Morehouse College	GA	40,064	C
Morgan State Univ	MD	17,190	LC
Morningside College	IA	36,865	C
Mount Holyoke College	MA	56,746	MC
Muhlenberg College	PA	56,645	VC+
Murray State Univ	KY	16,998	C
Muskingum Univ	OH	35,966	C
Nebr Wesleyan Univ	NE	38,140	C+
New College of Florida	FL	15,848	MC
New Jersey City Univ	NJ	21,456	LC
New Mexico Highlands Univ	NM	11,904	NC
New Mexico Inst of Mining and Technology	NM	14,833	HC
New Mexico State Univ	NM	14,050	C
New York Univ	NY	65,860	MC
Norfolk State Univ	VA	25,702	LC
N Car A&T State Univ	NC	13,365	LC
N Car Central Univ	NC	9,000	C
N Car State Univ	NC	19,515	HC+
North Central College	IL	48,712	VC
N Dak State Univ	ND	16,245	C
North Park Univ	IL	35,860	C
Northeastern Illinois Univ	IL	12,529	LC
Northeastern Univ	MA	62,703	MC
Northern Arizona Univ	AZ	20,246	VC
Northern Illinois Univ	IL	20,176	C
Northern Kentucky Univ	KY	16,486	C
Northern Mich Univ	MI	19,604	C
Northwest Missouri State Univ	MO	17,737	C
Northwest Nazarene Univ	ID	36,000	C
Northwestern Okla State Univ	OK	13,072	NC
Northwestern Univ	IL	66,344	MC
Norwich Univ	VT	28,212	C
Notre Dame of Maryland Univ	MD	46,465	VC
Oakland Univ	MI	20,763	C
Oberlin College	OH	66,012	MC
Occidental College	CA	65,530	MC
Oglethorpe Univ	GA	44,200	C+
Ohio Northern Univ	OH	44,050	VC
Ohio State Univ at Columbus	OH	21,703	HC+
Ohio Univ	OH	22,924	C
Ohio Wesleyan Univ	OH	49,460	VC
Okla Baptist Univ	OK	32,320	C
Okla City Univ	OK	40,476	VC
Okla State Univ	OK	17,180	VC
Old Dominion Univ	VA	20,910	C
Oral Roberts Univ	OK	34,316	C
Oregon State Univ	OR	22,519	VC
Otterbein Univ	OH	41,630	C
Ouachita Baptist Univ	AR	32,320	C
Pace Univ	NY	58,248	C
Pacific Lutheran Univ	WA	49,960	VC
Pacific Union College	CA	36,009	VC
Pacific Univ	OR	52,876	C
Penn State Erie/The Behrend College	PA	16,256	C
Pennsylvania State Univ - Univ Park	PA	29,760	HC
Pepperdine Univ	CA	74,460	HC+
Piedmont College	GA	32,512	C
Pittsburg State Univ	KS	13,880	NC
Pitzer College	CA	66,192	MC
Point Loma Nazarene Univ	CA	43,450	C
Pomona College	CA	64,957	MC
Pontifical Catholic Univ of PR	PR	10,534	
Portland State Univ	OR	19,443	C
Prairie View A&M Univ	TX	15,205	LC
Princeton Univ	NJ	57,610	MC
Principia College	IL	39,010	C+
Purdue Univ/Northwest	IN	15,038	C
Purdue Univ/West Lafayette	IN	20,032	MC
Radford Univ	VA	19,027	LC
Randolph College	VA	45,660	VC
Randolph-Macon College	VA	49,910	C
Reed College	OR	65,300	MC
Regis Univ	CO	44,520	C
Rensselaer Polytechnic Inst	NY	63,436	MC
Rhode Island College	RI	17,694	LC
Rhodes College	TN	51,900	HC
Rice Univ	TX	57,668	MC
Rider Univ	NJ	54,050	C
Ripon College	WI	46,911	C+
Roanoke College	VA	54,114	VC
Roberts Wesleyan College	NY	38,306	C
Rochester Inst of Technology	NY	50,842	HC
Rockhurst Univ	MO	29,220	C
Rollins College	FL	58,670	HC
Rose-Hulman Inst of Technology	IN	57,303	MC
Rowan Univ	NJ	24,491	VC+
Rutgers Univ - Camden	NJ	26,146	C
Rutgers Univ - New Brunswick	NJ	26,632	HC
Rutgers Univ - Newark	NJ	27,288	C
Saginaw Valley State Univ	MI	18,530	C
St. John's Univ	MN	51,624	C
St. Joseph's Univ	PA	57,544	VC+
St. Louis Univ	MO	49,866	HC
St. Mary's College	IN	50,600	C
St. Mary's College of Calif	CA	57,420	C
St. Mary's Univ of Minn	MN	41,210	VC
St. Michael's College	VT	51,725	VC+
St. Peter's Univ	NJ	49,192	C
St. Vincent College	PA	44,626	C
Salisbury Univ	MD	20,714	VC
Sam Houston State Univ	TX	18,792	C
Samford Univ	AL	39,232	VC
San Diego State Univ	CA	21,896	C+
San Francisco State Univ	CA	18,514	LC
San Jose State Univ	CA	21,540	C
Scripps College	CA	66,664	MC
Seattle Pacific Univ	WA	47,439	C+
Seattle Univ	WA	50,811	VC+
Seton Hall Univ	NJ	55,514	C
Seton Hill Univ	PA	46,972	C
Sewanee: The Univ of the South	TN	54,500	MC
Shaw Univ	NC	24,638	C
Shippensburg Univ of Pennsylvania	PA	23,208	C
Siena College	NY	48,916	C+
Simmons College	MA	53,090	VC
Simpson College	IA	43,839	VC
Skidmore College	NY	64,214	HC
Slippery Rock Univ of Pennsylvania	PA	10,360	C
Smith College	MA	63,914	MC
Sonoma State Univ	CA	27,806	C
S Car State Univ	SC	20,805	LC
S Dak School of Mines and Technology	SD	18,645	VC
S Dak State Univ	SD	15,634	C
Southeast Missouri State Univ	MO	15,498	C
Southeastern Louisiana Univ	LA	16,237	C
Southeastern Okla State Univ	OK	11,875	C
Southern Adventist Univ	TN	27,600	C
Southern Conn State Univ	CT	21,924	LC
Southern Illinois Univ Carbondale	IL	23,667	C
Southern Illinois Univ Edwardsville	IL	22,643	C
Southern Methodist Univ	TX	66,483	MC
Southern Nazarene Univ	OK	32,798	NC
Southern Univ and A&M College	LA	16,074	LC+
Southern Univ at New Orleans	LA	8,014	LC
Southwestern Adventist Univ	TX	27,756	LC
Southwestern Univ	TX	50,720	VC
Spelman College	GA	38,751	C
Spring Arbor Univ	MI	36,000	C
St. Bonaventure Univ	NY	44,237	C
St. Cloud State Univ	MN	10,600	C
St. John Fisher College	NY	43,620	C
St. John's College-Annapolis	MD	60,142	MC
St. John's Univ	NY	55,850	C
St. Lawrence Univ	NY	64,390	VC
St. Mary's College of Maryland	MD	26,634	VC
St. Mary's Univ	TX	37,500	C
St. Norbert College	WI	44,525	VC
St. Olaf College	MN	54,260	HC+
Stanford Univ	CA	60,409	MC
SUNY / Buffalo State College	NY	20,842	C
SUNY / SUNY Cortland	NY	20,706	VC
SUNY / SUNY Fredonia	NY	20,818	C
SUNY / SUNY Oneonta	NY	19,712	C+
SUNY / SUNY Plattsburgh	NY	18,814	C
SUNY / SUNY Potsdam	NY	20,404	C+
SUNY / Univ at Buffalo	NY	23,122	C+
SUNY at Binghamton	NY	22,861	MC
SUNY at Geneseo	NY	20,440	VC+
SUNY at New Paltz	NY	19,200	C
SUNY at Oswego	NY	21,351	C
SUNY SUNY Albany	NY	22,165	C
Stephen F. Austin State Univ	TX	18,406	LC
Stetson Univ	FL	53,544	VC
Stevens Inst of Technology	NJ	62,338	MC
Stockton Univ	NJ	25,059	
Stonehill College	MA	55,030	C+
Stony Brook Univ/The SUNY	NY	21,881	MC
Suffolk Univ	MA	50,308	C
Susquehanna Univ	PA	55,340	VC
Swarthmore College	PA	63,550	MC
Syracuse Univ	NY	60,239	VC
Talladega College	AL	19,215	C
Tarleton State Univ	TX	15,248	LC
Taylor Univ	IN	40,317	C+
Temple Univ	PA	24,392	VC
Tenn State Univ	TN	14,423	C
Tenn Tech Univ	TN	17,050	C
Texas A&M Univ	TX	20,521	VC+
Texas A&M Univ at Commerce	TX	10,496	C
Texas A&M Univ at Kingsville	TX	7,500	LC
Texas Christian Univ	TX	54,670	HC
Texas Lutheran Univ	TX	38,620	C
Texas State Univ	TX	19,350	C
Texas Tech Univ	TX	18,736	C+
The Catholic Univ of America	DC	56,356	VC
The Citadel, The Military College of S Car	SC	35,339	C
The College at Brockport - SUNY	NY	20,346	C
The College of New Jersey	NJ	31,909	HC
The College of Wooster	OH	57,900	VC+
The Lincoln Univ	PA	15,154	NC
The Univ of Akron	OH	21,477	C
The Univ of Tenn at Chattanooga	TN	16,744	C
The Univ of Tenn at Knoxville	TN	22,112	VC
The Univ of Utah	UT	17,924	VC
Thiel College	PA	41,590	C
Thomas More College	KY	36,720	C
Tougaloo College	MS	17,980	NC
Touro College	NY	28,950	VC
Towson Univ	MD	17,408	VC
Transylvania Univ	KY	45,690	VC+
Trevecca Nazarene Univ	TN	31,186	C
Trinity College	CT	63,920	HC+
Trinity Univ	TX	52,314	HC+
Truman State Univ	MO	16,014	HC
Tufts Univ	MA		MC
Tulane Univ	LA	63,396	HC+
Tuskegee Univ	AL	28,164	C
Union College	NE	23,270	C
Union College	NY	64,320	MC
Union Univ	TN	33,970	VC
United States Air Force Academy	CO		C
United States Military Academy at West Point	NY		HC+
United States Naval Academy	MD		MC
Univ of Alabama	AL	24,320	C+
Univ of Alabama at Birmingham	AL	19,906	C
Univ of Alabama in Huntsville	AL	19,445	VC
Univ of Alaska Fairbanks	AK	16,179	C
Univ of Arizona	AZ	23,100	C
Univ of Arkansas at Fayetteville	AR	19,152	C+
Univ of Arkansas at Little Rock	AR	18,211	C
Univ of Arkansas at Pine Bluff	AR	13,541	C
Univ of Calif at Berkeley	CA	28,853	MC
Univ of Calif at Davis	CA	28,468	HC
Univ of Calif at Irvine	CA	26,484	VC
Univ of Calif at Los Angeles	CA	30,162	MC
Univ of Calif at Riverside	CA	29,227	C+
Univ of Calif at Santa Barbara	CA	29,091	HC
Univ of Calif San Diego	CA	30,150	MC
Univ of Calif, Santa Cruz	CA	28,731	C+
Univ of Central Arkansas	AR	14,472	VC
Univ of Central Florida	FL	15,922	VC
Univ of Central Missouri	MO	18,982	C
Univ of Chicago	IL	67,584	MC
Univ of Cincinnati	OH	21,964	VC
Univ of Colo Boulder	CO	24,285	VC+
Univ of Colo Colo Springs	CO	19,663	C
Univ of Colo Denver	CO	23,230	C
Univ of Conn	CT	25,538	HC
Univ of Dallas	TX	45,500	VC+
Univ of Dayton	OH	53,620	C
Univ of Delaware	DE	24,976	VC+
Univ of Denver	CO	58,443	VC+
Univ of Evansville	IN	44,186	VC+
Univ of Florida	FL	16,291	HC+
Univ of Georgia	GA	21,250	HC
Univ of Hartford	CT	49,776	C
Univ of Hawaii at Hilo	HI	18,038	C
Univ of Hawaii at Manoa	HI	23,221	C
Univ of Houston	TX	21,483	VC
Univ of Idaho	ID	15,348	C
Univ of Illinois at Chicago	IL	25,006	VC
Univ of Illinois at Urbana-Champaign	IL	27,006	HC
Univ of Indianapolis	IN	36,480	C
Univ of Iowa	IA	18,683	VC+
Univ of Kansas	KS	20,135	C+
Univ of Kentucky	KY	33,306	C
Univ of La Verne	CA	55,600	C
Univ of Louisiana at Lafayette	LA	14,516	C
Univ of Louisville	KY	19,824	C
Univ of Maine	ME	20,792	C
Univ of Mary Washington	VA	24,764	VC
Univ of Maryland/Baltimore County	MD	21,296	VC
Univ of Maryland/College Park	MD	21,938	HC
Univ of Mass Amherst	MA	26,199	VC+
Univ of Mass Boston	MA	13,435	C
Univ of Mass Dartmouth	MA	25,658	C
Univ of Mass Lowell	MA	26,380	C
Univ of Memphis	TN	18,278	C
Univ of Miami	FL	63,494	MC
Univ of Mich/Ann Arbor	MI	24,410	MC
Univ of Mich/Dearborn	MI	11,757	VC
Univ of Mich-Flint	MI	17,607	C+
Univ of Minn/Duluth	MN	20,292	C+
Univ of Minn/Morris	MN	20,760	VC
Univ of Minn/Twin Cities	MN	23,519	HC+
Univ of Miss	MS	17,746	C+
Univ of Missouri/Columbia	MO	18,201	MC
Univ of Missouri-Kansas City	MO	19,563	VC
Univ of Missouri-St. Louis	MO		C
Univ of Montana	MT	14,105	C
Univ of Mount Union	OH	38,970	C
Univ of Nebr - Kearney	NE	16,546	LC
Univ of Nebr - Lincoln	NE	18,589	VC
Univ of Nebr - Omaha	NE	16,120	C
Univ of Nevada, Las Vegas	NV	17,553	C
Univ of Nevada/Reno	NV	18,010	C
Univ of New Hampshire	NH	28,562	VC
Univ of New Mexico	NM	15,404	C
Univ of New Orleans	LA	12,840	C
Univ of North Alabama	AL	15,398	C
Univ of N Car at Asheville	NC	15,723	VC+
Univ of N Car at Chapel Hill	NC	20,052	HC+
Univ of N Car at Charlotte	NC	15,547	C
Univ of N Car at Greensboro	NC	14,690	C
Univ of N Car at Pembroke	NC	14,388	LC
Univ of N Car at Wilmington	NC	14,590	VC
Univ of N Dak	ND	15,373	C
Univ of North Florida	FL	15,996	VC
Univ of North Georgia	GA	17,316	C
Univ of North Texas	TX	19,198	C
Univ of Northern Colo	CO	20,851	C
Univ of Notre Dame	IN	64,043	MC
Univ of Okla	OK	18,911	VC
Univ of Oregon	OR	22,972	C
Univ of Pennsylvania	PA	63,526	MC
Univ of Pittsburgh	PA	29,568	HC+
Univ of Portland	OR	52,152	VC
Univ of PR, at Humacao	PR	14,000	
Univ of PR, at Mayaguez	PR	13,995	
Univ of Puget Sound	WA	56,456	VC+
Univ of Redlands	CA	60,200	VC
Univ of Rhode Island	RI	24,906	C
Univ of Richmond	VA	60,880	MC
Univ of Rochester	NY	65,032	MC
Univ of San Diego	CA	58,442	VC+
Univ of San Francisco	CA	58,484	VC
Univ of Science and Arts of Okla	OK	11,140	VC
Univ of Scranton	PA	54,962	VC
Univ of South Alabama	AL	16,400	C
Univ of S Car at Columbia	SC	19,725	VC+
Univ of S Dak	SD	16,109	C
Univ of South Florida/Tampa	FL	16,110	VC+
Univ of Southern Calif	CA	66,631	C
Univ of Southern Indiana	IN	16,501	C
Univ of Southern Maine	ME	18,320	C
Univ of Southern Miss	MS	13,170	C
Univ of St. Thomas - Houston	TX	40,020	VC
Univ of Tampa	FL	36,944	C
Univ of Texas at Arlington	TX	18,026	LC
Univ of Texas at Austin	TX	26,102	HC
Univ of Texas at Dallas	TX	22,830	VC+
Univ of Texas at El Paso	TX	34,452	NC
Univ of Texas at San Antonio	TX	20,157	C
Univ of the Cumberlands	KY	32,000	C

ST = STATE $IS = IN-STATE COSTS SR = SELECTOR RATING

School	ST	$IS	SR
Univ of the District of Columbia	DC	21,044	LC
Univ of the Pacific	CA	57,006	VC
Univ of the Sciences	PA	54,038	VC
Univ of Toledo	OH	19,336	NC
Univ of Tulsa	OK	52,625	HC+
Univ of Vermont	VT	28,878	HC
Univ of Virginia	VA	25,891	MC
Univ of Washington	WA	23,149	VC
Univ of West Alabama	AL	15,516	NC
Univ of West Florida	FL	15,848	C
Univ of West Georgia	GA	16,360	LC
Univ of Wisc-Eau Claire	WI	15,797	VC
Univ of Wisc-La Crosse	WI	15,247	C+
Univ of Wisc-Madison	WI	20,934	MC
Univ of Wisc-Milwaukee	WI	21,496	C
Univ of Wisc-Oshkosh	WI	15,200	C
Univ of Wisc-Parkside	WI	15,193	C
Univ of Wisc-Platteville	WI	14,614	VC
Univ of Wisc-River Falls	WI	14,485	C
Univ of Wisc-Stevens Point	WI	14,043	C
Univ of Wisc-Whitewater	WI	13,976	C
Univ of Wyoming	WY	15,375	C+
Ursinus College	PA	61,690	VC
Utah State Univ	UT	12,736	C
Utica College	NY	30,430	C
Valparaiso Univ	IN	48,370	C+
Vanderbilt Univ	TN	60,572	MC
Vassar College	NY	65,491	MC
Villanova Univ	PA	62,523	MC
Virginia Commonwealth Univ	VA	23,049	C
Virginia Military Inst	VA	26,460	C+
Virginia Polytechnic Inst and State Univ	VA	21,276	HC
Virginia State Univ	VA	19,802	C+
Wabash College	IN	50,650	VC
Wagner College	NY	55,480	C+
Wake Forest Univ	NC	64,056	MC
Walla Walla Univ	WA	30,417	NC
Wartburg College	IA	47,840	C
Washburn Univ	KS	15,827	C
Washington & Jefferson College	PA	56,512	VC
Washington and Lee Univ	VA	59,647	MC
Washington College	MD	54,666	VC
Washington State Univ	WA	22,495	C
Washington Univ in St. Louis	MO	65,366	VC
Wayne State Univ	MI	22,016	C
Weber State Univ	UT	10,721	C
Wellesley College	MA	63,916	MC
Wells College	NY	50,500	C
Wesleyan College	GA	29,694	C+
Wesleyan Univ	CT	65,516	MC
West Chester Univ of Pennsylvania	PA	18,456	C
West Texas A&M Univ	TX	13,478	C
West Virginia Univ	WV	18,210	C
West Virginia Univ Inst of Technology	WV	16,462	NC
West Virginia Wesleyan College	WV	36,858	C
Western Illinois Univ	IL	20,825	C
Western Kentucky Univ	KY	16,850	C
Western Mich Univ	MI	21,054	C
Western Washington Univ	WA	18,003	C+
Westminster College	MO	32,820	C
Westminster College	PA	39,180	C+
Westminster College	UT	41,078	C+
Westmont College	CA	56,410	HC
Wheaton College	IL	43,610	MC
Wheaton College	MA	61,512	VC
Wheeling Jesuit Univ	WV	37,106	LC
Whitman College	WA	59,772	MC
Whittier College	CA	57,891	C
Whitworth Univ	WA	51,732	VC
Wichita State Univ	KS	21,643	C
Widener Univ	PA	56,486	C
Wiley College	TX	18,504	C
Wilkes Univ	PA	45,622	C
Willamette Univ	OR	61,817	VC+
William Jewell College	MO	41,210	C+
Williams College	MA	63,290	MC
Winona State Univ	MN	17,535	C
Wisc Lutheran College	WI	36,290	VC
Wittenberg Univ	OH	48,156	C+
Wofford College	SC	49,885	VC
Worcester Polytechnic Inst	MA	60,730	MC
Wright State Univ	OH	16,983	C
Xavier Univ	OH	47,880	C+
Xavier Univ of Louisiana	LA	31,689	C+
Yale Univ	CT	64,650	MC
Youngstown State Univ	OH	17,307	C

PHYSICS & PHYSICAL OCEANOGRAPHY

School	ST	$IS	SR
Millersville Univ of Pennsylvania	PA	23,782	C
Univ of Rhode Island	RI	24,906	C

PHYSICS AND MATHEMATICS

School	ST	$IS	SR
Bethany College	WV	36,300	NC
Bridgewater College	VA	44,510	C
Brown Univ	RI	64,566	MC
Ithaca College	NY	56,766	VC
Keene State College	NH	24,003	LC
Missouri Southern State Univ	MO	12,499	C
St. John's Univ	NY	55,850	C
Whitman College	WA	59,772	MC

PHYSICS SECONDARY EDUCATION

School	ST	$IS	SR
Arkansas Tech Univ	AR	15,484	C
Augustana College	IL	49,658	VC
Cedarville Univ	OH	34,990	VC
Colo State Univ	CO	22,162	VC
Grove City College	PA	25,692	VC
Indiana Univ Bloomington	IN	20,429	VC
Indiana Univ of Pennsylvania	PA	23,614	LC
Ithaca College	NY	56,766	VC
Providence College	RI	60,760	VC
St. John's Univ	NY	55,850	C
The Univ of Utah	UT	17,924	VC
Western Mich Univ	MI	21,054	C

PHYSICS WITH ASTROPHYSICS OPTION

School	ST	$IS	SR
Brown Univ	RI	64,566	MC
Univ of Nebr - Lincoln	NE	18,589	VC

PHYSICS/COMPUTER

School	ST	$IS	SR
Grove City College	PA	25,692	VC

PHYSICS/GEN SCIENCE SECONDARY EDUCATION

School	ST	$IS	SR
Grove City College	PA	25,692	VC
Lewis Univ	IL	40,370	C
Syracuse Univ	NY	60,239	VC

PHYSIOLOGY

School	ST	$IS	SR
Boston Univ	MA	65,110	MC
Brigham Young Univ	UT	12,748	HC
Cal State, Long Beach	CA	18,850	C
Florida State Univ	FL	16,771	HC
Hampshire College	MA	63,824	MC
Howard Univ	DC	37,616	C+
Marquette Univ	WI	48,390	VC+
Mich State Univ	MI	23,898	VC+
Missouri Southern State Univ	MO	12,499	C
Northern Mich Univ	MI	19,604	C
Okla Baptist Univ	OK	32,320	C
Okla State Univ	OK	17,180	VC
Rutgers Univ - New Brunswick	NJ	26,632	HC
San Francisco State Univ	CA	18,514	LC
Southern Illinois Univ Carbondale	IL	23,667	C
Texas State Univ	TX	19,350	C
The Evergreen State College	WA	16,599	C
Univ of Arizona	AZ	23,100	C
Univ of Calif at Davis	CA	28,468	HC
Univ of Calif at Los Angeles	CA	30,162	MC
Univ of Calif at Santa Barbara	CA	29,091	HC
Univ of Calif San Diego	CA	30,150	MC
Univ of Colo Boulder	CO	24,285	VC+
Univ of Conn	CT	25,538	HC
Univ of Great Falls	MT	38,524	C
Univ of Illinois at Urbana-Champaign	IL	27,006	HC
Univ of Minn/Twin Cities	MN	23,519	HC+
Univ of Montana-Western	MT	11,220	LC
Univ of Oregon	OR	22,972	C
Univ of Wyoming	WY	15,375	C+

PIANO PEDAGOGY

School	ST	$IS	SR
Ithaca College	NY	56,766	VC
Ohio Univ	OH	22,924	C
Okla Baptist Univ	OK	32,320	C
Okla City Univ	OK	40,476	VC
Samford Univ	AL	39,232	VC
Shorter Univ	GA	31,130	LC
Silver Lake College of the Holy Family	WI	36,290	LC
Texas Christian Univ	TX	54,670	HC
The Master's Univ	CA	43,870	C+

PIANO PERFORMANCE

School	ST	$IS	SR
Abilene Christian Univ	TX	41,800	C+
Aquinas College - Mich	MI	38,876	HC
Biola Univ	CA	46,402	C+
Boston Univ	MA	65,110	MC
Calif Baptist Univ	CA	41,392	C
Dallas Baptist Univ	TX	33,713	C
East Texas Baptist Univ	TX	33,134	C
Hope College	MI	39,940	VC
Madonna Univ	MI	29,050	C
Milligan College	TN	38,150	C
Missouri Southern State Univ	MO	12,499	C
New York Univ	NY	65,860	MC
Okla Baptist Univ	OK	32,320	C
Okla City Univ	OK	40,476	VC
Ouachita Baptist Univ	AR	32,320	C
Point Loma Nazarene Univ	CA	43,450	C
Roberts Wesleyan College	NY	38,306	C
Silver Lake College of the Holy Family	WI	36,290	LC
The Master's Univ	CA	43,870	C+
Univ of Central Okla	OK	13,486	C
Webster Univ	MO	37,490	C
West Chester Univ of Pennsylvania	PA	18,456	C
Youngstown State Univ	OH	17,307	C

PIANO/ORGAN

School	ST	$IS	SR
Bennington College	VT	63,960	MC
Calif Baptist Univ	CA	41,392	C
Calvin College	MI	41,570	VC+
Central Mich Univ	MI	20,330	C
Central Washington Univ	WA	16,803	C
Columbia College	SC	36,550	C
East Central Univ	OK	13,056	C
East Texas Baptist Univ	TX	33,134	C
Eastern Mich Univ	MI	19,761	C
Florida State Univ	FL	16,771	HC
Hardin-Simmons Univ	TX	33,966	C
Hope College	MI	39,940	VC
Illinois Wesleyan Univ	IL	56,430	VC+
Indiana Univ Bloomington	IN	20,429	VC
Indiana Univ-Purdue Univ Fort Wayne	IN	17,553	C
Jackson State Univ	MS	15,879	LC
Lenoir-Rhyne Univ	NC	43,200	C
Loyola Univ New Orleans	LA	51,708	VC+
Manhattan School of Music	NY	57,200	SP
Mannes School for Music	NY	44,500	SP
Marshall Univ	WV	17,242	C
Millikin Univ	IL	42,158	C
Miss College	MS	25,850	C
Northwestern Univ	IL	66,344	MC
Nyack College	NY	34,050	NC
Oberlin College	OH	66,012	MC
Ohio State Univ at Columbus	OH	21,703	HC+
Ohio Univ	OH	22,924	C
Okla City Univ	OK	40,476	VC
Ouachita Baptist Univ	AR	32,320	C
Pacific Lutheran Univ	WA	49,960	VC
Palm Beach Atlantic Univ	FL	39,720	C
Rider Univ	NJ	54,050	C
Roosevelt Univ	IL	40,651	VC
Samford Univ	AL	39,232	VC
San Francisco Conservatory of Music	CA	57,310	SP
Shorter Univ	GA	31,130	LC
Southern Methodist Univ	TX	66,483	MC
Stetson Univ	FL	53,544	VC
Syracuse Univ	NY	60,239	VC
Temple Univ	PA	24,392	VC
The Boston Conservatory at Berklee	MA	61,042	C+
The Catholic Univ of America	DC	56,356	VC
Union Univ	TN	33,970	VC
Univ of Cincinnati	OH	21,964	VC
Univ of Iowa	IA	18,683	VC+
Univ of Kansas	KS	20,135	C+
Univ of Northwestern - St. Paul	MN	38,160	C
Univ of Tulsa	OK	52,625	HC+
Weber State Univ	UT	10,721	C
Westminster Choir College	NJ	53,730	SP
Youngstown State Univ	OH	17,307	C

PLANETARY AND SPACE SCIENCE

School	ST	$IS	SR
Boston Univ	MA	65,110	MC
Brown Univ	RI	64,566	MC
Calif Inst of Technology	CA	58,761	MC
Florida Inst of Technology	FL	53,306	VC
Univ of Arizona	AZ	23,100	C
Virginia Polytechnic Inst and State Univ	VA	21,276	HC
Wilmington College	OH	34,600	C

PLANT GENETICS

School	ST	$IS	SR
Brigham Young Univ	UT	12,748	HC
Purdue Univ/West Lafayette	IN	20,032	MC
SUNY / The College of Environmental Science and Forestry	NY	23,853	VC
Univ of Calif at Berkeley	CA	28,853	MC
Univ of Calif at Riverside	CA	29,227	C+
Washington State Univ	WA	22,495	C

PLANT PATHOLOGY

School	ST	$IS	SR
Iowa State Univ	IA	17,570	C
Mich State Univ	MI	23,898	VC+
New Mexico State Univ	NM	14,050	C
SUNY / The College of Environmental Science and Forestry	NY	23,853	VC
Univ of Arizona	AZ	23,100	C
Univ of Calif at Riverside	CA	29,227	C+
Univ of Delaware	DE	24,976	VC+
Univ of Wisc-Madison	WI	20,934	MC
Washington State Univ	WA	22,495	C

PLANT PHYSIOLOGY

School	ST	$IS	SR
Brigham Young Univ	UT	12,748	HC
Ohio State Univ at Columbus	OH	21,703	HC+
Purdue Univ/West Lafayette	IN	20,032	MC
SUNY / The College of Environmental Science and Forestry	NY	23,853	VC
Univ of Illinois at Urbana-Champaign	IL	27,006	HC

PLANT PROTECTION (PEST MANAGEMENT)

School	ST	$IS	SR
Iowa State Univ	IA	17,570	C
Miss State Univ	MS	11,454	C+
N Dak State Univ	ND	16,245	C
Purdue Univ/West Lafayette	IN	20,032	MC
Univ of Hawaii at Manoa	HI	23,221	C
Washington State Univ	WA	22,495	C
West Texas A&M Univ	TX	13,478	C

PLANT SCIENCE

School	ST	$IS	SR
Arkansas State Univ	AR	16,190	C
Brigham Young Univ	UT	12,748	HC
Calif State Polytechnic Univ, Pomona	CA	21,541	C
Cal State, Fresno	CA	16,902	LC
Cornell Univ	NY	64,853	MC
Florida State Univ	FL	16,771	HC
Fort Valley State Univ	GA	17,988	VC
Iowa State Univ	IA	17,570	C
Louisiana State Univ and A&M College	LA	18,677	VC
Middle Tenn State Univ	TN	8,650	C
Missouri State Univ	MO	15,190	C+
Montana State Univ	MT	15,500	C+
N Dak State Univ	ND	16,245	C
Ohio State Univ at Columbus	OH	21,703	HC+
Okla State Univ	OK	17,180	VC
Pennsylvania State Univ - Univ Park	PA	29,760	HC
Purdue Univ/West Lafayette	IN	20,032	MC
Rutgers Univ - New Brunswick	NJ	26,632	HC
S Dak State Univ	SD	15,634	C
Southern Illinois Univ Carbondale	IL	23,667	C
SUNY / The College of Environmental Science and Forestry	NY	23,853	VC
SUNY /College of Agriculture and Tech at Cobleskill	NY	20,527	LC
Tarleton State Univ	TX	15,248	LC
Tenn Tech Univ	TN	17,050	C
Texas A&M Univ	TX	20,521	VC+
Texas A&M Univ at Kingsville	TX	7,500	LC
Texas Tech Univ	TX	18,736	C+
The Univ of Tenn at Knoxville	TN	22,112	VC
The Univ of Tenn at Martin	TN	14,876	C
Univ of Arizona	AZ	23,100	C
Univ of Calif at Davis	CA	28,468	HC
Univ of Calif, Santa Cruz	CA	28,731	C+
Univ of Delaware	DE	24,976	VC+
Univ of Florida	FL	16,291	HC+
Univ of Hawaii at Manoa	HI	23,221	C
Univ of Idaho	ID	15,348	C
Univ of Maryland/College Park	MD	21,938	HC
Univ of Mass Amherst	MA	26,199	VC+
Univ of Missouri/Columbia	MO	18,201	MC
Univ of Nebr - Lincoln	NE	18,589	VC
Univ of Rhode Island	RI	24,906	C
Univ of Vermont	VT	28,878	HC
Utah State Univ	UT	12,736	C
Washington State Univ	WA	22,495	C
Washington Univ in St. Louis	MO	65,366	VC
West Texas A&M Univ	TX	13,478	C
West Virginia Univ	WV	18,210	C

PLASTICS ENGINEERING

School	ST	$IS	SR
Ferris State Univ	MI	21,445	C
Pennsylvania College of Technology	PA	27,333	NC
Univ of Illinois at Urbana-Champaign	IL	27,006	HC
Univ of Mass Lowell	MA	26,380	C
Univ of Wisc-Stout	WI	19,667	C
Weber State Univ	UT	10,721	C
Western Washington Univ	WA	18,003	C+

PLASTICS TECHNOLOGY

School	ST	$IS	SR
Eastern Mich Univ	MI	19,761	C
Penn State Erie/The Behrend College	PA	16,256	C
Pittsburg State Univ	KS	13,880	NC
Weber State Univ	UT	10,721	C

PLAYWRITING/SCREENWRITING

School	ST	$IS	SR
Bennington College	VT	63,960	MC
Biola Univ	CA	46,402	C+
Chapman Univ	CA	63,078	VC+

School	ST	$IS	SR
DePaul Univ	IL	47,623	VC
Goddard College	VT	17,040	VC
Howard Univ	DC	37,616	C+
Loyola Marymount Univ	CA	58,038	HC
Metropolitan State Univ	MN	7,566	C
Ohio Univ	OH	22,924	C
Univ of Southern Calif	CA	66,631	C
Webster Univ	MO	37,490	C

POLICY ANALYSIS AND MANAGEMENT

School	ST	$IS	SR
Bloomfield College	NJ	39,100	LC
Carnegie Mellon Univ	PA	67,980	MC
Cornell Univ	NY	64,853	MC

POLISH

School	ST	$IS	SR
Univ of Illinois at Chicago	IL	25,006	VC
Univ of Pittsburgh	PA	29,568	HC+
Univ of Wisc-Madison	WI	20,934	MC

POLITICAL SCIENCE/ GOVERNMENT

School	ST	$IS	SR
Abilene Christian Univ	TX	41,800	C+
Adams State Univ	CO	17,703	LC
Adelphi Univ	NY	48,244	C
Adrian College	MI	42,400	C
Agnes Scott College	GA	51,930	VC+
Alabama A&M Univ	AL	18,796	C
Alabama State Univ	AL	14,142	NC
Albany State Univ	GA	19,462	C
Albertus Magnus College	CT	43,258	LC
Albion College	MI	52,650	C
Albright College	PA	46,660	C
Alcorn State Univ	MS	15,854	C
Alderson Broaddus Univ	WV	26,149	C
Alfred Univ	NY	42,296	C+
Allegheny College	PA	55,420	VC
Allen Univ	SC	19,300	NC
Alma College	MI	47,548	C
Alvernia Univ	PA	43,900	C
Alverno College	WI	33,294	LC
American International College	MA	46,300	LC
American Jewish Univ - College of A&S Campus	CA	44,234	C
American Univ	DC	59,379	HC+
Amherst College	MA		HC+
Anderson Univ	IN	38,200	C
Andrews Univ	MI	28,030	C+
Angelo State Univ	TX	15,263	NC
Anna Maria College	MA	48,186	C
Appalachian State Univ	NC	14,416	VC
Aquinas College - Mich	MI	38,876	HC
Arcadia Univ	PA	33,570	C+
Arizona State Univ at the Polytechnic Campus	AZ	21,360	VC
Arizona State Univ at the Tempe Campus	AZ	21,756	VC
Arizona State Univ at the West Campus	AZ	20,640	C
Arkansas State Univ	AR	16,190	C
Arkansas Tech Univ	AR	15,484	C
Armstrong State Univ	GA	16,962	C
Asbury Univ	KY	35,180	C+
Ashford Univ	CA	10,480	C
Ashland Univ	OH	21,440	C
Assumption College	MA	47,920	C+
Auburn Univ	AL	23,594	VC+
Auburn Univ at Montgomery	AL	15,290	C
Augsburg College	MN	43,929	C
Augusta Univ	GA	4,632	C
Augustana College	IL	49,658	VC
Augustana Univ	SD	38,424	VC
Aurora Univ	IL	33,970	C
Austin College	TX	45,875	VC
Austin Peay State Univ	TN	16,397	C
Averett Univ	VA	40,970	LC
Avila Univ	MO	35,480	C
Azusa Pacific Univ	CA	43,972	C
Baldwin Wallace Univ	OH	41,106	C
Ball State Univ	IN	19,590	C
Bard College	NY	64,024	HC
Bard College at Simon's Rock	MA	65,795	MC
Barnard College/Columbia Univ	NY	62,741	MC
Barry Univ	FL	37,830	C
Barton College	NC	38,686	LC
Bates College	ME	64,500	MC
Baylor Univ	TX	53,760	HC
Belhaven Univ	MS	31,016	C
Bellarmine Univ	KY	51,220	C
Bellevue Univ	NE	20,300	NC
Belmont Abbey College	NC	48,156	C
Belmont Univ	TN	40,970	VC
Beloit College	WI	55,206	HC
Bemidji State Univ	MN	16,056	VC
Benedict College	SC	28,238	NC
Benedictine College	KS	36,200	VC
Benedictine Univ	IL	38,300	C
Bennett College	NC	27,302	NC
Bennington College	VT	63,960	MC
Berea College	KY	7,042	C
Berry College	GA	45,286	C+
Bethany College	WV	36,300	NC
Bethel College	IN	35,860	C
Bethel Univ	MN	45,270	VC
Bethune-Cookman Univ	FL	22,970	C
Birmingham-Southern College	AL	44,478	VC
Black Hills State Univ	SD	15,899	C
Blackburn College	IL	28,526	LC
Bloomfield College	NJ	39,100	LC
Bloomsburg Univ of Pennsylvania	PA	19,066	LC
Boise State Univ	ID	14,860	C
Boston College	MA	65,737	MC
Boston Univ	MA	65,110	MC
Bowdoin College	ME	63,500	MC
Bowling Green State Univ	OH	19,747	C
Brandeis Univ	MA	65,925	MC
Brenau Univ - Women's College	GA	37,876	LC
Brewton-Parker College	GA	23,490	C
Briar Cliff Univ	IA	36,956	C
Bridgewater College	VA	44,510	C
Bridgewater State Univ	MA	21,810	C
Brigham Young Univ	UT	12,748	HC
Brigham Young Univ/Hawaii	HI	11,290	C
Brown Univ	RI	64,566	MC
Bryant Univ	RI	55,646	VC
Bryn Athyn College	PA	31,470	C
Bryn Mawr College	PA	59,890	MC
Bucknell Univ	PA	64,616	MC
Buena Vista Univ	IA	41,514	C
Butler Univ	IN	51,352	VC
Cabrini Univ	PA	42,591	LC
Caldwell Univ	NJ	42,165	NC
Calif Baptist Univ	CA	41,392	C
Calif Inst of Technology	CA	58,761	MC
Calif Lutheran Univ	CA	52,853	C
Calif Polytechnic State Univ	CA	17,979	HC+
Calif State Polytechnic Univ, Pomona	CA	21,541	C
Cal State, Bakersfield	CA	19,191	LC
Cal State, Chico	CA	21,440	C
Cal State, Dominguez Hills	CA	19,022	LC
Cal State, East Bay	CA	19,413	C
Cal State, Fresno	CA	16,902	LC
Cal State, Fullerton	CA	21,902	C
Cal State, Long Beach	CA	18,850	C
Cal State, Los Angeles	CA	17,186	LC
Cal State, Northridge	CA	16,859	LC
Cal State, San Bernardino	CA	12,000	C
Cal State, San Marcos	CA	24,184	LC
Cal State, Stanislaus	CA	16,212	C
Calif Univ of Pennsylvania	PA	14,217	LC
Calvin College	MI	41,570	VC+
Cameron Univ	OK	11,072	NC
Campbellsville Univ	KY	32,492	C
Capital Univ	OH	42,982	C
Carleton College	MN	64,071	MC
Carlow Univ	PA	38,549	LC
Carnegie Mellon Univ	PA	67,980	MC
Carroll College	MT	39,972	C+
Carroll Univ	WI	38,100	C+
Carthage College	WI	48,835	C
Case Western Reserve Univ	OH	60,304	MC
Castleton Univ	VT	20,186	C
Catawba College	NC	39,820	C
Cedar Crest College	PA	46,715	C
Cedarville Univ	OH	34,990	VC
Centenary College	NJ	43,602	C
Centenary College of Louisiana	LA	45,650	C+
Central College	IA	44,592	C
Central Conn State Univ	CT	21,203	C
Central Methodist Univ	MO	36,830	VC
Central State Univ	OH	18,564	C
Central Washington Univ	WA	16,803	C
Centre College	KY	49,250	HC
Chadron State College	NE	14,819	NC
Chapman Univ	CA	63,078	VC+
Charleston Southern Univ	SC	32,400	C
Chatham Univ	PA	46,517	C
Chestnut Hill College	PA	43,410	C
Cheyney Univ of Pennsylvania	PA	20,896	LC
Chicago State Univ	IL	20,144	C
Christendom College	VA	32,600	VC
Christopher Newport Univ	VA	23,968	VC+
CUNY/Baruch College	NY	21,609	HC
CUNY/Brooklyn College	NY	5,884	C+
CUNY/City College	NY	20,319	VC
CUNY/College of Staten Island	NY	17,840	NC
CUNY/Hunter College	NY	31,098	VC
CUNY/John Jay College of Criminal Justice	NY	6,359	NC
CUNY/Lehman College	NY	5,778	HC+
CUNY/Queens College	NY	27,896	C
CUNY/York College	NY	6,747	LC
Claflin Univ	SC	33,764	LC
Claremont McKenna College	CA	67,185	MC
Clarion Univ of Pennsylvania	PA	21,608	LC
Clark Atlanta Univ	GA	31,019	LC
Clark Univ	MA	51,600	HC+
Clarkson Univ	NY	60,392	HC
Clemson Univ	SC		HC
Cleveland State Univ	OH	22,196	C
Coastal Carolina Univ	SC	19,766	C
Coe College	IA	51,570	VC
Coker College	SC	34,810	LC
Colby College	ME	64,060	MC
Colgate Univ	NY	65,030	MC
College of Charleston	SC	22,699	C
College of St. Benedict	MN	52,806	C
College of the Holy Cross	MA	62,165	MC
College of William & Mary	VA		MC
Colo College	CO	62,560	MC
Colo Mesa Univ	CO	18,955	LC
Colo State Univ	CO	22,162	VC
Colo State Univ-Pueblo	CO	18,234	C
Columbia College	SC	36,550	C
Columbia College - Missouri	MO	27,803	C
Columbia Univ/ School of General Studies	NY	61,470	MC
Columbia Univ/City of New York	NY	62,958	MC
Columbus State Univ	GA	14,336	LC
Concord Univ	WV	14,954	C
Concordia College - Moorhead	MN	51,088	C+
Concordia Univ	CA	41,580	VC
Concordia Univ, Chicago	IL	39,694	C
Conn College	CT	65,000	MC
Converse College	SC	26,495	C
Coppin State Univ	MD	17,041	VC
Corban Univ	OR	40,306	C
Cornell College	IA	48,800	VC
Creighton Univ	NE	48,206	VC+
Culver-Stockton College	MO	33,525	C
Cumberland Univ	TN	27,710	C
Curry College	MA	51,815	C
Daemen College	NY	38,045	C
Dallas Baptist Univ	TX	33,713	C
Davidson College	NC	60,119	MC
Davis & Elkins College	WV	38,242	LC
Delaware State Univ	DE	19,376	NC
Delta State Univ	MS	13,176	C
Denison Univ	OH	58,860	MC
DePaul Univ	IL	47,623	VC
DePauw Univ	IN	58,688	HC+
DeSales Univ	PA	43,970	C
Dickinson College	PA	63,974	MC
Dickinson State Univ	ND	12,372	LC
Dillard Univ	LA	20,940	VC
Doane Univ	NE	39,184	VC
Dominican Univ	IL	41,222	C
Dominican Univ of Calif	CA	57,050	C
Dordt College	IA	37,860	C+
Drake Univ	IA	45,056	HC
Drew Univ/College of Liberal Arts	NJ	61,048	VC
Drexel Univ	PA	65,432	VC+
Drury Univ	MO	33,791	VC
Duke Univ	NC	64,188	
Duquesne Univ	PA	46,822	VC
Earlham College	IN	54,870	HC
East Carolina Univ	NC	16,937	C
East Central Univ	OK	13,056	C
East Stroudsburg Univ	PA	18,334	C
East Tenn State Univ	TN	13,994	C
East Texas Baptist Univ	TX	33,134	C
Eastern Conn State Univ	CT	23,059	C
Eastern Illinois Univ	IL	21,126	C
Eastern Kentucky Univ	KY	16,908	C
Eastern Mich Univ	MI	19,761	C
Eastern New Mexico Univ	NM	14,416	C
Eastern Univ	PA	39,540	C
Eastern Washington Univ	WA	25,572	LC
Eckerd College	FL	52,874	C
Edgewood College	WI	35,950	C
Edinboro Univ	PA	15,940	LC
Edward Waters College	FL	20,607	NC
Elizabeth City State Univ	NC	14,745	C
Elizabethtown College	PA	54,050	C
Elmhurst College	IL	45,428	C
Elmira College	NY	53,900	C
Elon Univ	NC	44,599	VC+
Emmanuel College	MA	52,110	C+
Emory and Henry College	VA	41,410	C
Emory Univ	GA	60,786	MC
Emporia State Univ	KS	14,570	C
Endicott College	MA	44,604	VC+
Eugene Lang College/The New School for Liberal Arts	NY	55,650	C
Eureka College	IL	30,220	C
Evangel Univ	MO	28,898	C
Excelsior College	NY	14,080	SP
Fairfield Univ	CT	59,860	VC+
Fairleigh Dickinson Univ/ College at Florham	NJ	52,062	C
Fairleigh Dickinson Univ/ Metropolitan Campus	NJ	40,254	C
Fairmont State Univ	WV	15,726	C
Fayetteville State Univ	NC	17,756	C
Ferris State Univ	MI	21,445	C
Ferrum College	VA	39,650	C
Fisk Univ	TN	32,066	LC
Fitchburg State Univ	MA	21,819	C
Flagler College	FL	27,620	C
Florida A&M Univ	FL	15,361	C
Florida Atlantic Univ	FL	17,339	C
Florida Gulf Coast Univ	FL	9,682	C
Florida International Univ	FL	19,854	C+
Florida Memorial Univ	FL	22,270	LC
Florida State Univ	FL	16,771	HC
Fordham Univ	NY	65,918	MC
Fort Hays State Univ	KS	12,131	C
Fort Lewis College	CO	18,980	C
Fort Valley State Univ	GA	17,988	VC
Framingham State Univ	MA	20,584	C
Francis Marion Univ	SC	16,464	LC
Franciscan Univ of Steubenville	OH	33,980	VC
Franklin and Marshall College	PA	63,170	HC
Franklin College	IN	39,380	C
Franklin Pierce Univ	NH	46,750	C
Friends Univ	KS	34,455	C
Frostburg State Univ	MD	17,280	LC
Furman Univ	SC	58,092	VC+
Gannon Univ	PA	42,032	C
Geneva College	PA	35,450	C
George Fox Univ	OR	42,938	C
George Mason Univ	VA	15,724	VC
George Washington Univ	DC	62,835	MC
Georgetown College	KY	41,440	C
Georgetown Univ	DC	65,926	MC
Georgia College & State Univ	GA	21,148	C+
Georgia Southern Univ	GA	16,596	C
Georgia Southwestern State Univ	GA	13,870	C
Georgia State Univ	GA	24,332	VC
Gettysburg College	PA	63,000	HC
Gonzaga Univ	WA	50,888	HC
Gordon College	MA	46,472	C+
Goucher College	MD	55,716	VC
Grambling State Univ	LA	15,701	C
Grand Valley State Univ	MI	22,250	C+
Grand View Univ	IA	32,302	C
Greensboro College	NC	42,400	LC
Grinnell College	IA	60,738	MC
Grove City College	PA	25,692	VC
Guilford College	NC	44,090	C
Gustavus Adolphus College	MN	52,433	HC
Hamilton College	NY	64,250	MC
Hamline Univ	MN	45,678	VC
Hampden-Sydney College	VA	56,248	C+
Hampshire College	MA	63,824	MC
Hampton Univ	VA	34,926	LC
Hanover College	IN	46,364	C+
Harding Univ	AR	25,421	C
Hardin-Simmons Univ	TX	33,966	C
Hartwick College	NY	51,270	C
Harvard College/Harvard Univ	MA	60,659	MC
Hastings College	NE	35,380	C+
Haverford College	PA	66,490	MC
Hawaii Pacific Univ	HI	33,420	C
Heidelberg Univ	OH	39,200	C
Henderson State Univ	AR	15,516	LC
Hendrix College	AR	54,020	VC+
High Point Univ	NC	45,977	C
Hilbert College	NY	30,850	C
Hillsdale College	MI	35,722	MC
Hiram College	OH	43,230	C
Hofstra Univ	NY	55,960	C+
Hollins Univ	VA	49,635	VC
Holy Family Univ	PA	43,326	LC
Hood College	MD	54,840	C
Hope College	MI	39,940	VC
Houghton College	NY	39,090	C
Houston Baptist Univ	TX	36,450	C
Howard Payne Univ	TX	34,320	C
Howard Univ	DC	37,616	C+
Humboldt State Univ	CA	20,514	C
Huntingdon College	AL	34,900	C
Huston-Tillotson Univ	TX	18,124	LC
Idaho State Univ	ID	13,619	NC
Illinois College	IL	40,850	VC
Illinois Inst of Technology	IL	56,826	HC+
Illinois State Univ	IL	23,418	VC
Illinois Wesleyan Univ	IL	56,430	VC+
Indiana State Univ	IN	23,223	LC
Indiana Univ Bloomington	IN	20,429	VC
Indiana Univ East	IN	7,072	C
Indiana Univ Northwest	IN	7,072	C
Indiana Univ of Pennsylvania	PA	23,614	LC
Indiana Univ South Bend	IN	14,242	C
Indiana Univ Southeast	IN	14,242	LC
Indiana Univ-Purdue Univ Fort Wayne	IN	17,553	C
Indiana Univ-Purdue Univ Indianapolis	IN	18,635	C
Indiana Wesleyan Univ	IN	33,674	C
Inter-American Univ of PR Ponce	PR	19,549	
Inter-American Univ of PR-Fajardo Campus	PR	18,336	
Inter-American Univ of PR-Metropolitan Campus	PR	20,045	
Inter-American Univ of PR-San Germán	PR	20,042	
Iona College	NY	50,984	C
Iowa State Univ	IA	17,570	C
Ithaca College	NY	56,766	VC
Jackson State Univ	MS	15,879	LC
Jacksonville State Univ	AL	14,628	LC
Jacksonville Univ	FL	46,230	C
James Madison Univ	VA	19,084	VC
John Brown Univ	AR	33,132	VC
John Carroll Univ	OH	49,740	C+
Johns Hopkins Univ	MD	65,386	MC
Johnson C. Smith Univ	NC	25,336	LC
Johnson State College	VT	20,752	C
Judson Univ	IL	37,700	C
Juniata College	PA	53,760	VC
Kalamazoo College	MI	53,931	HC+
Kansas State Univ	KS	17,780	VC
Kean Univ	NJ	24,650	C

ST = STATE $IS = IN-STATE COSTS SR = SELECTOR RATING

School	ST	$IS	SR
Keene State College	NH	24,003	LC
Kennesaw State Univ	GA	19,592	VC
Kent State Univ	OH	20,732	C
Kentucky State Univ	KY	13,364	LC
Kentucky Wesleyan College	KY	32,080	C
Kenyon College	OH	63,330	MC
Keuka College	NY	39,762	C
King's College	PA	46,858	C
Knox College	IL	52,615	VC+
Kutztown Univ of Pennsylvania	PA	19,056	LC
La Roche College	PA	37,924	LC
La Salle Univ	PA	55,790	C
La Sierra Univ	CA	39,690	VC
Lafayette College	PA	63,355	MC
LaGrange College	GA	39,930	C
Lake Erie College	OH	38,914	LC
Lake Forest College	IL	50,652	VC
Lamar Univ	TX	18,014	LC
Lander Univ	SC	43,994	C
Lawrence Univ	WI	54,498	HC
Le Moyne College	NY	46,000	C
Lebanon Valley College	PA	51,530	C
Lee Univ	TN	22,045	C
Lehigh Univ	PA	61,010	MC
LeMoyne-Owen College	TN	16,980	C
Lenoir-Rhyne Univ	NC	43,200	C
Lewis & Clark College	OR	58,434	HC+
Lewis Univ	IL	40,370	C
Liberty Univ	VA	19,101	C
Lincoln Univ	MO	13,602	NC
Lindenwood Univ	MO	25,132	C
Linfield College	OR	52,010	C
Lipscomb Univ	TN	41,296	VC
LIU Brooklyn	NY	49,682	C
LIU Post	NY	49,682	C
Livingstone College	NC	17,815	LC
Lock Haven Univ of Pennsylvania	PA	18,028	LC
Longwood Univ	VA	22,184	C
Loras College	IA	39,222	C
Louisiana State Univ and A&M College	LA	18,677	VC
Louisiana Tech Univ	LA	11,422	VC
Loyola Marymount Univ	CA	58,038	HC
Loyola Univ Chicago	IL	55,802	VC
Loyola Univ Maryland	MD	60,300	VC
Loyola Univ New Orleans	LA	51,708	VC+
Luther College	IA	48,540	C+
Lycoming College	PA	48,580	C
Lynchburg College	VA	46,740	C
Lyon College	AR	34,730	C+
Macalester College	MN	61,905	MC
MacMurray College	IL	33,620	C
Malone Univ	OH	38,448	C
Manchester Univ	IN	40,422	C
Manhattan College	NY	51,750	C+
Manhattanville College	NY	51,440	C+
Mansfield Univ	PA	23,376	LC
Marian Univ	IN	41,220	C
Marietta College	OH	46,190	C
Marist College	NY	49,860	VC
Marquette Univ	WI	48,390	VC+
Mars Hill Univ	NC	42,688	C
Marshall Univ	WV	17,242	C
Martin Univ	IN	20,264	LC
Mary Baldwin Univ	VA	39,865	C
Marygrove College	MI	28,926	NC
Marymount Manhattan College	NY	46,280	VC
Marymount Univ	VA	41,570	LC
Maryville College	TN	44,410	C
Marywood Univ	PA	46,900	C
Mass College of Liberal Arts	MA	20,128	C
Mass Inst of Technology	MA	62,662	MC
McDaniel College	MD	51,380	VC
McKendree Univ	IL	37,940	C+
McMurry Univ	TX	34,259	LC
McNeese State Univ	LA	7,838	C
Mercer Univ	GA	45,348	VC
Mercy College	NY	31,776	C
Mercyhurst Univ	PA	47,420	C
Meredith College	NC	45,297	C
Merrimack College	MA	52,770	C
Messiah College	PA	43,100	C+
Methodist Univ	NC	43,600	C
Metropolitan State Univ of Denver	CO	29,889	LC
Miami Univ	OH	27,190	HC+
Mich State Univ	MI	23,898	VC+
Middle Tenn State Univ	TN	8,650	C
Middlebury College	VT	64,332	MC
Midwestern State Univ	TX	17,572	C
Miles College	AL	18,646	NC
Millersville Univ of Pennsylvania	PA	23,782	C
Millikin Univ	IL	42,158	C
Mills College	CA	59,163	VC
Millsaps College	MS	50,080	C+
Minn State Univ, Mankato	MN	15,616	C
Minn State Univ, Moorhead	MN	15,941	C
Miss College	MS	25,850	C
Miss State Univ	MS	11,454	C+
Miss Univ for Women	MS	17,065	C
Miss Valley State Univ	MS	13,233	LC
Missouri Southern State Univ	MO	12,499	C
Missouri State Univ	MO	15,190	C+
Missouri Valley College	MO	28,150	C
Missouri Western State Univ	MO	16,741	
Molloy College	NY	40,440	C
Monmouth College	IL	42,260	C
Monmouth Univ	NJ	46,234	C
Montana State Univ	MT	15,500	C+
Montana State Univ-Billings	MT	22,960	C
Montclair State Univ	NJ	26,210	LC
Moravian College	PA	53,117	
Morehead State Univ	KY	17,422	C
Morehouse College	GA	40,064	C
Morgan State Univ	MD	17,190	LC
Morningside College	IA	36,865	C
Morris College	SC	18,500	LC
Mount Aloysius College	PA	29,976	C
Mount Holyoke College	MA	56,746	MC
Mount Mercy Univ	IA	36,826	C
Mount St. Mary College	NY	42,061	C
Mount St. Mary's Univ	MD	51,610	C
Mount St. Mary's Univ - Chalon Campus	CA	43,897	VC+
Mount Vernon Nazarene Univ	OH	34,500	C
Muhlenberg College	PA	56,645	VC+
Murray State Univ	KY	16,998	C
Muskingum Univ	OH	35,966	C
Nazareth College	NY	45,574	C
Nebr Wesleyan Univ	NE	38,140	C+
Neumann Univ	PA	40,678	LC
New College of Florida	FL	15,848	MC
New England College	NH	50,364	C
New Jersey City Univ	NJ	21,456	LC
New Mexico Highlands Univ	NM	11,904	NC
New Mexico State Univ	NM	14,050	C
New York Inst of Technology	NY	48,730	C
New York Univ	NY	65,860	MC
Newberry College	SC	34,550	C
Niagara Univ	NY	41,010	C
Nicholls State Univ	LA	10,534	C
Norfolk State Univ	VA	25,702	LC
N Car A&T State Univ	NC	13,365	LC
N Car Central Univ	NC	9,000	C
N Car State Univ	NC	19,515	HC+
N Car Wesleyan College	NC	39,200	C
North Central College	IL	48,712	VC
N Dak State Univ	ND	16,245	C
North Park Univ	IL	35,860	C
Northeastern Illinois Univ	IL	12,529	LC
Northeastern State Univ	OK	8,615	VC
Northeastern Univ	MA	62,703	MC
Northern Arizona Univ	AZ	20,246	VC
Northern Illinois Univ	IL	20,176	C
Northern Kentucky Univ	KY	16,486	C
Northern Mich Univ	MI	19,604	C
Northern State Univ	SD	14,505	C
Northwest Missouri State Univ	MO	17,737	C
Northwest Nazarene Univ	ID	36,000	C
Northwestern College of Iowa	IA	38,400	C+
Northwestern Okla State Univ	OK	13,072	NC
Northwestern Univ	IL	66,344	MC
Norwich Univ	VT	28,212	C
Notre Dame College	OH	37,150	VC
Notre Dame de Namur Univ	CA	46,526	LC
Notre Dame of Maryland Univ	MD	46,465	VC
Nova Southeastern Univ	FL	38,534	C+
Oakland Univ	MI	20,763	C
Oakwood Univ	AL	43,758	C
Oberlin College	OH	66,012	MC
Occidental College	CA	65,530	MC
Oglethorpe Univ	GA	44,200	C+
Ohio Dominican Univ	OH	41,340	C+
Ohio Northern Univ	OH	44,050	VC
Ohio State Univ at Columbus	OH	21,703	HC+
Ohio Univ	OH	22,924	C
Ohio Wesleyan Univ	OH	49,460	VC
Okla Baptist Univ	OK	32,320	C
Okla City Univ	OK	40,476	VC
Okla State Univ	OK	17,180	VC
Okla Wesleyan Univ	OK	33,206	C
Old Dominion Univ	VA	20,910	C
Olivet Nazarene Univ	IL	41,840	C
Oral Roberts Univ	OK	34,316	C
Oregon State Univ	OR	22,519	VC
Ottawa Univ	KS	36,074	VC
Otterbein Univ	OH	41,630	C
Ouachita Baptist Univ	AR	32,320	C
Our Lady of the Lake Univ	TX	35,012	LC
Pace Univ	NY	58,248	C
Pacific Lutheran Univ	WA	49,960	VC
Pacific Univ	OR	52,876	C
Palm Beach Atlantic Univ	FL	39,720	C
Park Univ	MO	20,329	C
Paul Quinn College	TX	25,350	LC
Penn State Erie/The Behrend College	PA	16,256	C
Pennsylvania State Univ - Univ Park	PA	29,760	HC
Pepperdine Univ	CA	74,460	HC+
Pfeiffer Univ	NC	39,695	LC
Philander Smith College	AR	20,814	LC
Piedmont College	GA	32,512	C
Pittsburg State Univ	KS	13,880	NC
Pitzer College	CA	66,192	MC
Plymouth State Univ	NH	23,180	LC
Point Loma Nazarene Univ	CA	43,450	C
Point Park Univ	PA	41,270	C
Pomona College	CA	64,957	MC
Pontifical Catholic Univ of PR	PR	10,534	
Portland State Univ	OR	19,443	C
Prairie View A&M Univ	TX	15,205	LC
Princeton Univ	NJ	57,610	MC
Principia College	IL	39,010	C+
Providence College	RI	60,760	VC
Purdue Univ/Northwest	IN	15,038	C
Purdue Univ/West Lafayette	IN	20,032	MC
Queens Univ of Charlotte	NC	39,543	C
Quincy Univ	IL	36,998	C
Quinnipiac Univ	CT	59,110	C
Radford Univ	VA	19,027	LC
Ramapo College of New Jersey	NJ	25,338	C
Randolph College	VA	45,660	VC
Randolph-Macon College	VA	49,910	C
Reed College	OR	65,300	MC
Regis College	MA	51,920	C
Regis Univ	CO	44,520	C
Rhode Island College	RI	17,694	LC
Rhodes College	TN	51,900	HC
Rice Univ	TX	57,668	MC
Rider Univ	NJ	54,050	C
Ripon College	WI	46,911	C+
Rivier Univ	NH	40,410	VC
Roanoke College	VA	54,114	VC
Rochester Inst of Technology	NY	50,842	HC
Rockford Univ	IL	36,030	C
Rockhurst Univ	MO	29,220	C
Rocky Mountain College	MT	34,270	C
Roger Williams Univ	RI	46,296	C+
Rollins College	FL	58,670	HC
Roosevelt Univ	IL	40,651	VC
Rosemont College	PA	30,980	C
Rowan Univ	NJ	24,491	VC+
Russell Sage College	NY	39,370	C
Rust College	MS	10,600	C
Rutgers Univ - Camden	NJ	26,146	C
Rutgers Univ - New Brunswick	NJ	26,632	HC
Rutgers Univ - Newark	NJ	27,288	C
Saginaw Valley State Univ	MI	18,530	C
St. Anselm College	NH	52,560	C+
St. Augustine's Univ	NC	26,048	C
St. Francis Univ	PA	42,268	NC
St. John's Univ	MN	51,624	C
St. Joseph's Univ	PA	57,544	VC+
St. Leo Univ	FL	31,650	C
St. Louis Univ	MO	49,866	HC
St. Martin's Univ	WA	45,056	C
St. Mary's College	IN	50,600	C
St. Mary's College of Calif	CA	57,420	C
St. Mary's Univ of Minn	MN	41,210	VC
St. Michael's College	VT	51,725	VC+
St. Peter's Univ	NJ	49,192	C
St. Vincent College	PA	44,626	C
St. Xavier Univ	IL	43,310	C
Salisbury Univ	MD	20,714	VC
Salve Regina Univ	RI	51,470	C
Sam Houston State Univ	TX	18,792	C
Samford Univ	AL	39,232	VC
San Diego State Univ	CA	21,896	C+
San Francisco State Univ	CA	18,514	LC
San Jose State Univ	CA	21,540	C
Sarah Lawrence College	NY	63,388	HC
Savannah State Univ	GA	15,631	C
Schreiner Univ	TX	34,626	LC
Scripps College	CA	66,664	MC
Seattle Pacific Univ	WA	47,439	C+
Seattle Univ	WA	50,811	VC+
Seton Hall Univ	NJ	55,514	C
Seton Hill Univ	PA	46,972	C
Sewanee: The Univ of the South	TN	54,500	MC
Shaw Univ	NC	24,638	C
Shenandoah Univ	VA	41,312	C
Shepherd Univ, West Virginia	WV	17,224	C
Shippensburg Univ of Pennsylvania	PA	23,208	C
Siena College	NY	48,916	C+
Simmons College	MA	53,090	VC
Simpson College	IA	43,839	VC
Skidmore College	NY	64,214	HC
Slippery Rock Univ of Pennsylvania	PA	10,360	C
Smith College	MA	63,914	MC
Sonoma State Univ	CA	27,806	C
S Car State Univ	SC	20,805	LC
S Dak State Univ	SD	15,634	C
Southeast Missouri State Univ	MO	15,498	C
Southeastern Louisiana Univ	LA	16,237	C
Southeastern Okla State Univ	OK	11,875	C
Southern Arkansas Univ	AR	21,532	C
Southern Conn State Univ	CT	21,924	LC
Southern Illinois Univ Carbondale	IL	23,667	C
Southern Illinois Univ Edwardsville	IL	22,643	C
Southern Methodist Univ	TX	66,483	MC
Southern Nazarene Univ	OK	32,798	NC
Southern New Hampshire Univ	NH	43,198	C
Southern Oregon Univ	OR	19,117	C
Southern Univ and A&M College	LA	16,074	LC+
Southern Univ at New Orleans	LA	8,014	LC
Southwest Baptist Univ	MO	29,900	LC
Southwest Minn State Univ	MN	17,783	C
Southwestern Okla State Univ	OK	11,790	C
Southwestern Univ	TX	50,720	VC
Spelman College	GA	38,751	C
Spring Hill College	AL	48,488	C
Springfield College	MA	45,995	C
St. Ambrose Univ	IA	39,019	C
St. Ambrose Univ	IA	39,019	C
St. Bonaventure Univ	NY	44,237	C
St. Catherine Univ	MN	45,630	VC
St. Cloud State Univ	MN	10,600	C
St. Edward's Univ	TX	53,100	VC
St. Francis College	NY	38,800	LC
St. John Fisher College	NY	43,620	C
St. John's College-Annapolis	MD	60,142	MC
St. John's Univ	NY	55,850	C
St. Joseph's College, New York/Brooklyn Campus	NY	25,114	LC
St. Joseph's College, New York/Long Island Campus	NY	25,124	C
St. Lawrence Univ	NY	64,390	VC
St. Mary's College of Maryland	MD	26,634	VC
St. Mary's Univ	TX	37,500	C
St. Norbert College	WI	44,525	VC
St. Olaf College	MN	54,260	HC+
St. Thomas Univ	FL	36,360	LC
Stanford Univ	CA	60,409	MC
SUNY / Buffalo State College	NY	20,842	C
SUNY / SUNY College at Old Westbury	NY	16,860	C
SUNY / SUNY Cortland	NY	20,706	VC
SUNY / SUNY Fredonia	NY	20,818	C
SUNY / SUNY Oneonta	NY	19,712	C+
SUNY / SUNY Plattsburgh	NY	18,814	C
SUNY / SUNY Potsdam	NY	20,404	C+
SUNY / Univ at Buffalo	NY	23,122	C+
SUNY at Binghamton	NY	22,861	MC
SUNY at Geneseo	NY	20,440	VC+
SUNY at New Paltz	NY	19,200	C
SUNY at Oswego	NY	21,351	C
SUNY at Purchase	NY	17,900	C
SUNY SUNY Albany	NY	22,165	C
Stephen F. Austin State Univ	TX	18,406	LC
Stetson Univ	FL	53,544	VC
Stockton Univ	NJ	25,059	
Stonehill College	MA	55,030	C+
Stony Brook Univ/The SUNY	NY	21,881	MC
Suffolk Univ	MA	50,308	C
Sul Ross State Univ	TX	15,021	LC
Susquehanna Univ	PA	55,340	VC
Swarthmore College	PA	63,550	MC
Syracuse Univ	NY	60,239	VC
Tarleton State Univ	TX	15,248	LC
Taylor Univ	IN	40,317	C+
Temple Univ	PA	24,392	VC
Tenn State Univ	TN	14,423	C
Tenn Tech Univ	TN	17,050	C
Texas A&M Univ	TX	20,521	VC+
Texas A&M Univ at Commerce	TX	10,496	C
Texas A&M Univ at Corpus Christi	TX	16,851	LC
Texas A&M Univ at Kingsville	TX	7,500	LC
Texas Christian Univ	TX	54,670	HC
Texas Lutheran Univ	TX	38,620	C
Texas Southern Univ	TX	18,212	LC
Texas State Univ	TX	19,350	C
Texas Tech Univ	TX	18,736	C+
Texas Wesleyan Univ	TX	35,134	C
Texas Woman's Univ	TX	15,302	LC
The Catholic Univ of America	DC	56,356	VC
The Citadel, The Military College of S Car	SC	35,339	C
The College at Brockport - SUNY	NY	20,346	C
The College of Idaho	ID	36,415	C
The College of New Jersey	NJ	31,909	HC
The College of New Rochelle	NY	46,300	VC
The College of St. Rose	NY	43,048	C
The College of Wooster	OH	57,900	VC+
The Evergreen State College	WA	16,599	C
The Lincoln Univ	PA	15,154	NC
The Master's Univ	CA	43,870	C+
The Univ of Akron	OH	21,477	C
The Univ of Tenn at Chattanooga	TN	16,744	C
The Univ of Tenn at Knoxville	TN	22,112	VC
The Univ of Tenn at Martin	TN	14,876	C
The Univ of Utah	UT	17,924	VC
The Univ of Virginia's College at Wise	VA	18,192	LC
Thiel College	PA	41,590	C
Thomas Edison State Univ	NJ	6,350	NC
Thomas More College	KY	36,720	C
Tougaloo College	MS	17,980	NC
Touro College	NY	28,950	VC
Towson Univ	MD	17,408	VC
Transylvania Univ	KY	45,690	VC+
Trevecca Nazarene Univ	TN	31,186	C
Trinity College	CT	63,920	HC+
Trinity Univ	TX	52,314	HC+
Trinity Washington Univ	DC	33,826	C+
Troy Univ	AL	16,171	C
Truman State Univ	MO	16,014	HC
Tufts Univ	MA		MC

ST = STATE $IS = IN-STATE COSTS SR = SELECTOR RATING

School	ST	$IS	SR
Tulane Univ	LA	63,396	HC+
Tusculum College	TN	31,625	C
Tuskegee Univ	AL	28,164	C
Union College	NY	64,320	MC
Union Univ	TN	33,970	VC
United States Air Force Academy	CO		C
United States Coast Guard Academy	CT	942	MC
United States Military Academy at West Point	NY		HC+
United States Naval Academy	MD		MC
Univ of Alabama	AL	24,320	C+
Univ of Alabama at Birmingham	AL	19,906	C
Univ of Alabama in Huntsville	AL	19,445	VC
Univ of Alaska Anchorage	AK	16,652	NC
Univ of Alaska Fairbanks	AK	16,179	C
Univ of Alaska Southeast	AK	11,493	C
Univ of Arizona	AZ	23,100	C
Univ of Arkansas at Fayetteville	AR	19,152	C+
Univ of Arkansas at Little Rock	AR	18,211	C
Univ of Arkansas at Monticello	AR	13,134	NC
Univ of Arkansas at Pine Bluff	AR	13,541	C
Univ of Calif at Berkeley	CA	28,853	MC
Univ of Calif at Davis	CA	28,468	HC
Univ of Calif at Irvine	CA	26,484	VC
Univ of Calif at Los Angeles	CA	30,162	MC
Univ of Calif at Riverside	CA	29,227	C+
Univ of Calif at Santa Barbara	CA	29,091	HC
Univ of Calif San Diego	CA	30,150	MC
Univ of Calif, Santa Cruz	CA	28,731	C+
Univ of Central Arkansas	AR	14,472	VC
Univ of Central Florida	FL	15,922	VC
Univ of Central Missouri	MO	18,982	C
Univ of Central Okla	OK	13,486	C
Univ of Charleston	WV	35,000	C
Univ of Chicago	IL	67,584	MC
Univ of Cincinnati	OH	21,964	VC
Univ of Colo Boulder	CO	24,285	VC+
Univ of Colo Colo Springs	CO	19,663	C
Univ of Colo Denver	CO	23,230	C
Univ of Conn	CT	25,538	HC
Univ of Dallas	TX	45,500	VC+
Univ of Dayton	OH	53,620	C
Univ of Delaware	DE	24,976	VC+
Univ of Denver	CO	58,443	VC+
Univ of Detroit Mercy	MI	48,816	C+
Univ of Evansville	IN	44,186	VC+
Univ of Findlay	OH	60,139	C
Univ of Florida	FL	16,291	HC+
Univ of Georgia	GA	21,250	HC
Univ of Great Falls	MT	38,524	C
Univ of Hartford	CT	49,776	C
Univ of Hawaii at Hilo	HI	18,038	C
Univ of Hawaii at Manoa	HI	23,221	C
Univ of Houston-Downtown	TX	7,241	C
Univ of Idaho	ID	15,348	C
Univ of Illinois at Chicago	IL	25,006	VC
Univ of Illinois at Urbana-Champaign	IL	27,006	HC
Univ of Indianapolis	IN	36,480	C
Univ of Iowa	IA	18,683	VC+
Univ of Kansas	KS	20,135	C+
Univ of Kentucky	KY	33,306	C
Univ of La Verne	CA	55,600	C
Univ of Louisiana at Lafayette	LA	14,516	C
Univ of Louisiana at Monroe	LA	15,970	C
Univ of Louisville	KY	19,824	C
Univ of Maine	ME	20,792	C
Univ of Maine at Farmington	ME	18,187	C
Univ of Mary Hardin-Baylor	TX	33,950	C+
Univ of Mary Washington	VA	24,764	VC
Univ of Maryland/Baltimore County	MD	21,296	VC
Univ of Maryland/College Park	MD	21,938	HC
Univ of Maryland/Univ College	MD	25,966	LC
Univ of Mass Amherst	MA	26,199	VC+
Univ of Mass Boston	MA	13,435	C
Univ of Mass Dartmouth	MA	25,658	C
Univ of Mass Lowell	MA	26,380	C
Univ of Memphis	TN	18,278	C
Univ of Miami	FL	63,494	MC
Univ of Mich/Ann Arbor	MI	24,410	MC
Univ of Mich/Dearborn	MI	11,757	VC
Univ of Mich-Flint	MI	17,607	C+
Univ of Minn/Duluth	MN	20,292	C+
Univ of Minn/Morris	MN	20,760	VC
Univ of Minn/Twin Cities	MN	23,519	HC+
Univ of Miss	MS	17,746	C+
Univ of Missouri/Columbia	MO	18,201	MC
Univ of Missouri-Kansas City	MO	19,563	VC
Univ of Missouri-St. Louis	MO		C
Univ of Mobile	AL	28,935	C
Univ of Montana	MT	14,105	C
Univ of Montana-Western	MT	11,220	LC
Univ of Montevallo	AL	19,502	C
Univ of Mount Union	OH	38,970	C
Univ of Nebr - Kearney	NE	16,546	LC
Univ of Nebr - Lincoln	NE	18,589	VC
Univ of Nebr - Omaha	NE	16,120	C
Univ of Nevada, Las Vegas	NV	17,553	C
Univ of Nevada/Reno	NV	18,010	C
Univ of New England	ME	48,880	C
Univ of New Hampshire	NH	28,562	VC
Univ of New Haven	CT	52,190	C
Univ of New Mexico	NM	15,404	C
Univ of New Orleans	LA	12,840	C
Univ of North Alabama	AL	15,398	C
Univ of N Car at Asheville	NC	15,723	VC+
Univ of N Car at Chapel Hill	NC	20,052	HC+
Univ of N Car at Charlotte	NC	15,547	C
Univ of N Car at Greensboro	NC	14,690	C
Univ of N Car at Pembroke	NC	14,388	LC
Univ of N Car at Wilmington	NC	14,590	VC
Univ of N Dak	ND	15,373	C
Univ of North Florida	FL	15,996	VC
Univ of North Georgia	GA	17,316	C
Univ of North Texas	TX	19,198	C
Univ of Northern Colo	CO	20,851	C
Univ of Notre Dame	IN	64,043	MC
Univ of Okla	OK	18,911	VC
Univ of Oregon	OR	22,972	C
Univ of Pennsylvania	PA	63,526	MC
Univ of Pikeville	KY	28,700	NC
Univ of Pittsburgh	PA	29,568	HC+
Univ of Pittsburgh at Greensburg	PA	23,132	C
Univ of Pittsburgh at Johnstown	PA	22,092	C
Univ of Portland	OR	52,152	VC
Univ of PR, at Mayaguez	PR	13,995	
Univ of PR-Rio Piedras campus	PR	13,327	
Univ of Puget Sound	WA	56,456	VC+
Univ of Redlands	CA	60,200	VC
Univ of Rhode Island	RI	24,906	C
Univ of Richmond	VA	60,880	MC
Univ of Rio Grande & Rio Grande Community College	OH	8,750	NC
Univ of Rochester	NY	65,032	MC
Univ of St. Francis	IN	37,400	C
Univ of St. Mary	KS	34,690	C
Univ of San Diego	CA	58,442	VC+
Univ of San Francisco	CA	58,484	VC
Univ of Science and Arts of Okla	OK	11,140	VC
Univ of Scranton	PA	54,962	VC
Univ of Sioux Falls	SD	34,330	C
Univ of South Alabama	AL	16,400	C
Univ of S Car Aiken	SC	16,712	C
Univ of S Car at Columbia	SC	19,725	VC+
Univ of S Car Upstate	SC	18,200	LC
Univ of S Dak	SD	16,109	C
Univ of South Florida/St. Petersburg	FL	15,980	C
Univ of South Florida/Tampa	FL	16,110	VC+
Univ of Southern Calif	CA	66,631	C
Univ of Southern Indiana	IN	16,501	C
Univ of Southern Maine	ME	18,320	C
Univ of Southern Miss	MS	13,170	C
Univ of St. Francis	IL	39,924	C
Univ of St. Thomas - Houston	TX	40,020	VC
Univ of Tampa	FL	36,944	C
Univ of Texas at Arlington	TX	18,026	LC
Univ of Texas at Austin	TX	26,102	HC
Univ of Texas at Dallas	TX	22,830	VC+
Univ of Texas at El Paso	TX	34,452	NC
Univ of Texas at San Antonio	TX	20,157	C
Univ of the Cumberlands	KY	32,000	C
Univ of the District of Columbia	DC	21,044	LC
Univ of the Incarnate Word	TX	39,162	LC
Univ of the Ozarks	AR	52,176	C
Univ of the Pacific	CA	57,006	VC
Univ of Toledo	OH	19,336	NC
Univ of Tulsa	OK	52,625	HC+
Univ of Vermont	VT	28,878	HC
Univ of Virginia	VA	25,891	MC
Univ of Washington	WA	23,149	VC
Univ of West Florida	FL	15,848	C
Univ of West Georgia	GA	16,360	LC
Univ of Wisc-Eau Claire	WI	15,797	VC
Univ of Wisc-Green Bay	WI	15,064	C
Univ of Wisc-La Crosse	WI	15,247	C+
Univ of Wisc-Madison	WI	20,934	MC
Univ of Wisc-Milwaukee	WI	21,496	C
Univ of Wisc-Oshkosh	WI	15,200	C
Univ of Wisc-Parkside	WI	15,193	C
Univ of Wisc-Platteville	WI	14,614	VC
Univ of Wisc-River Falls	WI	14,485	C
Univ of Wisc-Stevens Point	WI	14,043	C
Univ of Wisc-Superior	WI	14,446	C
Univ of Wisc-Whitewater	WI	13,976	C
Univ of Wyoming	WY	15,375	C+
Ursinus College	PA	61,690	VC
Utah State Univ	UT	12,736	C
Utica College	NY	30,430	C
Valparaiso Univ	IN	48,370	C+
Vanderbilt Univ	TN	60,572	MC
Vanguard Univ of Southern Calif	CA	40,740	VC
Vassar College	NY	65,491	MC
Villanova Univ	PA	62,523	MC
Virginia Commonwealth Univ	VA	23,049	C
Virginia Polytechnic Inst and State Univ	VA	21,276	HC
Virginia State Univ	VA	19,802	C+
Virginia Union Univ	VA	22,421	C
Virginia Wesleyan College	VA	43,728	LC
Wabash College	IN	50,650	VC
Wagner College	NY	55,480	C+
Wake Forest Univ	NC	64,056	MC
Walsh Univ	OH	39,010	C
Warren Wilson College	NC	44,220	VC
Wartburg College	IA	47,840	C
Washburn Univ	KS	15,827	C
Washington & Jefferson College	PA	56,512	VC
Washington Adventist Univ	MD	31,440	LC
Washington and Lee Univ	VA	59,647	MC
Washington College	MD	54,666	VC
Washington State Univ	WA	22,495	C
Washington Univ in St. Louis	MO	65,366	VC
Wayland Baptist Univ	TX	22,356	LC
Wayne State College	NE	12,802	C
Wayne State Univ	MI	22,016	C
Weber State Univ	UT	10,721	C
Webster Univ	MO	37,490	C
Wellesley College	MA	63,916	MC
Wells College	NY	50,500	C
Wesley College	DE	37,026	LC
Wesleyan College	GA	29,694	C+
Wesleyan Univ	CT	65,516	MC
West Chester Univ of Pennsylvania	PA	18,456	C
West Liberty Univ	WV	15,512	C
West Texas A&M Univ	TX	13,478	C
West Virginia State Univ	WV	8,378	NC
West Virginia Univ	WV	18,210	C
West Virginia Wesleyan College	WV	36,858	C
Western Carolina Univ	NC	13,965	C
Western Conn State Univ	CT	21,254	LC
Western Kentucky Univ	KY	16,850	C
Western Mich Univ	MI	21,054	C
Western New England Univ	MA	48,088	C
Western Oregon Univ	OR	15,021	LC
Western State Colo Univ	CO	18,639	C
Western Washington Univ	WA	18,003	C+
Westfield State Univ	MA	19,671	C
Westminster College	MO	32,820	C
Westminster College	PA	39,180	C+
Westminster College	UT	41,078	C+
Westmont College	CA	56,410	HC
Wheaton College	IL	43,610	MC
Wheaton College	MA	61,512	VC
Wheeling Jesuit Univ	WV	37,106	LC
Wheelock College	MA	49,225	C
Whitman College	WA	59,772	MC
Whittier College	CA	57,891	C
Whitworth Univ	WA	51,732	VC
Wichita State Univ	KS	21,643	C
Widener Univ	PA	56,486	C
Wilberforce Univ	OH	19,016	C
Wilkes Univ	PA	45,622	C
Willamette Univ	OR	61,817	VC+
William Jewell College	MO	41,210	C+
William Paterson Univ of New Jersey	NJ	23,133	C
William Peace Univ	NC	37,430	LC
William Penn Univ	IA	26,000	C
William Woods Univ	MO	32,040	C
Williams College	MA	63,290	MC
Wilmington College	OH	34,600	C
Wilson College	PA	35,620	C
Wingate Univ	NC	39,950	C
Winona State Univ	MN	17,535	C
Winston-Salem State Univ	NC	26,166	LC
Winthrop Univ	SC	23,082	C
Wittenberg Univ	OH	48,156	C+
Wofford College	SC	49,885	VC
Woodbury Univ	CA	46,958	C
Wright State Univ	OH	16,983	C
Xavier Univ	OH	47,880	C+
Xavier Univ of Louisiana	LA	31,689	C+
Yale Univ	CT	64,650	MC
Yeshiva Univ	NY	47,250	VC+
York College of Pennsylvania	PA	29,240	C
Youngstown State Univ	OH	17,307	C

POLYMER SCIENCE

School	ST	$IS	SR
Case Western Reserve Univ	OH	60,304	MC
Eastern Mich Univ	MI	19,761	C
Lynn Univ	FL	49,480	LC
Millersville Univ of Pennsylvania	PA	23,782	C
Murray State Univ	KY	16,998	C
Pittsburg State Univ	KS	13,880	NC
Rochester Inst of Technology	NY	50,842	HC
SUNY / The College of Environmental Science and Forestry	NY	23,853	VC
Univ of Calif at Davis	CA	28,468	HC
Univ of Southern Miss	MS	13,170	C
Western Washington Univ	WA	18,003	C+

POLYSOMNOGRAPHIC TECHNOLOGY

School	ST	$IS	SR
Stony Brook Univ/The SUNY	NY	21,881	MC

PORTUGUESE

School	ST	$IS	SR
Brigham Young Univ	UT	12,748	HC
Brown Univ	RI	64,566	MC
Dartmouth College	NH	66,174	MC
Florida International Univ	FL	19,854	C+
Georgetown Univ	DC	65,926	MC
Harvard College/Harvard Univ	MA	60,659	MC
Indiana Univ Bloomington	IN	20,429	VC
New York Univ	NY	65,860	MC
Ohio State Univ at Columbus	OH	21,703	HC+
Princeton Univ	NJ	57,610	MC
Rhode Island College	RI	17,694	LC
Rutgers Univ - New Brunswick	NJ	26,632	HC
Rutgers Univ - Newark	NJ	27,288	C
Tulane Univ	LA	63,396	HC+
Univ of Calif at Los Angeles	CA	30,162	MC
Univ of Calif at Santa Barbara	CA	29,091	HC
Univ of Florida	FL	16,291	HC+
Univ of Illinois at Urbana-Champaign	IL	27,006	HC
Univ of Iowa	IA	18,683	VC+
Univ of Mass Amherst	MA	26,199	VC+
Univ of Mass Dartmouth	MA	25,658	C
Univ of New Mexico	NM	15,404	C
Univ of Rhode Island	RI	24,906	C
Univ of Texas at Austin	TX	26,102	HC
Univ of Wisc-Madison	WI	20,934	MC
Wellesley College	MA	63,916	MC
Yale Univ	CT	64,650	MC

POULTRY SCIENCE

School	ST	$IS	SR
Auburn Univ	AL	23,594	VC+
Miss State Univ	MS	11,454	C+
N Car State Univ	NC	19,515	HC+
Stephen F. Austin State Univ	TX	18,406	LC
Texas A&M Univ	TX	20,521	VC+
Univ of Arkansas at Fayetteville	AR	19,152	C+
Univ of Georgia	GA	21,250	HC
Univ of Maryland/Eastern Shore	MD	17,013	C
Univ of Wisc-Madison	WI	20,934	MC
Virginia Polytechnic Inst and State Univ	VA	21,276	HC

PREALLIED HEALTH

School	ST	$IS	SR
Biola Univ	CA	46,402	C+
Ithaca College	NY	56,766	VC
La Salle Univ	PA	55,790	C
Lewis Univ	IL	40,370	C
Mount Aloysius College	PA	29,976	C
St. Michael's College	VT	51,725	VC+
The Master's Univ	CA	43,870	C+
Univ of Maine at Machias	ME	22,960	C
Xavier Univ	OH	47,880	C+

PRECISION PRODUCTION

School	ST	$IS	SR
Calif College of the Arts	CA	52,758	SP

PREDENTISTRY

School	ST	$IS	SR
Albertus Magnus College	CT	43,258	LC
American International College	MA	46,300	LC
Aquinas College - Mich	MI	38,876	HC
Arcadia Univ	PA	33,570	C+
Ashland Univ	OH	21,440	C
Auburn Univ	AL	23,594	VC+
Baldwin Wallace Univ	OH	41,106	C
Ball State Univ	IN	19,590	C
Barry Univ	FL	37,830	C
Baylor Univ	TX	53,760	HC
Bellarmine Univ	KY	51,220	C
Bemidji State Univ	MN	16,056	VC
Biola Univ	CA	46,402	C+
Boise State Univ	ID	14,860	C
Boston Univ	MA	65,110	MC
Brigham Young Univ/Hawaii	HI	11,290	C
Cabrini Univ	PA	42,591	LC
Calif Lutheran Univ	CA	52,853	C
Calvin College	MI	41,570	VC+
Campbellsville Univ	KY	32,492	C
Canisius College	NY	47,537	C
Capital Univ	OH	42,982	C
Cardinal Stritch Univ	WI	36,462	C
Carroll College	MT	39,972	C+
Chadron State College	NE	14,819	NC
Chicago State Univ	IL	20,144	C
Christopher Newport Univ	VA	23,968	VC+
CUNY/City College	NY	20,319	VC
CUNY/Hunter College	NY	31,098	VC
CUNY/Lehman College	NY	5,778	HC+
Clark Univ	MA	51,600	HC+
Clayton State Univ	GA	19,735	C
Clemson Univ	SC		HC
Coe College	IA	51,570	VC
College of St. Benedict	MN	52,806	C
Colo State Univ-Pueblo	CO	18,234	C
Concord Univ	WV	14,954	C
Concordia Univ Nebr	NE	36,280	VC
Concordia Univ, Ann Arbor	MI	35,945	VC

ST = STATE $IS = IN-STATE COSTS SR = SELECTOR RATING

School	ST	$IS	SR
Converse College	SC	26,495	C
Corban Univ	OR	40,306	C
Davis & Elkins College	WV	38,242	LC
Dominican Univ	IL	41,222	C
Dordt College	IA	37,860	C+
Drury Univ	MO	33,791	VC
Eastern Mennonite Univ	VA	42,550	C
Eastern Washington Univ	WA	25,572	LC
Eckerd College	FL	52,874	C
Elizabethtown College	PA	54,050	C
Elmira College	NY	53,900	C
Elms College	MA	45,646	VC
Fairmont State Univ	WV	15,726	C
Faulkner Univ	AL	26,410	C
Florida A&M Univ	FL	15,361	C
Florida State Univ	FL	16,771	HC
Fontbonne Univ	MO	33,717	C
Freed-Hardeman Univ	TN	29,450	C
Gannon Univ	PA	42,032	C
George Fox Univ	OR	42,938	C
Georgetown College	KY	41,440	C
Gettysburg College	PA	63,000	HC
Goshen College	IN	42,500	C
Grace College and Seminary	IN	31,524	C
Graceland Univ	IA	35,290	C
Grand Rapids Theological Seminary/Cornerstone Univ	MI	33,338	C
Grand Valley State Univ	MI	22,250	C+
Gustavus Adolphus College	MN	52,433	HC
Hardin-Simmons Univ	TX	33,966	C
Heidelberg Univ	OH	39,200	C
High Point Univ	NC	45,977	C
Hofstra Univ	NY	55,960	C+
Houghton College	NY	39,090	C
Howard Univ	DC	37,616	C+
Humboldt State Univ	CA	20,514	C
Indiana Univ-Purdue Univ Fort Wayne	IN	17,553	C
Iowa Wesleyan Univ	IA	39,200	C
Ithaca College	NY	56,766	VC
Johnson C. Smith Univ	NC	25,336	LC
Judson Univ	IL	37,700	C
Kent State Univ	OH	20,732	C
Kentucky Wesleyan College	KY	32,080	C
Keuka College	NY	39,762	C
King's College	PA	46,858	C
Kutztown Univ of Pennsylvania	PA	19,056	LC
Lamar Univ	TX	18,014	LC
Le Moyne College	NY	46,000	C
Lehigh Univ	PA	61,010	MC
Lenoir-Rhyne Univ	NC	43,200	C
Lewis Univ	IL	40,370	C
Lincoln Memorial Univ	TN	28,070	C
Lipscomb Univ	TN	41,296	VC
Louisiana College	LA	21,886	C
Loyola Univ New Orleans	LA	51,708	VC+
MacMurray College	IL	33,620	C
Madonna Univ	MI	29,050	C
Manhattan College	NY	51,750	C+
Mars Hill Univ	NC	42,688	C
Marshall Univ	WV	17,242	C
Maryville College	TN	44,410	C
MCPHS Univ	MA	45,470	SP
Mercer Univ	GA	45,348	VC
Mercyhurst Univ	PA	47,420	C
Merrimack College	MA	52,770	C
Methodist Univ	NC	43,600	C
Mich State Univ	MI	23,898	VC+
Mich Tech Univ	MI	24,739	VC+
Midland Univ	NE	37,468	
Midwestern State Univ	TX	17,572	C
Millikin Univ	IL	42,158	C
Minn State Univ, Mankato	MN	15,616	C
Minn State Univ, Moorhead	MN	15,941	C
Missouri Southern State Univ	MO	12,499	C
Montclair State Univ	NJ	26,210	LC
Mount Aloysius College	PA	29,976	C
Mount Mary Univ	WI	34,650	LC
Murray State Univ	KY	16,998	C
New York Univ	NY	65,860	MC
N Car State Univ	NC	19,515	HC+
North Central College	IL	48,712	VC
North Park Univ	IL	35,860	C
Northern Kentucky Univ	KY	16,486	C
Northern Mich Univ	MI	19,604	C
Northern State Univ	SD	14,505	C
Northwest Missouri State Univ	MO	17,737	C
Northwestern College of Iowa	IA	38,400	C+
Notre Dame of Maryland Univ	MD	46,465	VC
Ohio Univ	OH	22,924	C
Ohio Wesleyan Univ	OH	49,460	VC
Okla Wesleyan Univ	OK	33,206	C
Olivet College	MI	36,110	LC
Oral Roberts Univ	OK	34,316	C
Oregon State Univ	OR	22,519	VC
Ouachita Baptist Univ	AR	32,320	C
Quinnipiac Univ	CT	59,110	C
Rhode Island College	RI	17,694	LC
Rivier Univ	NH	40,410	VC
Roberts Wesleyan College	NY	38,306	C
Rochester Inst of Technology	NY	50,842	HC
Roosevelt Univ	IL	40,651	VC
Rosemont College	PA	30,980	C
Saginaw Valley State Univ	MI	18,530	C
St. Anselm College	NH	52,560	C+
St. John's Univ	MN	51,624	C
St. Mary-of-the-Woods College	IN	39,632	LC
St. Peter's Univ	NJ	49,192	C
St. Vincent College	PA	44,626	C
St. Xavier Univ	IL	43,310	C
Seton Hill Univ	PA	46,972	C
Simpson College	IA	43,839	VC
Spring Hill College	AL	48,488	C
Springfield College	MA	45,995	C
St. Cloud State Univ	MN	10,600	C
St. Edward's Univ	TX	53,100	VC
St. Mary's Univ	TX	37,500	C
St. Thomas Univ	FL	36,360	LC
SUNY / SUNY Fredonia	NY	20,818	C
SUNY / SUNY Oneonta	NY	19,712	C+
SUNY / The College of Environmental Science and Forestry	NY	23,853	VC
SUNY at Oswego	NY	21,351	C
SUNY SUNY Albany	NY	22,165	C
Syracuse Univ	NY	60,239	VC
Tarleton State Univ	TX	15,248	LC
Temple Univ	PA	24,392	VC
Texas A&M Univ at Commerce	TX	10,496	C
Texas A&M Univ at Kingsville	TX	7,500	LC
The Catholic Univ of America	DC	56,356	VC
The Master's Univ	CA	43,870	C+
The Univ of Tenn at Knoxville	TN	22,112	VC
Thiel College	PA	41,590	C
Touro College	NY	28,950	VC
Trinity Christian College	IL	35,580	C
Truman State Univ	MO	16,014	HC
Union Univ	TN	33,970	VC
Univ of Arkansas at Pine Bluff	AR	13,541	C
Univ of Bridgeport	CT	44,430	LC
Univ of Central Arkansas	AR	14,472	VC
Univ of Central Missouri	MO	18,982	C
Univ of Central Okla	OK	13,486	C
Univ of Cincinnati	OH	21,964	VC
Univ of Dayton	OH	53,620	C
Univ of Detroit Mercy	MI	48,816	C+
Univ of Evansville	IN	44,186	VC+
Univ of Great Falls	MT	38,524	C
Univ of Hartford	CT	49,776	C
Univ of Illinois at Chicago	IL	25,006	VC
Univ of Iowa	IA	18,683	VC+
Univ of Maine at Machias	ME	22,960	C
Univ of Maryland/College Park	MD	21,938	HC
Univ of Mass Amherst	MA	26,199	VC+
Univ of Miami	FL	63,494	MC
Univ of Minn/Twin Cities	MN	23,519	HC+
Univ of Nebr - Kearney	NE	16,546	LC
Univ of Nebr - Lincoln	NE	18,589	VC
Univ of New England	ME	48,880	C
Univ of N Car at Wilmington	NC	14,590	VC
Univ of North Georgia	GA	17,316	C
Univ of Rio Grande & Rio Grande Community College	OH	8,750	NC
Univ of St. Francis	IN	37,400	C
Univ of Southern Miss	MS	13,170	C
Univ of St. Francis	IL	39,924	C
Univ of the Cumberlands	KY	32,000	C
Univ of West Alabama	AL	15,516	NC
Univ of West Florida	FL	15,848	C
Univ of Wisc-Eau Claire	WI	15,797	VC
Utah State Univ	UT	12,736	C
Virginia Polytechnic Inst and State Univ	VA	21,276	HC
Walsh Univ	OH	39,010	C
Washington Adventist Univ	MD	31,440	LC
Washington State Univ	WA	22,495	C
Washington Univ in St. Louis	MO	65,366	VC
Waynesburg Univ	PA	32,290	C
Wellesley College	MA	63,916	MC
West Chester Univ of Pennsylvania	PA	18,456	C
West Liberty Univ	WV	15,512	C
West Texas A&M Univ	TX	13,478	C
Western Carolina Univ	NC	13,965	C
Western New Mexico Univ	NM	16,734	LC
Western State Colo Univ	CO	18,639	C
Westminster College	PA	39,180	C+
Whitworth Univ	WA	51,732	VC
Wilson College	PA	35,620	C
Wingate Univ	NC	39,950	C
Winona State Univ	MN	17,535	C
Wright State Univ	OH	16,983	C
Youngstown State Univ	OH	17,307	C

PREENGINEERING

School	ST	$IS	SR
Adams State Univ	CO	17,703	LC
Alice Lloyd College	KY	8,190	C
Aquinas College - Mich	MI	38,876	HC
Asbury Univ	KY	35,180	C+
Baldwin Wallace Univ	OH	41,106	C
Ball State Univ	IN	19,590	C
Bard College at Simon's Rock	MA	65,795	MC
Barry Univ	FL	37,830	C
Bellarmine Univ	KY	51,220	C
Beloit College	WI	55,206	HC
Bethany College	WV	36,300	NC
Bethel College	IN	35,860	C
Calif Baptist Univ	CA	41,392	C
Campbellsville Univ	KY	32,492	C
Canisius College	NY	47,537	C
CUNY/Hunter College	NY	31,098	VC
Clayton State Univ	GA	19,735	C
Coe College	IA	51,570	VC
College of St. Benedict	MN	52,806	C
College of the Ozarks	MO	7,230	C
Colo State Univ-Pueblo	CO	18,234	C
Concordia Univ, Ann Arbor	MI	35,945	VC
DePauw Univ	IN	58,688	HC+
Eastern Mennonite Univ	VA	42,550	C
Elizabethtown College	PA	54,050	C
Elmhurst College	IL	45,428	C
Ferris State Univ	MI	21,445	C
Freed-Hardeman Univ	TN	29,450	C
Furman Univ	SC	58,092	VC+
Georgetown College	KY	41,440	C
Goshen College	IN	42,500	C
Harvard College/Harvard Univ	MA	60,659	MC
Heidelberg Univ	OH	39,200	C
Houghton College	NY	39,090	C
Johnson C. Smith Univ	NC	25,336	LC
Judson Univ	IL	37,700	C
Kentucky Wesleyan College	KY	32,080	C
Kutztown Univ of Pennsylvania	PA	19,056	LC
Le Moyne College	NY	46,000	C
Lenoir-Rhyne Univ	NC	43,200	C
Lewis Univ	IL	40,370	C
Lipscomb Univ	TN	41,296	VC
Loyola Univ New Orleans	LA	51,708	VC+
MacMurray College	IL	33,620	C
Madonna Univ	MI	29,050	C
Marshall Univ	WV	17,242	C
Maryville College	TN	44,410	C
Midwestern State Univ	TX	17,572	C
Millikin Univ	IL	42,158	C
Minn State Univ, Mankato	MN	15,616	C
Mount Vernon Nazarene Univ	OH	34,500	C
North Central College	IL	48,712	VC
Northwest Missouri State Univ	MO	17,737	C
Notre Dame of Maryland Univ	MD	46,465	VC
Oral Roberts Univ	OK	34,316	C
Peru State College	NE	14,768	NC
Pfeiffer Univ	NC	39,695	LC
Providence College	RI	60,760	VC
Regis Univ	CO	44,520	C
Roberts Wesleyan College	NY	38,306	C
Saginaw Valley State Univ	MI	18,530	C
St. John's Univ	MN	51,624	C
St. Mary's College of Calif	CA	57,420	C
St. Michael's College	VT	51,725	VC+
Scripps College	CA	66,664	MC
Shaw Univ	NC	24,638	C
Simpson College	IA	43,839	VC
Southern Oregon Univ	OR	19,117	C
St. Edward's Univ	TX	53,100	VC
SUNY at Oswego	NY	21,351	C
Stockton Univ	NJ	25,059	
Texas A&M Univ at Commerce	TX	10,496	C
The College of Idaho	ID	36,415	C
Thiel College	PA	41,590	C
Truman State Univ	MO	16,014	HC
Union Univ	TN	33,970	VC
Univ of Arkansas at Pine Bluff	AR	13,541	C
Univ of Central Arkansas	AR	14,472	VC
Univ of N Car at Wilmington	NC	14,590	VC
Univ of North Georgia	GA	17,316	C
Univ of Rio Grande & Rio Grande Community College	OH	8,750	NC
Univ of the Cumberlands	KY	32,000	C
Wayland Baptist Univ	TX	22,356	LC
Wellesley College	MA	63,916	MC
West Liberty Univ	WV	15,512	C
West Texas A&M Univ	TX	13,478	C
Western Carolina Univ	NC	13,965	C
Western New England Univ	MA	48,088	C
Western State Colo Univ	CO	18,639	C
Whitman College	WA	59,772	MC
Widener Univ	PA	56,486	C
Wilberforce Univ	OH	19,016	C
Wingate Univ	NC	39,950	C
Winona State Univ	MN	17,535	C
Yeshiva Univ	NY	47,250	VC+

PRE-HEALTH BIOLOGICAL STUDIES

School	ST	$IS	SR
Bryant Univ	RI	55,646	VC
Elmhurst College	IL	45,428	C
John Carroll Univ	OH	49,740	C+
Lewis Univ	IL	40,370	C
Shippensburg Univ of Pennsylvania	PA	23,208	C
SUNY at Oswego	NY	21,351	C
Univ of Arkansas at Little Rock	AR	18,211	C
Urbana Univ	OH	30,820	C
Wilson College	PA	35,620	C

PRE-HEALTH STUDIES

School	ST	$IS	SR
Aquinas College - Mich	MI	38,876	HC
Asbury Univ	KY	35,180	C+
Augsburg College	MN	43,929	C
Averett Univ	VA	40,970	LC
Biola Univ	CA	46,402	C+
Bloomfield College	NJ	39,100	LC
Bryant Univ	RI	55,646	VC
Clayton State Univ	GA	19,735	C
Elmhurst College	IL	45,428	C
Ferris State Univ	MI	21,445	C
Fordham Univ	NY	65,918	MC
Grand Rapids Theological Seminary/Cornerstone Univ	MI	33,338	C
Hofstra Univ	NY	55,960	C+
Ithaca College	NY	56,766	VC
Johnson & Wales Univ/ Denver Campus	CO	42,707	C
Kalamazoo College	MI	53,931	HC+
Lewis Univ	IL	40,370	C
Marshall Univ	WV	17,242	C
Mass College of Liberal Arts	MA	20,128	C
Mayville State Univ	ND	18,371	NC
Messiah College	PA	43,100	C+
Milligan College	TN	38,150	C
Murray State Univ	KY	16,998	C
New York Univ	NY	65,860	MC
Okla City Univ	OK	40,476	VC
Point Park Univ	PA	41,270	C
Siena Heights Univ	MI	32,040	C
SUNY at Binghamton	NY	22,861	MC
SUNY at Oswego	NY	21,351	C
Texas Christian Univ	TX	54,670	HC
Univ of Arizona	AZ	23,100	C
Univ of Illinois at Chicago	IL	25,006	VC
Univ of Miami	FL	63,494	MC
Valparaiso Univ	IN	48,370	C+
Wilson College	PA	35,620	C

PRELAW

School	ST	$IS	SR
Adams State Univ	CO	17,703	LC
Albertus Magnus College	CT	43,258	LC
American International College	MA	46,300	LC
Aquinas College - Mich	MI	38,876	HC
Arcadia Univ	PA	33,570	C+
Ashland Univ	OH	21,440	C
Averett Univ	VA	40,970	LC
Ball State Univ	IN	19,590	C
Barry Univ	FL	37,830	C
Beloit College	WI	55,206	HC
Bemidji State Univ	MN	16,056	VC
Bennington College	VT	63,960	MC
Biola Univ	CA	46,402	C+
Blackburn College	IL	28,526	LC
Bryant Univ	RI	55,646	VC
Calif Lutheran Univ	CA	52,853	C
Calvin College	MI	41,570	VC+
Campbellsville Univ	KY	32,492	C
Canisius College	NY	47,537	C
Capital Univ	OH	42,982	C
Cardinal Stritch Univ	WI	36,462	C
Carroll College	MT	39,972	C+
Carroll Univ	WI	38,100	C+
Catawba College	NC	39,820	C
Cedarville Univ	OH	34,990	VC
Central Washington Univ	WA	16,803	C
Chadron State College	NE	14,819	NC
Chicago State Univ	IL	20,144	C
Christopher Newport Univ	VA	23,968	VC+
CUNY/City College	NY	20,319	VC
CUNY/Hunter College	NY	31,098	VC
CUNY/Lehman College	NY	5,778	HC+
Clark Univ	MA	51,600	HC+
Clemson Univ	SC		HC
Coe College	IA	51,570	VC
College of St. Benedict	MN	52,806	C
College of the Ozarks	MO	7,230	C
Colo State Univ-Pueblo	CO	18,234	C
Concord Univ	WV	14,954	C
Concordia Univ Nebr	NE	36,280	VC
Concordia Univ, Chicago	IL	39,694	C
Converse College	SC	26,495	C
Corban Univ	OR	40,306	C
Davis & Elkins College	WV	38,242	LC
Dominican Univ	IL	41,222	C
Dordt College	IA	37,860	C+
Drury Univ	MO	33,791	VC
East Central Univ	OK	13,056	C
Eastern Washington Univ	WA	25,572	LC
Eckerd College	FL	52,874	C
Edinboro Univ	PA	15,940	LC
Elmira College	NY	53,900	C
Elms College	MA	45,646	VC
Faulkner Univ	AL	26,410	C
Fitchburg State Univ	MA	21,819	C
Florida Inst of Technology	FL	53,306	VC
Florida State Univ	FL	16,771	HC
Fontbonne Univ	MO	33,717	C
Fordham Univ	NY	65,918	MC
Fresno Pacific Univ	CA	37,370	C
George Fox Univ	OR	42,938	C
Georgetown College	KY	41,440	C
Gettysburg College	PA	63,000	HC
Grace College and Seminary	IN	31,524	C

ST = STATE $IS = IN-STATE COSTS SR = SELECTOR RATING

School	ST	$IS	SR
Grand Valley State Univ	MI	22,250	C+
Gustavus Adolphus College	MN	52,433	HC
Hamline Univ	MN	45,678	VC
Hardin-Simmons Univ	TX	33,966	C
Heidelberg Univ	OH	39,200	C
High Point Univ	NC	45,977	C
Hofstra Univ	NY	55,960	C+
Houghton College	NY	39,090	C
Humboldt State Univ	CA	20,514	C
Huntington Univ	IN	33,996	C
Illinois College	IL	40,850	VC
Indiana Inst of Technology	IN	34,240	LC
Indiana Univ-Purdue Univ Fort Wayne	IN	17,553	C
Indiana Univ-Purdue Univ Indianapolis	IN	18,635	C
Indiana Wesleyan Univ	IN	33,674	C
Iowa Wesleyan Univ	IA	39,200	C
Ithaca College	NY	56,766	VC
Johnson C. Smith Univ	NC	25,336	LC
Johnson State College	VT	20,752	C
Judson Univ	IL	37,700	C
Kansas Wesleyan Univ	KS	36,600	C
Kentucky Wesleyan College	KY	32,080	C
Keuka College	NY	39,762	C
King's College	PA	46,858	C
Lafayette College	PA	63,355	MC
Lamar Univ	TX	18,014	LC
Le Moyne College	NY	46,000	C
Lenoir-Rhyne Univ	NC	43,200	C
LeTourneau Univ	TX	38,250	VC
Lewis Univ	IL	40,370	C
Limestone College	SC	32,100	C
Lincoln Memorial Univ	TN	28,070	C
Lindenwood Univ	MO	25,132	C
Lipscomb Univ	TN	41,296	VC
Louisiana College	LA	21,886	C
Lubbock Christian Univ	TX	28,426	C
MacMurray College	IL	33,620	C
Madonna Univ	MI	29,050	C
Manchester Univ	IN	40,422	C
Manhattan College	NY	51,750	C+
Mars Hill Univ	NC	42,688	C
Marshall Univ	WV	17,242	C
Maryville College	TN	44,410	C
Marywood Univ	PA	46,900	C
Mayville State Univ	ND	18,371	NC
Mercer Univ	GA	45,348	VC
Mercyhurst Univ	PA	47,420	C
Merrimack College	MA	52,770	C
Methodist Univ	NC	43,600	C
Mich State Univ	MI	23,898	VC+
Middle Tenn State Univ	TN	8,650	C
Midland Univ	NE	37,468	
Midwestern State Univ	TX	17,572	C
Millikin Univ	IL	42,158	C
Mills College	CA	59,163	VC
Minn State Univ, Mankato	MN	15,616	C
Minn State Univ, Moorhead	MN	15,941	C
Missouri Univ of Science and Technology	MO	18,655	HC
Monmouth Univ	NJ	46,234	C
Mount Aloysius College	PA	29,976	C
Mount Mary Univ	WI	34,650	LC
Mount Vernon Nazarene Univ	OH	34,500	C
National Univ	CA	14,730	LC
Neumann Univ	PA	40,678	LC
N Car State Univ	NC	19,515	HC+
North Central College	IL	48,712	VC
North Park Univ	IL	35,860	C
Northern Arizona Univ	AZ	20,246	VC
Northern Kentucky Univ	KY	16,486	C
Northern Mich Univ	MI	19,604	C
Northern State Univ	SD	14,505	C
Northwest Missouri State Univ	MO	17,737	C
Northwestern College of Iowa	IA	38,400	C+
Notre Dame of Maryland Univ	MD	46,465	VC
Oakland City Univ	IN	33,360	NC
Oberlin College	OH	66,012	MC
Ohio Univ	OH	22,924	C
Ohio Wesleyan Univ	OH	49,460	VC
Okla Baptist Univ	OK	32,320	C
Okla Christian Univ	OK	27,650	VC
Okla City Univ	OK	40,476	VC
Okla Wesleyan Univ	OK	33,206	C
Olivet College	MI	36,110	LC
Oral Roberts Univ	OK	34,316	C
Ouachita Baptist Univ	AR	32,320	C
Palm Beach Atlantic Univ	FL	39,720	C
Peru State College	NE	14,768	NC
Quinnipiac Univ	CT	59,110	C
Regis Univ	CO	44,520	C
Rensselaer Polytechnic Inst	NY	63,436	MC
Rhode Island College	RI	17,694	LC
Rider Univ	NJ	54,050	C
Rivier Univ	NH	40,410	VC
Roberts Wesleyan College	NY	38,306	C
Rochester Inst of Technology	NY	50,842	HC
Roosevelt Univ	IL	40,651	VC
Rosemont College	PA	30,980	C
Saginaw Valley State Univ	MI	18,530	C
St. Anselm College	NH	52,560	C+
St. Augustine's Univ	NC	26,048	C
St. John's Univ	MN	51,624	C
St. Mary-of-the-Woods College	IN	39,632	LC
St. Michael's College	VT	51,725	VC+
St. Peter's Univ	NJ	49,192	C
St. Vincent College	PA	44,626	C
St. Xavier Univ	IL	43,310	C
Schreiner Univ	TX	34,626	LC
Scripps College	CA	66,664	MC
Seattle Pacific Univ	WA	47,439	C+
Seton Hill Univ	PA	46,972	C
Simpson College	IA	43,839	VC
Southern Oregon Univ	OR	19,117	C
Springfield College	MA	45,995	C
St. Ambrose Univ	IA	39,019	C
St. Ambrose Univ	IA	39,019	C
St. Cloud State Univ	MN	10,600	C
St. Edward's Univ	TX	53,100	VC
St. Mary's Univ	TX	37,500	C
St. Thomas Aquinas College	NY	42,200	C
St. Thomas Univ	FL	36,360	LC
SUNY / SUNY Fredonia	NY	20,818	C
SUNY / SUNY Oneonta	NY	19,712	C+
SUNY / The College of Environmental Science and Forestry	NY	23,853	VC
SUNY at Oswego	NY	21,351	C
SUNY SUNY Albany	NY	22,165	C
Stetson Univ	FL	53,544	VC
Stillman College	AL	20,738	C
Syracuse Univ	NY	60,239	VC
Tarleton State Univ	TX	15,248	LC
Temple Univ	PA	24,392	VC
Texas A&M Univ at Commerce	TX	10,496	C
Texas A&M Univ at Kingsville	TX	7,500	LC
Texas Wesleyan Univ	TX	35,134	C
The Catholic Univ of America	DC	56,356	VC
The Master's Univ	CA	43,870	C+
Thiel College	PA	41,590	C
Touro College	NY	28,950	VC
Trinity Christian College	IL	35,580	C
Truman State Univ	MO	16,014	HC
Union Univ	TN	33,970	VC
Univ of Bridgeport	CT	44,430	LC
Univ of Central Missouri	MO	18,982	C
Univ of Cincinnati	OH	21,964	VC
Univ of Detroit Mercy	MI	48,816	C+
Univ of Evansville	IN	44,186	VC+
Univ of Findlay	OH	60,139	C
Univ of Great Falls	MT	38,524	C
Univ of Illinois at Urbana-Champaign	IL	27,006	HC
Univ of Iowa	IA	18,683	VC+
Univ of Mary	ND	23,180	C
Univ of Maryland/College Park	MD	21,938	HC
Univ of Miami	FL	63,494	MC
Univ of Minn/Duluth	MN	20,292	C+
Univ of Minn/Morris	MN	20,760	VC
Univ of Minn/Twin Cities	MN	23,519	HC+
Univ of Montana-Western	MT	11,220	LC
Univ of Nebr - Kearney	NE	16,546	LC
Univ of Nebr - Lincoln	NE	18,589	VC
Univ of N Car at Wilmington	NC	14,590	VC
Univ of North Georgia	GA	17,316	C
Univ of Rio Grande & Rio Grande Community College	OH	8,750	NC
Univ of Sioux Falls	SD	34,330	C
Univ of Southern Miss	MS	13,170	C
Univ of the Cumberlands	KY	32,000	C
Univ of the Incarnate Word	TX	39,162	LC
Univ of Tulsa	OK	52,625	HC+
Univ of West Alabama	AL	15,516	NC
Univ of West Florida	FL	15,848	C
Univ of Wisc-Eau Claire	WI	15,797	VC
Univ of Wisc-River Falls	WI	14,485	C
Univ of Wisc-Whitewater	WI	13,976	C
Urbana Univ	OH	30,820	C
Ursuline College	OH	41,076	LC
Utah State Univ	UT	12,736	C
Valparaiso Univ	IN	48,370	C+
Vassar College	NY	65,491	MC
Virginia Polytechnic Inst and State Univ	VA	21,276	HC
Walsh Univ	OH	39,010	C
Washington Adventist Univ	MD	31,440	LC
Washington State Univ	WA	22,495	C
Wayland Baptist Univ	TX	22,356	LC
Waynesburg Univ	PA	32,290	C
Webber International Univ	FL	31,904	C
Wellesley College	MA	63,916	MC
West Chester Univ of Pennsylvania	PA	18,456	C
West Liberty Univ	WV	15,512	C
West Texas A&M Univ	TX	13,478	C
Western Carolina Univ	NC	13,965	C
Western State Colo Univ	CO	18,639	C
Westminster College	PA	39,180	C+
Westminster College	UT	41,078	C+
Whitman College	WA	59,772	MC
Whitworth Univ	WA	51,732	VC
Wilberforce Univ	OH	19,016	C
William Peace Univ	NC	37,430	LC
Wilmington College	OH	34,600	C
Wilson College	PA	35,620	C
Wingate Univ	NC	39,950	C
Winona State Univ	MN	17,535	C
Wright State Univ	OH	16,983	C
Youngstown State Univ	OH	17,307	C

PREMEDICINE

School	ST	$IS	SR
Adams State Univ	CO	17,703	LC
Albertus Magnus College	CT	43,258	LC
American International College	MA	46,300	LC
American Jewish Univ - College of A&S Campus	CA	44,234	C
Aquinas College - Mich	MI	38,876	HC
Arcadia Univ	PA	33,570	C+
Ashland Univ	OH	21,440	C
Auburn Univ	AL	23,594	VC+
Augustana College	IL	49,658	VC
Avila Univ	MO	35,480	C
Baldwin Wallace Univ	OH	41,106	C
Ball State Univ	IN	19,590	C
Bard College at Simon's Rock	MA	65,795	MC
Barry Univ	FL	37,830	C
Bayamon Central Univ	PR	12,490	
Baylor Univ	TX	53,760	HC
Bellarmine Univ	KY	51,220	C
Beloit College	WI	55,206	HC
Bemidji State Univ	MN	16,056	VC
Bennington College	VT	63,960	MC
Bethel Univ	TN	24,738	C
Biola Univ	CA	46,402	C+
Blackburn College	IL	28,526	LC
Bloomfield College	NJ	39,100	LC
Bluffton Univ	OH	40,950	C
Boise State Univ	ID	14,860	C
Brigham Young Univ/Hawaii	HI	11,290	C
Bryant Univ	RI	55,646	VC
Cabrini Univ	PA	42,591	LC
Calif Lutheran Univ	CA	52,853	C
Cal State, San Bernardino	CA	12,000	C
Calvin College	MI	41,570	VC+
Campbellsville Univ	KY	32,492	C
Canisius College	NY	47,537	C
Capital Univ	OH	42,982	C
Cardinal Stritch Univ	WI	36,462	C
Carroll College	MT	39,972	C+
Chadron State College	NE	14,819	NC
Chicago State Univ	IL	20,144	C
Christopher Newport Univ	VA	23,968	VC+
CUNY/City College	NY	20,319	VC
CUNY/Hunter College	NY	31,098	VC
CUNY/Lehman College	NY	5,778	HC+
Clark Univ	MA	51,600	HC+
Clemson Univ	SC		HC
Cleveland State Univ	OH	22,196	C
Coe College	IA	51,570	VC
Coker College	SC	34,810	LC
College of St. Benedict	MN	52,806	C
College of the Ozarks	MO	7,230	C
Colo State Univ-Pueblo	CO	18,234	C
Concord Univ	WV	14,954	C
Concordia Univ	OR	35,000	C
Concordia Univ Nebr	NE	36,280	VC
Concordia Univ, Ann Arbor	MI	35,945	VC
Concordia Univ, Chicago	IL	39,694	C
Converse College	SC	26,495	C
Corban Univ	OR	40,306	C
Dakota State Univ	SD	13,811	C
Davis & Elkins College	WV	38,242	LC
Dominican Univ	IL	41,222	C
Dominican Univ of Calif	CA	57,050	C
Dordt College	IA	37,860	C+
Drexel Univ	PA	65,432	VC+
Drury Univ	MO	33,791	VC
Earlham College	IN	54,870	HC
East Central Univ	OK	13,056	C
Eastern Mennonite Univ	VA	42,550	C
Eastern Washington Univ	WA	25,572	LC
Eckerd College	FL	52,874	C
Edinboro Univ	PA	15,940	LC
Elizabethtown College	PA	54,050	C
Elmhurst College	IL	45,428	C
Elmira College	NY	53,900	C
Elms College	MA	45,646	VC
Faulkner Univ	AL	26,410	C
Florida A&M Univ	FL	15,361	C
Florida Inst of Technology	FL	53,306	VC
Florida State Univ	FL	16,771	HC
Fontbonne Univ	MO	33,717	C
Freed-Hardeman Univ	TN	29,450	C
Fresno Pacific Univ	CA	37,370	C
Friends Univ	KS	34,455	C
Gannon Univ	PA	42,032	C
George Fox Univ	OR	42,938	C
George Washington Univ	DC	62,835	MC
Georgetown College	KY	41,440	C
Gettysburg College	PA	63,000	HC
Goshen College	IN	42,500	C
Grace College and Seminary	IN	31,524	C
Graceland Univ	IA	35,290	C
Grand Rapids Theological Seminary/Cornerstone Univ	MI	33,338	C
Grand Valley State Univ	MI	22,250	C+
Gustavus Adolphus College	MN	52,433	HC
Hamline Univ	MN	45,678	VC
Hampshire College	MA	63,824	MC
Hardin-Simmons Univ	TX	33,966	C
Hawaii Pacific Univ	HI	33,420	C
Heidelberg Univ	OH	39,200	C
High Point Univ	NC	45,977	C
Hofstra Univ	NY	55,960	C+
Houghton College	NY	39,090	C
Howard Univ	DC	37,616	C+
Humboldt State Univ	CA	20,514	C
Huntington Univ	IN	33,996	C
Indiana Univ-Purdue Univ Fort Wayne	IN	17,553	C
Indiana Univ-Purdue Univ Indianapolis	IN	18,635	C
Indiana Wesleyan Univ	IN	33,674	C
Inter-American Univ of PR-San Germán	PR	20,042	
Iowa Wesleyan Univ	IA	39,200	C
Ithaca College	NY	56,766	VC
Jackson State Univ	MS	15,879	LC
Johnson C. Smith Univ	NC	25,336	LC
Johnson State College	VT	20,752	C
Judson Univ	IL	37,700	C
Kent State Univ	OH	20,732	C
Kentucky Wesleyan College	KY	32,080	C
Keuka College	NY	39,762	C
King's College	PA	46,858	C
Kutztown Univ of Pennsylvania	PA	19,056	LC
La Salle Univ	PA	55,790	C
Lamar Univ	TX	18,014	LC
Le Moyne College	NY	46,000	C
Lees-McRae College	NC	33,944	C
Lehigh Univ	PA	61,010	MC
Lenoir-Rhyne Univ	NC	43,200	C
LeTourneau Univ	TX	38,250	VC
Lewis Univ	IL	40,370	C
Lincoln Memorial Univ	TN	28,070	C
Lipscomb Univ	TN	41,296	VC
Louisiana College	LA	21,886	C
Loyola Univ New Orleans	LA	51,708	VC+
Lubbock Christian Univ	TX	28,426	C
MacMurray College	IL	33,620	C
Madonna Univ	MI	29,050	C
Manhattan College	NY	51,750	C+
Marquette Univ	WI	48,390	VC+
Mars Hill Univ	NC	42,688	C
Marshall Univ	WV	17,242	C
Marymount Manhattan College	NY	46,280	VC
Marymount Univ	VA	41,570	LC
Maryville College	TN	44,410	C
Marywood Univ	PA	46,900	C
Mayville State Univ	ND	18,371	NC
MCPHS Univ	MA	45,470	SP
Mercer Univ	GA	45,348	VC
Mercy College of Health Sciences	IA	16,920	C
Mercyhurst Univ	PA	47,420	C
Merrimack College	MA	52,770	C
Mich Tech Univ	MI	24,739	VC+
Midland Univ	NE	37,468	
Midwestern State Univ	TX	17,572	C
Milligan College	TN	38,150	C
Millikin Univ	IL	42,158	C
Minn State Univ, Mankato	MN	15,616	C
Minn State Univ, Moorhead	MN	15,941	C
Missouri Southern State Univ	MO	12,499	C
Missouri Univ of Science and Technology	MO	18,655	HC
Monmouth Univ	NJ	46,234	C
Montclair State Univ	NJ	26,210	LC
Mount Aloysius College	PA	29,976	C
Mount Mary Univ	WI	34,650	LC
Mount Vernon Nazarene Univ	OH	34,500	C
Murray State Univ	KY	16,998	C
Neumann Univ	PA	40,678	LC
New York Univ	NY	65,860	MC
N Car State Univ	NC	19,515	HC+
N Car Wesleyan College	NC	39,200	C
North Central College	IL	48,712	VC
North Park Univ	IL	35,860	C
Northern Kentucky Univ	KY	16,486	C
Northern Mich Univ	MI	19,604	C
Northern State Univ	SD	14,505	C
Northwest Missouri State Univ	MO	17,737	C
Northwestern College of Iowa	IA	38,400	C+
Northwestern Univ	IL	66,344	MC
Notre Dame of Maryland Univ	MD	46,465	VC
Oakland City Univ	IN	33,360	NC
Oberlin College	OH	66,012	MC
Ohio Univ	OH	22,924	C
Ohio Wesleyan Univ	OH	49,460	VC
Okla Baptist Univ	OK	32,320	C
Okla City Univ	OK	40,476	VC
Okla Wesleyan Univ	OK	33,206	C
Olivet College	MI	36,110	LC
Oral Roberts Univ	OK	34,316	C
Oregon State Univ	OR	22,519	VC
Ouachita Baptist Univ	AR	32,320	C
Pennsylvania State Univ - Univ Park	PA	29,760	HC
Peru State College	NE	14,768	NC
Pfeiffer Univ	NC	39,695	LC
Philadelphia Univ	PA	50,370	C
Pittsburg State Univ	KS	13,880	NC
Point Park Univ	PA	41,270	C
Providence College	RI	60,760	VC
Quinnipiac Univ	CT	59,110	C
Regis Univ	CO	44,520	C
Rensselaer Polytechnic Inst	NY	63,436	MC
Rhode Island College	RI	17,694	LC

ST = STATE $IS = IN-STATE COSTS SR = SELECTOR RATING

School	ST	$IS	SR
Rider Univ	NJ	54,050	C
Rivier Univ	NH	40,410	VC
Roberts Wesleyan College	NY	38,306	C
Rochester Inst of Technology	NY	50,842	HC
Roosevelt Univ	IL	40,651	VC
Rosemont College	PA	30,980	C
Saginaw Valley State Univ	MI	18,530	C
St. Anselm College	NH	52,560	C+
St. Augustine's Univ	NC	26,048	C
St. John's Univ	MN	51,624	C
St. Mary-of-the-Woods College	IN	39,632	LC
St. Peter's Univ	NJ	49,192	C
St. Vincent College	PA	44,626	C
St. Xavier Univ	IL	43,310	C
Sarah Lawrence College	NY	63,388	HC
Seton Hill Univ	PA	46,972	C
Siena Heights Univ	MI	32,040	C
Simpson College	IA	43,839	VC
Southern Oregon Univ	OR	19,117	C
Spring Hill College	AL	48,488	C
Springfield College	MA	45,995	C
St. Cloud State Univ	MN	10,600	C
St. Edward's Univ	TX	53,100	VC
St. Mary's Univ	TX	37,500	C
St. Thomas Aquinas College	NY	42,200	C
St. Thomas Univ	FL	36,360	LC
SUNY / SUNY Fredonia	NY	20,818	C
SUNY / SUNY Oneonta	NY	19,712	C+
SUNY / The College of Environmental Science and Forestry	NY	23,853	VC
SUNY at Oswego	NY	21,351	C
SUNY SUNY Albany	NY	22,165	C
Stillman College	AL	20,738	C
Syracuse Univ	NY	60,239	VC+
Tarleton State Univ	TX	15,248	LC
Taylor Univ	IN	40,317	C+
Temple Univ	PA	24,392	VC
Texas A&M Univ at Commerce	TX	10,496	C
Texas A&M Univ at Kingsville	TX	7,500	LC
The Catholic Univ of America	DC	56,356	VC
The Univ of Tenn at Knoxville	TN	22,112	VC
Thiel College	PA	41,590	C
Touro College	NY	28,950	VC
Trine Univ	IN	41,310	C
Trinity Christian College	IL	35,580	C
Trinity International Univ	IL	31,070	VC
Truman State Univ	MO	16,014	HC
Tusculum College	TN	31,625	C
Union Univ	TN	33,970	VC
Univ of Arkansas at Pine Bluff	AR	13,541	C
Univ of Bridgeport	CT	44,430	LC
Univ of Calif at Irvine	CA	26,484	VC+
Univ of Central Arkansas	AR	14,472	VC
Univ of Central Missouri	MO	18,982	C
Univ of Central Okla	OK	13,486	C
Univ of Cincinnati	OH	21,964	VC
Univ of Dayton	OH	53,620	C
Univ of Detroit Mercy	MI	48,816	C+
Univ of Evansville	IN	44,186	VC+
Univ of Findlay	OH	60,139	C
Univ of Great Falls	MT	38,524	C
Univ of Hartford	CT	49,776	C
Univ of Illinois at Chicago	IL	25,006	VC
Univ of Iowa	IA	18,683	VC+
Univ of Maine at Machias	ME	22,960	C
Univ of Mary	ND	23,180	C
Univ of Mass Amherst	MA	26,199	VC+
Univ of Miami	FL	63,494	MC
Univ of Minn/Morris	MN	20,760	VC
Univ of Minn/Twin Cities	MN	23,519	HC+
Univ of Nebr - Kearney	NE	16,546	LC
Univ of Nebr - Lincoln	NE	18,589	VC
Univ of New Orleans	LA	12,840	C
Univ of N Car at Wilmington	NC	14,590	VC
Univ of North Georgia	GA	17,316	C
Univ of PR, at Mayaguez	PR	13,995	
Univ of Rio Grande & Rio Grande Community College	OH	8,750	NC
Univ of St. Francis	IN	37,400	C
Univ of Sioux Falls	SD	34,330	C
Univ of Southern Miss	MS	13,170	C
Univ of St. Francis	IL	39,924	C
Univ of the Cumberlands	KY	32,000	C
Univ of Tulsa	OK	52,625	HC+
Univ of West Alabama	AL	15,516	NC
Univ of West Florida	FL	15,848	C
Univ of Wisc-Eau Claire	WI	15,797	VC
Univ of Wisc-Milwaukee	WI	21,496	C
Univ of Wisc-River Falls	WI	14,485	C
Urbana Univ	OH	30,820	C
Ursuline College	OH	41,076	LC
Utah State Univ	UT	12,736	C
Valparaiso Univ	IN	48,370	C+
Vanguard Univ of Southern Calif	CA	40,740	VC
Vassar College	NY	65,491	MC
Virginia Polytechnic Inst and State Univ	VA	21,276	HC
Walsh Univ	OH	39,010	C
Washington State Univ	WA	22,495	C
Washington Univ in St. Louis	MO	65,366	VC
Wayland Baptist Univ	TX	22,356	LC
Waynesburg Univ	PA	32,290	C
Wellesley College	MA	63,916	MC
West Chester Univ of Pennsylvania	PA	18,456	C
West Liberty Univ	WV	15,512	C
West Texas A&M Univ	TX	13,478	C
Western Carolina Univ	NC	13,965	C
Western New England Univ	MA	48,088	C
Western New Mexico Univ	NM	16,734	LC
Westminster College	PA	39,180	C+
Whitworth Univ	WA	51,732	VC
Wilmington College	OH	34,600	C
Wilson College	PA	35,620	C
Wingate Univ	NC	39,950	C
Winona State Univ	MN	17,535	C
Wright State Univ	OH	16,983	C
Xavier Univ of Louisiana	LA	31,689	C+
Youngstown State Univ	OH	17,307	C

PRE-OCCUPATIONAL THERAPY

School	ST	$IS	SR
Bay Path Univ	MA	45,349	C
Calvin College	MI	41,570	VC+
Eastern Mennonite Univ	VA	42,550	C
High Point Univ	NC	45,977	C
Indiana Univ-Purdue Univ Indianapolis	IN	18,635	C
Lewis Univ	IL	40,370	C
MCPHS Univ	MA	45,470	SP
Missouri Southern State Univ	MO	12,499	C
Murray State Univ	KY	16,998	C
Ohio Wesleyan Univ	OH	49,460	VC
Walsh Univ	OH	39,010	C
Wilson College	PA	35,620	C

PREOPTOMETRY

School	ST	$IS	SR
Adams State Univ	CO	17,703	LC
Arcadia Univ	PA	33,570	C+
Ashland Univ	OH	21,440	C
Auburn Univ	AL	23,594	VC+
Ball State Univ	IN	19,590	C
Calvin College	MI	41,570	VC+
Cardinal Stritch Univ	WI	36,462	C
Carroll College	MT	39,972	C+
College of St. Benedict	MN	52,806	C
Colo State Univ-Pueblo	CO	18,234	C
Corban Univ	OR	40,306	C
Dordt College	IA	37,860	C+
Drury Univ	MO	33,791	VC
East Central Univ	OK	13,056	C
Faulkner Univ	AL	26,410	C
Florida State Univ	FL	16,771	HC
Freed-Hardeman Univ	TN	29,450	C
Gannon Univ	PA	42,032	C
Hofstra Univ	NY	55,960	C+
Houghton College	NY	39,090	C
Indiana Univ-Purdue Univ Fort Wayne	IN	17,553	C
Iowa Wesleyan Univ	IA	39,200	C
Ithaca College	NY	56,766	VC
Le Moyne College	NY	46,000	C
Lehigh Univ	PA	61,010	MC
Lenoir-Rhyne Univ	NC	43,200	C
Lewis Univ	IL	40,370	C
Lipscomb Univ	TN	41,296	VC
Louisiana College	LA	21,886	C
Madonna Univ	MI	29,050	C
Marshall Univ	WV	17,242	C
MCPHS Univ	MA	45,470	SP
Millersville Univ of Pennsylvania	PA	23,782	C
Millikin Univ	IL	42,158	C
Missouri Southern State Univ	MO	12,499	C
Mount Aloysius College	PA	29,976	C
Murray State Univ	KY	16,998	C
Northern Kentucky Univ	KY	16,486	C
Oregon State Univ	OR	22,519	VC
Pittsburg State Univ	KS	13,880	NC
Rhode Island College	RI	17,694	LC
St. John's Univ	MN	51,624	C
Simpson College	IA	43,839	VC
SUNY / SUNY Fredonia	NY	20,818	C
SUNY at Oswego	NY	21,351	C
Trinity Christian College	IL	35,580	C
Univ of Central Arkansas	AR	14,472	VC
Univ of Central Okla	OK	13,486	C
Univ of Evansville	IN	44,186	VC+
Univ of Hartford	CT	49,776	C
Univ of Iowa	IA	18,683	VC+
Univ of N Car at Wilmington	NC	14,590	VC
Univ of St. Francis	IL	39,924	C
Univ of Wisc-Eau Claire	WI	15,797	VC
Walsh Univ	OH	39,010	C
Washington State Univ	WA	22,495	C
Wellesley College	MA	63,916	MC
Western Carolina Univ	NC	13,965	C
Western New England Univ	MA	48,088	C
Wilson College	PA	35,620	C
Winona State Univ	MN	17,535	C
Youngstown State Univ	OH	17,307	C

PREOSTEOPATHY

School	ST	$IS	SR
Colo State Univ-Pueblo	CO	18,234	C
Drury Univ	MO	33,791	VC
Eastern Mennonite Univ	VA	42,550	C
Hofstra Univ	NY	55,960	C+
Kent State Univ	OH	20,732	C
Madonna Univ	MI	29,050	C
Marshall Univ	WV	17,242	C
Marywood Univ	PA	46,900	C
MCPHS Univ	MA	45,470	SP
Mercyhurst Univ	PA	47,420	C
Mount Aloysius College	PA	29,976	C
Seton Hill Univ	PA	46,972	C
Wilson College	PA	35,620	C
Youngstown State Univ	OH	17,307	C

PREPHARMACY

School	ST	$IS	SR
Adams State Univ	CO	17,703	LC
Alabama A&M Univ	AL	18,796	C
Alice Lloyd College	KY	8,190	C
Baldwin Wallace Univ	OH	41,106	C
Barry Univ	FL	37,830	C
Biola Univ	CA	46,402	C+
Boise State Univ	ID	14,860	C
Cabrini Univ	PA	42,591	LC
Calvin College	MI	41,570	VC+
Campbellsville Univ	KY	32,492	C
Canisius College	NY	47,537	C
Carroll College	MT	39,972	C+
Carroll Univ	WI	38,100	C+
Christopher Newport Univ	VA	23,968	VC+
Clemson Univ	SC		HC
College of St. Benedict	MN	52,806	C
College of the Ozarks	MO	7,230	C
Colo State Univ-Pueblo	CO	18,234	C
Concord Univ	WV	14,954	C
Corban Univ	OR	40,306	C
Davis & Elkins College	WV	38,242	LC
Dominican Univ	IL	41,222	C
Dordt College	IA	37,860	C+
Drury Univ	MO	33,791	VC
East Central Univ	OK	13,056	C
Eastern Mennonite Univ	VA	42,550	C
Florida State Univ	FL	16,771	HC
Freed-Hardeman Univ	TN	29,450	C
Georgetown College	KY	41,440	C
Goshen College	IN	42,500	C
High Point Univ	NC	45,977	C
Houghton College	NY	39,090	C
Huntington Univ	IN	33,996	C
Husson Univ	ME	25,720	LC
Indiana Univ-Purdue Univ Fort Wayne	IN	17,553	C
Indiana Univ-Purdue Univ Indianapolis	IN	18,635	C
Le Moyne College	NY	46,000	C
Lewis Univ	IL	40,370	C
Lipscomb Univ	TN	41,296	VC
Lubbock Christian Univ	TX	28,426	C
Madonna Univ	MI	29,050	C
Mars Hill Univ	NC	42,688	C
Marshall Univ	WV	17,242	C
Mercer Univ	GA	45,348	VC
Mercyhurst Univ	PA	47,420	C
Mich Tech Univ	MI	24,739	VC+
Midwestern State Univ	TX	17,572	C
Millersville Univ of Pennsylvania	PA	23,782	C
Milligan College	TN	38,150	C
Millikin Univ	IL	42,158	C
Minn State Univ, Mankato	MN	15,616	C
Minn State Univ, Moorhead	MN	15,941	C
Missouri Southern State Univ	MO	12,499	C
Montclair State Univ	NJ	26,210	LC
Mount Aloysius College	PA	29,976	C
Mount Vernon Nazarene Univ	OH	34,500	C
Murray State Univ	KY	16,998	C
Neumann Univ	PA	40,678	LC
Northern Kentucky Univ	KY	16,486	C
Northwest Missouri State Univ	MO	17,737	C
Notre Dame of Maryland Univ	MD	46,465	VC
Ohio Univ	OH	22,924	C
Oregon State Univ	OR	22,519	VC
Peru State College	NE	14,768	NC
Pittsburg State Univ	KS	13,880	NC
Roberts Wesleyan College	NY	38,306	C
Roosevelt Univ	IL	40,651	VC
St. John's Univ	MN	51,624	C
St. Joseph's College of Maine	ME	46,485	C
St. Michael's College	VT	51,725	VC+
St. Vincent College	PA	44,626	C
St. Xavier Univ	IL	43,310	C
Simpson College	IA	43,839	VC
Southern Oregon Univ	OR	19,117	C
SUNY / The College of Environmental Science and Forestry	NY	23,853	VC
Tarleton State Univ	TX	15,248	LC
Texas A&M Univ at Commerce	TX	10,496	C
Texas A&M Univ at Kingsville	TX	7,500	LC
The Univ of Tenn at Knoxville	TN	22,112	VC
Thiel College	PA	41,590	C
Truman State Univ	MO	16,014	HC
Union Univ	TN	33,970	VC
Univ of Arkansas at Pine Bluff	AR	13,541	C
Univ of Central Arkansas	AR	14,472	VC
Univ of Cincinnati	OH	21,964	VC
Univ of Evansville	IN	44,186	VC+
Univ of Florida	FL	16,291	HC+
Univ of Illinois at Chicago	IL	25,006	VC
Univ of Iowa	IA	18,683	VC+
Univ of Miami	FL	63,494	MC
Univ of Minn/Twin Cities	MN	23,519	HC+
Univ of Nebr - Lincoln	NE	18,589	VC
Univ of New England	ME	48,880	C
Univ of N Car at Wilmington	NC	14,590	VC
Univ of North Georgia	GA	17,316	C
Univ of St. Francis	IL	39,924	C
Univ of the Cumberlands	KY	32,000	C
Univ of the Pacific	CA	57,006	VC
Univ of Wisc-Eau Claire	WI	15,797	VC
Univ of Wisc-River Falls	WI	14,485	C
Walsh Univ	OH	39,010	C
Washburn Univ	KS	15,827	C
Washington State Univ	WA	22,495	C
Washington Univ in St. Louis	MO	65,366	VC
West Liberty Univ	WV	15,512	C
West Texas A&M Univ	TX	13,478	C
Western Carolina Univ	NC	13,965	C
Western New England Univ	MA	48,088	C
Western New Mexico Univ	NM	16,734	LC
Wilkes Univ	PA	45,622	C
Wilson College	PA	35,620	C
Wingate Univ	NC	39,950	C
Winona State Univ	MN	17,535	C
Xavier Univ	OH	47,880	C+

PREPHYSICAL THERAPY

School	ST	$IS	SR
Asbury Univ	KY	35,180	C+
Baldwin Wallace Univ	OH	41,106	C
Bellarmine Univ	KY	51,220	C
Bethany College	WV	36,300	NC
Biola Univ	CA	46,402	C+
Boise State Univ	ID	14,860	C
Calif Baptist Univ	CA	41,392	C
Calvin College	MI	41,570	VC+
Christopher Newport Univ	VA	23,968	VC+
Coe College	IA	51,570	VC
College of St. Benedict	MN	52,806	C
Corban Univ	OR	40,306	C
Davis & Elkins College	WV	38,242	LC
Dordt College	IA	37,860	C+
Drury Univ	MO	33,791	VC
Eastern Mennonite Univ	VA	42,550	C
Elizabethtown College	PA	54,050	C
Elmhurst College	IL	45,428	C
Faulkner Univ	AL	26,410	C
Ferris State Univ	MI	21,445	C
Fontbonne Univ	MO	33,717	C
Georgetown College	KY	41,440	C
High Point Univ	NC	45,977	C
Hofstra Univ	NY	55,960	C+
Houghton College	NY	39,090	C
Huntington Univ	IN	33,996	C
Indiana Univ-Purdue Univ Indianapolis	IN	18,635	C
Iowa Wesleyan Univ	IA	39,200	C
Lewis Univ	IL	40,370	C
Lipscomb Univ	TN	41,296	VC
Lubbock Christian Univ	TX	28,426	C
Marshall Univ	WV	17,242	C
Marymount Univ	VA	41,570	LC
Mich Tech Univ	MI	24,739	VC+
Millikin Univ	IL	42,158	C
Missouri Southern State Univ	MO	12,499	C
Mount Aloysius College	PA	29,976	C
Mount Vernon Nazarene Univ	OH	34,500	C
Murray State Univ	KY	16,998	C
Northern Kentucky Univ	KY	16,486	C
Ohio Univ	OH	22,924	C
Oregon State Univ	OR	22,519	VC
Pittsburg State Univ	KS	13,880	NC
Roberts Wesleyan College	NY	38,306	C
Saginaw Valley State Univ	MI	18,530	C
St. John's Univ	MN	51,624	C
St. Mary's Univ of Minn	MN	41,210	VC
Simpson College	IA	43,839	VC
Southern Oregon Univ	OR	19,117	C
St. Edward's Univ	TX	53,100	VC
SUNY at Oswego	NY	21,351	C
The Master's Univ	CA	43,870	C+
Trinity International Univ	IL	31,070	VC
Univ of Dayton	OH	53,620	C
Univ of Iowa	IA	18,683	VC+
Univ of Miami	FL	63,494	MC
Univ of N Car at Wilmington	NC	14,590	VC
Univ of St. Francis	IL	39,924	C
Univ of the Cumberlands	KY	32,000	C
Univ of Wisc-Eau Claire	WI	15,797	VC
Walsh Univ	OH	39,010	C
Washington State Univ	WA	22,495	C
Waynesburg Univ	PA	32,290	C
West Chester Univ of Pennsylvania	PA	18,456	C
Western Carolina Univ	NC	13,965	C
Widener Univ	PA	56,486	C
Wilson College	PA	35,620	C
Wingate Univ	NC	39,950	C
Winona State Univ	MN	17,535	C

ST = STATE $IS = IN-STATE COSTS SR = SELECTOR RATING

PRE-PHYSICIAN ASSISTANT

School	ST	$IS	SR
Bryant Univ	RI	55,646	VC
Cabrini Univ	PA	42,591	LC
East Central Univ	OK	13,056	C
Eastern Mennonite Univ	VA	42,550	C
Hofstra Univ	NY	55,960	C+
Indiana Univ-Purdue Univ Indianapolis	IN	18,635	C
Lewis Univ	IL	40,370	C
Madonna Univ	MI	29,050	C
Millikin Univ	IL	42,158	C
Missouri Southern State Univ	MO	12,499	C
Murray State Univ	KY	16,998	C
Univ of Maine at Machias	ME	22,960	C
Univ of New England	ME	48,880	C
Wellesley College	MA	63,916	MC
Western New England Univ	MA	48,088	C
Wilson College	PA	35,620	C
Wingate Univ	NC	39,950	C

PREPODIATRY

School	ST	$IS	SR
Bloomfield College	NJ	39,100	LC
Colo State Univ-Pueblo	CO	18,234	C
Gannon Univ	PA	42,032	C
Hofstra Univ	NY	55,960	C+
Le Moyne College	NY	46,000	C
Lewis Univ	IL	40,370	C
Madonna Univ	MI	29,050	C
Marshall Univ	WV	17,242	C
MCPHS Univ	MA	45,470	SP
Millersville Univ of Pennsylvania	PA	23,782	C
Mount Aloysius College	PA	29,976	C
Oregon State Univ	OR	22,519	VC
Univ of Iowa	IA	18,683	VC+
Univ of N Car at Wilmington	NC	14,590	VC
Wellesley College	MA	63,916	MC
Wilson College	PA	35,620	C
Winona State Univ	MN	17,535	C

PREVENTIVE/WELLNESS HEALTH CARE

School	ST	$IS	SR
Appalachian State Univ	NC	14,416	VC
Daemen College	NY	38,045	C
Mount Aloysius College	PA	29,976	C
Oakland Univ	MI	20,763	C

PREVETERINARY SCIENCE

School	ST	$IS	SR
Adams State Univ	CO	17,703	LC
Alabama A&M Univ	AL	18,796	C
Albertus Magnus College	CT	43,258	LC
Andrews Univ	MI	28,030	C+
Arcadia Univ	PA	33,570	C+
Ashland Univ	OH	21,440	C
Auburn Univ	AL	23,594	VC+
Baldwin Wallace Univ	OH	41,106	C
Ball State Univ	IN	19,590	C
Becker College	MA	57,628	C
Bellarmine Univ	KY	51,220	C
Bethany College	WV	36,300	NC
Boise State Univ	ID	14,860	C
Calvin College	MI	41,570	VC+
Canisius College	NY	47,537	C
Cardinal Stritch Univ	WI	36,462	C
Carroll College	MT	39,972	C+
Christopher Newport Univ	VA	23,968	VC+
Clemson Univ	SC		HC
Coe College	IA	51,570	VC
College of St. Benedict	MN	52,806	C
College of the Ozarks	MO	7,230	C
Colo State Univ-Pueblo	CO	18,234	C
Corban Univ	OR	40,306	C
Davis & Elkins College	WV	38,242	LC
Dordt College	IA	37,860	C+
Drury Univ	MO	33,791	VC
Eastern Washington Univ	WA	25,572	LC
Elmhurst College	IL	45,428	C
Faulkner Univ	AL	26,410	C
Florida State Univ	FL	16,771	HC
Freed-Hardeman Univ	TN	29,450	C
Gannon Univ	PA	42,032	C
George Fox Univ	OR	42,938	C
Goshen College	IN	42,500	C
Graceland Univ	IA	35,290	C
Grand Rapids Theological Seminary/Cornerstone Univ	MI	33,338	C
High Point Univ	NC	45,977	C
Hofstra Univ	NY	55,960	C+
Houghton College	NY	39,090	C
Indiana Univ-Purdue Univ Fort Wayne	IN	17,553	C
Indiana Univ-Purdue Univ Indianapolis	IN	18,635	C
Iowa Wesleyan Univ	IA	39,200	C
Kansas State Univ	KS	17,780	VC
Kent State Univ	OH	20,732	C
Keuka College	NY	39,762	C
Le Moyne College	NY	46,000	C
Lees-McRae College	NC	33,944	C
Lenoir-Rhyne Univ	NC	43,200	C
LeTourneau Univ	TX	38,250	VC
Lewis Univ	IL	40,370	C
Lipscomb Univ	TN	41,296	VC
Louisiana College	LA	21,886	C
Loyola Univ New Orleans	LA	51,708	VC+
MacMurray College	IL	33,620	C
Madonna Univ	MI	29,050	C
Mars Hill Univ	NC	42,688	C
Mercyhurst Univ	PA	47,420	C
Mich State Univ	MI	23,898	VC+
Midwestern State Univ	TX	17,572	C
Millikin Univ	IL	42,158	C
Minn State Univ, Mankato	MN	15,616	C
Minn State Univ, Moorhead	MN	15,941	C
Missouri Southern State Univ	MO	12,499	C
Mount Aloysius College	PA	29,976	C
Mount Mary Univ	WI	34,650	LC
Murray State Univ	KY	16,998	C
N Car State Univ	NC	19,515	HC+
North Central College	IL	48,712	VC
N Dak State Univ	ND	16,245	C
Northern Kentucky Univ	KY	16,486	C
Northern Mich Univ	MI	19,604	C
Northwest Missouri State Univ	MO	17,737	C
Ohio Wesleyan Univ	OH	49,460	VC
Olivet College	MI	36,110	LC
Pennsylvania State Univ - Univ Park	PA	29,760	HC
Peru State College	NE	14,768	NC
Pittsburg State Univ	KS	13,880	NC
Rhode Island College	RI	17,694	LC
Rivier Univ	NH	40,410	VC
Roberts Wesleyan College	NY	38,306	C
Rochester Inst of Technology	NY	50,842	HC
Roosevelt Univ	IL	40,651	VC
St. John's Univ	MN	51,624	C
St. Mary-of-the-Woods College	IN	39,632	LC
St. Vincent College	PA	44,626	C
Seton Hill Univ	PA	46,972	C
Simpson College	IA	43,839	VC
Spring Hill College	AL	48,488	C
SUNY at Oswego	NY	21,351	C
Tarleton State Univ	TX	15,248	LC
Texas A&M Univ at Kingsville	TX	7,500	LC
The Catholic Univ of America	DC	56,356	VC
The Univ of Tenn at Knoxville	TN	22,112	VC
Thiel College	PA	41,590	C
Truman State Univ	MO	16,014	HC
Univ of Central Arkansas	AR	14,472	VC
Univ of Central Missouri	MO	18,982	C
Univ of Evansville	IN	44,186	VC+
Univ of Findlay	OH	60,139	C
Univ of Illinois at Urbana-Champaign	IL	27,006	HC
Univ of Iowa	IA	18,683	VC+
Univ of Maine at Machias	ME	22,960	C
Univ of Maryland/College Park	MD	21,938	HC
Univ of Mass Amherst	MA	26,199	VC+
Univ of Miami	FL	63,494	MC
Univ of Minn/Twin Cities	MN	23,519	HC+
Univ of Montana-Western	MT	11,220	LC
Univ of New Orleans	LA	12,840	C
Univ of N Car at Wilmington	NC	14,590	VC
Univ of North Georgia	GA	17,316	C
Univ of Rio Grande & Rio Grande Community College	OH	8,750	NC
Univ of St. Francis	IN	37,400	C
Univ of St. Francis	IL	39,924	C
Univ of the Cumberlands	KY	32,000	C
Univ of Wisc-Eau Claire	WI	15,797	VC
Walsh Univ	OH	39,010	C
Washington State Univ	WA	22,495	C
Washington Univ in St. Louis	MO	65,366	VC
Waynesburg Univ	PA	32,290	C
Wellesley College	MA	63,916	MC
West Texas A&M Univ	TX	13,478	C
Western Carolina Univ	NC	13,965	C
Wilmington College	OH	34,600	C
Wilson College	PA	35,620	C
Wingate Univ	NC	39,950	C
Winona State Univ	MN	17,535	C
Youngstown State Univ	OH	17,307	C

PRINTING MANAGEMENT

School	ST	$IS	SR
Ferris State Univ	MI	21,445	C

PRINTING TECHNOLOGY

School	ST	$IS	SR
Pennsylvania College of Technology	PA	27,333	NC
Rochester Inst of Technology	NY	50,842	HC

PRINTMAKING

School	ST	$IS	SR
Adams State Univ	CO	17,703	LC
Aquinas College - Mich	MI	38,876	HC
Art Academy of Cincinnati	OH	36,252	SP
Bennington College	VT	63,960	MC
Biola Univ	CA	46,402	C+
Boston Univ	MA	65,110	MC
Calif College of the Arts	CA	52,758	SP
Cal State, San Bernardino	CA	12,000	C
Cleveland Inst of Art	OH	51,439	C+
College for Creative Studies	MI	48,875	SP
Columbia College - Missouri	MO	27,803	C
Drake Univ	IA	45,056	HC
Escuela de Artes Plasticas de PR	PR	11,236	
Ferris State Univ	MI	21,445	C
Houghton College	NY	39,090	C
Howard Univ	DC	37,616	C+
Indiana Univ-Purdue Univ Fort Wayne	IN	17,553	C
Indiana Wesleyan Univ	IN	33,674	C
Kansas City Art Inst	MO	44,308	C+
Kutztown Univ of Pennsylvania	PA	19,056	LC
Maine College of Art	ME	43,794	SP
Maryland Inst College of Art	MD	56,795	SP
Mass College of Art and Design	MA	24,800	SP
Milwaukee Inst of Art and Design	WI	44,960	SP
Minneapolis College of Art and Design	MN	44,238	SP
Montserrat College of Art	MA	38,150	SP
Ohio Univ	OH	22,924	C
Old Dominion Univ	VA	20,910	C
Pacific Northwest College of Art	OR	38,494	SP
Rhode Island School of Design	RI	59,960	SP
San Francisco Art Inst	CA	58,505	SP
Savannah College of Art and Design	GA	49,595	C
School of the Art Inst of Chicago	IL	56,230	SP
St. Ambrose Univ	IA	39,019	C
St. Ambrose Univ	IA	39,019	C
SUNY / Buffalo State College	NY	20,842	C
SUNY at Binghamton	NY	22,861	MC
Syracuse Univ	NY	60,239	VC
Temple Univ	PA	24,392	VC
Texas A&M Univ at Commerce	TX	10,496	C
Texas Christian Univ	TX	54,670	HC
Univ of Dallas	TX	45,500	VC+
Univ of Hartford	CT	49,776	C
Univ of Iowa	IA	18,683	VC+
Univ of Kansas	KS	20,135	C+
Univ of Maine at Machias	ME	22,960	C
Univ of Miami	FL	63,494	MC
Univ of Mich/Ann Arbor	MI	24,410	MC
Univ of Oregon	OR	22,972	C
Univ of the Arts	PA	56,579	SP
Washington Univ in St. Louis	MO	65,366	VC
Webster Univ	MO	37,490	C
Youngstown State Univ	OH	17,307	C

PRODUCT DESIGN

School	ST	$IS	SR
Stanford Univ	CA	60,409	MC

PRODUCT DESIGN ENGINEERING TECHNOLOGY

School	ST	$IS	SR
Arizona State Univ at the Polytechnic Campus	AZ	21,360	VC
Ferris State Univ	MI	21,445	C
Keene State College	NH	24,003	LC

PRODUCTION AND OPERATIONS MANAGEMENT

School	ST	$IS	SR
San Diego State Univ	CA	21,896	C+

PROFESSIONAL GOLF MANAGEMENT

School	ST	$IS	SR
Ferris State Univ	MI	21,445	C
Univ of Idaho	ID	15,348	C

PROFESSIONAL PROGRAM IN ACCOUNTING

School	ST	$IS	SR
Black Hills State Univ	SD	15,899	C
Bloomfield College	NJ	39,100	LC
Bryant Univ	RI	55,646	VC
Texas Christian Univ	TX	54,670	HC

PROFESSIONAL STUDIES

School	ST	$IS	SR
Austin Peay State Univ	TN	16,397	C
College of Charleston	SC	22,699	C
Lewis Univ	IL	40,370	C
Old Dominion Univ	VA	20,910	C
Providence College	RI	60,760	VC
Shippensburg Univ of Pennsylvania	PA	23,208	C

PROFESSIONAL TENNIS MANAGEMENT

School	ST	$IS	SR
Carroll Univ	WI	38,100	C+
Ferris State Univ	MI	21,445	C

PROJECT MANAGEMENT

School	ST	$IS	SR
Ashford Univ	CA	10,480	C
Wingate Univ	NC	39,950	C

PRO-MO-TED-TECHNICAL EDUCATION

School	ST	$IS	SR
Ferris State Univ	MI	21,445	C

PROPERTY MANAGEMENT

School	ST	$IS	SR
New York Univ	NY	65,860	MC
Univ of Wisc-Stout	WI	19,667	C

PSYCHOBIOLOGY

School	ST	$IS	SR
Albright College	PA	46,660	C
Arcadia Univ	PA	33,570	C+
Centre College	KY	49,250	HC
Florida Atlantic Univ	FL	17,339	C
Hamilton College	NY	64,250	MC
Houghton College	NY	39,090	C
La Sierra Univ	CA	39,690	VC
Lebanon Valley College	PA	51,530	C
Lindsey Wilson College	KY	32,882	C
Quinnipiac Univ	CT	59,110	C
Ripon College	WI	46,911	C+
Simmons College	MA	53,090	VC
SUNY at Binghamton	NY	22,861	MC
Swarthmore College	PA	63,550	MC
Univ of Calif at Los Angeles	CA	30,162	MC
Utica College	NY	30,430	C
Wellesley College	MA	63,916	MC
Wilson College	PA	35,620	C

PSYCHOLOGY

School	ST	$IS	SR
Abilene Christian Univ	TX	41,800	C+
Adams State Univ	CO	17,703	LC
Adelphi Univ	NY	48,244	C
Adrian College	MI	42,400	C
Agnes Scott College	GA	51,930	VC+
Alabama A&M Univ	AL	18,796	C
Alabama State Univ	AL	14,142	NC
Alaska Pacific Univ	AK	26,680	VC
Albany State Univ	GA	19,462	C
Albertus Magnus College	CT	43,258	LC
Albion College	MI	52,650	C
Albright College	PA	46,660	C
Alcorn State Univ	MS	15,854	C
Alderson Broaddus Univ	WV	26,149	C
Alfred Univ	NY	42,296	C+
Allegheny College	PA	55,420	VC
Alma College	MI	47,548	C
Alvernia Univ	PA	43,900	C
Alverno College	WI	33,294	LC
American International College	MA	46,300	LC
American Jewish Univ - College of A&S Campus	CA	44,234	C
American Univ	DC	59,379	HC+
Amherst College	MA		HC+
Anderson Univ	IN	38,200	C
Andrews Univ	MI	28,030	C+
Angelo State Univ	TX	15,263	NC
Anna Maria College	MA	48,186	C
Appalachian State Univ	NC	14,416	VC
Aquinas College	TN	30,800	C+
Aquinas College - Mich	MI	38,876	HC
Arcadia Univ	PA	33,570	C+
Arizona State Univ at the Tempe Campus	AZ	21,756	VC
Arizona State Univ at the West Campus	AZ	20,640	C
Arkansas State Univ	AR	16,190	C
Arkansas Tech Univ	AR	15,484	C
Armstrong State Univ	GA	16,962	C
Asbury Univ	KY	35,180	C+
Ashford Univ	CA	10,480	C
Ashland Univ	OH	21,440	C
Assumption College	MA	47,920	C+
Atlantic Union College	MA	27,228	C
Auburn Univ	AL	23,594	VC+
Auburn Univ at Montgomery	AL	15,290	C
Augsburg College	MN	43,929	C
Augusta Univ	GA	4,632	C
Augustana College	IL	49,658	VC
Augustana Univ	SD	38,424	VC
Aurora Univ	IL	33,970	C
Austin College	TX	45,875	VC
Austin Peay State Univ	TN	16,397	C
Averett Univ	VA	40,970	LC
Avila Univ	MO	35,480	C
Azusa Pacific Univ	CA	43,972	C
Baker Univ	KS	33,350	C+
Baldwin Wallace Univ	OH	41,106	C
Ball State Univ	IN	19,590	C
Bard College	NY	64,024	HC
Bard College at Simon's Rock	MA	65,795	MC
Barnard College/Columbia Univ	NY	62,741	MC
Barry Univ	FL	37,830	C
Barton College	NC	38,686	LC
Bates College	ME	64,500	MC
Bay Path Univ	MA	45,349	C
Bayamon Central Univ	PR	12,490	
Baylor Univ	TX	53,760	HC
Becker College	MA	57,628	C
Belhaven Univ	MS	31,016	C
Bellarmine Univ	KY	51,220	C
Bellevue Univ	NE	20,300	NC
Belmont Abbey College	NC	48,156	C

ST = STATE $IS = IN-STATE COSTS SR = SELECTOR RATING

School	ST	$IS	SR
Belmont Univ	TN	40,970	VC
Beloit College	WI	55,206	HC
Bemidji State Univ	MN	16,056	VC
Benedictine College	KS	36,200	VC
Benedictine Univ	IL	38,300	C
Bennett College	NC	27,302	NC
Bennington College	VT	63,960	MC
Berea College	KY	7,042	C
Berry College	GA	45,286	C+
Bethany College	KS	46,100	NC
Bethany College	WV	36,300	NC
Bethel College	IN	35,860	C
Bethel College	KS	35,370	C
Bethel Univ	MN	45,270	VC
Bethel Univ	TN	24,738	C
Bethune-Cookman Univ	FL	22,970	C
Biola Univ	CA	46,402	C+
Birmingham-Southern College	AL	44,478	VC
Black Hills State Univ	SD	15,899	C
Blackburn College	IL	28,526	LC
Bloomfield College	NJ	39,100	LC
Bloomsburg Univ of Pennsylvania	PA	19,066	LC
Blue Mountain College	MS	15,949	VC
Bluefield College	VA	34,120	C+
Bluffton Univ	OH	40,950	C
Boise State Univ	ID	14,860	C
Boston College	MA	65,737	MC
Boston Univ	MA	65,110	MC
Bowdoin College	ME	63,500	MC
Bowie State Univ	MD	26,728	LC
Bowling Green State Univ	OH	19,747	C
Brandeis Univ	MA	65,925	MC
Brenau Univ - Women's College	GA	37,876	LC
Brescia Univ	KY	29,890	VC+
Brewton-Parker College	GA	23,490	C
Briar Cliff Univ	IA	36,956	C
Bridgewater College	VA	44,510	C
Bridgewater State Univ	MA	21,810	C
Brigham Young Univ	UT	12,748	HC
Brigham Young Univ/Hawaii	HI	11,290	C
Brown Univ	RI	64,566	MC
Bryan College	TN	31,440	C
Bryant Univ	RI	55,646	VC
Bryn Athyn College	PA	31,470	C
Bryn Mawr College	PA	59,890	MC
Bucknell Univ	PA	64,616	MC
Buena Vista Univ	IA	41,514	C
Butler Univ	IN	51,352	VC
Cabrini Univ	PA	42,591	LC
Cairn Univ	PA	36,296	C
Caldwell Univ	NJ	42,165	NC
Calif Baptist Univ	CA	41,392	C
Calif Lutheran Univ	CA	52,853	C
Calif Polytechnic State Univ	CA	17,979	HC+
Calif State Polytechnic Univ, Pomona	CA	21,541	C
Cal State, Bakersfield	CA	19,191	LC
Cal State, Chico	CA	21,440	C
Cal State, Dominguez Hills	CA	19,022	LC
Cal State, East Bay	CA	19,413	C
Cal State, Fresno	CA	16,902	LC
Cal State, Fullerton	CA	21,902	C
Cal State, Long Beach	CA	18,850	C
Cal State, Los Angeles	CA	17,186	LC
Cal State, Monterey Bay	CA	26,871	LC
Cal State, Northridge	CA	16,859	LC
Cal State, Sacramento	CA	20,332	C
Cal State, San Bernardino	CA	12,000	C
Cal State, San Marcos	CA	24,184	LC
Cal State, Stanislaus	CA	16,212	C
Calif Univ of Pennsylvania	PA	14,217	LC
Calumet College of St. Joseph	IN	22,735	C
Calvin College	MI	41,570	VC+
Cambridge College	MA	15,734	NC
Cameron Univ	OK	11,072	NC
Campbellsville Univ	KY	32,492	C
Canisius College	NY	47,537	C
Capital Univ	OH	42,982	C
Cardinal Stritch Univ	WI	36,462	C
Carleton College	MN	64,071	MC
Carlos Albizu Univ	FL		LC
Carlow Univ	PA	38,549	LC
Carnegie Mellon Univ	PA	67,980	MC
Carroll College	MT	39,972	C+
Carroll Univ	WI	38,100	C+
Carson-Newman Univ	TN	34,160	C
Carthage College	WI	48,835	C
Case Western Reserve Univ	OH	60,304	MC
Castleton Univ	VT	20,186	C
Catawba College	NC	39,820	C
Cazenovia College	NY	46,470	C
Cedar Crest College	PA	46,715	C
Cedarville Univ	OH	34,990	VC
Centenary College	NJ	43,602	C
Centenary College of Louisiana	LA	45,650	C+
Central College	IA	44,592	C
Central Conn State Univ	CT	21,203	C
Central Methodist Univ	MO	36,830	VC
Central Mich Univ	MI	20,330	C
Central State Univ	OH	18,564	C
Central Washington Univ	WA	16,803	C
Centre College	KY	49,250	HC
Chadron State College	NE	14,819	NC
Chaminade Univ of Honolulu	HI	36,000	C
Champlain College	VT	53,132	C+
Chapman Univ	CA	63,078	VC+
Charleston Southern Univ	SC	32,400	C
Charter Oak State College	CT	7,671	LC
Chatham Univ	PA	46,517	C
Chestnut Hill College	PA	43,410	C
Cheyney Univ of Pennsylvania	PA	20,896	LC
Chicago State Univ	IL	20,144	C
Christian Brothers Univ	TN	31,670	VC
Christopher Newport Univ	VA	23,968	VC+
CUNY/Baruch College	NY	21,609	HC
CUNY/Brooklyn College	NY	5,884	C+
CUNY/City College	NY	20,319	VC
CUNY/College of Staten Island	NY	17,840	NC
CUNY/Hunter College	NY	31,098	VC
CUNY/John Jay College of Criminal Justice	NY	6,359	NC
CUNY/Lehman College	NY	5,778	HC+
CUNY/Meger Evers College	NY	6,680	NC
CUNY/Queens College	NY	27,896	C
CUNY/York College	NY	6,747	LC
Claremont McKenna College	CA	67,185	MC
Clarion Univ of Pennsylvania	PA	21,608	LC
Clark Atlanta Univ	GA	31,019	LC
Clark Univ	MA	51,600	HC+
Clarke Univ	IA	38,940	C
Clarkson Univ	NY	60,392	HC
Clayton State Univ	GA	19,735	C
Clemson Univ	SC		HC
Cleveland State Univ	OH	22,196	C
Coastal Carolina Univ	SC	19,766	C
Coe College	IA	51,570	VC
Coker College	SC	34,810	LC
Colby College	ME	64,060	MC
Colby-Sawyer College	NH	50,790	C
Colgate Univ	NY	65,030	MC
College of Charleston	SC	22,699	C
College of Mount St. Vincent	NY	45,620	C
College of St. Benedict	MN	52,806	C
College of St. Elizabeth	NJ	44,432	LC
College of St. Mary	NE	35,184	C
College of St Joseph	VT	32,400	LC
College of St. Scholastica	MN	44,640	C
College of the Holy Cross	MA	62,165	MC
College of the Ozarks	MO	7,230	C
College of William & Mary	VA		MC
Colo Christian Univ	CO	39,940	VC
Colo College	CO	62,560	MC
Colo Mesa Univ	CO	18,955	LC
Colo State Univ	CO	22,162	VC
Colo State Univ-Pueblo	CO	18,234	C
Columbia College	SC	36,550	C
Columbia College - Missouri	MO	27,803	C
Columbia Univ/ School of General Studies	NY	61,470	MC
Columbia Univ/City of New York	NY	62,958	MC
Columbus State Univ	GA	14,336	LC
Concord Univ	WV	14,954	C
Concordia College - Moorhead	MN	51,088	C+
Concordia College - New York	NY	39,035	LC
Concordia Univ	CA	41,580	VC
Concordia Univ	OR	35,000	C
Concordia Univ Nebr	NE	36,280	VC
Concordia Univ St. Paul	MN	29,050	C
Concordia Univ Wisc	WI	35,910	C
Concordia Univ, Ann Arbor	MI	35,945	VC
Concordia Univ, Chicago	IL	39,694	C
Conn College	CT	65,000	MC
Converse College	SC	26,495	C
Coppin State Univ	MD	17,041	VC
Corban Univ	OR	40,306	C
Cornell College	IA	48,800	VC
Cornell Univ	NY	64,853	MC
Covenant College	GA	38,990	VC
Creighton Univ	NE	48,206	VC+
Culver-Stockton College	MO	33,525	C
Cumberland Univ	TN	27,710	C
Curry College	MA	51,815	C
Daemen College	NY	38,045	C
Dakota Wesleyan Univ	SD	32,850	C
Dallas Baptist Univ	TX	33,713	C
Daniel Webster College	NH	26,984	C
Dartmouth College	NH	66,174	MC
Davidson College	NC	60,119	MC
Davis & Elkins College	WV	38,242	LC
Defiance College	OH	41,630	C
Delaware State Univ	DE	19,376	NC
Delta State Univ	MS	13,176	C
Denison Univ	OH	58,860	MC
DePaul Univ	IL	47,623	VC
DePauw Univ	IN	58,688	HC+
DeSales Univ	PA	43,970	C
Dickinson College	PA	63,974	MC
Dillard Univ	LA	20,940	VC
Doane Univ	NE	39,184	VC
Dominican College	NY	31,270	LC
Dominican Univ	IL	41,222	C
Dominican Univ of Calif	CA	57,050	C
Dordt College	IA	37,860	C+
Drake Univ	IA	45,056	HC
Drew Univ/College of Liberal Arts	NJ	61,048	VC
Drexel Univ	PA	65,432	VC+
Drury Univ	MO	33,791	VC
Duke Univ	NC	64,188	
Duquesne Univ	PA	46,822	VC
D'Youville College	NY	36,780	C
Earlham College	IN	54,870	HC
East Carolina Univ	NC	16,937	C
East Central Univ	OK	13,056	C
East Stroudsburg Univ	PA	18,334	C
East Tenn State Univ	TN	13,994	C
East Texas Baptist Univ	TX	33,134	C
Eastern Conn State Univ	CT	23,059	C
Eastern Illinois Univ	IL	21,126	C
Eastern Kentucky Univ	KY	16,908	C
Eastern Mennonite Univ	VA	42,550	C
Eastern Mich Univ	MI	19,761	C
Eastern Nazarene College	MA	39,955	C
Eastern New Mexico Univ	NM	14,416	C
Eastern Oregon Univ	OR	17,715	C
Eastern Univ	PA	39,540	C
Eastern Washington Univ	WA	25,572	LC
Eckerd College	FL	52,874	C
Edgewood College	WI	35,950	C
Edinboro Univ	PA	15,940	LC
Edward Waters College	FL	20,607	NC
Elizabeth City State Univ	NC	14,745	C
Elizabethtown College	PA	54,050	C
Elmhurst College	IL	45,428	C
Elmira College	NY	53,900	C
Elms College	MA	45,646	VC
Elon Univ	NC	44,599	VC+
Embry-Riddle Aeronautical Univ - Worldwide	FL	17,480	C
Emmanuel College	MA	52,110	C+
Emory and Henry College	VA	41,410	C
Emory Univ	GA	60,786	MC
Emporia State Univ	KS	14,570	C
Endicott College	MA	44,604	VC+
Erskine College	SC	45,460	C
Eugene Lang College/The New School for Liberal Arts	NY	55,650	C
Eureka College	IL	30,220	C
Evangel Univ	MO	28,898	C
Excelsior College	NY	14,080	SP
Fairfield Univ	CT	59,860	VC+
Fairleigh Dickinson Univ/ College at Florham	NJ	52,062	C
Fairleigh Dickinson Univ/ Metropolitan Campus	NJ	40,254	C
Fairmont State Univ	WV	15,726	C
Fayetteville State Univ	NC	17,756	C
Felician Univ	NJ	45,370	LC
Ferris State Univ	MI	21,445	C
Ferrum College	VA	39,650	C
Fisk Univ	TN	32,066	LC
Fitchburg State Univ	MA	21,819	C
Flagler College	FL	27,620	C
Florida A&M Univ	FL	15,361	C
Florida Atlantic Univ	FL	17,339	C
Florida Gulf Coast Univ	FL	9,682	C
Florida Inst of Technology	FL	53,306	VC
Florida International Univ	FL	19,854	C+
Florida Memorial Univ	FL	22,270	LC
Florida State Univ	FL	16,771	HC
Fontbonne Univ	MO	33,717	C
Fordham Univ	NY	65,918	MC
Fort Hays State Univ	KS	12,131	C
Fort Lewis College	CO	18,980	C
Fort Valley State Univ	GA	17,988	VC
Framingham State Univ	MA	20,584	C
Francis Marion Univ	SC	16,464	LC
Franciscan Univ of Steubenville	OH	33,980	VC
Franklin and Marshall College	PA	63,170	HC
Franklin College	IN	39,380	C
Franklin Pierce Univ	NH	46,750	C
Freed-Hardeman Univ	TN	29,450	C
Fresno Pacific Univ	CA	37,370	C
Friends Univ	KS	34,455	C
Frostburg State Univ	MD	17,280	LC
Furman Univ	SC	58,092	VC+
Gallaudet Univ	DC	29,118	LC
Gannon Univ	PA	42,032	C
Gardner-Webb Univ	NC	39,200	C+
Geneva College	PA	35,450	C
George Fox Univ	OR	42,938	C
George Mason Univ	VA	15,724	VC
George Washington Univ	DC	62,835	MC
Georgetown College	KY	41,440	C
Georgetown Univ	DC	65,926	MC
Georgia College & State Univ	GA	21,148	C+
Georgia Inst of Technology	GA	23,360	MC
Georgia Southern Univ	GA	16,596	C
Georgia Southwestern State Univ	GA	13,870	C
Georgia State Univ	GA	24,332	VC
Georgian Court Univ	NJ	42,426	LC
Gettysburg College	PA	63,000	HC
Glenville State College	WV	17,386	NC
Goddard College	VT	17,040	VC
Goldey-Beacom College	DE	31,750	C
Gonzaga Univ	WA	50,888	HC
Gordon College	MA	46,472	C+
Goshen College	IN	42,500	C
Goucher College	MD	55,716	VC
Grace College and Seminary	IN	31,524	C
Graceland Univ	IA	35,290	C
Grambling State Univ	LA	15,701	C
Grand Canyon Univ	AZ	16,950	VC
Grand Rapids Theological Seminary/Cornerstone Univ	MI	33,338	C
Grand Valley State Univ	MI	22,250	C+
Grand View Univ	IA	32,302	C
Green Mountain College	VT	45,228	LC
Greensboro College	NC	42,400	LC
Greenville College	IL	27,012	C
Grinnell College	IA	60,738	MC
Grove City College	PA	25,692	VC
Guilford College	NC	44,090	C
Gustavus Adolphus College	MN	52,433	HC
Gwynedd Mercy Univ	PA	43,780	LC
Hamilton College	NY	64,250	MC
Hamline Univ	MN	45,678	VC
Hampden-Sydney College	VA	56,248	C+
Hampshire College	MA	63,824	MC
Hampton Univ	VA	34,926	LC
Hannibal-LaGrange Univ	MO	29,815	C
Hanover College	IN	46,364	C+
Harding Univ	AR	25,421	C
Hardin-Simmons Univ	TX	33,966	C
Hartwick College	NY	51,270	C
Harvard College/Harvard Univ	MA	60,659	MC
Hastings College	NE	35,380	C+
Haverford College	PA	66,490	MC
Hawaii Pacific Univ	HI	33,420	C
Heidelberg Univ	OH	39,200	C
Henderson State Univ	AR	15,516	LC
Hendrix College	AR	54,020	VC+
Heritage Univ	WA	19,825	NC
High Point Univ	NC	45,977	C
Hilbert College	NY	30,850	C
Hillsdale College	MI	35,722	MC
Hiram College	OH	43,230	C
Hofstra Univ	NY	55,960	C+
Hollins Univ	VA	49,635	VC
Holy Family Univ	PA	43,326	LC
Holy Names Univ	CA	46,630	LC
Hood College	MD	54,840	C
Hope College	MI	39,940	VC
Hope International Univ	CA	41,150	C
Houghton College	NY	39,090	C
Houston Baptist Univ	TX	36,450	C
Howard Payne Univ	TX	34,320	C
Howard Univ	DC	37,616	C+
Humboldt State Univ	CA	20,514	C
Huntingdon College	AL	34,900	C
Huntington Univ	IN	33,996	C
Husson Univ	ME	25,720	LC
Huston-Tillotson Univ	TX	18,124	LC
Idaho State Univ	ID	13,619	NC
Illinois College	IL	40,850	VC
Illinois Inst of Technology	IL	56,826	HC+
Illinois State Univ	IL	23,418	VC
Illinois Wesleyan Univ	IL	56,430	VC+
Indiana Inst of Technology	IN	34,240	LC
Indiana State Univ	IN	23,223	LC
Indiana Univ Bloomington	IN	20,429	VC
Indiana Univ East	IN	7,072	C
Indiana Univ Kokomo	IN	7,073	C
Indiana Univ Northwest	IN	7,072	C
Indiana Univ of Pennsylvania	PA	23,614	LC
Indiana Univ South Bend	IN	14,242	C
Indiana Univ Southeast	IN	14,242	LC
Indiana Univ-Purdue Univ Fort Wayne	IN	17,553	C
Indiana Univ-Purdue Univ Indianapolis	IN	18,635	C
Indiana Wesleyan Univ	IN	33,674	C
Inter-American Univ of PR Ponce	PR	19,549	
Inter-American Univ of PR- Aguadilla Campus	PR	21,657	
Inter-American Univ of PR- Fajardo Campus	PR	18,336	
Inter-American Univ of PR- Metropolitan Campus	PR	20,045	
Inter-American Univ of PR-San Germán	PR	20,042	
Iona College	NY	50,984	C
Iowa State Univ	IA	17,570	C
Iowa Wesleyan Univ	IA	39,200	C
Ithaca College	NY	56,766	VC
Jackson State Univ	MS	15,879	LC
Jacksonville State Univ	AL	14,628	LC
Jacksonville Univ	FL	46,230	C
James Madison Univ	VA	19,084	VC
John Brown Univ	AR	33,132	VC
John Carroll Univ	OH	49,740	C+
Johns Hopkins Univ	MD	65,386	MC
Johnson & Wales Univ/ Denver Campus	CO	42,707	C
Johnson C. Smith Univ	NC	25,336	LC
Johnson State College	VT	20,752	C
Judson College	AL	27,066	C
Judson Univ	IL	37,700	C
Juniata College	PA	53,760	VC
Kalamazoo College	MI	53,931	HC+
Kansas State Univ	KS	17,780	VC
Kansas Wesleyan Univ	KS	36,600	C
Kean Univ	NJ	24,650	C
Keene State College	NH	24,003	LC
Kennesaw State Univ	GA	19,592	VC
Kent State Univ	OH	20,732	C
Kentucky State Univ	KY	13,364	LC
Kentucky Wesleyan College	KY	32,080	C
Kenyon College	OH	63,330	MC

ST = STATE $IS = IN-STATE COSTS SR = SELECTOR RATING

School	ST	$IS	SR
Keuka College	NY	39,762	C
Keystone College	PA	28,680	LC
King Univ	TN	34,660	C
King's College	PA	46,858	C
Knox College	IL	52,615	VC+
Kutztown Univ of Pennsylvania	PA	19,056	LC
La Roche College	PA	37,924	LC
La Salle Univ	PA	55,790	C
La Sierra Univ	CA	39,690	VC
Lafayette College	PA	63,355	MC
LaGrange College	GA	39,930	C
Lake Erie College	OH	38,914	LC
Lake Forest College	IL	50,652	VC
Lakeland Univ	WI	35,130	C
Lamar Univ	TX	18,014	LC
Lander Univ	SC	43,994	C
Langston Univ	OK	14,314	C
Lasell College	MA	47,500	C
Lawrence Tech Univ	MI	39,770	VC
Lawrence Univ	WI	54,498	HC
Le Moyne College	NY	46,000	C
Lebanon Valley College	PA	51,530	C
Lee Univ	TN	22,045	C
Lees-McRae College	NC	33,944	C
Lehigh Univ	PA	61,010	MC
Lenoir-Rhyne Univ	NC	43,200	C
Lesley Univ	MA	41,550	C
LeTourneau Univ	TX	38,250	VC
Lewis & Clark College	OR	58,434	HC+
Lewis Univ	IL	40,370	C
Lewis-Clark State College	ID	14,202	C
Liberty Univ	VA	19,101	C
Limestone College	SC	32,100	C
Lincoln Memorial Univ	TN	28,070	C
Lincoln Univ	MO	13,602	NC
Lindenwood Univ	MO	25,132	C
Lindsey Wilson College	KY	32,882	C
Linfield College	OR	52,010	C
Lipscomb Univ	TN	41,296	VC
LIU Brooklyn	NY	49,682	C
LIU Post	NY	49,682	C
Livingstone College	NC	17,815	LC
Lock Haven Univ of Pennsylvania	PA	18,028	LC
Longwood Univ	VA	22,184	C
Loras College	IA	39,222	C
Louisiana College	LA	21,886	C
Louisiana State Univ and A&M College	LA	18,677	VC
Louisiana State Univ in Shreveport	LA	6,902	C
Louisiana Tech Univ	LA	11,422	VC
Lourdes Univ	OH	29,520	NC
Loyola Marymount Univ	CA	58,038	HC
Loyola Univ Chicago	IL	55,802	VC
Loyola Univ Maryland	MD	60,300	VC
Loyola Univ New Orleans	LA	51,708	VC+
Lubbock Christian Univ	TX	28,426	C
Luther College	IA	48,540	C+
Lycoming College	PA	48,580	C
Lynchburg College	VA	46,740	C
Lyndon State College	VT	20,714	C
Lyon College	AR	34,730	C+
Macalester College	MN	61,905	MC
MacMurray College	IL	33,620	C
Madonna Univ	MI	29,050	C
Malone Univ	OH	38,448	C
Manchester Univ	IN	40,422	C
Manhattan College	NY	51,750	C+
Manhattanville College	NY	51,440	C+
Mansfield Univ	PA	23,376	LC
Marian Univ	IN	41,220	C
Marian Univ	WI	32,420	LC
Marietta College	OH	46,190	C
Marist College	NY	49,860	VC
Marquette Univ	WI	48,390	VC+
Mars Hill Univ	NC	42,688	C
Marshall Univ	WV	17,242	C
Martin Univ	IN	20,264	LC
Mary Baldwin Univ	VA	39,865	C
Marygrove College	MI	28,926	NC
Marylhurst Univ	OR	20,295	NC
Marymount Manhattan College	NY	46,280	VC
Marymount Univ	VA	41,570	LC
Maryville College	TN	44,410	C
Maryville Univ of St. Louis	MO	38,046	VC+
Marywood Univ	PA	46,900	C
Mass College of Liberal Arts	MA	20,128	C
Mayville State Univ	ND	18,371	NC
McDaniel College	MD	51,380	VC
McKendree Univ	IL	37,940	C+
McMurry Univ	TX	34,259	LC
McNeese State Univ	LA	7,838	C
McPherson College	KS	34,909	C
Medaille College	NY	35,112	C
Menlo College	CA	51,380	LC
Mercer Univ	GA	45,348	VC
Mercy College	NY	31,776	C
Mercyhurst Univ	PA	47,420	C
Meredith College	NC	45,297	C
Merrimack College	MA	52,770	C
Messiah College	PA	43,100	C+
Methodist Univ	NC	43,600	C
Metropolitan State Univ	MN	7,566	C
Metropolitan State Univ of Denver	CO	29,889	LC
Miami Univ	OH	27,190	HC+
Mich State Univ	MI	23,898	VC+
Mich Tech Univ	MI	24,739	VC+
MidAmerica Nazarene Univ	KS	35,550	C
Middle Tenn State Univ	TN	8,650	C
Middlebury College	VT	64,332	MC
Midland Univ	NE	37,468	
Midway Univ	KY	31,640	LC
Midwestern State Univ	TX	17,572	C
Millersville Univ of Pennsylvania	PA	23,782	C
Milligan College	TN	38,150	C
Millikin Univ	IL	42,158	C
Mills College	CA	59,163	VC
Millsaps College	MS	50,080	C+
Minn State Univ, Mankato	MN	15,616	C
Minn State Univ, Moorhead	MN	15,941	C
Minot State Univ	ND	12,732	C
Misericordia Univ	PA	43,840	C
Miss College	MS	25,850	C
Miss State Univ	MS	11,454	C+
Miss Univ for Women	MS	17,065	C
Missouri Baptist Univ	MO	35,594	C
Missouri Southern State Univ	MO	12,499	C
Missouri Univ of Science and Technology	MO	18,655	HC
Missouri Valley College	MO	28,150	C
Missouri Western State Univ	MO	16,741	
Mitchell College	CT	43,280	C
Molloy College	NY	40,440	C
Monmouth College	IL	42,260	C
Monmouth Univ	NJ	46,234	C
Montana State Univ	MT	15,500	C+
Montana State Univ-Billings	MT	22,960	C
Montclair State Univ	NJ	26,210	LC
Montreat College	NC	31,298	LC
Moravian College	PA	53,117	
Morehead State Univ	KY	17,422	C
Morehouse College	GA	40,064	C
Morgan State Univ	MD	17,190	LC
Morningside College	IA	36,865	C
Mount Aloysius College	PA	29,976	C
Mount Holyoke College	MA	56,746	MC
Mount Mary Univ	WI	34,650	LC
Mount Mercy Univ	IA	36,826	C
Mount St. Mary College	NY	42,061	C
Mount St. Joseph Univ	OH	33,880	C
Mount St. Mary's Univ	MD	51,610	C
Mount St. Mary's Univ - Chalon Campus	CA	43,897	VC+
Mount Vernon Nazarene Univ	OH	34,500	C
Muhlenberg College	PA	56,645	VC+
Murray State Univ	KY	16,998	C
Muskingum Univ	OH	35,966	C
Naropa Univ	CO	42,826	NC
National Louis Univ	IL	16,920	LC
National Univ	CA	14,730	LC
Nazareth College	NY	45,574	C
Nebr Wesleyan Univ	NE	38,140	C+
Neumann Univ	PA	40,678	LC
New College of Florida	FL	15,848	MC
New England College	NH	50,364	C
New Jersey City Univ	NJ	21,456	LC
New Mexico Highlands Univ	NM	11,904	NC
New Mexico Inst of Mining and Technology	NM	14,833	HC
New Mexico State Univ	NM	14,050	C
New York Inst of Technology	NY	48,730	C
New York Univ	NY	65,860	MC
Newberry College	SC	34,550	C
Newbury College	MA	46,950	C
Newman Univ	KS	35,390	C
Niagara Univ	NY	41,010	C
Nicholls State Univ	LA	10,534	C
Nichols College	MA	46,800	LC
Norfolk State Univ	VA	25,702	LC
N Car A&T State Univ	NC	13,365	LC
N Car Central Univ	NC	9,000	C
N Car State Univ	NC	19,515	HC+
N Car Wesleyan College	NC	39,200	C
North Central College	IL	48,712	VC
N Dak State Univ	ND	16,245	C
North Greenville Univ	SC	25,930	C+
North Park Univ	IL	35,860	C
Northeastern Illinois Univ	IL	12,529	LC
Northeastern Univ	MA	62,703	MC
Northern Arizona Univ	AZ	20,246	VC
Northern Illinois Univ	IL	20,176	C
Northern Kentucky Univ	KY	16,486	C
Northern Mich Univ	MI	19,604	C
Northern State Univ	SD	14,505	C
Northland College	WI	41,103	C+
Northwest Christian Univ	OR	36,580	C
Northwest Missouri State Univ	MO	17,737	C
Northwest Nazarene Univ	ID	36,000	C
Northwest Univ	WA	35,876	VC
Northwestern College of Iowa	IA	38,400	C+
Northwestern Okla State Univ	OK	13,072	NC
Northwestern Univ	IL	66,344	MC
Norwich Univ	VT	28,212	C
Notre Dame College	OH	37,150	VC
Notre Dame de Namur Univ	CA	46,526	LC
Notre Dame of Maryland Univ	MD	46,465	VC
Nova Southeastern Univ	FL	38,534	C
Nyack College	NY	34,050	NC
Oakland Univ	MI	20,763	C
Oakwood Univ	AL	43,758	C
Oberlin College	OH	66,012	MC
Occidental College	CA	65,530	MC
Oglethorpe Univ	GA	44,200	C+
Ohio Dominican Univ	OH	41,340	C+
Ohio Northern Univ	OH	44,050	VC
Ohio State Univ at Columbus	OH	21,703	HC+
Ohio State Univ at Lima	OH	7,140	C
Ohio State Univ at Mansfield	OH	13,160	C
Ohio State Univ at Marion	OH	7,140	C
Ohio State Univ at Newark	OH	7,140	C
Ohio Univ	OH	22,924	C
Ohio Valley Univ	WV	29,480	C
Ohio Wesleyan Univ	OH	49,460	VC
Okla Baptist Univ	OK	32,320	C
Okla Christian Univ	OK	27,650	VC
Okla City Univ	OK	40,476	VC
Okla Panhandle State Univ	OK	6,152	NC
Okla State Univ	OK	17,180	VC
Old Dominion Univ	VA	20,910	C
Olivet College	MI	36,110	LC
Olivet Nazarene Univ	IL	41,840	C
Oral Roberts Univ	OK	34,316	C
Oregon State Univ	OR	22,519	VC
Ottawa Univ	KS	36,074	VC
Otterbein Univ	OH	41,630	C
Ouachita Baptist Univ	AR	32,320	C
Our Lady of the Lake Univ	TX	35,012	LC
Pace Univ	NY	58,248	C
Pacific Lutheran Univ	WA	49,960	VC
Pacific Union College	CA	36,009	VC
Pacific Univ	OR	52,876	C
Paine College	GA	19,506	LC
Palm Beach Atlantic Univ	FL	39,720	C
Park Univ	MO	20,329	C
Paul Quinn College	TX	25,350	LC
Penn State Erie/The Behrend College	PA	16,256	C
Pennsylvania State Univ - Univ Park	PA	29,760	HC
Pepperdine Univ	CA	74,460	HC+
Peru State College	NE	14,768	NC
Pfeiffer Univ	NC	39,695	LC
Philadelphia Univ	PA	50,370	C
Philander Smith College	AR	20,814	LC
Piedmont College	GA	32,512	C
Pine Manor College	MA	41,660	LC
Pittsburg State Univ	KS	13,880	NC
Pitzer College	CA	66,192	MC
Plymouth State Univ	NH	23,180	LC
Point Loma Nazarene Univ	CA	43,450	C
Point Park Univ	PA	41,270	C
Pomona College	CA	64,957	MC
Pontifical Catholic Univ of PR	PR	10,534	
Portland State Univ	OR	19,443	C
Post Univ	CT	41,150	C
Prairie View A&M Univ	TX	15,205	LC
Prescott College	AZ	33,284	C
Princeton Univ	NJ	57,610	MC
Providence College	RI	60,760	VC
Purdue Univ/Northwest	IN	15,038	C
Purdue Univ/West Lafayette	IN	20,032	MC
Queens Univ of Charlotte	NC	39,543	C
Quincy Univ	IL	36,998	C
Quinnipiac Univ	CT	59,110	C
Radford Univ	VA	19,027	LC
Ramapo College of New Jersey	NJ	25,338	C
Randolph College	VA	45,660	VC
Randolph-Macon College	VA	49,910	C
Reed College	OR	65,300	MC
Regis College	MA	51,920	C
Regis Univ	CO	44,520	C
Rensselaer Polytechnic Inst	NY	63,436	MC
Rhode Island College	RI	17,694	LC
Rhodes College	TN	51,900	HC
Rice Univ	TX	57,668	MC
Rider Univ	NJ	54,050	C
Ripon College	WI	46,911	C+
Rivier Univ	NH	40,410	VC
Roanoke College	VA	54,114	VC
Robert Morris Univ	PA	37,834	C
Roberts Wesleyan College	NY	38,306	C
Rochester College	MI	28,574	LC
Rochester Inst of Technology	NY	50,842	HC
Rockford Univ	IL	36,030	C
Rockhurst Univ	MO	29,220	C
Rocky Mountain College	MT	34,270	C
Roger Williams Univ	RI	46,296	C+
Rollins College	FL	58,670	HC
Roosevelt Univ	IL	40,651	VC
Rosemont College	PA	30,980	C
Rowan Univ	NJ	24,491	VC+
Russell Sage College	NY	39,370	C
Rutgers Univ - Camden	NJ	26,146	C
Rutgers Univ - New Brunswick	NJ	26,632	HC
Rutgers Univ - Newark	NJ	27,288	C
Sacred Heart Univ	CT	52,750	C
Saginaw Valley State Univ	MI	18,530	C
St. Anselm College	NH	52,560	C+
St. Augustine's Univ	NC	26,048	C
St. Francis Univ	PA	42,268	NC
St. John's Univ	MN	51,624	C
St. Joseph's College of Maine	ME	46,485	C
St. Joseph's Univ	PA	57,544	VC+
St. Leo Univ	FL	31,650	C
St. Louis Univ	MO	49,866	HC
St. Martin's Univ	WA	45,056	C
St. Mary-of-the-Woods College	IN	39,632	LC
St. Mary's College	IN	50,600	C
St. Mary's College of Calif	CA	57,420	C
St. Mary's Univ of Minn	MN	41,210	VC
St. Michael's College	VT	51,725	VC+
St. Peter's Univ	NJ	49,192	C
St. Vincent College	PA	44,626	C
St. Xavier Univ	IL	43,310	C
Salem College	NC	37,694	HC
Salem State Univ	MA	17,303	LC
Salisbury Univ	MD	20,714	VC
Salve Regina Univ	RI	51,470	C
Sam Houston State Univ	TX	18,792	C
Samford Univ	AL	39,232	VC
San Diego Christian College	CA	39,068	C
San Diego State Univ	CA	21,896	C+
San Francisco State Univ	CA	18,514	LC
San Jose State Univ	CA	21,540	C
Sarah Lawrence College	NY	63,388	HC
Schreiner Univ	TX	34,626	LC
Scripps College	CA	66,664	MC
Seattle Pacific Univ	WA	47,439	C+
Seattle Univ	WA	50,811	VC+
Seton Hall Univ	NJ	55,514	C
Seton Hill Univ	PA	46,972	C
Sewanee: The Univ of the South	TN	54,500	MC
Shaw Univ	NC	24,638	C
Shenandoah Univ	VA	41,312	C
Shepherd Univ, West Virginia	WV	17,224	C
Shippensburg Univ of Pennsylvania	PA	23,208	C
Shorter Univ	GA	31,130	LC
Siena College	NY	48,916	C+
Siena Heights Univ	MI	32,040	C
Silver Lake College of the Holy Family	WI	36,290	LC
Simmons College	MA	53,090	VC
Simpson College	IA	43,839	VC
Simpson Univ	CA	33,700	C
Skidmore College	NY	64,214	HC
Slippery Rock Univ of Pennsylvania	PA	10,360	C
Smith College	MA	63,914	MC
Sonoma State Univ	CA	27,806	C
S Car State Univ	SC	20,805	LC
S Dak State Univ	SD	15,634	C
Southeast Missouri State Univ	MO	15,498	C
Southeastern Louisiana Univ	LA	16,237	C
Southeastern Okla State Univ	OK	11,875	C
Southeastern Univ	FL	31,765	C
Southern Adventist Univ	TN	27,600	C
Southern Arkansas Univ	AR	21,532	C
Southern Conn State Univ	CT	21,924	LC
Southern Illinois Univ Carbondale	IL	23,667	C
Southern Illinois Univ Edwardsville	IL	22,643	C
Southern Methodist Univ	TX	66,483	MC
Southern Nazarene Univ	OK	32,798	NC
Southern New Hampshire Univ	NH	43,198	C
Southern Oregon Univ	OR	19,117	C
Southern Univ and A&M College	LA	16,074	LC+
Southern Univ at New Orleans	LA	8,014	LC
Southern Vermont College	VT	34,670	LC
Southern Wesleyan Univ	SC	32,130	LC
Southwest Baptist Univ	MO	29,900	LC
Southwest Minn State Univ	MN	17,783	C
Southwestern Adventist Univ	TX	27,756	LC
Southwestern College	KS	31,531	C
Southwestern Okla State Univ	OK	11,790	C
Southwestern Univ	TX	50,720	VC
Spalding Univ	KY	31,938	SP
Spelman College	GA	38,751	C
Spring Arbor Univ	MI	36,000	C
Spring Hill College	AL	48,488	C
Springfield College	MA	45,995	C
St. Ambrose Univ	IA	39,019	C
St. Ambrose Univ	IA	39,019	C
St. Andrews Univ	NC	44,634	LC
St. Bonaventure Univ	NY	44,237	C
St. Catherine Univ	MN	45,630	VC
St. Cloud State Univ	MN	10,600	C
St. Edward's Univ	TX	53,100	VC
St. Francis College	NY	38,800	LC
St. John Fisher College	NY	43,620	C
St. John's Univ	NY	55,850	C
St. Joseph's College, New York/Brooklyn Campus	NY	25,114	LC
St. Joseph's College, New York/Long Island Campus	NY	25,124	C
St. Lawrence Univ	NY	64,390	VC
St. Mary's College of Maryland	MD	26,634	VC
St. Mary's Univ	TX	37,500	C
St. Norbert College	WI	44,525	VC
St. Olaf College	MN	54,260	HC+
St. Thomas Aquinas College	NY	42,200	C
St. Thomas Univ	FL	36,360	LC
Stanford Univ	CA	60,409	MC
SUNY / Buffalo State College	NY	20,842	C
SUNY / Empire State College	NY	9,145	SP
SUNY / SUNY College at Old Westbury	NY	16,860	C

ST = STATE $IS = IN-STATE COSTS SR = SELECTOR RATING

School	ST	$IS	SR
SUNY / SUNY Cortland	NY	20,706	VC
SUNY / SUNY Fredonia	NY	20,818	C
SUNY / SUNY Oneonta	NY	19,712	C+
SUNY / SUNY Plattsburgh	NY	18,814	C
SUNY / SUNY Potsdam	NY	20,404	C+
SUNY / Univ at Buffalo	NY	23,122	C+
SUNY at Binghamton	NY	22,861	MC
SUNY at Geneseo	NY	20,440	VC+
SUNY at New Paltz	NY	19,200	C
SUNY at Oswego	NY	21,351	C
SUNY at Purchase	NY	17,900	C
SUNY Polytechnic Inst	NY	19,473	VC
SUNY SUNY Albany	NY	22,165	C
Stephen F. Austin State Univ	TX	18,406	LC
Sterling College	KS	32,830	C
Stetson Univ	FL	53,544	VC
Stevenson Univ	MD	72,770	C
Stockton Univ	NJ	25,059	
Stonehill College	MA	55,030	C+
Stony Brook Univ/The SUNY	NY	21,881	MC
Suffolk Univ	MA	50,308	C
Sul Ross State Univ	TX	15,021	LC
Susquehanna Univ	PA	55,340	VC
Swarthmore College	PA	63,550	MC
Syracuse Univ	NY	60,239	VC
Tabor College	KS	35,870	C
Talladega College	AL	19,215	C
Tarleton State Univ	TX	15,248	LC
Taylor Univ	IN	40,317	C+
Temple Univ	PA	24,392	VC
Tenn State Univ	TN	14,423	C
Tenn Tech Univ	TN	17,050	C
Texas A&M Univ	TX	20,521	VC+
Texas A&M Univ at Commerce	TX	10,496	C
Texas A&M Univ at Corpus Christi	TX	16,851	LC
Texas A&M Univ at Kingsville	TX	7,500	LC
Texas Christian Univ	TX	54,670	HC
Texas Lutheran Univ	TX	38,620	C
Texas Southern Univ	TX	18,212	LC
Texas State Univ	TX	19,350	C
Texas Tech Univ	TX	18,736	C+
Texas Wesleyan Univ	TX	35,134	C
Texas Woman's Univ	TX	15,302	LC
The Catholic Univ of America	DC	56,356	VC
The Citadel, The Military College of S Car	SC	35,339	C
The College at Brockport - SUNY	NY	20,346	C
The College of Idaho	ID	36,415	C
The College of New Jersey	NJ	31,909	HC
The College of New Rochelle	NY	46,300	VC
The College of St. Rose	NY	43,048	C
The College of Wooster	OH	57,900	VC+
The Univ of Akron	OH	21,477	C
The Univ of Tenn at Chattanooga	TN	16,744	C
The Univ of Tenn at Knoxville	TN	22,112	VC
The Univ of Tenn at Martin	TN	14,876	C
The Univ of Utah	UT	17,924	VC
The Univ of Virginia's College at Wise	VA	18,192	LC
Thiel College	PA	41,590	C
Thomas College	ME	35,268	LC
Thomas Edison State Univ	NJ	6,350	NC
Thomas More College	KY	36,720	C
Thomas Univ	GA	21,420	LC
Tiffin Univ	OH	31,380	C
Tougaloo College	MS	17,980	NC
Touro College	NY	28,950	VC
Towson Univ	MD	17,408	VC
Transylvania Univ	KY	45,690	VC+
Trevecca Nazarene Univ	TN	31,186	C
Trine Univ	IN	41,310	C
Trinity Christian College	IL	35,580	C
Trinity College	CT	63,920	HC+
Trinity International Univ	IL	31,070	VC
Trinity Univ	TX	52,314	HC+
Trinity Washington Univ	DC	33,826	C+
Troy Univ	AL	16,171	C
Truman State Univ	MO	16,014	HC
Tufts Univ	MA		MC
Tulane Univ	LA	63,396	HC+
Tusculum College	TN	31,625	C
Tuskegee Univ	AL	28,164	C
Union College	KY	32,310	C
Union College	NE	23,270	C
Union College	NY	64,320	MC
Union Inst & Univ	OH	8,912	SP
Union Univ	TN	33,970	VC
United States Air Force Academy	CO		C
Universidad del Turabo	PR	17,828	
Universidad Metropolitana	PR	17,828	
Univ of Alabama	AL	24,320	C+
Univ of Alabama at Birmingham	AL	19,906	C
Univ of Alabama in Huntsville	AL	19,445	VC
Univ of Alaska Anchorage	AK	16,652	NC
Univ of Alaska Fairbanks	AK	16,179	C
Univ of Arizona	AZ	23,100	C
Univ of Arkansas at Fayetteville	AR	19,152	C+
Univ of Arkansas at Little Rock	AR	18,211	C
Univ of Arkansas at Monticello	AR	13,134	NC
Univ of Arkansas at Pine Bluff	AR	13,541	C
Univ of Bridgeport	CT	44,430	LC
Univ of Calif at Berkeley	CA	28,853	MC
Univ of Calif at Davis	CA	28,468	HC
Univ of Calif at Irvine	CA	26,484	VC
Univ of Calif at Los Angeles	CA	30,162	MC
Univ of Calif at Riverside	CA	29,227	C+
Univ of Calif at Santa Barbara	CA	29,091	HC
Univ of Calif San Diego	CA	30,150	MC
Univ of Calif, Santa Cruz	CA	28,731	C+
Univ of Central Arkansas	AR	14,472	VC
Univ of Central Florida	FL	15,922	VC
Univ of Central Missouri	MO	18,982	C
Univ of Central Okla	OK	13,486	C
Univ of Charleston	WV	35,000	C
Univ of Chicago	IL	67,584	MC
Univ of Cincinnati	OH	21,964	VC
Univ of Colo Boulder	CO	24,285	VC+
Univ of Colo Colo Springs	CO	19,663	C
Univ of Colo Denver	CO	23,230	C
Univ of Conn	CT	25,538	HC
Univ of Dallas	TX	45,500	VC+
Univ of Dayton	OH	53,620	C
Univ of Delaware	DE	24,976	VC+
Univ of Denver	CO	58,443	VC+
Univ of Detroit Mercy	MI	48,816	C+
Univ of Dubuque	IA	37,824	C
Univ of Evansville	IN	44,186	VC+
Univ of Findlay	OH	60,139	C
Univ of Florida	FL	16,291	HC+
Univ of Georgia	GA	21,250	HC
Univ of Great Falls	MT	38,524	C
Univ of Hartford	CT	49,776	C
Univ of Hawaii at Hilo	HI	18,038	C
Univ of Hawaii at Manoa	HI	23,221	C
Univ of Houston-Downtown	TX	7,241	C
Univ of Idaho	ID	15,348	C
Univ of Illinois at Chicago	IL	25,006	VC
Univ of Illinois at Urbana-Champaign	IL	27,006	HC
Univ of Indianapolis	IN	36,480	C
Univ of Iowa	IA	18,683	VC+
Univ of Jamestown	ND	28,508	C
Univ of Kansas	KS	20,135	C+
Univ of Kentucky	KY	33,306	C
Univ of La Verne	CA	55,600	C
Univ of Louisiana at Lafayette	LA	14,516	C
Univ of Louisiana at Monroe	LA	15,970	C
Univ of Louisville	KY	19,824	C
Univ of Maine	ME	20,792	C
Univ of Maine at Farmington	ME	18,187	C
Univ of Maine at Machias	ME	22,960	C
Univ of Mary	ND	23,180	C
Univ of Mary Hardin-Baylor	TX	33,950	C+
Univ of Mary Washington	VA	24,764	VC
Univ of Maryland/Baltimore County	MD	21,296	VC
Univ of Maryland/College Park	MD	21,938	HC
Univ of Maryland/Univ College	MD	25,966	LC
Univ of Mass Amherst	MA	26,199	VC+
Univ of Mass Boston	MA	13,435	C
Univ of Mass Dartmouth	MA	25,658	C
Univ of Mass Lowell	MA	26,380	C
Univ of Memphis	TN	18,278	C
Univ of Miami	FL	63,494	MC
Univ of Mich/Ann Arbor	MI	24,410	MC
Univ of Mich/Dearborn	MI	11,757	VC
Univ of Mich-Flint	MI	17,607	C+
Univ of Minn/Duluth	MN	20,292	C+
Univ of Minn/Morris	MN	20,760	VC
Univ of Minn/Twin Cities	MN	23,519	HC+
Univ of Miss	MS	17,746	C+
Univ of Missouri/Columbia	MO	18,201	MC
Univ of Missouri-Kansas City	MO	19,563	VC
Univ of Missouri-St. Louis	MO		C
Univ of Mobile	AL	28,935	C
Univ of Montana	MT	14,105	C
Univ of Montevallo	AL	19,502	C
Univ of Mount Olive	NC	18,426	C
Univ of Mount Union	OH	38,970	C
Univ of Nebr - Kearney	NE	16,546	LC
Univ of Nebr - Lincoln	NE	18,589	VC
Univ of Nebr - Omaha	NE	16,120	C
Univ of Nevada, Las Vegas	NV	17,553	C
Univ of Nevada/Reno	NV	18,010	C
Univ of New England	ME	48,880	C
Univ of New Hampshire	NH	28,562	VC
Univ of New Hampshire - Manchester	NH	14,490	C
Univ of New Haven	CT	52,190	C
Univ of New Mexico	NM	15,404	C
Univ of New Orleans	LA	12,840	C
Univ of North Alabama	AL	15,398	C
Univ of N Car at Asheville	NC	15,723	VC+
Univ of N Car at Chapel Hill	NC	20,052	HC+
Univ of N Car at Charlotte	NC	15,547	C
Univ of N Car at Greensboro	NC	14,690	C
Univ of N Car at Pembroke	NC	14,388	LC
Univ of N Car at Wilmington	NC	14,590	VC
Univ of N Dak	ND	15,373	C
Univ of North Florida	FL	15,996	VC
Univ of North Georgia	GA	17,316	C
Univ of North Texas	TX	19,198	C
Univ of Northern Colo	CO	20,851	C
Univ of Northwestern - St. Paul	MN	38,160	C
Univ of Notre Dame	IN	64,043	MC
Univ of Okla	OK	18,911	VC
Univ of Oregon	OR	22,972	C
Univ of Pennsylvania	PA	63,526	MC
Univ of Pikeville	KY	28,700	NC
Univ of Pittsburgh	PA	29,568	HC+
Univ of Pittsburgh at Bradford	PA	22,402	C
Univ of Pittsburgh at Greensburg	PA	23,132	C
Univ of Pittsburgh at Johnstown	PA	22,092	C
Univ of Portland	OR	52,152	VC
Univ of PR, at Cayey	PR		
Univ of PR, at Mayaguez	PR	13,995	
Univ of PR-Rio Piedras campus	PR	13,327	
Univ of Puget Sound	WA	56,456	VC+
Univ of Redlands	CA	60,200	VC
Univ of Rhode Island	RI	24,906	C
Univ of Richmond	VA	60,880	MC
Univ of Rio Grande & Rio Grande Community College	OH	8,750	NC
Univ of Rochester	NY	65,032	MC
Univ of St. Francis	IN	37,400	C
Univ of St. Joseph	CT	49,550	C
Univ of St. Mary	KS	34,690	C
Univ of San Diego	CA	58,442	VC+
Univ of San Francisco	CA	58,484	VC
Univ of Science and Arts of Okla	OK	11,140	VC
Univ of Scranton	PA	54,962	VC
Univ of Sioux Falls	SD	34,330	C
Univ of South Alabama	AL	16,400	C
Univ of S Car Aiken	SC	16,712	C
Univ of S Car at Columbia	SC	19,725	VC+
Univ of S Car Upstate	SC	18,200	LC
Univ of S Dak	SD	16,109	C
Univ of South Florida/St. Petersburg	FL	15,980	C
Univ of South Florida/Tampa	FL	16,110	VC+
Univ of Southern Calif	CA	66,631	C
Univ of Southern Indiana	IN	16,501	C
Univ of Southern Maine	ME	18,320	C
Univ of Southern Miss	MS	13,170	C
Univ of St. Francis	IL	39,924	C
Univ of St. Thomas - Houston	TX	40,020	VC
Univ of Tampa	FL	36,944	C
Univ of Texas at Arlington	TX	18,026	LC
Univ of Texas at Austin	TX	26,102	HC
Univ of Texas at Dallas	TX	22,830	VC+
Univ of Texas at El Paso	TX	34,452	NC
Univ of the Cumberlands	KY	32,000	C
Univ of the District of Columbia	DC	21,044	LC
Univ of the Incarnate Word	TX	39,162	LC
Univ of the Ozarks	AR	52,176	C
Univ of the Pacific	CA	57,006	VC
Univ of the Sacred Heart	PR	17,932	
Univ of the Sciences	PA	54,038	VC
Univ of the Southwest	NM	22,766	C
Univ of Toledo	OH	19,336	NC
Univ of Tulsa	OK	52,625	HC+
Univ of Vermont	VT	28,878	HC
Univ of Virginia	VA	25,891	MC
Univ of Washington	WA	23,149	VC
Univ of West Alabama	AL	15,516	NC
Univ of West Florida	FL	15,848	C
Univ of West Georgia	GA	16,360	LC
Univ of Wisc-Eau Claire	WI	15,797	VC
Univ of Wisc-Green Bay	WI	15,064	C
Univ of Wisc-La Crosse	WI	15,247	C+
Univ of Wisc-Madison	WI	20,934	MC
Univ of Wisc-Milwaukee	WI	21,496	C
Univ of Wisc-Oshkosh	WI	15,200	C
Univ of Wisc-Parkside	WI	15,193	C
Univ of Wisc-Platteville	WI	14,614	VC
Univ of Wisc-River Falls	WI	14,485	C
Univ of Wisc-Stevens Point	WI	14,043	C
Univ of Wisc-Stout	WI	19,667	C
Univ of Wisc-Superior	WI	14,446	C
Univ of Wisc-Whitewater	WI	13,976	C
Univ of Wyoming	WY	15,375	C+
Upper Iowa Univ	IA	34,990	NC
Urbana Univ	OH	30,820	C
Ursinus College	PA	61,690	VC
Ursuline College	OH	41,076	LC
Utah State Univ	UT	12,736	C
Utica College	NY	30,430	C
Valparaiso Univ	IN	48,370	C+
Vanderbilt Univ	TN	60,572	MC
Vanguard Univ of Southern Calif	CA	40,740	VC
Vassar College	NY	65,491	MC
Villanova Univ	PA	62,523	MC
Virginia Commonwealth Univ	VA	23,049	C
Virginia Military Inst	VA	26,460	C+
Virginia Polytechnic Inst and State Univ	VA	21,276	HC
Virginia State Univ	VA	19,802	C+
Virginia Union Univ	VA	22,421	C
Virginia Wesleyan College	VA	43,728	LC
Viterbo Univ	WI	34,660	C
Wabash College	IN	50,650	VC
Wagner College	NY	55,480	C+
Wake Forest Univ	NC	64,056	MC
Walla Walla Univ	WA	30,417	NC
Walsh Univ	OH	39,010	C
Warner Univ	FL	28,216	C
Warren Wilson College	NC	44,220	VC
Wartburg College	IA	47,840	C
Washburn Univ	KS	15,827	C
Washington & Jefferson College	PA	56,512	VC
Washington Adventist Univ	MD	31,440	LC
Washington and Lee Univ	VA	59,647	MC
Washington College	MD	54,666	VC
Washington State Univ	WA	22,495	C
Washington Univ in St. Louis	MO	65,366	VC
Wayland Baptist Univ	TX	22,356	LC
Wayne State College	NE	12,802	C
Wayne State Univ	MI	22,016	C
Waynesburg Univ	PA	32,290	C
Weber State Univ	UT	10,721	C
Webster Univ	MO	37,490	C
Wellesley College	MA	63,916	MC
Wells College	NY	50,500	C
Wesley College	DE	37,026	LC
Wesleyan College	GA	29,694	C+
Wesleyan Univ	CT	65,516	MC
West Chester Univ of Pennsylvania	PA	18,456	C
West Liberty Univ	WV	15,512	C
West Texas A&M Univ	TX	13,478	C
West Virginia State Univ	WV	8,378	NC
West Virginia Univ	WV	18,210	C
West Virginia Wesleyan College	WV	36,858	C
Western Carolina Univ	NC	13,965	C
Western Conn State Univ	CT	21,254	LC
Western Illinois Univ	IL	20,825	C
Western Kentucky Univ	KY	16,850	C
Western Mich Univ	MI	21,054	C
Western New England Univ	MA	48,088	C
Western New Mexico Univ	NM	16,734	LC
Western Oregon Univ	OR	15,021	LC
Western State Colo Univ	CO	18,639	C
Western Washington Univ	WA	18,003	C+
Westfield State Univ	MA	19,671	C
Westminster College	MO	32,820	C
Westminster College	PA	39,180	C+
Westminster College	UT	41,078	C+
Westmont College	CA	56,410	HC
Wheaton College	IL	43,610	MC
Wheaton College	MA	61,512	VC
Wheeling Jesuit Univ	WV	37,106	LC
Wheelock College	MA	49,225	C
Whitman College	WA	59,772	MC
Whittier College	CA	57,891	C
Whitworth Univ	WA	51,732	VC
Wichita State Univ	KS	21,643	C
Widener Univ	PA	56,486	C
Wilberforce Univ	OH	19,016	C
Wilkes Univ	PA	45,622	C
Willamette Univ	OR	61,817	VC+
William Carey Univ	MS	23,950	LC
William Jewell College	MO	41,210	C+
William Paterson Univ of New Jersey	NJ	23,133	C
William Peace Univ	NC	37,430	LC
William Penn Univ	IA	26,000	C
William Woods Univ	MO	32,040	C
Williams Baptist College	AR	24,720	C
Williams College	MA	63,290	MC
Wilmington College	OH	34,600	C
Wilson College	PA	35,620	C
Wingate Univ	NC	39,950	C
Winona State Univ	MN	17,535	C
Winston-Salem State Univ	NC	26,166	LC
Winthrop Univ	SC	23,082	C
Wisc Lutheran College	WI	36,290	VC
Wittenberg Univ	OH	48,156	C+
Wofford College	SC	49,885	VC
Woodbury Univ	CA	46,958	C
Worcester State Univ	MA	20,977	C
Wright State Univ	OH	16,983	C
Xavier Univ	OH	47,880	C+
Xavier Univ of Louisiana	LA	31,689	C+
Yale Univ	CT	64,650	MC
Yeshiva Univ	NY	47,250	VC+
York College	NE	24,300	C
York College of Pennsylvania	PA	29,240	C
Youngstown State Univ	OH	17,307	C

PSYCHOLOGY EDUCATION

School	ST	$IS	SR
Bethany College	WV	36,300	NC
Bloomfield College	NJ	39,100	LC
Eastern Mich Univ	MI	19,761	C
Kutztown Univ of Pennsylvania	PA	19,056	LC
Lamar Univ	TX	18,014	LC
Mount Holyoke College	MA	56,746	MC
Nazareth College	NY	45,574	C
Pittsburg State Univ	KS	13,880	NC
Rocky Mountain College	MT	34,270	C
St. Vincent College	PA	44,626	C
Tulane Univ	LA	63,396	HC+
Univ of Arizona	AZ	23,100	C
Univ of Delaware	DE	24,976	VC+

ST = STATE **$IS** = IN-STATE COSTS **SR** = SELECTOR RATING

School	ST	$IS	SR
Univ of Rio Grande & Rio Grande Community College	OH	8,750	NC
Valparaiso Univ	IN	48,370	C+
Weber State Univ	UT	10,721	C
York College	NE	24,300	C

PUBLIC ADMINISTRATION

School	ST	$IS	SR
American International College	MA	46,300	LC
Anna Maria College	MA	48,186	C
Aquinas College - Mich	MI	38,876	HC
Ashford Univ	CA	10,480	C
Auburn Univ	AL	23,594	VC+
Auburn Univ at Montgomery	AL	15,290	C
Austin Peay State Univ	TN	16,397	C
Baldwin Wallace Univ	OH	41,106	C
Baylor Univ	TX	53,760	HC
Bentley Univ	MA	60,890	HC
Blackburn College	IL	28,526	LC
Bloomfield College	NJ	39,100	LC
Brown Univ	RI	64,566	MC
Bryant Univ	RI	55,646	VC
Calif Baptist Univ	CA	41,392	C
Cal State, Bakersfield	CA	19,191	LC
Cal State, Chico	CA	21,440	C
Cal State, Dominguez Hills	CA	19,022	LC
Cal State, Fresno	CA	16,902	LC
Cal State, Fullerton	CA	21,902	C
Cal State, Sacramento	CA	20,332	C
Cal State, San Bernardino	CA	12,000	C
Calvin College	MI	41,570	VC+
Carlow Univ	PA	38,549	LC
Carnegie Mellon Univ	PA	67,980	MC
Carroll College	MT	39,972	C+
Catawba College	NC	39,820	C
Cedarville Univ	OH	34,990	VC
Central State Univ	OH	18,564	C
Central Washington Univ	WA	16,803	C
CUNY/John Jay College of Criminal Justice	NY	6,359	NC
CUNY/Meger Evers College	NY	6,680	NC
Dakota Wesleyan Univ	SD	32,850	C
Defiance College	OH	41,630	C
DePaul Univ	IL	47,623	VC
Doane Univ	NE	39,184	VC
Dordt College	IA	37,860	C+
Eastern Mich Univ	MI	19,761	C
Elizabethtown College	PA	54,050	C
Elizabethtown College School of Continuing and Professional Studies	PA	18,900	C
Elon Univ	NC	44,599	VC+
Evangel Univ	MO	28,898	C
Fayetteville State Univ	NC	17,756	C
Flagler College	FL	27,620	C
Florida A&M Univ	FL	15,361	C
Florida Atlantic Univ	FL	17,339	C
Florida International Univ	FL	19,854	C+
Florida Memorial Univ	FL	22,270	LC
George Mason Univ	VA	15,724	VC
Grambling State Univ	LA	15,701	C
Grand Valley State Univ	MI	22,250	C+
Harding Univ	AR	25,421	C
Hawaii Pacific Univ	HI	33,420	C
Heidelberg Univ	OH	39,200	C
Henderson State Univ	AR	15,516	LC
Howard Univ	DC	37,616	C+
Indiana Univ Kokomo	IN	7,073	C
Indiana Univ-Purdue Univ Fort Wayne	IN	17,553	C
Inter-American Univ of PR Ponce	PR	19,549	
Inter-American Univ of PR-Fajardo Campus	PR	18,336	
Inter-American Univ of PR-San Germán	PR	20,042	
James Madison Univ	VA	19,084	VC
Juniata College	PA	53,760	VC
Kalamazoo College	MI	53,931	HC+
Kean Univ	NJ	24,650	C
Kentucky State Univ	KY	13,364	LC
Kutztown Univ of Pennsylvania	PA	19,056	LC
Lakeland Univ	WI	35,130	C
Lamar Univ	TX	18,014	LC
LeTourneau Univ	TX	38,250	VC
Lewis Univ	IL	40,370	C
Lincoln Univ	MO	13,602	NC
Lindenwood Univ	MO	25,132	C
LIU Post	NY	49,682	C
Louisiana College	LA	21,886	C
Mass College of Liberal Arts	MA	20,128	C
Metropolitan State Univ	MN	7,566	C
Miami Univ	OH	27,190	HC+
Mich State Univ	MI	23,898	VC+
Middle Tenn State Univ	TN	8,650	C
Mills College	CA	59,163	VC
Millsaps College	MS	50,080	C+
Miss Valley State Univ	MS	13,233	LC
Missouri Valley College	MO	28,150	C
Mount Aloysius College	PA	29,976	C
Murray State Univ	KY	16,998	C
New York Univ	NY	65,860	MC
Norfolk State Univ	VA	25,702	LC
Northern Arizona Univ	AZ	20,246	VC
Northern Kentucky Univ	KY	16,486	C
Northern Mich Univ	MI	19,604	C
Northland College	WI	41,103	C+
Northwest Missouri State Univ	MO	17,737	C
Nova Southeastern Univ	FL	38,534	C+
Oakland Univ	MI	20,763	C
Ohio Univ	OH	22,924	C
Ohio Wesleyan Univ	OH	49,460	VC
Otterbein Univ	OH	41,630	C
Park Univ	MO	20,329	C
Plymouth State Univ	NH	23,180	LC
Point Park Univ	PA	41,270	C
Pontifical Catholic Univ of PR	PR	10,534	
Regis Univ	CO	44,520	C
Rhode Island College	RI	17,694	LC
Roger Williams Univ	RI	46,296	C+
Roosevelt Univ	IL	40,651	VC
Rutgers Univ - Newark	NJ	27,288	C
Saginaw Valley State Univ	MI	18,530	C
St. Francis Univ	PA	42,268	NC
St. Joseph's Univ	PA	57,544	VC+
Samford Univ	AL	39,232	VC
San Diego State Univ	CA	21,896	C+
Seattle Univ	WA	50,811	VC+
Shaw Univ	NC	24,638	C
Shenandoah Univ	VA	41,312	C
Shippensburg Univ of Pennsylvania	PA	23,208	C
Siena Heights Univ	MI	32,040	C
Silver Lake College of the Holy Family	WI	36,290	LC
Slippery Rock Univ of Pennsylvania	PA	10,360	C
Southeastern Univ	FL	31,765	C
Southern Adventist Univ	TN	27,600	C
Southern Univ and A&M College	LA	16,074	LC+
Southwest Minn State Univ	MN	17,783	C
St. Cloud State Univ	MN	10,600	C
St. John's Univ	NY	55,850	C
Stanford Univ	CA	60,409	MC
Stephen F. Austin State Univ	TX	18,406	LC
Stonehill College	MA	55,030	C+
Talladega College	AL	19,215	C
Texas A&M Univ at Kingsville	TX	7,500	LC
Texas State Univ	TX	19,350	C
The Univ of Tenn at Knoxville	TN	22,112	VC
The Univ of Tenn at Martin	TN	14,876	C
Thomas Edison State Univ	NJ	6,350	NC
Union Inst & Univ	OH	8,912	SP
Universidad del Turabo	PR	17,828	
Univ of Alaska Southeast	AK	11,493	C
Univ of Arizona	AZ	23,100	C
Univ of Arkansas at Fayetteville	AR	19,152	C+
Univ of Arkansas at Little Rock	AR	18,211	C
Univ of Central Arkansas	AR	14,472	VC
Univ of Central Florida	FL	15,922	VC
Univ of Central Okla	OK	13,486	C
Univ of Illinois at Chicago	IL	25,006	VC
Univ of Kansas	KS	20,135	C+
Univ of La Verne	CA	55,600	C
Univ of Louisville	KY	19,824	C
Univ of Maine at Augusta	ME	7,812	C
Univ of Mich-Flint	MI	17,607	C+
Univ of Miss	MS	17,746	C+
Univ of Missouri/Columbia	MO	18,201	MC
Univ of Missouri-St. Louis	MO		C
Univ of Nebr - Omaha	NE	16,120	C
Univ of Nevada, Las Vegas	NV	17,553	C
Univ of N Dak	ND	15,373	C
Univ of North Florida	FL	15,996	VC
Univ of Okla	OK	18,911	VC
Univ of Oregon	OR	22,972	C
Univ of Pennsylvania	PA	63,526	MC
Univ of Pittsburgh	PA	29,568	HC+
Univ of San Francisco	CA	58,484	VC
Univ of Southern Indiana	IN	16,501	C
Univ of Texas at Dallas	TX	22,830	VC+
Univ of Texas at San Antonio	TX	20,157	C
Univ of the District of Columbia	DC	21,044	LC
Univ of Virginia	VA	25,891	MC
Univ of Wisc-Green Bay	WI	15,064	C
Univ of Wisc-La Crosse	WI	15,247	C+
Univ of Wisc-Stevens Point	WI	14,043	C
Univ of Wisc-Superior	WI	14,446	C
Univ of Wisc-Whitewater	WI	13,976	C
Virginia State Univ	VA	19,802	C+
Wagner College	NY	55,480	C+
Washburn Univ	KS	15,827	C
West Texas A&M Univ	TX	13,478	C
West Virginia Univ Inst of Technology	WV	16,462	NC
Western New Mexico Univ	NM	16,734	LC
Western Oregon Univ	OR	15,021	LC
Wilkes Univ	PA	45,622	C
Winona State Univ	MN	17,535	C
Winston-Salem State Univ	NC	26,166	LC

PUBLIC AFFAIRS

School	ST	$IS	SR
Albion College	MI	52,650	C
Bloomfield College	NJ	39,100	LC
Bryant Univ	RI	55,646	VC
Chatham Univ	PA	46,517	C
CUNY/Baruch College	NY	21,609	HC
College of William & Mary	VA		MC
Columbia College	SC	36,550	C
DePaul Univ	IL	47,623	VC
Dickinson College	PA	63,974	MC
Duke Univ	NC	64,188	
Emory and Henry College	VA	41,410	C
Georgia Inst of Technology	GA	23,360	MC
Hamilton College	NY	64,250	MC
Howard Univ	DC	37,616	C+
Indiana Univ Bloomington	IN	20,429	VC
Indiana Univ Northwest	IN	7,072	C
Indiana Univ-Purdue Univ Fort Wayne	IN	17,553	C
Indiana Univ-Purdue Univ Indianapolis	IN	18,635	C
Meredith College	NC	45,297	C
Mills College	CA	59,163	VC
Muskingum Univ	OH	35,966	C
New College of Florida	FL	15,848	MC
Ohio State Univ at Columbus	OH	21,703	HC+
Olivet Nazarene Univ	IL	41,840	C
Pomona College	CA	64,957	MC
Rice Univ	TX	57,668	MC
Rochester Inst of Technology	NY	50,842	HC
St. Vincent College	PA	44,626	C
Southern Methodist Univ	TX	66,483	MC
Southern New Hampshire Univ	NH	43,198	C
St. Mary's College of Maryland	MD	26,634	VC
SUNY / Empire State College	NY	9,145	SP
Stevenson Univ	MD	72,770	C
Texas Southern Univ	TX	18,212	LC
Trinity College	CT	63,920	HC+
Univ of Chicago	IL	67,584	MC
Univ of Denver	CO	58,443	VC+
Univ of Illinois at Chicago	IL	25,006	VC
Univ of Mich/Ann Arbor	MI	24,410	MC
Univ of Missouri/Columbia	MO	18,201	MC
Univ of N Car at Chapel Hill	NC	20,052	HC+
Univ of Pittsburgh	PA	29,568	HC+
Vanderbilt Univ	TN	60,572	MC
Virginia Polytechnic Inst and State Univ	VA	21,276	HC
Washington & Jefferson College	PA	56,512	VC
Washington and Lee Univ	VA	59,647	MC
Washington State Univ	WA	22,495	C
Wayne State Univ	MI	22,016	C
Western Washington Univ	WA	18,003	C+

PUBLIC HEALTH

School	ST	$IS	SR
Agnes Scott College	GA	51,930	VC+
Allegheny College	PA	55,420	VC
Allen College	IA	32,367	NC
American Univ	DC	59,379	HC+
Andrews Univ	MI	28,030	C+
Arizona State Univ at the Downtown Phoenix Campus	AZ	23,680	VC
Armstrong State Univ	GA	16,962	C
Augustana College	IL	49,658	VC
Baldwin Wallace Univ	OH	41,106	C
Benedict College	SC	28,238	NC
Bluffton Univ	OH	40,950	C
Bowling Green State Univ	OH	19,747	C
Brown Univ	RI	64,566	MC
Calif Baptist Univ	CA	41,392	C
Cal State, Fresno	CA	16,902	LC
Calvin College	MI	41,570	VC+
Carroll Univ	WI	38,100	C+
Central Mich Univ	MI	20,330	C
Central Washington Univ	WA	16,803	C
CUNY/Hunter College	NY	31,098	VC
Colby-Sawyer College	NH	50,790	C
College of Charleston	SC	22,699	C
Dillard Univ	LA	20,940	VC
Drexel Univ	PA	65,432	VC+
East Carolina Univ	NC	16,937	C
East Stroudsburg Univ	PA	18,334	C
East Tenn State Univ	TN	13,994	C
Edinboro Univ	PA	15,940	LC
Elon Univ	NC	44,599	VC+
Ferris State Univ	MI	21,445	C
Fort Lewis College	CO	18,980	C
Hawaii Pacific Univ	HI	33,420	C
Howard Univ	DC	37,616	C+
Indiana State Univ	IN	23,223	LC
Indiana Univ Bloomington	IN	20,429	VC
Indiana Univ of Pennsylvania	PA	23,614	LC
Indiana Univ-Purdue Univ Indianapolis	IN	18,635	C
Ithaca College	NY	56,766	VC
Johns Hopkins Univ	MD	65,386	MC
Kent State Univ	OH	20,732	C
LIU Brooklyn	NY	49,682	C
Malone Univ	OH	38,448	C
Mansfield Univ	PA	23,376	LC
Marian Univ	IN	41,220	C
Marshall Univ	WV	17,242	C
MCPHS Univ	MA	45,470	SP
Miami Univ	OH	27,190	HC+
Mills College	CA	59,163	VC
Minn State Univ, Mankato	MN	15,616	C
Miss Univ for Women	MS	17,065	C
Montclair State Univ	NJ	26,210	LC
New Jersey City Univ	NJ	21,456	LC
New York Univ	NY	65,860	MC
Northeastern Illinois Univ	IL	12,529	LC
Ohio Univ	OH	22,924	C
Old Dominion Univ	VA	20,910	C
Oregon State Univ	OR	22,519	VC
Regis College	MA	51,920	C
Rutgers Univ - New Brunswick	NJ	26,632	HC
St. Louis Univ	MO	49,866	HC
Samford Univ	AL	39,232	VC
San Jose State Univ	CA	21,540	C
Shenandoah Univ	VA	41,312	C
Simmons College	MA	53,090	VC
Southern Conn State Univ	CT	21,924	LC
St. Cloud State Univ	MN	10,600	C
St. Joseph's College, New York/Long Island Campus	NY	25,124	C
Stockton Univ	NJ	25,059	
Syracuse Univ	NY	60,239	VC
Tarleton State Univ	TX	15,248	LC
Taylor Univ	IN	40,317	C+
Temple Univ	PA	24,392	VC
Texas A&M Univ	TX	20,521	VC+
Truman State Univ	MO	16,014	HC
Tulane Univ	LA	63,396	HC+
Univ of Alabama at Birmingham	AL	19,906	C
Univ of Arizona	AZ	23,100	C
Univ of Arkansas at Fayetteville	AR	19,152	C+
Univ of Calif at Berkeley	CA	28,853	MC
Univ of Calif at Irvine	CA	26,484	VC
Univ of Colo Denver	CO	23,230	C
Univ of Evansville	IN	44,186	VC+
Univ of Illinois at Chicago	IL	25,006	VC
Univ of Illinois at Urbana-Champaign	IL	27,006	HC
Univ of Louisville	KY	19,824	C
Univ of Maryland/College Park	MD	21,938	HC
Univ of Mass Amherst	MA	26,199	VC+
Univ of Mass Lowell	MA	26,380	C
Univ of Miami	FL	63,494	MC
Univ of Missouri/Columbia	MO	18,201	MC
Univ of New England	ME	48,880	C
Univ of N Car at Charlotte	NC	15,547	C
Univ of N Car at Greensboro	NC	14,690	C
Univ of Rochester	NY	65,032	MC
Univ of St. Joseph	CT	49,550	C
Univ of S Car at Columbia	SC	19,725	VC+
Univ of Tampa	FL	36,944	C
Univ of the Cumberlands	KY	32,000	C
Univ of Wisc-Eau Claire	WI	15,797	VC
Utah State Univ	UT	12,736	C
Valparaiso Univ	IN	48,370	C+
Walla Walla Univ	WA	30,417	NC
Wayne State Univ	MI	22,016	C
West Chester Univ of Pennsylvania	PA	18,456	C
Western Illinois Univ	IL	20,825	C
Western Kentucky Univ	KY	16,850	C
Western New Mexico Univ	NM	16,734	LC
Winona State Univ	MN	17,535	C
Worcester State Univ	MA	20,977	C
Youngstown State Univ	OH	17,307	C

PUBLIC HISTORY/ARCHIVES

School	ST	$IS	SR
Arkansas Tech Univ	AR	15,484	C
Baldwin Wallace Univ	OH	41,106	C
East Carolina Univ	NC	16,937	C
Flagler College	FL	27,620	C
Northern Kentucky Univ	KY	16,486	C
Weber State Univ	UT	10,721	C
Western Mich Univ	MI	21,054	C

PUBLIC RELATIONS

School	ST	$IS	SR
Abilene Christian Univ	TX	41,800	C+
American Univ	DC	59,379	HC+
Andrews Univ	MI	28,030	C+
Appalachian State Univ	NC	14,416	VC
Ashford Univ	CA	10,480	C
Auburn Univ	AL	23,594	VC+
Baldwin Wallace Univ	OH	41,106	C
Barry Univ	FL	37,830	C
Belmont Univ	TN	40,970	VC
Bethany College	WV	36,300	NC
Biola Univ	CA	46,402	C+
Bluffton Univ	OH	40,950	C
Brigham Young Univ	UT	12,748	HC
Bryant Univ	RI	55,646	VC
Butler Univ	IN	51,352	VC
Calif Baptist Univ	CA	41,392	C
Cal State, Fresno	CA	16,902	LC
Cal State, Fullerton	CA	21,902	C
Capital Univ	OH	42,982	C
Cardinal Stritch Univ	WI	36,462	C
Carroll College	MT	39,972	C+
Central Mich Univ	MI	20,330	C
Central Washington Univ	WA	16,803	C
Champlain College	VT	53,132	C+
Chapman Univ	CA	63,078	VC+
Coe College	IA	51,570	VC
College of the Ozarks	MO	7,230	C
Columbia College - Missouri	MO	27,803	C
Columbia College Chicago	IL	43,168	C
Dallas Baptist Univ	TX	33,713	C
DePaul Univ	IL	47,623	VC

ST = STATE $IS = IN-STATE COSTS SR = SELECTOR RATING

School	ST	$IS	SR
Drake Univ	IA	45,056	HC
Drury Univ	MO	33,791	VC
Duquesne Univ	PA	46,822	VC
Eastern Kentucky Univ	KY	16,908	C
Eastern Mich Univ	MI	19,761	C
Emerson College	MA	54,736	HC
Fairfield Univ	CT	59,860	VC+
Ferris State Univ	MI	21,445	C
Flagler College	FL	27,620	C
Florida State Univ	FL	16,771	HC
Franklin College	IN	39,380	C
Freed-Hardeman Univ	TN	29,450	C
George Washington Univ	DC	62,835	MC
Georgia Southern Univ	GA	16,596	C
Gonzaga Univ	WA	50,888	HC
Goshen College	IN	42,500	C
Greenville College	IL	27,012	C
Gwynedd Mercy Univ	PA	43,780	LC
Hardin-Simmons Univ	TX	33,966	C
Hawaii Pacific Univ	HI	33,420	C
Heidelberg Univ	OH	39,200	C
Hofstra Univ	NY	55,960	C+
Howard Univ	DC	37,616	C+
Huntington Univ	IN	33,996	C
Illinois State Univ	IL	23,418	VC
Ithaca College	NY	56,766	VC
Keene State College	NH	24,003	LC
Kennesaw State Univ	GA	19,592	VC
Kent State Univ	OH	20,732	C
Lasell College	MA	47,500	C
Lee Univ	TN	22,045	C
Lewis Univ	IL	40,370	C
LIU Post	NY	49,682	C
Loras College	IA	39,222	C
Lynn Univ	FL	49,480	LC
Malone Univ	OH	38,448	C
Marietta College	OH	46,190	C
Marquette Univ	WI	48,390	VC+
Marshall Univ	WV	17,242	C
McKendree Univ	IL	37,940	C+
Mercyhurst Univ	PA	47,420	C
Messiah College	PA	43,100	C+
Middle Tenn State Univ	TN	8,650	C
Millersville Univ of Pennsylvania	PA	23,782	C
Millikin Univ	IL	42,158	C
Minn State Univ, Moorhead	MN	15,941	C
Missouri Baptist Univ	MO	35,594	C
Missouri Southern State Univ	MO	12,499	C
Montana State Univ-Billings	MT	22,960	C
Montclair State Univ	NJ	26,210	LC
Mount St. Mary College	NY	42,061	C
Mount Vernon Nazarene Univ	OH	34,500	C
Murray State Univ	KY	16,998	C
New York Univ	NY	65,860	MC
N Dak State Univ	ND	16,245	C
Northern Kentucky Univ	KY	16,486	C
Northern Mich Univ	MI	19,604	C
Northwest Missouri State Univ	MO	17,737	C
Northwestern College of Iowa	IA	38,400	C+
Northwestern Okla State Univ	OK	13,072	NC
Notre Dame College	OH	37,150	VC
Ohio Dominican Univ	OH	41,340	C+
Ohio Northern Univ	OH	44,050	VC
Ohio Univ	OH	22,924	C
Okla Christian Univ	OK	27,650	VC
Okla City Univ	OK	40,476	VC
Otterbein Univ	OH	41,630	C
Pace Univ	NY	58,248	C
Pacific Union College	CA	36,009	VC
Park Univ	MO	20,329	C
Pepperdine Univ	CA	74,460	HC+
Point Park Univ	PA	41,270	C
Pontifical Catholic Univ of PR	PR	10,534	
Purdue Univ/Northwest	IN	15,038	C
Purdue Univ/West Lafayette	IN	20,032	MC
Quinnipiac Univ	CT	59,110	C
Rider Univ	NJ	54,050	C
Rochester Inst of Technology	NY	50,842	HC
Roosevelt Univ	IL	40,651	VC
Rowan Univ	NJ	24,491	VC+
St. Mary's Univ of Minn	MN	41,210	VC
San Diego State Univ	CA	21,896	C+
San Jose State Univ	CA	21,540	C
Shorter Univ	GA	31,130	LC
Simpson College	IA	43,839	VC
Southeast Missouri State Univ	MO	15,498	C
Southeastern Univ	FL	31,765	C
Southern Adventist Univ	TN	27,600	C
Southern Illinois Univ Edwardsville	IL	22,643	C
Southern Methodist Univ	TX	66,483	MC
Spring Hill College	AL	48,488	C
St. John's Univ	NY	55,850	C
SUNY / SUNY Fredonia	NY	20,818	C
SUNY / SUNY Plattsburgh	NY	18,814	C
SUNY at Oswego	NY	21,351	C
Stephens College	MO	38,042	C
Suffolk Univ	MA	50,308	C
Syracuse Univ	NY	60,239	VC
Taylor Univ	IN	40,317	C+
Temple Univ	PA	24,392	VC
Texas State Univ	TX	19,350	C
Texas Tech Univ	TX	18,736	C+
The Univ of Akron	OH	21,477	C
The Univ of Tenn at Knoxville	TN	22,112	VC
Union College	NE	23,270	C
Union Univ	TN	33,970	VC
Univ of Alabama	AL	24,320	C+
Univ of Central Florida	FL	15,922	VC
Univ of Central Missouri	MO	18,982	C
Univ of Central Okla	OK	13,486	C
Univ of Florida	FL	16,291	HC+
Univ of Georgia	GA	21,250	HC
Univ of Idaho	ID	15,348	C
Univ of Indianapolis	IN	36,480	C
Univ of Louisiana at Lafayette	LA	14,516	C
Univ of Miami	FL	63,494	MC
Univ of Nebr - Lincoln	NE	18,589	VC
Univ of North Alabama	AL	15,398	C
Univ of Northwestern - St. Paul	MN	38,160	C
Univ of Oregon	OR	22,972	C
Univ of Pittsburgh at Bradford	PA	22,402	C
Univ of Rhode Island	RI	24,906	C
Univ of Rio Grande & Rio Grande Community College	OH	8,750	NC
Univ of S Car at Columbia	SC	19,725	VC+
Univ of Southern Calif	CA	66,631	C
Univ of Southern Indiana	IN	16,501	C
Univ of Texas at Austin	TX	26,102	HC
Univ of Wisc-Whitewater	WI	13,976	C
Ursuline College	OH	41,076	LC
Utica College	NY	30,430	C
Wartburg College	IA	47,840	C
Washington State Univ	WA	22,495	C
Wayne State Univ	MI	22,016	C
Waynesburg Univ	PA	32,290	C
Weber State Univ	UT	10,721	C
Webster Univ	MO	37,490	C
West Liberty Univ	WV	15,512	C
West Texas A&M Univ	TX	13,478	C
West Virginia Univ	WV	18,210	C
West Virginia Wesleyan College	WV	36,858	C
Western Kentucky Univ	KY	16,850	C
Western Mich Univ	MI	21,054	C
Western New England Univ	MA	48,088	C
Westminster College	PA	39,180	C+
William Penn Univ	IA	26,000	C
Wilmington College	OH	34,600	C
Wingate Univ	NC	39,950	C
Winthrop Univ	SC	23,082	C
Xavier Univ	OH	47,880	C+
York College of Pennsylvania	PA	29,240	C
Youngstown State Univ	OH	17,307	C

PUBLISHING

School	ST	$IS	SR
Benedictine Univ	IL	38,300	C
Biola Univ	CA	46,402	C+
Emerson College	MA	54,736	HC
Hofstra Univ	NY	55,960	C+
New York Univ	NY	65,860	MC
Rochester Inst of Technology	NY	50,842	HC
West Texas A&M Univ	TX	13,478	C

PUERTO RICAN STUDIES

School	ST	$IS	SR
CUNY/Brooklyn College	NY	5,884	C+
Rutgers Univ - Newark	NJ	27,288	C
Univ of Mich/Ann Arbor	MI	24,410	MC

PURCHASING/INVENTORY MANAGEMENT

School	ST	$IS	SR
Bloomfield College	NJ	39,100	LC
Central Mich Univ	MI	20,330	C
Univ of Illinois at Urbana-Champaign	IL	27,006	HC
Univ of North Texas	TX	19,198	C
Weber State Univ	UT	10,721	C
Xavier Univ	OH	47,880	C+

QUANTITATIVE METHODS

School	ST	$IS	SR
Bard College at Simon's Rock	MA	65,795	MC
Bryant Univ	RI	55,646	VC
Bucknell Univ	PA	64,616	MC
CUNY/City College	NY	20,319	VC
James Madison Univ	VA	19,084	VC
Millersville Univ of Pennsylvania	PA	23,782	C
Pace Univ	NY	58,248	C
Univ of Cincinnati	OH	21,964	VC
Univ of Washington	WA	23,149	VC
Whitworth Univ	WA	51,732	VC

RADIATION PROTECTION

School	ST	$IS	SR
Thomas Edison State Univ	NJ	6,350	NC

RADIATION THERAPY

School	ST	$IS	SR
Augusta Univ	GA	4,632	C
Benedictine Univ	IL	38,300	C
Gwynedd Mercy Univ	PA	43,780	LC
Howard Univ	DC	37,616	C+
Indiana Univ Kokomo	IN	7,073	C
Indiana Univ-Purdue Univ Indianapolis	IN	18,635	C
Lewis Univ	IL	40,370	C
MCPHS Univ	MA	45,470	SP
Mount Aloysius College	PA	29,976	C
North Central College	IL	48,712	VC
St. Louis Univ	MO	49,866	HC
Texas State Univ	TX	19,350	C
Thomas Edison State Univ	NJ	6,350	NC
Univ of Mich-Flint	MI	17,607	C+
Univ of St. Francis	IL	39,924	C
Univ of Vermont	VT	28,878	HC
Univ of Wisc-La Crosse	WI	15,247	C+
Wayne State Univ	MI	22,016	C
Weber State Univ	UT	10,721	C

RADIO/TELEVISION TECHNOLOGY

School	ST	$IS	SR
Arkansas State Univ	AR	16,190	C
Biola Univ	CA	46,402	C+
Cal State, Fullerton	CA	21,902	C
CUNY/Brooklyn College	NY	5,884	C+
Columbia College Chicago	IL	43,168	C
DeSales Univ	PA	43,970	C
Drury Univ	MO	33,791	VC
Emerson College	MA	54,736	HC
Hardin-Simmons Univ	TX	33,966	C
Hofstra Univ	NY	55,960	C+
Lyndon State College	VT	20,714	C
Marshall Univ	WV	17,242	C
Mount Ida College	MA	46,820	C
Murray State Univ	KY	16,998	C
New York Univ	NY	65,860	MC
Northern Kentucky Univ	KY	16,486	C
Northwestern Univ	IL	66,344	MC
Ohio Univ	OH	22,924	C
Pacific Union College	CA	36,009	VC
Rowan Univ	NJ	24,491	VC+
San Francisco State Univ	CA	18,514	LC
Southern Illinois Univ Edwardsville	IL	22,643	C
St. John's Univ	NY	55,850	C
Stephen F. Austin State Univ	TX	18,406	LC
Univ of Arkansas at Little Rock	AR	18,211	C
Univ of Central Florida	FL	15,922	VC
Univ of Montana	MT	14,105	C
Univ of North Texas	TX	19,198	C
Univ of Southern Indiana	IN	16,501	C
Univ of Southern Miss	MS	13,170	C
Vanguard Univ of Southern Calif	CA	40,740	VC

RADIO/TV

School	ST	$IS	SR
Bloomfield College	NJ	39,100	LC
Columbia College Chicago	IL	43,168	C
Lewis Univ	IL	40,370	C
LIU Post	NY	49,682	C
San Diego State Univ	CA	21,896	C+
Southern Illinois Univ Carbondale	IL	23,667	C
St. Ambrose Univ	IA	39,019	C
St. Ambrose Univ	IA	39,019	C
Univ of Cincinnati	OH	21,964	VC

RADIOGRAPH MEDICAL TECHNOLOGY

School	ST	$IS	SR
Alderson Broaddus Univ	WV	26,149	C
Clarkson College	NE	31,868	C
Henderson State Univ	AR	15,516	LC
Howard Univ	DC	37,616	C+
La Roche College	PA	37,924	LC
Lewis Univ	IL	40,370	C
Lewis-Clark State College	ID	14,202	C
Misericordia Univ	PA	43,840	C
Mount Aloysius College	PA	29,976	C
Ohio State Univ at Columbus	OH	21,703	HC+
Oregon Inst of Technology	OR	8,910	C
Pennsylvania College of Technology	PA	27,333	NC
St. Louis Univ	MO	49,866	HC
Univ of St. Francis	IL	39,924	C
Weber State Univ	UT	10,721	C

RADIOLOGIC IMAGING MODALITIES

School	ST	$IS	SR
St. Louis Univ	MO	49,866	HC
Thomas Edison State Univ	NJ	6,350	NC
Weber State Univ	UT	10,721	C

RADIOLOGICAL SCIENCE

School	ST	$IS	SR
Adventist Univ of Health Sciences	FL	26,430	NC
Arkansas State Univ	AR	16,190	C
Armstrong State Univ	GA	16,962	C
Austin Peay State Univ	TN	16,397	C
CUNY/College of Technology	NY	6,669	NC
Concordia Univ St. Paul	MN	29,050	C
Friends Univ	KS	34,455	C
George Washington Univ	DC	62,835	MC
Idaho State Univ	ID	13,619	NC
Indiana Univ Northwest	IN	7,072	C
Manhattan College	NY	51,750	C+
Midwestern State Univ	TX	17,572	C
Missouri State Univ	MO	15,190	C+
Mount Aloysius College	PA	29,976	C
Purdue Univ/West Lafayette	IN	20,032	MC
Quinnipiac Univ	CT	59,110	C
Regis College	MA	51,920	C
Southern Vermont College	VT	34,670	LC
St. Francis College	NY	38,800	LC
St. John's Univ	NY	55,850	C
Suffolk Univ	MA	50,308	C
Texas A&M Univ	TX	20,521	VC+
Univ of Central Arkansas	AR	14,472	VC
Univ of Charleston	WV	35,000	C
Univ of Iowa	IA	18,683	VC+
Univ of Mich/Ann Arbor	MI	24,410	MC
Univ of Miss	MS	17,746	C+
Univ of Missouri/Columbia	MO	18,201	MC
Univ of New Mexico	NM	15,404	C
Univ of N Car at Chapel Hill	NC	20,052	HC+
Univ of Pittsburgh at Bradford	PA	22,402	C
Univ of South Alabama	AL	16,400	C
Univ of Southern Indiana	IN	16,501	C
Weber State Univ	UT	10,721	C

RADIOLOGICAL TECHNOLOGY

School	ST	$IS	SR
Allen College	IA	32,367	NC
Austin Peay State Univ	TN	16,397	C
Averett Univ	VA	40,970	LC
Avila Univ	MO	35,480	C
Bloomsburg Univ of Pennsylvania	PA	19,066	LC
Boise State Univ	ID	14,860	C
Briar Cliff Univ	IA	36,956	C
Cal State, Northridge	CA	16,859	LC
Carroll Univ	WI	38,100	C+
Champlain College	VT	53,132	C+
Clarion Univ of Pennsylvania	PA	21,608	LC
Clarkson College	NE	31,868	C
College of St Joseph	VT	32,400	LC
Colo Mesa Univ	CO	18,955	LC
Concordia College - New York	NY	39,035	LC
Concordia Univ Wisc	WI	35,910	C
Fairleigh Dickinson Univ/ College at Florham	NJ	52,062	C
Fairleigh Dickinson Univ/ Metropolitan Campus	NJ	40,254	C
Fort Hays State Univ	KS	12,131	C
Friends Univ	KS	34,455	C
Gwynedd Mercy Univ	PA	43,780	LC
Henderson State Univ	AR	15,516	LC
Holy Family Univ	PA	43,326	LC
Howard Univ	DC	37,616	C+
Inter-American Univ of PR-Aguadilla Campus	PR	21,657	
LIU Post	NY	49,682	C
Mansfield Univ	PA	23,376	LC
Marian Univ	WI	32,420	LC
McNeese State Univ	LA	7,838	C
MCPHS Univ	MA	45,470	SP
Minot State Univ	ND	12,732	C
Missouri Southern State Univ	MO	12,499	C
Mount Aloysius College	PA	29,976	C
Mount Marty College	SD	32,972	C
Mount Mary Univ	WI	34,650	LC
Nebr Methodist College	NE	25,134	SP
N Dak State Univ	ND	16,245	C
Northern Kentucky Univ	KY	16,486	C
Presentation College	SD	25,454	NC
Purdue Univ/West Lafayette	IN	20,032	MC
Rhode Island College	RI	17,694	LC
Southern Illinois Univ Carbondale	IL	23,667	C
Southwestern Okla State Univ	OK	11,790	C
Univ of Hartford	CT	49,776	C
Univ of Jamestown	ND	28,508	C
Univ of Louisiana at Monroe	LA	15,970	C
Univ of Mary	ND	23,180	C
Univ of Nevada, Las Vegas	NV	17,553	C
Walla Walla Univ	WA	30,417	NC
Wayne State Univ	MI	22,016	C
William Carey Univ	MS	23,950	LC
Xavier Univ	OH	47,880	C+

RANCH MANAGEMENT

School	ST	$IS	SR
Texas Christian Univ	TX	54,670	HC
Univ of Nebr - Lincoln	NE	18,589	VC

RANGE/FARM MANAGEMENT

School	ST	$IS	SR
Colo State Univ	CO	22,162	VC
Eastern Oregon Univ	OR	17,715	C
Lake Erie College	OH	38,914	LC
New Mexico State Univ	NM	14,050	C
N Dak State Univ	ND	16,245	C
Oregon State Univ	OR	22,519	VC
S Dak State Univ	SD	15,634	C
Tarleton State Univ	TX	15,248	LC
Texas A&M Univ	TX	20,521	VC+
Texas A&M Univ at Kingsville	TX	7,500	LC
Unity College	ME	37,670	C
Univ of Calif at Davis	CA	28,468	HC
Univ of Idaho	ID	15,348	C
Univ of Illinois at Urbana-Champaign	IL	27,006	HC

ST = STATE $IS = IN-STATE COSTS SR = SELECTOR RATING

School	ST	$IS	SR
Univ of Nebr - Lincoln	NE	18,589	VC
Univ of Wyoming	WY	15,375	C+
Utah State Univ	UT	12,736	C
Washington State Univ	WA	22,495	C
Wilmington College	OH	34,600	C

READING EDUCATION

School	ST	$IS	SR
Ball State Univ	IN	19,590	C
Baylor Univ	TX	53,760	HC
Black Hills State Univ	SD	15,899	C
Calif Univ of Pennsylvania	PA	14,217	LC
Dallas Baptist Univ	TX	33,713	C
Defiance College	OH	41,630	C
Eastern Mich Univ	MI	19,761	C
Florida State Univ	FL	16,771	HC
Hardin-Simmons Univ	TX	33,966	C
Houston Baptist Univ	TX	36,450	C
Howard Univ	DC	37,616	C+
Missouri Southern State Univ	MO	12,499	C
Muskingum Univ	OH	35,966	C
Silver Lake College of the Holy Family	WI	36,290	LC
S Car State Univ	SC	20,805	LC
Southwestern Okla State Univ	OK	11,790	C
Univ of Arkansas at Little Rock	AR	18,211	C
Univ of Great Falls	MT	38,524	C
Univ of Mary Hardin-Baylor	TX	33,950	C+
Univ of Rio Grande & Rio Grande Community College	OH	8,750	NC
West Texas A&M Univ	TX	13,478	C
West Virginia Univ	WV	18,210	C
Western Washington Univ	WA	18,003	C+
Wingate Univ	NC	39,950	C

REAL ESTATE

School	ST	$IS	SR
Angelo State Univ	TX	15,263	NC
Ashford Univ	CA	10,480	C
Baylor Univ	TX	53,760	HC
Cal State, Sacramento	CA	20,332	C
Central Mich Univ	MI	20,330	C
CUNY/Baruch College	NY	21,609	HC
Clarion Univ of Pennsylvania	PA	21,608	LC
Colo State Univ	CO	22,162	VC
DePaul Univ	IL	47,623	VC
Florida Atlantic Univ	FL	17,339	C
Florida International Univ	FL	19,854	C+
Georgia State Univ	GA	24,332	VC
Indiana Univ Bloomington	IN	20,429	VC
Marquette Univ	WI	48,390	VC+
Marylhurst Univ	OR	20,295	NC
Menlo College	CA	51,380	LC
Miss State Univ	MS	11,454	C+
Monmouth Univ	NJ	46,234	C
Morehead State Univ	KY	17,422	C
New York Univ	NY	65,860	MC
Ohio State Univ at Columbus	OH	21,703	HC+
Old Dominion Univ	VA	20,910	C
Peirce College	PA	16,780	NC
San Diego State Univ	CA	21,896	C+
Southern Methodist Univ	TX	66,483	MC
Syracuse Univ	NY	60,239	VC
Temple Univ	PA	24,392	VC
Texas A&M Univ at Kingsville	TX	7,500	LC
Univ of Central Florida	FL	15,922	VC
Univ of Cincinnati	OH	21,964	VC
Univ of Conn	CT	25,538	HC
Univ of Denver	CO	58,443	VC+
Univ of Georgia	GA	21,250	HC
Univ of Illinois at Chicago	IL	25,006	VC
Univ of Illinois at Urbana-Champaign	IL	27,006	HC
Univ of Miami	FL	63,494	MC
Univ of Miss	MS	17,746	C+
Univ of Missouri/Columbia	MO	18,201	MC
Univ of Nebr - Omaha	NE	16,120	C
Univ of Nevada, Las Vegas	NV	17,553	C
Univ of N Car at Charlotte	NC	15,547	C
Univ of North Texas	TX	19,198	C
Univ of Pennsylvania	PA	63,526	MC
Univ of San Diego	CA	58,442	VC+
Univ of S Car at Columbia	SC	19,725	VC+
Univ of Texas at Arlington	TX	18,026	LC
Univ of West Georgia	GA	16,360	LC
Univ of Wisc-Madison	WI	20,934	MC
Univ of Wisc-Milwaukee	WI	21,496	C
Villanova Univ	PA	62,523	MC
Washington State Univ	WA	22,495	C

REAL ESTATE FINANCE

School	ST	$IS	SR
Calif State Polytechnic Univ, Pomona	CA	21,541	C
Southern Methodist Univ	TX	66,483	MC
Texas Christian Univ	TX	54,670	HC
Wright State Univ	OH	16,983	C

RECREATION ADMINISTRATION

School	ST	$IS	SR
Eastern Illinois Univ	IL	21,126	C
Kent State Univ	OH	20,732	C
Okla Baptist Univ	OK	32,320	C
San Diego State Univ	CA	21,896	C+
Southeast Missouri State Univ	MO	15,498	C

School	ST	$IS	SR
Univ of Maine at Machias	ME	22,960	C
Univ of New England	ME	48,880	C
Univ of New Hampshire	NH	28,562	VC

RECREATION AND LEISURE SERVICES

School	ST	$IS	SR
Alcorn State Univ	MS	15,854	C
Aquinas College - Mich	MI	38,876	HC
Asbury Univ	KY	35,180	C+
Aurora Univ	IL	33,970	C
Brigham Young Univ	UT	12,748	HC
Calif Polytechnic State Univ	CA	17,979	HC+
Cal State, East Bay	CA	19,413	C
Cal State, Long Beach	CA	18,850	C
Cal State, Northridge	CA	16,859	LC
Catawba College	NC	39,820	C
Central Washington Univ	WA	16,803	C
Chicago State Univ	IL	20,144	C
Colo State Univ-Pueblo	CO	18,234	C
Cumberland Univ	TN	27,710	C
East Central Univ	OK	13,056	C
East Stroudsburg Univ	PA	18,334	C
Eastern Washington Univ	WA	25,572	LC
Emporia State Univ	KS	14,570	C
Ferris State Univ	MI	21,445	C
Ferrum College	VA	39,650	C
Florida State Univ	FL	16,771	HC
Frostburg State Univ	MD	17,280	LC
Georgia College & State Univ	GA	21,148	C+
Gordon College	MA	46,472	C+
Graceland Univ	IA	35,290	C
Grambling State Univ	LA	15,701	C
Green Mountain College	VT	45,228	LC
Greenville College	IL	27,012	C
Hannibal-LaGrange Univ	MO	29,815	C
Henderson State Univ	AR	15,516	LC
Houghton College	NY	39,090	C
Indiana Inst of Technology	IN	34,240	LC
Indiana State Univ	IN	23,223	LC
Indiana Univ Bloomington	IN	20,429	VC
Ithaca College	NY	56,766	VC
James Madison Univ	VA	19,084	VC
Johnson & Wales Univ/North Miami Campus	FL	42,707	C
Johnson & Wales Univ/ Providence Campus	RI	42,248	C
Kutztown Univ of Pennsylvania	PA	19,056	LC
Lindsey Wilson College	KY	32,882	C
Lyndon State College	VT	20,714	C
Mars Hill Univ	NC	42,688	C
Maryville College	TN	44,410	C
Metropolitan State Univ of Denver	CO	29,889	LC
Middle Tenn State Univ	TN	8,650	C
Minn State Univ, Mankato	MN	15,616	C
Missouri State Univ	MO	15,190	C+
Montclair State Univ	NJ	26,210	LC
Morris College	SC	18,500	LC
Murray State Univ	KY	16,998	C
New England College	NH	50,364	C
New York Univ	NY	65,860	MC
N Car State Univ	NC	19,515	HC+
N Dak State Univ	ND	16,245	C
Northwest Missouri State Univ	MO	17,737	C
Northwest Nazarene Univ	ID	36,000	C
Ohio Univ	OH	22,924	C
Okla State Univ	OK	17,180	VC
Old Dominion Univ	VA	20,910	C
Olivet Nazarene Univ	IL	41,840	C
Oral Roberts Univ	OK	34,316	C
Ouachita Baptist Univ	AR	32,320	C
Pittsburg State Univ	KS	13,880	NC
Plymouth State Univ	NH	23,180	LC
Radford Univ	VA	19,027	LC
Rensselaer Polytechnic Inst	NY	63,436	MC
Shaw Univ	NC	24,638	C
Shepherd Univ, West Virginia	WV	17,224	C
Simpson Univ	CA	33,700	C
Southeastern Okla State Univ	OK	11,875	C
Southern Conn State Univ	CT	21,924	LC
Southern Illinois Univ Carbondale	IL	23,667	C
Southern Wesleyan Univ	SC	32,130	LC
Southwest Baptist Univ	MO	29,900	LC
St. Joseph's College, New York/Brooklyn Campus	NY	25,114	LC
St. Joseph's College, New York/Long Island Campus	NY	25,124	C
St. Thomas Aquinas College	NY	42,200	C
Texas A&M Univ at Galveston	TX	15,920	C
The College at Brockport - SUNY	NY	20,346	C
The Univ of Tenn at Chattanooga	TN	16,744	C
The Univ of Utah	UT	17,924	VC
Tougaloo College	MS	17,980	NC
Trine Univ	IN	41,310	C
Unity College	ME	37,670	C
Univ of Central Missouri	MO	18,982	C
Univ of Florida	FL	16,291	HC+
Univ of Georgia	GA	21,250	HC
Univ of Hawaii at Manoa	HI	23,221	C
Univ of Idaho	ID	15,348	C
Univ of Illinois at Urbana-Champaign	IL	27,006	HC

School	ST	$IS	SR
Univ of Iowa	IA	18,683	VC+
Univ of Maine at Farmington	ME	18,187	C
Univ of Maine at Machias	ME	22,960	C
Univ of Maine at Presque Isle	ME	14,870	C
Univ of Memphis	TN	18,278	C
Univ of Minn/Twin Cities	MN	23,519	HC+
Univ of Mount Olive	NC	18,426	C
Univ of Nebr - Omaha	NE	16,120	C
Univ of North Georgia	GA	17,316	C
Univ of North Texas	TX	19,198	C
Univ of Northern Colo	CO	20,851	C
Univ of South Alabama	AL	16,400	C
Univ of S Dak	SD	16,109	C
Univ of Toledo	OH	19,336	NC
Upper Iowa Univ	IA	34,990	NC
Voorhees College	SC	19,976	C
Wartburg College	IA	47,840	C
West Virginia Univ	WV	18,210	C
Western Kentucky Univ	KY	16,850	C
Western Mich Univ	MI	21,054	C
Western State Colo Univ	CO	18,639	C
William Penn Univ	IA	26,000	C
Winona State Univ	MN	17,535	C
York College of Pennsylvania	PA	29,240	C

RECREATION EDUCATION

School	ST	$IS	SR
Alderson Broaddus Univ	WV	26,149	C
Baylor Univ	TX	53,760	HC
Benedict College	SC	28,238	NC
Campbellsville Univ	KY	32,492	C
Claflin Univ	SC	33,764	LC
College of the Ozarks	MO	7,230	C
Eastern Washington Univ	WA	25,572	LC
Friends Univ	KS	34,455	C
Georgia Southern Univ	GA	16,596	C
Johnson State College	VT	20,752	C
Lyndon State College	VT	20,714	C
Northeastern Illinois Univ	IL	12,529	LC
Northwest Missouri State Univ	MO	17,737	C
Northwest Nazarene Univ	ID	36,000	C
Ohio Univ	OH	22,924	C
Oral Roberts Univ	OK	34,316	C
Plymouth State Univ	NH	23,180	LC
Prescott College	AZ	33,284	C
St. Mary's College of Calif	CA	57,420	C
San Francisco State Univ	CA	18,514	LC
San Jose State Univ	CA	21,540	C
Southern Adventist Univ	TN	27,600	C
Southern Oregon Univ	OR	19,117	C
Southern Univ at New Orleans	LA	8,014	LC
SUNY / SUNY Cortland	NY	20,706	VC
The Univ of Tenn at Knoxville	TN	22,112	VC
Toccoa Falls College	GA	27,920	C
Univ of Arkansas at Fayetteville	AR	19,152	C+
Univ of Conn	CT	25,538	HC
Univ of Maine at Machias	ME	22,960	C
Univ of Minn/Duluth	MN	20,292	C+
Univ of Nevada, Las Vegas	NV	17,553	C
Western Washington Univ	WA	18,003	C+

RECREATION THERAPY

School	ST	$IS	SR
Alderson Broaddus Univ	WV	26,149	C
Ashland Univ	OH	21,440	C
Cal State, Northridge	CA	16,859	LC
Calvin College	MI	41,570	VC+
Catawba College	NC	39,820	C
Central Mich Univ	MI	20,330	C
East Carolina Univ	NC	16,937	C
Eastern Mich Univ	MI	19,761	C
Eastern Washington Univ	WA	25,572	LC
Grand Valley State Univ	MI	22,250	C+
Hampton Univ	VA	34,926	LC
Houghton College	NY	39,090	C
Huntington Univ	IN	33,996	C
Indiana Inst of Technology	IN	34,240	LC
Indiana Univ Bloomington	IN	20,429	VC
Ithaca College	NY	56,766	VC
Longwood Univ	VA	22,184	C
Nova Southeastern Univ	FL	38,534	C+
Pittsburg State Univ	KS	13,880	NC
Shaw Univ	NC	24,638	C
Southern Univ and A&M College	LA	16,074	LC+
Springfield College	MA	45,995	C
Temple Univ	PA	24,392	VC
Unity College	ME	37,670	C
Univ of Iowa	IA	18,683	VC+
Univ of N Car at Wilmington	NC	14,590	VC
Univ of Southern Maine	ME	18,320	C
Univ of Wisc-La Crosse	WI	15,247	C+
Univ of Wisc-Milwaukee	WI	21,496	C
Utica College	NY	30,430	C
West Virginia State Univ	WV	8,378	NC
Western Carolina Univ	NC	13,965	C
Winston-Salem State Univ	NC	26,166	LC

RECREATION/LEISURE (ADVENTURE LEADERSHIP)

School	ST	$IS	SR
Davis & Elkins College	WV	38,242	LC
Murray State Univ	KY	16,998	C
Oregon State Univ	OR	22,519	VC

School	ST	$IS	SR
Univ of Maine at Machias	ME	22,960	C

RECREATION/LEISURE (COMMUNITY RECREATION)

School	ST	$IS	SR
MidAmerica Nazarene Univ	KS	35,550	C
Murray State Univ	KY	16,998	C
Univ of Maine at Machias	ME	22,960	C

RECREATIONAL FACILITIES MANAGEMENT

School	ST	$IS	SR
Alaska Pacific Univ	AK	26,680	VC
Alderson Broaddus Univ	WV	26,149	C
Appalachian State Univ	NC	14,416	VC
Aquinas College - Mich	MI	38,876	HC
Ashland Univ	OH	21,440	C
Bluffton Univ	OH	40,950	C
Cal State, Fresno	CA	16,902	LC
Central Methodist Univ	MO	36,830	VC
Central Mich Univ	MI	20,330	C
Colo State Univ	CO	22,162	VC
Dordt College	IA	37,860	C+
East Carolina Univ	NC	16,937	C
Eastern Mennonite Univ	VA	42,550	C
Florida Gulf Coast Univ	FL	9,682	C
Florida State Univ	FL	16,771	HC
Glenville State College	WV	17,386	NC
Graceland Univ	IA	35,290	C
Houghton College	NY	39,090	C
Indiana Wesleyan Univ	IN	33,674	C
Johnson & Wales Univ/ Providence Campus	RI	42,248	C
Johnson State College	VT	20,752	C
Kean Univ	NJ	24,650	C
Millikin Univ	IL	42,158	C
Missouri Valley College	MO	28,150	C
Ohio Univ	OH	22,924	C
Okla Baptist Univ	OK	32,320	C
San Francisco State Univ	CA	18,514	LC
Sierra Nevada College	NV	43,482	C
SUNY at Oswego	NY	21,351	C
Texas A&M Univ	TX	20,521	VC+
Texas State Univ	TX	19,350	C
Trine Univ	IN	41,310	C
Union College	KY	32,310	C
Univ of Iowa	IA	18,683	VC+
Univ of Maine at Machias	ME	22,960	C
Univ of Minn/Twin Cities	MN	23,519	HC+
Univ of Montana	MT	14,105	C
Univ of Nevada, Las Vegas	NV	17,553	C
Univ of St. Francis	IL	39,924	C
Univ of the Sciences	PA	54,038	VC

REHABILITATION THERAPY

School	ST	$IS	SR
Armstrong State Univ	GA	16,962	C
Cal State, Los Angeles	CA	17,186	LC
Central Mich Univ	MI	20,330	C
Clarion Univ of Pennsylvania	PA	21,608	LC
Coppin State Univ	MD	17,041	VC
East Carolina Univ	NC	16,937	C
Emporia State Univ	KS	14,570	C
Florida State Univ	FL	16,771	HC
Hilbert College	NY	30,850	C
Ithaca College	NY	56,766	VC
Maryville Univ of St. Louis	MO	38,046	VC+
Montana State Univ-Billings	MT	22,960	C
Pennsylvania State Univ - Univ Park	PA	29,760	HC
Rutgers Univ - New Brunswick	NJ	26,632	HC
Shaw Univ	NC	24,638	C
Southern Illinois Univ Carbondale	IL	23,667	C
Southern Univ and A&M College	LA	16,074	LC+
Springfield College	MA	45,995	C
St. Catherine Univ	MN	45,630	VC
Stephen F. Austin State Univ	TX	18,406	LC
The Univ of Tenn at Chattanooga	TN	16,744	C
Thomas Univ	GA	21,420	LC
Troy Univ	AL	16,171	C
Univ of Arizona	AZ	23,100	C
Univ of Arkansas at Pine Bluff	AR	13,541	C
Univ of Florida	FL	16,291	HC+
Univ of Illinois at Urbana-Champaign	IL	27,006	HC
Univ of Maine at Farmington	ME	18,187	C
Univ of Maryland/Eastern Shore	MD	17,013	C
Univ of North Texas	TX	19,198	C
Univ of Northern Colo	CO	20,851	C
Univ of Pittsburgh	PA	29,568	HC+
Univ of Wisc-Stout	WI	19,667	C
Western Washington Univ	WA	18,003	C+
Wilberforce Univ	OH	19,016	C
Wright State Univ	OH	16,983	C

REHABILITATIVE AND HUMAN SERVICES

School	ST	$IS	SR
East Stroudsburg Univ	PA	18,334	C

ST = STATE $IS = IN-STATE COSTS SR = SELECTOR RATING

RELIGION

School	ST	$IS	SR
Adrian College	MI	42,400	C
Agnes Scott College	GA	51,930	VC+
Albertus Magnus College	CT	43,258	LC
Albion College	MI	52,650	C
Albright College	PA	46,660	C
Allegheny College	PA	55,420	VC
Alma College	MI	47,548	C
Alverno College	WI	33,294	LC
Amherst College	MA		HC+
Anderson Univ	IN	38,200	C
Andrews Univ	MI	28,030	C+
Anna Maria College	MA	48,186	C
Appalachian State Univ	NC	14,416	VC
Aquinas College - Mich	MI	38,876	HC
Arkansas Baptist College	AR	20,280	NC
Asbury Univ	KY	35,180	C+
Ashland Univ	OH	21,440	C
Atlantic Union College	MA	27,228	C
Augsburg College	MN	43,929	C
Augustana College	IL	49,658	VC
Augustana Univ	SD	38,424	VC
Aurora Univ	IL	33,970	C
Austin College	TX	45,875	VC
Averett Univ	VA	40,970	LC
Azusa Pacific Univ	CA	43,972	C
Baker Univ	KS	33,350	C+
Baldwin Wallace Univ	OH	41,106	C
Ball State Univ	IN	19,590	C
Bard College	NY	64,024	HC
Barnard College/Columbia Univ	NY	62,741	MC
Barton College	NC	38,686	LC
Bayamon Central Univ	PR	12,490	
Baylor Univ	TX	53,760	HC
Belmont Univ	TN	40,970	VC
Beloit College	WI	55,206	HC
Benedict College	SC	28,238	NC
Benedictine College	KS	36,200	VC
Berea College	KY	7,042	C
Berry College	GA	45,286	C+
Bethany College	WV	36,300	NC
Bethel College	IN	35,860	C
Bethel College	KS	35,370	C
Bethune-Cookman Univ	FL	22,970	C
Birmingham-Southern College	AL	44,478	VC
Bloomfield College	NJ	39,100	LC
Bluefield College	VA	34,120	C+
Boston Univ	MA	65,110	MC
Bowdoin College	ME	63,500	MC
Brescia Univ	KY	29,890	VC+
Brown Univ	RI	64,566	MC
Bryan College	TN	31,440	C
Bryn Athyn College	PA	31,470	C
Bryn Mawr College	PA	59,890	MC
Bucknell Univ	PA	64,616	MC
Butler Univ	IN	51,352	VC
Calif Lutheran Univ	CA	52,853	C
Cal State, Bakersfield	CA	19,191	LC
Cal State, Fullerton	CA	21,902	C
Cal State, Long Beach	CA	18,850	C
Calumet College of St. Joseph	IN	22,735	C
Calvin College	MI	41,570	VC+
Capital Univ	OH	42,982	C
Cardinal Stritch Univ	WI	36,462	C
Carleton College	MN	64,071	MC
Carroll College	MT	39,972	C+
Carroll Univ	WI	38,100	C+
Carson-Newman Univ	TN	34,160	C
Carthage College	WI	48,835	C
Case Western Reserve Univ	OH	60,304	MC
Catawba College	NC	39,820	C
Centenary College of Louisiana	LA	45,650	C+
Central College	IA	44,592	C
Central Methodist Univ	MO	36,830	VC
Central Mich Univ	MI	20,330	C
Centre College	KY	49,250	HC
Chaminade Univ of Honolulu	HI	36,000	C
Chapman Univ	CA	63,078	VC+
Charleston Southern Univ	SC	32,400	C
CUNY/Brooklyn College	NY	5,884	C+
CUNY/Hunter College	NY	31,098	VC
CUNY/Queens College	NY	27,896	C
Claremont McKenna College	CA	67,185	MC
Clark Atlanta Univ	GA	31,019	LC
Clarke Univ	IA	38,940	C
Cleveland State Univ	OH	22,196	C
Coe College	IA	51,570	VC
Colby College	ME	64,060	MC
Colgate Univ	NY	65,030	MC
College of Mount St. Vincent	NY	45,620	C
College of St. Scholastica	MN	44,640	C
College of the Holy Cross	MA	62,165	MC
College of the Ozarks	MO	7,230	C
College of William & Mary	VA		MC
Colo College	CO	62,560	MC
Columbia College	SC	36,550	C
Columbia Univ/ School of General Studies	NY	61,470	MC
Columbia Univ/City of New York	NY	62,958	MC
Concordia College - Moorhead	MN	51,088	C+
Concordia College - New York	NY	39,035	LC
Concordia Univ St. Paul	MN	29,050	C
Concordia Univ Wisc	WI	35,910	C
Concordia Univ, Ann Arbor	MI	35,945	VC
Concordia Univ, Chicago	IL	39,694	C
Conn College	CT	65,000	MC
Converse College	SC	26,495	C
Cornell College	IA	48,800	VC
Culver-Stockton College	MO	33,525	C
Daemen College	NY	38,045	C
Dallas Baptist Univ	TX	33,713	C
Dartmouth College	NH	66,174	MC
Davidson College	NC	60,119	MC
Defiance College	OH	41,630	C
Denison Univ	OH	58,860	MC
DePaul Univ	IL	47,623	VC
DePauw Univ	IN	58,688	HC+
Dickinson College	PA	63,974	MC
Doane Univ	NE	39,184	VC
Dominican Univ	IL	41,222	C
Dominican Univ of Calif	CA	57,050	C
Dordt College	IA	37,860	C+
Drake Univ	IA	45,056	HC
Drew Univ/College of Liberal Arts	NJ	61,048	VC
Drury Univ	MO	33,791	VC
Duke Univ	NC	64,188	
Earlham College	IN	54,870	HC
East Texas Baptist Univ	TX	33,134	C
Eastern Mennonite Univ	VA	42,550	C
Eastern Nazarene College	MA	39,955	C
Eastern New Mexico Univ	NM	14,416	C
Eckerd College	FL	52,874	C
Edward Waters College	FL	20,607	NC
Elizabethtown College	PA	54,050	C
Elizabethtown College School of Continuing and Professional Studies	PA	18,900	C
Elmhurst College	IL	45,428	C
Elms College	MA	45,646	VC
Emmanuel College	MA	52,110	C+
Emory and Henry College	VA	41,410	C
Emory Univ	GA	60,786	MC
Erskine College	SC	45,460	C
Eugene Lang College/The New School for Liberal Arts	NY	55,650	C
Eureka College	IL	30,220	C
Evangel Univ	MO	28,898	C
Felician Univ	NJ	45,370	LC
Ferrum College	VA	39,650	C
Fisk Univ	TN	32,066	LC
Florida International Univ	FL	19,854	C+
Florida Memorial Univ	FL	22,270	LC
Florida State Univ	FL	16,771	HC
Fontbonne Univ	MO	33,717	C
Fordham Univ	NY	65,918	MC
Franklin and Marshall College	PA	63,170	HC
Franklin College	IN	39,380	C
Fresno Pacific Univ	CA	37,370	C
Friends Univ	KS	34,455	C
Furman Univ	SC	58,092	VC+
Gardner-Webb Univ	NC	39,200	C+
George Fox Univ	OR	42,938	C
George Mason Univ	VA	15,724	VC
George Washington Univ	DC	62,835	MC
Georgetown College	KY	41,440	C
Georgetown Univ	DC	65,926	MC
Gettysburg College	PA	63,000	HC
Gonzaga Univ	WA	50,888	HC
Goshen College	IN	42,500	C
Goucher College	MD	55,716	VC
Grace College and Seminary	IN	31,524	C
Graceland Univ	IA	35,290	C
Grand Rapids Theological Seminary/Cornerstone Univ	MI	33,338	C
Greensboro College	NC	42,400	LC
Greenville College	IL	27,012	C
Grinnell College	IA	60,738	MC
Guilford College	NC	44,090	C
Gustavus Adolphus College	MN	52,433	HC
Hamilton College	NY	64,250	MC
Hamline Univ	MN	45,678	VC
Hampden-Sydney College	VA	56,248	C+
Hampshire College	MA	63,824	MC
Harding Univ	AR	25,421	C
Hartwick College	NY	51,270	C
Harvard College/Harvard Univ	MA	60,659	MC
Hastings College	NE	35,380	C+
Haverford College	PA	66,490	MC
Heidelberg Univ	OH	39,200	C
Hellenic College/Holy Cross Greek Orthodox School of Theology	MA	39,906	C
Hendrix College	AR	54,020	VC+
High Point Univ	NC	45,977	C
Hillsdale College	MI	35,722	MC
Hiram College	OH	43,230	C
Hofstra Univ	NY	55,960	C+
Hollins Univ	VA	49,635	VC
Holy Family Univ	PA	43,326	LC
Holy Names Univ	CA	46,630	LC
Hood College	MD	54,840	C
Hope College	MI	39,940	VC
Houghton College	NY	39,090	C
Howard Univ	DC	37,616	C+
Humboldt State Univ	CA	20,514	C
Huntingdon College	AL	34,900	C
Huntington Univ	IN	33,996	C
Illinois College	IL	40,850	VC
Illinois Wesleyan Univ	IL	56,430	VC+
Indiana Wesleyan Univ	IN	33,674	C
Iona College	NY	50,984	C
Iowa State Univ	IA	17,570	C
Iowa Wesleyan Univ	IA	39,200	C
James Madison Univ	VA	19,084	VC
Jarvis Christian College	TX	20,160	NC
John Carroll Univ	OH	49,740	C+
Judson College	AL	27,066	C
Kalamazoo College	MI	53,931	HC+
Kansas Wesleyan Univ	KS	36,600	C
La Roche College	PA	37,924	LC
La Salle Univ	PA	55,790	C
La Sierra Univ	CA	39,690	VC
Lafayette College	PA	63,355	MC
LaGrange College	GA	39,930	C
Lake Forest College	IL	50,652	VC
Lakeland Univ	WI	35,130	C
Lane College	TN	16,550	C
Le Moyne College	NY	46,000	C
Lebanon Valley College	PA	51,530	C
Lees-McRae College	NC	33,944	C
Lehigh Univ	PA	61,010	MC
Lenoir-Rhyne Univ	NC	43,200	C
Lewis & Clark College	OR	58,434	HC+
Liberty Univ	VA	19,101	C
Lindenwood Univ	MO	25,132	C
Linfield College	OR	52,010	C
Loras College	IA	39,222	C
Louisiana College	LA	21,886	C
Loyola Univ New Orleans	LA	51,708	VC+
Luther College	IA	48,540	C+
Lycoming College	PA	48,580	C
Lynchburg College	VA	46,740	C
Lyon College	AR	34,730	C+
Macalester College	MN	61,905	MC
MacMurray College	IL	33,620	C
Manchester Univ	IN	40,422	C
Manhattan College	NY	51,750	C+
Manhattanville College	NY	51,440	C+
Marist College	NY	49,860	VC
Mars Hill Univ	NC	42,688	C
Martin Univ	IN	20,264	LC
Marygrove College	MI	28,926	NC
Marylhurst Univ	OR	20,295	NC
Maryville College	TN	44,410	C
Marywood Univ	PA	46,900	C
McDaniel College	MD	51,380	VC
McKendree Univ	IL	37,940	C+
McMurry Univ	TX	34,259	LC
McPherson College	KS	34,909	C
Mercer Univ	GA	45,348	VC
Mercyhurst Univ	PA	47,420	C
Meredith College	NC	45,297	C
Merrimack College	MA	52,770	C
Methodist Univ	NC	43,600	C
Miami Univ	OH	27,190	HC+
Mich State Univ	MI	23,898	VC+
Middlebury College	VT	64,332	MC
Midland Univ	NE	37,468	
Millsaps College	MS	50,080	C+
Missouri State Univ	MO	15,190	C+
Missouri Valley College	MO	28,150	C
Monmouth College	IL	42,260	C
Montclair State Univ	NJ	26,210	LC
Montreat College	NC	31,298	LC
Moravian College	PA	53,117	
Morehouse College	GA	40,064	C
Morgan State Univ	MD	17,190	LC
Morningside College	IA	36,865	C
Mount Aloysius College	PA	29,976	C
Mount Holyoke College	MA	56,746	MC
Mount Marty College	SD	32,972	C
Mount Mercy Univ	IA	36,826	C
Mount St. Joseph Univ	OH	33,880	C
Mount St. Mary's Univ - Chalon Campus	CA	43,897	VC+
Mount Vernon Nazarene Univ	OH	34,500	C
Muhlenberg College	PA	56,645	VC+
Muskingum Univ	OH	35,966	C
Naropa Univ	CO	42,826	NC
Nazareth College	NY	45,574	C
Nebr Wesleyan Univ	NE	38,140	C+
New College of Florida	FL	15,848	MC
New York Univ	NY	65,860	MC
Newberry College	SC	34,550	C
Niagara Univ	NY	41,010	C
N Car State Univ	NC	19,515	HC+
N Car Wesleyan College	NC	39,200	C
North Central College	IL	48,712	VC
North Central Univ	MN	26,400	C
Northeastern Univ	MA	62,703	MC
Northland College	WI	41,103	C+
Northwest Univ	WA	35,876	VC
Northwestern College of Iowa	IA	38,400	C+
Northwestern Univ	IL	66,344	MC
Notre Dame de Namur Univ	CA	46,526	LC
Notre Dame of Maryland Univ	MD	46,465	VC
Nyack College	NY	34,050	NC
Oakland City Univ	IN	33,360	NC
Oakwood Univ	AL	43,758	C
Oberlin College	OH	66,012	MC
Occidental College	CA	65,530	MC
Ohio Northern Univ	OH	44,050	VC
Ohio Univ	OH	22,924	C
Ohio Wesleyan Univ	OH	49,460	VC
Okla Baptist Univ	OK	32,320	C
Okla City Univ	OK	40,476	VC
Okla Wesleyan Univ	OK	33,206	C
Olivet Nazarene Univ	IL	41,840	C
Oral Roberts Univ	OK	34,316	C
Ottawa Univ	KS	36,074	VC
Otterbein Univ	OH	41,630	C
Ouachita Baptist Univ	AR	32,320	C
Our Lady of the Lake Univ	TX	35,012	LC
Pacific Lutheran Univ	WA	49,960	VC
Pacific Union College	CA	36,009	VC
Pepperdine Univ	CA	74,460	HC+
Pfeiffer Univ	NC	39,695	LC
Piedmont College	GA	32,512	C
Pontifical Catholic Univ of PR	PR	10,534	
Prescott College	AZ	33,284	C
Princeton Univ	NJ	57,610	MC
Principia College	IL	39,010	C+
Purdue Univ/West Lafayette	IN	20,032	MC
Queens Univ of Charlotte	NC	39,543	C
Randolph College	VA	45,660	VC
Randolph-Macon College	VA	49,910	C
Reed College	OR	65,300	MC
Regis Univ	CO	44,520	C
Rhodes College	TN	51,900	HC
Rice Univ	TX	57,668	MC
Ripon College	WI	46,911	C+
Roanoke College	VA	54,114	VC
Roberts Wesleyan College	NY	38,306	C
Rollins College	FL	58,670	HC
Rosemont College	PA	30,980	C
Rutgers Univ - Camden	NJ	26,146	C
Rutgers Univ - New Brunswick	NJ	26,632	HC
St. Francis Univ	PA	42,268	NC
St. Leo Univ	FL	31,650	C
St. Mary's College	IN	50,600	C
St. Mary's College of Calif	CA	57,420	C
St. Michael's College	VT	51,725	VC+
St. Xavier Univ	IL	43,310	C
Salem College	NC	37,694	HC
Salve Regina Univ	RI	51,470	C
Samford Univ	AL	39,232	VC
San Francisco State Univ	CA	18,514	LC
San Jose State Univ	CA	21,540	C
Sarah Lawrence College	NY	63,388	HC
Schreiner Univ	TX	34,626	LC
Scripps College	CA	66,664	MC
Seattle Univ	WA	50,811	VC+
Seton Hall Univ	NJ	55,514	C
Seton Hill Univ	PA	46,972	C
Sewanee: The Univ of the South	TN	54,500	MC
Shaw Univ	NC	24,638	C
Shenandoah Univ	VA	41,312	C
Shorter Univ	GA	31,130	LC
Siena College	NY	48,916	C+
Siena Heights Univ	MI	32,040	C
Silver Lake College of the Holy Family	WI	36,290	LC
Simpson College	IA	43,839	VC
Simpson Univ	CA	33,700	C
Skidmore College	NY	64,214	HC
Smith College	MA	63,914	MC
Southeastern Univ	FL	31,765	C
Southern Methodist Univ	TX	66,483	MC
Southern Wesleyan Univ	SC	32,130	LC
Southwestern Adventist Univ	TX	27,756	LC
Southwestern Univ	TX	50,720	VC
Spelman College	GA	38,751	C
St. Edward's Univ	TX	53,100	VC
St. Francis College	NY	38,800	LC
St. John Fisher College	NY	43,620	C
St. Lawrence Univ	NY	64,390	VC
St. Mary's College of Maryland	MD	26,634	VC
St. Norbert College	WI	44,525	VC
St. Olaf College	MN	54,260	HC+
St. Thomas Aquinas College	NY	42,200	C
St. Thomas Univ	FL	36,360	LC
Stanford Univ	CA	60,409	MC
SUNY / SUNY College at Old Westbury	NY	16,860	C
Stetson Univ	FL	53,544	VC
Stillman College	AL	20,738	C
Stonehill College	MA	55,030	C+
Susquehanna Univ	PA	55,340	VC
Swarthmore College	PA	63,550	MC
Syracuse Univ	NY	60,239	VC
Tabor College	KS	35,870	C
Temple Univ	PA	24,392	VC
Texas A&M Univ at Commerce	TX	10,496	C
Texas Christian Univ	TX	54,670	HC
Texas Wesleyan Univ	TX	35,134	C
The Catholic Univ of America	DC	56,356	VC
The College of Idaho	ID	36,415	C
The College of New Rochelle	NY	46,300	VC
The College of Wooster	OH	57,900	VC+
The Lincoln Univ	PA	15,154	NC
The Univ of Tenn at Knoxville	TN	22,112	VC
Thiel College	PA	41,590	C
Thomas Edison State Univ	NJ	6,350	NC
Tougaloo College	MS	17,980	NC

School	ST	$IS	SR
Towson Univ	MD	17,408	VC
Transylvania Univ	KY	45,690	VC+
Trevecca Nazarene Univ	TN	31,186	C
Trinity College	CT	63,920	HC+
Trinity Univ	TX	52,314	HC+
Truman State Univ	MO	16,014	HC
Tufts Univ	MA		MC
Tulane Univ	LA	63,396	HC+
Union College	KY	32,310	C
Union College	NE	23,270	C
Union College	NY	64,320	MC
Union Univ	TN	33,970	VC
Universidad Adventista de las Antillas	PR	16,606	
Univ of Alabama	AL	24,320	C+
Univ of Bridgeport	CT	44,430	LC
Univ of Calif at Berkeley	CA	28,853	MC
Univ of Calif at Davis	CA	28,468	HC
Univ of Calif at Irvine	CA	26,484	VC
Univ of Calif at Los Angeles	CA	30,162	MC
Univ of Calif at Riverside	CA	29,227	C+
Univ of Calif at Santa Barbara	CA	29,091	HC
Univ of Calif San Diego	CA	30,150	MC
Univ of Central Arkansas	AR	14,472	VC
Univ of Central Florida	FL	15,922	VC
Univ of Chicago	IL	67,584	MC
Univ of Dayton	OH	53,620	C
Univ of Denver	CO	58,443	VC+
Univ of Detroit Mercy	MI	48,816	C+
Univ of Dubuque	IA	37,824	C
Univ of Findlay	OH	60,139	C
Univ of Florida	FL	16,291	HC+
Univ of Georgia	GA	21,250	HC
Univ of Great Falls	MT	38,524	C
Univ of Hawaii at Manoa	HI	23,221	C
Univ of Illinois at Urbana-Champaign	IL	27,006	HC
Univ of Indianapolis	IN	36,480	C
Univ of Iowa	IA	18,683	VC+
Univ of Jamestown	ND	28,508	C
Univ of Kansas	KS	20,135	C+
Univ of La Verne	CA	55,600	C
Univ of Mary Hardin-Baylor	TX	33,950	C+
Univ of Mary Washington	VA	24,764	VC
Univ of Miami	FL	63,494	MC
Univ of Mich/Ann Arbor	MI	24,410	MC
Univ of Miss	MS	17,746	C+
Univ of Missouri/Columbia	MO	18,201	MC
Univ of Mobile	AL	28,935	C
Univ of Mount Olive	NC	18,426	C
Univ of Mount Union	OH	38,970	C
Univ of New Mexico	NM	15,404	C
Univ of N Car at Asheville	NC	15,723	VC+
Univ of N Car at Chapel Hill	NC	20,052	HC+
Univ of N Car at Greensboro	NC	14,690	C
Univ of N Car at Wilmington	NC	14,590	VC
Univ of N Dak	ND	15,373	C
Univ of North Florida	FL	15,996	VC
Univ of Okla	OK	18,911	VC
Univ of Oregon	OR	22,972	C
Univ of Pennsylvania	PA	63,526	MC
Univ of Pikeville	KY	28,700	NC
Univ of Pittsburgh	PA	29,568	HC+
Univ of Puget Sound	WA	56,456	VC+
Univ of Redlands	CA	60,200	VC
Univ of Richmond	VA	60,880	MC
Univ of Rochester	NY	65,032	MC
Univ of St. Joseph	CT	49,550	C
Univ of Sioux Falls	SD	34,330	C
Univ of S Car at Columbia	SC	19,725	VC+
Univ of South Florida/Tampa	FL	16,110	VC+
Univ of Southern Calif	CA	66,631	C
Univ of St. Thomas - Houston	TX	40,020	VC
Univ of Texas at Austin	TX	26,102	HC
Univ of the Cumberlands	KY	32,000	C
Univ of the Incarnate Word	TX	39,162	LC
Univ of the Ozarks	AR	52,176	C
Univ of the Pacific	CA	57,006	VC
Univ of Tulsa	OK	52,625	HC+
Univ of Vermont	VT	28,878	HC
Univ of Virginia	VA	25,891	MC
Univ of Washington	WA	23,149	VC
Univ of West Florida	FL	15,848	C
Univ of Wisc-Madison	WI	20,934	MC
Univ of Wisc-Milwaukee	WI	21,496	C
Univ of Wisc-Oshkosh	WI	15,200	C
Ursuline College	OH	41,076	LC
Valparaiso Univ	IN	48,370	C+
Vassar College	NY	65,491	MC
Villanova Univ	PA	62,523	MC
Virginia Commonwealth Univ	VA	23,049	C
Virginia Union Univ	VA	22,421	C
Virginia Wesleyan College	VA	43,728	LC
Wabash College	IN	50,650	VC
Wake Forest Univ	NC	64,056	MC
Walla Walla Univ	WA	30,417	NC
Warren Wilson College	NC	44,220	VC
Wartburg College	IA	47,840	C
Washburn Univ	KS	15,827	C
Washington Adventist Univ	MD	31,440	LC
Washington and Lee Univ	VA	59,647	MC
Washington State Univ	WA	22,495	C
Washington Univ in St. Louis	MO	65,366	VC
Wayland Baptist Univ	TX	22,356	LC
Webster Univ	MO	37,490	C
Wellesley College	MA	63,916	MC
Wesleyan College	GA	29,694	C+
Wesleyan Univ	CT	65,516	MC
West Virginia Wesleyan College	WV	36,858	C
Western Kentucky Univ	KY	16,850	C
Western Mich Univ	MI	21,054	C
Westminster College	MO	32,820	C
Westminster College	PA	39,180	C+
Westmont College	CA	56,410	HC
Wheaton College	MA	61,512	VC
Whitman College	WA	59,772	MC
Whittier College	CA	57,891	C
Wiley College	TX	18,504	C
Willamette Univ	OR	61,817	VC+
William Carey Univ	MS	23,950	LC
William Jewell College	MO	41,210	C+
Williams Baptist College	AR	24,720	C
Williams College	MA	63,290	MC
Wilmington College	OH	34,600	C
Wilson College	PA	35,620	C
Winthrop Univ	SC	23,082	C
Wittenberg Univ	OH	48,156	C+
Wofford College	SC	49,885	VC
Wright State Univ	OH	16,983	C
Yale Univ	CT	64,650	MC
Yeshiva Univ	NY	47,250	VC+
Youngstown State Univ	OH	17,307	C

RELIGIOUS EDUCATION

School	ST	$IS	SR
Andrews Univ	MI	28,030	C+
Baylor Univ	TX	53,760	HC
Bloomfield College	NJ	39,100	LC
Cal State, Northridge	CA	16,859	LC
Campbellsville Univ	KY	32,492	C
Cedarville Univ	OH	34,990	VC
Concordia Univ St. Paul	MN	29,050	C
Dallas Baptist Univ	TX	33,713	C
East Texas Baptist Univ	TX	33,134	C
Edgewood College	WI	35,950	C
Franciscan Univ of Steubenville	OH	33,980	VC
Georgia State Univ	GA	24,332	VC
Grace Bible College	MI	25,250	C
Grand Rapids Theological Seminary/Cornerstone Univ	MI	33,338	C
Houghton College	NY	39,090	C
Indiana Wesleyan Univ	IN	33,674	C
Kansas Wesleyan Univ	KS	36,600	C
Lenoir-Rhyne Univ	NC	43,200	C
Louisiana College	LA	21,886	C
Loyola Univ Chicago	IL	55,802	VC
Loyola Univ New Orleans	LA	51,708	VC+
Marian Univ	IN	41,220	C
Mercyhurst Univ	PA	47,420	C
Morris College	SC	18,500	LC
Mount Mary Univ	WI	34,650	LC
Mount St. Joseph Univ	OH	33,880	C
Mount Vernon Nazarene Univ	OH	34,500	C
Muskingum Univ	OH	35,966	C
North Central Univ	MN	26,400	C
Northwest Univ	WA	35,876	VC
Oakwood Univ	AL	43,758	C
Okla Christian Univ	OK	27,650	VC
Okla City Univ	OK	40,476	VC
Oral Roberts Univ	OK	34,316	C
Pfeiffer Univ	NC	39,695	LC
Simpson Univ	CA	33,700	C
Southern Adventist Univ	TN	27,600	C
Southwest Baptist Univ	MO	29,900	LC
Sterling College	KS	32,830	C
Texas Wesleyan Univ	TX	35,134	C
Thiel College	PA	41,590	C
Trinity Bible College	ND		
Union College	NE	23,270	C
Univ of Arizona	AZ	23,100	C
Univ of Calif at Riverside	CA	29,227	C+
Univ of Dayton	OH	53,620	C
Univ of Jamestown	ND	28,508	C
Univ of Northwestern - St. Paul	MN	38,160	C
Vanguard Univ of Southern Calif	CA	40,740	VC
Viterbo Univ	WI	34,660	C
Wayland Baptist Univ	TX	22,356	LC
West Virginia Wesleyan College	WV	36,858	C
Williams Baptist College	AR	24,720	C

RELIGIOUS MUSIC

School	ST	$IS	SR
Aquinas College - Mich	MI	38,876	HC
Baylor Univ	TX	53,760	HC
Belhaven Univ	MS	31,016	C
Bethel Univ	MN	45,270	VC
Calvin College	MI	41,570	VC+
Campbellsville Univ	KY	32,492	C
Centenary College of Louisiana	LA	45,650	C+
Charleston Southern Univ	SC	32,400	C
College of the Ozarks	MO	7,230	C
Columbia College	SC	36,550	C
Concordia College - New York	NY	39,035	LC
Concordia Univ St. Paul	MN	29,050	C
Concordia Univ Texas	TX	40,210	C
Concordia Univ Wisc	WI	35,910	C
Concordia Univ, Ann Arbor	MI	35,945	VC
Dallas Baptist Univ	TX	33,713	C
East Texas Baptist Univ	TX	33,134	C
Eastern Nazarene College	MA	39,955	C
Evangel Univ	MO	28,898	C
Franciscan Univ of Steubenville	OH	33,980	VC
Furman Univ	SC	58,092	VC+
Gardner-Webb Univ	NC	39,200	C+
Grove City College	PA	25,692	VC
Hannibal-LaGrange Univ	MO	29,815	C
Hardin-Simmons Univ	TX	33,966	C
Houghton College	NY	39,090	C
Houston Baptist Univ	TX	36,450	C
Huntington Univ	IN	33,996	C
Indiana Wesleyan Univ	IN	33,674	C
Johnson C. Smith Univ	NC	25,336	LC
Kentucky Christian Univ	KY	26,560	LC
Lee Univ	TN	22,045	C
Lenoir-Rhyne Univ	NC	43,200	C
Louisiana College	LA	21,886	C
Madonna Univ	MI	29,050	C
Malone Univ	OH	38,448	C
McKendree Univ	IL	37,940	C+
Milligan College	TN	38,150	C
Miss College	MS	25,850	C
Missouri Baptist Univ	MO	35,594	C
Mount Vernon Nazarene Univ	OH	34,500	C
North Central Univ	MN	26,400	C
Northwest Univ	WA	35,876	VC
Northwestern College of Iowa	IA	38,400	C+
Nyack College	NY	34,050	NC
Okla Wesleyan Univ	OK	33,206	C
Olivet Nazarene Univ	IL	41,840	C
Oral Roberts Univ	OK	34,316	C
Ouachita Baptist Univ	AR	32,320	C
Pfeiffer Univ	NC	39,695	LC
Samford Univ	AL	39,232	VC
Seton Hill Univ	PA	46,972	C
Shorter Univ	GA	31,130	LC
Southeastern Univ	FL	31,765	C
Southern Nazarene Univ	OK	32,798	NC
Southwest Baptist Univ	MO	29,900	LC
St. Olaf College	MN	54,260	HC+
Union Univ	TN	33,970	VC
Univ of Mobile	AL	28,935	C
Univ of the Cumberlands	KY	32,000	C
Valparaiso Univ	IN	48,370	C+
Warner Pacific College	OR	33,790	C
Warner Univ	FL	28,216	C
Wartburg College	IA	47,840	C
Wayland Baptist Univ	TX	22,356	LC
Westminster College	PA	39,180	C+
William Carey Univ	MS	23,950	LC
Williams Baptist College	AR	24,720	C

RELIGIOUS STUDIES

School	ST	$IS	SR
American Univ	DC	59,379	HC+
Aquinas College - Mich	MI	38,876	HC
Arizona State Univ at the Tempe Campus	AZ	21,756	VC
Ashland Univ	OH	21,440	C
Avila Univ	MO	35,480	C
Bates College	ME	64,500	MC
Beloit College	WI	55,206	HC
Biola Univ	CA	46,402	C+
Brown Univ	RI	64,566	MC
Bryn Athyn College	PA	31,470	C
Cabrini Univ	PA	42,591	LC
Cal State, Chico	CA	21,440	C
Cal State, Long Beach	CA	18,850	C
Cal State, Northridge	CA	16,859	LC
College of Charleston	SC	22,699	C
Concordia Univ, Ann Arbor	MI	35,945	VC
Cornell Univ	NY	64,853	MC
Dallas Baptist Univ	TX	33,713	C
Dordt College	IA	37,860	C+
Edgewood College	WI	35,950	C
Elon Univ	NC	44,599	VC+
Fairfield Univ	CT	59,860	VC+
Fontbonne Univ	MO	33,717	C
Georgian Court Univ	NJ	42,426	LC
Hardin-Simmons Univ	TX	33,966	C
Houghton College	NY	39,090	C
Indiana Univ Bloomington	IN	20,429	VC
Indiana Univ of Pennsylvania	PA	23,614	LC
Indiana Univ-Purdue Univ Indianapolis	IN	18,635	C
Kenyon College	OH	63,330	MC
King Univ	TN	34,660	C
Lebanon Valley College	PA	51,530	C
Madonna Univ	MI	29,050	C
Marian Univ	IN	41,220	C
McKendree Univ	IL	37,940	C+
MidAmerica Nazarene Univ	KS	35,550	C
New York Univ	NY	65,860	MC
Niagara Univ	NY	41,010	C
Okla Baptist Univ	OK	32,320	C
Old Dominion Univ	VA	20,910	C
Oregon State Univ	OR	22,519	VC
Pomona College	CA	64,957	MC
St. Joseph's Univ	PA	57,544	VC+
St. Martin's Univ	WA	45,056	C
San Diego State Univ	CA	21,896	C+
San Jose State Univ	CA	21,540	C
Stony Brook Univ/The SUNY	NY	21,881	MC
Syracuse Univ	NY	60,239	VC
The Univ of Utah	UT	17,924	VC
Univ of Arizona	AZ	23,100	C
Univ of Calif San Diego	CA	30,150	MC
Univ of Chicago	IL	67,584	MC
Univ of Colo Boulder	CO	24,285	VC+
Univ of Findlay	OH	60,139	C
Univ of Great Falls	MT	38,524	C
Univ of Miami	FL	63,494	MC
Univ of Nebr - Lincoln	NE	18,589	VC
Univ of N Car at Charlotte	NC	15,547	C
Univ of San Francisco	CA	58,484	VC
Univ of Wisc-Eau Claire	WI	15,797	VC
Univ of Wyoming	WY	15,375	C+
Ursinus College	PA	61,690	VC
Vanderbilt Univ	TN	60,572	MC
Viterbo Univ	WI	34,660	C
Washington State Univ	WA	22,495	C
Webster Univ	MO	37,490	C
Wheaton College	MA	61,512	VC
Wingate Univ	NC	39,950	C

RESORT MANAGEMENT

School	ST	$IS	SR
Ferris State Univ	MI	21,445	C

RESPIRATORY CARE

School	ST	$IS	SR
Stony Brook Univ/The SUNY	NY	21,881	MC

RESPIRATORY THERAPY

School	ST	$IS	SR
Armstrong State Univ	GA	16,962	C
Augusta Univ	GA	4,632	C
Ball State Univ	IN	19,590	C
Bellarmine Univ	KY	51,220	C
Boise State Univ	ID	14,860	C
Dakota State Univ	SD	13,811	C
Drury Univ	MO	33,791	VC
Gannon Univ	PA	42,032	C
Georgia State Univ	GA	24,332	VC
Gwynedd Mercy Univ	PA	43,780	LC
Indiana Univ Kokomo	IN	7,073	C
Indiana Univ of Pennsylvania	PA	23,614	LC
Indiana Univ-Purdue Univ Indianapolis	IN	18,635	C
Lewis Univ	IL	40,370	C
LIU Brooklyn	NY	49,682	C
Mansfield Univ	PA	23,376	LC
Marshall Univ	WV	17,242	C
Midwestern State Univ	TX	17,572	C
Millersville Univ of Pennsylvania	PA	23,782	C
Missouri Southern State Univ	MO	12,499	C
Missouri State Univ	MO	15,190	C+
Nebr Methodist College	NE	25,134	SP
N Dak State Univ	ND	16,245	C
Nova Southeastern Univ	FL	38,534	C+
Ohio State Univ at Columbus	OH	21,703	HC+
Point Park Univ	PA	41,270	C
Rhode Island College	RI	17,694	LC
Salisbury Univ	MD	20,714	VC
Samford Univ	AL	39,232	VC
Shenandoah Univ	VA	41,312	C
St. Catherine Univ	MN	45,630	VC
Stony Brook Univ/The SUNY	NY	21,881	MC
Tenn State Univ	TN	14,423	C
Texas Southern Univ	TX	18,212	LC
Texas State Univ	TX	19,350	C
The Univ of Akron	OH	21,477	C
Thomas Edison State Univ	NJ	6,350	NC
Univ of Alabama at Birmingham	AL	19,906	C
Univ of Cincinnati	OH	21,964	VC
Univ of Indianapolis	IN	36,480	C
Univ of Kansas	KS	20,135	C+
Univ of Mary	ND	23,180	C
Univ of Missouri/Columbia	MO	18,201	MC
Univ of N Car at Charlotte	NC	15,547	C
Univ of South Alabama	AL	16,400	C
Univ of Southern Indiana	IN	16,501	C
Univ of the Ozarks	AR	52,176	C
Washington Adventist Univ	MD	31,440	LC
Weber State Univ	UT	10,721	C
West Chester Univ of Pennsylvania	PA	18,456	C
Wheeling Jesuit Univ	WV	37,106	LC
York College of Pennsylvania	PA	29,240	C
Youngstown State Univ	OH	17,307	C

RETAILING

School	ST	$IS	SR
Bryant Univ	RI	55,646	VC
Central Mich Univ	MI	20,330	C
East Central Univ	OK	13,056	C
Johnson & Wales Univ/ Denver Campus	CO	42,707	C
Johnson & Wales Univ/ Providence Campus	RI	42,248	C
Marywood Univ	PA	46,900	C
Montclair State Univ	NJ	26,210	LC
Mount Ida College	MA	46,820	C
Ohio Univ	OH	22,924	C
Purdue Univ/West Lafayette	IN	20,032	MC
Simmons College	MA	53,090	VC
Southern New Hampshire Univ	NH	43,198	C
Syracuse Univ	NY	60,239	VC
Texas Tech Univ	TX	18,736	C+

ST = STATE **$IS** = IN-STATE COSTS **SR** = SELECTOR RATING

School	ST	$IS	SR
The Univ of Tenn at Knoxville	TN	22,112	VC
Univ of Arizona	AZ	23,100	C
Univ of Arkansas at Fayetteville	AR	19,152	C+
Univ of Minn/Twin Cities	MN	23,519	HC+
Univ of Pennsylvania	PA	63,526	MC
Univ of S Car at Columbia	SC	19,725	VC+
Univ of Wisc-Madison	WI	20,934	MC
Univ of Wisc-Stout	WI	19,667	C
Youngstown State Univ	OH	17,307	C

ROBOTIC & MECHATRONIC SYSTEMS ENGINEERING

School	ST	$IS	SR
Univ of Detroit Mercy	MI	48,816	C+

ROMANCE LANGUAGES AND LITERATURE

School	ST	$IS	SR
Boston College	MA	65,737	MC
Bowdoin College	ME	63,500	MC
Bowling Green State Univ	OH	19,747	C
Bryant Univ	RI	55,646	VC
Bryn Mawr College	PA	59,890	MC
Carleton College	MN	64,071	MC
CUNY/City College	NY	20,319	VC
Clark Univ	MA	51,600	HC+
Colo College	CO	62,560	MC
Dartmouth College	NH	66,174	MC
DePauw Univ	IN	58,688	HC+
Haverford College	PA	66,490	MC
Johns Hopkins Univ	MD	65,386	MC
Mount Holyoke College	MA	56,746	MC
New York Univ	NY	65,860	MC
Oberlin College	OH	66,012	MC
Pomona College	CA	64,957	MC
Queens Univ of Charlotte	NC	39,543	C
Rockford Univ	IL	36,030	C
St. Thomas Aquinas College	NY	42,200	C
SUNY SUNY Albany	NY	22,165	C
Truman State Univ	MO	16,014	HC
Univ of Chicago	IL	67,584	MC
Univ of Georgia	GA	21,250	HC
Univ of Maryland/College Park	MD	21,938	HC
Univ of Nevada, Las Vegas	NV	17,553	C
Univ of N Car at Chapel Hill	NC	20,052	HC+
Univ of Notre Dame	IN	64,043	MC
Univ of Oregon	OR	22,972	C
Univ of PR-Rio Piedras campus	PR	13,327	
Washington and Lee Univ	VA	59,647	MC
Washington Univ in St. Louis	MO	65,366	VC
Wayne State Univ	MI	22,016	C
Wesleyan Univ	CT	65,516	MC
Wheeling Jesuit Univ	WV	37,106	LC

RURAL ECONOMICS

School	ST	$IS	SR
Univ of Idaho	ID	15,348	C

RURAL SOCIOLOGY

School	ST	$IS	SR
Northland College	WI	41,103	C+
S Dak State Univ	SD	15,634	C
Univ of Missouri/Columbia	MO	18,201	MC
Univ of Wisc-Madison	WI	20,934	MC

RUSSIAN

School	ST	$IS	SR
American Univ	DC	59,379	HC+
Amherst College	MA		HC+
Arizona State Univ at the Tempe Campus	AZ	21,756	VC
Bard College	NY	64,024	HC
Barnard College/Columbia Univ	NY	62,741	MC
Bates College	ME	64,500	MC
Baylor Univ	TX	53,760	HC
Beloit College	WI	55,206	HC
Bowdoin College	ME	63,500	MC
Bowling Green State Univ	OH	19,747	C
Brigham Young Univ	UT	12,748	HC
Bryn Mawr College	PA	59,890	MC
Bucknell Univ	PA	64,616	MC
Cal State, Northridge	CA	16,859	LC
Carleton College	MN	64,071	MC
Central Washington Univ	WA	16,803	C
CUNY/Brooklyn College	NY	5,884	C+
CUNY/Hunter College	NY	31,098	VC
CUNY/Lehman College	NY	5,778	HC+
CUNY/Queens College	NY	27,896	C
Colgate Univ	NY	65,030	MC
College of the Holy Cross	MA	62,165	MC
Columbia Univ/City of New York	NY	62,958	MC
Cornell College	IA	48,800	VC
Dartmouth College	NH	66,174	MC
Dickinson College	PA	63,974	MC
Ferrum College	VA	39,650	C
Florida State Univ	FL	16,771	HC
George Washington Univ	DC	62,835	MC
Georgetown Univ	DC	65,926	MC
Goucher College	MD	55,716	VC
Grinnell College	IA	60,738	MC
Gustavus Adolphus College	MN	52,433	HC
Harvard College/Harvard Univ	MA	60,659	MC
Haverford College	PA	66,490	MC
Hofstra Univ	NY	55,960	C+
Indiana Univ Bloomington	IN	20,429	VC
Iowa State Univ	IA	17,570	C
Juniata College	PA	53,760	VC
La Salle Univ	PA	55,790	C
Lawrence Univ	WI	54,498	HC
Luther College	IA	48,540	C+
Macalester College	MN	61,905	MC
Miami Univ	OH	27,190	HC+
Mich State Univ	MI	23,898	VC+
Middlebury College	VT	64,332	MC
New York Univ	NY	65,860	MC
Northern Illinois Univ	IL	20,176	C
Oberlin College	OH	66,012	MC
Ohio State Univ at Columbus	OH	21,703	HC+
Ohio Univ	OH	22,924	C
Pomona College	CA	64,957	MC
Portland State Univ	OR	19,443	C
Purdue Univ/West Lafayette	IN	20,032	MC
Rider Univ	NJ	54,050	C
Rutgers Univ - New Brunswick	NJ	26,632	HC
San Diego State Univ	CA	21,896	C+
Sarah Lawrence College	NY	63,388	HC
Scripps College	CA	66,664	MC
Seattle Pacific Univ	WA	47,439	C+
Sewanee: The Univ of the South	TN	54,500	MC
Smith College	MA	63,914	MC
St. Olaf College	MN	54,260	HC+
Swarthmore College	PA	63,550	MC
Texas A&M Univ	TX	20,521	VC+
The Univ of Tenn at Knoxville	TN	22,112	VC
The Univ of Utah	UT	17,924	VC
Thomas Edison State Univ	NJ	6,350	NC
Trinity College	CT	63,920	HC+
Trinity Univ	TX	52,314	HC+
Truman State Univ	MO	16,014	HC
Tufts Univ	MA		MC
Tulane Univ	LA	63,396	HC+
Univ of Alabama	AL	24,320	C+
Univ of Alaska Fairbanks	AK	16,179	C
Univ of Arizona	AZ	23,100	C
Univ of Calif at Davis	CA	28,468	HC
Univ of Calif at Riverside	CA	29,227	C+
Univ of Calif San Diego	CA	30,150	MC
Univ of Chicago	IL	67,584	MC
Univ of Denver	CO	58,443	VC+
Univ of Florida	FL	16,291	HC+
Univ of Georgia	GA	21,250	HC
Univ of Hawaii at Manoa	HI	23,221	C
Univ of Illinois at Chicago	IL	25,006	VC
Univ of Iowa	IA	18,683	VC+
Univ of Kentucky	KY	33,306	C
Univ of Maryland/Baltimore County	MD	21,296	VC
Univ of Maryland/College Park	MD	21,938	HC
Univ of Mich/Ann Arbor	MI	24,410	MC
Univ of Minn/Twin Cities	MN	23,519	HC+
Univ of Missouri/Columbia	MO	18,201	MC
Univ of Montana	MT	14,105	C
Univ of Nebr - Lincoln	NE	18,589	VC
Univ of New Hampshire	NH	28,562	VC
Univ of New Mexico	NM	15,404	C
Univ of Notre Dame	IN	64,043	MC
Univ of Oregon	OR	22,972	C
Univ of Pennsylvania	PA	63,526	MC
Univ of Pittsburgh	PA	29,568	HC+
Univ of Rochester	NY	65,032	MC
Univ of S Car at Columbia	SC	19,725	VC+
Univ of South Florida/Tampa	FL	16,110	VC+
Univ of Southern Calif	CA	66,631	C
Univ of Texas at Arlington	TX	18,026	LC
Univ of Texas at Austin	TX	26,102	HC
Univ of Vermont	VT	28,878	HC
Univ of Wisc-Madison	WI	20,934	MC
Univ of Wyoming	WY	15,375	C+
Vanderbilt Univ	TN	60,572	MC
Wake Forest Univ	NC	64,056	MC
Washington State Univ	WA	22,495	C
Wellesley College	MA	63,916	MC
West Chester Univ of Pennsylvania	PA	18,456	C
Western Washington Univ	WA	18,003	C+
Wheaton College	MA	61,512	VC
Williams College	MA	63,290	MC
Yale Univ	CT	64,650	MC

RUSSIAN AND SLAVIC STUDIES

School	ST	$IS	SR
American Univ	DC	59,379	HC+
Augsburg College	MN	43,929	C
Bard College	NY	64,024	HC
Baylor Univ	TX	53,760	HC
Boston College	MA	65,737	MC
Brown Univ	RI	64,566	MC
Carnegie Mellon Univ	PA	67,980	MC
Colgate Univ	NY	65,030	MC
Colo College	CO	62,560	MC
Columbia Univ/City of New York	NY	62,958	MC
Conn College	CT	65,000	MC
Cornell College	IA	48,800	VC
Dartmouth College	NH	66,174	MC
DePauw Univ	IN	58,688	HC+
Eastern Mich Univ	MI	19,761	C
Emory Univ	GA	60,786	MC
Florida State Univ	FL	16,771	HC
George Mason Univ	VA	15,724	VC
Grand Valley State Univ	MI	22,250	C+
Hamilton College	NY	64,250	MC
Harvard College/Harvard Univ	MA	60,659	MC
Indiana Univ Bloomington	IN	20,429	VC
Lafayette College	PA	63,355	MC
Middlebury College	VT	64,332	MC
Mount Holyoke College	MA	56,746	MC
Muhlenberg College	PA	56,645	VC+
New York Univ	NY	65,860	MC
Oakland Univ	MI	20,763	C
Oberlin College	OH	66,012	MC
Pomona College	CA	64,957	MC
Purdue Univ/West Lafayette	IN	20,032	MC
Rhodes College	TN	51,900	HC
Rutgers Univ - New Brunswick	NJ	26,632	HC
San Diego State Univ	CA	21,896	C+
Sarah Lawrence College	NY	63,388	HC
Smith College	MA	63,914	MC
St. Olaf College	MN	54,260	HC+
Stetson Univ	FL	53,544	VC
Syracuse Univ	NY	60,239	VC
Texas Tech Univ	TX	18,736	C+
The College of Wooster	OH	57,900	VC+
Tufts Univ	MA		MC
Tulane Univ	LA	63,396	HC+
Univ of Calif at Los Angeles	CA	30,162	MC
Univ of Calif at Riverside	CA	29,227	C+
Univ of Calif San Diego	CA	30,150	MC
Univ of Illinois at Chicago	IL	25,006	VC
Univ of Illinois at Urbana-Champaign	IL	27,006	HC
Univ of Iowa	IA	18,683	VC+
Univ of Kansas	KS	20,135	C+
Univ of Maryland/College Park	MD	21,938	HC
Univ of Mass Amherst	MA	26,199	VC+
Univ of Mich/Ann Arbor	MI	24,410	MC
Univ of Minn/Twin Cities	MN	23,519	HC+
Univ of N Car at Chapel Hill	NC	20,052	HC+
Univ of Richmond	VA	60,880	MC
Univ of Rochester	NY	65,032	MC
Univ of Texas at Austin	TX	26,102	HC
Univ of Tulsa	OK	52,625	HC+
Univ of Vermont	VT	28,878	HC
Univ of Washington	WA	23,149	VC
Wesleyan Univ	CT	65,516	MC
West Chester Univ of Pennsylvania	PA	18,456	C
Yale Univ	CT	64,650	MC

RUSSIAN LANGUAGES AND LITERATURE

School	ST	$IS	SR
Boston Univ	MA	65,110	MC
Brandeis Univ	MA	65,925	MC
Brown Univ	RI	64,566	MC
Colby College	ME	64,060	MC
Emory Univ	GA	60,786	MC
Kent State Univ	OH	20,732	C
New College of Florida	FL	15,848	MC
Oberlin College	OH	66,012	MC
Okla State Univ	OK	17,180	VC
Pennsylvania State Univ - Univ Park	PA	29,760	HC
Reed College	OR	65,300	MC
St. Louis Univ	MO	49,866	HC
Stony Brook Univ/The SUNY	NY	21,881	MC
Syracuse Univ	NY	60,239	VC
The College of Wooster	OH	57,900	VC+
Univ of Calif at Los Angeles	CA	30,162	MC
Univ of Calif at Riverside	CA	29,227	C+
Univ of Colo Boulder	CO	24,285	VC+
Univ of Illinois at Chicago	IL	25,006	VC
Univ of Illinois at Urbana-Champaign	IL	27,006	HC
Univ of Mich/Ann Arbor	MI	24,410	MC
Univ of Okla	OK	18,911	VC
Univ of Wisc-Milwaukee	WI	21,496	C
Vassar College	NY	65,491	MC
Washington and Lee Univ	VA	59,647	MC
Wellesley College	MA	63,916	MC
West Chester Univ of Pennsylvania	PA	18,456	C
Wheaton College	MA	61,512	VC
Yale Univ	CT	64,650	MC

SAFETY AND SECURITY TECHNOLOGY

School	ST	$IS	SR
Davenport Univ	MI	25,896	LC
Embry-Riddle Aeronautical Univ - Worldwide	FL	17,480	C
Farmingdale State College	NY	20,624	C
Georgetown College	KY	41,440	C
Marshall Univ	WV	17,242	C
St. Louis Univ	MO	49,866	HC
Univ of Wisc-Whitewater	WI	13,976	C

SAFETY MANAGEMENT

School	ST	$IS	SR
Amridge Univ	AL	10,860	LC
CUNY/John Jay College of Criminal Justice	NY	6,359	NC
Concordia Univ, Ann Arbor	MI	35,945	VC
Embry-Riddle Aeronautical Univ - Worldwide	FL	17,480	C
Franklin Univ	OH	56,262	SP
Illinois State Univ	IL	23,418	VC
Indiana State Univ	IN	23,223	LC
Mansfield Univ	PA	23,376	LC
Marshall Univ	WV	17,242	C
Pittsburg State Univ	KS	13,880	NC
St. Louis Univ	MO	49,866	HC
S Dak State Univ	SD	15,634	C
Univ of Central Missouri	MO	18,982	C
Univ of Houston-Downtown	TX	7,241	C

SAFETY SCIENCE

School	ST	$IS	SR
Central Washington Univ	WA	16,803	C
Embry-Riddle Aeronautical Univ - Daytona Beach	FL	44,712	VC
Indiana Univ Bloomington	IN	20,429	VC
Indiana Univ of Pennsylvania	PA	23,614	LC
Virginia Commonwealth Univ	VA	23,049	C

SANSKRIT AND INDIAN STUDIES

School	ST	$IS	SR
Bard College	NY	64,024	HC
Brown Univ	RI	64,566	MC
Harvard College/Harvard Univ	MA	60,659	MC
Univ of Iowa	IA	18,683	VC+

SCANDINAVIAN LANGUAGES

School	ST	$IS	SR
Augsburg College	MN	43,929	C
Augustana College	IL	49,658	VC
Gustavus Adolphus College	MN	52,433	HC
North Park Univ	IL	35,860	C
Univ of Calif at Berkeley	CA	28,853	MC
Univ of Calif at Los Angeles	CA	30,162	MC
Univ of Minn/Twin Cities	MN	23,519	HC+
Univ of Texas at Austin	TX	26,102	HC
Univ of Washington	WA	23,149	VC

SCANDINAVIAN STUDIES

School	ST	$IS	SR
Augsburg College	MN	43,929	C
Concordia College - Moorhead	MN	51,088	C+
Minn State Univ, Mankato	MN	15,616	C
Pacific Lutheran Univ	WA	49,960	VC
Univ of Wisc-Madison	WI	20,934	MC
Univ of Wisc-Milwaukee	WI	21,496	C

SCENIC AND LIGHTING DESIGN

School	ST	$IS	SR
Boston Univ	MA	65,110	MC
Webster Univ	MO	37,490	C

SCHOOL PSYCHOLOGY

School	ST	$IS	SR
Adams State Univ	CO	17,703	LC
Calif Univ of Pennsylvania	PA	14,217	LC
Eastern Mich Univ	MI	19,761	C
Howard Univ	DC	37,616	C+
New York Univ	NY	65,860	MC
Radford Univ	VA	19,027	LC
Southwestern Okla State Univ	OK	11,790	C
Univ of Arizona	AZ	23,100	C

SCIENCE

School	ST	$IS	SR
Alfred Univ	NY	42,296	C+
Alvernia Univ	PA	43,900	C
Alverno College	WI	33,294	LC
American International College	MA	46,300	LC
Arcadia Univ	PA	33,570	C+
Bennington College	VT	63,960	MC
Black Hills State Univ	SD	15,899	C
Bowling Green State Univ	OH	19,747	C
Buena Vista Univ	IA	41,514	C
Caribbean Univ	PR	15,471	
Cedar Crest College	PA	46,715	C
Central Mich Univ	MI	20,330	C
Cheyney Univ of Pennsylvania	PA	20,896	LC
Coe College	IA	51,570	VC
Colo Christian Univ	CO	39,940	VC
Concordia Univ, Ann Arbor	MI	35,945	VC
Dallas Baptist Univ	TX	33,713	C
Drexel Univ	PA	65,432	VC+
East Stroudsburg Univ	PA	18,334	C
Eastern Mich Univ	MI	19,761	C
Eastern Nazarene College	MA	39,955	C
Fairleigh Dickinson Univ/Metropolitan Campus	NJ	40,254	C
Fordham Univ	NY	65,918	MC
Fort Hays State Univ	KS	12,131	C
Gannon Univ	PA	42,032	C
Grace College and Seminary	IN	31,524	C
Graceland Univ	IA	35,290	C
Grand Valley State Univ	MI	22,250	C+
Grinnell College	IA	60,738	MC
Hampshire College	MA	63,824	MC

School	ST	$IS	SR
Hawaii Pacific Univ	HI	33,420	C
Heritage Univ	WA	19,825	NC
Houghton College	NY	39,090	C
Indiana Wesleyan Univ	IN	33,674	C
Johnson C. Smith Univ	NC	25,336	LC
Keene State College	NH	24,003	LC
King's College	PA	46,858	C
La Salle Univ	PA	55,790	C
Le Moyne College	NY	46,000	C
Lee Univ	TN	22,045	C
LeMoyne-Owen College	TN	16,980	C
Lyndon State College	VT	20,714	C
Madonna Univ	MI	29,050	C
Marygrove College	MI	28,926	NC
Marylhurst Univ	OR	20,295	NC
Maryville Univ of St. Louis	MO	38,046	VC+
Marywood Univ	PA	46,900	C
Mayville State Univ	ND	18,371	NC
Middle Tenn State Univ	TN	8,650	C
Miss State Univ	MS	11,454	C+
Missouri Southern State Univ	MO	12,499	C
Montana Tech of the Univ of Montana	MT	15,447	C+
Mount Aloysius College	PA	29,976	C
Mount St. Mary College	NY	42,061	C
National Louis Univ	IL	16,920	LC
Northern Kentucky Univ	KY	16,486	C
Northwest Missouri State Univ	MO	17,737	C
Okla City Univ	OK	40,476	VC
Okla Wesleyan Univ	OK	33,206	C
Penn State Erie/The Behrend College	PA	16,256	C
Penn State Univ/Altoona	PA	24,584	C
Piedmont College	GA	32,512	C
Pitzer College	CA	66,192	MC
Pomona College	CA	64,957	MC
Purdue Univ/West Lafayette	IN	20,032	MC
Rochester Inst of Technology	NY	50,842	HC
Rockford Univ	IL	36,030	C
Rutgers Univ - Camden	NJ	26,146	C
Samford Univ	AL	39,232	VC
Seattle Univ	WA	50,811	VC+
Sierra Nevada College	NV	43,482	C
Southern Nazarene Univ	OK	32,798	NC
Southern Oregon Univ	OR	19,117	C
St. John's College, Santa Fe	NM	60,109	HC+
SUNY / Empire State College	NY	9,145	SP
The Lincoln Univ	PA	15,154	NC
Tiffin Univ	OH	31,380	C
Trevecca Nazarene Univ	TN	31,186	C
Troy Univ	AL	16,171	C
Tulane Univ	LA	63,396	HC+
Union College	NE	23,270	C
Union College	NY	64,320	MC
United States Air Force Academy	CO		C
United States Naval Academy	MD		MC
Univ of Alabama in Huntsville	AL	19,445	VC
Univ of Denver	CO	58,443	VC+
Univ of Findlay	OH	60,139	C
Univ of Great Falls	MT	38,524	C
Univ of Mass Amherst	MA	26,199	VC+
Univ of Mich/Dearborn	MI	11,757	VC
Univ of Mich-Flint	MI	17,607	C+
Univ of Nebr - Lincoln	NE	18,589	VC
Univ of N Dak	ND	15,373	C
Univ of Notre Dame	IN	64,043	MC
Univ of Oregon	OR	22,972	C
Univ of Texas at El Paso	TX	34,452	NC
Univ of Wisc-Parkside	WI	15,193	C
Univ of Wisc-River Falls	WI	14,485	C
Univ of Wisc-Stout	WI	19,667	C
Upper Iowa Univ	IA	34,990	NC
Urbana Univ	OH	30,820	C
Valley City State Univ	ND	13,267	C
Villanova Univ	PA	62,523	MC
Virginia Commonwealth Univ	VA	23,049	C
Walsh Univ	OH	39,010	C
Washburn Univ	KS	15,827	C
Washington State Univ	WA	22,495	C
Wayland Baptist Univ	TX	22,356	LC
West Virginia Univ	WV	18,210	C
Western New Mexico Univ	NM	16,734	LC
Westfield State Univ	MA	19,671	C
Widener Univ	PA	56,486	C
Wilberforce Univ	OH	19,016	C
Willamette Univ	OR	61,817	VC+
William Woods Univ	MO	32,040	C

SCIENCE AND MANAGEMENT

School	ST	$IS	SR
Claremont McKenna College	CA	67,185	MC
George Mason Univ	VA	15,724	VC
Philadelphia Univ	PA	50,370	C
Pitzer College	CA	66,192	MC
Scripps College	CA	66,664	MC
Texas A&M Univ at Galveston	TX	15,920	C
Univ of St. Francis	IN	37,400	C

SCIENCE AND SOCIETY

School	ST	$IS	SR
Bard College	NY	64,024	HC
Brown Univ	RI	64,566	MC
Butler Univ	IN	51,352	VC
CUNY/College of Staten Island	NY	17,840	NC
Northwestern Univ	IL	66,344	MC
Ramapo College of New Jersey	NJ	25,338	C
Rutgers Univ - Newark	NJ	27,288	C
Univ of Puget Sound	WA	56,456	VC+
Vassar College	NY	65,491	MC
Wesleyan Univ	CT	65,516	MC

SCIENCE AND TECHNOLOGY STUDIES

School	ST	$IS	SR
Cornell Univ	NY	64,853	MC
Georgia Inst of Technology	GA	23,360	MC
Kean Univ	NJ	24,650	C
Oglala Lakota College	SD	15,050	NC

SCIENCE EDUCATION

School	ST	$IS	SR
Adams State Univ	CO	17,703	LC
Alabama A&M Univ	AL	18,796	C
Albany State Univ	GA	19,462	C
Alfred Univ	NY	42,296	C+
Alverno College	WI	33,294	LC
American International College	MA	46,300	LC
Anderson Univ	IN	38,200	C
Andrews Univ	MI	28,030	C+
Appalachian State Univ	NC	14,416	VC
Aquinas College - Mich	MI	38,876	HC
Arkansas State Univ	AR	16,190	C
Arkansas Tech Univ	AR	15,484	C
Asbury Univ	KY	35,180	C+
Ashland Univ	OH	21,440	C
Auburn Univ	AL	23,594	VC+
Baldwin Wallace Univ	OH	41,106	C
Ball State Univ	IN	19,590	C
Bayamon Central Univ	PR	12,490	
Baylor Univ	TX	53,760	HC
Bemidji State Univ	MN	16,056	VC
Bennett College	NC	27,302	NC
Bethany College	KS	46,100	NC
Bethany College	WV	36,300	NC
Bethel College	IN	35,860	C
Bethel Univ	MN	45,270	VC
Bethune-Cookman Univ	FL	22,970	C
Black Hills State Univ	SD	15,899	C
Blackburn College	IL	28,526	LC
Bloomfield College	NJ	39,100	LC
Blue Mountain College	MS	15,949	VC
Boston Univ	MA	65,110	MC
Bowie State Univ	MD	26,728	LC
Bowling Green State Univ	OH	19,747	C
Brigham Young Univ	UT	12,748	HC
Brigham Young Univ/Hawaii	HI	11,290	C
Bryan College	TN	31,440	C
Buena Vista Univ	IA	41,514	C
Cal State, Long Beach	CA	18,850	C
Calvin College	MI	41,570	VC+
Canisius College	NY	47,537	C
Caribbean Univ	PR	15,471	
Carroll Univ	WI	38,100	C+
Carson-Newman Univ	TN	34,160	C
Catawba College	NC	39,820	C
Cedarville Univ	OH	34,990	VC
Central Washington Univ	WA	16,803	C
Chadron State College	NE	14,819	NC
Charleston Southern Univ	SC	32,400	C
CUNY/Brooklyn College	NY	5,884	C+
CUNY/Hunter College	NY	31,098	VC
CUNY/Lehman College	NY	5,778	HC+
Colo State Univ	CO	22,162	VC
Concord Univ	WV	14,954	C
Concordia Univ Nebr	NE	36,280	VC
Concordia Univ St. Paul	MN	29,050	C
Concordia Univ, Chicago	IL	39,694	C
Converse College	SC	26,495	C
Corban Univ	OR	40,306	C
Covenant College	GA	38,990	VC
Daemen College	NY	38,045	C
Dallas Baptist Univ	TX	33,713	C
Defiance College	OH	41,630	C
Delaware State Univ	DE	19,376	NC
Dickinson State Univ	ND	12,372	LC
Dominican College	NY	31,270	LC
Dordt College	IA	37,860	C+
East Carolina Univ	NC	16,937	C
East Texas Baptist Univ	TX	33,134	C
Eastern Illinois Univ	IL	21,126	C
Eastern Mich Univ	MI	19,761	C
Eastern Nazarene College	MA	39,955	C
Eastern Washington Univ	WA	25,572	LC
Edinboro Univ	PA	15,940	LC
Elizabethtown College	PA	54,050	C
Elmira College	NY	53,900	C
Elms College	MA	45,646	VC
Elon Univ	NC	44,599	VC+
Eureka College	IL	30,220	C
Evangel Univ	MO	28,898	C
Fairmont State Univ	WV	15,726	C
Faulkner Univ	AL	26,410	C
Florida A&M Univ	FL	15,361	C
Florida Inst of Technology	FL	53,306	VC
Florida International Univ	FL	19,854	C+
Florida State Univ	FL	16,771	HC
Franklin College	IN	39,380	C
Freed-Hardeman Univ	TN	29,450	C
Fresno Pacific Univ	CA	37,370	C
Friends Univ	KS	34,455	C
Gettysburg College	PA	63,000	HC
Glenville State College	WV	17,386	NC
Goshen College	IN	42,500	C
Grace College and Seminary	IN	31,524	C
Grand Rapids Theological Seminary/Cornerstone Univ	MI	33,338	C
Grand Valley State Univ	MI	22,250	C+
Greensboro College	NC	42,400	LC
Greenville College	IL	27,012	C
Gustavus Adolphus College	MN	52,433	HC
Gwynedd Mercy Univ	PA	43,780	LC
Hamline Univ	MN	45,678	VC
Hardin-Simmons Univ	TX	33,966	C
Hastings College	NE	35,380	C+
Heidelberg Univ	OH	39,200	C
Heritage Univ	WA	19,825	NC
Hofstra Univ	NY	55,960	C+
Holy Family Univ	PA	43,326	LC
Hood College	MD	54,840	C
Hope College	MI	39,940	VC
Houghton College	NY	39,090	C
Humboldt State Univ	CA	20,514	C
Huntington Univ	IN	33,996	C
Husson Univ	ME	25,720	LC
Illinois College	IL	40,850	VC
Indiana State Univ	IN	23,223	LC
Indiana Univ-Purdue Univ Fort Wayne	IN	17,553	C
Indiana Wesleyan Univ	IN	33,674	C
Inter-American Univ of PR-San Germán	PR	20,042	
Johnson State College	VT	20,752	C
Judson College	AL	27,066	C
Judson Univ	IL	37,700	C
Juniata College	PA	53,760	VC
Keene State College	NH	24,003	LC
Kent State Univ	OH	20,732	C
King's College	PA	46,858	C
Kutztown Univ of Pennsylvania	PA	19,056	LC
La Salle Univ	PA	55,790	C
Lamar Univ	TX	18,014	LC
Langston Univ	OK	14,314	C
Le Moyne College	NY	46,000	C
Lenoir-Rhyne Univ	NC	43,200	C
LeTourneau Univ	TX	38,250	VC
Lincoln Memorial Univ	TN	28,070	C
Lindenwood Univ	MO	25,132	C
LIU Brooklyn	NY	49,682	C
Livingstone College	NC	17,815	LC
Lock Haven Univ of Pennsylvania	PA	18,028	LC
Louisiana College	LA	21,886	C
Loyola Univ Chicago	IL	55,802	VC
Lyndon State College	VT	20,714	C
MacMurray College	IL	33,620	C
Malone Univ	OH	38,448	C
Manhattan College	NY	51,750	C+
Marian Univ	WI	32,420	LC
Mars Hill Univ	NC	42,688	C
Maryville College	TN	44,410	C
Marywood Univ	PA	46,900	C
Mayville State Univ	ND	18,371	NC
Mercyhurst Univ	PA	47,420	C
Messiah College	PA	43,100	C+
Miami Univ	OH	27,190	HC+
MidAmerica Nazarene Univ	KS	35,550	C
Midland Univ	NE	37,468	
Miles College	AL	18,646	NC
Millersville Univ of Pennsylvania	PA	23,782	C
Minn State Univ, Mankato	MN	15,616	C
Minn State Univ, Moorhead	MN	15,941	C
Minot State Univ	ND	12,732	C
Miss Valley State Univ	MS	13,233	LC
Missouri Southern State Univ	MO	12,499	C
Missouri State Univ	MO	15,190	C+
Monmouth Univ	NJ	46,234	C
Montana State Univ-Billings	MT	22,960	C
Montana State Univ-Northern	MT	11,370	NC
Morningside College	IA	36,865	C
Morris College	SC	18,500	LC
Mount Aloysius College	PA	29,976	C
Mount Mary Univ	WI	34,650	LC
Mount Vernon Nazarene Univ	OH	34,500	C
Muskingum Univ	OH	35,966	C
Nebr Wesleyan Univ	NE	38,140	C+
New Mexico Highlands Univ	NM	11,904	NC
New York Univ	NY	65,860	MC
Niagara Univ	NY	41,010	C
N Car State Univ	NC	19,515	HC+
Northeastern State Univ	OK	8,615	VC
Northern Mich Univ	MI	19,604	C
Northern State Univ	SD	14,505	C
Northwest Missouri State Univ	MO	17,737	C
Northwestern College of Iowa	IA	38,400	C+
Northwestern Okla State Univ	OK	13,072	NC
Notre Dame of Maryland Univ	MD	46,465	VC
Nova Southeastern Univ	FL	38,534	C+
Oakland City Univ	IN	33,360	NC
Oakwood Univ	AL	43,758	C
Ohio Univ	OH	22,924	C
Ohio Valley Univ	WV	29,480	C
Ohio Wesleyan Univ	OH	49,460	VC
Okla Baptist Univ	OK	32,320	C
Okla Christian Univ	OK	27,650	VC
Okla Wesleyan Univ	OK	33,206	C
Old Dominion Univ	VA	20,910	C
Olivet Nazarene Univ	IL	41,840	C
Oral Roberts Univ	OK	34,316	C
Ouachita Baptist Univ	AR	32,320	C
Palm Beach Atlantic Univ	FL	39,720	C
Peru State College	NE	14,768	NC
Pfeiffer Univ	NC	39,695	LC
Piedmont College	GA	32,512	C
Plymouth State Univ	NH	23,180	LC
Pontifical Catholic Univ of PR	PR	10,534	
Purdue Univ/Northwest	IN	15,038	C
Purdue Univ/West Lafayette	IN	20,032	MC
Rhode Island College	RI	17,694	LC
Rider Univ	NJ	54,050	C
Rocky Mountain College	MT	34,270	C
Rowan Univ	NJ	24,491	VC+
Rust College	MS	10,600	C
Saginaw Valley State Univ	MI	18,530	C
St. Augustine's Univ	NC	26,048	C
St. Louis Univ	MO	49,866	HC
St. Mary-of-the-Woods College	IN	39,632	LC
St. Michael's College	VT	51,725	VC+
St. Vincent College	PA	44,626	C
St. Xavier Univ	IL	43,310	C
Salem State Univ	MA	17,303	LC
Schreiner Univ	TX	34,626	LC
Seattle Pacific Univ	WA	47,439	C+
Seton Hill Univ	PA	46,972	C
Shaw Univ	NC	24,638	C
Shepherd Univ, West Virginia	WV	17,224	C
Siena Heights Univ	MI	32,040	C
Slippery Rock Univ of Pennsylvania	PA	10,360	C
Southeast Missouri State Univ	MO	15,498	C
Southeastern Okla State Univ	OK	11,875	C
Southern Arkansas Univ	AR	21,532	C
Southern Conn State Univ	CT	21,924	LC
Southern Illinois Univ Edwardsville	IL	22,643	C
Southern Nazarene Univ	OK	32,798	NC
Southern Univ at New Orleans	LA	8,014	LC
Southwest Minn State Univ	MN	17,783	C
Southwestern Okla State Univ	OK	11,790	C
Springfield College	MA	45,995	C
St. Cloud State Univ	MN	10,600	C
St. Edward's Univ	TX	53,100	VC
St. John Fisher College	NY	43,620	C
St. Mary's Univ	TX	37,500	C
St. Thomas Aquinas College	NY	42,200	C
SUNY / Buffalo State College	NY	20,842	C
SUNY / SUNY College at Old Westbury	NY	16,860	C
SUNY / SUNY Fredonia	NY	20,818	C
SUNY / SUNY Oneonta	NY	19,712	C+
SUNY / SUNY Potsdam	NY	20,404	C+
SUNY at New Paltz	NY	19,200	C
Suffolk Univ	MA	50,308	C
Taylor Univ	IN	40,317	C+
Texas A&M Univ at Commerce	TX	10,496	C
The College of New Jersey	NJ	31,909	HC
The College of St. Rose	NY	43,048	C
Toccoa Falls College	GA	27,920	C
Tougaloo College	MS	17,980	NC
Trevecca Nazarene Univ	TN	31,186	C
Trine Univ	IN	41,310	C
Troy Univ	AL	16,171	C
Union College	KY	32,310	C
Universidad del Turabo	PR	17,828	
Univ of Arizona	AZ	23,100	C
Univ of Arkansas at Pine Bluff	AR	13,541	C
Univ of Calif San Diego	CA	30,150	MC
Univ of Central Arkansas	AR	14,472	VC
Univ of Central Florida	FL	15,922	VC
Univ of Central Missouri	MO	18,982	C
Univ of Central Okla	OK	13,486	C
Univ of Charleston	WV	35,000	C
Univ of Cincinnati	OH	21,964	VC
Univ of Conn	CT	25,538	HC
Univ of Delaware	DE	24,976	VC+
Univ of Evansville	IN	44,186	VC+
Univ of Georgia	GA	21,250	HC
Univ of Great Falls	MT	38,524	C
Univ of Idaho	ID	15,348	C
Univ of Illinois at Urbana-Champaign	IL	27,006	HC
Univ of Indianapolis	IN	36,480	C
Univ of Iowa	IA	18,683	VC+
Univ of Kentucky	KY	33,306	C
Univ of Louisiana at Lafayette	LA	14,516	C
Univ of Louisville	KY	19,824	C
Univ of Mary Hardin-Baylor	TX	33,950	C+
Univ of Maryland/Eastern Shore	MD	17,013	C
Univ of Mich/Dearborn	MI	11,757	VC
Univ of Minn/Duluth	MN	20,292	C+
Univ of Minn/Twin Cities	MN	23,519	HC+
Univ of Miss	MS	17,746	C+
Univ of Missouri/Columbia	MO	18,201	MC

ST = STATE $IS = IN-STATE COSTS SR = SELECTOR RATING

School	ST	$IS	SR
Univ of Montana	MT	14,105	C
Univ of Montana-Western	MT	11,220	LC
Univ of Nebr - Kearney	NE	16,546	LC
Univ of Nebr - Lincoln	NE	18,589	VC
Univ of North Alabama	AL	15,398	C
Univ of N Car at Greensboro	NC	14,690	C
Univ of N Car at Pembroke	NC	14,388	LC
Univ of North Florida	FL	15,996	VC
Univ of North Georgia	GA	17,316	C
Univ of Northern Colo	CO	20,851	C
Univ of Notre Dame	IN	64,043	MC
Univ of Okla	OK	18,911	VC
Univ of Pittsburgh at Bradford	PA	22,402	C
Univ of Pittsburgh at Johnstown	PA	22,092	C
Univ of Rio Grande & Rio Grande Community College	OH	8,750	NC
Univ of Sioux Falls	SD	34,330	C
Univ of South Florida/Tampa	FL	16,110	VC+
Univ of Southern Indiana	IN	16,501	C
Univ of Southern Miss	MS	13,170	C
Univ of the Cumberlands	KY	32,000	C
Univ of Toledo	OH	19,336	NC
Univ of Vermont	VT	28,878	HC
Univ of West Alabama	AL	15,516	NC
Univ of Wisc-Eau Claire	WI	15,797	VC
Univ of Wisc-La Crosse	WI	15,247	C+
Univ of Wisc-Oshkosh	WI	15,200	C
Univ of Wisc-Stout	WI	19,667	C
Univ of Wisc-Superior	WI	14,446	C
Univ of Wisc-Whitewater	WI	13,976	C
Utah State Univ	UT	12,736	C
Valparaiso Univ	IN	48,370	C+
Vanguard Univ of Southern Calif	CA	40,740	VC
Virginia Polytechnic Inst and State Univ	VA	21,276	HC
Viterbo Univ	WI	34,660	C
Warner Univ	FL	28,216	C
Wartburg College	IA	47,840	C
Washington State Univ	WA	22,495	C
Washington Univ in St. Louis	MO	65,366	VC
Wayne State College	NE	12,802	C
Wayne State Univ	MI	22,016	C
Weber State Univ	UT	10,721	C
West Chester Univ of Pennsylvania	PA	18,456	C
West Liberty Univ	WV	15,512	C
West Texas A&M Univ	TX	13,478	C
Western Carolina Univ	NC	13,965	C
Western New Mexico Univ	NM	16,734	LC
Western State Colo Univ	CO	18,639	C
Western Washington Univ	WA	18,003	C+
Wheelock College	MA	49,225	C
Whitworth Univ	WA	51,732	VC
Widener Univ	PA	56,486	C
William Penn Univ	IA	26,000	C
Wilmington College	OH	34,600	C
Winona State Univ	MN	17,535	C
Wittenberg Univ	OH	48,156	C+
Wright State Univ	OH	16,983	C
Xavier Univ	OH	47,880	C+
Xavier Univ of Louisiana	LA	31,689	C+
York College	NE	24,300	C
York College of Pennsylvania	PA	29,240	C
Youngstown State Univ	OH	17,307	C

SCIENCE OF EARTH SYSTEMS

School	ST	$IS	SR
Bryant Univ	RI	55,646	VC
Cornell Univ	NY	64,853	MC
Univ of Illinois at Chicago	IL	25,006	VC

SCIENCE OF NATURAL AND ENVIRONMENTAL SYSTEMS

School	ST	$IS	SR
Bryant Univ	RI	55,646	VC
Cornell Univ	NY	64,853	MC

SCIENCE TECHNOLOGY

School	ST	$IS	SR
Arizona State Univ at the Polytechnic Campus	AZ	21,360	VC
Colby College	ME	64,060	MC
James Madison Univ	VA	19,084	VC
Lehigh Univ	PA	61,010	MC
Marshall Univ	WV	17,242	C
Mass Inst of Technology	MA	62,662	MC
Missouri Southern State Univ	MO	12,499	C
Pennsylvania State Univ - Univ Park	PA	29,760	HC
Rensselaer Polytechnic Inst	NY	63,436	MC
Scripps College	CA	66,664	MC
Stevens Inst of Technology	NJ	62,338	MC
Univ of Pennsylvania	PA	63,526	MC

SCIENTIFIC/MEDICAL MARKETING

School	ST	$IS	SR
Carlow Univ	PA	38,549	LC

SCULPTURE

School	ST	$IS	SR
Adams State Univ	CO	17,703	LC
Aquinas College - Mich	MI	38,876	HC
Art Academy of Cincinnati	OH	36,252	SP
Bennington College	VT	63,960	MC
Boston Univ	MA	65,110	MC
Calif College of the Arts	CA	52,758	SP
Cal State, San Bernardino	CA	12,000	C
Cleveland Inst of Art	OH	51,439	C+
College for Creative Studies	MI	48,875	SP
Colo State Univ	CO	22,162	VC
Escuela de Artes Plasticas de PR	PR	11,236	
Ferris State Univ	MI	21,445	C
Howard Univ	DC	37,616	C+
Indiana Univ Bloomington	IN	20,429	VC
Indiana Univ-Purdue Univ Fort Wayne	IN	17,553	C
Kansas City Art Inst	MO	44,308	C+
Kutztown Univ of Pennsylvania	PA	19,056	LC
Maine College of Art	ME	43,794	SP
Marshall Univ	WV	17,242	C
Maryland Inst College of Art	MD	56,795	SP
Marywood Univ	PA	46,900	C
Mass College of Art and Design	MA	24,800	SP
Milwaukee Inst of Art and Design	WI	44,960	SP
Minneapolis College of Art and Design	MN	44,238	SP
Montserrat College of Art	MA	38,150	SP
Moore College of Art and Design	PA	50,135	SP
Ohio Univ	OH	22,924	C
Pacific Northwest College of Art	OR	38,494	SP
Rhode Island School of Design	RI	59,960	SP
Rochester Inst of Technology	NY	50,842	HC
San Francisco Art Inst	CA	58,505	SP
Santa Fe Univ of Art and Design	NM	39,980	SP
Savannah College of Art and Design	GA	49,595	C
School of the Art Inst of Chicago	IL	56,230	SP
SUNY / Buffalo State College	NY	20,842	C
SUNY at Binghamton	NY	22,861	MC
SUNY at New Paltz	NY	19,200	C
SUNY SUNY Albany	NY	22,165	C
Syracuse Univ	NY	60,239	VC
Temple Univ	PA	24,392	VC
Texas Christian Univ	TX	54,670	HC
Univ of Dallas	TX	45,500	VC+
Univ of Hartford	CT	49,776	C
Univ of Illinois at Chicago	IL	25,006	VC
Univ of Illinois at Urbana-Champaign	IL	27,006	HC
Univ of Iowa	IA	18,683	VC+
Univ of Kansas	KS	20,135	C+
Univ of Mass Dartmouth	MA	25,658	C
Univ of Miami	FL	63,494	MC
Univ of Mich/Ann Arbor	MI	24,410	MC
Univ of Oregon	OR	22,972	C
Univ of the Arts	PA	56,579	SP
Univ of Washington	WA	23,149	VC
Virginia Commonwealth Univ	VA	23,049	C
Washington Univ in St. Louis	MO	65,366	VC
Webster Univ	MO	37,490	C
Western Washington Univ	WA	18,003	C+

SECONDARY EDUCATION

School	ST	$IS	SR
Abilene Christian Univ	TX	41,800	C+
Adams State Univ	CO	17,703	LC
Adrian College	MI	42,400	C
Alabama A&M Univ	AL	18,796	C
Alabama State Univ	AL	14,142	NC
Albright College	PA	46,660	C
Alderson Broaddus Univ	WV	26,149	C
Alfred Univ	NY	42,296	C+
Alice Lloyd College	KY	8,190	C
Alma College	MI	47,548	C
Alvernia Univ	PA	43,900	C
Alverno College	WI	33,294	LC
American International College	MA	46,300	LC
American Univ	DC	59,379	HC+
Andrews Univ	MI	28,030	C+
Appalachian State Univ	NC	14,416	VC
Aquinas College	TN	30,800	C+
Aquinas College - Mich	MI	38,876	HC
Arcadia Univ	PA	33,570	C+
Arizona State Univ at the Polytechnic Campus	AZ	21,360	VC
Arizona State Univ at the Tempe Campus	AZ	21,756	VC
Arizona State Univ at the West Campus	AZ	20,640	C
Armstrong State Univ	GA	16,962	C
Asbury Univ	KY	35,180	C+
Ashland Univ	OH	21,440	C
Auburn Univ	AL	23,594	VC+
Auburn Univ at Montgomery	AL	15,290	C
Augsburg College	MN	43,929	C
Augustana College	IL	49,658	VC
Aurora Univ	IL	33,970	C
Averett Univ	VA	40,970	LC
Baker Univ	KS	33,350	C+
Bayamon Central Univ	PR	12,490	
Baylor Univ	TX	53,760	HC
Bemidji State Univ	MN	16,056	VC
Benedictine College	KS	36,200	VC
Bennington College	VT	63,960	MC
Bethany College	KS	46,100	NC
Bethany College	WV	36,300	NC
Bethel College	IN	35,860	C
Bethel Univ	MN	45,270	VC
Birmingham-Southern College	AL	44,478	VC
Blackburn College	IL	28,526	LC
Bloomfield College	NJ	39,100	LC
Bloomsburg Univ of Pennsylvania	PA	19,066	LC
Bluefield College	VA	34,120	C+
Boise State Univ	ID	14,860	C
Boston College	MA	65,737	MC
Bowling Green State Univ	OH	19,747	C
Briar Cliff Univ	IA	36,956	C
Buena Vista Univ	IA	41,514	C
Butler Univ	IN	51,352	VC
Cabrini Univ	PA	42,591	LC
Calif Univ of Pennsylvania	PA	14,217	LC
Calumet College of St. Joseph	IN	22,735	C
Calvin College	MI	41,570	VC+
Capital Univ	OH	42,982	C
Cardinal Stritch Univ	WI	36,462	C
Caribbean Univ	PR	15,471	
Carlow Univ	PA	38,549	LC
Carroll College	MT	39,972	C+
Carson-Newman Univ	TN	34,160	C
Carthage College	WI	48,835	C
Centenary College	NJ	43,602	C
Central State Univ	OH	18,564	C
Central Washington Univ	WA	16,803	C
Chadron State College	NE	14,819	NC
Chaminade Univ of Honolulu	HI	36,000	C
Champlain College	VT	53,132	C+
Chicago State Univ	IL	20,144	C
CUNY/Brooklyn College	NY	5,884	C+
CUNY/City College	NY	20,319	VC
CUNY/College of Staten Island	NY	17,840	NC
CUNY/Hunter College	NY	31,098	VC
CUNY/Lehman College	NY	5,778	HC+
CUNY/Queens College	NY	27,896	C
Clarion Univ of Pennsylvania	PA	21,608	LC
Clarke Univ	IA	38,940	C
Clemson Univ	SC		HC
Cleveland State Univ	OH	22,196	C
Coe College	IA	51,570	VC
College of Charleston	SC	22,699	C
College of St Joseph	VT	32,400	LC
College of the Ozarks	MO	7,230	C
Colo Christian Univ	CO	39,940	VC
Columbia College - Missouri	MO	27,803	C
Columbus State Univ	GA	14,336	LC
Concord Univ	WV	14,954	C
Concordia College - Moorhead	MN	51,088	C+
Concordia Univ	OR	35,000	C
Concordia Univ Nebr	NE	36,280	VC
Concordia Univ St. Paul	MN	29,050	C
Concordia Univ Texas	TX	40,210	C
Concordia Univ Wisc	WI	35,910	C
Concordia Univ, Ann Arbor	MI	35,945	VC
Concordia Univ, Chicago	IL	39,694	C
Converse College	SC	26,495	C
Cornell College	IA	48,800	VC
Cumberland Univ	TN	27,710	C
Dakota State Univ	SD	13,811	C
Dallas Baptist Univ	TX	33,713	C
Defiance College	OH	41,630	C
Delaware Valley Univ	PA	49,796	C
DePaul Univ	IL	47,623	VC
Dickinson State Univ	ND	12,372	LC
Dominican College	NY	31,270	LC
Dominican Univ	IL	41,222	C
Dordt College	IA	37,860	C+
Drake Univ	IA	45,056	HC
Drury Univ	MO	33,791	VC
East Texas Baptist Univ	TX	33,134	C
Eastern Kentucky Univ	KY	16,908	C
Eastern Mennonite Univ	VA	42,550	C
Eastern Mich Univ	MI	19,761	C
Eastern Washington Univ	WA	25,572	LC
Edinboro Univ	PA	15,940	LC
Elizabethtown College	PA	54,050	C
Elmhurst College	IL	45,428	C
Elmira College	NY	53,900	C
Elms College	MA	45,646	VC
Elon Univ	NC	44,599	VC+
Emmanuel College	MA	52,110	C+
Emporia State Univ	KS	14,570	C
Eureka College	IL	30,220	C
Evangel Univ	MO	28,898	C
Fairmont State Univ	WV	15,726	C
Fayetteville State Univ	NC	17,756	C
Felician Univ	NJ	45,370	LC
Fitchburg State Univ	MA	21,819	C
Florida Gulf Coast Univ	FL	9,682	C
Florida Memorial Univ	FL	22,270	LC
Fontbonne Univ	MO	33,717	C
Fort Valley State Univ	GA	17,988	VC
Franklin College	IN	39,380	C
Franklin Pierce Univ	NH	46,750	C
Freed-Hardeman Univ	TN	29,450	C
Friends Univ	KS	34,455	C
Gallaudet Univ	DC	29,118	LC
Gardner-Webb Univ	NC	39,200	C+
Georgetown College	KY	41,440	C
Gettysburg College	PA	63,000	HC
Glenville State College	WV	17,386	NC
Goddard College	VT	17,040	VC
Gordon College	MA	46,472	C+
Goshen College	IN	42,500	C
Grace Bible College	MI	25,250	C
Grambling State Univ	LA	15,701	C
Grand Canyon Univ	AZ	16,950	VC
Grand Rapids Theological Seminary/Cornerstone Univ	MI	33,338	C
Grand Valley State Univ	MI	22,250	C+
Grand View Univ	IA	32,302	C
Green Mountain College	VT	45,228	LC
Greensboro College	NC	42,400	LC
Gustavus Adolphus College	MN	52,433	HC
Gwynedd Mercy Univ	PA	43,780	LC
Hamline Univ	MN	45,678	VC
Hannibal-LaGrange Univ	MO	29,815	C
Harding Univ	AR	25,421	C
Hardin-Simmons Univ	TX	33,966	C
Harris-Stowe State Univ	MO	14,360	NC
Hastings College	NE	35,380	C+
Heidelberg Univ	OH	39,200	C
Heritage Univ	WA	19,825	NC
Hofstra Univ	NY	55,960	C+
Holy Family Univ	PA	43,326	LC
Hood College	MD	54,840	C
Hope College	MI	39,940	VC
Hope International Univ	CA	41,150	C
Houghton College	NY	39,090	C
Houston Baptist Univ	TX	36,450	C
Howard Payne Univ	TX	34,320	C
Howard Univ	DC	37,616	C+
Humboldt State Univ	CA	20,514	C
Huntington Univ	IN	33,996	C
Idaho State Univ	ID	13,619	NC
Illinois College	IL	40,850	VC
Indiana State Univ	IN	23,223	LC
Indiana Univ Bloomington	IN	20,429	VC
Indiana Univ East	IN	7,072	C
Indiana Univ Kokomo	IN	7,073	C
Indiana Univ Northwest	IN	7,072	C
Indiana Univ South Bend	IN	14,242	C
Indiana Univ Southeast	IN	14,242	LC
Indiana Univ-Purdue Univ Fort Wayne	IN	17,553	C
Indiana Wesleyan Univ	IN	33,674	C
Inter-American Univ of PR Ponce	PR	19,549	
Inter-American Univ of PR-Aguadilla Campus	PR	21,657	
Inter-American Univ of PR-Arecibo Campus	PR	18,245	
Inter-American Univ of PR-Barranquitas	PR	18,336	
Inter-American Univ of PR-Fajardo Campus	PR	18,336	
Inter-American Univ of PR-Metropolitan Campus	PR	20,045	
Inter-American Univ of PR-San Germán	PR	20,042	
Iowa State Univ	IA	17,570	C
Iowa Wesleyan Univ	IA	39,200	C
Ithaca College	NY	56,766	VC
Jacksonville State Univ	AL	14,628	LC
Jarvis Christian College	TX	20,160	NC
John Carroll Univ	OH	49,740	C+
Johnson State College	VT	20,752	C
Judson Univ	IL	37,700	C
Juniata College	PA	53,760	VC
Kansas State Univ	KS	17,780	VC
Kansas Wesleyan Univ	KS	36,600	C
Kean Univ	NJ	24,650	C
Keene State College	NH	24,003	LC
Kentucky State Univ	KY	13,364	LC
Kentucky Wesleyan College	KY	32,080	C
Keuka College	NY	39,762	C
King's College	PA	46,858	C
Knox College	IL	52,615	VC+
Kutztown Univ of Pennsylvania	PA	19,056	LC
La Salle Univ	PA	55,790	C
La Sierra Univ	CA	39,690	VC
Lakeland Univ	WI	35,130	C
Lamar Univ	TX	18,014	LC
Lasell College	MA	47,500	C
Le Moyne College	NY	46,000	C
Lenoir-Rhyne Univ	NC	43,200	C
LeTourneau Univ	TX	38,250	VC
Lewis Univ	IL	40,370	C
Lewis-Clark State College	ID	14,202	C
Lincoln Memorial Univ	TN	28,070	C
Lindenwood Univ	MO	25,132	C
Lindsey Wilson College	KY	32,882	C
LIU Brooklyn	NY	49,682	C
Livingstone College	NC	17,815	LC
Lock Haven Univ of Pennsylvania	PA	18,028	LC
Louisiana College	LA	21,886	C
Louisiana State Univ in Shreveport	LA	6,902	C
Louisiana Tech Univ	LA	11,422	VC
Loyola Univ Chicago	IL	55,802	VC
Lubbock Christian Univ	TX	28,426	C
MacMurray College	IL	33,620	C
Madonna Univ	MI	29,050	C
Malone Univ	OH	38,448	C

ST = STATE　**$IS** = IN-STATE COSTS　**SR** = SELECTOR RATING

School	ST	$IS	SR
Manchester Univ	IN	40,422	C
Manhattan College	NY	51,750	C+
Mansfield Univ	PA	23,376	LC
Marian Univ	IN	41,220	C
Marian Univ	WI	32,420	LC
Marquette Univ	WI	48,390	VC+
Marshall Univ	WV	17,242	C
Maryville College	TN	44,410	C
Maryville Univ of St. Louis	MO	38,046	VC+
Marywood Univ	PA	46,900	C
Mass College of Liberal Arts	MA	20,128	C
Mayville State Univ	ND	18,371	NC
McMurry Univ	TX	34,259	LC
McPherson College	KS	34,909	C
Mercer Univ	GA	45,348	VC
Mercyhurst Univ	PA	47,420	C
Merrimack College	MA	52,770	C
Messiah College	PA	43,100	C+
Methodist Univ	NC	43,600	C
Miami Univ	OH	27,190	HC+
Mich Tech Univ	MI	24,739	VC+
Midland Univ	NE	37,468	
Miles College	AL	18,646	NC
Millikin Univ	IL	42,158	C
Minn State Univ, Mankato	MN	15,616	C
Miss State Univ	MS	11,454	C+
Missouri Baptist Univ	MO	35,594	C
Missouri Univ of Science and Technology	MO	18,655	HC
Missouri Western State Univ	MO	16,741	
Monmouth College	IL	42,260	C
Monmouth Univ	NJ	46,234	C
Montana State Univ	MT	15,500	C+
Montana State Univ-Billings	MT	22,960	C
Montana State Univ-Northern	MT	11,370	NC
Moravian College	PA	53,117	
Mount Aloysius College	PA	29,976	C
Mount Marty College	SD	32,972	C
Mount Mercy Univ	IA	36,826	C
Muskingum Univ	OH	35,966	C
New England College	NH	50,364	C
New Jersey City Univ	NJ	21,456	LC
New Mexico State Univ	NM	14,050	C
New York Univ	NY	65,860	MC
Newman Univ	KS	35,390	C
Niagara Univ	NY	41,010	C
Nicholls State Univ	LA	10,534	C
N Car State Univ	NC	19,515	HC+
North Central College	IL	48,712	VC
N Dak State Univ	ND	16,245	C
North Park Univ	IL	35,860	C
Northeastern Illinois Univ	IL	12,529	LC
Northeastern State Univ	OK	8,615	VC
Northern Arizona Univ	AZ	20,246	VC
Northern Kentucky Univ	KY	16,486	C
Northern Mich Univ	MI	19,604	C
Northern State Univ	SD	14,505	C
Northland College	WI	41,103	C+
Northwest Missouri State Univ	MO	17,737	C
Northwest Nazarene Univ	ID	36,000	C
Northwest Univ	WA	35,876	VC
Northwestern College of Iowa	IA	38,400	C+
Northwestern Okla State Univ	OK	13,072	NC
Northwestern Univ	IL	66,344	MC
Notre Dame College	OH	37,150	VC
Notre Dame of Maryland Univ	MD	46,465	VC
Nova Southeastern Univ	FL	38,534	C+
Nyack College	NY	34,050	NC
Oakland City Univ	IN	33,360	NC
Oglala Lakota College	SD	15,050	NC
Okla Baptist Univ	OK	32,320	C
Okla City Univ	OK	40,476	VC
Okla State Univ	OK	17,180	VC
Okla Wesleyan Univ	OK	33,206	C
Old Dominion Univ	VA	20,910	C
Olivet College	MI	36,110	LC
Ouachita Baptist Univ	AR	32,320	C
Pacific Lutheran Univ	WA	49,960	VC
Paine College	GA	19,506	LC
Palm Beach Atlantic Univ	FL	39,720	C
Pennsylvania State Univ - Univ Park	PA	29,760	HC
Pepperdine Univ	CA	74,460	HC+
Peru State College	NE	14,768	NC
Pfeiffer Univ	NC	39,695	LC
Piedmont College	GA	32,512	C
Pittsburg State Univ	KS	13,880	NC
Point Park Univ	PA	41,270	C
Pontifical Catholic Univ of PR	PR	10,534	
Prescott College	AZ	33,284	C
Providence College	RI	60,760	VC
Purdue Univ/Northwest	IN	15,038	C
Purdue Univ/West Lafayette	IN	20,032	MC
Quinnipiac Univ	CT	59,110	C
Rhode Island College	RI	17,694	LC
Rider Univ	NJ	54,050	C
Ripon College	WI	46,911	C+
Rivier Univ	NH	40,410	VC
Roberts Wesleyan College	NY	38,306	C
Rockhurst Univ	MO	29,220	C
Roger Williams Univ	RI	46,296	C+
Roosevelt Univ	IL	40,651	VC
Rosemont College	PA	30,980	C
Rust College	MS	10,600	C
St. Anselm College	NH	52,560	C+
St. Francis Univ	PA	42,268	NC
St. Leo Univ	FL	31,650	C
St. Louis Univ	MO	49,866	HC
St. Mary's Univ of Minn	MN	41,210	VC
St. Michael's College	VT	51,725	VC+
St. Peter's Univ	NJ	49,192	C
St. Xavier Univ	IL	43,310	C
Salem International Univ	WV	21,090	LC
Salem State Univ	MA	17,303	LC
Salve Regina Univ	RI	51,470	C
Samford Univ	AL	39,232	VC
Schreiner Univ	TX	34,626	LC
Seattle Pacific Univ	WA	47,439	C+
Seton Hall Univ	NJ	55,514	C
Seton Hill Univ	PA	46,972	C
Shaw Univ	NC	24,638	C
Shepherd Univ, West Virginia	WV	17,224	C
Shippensburg Univ of Pennsylvania	PA	23,208	C
Silver Lake College of the Holy Family	WI	36,290	LC
Simmons College	MA	53,090	VC
Simpson College	IA	43,839	VC
Simpson Univ	CA	33,700	C
Slippery Rock Univ of Pennsylvania	PA	10,360	C
S Dak State Univ	SD	15,634	C
Southeastern Okla State Univ	OK	11,875	C
Southeastern Univ	FL	31,765	C
Southern Conn State Univ	CT	21,924	LC
Southern New Hampshire Univ	NH	43,198	C
Southern Univ and A&M College	LA	16,074	LC+
Southern Univ at New Orleans	LA	8,014	LC
Southwest Baptist Univ	MO	29,900	LC
Southwestern Adventist Univ	TX	27,756	LC
Southwestern College	KS	31,531	C
Southwestern College	KS	31,531	C
Southwestern Okla State Univ	OK	11,790	C
Spalding Univ	KY	31,938	SP
Spring Hill College	AL	48,488	C
Springfield College	MA	45,995	C
St. Ambrose Univ	IA	39,019	C
St. Ambrose Univ	IA	39,019	C
St. Catherine Univ	MN	45,630	VC
St. Cloud State Univ	MN	10,600	C
St. Francis College	NY	38,800	LC
St. John Fisher College	NY	43,620	C
St. John's Univ	NY	55,850	C
St. Joseph's College, New York/Brooklyn Campus	NY	25,114	LC
St. Joseph's College, New York/Long Island Campus	NY	25,124	C
St. Mary's Univ	TX	37,500	C
St. Thomas Aquinas College	NY	42,200	C
St. Thomas Univ	FL	36,360	LC
SUNY / Buffalo State College	NY	20,842	C
SUNY / SUNY College at Old Westbury	NY	16,860	C
SUNY / SUNY Cortland	NY	20,706	VC
SUNY / SUNY Fredonia	NY	20,818	C
SUNY / SUNY Oneonta	NY	19,712	C+
SUNY at New Paltz	NY	19,200	C
SUNY at Oswego	NY	21,351	C
Tabor College	KS	35,870	C
Taylor Univ	IN	40,317	C+
Temple Univ	PA	24,392	VC
Tenn Tech Univ	TN	17,050	C
Texas A&M Univ	TX	20,521	VC+
Texas A&M Univ at Commerce	TX	10,496	C
Texas A&M Univ at Kingsville	TX	7,500	LC
Texas Christian Univ	TX	54,670	HC
The Catholic Univ of America	DC	56,356	VC
The Citadel, The Military College of S Car	SC	35,339	C
The Master's Univ	CA	43,870	C+
The Univ of Tenn at Chattanooga	TN	16,744	C
The Univ of Tenn at Martin	TN	14,876	C
Thiel College	PA	41,590	C
Thomas More College	KY	36,720	C
Thomas Univ	GA	21,420	LC
Trevecca Nazarene Univ	TN	31,186	C
Trine Univ	IN	41,310	C
Trinity International Univ	IL	31,070	VC
Troy Univ	AL	16,171	C
Tuskegee Univ	AL	28,164	C
Union College	KY	32,310	C
Union College	NE	23,270	C
Union Univ	TN	33,970	VC
Unity College	ME	37,670	C
Universidad Adventista de las Antillas	PR	16,606	
Universidad del Turabo	PR	17,828	
Universidad Metropolitana	PR	17,828	
Univ of Alabama	AL	24,320	C+
Univ of Alabama at Birmingham	AL	19,906	C
Univ of Alaska Fairbanks	AK	16,179	C
Univ of Arizona	AZ	23,100	C
Univ of Arkansas at Little Rock	AR	18,211	C
Univ of Central Arkansas	AR	14,472	VC
Univ of Central Missouri	MO	18,982	C
Univ of Central Okla	OK	13,486	C
Univ of Cincinnati	OH	21,964	VC
Univ of Dayton	OH	53,620	C
Univ of Delaware	DE	24,976	VC+
Univ of Detroit Mercy	MI	48,816	C+
Univ of Findlay	OH	60,139	C
Univ of Great Falls	MT	38,524	C
Univ of Hartford	CT	49,776	C
Univ of Hawaii at Manoa	HI	23,221	C
Univ of Holy Cross	LA	21,523	C
Univ of Idaho	ID	15,348	C
Univ of Illinois at Chicago	IL	25,006	VC
Univ of Illinois at Urbana-Champaign	IL	27,006	HC
Univ of Indianapolis	IN	36,480	C
Univ of Iowa	IA	18,683	VC+
Univ of Kansas	KS	20,135	C+
Univ of Kentucky	KY	33,306	C
Univ of Louisiana at Lafayette	LA	14,516	C
Univ of Louisiana at Monroe	LA	15,970	C
Univ of Louisville	KY	19,824	C
Univ of Maine	ME	20,792	C
Univ of Maine at Farmington	ME	18,187	C
Univ of Maine at Fort Kent	ME	15,165	LC
Univ of Maine at Presque Isle	ME	14,870	C
Univ of Mary Hardin-Baylor	TX	33,950	C+
Univ of Maryland/College Park	MD	21,938	HC
Univ of Maryland/Eastern Shore	MD	17,013	C
Univ of Mich/Dearborn	MI	11,757	VC
Univ of Mich-Flint	MI	17,607	C+
Univ of Minn/Duluth	MN	20,292	C+
Univ of Minn/Morris	MN	20,760	VC
Univ of Missouri/Columbia	MO	18,201	MC
Univ of Missouri-Kansas City	MO	19,563	VC
Univ of Missouri-St. Louis	MO		C
Univ of Montana	MT	14,105	C
Univ of Montana-Western	MT	11,220	LC
Univ of Mount Olive	NC	18,426	C
Univ of Nebr - Kearney	NE	16,546	LC
Univ of Nebr - Lincoln	NE	18,589	VC
Univ of Nebr - Omaha	NE	16,120	C
Univ of Nevada, Las Vegas	NV	17,553	C
Univ of Nevada/Reno	NV	18,010	C
Univ of New England	ME	48,880	C
Univ of New Mexico	NM	15,404	C
Univ of New Orleans	LA	12,840	C
Univ of North Alabama	AL	15,398	C
Univ of N Car at Wilmington	NC	14,590	VC
Univ of North Florida	FL	15,996	VC
Univ of North Georgia	GA	17,316	C
Univ of Pikeville	KY	28,700	NC
Univ of Pittsburgh at Johnstown	PA	22,092	C
Univ of Portland	OR	52,152	VC
Univ of PR, at Cayey	PR		
Univ of PR-Rio Piedras campus	PR	13,327	
Univ of Rhode Island	RI	24,906	C
Univ of Rio Grande & Rio Grande Community College	OH	8,750	NC
Univ of San Francisco	CA	58,484	VC
Univ of Scranton	PA	54,962	VC
Univ of Sioux Falls	SD	34,330	C
Univ of South Alabama	AL	16,400	C
Univ of S Car Aiken	SC	16,712	C
Univ of S Car Upstate	SC	18,200	LC
Univ of S Dak	SD	16,109	C
Univ of Southern Indiana	IN	16,501	C
Univ of Southern Miss	MS	13,170	C
Univ of St. Francis	IL	39,924	C
Univ of Tampa	FL	36,944	C
Univ of the Incarnate Word	TX	39,162	LC
Univ of the Southwest	NM	22,766	C
Univ of Toledo	OH	19,336	NC
Univ of Vermont	VT	28,878	HC
Univ of West Alabama	AL	15,516	NC
Univ of West Florida	FL	15,848	C
Univ of Wisc-Green Bay	WI	15,064	C
Univ of Wisc-La Crosse	WI	15,247	C+
Univ of Wisc-Madison	WI	20,934	MC
Univ of Wisc-Oshkosh	WI	15,200	C
Univ of Wisc-Platteville	WI	14,614	VC
Univ of Wisc-River Falls	WI	14,485	C
Univ of Wisc-Superior	WI	14,446	C
Univ of Wisc-Whitewater	WI	13,976	C
Univ of Wyoming	WY	15,375	C+
Urbana Univ	OH	30,820	C
Ursuline College	OH	41,076	LC
Utah State Univ	UT	12,736	C
Valparaiso Univ	IN	48,370	C+
Vanderbilt Univ	TN	60,572	MC
Vanguard Univ of Southern Calif	CA	40,740	VC
Villanova Univ	PA	62,523	MC
Virginia Polytechnic Inst and State Univ	VA	21,276	HC
Virginia Union Univ	VA	22,421	C
Virginia Wesleyan College	VA	43,728	LC
Wagner College	NY	55,480	C+
Walsh Univ	OH	39,010	C
Wartburg College	IA	47,840	C
Washburn Univ	KS	15,827	C
Washington State Univ	WA	22,495	C
Washington Univ in St. Louis	MO	65,366	VC
Wayne State Univ	MI	22,016	C
Weber State Univ	UT	10,721	C
Webster Univ	MO	37,490	C
Wellesley College	MA	63,916	MC
West Chester Univ of Pennsylvania	PA	18,456	C
West Liberty Univ	WV	15,512	C
West Virginia State Univ	WV	8,378	NC
West Virginia Wesleyan College	WV	36,858	C
Western Carolina Univ	NC	13,965	C
Western Conn State Univ	CT	21,254	LC
Western Mich Univ	MI	21,054	C
Western New England Univ	MA	48,088	C
Western New Mexico Univ	NM	16,734	LC
Western State Colo Univ	CO	18,639	C
Western Washington Univ	WA	18,003	C+
Westminster College	MO	32,820	C
Westminster College	PA	39,180	C+
Wheaton College	IL	43,610	MC
Wheaton College	MA	61,512	VC
Whitworth Univ	WA	51,732	VC
Wichita State Univ	KS	21,643	C
Wiley College	TX	18,504	C
William Jewell College	MO	41,210	C+
William Penn Univ	IA	26,000	C
Williams Baptist College	AR	24,720	C
Wilmington College	OH	34,600	C
Wilson College	PA	35,620	C
Winona State Univ	MN	17,535	C
Winthrop Univ	SC	23,082	C
Wisc Lutheran College	WI	36,290	VC
Wittenberg Univ	OH	48,156	C+
Wright State Univ	OH	16,983	C
York College	NE	24,300	C
York College of Pennsylvania	PA	29,240	C
Youngstown State Univ	OH	17,307	C

SECRETARIAL STUDIES/OFFICE MANAGEMENT

School	ST	$IS	SR
Caribbean Univ	PR	15,471	
Dordt College	IA	37,860	C+
Inter-American Univ of PR Ponce	PR	19,549	
Inter-American Univ of PR-Aguadilla Campus	PR	21,657	
Inter-American Univ of PR-Barranquitas	PR	18,336	
Inter-American Univ of PR-Bayamon	PR	18,785	
Inter-American Univ of PR-Fajardo Campus	PR	18,336	
Inter-American Univ of PR-Metropolitan Campus	PR	20,045	
Inter-American Univ of PR-San Germán	PR	20,042	
Johnson & Wales Univ/Providence Campus	RI	42,248	C
Southeastern Okla State Univ	OK	11,875	C
Southern Univ at New Orleans	LA	8,014	LC
Universidad del Turabo	PR	17,828	
Univ of PR, at Arecibo	PR	12,652	
Univ of PR, at Cayey	PR		
Univ of PR, at Humacao	PR	14,000	
Univ of PR-Rio Piedras campus	PR	13,327	
Univ of the Sacred Heart	PR	17,932	

SLAVIC LANGUAGES

School	ST	$IS	SR
Columbia Univ/ School of General Studies	NY	61,470	MC
Duke Univ	NC	64,188	
Indiana Univ Bloomington	IN	20,429	VC
New York Univ	NY	65,860	MC
Northwestern Univ	IL	66,344	MC
Princeton Univ	NJ	57,610	MC
Stanford Univ	CA	60,409	MC
Univ of Calif at Berkeley	CA	28,853	MC
Univ of Calif at Santa Barbara	CA	29,091	HC
Univ of Chicago	IL	67,584	MC
Univ of Illinois at Chicago	IL	25,006	VC
Univ of Kansas	KS	20,135	C+
Univ of Pittsburgh	PA	29,568	HC+
Univ of Texas at Austin	TX	26,102	HC
Univ of Virginia	VA	25,891	MC
Univ of Washington	WA	23,149	VC
Wayne State Univ	MI	22,016	C
Yale Univ	CT	64,650	MC

SMALL BUSINESS MANAGEMENT

School	ST	$IS	SR
Adams State Univ	CO	17,703	LC
Bay Path Univ	MA	45,349	C
Cal State, Chico	CA	21,440	C
Cal State, San Bernardino	CA	12,000	C
Calvin College	MI	41,570	VC+
Carroll Univ	WI	38,100	C+
Concord Univ	WV	14,954	C
Florida Atlantic Univ	FL	17,339	C
Florida State Univ	FL	16,771	HC
Hawaii Pacific Univ	HI	33,420	C
Huntington Univ	IN	33,996	C
Johnson & Wales Univ/Denver Campus	CO	42,707	C
Johnson & Wales Univ/Providence Campus	RI	42,248	C

School	ST	$IS	SR
Johnson State College	VT	20,752	C
Mount Aloysius College	PA	29,976	C
Mount Ida College	MA	46,820	C
Northern Arizona Univ	AZ	20,246	VC
Rowan Univ	NJ	24,491	VC+
Stetson Univ	FL	53,544	VC
Tusculum College	TN	31,625	C
Union College	NE	23,270	C
Univ of Maine at Machias	ME	22,960	C
Univ of Montana	MT	14,105	C
Univ of Montana-Western	MT	11,220	LC

SOCIAL FOUNDATIONS

School	ST	$IS	SR
Amridge Univ	AL	10,860	LC
Eastern Mich Univ	MI	19,761	C

SOCIAL PSYCHOLOGY

School	ST	$IS	SR
Bennington College	VT	63,960	MC
Clarion Univ of Pennsylvania	PA	21,608	LC
Florida Atlantic Univ	FL	17,339	C
Goddard College	VT	17,040	VC
Northwest Missouri State Univ	MO	17,737	C
Park Univ	MO	20,329	C
Univ of Calif at Irvine	CA	26,484	VC
Univ of Holy Cross	LA	21,523	C

SOCIAL SCIENCE

School	ST	$IS	SR
Adelphi Univ	NY	48,244	C
Anna Maria College	MA	48,186	C
Aquinas College - Mich	MI	38,876	HC
Arizona State Univ at the West Campus	AZ	20,640	C
Ashford Univ	CA	10,480	C
Ashland Univ	OH	21,440	C
Azusa Pacific Univ	CA	43,972	C
Ball State Univ	IN	19,590	C
Bellevue Univ	NE	20,300	NC
Bemidji State Univ	MN	16,056	VC
Benedict College	SC	28,238	NC
Benedictine College	KS	36,200	VC
Benedictine Univ	IL	38,300	C
Bennington College	VT	63,960	MC
Bethany College	KS	46,100	NC
Biola Univ	CA	46,402	C+
Black Hills State Univ	SD	15,899	C
Bluefield State College	WV	5,832	LC
Bluffton Univ	OH	40,950	C
Boise State Univ	ID	14,860	C
Bowling Green State Univ	OH	19,747	C
Brewton-Parker College	GA	23,490	C
Bryant Univ	RI	55,646	VC
Calif Baptist Univ	CA	41,392	C
Calif Lutheran Univ	CA	52,853	C
Cal State, Chico	CA	21,440	C
Cal State, Fresno	CA	16,902	LC
Cal State, Los Angeles	CA	17,186	LC
Cal State, Monterey Bay	CA	26,871	LC
Cal State, Sacramento	CA	20,332	C
Cal State, San Bernardino	CA	12,000	C
Cal State, San Marcos	CA	24,184	LC
Cal State, Stanislaus	CA	16,212	C
Calif Univ of Pennsylvania	PA	14,217	LC
Canisius College	NY	47,537	C
Cardinal Stritch Univ	WI	36,462	C
Caribbean Univ	PR	15,471	
Carnegie Mellon Univ	PA	67,980	MC
Carroll College	MT	39,972	C+
Carson-Newman Univ	TN	34,160	C
Carthage College	WI	48,835	C
Castleton Univ	VT	20,186	C
Cazenovia College	NY	46,470	C
Central Conn State Univ	CT	21,203	C
Central Mich Univ	MI	20,330	C
Central Washington Univ	WA	16,803	C
Chadron State College	NE	14,819	NC
Charleston Southern Univ	SC	32,400	C
Cheyney Univ of Pennsylvania	PA	20,896	LC
CUNY/Hunter College	NY	31,098	VC
Clarion Univ of Pennsylvania	PA	21,608	LC
Cleveland State Univ	OH	22,196	C
Colgate Univ	NY	65,030	MC
College of St. Benedict	MN	52,806	C
College of St. Mary	NE	35,184	C
College of the Ozarks	MO	7,230	C
Colo Christian Univ	CO	39,940	VC
Colo Mesa Univ	CO	18,955	LC
Colo State Univ-Pueblo	CO	18,234	C
Concord Univ	WV	14,954	C
Concordia Univ Wisc	WI	35,910	C
Concordia Univ, Ann Arbor	MI	35,945	VC
Concordia Univ, Chicago	IL	39,694	C
Coppin State Univ	MD	17,041	VC
Corban Univ	OR	40,306	C
Covenant College	GA	38,990	VC
Cumberland Univ	TN	27,710	C
Delta State Univ	MS	13,176	C
DePaul Univ	IL	47,623	VC
Dominican College	NY	31,270	LC
Dominican Univ	IL	41,222	C
Dordt College	IA	37,860	C+
Eastern Conn State Univ	CT	23,059	C
Eastern Mennonite Univ	VA	42,550	C
Eastern Washington Univ	WA	25,572	LC
Edinboro Univ	PA	15,940	LC
Elizabeth City State Univ	NC	14,745	C
Emporia State Univ	KS	14,570	C
Eureka College	IL	30,220	C
Evangel Univ	MO	28,898	C
Faulkner Univ	AL	26,410	C
Fayetteville State Univ	NC	17,756	C
Felician Univ	NJ	45,370	LC
Florida A&M Univ	FL	15,361	C
Florida Atlantic Univ	FL	17,339	C
Florida State Univ	FL	16,771	HC
Fordham Univ	NY	65,918	MC
Fresno Pacific Univ	CA	37,370	C
Frostburg State Univ	MD	17,280	LC
Gardner-Webb Univ	NC	39,200	C+
George Fox Univ	OR	42,938	C
Goddard College	VT	17,040	VC
Graceland Univ	IA	35,290	C
Grand Valley State Univ	MI	22,250	C+
Gustavus Adolphus College	MN	52,433	HC
Hamline Univ	MN	45,678	VC
Harding Univ	AR	25,421	C
Harvard College/Harvard Univ	MA	60,659	MC
Hastings College	NE	35,380	C+
Hawaii Pacific Univ	HI	33,420	C
Heidelberg Univ	OH	39,200	C
Hope International Univ	CA	41,150	C
Humboldt State Univ	CA	20,514	C
Illinois State Univ	IL	23,418	VC
Indiana Univ of Pennsylvania	PA	23,614	LC
Indiana Univ-Purdue Univ Fort Wayne	IN	17,553	C
James Madison Univ	VA	19,084	VC
Johns Hopkins Univ	MD	65,386	MC
Johnson C. Smith Univ	NC	25,336	LC
Juniata College	PA	53,760	VC
Kansas State Univ	KS	17,780	VC
Keystone College	PA	28,680	LC
Lake Erie College	OH	38,914	LC
Lamar Univ	TX	18,014	LC
Langston Univ	OK	14,314	C
LeMoyne-Owen College	TN	16,980	C
Lesley Univ	MA	41,550	C
Lewis-Clark State College	ID	14,202	C
Liberty Univ	VA	19,101	C
Lincoln Memorial Univ	TN	28,070	C
Lindsey Wilson College	KY	32,882	C
LIU Brooklyn	NY	49,682	C
LIU Post	NY	49,682	C
Lock Haven Univ of Pennsylvania	PA	18,028	LC
Loyola Univ New Orleans	LA	51,708	VC+
Lyndon State College	VT	20,714	C
Marquette Univ	WI	48,390	VC+
Marygrove College	MI	28,926	NC
Marylhurst Univ	OR	20,295	NC
Maryville College	TN	44,410	C
Marywood Univ	PA	46,900	C
Mayville State Univ	ND	18,371	NC
McKendree Univ	IL	37,940	C+
Medaille College	NY	35,112	C
Mercer Univ	GA	45,348	VC
Metropolitan State Univ	MN	7,566	C
Mich State Univ	MI	23,898	VC+
Mich Tech Univ	MI	24,739	VC+
Midland Univ	NE	37,468	
Minot State Univ	ND	12,732	C
Miss Univ for Women	MS	17,065	C
Missouri Baptist Univ	MO	35,594	C
Montana State Univ-Northern	MT	11,370	NC
Moravian College	PA	53,117	
Morehead State Univ	KY	17,422	C
Mount Marty College	SD	32,972	C
Mount St. Mary College	NY	42,061	C
Mount St. Mary's Univ - Chalon Campus	CA	43,897	VC+
Muskingum Univ	OH	35,966	C
National Louis Univ	IL	16,920	LC
Nazareth College	NY	45,574	C
New College of Florida	FL	15,848	MC
New York Univ	NY	65,860	MC
Niagara Univ	NY	41,010	C
N Car State Univ	NC	19,515	HC+
North Central College	IL	48,712	VC
N Dak State Univ	ND	16,245	C
Northeastern State Univ	OK	8,615	VC
Northern Kentucky Univ	KY	16,486	C
Northern State Univ	SD	14,505	C
Northwest Christian Univ	OR	36,580	C
Northwest Missouri State Univ	MO	17,737	C
Northwestern Okla State Univ	OK	13,072	NC
Notre Dame de Namur Univ	CA	46,526	LC
Ohio Wesleyan Univ	OH	49,460	VC
Okla Baptist Univ	OK	32,320	C
Olivet Nazarene Univ	IL	41,840	C
Oregon State Univ	OR	22,519	VC
Pace Univ	NY	58,248	C
Pepperdine Univ	CA	74,460	HC+
Peru State College	NE	14,768	NC
Piedmont College	GA	32,512	C
Plymouth State Univ	NH	23,180	LC
Point Loma Nazarene Univ	CA	43,450	C
Pontifical Catholic Univ of PR	PR	10,534	
Prescott College	AZ	33,284	C
Providence College	RI	60,760	VC
Quinnipiac Univ	CT	59,110	C
Radford Univ	VA	19,027	LC
Ramapo College of New Jersey	NJ	25,338	C
Rhode Island College	RI	17,694	LC
Robert Morris Univ	PA	37,834	C
Rockford Univ	IL	36,030	C
Roger Williams Univ	RI	46,296	C+
Roosevelt Univ	IL	40,651	VC
Rosemont College	PA	30,980	C
St. John's Univ	MN	51,624	C
St. Mary's Univ of Minn	MN	41,210	VC
St. Peter's Univ	NJ	49,192	C
St. Xavier Univ	IL	43,310	C
San Diego State Univ	CA	21,896	C+
San Jose State Univ	CA	21,540	C
Seattle Pacific Univ	WA	47,439	C+
Seton Hall Univ	NJ	55,514	C
Shimer College	IL	42,130	VC+
Shorter Univ	GA	31,130	LC
Siena Heights Univ	MI	32,040	C
Silver Lake College of the Holy Family	WI	36,290	LC
Simpson Univ	CA	33,700	C
Skidmore College	NY	64,214	HC
Slippery Rock Univ of Pennsylvania	PA	10,360	C
Southeast Missouri State Univ	MO	15,498	C
Southeastern Okla State Univ	OK	11,875	C
Southern Illinois Univ Carbondale	IL	23,667	C
Southern New Hampshire Univ	NH	43,198	C
Southern Oregon Univ	OR	19,117	C
Southwestern Adventist Univ	TX	27,756	LC
Spalding Univ	KY	31,938	SP
Spring Arbor Univ	MI	36,000	C
Spring Hill College	AL	48,488	C
St. Andrews Univ	NC	44,634	LC
St. Cloud State Univ	MN	10,600	C
St. Joseph's College, New York/Brooklyn Campus	NY	25,114	LC
St. Joseph's College, New York/Long Island Campus	NY	25,124	C
St. Thomas Aquinas College	NY	42,200	C
SUNY / Univ at Buffalo	NY	23,122	C+
SUNY at New Paltz	NY	19,200	C
Suffolk Univ	MA	50,308	C
Sul Ross State Univ	TX	15,021	LC
Temple Univ	PA	24,392	VC
The Catholic Univ of America	DC	56,356	VC
The Univ of Akron	OH	21,477	C
The Univ of Utah	UT	17,924	VC
The Univ of Virginia's College at Wise	VA	18,192	LC
Thomas Edison State Univ	NJ	6,350	NC
Thomas Univ	GA	21,420	LC
Touro College	NY	28,950	VC
Towson Univ	MD	17,408	VC
Trine Univ	IN	41,310	C
Trinity International Univ	IL	31,070	VC
Troy Univ	AL	16,171	C
Tulane Univ	LA	63,396	HC+
Union College	NE	23,270	C
Union College	NY	64,320	MC
Union Inst & Univ	OH	8,912	SP
United States Air Force Academy	CO		C
Universidad del Turabo	PR	17,828	
Universidad Metropolitana	PR	17,828	
Univ of Alaska Southeast	AK	11,493	C
Univ of Bridgeport	CT	44,430	LC
Univ of Calif at Berkeley	CA	28,853	MC
Univ of Calif at Davis	CA	28,468	HC
Univ of Calif at Irvine	CA	26,484	VC
Univ of Central Florida	FL	15,922	VC
Univ of Chicago	IL	67,584	MC
Univ of Cincinnati	OH	21,964	VC
Univ of Denver	CO	58,443	VC+
Univ of Great Falls	MT	38,524	C
Univ of Holy Cross	LA	21,523	C
Univ of Houston-Downtown	TX	7,241	C
Univ of Indianapolis	IN	36,480	C
Univ of Iowa	IA	18,683	VC+
Univ of La Verne	CA	55,600	C
Univ of Maine at Augusta	ME	7,812	C
Univ of Maine at Fort Kent	ME	15,165	LC
Univ of Mary	ND	23,180	C
Univ of Maryland/Univ College	MD	25,966	LC
Univ of Mich/Ann Arbor	MI	24,410	MC
Univ of Mich-Flint	MI	17,607	C+
Univ of Minn/Morris	MN	20,760	VC
Univ of Missouri/Columbia	MO	18,201	MC
Univ of Mobile	AL	28,935	C
Univ of Montana-Western	MT	11,220	LC
Univ of Montevallo	AL	19,502	C
Univ of Mount Union	OH	38,970	C
Univ of Nebr - Kearney	NE	16,546	LC
Univ of Nevada, Las Vegas	NV	17,553	C
Univ of N Dak	ND	15,373	C
Univ of North Georgia	GA	17,316	C
Univ of North Texas	TX	19,198	C
Univ of Northern Colo	CO	20,851	C
Univ of Oregon	OR	22,972	C
Univ of Pittsburgh	PA	29,568	HC+
Univ of Pittsburgh at Bradford	PA	22,402	C
Univ of Pittsburgh at Greensburg	PA	23,132	C
Univ of Pittsburgh at Johnstown	PA	22,092	C
Univ of PR, at Mayaguez	PR	13,995	
Univ of PR-Rio Piedras campus	PR	13,327	
Univ of Sioux Falls	SD	34,330	C
Univ of South Florida/St. Petersburg	FL	15,980	C
Univ of South Florida/Tampa	FL	16,110	VC+
Univ of Southern Calif	CA	66,631	C
Univ of Southern Indiana	IN	16,501	C
Univ of Southern Miss	MS	13,170	C
Univ of the Ozarks	AR	52,176	C
Univ of the Pacific	CA	57,006	VC
Univ of West Alabama	AL	15,516	NC
Univ of West Florida	FL	15,848	C
Univ of Wisc-Platteville	WI	14,614	VC
Univ of Wisc-Stevens Point	WI	14,043	C
Univ of Wyoming	WY	15,375	C+
Upper Iowa Univ	IA	34,990	NC
Valley City State Univ	ND	13,267	C
Valparaiso Univ	IN	48,370	C+
Virginia Wesleyan College	VA	43,728	LC
Warner Pacific College	OR	33,790	C
Washington State Univ	WA	22,495	C
Washington Univ in St. Louis	MO	65,366	VC
Wayland Baptist Univ	TX	22,356	LC
Wayne State College	NE	12,802	C
Waynesburg Univ	PA	32,290	C
Wesleyan College	GA	29,694	C+
West Liberty Univ	WV	15,512	C
West Texas A&M Univ	TX	13,478	C
West Virginia Wesleyan College	WV	36,858	C
Western Carolina Univ	NC	13,965	C
Western Conn State Univ	CT	21,254	LC
Western New Mexico Univ	NM	16,734	LC
Western Oregon Univ	OR	15,021	LC
Westminster College	PA	39,180	C+
Westminster College	UT	41,078	C+
Westmont College	CA	56,410	HC
Wheaton College	IL	43,610	MC
Wilberforce Univ	OH	19,016	C
Wiley College	TX	18,504	C
William Carey Univ	MS	23,950	LC
Wilmington College	OH	34,600	C
Wisc Lutheran College	WI	36,290	VC
Worcester Polytechnic Inst	MA	60,730	MC

SOCIAL SCIENCE EDUCATION

School	ST	$IS	SR
Appalachian State Univ	NC	14,416	VC
Aquinas College - Mich	MI	38,876	HC
Arkansas State Univ	AR	16,190	C
Auburn Univ	AL	23,594	VC+
Baylor Univ	TX	53,760	HC
Bethune-Cookman Univ	FL	22,970	C
Black Hills State Univ	SD	15,899	C
Blackburn College	IL	28,526	LC
Blue Mountain College	MS	15,949	VC
Boise State Univ	ID	14,860	C
Bowling Green State Univ	OH	19,747	C
Brigham Young Univ	UT	12,748	HC
Brigham Young Univ/Hawaii	HI	11,290	C
Campbellsville Univ	KY	32,492	C
Central Methodist Univ	MO	36,830	VC
Coker College	SC	34,810	LC
Colby-Sawyer College	NH	50,790	C
College of St. Scholastica	MN	44,640	C
Concordia College - New York	NY	39,035	LC
Delta State Univ	MS	13,176	C
Dordt College	IA	37,860	C+
Eastern Illinois Univ	IL	21,126	C
Eastern Nazarene College	MA	39,955	C
Eastern Washington Univ	WA	25,572	LC
Faulkner Univ	AL	26,410	C
Fayetteville State Univ	NC	17,756	C
Florida Gulf Coast Univ	FL	9,682	C
Florida State Univ	FL	16,771	HC
Fresno Pacific Univ	CA	37,370	C
Friends Univ	KS	34,455	C
Hope International Univ	CA	41,150	C
Humboldt State Univ	CA	20,514	C
Illinois State Univ	IL	23,418	VC
Ithaca College	NY	56,766	VC
Jackson State Univ	MS	15,879	LC
Knox College	IL	52,615	VC+
Kutztown Univ of Pennsylvania	PA	19,056	LC
Lincoln Univ	MO	13,602	NC
Marian Univ	WI	32,420	LC
Marywood Univ	PA	46,900	C
Mayville State Univ	ND	18,371	NC
Mercyhurst Univ	PA	47,420	C
Miles College	AL	18,646	NC
Millikin Univ	IL	42,158	C
Miss Valley State Univ	MS	13,233	LC
Missouri Southern State Univ	MO	12,499	C
Montana State Univ-Billings	MT	22,960	C
Montana State Univ-Northern	MT	11,370	NC
Nazareth College	NY	45,574	C
Nebr Wesleyan Univ	NE	38,140	C+
New York Univ	NY	65,860	MC

ST = STATE $IS = IN-STATE COSTS SR = SELECTOR RATING

School	ST	$IS	SR
N Car A&T State Univ	NC	13,365	LC
N Dak State Univ	ND	16,245	C
Oakwood Univ	AL	43,758	C
Oglala Lakota College	SD	15,050	NC
Okla Christian Univ	OK	27,650	VC
Olivet Nazarene Univ	IL	41,840	C
Piedmont College	GA	32,512	C
Prescott College	AZ	33,284	C
Rocky Mountain College	MT	34,270	C
Rust College	MS	10,600	C
St. Louis Univ	MO	49,866	HC
St. Mary-of-the-Woods College	IN	39,632	LC
Schreiner Univ	TX	34,626	LC
Seattle Pacific Univ	WA	47,439	C+
Seton Hill Univ	PA	46,972	C
Silver Lake College of the Holy Family	WI	36,290	LC
Simpson Univ	CA	33,700	C
S Car State Univ	SC	20,805	LC
Southeastern Louisiana Univ	LA	16,237	C
Southern Illinois Univ Edwardsville	IL	22,643	C
Southwestern Okla State Univ	OK	11,790	C
SUNY / SUNY Oneonta	NY	19,712	C+
Stetson Univ	FL	53,544	VC
Texas Wesleyan Univ	TX	35,134	C
The College of New Jersey	NJ	31,909	HC
The Univ of Utah	UT	17,924	VC
Trine Univ	IN	41,310	C
Troy Univ	AL	16,171	C
Union College	NE	23,270	C
Universidad del Turabo	PR	17,828	
Univ of Arkansas at Pine Bluff	AR	13,541	C
Univ of Central Florida	FL	15,922	VC
Univ of Mary	ND	23,180	C
Univ of Maryland/Eastern Shore	MD	17,013	C
Univ of Miss	MS	17,746	C+
Univ of Montana-Western	MT	11,220	LC
Univ of Nebr - Lincoln	NE	18,589	VC
Univ of North Alabama	AL	15,398	C
Univ of N Car at Greensboro	NC	14,690	C
Univ of North Georgia	GA	17,316	C
Univ of Northern Colo	CO	20,851	C
Univ of Pittsburgh at Johnstown	PA	22,092	C
Univ of Rio Grande & Rio Grande Community College	OH	8,750	NC
Univ of Southern Indiana	IN	16,501	C
Univ of Wisc-Oshkosh	WI	15,200	C
Univ of Wisc-Superior	WI	14,446	C
Valparaiso Univ	IN	48,370	C+
Warner Univ	FL	28,216	C
Washington Univ in St. Louis	MO	65,366	VC
Weber State Univ	UT	10,721	C
West Liberty Univ	WV	15,512	C
Western Carolina Univ	NC	13,965	C
Westmont College	CA	56,410	HC
Wiley College	TX	18,504	C
Wilmington College	OH	34,600	C
Wilson College	PA	35,620	C
Wright State Univ	OH	16,983	C
York College	NE	24,300	C
Youngstown State Univ	OH	17,307	C

SOCIAL STUDIES

School	ST	$IS	SR
Andrews Univ	MI	28,030	C+
Aquinas College - Mich	MI	38,876	HC
Arkansas Tech Univ	AR	15,484	C
Barton College	NC	38,686	LC
Bethel Univ	MN	45,270	VC
Bluefield College	VA	34,120	C+
Bluffton Univ	OH	40,950	C
Brescia Univ	KY	29,890	VC+
Caldwell Univ	NJ	42,165	NC
Central Mich Univ	MI	20,330	C
Chaminade Univ of Honolulu	HI	36,000	C
Cleveland State Univ	OH	22,196	C
Concordia Univ, Ann Arbor	MI	35,945	VC
DePaul Univ	IL	47,623	VC
Eastern Mich Univ	MI	19,761	C
Eastern Nazarene College	MA	39,955	C
Eastern New Mexico Univ	NM	14,416	C
Edgewood College	WI	35,950	C
Erskine College	SC	45,460	C
Ferris State Univ	MI	21,445	C
Ferrum College	VA	39,650	C
Hamline Univ	MN	45,678	VC
Harvard College/Harvard Univ	MA	60,659	MC
Indiana Wesleyan Univ	IN	33,674	C
Ithaca College	NY	56,766	VC
Madonna Univ	MI	29,050	C
Mayville State Univ	ND	18,371	NC
McMurry Univ	TX	34,259	LC
Methodist Univ	NC	43,600	C
Millersville Univ of Pennsylvania	PA	23,782	C
Minn State Univ, Mankato	MN	15,616	C
Miss College	MS	25,850	C
Missouri Southern State Univ	MO	12,499	C
Mount Aloysius College	PA	29,976	C
Mount Mary Univ	WI	34,650	LC
Mount St. Mary's Univ	MD	51,610	C
New York Univ	NY	65,860	MC
Northern Kentucky Univ	KY	16,486	C
Ohio Northern Univ	OH	44,050	VC
Okla Christian Univ	OK	27,650	VC
Okla Panhandle State Univ	OK	6,152	NC
Okla Wesleyan Univ	OK	33,206	C
Olivet College	MI	36,110	LC
Our Lady of the Lake Univ	TX	35,012	LC
Pacific Union College	CA	36,009	VC
Pfeiffer Univ	NC	39,695	LC
Purdue Univ/West Lafayette	IN	20,032	MC
S Car State Univ	SC	20,805	LC
Southern Wesleyan Univ	SC	32,130	LC
Southwestern Adventist Univ	TX	27,756	LC
Spring Arbor Univ	MI	36,000	C
St. Catherine Univ	MN	45,630	VC
St. Francis College	NY	38,800	LC
St. John's Univ	NY	55,850	C
Tulane Univ	LA	63,396	HC+
Univ of Great Falls	MT	38,524	C
Univ of Mich/Dearborn	MI	11,757	VC
Univ of Wisc-Eau Claire	WI	15,797	VC
Univ of Wisc-Madison	WI	20,934	MC
Univ of Wisc-River Falls	WI	14,485	C
Univ of Wisc-Superior	WI	14,446	C
Utica College	NY	30,430	C
Virginia Wesleyan College	VA	43,728	LC
Viterbo Univ	WI	34,660	C
Washington State Univ	WA	22,495	C
Wayland Baptist Univ	TX	22,356	LC
Wesleyan Univ	CT	65,516	MC
West Liberty Univ	WV	15,512	C
Western Kentucky Univ	KY	16,850	C
Western Washington Univ	WA	18,003	C+
Youngstown State Univ	OH	17,307	C

SOCIAL STUDIES EDUCATION

School	ST	$IS	SR
Adams State Univ	CO	17,703	LC
Alabama State Univ	AL	14,142	NC
Alfred Univ	NY	42,296	C+
Alice Lloyd College	KY	8,190	C
Anderson Univ	IN	38,200	C
Andrews Univ	MI	28,030	C+
Appalachian State Univ	NC	14,416	VC
Aquinas College - Mich	MI	38,876	HC
Asbury Univ	KY	35,180	C+
Augustana Univ	SD	38,424	VC
Baylor Univ	TX	53,760	HC
Bethany College	WV	36,300	NC
Bethel College	IN	35,860	C
Bethel Univ	MN	45,270	VC
Biola Univ	CA	46,402	C+
Bloomsburg Univ of Pennsylvania	PA	19,066	LC
Boston Univ	MA	65,110	MC
Cameron Univ	OK	11,072	NC
Canisius College	NY	47,537	C
Catawba College	NC	39,820	C
Cedarville Univ	OH	34,990	VC
Central Washington Univ	WA	16,803	C
CUNY/Brooklyn College	NY	5,884	C+
CUNY/City College	NY	20,319	VC
Colby-Sawyer College	NH	50,790	C
College of the Ozarks	MO	7,230	C
Colo State Univ	CO	22,162	VC
Concordia College - Moorhead	MN	51,088	C+
Concordia College - New York	NY	39,035	LC
Concordia Univ St. Paul	MN	29,050	C
Corban Univ	OR	40,306	C
Daemen College	NY	38,045	C
Defiance College	OH	41,630	C
Duquesne Univ	PA	46,822	VC
East Carolina Univ	NC	16,937	C
East Texas Baptist Univ	TX	33,134	C
Eastern Mich Univ	MI	19,761	C
Edinboro Univ	PA	15,940	LC
Elizabethtown College	PA	54,050	C
Ferris State Univ	MI	21,445	C
Franklin College	IN	39,380	C
Gannon Univ	PA	42,032	C
Glenville State College	WV	17,386	NC
Grambling State Univ	LA	15,701	C
Green Mountain College	VT	45,228	LC
Greensboro College	NC	42,400	LC
Gwynedd Mercy Univ	PA	43,780	LC
Hardin-Simmons Univ	TX	33,966	C
Hofstra Univ	NY	55,960	C+
Huntington Univ	IN	33,996	C
Indiana State Univ	IN	23,223	LC
Indiana Univ Bloomington	IN	20,429	VC
Indiana Univ Northwest	IN	7,072	C
Indiana Univ of Pennsylvania	PA	23,614	LC
Indiana Univ South Bend	IN	14,242	C
Indiana Univ Southeast	IN	14,242	LC
Indiana Univ-Purdue Univ Indianapolis	IN	18,635	C
Indiana Wesleyan Univ	IN	33,674	C
Ithaca College	NY	56,766	VC
John Brown Univ	AR	33,132	VC
Judson College	AL	27,066	C
Juniata College	PA	53,760	VC
Kentucky Christian Univ	KY	26,560	LC
Kentucky State Univ	KY	13,364	LC
Keystone College	PA	28,680	LC
King Univ	TN	34,660	C
Kutztown Univ of Pennsylvania	PA	19,056	LC
La Salle Univ	PA	55,790	C
Le Moyne College	NY	46,000	C
LIU Brooklyn	NY	49,682	C
LIU Post	NY	49,682	C
Louisiana College	LA	21,886	C
Malone Univ	OH	38,448	C
Mansfield Univ	PA	23,376	LC
Mars Hill Univ	NC	42,688	C
Marshall Univ	WV	17,242	C
Marygrove College	MI	28,926	NC
Messiah College	PA	43,100	C+
MidAmerica Nazarene Univ	KS	35,550	C
Millersville Univ of Pennsylvania	PA	23,782	C
Minn State Univ, Mankato	MN	15,616	C
Minn State Univ, Moorhead	MN	15,941	C
Missouri Southern State Univ	MO	12,499	C
Missouri Valley College	MO	28,150	C
Monmouth Univ	NJ	46,234	C
Montana State Univ-Billings	MT	22,960	C
Morningside College	IA	36,865	C
Morris College	SC	18,500	LC
Mount Aloysius College	PA	29,976	C
Mount Vernon Nazarene Univ	OH	34,500	C
New York Univ	NY	65,860	MC
Niagara Univ	NY	41,010	C
N Car State Univ	NC	19,515	HC+
North Greenville Univ	SC	25,930	C+
Ohio Univ	OH	22,924	C
Okla Baptist Univ	OK	32,320	C
Okla Christian Univ	OK	27,650	VC
Okla Wesleyan Univ	OK	33,206	C
Old Dominion Univ	VA	20,910	C
Oral Roberts Univ	OK	34,316	C
Ouachita Baptist Univ	AR	32,320	C
Pfeiffer Univ	NC	39,695	LC
Piedmont College	GA	32,512	C
Pittsburg State Univ	KS	13,880	NC
Pontifical Catholic Univ of PR	PR	10,534	
Prescott College	AZ	33,284	C
Purdue Univ/Northwest	IN	15,038	C
Purdue Univ/West Lafayette	IN	20,032	MC
Rider Univ	NJ	54,050	C
Rivier Univ	NH	40,410	VC
Rocky Mountain College	MT	34,270	C
Saginaw Valley State Univ	MI	18,530	C
St. Augustine's Univ	NC	26,048	C
St. Mary's Univ of Minn	MN	41,210	VC
Shaw Univ	NC	24,638	C
Shepherd Univ, West Virginia	WV	17,224	C
Shippensburg Univ of Pennsylvania	PA	23,208	C
Southeast Missouri State Univ	MO	15,498	C
Southeastern Okla State Univ	OK	11,875	C
Southern Nazarene Univ	OK	32,798	NC
Southern New Hampshire Univ	NH	43,198	C
Southern Univ and A&M College	LA	16,074	LC+
Southern Univ at New Orleans	LA	8,014	LC
Southwest Baptist Univ	MO	29,900	LC
St. Edward's Univ	TX	53,100	VC
St. John Fisher College	NY	43,620	C
St. Olaf College	MN	54,260	HC+
St. Thomas Univ	FL	36,360	LC
SUNY / SUNY College at Old Westbury	NY	16,860	C
SUNY / SUNY Fredonia	NY	20,818	C
SUNY / SUNY Potsdam	NY	20,404	C+
SUNY at New Paltz	NY	19,200	C
SUNY at Oswego	NY	21,351	C
Syracuse Univ	NY	60,239	VC
Taylor Univ	IN	40,317	C+
Texas Wesleyan Univ	TX	35,134	C
The College of New Jersey	NJ	31,909	HC
Thomas More College	KY	36,720	C
Tiffin Univ	OH	31,380	C
Union College	KY	32,310	C
Univ of Central Missouri	MO	18,982	C
Univ of Central Okla	OK	13,486	C
Univ of Charleston	WV	35,000	C
Univ of Conn	CT	25,538	HC
Univ of Evansville	IN	44,186	VC+
Univ of Georgia	GA	21,250	HC
Univ of Great Falls	MT	38,524	C
Univ of Indianapolis	IN	36,480	C
Univ of Kentucky	KY	33,306	C
Univ of Louisiana at Lafayette	LA	14,516	C
Univ of Maine at Machias	ME	22,960	C
Univ of Mary Hardin-Baylor	TX	33,950	C+
Univ of Mich/Dearborn	MI	11,757	VC
Univ of Minn/Duluth	MN	20,292	C+
Univ of Minn/Twin Cities	MN	23,519	HC+
Univ of Missouri/Columbia	MO	18,201	MC
Univ of Montana-Western	MT	11,220	LC
Univ of N Car at Charlotte	NC	15,547	C
Univ of N Car at Greensboro	NC	14,690	C
Univ of North Florida	FL	15,996	VC
Univ of Northwestern - St. Paul	MN	38,160	C
Univ of Okla	OK	18,911	VC
Univ of Pittsburgh at Bradford	PA	22,402	C
Univ of Rio Grande & Rio Grande Community College	OH	8,750	NC
Univ of S Car Upstate	SC	18,200	LC
Univ of South Florida/Tampa	FL	16,110	VC+
Univ of the Cumberlands	KY	32,000	C
Univ of Vermont	VT	28,878	HC
Univ of Wisc-La Crosse	WI	15,247	C+
Univ of Wisc-Whitewater	WI	13,976	C
Valparaiso Univ	IN	48,370	C+
Virginia Wesleyan College	VA	43,728	LC
Viterbo Univ	WI	34,660	C
Wartburg College	IA	47,840	C
Washington State Univ	WA	22,495	C
Washington Univ in St. Louis	MO	65,366	VC
Wayne State Univ	MI	22,016	C
Webster Univ	MO	37,490	C
West Chester Univ of Pennsylvania	PA	18,456	C
West Texas A&M Univ	TX	13,478	C
Whitworth Univ	WA	51,732	VC
Wilmington College	OH	34,600	C
Wilson College	PA	35,620	C
Winona State Univ	MN	17,535	C
Xavier Univ of Louisiana	LA	31,689	C+
York College of Pennsylvania	PA	29,240	C
Youngstown State Univ	OH	17,307	C

SOCIAL STUDIES SECONDARY SCHOOL EDUCATION

School	ST	$IS	SR
Aquinas College - Mich	MI	38,876	HC
Biola Univ	CA	46,402	C+
Concordia Univ St. Paul	MN	29,050	C
East Texas Baptist Univ	TX	33,134	C
Elizabethtown College	PA	54,050	C
Flagler College	FL	27,620	C
Georgetown College	KY	41,440	C
Grove City College	PA	25,692	VC
Kent State Univ	OH	20,732	C
Missouri Southern State Univ	MO	12,499	C
Monmouth Univ	NJ	46,234	C
Murray State Univ	KY	16,998	C
Neumann Univ	PA	40,678	LC
New York Univ	NY	65,860	MC
Niagara Univ	NY	41,010	C
Ouachita Baptist Univ	AR	32,320	C
St. John's Univ	NY	55,850	C
SUNY / SUNY Fredonia	NY	20,818	C
Taylor Univ	IN	40,317	C+
The College of St. Rose	NY	43,048	C
Univ of Maine at Machias	ME	22,960	C
Univ of Wisc-Superior	WI	14,446	C
Webster Univ	MO	37,490	C
Western Mich Univ	MI	21,054	C
Wilson College	PA	35,620	C
Youngstown State Univ	OH	17,307	C

SOCIAL WORK

School	ST	$IS	SR
Abilene Christian Univ	TX	41,800	C+
Adams State Univ	CO	17,703	LC
Adelphi Univ	NY	48,244	C
Adrian College	MI	42,400	C
Alabama A&M Univ	AL	18,796	C
Alabama State Univ	AL	14,142	NC
Albany State Univ	GA	19,462	C
Alcorn State Univ	MS	15,854	C
Alvernia Univ	PA	43,900	C
Anderson Univ	IN	38,200	C
Andrews Univ	MI	28,030	C+
Angelo State Univ	TX	15,263	NC
Anna Maria College	MA	48,186	C
Appalachian State Univ	NC	14,416	VC
Arizona State Univ at the Downtown Phoenix Campus	AZ	23,680	VC
Arizona State Univ at the West Campus	AZ	20,640	C
Arkansas State Univ	AR	16,190	C
Asbury Univ	KY	35,180	C+
Ashland Univ	OH	21,440	C
Atlantic Union College	MA	27,228	C
Auburn Univ	AL	23,594	VC+
Augsburg College	MN	43,929	C
Augusta Univ	GA	4,632	C
Augustana College	IL	49,658	VC
Aurora Univ	IL	33,970	C
Austin Peay State Univ	TN	16,397	C
Avila Univ	MO	35,480	C
Azusa Pacific Univ	CA	43,972	C
Ball State Univ	IN	19,590	C
Barton College	NC	38,686	LC
Bayamon Central Univ	PR	12,490	
Baylor Univ	TX	53,760	HC
Belhaven Univ	MS	31,016	C
Belmont Univ	TN	40,970	VC
Bemidji State Univ	MN	16,056	VC
Benedict College	SC	28,238	NC
Bennett College	NC	27,302	NC
Bethany College	WV	36,300	NC
Bethel College	KS	35,370	C
Bethel Univ	MN	45,270	VC
Biola Univ	CA	46,402	C+
Bloomfield College	NJ	39,100	LC
Bloomsburg Univ of Pennsylvania	PA	19,066	LC
Bluffton Univ	OH	40,950	C
Boise State Univ	ID	14,860	C
Bowie State Univ	MD	26,728	LC
Bowling Green State Univ	OH	19,747	C

ST = STATE $IS = IN-STATE COSTS SR = SELECTOR RATING

School	ST	$IS	SR
Brescia Univ	KY	29,890	VC+
Briar Cliff Univ	IA	36,956	C
Bridgewater State Univ	MA	21,810	C
Brigham Young Univ	UT	12,748	HC
Brigham Young Univ/Hawaii	HI	11,290	C
Buena Vista Univ	IA	41,514	C
Cabrini Univ	PA	42,591	LC
Cairn Univ	PA	36,296	C
Cal State, Chico	CA	21,440	C
Cal State, Fresno	CA	16,902	LC
Cal State, Long Beach	CA	18,850	C
Cal State, Los Angeles	CA	17,186	LC
Cal State, Sacramento	CA	20,332	C
Cal State, San Bernardino	CA	12,000	C
Calif Univ of Pennsylvania	PA	14,217	LC
Calvin College	MI	41,570	VC+
Campbellsville Univ	KY	32,492	C
Capital Univ	OH	42,982	C
Caribbean Univ	PR	15,471	
Carlow Univ	PA	38,549	LC
Carthage College	WI	48,835	C
Castleton Univ	VT	20,186	C
Cedar Crest College	PA	46,715	C
Cedarville Univ	OH	34,990	VC
Central Conn State Univ	CT	21,203	C
Central Mich Univ	MI	20,330	C
Central State Univ	OH	18,564	C
Central Washington Univ	WA	16,803	C
Chadron State College	NE	14,819	NC
Champlain College	VT	53,132	C+
Chapman Univ	CA	63,078	VC+
Chatham Univ	PA	46,517	C
Christopher Newport Univ	VA	23,968	VC+
CUNY/College of Staten Island	NY	17,840	NC
CUNY/Lehman College	NY	5,778	HC+
CUNY/York College	NY	6,747	LC
Clark Atlanta Univ	GA	31,019	LC
Clarke Univ	IA	38,940	C
Cleveland State Univ	OH	22,196	C
Coker College	SC	34,810	LC
College of St. Scholastica	MN	44,640	C
College of the Ozarks	MO	7,230	C
Colo Mesa Univ	CO	18,955	LC
Colo State Univ	CO	22,162	VC
Colo State Univ-Pueblo	CO	18,234	C
Columbia College	SC	36,550	C
Columbia College - Missouri	MO	27,803	C
Concord Univ	WV	14,954	C
Concordia College - Moorhead	MN	51,088	C+
Concordia College - New York	NY	39,035	LC
Concordia Univ	OR	35,000	C
Concordia Univ Wisc	WI	35,910	C
Concordia Univ, Chicago	IL	39,694	C
Coppin State Univ	MD	17,041	VC
Creighton Univ	NE	48,206	VC+
Daemen College	NY	38,045	C
Defiance College	OH	41,630	C
Delaware State Univ	DE	19,376	NC
Delta State Univ	MS	13,176	C
Dickinson State Univ	ND	12,372	LC
Dominican College	NY	31,270	LC
Dordt College	IA	37,860	C+
East Carolina Univ	NC	16,937	C
East Central Univ	OK	13,056	C
East Stroudsburg Univ	PA	18,334	C
East Tenn State Univ	TN	13,994	C
Eastern Conn State Univ	CT	23,059	C
Eastern Kentucky Univ	KY	16,908	C
Eastern Mennonite Univ	VA	42,550	C
Eastern Mich Univ	MI	19,761	C
Eastern Nazarene College	MA	39,955	C
Eastern New Mexico Univ	NM	14,416	C
Eastern Univ	PA	39,540	C
Eastern Washington Univ	WA	25,572	LC
Edinboro Univ	PA	15,940	LC
Elizabeth City State Univ	NC	14,745	C
Elizabethtown College	PA	54,050	C
Elms College	MA	45,646	VC
Evangel Univ	MO	28,898	C
Fayetteville State Univ	NC	17,756	C
Ferris State Univ	MI	21,445	C
Ferrum College	VA	39,650	C
Florida A&M Univ	FL	15,361	C
Florida Atlantic Univ	FL	17,339	C
Florida Gulf Coast Univ	FL	9,682	C
Florida International Univ	FL	19,854	C+
Florida State Univ	FL	16,771	HC
Fontbonne Univ	MO	33,717	C
Fordham Univ	NY	65,918	MC
Fort Hays State Univ	KS	12,131	C
Fort Valley State Univ	GA	17,988	VC
Franciscan Univ of Steubenville	OH	33,980	VC
Franklin Pierce Univ	NH	46,750	C
Freed-Hardeman Univ	TN	29,450	C
Fresno Pacific Univ	CA	37,370	C
Frostburg State Univ	MD	17,280	LC
Gallaudet Univ	DC	29,118	LC
Gannon Univ	PA	42,032	C
George Fox Univ	OR	42,938	C
George Mason Univ	VA	15,724	VC
Georgia State Univ	GA	24,332	VC
Georgian Court Univ	NJ	42,426	LC
Gordon College	MA	46,472	C+
Goshen College	IN	42,500	C
Grace College and Seminary	IN	31,524	C
Grambling State Univ	LA	15,701	C
Grand Rapids Theological Seminary/Cornerstone Univ	MI	33,338	C
Grand Valley State Univ	MI	22,250	C+
Greenville College	IL	27,012	C
Hannibal-LaGrange Univ	MO	29,815	C
Harding Univ	AR	25,421	C
Hardin-Simmons Univ	TX	33,966	C
Hawaii Pacific Univ	HI	33,420	C
Heritage Univ	WA	19,825	NC
Hood College	MD	54,840	C
Hope College	MI	39,940	VC
Howard Payne Univ	TX	34,320	C
Howard Univ	DC	37,616	C+
Humboldt State Univ	CA	20,514	C
Huntington Univ	IN	33,996	C
Idaho State Univ	ID	13,619	NC
Illinois State Univ	IL	23,418	VC
Indiana State Univ	IN	23,223	LC
Indiana Univ Bloomington	IN	20,429	VC
Indiana Univ East	IN	7,072	C
Indiana Univ Northwest	IN	7,072	C
Indiana Univ South Bend	IN	14,242	C
Indiana Univ-Purdue Univ Indianapolis	IN	18,635	C
Indiana Wesleyan Univ	IN	33,674	C
Inter-American Univ of PR Ponce	PR	19,549	
Inter-American Univ of PR-Aguadilla Campus	PR	21,657	
Inter-American Univ of PR-Arecibo Campus	PR	18,245	
Inter-American Univ of PR-Fajardo Campus	PR	18,336	
Inter-American Univ of PR-Metropolitan Campus	PR	20,045	
Iona College	NY	50,984	C
Jackson State Univ	MS	15,879	LC
Jacksonville State Univ	AL	14,628	LC
James Madison Univ	VA	19,084	VC
Jarvis Christian College	TX	20,160	NC
Johnson C. Smith Univ	NC	25,336	LC
Judson College	AL	27,066	C
Juniata College	PA	53,760	VC
Kansas State Univ	KS	17,780	VC
Kentucky Christian Univ	KY	26,560	LC
Kentucky State Univ	KY	13,364	LC
Keuka College	NY	39,762	C
King Univ	TN	34,660	C
Kutztown Univ of Pennsylvania	PA	19,056	LC
La Salle Univ	PA	55,790	C
La Sierra Univ	CA	39,690	VC
Lamar Univ	TX	18,014	LC
LeMoyne-Owen College	TN	16,980	C
Lewis Univ	IL	40,370	C
Lewis-Clark State College	ID	14,202	C
Limestone College	SC	32,100	C
Lincoln Memorial Univ	TN	28,070	C
Lincoln Univ	MO	13,602	NC
Lindenwood Univ	MO	25,132	C
Lipscomb Univ	TN	41,296	VC
LIU Brooklyn	NY	49,682	C
LIU Post	NY	49,682	C
Livingstone College	NC	17,815	LC
Lock Haven Univ of Pennsylvania	PA	18,028	LC
Longwood Univ	VA	22,184	C
Loras College	IA	39,222	C
Louisiana College	LA	21,886	C
Lourdes Univ	OH	29,520	NC
Loyola Univ Chicago	IL	55,802	VC
Lubbock Christian Univ	TX	28,426	C
Luther College	IA	48,540	C+
MacMurray College	IL	33,620	C
Madonna Univ	MI	29,050	C
Malone Univ	OH	38,448	C
Manchester Univ	IN	40,422	C
Mansfield Univ	PA	23,376	LC
Marian Univ	WI	32,420	LC
Marist College	NY	49,860	VC
Mars Hill Univ	NC	42,688	C
Marshall Univ	WV	17,242	C
Mary Baldwin Univ	VA	39,865	C
Marygrove College	MI	28,926	NC
Marywood Univ	PA	46,900	C
McDaniel College	MD	51,380	VC
McKendree Univ	IL	37,940	C+
Mercy College	NY	31,776	C
Mercyhurst Univ	PA	47,420	C
Meredith College	NC	45,297	C
Messiah College	PA	43,100	C+
Methodist Univ	NC	43,600	C
Metropolitan College of New York	NY		VC
Metropolitan State Univ	MN	7,566	C
Metropolitan State Univ of Denver	CO	29,889	LC
Miami Univ	OH	27,190	HC+
Mich State Univ	MI	23,898	VC+
Middle Tenn State Univ	TN	8,650	C
Midwestern State Univ	TX	17,572	C
Miles College	AL	18,646	NC
Millersville Univ of Pennsylvania	PA	23,782	C
Milligan College	TN	38,150	C
Minn State Univ, Mankato	MN	15,616	C
Minn State Univ, Moorhead	MN	15,941	C
Minot State Univ	ND	12,732	C
Misericordia Univ	PA	43,840	C
Miss College	MS	25,850	C
Miss State Univ	MS	11,454	C+
Miss Valley State Univ	MS	13,233	LC
Missouri State Univ	MO	15,190	C+
Missouri Western State Univ	MO	16,741	
Molloy College	NY	40,440	C
Monmouth Univ	NJ	46,234	C
Morehead State Univ	KY	17,422	C
Morgan State Univ	MD	17,190	LC
Mount Mary Univ	WI	34,650	LC
Mount Mercy Univ	IA	36,826	C
Mount St. Joseph Univ	OH	33,880	C
Mount St. Mary's Univ - Chalon Campus	CA	43,897	VC+
Mount Vernon Nazarene Univ	OH	34,500	C
Murray State Univ	KY	16,998	C
Nazareth College	NY	45,574	C
Nebr Wesleyan Univ	NE	38,140	C+
Neumann Univ	PA	40,678	LC
New Mexico Highlands Univ	NM	11,904	NC
New Mexico State Univ	NM	14,050	C
New York Inst of Technology	NY	48,730	C
New York Univ	NY	65,860	MC
Niagara Univ	NY	41,010	C
N Car A&T State Univ	NC	13,365	LC
N Car Central Univ	NC	9,000	C
N Car State Univ	NC	19,515	HC+
Northeastern Illinois Univ	IL	12,529	LC
Northeastern State Univ	OK	8,615	VC
Northern Arizona Univ	AZ	20,246	VC
Northern Kentucky Univ	KY	16,486	C
Northern Mich Univ	MI	19,604	C
Northwest Nazarene Univ	ID	36,000	C
Northwestern College of Iowa	IA	38,400	C+
Northwestern Okla State Univ	OK	13,072	NC
Nyack College	NY	34,050	NC
Oakland Univ	MI	20,763	C
Oakwood Univ	AL	43,758	C
Oglala Lakota College	SD	15,050	NC
Oglethorpe Univ	GA	44,200	C+
Ohio Dominican Univ	OH	41,340	C+
Ohio State Univ at Columbus	OH	21,703	HC+
Ohio Univ	OH	22,924	C
Okla Baptist Univ	OK	32,320	C
Olivet Nazarene Univ	IL	41,840	C
Oral Roberts Univ	OK	34,316	C
Our Lady of the Lake Univ	TX	35,012	LC
Pacific Lutheran Univ	WA	49,960	VC
Pacific Union College	CA	36,009	VC
Pacific Univ	OR	52,876	C
Park Univ	MO	20,329	C
Philander Smith College	AR	20,814	LC
Pittsburg State Univ	KS	13,880	NC
Plymouth State Univ	NH	23,180	LC
Point Loma Nazarene Univ	CA	43,450	C
Pontifical Catholic Univ of PR	PR	10,534	
Portland State Univ	OR	19,443	C
Prairie View A&M Univ	TX	15,205	LC
Prescott College	AZ	33,284	C
Presentation College	SD	25,454	NC
Providence College	RI	60,760	VC
Purdue Univ/Northwest	IN	15,038	C
Purdue Univ/West Lafayette	IN	20,032	MC
Quincy Univ	IL	36,998	C
Radford Univ	VA	19,027	LC
Ramapo College of New Jersey	NJ	25,338	C
Regis College	MA	51,920	C
Rhode Island College	RI	17,694	LC
Roberts Wesleyan College	NY	38,306	C
Rust College	MS	10,600	C
Rutgers Univ - Camden	NJ	26,146	C
Rutgers Univ - New Brunswick	NJ	26,632	HC
Rutgers Univ - Newark	NJ	27,288	C
Sacred Heart Univ	CT	52,750	C
Saginaw Valley State Univ	MI	18,530	C
St. Francis Univ	PA	42,268	NC
St. Leo Univ	FL	31,650	C
St. Louis Univ	MO	49,866	HC
St. Martin's Univ	WA	45,056	C
St. Mary's College	IN	50,600	C
Salem State Univ	MA	17,303	LC
Salisbury Univ	MD	20,714	VC
Salve Regina Univ	RI	51,470	C
San Diego State Univ	CA	21,896	C+
San Francisco State Univ	CA	18,514	LC
San Jose State Univ	CA	21,540	C
Savannah State Univ	GA	15,631	C
Seattle Univ	WA	50,811	VC+
Seton Hall Univ	NJ	55,514	C
Seton Hill Univ	PA	46,972	C
Shaw Univ	NC	24,638	C
Shepherd Univ, West Virginia	WV	17,224	C
Shippensburg Univ of Pennsylvania	PA	23,208	C
Siena College	NY	48,916	C+
Siena Heights Univ	MI	32,040	C
Silver Lake College of the Holy Family	WI	36,290	LC
Simmons College	MA	53,090	VC
Skidmore College	NY	64,214	HC
Slippery Rock Univ of Pennsylvania	PA	10,360	C
S Car State Univ	SC	20,805	LC
Southeast Missouri State Univ	MO	15,498	C
Southeastern Louisiana Univ	LA	16,237	C
Southeastern Univ	FL	31,765	C
Southern Adventist Univ	TN	27,600	C
Southern Conn State Univ	CT	21,924	LC
Southern Illinois Univ Carbondale	IL	23,667	C
Southern Illinois Univ Edwardsville	IL	22,643	C
Southern Univ and A&M College	LA	16,074	LC+
Southern Univ at New Orleans	LA	8,014	LC
Southwest Minn State Univ	MN	17,783	C
Southwestern Adventist Univ	TX	27,756	LC
Spalding Univ	KY	31,938	SP
Spring Arbor Univ	MI	36,000	C
St. Ambrose Univ	IA	39,019	C
St. Ambrose Univ	IA	39,019	C
St. Catherine Univ	MN	45,630	VC
St. Cloud State Univ	MN	10,600	C
St. Edward's Univ	TX	53,100	VC
St. Olaf College	MN	54,260	HC+
SUNY / Buffalo State College	NY	20,842	C
SUNY / SUNY Fredonia	NY	20,818	C
SUNY / SUNY Plattsburgh	NY	18,814	C
SUNY SUNY Albany	NY	22,165	C
Stephen F. Austin State Univ	TX	18,406	LC
Stockton Univ	NJ	25,059	
Stony Brook Univ/The SUNY	NY	21,881	MC
Syracuse Univ	NY	60,239	VC
Tabor College	KS	35,870	C
Talladega College	AL	19,215	C
Tarleton State Univ	TX	15,248	LC
Taylor Univ	IN	40,317	C+
Temple Univ	PA	24,392	VC
Tenn State Univ	TN	14,423	C
Texas A&M Univ at Commerce	TX	10,496	C
Texas Christian Univ	TX	54,670	HC
Texas Southern Univ	TX	18,212	LC
Texas State Univ	TX	19,350	C
Texas Tech Univ	TX	18,736	C+
Texas Woman's Univ	TX	15,302	LC
The Catholic Univ of America	DC	56,356	VC
The College at Brockport - SUNY	NY	20,346	C
The College of New Rochelle	NY	46,300	VC
The College of St. Rose	NY	43,048	C
The Univ of Akron	OH	21,477	C
The Univ of Tenn at Chattanooga	TN	16,744	C
The Univ of Tenn at Knoxville	TN	22,112	VC
The Univ of Tenn at Martin	TN	14,876	C
The Univ of Utah	UT	17,924	VC
Thomas Univ	GA	21,420	LC
Trevecca Nazarene Univ	TN	31,186	C
Trinity Christian College	IL	35,580	C
Troy Univ	AL	16,171	C
Tulane Univ	LA	63,396	HC+
Tuskegee Univ	AL	28,164	C
Union College	KY	32,310	C
Union College	NE	23,270	C
Union Inst & Univ	OH	8,912	SP
Union Univ	TN	33,970	VC
Univ of Alabama	AL	24,320	C+
Univ of Alabama at Birmingham	AL	19,906	C
Univ of Alaska Anchorage	AK	16,652	NC
Univ of Alaska Fairbanks	AK	16,179	C
Univ of Arkansas at Fayetteville	AR	19,152	C+
Univ of Arkansas at Little Rock	AR	18,211	C
Univ of Arkansas at Monticello	AR	13,134	NC
Univ of Arkansas at Pine Bluff	AR	13,541	C
Univ of Calif at Berkeley	CA	28,853	MC
Univ of Central Florida	FL	15,922	VC
Univ of Central Missouri	MO	18,982	C
Univ of Cincinnati	OH	21,964	VC
Univ of Detroit Mercy	MI	48,816	C+
Univ of Findlay	OH	60,139	C
Univ of Georgia	GA	21,250	HC
Univ of Hawaii at Manoa	HI	23,221	C
Univ of Houston-Downtown	TX	7,241	C
Univ of Indianapolis	IN	36,480	C
Univ of Iowa	IA	18,683	VC+
Univ of Kansas	KS	20,135	C+
Univ of Kentucky	KY	33,306	C
Univ of Louisiana at Monroe	LA	15,970	C
Univ of Louisville	KY	19,824	C
Univ of Maine	ME	20,792	C
Univ of Maine at Presque Isle	ME	14,870	C
Univ of Mary	ND	23,180	C
Univ of Mary Hardin-Baylor	TX	33,950	C+
Univ of Maryland/Baltimore County	MD	21,296	VC
Univ of Memphis	TN	18,278	C
Univ of Mich-Flint	MI	17,607	C+
Univ of Miss	MS	17,746	C+
Univ of Missouri/Columbia	MO	18,201	MC
Univ of Missouri-St. Louis	MO		C
Univ of Montana	MT	14,105	C
Univ of Montevallo	AL	19,502	C

ST = STATE $IS = IN-STATE COSTS SR = SELECTOR RATING

School	ST	$IS	SR
Univ of Nebr - Kearney	NE	16,546	LC
Univ of Nebr - Omaha	NE	16,120	C
Univ of Nevada, Las Vegas	NV	17,553	C
Univ of Nevada/Reno	NV	18,010	C
Univ of New England	ME	48,880	C
Univ of New Hampshire	NH	28,562	VC
Univ of North Alabama	AL	15,398	C
Univ of N Car at Charlotte	NC	15,547	C
Univ of N Car at Greensboro	NC	14,690	C
Univ of N Car at Pembroke	NC	14,388	LC
Univ of N Car at Wilmington	NC	14,590	VC
Univ of N Dak	ND	15,373	C
Univ of North Texas	TX	19,198	C
Univ of Okla	OK	18,911	VC
Univ of Pikeville	KY	28,700	NC
Univ of Pittsburgh	PA	29,568	HC+
Univ of Portland	OR	52,152	VC
Univ of PR, at Humacao	PR	14,000	
Univ of PR-Rio Piedras campus	PR	13,327	
Univ of Rio Grande & Rio Grande Community College	OH	8,750	NC
Univ of St. Francis	IN	37,400	C
Univ of St. Joseph	CT	49,550	C
Univ of Sioux Falls	SD	34,330	C
Univ of South Alabama	AL	16,400	C
Univ of S Car at Columbia	SC	19,725	VC+
Univ of S Dak	SD	16,109	C
Univ of South Florida/Tampa	FL	16,110	VC+
Univ of Southern Indiana	IN	16,501	C
Univ of Southern Maine	ME	18,320	C
Univ of Southern Miss	MS	13,170	C
Univ of St. Francis	IL	39,924	C
Univ of Texas at Arlington	TX	18,026	LC
Univ of Texas at Austin	TX	26,102	HC
Univ of Texas at El Paso	TX	34,452	NC
Univ of the Cumberlands	KY	32,000	C
Univ of the District of Columbia	DC	21,044	LC
Univ of the Sacred Heart	PR	17,932	
Univ of Toledo	OH	19,336	NC
Univ of Vermont	VT	28,878	HC
Univ of Washington	WA	23,149	VC
Univ of West Florida	FL	15,848	C
Univ of Wisc-Eau Claire	WI	15,797	VC
Univ of Wisc-Green Bay	WI	15,064	C
Univ of Wisc-Madison	WI	20,934	MC
Univ of Wisc-Milwaukee	WI	21,496	C
Univ of Wisc-Oshkosh	WI	15,200	C
Univ of Wisc-River Falls	WI	14,485	C
Univ of Wisc-Stevens Point	WI	14,043	C
Univ of Wisc-Superior	WI	14,446	C
Univ of Wisc-Whitewater	WI	13,976	C
Univ of Wyoming	WY	15,375	C+
Ursuline College	OH	41,076	LC
Utah State Univ	UT	12,736	C
Valparaiso Univ	IN	48,370	C+
Virginia Commonwealth Univ	VA	23,049	C
Virginia State Univ	VA	19,802	C+
Virginia Union Univ	VA	22,421	C
Virginia Wesleyan College	VA	43,728	LC
Viterbo Univ	WI	34,660	C
Walla Walla Univ	WA	30,417	NC
Warner Univ	FL	28,216	C
Warren Wilson College	NC	44,220	VC
Wartburg College	IA	47,840	C
Washburn Univ	KS	15,827	C
Washington State Univ	WA	22,495	C
Wayne State Univ	MI	22,016	C
Weber State Univ	UT	10,721	C
West Chester Univ of Pennsylvania	PA	18,456	C
West Texas A&M Univ	TX	13,478	C
West Virginia State Univ	WV	8,378	NC
West Virginia Univ	WV	18,210	C
Western Carolina Univ	NC	13,965	C
Western Conn State Univ	CT	21,254	LC
Western Illinois Univ	IL	20,825	C
Western Kentucky Univ	KY	16,850	C
Western Mich Univ	MI	21,054	C
Western New England Univ	MA	48,088	C
Western New Mexico Univ	NM	16,734	LC
Westfield State Univ	MA	19,671	C
Wheelock College	MA	49,225	C
Whittier College	CA	57,891	C
Wichita State Univ	KS	21,643	C
Widener Univ	PA	56,486	C
Wilberforce Univ	OH	19,016	C
William Woods Univ	MO	32,040	C
Wilmington College	OH	34,600	C
Winona State Univ	MN	17,535	C
Winthrop Univ	SC	23,082	C
Wright State Univ	OH	16,983	C
Xavier Univ	OH	47,880	C+
Youngstown State Univ	OH	17,307	C

SOCIOLOGY

School	ST	$IS	SR
Abilene Christian Univ	TX	41,800	C+
Adams State Univ	CO	17,703	LC
Adelphi Univ	NY	48,244	C
Adrian College	MI	42,400	C
Agnes Scott College	GA	51,930	VC+
Alabama A&M Univ	AL	18,796	C
Alabama State Univ	AL	14,142	NC
Albany State Univ	GA	19,462	C
Albertus Magnus College	CT	43,258	LC
Albion College	MI	52,650	C
Albright College	PA	46,660	C
Alcorn State Univ	MS	15,854	C
Alfred Univ	NY	42,296	C+
Allen Univ	SC	19,300	NC
Alma College	MI	47,548	C
Alverno College	WI	33,294	LC
American International College	MA	46,300	LC
American Univ	DC	59,379	HC+
Amherst College	MA		HC+
Anderson Univ	IN	38,200	C
Andrews Univ	MI	28,030	C+
Angelo State Univ	TX	15,263	NC
Anna Maria College	MA	48,186	C
Appalachian State Univ	NC	14,416	VC
Aquinas College - Mich	MI	38,876	HC
Arcadia Univ	PA	33,570	C+
Arizona State Univ at the Tempe Campus	AZ	21,756	VC
Arizona State Univ at the West Campus	AZ	20,640	C
Arkansas State Univ	AR	16,190	C
Arkansas Tech Univ	AR	15,484	C
Asbury Univ	KY	35,180	C+
Ashford Univ	CA	10,480	C
Ashland Univ	OH	21,440	C
Assumption College	MA	47,920	C+
Auburn Univ	AL	23,594	VC+
Auburn Univ at Montgomery	AL	15,290	C
Augsburg College	MN	43,929	C
Augusta Univ	GA	4,632	C
Augustana College	IL	49,658	VC
Augustana Univ	SD	38,424	VC
Aurora Univ	IL	33,970	C
Austin College	TX	45,875	VC
Austin Peay State Univ	TN	16,397	C
Averett Univ	VA	40,970	LC
Avila Univ	MO	35,480	C
Azusa Pacific Univ	CA	43,972	C
Baker Univ	KS	33,350	C+
Baldwin Wallace Univ	OH	41,106	C
Ball State Univ	IN	19,590	C
Bard College	NY	64,024	HC
Barnard College/Columbia Univ	NY	62,741	MC
Barry Univ	FL	37,830	C
Bates College	ME	64,500	MC
Bayamon Central Univ	PR	12,490	
Baylor Univ	TX	53,760	HC
Bellarmine Univ	KY	51,220	C
Bellevue Univ	NE	20,300	NC
Belmont Univ	TN	40,970	VC
Beloit College	WI	55,206	HC
Bemidji State Univ	MN	16,056	VC
Benedict College	SC	28,238	NC
Benedictine College	KS	36,200	VC
Benedictine Univ	IL	38,300	C
Bennington College	VT	63,960	MC
Berea College	KY	7,042	C
Berry College	GA	45,286	C+
Bethel College	IN	35,860	C
Bethel Univ	TN	24,738	C
Bethune-Cookman Univ	FL	22,970	C
Biola Univ	CA	46,402	C+
Birmingham-Southern College	AL	44,478	VC
Black Hills State Univ	SD	15,899	C
Bloomfield College	NJ	39,100	LC
Bloomsburg Univ of Pennsylvania	PA	19,066	LC
Bluffton Univ	OH	40,950	C
Boise State Univ	ID	14,860	C
Boston College	MA	65,737	MC
Boston Univ	MA	65,110	MC
Bowdoin College	ME	63,500	MC
Bowie State Univ	MD	26,728	LC
Bowling Green State Univ	OH	19,747	C
Brandeis Univ	MA	65,925	MC
Brewton-Parker College	GA	23,490	C
Briar Cliff Univ	IA	36,956	C
Bridgewater College	VA	44,510	C
Bridgewater State Univ	MA	21,810	C
Brigham Young Univ	UT	12,748	HC
Brown Univ	RI	64,566	MC
Bryant Univ	RI	55,646	VC
Bryn Athyn College	PA	31,470	C
Bryn Mawr College	PA	59,890	MC
Bucknell Univ	PA	64,616	MC
Butler Univ	IN	51,352	VC
Cabrini Univ	PA	42,591	LC
Caldwell Univ	NJ	42,165	NC
Calif Baptist Univ	CA	41,392	C
Calif Lutheran Univ	CA	52,853	C
Calif Polytechnic State Univ	CA	17,979	HC+
Calif State Polytechnic Univ, Pomona	CA	21,541	C
Cal State, Bakersfield	CA	19,191	LC
Cal State, Chico	CA	21,440	C
Cal State, Dominguez Hills	CA	19,022	LC
Cal State, East Bay	CA	19,413	C
Cal State, Fresno	CA	16,902	LC
Cal State, Long Beach	CA	18,850	C
Cal State, Los Angeles	CA	17,186	LC
Cal State, Northridge	CA	16,859	LC
Cal State, Sacramento	CA	20,332	C
Cal State, San Bernardino	CA	12,000	C
Cal State, San Marcos	CA	24,184	LC
Cal State, Stanislaus	CA	16,212	C
Calvin College	MI	41,570	VC+
Cameron Univ	OK	11,072	NC
Campbellsville Univ	KY	32,492	C
Canisius College	NY	47,537	C
Capital Univ	OH	42,982	C
Cardinal Stritch Univ	WI	36,462	C
Carleton College	MN	64,071	MC
Carlow Univ	PA	38,549	LC
Carroll College	MT	39,972	C+
Carroll Univ	WI	38,100	C+
Carson-Newman Univ	TN	34,160	C
Carthage College	WI	48,835	C
Case Western Reserve Univ	OH	60,304	MC
Castleton Univ	VT	20,186	C
Catawba College	NC	39,820	C
Centenary College	NJ	43,602	C
Centenary College of Louisiana	LA	45,650	C+
Central College	IA	44,592	C
Central Conn State Univ	CT	21,203	C
Central Methodist Univ	MO	36,830	VC
Central Mich Univ	MI	20,330	C
Central State Univ	OH	18,564	C
Central Washington Univ	WA	16,803	C
Centre College	KY	49,250	HC
Chadron State College	NE	14,819	NC
Chapman Univ	CA	63,078	VC+
Charleston Southern Univ	SC	32,400	C
Chestnut Hill College	PA	43,410	C
Chicago State Univ	IL	20,144	C
Christopher Newport Univ	VA	23,968	VC+
CUNY/Baruch College	NY	21,609	HC
CUNY/Brooklyn College	NY	5,884	C+
CUNY/City College	NY	20,319	VC
CUNY/College of Staten Island	NY	17,840	NC
CUNY/Hunter College	NY	31,098	VC
CUNY/Lehman College	NY	5,778	HC+
CUNY/Queens College	NY	27,896	C
CUNY/York College	NY	6,747	LC
Claflin Univ	SC	33,764	LC
Clarion Univ of Pennsylvania	PA	21,608	LC
Clark Atlanta Univ	GA	31,019	LC
Clark Univ	MA	51,600	HC+
Clemson Univ	SC		HC
Cleveland State Univ	OH	22,196	C
Coastal Carolina Univ	SC	19,766	C
Coe College	IA	51,570	VC
Coker College	SC	34,810	LC
Colby College	ME	64,060	MC
Colby-Sawyer College	NH	50,790	C
Colgate Univ	NY	65,030	MC
College of Charleston	SC	22,699	C
College of Mount St. Vincent	NY	45,620	C
College of St. Benedict	MN	52,806	C
College of St. Elizabeth	NJ	44,432	LC
College of the Holy Cross	MA	62,165	MC
College of the Ozarks	MO	7,230	C
College of William & Mary	VA		MC
Colo College	CO	62,560	MC
Colo Mesa Univ	CO	18,955	LC
Colo State Univ	CO	22,162	VC
Colo State Univ-Pueblo	CO	18,234	C
Columbia College	SC	36,550	C
Columbia College - Missouri	MO	27,803	C
Columbia Univ/ School of General Studies	NY	61,470	MC
Columbia Univ/City of New York	NY	62,958	MC
Columbus State Univ	GA	14,336	LC
Concord Univ	WV	14,954	C
Concordia College - Moorhead	MN	51,088	C+
Concordia College - New York	NY	39,035	LC
Concordia Univ St. Paul	MN	29,050	C
Concordia Univ, Ann Arbor	MI	35,945	VC
Concordia Univ, Chicago	IL	39,694	C
Conn College	CT	65,000	MC
Cornell College	IA	48,800	VC
Cornell Univ	NY	64,853	MC
Covenant College	GA	38,990	VC
Creighton Univ	NE	48,206	VC+
Cumberland Univ	TN	27,710	C
Curry College	MA	51,815	C
Dakota Wesleyan Univ	SD	32,850	C
Dallas Baptist Univ	TX	33,713	C
Dartmouth College	NH	66,174	MC
Davidson College	NC	60,119	MC
Delaware State Univ	DE	19,376	NC
Denison Univ	OH	58,860	MC
DePaul Univ	IL	47,623	VC
DePauw Univ	IN	58,688	HC+
Dickinson College	PA	63,974	MC
Dickinson State Univ	ND	12,372	LC
Dillard Univ	LA	20,940	VC
Doane Univ	NE	39,184	VC
Dominican Univ	IL	41,222	C
Dordt College	IA	37,860	C+
Drake Univ	IA	45,056	HC
Drew Univ/College of Liberal Arts	NJ	61,048	VC
Drexel Univ	PA	65,432	VC+
Drury Univ	MO	33,791	VC
Duke Univ	NC	64,188	
Duquesne Univ	PA	46,822	VC
D'Youville College	NY	36,780	C
Earlham College	IN	54,870	HC
East Carolina Univ	NC	16,937	C
East Central Univ	OK	13,056	C
East Stroudsburg Univ	PA	18,334	C
East Tenn State Univ	TN	13,994	C
East Texas Baptist Univ	TX	33,134	C
Eastern Conn State Univ	CT	23,059	C
Eastern Illinois Univ	IL	21,126	C
Eastern Kentucky Univ	KY	16,908	C
Eastern Mennonite Univ	VA	42,550	C
Eastern Mich Univ	MI	19,761	C
Eastern Nazarene College	MA	39,955	C
Eastern New Mexico Univ	NM	14,416	C
Eastern Oregon Univ	OR	17,715	C
Eastern Univ	PA	39,540	C
Eastern Washington Univ	WA	25,572	LC
Eckerd College	FL	52,874	C
Edgewood College	WI	35,950	C
Edward Waters College	FL	20,607	NC
Elizabeth City State Univ	NC	14,745	C
Elizabethtown College	PA	54,050	C
Elmhurst College	IL	45,428	C
Elmira College	NY	53,900	C
Elms College	MA	45,646	VC
Elon Univ	NC	44,599	VC+
Emmanuel College	MA	52,110	C+
Emory and Henry College	VA	41,410	C
Emory Univ	GA	60,786	MC
Emporia State Univ	KS	14,570	C
Eugene Lang College/The New School for Liberal Arts	NY	55,650	C
Eureka College	IL	30,220	C
Evangel Univ	MO	28,898	C
Excelsior College	NY	14,080	SP
Fairfield Univ	CT	59,860	VC+
Fairleigh Dickinson Univ/ College at Florham	NJ	52,062	C
Fairmont State Univ	WV	15,726	C
Fayetteville State Univ	NC	17,756	C
Ferris State Univ	MI	21,445	C
Fisk Univ	TN	32,066	LC
Fitchburg State Univ	MA	21,819	C
Flagler College	FL	27,620	C
Florida A&M Univ	FL	15,361	C
Florida Atlantic Univ	FL	17,339	C
Florida Gulf Coast Univ	FL	9,682	C
Florida International Univ	FL	19,854	C+
Florida Memorial Univ	FL	22,270	LC
Florida State Univ	FL	16,771	HC
Fontbonne Univ	MO	33,717	C
Fordham Univ	NY	65,918	MC
Fort Hays State Univ	KS	12,131	C
Fort Lewis College	CO	18,980	C
Fort Valley State Univ	GA	17,988	VC
Framingham State Univ	MA	20,584	C
Francis Marion Univ	SC	16,464	LC
Franciscan Univ of Steubenville	OH	33,980	VC
Franklin and Marshall College	PA	63,170	HC
Franklin College	IN	39,380	C
Frostburg State Univ	MD	17,280	LC
Furman Univ	SC	58,092	VC+
Gallaudet Univ	DC	29,118	LC
Gardner-Webb Univ	NC	39,200	C+
Geneva College	PA	35,450	C
George Fox Univ	OR	42,938	C
George Mason Univ	VA	15,724	VC
George Washington Univ	DC	62,835	MC
Georgetown College	KY	41,440	C
Georgetown Univ	DC	65,926	MC
Georgia College & State Univ	GA	21,148	C+
Georgia Southwestern State Univ	GA	13,870	C
Georgia State Univ	GA	24,332	VC
Gettysburg College	PA	63,000	HC
Gonzaga Univ	WA	50,888	HC
Gordon College	MA	46,472	C+
Goshen College	IN	42,500	C
Goucher College	MD	55,716	VC
Grace College and Seminary	IN	31,524	C
Graceland Univ	IA	35,290	C
Grambling State Univ	LA	15,701	C
Grand Canyon Univ	AZ	16,950	VC
Grand Valley State Univ	MI	22,250	C+
Green Mountain College	VT	45,228	LC
Greensboro College	NC	42,400	LC
Greenville College	IL	27,012	C
Grinnell College	IA	60,738	MC
Grove City College	PA	25,692	VC
Guilford College	NC	44,090	C
Gustavus Adolphus College	MN	52,433	HC
Hamilton College	NY	64,250	MC
Hamline Univ	MN	45,678	VC
Hampshire College	MA	63,824	MC
Hampton Univ	VA	34,926	LC
Hannibal-LaGrange Univ	MO	29,815	C
Hanover College	IN	46,364	C+
Hardin-Simmons Univ	TX	33,966	C
Hartwick College	NY	51,270	C
Harvard College/Harvard Univ	MA	60,659	MC
Hastings College	NE	35,380	C+
Haverford College	PA	66,490	MC
Hawaii Pacific Univ	HI	33,420	C
Henderson State Univ	AR	15,516	LC
Hendrix College	AR	54,020	VC+
High Point Univ	NC	45,977	C
Hillsdale College	MI	35,722	MC
Hiram College	OH	43,230	C

ST = STATE $IS = IN-STATE COSTS SR = SELECTOR RATING

School	ST	$IS	SR
Hofstra Univ	NY	55,960	C+
Hollins Univ	VA	49,635	VC
Holy Family Univ	PA	43,326	LC
Holy Names Univ	CA	46,630	LC
Hood College	MD	54,840	C
Hope College	MI	39,940	VC
Houghton College	NY	39,090	C
Houston Baptist Univ	TX	36,450	C
Howard Payne Univ	TX	34,320	C
Howard Univ	DC	37,616	C+
Humboldt State Univ	CA	20,514	C
Huntington Univ	IN	33,996	C
Huston-Tillotson Univ	TX	18,124	LC
Idaho State Univ	ID	13,619	NC
Illinois College	IL	40,850	VC
Illinois State Univ	IL	23,418	VC
Illinois Wesleyan Univ	IL	56,430	VC+
Indiana State Univ	IN	23,223	LC
Indiana Univ Bloomington	IN	20,429	VC
Indiana Univ East	IN	7,072	C
Indiana Univ Kokomo	IN	7,073	C
Indiana Univ Northwest	IN	7,072	C
Indiana Univ of Pennsylvania	PA	23,614	LC
Indiana Univ South Bend	IN	14,242	C
Indiana Univ Southeast	IN	14,242	LC
Indiana Univ-Purdue Univ Fort Wayne	IN	17,553	C
Indiana Univ-Purdue Univ Indianapolis	IN	18,635	C
Indiana Wesleyan Univ	IN	33,674	C
Inter-American Univ of PR Ponce	PR	19,549	
Inter-American Univ of PR-Fajardo Campus	PR	18,336	
Inter-American Univ of PR-Metropolitan Campus	PR	20,045	
Inter-American Univ of PR-San Germán	PR	20,042	
Iona College	NY	50,984	C
Iowa State Univ	IA	17,570	C
Iowa Wesleyan Univ	IA	39,200	C
Ithaca College	NY	56,766	VC
Jackson State Univ	MS	15,879	LC
Jacksonville State Univ	AL	14,628	LC
Jacksonville Univ	FL	46,230	C
James Madison Univ	VA	19,084	VC
Jarvis Christian College	TX	20,160	NC
John Carroll Univ	OH	49,740	C+
Johns Hopkins Univ	MD	65,386	MC
Johnson & Wales Univ/Denver Campus	CO	42,707	C
Johnson C. Smith Univ	NC	25,336	LC
Johnson State College	VT	20,752	C
Judson Univ	IL	37,700	C
Juniata College	PA	53,760	VC
Kalamazoo College	MI	53,931	HC+
Kansas State Univ	KS	17,780	VC
Kansas Wesleyan Univ	KS	36,600	C
Kean Univ	NJ	24,650	C
Keene State College	NH	24,003	LC
Kennesaw State Univ	GA	19,592	VC
Kent State Univ	OH	20,732	C
Kentucky State Univ	KY	13,364	LC
Kentucky Wesleyan College	KY	32,080	C
Kenyon College	OH	63,330	MC
Keuka College	NY	39,762	C
King's College	PA	46,858	C
Knox College	IL	52,615	VC+
Kutztown Univ of Pennsylvania	PA	19,056	LC
La Roche College	PA	37,924	LC
La Salle Univ	PA	55,790	C
La Sierra Univ	CA	39,690	VC
Lafayette College	PA	63,355	MC
LaGrange College	GA	39,930	C
Lake Forest College	IL	50,652	VC
Lakeland Univ	WI	35,130	C
Lamar Univ	TX	18,014	LC
Lander Univ	SC	43,994	C
Lane College	TN	16,550	C
Langston Univ	OK	14,314	C
Lasell College	MA	47,500	C
Le Moyne College	NY	46,000	C
Lebanon Valley College	PA	51,530	C
Lee Univ	TN	22,045	C
Lehigh Univ	PA	61,010	MC
LeMoyne-Owen College	TN	16,980	C
Lenoir-Rhyne Univ	NC	43,200	C
Lewis & Clark College	OR	58,434	HC+
Lewis Univ	IL	40,370	C
Lewis-Clark State College	ID	14,202	C
Lincoln Univ	MO	13,602	NC
Lindenwood Univ	MO	25,132	C
Linfield College	OR	52,010	C
LIU Brooklyn	NY	49,682	C
LIU Post	NY	49,682	C
Livingstone College	NC	17,815	LC
Lock Haven Univ of Pennsylvania	PA	18,028	LC
Longwood Univ	VA	22,184	C
Loras College	IA	39,222	C
Louisiana College	LA	21,886	C
Louisiana State Univ and A&M College	LA	18,677	VC
Louisiana State Univ in Shreveport	LA	6,902	C
Louisiana Tech Univ	LA	11,422	VC
Lourdes Univ	OH	29,520	NC
Loyola Marymount Univ	CA	58,038	HC
Loyola Univ Chicago	IL	55,802	VC
Loyola Univ Maryland	MD	60,300	VC
Loyola Univ New Orleans	LA	51,708	VC+
Luther College	IA	48,540	C+
Lycoming College	PA	48,580	C
Lynchburg College	VA	46,740	C
Macalester College	MN	61,905	MC
Madonna Univ	MI	29,050	C
Manchester Univ	IN	40,422	C
Manhattan College	NY	51,750	C+
Manhattanville College	NY	51,440	C+
Marian Univ	IN	41,220	C
Marquette Univ	WI	48,390	VC+
Mars Hill Univ	NC	42,688	C
Marshall Univ	WV	17,242	C
Martin Univ	IN	20,264	LC
Mary Baldwin Univ	VA	39,865	C
Marymount Manhattan College	NY	46,280	VC
Marymount Univ	VA	41,570	LC
Maryville College	TN	44,410	C
Maryville Univ of St. Louis	MO	38,046	VC+
Mass College of Liberal Arts	MA	20,128	C
Mayville State Univ	ND	18,371	NC
McDaniel College	MD	51,380	VC
McKendree Univ	IL	37,940	C+
McMurry Univ	TX	34,259	LC
McNeese State Univ	LA	7,838	C
McPherson College	KS	34,909	C
Mercer Univ	GA	45,348	VC
Mercy College	NY	31,776	C
Mercyhurst Univ	PA	47,420	C
Meredith College	NC	45,297	C
Merrimack College	MA	52,770	C
Messiah College	PA	43,100	C+
Methodist Univ	NC	43,600	C
Metropolitan State Univ of Denver	CO	29,889	LC
Miami Univ	OH	27,190	HC+
Mich State Univ	MI	23,898	VC+
MidAmerica Nazarene Univ	KS	35,550	C
Middle Tenn State Univ	TN	8,650	C
Middlebury College	VT	64,332	MC
Midland Univ	NE	37,468	
Midwestern State Univ	TX	17,572	C
Millersville Univ of Pennsylvania	PA	23,782	C
Milligan College	TN	38,150	C
Millikin Univ	IL	42,158	C
Mills College	CA	59,163	VC
Millsaps College	MS	50,080	C+
Minn State Univ, Mankato	MN	15,616	C
Minn State Univ, Moorhead	MN	15,941	C
Minot State Univ	ND	12,732	C
Miss College	MS	25,850	C
Miss State Univ	MS	11,454	C+
Miss Valley State Univ	MS	13,233	LC
Missouri Southern State Univ	MO	12,499	C
Missouri State Univ	MO	15,190	C+
Missouri Valley College	MO	28,150	C
Molloy College	NY	40,440	C
Monmouth College	IL	42,260	C
Monmouth Univ	NJ	46,234	C
Montana State Univ	MT	15,500	C+
Montana State Univ-Billings	MT	22,960	C
Montclair State Univ	NJ	26,210	LC
Moravian College	PA	53,117	
Morehead State Univ	KY	17,422	C
Morehouse College	GA	40,064	C
Morgan State Univ	MD	17,190	LC
Morris College	SC	18,500	LC
Mount Holyoke College	MA	56,746	MC
Mount Ida College	MA	46,820	C
Mount Mary Univ	WI	34,650	LC
Mount Mercy Univ	IA	36,826	C
Mount St. Mary College	NY	42,061	C
Mount St. Joseph Univ	OH	33,880	C
Mount St. Mary's Univ	MD	51,610	C
Mount St. Mary's Univ - Chalon Campus	CA	43,897	VC+
Mount Vernon Nazarene Univ	OH	34,500	C
Muhlenberg College	PA	56,645	VC+
Murray State Univ	KY	16,998	C
Muskingum Univ	OH	35,966	C
National Univ	CA	14,730	LC
Nazareth College	NY	45,574	C
Nebr Wesleyan Univ	NE	38,140	C+
New College of Florida	FL	15,848	MC
New England College	NH	50,364	C
New Jersey City Univ	NJ	21,456	LC
New Mexico Highlands Univ	NM	11,904	NC
New Mexico State Univ	NM	14,050	C
New York Inst of Technology	NY	48,730	C
New York Univ	NY	65,860	MC
Newberry College	SC	34,550	C
Newman Univ	KS	35,390	C
Niagara Univ	NY	41,010	C
Nicholls State Univ	LA	10,534	C
Norfolk State Univ	VA	25,702	LC
N Car A&T State Univ	NC	13,365	LC
N Car Central Univ	NC	9,000	C
N Car State Univ	NC	19,515	HC+
N Car Wesleyan College	NC	39,200	C
North Central College	IL	48,712	VC
N Dak State Univ	ND	16,245	C
North Park Univ	IL	35,860	C
Northeastern Illinois Univ	IL	12,529	LC
Northeastern State Univ	OK	8,615	VC
Northeastern Univ	MA	62,703	MC
Northern Arizona Univ	AZ	20,246	VC
Northern Illinois Univ	IL	20,176	C
Northern Kentucky Univ	KY	16,486	C
Northern Mich Univ	MI	19,604	C
Northern State Univ	SD	14,505	C
Northland College	WI	41,103	C+
Northwest Missouri State Univ	MO	17,737	C
Northwestern College of Iowa	IA	38,400	C+
Northwestern Okla State Univ	OK	13,072	NC
Northwestern Univ	IL	66,344	MC
Notre Dame de Namur Univ	CA	46,526	LC
Nova Southeastern Univ	FL	38,534	C+
Nyack College	NY	34,050	NC
Oakland Univ	MI	20,763	C
Oberlin College	OH	66,012	MC
Occidental College	CA	65,530	MC
Oglala Lakota College	SD	15,050	NC
Oglethorpe Univ	GA	44,200	C+
Ohio Dominican Univ	OH	41,340	C+
Ohio Northern Univ	OH	44,050	VC
Ohio State Univ at Columbus	OH	21,703	HC+
Ohio Univ	OH	22,924	C
Ohio Valley Univ	WV	29,480	C
Ohio Wesleyan Univ	OH	49,460	VC
Okla Baptist Univ	OK	32,320	C
Okla City Univ	OK	40,476	VC
Okla State Univ	OK	17,180	VC
Okla Wesleyan Univ	OK	33,206	C
Old Dominion Univ	VA	20,910	C
Olivet College	MI	36,110	LC
Olivet Nazarene Univ	IL	41,840	C
Oregon State Univ	OR	22,519	VC
Ottawa Univ	KS	36,074	VC
Otterbein Univ	OH	41,630	C
Ouachita Baptist Univ	AR	32,320	C
Our Lady of the Lake Univ	TX	35,012	LC
Pace Univ	NY	58,248	C
Pacific Lutheran Univ	WA	49,960	VC
Pacific Univ	OR	52,876	C
Paine College	GA	19,506	LC
Park Univ	MO	20,329	C
Pennsylvania State Univ - Univ Park	PA	29,760	HC
Pepperdine Univ	CA	74,460	HC+
Peru State College	NE	14,768	NC
Philander Smith College	AR	20,814	LC
Piedmont College	GA	32,512	C
Pittsburg State Univ	KS	13,880	NC
Pitzer College	CA	66,192	MC
Point Loma Nazarene Univ	CA	43,450	C
Pomona College	CA	64,957	MC
Pontifical Catholic Univ of PR	PR	10,534	
Portland State Univ	OR	19,443	C
Post Univ	CT	41,150	C
Prairie View A&M Univ	TX	15,205	LC
Prescott College	AZ	33,284	C
Princeton Univ	NJ	57,610	MC
Principia College	IL	39,010	C+
Providence College	RI	60,760	VC
Purdue Univ/Northwest	IN	15,038	C
Purdue Univ/West Lafayette	IN	20,032	MC
Queens Univ of Charlotte	NC	39,543	C
Quinnipiac Univ	CT	59,110	C
Radford Univ	VA	19,027	LC
Ramapo College of New Jersey	NJ	25,338	C
Randolph College	VA	45,660	VC
Randolph-Macon College	VA	49,910	C
Reed College	OR	65,300	MC
Regis College	MA	51,920	C
Regis Univ	CO	44,520	C
Rhode Island College	RI	17,694	LC
Rhodes College	TN	51,900	HC
Rice Univ	TX	57,668	MC
Rider Univ	NJ	54,050	C
Ripon College	WI	46,911	C+
Rivier Univ	NH	40,410	VC
Roanoke College	VA	54,114	VC
Robert Morris Univ	PA	37,834	C
Rochester Inst of Technology	NY	50,842	HC
Rockford Univ	IL	36,030	C
Rocky Mountain College	MT	34,270	C
Roger Williams Univ	RI	46,296	C+
Rollins College	FL	58,670	HC
Roosevelt Univ	IL	40,651	VC
Rosemont College	PA	30,980	C
Rowan Univ	NJ	24,491	VC+
Russell Sage College	NY	39,370	C
Rust College	MS	10,600	C
Rutgers Univ - Camden	NJ	26,146	C
Rutgers Univ - New Brunswick	NJ	26,632	HC
Rutgers Univ - Newark	NJ	27,288	C
Sacred Heart Univ	CT	52,750	C
Saginaw Valley State Univ	MI	18,530	C
St. Anselm College	NH	52,560	C+
St. Augustine's Univ	NC	26,048	C
St. Francis Univ	PA	42,268	NC
St. John's Univ	MN	51,624	C
St. Joseph's College of Maine	ME	46,485	C
St. Joseph's Univ	PA	57,544	VC+
St. Leo Univ	FL	31,650	C
St. Louis Univ	MO	49,866	HC
St. Martin's Univ	WA	45,056	C
St. Mary's College	IN	50,600	C
St. Mary's College of Calif	CA	57,420	C
St. Mary's Univ of Minn	MN	41,210	VC
St. Michael's College	VT	51,725	VC+
St. Peter's Univ	NJ	49,192	C
St. Vincent College	PA	44,626	C
St. Xavier Univ	IL	43,310	C
Salem College	NC	37,694	HC
Salem State Univ	MA	17,303	LC
Salisbury Univ	MD	20,714	VC
Salve Regina Univ	RI	51,470	C
Sam Houston State Univ	TX	18,792	C
Samford Univ	AL	39,232	VC
San Diego State Univ	CA	21,896	C+
San Francisco State Univ	CA	18,514	LC
San Jose State Univ	CA	21,540	C
Sarah Lawrence College	NY	63,388	HC
Savannah State Univ	GA	15,631	C
Scripps College	CA	66,664	MC
Seattle Pacific Univ	WA	47,439	C+
Seattle Univ	WA	50,811	VC+
Seton Hall Univ	NJ	55,514	C
Seton Hill Univ	PA	46,972	C
Shaw Univ	NC	24,638	C
Shenandoah Univ	VA	41,312	C
Shepherd Univ, West Virginia	WV	17,224	C
Shippensburg Univ of Pennsylvania	PA	23,208	C
Siena College	NY	48,916	C+
Simmons College	MA	53,090	VC
Simpson College	IA	43,839	VC
Skidmore College	NY	64,214	HC
Slippery Rock Univ of Pennsylvania	PA	10,360	C
Smith College	MA	63,914	MC
Sonoma State Univ	CA	27,806	C
S Car State Univ	SC	20,805	LC
S Dak State Univ	SD	15,634	C
Southeastern Louisiana Univ	LA	16,237	C
Southeastern Okla State Univ	OK	11,875	C
Southern Arkansas Univ	AR	21,532	C
Southern Conn State Univ	CT	21,924	LC
Southern Illinois Univ Carbondale	IL	23,667	C
Southern Illinois Univ Edwardsville	IL	22,643	C
Southern Methodist Univ	TX	66,483	MC
Southern Nazarene Univ	OK	32,798	NC
Southern Oregon Univ	OR	19,117	C
Southern Univ and A&M College	LA	16,074	LC+
Southern Univ at New Orleans	LA	8,014	LC
Southwest Baptist Univ	MO	29,900	LC
Southwest Minn State Univ	MN	17,783	C
Southwestern Univ	TX	50,720	VC
Spelman College	GA	38,751	C
Spring Arbor Univ	MI	36,000	C
Spring Hill College	AL	48,488	C
Springfield College	MA	45,995	C
St. Ambrose Univ	IA	39,019	C
St. Ambrose Univ	IA	39,019	C
St. Bonaventure Univ	NY	44,237	C
St. Catherine Univ	MN	45,630	VC
St. Cloud State Univ	MN	10,600	C
St. Edward's Univ	TX	53,100	VC
St. Francis College	NY	38,800	LC
St. John Fisher College	NY	43,620	C
St. John's Univ	NY	55,850	C
St. Joseph's College, New York/Brooklyn Campus	NY	25,114	LC
St. Joseph's College, New York/Long Island Campus	NY	25,124	C
St. Lawrence Univ	NY	64,390	VC
St. Mary's College of Maryland	MD	26,634	VC
St. Mary's Univ	TX	37,500	C
St. Norbert College	WI	44,525	VC
St. Olaf College	MN	54,260	HC+
Stanford Univ	CA	60,409	MC
SUNY / Buffalo State College	NY	20,842	C
SUNY / Empire State College	NY	9,145	SP
SUNY / SUNY College at Old Westbury	NY	16,860	C
SUNY / SUNY Cortland	NY	20,706	VC
SUNY / SUNY Fredonia	NY	20,818	C
SUNY / SUNY Oneonta	NY	19,712	C+
SUNY / SUNY Plattsburgh	NY	18,814	C
SUNY / SUNY Potsdam	NY	20,404	C+
SUNY / Univ at Buffalo	NY	23,122	C+
SUNY at Binghamton	NY	22,861	MC
SUNY at Geneseo	NY	20,440	VC+
SUNY at New Paltz	NY	19,200	C
SUNY at Oswego	NY	21,351	C
SUNY at Purchase	NY	17,900	C
SUNY Polytechnic Inst	NY	19,473	VC
SUNY SUNY Albany	NY	22,165	C
Stephen F. Austin State Univ	TX	18,406	LC
Stetson Univ	FL	53,544	VC
Stonehill College	MA	55,030	C+
Stony Brook Univ/The SUNY	NY	21,881	MC
Suffolk Univ	MA	50,308	C
Susquehanna Univ	PA	55,340	VC
Swarthmore College	PA	63,550	MC
Syracuse Univ	NY	60,239	VC
Talladega College	AL	19,215	C
Tarleton State Univ	TX	15,248	LC
Taylor Univ	IN	40,317	C+
Temple Univ	PA	24,392	VC
Tenn State Univ	TN	14,423	C

ST = STATE $IS = IN-STATE COSTS SR = SELECTOR RATING

School	ST	$IS	SR
Tenn Tech Univ	TN	17,050	C
Texas A&M Univ	TX	20,521	VC+
Texas A&M Univ at Commerce	TX	10,496	C
Texas A&M Univ at Corpus Christi	TX	16,851	LC
Texas A&M Univ at Kingsville	TX	7,500	LC
Texas Christian Univ	TX	54,670	HC
Texas Lutheran Univ	TX	38,620	C
Texas Southern Univ	TX	18,212	LC
Texas State Univ	TX	19,350	C
Texas Tech Univ	TX	18,736	C+
Texas Wesleyan Univ	TX	35,134	C
Texas Woman's Univ	TX	15,302	LC
The Catholic Univ of America	DC	56,356	VC
The College at Brockport - SUNY	NY	20,346	C
The College of New Jersey	NJ	31,909	HC
The College of New Rochelle	NY	46,300	VC
The College of Wooster	OH	57,900	VC+
The Evergreen State College	WA	16,599	C
The Lincoln Univ	PA	15,154	NC
The Univ of Akron	OH	21,477	C
The Univ of Tenn at Chattanooga	TN	16,744	C
The Univ of Tenn at Knoxville	TN	22,112	VC
The Univ of Tenn at Martin	TN	14,876	C
The Univ of Utah	UT	17,924	VC
Thiel College	PA	41,590	C
Thomas Edison State Univ	NJ	6,350	NC
Thomas More College	KY	36,720	C
Tougaloo College	MS	17,980	NC
Touro College	NY	28,950	VC
Towson Univ	MD	17,408	VC
Transylvania Univ	KY	45,690	VC+
Trevecca Nazarene Univ	TN	31,186	C
Trinity Christian College	IL	35,580	C
Trinity College	CT	63,920	HC+
Trinity Univ	TX	52,314	HC+
Trinity Washington Univ	DC	33,826	C+
Troy Univ	AL	16,171	C
Truman State Univ	MO	16,014	HC
Tufts Univ	MA		MC
Tulane Univ	LA	63,396	HC+
Tuskegee Univ	AL	28,164	C
Union College	KY	32,310	C
Union College	NY	64,320	MC
Union Univ	TN	33,970	VC
United States Military Academy at West Point	NY		HC+
Universidad del Turabo	PR	17,828	
Universidad Metropolitana	PR	17,828	
Univ of Alabama at Birmingham	AL	19,906	C
Univ of Alabama in Huntsville	AL	19,445	VC
Univ of Alaska Anchorage	AK	16,652	NC
Univ of Alaska Fairbanks	AK	16,179	C
Univ of Arizona	AZ	23,100	C
Univ of Arkansas at Fayetteville	AR	19,152	C+
Univ of Arkansas at Little Rock	AR	18,211	C
Univ of Arkansas at Pine Bluff	AR	13,541	C
Univ of Calif at Berkeley	CA	28,853	MC
Univ of Calif at Davis	CA	28,468	HC
Univ of Calif at Irvine	CA	26,484	VC
Univ of Calif at Los Angeles	CA	30,162	MC
Univ of Calif at Riverside	CA	29,227	C+
Univ of Calif at Santa Barbara	CA	29,091	HC
Univ of Calif San Diego	CA	30,150	MC
Univ of Calif, Santa Cruz	CA	28,731	C+
Univ of Central Arkansas	AR	14,472	VC
Univ of Central Florida	FL	15,922	VC
Univ of Central Missouri	MO	18,982	C
Univ of Central Okla	OK	13,486	C
Univ of Chicago	IL	67,584	MC
Univ of Cincinnati	OH	21,964	VC
Univ of Colo Boulder	CO	24,285	VC+
Univ of Colo Colo Springs	CO	19,663	C
Univ of Colo Denver	CO	23,230	C
Univ of Conn	CT	25,538	HC
Univ of Dayton	OH	53,620	C
Univ of Delaware	DE	24,976	VC+
Univ of Denver	CO	58,443	VC+
Univ of Detroit Mercy	MI	48,816	C+
Univ of Dubuque	IA	37,824	C
Univ of Evansville	IN	44,186	VC+
Univ of Findlay	OH	60,139	C
Univ of Florida	FL	16,291	HC+
Univ of Georgia	GA	21,250	HC
Univ of Great Falls	MT	38,524	C
Univ of Hartford	CT	49,776	C
Univ of Hawaii at Hilo	HI	18,038	C
Univ of Hawaii at Manoa	HI	23,221	C
Univ of Houston-Downtown	TX	7,241	C
Univ of Idaho	ID	15,348	C
Univ of Illinois at Chicago	IL	25,006	VC
Univ of Illinois at Urbana-Champaign	IL	27,006	HC
Univ of Indianapolis	IN	36,480	C
Univ of Iowa	IA	18,683	VC+
Univ of Kansas	KS	20,135	C+
Univ of Kentucky	KY	33,306	C
Univ of La Verne	CA	55,600	C
Univ of Louisiana at Lafayette	LA	14,516	C
Univ of Louisville	KY	19,824	C
Univ of Maine	ME	20,792	C
Univ of Maine at Farmington	ME	18,187	C
Univ of Mary Hardin-Baylor	TX	33,950	C+
Univ of Mary Washington	VA	24,764	VC
Univ of Maryland/Baltimore County	MD	21,296	VC
Univ of Maryland/College Park	MD	21,938	HC
Univ of Maryland/Eastern Shore	MD	17,013	C
Univ of Mass Amherst	MA	26,199	VC+
Univ of Mass Boston	MA	13,435	C
Univ of Mass Dartmouth	MA	25,658	C
Univ of Mass Lowell	MA	26,380	C
Univ of Memphis	TN	18,278	C
Univ of Miami	FL	63,494	MC
Univ of Mich/Ann Arbor	MI	24,410	MC
Univ of Mich/Dearborn	MI	11,757	VC
Univ of Mich-Flint	MI	17,607	C+
Univ of Minn/Duluth	MN	20,292	C+
Univ of Minn/Morris	MN	20,760	VC
Univ of Minn/Twin Cities	MN	23,519	HC+
Univ of Miss	MS	17,746	C+
Univ of Missouri/Columbia	MO	18,201	MC
Univ of Missouri-Kansas City	MO	19,563	VC
Univ of Missouri-St. Louis	MO		C
Univ of Mobile	AL	28,935	C
Univ of Montana	MT	14,105	C
Univ of Montana-Western	MT	11,220	LC
Univ of Montevallo	AL	19,502	C
Univ of Mount Union	OH	38,970	C
Univ of Nebr - Kearney	NE	16,546	LC
Univ of Nebr - Lincoln	NE	18,589	VC
Univ of Nebr - Omaha	NE	16,120	C
Univ of Nevada, Las Vegas	NV	17,553	C
Univ of Nevada/Reno	NV	18,010	C
Univ of New England	ME	48,880	C
Univ of New Hampshire	NH	28,562	VC
Univ of New Mexico	NM	15,404	C
Univ of New Orleans	LA	12,840	C
Univ of North Alabama	AL	15,398	C
Univ of N Car at Asheville	NC	15,723	VC+
Univ of N Car at Chapel Hill	NC	20,052	HC+
Univ of N Car at Charlotte	NC	15,547	C
Univ of N Car at Greensboro	NC	14,690	C
Univ of N Car at Pembroke	NC	14,388	LC
Univ of N Car at Wilmington	NC	14,590	VC
Univ of N Dak	ND	15,373	C
Univ of North Florida	FL	15,996	VC
Univ of North Georgia	GA	17,316	C
Univ of North Texas	TX	19,198	C
Univ of Northern Colo	CO	20,851	C
Univ of Notre Dame	IN	64,043	MC
Univ of Okla	OK	18,911	VC
Univ of Oregon	OR	22,972	C
Univ of Pennsylvania	PA	63,526	MC
Univ of Pikeville	KY	28,700	NC
Univ of Pittsburgh	PA	29,568	HC+
Univ of Pittsburgh at Bradford	PA	22,402	C
Univ of Pittsburgh at Johnstown	PA	22,092	C
Univ of Portland	OR	52,152	VC
Univ of PR, at Mayaguez	PR	13,995	
Univ of PR-Rio Piedras campus	PR	13,327	
Univ of Puget Sound	WA	56,456	VC+
Univ of Redlands	CA	60,200	VC
Univ of Rhode Island	RI	24,906	C
Univ of Richmond	VA	60,880	MC
Univ of Rio Grande & Rio Grande Community College	OH	8,750	NC
Univ of St. Francis	IN	37,400	C
Univ of St. Mary	KS	34,690	C
Univ of San Diego	CA	58,442	VC+
Univ of San Francisco	CA	58,484	VC
Univ of Science and Arts of Okla	OK	11,140	VC
Univ of Scranton	PA	54,962	VC
Univ of Sioux Falls	SD	34,330	C
Univ of South Alabama	AL	16,400	C
Univ of S Car Aiken	SC	16,712	C
Univ of S Car at Columbia	SC	19,725	VC+
Univ of S Car Upstate	SC	18,200	LC
Univ of S Dak	SD	16,109	C
Univ of South Florida/Tampa	FL	16,110	VC+
Univ of Southern Calif	CA	66,631	C
Univ of Southern Indiana	IN	16,501	C
Univ of Southern Maine	ME	18,320	C
Univ of Southern Miss	MS	13,170	C
Univ of Tampa	FL	36,944	C
Univ of Texas at Arlington	TX	18,026	LC
Univ of Texas at Austin	TX	26,102	HC
Univ of Texas at Dallas	TX	22,830	VC+
Univ of Texas at El Paso	TX	34,452	NC
Univ of Texas at San Antonio	TX	20,157	C
Univ of the District of Columbia	DC	21,044	LC
Univ of the Incarnate Word	TX	39,162	LC
Univ of the Ozarks	AR	52,176	C
Univ of the Pacific	CA	57,006	VC
Univ of the Southwest	NM	22,766	C
Univ of Toledo	OH	19,336	NC
Univ of Tulsa	OK	52,625	HC+
Univ of Vermont	VT	28,878	HC
Univ of Virginia	VA	25,891	MC
Univ of Washington	WA	23,149	VC
Univ of West Alabama	AL	15,516	NC
Univ of West Georgia	GA	16,360	LC
Univ of Wisc-Eau Claire	WI	15,797	VC
Univ of Wisc-La Crosse	WI	15,247	C+
Univ of Wisc-Madison	WI	20,934	MC
Univ of Wisc-Milwaukee	WI	21,496	C
Univ of Wisc-Oshkosh	WI	15,200	C
Univ of Wisc-Parkside	WI	15,193	C
Univ of Wisc-River Falls	WI	14,485	C
Univ of Wisc-Stevens Point	WI	14,043	C
Univ of Wisc-Superior	WI	14,446	C
Univ of Wisc-Whitewater	WI	13,976	C
Univ of Wyoming	WY	15,375	C+
Upper Iowa Univ	IA	34,990	NC
Urbana Univ	OH	30,820	C
Ursinus College	PA	61,690	VC
Ursuline College	OH	41,076	LC
Utah State Univ	UT	12,736	C
Utica College	NY	30,430	C
Valparaiso Univ	IN	48,370	C+
Vanderbilt Univ	TN	60,572	MC
Vanguard Univ of Southern Calif	CA	40,740	VC
Vassar College	NY	65,491	MC
Villanova Univ	PA	62,523	MC
Virginia Commonwealth Univ	VA	23,049	C
Virginia Polytechnic Inst and State Univ	VA	21,276	HC
Virginia State Univ	VA	19,802	C+
Virginia Union Univ	VA	22,421	C
Virginia Wesleyan College	VA	43,728	LC
Viterbo Univ	WI	34,660	C
Voorhees College	SC	19,976	C
Wagner College	NY	55,480	C+
Wake Forest Univ	NC	64,056	MC
Walla Walla Univ	WA	30,417	NC
Walsh Univ	OH	39,010	C
Warner Pacific College	OR	33,790	C
Warren Wilson College	NC	44,220	VC
Wartburg College	IA	47,840	C
Washburn Univ	KS	15,827	C
Washington & Jefferson College	PA	56,512	VC
Washington and Lee Univ	VA	59,647	MC
Washington College	MD	54,666	VC
Washington State Univ	WA	22,495	C
Wayland Baptist Univ	TX	22,356	LC
Wayne State College	NE	12,802	C
Wayne State Univ	MI	22,016	C
Waynesburg Univ	PA	32,290	C
Weber State Univ	UT	10,721	C
Webster Univ	MO	37,490	C
Wellesley College	MA	63,916	MC
Wells College	NY	50,500	C
Wesleyan Univ	CT	65,516	MC
West Chester Univ of Pennsylvania	PA	18,456	C
West Liberty Univ	WV	15,512	C
West Texas A&M Univ	TX	13,478	C
West Virginia State Univ	WV	8,378	NC
West Virginia Univ	WV	18,210	C
West Virginia Wesleyan College	WV	36,858	C
Western Carolina Univ	NC	13,965	C
Western Conn State Univ	CT	21,254	LC
Western Illinois Univ	IL	20,825	C
Western Kentucky Univ	KY	16,850	C
Western Mich Univ	MI	21,054	C
Western New England Univ	MA	48,088	C
Western New Mexico Univ	NM	16,734	LC
Western Oregon Univ	OR	15,021	LC
Western State Colo Univ	CO	18,639	C
Western Washington Univ	WA	18,003	C+
Westfield State Univ	MA	19,671	C
Westminster College	MO	32,820	C
Westminster College	PA	39,180	C+
Westminster College	UT	41,078	C+
Westmont College	CA	56,410	HC
Wheaton College	IL	43,610	MC
Wheaton College	MA	61,512	VC
Whitman College	WA	59,772	MC
Whittier College	CA	57,891	C
Whitworth Univ	WA	51,732	VC
Wichita State Univ	KS	21,643	C
Widener Univ	PA	56,486	C
Wilberforce Univ	OH	19,016	C
Wiley College	TX	18,504	C
Wilkes Univ	PA	45,622	C
Willamette Univ	OR	61,817	VC+
William Paterson Univ of New Jersey	NJ	23,133	C
William Penn Univ	IA	26,000	C
Williams College	MA	63,290	MC
Wilmington College	OH	34,600	C
Wilson College	PA	35,620	C
Wingate Univ	NC	39,950	C
Winona State Univ	MN	17,535	C
Winston-Salem State Univ	NC	26,166	LC
Winthrop Univ	SC	23,082	C
Wittenberg Univ	OH	48,156	C+
Wofford College	SC	49,885	VC
Worcester State Univ	MA	20,977	C
Wright State Univ	OH	16,983	C
Xavier Univ	OH	47,880	C+
Xavier Univ of Louisiana	LA	31,689	C+
Yale Univ	CT	64,650	MC
Yeshiva Univ	NY	47,250	VC+
York College of Pennsylvania	PA	29,240	C
Youngstown State Univ	OH	17,307	C

SOFTWARE ENGINEERING

School	ST	$IS	SR
Allegheny College	PA	55,420	VC
Arizona State Univ at the Polytechnic Campus	AZ	21,360	VC
Auburn Univ	AL	23,594	VC+
Baldwin Wallace Univ	OH	41,106	C
Butler Univ	IN	51,352	VC
Calif Baptist Univ	CA	41,392	C
Calif Polytechnic State Univ	CA	17,979	HC+
Central Washington Univ	WA	16,803	C
Chapman Univ	CA	63,078	VC+
Clarkson Univ	NY	60,392	HC
Drexel Univ	PA	65,432	VC+
Embry-Riddle Aeronautical Univ - Daytona Beach	FL	44,712	VC
Embry-Riddle Aeronautical Univ - Prescott Campus	AZ	44,054	VC
Fairfield Univ	CT	59,860	VC+
Florida Inst of Technology	FL	53,306	VC
Gannon Univ	PA	42,032	C
George Mason Univ	VA	15,724	VC
Husson Univ	ME	25,720	LC
Indiana Inst of Technology	IN	34,240	LC
Keene State College	NH	24,003	LC
Kennesaw State Univ	GA	19,592	VC
Kutztown Univ of Pennsylvania	PA	19,056	LC
Lipscomb Univ	TN	41,296	VC
Loyola Univ Chicago	IL	55,802	VC
Miami Univ	OH	27,190	HC+
Mich Tech Univ	MI	24,739	VC+
Milwaukee School of Engineering	WI	45,153	HC
Monmouth Univ	NJ	46,234	C
National Univ	CA	14,730	LC
Nova Southeastern Univ	FL	38,534	C+
Okla City Univ	OK	40,476	VC
Purdue Univ/West Lafayette	IN	20,032	MC
Quinnipiac Univ	CT	59,110	C
Rochester Inst of Technology	NY	50,842	HC
Rose-Hulman Inst of Technology	IN	57,303	MC
San Jose State Univ	CA	21,540	C
Shippensburg Univ of Pennsylvania	PA	23,208	C
S Dak State Univ	SD	15,634	C
SUNY at Oswego	NY	21,351	C
Univ of Calif at Irvine	CA	26,484	VC
Univ of Detroit Mercy	MI	48,816	C+
Univ of Mass Dartmouth	MA	25,658	C
Univ of Mich/Dearborn	MI	11,757	VC
Univ of Minn Crookston	MN	19,739	C
Univ of N Car at Charlotte	NC	15,547	C
Univ of Texas at Dallas	TX	22,830	VC+
Univ of Wisc-Platteville	WI	14,614	VC
Vermont Technical College	VT	23,838	C
Washington State Univ	WA	22,495	C

SOFTWARE PRODUCTION & MANAGEMENT

School	ST	$IS	SR
Univ of Detroit Mercy	MI	48,816	C+

SOIL SCIENCE

School	ST	$IS	SR
Alabama A&M Univ	AL	18,796	C
Auburn Univ	AL	23,594	VC+
Calif Polytechnic State Univ	CA	17,979	HC+
Clemson Univ	SC		HC
Colo State Univ	CO	22,162	VC
Eastern Oregon Univ	OR	17,715	C
Mich State Univ	MI	23,898	VC+
New Mexico State Univ	NM	14,050	C
N Car State Univ	NC	19,515	HC+
N Dak State Univ	ND	16,245	C
Okla State Univ	OK	17,180	VC
Oregon State Univ	OR	22,519	VC
Purdue Univ/West Lafayette	IN	20,032	MC
Southern Illinois Univ Carbondale	IL	23,667	C
SUNY / The College of Environmental Science and Forestry	NY	23,853	VC
Tenn Tech Univ	TN	17,050	C
Texas A&M Univ at Kingsville	TX	7,500	LC
The Univ of Tenn at Knoxville	TN	22,112	VC
Univ of Arizona	AZ	23,100	C
Univ of Arkansas at Fayetteville	AR	19,152	C+
Univ of Calif at Davis	CA	28,468	HC
Univ of Calif at Riverside	CA	29,227	C+
Univ of Delaware	DE	24,976	VC+
Univ of Florida	FL	16,291	HC+
Univ of Hawaii at Manoa	HI	23,221	C
Univ of Idaho	ID	15,348	C
Univ of Mass Amherst	MA	26,199	VC+
Univ of Missouri/Columbia	MO	18,201	MC
Univ of Wisc-Madison	WI	20,934	MC
Univ of Wisc-Platteville	WI	14,614	VC
Univ of Wisc-River Falls	WI	14,485	C
Univ of Wisc-Stevens Point	WI	14,043	C
Utah State Univ	UT	12,736	C

ST = STATE **$IS** = IN-STATE COSTS **SR** = SELECTOR RATING

School	ST	$IS	SR
Virginia Polytechnic Inst and State Univ	VA	21,276	HC
Washington State Univ	WA	22,495	C
West Texas A&M Univ	TX	13,478	C

SOUTH ASIAN STUDIES

School	ST	$IS	SR
Appalachian State Univ	NC	14,416	VC
Brown Univ	RI	64,566	MC
Indiana Univ Bloomington	IN	20,429	VC
Middlebury College	VT	64,332	MC
Mount Holyoke College	MA	56,746	MC
Oakland Univ	MI	20,763	C
SUNY at Binghamton	NY	22,861	MC
Univ of Calif at Berkeley	CA	28,853	MC
Univ of Calif at Los Angeles	CA	30,162	MC
Univ of Chicago	IL	67,584	MC
Univ of Minn/Twin Cities	MN	23,519	HC+
Univ of Pennsylvania	PA	63,526	MC
Univ of Washington	WA	23,149	VC
Washington Univ in St. Louis	MO	65,366	VC
Yale Univ	CT	64,650	MC

SOUTHWEST AMERICAN STUDIES

School	ST	$IS	SR
Colo College	CO	62,560	MC
Fort Lewis College	CO	18,980	C

SPACE PHYSICS

School	ST	$IS	SR
Embry-Riddle Aeronautical Univ - Daytona Beach	FL	44,712	VC
Embry-Riddle Aeronautical Univ - Prescott Campus	AZ	44,054	VC

SPANISH

School	ST	$IS	SR
Abilene Christian Univ	TX	41,800	C+
Adams State Univ	CO	17,703	LC
Adelphi Univ	NY	48,244	C
Adrian College	MI	42,400	C
Agnes Scott College	GA	51,930	VC+
Alabama State Univ	AL	14,142	NC
Albany State Univ	GA	19,462	C
Albion College	MI	52,650	C
Albright College	PA	46,660	C
Alfred Univ	NY	42,296	C+
Allegheny College	PA	55,420	VC
Alma College	MI	47,548	C
American International College	MA	46,300	LC
American Univ	DC	59,379	HC+
Amherst College	MA		HC+
Anderson Univ	IN	38,200	C
Andrews Univ	MI	28,030	C+
Angelo State Univ	TX	15,263	NC
Appalachian State Univ	NC	14,416	VC
Aquinas College - Mich	MI	38,876	HC
Arizona State Univ at the Tempe Campus	AZ	21,756	VC
Arizona State Univ at the West Campus	AZ	20,640	C
Armstrong State Univ	GA	16,962	C
Asbury Univ	KY	35,180	C+
Ashland Univ	OH	21,440	C
Assumption College	MA	47,920	C+
Auburn Univ	AL	23,594	VC+
Auburn Univ at Montgomery	AL	15,290	C
Augsburg College	MN	43,929	C
Augustana College	IL	49,658	VC
Augustana Univ	SD	38,424	VC
Aurora Univ	IL	33,970	C
Austin College	TX	45,875	VC
Azusa Pacific Univ	CA	43,972	C
Baker Univ	KS	33,350	C+
Baldwin Wallace Univ	OH	41,106	C
Ball State Univ	IN	19,590	C
Bard College	NY	64,024	HC
Barnard College/Columbia Univ	NY	62,741	MC
Barry Univ	FL	37,830	C
Bates College	ME	64,500	MC
Bayamon Central Univ	PR	12,490	
Baylor Univ	TX	53,760	HC
Bellarmine Univ	KY	51,220	C
Belmont Univ	TN	40,970	VC
Beloit College	WI	55,206	HC
Bemidji State Univ	MN	16,056	VC
Benedictine College	KS	36,200	VC
Benedictine Univ	IL	38,300	C
Bennington College	VT	63,960	MC
Berea College	KY	7,042	C
Berry College	GA	45,286	C+
Bethany College	WV	36,300	NC
Bethel Univ	MN	45,270	VC
Biola Univ	CA	46,402	C+
Birmingham-Southern College	AL	44,478	VC
Black Hills State Univ	SD	15,899	C
Blackburn College	IL	28,526	LC
Bluffton Univ	OH	40,950	C
Boise State Univ	ID	14,860	C
Boston Univ	MA	65,110	MC
Bowdoin College	ME	63,500	MC
Bowling Green State Univ	OH	19,747	C
Brandeis Univ	MA	65,925	MC
Brescia Univ	KY	29,890	VC+
Briar Cliff Univ	IA	36,956	C
Bridgewater College	VA	44,510	C
Bridgewater State Univ	MA	21,810	C
Brigham Young Univ	UT	12,748	HC
Bryan College	TN	31,440	C
Bryant Univ	RI	55,646	VC
Bryn Mawr College	PA	59,890	MC
Bucknell Univ	PA	64,616	MC
Buena Vista Univ	IA	41,514	C
Butler Univ	IN	51,352	VC
Cabrini Univ	PA	42,591	LC
Caldwell Univ	NJ	42,165	NC
Calif Baptist Univ	CA	41,392	C
Calif Lutheran Univ	CA	52,853	C
Calif State Polytechnic Univ, Pomona	CA	21,541	C
Cal State, Bakersfield	CA	19,191	LC
Cal State, Chico	CA	21,440	C
Cal State, Dominguez Hills	CA	19,022	LC
Cal State, East Bay	CA	19,413	C
Cal State, Fresno	CA	16,902	LC
Cal State, Fullerton	CA	21,902	C
Cal State, Long Beach	CA	18,850	C
Cal State, Los Angeles	CA	17,186	LC
Cal State, Monterey Bay	CA	26,871	LC
Cal State, Northridge	CA	16,859	LC
Cal State, Sacramento	CA	20,332	C
Cal State, San Bernardino	CA	12,000	C
Cal State, San Marcos	CA	24,184	LC
Cal State, Stanislaus	CA	16,212	C
Calif Univ of Pennsylvania	PA	14,217	LC
Calvin College	MI	41,570	VC+
Canisius College	NY	47,537	C
Capital Univ	OH	42,982	C
Cardinal Stritch Univ	WI	36,462	C
Carleton College	MN	64,071	MC
Carlow Univ	PA	38,549	LC
Carnegie Mellon Univ	PA	67,980	MC
Carroll College	MT	39,972	C+
Carroll Univ	WI	38,100	C+
Carson-Newman Univ	TN	34,160	C
Carthage College	WI	48,835	C
Case Western Reserve Univ	OH	60,304	MC
Castleton Univ	VT	20,186	C
Catawba College	NC	39,820	C
Cedarville Univ	OH	34,990	VC
Centenary College of Louisiana	LA	45,650	C+
Central College	IA	44,592	C
Central Conn State Univ	CT	21,203	C
Central Methodist Univ	MO	36,830	VC
Central Mich Univ	MI	20,330	C
Central Washington Univ	WA	16,803	C
Centre College	KY	49,250	HC
Chapman Univ	CA	63,078	VC+
Charleston Southern Univ	SC	32,400	C
Chatham Univ	PA	46,517	C
Chestnut Hill College	PA	43,410	C
Chicago State Univ	IL	20,144	C
Christopher Newport Univ	VA	23,968	VC+
CUNY/Baruch College	NY	21,609	HC
CUNY/Brooklyn College	NY	5,884	C+
CUNY/City College	NY	20,319	VC
CUNY/College of Staten Island	NY	17,840	NC
CUNY/Hunter College	NY	31,098	VC
CUNY/Lehman College	NY	5,778	HC+
CUNY/Queens College	NY	27,896	C
CUNY/York College	NY	6,747	LC
Claremont McKenna College	CA	67,185	MC
Clarion Univ of Pennsylvania	PA	21,608	LC
Clark Univ	MA	51,600	HC+
Clarke Univ	IA	38,940	C
Clemson Univ	SC		HC
Cleveland State Univ	OH	22,196	C
Coastal Carolina Univ	SC	19,766	C
Coe College	IA	51,570	VC
Coker College	SC	34,810	LC
Colby College	ME	64,060	MC
Colgate Univ	NY	65,030	MC
College of Charleston	SC	22,699	C
College of Mount St. Vincent	NY	45,620	C
College of St. Benedict	MN	52,806	C
College of St. Elizabeth	NJ	44,432	LC
College of St. Mary	NE	35,184	C
College of the Holy Cross	MA	62,165	MC
College of the Ozarks	MO	7,230	C
Colo Mesa Univ	CO	18,955	LC
Colo State Univ	CO	22,162	VC
Colo State Univ-Pueblo	CO	18,234	C
Columbia College	SC	36,550	C
Columbia Univ/ School of General Studies	NY	61,470	MC
Columbia Univ/City of New York	NY	62,958	MC
Columbus State Univ	GA	14,336	LC
Concordia College - Moorhead	MN	51,088	C+
Concordia Univ Texas	TX	40,210	C
Concordia Univ Wisc	WI	35,910	C
Concordia Univ, Ann Arbor	MI	35,945	VC
Converse College	SC	26,495	C
Cornell College	IA	48,800	VC
Cornell Univ	NY	64,853	MC
Covenant College	GA	38,990	VC
Daemen College	NY	38,045	C
Dartmouth College	NH	66,174	MC
Davidson College	NC	60,119	MC
Delaware State Univ	DE	19,376	NC
Denison Univ	OH	58,860	MC
DePaul Univ	IL	47,623	VC
DePauw Univ	IN	58,688	HC+
DeSales Univ	PA	43,970	C
Dickinson College	PA	63,974	MC
Dickinson State Univ	ND	12,372	LC
Doane Univ	NE	39,184	VC
Dominican College	NY	31,270	LC
Dominican Univ	IL	41,222	C
Dordt College	IA	37,860	C+
Drew Univ/College of Liberal Arts	NJ	61,048	VC
Drury Univ	MO	33,791	VC
Duke Univ	NC	64,188	
Duquesne Univ	PA	46,822	VC
Earlham College	IN	54,870	HC
East Stroudsburg Univ	PA	18,334	C
East Texas Baptist Univ	TX	33,134	C
Eastern Conn State Univ	CT	23,059	C
Eastern Kentucky Univ	KY	16,908	C
Eastern Mennonite Univ	VA	42,550	C
Eastern Mich Univ	MI	19,761	C
Eastern Nazarene College	MA	39,955	C
Eastern New Mexico Univ	NM	14,416	C
Eastern Univ	PA	39,540	C
Eastern Washington Univ	WA	25,572	LC
Eckerd College	FL	52,874	C
Edgewood College	WI	35,950	C
Elizabethtown College	PA	54,050	C
Elmhurst College	IL	45,428	C
Elms College	MA	45,646	VC
Elon Univ	NC	44,599	VC+
Emmanuel College	MA	52,110	C+
Emory Univ	GA	60,786	MC
Evangel Univ	MO	28,898	C
Fairfield Univ	CT	59,860	VC+
Fairmont State Univ	WV	15,726	C
Fayetteville State Univ	NC	17,756	C
Ferrum College	VA	39,650	C
Fisk Univ	TN	32,066	LC
Flagler College	FL	27,620	C
Florida Atlantic Univ	FL	17,339	C
Florida Gulf Coast Univ	FL	9,682	C
Florida International Univ	FL	19,854	C+
Florida State Univ	FL	16,771	HC
Fordham Univ	NY	65,918	MC
Fort Hays State Univ	KS	12,131	C
Fort Lewis College	CO	18,980	C
Framingham State Univ	MA	20,584	C
Franciscan Univ of Steubenville	OH	33,980	VC
Franklin and Marshall College	PA	63,170	HC
Franklin College	IN	39,380	C
Fresno Pacific Univ	CA	37,370	C
Friends Univ	KS	34,455	C
Furman Univ	SC	58,092	VC+
Gallaudet Univ	DC	29,118	LC
Gardner-Webb Univ	NC	39,200	C+
Geneva College	PA	35,450	C
George Fox Univ	OR	42,938	C
George Mason Univ	VA	15,724	VC
George Washington Univ	DC	62,835	MC
Georgetown College	KY	41,440	C
Georgetown Univ	DC	65,926	MC
Georgia State Univ	GA	24,332	VC
Georgian Court Univ	NJ	42,426	LC
Gettysburg College	PA	63,000	HC
Gonzaga Univ	WA	50,888	HC
Gordon College	MA	46,472	C+
Goshen College	IN	42,500	C
Goucher College	MD	55,716	VC
Grace College and Seminary	IN	31,524	C
Graceland Univ	IA	35,290	C
Grand Valley State Univ	MI	22,250	C+
Greensboro College	NC	42,400	LC
Greenville College	IL	27,012	C
Grinnell College	IA	60,738	MC
Grove City College	PA	25,692	VC
Guilford College	NC	44,090	C
Gustavus Adolphus College	MN	52,433	HC
Hamline Univ	MN	45,678	VC
Hampden-Sydney College	VA	56,248	C+
Hanover College	IN	46,364	C+
Harding Univ	AR	25,421	C
Hardin-Simmons Univ	TX	33,966	C
Hartwick College	NY	51,270	C
Harvard College/Harvard Univ	MA	60,659	MC
Hastings College	NE	35,380	C+
Haverford College	PA	66,490	MC
Heidelberg Univ	OH	39,200	C
Henderson State Univ	AR	15,516	LC
Hendrix College	AR	54,020	VC+
High Point Univ	NC	45,977	C
Hillsdale College	MI	35,722	MC
Hiram College	OH	43,230	C
Hofstra Univ	NY	55,960	C+
Hollins Univ	VA	49,635	VC
Hood College	MD	54,840	C
Hope College	MI	39,940	VC
Houghton College	NY	39,090	C
Houston Baptist Univ	TX	36,450	C
Howard Payne Univ	TX	34,320	C
Howard Univ	DC	37,616	C+
Humboldt State Univ	CA	20,514	C
Idaho State Univ	ID	13,619	NC
Illinois College	IL	40,850	VC
Illinois State Univ	IL	23,418	VC
Indiana State Univ	IN	23,223	LC
Indiana Univ Bloomington	IN	20,429	VC
Indiana Univ East	IN	7,072	C
Indiana Univ Northwest	IN	7,072	C
Indiana Univ of Pennsylvania	PA	23,614	LC
Indiana Univ South Bend	IN	14,242	C
Indiana Univ Southeast	IN	14,242	LC
Indiana Univ-Purdue Univ Fort Wayne	IN	17,553	C
Indiana Univ-Purdue Univ Indianapolis	IN	18,635	C
Indiana Wesleyan Univ	IN	33,674	C
Inter-American Univ of PR Ponce	PR	19,549	
Inter-American Univ of PR-Fajardo Campus	PR	18,336	
Inter-American Univ of PR-Metropolitan Campus	PR	20,045	
Inter-American Univ of PR-San Germán	PR	20,042	
Iona College	NY	50,984	C
Iowa State Univ	IA	17,570	C
Ithaca College	NY	56,766	VC
Jacksonville Univ	FL	46,230	C
John Brown Univ	AR	33,132	VC
John Carroll Univ	OH	49,740	C+
Johns Hopkins Univ	MD	65,386	MC
Johnson C. Smith Univ	NC	25,336	LC
Judson College	AL	27,066	C
Juniata College	PA	53,760	VC
Kalamazoo College	MI	53,931	HC+
Kansas Wesleyan Univ	KS	36,600	C
Kean Univ	NJ	24,650	C
Keene State College	NH	24,003	LC
Kentucky Wesleyan College	KY	32,080	C
Kenyon College	OH	63,330	MC
King Univ	TN	34,660	C
King's College	PA	46,858	C
Knox College	IL	52,615	VC+
Kutztown Univ of Pennsylvania	PA	19,056	LC
La Salle Univ	PA	55,790	C
La Sierra Univ	CA	39,690	VC
Lafayette College	PA	63,355	MC
LaGrange College	GA	39,930	C
Lake Forest College	IL	50,652	VC
Lakeland Univ	WI	35,130	C
Lamar Univ	TX	18,014	LC
Lander Univ	SC	43,994	C
Lawrence Univ	WI	54,498	HC
Le Moyne College	NY	46,000	C
Lebanon Valley College	PA	51,530	C
Lee Univ	TN	22,045	C
Lehigh Univ	PA	61,010	MC
Lenoir-Rhyne Univ	NC	43,200	C
Lewis Univ	IL	40,370	C
Liberty Univ	VA	19,101	C
Lincoln Univ	MO	13,602	NC
Lindenwood Univ	MO	25,132	C
Linfield College	OR	52,010	C
Lipscomb Univ	TN	41,296	VC
LIU Brooklyn	NY	49,682	C
LIU Post	NY	49,682	C
Lock Haven Univ of Pennsylvania	PA	18,028	LC
Loras College	IA	39,222	C
Louisiana State Univ and A&M College	LA	18,677	VC
Louisiana Tech Univ	LA	11,422	VC
Loyola Marymount Univ	CA	58,038	HC
Loyola Univ Chicago	IL	55,802	VC
Loyola Univ Maryland	MD	60,300	VC
Loyola Univ New Orleans	LA	51,708	VC+
Luther College	IA	48,540	C+
Lycoming College	PA	48,580	C
Lynchburg College	VA	46,740	C
Lyon College	AR	34,730	C+
Macalester College	MN	61,905	MC
MacMurray College	IL	33,620	C
Madonna Univ	MI	29,050	C
Manchester Univ	IN	40,422	C
Manhattan College	NY	51,750	C+
Manhattanville College	NY	51,440	C+
Marian Univ	IN	41,220	C
Marietta College	OH	46,190	C
Marist College	NY	49,860	VC
Marquette Univ	WI	48,390	VC+
Mars Hill Univ	NC	42,688	C
Marshall Univ	WV	17,242	C
Martin Univ	IN	20,264	LC
Maryville College	TN	44,410	C
Marywood Univ	PA	46,900	C
McDaniel College	MD	51,380	VC
McMurry Univ	TX	34,259	LC
McPherson College	KS	34,909	C
Mercer Univ	GA	45,348	VC
Mercy College	NY	31,776	C
Meredith College	NC	45,297	C
Methodist Univ	NC	43,600	C
Metropolitan State Univ of Denver	CO	29,889	LC
Miami Univ	OH	27,190	HC+
Mich State Univ	MI	23,898	VC+
Middle Tenn State Univ	TN	8,650	C
Middlebury College	VT	64,332	MC
Midwestern State Univ	TX	17,572	C
Millersville Univ of Pennsylvania	PA	23,782	C
Millikin Univ	IL	42,158	C

ST = STATE $IS = IN-STATE COSTS   SR = SELECTOR RATING

School	ST	$IS	SR
Mills College	CA	59,163	VC
Millsaps College	MS	50,080	C+
Minn State Univ, Mankato	MN	15,616	C
Minn State Univ, Moorhead	MN	15,941	C
Minot State Univ	ND	12,732	C
Miss College	MS	25,850	C
Miss Univ for Women	MS	17,065	C
Missouri State Univ	MO	15,190	C+
Missouri Western State Univ	MO	16,741	
Monmouth College	IL	42,260	C
Monmouth Univ	NJ	46,234	C
Montclair State Univ	NJ	26,210	LC
Moravian College	PA	53,117	
Morehouse College	GA	40,064	C
Morningside College	IA	36,865	C
Mount Holyoke College	MA	56,746	MC
Mount Mary Univ	WI	34,650	LC
Mount St. Mary's Univ	MD	51,610	C
Mount St. Mary's Univ - Chalon Campus	CA	43,897	VC+
Mount Vernon Nazarene Univ	OH	34,500	C
Muhlenberg College	PA	56,645	VC+
Murray State Univ	KY	16,998	C
Muskingum Univ	OH	35,966	C
Nazareth College	NY	45,574	C
Nebr Wesleyan Univ	NE	38,140	C+
New College of Florida	FL	15,848	MC
New Jersey City Univ	NJ	21,456	LC
New Mexico Highlands Univ	NM	11,904	NC
New York Univ	NY	65,860	MC
Newberry College	SC	34,550	C
Niagara Univ	NY	41,010	C
N Car Central Univ	NC	9,000	C
N Car State Univ	NC	19,515	HC+
North Central College	IL	48,712	VC
N Dak State Univ	ND	16,245	C
North Greenville Univ	SC	25,930	C+
North Park Univ	IL	35,860	C
Northeastern Illinois Univ	IL	12,529	LC
Northeastern State Univ	OK	8,615	VC
Northern Arizona Univ	AZ	20,246	VC
Northern Illinois Univ	IL	20,176	C
Northern Kentucky Univ	KY	16,486	C
Northern Mich Univ	MI	19,604	C
Northern State Univ	SD	14,505	C
Northwest Missouri State Univ	MO	17,737	C
Northwest Nazarene Univ	ID	36,000	C
Northwestern College of Iowa	IA	38,400	C+
Northwestern Univ	IL	66,344	MC
Oakland Univ	MI	20,763	C
Oakwood Univ	AL	43,758	C
Oberlin College	OH	66,012	MC
Occidental College	CA	65,530	MC
Oglethorpe Univ	GA	44,200	C+
Ohio Northern Univ	OH	44,050	VC
Ohio State Univ at Columbus	OH	21,703	HC+
Ohio Univ	OH	22,924	C
Ohio Wesleyan Univ	OH	49,460	VC
Okla Baptist Univ	OK	32,320	C
Okla Christian Univ	OK	27,650	VC
Okla City Univ	OK	40,476	VC
Okla State Univ	OK	17,180	VC
Old Dominion Univ	VA	20,910	C
Olivet Nazarene Univ	IL	41,840	C
Oral Roberts Univ	OK	34,316	C
Oregon State Univ	OR	22,519	VC
Otterbein Univ	OH	41,630	C
Ouachita Baptist Univ	AR	32,320	C
Our Lady of the Lake Univ	TX	35,012	LC
Pace Univ	NY	58,248	C
Pacific Lutheran Univ	WA	49,960	VC
Pacific Union College	CA	36,009	VC
Pacific Univ	OR	52,876	C
Park Univ	MO	20,329	C
Pepperdine Univ	CA	74,460	HC+
Piedmont College	GA	32,512	C
Pitzer College	CA	66,192	MC
Plymouth State Univ	NH	23,180	LC
Point Loma Nazarene Univ	CA	43,450	C
Pomona College	CA	64,957	MC
Pontifical Catholic Univ of PR	PR	10,534	
Portland State Univ	OR	19,443	C
Prairie View A&M Univ	TX	15,205	LC
Prescott College	AZ	33,284	C
Princeton Univ	NJ	57,610	MC
Principia College	IL	39,010	C+
Providence College	RI	60,760	VC
Purdue Univ/Northwest	IN	15,038	C
Purdue Univ/West Lafayette	IN	20,032	MC
Queens Univ of Charlotte	NC	39,543	C
Quinnipiac Univ	CT	59,110	C
Randolph College	VA	45,660	VC
Randolph-Macon College	VA	49,910	C
Regis College	MA	51,920	C
Regis Univ	CO	44,520	C
Rhode Island College	RI	17,694	LC
Rhodes College	TN	51,900	HC
Rider Univ	NJ	54,050	C
Ripon College	WI	46,911	C+
Roanoke College	VA	54,114	VC
Roberts Wesleyan College	NY	38,306	C
Rockford Univ	IL	36,030	C
Rockhurst Univ	MO	29,220	C
Rollins College	FL	58,670	HC
Roosevelt Univ	IL	40,651	VC
Rosemont College	PA	30,980	C
Rowan Univ	NJ	24,491	VC+
Russell Sage College	NY	39,370	C
Rutgers Univ - Camden	NJ	26,146	C
Rutgers Univ - New Brunswick	NJ	26,632	HC
Rutgers Univ - Newark	NJ	27,288	C
Sacred Heart Univ	CT	52,750	C
Saginaw Valley State Univ	MI	18,530	C
St. Anselm College	NH	52,560	C+
St. Augustine's Univ	NC	26,048	C
St. Francis Univ	PA	42,268	NC
St. John's Univ	MN	51,624	C
St. Joseph's Univ	PA	57,544	VC+
St. Louis Univ	MO	49,866	HC
St. Mary's College	IN	50,600	C
St. Mary's College of Calif	CA	57,420	C
St. Mary's Univ of Minn	MN	41,210	VC
St. Michael's College	VT	51,725	VC+
St. Peter's Univ	NJ	49,192	C
St. Vincent College	PA	44,626	C
St. Xavier Univ	IL	43,310	C
Salem College	NC	37,694	HC
Salisbury Univ	MD	20,714	VC
Salve Regina Univ	RI	51,470	C
Sam Houston State Univ	TX	18,792	C
Samford Univ	AL	39,232	VC
San Diego State Univ	CA	21,896	C+
San Francisco State Univ	CA	18,514	LC
San Jose State Univ	CA	21,540	C
Sarah Lawrence College	NY	63,388	HC
Scripps College	CA	66,664	MC
Seattle Pacific Univ	WA	47,439	C+
Seattle Univ	WA	50,811	VC+
Seton Hall Univ	NJ	55,514	C
Seton Hill Univ	PA	46,972	C
Sewanee: The Univ of the South	TN	54,500	MC
Shenandoah Univ	VA	41,312	C
Shepherd Univ, West Virginia	WV	17,224	C
Shippensburg Univ of Pennsylvania	PA	23,208	C
Shorter Univ	GA	31,130	LC
Siena College	NY	48,916	C+
Siena Heights Univ	MI	32,040	C
Simmons College	MA	53,090	VC
Simpson College	IA	43,839	VC
Skidmore College	NY	64,214	HC
Slippery Rock Univ of Pennsylvania	PA	10,360	C
Smith College	MA	63,914	MC
Sonoma State Univ	CA	27,806	C
S Car State Univ	SC	20,805	LC
S Dak State Univ	SD	15,634	C
Southeastern Louisiana Univ	LA	16,237	C
Southern Arkansas Univ	AR	21,532	C
Southern Conn State Univ	CT	21,924	LC
Southern Illinois Univ Edwardsville	IL	22,643	C
Southern Methodist Univ	TX	66,483	MC
Southern Nazarene Univ	OK	32,798	NC
Southern Oregon Univ	OR	19,117	C
Southern Univ and A&M College	LA	16,074	LC+
Southern Univ at New Orleans	LA	8,014	LC
Southwest Baptist Univ	MO	29,900	LC
Southwest Minn State Univ	MN	17,783	C
Southwestern Okla State Univ	OK	11,790	C
Southwestern Univ	TX	50,720	VC
Spelman College	GA	38,751	C
Spring Arbor Univ	MI	36,000	C
St. Ambrose Univ	IA	39,019	C
St. Ambrose Univ	IA	39,019	C
St. Bonaventure Univ	NY	44,237	C
St. Catherine Univ	MN	45,630	VC
St. Edward's Univ	TX	53,100	VC
St. Francis College	NY	38,800	LC
St. John Fisher College	NY	43,620	C
St. John's Univ	NY	55,850	C
St. Joseph's College, New York/Brooklyn Campus	NY	25,114	LC
St. Joseph's College, New York/Long Island Campus	NY	25,124	C
St. Lawrence Univ	NY	64,390	VC
St. Mary's Univ	TX	37,500	C
St. Norbert College	WI	44,525	VC
St. Olaf College	MN	54,260	HC+
St. Thomas Aquinas College	NY	42,200	C
Stanford Univ	CA	60,409	MC
SUNY / Buffalo State College	NY	20,842	C
SUNY / SUNY College at Old Westbury	NY	16,860	C
SUNY / SUNY Fredonia	NY	20,818	C
SUNY / SUNY Oneonta	NY	19,712	C+
SUNY / SUNY Plattsburgh	NY	18,814	C
SUNY / SUNY Potsdam	NY	20,404	C+
SUNY / Univ at Buffalo	NY	23,122	C+
SUNY at Binghamton	NY	22,861	MC
SUNY at Geneseo	NY	20,440	VC+
SUNY at New Paltz	NY	19,200	C
SUNY at Oswego	NY	21,351	C
SUNY SUNY Albany	NY	22,165	C
Stephen F. Austin State Univ	TX	18,406	LC
Stetson Univ	FL	53,544	VC
Stonehill College	MA	55,030	C+
Suffolk Univ	MA	50,308	C
Sul Ross State Univ	TX	15,021	LC
Susquehanna Univ	PA	55,340	VC
Swarthmore College	PA	63,550	MC
Tarleton State Univ	TX	15,248	LC
Taylor Univ	IN	40,317	C+
Temple Univ	PA	24,392	VC
Tenn Tech Univ	TN	17,050	C
Texas A&M Univ	TX	20,521	VC+
Texas A&M Univ at Commerce	TX	10,496	C
Texas A&M Univ at Corpus Christi	TX	16,851	LC
Texas A&M Univ at Kingsville	TX	7,500	LC
Texas Christian Univ	TX	54,670	HC
Texas Lutheran Univ	TX	38,620	C
Texas Southern Univ	TX	18,212	LC
Texas State Univ	TX	19,350	C
Texas Tech Univ	TX	18,736	C+
Texas Wesleyan Univ	TX	35,134	C
The Catholic Univ of America	DC	56,356	VC
The Citadel, The Military College of S Car	SC	35,339	C
The College at Brockport - SUNY	NY	20,346	C
The College of Idaho	ID	36,415	C
The College of New Jersey	NJ	31,909	HC
The College of New Rochelle	NY	46,300	VC
The College of Wooster	OH	57,900	VC+
The Lincoln Univ	PA	15,154	NC
The Univ of Akron	OH	21,477	C
The Univ of Tenn at Chattanooga	TN	16,744	C
The Univ of Tenn at Martin	TN	14,876	C
The Univ of Utah	UT	17,924	VC
The Univ of Virginia's College at Wise	VA	18,192	LC
Thomas Edison State Univ	NJ	6,350	NC
Thomas More College	KY	36,720	C
Towson Univ	MD	17,408	VC
Transylvania Univ	KY	45,690	VC+
Trinity Christian College	IL	35,580	C
Trinity College	CT	63,920	HC+
Trinity Univ	TX	52,314	HC+
Truman State Univ	MO	16,014	HC
Tufts Univ	MA		MC
Tulane Univ	LA	63,396	HC+
Union College	NE	23,270	C
Union Univ	TN	33,970	VC
Universidad Adventista de las Antillas	PR	16,606	
Universidad del Turabo	PR	17,828	
Univ of Alabama	AL	24,320	C+
Univ of Arizona	AZ	23,100	C
Univ of Arkansas at Fayetteville	AR	19,152	C+
Univ of Arkansas at Little Rock	AR	18,211	C
Univ of Calif at Berkeley	CA	28,853	MC
Univ of Calif at Davis	CA	28,468	HC
Univ of Calif at Irvine	CA	26,484	VC
Univ of Calif at Los Angeles	CA	30,162	MC
Univ of Calif at Riverside	CA	29,227	C+
Univ of Calif at Santa Barbara	CA	29,091	HC
Univ of Central Arkansas	AR	14,472	VC
Univ of Central Florida	FL	15,922	VC
Univ of Central Missouri	MO	18,982	C
Univ of Central Okla	OK	13,486	C
Univ of Cincinnati	OH	21,964	VC
Univ of Colo Boulder	CO	24,285	VC+
Univ of Colo Colo Springs	CO	19,663	C
Univ of Colo Denver	CO	23,230	C
Univ of Conn	CT	25,538	HC
Univ of Dallas	TX	45,500	VC+
Univ of Dayton	OH	53,620	C
Univ of Denver	CO	58,443	VC+
Univ of Evansville	IN	44,186	VC+
Univ of Findlay	OH	60,139	C
Univ of Florida	FL	16,291	HC+
Univ of Georgia	GA	21,250	HC
Univ of Hawaii at Manoa	HI	23,221	C
Univ of Houston	TX	21,483	VC
Univ of Houston-Downtown	TX	7,241	C
Univ of Idaho	ID	15,348	C
Univ of Illinois at Chicago	IL	25,006	VC
Univ of Illinois at Urbana-Champaign	IL	27,006	HC
Univ of Indianapolis	IN	36,480	C
Univ of Iowa	IA	18,683	VC+
Univ of Jamestown	ND	28,508	C
Univ of Kansas	KS	20,135	C+
Univ of Kentucky	KY	33,306	C
Univ of La Verne	CA	55,600	C
Univ of Louisiana at Lafayette	LA	14,516	C
Univ of Louisville	KY	19,824	C
Univ of Maine	ME	20,792	C
Univ of Mary Hardin-Baylor	TX	33,950	C+
Univ of Mary Washington	VA	24,764	VC
Univ of Maryland/Baltimore County	MD	21,296	VC
Univ of Maryland/College Park	MD	21,938	HC
Univ of Maryland/Univ College	MD	25,966	LC
Univ of Mass Amherst	MA	26,199	VC+
Univ of Mass Boston	MA	13,435	C
Univ of Mass Dartmouth	MA	25,658	C
Univ of Miami	FL	63,494	MC
Univ of Mich/Ann Arbor	MI	24,410	MC
Univ of Mich-Flint	MI	17,607	C+
Univ of Minn/Duluth	MN	20,292	C+
Univ of Minn/Morris	MN	20,760	VC
Univ of Minn/Twin Cities	MN	23,519	HC+
Univ of Miss	MS	17,746	C+
Univ of Missouri/Columbia	MO	18,201	MC
Univ of Missouri-Kansas City	MO	19,563	VC
Univ of Missouri-St. Louis	MO		C
Univ of Montana	MT	14,105	C
Univ of Montevallo	AL	19,502	C
Univ of Mount Union	OH	38,970	C
Univ of Nebr - Kearney	NE	16,546	LC
Univ of Nebr - Lincoln	NE	18,589	VC
Univ of Nebr - Omaha	NE	16,120	C
Univ of Nevada, Las Vegas	NV	17,553	C
Univ of Nevada/Reno	NV	18,010	C
Univ of New Hampshire	NH	28,562	VC
Univ of New Mexico	NM	15,404	C
Univ of New Orleans	LA	12,840	C
Univ of North Alabama	AL	15,398	C
Univ of N Car at Asheville	NC	15,723	VC+
Univ of N Car at Charlotte	NC	15,547	C
Univ of N Car at Greensboro	NC	14,690	C
Univ of N Car at Pembroke	NC	14,388	LC
Univ of N Car at Wilmington	NC	14,590	VC
Univ of N Dak	ND	15,373	C
Univ of North Florida	FL	15,996	VC
Univ of North Georgia	GA	17,316	C
Univ of North Texas	TX	19,198	C
Univ of Northern Colo	CO	20,851	C
Univ of Northwestern - St. Paul	MN	38,160	C
Univ of Notre Dame	IN	64,043	MC
Univ of Okla	OK	18,911	VC
Univ of Oregon	OR	22,972	C
Univ of Pikeville	KY	28,700	NC
Univ of Pittsburgh	PA	29,568	HC+
Univ of Portland	OR	52,152	VC
Univ of Puget Sound	WA	56,456	VC+
Univ of Redlands	CA	60,200	VC
Univ of Rhode Island	RI	24,906	C
Univ of Richmond	VA	60,880	MC
Univ of Rochester	NY	65,032	MC
Univ of St. Joseph	CT	49,550	C
Univ of San Diego	CA	58,442	VC+
Univ of San Francisco	CA	58,484	VC
Univ of Scranton	PA	54,962	VC
Univ of S Car at Columbia	SC	19,725	VC+
Univ of S Car Upstate	SC	18,200	LC
Univ of S Dak	SD	16,109	C
Univ of South Florida/Tampa	FL	16,110	VC+
Univ of Southern Calif	CA	66,631	C
Univ of Southern Indiana	IN	16,501	C
Univ of St. Thomas - Houston	TX	40,020	VC
Univ of Tampa	FL	36,944	C
Univ of Texas at Arlington	TX	18,026	LC
Univ of Texas at Austin	TX	26,102	HC
Univ of Texas at El Paso	TX	34,452	NC
Univ of Texas at San Antonio	TX	20,157	C
Univ of the Cumberlands	KY	32,000	C
Univ of the District of Columbia	DC	21,044	LC
Univ of the Incarnate Word	TX	39,162	LC
Univ of the Pacific	CA	57,006	VC
Univ of Toledo	OH	19,336	NC
Univ of Tulsa	OK	52,625	HC+
Univ of Vermont	VT	28,878	HC
Univ of Virginia	VA	25,891	MC
Univ of Washington	WA	23,149	VC
Univ of Wisc-Eau Claire	WI	15,797	VC
Univ of Wisc-Green Bay	WI	15,064	C
Univ of Wisc-La Crosse	WI	15,247	C+
Univ of Wisc-Madison	WI	20,934	MC
Univ of Wisc-Oshkosh	WI	15,200	C
Univ of Wisc-Parkside	WI	15,193	C
Univ of Wisc-Platteville	WI	14,614	VC
Univ of Wisc-Stevens Point	WI	14,043	C
Univ of Wisc-Whitewater	WI	13,976	C
Univ of Wyoming	WY	15,375	C+
Ursinus College	PA	61,690	VC
Utah State Univ	UT	12,736	C
Valley City State Univ	ND	13,267	C
Valparaiso Univ	IN	48,370	C+
Vanderbilt Univ	TN	60,572	MC
Vanguard Univ of Southern Calif	CA	40,740	VC
Villanova Univ	PA	62,523	MC
Virginia Polytechnic Inst and State Univ	VA	21,276	HC
Virginia Wesleyan College	VA	43,728	LC
Viterbo Univ	WI	34,660	C
Wabash College	IN	50,650	VC
Wake Forest Univ	NC	64,056	MC
Walla Walla Univ	WA	30,417	NC
Walsh Univ	OH	39,010	C
Wartburg College	IA	47,840	C
Washburn Univ	KS	15,827	C
Washington & Jefferson College	PA	56,512	VC
Washington and Lee Univ	VA	59,647	MC
Washington College	MD	54,666	VC
Washington State Univ	WA	22,495	C
Washington Univ in St. Louis	MO	65,366	VC
Wayland Baptist Univ	TX	22,356	LC
Wayne State College	NE	12,802	C
Weber State Univ	UT	10,721	C
Webster Univ	MO	37,490	C
Wellesley College	MA	63,916	MC
Wells College	NY	50,500	C

ST = STATE $IS = IN-STATE COSTS SR = SELECTOR RATING

School	ST	$IS	SR
Wesleyan College	GA	29,694	C+
West Chester Univ of Pennsylvania	PA	18,456	C
West Texas A&M Univ	TX	13,478	C
Western Carolina Univ	NC	13,965	C
Western Conn State Univ	CT	21,254	LC
Western Kentucky Univ	KY	16,850	C
Western Mich Univ	MI	21,054	C
Western New Mexico Univ	NM	16,734	LC
Western Oregon Univ	OR	15,021	LC
Western State Colo Univ	CO	18,639	C
Western Washington Univ	WA	18,003	C+
Westfield State Univ	MA	19,671	C
Westminster College	MO	32,820	C
Westminster College	PA	39,180	C+
Westmont College	CA	56,410	HC
Wheaton College	IL	43,610	MC
Wheeling Jesuit Univ	WV	37,106	LC
Whitman College	WA	59,772	MC
Whittier College	CA	57,891	C
Whitworth Univ	WA	51,732	VC
Wichita State Univ	KS	21,643	C
Widener Univ	PA	56,486	C
Wiley College	TX	18,504	C
Wilkes Univ	PA	45,622	C
Willamette Univ	OR	61,817	VC+
William Carey Univ	MS	23,950	LC
William Jewell College	MO	41,210	C+
William Paterson Univ of New Jersey	NJ	23,133	C
Williams College	MA	63,290	MC
Wilmington College	OH	34,600	C
Wilson College	PA	35,620	C
Winona State Univ	MN	17,535	C
Winston-Salem State Univ	NC	26,166	LC
Winthrop Univ	SC	23,082	C
Wisc Lutheran College	WI	36,290	VC
Wittenberg Univ	OH	48,156	C+
Wofford College	SC	49,885	VC
Worcester State Univ	MA	20,977	C
Wright State Univ	OH	16,983	C
Xavier Univ	OH	47,880	C+
Xavier Univ of Louisiana	LA	31,689	C+
Yale Univ	CT	64,650	MC
York College of Pennsylvania	PA	29,240	C
Youngstown State Univ	OH	17,307	C

SPANISH ADOLESCENSE EDUCATION

School	ST	$IS	SR
Augustana College	IL	49,658	VC
Bethany College	WV	36,300	NC
Blue Mountain College	MS	15,949	VC
Indiana Univ of Pennsylvania	PA	23,614	LC
King Univ	TN	34,660	C
LIU Post	NY	49,682	C
Messiah College	PA	43,100	C+
Nazareth College	NY	45,574	C
Niagara Univ	NY	41,010	C
Northern Kentucky Univ	KY	16,486	C
Old Dominion Univ	VA	20,910	C
St. Mary's Univ of Minn	MN	41,210	VC
St. John's Univ	NY	55,850	C
SUNY / SUNY Plattsburgh	NY	18,814	C
SUNY / SUNY Potsdam	NY	20,404	C+
SUNY at Oswego	NY	21,351	C
Youngstown State Univ	OH	17,307	C

SPANISH AND HISPANIC STUDIES

School	ST	$IS	SR
Bryant Univ	RI	55,646	VC
Creighton Univ	NE	48,206	VC+
Molloy College	NY	40,440	C
Oberlin College	OH	66,012	MC

SPANISH EDUCATION K-12

School	ST	$IS	SR
Aquinas College - Mich	MI	38,876	HC
Black Hills State Univ	SD	15,899	C
Cedarville Univ	OH	34,990	VC
CUNY/Queens College	NY	27,896	C
College of the Ozarks	MO	7,230	C
Colo State Univ	CO	22,162	VC
Edgewood College	WI	35,950	C
Grove City College	PA	25,692	VC
Indiana Univ South Bend	IN	14,242	C
Indiana Univ-Purdue Univ Indianapolis	IN	18,635	C
Lewis Univ	IL	40,370	C
Lubbock Christian Univ	TX	28,426	C
Madonna Univ	MI	29,050	C
Missouri Southern State Univ	MO	12,499	C
Monmouth Univ	NJ	46,234	C
Murray State Univ	KY	16,998	C
Niagara Univ	NY	41,010	C
St. Ambrose Univ	IA	39,019	C
St. Ambrose Univ	IA	39,019	C
Syracuse Univ	NY	60,239	VC
Univ of the Cumberlands	KY	32,000	C
Western Mich Univ	MI	21,054	C

SPANISH LANGUAGE AND LITERATURE

School	ST	$IS	SR
Messiah College	PA	43,100	C+
Stony Brook Univ/The SUNY	NY	21,881	MC

SPANISH STUDIES

School	ST	$IS	SR
American Univ	DC	59,379	HC+
Ashland Univ	OH	21,440	C
Bard College	NY	64,024	HC
Bard College at Simon's Rock	MA	65,795	MC
Barton College	NC	38,686	LC
Bentley Univ	MA	60,890	HC
Blue Mountain College	MS	15,949	VC
Bryant Univ	RI	55,646	VC
Cal State, San Bernardino	CA	12,000	C
Cedar Crest College	PA	46,715	C
Coe College	IA	51,570	VC
College of William & Mary	VA		MC
Dartmouth College	NH	66,174	MC
Drury Univ	MO	33,791	VC
Fairleigh Dickinson Univ/ College at Florham	NJ	52,062	C
Fairleigh Dickinson Univ/ Metropolitan Campus	NJ	40,254	C
Fordham Univ	NY	65,918	MC
Holy Names Univ	CA	46,630	LC
Howard Univ	DC	37,616	C+
Kent State Univ	OH	20,732	C
Lake Erie College	OH	38,914	LC
Lebanon Valley College	PA	51,530	C
Messiah College	PA	43,100	C+
Mills College	CA	59,163	VC
Minn State Univ, Moorhead	MN	15,941	C
Montana State Univ-Billings	MT	22,960	C
New College of Florida	FL	15,848	MC
Northern Mich Univ	MI	19,604	C
Olivet Nazarene Univ	IL	41,840	C
Pennsylvania State Univ - Univ Park	PA	29,760	HC
Purdue Univ/West Lafayette	IN	20,032	MC
Ramapo College of New Jersey	NJ	25,338	C
Reed College	OR	65,300	MC
Southern Nazarene Univ	OK	32,798	NC
Spring Hill College	AL	48,488	C
SUNY SUNY Albany	NY	22,165	C
Stony Brook Univ/The SUNY	NY	21,881	MC
Syracuse Univ	NY	60,239	VC
Texas A&M Univ	TX	20,521	VC+
The Catholic Univ of America	DC	56,356	VC
Union College	NY	64,320	MC
Univ of Calif at Los Angeles	CA	30,162	MC
Univ of Calif San Diego	CA	30,150	MC
Univ of Illinois at Chicago	IL	25,006	VC
Univ of Wisc-Milwaukee	WI	21,496	C
Vassar College	NY	65,491	MC
West Chester Univ of Pennsylvania	PA	18,456	C
Westminster College	UT	41,078	C+
Winthrop Univ	SC	23,082	C
Youngstown State Univ	OH	17,307	C

SPEC ED/EARLY CHILD DUAL PROG

School	ST	$IS	SR
East Stroudsburg Univ	PA	18,334	C
Lewis Univ	IL	40,370	C
Neumann Univ	PA	40,678	LC
Okla Baptist Univ	OK	32,320	C
Syracuse Univ	NY	60,239	VC
West Chester Univ of Pennsylvania	PA	18,456	C

SPECIAL ED / MIDDLE LEVEL EDUCATION

School	ST	$IS	SR
East Stroudsburg Univ	PA	18,334	C
Lewis Univ	IL	40,370	C
Syracuse Univ	NY	60,239	VC
West Chester Univ of Pennsylvania	PA	18,456	C

SPECIAL EDUCATION

School	ST	$IS	SR
Abilene Christian Univ	TX	41,800	C+
Adams State Univ	CO	17,703	LC
Alabama A&M Univ	AL	18,796	C
Alabama State Univ	AL	14,142	NC
Albany State Univ	GA	19,462	C
Albright College	PA	46,660	C
Alcorn State Univ	MS	15,854	C
Alma College	MI	47,548	C
American International College	MA	46,300	LC
Appalachian State Univ	NC	14,416	VC
Aquinas College - Mich	MI	38,876	HC
Arcadia Univ	PA	33,570	C+
Arizona State Univ at the Polytechnic Campus	AZ	21,360	VC
Arizona State Univ at the Tempe Campus	AZ	21,756	VC
Arizona State Univ at the West Campus	AZ	20,640	C
Arkansas State Univ	AR	16,190	C
Armstrong State Univ	GA	16,962	C
Auburn Univ	AL	23,594	VC+
Auburn Univ at Montgomery	AL	15,290	C
Augusta Univ	GA	4,632	C
Augustana Univ	SD	38,424	VC
Aurora Univ	IL	33,970	C
Austin Peay State Univ	TN	16,397	C
Avila Univ	MO	35,480	C
Ball State Univ	IN	19,590	C
Baylor Univ	TX	53,760	HC
Bellarmine Univ	KY	51,220	C
Benedictine College	KS	36,200	VC
Benedictine Univ	IL	38,300	C
Bennett College	NC	27,302	NC
Black Hills State Univ	SD	15,899	C
Bloomfield College	NJ	39,100	LC
Bloomsburg Univ of Pennsylvania	PA	19,066	LC
Bluffton Univ	OH	40,950	C
Boise State Univ	ID	14,860	C
Boston College	MA	65,737	MC
Boston Univ	MA	65,110	MC
Bowling Green State Univ	OH	19,747	C
Brenau Univ - Women's College	GA	37,876	LC
Brescia Univ	KY	29,890	VC+
Bridgewater State Univ	MA	21,810	C
Brigham Young Univ	UT	12,748	HC
Brigham Young Univ/Hawaii	HI	11,290	C
Buena Vista Univ	IA	41,514	C
Butler Univ	IN	51,352	VC
Cabrini Univ	PA	42,591	LC
Cal State, Long Beach	CA	18,850	C
Calif Univ of Pennsylvania	PA	14,217	LC
Calvin College	MI	41,570	VC+
Canisius College	NY	47,537	C
Cardinal Stritch Univ	WI	36,462	C
Caribbean Univ	PR	15,471	
Carlow Univ	PA	38,549	LC
Cedarville Univ	OH	34,990	VC
Central Methodist Univ	MO	36,830	VC
Central State Univ	OH	18,564	C
Central Washington Univ	WA	16,803	C
Cheyney Univ of Pennsylvania	PA	20,896	LC
Christian Brothers Univ	TN	31,670	VC
CUNY/City College	NY	20,319	VC
CUNY/Meger Evers College	NY	6,680	NC
Clarion Univ of Pennsylvania	PA	21,608	LC
Clarke Univ	IA	38,940	C
Clemson Univ	SC		HC
Cleveland State Univ	OH	22,196	C
Coastal Carolina Univ	SC	19,766	C
College of Charleston	SC	22,699	C
College of Mount St. Vincent	NY	45,620	C
College of St. Mary	NE	35,184	C
Columbia College	SC	36,550	C
Columbus State Univ	GA	14,336	LC
Concord Univ	WV	14,954	C
Concordia Univ Nebr	NE	36,280	VC
Concordia Univ St. Paul	MN	29,050	C
Coppin State Univ	MD	17,041	VC
Cumberland Univ	TN	27,710	C
Curry College	MA	51,815	C
Dakota Wesleyan Univ	SD	32,850	C
Delaware State Univ	DE	19,376	NC
DePaul Univ	IL	47,623	VC
Doane Univ	NE	39,184	VC
Dominican College	NY	31,270	LC
Dordt College	IA	37,860	C+
East Carolina Univ	NC	16,937	C
East Central Univ	OK	13,056	C
East Tenn State Univ	TN	13,994	C
Eastern Illinois Univ	IL	21,126	C
Eastern Kentucky Univ	KY	16,908	C
Eastern Mennonite Univ	VA	42,550	C
Eastern Mich Univ	MI	19,761	C
Eastern New Mexico Univ	NM	14,416	C
Edgewood College	WI	35,950	C
Edinboro Univ	PA	15,940	LC
Elizabeth City State Univ	NC	14,745	C
Elmhurst College	IL	45,428	C
Elmira College	NY	53,900	C
Elms College	MA	45,646	VC
Elon Univ	NC	44,599	VC+
Erskine College	SC	45,460	C
Evangel Univ	MO	28,898	C
Felician Univ	NJ	45,370	LC
Fitchburg State Univ	MA	21,819	C
Florida Atlantic Univ	FL	17,339	C
Florida Gulf Coast Univ	FL	9,682	C
Florida International Univ	FL	19,854	C+
Fontbonne Univ	MO	33,717	C
Freed-Hardeman Univ	TN	29,450	C
Gannon Univ	PA	42,032	C
Georgia College & State Univ	GA	21,148	C+
Georgia Southern Univ	GA	16,596	C
Georgia Southwestern State Univ	GA	13,870	C
Glenville State College	WV	17,386	NC
Gonzaga Univ	WA	50,888	HC
Gordon College	MA	46,472	C+
Goucher College	MD	55,716	VC
Grace College and Seminary	IN	31,524	C
Grambling State Univ	LA	15,701	C
Grand Valley State Univ	MI	22,250	C+
Greensboro College	NC	42,400	LC
Greenville College	IL	27,012	C
Grove City College	PA	25,692	VC
Gwynedd Mercy Univ	PA	43,780	LC
Hastings College	NE	35,380	C+
High Point Univ	NC	45,977	C
Holy Family Univ	PA	43,326	LC
Hood College	MD	54,840	C
Hope College	MI	39,940	VC
Houghton College	NY	39,090	C
Houston Baptist Univ	TX	36,450	C
Illinois State Univ	IL	23,418	VC
Indiana State Univ	IN	23,223	LC
Indiana Univ Bloomington	IN	20,429	VC
Indiana Univ South Bend	IN	14,242	C
Indiana Univ Southeast	IN	14,242	LC
Indiana Wesleyan Univ	IN	33,674	C
Inter-American Univ of PR Ponce	PR	19,549	
Inter-American Univ of PR-Aguadilla Campus	PR	21,657	
Inter-American Univ of PR-Arecibo Campus	PR	18,245	
Inter-American Univ of PR-Fajardo Campus	PR	18,336	
Inter-American Univ of PR-Metropolitan Campus	PR	20,045	
Inter-American Univ of PR-San Germán	PR	20,042	
Jackson State Univ	MS	15,879	LC
Jacksonville State Univ	AL	14,628	LC
Jarvis Christian College	TX	20,160	NC
Juniata College	PA	53,760	VC
Kansas Wesleyan Univ	KS	36,600	C
Kean Univ	NJ	24,650	C
Keene State College	NH	24,003	LC
Kent State Univ	OH	20,732	C
King's College	PA	46,858	C
Kutztown Univ of Pennsylvania	PA	19,056	LC
La Salle Univ	PA	55,790	C
Lake Erie College	OH	38,914	LC
Lamar Univ	TX	18,014	LC
Lander Univ	SC	43,994	C
Le Moyne College	NY	46,000	C
Lebanon Valley College	PA	51,530	C
Lee Univ	TN	22,045	C
LeMoyne-Owen College	TN	16,980	C
Lesley Univ	MA	41,550	C
Lewis Univ	IL	40,370	C
Lincoln Univ	MO	13,602	NC
Lock Haven Univ of Pennsylvania	PA	18,028	LC
Longwood Univ	VA	22,184	C
Louisiana College	LA	21,886	C
Louisiana State Univ and A&M College	LA	18,677	VC
Louisiana Tech Univ	LA	11,422	VC
Loyola Univ Chicago	IL	55,802	VC
MacMurray College	IL	33,620	C
Malone Univ	OH	38,448	C
Manhattan College	NY	51,750	C+
Marian Univ	IN	41,220	C
Marist College	NY	49,860	VC
Marshall Univ	WV	17,242	C
Marygrove College	MI	28,926	NC
Marymount Univ	VA	41,570	LC
Marywood Univ	PA	46,900	C
McKendree Univ	IL	37,940	C+
McPherson College	KS	34,909	C
Mercer Univ	GA	45,348	VC
Mercy College	NY	31,776	C
Mercyhurst Univ	PA	47,420	C
Methodist Univ	NC	43,600	C
Miami Univ	OH	27,190	HC+
Mich State Univ	MI	23,898	VC+
Middle Tenn State Univ	TN	8,650	C
Millersville Univ of Pennsylvania	PA	23,782	C
Milligan College	TN	38,150	C
Minn State Univ, Mankato	MN	15,616	C
Minn State Univ, Moorhead	MN	15,941	C
Miss College	MS	25,850	C
Miss State Univ	MS	11,454	C+
Missouri Baptist Univ	MO	35,594	C
Missouri Southern State Univ	MO	12,499	C
Missouri State Univ	MO	15,190	C+
Monmouth Univ	NJ	46,234	C
Montana State Univ-Billings	MT	22,960	C
Morehead State Univ	KY	17,422	C
Morningside College	IA	36,865	C
Mount Marty College	SD	32,972	C
Mount St. Joseph Univ	OH	33,880	C
Mount Vernon Nazarene Univ	OH	34,500	C
Muskingum Univ	OH	35,966	C
Nebr Wesleyan Univ	NE	38,140	C+
New England College	NH	50,364	C
New Jersey City Univ	NJ	21,456	LC
New Mexico Highlands Univ	NM	11,904	NC
New Mexico State Univ	NM	14,050	C
New York Univ	NY	65,860	MC
Niagara Univ	NY	41,010	C
Nicholls State Univ	LA	10,534	C
N Car A&T State Univ	NC	13,365	LC
Northeastern Illinois Univ	IL	12,529	LC
Northeastern State Univ	OK	8,615	VC
Northern Arizona Univ	AZ	20,246	VC
Northern Illinois Univ	IL	20,176	C
Northern Kentucky Univ	KY	16,486	C
Northern State Univ	SD	14,505	C
Northwest Missouri State Univ	MO	17,737	C
Northwest Univ	WA	35,876	VC
Northwestern College of Iowa	IA	38,400	C+
Northwestern Okla State Univ	OK	13,072	NC
Notre Dame College	OH	37,150	VC

School	ST	$IS	SR
Notre Dame of Maryland Univ	MD	46,465	VC
Ohio Dominican Univ	OH	41,340	C+
Ohio Univ	OH	22,924	C
Okla Baptist Univ	OK	32,320	C
Old Dominion Univ	VA	20,910	C
Oral Roberts Univ	OK	34,316	C
Our Lady of the Lake Univ	TX	35,012	LC
Pennsylvania State Univ - Univ Park	PA	29,760	HC
Peru State College	NE	14,768	NC
Pfeiffer Univ	NC	39,695	LC
Piedmont College	GA	32,512	C
Point Park Univ	PA	41,270	C
Pontifical Catholic Univ of PR	PR	10,534	
Prescott College	AZ	33,284	C
Providence College	RI	60,760	VC
Purdue Univ/West Lafayette	IN	20,032	MC
Quincy Univ	IL	36,998	C
Radford Univ	VA	19,027	LC
Rhode Island College	RI	17,694	LC
Roberts Wesleyan College	NY	38,306	C
Rockford Univ	IL	36,030	C
Saginaw Valley State Univ	MI	18,530	C
St. Joseph's Univ	PA	57,544	VC+
St. Martin's Univ	WA	45,056	C
St. Mary-of-the-Woods College	IN	39,632	LC
Salve Regina Univ	RI	51,470	C
Seattle Pacific Univ	WA	47,439	C+
Seton Hall Univ	NJ	55,514	C
Seton Hill Univ	PA	46,972	C
Shaw Univ	NC	24,638	C
Shippensburg Univ of Pennsylvania	PA	23,208	C
Siena Heights Univ	MI	32,040	C
Silver Lake College of the Holy Family	WI	36,290	LC
Simmons College	MA	53,090	VC
Slippery Rock Univ of Pennsylvania	PA	10,360	C
S Car State Univ	SC	20,805	LC
Southeastern Louisiana Univ	LA	16,237	C
Southern Conn State Univ	CT	21,924	LC
Southern Illinois Univ Carbondale	IL	23,667	C
Southern Illinois Univ Edwardsville	IL	22,643	C
Southern New Hampshire Univ	NH	43,198	C
Southern Univ and A&M College	LA	16,074	LC+
Southern Wesleyan Univ	SC	32,130	LC
Southwestern Okla State Univ	OK	11,790	C
Spring Arbor Univ	MI	36,000	C
St. Ambrose Univ	IA	39,019	C
St. Ambrose Univ	IA	39,019	C
St. Bonaventure Univ	NY	44,237	C
St. Edward's Univ	TX	53,100	VC
St. John Fisher College	NY	43,620	C
St. John's Univ	NY	55,850	C
St. Joseph's College, New York/Brooklyn Campus	NY	25,114	LC
St. Joseph's College, New York/Long Island Campus	NY	25,124	C
St. Thomas Aquinas College	NY	42,200	C
SUNY / Buffalo State College	NY	20,842	C
SUNY / SUNY College at Old Westbury	NY	16,860	C
SUNY / SUNY Plattsburgh	NY	18,814	C
SUNY at Geneseo	NY	20,440	VC+
Stephen F. Austin State Univ	TX	18,406	LC
Tenn State Univ	TN	14,423	C
Tenn Tech Univ	TN	17,050	C
Texas State Univ	TX	19,350	C
The College of New Jersey	NJ	31,909	HC
The College of St. Rose	NY	43,048	C
The Univ of Akron	OH	21,477	C
The Univ of Tenn at Chattanooga	TN	16,744	C
The Univ of Tenn at Knoxville	TN	22,112	VC
The Univ of Tenn at Martin	TN	14,876	C
The Univ of Utah	UT	17,924	VC
Thiel College	PA	41,590	C
Tougaloo College	MS	17,980	NC
Touro College	NY	28,950	VC
Towson Univ	MD	17,408	VC
Trevecca Nazarene Univ	TN	31,186	C
Trinity Christian College	IL	35,580	C
Troy Univ	AL	16,171	C
Tusculum College	TN	31,625	C
Tuskegee Univ	AL	28,164	C
Union College	KY	32,310	C
Union Univ	TN	33,970	VC
Universidad del Turabo	PR	17,828	
Univ of Alabama	AL	24,320	C+
Univ of Arizona	AZ	23,100	C
Univ of Arkansas at Fayetteville	AR	19,152	C+
Univ of Arkansas at Little Rock	AR	18,211	C
Univ of Arkansas at Pine Bluff	AR	13,541	C
Univ of Central Arkansas	AR	14,472	VC
Univ of Central Missouri	MO	18,982	C
Univ of Central Okla	OK	13,486	C
Univ of Charleston	WV	35,000	C
Univ of Cincinnati	OH	21,964	VC
Univ of Conn	CT	25,538	HC
Univ of Dayton	OH	53,620	C
Univ of Delaware	DE	24,976	VC+
Univ of Detroit Mercy	MI	48,816	C+
Univ of Evansville	IN	44,186	VC+
Univ of Georgia	GA	21,250	HC
Univ of Great Falls	MT	38,524	C
Univ of Hartford	CT	49,776	C
Univ of Kentucky	KY	33,306	C
Univ of Louisiana at Lafayette	LA	14,516	C
Univ of Louisiana at Monroe	LA	15,970	C
Univ of Maine at Farmington	ME	18,187	C
Univ of Maine at Machias	ME	22,960	C
Univ of Mary	ND	23,180	C
Univ of Mary Hardin-Baylor	TX	33,950	C+
Univ of Maryland/College Park	MD	21,938	HC
Univ of Memphis	TN	18,278	C
Univ of Mich/Dearborn	MI	11,757	VC
Univ of Miss	MS	17,746	C+
Univ of Missouri-St. Louis	MO		C
Univ of Montana-Western	MT	11,220	LC
Univ of Nebr - Kearney	NE	16,546	LC
Univ of Nebr - Lincoln	NE	18,589	VC
Univ of Nevada, Las Vegas	NV	17,553	C
Univ of Nevada/Reno	NV	18,010	C
Univ of New Mexico	NM	15,404	C
Univ of N Car at Charlotte	NC	15,547	C
Univ of N Car at Greensboro	NC	14,690	C
Univ of N Car at Wilmington	NC	14,590	VC
Univ of North Florida	FL	15,996	VC
Univ of North Georgia	GA	17,316	C
Univ of Northern Colo	CO	20,851	C
Univ of Okla	OK	18,911	VC
Univ of PR, at Cayey	PR		
Univ of PR-Rio Piedras campus	PR	13,327	
Univ of St. Francis	IN	37,400	C
Univ of St. Joseph	CT	49,550	C
Univ of South Alabama	AL	16,400	C
Univ of S Car Aiken	SC	16,712	C
Univ of S Car Upstate	SC	18,200	LC
Univ of S Dak	SD	16,109	C
Univ of South Florida/Tampa	FL	16,110	VC+
Univ of Southern Indiana	IN	16,501	C
Univ of St. Francis	IL	39,924	C
Univ of the Cumberlands	KY	32,000	C
Univ of the Southwest	NM	22,766	C
Univ of Toledo	OH	19,336	NC
Univ of Vermont	VT	28,878	HC
Univ of West Alabama	AL	15,516	NC
Univ of West Georgia	GA	16,360	LC
Univ of Wisc-Eau Claire	WI	15,797	VC
Univ of Wisc-Madison	WI	20,934	MC
Univ of Wisc-Milwaukee	WI	21,496	C
Univ of Wisc-Oshkosh	WI	15,200	C
Univ of Wisc-Stout	WI	19,667	C
Univ of Wisc-Whitewater	WI	13,976	C
Univ of Wyoming	WY	15,375	C+
Ursuline College	OH	41,076	LC
Utah State Univ	UT	12,736	C
Vanderbilt Univ	TN	60,572	MC
Virginia Union Univ	VA	22,421	C
Walla Walla Univ	WA	30,417	NC
Walsh Univ	OH	39,010	C
Washington State Univ	WA	22,495	C
Wayne State College	NE	12,802	C
Wayne State Univ	MI	22,016	C
Waynesburg Univ	PA	32,290	C
Weber State Univ	UT	10,721	C
Webster Univ	MO	37,490	C
West Chester Univ of Pennsylvania	PA	18,456	C
West Liberty Univ	WV	15,512	C
West Texas A&M Univ	TX	13,478	C
Western Carolina Univ	NC	13,965	C
Western Illinois Univ	IL	20,825	C
Western Mich Univ	MI	21,054	C
Western New Mexico Univ	NM	16,734	LC
Western Washington Univ	WA	18,003	C+
Westfield State Univ	MA	19,671	C
Westminster College	UT	41,078	C+
Wheelock College	MA	49,225	C
Wichita State Univ	KS	21,643	C
Widener Univ	PA	56,486	C
Wiley College	TX	18,504	C
William Paterson Univ of New Jersey	NJ	23,133	C
William Penn Univ	IA	26,000	C
William Woods Univ	MO	32,040	C
Wilson College	PA	35,620	C
Winona State Univ	MN	17,535	C
Winston-Salem State Univ	NC	26,166	LC
Winthrop Univ	SC	23,082	C
Wittenberg Univ	OH	48,156	C+
Wright State Univ	OH	16,983	C
Xavier Univ	OH	47,880	C+
York College	NE	24,300	C
York College of Pennsylvania	PA	29,240	C
Youngstown State Univ	OH	17,307	C

SPECIFIC LEARNING DISABILITIES

School	ST	$IS	SR
Aquinas College - Mich	MI	38,876	HC
Baldwin Wallace Univ	OH	41,106	C
Barton College	NC	38,686	LC
Florida International Univ	FL	19,854	C+
Florida State Univ	FL	16,771	HC
Idaho State Univ	ID	13,619	NC
Murray State Univ	KY	16,998	C
Northwest Missouri State Univ	MO	17,737	C
Univ of South Florida/Tampa	FL	16,110	VC+
Western Mich Univ	MI	21,054	C
Winona State Univ	MN	17,535	C

SPEECH AND THEATRE EDUCATION

School	ST	$IS	SR
College of the Ozarks	MO	7,230	C
MidAmerica Nazarene Univ	KS	35,550	C
Missouri Baptist Univ	MO	35,594	C
Missouri Southern State Univ	MO	12,499	C
Southwestern College	KS	31,531	C
Southwestern College	KS	31,531	C
St. Ambrose Univ	IA	39,019	C
St. Ambrose Univ	IA	39,019	C

SPEECH CORRECTION

School	ST	$IS	SR
Columbia College	SC	36,550	C
East Texas Baptist Univ	TX	33,134	C
Ithaca College	NY	56,766	VC
Kutztown Univ of Pennsylvania	PA	19,056	LC
New York Univ	NY	65,860	MC
Western Carolina Univ	NC	13,965	C

SPEECH PATHOLOGY/ AUDIOLOGY

School	ST	$IS	SR
Adelphi Univ	NY	48,244	C
Alabama A&M Univ	AL	18,796	C
Andrews Univ	MI	28,030	C+
Appalachian State Univ	NC	14,416	VC
Arizona State Univ at the Tempe Campus	AZ	21,756	VC
Auburn Univ	AL	23,594	VC+
Auburn Univ at Montgomery	AL	15,290	C
Ball State Univ	IN	19,590	C
Baylor Univ	TX	53,760	HC
Biola Univ	CA	46,402	C+
Bloomsburg Univ of Pennsylvania	PA	19,066	LC
Bluffton Univ	OH	40,950	C
Boston Univ	MA	65,110	MC
Brescia Univ	KY	29,890	VC+
Brigham Young Univ	UT	12,748	HC
Butler Univ	IN	51,352	VC
Cal State, East Bay	CA	19,413	C
Cal State, Fresno	CA	16,902	LC
Cal State, Fullerton	CA	21,902	C
Cal State, Los Angeles	CA	17,186	LC
Cal State, Northridge	CA	16,859	LC
Cal State, Sacramento	CA	20,332	C
Calvin College	MI	41,570	VC+
Case Western Reserve Univ	OH	60,304	MC
Central Mich Univ	MI	20,330	C
CUNY/Brooklyn College	NY	5,884	C+
CUNY/Lehman College	NY	5,778	HC+
CUNY/Queens College	NY	27,896	C
Clarion Univ of Pennsylvania	PA	21,608	LC
Clemson Univ	SC		HC
Cleveland State Univ	OH	22,196	C
Colo State Univ-Pueblo	CO	18,234	C
Delta State Univ	MS	13,176	C
Duquesne Univ	PA	46,822	VC
East Carolina Univ	NC	16,937	C
Eastern Mich Univ	MI	19,761	C
Eastern New Mexico Univ	NM	14,416	C
Eastern Washington Univ	WA	25,572	LC
Edinboro Univ	PA	15,940	LC
Elmhurst College	IL	45,428	C
Elmira College	NY	53,900	C
Elms College	MA	45,646	VC
Emerson College	MA	54,736	HC
Florida State Univ	FL	16,771	HC
Fontbonne Univ	MO	33,717	C
Fort Hays State Univ	KS	12,131	C
Geneva College	PA	35,450	C
George Washington Univ	DC	62,835	MC
Hampton Univ	VA	34,926	LC
Harding Univ	AR	25,421	C
Hardin-Simmons Univ	TX	33,966	C
Hofstra Univ	NY	55,960	C+
Howard Univ	DC	37,616	C+
Idaho State Univ	ID	13,619	NC
Illinois State Univ	IL	23,418	VC
Indiana State Univ	IN	23,223	LC
Indiana Univ Bloomington	IN	20,429	VC
Indiana Univ of Pennsylvania	PA	23,614	LC
Indiana Univ-Purdue Univ Fort Wayne	IN	17,553	C
Iona College	NY	50,984	C
Ithaca College	NY	56,766	VC
James Madison Univ	VA	19,084	VC
Kansas State Univ	KS	17,780	VC
Kean Univ	NJ	24,650	C
Kent State Univ	OH	20,732	C
Kutztown Univ of Pennsylvania	PA	19,056	LC
La Salle Univ	PA	55,790	C
Lamar Univ	TX	18,014	LC
LIU Post	NY	49,682	C
Louisiana State Univ and A&M College	LA	18,677	VC
Louisiana Tech Univ	LA	11,422	VC
Loyola Univ Maryland	MD	60,300	VC
Marquette Univ	WI	48,390	VC+
Marshall Univ	WV	17,242	C
Marymount Manhattan College	NY	46,280	VC
Maryville Univ of St. Louis	MO	38,046	VC+
Marywood Univ	PA	46,900	C
Mercy College	NY	31,776	C
Miami Univ	OH	27,190	HC+
Mich State Univ	MI	23,898	VC+
Minn State Univ, Mankato	MN	15,616	C
Minn State Univ, Moorhead	MN	15,941	C
Minot State Univ	ND	12,732	C
Miss Univ for Women	MS	17,065	C
Missouri State Univ	MO	15,190	C+
Molloy College	NY	40,440	C
Murray State Univ	KY	16,998	C
Nazareth College	NY	45,574	C
New Mexico State Univ	NM	14,050	C
New York Univ	NY	65,860	MC
Nicholls State Univ	LA	10,534	C
N Car State Univ	NC	19,515	HC+
Northeastern Univ	MA	62,703	MC
Northern Illinois Univ	IL	20,176	C
Northern Mich Univ	MI	19,604	C
Northern State Univ	SD	14,505	C
Northwestern Univ	IL	66,344	MC
Nova Southeastern Univ	FL	38,534	C+
Ohio State Univ at Columbus	OH	21,703	HC+
Okla State Univ	OK	17,180	VC
Old Dominion Univ	VA	20,910	C
Ouachita Baptist Univ	AR	32,320	C
Our Lady of the Lake Univ	TX	35,012	LC
Purdue Univ/West Lafayette	IN	20,032	MC
Radford Univ	VA	19,027	LC
Rockhurst Univ	MO	29,220	C
St. Louis Univ	MO	49,866	HC
St. Mary's College	IN	50,600	C
St. Xavier Univ	IL	43,310	C
San Diego State Univ	CA	21,896	C+
San Francisco State Univ	CA	18,514	LC
San Jose State Univ	CA	21,540	C
Shaw Univ	NC	24,638	C
S Car State Univ	SC	20,805	LC
Southern Illinois Univ Edwardsville	IL	22,643	C
Southern Univ and A&M College	LA	16,074	LC+
St. Ambrose Univ	IA	39,019	C
St. Ambrose Univ	IA	39,019	C
St. Cloud State Univ	MN	10,600	C
St. John's Univ	NY	55,850	C
SUNY / Buffalo State College	NY	20,842	C
SUNY / SUNY Cortland	NY	20,706	VC
SUNY / SUNY Fredonia	NY	20,818	C
SUNY / Univ at Buffalo	NY	23,122	C+
SUNY at New Paltz	NY	19,200	C
Stockton Univ	NJ	25,059	
Tenn State Univ	TN	14,423	C
Texas A&M Univ at Kingsville	TX	7,500	LC
Texas Christian Univ	TX	54,670	HC
Texas State Univ	TX	19,350	C
The College of Idaho	ID	36,415	C
The Univ of Akron	OH	21,477	C
The Univ of Utah	UT	17,924	VC
Thiel College	PA	41,590	C
Towson Univ	MD	17,408	VC
Truman State Univ	MO	16,014	HC
Univ of Arizona	AZ	23,100	C
Univ of Arkansas at Little Rock	AR	18,211	C
Univ of Central Arkansas	AR	14,472	VC
Univ of Central Florida	FL	15,922	VC
Univ of Central Missouri	MO	18,982	C
Univ of Central Okla	OK	13,486	C
Univ of Cincinnati	OH	21,964	VC
Univ of Colo Boulder	CO	24,285	VC+
Univ of Florida	FL	16,291	HC+
Univ of Hawaii at Manoa	HI	23,221	C
Univ of Iowa	IA	18,683	VC+
Univ of Louisiana at Lafayette	LA	14,516	C
Univ of Louisiana at Monroe	LA	15,970	C
Univ of Maine	ME	20,792	C
Univ of Maryland/College Park	MD	21,938	HC
Univ of Mass Amherst	MA	26,199	VC+
Univ of Minn/Twin Cities	MN	23,519	HC+
Univ of Montevallo	AL	19,502	C
Univ of Nebr - Lincoln	NE	18,589	VC
Univ of Nevada/Reno	NV	18,010	C
Univ of New Hampshire	NH	28,562	VC
Univ of New Mexico	NM	15,404	C
Univ of N Car at Greensboro	NC	14,690	C
Univ of North Texas	TX	19,198	C
Univ of Northern Colo	CO	20,851	C
Univ of Oregon	OR	22,972	C
Univ of Science and Arts of Okla	OK	11,140	VC
Univ of South Alabama	AL	16,400	C
Univ of S Dak	SD	16,109	C
Univ of Southern Miss	MS	13,170	C
Univ of Texas at Austin	TX	26,102	HC
Univ of Texas at Dallas	TX	22,830	VC+
Univ of the District of Columbia	DC	21,044	LC

ST = STATE $IS = IN-STATE COSTS SR = SELECTOR RATING

School	ST	$IS	SR
Univ of the Pacific	CA	57,006	VC
Univ of Toledo	OH	19,336	NC
Univ of Tulsa	OK	52,625	HC+
Univ of Vermont	VT	28,878	HC
Univ of Virginia	VA	25,891	MC
Univ of Washington	WA	23,149	VC
Univ of West Georgia	GA	16,360	LC
Univ of Wisc-Madison	WI	20,934	MC
Univ of Wisc-Milwaukee	WI	21,496	C
Univ of Wisc-Oshkosh	WI	15,200	C
Univ of Wisc-River Falls	WI	14,485	C
Univ of Wisc-Stevens Point	WI	14,043	C
Univ of Wyoming	WY	15,375	C+
Utah State Univ	UT	12,736	C
Washington State Univ	WA	22,495	C
Wayne State Univ	MI	22,016	C
West Chester Univ of Pennsylvania	PA	18,456	C
West Liberty Univ	WV	15,512	C
West Texas A&M Univ	TX	13,478	C
West Virginia Univ	WV	18,210	C
Western Kentucky Univ	KY	16,850	C
Western Mich Univ	MI	21,054	C
Western Washington Univ	WA	18,003	C+
Wichita State Univ	KS	21,643	C
Worcester State Univ	MA	20,977	C
Xavier Univ of Louisiana	LA	31,689	C+

SPEECH THERAPY

School	ST	$IS	SR
Baylor Univ	TX	53,760	HC
Biola Univ	CA	46,402	C+
Cal State, Fresno	CA	16,902	LC
Cleveland State Univ	OH	22,196	C
Ithaca College	NY	56,766	VC
Misericordia Univ	PA	43,840	C
Northern Mich Univ	MI	19,604	C
Ohio State Univ at Columbus	OH	21,703	HC+
Southern Univ and A&M College	LA	16,074	LC+
St. Ambrose Univ	IA	39,019	C
St. Ambrose Univ	IA	39,019	C
Stephen F. Austin State Univ	TX	18,406	LC
Temple Univ	PA	24,392	VC

SPEECH/DEBATE/RHETORIC

School	ST	$IS	SR
Albany State Univ	GA	19,462	C
Arkansas Tech Univ	AR	15,484	C
Ashland Univ	OH	21,440	C
Auburn Univ	AL	23,594	VC+
Augsburg College	MN	43,929	C
Bates College	ME	64,500	MC
Baylor Univ	TX	53,760	HC
Bellarmine Univ	KY	51,220	C
Black Hills State Univ	SD	15,899	C
Bloomsburg Univ of Pennsylvania	PA	19,066	LC
Bridgewater State Univ	MA	21,810	C
Bryant Univ	RI	55,646	VC
Butler Univ	IN	51,352	VC
Cal State, East Bay	CA	19,413	C
Cal State, Fresno	CA	16,902	LC
Cal State, Fullerton	CA	21,902	C
Cal State, Los Angeles	CA	17,186	LC
Cal State, Northridge	CA	16,859	LC
Calif Univ of Pennsylvania	PA	14,217	LC
Canisius College	NY	47,537	C
Capital Univ	OH	42,982	C
Central Mich Univ	MI	20,330	C
Central Washington Univ	WA	16,803	C
Chadron State College	NE	14,819	NC
Charleston Southern Univ	SC	32,400	C
Chicago State Univ	IL	20,144	C
CUNY/Brooklyn College	NY	5,884	C+
CUNY/Lehman College	NY	5,778	HC+
CUNY/York College	NY	6,747	LC
Clarion Univ of Pennsylvania	PA	21,608	LC
Clark Atlanta Univ	GA	31,019	LC
Concordia Univ Nebr	NE	36,280	VC
Concordia Univ Wisc	WI	35,910	C
Denison Univ	OH	58,860	MC
DePaul Univ	IL	47,623	VC
Dickinson State Univ	ND	12,372	LC
Dordt College	IA	37,860	C+
Drake Univ	IA	45,056	HC
Duquesne Univ	PA	46,822	VC
East Carolina Univ	NC	16,937	C
East Central Univ	OK	13,056	C
East Tenn State Univ	TN	13,994	C
East Texas Baptist Univ	TX	33,134	C
Eastern Kentucky Univ	KY	16,908	C
Eastern Mich Univ	MI	19,761	C
Eastern Nazarene College	MA	39,955	C
Eastern Washington Univ	WA	25,572	LC
Emerson College	MA	54,736	HC
Evangel Univ	MO	28,898	C
Fairmont State Univ	WV	15,726	C
Fayetteville State Univ	NC	17,756	C
Fisk Univ	TN	32,066	LC
Florida State Univ	FL	16,771	HC
Freed-Hardeman Univ	TN	29,450	C
Geneva College	PA	35,450	C
Georgia College & State Univ	GA	21,148	C+
Georgia State Univ	GA	24,332	VC
Gonzaga Univ	WA	50,888	HC
Graceland Univ	IA	35,290	C
Grand Rapids Theological Seminary/Cornerstone Univ	MI	33,338	C
Greenville College	IL	27,012	C
Gustavus Adolphus College	MN	52,433	HC
Hannibal-LaGrange Univ	MO	29,815	C
Hardin-Simmons Univ	TX	33,966	C
Hastings College	NE	35,380	C+
Hillsdale College	MI	35,722	MC
Hofstra Univ	NY	55,960	C+
Humboldt State Univ	CA	20,514	C
Illinois College	IL	40,850	VC
Illinois State Univ	IL	23,418	VC
Indiana Univ-Purdue Univ Fort Wayne	IN	17,553	C
Iona College	NY	50,984	C
Iowa State Univ	IA	17,570	C
Jackson State Univ	MS	15,879	LC
James Madison Univ	VA	19,084	VC
Kansas Wesleyan Univ	KS	36,600	C
Kutztown Univ of Pennsylvania	PA	19,056	LC
Lamar Univ	TX	18,014	LC
Lander Univ	SC	43,994	C
Langston Univ	OK	14,314	C
Lewis Univ	IL	40,370	C
Lock Haven Univ of Pennsylvania	PA	18,028	LC
Louisiana College	LA	21,886	C
Louisiana Tech Univ	LA	11,422	VC
Marietta College	OH	46,190	C
McKendree Univ	IL	37,940	C+
McPherson College	KS	34,909	C
Metropolitan State Univ of Denver	CO	29,889	LC
Miami Univ	OH	27,190	HC+
Minn State Univ, Mankato	MN	15,616	C
Minn State Univ, Moorhead	MN	15,941	C
Miss Valley State Univ	MS	13,233	LC
Missouri State Univ	MO	15,190	C+
Missouri Valley College	MO	28,150	C
Missouri Western State Univ	MO	16,741	
Montclair State Univ	NJ	26,210	LC
Morgan State Univ	MD	17,190	LC
Muskingum Univ	OH	35,966	C
New York Univ	NY	65,860	MC
N Car A&T State Univ	NC	13,365	LC
North Central College	IL	48,712	VC
Northeastern State Univ	OK	8,615	VC
Northern Kentucky Univ	KY	16,486	C
Northern Mich Univ	MI	19,604	C
Northwest Missouri State Univ	MO	17,737	C
Northwestern Okla State Univ	OK	13,072	NC
Ohio Univ	OH	22,924	C
Okla Baptist Univ	OK	32,320	C
Oral Roberts Univ	OK	34,316	C
Oregon State Univ	OR	22,519	VC
Otterbein Univ	OH	41,630	C
Ouachita Baptist Univ	AR	32,320	C
Pennsylvania State Univ - Univ Park	PA	29,760	HC
Pepperdine Univ	CA	74,460	HC+
Point Loma Nazarene Univ	CA	43,450	C
Portland State Univ	OR	19,443	C
Prairie View A&M Univ	TX	15,205	LC
Radford Univ	VA	19,027	LC
Rowan Univ	NJ	24,491	VC+
Sam Houston State Univ	TX	18,792	C
San Francisco State Univ	CA	18,514	LC
San Jose State Univ	CA	21,540	C
Shippensburg Univ of Pennsylvania	PA	23,208	C
Southeastern Okla State Univ	OK	11,875	C
Southern Illinois Univ Carbondale	IL	23,667	C
Southern Illinois Univ Edwardsville	IL	22,643	C
Southern Nazarene Univ	OK	32,798	NC
Southern Univ at New Orleans	LA	8,014	LC
Southwestern Adventist Univ	TX	27,756	LC
St. Catherine Univ	MN	45,630	VC
St. Cloud State Univ	MN	10,600	C
St. John's Univ	NY	55,850	C
St. Joseph's College, New York/Brooklyn Campus	NY	25,114	LC
St. Joseph's College, New York/Long Island Campus	NY	25,124	C
St. Mary's Univ	TX	37,500	C
SUNY at Binghamton	NY	22,861	MC
SUNY at New Paltz	NY	19,200	C
Stephen F. Austin State Univ	TX	18,406	LC
Suffolk Univ	MA	50,308	C
Tarleton State Univ	TX	15,248	LC
Temple Univ	PA	24,392	VC
Tenn State Univ	TN	14,423	C
Texas A&M Univ	TX	20,521	VC+
Texas A&M Univ at Corpus Christi	TX	16,851	LC
Touro College	NY	28,950	VC
Univ of Alaska Southeast	AK	11,493	C
Univ of Arkansas at Monticello	AR	13,134	NC
Univ of Arkansas at Pine Bluff	AR	13,541	C
Univ of Calif at Berkeley	CA	28,853	MC
Univ of Calif at Davis	CA	28,468	HC
Univ of Central Arkansas	AR	14,472	VC
Univ of Central Missouri	MO	18,982	C
Univ of Cincinnati	OH	21,964	VC
Univ of Dubuque	IA	37,824	C
Univ of Florida	FL	16,291	HC+
Univ of Hawaii at Manoa	HI	23,221	C
Univ of Illinois at Urbana-Champaign	IL	27,006	HC
Univ of Iowa	IA	18,683	VC+
Univ of Kansas	KS	20,135	C+
Univ of La Verne	CA	55,600	C
Univ of Mary Hardin-Baylor	TX	33,950	C+
Univ of Mich/Ann Arbor	MI	24,410	MC
Univ of Minn/Morris	MN	20,760	VC
Univ of Minn/Twin Cities	MN	23,519	HC+
Univ of Nebr - Kearney	NE	16,546	LC
Univ of Nebr - Lincoln	NE	18,589	VC
Univ of Nebr - Omaha	NE	16,120	C
Univ of N Car at Wilmington	NC	14,590	VC
Univ of Sioux Falls	SD	34,330	C
Univ of S Car at Columbia	SC	19,725	VC+
Univ of South Florida/Tampa	FL	16,110	VC+
Univ of Southern Indiana	IN	16,501	C
Univ of Southern Miss	MS	13,170	C
Univ of Texas at Arlington	TX	18,026	LC
Univ of Texas at Austin	TX	26,102	HC
Univ of Texas at El Paso	TX	34,452	NC
Univ of Washington	WA	23,149	VC
Univ of Wisc-La Crosse	WI	15,247	C+
Univ of Wisc-Oshkosh	WI	15,200	C
Univ of Wisc-River Falls	WI	14,485	C
Univ of Wisc-Superior	WI	14,446	C
Univ of Wisc-Whitewater	WI	13,976	C
Wabash College	IN	50,650	VC
Walla Walla Univ	WA	30,417	NC
Washburn Univ	KS	15,827	C
Wayne State College	NE	12,802	C
West Texas A&M Univ	TX	13,478	C
West Virginia Univ	WV	18,210	C
West Virginia Wesleyan College	WV	36,858	C
Western Carolina Univ	NC	13,965	C
Western Oregon Univ	OR	15,021	LC
Whitman College	WA	59,772	MC
Whitworth Univ	WA	51,732	VC
Willamette Univ	OR	61,817	VC+
Wilmington College	OH	34,600	C
Winona State Univ	MN	17,535	C
Yeshiva Univ	NY	47,250	VC+

SPORT & LIFESTYLE STUDIES

School	ST	$IS	SR
Bryant Univ	RI	55,646	VC
Lewis Univ	IL	40,370	C
Ohio Univ	OH	22,924	C
Univ of Maine at Machias	ME	22,960	C

SPORTS ADMINISTRATION

School	ST	$IS	SR
Ball State Univ	IN	19,590	C
Bethany College	WV	36,300	NC
Bryant Univ	RI	55,646	VC
East Central Univ	OK	13,056	C
Lewis-Clark State College	ID	14,202	C
Ohio Univ	OH	22,924	C
Samford Univ	AL	39,232	VC
Southern Illinois Univ Carbondale	IL	23,667	C
Southern Methodist Univ	TX	66,483	MC

SPORTS AND WELLNESS STUDIES

School	ST	$IS	SR
Adams State Univ	CO	17,703	LC
Aquinas College - Mich	MI	38,876	HC
Arizona State Univ at the Downtown Phoenix Campus	AZ	23,680	VC
Averett Univ	VA	40,970	LC
Bryant Univ	RI	55,646	VC
Corban Univ	OR	40,306	C
Dakota Wesleyan Univ	SD	32,850	C
Georgian Court Univ	NJ	42,426	LC
Ithaca College	NY	56,766	VC
Lewis Univ	IL	40,370	C
Mercy College	NY	31,776	C
Nova Southeastern Univ	FL	38,534	C+
Okla Christian Univ	OK	27,650	VC
Southwestern College	KS	31,531	C
SUNY / SUNY Plattsburgh	NY	18,814	C
Univ of Illinois at Chicago	IL	25,006	VC
Univ of Maine at Machias	ME	22,960	C
Univ of Montana-Western	MT	11,220	LC
Westminster College	MO	32,820	C
Winthrop Univ	SC	23,082	C

SPORTS COMMUNICATION

School	ST	$IS	SR
Bethany College	WV	36,300	NC
Bryant Univ	RI	55,646	VC
Ferris State Univ	MI	21,445	C
Indiana Univ Bloomington	IN	20,429	VC
Millikin Univ	IL	42,158	C
Neumann Univ	PA	40,678	LC

SPORTS MANAGEMENT

School	ST	$IS	SR
Adams State Univ	CO	17,703	LC
Adrian College	MI	42,400	C
Alvernia Univ	PA	43,900	C
Anderson Univ	IN	38,200	C
Anna Maria College	MA	48,186	C
Aquinas College - Mich	MI	38,876	HC
Arkansas State Univ	AR	16,190	C
Asbury Univ	KY	35,180	C+
Ashford Univ	CA	10,480	C
Ashland Univ	OH	21,440	C
Augustana Univ	SD	38,424	VC
Baker Univ	KS	33,350	C+
Baldwin Wallace Univ	OH	41,106	C
Ball State Univ	IN	19,590	C
Barry Univ	FL	37,830	C
Barton College	NC	38,686	LC
Becker College	MA	57,628	C
Belmont Abbey College	NC	48,156	C
Bethany College	KS	46,100	NC
Bethany College	WV	36,300	NC
Bethel College	IN	35,860	C
Blackburn College	IL	28,526	LC
Bluffton Univ	OH	40,950	C
Bowling Green State Univ	OH	19,747	C
Bryant Univ	RI	55,646	VC
Buena Vista Univ	IA	41,514	C
Calif Univ of Pennsylvania	PA	14,217	LC
Calvin College	MI	41,570	VC+
Cameron Univ	OK	11,072	NC
Campbellsville Univ	KY	32,492	C
Canisius College	NY	47,537	C
Castleton Univ	VT	20,186	C
Catawba College	NC	39,820	C
Cedarville Univ	OH	34,990	VC
Central Methodist Univ	MO	36,830	VC
Claflin Univ	SC	33,764	LC
Clarke Univ	IA	38,940	C
Coastal Carolina Univ	SC	19,766	C
Colby-Sawyer College	NH	50,790	C
College of St Joseph	VT	32,400	LC
Colo Mesa Univ	CO	18,955	LC
Columbia College - Missouri	MO	27,803	C
Concordia Univ Nebr	NE	36,280	VC
Concordia Univ St. Paul	MN	29,050	C
Coppin State Univ	MD	17,041	VC
Corban Univ	OR	40,306	C
Culver-Stockton College	MO	33,525	C
Dakota Wesleyan Univ	SD	32,850	C
Dallas Baptist Univ	TX	33,713	C
Daniel Webster College	NH	26,984	C
Davis & Elkins College	WV	38,242	LC
Defiance College	OH	41,630	C
Delaware Valley Univ	PA	49,796	C
DeSales Univ	PA	43,970	C
Dordt College	IA	37,860	C+
Drexel Univ	PA	65,432	VC+
Drury Univ	MO	33,791	VC
East Stroudsburg Univ	PA	18,334	C
Eastern Conn State Univ	CT	23,059	C
Edinboro Univ	PA	15,940	LC
Elmhurst College	IL	45,428	C
Elon Univ	NC	44,599	VC+
Emmanuel College	MA	52,110	C+
Endicott College	MA	44,604	VC+
Erskine College	SC	45,460	C
Farmingdale State College	NY	20,624	C
Faulkner Univ	AL	26,410	C
Ferrum College	VA	39,650	C
Flagler College	FL	27,620	C
Florida Inst of Technology	FL	53,306	VC
Florida State Univ	FL	16,771	HC
Fontbonne Univ	MO	33,717	C
Franklin Pierce Univ	NH	46,750	C
Fresno Pacific Univ	CA	37,370	C
Gannon Univ	PA	42,032	C
Gardner-Webb Univ	NC	39,200	C+
Georgetown College	KY	41,440	C
Georgia Southern Univ	GA	16,596	C
Glenville State College	WV	17,386	NC
Goldey-Beacom College	DE	31,750	C
Gonzaga Univ	WA	50,888	HC
Grand Canyon Univ	AZ	16,950	VC
Grand Rapids Theological Seminary/Cornerstone Univ	MI	33,338	C
Grand View Univ	IA	32,302	C
Guilford College	NC	44,090	C
Gwynedd Mercy Univ	PA	43,780	LC
Hampton Univ	VA	34,926	LC
Harding Univ	AR	25,421	C
Heidelberg Univ	OH	39,200	C
Hilbert College	NY	30,850	C
Hillsdale College	MI	35,722	MC
Holy Family Univ	PA	43,326	LC
Hope International Univ	CA	41,150	C
Howard Univ	DC	37,616	C+
Huntingdon College	AL	34,900	C
Huntington Univ	IN	33,996	C
Husson Univ	ME	25,720	LC
Indiana Inst of Technology	IN	34,240	LC
Indiana State Univ	IN	23,223	LC
Iowa Wesleyan Univ	IA	39,200	C
Ithaca College	NY	56,766	VC
Johnson & Wales Univ/ Charlotte Campus	NC	43,988	C
Johnson & Wales Univ/North Miami Campus	FL	42,707	C
Johnson & Wales Univ/ Providence Campus	RI	42,248	C
Johnson C. Smith Univ	NC	25,336	LC

ST = STATE **$IS** = IN-STATE COSTS **SR** = SELECTOR RATING

School	ST	$IS	SR
Judson Univ	IL	37,700	C
Keiser Univ	FL	35,010	LC
Kent State Univ	OH	20,732	C
Kentucky Wesleyan College	KY	32,080	C
Keystone College	PA	28,680	LC
King Univ	TN	34,660	C
Lake Erie College	OH	38,914	LC
Lasell College	MA	47,500	C
Lees-McRae College	NC	33,944	C
Lenoir-Rhyne Univ	NC	43,200	C
Lewis Univ	IL	40,370	C
Liberty Univ	VA	19,101	C
Limestone College	SC	32,100	C
Lindenwood Univ	MO	25,132	C
Lipscomb Univ	TN	41,296	VC
LIU Brooklyn	NY	49,682	C
Livingstone College	NC	17,815	LC
Loras College	IA	39,222	C
Louisiana State Univ and A&M College	LA	18,677	VC
Loyola Univ Chicago	IL	55,802	VC
Lubbock Christian Univ	TX	28,426	C
Lynchburg College	VA	46,740	C
Lyndon State College	VT	20,714	C
Lynn Univ	FL	49,480	LC
MacMurray College	IL	33,620	C
Madonna Univ	MI	29,050	C
Malone Univ	OH	38,448	C
Marian Univ	IN	41,220	C
Marian Univ	WI	32,420	LC
Marietta College	OH	46,190	C
Marshall Univ	WV	17,242	C
Maryville Univ of St. Louis	MO	38,046	VC+
Mayville State Univ	ND	18,371	NC
Medaille College	NY	35,112	C
Menlo College	CA	51,380	LC
Messiah College	PA	43,100	C+
Methodist Univ	NC	43,600	C
Miami Univ	OH	27,190	HC+
Mich Tech Univ	MI	24,739	VC+
MidAmerica Nazarene Univ	KS	35,550	C
Midway Univ	KY	31,640	LC
Millikin Univ	IL	42,158	C
Minn State Univ, Mankato	MN	15,616	C
Misericordia Univ	PA	43,840	C
Miss Univ for Women	MS	17,065	C
Missouri Baptist Univ	MO	35,594	C
Mitchell College	CT	43,280	C
Mount St. Joseph Univ	OH	33,880	C
Mount St. Mary's Univ	MD	51,610	C
Mount Vernon Nazarene Univ	OH	34,500	C
Nebr Wesleyan Univ	NE	38,140	C+
Neumann Univ	PA	40,678	LC
New England College	NH	50,364	C
New York Univ	NY	65,860	MC
Newbury College	MA	46,950	C
Niagara Univ	NY	41,010	C
Nichols College	MA	46,800	LC
North Central College	IL	48,712	VC
N Dak State Univ	ND	16,245	C
North Greenville Univ	SC	25,930	C+
Northern Kentucky Univ	KY	16,486	C
Northwood Univ - Mich	MI	35,010	LC
Ohio Dominican Univ	OH	41,340	C+
Ohio Northern Univ	OH	44,050	VC
Ohio Univ	OH	22,924	C
Ohio Valley Univ	WV	29,480	C
Okla Baptist Univ	OK	32,320	C
Old Dominion Univ	VA	20,910	C
Olivet Nazarene Univ	IL	41,840	C
Ouachita Baptist Univ	AR	32,320	C
Peru State College	NE	14,768	NC
Pfeiffer Univ	NC	39,695	LC
Point Park Univ	PA	41,270	C
Principia College	IL	39,010	C+
Queens Univ of Charlotte	NC	39,543	C
Quincy Univ	IL	36,998	C
Roanoke College	VA	54,114	VC
Robert Morris Univ	PA	37,834	C
Rochester College	MI	28,574	LC
Rocky Mountain College	MT	34,270	C
Sacred Heart Univ	CT	52,750	C
St. Leo Univ	FL	31,650	C
St. Mary's Univ of Minn	MN	41,210	VC
Salem International Univ	WV	21,090	LC
Seton Hall Univ	NJ	55,514	C
Seton Hill Univ	PA	46,972	C
Shenandoah Univ	VA	41,312	C
Shorter Univ	GA	31,130	LC
Simpson College	IA	43,839	VC
Southeast Missouri State Univ	MO	15,498	C
Southeastern Louisiana Univ	LA	16,237	C
Southeastern Univ	FL	31,765	C
Southern Nazarene Univ	OK	32,798	NC
Southern New Hampshire Univ	NH	43,198	C
Southern Vermont College	VT	34,670	LC
Southern Wesleyan Univ	SC	32,130	LC
Southwest Baptist Univ	MO	29,900	LC
Southwestern College	KS	31,531	C
Southwestern Okla State Univ	OK	11,790	C
Springfield College	MA	45,995	C
St. Ambrose Univ	IA	39,019	C
St. Ambrose Univ	IA	39,019	C
St. John Fisher College	NY	43,620	C
St. John's Univ	NY	55,850	C
St. Thomas Univ	FL	36,360	LC
SUNY / SUNY Cortland	NY	20,706	VC
SUNY / SUNY Fredonia	NY	20,818	C
Sterling College	KS	32,830	C
Stetson Univ	FL	53,544	VC
Syracuse Univ	NY	60,239	VC
Taylor Univ	IN	40,317	C+
Temple Univ	PA	24,392	VC
Texas Tech Univ	TX	18,736	C+
The College at Brockport - SUNY	NY	20,346	C
The Univ of Tenn at Knoxville	TN	22,112	VC
Thomas College	ME	35,268	LC
Tiffin Univ	OH	31,380	C
Towson Univ	MD	17,408	VC
Trevecca Nazarene Univ	TN	31,186	C
Trine Univ	IN	41,310	C
Trinity International Univ	IL	31,070	VC
Troy Univ	AL	16,171	C
Tusculum College	TN	31,625	C
Union College	KY	32,310	C
Union Univ	TN	33,970	VC
Univ of Arizona	AZ	23,100	C
Univ of Arkansas at Little Rock	AR	18,211	C
Univ of Charleston	WV	35,000	C
Univ of Cincinnati	OH	21,964	VC
Univ of Dayton	OH	53,620	C
Univ of Delaware	DE	24,976	VC+
Univ of Evansville	IN	44,186	VC+
Univ of Georgia	GA	21,250	HC
Univ of Indianapolis	IN	36,480	C
Univ of Kansas	KS	20,135	C+
Univ of Louisville	KY	19,824	C
Univ of Maine at Machias	ME	22,960	C
Univ of Mary Hardin-Baylor	TX	33,950	C+
Univ of Mass Amherst	MA	26,199	VC+
Univ of Miami	FL	63,494	MC
Univ of Mich/Ann Arbor	MI	24,410	MC
Univ of Minn Crookston	MN	19,739	C
Univ of Montana-Western	MT	11,220	LC
Univ of Mount Union	OH	38,970	C
Univ of New England	ME	48,880	C
Univ of New Haven	CT	52,190	C
Univ of North Florida	FL	15,996	VC
Univ of Pittsburgh at Bradford	PA	22,402	C
Univ of St. Mary	KS	34,690	C
Univ of S Car at Columbia	SC	19,725	VC+
Univ of S Dak	SD	16,109	C
Univ of Southern Indiana	IN	16,501	C
Univ of Tampa	FL	36,944	C
Univ of the Cumberlands	KY	32,000	C
Univ of the Incarnate Word	TX	39,162	LC
Univ of Tulsa	OK	52,625	HC+
Univ of West Georgia	GA	16,360	LC
Urbana Univ	OH	30,820	C
Valparaiso Univ	IN	48,370	C+
Virginia Commonwealth Univ	VA	23,049	C
Viterbo Univ	WI	34,660	C
Warner Univ	FL	28,216	C
Washington State Univ	WA	22,495	C
Wayne State College	NE	12,802	C
Webber International Univ	FL	31,904	C
Wesley College	DE	37,026	LC
West Virginia Univ	WV	18,210	C
Western Carolina Univ	NC	13,965	C
Western Mich Univ	MI	21,054	C
Western New England Univ	MA	48,088	C
Westminster College	MO	32,820	C
Wichita State Univ	KS	21,643	C
Wilkes Univ	PA	45,622	C
William Penn Univ	IA	26,000	C
Wilmington College	OH	34,600	C
Wilmington Univ	DE	8,546	NC
Wilson College	PA	35,620	C
Wingate Univ	NC	39,950	C
Winston-Salem State Univ	NC	26,166	LC
Winthrop Univ	SC	23,082	C
Wittenberg Univ	OH	48,156	C+
Xavier Univ	OH	47,880	C+
York College of Pennsylvania	PA	29,240	C

SPORTS MARKETING

School	ST	$IS	SR
Baylor Univ	TX	53,760	HC
Bryant Univ	RI	55,646	VC
Duquesne Univ	PA	46,822	VC
Indiana Univ Bloomington	IN	20,429	VC
Pace Univ	NY	58,248	C
St. Joseph's Univ	PA	57,544	VC+
Southern Nazarene Univ	OK	32,798	NC
St. Ambrose Univ	IA	39,019	C
St. Ambrose Univ	IA	39,019	C
Thomas More College	KY	36,720	C
Xavier Univ	OH	47,880	C+

SPORTS MEDIA

School	ST	$IS	SR
Arizona State Univ at the Downtown Phoenix Campus	AZ	23,680	VC
Bethany College	WV	36,300	NC
Bryant Univ	RI	55,646	VC
Ithaca College	NY	56,766	VC
Lasell College	MA	47,500	C
Marshall Univ	WV	17,242	C
Newman Univ	KS	35,390	C
Southern Nazarene Univ	OK	32,798	NC
Texas Christian Univ	TX	54,670	HC
Youngstown State Univ	OH	17,307	C

SPORTS MEDICINE

School	ST	$IS	SR
Alcorn State Univ	MS	15,854	C
Aquinas College - Mich	MI	38,876	HC
Avila Univ	MO	35,480	C
Belhaven Univ	MS	31,016	C
Briar Cliff Univ	IA	36,956	C
Campbellsville Univ	KY	32,492	C
Canisius College	NY	47,537	C
Capital Univ	OH	42,982	C
Central Mich Univ	MI	20,330	C
Concordia Univ Wisc	WI	35,910	C
Eastern Mich Univ	MI	19,761	C
Eastern Nazarene College	MA	39,955	C
Florida State Univ	FL	16,771	HC
Howard Univ	DC	37,616	C+
Ithaca College	NY	56,766	VC
King's College	PA	46,858	C
Lander Univ	SC	43,994	C
Mercyhurst Univ	PA	47,420	C
Merrimack College	MA	52,770	C
Norwich Univ	VT	28,212	C
Ohio Univ	OH	22,924	C
Pepperdine Univ	CA	74,460	HC+
Samford Univ	AL	39,232	VC
Southern Oregon Univ	OR	19,117	C
Towson Univ	MD	17,408	VC
Trinity International Univ	IL	31,070	VC
Tusculum College	TN	31,625	C
Union Univ	TN	33,970	VC
Univ of Kansas	KS	20,135	C+
Univ of Nevada, Las Vegas	NV	17,553	C
Univ of Pittsburgh at Bradford	PA	22,402	C
Univ of Southern Maine	ME	18,320	C
West Chester Univ of Pennsylvania	PA	18,456	C
Western Carolina Univ	NC	13,965	C

SPORTS PSYCHOLOGY

School	ST	$IS	SR
Faulkner Univ	AL	26,410	C
Hillsdale College	MI	35,722	MC
Lubbock Christian Univ	TX	28,426	C
Texas Christian Univ	TX	54,670	HC

SPORTS STUDIES

School	ST	$IS	SR
Bethel College	IN	35,860	C
Brewton-Parker College	GA	23,490	C
Bryant Univ	RI	55,646	VC
Guilford College	NC	44,090	C
Huntingdon College	AL	34,900	C
Huntington Univ	IN	33,996	C
Ithaca College	NY	56,766	VC
John Carroll Univ	OH	49,740	C+
Lake Erie College	OH	38,914	LC
Lasell College	MA	47,500	C
Manhattanville College	NY	51,440	C+
Southern Nazarene Univ	OK	32,798	NC
St. Andrews Univ	NC	44,634	LC
St. Bonaventure Univ	NY	44,237	C
Trinity Christian College	IL	35,580	C
Univ of Iowa	IA	18,683	VC+
Univ of Minn/Morris	MN	20,760	VC
Univ of Montana-Western	MT	11,220	LC
Vanguard Univ of Southern Calif	CA	40,740	VC

STAGE MANAGEMENT

School	ST	$IS	SR
Boston Univ	MA	65,110	MC
Iowa Wesleyan Univ	IA	39,200	C
Ohio Univ	OH	22,924	C
Pace Univ	NY	58,248	C
St. Ambrose Univ	IA	39,019	C
St. Ambrose Univ	IA	39,019	C
Syracuse Univ	NY	60,239	VC

STATISTICS

School	ST	$IS	SR
American Univ	DC	59,379	HC+
Amherst College	MA		HC+
Appalachian State Univ	NC	14,416	VC
Arizona State Univ at the West Campus	AZ	20,640	C
Barnard College/Columbia Univ	NY	62,741	MC
Biola Univ	CA	46,402	C+
Bowling Green State Univ	OH	19,747	C
Brigham Young Univ	UT	12,748	HC
Brown Univ	RI	64,566	MC
Bryant Univ	RI	55,646	VC
Calif Baptist Univ	CA	41,392	C
Calif Polytechnic State Univ	CA	17,979	HC+
Cal State, East Bay	CA	19,413	C
Cal State, Fullerton	CA	21,902	C
Cal State, Long Beach	CA	18,850	C
Carnegie Mellon Univ	PA	67,980	MC
Case Western Reserve Univ	OH	60,304	MC
Central Mich Univ	MI	20,330	C
CUNY/Baruch College	NY	21,609	HC
CUNY/Hunter College	NY	31,098	VC
Colo State Univ	CO	22,162	VC
Columbia Univ/ School of General Studies	NY	61,470	MC
Columbia Univ/City of New York	NY	62,958	MC
Cornell Univ	NY	64,853	MC
Eastern Kentucky Univ	KY	16,908	C
Eastern Mich Univ	MI	19,761	C
Elon Univ	NC	44,599	VC+
Florida International Univ	FL	19,854	C+
Florida State Univ	FL	16,771	HC
Fordham Univ	NY	65,918	MC
George Washington Univ	DC	62,835	MC
Georgia State Univ	GA	24,332	VC
Grand Valley State Univ	MI	22,250	C+
Harvard College/Harvard Univ	MA	60,659	MC
Idaho State Univ	ID	13,619	NC
Indiana Univ Bloomington	IN	20,429	VC
Indiana Univ-Purdue Univ Fort Wayne	IN	17,553	C
Iowa State Univ	IA	17,570	C
Jackson State Univ	MS	15,879	LC
James Madison Univ	VA	19,084	VC
Kansas State Univ	KS	17,780	VC
Le Moyne College	NY	46,000	C
Lehigh Univ	PA	61,010	MC
Loyola Univ Chicago	IL	55,802	VC
Luther College	IA	48,540	C+
Marquette Univ	WI	48,390	VC+
Miami Univ	OH	27,190	HC+
Mich State Univ	MI	23,898	VC+
Mich Tech Univ	MI	24,739	VC+
Millersville Univ of Pennsylvania	PA	23,782	C
Missouri Univ of Science and Technology	MO	18,655	HC
Montana Tech of the Univ of Montana	MT	15,447	C+
Mount Holyoke College	MA	56,746	MC
New York Univ	NY	65,860	MC
N Car State Univ	NC	19,515	HC+
N Dak State Univ	ND	16,245	C
Northern Kentucky Univ	KY	16,486	C
Northwest Missouri State Univ	MO	17,737	C
Northwestern Univ	IL	66,344	MC
Oakland Univ	MI	20,763	C
Ohio Northern Univ	OH	44,050	VC
Ohio Univ	OH	22,924	C
Okla State Univ	OK	17,180	VC
Old Dominion Univ	VA	20,910	C
Pennsylvania State Univ - Univ Park	PA	29,760	HC
Purdue Univ/West Lafayette	IN	20,032	MC
Rice Univ	TX	57,668	MC
Rochester Inst of Technology	NY	50,842	HC
Roosevelt Univ	IL	40,651	VC
Rutgers Univ - New Brunswick	NJ	26,632	HC
St. Mary's College	IN	50,600	C
San Diego State Univ	CA	21,896	C+
San Francisco State Univ	CA	18,514	LC
San Jose State Univ	CA	21,540	C
Southern Illinois Univ Edwardsville	IL	22,643	C
Southern Methodist Univ	TX	66,483	MC
St. Cloud State Univ	MN	10,600	C
St. John Fisher College	NY	43,620	C
SUNY / SUNY Oneonta	NY	19,712	C+
SUNY / Univ at Buffalo	NY	23,122	C+
The Univ of Akron	OH	21,477	C
The Univ of Tenn at Knoxville	TN	22,112	VC
Univ of Arizona	AZ	23,100	C
Univ of Arkansas at Fayetteville	AR	19,152	C+
Univ of Calif at Berkeley	CA	28,853	MC
Univ of Calif at Davis	CA	28,468	HC
Univ of Calif at Los Angeles	CA	30,162	MC
Univ of Calif at Riverside	CA	29,227	C+
Univ of Calif at Santa Barbara	CA	29,091	HC
Univ of Central Florida	FL	15,922	VC
Univ of Chicago	IL	67,584	MC
Univ of Conn	CT	25,538	HC
Univ of Delaware	DE	24,976	VC+
Univ of Denver	CO	58,443	VC+
Univ of Florida	FL	16,291	HC+
Univ of Georgia	GA	21,250	HC
Univ of Houston-Downtown	TX	7,241	C
Univ of Illinois at Chicago	IL	25,006	VC
Univ of Illinois at Urbana-Champaign	IL	27,006	HC
Univ of Iowa	IA	18,683	VC+
Univ of Louisiana at Lafayette	LA	14,516	C
Univ of Maryland/Baltimore County	MD	21,296	VC
Univ of Miami	FL	63,494	MC
Univ of Mich/Ann Arbor	MI	24,410	MC
Univ of Minn/Duluth	MN	20,292	C+
Univ of Minn/Morris	MN	20,760	VC
Univ of Minn/Twin Cities	MN	23,519	HC+
Univ of Missouri/Columbia	MO	18,201	MC
Univ of Nebr - Kearney	NE	16,546	LC
Univ of New Hampshire	NH	28,562	VC
Univ of New Mexico	NM	15,404	C
Univ of N Car at Wilmington	NC	14,590	VC
Univ of North Florida	FL	15,996	VC
Univ of Northern Colo	CO	20,851	C

ST = STATE **$IS** = IN-STATE COSTS **SR** = SELECTOR RATING

School	ST	$IS	SR
Univ of Notre Dame	IN	64,043	MC
Univ of Pennsylvania	PA	63,526	MC
Univ of Pittsburgh	PA	29,568	HC+
Univ of Rhode Island	RI	24,906	C
Univ of Rochester	NY	65,032	MC
Univ of S Car at Columbia	SC	19,725	VC+
Univ of Southern Miss	MS	13,170	C
Univ of Texas at El Paso	TX	34,452	NC
Univ of Texas at San Antonio	TX	20,157	C
Univ of Vermont	VT	28,878	HC
Univ of Washington	WA	23,149	VC
Univ of West Florida	FL	15,848	C
Univ of Wisc-Madison	WI	20,934	MC
Univ of Wyoming	WY	15,375	C+
Utah State Univ	UT	12,736	C
Villanova Univ	PA	62,523	MC
Virginia Polytechnic Inst and State Univ	VA	21,276	HC
Washington Univ in St. Louis	MO	65,366	VC
West Chester Univ of Pennsylvania	PA	18,456	C
Western Mich Univ	MI	21,054	C
Williams College	MA	63,290	MC
Winona State Univ	MN	17,535	C
Wright State Univ	OH	16,983	C
Xavier Univ of Louisiana	LA	31,689	C+
Yale Univ	CT	64,650	MC
Youngstown State Univ	OH	17,307	C

STRATEGIC COMMUNICATION

School	ST	$IS	SR
American Univ	DC	59,379	HC+
Arkansas State Univ	AR	16,190	C
Bryant Univ	RI	55,646	VC
Butler Univ	IN	51,352	VC
Calvin College	MI	41,570	VC+
Central Conn State Univ	CT	21,203	C
Chapman Univ	CA	63,078	VC+
Concordia Univ St. Paul	MN	29,050	C
Elon Univ	NC	44,599	VC+
Flagler College	FL	27,620	C
Neumann Univ	PA	40,678	LC
Northern Arizona Univ	AZ	20,246	VC
Texas Christian Univ	TX	54,670	HC
Univ of Denver	CO	58,443	VC+
Washington State Univ	WA	22,495	C

STRINGS

School	ST	$IS	SR
Bennington College	VT	63,960	MC
Central Washington Univ	WA	16,803	C
Eastern Mich Univ	MI	19,761	C
Florida State Univ	FL	16,771	HC
Hardin-Simmons Univ	TX	33,966	C
Indiana Univ-Purdue Univ Fort Wayne	IN	17,553	C
Manhattan School of Music	NY	57,200	SP
Mannes School for Music	NY	44,500	SP
Marshall Univ	WV	17,242	C
Northwestern Univ	IL	66,344	MC
Oberlin College	OH	66,012	MC
Roosevelt Univ	IL	40,651	VC
San Francisco Conservatory of Music	CA	57,310	SP
Seattle Univ	WA	50,811	VC+
Syracuse Univ	NY	60,239	VC
Texas Christian Univ	TX	54,670	HC
Univ of Iowa	IA	18,683	VC+
Univ of Kansas	KS	20,135	C+
Univ of Northwestern - St. Paul	MN	38,160	C
Weber State Univ	UT	10,721	C
Wright State Univ	OH	16,983	C
Youngstown State Univ	OH	17,307	C

STUDIO ART

School	ST	$IS	SR
Adrian College	MI	42,400	C
Agnes Scott College	GA	51,930	VC+
Albertus Magnus College	CT	43,258	LC
Allegheny College	PA	55,420	VC
American Univ	DC	59,379	HC+
Angelo State Univ	TX	15,263	NC
Anna Maria College	MA	48,186	C
Appalachian State Univ	NC	14,416	VC
Assumption College	MA	47,920	C+
Augsburg College	MN	43,929	C
Baker Univ	KS	33,350	C+
Baldwin Wallace Univ	OH	41,106	C
Bard College	NY	64,024	HC
Barton College	NC	38,686	LC
Baylor Univ	TX	53,760	HC
Bellarmine Univ	KY	51,220	C
Belmont Univ	TN	40,970	VC
Beloit College	WI	55,206	HC
Benedict College	SC	28,238	NC
Benedictine Univ	IL	38,300	C
Bennington College	VT	63,960	MC
Berry College	GA	45,286	C+
Bethany College	WV	36,300	NC
Bethel College	IN	35,860	C
Biola Univ	CA	46,402	C+
Birmingham-Southern College	AL	44,478	VC
Bloomsburg Univ of Pennsylvania	PA	19,066	LC
Boston College	MA	65,737	MC
Bowdoin College	ME	63,500	MC
Brandeis Univ	MA	65,925	MC
Brenau Univ - Women's College	GA	37,876	LC
Brigham Young Univ	UT	12,748	HC
Caldwell Univ	NJ	42,165	NC
Carleton College	MN	64,071	MC
Carthage College	WI	48,835	C
Cazenovia College	NY	46,470	C
Cedarville Univ	OH	34,990	VC
Centenary College of Louisiana	LA	45,650	C+
Central Washington Univ	WA	16,803	C
Christian Brothers Univ	TN	31,670	VC
CUNY/Queens College	NY	27,896	C
CUNY/York College	NY	6,747	LC
Clark Univ	MA	51,600	HC+
Clarke Univ	IA	38,940	C
Coastal Carolina Univ	SC	19,766	C
Colby College	ME	64,060	MC
Colby-Sawyer College	NH	50,790	C
Colgate Univ	NY	65,030	MC
College of Charleston	SC	22,699	C
College of the Holy Cross	MA	62,165	MC
College of the Ozarks	MO	7,230	C
Colo College	CO	62,560	MC
Columbia College	SC	36,550	C
Concordia Univ Nebr	NE	36,280	VC
Concordia Univ St. Paul	MN	29,050	C
Cornell College	IA	48,800	VC
Creighton Univ	NE	48,206	VC+
Dartmouth College	NH	66,174	MC
Denison Univ	OH	58,860	MC
DePauw Univ	IN	58,688	HC+
Drake Univ	IA	45,056	HC
East Carolina Univ	NC	16,937	C
East Central Univ	OK	13,056	C
Eastern Washington Univ	WA	25,572	LC
Elizabethtown College	PA	54,050	C
Emmanuel College	MA	52,110	C+
Endicott College	MA	44,604	VC+
Fairfield Univ	CT	59,860	VC+
Florida State Univ	FL	16,771	HC
Fordham Univ	NY	65,918	MC
Framingham State Univ	MA	20,584	C
Franklin and Marshall College	PA	63,170	HC
Franklin College	IN	39,380	C
Georgia State Univ	GA	24,332	VC
Gettysburg College	PA	63,000	HC
Graceland Univ	IA	35,290	C
Grinnell College	IA	60,738	MC
Hamilton College	NY	64,250	MC
Henderson State Univ	AR	15,516	LC
High Point Univ	NC	45,977	C
Hollins Univ	VA	49,635	VC
Houghton College	NY	39,090	C
Huntington Univ	IN	33,996	C
Indiana State Univ	IN	23,223	LC
Indiana Univ Bloomington	IN	20,429	VC
Indiana Univ of Pennsylvania	PA	23,614	LC
Indiana Wesleyan Univ	IN	33,674	C
Ithaca College	NY	56,766	VC
Jacksonville Univ	FL	46,230	C
Johnson State College	VT	20,752	C
Juniata College	PA	53,760	VC
Kansas Wesleyan Univ	KS	36,600	C
Kean Univ	NJ	24,650	C
Kentucky State Univ	KY	13,364	LC
Knox College	IL	52,615	VC+
Kutztown Univ of Pennsylvania	PA	19,056	LC
Lawrence Univ	WI	54,498	HC
Lewis & Clark College	OR	58,434	HC+
Limestone College	SC	32,100	C
Lindenwood Univ	MO	25,132	C
Linfield College	OR	52,010	C
Lipscomb Univ	TN	41,296	VC
LIU Brooklyn	NY	49,682	C
Louisiana College	LA	21,886	C
Louisiana State Univ and A&M College	LA	18,677	VC
Loyola Marymount Univ	CA	58,038	HC
Loyola Univ Chicago	IL	55,802	VC
Loyola Univ New Orleans	LA	51,708	VC+
Lycoming College	PA	48,580	C
Manhattanville College	NY	51,440	C+
Marian Univ	IN	41,220	C
Marietta College	OH	46,190	C
Marist College	NY	49,860	VC
Mary Baldwin Univ	VA	39,865	C
Maryville Univ of St. Louis	MO	38,046	VC+
Marywood Univ	PA	46,900	C
Mass College of Art and Design	MA	24,800	SP
Memphis College of Art	TN	39,750	C
Mercyhurst Univ	PA	47,420	C
Messiah College	PA	43,100	C+
Mich State Univ	MI	23,898	VC+
Middle Tenn State Univ	TN	8,650	C
Middlebury College	VT	64,332	MC
Millikin Univ	IL	42,158	C
Mills College	CA	59,163	VC
Millsaps College	MS	50,080	C+
Minneapolis College of Art and Design	MN	44,238	SP
Missouri Southern State Univ	MO	12,499	C
Montclair State Univ	NJ	26,210	LC
Moravian College	PA	53,117	
Mount Holyoke College	MA	56,746	MC
Murray State Univ	KY	16,998	C
Nazareth College	NY	45,574	C
Nebr Wesleyan Univ	NE	38,140	C+
New York Univ	NY	65,860	MC
North Central College	IL	48,712	VC
North Greenville Univ	SC	25,930	C+
Northeastern Univ	MA	62,703	MC
Northern Arizona Univ	AZ	20,246	VC
Northern Illinois Univ	IL	20,176	C
Northern Kentucky Univ	KY	16,486	C
Notre Dame College	OH	37,150	VC
Notre Dame of Maryland Univ	MD	46,465	VC
Oakland Univ	MI	20,763	C
Oberlin College	OH	66,012	MC
Ohio Univ	OH	22,924	C
Okla City Univ	OK	40,476	VC
Old Dominion Univ	VA	20,910	C
Oral Roberts Univ	OK	34,316	C
Pacific Lutheran Univ	WA	49,960	VC
Parsons The New School for Design	NY	56,610	SP
Pomona College	CA	64,957	MC
Prescott College	AZ	33,284	C
Principia College	IL	39,010	C+
Providence College	RI	60,760	VC
Randolph-Macon College	VA	49,910	C
Rhode Island College	RI	17,694	LC
Ripon College	WI	46,911	C+
Rivier Univ	NH	40,410	VC
Roberts Wesleyan College	NY	38,306	C
Rochester Inst of Technology	NY	50,842	HC
Rollins College	FL	58,670	HC
St. Louis Univ	MO	49,866	HC
St. Mary's Univ of Minn	MN	41,210	VC
St. Vincent College	PA	44,626	C
Salem College	NC	37,694	HC
Salve Regina Univ	RI	51,470	C
San Diego State Univ	CA	21,896	C+
Santa Fe Univ of Art and Design	NM	39,980	SP
Scripps College	CA	66,664	MC
Seton Hill Univ	PA	46,972	C
Siena Heights Univ	MI	32,040	C
Silver Lake College of the Holy Family	WI	36,290	LC
Smith College	MA	63,914	MC
Southern Conn State Univ	CT	21,924	LC
Southern Illinois Univ Edwardsville	IL	22,643	C
Southern Methodist Univ	TX	66,483	MC
Southern Oregon Univ	OR	19,117	C
Spalding Univ	KY	31,938	SP
Spring Hill College	AL	48,488	C
St. Joseph's College, New York/Long Island Campus	NY	25,124	C
St. Lawrence Univ	NY	64,390	VC
St. Olaf College	MN	54,260	HC+
Stanford Univ	CA	60,409	MC
SUNY / SUNY Potsdam	NY	20,404	C+
SUNY / Univ at Buffalo	NY	23,122	C+
SUNY at Binghamton	NY	22,861	MC
SUNY at New Paltz	NY	19,200	C
SUNY SUNY Albany	NY	22,165	C
Stetson Univ	FL	53,544	VC
Stony Brook Univ/The SUNY	NY	21,881	MC
Susquehanna Univ	PA	55,340	VC
Tabor College	KS	35,870	C
Taylor Univ	IN	40,317	C+
Texas Christian Univ	TX	54,670	HC
Texas State Univ	TX	19,350	C
The Catholic Univ of America	DC	56,356	VC
The College at Brockport - SUNY	NY	20,346	C
The College of St. Rose	NY	43,048	C
The Univ of Akron	OH	21,477	C
The Univ of Tenn at Knoxville	TN	22,112	VC
Transylvania Univ	KY	45,690	VC+
Trinity Christian College	IL	35,580	C
Trinity College	CT	63,920	HC+
Troy Univ	AL	16,171	C
Truman State Univ	MO	16,014	HC
Tulane Univ	LA	63,396	HC+
Union College	NE	23,270	C
Union College	NY	64,320	MC
Univ of Arizona	AZ	23,100	C
Univ of Calif at Davis	CA	28,468	HC
Univ of Calif at Irvine	CA	26,484	VC
Univ of Calif San Diego	CA	30,150	MC
Univ of Central Missouri	MO	18,982	C
Univ of Colo Boulder	CO	24,285	VC+
Univ of Findlay	OH	60,139	C
Univ of Georgia	GA	21,250	HC
Univ of Houston	TX	21,483	VC
Univ of Idaho	ID	15,348	C
Univ of Illinois at Chicago	IL	25,006	VC
Univ of Indianapolis	IN	36,480	C
Univ of Maine	ME	20,792	C
Univ of Mary Washington	VA	24,764	VC
Univ of Maryland/College Park	MD	21,938	HC
Univ of Mass Amherst	MA	26,199	VC+
Univ of Miami	FL	63,494	MC
Univ of Minn/Duluth	MN	20,292	C+
Univ of Minn/Morris	MN	20,760	VC
Univ of Minn/Twin Cities	MN	23,519	HC+
Univ of Missouri-Kansas City	MO	19,563	VC
Univ of Missouri-St. Louis	MO		C
Univ of Montevallo	AL	19,502	C
Univ of Nebr - Lincoln	NE	18,589	VC
Univ of New Hampshire	NH	28,562	VC
Univ of New Mexico	NM	15,404	C
Univ of New Orleans	LA	12,840	C
Univ of N Car at Chapel Hill	NC	20,052	HC+
Univ of N Car at Wilmington	NC	14,590	VC
Univ of North Texas	TX	19,198	C
Univ of Northwestern - St. Paul	MN	38,160	C
Univ of Notre Dame	IN	64,043	MC
Univ of Pittsburgh	PA	29,568	HC+
Univ of Redlands	CA	60,200	VC
Univ of Richmond	VA	60,880	MC
Univ of Rochester	NY	65,032	MC
Univ of St. Francis	IN	37,400	C
Univ of S Car at Columbia	SC	19,725	VC+
Univ of S Car Upstate	SC	18,200	LC
Univ of Southern Calif	CA	66,631	C
Univ of St. Thomas - Houston	TX	40,020	VC
Univ of Texas at Arlington	TX	18,026	LC
Univ of Texas at Austin	TX	26,102	HC
Univ of the Pacific	CA	57,006	VC
Univ of Washington	WA	23,149	VC
Univ of West Florida	FL	15,848	C
Univ of Wisc-Stout	WI	19,667	C
Univ of Wisc-Superior	WI	14,446	C
Viterbo Univ	WI	34,660	C
Wake Forest Univ	NC	64,056	MC
Washington & Jefferson College	PA	56,512	VC
Washington and Lee Univ	VA	59,647	MC
Washington Univ in St. Louis	MO	65,366	VC
Webster Univ	MO	37,490	C
Wellesley College	MA	63,916	MC
Wesleyan College	GA	29,694	C+
Wesleyan Univ	CT	65,516	MC
West Chester Univ of Pennsylvania	PA	18,456	C
West Texas A&M Univ	TX	13,478	C
Wheaton College	MA	61,512	VC
Wichita State Univ	KS	21,643	C
Willamette Univ	OR	61,817	VC+
William Paterson Univ of New Jersey	NJ	23,133	C
William Woods Univ	MO	32,040	C
Wilson College	PA	35,620	C
Wofford College	SC	49,885	VC
Wright State Univ	OH	16,983	C
Youngstown State Univ	OH	17,307	C

STUDIO ART CERAMICS

School	ST	$IS	SR
Bard College at Simon's Rock	MA	65,795	MC
College of the Ozarks	MO	7,230	C
Rochester Inst of Technology	NY	50,842	HC
Texas Christian Univ	TX	54,670	HC

STUDIO ART COMPUTER ART

School	ST	$IS	SR
College of the Ozarks	MO	7,230	C
Rochester Inst of Technology	NY	50,842	HC

STUDIO ART FIBERS

School	ST	$IS	SR
College of the Ozarks	MO	7,230	C
Old Dominion Univ	VA	20,910	C

STUDIO ART GRAPHIC DESIGN

School	ST	$IS	SR
College of the Ozarks	MO	7,230	C
Franklin College	IN	39,380	C
Georgian Court Univ	NJ	42,426	LC
Rochester Inst of Technology	NY	50,842	HC
Silver Lake College of the Holy Family	WI	36,290	LC
SUNY SUNY Albany	NY	22,165	C
Wellesley College	MA	63,916	MC

STUDIO ART PAINTING

School	ST	$IS	SR
Bard College at Simon's Rock	MA	65,795	MC
College of the Ozarks	MO	7,230	C
Franklin College	IN	39,380	C
Missouri Southern State Univ	MO	12,499	C
Oberlin College	OH	66,012	MC
Old Dominion Univ	VA	20,910	C
Rochester Inst of Technology	NY	50,842	HC
SUNY SUNY Albany	NY	22,165	C
Texas Christian Univ	TX	54,670	HC
Wellesley College	MA	63,916	MC

SUPPLY CHAIN MANAGEMENT

School	ST	$IS	SR
Arizona State Univ at the Tempe Campus	AZ	21,756	VC
Arkansas State Univ	AR	16,190	C
Ashford Univ	CA	10,480	C
Bloomfield College	NJ	39,100	LC
Boise State Univ	ID	14,860	C
Bryant Univ	RI	55,646	VC
Clarkson Univ	NY	60,392	HC
College of Charleston	SC	22,699	C
Duquesne Univ	PA	46,822	VC
Eastern Mich Univ	MI	19,761	C
Elmhurst College	IL	45,428	C

School	ST	$IS	SR
Fontbonne Univ	MO	33,717	C
Gannon Univ	PA	42,032	C
Hofstra Univ	NY	55,960	C+
Howard Univ	DC	37,616	C+
Lehigh Univ	PA	61,010	MC
Lipscomb Univ	TN	41,296	VC
Marquette Univ	WI	48,390	VC+
Miami Univ	OH	27,190	HC+
Mich State Univ	MI	23,898	VC+
Murray State Univ	KY	16,998	C
Old Dominion Univ	VA	20,910	C
Pennsylvania State Univ - Univ Park	PA	29,760	HC
Rutgers Univ - Newark	NJ	27,288	C
Shippensburg Univ of Pennsylvania	PA	23,208	C
Southeastern Louisiana Univ	LA	16,237	C
SUNY / SUNY Plattsburgh	NY	18,814	C
SUNY at Binghamton	NY	22,861	MC
Syracuse Univ	NY	60,239	VC
Texas A&M Univ	TX	20,521	VC+
Texas Christian Univ	TX	54,670	HC
Texas Tech Univ	TX	18,736	C+
Tuskegee Univ	AL	28,164	C
Univ of Houston	TX	21,483	VC
Univ of Houston-Downtown	TX	7,241	C
Univ of Kansas	KS	20,135	C+
Univ of Maryland/College Park	MD	21,938	HC
Univ of Mich/Dearborn	MI	11,757	VC
Univ of Nebr - Lincoln	NE	18,589	VC
Univ of N Car at Charlotte	NC	15,547	C
Univ of Pittsburgh	PA	29,568	HC+
Univ of Rhode Island	RI	24,906	C
Univ of Wisc-Stout	WI	19,667	C
Wayne State Univ	MI	22,016	C
Weber State Univ	UT	10,721	C
Western Illinois Univ	IL	20,825	C
Western Mich Univ	MI	21,054	C
Wright State Univ	OH	16,983	C
Youngstown State Univ	OH	17,307	C

SURVEY AND MAPPING TECHNOLOGY

School	ST	$IS	SR
Alfred State College	NY	19,895	C
East Tenn State Univ	TN	13,994	C
Glenville State College	WV	17,386	NC
Kennesaw State Univ	GA	19,592	VC
Metropolitan State Univ of Denver	CO	29,889	LC
Purdue Univ/Northwest	IN	15,038	C
SUNY / The College of Environmental Science and Forestry	NY	23,853	VC
The Univ of Akron	OH	21,477	C
Univ of Alaska Anchorage	AK	16,652	NC
Univ of Maine at Machias	ME	22,960	C

SURVEYING ENGINEERING

School	ST	$IS	SR
Cal State, Fresno	CA	16,902	LC
Ferris State Univ	MI	21,445	C
Metropolitan State Univ of Denver	CO	29,889	LC
Mich Tech Univ	MI	24,739	VC+
New Mexico State Univ	NM	14,050	C
Oregon Inst of Technology	OR	8,910	C
Purdue Univ/West Lafayette	IN	20,032	MC
Universidad Metropolitana	PR	17,828	
Universidad Politecnica de PR, Hato Rey campus	PR	23,514	
Univ of Arkansas at Little Rock	AR	18,211	C
Univ of Maine	ME	20,792	C
Univ of PR, at Mayaguez	PR	13,995	

SUSTAINABILITY

School	ST	$IS	SR
Davis & Elkins College	WV	38,242	LC
Univ of New Hampshire	NH	28,562	VC

SUSTAINABLE ENERGY

School	ST	$IS	SR
Bryant Univ	RI	55,646	VC
Creighton Univ	NE	48,206	VC+

SUSTAINABLE ENERGY SCIENCE

School	ST	$IS	SR
Bryant Univ	RI	55,646	VC
Creighton Univ	NE	48,206	VC+

SUSTAINABLE MANAGEMENT

School	ST	$IS	SR
Ashford Univ	CA	10,480	C
Aurora Univ	IL	33,970	C
Baldwin Wallace Univ	OH	41,106	C
Bentley Univ	MA	60,890	HC
Bryant Univ	RI	55,646	VC
Catawba College	NC	39,820	C
Chatham Univ	PA	46,517	C
Goddard College	VT	17,040	VC
Kean Univ	NJ	24,650	C
Lipscomb Univ	TN	41,296	VC
Marylhurst Univ	OR	20,295	NC
Messiah College	PA	43,100	C+
Miami Univ	OH	27,190	HC+
Northland College	WI	41,103	C+
St. Louis Univ	MO	49,866	HC
Taylor Univ	IN	40,317	C+
Univ of Maine at Machias	ME	22,960	C
Univ of Rhode Island	RI	24,906	C
Univ of Wisc-Green Bay	WI	15,064	C
Univ of Wisc-Stout	WI	19,667	C
Univ of Wisc-Superior	WI	14,446	C
Viterbo Univ	WI	34,660	C
Xavier Univ	OH	47,880	C+

SYSTEMS ANALYSIS

School	ST	$IS	SR
Baldwin Wallace Univ	OH	41,106	C
George Washington Univ	DC	62,835	MC
Johnson & Wales Univ/ Providence Campus	RI	42,248	C
Rochester Inst of Technology	NY	50,842	HC

SYSTEMS ENGINEERING

School	ST	$IS	SR
Azusa Pacific Univ	CA	43,972	C
Calif Baptist Univ	CA	41,392	C
Case Western Reserve Univ	OH	60,304	MC
Embry-Riddle Aeronautical Univ - Daytona Beach	FL	44,712	VC
Embry-Riddle Aeronautical Univ - Worldwide	FL	17,480	C
George Mason Univ	VA	15,724	VC
Indiana Univ Bloomington	IN	20,429	VC
Johns Hopkins Univ	MD	65,386	MC
Kennesaw State Univ	GA	19,592	VC
Missouri Univ of Science and Technology	MO	18,655	HC
Point Park Univ	PA	41,270	C
Southern Nazarene Univ	OK	32,798	NC
Stanford Univ	CA	60,409	MC
SUNY at Binghamton	NY	22,861	MC
Stevens Inst of Technology	NJ	62,338	MC
Taylor Univ	IN	40,317	C+
Texas A&M Univ at Galveston	TX	15,920	C
United States Military Academy at West Point	NY		HC+
United States Naval Academy	MD		MC
Univ of Arizona	AZ	23,100	C
Univ of New Haven	CT	52,190	C
Univ of N Car at Charlotte	NC	15,547	C
Univ of Southern Calif	CA	66,631	C
Univ of Virginia	VA	25,891	MC
Washington Univ in St. Louis	MO	65,366	VC
West Virginia Univ	WV	18,210	C
Wright State Univ	OH	16,983	C

SYSTEMS SCIENCE

School	ST	$IS	SR
Case Western Reserve Univ	OH	60,304	MC
Johnson & Wales Univ/ Providence Campus	RI	42,248	C
Stanford Univ	CA	60,409	MC
United States Military Academy at West Point	NY		HC+
Washington Univ in St. Louis	MO	65,366	VC

TEACHING ENGLISH AS A SECOND/FOREIGN LANGUAGE (TESOL/TEFOL)

School	ST	$IS	SR
Andrews Univ	MI	28,030	C+
Aquinas College - Mich	MI	38,876	HC
Bethel Univ	MN	45,270	VC
Brigham Young Univ/Hawaii	HI	11,290	C
Campbellsville Univ	KY	32,492	C
Canisius College	NY	47,537	C
Caribbean Univ	PR	15,471	
Carroll College	MT	39,972	C+
CUNY/Queens College	NY	27,896	C
Elms College	MA	45,646	VC
Goshen College	IN	42,500	C
Hawaii Pacific Univ	HI	33,420	C
Houghton College	NY	39,090	C
Houston Baptist Univ	TX	36,450	C
Howard Payne Univ	TX	34,320	C
Huntington Univ	IN	33,996	C
Inter-American Univ of PR-Arecibo Campus	PR	18,245	
Inter-American Univ of PR-San Germán	PR	20,042	
Kent State Univ	OH	20,732	C
Le Moyne College	NY	46,000	C
Mercy College	NY	31,776	C
Missouri Southern State Univ	MO	12,499	C
Murray State Univ	KY	16,998	C
Niagara Univ	NY	41,010	C
Northeastern Illinois Univ	IL	12,529	LC
Nyack College	NY	34,050	NC
Okla Christian Univ	OK	27,650	VC
Pontifical Catholic Univ of PR	PR	10,534	
San Jose State Univ	CA	21,540	C
Seattle Pacific Univ	WA	47,439	C+
Simmons College	MA	53,090	VC
SUNY at Oswego	NY	21,351	C
Taylor Univ	IN	40,317	C+
Texas Wesleyan Univ	TX	35,134	C
The Univ of Utah	UT	17,924	VC
Union Univ	TN	33,970	VC
Univ of Arizona	AZ	23,100	C
Univ of Louisville	KY	19,824	C
Univ of Minn/Twin Cities	MN	23,519	HC+
Univ of Nebr - Kearney	NE	16,546	LC
Univ of PR, at Mayaguez	PR	13,995	
Weber State Univ	UT	10,721	C
Western Carolina Univ	NC	13,965	C
Winona State Univ	MN	17,535	C

TECHNICAL & APPLIED STUDIES

School	ST	$IS	SR
Bloomsburg Univ of Pennsylvania	PA	19,066	LC
Ohio Univ	OH	22,924	C

TECHNICAL AND BUSINESS WRITING

School	ST	$IS	SR
Carlow Univ	PA	38,549	LC
Cedarville Univ	OH	34,990	VC
CUNY/College of Technology	NY	6,669	NC
Eastern Mich Univ	MI	19,761	C
Illinois Inst of Technology	IL	56,826	HC+
Indiana Univ-Purdue Univ Fort Wayne	IN	17,553	C
Lawrence Tech Univ	MI	39,770	VC
Madonna Univ	MI	29,050	C
Metropolitan State Univ	MN	7,566	C
Mich Tech Univ	MI	24,739	VC+
Milwaukee School of Engineering	WI	45,153	HC
Missouri Univ of Science and Technology	MO	18,655	HC
Mount Mary Univ	WI	34,650	LC
New Jersey Inst of Technology	NJ	29,569	VC
New Mexico Inst of Mining and Technology	NM	14,833	HC
New York Univ	NY	65,860	MC
Saginaw Valley State Univ	MI	18,530	C
Taylor Univ	IN	40,317	C+
Tenn Tech Univ	TN	17,050	C
Univ of Arkansas at Little Rock	AR	18,211	C
Univ of Findlay	OH	60,139	C
Univ of Hartford	CT	49,776	C
Univ of Houston-Downtown	TX	7,241	C
Univ of Montana-Western	MT	11,220	LC
Univ of Washington	WA	23,149	VC
Valparaiso Univ	IN	48,370	C+
Weber State Univ	UT	10,721	C
Winthrop Univ	SC	23,082	C
Worcester Polytechnic Inst	MA	60,730	MC
Youngstown State Univ	OH	17,307	C

TECHNICAL COMMUNICATION

School	ST	$IS	SR
Arizona State Univ at the Polytechnic Campus	AZ	21,360	VC
Bowling Green State Univ	OH	19,747	C
Carnegie Mellon Univ	PA	67,980	MC
Ferris State Univ	MI	21,445	C
Indiana Univ-Purdue Univ Indianapolis	IN	18,635	C
King Univ	TN	34,660	C
Mercer Univ	GA	45,348	VC
Minn State Univ, Mankato	MN	15,616	C
Texas Tech Univ	TX	18,736	C+

TECHNICAL EDUCATION

School	ST	$IS	SR
Bowling Green State Univ	OH	19,747	C
Brigham Young Univ	UT	12,748	HC
Central Conn State Univ	CT	21,203	C
CUNY/College of Technology	NY	6,669	NC
Eastern Illinois Univ	IL	21,126	C
Eastern Kentucky Univ	KY	16,908	C
Eastern Mich Univ	MI	19,761	C
Eastern New Mexico Univ	NM	14,416	C
Elizabeth City State Univ	NC	14,745	C
Ferris State Univ	MI	21,445	C
Fitchburg State Univ	MA	21,819	C
Fort Hays State Univ	KS	12,131	C
Illinois State Univ	IL	23,418	VC
Millersville Univ of Pennsylvania	PA	23,782	C
Miss State Univ	MS	11,454	C+
Montana State Univ	MT	15,500	C+
Murray State Univ	KY	16,998	C
Norfolk State Univ	VA	25,702	LC
N Car State Univ	NC	19,515	HC+
Ohio State Univ at Columbus	OH	21,703	HC+
Pittsburg State Univ	KS	13,880	NC
Purdue Univ/West Lafayette	IN	20,032	MC
Rhode Island College	RI	17,694	LC
Rochester College	MI	28,574	LC
S Dak State Univ	SD	15,634	C
SUNY at Oswego	NY	21,351	C
Temple Univ	PA	24,392	VC
Texas State Univ	TX	19,350	C
The College of New Jersey	NJ	31,909	HC
The Univ of Akron	OH	21,477	C
Thomas Edison State Univ	NJ	6,350	NC
Tuskegee Univ	AL	28,164	C
Univ of Arkansas at Fayetteville	AR	19,152	C+
Univ of Central Florida	FL	15,922	VC
Univ of Idaho	ID	15,348	C
Univ of New Mexico	NM	15,404	C
Univ of Southern Maine	ME	18,320	C
Univ of Wisc-Platteville	WI	14,614	VC
Univ of Wisc-Stout	WI	19,667	C
Univ of Wyoming	WY	15,375	C+
Valley City State Univ	ND	13,267	C
Western Kentucky Univ	KY	16,850	C
Western Washington Univ	WA	18,003	C+

TECHNICAL OPERATIONS MANAGEMENT

School	ST	$IS	SR
Embry-Riddle Aeronautical Univ - Worldwide	FL	17,480	C
Ohio Univ	OH	22,924	C

TECHNOLOGICAL MANAGEMENT

School	ST	$IS	SR
Alfred State College	NY	19,895	C
Arizona State Univ at the Polytechnic Campus	AZ	21,360	VC
Arkansas State Univ	AR	16,190	C
Brewton-Parker College	GA	23,490	C
Cameron Univ	OK	11,072	NC
Clayton State Univ	GA	19,735	C
Colo Technical Univ	CO	21,455	NC
Davenport Univ	MI	25,896	LC
Excelsior College	NY	14,080	SP
Franklin Univ	OH	56,262	SP
Golden Gate Univ	CA	32,110	C
Johnson & Wales Univ/ Providence Campus	RI	42,248	C
Lawrence Tech Univ	MI	39,770	VC
New Jersey Inst of Technology	NJ	29,569	VC
Northern Illinois Univ	IL	20,176	C
Ohio Northern Univ	OH	44,050	VC
Okla Panhandle State Univ	OK	6,152	NC
Pennsylvania College of Technology	PA	27,333	NC
Pittsburg State Univ	KS	13,880	NC
Roger Williams Univ	RI	46,296	C+
Southeast Missouri State Univ	MO	15,498	C
Southern Illinois Univ Carbondale	IL	23,667	C
Southern New Hampshire Univ	NH	43,198	C
Southern Univ at New Orleans	LA	8,014	LC
SUNY /College of Agriculture and Tech at Cobleskill	NY	20,527	LC
SUNY at Oswego	NY	21,351	C
Stony Brook Univ/The SUNY	NY	21,881	MC
Texas A&M Univ	TX	20,521	VC+
Troy Univ	AL	16,171	C
Univ of Alaska Anchorage	AK	16,652	NC
Univ of Findlay	OH	60,139	C
Univ of North Georgia	GA	17,316	C
Washburn Univ	KS	15,827	C
Wayne State College	NE	12,802	C
Wentworth Inst of Technology	MA	47,112	C

TECHNOLOGY & SCIENCE EDUCATION

School	ST	$IS	SR
Colo State Univ	CO	22,162	VC
Excelsior College	NY	14,080	SP
Univ of Wisc-Stout	WI	19,667	C
Viterbo Univ	WI	34,660	C

TECHNOLOGY AND PUBLIC AFFAIRS

School	ST	$IS	SR
Kent State Univ	OH	20,732	C
New Jersey Inst of Technology	NJ	29,569	VC
Pomona College	CA	64,957	MC
Washington Univ in St. Louis	MO	65,366	VC
Western Kentucky Univ	KY	16,850	C
Western Washington Univ	WA	18,003	C+
Worcester Polytechnic Inst	MA	60,730	MC

TELECOMMUNICATIONS

School	ST	$IS	SR
Alabama A&M Univ	AL	18,796	C
Baylor Univ	TX	53,760	HC
Bowling Green State Univ	OH	19,747	C
Cal State, Monterey Bay	CA	26,871	LC
Capitol Technology Univ	MD	31,410	C
CUNY/College of Technology	NY	6,669	NC
Colo Technical Univ	CO	21,455	NC
Concordia Univ Wisc	WI	35,910	C
Eastern Mich Univ	MI	19,761	C
Fort Hays State Univ	KS	12,131	C
Howard Univ	DC	37,616	C+
Illinois State Univ	IL	23,418	VC
Indiana Univ Bloomington	IN	20,429	VC
Indiana Univ-Purdue Univ Fort Wayne	IN	17,553	C
Ithaca College	NY	56,766	VC
Kutztown Univ of Pennsylvania	PA	19,056	LC
Lee Univ	TN	22,045	C
Mich State Univ	MI	23,898	VC+
Morgan State Univ	MD	17,190	LC
New York Inst of Technology	NY	48,730	C
Ohio Univ	OH	22,924	C

ST = STATE $IS = IN-STATE COSTS SR = SELECTOR RATING

School	ST	$IS	SR
Okla Baptist Univ	OK	32,320	C
Pepperdine Univ	CA	74,460	HC+
Rochester Inst of Technology	NY	50,842	HC
Roosevelt Univ	IL	40,651	VC
St. John's Univ	NY	55,850	C
Temple Univ	PA	24,392	VC
Texas A&M Univ	TX	20,521	VC+
Univ of PR, at Arecibo	PR	12,652	
Univ of Alabama	AL	24,320	C+
Univ of Florida	FL	16,291	HC+
Univ of Idaho	ID	15,348	C
Univ of Kentucky	KY	33,306	C
Univ of Louisiana at Lafayette	LA	14,516	C
Univ of Nebr - Kearney	NE	16,546	LC
Univ of North Texas	TX	19,198	C
Univ of Northern Colo	CO	20,851	C
Univ of Texas at Dallas	TX	22,830	VC+
Univ of the Sacred Heart	PR	17,932	
Univ of Wisc-Stout	WI	19,667	C
Western Mich Univ	MI	21,054	C
Youngstown State Univ	OH	17,307	C

TELECOMMUNICATIONS ENGINEERING TECHNOLOGY

School	ST	$IS	SR
Farmingdale State College	NY	20,624	C
Jackson State Univ	MS	15,879	LC
Kennesaw State Univ	GA	19,592	VC
Univ of Texas at Dallas	TX	22,830	VC+

TELECOMMUNICATIONS SYSTEMS MANAGEMENT

School	ST	$IS	SR
Kent State Univ	OH	20,732	C
Murray State Univ	KY	16,998	C

TELECOMMUNICATIONS SYSTEMS MGMT

School	ST	$IS	SR
Kent State Univ	OH	20,732	C
Murray State Univ	KY	16,998	C

TELEVISION & DIGITAL MEDIA PRODUCTION

School	ST	$IS	SR
Bloomfield College	NJ	39,100	LC
Drexel Univ	PA	65,432	VC+
Ferris State Univ	MI	21,445	C
Hofstra Univ	NY	55,960	C+
Kent State Univ	OH	20,732	C
Neumann Univ	PA	40,678	LC
Robert Morris Univ	PA	37,834	C
Syracuse Univ	NY	60,239	VC
Texas Tech Univ	TX	18,736	C+
Wisc Lutheran College	WI	36,290	VC

TEXTILE ENGINEERING

School	ST	$IS	SR
Auburn Univ	AL	23,594	VC+
N Car State Univ	NC	19,515	HC+
Philadelphia Univ	PA	50,370	C

TEXTILE MARKETING

School	ST	$IS	SR
Univ of Rhode Island	RI	24,906	C

TEXTILE TECHNOLOGY

School	ST	$IS	SR
Clemson Univ	SC		HC
Fashion Inst of Technology/ SUNY	NY	18,521	SP
Mich State Univ	MI	23,898	VC+
Philadelphia Univ	PA	50,370	C
Univ of Wisc-Madison	WI	20,934	MC

TEXTILE, FASHION MERCHANDISING & DESIGN

School	ST	$IS	SR
East Central Univ	OK	13,056	C
Univ of Rhode Island	RI	24,906	C
Western Mich Univ	MI	21,054	C

TEXTILES AND CLOTHING

School	ST	$IS	SR
Albright College	PA	46,660	C
Auburn Univ	AL	23,594	VC+
Calif College of the Arts	CA	52,758	SP
College for Creative Studies	MI	48,875	SP
Eastern Mich Univ	MI	19,761	C
Fashion Inst of Technology/ SUNY	NY	18,521	SP
Framingham State Univ	MA	20,584	C
Howard Univ	DC	37,616	C+
Indiana State Univ	IN	23,223	LC
Iowa State Univ	IA	17,570	C
Kansas State Univ	KS	17,780	VC
Lipscomb Univ	TN	41,296	VC
Louisiana State Univ and A&M College	LA	18,677	VC
Middle Tenn State Univ	TN	8,650	C
Moore College of Art and Design	PA	50,135	SP
New Mexico State Univ	NM	14,050	C
N Car State Univ	NC	19,515	HC+
N Dak State Univ	ND	16,245	C
Northern Illinois Univ	IL	20,176	C
Northwest Missouri State Univ	MO	17,737	C
Rhode Island School of Design	RI	59,960	SP
Univ of Calif at Davis	CA	28,468	HC
Univ of Central Missouri	MO	18,982	C
Univ of Idaho	ID	15,348	C
Univ of Illinois at Urbana-Champaign	IL	27,006	HC
Univ of Kentucky	KY	33,306	C
Univ of Minn/Twin Cities	MN	23,519	HC+
Univ of Missouri/Columbia	MO	18,201	MC
Univ of Nebr - Lincoln	NE	18,589	VC
Univ of Texas at Austin	TX	26,102	HC
Univ of Wisc-Madison	WI	20,934	MC
Western Kentucky Univ	KY	16,850	C
Western Mich Univ	MI	21,054	C

THEATER DESIGN

School	ST	$IS	SR
Adelphi Univ	NY	48,244	C
Alabama A&M Univ	AL	18,796	C
Arcadia Univ	PA	33,570	C+
Baldwin Wallace Univ	OH	41,106	C
Baylor Univ	TX	53,760	HC
Belmont Univ	TN	40,970	VC
Bennington College	VT	63,960	MC
Biola Univ	CA	46,402	C+
Boston Univ	MA	65,110	MC
Calif Inst of the Arts	CA	56,426	SP
Cal State, Fresno	CA	16,902	LC
Cal State, Fullerton	CA	21,902	C
Central Mich Univ	MI	20,330	C
College of the Ozarks	MO	7,230	C
Colo State Univ	CO	22,162	VC
Cornish College of the Arts	WA	47,750	SP
Davis & Elkins College	WV	38,242	LC
DePaul Univ	IL	47,623	VC
DeSales Univ	PA	43,970	C
Elon Univ	NC	44,599	VC+
Emerson College	MA	54,736	HC
Eugene Lang College/The New School for Liberal Arts	NY	55,650	C
Faulkner Univ	AL	26,410	C
Florida State Univ	FL	16,771	HC
Fordham Univ	NY	65,918	MC
Grand Canyon Univ	AZ	16,950	VC
Hofstra Univ	NY	55,960	C+
Huntington Univ	IN	33,996	C
Illinois Wesleyan Univ	IL	56,430	VC+
Ithaca College	NY	56,766	VC
Johnson State College	VT	20,752	C
Kean Univ	NJ	24,650	C
Keene State College	NH	24,003	LC
Lehigh Univ	PA	61,010	MC
Marshall Univ	WV	17,242	C
Mich Tech Univ	MI	24,739	VC+
Millikin Univ	IL	42,158	C
Montclair State Univ	NJ	26,210	LC
Niagara Univ	NY	41,010	C
Oberlin College	OH	66,012	MC
Ohio State Univ at Columbus	OH	21,703	HC+
Ohio Univ	OH	22,924	C
Okla City Univ	OK	40,476	VC
Old Dominion Univ	VA	20,910	C
Pace Univ	NY	58,248	C
Palm Beach Atlantic Univ	FL	39,720	C
Pennsylvania State Univ - Univ Park	PA	29,760	HC
Piedmont College	GA	32,512	C
Roosevelt Univ	IL	40,651	VC
Santa Fe Univ of Art and Design	NM	39,980	SP
Seton Hill Univ	PA	46,972	C
Shenandoah Univ	VA	41,312	C
Southern Illinois Univ Edwardsville	IL	22,643	C
SUNY / SUNY Fredonia	NY	20,818	C
SUNY at Binghamton	NY	22,861	MC
SUNY at Geneseo	NY	20,440	VC+
SUNY at New Paltz	NY	19,200	C
SUNY at Purchase	NY	17,900	C
Stephens College	MO	38,042	C
Syracuse Univ	NY	60,239	VC
Temple Univ	PA	24,392	VC
Texas Christian Univ	TX	54,670	HC
Texas Wesleyan Univ	TX	35,134	C
Towson Univ	MD	17,408	VC
Tulane Univ	LA	63,396	HC+
Univ of Central Missouri	MO	18,982	C
Univ of Central Okla	OK	13,486	C
Univ of Cincinnati	OH	21,964	VC
Univ of Conn	CT	25,538	HC
Univ of Florida	FL	16,291	HC+
Univ of Illinois at Chicago	IL	25,006	VC
Univ of Kansas	KS	20,135	C+
Univ of Maryland/Baltimore County	MD	21,296	VC
Univ of Miami	FL	63,494	MC
Univ of Mich/Ann Arbor	MI	24,410	MC
Univ of Nebr - Lincoln	NE	18,589	VC
Univ of New Mexico	NM	15,404	C
Univ of N Car at Wilmington	NC	14,590	VC
Univ of N Car School of the Arts	NC	18,040	SP
Univ of North Texas	TX	19,198	C
Univ of Southern Calif	CA	66,631	C
Wagner College	NY	55,480	C+
Washburn Univ	KS	15,827	C
Webster Univ	MO	37,490	C
West Chester Univ of Pennsylvania	PA	18,456	C
Western Mich Univ	MI	21,054	C
Western Washington Univ	WA	18,003	C+
Wright State Univ	OH	16,983	C

THEATER MANAGEMENT

School	ST	$IS	SR
Aquinas College - Mich	MI	38,876	HC
Baldwin Wallace Univ	OH	41,106	C
Barry Univ	FL	37,830	C
Benedictine College	KS	36,200	VC
Bethel Univ	TN	24,738	C
Biola Univ	CA	46,402	C+
Boston Univ	MA	65,110	MC
Cal State, Fullerton	CA	21,902	C
Catawba College	NC	39,820	C
CUNY/Brooklyn College	NY	5,884	C+
Colo Mesa Univ	CO	18,955	LC
DePaul Univ	IL	47,623	VC
DeSales Univ	PA	43,970	C
Emerson College	MA	54,736	HC
Fitchburg State Univ	MA	21,819	C
Fontbonne Univ	MO	33,717	C
Grand Canyon Univ	AZ	16,950	VC
Hofstra Univ	NY	55,960	C+
Illinois Wesleyan Univ	IL	56,430	VC+
Ithaca College	NY	56,766	VC
Johnson State College	VT	20,752	C
King Univ	TN	34,660	C
Marywood Univ	PA	46,900	C
Messiah College	PA	43,100	C+
Millikin Univ	IL	42,158	C
New York Univ	NY	65,860	MC
Ohio Univ	OH	22,924	C
Pace Univ	NY	58,248	C
Roosevelt Univ	IL	40,651	VC
St. Louis Univ	MO	49,866	HC
Santa Fe Univ of Art and Design	NM	39,980	SP
Seton Hill Univ	PA	46,972	C
Temple Univ	PA	24,392	VC
The Univ of Akron	OH	21,477	C
Trinity College	CT	63,920	HC+
Univ of Delaware	DE	24,976	VC+
Univ of Evansville	IN	44,186	VC+
Univ of Hartford	CT	49,776	C
Univ of Miami	FL	63,494	MC
Univ of North Texas	TX	19,198	C
Univ of Southern Calif	CA	66,631	C
Univ of Texas at El Paso	TX	34,452	NC
West Chester Univ of Pennsylvania	PA	18,456	C
Western Mich Univ	MI	21,054	C
Wright State Univ	OH	16,983	C

THEATRE ACTING

School	ST	$IS	SR
Asbury Univ	KY	35,180	C+
Baldwin Wallace Univ	OH	41,106	C
Bates College	ME	64,500	MC
Bethany College	WV	36,300	NC
Biola Univ	CA	46,402	C+
Colo State Univ	CO	22,162	VC
Columbus State Univ	GA	14,336	LC
DeSales Univ	PA	43,970	C
Dordt College	IA	37,860	C+
Eastern Conn State Univ	CT	23,059	C
Elon Univ	NC	44,599	VC+
Eugene Lang College/The New School for Liberal Arts	NY	55,650	C
Fairmont State Univ	WV	15,726	C
Fontbonne Univ	MO	33,717	C
Fordham Univ	NY	65,918	MC
Gonzaga Univ	WA	50,888	HC
Hiram College	OH	43,230	C
Illinois State Univ	IL	23,418	VC
Keene State College	NH	24,003	LC
Lycoming College	PA	48,580	C
Millersville Univ of Pennsylvania	PA	23,782	C
Nova Southeastern Univ	FL	38,534	C+
Oberlin College	OH	66,012	MC
Okla City Univ	OK	40,476	VC
Pace Univ	NY	58,248	C
Southeast Missouri State Univ	MO	15,498	C
St. Ambrose Univ	IA	39,019	C
St. Ambrose Univ	IA	39,019	C
SUNY at Oswego	NY	21,351	C
Texas A&M Univ	TX	20,521	VC+
Texas Christian Univ	TX	54,670	HC
The College at Brockport - SUNY	NY	20,346	C
Univ of Central Okla	OK	13,486	C
Univ of Detroit Mercy	MI	48,816	C+
Univ of Georgia	GA	21,250	HC
Univ of Illinois at Chicago	IL	25,006	VC
Univ of Miami	FL	63,494	MC
Univ of Tampa	FL	36,944	C
Univ of Wyoming	WY	15,375	C+
Western Mich Univ	MI	21,054	C
Wright State Univ	OH	16,983	C
Youngstown State Univ	OH	17,307	C

THEATRE ARTS

School	ST	$IS	SR
Adams State Univ	CO	17,703	LC
Albion College	MI	52,650	C
Alfred Univ	NY	42,296	C+
Alma College	MI	47,548	C
Alvernia Univ	PA	43,900	C
Angelo State Univ	TX	15,263	NC
Aquinas College - Mich	MI	38,876	HC
Arizona State Univ at the Tempe Campus	AZ	21,756	VC
Arkansas State Univ	AR	16,190	C
Armstrong State Univ	GA	16,962	C
Augustana College	IL	49,658	VC
Augustana Univ	SD	38,424	VC
Averett Univ	VA	40,970	LC
Azusa Pacific Univ	CA	43,972	C
Bard College	NY	64,024	HC
Belmont Univ	TN	40,970	VC
Berea College	KY	7,042	C
Berry College	GA	45,286	C+
Bethany College	KS	46,100	NC
Bethel College	IN	35,860	C
Biola Univ	CA	46,402	C+
Birmingham-Southern College	AL	44,478	VC
Bloomsburg Univ of Pennsylvania	PA	19,066	LC
Boise State Univ	ID	14,860	C
Boston Univ	MA	65,110	MC
Bowdoin College	ME	63,500	MC
Brandeis Univ	MA	65,925	MC
Brescia Univ	KY	29,890	VC+
Brown Univ	RI	64,566	MC
Bryan College	TN	31,440	C
Buena Vista Univ	IA	41,514	C
Butler Univ	IN	51,352	VC
Calif Baptist Univ	CA	41,392	C
Calif Lutheran Univ	CA	52,853	C
Calif Polytechnic State Univ	CA	17,979	HC+
Calif State Polytechnic Univ, Pomona	CA	21,541	C
Cal State, Chico	CA	21,440	C
Cal State, Fresno	CA	16,902	LC
Cal State, Long Beach	CA	18,850	C
Cameron Univ	OK	11,072	NC
Campbellsville Univ	KY	32,492	C
Canisius College	NY	47,537	C
Carroll Univ	WI	38,100	C+
Carthage College	WI	48,835	C
Case Western Reserve Univ	OH	60,304	MC
Castleton Univ	VT	20,186	C
Catawba College	NC	39,820	C
Cedarville Univ	OH	34,990	VC
Central College	IA	44,592	C
Central Conn State Univ	CT	21,203	C
Christopher Newport Univ	VA	23,968	VC+
Coe College	IA	51,570	VC
Colby College	ME	64,060	MC
College of Charleston	SC	22,699	C
College of St. Benedict	MN	52,806	C
College of the Holy Cross	MA	62,165	MC
College of William & Mary	VA		MC
Colo Mesa Univ	CO	18,955	LC
Columbia College Chicago	IL	43,168	C
Concordia Univ St. Paul	MN	29,050	C
Creighton Univ	NE	48,206	VC+
Dartmouth College	NH	66,174	MC
Davis & Elkins College	WV	38,242	LC
DePaul Univ	IL	47,623	VC
Dickinson College	PA	63,974	MC
Dominican Univ	IL	41,222	C
Dordt College	IA	37,860	C+
Drew Univ/College of Liberal Arts	NJ	61,048	VC
East Central Univ	OK	13,056	C
East Stroudsburg Univ	PA	18,334	C
East Texas Baptist Univ	TX	33,134	C
Eastern Illinois Univ	IL	21,126	C
Eastern Mennonite Univ	VA	42,550	C
Edgewood College	WI	35,950	C
Elmhurst College	IL	45,428	C
Elmira College	NY	53,900	C
Elon Univ	NC	44,599	VC+
Emporia State Univ	KS	14,570	C
Fairfield Univ	CT	59,860	VC+
Five Towns College	NY	35,350	C
Flagler College	FL	27,620	C
Fontbonne Univ	MO	33,717	C
Franklin College	IN	39,380	C
Franklin Pierce Univ	NH	46,750	C
Frostburg State Univ	MD	17,280	LC
Gallaudet Univ	DC	29,118	LC
Georgia College & State Univ	GA	21,148	C+
Goshen College	IN	42,500	C
Goucher College	MD	55,716	VC
Grand Canyon Univ	AZ	16,950	VC
Grinnell College	IA	60,738	MC
Guilford College	NC	44,090	C
Hamline Univ	MN	45,678	VC
Hampden-Sydney College	VA	56,248	C+
Henderson State Univ	AR	15,516	LC
High Point Univ	NC	45,977	C
Hillsdale College	MI	35,722	MC
Hollins Univ	VA	49,635	VC
Hope College	MI	39,940	VC
Howard Univ	DC	37,616	C+
Huntington Univ	IN	33,996	C

ST = STATE $IS = IN-STATE COSTS SR = SELECTOR RATING

School	ST	$IS	SR
Indiana Univ Bloomington	IN	20,429	VC
Indiana Univ Northwest	IN	7,072	C
Indiana Univ of Pennsylvania	PA	23,614	LC
Indiana Univ South Bend	IN	14,242	C
Indiana Univ Southeast	IN	14,242	LC
John Carroll Univ	OH	49,740	C+
Kean Univ	NJ	24,650	C
Kennesaw State Univ	GA	19,592	VC
Kent State Univ	OH	20,732	C
King Univ	TN	34,660	C
Knox College	IL	52,615	VC+
LaGrange College	GA	39,930	C
Lake Forest College	IL	50,652	VC
Lewis Univ	IL	40,370	C
Limestone College	SC	32,100	C
Linfield College	OR	52,010	C
Lipscomb Univ	TN	41,296	VC
LIU Post	NY	49,682	C
Loyola Marymount Univ	CA	58,038	HC
Loyola Univ Chicago	IL	55,802	VC
Lubbock Christian Univ	TX	28,426	C
Luther College	IA	48,540	C+
Lynchburg College	VA	46,740	C
Marquette Univ	WI	48,390	VC+
Marshall Univ	WV	17,242	C
Miami Univ	OH	27,190	HC+
Millikin Univ	IL	42,158	C
Missouri Baptist Univ	MO	35,594	C
Missouri Southern State Univ	MO	12,499	C
Missouri State Univ	MO	15,190	C+
Molloy College	NY	40,440	C
Montreat College	NC	31,298	LC
Murray State Univ	KY	16,998	C
Nazareth College	NY	45,574	C
New Mexico State Univ	NM	14,050	C
Niagara Univ	NY	41,010	C
North Central College	IL	48,712	VC
N Dak State Univ	ND	16,245	C
North Greenville Univ	SC	25,930	C+
Northeastern Illinois Univ	IL	12,529	LC
Northeastern Univ	MA	62,703	MC
Northern Arizona Univ	AZ	20,246	VC
Northern Kentucky Univ	KY	16,486	C
Northern Mich Univ	MI	19,604	C
Occidental College	CA	65,530	MC
Ohio State Univ at Columbus	OH	21,703	HC+
Ohio Wesleyan Univ	OH	49,460	VC
Okla City Univ	OK	40,476	VC
Ouachita Baptist Univ	AR	32,320	C
Pace Univ	NY	58,248	C
Pacific Lutheran Univ	WA	49,960	VC
Piedmont College	GA	32,512	C
Plymouth State Univ	NH	23,180	LC
Point Park Univ	PA	41,270	C
Pomona College	CA	64,957	MC
Providence College	RI	60,760	VC
Quinnipiac Univ	CT	59,110	C
Radford Univ	VA	19,027	LC
Rhodes College	TN	51,900	HC
Roanoke College	VA	54,114	VC
Rocky Mountain College	MT	34,270	C
Roger Williams Univ	RI	46,296	C+
Rollins College	FL	58,670	HC
Rowan Univ	NJ	24,491	VC+
St. John's Univ	MN	51,624	C
St. Joseph's Univ	PA	57,544	VC+
St. Louis Univ	MO	49,866	HC
St. Martin's Univ	WA	45,056	C
St. Mary's Univ of Minn	MN	41,210	VC
Salisbury Univ	MD	20,714	VC
Samford Univ	AL	39,232	VC
San Diego State Univ	CA	21,896	C+
Schreiner Univ	TX	34,626	LC
Seattle Univ	WA	50,811	VC+
Seton Hall Univ	NJ	55,514	C
Seton Hill Univ	PA	46,972	C
Sewanee: The Univ of the South	TN	54,500	MC
Siena Heights Univ	MI	32,040	C
Southern Oregon Univ	OR	19,117	C
Southwestern College	KS	31,531	C
Spring Hill College	AL	48,488	C
St. Edward's Univ	TX	53,100	VC
St. Norbert College	WI	44,525	VC
St. Olaf College	MN	54,260	HC+
SUNY / SUNY Fredonia	NY	20,818	C
SUNY / SUNY Potsdam	NY	20,404	C+
SUNY / Univ at Buffalo	NY	23,122	C+
SUNY at Binghamton	NY	22,861	MC
SUNY at Oswego	NY	21,351	C
Sterling College	KS	32,830	C
Stony Brook Univ/The SUNY	NY	21,881	MC
Susquehanna Univ	PA	55,340	VC
Swarthmore College	PA	63,550	MC
Tabor College	KS	35,870	C
Tarleton State Univ	TX	15,248	LC
Taylor Univ	IN	40,317	C+
Texas Christian Univ	TX	54,670	HC
Texas State Univ	TX	19,350	C
Texas Tech Univ	TX	18,736	C+
The College of Idaho	ID	36,415	C
The Univ of Tenn at Knoxville	TN	22,112	VC
The Univ of Utah	UT	17,924	VC
Thomas Edison State Univ	NJ	6,350	NC
Transylvania Univ	KY	45,690	VC+
Univ of Alaska Fairbanks	AK	16,179	C
Univ of Arizona	AZ	23,100	C
Univ of Arkansas at Little Rock	AR	18,211	C
Univ of Calif at Riverside	CA	29,227	C+
Univ of Central Florida	FL	15,922	VC
Univ of Central Okla	OK	13,486	C
Univ of Colo Boulder	CO	24,285	VC+
Univ of Illinois at Chicago	IL	25,006	VC
Univ of Iowa	IA	18,683	VC+
Univ of Kansas	KS	20,135	C+
Univ of Louisville	KY	19,824	C
Univ of Maryland/College Park	MD	21,938	HC
Univ of Miami	FL	63,494	MC
Univ of Miss	MS	17,746	C+
Univ of Nebr - Lincoln	NE	18,589	VC
Univ of New Hampshire	NH	28,562	VC
Univ of New Haven	CT	52,190	C
Univ of N Car at Charlotte	NC	15,547	C
Univ of Oregon	OR	22,972	C
Univ of Pittsburgh	PA	29,568	HC+
Univ of Rhode Island	RI	24,906	C
Univ of Richmond	VA	60,880	MC
Univ of Rochester	NY	65,032	MC
Univ of St. Mary	KS	34,690	C
Univ of San Diego	CA	58,442	VC+
Univ of Scranton	PA	54,962	VC
Univ of Southern Indiana	IN	16,501	C
Univ of Tulsa	OK	52,625	HC+
Univ of West Georgia	GA	16,360	LC
Univ of Wisc-Eau Claire	WI	15,797	VC
Univ of Wisc-Green Bay	WI	15,064	C
Univ of Wisc-Madison	WI	20,934	MC
Univ of Wisc-Milwaukee	WI	21,496	C
Univ of Wisc-Superior	WI	14,446	C
Valparaiso Univ	IN	48,370	C+
Vanderbilt Univ	TN	60,572	MC
Vanguard Univ of Southern Calif	CA	40,740	VC
Warren Wilson College	NC	44,220	VC
Washington State Univ	WA	22,495	C
Wayne State Univ	MI	22,016	C
Weber State Univ	UT	10,721	C
Wellesley College	MA	63,916	MC
West Chester Univ of Pennsylvania	PA	18,456	C
West Virginia Wesleyan College	WV	36,858	C
Western Illinois Univ	IL	20,825	C
Western Washington Univ	WA	18,003	C+
Westfield State Univ	MA	19,671	C
Whitman College	WA	59,772	MC
Whitworth Univ	WA	51,732	VC
Wichita State Univ	KS	21,643	C
William Peace Univ	NC	37,430	LC
Winthrop Univ	SC	23,082	C
Wisc Lutheran College	WI	36,290	VC
Wofford College	SC	49,885	VC
Xavier Univ	OH	47,880	C+
Youngstown State Univ	OH	17,307	C

THEATRE MINISTRY

School	ST	$IS	SR
College of the Ozarks	MO	7,230	C

THEATRE PRODUCTION

School	ST	$IS	SR
Aquinas College - Mich	MI	38,876	HC
Bethany College	WV	36,300	NC
Boston Univ	MA	65,110	MC
Carthage College	WI	48,835	C
Colo State Univ	CO	22,162	VC
DeSales Univ	PA	43,970	C
Elon Univ	NC	44,599	VC+
Fontbonne Univ	MO	33,717	C
Fordham Univ	NY	65,918	MC
Keene State College	NH	24,003	LC
Lamar Univ	TX	18,014	LC
Millikin Univ	IL	42,158	C
Neumann Univ	PA	40,678	LC
Okla City Univ	OK	40,476	VC
Pace Univ	NY	58,248	C
Shenandoah Univ	VA	41,312	C
Southern Oregon Univ	OR	19,117	C
SUNY / SUNY Fredonia	NY	20,818	C
SUNY at Oswego	NY	21,351	C
Texas Christian Univ	TX	54,670	HC
Univ of Arizona	AZ	23,100	C
Univ of Illinois at Chicago	IL	25,006	VC
West Chester Univ of Pennsylvania	PA	18,456	C
Youngstown State Univ	OH	17,307	C

THEATRE STUDIES

School	ST	$IS	SR
Amherst College	MA		HC+
Aquinas College - Mich	MI	38,876	HC
Aurora Univ	IL	33,970	C
Baker Univ	KS	33,350	C+
Baylor Univ	TX	53,760	HC
Bowling Green State Univ	OH	19,747	C
Capital Univ	OH	42,982	C
Chapman Univ	CA	63,078	VC+
Chatham Univ	PA	46,517	C
Colgate Univ	NY	65,030	MC
College of the Ozarks	MO	7,230	C
Colo State Univ	CO	22,162	VC
Cornell College	IA	48,800	VC
Elon Univ	NC	44,599	VC+
Eugene Lang College/The New School for Liberal Arts	NY	55,650	C
Faulkner Univ	AL	26,410	C
Hardin-Simmons Univ	TX	33,966	C
John Carroll Univ	OH	49,740	C+
Lewis Univ	IL	40,370	C
Lindsey Wilson College	KY	32,882	C
Malone Univ	OH	38,448	C
Mich State Univ	MI	23,898	VC+
Mich Tech Univ	MI	24,739	VC+
Mills College	CA	59,163	VC
Minn State Univ, Mankato	MN	15,616	C
Missouri Southern State Univ	MO	12,499	C
Oberlin College	OH	66,012	MC
Southern Oregon Univ	OR	19,117	C
SUNY / SUNY Fredonia	NY	20,818	C
Stephen F. Austin State Univ	TX	18,406	LC
Texas Christian Univ	TX	54,670	HC
Trinity Univ	TX	52,314	HC+
Univ of Central Florida	FL	15,922	VC
Univ of Central Okla	OK	13,486	C
Univ of Chicago	IL	67,584	MC
Univ of Dayton	OH	53,620	C
Univ of Denver	CO	58,443	VC+
Univ of Illinois at Chicago	IL	25,006	VC
Univ of Indianapolis	IN	36,480	C
Univ of New Mexico	NM	15,404	C
Univ of S Dak	SD	16,109	C
Viterbo Univ	WI	34,660	C
Wake Forest Univ	NC	64,056	MC
Wells College	NY	50,500	C
West Chester Univ of Pennsylvania	PA	18,456	C
Western Mich Univ	MI	21,054	C
Wright State Univ	OH	16,983	C
Xavier Univ	OH	47,880	C+
Youngstown State Univ	OH	17,307	C

THEATRE/DANCE

School	ST	$IS	SR
Austin Peay State Univ	TN	16,397	C
Wheaton College	MA	61,512	VC

THEOLOGICAL STUDIES

School	ST	$IS	SR
Alvernia Univ	PA	43,900	C
Andrews Univ	MI	28,030	C+
Aquinas College	TN	30,800	C+
Aquinas College - Mich	MI	38,876	HC
Assumption College	MA	47,920	C+
Atlantic Union College	MA	27,228	C
Avila Univ	MO	35,480	C
Bard College	NY	64,024	HC
Barry Univ	FL	37,830	C
Bellarmine Univ	KY	51,220	C
Belmont Abbey College	NC	48,156	C
Benedictine Univ	IL	38,300	C
Bethel Univ	MN	45,270	VC
Boston College	MA	65,737	MC
Briar Cliff Univ	IA	36,956	C
Caldwell Univ	NJ	42,165	NC
Calif Lutheran Univ	CA	52,853	C
Calumet College of St. Joseph	IN	22,735	C
Calvin College	MI	41,570	VC+
Carlow Univ	PA	38,549	LC
Cedarville Univ	OH	34,990	VC
Christendom College	VA	32,600	VC
College of St. Benedict	MN	52,806	C
College of St. Elizabeth	NJ	44,432	LC
College of St. Mary	NE	35,184	C
Colo Christian Univ	CO	39,940	VC
Concordia Univ	CA	41,580	VC
Concordia Univ	OR	35,000	C
Concordia Univ Nebr	NE	36,280	VC
Concordia Univ St. Paul	MN	29,050	C
Concordia Univ Wisc	WI	35,910	C
Concordia Univ, Chicago	IL	39,694	C
Corban Univ	OR	40,306	C
DeSales Univ	PA	43,970	C
Dominican Univ	IL	41,222	C
Duquesne Univ	PA	46,822	VC
Eastern Mennonite Univ	VA	42,550	C
Eastern Univ	PA	39,540	C
Elmhurst College	IL	45,428	C
Fordham Univ	NY	65,918	MC
Franciscan Univ of Steubenville	OH	33,980	VC
Gannon Univ	PA	42,032	C
Hanover College	IN	46,364	C+
Hardin-Simmons Univ	TX	33,966	C
John Carroll Univ	OH	49,740	C+
Juniata College	PA	53,760	VC
King's College	PA	46,858	C
Lenoir-Rhyne Univ	NC	43,200	C
Lewis Univ	IL	40,370	C
Livingstone College	NC	17,815	LC
Lourdes Univ	OH	29,520	NC
Loyola Univ Chicago	IL	55,802	VC
Loyola Univ Maryland	MD	60,300	VC
Malone Univ	OH	38,448	C
Marquette Univ	WI	48,390	VC+
Marymount Univ	VA	41,570	LC
Messiah College	PA	43,100	C+
Mount Mary Univ	WI	34,650	LC
Mount St. Mary's Univ	MD	51,610	C
Mount Vernon Nazarene Univ	OH	34,500	C
Newman Univ	KS	35,390	C
Northwest Univ	WA	35,876	VC
Notre Dame College	OH	37,150	VC
Nyack College	NY	34,050	NC
Ohio Dominican Univ	OH	41,340	C+
Ouachita Baptist Univ	AR	32,320	C
Pacific Union College	CA	36,009	VC
Pontifical Catholic Univ of PR	PR	10,534	
Providence College	RI	60,760	VC
Quincy Univ	IL	36,998	C
Rockhurst Univ	MO	29,220	C
St. Anselm College	NH	52,560	C+
St. John's Univ	MN	51,624	C
St. Joseph's College of Maine	ME	46,485	C
St. Joseph's Univ	PA	57,544	VC+
St. Louis Univ	MO	49,866	HC
St. Mary-of-the-Woods College	IN	39,632	LC
St. Peter's Univ	NJ	49,192	C
St. Vincent College	PA	44,626	C
Seattle Pacific Univ	WA	47,439	C+
Seattle Univ	WA	50,811	VC+
Seton Hall Univ	NJ	55,514	C
Southern Adventist Univ	TN	27,600	C
Southern Nazarene Univ	OK	32,798	NC
Southwestern Adventist Univ	TX	27,756	LC
Spring Arbor Univ	MI	36,000	C
Spring Hill College	AL	48,488	C
St. Ambrose Univ	IA	39,019	C
St. Ambrose Univ	IA	39,019	C
St. Bonaventure Univ	NY	44,237	C
St. Catherine Univ	MN	45,630	VC
St. John's College-Annapolis	MD	60,142	MC
St. Mary's Univ	TX	37,500	C
Sterling College	KS	32,830	C
Texas Lutheran Univ	TX	38,620	C
The Catholic Univ of America	DC	56,356	VC
Thomas More College	KY	36,720	C
Trinity Christian College	IL	35,580	C
Union College	NE	23,270	C
Universidad Adventista de las Antillas	PR	16,606	
Univ of Chicago	IL	67,584	MC
Univ of Dallas	TX	45,500	VC+
Univ of Evansville	IN	44,186	VC+
Univ of Great Falls	MT	38,524	C
Univ of Mary	ND	23,180	C
Univ of Mobile	AL	28,935	C
Univ of Portland	OR	52,152	VC
Univ of St. Mary	KS	34,690	C
Univ of San Diego	CA	58,442	VC+
Univ of San Francisco	CA	58,484	VC
Univ of Scranton	PA	54,962	VC
Univ of St. Francis	IL	39,924	C
Univ of St. Thomas - Houston	TX	40,020	VC
Valparaiso Univ	IN	48,370	C+
Vanguard Univ of Southern Calif	CA	40,740	VC
Villanova Univ	PA	62,523	MC
Walla Walla Univ	WA	30,417	NC
Walsh Univ	OH	39,010	C
Washington Adventist Univ	MD	31,440	LC
Wheeling Jesuit Univ	WV	37,106	LC
Whitworth Univ	WA	51,732	VC
Wisc Lutheran College	WI	36,290	VC
Xavier Univ	OH	47,880	C+
Xavier Univ of Louisiana	LA	31,689	C+

THEOLOGY

School	ST	$IS	SR
Aquinas College - Mich	MI	38,876	HC
Azusa Pacific Univ	CA	43,972	C
Calif Baptist Univ	CA	41,392	C
Calvin College	MI	41,570	VC+
Creighton Univ	NE	48,206	VC+
Lewis Univ	IL	40,370	C
Loyola Marymount Univ	CA	58,038	HC
Marian Univ	IN	41,220	C
Molloy College	NY	40,440	C
St. Louis Univ	MO	49,866	HC
St. Mary's Univ of Minn	MN	41,210	VC
Silver Lake College of the Holy Family	WI	36,290	LC
St. John's Univ	NY	55,850	C
The Master's Univ	CA	43,870	C+
Univ of Notre Dame	IN	64,043	MC
Univ of St. Francis	IN	37,400	C

THERAPEUTIC RIDING

School	ST	$IS	SR
St. Andrews Univ	NC	44,634	LC
Wilson College	PA	35,620	C

THIRD WORLD STUDIES

School	ST	$IS	SR
Appalachian State Univ	NC	14,416	VC
Bethel Univ	MN	45,270	VC
Brown Univ	RI	64,566	MC
Pitzer College	CA	66,192	MC
Univ of Calif San Diego	CA	30,150	MC

TOTAL QUALITY MANAGEMENT (TQM)

School	ST	$IS	SR
Cal State, Dominguez Hills	CA	19,022	LC

ST = STATE $IS = IN-STATE COSTS SR = SELECTOR RATING

TOURISM

School	ST	$IS	SR
Arizona State Univ at the Downtown Phoenix Campus	AZ	23,680	VC
Black Hills State Univ	SD	15,899	C
Bowling Green State Univ	OH	19,747	C
Brigham Young Univ	UT	12,748	HC
Brigham Young Univ/Hawaii	HI	11,290	C
Cal State, Dominguez Hills	CA	19,022	LC
Cal State, Fullerton	CA	21,902	C
Central Washington Univ	WA	16,803	C
Coastal Carolina Univ	SC	19,766	C
Colo State Univ	CO	22,162	VC
Eastern Mich Univ	MI	19,761	C
George Mason Univ	VA	15,724	VC
George Washington Univ	DC	62,835	MC
Hawaii Pacific Univ	HI	33,420	C
Indiana Univ Bloomington	IN	20,429	VC
Indiana Univ Kokomo	IN	7,073	C
Indiana Univ-Purdue Univ Indianapolis	IN	18,635	C
James Madison Univ	VA	19,084	VC
Johnson & Wales Univ/ Charlotte Campus	NC	43,988	C
Johnson & Wales Univ/ Denver Campus	CO	42,707	C
Johnson & Wales Univ/North Miami Campus	FL	42,707	C
Johnson & Wales Univ/ Providence Campus	RI	42,248	C
Johnson State College	VT	20,752	C
Kent State Univ	OH	20,732	C
Lasell College	MA	47,500	C
Mich State Univ	MI	23,898	VC+
Montclair State Univ	NJ	26,210	LC
New Mexico State Univ	NM	14,050	C
Niagara Univ	NY	41,010	C
Ohio Univ	OH	22,924	C
Plymouth State Univ	NH	23,180	LC
Purdue Univ/West Lafayette	IN	20,032	MC
Rochester Inst of Technology	NY	50,842	HC
Seton Hill Univ	PA	46,972	C
Southern New Hampshire Univ	NH	43,198	C
St. Joseph's College, New York/Brooklyn Campus	NY	25,114	LC
St. Joseph's College, New York/Long Island Campus	NY	25,124	C
St. Thomas Univ	FL	36,360	LC
Temple Univ	PA	24,392	VC
Texas State Univ	TX	19,350	C
Univ of Central Missouri	MO	18,982	C
Univ of Hawaii at Manoa	HI	23,221	C
Univ of Maine at Machias	ME	22,960	C
Univ of Missouri/Columbia	MO	18,201	MC
Univ of Montana-Western	MT	11,220	LC
Univ of New Haven	CT	52,190	C
Univ of New Orleans	LA	12,840	C
Univ of the Sacred Heart	PR	17,932	
Virginia Polytechnic Inst and State Univ	VA	21,276	HC
West Liberty Univ	WV	15,512	C
West Virginia Univ	WV	18,210	C
Western Mich Univ	MI	21,054	C

TOXICOLOGY

School	ST	$IS	SR
Ashland Univ	OH	21,440	C
Bloomfield College	NJ	39,100	LC
Nazareth College	NY	45,574	C
Pennsylvania State Univ - Univ Park	PA	29,760	HC
St. John's Univ	NY	55,850	C
Univ of Calif at Davis	CA	28,468	HC
Univ of Louisiana at Monroe	LA	15,970	C
Univ of the Sciences	PA	54,038	VC

TOY DESIGN

School	ST	$IS	SR
Fashion Inst of Technology/ SUNY	NY	18,521	SP
Otis College of Art and Design	CA	55,858	SP

TRADE AND INDUSTRIAL EDUCATION

School	ST	$IS	SR
Alabama A&M Univ	AL	18,796	C
Eastern Mich Univ	MI	19,761	C
Siena Heights Univ	MI	32,040	C
SUNY at Oswego	NY	21,351	C
Univ of Nevada, Las Vegas	NV	17,553	C
Univ of Wyoming	WY	15,375	C+
Virginia State Univ	VA	19,802	C+

TRADE AND INDUSTRIAL SUPERVISION AND MANAGEMENT

School	ST	$IS	SR
Cal State, Dominguez Hills	CA	19,022	LC
Eastern Mich Univ	MI	19,761	C
Metropolitan State Univ	MN	7,566	C
Miss State Univ	MS	11,454	C+
Washington Univ in St. Louis	MO	65,366	VC

TRANSPORTATION AND TRAVEL MARKETING

School	ST	$IS	SR
Johnson & Wales Univ/ Providence Campus	RI	42,248	C
Keiser Univ	FL	35,010	LC
Northwood Univ - Mich	MI	35,010	LC

TRANSPORTATION ENGINEERING

School	ST	$IS	SR
Calif Polytechnic State Univ	CA	17,979	HC+
Embry-Riddle Aeronautical Univ - Worldwide	FL	17,480	C
Lawrence Tech Univ	MI	39,770	VC
Texas A&M Univ at Galveston	TX	15,920	C

TRANSPORTATION MANAGEMENT

School	ST	$IS	SR
Auburn Univ	AL	23,594	VC+
Cal State, Maritime Academy	CA	19,450	LC
Embry-Riddle Aeronautical Univ - Worldwide	FL	17,480	C
Florida Memorial Univ	FL	22,270	LC
Iowa State Univ	IA	17,570	C
Niagara Univ	NY	41,010	C
Ohio State Univ at Columbus	OH	21,703	HC+
Southern Univ at New Orleans	LA	8,014	LC
SUNY /Maritime College	NY	16,020	C
Texas A&M Univ at Galveston	TX	15,920	C
Univ of Alaska Anchorage	AK	16,652	NC
Univ of Arkansas at Fayetteville	AR	19,152	C+
Univ of North Florida	FL	15,996	VC
Univ of Pennsylvania	PA	63,526	MC
Univ of Wisc-Superior	WI	14,446	C

TRANSPORTATION TECHNOLOGY

School	ST	$IS	SR
Maine Maritime Academy	ME	22,536	C
Missouri Southern State Univ	MO	12,499	C

TURFGRASS AND LANDSCAPE MANAGEMENT

School	ST	$IS	SR
New Mexico State Univ	NM	14,050	C
Pennsylvania State Univ - Univ Park	PA	29,760	HC
Univ of Georgia	GA	21,250	HC
Univ of Nebr - Lincoln	NE	18,589	VC
Washington State Univ	WA	22,495	C

ULTRASOUND TECHNOLOGY

School	ST	$IS	SR
Barry Univ	FL	37,830	C
Lewis Univ	IL	40,370	C
MCPHS Univ	MA	45,470	SP
Mount Aloysius College	PA	29,976	C
Newman Univ	KS	35,390	C
Oregon Inst of Technology	OR	8,910	C
Rochester Inst of Technology	NY	50,842	HC
Seattle Univ	WA	50,811	VC+
Washburn Univ	KS	15,827	C

UNIVERSITY STUDIES

School	ST	$IS	SR
East Texas Baptist Univ	TX	33,134	C
Shenandoah Univ	VA	41,312	C
Texas Tech Univ	TX	18,736	C+
Univ of Maine	ME	20,792	C
Western Mich Univ	MI	21,054	C

URBAN ADMINISTRATION

School	ST	$IS	SR
New York Inst of Technology	NY	48,730	C

URBAN AND REGIONAL STUDIES

School	ST	$IS	SR
Arizona State Univ at the Downtown Phoenix Campus	AZ	23,680	VC
Cornell Univ	NY	64,853	MC
Frostburg State Univ	MD	17,280	LC
Ohio Univ	OH	22,924	C
Texas A&M Univ	TX	20,521	VC+
Univ of Arizona	AZ	23,100	C

URBAN DESIGN

School	ST	$IS	SR
New York Univ	NY	65,860	MC
Parsons The New School for Design	NY	56,610	SP
SUNY SUNY Albany	NY	22,165	C
Univ of Virginia	VA	25,891	MC

URBAN ECOLOGY

School	ST	$IS	SR
Hofstra Univ	NY	55,960	C+
Seattle Univ	WA	50,811	VC+
Xavier Univ	OH	47,880	C+

URBAN PLANNING TECHNOLOGY

School	ST	$IS	SR
Ball State Univ	IN	19,590	C
Calif State Polytechnic Univ, Pomona	CA	21,541	C
Eastern Mich Univ	MI	19,761	C
Florida Atlantic Univ	FL	17,339	C
Mich State Univ	MI	23,898	VC+
San Jose State Univ	CA	21,540	C
Texas State Univ	TX	19,350	C
The Univ of Utah	UT	17,924	VC
Univ of Nevada, Las Vegas	NV	17,553	C
Univ of Wisc-Milwaukee	WI	21,496	C
West Chester Univ of Pennsylvania	PA	18,456	C

URBAN STUDIES

School	ST	$IS	SR
Albertus Magnus College	CT	43,258	LC
Arizona State Univ at the Tempe Campus	AZ	21,756	VC
Augsburg College	MN	43,929	C
Barnard College/Columbia Univ	NY	62,741	MC
Baylor Univ	TX	53,760	HC
Bellevue Univ	NE	20,300	NC
Boston Univ	MA	65,110	MC
Brown Univ	RI	64,566	MC
Bryn Mawr College	PA	59,890	MC
Calif State Polytechnic Univ, Pomona	CA	21,541	C
Cal State, Fresno	CA	16,902	LC
Cal State, Northridge	CA	16,859	LC
Calumet College of St. Joseph	IN	22,735	C
Canisius College	NY	47,537	C
Carnegie Mellon Univ	PA	67,980	MC
CUNY/City College	NY	20,319	VC
CUNY/Hunter College	NY	31,098	VC
CUNY/Queens College	NY	27,896	C
Cleveland State Univ	OH	22,196	C
College of Charleston	SC	22,699	C
College of Mount St. Vincent	NY	45,620	C
Columbia Univ/ School of General Studies	NY	61,470	MC
Columbia Univ/City of New York	NY	62,958	MC
Conn College	CT	65,000	MC
Coppin State Univ	MD	17,041	VC
DePaul Univ	IL	47,623	VC
Dillard Univ	LA	20,940	VC
Eastern Mich Univ	MI	19,761	C
Eastern Washington Univ	WA	25,572	LC
Elmhurst College	IL	45,428	C
Eugene Lang College/The New School for Liberal Arts	NY	55,650	C
Fordham Univ	NY	65,918	MC
Furman Univ	SC	58,092	VC+
Georgia State Univ	GA	24,332	VC
Hamline Univ	MN	45,678	VC
Hampshire College	MA	63,824	MC
Haverford College	PA	66,490	MC
Howard Univ	DC	37,616	C+
Jackson State Univ	MS	15,879	LC
Langston Univ	OK	14,314	C
LeMoyne-Owen College	TN	16,980	C
Lipscomb Univ	TN	41,296	VC
Loyola Marymount Univ	CA	58,038	HC
Manhattan College	NY	51,750	C+
Mass Inst of Technology	MA	62,662	MC
Metropolitan State Univ of Denver	CO	29,889	LC
Miami Univ	OH	27,190	HC+
Minn State Univ, Mankato	MN	15,616	C
Morehouse College	GA	40,064	C
New College of Florida	FL	15,848	MC
New York Univ	NY	65,860	MC
Northeastern Illinois Univ	IL	12,529	LC
Northwestern Univ	IL	66,344	MC
Occidental College	CA	65,530	MC
Ohio Univ	OH	22,924	C
Ohio Wesleyan Univ	OH	49,460	VC
Rhodes College	TN	51,900	HC
Roosevelt Univ	IL	40,651	VC
Rutgers Univ - Camden	NJ	26,146	C
Rutgers Univ - New Brunswick	NJ	26,632	HC
St. Augustine's Univ	NC	26,048	C
St. Louis Univ	MO	49,866	HC
St. Peter's Univ	NJ	49,192	C
San Diego State Univ	CA	21,896	C+
San Francisco State Univ	CA	18,514	LC
Smith College	MA	63,914	MC
Southern Nazarene Univ	OK	32,798	NC
St. Cloud State Univ	MN	10,600	C
Stanford Univ	CA	60,409	MC
SUNY / Buffalo State College	NY	20,842	C
The College of Wooster	OH	57,900	VC+
The Univ of Utah	UT	17,924	VC
Trinity Univ	TX	52,314	HC+
Tufts Univ	MA		MC
Univ of Calif at Berkeley	CA	28,853	MC
Univ of Calif at Irvine	CA	26,484	VC
Univ of Calif San Diego	CA	30,150	MC
Univ of Cincinnati	OH	21,964	VC
Univ of Conn	CT	25,538	HC
Univ of Illinois at Chicago	IL	25,006	VC
Univ of Mich/Dearborn	MI	11,757	VC
Univ of Mich-Flint	MI	17,607	C+
Univ of Minn/Duluth	MN	20,292	C+
Univ of Minn/Twin Cities	MN	23,519	HC+
Univ of Missouri-Kansas City	MO	19,563	VC
Univ of New Orleans	LA	12,840	C
Univ of Northwestern - St. Paul	MN	38,160	C
Univ of Pennsylvania	PA	63,526	MC
Univ of Pittsburgh	PA	29,568	HC+
Univ of Texas at Austin	TX	26,102	HC
Univ of the District of Columbia	DC	21,044	LC
Univ of the Sacred Heart	PR	17,932	
Univ of Wisc-Green Bay	WI	15,064	C
Univ of Wisc-Milwaukee	WI	21,496	C
Univ of Wisc-Oshkosh	WI	15,200	C
Vassar College	NY	65,491	MC
Virginia Commonwealth Univ	VA	23,049	C
Virginia Polytechnic Inst and State Univ	VA	21,276	HC
Washington Univ in St. Louis	MO	65,366	VC
Wayne State Univ	MI	22,016	C
Wheaton College	IL	43,610	MC
Worcester State Univ	MA	20,977	C
Wright State Univ	OH	16,983	C

VASCULAR SONOGRAPHY

School	ST	$IS	SR
Lewis Univ	IL	40,370	C
MCPHS Univ	MA	45,470	SP
Thomas Edison State Univ	NJ	6,350	NC
Weber State Univ	UT	10,721	C

VETERINARY SCIENCE

School	ST	$IS	SR
Becker College	MA	57,628	C
Fort Valley State Univ	GA	17,988	VC
Lincoln Memorial Univ	TN	28,070	C
Medaille College	NY	35,112	C
Mercy College	NY	31,776	C
Mich State Univ	MI	23,898	VC+
Mount Ida College	MA	46,820	C
Newberry College	SC	34,550	C
N Dak State Univ	ND	16,245	C
Pennsylvania State Univ - Univ Park	PA	29,760	HC
Tuskegee Univ	AL	28,164	C
Univ of Arizona	AZ	23,100	C
Univ of Idaho	ID	15,348	C
Univ of Maine	ME	20,792	C
Univ of Maryland/College Park	MD	21,938	HC
Univ of Missouri/Columbia	MO	18,201	MC
Univ of Montana-Western	MT	11,220	LC
Univ of Nebr - Lincoln	NE	18,589	VC
Utah State Univ	UT	12,736	C
Walla Walla Univ	WA	30,417	NC
West Virginia Univ	WV	18,210	C
Wilson College	PA	35,620	C

VETERINARY TECHNOLOGY

School	ST	$IS	SR
Murray State Univ	KY	16,998	C
Tarleton State Univ	TX	15,248	LC

VICTORIAN STUDIES

School	ST	$IS	SR
Bard College	NY	64,024	HC
Vassar College	NY	65,491	MC

VIDEO

School	ST	$IS	SR
Bennington College	VT	63,960	MC
Bloomfield College	NJ	39,100	LC
Calif Inst of the Arts	CA	56,426	SP
Calvin College	MI	41,570	VC+
CUNY/City College	NY	20,319	VC
Drexel Univ	PA	65,432	VC+
Fairleigh Dickinson Univ/ College at Florham	NJ	52,062	C
Fitchburg State Univ	MA	21,819	C
Five Towns College	NY	35,350	C
George Mason Univ	VA	15,724	VC
Grand Rapids Theological Seminary/Cornerstone Univ	MI	33,338	C
Hampshire College	MA	63,824	MC
Hofstra Univ	NY	55,960	C+
Ithaca College	NY	56,766	VC
Lasell College	MA	47,500	C
Madonna Univ	MI	29,050	C
Maryland Inst College of Art	MD	56,795	SP
Minneapolis College of Art and Design	MN	44,238	SP
New Mexico State Univ	NM	14,050	C
Ohio Univ	OH	22,924	C
Point Park Univ	PA	41,270	C
Rochester Inst of Technology	NY	50,842	HC
School of the Art Inst of Chicago	IL	56,230	SP
School of Visual Arts	NY	47,500	SP
Spring Arbor Univ	MI	36,000	C
SUNY / SUNY Fredonia	NY	20,818	C
Stevenson Univ	MD	72,770	C
Syracuse Univ	NY	60,239	VC
The Art Inst of Atlanta	GA	34,334	SP

School	ST	$IS	SR
Univ of Hartford	CT	49,776	C
Univ of Mich/Ann Arbor	MI	24,410	MC
Univ of Okla	OK	18,911	VC
Univ of Southern Calif	CA	66,631	C
Webster Univ	MO	37,490	C
Wilmington Univ	DE	8,546	NC

VISUAL AND PERFORMING ARTS

School	ST	$IS	SR
Albion College	MI	52,650	C
Alderson Broaddus Univ	WV	26,149	C
Andrews Univ	MI	28,030	C+
Anna Maria College	MA	48,186	C
Aquinas College - Mich	MI	38,876	HC
Arizona State Univ at the Tempe Campus	AZ	21,756	VC
Armstrong State Univ	GA	16,962	C
Belmont Univ	TN	40,970	VC
Bennett College	NC	27,302	NC
Bennington College	VT	63,960	MC
Bethel Univ	MN	45,270	VC
Bowling Green State Univ	OH	19,747	C
Brigham Young Univ	UT	12,748	HC
Brown Univ	RI	64,566	MC
Bucknell Univ	PA	64,616	MC
Calif Baptist Univ	CA	41,392	C
Calif College of the Arts	CA	52,758	SP
Calif Inst of the Arts	CA	56,426	SP
Cal State, Fullerton	CA	21,902	C
Cal State, Monterey Bay	CA	26,871	LC
Cal State, San Marcos	CA	24,184	LC
Central Mich Univ	MI	20,330	C
Central Washington Univ	WA	16,803	C
Chatham Univ	PA	46,517	C
CUNY/Brooklyn College	NY	5,884	C+
Clark Univ	MA	51,600	HC+
Columbia Univ/ School of General Studies	NY	61,470	MC
Columbia Univ/City of New York	NY	62,958	MC
Columbus State Univ	GA	14,336	LC
Coppin State Univ	MD	17,041	VC
Curry College	MA	51,815	C
Dordt College	IA	37,860	C+
Duke Univ	NC	64,188	
East Texas Baptist Univ	TX	33,134	C
Eastern Conn State Univ	CT	23,059	C
Eastern Mich Univ	MI	19,761	C
Eckerd College	FL	52,874	C
Erskine College	SC	45,460	C
Fayetteville State Univ	NC	17,756	C
Florida Atlantic Univ	FL	17,339	C
Fordham Univ	NY	65,918	MC
George Mason Univ	VA	15,724	VC
Goddard College	VT	17,040	VC
Grambling State Univ	LA	15,701	C
Grand View Univ	IA	32,302	C
Guilford College	NC	44,090	C
Hampden-Sydney College	VA	56,248	C+
Haverford College	PA	66,490	MC
Heritage Univ	WA	19,825	NC
Hofstra Univ	NY	55,960	C+
Indiana Univ Bloomington	IN	20,429	VC
Inter-American Univ of PR Ponce	PR	19,549	
Inter-American Univ of PR-Bayamon	PR	18,785	
Inter-American Univ of PR-Fajardo Campus	PR	18,336	
Ithaca College	NY	56,766	VC
Johnson State College	VT	20,752	C
Kean Univ	NJ	24,650	C
Kent State Univ	OH	20,732	C
Keystone College	PA	28,680	LC
Kutztown Univ of Pennsylvania	PA	19,056	LC
Lander Univ	SC	43,994	C
Lees-McRae College	NC	33,944	C
Lesley Univ	MA	41,550	C
Lipscomb Univ	TN	41,296	VC
LIU Brooklyn	NY	49,682	C
Longwood Univ	VA	22,184	C
Loyola Univ New Orleans	LA	51,708	VC+
Mass College of Liberal Arts	MA	20,128	C
Millikin Univ	IL	42,158	C
Naropa Univ	CO	42,826	NC
New England Conservatory of Music	MA	58,655	SP
New Mexico State Univ	NM	14,050	C
Notre Dame College	OH	37,150	VC
Ohio Univ	OH	22,924	C
Oregon State Univ	OR	22,519	VC
Otterbein Univ	OH	41,630	C
Ouachita Baptist Univ	AR	32,320	C
Penn State Univ/Altoona	PA	24,584	C
Pennsylvania State Univ - Univ Park	PA	29,760	HC
Prescott College	AZ	33,284	C
Purdue Univ/West Lafayette	IN	20,032	MC
Ramapo College of New Jersey	NJ	25,338	C
Regis Univ	CO	44,520	C
Rice Univ	TX	57,668	MC
Roger Williams Univ	RI	46,296	C+
Rutgers Univ - New Brunswick	NJ	26,632	HC
Rutgers Univ - Newark	NJ	27,288	C
St. Augustine's Univ	NC	26,048	C
St. Mary's College	IN	50,600	C
St. Peter's Univ	NJ	49,192	C
St. Vincent College	PA	44,626	C
Sarah Lawrence College	NY	63,388	HC
Savannah State Univ	GA	15,631	C
School of the Art Inst of Chicago	IL	56,230	SP
Schreiner Univ	TX	34,626	LC
Seattle Univ	WA	50,811	VC+
Shaw Univ	NC	24,638	C
Siena College	NY	48,916	C+
Siena Heights Univ	MI	32,040	C
Sonoma State Univ	CA	27,806	C
S Car State Univ	SC	20,805	LC
Southern Oregon Univ	OR	19,117	C
Spring Arbor Univ	MI	36,000	C
St. Andrews Univ	NC	44,634	LC
St. Bonaventure Univ	NY	44,237	C
St. Lawrence Univ	NY	64,390	VC
St. Mary's College of Maryland	MD	26,634	VC
St. Thomas Aquinas College	NY	42,200	C
SUNY / SUNY College at Old Westbury	NY	16,860	C
SUNY / SUNY Potsdam	NY	20,404	C+
SUNY at Binghamton	NY	22,861	MC
SUNY at New Paltz	NY	19,200	C
SUNY at Purchase	NY	17,900	C
Susquehanna Univ	PA	55,340	VC
Taylor Univ	IN	40,317	C+
Temple Univ	PA	24,392	VC
The Evergreen State College	WA	16,599	C
The Lincoln Univ	PA	15,154	NC
Univ of Alaska Anchorage	AK	16,652	NC
Univ of Arkansas at Little Rock	AR	18,211	C
Univ of Calif at Riverside	CA	29,227	C+
Univ of Calif San Diego	CA	30,150	MC
Univ of Chicago	IL	67,584	MC
Univ of Cincinnati	OH	21,964	VC
Univ of Colo Colo Springs	CO	19,663	C
Univ of Colo Denver	CO	23,230	C
Univ of Conn	CT	25,538	HC
Univ of Florida	FL	16,291	HC+
Univ of Hartford	CT	49,776	C
Univ of Illinois at Chicago	IL	25,006	VC
Univ of Maine at Farmington	ME	18,187	C
Univ of Maryland/Baltimore County	MD	21,296	VC
Univ of Montana-Western	MT	11,220	LC
Univ of New Haven	CT	52,190	C
Univ of N Dak	ND	15,373	C
Univ of North Texas	TX	19,198	C
Univ of Northern Colo	CO	20,851	C
Univ of Pennsylvania	PA	63,526	MC
Univ of San Diego	CA	58,442	VC+
Univ of San Francisco	CA	58,484	VC
Univ of Southern Calif	CA	66,631	C
Univ of St. Francis	IL	39,924	C
Univ of Texas at Austin	TX	26,102	HC
Univ of Texas at Dallas	TX	22,830	VC+
Univ of the Sacred Heart	PR	17,932	
Univ of Tulsa	OK	52,625	HC+
Univ of Wisc-Platteville	WI	14,614	VC
Univ of Wisc-Superior	WI	14,446	C
Virginia State Univ	VA	19,802	C+
Wagner College	NY	55,480	C+
Washington Univ in St. Louis	MO	65,366	VC
Weber State Univ	UT	10,721	C
Wells College	NY	50,500	C
West Chester Univ of Pennsylvania	PA	18,456	C
West Virginia Univ	WV	18,210	C
Western Kentucky Univ	KY	16,850	C
Western Washington Univ	WA	18,003	C+
Wichita State Univ	KS	21,643	C
Worcester State Univ	MA	20,977	C

VISUAL ARTS

School	ST	$IS	SR
Brown Univ	RI	64,566	MC
Univ of Chicago	IL	67,584	MC

VISUAL COMMUNICATION

School	ST	$IS	SR
Bryant Univ	RI	55,646	VC
Iowa Wesleyan Univ	IA	39,200	C
Neumann Univ	PA	40,678	LC
Northern Arizona Univ	AZ	20,246	VC
Purdue Univ/Northwest	IN	15,038	C
Rochester Inst of Technology	NY	50,842	HC
Univ of Okla	OK	18,911	VC

VISUAL DESIGN

School	ST	$IS	SR
Art Academy of Cincinnati	OH	36,252	SP
Bryant Univ	RI	55,646	VC
Calif Inst of the Arts	CA	56,426	SP
Cal State, Fullerton	CA	21,902	C
Cazenovia College	NY	46,470	C
Cedarville Univ	OH	34,990	VC
Drury Univ	MO	33,791	VC
Eastern New Mexico Univ	NM	14,416	C
Farmingdale State College	NY	20,624	C
High Point Univ	NC	45,977	C
Indiana Univ-Purdue Univ Fort Wayne	IN	17,553	C
Kent State Univ	OH	20,732	C
Loyola Univ Chicago	IL	55,802	VC
Nazareth College	NY	45,574	C
Ohio State Univ at Columbus	OH	21,703	HC+
Okla Christian Univ	OK	27,650	VC
Rochester Inst of Technology	NY	50,842	HC
San Francisco State Univ	CA	18,514	LC
Stevenson Univ	MD	72,770	C
Truman State Univ	MO	16,014	HC
Univ of Dayton	OH	53,620	C
Univ of Delaware	DE	24,976	VC+
Univ of Mary Hardin-Baylor	TX	33,950	C+
Univ of Mass Dartmouth	MA	25,658	C
Univ of New Haven	CT	52,190	C
Weber State Univ	UT	10,721	C
Whitworth Univ	WA	51,732	VC

VISUAL EFFECTS

School	ST	$IS	SR
Otis College of Art and Design	CA	55,858	SP
Ringling College of Art and Design	FL	57,430	SP
Savannah College of Art and Design	GA	49,595	C
School of Visual Arts	NY	47,500	SP

VITICULTURE AND ENOLOGY

School	ST	$IS	SR
Cornell Univ	NY	64,853	MC
Washington State Univ	WA	22,495	C

VOCAL MUSIC EDUCATION

School	ST	$IS	SR
Aquinas College - Mich	MI	38,876	HC
Calvin College	MI	41,570	VC+
Concordia Univ St. Paul	MN	29,050	C
Curtis Inst of Music	PA	20,944	SP
Dordt College	IA	37,860	C+
East Central Univ	OK	13,056	C
Hope College	MI	39,940	VC
Houghton College	NY	39,090	C
King Univ	TN	34,660	C
Marian Univ	IN	41,220	C
Murray State Univ	KY	16,998	C
Okla Baptist Univ	OK	32,320	C
Silver Lake College of the Holy Family	WI	36,290	LC
St. Ambrose Univ	IA	39,019	C
St. Ambrose Univ	IA	39,019	C
Texas Christian Univ	TX	54,670	HC
Webster Univ	MO	37,490	C
West Chester Univ of Pennsylvania	PA	18,456	C
Youngstown State Univ	OH	17,307	C

VOCAL PERFORMANCE

School	ST	$IS	SR
Abilene Christian Univ	TX	41,800	C+
Aquinas College - Mich	MI	38,876	HC
Arkansas State Univ	AR	16,190	C
Calif Baptist Univ	CA	41,392	C
Dallas Baptist Univ	TX	33,713	C
East Central Univ	OK	13,056	C
East Texas Baptist Univ	TX	33,134	C
Houghton College	NY	39,090	C
LIU Post	NY	49,682	C
Madonna Univ	MI	29,050	C
Marian Univ	IN	41,220	C
Missouri Southern State Univ	MO	12,499	C
New York Univ	NY	65,860	MC
Ohio Univ	OH	22,924	C
Okla Christian Univ	OK	27,650	VC
Okla City Univ	OK	40,476	VC
Point Loma Nazarene Univ	CA	43,450	C
Roberts Wesleyan College	NY	38,306	C
Taylor Univ	IN	40,317	C+
Texas Christian Univ	TX	54,670	HC
Univ of Miami	FL	63,494	MC
Webster Univ	MO	37,490	C
West Chester Univ of Pennsylvania	PA	18,456	C
Western Mich Univ	MI	21,054	C
Wingate Univ	NC	39,950	C
Wright State Univ	OH	16,983	C
Youngstown State Univ	OH	17,307	C

VOCATIONAL EDUCATION

School	ST	$IS	SR
Auburn Univ	AL	23,594	VC+
Cal State, Los Angeles	CA	17,186	LC
Cal State, San Bernardino	CA	12,000	C
Chicago State Univ	IL	20,144	C
CUNY/College of Technology	NY	6,669	NC
College of the Ozarks	MO	7,230	C
Fitchburg State Univ	MA	21,819	C
Indiana Univ of Pennsylvania	PA	23,614	LC
Martin Univ	IN	20,264	LC
N Car State Univ	NC	19,515	HC+
Okla State Univ	OK	17,180	VC
Pittsburg State Univ	KS	13,880	NC
S Dak State Univ	SD	15,634	C
Southern Illinois Univ Carbondale	IL	23,667	C
SUNY at Oswego	NY	21,351	C
Univ of Illinois at Urbana-Champaign	IL	27,006	HC
Univ of Toledo	OH	19,336	NC
Univ of Wisc-Stout	WI	19,667	C
Valley City State Univ	ND	13,267	C
Western Kentucky Univ	KY	16,850	C
Western Mich Univ	MI	21,054	C
Western New Mexico Univ	NM	16,734	LC
Westfield State Univ	MA	19,671	C
Youngstown State Univ	OH	17,307	C

VOICE

School	ST	$IS	SR
Aquinas College - Mich	MI	38,876	HC
Baldwin Wallace Univ	OH	41,106	C
Bennington College	VT	63,960	MC
Boston Univ	MA	65,110	MC
Bucknell Univ	PA	64,616	MC
Butler Univ	IN	51,352	VC
Calif Baptist Univ	CA	41,392	C
Calvin College	MI	41,570	VC+
Campbellsville Univ	KY	32,492	C
Central Mich Univ	MI	20,330	C
Central Washington Univ	WA	16,803	C
East Central Univ	OK	13,056	C
East Texas Baptist Univ	TX	33,134	C
Eastern Mich Univ	MI	19,761	C
Florida State Univ	FL	16,771	HC
Hardin-Simmons Univ	TX	33,966	C
Houghton College	NY	39,090	C
Illinois Wesleyan Univ	IL	56,430	VC+
Indiana Univ Bloomington	IN	20,429	VC
Indiana Univ-Purdue Univ Fort Wayne	IN	17,553	C
Juilliard School	NY	57,162	SP
Loyola Univ New Orleans	LA	51,708	VC+
Manhattan School of Music	NY	57,200	SP
Mannes School for Music	NY	44,500	SP
Marshall Univ	WV	17,242	C
Millikin Univ	IL	42,158	C
Miss College	MS	25,850	C
Mount Aloysius College	PA	29,976	C
New York Univ	NY	65,860	MC
Northwestern Univ	IL	66,344	MC
Nyack College	NY	34,050	NC
Ohio Univ	OH	22,924	C
Ouachita Baptist Univ	AR	32,320	C
Pacific Lutheran Univ	WA	49,960	VC
Palm Beach Atlantic Univ	FL	39,720	C
Rider Univ	NJ	54,050	C
Roosevelt Univ	IL	40,651	VC
Samford Univ	AL	39,232	VC
San Francisco Conservatory of Music	CA	57,310	SP
Shorter Univ	GA	31,130	LC
Silver Lake College of the Holy Family	WI	36,290	LC
St. Ambrose Univ	IA	39,019	C
St. Ambrose Univ	IA	39,019	C
Stetson Univ	FL	53,544	VC
Syracuse Univ	NY	60,239	VC
The Catholic Univ of America	DC	56,356	VC
Union Univ	TN	33,970	VC
Univ of Cincinnati	OH	21,964	VC
Univ of Illinois at Urbana-Champaign	IL	27,006	HC
Univ of Iowa	IA	18,683	VC+
Univ of Kansas	KS	20,135	C+
Univ of Mobile	AL	28,935	C
Univ of Northwestern - St. Paul	MN	38,160	C
Univ of Tulsa	OK	52,625	HC+
Valparaiso Univ	IN	48,370	C+
Weber State Univ	UT	10,721	C
Webster Univ	MO	37,490	C
West Chester Univ of Pennsylvania	PA	18,456	C
Westminster Choir College	NJ	53,730	SP
York College	NE	24,300	C
Youngstown State Univ	OH	17,307	C

WATER AND WASTEWATER TECHNOLOGY

School	ST	$IS	SR
Northland College	WI	41,103	C+
Texas State Univ	TX	19,350	C
Wright State Univ	OH	16,983	C

WATER RESOURCES

School	ST	$IS	SR
Bryant Univ	RI	55,646	VC
Central State Univ	OH	18,564	C
Colo State Univ	CO	22,162	VC
Heidelberg Univ	OH	39,200	C
Northern Mich Univ	MI	19,604	C
Prescott College	AZ	33,284	C
SUNY / SUNY Oneonta	NY	19,712	C+
Tarleton State Univ	TX	15,248	LC
Texas A&M Univ at Galveston	TX	15,920	C
The College at Brockport - SUNY	NY	20,346	C
Univ of Georgia	GA	21,250	HC
Univ of Nebr - Lincoln	NE	18,589	VC

WEB SERVICES

School	ST	$IS	SR
Bloomfield College	NJ	39,100	LC
Champlain College	VT	53,132	C+
Idaho State Univ	ID	13,619	NC
Indiana Inst of Technology	IN	34,240	LC

ST = STATE $IS = IN-STATE COSTS SR = SELECTOR RATING

School	ST	$IS	SR
Johnson & Wales Univ/ Providence Campus	RI	42,248	C
Keene State College	NH	24,003	LC
Limestone College	SC	32,100	C
Lipscomb Univ	TN	41,296	VC
Marymount Univ	VA	41,570	LC
Mercyhurst Univ	PA	47,420	C
Roger Williams Univ	RI	46,296	C+
Southern Adventist Univ	TN	27,600	C
Taylor Univ	IN	40,317	C+
Thiel College	PA	41,590	C
Univ of Wisc-Milwaukee	WI	21,496	C
Univ of Wisc-Stevens Point	WI	14,043	C

WEB TECHNOLOGY

School	ST	$IS	SR
Belmont Univ	TN	40,970	VC
Bloomfield College	NJ	39,100	LC
Cogswell Polytechnical College	CA	30,531	C
Davenport Univ	MI	25,896	LC
Drexel Univ	PA	65,432	VC+
Edgewood College	WI	35,950	C
Illinois Inst of Technology	IL	56,826	HC+
Lasell College	MA	47,500	C
Limestone College	SC	32,100	C
Mercyhurst Univ	PA	47,420	C
Mount Aloysius College	PA	29,976	C
Pennsylvania College of Technology	PA	27,333	NC
Quinnipiac Univ	CT	59,110	C
Roger Williams Univ	RI	46,296	C+
Seattle Univ	WA	50,811	VC+
Tenn Tech Univ	TN	17,050	C
Tulane Univ	LA	63,396	HC+
Univ of St. Francis	IL	39,924	C

WELDING ENGINEERING

School	ST	$IS	SR
Ferris State Univ	MI	21,445	C
Idaho State Univ	ID	13,619	NC
LeTourneau Univ	TX	38,250	VC
Lewis-Clark State College	ID	14,202	C
Ohio State Univ at Columbus	OH	21,703	HC+
Pennsylvania College of Technology	PA	27,333	NC
Weber State Univ	UT	10,721	C

WESTERN CIVILIZATION/ CULTURE

School	ST	$IS	SR
St. John's College-Annapolis	MD	60,142	MC
Univ of Montana-Western	MT	11,220	LC

WESTERN EUROPEAN STUDIES

School	ST	$IS	SR
Denison Univ	OH	58,860	MC
St. John's College-Annapolis	MD	60,142	MC
The College of Wooster	OH	57,900	VC+
Univ of Mich/Ann Arbor	MI	24,410	MC
Washington Univ in St. Louis	MO	65,366	VC

WILDLIFE BIOLOGY

School	ST	$IS	SR
Adams State Univ	CO	17,703	LC
Arkansas Tech Univ	AR	15,484	C
Auburn Univ	AL	23,594	VC+
Colo State Univ	CO	22,162	VC
Friends Univ	KS	34,455	C
Humboldt State Univ	CA	20,514	C
Kansas State Univ	KS	17,780	VC
Lees-McRae College	NC	33,944	C
Murray State Univ	KY	16,998	C
Ohio Univ	OH	22,924	C
Oregon State Univ	OR	22,519	VC
Prescott College	AZ	33,284	C
Purdue Univ/West Lafayette	IN	20,032	MC
S Dak State Univ	SD	15,634	C
SUNY / The College of Environmental Science and Forestry	NY	23,853	VC
Tarleton State Univ	TX	15,248	LC
Texas State Univ	TX	19,350	C
The Univ of Tenn at Knoxville	TN	22,112	VC
Unity College	ME	37,670	C
Univ of Calif at Davis	CA	28,468	HC
Univ of Florida	FL	16,291	HC+
Univ of Illinois at Urbana-Champaign	IL	27,006	HC
Univ of Maine at Machias	ME	22,960	C
Univ of Minn/Twin Cities	MN	23,519	HC+
Univ of Montana	MT	14,105	C
Univ of Montana-Western	MT	11,220	LC
Univ of New Hampshire	NH	28,562	VC
Univ of Vermont	VT	28,878	HC
Univ of Wisc-Madison	WI	20,934	MC
Univ of Wisc-Stevens Point	WI	14,043	C
Univ of Wyoming	WY	15,375	C+
Washington State Univ	WA	22,495	C
West Texas A&M Univ	TX	13,478	C

WILDLIFE CONSERVATION BIOLOGY

School	ST	$IS	SR
Bryant Univ	RI	55,646	VC
Univ of Alaska Fairbanks	AK	16,179	C
Univ of Maine at Machias	ME	22,960	C
Univ of Rhode Island	RI	24,906	C

WILDLIFE MANAGEMENT

School	ST	$IS	SR
Arkansas State Univ	AR	16,190	C
Brigham Young Univ	UT	12,748	HC
Dakota Wesleyan Univ	SD	32,850	C
Delaware Valley Univ	PA	49,796	C
Eastern Kentucky Univ	KY	16,908	C
Eastern New Mexico Univ	NM	14,416	C
Frostburg State Univ	MD	17,280	LC
Kansas State Univ	KS	17,780	VC
Lincoln Memorial Univ	TN	28,070	C
Louisiana Tech Univ	LA	11,422	VC
Mich State Univ	MI	23,898	VC+
Mich Tech Univ	MI	24,739	VC+
Miss State Univ	MS	11,454	C+
Missouri State Univ	MO	15,190	C+
Northern Mich Univ	MI	19,604	C
Northwest Missouri State Univ	MO	17,737	C
Peru State College	NE	14,768	NC
Prescott College	AZ	33,284	C
SUNY /College of Agriculture and Tech at Cobleskill	NY	20,527	LC
Stephen F. Austin State Univ	TX	18,406	LC
Sul Ross State Univ	TX	15,021	LC
Tarleton State Univ	TX	15,248	LC
Tenn Tech Univ	TN	17,050	C
Texas A&M Univ at Commerce	TX	10,496	C
Unity College	ME	37,670	C
Univ of Arkansas at Monticello	AR	13,134	NC
Univ of Delaware	DE	24,976	VC+
Univ of Idaho	ID	15,348	C
Univ of Illinois at Urbana-Champaign	IL	27,006	HC
Univ of Maine	ME	20,792	C
Univ of Nebr - Lincoln	NE	18,589	VC
Univ of Nevada/Reno	NV	18,010	C
Univ of PR, at Humacao	PR	14,000	
Utah State Univ	UT	12,736	C
Washington State Univ	WA	22,495	C
West Virginia Univ	WV	18,210	C

WILDLIFE SCIENCE

School	ST	$IS	SR
Embry-Riddle Aeronautical Univ - Prescott Campus	AZ	44,054	VC
New Mexico State Univ	NM	14,050	C
Texas A&M Univ	TX	20,521	VC+

WINDS

School	ST	$IS	SR
Eastern Mich Univ	MI	19,761	C
Florida State Univ	FL	16,771	HC
Mannes School for Music	NY	44,500	SP
Miss College	MS	25,850	C
Northwestern Univ	IL	66,344	MC
Oberlin College	OH	66,012	MC
Roosevelt Univ	IL	40,651	VC
San Francisco Conservatory of Music	CA	57,310	SP
Stetson Univ	FL	53,544	VC
Syracuse Univ	NY	60,239	VC
Texas Tech Univ	TX	18,736	C+
Univ of Kansas	KS	20,135	C+
Univ of Mich/Ann Arbor	MI	24,410	MC
Wright State Univ	OH	16,983	C
Youngstown State Univ	OH	17,307	C

WINE AND VITICULTURE

School	ST	$IS	SR
Calif Polytechnic State Univ	CA	17,979	HC+

WOMEN & GENDER STUDIES

School	ST	$IS	SR
Allegheny College	PA	55,420	VC
Amherst College	MA		HC+
Aquinas College - Mich	MI	38,876	HC
Arizona State Univ at the West Campus	AZ	20,640	C
Armstrong State Univ	GA	16,962	C
Austin College	TX	45,875	VC
Bates College	ME	64,500	MC
Brown Univ	RI	64,566	MC
Bryant Univ	RI	55,646	VC
Cabrini Univ	PA	42,591	LC
Cal State, Chico	CA	21,440	C
Cal State, Long Beach	CA	18,850	C
Case Western Reserve Univ	OH	60,304	MC
Castleton Univ	VT	20,186	C
CUNY/College of Staten Island	NY	17,840	NC
Cornell College	IA	48,800	VC
Delaware State Univ	DE	19,376	NC
Duquesne Univ	PA	46,822	VC
Eastern Conn State Univ	CT	23,059	C
Elon Univ	NC	44,599	VC+
Goddard College	VT	17,040	VC
Illinois Wesleyan Univ	IL	56,430	VC+
Indiana Univ South Bend	IN	14,242	C
Keene State College	NH	24,003	LC
Kenyon College	OH	63,330	MC
Knox College	IL	52,615	VC+
Loyola Marymount Univ	CA	58,038	HC
Lycoming College	PA	48,580	C
Mills College	CA	59,163	VC
New Jersey City Univ	NJ	21,456	LC
N Dak State Univ	ND	16,245	C
Northern Arizona Univ	AZ	20,246	VC
Oberlin College	OH	66,012	MC
Ohio Univ	OH	22,924	C
Otterbein Univ	OH	41,630	C
Pace Univ	NY	58,248	C
Pacific Lutheran Univ	WA	49,960	VC
St. Mary's College	IN	50,600	C
Seattle Univ	WA	50,811	VC+
Seton Hill Univ	PA	46,972	C
Southern Oregon Univ	OR	19,117	C
St. Ambrose Univ	IA	39,019	C
St. Ambrose Univ	IA	39,019	C
SUNY at Oswego	NY	21,351	C
SUNY SUNY Albany	NY	22,165	C
Stony Brook Univ/The SUNY	NY	21,881	MC
Syracuse Univ	NY	60,239	VC
Univ of Colo Boulder	CO	24,285	VC+
Univ of Illinois at Chicago	IL	25,006	VC
Univ of Kansas	KS	20,135	C+
Univ of Maine	ME	20,792	C
Univ of Maryland/Baltimore County	MD	21,296	VC
Univ of Mass Boston	MA	13,435	C
Univ of Mass Dartmouth	MA	25,658	C
Univ of Mich/Dearborn	MI	11,757	VC
Univ of Nebr - Lincoln	NE	18,589	VC
Univ of N Car at Chapel Hill	NC	20,052	HC+
Univ of S Dak	SD	16,109	C
Univ of Tulsa	OK	52,625	HC+
Univ of Wyoming	WY	15,375	C+
Vanderbilt Univ	TN	60,572	MC
Wellesley College	MA	63,916	MC
Wells College	NY	50,500	C
West Chester Univ of Pennsylvania	PA	18,456	C
Western Washington Univ	WA	18,003	C+
Wheaton College	MA	61,512	VC
Wichita State Univ	KS	21,643	C
Winona State Univ	MN	17,535	C

WOMEN'S STUDIES

School	ST	$IS	SR
Agnes Scott College	GA	51,930	VC+
Albion College	MI	52,650	C
Albright College	PA	46,660	C
Alverno College	WI	33,294	LC
American Univ	DC	59,379	HC+
Appalachian State Univ	NC	14,416	VC
Aquinas College - Mich	MI	38,876	HC
Arizona State Univ at the Tempe Campus	AZ	21,756	VC
Arizona State Univ at the West Campus	AZ	20,640	C
Augsburg College	MN	43,929	C
Augustana College	IL	49,658	VC
Ball State Univ	IN	19,590	C
Barnard College/Columbia Univ	NY	62,741	MC
Beloit College	WI	55,206	HC
Bennington College	VT	63,960	MC
Berea College	KY	7,042	C
Bloomfield College	NJ	39,100	LC
Bowdoin College	ME	63,500	MC
Bowling Green State Univ	OH	19,747	C
Brandeis Univ	MA	65,925	MC
Brown Univ	RI	64,566	MC
Bryant Univ	RI	55,646	VC
Bucknell Univ	PA	64,616	MC
Cal State, Fresno	CA	16,902	LC
Cal State, Fullerton	CA	21,902	C
Cal State, Long Beach	CA	18,850	C
Cal State, Northridge	CA	16,859	LC
Cal State, San Marcos	CA	24,184	LC
Canisius College	NY	47,537	C
Carleton College	MN	64,071	MC
Central Mich Univ	MI	20,330	C
Chatham Univ	PA	46,517	C
CUNY/Brooklyn College	NY	5,884	C+
CUNY/Hunter College	NY	31,098	VC
CUNY/Queens College	NY	27,896	C
Clark Univ	MA	51,600	HC+
Cleveland State Univ	OH	22,196	C
Coe College	IA	51,570	VC
Colby College	ME	64,060	MC
Colgate Univ	NY	65,030	MC
College of Charleston	SC	22,699	C
College of William & Mary	VA		MC
Colo College	CO	62,560	MC
Columbia Univ/ School of General Studies	NY	61,470	MC
Columbia Univ/City of New York	NY	62,958	MC
Dartmouth College	NH	66,174	MC
Denison Univ	OH	58,860	MC
DePaul Univ	IL	47,623	VC
DePauw Univ	IN	58,688	HC+
Dickinson College	PA	63,974	MC
Dominican Univ	IL	41,222	C
Dominican Univ of Calif	CA	57,050	C
Drew Univ/College of Liberal Arts	NJ	61,048	VC
Duke Univ	NC	64,188	
Earlham College	IN	54,870	HC
East Carolina Univ	NC	16,937	C
Eastern Mich Univ	MI	19,761	C
Eckerd College	FL	52,874	C
Emory Univ	GA	60,786	MC
Florida International Univ	FL	19,854	C+
Florida State Univ	FL	16,771	HC
Fordham Univ	NY	65,918	MC
Georgia State Univ	GA	24,332	VC
Gettysburg College	PA	63,000	HC
Goucher College	MD	55,716	VC
Guilford College	NC	44,090	C
Gustavus Adolphus College	MN	52,433	HC
Hamilton College	NY	64,250	MC
Hamline Univ	MN	45,678	VC
Hampshire College	MA	63,824	MC
Harvard College/Harvard Univ	MA	60,659	MC
Hofstra Univ	NY	55,960	C+
Hope College	MI	39,940	VC
Howard Univ	DC	37,616	C+
Indiana Univ-Purdue Univ Fort Wayne	IN	17,553	C
John Carroll Univ	OH	49,740	C+
Kansas State Univ	KS	17,780	VC
Lehigh Univ	PA	61,010	MC
Loyola Univ Chicago	IL	55,802	VC
Luther College	IA	48,540	C+
Macalester College	MN	61,905	MC
Marshall Univ	WV	17,242	C
Mercer Univ	GA	45,348	VC
Metropolitan State Univ	MN	7,566	C
Miami Univ	OH	27,190	HC+
Mich State Univ	MI	23,898	VC+
Middlebury College	VT	64,332	MC
Minn State Univ, Mankato	MN	15,616	C
Minn State Univ, Moorhead	MN	15,941	C
Montclair State Univ	NJ	26,210	LC
Moravian College	PA	53,117	
Mount Aloysius College	PA	29,976	C
Nazareth College	NY	45,574	C
Nebr Wesleyan Univ	NE	38,140	C+
New Mexico State Univ	NM	14,050	C
Northeastern Illinois Univ	IL	12,529	LC
Northern Kentucky Univ	KY	16,486	C
Oakland Univ	MI	20,763	C
Oberlin College	OH	66,012	MC
Ohio State Univ at Columbus	OH	21,703	HC+
Ohio Univ	OH	22,924	C
Ohio Wesleyan Univ	OH	49,460	VC
Old Dominion Univ	VA	20,910	C
Oregon State Univ	OR	22,519	VC
Pennsylvania State Univ - Univ Park	PA	29,760	HC
Pitzer College	CA	66,192	MC
Pomona College	CA	64,957	MC
Portland State Univ	OR	19,443	C
Prescott College	AZ	33,284	C
Providence College	RI	60,760	VC
Purdue Univ/West Lafayette	IN	20,032	MC
Randolph-Macon College	VA	49,910	C
Regis Univ	CO	44,520	C
Rhode Island College	RI	17,694	LC
Rice Univ	TX	57,668	MC
Roosevelt Univ	IL	40,651	VC
Rosemont College	PA	30,980	C
Rutgers Univ - New Brunswick	NJ	26,632	HC
Rutgers Univ - Newark	NJ	27,288	C
St. Louis Univ	MO	49,866	HC
San Diego State Univ	CA	21,896	C+
San Francisco State Univ	CA	18,514	LC
Sarah Lawrence College	NY	63,388	HC
Scripps College	CA	66,664	MC
Sewanee: The Univ of the South	TN	54,500	MC
Simmons College	MA	53,090	VC
Smith College	MA	63,914	MC
Sonoma State Univ	CA	27,806	C
Southwestern Univ	TX	50,720	VC
Spelman College	GA	38,751	C
St. Bonaventure Univ	NY	44,237	C
St. Catherine Univ	MN	45,630	VC
St. Olaf College	MN	54,260	HC+
Stanford Univ	CA	60,409	MC
SUNY / SUNY Fredonia	NY	20,818	C
SUNY / SUNY Plattsburgh	NY	18,814	C
SUNY / SUNY Potsdam	NY	20,404	C+
SUNY at New Paltz	NY	19,200	C
SUNY at Oswego	NY	21,351	C
SUNY at Purchase	NY	17,900	C
SUNY SUNY Albany	NY	22,165	C
Suffolk Univ	MA	50,308	C
Temple Univ	PA	24,392	VC
The College at Brockport - SUNY	NY	20,346	C
The College of New Jersey	NJ	31,909	HC
The College of New Rochelle	NY	46,300	VC
The College of Wooster	OH	57,900	VC+
Towson Univ	MD	17,408	VC
Trinity College	CT	63,920	HC+
Tulane Univ	LA	63,396	HC+
Union College	NY	64,320	MC
Univ of Arizona	AZ	23,100	C
Univ of Calif at Berkeley	CA	28,853	MC
Univ of Calif at Davis	CA	28,468	HC
Univ of Calif at Irvine	CA	26,484	VC
Univ of Calif at Los Angeles	CA	30,162	MC
Univ of Calif at Riverside	CA	29,227	C+
Univ of Calif at Santa Barbara	CA	29,091	HC
Univ of Calif, Santa Cruz	CA	28,731	C+
Univ of Cincinnati	OH	21,964	VC

ST = STATE $IS = IN-STATE COSTS SR = SELECTOR RATING

School	ST	$IS	SR
Univ of Colo Colo Springs	CO	19,663	C
Univ of Conn	CT	25,538	HC
Univ of Dayton	OH	53,620	C
Univ of Delaware	DE	24,976	VC+
Univ of Denver	CO	58,443	VC+
Univ of Georgia	GA	21,250	HC
Univ of Hawaii at Manoa	HI	23,221	C
Univ of Illinois at Urbana-Champaign	IL	27,006	HC
Univ of Iowa	IA	18,683	VC+
Univ of Kansas	KS	20,135	C+
Univ of Louisville	KY	19,824	C
Univ of Maryland/Baltimore County	MD	21,296	VC
Univ of Maryland/College Park	MD	21,938	HC
Univ of Mass Amherst	MA	26,199	VC+
Univ of Miami	FL	63,494	MC
Univ of Mich/Ann Arbor	MI	24,410	MC
Univ of Mich/Dearborn	MI	11,757	VC
Univ of Minn/Duluth	MN	20,292	C+
Univ of Minn/Morris	MN	20,760	VC
Univ of Minn/Twin Cities	MN	23,519	HC+
Univ of Montana-Western	MT	11,220	LC
Univ of Nebr - Omaha	NE	16,120	C
Univ of Nevada, Las Vegas	NV	17,553	C
Univ of Nevada/Reno	NV	18,010	C
Univ of New Hampshire	NH	28,562	VC
Univ of New Mexico	NM	15,404	C
Univ of N Car at Asheville	NC	15,723	VC+
Univ of N Car at Greensboro	NC	14,690	C
Univ of Okla	OK	18,911	VC
Univ of Oregon	OR	22,972	C
Univ of Pennsylvania	PA	63,526	MC
Univ of Pittsburgh	PA	29,568	HC+
Univ of Richmond	VA	60,880	MC
Univ of Rochester	NY	65,032	MC
Univ of St. Joseph	CT	49,550	C
Univ of Scranton	PA	54,962	VC
Univ of S Car at Columbia	SC	19,725	VC+
Univ of Southern Calif	CA	66,631	C
Univ of Southern Maine	ME	18,320	C
Univ of Texas at San Antonio	TX	20,157	C
Univ of Toledo	OH	19,336	NC
Univ of Tulsa	OK	52,625	HC+
Univ of Washington	WA	23,149	VC
Univ of Wisc-Eau Claire	WI	15,797	VC
Univ of Wisc-Green Bay	WI	15,064	C
Univ of Wisc-Madison	WI	20,934	MC
Univ of Wisc-Milwaukee	WI	21,496	C
Univ of Wisc-Whitewater	WI	13,976	C
Vassar College	NY	65,491	MC
Virginia Wesleyan College	VA	43,728	LC
Washington State Univ	WA	22,495	C
Washington Univ in St. Louis	MO	65,366	VC
Wayne State Univ	MI	22,016	C
Webster Univ	MO	37,490	C
Wellesley College	MA	63,916	MC
West Chester Univ of Pennsylvania	PA	18,456	C
Western Mich Univ	MI	21,054	C
Western Washington Univ	WA	18,003	C+
Wheaton College	MA	61,512	VC
Whitworth Univ	WA	51,732	VC
Wichita State Univ	KS	21,643	C
Widener Univ	PA	56,486	C
Willamette Univ	OR	61,817	VC+
Williams College	MA	63,290	MC
Yale Univ	CT	64,650	MC

WOOD SCIENCE

School	ST	$IS	SR
N Car State Univ	NC	19,515	HC+
Pittsburg State Univ	KS	13,880	NC
Purdue Univ/West Lafayette	IN	20,032	MC
SUNY / The College of Environmental Science and Forestry	NY	23,853	VC
Univ of Maine	ME	20,792	C
Univ of Mass Amherst	MA	26,199	VC+
West Virginia Univ	WV	18,210	C

WOODWORKING

School	ST	$IS	SR
Rochester Inst of Technology	NY	50,842	HC
SUNY at New Paltz	NY	19,200	C
Univ of Rio Grande & Rio Grande Community College	OH	8,750	NC

WORLD CULTURAL STUDIES

School	ST	$IS	SR
Calif Baptist Univ	CA	41,392	C
Georgia College & State Univ	GA	21,148	C+
Univ of Okla	OK	18,911	VC

WORLD LANGUAGE EDUCATION

School	ST	$IS	SR
Indiana Univ Bloomington	IN	20,429	VC
Univ of Georgia	GA	21,250	HC
Univ of Okla	OK	18,911	VC

WRITING

School	ST	$IS	SR
Aquinas College - Mich	MI	38,876	HC
Bay Path Univ	MA	45,349	C
Bloomfield College	NJ	39,100	LC
Cabrini Univ	PA	42,591	LC
Calif College of the Arts	CA	52,758	SP
Calvin College	MI	41,570	VC+
Carroll Univ	WI	38,100	C+
Catawba College	NC	39,820	C
Champlain College	VT	53,132	C+
Coe College	IA	51,570	VC
Columbia College Chicago	IL	43,168	C
Concordia College - New York	NY	39,035	LC
Eastern Mennonite Univ	VA	42,550	C
Elon Univ	NC	44,599	VC+
Fontbonne Univ	MO	33,717	C
Georgia Southern Univ	GA	16,596	C
Goshen College	IN	42,500	C
Houghton College	NY	39,090	C
Johnson State College	VT	20,752	C
Madonna Univ	MI	29,050	C
Marquette Univ	WI	48,390	VC+
New York Univ	NY	65,860	MC
Northland College	WI	41,103	C+
Okla Christian Univ	OK	27,650	VC
Old Dominion Univ	VA	20,910	C
Point Loma Nazarene Univ	CA	43,450	C
Savannah College of Art and Design	GA	49,595	C
Southern Oregon Univ	OR	19,117	C
Taylor Univ	IN	40,317	C+
Texas Christian Univ	TX	54,670	HC
The Univ of Utah	UT	17,924	VC
Univ of Central Florida	FL	15,922	VC
Univ of Maine at Machias	ME	22,960	C
Univ of Tampa	FL	36,944	C
Univ of Wisc-Superior	WI	14,446	C

WRITING & RHETORIC

School	ST	$IS	SR
Syracuse Univ	NY	60,239	VC
Univ of Rhode Island	RI	24,906	C
Western Mich Univ	MI	21,054	C

YIDDISH

School	ST	$IS	SR
Thomas Edison State Univ	NJ	6,350	NC

YOUTH MINISTRY

School	ST	$IS	SR
Andrews Univ	MI	28,030	C+
Asbury Univ	KY	35,180	C+
Augsburg College	MN	43,929	C
Azusa Pacific Univ	CA	43,972	C
Benedictine College	KS	36,200	VC
Bethel Univ	MN	45,270	VC
Bluffton Univ	OH	40,950	C
Cairn Univ	PA	36,296	C
Campbellsville Univ	KY	32,492	C
Cedarville Univ	OH	34,990	VC
Charleston Southern Univ	SC	32,400	C
Colo Christian Univ	CO	39,940	VC
Concordia Univ	OR	35,000	C
Corban Univ	OR	40,306	C
Dallas Baptist Univ	TX	33,713	C
Dordt College	IA	37,860	C+
East Texas Baptist Univ	TX	33,134	C
Eastern Univ	PA	39,540	C
Faulkner Univ	AL	26,410	C
Gordon College	MA	46,472	C+
Grace Bible College	MI	25,250	C
Grace College and Seminary	IN	31,524	C
Grand Rapids Theological Seminary/Cornerstone Univ	MI	33,338	C
Greenville College	IL	27,012	C
Harding Univ	AR	25,421	C
Hardin-Simmons Univ	TX	33,966	C
Hope International Univ	CA	41,150	C
Huntington Univ	IN	33,996	C
Judson Univ	IL	37,700	C
Kentucky Christian Univ	KY	26,560	LC
King Univ	TN	34,660	C
Lee Univ	TN	22,045	C
Lenoir-Rhyne Univ	NC	43,200	C
Lipscomb Univ	TN	41,296	VC
Lubbock Christian Univ	TX	28,426	C
MacMurray College	IL	33,620	C
Malone Univ	OH	38,448	C
MidAmerica Nazarene Univ	KS	35,550	C
Milligan College	TN	38,150	C
Mount Vernon Nazarene Univ	OH	34,500	C
North Greenville Univ	SC	25,930	C+
North Park Univ	IL	35,860	C
Northwest Nazarene Univ	ID	36,000	C
Northwest Univ	WA	35,876	VC
Northwestern College of Iowa	IA	38,400	C+
Nyack College	NY	34,050	NC
Ohio Northern Univ	OH	44,050	VC
Okla Baptist Univ	OK	32,320	C
Okla Christian Univ	OK	27,650	VC
Okla Wesleyan Univ	OK	33,206	C
Olivet Nazarene Univ	IL	41,840	C
Ouachita Baptist Univ	AR	32,320	C
Point Loma Nazarene Univ	CA	43,450	C
Rochester College	MI	28,574	LC
St. Mary's Univ of Minn	MN	41,210	VC
Shorter Univ	GA	31,130	LC
Simpson Univ	CA	33,700	C
Southern Nazarene Univ	OK	32,798	NC
Spring Arbor Univ	MI	36,000	C
Toccoa Falls College	GA	27,920	C
Trinity International Univ	IL	31,070	VC
Union Univ	TN	33,970	VC
Univ of Northwestern - St. Paul	MN	38,160	C
Vanguard Univ of Southern Calif	CA	40,740	VC
York College	NE	24,300	C

ZOOLOGY

School	ST	$IS	SR
Alabama A&M Univ	AL	18,796	C
Andrews Univ	MI	28,030	C+
Auburn Univ	AL	23,594	VC+
Bennington College	VT	63,960	MC
Calif State Polytechnic Univ, Pomona	CA	21,541	C
Cal State, Long Beach	CA	18,850	C
Canisius College	NY	47,537	C
Colo State Univ	CO	22,162	VC
Delaware Valley Univ	PA	49,796	C
Florida State Univ	FL	16,771	HC
Fort Valley State Univ	GA	17,988	VC
Friends Univ	KS	34,455	C
Humboldt State Univ	CA	20,514	C
Idaho State Univ	ID	13,619	NC
Kent State Univ	OH	20,732	C
Kentucky Wesleyan College	KY	32,080	C
Malone Univ	OH	38,448	C
Mars Hill Univ	NC	42,688	C
Miami Univ	OH	27,190	HC+
Mich State Univ	MI	23,898	VC+
N Car State Univ	NC	19,515	HC+
Northern Mich Univ	MI	19,604	C
Northwest Missouri State Univ	MO	17,737	C
Ohio State Univ at Columbus	OH	21,703	HC+
Ohio Univ	OH	22,924	C
Ohio Wesleyan Univ	OH	49,460	VC
Okla State Univ	OK	17,180	VC
Olivet Nazarene Univ	IL	41,840	C
Oregon State Univ	OR	22,519	VC
Otterbein Univ	OH	41,630	C
Rutgers Univ - Newark	NJ	27,288	C
San Diego State Univ	CA	21,896	C+
San Francisco State Univ	CA	18,514	LC
San Jose State Univ	CA	21,540	C
Southern Illinois Univ Carbondale	IL	23,667	C
SUNY at Oswego	NY	21,351	C
Texas A&M Univ	TX	20,521	VC+
Texas State Univ	TX	19,350	C
Texas Tech Univ	TX	18,736	C+
The Evergreen State College	WA	16,599	C
Univ of Calif at Davis	CA	28,468	HC
Univ of Calif at Santa Barbara	CA	29,091	HC
Univ of Florida	FL	16,291	HC+
Univ of Hawaii at Manoa	HI	23,221	C
Univ of Kentucky	KY	33,306	C
Univ of Maine	ME	20,792	C
Univ of Montana	MT	14,105	C
Univ of New Hampshire	NH	28,562	VC
Univ of Okla	OK	18,911	VC
Univ of Vermont	VT	28,878	HC
Univ of Washington	WA	23,149	VC
Univ of Wisc-Madison	WI	20,934	MC
Univ of Wyoming	WY	15,375	C+
Washington State Univ	WA	22,495	C
Weber State Univ	UT	10,721	C
Western New Mexico Univ	NM	16,734	LC

ST = STATE $IS = IN-STATE COSTS SR = SELECTOR RATING

PART IV

A CLOSE LOOK AT THE COLLEGES

This section will help you understand the college Profiles that are at the heart of this directory, so you can get the most out of them.

The College Admissions Selector explains Barron's unique system of comparing every school's degree of admissions competitiveness. Colleges are rated from Most Competitive to Less Competitive, and more.

Explanations of the ratings are followed by an in-depth look at the college capsule and essay.

Next come the Profiles—over 1600 four-year accredited colleges and universities in the United States—followed by encapsulated descriptions of about fifty religious schools. Universities outside the boundaries of this country are profiled here, too, including Canadian, European, and more.

COLLEGE ADMISSIONS SELECTOR

This index groups all the colleges listed in this book according to degree of admissions competitiveness. The *Selector* is not a rating of colleges by academic standards or quality of education; it is rather an attempt to describe, in general terms, the situation a prospective student will meet when applying for admission.

THE CRITERIA USED

The factors used in determining the category for each college were: median entrance examination scores for the 2016–2017 freshman class (the SAT score used was derived by averaging the median critical reading, math, and writing scores; the ACT score used was the median composite score); percentages of 2016–2017 freshmen scoring 500 and above and 600 and above on the critical reading, math, and writing sections of the SAT; percentages of 2016–2017 freshmen scoring 21 and above and 27 and above on the ACT; percentage of 2016–2017 freshmen who ranked in the upper fifth and the upper two-fifths of their high school graduating classes; minimum class rank and grade point average required for admission (if any); and percentage of applicants to the 2016–2017 freshman class who were accepted. The *Selector* cannot and does not take into account all the other factors that each college considers when making admissions decisions. Colleges place varying degrees of emphasis on the factors that comprise each of these categories.

USING THE SELECTOR

To use the *Selector* effectively, the prospective student's records should be compared realistically with the freshmen enrolled by the colleges in each category, as shown by the SAT or ACT scores, the quality of high school record emphasized by the colleges in each category, and the kinds of risks that the applicant wishes to take.

The student should also be aware of what importance a particular school places on various nonacademic factors; when available, this information is presented in the profile of the school. If a student has unusual qualifications that may compensate for exam scores or high school record, the student should examine admissions policies of the colleges in the next higher category than the one that encompasses his or her score and consider those colleges that give major consideration to factors other than exam scores and high school grades. The "safety" college should usually be chosen from the next lower category, where the student can be reasonably sure that his or her scores and high school record will fall above the median scores and records of the freshmen enrolled in the college.

The listing within each category is alphabetical and not in any qualitative order. State-supported institutions have been classified according to the requirements for state residents, but standards for admission of out-of-state students are usually higher. Colleges that are experimenting with the admission of students of higher potential but lower achievement may appear in a less competitive category because of this fact.

A WORD OF CAUTION

The *Selector* is intended primarily for preliminary screening, to eliminate the majority of colleges that are not suitable for a particular student. Be sure to examine the admissions policies spelled out in the *Admissions* section of each profile. And remember that many colleges have to reject *qualified* students; the *Selector* will tell you what your chances are, not which college will accept you.

MOST COMPETITIVE

Even superior students will encounter a great deal of competition for admission to the colleges in this category. In general, these colleges require high school rank in the top 10% to 20% and grade averages of A to B+. Median freshman test scores at these colleges are generally between 655 and 800 on the SAT and 29 and above on the ACT. In addition, many of these colleges admit only a small percentage of those who apply—usually fewer than one third.

Bard College at Simon's Rock, MA
Barnard College/Columbia University, NY
Bates College, ME
Bennington College, VT
Boston College, MA
Boston University, MA
Bowdoin College, ME
Brandeis University, MA
Brown University, RI
Bryn Mawr College, PA
Bucknell University, PA
California Institute of Technology, CA
Carleton College, MN
Carnegie Mellon University, PA
Case Western Reserve University, OH
Claremont McKenna College, CA
Colby College, ME
Colgate University, NY
College of the Holy Cross, MA
College of William & Mary, VA
Colorado College, CO
Colorado School of Mines, CO
Columbia University/School of General Studies, NY
Columbia University/City of New York, NY
Connecticut College, CT
Cooper Union for the Advancement of Science and Art, NY
Cornell University, NY
Dartmouth College, NH
Davidson College, NC
Denison University, OH
Dickinson College, PA
Emory University, GA
Fordham University, NY
Franklin W. Olin College of Engineering, MA
George Washington University, DC
Georgetown University, DC
Georgia Institute of Technology, GA
Grinnell College, IA
Hamilton College, NY
Hampshire College, MA
Harvard College/Harvard University, MA
Harvey Mudd College, CA
Haverford College, PA
Hillsdale College, MI
Johns Hopkins University, MD
Kenyon College, OH
Lafayette College, PA
Lehigh University, PA
Macalester College, MN
Massachusetts Institute of Technology, MA
Middlebury College, VT
Mount Holyoke College, MA
New College of Florida, FL
New York University, NY
Northeastern University, MA
Northwestern University, IL
Oberlin College, OH
Occidental College, CA
Pitzer College, CA
Pomona College, CA
Princeton University, NJ
Purdue University/West Lafayette, IN
Reed College, OR
Rensselaer Polytechnic Institute, NY
Rice University, TX
Rose-Hulman Institute of Technology, IN

Scripps College, CA
Sewanee: The University of the South, TN
Smith College, MA
Southern Methodist University, TX
St. John's College-Annapolis, MD
Stanford University, CA
State University of New York at Binghamton, NY
Stevens Institute of Technology, NJ
Stony Brook University/The State University of New York, NY
Swarthmore College, PA
Tufts University, MA
Union College, NY
United States Coast Guard Academy, CT
United States Naval Academy, MD
University of California at Berkeley, CA
University of California at Los Angeles, CA
University of California San Diego, CA
University of Chicago, IL
University of Miami, FL
University of Michigan/Ann Arbor, MI
University of Missouri/Columbia, MO
University of Notre Dame, IN
University of Pennsylvania, PA
University of Richmond, VA
University of Rochester, NY
University of Virginia, VA
University of Wisconsin-Madison, WI
Vanderbilt University, TN
Vassar College, NY
Villanova University, PA
Wake Forest University, NC
Washington and Lee University, VA
Webb Institute, NY
Wellesley College, MA
Wesleyan University, CT
Wheaton College, IL
Whitman College, WA
Williams College, MA
Worcester Polytechnic Institute, MA
Yale University, CT

HIGHLY COMPETITIVE

Colleges in this group generally look for students with grade averages of B+ to B and accept most of their students from the top 20% to 35% of the high school class. Median freshman test scores at these colleges generally range from 620 to 654 on the SAT and 27 or 28 on the ACT. These schools generally accept between one third and one half of their applicants.

To provide for finer distinctions within this admissions category, a plus (+) symbol has been placed before some entries. These are colleges with median freshman scores of 645 or more on the SAT or 28 or more on the ACT (depending on which test the college prefers), and colleges that accept fewer than one quarter of their applicants.

+American University, DC
+Amherst College, MA
Aquinas College - Michigan, MI
Babson College, MA
Bard College, NY
Baylor University, TX
Beloit College, WI
Bentley University, MA
Brigham Young University, UT
+California Polytechnic State University, CA
Centre College, KY
City University of New York/Baruch College, NY
+Clark University, MA
Clarkson University, NY
Clemson University, SC
The College of New Jersey, NJ
+College of the Atlantic, ME
+DePauw University, IN
Drake University, IA
Earlham College, IN
Emerson College, MA
Florida State University, FL
Franklin and Marshall College, PA
Gettysburg College, PA
Gonzaga University, WA
Gustavus Adolphus College, MN
Hobart and William Smith Colleges, NY
+Illinois Institute of Technology, IL
+Kalamazoo College, MI
Kettering University, MI
Lawrence University, WI
+Lewis & Clark College, OR
Loyola Marymount University, CA
+Miami University, OH
Milwaukee School of Engineering, WI
Missouri University of Science and Technology, MO
New Mexico Institute of Mining and Technology, NM
+North Carolina State University, NC
+Ohio State University at Columbus, OH
Pennsylvania State University - University Park, PA
+Pepperdine University, CA
Rhodes College, TN
Rochester Institute of Technology, NY
Rollins College, FL
Rutgers University - New Brunswick, NJ
Saint Louis University, MO
Salem College, NC
Sarah Lawrence College, NY
Skidmore College, NY
+St. John's College, Santa Fe, NM
+St. Olaf College, MN
Texas Christian University, TX
Thomas Aquinas College, CA
+Trinity College, CT
+Trinity University, TX
Truman State University, MO
+Tulane University, LA
United States Merchant Marine Academy, NY
+United States Military Academy at West Point, NY
University of California at Davis, CA
University of California at Santa Barbara, CA
University of Connecticut, CT
+University of Florida, FL
University of Georgia, GA
University of Illinois at Urbana-Champaign, IL
University of Maryland/College Park, MD
+University of Minnesota/Twin Cities, MN
+University of North Carolina at Chapel Hill, NC
+University of Pittsburgh, PA
University of Texas at Austin, TX
+University of Tulsa, OK
University of Vermont, VT
Virginia Polytechnic Institute and State University, VA
Westmont College, CA

VERY COMPETITIVE

The colleges in this category generally admit students whose averages are no less than B- and who rank in the top 35% to 50% of their graduating class. They generally report median freshman test scores in the 573 to 619 range on the SAT and from 24 to 26 on the ACT. These schools generally accept between one half and three quarters of their applicants.

The plus (+) has been placed before colleges with median freshman scores of 610 or above on the SAT or 26 or better on the ACT (depending on which test the college prefers), and colleges that accept fewer than one third of their applicants.

+Agnes Scott College, GA
Alaska Pacific University, AK
Allegheny College, PA
Appalachian State University, NC
Arizona State University at the Downtown Phoenix Campus, AZ
Arizona State University at the Polytechnic Campus, AZ
Arizona State University at the Tempe Campus, AZ
+Auburn University, AL
Augustana College, IL
Augustana University, SD
Austin College, TX
Belmont University, TN
Bemidji State University, MN
Benedictine College, KS
Bethel University, MN
Birmingham-Southern College, AL
Blue Mountain College, MS
Bradley University, IL
+Brescia University, KY
Bryant University, RI
Butler University, IN
+Calvin College, MI
Campbell University, NC
The Catholic University of America, DC
Cedarville University, OH
Central Methodist University, MO
+Chapman University, CA
Christendom College, VA
Christian Brothers University, TN
+Christopher Newport University, VA
City University of New York/City College, NY
City University of New York/Hunter College, NY
Coe College, IA
The College of New Rochelle, NY
+The College of Wooster, OH
Colorado Christian University, CO
Colorado State University, CO
Concordia University, CA
Concordia University Nebraska, NE
Concordia University, Ann Arbor, MI
Coppin State University, MD
Cornell College, IA
Covenant College, GA
+Creighton University, NE
DePaul University, IL
Dillard University, LA
Doane University, NE
Drew University/College of Liberal Arts, NJ
+Drexel University, PA
Drury University, MO
Duquesne University, PA
Elms College, MA
+Elon University, NC
Embry-Riddle Aeronautical University - Daytona Beach, FL
Embry-Riddle Aeronautical University - Prescott Campus, AZ
+Endicott College, MA
+Fairfield University, CT
Florida Institute of Technology, FL
Fort Valley State University, GA
Franciscan University of Steubenville, OH
+Furman University, SC
George Mason University, VA
Georgia State University, GA
Goddard College, VT
Goucher College, MD
Grand Canyon University, AZ
Grove City College, PA
Hamline University, MN
+Hendrix College, AR
Hollins University, VA
Hope College, MI
Illinois College, IL
Illinois State University, IL
+Illinois Wesleyan University, IL
Indiana University Bloomington, IN
Ithaca College, NY
James Madison University, VA
John Brown University, AR
Juniata College, PA
Kansas State University, KS
Kennesaw State University, GA
+Knox College, IL
La Sierra University, CA
Lake Forest College, IL
Lawrence Technological University, MI
LeTourneau University, TX
Lipscomb University, TN
Louisiana State University and A&M College, LA
Louisiana Tech University, LA
Loyola University Chicago, IL
Loyola University Maryland, MD
+Loyola University New Orleans, LA
Maharishi University of Management, IA
Marist College, NY
+Marlboro College, VT
+Marquette University, WI
Marymount Manhattan College, NY
+Maryville University of Saint Louis, MO
McDaniel College, MD
Mercer University, GA
Metropolitan College of New York, NY
+Michigan State University, MI
+Michigan Technological University, MI
Mills College, CA
+Mount St. Mary's University - Chalon Campus, CA
+Muhlenberg College, PA
New Jersey Institute of Technology, NJ
North Central College, IL
Northeastern State University, OK
Northern Arizona University, AZ
Northwest University, WA
Notre Dame College, OH
Notre Dame of Maryland University, MD
Ohio Northern University, OH
Ohio Wesleyan University, OH
Oklahoma Christian University, OK
Oklahoma City University, OK
Oklahoma State University, OK
Oregon State University, OR
Ottawa University, KS
Pacific Lutheran University, WA
Pacific Union College, CA
Pratt Institute, NY
Presbyterian College, SC
Providence College, RI
Rivier University, NH
Roanoke College, VA
Roosevelt University, IL
+Rowan University, NJ
Saint Joseph's University, PA
+Saint Michael's College, VT
Salisbury University, MD
Samford University, AL
+Seattle University, WA
+Shimer College, IL
Simmons College, MA
Simpson College, IA
South Dakota School of Mines and Technology, SD

Southwestern University, TX
St. Catherine University, MN
St. Edward's University, TX
St. Lawrence University, NY
St. Mary's College of Maryland, MD
St. Norbert College, WI
State University of New York/SUNY Cortland, NY
State University of New York/The College of Environmental Science and Forestry, NY
+State University of New York at Geneseo, NY
State University of New York Polytechnic Institute, NY
Sterling College, VT
Stetson University, FL
Susquehanna University, PA
Syracuse University, NY
Temple University, PA
+Texas A&M University, TX
Touro College, NY
Towson University, MD
+Transylvania University, KY
Trinity International University, IL
Union University, TN
University of Alabama in Huntsville, AL
University of California at Irvine, CA
University of Central Arkansas, AR
University of Central Florida, FL
University of Cincinnati, OH
+University of Colorado Boulder, CO
+University of Dallas, TX
+University of Delaware, DE
+University of Denver, CO
+University of Evansville, IN
University of Houston, TX
University of Illinois at Chicago, IL
+University of Iowa, IA
University of Mary Washington, VA
University of Maryland/Baltimore County, MD
+University of Massachusetts Amherst, MA
University of Michigan/Dearborn, MI
University of Minnesota/Morris, MN
University of Missouri-Kansas City, MO
University of Nebraska - Lincoln, NE
University of New Hampshire, NH
+University of North Carolina at Asheville, NC
University of North Carolina at Wilmington, NC
University of North Florida, FL
University of Oklahoma, OK
University of Portland, OR
+University of Puget Sound, WA
University of Redlands, CA
+University of San Diego, CA
University of San Francisco, CA
University of Science and Arts of Oklahoma, OK
University of Scranton, PA
+University of South Carolina at Columbia, SC
+University of South Florida/Tampa, FL
+University of St. Thomas, MN
University of St. Thomas - Houston, TX
The University of Tennessee at Knoxville, TN
+University of Texas at Dallas, TX
University of the Pacific, CA
University of the Sciences , PA
The University of Utah, UT
University of Washington, WA
University of Wisconsin-Eau Claire, WI
University of Wisconsin-Platteville, WI
Ursinus College, PA
Vanguard University of Southern California, CA
Wabash College, IN
Warren Wilson College, NC
Washington & Jefferson College, PA
Washington College, MD
Washington University in St. Louis, MO
Wheaton College, MA
Whitworth University, WA
+Willamette University, OR
Wisconsin Lutheran College, WI
Wofford College, SC
+Yeshiva University, NY

COMPETITIVE

This category is a very broad one, covering colleges that generally have median freshman test scores between 500 and 572 on the SAT and between 21 and 23 on the ACT. Some of these colleges require that students have high school averages of B- or better, although others state a minimum of C+ or C. Generally, these colleges prefer students in the top 50% to 65% of the graduating class and accept between 75% and 85% of their applicants.

Colleges with a plus (+) are those with median freshman SAT scores of 563 or more or median freshman ACT scores of 24 or more (depending on which test the colleges prefers), and those that admit fewer than half of their applicants.

+Abilene Christian University, TX
Adelphi University, NY
Adrian College, MI
Alabama A&M University, AL
Albany State University, GA
Albion College, MI
Albright College, PA
Alcorn State University, MS
Alderson Broaddus University, WV
Alfred State College, NY
+Alfred University, NY
Alice Lloyd College, KY
Alma College, MI
Alvernia University, PA
American Jewish University - College of Arts and Sciences Campus, CA
Anderson University, IN
+Andrews University, MI
Anna Maria College, MA
+Aquinas College, TN
+Arcadia University, PA
Arizona State University at the West Campus, AZ
Arkansas State University, AR
Arkansas Tech University, AR
Armstrong State University, GA
+Asbury University, KY
Ashford University, CA
Ashland University, OH
+Assumption College, MA
Atlantic Union College, MA
Auburn University at Montgomery, AL
Augsburg College, MN
Augusta University, GA
Aurora University, IL
Austin Peay State University, TN
Avila University, MO
Azusa Pacific University, CA
+Baker University, KS
Baldwin Wallace University, OH
Ball State University, IN
Barry University, FL
Bay Path University, MA
Beacon College, FL
Becker College, MA
Belhaven University, MS
Bellarmine University, KY
Belmont Abbey College, NC
Benedictine University, IL
Benjamin Franklin Institute of Technology, MA
Berea College, KY
+Berry College, GA
Bethel College, IN
Bethel College, KS
Bethel University, TN
Bethune-Cookman University, FL
+Biola University, CA
Black Hills State University, SD
+Bluefield College, VA
Bluffton University, OH
Boise State University, ID
Boricua College, NY
+The Boston Conservatory at Berklee, MA
Bowling Green State University, OH
Brewton-Parker College, GA
Briar Cliff University, IA
Bridgewater College, VA
Bridgewater State University, MA
Brigham Young University/Hawaii, HI
Bryan College, TN
Bryn Athyn College, PA
Buena Vista University, IA
Cairn University, PA
California Baptist University, CA
California Lutheran University, CA
California State Polytechnic University, Pomona, CA
California State University, Chico, CA
California State University, East Bay, CA
California State University, Fullerton, CA
California State University, Long Beach, CA
California State University, Sacramento, CA
California State University, San Bernardino, CA
California State University, Stanislaus, CA
Calumet College of St. Joseph, IN
Campbellsville University, KY
Canisius College, NY
Capital University, OH
Capitol Technology University, MD
Cardinal Stritch University, WI
+Carroll College, MT
+Carroll University, WI
Carson-Newman University, TN
Carthage College, WI
Castleton University, VT
Cazenovia College, NY
Cedar Crest College, PA
Centenary College, NJ
+Centenary College of Louisiana, LA
Central College, IA
Central Connecticut State University, CT
Central Michigan University, MI
Central State University, OH
Central Washington University, WA
Chaminade University of Honolulu, HI
+Champlain College, VT
Charleston Southern University, SC
Chatham University, PA
Chicago State University, IL
The Citadel, The Military College of South Carolina, SC
+City University of New York/Brooklyn College, NY
City University of New York/Queens College, NY
Clarke University, IA
Clarkson College, NE
Clayton State University, GA
+Cleveland Institute of Art, OH
Cleveland State University, OH
Coastal Carolina University, SC
Cogswell Polytechnical College, CA
Colby-Sawyer College, NH
The College at Brockport - State University of New York, NY
College of Charleston, SC
The College of Idaho, ID
College of Mount Saint Vincent, NY
College of Saint Benedict , MN
College of Saint Mary, NE
The College of Saint Rose, NY
College of St. Scholastica, MN
College of the Ozarks, MO
Colorado State University-Pueblo, CO
Columbia College, SC
Columbia College - Missouri, MO
Columbia College Chicago, IL
Columbus College of Art and Design, OH
Concord University, WV
+Concordia College - Moorhead, MN
Concordia University, OR
Concordia University Saint Paul, MN
Concordia University Texas, TX
Concordia University Wisconsin, WI

Concordia University, Chicago, IL
Converse College, SC
Corban University, OR
Culver-Stockton College, MO
Cumberland University, TN
Curry College, MA
Daemen College, NY
Dakota State University, SD
Dakota Wesleyan University, SD
Dallas Baptist University, TX
Daniel Webster College, NH
Defiance College, OH
Delaware Valley University, PA
Delta State University, MS
DeSales University, PA
Dominican University, IL
Dominican University of California, CA
+Dordt College, IA
D'Youville College, NY
East Carolina University, NC
East Central University, OK
East Stroudsburg University, PA
East Tennessee State University, TN
East Texas Baptist University, TX
Eastern Connecticut State University, CT
Eastern Illinois University, IL
Eastern Kentucky University, KY
Eastern Mennonite University, VA
Eastern Michigan University, MI
Eastern Nazarene College, MA
Eastern New Mexico University, NM
Eastern Oregon University, OR
Eastern University, PA
Eckerd College, FL
Edgewood College, WI
Elizabeth City State University, NC
Elizabethtown College, PA
Elizabethtown College School of Continuing and Professional Studies, PA
Elmhurst College, IL
Elmira College, NY
Embry-Riddle Aeronautical University - Worldwide, FL
+Emmanuel College, MA
Emory and Henry College, VA
Emporia State University, KS
Erskine College, SC
Eugene Lang College/The New School for Liberal Arts, NY
Eureka College, IL
Evangel University, MO
The Evergreen State College, WA
Fairleigh Dickinson University/College at Florham, NJ
Fairleigh Dickinson University/Metropolitan Campus, NJ
Fairmont State University, WV
Farmingdale State College, NY
Faulkner University, AL
Fayetteville State University, NC
Ferris State University, MI
Ferrum College, VA
Fitchburg State University, MA
Five Towns College, NY
Flagler College, FL
Florida Agricultural and Mechanical University, FL
Florida Atlantic University, FL
Florida Gulf Coast University, FL
+Florida International University, FL
+Florida Southern College, FL
Fontbonne University, MO
Fort Hays State University, KS
Fort Lewis College, CO
Framingham State University, MA
Franklin College, IN
Franklin Pierce University, NH
Freed-Hardeman University, TN
Fresno Pacific University, CA
Friends University, KS
Gannon University, PA
+Gardner-Webb University, NC
Geneva College, PA
George Fox University, OR
Georgetown College, KY
+Georgia College & State University, GA
Georgia Southern University, GA
Georgia Southwestern State University, GA
Golden Gate University, CA
Goldey-Beacom College, DE
+Gordon College, MA
Goshen College, IN
Grace Bible College, MI
Grace College and Seminary, IN
Graceland University, IA
Grambling State University, LA
Grand Rapids Theological Seminary/Cornerstone University, MI
+Grand Valley State University, MI
Grand View University, IA
Greenville College, IL
Guilford College, NC
+Hampden-Sydney College, VA
Hannibal-LaGrange University, MO
+Hanover College, IN
Harding University, AR
Hardin-Simmons University, TX
Hartwick College, NY
+Hastings College, NE
Hawaii Pacific University, HI
Heidelberg University, OH
Hellenic College/Holy Cross Greek Orthodox School of Theology, MA
High Point University, NC
Hilbert College, NY
Hiram College, OH
+Hofstra University, NY
Hood College, MD
Hope International University, CA
Houghton College, NY
Houston Baptist University, TX
Howard Payne University, TX
+Howard University, DC
Humboldt State University, CA
Humphreys College, CA
Huntingdon College, AL
Huntington University, IN
Immaculata University, PA
Indiana University East, IN
Indiana University Kokomo, IN
Indiana University Northwest, IN
Indiana University South Bend, IN
Indiana University-Purdue University Fort Wayne, IN
Indiana University-Purdue University Indianapolis, IN
Indiana Wesleyan University, IN
Iona College, NY
Iowa State University, IA
Iowa Wesleyan University, IA
Jacksonville University, FL
+John Carroll University, OH
Johnson & Wales University/Charlotte Campus, NC
Johnson & Wales University/Denver Campus, CO
Johnson & Wales University/North Miami Campus, FL
Johnson & Wales University/Providence Campus, RI
Johnson State College, VT
Judson College, AL
Judson University, IL
+Kansas City Art Institute, MO
Kansas Wesleyan University, KS
Kean University, NJ
Kendall College, IL
Kent State University, OH
Kentucky Wesleyan College, KY
Keuka College, NY
King University, TN
King's College, PA
La Salle University, PA
LaGrange College, GA
Lake Superior State University, MI
Lakeland University, WI
Lander University, SC
Lane College, TN
Langston University, OK
Lasell College, MA
Le Moyne College, NY
Lebanon Valley College, PA
Lee University, TN
Lees-McRae College, NC
LeMoyne-Owen College, TN

Lenoir-Rhyne University, NC
Lesley University, MA
Lewis University, IL
Lewis-Clark State College, ID
Liberty University, VA
Limestone College, SC
Lincoln Memorial University, TN
Lindenwood University, MO
Lindsey Wilson College, KY
Linfield College, OR
List College, NY
LIU Brooklyn, NY
LIU Post, NY
Longwood University, VA
Loras College, IA
Louisiana College, LA
Louisiana State University in Shreveport, LA
Lubbock Christian University, TX
+Luther College, IA
Lycoming College, PA
Lynchburg College, VA
Lyndon State College, VT
+Lyon College, AR
MacMurray College, IL
Madonna University, MI
Maine Maritime Academy, ME
Malone University, OH
Manchester University, IN
+Manhattan College, NY
+Manhattanville College, NY
Marian University, IN
Marietta College, OH
Mars Hill University, NC
Marshall University, WV
Mary Baldwin University, VA
Maryville College, TN
Marywood University, PA
Massachusetts College of Liberal Arts, MA
Massachusetts Maritime Academy, MA
+The Master's University, CA
+McKendree University, IL
McNeese State University, LA
McPherson College, KS
Medaille College, NY
Memphis College of Art, TN
Mercy College, NY
Mercy College of Health Sciences, IA
Mercyhurst University, PA
Meredith College, NC
Merrimack College, MA
+Messiah College, PA
Methodist University, NC
Metropolitan State University, MN
MidAmerica Nazarene University, KS
Middle Tennessee State University, TN
Midwestern State University, TX
Millersville University of Pennsylvania, PA
Milligan College, TN
Millikin University, IL
+Millsaps College, MS
Minnesota State University, Mankato, MN
Minnesota State University, Moorhead, MN
Minot State University, ND
Misericordia University, PA
Mississippi College, MS
+Mississippi State University, MS
Mississippi University for Women, MS
Missouri Baptist University, MO
Missouri Southern State University, MO
+Missouri State University, MO
Missouri Valley College, MO
Mitchell College, CT
Molloy College, NY
Monmouth College, IL
Monmouth University, NJ
Monroe College, NY
+Montana State University, MT
Montana State University-Billings, MT
+Montana Tech of the University of Montana, MT
Morehead State University, KY
Morehouse College, GA
Morningside College, IA
Mount Aloysius College, PA
Mount Ida College, MA
Mount Marty College, SD
Mount Mercy University, IA
Mount Saint Mary College, NY
Mount St. Joseph University, OH
Mount St. Mary's University, MD
Mount Vernon Nazarene University, OH
Murray State University, KY
Muskingum University, OH
Nazareth College, NY
+Nebraska Wesleyan University, NE
New England College, NH
New Mexico State University, NM
New York Institute of Technology, NY
Newberry College, SC
Newbury College, MA
Newman University, KS
Niagara University, NY
Nicholls State University, LA
North Carolina Central University, NC
North Carolina Wesleyan College, NC
North Central University, MN
North Dakota State University, ND
+North Greenville University, SC
North Park University, IL
Northern Illinois University, IL
Northern Kentucky University, KY
Northern Michigan University, MI
Northern State University, SD
+Northland College, WI
Northwest Christian University, OR
Northwest Missouri State University, MO
Northwest Nazarene University, ID
+Northwestern College of Iowa, IA
Northwestern State University of Louisiana, LA
Norwich University, VT
+Nova Southeastern University, FL
Oakland University, MI
Oakwood University, AL
+Oglethorpe University, GA
+Ohio Dominican University, OH
Ohio State University at Lima, OH
Ohio State University at Mansfield, OH
Ohio State University at Marion, OH
Ohio State University at Newark, OH
Ohio University, OH
Ohio Valley University, WV
Oklahoma Baptist University, OK
Oklahoma Wesleyan University, OK
Old Dominion University, VA
Olivet Nazarene University, IL
Oral Roberts University, OK
Oregon Institute of Technology, OR
Otterbein University, OH
Ouachita Baptist University, AR
Pace University, NY
Pacific University, OR
Palm Beach Atlantic University, FL
Park University, MO
Penn State Erie/The Behrend College, PA
Penn State University/Altoona, PA
Philadelphia University, PA
Piedmont College, GA
Point Loma Nazarene University, CA
Point Park University, PA
Portland State University, OR
Post University, CT
Prescott College, AZ
+Principia College, IL
Purdue University/Northwest, IN
Queens University of Charlotte, NC
Quincy University, IL
Quinnipiac University, CT
Ramapo College of New Jersey, NJ
Randolph College, VA
Randolph-Macon College, VA
Regis College, MA
Regis University, CO
Reinhardt University, GA
Rider University, NJ
+Ripon College, WI

Robert Morris University, PA
Roberts Wesleyan College, NY
Rockford University, IL
Rockhurst University, MO
Rocky Mountain College, MT
+Roger Williams University, RI
Rosemont College, PA
Russell Sage College, NY
Rust College, MS
Rutgers University - Camden, NJ
Rutgers University - Newark, NJ
Sacred Heart University, CT
Saginaw Valley State University, MI
SAGU American Indian College, AZ
+Saint Anselm College, NH
Saint Augustine's University, NC
Saint John's University, MN
Saint Joseph's College, IN
Saint Joseph's College of Maine, ME
Saint Leo University, FL
Saint Martin's University, WA
Saint Mary's College, IN
Saint Mary's College of California, CA
Saint Mary's University of Minnesota, MN
Saint Peter's University, NJ
Saint Vincent College, PA
Saint Xavier University, IL
Salve Regina University, RI
Sam Houston State University, TX
San Diego Christian College, CA
+San Diego State University, CA
San Jose State University, CA
Savannah College of Art and Design, GA
Savannah State University, GA
+Seattle Pacific University, WA
Seton Hall University, NJ
Seton Hill University, PA
Shaw University, NC
Shawnee State University, OH
Shenandoah University, VA
Shepherd University, West Virginia, WV
Shippensburg University of Pennsylvania, PA
+Siena College, NY
Siena Heights University, MI
Sierra Nevada College, NV
Simpson University, CA
Slippery Rock University of Pennsylvania, PA
Sonoma State University, CA
South Dakota State University, SD
Southeast Missouri State University, MO
Southeastern Louisiana University, LA
Southeastern Oklahoma State University, OK
Southeastern University, FL
Southern Adventist University, TN
Southern Arkansas University, AR
Southern Illinois University Carbondale, IL
Southern Illinois University Edwardsville, IL
Southern New Hampshire University, NH
Southern Oregon University, OR
Southern Utah University, UT
Southwest Minnesota State University, MN
Southwestern College, KS
Southwestern Oklahoma State University, OK
Spelman College, GA
Spring Arbor University, MI
Spring Hill College, AL
Springfield College, MA
St. Ambrose University, IA
St. Bonaventure University, NY
St. Cloud State University, MN
St. John Fisher College, NY
St. John's University, NY
St. Joseph's College, New York/Long Island Campus, NY
St. Mary's University, TX
St. Thomas Aquinas College, NY
State University of New York/Buffalo State College, NY
State University of New York/SUNY College at Old Westbury, NY
State University of New York/SUNY Fredonia, NY
+State University of New York/SUNY Oneonta, NY
State University of New York/SUNY Plattsburgh, NY
+State University of New York/SUNY Potsdam, NY
+State University of New York/University at Buffalo, NY
State University of New York/Maritime College, NY
State University of New York at New Paltz, NY
State University of New York at Oswego, NY
State University of New York at Purchase, NY
State University of New York SUNY Albany, NY
Stephens College, MO
Sterling College, KS
Stevenson University, MD
Stillman College, AL
+Stonehill College, MA
Suffolk University, MA
Tabor College, KS
Talladega College, AL
+Taylor University, IN
Tennessee State University, TN
Tennessee Technological University, TN
Tennessee Wesleyan University, TN
Texas A&M University at Commerce, TX
Texas A&M University at Galveston, TX
Texas Lutheran University, TX
Texas State University, TX
+Texas Tech University, TX
Texas Wesleyan University, TX
Thiel College, PA
Thomas More College, KY
Thomas More College of Liberal Arts, NH
Tiffin University, OH
Toccoa Falls College, GA
Trevecca Nazarene University, TN
Trine University, IN
Trinity Christian College, IL
+Trinity Washington University, DC
Troy University, AL
Tusculum College, TN
Tuskegee University, AL
Union College, KY
Union College, NE
United States Air Force Academy, CO
Unity College, ME
The University of Akron, OH
+University of Alabama, AL
University of Alabama at Birmingham, AL
University of Alaska Fairbanks, AK
University of Alaska Southeast, AK
University of Arizona, AZ
+University of Arkansas at Fayetteville, AR
University of Arkansas at Little Rock, AR
University of Arkansas at Pine Bluff, AR
+University of California at Riverside, CA
+University of California, Santa Cruz, CA
University of Central Missouri, MO
University of Central Oklahoma, OK
University of Charleston, WV
University of Colorado Colorado Springs, CO
University of Colorado Denver, CO
University of Dayton, OH
+University of Detroit Mercy, MI
University of Dubuque, IA
University of Findlay, OH
University of Great Falls, MT
University of Hartford, CT
University of Hawaii at Hilo, HI
University of Hawaii at Manoa, HI
University of Holy Cross, LA
University of Idaho, ID
University of Indianapolis, IN
University of Jamestown, ND
+University of Kansas, KS
University of Kentucky, KY
University of La Verne, CA
University of Louisiana at Lafayette, LA
University of Louisiana at Monroe, LA
University of Louisville, KY
University of Maine, ME
University of Maine at Augusta, ME
University of Maine at Farmington, ME
University of Maine at Machias, ME
University of Maine at Presque Isle, ME
University of Mary, ND
+University of Mary Hardin-Baylor, TX
University of Maryland/Eastern Shore, MD

University of Massachusetts Boston, MA
University of Massachusetts Dartmouth, MA
University of Massachusetts Lowell, MA
University of Memphis, TN
+University of Michigan-Flint, MI
University of Minnesota Crookston, MN
+University of Minnesota/Duluth, MN
+University of Mississippi, MS
University of Missouri-St. Louis, MO
University of Mobile, AL
University of Montana, MT
University of Montevallo, AL
University of Mount Olive, NC
University of Mount Union, OH
University of Nebraska - Omaha, NE
University of Nevada, Las Vegas, NV
University of Nevada/Reno, NV
University of New England, ME
University of New Hampshire - Manchester, NH
University of New Haven, CT
University of New Mexico, NM
University of New Orleans, LA
University of North Alabama, AL
University of North Carolina at Charlotte, NC
University of North Carolina at Greensboro, NC
University of North Dakota, ND
University of North Georgia, GA
University of North Texas, TX
University of Northern Colorado, CO
University of Northern Iowa, IA
University of Northwestern - St. Paul, MN
University of Oregon, OR
University of Pittsburgh at Bradford, PA
University of Pittsburgh at Greensburg, PA
University of Pittsburgh at Johnstown, PA
University of Rhode Island, RI
University of Saint Francis, IN
University of Saint Joseph, CT
University of Saint Mary, KS
University of Sioux Falls, SD
University of South Alabama, AL
University of South Carolina Aiken, SC
University of South Dakota, SD
University of South Florida/St. Petersburg, FL
University of Southern California, CA
University of Southern Indiana, IN
University of Southern Maine, ME
University of Southern Mississippi, MS
University of St. Francis, IL
University of Tampa, FL
The University of Tennessee at Chattanooga, TN
The University of Tennessee at Martin, TN
University of Texas at San Antonio, TX
University of the Cumberlands, KY
University of the Ozarks, AR
University of the Southwest, NM
University of West Florida, FL
University of Wisconsin-Green Bay, WI
+University of Wisconsin-La Crosse, WI
University of Wisconsin-Milwaukee, WI
University of Wisconsin-Oshkosh, WI
University of Wisconsin-Parkside, WI
University of Wisconsin-River Falls, WI
University of Wisconsin-Stevens Point, WI
University of Wisconsin-Stout, WI
University of Wisconsin-Superior, WI
University of Wisconsin-Whitewater, WI
+University of Wyoming, WY
Urbana University, OH
Utah State University, UT
Utica College, NY
Valdosta State University, GA
Valley City State University, ND
+Valparaiso University, IN
Vaughn College of Aeronautics and Technology, NY
Vermont Technical College, VT
Virginia Commonwealth University, VA
+Virginia Military Institute, VA
+Virginia State University, VA
Virginia Union University, VA
Viterbo University, WI
Voorhees College, SC
+Wagner College, NY
Walsh University, OH
Warner Pacific College, OR
Warner University, FL
Wartburg College, IA
Washburn University, KS
Washington State University, WA
Wayne State College, NE
Wayne State University, MI
Waynesburg University, PA
Webber International University, FL
Weber State University, UT
Webster University, MO
Wells College, NY
Wentworth Institute of Technology, MA
+Wesleyan College, GA
West Chester University of Pennsylvania, PA
West Liberty University, WV
West Texas A&M University, TX
West Virginia University, WV
West Virginia Wesleyan College, WV
Western Carolina University, NC
Western Illinois University, IL
Western Kentucky University, KY
Western Michigan University, MI
Western New England University, MA
Western State Colorado University, CO
+Western Washington University, WA
Westfield State University, MA
Westminster College, MO
+Westminster College, PA
+Westminster College, UT
Wheelock College, MA
Whittier College, CA
Wichita State University, KS
Widener University, PA
Wilberforce University, OH
Wiley College, TX
Wilkes University, PA
+William Jewell College, MO
William Paterson University of New Jersey, NJ
William Penn University, IA
William Woods University, MO
Williams Baptist College, AR
Wilmington College, OH
Wilson College, PA
Wingate University, NC
Winona State University, MN
Winthrop University, SC
+Wittenberg University, OH
Woodbury University, CA
Worcester State University, MA
Wright State University, OH
+Xavier University, OH
+Xavier University of Louisiana, LA
York College, NE
York College of Pennsylvania, PA
Youngstown State University, OH

LESS COMPETITIVE

Included in this category are colleges with median freshman test scores generally below 500 on the SAT and below 21 on the ACT; some colleges that require entrance examinations but do not report median scores; and colleges that admit students with averages generally below C who rank in the top 65% of the graduating class. These colleges usually admit 85% or more of their applicants. For detailed profiles of these colleges, please go to barronspac.com.

Adams State University, CO
Albertus Magnus College, CT
Alverno College, WI
American International College, MA
Amridge University, AL
Averett University, VA
Barton College, NC
Berkeley College/New Jersey, NJ
Berkeley College/New York City Campus, NY
Berkeley College/White Plains Campus, NY
Blackburn College, IL
Bloomfield College, NJ
Bloomsburg University of Pennsylvania, PA
Bluefield State College, WV
Bowie State University, MD
Brenau University - Women's College, GA
Cabrini University, PA
California State University, Maritime Academy, CA
California State University, Bakersfield, CA
California State University, Dominguez Hills, CA
California State University, Fresno, CA
California State University, Los Angeles, CA
California State University, Monterey Bay, CA
California State University, Northridge, CA
California State University, San Marcos, CA
California University of Pennsylvania, PA
Carlos Albizu University, FL
Carlow University, PA
Catawba College, NC
Charter Oak State College, CT
Chestnut Hill College, PA
Cheyney University of Pennsylvania, PA
City University of New York/Lehman College, NY
City University of New York/York College, NY
Claflin University, SC
Clarion University of Pennsylvania, PA
Clark Atlanta University, GA
Coker College, SC
College of Saint Elizabeth, NJ
College of St Joseph, VT
Colorado Mesa University, CO
Columbus State University, GA
Concordia College - New York, NY
Davenport University, MI
Davis & Elkins College, WV
Dickinson State University, ND
Dominican College, NY
Eastern Washington University, WA
Edinboro University, PA
Felician University, NJ
Fisk University, TN
Florida Memorial University, FL
Francis Marion University, SC
Frostburg State University, MD
Gallaudet University, DC
Georgian Court University, NJ
Goodwin College, CT
Green Mountain College, VT
Greensboro College, NC
Gwynedd Mercy University, PA
Hampton University, VA
Henderson State University, AR
Hodges University, FL
Holy Family University, PA
Holy Names University, CA
Husson University, ME
Huston-Tillotson University, TX
Indiana Institute of Technology, IN
Indiana State University, IN
Indiana University of Pennsylvania, PA
Indiana University Southeast, IN
Jackson State University, MS
Jacksonville State University, AL
Johnson C. Smith University, NC
Keene State College, NH
Keiser University, FL
Kentucky Christian University, KY
Kentucky State University, KY
Keystone College, PA
Kutztown University of Pennsylvania, PA
La Roche College, PA
Laguna College of Art and Design, CA
Lake Erie College, OH
Lamar University, TX
LIM College, NY
Livingstone College, NC
Lock Haven University of Pennsylvania, PA
Lynn University, FL
Mansfield University, PA
Marian University, WI
Martin University, IN
Marymount University, VA
McMurry University, TX
Menlo College, CA
Metropolitan State University of Denver, CO
Midway University, KY
Mississippi Valley State University, MS
Montclair State University, NJ
Montreat College, NC
Morgan State University, MD
Morris College, SC
Mount Mary University, WI
National Louis University, IL
National University, CA
Neumann University, PA
New Jersey City University, NJ
Nichols College, MA
Norfolk State University, VA
North Carolina A&T State University, NC
Northeastern Illinois University, IL
Northwood University - Michigan, MI
Notre Dame de Namur University, CA
Olivet College, MI
Our Lady of the Lake University, TX
Paine College, GA
Paul Quinn College, TX
Pfeiffer University, NC
Philander Smith College, AR
Pine Manor College, MA
Plymouth State University, NH
Prairie View A&M University, TX
Radford University, VA
Rhode Island College, RI
Rochester College, MI
Saint Mary-of-the-Woods College, IN
Salem International University, WV
Salem State University, MA
San Francisco State University, CA
Schreiner University, TX
Shepherd University, CA
Shorter University, GA
Silver Lake College of the Holy Family, WI
South Carolina State University, SC
South University, GA
Southern Connecticut State University, CT
+Southern University and A&M College, LA
Southern University at New Orleans, LA
Southern Vermont College, VT
Southern Wesleyan University, SC
Southwest Baptist University, MO
Southwestern Adventist University, TX
St. Andrews University, NC

St. Francis College, NY
St. Joseph's College, New York/Brooklyn Campus, NY
St. Thomas University, FL
State University of New York/College of Agriculture and Tech at Cobleskill, NY
Stephen F. Austin State University, TX
Sul Ross State University, TX
Tarleton State University, TX
Texas A&M University at Corpus Christi, TX
Texas A&M University at Kingsville, TX
Texas Southern University, TX
Texas Woman's University, TX
Thomas College, ME
Thomas University, GA
University of Bridgeport, CT
University of Houston-Downtown, TX
University of Maine at Fort Kent, ME
University of Maryland/University College, MD
University of Montana-Western, MT
University of Nebraska - Kearney, NE
University of North Carolina at Pembroke, NC
University of South Carolina Upstate, SC
University of Texas at Arlington, TX
University of the District of Columbia, DC
University of the Incarnate Word, TX
The University of Virginia's College at Wise, VA
University of West Georgia, GA
Ursuline College, OH
Virginia Wesleyan College, VA
Washington Adventist University, MD
Wayland Baptist University, TX
Wesley College, DE
Western Connecticut State University, CT
Western New Mexico University, NM
Western Oregon University, OR
Wheeling Jesuit University, WV
William Carey University, MS
William Peace University, NC
Winston-Salem State University, NC

NONCOMPETITIVE

The colleges in this category generally only require evidence of graduation from an accredited high school (although they may also require completion of a certain number of high school units). Some require that entrance examinations be taken for placement purposes only, or only by graduates of unaccredited high schools or only by out-of-state students. In some cases, insufficient capacity may compel a college in this category to limit the number of students that are accepted; generally, however, if a college accepts 98% or more of its applicants, it automatically falls in this category. Colleges are also rated Noncompetitive if they admit all state residents, but have some requirements for nonresidents. For detailed profiles of these colleges, please go to barronspac.com.

Adventist University of Health Sciences, FL
Alabama State University, AL
Allen College, IA
Allen University, SC
Angelo State University, TX
Arkansas Baptist College, AR
Baker College of Flint, MI
Bellevue University, NE
Benedict College, SC
Bennett College, NC
Bethany College, KS
Bethany College, WV
Boston Architectural College, MA
Caldwell University, NJ
Cambridge College, MA
Cameron University, OK
Chadron State College, NE
City University of New York/College of Staten Island, NY
City University of New York/College of Technology, NY
City University of New York/John Jay College of Criminal Justice, NY
City University of New York/Meger Evers College, NY
City University of Seattle, WA
Colorado Technical University, CO
Concordia College - Alabama, AL
Cox College, MO
Delaware State University, DE
Edward Waters College, FL
Glenville State College, WV
Harris-Stowe State University, MO
Heritage University, WA
Idaho State University, ID
Jarvis Christian College, TX
Lincoln University, MO
The Lincoln University, PA
Lourdes University, OH
Marygrove College, MI
Marylhurst University, OR
Mayville State University, ND
Miles College, AL
Montana State University-Northern, MT
Naropa University, CO
New Mexico Highlands University, NM
Northwestern Oklahoma State University, OK
Nyack College, NY
Oakland City University, IN
Oglala Lakota College, SD
Oklahoma Panhandle State University, OK
Peirce College, PA
Pennsylvania College of Technology, PA
Peru State College, NE
Pittsburg State University, KS
Presentation College, SD
Saint Francis University, PA
Sinte Gleska University, SD
Southern Nazarene University, OK
St. Gregory's University, OK
Thomas Edison State University, NJ
Tougaloo College, MS
University of Alaska Anchorage, AK
University of Arkansas at Monticello, AR
University of Pikeville, KY
University of Rio Grande & Rio Grande Community College, OH
University of Texas at El Paso, TX
University of Texas Rio Grande Valley, TX
University of Toledo, OH
University of West Alabama, AL
Upper Iowa University, IA
VanderCook College of Music, IL
Walla Walla University, WA
West Virginia State University, WV
West Virginia University Institute of Technology, WV
Wilmington University, DE

SPECIAL

Listed here are colleges whose programs of study are specialized; professional schools of art, music, nursing, and other disciplines. In general, the admissions requirements are not based primarily on academic criteria, but on evidence of talent or special interest in the field. Many other colleges and universities offer special-interest programs *in addition* to regular academic curricula, but such institutions have been given a regular competitive rating based on academic criteria. Schools oriented toward working adults have also been assigned this rating. For detailed profiles of these colleges, please go to barronspac.com.

Albany College of Pharmacy and Health Sciences, NY
Art Academy of Cincinnati, OH
The Art Institute of Atlanta, GA
Art Institute of Portland, OR
ArtCenter College of Design, CA
Berklee College of Music, MA
Cabarrus College of Health Sciences, NC
California College of the Arts, CA
California Institute of the Arts, CA
Cleveland Institute of Music, OH
College for Creative Studies, MI
College of Art and Design at Lesley University, MA
Cornish College of the Arts, WA
Curtis Institute of Music, PA
Eastman School of Music/University of Rochester, NY
Excelsior College, NY
Fashion Institute of Technology/State University of New York, NY
Franklin University, OH
Granite State College, NH
Juilliard School, NY
Maine College of Art, ME
Manhattan School of Music, NY
Mannes School for Music, NY
Maryland Institute College of Art, MD
Massachusetts College of Art and Design, MA
MCPHS University, MA
Milwaukee Institute of Art and Design, WI
Minneapolis College of Art and Design, MN
Montserrat College of Art, MA
Moore College of Art and Design, PA
Nebraska Methodist College, NE
New England Conservatory of Music, MA
NewSchool of Architecture & Design, CA
Otis College of Art and Design, CA
Pacific Northwest College of Art, OR
Parsons The New School for Design, NY
Research College of Nursing, MO
Rhode Island School of Design, RI
Ringling College of Art and Design, FL
Rocky Mountain College of Art and Design, CO
San Francisco Art Institute, CA
San Francisco Conservatory of Music, CA
Santa Fe University of Art and Design, NM
School of the Art Institute of Chicago, IL
School of Visual Arts, NY
Spalding University, KY
State University of New York/Empire State College, NY
Trinity College of Nursing and Health Sciences, IL
Union Institute & University, OH
University of North Carolina School of the Arts, NC
University of the Arts, PA
Westminster Choir College, NJ

AN EXPLANATION OF THE COLLEGE ENTRIES

THE BASICS

Over 1600 U.S. colleges and universities and Canadian and other foreign universities are described in detail in the Profiles that follow, as well as our web site, *www.barronspac.com*.

The Choice of Schools

Colleges and universities in this country may achieve recognition from a number of professional organizations, but we have based our choice of U.S. colleges on accreditation from the U.S. regional accrediting associations.

Accreditation amounts to a stamp of approval given to a college. The accreditation process evaluates institutions and programs to determine whether they meet established standards of educational quality. The regional associations listed below supervise an aspect of the accrediting procedure—the study of a detailed report submitted by the institution applying for accreditation, and then an inspection visit by members of the accrediting agency. The six agencies are associated with the Commission on Recognition of Postsecondary Accreditation (CORPA). They include:

Middle States Association of Colleges and Schools
New England Association of Schools and Colleges
North Central Association of Colleges and Schools
Northwest Commission on Colleges and Universities
Southern Association of Colleges and Schools
Western Association of Schools and Colleges

Getting accreditation for the first time can take a school several years. To acknowledge that schools have begun this process, the agencies accord them candidate status. Most candidates eventually are awarded full accreditation.

The U.S. schools included in this book are fully accredited or are candidates for that status. If the latter is the case, it is indicated below the address of the school. Because the U.S. regional accrediting bodies do not officially accredit Canadian colleges and universities, and because there is no equivalent accrediting system in Canada, we have chosen to include only the larger, English-language Canadian schools—those with total full-time undergraduate enrollment of more than 10,000. It should be understood that size in no way relates to quality; there are many excellent Canadian colleges and universities with fewer than 10,000 students.

Four-Year Colleges Only

This book presents Profiles for all accredited four-year colleges that grant bachelor's degrees and admit freshmen with no previous college experience. Most of these colleges also accept transfer students. Profiles of upper-division schools, which offer only the junior or senior year of undergraduate study, are not included, nor are junior or community colleges.

Consistent Entries

Each Profile of a U.S. college is organized in the same way; the only Profiles that vary are those of Canada, schools abroad, and religious schools. The following discussion applies to the U.S. college Profiles, but refers to the other Profiles as well.

Every Profile begins with a capsule and is followed by separate sections covering the campus environment, student life, programs of study, admissions, financial aid, information for international students, computers, graduates, and the admissions contact. These categories are always introduced in the same sequence, so you can find data and compare specific points easily. The following commentary will help you evaluate and interpret the information given for each college.

Data Collection

Barron's *Profiles of American Colleges* was first published in 1964. Since then, it has been revised every year online; comprehensive revisions are undertaken every year for the print edition. Such frequent updating is necessary because so much information about colleges—particularly enrollment figures, costs, programs of study, and admissions standards—changes rapidly.

The facts in the capsule portion of each Profile in this edition were gathered in the fall of 2016 and apply to the 2016–2017 academic year. Figures on tuition and room-and-board costs generally change soon after the book is published. For the most up-to-date information on such items, you should always check with the colleges. Other information—such as the basic nature of the school, its campus, and the educational goals of its students—changes less rapidly. A few new programs of study might be added or new services made available, but the basic educational offerings generally will remain constant.

THE CAPSULE

The capsule of each Profile provides basic information about the college at a glance. An explanation of the standard capsule is shown in the accompanying box.

All toll-free phone numbers are presumed to be out-of-state or both in-state and out-of-state, unless noted.

A former name is given if the name has been changed recently. To use the map code to the right of the college name, turn to the appropriate college-locator map at the beginning of each chapter. Wherever "n/av" is used in the capsule, it means the information was not available. The abbreviation "n/app" means not applicable.

Full-time, Part-time, Graduate

Enrollment figures are the clearest indication of the size of a college, and show whether or not it is coeducational and what the

---

COMPLETE NAME OF SCHOOL **MAP CODE**
(Former Name, if any)
City, State, Zip Code **Phone Numbers, Fax and E-mail**

Full-time: Full-time undergraduate enrollment
Part-time: Part-time undergraduate enrollment
Graduate: Graduate enrollment
Year: Semesters, quarters, summer sessions
Room & Board: Yearly room-and-board costs
Faculty: Number of full-time faculty; AAUP category of school, salary-level symbol
Ph.D.s: Percentage of faculty holding Ph.D.
Student/Faculty: Full-time student/full-time faculty ratio
Tuition: Yearly tuition and fees (out-of-state if different)
Freshman Class: Number of students who applied, number accepted, number enrolled
SAT: Median Critical Reading, Median Math, Median Writing (abbreviated CR/M/W)
ACT: Median composite ACT
Application Deadline: Fall admission deadline
CEEB Code: 0101
ADMISSIONS SELECTOR RATING

male-female ratio is. Graduate enrollment is presented to give a better idea of the size of the entire student body; some schools have far more graduate students enrolled than undergraduates.

Year
Some of the more innovative college calendars include the 4-1-4, 3-2-3, 3-3-1, and 1-3-1-4-3 terms. College administrators sometimes utilize various intersessions or interims—special short terms—for projects, independent study, short courses, or travel programs. The early semester calendar, which allows students to finish spring semesters earlier than those of the traditional semester calendar, gives students a head start on finding summer jobs. A modified semester (4-1-4) system provides a January or winter term, approximately four weeks long, for special projects that usually earn the same credit as one semester-long course. The trimester calendar divides the year into three equal parts; students may attend college during all three but generally take a vacation during any one. The quarter calendar divides the year into four equal parts; students usually attend for three quarters each year. The capsule also indicates schools that offer a summer session.

Application Deadline
Indicated here is the deadline for applications for admission to the fall semester. If there are no specific deadlines, it will say "open." Application deadlines for admission to other semesters are, where available, given in the admissions section of the profile.

CEEB Code
This is a standardized identification number assigned to a college or university by the Educational Testing Service (ETS).

Faculty
The first number given refers to the number of full-time faculty members at the college or university.

The Roman numeral and symbol that follow represent the salary level of faculty at the entire institution as compared with faculty salaries nationally. This information is based on the salary report* published by the American Association of University Professors (AAUP). The Roman numeral refers to the AAUP category to which the particular college or university is assigned. (This allows for comparison of faculty salaries at the same types of schools.) Category I includes "institutions that offer the doctorate degree, and that conferred in the most recent three years an annual average of fifteen or more earned doctorates covering a minimum of three nonrelated disciplines." Category IIA includes "institutions awarding degrees above the baccalaureate, but not included in Category I." Category IIB includes "institutions awarding only the baccalaureate or equivalent degree." Category III includes "institutions with academic ranks, mostly two-year institutions." Category IV includes "institutions without academic ranks." (With the exception of a few liberal arts colleges, this category includes mostly two-year institutions.)

The symbol that follows the Roman numeral indicates into which percentile range the average salary of professors, associate professors, assistant professors, and instructors at the school falls, as compared with other schools in the same AAUP category. The symbols used in this book represent the following:

++$	95th percentile and above
+$	80th–94.9th percentile
av$	60th–79.9th percentile
–$	40th–59.9th percentile
––$	39.9th percentile and below

If the school is not a member of AAUP, nothing will appear.

*Source: Annual Report on the Economic Status of the Profession published in the March-April 2016 issue of *Academe:* Bulletin of the AAUP, American Association of University Professors, 1133 Nineteenth Street N.W., Suite 200, Washington, DC 20036

Ph.D.s
The figure here indicates the percentage of full-time faculty who have Ph.D.s or the highest terminal degree.

Student/Faculty
Student/faculty ratios may be deceptive because the faculties of many large universities include scholars and scientists who do little or no teaching. Nearly every college has some large lecture classes, usually in required or popular subjects, and many small classes in advanced or specialized fields. Here, the ratio reflects full-time students and full-time faculty, and some colleges utilize the services of a large part-time faculty. Additionally, some institutions factor in an FTE component in determining this ratio. We do not, and thus the Student/Faculty ratio that we report may differ somewhat from what the college reports. In general, a student/faculty ratio of 10 to 1 is very good.

If the faculty and student body are both mostly part-time, the entry will say "n/app."

Tuition
It is important to remember that tuition costs change continually and that in many cases, these changes are substantial. Particularly heavy increases have occurred recently and will continue to occur. On the other hand, some smaller colleges are being encouraged to lower tuitions, in order to make higher education more affordable. Students are therefore urged to contact individual colleges for the most current tuition figures.

The figure given here includes tuition and student fees for the school's standard academic year. If costs differ for state residents and out-of-state residents, the figure for nonresidents is given in parentheses. Where tuition costs are listed per credit hour (p/c), per course (p/course), or per unit (p/unit), student fees are not included. In some university systems, tuition is the same for all schools. However, student fees, and therefore the total tuition figure, may vary from school to school.

Room and Board
It is suggested that students check with individual schools for the most current room-and-board figures because, like tuition figures, they increase continually. The room-and-board figures given here represent the annual cost of a double room and all meals. The word "none" indicates that the college does not charge for room and board; "n/app" indicates that room and board are not provided.

Freshman Class
The numbers apply to the number of students who applied, were accepted, and enrolled in the 2016–2017 freshman class or in a recent class.

SAT, ACT
Whenever available, the median SAT scores—Critical Reading, Math, and Writing--and the median ACT composite score for the 2016–2017 freshmen class are given. If the school has not reported median SAT or ACT scores, the capsule indicates whether the SAT or ACT is required. Note: New SAT scores have been established, but not all schools have adjusted to the new standards. The new procedure is as follows: SAT: Evidence-Based Reading and Writing; SAT: Math. Please refer to our website in late 2017 for any updates.

Admissions Selector Rating
The College Admissions Selector Rating indicates the degree of competitiveness of admission to the college.

THE GENERAL DESCRIPTION

The Introductory Paragraph

This paragraph indicates, in general, what types of programs the college offers, when it was founded, whether it is public or private, and its religious affiliation. Baccalaureate program accreditation and information on the size of the school's library collection are also provided.

In evaluating the size of the collection, keep in mind the difference between college and university libraries: A university's graduate and professional schools require many specialized books that would be of no value to an undergraduate. For a university, a ratio of one undergraduate to 500 books generally means an outstanding library, one to 200 an adequate library, one to 100 an inferior library. For a college, a ratio of one to 400 is outstanding, one to 300 superior, one to 200 adequate, one to 50 inferior.

These figures are somewhat arbitrary, because a large university with many professional schools or campuses requires more books than a smaller university. Furthermore, a recently founded college would be expected to have fewer books than an older school, since it has not inherited from the past what might be a great quantity of outdated and useless books. Most libraries can make up for deficiencies through interlibrary loans.

The ratio of students to the number of subscriptions to periodicals is less meaningful, and again, a university requires more periodicals than a college. But for a university, subscription to more than 15,000 periodicals is outstanding, and 6000 is generally more than adequate. For a college, 1500 subscriptions is exceptional, 700 very good, and 400 adequate. Subscription to fewer than 200 periodicals generally implies an inferior library with a very tight budget. Microform items are assuming greater importance within a library's holdings, and this information is included when available. Services of a Learning Resource Center and special facilities, such as a museum, radio or TV station, and Internet access are also described in this paragraph.

This paragraph also provides information on the campus: its size, the type of area in which it is located, and its proximity to a large city.

At most institutions, the existence of classrooms, administrative offices, and dining facilities may be taken for granted, and they generally are not mentioned in the entries unless they have been recently constructed or are considered exceptional.

Student Life

This section, with subdivisions that detail housing, campus activities, sports, facilities for disabled students, services offered to students, and campus safety concentrates on the everyday life of students.

The introductory paragraph, which includes various characteristics of the student body, gives an idea of the mix of attitudes and backgrounds. It includes, where available, percentages of students from out-of-state and from private or public high schools. It also indicates what percentage of the students belong to minority groups and what percentages are Protestant, Catholic, and Jewish. Finally, it tells the average age of all enrolled freshmen and of all undergraduates, and gives data on the freshman dropout rate and the percentage of freshmen who remain to graduate.

Male to Female Ratio. When available, the ratio of male to female students on the college campus is provided for the school.

Housing. Availability of on-campus housing is described here. If you plan to live on campus, note the type, quantity, and capacity of the dormitory accommodations. Some colleges provide dormitory rooms for freshmen, but require upperclass students to make their own arrangements to live in fraternity or sorority houses, off-campus apartments, or rented rooms in private houses. Some small colleges require all students who do not live with parents or other relatives to live on campus. And some colleges have no residence halls.

This paragraph tells whether special housing is available and whether campus housing is single-sex or coed. It gives the percentage of those who live on campus and those who remain on campus on weekends. Finally, it states if alcohol is not permitted on campus and whether students may keep cars on campus.

Faculty/Classrooms. The percentage of male and female faculty is mentioned here if provided by the college, along with the percentage of introductory courses taught by graduate students (if any). The average class size in an introductory lecture, laboratory, and regular class offering may also be indicated.

Programs of Study

Listed here are the bachelor's degrees granted, strongest and most popular majors, and whether associate, master's, and doctoral degrees are awarded. Major areas of study have been included under broader general areas (shown in capital letters in the profiles) for quicker reference; however, the general areas do not necessarily correspond to the academic divisions of the college or university but are more career-oriented.

Activities

Campus organizations play a vital part in students' social lives. This subsection lists types of activities, including student government, special interest or academic clubs, fraternities and sororities, and cultural and popular campus events sponsored at the college.

Sports. Sports are important on campus, so we indicate the extent of the athletic program by giving the number of intercollegiate and intramural sports offered for men and for women. We have also included the athletic and recreation facilities and campus stadium seating capacity.

Graduates. This section gives the number of graduates in the 2016–2017 class, the most popular majors and percentage of graduates earning degrees in those fields, and the percentages of graduates in the 2016 class who enrolled in graduate school or found employment within 6 months of graduation.

Services

Services that may be available to students—free or for a fee—include counseling, tutoring, remedial instruction, and reader service for the blind.

Library/Resources. This section describes the number of publications and media in the library collection of the college. In addition, you will also find computerized library services available to students, as well as any special learning facilities.

Physically Challenged Students. The colleges' own estimates of how accessible their campuses are to the physically disabled are provided. This information should be considered along with the specific kinds of special facilities available. If a Profile does not include a subsection on the disabled, the college did not provide the information.

Special. Special programs are described here. Students at almost every college now have the opportunity to study abroad, either through their college or through other institutions. Internships with businesses, schools, hospitals, and public agencies permit students to gain work experience as they learn. The pass/fail grading option, now quite prevalent, allows students to take courses in unfamiliar areas without threatening their academic average. Many schools offer students the opportunity to earn a combined B.A.-B.S. degree, pursue a general studies (no major) degree, or design their own major. Frequently students may take advantage of a cooperative program offered by two or more universities. Such a program might be referred to, for instance, as a 3-2 engineering program; a student in this program would spend three years at one institution and two at another. The number of national honor societies represented on campus is included. Schools also may conduct honors programs for qualified students, either university-wide or in specific major fields, and these also are listed.

Visiting. Some colleges hold special orientation programs for prospective students to give them a better idea of what the school is like. Many also will provide guides for informal visits, often allowing students to spend a night in the residence halls. You should make arrangements with the college before visiting.

Campus Safety and Security. This section lists the safety and security measures that are in place on the campus. These vary among schools, but may include 24-hour foot and vehicle patrol, self-defense education, security escort services, shuttle buses, informal discussions, pamphlets/posters/films, emergency telephones, and lighted pathways/sidewalks.

Requirements

Wherever possible, information on specific required courses and distribution requirements is supplied, in addition to the number of credits or hours required for graduation. If the college requires students to maintain a certain grade point average (GPA) or pass comprehensive exams to graduate, that also is given.

This section also specifies the minimum high school class rank and GPA, if any, required by the college for freshman applicants. It indicates what standardized tests (if any) are required, specifically the SAT or ACT, or for Puerto Rican schools, SAT Spanish Test, and the Spanish-language version of the SAT. Additional requirements are given such as whether an essay, interview, or audition is necessary, and if AP*/CLEP credit is given. If a college accepts applications on computer disk or on-line, those facts are so noted and described. Other factors used by the school in the admissions decision are also listed.

Procedures. This subsection indicates when you should take entrance exams, the application deadlines for various sessions, the application fee, and when students are notified of the admissions decision. Some schools note that their application deadlines are open; this can mean either that they will consider applications until a class is filled, or that applications are considered right up until registration for the term in which the student wishes to enroll. If a waiting list is an active part of the admissions procedure, the college may indicate the number of applicants placed on that list and the number of wait-listed applicants accepted.

Transfer Students. Nearly every college admits some transfer students. These students may have earned associate degrees at two-year colleges and want to continue their education at a four-year college or wish to attend a different school. One important thing to consider when transferring is how many credits earned at one school will be accepted at another, so entire semesters won't be spent making up lost work. Because most schools require students to spend a specified number of hours in residence to earn a degree, it is best not to wait too long to transfer if you decide to do so.

International Students. This section begins by telling how many of the school's students come from outside the United States. It tells which English proficiency exam, if any, applicants must take. Any necessary college entrance exams, including SAT Subject tests, are listed.

Admissions

The admissions section gives detailed information on standards so you can evaluate your chances for acceptance. Where the SAT or ACT scores of the 2015–2016 freshman class are broken down, you may compare your own scores. Because the role of standardized tests in the admissions process has been subject to criticism, more colleges are considering other factors such as recommendations from high school officials, leadership record, special talents, extracurricular activities, and advanced placement or honors courses completed. A few schools may consider education of parents, ability to pay for college, and relationship to alumni. Some give preference to state residents; others seek a geographically diverse student body.

If a college indicates that it follows an open admissions policy, it is noncompetitive and generally accepts all applicants who meet certain basic requirements, such as graduation from an accredited high school. If a college has rolling admissions, it decides on each application as soon as possible if the applicant's file is complete and does not specify a notification deadline. As a general rule, it is best to submit applications as early as possible.

Some colleges offer special admissions programs for nontraditional applicants. Early admissions programs allow students to begin college either during the summer before their freshman year or during what would have been their last year of high school; in the latter case, a high school diploma is not required. These programs are designed for students who are emotionally and educationally prepared for college at an earlier age than usual.

Deferred admissions plans permit students to spend a year at another activity, such as working or traveling, before beginning college. Students who take advantage of this option can relax during the year off, because they already have been accepted at a college and have a space reserved. During the year off from study, many students become clearer about their educational goals, and they perform better when they do begin study.

Early decision plans allow students to be notified by their first-choice school during the first term of the senior year. This plan may eliminate the anxiety of deciding whether or not to send a deposit to a second-choice college that offers admission before the first-choice college responds.

Admissions Contact. When provided, this is the name or title of the person to whom all correspondence regarding your application should be sent. In addition, internet addresses are included here.

Financial Aid

This paragraph in each Profile describes the availability of financial aid. It includes the percentage of freshmen and continuing students who receive aid, the average freshman award, and average and maximum amounts for various types of need-based and non-need-based financial aid. Aid application deadlines and required forms are also indicated. The schools' FAFSA Code is also included.

* Advanced Placement and AP are registered trademarks owned by the College Entrance Examination Board. No endorsement of this product is implied or given.

PROFILES OF AMERICAN COLLEGES

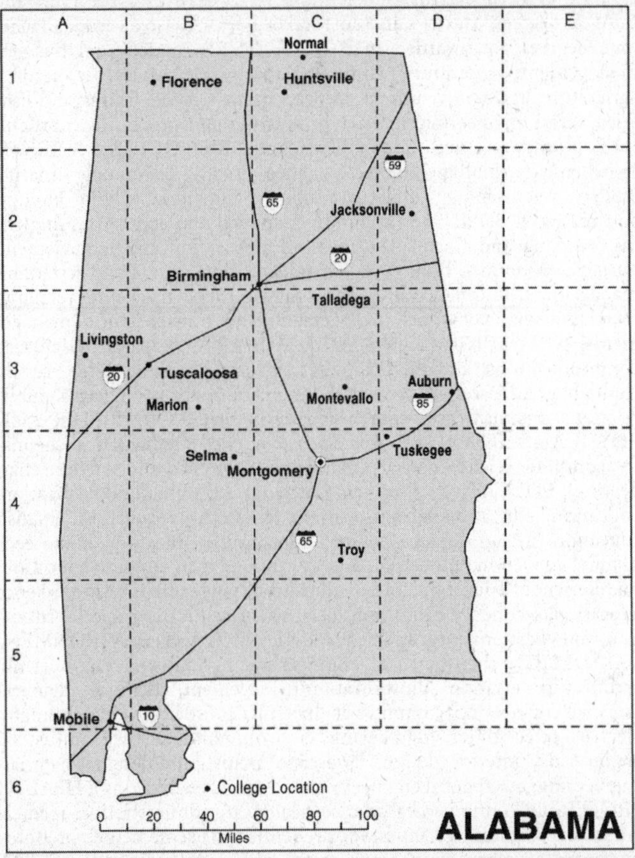

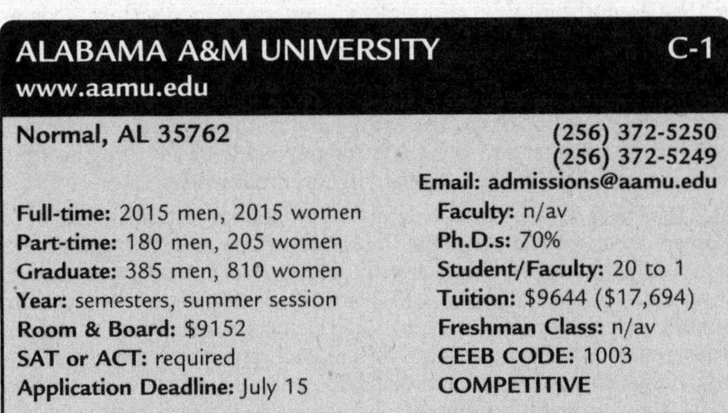

ALABAMA A&M UNIVERSITY C-1

www.aamu.edu

Normal, AL 35762

(256) 372-5250
(256) 372-5249
Email: admissions@aamu.edu

Full-time: 2015 men, 2015 women
Part-time: 180 men, 205 women
Graduate: 385 men, 810 women
Year: semesters, summer session
Room & Board: $9152
SAT or ACT: required
Application Deadline: July 15

Faculty: n/av
Ph.D.s: 70%
Student/Faculty: 20 to 1
Tuition: $9644 ($17,694)
Freshman Class: n/av
CEEB CODE: 1003
COMPETITIVE

Alabama A&M University, founded in 1875, is a public land-grant institution offering undergraduate and graduate studies. Reflecting its heritage as a traditional 1890 land-grant institution. AAMU functions as a teaching, research, and public service institution, including extension. There are 4 undergraduate schools and one graduate school. In addition to regional accreditation, A&M has baccalaureate program accreditation with ABET, ADA, AHEA, CSWE, FIDER, and NCATE. The 2300-acre campus is in a suburban area 90 miles north of Birmingham and 95 miles south of Nashville. Including any residence halls, there are 55 buildings.

STUDENT LIFE: 70% of undergraduates are from Alabama. Others are from 44 states, 11 foreign countries, and Canada. 90% are from public schools. 90% are African American; 6% White; 4% Foreign; 1% Asian American; 1% American Indian/Alaska Native; 1% Hispanic. 98% are Protestant. **Female To Male Ratio:** 1.2:1. The average age of freshmen is 18; all undergraduates, 20. **Housing:** 3100 students can be accommodated in college housing, which includes single-sex dorms. On-campus housing is guaranteed for all 4 years. 60% of students live on campus; of those, 60% remain on campus on weekends. Alcohol is not permitted. All students may keep cars.

FACULTY/CLASSROOMS: 50% teach undergraduates and 30% do research. No introductory courses are taught by graduate students. The average class size in an introductory lecture is 90; in a laboratory is 20; and in a regular course is 30.

PROGRAMS OF STUDY: A&M confers B.A., B.G.S., B.S., B.S.C.E., B.S.E.E., B.S.E.T., and B.S.M.E. degrees. Associate, master's, and doctoral degrees are also awarded. Bachelor's degrees are awarded in AGRICULTURE (agricultural business management, agricultural economics, agronomy, animal science, forestry and related sciences, horticulture, and soil science), BIOLOGICAL SCIENCE (biology/biological science, neurosciences, nutrition, and zoology), BUSINESS (accounting, banking and finance, business administration and management, management science, marketing/retailing/merchandising, and office supervision and management), COMMUNICATIONS AND THE ARTS (art, classics, dramatic arts, English, French, German, graphic design, jazz, journalism, linguistics, telecommunications, and theater design), COMPUTER AND PHYSICAL SCIENCE (chemistry, computer science, mathematics, and physics), EDUCATION (agricultural education, art education, early childhood education, elementary education, home economics education, industrial arts education, middle school education, music education, physical education, science education, secondary education, special education, and trade and industrial education), ENGINEERING AND ENVIRONMENTAL DESIGN (city/community/regional planning, civil engineering, civil engineering technology, drafting and design technology, electrical/electronics engineering, electrical/electronics engineering technology, environmental engineering, industrial engineering, industrial engineering technology, mechanical engineering, and mechanical engineering technology), HEALTH PROFESSIONS (medical laboratory technology, nursing, prepharmacy, preveterinary science, and speech pathology/audiology), SOCIAL SCIENCE (criminology, economics, family/consumer studies, food science, history, human development, humanities and social science, political science/government, psychology, social work, and sociology). Physics, food science, and teacher education are the strongest academically. Business administration, education, and computer science have the largest enrollments.

ACTIVITIES: 7% of men belong to 4 national fraternities; 9% of women belong to 4 national sororities. There are 109 groups on campus, including band, cheerleading, choir, chorus, computers, dance, debate, drama, drill team, ethnic, forensics, honors, international, jazz band, LGBT, marching band, newspaper, orchestra, pep band, political, professional, radio and TV, religious, social, student government, symphony, and yearbook. Popular campus events include Magic City Classic, Women's Week, and Men's Week. **Sports:** There are 7 intercollegiate sports for men and 7 for women, and 7 intramural sports for men and 7 for women. Facilities include a gym, an Olympic-size pool, bowling alley, an outdoor volley court, gyms, suspended 4-lane walking track, racquetball courts, weight room and cardio training area, multi-purpose activity rooms, and aerobic rooms. **Graduates:** The most popular majors were business administration, education, and computer science.

SERVICES: Counseling and information services are available, as is tutoring in most subjects. There is a reader service for the blind. **Library/Resources:** The library contains 253,620 volumes, 48,300 microform items, 3,010 audio/video tapes/CDs/DVDs, and subscribes to 2,070 periodicals including electronic. Computerized library services include interlibrary loans and database searching. Special learning facilities include an art gallery, radio station, TV station, and the State Black Archives Research Center and Museum. **Physically Challenged Students:** 85% of the campus is accessible. Facilities include wheelchair ramps, elevators, special parking, specially equipped restrooms, and lowered drinking fountains. **Special:** Co-op programs with Georgia Institute of Technology and Tuskegee University, cross-registration with the University of Alabama in Huntsville, Oakwood College, Calhoun Community College, and Athens State College, internships with various government agencies, dual majors, and work-study programs are available. There is a 3-2 engineering degree program with Georgia Institute of Technology. There are 5 national honor societies, a freshman honors program, and 5 departmental honors programs. **Visiting:** There are regularly scheduled orientations for prospective students, consisting of sessions in June, July, and November. Tours are not available during Spring break. The school hosts an Open House in March. There are guides for informal visits and visitors may stay overnight. To schedule a visit, contact the Office of Admissions at www.aamu.edu/admissions. **Campus Safety and Security:** Measures include 24-hour foot and vehicle patrol, self-defense education, and security escort services. There are lighted pathways/sidewalks.

REQUIREMENTS: The SAT or ACT is required, with a satisfactory score on the ACT. Applicants must have 4 years each of English, math, science, social studies, and history. An interview is recommended. The GED is accepted. A GPA of 2.0 is required. AP and CLEP credits are accepted. Important factors in the admissions decision are advanced placement or honors courses, leadership record, and recommendations by school officials. All students are required to take at least 52 hours of general studies, including phys ed, music, and art, and to maintain a minimum GPA of 2.0. Students must complete a total of 120 to 126 credit hours, with 30 to 36 in the major. A comprehensive exam is required for some majors. **Procedure:** Freshmen are admitted to all sessions. There are early decision, early admissions, deferred admissions, and rolling admissions plans. Applications should be filed by July 15 for fall entry; December 1 for spring entry; and May 15 for summer entry, along with a $30 fee. Applications are accepted on-line. **Transfer Students:** Transfer students must have a minimum GPA of 2.0 and have earned at least 12 semester credit hours. 30 of 128 credits required for the bachelor's degree must be completed at A&M. **International Students:** The school actively recruits these students. They must take the TOEFL.

Admissions Contact: Venita Clisby King, Director of Admissions. Email: *admissions@aamu.edu* Web: *www.aamu.edu*

FINANCIAL AID: In 2016-2017, 72% of all full-time freshmen received some form of financial aid. 75% of all full-time freshmen received need-based aid. The CCS/Profile, FAFSA, FFS, or SFS and the college's own financial statement are required. The FAFSA code is 001002. The priority date for freshman financial aid applications for fall entry is March 1.

ALABAMA STATE UNIVERSITY *(The complete profile is made available exclusively on our website, www.barronspac.com)*

AMRIDGE UNIVERSITY *(The complete profile is made available exclusively on our website, www.barronspac.com)*

AUBURN UNIVERSITY — D-3
www.auburn.edu

Auburn, AL 36849 — **(334) 844-4080**

Fax: (334) 844-4773	**Email:** admissions@auburn.edu
Full-time: 10,129 men, 10,267 women	**Faculty:** I, -$
	Ph.D.s: 89%
Part-time: 1484 men, 778 women	**Student/Faculty:** 19 to 1
Graduate: 2696 men, 2936 women	**Tuition:** $10,696 ($28,840)
Year: semesters, summer session	**Freshman Class:** 18,256 applied, 14,704 accepted, 4529 enrolled
Room & Board: $12,898	
SAT CR/M/W: 570/580/560 **ACT:** 27	**CEEB CODE:** 1005
Application Deadline: February 1	**VERY COMPETITIVE+**

Auburn University, founded in 1856, is a public land-grant institution awarding undergraduate and graduate programs in agriculture, business, education, engineering, forestry, and wildlife sciences, human sciences, liberal arts, nursing and sciences and math, with professional schools of pharmacy and veterinary medicine, and a graduate school. There are 11 undergraduate schools and 3 graduate schools. In addition to regional accreditation, Auburn has baccalaureate program accreditation with AACSB, ABET, ACCE, ACEJMC, ACPE, ADA, AHEA, ASLA, CSAB, CSWE, FIDER, NAAB, NASAD, NASM, NCATE, NLN, SAF, AABI, ACEND, ACEN, APA, ASHA, AVMA, CACREP, CCNE, CIDA, COAMFTE, CORE, NASPAA, NAST, and PAB. The 1875-acre campus is in a small town 110 miles southwest of Atlanta, GA. Including any residence halls, there are 452 buildings.

STUDENT LIFE: 63% of undergraduates are from Alabama. Others are from 51 states, 93 foreign countries, and Canada. 86% are from public schools. 84% are White. **Male To Female Ratio:** 1.0:1. The average age of freshmen is 18; all undergraduates, 20. 9% do not continue beyond their first year; 75% remain to graduate. **Housing:** 4798 students can be accommodated in college housing, which includes single-sex and coed dorms, on-campus apartments, and married student housing. In addition, there are honors houses, fraternity houses, and living and learning communities. On-campus housing is available on a first-come and first-served basis. 80% of students commute. Alcohol is not permitted. All students may keep cars.

FACULTY/CLASSROOMS: 62% of faculty are male; 38% are female. Graduate students teach 17% of introductory courses.

PROGRAMS OF STUDY: Auburn confers B.A., B.S., B.A.E., B.Arch., B.B.E., B.C.E., B.Che.E., B.E.E., B.F.A., B.Int. Arch., B.Int.Design, B.I.S.E., B.M.E., B.Mus.Ed., B.M., B.W.E., B.Mtl.E., B.P.F.E., and B.SW.E. degrees. Master's and doctoral degrees are also awarded. Bachelor's degrees are awarded in AGRICULTURE (agricultural business management, agricultural communications, agricultural economics, agriculture, agronomy, animal science, equine science, fishing and fisheries, forest engineering, forestry production and processing, horticulture, poultry science, and soil science), BIOLOGICAL SCIENCE (biochemistry, biology/biological science, botany, cell biology, marine biology, microbiology, molecular biology, nutrition, wildlife biology, and zoology), BUSINESS (accounting, apparel and accessories marketing, banking and finance, business administration and management, business economics, fashion merchandising, hotel/motel and restaurant management, international business management, marketing/retailing/merchandising, personnel management, and transportation management), COMMUNICATIONS AND THE ARTS (apparel design, art, communications, design, dramatic arts, English, fine arts, French, German, graphic design, industrial design, journalism, languages, public relations, Spanish, and speech/debate/rhetoric), COMPUTER AND PHYSICAL SCIENCE (actuarial science, applied mathematics, chemistry, computer science, geology, mathematics, physics, and software engineering), EDUCATION (business education, early childhood education, education, education administration, elementary education, English education, foreign languages education, health education, home economics education, industrial arts education, mathematics education, middle school education, music education, physical education, science education, secondary education, social science education, special education, and vocational education), ENGINEERING AND ENVIRONMENTAL DESIGN (aeronautical engineering, agricultural engineering, architecture, aviation administration/management, chemical engineering, civil engineering, computer engineering, construction management, electrical/electronics engineering, environmental science, industrial engineering, interior design, landscape architecture/design, materials engineering, mechanical engineering, and textile engineering), HEALTH PROFESSIONS (biomedical science, health care administration, medical laboratory technology, nursing, predentistry, premedicine, preoptometry, preveterinary science, and speech pathology/audiology), SOCIAL SCIENCE (anthropology, criminology, economics, food science, geography, history, home furnishings and equipment management/production/services, human development, philosophy, physical fitness/movement, political science/government, psychology, public administration, social work, sociology, and textiles and clothing). Engineering, education, and architecture are the strongest academically. Engineering, business, and liberal arts have the largest enrollments.

ACTIVITIES: 28% of men belong to 32 national fraternities; 43% of women belong to 20 national sororities. There are 479 groups on campus, including art, band, cheerleading, chess, choir, chorale, chorus, computers, dance, drama, drill team, environmental, ethnic, film, honors, international, jazz band, LGBT, literary magazine, marching band, musical theater, newspaper, opera, orchestra, pep band, photography, political, professional, radio and TV, religious, social, social service, student government, symphony, and yearbook. Popular campus events include A Day, Pep Rallies, and Tiger Nights. **Sports:** There are 8 intercollegiate sports for men and 11 for women, and 18 intramural sports for men and 18 for women. Facilities include an 87,451-seat stadium, 10,500-seat coliseum, baseball and softball stadiums, a women's athletics center, tennis center, aquatics center, soccer complex, track, intramural field houses, golf course, 2 equestrian arenas, student activities center with a volleyball arena, racquetball, tennis, basketball courts, fitness/weight room, and an aerobics/cardio theater. **Graduates:** From July 1, 2015 to June 30, 2016, 4420 bachelor's degrees were awarded. The most popular majors were business (20%), engineering (18%), and education (9%). 326 companies recruited on campus in 2015-2016. In an average class, 1% graduate in 3 years or less, 47% graduate in 4 years or less, 70% graduate in 5 years or less, and 75% graduate in 6 years or less. Of the 2015 graduating class, 42% were enrolled in graduate school within 6 months of graduation, and 83% were employed.

SERVICES: Counseling and information services are available, as is tutoring in most subjects. There is a reader service for the blind, and remedial writing. Auburn's Academic Support Services provides supplemental instruction and study partners through regularly scheduled peer-review sessions by students selected by the faculty. **Library/Resources:** The 3 libraries contain 4.5 million volumes, 2.6 million microform items, and 124,626 audio/video tapes/CDs/DVDs, and subscribe to 50,568 periodicals including electronic. Computerized library services include interlibrary loans, database searching, Internet access, and Wi-Fi capability. Special learning facilities include an art gallery, radio station, TV station, a nuclear science center, an arboretum, electron microscope laboratory, MRI research center, and a museum of fine arts. **Physically Challenged Students:** All of the campus is accessible. Facilities include wheelchair ramps, elevators, special parking, specially equipped restrooms, special class scheduling, lowered drinking fountains, special housing, elevators with Braille controls, wheelchair lifts, and asstistive technology lab. **Special:** An Honors College provides enhanced academic opportunities for qualified students, and a University College is available for students with still-developing or wide-ranging academic interests. Opportunities are available for co-op programs, internships, work-study, and dual majors on a program-by-program basis; students should contact their advisers for specific information. 3+2 engineering degrees are offered with numerous other liberal arts colleges or with Auburn's colleges of agriculture, liberal arts, or sciences and mathematics. Other options available to students include study abroad in more than 47 countries, credit by exam, non-degree study, and pass/fail grading on select courses. There are 42 national honor societies, Phi Beta Kappa, a freshman honors program, and 26 departmental honors programs. **Visiting:** There are regularly scheduled orientations for prospective students, including War Eagle Days, held in the fall and spring and offering students and their families an opportunity to meet with representatives from admissions, financial aid, housing, residence life, and various academic departments. There are guides for informal visits and visitors may sit in on classes. To schedule a visit, contact the Office of Admissions. **Campus Safety and Security:** Measures include 24-hour foot and vehicle patrol, emergency notification system, self-defense education, and security escort services. There are shuttle buses, emergency telephones, lighted pathways/sidewalks, and controlled access to dorms/residences.

REQUIREMENTS: The SAT or ACT is required. Favorable consideration for admission will be given to accredited secondary school graduates whose college ability test scores and high school grades give promise of the greatest level of success in college courses. Secondary school students planning to apply for admission are required to complete 4 years of English, 3 years each of social studies and math, and 2 years of science. Applicants of a mature age who are not high school graduates may be considered for admission if their educational attainments are shown through testing to be equivalent to those of high school graduates. Tests include the USAFI General Education Development Test, the American College Test, or other tests recommended by the Admissions Committee. AP credits are accepted. To graduate, students must complete a minimum of 120 credit hours with a cumulative GPA of at least 2.0. All students must complete Auburn's Core Curriculum. These 41-42 credit hours of courses in writing, the humanities, the social sciences, and mathematics and the natural sciences provide students with a broad foundation for attainment of 11 shared general education competencies. Students must also choose a major curriculum and complete its requirements and those of their college or school. **Procedure:** Freshmen are admitted to all sessions. There are deferred admissions and rolling admissions plans. Applications should be filed by February 1 for fall entry; October 1 for spring entry; and February 1 for summer entry, along with a $50 fee. Notification is sent on a rolling basis. Applications are accepted on-line. **Transfer Students:** 1250 transfer students enrolled in 2015-2016. Transfer applicants must provide official transcripts from each college attended. A satisfactory citizenship record, a minimum 2.5 GPA on all college work, and eligibility to re-enter the institution last attended are required for transfer admission. All transfer students who have attempted 32 semester hours of college work must have earned a cumulative 2.5 GPA in at least 20 semester hours of standard academic courses, in addition to the overall 2.5 cumulative average. These 20 semester hours must include at least 1 course in English (college-level composition or literature) and 1 in natural science with a lab. 30 of 120 credits required for the bachelor's degree must be completed at Auburn. **International Students:** There are 584 international students enrolled. The school actively recruits these students. They must take the TOEFL with a minimum score of 550 on the paper-based TOEFL (PBT) or 79 on the Internet-based version (iBT). They must also take the SAT or ACT.

ADMISSIONS: 81% of the 2016-2017 applicants were accepted. The SAT scores for the 2016-2017 freshman class were: Critical Reading-- 11% below 500, 53% between 500 and 599, 28% between 600 and 699, and 8% between 700 and 800. Math-- 11% below 500, 45% between 500 and 599, 32% between 600 and 699, and 12% between 700 and 800. Writing-- 18% below 500, 52% between 500 and 599, 26% between 600 and 699, and 5% between 700 and 800. The ACT scores were 15% between 18 and 23, 52% between 24 and 29, and 32% above 30. 53% of the current freshmen were in the top fifth of their class; 82% were in the top two fifths. There were 59 National Merit finalists. **Admissions Contact:** Dr. Wayne Alderman, Dean of Enrollment Services. E-Mail: *admissions@auburn.edu* Web: *www.auburn.edu*

FINANCIAL AID: In 2016-2017, 75% of all full-time freshmen and 68% of continuing full-time students received some form of financial aid. 36% of all full-time freshmen and 36% of continuing full-time students received need-based aid. The average freshman award was $15,045. Need-based scholarships or need-based grants averaged $9,078; need-based self-help aid (loans and jobs) averaged $3,698; and non-need-based athletic scholarships averaged $37,285. 13% of undergraduate students work part-time. Average annual earnings from campus work are $4500. The average financial indebtedness of the 2016 graduate was $28,170. Auburn is a member of CSS. The FAFSA code is 001009. The priority date for freshman financial aid applications for fall entry is February 10. The deadline for filing freshman financial aid applications for fall entry is March 1.

AUBURN UNIVERSITY AT MONTGOMERY C-4

www.aum.edu

Montgomery, AL 36124 (334) 244-3668

Fax: (334) 244-3795
Full-time: 1086 men, 2009 women
Part-time: 433 men, 745 women
Graduate: 192 men, 413 women
Year: semesters, summer session
Room & Board: $5650
SAT: required **ACT:** 21
Application Deadline: August 1

Email: admissions@aum.edu
Faculty: IIA, -$
Ph.D.s: n/av
Student/Faculty: n/av
Tuition: $9640 ($20,710)
Freshman Class: 2905 applied, 2225 accepted, 594 enrolled
CEEB CODE: 1036
COMPETITIVE

Auburn University at Montgomery, was founded in 1967. There are 5 academic units: college of arts and sciences, college of business, college of education, college of nursing and health sciences, and college of public policy and justice. In addition to regional accreditation, AUM has a baccalaureate program accreditation with AACSB, NCATE, CCNE, and NAACLS. The figures in the above capsule are approximate. There are 5 undergraduate schools and 4 graduate schools. The 500-acre campus is in a suburban area 7 miles east of downtown Montgomery. Including any residence halls, there are 51 buildings.

STUDENT LIFE: 94% of undergraduates are from Alabama. Others are from 33 states, 31 foreign countries, and Canada. 52% are White; 36% African American. **Female To Male Ratio:** 1.9:1. The average age of freshmen is 19; all undergraduates, 23. 34% do not continue beyond their first year; 27% remain to graduate. **Housing:** 996 students can be accommodated in college housing, which includes coed dorms, on-campus apartments, and married student housing. In addition, there are special-interest houses, and gender-neutral housing. On-campus housing is available on a first-come and first-served basis. 77% of students commute. All students may keep cars.

FACULTY/CLASSROOMS: 45% of faculty are male; 55% are female. No introductory courses are taught by graduate students. The average class size in an introductory lecture is 46; in a laboratory is 23; and in a regular course is 25.

PROGRAMS OF STUDY: AUM confers B.A., B.S., B.L.A., B.S.B.A., B.I.S. and B.S.N. degrees. Master's and doctoral degrees are also awarded. Bachelor's degrees are awarded in BIOLOGICAL SCIENCE (biology/biological science), BUSINESS (accounting, applied economics / management, business administration and management, entrepreneurial studies, finance, marketing management, marketing/retailing/merchandising, organizational leadership and management, and personnel management), COMMUNICATIONS AND THE ARTS (communications, English, fine arts, and Spanish), COMPUTER AND PHYSICAL SCIENCE (chemistry, computer science, information sciences and systems, mathematics, and physical sciences), EDUCATION (elementary education, secondary education, and special education), ENGINEERING AND ENVIRONMENTAL DESIGN (environmental science), HEALTH PROFESSIONS (kinesiology, medical laboratory science, nursing, and speech pathology/audiology), SOCIAL SCIENCE (criminal justice, economics, geography information science, history, homeland security/emergency preparedness, international studies, legal studies, liberal arts/general studies, political science/government, psychology, public administration, and sociology). Accounting, management information systems, psychology, nursing, kinesiology, and political science are the strongest academically. Nursing, biology, and kinesiology have the largest enrollments.

ACTIVITIES: 2% of men belong to 3 national fraternities; 5% of women belong to 6 national sororities. There are 52 groups on campus, including art, cheerleading, computers, dance, drama, environmental, ethnic, honors, international, LGBT, literary magazine, musical theater, newspaper, political, radio and TV, religious, social, social service, and student government. Popular campus events include AUM Fest, Welcome Week, Spring Fest, Mardi Gras, Shriek Week, Dances, and Band Parties. **Sports:** There are 5 intercollegiate sports for men and 5 for women, and 12 intramural sports for men and 12 for women. Facilities include a multipurpose gym-auditorium, an indoor jogging and walking track, baseball and soccer fields, tennis courts, and softball field. A wellness center is available as part of students fees. **Graduates:** From July 1, 2015 to June 30, 2016, 594 bachelor's degrees were awarded. The most popular majors were business (27%), nursing (26%), and psychology (7%). In an average class, 7% graduate in 4 years or less, 17% graduate in 5 years or less, and 23% graduate in 6 years or less.

SERVICES: Counseling and information services are available, as is tutoring in most subjects. Assistive technology services are also available. There is a reader service for the blind, and remedial math, reading, and writing, study skills, Plagiarism Bootcamp, classroom workshops, plagiarism workshops, test prep workshops. **Library/Resources:** The library contains 341,612 volumes, 2.4 million microform items, and 2,971 audio/video tapes/CDs/DVDs, and subscribes to 209 periodicals including electronic. Computerized library services include interlibrary loans, database searching, Internet access, and Wi-Fi capability. Special learning facilities include an art gallery, radio station, TV station, geographic information systems and computer, cartography lab technology, liberal arts Taylor center, Goodwyn Hall, sciences Clement Hall, business education, developmental math lab, and the AUM library. There is also the learning center/instructional support lab, one-on-one appointments in writing across the curriculum, math, business topics, accounting, economics, history, and conversational English for ESL students instructional support lab. There is individual and small group tutoring in math and science. In the Quality Enhancement Programs (SACS) we offer writing for success, writing across the curriculum program which provides faculty development for certified Writing Intensive (WI) courses. Students are required to pass 5 WI courses in order to graduate writing in the disciplines (WID), interns offer writing tutoring attached to specific WI courses Center for Excellence in Learning and Teaching (CELT) Office of Global Initiatives: Global Education Office offers educational events to promote learning about world cultures; Global Learning Communities Study Abroad Program Enrollment Management: UNIV 1000 first year success course AUM Bridge Program student support program for incoming students lacking full admissions requirements; includes receiving case-managed academic advising and personalized tutoring; opportunity to participate in a residential living and learning; Warhawk Warning Program-- provides a way for faculty, staff, and administrators to bring a student that they perceive as struggling to the attention of another caring AUM employee in order to connect the student with services that may support their future success. AUM Common Reading Program (CRP)--provides students, faculty, staff, and members of the local community with opportunities to interact in meaningful conversations relating to contemporary social and cultural issues via an annual common reading selection. **Physically Challenged Students:** 95% of the campus is accessible. Facilities include wheelchair ramps, elevators, special parking, specially equipped restrooms, special class scheduling, lowered drinking fountains, lowered telephones, and special housing. **Special:** AUM offers study abroad opportunities, co-op program opportunities, internships, and cross-registration with Huntingdon College and Faulkner University. Our study abroad programs are located in eight different countries including China, Costa Rica, England (Oxford and Northampton), France, Japan, Mexico, South Korea, and Sri Lanka. AUM also has a cooperative program with Rheem Manufacturing through the Department of Information Systems. Numerous department-specific internships are also available. There are 10 national honor societies, a freshman honors program, and 1 departmental honors program. **Visiting:** There are regularly scheduled orientations for prospective students, including meetings with faculty, staff, advising, and registration. There are guides for informal visits and visitors may sit in on classes. To schedule a visit, contact Amanda Brasington at admissions@aum.edu. **Campus Safety and Security:** Measures include 24-hour foot and vehicle patrol, emergency notification system, and security escort services. There are emergency telephones, lighted pathways/sidewalks, controlled access to dorms/residences, personal safety seminars, and emergency preparedness seminars.

REQUIREMENTS: The SAT or ACT is required. High school preparation should include English, math, social studies, science, and foreign language. The GED may be used for admission. AP and CLEP credits are accepted. To graduate, students must complete a minimum of 120 credit hours with a minimum GPA of 2.0 in the major and overall. All students must fulfill English composition requirements and liberal education program requirements. All students must complete five writing intensive courses. **Procedure:** Freshmen are admitted to all sessions. Entrance exams should be taken in the junior year. There is a rolling admissions plan. Applications should be filed by August 1 for fall entry. Applications are accepted on-line. **Transfer Students:** Applicants for transfer must have a C average and be in good standing at their last school. 30 of 120 credits required for the bachelor's degree must be completed at AUM. **International Students:** There are 166 international students enrolled. The school actively recruits these students. They must take the TOEFL with a minimum score of 500 on the paper-based TOEFL (PBT) or 61 on the Internet-based version (iBT), or take the IELTS.

ADMISSIONS: 77% of the 2016-2017 applicants were accepted. The SAT scores for the 2016-2017 freshman class were: Critical Reading-- 78% below 500, 11% between 500 and 599, and 11% between 600 and 699. Math-- 67% below 500 and 33% between 500 and 599. Writing-- 88% below 500 and 13% between 500 and 599. The ACT scores were 74% between 18 and 23, and 26% between 24 and 29. **Admissions Contact:** Rahmel Cowen, Director of Admissions & Recruiting. Email: *admissions@aum.edu* Web: *www.aum.edu*

FINANCIAL AID: In 2016-2017, 83% of all full-time freshmen received some form of financial aid. The average freshman award was $10,914. Need-based scholarships or need-based grants averaged $5,002 ($7,215 maximum); and need-based self-help aid (loans and jobs) averaged $3,673 ($10,000 maximum). Average annual earnings from campus work are $4441. The FAFSA code is 36124. The priority date for freshman financial aid applications for fall entry is March 1.

BIRMINGHAM-SOUTHERN COLLEGE C-2
www.bsc.edu

Birmingham, AL 35254	**(205) 226-4696 (800) 523-5793**
Fax: (205) 523-3074	**Email: admission@bsc.edu**
Full-time: 673 men, 664 women	**Faculty:** IIB, av$
Part-time: 3 men, 6 women	**Ph.D.s:** 96%
Graduate: n/av	**Student/Faculty:** 13 to 1
Year: 4-1-4, summer session	**Tuition:** $33,128
Room & Board: $11,350	**Freshman Class:** 2005 accepted, 441 enrolled
SAT CR/M: required **ACT:** 26	**CEEB CODE:** 1064
Application Deadline: February 1	**VERY COMPETITIVE**

Birmingham-Southern College, founded in 1856, is a private liberal arts college affiliated with the United Methodist Church. BSC offers 30 undergraduate majors, 23 minors, and 10 special programs. The figures in the above capsule and in this profile are approximate. There is 1 undergraduate school and 1 graduate school. In addition to regional accreditation, BSC has baccalaureate program accreditation with NASM and NCATE. The 192-acre campus is in an urban area 3 miles west of downtown Birmingham. Including any residence halls, there are 50 buildings.

STUDENT LIFE: 54% of undergraduates are from out of state, mostly the South. Students are from 38 states, 21 foreign countries, and Canada. 65% are from public schools. 79% are White; 5% Asian American; 2% Hispanic; 11% African American; 1% American Indian/Alaska Native; 1% two or more races; 1% race unknown. 54% are Protestant; 16% claim no religious affiliation; 13% Catholic. **Male To Female Ratio:** 1.0:1. The average age of freshmen is 18; all undergraduates, 21. 19% do not continue beyond their first year; 71% remain to graduate. **Housing:** 1624 students can be accommodated in college housing, which includes single-sex dorms, on-campus apartments, and married student housing. In addition, there are honors houses, fraternity houses, and sorority houses. On-campus housing is guaranteed for all 4 years. 90% of students live on campus; of those, 80% remain on campus on weekends. All students may keep cars.

FACULTY/CLASSROOMS: 54% of faculty are male; 46% are female. All teach undergraduates. No introductory courses are taught by graduate students. The average class size in an introductory lecture is 16 and in a laboratory is 20.

PROGRAMS OF STUDY: BSC confers B.A., B.F.A., and B.S. degrees. Bachelor's degrees are awarded in AGRICULTURE (environmental studies), BIOLOGICAL SCIENCE (biology/biological science), BUSINESS (accounting and business administration and management), COMMUNICATIONS AND THE ARTS (art, art history and appreciation, English, film and media studies, music, musical theater, Spanish, studio art, and theatre arts), COMPUTER AND PHYSICAL SCIENCE (chemistry, mathematics, and physics), EDUCATION (collaborative education, education, and secondary education), ENGINEERING AND ENVIRONMENTAL DESIGN (engineering), HEALTH PROFESSIONS (nursing), SOCIAL SCIENCE (Asian/Oriental studies, biopsychology, economics, history, interdisciplinary studies, philosophy, political science/government, psychology, religion, and sociology). Biology, business administration, and English have the largest enrollments.

ACTIVITIES: 43% of men belong to 7 national fraternities; 52% of women belong to 7 national sororities. There are 81 groups on campus, including art, band, cheerleading, choir, chorale, chorus, computers, dance, debate, drama, environmental, ethnic, film, honors, international, jazz band, LGBT, literary magazine, marching band, musical theater, newspaper, opera, orchestra, pep band, political, professional, religious, social, social service, student government, symphony, and yearbook. Popular campus events include Halloween on the Hilltop, and E-Fest. **Sports:** There are 10 intercollegiate sports for men and 10 for women, and 10 intramural sports for men and 10 for women. Facilities include a football stadium, urban environmental park, a basketball and volleyball coliseum, baseball field, softball field, racquetball and tennis courts, 2 soccer fields, weight room, intramural athletic field, indoor pool, game room, indoor jogging track, 3 gyms, golf simulator, and an aerobics studio. **Graduates:** From July 1, 2015 to June 30, 2016, 220 bachelor's degrees were awarded. The most popular majors were biology, business administration, and English. 250 companies recruited on campus in 2015-2016. Of the 2015 graduating class, 42% were enrolled in graduate school within 6 months of graduation, and 52% were employed.

SERVICES: Counseling and information services are available, as is tutoring in most subjects. Through the use of peer tutors and one-on-one assistance, the Academic Resource Center also promotes the Foundation's general education goal of collaborative learning and peer-teaching in most subjects, including a specific emphasis on math and writing. **Library/Resources:** The library contains 263,024 volumes, 90,675 microform items, and 38,261 audio/video tapes/CDs/DVDs, and subscribes to 40,000 periodicals including electronic. Computerized library services include interlibrary loans, database searching, Internet access, and Wi-Fi capability. Special learning facilities include an art gallery, planetarium, an environmental center, an outdoor educational center, and two digital classrooms. **Physically Challenged Students:** 90% of the campus is accessible. Facilities include wheelchair ramps, elevators, special parking, specially equipped restrooms, special class scheduling, lowered drinking fountains, lowered telephones, and special housing. **Special:** There is cross-registration with the University of Alabama at Birmingham, Miles College, the University of Montevallo, and Samford University. Student-designed, dual, and interdisciplinary majors, internships, work-study programs, and study abroad are offered. There is a 3-2 nursing program with Vanderbilt University and a 3-2 environmental studies program wih Duke University. A 3-2 engineering degree is offered with the University of Alabama at Birmingham, Auburn University, Columbia University, and Washington University. There are 19 national honor societies, Phi Beta Kappa, a freshman honors program, and 5 departmental honors programs. **Visiting:** There are regularly scheduled orientations for prospective students. We're here to plan every aspect of your visit! Each visit will include a tour of campus and an information session with a member of our staff. From there, you can customize your visit with additional experiences. There are guides for informal visits, visitors may sit in on classes, and stay overnight. **Campus Safety and Security:** Measures include 24-hour foot and vehicle patrol, emergency notification system, self-defense education, and security escort services. There are shuttle buses, emergency telephones, lighted pathways/sidewalks, and controlled access to dorms/residences.

REQUIREMENTS: The SAT or ACT is required. We know you're more than a set of test scores, so when you apply, we'll get to know you no matter your numbers. Your engagement and accomplishments outside the classroom, leadership potential, course preparation, class rank, and more will be taken into consideration by our holistic review process. Applicants should have graduated from an accredited secondary school with 4 courses in English, 4 each in math, science, and social studies, and a recommended 2 in foreign language. The GED is also accepted. An essay is required and an interview is recommended. Fine arts majors are advised to submit a portfolio or arrange an interview with the fine arts department. BSC requires applicants to be in the upper 50% of their class. A GPA of 2.3 is required. AP and CLEP credits are accepted. Important factors in the admissions decision are advanced placement or honors courses, leadership record, and recommendations by school officials. All students must complete 32 units, including 2 Exploration terms. A GPA of at least 2.0 is required to graduate. **Procedure:** Freshmen are admitted fall, winter, spring, and summer. Entrance exams should be taken in the spring of the junior year or fall of senior year. There are early admissions and deferred admissions plans. Applications should be filed by February 1 for fall entry, along with a $50 fee. Notifications are sent March 1. Applications are accepted on-line. **Transfer Students:** 23 transfer students enrolled in 2015-2016. Transfer applicants must have a minimum GPA of 2.0 and leave their former school in good standing. An essay and a school recommendation are required. An interview is recommended. 16 of 32 credits required for the bachelor's degree must be completed at BSC. **International Students:** There are 39 international students enrolled. The school actively recruits these students. They must take the TOEFL with a minimum score of 500 on the paper-based TOEFL (PBT) or 61 on the Internet-based version (iBT). The SAT or ACT is required instead of the TOEFL for students whose primary language is English, with minimum English or verbal scores of 21 or 475.

ADMISSIONS: The SAT scores for the 2016-2017 freshman class were: Critical Reading-- 31% below 500, 45% between 500 and 599, 21% between 600 and 699, and 3% between 700 and 800. Math-- 20% below 500, 47% between 500 and 599, 28% between 600 and 699, and 5% between 700 and 800. Writing-- 16% below 500, 45% between 500 and 599, 28% between 600 and 699, and 12% between 700 and 800. The ACT scores were 29% between 18 and 23, 50% between 24 and 29, and 21% above 30. 52% of the current freshmen were in the top fifth of their class; 76% were in the top two fifths. There was 1 National Merit finalist. 5 freshmen graduated first in their class. **Admissions Contact:** Sara H. Newhouse, Assoc VP, Admission/Financial Planning. Email: *admission@bsc.edu* Web: *www.bsc.edu*

FINANCIAL AID: In 2016-2017, 100% of all full-time freshmen and 99% of continuing full-time students received some form of financial aid. 30% of all full-time freshmen and 39% of continuing full-time students received need-based aid. The average freshman award was $23,452. Average annual earnings from campus work are $2000. The average financial indebtedness of the 2016 graduate was $28,000. The FAFSA code is 001012. The priority date for freshman financial aid applications for fall entry is March 1.

CONCORDIA COLLEGE - ALABAMA *(The complete profile is made available exclusively on our website, www.barronspac.com)*

FAULKNER UNIVERSITY — C-4

www.faulkner.edu

Montgomery, AL 36109	(334) 386-7200 (800) 879-9816
Fax: (334) 386-7137	**Email:** admissions@faulkner.edu
Full-time: 745 men, 1026 women	**Faculty:** 98
Part-time: 256 men, 537 women	**Ph.D.s:** 66%
Graduate: 278 men, 420 women	**Student/Faculty:** 18 to 1
Year: semesters, summer session	**Tuition:** $19,280
Room & Board: $7130	**Freshman Class:** 1712 applied, 981 accepted, 297388 enrolled
SAT CR/M/W: required **ACT:** 21	**CEEB CODE:** 1034
Application Deadline: n/av	**COMPETITIVE**

Faulkner University, founded in 1942, is a private, multicampus university affiliated with the Church of Christ, offering undergraduate programs in Bible studies, business, education, and liberal arts and sciences.

The figures in the above capsule and in this profile are from a recent year. There are 4 undergraduate schools and 4 graduate schools. In addition to regional accreditation, Faulkner has baccalaureate program accreditation with NCATE and ABA. The 92-acre campus is in an urban area 6.4 miles east of the Alabama State Capital in Montgomery, AL. Including any residence halls, there are 26 buildings.

STUDENT LIFE: 85% of undergraduates are from Alabama. Others are from 26 states, 31 foreign countries, and Canada. 75% are from public schools. 46% are White; 45% African American. 59% are Protestant. **Female To Male Ratio:** 1.6:1. The average age of freshmen is 19; all undergraduates, 28. 40% do not continue beyond their first year; 33% remain to graduate. **Housing:** 652 students can be accommodated in college housing, which includes single-sex dorms and on-campus apartments. On-campus housing is available on a first-come and first-served basis. Priority is given to out-of-town students. 72% of students commute. Alcohol is not permitted. All students may keep cars.

FACULTY/CLASSROOMS: 61% of faculty are male; 39% are female. 85% teach undergraduates. No introductory courses are taught by graduate students. The average class size in an introductory lecture is 19; in a laboratory is 14; and in a regular course is 13.

PROGRAMS OF STUDY: Faulkner confers B.A., and B.S. degrees. Associate, master's, and doctoral degrees are also awarded. Bachelor's degrees are awarded in BIOLOGICAL SCIENCE (biochemistry, biology/adolescence education, biology/biological science, environmental biology, and forensic psychology), BUSINESS (accounting, business administration and management, business information systems, human resources, management information systems, management science, and sports management), COMMUNICATIONS AND THE ARTS (choral music, English, information technology, literature, music, musical theater, theater design, and theatre studies), COMPUTER AND PHYSICAL SCIENCE (chemistry, computer information systems, computer science, industrial psychology/safety, information sciences and systems, informatics and computer science, and mathematics), EDUCATION (early childhood education, education, elementary education, English education, mathematics education, music education, physical education, science education, and social science education), HEALTH PROFESSIONS (predentistry, premedicine, preoptometry, prephysical therapy, preveterinary science, and sports psychology), SOCIAL SCIENCE (biblical languages, biblical studies, clinical psychology, counseling/psychology, criminal justice, criminology, history, humanities, law, law enforcement and corrections, legal studies, liberal arts/general studies, ministries, missions, philosophy, prelaw, social science, and youth ministry). Criminal justice, biology, and elementary education are the strongest academically. Biology, education, and sports management have the largest enrollments.

ACTIVITIES: 21% of men belong to 5 local fraternities; 34% of women belong to 5 local sororities. There are 26 groups on campus, including band, cheerleading, chorus, drama, honors, jazz band, literary magazine, marching band, musical theater, newspaper, pep band, religious, social, social service, student government, and yearbook. Popular campus events include Annual Bible Lectureship, Jamboree, and Fall Visitation Weekend. **Sports:** There are 5 intercollegiate sports for men and 5 for women, and 6 intramural sports for men and 6 for women. Facilities include a gym, multiplex, weight room, athletic weight room, walk/run track, exercise room, aerobics room, racquetball courts, game room, baseball and softball fields, and lighted tennis courts. **Graduates:** From July 1, 2015 to June 30, 2016, 452 bachelor's degrees were awarded. The most popular majors were business administration (35%), human resource management (21%), and criminal justice (17%). 26 companies recruited on campus in 2015-2016. In an average class, 10% graduate in 4 years or less, 33% graduate in 5 years or less, and 37% graduate in 6 years or less.

SERVICES: Counseling and information services are available, as is tutoring in most subjects. Attempts are made to fulfill all requests for tutoring, sometimes with peers. There is a reader service for the blind, and remedial math, reading, and writing. **Library/Resources:** The 2 libraries contain 769,046 volumes, 391,849 microform items, and 3,575 audio/video tapes/CDs/DVDs, and subscribe to 1,211 periodicals including electronic. Computerized library services include interlibrary loans, database searching, Internet access, and Wi-Fi capability. **Physically Challenged Students:** All of the campus is accessible. Facilities include wheelchair ramps, elevators, special parking, specially equipped restrooms, special class scheduling, and special housing. **Special:** A second bachelor's degree in a separate major may be completed with a minimum of 24 semester hours earned beyond the first degree. Cross-registration with Auburn University at Montgomery and Huntingdon College, dual majors, credit for life/military/work experience, and nondegree study are offered. Internships in education, psychology, criminal justice, Bible, and sports management are available, as are accelerated degree programs in some majors. There are 8 national honor societies, Phi Beta Kappa, a freshman honors program, and 1 departmental honors program. **Visiting:** There are regularly scheduled orientations for prospective students, we have three College Bound events (April, June, July) over a two day period that culminate in student registration. The week preceding the fall term is dedicated for an in-depth orientation we call Freshman Experience. There are guides for informal visits, visitors may sit in on classes, and stay overnight. To schedule a visit, contact Robin Byrd at (334) 386-7200. **Campus Safety and Security:** Measures include 24-hour foot and vehicle patrol and security escort services. There are lighted pathways/sidewalks and controlled access to dorms/residences.

REQUIREMENTS: The SAT is recommended. The ACT is required with a satisfactory score. Candidates must be graduates of an accredited secondary school, or have the GED equivalent, with a minimum of 15 academic units, including 3 in English. A GPA of 2.0 is required. AP and CLEP credits are accepted. Important factors in the admissions decision are leadership record, extracurricular activities record, recommendations by alumni, recommendations by school officials, advanced placement or honors courses, parents or siblings attended your school, and personality/intangible qualities. Students must complete a 52-semester-hour core curriculum, including courses in Bible, history, social science, English composition, literature, speech communication, physical and natural science, math, computer literacy, and phys ed. B.A. students must take 2 semesters of foreign language. At least 120 semester hours with a minimum GPA of 2.0 are required to graduate. **Procedure:** Freshmen are admitted fall, spring, and summer. Entrance exams should be taken during December. There is a rolling admissions plan. Application deadlines are open. Application fee is $25. Notification is sent on a rolling basis. Applications are accepted on-line. **Transfer Students:** 479 transfer students enrolled in 2015-2016. Applicants must be in good academic standing from another accredited college. 30 of 120 credits required for the bachelor's degree must be completed at Faulkner. **International Students:** There are 49 international students enrolled. They must take the TOEFL with a minimum score of 500 on the paper-based TOEFL (PBT) or 61 on the Internet-based version (iBT). They must also take the SAT or ACT, scoring 18.

ADMISSIONS: 57% of the 2016-2017 applicants were accepted. The SAT scores for the 2016-2017 freshman class were: Critical Reading-- 67% below 500, 26% between 500 and 599, and 7% between 600 and 699. Math-- 59% below 500, 37% between 500 and 599, and 4% between 600 and 699. Writing-- 70% below 500, 26% between 500 and 599, and 4% between 600 and 699. The ACT scores were 1% between 12 and 17, 70% between 18 and 23, 28% between 24 and 29, and 1% above 30. **Admissions Contact:** Neil Scott, Director of Admissions. Email: *admissions@faulkner.edu* Web: *www.faulkner.edu*

FINANCIAL AID: In 2016-2017, 98% of all full-time freshmen and 95% of continuing full-time students received some form of financial aid. 70% of all full-time freshmen and 63% of continuing full-time students received need-based aid. The average freshman award was $9,500. Need-based scholarships or need-based grants averaged $5,100; need-based self-help aid (loans and jobs) averaged $3,722; non-need-based athletic scholarships averaged $5,900; and other non-need-based awards and non-need-based scholarships averaged $9,200. 10% of undergraduate students work part-time. Average annual earnings from campus work are $1800. Faulkner is a member of CSS. The the state aid form and the college's own financial statement are required. The FAFSA code is 001003. The priority date for freshman financial aid applications for fall entry is February 10. The deadline for filing freshman financial aid applications for fall entry is March 10.

HUNTINGDON COLLEGE — C-4

www.huntingdon.edu

Montgomery, AL 36106	**(334) 833-4497** **(800) 763-0313**
Fax: (334) 833-4347	**Email: admiss@hawks.huntingdon.edu**
Full-time: 505 men, 376 women	**Faculty:** 46; IIB, --$
Part-time: 82 men, 185 women	**Ph.D.s:** 80%
Graduate: n/av	**Student/Faculty:** 19 to 1
Year: semesters, summer session	**Tuition:** $25,800
Room & Board: $9100	**Freshman Class:** 1716 applied, 974 accepted, 277 enrolled
SAT CR/M: required **ACT:** 21	**CEEB CODE:** 1303
Application Deadline: n/av	**COMPETITIVE**

Huntingdon College, founded in 1854, and affiliated with the United Methodist Church, is a private institution offering a liberal arts curriculum. Through its Huntingdon plan, the college provides hands-on experience through internships, service, and student-faculty research and exploration of the world through travel/study with faculty and fellow students; each student is also provided with a laptop computer. There is 1 undergraduate school. In addition to regional accreditation, Huntingdon has baccalaureate program accreditation with NASM and CAATE. The 71-acre campus is in a suburban area 90 miles south of Birmingham. Including any residence halls, there are 23 buildings.

STUDENT LIFE: 80% of undergraduates are from Alabama. Others are from 21 states, 3 foreign countries, and Canada. 86% are from public schools. 64% are White; 21% African American; 5% race unknown; 4% Hispanic; 4% two or more races; 1% Asian American; 1% American Indian/Alaska Native. 31% are Protestant; 28% Christian, Nondenominational, Pentecostal, Church of Christ and others; 19% claim no religious affiliation. **Male To Female Ratio:** 1.0:1. The average age of freshmen is 18; all undergraduates, 23. 38% do not continue beyond their first year; 39% remain to graduate. **Housing:** 627 students can be accommodated in college housing, which includes single-sex and coed dorms. In addition, there are fraternity houses and sorority houses. On-campus housing is guaranteed for all 4 years. 62% of students live on campus; of those, 70% remain on campus on weekends. Alcohol is not permitted. All students may keep cars.

FACULTY/CLASSROOMS: 55% of faculty are male; 54% are female. All teach undergraduates. No introductory courses are taught by graduate students. The average class size in an introductory lecture is 24; in a laboratory is 20; and in a regular course is 13.

PROGRAMS OF STUDY: Huntingdon confers B.A. and B.S. degrees (B.S. degrees can be earned in the Evening Studies program only) degrees. Bachelor's degrees are awarded in BIOLOGICAL SCIENCE (biochemistry, biology/adolescence education, biology/biological science, and cell biology), BUSINESS (accounting, business administration and management, and sports management), COMMUNICATIONS AND THE ARTS (art, communication rhetoric/communication, English, and music), COMPUTER AND PHYSICAL SCIENCE (chemistry, chemistry/adolescence education, chemistry/gen science second education, digital arts/technology, and mathematics), EDUCATION (collaborative education, elementary education, English education, history education, mathematics education, music education, physical education, and sports studies), HEALTH PROFESSIONS (exercise science), SOCIAL SCIENCE (Christian studies, criminal justice, history, political science/government, psychology, and religion). Biology and chemistry are the strongest academically. Sport studies, business administration, and biology have the largest enrollments.

ACTIVITIES: 18% of men belong to 3 national fraternities; 47% of women belong to 4 national sororities. There are 50 groups on campus, including art, band, cheerleading, choir, chorale, chorus, communications, drama, environmental, ethnic, honors, jazz band, literary magazine, marching band, newspaper, pep band, political, professional, religious, social, social service, student government, and yearbook. Popular campus events include Big Red Weekend, Presidential Convocation, Welcome Back Week, Homecoming Week, Countess of Huntingdon Ball, Home Football Games, Service of Lessons and Carols, Stallworth Lecture Series, Miss Huntingdon, CloverJam, Awards Convocation, and Baccalaureate. **Sports:** There are 8 intercollegiate sports for men and 8 for women, and 12 intramural sports for men and 12 for women. Facilities include a multipurpose student center with a refurbished gym for basketball and a fitness training facility with fixed and free weight machines, an athletic center with a gym used primarily for volleyball, sports medicine and athletic training facilities, a 3,000-seat football stadium, and state-of-the-art weight training and conditioning facilities. There are also outdoor tennis courts, softball, baseball, and soccer fields, an outdoor basketball court, and a sand volleyball court. **Graduates:** From July 1, 2015 to June 30, 2016, 249 bachelor's degrees were awarded. The most popular majors were business administration/business management (41%), human performance/sport studies (12%), and biology/cell biology (7%).

SERVICES: Counseling and information services are available, as is tutoring in some subjects, such as writing, mathematics, history, English, business, accounting, political science, religion, biology, and psychology. **Library/Resources:** The library contains 97,616 volumes, 61,402 microform items, and 4,569 audio/video tapes/CDs/DVDs, and subscribes to 190 periodicals including electronic. Computerized library services include interlibrary loans, database searching, Internet access, and Wi-Fi capability. Special learning facilities include an art gallery, the Bowman Ecological Study Center, Sybil Smith Hall, the Dr. Laurie Jean Weil Center for human performance and Archives for the Alabama-West Florida Conference of the United Methodist Church. **Physically Challenged Students:** 85% of the campus is accessible. Facilities include wheelchair ramps, elevators, special parking, specially equipped restrooms, special class scheduling, lowered drinking fountains, lowered telephones, and special housing. **Special:** Huntingdon currently offers more than 20 majors, the opportunity for travel/study experiences offered as part of regular educational costs, hands-on learning experiences in every program of study, dual majors, internships, and preprofessional advising. Cross-registration is available with Auburn University Montgomery, Faulkner University, and the Marine Environmental Sciences Consortium in Dauphin Island, Alabama. Work-study options are also available to qualifying students. There are 17 national honor societies, a freshman honors program, and 12 departmental honors programs. **Visiting:** There are regularly scheduled orientations for prospective students, and the Office of Admissions offers personal campus visits during the week (Monday-Friday) and select Saturdays. There are guides for informal visits, visitors may sit in on classes, and stay overnight. To schedule a visit, contact the Office of Admission. **Campus Safety and Security:** Measures include 24-hour foot and vehicle patrol, emergency notification system, self-defense education, and security escort services. There are emergency telephones, lighted pathways/sidewalks, controlled access to dorms/residences, weather alert broadcasts, and parking lot cameras in most lots.

REQUIREMENTS: The SAT or ACT is required. Prospective students must have received a high school diploma or its equivalency. AP, CLEP, IB, and dual enrollment credits are considered for acceptance. AP and CLEP credits are accepted. Huntingdon's core curriculum includes 39 hours of required courses, including 9 hours of religion/history of the church, 9 hours of writing/communication, and 3 hours each of fine art appreciation, history, literature, mathematics, natural sciences, social science and critical thinking (PACT). Students must maintain a minimum GPA of 2.0 over 120 credits for the bachelor's degree. Major requirements range from 30 to 60+ hours. **Procedure:** Freshmen are admitted fall, spring, and summer. Entrance exams should be taken in the spring of the junior year. There are deferred admissions and rolling admissions plans. Application deadlines are open. Applications are accepted on-line. **Transfer Students:** 55 transfer students enrolled in 2015-2016. Transfer students must have successfully completed 24 semester hours of non-remedial courses at a regionally accredited college or university and be in good standing at previously attended institutions, otherwise, students must meet the regular freshman admission requirements. Transfer admission to the Evening Studies Program should be referenced in the college catalog. 30 of 120 credits required for the bachelor's degree must be completed at Huntingdon. **International Students:** There are 5 international students enrolled. They must take the TOEFL with a minimum score of 500 on the paper-based TOEFL (PBT) or 45 on the Internet-based version (iBT). They must also take the SAT or ACT, scoring SAT 930/VERB 490 or ACT 20/ENGL 20.

ADMISSIONS: 57% of the 2016-2017 applicants were accepted. The SAT scores for the 2016-2017 freshman class were: Critical Reading-- 58% below 500, 37% between 500 and 599, and 5% between 600 and 699. Math-- 60% below 500, 33% between 500 and 599, and 7% between 600 and 699. The ACT scores were 11% between 12 and 17, 63% between 18 and 23, 24% between 24 and 29, and 2% above 30. 23% of the current freshmen were in the top fifth of their class; 54% were in the top two fifths. **Admissions Contact:** Laura Duncan, VP for Enrollment Management. Email: *admiss@hawks.huntingdon.edu* Web: *www.huntingdon.edu*

FINANCIAL AID: In 2016-2017, 100% of all full-time freshmen and 100% of continuing full-time students received some form of financial aid. 71% of all full-time freshmen and 68% of continuing full-time students received need-based aid. The average freshman award was $21,978. Need-based scholarships or need-based grants averaged $3,494; need-based self-help aid (loans and jobs) averaged $2,483; and other non-need-based awards and non-need-based scholarships averaged $16,213. The average financial indebtedness of the 2016 graduate was $33,503. The college's own financial statement is required. The FAFSA code is 001019. The priority date for freshman financial aid applications for fall entry is March 1. The deadline for filing freshman financial aid applications for fall entry is rolling.

JACKSONVILLE STATE UNIVERSITY *(The complete profile is made available exclusively on our website, www.barronspac.com)*

JUDSON COLLEGE B-3

www.judson.edu

Marion, AL 36756 (334) 683-5110
(800) 447-9472
Fax: (334) 683-5282 Email: admissions@judson.edu

Full-time: 1 men, 261 women	**Faculty:** 31
Part-time: 15 men, 70 women	**Ph.D.s:** 81%
Graduate: n/av	**Student/Faculty:** 9 to 1
Year: semesters, summer session	**Tuition:** $17,088
Room & Board: $9978	**Freshman Class:** 268 applied, 198 accepted, 68 enrolled
SAT or ACT: required	**CEEB CODE:** 1349
Application Deadline: open	**COMPETITIVE**

Judson College, founded in 1838, is a private women's liberal arts college affiliated with the Alabama Baptist Convention. Men are accepted only in the Distance Learning division of the college. Figures in the above capsule and in this profile are approximate. There is 1 undergraduate school. In addition to regional accreditation, Judson has baccalaureate program accreditation with NASM. The 118-acre campus is in a small town 75 miles southwest of Birmingham. Including any residence halls, there are 18 buildings.

STUDENT LIFE: 82% of undergraduates are from Alabama. Others are from 19 states, and 4 foreign countries. 77% are from public schools. 75% are White; 14% African American. 90% are Protestant. **Female To Male Ratio:** 20.7:1. The average age of freshmen is 18; all undergraduates, 25. 39% do not continue beyond their first year; 37% remain to graduate. **Housing:** 264 students can be accommodated in college housing, which includes single-sex dorms. On-campus housing is guaranteed for all 4 years. 57% of students live on campus; of those, 25% remain on campus on weekends. Alcohol is not permitted. All students may keep cars.

FACULTY/CLASSROOMS: 53% of faculty are male; 47% are female. All teach undergraduates. No introductory courses are taught by graduate students. The average class size in an introductory lecture is 23; in a laboratory is 12; and in a regular course is 7.

PROGRAMS OF STUDY: Judson confers B.A, B.Min., B.S. and B.S.W. degrees. Associate degrees are also awarded. Bachelor's degrees are awarded in AGRICULTURE (equine science), BIOLOGICAL SCIENCE (biology/biological science), BUSINESS (business administration and management), COMMUNICATIONS AND THE ARTS (applied music, art, English, and Spanish), COMPUTER AND PHYSICAL SCIENCE (chemistry and mathematics), EDUCATION (elementary education, English education, mathematics education, music education, science education, and social studies education), HEALTH PROFESSIONS (nursing), SOCIAL SCIENCE (criminal justice, history, interdisciplinary studies, psychology, religion, and social work). Biology, education, and business are the strongest academically. Biology, nursing, and psychology have the largest enrollments.

ACTIVITIES: There are no fraternities or sororities. There are 26 groups on campus, including art, band, choir, chorale, chorus, computers, departmental clubs, drama, environmental, honors, literary magazine, marching band, musical theater, newspaper, orchestra, photography, political, professional, religious, social, social service, student government, and yearbook. Popular campus events include Hockey Day, Junior-Sophomore Dance, Pageant, Christmas Tea and Vespers, and Rose Sunday. **Sports:** There are 6 intercollegiate sports for women, and 3 intramural sports for women. Facilities include an indoor swimming pool, equine center with class rooms, tack rooms, stalls, and a covered riding arena, tennis courts, wellness center, gym with an aerobics room and weight training facility, hockey field, softball field, soccer field, and a game room. **Graduates:** From July 1, 2015 to June 30, 2016, 58 bachelor's degrees were awarded. The most popular majors were nursing (34%), biology (12%), and English (9%). 10 companies recruited on campus in 2015-2016. In an average class, 3% graduate in 3 years or less, 10% graduate in 4 years or less, and 68% graduate in 5 years or less. Of the 2015 graduating class, 9% were enrolled in graduate school within 6 months of graduation, and 47% were employed.

SERVICES: Counseling and information services are available, as is tutoring in most subjects, such as math, English, history, business and others on request. There is remedial math and writing. **Library/Resources:** The library contains 59,096 volumes, 2,012 microform items, and 1,359 audio/video tapes/CDs/DVDs, and subscribes to 32,679 periodicals including electronic. Computerized library services include interlibrary loans, database searching, Internet access, and Wi-Fi capability. **Physically Challenged Students:** 75% of the campus is accessible. Facilities include wheelchair ramps, elevators, special parking, specially equipped restrooms, lowered drinking fountains, lowered telephones, and special housing. **Special:** Cross-registration with the Marion Military Institute is available for ROTC students. B.A.-B.S. degrees are offered in criminal justice, math, business, biology, psychology, and chemistry. Students study abroad in such places as Salzburg, China, India, Oxford, Uganda, Australia, Latin America, and the Middle East. Dual majors, an equine science program, an accelerated degree program, an interdisciplinary major, work-study programs, and internships are offered. Students may combine their Associate Degree in Nursing with Biology for a B.S. degree. There are preprofessional programs in health areas, engineering, and law. The Distance Learning program offers credit for prior learning experience and provides individually paced instruction leading to a baccalaureate degree. There are 7 national honor societies, a freshman honors program, and 19 departmental honors programs. **Visiting:** There are regularly scheduled orientations for prospective students, consisting of 3 college Scholarship Days, 1 in September, 1 in November and 1 in February, and a Junior Day in May. Activities include scholarship testing, an equine show, campus tours, faculty meetings, and financial aid planning. There are guides for informal visits, visitors may sit in on classes, and stay overnight. To schedule a visit, contact the Admissions Office. **Campus Safety and Security:** Measures include 24-hour foot and vehicle patrol, emergency notification system, self-defense education, and security escort services. There are emergency telephones, lighted pathways/sidewalks, controlled access to dorms/residences, and card access systems, are on classroom and administrative buildings.

REQUIREMENTS: Judson requires either the SAT or the ACT, along with a minimum composite score of 18. SAT applicants should have completed 17 high school credits, including 4 in English. Non-high school graduates must provide the GED equivalent. A GPA of 2.0 is required. AP and CLEP credits are accepted. All students are required to complete courses in English, history, multicultural studies, speech, religion, social science, math, science, humanities, computer literacy, health/phys ed, and women's studies. A total of 128 credit hours, with a minimum GPA of 2.0 (2.5 for education majors) is required to graduate. B.A. students must also complete at least 6 hours of foreign languages at the 200-level or above; B.S. students must complete at least 12 hours of math or science electives in addition to the core competency. A passing score is required on the English Language Usage Test and on the senior essay that meets the requirements of the Judson Quality Enhancement Plan. **Procedure:** Freshmen are admitted fall, winter, and summer. Entrance exams should be taken in the spring of the junior year. There are early admissions, deferred admissions, and rolling admissions plans. Application deadlines are open. The fall 2016 application fee was $35. Notification is sent on a rolling basis. Applications are accepted on-line. **Transfer Students:** 56 transfer students enrolled in 2015-2016. Transfer students must have a minimum GPA of 2.0 and be eligible to return to the school from which they transfer. 32 of 128 credits required for the bachelor's degree must be completed at Judson. **International Students:** There are 4 international students enrolled. The school actively recruits these students. They must take the TOEFL, with a minimum score of 500 on the paper-based TOEFL (PBT) or 61 on the Internet-based version (iBT), and the college's own test.

ADMISSIONS: 74% of the 2016-2017 applicants were accepted. 42% of the current freshmen were in the top fifth of their class; 67% were in the top two fifths. **Admissions Contact:** Layne Calhoun, Executive Director of Enrollment Service. Email: *admissions@judson.edu* Web: *www.judson.edu*

FINANCIAL AID: In 2016-2017, 100% of all full-time freshmen and 99% of continuing full-time students received some form of financial aid. 89% of all full-time freshmen and 87% of continuing full-time students received need-based aid. The average freshman award was $10,512. Need-based scholarships or need-based grants averaged $5,812 ($35,222 maximum); need-based self-help aid (loans and jobs) averaged $7,416 ($26,250 maximum); non-need-based athletic scholarships averaged $3,990 ($9,000 maximum); and other non-need-based awards and non-need-based scholarships averaged $8,037 ($35,222 maximum). 31% of undergraduate students work part-time. Average annual earnings from campus work are $899. The average financial indebtedness of the 2016 graduate was $24,374. The FAFSA code is 001023. The priority date for freshman financial aid applications for fall entry is March 1. The deadline for filing freshman financial aid applications for fall entry is July 1.

MILES COLLEGE *(The complete profile is made available exclusively on our website, www.barronspac.com)*

OAKWOOD UNIVERSITY C-1
www.oakwood.edu

Huntsville, AL 35896 (256) 726-7356 (800) 824-5312
Fax: (256) 726-7154 **Email:** admission@oakwood.edu
Full-time: 855 men, 857 women **Faculty:** n/av
Part-time: 143 men, 145 women **Ph.D.s:** 54%
Graduate: n/av **Student/Faculty:** n/av
Year: semesters, summer session **Tuition:** $27,038
Room & Board: $16,720 **Freshman Class:** n/av
SAT or ACT: recommended **CEEB CODE:** 1586
Application Deadline: open **COMPETITIVE**

Oakwood University, founded in 1896, is a private, historically black, Seventh-day Adventist institution, that aims to transform students through biblically-based education for service to God and humanity. The figures in the above capsule and in this profile are approximate. There is 1 undergraduate school. In addition to regional accreditation, Oakwood has baccalaureate program accreditation with ACBSP, ADA, CSWE, NCATE, AAADE, CADE, and NLNAC. The 1186-acre campus is in a suburban area 5 miles northwest of Huntsville. Including any residence halls, there are 30 buildings.

STUDENT LIFE: 79% of undergraduates are from out of state, mostly the South. Students are from 39 states, 22 foreign countries, and Canada. 52% are from public schools. 79% are African American; 12% Foreign. **Female To Male Ratio:** 1.0:1. The average age of freshmen is 19; all undergraduates, 23. 27% do not continue beyond their first year. **Housing:** 1173 students can be accommodated in college housing, which includes single-sex dorms and married student housing. On-campus housing is available on a first-come and first-served basis. Priority is given to out-of-town students. 71% of students live on campus; of those, 98% remain on campus on weekends. Alcohol is not permitted. Upperclassmen may keep cars.

FACULTY/CLASSROOMS: 51% of faculty are male; 49% are female. All teach undergraduates. No introductory courses are taught by graduate students. The average class size in an introductory lecture is 30; in a laboratory is 30; and in a regular course is 40.

PROGRAMS OF STUDY: Oakwood confers B.A., B.S., B.B.A., B.M. and B.S.W. degrees. Associate degrees are also awarded. Bachelor's degrees are awarded in BIOLOGICAL SCIENCE (biochemistry and biology/biological science), BUSINESS (accounting and business administration and management), COMMUNICATIONS AND THE ARTS (communications, English, foreign language, French, music, music business management, music performance, and Spanish), COMPUTER AND PHYSICAL SCIENCE (chemistry, chemistry education, computer mathematics, computer science, information sciences and systems, mathematics, and natural sciences), EDUCATION (business education, education, elementary education, English education, health and physical education, home economics education, mathematics education, music education, physical education, science education, and social science education), HEALTH PROFESSIONS (allied health, medical technology, and nursing), SOCIAL SCIENCE (dietetics, family/consumer studies, history, home economics, human development, international studies, ministries, physical fitness/movement, political science/government, psychology, religion, religious education, and social work). Biochemistry, chemistry, and nursing are the strongest academically. Business and biology have the largest enrollments.

ACTIVITIES: There are no fraternities or sororities. There are 20 groups on campus, including band, choir, chorale, drama, honors, international, newspaper, professional, radio and TV, religious, student government, United Nations children emergency fund social work club, and yearbook. Popular campus events include Convocations, Arts and Lecture Series and Centennial. **Sports:** There are 4 intramural sports for men and 3 for women. Facilities include a gym, skating rink, Olympic-size pool, tennis courts, playing fields, racquetball courts, and a weight room.

SERVICES: Counseling and information services are available, as is tutoring in most subjects. There is remedial math, reading, and writing. Testing, counseling, and developmental guidance services are available through the counseling center. **Library/Resources:** The library contains 125,373 volumes, 2,140 microform items, and 4,816 audio/video tapes/CDs/DVDs, and subscribes to 630 periodicals including electronic. Computerized library services include database searching. Special learning facilities include a radio station, and a Black History Museum. **Physically Challenged Students:** 80% of the campus is accessible. Facilities include wheelchair ramps, elevators, special parking, and specially equipped restrooms. **Special:** Students may cross-register with Alabama A&M, Athens State, or the University of Alabama at Huntsville. The college offers a student missionary abroad program as well as a study abroad program through the Adventist College Consortium. Internships, work-study, dual majors, independent study, life experience credit, and pass/fail options are also available. A second bachelor's degree is offered to students completing at least 160 semester credits. There are 1 national honor societies, Phi Beta Kappa, a freshman honors program, and 2 departmental honors programs. **Visiting:** There are guides for informal visits, visitors may sit in on classes, and stay overnight. To schedule a visit, contact the Enrollment Management. **Campus Safety and Security:** Measures include 24-hour foot and vehicle patrol and security escort services. There are lighted pathways/sidewalks.

REQUIREMENTS: The SAT or ACT is recommended. Applicants should be high school graduates with a minimum GPA of 2.0 and at least 11 academic units, distributed as follows: 4 in English, 2 each in math, science, and social studies, and 1 in typing. The GED is accepted. Two character references are required. Students with GPAs between 1.7 and 2.0 may be admitted on probation. Applicants admitted without test scores must take the ACT during freshman orientation. A GPA of 2.0 is required. AP and CLEP credits are accepted. Important factors in the admissions decision are recommendations by school officials, ability to finance college education, and leadership record. To graduate, students must complete 128 semester hours, including 30 in the major and 40 in upper-division courses, with a GPA of 2.0. Regular chapel attendance is required. All students must complete a liberal arts core, and must meet English oral and written proficiency requirements. **Procedure:** Freshmen are admitted to all sessions. Entrance exams should be taken before high school graduation. There are early decision and rolling admissions plans. Application deadlines are open. Application fee is $20. **Transfer Students:** Applicants must submit a college transcript and a statement of honorable dismissal. Grades of C minus or better transfer for credit. 32 of 128 credits required for the bachelor's degree must be completed at Oakwood. **International Students:** They must take the TOEFL and the college's own test. They must also take the SAT or ACT. Students may take the ACT on campus prior to registration.

Admissions Contact: Tracy Moore, Assistant Director of Admissions. Email: *admission@oakwood.edu* Web: *www.oakwood.edu*

FINANCIAL AID: Oakwood is a member of CSS. The college's own financial statement and student and parent federal income tax returns are required. The FAFSA code is 001033. The priority date for freshman financial aid applications for fall entry is March 1.

SAMFORD UNIVERSITY C-2
www.samford.edu

Birmingham, AL 35229 (205) 726-2871 (800) 888-7218
Fax: (205) 726-2171 **Email:** admission@samford.edu
Full-time: 1114 men, 2093 women **Faculty:** IIA, +$
Part-time: 46 men, 88 women **Ph.D.s:** n/av
Graduate: 820 men, 1310 women **Student/Faculty:** n/av
Year: 4-1-4, summer session **Tuition:** $29,402
Room & Board: $9830 **Freshman Class:** n/av
SAT CR/M/W: required **ACT:** required **CEEB CODE:** 1302
Application Deadline: July 1 **VERY COMPETITIVE**

Samford University, founded in 1841, is Alabama's top-ranked private university with nationally-ranked academic programs rooted in the university's historic Christian mission. Samford offers 30 undergraduate and graduate degree programs through 10 academic units: arts, arts and sciences, business, divinity, education, health professions, law, nursing, pharmacy and public health. There are 9 undergraduate schools and 10 graduate schools. In addition to regional accreditation, Samford has baccalaureate program accreditation with AACSB, ACPE, NASM, NCATE, CIDA, CCNE, and NAST. The 247-acre campus is in a suburban area

4 miles south of Birmingham, AL. Including any residence halls, there are 72 buildings.

STUDENT LIFE: 67% of undergraduates are from out of state, mostly the South. Students are from 39 states, 21 foreign countries, and Canada. 83% are White. 42% claim no religious affiliation; 20% Protestant. **Female To Male Ratio:** 1.8:1. The average age of freshmen is 19; all undergraduates, 20. 11% do not continue beyond their first year; 72% remain to graduate. **Housing:** 2315 students can be accommodated in college housing, which includes single-sex dorms and on-campus apartments. In addition, there are fraternity houses and sorority houses. On-campus housing is guaranteed for all 4 years, and is available on a first-come, and first-served basis. 69% of students live on campus. Alcohol is not permitted. All students may keep cars.

FACULTY/CLASSROOMS: 48% of faculty are male; 52% are female. No introductory courses are taught by graduate students. The average class size in an introductory lecture is 23 and in a laboratory is 13.

PROGRAMS OF STUDY: Samford confers B.S.B.A., B.S.E., B.S.N., B.A., B.F.A., B.M., B.M.E. and B.S degrees. Master's and doctoral degrees are also awarded. Bachelor's degrees are awarded in BIOLOGICAL SCIENCE (biochemistry, biology/biological science, marine science, and nutrition), BUSINESS (accounting, entrepreneurial studies, finance, management science, marketing management, and organizational leadership and management), COMMUNICATIONS AND THE ARTS (art, classics, communications, communication science, composition, English, French, German, graphic design, Greek, journalism, languages, Latin, music, music ministry, music performance, music theory and composition, musical theater, organ performance, piano/organ, piano pedagogy, Spanish, sports administration, theatre arts, and voice), COMPUTER AND PHYSICAL SCIENCE (chemistry, computer science, mathematics, physics, and science), EDUCATION (athletic training, early childhood education, elementary education, English education, global studies, music education, and secondary education), ENGINEERING AND ENVIRONMENTAL DESIGN (engineering physics, environmental science, and interior design), HEALTH PROFESSIONS (exercise science, health care administration, health promotion, healthy lifestyle management, health science, nursing, nutrition and dietetics, nutrition and wellness, pharmacy, public health, respiratory therapy, and sports medicine), SOCIAL SCIENCE (counseling/psychology, criminal justice, economics, geography, history, human development, international relations, Latin American studies, liberal arts/general studies, paralegal studies, philosophy, philosophy and religion, political science/government, psychology, public administration, religion, religious music, and sociology). Business, nursing, and liberal arts are the strongest academically. Nursing, journalism & mass communications, and early childhood/elementary/special education have the largest enrollments.

ACTIVITIES: 36% of men belong to 6 national fraternities; 57% of women belong to 8 national sororities. There are 130 groups on campus, including academic organizations/clubs and university sponsored organizations/clubs, art, band, cheerleading, choir, chorale, chorus, computers, dance, debate, drama, environmental, ethnic, film, honors, international, jazz band, literary magazine, marching band, musical theater, newspaper, opera, orchestra, pep band, photography, political, professional, radio and TV, religious, social, social service, student government, symphony, and yearbook. Popular campus events include Homecoming, Family Weekend, Hanging of the Green, Lighting of the Way,Welcome Back Week, Your School/Your City, Samford Arts, Connections, Step Sing, NCAA Division I Athletics, Samford Gives Back, Harry's Coffeehouse series, and Leadership Lunches. **Sports:** There are 8 intercollegiate sports for men and 9 for women, and 16 intramural sports for men and 16 for women. Facilities include football stadium, basketball courts, track and soccer stadium, baseball field, softball field, tennis pavilion and courts, volleyball court, four racquetball courts, a game room with two pool tables and two ping-pong tables, indoor walking track, dance studio, indoor pool and locker facilities, Alpine Tower is a 50-foot high structure, offering over 30 different climbing routes with varying degrees of difficulty, The Carolina Climbing Wall is a 50-foot high structure with windows that allows social climbing on both sides of the wall. **Graduates:** From July 1, 2015 to June 30, 2016, 803 bachelor's degrees were awarded. The most popular majors were health professions and related programs (6%). 163 companies recruited on campus in 2015-2016. In an average class, 59% graduate in 4 years or less, 70% graduate in 5 years or less, and 72% graduate in 6 years or less.

SERVICES: Counseling and information services are available, as is tutoring in most subjects. There is a reader service for the blind. **Library/Resources:** The 2 libraries contain 761,751 volumes, 678,778 microform items, and 13,244 audio/video tapes/CDs/DVDs, and subscribe to 31,549 periodicals including electronic. Computerized library services include interlibrary loans, database searching, Internet access, and Wi-Fi capability. Special learning facilities include an art gallery, planetarium, radio station, Center for Advocacy and Clinical Education, Center for Congregational Resources, Center for Children, Law, and Ethics, Center for Faith and Health, Center for Healthcare Innovations and Patient Outcomes Research, Center for Law and Civic Education, Center for Science and Religion, EDiscovery Institute and Review Center, Frances Marlin Mann Center for Ethics Leadership, Global Center, Health Care Ethics and Law Institute, Nursing School State of the Art Human Simulation Center, Business School Investment Center, and Conservatory. **Physically Challenged Students:** All of the campus is accessible. Facilities include wheelchair ramps, elevators, special parking, specially equipped restrooms, special class scheduling, lowered drinking fountains, and lowered telephones. **Special:** The Department of Physics offers a dual-degree engineering program jointly with the following universities: University of Alabama at Birmingham, Auburn University, and Mercer University (Georgia). The five-year program leads to two degrees: a bachelor of science degree from Samford with a major in engineering physics, and a bachelor of engineering degree from the participating university. Students in this five-year program will first pursue a three-year general curriculum at Samford, followed by a two-year general technical curriculum at one of the participating engineering schools. Samford University cooperates with the University of Alabama at Birmingham (UAB), Miles College, University of Montevallo, and Birmingham-Southern College in a student exchange program known as the Birmingham Area Consortium for Higher Education (BACHE). The program is designed to expand the undergraduate educational opportunities for students at these institutions. As part of its commitment to internationalization of the curriculum, Samford University provides a special opportunity for students and faculty to live and study in one of the most cosmopolitan and culturally rich cities of the world—London. Daniel House, Samford's London Study Centre, serves as home and classroom to students and faculty throughout the year in a variety of academic programs. Samford offers opportunities to travel and study in foreign countries for credit. The purpose of these programs is to prepare Samford students for global citizenship in the 21st century. More specifically, Samford seeks to expose students and faculty to the peoples and cultures of other nations; to provide on-site observation of historical, scientific, and cultural phenomena; and to provide opportunities for foreign language study within the cultural context of the target languages. There are 31 national honor societies, a freshman honors program, and 28 departmental honors programs. **Visiting:** There are regularly scheduled orientations for prospective students, and campus tours offered 6 days a week. Tours last 90 minutes followed by a 30-minute information session. Special arrangements can be made for overnight stay, class visitation, and/or meeting with Admission and Financial Aid counselors. There are guides for informal visits, visitors may sit in on classes, and stay overnight. To schedule a visit, contact the Office of Admission. **Campus Safety and Security:** Measures include 24-hour foot and vehicle patrol, emergency notification system, self-defense education, and security escort services. There are shuttle buses, emergency telephones, lighted pathways/sidewalks, controlled access to dorms/residences, and restricted access to campus during nighttime hours.

REQUIREMENTS: The SAT or ACT is required. Samford University seeks to enroll students capable of success in a challenging academic environment. Every applicant is evaluated individually on the basis of academic preparedness and potential, as well as personal fit with the mission and purpose of the university. The Admission Committee considers factors such as the rigor of the high school curriculum, grade point average, standardized test scores, and recommendations. AP and CLEP credits are accepted. Important factors in the admissions decision are advanced placement or honors courses, leadership record, and recommendations by school officials. The academic requirements for all students are to earn a minimum of 128 successfully completed credits, at least 50% of the credit for the first undergraduate degree from Samford. All undergraduates are required to take the University Core Curriculum at Samford (22 credits). **Procedure:** Freshmen are admitted fall, winter, spring, and summer. Entrance exams should be taken in the junior year. There are deferred admissions and rolling admissions plans. Applications should be filed by July 1 for fall entry, along with a $40 fee. Notifications are sent November 7. 236 applicants were on the 2016 waiting list; 40 were admitted. Applications are accepted on-line. Application fees are waived if application is completed on-line. **Transfer Students:**

113 transfer students enrolled in 2015-2016. Transfer students generally receive favorable admission review when they present a minimum cumulative 2.50 grade point average on all college-level coursework, provided they have attempted at least 24 credits, or 36 quarter credits, at institutions accredited by one of the regional accrediting agencies. If a student has attempted less than 24 credits of college-level coursework, an official high school transcript and official test scores must also be submitted in order to be considered for admission. 64 of 128 credits required for the bachelor's degree must be completed at Samford. **International Students:** There are 82 international students enrolled. The school actively recruits these students. They must also take the SAT or ACT.

ADMISSIONS: 91% of the 2016-2017 applicants were accepted. The SAT scores for the 2016-2017 freshman class were: Critical Reading--16% below 500, 45% between 500 and 599, 31% between 600 and 699, and 8% between 700 and 800. Math-- 22% below 500, 44% between 500 and 599, 27% between 600 and 699, and 5% between 700 and 800. Writing-- 18% below 500, 48% between 500 and 599, 28% between 600 and 699, and 5% between 700 and 800. The ACT scores were 1% between 12 and 17, 26% between 18 and 23, 54% between 24 and 29, and 19% above 30. 49% of the current freshmen were in the top fifth of their class; 76% were in the top two fifths. There were 4 National Merit finalists. **Admissions Contact:** Jason E. Black, Dean of Admission. Email: *admission@samford.edu* Web: *www.samford.edu*

FINANCIAL AID: In 2016-2017, 98% of all full-time freshmen and 93% of continuing full-time students received some form of financial aid. 49% of all full-time freshmen and 44% of continuing full-time students received need-based aid. The average freshman award was $20,049. Need-based scholarships or need-based grants averaged $4,321 ($39,544 maximum); need-based self-help aid (loans and jobs) averaged $2,904 ($25,000 maximum); non-need-based athletic scholarships averaged $14,165 ($41,000 maximum); and other non-need-based awards and non-need-based scholarships averaged $5,134 ($34,423 maximum). 16% of undergraduate students work part-time. Average annual earnings from campus work are $2459. The average financial indebtedness of the 2016 graduate was $29,794. The state aid form is required. The FAFSA code is 001036. The priority date for freshman financial aid applications for fall entry is March 1.

SPRING HILL COLLEGE A-5

www.shc.edu

Mobile, AL 36608	(251) 380-3030 (800) 742-6704
Fax: (251) 460-2186	Email: admit@shc.edu
Full-time: 508 men, 874 women	**Faculty:** 88
Part-time: 3 men, 11 women	**Ph.D.s:** 91%
Graduate: 50 men, 45 women	**Student/Faculty:** 16 to 1
Year: semesters, summer session	**Tuition:** $35,798
Room & Board: $12,690	**Freshman Class:** 8534 applied, 3715 accepted, 392 enrolled
SAT CR/M: 553/547 **ACT:** 24	**CEEB CODE:** 1733
Application Deadline: July 15	**COMPETITIVE**

Spring Hill College, founded in 1830, is the oldest Catholic college in the Southeast as well as the third oldest Jesuit college and fifth oldest Catholic college in the United States. Ranked among the top 20 Southern colleges and universities as "America's Best Colleges," its mission is to form students to become responsible leaders in service to others. The figures in the above capsule and in this profile are approximate. There are 8 undergraduate schools and 5 graduate schools. In addition to regional accreditation, Spring Hill has baccalaureate program accreditation with CCNE. The 381-acre campus is in a suburban area in Mobile, Alabama. Including any residence halls, there are 34 buildings.

STUDENT LIFE: 60% of undergraduates are from out of state, mostly the South. Students are from 32 states, 21 foreign countries, and Canada. 69% are White; 14% African American; 5% race unknown; 3% Hispanic; 3% Foreign; 3% two or more races; 2% Asian American; 1% American Indian/Alaska Native. 45% are Catholic; 30% Protestant; 23% claim no religious affiliation. **Female To Male Ratio:** 1.7:1. The average age of freshmen is 18; all undergraduates, 20. 24% do not continue beyond their first year; 53% remain to graduate. **Housing:** 1144 students can be accommodated in college housing, which includes coed dorms and on-campus apartments. In addition, there are special-interest houses. On-campus housing is guaranteed for all 4 years. 75% of students live on campus. All students may keep cars.

FACULTY/CLASSROOMS: 46% of faculty are male; 54% are female. 97% teach undergraduates. No introductory courses are taught by graduate students. The average class size in an introductory lecture is 23; in a laboratory is 15; and in a regular course is 18.

PROGRAMS OF STUDY: Spring Hill confers B.A., B.S. and B.S.N. degrees. Master's degrees are also awarded. Bachelor's degrees are awarded in BIOLOGICAL SCIENCE (biochemistry, biology/biological science, and marine biology), BUSINESS (accounting, business administration and management, international business management, marketing management, and organizational leadership and management), COMMUNICATIONS AND THE ARTS (arts administration/management, communications, digital communications, English, English writing, graphic design, journalism, public relations, studio art, and theatre arts), COMPUTER AND PHYSICAL SCIENCE (chemistry, computer science, and mathematics), EDUCATION (early childhood education, elementary education, and secondary education), ENGINEERING AND ENVIRONMENTAL DESIGN (engineering), HEALTH PROFESSIONS (health care administration, nursing, predentistry, premedicine, and preveterinary science), SOCIAL SCIENCE (biopsychology, economics, history, humanities, interdisciplinary studies, international studies, liberal arts/general studies, philosophy, political science/government, psychology, social science, sociology, Spanish studies, and theological studies). Business, biology, and nursing have the largest enrollments.

ACTIVITIES: 34% of men belong to 4 national fraternities; 38% of women belong to 6 national sororities. There are 57 groups on campus, including art, cheerleading, chorale, communications, computers, dance, drama, environmental, ethnic, film, honors, international, LGBT, literary magazine, newspaper, pep band, photography, political, professional, radio and TV, religious, social, social service, and student government. Popular campus events include Weeks of Welcome, Badger Expo, Christmas on the Hill, Free Art Fridays, Mardi Gras Week/Ball, Badger Brawl, Cajun Fest, McKinney Mixers, Family Weekend, and Badger Fest. **Sports:** There are 7 intercollegiate sports for men and 9 for women, and 12 intramural sports for men and 12 for women. Facilities include an 18-hole golf course, basketball courts, outdoor sand volleyball area, baseball, softball, rugby, and soccer fields. A recreation center houses the intercollegiate basketball arena, racquetball courts, weight-training and exercise facilities, an aerobic exercise room, and a running track. **Graduates:** From July 1, 2015 to June 30, 2016, 209 bachelor's degrees were awarded. The most popular majors were business (23%), psychology (12%), and communication arts (11%). In an average class, 46% graduate in 4 years or less, 52% graduate in 5 years or less, and 53% graduate in 6 years or less.

SERVICES: Counseling and information services are available, as is tutoring in some subjects, such as English, theology, math, languages, philosophy, economics, biology, chemistry, psychology, history and accounting. There is remedial math, reading, and writing. **Library/Resources:** The 2 libraries contain 188,926 volumes, 314,686 microform items, and 3,315 audio/video tapes/CDs/DVDs, and subscribe to 4,847 periodicals including electronic. Computerized library services include interlibrary loans, database searching, Internet access, and Wi-Fi capability. Special learning facilities include an art gallery, radio station, and a theater. **Physically Challenged Students:** 90% of the campus is accessible. Facilities include wheelchair ramps, elevators, special parking, specially equipped restrooms, special class scheduling, and special housing. **Special:** SHC offers dual degree engineering programs with the University of Alabama-Birmingham, Auburn University, the University of Florida, Marquette University, and Texas A & M University. The college is a member of the Marine Environmental Sciences Consortium and offers marine biology courses at the Dauphin Island Sea Lab. The college offers a study-abroad experience at its Italy Center in Bologna, Italy; other study abroad options are available through the CCSA (Cooperative Center for Study Abroad) consortium and the foreign study programs of other American Jesuit and non-Jesuit colleges and universities. Internships are available in many majors. There are 18 national honor societies and a freshman honors program. **Visiting:** There are regularly scheduled orientations for prospective students, campus tour, faculty appointment, attending a class, interview with an admission counselor. There are guides for informal visits, visitors may sit in on classes, and stay overnight. To schedule a visit, contact the Office of Admissions. **Campus**

Safety and Security: Measures include 24-hour foot and vehicle patrol, emergency notification system, self-defense education, and security escort services. There are emergency telephones, lighted pathways/sidewalks, and controlled access to dorms/residences.

REQUIREMENTS: The SAT is required, with the ACT is preferred. Applicants should have completed at least 16 high school units, including 4 in English, 3 each in math, science, and social studies, 2 in foreign languages, and 1 academic elective. The GED equivalent is accepted. AP and CLEP credits are accepted. All students must take core curriculum courses in English composition and literature, history, philosophy, theology, math, science, social science, fine art, and foreign language. Students must also take: one cultural diversity course; at least 3 writing-enriched courses (including one in the major) beyond the required 4 core curriculum English courses; and one LEAP (Learning, Engagement and Awareness, Personal Growth) course. Graduation requirements include completion of a minimum of 128 semester hours with a minimum GPA of 2.0 and 30 to 36 upper-division semester hours in the major with a minimum grade of C/C- (see department policy) in each of the major courses and prerequisites. **Procedure:** Freshmen are admitted fall, spring, and summer. Entrance exams should be taken in spring of the junior year or fall of the senior year. There are deferred admissions and rolling admissions plans. Applications should be filed by July 15 for fall entry; December 1 for spring entry, along with a $25 fee. Notification is sent on a rolling basis. Applications are accepted on-line. **Transfer Students:** 40 transfer students enrolled in 2015-2016. Transfer applicants must have at least 20 semester hours of college credit, a minimum college cumulative GPA of 2.5, good academic standing at the last college or university attended, and satisfactory recommendations. 32 of 128 credits required for the bachelor's degree must be completed at Spring Hill. **International Students:** There are 39 international students enrolled. The school actively recruits these students. They must take the TOEFL with a minimum score of 550 on the paper-based TOEFL (PBT) or 80 on the Internet-based version (iBT) or take the MELAB, or the IELTS. Students whose first language is English must take the ACT or SAT.

ADMISSIONS: 44% of the 2016-2017 applicants were accepted. The SAT scores for the 2016-2017 freshman class were: Critical Reading-- 20% below 500, 49% between 500 and 599, 29% between 600 and 699, and 2% between 700 and 800. Math-- 22% below 500, 60% between 500 and 599, 16% between 600 and 699, and 2% between 700 and 800. The ACT scores were 43% between 18 and 23, 49% between 24 and 29, and 8% above 30. 53% of the current freshmen were in the top fifth of their class; 80% were in the top two fifths. 8 freshmen graduated first in their class. **Admissions Contact:** Robert Stewart, Vice Pres for Admissions & Financial Aid. Email: *admit@shc.edu* Web: *www.shc.edu*

FINANCIAL AID: Spring Hill is a member of CSS. The the state aid form is required. The FAFSA code is 001041. The priority date for freshman financial aid applications for fall entry is March 1.

STILLMAN COLLEGE — B-3

www.stillman.edu

Tuscaloosa, AL 35403 — (404) 679-4501, (800) 841-5722

Fax: (205) 366-8817 — **Email:** admissions@stillman.edu

Full-time: 700 men, 800 women	**Faculty:** n/av
Part-time: 40 men, 40 women	**Ph.D.s:** 70%
Graduate: n/av	**Student/Faculty:** n/av
Year: semesters, summer session	**Tuition:** $13,682
Room & Board: $7056	**Freshman Class:** n/av
SAT or ACT: required	**CEEB CODE:** 1739
Application Deadline: n/av	**COMPETITIVE**

Stillman College, founded in 1876, is a small, private liberal arts institution affiliated with the Presbyterian Church. The figures in the above capsule and in this profile are approximate. There is 1 undergraduate school. In addition to regional accreditation, Stillman has baccalaureate program accreditation with NASM, NCATE, NCAA, and SIAC. The 105-acre campus is in a small town in Tuscaloosa, Alabama, just 52 miles from Birmingham. Including any residence halls, there are 26 buildings.

STUDENT LIFE: 70% of undergraduates are from Alabama. Others are from 27 states, and 8 foreign countries. 95% are from public schools. 98% are African American. 99% are Protestant. **Female To Male Ratio:** 1.1:1. The average age of freshmen is 19. **Housing:** 750 students can be accommodated in college housing, which includes single-sex dorms and off-campus apartments. On-campus housing is available on a first-come and first-served basis. 50% of students commute. Alcohol is not permitted. All students may keep cars.

FACULTY/CLASSROOMS: 40% of faculty are male; 60% are female. All teach undergraduates. No introductory courses are taught by graduate students. The average class size in an introductory lecture is 40; in a laboratory is 40; and in a regular course is 35.

PROGRAMS OF STUDY: Stillman confers B.A., and B.S. degrees. Bachelor's degrees are awarded in BIOLOGICAL SCIENCE (biology/biological science), BUSINESS (business administration and management), COMMUNICATIONS AND THE ARTS (art, English, and music), COMPUTER AND PHYSICAL SCIENCE (computer science and mathematics), EDUCATION (elementary education and physical education), HEALTH PROFESSIONS (premedicine), SOCIAL SCIENCE (history, prelaw, and religion).

ACTIVITIES: 10% of men belong to 4 national fraternities; 20% of women belong to 4 national sororities. There are 19 groups on campus, including art, band, cheerleading, choir, chorus, dance, debate, drama, honors, international, jazz band, marching band, newspaper, pep band, radio and TV, religious, social, social service, student government, and yearbook. **Sports:** There are 6 intercollegiate sports for men and 6 for women. Facilities include a college center, tennis courts, stress center, bowling lanes, billiards, swimming pool, gym, football field, and a weight room.

SERVICES: Counseling and information services are available, as is tutoring in some subjects, including reading, writing, math, physics, and chemistry. There is remedial math, reading, and writing. **Library/Resources:** The library contains 113,120 volumes, 7,240 microform items, and 3,550 audio/video tapes/CDs/DVDs, and subscribes to 360 periodicals including electronic. Computerized library services include interlibrary loans and database searching. Special learning facilities include an art gallery and radio station. **Physically Challenged Students:** Facilities include wheelchair ramps, elevators, special parking, and specially equipped restrooms. **Special:** Stillman offers local, national, and international opportunites for cooperative education and internships. Cross-registration is possible with the University of Alabama at Birmingham, with which there also are cooperative degree programs in nursing and allied health. Federal work-study is available on and off campus, and students may earn credit for prior learning experiences. There are 3 national honor societies. **Visiting:** There are regularly scheduled orientations for prospective students. To schedule a visit, contact the Director of Recruitment. **Campus Safety and Security:** Measures include 24-hour foot and vehicle patrol, self-defense education, and security escort services. There are lighted pathways/sidewalks.

REQUIREMENTS: The SAT or ACT is required. Applicants should be high school graduates or have earned the GED. Secondary preparation should include 4 units of English and 1 unit each of math, science, and history. All applicants must have an interview. Music majors must audition. AP and CLEP credits are accepted. To graduate, students must complete a minimum of 124 credit hours, with at least 30 in the major, and maintain a minimum GPA of 2.0 overall and in the major. The 53-credit-hour general education core includes courses in religion, logic, English composition, public speaking, African heritage, African American experience, history, social science, physical and life sciences, math, computer literacy, health, and phys ed. All students must submit a senior thesis and take a senior departmental exam. **Procedure:** Freshmen are admitted to all sessions. There is a rolling admissions plan. Check with the school for current application deadlines. The fall 2016 application fee was $25. **Transfer Students:** Transfer applicants should present at least a C average in previous college work and must plan to spend at least a year in residence. 64 of 124 credits required for the bachelor's degree must be completed at Stillman. **International Students:** The school actively recruits these students. They must take the TOEFL. They must also take the SAT or ACT.

Admissions Contact: Lu Ann Baker, Director of Admissions. Email: *admissions@stillman.edu* Web: *www.stillman.edu*

FINANCIAL AID: The CCS/Profile, FAFSA, FFS, or SFS and the college's own financial statement are required. The FAFSA code is 001044. The priority date for freshman financial aid applications for fall entry is March 1.

TALLADEGA COLLEGE C-2
www.talladega.edu

Talladega, AL 35160 (256) 761-6416
(800) 633-2440
Email: admissions@talladega.edu

Full-time: 270 men, 420 women
Part-time: 20 men, 30 women
Graduate: n/av
Year: semesters
Room & Board: $6704
SAT or ACT: required
Application Deadline: open
Faculty: n/av
Ph.D.s: 60%
Student/Faculty: 12 to 1
Tuition: $12,511 ($17,996)
Freshman Class: n/av
CEEB CODE: 1800
COMPETITIVE

Talladega College, founded in 1867, is a private liberal arts institution offering emphases on business, sciences, and social work. The figures in above capsule and in this profile are approximate. There is 1 undergraduate school. In addition to regional accreditation, Dega has baccalaureate program accreditation with CSWE. The 50-acre campus is in a small town 55 miles east of Birmingham and 115 miles west of Atlanta. Including any residence halls, there are 41 buildings.

STUDENT LIFE: 60% of undergraduates are from Alabama. Others are from 29 states, and 2 foreign countries. 99% are African American. 90% are Protestant. **Female To Male Ratio:** 1.6:1. The average age of freshmen is 18; all undergraduates, 20. 22% do not continue beyond their first year; 45% remain to graduate. **Housing:** 580 students can be accommodated in college housing, which includes single-sex dorms and on-campus apartments. In addition, there are honors houses. On-campus housing is guaranteed for all 4 years. 70% of students live on campus; of those, 90% remain on campus on weekends. Alcohol is not permitted. All students may keep cars.

FACULTY/CLASSROOMS: 60% of faculty are male; 40% are female. All teach undergraduates. No introductory courses are taught by graduate students. The average class size in an introductory lecture is 30; in a laboratory is 20; and in a regular course is 18.

PROGRAMS OF STUDY: Dega confers B.A. degrees. Bachelor's degrees are awarded in BIOLOGICAL SCIENCE (biology/biological science), BUSINESS (accounting, banking and finance, and business administration and management), COMMUNICATIONS AND THE ARTS (English and music performance), COMPUTER AND PHYSICAL SCIENCE (chemistry, computer science, mathematics, and physics), EDUCATION (music education), SOCIAL SCIENCE (economics, history, psychology, public administration, social work, and sociology). Business, biology, and chemistry are the strongest academically. Biology has the largest enrollment.

ACTIVITIES: 14% of men belong to 4 national fraternities; 40% of women belong to 4 national sororities. There are 23 groups on campus, including art, cheerleading, choir, chorus, computers, dance, drama, honors, jazz band, newspaper, professional, social, student government, and yearbook. Popular campus events include Spring Concert, Carnival and Coronation. **Sports:** There are 4 intercollegiate sports for men and 4 for women, and 8 intramural sports for men and 3 for women. Facilities include a swimming pool, a 150-seat gym, lounges, game rooms, tennis courts, and a baseball field.

SERVICES: Counseling and information services are available, as is tutoring in every subject. There is remedial math, reading, and writing. **Library/Resources:** The library contains 87,960, and 350 audio/video tapes/CDs/DVDs, and subscribes to 330 periodicals including electronic. Computerized library services include interlibrary loans. Special learning facilities include an art gallery, science drop-in center, curriculum and writing labs, and financial computer lab. **Physically Challenged Students:** 50% of the campus is accessible. Facilities include wheelchair ramps, elevators, special parking, and specially equipped restrooms. **Special:** Talladega offers co-op programs with other schools through individual departments, a 3-2 engineering degree with Auburn University, internships involving historic preservation work, work-study plans with Adopt-a-Family and Adult Literacy, and B.A.-B.S. degrees in biology, business administration, chemistry, and computer science. There are dual majors available in law, nursing, engineering, and allied health. There are 4 national honor societies. **Visiting:** There are guides for informal visits, visitors may sit in on classes, and stay overnight. To schedule a visit, contact the Admissions Office. **Campus Safety and Security:** Measures include 24-hour foot and vehicle patrol and security escort services. There are lighted pathways/sidewalks.

REQUIREMENTS: The SAT or ACT is required. Applicants must be graduates of an accredited secondary school with 22 academic units, including 4 in English, 3 in social studies, and 2 each in math, science, health/phys ed, and electives. The GED is considered. An essay and interview are recommended. An audition is required for music majors. A GPA of 2.5 is required. CLEP credits are accepted. Important factors in the admissions decision are advanced placement or honors courses, recommendations by school officials, and recommendations by alumni. To graduate, students must maintain a minimum GPA of 2.5 while taking 124 to 127 total semester hours, including 60 in the major and completion of a core curriculum. Distribution requirements at the freshman level include 8 semester hours in natural sciences, 6 each in communications, social sciences, and humanities, 2 in phys ed, and 1 in freshman orientation; additional hours in these subjects vary by major at the sophomore level. **Procedure:** Freshmen are admitted fall and spring. Entrance exams should be taken in the junior year. There are deferred admissions and rolling admissions plans. Application deadlines are open. The fall 2016 application fee was $10. Applications are accepted on-line. **Transfer Students:** Applicants must have a cumulative GPA of 2.0 in college work. The SAT or ACT is recommended. 60 of 124 credits required for the bachelor's degree must be completed at Dega. **International Students:** The school actively recruits these students. They must take the TOEFL and the college's own test. They must also take the SAT or ACT.

Admissions Contact: Monroe Thornton, Admissions Office. Email: *admissions@talladega.edu* Web: *www.talladega.edu*

FINANCIAL AID: The CCS/Profile, FAFSA, FFS, or SFS and the college's own financial statement are required. The FAFSA code is 001046. The priority date for freshman financial aid applications for fall entry is March 1.

TROY UNIVERSITY C-4
www.troy.edu

Troy, AL 36082 (334) 670-3179
(800) 551-9716
Fax: (334) 670-3733 Email: ask@troy.edu

Full-time: 3534 men, 5417 women
Part-time: 2175 men, 2438 women
Graduate: 1120 men, 3246 women
Year: semesters, summer session
Room & Board: $6526
SAT or ACT: required
Application Deadline: open
Faculty: IIA, --$
Ph.D.s: n/av
Student/Faculty: n/av
Tuition: $9646 ($18,256)
Freshman Class: n/av
CEEB CODE: 1738
COMPETITIVE

Troy University, founded in 1887, is a public institution composed of a network of campuses throughout Alabama and worldwide. International in scope, Troy University provides a variety of educational programs at the undergraduate and graduate levels for a diverse student body. Academic programs are offered in traditional, nontraditional and emerging electronic formats. Information in this profile applies to the Troy, Phenix City, Dothan, and Montgomery campuses and University College sites. There are 5 undergraduate schools and 5 graduate schools. In addition to regional accreditation, Troy has baccalaureate program accreditation with ACBSP, CSWE, NASM, NCATE, NLN, and CAAHEP. The 768-acre campus is in a rural area 50 miles south of Montgomery. Including any residence halls, there are 111 buildings.

STUDENT LIFE: 59% of undergraduates are from Alabama. Others are from 49 states, 72 foreign countries, and Canada. 53% are White; 31% African American. **Female To Male Ratio:** 1.6:1. The average age of freshmen is 22; all undergraduates, 27. 18% do not continue beyond their first year; 34% remain to graduate. **Housing:** 2377 students can be accommodated in college housing, which includes single-sex and coed dorms, on-campus apartments, off-campus apartments, and married student housing. In addition, there are honors houses, special-interest houses, fraternity houses, sorority houses, an international house, and substance-free housing. On-campus housing is guaranteed for all 4 years. 66% of students commute. Alcohol is not permitted. All students may keep cars.

FACULTY/CLASSROOMS: All teach undergraduates. No introductory courses are taught by graduate students.

PROGRAMS OF STUDY: Troy confers B.A., B.S., B.A.B.A., B.A.Ed., B.Applied Sc., B.F.A., B.M.Ed., B.S.B.A., B.S.Ed. and B.S.N. degrees. Associate and master's degrees are also awarded. Bachelor's degrees are awarded in BIOLOGICAL SCIENCE (biology/biological science and marine biology), BUSINESS (accounting, banking and finance, business administration and management, business economics, insurance, management science, marketing management, marketing/retailing/merchandising, personnel management, and sports management), COMMUNICATIONS AND THE ARTS (art, art history and appreciation, broadcasting, communications, design, dramatic arts, English, journalism, and studio art), COMPUTER AND PHYSICAL SCIENCE (chemistry, computer science, information sciences and systems, mathematics, and science), EDUCATION (art education, athletic training, collaborative education, early childhood education, elementary education, English education, health education, mathematics education, music education, physical education, science education, secondary education, social science education, and special education), ENGINEERING AND ENVIRONMENTAL DESIGN (environmental science and technological management), HEALTH PROFESSIONS (nursing and rehabilitation therapy), SOCIAL SCIENCE (criminal justice, history, human services, political science/government, psychology, social science, social work, and sociology). Business and education are the strongest academically. Business has the largest enrollment.

ACTIVITIES: 19% of men belong to 13 national fraternities; 18% of women belong to 9 national sororities. There are 197 groups on campus, including art, band, cheerleading, choir, chorale, chorus, computers, dance, debate, drama, drill team, ethnic, film, forensics, honors, international, jazz band, LGBT, literary magazine, marching band, musical theater, newspaper, opera, orchestra, pep band, photography, political, professional, radio and TV, religious, social, social service, student government, and symphony. Popular campus events include ISCO Festival, Spring Picnic and Heritage Week. **Sports:** There are 10 intercollegiate sports for men and 8 for women, and 15 intramural sports for men and 15 for women. Facilities include a 150-seat auditorium, a 3,000-square-foot weight training center, the 2,250-seat Pace-Riddle baseball stadium, a 9-hole golf course, the 30,000-seat Movie Gallery Veteran's Stadium, and 2 football practice fields. Other nearby facilities include a softball and soccer/track complex. The 4,000-seat Trojan Arena is home to both basketball teams and the volleyball team. Also available for student use is the natatorium with an indoor swimming pool, the recreational gym with an outdoor swimming pool, fitness centers, and intramural fields. **Graduates:** From July 1, 2015 to June 30, 2016, 2821 bachelor's degrees were awarded. The most popular majors were psychology (16%), computer information systems (4%), and social sciences (4%).

SERVICES: Counseling and information services are available, as is tutoring in some subjects. There is a reader service for the blind, and remedial math, reading, and writing. Tutors may be provided for students upon request. **Library/Resources:** The 4 libraries contain 594,716 volumes, 2.1 million microform items, and 19,532 audio/video tapes/CDs/DVDs, and subscribe to 3,263 periodicals including electronic. Computerized library services include interlibrary loans, database searching, Internet access, and Wi-Fi capability. Special learning facilities include an art gallery, planetarium, radio station, TV station, an arboretum, the Davis Theater, and the Rosa L. Parks Library, a museum and children's annex. **Physically Challenged Students:** 95% of the campus is accessible. Facilities include wheelchair ramps, elevators, special parking, specially equipped restrooms, special class scheduling, lowered drinking fountains, and lowered telephones. **Special:** Cross-registration with the Marine Biological Consortium, internships in education, journalism, and nursing, study abroad in 5 countries, work-study programs at the university, and student-designed majors in public relations, advertising, and other fields are offered. Credit for life experience and nondegree study are also offered. There is a dual-degree program with Vyatka State University of Humanities in Kirov, Russia. There are 29 national honor societies, Phi Beta Kappa, a freshman honors program, and 14 departmental honors programs. **Visiting:** There are regularly scheduled orientations for prospective students, including a campus tour, classroom visitation, academic consultation, and interviews. There are guides for informal visits and visitors may sit in on classes. To schedule a visit, contact the Office of Enrollment Services. **Campus Safety and Security:** Measures include 24-hour foot and vehicle patrol, self-defense education, and security escort services. There are lighted pathways/sidewalks, foot and vehicle patrols during class hours.

REQUIREMENTS: The SAT or ACT is required. Applicants must have earned at least 15 Carnegie units, with 11 in academic courses and 3 to 4 in English. An interview is recommended, along with a portfolio or audition for some programs. The GED is accepted. A GPA of 2.0 is required. AP and CLEP credits are accepted. Important factors in the admissions decision are ability to finance college education, evidence of special talent, and extracurricular activities record. All students must maintain a minimum GPA of 2.0 while taking 120 to 140 semester credit hours, 54 of which must be in their major field. Distribution requirements include 48 hours of general studies, covering such subjects as English, math, history, science, and fine arts. **Procedure:** Freshmen are admitted fall, spring, and summer. Entrance exams should be taken in the spring of junior year of high school. There is a rolling admissions plan. Application deadlines are open. Application fee is $30. Applications are accepted on-line. **Transfer Students:** Transfer applicants need 20 semester hours attempted at their previous institution, with a GPA of 2.0. **International Students:** The school actively recruits these students. They must take the TOEFL with a minimum score of 500 on the paper-based TOEFL (PBT) or 61 on the Internet-based version (iBT), or take the IELTS. They must also take the SAT, scoring 18.

Admissions Contact: Buddy Starling, Dean of Enrollment Services. Email: *ask@troy.edu* Web: *www.troy.edu*

FINANCIAL AID: The average freshman award was $4,467. Need-based scholarships or need-based grants averaged $4,622 ($5,775 maximum); need-based self-help aid (loans and jobs) averaged $3,628 ($950,000 maximum); non-need-based athletic scholarships averaged $6,204 ($29,444 maximum); and other non-need-based awards and non-need-based scholarships averaged $4,906 ($24,608 maximum). Average annual earnings from campus work are $2050. The college's own financial statement is required. The FAFSA code is 001047. The priority date for freshman financial aid applications for fall entry is March 1.

TUSKEGEE UNIVERSITY D-4

www.tuskegee.edu

Tuskegee, AL 36088 (334) 727-8289 (800) 622-6531

Fax: (334) 727 5750 **Email:** admissions@tuskegee.edu

Full-time: 1085 men, 1436 women	**Faculty:** 280
Part-time: 38 men, 39 women	**Ph.D.s:** 70%
Graduate: 161 men, 358 women	**Student/Faculty:** 12 to 1
Year: semesters, summer session	**Tuition:** $19,060
Room & Board: $9104	**Freshman Class:** 5147 applied, 3519 accepted, 650 enrolled
SAT CR/M: 500/480 **ACT:** 21	**CEEB CODE:** 1813
Application Deadline: open	**COMPETITIVE**

Tuskegee University, founded in 1881, is an independent professional and technical institution offering degree programs in liberal arts and sciences, agriculture, architecture, business, education, engineering, and health professions. There are 7 undergraduate schools and 4 graduate schools. In addition to regional accreditation, Tuskegee has baccalaureate program accreditation with ABET, CSWE, NAAB, NCATE, and NLN. The 5200-acre campus is in a rural area 40 miles east of Montgomery, AL, and 20 miles west of Auburn, AL. Including any residence halls, there are 160 buildings.

STUDENT LIFE: 67% of undergraduates are from out of state, mostly the South. Students are from 42 states, 31 foreign countries, and Canada. 90% are from public schools. 80% are African American. **Female To Male Ratio:** 1.4:1. The average age of freshmen is 19; all undergraduates, 22. 22% do not continue beyond their first year; 46% remain to graduate. **Housing:** 2300 students can be accommodated in college housing, which includes single-sex dorms, on-campus apartments, and married student housing. In addition, there are honors houses. On-campus housing is guaranteed for the freshman year only, is available on a first-come, and first-served basis. Alcohol is not permitted. All students may keep cars.

FACULTY/CLASSROOMS: 70% of faculty are male; 30% are female. No introductory courses are taught by graduate students.

PROGRAMS OF STUDY: Tuskegee confers B.A., B.S. and B.S.N. degrees. Master's and doctoral degrees are also awarded. Bachelor's degrees are awarded in AGRICULTURE (agricultural economics, animal science, and horticulture), BIOLOGICAL SCIENCE (biology/biological science), BUSINESS (accounting, banking and finance, business administration and management, business economics, hospitality management services, management science, marketing/retailing/merchandising, and supply chain management), COMMUNICATIONS AND THE ARTS (English), COMPUTER AND PHYSICAL SCIENCE (chemistry, computer science, mathematics, and physics), EDUCATION (early childhood education, elementary education, physical education, secondary education, special education, and technical education), ENGINEERING AND ENVIRONMENTAL DESIGN (aeronautical engineering, architecture, biomedical engineering, chemical engineering, construction management, electrical/electronics engineering, electrical/electronics engineering technology, and mechanical engineering), HEALTH PROFESSIONS (allied health, nursing, occupational therapy, and veterinary science), SOCIAL SCIENCE (dietetics, economics, food science, history, political science/government, psychology, social work, and sociology). Engineering, nursing, and veterinary science are the strongest academically. Engineering, biology, and veterinary science have the largest enrollments.

ACTIVITIES: 4% of men belong to 6 local and 4 national fraternities; 4% of women belong to 5 local and 4 national sororities. There are 60 groups on campus, including band, cheerleading, choir, chorus, drama, honors, international, jazz band, marching band, newspaper, orchestra, religious, social service, and student government. Popular campus events include Spring Pageant, Campus All-Star Challenge and Student Leadership Retreat. **Sports:** There are 5 intercollegiate sports for men and 5 for women, and 7 intramural sports for men and 6 for women. Facilities include a 10,000-seat stadium, a 5000-seat arena, a student center, tennis courts, a rifle range, playing fields, and an Olympic-size natatorium. **Graduates:** From July 1, 2015 to June 30, 2016, 356 bachelor's degrees were awarded. The most popular majors were engineering (11%), biology (11%), and business (8%). 87 companies recruited on campus in 2015-2016. In an average class, 17% graduate in 4 years or less, 28% graduate in 5 years or less, and 43% graduate in 6 years or less.

SERVICES: Counseling and information services are available, as is tutoring in some subjects. There is a reader service for the blind. **Library/Resources:** The 4 libraries contain 380,000 volumes, 2,500 microform items, and 3,000 audio/video tapes/CDs/DVDs, and subscribe to 1,150 periodicals including electronic. Computerized library services include interlibrary loans, database searching, Internet access, and Wi-Fi capability. **Physically Challenged Students:** Facilities include wheelchair ramps, elevators, special parking, specially equipped restrooms, special class scheduling, lowered drinking fountains, and lowered telephones. **Special:** Cooperative programs, internships, work-study programs, dual majors, nondegree study, and a B.A.-B.S. degree are offered. There are 17 national honor societies, a freshman honors program, and 9 departmental honors programs. **Visiting:** There are guides for informal visits, visitors may sit in on classes, and stay overnight. To schedule a visit, contact the Office of Admissions. **Campus Safety and Security:** Measures include 24-hour foot and vehicle patrol and security escort services. There are lighted pathways/sidewalks.

REQUIREMENTS: The SAT or ACT is required. A GPA of 3.0 is recommended. Applicants should be graduates of an accredited secondary school or hold the GED. They should have completed 4 units of English, 3 each of social science and math, and 1 each of physical science and biological science. SAT: Subject tests in mathematics (level I or II) and 1 other subject are recommended. An essay is not required. A GPA of 3.0 is required. AP and CLEP credits are accepted. Important factors in the admissions decision are advanced placement or honors courses, ability to finance college education, and geographical diversity. All students must complete a general education curriculum, including courses in history, sociology, philosophy, art, English, humanities, political science, math, natural sciences, and phys ed. A minimum of 124 semester credits with a GPA of 2.0 is required for graduation. **Procedure:** Freshmen are admitted to all sessions. Entrance exams should be taken starting in the junior year. There are early admissions and rolling admissions plans. Application deadlines are open. Application fee is $25. Applications are accepted on-line. **Transfer Students:** 166 transfer students enrolled in 2015-2016. Applicants must be in good standing at all previously attended institutions and have completed 12 or more semester hours with a GPA of 2.5. 44 of 124 credits required for the bachelor's degree must be completed at Tuskegee. **International Students:** There are 27 international students enrolled. They must take the TOEFL with a minimum score of 500 on the paper-based TOEFL (PBT) or 62 on the Internet-based version (iBT). They must also take the SAT or ACT, scoring 1000.

ADMISSIONS: 68% of the 2016-2017 applicants were accepted. The SAT scores for the 2016-2017 freshman class were: Critical Reading--67% below 500, 27% between 500 and 599, and 4% between 600 and 699. Math-- 64% below 500, 26% between 500 and 599, and 8% between 600 and 699. The ACT scores were 17% below 12, 61% between 12 and 17, 15% between 18 and 23, 6% between 24 and 29, and 1% above 30. 60% of the current freshmen were in the top fifth of their class; 80% were in the top two fifths. **Admissions Contact:** Elizabeth Dadzie, Associate VP of Admissions. Email: *admissions@tuskegee.edu* Web: *www.tuskegee.edu*

FINANCIAL AID: In 2016-2017, 87% of all full-time freshmen and 91% of continuing full-time students received some form of financial aid. 71% of all full-time freshmen and 74% of continuing full-time students received need-based aid. 59% of undergraduate students work part-time. Tuskegee is a member of CSS. The CSS/Profile, and federal tax returns are required. The FAFSA code is 001050. The priority date for freshman financial aid applications for fall entry is March 1. The deadline for filing freshman financial aid applications for fall entry is March 31.

UNIVERSITY OF ALABAMA — B-3

www.ua.edu

Tuscaloosa, AL 35487 — (205) 348-6010, (800) 933-BAMA

Fax: (205) 348-9046 — **Email:** admissions@ua.edu

Full-time: 11,253 men, 12,692 women
Part-time: 1022 men, 1267 women
Graduate: 2244 men, 3169 women
Year: semesters, summer session
Room & Board: $13,050

SAT or ACT: required
Application Deadline: March 1

Faculty: I, -$
Ph.D.s: n/av
Student/Faculty: 19 to 1
Tuition: $11,270 ($27,750)
Freshman Class: 22136 applied, 9636 accepted, 5728 enrolled
CEEB CODE: 1830
COMPETITIVE+

University of Alabama, is the first public university in Alabama that is a senior comprehensive doctoral level institution. The university was established by constitutional provision under statutory mandates and authorizations. Its mission is to advance the intellectual and social condition of the people of the state through quality programs of teaching, research and service. The figures in the above capsule and in this profile are approximate. There are 9 undergraduate schools and 2 graduate schools. In addition to regional accreditation, UA has baccalaureate program accreditation with AACSB, ABET, ACEJMC, ADA, CSWE, FIDER, NASAD, NASM, NCATE, AAFCS, CAAHEP, CCNE, NASD, and NAST. The 1000-acre campus is in a suburban area in Tuscaloosa, 50 miles southwest of Birmingham. Including any residence halls, there are 216 buildings.

STUDENT LIFE: 50% of undergraduates are from out of state, mostly the South. Students are from 50 states, 79 foreign countries, and Canada. 89% are from public schools. 81% are White; 12% African American. 56% are Protestant; 32% claim no religious affiliation. **Female To Male Ratio:** 1.2:1. The average age of freshmen is 18; all undergraduates, 21. 14% do not continue beyond their first year; 87% remain to graduate. **Housing:** 5800 students can be accommodated in college housing, which includes single-sex and coed dorms, on-campus apartments, and married student housing. In addition, there are honors houses, language houses, special-interest houses, fraternity houses, and sorority houses. On-campus housing is guaranteed for the freshman year only, and is available on a first-come, and first-served basis. 92% of students live on campus; of those, 35% remain on campus on weekends. All students may keep cars.

FACULTY/CLASSROOMS: 60% of faculty are male; 40% are female. 71% teach undergraduates, 5% do research, and 4% do both. Graduate students teach 28% of introductory courses. The average class size in an introductory lecture is 52; in a laboratory is 19; and in a regular course is 26.

PROGRAMS OF STUDY: UA confers B.A., B.S., B.A.Com., B.F.A., B.M., B.S.A.E., B.S.C.B.A., B.S.C.E., B.S.Che.E., B.S.Chem., B.S.C.S., B.S.Ed., B.S.E.E., B.S.Geo., B.S.H.E.S., B.S.I.E., B.S.M.E., B.S.Met., B.S. Micr., B.S.N. and B.S.W. degrees. Master's and doctoral degrees are also awarded. Bachelor's degrees are awarded in BIOLOGICAL SCIENCE (biology/biological science, marine science, and microbiology), BUSINESS (accounting and management information systems), COMMUNICATIONS AND THE ARTS (advertising, art history and appreciation, classics, communications, dance, English, French, German, journalism, music, public relations, Russian, Spanish, and telecommunications), COMPUTER AND PHYSICAL SCIENCE (chemistry, computer science, geology, mathematics, and physics), EDUCATION (athletic training, early childhood education, elementary education, music education, physical education, secondary education, and special education), ENGINEERING AND ENVIRONMENTAL DESIGN (aerospace studies, chemical engineering, civil engineering, electrical/electronics engineering, environmental science, industrial administration/management, industrial engineering, interior design, mechanical engineering, and metallurgical engineering), HEALTH PROFESSIONS (music therapy and nursing), SOCIAL SCIENCE (American studies, anthropology, clothing and textiles management/production/services, criminal justice, economics, food science, geography, history, human development, interdisciplinary studies, international studies, philosophy, political science/government, psychology, religion, and social work). Advertising, accounting, and engineering are the strongest academically. Business, elementary education, and nursing have the largest enrollments.

ACTIVITIES: 28% of men belong to 1 local and 26 national fraternities; 43% of women belong to 1 local and 20 national sororities. There are 391 groups on campus, including leadership and other national honoraries, academic service, art, band, cheerleading, chess, choir, chorale, chorus, computers, dance, debate, drama, drill team, ethnic, film, forensics, honors, international, jazz band, LGBT, literary magazine, marching band, musical theater, newspaper, opera, orchestra, pep band, photography, political, professional, radio and TV, religious, social, social service, student government, symphony, and yearbook. Popular campus events include Honors Week, Get on Board Day and Family Weekend. **Sports:** There are 9 intercollegiate sports for men and 12 for women, and 17 intramural sports for men and 16 for women. Facilities include an 83,000-seat football stadium, a 15,000-seat basketball arena, a track and field facility, a 6,100-seat baseball stadium, a 1,600-foot softball stadium, an indoor football practice facility, lighted varsity and public tennis courts, an aquatic complex with Olympic-size and standard pools and a weight-lifting facility, a soccer field, racquetball, basketball, and volleyball courts, weight and exercise rooms, an indoor/outdoor pool, and an 18-hole golf course with clubhouse and driving range. **Graduates:** From July 1, 2015 to June 30, 2016, 4463 bachelor's degrees were awarded. The most popular majors were business/marketing (29%), health professions and related programs (10%), and communication/journalism (9%). In an average class, 59% graduate in 3 years or less, 24% graduate in 5 years or less, and 67% graduate in 6 years or less. Of the 2015 graduating class, 87% were enrolled in graduate school within 6 months of graduation.

SERVICES: Counseling and information services are available, as is tutoring in some subjects, such as statistics math, chemistry, physics, computer science, accounting, finance, economics, and foreign languages. There is a reader service for the blind, remedial math, reading, and writing, center for teaching and learning, a writing lab, a career center, computer-based self-tutoring and a math computer lab. **Library/Resources:** The 10 libraries contain 2.5 million volumes, 4.0 million microform items, and 526,856 audio/video tapes/CDs/DVDs, and subscribe to 23,222 periodicals including electronic. Computerized library services include interlibrary loans, database searching, and Internet access. Special learning facilities include an art gallery, natural history museum, radio station, TV station, special collections department, map library, observatory, specialized computer labs, and archeological site. **Physically Challenged Students:** 90% of the campus is accessible. Facilities include wheelchair ramps, elevators, special parking, specially equipped restrooms, special class scheduling, lowered drinking fountains, lowered telephones, special housing. automatic doors, TDD, adaptive technology, and areas of rescue assistance. **Special:** UA offers cross-registration with Stillman College and Shelton State Community College, internships, international study programs, a Washington semester, a 3-week May-June interim term, exchange study within the United States, work-study, co-op programs, accelerated programs, B.A.-B.S. degrees, dual majors, student-designed majors, interdisciplinary majors in the New College arts and sciences program, credit for life experiences, nondegree study, and pass/fail options. There are 27 national honor societies, Phi Beta Kappa, a freshman honors program, and 17 departmental honors programs. **Visiting:** There are regularly scheduled orientations for prospective students, consisting of a campus tour followed by meetings with admissions counselors and faculty and staff. Customized visits to suit student and parent needs are possible. University Day (4 times a year) offers tours and information sessions. There are guides for informal visits, visitors may sit in on classes, and stay overnight. To schedule a visit, contact the Office of Undergraduate Admissions. **Campus Safety and Security:** Measures include 24-hour foot and vehicle patrol, self-defense education, and security escort services. There are emergency telephones, lighted pathways/sidewalks, community-oriented police service, UA police bike patrol, educational awareness for personal safety, alcohol awareness, child seat installations and domestic violence awareness programs.

REQUIREMENTS: The SAT or ACT is required. A minimum GPA of 2.0 is required; admission is based on a sliding scale of test scores and high school GPA. The GED is accepted. High school preparation should include 4 units each of English and social studies, 3 each of math and science, 1 of foreign language, and history and 5 of academic electives. Students with a 3.0 cumulative GPA and a satisfactory ACT or SAT (verbal and math only) score will generally be admitted. A GPA of 2.0 is required. AP and CLEP credits are accepted. Important factors in the admissions decision are advanced placement or honors courses, evidence of special talent, and leadership record. To graduate, all students must complete a minimum of 120 semester hours, including at least 27 in the major, with a minimum GPA of 2.0. Core curriculum requirements include 12 hours each of humanities/fine arts and history/social science, 11 of natural science/math, 6 of computer studies or a foreign language, 6 of English composition, and 6 of upper-level courses with a writing component. **Procedure:** Freshmen are admitted fall, spring, and summer. Entrance exams should be taken in the spring of the junior year. There are early admissions and rolling admissions plans. Applications should be filed by March 1 for fall entry; December 1 for spring entry; and March 1 for summer entry, along with a $40 fee. Notification is sent on a rolling basis. Applications are accepted on-line. **Transfer Students:** 1463 transfer students enrolled in 2015-2016. Applicants need an overall minimum GPA of 2.0 with at least 24 semester hours earned. Those with fewer than 24 hours must meet freshman standards. 30 of 120 credits required for the bachelor's degree must be completed at UA. **International Students:** The school actively recruits these students. They must take the TOEFL or earn a proficiency certificate from the university's English Language Institute. They must also take the SAT or ACT.

ADMISSIONS: 44% of the 2016-2017 applicants were accepted. **Admissions Contact:** Mary K. Spiegel, Director of Undergraduate Admissions. Email: *admissions@ua.edu* Web: *www.ua.edu*

FINANCIAL AID: The FAFSA code is 001051. The priority date for freshman financial aid applications for fall entry is March 1.

UNIVERSITY OF ALABAMA AT BIRMINGHAM — C-2

www.uab.edu

Birmingham, AL 35294	**(205) 934-8221** **(800) 421-8743**
Fax: (205) 975-7114	**Email: chooseuab@uab.edu**
Full-time: 3688 men, 5283 women	**Faculty:** I, av$
Part-time: 1371 men, 2027 women	**Ph.D.s:** 86%
Graduate: 2531 men, 4635 women	**Student/Faculty:** 18 to 1
Year: semesters, summer session	**Tuition:** $9936 ($22,844)
Room & Board: $9970	**Freshman Class:** n/av
SAT or ACT: required	**CEEB CODE:** 1856
Application Deadline: June 1	**COMPETITIVE**

University of Alabama at Birmingham, founded in 1969, is a public institution offering degrees in the arts and sciences, business, dentistry, education, engineering, health professions, joint health sciences, medicine, nursing, optometry and public health. There are 9 undergraduate schools and 11 graduate schools. In addition to regional accreditation, UAB has baccalaureate program accreditation with AACSB, ABET, CSWE, NASAD, NASM, NCATE, CCNE, CAHME, and CAAHEP. The 323-acre campus is in an urban area in Birmingham, Alabama. Including any residence halls, there are 246 buildings.

STUDENT LIFE: 87% of undergraduates are from Alabama. Others are from 50 states, 81 foreign countries, and Canada. 92% are from public schools. 61% are White; 6% Asian American; 4% Foreign; 3% Hispanic; 3% two or more races; 21% African American; and 1% race unknown. **Female To Male Ratio:** 1.6:1. The average age of freshmen is 18; all undergraduates, 23. 18% do not continue beyond their first year; 55% remain to graduate. **Housing:** 2796 students can be accommodated in college housing, which includes single-sex and coed dorms, on-campus apartments, and married student housing. On-campus housing is available on a first-come and first-served basis. 78% of students commute. Alcohol is not permitted. All students may keep cars.

FACULTY/CLASSROOMS: 52% of faculty are male; 48% are female. No introductory courses are taught by graduate students.

PROGRAMS OF STUDY: UAB confers B.A., B.S., B.F.A., B.S.B.M.E., B.S.C.E., B.S.E.E., B.S.M.E., B.S.Mt.E., B.S.N. and B.S.S.W. degrees. Master's and doctoral degrees are also awarded. Bachelor's degrees are awarded in BIOLOGICAL SCIENCE (biology/biological science and neurosciences), BUSINESS (accounting, banking and finance, and marketing/retailing/merchandising), COMMUNICATIONS AND THE ARTS (art, communications, dramatic arts, English, foreign language, music, and musical theater), COMPUTER AND PHYSICAL SCIENCE (chemistry, computer science, information sciences and systems, mathematics, natural sciences, and physics), EDUCATION (early childhood education, elementary education, health education, and secondary education), ENGINEERING AND ENVIRONMENTAL DESIGN (biomedical engineering, civil engineering, electrical/electronics engineering, industrial administration/management, materials engineering, and mechanical engineering), HEALTH PROFESSIONS (biomedical science, health science, kinesiology, medical records administration/services, medical technology, nuclear medical technology, nursing, public health, and respiratory therapy), SOCIAL SCIENCE (African American studies, anthropology, criminal justice, economics, history, international studies, philosophy, political science/government, psychology, social work, and sociology). Biology, accounting, and psychology have the largest enrollments.

ACTIVITIES: 10% of men belong to 12 national fraternities; 9% of women belong to 10 national sororities. There are 275 groups on campus, including band, cheerleading, chess, choir, chorale, chorus, computers, dance, drama, environmental, ethnic, honors, international, jazz band, LGBT, literary magazine, marching band, musical theater, newspaper, opera, orchestra, pep band, political, professional, radio and TV, religious, social, social service, and student government. Popular campus events include Springfest, Homecoming, Camille Armstrong Memorial Scholarship Stepshow, and Talent Search. **Sports:** There are 6 intercollegiate sports for men and 11 for women, and 35 intramural sports for men and 35 for women. Facilities include a 150,000-square-foot recreation center with 4 basketball/volleyball courts, 5 racquetball courts (1 of which can be converted to squash and 4 for wallyball), 4 aerobics studios, 18,000 square feet of weight and cardio-fitness areas, a game room, a KidsZone, an aquatics center with both lap and leisure components, a gym used for indoor soccer, floor hockey, badminton, a juice bar, an indoor track, and a climbing wall. **Graduates:** From July 1, 2015 to June 30, 2016, 2295 bachelor's degrees were awarded. The most popular majors were nursing (14%), psychology (8%), and biology (6%). 254 companies recruited on campus in 2015-2016. In an average class, 35% graduate in 4 years or less, 48% graduate in 5 years or less, and 53% graduate in 6 years or less.

SERVICES: Counseling and information services are available, as is tutoring in some subjects, such as biology, chemistry, physics, psychology, and mathematics. There is a reader service for the blind, and remedial math, reading, and writing, academic success center, university writing center, and math learning lab. **Library/Resources:** The 3 libraries contain 2.2 million volumes, 1.3 million microform items, and 29,744 audio/video tapes/CDs/DVDs, and subscribe to 39,256 periodicals including electronic. Computerized library services include interlibrary loans, database searching, Internet access, and Wi-Fi capability. Special learning facilities include an art gallery, radio station, TV station, Reynolds Historical Library, Alabama Museum of the Health Sciences, and Alys Stephens Performing Art Center. **Physically Challenged Students:** All of the campus is accessible. Facilities include wheelchair ramps, elevators, special parking, specially equipped restrooms, lowered drinking fountains, lowered telephones, and special housing. **Special:** UAB offers student-designed majors, cross-registration with the Birmingham Area Consortium for Higher Education, internships, study abroad in 32 countries, work-study programs, nondegree study, pass/fail options, and credit by exam and for life experience. Cooperative education programs in the student's area of interest provide full- or part-time work. Additionally, there are several special programs such as the Industrial Scholars Program (provides financial support and industry experience for engineering students), Fifth Year Master of Science program in biology, Mathematics Fast Track Program, and the Early Medical School Acceptance Program. There are 32 national honor societies, a freshman honors program, and 33 departmental honors programs. **Visiting:** There are regularly scheduled orientations for prospective students, including a question-and-answer session, academic advising, sessions for parents, and presentations on student life, financial aid, housing, and student development. There are guides for informal visits and visitors may sit in on classes. To schedule a visit, contact Hilary Murrell at campustour@uab.edu. **Campus Safety and Security:** Measures include 24-hour foot and vehicle patrol, emergency notification system, self-defense education, and security escort services. There are shuttle buses, emergency telephones, and lighted pathways/sidewalks.

REQUIREMENTS: The SAT or ACT is required. Applicants should have completed 17 Carnegie units and a college prep diploma, including 4 units in English, 3 units each in math, science, and social studies, 1 unit in foreign language, and 3 units in electives. The GED is accepted. A GPA of 2.0 is required. AP and CLEP credits are accepted. All students must complete a core curriculum that includes courses in math, computers, English, history, science and technology, social sciences, philosophy, fine arts, foreign language or culture, and literature. To receive a bachelor's degree, students must complete 128 semester hours for most programs, with a GPA of at least 2.0. **Procedure:** Freshmen are admitted to all sessions. Entrance exams should be taken during the beginning of the senior year. There are early admissions, deferred admissions, and rolling admissions plans. Applications should be filed by June 1 for fall entry, along with a $30 fee. Notification is sent on a rolling basis. Applications are accepted on-line. **Transfer Students:** 1598 transfer students enrolled in 2015-2016. Transfer applicants must have a GPA of 2.0 after completing 24 semester hours (or 36 quarter hours) of college-level work. College transcripts are required of all students. Applicants who have completed fewer than 24 semester hours must meet the requirements of beginning freshmen. **International Students:** There are 206 international students enrolled. The school actively recruits these students. They must take the TOEFL with a minimum score of 77 on the Internet-based version (iBT), or take the IELTS. They must also take the SAT or ACT.

ADMISSIONS: 89% of the 2016-2017 applicants were accepted. 47% of the current freshmen were in the top fifth of their class; 74% were in the top two fifths. There were 24 National Merit finalists. 24 freshmen graduated first in their class. **Admissions Contact:** Sean Kerins, Sr. Institutional Research Analyst. Email: *chooseuab@uab.edu* Web: *www.uab.edu*

FINANCIAL AID: In 2016-2017, 93% of all full-time freshmen and 70% of continuing full-time students received some form of financial aid. 52% of all full-time freshmen and 36% of continuing full-time students received need-based aid. The average freshman award was $6,306. Need-based scholarships or need-based grants averaged $2,607 ($15,651 maximum); need-based self-help aid (loans and jobs) averaged $1,989 ($4,354 maximum); non-need-based athletic scholarships averaged $8,864 ($20,171 maximum); and other non-need-based awards and non-need-based scholarships averaged $4,210 ($21,917 maximum). The average financial indebtedness of the 2016 graduate was $40,859. The FAFSA code is 001052. The priority date for freshman financial aid applications for fall entry is March 1.

UNIVERSITY OF ALABAMA IN HUNTSVILLE — C-1

www.uah.edu

Huntsville, AL 35899	(256) 824-2771 (800) UAH-CALL
Fax: (256) 824-4539	Email: uahadmissions@uah.edu
Full-time: 3036 men, 2221 women	**Faculty:** n/av
Part-time: 745 men, 505 women	**Ph.D.s:** 82%
Graduate: 1052 men, 909 women	**Student/Faculty:** 15 to 1
Year: semesters, summer session	**Tuition:** $9973 ($21,467)
Room & Board: $9603	**Freshman Class:** 4545 applied, 3467 accepted, 1216 enrolled
SAT or ACT: required	**CEEB CODE:** 1854
Application Deadline: August 20	**VERY COMPETITIVE**

University of Alabama at Huntsville, founded in 1950 and part of the University of Alabama system, is a public institution offering programs in liberal arts, sciences, business administration, nursing, and engineering. Figures in the above capsule and in this profile are approximate. There are 6 undergraduate schools and 1 graduate school. In addition to regional accreditation, UAHuntsville has baccalaureate program accreditation with AACSB, ABET, ACCE, CSAB, NASAD, NASM, NCATE, CCNE, and ACS. The 432-acre campus is in a suburban area 100 miles north of Birmingham and 90 miles south of Nashville. Including any residence halls, there are 59 buildings.

STUDENT LIFE: 84% of undergraduates are from Alabama. Others are from 44 states, 84 foreign countries, and Canada. 71% are White; 11%

African American; 4% Asian American; 4% Hispanic; 3% Foreign; 3% race unknown; 2% two or more races; 1% American Indian/Alaska Native. **Male To Female Ratio:** 1.3:1. The average age of freshmen is 18; all undergraduates, 22. 17% do not continue beyond their first year; 49% remain to graduate. **Housing:** 1652 students can be accommodated in college housing, which includes coed dorms, on-campus apartments, and married student housing. In addition, there are honors houses, fraternity houses, sorority houses, athletics teammates, freshman leadership and involvement, engineering, academic success and discovery. On-campus housing is guaranteed for the freshman year only, is available on a first-come, and first-served basis. 75% of students commute. Alcohol is not permitted. All students may keep cars.

FACULTY/CLASSROOMS: 56% of faculty are male; 44% are female. No introductory courses are taught by graduate students.

PROGRAMS OF STUDY: UAHuntsville confers B.A., B.F.A., B.S., B.S.B.A., B.S.A.E., B.S.Che.E., B.S.C.E., B.S.Cp.E., B.S.E.E., B.S.M.E., B.S.I.S.E., B.S.O.E. and B.S.N. degrees. Master's and doctoral degrees are also awarded. Bachelor's degrees are awarded in BIOLOGICAL SCIENCE (biology/biological science), BUSINESS (accounting, banking and finance, business administration and management, economics – statistics, and marketing/retailing/merchandising), COMMUNICATIONS AND THE ARTS (art, communications, English, languages, and music), COMPUTER AND PHYSICAL SCIENCE (chemistry, computer science, earth science, information sciences and systems, mathematics, physics, and science), EDUCATION (elementary education), ENGINEERING AND ENVIRONMENTAL DESIGN (chemical engineering, civil engineering, computer engineering, electrical/electronics engineering, industrial engineering, mechanical engineering, and optical engineering), HEALTH PROFESSIONS (nursing), SOCIAL SCIENCE (history, philosophy, political science/government, psychology, and sociology). Nursing, mechanical engineering, and computer science have the largest enrollments.

ACTIVITIES: There are 125 groups on campus, including academic club, art, band, cheerleading, choir, chorale, chorus, community service, computers, dance, drama, environmental, ethnic, honors, international, jazz band, LGBT, musical theater, multicultural club, newspaper, opera, pep band, political, professional, religious, social, social service, special interest, student government, and symphony. Popular campus events include Week of Welcome, Homecoming, Family Weekend, Late Night Breakfast, ChargerCon, The Big Event, Sandella Sounds, and Spring Fling. **Sports:** There are 9 intercollegiate sports for men and 9 for women, and 11 intramural sports for men and 11 for women. Facilities include a 2800-seat gym, swimming pool, racquetball and tennis courts, disc golf course, soccer fields, softball diamonds, a fitness center with cardio equipment, indoor track, weight room, fitness classes, aquatics, sand volleyball, basketball courts and a sports nutrition center. . **Graduates:** From July 1, 2015 to June 30, 2016, 1065 bachelor's degrees were awarded. The most popular majors were nursing (19%), management (7%), and mechanical engineering (7%). In an average class, 22% graduate in 4 years or less, 45% graduate in 5 years or less, and 49% graduate in 6 years or less.

SERVICES: Counseling and information services are available, as is tutoring in most subjects, such as tutoring services are available for most 100-200 level classes, most undergraduate math classes, and undergraduate writing in any discipline. **Library/Resources:** The library contains 289,500 volumes, 571,000 microform items, and 1,489 audio/video tapes/CDs/DVDs, and subscribes to 339 periodicals including electronic. Computerized library services include interlibrary loans, database searching, Internet access, and Wi-Fi capability. Special learning facilities include an art gallery, an optical observatory and a radio telescope; the National Space Science and Technology center, shared between UAHuntsville, NASA and the National Weather Service; and a rooftop greenhouse used for research and laboratory experiences. **Physically Challenged Students:** 98% of the campus is accessible. Facilities include wheelchair ramps, elevators, special parking, specially equipped restrooms, special class scheduling, lowered drinking fountains, special housing, a swimming pool lift, and sign language interpreters. **Special:** UAHuntsville offers co-op programs in all majors, cross-registration with Alabama Agricultural and Mechanical University, Athens State University, and Calhoun Community College, and internships in business, communications, education, and political science. A 3-2 engineering degree is available with Oakwood College. Dual majors, B.A.-B.S. degrees in math and biology, study abroad in 28 countries, nondegree study, and a pass/fail option are also offered. The Joint Undergraduate Masters Program (JUMP) is available in ten majors including atmospheric science, biology, business, chemistry, civil engineering, computer science, earth systems science, electrical and computer engineering, math and physics. There are 15 national honor societies and a freshman honors program. **Visiting:** There are regularly scheduled orientations for prospective students, including sessions on academics, campus life, financial aid and other important topics as well as time dedicated to advising and class registration. Social activities are available for participants to meet both new and current students. There are guides for informal visits, visitors may sit in on classes, and stay overnight. To schedule a visit, contact Vangie Harris at (800) 824-2773. **Campus Safety and Security:** Measures include 24-hour foot and vehicle patrol, emergency notification system, self-defense education, and security escort services. There are emergency telephones, lighted pathways/sidewalks, controlled access to dorms/residences, emergency management plan, 911 system and digitally recorded security cameras.

REQUIREMENTS: The SAT or ACT is required. A sliding scale with the GPA determines the minimum test score needed. The GED is accepted. Students should present a minimum of 20 Carnegie units, including 4 years of English and social studies, and 3 each of math and science. A GPA of 2.0 is required. AP and CLEP credits are accepted. All students must earn a minimum GPA of 2.0 over 120 to 134 credit hours, including 21 to 36 in their major. The core curriculum includes courses in English composition, literature, world history, foreign language and communications, fine arts, math, science and social sciences. **Procedure:** Freshmen are admitted fall, spring, and summer. Entrance exams should be taken during the junior year. There are early admissions, deferred admissions, and rolling admissions plans. Applications should be filed by August 20 for fall entry; December 15 for spring entry; and May 15 for summer entry, along with a $30 fee. Applications are accepted online. **Transfer Students:** 778 transfer students enrolled in 2015-2016. Applicants need a minimum cumulative GPA of 2.0, over at least 24 hours of credit from a regionally accredited college or university. 32 of 128 credits required for the bachelor's degree must be completed at UAHuntsville. **International Students:** There are 190 international students enrolled. The school actively recruits these students. They must take the TOEFL with a minimum score of 65 on the Internet-based version (iBT) and the college's own test. They must also take the SAT or ACT.

ADMISSIONS: 76% of the 2016-2017 applicants were accepted. The SAT scores for the 2016-2017 freshman class were: Critical Reading-- 13% below 500, 38% between 500 and 599, 35% between 600 and 699, and 13% between 700 and 800. Math-- 9% below 500, 34% between 500 and 599, 38% between 600 and 699, and 19% between 700 and 800. The ACT scores were 23% between 18 and 23, 43% between 24 and 29, and 34% above 30. 31% of the current freshmen were in the top fifth of their class; 58% were in the top two fifths. 7 freshmen graduated first in their class. **Admissions Contact:** Peggy Masters, Director of Admissions. Email: *uahadmissions@uah.edu* Web: *www.uah.edu*

FINANCIAL AID: In 2016-2017, 90% of all full-time freshmen and 77% of continuing full-time students received some form of financial aid. 50% of all full-time freshmen and 51% of continuing full-time students received need-based aid. The average freshman award was $12,111. Need-based scholarships or need-based grants averaged $9,701 ($34,421 maximum); need-based self-help aid (loans and jobs) averaged $9,371 ($32,421 maximum); non-need-based athletic scholarships averaged $7,700 ($32,496 maximum); and other non-need-based awards and non-need-based scholarships averaged $9,739 ($36,012 maximum). The average financial indebtedness of the 2016 graduate was $35,009. The FAFSA code is 001055. The priority date for freshman financial aid applications for fall entry is April 1. The deadline for filing freshman financial aid applications for fall entry is July 31.

UNIVERSITY OF MOBILE — A-5

www.umobile.edu

Mobile, AL 36613	**(251) 442-2249** **(800) 946-7267**
Fax: (251) 675-6329	**Email: cwittner@umobile.edu**
Full-time: 473 men, 809 women	**Faculty:** 84
Part-time: 40 men, 144 women	**Ph.D.s:** 62%
Graduate: 25 men, 109 women	**Student/Faculty:** 12 to 1
Year: semesters, summer session	**Tuition:** $19,385
Room & Board: $9550	**Freshman Class:** 1009 applied, 590 accepted, 275 enrolled
ACT: 22	**CEEB CODE:** 1515
Application Deadline: August 1	**COMPETITIVE**

University of Mobile, founded in 1961, is a private liberal arts institution affiliated with the Southern Baptists. There are 7 undergraduate schools and 5 graduate schools. In addition to regional accreditation, UMobile has baccalaureate program accreditation with ACBSP, NASM, CAATE, CCNE, and ACEN. The 880-acre campus is in a suburban area 10 miles northwest of Mobile. Including any residence halls, there are 60 buildings.

STUDENT LIFE: 74% of undergraduates are from Alabama. Others are from 39 states, 23 foreign countries, and Canada. 63% are White; 24% African American. **Female To Male Ratio:** 2.0:1. The average age of freshmen is 18; all undergraduates, 24. 23% do not continue beyond their first year; 46% remain to graduate. **Housing:** 734 students can be accommodated in college housing, which includes single-sex dorms and on-campus apartments. On-campus housing is guaranteed for the freshman year only, is available on a first-come, and first-served basis. 51% of students commute. Alcohol is not permitted. All students may keep cars.

FACULTY/CLASSROOMS: 50% of faculty are male; 50% are female. 98% teach undergraduates. No introductory courses are taught by graduate students. The average class size in an introductory lecture is 16; in a laboratory is 16; and in a regular course is 16.

PROGRAMS OF STUDY: UMobile confers B.A., B.S., B.B.A., B.M. and B.S.N. degrees. Associate and master's degrees are also awarded. Bachelor's degrees are awarded in BIOLOGICAL SCIENCE (biology/biological science and marine science), BUSINESS (accounting and business administration and management), COMMUNICATIONS AND THE ARTS (art, communications, English, music, music performance, and voice), COMPUTER AND PHYSICAL SCIENCE (information sciences and systems and mathematics), EDUCATION (athletic training, early childhood education, elementary education, and physical education), HEALTH PROFESSIONS (nursing), SOCIAL SCIENCE (history, humanities, liberal arts/general studies, political science/government, psychology, religion, religious music, social science, sociology, and theological studies). Business, education, and nursing are the strongest academically. Business administration, education, and nursing have the largest enrollments.

ACTIVITIES: There are no fraternities or sororities. There are 52 groups on campus, including art, band, cheerleading, choir, chorale, chorus, computers, dance, drama, drum and bugle corps, honors, international, jazz band, musical theater, opera, orchestra, pep band, political, professional, religious, social, social service, student government, and symphony. Popular campus events include College Preview Day and Christmas Spectacular. **Sports:** There are 7 intercollegiate sports for men and 8 for women, and 5 intramural sports for men and 5 for women. Facilities include an 800-seat gym, tennis complex with 10 courts, swimming pool, track, baseball, softball, 2 soccer fields, and a golf driving range with 2 putting greens. **Graduates:** From July 1, 2015 to June 30, 2016, 272 bachelor's degrees were awarded. The most popular majors were education (22%), nursing (21%), and business (15%). In an average class, 26% graduate in 4 years or less, 14% graduate in 5 years or less, and 42% graduate in 6 years or less. Of the 2015 graduating class, 26% were enrolled in graduate school within 6 months of graduation, and 72% were employed.

SERVICES: Counseling and information services are available, as is tutoring in some subjects, such as writing, English and math. There is also remedial math, reading, and writing available. Additional tutoring provided in other subjects as needed. **Library/Resources:** The library contains 110,005 volumes, and 1,733 audio/video tapes/CDs/DVDs, and subscribes to 258 periodicals including electronic. Computerized library services include interlibrary loans, database searching, Internet access, and Wi-Fi capability. Special learning facilities include an art gallery. **Physically Challenged Students:** All of the campus is accessible. Facilities include wheelchair ramps, elevators, special parking, specially equipped restrooms, special class scheduling, lowered drinking fountains, and special housing that can be arranged as-needed basis. **Special:** A variety of internships and work-study programs, a five-year B.S./M.B.A. degree, adult programs in business, education, nursing, and leadership/cultural studies, and dual majors are available, as is a 3-2 engineering degree with the University of South Alabama. There are 13 national honor societies, a freshman honors program, and 1 departmental honors program. **Visiting:** There are regularly scheduled orientations for prospective students, including financial aid seminars, academic seminars, faculty advising, campus tours, and admissions counseling. There are guides for informal visits, visitors may sit in on classes, and stay overnight. To schedule a visit, contact Justin McGehee at (251) 442-2638. **Campus Safety and Security:** Measures include 24-hour foot and vehicle patrol and emergency notification system. There are lighted pathways/sidewalks, controlled access to dorms/residences. A professional campus security service is available 24 hours per day.

REQUIREMENTS: Applicants must have 22 Carnegie units and a minimum composite score of 21 on the ACT. The GED is accepted. The ACT is not required of applicants over age 25. A GPA of 2.8 is required. AP and CLEP credits are accepted. Important factors in the admissions decision are advanced placement or honors courses, ability to finance college education, and leadership record. All students are required to complete 123 credit hours, with at least 30 in their major field, and earn a minimum GPA of 2.0. Distribution requirements include 9 hours in English, 4 hours in lab science, 6 hours in Christian ministries, and 3 hours each in math, history, and public speaking or philosophy. Students select an additional 18 hours of electives from among art, literature, psychology, sociology, political science, philosophy, science, history, economics, music, and Christian ministries. Chapel attendance is also required. **Procedure:** Freshmen are admitted fall, spring, and summer. Entrance exams should be taken in August before the junior year. There are deferred admissions and rolling admissions plans. Applications should be filed by August 1 for fall entry; January 4 for spring entry; and May 1 for summer entry. The fall 2016 application fee was $25. Notification is sent on a rolling basis. Applications are accepted on-line. **Transfer Students:** 113 transfer students enrolled in 2015-2016. Transfer students need to have earned a minimum GPA of 2.0 for previous college work. If fewer than 24 semester hours are accepted, a minimum score of 21 on the ACT and a high school transcript, or GED, are required. 32 of 123 credits required for the bachelor's degree must be completed at UMobile. **International Students:** There are 64 international students enrolled. The school actively recruits these students. They must take the TOEFL with a minimum score of 500 on the paper-based TOEFL (PBT) or 61 on the Internet-based version (iBT). They must also take the SAT or ACT, scoring 21.

ADMISSIONS: 58% of the 2016-2017 applicants were accepted. The SAT scores for the 2016-2017 freshman class were: Critical Reading-- 67% below 500, 24% between 500 and 599, and 9% between 600 and 699. Math-- 64% below 500, 33% between 500 and 599, and 3% between 600 and 699. 50% of the current freshmen were in the top fifth of their class; 84% were in the top two fifths. **Admissions Contact:** Charity Wittner, Director of Enrollment & Admissions. Email: *cwittner@umobile.edu* Web: *www.umobile.edu*

FINANCIAL AID: In 2016-2017, 82% of all full-time freshmen and 76% of continuing full-time students received some form of financial aid. 58% of all full-time freshmen and 45% of continuing full-time students received need-based aid. The average freshman award was $18,602. Need-based scholarships or need-based grants averaged $5,219; need-based self-help aid (loans and jobs) averaged $2,175; non-need-based athletic scholarships averaged $16,508; and other non-need-based awards and non-need-based scholarships averaged $9,377. Average annual earnings from campus work are $2175. The average financial indebtedness of the 2016 graduate was $28,250. The state aid form and the college's own financial statement are required. The FAFSA code is 001029. The deadline for filing freshman financial aid applications for fall entry is August 1.

UNIVERSITY OF MONTEVALLO C-3

www.montevallo.edu

Montevallo, AL 35115 (205) 665-6034

Fax: (205) 665-6032	**Email:** admissions@montevallo.edu
Full-time: 689 men, 1489 women	**Faculty:** IIA, -$
Part-time: 84 men, 147 women	**Ph.D.s:** 70%
Graduate: 99 men, 292 women	**Student/Faculty:** 16 to 1
Year: semesters, summer session	**Tuition:** $12,040 ($24,310)
Room & Board: $7462	**Freshman Class:** 2024 applied, 1417 accepted, 505 enrolled
ACT: 23	**CEEB CODE:** 1004
Application Deadline: August 1	**COMPETITIVE**

University of Montevallo, founded in 1896, is a public, liberal arts institution offering courses in business, fine arts, music, teacher preparation and preprofessional training. Figures in the above capsule and in this profile are approximate. There are 4 undergraduate schools and 2 graduate schools. In addition to regional accreditation, UM has baccalaureate program accreditation with AACSB, ADA, AHEA, CSWE, NASAD, NASM, NCATE, SACS, CACREP, and ACS. The 160-acre campus is in a small town 35 miles south of Birmingham. Including any residence halls, there are 40 buildings.

STUDENT LIFE: 93% of undergraduates are from Alabama. Others are from 6 states, 17 foreign countries, and Canada. 71% are White; 15% African American; 5% race unknown; 4% Hispanic; 2% two or more races; 1% Asian American; 1% American Indian/Alaska Native; 1% Foreign. **Female To Male Ratio:** 2.1:1. The average age of freshmen is 18; all undergraduates, 20. 23% do not continue beyond their first year; 45% remain to graduate. **Housing:** 1340 students can be accommodated in college housing, which includes single-sex and coed dorms and on-campus apartments. In addition, there are fraternity houses. On-campus housing is available on a first-come and first-served basis. 50% of students commute. All students may keep cars.

FACULTY/CLASSROOMS: 46% of faculty are male; 54% are female. 99% teach undergraduates. No introductory courses are taught by graduate students. The average class size in an introductory lecture is 24; in a laboratory is 23; and in a regular course is 24.

PROGRAMS OF STUDY: UM confers B.A., B.S., B.B.A., B.F.A., B.M. and B.M.E. degrees. Master's degrees are also awarded. Bachelor's degrees are awarded in BIOLOGICAL SCIENCE (biology/biological science), BUSINESS (accounting, banking and finance, business administration and management, management science, and marketing/retailing/merchandising), COMMUNICATIONS AND THE ARTS (art, communications, dramatic arts, English, French, German, journalism, music, music performance, Spanish, and studio art), COMPUTER AND PHYSICAL SCIENCE (chemistry and mathematics), EDUCATION (art education, education of the deaf and hearing impaired, elementary education, home economics education, music education, and physical education), ENGINEERING AND ENVIRONMENTAL DESIGN (environmental science), HEALTH PROFESSIONS (speech pathology/audiology), SOCIAL SCIENCE (family/consumer studies, history, political science/government, psychology, social science, social work, and sociology). Elementary/early childhood education, business, and art have the largest enrollments.

ACTIVITIES: 13% of men belong to 7 national fraternities; 19% of women belong to 8 national sororities. There are 93 groups on campus, including art, cheerleading, choir, chorus, computers, dance, debate, drama, environmental, ethnic, forensics, honors, international, jazz band, LGBT, literary magazine, musical theater, newspaper, pep band, photography, political, professional, radio and TV, religious, social, social service, student government, and yearbook. Popular campus events include College Night, and Honors Day. **Sports:** There are 4 intercollegiate sports for men and 7 for women, and 7 intramural sports for men and 4 for women. Facilities include a 97,000-square-foot student activity center with a 6-lane collegiate competition size pool, 6000-square-foot weight training and cardio-conditioning theater, 3500-seat arena, several athletic fields, tennis courts, sand volleyball facility, a lake, camping area, and an 18-hole golf course and driving range. **Graduates:** From July 1, 2015 to June 30, 2016, 326 bachelor's degrees were awarded. The most popular majors were business/marketing (17%), education (13%), and visual and performing arts (12%). In an average class, 21% graduate in 4 years or less, 41% graduate in 5 years or less, and 47% graduate in 6 years or less.

SERVICES: Counseling and information services are available, as is tutoring in some subjects. There is a reader service for the blind, and remedial math, reading, and writing, a study skill center, and speech and hearing center. **Library/Resources:** The library contains 266,236 volumes, 795,344 microform items, and 4,673 audio/video tapes/CDs/DVDs, and subscribes to 27,962 periodicals including electronic. Computerized library services include interlibrary loans, database searching, Internet access, and Wi-Fi capability. Special learning facilities include an art gallery, radio station, TV station, All-Steinway Music Department, Center for Innovative Teaching and Technology, Digital Cafe, Distance Learnin Classroom, Glass-blowing Studio, Painting and Drawing Studios, Ebeneezer Swamp Ecological Preserve, Speech and Hearing Center, Observatory, and Traffic Safety Center. **Physically Challenged Students:** Facilities include wheelchair ramps, elevators, special parking, specially equipped restrooms, special class scheduling, lowered drinking fountains, and lowered telephones. **Special:** A 3-2 engineering degree is offered with Auburn University, the University of Alabama at Birmingham, and the University of Alabama at Tuscaloosa. Internships are required for some majors. Study abroad, B.A.-B.S. degrees, dual degrees, a Washington semester, and pass/fail options are available. There are 26 national honor societies, a freshman honors program, and 1 departmental honors program. **Visiting:** There are regularly scheduled orientations for prospective students, consisting of a program of orientation, advising, and academic counseling prior to enrollment. There are guides for informal visits, visitors may sit in on classes, and stay overnight. To schedule a visit, contact the Office of Admissions. **Campus Safety and Security:** Measures include 24-hour foot and vehicle patrol, emergency notification system, self-defense education, and security escort services. There are emergency telephones, lighted pathways/sidewalks, controlled access to dorms/residences, campus lighting, and electronic access into residence halls.

REQUIREMENTS: The ACT is required. Applicants must present a high school transcript with a minimum GPA of 2.5 and successful completion of a minimum of 16 academic or college-preparatory credits from 9th to 12th grade, including 4 units each of English, social studies, and math, 2 units of science, and 4 units of foreign language or electives. Applicants who have earned a GED should have an official copy of their score report sent in lieu of a high school transcript. AP and CLEP credits are accepted. Important factors in the admissions decision are advanced placement or honors courses, evidence of special talent, and geographical diversity. To graduate, students must complete a minimum of 130 semester hours with an overall 2.0 GPA while meeting core, major, and minor requirements. Core requirements include 12 hours of writing reinforcement courses (usually met with literature and major/minor courses), 7 hours of sciences (2 branches), 6 hours each in foundations in writing, world literature, world civilizations, and institutions and issues courses, 4 hours of health/phys ed, 3 hours each of oral communications, math, computer science, fine arts, and humanities, and 1 additional fine arts or humanity elective. **Procedure:** Freshmen are admitted to all sessions. Entrance exams should be taken in spring of the junior year or fall of the senior year. There are deferred admissions and rolling admissions plans. Applications should be filed by August 1 for fall entry; December 1 for spring entry; and May 1 for summer entry. The fall 2016 application fee was $30. Notification is sent on a rolling basis. Applications are accepted on-line. **Transfer Students:** 157 transfer students enrolled in 2015-2016. A minimum of a cumulative C average on all college-level study attempted must have been attained. This is a cumulative GPA of 2.0 or better on a 4.0 scale. Applicants must be a student in good standing -- neither probation nor suspension can be in effect at the previous or current college of university attended. Transcripts of all previous study attempted must be submitted and evaluated before an application review can be conducted. Collegiate work from post-secondary institutions not accredited nor in candidacy status for accreditation by a regional accrediting association is not transferable to the University of Montevallo. Students who have completed less than 24 semester hours (or 36 quarter hours) of college-level study must also submit a secondary-school transcript and either an ACT or SAT score report and must satisfy all requirements for freshman admission. A maximum of 64 semester hours (or 96 quarter hours) may be transferred for credit from either a community or junior college. 33 of 130 credits required for the bachelor's degree must be completed at UM. **International Students:** There are 35 international students enrolled. They must take the TOEFL with a minimum score of 525 on the paper-based TOEFL (PBT) or 71 on the Internet-based version (iBT). They must also take the SAT or ACT.

ADMISSIONS: 70% of the 2016-2017 applicants were accepted. **Admissions Contact:** Greg Embry, Director of Admissions. Email: *admissions@montevallo.edu* Web: *www.montevallo.edu*

FINANCIAL AID: 17% of undergraduate students work part-time. Average annual earnings from campus work are $4640. The FAFSA code is 001004. The priority date for freshman financial aid applications for fall entry is March 1.

UNIVERSITY OF NORTH ALABAMA — B-1

www.una.edu

Florence, AL 35632	**(256) 765-4680** **(800) TALKUNA** **Email: admissions@una.edu**
Full-time: 2109 men, 3054 women	**Faculty:** IIA, --$
Part-time: 466 men, 684 women	**Ph.D.s:** n/av
Graduate: 482 men, 697 women	**Student/Faculty:** n/av
Year: semesters, summer session	**Tuition:** $8114 ($14,450)
Room & Board: $7284	**Freshman Class:** 4758 applied, 2456 accepted, 1196 enrolled
SAT or ACT: required	**CEEB CODE:** 1735
Application Deadline: n/av	**COMPETITIVE**

University of North Alabama was founded as LaGrange College in 1830. It was reestablished in 1872 as the first state-supported teachers college south of the Ohio River. There are 4 undergraduate schools and one graduate school. In addition to regional accreditation, UNA has baccalaureate program accreditation with AACSB, ABET, ACBSP, ACEJMC, CSWE, NASAD, NASM, NCATE, ACBSP, ASAC, CAC, CACREP, CAEP, CCNE, CIDA, and NKBA. The 130-acre campus is in an urban area 116 miles north of Birmingham. Including any residence halls, there are 80 buildings.

STUDENT LIFE: 79% of undergraduates are from Alabama. Others are from 35 states, 39 foreign countries, and Canada. 71% are White; 14% African American. **Female To Male Ratio:** 1.5:1. The average age of freshmen is 19; all undergraduates, 22. 25% do not continue beyond their first year; 43% remain to graduate. **Housing:** 1701 students can be accommodated in college housing, which includes single-sex and coed dorms, on-campus apartments, and off-campus apartments. In addition, there are fraternity houses, sorority houses, theme and wellness housing, and international housing. On-campus housing is guaranteed for the freshman year only, and is available on a first-come, and first-served basis. 75% of students commute. Alcohol is not permitted. All students may keep cars.

FACULTY/CLASSROOMS: All teach undergraduates. No introductory courses are taught by graduate students. The average class size in an introductory lecture is 18 and in a laboratory is 26.

PROGRAMS OF STUDY: UNA confers B.A., B.S., B.S.C.S., B.A.M., B.I.S., B.B.A., B.F.A., B.S.Ed., B.S.M., B.M., B.S.N. and B.S.W. degrees. Master's degrees are also awarded. Bachelor's degrees are awarded in BIOLOGICAL SCIENCE (biology/biological science and environmental biology), BUSINESS (accounting, banking and finance, business economics, and marketing/retailing/merchandising), COMMUNICATIONS AND THE ARTS (art, communications, dramatic arts, English, French, German, journalism, music, public relations, and Spanish), COMPUTER AND PHYSICAL SCIENCE (chemistry, computer science, geology, information sciences and systems, mathematics, and physics), EDUCATION (art education, business education, early childhood education, elementary education, foreign languages education, home economics education, music education, physical education, science education, secondary education, and social science education), ENGINEERING AND ENVIRONMENTAL DESIGN (interior design), HEALTH PROFESSIONS (industrial hygiene and nursing), SOCIAL SCIENCE (criminal justice, geography, history, liberal arts/general studies, political science/government, psychology, social work, and sociology). Physical sciences, biological sciences, nursing, and math are the strongest academically.

ACTIVITIES: 12% of men belong to 8 national fraternities; 8% of women belong to 7 national sororities. There are 139 groups on campus, including Diversity Student Ambassadors, UNA Nerd Pop Culture, art, band, cheerleading, choir, chorale, chorus, computers, debate, drama, drill team, environmental, ethnic, film, honors, international, jazz band, LGBT, literary magazine, marching band, musical theater, newspaper, opera, orchestra, pep band, photography, political, professional, religious, social, social service, student government, symphony, UNA Video Game Association, and yearbook. Popular campus events include Spring Fling and the George Lindsey Film Festival. **Sports:** There are 6 intercollegiate sports for men and 7 for women, and 20 intramural sports for men and 20 for women. Facilities include a 13,500-seat football stadium, a 4000-seat gym, baseball and softball fields, an outdoor track, indoor swimming pool, tennis courts, fitness center with a cardio theater, weights and machines, aerobics studio, gaming lounge, intramural field with 3 multipurpose courts, 2-lane track, and equipment checkout. **Graduates:** From July 1, 2015 to June 30, 2016, 1361 bachelor's degrees were awarded. The most popular majors were nursing (16%), professional management (7%), and elementary ed K-6 (6%). In an average class, 23% graduate in 4 years or less, 39% graduate in 5 years or less, and 43% graduate in 6 years or less.

SERVICES: Counseling and information services are available, as is tutoring in some subjects, such as physics, computer science, writing, math, English, history, biology, chemistry, accounting, finance, and economics, qualitative methods, and psychology. There is a reader service for the blind, and remedial math and writing. The academic resource center features computer-assisted tutoring and faculty mentoring **Library/Resources:** The 4 libraries contain 364,223 volumes, 1.1 million microform items, and 38,812 audio/video tapes/CDs/DVDs, and subscribe to 31,404 periodicals including electronic. Computerized library services include interlibrary loans, database searching, Internet access, and Wi-Fi capability. Special learning facilities include an art gallery and planetarium. **Physically Challenged Students:** 96% of the campus is accessible. Facilities include wheelchair ramps, elevators, special parking, specially equipped restrooms, special class scheduling, lowered drinking fountains, lowered telephones, and special housing. **Special:** University of North Alabama, offers cooperative programs in all majors, work-study programs, various B.A.-B.S. degrees, dual majors and a general studies degree. Nondegree study is possible. There are 13 national honor societies, Phi Beta Kappa, a freshman honors program, and 2 departmental honors programs. **Visiting:** There are regularly scheduled orientations for prospective students, including orientation programs conducted each summer prior to the fall semester. There are guides for informal visits. To schedule a visit, contact the Office of Admissions. **Campus Safety and Security:** Measures include 24-hour foot and vehicle patrol, emergency notification system, self-defense education, and security escort services. There are shuttle buses, emergency telephones, lighted pathways/sidewalks, and controlled access to dorms/residences.

REQUIREMENTS: The SAT or ACT is required. Applicants should be graduates of an accredited high school or have earned a GED. 13 High school united required are 4 in English, 3 in social studies, and 2 each in math, and science, and any 2 in foreign languages, history, or computer sciences. A GPA of 2.0 is required. AP and CLEP credits are accepted. Students must complete a core curriculum, which includes 12 semester hours in history, social and behavioral sciences, humanities, and fine arts, 11 in natural sciences and math, and 6 in language composition. Total number of hours in majors vary. Passing grades in 1 writing emphasis and 1 computer course also are needed. A minimum of 120 semester hours and a minimum GPA of 2.0 are required to graduate. **Procedure:** Freshmen are admitted fall, spring, and summer. Entrance exams should be taken in the senior year. There are deferred admissions and rolling admissions plans. Application deadlines are open. Application fee is $25. Applications are accepted on-line. Application fees are waived if application is completed on-line. **Transfer Students:** Applicants should be eligible to return to the school last attended. 30 of 120 credits required for the bachelor's degree must be completed at UNA. **International Students:** The school actively recruits these students.

ADMISSIONS: 52% of the 2016-2017 applicants were accepted. **Admissions Contact:** Julie Taylor, Interim Director of Admissions. Email: *admissions@una.edu* Web: *www.una.edu*

FINANCIAL AID: In 2016-2017, 73% of all full-time freshmen and 63% of continuing full-time students received some form of financial aid. 47% of all full-time freshmen and 44% of continuing full-time students received need-based aid. The average freshman award was $5,635. Need-based scholarships or need-based grants averaged $4,914 ($5,816 maximum); need-based self-help aid (loans and jobs) averaged $3,318 ($3,500 maximum); non-need-based athletic scholarships averaged $6,330 ($10,000 maximum); and other non-need-based awards and non-need-based scholarships averaged $5,742. 8% of undergraduate students work part-time. Average annual earnings from campus work are $2500. The FAFSA code is 001016. The priority date for freshman financial aid applications for fall entry is June 1.

UNIVERSITY OF SOUTH ALABAMA A-5
www.southalabama.edu

Mobile, AL 36688 (251) 460-6141
(800) 872-5247
Fax: (251) 460-7876 **Email:** recruitment@southalabama.edu

Full-time: 4449 men, 5155 women	**Faculty:** 568; IIA, -$
Part-time: 965 men, 1186 women	**Ph.D.s:** 76%
Graduate: 1097 men, 3584 women	**Student/Faculty:** 20 to 1
Year: semesters, summer session	**Tuition:** $9060 ($18,120)
Room & Board: $7340	**Freshman Class:** 6087 applied, 4882 accepted, 1904 enrolled
SAT CR/M/W: 512/502/507 **ACT:** 24	**CEEB CODE:** 1880
Application Deadline: July 15	**COMPETITIVE**

University of South Alabama, a state-supported institution established in 1963, offers undergraduate and graduate degrees. The figures in the above capsule and in this profile are approximate. There are 8 undergraduate schools and 9 graduate schools. In addition to regional accreditation, USA has baccalaureate program accreditation with AACSB,

ABET, CSAB, CSWE, NASM, NCATE, TEAC, JRCERT, CAAHEP, and CCNE. The 1224-acre campus is in a suburban area near the Gulf of Mexico in Mobile, Alabama, and 150 miles east of New Orleans. Including any residence halls, there are 117 buildings.

STUDENT LIFE: 82% of undergraduates are from Alabama. Others are from 51 states, 81 foreign countries, and Canada. 60% are White; 20% African American. 14% claim no religious affiliation. **Female To Male Ratio:** 1.5:1. The average age of freshmen is 19; all undergraduates, 22. 27% do not continue beyond their first year; 36% remain to graduate. **Housing:** 3324 students can be accommodated in college housing, which includes coed dorms, on-campus apartments, and off-campus apartments. In addition, there are special-interest houses, fraternity houses, sorority houses, and wellness and themed housing. On-campus housing is available on a first-come and first-served basis. 71% of students commute. Alcohol is not permitted. All students may keep cars.

FACULTY/CLASSROOMS: 51% of faculty are male; 49% are female. 68% teach undergraduates. No introductory courses are taught by graduate students.

PROGRAMS OF STUDY: USA confers B.A., B.S., B.F.A., B.M., B.S.B.A., B.S.N., B.P.H.S., B.S.R.S., B.S.I.T., B.S.I.S., B.S.C.S., B.S.C.A. and B.S.W. degrees. Master's and doctoral degrees are also awarded. Bachelor's degrees are awarded in BIOLOGICAL SCIENCE (biology/biological science), BUSINESS (accounting, banking and finance, business administration and management, business economics, hospitality management services, marketing/retailing/merchandising, and recreation and leisure services), COMMUNICATIONS AND THE ARTS (communications, dramatic arts, English, fine arts, information technology, languages, and music), COMPUTER AND PHYSICAL SCIENCE (atmospheric sciences and meteorology, chemistry, computer science, cyber intelligence/security studies, geology, information science, mathematics, and physics), EDUCATION (early childhood education, education, educational studies, elementary education, health education, health information management, physical education, secondary education, and special education), ENGINEERING AND ENVIRONMENTAL DESIGN (chemical engineering, civil engineering, computer engineering, electrical/electronics engineering, and mechanical engineering), HEALTH PROFESSIONS (biomedical science, emergency medical services, nursing, radiological science, respiratory therapy, and speech pathology/audiology), SOCIAL SCIENCE (anthropology, criminal justice, geography, history, interdisciplinary studies, international studies, philosophy, political science/government, psychology, social work, and sociology). Health professions, business, and engineering are the strongest academically. Business administration, nursing, and mechanical engineering have the largest enrollments.

ACTIVITIES: There are 205 groups on campus, including art, band, cheerleading, chess, choir, chorale, chorus, computers, dance, debate, drama, ethnic, film, honors, international, jazz band, LGBT, literary magazine, marching band, musical theater, newspaper, opera, orchestra, pep band, political, professional, radio and TV, religious, social, social service, student government, and symphony. Popular campus events include Club South, Greek Week and Chi Omega Songfest. **Sports:** There are 8 intercollegiate sports for men and 9 for women, and 15 intramural sports for men and 15 for women. Facilities include a 10,000-seat arena, 49,000-square-foot student recreation center, including 6 handball courts, fitness rooms, 2 basketball/volleyball courts, and an indoor track, several intramural fields, and an outdoor swimming pool. **Graduates:** From July 1, 2015 to June 30, 2016, 1996 bachelor's degrees were awarded. The most popular majors were nursing (17%), professional health sciences (5%), and interdisciplinary studies (5%). In an average class, 16% graduate in 4 years or less, 30% graduate in 5 years or less, and 38% graduate in 6 years or less.

SERVICES: **Library/Resources:** The 2 libraries contain 429,788 volumes, 1.2 million microform items, and 20,327 audio/video tapes/CDs/DVDs. Computerized library services include interlibrary loans, database searching, Internet access, and Wi-Fi capability. Special learning facilities include an art gallery, radio station, TV station, and the Archaeology Museum. **Physically Challenged Students:** Facilities include wheelchair ramps, elevators, special parking, specially equipped restrooms, lowered drinking fountains, and special housing. **Special:** University of South Alabama, offers co-op programs in most majors, federal work-study, internships, study abroad in many countries, dual majors, an adult degree program, and a personalized studies program. There are 20 national honor societies and a freshman honors program. **Visiting:** There are regularly scheduled orientations for prospective students, Orientation includes a campus tour, class registration, reserving textbooks, team building activities and obtaining a student ID. There are guides for informal visits. To schedule a visit, contact Scott Henne at recruitment@southalabama.edu. **Campus Safety and Security:** Measures include 24-hour foot and vehicle patrol, emergency notification system, self-defense education, and security escort services. There are shuttle buses, emergency telephones, lighted pathways/sidewalks, and controlled access to dorms/residences.

REQUIREMENTS: Applicants should be high school graduates or have a GED certificate. A minimum ACT score of 19 is required for regular admission. 16 academic units recommended for admissions are 4 in English, 3 each in math, social studies, and science; of those 2 units must be lab, and 3 academic electives. A GPA of 2.5 is required. AP and CLEP credits are accepted. General education requirements consist of 12 hours in written composition, 12 hours in humanities and fine arts, at least 12 hours in history and the social and behavioral sciences, and 11 hours in natural science and math. A minimum of 128 semester hours, with a minimum GPA of 2.0, is required for graduation. **Procedure:** Freshmen are admitted to all sessions. Entrance exams should be taken during the junior year or early in the senior year. There is a rolling admissions plan. Applications should be filed by July 15 for fall entry; December 1 for spring entry; and May 1 for summer entry, along with a $35 fee. Applications are accepted on-line. **Transfer Students:** 833 transfer students enrolled in 2015-2016. Transfer applicants must have at least a 2.0 GPA on all college work attempted for regular admission. An official transcript from each college or university attended is required. (If the student has earned less than 30 semester or 40 quarter hours, then an official high school transcript is required. If the student graduated from high school less than five years prior to matriculation at USA or is not at least 23 years of age, then ACT or SAT scores are required in addition to the high school transcript). 32 of 120 credits required for the bachelor's degree must be completed at USA. **International Students:** There are 968 international students enrolled. The school actively recruits these students. They must take the TOEFL with a minimum score of 61 on the Internet-based version (iBT) and the college's own test. They must also take the SAT or ACT, scoring 19.

ADMISSIONS: 80% of the 2016-2017 applicants were accepted. The SAT scores for the 2016-2017 freshman class were: Critical Reading--42% below 500, 37% between 500 and 599, 19% between 600 and 699, and 2% between 700 and 800. Math-- 42% below 500, 40% between 500 and 599, and 18% between 600 and 699. Writing-- 52% below 500, 34% between 500 and 599, 13% between 600 and 699, and 1% between 700 and 800. The ACT scores were 6% between 12 and 17, 53% between 18 and 23, 35% between 24 and 29, and 5% above 30. **Admissions Contact:** Scott Henne, Director, New Student Recruitment. Email: *recruitment@southalabama.edu* Web: *www.southalabama.edu*

FINANCIAL AID: In 2016-2017, 67% of all full-time freshmen and 63% of continuing full-time students received some form of financial aid. 61% of all full-time freshmen and 52% of continuing full-time students received need-based aid. The average freshman award was $9,869. Need-based scholarships or need-based grants averaged $7,057; need-based self-help aid (loans and jobs) averaged $3,694; non-need-based athletic scholarships averaged $18,648; other non-need-based awards and non-need-based scholarships averaged $3,454; and $5,257 from other forms of aid. The FAFSA code is 001057. The priority date for freshman financial aid applications for fall entry is May 31.

UNIVERSITY OF WEST ALABAMA *(The complete profile is made available exclusively on our website, www.barronspac.com)*

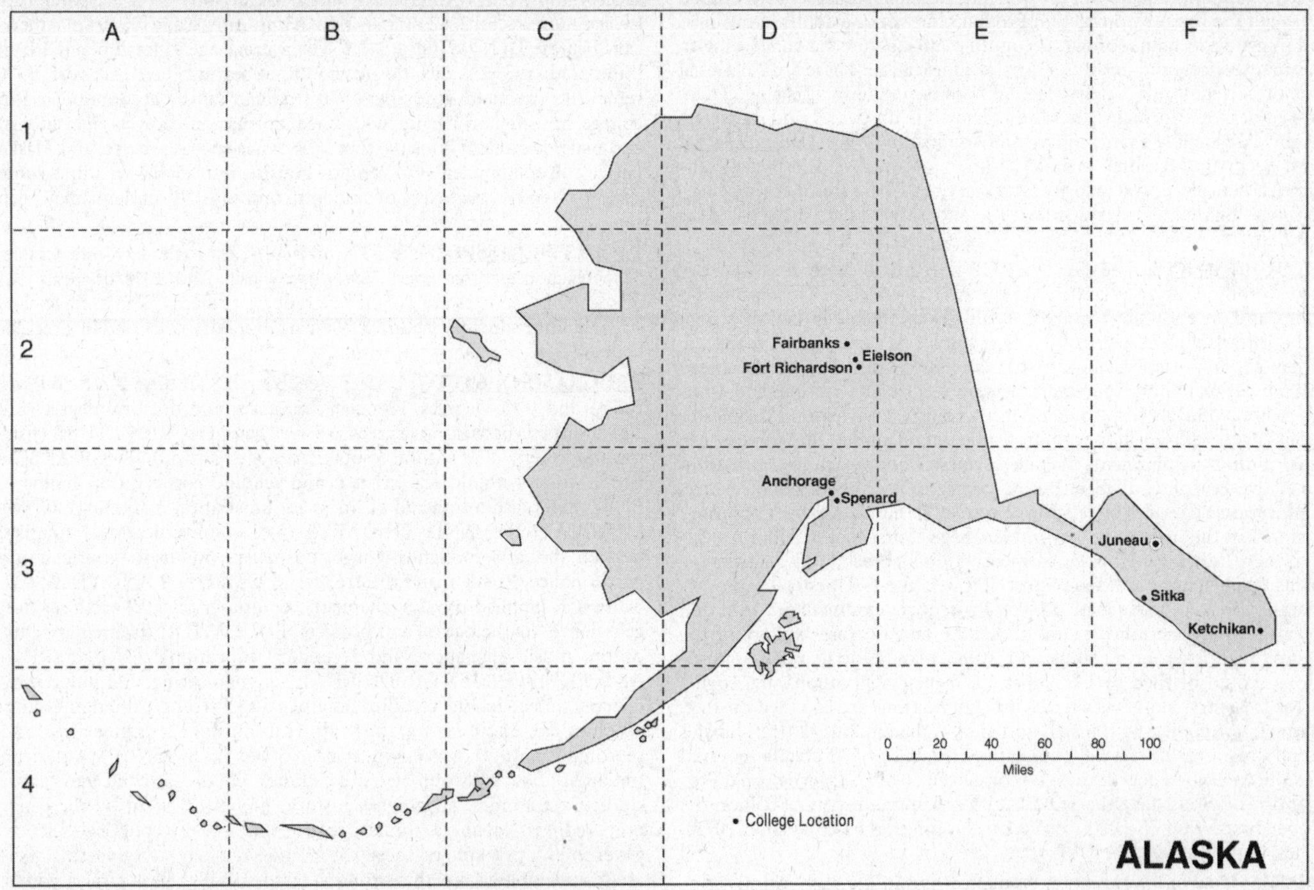

ALASKA PACIFIC UNIVERSITY D-3

www.alaskapacific.edu

Anchorage, AK 99508 (907) 564-8248
(800) 252-7528

Fax: (907) 564-8317 Email: admissions@alaskapacific.edu

Full-time: 125 men, 200 women	**Faculty:** n/av
Part-time: 60 men, 160 women	**Ph.D.s:** 60%
Graduate: 85 men, 190 women	**Student/Faculty:** 12 to 1
Year: 4-1-4, summer session	**Tuition:** $19,680
Room & Board: $7000	**Freshman Class:** n/av
SAT or ACT: required	**CEEB CODE:** 4201
Application Deadline: August 1	**VERY COMPETITIVE**

Alaska Pacific University, founded in 1957 and affiliated with the United Methodist Church, is a private institution offering undergraduate, graduate, and adult degree-completion programs. The figures in the above capsule and in this profile are approximate. There are 6 undergraduate schools and 6 graduate schools. In addition to regional accreditation, APU has baccalaureate program accreditation with NCATE. The 170-acre campus is in a suburban area in midtown Anchorage. Including any residence halls, there are 13 buildings.

STUDENT LIFE: 73% of undergraduates are from Alaska. Others are from 37 states, and 2 foreign countries. 68% are White; 18% American Indian/Alaska Native. **Female To Male Ratio:** 2.0:1. The average age of freshmen is 25; all undergraduates, 30. 25% do not continue beyond their first year; 36% remain to graduate. **Housing:** 170 students can be accommodated in college housing, which includes coed dorms and on-campus apartments. In addition, there are special-interest houses. On-campus housing is guaranteed for the freshman year only, and is available on a first-come, first-served basis, and is available on a lottery system for upperclassmen. 73% of students commute. Alcohol is not permitted. All students may keep cars.

FACULTY/CLASSROOMS: 42% of faculty are male; 58% are female. 98% teach undergraduates. No introductory courses are taught by graduate students. The average class size in an introductory lecture is 12; in a laboratory is 9; and in a regular course is 10.

PROGRAMS OF STUDY: APU confers B.A. and B.S. degrees. Associate and master's degrees are also awarded. Bachelor's degrees are awarded in AGRICULTURE (environmental studies and natural resource management), BIOLOGICAL SCIENCE (marine biology), BUSINESS (business administration and management and recreational facilities management), COMPUTER AND PHYSICAL SCIENCE (earth science), EDUCATION (elementary education), ENGINEERING AND ENVIRONMENTAL DESIGN (environmental science), HEALTH PROFESSIONS (health care administration), SOCIAL SCIENCE (human services, liberal arts/general studies, and psychology). Environmental science, outdoor studies, and psychology have the largest enrollments.

ACTIVITIES: There are no fraternities or sororities. There are 18 groups on campus, including art, band, chorus, drama, ethnic, international, newspaper, photography, professional, religious, social service, student government, and students in free enterprise. Popular campus events include Earth Day, Spring Honors Convocation and Fall Academic Convocation. **Sports:** There is no sports program at APU. Facilities include a 300-seat sports center, an indoor swimming pool, cross-country skiing and running trails, climbing wall, soccer fields, lake for boating, a disc golf course, and a weight/exercise room. **Graduates:** The most popular majors were business/marketing (19%), health professions and related programs (16%), social sciences, psychology, and engineering (7%).

SERVICES: Counseling and information services are available, as is tutoring in some subjects, such as math, writing, and other subjects as needed. There is remedial math and writing. **Library/Resources:** The library contains 891,103 volumes, 627,916 microform items, and 13,324 audio/video tapes/CDs/DVDs, and subscribes to 3,840 periodicals including electronic. Computerized library services include interlibrary loans and Internet access. Special learning facilities include an art gallery, TV station, the Alaskana collection located in the Consortium Library. **Physically Challenged Students:** 75% of the campus is accessible. Facilities include wheelchair ramps, elevators, special parking, specially equipped restrooms, lowered drinking fountains, and lowered telephones. **Special:** Internships are required, and study abroad, student-designed majors, and B.A.-B.S. degrees in earth sciences, environmental science, and marine biology are possible. Accelerated degrees are offered through the Degree Completion Program for working adults in business administration management, accounting information for management, human services, and health services administration. There are 2 national honor societies and 2 departmental honors programs. **Visiting:** There are guides for informal visits, visitors may sit in on classes, and stay overnight. To schedule a visit, contact the Admissions Office. **Campus Safety and Security:** Measures include 24-hour foot and vehicle patrol, self-defense education, and security escort services. There are emergency telephones, lighted pathways/sidewalks, and safety signs are posted as needed.

REQUIREMENTS: The SAT or ACT is required, with a satisfactory score on the SAT or at least 19 on the ACT. Two teacher recommendations and an essay are required. A GED is acceptable in lieu of a high school transcript. A GPA of 2.5 is required. AP and CLEP credits are accepted. Important factors in the admissions decision are advanced placement or honors courses, leadership record, and recommendations by school officials. All students must complete at least 128 semester hours, with 39 to 61 in the major, and maintain a minimum GPA of 2.0. Distribution requirements include 4 semester hours each in Orientation to Active Learning, a lab science, a course in social/behavioral science, and a course in ethics or religion, 2 courses in humanities, a sophomore seminar in the major, and a world language course that includes American Sign Language. Courses to meet writing, speech, and quantitative skills competencies are also required, as well as a 3-semester-hour practicum, portfolio, and senior project. **Procedure:** Freshmen are admitted to all sessions. Entrance exams should be taken before January of the senior year. There is a rolling admissions plan. Early decision applications should be filed by December 12; regular applications, by August 1 for fall entry, along with a $25 fee. Applications are accepted on-line. **Transfer Students:** 80 transfer students enrolled in 2015-2016. Transfer applicants must have a 2.0 cumulative GPA. 32 of 128 credits required for the bachelor's degree must be completed at APU. **International Students:** They must take the TOEFL with a minimum score of 550 on the paper-based TOEFL (PBT) or 79 on the Internet-based version (iBT). They must also take the SAT or ACT.

ADMISSIONS: One freshman graduated first in the class. **Admissions Contact:** Brian McDermott, Assistant Director of Admissions. Email: *admissions@alaskapacific.edu* Web: *www.alaskapacific.edu*

FINANCIAL AID: APU is a member of CSS. The FAFSA code is 001061. The priority date for freshman financial aid applications for fall entry is September 19.

UNIVERSITY OF ALASKA ANCHORAGE *(The complete profile is made available exclusively on our website, www.barronspac.com)*

UNIVERSITY OF ALASKA FAIRBANKS D-2
www.uaf.edu

Fairbanks, AK 99775	**(907) 474-7500** **(800) 478-1823**
Fax: (907) 474-7097	**Email: admissions@uaf.edu**
Full-time: 1259 men, 1209 women	**Faculty:** 328; I, --$
Part-time: 485 men, 644 women	**Ph.D.s:** 71%
Graduate: 467 men, 654 women	**Student/Faculty:** 8 to 1
Year: semesters, summer session	**Tuition:** $7799 ($23,084)
Room & Board: $8380	**Freshman Class:** 873 applied, 549 accepted, 450 enrolled
SAT CR/M/W: 560/550/530 **ACT:** 24	**CEEB CODE:** 4866
Application Deadline: June 15	**COMPETITIVE**

University of Alaska Fairbanks, founded in 1917 is the nation's northernmost Land, Sea, and Space Grant university and international research center. The institution advances and disseminates knowledge through teaching, research, and public service with an emphasis on Alaska and circumpolar regions. There are 8 undergraduate schools and 8 graduate schools. In addition to regional accreditation, UAF has baccalaureate program accreditation with AACSB, ABET, ACEJMC, CSWE, NASM, SAF, ACS, and CAEP. The 2250-acre campus is in a small town 4 miles northwest of Fairbanks. Including any residence halls, there are 68 buildings.

STUDENT LIFE: 81% of undergraduates are from Alaska. Others are from 47 states, 20 foreign countries, and Canada. 50% are White; 26% race unknown; 8% American Indian/Alaska Native; 7% Hispanic; 5% two or more races; 2% Foreign; 1% African American; 1% Asian American. **Female To Male Ratio:** 1.1:1. The average age of freshmen is 18; all undergraduates, 23. 25% do not continue beyond their first year; 39% remain to graduate. **Housing:** 1578 students can be accommodated in college housing, which includes coed dorms, on-campus apartments, and married student housing. first-year experience residence, and Alaska native cultural housing. On-campus housing is available on a first-come and first-served basis. 61% of students commute. All students may keep cars.

FACULTY/CLASSROOMS: 58% of faculty are male; 42% are female. 58% teach undergraduates, 72% do research, and 40% do both. No introductory courses are taught by graduate students. The average class size in an introductory lecture is 20; in a laboratory is 15; and in a regular course is 18.

PROGRAMS OF STUDY: UAF confers B.A., B.S., B.B.A., B.A.S., B.E.M., B.F.A. and B.M. degrees. Associate, master's, and doctoral degrees are also awarded. Bachelor's degrees are awarded in AGRICULTURE (fishing and fisheries and natural resource management), BIOLOGICAL SCIENCE (biology/biological science and wildlife conservation biology), BUSINESS (accounting and business administration marketing), COMMUNICATIONS AND THE ARTS (art, communications, English, Eskimo, film arts, foreign language, journalism, linguistics, music, music performance, Russian, and theatre arts), COMPUTER AND PHYSICAL SCIENCE (applied physics, chemistry, computer science, earth science, geoscience, mathematics, and physics), EDUCATION (elementary education, music education, and secondary education), ENGINEERING AND ENVIRONMENTAL DESIGN (civil engineering, computer engineering, electrical/electronics engineering, geological engineering, mechanical engineering, mining and mineral engineering, and petroleum/natural gas engineering), SOCIAL SCIENCE (American Indian studies, anthropology, area studies, child care/child and family studies, economics, geography, history, homeland security/emergency preparedness, Japanese studies, justice and society, political science/government, psychology, social work, and sociology). Engineering, fisheries, and biology are the strongest academically. Biological sciences, business administration, and mechanical engineering have the largest enrollments.

ACTIVITIES: There are 176 groups on campus, including art, band, chess, choir, chorus, communications, computers, dance, drama, environmental, ethnic, film, honors, international, jazz band, LGBT, literary magazine, newspaper, orchestra, photography, political, professional, radio and TV, religious, social, student government, and symphony. Popular campus events include Starvation Gulch, All-Campus Day, and Meltdown. **Sports:** There are 5 intercollegiate sports for men and 6 for women, and 8 intramural sports for men and 8 for women. Facilities include a 4500-seat arena, 2000-seat gym, 1500-seat skating rink, 2 racquetball courts, 2 weight rooms, 4 basketball courts, an Olympic-size swimming pool, small-bore rifle range, and a lighted 30-mile ski trail. **Graduates:** From July 1, 2015 to June 30, 2016, 572 bachelor's degrees were awarded. The most popular majors were biological sciences (10%), business administration (7%), and accounting (6%). 113 companies recruited on campus in 2015-2016. In an average class, 15% graduate in 4 years or less, 31% graduate in 5 years or less, and 39% graduate in 6 years or less.

SERVICES: Counseling and information services are available, as is tutoring in some subjects, such as chemistry, calculus, languages, biology, math, physics, geology and English. There is a reader service for the blind, and remedial math, reading, and writing. **Library/Resources:** The 3 libraries contain 831,082 volumes, 134,215 microform items, and 99,455 audio/video tapes/CDs/DVDs, and subscribe to 62,484 periodicals including electronic. Computerized library services include interlibrary loans, database searching, Internet access, and Wi-Fi capability. Special learning facilities include an art gallery, natural history museum, radio station, TV station, and several research institutes and labs for study in the physical and natural sciences that are associated with the university. **Physically Challenged Students:** 90% of the campus is accessible. Facilities include wheelchair ramps, elevators, special parking, specially equipped restrooms, special class scheduling, lowered drinking fountains, lowered telephones, special housing. **Special:** The university's Office of eLearning and Distance Education offers satellite education programs to Alaska residents to reach students at remote sites. Study abroad is offered in 42 countries. Internships are offered through the Rural Alaska Honors Institute. Student-designed majors, credit/no credit options, nondegree study, and credit for life, military, and work experience are also available. There are 8 national honor societies and a freshman honors program. **Visiting:** There are regularly scheduled orientations for prospective students. Tours generally include academic facilities, dorms, and student recreation center, and may also include meeting with an admissions counselor, professors, advisors, and students, and classroom visits. There are guides for informal visits, visitors may sit in on classes, and stay overnight. To schedule a visit, contact the Office of Admissions. **Campus Safety and Security:** Measures include 24-hour foot and vehicle patrol, emergency notification system, self-defense education, and security escort services. There are shuttle buses, emergency telephones, lighted pathways/sidewalks, controlled access to dorms/residences, 24-hour crisis line, and evening patrols inside dorms.

REQUIREMENTS: The SAT or ACT is required. Applicants should be graduates of an accredited secondary school with 16 academic credits, including 4 in English and 3 each in math, natural or physical sciences, and social sciences, with a minimum GPA of 2.5 in these courses. Applicants should have an overall high school GPA of at least 3.0 or an overall GPA of at least 2.5 along with an ACT Plus Writing score of at least 18 or SAT total score of at least 1290. The GED is not accepted. A GPA of 2.5 is required. AP and CLEP credits are accepted. All students must complete core courses in English and oral communication, library skills, humanities, social science, natural science, and math. A minimum of 120 credit hours, with 27 to 30 in the major, and a 2.0 GPA are required for graduation. **Procedure:** Freshmen are admitted to all sessions. Entrance exams should be taken within two years of the start of term. There are early admissions, deferred admissions, and rolling admissions plans. Applications should be filed by June 15 for fall entry; November 1 for spring entry; and May 1 for summer entry, along with a $50 fee. Notification is sent on a rolling basis. Applications are accepted on-line. Application fees are waived if application is completed on-line. **Transfer Students:** 246 transfer students enrolled in 2015-2016. A GPA of 2.0 in all previous college work and an honorable dismissal from all schools attended are required. Applicants with fewer than 30 semester hours of transferable credit also must have a high school GPA of 2.0 and ACT or SAT scores. 30 of 120 credits required for the bachelor's degree must be completed at UAF. **International Students:** There are 40 international students enrolled. The school actively recruits these students. They must take the TOEFL with a minimum score of 550 on the paper-based TOEFL (PBT) or 79 on the Internet-based version (iBT), or take the IELTS. They must also take the SAT or ACT.

ADMISSIONS: 63% of the 2016-2017 applicants were accepted. The SAT scores for the 2016-2017 freshman class were: Critical Reading-- 23% below 500, 45% between 500 and 599, 27% between 600 and 699, and 5% between 700 and 800. Math-- 26% below 500, 41% between 500 and 599, 25% between 600 and 699, and 7% between 700 and 800. Writing-- 32% below 500, 43% between 500 and 599, 22% between 600 and 699, and 3% between 700 and 800. The ACT scores were 7% between 12 and 17, 42% between 18 and 23, 41% between 24 and 29, and 10% above 30. 46% of the current freshmen were in the top fifth of their class; 75% were in the top two fifths. 25 freshmen graduated first in their class. **Admissions Contact:** Mary Kreta, Director of Admissions. Email: *admissions@uaf.edu* Web: *www.uaf.edu*

FINANCIAL AID: In 2016-2017, 90% of all full-time freshmen and 80% of continuing full-time students received some form of financial aid. 49% of all full-time freshmen and 51% of continuing full-time students received need-based aid. The average freshman award was $9,547. Need-based scholarships or need-based grants averaged $7,286 ($25,214 maximum); need-based self-help aid (loans and jobs) averaged $6,065 ($8,908 maximum); non-need-based athletic scholarships averaged $17,214 ($38,146 maximum); and other non-need-based awards and non-need-based scholarships averaged $8,922 ($44,755 maximum). 16% of undergraduate students work part-time. Average annual earnings from campus work are $5320. The average financial indebtedness of the 2016 graduate was $21,780. The FAFSA code is 001063. The deadline for filing freshman financial aid applications for fall entry is February 15.

UNIVERSITY OF ALASKA SOUTHEAST F-3

www.usa.alaska.edu

Juneau, AK 99801 (907) 465-6457
(877) 465-4827

Fax: (907) 465-6365 **Email: admissions@uas.alaska.edu**

Full-time: 270 men, 325 women	**Faculty:** n/av
Part-time: 625 men, 875 women	**Ph.D.s:** n/av
Graduate: 70 men, 80 women	**Student/Faculty:** n/av
Year: semesters, summer session	**Tuition:** $5693
Room & Board: $8317	**Freshman Class:** n/av
SAT or ACT: recommended	**CEEB CODE:** 4897
Application Deadline: August 1	**COMPETITIVE**

University of Alaska Southeast, a multicampus institution founded in 1972, is part of the University of Alaska statewide system, with baccalaureate programs offered in business and public administration, education, and liberal arts and science. The figures in the above capsule and in this profile are approximate. There are 4 undergraduate schools and 2 graduate schools. In addition to regional accreditation, UAS has baccalaureate program accreditation with NCATE. The 198-acre campus is in a suburban area 10 miles north of Juneau. Including any residence halls, there are 18 buildings.

STUDENT LIFE: 75% of undergraduates are from Alaska. Others are from 37 states, 12 foreign countries, and Canada. 95% are from public schools. 70% are White; 17% American Indian/Alaska Native. **Female To Male Ratio:** 1.3:1. The average age of freshmen is 18; all undergraduates, 24. **Housing:** 400 students can be accommodated in college housing, which includes single-sex dorms, on-campus apartments, and married student housing. On-campus housing is available on a first-come and first-served basis. Priority is given to out-of-town students. 90% of students commute. All students may keep cars.

FACULTY/CLASSROOMS: 98% teach undergraduates. No introductory courses are taught by graduate students. The average class size in an introductory lecture is 20 and in a laboratory is 12.

PROGRAMS OF STUDY: UAS confers B.A., B.S., B.B.A., B.Ed. and B.L.A. degrees. Associate and master's degrees are also awarded. Bachelor's degrees are awarded in BIOLOGICAL SCIENCE (biology/biological science and marine biology), BUSINESS (accounting and business administration and management), COMMUNICATIONS AND THE ARTS (art, communications, literature, and speech/debate/rhetoric), COMPUTER AND PHYSICAL SCIENCE (mathematics), EDUCATION (elementary education), ENGINEERING AND ENVIRONMENTAL DESIGN (environmental science), SOCIAL SCIENCE (liberal arts/general studies, political science/government, public administration, and social science). Accounting, marine biology, and environmental science are the strongest academically. Liberal arts has the largest enrollment.

ACTIVITIES: There are no fraternities or sororities. There are 16 groups on campus, including choir, ethnic, honors, LGBT, literary magazine, newspaper, political, professional, religious, and student government. Popular campus events include Ski Day, Whale-watching, and Eagle Preserve Field Trips. **Sports:** There are 3 intramural sports for men and 3 for women. Facilities include a community gym and pool, an activity center, and access to health club facilities.

SERVICES: Counseling and information services are available, as is tutoring in most subjects. There is a reader service for the blind, and remedial math, reading, and writing. **Library/Resources:** The library contains 250,000 volumes, 250,000 microform items, and 1,850 audio/video tapes/CDs/DVDs, and subscribes to 1,500 periodicals including electronic. Computerized library services include interlibrary loans, database searching, and Internet access. **Physically Challenged Students:** 95% of the campus is accessible. Facilities include wheelchair ramps, elevators, special parking, specially equipped restrooms, lowered drinking fountains, and lowered telephones. **Special:** UAS offers cross-registration through the National Student Exchange, and internships with federal and state agencies. Study abroad, work-study, dual and student-designed majors, credit/no credit options, and credit for military experience are also available. The School of Career and Continuing Education offers courses and certificate programs in technological skills. **Visiting:** There are regularly scheduled orientations for prospective students. There are guides for informal visits and visitors may sit in on classes. **Campus Safety and Security:** There are shuttle buses, emergency telephones, lighted pathways/sidewalks, and late-night security at student housing.

REQUIREMENTS: The SAT or ACT is recommended. Applicants

should be graduates of an accredited secondary school or have the GED. A GPA of 2.0 is required. AP and CLEP credits are accepted. All students are required to complete general education courses, including 15 credits in humanities and social science, 10 in math and natural sciences, 6 in written communication skills, and 3 in speech. A total of 120 semester credits, with at least 36 in the major, and a minimum GPA of 2.0 are required in order to graduate. In the liberal arts program, a portfolio is required. **Procedure:** Freshmen are admitted fall and spring. There are early admissions, deferred admissions, and rolling admissions plans. Applications should be filed by August 1 for fall entry. The fall 2016 application fee was $35. **Transfer Students:** A minimum GPA of 2.0 from an accredited institution is required. 30 of 120 credits required for the bachelor's degree must be completed at UAS. **International Students:** They must take the TOEFL. They must also take the SAT or ACT.

Admissions Contact: Joe G. Nelson J.D., Vice Chancellor of Enrollment/ Student Affairs. Email: *admissions@uas.alaska.edu* Web: *www.usa.alaska .edu*

FINANCIAL AID: UAS is a member of CSS. The college's own financial statement is required. The FAFSA code is 001065. The deadline for filing freshman financial aid applications for fall entry is February 15.

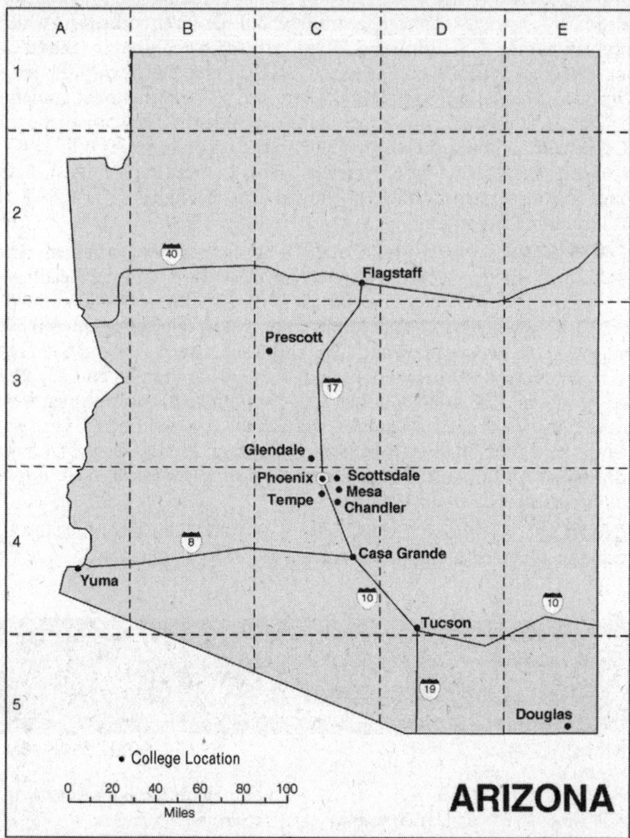

ARIZONA STATE UNIVERSITY AT THE DOWNTOWN PHOENIX CAMPUS C-4

www.campus.asu.edu/downtown-phoenix

Phoenix, AZ 85004 **(480) 965-7788**

Fax: (480) 965-3610
Full-time: 2745 men, 5493 women
Part-time: 374 men, 626 women
Graduate: 938 men, 1561 women
Year: semesters, summer session
Room & Board: $13,310

SAT CR/M: 540/530 **ACT:** 23
Application Deadline: February 1

Email: admissions@asu.edu
Faculty: IIA, av$
Ph.D.s: n/av
Student/Faculty: n/av
Tuition: $10,370 ($26,470)
Freshman Class: 5224 applied, 4007 accepted, 1298 enrolled
CEEB CODE: 4007
VERY COMPETITIVE

Arizona State University at the Downtown Phoenix Campus, in the nation's sixth-largest city, creates strong academic and career connections for students with media, health care, corporate, and government organizations. State-of-the-art living and learning facilities offer students a high-quality academic experience woven into the Valley's metropolitan core. The campus is near Phoenix's major sports, performing arts and cultural venues, and the city's burgeoning arts and dining scene. ASU was recently named the #1 school for innovation in the country by U.S. News & World Report for the second year in a row. ASU is a comprehensive public research university, measured not by whom we exclude, but rather by whom we include and how they succeed; advancing research and discovery of public value; and assuming fundamental responsibility for the economic, social, cultural, and overall health of the communities it serves. ASU champions intellectual and cultural diversity. Its research is inspired by real-world application, blurring the boundaries that traditionally separate academic disciplines. There are 7 undergraduate schools and 5 graduate schools. In addition to regional accreditation, ASU at the Downtown Phoenix campus has baccalaureate program accreditation with ACEJMC, ADA, CSWE, ACEND, CCNE, COAPRT, and NAACLS. The 18-acre campus is in an urban area in Phoenix, AZ. Including any residence halls, there are 21 buildings.

STUDENT LIFE: 72% of undergraduates are from Arizona. Others are from 38 foreign countries, and Canada. 94% are from public schools. 50% are White; 29% Hispanic; 6% African American; 5% Asian American; 4% two or more races; 2% American Indian/Alaska Native; 2% Foreign; 1% race unknown. **Female To Male Ratio:** 1.9:1. The average age of freshmen is 18; all undergraduates, 22. **Housing:** 1284 students can be accommodated in college housing, which includes coed dorms and off-campus apartments. In addition, there are honors houses, special-interest houses, and residence is available for freshmen and students in particular academic areas. On-campus housing is guaranteed for the freshman year only, is available on a first-come, first-served basis, and is available on a lottery system for upperclassmen. 85% of students commute. Alcohol is not permitted. All students may keep cars.

FACULTY/CLASSROOMS: No introductory courses are taught by graduate students.

PROGRAMS OF STUDY: ASU-Downtown Phoenix campus confers B.A., B.A.S., B.S., B.S.N. and B.S.W. degrees. Master's and doctoral degrees are also awarded. Bachelor's degrees are awarded in BIOLOGICAL SCIENCE (nutrition), BUSINESS (nonprofit/public organization management and tourism), COMMUNICATIONS AND THE ARTS (communications, journalism & technical communications, and sports media), COMPUTER AND PHYSICAL SCIENCE (applied science), EDUCATION (general studies, health education, and sports and wellness studies), HEALTH PROFESSIONS (community health work, exercise science, health science, kinesiology, nursing, and public health), SOCIAL SCIENCE (criminal justice, criminology, interdisciplinary studies, parks and recreation management, social work, and urban and regional studies). Criminal justice, journalism, and exercise & wellness have the largest enrollments.

ACTIVITIES: There are no fraternities or sororities. There are 92 groups on campus, including entrepreneurship, health, technology and sports, art, band, communications, cooking, debate, environmental, ethnic, film, honors, international, LGBT, musical theater, newspaper, photography, political, professional, radio and TV, religious, social, social service, and student government. Popular campus events include Taylor Fest, Sparky's Carnival, Devils in Disguise, FestDevil, Welcome Back BBQ, Homecoming Dance, Fall Fest, PitchFork Awards, Passport to Phoenix, Spring Bash, Spring Luau, Movies in the Park, and Finals Breakfast. **Sports:** There are 11 intercollegiate sports for men and 15 for women, and 11 intramural sports for men and 11 for women. Facilities include the Sun Devil Fitness Complex Downtown Phoenix, which includes state-of-the-art weight and fitness areas, cardiovascular and strength equipment, and free weights, gymnasium, indoor running track, a rooftop swimming pool, classrooms, and multipurpose area. **Graduates:** From July 1, 2015 to June 30, 2016, 2296 bachelor's degrees were awarded. The most popular majors were health professions (22%), homeland security, law enforcement, and firefighting (18%), parks, recreation, and leisure and fitness studies (17%). 212 companies recruited on campus in 2015-2016. Of the 2015 graduating class, 14% were enrolled in graduate school within 6 months of graduation, and 83% were employed.

SERVICES: Counseling and information services are available, as is tutoring in most subjects. ASU's University Academic Success Programs offers a range of free academic resources to support ASU students, both in-person and online. Services include: subject area tutoring, writing tutoring, graduate writing tutoring, graduate statistics tutoring, supplemental instruction (structured study groups), and academic mentoring (a peer mentoring program). ASU's Disability Resource Center (DRC) provides accommodations when needed for tutoring/services that the university provides. The DRC converts print or electronic materials that are not accessible into an accessible format for students who are blind or visually impaired, or who generally have a print related disability which includes learning disabilities. TRiO student support services (extended to those who are accepted into the TRiO program) provides tutoring as well that is more one on one. **Library/Resources:** The 2 libraries contain 4.8 million volumes, 7.8 million microform items, and 180,428 audio/video tapes/CDs/DVDs, and subscribe to 63,322 periodicals including electronic. Computerized library services include interlibrary loans, database searching, Internet access, and Wi-Fi capability. Special learning facilities include a radio station, TV station, writing labs, tutoring, research centers, instructional kitchen, news studio, and news museum. **Physically Challenged Students:** 99% of the campus is accessible. Facilities include wheelchair ramps, elevators, special parking, specially equipped restrooms, special class scheduling, lowered drinking fountains, lowered telephones, and special housing. There are flashing alarms for the deaf, modified residence hall rooms and an adaptive exercise program and facility. **Special:** Students on ASU's Downtown Phoenix Campus enjoy a variety of academic programs and opportunities to enhance their learning. For example, students in the journalism program produce and broadcast their own televised nightly newscast in an on-campus, state-of-the-art newsroom as part of the Phoenix PBS channel. And nursing students work at the ASU-Mayo Clinic Campus, as well as at nearby hospitals, gaining practical experience as they help heal patients. All students on the Downtown Phoenix campus can take on an internship in their field of study, as well as have the opportunity to study abroad in one of 55 countries. And choices such as concurrent degree programs, accelerated degree options, and the selection of 7.5- or 15-week semesters allow students to customize their college experience to exactly what they want it to be. There are 2 national honor societies and a freshman honors program. **Visiting:** There are regularly scheduled orientations for prospective students. There are guides for informal visits and visitors may sit in on classes. **Campus Safety and Security:** Measures include 24-hour foot and vehicle patrol, emergency notification system, self-defense education, and security escort services. There are shuttle buses, emergency telephones, lighted pathways/sidewalks, controlled access to dorms/residences, in-room safes, LiveSafe smartphone application, and surveillance cameras in some residence halls.

REQUIREMENTS: The SAT or ACT is recommended. Applicants must successfully complete ASU competency requirement; 4 years each of English (composition/literature based), math (algebra I, geometry, algebra II and one course requiring algebra II as a prerequisite), laboratory science - 3 years total (1 year each from any of the following areas are accepted: biology, chemistry, earth science, integrated sciences, and physics), social science - 2 years (including one year American history), second language - 2 years (same language), and fine arts or career and technical education - 1 year. Applicants must also meet at least one of the following: top 25% in high school graduating class, 3.0 GPA in competency courses (4.0 = A), ACT 22 (24 nonresidents), SAT 1120 (1180 nonresidents). Admission may be granted with one deficiency in no more than two competency areas. Deficiencies cannot be in both math and laboratory science. Students must earn a minimum 2.00 in any subject area. Most competencies may also be met by test scores or college courses. ASU admission decisions begin the first week of Sept. Submission of an ACT or SAT score is highly recommended for merit-based scholarship consideration. Some schools and colleges have higher requirements for admission to their majors. All students who don't meet the above standards will be evaluated through a process called Individual Review. Through this process Admission Services will review all available information about a student's application, carefully considering all aspects of a student's academic background and accomplishments. In some cases, additional information might be requested. ASU welcomes homeschool students and recognizes the unique academic experiences they contribute to our rich community of scholars. Students may also meet admission requirements by submitting an official GED score of 500 or above for tests taken before January 2014 or a GED score of 170 or above for tests taken after January 2014. AP and CLEP credits are accepted. To receive a degree from Arizona State University, students must have a minimum cumulative grade point average of 2.00 (some programs may require a higher GPA) and a minimum total of 120 credit hours, including a minimum of 45 hours of upper-division course work. The number of hours in the major varies by degree program, and some programs may require more upper-division work. All students must satisfy a minimum of 35 credit hours of approved General Studies coursework in five core areas and three awareness areas: mathematics studies, literacy and critical inquiry; humanities, arts and design and social and behavioral sciences, natural sciences, global awareness; historical awareness, and cultural diversity in the United States. **Procedure:** Freshmen are admitted fall and spring. There is a rolling admissions plan. Applications should be filed by February 1 for fall entry; December 1 for spring entry, along with a $50 fee. Notification is sent on a rolling basis. Applications are accepted on-line. **Transfer Students:** 1102 transfer students enrolled in 2015-2016. Requirements for general admission to Arizona State University: applicant must meet one of the following requirements (1) graduated from high school, (2) earned a GED, (3) completed an associate degree or be in progress toward an associate degree. Transfer students must meet one of the following requirements: less than 24 transferable credit hours - minimum 2.50 cumulative GPA and meet freshman aptitude requirements; 24 or more transferable credit hours - minimum 2.50 cumulative GPA; AGEC from an Arizona community college with a 2.00 or higher cumulative GPA; associate degree from a regionally accredited higher education institution with - 2.00 or higher cumulative GPA (residents) or 2.50 or higher cumulative GPA (nonresidents). "A" = 4.0; ASU accepts transfer college-level courses in which you have earned a "C-" or better. 30 of 120 credits required for the bachelor's degree must be completed at ASU at the Downtown Phoenix Campus. **International Students:** There are 171 international students enrolled. The school actively recruits these students. They must take the TOEFL with a minimum score of 500 on the paper-based TOEFL (PBT) or 61 on the Internet-based version (iBT), International English Language Testing Systems (IELTS); Pearson Test of English (PTE). SAT or ACT required for some.

ADMISSIONS: 77% of the 2016-2017 applicants were accepted. The SAT scores for the 2016-2017 freshman class were: Critical Reading-- 30% below 500, 46% between 500 and 599, 22% between 600 and 699, and 2% between 700 and 800. Math-- 32% below 500, 45% between 500 and 599, 21% between 600 and 699, and 3% between 700 and 800. The ACT scores were 6% between 12 and 17, 45% between 18 and 23, 42% between 24 and 29, and 7% above 30. 54% of the current freshmen were in the top fifth of their class; 86% were in the top two fifths. There was 1 National Merit finalists. **Admissions Contact:** Melissa Pizzo, Dean of Admissions and Financial Aid. Email: *admissions@asu.edu* Web: *https:/campus.asu.edu/downtown-phoenix*

FINANCIAL AID: The FAFSA code is 001081. The priority date for freshman financial aid applications for fall entry is January 1.

ARIZONA STATE UNIVERSITY AT THE POLYTECHNIC CAMPUS — C-4

www.campus.asu.edu/polytechnic

Mesa, AZ 85212 — **(480) 965-7788**

Fax: (480) 965-3610	**Email:** admissions@asu.edu
Full-time: 2397 men, 957 women	**Faculty:** IIA, av$
Part-time: 353 men, 162 women	**Ph.D.s:** n/av
Graduate: 338 men, 173 women	**Student/Faculty:** n/av
Year: semesters, summer session	**Tuition:** $9886 ($25,181)
Room & Board: $11,474	**Freshman Class:** 1974 applied, 1501 accepted, 494 enrolled
SAT CR/M: 550/580 **ACT:** 25	**CEEB CODE:** 4007
Application Deadline: February 1	**VERY COMPETITIVE**

Arizona State University at the Polytechnic Campus, is home to a tight-knit academic community in the fields of interdisciplinary science, engineering and technology, management and business, education and liberal arts. Thousands of square feet of innovative laboratory space make way for exciting hands-on, project-based learning. A new freshman residence hall, dining facility and student recreation center complement the growing campus community. ASU was recently named the #1 school in the country for innovation by U.S. News & World Report for the second year in a row. ASU is a comprehensive public research university, measured not by whom we exclude, but rather by whom we include and how they succeed; advancing research and discovery of public value; and assuming fundamental responsibility for the economic, social, cultural and overall health of the communities it serves. ASU champions intellectual and cultural diversity. Its research is inspired by real-world application, blurring the boundaries that traditionally separate academic disciplines. There are 7 undergraduate schools and 4 graduate schools. In addition to regional accreditation, ASU at the Polytechnic campus has baccalaureate program accreditation with ABET, ACCE, AABI, CAC, and EAC. The 575-acre campus is in a suburban area in Mesa, AZ. Including any residence halls, there are 85 buildings.

STUDENT LIFE: 72% of undergraduates are from Arizona. 47 foreign countries, and Canada. 95% are from public schools. 55% are White; 20% Hispanic; 8% Foreign; 6% Asian American; 4% African American; 4% two or more races; 1% American Indian/Alaska Native; 1% race unknown. **Male To Female Ratio:** 2.4:1. The average age of freshmen is 18; all undergraduates, 23. **Housing:** 1197 students can be accommodated in college housing, which includes coed dorms and married student housing. In addition, there are honors houses, special-interest houses, and on-campus houses available. Residence is available for freshmen and students in particular academic areas. On-campus housing is guaranteed for the freshman year only, and is available on a first-come, first-served basis, and is available on a lottery system for upperclassmen. 77% of students commute. Alcohol is not permitted. All students may keep cars.

FACULTY/CLASSROOMS: No introductory courses are taught by graduate students.

PROGRAMS OF STUDY: ASU-Polytechnic campus confers B.A., B.A.E., B.A.S., B.S. and B.S.E degrees. Master's and doctoral degrees are also awarded. Bachelor's degrees are awarded in AGRICULTURE (agricultural business management), BUSINESS (business administration and management, environment & natnl resource economics, information & communication technology, management, and organizational leadership and management), COMMUNICATIONS AND THE ARTS (communications, English, and technical communication), COMPUTER AND PHYSICAL SCIENCE (applied mathematics, applied science, computer information systems, science technology, and software engineering), EDUCATION (educational studies, elementary education, health information management, secondary education, and special education), ENGINEERING AND ENVIRONMENTAL DESIGN (aeronautical technology, air traffic management, electrical/electronics engineering technology, engineering, graphic arts technology, manufacturing engineering, manufacturing technology, mechanical engineering technology, product design engineering technology, and technological management), SOCIAL SCIENCE (food production/management/services, history, industrial and organizational psychology, interdisciplinary studies, liberal arts/general studies, and political science/government). Engineering, applied biological science, and business have the largest enrollments.

ACTIVITIES: There are no fraternities or sororities. There are 91 groups on campus, including art, band, computers, dance, environmental, ethnic, honors, international, newspaper, photography, professional, religious, social, social service, and student government. Popular campus events include Drumstix Dash, Fall Fest, Devils Royale, Boo Bash, Boat Races, and Innovation Showcase. **Sports:** There are 11 intercollegiate sports for men and 15 for women, and 7 intramural sports for men and 7 for women. Facilities include the Sun Devil Fitness Complex which has a 65,000 square feet of recreation space with basketball/badminton/volleyball courts, racquetball courts, tennis courts, sand volleyball courts, multipurpose soccer fields, softball field, cardio and strength equipment, bike co-op and a heated pool. **Graduates:** From July 1, 2015 to June 30, 2016, 755 bachelor's degrees were awarded. The most popular majors were engineering (27%), biological and biomedical sciences (12%), business, and management and marketing (11%). 72 companies recruited on campus in 2015-2016. Of the 2015 graduating class, 14% were enrolled in graduate school within 6 months of graduation, and 79% were employed.

SERVICES: Counseling and information services are available, as is tutoring in most subjects. ASU's University Academic Success Programs offers a range of free academic resources to support ASU students, both in-person and online. Services include: subject area tutoring, writing tutoring, graduate writing tutoring, graduate statistics tutoring, supplemental instruction (structured study groups), and academic mentoring (a peer mentoring program). ASU's Disability Resource Center (DRC) provides accommodations when needed for tutoring/services that the university provides. The DRC converts print or electronic materials that are not accessible into an accessible format for students who are blind or visually impaired, or who generally have a print related disability which includes learning disabilities. TRiO student support services (extended to those who are accepted into the TRiO program) provides tutoring as well that is more one on one. **Library/Resources:** The library contains 4.8 million volumes, 7.8 million microform items, and 180,428 audio/video tapes/CDs/DVDs, and subscribes to 63,322 periodicals including electronic. Computerized library services include interlibrary loans, database searching, Internet access, and Wi-Fi capability. **Physically Challenged Students:** 99% of the campus is accessible. Facilities include wheelchair ramps, elevators, special parking, specially equipped restrooms, special class scheduling, lowered drinking fountains, lowered telephones, and special housing. There are flashing alarms for the deaf, modified residence hall rooms and an adaptive exercise program and facility. **Special:** Students on ASU's Polytechnic Campus enjoy a variety of academic programs and opportunities to enhance their learning. For example, students in the aviation and air traffic control programs hone their flying skills in on-campus flight simulators and log flight hours at the adjacent Phoenix-Mesa Gateway Airport. And engineering students work in labs like the ASU Startup Labs, filled with equipment such as 3-D printers, laser cutters, CNC routers, and more. All students on the Polytechnic Campus can take on an internship in their field of study, as well as have the opportunity to study abroad in one of 55 countries. And choices such as concurrent degree programs, accelerated degree options, and the selection of 7.5- or 15-week semesters allow students to customize their college experience to exactly what they want it to be. There is 1 national honor society and a freshman honors program. **Visiting:** There are regularly scheduled orientations for prospective students. There are guides for informal visits and visitors may sit in on classes. **Campus Safety and Security:** Measures include 24-hour foot and vehicle patrol, emergency notification system, self-defense education, and security escort services. There are shuttle buses, emergency telephones, lighted pathways/sidewalks, controlled access to dorms/residences, in-room safes, LiveSafe smart phone application; surveillance cameras in some residence halls.

REQUIREMENTS: The SAT or ACT is recommended. Applicants must successfully complete ASU competency requirement; English - 4 years (composition/literature based), math - 4 years (algebra I, geometry, algebra II, and one course requiring algebra II as a prerequisite), laboratory science - 3 years total (1 year each from any of the following areas are accepted: biology, chemistry, earth science, integrated sciences, and physics), social science - 2 years (including one year American history), second language - 2 years (same language), and fine arts or career and technical education - 1 year. Applicants must also meet at least one of the following: top 25% in high school graduating class, 3.0 GPA in competency courses (4.0 = A), ACT 22 (24 nonresidents), SAT 1120 (1180 nonresidents). Admission may be granted with one deficiency in no more than two competency areas. Deficiencies cannot be in both math and laboratory science. Students must earn a minimum 2.00 in any subject area. Most competencies may also be met by test scores or college courses. ASU admission decisions begin the first week of Sept. Submission of an ACT or SAT score is highly recommended for merit-based scholarship consideration. Some schools and colleges have higher requirements for admission to their majors. All students who don't meet the above standards will be evaluated through a process called Individual Review. Through this process Admission Services will review all available information about a student's application, carefully considering all aspects of a student's academic background and accomplishments. In some cases, additional information might be requested. ASU welcomes homeschool students and recognizes the unique academic experiences they contribute to our rich community of scholars. Students may also meet admission requirements by submitting an official GED score of 500 or above for tests taken before January 2014 or a GED score of 170 or above for tests taken after January 2014. A GPA of 3.0 is required. AP and CLEP credits are accepted. To receive a degree from Arizona State University, students must have a minimum cumulative grade point average of 2.00 (some programs may require a higher GPA) and a minimum total of 120 credit hours, including a minimum of 45 hours of upper-division course work. The number of hours in the major varies by degree program, and some programs may require more upper-division work. All students must satisfy a minimum of 35 credit hours of approved General Studies course work in five core areas and three awareness areas: mathematics studies; literacy and critical inquiry; humanities, arts and design and social and behavioral sciences; natural sciences; global awareness; historical awareness; and cultural diversity in the United States. **Procedure:** Freshmen are admitted fall and spring. There is a rolling admissions plan. Applications should be filed by February 1 for fall entry; December 1 for spring entry, along with a $50 fee. Notification is sent on a rolling basis. Applications are accepted on-line. **Transfer Students:** 471 transfer students enrolled in 2015-2016. Requirements for general admission to Arizona State University: applicant must meet one of the following requirements (1) graduated from high school, (2) earned a GED, (3) completed an associate degree or be in progress toward an associate degree. Transfer students must meet one of the following requirements: less than 24 transferable credit hours - minimum 2.50 cumulative GPA and meet freshman aptitude requirements; 24 or more transferable credit hours - minimum 2.50 cumulative GPA; AGEC from an Arizona community college with a 2.00 or higher cumulative GPA; associate degree from a regionally accredited higher education institution with - 2.00 or higher cumulative GPA (residents) or 2.50 or higher cumulative GPA (nonresidents). "A" = 4.0; ASU accepts transfer college-level courses in which you have earned a "C-" or better. 30 of 120 credits required for the bachelor's degree must be completed at ASU at the Polytechnic Campus. **International Students:** There are 300 international students enrolled. The school actively recruits these students. They must take the TOEFL with a minimum score of 500 on the paper-based TOEFL (PBT) or 61 on the Internet-based version (iBT), International

English Language Testing Systems (IELTS); Pearson Tesk of English (PTE). SAT or ACT required for some.

ADMISSIONS: 76% of the 2016-2017 applicants were accepted. The SAT scores for the 2016-2017 freshman class were: Critical Reading-- 26% below 500, 45% between 500 and 599, 19% between 600 and 699, and 9% between 700 and 800. Math-- 17% below 500, 38% between 500 and 599, 35% between 600 and 699, and 10% between 700 and 800. The ACT scores were 3% between 12 and 17, 35% between 18 and 23, 46% between 24 and 29, and 16% above 30. 51% of the current freshmen were in the top fifth of their class; 78% were in the top two fifths. There were 5 National Merit finalists. **Admissions Contact:** Melissa Pizzo, Dean of Admissions and Financial Aid. Email: *admissions@asu.edu* Web: *https:/ campus.asu.edu/polytechnic*

FINANCIAL AID: The FAFSA code is 001081. The priority date for freshman financial aid applications for fall entry is January 1.

ARIZONA STATE UNIVERSITY AT THE TEMPE CAMPUS C-4

www.asu.edu

Tempe, AZ 85287 **(480) 965-7788**

Fax: (480) 965-3610
Email: admissions@asu.edu
Full-time: 22,101 men, 16,845 women
Faculty: I, av$
Ph.D.s: n/av
Part-time: 2145 men, 1386 women
Student/Faculty: n/av
Graduate: 5582 men, 3810 women
Tuition: $10,370 ($26,470)
Year: semesters, summer session
Freshman Class: 24764 applied, 20428 accepted, 8227 enrolled
Room & Board: $11,386
SAT CR/M: 560/580 **ACT:** 25
CEEB CODE: 4007
Application Deadline: February 1
VERY COMPETITIVE

Arizona State University at the Tempe Campus, welcomes students pursuing a wide range of majors including business, liberal arts, engineering and the sciences. Modern classrooms and high-tech laboratories create a dynamic and engaging learning environment. ASU was recently named the #1 school in the country for innovation for the second year in a row, and the top U.S. public university for international students by the Institute of International Education. ASU is a comprehensive public research university, measured not by whom we exclude, but rather by whom we include and how they succeed; advancing research and discovery of public value; and assuming fundamental responsibility for the economic, social, cultural, and overall health of the communities it serves. ASU champions intellectual and cultural diversity. Its research is inspired by real-world application, blurring the boundaries that traditionally separate academic disciplines. There are 10 undergraduate schools and 9 graduate schools. In addition to regional accreditation, ASU at the Tempe Campus has baccalaureate program accreditation with AACSB, ABET, ACCE, NAAB, NASAD, NASM, AABI, CAC, CAHME, CIDA, and LAAB. The 661-acre campus is in an urban area in Tempe, AZ. Including any residence halls, there are 198 buildings.

STUDENT LIFE: 65% of undergraduates are from Arizona. Others are from 113 foreign countries, and Canada. 93% are from public schools. 51% are White; 19% Hispanic; 13% Foreign; 7% Asian American; 4% African American; 4% two or more races; 1% American Indian/Alaska Native; 1% race unknown. **Male To Female Ratio:** 1.4:1. The average age of freshmen is 18; all undergraduates, 21. **Housing:** 10,073 students can be accommodated in college housing, which includes coed dorms, on-campus apartments, and off-campus apartments. In addition, there are honors houses, and residence is available for freshmen and students in particular academic areas. On-campus housing is guaranteed for the freshman year only, and is available on a first-come, first-served basis, and is available on a lottery system for upperclassmen. 79% of students commute. Alcohol is not permitted. All students may keep cars.

FACULTY/CLASSROOMS: No introductory courses are taught by graduate students.

PROGRAMS OF STUDY: ASU-Tempe campus confers B.A., B.A.E., B.F.A., B.Mus., B.S., B.S.D., B.S.E., B.S.LA. and B.S.P. degrees. Master's and doctoral degrees are also awarded. Bachelor's degrees are awarded in AGRICULTURE (environmental studies), BIOLOGICAL SCIENCE (biochemistry, biological sciences, biophysics, microbiology, and molecular biology), BUSINESS (accounting, business administration and management, finance, management, marketing/retailing/merchandising, and supply chain management), COMMUNICATIONS AND THE ARTS (art, communications, composition, dance, design, English, film arts, French, German, graphic design, industrial design, Italian, music, music performance, musical theater, performing arts, Russian, Spanish, theatre arts, and visual and performing arts), COMPUTER AND PHYSICAL SCIENCE (actuarial science, applied mathematics, chemistry, computer information systems, computer science, earth science, earth & space science, informatics and computer science, mathematics, and physics), EDUCATION (Asian studies, early childhood education, education, educational studies, elementary education, general studies, music education, secondary education, and special education), ENGINEERING AND ENVIRONMENTAL DESIGN (aerospace engineering, biomedical engineering, chemical engineering, civil engineering, computational sciences, construction engineering, construction management, electrical/electronics engineering, engineering management, environmental design, industrial engineering, interior design, landscape architecture, materials science, and mechanical engineering), HEALTH PROFESSIONS (music therapy and speech pathology/audiology), SOCIAL SCIENCE (African American studies, American Indian studies, anthropology, architectural studies, Asian/American studies, economics, geography, geography information science, history, human development, interdisciplinary studies, philosophy, political science/ government, psychology, religious studies, sociology, urban studies, and women's studies). Business, biological science, and computer science have the largest enrollments.

ACTIVITIES: 9% of men belong to 38 national fraternities; 17% of women belong to 28 national sororities. There are 852 groups on campus, including health, technology and sports, art, band, cheerleading, chess, choir, chorale, chorus, communications, computers, dance, debate, drama, drill team, entrepreneurship, environmental, ethnic, film, forensics, honors, international, jazz band, LGBT, literary magazine, marching band, musical theater, newspaper, orchestra, pep band, photography, political, professional, radio and TV, religious, social, social service, student government, and symphony. Popular campus events include Devils on Mill, Sorority and Fraternity Recruitment, Passport to ASU, Homecoming, MU After Dark, MU Takeover, Finals Breakfast, Sun Devils UNITE, and Devilpalooza. **Sports:** There are 11 intercollegiate sports for men and 15 for women, and 21 intramural sports for men and 21 for women. Facilities include the Sun Devil Fitness Complex consists of indoor activity space, as well as outdoor fields, sand volleyball courts and aquatics center. The complex has a state-of-the-art weight and fitness areas, including cardiovascular and strength equipment, and free weights; several multipurpose studios for group fitness classes and student sport/activity clubs; an indoor and outdoor tracks; gymnasium courts for sports and campus events; a multi-activity court gymnasium; a wellness suite for massage, meditation, and other wellness programs and services. The Tempe Campus has softball and baseball stadiums, athletic centers, golf course, aquatic complex, wrestling complex, soccer stadium, gymnastics training facility, track fields, football stadium, basketball arena, and tennis center. **Graduates:** From July 1, 2015 to June 30, 2016, 9050 bachelor's degrees were awarded. The most popular majors were business, management, and marketing (23%), engineering (12%), and social science (9%). 2628 companies recruited on campus in 2015-2016. Of the 2015 graduating class, 18% were enrolled in graduate school within 6 months of graduation, and 83% were employed.

SERVICES: Counseling and information services are available, as is tutoring in most subjects. ASU's University Academic Success Programs offers a range of free academic resources to support ASU students, both in-person and online. Services include subject area tutoring, writing tutoring, graduate writing tutoring, graduate statistics tutoring, supplemental instruction (structured study groups), and academic mentoring (a peer mentoring program). ASU's Disability Resource Center (DRC) provides accommodations when needed for tutoring/services that the university provides. The DRC converts print or electronic materials that are not accessible into an accessible format for students who are blind or visually impaired, or who generally have a print related disability which includes learning disabilities. TRiO student support services (extended to those who are accepted into the TRiO program) provides tutoring as well that is more one on one. **Library/Resources:** The 4 libraries contain 4.8 million volumes, 7.8 million microform items, and 180,428 audio/video tapes/CDs/DVDs, and subscribe to 63,322 periodicals including electronic. Computerized library services include interlibrary loans, database searching, Internet access, and Wi-Fi capability. Special learning facilities include an art gallery, natural history museum, planetarium, radio station, museums, galleries, collections, research labs, digital labs, art, dance and development studios, and research institutes. **Physically Challenged Students:** 99% of the campus is accessible. Facilities include wheelchair ramps, elevators, special parking, specially equipped restrooms, special class scheduling, lowered drinking fountains, lowered telephones, and special housing. There are flashing alarms for the deaf, modified residence hall rooms, and an adaptive exercise program and facility. **Special:** Students on ASU's Tempe Campus enjoy a variety of academic programs and opportunities to enhance their learning. For example, Tempe Campus is home to the first school entirely dedicated to undergraduate and graduate degrees and research in sustainability. And engineering, design and arts students have access to InnovationSpace, a sustainable product-development program. Students also have opportunities to participate in pioneering research in the Biodesign Institute and other centers, perform in Frank Lloyd Wright-designed ASU Gammage, and to pursue entrepreneurial interests through innovative programs embedded in each college. All students on the Tempe campus can take on an internship in their field of study, as well as have the opportunity to study abroad in one of 55 countries. And choices such as concurrent degree programs, accelerated degree options, and the selection of 7.5- or 15-week semesters allow students to customize their college experience to exactly what they want it to be. There are 26 national honor societies and a freshman honors program. **Visiting:** There are regularly scheduled orientations for prospective students. There are guides for informal visits and visitors may sit in on classes. **Campus Safety and Security:** Measures include 24-hour foot and vehicle patrol, emergency notification system, self-defense education, and security escort services. There are shuttle buses, emergency telephones, lighted pathways/sidewalks, controlled access to dorms/residences, in-room safes, LiveSafe smartphone application, and surveillance cameras in some residence halls.

REQUIREMENTS: The SAT or ACT is recommended. Applicants must successfully complete ASU competency requirement; English - 4 years (composition/literature based), math - 4 years (algebra I, geometry, algebra II, and one course requiring algebra II as a prerequisite), laboratory science - 3 years total (1 year each from any of the following areas are accepted: biology, chemistry, earth science, integrated sciences, and physics), social science - 2 years (including one year American history), second language - 2 years (same language), and fine arts or career and technical education - 1 year. Applicants must also meet at least one of the following: top 25% in high school graduating class, 3.0 GPA in competency courses (4.0 = A), ACT 22 (24 nonresidents), SAT 1120 (1180 nonresidents). Admission may be granted with one deficiency in no more than two competency areas. Deficiencies cannot be in both math and laboratory science. Students must earn a minimum 2.00 in any subject area. Most competencies may also be met by test scores or college courses. ASU admission decisions begin the first week of Sept. Submission of an ACT or SAT score is highly recommended for merit-based scholarship consideration. Some schools and colleges have higher requirements for admission to their majors. All students who don't meet the above standards will be evaluated through a process called Individual Review. Through this process Admission Services will review all available information about a student's application, carefully considering all aspects of a student's academic background and accomplishments. In some cases, additional information might be requested. ASU welcomes homeschool students and recognizes the unique academic experiences they contribute to our rich community of scholars. Students may also meet admission requirements by submitting an official GED score of 500 or above for tests taken before January 2014 or a GED score of 170 or above for tests taken after January 2014. A GPA of 3.0 is required. AP and CLEP credits are accepted. To receive a degree from Arizona State University, students must have a minimum cumulative grade point average of 2.00 (some programs may require a higher GPA) and a minimum total of 120 credit hours, including a minimum of 45 hours of upper-division coursework. The number of hours in the major varies by degree program, and some programs may require more upper-division work. All students must satisfy a minimum of 35 credit hours of approved General Studies coursework in five core areas and three awareness areas: mathematics studies; literacy and critical inquiry; humanities, arts and design and social and behavioral sciences; natural sciences; global awareness; historical awareness; and cultural diversity in the United States. **Procedure:** Freshmen are admitted fall and spring. There is a rolling admissions plan. Applications should be filed by February 1 for fall entry; December 1 for spring entry, along with a $50 fee. Notification is sent on a rolling basis. Applications are accepted on-line. Application fees are waived if application is completed on-line. **Transfer Students:** 3256 transfer students enrolled in 2015-2016. Requirements for general admission to Arizona State University: applicant must meet one of the following requirements (1) graduated from high school, (2) earned a GED, (3) completed an associate degree or be in progress toward an associate degree. Transfer students must meet one of the following requirements: less than 24 transferable credit hours - minimum 2.50 cumulative GPA and meet freshman aptitude requirements; 24 or more transferable credit hours - minimum 2.50 cumulative GPA; AGEC from an Arizona community college with a 2.00 or higher cumulative GPA; associate degree from a regionally accredited higher education institution with - 2.00 or higher cumulative GPA (residents) or 2.50 or higher cumulative GPA (nonresidents). "A" = 4.0; ASU accepts transfer college-level courses in which you have earned a "C-" or better. 30 of 120 credits required for the bachelor's degree must be completed at ASU at the Tempe Campus. **International Students:** There are 5369 international students enrolled. The school actively recruits these students. They must take the TOEFL with a minimum score of 500 on the paper-based TOEFL (PBT) or 61 on the Internet-based version (iBT), International English Language Testing Systems (IELTS); Pearson Test of English (PTE). SAT or ACT is required for the W.P. Carey school of business.

ADMISSIONS: 82% of the 2016-2017 applicants were accepted. The SAT scores for the 2016-2017 freshman class were: Critical Reading-- 22% below 500, 41% between 500 and 599, 28% between 600 and 699, and 9% between 700 and 800. Math-- 17% below 500, 39% between 500 and 599, 34% between 600 and 699, and 11% between 700 and 800. The ACT scores were 2% between 12 and 17, 32% between 18 and 23, 49% between 24 and 29, and 17% above 30. 51% of the current freshmen were in the top fifth of their class; 80% were in the top two fifths. There were 97 National Merit finalists. **Admissions Contact:** Melissa Pizzo , Dean of Admissions and Financial Aid. Email: *admissions@asu.edu* Web: *www.asu.edu*

FINANCIAL AID: The FAFSA code is 001081. The priority date for freshman financial aid applications for fall entry is January 1.

ARIZONA STATE UNIVERSITY AT THE WEST CAMPUS C-4

www.campus.asu.edu/west

Glendale, AZ 85036 **(480) 965-7788**

Fax: (480) 965-3610	**Email: admissions@asu.edu**
Full-time: 1050 men, 1674 women	**Faculty:** IIA, av$
Part-time: 227 men, 285 women	**Ph.D.s:** n/av
Graduate: 128 men, 255 women	**Student/Faculty:** n/av
Year: semesters, summer session	**Tuition:** $9684 ($24,219)
Room & Board: $10,474	**Freshman Class:** 1357 applied, 1025 accepted, 322 enrolled
SAT CR/M: 540/540 **ACT:** 23	**CEEB CODE:** 4007
Application Deadline: February 1	**COMPETITIVE**

Arizona State University's West Campus welcomes students studying business, education, and interdisciplinary arts and sciences. Undergraduate and graduate programs offer the resources of one of the top public research universities in the country within a community-based learning environment. Patterned after the University of Oxford's architecture, this inviting campus creates a close-knit community. Students become master learners, able to learn anything throughout their lives, on this classic-style campus. ASU was recently named the #1 innovative school in the country, and the top U.S. public university for international students by the International Institute of Education. ASU is a comprehensive public research university, measured not by whom we exclude, but rather by whom we include and how they succeed; advancing research and discovery of public value; and assuming fundamental responsibility for the economic, social, cultural and overall health of the communities it serves. ASU champions intellectual and cultural diversity. Its research is inspired by real-world application, blurring the boundaries that traditionally separate academic disciplines. There are 4 undergraduate schools and 3 graduate schools. The 278-acre campus is in an urban area in Phoenix, AZ. Including any residence halls, there are 21 buildings.

STUDENT LIFE: 82% of undergraduates are from Arizona. Others are from 22 foreign countries, and Canada. 95% are from public schools. 51% are White; 28% Hispanic. **Female To Male Ratio:** 1.6:1. The average age of freshmen is 18; all undergraduates, 24. **Housing:** 536 students can be accommodated in college housing, which includes coed dorms and on-campus apartments. In addition, there are honors houses, residence is available for freshmen and students in particular academic areas. On-campus housing is guaranteed for the freshman year only, and is available on a first-come, first-served basis, and is available on a lottery system for upperclassmen. 88% of students commute. Alcohol is not permitted. All students may keep cars.

FACULTY/CLASSROOMS: No introductory courses are taught by graduate students.

PROGRAMS OF STUDY: ASU at the West Campus confers B.A., B.A.E., B.A.S., B.G.M. and B.S. degrees. Master's and doctoral degrees are also awarded. Bachelor's degrees are awarded in BIOLOGICAL SCIENCE (biology (pre-physician assistant) and forensic science), BUSINESS (accounting, business administration and management, and sustainable management), COMMUNICATIONS AND THE ARTS (communication studies, communications, English, and Spanish), COMPUTER AND PHYSICAL SCIENCE (applied mathematics, applied science, and statistics), EDUCATION (educational studies, elementary education, secondary education, and special education), ENGINEERING AND ENVIRONMENTAL DESIGN (environmental science), HEALTH PROFESSIONS (community health work), SOCIAL SCIENCE (American studies, ethnic studies, history, interdisciplinary studies, Latin American studies, philosophy and religion, political science/government, psychology, social science, sociology, women & gender studies, and women's studies). Psychology, business, and biology have the largest enrollments.

ACTIVITIES: There are no fraternities or sororities. There are 53 groups on campus, including art, chess, chorale, communications, computers, dance, environmental, ethnic, film, forensics, LGBT, honors, international, newspaper, political, professional, radio and TV, religious, social, social service, and student government. Popular campus events include Sparky's Carnival and Fun Run, Finals Breakfast, and Market on the Move. **Sports:** There are 10 intercollegiate sports for men and 15 for women, and 20 intramural sports for men and 20 for women. Facilities include the Sun Devil Fitness Complex West a three story, state-of-the-art facility that includes a free weight fitness area overlooking a two-court gymnasium for sports and campus events. Other features include a weight machine area, a cardio loft, 2 racquetball courts, 3 lane indoor running track, and 2 multipurpose studios for group fitness, mind/body classes, and student sport/activity clubs. This complex also includes a wellness space, social gaming area, and a 6 lane pool complete with a shallow hangout area. Just outside of the complex are 2 sand volleyball courts, outdoor basketball courts, a green quad for campus activities, and a 6-acre multipurpose field, which hosts intramural and sport club programs. **Graduates:** From July 1, 2014 to June 30, 2015, 941 bachelor's degrees were awarded. The most popular majors were psychology (19%), education (18%), business, management, marketing, and related support services (13%). 136 companies recruited on campus in 2014-2015. Of the 2014 graduating class, 15% were enrolled in graduate school within 6 months of graduation, and 87% were employed.

SERVICES: Counseling and information services are available, as is tutoring in most subjects. There is a reader service for the blind. Face-to-face and online tutoring are free to students on all campuses. ASU offers supplemental instruction and academic mentoring. Academic success courses and graduate test preparation are also available. Disability Resource Centers support the learning needs of students with documented disabilities. **Library/Resources:** The library contains 4.8 million volumes, 7.8 million microform items, and 170,839 audio/video tapes/CDs/DVDs, and subscribes to 59,942 periodicals including electronic. Computerized library services include interlibrary loans, database searching, Internet access, and Wi-Fi capability. Special learning facilities include an art gallery, radio station, Herberger Young Scholars Academy school for 7th grade through 12th grade, art collections, galleries, dance studios, little theatre/black box, communications assessment learning lab, research labs, digital labs, music labs, cooking labs, performing arts studios, and writing labs. **Physically Challenged Students:** 99% of the campus is accessible. Facilities include wheelchair ramps, elevators, special parking, specially equipped restrooms, special class scheduling, lowered drinking fountains, lowered telephones, and special housing. There are flashing alarms for the deaf, modified residence hall rooms, and an adaptive exercise program and facility. **Special:** ASU's many undergraduate programs offer students a variety of special academic opportunities. ASU offers domestic and international internships in a variety of disciplines, more than 250 study abroad programs in over 55 countries, and work study programs. Students gain interdisciplinary skills through combining two areas of study from a list of more than 160 disciplines in the Interdisciplinary Studies program. ASU also offers students two ways to earn concurrent degrees; students can choose to create their own combination degree programs to match their personal or professional interest or choose from special, predetermined combinations. Accelerated degree options are also available for more than 55 degree programs. ASU has semesters (15 week schedule) and sessions (7.5 week schedule) allowing students flexibility in choosing their schedule. There are 2 national honor societies and a freshman honors program. **Visiting:** There are regularly scheduled orientations for prospective students. There are guides for informal visits and visitors may sit in on classes. **Campus Safety and Security:** Measures include 24-hour foot and vehicle patrol, emergency notification system, self-defense education, and security escort services. There are shuttle buses, emergency telephones, lighted pathways/sidewalks, controlled access to dorms/residences, in-room safes, LiveSafe smart phone application, and surveillance cameras in some residence halls.

REQUIREMENTS: The SAT or ACT is recommended. ASU requirements are, 4 years of English, 4 years of math, 3 years total (1 year each from any of the following) biology, chemistry, earth science, integrated science, and physics, 2 years of social studies (including 1 year of American history), 2 years of foreign language (same language), and 1 year of fine arts or career and technical education. Applicants must also meet at least one of the following: top 25% in high school graduating class, 3.0 GPA in competency courses (4.0=A), ACT 22 (24 nonresidents), SAT Reasoning 1040 (1110 nonresidents). All students who don't meet the above standards will be evaluated through a process called Individual Review. Through this process Undergraduate Admissions will review all available information about a student's application, carefully considering all aspects of a student's academic background and accomplishments. Submission of an ACT or SAT test score is highly recommended, In some cases, additional information might be requested. ASU welcomes homeschool students and recognizes the unique academic experiences they contribute to our rich community of scholars. AP and CLEP credits are accepted. To graduate, students must have a minimum cumulative grade point average of 2.0 (some programs may require a higher GPA) and a minimum total of 120 credit hours, including a minimum of 45 hours in upper division courses. The number of hours in the major varies by degree program, and some programs may require more upper-division work. All students must satisfy a minimum of 35 credit hours of approved General Studies coursework in five core areas and three awareness areas: mathematics studies, literacy and critical inquiry, humanities, fine arts, design, social and behavioral sciences, natural sciences, global awareness, historical awareness, and cultural diversity in the United States. **Procedure:** Freshmen are admitted fall and spring. There is a rolling admissions plan. Applications should be filed by February 1 for fall entry; December 1 for spring entry, along with a $50 fee. Applications are accepted on-line. **Transfer Students:** 526 transfer students enrolled in 2014-2015. All transfer students must meet ASU's graduation requirement by providing one of the following: official high school transcript with high school graduation date; GED with acceptable score of 500 or above; official college transcript with Associate degree posted (including award date); official college transcript with Associate degree in progress posted (including expected award date). Transfer applicants must meet at least one of the following requirements for admission to ASU. Please note that some ASU colleges and schools have higher requirements for admission to their majors. Arizona transfer students must meet one of the following requirements: Associate degree with a 2.00 cumulative GPA or higher (4.00=A); Arizona General Education Curriculum (AGEC) with a 2.50 cumulative GPA or higher (4.00=A); complete a transfer pathway program through an accredited Arizona community college. Nonresident transfer students must meet one of the following requirements: Associate degree with a 2.50 cumulative GPA or higher (4.00=A); AGEC with a 2.50 cumulative GPA or higher (4.00=A). (For those students transferring from a California community college, ASU accepts the Intersegmental General Education Transfer Curriculum/California State University General Education [IGETC/CSU GE] patterns). Students with fewer than 24 transferable credit hours must have a minimum 2.50 cumulative GPA and meet freshman aptitude requirements to be considered through individual review. 30 of 120 credits required for the bachelor's degree must be completed at ASU at the West campus. **International Students:** There are 109 international students enrolled. The school actively recruits these students. They must take the TOEFL with a minimum score of 500 on the paper-based TOEFL (PBT), or 61 on the Internet-based version (iBT). Students must take the IELTS. SAT or ACT required for some.

ADMISSIONS: 76% of the 2015-2016 applicants were accepted. The

SAT scores for the 2015-2016 freshman class were: Critical Reading-- 30% below 500, 42% between 500 and 599, 24% between 600 and 699, and 4% between 700 and 800. Math-- 34% below 500, 38% between 500 and 599, 23% between 600 and 699, and 5% between 700 and 800. The ACT scores were 8% between 12 and 17, 45% between 18 and 23, 40% between 24 and 29, and 7% above 30. 57% of the current freshmen were in the top fifth of their class; 85% were in the top two fifths. There were 2 National Merit finalists. **Admissions Contact:** Melissa Pizzo, Dean of Admissions and Financial Aid. E-Mail: *admissions@asu.edu* Web: *www.campus.asu.edu/west*

FINANCIAL AID: The FAFSA is required. The priority date for freshman financial aid applications for fall entry is March 1.

EMBRY-RIDDLE AERONAUTICAL UNIVERSITY - PRESCOTT CAMPUS C-3

www.prescott.erau.edu

Prescott, AZ 86301	(928) 777-6600 (800) 888-3728 **Email:** Prescott@erau.edu
Full-time: 1700 men, 555 women	**Faculty:** n/av
Part-time: 93 men, 29 women	**Ph.D.s:** 81%
Graduate: 46 men, 16 women	**Student/Faculty:** n/av
Year: semesters, summer session	**Tuition:** $33,826
Room & Board: $10,228	**Freshman Class:** 2130 applied, 1626 accepted, 604 enrolled
SAT CR/M/W: 570/600/535 **ACT:** 27	**CEEB CODE:** 4305
Application Deadline: July 1	**VERY COMPETITIVE**

Embry-Riddle Aeronautical University - Prescott Campus is a private institution offering undergraduate programs in aviation, engineering, business, and security & intelligence and graduate programs in safety science and security & intelligence studies. There are 4 undergraduate schools and 2 graduate schools. In addition to regional accreditation, ERAU has baccalaureate program accreditation with ABET, ACBSP, and AABI. The 539-acre campus is in a rural area 100 miles north of Phoenix. Including any residence halls, there are 71 buildings.

STUDENT LIFE: 78% of undergraduates are from out of state, mostly the Southwest. Students are from 48 states, 34 foreign countries, and Canada. 9% are race unknown; 8% Foreign; 61% White; 6% Asian American; 4% Hispanic; 2% African American; 11% two or more races. **Male To Female Ratio:** 3.1:1. The average age of freshmen is 18; all undergraduates, 21. 22% do not continue beyond their first year; 63% remain to graduate. **Housing:** 863 students can be accommodated in college housing, which includes coed dorms and on-campus apartments. Students in First Year Experience housing are grouped together by major if possible, and reside with a staff that is specially trained to handle first-year transitional issues. On-campus housing is guaranteed for the freshman year only, is available on a first-come, and first-served basis. 54% of students commute. All students may keep cars.

FACULTY/CLASSROOMS: 72% of faculty are male; 28% are female. No introductory courses are taught by graduate students.

PROGRAMS OF STUDY: ERAU confers B.S. degrees. Master's degrees are also awarded. Bachelor's degrees are awarded in AGRICULTURE (wildlife science), BIOLOGICAL SCIENCE (forensic psychology and forensic science), BUSINESS (business administration and management and business administration - international), COMMUNICATIONS AND THE ARTS (illustration), COMPUTER AND PHYSICAL SCIENCE (applied meteorology, astronomy, cyber operations, cyber intelligence/security studies, industrial psychology/safety, space physics, and software engineering), ENGINEERING AND ENVIRONMENTAL DESIGN (aeronautical science, aerospace engineering, air traffic management, aviation business administration, computer engineering, electrical/electronics engineering, and mechanical engineering), SOCIAL SCIENCE (forensic studies and interdisciplinary studies). Aerospace engineering, aeronautical science (flight), and global security & intelligence studies are the strongest academically. Aerospace engineering, global security & intelligence studies, and aeronautics have the largest enrollments.

ACTIVITIES: There are 100 groups on campus, including academic, jet dragster, military, band, choir, computers, dance, debate, drum and bugle corps, environmental, ethnic, forensics, honors, international, jazz band, LGBT, literary magazine, newspaper, orchestra, political, professional, radio and TV, religious, social, social service, special interest: UAV, and student government. Popular campus events include Hypnotist, Casino Night, OctoberWest, Activity Fair, GreekWeek, Finals Breakfast, Carpe Notcem Events, Smores, and Friday Night Entertainment. **Sports:** There are 6 intercollegiate sports for men and 7 for women. Facilities include a fitness center, gym/weight room, multipurpose athletic playing fields, game room, swimming pool complex, courts for racquetball, tennis and sand volleyball, gym equipped for basketball and indoor soccer, and indoor climbing wall. **Graduates:** From July 1, 2015 to June 30, 2016, 362 bachelor's degrees were awarded. The most popular majors were aerospace engineering (29%), global security & intelligence studies (19%), and aeronautics (14%). In an average class, 1% graduate in 3 years or less, 33% graduate in 4 years or less, 60% graduate in 5 years or less, and 63% graduate in 6 years or less.

SERVICES: Counseling and information services are available, as is tutoring in most subjects. There is remedial math, reading, and writing. **Library/Resources:** The library contains 34,177 volumes, 100,077 microform items, and 2,959 audio/video tapes/CDs/DVDs, and subscribes to 167 periodicals including electronic. Computerized library services include interlibrary loans, database searching, Internet access, and Wi-Fi capability. Special learning facilities include a radio station, The Flight Training Center at Ernest A. Love Field offers a simulator lab and flight operations center; the Academic Complex (AC1) is the primary residence of professors and houses design labs, the Weather Center lab and Airway Science Lab; Aerospace Experimentation and Fabrication Building (AXFAB); King Engineering and Technology Center (KEC) houses electrical and computer designs labs; Prescott Observatory Complex; Robertson Aviation Safety Center (RASC) is home to the most thorough accident investigation facility and a second building, RASCII, houses the large collection of Aviation Safety and Security Archives as well as the Industrial Hygiene and Ergonomics labs. **Physically Challenged Students:** 95% of the campus is accessible. Facilities include wheelchair ramps, special parking, specially equipped restrooms, lowered drinking fountains, lowered telephones, special housing, and pneumatic doors. **Special:** Cooperative and work-study programs, nondegree study, internships in all majors, and study abroad in 21 countries are offered. Flight training may be taken in conjunction with aeronautical science and other degree programs. Credit is given for life and military experience. There is a freshman honors program. **Visiting:** There are regularly scheduled orientations for prospective students, tours are offered at 9 a.m. and 1:00 p.m. Monday - Friday (Mon - Thur during summer). There are a variety of options including sitting in on an ERAU class, one-on-one meeting with a professor, and a tour of our Crash Lab. There are guides for informal visits and visitors may sit in on classes. **Campus Safety and Security:** Measures include 24-hour foot and vehicle patrol, emergency notification system, self-defense education, and security escort services. There are emergency telephones, lighted pathways/sidewalks, and controlled access to dorms/residences.

REQUIREMENTS: The SAT or ACT is recommended. AP and CLEP credits are accepted. All students must complete 36 credits of general education requirements, including courses in communication skills, technical report writing, humanities/social sciences, math, physical science, economics, and computer science. A total of 120 to 136 credit hours with a minimum GPA of 2.0 is required to graduate. **Procedure:** Freshmen are admitted fall, spring, and summer. Entrance exams should be taken by the fall of the senior year. There are deferred admissions and rolling admissions plans. Early decision applications should be filed by December 1; regular applications, by July 1 for fall entry; November 1 for spring entry; and April 1 for summer entry, along with a $50 fee. Notification is sent on a rolling basis. Applications are accepted on-line. **Transfer Students:** 164 transfer students enrolled in 2015-2016. A GPA of 2.5 is preferred. 30 of 120 credits required for the bachelor's degree must be completed at ERAU. **International Students:** There are 161 international students enrolled. The school actively recruits these students. They must take the TOEFL with a minimum score of 550 on the paper-based TOEFL (PBT) or 79 on the Internet-based version (iBT). SAT or ACT is strongly recommended.

ADMISSIONS: 76% of the 2016-2017 applicants were accepted. The SAT scores for the 2016-2017 freshman class were: Critical Reading-- 21% below 500, 38% between 500 and 599, 33% between 600 and 699, and 8% between 700 and 800. Math-- 15% below 500, 30% between 500 and 599, 45% between 600 and 699, and 10% between 700 and 800. Writing-- 31% below 500, 43% between 500 and 599, 21% between 600 and 699, and 4% between 700 and 800. The ACT scores were 2%

between 12 and 17, 23% between 18 and 23, 47% between 24 and 29, and 28% above 30. 44% of the current freshmen were in the top fifth of their class; 71% were in the top two fifths. 12 freshmen graduated first in their class. **Admissions Contact:** Sara Bofferding, Director, Prescott Admissions. Email: *Prescott@erau.edu* Web: *https:/prescott.erau.edu/admissions*

FINANCIAL AID: In 2016-2017, 97% of all full-time freshmen and 88% of continuing full-time students received some form of financial aid. 94% of all full-time freshmen and 84% of continuing full-time students received need-based aid. The average freshman award was $19,661. Need-based scholarships or need-based grants averaged $16,368; need-based self-help aid (loans and jobs) averaged $3,608; and non-need-based athletic scholarships averaged $10,826. 15% of undergraduate students work part-time. Average annual earnings from campus work are $1719. The priority date for freshman financial aid applications for fall entry is March 1.

GRAND CANYON UNIVERSITY C-4

www.gcu.edu

Phoenix, AZ 85017	(855) GCU-LOPE
	Email: admissions@gcu.edu
Full-time: 1767 men, 3568 women	Faculty: 223; IIB, av$
Part-time: 4997 men, 17348 women	Ph.D.s: 19%
Graduate: 3052 men, 10025 women	Student/Faculty: 25 to 1
Year: semesters, summer session	Tuition: $8300
Room & Board: $8650	Freshman Class: n/av
SAT or ACT: recommended	CEEB CODE: 4331
Application Deadline: August 22	VERY COMPETITIVE

Grand Canyon University is a Christian University, founded in 1949, and is a small, private, publicly traded nonsectarian liberal arts institution. The figures in the above capsule and in this profile are approximate. There are 5 undergraduate schools and 5 graduate schools. In addition to regional accreditation, GCU has baccalaureate program accreditation with ACBSP, CAATE, and CCNE. The 179-acre campus is in a suburban area in Phoenix, AZ. Including any residence halls, there are 50 buildings.

STUDENT LIFE: 73% of undergraduates are from out of state, mostly the Southwest. Students are from 50 states, 12 foreign countries, and Canada. 41% are White; 4% Asian American; 25% African American; 10% Hispanic; 1% American Indian/Alaska Native; 1% Foreign. 98% claim no religious affiliation. **Female To Male Ratio:** 3.2:1. The average age of freshmen is 18; all undergraduates, 33. **Housing:** 1600 students can be accommodated in college housing, which includes single-sex dorms, on-campus apartments, and married student housing. On-campus housing is available on a first-come and first-served basis. 52% of students commute. Alcohol is not permitted. All students may keep cars.

FACULTY/CLASSROOMS: 85% teach undergraduates. No introductory courses are taught by graduate students. The average class size in an introductory lecture is 18; in a laboratory is 14; and in a regular course is 18.

PROGRAMS OF STUDY: GCU confers B.A., B.S. and B.S.N. degrees. Master's and doctoral degrees are also awarded. Bachelor's degrees are awarded in BIOLOGICAL SCIENCE (biology/biological science), BUSINESS (accounting, business administration and management, entrepreneurial studies, management science, marketing/retailing/merchandising, and sports management), COMMUNICATIONS AND THE ARTS (communications, communications technology, English, music, music performance, theatre arts, theater design, and theater management), COMPUTER AND PHYSICAL SCIENCE (digital arts/technology), EDUCATION (athletic training, dance education, education, elementary education, music education, physical education, and secondary education), ENGINEERING AND ENVIRONMENTAL DESIGN (engineering technology), HEALTH PROFESSIONS (exercise science, health science, and nursing), SOCIAL SCIENCE (addiction studies, Christian studies, forensic studies, history, interdisciplinary studies, international studies, physical fitness/movement, psychology, and sociology). Education, business, and nursing are the strongest academically, and have the largest enrollments.

ACTIVITIES: There are no fraternities or sororities. There are 12 groups on campus, including art, band, cheerleading, choir, chorale, chorus, dance, drama, ethnic, film, honors, international, literary magazine, musical theater, newspaper, pep band, photography, political, professional, religious, social, social service, and student government. Popular campus events include Spiritual Emphasis Week, Harvest Festival, and Spring Formal. **Sports:** There are 10 intercollegiate sports for men and 11 for women, and 6 intramural sports for men and 6 for women. Facilities include an arena, intramural fields, baseball stadium, gymnasium, athlete performance center, soccer/track and field venue, a 150-seat softball venue, 55,000 square foot student recreation center (includes recreational basketball courts-2, a student fitness center, aerobics/dance room, cardio/weight facilities, locker facilities, wrestling and basketball intercollegiate training areas). **Graduates:** From July 1, 2015 to June 30, 2016, 2279 bachelor's degrees were awarded. The most popular majors were nusing (17%), curriculum and instruction (5%), and special education (4%). 100 companies recruited on campus in 2015-2016.

SERVICES: Counseling and information services are available, as is tutoring in every subject. There is remedial math, reading, and writing. Tutors are also trained in test-taking techniques, study skills, and time management. **Library/Resources:** The library contains 140,456 volumes, 53,459 microform items, and 527 audio/video tapes/CDs/DVDs, and subscribes to 9,502 periodicals including electronic. Computerized library services include interlibrary loans, database searching, Internet access, and Wi-Fi capability. Special learning facilities include an art gallery, a center for Learning and Advancement and a center for Innovation in Research and Teaching. **Physically Challenged Students:** 99% of the campus is accessible. Facilities include wheelchair ramps, elevators, special parking, specially equipped restrooms, lowered drinking fountains, and special housing. **Special:** Internships are ofered for most majors through organizatons, corporations, and agencies in the Phoenix area. Study abroad in 5 countries and a Washington semester are possible. There are 3 national honor societies and a freshman honors program. **Visiting:** There are regularly scheduled orientations for prospective students, including student orientation and registration in the summer. There are guides for informal visits, visitors may sit in on classes, and stay overnight. To schedule a visit, contact the Admission Office. **Campus Safety and Security:** Measures include 24-hour foot and vehicle patrol, emergency notification system, self-defense education, and security escort services. There are emergency telephones, lighted pathways/sidewalks, and controlled access to dorms/residences.

REQUIREMENTS: The SAT or ACT is recommended. Applicants need to be graduates of an accredited high school or have a GED. A GPA of 3.0 is required. AP and CLEP credits are accepted. Important factors in the admissions decision are evidence of special talent, extracurricular activities record, and leadership record. All students are required to complete 40 hours of general studies, including 12 hours each in Effective Communication and Critical Thinking, 8 hours in Global Awareness, and 4 hours each in University Foundation and Christian Worldview. A total of 120 semester hours, with a minimum GPA of 2.0, are required to graduate. **Procedure:** Freshmen are admitted to all sessions. Entrance exams should be taken during the junior or senior year of high school. There are early decision and rolling admissions plans. Applications should be filed by August 22 for fall entry. Applications are accepted on-line. **Transfer Students:** 30 of 120 credits required for the bachelor's degree must be completed at GCU. **International Students:** There are 102 international students enrolled. The school actively recruits these students. They must take the TOEFL with a minimum score of 500 on the paper-based TOEFL (PBT) or 61 on the Internet-based version (iBT) and the college's own test.

Admissions Contact: Dr. Antoinette Farmer, Executive Director. Email: *admissions@gcu.edu* Web: *www.gcu.edu*

FINANCIAL AID: 14% of undergraduate students work part-time. Average annual earnings from campus work are $4800. The FAFSA code is 001074. The priority date for freshman financial aid applications for fall entry is March 1.

NORTHERN ARIZONA UNIVERSITY C-2

www.nau.edu

Flagstaff, AZ 86011 (928) 523-5511 (888) 628-2968
Email: David.Dollins@nau.edu

Full-time: 8892 men, 12,602 women
Part-time: 1915 men, 3097 women
Graduate: 1209 men, 2653 women
Year: semesters, summer session
Room & Board: $9482

SAT: recommended **ACT:** 23
Application Deadline: March 1

Faculty: n/av
Ph.D.s: n/av
Student/Faculty: n/av
Tuition: $10,764 ($24,144)
Freshman Class: 36526 applied, 28521 accepted, 5607 enrolled
CEEB CODE: 4006
VERY COMPETITIVE

Northern Arizona University, founded in 1899, is a comprehensive public university. At NAU, we fully prepare students for meaningful life and work through our commitment to learning and teaching in an unparalleled environment. Through our main campus in Flagstaff and our distance-education opportunities throughout Arizona and online, we offer excellence in teaching, research, and public service to the citizens of Arizona and beyond. Northern Arizona University is a doctoral, higher research institution with undergraduate education at our core and significant research opportunities as well as select master's and doctoral programs. We offer undergraduate and graduate degrees in a full range of disciplines from liberal arts and sciences to professional and career-related fields. Our commitment to high-quality education at all levels is exemplified by small class size and close interaction between students and faculty. The figures in the above capsule and in this profile are approximate. There are 6 undergraduate schools and 1 graduate school. In addition to regional accreditation, NAU has baccalaureate program accreditation with AACSB, ABET, ACBSP, ACCE, ADA, CSWE, NASM, NCATE, NRPA, SAF, ACPHA, CCNE, and CODA. The 708-acre campus is in a small town 140 miles north of Phoenix and 80 miles from the Grand Canyon's South Rim. Including any residence halls, there are 116 buildings.

STUDENT LIFE: 68% of undergraduates are from Arizona. Others are from 50 states, 79 foreign countries, and Canada. 59% are White; 22% Hispanic; 5% two or more races; 4% Foreign; 3% African American; 3% American Indian/Alaska Native; 2% Asian American; 1% race unknown. **Female To Male Ratio:** 1.5:1. The average age of freshmen is 18; all undergraduates, 23. 24% do not continue beyond their first year; 53% remain to graduate. **Housing:** 9173 students can be accommodated in college housing, which includes single-sex and coed dorms, on-campus apartments, off-campus apartments, and married student housing. In addition, there are honors houses, language houses, special-interest houses, fraternity houses, and sorority houses. On-campus housing is available on a first-come, first-served basis, and is available on a lottery system for upperclassmen. 57% of students commute. All students may keep cars.

FACULTY/CLASSROOMS: 50% of faculty are male; 50% are female. No introductory courses are taught by graduate students. The average class size in an introductory lecture is 33 and in a laboratory is 21.

PROGRAMS OF STUDY: NAU confers B.A., B.A.S., B.A.S.W., B.B.A., B.F.A., B.M.Ed., B.Mus., B.S., B.S.Accy., B.S.B.A., B.S.C.S., B.S.D.H., B.S.E., B.S.Ed., B.S.F., B.S.Jour., B.S.N., B.S.W. and B.U.S. degrees. Master's and doctoral degrees are also awarded. Bachelor's degrees are awarded in AGRICULTURE (environmental studies and forestry and related sciences), BIOLOGICAL SCIENCE (biology/biological science and microbiology), BUSINESS (accounting, business administration and management, business economics, finance, hotel/motel and restaurant management, management science, marketing management, and small business management), COMMUNICATIONS AND THE ARTS (communications, English, film, television and digital media, journalism, modern language, music, music performance, photography, Spanish, strategic communication, studio art, theatre arts, and visual communication), COMPUTER AND PHYSICAL SCIENCE (applied science, astronomy, chemistry, computer information technology, computer information systems, computer science, geology, mathematics, and physics), EDUCATION (early childhood education, elementary education, music education, secondary education, and special education), ENGINEERING AND ENVIRONMENTAL DESIGN (civil engineering, construction management, environmental engineering, environmental science, interior design, and mechanical engineering), HEALTH PROFESSIONS (biomedical science, dental hygiene, electrical engineering, exercise science, health science, and nursing), SOCIAL SCIENCE (anthropology, criminal justice, criminology, geography, history, humanities, interdisciplinary studies, international relations, liberal arts/general studies, Native American studies, parks and recreation management, philosophy, political science/government, prelaw, psychology, public administration, social work, sociology, and women & gender studies). Criminology and criminal justice, biomedical science, and nursing have the largest enrollments.

ACTIVITIES: There are 350 groups on campus, including art, band, cheerleading, chess, choir, chorale, chorus, computers, dance, debate, drama, environmental, ethnic, film, forensics, honors, international, jazz band, LGBT, literary magazine, marching band, musical theater, newspaper, opera, orchestra, pep band, photography, political, professional, radio and TV, religious, social, social service, student government, and symphony. Popular campus events include Welcome Week, Family Weekend and Homecoming. **Sports:** There are 6 intercollegiate sports for men and 9 for women, and 11 intramural sports for men and 9 for women. Facilities include football, indoor track and field, three recreation centers with basketball and racquetball courts and weight rooms, indoor swimming pool with diving facilities, soccer, rugby, and lacrosse. The Health Learning Center engages students in holistic learning by integrating recreation, health services, and athletics. **Graduates:** From July 1, 2015 to June 30, 2016, 5119 bachelor's degrees were awarded. The most popular majors were nursing (6%), hotel and resturant management (4%), and criminology and criminal justice (4%). 200 companies recruited on campus in 2015-2016. In an average class, 33% graduate in 4 years or less, 48% graduate in 5 years or less, and 52% graduate in 6 years or less.

SERVICES: Counseling and information services are available, as is tutoring in most subjects. There is a reader service for the blind, and remedial math, reading, and writing. **Library/Resources:** The library contains 1.4 million volumes, and subscribes to 88,412 periodicals including electronic. Computerized library services include interlibrary loans, database searching, Internet access, and Wi-Fi capability. Special learning facilities include an art gallery, radio station, TV station, An observatory, research centers, and the Centennial Forest. **Physically Challenged Students:** 90% of the campus is accessible. Facilities include wheelchair ramps, elevators, special parking, specially equipped restrooms, special class scheduling, lowered drinking fountains, lowered telephones, and special housing. **Special:** NAU offers co-op programs in business and hotel/restaurant management, cross-registration with many universities through the National Student Exchange, and internships in most majors. Legislative internships are offered through the Arizona State Senate and House of Representatives. Students may study abroad in over 50 countries. Work-study programs are available in numerous fields, including engineering, business, and park services. NAU also offers a Personalized Learning competency based program. There are 16 national honor societies and a freshman honors program. **Visiting:** There are regularly scheduled orientations for prospective students. There are guides for informal visits and visitors may sit in on classes. To schedule a visit, contact Office of Undergraduate Admissions and Orientation at (928) 523-0922. **Campus Safety and Security:** Measures include 24-hour foot and vehicle patrol, emergency notification system, self-defense education, and security escort services. There are shuttle buses, emergency telephones, lighted pathways/sidewalks, and controlled access to dorms/residences.

REQUIREMENTS: The SAT or ACT is recommended. Students will be offered admission if they have a 3.0 or higher core GPA and have no deficiencies in the required college preparatory courses. You will be considered for admission if you have a 2.5 core GPA and have no more than one deficiency in any two areas in the college preparatory courses. If you have a combination of a math and lab science deficiency, you are not admissible. GPA is calculated on a 4.0 scale using only the 16 required core courses. Home schooled students must provide a high school transcript, college transcripts if there is college coursework. AP and CLEP credits are accepted. To receive a bachelor's degree at Northern Arizona University, you must complete a least 120 units of credit. Within those total units, you must complete: A. All of Northern Arizona University's liberal studies, diversity, junior-level writing, and capstone requirements. B. All requirements for your specific academic plan(s). C. At least 30 units of upper-division courses, which may include transfer work. D. At least 30 units of coursework taken through Northern Arizona University, of which at least 18 must be upper-division courses (300 level or above).

This requirement is not met by credit-by-exam, retro-credits, transfer coursework, etc. E. A cumulative grade point average of at least 2.0 on all work attempted at Northern Arizona University. **Procedure:** Freshmen are admitted fall, spring, and summer. Entrance exams should be taken Before the last semester of the senior year. There are deferred admissions and rolling admissions plans. Application deadlines are open. Application fee is $25. Applications are accepted on-line. **Transfer Students:** 2896 transfer students enrolled in 2015-2016. Transfer students are considered as high school graduates who have enrolled at a college, university or any other school since graduating from high school and have earned at least 12 college credits. If you are 22 or older, provide a posted high school degree or equivalent, or demonstrate the completion of a minimum of 12 transferrable college credits. At least six of those credits should be from academic subjects requiring college-level skill in reading, writing and/or analysis. Students applying to NAU's Personalized Learning program who are 22 or older must pass a readiness assessment and provide official copies of transcripts for all college-level coursework. The Office of Undergraduate Admissions and Orientation will evaluate transcripts to determine the number of transfer credits accepted. Northern Arizona University will accept college-level transfer coursework with grades of C or better or P from an institution that is accredited by one of the following: Northwest Commission on Colleges and Universities, Western Association of Schools and Colleges, Southern Association of Colleges and Schools, The Higher Learning Commission, New England Association of Schools and Colleges, Middle States Association of Colleges and Schools. You will be offered admission if you have earned a minimum of 35 credits and the Arizona AGEC or the California IGETC with a cumulative GPA of 2.5, or you have earned an associate's degree with a cumulative GPA of 2.0. You will be considered for admission if you have a 2.0 or higher overall college GPA (on a 4.0 scale) and at least 24 transferable academic college credits. 30 of 120 credits required for the bachelor's degree must be completed at NAU. **International Students:** There are 1070 international students enrolled. The school actively recruits these students. They must take the TOEFL with a minimum score of 525 on the paper-based TOEFL (PBT) or 70 on the Internet-based version (iBT), IELTS, ACT, or SAT.

ADMISSIONS: 78% of the 2016-2017 applicants were accepted. The SAT scores for the 2016-2017 freshman class were: Critical Reading-- 39% below 500, 42% between 500 and 599, 17% between 600 and 699, and 2% between 700 and 800. Math-- 38% below 500, 44% between 500 and 599, 16% between 600 and 699, and 2% between 700 and 800. Writing-- 47% below 500, 40% between 500 and 599, 12% between 600 and 699, and 1% between 700 and 800. The ACT scores were 11% between 12 and 17, 48% between 18 and 23, 36% between 24 and 29, and 5% above 30. **Admissions Contact:** David Dollins, Executive Director of Admissions. Email: *David.Dollins@nau.edu* Web: *www.nau.edu*

FINANCIAL AID: 63% of all full-time freshmen and 60% of continuing full-time students received need-based aid. The average freshman award was $12,205. Need-based scholarships or need-based grants averaged $7,010; need-based self-help aid (loans and jobs) averaged $3,393; and other non-need-based awards and non-need-based scholarships averaged $5,897. The FAFSA code is 001082. The priority date for freshman financial aid applications for fall entry is February 14.

PRESCOTT COLLEGE C-3

www.prescott.edu

Prescott, AZ 86301	(928) 350-2100 (800) 628-6364
Fax: (928) 776-5242	Email: admissions@prescott.edu
Full-time: 204 men, 240 women	**Faculty:** 60
Part-time: 40 men, 61 women	**Ph.D.s:** 58%
Graduate: 90 men, 308 women	**Student/Faculty:** 9 to 1
Year: semesters, summer session	**Tuition:** $26,819
Room & Board: $6465	**Freshman Class:** 399 applied, 291 accepted, 49 enrolled
SAT CR/M/W: 565/520/534 **ACT:** 23	**CEEB CODE:** 0484
Application Deadline: August 15	**COMPETITIVE**

Prescott College, founded in 1960, is a private liberal arts institution offering a nontraditional undergraduate program complemented with experiential learning focused on sustainability, the environment, and social justice. The curriculum is organized into multidisciplinary courses that allow students to pursue individual areas of competency. Evaluations of a student's work are conducted through a portfolio/contract system and an ongoing series of student self-evaluations. Grades are optional. The figures in the above capsule and in this profile are approximate. There are 2 undergraduate schools and 2 graduate schools. In addition to regional accreditation, Prescott has baccalaureate program accreditation with NASDTEC. The 13-acre campus is in a small town 100 miles northwest of Phoenix. Including any residence halls, there are 29 buildings.

STUDENT LIFE: 75% of undergraduates are from out of state, mostly the West. Students are from 42 states, 6 foreign countries, and Canada. 73% are White; 12% race unknown; 6% Hispanic; 4% two or more races; 2% African American; 2% American Indian/Alaska Native; 2% Foreign; 1% Asian American. **Female To Male Ratio:** 1.8:1. The average age of freshmen is 19; all undergraduates, 23. 27% do not continue beyond their first year; 37% remain to graduate. **Housing:** 120 students can be accommodated in college housing, which includes coed dorms and on-campus apartments. On-campus housing is guaranteed for the freshman year only, and is available on a first-come, and first-served basis. 80% of students commute. Alcohol is not permitted. All students may keep cars.

FACULTY/CLASSROOMS: 44% of faculty are male; 56% are female. 82% teach undergraduates. No introductory courses are taught by graduate students. The average class size in an introductory lecture is 12; in a laboratory is 12; and in a regular course is 12.

PROGRAMS OF STUDY: Prescott confers B.A., B.S. and B.F.A degrees. Master's and doctoral degrees are also awarded. Bachelor's degrees are awarded in AGRICULTURE (agriculture, environmental studies, forestry and related sciences, and wildlife management), BIOLOGICAL SCIENCE (biology/biological science, ecology, environmental biology, marine biology, marine science, and wildlife biology), BUSINESS (management science, nonprofit/public organization management, and organizational leadership and management), COMMUNICATIONS AND THE ARTS (art, arts administration/management, communications, creative writing, dance, dramatic arts, English, fine arts, journalism, literature, music, performing arts, photography, Spanish, studio art, and visual and performing arts), COMPUTER AND PHYSICAL SCIENCE (earth science, environmental geology, geology, mathematics, natural sciences, and oceanography), EDUCATION (agricultural education, art education, early childhood education, education, education of the emotionally handicapped, education of the exceptional child, education of the mentally handicapped, elementary education, environmental education, foreign languages education, guidance education, middle school education, music education, physical education, recreation education, secondary education, social science education, social studies education, and special education), ENGINEERING AND ENVIRONMENTAL DESIGN (environmental design, environmental science, and land use management and reclamation), HEALTH PROFESSIONS (art therapy, community health work, and mental health/human services), SOCIAL SCIENCE (addiction studies, anthropology, archeology, area studies, community services, counseling/psychology, economics, ethics, politics, and social policy, experimental psychology, gender studies, geography, history, human development, human ecology, human services, humanities, humanities and social science, international relations, international studies, Latin American studies, liberal arts/general studies, parks and recreation management, peace studies, philosophy and religion, psychology, religion, social science, social work, sociology, water resources, and women's studies). Environmental studies, and adventure education are the strongest academically. Environmental studies has the largest enrollment.

ACTIVITIES: There are no fraternities or sororities. There are 12 groups on campus, including bicycle, book club, dance and garden club, jugglers and hoopers, meditation club, agriculture, art, dance, drama, environmental, film, international, LGBT, literary magazine, newspaper, photography, political, social, social service, and student government. Popular campus events include Earth Day, and Southwest Writers Series. **Sports:** There is no sports program at Prescott. There are no sports facilities on campus, but students have access to the local community pool, a weight room, gym, and city league sports. **Graduates:** From July 1, 2015 to June 30, 2016, 196 bachelor's degrees were awarded. The most popular majors were human development (23%), environmental studies/natural resources (22%), and education (16%). In an average class, 23% graduate in 4 years or less, 34% graduate in 5 years or less, and 37% graduate in 6 years or less.

SERVICES: Counseling and information services are available, as is

tutoring in every subject. There is a learning specialist on staff, and untimed tests are available. There are recordings for the blind and dyslexic. **Library/Resources:** The library contains 131,524 volumes, 155 microform items, and 1,732 audio/video tapes/CDs/DVDs, and subscribes to 96,521 periodicals including electronic. Computerized library services include interlibrary loans, database searching, Internet access, and Wi-Fi capability. Special learning facilities include an art gallery, a library annex at Kino Bay, Mexico and Tucson Center, an experimental agroecology farm, a field station in Kino Bay, Mexico, a GIS station, state of the art visual arts classrooms and a functioning gallery, equipment gear warehouse, and a recycling center. In the library, there is access to a learning commons for writing and math. **Physically Challenged Students:** 90% of the campus is accessible. Facilities include wheelchair ramps, elevators, special parking, specially equipped restrooms, and special housing. **Special:** Cross-registration with EcoLeague colleges and the Consortium for Innovative Environments in Learning is possible. Student-coordinated internships, study abroad in almost any country, dual majors, a general studies degree, pass/fail options, and credit for life experience are offered. All majors are student-designed. **Visiting:** There are regularly scheduled orientations for prospective students, including a campus tour, an interview with an admissions counselor, opportunities to sit in classes, faculty interviews, and informational meetings with financial aid and library staff. There are guides for informal visits and visitors may sit in on classes. To schedule a visit, contact the Admissions Office at admissions@prescott.edu. **Campus Safety and Security:** Measures include emergency notification system and security escort services. There are emergency telephones, controlled access to dorms/residences, after hours patrol.

REQUIREMENTS: The SAT is required. The ACT is recommended. In addition, a high school diploma is required, and the GED is accepted. The school requires a completed application form, 1 essay, official transcripts, and 1 letter of recommendation. Students may also submit portfolios and writing samples. A GPA of 2.0 is required. AP and CLEP credits are accepted. Important factors in the admissions decision are extracurricular activities record, leadership record, and evidence of special talent. Students must complete an orientation course, fulfill a minimum residency requirement, demonstrate proficiency in college-level writing and math, and meet course and credit requirements. Students design an individual program of studies within 7 multidisciplinary areas: adventure education, arts and letters, cultural and regional studies, education, environmental studies, humanities, and human development. Each student is required to submit a graduation proposal at the end of the junior year to a graduation review committee. **Procedure:** Freshmen are admitted fall and spring. There are early decision, deferred admissions, and rolling admissions plans. Early decision applications should be filed by December 1; regular applications, by August 15 for fall entry; and December 15 for spring entry. Notification of early decision is sent December 15; regular decision, on a rolling basis. 11 early decision candidates were accepted for the 2016-2017 class. Applications are accepted on-line. **Transfer Students:** 119 transfer students enrolled in 2015-2016. Transfer applicants must meet the same requirements as entering freshmen and must also submit official college transcripts and an essay or personal statement. Students who successfully completed 2 years of college work (60 semester hours or 90 quarter credits) need not submit high school transcripts. There is a 2-year residency requirement. 60 of 120 credits required for the bachelor's degree must be completed at Prescott. **International Students:** There are 8 international students enrolled. They must take the TOEFL with a minimum score of 500 on the paper-based TOEFL (PBT) or 61 on the Internet-based version (iBT).

ADMISSIONS: 73% of the 2016-2017 applicants were accepted. The SAT scores for the 2016-2017 freshman class were: Critical Reading-- 29% below 500, 41% between 500 and 599, 18% between 600 and 699, and 12% between 700 and 800. Math-- 44% below 500, 26% between 500 and 599, 24% between 600 and 699, and 6% between 700 and 800. Writing-- 33% below 500, 50% between 500 and 599, 11% between 600 and 699, and 6% between 700 and 800. The ACT scores were 8% below 12, 42% between 12 and 17, 33% between 24 and 29, and 17% above 30. **Admissions Contact:** Paul Burkhardt, Executive VP & Provost. Email: *admissions@prescott.edu* Web: *www.prescott.edu*

FINANCIAL AID: In 2016-2017, 78% of all full-time freshmen and 70% of continuing full-time students received some form of financial aid. 77% of all full-time freshmen and 69% of continuing full-time students received need-based aid. The average freshman award was $19,706. Need-based scholarships or need-based grants averaged $14,569; need-based self-help aid (loans and jobs) averaged $5,493; other non-need-based awards and non-need-based scholarships averaged $8,642; and $4,821 from other forms of aid. 31% of undergraduate students work part-time. Average annual earnings from campus work are $800. The average financial indebtedness of the 2016 graduate was $27,213. The FAFSA code is 013659. The priority date for freshman financial aid applications for fall entry is March 1.

SAGU AMERICAN INDIAN COLLEGE C-4

www.aicag.edu

Phoenix, AZ 85021	(602) 944-3335 (800) 933-3828
Fax: (602) 943-8299	**Email:** ALCinfo@sagu.edu
Full-time: 50 men, 45 women	**Faculty:** n/av
Part-time: 15 men, 20 women	**Ph.D.s:** n/av
Graduate: n/av	**Student/Faculty:** n/av
Year: semesters	**Tuition:** $11,940
Room & Board: $6202	**Freshman Class:** n/av
SAT or ACT: required	**CEEB CODE:** 2597
Application Deadline: August 14	**COMPETITIVE**

SAGU American Indian College (AIC) founded in 1957, is a Christian college and Bible college with a specific mission of preparing American Indians for leadership in churches, education, and the community. AIC serves nearly 25 tribes as well as other ethnicities. AIC is a campus within the Southwestern Assemblies of God University. The figures in the above capsule and in this profile are approximate. There is 1 undergraduate school. In addition to regional accreditation, AIC has baccalaureate program accreditation with IACBE and SACSCOC. The 10-acre campus is in a small town in north Phoenix, just east of I17 and the Metrocenter area. Including any residence halls, there are 9 buildings.

STUDENT LIFE: 72% of undergraduates are from Arizona. Others are from 10 states, and 1 foreign country. 85% are from public schools. 7% are Hispanic; 67% American Indian/Alaska Native; 4% Asian American; 3% African American; 18% White; 1% Foreign. 100% are Protestant. **Male To Female Ratio:** Is 1:1. The average age of freshmen is 23; all undergraduates, 26. **Housing:** 80 students can be accommodated in college housing, which includes single-sex dorms and off-campus apartments. 52% of students live on campus; of those, 100% remain on campus on weekends. Alcohol is not permitted. All students may keep cars.

FACULTY/CLASSROOMS: 65% of faculty are male; 35% are female. All teach undergraduates. No introductory courses are taught by graduate students. The average class size in an introductory lecture is 11; in a laboratory is 6; and in a regular course is 6.

PROGRAMS OF STUDY: AIC confers B.A. degrees. Associate degrees are also awarded. Bachelor's degrees are awarded in EDUCATION (business education and elementary education), SOCIAL SCIENCE (ministries). Christian ministry, elementary education, and business are the strongest academically.

ACTIVITIES: There are no fraternities or sororities. Groups on campus include band, cheerleading, drama, ethnic, religious, student government, and yearbook. Popular campus events include Missions Conventions, and College Days. **Sports:** There is no sports program at AIC. Facilities include a full-size gym with a locker room and a weight room.

SERVICES: Counseling and information services are available, as is tutoring in most subjects. There is remedial math, reading, and writing. **Library/Resources:** The library contains 21,015 volumes, and 35 audio/video tapes/CDs/DVDs, and subscribes to 102 periodicals including electronic. Computerized library services include Internet access. **Physically Challenged Students:** All of the campus is accessible. Facilities include wheelchair ramps, special parking, specially equipped restrooms, and lowered drinking fountains. **Special:** Internships and dual majors are available. **Visiting:** There are regularly scheduled orientations for prospective students, consisting of College Days in the fall and spring semesters that include class visits, overnight stays in dorms, and meals in the cafeteria for 2 days. There are guides for informal visits, visitors may sit in on classes, and stay overnight. To schedule a visit, contact the Admissions Office. **Campus Safety and Security:** There are lighted pathways/sidewalks, and night security.

REQUIREMENTS: The SAT or ACT is required. Transcripts from high school and any other secondary schools attended are required along with a pastor's reference form. Applicants are required to take placement tests with satisfactory results. The GED is accepted. AP and CLEP credits are accepted. Important factors in the admissions decision are advanced placement or honors courses, evidence of special talent, and extracurricular activities record. To graduate, all students must maintain a GPA of 2.0 and complete 128 total credits. Students must complete courses in history, science, math, computer, and bible studies. A comprehensive bible exam is required. **Procedure:** Freshmen are admitted to all sessions. Entrance exams should be taken prior to acceptance. There are early decision, early admissions, and deferred admissions plans. Applications should be filed by August 14 for fall entry. **Transfer Students:** Official transcripts from high school and each college attended, plus a pastor's reference form are required. Students must demonstrate proficiency in English, writing, math, and reading. 30 of 128 credits required for the bachelor's degree must be completed at AIC. **International Students:** They must take the TOEFL. They must also take the SAT or ACT.

Admissions Contact: Erica Zamorano, Director of Student Services. Email: *ALCinfo@sagu.edu* Web: *www.aicag.edu*

FINANCIAL AID: The FAFSA code is 015550. The priority date for freshman financial aid applications for fall entry is March 1.

UNIVERSITY OF ARIZONA D-4

www.arizona.edu

Tucson, AZ 85721 (520) 621-3705

Email: admissions@email.arizona.edu

Full-time: 14,049 men, 15,292 women	**Faculty:** 1589; I, -$
	Ph.D.s: 90%
Part-time: 2428 men, 2303 women	**Student/Faculty:** 18 to 1
Graduate: 4534 men, 5019 women	**Tuition:** $11,800 ($35,000)
Year: semesters, summer session	**Freshman Class:** 36166 applied, 28433 accepted, 7753 enrolled
Room & Board: $11,300	
SAT CR/M/W: 515/525/515 **ACT:** 22	**CEEB CODE:** 4832
Application Deadline: November 5	**COMPETITIVE**

University of Arizona, founded in 1885, is a public land-grant institution controlled by the state of Arizona. Both traditional and online undergraduate programs are offered in agriculture, architecture, arts and sciences, business and public administration, education, engineering and mines, nursing, pharmacy and other health-related professions. There are 43 undergraduate schools and 1 graduate school. In addition to regional accreditation, UA has baccalaureate program accreditation with AACSB, ACPE, ADA, NASAD, NASM, and CCNE. The 393-acre campus is in an urban area in Tucson, AZ. Including any residence halls, there are 103 buildings.

STUDENT LIFE: 69% of undergraduates are from Arizona. Others are from 50 states, 138 foreign countries, and Canada. 86% are from public schools. 9% are Foreign; 6% Asian American; 53% White; 4% African American; 4% two or more races; 23% Hispanic; 1% American Indian/Alaska Native. **Female To Male Ratio:** 1.1:1. The average age of freshmen is 18; all undergraduates, 21. **Housing:** 7266 students can be accommodated in college housing, which includes single-sex and coed dorms, on-campus apartments, and off-campus apartments. In addition, there are honors houses, special-interest houses, fraternity houses, and sorority houses. On-campus housing is available on a first-come and first-served basis. 80% of students commute. Alcohol is not permitted. All students may keep cars.

FACULTY/CLASSROOMS: 61% of faculty are male; 39% are female. No introductory courses are taught by graduate students.

PROGRAMS OF STUDY: UA confers B.A., B.A.E., B.Arch., B.A.S., B.E.S., B.F.A., B.G.S., B.Mu., B.S., B.S.Ae.E., B.S.B.A., B.S.Bm.E., B.S.Bs.E., B.S.Ch.E., B.S.Cv.E., B.S.E., B.S.E.C.E., B.S.E.Mg., B.S.H.S., B.S.In.E., B.S.Me.E., B.S.Mn.E., B.S.M.S.E., B.S.N., B.S.O.S.E., B.S.S.B.E., B.S.S.Ed. and B.S.Sy.E. degrees. Master's and doctoral degrees are also awarded. Bachelor's degrees are awarded in AGRICULTURE (agricultural business management, agricultural economics, animal science, environmental studies, natural resource management, plant science, and soil science), BIOLOGICAL SCIENCE (biochemistry, biology/biological science, biometrics and biostatistics, cell biology, ecology, entomology, genetics, microbiology, molecular biology, neurosciences, nutrition, physiology, and plant pathology), BUSINESS (accounting, business administration and management, business economics, entrepreneurial studies, finance, management information systems, management science, marketing and distribution, operations management, and retailing), COMMUNICATIONS AND THE ARTS (art history, art, classics, communications, creative writing, dance, English, English as a second/foreign language, film arts, fine arts, French, Italian, journalism, linguistics, music, musical theater, performing arts, Russian, Spanish, studio art, and theatre arts), COMPUTER AND PHYSICAL SCIENCE (applied mathematics, applied science, astronomy, atmospheric sciences and meteorology, chemistry, computer science, geology, geoscience, hydrology, information sciences and systems, mathematics, medical physics, natural sciences, optics, physics, planetary and space science, and statistics), EDUCATION (agricultural education, art education, early childhood education, education, elementary education, library science, middle school education, music education, psychology education, school psychology, science education, secondary education, special education, and teaching English as a second/foreign language (TESOL/TEFOL)), ENGINEERING AND ENVIRONMENTAL DESIGN (aeronautical engineering, agricultural engineering, architecture, biomedical engineering, chemical engineering, civil engineering, electrical/electronics engineering, engineering, environmental engineering, environmental science, industrial engineering, landscape architecture/design, materials engineering, materials science, mechanical engineering, mining and mineral engineering, optical engineering, and systems engineering), HEALTH PROFESSIONS (environmental health science, medical science, nursing, pharmaceutical science, pharmacology, pharmacy, pre-health studies, public health, rehabilitation therapy, speech pathology/audiology, and veterinary science), SOCIAL SCIENCE (African studies, American Indian studies, anthropology, counseling/psychology, East Asian studies, economics, family/consumer studies, gender studies, geography, German area studies, history, human development, interdisciplinary studies, Judaic studies, Latin American studies, law, Mexican-American/Chicano studies, Middle Eastern studies, philosophy, political science/government, psychology, public administration, religious education, sociology, and women's studies). Sciences, social sciences, and business administration are the strongest academically. Business, and sciences have the largest enrollments.

ACTIVITIES: 12% of men belong to 25 national fraternities; 20% of women belong to 25 national sororities. There are 586 groups on campus, including art, band, cheerleading, chess, choir, chorale, chorus, computers, dance, debate, drama, drill team, environmental, ethnic, film, honors, international, jazz band, LGBT, literary magazine, marching band, musical theater, newspaper, orchestra, pep band, photography, political, professional, radio and TV, religious, social, student government, and yearbook. Popular campus events include Spring Fling Carnival, Cultural Programs and Family Weekend. **Sports:** There are 7 intercollegiate sports for men and 10 for women. Facilities include an athletic center, a stadium, arena, recreation facility with a weight room, a wave-less swimming pool, two gyms, aerobics facilities, treadmills, stair climbers, stationary bicycles, racquetball, squash, handball courts, hiking, backpacking, skiing trails as well as kayaking, caving, and scuba diving are available. **Graduates:** From July 1, 2015 to June 30, 2016, 7493 bachelor's degrees were awarded. The most popular majors were business/marketing (16%), biological/life sciences (11%), and social sciences (9%). In an average class, 42% graduate in 4 years or less, 14% graduate in 5 years or less, and 4% graduate in 6 years or less.

SERVICES: Counseling and information services are available, as is tutoring in most subjects. There is a reader service for the blind, and remedial math, reading, and writing. **Library/Resources:** The 7 libraries contain 6.6 million volumes, 5.6 million microform items, and 117,170 audio/video tapes/CDs/DVDs, and subscribe to 79,058 periodicals including electronic. Computerized library services include interlibrary loans, database searching, Internet access, and Wi-Fi capability. Special learning facilities include an art gallery, natural history museum, planetarium, radio station, TV station, the Ansel Adams center for creative photography, and the integrated learning center. **Physically Challenged Students:** All of the campus is accessible. Facilities include wheelchair ramps, elevators, special parking, specially equipped restrooms, special class scheduling, lowered drinking fountains, lowered telephones, and special housing. physical therapy, counseling, interpreters, equipment maintenance and an adaptive athletics program. **Special:** Co-op programs are available in almost all majors. Internships in almost all disciplines. Washington semester for certain internships related to government. Accelerated Masters programs-MBA, MIS, and Entrepreneurship programs. 119 B.A.-B.S. degrees, dual majors, interdisciplinary degrees such as engineering-math and theater arts-education, a 3-2 arts and sciences-business degree, and student designed majors are offered. Study abroad in numerous countries, work-study programs on campus, a general studies degree, and pass/fail options are offered. Non-degree study is possible. There are 33 national honor societies, Phi Beta Kappa, and a freshman honors program. **Visiting:** There are regularly scheduled orientations for prospective students, consisting of an admissions presentation and tour. There are guides for informal visits and visitors may sit in on classes. To schedule a visit, contact the Admissions Office. **Campus Safety and Security:** Measures include 24-hour foot and vehicle patrol, emergency notification system, self-defense education, and security escort services. There are shuttle buses, emergency telephones, lighted pathways/sidewalks, and controlled access to dorms/residences.

REQUIREMENTS: The SAT or ACT is recommended. Applicants should have completed 4 years each in high school English and math, 3 in science, 2 of a foreign language, and 1 each in history, fine arts, and social studies. A GED may be considered in place of a high school diploma. Some fine arts programs require auditions prior to admission. AP and CLEP credits are accepted. The University of Arizona offers a research-extensive curriculum and opportunities for all students to engage in real-world experiences designed to enhance classroom learning and meet workforce needs. Engagement experiences include internships, research projects, practicums, work options, study abroad and exchange programs. The UA also offers accelerated master's programs in a variety of disciplines including numerous online degree offerings through UA Online. Dual majors, interdisciplinary degrees, and minors are also available for preparing new generations of college students to address the world's most critical issues. On average, students see a huge ROI from the UA; its graduates are some of the world's most employable, collecting job offers at a 4% higher rate than the national average. **Procedure:** Freshmen are admitted to all sessions. There is a rolling admissions plan. Applications should be filed by November 5 for fall entry, along with a $50 fee. Notification is sent on a rolling basis. Applications are accepted on-line. **Transfer Students:** 2175 transfer students enrolled in 2015-2016. Resident transfer applicants must have a minimum GPA of 2.0; and nonresidents must have a minimum GPA of 2.5. Some university divisions have higher requirements. Admission is competitive for out-of-state students. 30 of 120 credits required for the bachelor's degree must be completed at UA. **International Students:** There are 2358 international students enrolled. The school actively recruits these students. They must take the TOEFL with a minimum score of 550 on the paper-based TOEFL (PBT) or 70 on the Internet-based version (iBT) and the Comprehensive English Language Test. They must also take the SAT or ACT, scoring 1110 only if the applicant is a graduate of a U.S. high school.

ADMISSIONS: 79% of the 2016-2017 applicants were accepted. The SAT scores for the 2016-2017 freshman class were: Critical Reading-- 31% below 500, 41% between 500 and 599, 23% between 600 and 699, and 5% between 700 and 800. Math-- 27% below 500, 41% between 500 and 599, 26% between 600 and 699, and 6% between 700 and 800. Writing-- 37% below 500, 42% between 500 and 599, 17% between 600 and 699, and 4% between 700 and 800. The ACT scores were 7% between 12 and 17, 37% between 18 and 23, 43% between 24 and 29, and 13% above 30. 38% of the current freshmen were in the top fifth of their class; 52% were in the top two fifths. There were 68 National Merit finalists. **Admissions Contact:** Kasandra Urquidez, Dean of Undergraduate Admissions. Email: *admissions@email.arizona.edu* Web: *www.arizona.edu*

FINANCIAL AID: In 2016-2017, 82% of all full-time freshmen and 74% of continuing full-time students received some form of financial aid. 54% of all full-time freshmen and 49% of continuing full-time students received need-based aid. UA is a member of CSS. The FAFSA code is 001083. The priority date for freshman financial aid applications for fall entry is March 1.

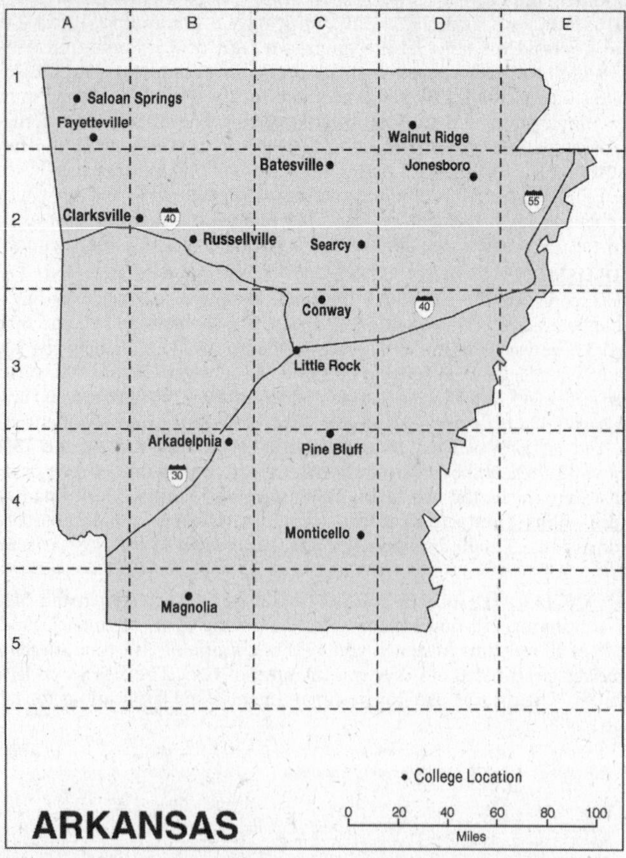

ARKANSAS BAPTIST COLLEGE *(The complete profile is made available exclusively on our website, www.barronspac.com)*

ARKANSAS STATE UNIVERSITY D-2

www.astate.edu

State University, AR 72467 **(870) 972-2782**

Fax: (870) 972-3545 **Email: admissions@astate.edu**

Full-time: 3193 men, 4102 women
Part-time: 919 men, 1378 women
Graduate: 1334 men, 2484 women
Year: semesters, summer session
Room & Board: $8140

SAT CR/M/W: 420/500/450 **ACT:** 24
Application Deadline: August 18

Faculty: 443; IIA, --$
Ph.D.s: 85%
Student/Faculty: 17 to 1
Tuition: $8050 ($14,050)
Freshman Class: 5346 applied, 3755 accepted, 1577 enrolled
CEEB CODE: 6011
COMPETITIVE

Arkansas State University, founded in 1909, is part of the Arkansas State University System and is a state-supported institution offering undergraduate and graduate degrees in agriculture and technology, business, education and behavioral sciences, engineering, fine arts, humanities and social sciences, media and communication, nursing and health professions, sciences, and mathematics. There are 6 undergraduate schools and one graduate school. In addition to regional accreditation, A-State has baccalaureate program accreditation with AACSB, ABET, ACEJMC, ADA, CSWE, NASAD, NASM, NCATE, NLN, AAM, ACEND, ACS, CAAASLP, CAATE, CACREP, CAEPNET, CALEA, CAPTE, COA, CORE, CSMA, JCERT, JRCDMS, JRCNMT, NAACLS, NACEP, NASP, NASPAA, NAST, and NIBS. The 1376-acre campus is in a small town 70 miles west of Memphis, TN. Including any residence halls, there are 157 buildings.

STUDENT LIFE: 85% of undergraduates are from Arkansas. Others are from 41 states, 50 foreign countries, and Canada. 93% are from public schools. 75% are White; 5% Foreign; 3% Hispanic; 2% two or more races; 13% African American; 1% Asian American; 1% race unknown. **Female To Male Ratio:** 1.5:1. The average age of freshmen is 18; all undergraduates, 23. 24% do not continue beyond their first year; 39% remain to graduate. **Housing:** 3217 students can be accommodated in college housing, which includes single-sex and coed dorms, on-campus apartments, and married student housing. In addition, there are honors houses, special-interest houses, fraternity houses, sorority houses, living learning communities (Honors, STEM, ROTC) and first-year residential experience wing. On-campus housing is available on a first-come and first-served basis. 70% of students commute. Alcohol is not permitted. All students may keep cars.

FACULTY/CLASSROOMS: 47% of faculty are male; 53% are female. 90% teach undergraduates, 20% do research, and 20% do both. Graduate students teach 5% of introductory courses. The average class size in an introductory lecture is 30; in a laboratory is 24; and in a regular course is 27.

PROGRAMS OF STUDY: A-State confers B.A., B.G.S., B.S., B.A.S., B.F.A., B.M., B.M.E., B.S.A., B.S.E., B.S.C.E., B.S.E.E., B.S.M.E., B.S.N., B.S.E.N., B.S.R.S. and B.S.W. degrees. Associate, master's, and doctoral degrees are also awarded. Bachelor's degrees are awarded in AGRICULTURE (agricultural business management, agriculture, animal science, plant science, and wildlife management), BIOLOGICAL SCIENCE (biology/adolescence education, biological sciences, and biotechnology), BUSINESS (accounting, banking and finance, business administration and management, business economics, international business, marketing, sports management, and supply chain management), COMMUNICATIONS AND THE ARTS (art, communications, English, foreign language, graphic design, information technology, instrumental music education, journalism, multimedia, music, radio/television technology, strategic communication, theatre arts, and vocal performance), COMPUTER AND PHYSICAL SCIENCE (chemistry, clinical laboratory science, chemistry education, computer science, mathematics, and physics), EDUCATION (athletic training, business education, early childhood education, elementary education, English education, foreign languages education, general studies, health education, mathematics education, middle school education, physical education, science education, social science education, and special education), ENGINEERING AND ENVIRONMENTAL DESIGN (civil engineering technology, electrical/electronics engineering, emergency/disaster science, engineering, manufacturing technology, mechanical engineering, and technological management), HEALTH PROFESSIONS (exercise science, health promotion, nursing, and radiological science), SOCIAL SCIENCE (communication sciences & disorders, criminology, dietetics, economics, history, interdisciplinary studies, philosophy, political science/government, psychology, social work, and sociology). Engineering, nursing, and biological sciences are the strongest academically. Nursing, early childhood education, and interdisciplinary studies have the largest enrollments.

ACTIVITIES: 16% of men belong to 13 national fraternities; 13% of women belong to 7 national sororities. There are 175 groups on campus, including academic clubs, art, cheerleading, choir, computers, dance, debate, drama, drill team, environmental, ethnic, forensics, honors, international, jazz band, LGBT, marching band, musical theater, newspaper, pep band, photography, political, professional, radio and TV, religious, social, social service, student government, symphony, and yearbook. Popular campus events include Welcome Week, Order of the Pack, Homecoming, Residence Life Back to School Luau, Springfest, and Black History Month Celebration. **Sports:** There are 7 intercollegiate sports for men and 9 for women, and 20 intramural sports for men and 20 for women. Facilities include a 10,038-seat convocation center for basketball games or 10,252 seat for concerts, a 30,382-seat football stadium, 1,200-seat baseball complex, 400+-seat track facility, and a 750-seat soccer field. **Graduates:** From July 1, 2015 to June 30, 2016, 1766 bachelor's degrees were awarded. The most popular majors were interdisciplinary studies (11%), nursing (8%), and early childhood education (7%). 718 companies recruited on campus in 2015-2016. In an average class, 11% graduate in 3 years or less, 28% graduate in 4 years or less, 37% graduate in 5 years or less, and 39% graduate in 6 years or less. Of the 2015 graduating class, 19% were enrolled in graduate school within 6 months of graduation, and 34% were employed.

SERVICES: Counseling and information services are available, as is tutoring in most subjects. There is a reader service for the blind, and remedial math, reading, and writing. Tutoring is provided in virtually all general education subjects. Student Support Services tries to provide as much tutoring as possible for upper level courses when tutors are available for the subject areas. **Library/Resources:** The library contains 838,243 volumes, and 112,847 audio/video tapes/CDs/DVDs, and subscribes to 40,822 periodicals including electronic. Computerized library services include interlibrary loans, database searching, Internet access, and Wi-Fi capability. Special learning facilities include an art gallery, natural history museum, radio station, TV station, Agriculture and Environmental Ecotoxicology Research, the Arkansas Biosciences Institute, the Fowler Center for Performing Arts, distance learning, the Hemingway-Pfeiffer Museum and Educational Center, a geographic information system facility, an electron microscope lab, and the Delta Studies Center. **Physically Challenged Students:** 90% of the campus is accessible. Facilities include wheelchair ramps, elevators, special parking, specially equipped restrooms, special class scheduling, lowered drinking fountains, and lowered telephones. **Special:** An interdisciplinary studies degree, study abroad, and work-study programs are offered. Dual majors and internships are available in many areas. Non-degree study is possible. There are 10 national honor societies and a freshman honors program. **Visiting:** There are regularly scheduled orientations for prospective students, consisting of various sessions held throughout the year. There are guides for informal visits, visitors may sit in on classes, and stay overnight. To schedule a visit, contact the Office of Recruitment at (870) 972-2782. **Campus Safety and Security:** Measures include 24-hour foot and vehicle patrol, emergency notification system, self-defense education, and security escort services. There are shuttle buses, emergency telephones, and lighted pathways/sidewalks.

REQUIREMENTS: SAT, ASSET, or COMPASS scores are required, with ACT scores recommended. Applicants should have completed 14 academic high school units, including 4 each in English and math, 3 in social studies, 3 in science (must be labs), and it is recommended to take 2 in 1 foreign language. Applicants must have an ACT composite score of 21 and a high school GPA of 2.75 for unconditional admission. AP and CLEP credits are accepted. All students must complete a 35 hour credit distribution of general education courses. A total of at least 120 credits, with a minimum GPA of 2.0, is required to graduate. **Procedure:** Freshmen are admitted fall, spring, and summer. Entrance exams should be taken before April 1 of the high school senior year. There are early admissions and rolling admissions plans. Applications should be filed by August 18 for fall entry; January 15 for spring entry; and May 27 for summer entry, along with a $15 fee. Applications are accepted on-line. **Transfer Students:** 897 transfer students enrolled in 2015-2016. Transfer applicants should have a minimum GPA of 2.0. Those having completed 12 or fewer credit hours will be admitted on the same basis as freshmen. Official transcripts from every institution attended are required. 32 of 120 credits required for the bachelor's degree must be completed at A-State. **International Students:** There are 441 international students enrolled. The school actively recruits these students. They must take the TOEFL with a minimum score of 500 on the paper-based TOEFL (PBT) or 61 on the Internet-based version (iBT).

ADMISSIONS: 70% of the 2016-2017 applicants were accepted. The SAT scores for the 2016-2017 freshman class were: Critical Reading-- 64% below 500 and 36% between 500 and 599. Math-- 44% below 500, 36% between 500 and 599, and 20% between 600 and 699. Writing-- 80% below 500 and 20% between 500 and 599. The ACT scores were 20% below 12, 30% between 12 and 17, 26% between 18 and 23, 14% between 24 and 29, and 11% above 30. 43% of the current freshmen were in the top fifth of their class; 66% were in the top two fifths. 49 freshmen graduated first in their class. **Admissions Contact:** Tammy Fowler, Director of Recruitment. Email: *admissions@astate.edu* Web: *www.astate.edu*

FINANCIAL AID: In 2016-2017, 93% of all full-time freshmen and 75% of continuing full-time students received some form of financial aid. 82% of all full-time freshmen and 74% of continuing full-time students received need-based aid. The average freshman award was $13,250. Need-based scholarships or need-based grants averaged $7,800 ($9,000 maximum); need-based self-help aid (loans and jobs) averaged $6,200 ($8,500 maximum); non-need-based athletic scholarships averaged $9,500 ($10,000 maximum); and other non-need-based awards and non-need-based scholarships averaged $6,000 ($12,000 maximum). 9% of undergraduate students work part-time. Average annual earnings from campus work are $5880. The average financial indebtedness of the 2016 graduate was $25,000. A-State is a member of CSS. The college's own financial statement is required. The FAFSA code is 001090. The priority date for freshman financial aid applications for fall entry is February 15. The deadline for filing freshman financial aid applications for fall entry is July 1.

ARKANSAS TECH UNIVERSITY B-2

www.atu.edu

Russellville, AR 72801 (479) 968-0343
(800) 582-6953

Fax: (479) 964-0522
Email: tech.enroll@atu.edu
Full-time: 3197 men, 3588 women
Faculty: 323
Part-time: 1774 men, 2494 women
Ph.D.s: 60%
Graduate: 288 men, 553 women
Student/Faculty: 20 to 1
Year: semesters, summer session
Tuition: $8280 ($14,850)
Room & Board: $7204
Freshman Class: 5232 applied, 3344 accepted, 1892 enrolled
SAT CR/M: 465/500 **ACT:** 22
CEEB CODE: 3010
Application Deadline: open
COMPETITIVE

Arkansas Tech University, founded in 1909, is a state-supported institution offering undergraduate instruction in arts and humanities, business, education, natural and health sciences, information technology, engineering, applied sciences, and other technical fields. Graduate instruction is offered in education, arts and humanities, instructional technology, information technology, fisheries and wildlife, nursing, emergency management, business administration, and engineering. There are 7 undergraduate schools and 1 graduate school. In addition to regional accreditation, Tech has baccalaureate program accreditation with AACSB, ABET, CAHEA, NASM, NCATE, NLN, NRPA, ACS, ACPHA, AHIMA, and FOHE. The 559-acre campus is in a small town 75 miles west of Little Rock. Including any residence halls, there are 125 buildings.

STUDENT LIFE: 93% of undergraduates are from Arkansas. Others are from 36 states, 45 foreign countries, and Canada. 8% are African American; 76% White; 7% Hispanic; 4% Foreign; 3% two or more races; 1% Asian American; 1% American Indian/Alaska Native. **Female To Male Ratio:** 1.3:1. The average age of freshmen is 18; all undergraduates, 22. 33% do not continue beyond their first year; 36% remain to graduate. **Housing:** 2852 students can be accommodated in college housing, which includes single-sex and coed dorms, on-campus apartments, and off-campus apartments. In addition, there are sorority houses. 69% of students commute. Alcohol is not permitted. All students may keep cars.

FACULTY/CLASSROOMS: 45% of faculty are male; 55% are female. No introductory courses are taught by graduate students.

PROGRAMS OF STUDY: Tech confers B.A., B.F.A., B.M.E., B.P.S., B.S., B.S.B.A., B.S.E.E., B.S.M.E. and B.S.N degrees. Associate, master's, and doctoral degrees are also awarded. Bachelor's degrees are awarded in AGRICULTURE (agricultural business management and fishing and fisheries), BIOLOGICAL SCIENCE (biology/biological science, life science, and wildlife biology), BUSINESS (accounting, business intelligence and analytics, finance, hospitality management services, management, and marketing), COMMUNICATIONS AND THE ARTS (art, communications, creative writing, English, fine arts, game design and development, journalism, languages, music, and speech/debate/rhetoric), COMPUTER AND PHYSICAL SCIENCE (chemistry, chemistry/adolescence education, computer game design/development, computer science, geology, information sciences and systems, mathematics, physical sciences, physics secondary education, and physics), EDUCATION (agricultural education, art education, business education, computer education, early childhood education, education, elementary education, foreign languages education, health education, health information management, middle school education, music education, physical education, and science education), ENGINEERING AND ENVIRONMENTAL DESIGN (electrical/electronics engineering, emergency/disaster science, engineering physics, environmental science, and mechanical engineering), HEALTH PROFESSIONS (biology, medical laboratory technology, and nursing), SOCIAL SCIENCE (cultural studies/critical theory & analysis, economics, history, international studies, parks and recreation management, political science/government, psychology, public history/archives, social studies, and sociology).

ACTIVITIES: 4% of men belong to 10 national fraternities; 8% of women belong to 4 national sororities. There are 190 groups on campus, including art, band, cheerleading, choir, chorale, chorus, computers, dance, debate, drama, drill team, environmental, ethnic, honors, international, jazz band, literary magazine, marching band, musical theater, newspaper, opera, orchestra, pep band, political, professional, radio and TV, religious, social, social service, and student government. Popular campus events include Greek Week, Family Day, and Spring Fling. **Sports:** There are 4 intercollegiate sports for men and 6 for women, and 11 intramural sports for men and 11 for women. Facilities include a coliseum, fields, racquetball courts, and a 10,000-seat stadium. **Graduates:** From July 1, 2015 to June 30, 2016, 1411 bachelor's degrees were awarded. The most popular majors were professional studies (19%), nursing (11%), and management and marketing (6%).

SERVICES: Counseling and information services are available, as is tutoring in most subjects. There is a reader service for the blind, and remedial math, reading, and writing. **Library/Resources:** The library contains 313,011 volumes, 905,816 microform items, and 16,178 audio/video tapes/CDs/DVDs, and subscribes to 756 periodicals including electronic. Computerized library services include interlibrary loans, database searching, Internet access, and Wi-Fi capability. Special learning facilities include an art gallery, radio station, TV station, an energy center, and a library with distance learning classrooms, satellite downlink, and 400 data drops for laptop computers. **Physically Challenged Students:** All of the campus is accessible. Facilities include wheelchair ramps, elevators, special parking, specially equipped restrooms, special class scheduling, lowered drinking fountains, lowered telephones, and special housing. **Special:** Special academic features include internships and work-study programs, as well as study abroad, accelerated programs, B.A.-B.S. degrees, and dual degree. Independent study is available to seniors. Off-campus courses and on-line telecourses are also offered. There are 4 national honor societies and a freshman honors program. **Visiting:** There are regularly scheduled orientations for prospective students. There are guides for informal visits and visitors may sit in on classes. To schedule a visit, contact the Admissions Office. **Campus Safety and Security:** Measures include 24-hour foot and vehicle patrol, emergency notification system, self-defense education, and security escort services. There are emergency telephones, lighted pathways/sidewalks, and controlled access to dorms/residences.

REQUIREMENTS: The ACT is required, with a composite score of 15 or above. The SAT is recommended, with a composite score of 1060 or above, or a composite COMPASS score of 47 (averaging scores in algebra, writing, and reading) or above for students who graduate from a public secondary school; composite ACT score of 19 or above, composite SAT score of 1330 or above, or a composite COMPASS score of 68 (averaging scores in algebra, writing, and reading) or above for students who graduate from a private secondary school, home school, or received a GED. Note: The ACT Writing exam is not required for admission purposes. A GPA of 2.0 is required. AP and CLEP credits are accepted. Students must complete at least 120 semester hours, including 40 hours of upper-level courses to fulfill a major, and maintain a minimum GPA of 2.0. General education requirements include 15 hours of social sciences, fine arts, and humanities, 8 of science, 6 of English, and 3 of math. No more than four semester hours of activity credit may be counted toward graduation. **Procedure:** Freshmen are admitted to all sessions. Entrance exams should be taken no later than the second semester of the senior year of high school. There are deferred admissions and rolling admissions plans. Application deadlines are open. Notification is sent on a rolling basis. Applications are accepted on-line. **Transfer Students:** 521 transfer students enrolled in 2015-2016. Transfer students making application for admission to Arkansas Tech University must submit official transcripts from all colleges/universities where they have been officially registered. Students seeking transfer of credit from other institutions may be asked to provide a catalog or course description from the transfer institution. Students with fewer than 24 semester hours of earned college-level credit must also submit a high school transcript and must request current transferable ACT or SAT scores be sent to the University. ACT, SAT, or COMPASS scores will not be required if the English and mathematics general education requirements have been satisfied with grades of "C" or better. In the event that receipt of a student's transcript is unavoidably delayed, as may frequently occur at midyear, a transfer student may be admitted provisionally pending receipt of the official transcript. However, the University reserves the right to require immediate withdrawal if the previous record does not meet admission requirements. Applicants for transfer must have earned a GPA of 2.00 (on a 4.00 scale) on all college-level courses attempted and be eligible to re-enroll at the last college or university attended. 30 of 120 credits required for the bachelor's degree must be completed at Tech. **International Students:** There are 361 international students enrolled. The school actively recruits these students. They must take the TOEFL with a minimum score of 500 on the paper-based TOEFL (PBT) or 61 on the Internet-based version (iBT), or take the IELTS or EIKEN. They must also take the SAT or ACT, scoring 15.

ADMISSIONS: 64% of the 2016-2017 applicants were accepted. The SAT scores for the 2016-2017 freshman class were: Critical Reading-- 67% below 500 and 33% between 500 and 599. Math-- 47% below 500, 47% between 500 and 599, and 7% between 600 and 699. The ACT scores were 17% between 12 and 17, 47% between 18 and 23, 32% between 24 and 29, and 4% above 30. 28% of the current freshmen were in the top fifth of their class; 57% were in the top two fifths. 5 freshmen graduated first in their class. **Admissions Contact:** Shauna Donnell, Director of Enrollment Management. Email: *tech.enroll@atu.edu* Web: *www.atu.edu*

FINANCIAL AID: In 2016-2017, 69% of all full-time freshmen and 67% of continuing full-time students received some form of financial aid. 56% of all full-time freshmen and 55% of continuing full-time students received need-based aid. The average freshman award was $9,187. Need-based scholarships or need-based grants averaged $4,467; need-based self-help aid (loans and jobs) averaged $2,929; and non-need-based athletic scholarships averaged $4,697. The average financial indebtedness of the 2016 graduate was $27,156. The college's own financial statement is required. The FAFSA code is 001089. The priority date for freshman financial aid applications for fall entry is March 15.

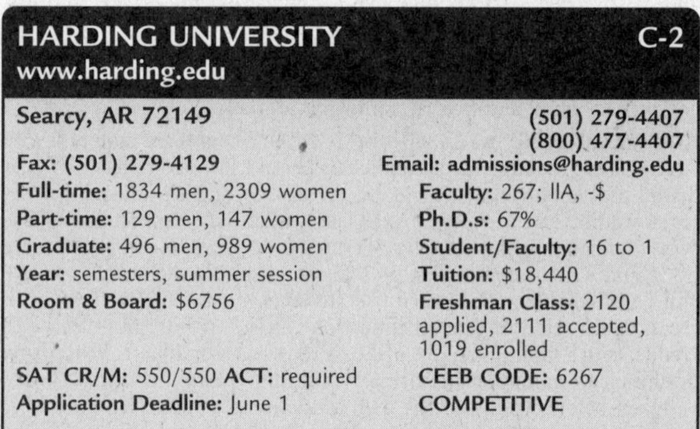

HARDING UNIVERSITY C-2
www.harding.edu

Searcy, AR 72149	(501) 279-4407 (800) 477-4407
Fax: (501) 279-4129	Email: admissions@harding.edu
Full-time: 1834 men, 2309 women	Faculty: 267; IIA, -$
Part-time: 129 men, 147 women	Ph.D.s: 67%
Graduate: 496 men, 989 women	Student/Faculty: 16 to 1
Year: semesters, summer session	Tuition: $18,440
Room & Board: $6756	Freshman Class: 2120 applied, 2111 accepted, 1019 enrolled
SAT CR/M: 550/550 ACT: required	CEEB CODE: 6267
Application Deadline: June 1	COMPETITIVE

Harding University, founded in 1924, is a private Christian institution comprised of the Colleges of Allied Health, Arts and Humanities, Sciences, Bible and Religion, Business, Education, Nursing, Honors and Pharmacy. There are 8 undergraduate schools and 5 graduate schools. In addition to regional accreditation, Harding has baccalaureate program accreditation with ABET, ACBSP, CSWE, NASM, NCATE, NLN, and CADE. The 350-acre campus is in a small town 50 miles northeast of Little Rock and 105 miles west of Memphis, TN. Including any residence halls, there are 59 buildings.

STUDENT LIFE: 73% of undergraduates are from out of state, mostly the South. Students are from 50 states, 54 foreign countries, and Canada. 65% are from public schools. 82% are White; 6% Foreign; 5% African American; 3% Hispanic; 2% two or more races; 1% Asian American; 1% American Indian/Alaska Native. 93% are Protestant. **Female To Male Ratio:** 1.4:1. The average age of freshmen is 18; all undergraduates, 21. 18% do not continue beyond their first year; 64% remain to graduate. **Housing:** 3247 students can be accommodated in college housing, which includes single-sex dorms, on-campus apartments, off-campus apartments, and married student housing. On-campus housing is guaranteed for all 4 years, and is available on a first-come, and first-served basis. 70% of students live on campus; of those, 75% remain on campus on weekends. Alcohol is not permitted. All students may keep cars.

FACULTY/CLASSROOMS: 68% of faculty are male; 32% are female. 78% teach undergraduates. No introductory courses are taught by graduate students. The average class size in an introductory lecture is 16 and in a laboratory is 14.

PROGRAMS OF STUDY: Harding confers B.A., B.S., B.B.A., B.F.A., B.M.E., B.M.N., B.S.N., B.S.W., M.S., M.A.T., M.B.A., M.S.E., M.S.N., M.E.D., E.D.D. and E.D.S. degrees. Master's and doctoral degrees are also awarded. Bachelor's degrees are awarded in BIOLOGICAL SCIENCE (biochemistry and biology/biological science), BUSINESS (accounting, banking and finance, business administration and management, fashion merchandising, international business management, marketing/retailing/merchandising, and sports management), COMMUNICATIONS AND THE ARTS (advertising, art, broadcasting, communications, design, dramatic arts, English, fine arts, French, graphic design, journalism, media arts, music, painting, and Spanish), COM-

PUTER AND PHYSICAL SCIENCE (chemistry, computer science, information sciences and systems, mathematics, and physics), EDUCATION (athletic training, Christian education, early childhood education, elementary education, foreign languages education, music education, and secondary education), ENGINEERING AND ENVIRONMENTAL DESIGN (biomedical engineering, computer engineering, electrical/electronics engineering, interior design, and mechanical engineering), HEALTH PROFESSIONS (exercise science, health, health care administration, health science, medical technology, nursing, and speech pathology/audiology), SOCIAL SCIENCE (American studies, biblical languages, biblical studies, child care/child and family studies, criminal justice, dietetics, economics, history, home economics, humanities, international studies, legal studies, liberal arts/general studies, ministries, missions, political science/government, psychology, public administration, religion, social science, social work, and youth ministry). Engineering, pharmacy, and physical theraphy are the strongest academically. Business, education, and nursing have the largest enrollments.

ACTIVITIES: There are no fraternities or sororities. There are 106 groups on campus, including art, band, cheerleading, choir, chorale, chorus, computers, debate, drama, ethnic, film, honors, international, jazz band, literary magazine, marching band, musical theater, newspaper, orchestra, pep band, photography, political, professional, radio and TV, religious, social, social service, student government, symphony, and yearbook. Popular campus events include Spring Sing, Homecoming, Bison Days, Family Weekend, and Lectureship. **Sports:** There are 9 intercollegiate sports for men and 9 for women, and 11 intramural sports for men and 9 for women. Facilities include baseball and softball fields, racquetball, handball, tennis courts, a football stadium, indoor and outdoor track, golf practice range, gymnastics room, weight rooms, an Olympic-size swimming pool, and 2 gyms. The football and athletic training complex provides state of the art weight room, locker room, office space, as well as rehabilitation area and hydrotherapy area. Harding owns a 2000-acre camp in the Ozark Mountains with horses, 25 rustic cabins, streams, and hiking trails. **Graduates:** From July 1, 2015 to June 30, 2016, 937 bachelor's degrees were awarded. The most popular majors were business/marketing (15%), early childhood licensure (14%), and health professions and related programs (12%). 145 companies recruited on campus in 2015-2016. In an average class, 43% graduate in 4 years or less, 61% graduate in 5 years or less, and 64% graduate in 6 years or less. Of the 2015 graduating class, 30% were enrolled in graduate school within 6 months of graduation, and 21% were employed.

SERVICES: Counseling and information services are available, as is tutoring in most subjects. There is a reader service for the blind, and remedial math, reading, and writing. **Library/Resources:** The library contains 367,438 volumes, and subscribes to 174,162 periodicals including electronic. Computerized library services include interlibrary loans, database searching, Internet access, and Wi-Fi capability. Special learning facilities include an art gallery, radio station, and TV station. **Physically Challenged Students:** 95% of the campus is accessible. Facilities include wheelchair ramps, elevators, special parking, specially equipped restrooms, special class scheduling, lowered drinking fountains, lowered telephones, and special housing. **Special:** The Harding campus in Florence, Italy, and Athens, Greece and programs in England, Latin America, France/Switzerland, Australia, and Zambia offer international studies. Internships are given in social work, teaching, nursing, and international missions. Co-op programs in all majors, work-study programs, dual majors, a general studies degree, and non-degree study are available. There are 11 national honor societies and a freshman honors program. **Visiting:** There are regularly scheduled orientations for prospective students. There are guides for informal visits, visitors may sit in on classes, and stay overnight. To schedule a visit, contact the Admissions Office. **Campus Safety and Security:** Measures include 24-hour foot and vehicle patrol, emergency notification system, self-defense education, and security escort services. There are emergency telephones, lighted pathways/sidewalks, and controlled access to dorms/residences.

REQUIREMENTS: The SAT or ACT is required. In addition, a lower GPA can be offset by higher test scores. Applicants should be graduates of an accredited secondary school and have completed 15 high school hours: 4 in English, 3 each in math, social studies, art, history, or music, and 2 in a science. An interview is highly recommended. AP and CLEP credits are accepted. Important factors in the admissions decision are leadership record, recommendations by school officials, and advanced placement or honors courses. All students must complete 53 hours of general education courses, including religion, English composition, history, speech communications, social sciences, biology, physical science, math, Western literature, music and art appreciation, and phys ed. A total of 128 semester hours, with a minimum GPA of 2.0, is required to graduate. 32 hours must be completed in residence and 45 must be upper level. **Procedure:** Freshmen are admitted to all sessions. Entrance exams should be taken in the junior year or early in the senior year. There are early admissions, deferred admissions, and rolling admissions plans. Applications should be filed by June 1 for fall entry; November 1 for spring entry, along with a $50 fee. Notifications are sent May 1. Applications are accepted on-line. **Transfer Students:** 190 transfer students enrolled in 2015-2016. Applicants with a minimum GPA of 2.0 and at least 14 semester hours earned are considered for admission. An interview is highly recommended. 32 of 128 credits required for the bachelor's degree must be completed at Harding. **International Students:** There are 284 international students enrolled. The school actively recruits these students. They must take the TOEFL with a minimum score of 550 on the paper-based TOEFL (PBT) or 79 on the Internet-based version (iBT). They must also take the SAT or ACT.

ADMISSIONS: 100% of the 2016-2017 applicants were accepted. The SAT scores for the 2016-2017 freshman class were: Critical Reading-- 23% below 500, 43% between 500 and 599, 25% between 600 and 699, and 9% between 700 and 800. Math-- 32% below 500, 38% between 500 and 599, 26% between 600 and 699, and 4% between 700 and 800. The ACT scores were 4% between 12 and 17, 34% between 18 and 23, 43% between 24 and 29, and 19% above 30. 26% of the current freshmen were in the top fifth of their class; 47% were in the top two fifths. There were 7 National Merit finalists. 38 freshmen graduated first in their class. **Admissions Contact:** Glen Dillard, Assistant Vice President for Enrollment Management. Email: *admissions@harding.edu* Web: *www.harding.edu*

FINANCIAL AID: In 2016-2017, 88% of all full-time freshmen and 77% of continuing full-time students received some form of financial aid. 82% of all full-time freshmen received need-based aid. The average freshman award was $17,864. Need-based scholarships or need-based grants averaged $8,447; and need-based self-help aid (loans and jobs) averaged $8,409. 33% of undergraduate students work part-time. Average annual earnings from campus work are $1281. The average financial indebtedness of the 2016 graduate was $26,352. The FAFSA code is 001097. The priority date for freshman financial aid applications for fall entry is February 15. The deadline for filing freshman financial aid applications for fall entry is April 1.

HENDERSON STATE UNIVERSITY *(The complete profile is made available exclusively on our website, www.barronspac.com)*

HENDRIX COLLEGE — C-3

www.hendrix.edu

Conway, AR 72032	**(501) 450-1362** **(800) 277-9017**
Fax: (501) 450-3843	**Email: adm@hendrix.edu**
Full-time: 621 men, 689 women	**Faculty:** 108; IIB, av$
Part-time: 6 men, 5 women	**Ph.D.s:** 93%
Graduate: 6 men, 1 women	**Student/Faculty:** 11 to 1
Year: semesters	**Tuition:** $42,440
Room & Board: $11,580	**Freshman Class:** 1516 applied, 1412 accepted, 399 enrolled
SAT CR/M: 603/606 **ACT:** 28	**CEEB CODE:** 6273
Application Deadline: November 15	**VERY COMPETITIVE+**

Hendrix College, founded in 1876, is a private liberal arts college affiliated with the United Methodist Church. The figures in the above capsule and in this profile are approximate. There is 1 undergraduate school and 1 graduate school. In addition to regional accreditation, Hendrix has baccalaureate program accreditation with NASM, NCATE, ACA, and ASBMB. The 180-acre campus is in a suburban area 25 miles northwest of Little Rock. Including any residence halls, there are 65 buildings.

STUDENT LIFE: 53% of undergraduates are from Arkansas. Others are from 44 states, and 50 foreign countries. 80% are from public schools. 55% are White; 4% African American; 4% Asian American; 4% Foreign; 3% Hispanic; 28% race unknown; 2% two or more races. 42% claim no religious affiliation; 27% Protestant; 11% Catholic. **Female To Male Ratio:** 1.1:1. The average age of freshmen is 18; all undergraduates, 20.

13% do not continue beyond their first year. **Housing:** 1257 students can be accommodated in college housing, which includes single-sex and coed dorms and on-campus apartments. In addition, there are language houses, a substance-free house, and ecology floor. On-campus housing is guaranteed for all 4 years, and is available on a first-come, first-served basis, and is available on a lottery system for upperclassmen. 94% of students live on campus; of those, 80% remain on campus on weekends. All students may keep cars.

FACULTY/CLASSROOMS: 53% of faculty are male; 47% are female. All teach undergraduates, 75% do research, and 75% do both. No introductory courses are taught by graduate students. The average class size in an introductory lecture is 16; in a laboratory is 18; and in a regular course is 36.

PROGRAMS OF STUDY: Hendrix confers B.A. degrees. Master's degrees are also awarded. Bachelor's degrees are awarded in AGRICULTURE (environmental studies), BIOLOGICAL SCIENCE (biochemistry and biology/biological science), BUSINESS (accounting and business economics), COMMUNICATIONS AND THE ARTS (art, dramatic arts, English, French, German, music, and Spanish), COMPUTER AND PHYSICAL SCIENCE (chemical physics, chemistry, computer science, mathematics, and physics), EDUCATION (early childhood education), HEALTH PROFESSIONS (allied health and exercise science), SOCIAL SCIENCE (American studies, anthropology, economics, history, interdisciplinary studies, international relations, philosophy, philosophy and religion, political science/government, psychology, religion, and sociology). English, and economics & business are the strongest academically. Psychology, English, and biochemistry & molecular biology have the largest enrollments.

ACTIVITIES: There are no fraternities or sororities. There are 70 groups on campus, including art, band, cheerleading, chess, choir, chorale, chorus, dance, debate, drama, environmental, ethnic, film, honors, international, jazz band, LGBT, literary magazine, musical theater, newspaper, orchestra, pep band, photography, political, professional, radio and TV, religious, social, social service, student government, and yearbook. Popular campus events include Campus Kitty, Themed Dance Parties, Shirttails, and Dance Competition. **Sports:** There are 10 intercollegiate sports for men and 11 for women, and 10 intramural sports for men and 10 for women. Facilities include the Wellness and Athletic center which includes a gym, fitness center with free weights/weight equipment as well as cardiovascular machines, indoor climbing wall, dance/movement studio, indoor track, pool with diving boards, baseball, softball, and soccer fields, multi-purpose turf field, outdoor tennis courts, a stadium, weight room, and tennis with indoor courts. **Graduates:** From July 1, 2015 to June 30, 2016, 281 bachelor's degrees were awarded. The most popular majors were biochemistry, biophysics, and molecular biology (11%), psychology (10%), and English (9%). 92 companies recruited on campus in 2015-2016. In an average class, 67% graduate in 4 years or less, 69% graduate in 5 years or less, and 68% graduate in 6 years or less. Of the 2015 graduating class, 32% were enrolled in graduate school within 6 months of graduation.

SERVICES: Counseling and information services are available, as is tutoring in some subjects, such as math, biology, writing, chemistry, foreign languanges, accounting, physics, genetics and zoology. There is a reader service for the blind. **Library/Resources:** The library contains 264,400 volumes, 67,497 microform items, and 4,088 audio/video tapes/CDs/DVDs, and subscribes to 65,518 periodicals including electronic. Computerized library services include interlibrary loans, database searching, Internet access, and Wi-Fi capability. Special learning facilities include an art gallery, radio station, and a writing lab. **Physically Challenged Students:** 90% of the campus is accessible. Facilities include wheelchair ramps, elevators, special parking, specially equipped restrooms, and lowered drinking fountains. **Special:** Internships and work-study may be arranged in all fields. The college offers 3-2 engineering programs with Columbia, Vanderbilt, and Washington Universities. Also available The Washington Center Program, study abroad, dual majors, and student-designed interdisciplinary studies. Students can pursue minors in all academic departments, as well as African studies, art history, Asian studies, dance, secondary education, gender studies, international business, medical humanities, neuroscience,public health, and applied mathmatics. There are 13 national honor societies and a chapter of Phi Beta Kappa. **Visiting:** There are regularly scheduled orientations for prospective students, Student visits include attending a class, visits with current students and faculty, a campus tour, and a luncheon with speakers. Students may also stay overnight in a residence hall. There are guides for informal visits, visitors may sit in on classes, and stay overnight. To schedule a visit, contact Jennifer McKenzie at (501) 450-1362. **Campus Safety and Security:** Measures include 24-hour foot and vehicle patrol, emergency notification system, self-defense education, and security escort services. There are emergency telephones, lighted pathways/sidewalks, and controlled access to dorms/residences.

REQUIREMENTS: The SAT or ACT is required. Students must have completed 4 high school units in English, 3 to 4 each in math and social studies, 2 in science, and 2 or more in a foreign language. The GED is accepted. AP and CLEP credits are accepted. Important factors in the admissions decision are extracurricular activities record, advanced placement or honors courses, and leadership record. The Collegiate Center is the general education program at Hendrix College and it has four distinct parts: First-Year Experience (consists of The Engaged Citizen course that is grouped in faculty dyads and an Explorations seminar that meets weekly), Capacities (consists of a bi-level writing program, foreign language (equivalent to two semesters), a quantitative skills course, and two physical activities), Learning Domains consists of 7 courses across 7 disciplines including one course in Expressive Arts, one course in Historical Perspectives, one course in Literary Studies, two courses (one a lab) in Natural Science Inquiry, one course in Social and Behavioral Analysis, and one course in Values, Beliefs and Ethics, The Odyssey Program (consists of 3 reflective, engaged experiences across the six categories of Artistic Creativity, Global Awareness, Professional and Leadership Development, Service to the World, Undergraduate Research, and Special Programs). All majors include a senior capstone experience that varies by major and 32 courses are required for graduation. **Procedure:** Freshmen are admitted fall and spring. Entrance exams should be taken during the junior and senior years. There is an early admissions plan. Applications should be filed by November 15 for fall entry, along with a $40 fee. Notification of early decision is sent December 15; regular decision, March 1. Applications are accepted on-line. **Transfer Students:** 15 transfer students enrolled in 2015-2016. Complete the Common Application online for free, or mail a completed Common Application along with $40 nonrefundable applicaiton fee. Submit an offical transcript starting in 9th grade. Request your ACT or SAT scores be sent to Hendrix. Have each college or university previously or currently attended send official transcript and a Dean of Student Affairs Recommendation Form. 16 of 32 credits required for the bachelor's degree must be completed at Hendrix. **International Students:** There are 64 international students enrolled. The school actively recruits these students. They must take the TOEFL with a minimum score of 550 on the paper-based TOEFL (PBT) or 79 on the Internet-based version (iBT).

ADMISSIONS: 93% of the 2016-2017 applicants were accepted. The SAT scores for the 2016-2017 freshman class were: Critical Reading-- 10% below 500, 35% between 500 and 599, 34% between 600 and 699, and 21% between 700 and 800. Math-- 7% below 500, 36% between 500 and 599, 43% between 600 and 699, and 14% between 700 and 800. The ACT scores were 1% below 12, 12% between 12 and 17, 18% between 18 and 23, 18% between 24 and 29, and 51% above 30. 68% of the current freshmen were in the top fifth of their class; 92% were in the top two fifths. There were 11 National Merit finalists. 21 freshmen graduated first in their class. **Admissions Contact:** Karen Foust, Executive VP for Enrollment. Email: *adm@hendrix.edu* Web: *www.hendrix.edu*

FINANCIAL AID: In 2016-2017, 100% of all full-time freshmen and 100% of continuing full-time students received some form of financial aid. 74% of all full-time freshmen and 63% of continuing full-time students received need-based aid. The average freshman award was $36,552. Need-based scholarships or need-based grants averaged $32,799 ($52,114 maximum); and need-based self-help aid (loans and jobs) averaged $5,463 ($7,500 maximum). 43% of undergraduate students work part-time. Average annual earnings from campus work are $853. The average financial indebtedness of the 2016 graduate was $30,151. The FAFSA code is 001099. The priority date for freshman financial aid applications for fall entry is March 1.

JOHN BROWN UNIVERSITY — A-1
www.jbu.edu

Siloam Springs, AR 72761	**(479) 524-7150** **(877) JBU-INFO**
Fax: (479) 524-4196	**Email: jbuinfo@jbu.edu**
Full-time: 627 men, 894 women	**Faculty:** IIB, --$
Part-time: 65 men, 84 women	**Ph.D.s:** 57%
Graduate: 217 men, 463 women	**Student/Faculty:** 14 to 1
Year: semesters, summer session	**Tuition:** $25,324
Room & Board: $8840	**Freshman Class:** 1206 applied, 930 accepted, 322 enrolled
SAT CR/M/W: 600/540/530 **ACT:** 26	**CEEB CODE:** 6311
Application Deadline: May 1	**VERY COMPETITIVE**

John Brown University, founded in 1919, is a private, interdenominational Christian university offering more than 39 undergraduate degree programs, 5 degree completion programs, and 10 graduate degree programs. There are 2 undergraduate schools and 4 graduate schools. In addition to regional accreditation, JBU has baccalaureate program accreditation with ABET, ACBSP, ACCE, and NCATE. The 200-acre campus is in a small town in Siloam Springs, AR, 25 miles west of Rogers, AK and 80 miles east of Tulsa, OK. Including any residence halls, there are 31 buildings.

STUDENT LIFE: 53% of undergraduates are from Arkansas. Others are from 40 states, 37 foreign countries, and Canada. 68% are from public schools. 73% are White; 6% Hispanic; 5% African American; 4% Foreign; 3% two or more races; 3% race unknown; 2% Asian American; 2% American Indian/Alaska Native. **Female To Male Ratio:** 1.6:1. The average age of freshmen is 18; all undergraduates, 20. 15% do not continue beyond their first year; 65% remain to graduate. **Housing:** 1100 students can be accommodated in college housing, which includes single-sex and coed dorms, on-campus apartments, and off-campus apartments. On-campus housing is guaranteed for all 4 years. 58% of students live on campus. Alcohol is not permitted. All students may keep cars.

FACULTY/CLASSROOMS: 67% of faculty are male; 34% are female. No introductory courses are taught by graduate students.

PROGRAMS OF STUDY: JBU confers B.A., B.S., B.S.N., B.Mus.Ed., B.S.E. and B.S.Eng. degrees. Associate and master's degrees are also awarded. Bachelor's degrees are awarded in BIOLOGICAL SCIENCE (biochemistry and biology/biological science), BUSINESS (accounting, business administration and management, international business, management, and marketing management), COMMUNICATIONS AND THE ARTS (art/art studies, communications, English, graphic design, illustration, music, photography, and Spanish), COMPUTER AND PHYSICAL SCIENCE (chemistry, digital arts/technology, and mathematics), EDUCATION (early childhood education, educational studies, elementary education, English education, music education, and social studies education), ENGINEERING AND ENVIRONMENTAL DESIGN (construction management, electrical/electronics engineering, and engineering), HEALTH PROFESSIONS (exercise science and nursing), SOCIAL SCIENCE (biblical studies, Christian studies, family and community services, history, interdisciplinary studies, ministries, philosophy, political science/government, and psychology). Engineering, nursing, teacher education, and visual arts are the strongest academically. Business, nursing, engineering, and graphic design have the largest enrollments.

ACTIVITIES: There are no fraternities or sororities. Groups on campus include art, cheerleading, choir, chorale, chorus, dance, debate, drama, ethnic, forensics, honors, international, jazz band, musical theater, newspaper, orchestra, pep band, photography, radio and TV, religious, student government, and yearbook. Popular campus events include Fall Breakway, Christmas Candlelight Service and Toilet Paper Game. **Sports:** There are 6 intercollegiate sports for men and 6 for women, and 10 intramural sports for men and 8 for women. Facilities include a 2000-seat gym, soccer and softball fields, a baseball diamond, training room and a swimming pool. The Lifetime Health Complex includes an indoor track, 4 racquetball courts, a nautilus fitness center, an aerobics room, tennis courts, a rugby pitch and a 3-court recreation center. **Graduates:** From July 1, 2015 to June 30, 2016, 318 bachelor's degrees were awarded. The most popular majors were business/marketing (48%), visual and performing arts (9%), and family and consumer sciences (7%). 93 companies recruited on campus in 2015-2016. In an average class, 1% graduate in 3 years or less, 55% graduate in 4 years or less, 63% graduate in 5 years or less, and 65% graduate in 6 years or less. Of the 2015 graduating class, 27% were enrolled in graduate school within 6 months of graduation, and 98% were employed.

SERVICES: Counseling and information services are available, as is tutoring in most subjects. There is a reader service for the blind, and remedial math and writing. **Library/Resources:** The library contains 287,410 volumes, 67,763 microform items, and 9,376 audio/video tapes/CDs/DVDs, and subscribes to 41,955 periodicals including electronic. Computerized library services include interlibrary loans, database searching, Internet access, and Wi-Fi capability. Special learning facilities include an art gallery, radio station, TV station, and a wellness assessment laboratory. **Physically Challenged Students:** 95% of the campus is accessible. Facilities include wheelchair ramps, elevators, special parking, specially equipped restrooms, special class scheduling, lowered drinking fountains, lowered telephones, and special housing. **Special:** Internships or field experiences are available in most majors. Study abroad in 15 countries, a Washington semester, work-study, and accelerated degree programs in organizational management and early childhood education are offered. There is a freshman honors program and 12 departmental honors programs. **Visiting:** There are regularly scheduled orientations for prospective students, including campus tours, consultations with faculty and coaches, and examination of financial aid opportunities. There are guides for informal visits, visitors may sit in on classes, and stay overnight. To schedule a visit, contact the Admissions Office at (479) 524-7190. **Campus Safety and Security:** Measures include 24-hour foot and vehicle patrol, emergency notification system, self-defense education, and security escort services. There are lighted pathways/sidewalks and controlled access to dorms/residences.

REQUIREMENTS: Applicants should have completed 14 high school units, including 4 in English, 3 in math, 2 each in science, social studies, and foreign language, and 1 in history. 2 references are required: 1 from a high school counselor or teacher, the other from a pastor or church leader. An essay and an interview are recommended. Applicants 21 years of age or older may be admitted without ACT or SAT scores. A GPA of 2.5 is required. AP and CLEP credits are accepted. All students must complete 25 hours of lower-level core courses, 19 to 22 of elective courses in wellness, natural science, mathematics, philosophy, arts, social studies, and global studies, and 8 hours in upper-level core courses. A total of 142 to 145 credit hours (includes hours for minor) with a minimum GPA of 2.25 (2.5 in profession education, teaching, and other state-required courses) is required to graduate. Students must complete an exit assessment before graduation. **Procedure:** Freshmen are admitted fall and spring. Entrance exams should be taken during the spring of the junior year or fall of the senior year. There is a rolling admissions plan. Applications should be filed by May 1 for fall entry, along with a $25 fee. Notifications are sent November 1. Applications are accepted on-line. **Transfer Students:** 65 transfer students enrolled in 2015-2016. Transfer applicants must have completed at least 12 units of college work, with a minimum 2.5 GPA. 36 of 124 credits required for the bachelor's degree must be completed at JBU. **International Students:** There are 94 international students enrolled. The school actively recruits these students. They must take the TOEFL with a minimum score of 80 on the Internet-based version (iBT).

ADMISSIONS: 77% of the 2016-2017 applicants were accepted. The SAT scores for the 2016-2017 freshman class were: Critical Reading-- 18% below 500, 32% between 500 and 599, 41% between 600 and 699, and 10% between 700 and 800. Math-- 29% below 500, 43% between 500 and 599, 23% between 600 and 699, and 5% between 700 and 800. Writing-- 22% below 500, 48% between 500 and 599, 27% between 600 and 699, and 4% between 700 and 800. The ACT scores were 3% between 12 and 17, 26% between 18 and 23, 52% between 24 and 29, and 19% above 30. 30% of the current freshmen were in the top fifth of their class; 59% were in the top two fifths. **Admissions Contact:** Don Crandall, Vice President for Enrollment. Email: *jbuinfo@jbu.edu* Web: *www.jbu.edu*

FINANCIAL AID: In 2016-2017, 98% of all full-time freshmen and 95% of continuing full-time students received some form of financial aid. 70% of all full-time freshmen and 67% of continuing full-time students received need-based aid. The average freshman award was $23,467. Need-based scholarships or need-based grants averaged $7,786; need-based self-help aid (loans and jobs) averaged $6,967; non-need-based athletic scholarships averaged $12,543; and other non-need-based awards and non-need-based scholarships averaged $10,369. The average financial indebtedness of the 2016 graduate was $23,148. The CSS/Profile and FFS are required. The FAFSA code is 001100. The priority date for freshman financial aid applications for fall entry is March 1.

LYON COLLEGE — C-2

www.lyon.edu

Batesville, AR 72501	**(870) 307-7204** **(800) 423-2542**
Fax: (870) 307-7593	**Email: admissions@lyon.edu**
Full-time: 361 men, 312 women	**Faculty:** 45; IIB, --$
Part-time: 8 men, 9 women	**Ph.D.s:** 100%
Graduate: n/av	**Student/Faculty:** 15 to 1
Year: semesters, summer session	**Tuition:** $26,290
Room & Board: $8440	**Freshman Class:** n/av
SAT CR/M/W: required **ACT:** required	**CEEB CODE:** 6009
Application Deadline: August 1	**COMPETITIVE+**

Lyon College, founded in 1872, is a selective, private, residential, liberal arts college affiliated with the Presbyterian Church. There is 1 undergraduate school. In addition to regional accreditation, Lyon has baccalaureate program accreditation with NCATE. The 136-acre campus is in a small town 90 miles north of Little Rock. Including any residence halls, there are 34 buildings.

STUDENT LIFE: 69% of undergraduates are from Arkansas. Others are from 23 states, and 10 foreign countries. 8% are Hispanic; 8% race unknown; 71% White; 6% African American; 3% American Indian/Alaska Native; 2% Asian American; 1% Foreign. **Male To Female Ratio:** 1.1:1. The average age of freshmen is 18; all undergraduates, 20. 34% do not continue beyond their first year; 50% remain to graduate. **Housing:** 496 students can be accommodated in college housing, which includes single-sex and coed dorms, on-campus apartments, off-campus apartments, and married student housing. In addition, there are special-interest houses, and freshman-only housing. On-campus housing is guaranteed for all 4 years. 75% of students live on campus. All students may keep cars.

FACULTY/CLASSROOMS: 66% of faculty are male; 34% are female. All teach undergraduates, and all do research. No introductory courses are taught by graduate students. The average class size in an introductory lecture is 16; in a laboratory is 17; and in a regular course is 16.

PROGRAMS OF STUDY: Lyon confers B.A., and B.S. degrees. Bachelor's degrees are awarded in AGRICULTURE (environmental studies), BIOLOGICAL SCIENCE (biology/biological science), BUSINESS (accounting, business administration and management, and business administration - international), COMMUNICATIONS AND THE ARTS (art, dramatic arts, English, music, and Spanish), COMPUTER AND PHYSICAL SCIENCE (chemistry and mathematics), EDUCATION (early childhood education), SOCIAL SCIENCE (anthropology, economics, history, political science/government, psychology, and religion). Psychology and biology are the strongest academically. Psychology, biology, and English have the largest enrollments.

ACTIVITIES: 18% of men belong to 3 national fraternities; 26% of women belong to 3 national sororities. There are 51 groups on campus, including art, bagpipe, band, cheerleading, chess, choir, drama, ethnic, film, honors, international, LGBT, literary magazine, marching band, newspaper, orchestra, photography, political, professional, religious, social, social service, student government, and yearbook. Popular campus events include Arkansas Scottish Festival, Service Day and Baccalaureate Day. **Sports:** There are 6 intercollegiate sports for men and 7 for women, and 14 intramural sports for men and 14 for women. Facilities include an 1100-seat gym, softball, baseball, soccer fields, cross-country trail, indoor swimming pool, 6 tennis courts, indoor baseball practice facility, indoor wrestling facility, indoor football practice facility, and a weight room. **Graduates:** From July 1, 2015 to June 30, 2016, 109 bachelor's degrees were awarded. The most popular majors were psychology (25%), biology (23%), and history (10%). In an average class, 45% graduate in 4 years or less, and 50% graduate in 5 years or less. Of the 2015 graduating class, 26% were enrolled in graduate school within 6 months of graduation, and 44% were employed.

SERVICES: Counseling and information services are available, as is tutoring in every subject, foreign language, chemistry, math, English, political science, history, economics, biology, religion & philosophy. There is remedial reading and writing. Writing and math labs are also available. **Library/Resources:** The library contains 225,191 volumes, 2,928 microform items, and 6,233 audio/video tapes/CDs/DVDs, and subscribes to 43,146 periodicals including electronic. Computerized library services include interlibrary loans, database searching, Internet access, and Wi-Fi capability. Special learning facilities include an art gallery, a writing lab, collaborative learning workstations, and a computer lab. **Physically Challenged Students:** 80% of the campus is accessible. Facilities include wheelchair ramps, elevators, special parking, specially equipped restrooms, and special housing. **Special:** Internships are offered as is cross-registration (for certain courses) with the University of Arkansas Community College at Batesville. A 2-2 engineering program is offered with the University of Missouri in Rolla, and a 3-2 program is offered with the University of Arkansas at Fayetteville. Work-study courses, study abroad in 4 countries, dual majors, student-designed majors, pass/fail options, a Washington semester, and credit for military experience are available. A 3-2 program is available with the University of Minnesota. There are 14 national honor societies and a freshman honors program. **Visiting:** There are regularly scheduled orientations for prospective students, consisting of a campus tour, admission and financial aid orientation, and information sessions with faculty and students. There are guides for informal visits and visitors may sit in on classes. To schedule a visit, contact the Admission Office. **Campus Safety and Security:** Measures include 24-hour foot and vehicle patrol, emergency notification system, self-defense education, and security escort services. There are lighted pathways/sidewalks and controlled access to dorms/residences.

REQUIREMENTS: The SAT or ACT is required. Applicants should have completed a minimum of 16 high school units, including 4 in English, 3 each in science, math, and social sciences, and 2 in a foreign language. A letter of recommendation and an admission interview are recommended. AP credits are accepted. All students are required to demonstrate proficiency in English composition, math, and foreign language, meet distribution requirements in social sciences, arts and literature, natural science and math, and religion and philosophy, complete the freshman orientation program, and take 1 semester of phys ed in each of the 4 years. The core curriculum requires 31 to 49 credit hours. A total of 120 credits, with a minimum GPA of 2.0, is required to graduate. **Procedure:** Freshmen are admitted fall and spring. Entrance exams should be taken in spring of the junior year and fall of the senior year. There are deferred admissions and rolling admissions plans. Applications should be filed by August 1 for fall entry; January 1 for spring entry, along with a $25 fee. Notification is sent on a rolling basis. Applications are accepted on-line. **Transfer Students:** 54 transfer students enrolled in 2015-2016. Transfer applicants with 24 or more semester hours must submit a transcript and statement of good standing from each institution attended. Students with fewer than 24 semester hours must submit their final high school transcript and ACT or SAT scores. 30 of 120 credits required for the bachelor's degree must be completed at Lyon. **International Students:** There are 23 international students enrolled. The school actively recruits these students. They must take the TOEFL with a minimum score of 550 on the paper-based TOEFL (PBT) or 79 on the Internet-based version (iBT), or take the IELTS. They must also take the SAT or ACT.

ADMISSIONS: 57% of the current freshmen were in the top fifth of their class; 85% were in the top two fifths. **Admissions Contact:** Donald Taylor, Director of Admissions. Email: *admissions@lyon.edu* Web: *www.lyon.edu*

FINANCIAL AID: In 2016-2017, 100% of all full-time freshmen and 99% of continuing full-time students received some form of financial aid. The average freshman award was $20,826. 16% of undergraduate students work part-time. Average annual earnings from campus work are $1000. The average financial indebtedness of the 2016 graduate was $27,136. The FAFSA code is 001088. The priority date for freshman financial aid applications for fall entry is March 1.

OUACHITA BAPTIST UNIVERSITY — B-4

www.obu.edu

Arkadelphia, AR 71998	(870) 245-5110 (800) 342-5628
Fax: (870) 245-5500	**Email:** admissions@obu.edu
Full-time: 684 men, 785 women	**Faculty:** 104; IIB, --$
Part-time: 15 men, 10 women	**Ph.D.s:** 87%
Graduate: n/av	**Student/Faculty:** 14 to 1
Year: semesters, summer session	**Tuition:** $24,940
Room & Board: $7380	**Freshman Class:** 1712 applied, 1145 accepted, 396 enrolled
SAT CR/M: 539/539 **ACT:** 24	**CEEB CODE:** 6549
Application Deadline: open	**COMPETITIVE**

Ouachita Baptist University, founded in 1886, is a private liberal arts institution affiliated with the Arkansas Baptist State Convention. There are 7 undergraduate schools. In addition to regional accreditation, Ouachita has baccalaureate program accreditation with AACSB, NASM, and NCATE. The 200-acre campus is in a small town 65 miles southwest of Little Rock. Including any residence halls, there are 38 buildings.

STUDENT LIFE: 67% of undergraduates are from Arkansas. Others are from 32 states, 30 foreign countries, and Canada. 90% are from public schools. 83% are White; 8% African American; 4% Hispanic; 2% Foreign; 1% Asian American; 1% American Indian/Alaska Native. 80% are Protestant; 15% unknown denominations. **Female To Male Ratio:** 1.1:1. The average age of freshmen is 18; all undergraduates, 21. 20% do not continue beyond their first year; 63% remain to graduate. **Housing:** 1587 students can be accommodated in college housing, which includes single-sex dorms, on-campus apartments, off-campus apartments, and married student housing. On-campus housing is guaranteed for all 4 years. 94% of students live on campus; of those, 50% remain on campus on weekends. Alcohol is not permitted. All students may keep cars.

FACULTY/CLASSROOMS: 58% of faculty are male; 42% are female. All teach undergraduates, 50% do research, and 50% do both. No introductory courses are taught by graduate students. The average class size in an introductory lecture is 30; in a laboratory is 12; and in a regular course is 17.

PROGRAMS OF STUDY: Ouachita confers B.A., B.F.A., B.S., B.M. and B.M.E. degrees. Associate degrees are also awarded. Bachelor's degrees are awarded in BIOLOGICAL SCIENCE (biology/biological science), BUSINESS (accounting, business administration and management, recreation and leisure services, and sports management), COMMUNICATIONS AND THE ARTS (applied music, art, church music, communications, dramatic arts, English, graphic design, instrumental performance, instrumental music education, keyboard - piano concentration, music, music composition, musical theater, piano/organ, piano performance, Spanish, speech/debate/rhetoric, theatre arts, visual and performing arts, and voice), COMPUTER AND PHYSICAL SCIENCE (chemistry, computer science, mathematics, and physics), EDUCATION (art education, business education, early childhood education, elementary education, foreign languages education, mathematics education, middle school education, music education, science education, secondary education, social studies education, and social studies secondary school education), HEALTH PROFESSIONS (predentistry, premedicine, and speech pathology/audiology), SOCIAL SCIENCE (biblical languages, biblical studies, Christian studies, dietetics, history, ministries, philosophy, philosophy and religion, political science/government, prelaw, psychology, religion, religious music, sociology, theological studies, and youth ministry). Biology, business administration, and Christian studies have the largest enrollments.

ACTIVITIES: 20% of men belong to 4 local fraternities; 35% of women belong to 4 local sororities. There are 60 groups on campus, including band, cheerleading, choir, chorale, chorus, computers, drama, drill team, ethnic, film, honors, international, jazz band, literary magazine, marching band, musical theater, newspaper, opera, orchestra, pep band, photography, political, professional, radio and TV, religious, social, social service, student government, and yearbook. Popular campus events include International Student Fair, Tiger Tunes and Tiger Traks. **Sports:** There are 7 intercollegiate sports for men and 7 for women, and 5 intramural sports for men and 5 for women. Facilities include a 6000-seat football stadium, an indoor & outdoor tennis center, indoor complex featuring a 2500-seat basketball arena, a swimming pool, a weight room, racquetball courts, and volleyball courts. **Graduates:** From July 1, 2015 to June 30, 2016, 338 bachelor's degrees were awarded. The most popular majors were business (19%), biology (13%), and visual and performing arts (9%). 35 companies recruited on campus in 2015-2016. In an average class, 1% graduate in 3 years or less, 52% graduate in 4 years or less, 61% graduate in 5 years or less, and 63% graduate in 6 years or less. Of the 2015 graduating class, 45% were enrolled in graduate school within 6 months of graduation, and 93% were employed.

SERVICES: Counseling and information services are available, as is tutoring in most subjects. There is a reader service for the blind, and remedial math, reading, and writing. **Library/Resources:** The 2 libraries contain 854,837 volumes, 325,598 microform items, and 3,612 audio/video tapes/CDs/DVDs, and subscribe to 21,500 periodicals including electronic. Computerized library services include interlibrary loans, database searching, and Wi-Fi capability. Special learning facilities include an art gallery and radio station. **Physically Challenged Students:** 95% of the campus is accessible. Facilities include wheelchair ramps, elevators, special parking, specially equipped restrooms, special class scheduling, and lowered drinking fountains. **Special:** Ouachita offers cross-registration with Henderson State University, a Washington semester for political science majors, internships for business majors and some mass communications and Christian studies majors, B.A.-B.S. degrees, dual majors, pass/fail options, and non-degree study. Study-abroad opportunities are available in Germany, England, France, Italy, Russia, Japan, China, Hong Kong, Australia, Austria, Belize, Scotland, Spain, South Africa, Costa Rica, and Morocco. There are 8 national honor societies and a freshman honors program. **Visiting:** There are regularly scheduled orientations for prospective students, include a campus tour, a question-and-answer session, and meetings with professors and students. There are guides for informal visits, visitors may sit in on classes, and stay overnight. To schedule a visit, contact the Admissions Counseling Office at admissions@obu.edu. **Campus Safety and Security:** Measures include 24-hour foot and vehicle patrol and emergency notification system. There are emergency telephones, lighted pathways/sidewalks, and controlled access to dorms/residences.

REQUIREMENTS: The SAT or ACT is required. Applicants should have completed 19 high school units, including 4 in English, 3 in social science, and 2 each in natural science and math. 2 in a foreign language and 1/2 in computer science are also recommended. A GPA of 2.8 is required. AP and CLEP credits are accepted. All students must fulfill 48 semester hours of general education courses, including 2 semesters of 1 foreign language and 7 chapel credits. A total of 120 semester hours, with a minimum GPA of 2.0, is required for graduation. **Procedure:** Freshmen are admitted fall, spring, and summer. Entrance exams should be taken in the junior year. There are deferred admissions and rolling admissions plans. Application deadlines are open. Applications are accepted on-line. **Transfer Students:** 55 transfer students enrolled in 2015-2016. Applicants must be eligible to return to their previous school. 60 of 120 credits required for the bachelor's degree must be completed at Ouachita. **International Students:** There are 37 international students enrolled. The school actively recruits these students. They must take the TOEFL with a minimum score of 550 on the paper-based TOEFL (PBT) or 80 on the Internet-based version (iBT).

ADMISSIONS: 67% of the 2016-2017 applicants were accepted. The SAT scores for the 2016-2017 freshman class were: Critical Reading-- 32% below 500, 35% between 500 and 599, 29% between 600 and 699, and 4% between 700 and 800. Math-- 33% below 500, 43% between 500 and 599, 23% between 600 and 699, and 1% between 700 and 800. The ACT scores were 6% between 12 and 17, 40% between 18 and 23, 38% between 24 and 29, and 16% above 30. 60% of the current freshmen were in the top fifth of their class; 80% were in the top two fifths. There were 18 National Merit finalists. 20 freshmen graduated first in their class. **Admissions Contact:** Lori Motl, Director of Admissions Counseling. Email: *admissions@obu.edu* Web: *www.obu.edu*

FINANCIAL AID: In 2016-2017, 98% of all full-time freshmen and 97% of continuing full-time students received some form of financial aid. 70% of all full-time freshmen and 80% of continuing full-time students received need-based aid. The average freshman award was $20,358. Need-based scholarships or need-based grants averaged $14,158; need-based self-help aid (loans and jobs) averaged $4,223; and other non-need-based awards and non-need-based scholarships averaged $1,977. 50% of undergraduate students work part-time. Average annual earnings from campus work are $1800. The average financial indebtedness of the 2016 graduate was $25,823. The college's own financial statement is required. The FAFSA code is 001102. The priority date for freshman financial aid applications for fall entry is January 15.

PHILANDER SMITH COLLEGE *(The complete profile is made available exclusively on our website, www.barronspac.com)*

SOUTHERN ARKANSAS UNIVERSITY — B-5

www.saumag.edu

Magnolia, AR 71754	**(870) 235-4040**
	(800) 332-SAUM
Fax: (870) 235-4931	**Email: muleriders@saumag.edu**
Full-time: 1298 men, 1536 women	**Faculty:** IIB, --$
Part-time: 77 men, 125 women	**Ph.D.s:** n/av
Graduate: 989 men, 495 women	**Student/Faculty:** n/av
Year: semesters, summer session	**Tuition:** $14,864 ($18,524)
Room & Board: $6668	**Freshman Class:** n/av
ACT: required	**CEEB CODE:** 6661
Application Deadline: August 27	**COMPETITIVE**

Southern Arkansas University, founded in 1909, is a state-supported liberal arts institution. There are 4 undergraduate schools and 1 graduate school. In addition to regional accreditation, SAU has baccalaureate program accreditation with AACSB, CSWE, NASAD, NASM, and CAEP. The 781-acre campus is in a small town in Magnolia, in Columbia County, Arkansas, situated less than 20 miles north of the Louisiana state line. Including any residence halls, there are 31 buildings.

STUDENT LIFE: 73% of undergraduates are from Arkansas. Others are from 38 states, 40 foreign countries, and Canada. 97% are from public schools. 51% are White; 24% Foreign; 21% African American; 2% Hispanic; 1% Asian American; 1% American Indian/Alaska Native. **Male To Female Ratio:** 1.1:1. The average age of freshmen is 18; all undergraduates, 28. 32% do not continue beyond their first year. **Housing:** 1842 students can be accommodated in college housing, which includes single-sex and coed dorms and on-campus apartments. In addition, there are honors houses. On-campus housing is guaranteed for all 4 years. 64% of students commute. Alcohol is not permitted. All students may keep cars.

FACULTY/CLASSROOMS: 56% of faculty are male; 44% are female. 97% teach undergraduates, 10% do research, and 10% do both. No introductory courses are taught by graduate students. The average class size in an introductory lecture is 23; in a laboratory is 18; and in a regular course is 20.

PROGRAMS OF STUDY: SAU confers B.A., B.S., B.A.S., B.B.A., B.M.E., B.S.E. and B.S.W. degrees. Associate and master's degrees are also awarded. Bachelor's degrees are awarded in AGRICULTURE (agricultural business management and agriculture), BIOLOGICAL SCIENCE (biology/biological science), BUSINESS (accounting and business administration and management), COMMUNICATIONS AND THE ARTS (art, broadcasting, communications, English, journalism, and Spanish), COMPUTER AND PHYSICAL SCIENCE (chemistry, computer science, and mathematics), EDUCATION (agricultural education, art education, business education, elementary education, health education, middle school education, music education, and science education), ENGINEERING AND ENVIRONMENTAL DESIGN (manufacturing technology), HEALTH PROFESSIONS (medical laboratory technology), SOCIAL SCIENCE (community services, history, are the strongest academically. Business administration and health education/kinesiology have the largest enrollment.

ACTIVITIES: 6% of men belong to 7 national fraternities; 5% of women belong to 7 national sororities. There are 80 groups on campus, including art, band, cheerleading, choir, chorale, computers, dance, drama, drill team, ethnic, honors, international, jazz band, literary magazine, marching band, musical theater, newspaper, pep band, photography, political, professional, religious, social, and student government. Popular campus events include Spring Fling, and Celebration of Lights. **Sports:** There are 8 intercollegiate sports for men and 8 for women, and 7 intramural sports for men and 7 for women. Facilities include a 6500-seat stadium, 1450-seat gym, 10 lighted tennis courts, baseball and softball fields, a track, indoor pool, a dance studio, basketball and volleyball courts, and a wellness center.

SERVICES: Counseling and information services are available, as is tutoring in most subjects. There is remedial math, reading, and writing. There is supplemental instruction in courses with high drop/failure rates. **Library/Resources:** The library contains 176,437 volumes, 669,721 microform items, and 12,214 audio/video tapes/CDs/DVDs, and subscribes to 725 periodicals including electronic. Computerized library services include interlibrary loans, database searching, and Internet access. Special learning facilities include an art gallery, biological field station, and a university working farm. **Physically Challenged Students:** 95% of the campus is accessible. Facilities include wheelchair ramps, elevators, special parking, specially equipped restrooms, special class scheduling, lowered drinking fountains, and lowered telephones. **Special:** Work-study programs at SAU, business and Spanish internships, study abroad in Russia and Mexico, and a general studies degree are offered. There is 1 national honor society, a freshman honors program, and 6 departmental honors programs. **Visiting:** There are regularly scheduled orientations for prospective students. There are guides for informal visits, visitors may sit in on classes, and stay overnight. To schedule a visit, contact the Admissions Office. **Campus Safety and Security:** Measures include 24-hour foot and vehicle patrol and security escort services. There are lighted pathways/sidewalks.

REQUIREMENTS: The ACT is required, with a minimum composite of 19. Applicants should have completed 4 high school units in English, 3 each in math and social studies, and 2 each in natural science and a foreign language. The GED is accepted. AP and CLEP credits are accepted. All students must complete 43 semester hours of general education courses, including 18 in humanities, 12 in social sciences, 4 each in biological and physical science, 3 in math, and 2 to 3 in physical and health education. A minimum of 124 total semester hours, with a minimum GPA of 2.0, is required to graduate. **Procedure:** Freshmen are admitted to all sessions. Entrance exams should be taken in the fall prior to enrollment. There are deferred admissions and rolling admissions plans. Application deadlines are open. Notification is sent on a rolling basis. Applications are accepted on-line. **Transfer Students:** Applicants must be eligible to return to their previous school and meet GPA requirements. Those with fewer than 24 credit hours must submit ACT or SAT scores and a high school transcript or GED. 30 of 124 credits required for the bachelor's degree must be completed at SAU. **International Students:** The school actively recruits these students. They must take the TOEFL. They must also take the ACT.

Admissions Contact: Sarah Jennings, Dean of Enrollment Services. Email: *muleriders@saumag.edu* Web: *www.saumag.edu*

FINANCIAL AID: The FAFSA code is 001107. The priority date for freshman financial aid applications for fall entry is February.

UNIVERSITY OF ARKANSAS AT FAYETTEVILLE — A-1

www.uark.edu

Fayetteville, AR 72701	**(479) 575-5346** **(800) 377-8632**
Fax: (479) 575-7515	**Email: uofa@uark.edu**
Full-time: 9326 men, 10,527 women	**Faculty:** 1146; I, -$
Part-time: 1375 men, 1320 women	**Ph.D.s:** 84%
Graduate: 2351 men, 2295 women	**Student/Faculty:** 19 to 1
Year: semesters, summer session	**Tuition:** $8820 ($23,168)
Room & Board: $10,332	**Freshman Class:** 15060 applied, 13627 accepted, 4993 enrolled
SAT CR/M: 550/560 **ACT:** 26	**CEEB CODE:** 6866
Application Deadline: August 1	**COMPETITIVE+**

Guided by a students-first philosophy, the University of Arkansas offers high-caliber teaching and hands-on research experiences to undergraduate and graduate students. In 2016 the Carnegie Foundation for the Advancement of Teaching confirmed the university's classification as a top tier research institution placing the U of A among the top 2 percent of universities and colleges nationwide with the highest level of research activity. Since its founding, the University of Arkansas has compiled a remarkable record of scientific, technological, intellectual and creative accomplishments. This achievement is exemplified by the late U.S. Senator J. William Fulbright, a Rhodes Scholar as a student and eventual president of the university. In 1946, Fulbright authored what became known as the Fulbright Program, the nation's primary international educational exchange program for scholars, students, educators, artists and professionals. There are 9 undergraduate schools and 2 graduate schools. In addition to regional accreditation, U of A has baccalaureate program accreditation with AACSB, ABET, ACEJMC, ADA, CSWE, FIDER, NAAB, NASM, NCATE, TEAC, ABA, CCNE, and AAFCS. The 718-acre campus is in an urban area Fayetteville, AR. Including any residence halls, there are 219 buildings.

STUDENT LIFE: 54% of undergraduates are from Arkansas. Others are from 50 states, 83 foreign countries, and Canada. 84% are from public schools. 76% are White; 8% Hispanic; 5% African American; 3% Foreign; 3% two or more races; 2% Asian American; 1% American Indian/Alaska Native; 1% race unknown. **Female To Male Ratio:** 1.1:1. The average age of freshmen is 18; all undergraduates, 21. 18% do not continue beyond their first year. **Housing:** 5729 students can be accommodated in college housing, which includes single-sex and coed dorms and on-campus apartments. In addition, there are honors houses, special-interest houses, fraternity houses, sorority houses, International living/learning community, and first-year experience program. On-campus housing is guaranteed for the freshman year only, and is available on a first-come, and first-served basis. 77% of students commute. All students may keep cars.

FACULTY/CLASSROOMS: 59% of faculty are male; 41% are female. 96% teach undergraduates. Graduate students teach 26% of introductory courses. The average class size in an introductory lecture is 43; in a laboratory is 20; and in a regular course is 36.

PROGRAMS OF STUDY: U of A confers B.A., B.Arch., B.F.A., B.I.D., B.L.A., B.M., B.S., B.S.A., B.S.B.A., B.S.B.E., B.S.B.M.E., B.S.C.E., B.S.ChE., B.S.CmpE., B.S.E., B.S.E.E., B.S.H.E.S., B.S.I.B., B.S.I.E., B.S.M.E., B.S.N. and B.S.W. degrees. Master's and doctoral degrees are also awarded. Bachelor's degrees are awarded in AGRICULTURE (agricultural business management, agricultural communications, animal science, horticulture, poultry science, and soil science), BIOLOGICAL SCIENCE (biology/biological science and nutrition), BUSINESS (accounting, apparel and accessories marketing, banking and finance, business administration and management, business administration marketing, business economics, business information systems, finance, hospitality management services, human resources, international business management, marketing management, marketing/retailing/merchandising, retailing, and transportation management), COMMUNICATIONS AND THE ARTS (art, communications, dramatic arts, English, French, German, graphic design, journalism, music, and Spanish), COMPUTER AND PHYSICAL SCIENCE (chemistry, computer science, earth science, geology, mathematics, physics, and statistics), EDUCATION (agricultural education, Asian studies, business education, childhood education, career, technical education & training, early childhood education, educational studies, elementary education, middle school education, music education, recreation education, special education, and technical education), ENGINEERING AND ENVIRONMENTAL DESIGN (architecture, bioengineering, chemical engineering, civil engineering, computer engineering, electrical/electronics engineering, environmental science, industrial engineering, interior design, landscape architecture, landscape architecture/design, and mechanical engineering), HEALTH PROFESSIONS (exercise science, health science, medical science, nursing, and public health), SOCIAL SCIENCE (African studies, African American studies, American studies, anthropology, architectural studies, classical/ancient civilization, criminal justice, dietetics, economics, European studies, food science, geography, history, human development, international relations, Latin American studies, Middle Eastern studies, philosophy, political science/government, psychology, public administration, social work, and sociology). Business, chemical, electrical, & biomedical engineering, creative writing, middle eastern studies, and computer science are the strongest academically. Business, engineering, and health professions have the largest enrollments.

ACTIVITIES: 21% of men belong to 19 national fraternities; 38% of women belong to 15 national sororities. There are 421 groups on campus, including art, band, cheerleading, chess, choir, chorale, chorus, computers, dance, drama, drill team, environmental, ethnic, honors, international, jazz band, LGBT, literary magazine, marching band, musical theater, newspaper, opera, orchestra, pep band, photography, political, professional, radio and TV, religious, social, social service, student government, symphony, and yearbook. Popular campus events include New Student Welcome, ROCK Camp, Welcome Weeks, Campus Blood Drive, MLK Vigil, Black History Month, Student Involvement Awards, Make a Difference Day, Emerging Leaders, Razorbash, Campus Drama Productions, Distinguished Lecture Series. **Sports:** There are 8 intercollegiate sports for men and 11 for women, and 25 intramural sports for men and 25 for women. Facilities include a 72,000-seat stadium, 19,200-seat basketball arena, 10,737-seat baseball stadium, 8,500-seat volleyball/gymnastics competition arena, 1,500-seat soccer stadium, 10 outdoor and 6 indoor tennis courts, an indoor practice football field, a 5000-seat indoor running track, outdoor track, a 1,500-seat softball stadium. In addition, we use the pool in the HPER Rec Center and we have privileges at Blessings Golf Course (men's and women's golf). **Graduates:** From July 1, 2015 to June 30, 2016, 4615 bachelor's degrees were awarded. The most popular majors were business/marketing (23%), engineering (10%), and health professions (8%). 531 companies recruited on campus in 2015-2016. In an average class, 42% graduate in 4 years or less, 59% graduate in 5 years or less, and 64% graduate in 6 years or less.

SERVICES: Counseling and information services are available, as is tutoring in some subjects, such as accounting, anthropology, biology, business law, chemical engineering, chemistry, economics, finance, geosciences, mechanical engineering, mathematics, music, philosophy, political science, psychology, physics, sociology, business, and world languages. There is a reader service for the blind, and remedial math, reading, and writing. There is a math resource center and a writing center. Student Support Services and individual colleges have labs and other facilities. **Library/Resources:** The 5 libraries contain 2.4 million volumes, 5.6 million microform items, and 41,823 audio/video tapes/CDs/DVDs, and subscribe to 83,532 periodicals including electronic. Computerized library services include interlibrary loans, database searching, Internet access, and Wi-Fi capability. Special learning facilities include a radio station, TV station, numerous research centers. **Physically Challenged Students:** All of the campus is accessible. Facilities include wheelchair ramps, elevators, special parking, specially equipped restrooms, special class scheduling, lowered drinking fountains, and lowered telephones. **Special:** Co-op programs and internships are available, as well as dual majors and B.A.-B.S. degrees in many majors, and study abroad in 26 countries. 3-3 Program: College of Arts and Sciences / School of Law, Dale Bumpers College/School of Law Law: JD/MBA, JD/MPA (Public Administration), Ag Law: LLM/MS (Ag Econ), Combined Academic - Medical or Dental Degree: Fulbright College of Arts and Sciences, JD/MA in Political Science, MBA/M.P.S. (public service) in conjunction with the Clinton School of Public Service, 5-year BA-MA in Journalism JD/MSW (Social Work). There are 47 national honor societies, Phi Beta Kappa, a freshman honors program, and 57 departmental honors programs. **Visiting:** There are regularly scheduled orientations for prospective students, visit consists of individual or group campus tours, meetings with an academic adviser, residence hall tours, and a meeting with an admissions counselor. Appointments are strongly encouraged for the best experience but not required. There are guides for informal visits and visitors may sit in on classes. To schedule a visit, contact Kristen Davidson at visit@uark.edu. **Campus Safety and Security:** Measures include 24-hour foot and vehicle patrol, emergency notification system, self-defense education, and security escort services. There are shuttle buses, emergency telephones, lighted pathways/sidewalks, controlled access to dorms/residences, crime prevention lectures, rape defense program, property engraving, bicycle patrol, and electronic card access in residence halls.

REQUIREMENTS: The SAT or ACT is required. Admissions requirements: 4 years of English and math, 3 years each of social science and natural science. Secondary school record, class rank, essay, recommendations, character, first generation, alumni relations, geographic residence, volunteer work and work experience considered. A GPA of 3.0 is required. AP and CLEP credits are accepted. Important factors in the admissions decision are leadership record, advanced placement or honors courses, evidence of special talent, personality/intangible qualities, extracurricular activities record, recommendations by alumni, and geographical diversity. To graduate, all students must complete 35 hours of general education courses, including 9 in social sciences, 8 in science, 6 in English, and 3 each in fine arts, math, humanities, and history/government. Students must have a minimum cumulative GPA of 2.0 and no more than 25% of the minimum total of 120 hours may be D or below. **Procedure:** Freshmen are admitted fall, spring, and summer. Entrance exams should be taken in the junior year or early in the senior year. There are early admissions and rolling admissions plans. Applications should be filed by August 1 for fall entry; December 20 for spring entry; and May 1 for summer entry, along with a $40 fee. Notification of early decision is sent December 15; regular decision, on a rolling basis. 352 applicants were on the 2016 waiting list; 21 were admitted. Applications are accepted online. Application fees are waived if application is completed online. **Transfer Students:** 1385 transfer students enrolled in 2015-2016. Applicants must present a GPA of 2.0 on all college coursework attempted and be in good standing at the last institution attended. Those with fewer than 24 transferable semester credits must meet the requirements of entering freshmen in addition to those of transfer students. 30 of 120 credits required for the bachelor's degree must be completed at U of A. **International Students:** There are 757 international students enrolled. The school actively recruits these students. They must take the TOEFL with a minimum score of 550 on the paper-based TOEFL (PBT) or 79 on the Internet-based version (iBT) and the college's own test, IELTS, and PTE-A. They must also take the SAT or ACT.

ADMISSIONS: 90% of the 2016-2017 applicants were accepted. The SAT scores for the 2016-2017 freshman class were: Critical Reading-- 22% below 500, 49% between 500 and 599, 25% between 600 and 699, and 4% between 700 and 800. Math-- 19% below 500, 45% between 500 and 599, 31% between 600 and 699, and 5% between 700 and 800. The ACT scores were 26% between 18 and 23, 54% between 24 and 29, and 20% above 30. 44% of the current freshmen were in the top fifth of their class; 75% were in the top two fifths. There were 48 National Merit finalists. **Admissions Contact:** Suzanne McCray, Vice Provost of Enrollment. Email: *uofa@uark.edu* Web: *application.uark.edu*

FINANCIAL AID: 11% of undergraduate students work part-time. Average annual earnings from campus work are $5410. The SFS is required. The FAFSA code is 001108. The priority date for freshman financial aid applications for fall entry is March 15.

UNIVERSITY OF ARKANSAS AT LITTLE ROCK C-3

www.ualr.edu

Little Rock, AR 72204	(501) 569-3492 (800) 482-8892
Fax: (501) 569-8956	Email: admissions@ualr.edu
Full-time: 2457 men, 3095 women	Faculty: 408; IIA, av$
Part-time: 1678 men, 2740 women	Ph.D.s: 66%
Graduate: 894 men, 1513 women	Student/Faculty: 14 to 1
Year: semesters, summer session	Tuition: $8129 ($19,199)
Room & Board: $9945	Freshman Class: 1344 applied, 864 accepted, 589 enrolled
SAT CR/M: required ACT: 21	CEEB CODE: 6368
Application Deadline: September 1	COMPETITIVE

The University of Arkansas, founded in 1927 as Little Rock Junior College, took the name of Little Rock University in 1957, and joined the University of Arkansas system in 1969. There are 7 undergraduate schools and 2 graduate schools. In addition to regional accreditation, UALR has baccalaureate program accreditation with AACSB, ABET, ACEJMC, ASLA, CSWE, NASAD, NASM, NCATE, and NLN. The 283-acre campus is in an urban area in Little Rock, AR. A second campus located in Benton, AK. Including any residence halls, there are 77 buildings.

STUDENT LIFE: 92% of undergraduates are from Arkansas. Others are from 49 states, 62 foreign countries, and Canada. 91% are from public schools. 58% are White; 22% African American; 6% Hispanic; 6% two or more races; 4% Foreign; 2% Asian American; 1% American Indian/Alaska Native; 1% race unknown. **Female To Male Ratio:** 1.5:1. The average age of freshmen is 19; all undergraduates, 19. 41% do not continue beyond their first year; 21% remain to graduate. **Housing:** 1376 students can be accommodated in college housing, which includes coed dorms, on-campus apartments, off-campus apartments, and married student housing. University-owned rental houses, and special housing for disabled students. On-campus housing is available on a first-come and first-served basis. 85% of students commute. Alcohol is not permitted. All students may keep cars.

FACULTY/CLASSROOMS: 52% of faculty are male; 48% are female. 80% teach undergraduates. Graduate students teach 4% of introductory courses. The average class size in an introductory lecture is 30; in a laboratory is 20; and in a regular course is 27.

PROGRAMS OF STUDY: UALR confers B.A., B.S., B.B.A., B.S.W., B.S.E. and B.S.N. degrees. Associate, master's, and doctoral degrees are also awarded. Bachelor's degrees are awarded in BIOLOGICAL SCIENCE (bioinformatics and biology/biological science), BUSINESS (accounting, banking and finance, business administration and management, management science, marketing/retailing/merchandising, and sports management), COMMUNICATIONS AND THE ARTS (advertising, American Sign Language, applied art, art, art history and appreciation, dance, dramatic arts, English, French, journalism, music, radio/television technology, Spanish, technical and business writing, theatre arts, and visual and performing arts), COMPUTER AND PHYSICAL SCIENCE (applied mathematics, applied science, chemistry, computer programming, computer science, geology, information sciences and systems, mathematics, and physics), EDUCATION (early childhood education, education administration, education of the deaf and hearing impaired, elementary education, health education, reading education, secondary education, and special education), ENGINEERING AND ENVIRONMENTAL DESIGN (computer technology, construction engineering, construction management, construction technology, electrical/electronics engineering technology, engineering mechanics, engineering technology, industrial administration/management, manufacturing engineering, mechanical engineering technology, and surveying engineering), HEALTH PROFESSIONS (environmental health science, health science, nursing, Pre-Health Biological studies, and speech pathology/audiology), SOCIAL SCIENCE (criminal justice, economics, history, international studies, interpreter for the deaf, law, liberal arts/general studies, philosophy, political science/government, psychology, public administration, social work, and sociology). Systems engineering, construction management, and computer science are the strongest academically. Psychology, management, and criminal justice have the largest enrollments.

ACTIVITIES: 2% of men and 2% of women belong to 5 national fraternities; 1% of women belong to 6 national sororities. There are 151 groups on campus, including student government and international students, art, cheerleading, chess, chorale, dance, drama, ethnic, honors, international, jazz band, LGBT, literary magazine, musical theater, newspaper, opera, pep band, political, professional, radio and TV, religious, social, social service, student government, and university program council. Popular campus events include International Week, Sunshine Days and Art Spree. **Sports:** There are 6 intercollegiate sports for men and 7 for women, and 18 intramural sports for men and 18 for women. Facilities include an 8,500-seat gym, swimming pool, tennis courts, baseball and intramural fields, soccer field/stadium, indoor/outdoor track facility, fitness & weight room, indoor jogging track, basketball, volleyball, golf, racquetball courts, and steam room with sauna. **Graduates:** From July 1, 2015 to June 30, 2016, 1310 bachelor's degrees were awarded. The most popular majors were health professions and related programs (15%), homeland security, law enforcement, firefighting, and protective services (9%), and psychology (7%). In an average class, 12% graduate in 4 years or less, 11% graduate in 5 years or less, and 21% graduate in 6 years or less. Of the 2015 graduating class, 6% were enrolled in graduate school within 6 months of graduation.

SERVICES: Counseling and information services are available, as is tutoring in every subject. There is a reader service for the blind, and remedial math, reading, and writing. Also available are a braille dictionary, typewriter, and reading machine and interpreters. **Library/Resources:** The library contains 674,979 volumes, 179,770 microform items, and 11,682 audio/video tapes/CDs/DVDs, and subscribes to 95,870 periodicals including electronic. Computerized library services include interlibrary loans and database searching. Special learning facilities include an art gallery, planetarium, radio station, TV station, including a speech and hearing clinic, study rooms, and Arkansas history and its region. **Physically Challenged Students:** 85% of the campus is accessible. Facilities include wheelchair ramps, elevators, special parking, specially equipped restrooms, special class scheduling, and lowered drinking fountains. **Special:** The University coordinates study abroad programs in China, Germany, Ghana, Great Britain, India, Norway, Poland, Romania, Taiwan, Turkey, Mexico, France, Spain, Hong Kong, and Austria. UALR has exchange relationships with more than 30 countries. In addition, more than 100 internships and work-study positions are available in various academic departments. Cross-registration with the University of Arkansas Medical School in the area of Communication Disorders is offered at the graduate level. B.A. and B.S. degrees, a general studies degree, student-designed majors, nondegree study, and pass/fail options are offered. UALR offers Accelerated Online courses/degree programs and regular semester online degree programs. There are 3 national honor societies, a freshman honors program, and 5 departmental honors programs. **Visiting:** There are regularly scheduled orientations for prospective students. Orientation takes place before each semester attendance is required. Online orientation is offered. There are guides for informal visits and visitors may sit in on classes. To schedule a visit, contact Office of Admissions. **Campus Safety and Security:** Measures include 24-hour foot and vehicle patrol, emergency notification system, self-defense education, and security escort services. There are shuttle buses, emergency telephones, lighted pathways/sidewalks, controlled access to dorms/residences, emergency phones, and a student patrol crime prevention unit.

REQUIREMENTS: The SAT or ACT is required. Two or more of the following criteria must be met: a high school GPA of at least 2.5 or a passing GED test score; an ACT composite score of at least 21 or a combined verbal/math SAT I score of 990 taken within the past 5 years; completion of a college preparatory core in high school that includes 4 units of English, 3 each of math and social studies, and 2 each of natural science and a single foreign language. Students with test subscores below the state minimum requirement will be placed in the appropriate development courses. A GPA of 2.5 is required. AP and CLEP credits are accepted. All undergraduate students must complete a minimum of 120 credit hours, including 45 at the upper level, while maintaining a GPA of 2.0. A minimum 44-hour core curriculum must be completed. Required categories include: English/Communications (9 hours), Math/Statistics (3 hours), Fine Arts/Humanities (9 hours), World Humanities (3 hours), Science (8 hours), and Social Sciences (15 hours). A second language requirement applies to students seeking a B.A. degree. Students must complete 30 hours in residence. Each student must complete a major and a minor or a double major. **Procedure:** Freshmen are admitted to all sessions. Entrance exams should be taken during the fall of the senior year. There are early admissions, deferred admissions, and rolling admissions plans. Application deadlines are open. Application fee is $40.

Applications are accepted on-line. **Transfer Students:** 1183 transfer students enrolled in 2015-2016. Applicants must have a minimum college GPA of 2.0. Applicants must submit official transcripts from each college previously attended. Students who have 12 or fewer acceptable transfer credits must meet all the admission requirements for entering freshmen. 30 of 124 credits required for the bachelor's degree must be completed at UALR. **International Students:** There are 279 international students enrolled. They must take the TOEFL with a minimum score of 525 on the paper-based TOEFL (PBT) or 71 on the Internet-based version (iBT) and the college's own test, Test of Written English, with a score of at least 4 points. For entering freshmen and transfers with less than 12 credit hours, ACT, SAT or COMPASS is required for placement only.

ADMISSIONS: 64% of the 2016-2017 applicants were accepted. The SAT scores for the 2016-2017 freshman class were: Critical Reading-- 95% below 500 and 5% between 500 and 599. Math-- 5% below 500, 58% between 500 and 599, and 11% between 600 and 699. The ACT scores were 10% below 12, 55% between 12 and 17, and 35% above 30. 2 freshmen graduated first in their class. **Admissions Contact:** Katie Young, Director. Email: *admissions@ualr.edu* Web: *www.ualr.edu*

FINANCIAL AID: In 2016-2017, 82% of all full-time freshmen and 84% of continuing full-time students received some form of financial aid. 60% of all full-time freshmen and 51% of continuing full-time students received need-based aid. The FAFSA code is 001101. The priority date for freshman financial aid applications for fall entry is March 1. The deadline for filing freshman financial aid applications for fall entry is November 1.

UNIVERSITY OF ARKANSAS AT MONTICELLO *(The complete profile is made available exclusively on our website, www.barronspac.com)*

UNIVERSITY OF ARKANSAS AT PINE BLUFF C-4

www.uapb.edu

Pine Bluff, AR 71601 (870) 575-8492

Fax: (870) 575-4607	**Email:** webadmin@uapb.edu
Full-time: 1018 men, 1294 women	**Faculty:** n/av
Part-time: 93 men, 140 women	**Ph.D.s:** n/av
Graduate: 55 men, 58 women	**Student/Faculty:** n/av
Year: semesters, summer session	**Tuition:** $6271 ($11,941)
Room & Board: $7270	**Freshman Class:** n/av
SAT: required	**CEEB CODE:** 6004
Application Deadline: August 1	**COMPETITIVE**

The University of Arkansas at Pine Bluff, established in 1873, is a historically black land-grant institution providing a liberal arts education as part of the public University of Arkansas system. There are 5 undergraduate schools and 1 graduate school. In addition to regional accreditation, UAPB has baccalaureate program accreditation with ACBSP, AHEA, CSWE, NASAD, NASM, and NCATE. The 318-acre campus is in a small town 40 miles southeast of Little Rock, AR and approximately 142 miles southwest of Memphis, TN. Including any residence halls, there are 49 buildings.

STUDENT LIFE: 61% of undergraduates are from Arkansas. Others are from 38 states, 20 foreign countries, and Canada. 91% are African American; 5% White; 2% Foreign; 1% Hispanic. **Female To Male Ratio:** 1.3:1. The average age of freshmen is 18; all undergraduates, 22. 29% do not continue beyond their first year; 27% remain to graduate. **Housing:** 1495 students can be accommodated in college housing, which includes single-sex dorms. There are honors clusters in the dorms. On-campus housing is guaranteed for all 4 years. 65% of students commute. Alcohol is not permitted. All students may keep cars.

FACULTY/CLASSROOMS: 54% of faculty are male; 46% are female. No introductory courses are taught by graduate students. The average class size in a laboratory is 20 and in a regular course is 21.

PROGRAMS OF STUDY: UAPB confers B.A.,B.S., BGS, and BSN degrees. Associate, master's, and doctoral degrees are also awarded. Bachelor's degrees are awarded in AGRICULTURE (agricultural sciences, agriculture, conservation and regulation, and fishing and fisheries), BIOLOGICAL SCIENCE (biology/biological science), BUSINESS (accounting and business administration and management), COMMUNICATIONS AND THE ARTS (art, English, journalism, music, and speech/debate/rhetoric), COMPUTER AND PHYSICAL SCIENCE (chemistry, computer science, mathematics, and physics), EDUCATION (agricultural education, art education, business education, early childhood education, English education, health and physical education, home economics education, industrial arts education, mathematics education, middle school education, music education, physical education, science education, social science education, and special education), ENGINEERING AND ENVIRONMENTAL DESIGN (industrial engineering technology and preengineering), HEALTH PROFESSIONS (nursing, predentistry, premedicine, prepharmacy, and rehabilitation therapy), SOCIAL SCIENCE (criminal justice, family/consumer studies, gerontology, history, liberal arts/general studies, parks and recreation management, political science/government, psychology, social work, and sociology). STEM disciplines are the strongest academically. Biology, business administration, and criminal justice have the largest enrollments.

ACTIVITIES: There are 104 groups on campus, including art, band, cheerleading, choir, computers, debate, drama, drill team, honors, jazz band, marching band, newspaper, orchestra, photography, political, professional, radio and TV, religious, social, social service, student government, and yearbook. Popular campus events include Founders Day, Messiah, Spring Emphasis, and Unity Fest. **Sports:** There are 7 intercollegiate sports for men and 8 for women, and 20 intramural sports for men and 19 for women. Facilities include a phys ed complex for flag football, basketball, volleyball, softball, tennis, handball, racquetball, track and field, badminton, swimming pool, and 6,000-seat football stadium.

SERVICES: Counseling and information services are available, as is tutoring in most subjects. There is a reader service for the blind, and remedial math, reading, and writing. **Library/Resources:** The library contains 271,547 volumes, 119,205 microform items, and 4,299 audio/video tapes/CDs/DVDs, and subscribes to 1,050 periodicals including electronic. Computerized library services include interlibrary loans and database searching. Special learning facilities include an art gallery, radio station, and TV station. **Physically Challenged Students:** 98% of the campus is accessible. Facilities include wheelchair ramps, elevators, special parking, specially equipped restrooms, special class scheduling, lowered drinking fountains, and lowered telephones. **Special:** The university offers formal co-op education and work-study programs, concurrent registration with members of the University of Arkansas system, internships, B.A.-B.S. degrees, and dual and student-designed majors. Also offered are credit for military experience, nondegree study, individualized programs of study for honors college students, and study abroad. There are 4 national honor societies, a freshman honors program, and 6 departmental honors programs. **Visiting:** There are regularly scheduled orientations for prospective students. There are guides for informal visits, visitors may sit in on classes, and stay overnight. To schedule a visit, contact the Director of Recruitment (800) 525-5272. **Campus Safety and Security:** Measures include 24-hour foot and vehicle patrol, self-defense education, and security escort services. There are emergency telephones, and lighted pathways/sidewalks. There is a department of public safety and security on campus.

REQUIREMENTS: The SAT is required. The ACT, with a satisfactory score is preferred. Applicants must have earned 22 credits, including 4 units of English and 3 each in social studies, math, and science. The GED is accepted. Students not meeting these requirements may apply for conditional admission. A GPA of 2.0 is required. AP and CLEP credits are accepted. All students must complete at least 120 hours of credit, including 30 hours in their major, while earning an overall 2.0 GPA (2.5 for teacher education majors) and a C or better in all major courses. Distribution requirements include English, math, social and natural science, and phys ed courses. Students must pass a comprehensive exam in their major. **Procedure:** Freshmen are admitted fall, spring, and summer. Entrance exams should be taken during the junior or senior year. There are early admissions, deferred admissions, and rolling admissions plans. Applications should be filed by August 1 for fall entry; January 1 for spring entry. **Transfer Students:** Transfer students must have a minimum GPA of 2.0. Applicants with fewer than 60 semester hours of college credit must submit an application, ACT or SAT I scores, and all college transcripts. 30 of 120 credits required for the bachelor's degree must be completed at UAPB. **International Students:** They must take the TOEFL with a minimum score of 550 on the paper-based TOEFL (PBT) or 79 on the Internet-based version (iBT). The ACT is preferred. SAT scores may be used.

Admissions Contact: Philomena Owasoyo, Director of Admissions. Email: *webadmin@uapb.edu* Web: *www.uapb.edu*

FINANCIAL AID: UAPB is a member of CSS. The FAFSA code is 001086. The priority date for freshman financial aid applications for fall entry is January 1.

UNIVERSITY OF CENTRAL ARKANSAS C-3

www.uca.edu

Conway, AR 72035	(501) 450-3663 (800) 243-8245 Email: helpdesk@uca.edu
Full-time: 3193 men, 4817 women	**Faculty:** IIA, --$
Part-time: 724 men, 882 women	**Ph.D.s:** n/av
Graduate: 489 men, 1382 women	**Student/Faculty:** n/av
Year: semesters, summer session	**Tuition:** $8224 ($14,447)
Room & Board: $6248	**Freshman Class:** 4922 applied, 4419 accepted, 1880 enrolled
SAT or ACT: required	**CEEB CODE:** 6012
Application Deadline: n/av	**VERY COMPETITIVE**

The University of Central Arkansas, established in 1907, is a comprehensive public institution offering undergraduate and graduate degrees in liberal arts, business, health-related sciences, and education. The figures given in the above capsule and in this profile are approximate. There are 6 undergraduate schools and 1 graduate school. In addition to regional accreditation, UCA has baccalaureate program accreditation with AACSB, ADA, APTA, CAHEA, NASAD, NASM, NCATE, and NLN. The 356-acre campus is in a small town 29 miles north of Little Rock. Including any residence halls, there are 124 buildings.

STUDENT LIFE: 85% of undergraduates are from Arkansas. Others are from 43 states, 73 foreign countries, and Canada. 68% are White; 16% African American; 5% Hispanic; 5% Foreign; 3% two or more races; 2% Asian American; 1% American Indian/Alaska Native; 1% race unknown. **Female To Male Ratio:** 1.6:1. The average age of freshmen is 18; all undergraduates, 20. 28% do not continue beyond their first year; 45% remain to graduate. **Housing:** 3867 students can be accommodated in college housing, which includes single-sex and coed dorms, on-campus apartments, off-campus apartments, and married student housing. In addition, there are honors houses, international students' residence hall, as well as residential colleges. On-campus housing is guaranteed for all 4 years. Alcohol is not permitted. All students may keep cars.

FACULTY/CLASSROOMS: No introductory courses are taught by graduate students.

PROGRAMS OF STUDY: UCA confers B.A., B.S., B.S.E., B.P.S., B.B.A., B.F.A., B.M. and B.S.N. degrees. Associate, master's, and doctoral degrees are also awarded. Bachelor's degrees are awarded in BIOLOGICAL SCIENCE (biology/biological science), BUSINESS (accounting, banking and finance, business administration and management, business economics, finance, insurance and risk management, and marketing/retailing/merchandising), COMMUNICATIONS AND THE ARTS (communications, creative writing, English, French, journalism, music, Spanish, and speech/debate/rhetoric), COMPUTER AND PHYSICAL SCIENCE (applied computing, applied mathematics, chemistry, computer science, information sciences and systems, mathematics, and physics), EDUCATION (art education, athletic training, early childhood education, education, education of the exceptional child, elementary education, foreign languages education, guidance education, library science, middle school education, music education, physical education, science education, secondary education, and special education), ENGINEERING AND ENVIRONMENTAL DESIGN (environmental science, interior design, and preengineering), HEALTH PROFESSIONS (exercise science, health care administration, health science, kinesiology, medical technology, nuclear medical technology, nursing, occupational therapy, physical therapy, predentistry, premedicine, preoptometry, prepharmacy, preveterinary science, radiological science, and speech pathology/audiology), SOCIAL SCIENCE (addiction studies, African American studies, anthropology, communication sciences & disorders, criminology, dietetics, economics, family/consumer studies, geography, geography information science, gerontology, history, philosophy, political science/government, psychology, public administration, religion, and sociology). Business, health-related sciences, and education are the strongest academically. Health professions & related sciences, business & marketing, and education have the largest enrollments.

ACTIVITIES: There are 230 groups on campus, including art, band, cheerleading, choir, chorale, chorus, computers, dance, debate, drama, environmental, ethnic, film, forensics, honors, international, jazz band, LGBT, literary magazine, marching band, musical theater, newspaper, orchestra, pep band, photography, political, professional, radio and TV, religious, social, social service, student government, symphony, and yearbook. Popular campus events include Bear Facts Day, Greek God and Miss UCA. **Sports:** There are 7 intercollegiate sports for men and 8 for women, and 14 intramural sports for men and 14 for women. Facilities include a gym, swimming pool, fitness center, racquetball and tennis courts, a track, soccer fields, football field, basketball court, softball fields, and an indoor athletic facility. **Graduates:** From July 1, 2015 to June 30, 2016, 1470 bachelor's degrees were awarded. The most popular majors were health professions and related sciences (21%), business/marketing (21%), and education (9%).

SERVICES: Counseling and information services are available, as is tutoring in some subjects, such as biology, chemistry, physics, algebra, trigonometry, calculus, geometry, sociology, writing, literature, Spanish, accounting, business statistics, French, German, writing and technology There is a reader service for the blind, and remedial math, reading, and writing. **Library/Resources:** The library contains 446,575 volumes, 618,347 microform items, and 3,173 audio/video tapes/CDs/DVDs, and subscribes to 59,937 periodicals including electronic. Computerized library services include interlibrary loans, database searching, Internet access, and Wi-Fi capability. Special learning facilities include an art gallery, planetarium, radio station, and TV station. **Physically Challenged Students:** Facilities include wheelchair ramps, elevators, special parking, specially equipped restrooms, special class scheduling, lowered drinking fountains, lowered telephones, and special housing. **Special:** Study abroad, work-study programs, a B.S.-B.A. degree, a 3-2 engineering degree with the University of Arkansas at Fayetteville, dual majors, nondegree study, and pass/fail options are available. Co-op programs in business, computer science, and health sciences and internships in education are also possible. There is a freshman honors program. **Visiting:** There are regularly scheduled orientations for prospective students, including tours at 11 a.m. and 2 p.m.; departments and dormitories may be visited. There are also special visitation days that include a campus tour, departmental session, lunch, parents' session, optional residence hall tour, and classroom visit or planetarium show. Visitors may sit in on classes. To schedule a visit, contact the Admissions Office at admissions@uca.edu. **Campus Safety and Security:** Measures include 24-hour foot and vehicle patrol, emergency notification system, self-defense education, and security escort services. There are shuttle buses, emergency telephones, lighted pathways/sidewalks, and controlled access to dorms/residences.

REQUIREMENTS: The SAT or ACT is required. A GPA of 2.8 is required. AP and CLEP credits are accepted. Important factors in the admissions decision are advanced placement or honors courses, evidence of special talent, and recommendations by school officials. All students must earn a minimum of 124 semester hours, including 40 in upper-division courses. A minimum GPA of 2.25 is needed for the B.B.A., 2.5 for most education programs. Minimum requirements also include 3 semester hours in phys ed. **Procedure:** Freshmen are admitted to all sessions. There is a rolling admissions plan. Application deadlines are open. Applications are accepted on-line. **Transfer Students:** Applicants need, on UCA's scale, a minimum cumulative GPA of 2.0. 15 of 120 credits required for the bachelor's degree must be completed at UCA. **International Students:** There are 469 international students enrolled. The school actively recruits these students. They must take the TOEFL.

ADMISSIONS: 90% of the 2016-2017 applicants were accepted. The SAT scores for the 2016-2017 freshman class were: Critical Reading-- 59% below 500, 29% between 500 and 599, and 12% between 600 and 699. Math-- 46% below 500, 42% between 500 and 599, and 13% between 600 and 699. Writing-- 68% below 500, 21% between 500 and 599, and 12% between 600 and 699. The ACT scores were 3% between 12 and 17, 45% between 18 and 23, 40% between 24 and 29, and 12% above 30. **Admissions Contact:** Amber Hall, Director of Institutional Research. Email: *helpdesk@uca.edu* Web: *www.uca.edu*

FINANCIAL AID: The FAFSA code is 001092. Check with the school for current application deadlines.

UNIVERSITY OF THE OZARKS B-2
www.ozarks.edu

Clarksville, AR 72830	(479) 979-1227 (800) 264-8636
Fax: (479) 979-1417	Email: admiss@ozarks.edu
Full-time: 280 men, 325 women	**Faculty:** n/av
Part-time: 20 men, 35 women	**Ph.D.s:** 77%
Graduate: n/av	**Student/Faculty:** 12 to 1
Year: semesters, summer session	**Tuition:** $24,440
Room & Board: $7450	**Freshman Class:** n/av
SAT or ACT: required	**CEEB CODE:** 6111
Application Deadline: April 1	**COMPETITIVE**

The University of the Ozarks, founded in 1834, is a private, comprehensive liberal arts, and professional programs school affiliated with the Presbyterian Church. The figures in the above capsule and in this profile are approximate. There are 4 undergraduate schools. In addition to regional accreditation, Ozarks has baccalaureate program accreditation with NCATE and IACBE. The 30-acre campus is in a small town in Clarksville, Arkansas, 1 hour east of Fort Smith, and 100 miles northwest of Little Rock. Including any residence halls, there are 16 buildings.

STUDENT LIFE: 59% of undergraduates are from Arkansas. Others are from 22 states, 20 foreign countries, and Canada. 93% are from public schools. 69% are White; 5% African American; 3% American Indian/Alaska Native; 3% Hispanic; 18% Foreign; 1% Asian American. 60% are Protestant; 20% claim no religious affiliation; 18% Catholic. **Female To Male Ratio:** 1.2:1. The average age of freshmen is 18; all undergraduates, 20. 33% do not continue beyond their first year; 46% remain to graduate. **Housing:** 447 students can be accommodated in college housing, which includes single-sex and coed dorms. On-campus housing is guaranteed for the freshman year only, and is available on a first-come, and first-served basis. Priority is given to out-of-town students. 64% of students live on campus; of those, 51% remain on campus on weekends. Alcohol is not permitted. All students may keep cars.

FACULTY/CLASSROOMS: 70% of faculty are male; 30% are female. All teach undergraduates. No introductory courses are taught by graduate students. The average class size in an introductory lecture is 14; in a laboratory is 11; and in a regular course is 15.

PROGRAMS OF STUDY: Ozarks confers B.A., B.S. and B.G.S. degrees. Bachelor's degrees are awarded in BIOLOGICAL SCIENCE (biology/biological science), BUSINESS (accounting, business administration and management, and marketing/retailing/merchandising), COMMUNICATIONS AND THE ARTS (art, communications, dramatic arts, English, and music), COMPUTER AND PHYSICAL SCIENCE (chemistry and mathematics), EDUCATION (business education, early childhood education, middle school education, and physical education), ENGINEERING AND ENVIRONMENTAL DESIGN (environmental science and materials science), HEALTH PROFESSIONS (respiratory therapy), SOCIAL SCIENCE (economics, history, liberal arts/general studies, political science/government, psychology, religion, social science, and sociology). Business and biology have the largest enrollment.

ACTIVITIES: There are no fraternities or sororities. There are 30 groups on campus, including special interest groups, university-sponsored groups, art, cheerleading, choir, chorale, chorus, dance, debate, drama, environmental, film, forensics, honors, international, literary magazine, newspaper, political, professional, radio and TV, recreational organizations, religious, social, social service, and student government. Popular campus events include International Fair and Banquet, Family Weekend and Freshman Matriculation Ceremony. **Sports:** There are 5 intercollegiate sports for men and 5 for women, and 6 intramural sports for men and 5 for women. Facilities include a sports complex housing racquetball courts, a pool, basketball arena, badminton, dodgeball, flag football, golf, volleyball, ping pong, sand vollyball, softball, soccer, and weight room, wrestling, and shooting sports, baseball fields, tennis courts, and a soccer stadium. **Graduates:** From July 1, 2015 to June 30, 2016, 106 bachelor's degrees were awarded. The most popular majors were business administration/management (15%), biology (13%), and marketing (11%). 50 companies recruited on campus in 2015-2016. In an average class, 32% graduate in 4 years or less, 45% graduate in 5 years or less, and 46% graduate in 6 years or less. Of the 2015 graduating class, 11% were enrolled in graduate school within 6 months of graduation, and 68% were employed.

SERVICES: Counseling and information services are available, as is tutoring in every subject. There is remedial math, reading, and writing. **Library/Resources:** The library contains 69,960 volumes, 6,927 microform items, and 2,955 audio/video tapes/CDs/DVDs, and subscribes to 611 periodicals including electronic. Computerized library services include interlibrary loans, database searching, Internet access, and Wi-Fi capability. Special learning facilities include an art gallery, radio station, TV station, and the Jones Learning Center which is for students with diagnosed learning disabilities. **Physically Challenged Students:** 90% of the campus is accessible. Facilities include elevators, special parking, specially equipped restrooms, special class scheduling, and lowered drinking fountains. **Special:** Internships, study abroad in 8 countries including Japan, numerous work-study programs, dual majors, a general studies degree, and a 3-2 engineering degree with the University of Arkansas are available. There are 3 national honor societies. **Visiting:** There are regularly scheduled orientations for prospective students, including a campus tour and meetings with faculty and students, admissions, and financial aid. In most cases, prospective students may meet with the president and coaches as requested. There are guides for informal visits, visitors may sit in on classes, and stay overnight. To schedule a visit, contact the Admissions Office. **Campus Safety and Security:** Measures include 24-hour foot and vehicle patrol. There are emergency telephones and lighted pathways/sidewalks.

REQUIREMENTS: The SAT or ACT is required, with a satisfactory score on the SAT or on the ACT. An interview is recommended. The GED is accepted. A GPA of 2.0 is required. AP and CLEP credits are accepted. Important factors in the admissions decision are personality/intangible qualities, advanced placement or honors courses, and evidence of special talent. Students are required to earn 124 hours, with 30 to 54 in the major, and maintain a minimum GPA of 2.0. Distribution requirements include 9 hours in civic awareness and social science, 7 to 10 hours in math and science, 4 hours in phys ed and wellness, 3 hours in literature, fine arts, and religion, and up to 6 hours in global awareness. **Procedure:** Freshmen are admitted to all sessions. Entrance exams should be taken as early as possible. There are deferred admissions and rolling admissions plans. Applications should be filed by April 1 for fall entry; December 1 for spring entry, along with a $30 fee. Applications are accepted on-line. **Transfer Students:** 41 transfer students enrolled in 2015-2016. A GPA of 2.0 and college transcripts are required. Applicants with a GPA of less than 2.0 or fewer than 30 hours of college work must furnish high school transcripts and ACT or SAT results. 30 of 124 credits required for the bachelor's degree must be completed at Ozarks. **International Students:** There are 118 international students enrolled. The school actively recruits these students. They must take the TOEFL and the college's own test.

Admissions Contact: Emma Lee Morrow, Admissions Coordinator. Email: *admiss@ozarks.edu*. Web: *www.ozarks.edu*

FINANCIAL AID: In 2016-2017, 99% of all full-time freshmen and 91% of continuing full-time students received some form of financial aid. 66% of all full-time freshmen and 47% of continuing full-time students received need-based aid. The average freshman award was $11,800. 41% of undergraduate students work part-time. Average annual earnings from campus work are $4900. The average financial indebtedness of the 2016 graduate was $16,000. The FAFSA code is 001094. Check with the school for current application deadlines.

WILLIAMS BAPTIST COLLEGE D-1
www.wbcoll.edu

Walnut Ridge, AR 72476	(870) 759-4120 (800) 722-4434
Fax: (870) 886-3924	Email: admissions@wbcoll.edu
Full-time: 241 men, 239 women	**Faculty:** 26
Part-time: 14 men, 33 women	**Ph.D.s:** 69%
Graduate: n/av	**Student/Faculty:** 15 to 1
Year: semesters, summer session	**Tuition:** $17,320
Room & Board: $7400	**Freshman Class:** 584 applied, 396 accepted, 164 enrolled
SAT: required **ACT:** 21	**CEEB CODE:** 6658
Application Deadline: rolling	**COMPETITIVE**

Williams Baptist College, founded in 1941, is a private liberal arts institution providing undergraduate education in business, education, humanities, natural sciences, religion, and social sciences. WBC is affiliated with the Southern Baptist Church and is sponsored by the Arkansas Baptist Convention. Figures in the above capsule and in this profile are approximate. There is 1 undergraduate school. In addition to regional accreditation, WBC has baccalaureate program accreditation with NCATE. The 180-acre campus is in a rural area 100 miles northwest of Memphis, TN, and 125 miles north of Little Rock. Including any residence halls, there are 54 buildings.

STUDENT LIFE: 71% of undergraduates are from Arkansas. Others are from 23 states, and 7 foreign countries. 80% are from public schools. 82% are White; 8% African American; 5% Hispanic; 3% Foreign; 2% American Indian/Alaska Native. 93% are Protestant. **Female To Male Ratio:** 1.1:1. The average age of freshmen is 18; all undergraduates, 23. 40% do not continue beyond their first year. **Housing:** 473 students can be accommodated in college housing, which includes single-sex dorms, on-campus apartments, and married student housing. On-campus housing is guaranteed for all 4 years. 74% of students live on campus; of those, 40% remain on campus on weekends. Alcohol is not permitted. All students may keep cars.

FACULTY/CLASSROOMS: 46% of faculty are male; 54% are female. All teach undergraduates, and all do research. No introductory courses are taught by graduate students. The average class size in an introductory lecture is 14; in a laboratory is 16; and in a regular course is 14.

PROGRAMS OF STUDY: WBC confers B.A., B.S. and B.S.Ed. degrees. Associate degrees are also awarded. Bachelor's degrees are awarded in BIOLOGICAL SCIENCE (biology/biological science), BUSINESS (business administration and management), COMMUNICATIONS AND THE ARTS (art, English, and music), COMPUTER AND PHYSICAL SCIENCE (computer science), EDUCATION (elementary education, physical education, and secondary education), SOCIAL SCIENCE (counseling/psychology, history, psychology, religion, religious education, and religious music). Education, business, and biology have the largest enrollments.

ACTIVITIES: There are no fraternities or sororities. There are 32 groups on campus, including art, cheerleading, choir, chorale, drama, international, literary magazine, professional, religious, social, social service, and student government. Popular campus events include Harvest Fest, Christmas in the Cove, and Spring Fling. **Sports:** There are 3 intercollegiate sports for men and 4 for women, and 4 intramural sports for men and 4 for women. Facilities include a gym, weight room, racquetball and tennis courts, a jogging track, sand volleyball, disc golf, and a student center. **Graduates:** From July 1, 2015 to June 30, 2016, 101 bachelor's degrees were awarded. The most popular majors were psychology (18%), early childhood education (18%), and business/finance (16%). In an average class, 29% graduate in 4 years or less, 37% graduate in 5 years or less, and 40% graduate in 6 years or less.

SERVICES: Counseling and information services are available, as is tutoring in most subjects such as remedial math. **Library/Resources:** The library contains 101,214 volumes, 119 microform items, and 172 audio/video tapes/CDs/DVDs, and subscribes to 31 periodicals including electronic. Computerized library services include interlibrary loans, database searching, Internet access, and Wi-Fi capability. Special learning facilities include an art gallery, and an education curriculum lab. **Physically Challenged Students:** 90% of the campus is accessible. Facilities include wheelchair ramps, elevators, special parking, specially equipped restrooms, lowered drinking fountains, and special housing. **Special:** WBC offers study abroad in England, Latin America, the Middle East, and Russia, a Washington semester through the American Studies Program, and general studies major. There are 9 national honor societies and 10 departmental honors programs. **Visiting:** There are regularly scheduled orientations for prospective students, tour the campus, visit with professors, and visit with current students. There are guides for informal visits, visitors may sit in on classes, and stay overnight. To schedule a visit, contact Andrew Watson at (800) 722-4434. **Campus Safety and Security:** Measures include 24-hour foot and vehicle patrol and emergency notification system. There are lighted pathways/sidewalks and controlled access to dorms/residences.

REQUIREMENTS: The SAT or ACT is required. First-time freshmen must have a minimum composite score of 19 and 2.5 cumulative high school GPA for unconditional admission. A GPA of 2.5 is required. AP and CLEP credits are accepted. To graduate, all students must follow a core curriculum including humanities, social science and religion, natural science and math, and physical activity. Chapel attendance is mandatory. A total of 123 credits, with 36 to 64 hours in the major, and a minimum GPA of 2.0 are required to graduate. **Procedure:** Freshmen are admitted to all sessions. There is a rolling admissions plan. Application deadlines are open. Applications are accepted on-line. Application fees are waived if application is completed on-line. **Transfer Students:** 58 transfer students enrolled in 2015-2016. Transfer students must have a GPA of 2.0 for unconditional admission. 32 of 123 credits required for the bachelor's degree must be completed at WBC. **International Students:** There are 19 international students enrolled. The school actively recruits these students. They must take the TOEFL with a minimum score of 500 on the paper-based TOEFL (PBT) or 61 on the Internet-based version (iBT). They must also take the SAT or ACT, scoring 19.

ADMISSIONS: 2 freshmen graduated first in their class. **Admissions Contact:** Andrew Watson, Director of Admissions. Email: *admissions@wbcoll.edu* Web: *www.wbcoll.edu*

FINANCIAL AID: In 2016-2017, 100% of all full-time freshmen and 100% of continuing full-time students received some form of financial aid. 62% of all full-time freshmen and 68% of continuing full-time students received need-based aid. The average freshman award was $14,931. Need-based scholarships or need-based grants averaged $4,260 ($7,330 maximum); need-based self-help aid (loans and jobs) averaged $3,257 ($5,787 maximum); non-need-based athletic scholarships averaged $4,430 ($16,459 maximum); and other non-need-based awards and non-need-based scholarships averaged $5,428 ($22,000 maximum). 39% of undergraduate students work part-time. Average annual earnings from campus work are $1280. The average financial indebtedness of the 2016 graduate was $19,197. The FAFSA code is 001106. The priority date for freshman financial aid applications for fall entry is February 1. The deadline for filing freshman financial aid applications for fall entry is May 1.

AMERICAN JEWISH UNIVERSITY - COLLEGE OF ARTS AND SCIENCES CAMPUS C-5

www.ajula.edu

Los Angeles, CA 90077	(310) 440-1247 (877) GO-2-AJULA
Fax: (310) 471-3657	**Email:** admissions@ajula.edu
Full-time: 40 men, 60 women	**Faculty:** n/av
Part-time: 5 men, 5 women	**Ph.D.s:** 100%
Graduate: 65 men, 75 women	**Student/Faculty:** n/av
Year: semesters	**Tuition:** $29,132
Room & Board: $15,102	**Freshman Class:** n/av
SAT or ACT: required	**CEEB CODE:** 4876
Application Deadline: May 31	**COMPETITIVE**

American Jewish University, College of Arts & Sciences Campus founded in 2007, is distinguished by its core curriculum integrating social justice and ethical leadership. It prepares students for careers and graduate studies in law, business, psychology, education, and other fields. The figures in the above capsule and in this profile are approximate. There is 1 undergraduate school and 3 graduate schools. In addition to regional accreditation, AJU has baccalaureate program accreditation with WASC. The 2700-acre campus is in a suburban area in Los Angeles and Simi Valley. Including any residence halls, there are 9 buildings.

STUDENT LIFE: 71% of undergraduates are from California. Others are from 22 states, and 2 foreign countries. 70% are from public schools. 81% are White; 6% Foreign; 3% African American. 94% are Jewish. **Female To Male Ratio:** 1.3:1. The average age of freshmen is 18; all undergraduates, 23. 5% do not continue beyond their first year; 90% remain to graduate. **Housing:** 192 students can be accommodated in college housing, which includes coed dorms, on-campus apartments, and married student housing. On-campus housing is guaranteed for all 4 years. 70% of students live on campus; of those, 70% remain on campus on weekends. All students may keep cars.

FACULTY/CLASSROOMS: 45% of faculty are male; 55% are female. All teach undergraduates and do research. No introductory courses are taught by graduate students. The average class size in an introductory lecture is 7 and in a laboratory is 7.

PROGRAMS OF STUDY: AJU confers B.A. degrees. Master's degrees are also awarded. Bachelor's degrees are awarded in BUSINESS (business administration and management), COMMUNICATIONS AND THE ARTS (journalism and literature), HEALTH PROFESSIONS (premedicine), SOCIAL SCIENCE (ethics, politics, and social policy, Judaic studies, liberal arts/general studies, political science/government, and psychology)..

ACTIVITIES: There are no fraternities or sororities. There are 15 groups on campus, including Tikkum Olam, bioethics, Hillel, peer mentoring, psychology, art, choir, dance, drama, Israel action, literary magazine, newspaper, political, radio and TV, religious, social, social service, and student government. Popular campus events include Israel Memorial Day (Yom Hazikaron), and Israel Independence Day (Yom Ha'atzmaut). **Sports:** There are no sports program at AJU. Facilities include a gym, basketball court, and a soccer field at the Familian campus in Los Angeles and horseback riding, swimming pools, and a ropes course at the Brandeis-Bardin campus in Simi Valley.

SERVICES: Counseling and information services are available, as is tutoring in most subjects. There is remedial math and writing. **Library/Resources:** The library contains 105,000 volumes, and subscribes to 400 periodicals including electronic. Computerized library services include interlibrary loans, database searching, Internet access, and Wi-Fi capability. Special learning facilities include an art gallery, radio station, and TV station. **Physically Challenged Students:** All of the campus is accessible. Facilities include elevators, special parking, specially equipped restrooms, lowered drinking fountains, and lowered telephones. **Special:** There is a 5-year joint business management program with American Jewish University's Lieber School of Graduate Studies and a 5-year joint master's degree in Jewish education with AJU's Fingerhut School of Education. Student designed and dual majors are available. Internships in all available majors, study abroad, work-study programs, accelerated degree programs, and pass/fail options are offered. Students may apply for independent study projects. There is 1 national honor society. **Visiting:** There are regularly scheduled orientations for prospective students, including meeting with admissions representatives, department chairs, and the Dean of the College of Arts and Sciences, sitting in on classes, sleeping over in the doms, eating meals in the Berg dining hall, meeting current students and touring the campus. There are guides for informal visits, visitors may sit in on classes, and stay overnight. To schedule a visit, contact the Director of Undergraduate Admissions. **Campus Safety and Security:** Measures include 24-hour foot and vehicle patrol, self-defense education, and security escort services. There are emergency telephones and lighted pathways/sidewalks.

REQUIREMENTS: The SAT or ACT is required. Applicants must be graduates of an accredited secondary school or have a GED. A visit and an interview are recommeded for all students. 2 letters of recommendation, an autobiographical essay, and official high school transcripts are required. A GPA of 2.0 is required. AP credits are accepted. Important factors in the admissions decision are extracurricular activities record. All students must complete a core curriculum combining the study of Jewish and Western civilizations, as well as courses in communications and foreign language and 1 in computer science. There are distribution requirements in math, natural and behavioral sciences, English, and fine arts. Other requirements vary according to the major, with at least 32 to 36 upper-division credits needed. A total of 120 semester units, with a minimum GPA of 2.0, is required to graduate. **Procedure:** Freshmen are admitted fall and spring. Entrance exams should be taken no later than November of the year prior to enrollment. There are early decision, deferred admissions, and rolling admissions plans. Applications should be filed by May 31 for fall entry; November 30 for spring entry. The fall 2016 application fee was $35. Notification is sent on a rolling basis. Applications are accepted on-line. **Transfer Students:** 19 transfer students enrolled in 2015-2016. Previous college work should be at the B level to transfer. Students with fewer than 60 college credits should also have a minimum 3.0 high school GPA, at least 1700 on the SAT or 24 on the ACT, recommendations, and an autobiographical essay. The SAT or ACT requirement is waived if the applicant has 60 or more transferable credits. A visit and an interview are recommended. 34 of 120 credits required for the bachelor's degree must be completed at AJU. **International Students:** They must take the TOEFL with a minimum score of 79 on the Internet-based version (iBT). They must also take the SAT or ACT.

Admissions Contact: Jyllian Siegal, Director of Undergraduate Admissions. Email: *mdavidson@ajula.edu* Web: *www.ajula.edu*

FINANCIAL AID: The college's own financial statement, and tax returns, and W2s are required. The deadline for filing freshman financial aid applications for fall entry is March 2.

ARTCENTER COLLEGE OF DESIGN *(The complete profile is made available exclusively on our website, www.barronspac.com)*

ASHFORD UNIVERSITY F-3
www.ashford.edu

San Diego, CA 92123 (866) 711-1700

Email: admissions@ashford.edu

Full-time: 13,608 men, 31,716 women
Part-time: 8 men, 16 women
Graduate: 1505 men, 4384 women
Year: varies, summer session
Room & Board: n/app
SAT or ACT: recommended
Application Deadline: n/av

Faculty: n/av
Ph.D.s: n/av
Student/Faculty: n/av
Tuition: $10,480
Freshman Class: n/av

CEEB CODE: 6418
COMPETITIVE

Ashford University, is a private liberal arts college founded in 1918. There are 4 undergraduate schools and 3 graduate schools. In addition to regional accreditation, AU has baccalaureate program accreditation with IACBE. The 25-acre campus is in a small town 135 miles west of Chicago, IL. Including any residence halls, there are 12 buildings.

STUDENT LIFE: 98% of undergraduates are from out of state, mostly the South. Students are from 50 states, 1 foreign country, and Canada. 47% are White; 35% African American; 3% two or more races; 2% race unknown; 10% Hispanic; 1% Asian American; 1% American Indian/Alaska Native. **Female To Male Ratio:** 2.4:1. The average age of all undergraduates is 35. **Housing:** 573 students can be accommodated in college housing, which includes single-sex and coed dorms. On-campus housing is guaranteed for all 4 years. Alcohol is not permitted. All students may keep cars.

FACULTY/CLASSROOMS: No introductory courses are taught by graduate students.

PROGRAMS OF STUDY: AU confers B.A., and B.S. degrees. Associate and master's degrees are also awarded. Bachelor's degrees are awarded in AGRICULTURE (environmental studies), BIOLOGICAL SCIENCE (biology/biological science), BUSINESS (accounting, business administration and management, business economics, business information systems, business leadership, entrepreneurial studies, finance, hospitality management services, human resources/organizational mgmt, international business, marketing, operations management, organizational leadership and management, real estate, sports management, supply chain management, sustainable management, and project management), COMMUNICATIONS AND THE ARTS (communication studies, English, journalism, linguistics, and public relations), COMPUTER AND PHYSICAL SCIENCE (computer science and natural sciences), EDUCATION (early childhood education, education, education administration, educational studies, elementary education, English education, health education, health information management, library science, and physical education), ENGINEERING AND ENVIRONMENTAL DESIGN (computer graphics, instructional design, and military science), HEALTH PROFESSIONS (community health work, complementary/alternative health, health care administration, health promotion, and health science), SOCIAL SCIENCE (anthropology, behavioral science, child psychology/development, cognitive science, criminal justice, family/consumer studies, gerontology, history, homeland security/emergency preparedness, law enforcement and corrections, liberal arts/general studies, political science/government, psychology, public administration, social science, and sociology). Organizational management, psychology, early childhood education have the largest enrollments.

ACTIVITIES: There are no fraternities or sororities. Groups on campus include art, band, choir, computers, dance, drama, environmental, ethnic, honors, international, LGBT, literary magazine, musical theater, newspaper, professional, religious, SISEA (Iowa State Education Association), social, social service, and student government. Popular campus events include Family Weekend, Matriculation Ceremony, Earth Day, and Commencement. **Sports:** There are 8 intercollegiate sports for men and 9 for women, and 11 intramural sports for men and 11 for women. Facilities include an arena with 2 regulation-size basketball courts, a fitness center, 4-lane perimeter track, 2 locker rooms plus 2 rooms and 1 training room. A state-of-the-art artificial turf soccer field and an outdoor all-weather track exists on the lower portion of the campus and hosts the AU men's and women's soccer programs and well as the men's and women's outdoor track and field teams.**Graduates:** From July 1, 2015 to June 30, 2016, 11850 bachelor's degrees were awarded. The most popular majors were organizational management (12%), psychology (9%), and early childhood education (9%).

SERVICES: Counseling and information services are available, as is tutoring in every subject. There is also voice-activated computer software, proctoring exams, and prep courses for the GRE and MCAT. **Library/Resources:** The library contains 103,569 volumes, 73,405 microform items, and 2,509 audio/video tapes/CDs/DVDs, and subscribes to 129,376 periodicals including electronic. Computerized library services include interlibrary loans, database searching, Internet access, and Wi-Fi capability. Special learning facilities include an art gallery, a living lab adjacent to the campus. **Physically Challenged Students:** 95% of the campus is accessible. Facilities include wheelchair ramps, elevators, special parking, specially equipped restrooms, lowered drinking fountains, and special housing. **Special:** There are 2 national honor societies, a freshman honors program, and 1 departmental honors program. **Visiting:** There are regularly scheduled orientations for prospective students, including 2-day orientation sessions held prior to the first week of classes for students and parents on campus and an online orientation offered for online students.. There are guides for informal visits, visitors may sit in on classes, and stay overnight. To schedule a visit, contact the Admissions Office. **Campus Safety and Security:** Measures include self-defense education and security escort services. There are shuttle buses, emergency telephones, lighted pathways/sidewalks. The campus has 24-hour security through the Clinton police department. On-campus security is also available.

REQUIREMENTS: The ACT is recommended. The SAT is accepted. Applicants must be graduates of an accredited secondary school or have earned a GED and must meet 2 of the following requirements: a GPA of 2.0 in college preparatory or regular high school courses, rank in the upper half of the graduating class, and a minimum ACT composite score of 18 or a satisfactory SAT score. AU requires applicants to be in the upper 50% of their class. AP and CLEP credits are accepted. Students must complete 120 semester hours, including 25 semester hours of general education subject areas, plus 24 hours of genereal education competencies (communication, critical thinking, mathematical, etc.); 30 hours of upper division coursework, 18-21 of these hours must be in the major (depends on program); minimum GPA of 2.00 although a higher GPA is required for some programs; minimum of 30 credits earned at the University; completion of all major, minor, and specialization course requirements; and a final exam, report, or project is required in every course. **Procedure:** Freshmen are admitted to all sessions. Entrance exams should be taken before enrolling. There are deferred admissions and rolling admissions plans. Check with the school for current application deadlines. Application fees are waived if application is completed online. **Transfer Students:** 5789 transfer students enrolled in 2015-2016. Applicants may apply up to a maximum of 90 semester credit hours 30 of 120 credits required for the bachelor's degree must be completed at AU. **International Students:** They must take the TOEFL with a minimum score of 500 on the paper-based TOEFL (PBT) or 61 on the Internet-based version (iBT).

Admissions Contact: Office of Admissions. Email: *admissions@ashford.edu* Web: *www.ashford.edu*

FINANCIAL AID: The college's own financial statement is required. Check with the school for current application deadlines.

AZUSA PACIFIC UNIVERSITY D-5
www.apu.edu

Azusa, CA 91702	626-812-3073 (800) TALK-APU
Fax: (626) 812-3096	**Email:** admissions@apu.edu
Full-time: 1893 men, 3463 women	**Faculty:** 272; I, -$
Part-time: 151 men, 376 women	**Ph.D.s:** 64%
Graduate: 1188 men, 2904 women	**Student/Faculty:** 20 to 1
Year: semesters, summer session	**Tuition:** $34,754
Room & Board: $9218	**Freshman Class:** 6084 applied, 4922 accepted, 1192 enrolled
SAT CR/M: 530/540 **ACT:** 24	**CEEB CODE:** 4596
Application Deadline: May 1	**COMPETITIVE**

Azusa Pacific University, founded in 1899, is a private (non-profit), interdenominational Christian institution offering undergraduate and graduate programs in the liberal arts and emphasizing spiritual growth. There are 7 undergraduate schools and 8 graduate schools. In addition to regional accreditation, APU has baccalaureate program accreditation with CSWE, NASAD, NASM, NCATE, NLN, IACBE, ATS, and CAPTE. The 105-acre campus is in a small town 26 miles notheast of Los Angeles. Including any residence halls, there are 67 buildings.

STUDENT LIFE: Students are from 44 states, 41 foreign countries, and Canada. 9% are Asian American; 8% two or more races; 43% White; 4% African American; 29% Hispanic; 17% race unknown. **Female To Male Ratio:** 2.1:1. The average age of freshmen is 18; all undergraduates, 21. 12% do not continue beyond their first year; 88% remain to graduate. **Housing:** 3101 students can be accommodated in college housing, which includes single-sex and coed dorms, on-campus apartments, and off-campus apartments. In addition, there are honors houses and special-interest houses. On-campus housing is available on a first-come, first-served basis, and is available on a lottery system for upperclassmen. 62% of students live on campus. Alcohol is not permitted. All students may keep cars.

FACULTY/CLASSROOMS: 43% of faculty are male; 56% are female. No introductory courses are taught by graduate students.

PROGRAMS OF STUDY: APU confers B.A., B.S., B.M., B.F.A, B.S.N. and B.S.W. degrees. Master's and doctoral degrees are also awarded. Bachelor's degrees are awarded in BIOLOGICAL SCIENCE (biochemistry and biology/biological science), BUSINESS (accounting, business administration and management, international business, and marketing/retailing/merchandising), COMMUNICATIONS AND THE ARTS (acting, communications, English, fine arts, graphic design, journalism, music, Spanish, and theatre arts), COMPUTER AND PHYSICAL SCIENCE (chemistry, computer science, information sciences and systems, mathematics, and physics), EDUCATION (art education, athletic training, music education, and physical education), ENGINEERING AND ENVIRONMENTAL DESIGN (systems engineering), HEALTH PROFESSIONS (allied health, biology, and nursing), SOCIAL SCIENCE (biblical studies, criminal justice, history, international studies, liberal arts/general studies, liberal arts, sciences, general studies, humanities, ministries, philosophy, political science/government, psychology, religion, social science, social work, sociology, theology, and youth ministry). Nursing, education, and religion are the strongest academically. Business, nursing, and psychology have the largest enrollments.

ACTIVITIES: There are no fraternities or sororities. There are 50 groups on campus, including art, band, cheerleading, choir, chorale, chorus, computers, dance, debate, drama, ethnic, film, honors, international, jazz band, literary magazine, marching band, musical theater, newspaper, opera, orchestra, pep band, photography, political, professional, radio and TV, religious, social, social service, student government, and yearbook. Popular campus events include Missions Week, Mega Weekend-Homecoming/Dinner Rally and Night of Champions. **Sports:** Facilities include an all-weather track, football stadium, a baseball field, gym, residence hall lounge, turf recreation field, sand volleyball courts, indoor/outdoor basketball courts, and a recreation room. **Graduates:** From July 1, 2015 to June 30, 2016, 1783 bachelor's degrees were awarded. The most popular majors were health professions and related programs (23%), business/marketing (21%), and visual and performing arts (9%). In an average class, 8% graduate in 4 years or less, 50% graduate in 5 years or less, and 68% graduate in 6 years or less.

SERVICES: Counseling and information services are available, as is tutoring in most subjects. There is remedial math, reading, and writing. **Library/Resources:** The 3 libraries contain 386,074 volumes, 703,979 microform items, and subscribe to 93,873 periodicals including electronic. Computerized library services include interlibrary loans, database searching, Internet access, and Wi-Fi capability. Special learning facilities include an art gallery, radio station, and TV station. **Physically Challenged Students:** All of the campus is accessible. Facilities include wheelchair ramps, elevators, special parking, specially equipped restrooms, lowered drinking fountains, lowered telephones, and special housing. **Special:** Internships in ministerial and American studies, study abroad in Japan, Latin America, Taiwan, England, Australia, China, Tanzania, Italy, Israel, France, Lithuania, Spain, Uganda, and South Africa, and a Washington semester are available. In addition work-study with the university, a B.A.-B.S. degree, dual majors in all programs, and a 3-2 engineering degree are offered. Accelerated degree programs are available in Christian leadership, computer information systems, management information systems, human development, and organizational leadership; there is also a Registered Nurse to Bachelor of Science in Nursing Program. APU awards credit for life experience and allows nondegree study. There are 13 national honor societies and a freshman honors program. **Visiting:** There are regularly scheduled orientations for prospective students, including Seniors Only Day in November, and a brother/sister weekend in February that is open to both juniors and seniors. There are guides for informal visits, visitors may sit in on classes, and stay overnight. To schedule a visit, contact the Admissions Office. **Campus Safety and Security:** Measures include 24-hour foot and vehicle patrol, emergency notification system, self-defense education, and security escort services. There are shuttle buses, emergency telephones, lighted pathways/sidewalks, and controlled access to dorms/residences.

REQUIREMENTS: The SAT and ACT are required, but no minimum score is necessary. An essay is required. A portfolio and an interview are recommended for certain programs. The GED is accepted. A GPA of 3.0 is required. AP and CLEP credits are accepted. Important factors in the admissions decision are personality/intangible qualities, recommendations by school officials, evidence of special talent, and advanced placement or honors courses. All students must take 120 semester units and earn a minimum GPA of 2.0. 18 units of Bible courses, 120 hours of community ministry, and 2 units of health are required. General education requirements include courses in public speaking, fine arts, religion & philosophy, English, algebra, foreign language, phys ed., heritage & institution, identity & relationships, and nature are also required courses. **Procedure:** Freshmen are admitted to all sessions. Entrance exams should be taken prior to enrollment. There are early admissions, deferred admissions, and rolling admissions plans. Early decision applications should be filed by February 15; regular applications, by May 1 for fall entry; and October 15 for spring entry, along with a $45 fee. Notification of early decision is sent October 1; regular decision, April 1. Application fees are waived if application is completed online. **Transfer Students:** 534 transfer students enrolled in 2015-2016. Applicants must have a minimum GPA of 2.20 on previous college work. The SAT or ACT is not required if 30 or more semester units have been completed. An associate degree and an interview are recommended. 30 of 120 credits required for the bachelor's degree must be completed at APU. **International Students:** There are 130 international students enrolled. The school actively recruits these students. They must take the TOEFL with a minimum score of 587 on the paper-based TOEFL (PBT) or 94 on the Internet-based version (iBT). They must also take the SAT or ACT.

ADMISSIONS: 81% of the 2016-2017 applicants were accepted. The SAT scores for the 2016-2017 freshman class were: Critical Reading-- 32% below 500, 45% between 500 and 599, 21% between 600 and 699, and 3% between 700 and 800. Math-- 4% below 500, 34% between 500 and 599, 21% between 600 and 699, and 2% between 700 and 800. The ACT scores were 4% between 12 and 17, 42% between 18 and 23, 44% between 24 and 29, and 10% above 30. **Admissions Contact:** Kimberley Wiedefeld, Senior Director Undergraduate Admissions. Email: *admissions@apu.edu* Web: *www.apu.edu*

FINANCIAL AID: In 2016-2017, 93% of all full-time freshmen received some form of financial aid. The average freshman award was $21,492. Need-based scholarships or need-based grants averaged $10,581; need-based self-help aid (loans and jobs) averaged $3,659; non-need-based athletic scholarships averaged $20,225; and other non-need-based awards and non-need-based scholarships averaged $9,432. The average financial indebtedness of the 2016 graduate was $30,516. The college's own financial statement is required. The FAFSA code is 001117. Check with the school for current application deadlines.

BIOLA UNIVERSITY D-5

www.biola.edu

La Mirada, CA 90639	(562) 903-4752 (800) OK-BIOLA
Fax: (562) 903-4709	Email: admissions@biola.edu
Full-time: 1582 men, 2575 women	**Faculty:** IIA, --$
Part-time: 88 men, 92 women	**Ph.D.s:** 74%
Graduate: 1294 men, 671 women	**Student/Faculty:** 16 to 1
Year: 4-1-4, summer session	**Tuition:** $36,696
Room & Board: $10,016	**Freshman Class:** 3528 applied, 2634 accepted, 930 enrolled
SAT CR/M/W: 556/559/550 **ACT:** 24	**CEEB CODE:** 4017
Application Deadline: March 1	**COMPETITIVE+**

Biola University, founded in 1908, is a private, Interdenominational Christian institution offering undergraduate and graduate degrees in arts and sciences, psychology, theology, intercultural studies, and business. The figures in the above capsule and in this profile are approximate. There are 7 undergraduate schools and 6 graduate schools. In addition to regional accreditation, Biola has baccalaureate program accreditation with ACBSP, NASAD, NASM, NLN, APA, and and ATS. The 95-acre campus is in a suburban area in La Mirada, CA, located on the border of Los Angeles and Orange counties. Including any residence halls, there are 53 buildings.

STUDENT LIFE: 78% of undergraduates are from California. Others are from 40 states, 28 foreign countries, and Canada. 69% are from public schools. 6% are two or more races; 56% White; 2% African American; 2% Foreign; 2% race unknown; 17% Hispanic; 15% Asian American. 99% are Protestant. **Female To Male Ratio:** 1.1:1. The average age of freshmen is 18; all undergraduates, 20. 14% do not continue beyond their first year; 65% remain to graduate. **Housing:** 2307 students can be accommodated in college housing, which includes single-sex and coed dorms, on-campus apartments, and off-campus apartments. On-campus housing is guaranteed for the freshman year only, is available on a first-come, first-served basis, and is available on a lottery system for upperclassmen. 61% of students live on campus; of those, 73% remain on campus on weekends. Alcohol is not permitted. All students may keep cars.

FACULTY/CLASSROOMS: 63% of faculty are male; 37% are female. No introductory courses are taught by graduate students.

PROGRAMS OF STUDY: Biola confers B.A., B.S., B.F.A. and B.M. degrees. Master's and doctoral degrees are also awarded. Bachelor's degrees are awarded in BIOLOGICAL SCIENCE (biochemistry, biology/adolescence education, biology/biological science, and life science), BUSINESS (accounting, business administration and management, business communications, business economics, business information systems, economics – statistics, international business management, management information systems, management science, and marketing management), COMMUNICATIONS AND THE ARTS (advertising, American literature, American sign language, art, broadcasting, communications, dramatic arts, drawing, English, film arts, fine arts, graphic design, journalism, music, music composition, music performance, music theory and composition, painting, performing arts, photography, piano performance, playwriting/screenwriting, printmaking, public relations, publishing, radio/television technology, Spanish, studio art, theatre acting, theatre arts, theater design, and theater management), COMPUTER AND PHYSICAL SCIENCE (applied mathematics, chemistry, computer mathematics, computer information technology, computer science, information sciences and systems, mathematics, mathematics/theoretical, natural sciences, physical sciences, physics, and statistics), EDUCATION (Christian education, early childhood education, mathematics education, music education, physical education, social studies education, and social studies secondary school education), ENGINEERING AND ENVIRONMENTAL DESIGN (computational sciences, computer technology, engineering, and environmental science), HEALTH PROFESSIONS (nursing, physical therapy, preallied health, pre-health studies, predentistry, premedicine, prepharmacy, prephysical therapy, speech pathology/audiology, and speech therapy), SOCIAL SCIENCE (anthropology, applied psychology, archeology, biblical studies, counseling/psychology, crosscultural studies, early childhood studies, economics, history, humanities, liberal arts/general studies, ministries, missions, philosophy, philosophy and religion, prelaw, psychology, religious studies, social science, social work, and sociology). Biblical studies, business administration, and journalism/communication are the strongest academically. Biblical studies, business, and psychology have the largest enrollments.

ACTIVITIES: There are no fraternities or sororities. There are 52 groups on campus, including adventure club, art, band, cheerleading, chess, choir, chorale, dance, debate, drama, environmental, ethnic, film, forensics, honors, international, jazz band, literary magazine, musical theater, newspaper, opera, orchestra, political, professional, radio and TV, religious, social, social service, student government, symphony, and yearbook. Popular campus events include Multicultural Week, Christmas Celebration, Biola Weekend, Missions Conference and Torrey Conference. **Sports:** There are 12 intercollegiate sports for men and 12 for women, and 10 intramural sports for men and 10 for women. Facilities include a gym/swimming complex, a 450-seat auditorium, athletic fields for soccer, a quarter-mile track, a baseball diamond, tennis, sand volleyball, and basketball courts, and a fitness center. **Graduates:** From July 1, 2015 to June 30, 2016, 898 bachelor's degrees were awarded. The most popular majors were business/marketing (19%), theology and religious vocations (14%), and visual and performing arts (11%). In an average class, 47% graduate in 4 years or less, 62% graduate in 5 years or less, and 65% graduate in 6 years or less. Of the 2015 graduating class, 50% were employed within 6 months of graduation.

SERVICES: Counseling and information services are available, as is tutoring in most subjects. There is a reader service for the blind, and a writing center is available to all students. **Library/Resources:** The library contains 315,000 volumes, 580,000 microform items, and 9,232 audio/video tapes/CDs/DVDs, and subscribes to 30,000 periodicals including electronic. Computerized library services include interlibrary loans, database searching, Internet access, and Wi-Fi capability. Special learning facilities include an art gallery, radio station, TV station, film studio, 3-D art facility, MIDI lab for music composition majors, electronic piano lab, listening lab with music archives, physical science labs, scanning electron microscope, and an archeological dig-site. **Physically Challenged Students:** 90% of the campus is accessible. Facilities include wheelchair ramps, elevators, special parking, specially equipped restrooms, special class scheduling, lowered drinking fountains, and lowered telephones. **Special:** Cross-registration with the Au Sable Institute of Environmental Studies is possible. Biola offers internships, summer travel tours, study abroad in 11 countries, and an American studies program in Washington D.C., sponsored by the Christian College Coalition. Special programs include L.A. Film Studies, a semester in Hollywood working in the film industry; Biola Baja, a 3-week program at Vermillion Sea Field, Baja; a family studies course at Focus on the Family Institute in Colorado Springs; a China studies program at Fudan University in Shanghai, China, and a development theory studies program in Honduras. Also available are on- and off-campus work-study programs, a B.A.-B.S. degree, a 3-2 engineering degree with the University of Southern California, dual majors, and nondegree study. There are several preprofessional programs available, including prelaw, prephysical therapy, and prechiropractic. A 3-1 program with Los Angeles College of Chiropractic is offered. Students can also attend a semester at Martha's Vineyard with the Contemporary Music Center and explore the many areas of the Christian music industry. There are 2 national honor societies, a freshman honors program, and 7 departmental honors programs. **Visiting:** There are regularly scheduled orientations for prospective students, including class visits; orientation with the departments of admissions, financial aid, and student affairs; chapel; a sporting event; and a Disneyland or Knott's Berry Farm visit. There are guides for informal visits, visitors may sit in on classes, and stay overnight. To schedule a visit, contact the Admissions Office. **Campus Safety and Security:** Measures include 24-hour foot and vehicle patrol, emergency notification system, self-defense education, and security escort services. There are shuttle buses, emergency telephones, lighted pathways/sidewalks, controlled access to dorms/residences, bicycle patrol, and Segway patrol.

REQUIREMENTS: The SAT or ACT is required. Applicants need not be graduates of an accredited secondary school. The GED is accepted. Students should have completed 15 academic credits, including 4 years of English and foreign language, 3 years of math, and 2 each of social studies and science. All students must be evangelical Christians who can demonstrate Christian character, leadership ability, and the aptitude for possible success in college. Applicants must submit 1 reference from their pastor or someone on the pastoral staff. A personal essay is required. A GPA of 3.0 is required. AP and CLEP credits are accepted. Important factors in the admissions decision are personality/intangible qualities, recommendations by school officials, and leadership record. To graduate, students must pass a writing competency exam, complete 30 units of biblical studies and theology, and fulfill the general education and phys ed requirements. At least 130 semester hours must be completed, with 30 hours in the major and 24 of these in upper-division work. Other requirements vary by major. A minimum 2.0 GPA is required. **Procedure:** Freshmen are admitted to all sessions. There are early decision and rolling admissions plans. Early decision applications should be filed by November 15; regular applications, by March 1 for fall entry; and November 15 for spring entry, along with a $45 fee. Notification of early decision is sent January 15; regular decision, April 1. Applications are accepted on-line. **Transfer Students:** 322 transfer students enrolled in 2015-2016. Applicants with fewer than 15 credit hours must submit both college transcripts and SAT scores. All students must provide high school transcripts. A minimum 2.0 GPA and an interview are required. 30 of 130 credits required for the bachelor's degree must be completed at Biola. **International Students:** There are 180 international students enrolled. The school actively recruits these students. They must take the TOEFL with a minimum score of 600 on the paper-based TOEFL (PBT) or 100 on the Internet-based version (iBT). They must also take the SAT or ACT.

ADMISSIONS: 75% of the 2016-2017 applicants were accepted. The SAT scores for the 2016-2017 freshman class were: Critical Reading-- 24% below 500, 42% between 500 and 599, 27% between 600 and 699, and 7% between 700 and 800. Math-- 26% below 500, 42% between 500 and 599, 29% between 600 and 699, and 3% between 700 and 800. Writing-- 25% below 500, 44% between 500 and 599, 25% between 600 and 699, and 6% between 700 and 800. The ACT scores were 7% below 12, 35% between 12 and 17, 28% between 18 and 23, 19% between 24 and 29, and 11% above 30. **Admissions Contact:** André Stephens, Senior Director/Undergraduate Admissions. Email: *admissions@biola.edu* Web: *www.biola.edu*

FINANCIAL AID: In 2016-2017, 69% of all full-time freshmen and 70% of continuing full-time students received some form of financial aid. 68% of all full-time freshmen and 67% of continuing full-time students received need-based aid. The average freshman award was $16,773. Need-based scholarships or need-based grants averaged $12,990; need-based self-help aid (loans and jobs) averaged $7,011; non-need-based athletic scholarships averaged $11,165; and other non-need-based awards and non-need-based scholarships averaged $6,523. 34% of undergraduate students work part-time. The average financial indebtedness of the 2016 graduate was $34,587. Biola is a member of CSS. The college's own financial statement, California residents should submit the Cal Grant GPA verification form are required. The FAFSA code is 001122. The priority date for freshman financial aid applications for fall entry is May 15. The deadline for filing freshman financial aid applications for fall entry is June 15.

CALIFORNIA BAPTIST UNIVERSITY D-5

www.calbaptist.edu

Riverside, CA 92504 **(951) 343-4212** **(877) 228-8866**

Fax: (951) 343-4525 **Email: admissions@calbaptist.edu**

Full-time: 2168 men, 3717 women	**Faculty:** 309
Part-time: 382 men, 670 women	**Ph.D.s:** 75%
Graduate: 635 men, 1585 women	**Student/Faculty:** 19 to 1
Year: semesters, summer session	**Tuition:** $31,372
Room & Board: $10,020	**Freshman Class:** 4971 applied, 3181 accepted, 1146 enrolled
SAT CR/M/W: required **ACT:** 22	**CEEB CODE:** 4094
Application Deadline: rolling	**COMPETITIVE**

California Baptist University (CBU) is one of the top private Christian colleges and universities in Southern California. CBU offers bachelor's, master's and credential programs in Riverside, San Bernardino and online. California Baptist University believes each person has been created for a purpose. CBU strives to help students understand and engage this purpose by providing a Christ-centered educational experience that integrates academics with spiritual and social development opportunities. Graduates are challenged to become individuals whose skills, integrity and sense of purpose glorify God and distinguish them in the workplace and in the world. There are 11 undergraduate schools and 10 graduate schools. In addition to regional accreditation, CBU has baccalaureate program accreditation with ABET, ACBSP, NAAB, NASM, CAATE, CCNE, and CCTC. The 160-acre campus is in a suburban area 60 miles east of Los Angeles. Including any residence halls, there are 138 buildings.

STUDENT LIFE: 91% of undergraduates are from California. Others are from 46 states, 29 foreign countries, and Canada. 90% are from public schools. 38% are White; 36% Hispanic; 8% African American; 6% two or more races; 5% Asian American; 4% race unknown; 2% Foreign; 1% American Indian/Alaska Native. 45% are Protestant; 32% Orthodox, Latter Day Saints, Buddhist, Jehovah Witness, Muslim, Islam, and Unknown; 11% Catholic. **Female To Male Ratio:** 1.9:1. The average age of freshmen is 18; all undergraduates, 23. 25% do not continue beyond their first year; 60% remain to graduate. **Housing:** 2865 students can be accommodated in college housing, which includes single-sex and coed dorms, on-campus apartments, and married student housing. In addition, there are special-interest houses, and Global Village for students interested in living with multicultural residents. On-campus housing is guaranteed for the freshman year only, and is available on a first-come, and first-served basis. 61% of students commute. Alcohol is not permitted. All students may keep cars.

FACULTY/CLASSROOMS: 51% of faculty are male; 49% are female. 95% teach undergraduates, 10% do research, and 10% do both. No introductory courses are taught by graduate students. The average class size in an introductory lecture is 21 and in a laboratory is 14.

PROGRAMS OF STUDY: CBU confers B.A., B.C.S., B.S., B.S.Ch.E., B.S.C.E., B.S.E.C.E., B.S.E., B.S.M.E., B.S.N., B.A.T., B.M., B.C.S., B.S.B.M.E., B.Sw.E., B.S.I.S.E. and B.F.A. degrees. Associate, master's, and doctoral degrees are also awarded. Bachelor's degrees are awarded in BIOLOGICAL SCIENCE (biochemistry, biology/biological science, and nutritional sciences), BUSINESS (accounting, business administration and management, entrepreneurial studies, leadership, marketing/retailing/merchandising, and organizational leadership and management), COMMUNICATIONS AND THE ARTS (communication studies, communications, creative writing, digital media, English, film arts, graphic design, information technology, journalism, journalism - news & information, music, music composition, music performance, performing arts, photography, piano/organ, piano performance, public relations, Spanish, theatre arts, visual and performing arts, vocal performance, and voice), COMPUTER AND PHYSICAL SCIENCE (actuarial science, chemistry, combined science, computer engineering technology, computer science, digital arts/technology, mathematics, software engineering, and statistics), EDUCATION (health education, mathematics education, and music education), ENGINEERING AND ENVIRONMENTAL DESIGN (applied aviation, architecture, aviation administration/management, aviation flight technology, bioengineering, biomedical engineering, chemical engineering, civil engineering, construction management, electrical and computer engineering, electrical/electronics engineering, engineering, environmental science, industrial engineering, mechanical engineering, preengineering, and systems engineering), HEALTH PROFESSIONS (communicative disorders, exercise science, health care administration, health science, kinesiology, nursing, prephysical therapy, and public health), SOCIAL SCIENCE (anthropology, behavioral science, Christian studies, communication sciences & disorders, criminal justice, early childhood studies, history, interdisciplinary studies, international studies, liberal arts/general studies, philosophy, political science/government, psychology, public administration, social science, sociology, theology, and world cultural studies). Engineering, nursing, business administration, psychology and education are the strongest academically. Business administration, nursing/pre-nursing, and psychology have the largest enrollments.

ACTIVITIES: There are no fraternities or sororities. There are 81 groups on campus, including art, band, cheerleading, choir, chorale, chorus, communications, computers, debate, drama, drill team, environmental, ethnic, film, forensics, honors, international, jazz band, literary magazine, musical theater, newspaper, orchestra, pep band, photography, political, professional, religious, social, social service, student government, symphony, and yearbook. Popular campus events include Lancer Cup soccer championship, Basketball Midnight Madness, Homecoming Block Party and Fortuna Bowl Flag Football, Yule Festival, Kugel Walk (symbol of Christ's Great Commission), and TWIRP Week-The Woman Is Required to Pay. **Sports:** There are 10 intercollegiate sports for men and 10 for women, and 6 intramural sports for men and 6 for women. Facilities include a gymnasium, recreation center with indoor basketball courts, racquetball courts, climbing wall, and rooftop running track and soccer field, aquatics center with Olympic-size pool, outdoor athletic complex with baseball, softball, and soccer fields, athletic performance center, athletic training clinic, tennis center, and sand volleyball courts. **Graduates:** From July 1, 2015 to June 30, 2016, 1335 bachelor's degrees were awarded. The most popular majors were business administration (14%), nursing (11%), and psychology (9%). 500 companies recruited on campus in 2015-2016. In an average class, 1% graduate in 3 years or less, 44% graduate in 4 years or less, 58% graduate in 5 years or less, and 60% graduate in 6 years or less.

SERVICES: Counseling and information services are available, as is tutoring in most subjects. There is remedial math, reading, and writing. **Library/Resources:** The library contains 329,030 volumes, 54,853 microform items, and 24,892 audio/video tapes/CDs/DVDs, and subscribes to 38,320 periodicals including electronic. Computerized library services include interlibrary loans, database searching, Internet access, and Wi-Fi capability. Special learning facilities include an art gallery, music production and recording studios, language lab, digital design and photography studio, architecture studios, theater arts stage production workshop, and Bourns engineering laboratories. **Physically Challenged Students:** 95% of the campus is accessible. Facilities include wheelchair ramps, elevators, special parking, specially equipped restrooms, and lowered drinking fountains. **Special:** California Baptist University offers accelerated programs in accounting, business administration, christian ministries, communication studies, computer information technology, criminal justice, early childhood studies, English, graphic design and digital media, kinesiology, liberal studies, marketing, nursing RN to BSN, organizational leadership, psychology, public administration, public health, public relations, and sociology. In addition, CBU offers Study abroad, internships, work-study programs, a Washington semester, double majors, and credit for military/work experience are available. There are 7 national honor societies, a freshman honors program, and 4 departmental honors programs. **Visiting:** There are regularly scheduled orientations for prospective students, a campus tour, academic fair, meet deans/professors, sit in on a class and chapel, spend the night in residence housing, and meet current students. There are guides for informal visits, visitors may sit in on classes, and stay overnight. To schedule a visit, contact Allen Johnson at (877) 228-8866. **Campus Safety and Security:** Measures include 24-hour foot and vehicle patrol, emergency notification system, self-defense education, and security escort services. There are shuttle buses, emergency telephones, lighted pathways/sidewalks, and controlled access to dorms/residences.

REQUIREMENTS: Applicants should be graduates of an accredited high school or have a GED. Official high school transcripts are required. Standard admission requires a minimum high school GPA of 2.5. and a composite score of 920 on the SAT Critical Reading and Math or 19 on the ACT Composite. Required academic units: 4 years of English, 3 years of mathematics, 2 years each of lab science, foreign language, social studies, and history. Additional recommended courses include 1 year of fine and performing arts; 1 year of psychology or sociology; and 1 year of religion. An essay and two letters of recommendation are required. One of the letters must be an academic reference (from teacher or professor). The second reference is a personal reference and can be completed by a pastor, co-worker or friend. We do not accept recommendations from family or university employees. A GPA of 2.5 is required. AP and CLEP credits are accepted. Important factors in the admissions decision are evidence of special talent, leadership record, and advanced placement or honors courses. Complete at least 124 semester units of credit, at least 39 or which are upper division courses. Complete at least 36 units in residence at CBU, at least 30 or which are upper division courses. Earn a cummulative grade point average of at least 2.0 overall with no grade below C- in the major field of study. Students must also complete competency requirements in English Composition, mathematics, technology coursework, and two semesters of the same foreign language, 3 units in Intermediate Composition, 4 units in Lab Science; 9 units in Biblical and Theological Core, 6 units in Natural World courses, 6 units in Social World courses, 6 units in Political World courses, and 6 units in Cultural World courses. **Procedure:** Freshmen are admitted fall, spring, and summer. Entrance exams should be taken during the junior year. There are deferred admissions and rolling admissions plans. Application deadlines are open. The fall 2016 application fee was $45. Notification of early decision is sent January 31; regular decision, Nov 9. Applications are accepted on-line. **Transfer Students:** 1384 transfer students enrolled in 2015-2016. Students who have completed 24 or more units from a regionally accredited college or university will be evaluated on the basis of their official college transcripts. Standard admission requires a minimum cumulative GPA of 2.0 for all college work. Only courses with a grade of C- or better may transfer. 36 of 124 credits required for the bachelor's degree must be completed at CBU. **International Students:** There are 137 international students enrolled. The school actively recruits these students. They must take the TOEFL with a minimum score of 527 on the paper-based TOEFL (PBT) or 71 on the Internet-based version (iBT). They must also take the SAT or ACT, scoring 920 SAT Rdg & Math; 21 ACT Composite.

ADMISSIONS: 64% of the 2016-2017 applicants were accepted. The SAT scores for the 2016-2017 freshman class were: Critical Reading-- 54% below 500, 32% between 500 and 599, 13% between 600 and 699, and 1% between 700 and 800. Math-- 55% below 500, 32% between 500 and 599, 12% between 600 and 699, and 1% between 700 and 800. Writing-- 57% below 500, 35% between 500 and 599, 7% between 600 and 699, and 1% between 700 and 800. The ACT scores were 16% between 12 and 17, 52% between 18 and 23, 29% between 24 and 29, and 3% above 30. **Admissions Contact:** Allen Johnson, Dean of Admissions. Email: *admissions@calbaptist.edu* Web: *www.calbaptist.edu*

FINANCIAL AID: In 2016-2017, 92% of all full-time freshmen and 89% of continuing full-time students received some form of financial aid. 83% of all full-time freshmen and 81% of continuing full-time students received need-based aid. The average freshman award was $29,792. Need-based scholarships or need-based grants averaged $10,328; need-based self-help aid (loans and jobs) averaged $3,850; non-need-based athletic scholarships averaged $23,262; and other non-need-based awards and non-need-based scholarships averaged $11,070. 15% of undergraduate students work part-time. Average annual earnings from campus work are $3900. The average financial indebtedness of the 2016 graduate was $23,018. The FAFSA code is 001125. The priority date for freshman financial aid applications for fall entry is March 2.

CALIFORNIA COLLEGE OF THE ARTS *(The complete profile is made available exclusively on our website, www.barronspac.com)*

CALIFORNIA INSTITUTE OF TECHNOLOGY C-5

www.caltech.edu

Pasadena, CA 91125	**(626) 395-6341**
Fax: (626) 683-3026	**Email:** ugadmissions@caltech.edu
Full-time: 625 men, 358 women	**Faculty:** I, ++$
Part-time: n/av	**Ph.D.s:** 97%
Graduate: 905 men, 321 women	**Student/Faculty:** 3 to 1
Year: quarters	**Tuition:** $45,390
Room & Board: $13,371	**Freshman Class:** 6525 applied, 576 accepted, 226 enrolled
SAT or ACT: required	**CEEB CODE:** 4034
Application Deadline: January 3	**MOST COMPETITIVE**

California Institute of Technology, founded in 1891, is a private institution offering programs in engineering, science, and math. The figures in the above capsule and in this profile are approximate. There are 2 undergraduate schools and 6 graduate schools. In addition to regional accreditation, Caltech has baccalaureate program accreditation with ABET and ACS. The 124-acre campus is in a suburban area 12 miles northeast of Los Angeles. Including any residence halls, there are 105 buildings.

STUDENT LIFE: 63% of undergraduates are from out of state, mostly the West. Students are from 46 states, 28 foreign countries, and Canada. 85% are from public schools. 40% are Asian American; 31% White; 2% African American; 11% Foreign; 10% Hispanic; 1% American Indian/Alaska Native. **Male To Female Ratio:** 2.3:1. The average age of freshmen is 18; all undergraduates, 20. 2% do not continue beyond their first year; 90% remain to graduate. **Housing:** 879 students can be accommodated in college housing, which includes coed dorms, on-campus apartments, off-campus apartments, and married student housing. On-campus housing is guaranteed for the freshman year only. 85% of students live on campus. Alcohol is not permitted. All students may keep cars.

FACULTY/CLASSROOMS: 82% of faculty are male; 18% are female. All teach undergraduates, and do research. No introductory courses are taught by graduate students. The average class size in an introductory lecture is 200 and in a regular course is 15.

PROGRAMS OF STUDY: Caltech confers B.S. degrees. Master's and doctoral degrees are also awarded. Bachelor's degrees are awarded in BIOLOGICAL SCIENCE (biology/biological science), BUSINESS (business administration and management), COMPUTER AND PHYSICAL SCIENCE (applied mathematics, astrophysics, chemistry, computer mathematics, computer science, geochemistry, geology, geophysics and seismology, mathematics, physics, and planetary and space science), ENGINEERING AND ENVIRONMENTAL DESIGN (chemical engineering, computer engineering, electrical/electronics engineering, engineering and applied science, materials science, and mechanical engineering), HEALTH PROFESSIONS (environmental health science), SOCIAL SCIENCE (economics, history, history of science, philosophy, and political science/government). Engineering, physical science, and computer science have the largest enrollments.

ACTIVITIES: There are no fraternities or sororities. There are 150 groups on campus, including art, band, cheerleading, chess, choir, chorale, chorus, computers, dance, drama, ethnic, film, honors, international, jazz band, LGBT, literary magazine, musical theater, newspaper, orchestra, pep band, photography, political, professional, religious, social, social service, student government, symphony, and yearbook. Popular campus events include Ditch Day, International Day, and Pre-Frosh Weekend. **Sports:** There are 9 intercollegiate sports for men and 8 for women, and 19 intramural sports for men and 15 for women. Facilities include 2 Olympic-size swimming pools, a gym, a track, a football field, 4 baseball fields, and 8 tennis courts. Another athletic facility includes a gym, exercise room with equipment, and racquetball courts. **Graduates:** From July 1, 2015 to June 30, 2016, 197 bachelor's degrees were awarded. The most popular majors were engineering (36%), physical sciences (22%), and computer and information sciences (18%). 85 companies recruited on campus in 2015-2016. In an average class, 82% graduate in 4 years or less and 89% graduate in 6 years or less. Of the 2015 graduating class, 55% were enrolled in graduate school within 6 months of graduation.

SERVICES: Counseling and information services are available, as is tutoring in every subject. There is a reader service for the blind. **Library/Resources:** The 7 libraries contain 624,136 volumes, 10,586 microform items, and 3,033 audio/video tapes/CDs/DVDs, and subscribe to 2,641 periodicals including electronic. Computerized library services include interlibrary loans, database searching, and Internet access. **Physically Challenged Students:** 98% of the campus is accessible. Facilities include wheelchair ramps, elevators, special parking, specially equipped restrooms, lowered telephones, and special housing. **Special:** Caltech offers cross-registration with Scripps College, Occidental College, and Art Center College of Design, as well as various work-study programs, including those with NASA's Jet Propulsion Laboratory, dual majors in any major, and independent studies degrees with faculty-approved student-designed majors. A 3-2 engineering degree is possible with several institutions. Pass/fail options are available for freshmen. A summer undergraduate research fellowship program is offered. Study abroad at University College in London, Cambridge University, and University of Copenhagen, in Denmark. **Visiting:** There are regularly scheduled orientations for prospective students, including a student-led campus tour followed by an information session. There are guides for informal visits and visitors may sit in on classes. To schedule a visit, contact the Undergaduate Admissions Office. **Campus Safety and Security:** Measures include 24-hour foot and vehicle patrol, emergency notification system, self-defense education, and security escort services. There are emergency telephones, lighted pathways/sidewalks, and controlled access to dorms/residences.

REQUIREMENTS: The SAT or ACT is required. SAT II: Subject tests in math level II and 1 in physics, biology, or chemistry are required. Applicants should have completed 4 years of high school math (including a year of calculus), 3 years of English, 1 year of chemistry, 1 year of physics, and 1 year of U.S. History or Government (waived for international students). Important factors in the admissions decision are advanced placement or honors courses, leadership record, personality/intangible qualities, extracurricular activities record, recommendations by school officials, parents or siblings attended your school, evidence of special talent, and geographical diversity. All grades are issued pass/fail. **Procedure:** Freshmen are admitted fall. Entrance exams should be taken through December of the senior year. There are early admissions and deferred admissions plans. Early decision applications should be filed by November 1; regular applications, by January 3 for fall entry, along with a $65 fee. Notification of early decision is sent December 15; regular decision, April 1. 482 applicants were on the 2016 waiting list; 47 were admitted. Applications are accepted on-line. **Transfer Students:** 3 transfer students enrolled in 2015-2016. Transfers, admitted only into sophomore and junior classes, need a minimum GPA of 3.0. Applicants must have completed 1 year (2 years for juniors) of calculus and calculus-based physics, and must take Caltech's entrance exams in math and physics. Chemistry or chemical engineering majors also should have completed 1 year of chemistry and must take an additional entrance exam. 216 of 780 credits required for the bachelor's degree must be completed at Caltech. **International Students:** There are 116 international students enrolled. The school actively recruits these students. They must also take the SAT or ACT.

ADMISSIONS: 100% of the current freshmen were in the top fifth of their class; 100% were in the top two fifths. **Admissions Contact:** Jarrid Whitney, Executive Director of Admissions and Financial Aid. Email: *ugadmissions@caltech.edu* Web: *www.caltech.edu*

FINANCIAL AID: In 2016-2017, 56% of all full-time freshmen and 54% of continuing full-time students received some form of financial aid. 56% of all full-time freshmen and 54% of continuing full-time students received need-based aid. The average freshman award was $41,669. Need-based scholarships or need-based grants averaged $37,557; need-based self-help aid (loans and jobs) averaged $5,964; and other non-need-based awards and non-need-based scholarships averaged $4,624. The average financial indebtedness of the 2016 graduate was $12,104. Caltech is a member of CSS. The CSS/Profile, the state aid form, the college's own financial statement, noncustodial profile, and business/farm supplement are required. The FAFSA code is 001131. The priority date for freshman financial aid applications for fall entry is March 2.

CALIFORNIA INSTITUTE OF THE ARTS *(The complete profile is made available exclusively on our website, www.barronspac.com)*

CALIFORNIA LUTHERAN UNIVERSITY C-5

www.callutheran.edu

Thousand Oaks, CA 91360 (805) 493-3049 (877) 258-3678

Fax: (805) 493-3645 **Email:** admissions@callutheran.edu

Full-time: 1189 men, 1579 women	**Faculty:** 144; IIA, +$
Part-time: 52 men, 72 women	**Ph.D.s:** 85%
Graduate: 496 men, 785 women	**Student/Faculty:** 14 to 1
Year: semesters, summer session	**Tuition:** $39,793
Room & Board: $13,060	**Freshman Class:** 6013 applied, 3860 accepted, 638 enrolled

SAT CR/M/W: 545/553/541 **ACT:** required

CEEB CODE: 4088

Application Deadline: January 1 **COMPETITIVE**

California Lutheran University is a diverse, scholarly community dedicated to excellence in the liberal arts and sciences and professional studies. Rooted in the Lutheran tradition of Christian faith, the University encourages critical inquiry into matters of both faith and reason. The mission of the University is to educate leaders for a global society who are strong in character and judgment, confident in their identity and vocation, and committed to service and justice. There are 2 undergraduate schools and 4 graduate schools. In addition to regional accreditation, Cal Lutheran has baccalaureate program accreditation with WSCUC. The 225-acre campus is in a suburban area 45 miles north of downtown Los Angeles in Ventura County, and 50 miles south of Santa Barbara. Including any residence halls, there are 53 buildings.

STUDENT LIFE: 84% of undergraduates are from California. Others are from 34 states, 45 foreign countries, and Canada. 75% are from public schools. 48% are White; 28% Hispanic; 8% two or more races; 5% Asian American; 4% Foreign; 3% African American; 3% race unknown; 1% American Indian/Alaska Native. 40% claim no religious affiliation; 22% Catholic; 20% Protestant. **Female To Male Ratio:** 1.4:1. The average age of freshmen is 18; all undergraduates, 22. 15% do not continue beyond their first year; 85% remain to graduate. **Housing:** 1448 students can be accommodated in college housing, which includes coed dorms and on-campus apartments. On-campus housing is guaranteed for all 4 years. 52% of students live on campus; of those, 60% remain on campus on weekends. Alcohol is not permitted. All students may keep cars.

FACULTY/CLASSROOMS: 51% of faculty are male; 49% are female. 67% teach undergraduates. No introductory courses are taught by graduate students.

PROGRAMS OF STUDY: Cal Lutheran confers B.A., and B.S. degrees. Master's and doctoral degrees are also awarded. Bachelor's degrees are awarded in AGRICULTURE (environmental studies), BIOLOGICAL SCIENCE (biochemistry and biology/biological science), BUSINESS (accounting and business administration and management), COMMUNICATIONS AND THE ARTS (art, communications, English, French, German, multimedia, music, music production/recording technology, music performance, Spanish, and theatre arts), COMPUTER AND PHYSICAL SCIENCE (chemistry, computer science, geology, information sciences and systems, mathematics, and physics), HEALTH PROFESSIONS (exercise science, predentistry, and premedicine), SOCIAL SCIENCE (criminal justice, economics, history, interdisciplinary studies, international studies, liberal arts/general studies, philosophy, political science/government, prelaw, psychology, religion, social science, sociology, and theological studies). Biology, accounting, and exercise science are the strongest academically. Business, psychology, and exercise science have the largest enrollments.

ACTIVITIES: There are no fraternities or sororities. There are 80 groups on campus, including Model United Nations, art, band, cheerleading, choir, chorale, chorus, computers, dance, debate, drama, environmental, ethnic, film, forensics, honors, international, jazz band, LGBT, literary magazine, musical theater, newspaper, orchestra, pep band, photography, political, professional, radio and TV, religious, social, social service, student alumni, student government, and symphony. Popular campus events include Santa Lucia, Scandinavian Festival, Chinese New Year, World Fair and Service Day. **Sports:** There are 11 intercollegiate sports for men and 10 for women, and 11 intramural sports for men and 11 for women. Facilities include a sports and fitness center, an arena for home basketball and volleyball games, dance studio, training room and the Cal Lutheran Athletic Hall of Fame, football and soccer teams, a 50-meter pool and diving, cross-country, golf, softball, volleyball, track and field, and water polo. **Graduates:** From July 1, 2015 to June 30, 2016, 817 bachelor's degrees were awarded. The most popular majors were business (22%), communication (15%), and psychology (12%). 146 companies recruited on campus in 2015-2016. In an average class, 2% graduate in 3 years or less, 67% graduate in 4 years or less, 73% graduate in 5 years or less, and 73% graduate in 6 years or less. Of the 2015 graduating class, 29% were enrolled in graduate school within 6 months of graduation, and 60% were employed.

SERVICES: Counseling and information services are available, as is tutoring in every subject. The learning resources and writing centers offer help with study and writing skills. There is a reader service for the blind, and remedial math, reading, and writing. A student support services program helps low-income first-generation students adapt to the academic and social life of the campus. We have a coordinator for students with disabilities. **Library/Resources:** The library contains 334,453 volumes, 22,000 microform items, and 2,957 audio/video tapes/CDs/DVDs, and subscribes to 80 periodicals including electronic. Computerized library services include interlibrary loans, database searching, Internet access, and Wi-Fi capability. Special learning facilities include an art gallery, radio station, TV station, a human performance lab, and SEEd project garden. **Physically Challenged Students:** 95% of the campus is accessible. Facilities include wheelchair ramps, elevators, special parking, specially equipped restrooms, lowered drinking fountains, lowered telephones, and special housing. **Special:** Cal Lutheran offers co-op programs, internships, a Washington semester, and study abroad in over 80 countries. Also available are work-study and student-designed interdisciplinary degree majors, redit for experiential learning, special student status for non degree study, pass/fail options and continuing education. A bachelor's degree for professionals program offers accelerated degrees in accounting, business, computer science, communication, liberal studies, organizational leadership and psychology. There are 9 national honor societies and a freshman honors program. **Visiting:** There are regularly scheduled orientations for prospective students, including an admission and financial aid interview, a tour, visits with faculty or coaches, and lunch. There are guides for informal visits, visitors may sit in on classes, and stay overnight. To schedule a visit, contact the Presidential Host Coordinators at prehost@callutheran.edu. **Campus Safety and Security:** Measures include 24-hour foot and vehicle patrol, emergency notification system, self-defense education, and security escort services. There are emergency telephones, lighted pathways/sidewalks, controlled access to dorms/residences, All residence halls are equipped with security systems.

REQUIREMENTS: The SAT or ACT is required. Applicants must be graduates of an accredited secondary school and have completed a minimum of four years of English, two years of math, and two years each of foreign language, social studies, and lab science. The GED is accepted. An essay is required and an interview is recommended. AP and CLEP credits are accepted. Important factors in the admissions decision are advanced placement or honors courses, recommendations by school officials, and evidence of special talent. To graduate, all students must complete a core curriculum including 16 to 20 units in social science, 8 each in religion, foreign language, and science, 7 in English, 4 to 6 in creative arts, 4 in math, and 1 in phys ed. Students must also fulfill content requirements of a freshman cluster and take one course of each: writing-intensive, speaking intensive, global studies, U.S diversity, and senior level capstone. Also needed are a total of 124 units, 40 of which must be upper division with 32 hours in the major for a B.A. and a minimum of 36 hours for a B.S. The final 30 credits before graduation must be completed at Cal Lutheran. Students must have a minimum 2.0 GPA. **Procedure:** Freshmen are admitted fall and spring. Entrance exams should be taken during spring of junior year, or early fall of senior year. There is an early admissions plan. Early decision applications should be filed by November 1; regular applications, by January 1 for fall entry; and October 1 for spring entry, along with a $25 fee. Notification of early decision is sent January 15; regular decision, on a Rolling basis. 328 applicants were on the 2016 waiting list; 41 were admitted. Applications are accepted on-line. **Transfer Students:** 270 transfer students enrolled in 2015-2016. Transfers should have at least a 2.75 transferable GPA and 28 transferable units. An application is required. An interview is recommended. Applicants must be in good standing at the previous college and may submit a recommendation from a college professor in lieu of a high school recommendation. 30 of 124 credits required for the bachelor's degree must be completed at Cal Lutheran. **International Students:** There are 97 international students enrolled. The school actively recruits these students. They must take the TOEFL with a minimum score of 550 on the paper-based TOEFL (PBT) or 79 on the Internet-based version (iBT). They must also take the SAT or ACT.

ADMISSIONS: 64% of the 2016-2017 applicants were accepted. The SAT scores for the 2016-2017 freshman class were: Critical Reading-- 25% below 500, 51% between 500 and 599, 22% between 600 and 699, and 2% between 700 and 800. Math-- 22% below 500, 48% between 500 and 599, 27% between 600 and 699, and 3% between 700 and 800. Writing-- 26% below 500, 51% between 500 and 599, 23% between 600 and 699, and 1% between 700 and 800. The ACT scores were 1% between 12 and 17, 37% between 18 and 23, 52% between 24 and 29, and 9% above 30. 68% of the current freshmen were in the top fifth of their class; 93% were in the top two fifths. 4 freshmen graduated first in their class. **Admissions Contact:** Michael Elgarico, Director of Undergraduate Admissions. Email: *admissions@callutheran.edu* Web: *www.callutheran.edu*

FINANCIAL AID: In 2016-2017, 97% of all full-time freshmen and 95% of continuing full-time students received some form of financial aid. 75% of all full-time freshmen and 59% of continuing full-time students received need-based aid. The average freshman award was $32,490. Need-based scholarships or need-based grants averaged $29,830 ($57,800 maximum); need-based self-help aid (loans and jobs) averaged $6,900 ($14,500 maximum); and other non-need-based awards and non-need-based scholarships averaged $20,530 ($50,500 maximum). 26% of undergraduate students work part-time. Average annual earnings from campus work are $2500. The average financial indebtedness of the 2016 graduate was $20,000. The FAFSA code is 001133. The priority date for freshman financial aid applications for fall entry is March 1.

CALIFORNIA POLYTECHNIC STATE UNIVERSITY — B-4

www.calpoly.edu

San Luis Obispo, CA 93407 — **(805) 756-2311**

Fax: (805) 756-5400
Full-time: 10,301 men, 9349 women
Part-time: 482 men, 235 women
Graduate: 426 men, 454 women
Year: quarters, summer session
Room & Board: $12,507

SAT CR/M: 610/645 **ACT:** 29
Application Deadline: November 30

Email: admissions@calpoly.edu
Faculty: 328; IIA, +$
Ph.D.s: n/av
Student/Faculty: 19 to 1
Tuition: $9075 ($20,235)
Freshman Class: 48162 applied, 14202 accepted, 4341 enrolled
CEEB CODE: 4038
HIGHLY COMPETITIVE+

California Polytechnic State University, founded in 1901, is a public institution that is part of the California State University system. It offers programs in agriculture, architecture and environmental design, business, education, engineering, liberal arts, sciences, math, and preprofessional studies. There are 6 undergraduate schools. In addition to regional accreditation, Cal Poly has baccalaureate program accreditation with AACSB, ABET, ACCE, ASLA, NAAB, NASAD, NASM, NRPA, SAF, ACEND, CAC, CCTC, COAPRT, ACCGC, AAPAR, ATMAE, EAC, LAAB, and PAB (AICP). The 6000-acre campus is in a suburban area 200 miles north of Los Angeles, and 230 miles south of San Francisco. Including any residence halls, there are 125 buildings.

STUDENT LIFE: 86% of undergraduates are from California. 7% are two or more races; 57% White; 2% race unknown; 16% Hispanic; 13% Asian American. **Male To Female Ratio:** 1.1:1. The average age of freshmen is 18; all undergraduates, 20. 7% do not continue beyond their first year. **Housing:** 6239 students can be accommodated in college housing, which includes single-sex and coed dorms, on-campus apartments, and off-campus apartments. In addition, there are honors houses, special-interest houses, apartments for single students, international students, theme housing, and gender inclusive housing. On-campus housing is available on a first-come, first-served basis, and on a lottery system for upperclassmen. 64% of students commute. All students may keep cars. Alcohol is not permitted.

FACULTY/CLASSROOMS: No introductory courses are taught by graduate students.

PROGRAMS OF STUDY: Cal Poly confers B.A., B.S., B.Arch., B.F.A. and B.L.A. degrees. Master's degrees are also awarded. Bachelor's degrees are awarded in AGRICULTURE (agricultural business management, agricultural communications, agricultural mechanics, agricultural sciences, agronomy, animal science, dairy science, forestry and related sciences, natural resource management, soil science, and wine and viticulture), BIOLOGICAL SCIENCE (biochemistry, biology/biological science, microbiology, and nutrition), BUSINESS (business administration and management and recreation and leisure services), COMMUNICATIONS AND THE ARTS (art and design, communication studies, English, graphic communications, journalism, modern language, music, and theatre arts), COMPUTER AND PHYSICAL SCIENCE (chemistry, computer science, earth science, industrial technology, mathematics, physics, software engineering, and statistics), EDUCATION (agricultural education and education), ENGINEERING AND ENVIRONMENTAL DESIGN (aeronautical engineering, architectural engineering, architecture, biomedical engineering, bioresource engineering, city/community/regional planning, civil engineering, computer engineering, construction management, electrical/electronics engineering, engineering science, environmental engineering, environmental science, industrial engineering, landscape architecture, manufacturing engineering, materials engineering, mechanical engineering, and transportation engineering), HEALTH PROFESSIONS (kinesiology), SOCIAL SCIENCE (anthropology, child psychology/development, economics, ethnic studies, food science, history, interdisciplinary studies, liberal arts/general studies, liberal arts/engineering studies, philosophy, political science/government, psychology, and sociology).

ACTIVITIES: Groups on campus include art, band, cheerleading, chess, choir, chorale, chorus, computers, dance, debate, drama, environmental, ethnic, film, honors, international, jazz band, LGBT, literary magazine, marching band, musical theater, newspaper, opera, orchestra, pep band, photography, political, professional, radio and TV, religious, social, social service, student government, symphony, and various engineering clubs. Popular campus events include Rose Float, Open House, Week of Welcome, and SOAR. **Sports:** There are 10 intercollegiate sports for men and 10 for women, and 7 intramural sports for men and 7 for women. Facilities include outdoor track, outdoor swimming pools, sand volleyball, tennis, basketball and racquetball courts, weight rooms, cardio exercise rooms, martial arts room, synthetic & natural turf playing fields, baseball stadium, softball stadium, and a football/soccer stadium. **Graduates:** From July 1, 2015 to June 30, 2016, 4147 bachelor's degrees were awarded. The most popular majors were engineering (27%), agriculture (13%), and busiess/marketing (12%). In an average class, 79% graduate in 6 years or less.

SERVICES: Counseling and information services are available, as is tutoring in most subjects. There is a reader service for the blind. Writing skills lab, psychological and career services are also available. **Library/Resources:** The library contains 795,216 volumes, 1.8 million microform items, 3,000 audio/video tapes/CDs/DVDs, and subscribes to 60,000 periodicals including electronic. Computerized library services include interlibrary loans, database searching, Internet access, and Wi-Fi capability. Special learning facilities include an art gallery, radio station, and TV station. **Physically Challenged Students:** 80% of the campus is accessible. Facilities include wheelchair ramps, elevators, special parking, specially equipped restrooms, special class scheduling, lowered drinking fountains, lowered telephones, and special housing. **Special:** Cal Poly offers work-study programs, co-op programs in numerous majors, study abroad, and dual majors. Credit for military experience and pass/fail options are available. There is also a freshman honors program. **Visiting:** There are regularly scheduled orientations for prospective students, campus tours are offered Monday through Friday. There are guides for informal visits. To schedule a visit, contact the Admissions Office. **Campus Safety and Security:** Measures include 24-hour foot and vehicle patrol, emergency notification system, self-defense education, and security escort services. There are emergency telephones, lighted pathways/sidewalks, and controlled access to dorms/residences.

REQUIREMENTS: The SAT or ACT is required. Applicants must be graduates of an accredited high school or have a GED. Required are 15 academic credits, (units recommended 21-23) including 4-5 years of English, 3 units of math, (recommended 4-5), 2 of science (2 lab), (recommended 4 with 2 lab), 2 of foreign language, (recommended 4), and 1 each of social studies, history, and 1 unit of visual and performing arts, (recommended 2), and 1 unit of academic electives. AP and CLEP credits are accepted. Students must have a minimum 2.0 GPA, 72 quarter units of general education, a minimum of 180 total units, a United States Cultural Pluralism course, completion of the Graduation Writing Requirement, a minimum of 50 units in residence and a senior project are required. **Procedure:** Freshmen are admitted in the fall. Entrance exams should be taken mid-June every year. There are early decision and early admissions plans. Early decision applications should be filed by October 31; regular applications, by November 30 for fall entry, along with a $55 fee. Notification of early decision is sent December 15. 1343 early decision candidates were accepted for the 2016-2017 class. 1011 applicants were on the 2016 waiting list; 675 were admitted. Applications are accepted online. **Transfer Students:** 779 transfer students enrolled in 2015-2016. Applicants must meet general education and breadth requirements and submit college transcripts with a minimum GPA of 2.0. Students may enroll in the fall. 50 credits required for the bachelor's degree must be completed at Cal Poly. **International Students:** There are 211 international students enrolled. The school actively recruits these students. They must take the TOEFL with a minimum score of 550 on the paper-based TOEFL (PBT) or 80 on the Internet-based version (iBT). Student must also take the IELTS.

ADMISSIONS: 29% of the 2016-2017 applicants were accepted. The SAT scores for the 2016-2017 freshman class were: Critical Reading-- 6% below 500, 36% between 500 and 599, 44% between 600 and 699, and 14% between 700 and 800. Math-- 1% below 500, 27% between 500 and 599, 46% between 600 and 699, and 25% between 700 and 800. 83% of the current freshmen were in the top fifth of their class; 98% were in the top two fifths. **Admissions Contact:** Mauricio Saavedra, Executive Director of Institutional Research. Email: *admissions@calpoly.edu* Web: *www.calpoly.edu*

FINANCIAL AID: The average freshman award was $9,585. Need-based scholarships or need-based grants averaged $3,287; need-based self-help aid (loans and jobs) averaged $3,106; non-need-based athletic scholarships averaged $3,241; other non-need-based awards and non-need-based scholarships averaged $3,291; and $2,303 from other forms of aid. The average financial indebtedness of the 2016 graduate was $22,413. The priority date for freshman financial aid applications for fall entry is March 15.

CALIFORNIA STATE POLYTECHNIC UNIVERSITY, POMONA D-5

www.cpp.edu

Pomona, CA 91768 **(909) 869-5299**

Fax: (909) 869-4529
Full-time: 11,458 men, 9690 women
Part-time: 1580 men, 1003 women
Graduate: 781 men, 814 women
Year: quarters, summer session
Room & Board: $14,514

SAT CR/M: 500/530 **ACT:** 23
Application Deadline: November 1

Email: admissions@cpp.edu
Faculty: IIA, +$
Ph.D.s: 80%
Student/Faculty: 23 to 1
Tuition: $7027 ($18,187)
Freshman Class: 32920 applied, 19474 accepted, 4204 enrolled
CEEB CODE: 4082
COMPETITIVE

California State Polytechnic University, Pomona, an occupationally oriented institution founded in 1938, is part of the state-supported university system. It offers undergraduate and graduate programs in agriculture, liberal arts and sciences, business, engineering, and technical and professional training. There are 8 undergraduate schools and 7 graduate schools. In addition to regional accreditation, Cal Poly Pomona has baccalaureate program accreditation with AACSB, ABET, ADA, ASLA, CSAB, and NAAB. The 1438-acre campus is in a suburban area 30 miles east of Los Angeles. Including any residence halls, there are 80 buildings.

STUDENT LIFE: 97% of undergraduates are from California. Others are from 35 states, 62 foreign countries, and Canada. 90% are from public schools. 6% are Foreign; 41% Hispanic; 4% two or more races; 4% race unknown; 3% African American; 23% Asian American; 18% White. **Male To Female Ratio:** 1.2:1. The average age of freshmen is 18; all undergraduates, 22. 11% do not continue beyond their first year; 63% remain to graduate. **Housing:** 2400 students can be accommodated in college housing, which includes coed dorms and on-campus apartments. In addition, there are honors houses, special-interest houses, and a center for regenerative studies. On-campus housing is available on a first-come and first-served basis. 90% of students commute. All students may keep cars.

FACULTY/CLASSROOMS: 59% of faculty are male; 41% are female. No introductory courses are taught by graduate students. The average class size in an introductory lecture is 37; in a laboratory is 33; and in a regular course is 35.

PROGRAMS OF STUDY: Cal Poly Pomona confers B.A., B.S., BArch., and B.F.A. degrees. Master's and doctoral degrees are also awarded. Bachelor's degrees are awarded in AGRICULTURE (agricultural business management, agricultural sciences, animal science, and plant science), BIOLOGICAL SCIENCE (biology/biological science, biotechnology, botany, environmental biology, microbiology, and zoology), BUSINESS (accounting, apparel and accessories marketing, business administration and management, business administration, management operations, business administration marketing, hotel/motel and restaurant management, human resources/organizational management, international business management, and real estate finance), COMMUNICATIONS AND THE ARTS (art history and appreciation, communications, English, graphic design, music, Spanish, and theatre arts), COMPUTER AND PHYSICAL SCIENCE (chemistry, computer information systems, computer science, geology, mathematics, and physics), ENGINEERING AND ENVIRONMENTAL DESIGN (aerospace engineering, architecture, chemical engineering, civil engineering, computer engineering, construction engineering, electrical and computer engineering, electrical/electronics engineering, engineering technology, industrial engineering, landscape architecture/design, manufacturing engineering, mechanical engineering, and urban planning technology), HEALTH PROFESSIONS (nutrition and dietetics), SOCIAL SCIENCE (anthropology, economics, food science, gender studies, geography, history, liberal arts/general studies, philosophy, physical fitness/movement, political science/government, psychology, sociology, and urban studies). Engineering, architecture, agriculture, and business administration are the strongest academically. Hospitality management, mechanical engineering, and civil engineering have the largest enrollments.

ACTIVITIES: 2% of men belong to 10 national fraternities; 1% of women belong to 5 national sororities. There are 551 groups on campus, including art, band, cheerleading, choir, chorale, chorus, communications, computers, dance, drama, ethnic, film, honors, international, jazz band, LGBT, literary magazine, musical theater, newspaper, opera, orchestra, pep band, photography, political, professional, religious, Rose Float Club, social, social service, student government, and symphony. Popular campus events include BroncoFusion, Hot Dog Caper, Pumpkin Festival, Unity Luncheon, Homecoming and Commencement. **Sports:** There are 5 intercollegiate sports for men and 5 for women. Facilities include a 5000-seat stadium, tennis and racquetball courts, basketball and volleyball courts, soccer, baseball, and softball fields, a track, swimming pool, gymnastics and weight rooms, a horse arena, and dance studios. Bronco Recreation and Intramural Complex (BRIC) rock wall, fitness studios, basketball courts, MAC, racquetball courts, running track, lap pool, cardio and strength equipment. **Graduates:** From July 1, 2015 to June 30, 2016, 4830 bachelor's degrees were awarded. The most popular majors were hospitality management (8%), management & human resources (6%), and accounting (5%). 840 companies recruited on campus in 2015-2016. In an average class, 18% graduate in 4 years or less, 53% graduate in 5 years or less, and 69% graduate in 6 years or less.

SERVICES: Counseling and information services are available, as is tutoring in most subjects. There is a reader service for the blind, and remedial math and writing. **Library/Resources:** The library contains 855,565 volumes, 1.4 million microform items, and 11,390 audio/video tapes/CDs/DVDs, and subscribes to 89,315 periodicals including electronic. Computerized library services include interlibrary loans, database searching, Internet access, and Wi-Fi capability. Special learning facilities include an art gallery, an interactive TV studio, Arabian Horse Center and Equine Research Facility, BioTrek Project (featuring the Rainforest Learning Center, Ethnobotany Gardening Learning Center, Aquatic Biology Learning Center, Mesozoic Garden and Learning Center, and Cal Poly Wildlands), Restaurant at Kellogg Ranch, AGRIscapes Agricultural Outreach Center, and the Lyle Center for Regenerative Studies. **Physically Challenged Students:** 96% of the campus is accessible. Facilities include wheelchair ramps, elevators, special parking, specially equipped restrooms, special class scheduling, lowered drinking fountains, lowered telephones. There is avaliable a specialized tram, van and shuttle transportation. **Special:** Cross-registration is possible with any California State University school. Internships and co-op programs are available in agriculture, business, environmental design, engineering, science, political science, behavioral science, and phys ed. An international study program in 17 countries, work-study programs, B.A.-B.S. degrees, a liberal studies degree, credit for military experience, an external degree program, and credit/no credit options are offered. Nondegree study is possible. There are 24 national honor societies and a freshman honors program. **Visiting:** There are regularly scheduled orientations for prospective students, consisting of tours of the campus led by current undergraduate students and a 90-minute walking tour. There are guides for informal visits, visitors may sit in on classes, and stay overnight. To schedule a visit, contact Campus Tours at (909) 869-3529. **Campus Safety and Security:** Measures include 24-hour foot and vehicle patrol, emergency notification system, self-defense education, and security escort services. There are shuttle buses, emergency telephones, lighted pathways/sidewalks, vehicle assists, and crime prevention programs.

REQUIREMENTS: The SAT or ACT is recommended. Applicants must be graduates of an accredited secondary school or have a GED equivalent. Secondary school courses must include 4 years of high school English, 3 each of math and electives, 2 of foreign language, and 1 each of science, history, and art. A GPA of 2.0 is required. AP and CLEP credits are accepted. All students must complete general education requirements, including courses in written and oral communications, critical thinking, math, humanities, natural sciences, and social sciences, and must pass a graduation writing test. A total of 180 (B.A.) to 246 (B.S.) quarter units with a minimum GPA of 2.0 is required to graduate. **Procedure:** Freshmen are admitted fall. Entrance exams should be taken during the fall of the senior year. There is a rolling admissions plan. Applications should be filed by November 1 for fall entry; June 1 for winter entry; August 1 for spring entry; and February 1 for summer entry, along with a $55 fee. Notification is sent on a rolling basis. Applications are accepted on-line. **Transfer Students:** 2328 transfer students enrolled in 2015-2016. Applicants must have completed 56 semester or 90 quarter units including college preparatory subjects. A 2.0 GPA (2.4 for nonresidents) is required. 50 of 180 credits required for the bachelor's degree must be completed at Cal Poly Pomona. **International Students:** There are 1210 international students enrolled. They must take the TOEFL with a minimum score of 525 on the paper-based TOEFL (PBT) or 70 on the Internet-based version (iBT). They must also take the SAT or ACT.

ADMISSIONS: 59% of the 2016-2017 applicants were accepted. The SAT scores for the 2016-2017 freshman class were: Critical Reading--49% below 500, 35% between 500 and 599, 14% between 600 and 699, and 2% between 700 and 800. Math-- 37% below 500, 36% between 500 and 599, 22% between 600 and 699, and 5% between 700 and 800. The ACT scores were 10% between 12 and 17, 40% between 18 and 23, 40% between 24 and 29, and 10% above 30. **Admissions Contact:** Andrew M. Wright, Director of Admissions. Email: *admissions@cpp.edu* Web: *www.cpp.edu*

FINANCIAL AID: In 2016-2017, 57% of all full-time freshmen and 60% of continuing full-time students received some form of financial aid. 49% of all full-time freshmen and 50% of continuing full-time students received need-based aid. The average freshman award was $9,943. Need-based scholarships or need-based grants averaged $9,413; need-based self-help aid (loans and jobs) averaged $3,557; non-need-based athletic scholarships averaged $1,000; and other non-need-based awards and non-need-based scholarships averaged $1,194. Average annual earnings from campus work are $2000. The average financial indebtedness of the 2016 graduate was $22,235. The deadline for filing freshman financial aid applications for fall entry is March 2.

CALIFORNIA STATE UNIVERSITY, MARITIME ACADEMY *(The complete profile is made available exclusively on our website, www.barronspac.com)*

CALIFORNIA STATE UNIVERSITY, BAKERSFIELD *(The complete profile is made available exclusively on our website, www.barronspac.com)*

CALIFORNIA STATE UNIVERSITY, CHICO B-2

www.csuchico.edu

Chico, CA 95929 (530) 898-4428 (800) 542-4426
Fax: (530) 898-6456 **Email:** info@csuchico.edu

Full-time: 5494 men, 5942 women
Part-time: 536 men, 526 women
Graduate: 184 men, 315 women
Year: semesters, summer session
Room & Board: $12,824
SAT CR/M: 495/500 **ACT:** 21
Application Deadline: November 30

Faculty: 496; IIA, av$
Ph.D.s: 84%
Student/Faculty: 23 to 1
Tuition: $8616 ($10,481)
Freshman Class: 23124 applied, 15393 accepted, 2313 enrolled
CEEB CODE: 4048
COMPETITIVE

California State University, Chico, founded in 1887, is a public institution offering undergraduate programs in behavioral and social sciences, business, communication and education, engineering, computer science and technology, humanities and fine arts, natural sciences, agriculture, and nursing. The university also offers web-based classes. There are 7 undergraduate schools and 1 graduate school. In addition to regional accreditation, Chico State has baccalaureate program accreditation with AACSB, ABET, ACCE, ACEJMC, ADA, CSAB, CSWE, NASAD, NASM, NRPA, AAAHC, AACN, NASP, COAPRT, ACS, ASHA, ATMAE, AUPHA, and NASPAA. The 130-acre campus is in a small town 90 miles north of Sacramento, and 174 miles northeast of San Francisco. Including any residence halls, there are 65 buildings.

STUDENT LIFE: 96% of undergraduates are from California. Others are from 35 states, 43 foreign countries, and Canada. 91% are from public schools. 44% are White; 30% Hispanic; 6% Asian American; 5% two or more races; 4% Foreign; 4% race unknown; 2% African American; 1% American Indian/Alaska Native. **Female To Male Ratio:** 1.1:1. The average age of freshmen is 18; all undergraduates, 24. 15% do not continue beyond their first year; 85% remain to graduate. **Housing:** 2222 students can be accommodated in college housing, which includes coed dorms, on-campus apartments, and off-campus apartments. In addition, there are honors houses, language houses, special-interest houses, fraternity houses, sorority houses, thematic housing for minorities in engineering and science, math, and business. Theme floors include community service, recreational sports, leadership, adventure outings, and sustainability. On-campus housing is available on a first-come and first-served basis. 99% of students commute. Alcohol is not permitted. All students may keep cars.

FACULTY/CLASSROOMS: 50% of faculty are male; 50% are female. 97% teach undergraduates, and 21% do research. No introductory courses are taught by graduate students. The average class size in an introductory lecture is 30; in a laboratory is 21; and in a regular course is 22.

PROGRAMS OF STUDY: Chico State confers B.A., B.S. and B.F.A. degrees. Master's degrees are also awarded. Bachelor's degrees are awarded in AGRICULTURE (agricultural business management, agriculture, and animal science), BIOLOGICAL SCIENCE (biochemistry, biology/biological science, and microbiology), BUSINESS (business administration and management and small business management), COMMUNICATIONS AND THE ARTS (art, communication design , communications, English, fine arts, German, graphic design, journalism, music, music industry, musical theater, Spanish, and theatre arts), COMPUTER AND PHYSICAL SCIENCE (chemistry, computer information systems, computer science, geology, mathematics, natural sciences, and physics), EDUCATION (art education and Asian studies), ENGINEERING AND ENVIRONMENTAL DESIGN (civil engineering, computer engineering, computer graphics, construction management, electrical/electronics engineering, environmental science, mechanical engineering, and mechatronics engineering), HEALTH PROFESSIONS (health care administration, health science, and nursing), SOCIAL SCIENCE (anthropology, child psychology/development, communication sciences & disorders, criminal justice, dietetics, economics, French studies, gender studies, geography, history, humanities, international relations, Latin American studies, liberal arts/general studies, philosophy, political science/government, psychology, public administration, religious studies, social science, social work, sociology, and women & gender studies). Business administration, nursing, and psychology are the strongest academically. Business administration, psychology, and pre-nursing have the largest enrollments.

ACTIVITIES: 2% of men belong to 3 local and 11 national fraternities; 5% of women belong to 1 local and 11 national sororities. There are 240 groups on campus, including art, band, cheerleading, choir, chorale, chorus, computers, dance, debate, drama, environmental, ethnic, film, forensics, honors, international, jazz band, LGBT, literary magazine, musical theater, newspaper, opera, orchestra, pep band, political, professional, radio and TV, religious, social, social service, student government, symphony, and yearbook. Popular campus events include Cesar Chavez Day Cats in the community clean-up, Wildcat Welcome, Up 'Til Dawn, and St. Jude Hospital Fund-raiser. **Sports:** There are 6 intercollegiate sports for men and 7 for women, and 8 intramural sports for men and 8 for women. Facilities include 2 gyms, athletic training rooms, a dance studio, swimming and diving pools, a par course, putting greens and sand trap, handball/racquetball courts, baseball/softball fields, an all-weather track, a soccer stadium, 7500-seat athletic stadium, a residence hall sports center. A recreation center includes a climbing wall, pool, fitness and weight rooms, a concert/events facility, and a computer lab. **Graduates:** From July 1, 2015 to June 30, 2016, 3415 bachelor's degrees were awarded. The most popular majors were business administration (16%), psychology (7%), and liberal studies (5%). 494 companies recruited on campus in 2015-2016. In an average class, 24% graduate in 4 years or less, 53% graduate in 5 years or less, and 59% graduate in 6 years or less.

SERVICES: Counseling and information services are available, as is tutoring in most subjects, such as accounting, anthropology, Arabic, business administration, biology, chemistry, economics, finance, French, German, history, Italian, Japanese, math, management information systems, music, philosophy, physics, political science, and psychology. There is a reader service for the blind, and remedial math and writing. A student learning center offers a tutorial program, study skills development, learning assistance workshops, and writing resources. **Library/Resources:** The library contains 924,281 volumes, 1.2 million microform items, and 23,725 audio/video tapes/CDs/DVDs, and subscribes to 600 periodicals including electronic. Computerized library services include interlibrary loans, database searching, and Internet access. Special learning facilities include an art gallery, planetarium, radio station, instructional media center, university farm, biological field station, anthropology museum, media preparation lab, computer graphics lab, recording arts studio, writing center, distributed learning technologies, Gateway science museum, and a Wildcat Recreation Center. **Physically Challenged Students:** 95% of the campus is accessible. Facilities include wheelchair ramps, elevators, special parking, specially equipped restrooms, special class scheduling, lowered drinking fountains, lowered telephones, and special housing. **Special:** The university offers co-op programs and cross-registration as part of the National Student Exchange. In addition, internships, distance learning, teacher certification, study abroad in 32 countries, work-study, student-designed majors, independent study, credit for experience, non-degree study, and pass/fail options are available. Chico State has a nationally recognized sustainability program and an established Institute for Sustainable Development. There are 16 national honor societies, Phi Beta Kappa, a freshman honors program, and 40 departmental honors programs. **Visiting:** There are regularly scheduled orientations for prospective students, consisting of a 1-hour tour given at 11:30 a.m. Monday through Saturday. There are guides for informal visits and visitors may sit in on classes. To schedule a visit, contact the Office of Admissions. **Campus Safety and Security:** Measures include 24-hour foot and vehicle patrol, emergency notification system, self-defense education, and security escort services. There are shuttle buses, emergency telephones, lighted pathways/sidewalks, controlled access to dorms/residences, a freshman safe start program, a victim awareness program, and crime prevention workshops.

REQUIREMENTS: An index combining GPA and SAT and ACT scores is used to determine eligibility for admission. Applicants must be graduates of a secondary school or have a GED and completed 4 years of English, 3 years of math, 2 years of lab sciences (1 physical and 1 life), 2 years of the same foreign language, 2 years of social science, 1 year of a visual or performing art course, and 1 year of electives. A GPA of 2.0 is required. AP and CLEP credits are accepted. Graduation requirements include: complete a total of 120 to 132 units, 40 units of upper division coursework, a minimum of 12 units must be in their major, 30 units in residence at California State University, Chico, 48 units of prescribed General Education (9 units as a resident at Chico State), minimum of two courses with focus on cultural diversity, demonstrate competent understanding of the Constitution of the United States, U.S. History, mathematics and writing, complete an approved major, and maintain a G.P.A of 2.0 or better. General education coursework includes: oral communications, writing, critical thinking, mathematics, two laboratory sciences (one physical science and one in the life sciences), U.S. History, U.S. Governmental Institutions, four writing intensive courses, and a GE Capstone course. In addition, each student must complete a Pathway, which consists of 18 units of lower division and 9 units of upper division coursework. **Procedure:** Freshmen are admitted fall and spring. Entrance exams should be taken in fall of the senior year. There are deferred admissions and rolling admissions plans. Early decision applications should be filed by October 1; regular applications, by November 30 for fall entry, along with a $55 fee. Notifications are sent March 1. Applications are accepted on-line. **Transfer Students:** 1468 transfer students enrolled in 2015-2016. Transfer students who are California residents must have a minimum 2.0 GPA, and nonresidents need 2.4. Students must have made up any missing college preparatory subjects and provide a statement of good standing and transcripts from prior institutions. 30 of 124 credits required for the bachelor's degree must be completed at Chico State. **International Students:** There are 589 international students enrolled. The school actively recruits these students. They must take the TOEFL with a minimum score of 500 on the paper-based TOEFL (PBT) or 61 on the Internet-based version (iBT), and take the IELTS. They must also take the SAT or ACT.

ADMISSIONS: 67% of the 2016-2017 applicants were accepted. The SAT scores for the 2016-2017 freshman class were: Critical Reading--42% below 500, 38% between 500 and 599, 10% between 600 and 699, and 1% between 700 and 800. Math-- 40% below 500, 39% between 500 and 599, 11% between 600 and 699, and 1% between 700 and 800. The ACT scores were 1% below 12, 16% between 12 and 17, 54% between 18 and 23, 27% between 24 and 29, and 2% above 30. **Admissions Contact:** Barbara Fortin, Interim Director of Admissions. Email: *info@csuchico.edu* Web: *www.csuchico.edu*

FINANCIAL AID: In 2016-2017, 41% of all full-time freshmen and 44% of continuing full-time students received some form of financial aid. 72% of all full-time freshmen and 71% of continuing full-time students received need-based aid. The average freshman award was $17,380. Need-based scholarships or need-based grants averaged $10,538; need-based self-help aid (loans and jobs) averaged $3,570; non-need-based athletic scholarships averaged $2,560; and other non-need-based awards and non-need-based scholarships averaged $1,536. The priority date for freshman financial aid applications for fall entry is March 2. The deadline for filing freshman financial aid applications for fall entry is rolling.

CALIFORNIA STATE UNIVERSITY, DOMINGUEZ HILLS *(The complete profile is made available exclusively on our website, www.barronspac.com)*

CALIFORNIA STATE UNIVERSITY, EAST BAY — B-3

www.csueastbay.edu

Hayward, CA 94542 — **(510) 885-2310**

Email: admissions@csueastbay.edu

Full-time: 3985 men, 6313 women	**Faculty:** IIA, +$
Part-time: 617 men, 938 women	**Ph.D.s:** n/av
Graduate: 738 men, 1260 women	**Student/Faculty:** n/av
Year: quarters, summer session	**Tuition:** $6564 ($15,492)
Room & Board: $12,849	**Freshman Class:** n/av
SAT or ACT: recommended	**CEEB CODE:** 4011
Application Deadline: December 15	**COMPETITIVE**

California State University/East Bay, founded in 1957, is part of the California State University system. The institution offers degree programs in the arts, sciences, business and economics, and education to a primarily commuter student body. The figures given in the above capsule and in this profile are approximate. There are 4 undergraduate schools and 4 graduate schools. In addition to regional accreditation, Cal. State East Bay has baccalaureate program accreditation with AACSB, NASAD, NASM, NCATE, and NLN. The 342-acre campus is in a small town 20 miles southeast of San Francisco in the Hayward Hills. Including any residence halls, there are 19 buildings.

STUDENT LIFE: 92% of undergraduates are from California. Others are from 31 states, 63 foreign countries, and Canada. 85% are from public schools. 8% are Foreign; 23% Asian American; 23% Hispanic; 21% White; 11% African American; 1% American Indian/Alaska Native. **Female To Male Ratio:** 1.6:1. The average age of all undergraduates is 25. 25% do not continue beyond their first year; 50% remain to graduate. **Housing:** 1300 students can be accommodated in college housing, which includes coed on-campus apartments. In addition, there are special-interest houses. On-campus housing is available on a first-come and first-served basis. 90% of students commute. All students may keep cars.

FACULTY/CLASSROOMS: 45% of faculty are male; 55% are female. No introductory courses are taught by graduate students.

PROGRAMS OF STUDY: Cal. State East Bay confers B.A., and B.S. degrees. Master's and doctoral degrees are also awarded. Bachelor's degrees are awarded in AGRICULTURE (environmental studies), BIOLOGICAL SCIENCE (biology/biological science), BUSINESS (accounting, business administration and management, and recreation and leisure services), COMMUNICATIONS AND THE ARTS (advertising, art, communications, dramatic arts, English, music, Spanish, and speech/debate/rhetoric), COMPUTER AND PHYSICAL SCIENCE (chemistry, computer science, geology, mathematics, physical sciences, physics, and statistics), ENGINEERING AND ENVIRONMENTAL DESIGN (engineering, environmental science, and industrial engineering), HEALTH PROFESSIONS (health science, nursing, and speech pathology/audiology), SOCIAL SCIENCE (anthropology, criminal justice, economics, ethnic studies, geography, history, human development, international studies, Latin American studies, liberal arts/general studies, philosophy, physical fitness/movement, political science/government, psychology, and sociology).

ACTIVITIES: 1% of men belong to 4 national fraternities; 1% of women belong to 3 national sororities. There are 90 groups on campus, including art, cheerleading, choir, chorale, chorus, computers, dance, drama, environmental, ethnic, film, honors, international, jazz band, LGBT, literary magazine, musical theater, newspaper, opera, orchestra, pep band, photography, political, professional, radio and TV, religious, social, social service, student government, and symphony. Popular campus events include Science Fair, Leadership Conferences and Al Fresco. **Sports:** There are 5 intercollegiate sports for men and 8 for women. Facilities include tennis and racquetball courts, 2 swimming pools, track, soccer field, a martial arts facility, a dance studio, baseball & softball diamonds, a 9000-seat stadium, a 500-seat gym, and a 500-seat theater. **Graduates:** From July 1, 2015 to June 30, 2016, 2700 bachelor's degrees were awarded. The most popular majors were business administration (30%), health sciences (7%), and nursing (7%). In an average class, 25% graduate in 4 years or less, 35% graduate in 5 years or less, and 45% graduate in 6 years or less.

SERVICES: Counseling and information services are available, as is tutoring in most subjects. There is a reader service for the blind, and remedial math, reading, and writing. **Library/Resources:** The 2 libraries contain 912,912 volumes, 873,177 microform items, and 29,768 audio/video tapes/CDs/DVDs, and subscribe to 2,000 periodicals including electronic. Computerized library services include interlibrary loans, database searching, Internet access, and Wi-Fi capability. Special learning facilities include an art gallery, natural history museum, radio station, TV station, a marine biology lab, and geology summer field camp. **Physically Challenged Students:** 95% of the campus is accessible. Facilities include wheelchair ramps, elevators, special parking, specially equipped restrooms, special class scheduling, lowered drinking fountains, lowered telephones, and special housing. The Disabled Student Services Center provides scribe, interpretive, and translation services. **Special:** California State East Bay offers cross-registration with local community colleges, other CSU campuses, and the University of California, Berkeley. Internships, study abroad in 20 countries, work-study programs, and student-designed majors are also available. The PACE program provides degree opportunities in liberal studies, hospitality and leisure services, and in human development to working adults. There is 1 national honor society, a freshman honors program, and 1 departmental honors program. **Visiting:** There are regularly scheduled orientations for prospective students. There are guides for informal visits and visitors may sit in on classes. To schedule a visit, contact the Welcome Center at admissions@csueastbay.edu. **Campus Safety and Security:** Measures include 24-hour foot and vehicle patrol, self-defense education, and security escort services. There are shuttle buses, emergency telephones, and lighted pathways/sidewalks.

REQUIREMENTS: All students must meet the eligibility index, a combination of the high school GPA and SAT or ACT scores. Applicants must be graduates of an accredited secondary school or have a GED certificate. Secondary school courses must include 4 years of English, 3 of math, 2 each of a language other than English, social science, and science with a lab, and 1 elective. A GPA of 2.0 is required. AP and CLEP credits are accepted. In order to graduate, students must fulfill the university writing skills requirement, have a 2.0 minimum GPA, and complete 186 quarter units. **Procedure:** Freshmen are admitted to all sessions. Entrance exams should be taken prior to orientation. There is a rolling admissions plan. Applications should be filed by December 15 for fall entry, along with a $55 fee. Notification is sent on a rolling basis. Applications are accepted on-line. **Transfer Students:** Applicants must have a minimum 2.0 GPA (2.45 for nonresidents), be in good standing at the last college attended, and either meet freshman admission requirements or have completed at least 56 transferable semester (84 quarter) units. 45 of 186 credits required for the bachelor's degree must be completed at Cal. State East Bay. **International Students:** The school actively recruits these students. They must take the TOEFL. They must also take the SAT or ACT.

Admissions Contact: Office of Admissions. Email: *admissions@csueastbay.edu* Web: *www.csueastbay.edu*

FINANCIAL AID: Cal. State East Bay is a member of CSS. The FAFSA code is 001138. Check with the school for current application deadlines.

CALIFORNIA STATE UNIVERSITY, FRESNO *(The complete profile is made available exclusively on our website, www.barronspac.com)*

CALIFORNIA STATE UNIVERSITY, FULLERTON — D-5

www.fullerton.edu

Fullerton, CA 92834 — (657) 278-2371

Fax: (657) 278-2356	**Email:** admissions@fullerton.edu
Full-time: 12213 men, 15781 women	**Faculty:** 850; IIA, +$
	Ph.D.s: 82%
Part-time: 3119 men, 3463 women	**Student/Faculty:** 32 to 1
Graduate: 2293 men, 3366 women	**Tuition:** $6560 ($15,488)
Year: semesters, summer session	**Freshman Class:** 44493 applied, 21459 accepted, 4426 enrolled
Room & Board: $15,342	
SAT CR/M: 520/550 **ACT:** 23	**CEEB CODE:** 4589
Application Deadline: November 30	**COMPETITIVE**

California State University/Fullerton, founded in 1957, is part of the California State University system. The figures in the above capsule and in this profile are approximate. The school offers programs in the arts, business and economics, communications, engineering and computer science, education, health and human development, humanities and social science, natural science and math. The institution provides a comprehensive teaching credential program. There are 8 undergraduate schools and 8 graduate schools. In addition to regional accreditation, Cal State Fullerton has baccalaureate program accreditation with AACSB, ABET, ACEJMC, NASAD, NASM, NCATE, NLN, ACS, ASHA, CAAHEP, CCNE, CCTE, CSWE, NASD, NASPAA, and NAST. The 240-acre campus is in a suburban area 30 miles southeast of Los Angeles. Including any residence halls, there are 29 buildings.

STUDENT LIFE: 97% of undergraduates are from California. Others are from 39 states, 65 foreign countries, and Canada. 96% are from public schools. 6% are Foreign; 42% Hispanic; 4% two or more races; 4% race unknown; 21% Asian American; 20% White; 2% African American. **Female To Male Ratio:** 1.3:1. The average age of freshmen is 18; all undergraduates, 22. 11% do not continue beyond their first year; 89% remain to graduate. **Housing:** 2000 students can be accommodated in college housing, which includes coed on-campus apartments and off-campus apartments. In addition, there are fraternity houses and sorority houses. On-campus housing is available on a first-come and first-served basis. 94% of students commute. All students may keep cars.

FACULTY/CLASSROOMS: 50% of faculty are male; 50% are female. 85% teach undergraduates, and do research. Graduate students teach 15% of introductory courses. The average class size in an introductory lecture is 37; in a laboratory is 22; and in a regular course is 34.

PROGRAMS OF STUDY: Cal State Fullerton confers B.A., B.S., B.F.A. and B.M. degrees. Master's and doctoral degrees are also awarded. Bachelor's degrees are awarded in BIOLOGICAL SCIENCE (biochemistry and biology/biological science), BUSINESS (business administration and management, business economics, entrepreneurial studies, finance, international business management, management science, marketing/retailing/merchandising, and tourism), COMMUNICATIONS AND THE ARTS (advertising, art history, art, communications, comparative literature, dance, dramatic arts, English, fine arts, French, Japanese, journalism, linguistics, music, music performance, public relations, radio/television technology, Spanish, speech/debate/rhetoric, theater design, theater management, visual and performing arts, and visual design), COMPUTER AND PHYSICAL SCIENCE (applied mathematics, chemistry, computer science, geology, information sciences and systems, mathematics, physics, and statistics), EDUCATION (athletic training and music education), ENGINEERING AND ENVIRONMENTAL DESIGN (civil engineering, computer engineering, electrical/electronics engineering, engineering and applied science, and mechanical engineering), HEALTH PROFESSIONS (exercise science, health science, kinesiology, nursing, and speech pathology/audiology), SOCIAL SCIENCE (African American studies, American studies, anthropology, Asian/American studies, child care/child and family studies, criminal justice, economics, ethnic studies, European studies, geography, history, human services, Latin American studies, liberal arts/general studies, Mexican-American/Chicano studies, philosophy, political science/government, psychology, public administration, religion, and women's studies). Business, economics, and teacher credential program are the strongest academically. Business, economics, and humanities have the largest enrollments.

ACTIVITIES: 2% of men belong to 5 local and 13 national fraternities; 3% of women belong to 1 local and 8 national sororities. There are 324 groups on campus, including art, band, cheerleading, choir, chorus, communications, computers, dance, debate, drama, ethnic, film, forensics, honors, international, jazz band, LGBT, literary magazine, musical theater, newspaper, opera, orchestra, pep band, photography, political, professional, radio and TV, religious, social, social service, and student government. Popular campus events include Block Party, Spring Concert, and Snow Day. **Sports:** There are 6 intercollegiate sports for men and 9 for women, and 15 intramural sports for men and 11 for women. Facilities include a gym, a swimming pool, tennis and racquetball courts, baseball/softball, track, and soccer fields, a bowling alley, and a stadium. **Graduates:** From July 1, 2015 to June 30, 2016, 8034 bachelor's degrees were awarded. The most popular majors were business administration (25%), communication/journalism (9%), and psychology (7%). In an average class, 3% graduate in 3 years or less, 42% graduate in 4 years or less, 78% graduate in 5 years or less, and 91% graduate in 6 years or less.

SERVICES: Counseling and information services are available, as is tutoring in most subjects. There is a reader service for the blind, and remedial math, reading, and writing. **Library/Resources:** The library contains 1.3 million volumes, 1.2 million microform items, and 35,016 audio/video tapes/CDs/DVDs. Computerized library services include interlibrary loans, database searching, Internet access, and Wi-Fi capability. Special learning facilities include an art gallery, radio station, TV station, a wildlife sanctuary, an arboretum, a desert studies center, a demographic research center, and a number of centers for studies in economics and business, the environment, aging, education, land use, oral and public history, and religion in America. **Physically Challenged Students:** All of the campus is accessible. Facilities include wheelchair ramps, elevators, special parking, specially equipped restrooms, lowered drinking fountains, lowered telephones, and automatic doors. **Special:** The university offers distance learning, honors program, freshman program, internships and co-op programs in 45 academic areas, study abroad in 18 countries, and work-study programs both on and off campus. Double majors, and pass/fail options, teacher credential programs, and service learning are also available. There is a freshman honors program. **Visiting:** There are regularly scheduled orientations for prospective students, consisting of daily campus tours and information on academic colleges, student services, student life, and the history of Cal State Fullerton. There are guides for informal visits. To schedule a visit, contact New Student & Parent Programs at (657) 278-2501. **Campus Safety and Security:** Measures include 24-hour foot and vehicle patrol, emergency notification system, self-defense education, and security escort services. There are shuttle buses, emergency telephones, and lighted pathways/sidewalks.

REQUIREMENTS: The SAT or ACT is required. Applicants must be graduates of an accredited secondary school or have a GED certificate. Secondary school courses must include 4 years of English, 3 of math, 2 each of a foreign language, science, and history, and 1 of visual or performing arts. Admission is based on the Qualifiable Eligibility Index, a combination of the high school GPA and either the SAT or ACT score. Auditions are required for music majors. AP and CLEP credits are accepted. Graduation requirements for all students include completion of a minimum of 51 units of general education courses, a 2.0 GPA, and an upper-division writing course designated by the major department. 120 to 135 credit hours must be completed for graduation. **Procedure:** Freshmen are admitted fall. Entrance exams should be taken during the senior year of high school. There is a rolling admissions plan. Applications should be filed by November 30 for fall entry, along with a $55 fee. Notification is sent on a rolling basis. Applications are accepted on-line. **Transfer Students:** 4123 transfer students enrolled in 2015-2016. Applicants must have a minimum 2.0 GPA. The SAT or ACT is required for students with fewer than 60 transferable units earned. Students with 60 transferable units or more must have 30 units of general education completed with a C or better, including English composition, math, speech, and critical thinking. 30 of 120 credits required for the bachelor's degree must be completed at Cal State Fullerton. **International Students:** There are 1121 international students enrolled. They must take the TOEFL with a minimum score of 500 on the paper-based TOEFL (PBT) or 61 on the Internet-based version (iBT).

ADMISSIONS: 48% of the 2016-2017 applicants were accepted. The SAT scores for the 2016-2017 freshman class were: Critical Reading-- 32% below 500, 52% between 500 and 599, 15% between 600 and 699, and 1% between 700 and 800. Math-- 25% below 500, 51% between 500 and 599, 22% between 600 and 699, and 2% between 700 and 800. The ACT scores were 4% between 12 and 17, 52% between 18 and 23, 41% between 24 and 29, and 4% above 30. 54% of the current freshmen were in the top fifth of their class; 90% were in the top two fifths. 9 freshmen graduated first in their class. **Admissions Contact:** Admissions Office. Email: *admissions@fullerton.edu* Web: *www.fullerton.edu*

FINANCIAL AID: In 2016-2017, 67% of all full-time freshmen and 66% of continuing full-time students received some form of financial aid. 55% of all full-time freshmen and 51% of continuing full-time students received need-based aid. The average freshman award was $6,717. Need-based scholarships or need-based grants averaged $3,615; need-based self-help aid (loans and jobs) averaged $4,036; non-need-based athletic scholarships averaged $2,538; and other non-need-based awards and non-need-based scholarships averaged $1,287. The priority date for freshman financial aid applications for fall entry is March 2. The deadline for filing freshman financial aid applications for fall entry is June 6.

CALIFORNIA STATE UNIVERSITY, LONG BEACH D-5

www.csulb.edu

Long Beach, CA 90840	(562) 985-5471
Fax: (562) 985-4973	Email: eslb@csulb.edu
Full-time: 11,715 men, 15,227 women	Faculty: IIA, +$
Part-time: 2333 men, 2971 women	Ph.D.s: 87%
Graduate: 2055 men, 3475 women	Student/Faculty: n/av
Year: semesters, summer session	Tuition: $6452 ($16,124)
Room & Board: $12,398	Freshman Class: 60744 applied, 19711 accepted, 4253 enrolled
SAT CR/M: 514/531 ACT: 23	CEEB CODE: 4389
Application Deadline: November 30	COMPETITIVE

California State University Long Beach, is a diverse, student-centered, globally-engaged public university committed to providing highly-valued undergraduate and graduate educational opportunities through superior teaching, research, creative activity and service for the people of California and the world. Long Beach is one of the largest campuses in the CSU system and in the state of California. It is nationally recognized as one of the nations' best values in higher education, offering a high-quality, low-cost education. There are 7 undergraduate schools and 7 graduate schools. In addition to regional accreditation, CSULB has baccalaureate program accreditation with AACSB, AALE, ABET, ACEJMC, AHEA, APTA, CAHEA, CSAB, CSWE, FIDER, NASAD, NASM, NCATE, NLN, and NRPA. The 322-acre campus is in an urban area about three miles from the ocean, 25 miles southeast of Los Angeles and a short drive to Orange County. Including any residence halls, there are 95 buildings.

STUDENT LIFE: 95% of undergraduates are from California. Others are from 45 states, 99 foreign countries, and Canada. 46% are from public schools. 8% are Foreign; 4% African American; 4% two or more races; 4% race unknown; 37% Hispanic; 22% Asian American; 20% White. **Female To Male Ratio:** 1.3:1. The average age of freshmen is 18; all undergraduates, 23. 11% do not continue beyond their first year; and 89% remain to graduate. **Housing:** 2728 students can be accommodated in college housing, which includes single-sex and coed dorms. In addition, there are honors houses, special-interest houses, 4 living/learning communities. On-campus housing is available on a first-come and first-served basis. 91% of students commute. Alcohol is not permitted. All students may keep cars.

FACULTY/CLASSROOMS: 50% of faculty are male; 50% are female. No introductory courses are taught by graduate students.

PROGRAMS OF STUDY: CSULB confers B.A., B.S., B.F.A. and B.M. degrees. Master's and doctoral degrees are also awarded. Bachelor's degrees are awarded in BIOLOGICAL SCIENCE (biochemistry, biology/biological science, botany, cell biology, ecology, marine biology, microbiology, nutritional sciences, physiology, and zoology), BUSINESS (accounting, banking and finance, business administration and management, business economics, finance, international business, international business management, management information systems, marketing/retailing/merchandising, personnel management, and recreation and leisure services), COMMUNICATIONS AND THE ARTS (art history, art, Chinese, classics, communications, comparative literature, creative writing, dance, design, dramatic arts, English, film arts, French, French and Francophone studies, German, Japanese, journalism, music, Spanish, and theatre arts), COMPUTER AND PHYSICAL SCIENCE (applied mathematics, chemistry, computer engineering technology, computer science, earth science, geology, mathematics, physics, and statistics), EDUCATION (elementary education, mathematics education, science education, and special education), ENGINEERING AND ENVIRONMENTAL DESIGN (aerospace engineering, chemical engineering, civil engineering, computer engineering, electrical/electronics engineering, engineering technology, environmental science, and mechanical engineering), HEALTH PROFESSIONS (health care administration, health science, kinesiology, and nursing), SOCIAL SCIENCE (African studies, American studies, anthropology, Asian/Oriental studies, child care/child and family studies, child psychology/development, criminal justice, criminology, economics, family/consumer studies, geography, Hispanic American studies, history, human development, interdisciplinary studies, international studies, philosophy, political science/government, psychology, religion, religious studies, social work, sociology, women & gender studies, and women's studies). Art, biological sciences, and music are the strongest academically. Business administration, psychology, and speech communication have the largest enrollments.

ACTIVITIES: 7% of men belong to 24 national fraternities; 6% of women belong to 17 national sororities. There are 395 groups on campus, including art, band, cheerleading, choir, chorale, chorus, communications, computers, dance, debate, drama, drill team, ethnic, film, forensics, honors, international, jazz band, LGBT, literary magazine, musical theater, newspaper, opera, orchestra, pep band, photography, political, professional, radio and TV, religious, social, social service, student government, and symphony. Popular campus events include Homecoming, and Smorgasport. **Sports:** There are 7 intercollegiate sports for men and 11 for women, and 14 intramural sports for men and 12 for women. Facilities include volleyball courts, basketball courts, softball complex, women's soccer, all-weather track and runways and grass turf throughout the infield, the Rhodes Tennis Center is a 12-court complex women's tennis program. There is also a recreation facility with three-court gym, a multi-activity court gym, indoor jogging track, weight lifting and cardio equipment, racquetball courts, activity rooms, a climbing wall, and outdoor pool and spa. **Graduates:** From July 1, 2015 to June 30, 2016, 8679 bachelor's degrees were awarded. The most popular majors were psychology (5%), family & consumer sciences (5%), and communication (5%). In an average class, 16% graduate in 4 years or less and 68% graduate in 6 years or less.

SERVICES: Counseling and information services are available, as is tutoring in most subjects. There is a reader service for the blind, and remedial math, reading, and writing. **Library/Resources:** The library contains 1.1 million volumes, 1.5 million microform items, and 29,948 audio/video tapes/CDs/DVDs, and subscribes to 21,002 periodicals including electronic. Computerized library services include interlibrary loans, database searching, and Internet access. Special learning facilities include an art gallery, radio station, and TV station. **Physically Challenged Students:** 95% of the campus is accessible. Facilities include wheelchair ramps, elevators, special parking, specially equipped restrooms, special class scheduling, lowered drinking fountains, and lowered telephones. **Special:** There are 23 national honor societies, Phi Beta Kappa, and a freshman honors program. **Visiting:** There are regularly scheduled orientations for prospective students, consisting of a one hour walking tour which showcases campus distinctions and facilities, provides a general overview of campus academic programs, student support services and campus life. There are guides for informal visits. To schedule a visit, contact The Office of University Outreach and School Relations at (562) 985-5358. **Campus Safety and Security:** Measures include 24-hour foot and vehicle patrol, emergency notification system, and security escort services. There are shuttle buses, emergency telephones, and lighted pathways/sidewalks.

REQUIREMENTS: The SAT or ACT is required. Applicants must be graduates of an accredited secondary school and have completed 4 years of English, 3 years of math, 2 years of the same foreign language, 2 years of lab science,2 years of history and social science, 1 year of visual and performing arts and 1 year of electives. Students are admitted on the basis of the eligibility index, a formula that combines students' achievement in high school college preparatory courses with the results of the SAT I or ACT. California residents with a minimum 3.0 GPA are automatically admissible. A portfolio is required for art and design students. An audition is required for dance, music, and theater students. AP and CLEP credits are accepted. Graduation requirements for all students include the completion of 40 units of upper-division course work and 30 units in residence at the university. Students must have a minimum 2.0 GPA and a total of 120 to 132 units, depending on the major. Students must also satisfy the Graduation Writing Assessment Requirement. **Procedure:** Freshmen are admitted fall and spring. Entrance exams should be taken during the fall semester of 12th grade. There is a rolling admissions plan. Applications should be filed by November 30 for fall entry; August 31 for spring entry. The fall 2016 application fee was $55. Applications are accepted on-line. **Transfer Students:** 3284 transfer students enrolled in 2015-2016. Upper-division students must have completed a minimum of 56 semester units and have a minimum 2.0 GPA; lower-division students must meet the same requirements as entering freshmen. 30 of 120 credits required for the bachelor's degree must be completed at CSULB. **International Students:** There are 1921 international students enrolled. The school actively recruits these students. They must take the TOEFL with a minimum score of 500 on the paper-based TOEFL (PBT) or 61 on the Internet-based version (iBT).

ADMISSIONS: 34% of the 2016-2017 applicants were accepted. The SAT scores for the 2016-2017 freshman class were: Critical Reading-- 42% below 500, 44% between 500 and 599, 13% between 600 and 699, and 2% between 700 and 800. Math-- 32% below 500, 42% between 500 and 599, 24% between 600 and 699, and 3% between 700 and 800. The ACT scores were 42% below 12, 25% between 12 and 17, 20% between 18 and 23, 7% between 24 and 29, and 6% above 30. **Admissions Contact:** Tom Enders, Associate Vice Pres. Enrollment Services. Email: *eslb@csulb.edu* Web: *www.csulb.edu*

FINANCIAL AID: CSU-Long Beach is a member of CSS. The deadline for filing freshman financial aid applications for fall entry is March 2.

CALIFORNIA STATE UNIVERSITY, LOS ANGELES *(The complete profile is made available exclusively on our website, www.barronspac.com)*

CALIFORNIA STATE UNIVERSITY, MONTEREY BAY *(The complete profile is made available exclusively on our website, www.barronspac.com)*

CALIFORNIA STATE UNIVERSITY, NORTHRIDGE *(The complete profile is made available exclusively on our website, www.barronspac.com)*

CALIFORNIA STATE UNIVERSITY, SACRAMENTO — B-3

www.csus.edu

Sacramento, CA 95819 — **(916) 278-7362**, **(800) 722-4748**

Fax: (916) 278-5603	**Email: admissions@csus.edu**
Full-time: 8697 men, 11,713 women	**Faculty:** IIA, +$
Part-time: 1971 men, 2320 women	**Ph.D.s:** n/av
Graduate: 1071 men, 2244 women	**Student/Faculty:** n/av
Year: semesters, summer session	**Tuition:** $6872 ($17,732)
Room & Board: $13,460	**Freshman Class:** 18617 applied, 12496 accepted, 4671 enrolled
SAT or ACT: required	**CEEB CODE:** 4671
Application Deadline: November 30	**COMPETITIVE**

California State University/Sacramento, founded in 1947, is an integral part of the community, committed to access, excellence and diversity. The figures given in the above capsule and in this profile are approximate. CSUS is dedicated to the life-altering potential of learning that balances a liberal arts education with depth of knowledge in a discipline. We are committed to providing an excellent education to all eligible applicants who aspire to expand their knowledge and prepare themselves for meaningful lives, careers, and service to their community. Reflecting the metropolitan character of the area, CSU-Sacramento is a richly diverse community. As such, the University is committed to fostering in all its members a sense of inclusiveness, respect for human differences, and concern for others. In doing so, we strive to create a pluralistic community in which members participate collaboratively in all aspects of university life. There are 7 undergraduate schools and 7 graduate schools. In addition to regional accreditation, Sacramento State has baccalaureate program accreditation with AACSB, ABET, ACBSP, ACCE, ADA, AHEA, APTA, ASLA, CSWE, FIDER, NASAD, NASM, NCATE, NLN, NRPA, and TEAC. The 300-acre campus is in a suburban area in Sacramento, California, 90 miles northeast of San Francisco. Including any residence halls, there are 52 buildings.

STUDENT LIFE: 99% of undergraduates are from California. Others are from 37 states, 36 foreign countries, and Canada. 96% are from public schools. 6% are African American; 35% White; 3% Foreign; 22% Hispanic; 21% Asian American; 11% race unknown; 1% American Indian/Alaska Native. **Female To Male Ratio:** 1.4:1. **Housing:** 1100 students can be accommodated in college housing, which includes coed dorms and off-campus apartments. On-campus housing is available on a first-come and first-served basis. 95% of students commute. All students may keep cars.

FACULTY/CLASSROOMS: 51% of faculty are male; 49% are female. All teach undergraduates, and all do research. No introductory courses are taught by graduate students. The average class size in an introductory lecture is 38; in a laboratory is 19; and in a regular course is 34.

PROGRAMS OF STUDY: Sacramento State confers B.A., B.S., B.M. and B.V.E. degrees. Master's and doctoral degrees are also awarded. Bachelor's degrees are awarded in AGRICULTURE (natural resource management), BIOLOGICAL SCIENCE (biology/biological science and microbiology), BUSINESS (accounting, banking and finance, business administration and management, insurance, international business management, management information systems, marketing/retailing/merchandising, and real estate), COMMUNICATIONS AND THE ARTS (communications, dramatic arts, English, French, German, journalism, music, and Spanish), COMPUTER AND PHYSICAL SCIENCE (chemistry, computer science, geology, mathematics, physical sciences, and physics), EDUCATION (business education, early childhood education, and health education), ENGINEERING AND ENVIRONMENTAL DESIGN (civil engineering, computer engineering, electrical/electronics engineering, engineering technology, and mechanical engineering), HEALTH PROFESSIONS (environmental health science, medical laboratory technology, nursing, physical therapy, and speech pathology/audiology), SOCIAL SCIENCE (anthropology, criminal justice, economics, geography, history, homeland security, international relations, parks and recreation management, philosophy, psychology, public administration, social science, social work, and sociology). Nursing, criminal justice, and business administration are the strongest academically. Business administration, and communications have the largest enrollments.

ACTIVITIES: 7% of men belong to 3 local and 18 national fraternities;

5% of women belong to 1 local and 20 national sororities. There are 230 groups on campus, including art, band, cheerleading, chess, choir, chorale, chorus, computers, dance, debate, drama, ethnic, film, honors, international, jazz band, LGBT, literary magazine, marching band, musical theater, newspaper, opera, orchestra, pep band, photography, political, professional, radio and TV, religious, social, social service, student government, and symphony. Popular campus events include Greek Week, Festival of New American Music, and River City Days. **Sports:** Facilities include a 17000-seat stadium, 2 gyms, 2 swimming pools, an all-weather outdoor track, 16 tennis courts, baseball, softball, soccer fields, and an aquatic center, with sailing, wind-surfing, rowing, and canoeing. **Graduates:** From July 1, 2015 to June 30, 2016, 5787 bachelor's degrees were awarded. The most popular majors were business/marketing (21%), homeland security (11%), and communication/journalism (8%).

SERVICES: Counseling and information services are available, as is tutoring in most subjects. There is a reader service for the blind, and remedial math, reading, and writing. **Library/Resources:** The library contains 1.4 million volumes, 2.4 million microform items, and 53,515 audio/video tapes/CDs/DVDs, and subscribes to 2,171 periodicals including electronic. Computerized library services include interlibrary loans, database searching, and Internet access. Special learning facilities include an art gallery, radio station, an aquatic center, an anthropology museum, several art galleries, and a wellness center. **Physically Challenged Students:** 90% of the campus is accessible. Facilities include wheelchair ramps, elevators, special parking, specially equipped restrooms, special class scheduling, lowered drinking fountains, and lowered telephones. **Special:** The university offers cross-registration with other California State University schools, co-op programs in many academic programs, internships, a Washington semester, study abroad in 12 countries, and dual and student-designed majors. A joint Ph.D. program in public history is available with the University of California at Santa Barbara. There is a chapter of Phi Beta Kappa and a freshman honors program. **Visiting:** There are regularly scheduled orientations for prospective students. There are guides for informal visits and visitors may sit in on classes. To schedule a visit, contact the University Outreach Services Office. **Campus Safety and Security:** Measures include 24-hour foot and vehicle patrol, self-defense education, and security escort services. There are shuttle buses, emergency telephones, and lighted pathways/sidewalks.

REQUIREMENTS: The SAT or ACT is required of applicants with a high school GPA below 3.0. Applicants should have completed 4 years of high school English, 3 years of math, 2 years of a foreign language, 1 year each of lab science, history, and visual/performing arts and 3 years of college preparatory electives. AP and CLEP credits are accepted. In order to graduate, students must complete a minimum of 120 semester hours, including 30 to 86 hours in the major, with a minimum 2.0 GPA. Students must complete 51 units in general education requirements and take proficiency exams in writing and a foreign language. Distribution requirements include 15 units in the individual and society; 12 each in arts and humanities and physical universe/life forms, 9 in English language communication, and 3 in understanding personal development. A course in race and ethnicity in American society is required. **Procedure:** Freshmen are admitted fall and spring. Entrance exams should be taken before December of the senior year. There are deferred admissions and rolling admissions plans. Applications should be filed by November 30 for fall entry. The fall 2016 application fee was $55. Notifications are sent November 1. Applications are accepted on-line. **Transfer Students:** 3556 transfer students enrolled in 2015-2016. Applicants must have a 2.0 GPA and 56 transferable semester units, including 30 units of specific general education courses to include oral and written communication, critical thinking, and math. 30 of 120 credits required for the bachelor's degree must be completed at Sacramento State. **International Students:** There are 333 international students enrolled. The school actively recruits these students. They must take the TOEFL. They must also take the SAT or ACT.

ADMISSIONS: 67% of the 2016-2017 applicants were accepted. **Admissions Contact:** Emiliano Diaz, Director of University Outreach Services. Email: *admissions@csus.edu* Web: *www.csus.edu*

FINANCIAL AID: CSU-Sacramento is a member of CSS. Check with the school for current application deadlines.

CALIFORNIA STATE UNIVERSITY, SAN BERNARDINO — D-5

www.csusb.edu

San Bernardino, CA 92407 — **(909) 537-5188**

Fax: (909) 537-7034	**Email:** moreinfo@csusb.edu
Full-time: 4817 men, 8163 women	**Faculty:** IIA, +$
Part-time: 707 men, 1045 women	**Ph.D.s:** n/av
Graduate: 919 men, 1599 women	**Student/Faculty:** n/av
Year: quarters, summer session	**Tuition:** $6453 ($12,150)
Room & Board: $9796	**Freshman Class:** n/av **CEEB CODE:** 4099
Application Deadline: open	**COMPETITIVE**

California State University/San Bernardino, founded in 1965, is a public, comprehensive regional university offering programs in business and public administration, natural sciences, education, arts and letters, and social and behavioral sciences. The figures in the above capsule and in this profile are approximate. There are 5 undergraduate schools and 19 graduate schools. In addition to regional accreditation, CSUSB has baccalaureate program accreditation with AACSB, ABET, ADA, CSAB, CSWE, NASAD, NASM, NCATE, NLN, NAST, CORE, and CCNE. The 430-acre campus is in a suburban area 60 miles east of Los Angeles and 60 miles west of Palm Springs. Including any residence halls, there are 45 buildings.

STUDENT LIFE: 99% of undergraduates are from California. Others are from states, and Canada. 9% are African American; 7% Asian American; 5% Foreign; 46% Hispanic; 24% White. **Female To Male Ratio:** 1.7:1. The average age of freshmen is 18; all undergraduates, 22. 18% do not continue beyond their first year; 82% remain to graduate. **Housing:** College-sponsored housing includes single-sex and coed dorms and on-campus apartments. In addition, there are special-interest houses, an all-women dorm. On-campus housing is available on a first-come and first-served basis. All students may keep cars.

FACULTY/CLASSROOMS: No introductory courses are taught by graduate students. The average class size in an introductory lecture is 40; in a laboratory is 18; and in a regular course is 24.

PROGRAMS OF STUDY: CSUSB confers B.A., B.S. and B.V.E. degrees. Master's degrees are also awarded. Bachelor's degrees are awarded in AGRICULTURE (environmental studies), BIOLOGICAL SCIENCE (biochemistry and biology/biological science), BUSINESS (accounting, banking and finance, business administration and management, business economics, human resources, international business management, management information systems, management science, and small business management), COMMUNICATIONS AND THE ARTS (art, art history and appreciation, ceramic art and design, communications, dance, dramatic arts, English, French, graphic design, music, music history and appreciation, music performance, music technology, musicology/ethnomusicology, painting, photography, printmaking, sculpture, and Spanish), COMPUTER AND PHYSICAL SCIENCE (applied physics, chemistry, computer science, geology, mathematics, and physics), EDUCATION (bilingual/bicultural education, health education, music education, and vocational education), HEALTH PROFESSIONS (environmental health science, exercise science, health care administration, health science, nursing, and premedicine), SOCIAL SCIENCE (American studies, anthropology, child psychology/development, criminal justice, economics, ethnic studies, food science, geography, gerontology, history, human development, human services, humanities, liberal arts/general studies, paralegal studies, philosophy, political science/government, psychology, public administration, social science, social work, sociology, and Spanish studies). Liberal studies, nursing, and psychology have the largest enrollments.

ACTIVITIES: 4% of men belong to 1 local and 8 national fraternities; 3% of women belong to 6 national sororities. There are 80 groups on campus, including art, cheerleading, choir, chorale, chorus, computers, dance, drama, ethnic, honors, international, jazz band, LGBT, musical theater, newspaper, orchestra, political, professional, radio and TV, religious, social, social service, and student government. Popular campus events include Annual Picnic, and California Indian Cultural Awareness Conference. **Sports:** There are 4 intercollegiate sports for men and 7 for women. Facilities include an arena for basketball and volleyball, baseball, softball, soccer fields, tennis courts, swimming pools for water polo and recreational swimming, and a gym for recreational workouts. **Graduates:**

From July 1, 2015 to June 30, 2016, 2868 bachelor's degrees were awarded. The most popular majors were psychology (10%), criminal justice (7%), and liberal studies (7%).

SERVICES: Counseling and information services are available, as is tutoring in most subjects. There is a reader service for the blind, and remedial math and writing. **Library/Resources:** Computerized library services include interlibrary loans and database searching. Special learning facilities include an art gallery, radio station, an observatory. **Physically Challenged Students:** 95% of the campus is accessible. Facilities include wheelchair ramps, elevators, special parking, specially equipped restrooms, lowered drinking fountains, and lowered telephones. **Special:** The university offers cross-registration with other CSU campuses and study abroad in 18 countries. Also available are internships, accelerated study, campus and community work-study programs, B.A.-B.S. degrees, dual and student-designed majors, credit for vocational education and military experience, and nondegree study. There are 3 national honor societies, Phi Beta Kappa, and a freshman honors program. **Visiting:** There are regularly scheduled orientations for prospective students, including sessions on admissions requirements, financial aid information, and campus (student) life information. There are guides for informal visits, visitors may sit in on classes, and stay overnight. To schedule a visit, contact the Outreach Services Office. **Campus Safety and Security:** Measures include 24-hour foot and vehicle patrol, self-defense education, and security escort services. There are emergency telephones, lighted pathways/sidewalks, Email and web site alerts.

REQUIREMENTS: Applicants must be graduates of an accredited secondary school. Preparatory work should include 4 years of English, 3 of math, 2 of foreign language, 1 each of U.S. history/government, lab science, and visual and performing arts, and 3 of electives. Admission is based on an eligibility index that weighs the high school GPA and the SAT or ACT score. Students with GPAs of 3.0 or better (3.6 for nonresidents) are exempt from test score requirements. AP and CLEP credits are accepted. Important factors in the admissions decision are advanced placement or honors courses, recommendations by school officials, and leadership record. To graduate, students must complete 180 to 198 quarter hours, including 60 in upper-division courses and requirements for the major, with a minimum GPA of 2.0. The 82-credit general education program includes courses in basic skills, natural sciences, humanities, social and behavioral sciences, lifelong understanding, upper-division writing, multicultural/gender studies, and electives. Students must also demonstrate an understanding of the U.S. Constitution, American history, and California government. **Procedure:** Freshmen are admitted to all sessions. Entrance exams should be taken prior to applying. There is a rolling admissions plan. Application deadlines are open. The fall 2016 application fee was $55. Notification is sent on a rolling basis. Applications are accepted on-line. **Transfer Students:** 1676 transfer students enrolled in 2015-2016. Applicants must have a minimum college GPA of 2.0 (2.4 for nonresidents) and be in good standing at the previously attended institution. Those with fewer than 56 transferable semester units must submit ACT or SAT scores. 45 of 180 credits required for the bachelor's degree must be completed at CSUSB. **International Students:** There are 557 international students enrolled. The school actively recruits these students.

Admissions Contact: Olivia Rosas, Director. Email: *moreinfo@csusb.edu* Web: *www.csusb.edu*

FINANCIAL AID: Check with the school for current application deadlines.

CALIFORNIA STATE UNIVERSITY, SAN MARCOS *(The complete profile is made available exclusively on our website, www.barronspac.com)*

CALIFORNIA STATE UNIVERSITY, STANISLAUS — B-3

www.csustan.edu

Turlock, CA 95382 — **(209) 667-3070**

Fax: (209) 667-3788 — **Email:** outreach_help_desk@csustan.edu

Full-time: 1610 men, 3010 women	**Faculty:** IIA, av$
Part-time: 665 men, 1355 women	**Ph.D.s:** n/av
Graduate: 520 men, 1190 women	**Student/Faculty:** n/av
Year: 4-1-4, summer session	**Tuition:** $6704
Room & Board: $9508	**Freshman Class:** n/av **CEEB CODE:** 4713
Application Deadline: August 18	**COMPETITIVE**

California State University/Stanislaus, founded in 1957, is a state-supported institution offering undergraduate and graduate programs in liberal and fine arts, business, health science, and teacher preparation. The figures in the above capsule and in this survey are approximate. There are 3 undergraduate schools and 1 graduate school. In addition to regional accreditation, CSU Stanislaus has baccalaureate program accreditation with AACSB, CSWE, NASAD, NASM, NCATE, ABA, ACS, CCNE, CCTC, NASPAA, and NAST. The 228-acre campus is in a suburban area in the San Joaquin Valley, about 100 miles south of San Francisco. Including any residence halls, there are 26 buildings.

STUDENT LIFE: 94% of undergraduates are from California. Others are from 21 states, 46 foreign countries, and Canada. 95% are from public schools. 43% are White; 4% African American; 27% Hispanic; 11% Asian American; 1% American Indian/Alaska Native. **Female To Male Ratio:** 2.0:1. The average age of freshmen is 18; all undergraduates, 25. 18% do not continue beyond their first year; 50% remain to graduate. **Housing:** 650 students can be accommodated in college housing, which includes coed dorms and on-campus apartments. On-campus housing is available on a first-come and first-served basis. 90% of students commute. All students may keep cars.

FACULTY/CLASSROOMS: 53% of faculty are male; 47% are female. All teach undergraduates. No introductory courses are taught by graduate students.

PROGRAMS OF STUDY: CSU Stanislaus confers B.A., B.S., B.F.A. and B.M. degrees. Master's degrees are also awarded. Bachelor's degrees are awarded in AGRICULTURE (agriculture), BIOLOGICAL SCIENCE (biology/biological science), BUSINESS (business administration and management), COMMUNICATIONS AND THE ARTS (art, art history and appreciation, communications, dramatic arts, English, fine arts, French, music, music performance, and Spanish), COMPUTER AND PHYSICAL SCIENCE (applied physics, chemistry, computer science, geology, information sciences and systems, mathematics, physical sciences, and physics), EDUCATION (health education and physical education), HEALTH PROFESSIONS (nursing), SOCIAL SCIENCE (anthropology, child psychology/development, cognitive science, criminal justice, developmental psychology, economics, ethnic studies, geography, history, interdisciplinary studies, liberal arts/general studies, philosophy, political science/government, psychology, social science, and sociology). Liberal studies, business administration, and psychology have the largest enrollments.

ACTIVITIES: 3% of men belong to 1 local and 4 national fraternities; 3% of women belong to 5 local and 3 national sororities. There are 64 groups on campus, including art, band, cheerleading, choir, chorale, chorus, computers, dance, drama, ethnic, honors, international, jazz band, LGBT, newspaper, opera, orchestra, photography, political, professional, radio and TV, religious, social, social service, student government, and symphony. Popular campus events include Warrior Day, College Day, and Wellness Day. **Sports:** There are 6 intercollegiate sports for men and 6 for women, and 9 intramural sports for men and 9 for women. Facilities include a field house, 2300-seat gym, softball and baseball diamonds, soccer field, tennis courts, an all-weather track, swimming pool, and a weight room.

SERVICES: Counseling and information services are available, as is tutoring in most subjects. There is a reader service for the blind, and remedial math, reading, and writing. **Library/Resources:** The library contains 363,479 volumes, 1.3 million microform items, and 4,288 audio/video tapes/CDs/DVDs, and subscribes to 1,398 periodicals including electronic. Computerized library services include interlibrary loans, database searching, Internet access, and Wi-Fi capability. Special learning facilities include an art gallery, radio station, laser lab, marine sciences station, greenhouse, art gallery, main stage theater, recital hall, observatory, art complex, and distance learning studios. **Physically Challenged Students:** 99% of the campus is accessible. Facilities include wheelchair ramps, elevators, special parking, specially equipped restrooms, lowered drinking fountains, lowered telephones, and special housing. **Special:** Numerous co-op programs and internships are offered. Cross-registration with the Higher Education Consortium of Central California, study abroad, work-study programs, nondegree study, an accelerated degree program, B.A.-B.S. degrees, dual majors, student-designed majors, and pass/fail options are also available. There are 10 national honor societies, Phi Beta Kappa, a freshman honors program, and 99 departmental honors programs. **Visiting:** There are regularly scheduled orientations for prospective students. There are guides for informal visits and visitors may sit in on classes. To schedule a visit, contact the University Outreach. **Campus Safety and Security:** Measures include 24-hour foot and vehicle patrol, self-defense education, and security escort services. There are shuttle buses, emergency telephones, lighted pathways/sidewalks, and CPR and first-aid training.

REQUIREMENTS: Admission is based on an eligibility index that weights GPA and SAT or ACT scores. Applicants with a GPA of 3.0 (3.4 for nonresidents) are exempt from test score requirements. Applicants should be graduates of an accredited secondary school. Preparatory course work should include 4 years of English, 3 of math, 2 each of foreign language, history/social sciences, and lab science, 1 of visual and performing arts, and 1 academic elective. AP and CLEP credits are accepted. Important factors in the admissions decision are advanced placement or honors courses, evidence of special talent, and geographical diversity. To graduate, students must complete at least 120 semester units, including 51 in the general education program and 40 in upper-division courses, with a minimum GPA of 2.0. Distribution requirements consist of 12 units of Social, Economic, and Political Institutions and Human Behavior, 9 each of Communication Skills, Natural Sciences and Mathematics, and Humanities, and 3 of Individual Resources for Modern Living. **Procedure:** Freshmen are admitted to all sessions. Entrance exams should be taken in fall of the senior year. There is a rolling admissions plan. Applications should be filed by August 18 for fall entry, along with a $55 fee. Notification is sent on a rolling basis. Applications are accepted online. **Transfer Students:** Applicants must have a college GPA of 2.0 (2.4 for nonresidents) and have completed their lower-division general education English and math courses. Those with fewer than 60 transferable semester credits must meet freshman entrance requirements. 30 of 120 credits required for the bachelor's degree must be completed at CSU Stanislaus. **International Students:** They must take the TOEFL. They must also take the SAT or ACT.

Admissions Contact: Lisa Bernardo, Director of Admissions and Records. Email: *outreach_help_desk@csustan.edu* Web: *www.csustan.edu*

FINANCIAL AID: The priority date for freshman financial aid applications for fall entry is March 2.

CHAPMAN UNIVERSITY — D-5

www.chapman.edu/admission

Orange, CA 92866	**(714) 997-6711** **(888) CU-APPLY**
Fax: (714) 997-6713	**Email: admit@chapman.edu**
Full-time: 2393 men, 3611 women	**Faculty:** 348; IIA, ++$
Part-time: 144 men, 133 women	**Ph.D.s:** 87%
Graduate: 775 men, 1076 women	**Student/Faculty:** 14 to 1
Year: 4-1-4, summer session	**Tuition:** $45,393
Room & Board: $12,954	**Freshman Class:** 12507 applied, 5883 accepted, 1422 enrolled
SAT CR/M/W: 600/600/610 **ACT:** 27	**CEEB CODE:** 4047
Application Deadline: January 15	**VERY COMPETITIVE+**

Chapman University, founded in 1861, is one of the oldest, and most prestigious private universities in California. Known for its blend of liberal arts and professional programs. The university's mission is to provide personalized education of distinction that leads to inquiring, ethical and productive lives as global citizens. There are 7 undergraduate schools and 8 graduate schools. In addition to regional accreditation, Chapman has baccalaureate program accreditation with AACSB, NASM, CAATE, NASD, and NAST. The 79-acre campus is in a suburban area 35 miles southeast of Los Angeles. Including any residence halls, there are 52 buildings.

STUDENT LIFE: 74% of undergraduates are from California. Others are from 45 states, 84 foreign countries, and Canada. 60% are White; 6% two or more races; 4% Foreign; 3% race unknown; 14% Hispanic; 10% Asian American; 1% African American. 30% are Catholic; 25% Protestant; 18% claim no religious affiliation; 17% Christian, Buddhist, Baha'i, Hindu, and Muslim. **Female To Male Ratio:** 1.5:1. The average age of freshmen is 18; all undergraduates, 20. 9% do not continue beyond their first year; 74% remain to graduate. **Housing:** 1958 students can be accommodated in college housing, which includes coed dorms, on-campus apartments, off-campus apartments, and married student housing. In addition, there are special-interest houses. On-campus housing is guaranteed for the freshman year only, and is available on a first-come, first-served basis, and is available on a lottery system for upperclassmen. Priority is given to out-of-town students. 68% of students commute. All students may keep cars.

FACULTY/CLASSROOMS: 58% of faculty are male; 42% are female. 89% teach undergraduates. Graduate students teach 2% of introductory courses. The average class size in an introductory lecture is 24 and in a laboratory is 24.

PROGRAMS OF STUDY: Chapman confers B.A., B.S., B.F.A. and B.M. degrees. Master's and doctoral degrees are also awarded. Bachelor's degrees are awarded in BIOLOGICAL SCIENCE (biochemistry and biology/biological science), BUSINESS (accounting and business administration and management), COMMUNICATIONS AND THE ARTS (acting, art, art history and appreciation, broadcasting, communications, creative writing, dance, dramatic arts, English, film arts, film, television and digital media, French, graphic design, keyboard - piano concentration, music, music performance, music theory and composition, playwriting/screenwriting, public relations, Spanish, strategic communication, and theatre studies), COMPUTER AND PHYSICAL SCIENCE (chemistry, computer science, digital arts/technology, information sciences and systems, mathematics, physics, and software engineering), EDUCATION (athletic training, education, and music education), ENGINEERING AND ENVIRONMENTAL DESIGN (environmental science), HEALTH PROFESSIONS (health science and kinesiology), SOCIAL SCIENCE (economics, history, peace studies, philosophy, political science/government, psychology, religion, social work, and sociology). business, computational science, and history are the strongest academically. business, communication studies, and psychology have the largest enrollments.

ACTIVITIES: 28% of men belong to 9 national fraternities; 38% of women belong to 8 national sororities. Groups on campus include art, band, cheerleading, choir, chorale, chorus, computers, dance, debate, drama, environmental, ethnic, film, forensics, honors, international, jazz band, LGBT, literary magazine, musical theater, newspaper, opera, orchestra, pep band, photography, political, professional, radio and TV, religious, social, social service, student government, symphony, and yearbook. **Sports:** There are 11 intercollegiate sports for men and 11 for women, and 4 intramural sports for men and 4 for women. Facilities include a gym, a weight room, soccer/football field, aquatic center, tennis courts, baseball and softball fields. **Graduates:** From July 1, 2015 to June 30, 2016, 1352 bachelor's degrees were awarded. The most popular majors were business administration (17%), communication studies (10%), and film studies (10%). In an average class, 2% graduate in 3 years or less, 58% graduate in 4 years or less, 71% graduate in 5 years or less, and 74% graduate in 6 years or less.

SERVICES: Counseling and information services are available, as is tutoring in most subjects. There is a reader service for the blind, and remedial math, reading, and writing. **Library/Resources:** The 2 libraries contain 322,793 volumes, 689,946 microform items, and 25,594 audio/video tapes/CDs/DVDs, and subscribe to 62,917 periodicals including electronic. Computerized library services include interlibrary loans, database searching, Internet access, and Wi-Fi capability. Special learning facilities include a radio station, food science sensory lab, and economic sciences lab. **Physically Challenged Students:** 75% of the campus is accessible. Facilities include wheelchair ramps, elevators, special parking, specially equipped restrooms, special class scheduling, lowered drinking fountains, lowered telephones, and special housing. **Special:** Internship programs are available. Students are encouraged to study abroad for a semester or spend a semester in Washington, D.C. Dual and student-designed majors are possible. A general studies degree, B.A.-B.S. degrees, nondegree study options, and pass/fail options are also permitted. A 3-2 engineering degree with the University of California, Irvine, is also available. There are 13 national honor societies and a freshman honors program. **Visiting:** There are regularly scheduled orientations for prospective students, consisting of Fall and Spring Campus Exploration Day events. Weekday appointments and campus tours are also available. There are guides for informal visits and visitors may sit in on classes. To schedule a visit, contact the Office of Admissions. **Campus Safety and Security:** Measures include 24-hour foot and vehicle patrol, emergency notification system, self-defense education, and security escort services. There are shuttle buses, emergency telephones, lighted pathways/sidewalks, controlled access to dorms/residences, rape awareness, and victim assistance programs.

REQUIREMENTS: The SAT or ACT is required. The ACT Optional Writing test is also required. Applicants should be graduates of accredited high schools or have earned the GED. Secondary preparation should include 4 years of English, foreign language, math, and social science;

and 2 years of science. Prospective art or music majors should show some preparation in those fields. A personal essay is required. An on-campus interview is recommended. Entry to the film school requires portfolio acceptance. Dance performance and theater performance require auditions. AP and CLEP credits are accepted. Important factors in the admissions decision are advanced placement or honors courses, evidence of special talent, and leadership record. Students in the baccalaureate program must complete a total of 124 credits with at least a 2.0 GPA. The general education program includes courses in artistic inquiry, natural science inquiry, quantitative inquiry, social inquiry, values and ethical inquiry, and written inquiry. Freshman foundation, global citizenship, and interdisciplinary courses are also required. **Procedure:** Freshmen are admitted in the fall and spring. Entrance exams should be taken by fall of the senior year. Applications should be filed by January 15 for fall entry; November 1 for spring entry, along with a $65 fee. Notifications are sent March 15. 455 applicants were on the 2016 waiting list; 92 were admitted. Applications are accepted on-line. **Transfer Students:** 358 transfer students enrolled in 2015-2016. Transfer applicants should have completed at least 12 credits of transferable college work with a 2.25 minimum GPA. High school records and SAT or ACT scores should be submitted if fewer than 30 transferable credits have been completed. 48 of 124 credits required for the bachelor's degree must be completed at Chapman. **International Students:** There are 256 international students enrolled. The school actively recruits these students. They must take the TOEFL with a minimum score of 550 on the paper-based TOEFL (PBT) or 80 on the Internet-based version (iBT). They must also take the SAT or ACT.

ADMISSIONS: 47% of the 2016-2017 applicants were accepted. The SAT scores for the 2016-2017 freshman class were: Critical Reading-- 6% below 500, 41% between 500 and 599, 45% between 600 and 699, and 8% between 700 and 800. Math-- 4% below 500, 41% between 500 and 599, 45% between 600 and 699, and 10% between 700 and 800. Writing-- 4% below 500, 38% between 500 and 599, 46% between 600 and 699, and 12% between 700 and 800. The ACT scores were 2% below 12, 12% between 12 and 17, 28% between 18 and 23, 26% between 24 and 29, and 33% above 30. **Admissions Contact:** Mike Drummy, Assistant Vice President and Chief Admission Officer. Email: *admit@chapman.edu* Web: *www.chapman.edu*

FINANCIAL AID: Chapman is a member of CSS. The state aid form is required. The FAFSA code is 001164. The priority date for freshman financial aid applications for fall entry is March 2.

CLAREMONT MCKENNA COLLEGE D-5

www.cmc.edu

Claremont, CA 91711	(909) 621-8088
Fax: (909) 621-8516	**Email:** admission@cmc.edu
Full-time: 673 men, 625 women	**Faculty:** 145; IIB, ++$
Part-time: 3 women	**Ph.D.s:** 98%
Graduate: 21 men, 2 women	**Student/Faculty:** 8 to 1
Year: semesters	**Tuition:** $49,045
Room & Board: $16,360	**Freshman Class:** 6043 applied, 651 accepted, 327 enrolled
SAT CR/M/W: 710/740/710 **ACT:** 32	**CEEB CODE:** 4054
Application Deadline: January 1	**MOST COMPETITIVE**

Claremont McKenna College, founded in 1946, is a highly selective, independent, coeducational, residential, undergraduate liberal arts college with a curricular emphasis on economics, government, and public affairs. By combining the intellectual breadth of the liberal arts with the more pragmatic concerns of public affairs, based on principles established by founding President George C. S. Benson, CMC helps students acquire the vision, skills, and values they will need to lead society. There are 2 undergraduate schools and 1 graduate school. The 69-acre campus is in a suburban area 35 miles east of downtown Los Angeles.

STUDENT LIFE: 63% of undergraduates are from out of state, mostly the West. Students are from 46 states, 31 foreign countries, and Canada. 43% are White; 17% Foreign; 12% Hispanic. **Male To Female Ratio:** 1.1:1. The average age of freshmen is 18; all undergraduates, 20. 4% do not continue beyond their first year; 96% remain to graduate. **Housing:** 1183 students can be accommodated in college housing, which includes single-sex and coed dorms and on-campus apartments, and substance-free housing. On-campus housing is guaranteed for the freshman year only and is available on a lottery system for upperclassmen. 97% of students live on campus. Upperclassmen may keep cars.

FACULTY/CLASSROOMS: 67% of faculty are male; 33% are female. No introductory courses are taught by graduate students. The average class size in a regular course is 18.

PROGRAMS OF STUDY: CMC confers B.A. degrees. Master's degrees are also awarded. Bachelor's degrees are awarded in AGRICULTURE (environmental studies), BIOLOGICAL SCIENCE (biochemistry, biology/biological science, biophysics, molecular biology, and neurosciences), BUSINESS (accounting and management engineering), COMMUNICATIONS AND THE ARTS (classics, film arts, French, literature, media arts, Spanish, and theatre arts), COMPUTER AND PHYSICAL SCIENCE (chemistry, mathematics, physics, and science and management), ENGINEERING AND ENVIRONMENTAL DESIGN (environmental science), SOCIAL SCIENCE (African studies, American studies, Asian/Oriental studies, economics, Hispanic American studies, history, interdisciplinary studies, international relations, legal studies, Middle Eastern studies, philosophy, political science/government, psychology, and religion). Economics, international relations, and government have the largest enrollments.

ACTIVITIES: There are no fraternities or sororities. There are 48 groups on campus, including Army ROTC, band, chorale, communications, computers, dance, debate, drama, environmental, ethnic, film, honors, international, jazz band, LGBT, literary magazine, musical theater, newspaper, political, professional, religious, social, social service, student government, symphony, and yearbook. Popular campus events include International Festival, Athenaeum Speakers, and Monte Carlo Night (Homecoming). **Sports:** There are 10 intercollegiate sports for men and 11 for women, and 8 intramural sports for men and 8 for women. Facilities include basketball courts, weight room, fitness center, squash, volleyball, track and football field, aquatic center, tennis courts, baseball, softball, lacrosse, soccer fields, archery range, squash and volleyball courts. **Graduates:** From July 1, 2014 to June 30, 2015, 319 bachelor's degrees were awarded. The most popular majors were economics (27%), government (15%), and psychology (13%). 106 companies recruited on campus in 2014-2015. In an average class, 84% graduate in 4 years or less, 92% graduate in 5 years or less, and 92% graduate in 6 years or less.

SERVICES: The Center for Writing and Public Discourse offers writing assistance and specialized workshops. **Library/Resources:** The library contains 1.1 million volumes, 980,340 microform items, and 13,171 audio/video tapes/CDs/DVDs. Computerized library services include interlibrary loans, database searching, Internet access, and Wi-Fi capability. **Physically Challenged Students:** All of the campus is accessible. Facilities include wheelchair ramps, elevators, special parking, and specially equipped restrooms. The campus complies with ADA requirements and reasonably accommodates students with physical disabilities as necessary to meet their access needs. **Special:** Internships, Washington DC and Silicon Valley programs, BA/MA program in Finance, 3-2 engineering degree, cross registration with the Claremont Colleges, study abroad programs, ten research institutes, and the Robert Day Scholars program. There is a chapter of Phi Beta Kappa. **Visiting:** There are regularly scheduled orientations for prospective students. There are guides for informal visits, visitors may sit in on classes, and stay overnight. To schedule a visit, contact the Office of Admission. **Campus Safety and Security:** Measures include 24-hour foot and vehicle patrol, emergency notification system, and security escort services. There are emergency telephones, lighted pathways/sidewalks, and controlled access to dorms/residences.

REQUIREMENTS: The SAT or ACT is required. The ACT Optional Writing test is also required. AP credits are accepted. All students must complete 32 courses (128 semester hours), including general education, major and grade-point requirements. **Procedure:** Freshmen are admitted fall. Entrance exams should be taken no later than the fall of your senior year. There is a early decision plan. Early decision applications should be filed by November 1; regular applications, by January 1 for fall entry; and November 1 for spring entry, along with a $60 fee. Notification of early decision is sent December 15; regular decision, April 1. 181 early decision candidates were accepted for the 2015-2016 class. 614 applicants were on the 2015 waiting list; 38 were admitted. Applications are accepted on-line. **Transfer Students:** 21 transfer students enrolled in 2014-2015. 64 of 128 credits required for the bachelor's degree must be completed at CMC. **International Students:** There are 215 international students enrolled. The school actively recruits these students. They must take the TOEFL with a minimum score of 600 on the paper-based TOEFL (PBT) or 100 on the Internet-based version (iBT). They must also take the SAT or ACT.

ADMISSIONS: 11% of the 2015-2016 applicants were accepted. The SAT scores for the 2015-2016 freshman class were: Critical Reading-- 1% between 500 and 599, 38% between 600 and 699, and 61% between 700 and 800. Math-- 2% between 500 and 599, 33% between 600 and 699, and 65% between 700 and 800. Writing-- 2% between 500 and 599, 25% between 600 and 699, and 73% between 700 and 800. The ACT scores were 19% between 24 and 29, and 81% above 30. **Admissions Contact:** Georgette R. DeVeres, AVP and Dean of Admission & Financial Aid. E-Mail: *admission@cmc.edu* Web: *www.cmc.edu*

FINANCIAL AID: In 2015-2016, 41% of all full-time freshmen received some form of financial aid. 40% of all full-time freshmen received need-based aid. The average freshman award was $41,971. Need-based scholarships or need-based grants averaged $39,775; need-based self-help aid (loans and jobs) averaged $4,797; and other non-need-based awards and non-need-based scholarships averaged $15,713. The average financial indebtedness of the 2015 graduate was $25,462. CMC is a member of CSS. The CSS/Profile, FAFSA, and the state aid form are required. The priority date for freshman financial aid applications for fall entry is January 1. The deadline for filing freshman financial aid applications for fall entry is February 1.

COGSWELL POLYTECHNICAL COLLEGE B-3
www.cogswell.edu

San Jose, CA 95134 | **(408) 541-0100** | **(800)-264-7955**
Fax: (408) 747-0764 | **Email: admissions@cogswell.edu**

Full-time: 142 men, 45 women	**Faculty:** 11; IIB, --$
Part-time: 87 men, 14 women	**Ph.D.s:** 35%
Graduate: n/av	**Student/Faculty:** 12 to 1
Year: semesters, summer session	**Tuition:** $19,668
Room & Board: $10,863	**Freshman Class:** n/av
SAT or ACT: recommended	**CEEB CODE:** 4057
Application Deadline: n/av	**COMPETITIVE**

With over one hundred and twenty years of academic history, Cogswell College provides accredited higher education that empowers students to innovate through the integration of art, engineering and entrepreneurship. The figures in the above capsule and in this profile are approximate. There is 1 undergraduate school and 1 graduate school. In addition to regional accreditation, Cogswell College has baccalaureate program accreditation with WASC. The 4-acre campus is in a suburban area 40 miles south of San Francisco in California's Silicon Valley. Including any residence halls, there is 1 building.

STUDENT LIFE: 88% of undergraduates are from California. Others are from 13 states, and 2 foreign countries. 65% are from public schools. 49% are White; 4% African American; 2% Foreign; 15% Hispanic; 10% Asian American; 1% American Indian/Alaska Native. **Male To Female Ratio:** 3.9:1. The average age of freshmen is 19; all undergraduates, 28. 29% do not continue beyond their first year; 71% remain to graduate. **Housing:** 70 students can be accommodated in college housing. Arrangements can be made to accommodate students in private houses or at nearby corporate apartments. Alcohol is not permitted. All students commute. All students may keep cars.

FACULTY/CLASSROOMS: 65% of faculty are male; 35% are female. No introductory courses are taught by graduate students. The average class size in an introductory lecture is 15; in a laboratory is 8; and in a regular course is 25.

PROGRAMS OF STUDY: Cogswell College confers B.A.D.A.A., B.S.D.A.T., B.S.D.A.E., B.S.(Comp Eng), B.S.S.E., B.S.F.A., B.S.F.P.T. and B.A.E.I. degrees. Master's degrees are also awarded. Bachelor's degrees are awarded in BUSINESS (entrepreneurial studies), COMMUNICATIONS AND THE ARTS (animation, audio technology, and music technology), COMPUTER AND PHYSICAL SCIENCE (computer programming, digital arts/technology, and web technology), ENGINEERING AND ENVIRONMENTAL DESIGN (computer engineering and computer graphics), SOCIAL SCIENCE (fire control and safety technology and fire protection). Digital art & animation, and digital audio technology, are the strongest academically, and have the largest enrollments.

ACTIVITIES: There are no fraternities or sororities. Groups on campus include art, computers, honors, international, jazz band, radio and TV, and student government. Popular campus events include Founders Day, Club Competitions, and Friday Concerts. **Sports:** There is no sports program at Cogswell College. Facilities include a game room, a student lounge, and access to community athletic facilities. **Graduates:** From July 1, 2015 to June 30, 2016, 47 bachelor's degrees were awarded. The most popular majors were digital art and animation (43%), fire administration (34%), and digital audio technology (15%). In an average class, 33% graduate in 4 years or less, 44% graduate in 5 years or less, and 55% graduate in 6 years or less.

SERVICES: On campus tutoring is available if needed for any subjects **Library/Resources:** The library contains 103,000 volumes, 250 microform items, and 831 audio/video tapes/CDs/DVDs, and subscribes to 16 periodicals including electronic. Computerized library services include database searching. Special learning facilities include an art gallery, radio station, drawing and sculpture studios, digital arts labs, audio labs, and a recording studio. **Physically Challenged Students:** Facilities include wheelchair ramps, special parking, specially equipped restrooms, special class scheduling, lowered drinking fountains, and lowered telephones. **Special:** Cogswell offers various internships and work-study programs. The college administers the Degree at a Distance Program (DDP) for the Fire Service program for Arizona, California, and Nevada, through which nonresident students can earn a B.S. in Fire Administration or Fire Prevention and Technology. There is a freshman honors program. **Visiting:** Visitors may sit in on classes. **Campus Safety and Security:** Measures include emergency notification system. There are emergency telephones, lighted pathways/sidewalks, controlled access to dorms/residences, an emergency evacuation plan, and maps in the classrooms.

REQUIREMENTS: The SAT or ACT is recommended. Applicants must be high school graduates or have the GED. Secondary preparation must include 3 years of English, 2 to 3 of math, including algebra, geometry, and trigonometry, and 1 year of science. Cogswell requires a personal essay and recommends a personal interview. A portfolio is required for computer and video imaging programs. AP and CLEP credits are accepted. Important factors in the admissions decision are evidence of special talent, recommendations by school officials, and ability to finance your college education. To graduate, students must complete a total of 120 to 131 credits with 18 to 27 in the major and have a 2.0 GPA. 45 to 56 credits in general education core courses are required, depending on the major, and include courses in English, math, natural sciences, social sciences, and humanities. **Procedure:** Freshmen are admitted to all sessions. There is a rolling admissions plan. Application deadlines are open. Applications are accepted online. **Transfer Students:** Applicants must have completed at least 12 college credits with a 2.2 GPA. An interview is recommended. 40 of 120 credits required for the bachelor's degree must be completed at Cogswell College. **International Students:** There are 11 international students enrolled. They must take the TOEFL with a minimum score of 525 on the paper-based TOEFL (PBT).

Admissions Contact: Aaron Kark, Director of Amnissions. Email: *admissions@cogswell.edu* Web: *www.cogswell.edu*

FINANCIAL AID: In 2016-2017, 77% of all full-time freshmen and 75% of continuing full-time students received some form of financial aid. 75% of all full-time freshmen and 72% of continuing full-time students received need-based aid. 4% of undergraduate students work part-time. Average annual earnings from campus work are $2500. The average financial indebtedness of the 2016 graduate was $22,352. Cogswell College is a member of CSS. The college's own financial statement is required. The FAFSA code is 001177. The deadline for filing freshman financial aid applications for fall entry is March 1.

CONCORDIA UNIVERSITY D-5
www.cui.edu

Irvine, CA 92612 | **(949) 214-3010** | **(800) 229-1200**
Fax: (949) 214-3520 | **Email: admissions@cui.edu**

Full-time: 618 men, 974 women	**Faculty:** n/av
Part-time: 39 men, 107 women	**Ph.D.s:** n/av
Graduate: 837 men, 944 women	**Student/Faculty:** n/av
Year: semesters, summer session	**Tuition:** $31,690
Room & Board: $9890	**Freshman Class:** n/av
SAT or ACT: required	**CEEB CODE:** 4069
Application Deadline: n/av	**VERY COMPETITIVE**

Concordia University, founded in 1972, is a private liberal arts college affiliated with the Lutheran Church-Missouri Synod. The figures in the above capsule and in this profile are approximate. There are 5 undergraduate schools and 4 graduate schools. In addition to regional accreditation, Concordia Irvine has baccalaureate program accreditation with WASC and CTC. The 70-acre campus is in a suburban area 40 miles south of Los Angeles. Including any residence halls, there are 26 buildings.

STUDENT LIFE: 89% of undergraduates are from California. Others are from 34 states, 18 foreign countries, and Canada. 66% are White; 6% Foreign; 4% African American; 4% Asian American; 13% Hispanic; 1% American Indian/Alaska Native. 16% are Catholic; 15% nondenominational . **Female To Male Ratio:** 1.4:1. The average age of freshmen is 18; all undergraduates, 22. 73% remain to graduate. **Housing:** 1077 students can be accommodated in college housing, which includes single-sex dorms. On-campus housing is guaranteed for all 4 years. 69% of students live on campus; of those, 95% remain on campus on weekends. All students may keep cars.

FACULTY/CLASSROOMS: 63% of faculty are male; 37% are female. No introductory courses are taught by graduate students.

PROGRAMS OF STUDY: Concordia Irvine confers B.A. degrees. Associate and master's degrees are also awarded. Bachelor's degrees are awarded in BIOLOGICAL SCIENCE (biology/biological science), BUSINESS (business administration and management), COMMUNICATIONS AND THE ARTS (art, communications, dramatic arts, English, film arts, and music), COMPUTER AND PHYSICAL SCIENCE (chemistry and mathematics), EDUCATION (Christian education and early childhood education), HEALTH PROFESSIONS (exercise science), SOCIAL SCIENCE (behavioral science, biblical languages, history, humanities, international studies, liberal arts/general studies, political science/government, psychology, and theological studies). Business administration, education and social science are the strongest academically.

ACTIVITIES: There are no fraternities or sororities. There are 20 groups on campus, including art, choir, chorale, chorus, communications, dance, debate, drama, ethnic, film, forensics, honors, literary magazine, newspaper, political, radio and TV, religious, social, social service, student government, and yearbook. Popular campus events include Closing Banquet, Christmas Dance and Oktoberfest. **Sports:** There are 9 intercollegiate sports for men and 10 for women, and 7 intramural sports for men and 6 for women. Facilities include a 1800-seat gym, soccer field, baseball/softball diamond, volleyball, tennis, racquetball courts, track field, weight room, dance room, and team rooms.

SERVICES: Counseling and information services are available, as is tutoring in some subjects, such as math, chemistry, critical thinking, Spanish, biology and calculus. **Library/Resources:** The library contains 82,600 volumes, 54,550 microform items, and 2,000 audio/video tapes/CDs/DVDs, and subscribes to 10,513 periodicals including electronic. Computerized library services include interlibrary loans, database searching, and Internet access. Special learning facilities include an art gallery and radio station. **Physically Challenged Students:** 90% of the campus is accessible. Facilities include wheelchair ramps, elevators, special parking, and specially equipped restrooms. **Special:** Cross-registration is possible with 9 Concordia University institutions nationwide. An accelerated degree program in either applied liberal arts or business administration and leadership. Internships, study abroad, and dual and student-designed majors are available. There are 6 national honor societies, a freshman honors program, and 2 departmental honors programs. **Visiting:** There are regularly scheduled orientations for prospective students. There are guides for informal visits, visitors may sit in on classes, and stay overnight. To schedule a visit, contact the Admission Office. **Campus Safety and Security:** Measures include 24-hour foot and vehicle patrol and security escort services. There are lighted pathways/sidewalks.

REQUIREMENTS: The SAT or ACT is required. Applicants should be high school graduates with 4 years of English, 3 each of math and science, and 2 each of social studies and a foreign language. The GED is accepted. A school reference is also required. A GPA of 2.8 is required. AP and CLEP credits are accepted. All students must complete 49 semester hours of general education requirements, including courses in humanities and fine arts, math and science, social science, religion, and exercise and sport science. A total of 128 credits is required to graduate. A GPA of 2.0 in major and program course work must be maintained. For the CU Accelerate program, 120 semester units are required to graduate. **Procedure:** Freshmen are admitted fall and spring. Entrance exams should be taken by the fall of the senior year. There are deferred admissions and rolling admissions plans. Check with the school for current application deadlines. The fall 2016 application fee was $50. Notifications are sent April 15. Applications are accepted online. **Transfer Students:** A GPA of 2.3 is required and a minimum of 24 semester or 36 quarter units completed. An academic reference is required, as are official high school transcripts. 32 of 128 credits required for the bachelor's degree must be completed at Concordia Irvine. **International Students:** The school actively recruits these students. They must take the TOEFL, and SAT or ACT.

Admissions Contact: Doug Wible, Director of Undergraduate Admissions. Email: *admissions@cui.edu* Web: *www.cui.edu*

FINANCIAL AID: The the college's own financial statement is required. The FAFSA code is 013885. Check with the school for current application deadlines.

DOMINICAN UNIVERSITY OF CALIFORNIA — B-3

www.dominican.edu

San Rafael, CA 94901 — **(888) 323-6763**

Fax: (415) 485-3214	**Email: enroll@dominican.edu**
Full-time: 350 men, 1000 women	**Faculty:** IIA, +$
Part-time: 75 men, 200 women	**Ph.D.s:** 74%
Graduate: 215 men, 500 women	**Student/Faculty:** n/av
Year: semesters, summer session	**Tuition:** $43,400
Room & Board: $13,650	**Freshman Class:** n/av
SAT or ACT: required	**CEEB CODE:** 4284
Application Deadline: open	**COMPETITIVE**

Dominican University of California, founded in 1890, is an independent, international, learner-centered university of Catholic heritage. The figures in the above capsule and in this profile are approximate. There are 4 undergraduate schools and 4 graduate schools. In addition to regional accreditation, Dominican has baccalaureate program accreditation with AOTA, CCNE, and CCTE. The 80-acre campus is in a suburban area 12 miles north of San Francisco. Including any residence halls, there are 25 buildings.

STUDENT LIFE: 91% of undergraduates are from California. Others are from 31 states, 15 foreign countries, and Canada. 48% are from public schools. 6% are African American; 33% White; 3% Foreign; 25% Asian American; 18% Hispanic; 1% American Indian/Alaska Native. 38% are Catholic. **Female To Male Ratio:** 2.7:1. The average age of freshmen is 18; all undergraduates, 24. 16% do not continue beyond their first year; 34% remain to graduate. **Housing:** 600 students can be accommodated in college housing, which includes coed dorms. On-campus housing is available on a first-come, first-served basis, and is available on a lottery system for upperclassmen. 55% of students commute. Upperclassmen may keep cars.

FACULTY/CLASSROOMS: 47% of faculty are male; 53% are female. All teach undergraduates, 75% do research, and 75% do both. No introductory courses are taught by graduate students. The average class size in an introductory lecture is 19; in a laboratory is 15; and in a regular course is 15.

PROGRAMS OF STUDY: Dominican confers B.A., B.S., B.F.A. and B.S.N. degrees. Master's degrees are also awarded. Bachelor's degrees are awarded in AGRICULTURE (environmental studies), BIOLOGICAL SCIENCE (biology/biological science), BUSINESS (business administration and management and international business management), COMMUNICATIONS AND THE ARTS (art, art history and appreciation, communications, creative writing, dance, English literature, graphic design, and music), HEALTH PROFESSIONS (nursing, occupational therapy, and premedicine), SOCIAL SCIENCE (history, humanities, international studies, liberal arts/general studies, political science/government, psychology, religion, and women's studies). Nursing, biology, and psychology have the largest enrollments.

ACTIVITIES: There are no fraternities or sororities. There are 27 groups on campus, including art, band, cheerleading, choir, chorale, dance, drama, environmental, ethnic, film, honors, international, jazz band, LGBT, literary magazine, musical theater, newspaper, orchestra, photography, political, professional, radio and TV, religious, social service, and student government. Popular campus events include Shield Day (welcoming the freshman class), Boat Dance and Penguin Ball. **Sports:** There are 5 intercollegiate sports for men and 7 for women, and 5 intramural sports for men and 5 for women. Facilities include a gym, fitness center, swimming pool, 2 basketball courts, a multipurpose room for dance and exercise classes, tennis courts, and a soccer field. **Graduates:** From July 1, 2015 to June 30, 2016, 283 bachelor's degrees were awarded. The most popular majors were nursing (27%), psychology (15%), and business (11%). In an average class, 44% graduate in 4 years or less, 46% graduate in 5 years or less, and 51% graduate in 6 years or less.

SERVICES: Counseling and information services are available, as is tutoring in some subjects, such as writing, math, chemistry, economics, time management, study skills, anatomy, physiology, algebra, and physics. There is a reader service for the blind, and remedial math and writing. **Library/Resources:** The library contains 92,536 volumes, 3,500 microform items, and 1,640 audio/video tapes/CDs/DVDs, and subscribes to 597 periodicals including electronic. Computerized library services include interlibrary loans, database searching, Internet access, and Wi-Fi capability. Special learning facilities include an art gallery, radio station, music library, and an art history slide and print collection. **Physically Challenged Students:** 50% of the campus is accessible. Facilities include wheelchair ramps, elevators, special parking, specially equipped restrooms, special class scheduling, and lowered drinking fountains. **Special:** There is a semester interchange program with colleges in Michigan, Florida, or New York. Dominican also offers study abroad, dual majors for students with a 3.0 GPA or better, B.A.-B.S. degrees, student-designed majors, a Washington semester, internships, pass/fail options outside of major and general education courses, and an evening/weekend bachelor's degree program. There are 3 national honor societies, Phi Beta Kappa, a freshman honors program, and 3 departmental honors programs. **Visiting:** There are regularly scheduled orientations for prospective students, including financial aid conferences, lunch on campus, meeting with the prospective academic adviser, and a campus tour. There are guides for informal visits and visitors may sit in on classes. To schedule a visit, contact the Admissions Office. **Campus Safety and Security:** Measures include 24-hour foot and vehicle patrol, emergency notification system, and security escort services. There are emergency telephones, lighted pathways/sidewalks, and controlled access to dorms/residences.

REQUIREMENTS: The SAT or ACT is required. Applicants must be graduates of an accredited high school or have earned the GED. Secondary preparation must include 4 years of English, 2 each of math and a foreign language, and 1 each of lab science and history. An essay and a recommendation are required. An interview and a visit to the campus are highly recommended. Prospective music majors are encouraged to schedule an audition. AP and CLEP credits are accepted. Important factors in the admissions decision are recommendations by school officials, extracurricular activities record, and evidence of special talent. All students must complete 124 credit hours including at least 24 in upper-division work, with a minimum 2.0 GPA. Core requirements include a cultural heritage colloquium of 9 units, 6 units each in religion and first-year interdisciplinary studies, 3 to 4 units each of math and quantitative reasoning, natural science, social science, moral philosophy and ethics, and creative and performing arts, and 1 unit of information and research. Students must pass a computer competency test, and a senior thesis, project, recital, or comprehensive exam. **Procedure:** Freshmen are admitted fall and spring. Entrance exams should be taken in the fall or early spring of the senior year. There are deferred admissions and rolling admissions plans. Application deadlines are open. Application fee is $50. Applications are accepted online. **Transfer Students:** 110 transfer students enrolled in 2015-2016. Applicants must have a 2.0 GPA at an accredited college. They must also submit official high school and college transcripts and a letter of recommendation from a professor, academic dean, or counselor. 30 of 124 credits required for the bachelor's degree must be completed at Dominican. **International Students:** There are 30 international students enrolled. The school actively recruits these students. They must take the TOEFL with a minimum score of 550 on the paper-based TOEFL (PBT) or 80 on the Internet-based version (iBT). They must also take the SAT or ACT.

Admissions Contact: Rebecca Finn Kenney, Asst. VP of Undergraduate Admissions. Email: *enroll@dominican.edu* Web: *www.dominican.edu*

FINANCIAL AID: In 2016-2017, 97% of all full-time freshmen and 85% of continuing full-time students received some form of financial aid. 70% of all full-time freshmen and 72% of continuing full-time students received need-based aid. The average freshman award was $34,561. Need-based scholarships or need-based grants averaged $14,006 ($28,922 maximum); need-based self-help aid (loans and jobs) averaged $4,646 ($7,375 maximum); non-need-based athletic scholarships averaged $2,567 ($6,000 maximum); and other non-need-based awards and non-need-based scholarships averaged $7,660 ($15,500 maximum). 17% of undergraduate students work part-time. Average annual earnings from campus work are $2254. The average financial indebtedness of the 2016 graduate was $19,092. Dominican is a member of CSS. The college's own financial statement is required. The FAFSA code is 001196. Check with the school for current application deadlines.

FRESNO PACIFIC UNIVERSITY — C-3

www.fresno.edu

Fresno, CA 93702	**(559) 453-2039** **(800) 660-6089**
Fax: (559) 453-2007	**Email: ugadmis@fresno.edu**
Full-time: 701 men, 1448 women	**Faculty:** IIA, --$
Part-time: 108 men, 182 women	**Ph.D.s:** n/av
Graduate: 320 men, 701 women	**Student/Faculty:** n/av
Year: semesters, summer session	**Tuition:** $29,335
Room & Board: $8035	**Freshman Class:** n/av
SAT or ACT: required	**CEEB CODE:** 4616
Application Deadline: July 31	**COMPETITIVE**

Fresno Pacific University, founded in 1944, is a private Christian liberal arts college offering undergraduate and graduate degrees, and is affiliated with the Mennonite Brethren. The figures in the above capsule and in this profile are approximate. There are 4 undergraduate schools and 5 graduate schools. In addition to regional accreditation, FPU has baccalaureate program accreditation with WASC. The 42-acre campus is in a suburban area 150 miles southeast of San Francisco. Including any residence halls, there are 20 buildings.

STUDENT LIFE: 97% of undergraduates are from California. Others are from 14 states, 12 foreign countries, and Canada. 86% are from public schools. 50% are White; 4% African American; 4% Asian American; 4% Foreign; 29% Hispanic; 1% American Indian/Alaska Native. 79% are Protestant; 15% Catholic. **Female To Male Ratio:** 2.1:1. The average age of freshmen is 20; all undergraduates, 21. 20% do not continue beyond their first year; 62% remain to graduate. **Housing:** 550 students can be accommodated in college housing, which includes single-sex dorms, on-campus apartments, and off-campus apartments. In addition, there are special-interest houses. On-campus housing is available on a first-come, first-served basis, and is available on a lottery system for upperclassmen. Priority is given to out-of-town students. 51% of students commute. Alcohol is not permitted. All students may keep cars.

FACULTY/CLASSROOMS: 66% of faculty are male; 34% are female. 78% teach undergraduates. No introductory courses are taught by graduate students. The average class size in a laboratory is 14 and in a regular course is 18.

PROGRAMS OF STUDY: FPU confers B.A., and B.S. degrees. Associate and master's degrees are also awarded. Bachelor's degrees are awarded in BIOLOGICAL SCIENCE (biology/biological science), BUSINESS (accounting, business administration and management, and sports management), COMMUNICATIONS AND THE ARTS (English, music, and Spanish), COMPUTER AND PHYSICAL SCIENCE (chemistry, mathematics, and natural sciences), EDUCATION (English education, mathematics education, music education, physical education, science education, and social science education), ENGINEERING AND ENVIRONMENTAL DESIGN (environmental science), HEALTH PROFESSIONS (premedicine), SOCIAL SCIENCE (history, ministries, missions, philosophy, prelaw, psychology, religion, social science, and social work). Business, education, and religion are the strongest academically. Business, education, and psychology have the largest enrollments.

ACTIVITIES: There are no fraternities or sororities. There are 20 groups on campus, including art, cheerleading, choir, chorale, chorus, communications, dance, drama, ethnic, honors, international, jazz band, newspaper, pep band, political, professional, religious, social, social service, and student government. Popular campus events include Carol Sing, Winter Ball, and Junior/Senior Banquet. **Sports:** There are 8 intercollegiate sports for men and 8 for women, and 9 intramural sports for men and 9 for women. Facilities include a gym, soccer fields, swimming pool, track & field facility, weight room, racquetball courts, and tennis courts.

SERVICES: Counseling and information services are available, as is

tutoring in every subject. There is a reader service for the blind, and remedial math, reading, and writing. **Library/Resources:** The library contains 197,532 volumes, 315,000 microform items, and 7,840 audio/video tapes/CDs/DVDs, and subscribes to 3,200 periodicals including electronic. Computerized library services include interlibrary loans, database searching, and Internet access. **Physically Challenged Students:** All of the campus is accessible. Facilities include wheelchair ramps, elevators, special parking, specially equipped restrooms, lowered drinking fountains, lowered telephones, and special housing. **Special:** Accelerated degrees and internships are available as is a 1-semester cooperative program with the University of California, Davis. Cross-registration is possible with San Joaquin College of Law and California State University, Fresno. A B.A. in management and organizational development is offered to working adults. Other off-campus learning opportunities include programs in American studies in Washington, D.C., urban studies in Chicago, and study abroad in Israel, Japan, and Costa Rica, and at Brethren Colleges in England, Spain, France, Germany, or China. There are 2 national honor societies, a freshman honors program, and 1 departmental honors program. **Visiting:** There are regularly scheduled orientations for prospective students. There are guides for informal visits, visitors may sit in on classes, and stay overnight. To schedule a visit, contact the Admissions Office. **Campus Safety and Security:** Measures include 24-hour foot and vehicle patrol, self-defense education, and security escort services. There are shuttle buses, emergency telephones, lighted pathways/sidewalks, 24-hour CCTV monitored in real-time closed-circuit security cameras. 16 cameras create a virtual perimeter patrol of the campus with 5 emergency telephones and 8 regular telephones.

REQUIREMENTS: The SAT or ACT is required. Applicants should be graduates of an accredited high school or have the GED. Required secondary preparation includes 4 years of college prep English, 2 years of social studies, algebra 1 and 2, and geometry, and at least 1 year of a lab science. The college recommends that applicants also take courses in art, music, and 2 years of the same foreign language, all with a grade of C or better. An essay is required, and an audition is recommended for prospective music majors. A GPA of 3.1 is required. AP and CLEP credits are accepted. Important factors in the admissions decision are recommendations by school officials, advanced placement or honors courses, and extracurricular activities record. Students must complete 124 semester units, 40 of which are in upper-division courses, with at least a 2.0 GPA. General education requirements include a biblical studies/world civilization series, and 2 courses each in humanities, natural sciences, social sciences, and phys ed and math. Students are required to attend College Hour, a twice-weekly program of lectures, films, and concerts. Students are also encouraged to volunteer 2 hours of community service per week. Several majors require internships. **Procedure:** Freshmen are admitted fall and spring. Entrance exams should be taken during the fall of their senior year. There are early admissions and rolling admissions plans. Applicants should apply by July 31 for fall entry, along with a $40 fee. Notification is sent on a rolling basis. Applications are accepted online. **Transfer Students:** Applicants should have completed at least 24 transferable units of college work with a 2.4 GPA. Those with fewer credits may apply any time but must meet freshman admission requirements. The SAT or ACT scores are recommended. 30 of 124 credits required for the bachelor's degree must be completed at FPU. **International Students:** The school actively recruits these students. They must take the TOEFL.

ADMISSIONS: 4 freshmen graduated first in their class. **Admissions Contact:** Yammilette Rodriguez, Undergraduate College Admission. Email: *ugadmis@fresno.edu* Web: *www.fresno.edu*

FINANCIAL AID: The FAFSA code is 001253. Check with the school for current application deadlines.

GOLDEN GATE UNIVERSITY B-3

www.ggu.edu

San Francisco, CA 94105	(415) 442-7800 (800) 448-4968
Fax: (415) 442-7807	**Email:** info@ggu.edu
Full-time: 85 men, 110 women	**Faculty:** n/av
Part-time: 215 men, 235 women	**Ph.D.s:** n/av
Graduate: 1555 men, 1795 women	**Student/Faculty:** n/av
Year: varies, summer session	**Tuition:** $18,910
Room & Board: $13,200	**Freshman Class:** n/av **CEEB CODE:** 4329
Application Deadline: n/av	**COMPETITIVE**

Golden Gate University, founded in 1901, is a private, independent, commuter institution offering undergraduate and graduate degrees in business administration, accounting, human and social sciences. The figures given in the above capsule and in this profile are approximate. Tuition cost varies by program chosen by student. There are 3 undergraduate schools and 4 graduate schools. In addition to regional accreditation, Golden Gate has baccalaureate program accreditation with WASC. The 1-acre campus is in an urban area in San Francisco. Including any residence halls, there are 2 buildings.

STUDENT LIFE: 51% are White; 19% Asian American; 18% Foreign; 10% African American; 10% Hispanic. **Female To Male Ratio:** 1.2:1. The average age of freshmen is 21; all undergraduates, 37. 12% do not continue beyond their first year. **Housing:** Alcohol is not permitted. All students commute.

FACULTY/CLASSROOMS: All teach undergraduates. No introductory courses are taught by graduate students. The average class size in an introductory lecture is 25; in a laboratory is 15; and in a regular course is 20.

PROGRAMS OF STUDY: Golden Gate confers B.S., and B.B.A. degrees. Master's and doctoral degrees are also awarded. Bachelor's degrees are awarded in BUSINESS (accounting, banking and finance, human resources, and international business management), ENGINEERING AND ENVIRONMENTAL DESIGN (technological management). Accounting, finance, and information systems are the strongest academically. Finance, accounting, and management have the largest enrollments.

ACTIVITIES: There are no fraternities or sororities. There are 5 groups on campus, including ethnic, international, newspaper, professional, and social. A popular campus event is the Commencement Ball. **Sports:** There is no sports program at Golden Gate.

SERVICES: Counseling and information services are available, as is tutoring in some subjects. There is remedial math, reading, and writing. **Library/Resources:** The 2 libraries contain 300,000 volumes, and subscribe to 2,500 periodicals including electronic. Computerized library services include interlibrary loans and database searching. **Physically Challenged Students:** All of the campus is accessible. Facilities include wheelchair ramps, elevators, special parking, and specially equipped restrooms. **Special:** The university offers cooperative programs, cross-registration with the San Francisco Consortium, internships, an accelerated degree program, dual majors, credit for military experience, nondegree study, and credit/no credit options. Also available are weekend classes and 10-week terms. **Visiting:** Visitors may sit in on classes. To schedule a visit, contact the Student Affairs Office. **Campus Safety and Security:** Measures include security escort services.

REQUIREMENTS: Applicants must be graduates of an accredited secondary school or have a GED. A GPA of 3.0 is required. AP and CLEP credits are accepted. A total of 123 trimester hours, with 21 to 33 in the major, are required to graduate. **Procedure:** Freshmen are admitted fall, spring, and summer. There is a rolling admissions plan. Check with the school for current application deadlines. Notification is sent on a rolling basis. Applications are accepted online. **Transfer Students:** At least 24 transferable units and a 2.0 overall GPA are required. A minimum of 30 units out of 123, including 21 in the major, must be completed at GGU. **International Students:** The school actively recruits these students. They must take the TOEFL.

Admissions Contact: Office of Admissions and Student Affairs. Email: *info@ggu.edu* Web: *www.ggu.edu*

FINANCIAL AID: The FAFSA code is 001205. Check with the school for current application deadlines.

HARVEY MUDD COLLEGE D-5

www.hmc.edu

Claremont, CA 91711	(909) 621-8011
Fax: (909) 607-7046	**Email:** admission@hmc.edu
Full-time: 432 men, 380 women	**Faculty:** 93; IIB, ++$
Part-time: 1 men, 1 women	**Ph.D.s:** 100%
Graduate: n/av	**Student/Faculty:** 9 to 1
Year: semesters	**Tuition:** $50,649
Room & Board: $16,506	**Freshman Class:** 4119 applied, 534 accepted, 214 enrolled
SAT CR/M/W: 720/770/720 **ACT:** 34	**CEEB CODE:** 4341
Application Deadline: January 5	**MOST COMPETITIVE**

Harvey Mudd College, founded in 1955, is one of the Claremont Colleges. It is a private institution specializing in a math, science, and engineering education within a liberal arts tradition. There are 5 undergraduate schools and 2 graduate schools. In addition to regional accreditation, Harvey Mudd College has baccalaureate program accreditation with ABET and WASC. The 33-acre campus is in a suburban area 35 miles east of Los Angeles. Including any residence halls, there are 20 buildings.

STUDENT LIFE: 59% of undergraduates are from out of state, mostly the Middle Atlantic. Students are from 41 states, 24 foreign countries, and Canada. 65% are from public schools. 44% are White; 21% Asian American; 13% Foreign; 10% Hispanic; 6% two or more races; 4% race unknown; 2% African American; 1% American Indian/Alaska Native. **Male To Female Ratio:** 1.1:1. The average age of freshmen is 18; all undergraduates, 19. 3% do not continue beyond their first year; 90% remain to graduate. **Housing:** College-sponsored housing includes single-sex and coed dorms, on-campus apartments, off-campus apartments, and married student housing. On-campus housing is guaranteed for the freshman year only and is available on a lottery system for upperclassmen. Upperclassmen may keep cars.

FACULTY/CLASSROOMS: 62% of faculty are male; 38% are female. All teach undergraduates, and all do research. No introductory courses are taught by graduate students. The average class size in an introductory lecture is 65; in a laboratory is 20; and in a regular course is 20.

PROGRAMS OF STUDY: Harvey Mudd College confers B.S. degrees. Bachelor's degrees are awarded in BIOLOGICAL SCIENCE (biology/biological science), COMPUTER AND PHYSICAL SCIENCE (chemistry, computer science, mathematics, and physics), ENGINEERING AND ENVIRONMENTAL DESIGN (engineering). Engineering, computer science, and mathematics have the largest enrollments.

ACTIVITIES: There are no fraternities or sororities. There are 46 groups on campus, including art, band, chess, choir, chorale, chorus, computers, dance, drama, environmental, ethnic, film, international, jazz band, LGBT, literary magazine, musical theater, newspaper, orchestra, photography, political, professional, radio and TV, religious, social, social service, student government, symphony, and yearbook. Popular campus events include 5-Class Competition, Wednesday Nighters, Crib Races, Frosh Soph Games, and Inner Tube Water Polo. **Sports:** There are 10 intercollegiate sports for men and 11 for women, and 9 intramural sports for men and 9 for women. Facilities include sharing an athletic facility housing with The Clarmont McKenna College and Scripps College, which has 2 gym floors, weight room, track, swimming pool, tennis courts, and sports fields. The HMC campus recreation facility houses a full-size gym floor, an aerobics/dance room, and a fitness room with cardio and weight equipment. **Graduates:** From July 1, 2015 to June 30, 2016, 184 bachelor's degrees were awarded. The most popular majors were computer science (30%), engineering (29%), and joint computer science and mathematics (12%). 185 companies recruited on campus in 2015-2016. In an average class, 85% graduate in 4 years or less, 88% graduate in 5 years or less, and 90% graduate in 6 years or less. Of the 2015 graduating class, 27% were enrolled in graduate school within 6 months of graduation, and 64% were employed.

SERVICES: Counseling and information services are available, as is tutoring in most subjects. Additional support is offered on a case-by-case basis in coordination with the Associate Dean of Academic Affairs, the Associate Dean of Student Life, the Academic Excellence Program, and our faculty. **Library/Resources:** The library contains 2.0 million volumes, and subscribes to 70,000 periodicals including electronic. Computerized library services include interlibrary loans, database searching, Internet access, and Wi-Fi capability. Special learning facilities include an art gallery, planetarium, radio station, and TV station. **Physically Challenged Students:** Facilities include wheelchair ramps, elevators, special parking, specially equipped restrooms, special class scheduling, and lowered drinking fountains. **Special:** Students may cross-register at any of the other Claremont Colleges. Industry-sponsored projects (the Clinic Program) are available for all students, and required for Engineering and Computer Science majors. All students may choose to study abroad and an on-campus office supports these students. We offer dual and special majors in computer science and math, and computational biology, chemistry and biology, and student-designed majors are also available. A 3-2 engineering degree with Claremont McKenna College or Scripps College is possible. The first semester for freshmen is taken on a pass/fail basis. There is 1 national honor society and 7 departmental honors programs. **Visiting:** There are regularly scheduled orientations for prospective students, campus tours and admission interviews are offered Monday through Friday and some Saturday mornings during the fall. Visitors may sit in on classes and stay overnight. To schedule a visit, contact the Office of Admission. **Campus Safety and Security:** Measures include 24-hour foot and vehicle patrol, emergency notification system, self-defense education, and security escort services. There are emergency telephones, lighted pathways/sidewalks, and controlled access to dorms/residences.

REQUIREMENTS: Applicants must have completed 4 years each of English and mathematics (including algebra, demonstrative and analytic geometry, trigonometry, and calculus), 3 years of science (including 1 year each of physics and chemistry), and 1 year of history. The college recommends applicants take 2 years of a foreign language and 2 additional years each of history and social sciences. Students are required to take the SAT or ACT, and SAT subject tests in Math (level 2) and 1 other subject. Letters of recommendation are required from the student's counselor, a math or science teacher, and an English, social science, or foreign language teacher. Applicants must submit 2 personal essays and are encouraged to seek an interview. Important factors in the admissions decision are advanced placement or honors courses, personality/intangible qualities, and extracurricular activities record. The required curriculum, is divided into three components: the Common Core, which provides the foundation for advanced study, the program in Humanities, Social Sciences, and the Arts, which completes the liberal arts nature of a Harvey Mudd College education by providing humanistic, social scientific, and aesthetic perspectives; and the Major, which builds depth and technical competence. Unifying all of these is an emphasis on strong oral and written communications, the development of computational skills, and direct experience with a research or design project. In order to be recommended by the faculty for the Bachelor of Science degree, students are required to complete satisfactorily a minimum of 128 credit hours of courses (including approved transfer credits for courses taken at other colleges). **Procedure:** Freshmen are admitted fall. Entrance exams should be taken ED I- Nov test date, ED II- Dec test date, RD- Jan test date. There are early decision and deferred admissions plans. Early decision applications should be filed by November 15; regular applications, by January 5 for fall entry, along with a $70 fee. Notification of early decision is sent December 15; regular decision, April 1. 77 early decision candidates were accepted for the 2016-2017 class. 534 applicants were on the 2016 waiting list; 11 were admitted. Applications are accepted online. **Transfer Students:** 4 transfer students enrolled in 2015-2016. Applicants must submit high school and college transcripts, course descriptions, and references from a counselor, a college math, science, or engineering teacher, and a college humanities or social science teacher. Test scores for already completed SAT, ACT, and SAT subject tests are highly recommended. Students should aim to complete courses equivalent to the courses in our Common Core. 64 of 128 credits required for the bachelor's degree must be completed at Harvey Mudd College. **International Students:** There are 104 international students enrolled. The school actively recruits these students. They must take the TOEFL with a minimum score of 600 on the paper-based TOEFL (PBT) or 100 on the Internet-based version (iBT), or take the IELTS if English has not been their primary language of instruction for the last 5 years. They must also take the SAT or ACT.

ADMISSIONS: 13% of the 2016-2017 applicants were accepted. The SAT scores for the 2016-2017 freshman class were: Critical Reading-- 4% between 500 and 599, 31% between 600 and 699, and 65% between 700 and 800. Math-- 12% between 600 and 699 and 88% between 700 and 800. Writing-- 4% between 500 and 599, 33% between 600 and 699, and 63% between 700 and 800. The ACT scores were 6% between 24 and 29, and 94% above 30. 98% of the current freshmen were in the top fifth of their class; 100% were in the top two fifths. 13 freshmen graduated first in their class. **Admissions Contact:** Peter Osgood, Director of Admission. Email: *admission@hmc.edu* Web: *www.hmc.edu*

FINANCIAL AID: In 2016-2017, 79% of all full-time freshmen and 73% of continuing full-time students received some form of financial aid. 52% of all full-time freshmen and 47% of continuing full-time students received need-based aid. The average freshman award was $39,515. Need-based scholarships or need-based grants averaged $42,553 ($73,143 maximum); need-based self-help aid (loans and jobs) averaged $5,062 ($11,400 maximum); and other non-need-based awards and non-need-based scholarships averaged $8,891 ($55,868 maximum). The average financial indebtedness of the 2016 graduate was $27,483. Harvey Mudd College is a member of CSS. The CSS/Profile and the state aid form are required. The FAFSA code is 001171. The deadline for filing freshman financial aid applications for fall entry is February 1.

HOLY NAMES UNIVERSITY *(The complete profile is made available exclusively on our website, www.barronspac.com)*

HOPE INTERNATIONAL UNIVERSITY D-5
www.hiu.edu

Fullerton, CA 92831 (714) 879-3901
(800) 762-1294
Fax: (714) 524-0231 Email: undergradadmissions@hiu.edu

Full-time: 339 men, 393 women	**Faculty:** 42
Part-time: 77 men, 105 women	**Ph.D.s:** 74%
Graduate: 163 men, 263 women	**Student/Faculty:** 14 to 1
Year: 4-1-4, summer session	**Tuition:** $31,600
Room & Board: $9550	**Freshman Class:** n/av
SAT or ACT: required	**CEEB CODE:** 4614
Application Deadline: December 1	**COMPETITIVE**

Hope International University, founded in 1928, is a private liberal arts institution affiliated with the Independent Christian Churches and Churches of Christ. There are 5 undergraduate schools and 4 graduate schools. In addition to regional accreditation, HIU has baccalaureate program accreditation with ABHE. The 15-acre campus is in an urban area 45 miles southeast of Los Angeles. Including any residence halls, there are 9 buildings.

STUDENT LIFE: 76% of undergraduates are from California. Others are from 43 states, 13 foreign countries, and Canada. 45% are White; 21% Hispanic; 11% two or more races; 10% race unknown; 6% African American; 4% Foreign; 2% Asian American; 1% American Indian/Alaska Native. 65% are Protestant; 20% Catholic; 15% claim no religious affiliation. **Female To Male Ratio:** 1.3:1. The average age of freshmen is 18; all undergraduates, 25. 30% do not continue beyond their first year; 42% remain to graduate. **Housing:** 530 students can be accommodated in college housing, which includes single-sex dorms and on-campus apartments. On-campus housing is guaranteed for all 4 years, and is available on a first-come, and first-served basis. 54% of students commute. Alcohol is not permitted. All students may keep cars.

FACULTY/CLASSROOMS: 60% of faculty are male; 40% are female. All teach undergraduates. No introductory courses are taught by graduate students. The average class size in an introductory lecture is 16; in a laboratory is 7; and in a regular course is 16.

PROGRAMS OF STUDY: HIU confers B.A., B.S. and B.Mus. degrees. Associate and master's degrees are also awarded. Bachelor's degrees are awarded in BUSINESS (business administration and management and sports management), COMMUNICATIONS AND THE ARTS (church music, English literature, and music ministry), EDUCATION (education, elementary education, secondary education, and social science education), SOCIAL SCIENCE (biblical studies, child psychology/development, criminal justice, crosscultural studies, human development, human services, liberal arts/general studies, ministries, pastoral studies, psychology, social science, and youth ministry). Psychology is the strongest academically. Ministry/Biblical studies, psychology & counseling, and business have the largest enrollments.

ACTIVITIES: There are no fraternities or sororities. There are 17 groups on campus, including cheerleading, choir, chorale, communications, drama, international, jazz band, musical theater, newspaper, religious, social service, student government, Model UN at Harvard and Security Council at Yale, and yearbook. Popular campus events include Spring Formal and Intercultural Awareness Events. **Sports:** There are 8 intercollegiate sports for men and 8 for women, and 4 intramural sports for men and 4 for women. Facilities include a gym with basketball and volleyball courts, fitness center, and recreation room. An outdoor swimming pool is adjacent to the residence halls. **Graduates:** From July 1, 2015 to June 30, 2016, 185 bachelor's degrees were awarded. The most popular majors were psychology, social science and human services (36%), ministries and biblical studies (31%), and business (19%). In an average class, 21% graduate in 4 years or less, 39% graduate in 5 years or less, and 47% graduate in 6 years or less.

SERVICES: Counseling and information services are available, as is tutoring in some subjects, such as history, English, mathematics, science, Bible, and financial accounting. There is a reader service for the blind, and remedial math, reading, and writing. **Library/Resources:** The library contains 193,398 volumes, 100 microform items, and 2,287 audio/video tapes/CDs/DVDs, and subscribes to 500 periodicals including electronic. Computerized library services include interlibrary loans, database searching, Internet access, and Wi-Fi capability. **Physically Challenged Students:** 95% of the campus is accessible. Facilities include elevators, special parking, specially equipped restrooms. Priority is given to disabled students for first-floor housing. **Special:** Hope International offers cross-registration with California State University, Fullerton. Internships, study abroad in 7 countries, work-study programs, dual and student-designed majors, non-degree study, pass/fail options, and credit for life, military, and work experience are also offered. Most Leadership and Ethics Curriculum courses are available in the online modality as well. There is 1 national honor society and 1 departmental honors program. **Visiting:** There are guides for informal visits, visitors may sit in on classes, and stay overnight. To schedule a visit, contact Amanda Matthews at ajmatthews@hiu.edu. **Campus Safety and Security:** Measures include 24-hour foot and vehicle patrol, emergency notification system, and security escort services. There are emergency telephones, lighted pathways/sidewalks, and controlled access to dorms/residences.

REQUIREMENTS: The SAT or ACT is required. Applicants must be high school graduates. The GED is accepted. A personal essay and references from a church leader and an academic counselor are required. AP and CLEP credits are accepted. Regular attendance at chapel and participation in Christian service is required. To graduate, students must complete at least 120 credit units with 36 to 51 in the major. A minimum GPA of 2.0 must be maintained. The Leadership and Ethics Core curriculum includes required and elective courses in biblical studies, leadership, written and oral communication, social sciences, humanities, natural sciences, and math. **Procedure:** Freshmen are admitted fall and spring. There are early admissions, deferred admissions, and rolling admissions plans. Application deadlines are open. Application fee is $40. Applications are accepted online. **Transfer Students:** 40 transfer students enrolled in 2015-2016. Transfer students must submit copies of college transcripts and SAT or ACT scores if fewer than 30 college units have been completed. A minimum GPA of 2.0 is required. 30 of 120 credits required for the bachelor's degree must be completed at HIU. **International Students:** There are 22 international students enrolled. The school actively recruits these students. They must take the TOEFL with a minimum score of 83 on the Internet-based version (iBT).

Admissions Contact: Dionne Butler, Director of Undergraduate Admissions. Email: *undergradadmissions@hiu.edu* Web: *www.hiu.edu*

FINANCIAL AID: The college's own financial statement is required. The FAFSA code is 001252. Check with the school for current application deadlines.

HUMBOLDT STATE UNIVERSITY A-1
www.humboldt.edu

Arcata, CA 95521 (707) 826-4402
(866) 850-9556
Fax: (707) 826-6194 Email: hsuinfo@.humboldt.edu

Full-time: 2855 men, 3255 women	**Faculty:** IIA, av$
Part-time: 355 men, 365 women	**Ph.D.s:** n/av
Graduate: 415 men, 635 women	**Student/Faculty:** n/av
Year: semesters, summer session	**Tuition:** $8400 ($16,200)
Room & Board: $12,114	**Freshman Class:** n/av
SAT or ACT: recommended	**CEEB CODE:** 4345
Application Deadline: rolling	**COMPETITIVE**

Humboldt State University, founded in 1913, is a liberal arts institution and is part of the California State University system. Humboldt offers 48 majors, and 11 graduate programs in 3 colleges. The figures given in the above capsule and in this profile are approximate. There are 3 undergraduate schools and 1 graduate school. In addition to regional accreditation, Humboldt has baccalaureate program accreditation with ABET, CSWE, NASAD, NASM, NLN, SAF, and NAST. The 161-acre campus is in a small town 275 miles north of San Francisco. Including any residence halls, there are 93 buildings.

STUDENT LIFE: 83% of undergraduates are from California. Others are from 50 states, 28 foreign countries, and Canada. 95% are from public schools. 53% are White; 4% African American; 4% Asian American; 3% American Indian/Alaska Native; 10% Hispanic. **Female To Male Ratio:** 1.2:1. The average age of freshmen is 19; all undergraduates, 24. 25% do not continue beyond their first year; 49% remain to graduate. **Housing:** 1400 students can be accommodated in college housing, which includes single-sex and coed dorms and on-campus apartments. In addition, there are special-interest houses, and living learning houses. On-campus housing is available on a first-come and first-served basis. 82% of students commute. All students may keep cars.

FACULTY/CLASSROOMS: 53% of faculty are male; 47% are female. All

teach undergraduates. No introductory courses are taught by graduate students. The average class size in an introductory lecture is 33; in a laboratory is 21; and in a regular course is 24.

PROGRAMS OF STUDY: Humboldt confers B.A., and B.S. degrees. Master's degrees are also awarded. Bachelor's degrees are awarded in AGRICULTURE (fishing and fisheries, forestry and related sciences, and natural resource management), BIOLOGICAL SCIENCE (biology/biological science, botany, wildlife biology, and zoology), BUSINESS (business administration and management and business economics), COMMUNICATIONS AND THE ARTS (art, communications, dramatic arts, English, fine arts, French, German, journalism, music, Spanish, and speech/debate/rhetoric), COMPUTER AND PHYSICAL SCIENCE (chemistry, geology, information sciences and systems, mathematics, oceanography, and physics), EDUCATION (business education, elementary education, English education, industrial arts education, mathematics education, middle school education, music education, physical education, science education, secondary education, and social science education), ENGINEERING AND ENVIRONMENTAL DESIGN (environmental engineering, environmental science, industrial engineering technology, and land use management and reclamation), HEALTH PROFESSIONS (nursing, predentistry, and premedicine), SOCIAL SCIENCE (anthropology, child psychology/development, geography, history, liberal arts/general studies, Native American studies, parks and recreation management, philosophy, physical fitness/movement, political science/government, prelaw, psychology, religion, social science, social work, and sociology). Environmental resources engineering, natural resources, and performing arts are the strongest academically. Biological sciences has the largest enrollment.

ACTIVITIES: There are 178 groups on campus, including art, band, cheerleading, chorale, chorus, computers, dance, debate, drama, environmental, ethnic, film, honors, international, jazz band, LGBT, literary magazine, marching band, musical theater, newspaper, opera, orchestra, pep band, photography, political, professional, radio and TV, religious, social, social service, student government, and symphony. Popular campus events include Campus Dialogue on Race, International Education week and International Cultural Festival. **Sports:** There are 5 intercollegiate sports for men and 7 for women, and 4 intramural sports for men and 4 for women. Facilities include a stadium, all-weather track, a swimming pool, tennis and racquetball courts, playing fields, 2 gyms, student recreation center with exercise equipment and weight room, and a rock-climbing wall.

SERVICES: Counseling and information services are available, as is tutoring in every subject. There is a reader service for the blind, and remedial math, reading, and writing. **Library/Resources:** The library contains 566,531 volumes, 610,992 microform items, and 21,955 audio/video tapes/CDs/DVDs, and subscribes to 1,413 periodicals including electronic. Computerized library services include interlibrary loans, database searching, Internet access, and Wi-Fi capability. Special learning facilities include an art gallery, natural history museum, radio station, observatory, greenhouse, solar hydrogen project, wildlife sanctuaries, the center for Appropriate Technology, child development lab, ceramics lab, jewelry lab, marine lab, marine research vessel, fish hatchery, and wildlife care center. **Physically Challenged Students:** 60% of the campus is accessible. Facilities include wheelchair ramps, elevators, special parking, specially equipped restrooms, special class scheduling, lowered drinking fountains, and lowered telephones. Wheelchair-accessible transportation, and a study center. **Special:** HSU offers campus work-study programs and co-op programs with a variety of public and private agencies, fisheries, biology, geology, botany, engineering, soil science, hydrology, and range and soil conservation. Internships and study abroad in 25 countries, with semesters in London, China, and Greece, are also offered. Dual majors, student-designed majors, credit for life and military experience, and credit/no credit grading options are also available. **Visiting:** There are regularly scheduled orientations for prospective students, including Preview Day in the spring and mandatory summer orientation for new students, which provides peer and academic counseling, registration, and a variety of social activities. There are guides for informal visits, visitors may sit in on classes, and stay overnight. To schedule a visit, contact the Office of Admissions. **Campus Safety and Security:** Measures include 24-hour foot and vehicle patrol, emergency notification system, self-defense education, and security escort services. There are emergency telephones, lighted pathways/sidewalks, and emergency transportation services.

REQUIREMENTS: The SAT or ACT is recommended. Applicants must be high school graduates with a minimum of 15 academic credits, to include 4 years in English, 3 years in college prep math, 2 years each in foreign language, social science, and lab science, including 1 year each in physical, life science, and U.S. history/government and visual and performing arts. The GED is accepted. HSU uses an eligibility index that combines GPA and ACT or SAT scores for admission. Requirements are higher for out-of-state applicants. Contact the Office of Admissions for further information. A GPA of 2.0 is required. AP and CLEP credits are accepted. To graduate, students must complete 120 to 132 semester credits, including 48 in general education courses, 24 to 36 in the major, and up to 40 in electives, with a minimum overall GPA of 2.0. Requirements include freshman reading and composition, diversity and common ground course work, and U.S. history course work as required by the California legislature. **Procedure:** Freshmen are admitted fall and spring. Entrance exams should be taken prior to admission. There are early decision and rolling admissions plans. Check with the school for current application deadlines. The application fee is $55. Notification is sent on a rolling basis. Applications are accepted on-line. **Transfer Students:** Applicants must have a minimum college GPA of 2.0 (2.4 for nonresidents). To enter, students need 30 general education units with a grade of C or better, including courses in written and speech communication, critical thinking, and math. Students with fewer than 56 transferable semester units must meet freshman requirements. 30 of 132 credits required for the bachelor's degree must be completed at Humboldt. **International Students:** There are 61 international students enrolled. The school actively recruits these students. They must take the TOEFL.

Admissions Contact: Rebecca Kalal, Assistant Director of Admissions. Email: *hsuinfo@.humboldt.edu* Web: *www.humboldt.edu*

FINANCIAL AID: The FAFSA code is 001149. Check with the school for current application deadlines.

HUMPHREYS COLLEGE — B-3

www.humphreys.edu

Stockton, CA 95207 — **(209) 478-0800**

Fax: (209) 478-8721	**Email: ugadmission@humphreys.edu**
Full-time: 300 men, 320 women	**Faculty:** n/av
Part-time: n/av	**Ph.D.s:** n/av
Graduate: n/av	**Student/Faculty:** n/av
Year: trimesters, summer session	**Tuition:** $15,323
Room & Board: $12,467	**Freshman Class:** n/av **CEEB CODE:** 4346
Application Deadline: open	**COMPETITIVE**

Humphreys College, founded in 1896, is an independent institution offering undergraduate degrees in business management, accounting, paralegal studies, computer management, law, early childhood education, and liberal arts to a primarily commuter student body. The figures given in the above capsule and in this profile are approximate. There is 1 undergraduate school and 1 graduate school. In addition to regional accreditation, Humphreys has baccalaureate program accreditation with WASC. The 10-acre campus is in a suburban area 40 miles south of Sacramento. Including any residence halls, there are 9 buildings.

STUDENT LIFE: 97% of undergraduates are from California. Others are from 4 states, and 5 foreign countries. 97% are from public schools. 70% are White; 7% African American; 4% Asian American; 17% Hispanic; 1% American Indian/Alaska Native; 1% Foreign. **Female To Male Ratio:** 1.1:1. The average age of freshmen is 23; all undergraduates, 25. 20% do not continue beyond their first year; 50% remain to graduate. **Housing:** 64 students can be accommodated in college housing, which includes single-sex on-campus apartments and married student housing. On-campus housing is available on a first-come and first-served basis. Priority is given to out-of-town students. 90% of students commute. Alcohol is not permitted. All students may keep cars.

FACULTY/CLASSROOMS: 51% of faculty are male; 49% are female. All teach undergraduates. No introductory courses are taught by graduate students. The average class size in an introductory lecture is 17.

PROGRAMS OF STUDY: Humphreys confers B.S. degrees. Associate and doctoral degrees are also awarded. Bachelor's degrees are awarded in BUSINESS (accounting, business administration and management, court reporting, and management information systems), EDUCATION (early childhood education), SOCIAL SCIENCE (community services and paralegal studies). Paralegal studies has the largest enrollment.

ACTIVITIES: There are no fraternities or sororities. There are 4 groups

on campus, including professional and student government. Popular campus events include Halloween Party, Christmas Dinner, and a quarterly Hot Dog Day Barbecue. **Sports:** There is no sports program at Humphreys. Facilities include a swimming pool, basketball court, tennis court, and sports fields.

SERVICES: Counseling and information services are available, as is tutoring in some subjects. There is remedial math and writing. **Library/Resources:** The 2 libraries contain 21,000 volumes, and 1,000 audio/video tapes/CDs/DVDs, and subscribe to 110 periodicals including electronic. Computerized library services include database searching. **Physically Challenged Students:** All of the campus is accessible. Facilities include wheelchair ramps, special parking, specially equipped restrooms, special class scheduling, lowered drinking fountains, and lowered telephones. **Special:** Local internship positions are available for students of paralegal studies and business administration. Dual majors in business studies are possible. **Visiting:** There are regularly scheduled orientations for prospective students, including a campus tour, classroom visits, and meetings with admissions, financial aid, and academic advisers. There are guides for informal visits and visitors may sit in on classes. To schedule a visit, contact the Admissions Office. **Campus Safety and Security:** Measures include 24-hour foot and vehicle patrol and security escort services. There are lighted pathways/sidewalks.

REQUIREMENTS: Applicants must be graduates of an accredited secondary school or have earned a GED. AP and CLEP credits are accepted. To graduate, students must complete a total of 180 quarter units, including 56 in the major and 72 in general education courses, with a minimum GPA of 2.0. **Procedure:** Freshmen are admitted to all sessions. Entrance exams should be taken at any time. There are deferred admissions and rolling admissions plans. Application deadlines are open. Application fee is $40. **Transfer Students:** Applicants must submit official transcripts and have a GPA of at least 2.0. 36 of 180 credits required for the bachelor's degree must be completed at Humphreys. **International Students:** They must take the TOEFL or MELAB.

Admissions Contact: Santa Lopez-Minatre, Director of Admissions. Email: *ugadmission@humphreys.edu* Web: *www.humphreys.edu*

FINANCIAL AID: Humphreys is a member of CSS. The FAFSA code is 001212. Check with the school for current application deadlines.

LA SIERRA UNIVERSITY — D-5

www.lasierra.edu

Riverside, CA 92515	(951) 785-2957 (800) 874-5587
Fax: (951) 785-2447	Email: admissions@lasierra.edu
Full-time: 615 men, 865 women	Faculty: n/av
Part-time: 90 men, 110 women	Ph.D.s: n/av
Graduate: 160 men, 175 women	Student/Faculty: n/av
Year: trimesters, summer session	Tuition: $31,590
Room & Board: $8100	Freshman Class: n/av
SAT or ACT: required	CEEB CODE: 4380
Application Deadline: n/av	VERY COMPETITIVE

La Sierra University, founded originally as La Sierra Academy in 1922, is a Seventh-day Adventist, private university, offering undergraduate and graduate programs in applied and liberal arts and sciences, business and management, religion, and education. The figures given in the above capsule and in this profile are approximate. There are 5 undergraduate schools and 4 graduate schools. In addition to regional accreditation, La Sierra has baccalaureate program accreditation with ABET, CSWE, NASM, CCTC, ATS, and AAA. The 300-acre campus is in a suburban area 40 miles east of Los Angeles. Including any residence halls, there are 48 buildings.

STUDENT LIFE: 21% of undergraduates are from California. Others are from 34 states, 58 foreign countries, and Canada. 39% are from public schools. 8% are Foreign; 7% African American; 35% White; 31% Asian American; 19% Hispanic; 1% American Indian/Alaska Native. 90% are Protestant; 12% claim no religious affiliation. **Female To Male Ratio:** 1.3:1. The average age of freshmen is 19; all undergraduates, 22. **Housing:** 850 students can be accommodated in college housing, which includes single-sex dorms, on-campus apartments, off-campus apartments, and married student housing. In addition, there are honors houses. On-campus housing is guaranteed for the freshman year only, and is available on a first-come, and first-served basis. Priority is given to out-of-town students. 56% of students commute. Alcohol is not permitted. All students may keep cars.

FACULTY/CLASSROOMS: All teach undergraduates, 70% do research, and 70% do both. Graduate students teach 1% of introductory courses. The average class size in an introductory lecture is 30; in a laboratory is 21; and in a regular course is 20.

PROGRAMS OF STUDY: La Sierra confers B.A., B.S., B.F.A., B.Mus. and B.S.W. degrees. Master's and doctoral degrees are also awarded. Bachelor's degrees are awarded in BIOLOGICAL SCIENCE (biochemistry, biology/biological science, biometrics and biostatistics, and biophysics), BUSINESS (accounting, banking and finance, business administration and management, electronic business, international business management, and marketing management), COMMUNICATIONS AND THE ARTS (art, communications, English, English as a second/foreign language, fine arts, graphic design, music, music performance, and Spanish), COMPUTER AND PHYSICAL SCIENCE (chemistry, computer science, information sciences and systems, mathematics, and physics), EDUCATION (elementary education, music education, physical education, and secondary education), HEALTH PROFESSIONS (exercise science and health science), SOCIAL SCIENCE (history, liberal arts/general studies, political science/government, psychobiology, psychology, religion, social work, and sociology). Biology, criminal justice, and business are the strongest academically and have the largest enrollments.

ACTIVITIES: There are no fraternities or sororities. There are 30 groups on campus, including art, band, choir, chorale, chorus, computers, debate, drama, environmental, ethnic, film, honors, international, literary magazine, newspaper, orchestra, photography, professional, religious, social service, student government, symphony, and yearbook. Popular campus events include University Experience, Academic Expo and Community Service Day. **Sports:** There are 3 intercollegiate sports for men and 3 for women, and 9 intramural sports for men and 9 for women. Facilities include a gym, soccer and flag football fields, running track, swimming pool, and a fitness center. **Graduates:** From July 1, 2015 to June 30, 2016, 208 bachelor's degrees were awarded. The most popular majors were biomedical science (9%), management (7%), and exercise science/scientific basis (5%). In an average class, 35% graduate in 4 years or less and 45% graduate in 6 years or less.

SERVICES: Counseling and information services are available, as is tutoring in most subjects. There is a reader service for the blind, and remedial math, reading, and writing, and a learning support center. **Library/Resources:** The library contains 255,694 volumes, 386,372 microform items, and 118,844 audio/video tapes/CDs/DVDs, and subscribes to 792 periodicals including electronic. Computerized library services include interlibrary loans, database searching, Internet access, and Wi-Fi capability. Special learning facilities include an art gallery, natural history museum, an observatory, Missionary Museum, and arboretum. **Physically Challenged Students:** 99% of the campus is accessible. Facilities include wheelchair ramps, elevators, special parking, specially equipped restrooms, and special class scheduling. **Special:** Cross-registration with Walla Walla College is necessary for engineering students. Study abroad is available in 3 countries through the Adventist Colleges Abroad Consortium. Liberal studies students work with an adviser to design their own major. There is a freshman honors program. **Visiting:** There are regularly scheduled orientations for prospective students, including a tour and meetings with faculty and administrators. There are guides for informal visits, visitors may sit in on classes, and stay overnight. To schedule a visit, contact the Admissions Office. **Campus Safety and Security:** Measures include 24-hour foot and vehicle patrol, emergency notification system, and security escort services. There are emergency telephones, lighted pathways/sidewalks, and controlled access to dorms/residences.

REQUIREMENTS: The SAT or ACT is required. Prospective students should have a high school diploma or equivalent. Completion of college preparatory work is required. A recommendation is also required. A GPA of 2.5 is required. AP and CLEP credits are accepted. Important factors in the admissions decision are recommendations by school officials, leadership record, and evidence of special talent. To graduate, students must complete 190 units, at least 60 of which must be upper-division, with a GPA of 2.0. All students must complete a University Studies curriculum requirements and 3 community service courses. **Procedure:** Freshmen are admitted to all sessions. Entrance exams should be taken during the senior year. There are deferred admissions and rolling admissions plans. Check with the school for current application deadlines. The fall 2016 application fee was $30. **Transfer Students:** Transcripts from all previous colleges are required. 36 of 190 credits required for the bachelor's degree must be completed at La Sierra. **International Students:** There are 283 international students enrolled. The school actively recruits these students. They must take the TOEFL with a minimum score of 500 on the paper-based TOEFL (PBT). They must also take the SAT or ACT.

Admissions Contact: Ivy Tejeda, Associate Director of Admissions. Email: *admissions@lasierra.edu* Web: *www.lasierra.edu*

FINANCIAL AID: La Sierra is a member of CSS. The FAFSA code is 001215. Check with the school for current application deadlines.

LAGUNA COLLEGE OF ART AND DESIGN *(The complete profile is made available exclusively on our website, www.barronspac.com)*

LOYOLA MARYMOUNT UNIVERSITY C-5

www.lmu.edu

Los Angeles, CA 90045	(310) 338-2750 (800) LMU-INFO Email: admissions@lmu.edu
Full-time: 2631 men, 3413 women	**Faculty:** 441
Part-time: 125 men, 92 women	**Ph.D.s:** 96%
Graduate: 1122 men, 1947 women	**Student/Faculty:** 11 to 1
Year: semesters, summer session	**Tuition:** $44,230
Room & Board: $13,808	**Freshman Class:** 13506 applied, 7276 accepted, 1331 enrolled
SAT CR/M/W: 600/620/600 **ACT:** 28	**CEEB CODE:** 4403
Application Deadline: January 15	**HIGHLY COMPETITIVE**

Loyola Marymount University is one of the largest Catholic universities in the West and one of 28 Jesuit universities in the United States. At LMU the city becomes an extension of the classroom, offering a rich diversity of culture, interests, access and opportunities. That diversity is being put to work at the university's World Policy Institute @LMU, a think-tank idea incubator launched in partnership with the WPI based in New York City. Founded in 1911, LMU is a comprehensive university offering 58 major programs and 53 minor programs for undergraduates; 46 master's degrees; two research level doctoral degrees; one professional practice doctoral degree; and 13 credential programs. Colleges and schools include: Bellarmine College of Liberal Arts, College of Business Administration, College of Communication and Fine Arts, Frank R. Seaver College of Science and Engineering, Loyola Law School, School of Education and School of Film and Television. Community-based learning has been integrated into many courses, giving students experience in being of service as they work on their academic goals. LMU's academic rigor and demand for excellence places it among the 25 "cutting-edge schools with an eye toward the future" and a "top producer" of Fulbright awardees. There are 5 undergraduate schools and 2 graduate schools. In addition to regional accreditation, LMU has baccalaureate program accreditation with AACSB, ABET, NASAD, NASM, NCATE, ACS, NAST, and NASD. The 142-acre campus is in a suburban area 15 miles southwest of downtown Los Angeles. Including any residence halls, there are 66 buildings.

STUDENT LIFE: 74% of undergraduates are from California. Others are from 48 states, 64 foreign countries, and Canada. 52% are from public schools. 8% are two or more races; 6% African American; 44% White; 21% Hispanic; 11% Asian American; 10% Foreign. 38% are Catholic; 17% Christian, Muslim, Buddhist, Armenian Orthodox, Greek Orthodox, Mormon, and Seventh Day Adventist. **Female To Male Ratio:** 1.4:1. The average age of freshmen is 18; all undergraduates, 20. 12% do not continue beyond their first year; 83% remain to graduate. **Housing:** 3210 students can be accommodated in college housing, which includes single-sex and coed dorms and on-campus apartments. In addition, there are honors houses and special-interest houses. On-campus housing is guaranteed for the freshman year only and is available on a lottery system for upperclassmen. 52% of students live on campus. All students may keep cars.

FACULTY/CLASSROOMS: 54% of faculty are male; 46% are female. All teach undergraduates, and all do research. Graduate students teach 1% of introductory courses. The average class size in an introductory lecture is 26 and in a laboratory is 57.

PROGRAMS OF STUDY: LMU confers B.A., B.S., B.B.A., B.S.A. and B.S.E. degrees. Master's and doctoral degrees are also awarded. Bachelor's degrees are awarded in BIOLOGICAL SCIENCE (biochemistry and biology/biological science), BUSINESS (accounting, entrepreneurial studies, finance, management information systems, management, and marketing), COMMUNICATIONS AND THE ARTS (animation, art history, communication studies, dance, English, film, television and digital media, French, modern language, music, music production/recording technology, playwriting/screenwriting, Spanish, studio art, and theatre arts), COMPUTER AND PHYSICAL SCIENCE (applied mathematics, chemistry, computer science, mathematics, and physics), EDUCATION (Asian studies), ENGINEERING AND ENVIRONMENTAL DESIGN (civil engineering, electrical/electronics engineering, engineering physics, environmental science, and mechanical engineering), HEALTH PROFESSIONS (health science), SOCIAL SCIENCE (African American studies, classical/ancient civilization, economics, European studies, Hispanic American studies, history, humanities, interdisciplinary studies, international relations, liberal arts/general studies, philosophy, political science/government, psychology, sociology, theology, urban studies, and women & gender studies). The school of film and television, entrepreneurship, and marketing are the strongest academically. Marketing, communication studies, and psychology have the largest enrollments.

ACTIVITIES: 17% of men belong to 10 national fraternities; 33% of women belong to 12 national sororities. There are 173 groups on campus, including art, cheerleading, chess, choir, chorale, chorus, communications, computers, dance, debate, drama, environmental, ethnic, film, honors, international, LGBT, literary magazine, newspaper, orchestra, pep band, political, professional, radio and TV, religious, social, social justice, comedy, social service, student government, and yearbook. Popular campus events include Fallapalooza, After Sunset, Greek Life Lip Sync & Stroll Off, Na Kolea's Luau, Charity Ball, Philipino Cultural Night, Fright Night, and Sunken Garden Festival. **Sports:** There are 10 intercollegiate sports for men and 12 for women, and 6 intramural sports for men and 5 for women. Facilities include The Fritz B. Burns Recreation Center, which houses a fitness center, 3 basketball courts, 2 group-exercise/fitness studios, fitness/wellness center, men's/women's lockers, a pro shop, and a classroom. There is also a 50-meter, outdoor swimming pool and pool deck for recreational usage. Additionally, there are two recreational fields for outdoor recreational programming (mainly Intramural Sports and Club Sports). NCAA Intercollegiate athletics facilities include: Gersten Pavilion which seats 4,156 spectators in the sports of men's and women's basketball and women's volleyball, Burns Aquatics center which serves men's and women's water polo and women's swimming, tennis courts, Smith Field for women's softball, Indoor Batting Cage for softball, Page Stadium for men's baseball, Lions Indoor Batting Cage for baseball, Jane Brown Bove floating boathouse for women's rowing and men's crew, Higgins Golf Practice Center for men's golf, and Sullivan Field for men's and women's soccer. **Graduates:** From July 1, 2015 to June 30, 2016, 1589 bachelor's degrees were awarded. The most popular majors were marketing (11%), psychology (8%), and communication studies (7%). 166 companies recruited on campus in 2015-2016. In an average class, 1% graduate in 3 years or less, 74% graduate in 4 years or less, 82% graduate in 5 years or less, and 83% graduate in 6 years or less. Of the 2015 graduating class, 26% were enrolled in graduate school within 6 months of graduation, and 60% were employed.

SERVICES: Counseling and information services are available, as is tutoring in most subjects. There is a reader service for the blind, and remedial math, reading, and writing. There is an extensive learning resource center with full-time specialists in reading, writing, and study skills, as well as a peer tutoring staff and computer-aided instruction. **Library/Resources:** The library contains 669,849 volumes, 1,284 microform items, and 25,771 audio/video tapes/CDs/DVDs, and subscribes to 46,440 periodicals including electronic. Computerized library services include interlibrary loans, database searching, Internet access, and Wi-Fi capability. Special learning facilities include an art gallery, radio station, TV station, computer graphics lab, theater, and the Thomas and Dorothy Leavey Center for the study of Los Angeles. **Physically Challenged Students:** 95% of the campus is accessible. Facilities include wheelchair ramps, elevators, special parking, specially equipped restrooms, special class scheduling, lowered drinking fountains, lowered telephones, special housing. Special test arrangements, adaptive equipment, braille services, interpreters for hearing impaired, note-taking services, talking books, and tape recorders. **Special:** LMU offers internships and volunteer work experience with local firms, study abroad in over 20 countries, global immersion courses that include intensive spring break study trips, a Washington semester, dual majors, work-study, student-designed and individualized studies majors, a general studies degree, non-degree study, 4+1 master's programs, and some pass/fail options for electives. There are 25 national honor societies and a freshman honors program. **Visiting:** There are regularly scheduled orientations for prospective students, Student visits consist of an open house in the fall. There are guides for informal visits and visitors may sit in on classes. To schedule a visit, contact Alice Johnson at admissions@lmu.edu. **Campus Safety and Security:** Measures include 24-hour foot and vehicle patrol, emergency notification system, self-defense education, and security escort services. There are shuttle buses, emergency telephones, lighted pathways/sidewalks, controlled access to dorms/residences, Personal property engraving program, emergency preparedness program, and safe ride home program.

REQUIREMENTS: The SAT is required. The ACT is recommended. Prospective students must be graduates of an accredited secondary school and have completed 4 years of English, 3 each of a foreign language, math, and social studies, 2 of science, and 1 of an academic elective. A recommendation from an official of a previous school and essays are required. AP credits are accepted. Important factors in the admissions decision are parents or siblings attended your school, leadership record, and evidence of special talent. Regardless of major, all undergraduates must take courses in the following core areas: First year seminar, rhetorical arts, quantitative reasoning, theological inquiry, philisophical inquiry, studies in American diversity, creative experience, historical analysis and perspectives, understanding human behavior, faith and reason, ethics and justice, interdisciplinary connections, and the nature of science, technology and mathematics. A minimum 2.0 GPA is required, as are at least 120 semester hours, with at least 45 semester hours in upper-division courses. At least 30 of the last 36 semester hours of academic work and at least two thirds of the upper-division semester hours of the major must be completed at LMU. **Procedure:** Freshmen are admitted fall and spring. Entrance exams should be taken during the spring of the junior year or fall of senior year. There are early decision, early admissions, deferred admissions, and rolling admissions plans. Early decision applications should be filed by November 1; regular applications, by January 15 for fall entry; and October 15 for spring entry, along with a $60 fee. Notification of early decision is sent December 1; regular decision, 1997 applicants were on the 2016 waiting list; 206 were admitted. Applications are accepted on-line. Application fees are waived if application is completed on-line. **Transfer Students:** 503 transfer students enrolled in 2015-2016. Applicants must have a minimum 3.00 GPA in college work and most recent college work. Students who were not academically eligible for admission as freshmen must have at least 30 semester hours of college work with at least a 3.00 cumulative average. Grades below C (2.0) do not transfer. No minimum credit hours are necessary for students who meet freshman requirements. Standardized test scores (SAT or ACT) are required for those with fewer than 30 transfer hours, and letters of recommendation are recommended for all transfer students. 30 of 120 credits required for the bachelor's degree must be completed at LMU. **International Students:** There are 574 international students enrolled. The school actively recruits these students. They must take the TOEFL with a minimum score of 550 on the paper-based TOEFL (PBT) or 80 on the Internet-based version (iBT). The IELTS may place the TOEFL.

ADMISSIONS: 5% of the 2016-2017 applicants were accepted. The SAT scores for the 2016-2017 freshman class were: Critical Reading-- 7% below 500, 39% between 500 and 599, 40% between 600 and 699, and 14% between 700 and 800. Math-- 5% below 500, 34% between 500 and 599, 46% between 600 and 699, and 15% between 700 and 800. Writing-- 7% below 500, 37% between 500 and 599, 43% between 600 and 699, and 13% between 700 and 800. The ACT scores were 5% between 18 and 23, 62% between 24 and 29, and 33% above 30. 62% of the current freshmen were in the top fifth of their class; 95% were in the top two fifths. **Admissions Contact:** Matthew Fissinger, Assistant Vice Provost for Undergraduate. Email: *admissions@lmu.edu* Web: *www.lmu.edu*

FINANCIAL AID: In 2016-2017, 90% of all full-time freshmen and 86% of continuing full-time students received some form of financial aid. 49% of all full-time freshmen and 51% of continuing full-time students received need-based aid. The average freshman award was $25,371. Need-based scholarships or need-based grants averaged $10,830 ($61,269 maximum); need-based self-help aid (loans and jobs) averaged $3,280 ($36,788 maximum); non-need-based athletic scholarships averaged $855 ($60,784 maximum); other non-need-based awards and non-need-based scholarships averaged $4,061 ($60,000 maximum); and $6,434 from other forms of aid. 52% of undergraduate students work part-time. Average annual earnings from campus work are $2703. The average financial indebtedness of the 2016 graduate was $30,698. The FAFSA code is 001234. The priority date for freshman financial aid applications for fall entry is February 1.

MENLO COLLEGE *(The complete profile is made available exclusively on our website, www.barronspac.com)*

MILLS COLLEGE — B-3
www.mills.edu

Oakland, CA 94613	**(510) 430-2135** **(800) 87-MILLS**
Fax: (510) 430-3314	**Email: admission@mills.edu**
Full-time: 775 women	**Faculty:** 97; IIA, ++$
Part-time: 33 women	**Ph.D.s:** 90%
Graduate: 106 men, 418 women	**Student/Faculty:** 10 to 1
Year: semesters	**Tuition:** $45,635
Room & Board: $13,528	**Freshman Class:** 1129 applied, 888 accepted, 169 enrolled
SAT CR/M/W: 580/510/560 **ACT:** 27	**CEEB CODE:** 4485
Application Deadline: January 15	**VERY COMPETITIVE**

Mills College offers a challenging liberal arts curriculum that encourages you to think creatively, prepares you to take well-calculated risks, and equips you to put your passions into practice. We are driven by a determination to improve ourselves and the world around us and to work smarter by working together. At Mills, you will be encouraged to stand out, emboldened to think big, and empowered to make a statement. There is 1 undergraduate school and 4 graduate schools. The 135-acre campus is in an urban area in the San Francisco Bay area, 12 miles east of San Francisco and 8 miles from Berkeley. Including any residence halls, there are 64 buildings.

STUDENT LIFE: 81% of undergraduates are from California. Others are from 37 states, and 8 foreign countries. 88% are from public schools. 45% are White; 27% Hispanic; 9% African American; 9% Asian American; 8% two or more races; 2% Foreign; 1% American Indian/Alaska Native; 1% race unknown. 42% are Atheist, and Agnostic; 21% claim no religious affiliation; 15% Protestant; 11% Catholic. **Female To Male Ratio:** 11.6:1. The average age of freshmen is 18; all undergraduates, 22. 19% do not continue beyond their first year; 68% remain to graduate. **Housing:** 690 students can be accommodated in college housing, which includes single-sex and coed dorms and on-campus apartments. In addition, there are language houses, special-interest houses, married-student housing is offered on an equal basis to domestic partners of lesbian and gay students, and a student co-op house is available for juniors and seniors. On-campus housing is guaranteed for all 4 years, and is available on a first-come, and first-served basis. 60% of students live on campus; of those, 77% remain on campus on weekends. All students may keep cars.

FACULTY/CLASSROOMS: 31% of faculty are male; 69% are female. 97% teach undergraduates, 97% do research, and 97% do both. No introductory courses are taught by graduate students. The average class size in an introductory lecture is 25; in a laboratory is 15; and in a regular course is 16.

PROGRAMS OF STUDY: Mills confers B.A. and B.S. degrees. Master's and doctoral degrees are also awarded. Bachelor's degrees are awarded in AGRICULTURE (environmental studies), BIOLOGICAL SCIENCE (biochemistry, biology/biological science, microbiology, and molecular biology), BUSINESS (business economics), COMMUNICATIONS AND THE ARTS (art history, creative writing, dance, English, English literature, English Writing, French, media arts, modern language, music, Spanish, studio art, and theatre studies), COMPUTER AND PHYSICAL SCIENCE (chemistry, computer information technology, computer science, and mathematics), ENGINEERING AND ENVIRONMENTAL DESIGN (environmental science), HEALTH PROFESSIONS (nursing and public health), SOCIAL SCIENCE (anthropology, biopsychology, child psychology/development, early childhood studies, economics, ethnic studies, government, French studies, Hispanic American studies, history, international relations, philosophy, political science/government, prelaw, psychology, public administration, public affairs, sociology, Spanish studies, and women & gender studies). Music, studio art, English, and computer science are the strongest academically. Psychology, English, and biology have the largest enrollments.

ACTIVITIES: There are no fraternities or sororities. There are 63 groups on campus, including art, cheerleading, choir, dance, drama, environmental, ethnic, film, honors, international, LGBT, literary magazine, newspaper, political, professional, religious, social, social service, student government, and yearbook. Popular campus events include Black and White Ball, Spring Fling, Heritage Months, Fetish Ball, Choir Winter Celebration, Vagina Monologues, Final Snacks & Midnight Breakfast, Final Fridays, and Second Saturdays. **Sports:** There are 6 intercollegiate sports for women, and 9 intramural sports for women. Facilities include facilities include a multi-purpose gymnasium, fitness center with cardio-fitness and strength training equipment, training room, activity rooms, dance studios, aquatic center, therapy spa, lighted tennis courts, soccer field, wooded trails for hiking and running, boathouse for rowing. **Graduates:** From July 1, 2015 to June 30, 2016, 262 bachelor's degrees were awarded. The most popular majors were English (15%), psychology (9%), and biology (9%). 63 companies recruited on campus in 2015-2016. In an average class, 5% graduate in 3 years or less, 62% graduate in 4 years or less, 64% graduate in 5 years or less, and 67% graduate in 6 years or less. Of the 2015 graduating class, 10% were enrolled in graduate school within 6 months of graduation, and 79% were employed.

SERVICES: Counseling and information services are available, as is tutoring in every subject. There is a reader service for the blind, and remedial math and writing. **Library/Resources:** The library contains 246,312 volumes, 199 microform items, and 14,609 audio/video tapes/CDs/DVDs, and subscribes to 46,256 periodicals including electronic. Computerized library services include interlibrary loans, database searching, Internet access, and Wi-Fi capability. Special learning facilities include art gallery, children's school, small book press, electronic/computer music studio, dance and fine arts studios, botanical garden, urban farm, electronic collaborative learning center, and innovation lab. **Physically Challenged Students:** All of the campus is accessible. Facilities include wheelchair ramps, elevators, special parking, specially equipped restrooms, special class scheduling, lowered drinking fountains, lowered telephones, and special housing. **Special:** Cross-registration is available for students to attend classes at the University of California at Berkeley, California State University, and California College of the Arts, among others. Mills offers the opportunity to study at other women's colleges in the U.S. Mills also offers co-op programs, internships, study abroad, and a Washington semester. Students can participate in work-study programs and can declare a dual major, a student-designed major, or an interdisciplinary major such as Public Health and Health Equity. Accelerated degree programs include a 5 year M.B.A., Masters in Public Policy (MPP) or combination MBA/MPP; as well as a B.A./M.A. program in which students graduate in 5 years with a bachelor's degree in psychology and a master's in infant mental health, or in five years. There is also an option to earn a B.A., an M.A. in education, and complete a program qualifying them for a teaching credential. Mills also offers a a 3-2 engineering degree with USC and a prenursing program leading to a bachelor's degree in nursing at Simmons College. Credit by exam, and pass/fail options are also available. There are 5 national honor societies and a chapter of Phi Beta Kappa. **Visiting:** There are regularly scheduled orientations for prospective students, consisting of class visits, campus tours, lunch with faculty, financial aid workshops, an admissions interview, and an overnight stay. There are guides for informal visits, visitors may sit in on classes, and stay overnight. **Campus Safety and Security:** Measures include 24-hour foot and vehicle patrol, emergency notification system, self-defense education, and security escort services. There are shuttle buses, emergency telephones, lighted pathways/sidewalks, controlled access to dorms/residences, AED units, and vehicle jumps.

REQUIREMENTS: The SAT or ACT is recommended. Students are required to submit a high school transcript, two letters of recommendation, a school report, and a writing sample or personal statement. Official SAT or ACT test scores are optional. Interviews are recommended but not required. GED or High School Proficiency are accepted in lieu of a high school transcript. We recommend a cumulative GPA of 3.0 or higher and SAT scores above 1500 combined. AP and CLEP credits are accepted. Important factors in the admissions decision are advanced placement or honors courses, personality/intangible qualities, and recommendations by school officials. To graduate, students must fulfill Core Curriculum requirements, earn a total of 120 semester units, with at least 30 in the major, and maintain a minimum GPA of 2.0. Students are required to fulfill the following core curriculum areas: written and oral communication, information literacy, quantitative literacy, critical analysis, race, gender & power, language other than English, scientific inquiry, international perspectives, community engagement, creativity, innovation and experimentation. **Procedure:** Freshmen are admitted fall and spring. Entrance exams should be taken at least 1 month prior to application. There are early decision and deferred admissions plans. Early decision applications should be filed by November 15; regular applications by January 15 for fall entry; and November 1 for spring entry, along with a $50 fee. Notification of early decision is sent December 1; regular decision, February 15. 217 early decision candidates were accepted for the 2016-2017 class. Applications are accepted on-line. **Transfer Students:** 136 transfer students enrolled in 2015-2016. A writing sample, two letters of recommendation, a high school transcript, and official transcripts from all colleges attended are required.The recommended minimum GPA to apply to Mills is 3.0. We consider other factors such as writing skills, strength of curriculum, and number of credit hours. 40 of 120 credits required for the bachelor's degree must be completed at Mills. **International Students:** There are 8 international students enrolled. They must take the TOEFL with a minimum score of 550 on the paper-based TOEFL (PBT) or 80 on the Internet-based version (iBT).

ADMISSIONS: 79% of the 2016-2017 applicants were accepted. The SAT scores for the 2016-2017 freshman class were: Critical Reading-- 28% below 500, 23% between 500 and 599, 36% between 600 and 699, and 12% between 700 and 800. Math-- 43% below 500, 32% between 500 and 599, 20% between 600 and 699, and 4% between 700 and 800. Writing-- 33% below 500, 29% between 500 and 599, 25% between 600 and 699, and 12% between 700 and 800. The ACT scores were 2% below 12, 3% between 12 and 17, 23% between 18 and 23, 51% between 24 and 29, and 23% above 30. 52% of the current freshmen were in the top fifth of their class; 90% were in the top two fifths. There was 1 National Merit finalist. 2 freshmen graduated first in their class. **Admissions Contact:** Robyn Royster, Director of Undergraduate Admission. Email: *admission@mills.edu* Web: *www.mills.edu*

FINANCIAL AID: In 2016-2017, 100% of all full-time freshmen and 92% of continuing full-time students received some form of financial aid. 72% of all full-time freshmen and 68% of continuing full-time students received need-based aid. The average freshman award was $46,864. Need-based scholarships or need-based grants averaged $40,957; need-based self-help aid (loans and jobs) averaged $7,491; and other non-need-based awards and non-need-based scholarships averaged $30,573. 97% of undergraduate students work part-time. Average annual earnings from campus work are $2379. The average financial indebtedness of the 2016 graduate was $33,175. The the college's own financial statement is required. The FAFSA code is 001238. The priority date for freshman financial aid applications for fall entry is February 1. The deadline for filing freshman financial aid applications for fall entry is February 15.

MOUNT ST. MARY'S UNIVERSITY - CHALON CAMPUS C-5

www.msmu.edu

Los Angeles, CA 90049

(310) 954-4250
(800) 999-9893

Fax: (310) 954-4259
Email: admissions@msmu.edu

Full-time: 91 men, 1712 women	**Faculty:** 88; IIA, +$
Part-time: 83 men, 402 women	**Ph.D.s:** 61%
Graduate: 126 men, 448 women	**Student/Faculty:** 12 to 1
Year: semesters	**Tuition:** $33,367
Room & Board: $10,530	**Freshman Class:** 1799 applied, 309 accepted, 528 enrolled
SAT or ACT: required	**CEEB CODE:** 4493
Application Deadline: February 15	**VERY COMPETITIVE+**

Mount St. Mary's University, Chalon Campus, founded in 1925 and affiliated with the Catholic Church, is a private, primarily women's institution. The traditional baccalaureate program is offered at the Chalon campus and associate programs are offered at the Doheny campus. The figures in the above capsule and in this profile are approximate. There is 1 undergraduate school and 1 graduate school. In addition to regional accreditation, The Mount has baccalaureate program accreditation with NLN, CSC, UWASC, California Commission on Teacher Credentialing,

Collegiate Nursing Ed, and Physical Therapy Ed. The 72-acre campus is in an urban area 10 miles west of Los Angeles, and the Dohney campus is near downtown Los Angeles. Including any residence halls, there are 31 buildings.

STUDENT LIFE: 97% of undergraduates are from California. Others are from 19 states, 5 foreign countries, and Canada. 70% are from public schools. 8% are African American; 7% two or more races; 57% Hispanic; 15% Asian American; 12% White; 1% American Indian/Alaska Native; 1% Foreign. 53% are Catholic; 14% Protestant; 13% claim no religious affiliation. **Female To Male Ratio:** 8.5:1. The average age of freshmen is 18; all undergraduates, 23. 16% do not continue beyond their first year; 84% remain to graduate. **Housing:** 668 students can be accommodated in college housing, which includes single-sex dorms. On-campus housing is available on a first-come and first-served basis. 71% of students commute. All students may keep cars.

FACULTY/CLASSROOMS: 27% of faculty are male; 73% are female. 92% teach undergraduates. No introductory courses are taught by graduate students. The average class size in an introductory lecture is 23; in a laboratory is 18; and in a regular course is 23.

PROGRAMS OF STUDY: The Mount confers B.A., B.S. and B.S.N. degrees. Associate, master's, and doctoral degrees are also awarded. Bachelor's degrees are awarded in BIOLOGICAL SCIENCE (biochemistry and biology/biological science), BUSINESS (business administration and management), COMMUNICATIONS AND THE ARTS (art, English, film arts, French, music, and Spanish), COMPUTER AND PHYSICAL SCIENCE (chemistry and mathematics), EDUCATION (elementary education), HEALTH PROFESSIONS (health care administration and nursing), SOCIAL SCIENCE (American studies, child psychology/development, counseling/psychology, gerontology, history, liberal arts/general studies, philosophy, political science/government, psychology, religion, social science, social work, and sociology). Nursing, Pre-nursing, psychology, business, biology, sociology, Pre-health, and liberal arts is the strongest academically and have the largest enrollments.

ACTIVITIES: There are no fraternities; 1% of women belong to 2 local and 1 national sororities. There are 28 groups on campus, including art, choir, drama, environmental, ethnic, film, honors, international, LGBT, newspaper, political, professional, religious, social, social service, student government, and yearbook. Popular campus events include Leadership Boot Camp, Charity Ball and Spring Carnival. **Sports:** There is 1 intramural sport for men and 2 for women. Facilities include a basketball court, tennis courts, volleyball court, swimming pool, fitness workout room, and dance studio. **Graduates:** From July 1, 2015 to June 30, 2016, 516 bachelor's degrees were awarded. The most popular majors were nursing (50%), sociology (13%), and business (11%). In an average class, 54% graduate in 4 years or less, 59% graduate in 5 years or less, and 62% graduate in 6 years or less. Of the 2015 graduating class, 26% were enrolled in graduate school within 6 months of graduation, and 31% were employed.

SERVICES: Counseling and information services are available, as is tutoring in most subjects. A peer tutoring program is available. **Library/Resources:** The 2 libraries contain 140,000 volumes, and 2,520 audio/video tapes/CDs/DVDs, and subscribe to 25,000 periodicals including electronic. Computerized library services include interlibrary loans, database searching, Internet access, and Wi-Fi capability. Special learning facilities include an art gallery, and film studio. **Physically Challenged Students:** All of the campus is accessible. Facilities include wheelchair ramps, elevators, special parking, specially equipped restrooms, lowered drinking fountains, lowered telephones, and special housing. **Special:** The Mount offers cross-registration with UCLA, the University of Judaism, internships, study abroad in 17 countries, a Washington semester through American University, dual and student-designed majors, work-study programs, and an accelerated degree program in nursing. There are 20 national honor societies, Phi Beta Kappa, and a freshman honors program. **Visiting:** There are regularly scheduled orientations for prospective students, including workshops, student panels, tours, class visits, and faculty presentations. There are guides for informal visits, visitors may sit in on classes, and stay overnight. To schedule a visit, contact the Admissions Office. **Campus Safety and Security:** Measures include 24-hour foot and vehicle patrol, emergency notification system, self-defense education, and security escort services. There are shuttle buses, emergency telephones, lighted pathways/sidewalks, and controlled access to dorms/residences.

REQUIREMENTS: The SAT or ACT is required. Applicants must be graduates of an accredited secondary school or have earned the GED, with 16 academic credits and 16 Carnegie units, including 4 years of English literature and composition, 2 or 3 years each of math, science, and social studies, and 1 or 2 years of history. An essay is required, and an interview is recommended. A GPA of 2.5 is required. AP and CLEP credits are accepted. Important factors in the admissions decision are advanced placement or honors courses, extracurricular activities record, and leadership record. To graduate, students must complete at least 124 semester units with a GPA of 2.0 (C average); a minimum of 45 semester units must be in upper-division work. The total number of hours students must complete in their major varies. All students must satisfy a senior residence requirement and complete a general studies program. Freshmen entering the college with fewer than 24 units must complete Introduction to College Studies. Students must file a graduation application in the Registrar's Office by the end of the term prior to the term of projected completion. **Procedure:** Freshmen are admitted fall and spring. Entrance exams should be taken at the end of the junior year or the beginning of the senior year. There is a rolling admissions plan. Applications should be filed by February 15 for fall entry; November 1 for spring entry, along with a $50 fee. Notification is sent on a rolling basis. Applications are accepted on-line. **Transfer Students:** 254 transfer students enrolled in 2015-2016. Transfer students must have a minimum 2.40 GPA with at least 24 completed credit hours. 30 of 124 credits required for the bachelor's degree must be completed at The Mount. **International Students:** There are 22 international students enrolled. They must take the TOEFL with a minimum score of 530 on the paper-based TOEFL (PBT) or 75 on the Internet-based version (iBT). They must also take the SAT or ACT.

ADMISSIONS: 17% of the 2016-2017 applicants were accepted. **Admissions Contact:** Yvonne Berumen, Director of Admissions. Email: *admissions@msmu.edu* Web: *www.msmu.edu*

FINANCIAL AID: In 2016-2017, 92% of all full-time freshmen and 80% of continuing full-time students received some form of financial aid. 86% of all full-time freshmen and 77% of continuing full-time students received need-based aid. 45% of undergraduate students work part-time. Average annual earnings from campus work are $2723. The Mount is a member of CSS. The college's own financial statement is required. The FAFSA code is 001243. The priority date for freshman financial aid applications for fall entry is February 15.

NATIONAL UNIVERSITY *(The complete profile is made available exclusively on our website, www.barronspac.com)*

NEWSCHOOL OF ARCHITECTURE & DESIGN *(The complete profile is made available exclusively on our website, www.barronspac.com)*

NOTRE DAME DE NAMUR UNIVERSITY *(The complete profile is made available exclusively on our website, www.barronspac.com)*

OCCIDENTAL COLLEGE — C-5

www.oxy.edu

Los Angeles, CA 90041 — **(323) 259-2700**, **(800) 825-5262**

Fax: (323) 341-4875 — **Email: admission@oxy.edu**

Full-time: 883 men, 1186 women	**Faculty:** 172; IIB, ++$
Part-time: 11 men, 8 women	**Ph.D.s:** 95%
Graduate: n/av	**Student/Faculty:** 12 to 1
Year: semesters	**Tuition:** $51,070
Room & Board: $14,460	**Freshman Class:** 5911 applied, 2652 accepted, 518 enrolled
SAT CR/M/W: 645/645/648 **ACT:** 30	**CEEB CODE:** 4581
Application Deadline: January 15	**MOST COMPETITIVE**

Occidental College, founded in 1887, is a private, nonsectarian school of liberal arts and sciences, one of the few top liberal arts colleges in a major city. Even more distinctive is Occidental's ability to sustain its traditional commitment to high achievement while enrolling a diverse student body and faculty. The figures in the above capsule and in this profile are approximate. There is 1 undergraduate school. In addition to regional accreditation, Oxy has baccalaureate program accreditation with WASC. The 120-acre campus is in an urban area in the city of Los Angeles. Including any residence halls, there are 44 buildings.

STUDENT LIFE: 52% of undergraduates are from out of state, mostly

the Northwest. Students are from 45 states, 34 foreign countries, and Canada. 58% are from public schools. 6% are Foreign; 51% White; 5% African American; 15% Hispanic; 12% Asian American; 10% two or more races; 1% race unknown. 35% are Protestant; 30% claim no religious affiliation; 19% Catholic; 11% Jewish. **Female To Male Ratio:** 1.3:1. The average age of freshmen is 18; all undergraduates, 20. 7% do not continue beyond their first year; 88% remain to graduate. **Housing:** 1671 students can be accommodated in college housing, which includes coed dorms. In addition, there are special-interest houses, fraternity houses, multicultural, pets, all-women, theme housing, and gender neutral. On-campus housing is available on a lottery system for upperclassmen. 82% of students live on campus; of those, 60% remain on campus on weekends. All students may keep cars.

FACULTY/CLASSROOMS: 50% of faculty are male; 50% are female. All teach undergraduates, and all do research. No introductory courses are taught by graduate students. The average class size in an introductory lecture is 20; in a laboratory is 12; and in a regular course is 15.

PROGRAMS OF STUDY: Oxy confers A.B. degrees. Master's degrees are also awarded. Bachelor's degrees are awarded in BIOLOGICAL SCIENCE (biochemistry and biology/biological science), COMMUNICATIONS AND THE ARTS (art history, Chinese, English, French, Japanese, languages, music, Spanish, and theatre arts), COMPUTER AND PHYSICAL SCIENCE (chemistry, geology, mathematics, and physics), EDUCATION (Asian studies), SOCIAL SCIENCE (American studies, cognitive science, cultural studies/critical theory & analysis, East Asian studies, economics, history, international relations, Latin American studies, philosophy, physical fitness/movement, political science/government, psychology, religion, sociology, and urban studies). Social sciences, biology, and chemistry are the strongest academically. Economics, diplomacy & world affairs, and biology have the largest enrollments.

ACTIVITIES: 10% of men belong to 4 national fraternities; 13% of women belong to 2 local and 2 national sororities. There are 116 groups on campus, including art, cheerleading, choir, chorus, dance, debate, drama, environmental, ethnic, honors, international, LGBT, literary magazine, musical theater, newspaper, orchestra, photography, political, professional, religious, social, social service, student government, student investment fund; entrepreneurs, symphony, and yearbook. Popular campus events include Dance Production, New Play Festival, and Taste of Oxy. **Sports:** There are 10 intercollegiate sports for men and 11 for women, and 6 intramural sports for men and 6 for women. Facilities include a football, soccer, baseball, softball fields, all-weather track, tennis courts, outdoor pool, outdoor basketball courts, dance studio, sports medicine center, gym, weight room, and a fitness center. **Graduates:** From July 1, 2015 to June 30, 2016, 504 bachelor's degrees were awarded. The most popular majors were economics (15%), diplomacy and world affairs (8%), and biology (7%). 50 companies recruited on campus in 2015-2016. In an average class, 85% graduate in 6 years or less. Of the 2015 graduating class, 22% were enrolled in graduate school within 6 months of graduation, and 64% were employed.

SERVICES: There are peer tutors available in biology, chemistry, geology, kinesiology, mathematics and physics. Peer and faculty advisers are available through the Center for Academic Excellence. **Library/Resources:** The library contains 431,586 volumes, 6,839 microform items, and 12,338 audio/video tapes/CDs/DVDs, and subscribes to 55,322 periodicals including electronic. Computerized library services include interlibrary loans, database searching, Internet access, and Wi-Fi capability. Special learning facilities include an art gallery, student newspaper and yearbook, theater, art studio and gallery, ornithology, conchology and geology collections, physics, plasma, paleomagnetic and optic labs, and library special collections. **Physically Challenged Students:** 80% of the campus is accessible. Facilities include wheelchair ramps, elevators, special parking, specially equipped restrooms, lowered drinking fountains. Occidental also has a hillside campus. **Special:** Cross-registration is permitted with the California Institute of Technology and the Art Center College of Design. Students may study abroad in 41 countries in Europe, Asia, Africa, and Latin America. Opportunities are provided for internships, a Washington semester, a residential U.N. semester in New York City, dual and student-designed majors, a 3-2 engineering degree with the California Institute of Technology, a 3-3 law program with Columbia, and a 4-2 biotech program with Keck. There are 8 national honor societies, Phi Beta Kappa, and 32 departmental honors programs. **Visiting:** There are regularly scheduled orientations for prospective students, including campus tours and info sessions with an admission officer at 11:30 a.m. and 4 p.m. There are guides for informal visits, visitors may sit in on classes, and stay overnight. To schedule a visit, contact the Office of Admission at admission@oxy.edu. **Campus Safety and Security:** Measures include 24-hour foot and vehicle patrol, emergency notification system, self-defense education, and security escort services. There are shuttle buses, emergency telephones, lighted pathways/sidewalks, controlled access to dorms/residences, and whistle alert program.

REQUIREMENTS: The SAT or ACT is required. Applicants should be high school graduates of high academic standing with units recommended 4 years of English, 3 each of math, foreign language and science, and history, 2 of social studies. The GED is accepted. An essay is required and an interview is recommended. A GPA of 3.6 is required. AP credits are accepted. Important factors in the admissions decision are advanced placement or honors courses, personality/intangible qualities, extracurricular activities record, and recommendations by school officials. To graduate, students must complete 32 courses of 4 semester hours each and maintain a minimum GPA of 2.0. In addition, all students must fulfill core course requirements in foreign language, fine arts, writing proficiency, 12 units are required in science and mathematics, foreign language, and cultural studies. To graduate, all students must complete a comprehensive exam; some majors require a thesis. **Procedure:** Freshmen are admitted fall. Entrance exams should be taken during your senior year, and test scores must be received by Feb 1. There are early decision and deferred admissions plans. Early decision applications should be filed by November 15; regular applications, by January 15 for fall entry, along with a $60 fee. Notification of early decision is sent December 15; regular decision, March 25. 130 early decision candidates were accepted for the 2016-2017 class. 359 applicants were on the 2016 waiting list; 26 were admitted. Applications are accepted on-line. **Transfer Students:** 36 transfer students enrolled in 2015-2016. Students must have at least a B average (3.0 GPA) in all courses submitted for transfer credit. The SAT or ACT is required. All high school and college transcripts, statement of good standing from prior institution(s), and an interview is recommended. The application deadline is April 1 for fall, and November 1 for spring. 64 of 128 credits required for the bachelor's degree must be completed at Oxy. **International Students:** There are 121 international students enrolled. The school actively recruits these students. They must take the TOEFL with a minimum score of 600 on the paper-based TOEFL (PBT). They must also take the SAT or ACT.

ADMISSIONS: 45% of the 2016-2017 applicants were accepted. The SAT scores for the 2016-2017 freshman class were: Critical Reading-- 2% below 500, 22% between 500 and 599, 56% between 600 and 699, and 20% between 700 and 800. Math-- 1% below 500, 23% between 500 and 599, 53% between 600 and 699, and 24% between 700 and 800. Writing-- 1% below 500, 21% between 500 and 599, 55% between 600 and 699, and 23% between 700 and 800. The ACT scores were 2% between 18 and 23, 51% between 24 and 29, and 46% above 30. **Admissions Contact:** M. Teresa Kaldor, PhD., Director of Institutional Research. Email: *admission@oxy.edu* Web: *www.oxy.edu*

FINANCIAL AID: In 2016-2017, 73% of all full-time freshmen and 70% of continuing full-time students received some form of financial aid. 58% of all full-time freshmen and 55% of continuing full-time students received need-based aid. The average freshman award was $43,019. Need-based scholarships or need-based grants averaged $34,600 ($63,194 maximum); need-based self-help aid (loans and jobs) averaged $7,320 ($13,500 maximum); and other non-need-based awards and non-need-based scholarships averaged $11,113 ($49,248 maximum). The average financial indebtedness of the 2016 graduate was $29,940. Oxy is a member of CSS. The CSS/Profile, state aid form, and non-custodial parent's statement are required. The FAFSA code is 001249. The priority date for freshman financial aid applications for fall entry is January 15.

OTIS COLLEGE OF ART AND DESIGN *(The complete profile is made available exclusively on our website, www.barronspac.com)*

PACIFIC UNION COLLEGE — B-2
www.puc.edu

Angwin, CA 94508	**(707) 965-6336** **(800) 862-7080**
Fax: (707) 965-6432	**Email: enroll@puc.edu**
Full-time: 500 men, 575 women	**Faculty:** n/av
Part-time: 135 men, 165 women	**Ph.D.s:** n/av
Graduate: 1 women	**Student/Faculty:** n/av
Year: trimesters, summer session	**Tuition:** $28,314
Room & Board: $7695	**Freshman Class:** n/av
SAT or ACT: recommended	**CEEB CODE:** 4600
Application Deadline: open	**VERY COMPETITIVE**

Pacific Union College, founded in 1888, is a private college affiliated with the Seventh-day Adventist Church, offering programs in liberal arts, religion, business, health science, and teacher preparation. The figures in the above capsule and in this profile are approximate. There is 1 undergraduate school and 1 graduate school. In addition to regional accreditation, PUC has baccalaureate program accreditation with CSWE, NASM, NLN, CCTC, and IACBE. The 1500-acre campus is in a rural area 70 miles north of San Francisco. Including any residence halls, there are 60 buildings.

STUDENT LIFE: 76% of undergraduates are from California. Others are from 42 states, 26 foreign countries, and Canada. 7% are Foreign; 40% White; 4% African American; 29% Asian American; 15% Hispanic; 1% American Indian/Alaska Native. **Female To Male Ratio:** 1.2:1. The average age of freshmen is 19; all undergraduates, 21. 32% do not continue beyond their first year; 40% remain to graduate. **Housing:** 1344 students can be accommodated in college housing, which includes single-sex dorms and married student housing. On-campus housing is guaranteed for the freshman year only. 76% of students live on campus. Alcohol is not permitted. All students may keep cars.

FACULTY/CLASSROOMS: 56% of faculty are male; 44% are female. All teach undergraduates. No introductory courses are taught by graduate students. The average class size in an introductory lecture is 19; in a laboratory is 18; and in a regular course is 17.

PROGRAMS OF STUDY: PUC confers B.A., B.S., B.B.A., B.Mus. and B.S.W. degrees. Associate and master's degrees are also awarded. Bachelor's degrees are awarded in BIOLOGICAL SCIENCE (biology/biological science and biophysics), BUSINESS (business administration and management), COMMUNICATIONS AND THE ARTS (communications, English, fine arts, French, graphic design, journalism, music, photography, public relations, radio/television technology, and Spanish), COMPUTER AND PHYSICAL SCIENCE (applied mathematics, chemistry, computer science, mathematics, natural sciences, and physics), EDUCATION (early childhood education and physical education), ENGINEERING AND ENVIRONMENTAL DESIGN (airline piloting and navigation and graphic arts technology), HEALTH PROFESSIONS (nursing), SOCIAL SCIENCE (history, psychology, religion, social studies, social work, and theological studies). Sciences and behavioral science is the strongest academically. Nursing and business administration have the largest enrollment.

ACTIVITIES: There are no fraternities or sororities. There are 50 groups on campus, including campus ministries, academic groups, art, band, chess, choir, chorale, computers, drama, ethnic, film, honors, jazz band, literary magazine, newspaper, orchestra, photography, political, radio and TV, religious, social, student government, symphony, and yearbook. Popular campus events include Picnic and Ski Days, All-College Get-Acquainted Party, and Fall and Spring Festivals. **Sports:** There are 3 intercollegiate sports for men and 3 for women, and 6 intramural sports for men and 6 for women. Facilities include a gym, pool, tennis courts, and athletic fields for softball, soccer, volleyball, flag ball, and track and field. **Graduates:** From July 1, 2015 to June 30, 2016, 325 bachelor's degrees were awarded. The most popular majors were nursing (36%), business (19%), and chemistry (5%). In an average class, 12% graduate in 4 years or less, 19% graduate in 5 years or less, and 36% graduate in 6 years or less.

SERVICES: Counseling and information services are available, as is tutoring in most subjects. There is a reader service for the blind, and remedial math and writing. **Library/Resources:** The library contains 148,218 volumes, 125,268 microform items, and 6,623 audio/video tapes/CDs/DVDs, and subscribes to 10,637 periodicals including electronic. Computerized library services include interlibrary loans, database searching, Internet access, and Wi-Fi capability. Special learning facilities include an art gallery, natural history museum, radio station, video production studio, observatory, and marine field station. **Physically Challenged Students:** 95% of the campus is accessible. Facilities include wheelchair ramps, elevators, special parking, specially equipped restrooms, and special class scheduling. **Special:** Students may study abroad in Austria, Spain, France, Argentina, and Italy, earn B.A.-B.S. degrees, take dual majors, and pursue a major in interdisciplinary studies. Internships, social work, education, and ministerial field experiences, and accelerated degree programs in business management and early childhood education are also offered. The college offers nondegree study and credit for life, military, and work experience. There are 2 national honor societies and a freshman honors program. **Visiting:** There are regularly scheduled orientations for prospective students. There are guides for informal visits, visitors may sit in on classes, and stay overnight. To schedule a visit, contact the Admissions Office. **Campus Safety and Security:** Measures include 24-hour foot and vehicle patrol, emergency notification system, self-defense education, and security escort services. There are emergency telephones, lighted pathways/sidewalks, and a safety committee.

REQUIREMENTS: The SAT or ACT is recommended. Scores are used only for advising purposes. Candidates for admission should have completed 4 years of English, 2 of math, and 1 each of science and history. A GPA of 2.3 is required. AP and CLEP credits are accepted. Important factors in the admissions decision are recommendations by school officials, leadership record, and advanced placement or honors courses. To graduate, a student must complete a minimum of 192 quarter hours, including 60 in upper-level courses, maintain a minimum GPA of 2.0. Distribution requirements include courses in rhetoric, statistics, historic, philosophy, social science, foreign language, literature, visual and applied arts, music, math, science, and health and fitness. A religion course is required, and a thesis in some programs. **Procedure:** Freshmen are admitted to all sessions. Entrance exams should be taken in the junior or senior year. There is a rolling admissions plan. Application deadlines are open. Application fee is $30. Applications are accepted on-line. **Transfer Students:** Admission requirements are the same as for non-transfer students. 36 of 192 credits required for the bachelor's degree must be completed at PUC. **International Students:** There are 92 international students enrolled. They must take the TOEFL. They must also take the SAT or ACT.

Admissions Contact: Darren Hagen, Director of Enrollment Services. Email: *enroll@puc.edu* Web: *www.puc.edu*

FINANCIAL AID: In 2016-2017, 100% of all full-time freshmen and 99% of continuing full-time students received some form of financial aid. 95% of all full-time freshmen and 64% of continuing full-time students received need-based aid. 80% of undergraduate students work part-time. Average annual earnings from campus work are $1500. The college's own financial statement is required. The FAFSA code is 001258. Check with the school for current application deadlines.

PEPPERDINE UNIVERSITY — C-4

www.pepperdine.edu

Malibu, CA 90263 — **(310) 506-4369**

Fax: (310) 506-4861 — **Email: admission-seaver@pepperdine.edu**

Full-time: 1262 men, 1824 women	**Faculty:** IIA, ++$
Part-time: 232 men, 170 women	**Ph.D.s:** 100%
Graduate: 1499 men, 2332 women	**Student/Faculty:** 15 to 1
Year: semesters, summer session	**Tuition:** $56,460
Room & Board: $18,000	**Freshman Class:** 9222 applied, 3497 accepted, 777 enrolled
SAT CR/M/W: 604/623/610 **ACT:** 29	**CEEB CODE:** 4630
Application Deadline: January 5	**HIGHLY COMPETITIVE+**

Pepperdine University, founded in 1937, is a private liberal arts university affiliated with the Church of Christ. Figures in the above capsule and in this profile are approximate. Tuition costs varies by programs chosen. There are 5 undergraduate schools and 5 graduate schools. In addition to regional accreditation, Pepperdine has baccalaureate program accreditation with AACSB and NCATE. The 830-acre campus is in a suburban area 35 miles northwest of Los Angeles, overlooking the Pacific Ocean. Including any residence halls, there are 76 buildings.

STUDENT LIFE: 53% of undergraduates are from California. Others are from 50 states, 60 foreign countries, and Canada. 65% are from public schools. 9% are Foreign; 7% African American; 45% White; 15% Hispanic; 12% Asian American; 1% American Indian/Alaska Native. 16% are Catholic. **Female To Male Ratio:** 1.4:1. The average age of freshmen is 18; all undergraduates, 20. **Housing:** College-sponsored housing includes single-sex dorms, on-campus apartments, off-campus apartments, and married student housing. In addition, there are honors houses and special-interest houses. On-campus housing is guaranteed for the freshman year only and is available on a lottery system for upperclassmen. Alcohol is not permitted. All students may keep cars.

FACULTY/CLASSROOMS: 58% of faculty are male; 42% are female. All teach undergraduates, and all do research. No introductory courses are taught by graduate students. The average class size in an introductory lecture is 18; in a laboratory is 15; and in a regular course is 17.

PROGRAMS OF STUDY: Pepperdine confers B.A., B.S. and B.S.M. degrees. Master's and doctoral degrees are also awarded. Bachelor's degrees are awarded in BIOLOGICAL SCIENCE (biology/biological science and nutrition), BUSINESS (accounting, business administration and management, international business management, management science, and marketing management), COMMUNICATIONS AND THE ARTS (advertising, art, art history and appreciation, communications, creative writing, dramatic arts, English, film arts, French, German, Italian, journalism, media arts, music, public relations, Spanish, speech/debate/rhetoric, and telecommunications), COMPUTER AND PHYSICAL SCIENCE (chemistry, computer science, mathematics, natural sciences, and physics), EDUCATION (elementary education, mathematics education, physical education, and secondary education), ENGINEERING AND ENVIRONMENTAL DESIGN (engineering), HEALTH PROFESSIONS (sports medicine), SOCIAL SCIENCE (economics, Hispanic American studies, history, humanities, international studies, liberal arts/general studies, philosophy, political science/government, psychology, religion, social science, and sociology). Natural sciences (premedical), sports medicine, and business administration are the strongest academically. Communication and business have the largest enrollment.

ACTIVITIES: There are 60 groups on campus, including Hawaiian club, women's leadership, art, band, cheerleading, chess, choir, chorale, chorus, computers, dance, debate, drama, environmental, ethnic, film, honors, international, jazz band, literary magazine, medical club, musical theater, newspaper, opera, orchestra, pep band, photography, political, professional, radio and TV, religious, social, social service, student government, and symphony. Popular campus events include Waves Weekend, C2F (Culture and Club Fair), Songfest and REEL Stories Student Film Festival. **Sports:** There are 8 intercollegiate sports for men and 9 for women, and 7 intramural sports for men and 7 for women. Facilities include a field house, pool, weight room, basketball, racquetball, tennis courts, playing fields, all-weather track, and aerobics room. **Graduates:** From July 1, 2015 to June 30, 2016, 891 bachelor's degrees were awarded. The most popular majors were business administration (9%), international business (6%), and advertising (4%). In an average class, 3% graduate in 3 years or less, 69% graduate in 4 years or less, 80% graduate in 5 years or less, and 81% graduate in 6 years or less.

SERVICES: Counseling and information services are available, as is tutoring in most subjects. **Library/Resources:** The 4 libraries contain 551,502 volumes, 505,458 microform items, and 15,402 audio/video tapes/CDs/DVDs, and subscribe to 51,798 periodicals including electronic. Computerized library services include interlibrary loans, database searching, and Internet access. Special learning facilities include an art gallery, radio station, TV station, writing center, and academic center for excellence. **Physically Challenged Students:** 90% of the campus is accessible. Facilities include wheelchair ramps, elevators, special parking, specially equipped restrooms, special class scheduling, lowered drinking fountains, lowered telephones, and special housing. **Special:** Students may earn 1 to 4 units for an internship, available in most majors, participate in a Washington semester, and study abroad in 8 countries. The school offers a 3-2 engineering degree with Washington University in St. Louis and the University of Southern California. There are dual majors in any discipline, student-designed contract majors, federal work-study programs, nondegree study, and pass/fail options. There are 14 national honor societies and 6 departmental honors programs. **Visiting:** There are regularly scheduled orientations for prospective students, Information sessions, campus tours, classroom visits, admission counselor meetings, and meeting faculty member. There are guides for informal visits, visitors may sit in on classes, and stay overnight. To schedule a visit, contact the Housing and Residence Life Office at (310) 506-7586. **Campus Safety and Security:** Measures include 24-hour foot and vehicle patrol, emergency notification system, self-defense education, and security escort services. There are shuttle buses, emergency telephones, lighted pathways/sidewalks, in-room safes, guarded entrances to campus, security cameras, and a campus crimewatch program.

REQUIREMENTS: The SAT or ACT is required. It is strongly recommended that candidates for admission present a college preparatory program that includes 4 years of English, 3 of math, 2 each of foreign language and science, and courses in speech communication, humanities, and social science. AP and CLEP credits are accepted. Important factors in the admissions decision are advanced placement or honors courses, recommendations by school officials, and evidence of special talent. To graduate, students must complete 128 units, including 64 units of general education requirements. 2 years of a broad liberal arts core curriculum are needed. Courses are required in English, religion, Western heritage, non-Western heritage, American heritage, behavioral science, foreign language, lab science, math, speech and rhetoric, freshman seminar, and phys ed. Students must take at least 40 upper-division units and complete a 28-unit residency requirement. Pepperdine requires a minimum GPA of 2.0 for graduation. **Procedure:** Freshmen are admitted fall and spring. Entrance exams should be taken in the fall. There is a deferred admissions plan. Applications should be filed by January 5 for fall entry; October 15 for spring entry, along with a $65 fee. Notifications are sent April 1. Applications are accepted on-line. **Transfer Students:** Transfer applicants should have a minimum GPA of 3.0 from an accredited college. SAT or ACT scores are required for applicants who have completed fewer than 30 transferable semester hours at an accredited college. 28 of 128 credits required for the bachelor's degree must be completed at Pepperdine. **International Students:** There are 290 international students enrolled. The school actively recruits these students. They must take the TOEFL with a minimum score of 550 on the paper-based TOEFL (PBT) or 80 on the Internet-based version (iBT) and the college's own test. They must also take the SAT.

ADMISSIONS: 38% of the 2016-2017 applicants were accepted. The SAT scores for the 2016-2017 freshman class were: Critical Reading-- 6% below 500, 39% between 500 and 599, 42% between 600 and 699, and 13% between 700 and 800. Math-- 5% below 500, 28% between 500 and 599, 46% between 600 and 699, and 21% between 700 and 800. Writing-- 5% below 500, 34% between 500 and 599, 43% between 600 and 699, and 18% between 700 and 800. The ACT scores were 6% below 12, 8% between 12 and 17, 19% between 18 and 23, 21% between 24 and 29, and 46% above 30. 74% of the current freshmen were in the top fifth of their class; 93% were in the top two fifths. **Admissions Contact:** Michael Truschke, Dean of Admission and Enrollment Management. Email: *admission-seaver@pepperdine.edu* Web: *www.pepperdine.edu*

FINANCIAL AID: In 2016-2017, 76% of all full-time freshmen and 73% of continuing full-time students received some form of financial aid. 53% of all full-time freshmen and 53% of continuing full-time students received need-based aid. 40% of undergraduate students work part-time. Average annual earnings from campus work are $2100. The college's own financial statement, and the federal income tax form, the state scholarship/grant form (California residents), and W-2 wage statements are required. The priority date for freshman financial aid applications for fall entry is February 15.

PITZER COLLEGE — D-5
www.pitzer.edu

Claremont, CA 91711	(909) 621-8129 (800) PITZER-1
Fax: (909) 621-8770	Email: admission@pitzer.edu
Full-time: 411 men, 647 women	**Faculty:** 74; IIB, ++$
Part-time: 12 men, 29 women	**Ph.D.s:** 100%
Graduate: n/av	**Student/Faculty:** 12 to 1
Year: semesters, summer session	**Tuition:** $50,430
Room & Board: $15,762	**Freshman Class:** 3743 applied, 903 accepted, 272 enrolled
SAT CR/M: 652/641 **ACT:** 30	**CEEB CODE:** 4619
Application Deadline: January 1	**MOST COMPETITIVE**

Pitzer College, founded in 1963, is a private liberal arts college that through an interdisciplinary approach emphasizes social justice, intercultural understanding, and environmental sensitivity. Pitzer is one of the Claremont Colleges. The figures in the above capsule and in this profile are approximate. Tuition cost varies by programs chosen. There are 2 undergraduate schools. In addition to regional accreditation, Pitzer has baccalaureate program accreditation with WASC. The 31-acre campus is in a suburban area 35 miles east of Los Angeles. Including any residence halls, there are 17 buildings.

STUDENT LIFE: 50% of undergraduates are from out of state, mostly the Northwest. Students are from 42 states, 14 foreign countries, and Canada. 8% are Asian American; 6% African American; 46% White; 3% Foreign; 16% Hispanic; 1% American Indian/Alaska Native. **Female To Male Ratio:** 1.6:1. The average age of freshmen is 18; all undergraduates, 21. 7% do not continue beyond their first year; 80% remain to graduate. **Housing:** 734 students can be accommodated in college housing, which includes coed dorms and off-campus apartments. In addition, there are special-interest houses, quiet hall, involvement tower, food co-op, substance-free, and all-female floors. On-campus housing is guaranteed for the freshman year only. 75% of students live on campus; of those, 75% remain on campus on weekends. Upperclassmen may keep cars.

FACULTY/CLASSROOMS: 54% of faculty are male; 46% are female. All teach undergraduates, and do research. No introductory courses are taught by graduate students. The average class size in an introductory lecture is 20; in a laboratory is 18; and in a regular course is 18.

PROGRAMS OF STUDY: Pitzer confers B.A. degrees. Bachelor's degrees are awarded in BIOLOGICAL SCIENCE (biochemistry, biology/biological science, and neurosciences), BUSINESS (management engineering and organizational behavior), COMMUNICATIONS AND THE ARTS (art, classics, dance, dramatic arts, English, film arts, French, linguistics, media arts, music, and Spanish), COMPUTER AND PHYSICAL SCIENCE (chemistry, mathematics, physics, science, and science and management), ENGINEERING AND ENVIRONMENTAL DESIGN (environmental science), SOCIAL SCIENCE (African American studies, American studies, anthropology, Asian/American studies, Asian/Oriental studies, Caribbean studies, economics, European studies, history, international relations, Latin American studies, Mexican-American/Chicano studies, philosophy, political science/government, psychology, sociology, Third World studies, and women's studies). Social and behavioral sciences are the strongest academically and have the largest enrollments is the strongest academically.

ACTIVITIES: There are no fraternities or sororities. There are 50 groups on campus, including art, band, chess, choir, chorale, chorus, computers, dance, debate, drama, environmental, ethnic, film, honors, international, jazz band, LGBT, literary magazine, newspaper, orchestra, photography, political, professional, radio and TV, religious, social, social service, student government, and symphony. Popular campus events include the Kohoutek Festival, Hammock on the Mounds and Reggae Festival. **Sports:** There are 10 intercollegiate sports for men and 11 for women. Facilities include gyms, swimming pools, tennis courts, playing fields, and lighted volleyball courts, and campus stadium. There are also shared intercollegiate sports with Pomona College. The Gold Student Center features a fitness room, lap pool, Frisbee field, basketball and volleyball courts. **Graduates:** From July 1, 2015 to June 30, 2016, 244 bachelor's degrees were awarded. The most popular majors were psychology (17%), political studies, and and sociology (11%). 25 companies recruited on campus in 2015-2016. In an average class, 75% graduate in 4 years or less, 80% graduate in 5 years or less, and 85% graduate in 6 years or less. Of the 2015 graduating class, 17% were enrolled in graduate school within 6 months of graduation, and 56% were employed.

SERVICES: Counseling and information services are available, as is tutoring in most subjects, such as tutoring software and programs for the learning disabled. There is a reader service for the blind, and remedial writing. **Library/Resources:** The library contains 250,000 volumes, 1.2 million microform items, and 17,000 audio/video tapes/CDs/DVDs, and subscribes to 35,000 periodicals including electronic. Computerized library services include interlibrary loans, database searching, Internet access, and Wi-Fi capability. Special learning facilities include an art gallery, radio station, social science lab, arboretum, and a farm in Costa Rica. **Physically Challenged Students:** 95% of the campus is accessible. Facilities include wheelchair ramps, elevators, special parking, specially equipped restrooms, lowered drinking fountains, lowered telephones, and special housing. **Special:** Students may cross-register at any of the other Claremont Colleges, or study abroad in 60 countries in Africa, Asia, Europe, Latin America, North America, or Oceania. There are co-op programs, work-study, internships, dual majors, student-designed majors, an extensive first-year seminar program, and interdisciplinary study offered in science and technology, and international or intercultural studies. Joint advanced degrees are offered in math, economics, M.I.S., psychology, and public policy, as is a 7-year B.A./D.O. program with the College of Western Health Sciences. There are independent study and limited pass/fail options. There is 1 national honor society and 18 departmental honors programs. **Visiting:** There are regularly scheduled orientations for prospective students. There are guides for informal visits, visitors may sit in on classes, and stay overnight. To schedule a visit, contact the Office of Admissions. **Campus Safety and Security:** Measures include 24-hour foot and vehicle patrol, emergency notification system, self-defense education, and security escort services. There are emergency telephones and lighted pathways/sidewalks.

REQUIREMENTS: Applicants must be graduates of an accredited secondary school or have earned the GED. Secondary school courses must include 4 years of English courses requiring extensive writing, and 3 years each of social and behavioral sciences including history, lab science, foreign language, and math. A personal essay is required and a personal interview is recommended. Students in the top 10% of their class or those with an unweighted GPA in academic subjects of 3.5 are not required to submit ACT or SAT scores. Students without these qualifications must submit either ACT or SAT scores, 2 SAT subject tests, 2 AP test scores of at least 4 (1 in English, 1 in math or science), 2 IB exams (English 1A and Mathematics Methods Standard Level or a higher-level course), or a recent analytical writing sample from a humanities or social science course and a math exam from a course at the algebra II level or higher, both including teacher's comments and grades. AP credits are accepted. Important factors in the admissions decision are advanced placement or honors courses, leadership record, and evidence of special talent. Students must complete a total of 32 courses with a 2.0 GPA. Although requirements vary according to major, most students take introductory or preparatory courses in their first 2 years and courses in or related to their major in the last 2 years. All students must fulfill educational objectives in the following areas: interdisciplinary and intercultural exploration, social responsibility and the ethical implications of knowledge and action, breadth of knowledge, and written expression. More than 10 courses are required in the major. **Procedure:** Freshmen are admitted fall and spring. Entrance exams should be taken by January 1. There are early decision and deferred admissions plans. Early decision applications should be filed by November 1; regular applications, by January 1 for fall entry; and October 15 for spring entry. The fall 2016 application fee was $50. Notifications are sent April 1. Applications are accepted on-line. **Transfer Students:** 21 transfer students enrolled in 2015-2016. No more than 2 years of previous credits may be transferred. 64 of 128 credits required for the bachelor's degree must be completed at Pitzer. **International Students:** There are 36 international students enrolled. The school actively recruits these students. They must take the TOEFL with a minimum score of 520 on the paper-based TOEFL (PBT) or 70 on the Internet-based version (iBT).

ADMISSIONS: 24% of the 2016-2017 applicants were accepted. The SAT scores for the 2016-2017 freshman class were: Critical Reading--15% between 500 and 599, 60% between 600 and 699, and 25% between 700 and 800. Math-- 24% between 500 and 599, 60% between 600 and 699, and 16% between 700 and 800. 75% of the current freshmen were in the top fifth of their class; 98% were in the top two fifths. **Admissions Contact:** Angel Perez, Vice President, Admission and Financial Aid. Email: *admission@pitzer.edu* Web: *www.pitzer.edu*

FINANCIAL AID: In 2016-2017, 34% of all full-time freshmen and 40% of continuing full-time students received some form of financial aid. 32% of all full-time freshmen and 39% of continuing full-time students received need-based aid. The average freshman award was $35,509. Need-based scholarships or need-based grants averaged $32,873; need-based self-help aid (loans and jobs) averaged $4,914; and other non-need-based awards and non-need-based scholarships averaged $5,000. Pitzer is a member of CSS. The CSS/Profile and the state aid form are required. The FAFSA code is 001172. The deadline for filing freshman financial aid applications for fall entry is February 1.

POINT LOMA NAZARENE UNIVERSITY D-5

www.pointloma.edu

San Diego, CA 92106 (619) 849-2541 (800) 733-7770

Fax: (619) 849-2601 **Email:** admissions@pointloma.edu

Full-time: 935 men, 1657 women	**Faculty:** n/av
Part-time: 140 men, 321 women	**Ph.D.s:** 87%
Graduate: 313 men, 790 women	**Student/Faculty:** 15 to 1
Year: semesters, summer session	**Tuition:** $33,500
Room & Board: $9950	**Freshman Class:** 3162 applied, 2195 accepted, 594 enrolled
SAT CR/M/W: 560/565/560 **ACT:** 26	**CEEB CODE:** 4605
Application Deadline: February 15	**COMPETITIVE**

Point Loma Nazarene University, founded in 1902, is a private liberal arts university affiliated with the Church of the Nazarene. There are 6 undergraduate schools and 7 graduate schools. In addition to regional accreditation, PLNU has baccalaureate program accreditation with ACBSP, CSWE, NASM, NCATE, ACEND, CCTC, CAATE, and CCNE. The 90-acre campus is in a suburban area in San Diego. Including any residence halls, there are 51 buildings.

STUDENT LIFE: 83% of undergraduates are from California. 55% are White; 24% Hispanic; 7% two or more races; 6% Asian American; 2% African American; 2% race unknown; 1% American Indian/Alaska Native; 1% Foreign. **Female To Male Ratio:** 2.0:1. The average age of freshmen is 18; all undergraduates, 22. 14% do not continue beyond their first year; 71% remain to graduate. **Housing:** 1762 students can be accommodated in college housing, which includes single-sex and coed dorms, on-campus apartments, and off-campus apartments. On-campus housing is available on a first-come, first-served basis, and is available on a lottery system for upperclassmen. 56% of students live on campus. Alcohol is not permitted. Upperclassmen may keep cars.

FACULTY/CLASSROOMS: 47% of faculty are male; 53% are female. No introductory courses are taught by graduate students. The average class size in an introductory lecture is 24 and in a laboratory is 19.

PROGRAMS OF STUDY: PLNU confers B.A., B.S., B.Mus. B.S.N. and B.S.Bus Admin degrees. Master's degrees are also awarded. Bachelor's degrees are awarded in BIOLOGICAL SCIENCE (biochemistry, biology/biological science, and nutrition), BUSINESS (accounting, business administration and management, business administration - international, business communications, business information systems, finance, marketing, and organizational leadership and management), COMMUNICATIONS AND THE ARTS (art history, art, art and design, art history and appreciation, broadcasting, communications, French, graphic design, graphic design & media, journalism, literature, media arts, music, music composition, music ministry, music performance, piano performance, Spanish, speech/debate/rhetoric, vocal performance, and writing), COMPUTER AND PHYSICAL SCIENCE (chemistry, computer information technology, computer science, mathematics, and physics), EDUCATION (art education, athletic training, education, and music education), ENGINEERING AND ENVIRONMENTAL DESIGN (engineering physics and environmental science), HEALTH PROFESSIONS (exercise science, health science, and nursing), SOCIAL SCIENCE (biblical studies, child psychology/development, Christian studies, criminal justice, dietetics, economics, history, international studies, ministries, philosophy, political science/government, psychology, social science, social work, sociology, and youth ministry). Nursing, business administration, and biology are the strongest academically and have the largest enrollments.

ACTIVITIES: There are no fraternities or sororities. Groups on campus include art, band, cheerleading, choir, chorale, chorus, communications, computers, debate, drama, ethnic, film, forensics, honors, international, jazz band, literary magazine, musical theater, newspaper, opera, orchestra, photography, political, professional, radio and TV, religious, social, social service, student government, and yearbook. Popular campus events include Spiritual Emphasis Week and Christmas Messiah Concert. **Sports:** There are 4 intercollegiate sports for men and 7 for women. Facilities include a gym, baseball and soccer fields, track, tennis courts, dorm lounges, table tennis and pool tables. **Graduates:** From July 1, 2015 to June 30, 2016, 658 bachelor's degrees were awarded. The most popular majors were business/marketing (25%), health professions and related programs (23%), and psychology (9%). In an average class, 70% graduate in 4 years or less, 74% graduate in 5 years or less, and 71% graduate in 6 years or less.

SERVICES: Counseling and information services are available, as is tutoring in most subjects. There is a reader service for the blind, and remedial math, reading, and writing. **Library/Resources:** Computerized library services include interlibrary loans, database searching, and Internet access. Special learning facilities include an art gallery, radio station, TV station, and a lab preschool. **Physically Challenged Students:** All of the campus is accessible. Facilities include wheelchair ramps, elevators, special parking, specially equipped restrooms, special class scheduling, lowered drinking fountains, and lowered telephones. **Special:** PLNU offers internships in the church, state and national governments, journalism, small business, and the film industry. Students may study abroad in several world capitals and in more than 40 countries. There are Washington and United Nations semester programs. Various dual or interdepartmental majors are offered, including biology-chemistry, graphic communications, human environmental science-business, and church music-youth ministries. There are pre-professional programs in medicine/dentistry, law, and engineering. A general studies degree in liberal studies is available, as is credit for life, military, and work experience for nursing students. There is a freshman honors program. **Visiting:** There are regularly scheduled orientations for prospective students, including campus tours and appointments with major advisers. There are guides for informal visits, visitors may sit in on classes, and stay overnight. To schedule a visit, contact the Admissions Office. **Campus Safety and Security:** Measures include 24-hour foot and vehicle patrol, emergency notification system, self-defense education, and security escort services. There are shuttle buses, emergency telephones, and lighted pathways/sidewalks.

REQUIREMENTS: The SAT or ACT is required. Candidates for admission should have completed 4 years of English, 3 of math, 2 each of a lab science and the same foreign language, and 1 of history. AP and CLEP credits are accepted. Important factors in the admissions decision are personality/intangible qualities, leadership record, and advanced placement or honors courses. To graduate, students must complete a minimum of 128 semester units. At least 24 upper-division semester units are needed for the major. A minimum GPA of 2.0 is required. Students must complete the general education requirements, though B.S.N. candidates need not take a foreign language. General education requirements include 9 courses in cultural studies, 5 in the sciences, 4 in cognitive studies, and 3 in religious studies. Students must demonstrate proficiency in writing and math. **Procedure:** Freshmen are admitted fall. Entrance exams should be taken in the junior year or early in the senior year. Applications should be filed by February 15 for fall entry, along with a $55 fee. Notifications are sent April 1. Applications are accepted on-line. **Transfer Students:** 352 transfer students enrolled in 2015-2016. Transfer students must have a minimum cumulative GPA of 2.0 (based on transferable units) to be considered for admission. Applicants with at least 36 transferable units at the time of application need only submit college transcripts (high school transcripts are not required for these applicants). 24 of 128 credits required for the bachelor's degree must be completed at PLNU. **International Students:** There are 35 international students enrolled. They must take the TOEFL with a minimum score of 550 on the paper-based TOEFL (PBT) or 80 on the Internet-based version (iBT).

ADMISSIONS: 69% of the 2016-2017 applicants were accepted. The SAT scores for the 2016-2017 freshman class were: Critical Reading-- 17% below 500, 47% between 500 and 599, 32% between 600 and 699, and 4% between 700 and 800. Math-- 16% below 500, 48% between 500 and 599, 32% between 600 and 699, and 5% between 700 and 800. Writing-- 23% below 500, 47% between 500 and 599, 27% between 600 and 699, and 4% between 700 and 800. The ACT scores were 1% between 12 and 17, 26% between 18 and 23, 57% between 24 and 29, and 16% above 30. **Admissions Contact:** Shannon Hutchison, Director, Undergrad Admissions. Email: *admissions@pointloma.edu* Web: *www.pointloma.edu*

FINANCIAL AID: The average financial indebtedness of the 2016 graduate was $34,844. PLNU is a member of CSS. The FAFSA code is 001262. The priority date for freshman financial aid applications for fall entry is March 2.

POMONA COLLEGE — D-5

www.pomona.edu

Claremont, CA 91711 — **(909) 621-8134**

Fax: (909) 621-8952	**Email:** admissions@pomona.edu
Full-time: 810 men, 832 women	**Faculty:** 188; IIB, ++$
Part-time: n/av	**Ph.D.s:** 92%
Graduate: n/av	**Student/Faculty:** 8 to 1
Year: semesters	**Tuition:** $49,352
Room & Board: $15,605	**Freshman Class:** 8102 applied, 765 accepted, 411 enrolled
SAT CR/M/W: 720/720/730 **ACT:** 32	**CEEB CODE:** 4607
Application Deadline: January 1	**MOST COMPETITIVE**

Pomona College, founded in 1887, is one of the nation's leading liberal arts colleges and the founding member of The Claremont Colleges, a consortium of five undergraduate and 2 graduate schools. In addition to regional accreditation, Pomona has baccalaureate program accreditation with WASC. The 140-acre campus is in a suburban area 35 miles east of Los Angeles, and 20 miles east of Pasadena. Including any residence halls, there are 63 buildings.

STUDENT LIFE: 74% of undergraduates are from out of state, mostly the Midwest. Students are from 49 states, 63 foreign countries, and Canada. 55% are from public schools. 8% are African American; 7% two or more races; 5% race unknown; 38% White; 15% Hispanic; 14% Asian American; 11% Foreign. **Female To Male Ratio:** 1.0:1. The average age of freshmen is 18; all undergraduates, 20. 3% do not continue beyond their first year; 96% remain to graduate. **Housing:** 1660 students can be accommodated in college housing, which includes coed dorms and on-campus apartments. In addition, there are language houses. On-campus housing is guaranteed for all 4 years. 98% of students live on campus. Upperclassmen may keep cars.

FACULTY/CLASSROOMS: 54% of faculty are male; 46% are female. All teach undergraduates, and all do research. No introductory courses are taught by graduate students. The average class size in a regular course is 15.

PROGRAMS OF STUDY: Pomona confers B.A. degrees. Bachelor's degrees are awarded in AGRICULTURE (environmental studies), BIOLOGICAL SCIENCE (biology/biological science, molecular biology, and neurosciences), COMMUNICATIONS AND THE ARTS (Africana studies, art history and appreciation, Chinese, classics, dance, English, fine arts, French, Japanese, languages, linguistics, literature, media arts, music, romance languages and literature, Russian, Spanish, studio art, and theatre arts), COMPUTER AND PHYSICAL SCIENCE (chemistry, computer science, geology, mathematics, physics, and science), ENGINEERING AND ENVIRONMENTAL DESIGN (technology and public affairs), SOCIAL SCIENCE (American studies, anthropology, Asian/American studies, Asian/Oriental studies, cognitive science, economics, German area studies, Hispanic American studies, history, international relations, Latin American studies, medieval studies, Mexican-American/Chicano studies, Middle Eastern studies, philosophy, political science/government, psychology, public affairs, religious studies, Russian and Slavic studies, sociology, and women's studies).

ACTIVITIES: There are 200 groups on campus, including Outdoors Club of the Claremont Colleges, art, band, chess, choir, chorus, dance, debate, drama, environmental, ethnic, film, honors, international, jazz band, LGBT, literary magazine, musical theater, newspaper, orchestra, pep band, photography, political, professional, radio and TV, religious, social, social service, student government, symphony, and yearbook. **Sports:** There are 10 intercollegiate sports for men and 11 for women, and 13 intramural sports for men and 13 for women. Facilities include a track, swimming pools, weight room, fitness center, dance studio, playing fields, tennis, squash, racquetball, basketball, volleyball, and badminton. **Graduates:** From July 1, 2015 to June 30, 2016, 380 bachelor's degrees were awarded. The most popular majors were economics (12%), mathematics (10%), and computer science (8%). 500 companies recruited on campus in 2015-2016. In an average class, 92% graduate in 4 years or less, 96% graduate in 5 years or less, and 97% graduate in 6 years or less. Of the 2015 graduating class, 20% were enrolled in graduate school within 6 months of graduation, and 35% were employed.

SERVICES: Counseling and information services are available, as is tutoring in most subjects. There is a reader service for the blind. **Library/Resources:** The 3 libraries contain 2.0 million volumes, 1.4 million microform items, and 777 audio/video tapes/CDs/DVDs, and subscribe to 6,624 periodicals including electronic. Computerized library services include interlibrary loans, database searching, and Internet access. Special learning facilities include an art gallery, planetarium, radio station, observatory, modern languages and international relations center, and organic farm. **Physically Challenged Students:** 80% of the campus is accessible. Facilities include wheelchair ramps, elevators, special parking, specially equipped restrooms, special class scheduling, lowered drinking fountains, and lowered telephones. **Special:** Students may cross-register at any of The Claremont Colleges, which are on adjacent campuses and follow the same academic schedule. Study abroad is offered through 49 programs in 31 countries. The Pomona College Internship Program provides students with paid part-time internships in the greater Los Angeles area. Paid internship opportunities are also offered in the summer. The college's Summer Undergraduate Research Program enables students to conduct extended, focused research in close cooperation with a Pomona faculty member. SURP funding includes room and board, a supply budget, and a stipend. Other opportunities include spending a semester in Washington, D.C., a 3-2 engineering program offered with the California Institute of Technology, Washington University in St. Louis, and Dartmouth College, spending one semester at Colby, Smith, Spelman, or Swarthmore colleges, independent study options, and dual and student-designed majors. There is a chapter of Phi Beta Kappa. **Visiting:** There are regularly scheduled orientations for prospective students, including interviews, information sessions, and guided tours. Visitors may sit in on classes and stay overnight. To schedule a visit, contact the Office of Admissions. **Campus Safety and Security:** Measures include 24-hour foot and vehicle patrol, emergency notification system, self-defense education, and security escort services. There are emergency telephones, lighted pathways/sidewalks, and controlled access to dorms/residences.

REQUIREMENTS: The SAT or ACT is required. Although applicants need not be graduates of accredited high schools (some may be admitted after the junior year), most are, or have earned the GED. Secondary preparation must include 4 years of English, 3 years each of math and foreign languages, and 2 years each of lab and social sciences. An interview is strongly recommended. AP credits are accepted. Important factors in the admissions decision are advanced placement or honors courses, recommendations by school officials, and extracurricular activities record. The B.A. requires 32 credits, 30 of which must be completed post-matriculation. Students must satisfy the breadth of study requirements (one course in each of five areas), complete a first-year Critical Inquiry seminar, take one P.E. course in the first year, demonstrate proficiency in 3 semesters of the same foreign language, and satisfy the requirements for a major (including a senior exercise). **Procedure:** Freshmen are admitted in the fall. Entrance exams should be taken before December of the senior year. There is a early decision plan. Early decision applications should be filed by November 1; regular applications, by January 1 for fall entry, along with a $70 fee. Notification of early decision is sent December 15; regular decision, April 1. 196 early decision candidates were accepted for the 2016-2017 class. 608 applicants were on the 2016 waiting list; 26 were admitted. Applications are accepted on-line. Application fees are waived if application is completed online. **Transfer Students:** 13 transfer students enrolled in 2015-2016. Applicants must have completed at least 1 year (24 semester hours) of college-level courses at the time of enrollment. 16 of 32 credits required for the bachelor's degree must be completed at Pomona. **International Students:** There are 180 international students enrolled. The school actively recruits these students. They must take the TOEFL with a minimum score of 600 on the paper-based TOEFL (PBT) or 100 on the Internet-based version (iBT). They must also take the SAT or ACT.

ADMISSIONS: 9% of the 2016-2017 applicants were accepted. The SAT scores for the 2016-2017 freshman class were: Critical Reading-- 6% between 500 and 599, 31% between 600 and 699, and 63% between 700 and 800. Math-- 6% between 500 and 599, 29% between 600 and 699, and 65% between 700 and 800. Writing-- 6% between 500 and 599, 28% between 600 and 699, and 67% between 700 and 800. The ACT scores were 1% between 18 and 23, 16% between 24 and 29, and 82% above 30. 97% of the current freshmen were in the top fifth of their class; 100% were in the top two fifths. **Admissions Contact:** Seth Allen, Vice President and Dean of Admissions. Email: *admissions@pomona.edu* Web: *www.pomona.edu*

FINANCIAL AID: In 2016-2017, 57% of all full-time freshmen and 56% of continuing full-time students received some form of financial aid. 57% of all full-time freshmen and 56% of continuing full-time students received need-based aid. The average freshman award was $47,430. Need-based scholarships or need-based grants averaged $45,689; and need-based self-help aid (loans and jobs) averaged $1,741. The average financial indebtedness of the 2016 graduate was $13,381. Pomona is a member of CSS. The CSS/Profile is required. The priority date for freshman financial aid applications for fall entry is February 1. The deadline for filing freshman financial aid applications for fall entry is June 1.

SAINT MARY'S COLLEGE OF CALIFORNIA B-3

www.stmarys-ca.edu

Moraga, CA 94575	**(925) 631-4224** **(800) 800-4SMC**
Fax: (925) 376-7193	**Email: smcadmit@stmarys-ca.edu**
Full-time: 1106 men, 1675 women	**Faculty:** 194; IIA, av$
Part-time: 101 men, 153 women	**Ph.D.s:** 95%
Graduate: 396 men, 797 women	**Student/Faculty:** 14 to 1
Year: 4-1-4, summer session	**Tuition:** $42,930
Room & Board: $14,490	**Freshman Class:** 5256 applied, 3448 accepted, 623 enrolled
SAT CR/M: 552/558 **ACT:** 24	**CEEB CODE:** 4675
Application Deadline: February 1	**COMPETITIVE**

Saint Mary's College of California, founded in 1863, is a private, independent, liberal arts college affiliated with the Roman Catholic Church. The school offers undergraduate and graduate programs in liberal arts, nursing, economics and business administration, education, and preprofessional studies. There are 4 undergraduate schools and 3 graduate schools. In addition to regional accreditation, SMC has baccalaureate program accreditation with NLN. The 420-acre campus is in a suburban area 20 miles east of San Francisco. Including any residence halls, there are 77 buildings.

STUDENT LIFE: 84% of undergraduates are from California. Others are from 40 states, 18 foreign countries, and Canada. 57% are from public schools. 5% are African American; 48% White; 24% Hispanic; 2% Foreign; 11% Asian American; 1% American Indian/Alaska Native. 43% are Catholic; 39% claim no religious affiliation; 13% Protestant. **Female To Male Ratio:** 1.6:1. The average age of freshmen is 19; all undergraduates, 21. 13% do not continue beyond their first year; 87% remain to graduate. **Housing:** 1557 students can be accommodated in college housing, which includes single-sex and coed dorms, on-campus apartments, and off-campus apartments. In addition, there are honors houses, special-interest houses, and Lasallian and Santiago living communities. On-campus housing is guaranteed for the freshman year only and is available on a lottery system for upperclassmen. 62% of students live on campus; of those, 50% remain on campus on weekends. All students may keep cars.

FACULTY/CLASSROOMS: 48% of faculty are male; 52% are female. All teach undergraduates, and do research. No introductory courses are taught by graduate students. The average class size in an introductory lecture is 25; in a laboratory is 16; and in a regular course is 20.

PROGRAMS OF STUDY: SMC confers B.A. and B.S. degrees. Master's and doctoral degrees are also awarded. Bachelor's degrees are awarded in AGRICULTURE (environmental studies), BIOLOGICAL SCIENCE (biology/biological science), BUSINESS (accounting and business administration and management), COMMUNICATIONS AND THE ARTS (art, classical languages, communications, English, French, performing arts, and Spanish), COMPUTER AND PHYSICAL SCIENCE (chemistry, computer science, mathematics, and physics), EDUCATION (health education, physical education, and recreation education), ENGINEERING AND ENVIRONMENTAL DESIGN (environmental science and preengineering), HEALTH PROFESSIONS (health science), SOCIAL SCIENCE (anthropology, economics, history, international studies, liberal arts/general studies, philosophy, political science/government, psychology, religion, and sociology). Business administration, communications, and psychology have the largest enrollments.

ACTIVITIES: There are no fraternities or sororities. There are 41 groups on campus, including art, cheerleading, choir, chorale, chorus, dance, debate, drama, environmental, ethnic, forensics, honors, international, jazz band, LGBT, literary magazine, musical theater, newspaper, pep band, political, professional, radio and TV, religious, social, social service, and student government. Popular campus events include Cultural Nights, and Coffee House events. **Sports:** There are 7 intercollegiate sports for men and 9 for women, and 7 intramural sports for men and 7 for women. Facilities include a gym, football, baseball, recreational fields, swimming pool, tennis courts, soccer field, rugby pitch, weight room, and workout facility. **Graduates:** From July 1, 2015 to June 30, 2016, 598 bachelor's degrees were awarded. The most popular majors were business administration (19%), communication (12%), and psychology (10%). 92 companies recruited on campus in 2015-2016. In an average class, 52% graduate in 4 years or less, 56% graduate in 5 years or less, and 57% graduate in 6 years or less. Of the 2015 graduating class, 14% were enrolled in graduate school within 6 months of graduation, and 64% were employed.

SERVICES: Counseling and information services are available, as is tutoring in most subjects. There is a reader service for the blind, and remedial writing. Tutoring is available for 1-on-1 sessions or group workshops. Readers, note takers, and other services are provided to learning or physically disabled students. **Library/Resources:** The library contains 412,735 volumes, 8,003 microform items, and 9,981 audio/video tapes/CDs/DVDs, and subscribes to 92,291 periodicals including electronic. Computerized library services include interlibrary loans, database searching, Internet access, and Wi-Fi capability. Special learning facilities include an art gallery, radio station, and an observatory. **Physically Challenged Students:** 90% of the campus is accessible. Facilities include wheelchair ramps, elevators, special parking, specially equipped restrooms, special class scheduling, lowered drinking fountains, lowered telephones, and special housing. **Special:** The college offers seminars in all fields, dual and student-designed majors, study abroad in 8 countries, a Washington semester, work-study, cross-registration with the Regional Association of East Bay Colleges and Universities, and B.A.-B.S. liberal arts degree. There are 3-2 engineering programs with Washington University, the University of Southern California, and Boston University. There are a freshman honors program and 2 departmental honors programs. **Visiting:** There are regularly scheduled orientations for prospective students, and tours. There are guides for informal visits, visitors may sit in on classes, and stay overnight. **Campus Safety and Security:** Measures include 24-hour foot and vehicle patrol, emergency notification system, and security escort services. There are emergency telephones, lighted pathways/sidewalks, controlled access to dorms/residences, and late night transport/escort service.

REQUIREMENTS: The SAT or ACT is required, with the SAT preferred. Candidates should be graduates of an accredited secondary school, with 16 academic units, including 4 units in English and 1 unit each in algebra, advanced algebra, geometry, and U.S. history. It is recommended that the remaining units be made up of foreign language, lab science, and additional academic electives in the student's areas of strength. The GED is accepted. An essay is required. A GPA of 2.0 is required. AP and CLEP credits are accepted. Important factors in the admissions decision are recommendations by school officials, advanced placement or honors courses, and parents or siblings attended your school. To graduate, students must complete 36 course credits, including 17 at the upper-division level, with a GPA of 2.0 overall and in the major. Specific requirements include a 4-course Great Books seminar and 2 courses each in religious studies, humanities, math/science, written English, and social sciences. All students must demonstrate proficiency in a second language. **Procedure:** Freshmen are admitted to all sessions. Entrance exams should be taken by December of the senior year. There are early admissions and deferred admissions plans. Early decision applications should be filed by November 15; regular applications, by February 1 for fall entry; and January 1 for spring entry, along with a $55 fee. Notification of early decision is sent December 15; regular decision, March 15. 894 applicants were on the 2016 waiting list; 167 were admitted. Applications are accepted on-line. **Transfer Students:** 199 transfer students enrolled in 2015-2016. Applicants must have a GPA of 2.3 and a minimum of 23 transferable academic semester units. 9 of 36 credits required for the bachelor's degree must be completed at SMC. **International Students:** There are 70 international students enrolled. The school actively recruits these students. They must take the TOEFL with a minimum score of 550 on the paper-based TOEFL (PBT) or 79 on the Internet-based version (iBT) and the Comprehensive English Language Test, Nonactive English speakers who submit a minimum score or higher on the TOEFL may be admitted as full-time undergraduates.

ADMISSIONS: 66% of the 2016-2017 applicants were accepted. The SAT scores for the 2016-2017 freshman class were: Critical Reading-- 23% below 500, 49% between 500 and 599, 23% between 600 and 699, and 5% between 700 and 800. Math-- 23% below 500, 46% between 500 and 599, 29% between 600 and 699, and 4% between 700 and 800. The ACT scores were 13% below 12, 33% between 12 and 17, 27% between 18 and 23, 14% between 24 and 29, and 11% above 30. 51% of the current freshmen were in the top fifth of their class; 79% were in the top two fifths. 6 freshmen graduated first in their class. **Admissions Contact:** Michael McKeon, Asst. Vice Provost & Dean of Admissions. Email: *smcadmit@stmarys-ca.edu* Web: *www.stmarys-ca.edu*

FINANCIAL AID: In 2016-2017, 94% of all full-time freshmen and 96% of continuing full-time students received some form of financial aid. 89% of all full-time freshmen and 76% of continuing full-time students received need-based aid. The average freshman award was $31,979. Need-based scholarships or need-based grants averaged $24,082 ($31,200 maximum); need-based self-help aid (loans and jobs) averaged $6,640 ($7,500 maximum); non-need-based athletic scholarships averaged $36,486 ($59,470 maximum); and other non-need-based awards and non-need-based scholarships averaged $14,946 ($39,740 maximum). 60% of undergraduate students work part-time. Average annual earnings from campus work are $2007. The average financial indebtedness of the 2016 graduate was $33,000. SMC is a member of CSS. The priority date for freshman financial aid applications for fall entry is February 15.

SAN DIEGO CHRISTIAN COLLEGE D-5
www.sdcc.edu

Santee, CA 92071	**(619) 588-8700** **(800) 676-2242**
Fax: (619) 590-1739	**Email: admissions@sdcc.com**
Full-time: 330 men, 335 women	**Faculty:** n/av
Part-time: 40 men, 47 women	**Ph.D.s:** n/av
Graduate: n/av	**Student/Faculty:** n/av
Year: semesters, summer session	**Tuition:** $28,100
Room & Board: $10,968	**Freshman Class:** n/av
SAT or ACT: required	**CEEB CODE:** 4150
Application Deadline: open	**COMPETITIVE**

San Diego Christian College is a small, private institution founded in 1970 by the Scott Memorial Baptist Church of San Diego, with which it is still affiliated. It offers programs in the liberal arts, business, and education. The figures given in the above capsule and in this profile are approximate. There is 1 undergraduate school. In addition to regional accreditation, SDCC has baccalaureate program accreditation with WASC and ACSI. The 32-acre campus is in a suburban area 15 miles east of San Diego. Including any residence halls, there are 14 buildings.

STUDENT LIFE: 80% of undergraduates are from California. Others are from states. 75% are from public schools. 70% are White; 4% Asian American; 2% Foreign; 10% African American; 10% Hispanic; 1% American Indian/Alaska Native. 100% are Protestant. **Female To Male Ratio:** 1.0:1. The average age of freshmen is 18; all undergraduates, 21. 40% do not continue beyond their first year; 30% remain to graduate. **Housing:** 200 students can be accommodated in college housing, which includes single-sex dorms and off-campus apartments. In addition, there are language houses. On-campus housing is guaranteed for all 4 years, and is available on a first-come, and first-served basis. 50% of students commute. Alcohol is not permitted. All students may keep cars.

FACULTY/CLASSROOMS: 60% of faculty are male; 40% are female. All teach undergraduates. No introductory courses are taught by graduate students. The average class size in an introductory lecture is 40; in a laboratory is 15; and in a regular course is 16.

PROGRAMS OF STUDY: SDCC confers B.A., and B.S. degrees. Associate degrees are also awarded. Bachelor's degrees are awarded in BIOLOGICAL SCIENCE (biology/biological science), BUSINESS (business administration and management), COMMUNICATIONS AND THE ARTS (communications, English, and music), COMPUTER AND PHYSICAL SCIENCE (mathematics), EDUCATION (education), ENGINEERING AND ENVIRONMENTAL DESIGN (aviation administration/management), SOCIAL SCIENCE (biblical studies, history, human development, interdisciplinary studies, liberal arts/general studies, physical fitness/movement, and psychology). Counseling psychology, education, and business are the strongest academically. Business, education, and human development have the largest enrollments.

ACTIVITIES: There are no fraternities or sororities. There are 16 groups on campus, including art, cheerleading, choir, chorale, chorus, computers, drama, honors, international, musical theater, newspaper, pep band, political, religious, social, student government, and yearbook. Popular campus events include Spring, Winter, and Valentine's Day Banquets and the Missions Conference. **Sports:** There are 3 intercollegiate sports for men and 4 for women, and 5 intramural sports for men and 4 for women. Facilities include a swimming pool, gym, outdoor courts for tennis, volleyball, and basketball, soccer and softball fields.

SERVICES: Counseling and information services are available, as is tutoring in some subjects, such as tutors recruited as needed for most general education courses. There is remedial math, reading, and writing. **Library/Resources:** The library contains 69,435 volumes, 80 microform items, and 61,522 audio/video tapes/CDs/DVDs, and subscribes to 30,475 periodicals including electronic. Computerized library services include interlibrary loans, database searching, and Internet access. **Physically Challenged Students:** 90% of the campus is accessible. Facilities include wheelchair ramps, elevators, special parking, and special class scheduling. **Special:** Students attend chapel 3 times each week, participate in an annual Bible conference, and complete a student ministry assignment each semester. Independent study for 1 to 3 credits can be arranged. There are internships in psychology, pastoral studies, and education. **Visiting:** There are regularly scheduled orientations for prospective students, including a campus tour, cafeteria meal, and class and chapel attendance. There are guides for informal visits, visitors may sit in on classes, and stay overnight. To schedule a visit, contact the Admissions Office. **Campus Safety and Security:** Measures include 24-hour foot and vehicle patrol and emergency notification system. There are lighted pathways/sidewalks, and a fenced campus.

REQUIREMENTS: The SAT or ACT is required, with the ACT preferred. Applicants must have a high school diploma or the GED, or have successfully completed the California State High School Proficiency Exam. Secondary preparation should include 4 units of English, 3 each of math, natural science, and social studies, and 2 of a single foreign language. A personal essay is also required. In addition, applicants must meet certain spiritual requirements. AP and CLEP credits are accepted. Important factors in the admissions decision are recommendations by school officials, leadership record, and extracurricular activities record. The required credits for graduation vary by degree program and major. All students must take 46 to 52 credits in sciences and math, social science, and humanities, 20 credits in personal Christian development and biblical studies, and the balance in major field requirements and electives. A 2.0 GPA is required for graduation. **Procedure:** Freshmen are admitted fall and spring. Entrance exams should be taken during the junior year. There is a rolling admissions plan. Application deadlines are open. The fall 2016 application fee was $25. Notification is sent on a rolling basis. **Transfer Students:** 30 of 124 credits required for the bachelor's degree must be completed at SDCC. **International Students:** The school actively recruits these students. They must take the TOEFL and the college's own test. They must also take the SAT or ACT, scoring 900.

Admissions Contact: Christine Roberts, Director of Admissions. Email: *admissions@sdcc.com* Web: *www.sdcc.edu*

FINANCIAL AID: SDCC is a member of CSS. The college's own financial statement is required. The FAFSA code is 012031. Check with the school for current application deadlines.

SAN DIEGO STATE UNIVERSITY D-5
www.sdsu.edu

San Diego, CA 92182	**(619) 594-6336** **(855) 594-3983**
	Email: admissions@sdsu.edu
Full-time: 12,180 men, 14,608 women	**Faculty:** IIA, +$
	Ph.D.s: 89%
Part-time: 1469 men, 1596 women	**Student/Faculty:** n/av
Graduate: 1897 men, 2938 women	**Tuition:** $7084 ($11,160)
Year: semesters, summer session	**Freshman Class:** 60691 applied, 20943 accepted, 5077 enrolled
Room & Board: $14,812	
SAT CR/M: 548/566 **ACT:** 25	**CEEB CODE:** 4682
Application Deadline: November 30	**COMPETITIVE+**

San Diego State University, founded in 1897, is a public research university that is part of the California State University system. There are 8 undergraduate schools. In addition to regional accreditation, SDSU has baccalaureate program accreditation with AACSB, ABET, ACEJMC, CSWE, NASAD, NRPA, ACS, APA, ACGME, ACME, CAATE, CAHME, CORE, NCRE, CAA, CTC, WAGS, CIDA, CGS, CEPH, NASP, NAEYC, CCNE, NASPAA, NAST, BRN, ACEND, COAMFTE, and NCATE. The 283-acre campus is in an urban area 8 miles east of downtown San Diego. Including any residence halls, there are 108 buildings.

STUDENT LIFE: 91% of undergraduates are from California. Others are from 49 states, 115 foreign countries, and Canada. 92% are from public schools. 7% are Foreign; 7% two or more races; 4% African American; 4% race unknown; 33% White; 31% Hispanic; 14% Asian American. **Female To Male Ratio:** 1.2:1. The average age of freshmen is 19; all undergraduates, 22. 10% do not continue beyond their first year. **Housing:** 4803 students can be accommodated in college housing, which includes coed dorms and on-campus apartments. In addition, there are honors houses, language houses, special-interest houses, gender neutral housing, international housing, a living/learning center, Aztec engineering residence, substance-free and quiet-study housing, and apartments for single students. On-campus housing is available on a first-come and first-served basis. 85% of students commute. All students may keep cars.

FACULTY/CLASSROOMS: 50% of faculty are male; 50% are female. No introductory courses are taught by graduate students. The average class size in an introductory lecture is 76; in a laboratory is 18; and in a regular course is 54.

PROGRAMS OF STUDY: SDSU confers B.A., B.F.A., B.S., and B.M.

degrees. Master's and doctoral degrees are also awarded. Bachelor's degrees are awarded in AGRICULTURE (environmental studies), BIOLOGICAL SCIENCE (biology/biological science, ecology, microbiology, nutrition, and zoology), BUSINESS (accounting, business administration and management, finance, financial services, hospitality management services, human resources/organizational mgmt, international business management, international security/conflict resolution mgmt, management & strategic leadership, marketing/retailing/merchandising, real estate, and production and operations management), COMMUNICATIONS AND THE ARTS (advertising, art history, art, classics, communications, comparative literature, dance, English, English Writing, French, German, graphic design, Japanese, journalism, linguistics, media management, multimedia, music, music performance, public relations, radio/tv, recreation administration, Russian, Spanish, communication arts - speech, studio art, and theatre arts), COMPUTER AND PHYSICAL SCIENCE (applied mathematics, astronomy, chemical physics, chemistry, computer science, geology, information sciences and systems, mathematics, physical sciences, physics, and statistics), EDUCATION (athletic training and music education), ENGINEERING AND ENVIRONMENTAL DESIGN (aerospace engineering, civil engineering, computer engineering, construction engineering, electrical/electronics engineering, engineering, environmental engineering, environmental science, interior design, and mechanical engineering), HEALTH PROFESSIONS (communicative disorders, exercise science, health communication, health science, kinesiology, nursing, and speech pathology/audiology), SOCIAL SCIENCE (African American studies, American Indian studies, anthropology, Asian/Oriental studies, child psychology/development, criminal justice, economics, European studies, gender studies, geography, gerontology, history, humanities, interdisciplinary studies, international studies, Latin American studies, liberal arts/general studies, Mexican-American/Chicano studies, modern jewish studies, philosophy, political science/government, psychology, public administration, religious studies, Russian and Slavic studies, social science, social work, sociology, urban studies, and women's studies). Psychology, physical education/kinesiology, and biology have the largest enrollments.

ACTIVITIES: 8% of men belong to 22 national fraternities; 9% of women belong to 22 national sororities. There are 231 groups on campus, including art, band, cheerleading, choir, chorale, chorus, dance, debate, drama, drill team, environmental, ethnic, film, honors, international, jazz band, LGBT, literary magazine, marching band, musical theater, newspaper, opera, orchestra, pep band, political, professional, radio and TV, religious, social, social service, student government, and symphony. Popular campus events include Student Involvement Expo, Welcome Week, Aztec Nights, Midnight Breakfast Finals Week, and Explore SDSU. **Sports:** There are 6 intercollegiate sports for men and 13 for women, and 8 intramural sports for men and 8 for women. Facilities include a gym, basketball, racquetball, tennis, volleyball courts, swimming pool/aquaplex, track, soccer, softball, baseball, football fields, aquatic center, weight room, bowling, gymnastic equipment, cardio room, and a climbing wall. **Graduates:** From July 1, 2015 to June 30, 2016, 6840 bachelor's degrees were awarded. The most popular majors were psychology (8%), criminal justice administration (5%), and management (5%). 834 companies recruited on campus in 2015-2016. In an average class, 34% graduate in 4 years or less, 65% graduate in 5 years or less, and 74% graduate in 6 years or less.

SERVICES: Counseling and information services are available, as is tutoring in most subjects. There is a reader service for the blind. **Library/Resources:** Computerized library services include interlibrary loans, database searching, Internet access, and Wi-Fi capability. Special learning facilities include an art gallery, planetarium, radio station, TV station, performing arts theatres, recital halls, seismology and weather stations. **Physically Challenged Students:** 99% of the campus is accessible. Facilities include wheelchair ramps, elevators, special parking, specially equipped restrooms, special class scheduling, lowered drinking fountains, lowered telephones, and special housing. **Special:** SDSU has opportunities for cross-registration, distance learning, double major, English as a second language (ESL), exchange student program (domestic), external degree program, honors program, independent study, internships, liberal arts/career combination, student-designed major, study abroad, and teacher certification program. There are 27 national honor societies, Phi Beta Kappa, and a freshman honors program. **Visiting:** There are regularly scheduled orientations for prospective students, including tours that can be scheduled with SDSU ambassadors. **Campus Safety and Security:** Measures include 24-hour foot and vehicle patrol, emergency notification system, self-defense education, and security escort services. There are shuttle buses, emergency telephones, lighted pathways/sidewalks, and controlled access to dorms/residences.

REQUIREMENTS: The SAT or ACT is required. Applicants must have a qualifying CSU eligibility index, based on a combination of GPA and standardized test scores. Candidates for admission should have completed 4 years of English, 3 years of math (4 recommended), 2 years each of science and foreign language, and 1 year each of social studies, U.S. history, visual/performing arts, and academic elective. AP and CLEP credits are accepted. To graduate, students must complete a minimum of 120 units, including 49 general education units. The number of units in the major varies by program. A 2.0 or higher GPA must be maintained, depending on the major. Students must demonstrate math and writing competency and fulfill requirements in upper-division writing and in American Institutions. Certain majors require a senior thesis. **Procedure:** Freshmen are admitted fall. Entrance exams should be taken by October of the senior year. Applications should be filed by November 30 for fall entry, along with a $55 fee. Notifications are sent in March. 1170 applicants were on the 2016 waiting list; 565 were admitted. Application fees are waived if application is completed online. **Transfer Students:** 3673 transfer students enrolled in 2015-2016. Transfer applicants are required to declare a major and have completed all preparation for the major courses and pre-major requirements if applicable. In addition, all lower division general education (GE) courses must be completed. Must have "C-" grades in four required classes: GE oral communication, GE written communication, GE critical thinking, and GE mathematics (above the level of intermediate algebra). Different application policies apply for applicants in and out of SDSU service area and for applicants in impacted majors. Refer to the Office of Admission website for more information. 30 of 120 credits required for the bachelor's degree must be completed at SDSU. **International Students:** There are 2761 international students enrolled. The school actively recruits these students. They must take the TOEFL with a minimum score of 550 on the paper-based TOEFL (PBT) or 80 on the Internet-based version (iBT) and the college's own test, take the IELTS, scoring 6.5 or higher. They must also take the SAT or ACT.

ADMISSIONS: 35% of the 2016-2017 applicants were accepted. The SAT scores for the 2016-2017 freshman class were: Critical Reading-- 25% below 500, 46% between 500 and 599, 25% between 600 and 699, and 3% between 700 and 800. Math-- 19% below 500, 44% between 500 and 599, 33% between 600 and 699, and 4% between 700 and 800. Writing-- 30% below 500, 46% between 500 and 599, 22% between 600 and 699, and 2% between 700 and 800. The ACT scores were 3% between 12 and 17, 28% between 18 and 23, 56% between 24 and 29, and 13% above 30. 62% of the current freshmen were in the top fifth of their class; 90% were in the top two fifths. **Admissions Contact:** Sabrina Cortell, Director of Admissions. Email: *admissions@sdsu.edu* Web: *www.sdsu.edu/apply*

FINANCIAL AID: In 2016-2017, 61% of all full-time freshmen and 63% of continuing full-time students received some form of financial aid. 52% of all full-time freshmen and 42% of continuing full-time students received need-based aid. The average freshman award was $8,000. Need-based scholarships or need-based grants averaged $9,600; need-based self-help aid (loans and jobs) averaged $3,400; non-need-based athletic scholarships averaged $20,500; and other non-need-based awards and non-need-based scholarships averaged $3,800. The average financial indebtedness of the 2016 graduate was $18,000. SDSU is a member of CSS. The state aid form is required. The FAFSA code is 001151. The priority date for freshman financial aid applications for fall entry is April 1. The deadline for filing freshman financial aid applications for fall entry is March 2.

SAN FRANCISCO ART INSTITUTE *(The complete profile is made available exclusively on our website, www.barronspac.com)*

SAN FRANCISCO CONSERVATORY OF MUSIC *(The complete profile is made available exclusively on our website, www.barronspac.com)*

SAN FRANCISCO STATE UNIVERSITY *(The complete profile is made available exclusively on our website, www.barronspac.com)*

SAN JOSE STATE UNIVERSITY B-3

www.sjsu.edu

San Jose, CA 95192 **(408) 283-7500**

Email: admissions@sjsu.edu

Full-time: 11,322 men, 10,291 women	**Faculty:** IIA, +$
	Ph.D.s: n/av
Part-time: 2537 men, 2282 women	**Student/Faculty:** 26 to 1
Graduate: 2436 men, 2836 women	**Tuition:** $7323 ($16,251)
Year: semesters, summer session	**Freshman Class:** 31555 applied, 16862 accepted, 3208 enrolled
Room & Board: $14,217	
SAT CR/M/W: 502/522/497 **ACT:** 23	**CEEB CODE:** 4687
Application Deadline: November 30	**COMPETITIVE**

San Jose State University, founded in 1857 and part of the California State University system, is a public institution offering undergraduate and graduate programs in applied arts and science, social science, and social work to a primarily commuter student body. The figures in the above capsule and in this profile are approximate. There are 8 undergraduate schools and 8 graduate schools. In addition to regional accreditation, SJSU has baccalaureate program accreditation with AACSB, ABET, ADA, APTA, CSWE, NASAD, NASM, NCATE, NRPA, and TEAC. The 154-acre campus is in an urban area in the center of the city of San Jose, CA. Including any residence halls, there are 64 buildings.

STUDENT LIFE: 96% of undergraduates are from California. Others are from states, 125 foreign countries, and Canada. 93% are from public schools. 9% are race unknown; 32% Asian American; 3% African American; 24% Hispanic; 19% White; 12% Foreign. **Male To Female Ratio:** 1.1:1. The average age of freshmen is 19; all undergraduates, 23. 86% do not continue beyond their first year; 56% remain to graduate. **Housing:** 4000 students can be accommodated in college housing, which includes coed dorms and on-campus apartments. In addition, there are special-interest houses, fraternity houses, and sorority houses. On-campus housing is available on a first-come and first-served basis. Alcohol is not permitted. All students may keep cars.

FACULTY/CLASSROOMS: 49% of faculty are male; 51% are female. No introductory courses are taught by graduate students.

PROGRAMS OF STUDY: SJSU confers B.A., B.S., B.F.A. and B.Mus. degrees. Master's and doctoral degrees are also awarded. Bachelor's degrees are awarded in AGRICULTURE (environmental studies), BIOLOGICAL SCIENCE (biochemistry, biology/biological science, botany, forensic science, marine science, microbiology, nutritional sciences, and zoology), BUSINESS (accounting, banking and finance, business administration and management, international business management, and marketing/retailing/merchandising), COMMUNICATIONS AND THE ARTS (advertising, art history, broadcasting, Chinese, communication studies, dance, design, dramatic arts, English, film arts, fine arts, French, German, Japanese, jazz, journalism, literature, music, public relations, Spanish, and speech/debate/rhetoric), COMPUTER AND PHYSICAL SCIENCE (applied mathematics, chemistry, computer science, geology, mathematics, natural sciences, physics, software engineering, and statistics), EDUCATION (early childhood education, education administration, education of the deaf and hearing impaired, music education, recreation education, and teaching English as a second/foreign language (TESOL/TEFOL)), ENGINEERING AND ENVIRONMENTAL DESIGN (aeronautical engineering, biomedical engineering, chemical engineering, civil engineering, computer engineering, electrical/electronics engineering, engineering, industrial engineering, interior design, materials engineering, mechanical engineering, and urban planning technology), HEALTH PROFESSIONS (health science, nursing, occupational therapy, public health, and speech pathology/audiology), SOCIAL SCIENCE (anthropology, criminal justice, economics, food science, geography, history, Mexican-American/Chicano studies, philosophy, political science/government, psychology, religion, religious studies, social science, social work, and sociology). Accounting is the strongest academically. Psychology, accounting, and electrical engineering have the largest enrollments.

ACTIVITIES: There are 394 groups on campus, including art, cheerleading, choir, chorale, communications, dance, debate, drama, ethnic, film, forensics, international, LGBT, literary magazine, marching band, newspaper, opera, orchestra, pep band, radio and TV, social, student government, and symphony. Popular campus events include International Food Bazaar, Fall Welcome Day, and National Collegiate Alcohol Awareness Week. **Sports:** There are 7 intercollegiate sports for men and 12 for women, and 13 intramural sports for men and 13 for women. Facilities include a gym, pool, track, football field, baseball field, recreation center with racquetball courts and a bowling alley. **Graduates:** From July 1, 2015 to June 30, 2016, 6011 bachelor's degrees were awarded. The most popular majors were psychology (5%), accounting (5%), and communication studies (4%).

SERVICES: Counseling and information services are available, as is tutoring in most subjects. There is a reader service for the blind, and remedial math and writing. There are also test accommodations, sign-language interpreters, liaisons to faculty, and note takers. **Library/Resources:** The library contains 920,971 volumes, and 24,527 audio/video tapes/CDs/DVDs, and subscribes to 375,676 periodicals including electronic. Computerized library services include interlibrary loans, database searching, Internet access, and Wi-Fi capability. Special learning facilities include an art gallery and radio station. **Physically Challenged Students:** Facilities include wheelchair ramps, elevators, special parking, specially equipped restrooms, special class scheduling, lowered drinking fountains, lowered telephones. preadmission assistance. **Special:** SJSU has opportunities for cooperative programs in business, science, engineering, arts, and the humanities, work-study with many employers, internships (some required, some optional), study abroad in 16 countries, field experiences, and student teaching. An accelerated program is offered in nursing, and the B.A.-B.S. degree and dual majors are available in various areas of study. A general studies degree, student-designed majors, nondegree study, and credit/no-credit options are possible. There is a freshman honors program. **Visiting:** There are regularly scheduled orientations for prospective students. There are guides for informal visits and visitors may sit in on classes. To schedule a visit, contact the Office of Relations at (408) 924-2564. **Campus Safety and Security:** Measures include 24-hour foot and vehicle patrol, emergency notification system, self-defense education, and security escort services. There are shuttle buses, emergency telephones, lighted pathways/sidewalks, controlled access to dorms/residences, and canine patrol.

REQUIREMENTS: The SAT or ACT is required. Scores are used to calculate an eligibility index rating, which determines qualification for admission. Graduation from an accredited secondary school is required; the GED is accepted. Applicants must have completed 4 years of English, 3 each of math and electives, 2 of a foreign language, and 1 each of history, science, and art. A GPA of 2.0 is required. AP and CLEP credits are accepted. Students must complete 39 units of core general education, including 12 units of upper-division courses in residence and 6 units of history and institutions. A minimum of 124 credits, with at least 24 in the major, a minimum GPA of 2.0, and the successful completion of writing, English, and entry-level math tests are required to graduate. **Procedure:** Freshmen are admitted fall and spring. Entrance exams should be taken prior to the fall semester. There are deferred admissions and rolling admissions plans. Applications should be filed by November 30 for fall entry. The fall 2016 application fee was $55. Applications are accepted on-line. **Transfer Students:** Applicants must have a minimum GPA of 2.0. The student's rating in the eligibility index is also considered in determining qualification for transfer. 30 of 120 credits required for the bachelor's degree must be completed at SJSU. **International Students:** The school actively recruits these students. They must take the TOEFL. They must also take the SAT or ACT.

ADMISSIONS: 53% of the 2016-2017 applicants were accepted. The SAT scores for the 2016-2017 freshman class were: Critical Reading-- 46% below 500, 40% between 500 and 599, 13% between 600 and 699, and 2% between 700 and 800. Math-- 52% below 500, 34% between 500 and 599, 12% between 600 and 699, and 2% between 700 and 800. Writing-- 37% below 500, 38% between 500 and 599, 20% between 600 and 699, and 4% between 700 and 800. The ACT scores were 12% between 12 and 17, 48% between 18 and 23, 34% between 24 and 29, and 5% above 30. **Admissions Contact:** Deanna Gonzales, Director of Undergraduate Admission. Email: *admissions@sjsu.edu* Web: *www.sjsu.edu*

FINANCIAL AID: In 2016-2017, 62% of all full-time freshmen received some form of financial aid. The average freshman award was $18,045. The average financial indebtedness of the 2016 graduate was $18,513. SJSU is a member of CSS. The FAFSA code is 001155. Check with the school for current application deadlines.

SCRIPPS COLLEGE D-5
www.scrippscollege.edu

Claremont, CA 91711 (909) 621-8578
(800) 770-1333
Fax: (909) 607-7508 Email: admission@scrippscollege.edu

Full-time: 1026 women	**Faculty:** IIB, ++$
Part-time: 4 women	**Ph.D.s:** n/av
Graduate: n/av	**Student/Faculty:** 10 to 1
Year: semesters	**Tuition:** $50,982
Room & Board: $15,682	**Freshman Class:** 3032 applied, 903 accepted, 270 enrolled
SAT CR/M/W: 700/665/700 **ACT:** 30	**CEEB CODE:** 4693
Application Deadline: January 1	**MOST COMPETITIVE**

Scripps College, founded in 1926, is a private liberal arts institution for women. A member of the Claremont Colleges, Scripps emphasizes a challenging core curriculum based on interdisciplinary humanistic studies. There are 5 undergraduate schools. In addition to regional accreditation, Scripps has baccalaureate program accreditation with WASC. The 33-acre campus is in a suburban area 35 miles east of Los Angeles. Including any residence halls, there are 28 buildings.

STUDENT LIFE: 6% are two or more races; 6% race unknown; 52% White; 5% Foreign; 4% African American; 15% Asian American; 11% Hispanic. The student base is all female. **Housing:** 947 students can be accommodated in college housing, which includes coed dorms, on-campus apartments, and off-campus apartments. foreign language corridors, and living-learning communities. On-campus housing is guaranteed for all 4 years. All students may keep cars.

FACULTY/CLASSROOMS: All teach undergraduates and do research. No introductory courses are taught by graduate students.

PROGRAMS OF STUDY: Scripps confers B.A. and B.S. degrees. Bachelor's degrees are awarded in AGRICULTURE (environmental studies), BIOLOGICAL SCIENCE (biology/biological science, molecular biology, and neurosciences), COMMUNICATIONS AND THE ARTS (art history and appreciation, Chinese, classical languages, communications, dance, dramatic arts, English, Germanic languages and literature, Italian, Japanese, languages, music, Russian, Spanish, and studio art), COMPUTER AND PHYSICAL SCIENCE (chemistry, computer science, geology, mathematics, physics, science and management, and science technology), ENGINEERING AND ENVIRONMENTAL DESIGN (environmental science and preengineering), SOCIAL SCIENCE (African American studies, American studies, anthropology, Asian/American studies, Asian/Oriental studies, classical/ancient civilization, economics, European studies, French studies, German area studies, Hispanic American studies, history, humanities, Italian studies, Judaic studies, Latin American studies, law, Mexican-American/Chicano studies, philosophy, political science/government, prelaw, psychology, religion, sociology, and women's studies). Psychology, media studies, and economics have the largest enrollments.

ACTIVITIES: There are no fraternities or sororities. There are 200 groups on campus, including art, choir, chorale, chorus, computers, dance, debate, drama, environmental, ethnic, film, honors, international, LGBT, literary magazine, musical theater, newspaper, orchestra, photography, political, professional, religious, social, social service, student government, symphony, and yearbook. Popular campus events include Spring Fling Carnival, Levitt on the Lawn, Weekly Tea, Scripps Outdoor Adventure Program. **Sports:** There are 11 intercollegiate sports for women, and 6 intramural sports. Facilities include an aerobics studio, cardio machine room, weight room, swimming pool and soccer/lacrosse fields, tennis courts, climbing wall, outdoor track, and fields for baseball and softball. **Graduates:** From July 1, 2015 to June 30, 2016, 205 bachelor's degrees were awarded. 300 companies recruited on campus in 2015-2016. In an average class, 80% graduate in 4 years or less, 84% graduate in 5 years or less, and 84% graduate in 6 years or less.

SERVICES: Counseling and information services are available, as is tutoring in every subject. There is a reader service for the blind. **Library/Resources:** The library contains 1.4 million volumes, and 93,616 audio/video tapes/CDs/DVDs. Computerized library services include interlibrary loans, database searching, Internet access, and Wi-Fi capability. Special learning facilities include an art gallery, humanities museum and biological field station. **Physically Challenged Students:** Facilities include wheelchair ramps, elevators, special parking, specially equipped restrooms, special class scheduling, lowered drinking fountains, and special housing. **Special:** Students may cross-register with any of the other Claremont Colleges. Scripps also offers study abroad in 36 countries, a Washington semester, and student-designed, dual, and interdisciplinary majors, including organizational studies and science, technology, and society. Many courses are offered as seminars. There are 4-1 accelerated degree programs in the arts and business administration. A 3-2 engineering program (B.A.-B.S.) is offered with Harvey Mudd College. There are 7 national honor societies and a chapter of Phi Beta Kappa. **Visiting:** There are guides for informal visits, visitors may sit in on classes, and stay overnight. To schedule a visit, contact the Admission Office. **Campus Safety and Security:** Measures include 24-hour foot and vehicle patrol, emergency notification system, self-defense education, and security escort services. There are emergency telephones, lighted pathways/sidewalks, and controlled access to dorms/residences.

REQUIREMENTS: The SAT or ACT is required. Applicants must have completed 4 units each of high school English and math, 3 each of lab science and social studies, and either 3 of a single foreign language or 2 each of 2 languages. SAT Subject Tests and an interview are recommended. An essay and a graded writing assignment from the junior or senior year are required. AP and CLEP credits are accepted. Students must complete a total of 32 courses, or 128 units, with at least a C average. Requirements include a 3-semester humanities core, a first-year writing/critical thinking course, and 1 course each in fine arts, letters, natural science, social science, gender and women's studies, and race and ethnic studies. A senior thesis or project is also required. **Procedure:** Freshmen are admitted fall and spring. Entrance exams should be taken by December of the senior year. There are early decision, early admissions, and deferred admissions plans. Early decision applications should be filed by November 15; regular applications, by January 1 for fall entry; and November 1 for spring entry, along with a $60 fee. Notification of early decision is sent December 15; regular decision, April 1. 119 early decision candidates were accepted for the 2016-2017 class. 290 applicants were on the 2016 waiting list; 33 were admitted. Application fees are waived if application is completed on-line. **Transfer Students:** 1 transfer students enrolled in 2015-2016. A cumulative college GPA of 3.0 is recommended 16 credits required for the bachelor's degree must be completed at Scripps. **International Students:** There are 50 international students enrolled. The school actively recruits these students. They must take the TOEFL with a minimum score of 600 on the paper-based TOEFL (PBT) or 100 on the Internet-based version (iBT). They must also take the SAT or ACT.

ADMISSIONS: 30% of the 2016-2017 applicants were accepted. The SAT scores for the 2016-2017 freshman class were: Critical Reading-- 4% between 500 and 599, 42% between 600 and 699, and 55% between 700 and 800. Math-- 12% between 500 and 599, 58% between 600 and 699, and 29% between 700 and 800. Writing-- 4% between 500 and 599, 43% between 600 and 699, and 53% between 700 and 800. The ACT scores were 2% between 18 and 23, 35% between 24 and 29, and 63% above 30. **Admissions Contact:** Victoria Romero, VP for Enrollment. Email: *admission@scrippscollege.edu* Web: *www.scrippscollege.edu*

FINANCIAL AID: Scripps is a member of CSS. The CSS/Profile and the state aid form are required. The FAFSA code is 001174. The deadline for filing freshman financial aid applications for fall entry is February 1.

SIMPSON UNIVERSITY B-2
www.simpsonu.edu

Redding, CA 96003 (530) 224-5600
(888) 9-SIMPSON
Fax: (530) 226-4861 Email: admissions@simpsonu.edu

Full-time: 322 men, 665 women	**Faculty:** 43
Part-time: 12 men, 20 women	**Ph.D.s:** 56%
Graduate: 102 men, 176 women	**Student/Faculty:** 15 to 1
Year: semesters, summer session	**Tuition:** $25,950
Room & Board: $7750	**Freshman Class:** 533 applied, 317 accepted, 158 enrolled
SAT CR/M/W: 500/500/490 **ACT:** 21	**CEEB CODE:** 4698
Application Deadline: open	**COMPETITIVE**

Simpson University, founded in 1921, is a Christian university offering undergraduate, graduate, and teaching credential programs. The university is an official institution of the Christian and Missionary Alliance, and the student population represents more than 25 evangelical denominations. The figures in the above capsule and in this profile are approximate. There is 1 undergraduate school and 3 graduate schools. In addition to regional accreditation, Simpson has baccalaureate program accreditation with WASC. The 92-acre campus is in a suburban area in the northeast city limits of Redding. Including any residence halls, there are 17 buildings.

STUDENT LIFE: 87% of undergraduates are from California. Others are from 27 states, and 7 foreign countries. 59% are from public schools. 9% are Hispanic; 7% Asian American; 60% White; 4% African American; 2% American Indian/Alaska Native; 1% Foreign. 99% are Protestant. **Female To Male Ratio:** 2.0:1. The average age of freshmen is 18; all undergraduates, 25. 35% do not continue beyond their first year; 45% remain to graduate. **Housing:** 590 students can be accommodated in college housing, which includes single-sex dorms, off-campus apartments, and married student housing. In addition, there are special-interest houses, including Gatehouse- Missionary Kid housing. On-campus housing is guaranteed for all 4 years. 55% of students commute. Alcohol is not permitted. All students may keep cars.

FACULTY/CLASSROOMS: 52% of faculty are male; 48% are female. 65% teach undergraduates. No introductory courses are taught by graduate students. The average class size in an introductory lecture is 42; in a laboratory is 11; and in a regular course is 11.

PROGRAMS OF STUDY: Simpson confers B.A. and B.S. degrees. Associate and master's degrees are also awarded. Bachelor's degrees are awarded in BIOLOGICAL SCIENCE (biology/biological science), BUSINESS (accounting, business administration and management, human resources, organizational leadership and management, and recreation and leisure services), COMMUNICATIONS AND THE ARTS (communications, English, and music), COMPUTER AND PHYSICAL SCIENCE (mathematics), EDUCATION (elementary education, English education, mathematics education, music education, secondary education, and social science education), HEALTH PROFESSIONS (health care administration and nursing), SOCIAL SCIENCE (biblical studies, crosscultural studies, history, liberal arts/general studies, ministries, missions, pastoral studies, psychology, religion, religious education, social science, and youth ministry). Biology, nursing, and music are the strongest academically. Psychology, business administration, and liberal studies have the largest enrollments.

ACTIVITIES: There are no fraternities or sororities. There are 20 groups on campus, including commuter students association, psychology, band, choir, chorale, computers, drama, ethnic, film, golf, international, jazz band, newspaper, orchestra, photography, professional, religious, social, social service, student government, symphony, and yearbook. Popular campus events include Spring Banquet, Missions Emphasis Week and Airband. **Sports:** There are 5 intercollegiate sports for men and 6 for women, and 2 intramural sports for men and 1 for women. Facilities include a soccer field, a gym, weight and training rooms, softball field, outdoor volleyball and basketball courts. Students have access to nearby facilities for swimming, boating, mountain climbing, and skiing. **Graduates:** From July 1, 2015 to June 30, 2016, 300 bachelor's degrees were awarded. The most popular majors were liberal arts (18%), psychology (18%), and human resources management (9%). In an average class, 1% graduate in 3 years or less, 32% graduate in 4 years or less, 43% graduate in 5 years or less, and 45% graduate in 6 years or less.

SERVICES: Counseling and information services are available, as is tutoring in every subject. There is remedial math and writing. **Library/Resources:** The library contains 176,640 volumes, 242,910 microform items, and 3,253 audio/video tapes/CDs/DVDs, and subscribes to 24,334 periodicals including electronic. Computerized library services include interlibrary loans, database searching, Internet access, and Wi-Fi capability. **Physically Challenged Students:** 95% of the campus is accessible. Facilities include wheelchair ramps, elevators, special parking, specially equipped restrooms, lowered drinking fountains, lowered telephones, and special housing. **Special:** Off-campus educational programs are offered through the China Studies Program, Contemporary Music Program in Martha's Vineyard, Latin American Studies Program, Los Angeles Film Studies Center, Middle East Studies Program, Oxford Honors Program, and the Russian Studies Program. Students may study abroad in a variety of countries. Internships are available in Christian education, pastoral studies, youth ministries, business, and psychology. Work-study programs in elementary education and with the federal government are also available. There is also a 1-year, nondegree certificate program in Bible and contemporary church music. There are 2 national honor societies and 1 departmental honors program. **Visiting:** There are regularly scheduled orientations for prospective students, and Genesis Weekend. There are guides for informal visits, visitors may sit in on classes, and stay overnight. To schedule a visit, contact the Visit Coordinator at (530) 226-4769. **Campus Safety and Security:** Measures include 24-hour foot and vehicle patrol, emergency notification system, and security escort services. There are emergency telephones, lighted pathways/sidewalks, controlled access to dorms/residences, emergency whistle program, local police patrols, and monthly campus safety meetings.

REQUIREMENTS: The SAT or ACT is required. Applicants must be graduates of an accredited high school or have a GED. It is recommended that applicants have completed 4 years of high school English, 3 each of math, science, and social studies/history, and 2 of a foreign language. A GPA of 2.0 is required. AP and CLEP credits are accepted. Important factors in the admissions decision are leadership record, personality/intangible qualities, and recommendations by school officials. Students must complete at least 124 credits, with a minimum of 36 upper-division credits and at least 42 major credits (of which 24 must be upper division). A minimum GPA of 2.0 must be maintained. Foundational studies requirements include 24 credits in biblical studies and theology and 41 credits in human expression, human history and behavior, and global environment. **Procedure:** Freshmen are admitted to all sessions. Entrance exams should be taken during the junior year or in the fall of the senior year. There are deferred admissions and rolling admissions plans. Application deadlines are open. Application fee is $25. Notification is sent on a rolling basis. Applications are accepted on-line. **Transfer Students:** 98 transfer students enrolled in 2015-2016. Transfer applicants with at least 30 semester college credits need not submit SAT or ACT scores. 30 of 124 credits required for the bachelor's degree must be completed at Simpson. **International Students:** There are 7 international students enrolled. They must take the TOEFL with a minimum score of 500 on the paper-based TOEFL (PBT) or 79 on the Internet-based version (iBT). They must also take the SAT or ACT.

ADMISSIONS: 59% of the 2016-2017 applicants were accepted. The SAT scores for the 2016-2017 freshman class were: Critical Reading-- 35% below 500, 41% between 500 and 599, 22% between 600 and 699, and 2% between 700 and 800. Math-- 36% below 500, 50% between 500 and 599, and 14% between 600 and 699. Writing-- 42% below 500, 43% between 500 and 599, and 15% between 600 and 699. The ACT scores were 44% below 12, 26% between 12 and 17, 13% between 18 and 23, 11% between 24 and 29, and 4% above 30. 53% of the current freshmen were in the top fifth of their class; 71% were in the top two fifths. **Admissions Contact:** Kendell Kluttz, Director of Admissions. Email: *admissions@simpsonu.edu* Web: *www.simpsonu.edu*

FINANCIAL AID: In 2016-2017, 100% of all full-time freshmen and 99% of continuing full-time students received some form of financial aid. 91% of all full-time freshmen and 94% of continuing full-time students received need-based aid. The average freshman award was $14,815. Need-based scholarships or need-based grants averaged $15,600 ($25,400 maximum); need-based self-help aid (loans and jobs) averaged $4,300 ($9,000 maximum); non-need-based athletic scholarships averaged $7,227 ($9,000 maximum); and other non-need-based awards and non-need-based scholarships averaged $7,610 ($21,600 maximum). 27% of undergraduate students work part-time. Average annual earnings from campus work are $3452. The average financial indebtedness of the 2016 graduate was $17,524. Simpson is a member of CSS. The college's own financial statement is required. The FAFSA code is 001291. The priority date for freshman financial aid applications for fall entry is March 2.

SONOMA STATE UNIVERSITY B-3

www.sonoma.edu

Rohnert Park, CA 94928 **(707) 664-2874**

Email: student.outreach@sonoma.edu

Full-time: 2799 men, 4996 women	**Faculty:** IIA, av$
Part-time: 386 men, 425 women	**Ph.D.s:** n/av
Graduate: 185 men, 532 women	**Student/Faculty:** n/av
Year: semesters, summer session	**Tuition:** $14,660 ($18,490)
Room & Board: $13,146	**Freshman Class:** 16487 applied, 12575 accepted, 1806 enrolled
SAT CR/M: required **ACT:** 21	**CEEB CODE:** 4723
Application Deadline: November 30	**COMPETITIVE**

Sonoma State University, founded in 1960, and part of the California State University system, offers undergraduate programs in business and economics, natural sciences, social sciences, and arts and humanities, and graduate programs in education, counseling, public administration, biology and business. There are 6 undergraduate schools and 1 graduate school. In addition to regional accreditation, Sonoma State has baccalaureate program accreditation with AACSB, NASAD, NASM, NCATE, NLN, ACS, CTC, and NLNAC. The 269-acre campus is in a suburban area 45 miles north of San Francisco.

STUDENT LIFE: 99% of undergraduates are from California. 7% are two or more races; 7% race unknown; 5% Asian American; 46% White; 31% Hispanic; 2% African American; 2% Foreign. **Female To Male Ratio:** 1.8:1. The average age of freshmen is 18; all undergraduates, 21. **Housing:** College-sponsored housing includes single-sex and coed dorms and on-campus apartments. In addition, there are special-interest houses, women in math/science, housing for focused learning communities- freshman seminar dorms, special housing for disabled students, wellness housing, substance-free and intensive-study houses. On-campus housing is available on a first-come and first-served basis. All students may keep cars.

FACULTY/CLASSROOMS: 46% of faculty are male; 54% are female. No introductory courses are taught by graduate students.

PROGRAMS OF STUDY: Sonoma State confers B.A., B.F.A. and B.S. degrees. Master's degrees are also awarded. Bachelor's degrees are awarded in BIOLOGICAL SCIENCE (biochemistry and biology/biological science), BUSINESS (business administration and management), COMMUNICATIONS AND THE ARTS (art, communications, English, fine arts, French, music, Spanish, and visual and performing arts), COMPUTER AND PHYSICAL SCIENCE (chemistry, computer science, geology, mathematics, and physics), ENGINEERING AND ENVIRONMENTAL DESIGN (environmental science), HEALTH PROFESSIONS (nursing), SOCIAL SCIENCE (African American studies, American Indian studies, anthropology, criminal justice, economics, ethnic studies, gender studies, geography, history, human development, interdisciplinary studies, international studies, Latin American studies, liberal arts/general studies, Mexican-American/Chicano studies, philosophy, physical fitness/movement, political science/government, psychology, sociology, and women's studies). Business, psychology, and liberal studies have the largest enrollments.

ACTIVITIES: Groups on campus include art, cheerleading, chess, choir, chorale, chorus, computers, dance, drama, ethnic, honors, jazz band, LGBT, literary magazine, musical theater, newspaper, opera, orchestra, pep band, political, professional, religious, social, social service, student government, and symphony. Popular campus events include Big Night, Science Night, Parents Day, and Unity Through Diversity Week. **Sports:** There are 5 intercollegiate sports for men and 9 for women. Facilities include a stadium, gym, field house, tennis courts, pool, auditorium, and playing fields, two-court gymnasium, one-court gymnasium/soccer arena, fitness center, climbing wall, outdoor adventure resource and equipment rental area, game room, exercise studios, and spa. **Graduates:** From July 1, 2015 to June 30, 2016, 1949 bachelor's degrees were awarded. The most popular majors were business administration (18%), psychology (10%), and sociology (7%). In an average class, 28% graduate in 4 years or less, 56% graduate in 5 years or less, and 61% graduate in 6 years or less.

SERVICES: Counseling and information services are available, as is tutoring in most subjects. There is a reader service for the blind, and remedial math, reading, and writing. Learning disability assessment is also available. **Library/Resources:** The library contains 44,242 audio/video tapes/CDs/DVDs. Computerized library services include interlibrary loans, database searching, Internet access, and Wi-Fi capability. Special learning facilities include an art gallery, performing arts center, observatory, electron microscope, seismograph, environmental technology center, green music center and natural preserves. **Physically Challenged Students:** All of the campus is accessible. Facilities include wheelchair ramps, elevators, special parking, specially equipped restrooms, special class scheduling, lowered drinking fountains, and lowered telephones. Including a reading machine, phonic listening devices, PC and mainframe access, and interpreters are also available. **Special:** Students may cross-register at Mills College, Oakland, and University of California, Berkeley. Study-abroad programs are available in 17 countries. Community service internships, work-study, nondegree study through Open University, and pass/fail grading options are available. B.A. and B.S. options in biology, chemistry, environmental studies, geology, interdisciplinary studies, math, and physics are offered. The Hutchins School B.A. in liberal studies offers small seminar classes and an interdisciplinary curriculum. Distance learning programs in nursing are available at 3 off-site centers. **Visiting:** There are regularly scheduled orientations for prospective students, consisting of programs in the spring and summer. There are guides for informal visits and visitors may sit in on classes. To schedule a visit, contact the Admissions Development Office. **Campus Safety and Security:** Measures include 24-hour foot and vehicle patrol, emergency notification system, self-defense education, and security escort services. There are emergency telephones and lighted pathways/sidewalks.

REQUIREMENTS: The SAT is required. Applicants should be graduates of accredited high school or have earned the GED. Secondary school preparation should include 4 years of English, 3 year of math, 2 years each of science, foreign language and history, and 1 each of visual/performing arts, academic electives, science with lab. A GPA of 2.0 is required. AP and CLEP credits are accepted. Undergraduate students must complete 120 to 132 units, depending on the degree program, consisting of 48 to 51 units of general education, a concentration of study in a specific major, and electives. General education programs require experience in oral and written communications, critical thinking, natural science and math, arts and humanities, social sciences, and personal integration. All students must take an ethnic studies course and the equivalent of courses in U.S. government, U.S. history, and California government. **Procedure:** Freshmen are admitted fall and spring. There is a rolling admissions plan. Applications should be filed by November 30 for fall entry, along with a $55 fee. Applications are accepted on-line. **Transfer Students:** Applicants must have a minimum 2.0 GPA. The maximum number of transferable credits is 70. 30 of 120 credits required for the bachelor's degree must be completed at Sonoma State. **International Students:** There are 189 international students enrolled. The school actively recruits these students. They must take the TOEFL with a minimum score of 500 on the paper-based TOEFL (PBT) or 61 on the Internet-based version (iBT). They must also take the SAT or ACT.

ADMISSIONS: 76% of the 2016-2017 applicants were accepted. The SAT scores for the 2016-2017 freshman class were: Critical Reading-- 51% below 500, 38% between 500 and 599, 10% between 600 and 699, and 1% between 700 and 800. Math-- 52% below 500, 39% between 500 and 599, 8% between 600 and 699, and 1% between 700 and 800. Writing-- 56% below 500, 37% between 500 and 599, 6% between 600 and 699, and 1% between 700 and 800. The ACT scores were 16% between 12 and 17, 52% between 18 and 23, 30% between 24 and 29, and 2% above 30. **Admissions Contact:** Natalie Kalogiannis, Director of Admissions. Email: *student.outreach@sonoma.edu* Web: *www.sonoma.edu*

FINANCIAL AID: The average freshman award was $10,004. Need-based scholarships or need-based grants averaged $10,498; and need-based self-help aid (loans and jobs) averaged $3,145. The FAFSA code is 001156. The priority date for freshman financial aid applications for fall entry is January 31. The deadline for filing freshman financial aid applications for fall entry is rolling.

STANFORD UNIVERSITY — B-3

www.stanford.edu

Stanford, CA 94305 — **(650) 723-2091**

Fax: (650) 723-6050 — **Email:** admission@stanford.edu

Full-time: 3704 men, 3315 women	**Faculty:** I, ++$
Part-time: 30 men, 40 women	**Ph.D.s:** 99%
Graduate: 6687 men, 4693 women	**Student/Faculty:** 4 to 1
Year: quarters, summer session	**Tuition:** $46,302
Room & Board: $14,107	**Freshman Class:** 42167 applied, 2145 accepted, 1678 enrolled
SAT or ACT: required	**CEEB CODE:** 4704
Application Deadline: January 3	**MOST COMPETITIVE**

Stanford University is a research institution, with seven schools: business, earth sciences, education, engineering, humanities & sciences, law and medicine. Areas of academic excellence cross disciplines, ranging from humanities to social sciences to engineering and the sciences. Students, distinguished by initiative, love of learning and commitment to public service, are talented in many areas, including academics, art, music and athletics. There are 7 undergraduate schools and 3 graduate schools. In addition to regional accreditation, Stanford has baccalaureate program accreditation with AACSB and ABET. The 8180-acre campus is in an urban area 30 miles south of San Francisco, 20 miles north of San Jose and adjacent to the cities of Palo Alto and Menlo Park. Including any residence halls, there are 700 buildings.

STUDENT LIFE: 53% of undergraduates are from out of state, mostly the South. Students are from 50 states, 90 foreign countries, and Canada. 58% are from public schools. 8% are African American; 8% Foreign; 43% White; 3% race unknown; 23% Asian American; 2% American Indian/Alaska Native; 13% Hispanic. **Male To Female Ratio:** 1.3:1. The average age of freshmen is 18; all undergraduates, 20. 1% do not continue beyond their first year; 95% remain to graduate. **Housing:** 6503 students can be accommodated in college housing, which includes single-sex and coed dorms, on-campus apartments, off-campus apartments, and married student housing. In addition, there are language houses, special-interest houses, fraternity houses, sorority houses, Ethnic theme houses, substance free housing, and academic interest. On-campus housing is guaranteed for all 4 years. 92% of students live on campus; of those, 95% remain on campus on weekends. Upperclassmen may keep cars.

FACULTY/CLASSROOMS: 73% of faculty are male; 27% are female. All teach undergraduates, and do research. No introductory courses are taught by graduate students.

PROGRAMS OF STUDY: Stanford confers A.B., B.S. and B.A.S. degrees. Master's and doctoral degrees are also awarded. Bachelor's degrees are awarded in BIOLOGICAL SCIENCE (biology/biological science), BUSINESS (management engineering and product design), COMMUNICATIONS AND THE ARTS (art, art history and appreciation, Chinese, classics, communications, comparative literature, dramatic arts, English, film arts, fine arts, French, Italian, Japanese, linguistics, music, Slavic languages, Spanish, and studio art), COMPUTER AND PHYSICAL SCIENCE (chemistry, computer science, earth science, geology, geophysics and seismology, geoscience, mathematics, mathematics/computational, and physics), ENGINEERING AND ENVIRONMENTAL DESIGN (aeronautical engineering, architectural engineering, bioengineering, chemical engineering, civil engineering, electrical/electronics engineering, engineering, engineering physics, environmental engineering, industrial engineering, materials science, mechanical engineering, petroleum/natural gas engineering, and systems engineering), SOCIAL SCIENCE (African American studies, American studies, anthropology, archeology, area studies, Asian/American studies, crosscultural studies, East Asian studies, economics, German area studies, Hispanic American studies, history, Iberian studies, international relations, Judaic studies, Latin American studies, Native American studies, philosophy, political science/government, psychology, public administration, religion, sociology, systems science, urban studies, and women's studies). Computer science, human biology, and engineering have the largest enrollments.

ACTIVITIES: 24% of men belong to 16 national fraternities; 28% of women belong to 14 national sororities. There are 625 groups on campus, including art, band, cheerleading, chess, choir, chorale, chorus, computers, dance, debate, drama, environmental, ethnic, film, honors, international, jazz band, LGBT, literary magazine, marching band, musical theater, newspaper, opera, orchestra, pep band, photography, political, professional, radio and TV, religious, social, social service, student government, symphony, and yearbook. Popular campus events include The Big Game, Full Moon on the Quad, Gaities, Fountain Hopping, and Viennese Ball. **Sports:** There are 16 intercollegiate sports for men and 20 for women. Facilities include athletic fields, gyms, swimming pools, volleyball courts, lighted tennis courts, dance studios, climbing wall, weight rooms, golf course, sailing facility, rowing facility, handball, racquetball, squash courts, baseball diamond, football stadium, softball stadium, soccer stadium, field hockey, and lacrosse. **Graduates:** From July 1, 2015 to June 30, 2016, 1723 bachelor's degrees were awarded. The most popular majors were interdisciplinary studies (18%), engineering (16%), and social sciences (15%). 350 companies recruited on campus in 2015-2016. In an average class, 95% graduate in 6 years or less.

SERVICES: Counseling and information services are available, as is tutoring in most subjects. There is a reader service for the blind. Schwab Learning Center offers services for students with learning disabilities and attention-deficit hyperactivity disorder. **Library/Resources:** The 20 libraries contain 9.3 million volumes, 6.0 million microform items, and 2.5 million audio/video tapes/CDs/DVDs, and subscribe to 77,000 periodicals including electronic. Computerized library services include interlibrary loans, database searching, Internet access, and Wi-Fi capability. Special learning facilities include an art gallery, radio station, TV station, 3 art museums, concert hall, biological preserve, linear accelerator, and an observatory. **Physically Challenged Students:** 98% of the campus is accessible. Facilities include wheelchair ramps, elevators, special parking, specially equipped restrooms, special class scheduling, lowered drinking fountains, lowered telephones, special housing. Stanford has a Diversity and Access Office and an Office of Accessible Education to provide help. **Special:** Internships, study abroad, a Washington semester, a New York City program, Marine research center, semester at sea, 12 overseas study programs, dual majors, a B.A.-B.S. degree, research opportunities, honors programs and co-terminal bachelor's and master's programs. Also offered on a pilot basis are joint majors that integrate humanities, and computer science. There is a chapter of Phi Beta Kappa. **Visiting:** There are regularly scheduled orientations for prospective students, including group information sessions and campus tours. There are guides for informal visits, visitors may sit in on classes, and stay overnight. To schedule a visit, contact the Office of Undergraduate Admission at admission@stanford.edu. **Campus Safety and Security:** Measures include 24-hour foot and vehicle patrol, emergency notification system, self-defense education, and security escort services. There are shuttle buses, emergency telephones, lighted pathways/sidewalks, controlled access to dorms/residences, and AlertSU notifies students immediately of safety threats on campus.

REQUIREMENTS: The SAT (Critical Reading, Math and Writing) or ACT Plus Writing is required. SAT Subject Tests are recommended. The university also recommends that applicants have strong preparation in high school English, math, a foreign language, science and social studies. If English is not your native language, we recommend, but do not require, the Test of English as a Foreign Language. Generally speaking, Stanford students have taken the most rigorous classes available to them. Applicants must complete the Common Application, the Stanford University Questions and arrange for recommendations. Candidates choose one topic from the Common Application, as well as complete three Stanford short essays. AP credits are accepted. Important factors in the admissions decision are advanced placement or honors courses, personality/intangible qualities, and recommendations by school officials. To graduate, students must complete 180 units, including requirements for the major, a writing and rhetoric requirement, and 1 year of a foreign language. General education requirements include the one-quarter freshman class Thinking Matters. Also required is Ways of Thinking, Ways of Doing, which includes eleven courses in eight subject areas, including aesthetic and interpretive inquiry, applied quantitative reasoning, creative expression, engaging diversity, ethical reasoning, formal reasoning, scientific method and analysis and social inquiry **Procedure:** Freshmen are admitted fall. Entrance exams should be taken by Nov. 1 for early decision; Jan. 15 for regular admission. There are early decision and deferred admissions plans. Early decision applications should be filed by November 1; regular applications, by January 3 for fall entry, along with a $90 fee. Notification of early decision is sent December 15; regular decision, April 1. 748 early decision candidates were accepted for the 2016-2017 class. 958 applicants were on the 2016 waiting list; 7 were admitted. Applications are accepted on-line. **Transfer Students:** 29 transfer students enrolled in 2015-2016. Transfer students must complete 1 full year of academic work prior to enrollment. There is only fall quarter enrollment for transfer students. The application deadline is March 15. 90 of 180 credits required for the bachelor's degree must be completed at Stanford. **International Students:** There are 574 international students enrolled. The school actively recruits these students. They must take the SAT or ACT. SAT Subject tests are recommended.

ADMISSIONS: 5% of the 2016-2017 applicants were accepted. The SAT scores for the 2016-2017 freshman class were: Critical Reading-- 5% between 500 and 599, 26% between 600 and 699, and 69% between 700 and 800. Math-- 3% between 500 and 599, 19% between 600 and 699, and 78% between 700 and 800. Writing-- 4% between 500 and 599, 22% between 600 and 699, and 74% between 700 and 800. The ACT scores were 1% below 12, 11% between 18 and 23, and 88% above 30. 99% of the current freshmen were in the top fifth of their class; 100% were in the top two fifths. **Admissions Contact:** Richard H. Shaw, Dean of Admissions. Email: *admission@stanford.edu* Web: *www.stanford.edu*

FINANCIAL AID: In 2016-2017, 82% of continuing full-time students received some form of financial aid. The average freshman award was $42,514. Need-based scholarships or need-based grants averaged $44,790; need-based self-help aid (loans and jobs) averaged $2,168; and non-need-based athletic scholarships averaged $41,935. The average financial indebtedness of the 2016 graduate was $19,230. Stanford is a member of CSS. The CSS/Profile is required. The FAFSA code is 001305. The priority date for freshman financial aid applications for fall entry is February 15.

THE MASTER'S UNIVERSITY D-4

www.masters.edu

Santa Clarita, CA 91321	(661) 362-2209 (800) 568-6248
Fax: (661) 362-2718	**Email:** admissions@masters.edu
Full-time: 486 men, 460 women	**Faculty:** 67
Part-time: 139 men, 69 women	**Ph.D.s:** 75%
Graduate: 467 men, 79 women	**Student/Faculty:** 10 to 1
Year: semesters, summer session	**Tuition:** $33,020
Room & Board: $10,850	**Freshman Class:** 446 applied, 371 accepted, 173 enrolled
SAT CR/M/W: 560/520/550 **ACT:** 25	**CEEB CODE:** 4411
Application Deadline: n/av	**COMPETITIVE+**

The Master's University, founded in 1927, is a Christ-centered liberal arts college that exists to advance the kingdom of God by equipping students for moral integrity and lives of service in strategic fields of ministry and vocation. Within this authentic and life-changing community students from around the globe gather to be academically challenged, culturally engaged, and to embrace Biblical fidelity in all things. There is 1 undergraduate school and 1 graduate school. In addition to regional accreditation, Master's has baccalaureate program accreditation with ABHES, NASM, and WSCUC. The 110-acre campus is in a suburban area 35 miles north of Los Angeles. Including any residence halls, there are 32 buildings.

STUDENT LIFE: 67% of undergraduates are from California. Others are from 40 states, 23 foreign countries, and Canada. 40% are from public schools. 9% Hispanic; 7% two or more races; 66% White; 6% Asian American; 5% Race Unknown; 4% Foreign; 3% African American; and 100% Protestant. **Male To Female Ratio:** 1.8:1. The average age of freshmen is 18; all undergraduates, 20. 18% do not continue beyond their first year; 62% remain to graduate. **Housing:** 800 students can be accommodated in college housing, which includes single-sex dorms and off-campus apartments. On-campus housing is guaranteed for all 4 years, and is available on a first-come, and first-served basis. 75% of students live on campus; of those, 80% remain on campus on weekends. Alcohol is not permitted. All students may keep cars.

FACULTY/CLASSROOMS: 73% of faculty are male; 27% are female. All teach undergraduates. No introductory courses are taught by graduate students. The average class size in an introductory lecture is 30; in a laboratory is 11; and in a regular course is 13.

PROGRAMS OF STUDY: Master's confers B.A., B.S. and B.Mus. degrees. Master's and doctoral degrees are also awarded. Bachelor's degrees are awarded in BIOLOGICAL SCIENCE (biology/biological science and biological sciences), BUSINESS (accounting, accounting (finance), business administration w/legal studies, business administration and management, business (dual major program), business administration - international, business administration, management, operations, business administration marketing, and business information systems), COMMUNICATIONS AND THE ARTS (church music, communication studies, communications, English, film, television and digital media, instrumental performance, music, music composition, music ministry, music production/recording technology, music theory and composition, organ performance, piano pedagogy, and piano performance), COMPUTER AND PHYSICAL SCIENCE (applied mathematics, computer information systems, information sciences and systems, mathematics, and natural sciences), EDUCATION (Christian education, elementary education, music education, physical education, and secondary education), HEALTH PROFESSIONS (biology, kinesiology, preallied health, predentistry, and prephysical therapy), SOCIAL SCIENCE (biblical languages, biblical studies, Christian studies, family/consumer studies, history, home economics, liberal arts/general studies, liberal arts, sciences, general studies, humanities, missions, pastoral studies, political science/government, prelaw, and theology). Biblical studies, business administration, and biological sciences are the strongest academically. Business administration, biblical studies, and communication have the largest enrollments.

ACTIVITIES: There are no fraternities or sororities. There are 15 groups on campus, including band, choir, chorale, chorus, drama, ethnic, Evangelism, film, international justice mission, jazz band, musical theater, newspaper, opera, orchestra, pep band, photography, political, religious, social, social service, and student government. Popular campus events include Outreach Week, Truth & Life Conference, Disney Week, Week of Welcome, TMC Blend Coffeehouse, and Brother-Sister Dorm Events. **Sports:** There are 7 intercollegiate sports for men and 6 for women, and 6 intramural sports for men and 6 for women. Facilities include MacArthur Center Gymnasium (Bross Court), Reese Field (baseball and soccer), tennis and volleyball courts, batting cages, intramural field, swimming pool, team clubhouses, and fully-equipped fitness facility. **Graduates:** From July 1, 2015 to June 30, 2016, 267 bachelor's degrees were awarded. The most popular majors were business marketing (22%), theology and religious vocations (16%), and communications (13%). In an average class, 68% graduate in 6 years or less. Of the 2015 graduating class, 10% were enrolled in graduate school within 6 months of graduation.

SERVICES: Counseling and information services are available, as is tutoring in most subjects. There is remedial math and writing. **Library/Resources:** The library contains 194,000 volumes, 38,500 microform items, and 2,750 audio/video tapes/CDs/DVDs, and subscribes to 35,000 periodicals including electronic. Computerized library services include interlibrary loans, database searching, Internet access, and Wi-Fi capability. **Physically Challenged Students:** 90% of the campus is accessible. Facilities include wheelchair ramps, elevators, special parking, specially equipped restrooms, and lowered drinking fountains. **Special:** Students may cross-register with the Council for Christian Colleges and Universities (CCCU) for additional study abroad programs. Internships are offered with local businesses, churches, radio stations, and newspapers. **Visiting:** There are regularly scheduled orientations for prospective students, chapel, meetings with faculty, interviews, athletic events, financial aid seminar, and college activities. There are guides for informal visits, visitors may sit in on classes, and stay overnight. To schedule a visit, contact Taylor Patrick at tpatrick@masters.edu. **Campus Safety and Security:** Measures include 24-hour foot and vehicle patrol, emergency notification system, and security escort services. There are shuttle buses, lighted pathways/sidewalks, and controlled access to dorms/residences.

REQUIREMENTS: The SAT or ACT is required. Applicants must have completed 4 years of English, 2 years each of science, and history, 3 years of math, and 3 units of electives are recommended. A GPA of 2.8 is required. AP and CLEP credits are accepted. Important factors in the admissions decision are personality/intangible qualities, recommendations by school officials, and leadership record. Students must complete at least 122 semester hours, including a minimum of 61 GE units distributed as follows: 21 in the Scripture Set, 27 in the Worldview Set, and 13 in the Skills Set. Students must complete at least 40 semester hours in upper-division courses and at least 40 in the major and must maintain a minimum GPA of 2.0. **Procedure:** Freshmen are admitted fall and spring. There are early admissions, deferred admissions, and rolling admissions plans. Early decision applications should be filed by November 15, along with a $40 fee. Notification of early decision is sent December 1; regular decision, Applications are accepted on-line. **Transfer Students:** 77 transfer students enrolled in 2015-2016. Applicants must meet freshman requirements. A maximum of 70 units can be transferred from a junior college and 94 units from a 4-year college. 28 of 122 credits required for the bachelor's degree must be completed at Master's. **International Students:** There are 50 international students enrolled. They must take the TOEFL with a minimum score of 550 on the paper-based TOEFL (PBT) or 80 on the Internet-based version (iBT).

ADMISSIONS: 83% of the 2016-2017 applicants were accepted. The SAT scores for the 2016-2017 freshman class were: Critical Reading-- 25% below 500, 39% between 500 and 599, 28% between 600 and 699, and 8% between 700 and 800. Math-- 40% below 500, 38% between 500 and 599, 19% between 600 and 699, and 3% between 700 and 800. Writing-- 37% below 500, 34% between 500 and 599, 24% between 600 and 699, and 5% between 700 and 800. The ACT scores were 5% between 12 and 17, 43% between 18 and 23, 39% between 24 and 29, and 13% above 30. 43% of the current freshmen were in the top fifth of their class; 67% were in the top two fifths. 2 freshmen graduated first in their class. **Admissions Contact:** Hollie Jackson, Director of Admissions. Email: *admissions@masters.edu* Web: *www.masters.edu*

FINANCIAL AID: In 2016-2017, 98% of all full-time freshmen and 96% of continuing full-time students received some form of financial aid. 78% of all full-time freshmen and 77% of continuing full-time students received need-based aid. The average freshman award was $23,733.

Need-based scholarships or need-based grants averaged $19,981 ($9,084 maximum); need-based self-help aid (loans and jobs) averaged $4,555 ($5,000 maximum); non-need-based athletic scholarships averaged $16,588 ($40,860 maximum); and other non-need-based awards and non-need-based scholarships averaged $9,585 ($14,000 maximum). 21% of undergraduate students work part-time. Average annual earnings from campus work are $2943. The average financial indebtedness of the 2016 graduate was $19,233. Master's is a member of CSS. The college's own financial statement is required. The priority date for freshman financial aid applications for fall entry is March 2. The deadline for filing freshman financial aid applications for fall entry is August 28.

THOMAS AQUINAS COLLEGE C-4
www.thomasaquinas.edu

Santa Paula, CA 93060 **(800) 634-9797**

Fax: (805) 421-5905 **Email:** admissions@thomasaquinas.edu

Full-time: 197 men, 192 women	**Faculty:** 33
Part-time: n/av	**Ph.D.s:** 87%
Graduate: n/av	**Student/Faculty:** 11 to 1
Year: semesters	**Tuition:** $24,500
Room & Board: $7950	**Freshman Class:** 216 applied, 157 accepted, 102 enrolled
SAT CR/M/W: 660/600/620 **ACT:** 28	**CEEB CODE:** 4828
Application Deadline: December 15	**HIGHLY COMPETITIVE**

Thomas Aquinas College, founded in 1971 and affiliated with the Roman Catholic Church, is a small, private, liberal arts college offering an integrated studies curriculum based on the Great Books. All classes are conducted as conversations directed by teachers using the Socratic method. Figures in the above capsule and in this profile are approximate. There is 1 undergraduate school. The 131-acre campus is in a rural area 70 miles northwest of Los Angeles. Including any residence halls, there are 20 buildings.

STUDENT LIFE: 59% of undergraduates are from out of state, mostly the Midwest. Students are from 40 states, 9 foreign countries, and Canada. 21% are from public schools. 71% are White; 7% two or more races; 3% Foreign; 2% Asian American; 2% race unknown; 15% Hispanic; 1% African American. 97% are Catholic. **Male To Female Ratio:** 1.0:1. The average age of freshmen is 18; all undergraduates, 20. 8% do not continue beyond their first year; 92% remain to graduate. **Housing:** 398 students can be accommodated in college housing, which includes single-sex dorms. On-campus housing is guaranteed for all 4 years. 99% of students live on campus; of those, 85% remain on campus on weekends. Alcohol is not permitted. All students may keep cars.

FACULTY/CLASSROOMS: 92% of faculty are male; 8% are female. All teach undergraduates. No introductory courses are taught by graduate students. The average class size in a laboratory and in a regular course is 17.

PROGRAMS OF STUDY: TAC confers B.A. degrees. Bachelor's degrees are awarded in SOCIAL SCIENCE (liberal arts/general studies).

ACTIVITIES: There are no fraternities or sororities. There are 6 groups on campus, including art, choir, chorale, chorus, drama, literary magazine, Medical Society, and orchestra. Popular campus events include St. Thomas Aquinas Day, President's Day, St. Patrick's Day and Easter. **Sports:** There are 7 intramural sports for men and 6 for women. Facilities include a tennis, basketball, and volleyball courts, soccer field, swimming pool, weight-lifting rooms, and a softball field. **Graduates:** From July 1, 2015 to June 30, 2016, 80 bachelor's degrees were awarded. The most popular majors were liberal arts (100%). 19 companies recruited on campus in 2015-2016. In an average class, 82% graduate in 4 years or less, 75% graduate in 5 years or less, and 82% graduate in 6 years or less. Of the 2015 graduating class, 9% were enrolled in graduate school within 6 months of graduation, and 100% were employed.

SERVICES: There is remedial writing. All students may be tutored by the full-time teaching faculty. **Library/Resources:** The library contains 63,106 volumes, and 5,875 audio/video tapes/CDs/DVDs, and subscribes to 66 periodicals including electronic. Computerized library services include database searching, Internet access, and Wi-Fi capability. **Physically Challenged Students:** All of the campus is accessible. Facilities include wheelchair ramps, elevators, special parking, specially equipped restrooms, special class scheduling, lowered drinking fountains, lowered telephones, and special housing. **Visiting:** There are regularly scheduled orientations for prospective students, including a campus tour and hosting of prospective students by current students. Visits are for up to 3 days and consist of observing classes, attending lectures and concerts, enjoying community meals and events. There are guides for informal visits, visitors may sit in on classes, and stay overnight. To schedule a visit, contact The Admissions Office.

REQUIREMENTS: The SAT or ACT is required. Candidates for admission are expected to have completed four years of English and a minimum of two years each of natural science, foreign language, algebra, and one year of geometry. Additional work in science, mathematics and language study is recommended. Important factors in the admissions decision are personality/intangible qualities, advanced placement or honors courses, and recommendations by school officials. The entire curriculum is required of all students to graduate: four years each of philosophy, theology, mathematics, science and seminar (seminar covers philosophical works not covered in the philosophy courses, literature, history, and social science, among others), two years of language (Latin), and one year of music. Seniors are required to write and defend a thesis. A total of 146 semester hours, with a minimum GPA of 2.0. **Procedure:** Freshmen are admitted in the fall. There is a rolling admissions plan. Application deadlines are open. 15 applicants were on the 2016 waiting list; 10 were admitted. Applications are accepted online. **Transfer Students:** The integrated nature of the program requires that all students start as freshmen, and so, regardless of past education Thomas Aquinas College only admits students as freshmen. 15-20% of each freshman class has attended College elswhere prior to enrolling in Thomas Aquinas College. 146 of 146 credits required for the bachelor's degree must be completed at TAC. **International Students:** There are 12 international students enrolled. They must take the TOEFL with a minimum score of 570 on the paper-based TOEFL (PBT). They must also take the SAT or ACT.

ADMISSIONS: 73% of the 2016-2017 applicants were accepted. The SAT scores for the 2016-2017 freshman class were: Critical Reading-- 3% below 500, 19% between 500 and 599, 41% between 600 and 699, and 37% between 700 and 800. Math-- 3% below 500, 49% between 500 and 599, 37% between 600 and 699, and 11% between 700 and 800. Writing-- 3% below 500, 31% between 500 and 599, 51% between 600 and 699, and 14% between 700 and 800. The ACT scores were 4% between 18 and 23, 67% between 24 and 29, and 30% above 30. 43% of the current freshmen were in the top fifth of their class; 86% were in the top two fifths. There was 1 National Merit finalist. **Admissions Contact:** Jonathan P. Daly, Director of Admissions. Email: *admissions@thomasaquinas.edu* Web: *www.thomasaquinas.edu*

FINANCIAL AID: In 2016-2017, 79% of all full-time freshmen and 79% of continuing full-time students received some form of financial aid. 75% of all full-time freshmen and 74% of continuing full-time students received need-based aid. The average freshman award was $19,604. Need-based scholarships or need-based grants averaged $11,543 ($22,534 maximum); need-based self-help aid (loans and jobs) averaged $7,403 ($9,200 maximum); and other non-need-based awards and non-need-based scholarships averaged $49 ($3,000 maximum). 75% of undergraduate students work part-time. Average annual earnings from campus work are $4632. The average financial indebtedness of the 2016 graduate was $11,826. The college's own financial statement, and parent and student federal tax returns are required. The FAFSA code is 023580. The deadline for filing freshman financial aid applications for fall entry is March 2.

UNIVERSITY OF CALIFORNIA AT BERKELEY B-3
www.berkeley.edu

Berkeley, CA 94720 **(510) 642-2316**

Email: admissions@berkeley.edu

Full-time: 12756 men, 13866 women	**Faculty:** 1623; I, ++$
	Ph.D.s: 99%
Part-time: 427 men, 447 women	**Student/Faculty:** 17 to 1
Graduate: 5785 men, 4923 women	**Tuition:** $13,431 ($38,139)
Year: semesters, summer session	**Freshman Class:** 78924 applied, 12048 accepted, 5550 enrolled
Room & Board: $15,422	
SAT CR/M/W: 670/705/685 **ACT:** 32	**CEEB CODE:** 4833
Application Deadline: November 30	**MOST COMPETITIVE**

University of California at Berkeley, founded in 1868, is a public institution offering a wide variety of programs in the social and physical sciences, liberal arts, and professional fields. It is the oldest campus of the University of California system. The Berkeley Middle Class Access Plan (MCAP) is a new financial aid program to help middle-class families pay for cost for undergraduate degree programs. MCAP will not cover nonresident tuition. Under the Blue and Gold Opportunity Plan the university will cover tuition and fee cost for low-income California residents. There are 7 undergraduate schools and 14 graduate schools. In addition to regional accreditation, Cal has baccalaureate program accreditation with AACSB, ABET, ADA, ASLA, SAF, and ACS. The 1232-acre campus is in an urban area 10 miles east of San Francisco. Including any residence halls, there are 300 buildings.

STUDENT LIFE: 85% of undergraduates are from California. Others are from 50 states, 80 foreign countries, and Canada. 85% are from public schools. 43% are Asian American; 4% African American; 32% White; 2% two or more races; 2% race unknown; 13% Hispanic; 1% American Indian/Alaska Native. **Female To Male Ratio:** 1.0:1. The average age of freshmen is 18; all undergraduates, 20. 4% do not continue beyond their first year; 90% remain to graduate. **Housing:** 8800 students can be accommodated in college housing, which includes single-sex and coed dorms, off-campus apartments, and married student housing. In addition, there are honors houses, language houses, special-interest houses, fraternity houses, sorority houses, substance-free housing, an international house, theme housing, wellness housing, apartments for student with children, and co-op housing. On-campus housing is guaranteed for the freshman year only and is available on a lottery system for upperclassmen. 74% of students commute. All students may keep cars.

FACULTY/CLASSROOMS: 65% of faculty are male; 35% are female. No introductory courses are taught by graduate students.

PROGRAMS OF STUDY: Cal confers A.B. and B.S. degrees. Master's and doctoral degrees are also awarded. Bachelor's degrees are awarded in AGRICULTURE (conservation and regulation and forestry and related sciences), BIOLOGICAL SCIENCE (biology/biological science, microbiology, molecular biology, nutrition, and plant genetics), BUSINESS (business administration and management, management science, and operations research), COMMUNICATIONS AND THE ARTS (art, art history and appreciation, Chinese, classical languages, communications, comparative literature, dance, dramatic arts, Dutch, English, film arts, French, German, Greek, Italian, Japanese, Latin, linguistics, music, Scandinavian languages, Slavic languages, Spanish, and speech/debate/rhetoric), COMPUTER AND PHYSICAL SCIENCE (applied mathematics, astrophysics, chemistry, computer science, earth science, mathematics, physical sciences, physics, and statistics), ENGINEERING AND ENVIRONMENTAL DESIGN (architecture, bioengineering, chemical engineering, civil engineering, computer engineering, electrical/electronics engineering, engineering and applied science, engineering physics, environmental engineering, environmental science, industrial engineering, landscape architecture/design, manufacturing engineering, materials engineering, materials science, mechanical engineering, and nuclear engineering), HEALTH PROFESSIONS (optometry and public health), SOCIAL SCIENCE (African American studies, American studies, anthropology, Asian/American studies, Asian/Oriental studies, Celtic studies, classical/ancient civilization, cognitive science, economics, ethnic studies, geography, Hispanic American studies, history, interdisciplinary studies, Latin American studies, law, Middle Eastern studies, Native American studies, Near Eastern studies, peace studies, political science/government, psychology, religion, social science, social work, sociology, South Asian studies, urban studies, and women's studies). Electrical engineering & computer science, political science, and economics have the largest enrollments.

ACTIVITIES: There are 400 groups on campus, including art, band, cheerleading, chess, choir, chorale, chorus, computers, dance, debate, drama, ethnic, film, forensics, honors, international, jazz band, LGBT, literary magazine, marching band, model UN, musical theater, newspaper, opera, orchestra, pep band, photography, political, professional, radio and TV, religious, social, social service, student government, symphony, and yearbook. Popular campus events include The Big Game, Cal Performances, and E-Week. **Sports:** Facilities include a football stadium, track, basketball pavilion, gyms, martial arts room, swimming pools, weight rooms, squash, racquetball, handball, volleyball, tennis courts, and baseball and softball fields. **Graduates:** From July 1, 2015 to June 30, 2016, 7647 bachelor's degrees were awarded. The most popular majors were social sciences (20%), biological/life sciences, and engineering (12%), business/marketing, natural resources and conservation, English, and interdisciplinary studies (5%). 600 companies recruited on campus in 2015-2016. In an average class, 3% graduate in 3 years or less, 69% graduate in 4 years or less, 88% graduate in 5 years or less, and 91% graduate in 6 years or less.

SERVICES: Counseling and information services are available, as is tutoring in most subjects. There is a reader service for the blind. **Library/Resources:** The 35 libraries contain 10.4 million volumes, 6.6 million microform items, and 46,162 audio/video tapes/CDs/DVDs, and subscribe to 82,151 periodicals including electronic. Computerized library services include interlibrary loans and database searching. Special learning facilities include an art gallery, natural history museum, radio station, botanical garden, anthropology museum, hall of science, the University Art Museum and Pacific Film Archive, seismographic station, herbaria, the Hall for the Performing Arts, and observatory. **Physically Challenged Students:** 95% of the campus is accessible. Facilities include wheelchair ramps, elevators, special parking, specially equipped restrooms, special class scheduling, lowered drinking fountains, and lowered telephones. **Special:** Co-op programs, cross-registration with area schools, internships, work-study programs, and study abroad in 35 countries are available. Interdisciplinary majors are also available, as are pass/fail options, independent study, an independent research and undergraduate research program, and a freshman seminar program, in which 15 to 25 students meet with professors to explore a wide range of majors. There is a 3-2 engineering program with the University of California, Santa Cruz. There is a chapter of Phi Beta Kappa and a freshman honors program. **Visiting:** There are regularly scheduled orientations for prospective students, including 1 1/2 hour student-led walking tours, usually followed by an admissions information presentation; self-guided tours are also available. There are guides for informal visits and visitors may sit in on classes. To schedule a visit, contact the Visitor Services at (510) 642-5215. **Campus Safety and Security:** Measures include 24-hour foot and vehicle patrol, emergency notification system, self-defense education, and security escort services. There are shuttle buses, emergency telephones, lighted pathways/sidewalks, controlled access to dorms/residences, a rape prevention peer education program, an earthquake emergency preparedness program, and safety, threats and alerts reports via computer.

REQUIREMENTS: The SAT or ACT is required. Applicants must submit scores from 2 SAT Subject Tests, these are recommended for applicants to chemistry and engineering. High school units required are 4 years of English, 3 of math (4 recommended), 2 each of history/social studies, 2 each of science with lab science (3 recommended), 2 of foreign language (3 recommended), and 1 of college preparatory electives, and or other 1 of visual or performing arts. AP credits are accepted. Important factors in the admissions decision are advanced placement or honors courses, evidence of special talent, leadership record, parents or siblings attended your school, and geographical diversity. All undergraduate students are required to satisfy the general university requirements of English and writing proficiency and take integrative and comparative courses in American history, institutions, and cultures. Students must complete 120 units with a minimum GPA of 2.0. **Procedure:** Freshmen are admitted fall. Entrance exams should be taken no later than the December test dates in the senior year. There is a deferred admissions plan. Applications should be filed by November 30 for fall entry, along with a $70 fee. Notifications are sent March 31. Applications are accepted online. **Transfer Students:** 2170 transfer students enrolled in 2015-2016. Requirements are all college transcripts, and an essay or personal statement. An 2.4 GPA on a scale of 4.0. Students may enroll in the fall-November 30. Notification is April 30, and must reply by June 1. 24 of 120 credits required for the bachelor's degree must be completed at Cal. **International Students:** There are 1073 international students enrolled. They must take the TOEFL with a minimum score of 550 on the paper-based TOEFL (PBT) or 83 on the Internet-based version (iBT). They must also take the SAT or ACT.

ADMISSIONS: 15% of the 2016-2017 applicants were accepted. 98% of the current freshmen were in the top fifth of their class; 100% were in the top two fifths. **Admissions Contact:** Walter A. Robinson, Director of Undergraduate Admission. Email: admissions@berkeley.edu Web: *www.berkeley.edu*

FINANCIAL AID: In 2016-2017, 65% of all full-time freshmen received some form of financial aid or need-based aid. The average freshman award was $23,948. Need-based scholarships or need-based grants averaged $20,864; need-based self-help aid (loans and jobs) averaged $6,839; non-need-based athletic scholarships averaged $26,155; other non-need-based awards and non-need-based scholarships averaged $6,686; and

$6,737 from other forms of aid. The average financial indebtedness of the 2016 graduate was $17,869. The FAFSA code is 001312. The deadline for filing freshman financial aid applications for fall entry is March 2.

UNIVERSITY OF CALIFORNIA AT DAVIS B-2

www.ucdavis.edu

Davis, CA 95616	**(530) 752-2971**
Fax: (530) 752-1280	**Email: undergraduateadmissions@ucdavis**
Full-time: 11,456 men, 16,510 women	**Faculty:** I, +$
	Ph.D.s: 98%
Part-time: 202 men, 216 women	**Student/Faculty:** 18 to 1
Graduate: 3235 men, 3567 women	**Tuition:** $13,950 ($38,659)
Year: quarters, summer session	**Freshman Class:** 64510 applied, 24614 accepted, 5369 enrolled
Room & Board: $14,517	
SAT or ACT: required	**CEEB CODE:** 4834
Application Deadline: November 30	**HIGHLY COMPETITIVE**

University of California at Davis, founded in 1908, is a land-grant, comprehensive institution offering programs in arts and science, agricultural and environmental sciences, and engineering. There are 4 undergraduate schools and 5 graduate schools. In addition to regional accreditation, UC Davis has baccalaureate program accreditation with ABET, ADA, and ASLA. The 5300-acre campus is in a suburban area 15 miles west of Sacramento, and 72 miles northeast of San Francisco. Including any residence halls, there are 1186 buildings.

STUDENT LIFE: 96% of undergraduates are from California. Others are from states. 5% are two or more races; 32% Asian American; 28% White; 2% African American; 2% race unknown; 19% Hispanic; 11% Foreign. **Female To Male Ratio:** 1.4:1. The average age of freshmen is 19; all undergraduates, 21. 8% do not continue beyond their first year; 83% remain to graduate. **Housing:** College-sponsored housing includes single-sex and coed dorms, on-campus apartments, off-campus apartments, and married student housing. In addition, there are honors houses, language houses, and special-interest houses. On-campus housing is guaranteed for the freshman year only. 75% of students commute. Alcohol is not permitted. No one may keep cars.

FACULTY/CLASSROOMS: 61% of faculty are male; 39% are female. No introductory courses are taught by graduate students.

PROGRAMS OF STUDY: UC Davis confers B.S., A.B. and B.A.S. degrees. Master's and doctoral degrees are also awarded. Bachelor's degrees are awarded in AGRICULTURE (agricultural business management, agricultural economics, animal science, international agriculture, plant science, range/farm management, and soil science), BIOLOGICAL SCIENCE (avian sciences, bacteriology, biochemistry, biology/biological science, botany, ecology, entomology, environmental biology, genetics, microbiology, nutrition, physiology, toxicology, wildlife biology, and zoology), BUSINESS (organizational behavior), COMMUNICATIONS AND THE ARTS (art history and appreciation, Chinese, communications, comparative literature, design, dramatic arts, English, fine arts, French, German, Greek, Italian, Japanese, Latin, linguistics, music, Russian, Spanish, speech/debate/rhetoric, and studio art), COMPUTER AND PHYSICAL SCIENCE (atmospheric sciences and meteorology, chemistry, computer science, geology, hydrology, mathematics, physics, polymer science, and statistics), EDUCATION (physical education), ENGINEERING AND ENVIRONMENTAL DESIGN (aeronautical engineering, agricultural engineering, bioengineering, chemical engineering, civil engineering, computer engineering, electrical/electronics engineering, environmental design, environmental science, landscape architecture/design, materials engineering, and mechanical engineering), HEALTH PROFESSIONS (community health work and environmental health science), SOCIAL SCIENCE (African studies, American studies, anthropology, behavioral science, classical/ancient civilization, dietetics, East Asian studies, economics, food science, geography, history, human development, human ecology, international relations, medieval studies, Mexican-American/Chicano studies, Native American studies, philosophy, political science/government, psychology, religion, social science, sociology, textiles and clothing, and women's studies). Agricultural, biological, and biotechnical sciences are the strongest academically. Biological science, biochemistry, and psychology have the largest enrollments.

ACTIVITIES: Groups on campus include art, band, cheerleading, chess, choir, chorus, communications, computers, dance, debate, drama, ethnic, film, honors, international, jazz band, LGBT, literary magazine, marching band, musical theater, newspaper, orchestra, pep band, photography, political, professional, radio and TV, religious, social, social service, student government, and symphony. Popular campus events include Picnic Day, Whole Earth Festival, and Asian Pacific Cultural Week. **Sports:** There are 9 intercollegiate sports for men and 14 for women. **Graduates:** From July 1, 2015 to June 30, 2016, 7120 bachelor's degrees were awarded. The most popular majors were psychology (9%), economics (7%), and managerial economics (5%). In an average class, 2% graduate in 3 years or less, 54% graduate in 4 years or less, 79% graduate in 5 years or less, and 83% graduate in 6 years or less.

SERVICES: Counseling and information services are available, as is tutoring in most subjects. There is a reader service for the blind, and remedial math and writing. **Library/Resources:** The 6 libraries contain 4.5 million volumes, 4.3 million microform items, and 12,977 audio/video tapes/CDs/DVDs, and subscribe to 120,531 periodicals including electronic. Computerized library services include interlibrary loans, database searching, Internet access, and Wi-Fi capability. Special learning facilities include an art gallery, radio station, experimental farm, arboretum, raptor center, equestrian center, primate research center, and the Crocker Nuclear Laboratory. **Physically Challenged Students:** All of the campus is accessible. Facilities include wheelchair ramps, elevators, special parking, specially equipped restrooms, special class scheduling, lowered drinking fountains, lowered telephones, and lowered automatic teller machines. **Special:** There are credit and noncredit internship programs. Study abroad in more than 32 countries and a Washington semester are offered. Students may participate in college work-study, federal work-study, and California work-study programs. Several A.B.-B.S. degrees are offered. Students may design their own majors, take dual majors, and elect pass/fail options. Interdisciplinary majors are offered in African American and African studies, American studies, Mexican American studies, comparative literature, East Asian studies, exercise science, international relations, linguistics, medieval studies, Native American studies, religious studies, and women's studies. There is a chapter of Phi Beta Kappa and a freshman honors program. **Visiting:** There are regularly scheduled orientations for prospective students, including weekend tours of the campus, weekday tours by appointment, and drop-in counseling with staff and faculty. The campus also offers a 1-day preview for prospective students and their families. There are guides for informal visits, visitors may sit in on classes, and stay overnight. To schedule a visit, contact UC Davis Visitor Services at visit@ucdavis.edu. **Campus Safety and Security:** Measures include 24-hour foot and vehicle patrol, emergency notification system, self-defense education, and security escort services. There are shuttle buses, emergency telephones, lighted pathways/sidewalks, There is also a rape prevention program, a crime prevention unit, a bike patrol unit, and a K-9 program.

REQUIREMENTS: The SAT or ACT is required. Candidates for admission should have completed 4 units of English, 3 of math, and 2 each of foreign language, history/social science, lab science, and college preparatory electives, for a total of 15 units. Two SAT Subject Tests are required in two different areas. AP credits are accepted. General education requirements vary by college but are based on 3 components: topical breadth, social-cultural diversity, and writing experience. A minimum of 180 quarter units with a minimum GPA of 2.0 are required for graduation, as is proficiency in English composition and American History and Institutions requirement. **Procedure:** Freshmen are admitted fall, winter, and spring. Entrance exams should be taken by December of the senior year. There is a deferred admissions plan. Applications should be filed by November 30 for fall entry. The fall 2016 application fee was $70. Notifications are sent March 15. 2733 applicants were on the 2016 waiting list; 2030 were admitted. Applications are accepted on-line. **Transfer Students:** 2932 transfer students enrolled in 2015-2016. Junior-level transfers have priority. Requirements vary by college, discipline, and major. 35 of 180 credits required for the bachelor's degree must be completed at UC Davis. **International Students:** They must take the TOEFL with a minimum score of 550 on the paper-based TOEFL (PBT) or 60 on the Internet-based version (iBT). They must also take the SAT or ACT.

ADMISSIONS: 38% of the 2016-2017 applicants were accepted. The SAT scores for the 2016-2017 freshman class were: Critical Reading-- 20% below 500, 39% between 500 and 599, 31% between 600 and 699, and 10% between 700 and 800. Math-- 11% below 500, 23% between 500 and 599, 36% between 600 and 699, and 29% between 700 and 800. Writing-- 16% below 500, 33% between 500 and 599, 38% between 600 and 699, and 13% between 700 and 800. The ACT scores were 1% between 12 and 17, 18% between 18 and 23, 48% between 24 and 29, and 33% above 30. **Admissions Contact:** Walter Robinson, Director, Undergraduate Admissions. Email: *undergraduateadmissions@ucdavis* Web: *www.ucdavis.edu*

FINANCIAL AID: UC Davis is a member of CSS. The FAFSA code is 001313. The deadline for filing freshman financial aid applications for fall entry is March 2.

UNIVERSITY OF CALIFORNIA AT IRVINE D-5

www.uci.edu

Irvine, CA 92697	(949) 824-6703
Fax: (949) 824-2951	Email: admissions@uci.edu
Full-time: 9965 men, 11,913 women	**Faculty:** 1467; I, +$
Part-time: 196 men, 142 women	**Ph.D.s:** 98%
Graduate: 3108 men, 2155 women	**Student/Faculty:** 19 to 1
Year: quarters, summer session	**Tuition:** $14,749 ($37,104)
Room & Board: $11,735	**Freshman Class:** 56508 applied, 23956 accepted, 5077 enrolled
SAT CR/M/W: 540/610/550 **ACT:** required	**CEEB CODE:** 4859
Application Deadline: November 30	**VERY COMPETITIVE**

University of California, Irvine, founded in 1965, is a public research university and part of the University of California System. The figures in the above capsule and in this profile are approximate. There are 13 undergraduate schools and 15 graduate schools. In addition to regional accreditation, UCI has baccalaureate program accreditation with AACSB, ABET, ABA, and AAMC. The 1489-acre campus is in a suburban area 40 miles south of Los Angeles. Including any residence halls, there are 492 buildings.

STUDENT LIFE: 91% of undergraduates are from California. Others are from 40 states, 70 foreign countries, and Canada. 86% are from public schools. 52% are Asian American; 3% African American; 3% Foreign; 20% Hispanic; 19% White; 1% American Indian/Alaska Native. **Female To Male Ratio:** 1.1:1. The average age of freshmen is 18; all undergraduates, 21. 7% do not continue beyond their first year; 93% remain to graduate. **Housing:** 10199 students can be accommodated in college housing, which includes single-sex and coed dorms, on-campus apartments, and married student housing. In addition, there are honors houses, special-interest houses, fraternity houses, and sorority houses. On-campus housing is available on a first-come, first-served basis, and is available on a lottery system for upperclassmen. 62% of students commute. All students may keep cars.

FACULTY/CLASSROOMS: 64% of faculty are male; 36% are female. All teach undergraduates, and do research. No introductory courses are taught by graduate students. The average class size in an introductory lecture is 107; in a laboratory is 20; and in a regular course is 31.

PROGRAMS OF STUDY: UCI confers B.A., B.S., B.F.A. and B.Mus. degrees. Master's and doctoral degrees are also awarded. Bachelor's degrees are awarded in AGRICULTURE (environmental studies), BIOLOGICAL SCIENCE (biochemistry, bioinformatics, biology/biological science, botany, cell biology, ecology, genetics, microbiology, and neurosciences), BUSINESS (business administration and management, business economics, and economics – statistics), COMMUNICATIONS AND THE ARTS (art history, classics, comparative literature, creative writing, dance, dramatic arts, English, film arts, French, Japanese, journalism, Korean, media arts, music, music performance, musical theater, Spanish, and studio art), COMPUTER AND PHYSICAL SCIENCE (chemistry, computer science, earth science, environmental geology, geology, information sciences and systems, mathematics, physics, and software engineering), EDUCATION (global studies), ENGINEERING AND ENVIRONMENTAL DESIGN (aeronautical engineering, biomedical engineering, chemical engineering, civil engineering, computer engineering, electrical/electronics engineering, engineering, environmental engineering, environmental science, materials engineering, and mechanical engineering), HEALTH PROFESSIONS (nursing, pharmaceutical science, premedicine, and public health), SOCIAL SCIENCE (African American studies, anthropology, Asian/American studies, Chinese Studies, classical/ancient civilization, criminology, East Asian studies, economics, European studies, German area studies, Hispanic American studies, history, humanities, interdisciplinary studies, international studies, philosophy, political science/government, psychology, religion, social psychology, social science, sociology, urban studies, and women's studies). Biological sciences, psychology and social behavior, and business economics have the largest enrollments.

ACTIVITIES: 9% of men belong to 21 national fraternities; 10% of women belong to 3 local and 23 national sororities. There are 543 groups on campus, including art, band, cheerleading, chess, choir, chorus, communications, computers, dance, debate, drama, environmental, ethnic, film, honors, international, jazz band, LGBT, literary magazine, marching band, musical theater, newspaper, opera, orchestra, pep band, political, professional, radio and TV, religious, social, social service, student government, symphony, and yearbook. Popular campus events include Celebrate UCI, Shocktoberfest, Homecoming, Reggae & Wayzgoose Festivals, and Welcome Week's All-UCI Dance Battle. **Sports:** There are 35 intercollegiate sports for men and 33 for women, and 23 intramural sports for men and 23 for women. Facilities include a track stadium, events center, soccer field, tennis stadium, baseball, swimming pool, indoor handball/racquetball/squash courts, and an activities hall with areas for badminton, basketball, volleyball, combatives, fencing, and weight training. Sailing and crew base is located in nearby Newport Beach. **Graduates:** From July 1, 2015 to June 30, 2016, 6766 bachelor's degrees were awarded. The most popular majors were biological sciences (14%), business economics (8%), and pyschology and social behavior (6%). In an average class, 4% graduate in 3 years or less, 68% graduate in 4 years or less, 84% graduate in 5 years or less, and 86% graduate in 6 years or less.

SERVICES: Counseling and information services are available, as is tutoring in some subjects. There is a reader service for the blind, and remedial reading and writing. **Library/Resources:** The 4 libraries contain 3.2 million volumes, 2.2 million microform items, and 123,396 audio/video tapes/CDs/DVDs, and subscribe to 132,134 periodicals including electronic. Computerized library services include interlibrary loans, database searching, and Internet access. Special learning facilities include an art gallery, planetarium, radio station, freshwater marsh reserve, arboretum, laser institute, and numerous research centers. **Physically Challenged Students:** 95% of the campus is accessible. Facilities include wheelchair ramps, elevators, special parking, specially equipped restrooms, special class scheduling, lowered drinking fountains, lowered telephones, and special housing. **Special:** Students may study abroad in dozens of locations. UCI also offers internships, a Washington semester, semester at sea, work-study programs with the university, B.A.-B.S. degrees, dual majors, and pass/fail options. There are 7 national honor societies, Phi Beta Kappa, and a freshman honors program. **Visiting:** There are regularly scheduled orientations for prospective students. There are guides for informal visits, visitors may sit in on classes, and stay overnight. To schedule a visit, contact the Visitor Center at (949) 824-4636. **Campus Safety and Security:** Measures include 24-hour foot and vehicle patrol, emergency notification system, self-defense education, and security escort services. There are shuttle buses, emergency telephones, and lighted pathways/sidewalks.

REQUIREMENTS: The SAT or ACT is required. Required minimum scores are determined by an eligibility index. Applicants need 15 academic credits, including 4 years of English, 3 in math, and 2 each in foreign language, history/social science, lab science, and electives. An additional year each in foreign language, math, and science is recommended. An essay is also required. The GED is accepted. AP credits are accepted. To graduate, students must maintain a GPA of at least 2.0, earn 180 quarter units, satisfy all the requirements for their majors, and fulfill requirements in English composition and in American history and institutions. Further, students must also meet the following General Education requirements: Writing (two lower-division plus one upper-division course), Science and Technology (three courses), Social and Behavioral Sciences (three courses), Arts and Humanities (three courses), Quantitative, Symbolic, and Computational Reasoning(three courses that may also satisfy another GE category), Language other than English (one course), Multicultural Studies (one course that may also satisfy another GE category), International/Global Issues (one course that may also satisfy another GE category). **Procedure:** Freshmen are admitted fall. Entrance exams should be taken no later than December of the senior year. Applications should be filed by November 30 for fall entry, along with a $70 fee. Notifications are sent March 31. Applications are accepted on-line. **Transfer Students:** 1727 transfer students enrolled in 2015-2016. UC requirements for admission as a tranfer applicant vary according to the high school record. Please see catalog for full details. 36 of 180 credits required for the bachelor's degree must be completed at UCI. **International Students:** There are 1292 international students enrolled. They must take the TOEFL with a minimum score of 550 on the paper-based TOEFL (PBT) or 80 on the Internet-based version (iBT). They must also take the SAT or ACT.

ADMISSIONS: 42% of the 2016-2017 applicants were accepted. The SAT scores for the 2016-2017 freshman class were: Critical Reading-- 34% below 500, 37% between 500 and 599, 24% between 600 and 699, and 5% between 700 and 800. Math-- 15% below 500, 30% between 500 and 599, 40% between 600 and 699, and 15% between 700 and 800. Writing-- 27% below 500, 40% between 500 and 599, 28% between 600 and 699, and 5% between 700 and 800. **Admissions Contact:** Brent Yunek, Assistant Vice Chancellor, Enrollment Services. Email: *admissions@uci.edu* Web: *www.uci.edu*

FINANCIAL AID: UCI is a member of CSS. The FAFSA code is 001314. The priority date for freshman financial aid applications for fall entry is March 2. The deadline for fall entry is May 2.

UNIVERSITY OF CALIFORNIA AT LOS ANGELES C-5

www.ucla.edu

Los Angeles, CA 90095 **(310) 825-3101**

Fax: (310) 206-1206 **Email:** ugadm@admissions.ucla.edu

Full-time: 11,378 men, 14,056 women
Part-time: 386 men, 342 women
Graduate: 7128 men, 6303 women
Year: quarters, summer session
Room & Board: $15,069

Faculty: I, ++$
Ph.D.s: 98%
Student/Faculty: n/av
Tuition: $15,093 ($34,496)
Freshman Class: 57,670 applied, 13,088 accepted, 4636 enrolled

SAT CR/M/W: 640/680/660 **ACT:** 29
Application Deadline: November 30

CEEB CODE: 4837
MOST COMPETITIVE

University of California at Los Angeles (UCLA), founded in 1919, is a public research university offering undergraduate and graduate degrees. Its disciplines include arts and sciences, engineering, applied science, health sciences, law, management, and theater, film, and television. The figures in the above capsule and in this profile are approximate. There are 5 undergraduate schools and 12 graduate schools. In addition to regional accreditation, UCLA has baccalaureate program accreditation with AACSB, ABET, ADA, CSAB, CSWE, FIDER, NAAB, NLN, CCNE, and NAST. The 419-acre campus is in an urban area in Los Angeles. Including any residence halls, there are 190 buildings.

STUDENT LIFE: 89% of undergraduates are from California. Others are from 46 states, 71 foreign countries, and Canada. 77% are from public schools. 6% are Foreign; 4% African American; 36% Asian American; 32% White; 16% Hispanic. **Female To Male Ratio:** 1.1:1. The average age of freshmen is 18; all undergraduates, 21. 3% do not continue beyond their first year; 92% remain to graduate. **Housing:** 13300 students can be accommodated in college housing, which includes coed dorms, off-campus apartments, and married student housing. In addition, there are special-interest houses, fraternity houses, and sorority houses. On-campus housing is available on a lottery system for upperclassmen. 64% of students commute. Alcohol is not permitted. Some may keep cars.

FACULTY/CLASSROOMS: 65% of faculty are male; 35% are female. All teach undergraduates, and do research. No introductory courses are taught by graduate students.

PROGRAMS OF STUDY: UCLA confers B.A., and B.S degrees. Master's and doctoral degrees are also awarded. Bachelor's degrees are awarded in AGRICULTURE (environmental studies), BIOLOGICAL SCIENCE (biochemistry, biology/biological science, biophysics, cell biology, ecology, marine biology, microbiology, molecular biology, neurosciences, and physiology), BUSINESS (business economics), COMMUNICATIONS AND THE ARTS (American literature, Arabic, art, art history and appreciation, Chinese, classics, communications, dramatic arts, English, film arts, French, German, Greek, Hebrew, Italian, Japanese, Korean, Latin, linguistics, music, music history and appreciation, musicology/ethnomusicology, Portuguese, Russian languages and literature, Scandinavian languages, and Spanish), COMPUTER AND PHYSICAL SCIENCE (applied mathematics, astrophysics, atmospheric sciences and meteorology, chemistry, computer science, earth science, geology, geophysics and seismology, mathematics, physics, and statistics), EDUCATION (mathematics education), ENGINEERING AND ENVIRONMENTAL DESIGN (aeronautical engineering, aerospace studies, architecture, bioengineering, biomedical engineering, chemical engineering, civil engineering, computer engineering, electrical/electronics engineering, environmental science, geological engineering, materials engineering, materials science, and mechanical engineering), HEALTH PROFESSIONS (nursing), SOCIAL SCIENCE (African studies, African American studies, American Indian studies, anthropology, Asian/American studies, Asian/Oriental studies, classical/ancient civilization, cognitive science, East Asian studies, economics, European studies, French studies, geography, history, international studies, Italian studies, Judaic studies, Latin American studies, Mexican-American/Chicano studies, Middle Eastern studies, Near Eastern studies, philosophy, political science/government, psychobiology, psychology, religion, Russian and Slavic studies, sociology, South Asian studies, Spanish studies, and women's studies). Economics, psychology, and political science have the largest enrollments.

ACTIVITIES: 13% of men belong to 32 national fraternities; 13% of women belong to 33 national sororities. There are 1000 groups on campus, including art, band, cheerleading, chess, choir, chorale, chorus, computers, dance, debate, drama, environmental, ethnic, film, forensics, honors, international, jazz band, LGBT, literary magazine, marching band, musical theater, newspaper, opera, orchestra, pep band, photography, political, professional, radio and TV, religious, social, social service, student government, symphony, and yearbook. Popular campus events include Career Week, Casino Night, and Welcome Week. **Sports:** There are 10 intercollegiate sports for men and 12 for women, and 21 intramural sports for men and 19 for women. Facilities include a pavilion, stadium, tennis center, and a recreation & sports center. **Graduates:** From July 1, 2015 to June 30, 2016, 7518 bachelor's degrees were awarded. The most popular majors were political science (9%), history (8%), and psychology (8%). In an average class, 3% graduate in 3 years or less, 70% graduate in 4 years or less, 87% graduate in 5 years or less, and 90% graduate in 6 years or less.

SERVICES: Counseling and information services are available, as is tutoring in most subjects. There is a reader service for the blind. **Library/Resources:** The 13 libraries contain 9.2 million volumes, 6.2 million microform items, and 5.0 million audio/video tapes/CDs/DVDs, and subscribe to 78,463 periodicals including electronic. Computerized library services include interlibrary loans, database searching, and Internet access. Special learning facilities include an art gallery, natural history museum, planetarium, radio station, TV station, air photo archives, arts library, biomed library, young research library, Clark Memorial Library, College Library, Cuneiform Digital Library, Darling Biomedical Library, Darling Law Library, Film and Television Archive, Folklore and Mythology Archive, Ethnomusicology Archive, Institute for Social Science Library, Libraries of the Ethnic Studies Centers, music library, Rudolph East Asian Library, Rosenfeld Management Library, Science and Engineering Library, UES Gonda Library, University Archives, and the Performing Arts Special Collections. MUSEUMS--Fowler Museum, Hammer Museum of Art and Culture Center, Grunwald Center for Graphic Arts, New Wright Gallery, GARDENS--Mildred E. Mathias Botanical Garden, Franklin D. Murphy Sculpture Garden, Hannah Carter Japanese Garden, ART--Eli and Edythe Broad Art Center, DANCE--Glorya Kaufman Hall, THEATER--Geffen Playhouse, Macgowan Little Theater, Freud Playhouse, Billy Wilder Theater, MUSIC--Royce Hall, Schoenberg Hall, Pauley Pavilion, Los Angeles Tennis Center, and the FILM--James Bridges Theater. **Physically Challenged Students:** All of the campus is accessible. Facilities include wheelchair ramps, elevators, special parking, specially equipped restrooms, special class scheduling, lowered drinking fountains, and lowered telephones. **Special:** Opportunities are provided for internships, work-study programs, study abroad in 33 countries, student-designed majors, dual majors, and interdisciplinary majors, including chemistry and materials science, Chicana and Chicano studies, and math and engineering. There is a Washington, D.C., program for 20 to 30 students selected each fall and spring. There are 21 national honor societies, Phi Beta Kappa, a freshman honors program, and 100 departmental honors programs. **Visiting:** There are regularly scheduled orientations for prospective students, including campus tours by current UCLA students. Reservations are required. Visitors may sit in on classes. To schedule a visit, contact Undergraduate Admissions. **Campus Safety and Security:** Measures include 24-hour foot and vehicle patrol, emergency notification system, self-defense education, and security escort services. There are shuttle buses, emergency telephones, lighted pathways/sidewalks, and controlled access to dorms/residences.

REQUIREMENTS: The ACT Optional Writing test is also required. For freshmen applicants applying for admission to fall quarter 2012 or later, we will no longer require two SAT subject exams. (We will still review these exams if applicants choose to send them to us, and certain SAT subject exams may be recommended for some majors). We will continue to require either the SAT Reasoning or ACT with Writing examination. AP credits are accepted. Important factors in the admissions decision are advanced placement or honors courses, evidence of special talent, and leadership record. Students must complete a minimum of 180 quarter units and maintain a minimum GPA of 2.0 in all courses. All students must demonstrate a proficiency in English composition, or take specific courses to achieve this proficiency, and must also meet course requirements in American history and institutions. Other requirements vary by major and college or school. **Procedure:** Freshmen are admitted fall. Entrance exams should be taken preferably in the junior year, but no later than December of the senior year. Applications should be filed by November 30 for fall entry. The fall 2016 application fee was $60. Notifications are sent March 15. Applications are accepted on-line. **Transfer Students:** 3229 transfer students enrolled in 2015-2016. For minimum requirements, transfer students must have earned 90 quarter units at the previous college and have completed preparatory courses for the selected major. Most students selected present a GPA of 3.0 or better. 68 of 180 credits required for the bachelor's degree must be completed at UCLA. **International Students:** There are 1498 international students enrolled. They must take the TOEFL with a minimum score of 550 on the paper-based TOEFL (PBT) or 83 on the Internet-based version (iBT), or take the IELTS, scoring at least 7. They must also take the SAT or ACT.

ADMISSIONS: 23% of the 2016-2017 applicants were accepted. The SAT scores for the 2016-2017 freshman class were: Critical Reading-- 8% below 500, 24% between 500 and 599, 45% between 600 and 699, and 23% between 700 and 800. Math-- 6% below 500, 16% between 500 and 599, 36% between 600 and 699, and 42% between 700 and 800. Writing-- 6% below 500, 21% between 500 and 599, 40% between 600 and 699, and 33% between 700 and 800. The ACT scores were 8% below 12, 13% between 12 and 17, 16% between 18 and 23, 14% between 24 and 29, and 53% above 30. **Admissions Contact:** Gary Clark, Director of Admissions. Email: *ugadm@admissions@ucla.edu* Web: *www.ucla.edu*

FINANCIAL AID: In 2016-2017, 56% of all full-time freshmen and 55% of continuing full-time students received some form of financial aid. 54% of all full-time freshmen and 52% of continuing full-time students received need-based aid. The average freshman award was $19,561. Need-based scholarships or need-based grants averaged $16,080; need-based self-help aid (loans and jobs) averaged $6,144; non-need-based athletic scholarships averaged $18,580; and other non-need-based awards and non-need-based scholarships averaged $5,493. The average financial indebtedness of the 2016 graduate was $18,203. The college's own financial statement is required. The deadline for filing freshman financial aid applications for fall entry is March 2.

UNIVERSITY OF CALIFORNIA AT RIVERSIDE D-5

www.ucr.edu

Riverside, CA 92521 (951) 827-4531

Fax: (951) 827-6346	Email: admissions@ucr.edu
Full-time: 8817 men, 9380 women	**Faculty:** 751; I, +$
Part-time: 248 men, 167 women	**Ph.D.s:** 98%
Graduate: 1470 men, 1206 women	**Student/Faculty:** 21 to 1
Year: quarters, summer session	**Tuition:** $15,210 ($41,832)
Room & Board: $16,400	**Freshman Class:** 34816 applied, 20973 accepted, 4201 enrolled
SAT CR/M/W: 540/540/580 **ACT:** 23	**CEEB CODE:** 4839
Application Deadline: November 30	**COMPETITIVE+**

University of California at Riverside, founded in 1954, is a public research university with undergraduate and graduate programs in engineering, humanities, arts, social sciences, natural and agricultural sciences, medicine, public policy, health sciences, education and business. The figures in the above capsule and in this profile are in a recent year. There are 3 undergraduate schools and 9 graduate schools. In addition to regional accreditation, UCR has baccalaureate program accreditation with AACSB, ABET, and ACS. The 1200-acre campus is in a suburban area 50 miles east of Los Angeles. Including any residence halls, there are 668 buildings.

STUDENT LIFE: 98% of undergraduates are from California. Others are from 35 states, 43 foreign countries, and Canada. 92% are from public schools. 9% are Foreign; 6% African American; 35% Asian American; 32% Hispanic; 2% race unknown; 17% White; 1% American Indian/Alaska Native. **Female To Male Ratio:** 1.0:1. The average age of freshmen is 18; all undergraduates, 20.3. 11% do not continue beyond their first year; 89% remain to graduate. **Housing:** 6045 students can be accommodated in college housing, which includes coed dorms, on-campus apartments, and married student housing. In addition, there are honors houses, special-interest houses, and international village. On-campus housing is guaranteed for the freshman year only, and is available on a first-come, first-served basis, and is available on a lottery system for upperclassmen. 70% of students commute. All students may keep cars.

FACULTY/CLASSROOMS: 65% of faculty are male; 35% are female. All teach undergraduates, and 74% do research. No introductory courses are taught by graduate students.

PROGRAMS OF STUDY: UCR confers B.A., and B.S. degrees. Master's and doctoral degrees are also awarded. Bachelor's degrees are awarded in AGRICULTURE (soil science), BIOLOGICAL SCIENCE (biochemistry, biology/biological science, cell biology, entomology, genetics, microbiology, neurosciences, plant genetics, and plant pathology), BUSINESS (business administration and management, business economics, and management science), COMMUNICATIONS AND THE ARTS (art history, art, art history and appreciation, Chinese, classical languages, comparative literature, creative writing, dance, dramatic arts, English, film arts, French, German, Germanic languages and literature, Japanese, languages, linguistics, music, Russian, Russian languages and literature, Spanish, theatre arts, and visual and performing arts), COMPUTER AND PHYSICAL SCIENCE (chemistry, computer science, geology, geophysics and seismology, geoscience, information sciences and systems, mathematics, physical sciences, physics, and statistics), EDUCATION (mathematics education), ENGINEERING AND ENVIRONMENTAL DESIGN (bioengineering, chemical engineering, electrical/electronics engineering, engineering and applied science, engineering mechanics, environmental engineering, environmental science, materials engineering, and mechanical engineering), HEALTH PROFESSIONS (biomedical science), SOCIAL SCIENCE (African American studies, anthropology, Asian/American studies, Asian/Oriental studies, classical/ancient civilization, economics, ethnic studies, history, humanities and social science, interdisciplinary studies, Latin American studies, liberal arts/general studies, Mexican-American/Chicano studies, Middle Eastern studies, Native American studies, philosophy, political science/government, psychology, religion, religious education, Russian and Slavic studies, sociology, and women's studies). Engineering is the strongest academically. Business administration, biology, and psychology have the largest enrollments.

ACTIVITIES: 1% of men belong to 6 local and 14 national fraternities; 1% of women belong to 8 local and 12 national sororities. There are 470 groups on campus, including art, bagpipe, cheerleading, computers, dance, drama, ethnic, film, honors, international, LGBT, literary magazine, musical theater, newspaper, pep band, photography, political, professional, radio and TV, social, social service, and student government. Popular campus events include HEAT Festival, Block Party and Spring Splash. **Sports:** There are 7 intercollegiate sports for men and 8 for women, and 8 intramural sports for men and 9 for women. UCR competes in the NCAA Division I. The campus has a heated Olympic-size pool, student recreation center with a weight room/fitness center, indoor multi-use courts, racquetball courts, squash court, fitness studios, tennis courts, roller hockey rink, challenge ropes course, and a jogging trail. **Graduates:** From July 1, 2015 to June 30, 2016, 4196 bachelor's degrees were awarded. The most popular majors were business/marketing (15%), psychology (10%), and biology (7%). 248 companies recruited on campus in 2015-2016. In an average class, 2% graduate in 3 years or less, 42% graduate in 4 years or less, 62% graduate in 5 years or less, and 69% graduate in 6 years or less. Of the 2015 graduating class, 39% were enrolled in graduate school within 6 months of graduation, and 78% were employed.

SERVICES: Counseling and information services are available, as is tutoring in most subjects, and a reader service for the blind. There are also study skills classes, preparation sessions for graduate entrance exams, study groups, individual counseling and lab work, and speed-reading classes. **Library/Resources:** The 4 libraries contain 3.2 million volumes, 2.3 million microform items, and subscribe to 97,678 periodicals including electronic. Computerized library services include interlibrary loans, database searching, Internet access, and Wi-Fi capability. Special learning facilities include an art gallery, radio station, Culver Center for the Arts, Sweeney Art Gallery, UCR/California Museum of Photography, College of Engineering-Center for Environmental Research and Technology, Air Pollution Research Center, Agricultural Research Institute for Deserts, Citrus Variety Collection, Agricultural Experiment Station, Botanic Gardens, Entomology Museum, George E. Brown Salinity Lab, and Core Instrumentation Facility for genomics research. **Physically Challenged Students:** Facilities include wheelchair ramps, elevators, special parking, specially equipped restrooms, special class scheduling, lowered drinking fountains, lowered telephones, special housing, and automatic doors. **Special:** Internships, work-study programs with various agencies and employers on and off campus, study abroad in 35 countries, and a semester in Washington are available. The campus also has a School of Medicine and a School of Public Policy. Student-dual majors, opportunities for undergraduate research, and pass/fail options in elective subjects are possible. Grants are available for research, fieldwork, or other creative activity. Academic internships and co-op programs are offered in all majors. There are 14 national honor societies, Phi Beta Kappa, a freshman honors program, and 13 departmental honors programs. **Visiting:** There are regularly scheduled orientations for prospective students, Discover Days, Highlander Day: College Week Live Virtual UCR Day, Chancellor's receptions in the spring, tours are available throughout the year on weekdays and some Saturdays. There are guides for informal visits, visitors may sit in on classes, and stay overnight. To schedule a visit, contact Visitor Relations Manager at (951) 827-4531. **Campus Safety and Security:** Measures include 24-hour foot and vehicle patrol, emergency notification system, self-defense education, and security escort services. There are emergency telephones, lighted pathways/sidewalks, off campus point to point shuttle service; 24/7 University of California police department.

REQUIREMENTS: The SAT or ACT is required, as is the ACT Optional Writing test. In addition, the minimum GPA varies depending on SAT or ACT scores. Candidates for admission should have completed 4 years of English, 3 of math, and 2 of foreign language, history, science, 1 visual/performing arts and electives. UCR requires applicants to be in the upper 25% of their class. AP credits are accepted. Students must demonstrate proficiency in English and a knowledge of American history and institutions. A total of 180 quarter credit hours with a minimum GPA of 2.0 is required in order to graduate. The number of hours in the major varies. All students must complete a 1-year sequence in English composition, in computers, math, or statistics, and in concepts/issues of ethnicity. There are breadth requirements in humanities, social sciences, and natural sciences/math. For all students; the number of units/courses in each group depends on the student's college and major. A thesis is required for honors program students. **Procedure:** Freshmen are admitted fall. Entrance exams should be taken by December of the senior year. Applications should be filed by November 30 for fall entry, along with a $70 fee. Notifications are sent February 1. 3748 applicants were on the 2016 waiting list; 1412 were admitted. Applications are accepted on-line. **Transfer Students:** 1235 transfer students enrolled in 2015-2016. Transfer students applying to selecting majors must meet major preparation and GPA requirements for that major. 45 of 180 credits required for the bachelor's degree must be completed at UCR. **International Students:** There are 586 international students enrolled. The school actively recruits these students. They must take the TOEFL with a minimum score of 550 on the paper-based TOEFL (PBT) or 80 on the Internet-based version (iBT), take the IELTS. They must also take the SAT or ACT.

ADMISSIONS: 60% of the 2016-2017 applicants were accepted. The SAT scores for the 2016-2017 freshman class were: Critical Reading-- 26% below 500, 45% between 500 and 599, 22% between 600 and 699, and 6% between 700 and 800. Math-- 17% below 500, 39% between 500 and 599, 34% between 600 and 699, and 9% between 700 and 800. Writing-- 26% below 500, 48% between 500 and 599, 23% between 600 and 699, and 2% between 700 and 800. The ACT scores were 27% below 12, 29% between 12 and 17, 25% between 18 and 23, 10% between 24 and 29, and 9% above 30. 100% of the current freshmen were in the top fifth of their class. **Admissions Contact:** Emily Engelschall, Director, Undergraduate Admissions. Email: *admissions@ucr.edu* Web: *www.ucr.edu*

FINANCIAL AID: In 2016-2017, 89% of all full-time freshmen and 85% of continuing full-time students received some form of financial aid. 77% of all full-time freshmen and 78% of continuing full-time students received need-based aid. 27% of undergraduate students work part-time. The FAFSA code is 001316. The priority date for freshman financial aid applications for fall entry is March 2. The deadline for filing freshman financial aid applications for fall entry is May 1.

UNIVERSITY OF CALIFORNIA AT SANTA BARBARA C-5

www.ucsb.edu

Santa Barbara, CA 93106	(805) 893-2881
Fax: (805) 893-8779	**Email:** ucinfo@applyucsupport.net
Full-time: 9065 men, 10,011 women	**Faculty:** 885; I, ++$
Part-time: 172 men, 114 women	**Ph.D.s:** 100%
Graduate: 1611 men, 1252 women	**Student/Faculty:** 17 to 1
Year: quarters, summer session	**Tuition:** $14,022 ($35,767)
Room & Board: $15,069	**Freshman Class:** 62427 applied, 24813 accepted, 4624 enrolled
SAT CR/M/W: 610/640/630 **ACT:** 27	**CEEB CODE:** 4835
Application Deadline: November 30	**HIGHLY COMPETITIVE**

University of California at Santa Barbara, founded in 1891, is a public liberal arts institution offering programs in creative studies, engineering, and letters and science. The figures given in the above capaule and in this profile are approximate. There are 3 undergraduate schools and 1 graduate school. In addition to regional accreditation, UCSB has baccalaureate program accreditation with ABET, CSAB, APA, and NASD. The 1055-acre campus is in a suburban area 10 miles north of Santa Barbara. Including any residence halls, there are 399 buildings.

STUDENT LIFE: 93% of undergraduates are from California. Others are from 48 states, 80 foreign countries, and Canada. 86% are from public schools. 40% are White; 4% African American; 4% Foreign; 24% Asian American; 24% Hispanic; 1% American Indian/Alaska Native. **Female To Male Ratio:** 1.0:1. The average age of freshmen is 18; all undergraduates, 20. 9% do not continue beyond their first year; 91% remain to graduate. **Housing:** 6300 students can be accommodated in college housing, which includes coed dorms, on-campus apartments, off-campus apartments, and married student housing. In addition, there are special-interest houses. On-campus housing is guaranteed for the freshman year only, and is available on a first-come, and first-served basis. 66% of students commute. All students may keep cars.

FACULTY/CLASSROOMS: 63% of faculty are male; 37% are female. All teach undergraduates, and do research. No introductory courses are taught by graduate students. The average class size in an introductory lecture is 100; in a laboratory is 17; and in a regular course is 40.

PROGRAMS OF STUDY: UCSB confers B.A., B.F.A., B.M. and B.S. degrees. Master's and doctoral degrees are also awarded. Bachelor's degrees are awarded in BIOLOGICAL SCIENCE (biochemistry, biology/biological science, cell biology, ecology, evolutionary biology, marine biology, microbiology, molecular biology, physiology, and zoology), BUSINESS (accounting), COMMUNICATIONS AND THE ARTS (art, art history and appreciation, Chinese, classics, communications, comparative literature, dance, dramatic arts, English, film arts, French, German, Germanic languages and literature, Japanese, linguistics, literature, music, music performance, music theory and composition, Portuguese, Slavic languages, and Spanish), COMPUTER AND PHYSICAL SCIENCE (actuarial science, chemistry, computer science, earth science, geology, geophysics and seismology, hydrology, mathematics, physics, and statistics), ENGINEERING AND ENVIRONMENTAL DESIGN (chemical engineering, computer engineering, electrical/electronics engineering, environmental science, and mechanical engineering), HEALTH PROFESSIONS (pharmacy), SOCIAL SCIENCE (African American studies, anthropology, Asian/American studies, Asian/Oriental studies, biopsychology, economics, geography, history, interdisciplinary studies, international studies, Islamic studies, Italian studies, Latin American studies, medieval studies, Mexican-American/Chicano studies, Middle Eastern studies, philosophy, political science/government, psychology, religion, sociology, and women's studies). Economics, biological science, and psychology have the largest enrollments.

ACTIVITIES: 8% of men belong to 20 national fraternities; 12% of

women belong to 24 national sororities. There are 455 groups on campus, including art, band, cheerleading, chess, choir, chorale, chorus, computers, dance, drama, environmental, ethnic, film, honors, international, jazz band, LGBT, literary magazine, musical theater, newspaper, opera, pep band, photography, political, professional, radio and TV, religious, social, social service, student government, symphony, and yearbook. Popular campus events include Club Day, Activities Fair, and UCEN Cultural Festival, and Exxtravaganza. **Sports:** There are 10 intercollegiate sports for men and 10 for women, and 19 intramural sports for men and 19 for women. Facilities include gyms, rock-climbing walls, indoor and outdoor basketball courts, outdoor tennis, sand volleyball courts, swimming pools, including 1 Olympic-sized pool, football/soccer stadium, softball diamond, baseball stadium, indoor/outdoor racquetball/squash courts, extensive playing fields, weight rooms, fitness center, and a synthetic track. **Graduates:** From July 1, 2015 to June 30, 2016, 5775 bachelor's degrees were awarded. The most popular majors were biological sciences (15%), economics (9%), and psychology (8%). 475 companies recruited on campus in 2015-2016. In an average class, 69% graduate in 4 years or less, 83% graduate in 5 years or less, and 86% graduate in 6 years or less.

SERVICES: Counseling and information services are available, as is tutoring in most subjects. There is a reader service for the blind, and remedial reading and writing. **Library/Resources:** The library contains 3.0 million volumes, 3.8 million microform items, and 5.5 million audio/video tapes/CDs/DVDs, and subscribes to 92,139 periodicals including electronic. Computerized library services include interlibrary loans, database searching, Internet access, and Wi-Fi capability. Special learning facilities include an art gallery, radio station, a language and learning lab, and numerous national and multicampus research institutes. **Physically Challenged Students:** All of the campus is accessible. Facilities include wheelchair ramps, elevators, special parking, specially equipped restrooms, special class scheduling, lowered drinking fountains, and lowered telephones. **Special:** A Washington semester, internships, cross-registration with all University of California campuses, study abroad in 34 countries, work-study programs, dual majors, student-designed majors, the B.A.-B.S. degree, and an accelerated degree program in electrical engineering are offered. There are 3 national honor societies, including Phi Beta Kappa, and a freshman honors program. **Visiting:** There are regularly scheduled orientations for prospective students, consisting of a campus film, an information session, and a walking tour of the campus led by a student guide. There are guides for informal visits, visitors may sit in on classes, and stay overnight. To schedule a visit, contact the Office of Relations at (805) 893-2485. **Campus Safety and Security:** Measures include 24-hour foot and vehicle patrol, emergency notification system, self-defense education, and security escort services. There are emergency telephones and lighted pathways/sidewalks.

REQUIREMENTS: The SAT is required. The ACT and ACT Writing Test are recommended, to SAT Subject tests in math and 1 other choice. Candidates for admission must have completed 4 years of English, 3 of math, and 2 each of foreign language, lab science, history/social science, and college-preparatory electives. An additional year each in foreign language, math, and science is recommended. A GPA of 3.3 is required. AP credits are accepted. Graduation requirements vary by college. Generally, students will take one third of their distribution in the major subject, one third in general education courses, and one third in elective courses. General subject requirements include courses in English, foreign language, science/math/technology, social sciences, civilization and thought, literature, and the arts. Specific subject requirements include 6 writing-intensive courses and 1 course each in non-Western culture, quantitative relationships, and ethnic studies. To graduate, students must earn at least 180 quarter units, with a minimum GPA of 2.0, and have completed the American History and Institutions requirement. **Procedure:** Freshmen are admitted in the fall. Entrance exams should be taken by December of the senior year. Applications should be filed by November 30 for fall entry, along with a $70 fee. Notifications are sent March 1. Applications are accepted on-line. **Transfer Students:** 1651 transfer students enrolled in 2015-2016. High school transcripts, college transcripts, and an essay or personal statement are required for all transfer applicants. Standardized test scores are required of all lower division transfers. An applicant must be in good standing at prior institution but no statement to this request is required. Preference is given to students who have completed 90 quarter (60 a semester) units and who transfer from community colleges. California residents should have a minimum 2.0 GPA in transferable course work; nonresidents, a 2.8 GPA. Students with fewer than 12 quarter or semester units of transferable course work must provide standardized test scores. 35 of 180 credits required for the bachelor's degree must be completed at UCSB. **International Students:** There are 552 international students enrolled. They must take the TOEFL with a minimum score of 550 on the paper-based (PBT) or 80 on the Internet-based version (iBT). They must also take the SAT or ACT.

ADMISSIONS: 40% of the 2016-2017 applicants were accepted. The SAT scores for the 2016-2017 freshman class were: Critical Reading-- 10% below 500, 32% between 500 and 599, 42% between 600 and 699, and 16% between 700 and 800. Math-- 6% below 500, 23% between 500 and 599, 45% between 600 and 699, and 27% between 700 and 800. Writing-- 6% below 500, 29% between 500 and 599, 45% between 600 and 699, and 19% between 700 and 800. The ACT scores were 7% below 12, 14% between 12 and 17, 21% between 18 and 23, 17% between 24 and 29, and 41% above 30. 100% of the current freshmen were in the top fifth of their class; 100% were in the top two fifths. **Admissions Contact:** Office of Admissions Email: *ucinfo@applyucsupport.net* Web: *www.ucsb.edu*

FINANCIAL AID: In 2016-2017, 62% of all full-time freshmen and 58% of continuing full-time students received some form of financial aid. 58% of all full-time freshmen and 53% of continuing full-time students received need-based aid. 19% of undergraduate students work part-time. UCSB is a member of CSS. The FAFSA code is 001320. The deadline for filing freshman financial aid applications for fall entry is March 2.

UNIVERSITY OF CALIFORNIA SAN DIEGO D-5
www.ucsd.edu

La Jolla, CA 92093 (858) 534-4831

Fax: (858) 534-5629
Email: admissionsreply@ucsd.edu
Full-time: 13,956 men, 12,634 women
Faculty: I, ++$
Ph.D.s: 98%
Part-time: n/av
Student/Faculty: 19 to 1
Graduate: n/av
Tuition: $17,605 ($44,287)
Year: quarters, summer session
Freshman Class: 84209 applied, 28285 accepted, 5660 enrolled
Room & Board: $12,545
SAT CR/M/W: 648/689/660 **ACT:** 30
CEEB CODE: 4836
Application Deadline: November 30
MOST COMPETITIVE

University of California San Diego, founded in 1960, is a public institution. There are 6 undergraduate schools and 5 graduate schools. In addition to regional accreditation, UC San Diego has baccalaureate program accreditation with ABET. The 2100-acre campus is in a suburban area just off the California coast in La Jolla, about 12 miles north of downtown San Diego. Including any residence halls, there are 772 buildings.

STUDENT LIFE: 77% of undergraduates are from California. Others are from 50 states, 92 foreign countries, and Canada. 88% are from public schools. 9% are race unknown; 6% Foreign; 46% Asian American; 21% White; 2% African American; 16% Hispanic. **Male To Female Ratio:** 1.1:1. The average age of freshmen is 18; all undergraduates, 21. 5% do not continue beyond their first year; 95% remain to graduate. **Housing:** 11500 students can be accommodated in college housing, which includes single-sex and coed dorms, on-campus apartments, and married student housing. In addition, there are language houses, special-interest houses, and identity housing. On-campus housing is available on a lottery system for upperclassmen. 57% of students commute. Upperclassmen may keep cars.

FACULTY/CLASSROOMS: 71% of faculty are male; 29% are female. No introductory courses are taught by graduate students. The average class size in an introductory lecture is 350 and in a laboratory is 40.

PROGRAMS OF STUDY: UC San Diego confers B.A., and B.S. degrees. Master's and doctoral degrees are also awarded. Bachelor's degrees are awarded in AGRICULTURE (environmental studies), BIOLOGICAL SCIENCE (biochemistry, bioinformatics, biology/biological science, biological sciences, biophysics, biotechnology, ecology, environmental biology, marine biology, marine science, microbiology, molecular biology, and physiology), BUSINESS (economics – statistics and management science), COMMUNICATIONS AND THE ARTS (art history, art, art history and appreciation, Chinese, classics, communications, dance, dramatic arts, English literature, Germanic languages and literature, Italian, Japanese, linguistics, literature, music, music history and appreciation, music technology, Russian, studio art, and visual and performing arts),

COMPUTER AND PHYSICAL SCIENCE (applied mathematics, applied physics, chemistry, computer science, earth science, environmental chemistry, information sciences and systems, mathematics, physical chemistry, and physics), EDUCATION (mathematics education and science education), ENGINEERING AND ENVIRONMENTAL DESIGN (aerospace engineering, aerospace studies, bioengineering, chemical engineering, chemical engineering technology, computer engineering, electrical/electronics engineering, engineering, engineering physics, environmental engineering, environmental engineering technology, environmental science, and mechanical engineering), HEALTH PROFESSIONS (global & public health sciences and human biology), SOCIAL SCIENCE (African studies, anthropology, cognitive science, economics, ethnic studies, French studies, gender studies, history, human development, international studies, Italian studies, Japanese studies, Judaic studies, Latin American studies, philosophy, political science/government, psychology, religion, religious studies, Russian and Slavic studies, sociology, Spanish studies, Third World studies, and urban studies). Sciences, engineering, and the arts are the strongest academically. Biology, economics, and psychology have the largest enrollments.

ACTIVITIES: 12% of men belong to 23 national fraternities; 12% of women belong to 20 national sororities. There are 600 groups on campus, including enterprise club, academic, art, band, cheerleading, chess, choir, chorale, chorus, computers, dance, debate, drama, environmental, ethnic, film, honors, international, jazz band, LGBT, literary magazine, musical theater, newspaper, opera, orchestra, pep band, photography, political, professional, radio and TV, religious, social, social service, student government, symphony, and yearbook. Popular campus events include Sun God Festival and Founders Day Celebration. **Sports:** There are 12 intercollegiate sports for men and 11 for women, and 11 intramural sports for men and 11 for women. Facilities include all-weather track, soccer and softball fields, athletic training facility, pools, spa, weight room, tennis courts, playing fields, and a golf driving range. An recreation complex features a arena, handball/racquetball courts, squash courts, weight-training facility, climbing wall, basketball, volleyball, and badminton courts. **Graduates:** From July 1, 2015 to June 30, 2016, 6000 bachelor's degrees were awarded. The most popular majors were social sciences, engineering technology, and biology.

SERVICES: Counseling and information services are available, as is tutoring in most subjects. There is a reader service for the blind. There is also the Office of Acadamic Support and Instructional Services (OASIS), and a writing lab. **Library/Resources:** The library contains 7.0 million volumes, 2.9 million microform items, and 87,625 audio/video tapes/CDs/DVDs, and subscribes to 42,000 periodicals including electronic. Computerized library services include interlibrary loans, database searching, Internet access, and Wi-Fi capability. Special learning facilities include an art gallery, radio station, TV station, aquarium-museum, supercomputer center, theater, and myriad labs. **Physically Challenged Students:** Facilities include wheelchair ramps, elevators, special parking, specially equipped restrooms, special class scheduling, lowered drinking fountains, and lowered telephones. Special accommodations, and administrative support services. **Special:** Internships in many fields, work-study, study abroad in more than 30 countries, and a Washington semester are offered. B.A.-B.S. degrees, an accelerated degree, dual majors, student-designed majors, and exchange programs with Dartmouth College, Spelman College, and Morehouse College are available. Nondegree study, credit for military experience, and pass/fail options are possible. There is a chapter of Phi Beta Kappa and a freshman honors program. **Visiting:** There are regularly scheduled orientations for prospective students. Triton Tour includes: 30-minute Admission Information Session, conducted by an Admissions Officer and a 90-minute walking tour led by current students. There are guides for informal visits and visitors may sit in on classes. To schedule a visit, contact Campus Tours at (858) 822-1455. **Campus Safety and Security:** Measures include 24-hour foot and vehicle patrol, emergency notification system, self-defense education, and security escort services. There are shuttle buses, emergency telephones, lighted pathways/sidewalks, Student safety awareness program, peer educators, and an on-campus police department.

REQUIREMENTS: The SAT or ACT are recommended. The ACT Optional Writing test is required. Students must submit scores from either: ACT plus Writing or SAT Reasoning Test with critical reading, math and writing; scores must be from same sitting. Recommended for engineering, biological or physical sciences majors: 2 SAT Subject Tests closely related to your major. Tests must be taken by December of senior year. A GPA of 3.0 is required. AP credits are accepted. Important factors in the admissions decision are advanced placement or honors courses, leadership record, and extracurricular activities record. Graduation requirements vary by undergraduate college but students must complete 180 to 184 total quarter units or 45 to 46 courses, with a minimum of 60 credit hours or 12 to 22 courses in the major. Students must maintain a minimum GPA of 2.0. **Procedure:** Freshmen are admitted in the fall. Entrance exams should be taken by December of the senior year. Applications should be filed by November 30 for fall entry, along with a $70 fee. Notifications are sent March 30. Applications are accepted on-line. **Transfer Students:** 2933 transfer students enrolled in 2015-2016. A minimum of 60 UC-transferable semester (90 quarter) units are required. In addition, students must complete the UC-transferable college courses below with a C grade or better in each course. Each course must be 3 semester (4-5 quarter) units. 2 English composition, 1 mathematical concepts and quantitative reasoning, 4 courses from at least 2 of the following: arts and humanities, physical and biological sciences, and social and behavioral sciences. UC San Diego requires a competitive GPA in UC-transferable courses and good academic standing. 36 of 180 credits required for the bachelor's degree must be completed at UC San Diego. **International Students:** They must take the TOEFL with a minimum score of 550 on the paper-based TOEFL (PBT) or 80 on the Internet-based version (iBT). They must also take the SAT or ACT.

ADMISSIONS: 34% of the 2016-2017 applicants were accepted. The SAT scores for the 2016-2017 freshman class were: Critical Reading-- 7% below 500, 32% between 500 and 599, 44% between 600 and 699, and 16% between 700 and 800. Math-- 3% below 500, 15% between 500 and 599, 33% between 600 and 699, and 49% between 700 and 800. **Admissions Contact:** Kris Wong Davis, Admission Director. Email: *admissionsreply@ucsd.edu* Web: *www.admissions.ucsd.edu*

FINANCIAL AID: In 2016-2017, 68% of continuing full-time students received some form of financial aid. 70% of undergraduate students work part-time. UC San Diego is a member of CSS. The state aid form is required. The FAFSA code is 001317. The deadline for filing freshman financial aid applications for fall entry is March 2.

UNIVERSITY OF CALIFORNIA, SANTA CRUZ B-3

www.ucsc.edu

Santa Cruz, CA 95064	(831) 459-4008 (831) 459-0111
Fax: (831) 459-4452	Email: admissions@ucsc.edu
Full-time: 7197 men, 8253 women	**Faculty:** I, +$
Part-time: 114 men, 131 women	**Ph.D.s:** 98%
Graduate: 818 men, 690 women	**Student/Faculty:** 18 to 1
Year: trimesters, summer session	**Tuition:** $13,398
Room & Board: $14,730	**Freshman Class:** 38640 applied, 20039 accepted, 3303 enrolled
SAT CR/M/W: 550/560/550 **ACT:** 24	**CEEB CODE:** 4860
Application Deadline: November 30	**COMPETITIVE+**

The University of California, Santa Cruz, is a public university, founded in 1965. UC Santa Cruz began as a showcase for progressive, cross-disciplinary undergraduate education, innovative teaching methods and contemporary architecture. Since then, it has evolved into a modern research university with a wide variety of undergraduate and graduate programs, while retaining its reputation for strong undergraduate support and political activism. The residential college system, consisting of 10 small colleges, combines the student support of a small college with the resources of a major university. There are 10 undergraduate schools and 1 graduate school. In addition to regional accreditation, UCSC has baccalaureate program accreditation with ABET. The campus is in a small town. Including any residence halls, there are 559 buildings.

STUDENT LIFE: 96% of undergraduates are from California. Others are from 46 states, 79 foreign countries, and Canada. 90% are from public schools. 37% are White; 30% Hispanic; 20% Asian American. **Female To Male Ratio:** 1.1:1. The average age of freshmen is 19; all undergraduates, 21. 9% do not continue beyond their first year; 75% remain to graduate. **Housing:** 8415 students can be accommodated in college housing, which includes single-sex and coed dorms, on-campus apartments, off-campus apartments, and married student housing. In addition, there are language houses, special-interest houses, and multicultural residence halls. On-campus housing is available on a lottery system for upperclassmen. 53% of students commute. Alcohol is not permitted. Upperclassmen may keep cars.

FACULTY/CLASSROOMS: 58% of faculty are male; 42% are female. All teach and do research. Graduate students teach 1% of introductory courses.

PROGRAMS OF STUDY: UCSC confers B.A., B.S. and B.M. degrees. Master's and doctoral degrees are also awarded. Bachelor's degrees are awarded in AGRICULTURE (environmental studies and plant science), BIOLOGICAL SCIENCE (biochemistry, bioinformatics, biology/biological science, cell biology, ecology, evolutionary biology, marine biology, molecular biology, and neurosciences), BUSINESS (business economics and international economics), COMMUNICATIONS AND THE ARTS (art, art history and appreciation, classical languages, dramatic arts, film arts, language arts, linguistics, literature, and music), COMPUTER AND PHYSICAL SCIENCE (chemistry, computer game design/development, computer science, earth science, geology, information sciences and systems, mathematics, and physics), ENGINEERING AND ENVIRONMENTAL DESIGN (computer engineering and electrical/electronics engineering), HEALTH PROFESSIONS (health science), SOCIAL SCIENCE (American studies, anthropology, community services, economics, German area studies, history, Italian studies, Latin American studies, law, philosophy, political science/government, psychology, sociology, and women's studies). Psychology, business management economics and biology have the largest enrollments.

ACTIVITIES: There are 157 groups on campus, including art, band, cheerleading, chess, choir, chorale, chorus, computers, dance, debate, drama, ethnic, film, honors, international, jazz band, LGBT, literary magazine, musical theater, newspaper, opera, orchestra, photography, political, professional, radio and TV, religious, social, social service, student government, and symphony. Popular campus events include Multicultural Festival and Martin Luther King Convocation. **Sports:** There are 5 intercollegiate sports for men and 7 for women, and 10 intramural sports for men and 6 for women. Facilities include a pool, playing fields, weight room, jogging track, gyms, fitness course, racquetball, tennis, basketball courts, and a fitness center. **Graduates:** From July 1, 2014 to June 30, 2015, 3958 bachelor's degrees were awarded. The most popular majors were biological and life sciences (16%), social sciences (15%), and psychology (13%). In an average class, 4% graduate in 3 years or less, 55% graduate in 4 years or less, 70% graduate in 5 years or less, and 74% graduate in 6 years or less.

SERVICES: Counseling and information services are available, as is tutoring in most subjects. There is a reader service for the blind. A learning center helps SAA/EOP students with math and writing skills. There is also a program to help any student who is having trouble with certain courses. **Library/Resources:** The 2 libraries contain 2.3 million volumes, 68,573 microform items, and 56,757 audio/video tapes/CDs/DVDs, and subscribe to 46,433 periodicals including electronic. Computerized library services include interlibrary loans, database searching, and Internet access. Special learning facilities include an art gallery, natural history museum, radio and TV station. Under the Agroecology Program, there is a farm, arboretum, marine lab, Seymour Marine Discovery Center, Lick Observatory on Mt. Hamilton, Silicon Valley Center, Digital Arts Research Center, Genome Bioinformatics Project, and a computer game design. **Physically Challenged Students:** 90% of the campus is accessible. Facilities include wheelchair ramps, elevators, special parking, specially equipped restrooms, special class scheduling, lowered drinking fountains, lowered telephones. Wheelchair lift-equipped transportation. **Special:** Cross-registration is possible with other University of California campuses, Hampshire College, the University of New Hampshire, and the University of New Mexico. UCSC also offers work-study, a Washington semester, internships in many arenas, study abroad in 34 countries, student-designed majors, dual majors, and a B.A.-B.S. degree in earth sciences, chemistry, and computer science. There is a chapter of Phi Beta Kappa and a freshman honors program. **Visiting:** There are regularly scheduled orientations for prospective students. There are guides for informal visits and visitors may sit in on classes. To schedule a visit, contact the Office of Admissions. **Campus Safety and Security:** Measures include 24-hour foot and vehicle patrol, emergency notification system, self-defense education, and security escort services. There are shuttle buses, emergency telephones, lighted pathways/sidewalks, a rape prevention program, seminars for residential staff, and guards at each entrance from 8 p.m. until dawn.

REQUIREMENTS: The SAT or ACT is required. The ACT Optional Writing test is also required. Applicants must be graduates of an accredited secondary school or have a GED certificate. They should have completed 15 academic credits, including 4 years of English, 3 years of math, and 2 years each of foreign language, history, lab science, visual or performing arts, and college preparatory electives. Auditions are required for music majors, and portfolios are required for art majors. All students must submit a personal statement. Nonresidents must meet additional requirements. A GPA of 2.8 is required. AP credits are accepted. Important factors in the admissions decision are advanced placement or honors courses, evidence of special talent, and extracurricular activities record. To graduate, all students must complete 36 full-credit courses (180 quarter units) with a minimum GPA of 2.0. Courses are required in arts, English, history, writing-intensive, U.S. ethnic minorities/non-Western society, humanities, math, sciences, and social sciences. They must satisfy university requirements in U.S. history and institutions and in English composition, the residence requirement, the core course, and a comprehensive exam or equivalent body of work, or a senior thesis. Particular college requirements and those of an approved major vary. All students must also satisfy each of the UCSC general education requirements with a course graded C or better. **Procedure:** Freshmen are admitted fall and winter. Entrance exams should be taken by December of the senior year. Applications should be filed by November 30 for fall entry, along with a $70 fee. Notifications are sent March 31. Applications are accepted on-line. **Transfer Students:** 1005 transfer students enrolled in 2014-2015. Applicants should have completed 84 quarter credits, with a GPA of 2.4 required for California residents and 2.8 for nonresidents, and all subject areas must be completed. No senior transfers are accepted. 35 of 180 credits required for the bachelor's degree must be completed at UCSC. **International Students:** There are 806 international students enrolled. They must take the TOEFL with a minimum score of 550 on the paper-based (PBT) or 83 on the Internet-based version (iBT). They must also take the SAT or ACT.

ADMISSIONS: 52% of the 2015-2016 applicants were accepted. The SAT scores for the 2015-2016 freshman class were: Critical Reading-- 27% below 500, 36% between 500 and 599, 29% between 600 and 699, and 8% between 700 and 800. Math-- 21% below 500, 34% between 500 and 599, 33% between 600 and 699, and 11% between 700 and 800. Writing-- 26% below 500, 38% between 500 and 599, 30% between 600 and 699, and 6% between 700 and 800. The ACT scores were 23% below 12, 21% between 12 and 17, 24% between 18 and 23, 12% between 24 and 29, and 18% above 30. 100% of the current freshmen were in the top fifth of their class; 100% were in the top two fifths. **Admissions Contact:** Michael Mc Cawley, Director of Admissions. E-Mail: *admissions@ucsc.edu* Web: *www.ucsc.edu*

FINANCIAL AID: In 2015-2016, 68% of continuing full-time students received some form of financial aid. The FAFSA is required. The priority date for freshman financial aid applications for fall entry is January 1. The deadline for filing freshman financial aid applications for fall entry is March 2.

UNIVERSITY OF LA VERNE — D-5

www.laverne.edu

La Verne, CA 91750	(909) 392-2800 (800) 876-4858
Fax: (909) 392-2714	Email: admission@laverne.edu
Full-time: 1130 men, 1643 women	Faculty: 245
Part-time: 41 men, 45 women	Ph.D.s: 81%
Graduate: 692 men, 1326 women	Student/Faculty: 13 to 1
Year: 4-1-4, summer session	Tuition: $39,900
Room & Board: $15,700	Freshman Class: 8179 applied, 3859 accepted, 724 enrolled
SAT CR/M/W: 520/520/510 ACT: 22	CEEB CODE: 4381
Application Deadline: February 1	COMPETITIVE

University of La Verne, founded in 1891, has been dedicated to the belief that a quality, values-based education enriches the human condition by engendering service, scholarly accomplishment, and professionalism. Though decades of growth have changed its appearance and reach, La Verne has retained its sense of purpose, seeking to provide students with individual attention to spark personal growth through intellectual challenge and development. The figures in the above capsule and in this profile are approximate. There are 3 undergraduate schools and 4 graduate schools. In addition to regional accreditation, La Verne has baccalaureate program accreditation with NCATE, CCTC, and CAATE. The 38-acre campus is in a suburban area on the eastern edge of Los Angeles County, some 30 miles from downtown Los Angeles. Including any residence halls, there are 35 buildings.

STUDENT LIFE: 96% of undergraduates are from California. Others are from 19 states, and 10 foreign countries. 7% are Asian American; 51% Hispanic; 5% African American; 5% Foreign; 4% two or more races; 26% White; 2% race unknown. **Female To Male Ratio:** 1.6:1. The average age of freshmen is 18; all undergraduates, 20. 13% do not continue beyond their first year; 59% remain to graduate. **Housing:** 837 students can be accommodated in college housing, which includes single-sex and coed dorms. In addition, there are special-interest houses, internatinal housing and theme housing. On-campus housing is available on a first-come, first-served basis, and is available on a lottery system for upperclassmen. Priority is given to out-of-town students. 69% of students commute. Alcohol is not permitted. All students may keep cars.

FACULTY/CLASSROOMS: 50% of faculty are male; 50% are female. No introductory courses are taught by graduate students. The average class size in an introductory lecture is 17 and in a regular course is 17.

PROGRAMS OF STUDY: La Verne confers B.A., and B.S. degrees. Associate, master's, and doctoral degrees are also awarded. Bachelor's degrees are awarded in BIOLOGICAL SCIENCE (biology/biological science and environmental biology), BUSINESS (accounting, business administration and management, business economics, electronic business, institutional management, and international business management), COMMUNICATIONS AND THE ARTS (art, art history and appreciation, broadcasting, communications, comparative literature, dramatic arts, English, French, German, journalism, music, photography, Spanish, and speech/debate/rhetoric), COMPUTER AND PHYSICAL SCIENCE (chemistry, computer science, mathematics, natural sciences, and physics), EDUCATION (athletic training and education), ENGINEERING AND ENVIRONMENTAL DESIGN (computer engineering and environmental science), HEALTH PROFESSIONS (health care administration), SOCIAL SCIENCE (anthropology, behavioral science, child psychology/development, criminology, history, international studies, liberal arts/general studies, paralegal studies, philosophy, physical fitness/movement, political science/government, psychology, public administration, religion, social science, and sociology). Business administration, natural science, and education are the strongest academically. Business administration, organizational management, and liberal studies have the largest enrollments.

ACTIVITIES: 8% of men belong to 1 local and 2 national fraternities; 12% of women belong to 2 local and 3 national sororities. There are 66 groups on campus, including art, band, choir, chorale, chorus, communications, computers, dance, debate, drama, environmental, ethnic, forensics, honors, international, jazz band, LGBT, literary magazine, musical theater, newspaper, pep band, photography, political, professional, radio and TV, religious, social, social service, and student government. Popular campus events include Homecoming, Club Day, and Greek Week. **Sports:** There are 11 intercollegiate sports for men and 9 for women. Facilities include a football field, soccer field, track, and an indoor gym with weight and fitness centers. **Graduates:** From July 1, 2015 to June 30, 2016, 549 bachelor's degrees were awarded. The most popular majors were business/marketing (21%), social sciences (16%), and psychology (14%). In an average class, 64% graduate in 6 years or less.

SERVICES: Counseling and information services are available, as is tutoring in most subjects. There is a reader service for the blind, and remedial math and writing. Students may use the Learning Enhancement Center or schedule tutoring free of charge. **Library/Resources:** The library contains 181,576 volumes, 1,068 microform items, and 1,640 audio/video tapes/CDs/DVDs, and subscribes to 37,287 periodicals including electronic. Computerized library services include interlibrary loans, database searching, Internet access, and Wi-Fi capability. Special learning facilities include an art gallery, natural history museum, radio station, TV station, a theater, archeology lab, and nuclear magnetic resonance (NMR) facility. **Physically Challenged Students:** Facilities include wheelchair ramps, elevators, special parking, specially equipped restrooms, lowered drinking fountains, and lowered telephones. **Special:** La Verne offers study abroad programs, work-study programs, student-designed majors, exchange student programs (domestic) distance learning and double major, liberal arts/career combination, and accelerated programs for adults. There are 9 national honor societies and a freshman honors program. **Visiting:** There are regularly scheduled orientations for prospective students, Student visits include campus tours, faculty and student panels, and meals. There are guides for informal visits, visitors may sit in on classes, and stay overnight. To schedule a visit, contact the Admissions Office. **Campus Safety and Security:** Measures include 24-hour foot and vehicle patrol, emergency notification system, and security escort services. There are shuttle buses, emergency telephones, lighted pathways/sidewalks, and controlled access to dorms/residences.

REQUIREMENTS: The ACT Optional Writing test is required. The SAT or ACT is recommended. Applicants must be graduates of an accredited secondary school. To apply for admission to the university, the following documents must be submitted to the Office of Admission: application for admission and application fee (using the La Verne Application for Admission or the Common Application), personal statement, high school transcripts, SAT I or ACT test scores, letter of recommendation. AP and CLEP credits are accepted. Important factors in the admissions decision are leadership record, advanced placement or honors courses, personality/intangible qualities, extracurricular activities record, geographical diversity, and recommendations by school officials. 128 semester hours, 44 must be taken at La Verne. At least 16 semester hours of the last 32 must be taken at La Verne. The La Verne Experience integrates curricular, co-curricular, and community engagement activities for traditional undergraduates and spans throughout their four years at La Verne. **Procedure:** Freshmen are admitted fall and spring. Entrance exams should be taken during the junior or senior year. There are deferred admissions and rolling admissions plans. Applications should be filed by February 1 for fall entry; December 1 for spring entry, along with a $50 fee. Notifications are sent December 1. Applications are accepted on-line. **Transfer Students:** 175 transfer students enrolled in 2015-2016. Transfer requirements include: 28 college semester units completed upon enrollment at La Verne, 2.7 GPA, College-level English and college-level math (typically college algebra or statistics or pre-calculus and higher). Students may enroll in the fall, April 1, and spring, December 1. 44 of 128 credits required for the bachelor's degree must be completed at La Verne. **International Students:** There are 123 international students enrolled. The school actively recruits these students. They must take the TOEFL with a minimum score of 550 on the paper-based TOEFL (PBT) or 80 on the Internet-based version (iBT), the Comprehensive English Language Test, and the college's own test, SAT critical reading score of 550, a minimum score of 6.5 on IELTS. They must also take the SAT or ACT.

ADMISSIONS: 47% of the 2016-2017 applicants were accepted. The SAT scores for the 2016-2017 freshman class were: Critical Reading-- 39% below 500, 48% between 500 and 599, 12% between 600 and 699, and 1% between 700 and 800. Math-- 37% below 500, 45% between 500 and 599, 17% between 600 and 699, and 1% between 700 and 800. Writing-- 44% below 500, 44% between 500 and 599, 11% between 600 and 699, and 1% between 700 and 800. The ACT scores were 3% between 12 and 17, 58% between 18 and 23, 34% between 24 and 29, and 5% above 30. 54% of the current freshmen were in the top fifth of their class; 86% were in the top two fifths. 3 freshmen graduated first in their class. **Admissions Contact:** Ana Liza V. Zell, Associate Dean of Undergraduate Admissions. Email: *admission@laverne.edu* Web: *www.laverne.edu*

FINANCIAL AID: In 2016-2017, 86% of all full-time freshmen and 83% of continuing full-time students received some form of financial aid. 82% of all full-time freshmen and 77% of continuing full-time students received need-based aid. The average freshman award was $34,418. Need-based scholarships or need-based grants averaged $11,116; need-based self-help aid (loans and jobs) averaged $3,904; non-need-based athletic scholarships averaged $20,998; and $3,749 from other forms of aid. The average financial indebtedness of the 2016 graduate was $30,844. The state aid form, and the Cal Grant Application if available are required. The FAFSA code is 001216. The priority date for freshman financial aid applications for fall entry is March 2.

UNIVERSITY OF REDLANDS E-5

www.redlands.edu

Redlands, CA 92373 (909) 335-4074
(800) 455-5064

Fax: (909) 335-4089 **Email: admissions@redlands.edu**

Full-time: 975 men, 1375 women	**Faculty:** IIA, ++$
Part-time: 10 men, 15 women	**Ph.D.s:** 86%
Graduate: 30 men, 20 women	**Student/Faculty:** n/av
Year: 4-1-4	**Tuition:** $46,720
Room & Board: $13,480	**Freshman Class:** n/av
SAT or ACT: required	**CEEB CODE:** 4848
Application Deadline: January 15	**VERY COMPETITIVE**

University of Redlands, founded in 1907, is a private institution that offers programs in liberal and fine arts, business, and teacher preparation. The figures in the above capsule and in this profile are approximate. There are 2 undergraduate schools and 4 graduate schools. In addition to regional accreditation, Redlands has baccalaureate program accreditation with WASC. The 160-acre campus is in a suburban area 60 miles east of Los Angeles. Including any residence halls, there are 86 buildings.

STUDENT LIFE: 71% of undergraduates are from California. Others are from 45 states, 8 foreign countries, and Canada. 60% are White; 6% Asian American; 2% African American; 12% Hispanic; 1% American Indian/Alaska Native; 1% Foreign. **Female To Male Ratio:** 1.4:1. The average age of freshmen is 18; all undergraduates, 20. 15% do not continue beyond their first year; 60% remain to graduate. **Housing:** 1621 students can be accommodated in college housing, which includes single-sex and coed dorms, on-campus apartments, and off-campus apartments. In addition, there are honors houses, special-interest houses, fraternity houses, and sorority houses. On-campus housing is guaranteed for all 4 years. 70% of students live on campus. All students may keep cars.

FACULTY/CLASSROOMS: 48% of faculty are male; 52% are female. All teach undergraduates. No introductory courses are taught by graduate students. The average class size in an introductory lecture is 20; in a laboratory is 10; and in a regular course is 12.

PROGRAMS OF STUDY: Redlands confers B.A., B.S. and B.Mus. degrees. Master's degrees are also awarded. Bachelor's degrees are awarded in AGRICULTURE (environmental studies), BIOLOGICAL SCIENCE (biochemistry and biology/biological science), BUSINESS (accounting and business administration and management), COMMUNICATIONS AND THE ARTS (art, creative writing, dramatic arts, English, English literature, French, German, music, Spanish, and studio art), COMPUTER AND PHYSICAL SCIENCE (chemistry, computer science, information sciences and systems, mathematics, and physics), EDUCATION (music education), ENGINEERING AND ENVIRONMENTAL DESIGN (environmental science), SOCIAL SCIENCE (anthropology, Asian/Oriental studies, economics, history, interdisciplinary studies, international relations, liberal arts/general studies, philosophy, political science/government, psychology, religion, and sociology). Liberal arts is the strongest academically. Business has the largest enrollment.

ACTIVITIES: 3% of men belong to 6 local fraternities; 6% of women belong to 5 local sororities. There are 105 groups on campus, including art, band, cheerleading, chess, choir, chorale, chorus, dance, debate, drama, drill team, ethnic, film, honors, international, jazz band, LGBT, literary magazine, musical theater, newspaper, opera, orchestra, pep band, photography, political, professional, radio and TV, religious, social, social service, student government, symphony, and yearbook. Popular campus events include Mayfest, Multicultural Festival, and Feast of Lights. **Sports:** There are 10 intercollegiate sports for men and 10 for women, and 7 intramural sports for men and 7 for women. Facilities include a fitness center, an aquatic center, a football stadium, tennis courts, and baseball, softball, soccer, and lacrosse fields.

SERVICES: Counseling and information services are available, as is tutoring in every subject. There is a reader service for the blind. **Library/ Resources:** The library contains 421,219 volumes, 317,465 microform items, and 6,091 audio/video tapes/CDs/DVDs, and subscribes to 12,800 periodicals including electronic. Computerized library services include interlibrary loans, database searching, and Internet access. Special learning facilities include an art gallery, radio station, language lab, computer center, and a geographic information systems lab. **Physically Challenged Students:** 25% of the campus is accessible. Facilities include wheelchair ramps, elevators, special parking, specially equipped restrooms, special class scheduling, lowered drinking fountains, and lowered telephones. **Special:** Cross-registration with sister colleges, various internships, and study abroad in 50 countries are offered. A Washington semester, a Sacramento program, various work-study programs, B.A.-B.S. degrees, a liberal studies degree, dual majors, and accelerated degree programs are available. Students may pursue nondegree study, take advantage of pass/ fail options, and receive credit for life or work experience. At the Johnston Center for Integrative Studies, students design their own majors and courses of study. There are 4 national honor societies, Phi Beta Kappa, a freshman honors program, and 23 departmental honors programs. **Visiting:** There are regularly scheduled orientations for prospective students, including campus tours on Saturdays during the school year, interviews with counselors, department heads, and coaches, and sitting in on classes. There are guides for informal visits, visitors may sit in on classes, and stay overnight. To schedule a visit, contact the Admissions office. **Campus Safety and Security:** Measures include 24-hour foot and vehicle patrol, self-defense education, and security escort services. There are shuttle buses, emergency telephones, lighted pathways/sidewalks, and safety whistles.

REQUIREMENTS: The SAT or ACT is required. Applicants should complete at least 16 credits in academic areas, including 4 years of English, 3 years of math, up to and including Algebra II, and 2 to 3 years of foreign language, sciences, and social studies. AP and CLEP credits are accepted. Important factors in the admissions decision are advanced placement or honors courses, leadership record, and personality/ intangible qualities. Requirements for graduation vary according to the degree and major. Students must complete at least 128 units with at least 32 in residence and maintain a minimum GPA of 2.0. Students pursuing a B.S. degree must fulfill an additional field requirement or a minor. A comprehensive exam is required for some programs. A liberal arts core curriculum, first-year seminar, community service, and participation in 2 May terms are required. **Procedure:** Freshmen are admitted fall and spring. Entrance exams should be taken prior to application. There are deferred admissions and rolling admissions plans. Early decision applications should be filed by November 15; regular applications, by January 15 for fall entry. The fall 2016 application fee was $45. Applications are accepted on-line. **Transfer Students:** The SAT or the ACT may be required of transfer applicants, depending on how many units are accepted. 32 of 128 credits required for the bachelor's degree must be completed at Redlands. **International Students:** The school actively recruits these students. They must take the TOEFL. They must also take the SAT or ACT.

Admissions Contact: Paul M. Driscoll, Dean of Admissions. Email: *admissions@redlands.edu* Web: *www.redlands.edu*

FINANCIAL AID: The college's own financial statement, and the GPA verification form for California residents are required. The FAFSA code is 001322. Check with the school for current application deadlines.

UNIVERSITY OF SAN DIEGO — D-5

www.sandiego.edu

San Diego, CA 92110	**(619) 260-4506** **(800) 248-4873**
Fax: (619) 260-6836	**Email: admissions@sandiego.edu**
Full-time: 2527 men, 2972 women	**Faculty:** 319; I, ++$
Part-time: 100 men, 112 women	**Ph.D.s:** 95%
Graduate: 1135 men, 1662 women	**Student/Faculty:** 15 to 1
Year: 4-1-4, summer session	**Tuition:** $46,140
Room & Board: $12,302	**Freshman Class:** 14413 applied, 7406 accepted, 1133 enrolled
SAT CR/M/W: 600/610/600 **ACT:** 28	**CEEB CODE:** 4849
Application Deadline: December 15	**VERY COMPETITIVE+**

University of San Diego, founded in 1949, is a private, Catholic liberal arts university. There are 3 undergraduate schools and 8 graduate schools. In addition to regional accreditation, USD has baccalaureate program accreditation with AACSB, ABET, and NCATE. The 180-acre campus is in an urban area 5 miles north of downtown San Diego. Including any residence halls, there are 85 buildings.

STUDENT LIFE: 62% of undergraduates are from California. Others are from 49 states, 62 foreign countries, and Canada. 58% are from public schools. 51% are White; 19% Hispanic; 9% Foreign; 8% Asian American; 6% two or more races; 3% African American; 3% race unknown; 1% American Indian/Alaska Native. 43% are Catholic; 29% claim no religious affiliation; 20% Protestant. **Female To Male Ratio:** 1.3:1. The average age of freshmen is 18; all undergraduates, 20. 13% do not continue beyond their first year; 79% remain to graduate. **Housing:** 2675 students can be accommodated in college housing, which includes single-sex and coed dorms and on-campus apartments. In addition, there are special-interest houses. On-campus housing is available on a first-come, first-served basis, and is available on a lottery system for upperclassmen. 56% of students commute. All students may keep cars.

FACULTY/CLASSROOMS: 51% of faculty are male; 49% are female. No introductory courses are taught by graduate students. The average class size in a laboratory is 16 and in a regular course is 22.

PROGRAMS OF STUDY: USD confers B.A., B.A./B.S., B.Acc. and

B.B.A. degrees. Master's and doctoral degrees are also awarded. Bachelor's degrees are awarded in AGRICULTURE (environmental studies), BIOLOGICAL SCIENCE (biochemistry, biology/biological science, biophysics, and marine science), BUSINESS (accounting, business administration and management, business economics, finance, international business management, marketing management, and real estate), COMMUNICATIONS AND THE ARTS (art history, art and design, communications, English, French, music, Spanish, theatre arts, and visual and performing arts), COMPUTER AND PHYSICAL SCIENCE (chemistry, computer science, mathematics, and physics), ENGINEERING AND ENVIRONMENTAL DESIGN (electrical/electronics engineering, industrial engineering, and mechanical engineering), SOCIAL SCIENCE (anthropology, architectural studies, behavioral science, economics, ethnic studies, history, humanities, international relations, Italian studies, liberal arts/general studies, philosophy, political science/government, psychology, sociology, and theological studies). Business administration, finance and communication studies have the largest enrollments.

ACTIVITIES: 25% of men belong to 9 national fraternities; 32% of women belong to 9 national sororities. There are 165 groups on campus, including sports and outreach/diversity clubs, academic, cheerleading, choir, chorale, dance, debate, drama, environmental, ethnic, film, honors, international, LGBT, musical theater, newspaper, pep band, political, professional, radio and TV, religious, social, social service, and student government. Popular campus events include Involvement Fair, International Student Organization Expo, Multicultural Night, Gender Expression Supreme Drag Superstar, Greek Week, Changemaker Fest. **Sports:** There are 8 intercollegiate sports for men and 9 for women, and 10 intramural sports for men and 10 for women. Facilities include a sports center, football and soccer stadium, tennis courts, swimming pools, baseball facility, and an aquatic center. **Graduates:** From July 1, 2015 to June 30, 2016, 1345 bachelor's degrees were awarded. The most popular majors were finance (11%), business administration (9%), and communications (8%). 221 companies recruited on campus in 2015-2016. In an average class, 66% graduate in 4 years or less, 77% graduate in 5 years or less, and 78% graduate in 6 years or less. Of the 2015 graduating class, 15% were enrolled in graduate school within 6 months of graduation, and 99% were employed.

SERVICES: Counseling and information services are available, as is tutoring in most subjects. **Library/Resources:** Computerized library services include interlibrary loans, database searching, Internet access, and Wi-Fi capability. Special learning facilities include an art gallery, radio station, TV station, media center, child development center, and a greenhouse. **Physically Challenged Students:** 85% of the campus is accessible. Facilities include wheelchair ramps, elevators, special parking, specially equipped restrooms, lowered drinking fountains. Individual needs can be accommodated. **Special:** A B.A.-B.S. degree is offered in electrical, industrial and mechanical engineering. Internships in all disciplines, study abroad in over 30 countries and work-study programs on campus are available. Undergraduate research is a focus and available in many disciplines. The Washington Center Academic Seminar takes place each January in Washington, DC. The Department of Political Science and International Relations offers an intersession course (PS434) which enables students to earn 3 units for attending the seminar. There are 22 national honor societies, Phi Beta Kappa, and a freshman honors program. **Visiting:** There are regularly scheduled orientations for prospective students, tours and information sessions offered by the Admissions Office Monday through Friday and most Saturdays from November through April. There are guides for informal visits, visitors may sit in on classes, and stay overnight. To schedule a visit, contact the Undergraduate Admissions Office. **Campus Safety and Security:** Measures include 24-hour foot and vehicle patrol, emergency notification system, self-defense education, and security escort services. There are shuttle buses, emergency telephones, lighted pathways/sidewalks, and controlled access to dorms/residences.

REQUIREMENTS: Applicants should present a well-balanced secondary school program of college preparatory courses in English, foreign language, math, laboratory science, history, and social science. Both the content of the academic program as well as the quality of performance is considered. In addition, SAT/ACT results are used to broaden understanding of the applicant's potential. Participation in extracurricular activities at the school and in the community or church is taken into consideration in the admission decision. AP and CLEP credits are accepted. Important factors in the admissions decision are advanced placement or honors courses, parents or siblings attended your school, and personality/intangible qualities. All students must take 124 credit hours,including 36 to 72 in their major, while maintaining a minimum GPA of 2.0. Distribution requirements include 9 units each of religious studies and humanities and fine arts, 6 each of philosophy, natural sciences, and social sciences, 3 or 4 of math, 3 of composition and literature, 3 semesters of foreign language., as well as 3 units upper division writing and 3 units in diversity of the human experience. **Procedure:** Freshmen are admitted fall, spring, and summer. Applications should be filed by December 15 for fall entry; October 1 for spring entry, along with a $55 fee. 1756 applicants were on the 2016 waiting list; 626 were admitted. Applications are accepted on-line. **Transfer Students:** 504 transfer students enrolled in 2015-2016. Transfer students must have a minimum GPA of 3.0 and have earned 24 credit hours. 30 of 124 credits required for the bachelor's degree must be completed at USD. **International Students:** There are 537 international students enrolled. The school actively recruits these students. They must take the TOEFL with a minimum score of 550 on the paper-based TOEFL (PBT) or 80 on the Internet-based version (iBT). They must also take the SAT or ACT.

ADMISSIONS: 51% of the 2016-2017 applicants were accepted. The SAT scores for the 2016-2017 freshman class were: Critical Reading-- 11% below 500, 35% between 500 and 599, 45% between 600 and 699, and 9% between 700 and 800. Math-- 6% below 500, 34% between 500 and 599, 51% between 600 and 699, and 9% between 700 and 800. Writing-- 9% below 500, 36% between 500 and 599, 45% between 600 and 699, and 9% between 700 and 800. The ACT scores were 1% between 12 and 17, 9% between 18 and 23, 57% between 24 and 29, and 33% above 30. 70% of the current freshmen were in the top fifth of their class; 93% were in the top two fifths. **Admissions Contact:** Minh-Ha Hoang, Director of Admissions. Email: *admissions@sandiego.edu* Web: *www.sandiego.edu*

FINANCIAL AID: In 2016-2017, 80% of all full-time freshmen and 73% of continuing full-time students received some form of financial aid. 50% of all full-time freshmen and 51% of continuing full-time students received need-based aid. The average freshman award was $32,725. Need-based scholarships or need-based grants averaged $26,943; need-based self-help aid (loans and jobs) averaged $6,159; non-need-based athletic scholarships averaged $38,759; and other non-need-based awards and non-need-based scholarships averaged $11,949. 17% of undergraduate students work part-time. Average annual earnings from campus work are $2500. The average financial indebtedness of the 2016 graduate was $29,646. The FAFSA code is 010395. The priority date for freshman financial aid applications for fall entry is March 2.

UNIVERSITY OF SAN FRANCISCO B-3

www.usfca.edu

San Francisco, CA 94117 | (415) 422-6563 | (800) CALL USF

Fax: (415) 422-2217 | **Email:** admissions@usfca.edu

Full-time: 2452 men, 3998 women	**Faculty:** I, +$
Part-time: 126 men, 169 women	**Ph.D.s:** n/av
Graduate: 1429 men, 2844 women	**Student/Faculty:** n/av
Year: 4-1-4, summer session	**Tuition:** $9400
Room & Board: $4590	**Freshman Class:** 15441 applied, 10907 accepted, 1587 enrolled
SAT CR/M/W: required **ACT:** required	**CEEB CODE:** 4850
Application Deadline: January 15	**VERY COMPETITIVE**

University of San Francisco, founded in 1855, is a private Roman Catholic institution run by the Jesuit Fathers and offering degree programs in the arts and sciences, business, education, nursing, and law. There are 3 undergraduate schools and 5 graduate schools. In addition to regional accreditation, USF has baccalaureate program accreditation with AACSB, CSAB, NLN, NASPAA, CCNE, and ABA. The 55-acre campus is in an urban area in the heart of the city. Including any residence halls, there are 21 buildings.

STUDENT LIFE: 77% of undergraduates are from California. Others are from 49 states, 69 foreign countries, and Canada. 26% are White; 22% Asian American; 20% Hispanic; 18% Foreign; 7% two or more races; 3% African American; 2% race unknown; 1% American Indian/Alaska Native. 42% are Buddhist, Hindu, Muslim, and unknown; 27% Catholic; 23% claim no religious affiliation. **Female To Male Ratio:** 1.7:1. The average age of freshmen is 18; all undergraduates, 21. 14% do not continue beyond their first year; 72% remain to graduate. **Housing:** 2250 students can be accommodated in college housing, which includes single-sex and coed dorms, on-campus apartments, and off-campus apartments. In addition, there are special-interest houses, multicultural floor, an academic interest floor, a freshman experiences floor, and a quiet floor. On-campus housing is guaranteed for the freshman year only. 63% of students commute. Alcohol is not permitted. All students may keep cars.

FACULTY/CLASSROOMS: No introductory courses are taught by graduate students. The average class size in an introductory lecture is 22; in a laboratory is 14; and in a regular course is 27.

PROGRAMS OF STUDY: USF confers B.B.A., B.A., B.S., B.Arch., B.F.A., B.P.A., B.S.B.A., B.H.S. and B.S.N. degrees. Master's and doctoral degrees are also awarded. Bachelor's degrees are awarded in AGRICULTURE (environmental studies), BIOLOGICAL SCIENCE (biology/biological science and biophysics), BUSINESS (accounting, applied economics / management, business administration and management, business economics, entrepreneurial studies, finance, hospitality management services, hotel/motel and restaurant management, human resources/organizational mgmt, international business, international economics, management information systems, marketing, and organizational behavior), COMMUNICATIONS AND THE ARTS (advertising, art history and appreciation, arts administration/management, communication studies, communications, comparative literature, design, drawing, English, fine arts, French, graphic design, illustration, media arts, painting, performing arts, photography, Spanish, and visual and performing arts), COMPUTER AND PHYSICAL SCIENCE (applied science, chemistry, computer information systems, computer science, information sciences and systems, mathematics, and physics), EDUCATION (art education, Asian studies, and secondary education), ENGINEERING AND ENVIRONMENTAL DESIGN (architecture, engineering physics, environmental science, interior architecture, and interior design), HEALTH PROFESSIONS (exercise science, health services administration, and nursing), SOCIAL SCIENCE (American studies, economics, history, international studies, Latin American studies, law enforcement and corrections, liberal arts/general studies, philosophy, political science/government, psychology, public administration, religious studies, sociology, and theological studies). Sciences and business is the strongest academically. Business, nursing, and psychology have the largest enrollments.

ACTIVITIES: There are 117 groups on campus, including art, band, cheerleading, choir, chorale, chorus, communications, computers, dance, drama, environmental, ethnic, film, honors, international, jazz band, literary magazine, marching band, musical theater, newspaper, orchestra, pep band, political, professional, radio and TV, religious, social, social service, student government, and yearbook. There are 8 intercollegiate sports for women, and 6 intramural sports for men and 6 for women. Facilities include a soccer stadium, recreation center, swimming pool, multipurpose gym, weight room, dance and aerobics room, martial arts room and racquetball/handball courts. Popular campus events include Founders Day and International Week. **Graduates:** From July 1, 2015 to June 30, 2016, 1699 bachelor's degrees were awarded. The most popular majors were nursing (9%), finance (9%), and psychology (7%). In an average class, 3% graduate in 3 years or less, 62% graduate in 4 years or less, 71% graduate in 5 years or less, and 72% graduate in 6 years or less.

SERVICES: Counseling and information services are available, as is tutoring in every subject. There is a reader service for the blind, and a full-time counselor for learning-disabled students. In addition a learning and writing center is available for students in need of academic assistance. **Library/Resources:** The 2 libraries contain 1,000,000 volumes, 900,000 microform items, and 6,000 audio/video tapes/CDs/DVDs, and subscribe to 2,500 periodicals including electronic. Computerized library services include interlibrary loans, database searching, Internet access, and Wi-Fi capability. Special learning facilities include an art gallery, radio station, TV station, a rare book room, the Institute for Chinese-Western Cultural History, and the Center for Pacific Rim Studies. **Physically Challenged Students:** 95% of the campus is accessible. Facilities include wheelchair ramps, elevators, special parking, specially equipped restrooms, lowered drinking fountains. **Special:** Cross-registration with the San Francisco Consortium, internships with local business, social services, and research opportunities are available. Study abroad in Europe and Japan, work-study programs on and off campus and with social service agencies, a B.A.-B.S. degree in exercise and sports science, dual majors in liberal arts and education, 3-2 engineering degrees with the University of Southern California, student-designed majors, nondegree study, and limited pass/fail options are also available. The College of Professional Studies is a degree completion program for working adults. There are 13 national honor societies and a freshman honors program. **Visiting:** There are regularly scheduled orientations for prospective students, including a tour of campus, academic buildings, library, residence halls, recreation centers, and a group information session hosted by an admissions staff member. There are guides for informal visits, visitors may sit in on classes, and stay overnight. To schedule a visit, contact the Office of Admissions at admission@usfca.edu. **Campus Safety and Security:** Measures include 24-hour foot and vehicle patrol, emergency notification system, self-defense education, and security escort services. There are shuttle buses, emergency telephones, lighted pathways/sidewalks, and controlled access to dorms/residences.

REQUIREMENTS: The SAT or ACT is required. Applicants are required to have 20 academic units, based on 6 years of academic electives, 4 of English, 3 each of math and social studies, and 2 each of foreign language and lab science. An essay is required. The GED is accepted. A GPA of 3.0 is required. AP and CLEP credits are accepted. Important factors in the admissions decision are extracurricular activities record, evidence of special talent, and leadership record. All students must maintain a GPA of at least 2.0 and take 128 credit hours, including 58 in upper-division courses. 36 to 58 hours are required in the major. The current general education requirements include 9 units each of basic skills and history/social science, 6 each of philosophy, religious studies, cultural perspectives, natural science, and literature and fine arts, and 3 of ethics. **Procedure:** Freshmen are admitted fall and spring. Entrance exams should be taken during the first half of the senior year. There are early decision, early admissions, deferred admissions, and rolling admissions plans. Early decision applications should be filed by November 15; regular applications, by January 15 for fall entry, along with a $65 fee. Notification of early decision is sent January 1; regular decision, on a rolling basis. 198 applicants were on the 2016 waiting list. Applications are accepted on-line. **Transfer Students:** 462 transfer students enrolled in 2015-2016. Applicants need a GPA of 3.0 or higher to be competitive for admission. 45 of 128 credits required for the bachelor's degree must be completed at USF. **International Students:** There are 1200 international students enrolled. The school actively recruits these students. They must take the TOEFL with a minimum score of 550 on the paper-based TOEFL (PBT) or 80 on the Internet-based version (iBT).

ADMISSIONS: 71% of the 2016-2017 applicants were accepted.; 3% were in the top two fifths. 5 freshmen graduated first in their class. **Admissions Contact:** April Crabtree, Director, Undergraduate Admissions. Email: *admissions@usfca.edu* Web: *www.usfca.edu*

FINANCIAL AID: In 2016-2017, 83% of all full-time freshmen and 73% of continuing full-time students received some form of financial aid. 62% of all full-time freshmen and 55% of continuing full-time students received need-based aid. The average freshman award was $35,575. Need-based scholarships or need-based grants averaged $21,677 ($51,484 maximum); need-based self-help aid (loans and jobs) averaged $13,047 ($68,084 maximum); non-need-based athletic scholarships averaged $43,498 ($63,214 maximum); and other non-need-based awards and non-need-based scholarships averaged $16,075 ($66,040 maximum). 47% of undergraduate students work part-time. The average financial indebtedness of the 2016 graduate was $47,322. The CSS/Profile is required. The FAFSA code is 001325. The deadline for filing freshman financial aid applications for fall entry is February 15.

UNIVERSITY OF SOUTHERN CALIFORNIA C-5

www.usc.edu

Los Angeles, CA 90089 **(213) 740-1111**

Fax: (213) 740-6364	**Email:** admdean@usc.edu
Full-time: 8687 men, 9383 women	**Faculty:** 1572; I, +$
Part-time: 258 men, 229 women	**Ph.D.s:** 90%
Graduate: 11,545 men, 13,532 women	**Student/Faculty:** 9 to 1
	Tuition: $38,000
Year: semesters, summer session	**Freshman Class:** 51924 applied, 9181 accepted, 2949 enrolled
Room & Board: $13,855	
SAT or ACT: required	**CEEB CODE:** 4852
Application Deadline: January 10	**COMPETITIVE**

University of Southern California, founded in 1880, is a private institution offering undergraduate and graduate programs in liberal arts, fine arts, education, business, law, dentistry, engineering, communications, and health professions. There are 13 undergraduate schools and 18 graduate schools. In addition to regional accreditation, USC has baccalaureate program accreditation with AACSB, ABET, ACEJMC, ACPE, ADA, APTA, CSWE, NAAB, NASM, NCATE, NLN, ACS, AOTA, ACPOTE, CODA, and CAPTE. The 226-acre campus is in an urban area 3 miles south of the Los Angeles Civic Center. Including any residence halls, there are 275 buildings.

STUDENT LIFE: **Female To Male Ratio:** 1.1:1. **Housing:** College-sponsored housing includes coed dorms, on-campus apartments, off-campus apartments, and married student housing. In addition, there are honors houses, special-interest houses, fraternity houses, sorority houses, multicultural floors, substance-free housing, and international housing. On-campus housing is guaranteed for the freshman year only, is available on a first-come, first-served basis, and is available on a lottery system for upperclassmen. All students may keep cars.

FACULTY/CLASSROOMS: 60% of faculty are male; 40% are female. 83% teach undergraduates. No introductory courses are taught by graduate students.

PROGRAMS OF STUDY: USC confers B.A., B.S., B.Arch., B.F.A., B.Land.Arch. and B.M. degrees. Master's and doctoral degrees are also awarded. Bachelor's degrees are awarded in AGRICULTURE (environmental studies), BIOLOGICAL SCIENCE (biology/biological science, biophysics, and neurosciences), BUSINESS (accounting, business administration and management, and international business management), COMMUNICATIONS AND THE ARTS (art history and appreciation, broadcasting, classics, communications, comparative literature, creative writing, dramatic arts, East Asian languages and literature, English, English literature, film arts, fine arts, French, Italian, jazz, journalism, linguistics, music, music performance, playwriting/screenwriting, public relations, Russian, Spanish, studio art, theater design, theater management, video, and visual and performing arts), COMPUTER AND PHYSICAL SCIENCE (applied mathematics, astronomy, chemistry, computer science, geology, mathematics, physical sciences, and physics), ENGINEERING AND ENVIRONMENTAL DESIGN (aeronautical engineering, aerospace studies, architecture, biomedical engineering, chemical engineering, civil engineering, computer engineering, construction engineering, electrical/electronics engineering, environmental engineering, environmental science, industrial engineering, mechanical engineering, petroleum/natural gas engineering, and systems engineering), HEALTH PROFESSIONS (dental hygiene, exercise science, and occupational therapy), SOCIAL SCIENCE (African American studies, American studies, anthropology, Asian/American studies, classical/ancient civilization, East Asian studies, economics, ethics, politics, and social policy, geography, gerontology, history, international relations, Judaic studies, Latin American studies, philosophy, political science/government, psychology, religion, social science, sociology, and women's studies). Business, communications, and biological sciences have the largest enrollments.

ACTIVITIES: Groups on campus include art, band, cheerleading, chess, choir, chorale, chorus, computers, dance, debate, drama, drill team, environmental, ethnic, film, forensics, honors, international, jazz band, LGBT, literary magazine, marching band, musical theater, newspaper, opera, orchestra, pep band, photography, political, professional, radio and TV, religious, social, social service, student government, symphony, and yearbook. Popular campus events include Springfest, International Food and Cultural Fair, and Spectrum Concert Series. **Sports:** There are 10 intercollegiate sports for men and 12 for women, and 30 intramural sports for men and 23 for women. Facilities include a student athletic center, track, gym, 2 Olympic pools, tennis, swimming, and baseball stadiums. **Graduates:** From July 1, 2015 to June 30, 2016, 5487 bachelor's degrees were awarded. The most popular majors were business (24%), communication (7%), and accounting (5%). In an average class, 3% graduate in 3 years or less, 75% graduate in 4 years or less, 89% graduate in 5 years or less, and 90% graduate in 6 years or less.

SERVICES: Counseling and information services are available, as is tutoring in every subject. There is a reader service for the blind. Accommodations are made for students with disabilities. **Library/Resources:** The 23 libraries contain 4.8 million volumes, 6.6 million microform items, and 84,953 audio/video tapes/CDs/DVDs, and subscribe to 0 periodicals including electronic. Computerized library services include interlibrary loans, database searching, Internet access, and Wi-Fi capability. Special learning facilities include an art gallery, natural history museum, radio station, TV station, state-of-the-art cinema/film-making facilities, labs, wind tunnel, and a marine science center. **Physically Challenged Students:** 97% of the campus is accessible. Facilities include wheelchair ramps, elevators, special parking, specially equipped restrooms, special class scheduling, and special housing. There is also shuttle service for students with temporary disabilities. **Special:** Cross-registration is permitted with Hebrew Union College and Howard University. Internships in various majors, a Washington semester, work-study programs, study abroad in 29 countries, dual majors, a general studies degree, student-designed majors, a 3-2 engineering degree, and pass/fail options are available. Students are encouraged to pursue interdisciplinary study linking core art and science disciplines to professional programs. There are 39 national honor societies, Phi Beta Kappa, and a freshman honors program. **Visiting:** There are regularly scheduled orientations for prospective students. There are guides for informal visits, visitors may sit in on classes, and stay overnight. To schedule a visit, contact the Admission Office. **Campus Safety and Security:** Measures include 24-hour foot and vehicle patrol, emergency notification system, self-defense education, and security escort services. There are shuttle buses, emergency telephones, and lighted pathways/sidewalks. The safety department responds to calls for service on and off campus.

REQUIREMENTS: The SAT or ACT is required, as well as the ACT Optional Writing test. In addition, 3 SAT Subject Tests are recommended. Graduation from an accredited secondary school is required. Applicants must have completed at least 13 year-long courses in English, humanities, math, natural sciences, social sciences, and foreign languages, plus 3 additional year-long courses in those areas or in computer science and, with some exceptions, theater, fine arts, journalism, music or speech. AP credits are accepted. Important factors in the admissions decision are advanced placement or honors courses, recommendations by school officials, and evidence of special talent. All students must satisfy requirements in foreign language, freshman writing, general education, and take 1 multicultural course. Graduation requirements include a minimum of 128 credit hours and a minimum GPA of 2.0. **Procedure:** Freshmen are admitted fall and spring. Entrance exams should be taken by November of the senior year for scholarship applicants; by December for all others. Applications should be filed by January 10 for fall entry, along with a $80 fee. Notifications are sent April 1. Applications are accepted on-line. **Transfer Students:** 1658 transfer students enrolled in 2015-2016. Transfer applicants must submit 30 units of transferable work with a strong GPA in a rigorous selection of courses. SAT or ACT scores are considered if 30 units have not been completed. 64 of 128 credits required for the bachelor's degree must be completed at USC. **International Students:** There are 2604 international students enrolled. The school actively recruits these students. They must take the TOEFL, Undergraduate students who score 500 or better on the verbal portion of the SAT are exempted from providing TOEFL scores. Upon arrival students with low TOEFL scores are required to take our local English proficiency examination. They must also take the SAT or ACT.

ADMISSIONS: 18% of the 2016-2017 applicants were accepted. The SAT scores for the 2016-2017 freshman class were: Critical Reading-- 2% below 500, 14% between 500 and 599, 48% between 600 and 699, and 36% between 700 and 800. Math-- 2% below 500, 10% between 500 and 599, 32% between 600 and 699, and 57% between 700 and 800. Writing-- 2% below 500, 9% between 500 and 599, 38% between 600 and 699, and 50% between 700 and 800. There were 251 National Merit finalists. **Admissions Contact:** Timothy Brunold, Dean of Admission. Email: *admdean@usc.edu* Web: *www.usc.edu*

FINANCIAL AID: In 2016-2017, 61% of all full-time freshmen and 61% of continuing full-time students received some form of financial aid. 36% of all full-time freshmen and 41% of continuing full-time students received need-based aid. The average freshman award was $45,044. Need-based scholarships or need-based grants averaged $31,962; need-based self-help aid (loans and jobs) averaged $6,804; non-need-based athletic scholarships averaged $39,380; and other non-need-based awards and non-need-based scholarships averaged $21,460. The average financial indebtedness of the 2016 graduate was $28,541. USC is a member of CSS. The CSS/Profile, parent and student federal income tax forms and all schedules are required. The FAFSA code is 001328. The priority date for freshman financial aid applications for fall entry is February 2.

UNIVERSITY OF THE PACIFIC B-3
www.pacific.edu

Stockton, CA 95211	(209) 946-2211 (800) 959-2867
Fax: (209) 946-2413	Email: admission@pacific.edu
Full-time: 1811 men, 1969 women	**Faculty:** IIA, ++$
Part-time: 48 men, 49 women	**Ph.D.s:** 74%
Graduate: 1101 men, 1443 women	**Student/Faculty:** 14 to 1
Year: semesters, summer session	**Tuition:** $44,688
Room & Board: $12,318	**Freshman Class:** 14,222 applied, 10,332 accepted, 958 enrolled
SAT CR/M/W: 570/605/570 **ACT:** 25	**CEEB CODE:** 4065
Application Deadline: February 15	**VERY COMPETITIVE**

University of the Pacific, founded in 1851, is a private institution that offers undergraduate and graduate programs in the arts and sciences, and professional programs in pharmacy, law, and dentistry. The figures in the above capsule and in this profile are approximate. There are 8 undergraduate schools and 1 graduate school. In addition to regional accreditation, Pacific has baccalaureate program accreditation with AACSB, ABET, NASAD, NASM, NCATE, ACS, and CAAHEP. The 175-acre campus is in a suburban area 80 miles east of San Francisco, and 40 miles south of Sacramento. Including any residence halls, there are 68 buildings.

STUDENT LIFE: 85% of undergraduates are from California. Others are from states, and Canada. 4% are Foreign; 36% Asian American; 35% White; 3% African American; 12% Hispanic; 1% American Indian/Alaska Native. **Female To Male Ratio:** 1.2:1. The average age of freshmen is 18; all undergraduates, 20. 13% do not continue beyond their first year; 82% remain to graduate. **Housing:** 2208 students can be accommodated in college housing, which includes coed dorms, on-campus apartments, and married student housing. In addition, there are honors houses, special-interest houses, fraternity houses, sorority houses, intercultural, wellness, pharmacy, honors, and learning involvement theme houses. On-campus housing is guaranteed for the freshman year only, and is available on a first-come, first-served basis, and is available on a lottery system for upperclassmen. Priority is given to out-of-town students. 57% of students live on campus. Alcohol is not permitted. All students may keep cars.

FACULTY/CLASSROOMS: 55% of faculty are male; 45% are female. All teach undergraduates. No introductory courses are taught by graduate students. The average class size in a regular course is 19.

PROGRAMS OF STUDY: Pacific confers B.A., B.S., B.F.A., B.M., B.S.B.A., B.S.B.E., B.S.C.E., B.S.E.E., B.S.E.M., B.S.E.P. and B.S.M.E. degrees. Master's and doctoral degrees are also awarded. Bachelor's degrees are awarded in BIOLOGICAL SCIENCE (biochemistry and biology/biological science), BUSINESS (business administration and management), COMMUNICATIONS AND THE ARTS (art, communications, dramatic arts, English, French, German, graphic design, Japanese, music, music business management, music history and appreciation, music performance, music theory and composition, Spanish, and studio art), COMPUTER AND PHYSICAL SCIENCE (applied mathematics, chemistry, computer science, geology, geophysics and seismology, information sciences and systems, mathematics, and physics), EDUCATION (education, music education, and physical education), ENGINEERING AND ENVIRONMENTAL DESIGN (civil engineering, computer engineering, electrical/electronics engineering, engineering management, engineering physics, environmental science, and mechanical engineering), HEALTH PROFESSIONS (music therapy, prepharmacy, and speech pathology/audiology), SOCIAL SCIENCE (economics, history, international relations, international studies, liberal arts/general studies, philosophy, political science/government, psychology, religion, social science, and sociology). Natural sciences, and the professions are the strongest academically. Arts and sciences, pharmacy, and business have the largest enrollments.

ACTIVITIES: 15% of men and 16% of women belong to 1 local and 7 national fraternities; 22% of women belong to 1 local and 6 national sororities. There are 100 groups on campus, including resident hall association, intramurals, model UN, residential learning, band, cheerleading, choir, chorale, chorus, club sports, computers, dance, debate, drama, ethnic, forensics, honors, international, jazz band, LGBT, literary magazine, musical theater, newspaper, opera, orchestra, pep band, photography, political, professional, radio and TV, religious, social, social service, student government, symphony, and yearbook. Popular campus events include Alumni Weekend, Pacific Boardwalk Carnival and Cultural Diversity Week. **Sports:** There are 7 intercollegiate sports for men and 9 for women, and 30 intramural sports for men and 30 for women. Facilities include a sports arena, an Olympic-size pool, tennis courts, softball field, and a fitness center. **Graduates:** From July 1, 2015 to June 30, 2016, 823 bachelor's degrees were awarded. The most popular majors were business/marketing (24%), biological/life sciences (16%), and engineering/engineering tech (8%).

SERVICES: Counseling and information services are available, as is tutoring in every subject. There is a reader service for the blind, and remedial math, reading, and writing. **Library/Resources:** The 2 libraries contain 381,686 volumes, 691,985 microform items, and 12,732 audio/video tapes/CDs/DVDs, and subscribe to 12,732 periodicals including electronic. Computerized library services include interlibrary loans, database searching, and Internet access. Special learning facilities include an art gallery, radio station, and the Brubeck Institute. **Physically Challenged Students:** 90% of the campus is accessible. Facilities include wheelchair ramps, elevators, special parking, specially equipped restrooms, special class scheduling, lowered drinking fountains, and lowered telephones. **Special:** The engineering school requires and guarantees a co-op program for specialized training in the field. Internships for credit or pay in all majors, more than 230 study-abroad programs in more than 80 countries, a Washington semester, and more than 20 work-study programs also are available. Student-designed majors, B.A./B.S. degrees, dual majors in most disciplines, and pass/fail options are possible. There are 18 national honor societies, a freshman honors program, and 42 departmental honors programs. **Visiting:** There are regularly scheduled orientations for prospective students, visiting students can take a tour, and schedule appointments with faculty, admissions, financial aid personnel, and class visits. There are guides for informal visits, visitors may sit in on classes, and stay overnight. To schedule a visit, contact the Admissions Office. **Campus Safety and Security:** Measures include 24-hour foot and vehicle patrol and security escort services. There are emergency telephones and lighted pathways/sidewalks.

REQUIREMENTS: The SAT or ACT is required. Applicants must have 16 academic credits, including a recommended 4 years of high school English, 3 of math, 2 in the same foreign language, 2 of lab science, 1 of U.S history or government, 1 of fine or performing arts, and 4 additional academic courses. An essay is required and an interview is recommended. In addition, music students must audition. The GED is accepted plus one year of math and science for science and health related majors. A GPA of 2.5 is required. AP and CLEP credits are accepted. Important factors in the admissions decision are advanced placement or honors courses, leadership record, and extracurricular activities record. Students must complete at least 124 credit hours to graduate. The required general education program consists of 3 "mentor seminars" and 6 to 9 other courses chosen from categories such as the Individual and Society, the Human Heritage, and the Natural World and Formal Systems of Thought. **Procedure:** Freshmen are admitted fall and spring. Entrance exams should be taken in the spring of the junior year or fall of the senior year. There are early decision, early admissions, deferred admissions, and rolling admissions plans. Early decision applications should be filed by November 15; regular applications, by February 15 for fall entry; and November 15 for spring entry, along with a $35 fee. Notification of early decision is sent January 15; regular decision, March 15. 1100 applicants were on the 2016 waiting list; 34 were admitted. Applications are accepted on-line. **Transfer Students:** 178 transfer students enrolled in 2015-2016. Applicants should have a minimum GPA of 3.0 and at least 16 credit hours. The SAT or ACT and high school transcripts are required if fewer than 30 units of college work have been completed. 32 of 124 credits required for the bachelor's degree must be completed at Pacific. **International Students:** There are 125 international students enrolled. The school actively recruits these students. They must take the TOEFL. The SAT or ACT is required if the student has attended a U.S.-style high school.

ADMISSIONS: 73% of the 2016-2017 applicants were accepted. The SAT scores for the 2016-2017 freshman class were: Critical Reading-- 21% below 500, 38% between 500 and 599, 31% between 600 and 699, and 10% between 700 and 800. Math-- 15% below 500, 29% between 500 and 599, 34% between 600 and 699, and 22% between 700 and 800. Writing-- 23% below 500, 37% between 500 and 599, 29% between 600 and 699, and 11% between 700 and 800. The ACT scores were 4% below 12, 30% between 18 and 23, and 66% above 30. **Admissions Contact:**

Margaret Adkins, Director of Admissions. Email: *admission@pacific.edu* Web: *www.pacific.edu*

FINANCIAL AID: Pacific is a member of CSS. The FAFSA code is 001329. The deadline for filing freshman financial aid applications for fall entry is February 15.

VANGUARD UNIVERSITY OF SOUTHERN CALIFORNIA D-5

www.vanguard.edu

Costa Mesa, CA 92626	(714) 556-3610 (800) 722-6279
Fax: (714) 966-5471	Email: admissions@vanguard.edu
Full-time: 532 men, 962 women	**Faculty:** n/av
Part-time: 156 men, 391 women	**Ph.D.s:** 81%
Graduate: 79 men, 189 women	**Student/Faculty:** 19 to 1
Year: semesters, summer session	**Tuition:** $31,430
Room & Board: $9310	**Freshman Class:** 1244 applied, 917 accepted, 412 enrolled
SAT or ACT: required	**CEEB CODE:** 4701
Application Deadline: March 2	**VERY COMPETITIVE**

Vanguard University of Southern California, founded in 1920, is a private Christian comprehensive university of liberal arts and professional studies affiliated with the Assemblies of God. The figures in the above capsule and in this profile are approximate. There is 1 undergraduate school and 4 graduate schools. In addition to regional accreditation, VUSC has baccalaureate program accreditation with WASC. The 38-acre campus is in a suburban area 40 miles southeast of Los Angeles, and 5 miles north of Newport Beach. Including any residence halls, there are 25 buildings.

STUDENT LIFE: 95% of undergraduates are from California. Others are from 29 states, 8 foreign countries, and Canada. 75% are from public schools. 7% are Asian American; 6% African American; 56% White; 27% Hispanic; 2% American Indian/Alaska Native; 1% Foreign. 74% are Protestant; 22% unknown denominations. **Female To Male Ratio:** 2.0:1. The average age of freshmen is 22; all undergraduates, 24. 25% do not continue beyond their first year; 55% remain to graduate. **Housing:** 1074 students can be accommodated in college housing, which includes single-sex and coed dorms, on-campus apartments, off-campus apartments, and married student housing. On-campus housing is available on a first-come, first-served basis, and is available on a lottery system for upperclassmen. Priority is given to out-of-town students. 74% of students live on campus; of those, 75% remain on campus on weekends. Alcohol is not permitted. All students may keep cars.

FACULTY/CLASSROOMS: 54% of faculty are male; 46% are female. 57% teach undergraduates. No introductory courses are taught by graduate students. The average class size in an introductory lecture is 40; in a laboratory is 12; and in a regular course is 19.

PROGRAMS OF STUDY: VUSC confers B.A., and B.S. degrees. Associate and master's degrees are also awarded. Bachelor's degrees are awarded in BIOLOGICAL SCIENCE (biochemistry and biology/biological science), BUSINESS (accounting, business administration and management, international business management, and marketing/retailing/merchandising), COMMUNICATIONS AND THE ARTS (broadcasting, communications, digital communications, dramatic arts, English, music, radio/television technology, Spanish, and theatre arts), COMPUTER AND PHYSICAL SCIENCE (chemistry and mathematics), EDUCATION (athletic training, education, elementary education, physical education, science education, secondary education, and sports studies), HEALTH PROFESSIONS (exercise science, nursing, physical therapy, and premedicine), SOCIAL SCIENCE (anthropology, biblical studies, Christian studies, history, liberal arts/general studies, ministries, missions, pastoral studies, political science/government, psychology, religious education, sociology, theological studies, and youth ministry). Religion, social sciences, natural sciences, and kinesiology are the strongest academically. Business, psychology, and communication have the largest enrollments.

ACTIVITIES: There are no fraternities or sororities. There are 30 groups on campus, including art, band, choir, chorale, chorus, computers, dance, debate, drama, ethnic, film, forensics, international, jazz band, literary magazine, musical theater, newspaper, opera, orchestra, photography, political, professional, radio and TV, religious, social, social service, student government, symphony, and yearbook. Popular campus events include Harvest Party, International Missions Week and Christmas Party. **Sports:** There are 7 intercollegiate sports for men and 8 for women, and 4 intramural sports for men and 4 for women. Facilities include a gym, baseball, softball, soccer fields, a weight room, and contracted off-campus tennis courts and track course. **Graduates:** From July 1, 2015 to June 30, 2016, 432 bachelor's degrees were awarded. The most popular majors were psychology (20%), business administration (17%), and communications (11%). In an average class, 45% graduate in 4 years or less and 54% graduate in 6 years or less.

SERVICES: Counseling and information services are available, as is tutoring in most subjects such as time management, organization skill, a writing center, and learning strategy. **Library/Resources:** The library contains 175,877 volumes, 20,795 microform items, and 7,962 audio/video tapes/CDs/DVDs, and subscribes to 10,000 periodicals including electronic. Computerized library services include interlibrary loans, database searching, and Internet access. Special learning facilities include a radio station. **Physically Challenged Students:** 95% of the campus is accessible. Facilities include wheelchair ramps, elevators, special parking, specially equipped restrooms, special class scheduling, and special housing. **Special:** Study abroad in cooperation with Assemblies of God programs and programs in the CCCU with placement in over 100 countries, a general studies degree, work-study, accelerated degree programs in business, psychology, and religion, and pass/fail options are available. 3 summer sessions are offered. There are 9 national honor societies and 6 departmental honors programs. **Visiting:** There are regularly scheduled orientations for prospective students, during fall and spring university for students and parents. There are guides for informal visits, visitors may sit in on classes, and stay overnight. To schedule a visit, contact the Undergraduate Admissions. **Campus Safety and Security:** Measures include 24-hour foot and vehicle patrol, emergency notification system, and security escort services. There are emergency telephones, lighted pathways/sidewalks, controlled access to dorms/residences, room locks, and vehicle locks.

REQUIREMENTS: The SAT or ACT is required. High school courses should include 4 years of English, 3 of social studies, and 2 of math and science. Applicants are required to write an application essay and submit 2 references (1 academic and 1 from a pastor/minister). A GPA of 2.8 is required. AP and CLEP credits are accepted. Important factors in the admissions decision are leadership record, advanced placement or honors courses, and evidence of special talent. Students must complete a minimum of 124 credits, with 40 to 70 in the major. General education requirements include 16 credits in religion, 15 in humanities and fine arts, 12 in social science, 7 in natural sciences and math, and 2 in phys ed. **Procedure:** Freshmen are admitted fall and spring. Entrance exams should be taken in the junior year. There is a rolling admissions plan. Early decision applications should be filed by December 1; regular applications, by March 2 for fall entry; and December 1 for spring entry, along with a $45 fee. **Transfer Students:** 173 transfer students enrolled in 2015-2016. Transfer applicants must submit college transcripts and have a minimum college GPA of 2.5. 24 of 124 credits required for the bachelor's degree must be completed at VUSC. **International Students:** They must take the TOEFL with a minimum score of 550 on the paper-based TOEFL (PBT) or 80 on the Internet-based version (iBT).

ADMISSIONS: 74% of the 2016-2017 applicants were accepted. There was 1 National Merit finalist. 5 freshmen graduated first in their class. **Admissions Contact:** Katy Neric, Assoc Director Admissions Marketing. Email: *admissions@vanguard.edu* Web: *www.vanguard.edu*

FINANCIAL AID: In 2016-2017, 92% of all full-time freshmen received some form of financial aid. The FAFSA code is 001293. Check with the school for current application deadlines.

WESTMONT COLLEGE C-5

www.westmont.edu

Santa Barbara, CA 93108	(805) 565-6005 (800) 777-9011
Fax: (805) 565-6234	Email: admissions@westmont.edu
Full-time: 515 men, 800 women	**Faculty:** IIB, +$
Part-time: 5 men, 20 women	**Ph.D.s:** 89%
Graduate: n/av	**Student/Faculty:** n/av
Year: semesters, summer session	**Tuition:** $42,900
Room & Board: $13,510	**Freshman Class:** n/av
SAT or ACT: required	**CEEB CODE:** 4950
Application Deadline: August 15	**HIGHLY COMPETITIVE**

Westmont College, founded in 1937, is a private, nondenominational Christian institution offering undergraduate liberal arts degrees. The figures in the above capsule and in this profile are approximate. There is 1 undergraduate school. In addition to regional accreditation, Westmont has baccalaureate program accreditation with WASC. The 111-acre campus is in a suburban area 90 miles north of Los Angeles. Including any residence halls, there are 30 buildings.

STUDENT LIFE: 69% of undergraduates are from California. Others are from 41 states, 8 foreign countries, and Canada. 70% are from public schools. 9% are Asian American; 69% White; 10% Hispanic; 1% African American; 1% American Indian/Alaska Native; 1% Foreign. 95% are Protestant. **Female To Male Ratio:** 1.6:1. The average age of freshmen is 18; all undergraduates, 20. 13% do not continue beyond their first year; 70% remain to graduate. **Housing:** 1113 students can be accommodated in college housing, which includes single-sex and coed dorms and off-campus apartments. On-campus housing is guaranteed for all 4 years. 84% of students live on campus; of those, 65% remain on campus on weekends. Alcohol is not permitted. Upperclassmen may keep cars.

FACULTY/CLASSROOMS: 67% of faculty are male; 33% are female. All teach undergraduates, and do research. No introductory courses are taught by graduate students. The average class size in an introductory lecture is 30; in a laboratory is 15; and in a regular course is 20.

PROGRAMS OF STUDY: Westmont confers B.A., and B.S. degrees. Bachelor's degrees are awarded in BIOLOGICAL SCIENCE (biology/biological science), BUSINESS (business economics), COMMUNICATIONS AND THE ARTS (art, communications, dramatic arts, English, French, modern language, music, and Spanish), COMPUTER AND PHYSICAL SCIENCE (chemistry, computer science, mathematics, and physics), EDUCATION (art education, English education, mathematics education, music education, and social science education), ENGINEERING AND ENVIRONMENTAL DESIGN (engineering physics), HEALTH PROFESSIONS (exercise science), SOCIAL SCIENCE (European studies, history, liberal arts/general studies, philosophy, political science/government, psychology, religion, social science, and sociology). Biology, communication studies, and economics/business have the largest enrollments.

ACTIVITIES: There are no fraternities or sororities. There are 50 groups on campus, including art, band, chess, choir, chorale, chorus, computers, dance, debate, drama, ethnic, film, honors, international, jazz band, leadership club, literary magazine, musical theater, newspaper, opera, orchestra, pep band, photography, political, professional, radio and TV, religious, social, social service, student government, symphony, and yearbook. Popular campus events include Spring Sing Musical/Talent Show, Multicultural Fellowship Week, and Theatrical and Musical Productions. **Sports:** There are 6 intercollegiate sports for men and 6 for women, and 10 intramural sports for men and 10 for women. Facilities include a gym, soccer/baseball field, swimming pool, fitness room, dance studio, track, volleyball, tennis, basketball, and racquetball courts. **Graduates:** From July 1, 2015 to June 30, 2016, 326 bachelor's degrees were awarded. The most popular majors were business/economics (14%), English (12%), and social sciences (9%). 50 companies recruited on campus in 2015-2016. In an average class, 73% graduate in 4 years or less. Of the 2015 graduating class, 48% were enrolled in graduate school within 6 months of graduation, and 85% were employed.

SERVICES: Counseling and information services are available, as is tutoring in every subject. There is a reader service for the blind, and remedial math. A writers' corner supervised by tutors is also available. **Library/Resources:** The library contains 162,274 volumes, 20,687 microform items, and 7,926 audio/video tapes/CDs/DVDs, and subscribes to 3,211 periodicals including electronic. Computerized library services include interlibrary loans, database searching, and Internet access. Special learning facilities include an art gallery, radio station, an observatory, a science center with a premedical center, and a physiology lab. **Physically Challenged Students:** 60% of the campus is accessible. Facilities include wheelchair ramps, elevators, special parking, specially equipped restrooms, special class scheduling, lowered drinking fountains, lowered telephones, and special housing. **Special:** Westmont offers cross-registration with 12 Christian colleges in the Christian College Consortium, internships in local businesses and social agencies, study abroad in 11 countries, and semesters in Washington, D.C., San Francisco, and Los Angeles. B.A.-B.S. degrees, student-designed majors, work-study programs, a 3-2 engineering program with several California universities, the University of Washington, and Boston University, and pass/fail options are also available. There are preprofessional programs in sports medicine, dentistry, engineering, law, medicine, ministry/missions, optometry, pharmacology, physical therapy, teaching, and veterinary medicine. There are 8 national honor societies, a freshman honors program, and 9 departmental honors programs. **Visiting:** There are regularly scheduled orientations for prospective students, consisting of meeting faculty and administrators attending classes, academic seminars, student/parent panels, academic open houses, admission and financial aid sessions, student led small groups, campus tours, and various cultural events. There are guides for informal visits, visitors may sit in on classes, and stay overnight. To schedule a visit, contact Admissions/Campus Visit Coordinator. **Campus Safety and Security:** Measures include 24-hour foot and vehicle patrol, self-defense education, and security escort services. There are shuttle buses, emergency telephones, and lighted pathways/sidewalks.

REQUIREMENTS: The SAT or ACT is required. The ACT Optional Writing test is also required. In addition, Applicants need 16 academic credits, including 4 years of high school English, 3 of math, 2 each of a foreign language, social science, and physical science, and 1 each of history and biological science. Interviews are recommended. Essays are required. The GED is accepted. AP and CLEP credits are accepted. Important factors in the admissions decision are advanced placement or honors courses, leadership record, and extracurricular activities record. Of the 124 semester units required for graduation, the college's general education requirements include 20 semester units of Common Context courses and 32 semester units of Common Inquiries courses. In addition, students must complete Common Skills courses and courses relating to Competent and Compassionate Action. Courses in religions studies and phys ed are required, as are courses in the history of Western civilization and English composition. Math proficiency is also required. There are distribution requirements in social sciences, humanities, and natural sciences. The total number of hours in the major varies from 36 to 66. A GPA of 2.0 must be maintained. **Procedure:** Freshmen are admitted fall and spring. Entrance exams should be taken during the spring of the junior year or the beginning of the senior year. Applications should be filed by August 15 for fall entry. The fall 2016 application fee was $35. Applications are accepted on-line. **Transfer Students:** 55 transfer students enrolled in 2015-2016. Transfer students from 2-year colleges should have a minimum GPA of 2.8 and students from 4-year colleges or universities, a 2.5. The college will not accept more than 64 transferable units from a community college; there is no maximum number of transferable units from a 4-year college. High school transcripts and test scores are required if the student has fewer than 24 transferable units. 32 of 124 credits required for the bachelor's degree must be completed at Westmont. **International Students:** There are 9 international students enrolled. The school actively recruits these students. They must take the TOEFL with a minimum score of 560 on the paper-based TOEFL (PBT) or 83 on the Internet-based version (iBT). They must also take the SAT or ACT.

Admissions Contact: Joyce M. Luy, Dean of Admissions. Email: *admissions@westmont.edu* Web: *www.westmont.edu*

FINANCIAL AID: In 2016-2017, 83% of all full-time freshmen and 85% of continuing full-time students received some form of financial aid. 83% of all full-time freshmen and 85% of continuing full-time students received need-based aid. 54% of undergraduate students work part-time. Average annual earnings from campus work are $909. The FAFSA code is 001341. Check with the school for current application deadlines.

WHITTIER COLLEGE — D-5

www.whittier.edu

Whittier, CA 90608 — **(562) 907-4238**

Fax: (562) 907-4870	**Email:** admissions@whittier.edu
Full-time: 634 men, 720 women	**Faculty:** 92; IIB, +$
Part-time: 7 men, 7 women	**Ph.D.s:** 100%
Graduate: 258 men, 286 women	**Student/Faculty:** 15 to 1
Year: 4-1-4, summer session	**Tuition:** $46,604
Room & Board: $11,287	**Freshman Class:** 1970 applied, 1639 accepted, 358 enrolled
SAT CR/M: 526/532 **ACT:** 22	**CEEB CODE:** 4952
Application Deadline: February 1	**COMPETITIVE**

Whittier College, founded in 1887 by the Society of Friends and chartered by the state of California in 1901, is an independent, secular, liberal arts institution. The figures in the above capsule and in this profile are approximate. There is 1 undergraduate school and 2 graduate schools. In addition to regional accreditation, Whittier has baccalaureate program accreditation with CSWE. The 75-acre campus is in a suburban area 18 miles southeast of Los Angeles, in the foothills of the San Gabriel Mountains. Including any residence halls, there are 51 buildings.

STUDENT LIFE: 71% of undergraduates are from California. Others are from 25 states, 16 foreign countries, and Canada. 8% are Asian American; 6% African American; 40% White; 29% Hispanic; 2% Foreign; 1% American Indian/Alaska Native. **Female To Male Ratio:** 1.1:1. The average age of freshmen is 18; all undergraduates, 20. 26% do not continue beyond their first year; 54% remain to graduate. **Housing:** 840 students can be accommodated in college housing, which includes coed dorms. In addition, there are special-interest houses. On-campus housing is guaranteed for all 4 years. 61% of students live on campus; of those, 85% remain on campus on weekends. All students may keep cars.

FACULTY/CLASSROOMS: 47% of faculty are male; 53% are female. All teach undergraduates, and do research. No introductory courses are taught by graduate students. The average class size in an introductory lecture is 20; in a laboratory is 24; and in a regular course is 22.

PROGRAMS OF STUDY: Whittier confers B.A. degrees. Master's and doctoral degrees are also awarded. Bachelor's degrees are awarded in BIOLOGICAL SCIENCE (biochemistry and biology/biological science), BUSINESS (business administration and management), COMMUNICATIONS AND THE ARTS (art, Chinese, dramatic arts, English, French, music, and Spanish), COMPUTER AND PHYSICAL SCIENCE (chemistry, mathematics, and physics), ENGINEERING AND ENVIRONMENTAL DESIGN (environmental science), SOCIAL SCIENCE (child psychology/development, economics, history, international studies, philosophy, physical fitness/movement, political science/government, psychology, religion, social work, and sociology). Business administration, political science, and English have the largest enrollments.

ACTIVITIES: 13% of men belong to 4 local fraternities; 21% of women belong to 6 local sororities. There are 90 groups on campus, including art, band, cheerleading, choir, chorale, chorus, computers, dance, drama, ethnic, film, honors, international, jazz band, LGBT, literary magazine, musical theater, newspaper, photography, political, professional, radio and TV, religious, social, social service, and student government. Popular campus events include Helping Hands Day, Tardeada-Latino Cultural Celebration, and MLK Jr. Oratorical Contest. **Sports:** There are 11 intercollegiate sports for men and 10 for women, and 5 intramural sports for men and 5 for women. Facilities include a stadium, gym, playing fields, athletics center, aquatics center, fitness center, and tennis courts. **Graduates:** From July 1, 2015 to June 30, 2016, 259 bachelor's degrees were awarded. The most popular majors were business (12%), political science (10%), and English (10%). 38 companies recruited on campus in 2015-2016. In an average class, 49% graduate in 4 years or less, 62% graduate in 5 years or less, and 64% graduate in 6 years or less. Of the 2015 graduating class, 37% were enrolled in graduate school within 6 months of graduation, and 57% were employed.

SERVICES: Counseling and information services are available, as is tutoring in every subject. **Library/Resources:** The library contains 127,410 volumes, 6,877 microform items, and 1,793 audio/video tapes/CDs/DVDs, and subscribes to 26,365 periodicals including electronic. Computerized library services include interlibrary loans, database searching, Internet access, and Wi-Fi capability. Special learning facilities include an art gallery, radio station, performing arts center, and writing center. **Physically Challenged Students:** 75% of the campus is accessible. Facilities include wheelchair ramps, elevators, special parking, specially equipped restrooms, special class scheduling, lowered drinking fountains, lowered telephones, and special housing. **Special:** Internships are possible fall, spring, and summer. Study abroad is offered in 30 countries. The Whittier Scholars Program offers self-designed interdisciplinary curricula, and dual majors are possible in all majors. Nondegree study and pass/fail options are available. Whittier offers a 3-2 engineering program with the Universities of Southern California and Minnesota, and a 3-3 law degree with Whittier Law School. There are 17 national honor societies and 16 departmental honors programs. **Visiting:** There are regularly scheduled orientations for prospective students, consisting of an interview with an admission officer and a campus tour. Customized visits can be arranged to include faculty, coaches, extracurricular activities, class visits, and residence hall tours. There are guides for informal visits, visitors may sit in on classes, and stay overnight. To schedule a visit, contact the Office of Admissions. **Campus Safety and Security:** Measures include 24-hour foot and vehicle patrol, emergency notification system, self-defense education, and security escort services. There are emergency telephones and lighted pathways/sidewalks.

REQUIREMENTS: The SAT or ACT is required. The SAT I is preferred. The college recommends that applicants have 4 years of high school English, 3 years each of history, math, and science, and 2 years of a foreign language. An essay is required. An interview is recommended. A GPA of 2.5 is required. AP credits are accepted. Important factors in the admissions decision are advanced placement or honors courses, recommendations by school officials, and leadership record. All students must take a total of 120 credits, including at least 30 in the major field, with a minimum GPA of 2.0. Distribution requirements include 4 courses in 4 distinct areas of communication, 4 courses in culture from 4 distinct areas, and a pair of courses in science and society. **Procedure:** Freshmen are admitted fall and spring. Entrance exams should be taken during the junior year or fall of the senior year. There are early admissions, deferred admissions, and rolling admissions plans. Early decision applications should be filed by December 1; regular applications, by February 1 for fall entry; and December 1 for spring entry, along with a $50 fee. Notification of early decision is sent December 29; regular decision, March 1. Applications are accepted on-line. **Transfer Students:** 95 transfer students enrolled in 2015-2016. Transfer applicants are considered on a case-by-case basis, but a minimum GPA of 2.5 is recommended in academic course work. The SAT or the ACT is required for students with fewer than 30 academic units. The GED is accepted for transfer applicants with at least 30 academic units. 30 of 120 credits required for the bachelor's degree must be completed at Whittier. **International Students:** There are 32 international students enrolled. The school actively recruits these students. They must take the TOEFL. They must also take the SAT or ACT.

ADMISSIONS: 83% of the 2016-2017 applicants were accepted. The SAT scores for the 2016-2017 freshman class were: Critical Reading-- 38% below 500, 42% between 500 and 599, 17% between 600 and 699, and 3% between 700 and 800. Math-- 36% below 500, 41% between 500 and 599, 21% between 600 and 699, and 2% between 700 and 800. Writing-- 40% below 500, 42% between 500 and 599, 16% between 600 and 699, and 2% between 700 and 800. The ACT scores were 36% below 12, 27% between 12 and 17, 23% between 18 and 23, 8% between 24 and 29, and 6% above 30. 54% of the current freshmen were in the top fifth of their class; 75% were in the top two fifths. 16 freshmen graduated first in their class. **Admissions Contact:** Lisa Meyer, Vice President of Enrollment. Email: *admissions@whittier.edu* Web: *www.whittier.edu*

FINANCIAL AID: In 2016-2017, 83% of all full-time freshmen and 75% of continuing full-time students received some form of financial aid. 67% of all full-time freshmen and 64% of continuing full-time students received need-based aid. The average freshman award was $31,970. 64% of undergraduate students work part-time. Average annual earnings from campus work are $1280. The average financial indebtedness of the 2016 graduate was $30,970. Whittier is a member of CSS. The college's own financial statement is required. The FAFSA code is 001342. The deadline for filing freshman financial aid applications for fall entry is February 15.

WOODBURY UNIVERSITY C-5

www.woodbury.edu

Burbank, CA 91510	**(818) 252-5221** **(800) 784-9663**
Fax: (818) 767-7520	**Email: info@woodbury.edu**
Full-time: 465 men, 585 women	**Faculty:** n/av
Part-time: 110 men, 145 women	**Ph.D.s:** 58%
Graduate: 110 men, 140 women	**Student/Faculty:** n/av
Year: semesters, summer session	**Tuition:** $36,408
Room & Board: $10,550	**Freshman Class:** n/av
SAT: required	**CEEB CODE:** 4955
Application Deadline: n/av	**COMPETITIVE**

Woodbury University, founded in 1884, is a private institution that emphasizes business and professional design education. The figures in the above capsule and in this profile are approximate. There are 4 undergraduate schools and 3 graduate schools. In addition to regional accreditation, Woodbury has baccalaureate program accreditation with ACBSP,

FIDER, and NAAB. The 22-acre campus is in a suburban area 17 miles north of Los Angeles. Including any residence halls, there are 22 buildings.

STUDENT LIFE: Students are from 41 foreign countries, and Canada. 7% are Foreign; 6% African American; 45% White; 30% Hispanic; 10% Asian American. **Female To Male Ratio:** 1.3:1. The average age of freshmen is 18; all undergraduates, 22. 24% do not continue beyond their first year; 53% remain to graduate. **Housing:** 227 students can be accommodated in college housing, which includes single-sex and coed dorms and off-campus apartments, and nonsmoking suites. On-campus housing is available on a first-come and first-served basis. 80% of students commute. Alcohol is not permitted. All students may keep cars.

FACULTY/CLASSROOMS: 51% of faculty are male; 49% are female. No introductory courses are taught by graduate students. The average class size in an introductory lecture is 25; in a laboratory is 15; and in a regular course is 15.

PROGRAMS OF STUDY: Woodbury confers B.A., B.S., B.Arch. and B.F.A. degrees. Master's degrees are also awarded. Bachelor's degrees are awarded in BUSINESS (accounting, business administration and management, fashion merchandising, marketing/retailing/merchandising, and organizational behavior), COMMUNICATIONS AND THE ARTS (animation, communications, and graphic design), COMPUTER AND PHYSICAL SCIENCE (information sciences and systems), ENGINEERING AND ENVIRONMENTAL DESIGN (architecture and interior design), SOCIAL SCIENCE (fashion design and technology, history, interdisciplinary studies, political science/government, and psychology). Business, and architecture are the strongest academically and have the largest enrollments.

ACTIVITIES: 1% of men belong to 1 local and 1 national fraternities; 1% of women belong to 2 local and 1 national sororities. There are 25 groups on campus, including drama, ethnic, fashion club, international, newspaper, professional, religious, social, social service, and student government. Popular campus events include University Gala, Winter Formal and Springfest. **Sports:** There are 4 intramural sports for men and 4 for women. Facilities include basketball and volleyball courts, weight training and aerobics rooms, outdoor swimming pool, track, and a field for soccer. **Graduates:** From July 1, 2015 to June 30, 2016, 233 bachelor's degrees were awarded. The most popular majors were architecture (30%), business management (16%), and fashion design (10%). In an average class, 34% graduate in 4 years or less, 49% graduate in 5 years or less, and 53% graduate in 6 years or less.

SERVICES: Counseling and information services are available, as is tutoring in some subjects, accounting, physics, structures, economics, and math. There is remedial math, reading, and writing. Books on tape are available for the blind. **Library/Resources:** The library contains 71,178 volumes, 93,770 microform items, and 20,065 audio/video tapes/CDs/DVDs, and subscribes to 358 periodicals including electronic. Computerized library services include interlibrary loans, database searching, and Internet access. Special learning facilities include an art gallery, an architecture gallery, art/design gallery, and fashion center. **Physically Challenged Students:** 95% of the campus is accessible. Facilities include wheelchair ramps, elevators, special parking, specially equipped restrooms, special class scheduling, and special housing. **Special:** Internships or verified work experience is required for all majors with the exception of organizational leadership and interdisciplinary studies. Concurrent registration with area institutions, work-study programs, study abroad in France, Spain, China, Korea, England, and Germany, dual majors, and pass/fail options also are offered. **Visiting:** There are regularly scheduled orientations for prospective students, consisting of meeting with admissions counselors, the president, faculty members, students, financial aid counselors, and student services staff. There are guides for informal visits, visitors may sit in on classes, and stay overnight. To schedule a visit, contact the Admissions Office. **Campus Safety and Security:** Measures include 24-hour foot and vehicle patrol, self-defense education, and security escort services. There are emergency telephones and lighted pathways/sidewalks.

REQUIREMENTS: Application form, essay, 2 academic references, high school transcripts, and SAT or ACT scores are required for all applicants. A GPA of 2.0 is required. AP and CLEP credits are accepted. Important factors in the admissions decision are advanced placement or honors courses, evidence of special talent, and recommendations by school officials. To graduate with a B.S., students must complete 126 semester units, including 61 to 66 in the major with a B.A., 120 including 45 to 54 in the major with a B.F.A., 128 including 68 in the major with a B.Arch., 160 semester units, including 98 in the major. All students must maintain a minimum GPA of 2.0 and take freshman composition, computer literacy, and public speaking courses. Course work in behavioral and social sciences, fine arts, humanities, physical and biological sciences, and math are also part of the curriculum. **Procedure:** Freshmen are admitted fall, spring, and summer. Entrance exams should be taken prior to application. There are deferred admissions and rolling admissions plans. Application deadlines are open. The fall 2016 application fee was $35. Notification is sent on a rolling basis. Applications are accepted on-line. **Transfer Students:** 152 transfer students enrolled in 2015-2016. Applicants are required to have maintained a minimum GPA of 2.0 and to take the SAT or ACT if they have completed fewer than 30 semester units. 45 credits required for the bachelor's degree must be completed at Woodbury. **International Students:** There are 74 international students enrolled. The school actively recruits these students. They must take the TOEFL with a minimum score of 500 on the paper-based TOEFL (PBT). They must also take the SAT or ACT.

Admissions Contact: Ruth Lorenzana, Director of Admissions. Email: *info@woodbury.edu* Web: *www.woodbury.edu*

FINANCIAL AID: In 2016-2017, 88% of all full-time freshmen and 90% of continuing full-time students received some form of financial aid. 88% of all full-time freshmen and 88% of continuing full-time students received need-based aid. The average freshman award was $17,417. Need-based scholarships or need-based grants averaged $14,448; need-based self-help aid (loans and jobs) averaged $3,543; and other non-need-based awards and non-need-based scholarships averaged $12,706. 10% of undergraduate students work part-time. Average annual earnings from campus work are $1200. The average financial indebtedness of the 2016 graduate was $38,660. Woodbury is a member of CSS. The college's own financial statement is required. The FAFSA code is 001343. Check with the school for current application deadlines.

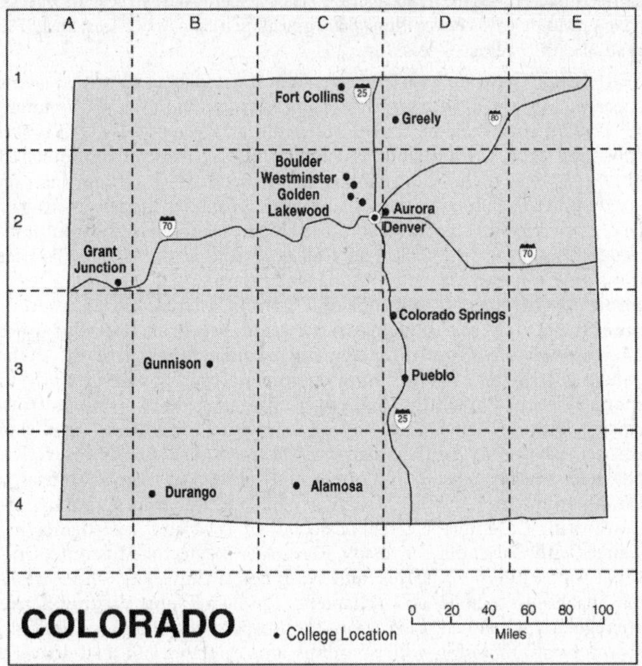

ADAMS STATE UNIVERSITY *(The complete profile is made available exclusively on our website, www.barronspac.com)*

COLORADO CHRISTIAN UNIVERSITY C-2

www.ccu.edu

Lakewood, CO 80226 **(303) 963-3207**
(800) 44 FAITH
Fax: (303) 963-3401 **Email: ccuadmissions@ccu.edu**

Full-time: 425 men, 700 women	**Faculty:** n/av
Part-time: 175 men, 175 women	**Ph.D.s:** 85%
Graduate: 55 men, 80 women	**Student/Faculty:** n/av
Year: semesters, summer session	**Tuition:** $29,360
Room & Board: $10,580	**Freshman Class:** n/av
SAT or ACT: required	**CEEB CODE:** 4659
Application Deadline: August 1	**VERY COMPETITIVE**

Colorado Christian University, founded in 1914, is a private, Christian interdenominational institution offering undergraduate and graduate programs in the arts and sciences, biblical studies, music, and education. The figures in the above capsule and in this profile are approximate. There are 4 undergraduate schools and 3 graduate schools. In addition to regional accreditation, CCU has baccalaureate program accreditation with NCA. The 29-acre campus is in a suburban area 10 miles west of Denver. Including any residence halls, there are 21 buildings.

STUDENT LIFE: 55% of undergraduates are from Colorado. Others are from 50 states, 16 foreign countries, and Canada. 81% are White; 7% African American; 6% Hispanic; 1% Asian American; 1% American Indian/Alaska Native; 1% Foreign. 99% are Protestant. **Female To Male Ratio:** 1.5:1. The average age of freshmen is 19; all undergraduates, 20. 33% do not continue beyond their first year. **Housing:** 732 students can be accommodated in college housing, which includes single-sex dorms, on-campus apartments, off-campus apartments, and married student housing. In addition, there are special-interest houses. On-campus housing is guaranteed for the freshman year only, and is available on a first-come, first-served basis, and is available on a lottery system for upperclassmen. Priority is given to out-of-town students. 65% of students live on campus; of those, 38% remain on campus on weekends. Alcohol is not permitted. All students may keep cars.

FACULTY/CLASSROOMS: 65% of faculty are male; 35% are female. No introductory courses are taught by graduate students. The average class size in an introductory lecture is 25; in a laboratory is 18; and in a regular course is 30.

PROGRAMS OF STUDY: CCU confers B.A., B.S. and B.M. degrees. Associate and master's degrees are also awarded. Bachelor's degrees are awarded in BIOLOGICAL SCIENCE (biology/biological science), BUSINESS (accounting, business administration and management, human resources, management information systems, and management science), COMMUNICATIONS AND THE ARTS (art, communications, English, and music), COMPUTER AND PHYSICAL SCIENCE (computer management and science), EDUCATION (elementary education, music education, and secondary education), SOCIAL SCIENCE (biblical studies, history, liberal arts/general studies, psychology, social science, theological studies, and youth ministry). Science, biology, and education are the strongest academically. Human resources management, computer/information technology, and liberal arts have the largest enrollments.

ACTIVITIES: There are no fraternities or sororities. There are 21 groups on campus, including band, cheerleading, choir, chorus, computers, drama, honors, international, jazz band, literary magazine, musical theater, newspaper, orchestra, photography, professional, religious, social, social service, student government, symphony, and yearbook. Popular campus events include Preview Days, Spring Retreat, and New Student Retreat. **Sports:** There are 5 intercollegiate sports for men and 5 for women, and 6 intramural sports for men and 6 for women. Facilities include a gym, and soccer and practice fields.

SERVICES: Counseling and information services are available, as is tutoring in every subject. There is remedial math, reading, and writing. **Library/Resources:** The library contains 53,532 volumes, 281,234 microform items, and 3,917 audio/video tapes/CDs/DVDs, and subscribes to 415 periodicals including electronic. Computerized library services include interlibrary loans, database searching, and Internet access. Special learning facilities include an art gallery. **Physically Challenged Students:** 85% of the campus is accessible. Facilities include wheelchair ramps, special parking, specially equipped restrooms, special class scheduling, lowered drinking fountains, lowered telephones, and special housing. **Special:** The school offers an ROTC program in cooperation with CU Boulder, cross-registration with the Focus on the Family Institute, internships, study abroad in 7 countries, a Washington semester, and work-study programs. Accelerated degree programs are available in Christian leadership, organizational management, and management of information systems. Dual and student-designed majors, nondegree study, pass/fail options, and credit for life, military, and work experience are also available. There are 2 national honor societies, a freshman honors program, and 1 departmental honors program. **Visiting:** There are regularly scheduled orientations for prospective students. There are guides for informal visits, visitors may sit in on classes, and stay overnight. To schedule a visit, contact the Office of Admissions. **Campus Safety and Security:** Measures include 24-hour foot and vehicle patrol and security escort services. There are emergency telephones and lighted pathways/sidewalks.

REQUIREMENTS: The SAT or ACT is required. Applicants must be graduates of an accredited secondary school, and have completed 4 years of English, 3 years of math, 2-3 years of science, and 2 years of a foreign language. The GED is accepted. Two essay are required. If you don't meet the admission requirements, your application file will be reviewed by a committee. A campus visit is recommended. A GPA of 2.8 is required. AP and CLEP credits are accepted. To graduate, students must complete at least 128 semester hours, including the 48-hour general education requirement and courses specified for the major, with a minimum cumulative GPA of 2.0, 2.5 in the major. The university requires 4 semesters of Christian service and regular chapel attendance. All students must complete 12 credits in biblical studies. **Procedure:** Freshmen are admitted to all sessions. There are deferred admissions and rolling admissions plans. Applications should be filed by August 1 for fall entry. The fall 2016 application fee was $40. Applications are accepted on-line. **Transfer Students:** Applicants for transfer should have completed 12 college credits with a minimum GPA of 2.0. 30 of 128 credits required for the bachelor's degree must be completed at CCU. **International Students:** The school actively recruits these students. They must take the TOEFL and the college's own test. They must also take the SAT or ACT.

Admissions Contact: Simeon Turner, Assoc. Director of Admissions. Email: *ccuadmissions@ccu.edu* Web: *www.ccu.edu*

FINANCIAL AID: The FAFSA code is 009401. Check with the school for current application deadlines.

COLORADO COLLEGE D-3
www.coloradocollege.edu

Colorado Springs, CO 80903 (719) 389-6344
(800) 542-7214
Fax: (719) 389-6816 Email: admission@coloradocollege.edu

Full-time: 957 men, 1127 women	**Faculty:** IIB, +$
Part-time: 4 men, 13 women	**Ph.D.s:** 99%
Graduate: 5 men, 8 women	**Student/Faculty:** 10 to 1
Year: other, summer session	**Tuition:** $50,892
Room & Board: $11,668	**Freshman Class:** 7894 applied, 1262 accepted, 533 enrolled
SAT CR/M/W: 670/660/660 **ACT:** 30	**CEEB CODE:** 4072
Application Deadline: January 15	**MOST COMPETITIVE**

Colorado College, founded in 1874, is an independent liberal arts and sciences institution. The academic year is based on the "Block Plan," under which students take one course during each of the eight three-and-a-half-week-long blocks of study. There is also a two-block Summer Session. There is 1 undergraduate school and 1 graduate school. In addition to regional accreditation, CC has baccalaureate program accreditation with NCA. The 90-acre campus is in an urban area in Colorado Springs, 70 miles south of Denver. Including any residence halls, there are 77 buildings.

STUDENT LIFE: 83% of undergraduates are from out of state, mostly the Northeast. Students are from 48 states, 65 foreign countries, and Canada. 9% are Hispanic; 9% two or more races; 8% Foreign; 66% White; 4% Asian American; 3% African American; 1% race unknown. **Female To Male Ratio:** 1.2:1. The average age of freshmen is 18; all undergraduates, 20. 4% do not continue beyond their first year; 87% remain to graduate. **Housing:** 1555 students can be accommodated in college housing, which includes single-sex and coed dorms, on-campus apartments, and off-campus apartments. In addition, there are language houses, fraternity houses, substance-free, smoke-free, diversity, community arts, and sustainable living houses. On-campus housing is guaranteed for all 4 years. 75% of students live on campus. Upperclassmen may keep cars.

FACULTY/CLASSROOMS: 52% of faculty are male; 48% are female. All teach undergraduates. No introductory courses are taught by graduate students. The average class size in a regular course is 15.

PROGRAMS OF STUDY: CC confers B.A. degrees. Master's degrees are also awarded. Bachelor's degrees are awarded in BIOLOGICAL SCIENCE (biology ecology and field biology, biochemistry, molecular biology, and neurosciences), BUSINESS (international economics), COMMUNICATIONS AND THE ARTS (art history and appreciation, classics, comparative literature, creative writing, dance, dramatic arts, English, film arts, Germanic languages and literature, music, romance languages and literature, and studio art), COMPUTER AND PHYSICAL SCIENCE (chemistry, computer science, geology, mathematics, and physics), EDUCATION (education), ENGINEERING AND ENVIRONMENTAL DESIGN (environmental science), SOCIAL SCIENCE (anthropology, Asian/Oriental studies, economics, French studies, gender studies, Hispanic American studies, history, history of philosophy, interdisciplinary studies, Italian studies, liberal arts/general studies, philosophy, political science/government, psychology, religion, Russian and Slavic studies, sociology, Southwest American studies, and women's studies). Economics, sociology, and political science have the largest enrollments.

ACTIVITIES: There are 140 groups on campus, including art, band, chess, choir, chorale, chorus, communications, computers, dance, debate, drama, environmental, ethnic, film, forensics, health awareness, honors, international, jazz band, LGBT, literary magazine, musical theater, newspaper, orchestra, other major clubs are outdoor, photography, political, professional, religious, science, social, social service, student government, symphony, and yearbook. Popular campus events include Afternoon and Evening Blues, Rock, Folk, Jazz, World Music Concerts, Annual Arts and Crafts Sale, Winter Ball, and Homecoming. **Sports:** There are 8 intercollegiate sports for men and 8 for women, and 14 intramural sports for men and 12 for women. Facilities include a sports center with two gyms, weight & exercise rooms, squash, tennis, racquetball courts, a pool, ice rink, and playing fields. **Graduates:** From July 1, 2015 to June 30, 2016, 539 bachelor's degrees were awarded. The most popular majors were economics (10%), organismal, evolutionary, and ecological biology (7%), and political science (7%). 27 companies recruited on campus in 2015-2016. In an average class, 2% graduate in 3 years or less, 82% graduate in 4 years or less, 86% graduate in 5 years or less, and 87% graduate in 6 years or less.

SERVICES: There are a variety of services and resources to help students succeed. **Library/Resources:** The 2 libraries contain 542,347 volumes, 131,550 microform items, and 36,367 audio/video tapes/CDs/DVDs, and subscribe to 61,793 periodicals including electronic. Computerized library services include interlibrary loans, database searching, Internet access, and Wi-Fi capability. Special learning facilities include an art gallery, an electronic music studio, music library, telescope dome, multimedia computer lab, the Colorado College Press, an herbarium, Fourier transform nuclear magnetic resonance spectrometer, a scanning electronic microscope and transmission electronic microscope, an environmental service van equipped for field research, petrographic microscopes, an X-ray diffractometer, sedimentology lab, metabolic equipment, hydrostatic weighing equipment, and a cadaver study in sports science. **Physically Challenged Students:** Staff members work closely with students who have documented disabilities requiring accommodation to ensure equal access to the college's programs, activities, and services. **Special:** CC offers study abroad in many countries, a Washington semester, student-designed majors, 3-3 law program opportunity with Columbia University School of Law, and 3-2 engineering degrees with Columbia University, Rensselaer Polytechnic Institute, University of Southern California, and Washington University. There are 12 national honor societies and a chapter of Phi Beta Kappa. **Visiting:** There are regularly scheduled orientations for prospective students, a class visit, an information session with an admissions director, and a student-led tour. There are guides for informal visits, visitors may sit in on classes, and stay overnight. To schedule a visit, contact Admission Office. **Campus Safety and Security:** Measures include 24-hour foot and vehicle patrol, emergency notification system, self-defense education, and security escort services. There are emergency telephones, lighted pathways/sidewalks, controlled access to dorms/residences, whistle stop program, and fire safety inspections.

REQUIREMENTS: Applicants should have completed at least 16 (18 to 20 recommended) high school academic credits. The GED is accepted. An essay is required. Colorado College has adopted a flexible testing policy that allows applicants an expanded set of choices for meeting standardized test requirements. AP credits are accepted. Important factors in the admissions decision are advanced placement or honors courses, extracurricular activities record, and evidence of special talent. To graduate, students must complete 32 units with a cumulative GPA of 2.0. No major may require more than 14 units in any one department and no more than 16 overall (including prerequisites). Students must take and pass at least one full unit in each academic division. They must complete a Critical Perspectives requirement, consisting of "West in Time" units (one two-block course, two units); a "Global Cultures" unit (one unit); a "Social Inequality" unit (one unit); "Scientific Investigation of the Natural World" (two units, including at least one lab or field course); "Quantitative Reasoning" (one unit). Courses may meet more than one designation (for example, a course may be designated both "West in Time" and "Global Cultures") but students must choose one designation or the other, except in the case of "Quantitative Reasoning," which may be fulfilled along with any of the other Critical Perspectives requirements. Basic competency in a foreign language is also required, as are two units of a First-Year Experience course. **Procedure:** Freshmen are admitted fall and spring. Entrance exams must be received by January 15 for fall entry. There are early decision, early admissions, and deferred admissions plans. Early decision applications should be filed by November 10; regular applications, by January 15 for fall entry, along with a $60 fee. Notification of early decision is sent December 15; regular decision, April 1. 280 early decision candidates were accepted for the 2016-2017 class. 213 applicants were on the 2016 waiting list; 21 were admitted. Applications are accepted on-line. **Transfer Students:** 31 transfer students enrolled in 2015-2016. 64 of 128 credits required for the bachelor's degree must be completed at CC. **International Students:** There are 162 international students enrolled. The school actively recruits these students. Applicants must submit either the SAT Reasoning, ACT test, or three exams of the applicant's choice selected from a list.

ADMISSIONS: 16% of the 2016-2017 applicants were accepted. The SAT scores for the 2016-2017 freshman class were: Critical Reading-- 3% below 500, 19% between 500 and 599, 38% between 600 and 699, and 40% between 700 and 800. Math-- 1% below 500, 13% between 500 and 599, 54% between 600 and 699, and 32% between 700 and 800. Writing-- 4% below 500, 12% between 500 and 599, 56% between 600 and 699, and 28% between 700 and 800. The ACT scores were 2% between 18 and 23, 33% between 24 and 29, and 65% above 30. 86% of the current freshmen were in the top fifth of their class; 98% were in the top two fifths. **Admissions Contact:** Carlos Jiminez, Director of Admissions - Outreach and Recruitment. Email: *admission@coloradocollege.edu* Web: *www.coloradocollege.edu*

FINANCIAL AID: In 2016-2017, 42% of all full-time freshmen and 45% of continuing full-time students received some form of financial aid. 32% of all full-time freshmen and 30% of continuing full-time students received need-based aid. The average freshman award was $39,182. Need-based scholarships or need-based grants averaged $41,763 ($66,158 maximum); need-based self-help aid (loans and jobs) averaged $8,071 ($13,100 maximum); non-need-based athletic scholarships averaged $52,455 ($66,744 maximum); and other non-need-based awards and non-need-based scholarships averaged $14,890 ($62,560 maximum). 49% of undergraduate students work part-time. Average annual earnings from campus work are $1321. The average financial indebtedness of the 2016 graduate was $20,742. CC is a member of CSS. The CSS/Profile, noncustodial parents' form, parent and student tax return are required. The FAFSA code is 001347. The priority date for freshman financial aid applications for fall entry is November 10. The deadline for filing freshman financial aid, and applications for fall entry is January 15.

COLORADO MESA UNIVERSITY *(The complete profile is made available exclusively on our website, www.barronspac.com)*

COLORADO SCHOOL OF MINES — C-2

www.mines.edu

Golden, CO 80401	**(303) 273-3220** **(888) 446-9489**
Fax: (303) 273-3509	**Email: admit@mines.edu**
Full-time: 3080 men, 1129 women	**Faculty:** I, av$
Part-time: 136 men, 38 women	**Ph.D.s:** 90%
Graduate: 936 men, 354 women	**Student/Faculty:** n/av
Year: semesters, summer session	**Tuition:** $17,842 ($36,148)
Room & Board: $11,477	**Freshman Class:** 12340 applied, 4501 accepted, 999 enrolled
SAT CR/M/W: 635/680/605 **ACT:** 30	**CEEB CODE:** 4073
Application Deadline: n/av	**MOST COMPETITIVE**

Colorado School of Mines, founded in 1874, is a public institution offering programs in math, science, economics, and engineering. Figures in the above capsule and in this profile are approximate. There is 1 undergraduate school. In addition to regional accreditation, Mines has baccalaureate program accreditation with ABET. The 373-acre campus is in a small town 20 miles west of Denver. Including any residence halls, there are 40 buildings.

STUDENT LIFE: 76% of undergraduates are from Colorado. Others are from 44 states, 52 foreign countries, and Canada. 90% are from public schools. 79% are White; 7% Hispanic; 7% Foreign; 5% Asian American; 2% African American; 1% American Indian/Alaska Native. 52% are Protestant; 21% Catholic; 20% claim no religious affiliation. **Male To Female Ratio:** 2.7:1. The average age of freshmen is 18; all undergraduates, 20. 14% do not continue beyond their first year; 67% remain to graduate. **Housing:** 855 students can be accommodated in college housing, which includes single-sex and coed dorms, on-campus apartments, and married student housing. In addition, there are fraternity houses and sorority houses. On-campus housing is guaranteed for the freshman year only, and is available on a first-come, and first-served basis. 10% of students commute. All students may keep cars.

FACULTY/CLASSROOMS: 80% of faculty are male; 20% are female. 93% teach undergraduates, 50% do research, and 50% do both. No introductory courses are taught by graduate students. The average class size in an introductory lecture is 100; in a laboratory is 22; and in a regular course is 29.

PROGRAMS OF STUDY: Mines confers B.S. degrees. Master's and doctoral degrees are also awarded. Bachelor's degrees are awarded in COMPUTER AND PHYSICAL SCIENCE (chemistry, mathematics, and physics), ENGINEERING AND ENVIRONMENTAL DESIGN (chemical engineering, engineering, geological engineering, geophysical engineering, metallurgical engineering, mining and mineral engineering, and petroleum/natural gas engineering), SOCIAL SCIENCE (economics). Chemical engineering, geological engineering, and petroleum engineering are the strongest academically. General engineering, chemical engineering, and engineering physics have the largest enrollments.

ACTIVITIES: 19% of men belong to 7 national fraternities; 19% of women belong to 3 national sororities. There are 95 groups on campus, including band, cheerleading, choir, chorus, computers, drama, ethnic, honors, international, jazz band, literary magazine, marching band, musical theater, newspaper, pep band, political, professional, radio station, religious, social, social service, student government, symphony, and yearbook. Popular campus events include International Day and Parents Day. **Sports:** There are 9 intercollegiate sports for men and 7 for women, and 20 intramural sports for men and 20 for women. Facilities include a 10,000-seat stadium, a recreation center, gym, numerous intramural fields, tennis courts, and a field house. **Graduates:** From July 1, 2015 to June 30, 2016, 889 bachelor's degrees were awarded. The most popular majors were general engineering (34%), petroleum engineering (12%), and chemical engineering (11%). 267 companies recruited on campus in 2015-2016. In an average class, 1% graduate in 3 years or less, 40% graduate in 4 years or less, 66% graduate in 5 years or less, and 69% graduate in 6 years or less.

SERVICES: Counseling and information services are available, as is tutoring in most subjects. There is a reader service for the blind, and remedial math and writing. **Library/Resources:** The library contains 356,000 volumes, 236,000 microform items, and subscribes to 2,700 periodicals including electronic. Computerized library services include interlibrary loans, database searching, and Internet access. **Physically Challenged Students:** All of the campus is accessible. Facilities include wheelchair ramps, elevators, special parking, specially equipped restrooms, special class scheduling, lowered drinking fountains, lowered telephones, and special housing. **Special:** Co-op programs, internships in the McBride honors program, and in humanities, accelerated degree programs in all majors, dual majors, study abroad in 20 countries, and nondegree study are offered. There is 1 national honor society, a freshman honors program, and 3 departmental honors programs. **Visiting:** There are regularly scheduled orientations for prospective students, including a half-day-long visitation program twice each fall where students may visit departments and talk with faculty. Sessions in admissions and financial aid also are given. There are guides for informal visits and visitors may sit in on classes. To schedule a visit, contact the Admissions Office. **Campus Safety and Security:** Measures include 24-hour foot and vehicle patrol, emergency notification system, and self-defense education. There are emergency telephones and lighted pathways/sidewalks.

REQUIREMENTS: The SAT or ACT is required. Applicants must be graduates of an accredited secondary school. The GED is accepted. Students should have completed 17 high school academic credits, including 4 units each of English and math, 3 units of science (all of these units including lab), 1 unit of foreign language, 3 units of social studies, and 2 units of academic electives. AP credits are accepted. Important factors in the admissions decision are advanced placement or honors courses, leadership record, evidence of special talent, personality/intangible qualities, extracurricular activities record, recommendations by alumni, geographical diversity, and recommendations by school officials. Students must complete 138 to 148 credit hours, with 35 to 40 hours in the major and a GPA of 2.0. Required courses include humanities, calculus, physics, computer science, chemistry, and phys ed. **Procedure:** Freshmen are admitted to all sessions. Entrance exams should be taken by late in the junior year or early in the senior year. There are deferred admissions and rolling admissions plans. Check with the school for current application deadlines. The application fee is $45. Applications are accepted on-line. **Transfer Students:** 159 transfer students enrolled in 2015-2016. Transfer applicants must have a minimum GPA of 2.75. 30 of 138 credits required for the bachelor's degree must be completed at Mines. **International Students:** There are 204 international students enrolled. The school actively recruits these students. They must take the TOEFL with a minimum score of 550 on the paper-based TOEFL (PBT) or 79 on the Internet-based version (iBT) and the Comprehensive English Language Test.

ADMISSIONS: 36% of the 2016-2017 applicants were accepted. 75 freshmen graduated first in their class. **Admissions Contact:** Bruce Goetz, Director of Admissions. Email: *admit@mines.edu* Web: *www.mines.edu*

FINANCIAL AID: In 2016-2017, 85% of all full-time freshmen received some form of financial aid. The average freshman award was $12,181.

Need-based scholarships or need-based grants averaged $4,835; need-based self-help aid (loans and jobs) averaged $5,263; non-need-based athletic scholarships averaged $7,129; other non-need-based awards and non-need-based scholarships averaged $4,764; and $7,666 from other forms of aid. The average financial indebtedness of the 2016 graduate was $23,667. Mines is a member of CSS. The FAFSA code is 001348. Check with the school for current application deadlines.

COLORADO STATE UNIVERSITY C-1

www.colostate.edu

Fort Collins, CO 80523 **(970) 491-6909**

Fax: (970) 491-7799
Email: admissions@colostate.edu
Full-time: 10,791 men, 11,305 women
Faculty: 1026
Ph.D.s: 99%
Part-time: 929 men, 743 women
Student/Faculty: 18 to 1
Graduate: 2070 men, 2459 women
Tuition: $11,052 ($28,346)
Year: semesters, summer session
Freshman Class: 21759 applied, 16963 accepted, 4956 enrolled
Room & Board: $11,110
SAT CR/M: 570/570 **ACT:** 25
CEEB CODE: 4075
Application Deadline: February 1
VERY COMPETITIVE

Colorado State University, founded in 1870 and part of the Colorado State University system, is a public land-grant institution offering 72 undergraduate degrees in 53 departments within 8 colleges. There are 8 undergraduate schools and 1 graduate school. In addition to regional accreditation, Colorado State has baccalaureate program accreditation with AACSB, ABET, ACCE, ACEJMC, CSWE, NASM, SAF, TEAC, LAAB, SRM, CIDA, ACEND, NEHSPAC, CACREP, EHAC, AAFMT, ACOTE, APA, and AVMA. The 586-acre campus is in a suburban area about 65 miles north of Denver. Including any residence halls, there are 157 buildings.

STUDENT LIFE: 74% of undergraduates are from Colorado. Others are from 50 states, 109 foreign countries, and Canada. 70% are White; 11% Hispanic; 7% Foreign; 3% Asian American; 3% two or more races; 3% race unknown; 2% African American; 1% American Indian/Alaska Native. **Female To Male Ratio:** 1.1:1. The average age of freshmen is 18; all undergraduates, 21. 14% do not continue beyond their first year; 67% remain to graduate. **Housing:** 6659 students can be accommodated in college housing, which includes coed dorms, on-campus apartments, off-campus apartments, and married student housing. In addition, there are special-interest houses, honors floors, and more than 10 different residential learning communities. On-campus housing is guaranteed for the freshman year only, and is available on a first-come, first-served basis. 71% of students commute. All students may keep cars.

FACULTY/CLASSROOMS: 63% of faculty are male; 37% are female. All teach undergraduates, and all do research. Graduate students teach 15% of introductory courses. The average class size in an introductory lecture is 57; in a laboratory is 23; and in a regular course is 38.

PROGRAMS OF STUDY: Colorado State confers B.A., B.S., B.F.A., B.S.W., and B.M. degrees. Master's and doctoral degrees are also awarded. Bachelor's degrees are awarded in AGRICULTURE (agricultural business management, agricultural economics, agronomy, animal science, equine science, fishing and fisheries, forestry and related sciences, horticulture, natural resources, natural resource management, range/farm management, and soil science), BIOLOGICAL SCIENCE (biochemistry, biology/biological science, botany, ecology, microbiology, neurosciences, nutrition, wildlife biology, and zoology), BUSINESS (accounting, apparel and accessories marketing, banking and finance, business administration and management, hospitality management services, hotel/motel and restaurant management, management information systems, marketing/retailing/merchandising, real estate, recreational facilities management, and tourism), COMMUNICATIONS AND THE ARTS (apparel design, art, art history and appreciation, communications, creative writing, dance, dramatic arts, drawing, English, fiber/textiles/weaving, fine arts, foreign language, French, German, graphic design, journalism, languages, metal/jewelry, music, music performance, music theory and composition, painting, performing arts, photography, sculpture, Spanish, theatre acting, theater design, theatre production, and theatre studies), COMPUTER AND PHYSICAL SCIENCE (applied mathematics, chemistry, computer science, geology, information sciences and systems, mathematics, natural sciences, physical sciences, physics secondary education, physics, and statistics), EDUCATION (agricultural education, art education, early childhood education, education, English education, foreign languages education, French studies K-12 education, mathematics education, music education, science education, social studies education, Spanish education K-12, and technology & science education), ENGINEERING AND ENVIRONMENTAL DESIGN (biomedical engineering, chemical engineering, civil engineering, computer engineering, computer technology, construction management, electrical/electronics engineering, engineering, engineering and applied science, engineering physics, environmental engineering, interior design, landscape architecture/design, and mechanical engineering), HEALTH PROFESSIONS (biomedical science, environmental health science, exercise science, health science, and music therapy), SOCIAL SCIENCE (anthropology, economics, ethnic studies, family/consumer studies, fire services administration, food science, history, human development, interdisciplinary studies, international studies, liberal arts/general studies, philosophy, political science/government, psychology, social work, sociology, and water resources). Engineering, journalism & technical communication, business, and computer science are the strongest academically. Biology, psychology, and health & exercise science have the largest enrollments.

ACTIVITIES: 9% of men belong to 26 national fraternities; 13% of women belong to 19 national sororities. There are 465 groups on campus, including art, band, cheerleading, chess, choir, chorale, chorus, computers, dance, drama, drill team, environmental, ethnic, film, honors, international, jazz band, LGBT, literary magazine, marching band, musical theater, newspaper, opera, orchestra, pep band, photography, political, professional, radio and TV, religious, social, social service, student government, and symphony. Popular campus events include Homecoming, Ag Day, and President's Annual Address and Picnic. **Sports:** There are 5 intercollegiate sports for men and 9 for women, and 24 intramural sports for men and 24 for women. Facilities include a 30,000-seat stadium, an 8745-seat arena, indoor and outdoor tracks, tennis complex, intramural fields, indoor swimming pools, a comprehensive student recreation center (featuring free weights, state-of-the-art fitness equipment, climbing wall and sports courts), and a ropes course. **Graduates:** From July 1, 2015 to June 30, 2016, 4995 bachelor's degrees were awarded. The most popular majors were business/marketing (14%), biological/life sciences (10%), and social sciences (9%). 840 companies recruited on campus in 2015-2016. In an average class, 2% graduate in 3 years or less, 41% graduate in 4 years or less, 63% graduate in 5 years or less, and 66% graduate in 6 years or less. Of the 2015 graduating class, 24% were enrolled in graduate school within 6 months of graduation, and 62% were employed.

SERVICES: Counseling and information services are available, as is tutoring in most subjects. There is a reader service for the blind. Interpreters and note takers are available. **Library/Resources:** The 2 libraries contain 2.8 million volumes, 86,614 microform items, and 2,890 audio/video tapes/CDs/DVDs, and subscribe to 77,181 periodicals including electronic. Computerized library services include interlibrary loans, database searching, Internet access, and Wi-Fi capability. Special learning facilities include an art gallery, radio station, and TV station. Colorado State University boasts many unique, state-of-the-art learning facilities including a concert hall, a Thrust theatre, a music hall, engineering research center, equine center, veterinary teaching hospital, environmental learning center, and a plant environmental research center. These are just a few of the cutting-edge learning facilities that serve the many disciplines at CSU. **Physically Challenged Students:** 98% of the campus is accessible. Facilities include wheelchair ramps, elevators, special parking, specially equipped restrooms, special class scheduling, lowered drinking fountains, lowered telephones, and special housing. **Special:** Colorado State offers a co-op program in Engineering, study abroad, a semester at sea, work-study programs, internships, B.A.-B.S. degrees, dual majors, and pass/fail options. Teaching certification students receive a bachelor's degree in their chosen subject and also complete a certification sequence through the School of Education. There are 41 national honor societies, Phi Beta Kappa, a freshman honors program, and 28 departmental honors programs. **Visiting:** There are regularly scheduled orientations for prospective students, and regularly scheduled visit days provide specialized information for particular groups including high school seniors and juniors, transfer students, special interests, and others. A daily information session and campus tour are presented each weekday. There are guides for informal visits and visitors may sit in on classes. To schedule a visit, contact Office of Admissions. **Campus Safety and Security:** Measures include 24-hour foot and vehicle patrol, emergency notification system, self-defense education, and security escort services. There are shuttle buses, emergency telephones, lighted pathways/sidewalks, controlled access to dorms/residences, lectures by campus police on a variety of safety issues, a crime victim support unit, safe walk escort, and a bike patrol.

REQUIREMENTS: The SAT or ACT is required. Graduation from secondary school is required. The GED is accepted. Priority consideration is given to applicants who have earned a minimum 3.25 GPA with no D/F grades and who will have successfully satisfied our academic course work standards before enrolling at CSU. Applicants with a GPA below 3.25, occasional D/F grades, and/or fewer than the 18 recommended high school units are encouraged to apply, since many factors are considered in the holistic review process. The 18 recommended high school credits are to include 4 English, 4 math, 3 science (at least 2 must include a lab), 2 social studies, 1 history, 2 foreign language (must be the same language), and 2 academic electives. An essay (minimum 250 words) and 1 recommendation are required. The most recent freshman class entered with an average GPA of 3.61; ACT Composite score of 25.2; SAT Critical Reading score of 568; and SAT Math score of 572. AP and CLEP credits are accepted. In order to graduate, students must complete a minimum of 120 credit hours (more for some programs), 42 of which must be upper division. The minimum GPA required for graduation is 2.0. Students must complete the All University Core and all curricular requirements as described in the current catalog. **Procedure:** Freshmen are admitted to all sessions. Entrance exams should be taken during the junior year or early fall of the senior year. There are deferred admissions and rolling admissions plans. Applications should be filed by February 1 for fall entry; November 1 for spring entry, along with a $50 fee. Notification is sent on a rolling basis. Applications are accepted on-line. **Transfer Students:** 2292 transfer students enrolled in 2015-2016. Strong candidates for transfer admission have earned a minimum 2.5 cumulative GPA in 30 or more college-level academic semester credits and have satisfied the transfer admissions requirement in mathematics. Students holding an Associate Degree from an accredited Colorado institution are guaranteed admission provided that it is the last institution attended and that a cumulative 2.0 GPA has been achieved from all institutions attended. Specific majors may require additional course-work and a higher GPA. 30 of 120 credits required for the bachelor's degree must be completed at Colorado State. **International Students:** There are 951 international students enrolled. The school actively recruits these students. They must take the TOEFL with a minimum score of 550 on the paper-based TOEFL (PBT) or 79 on the Internet-based version (iBT). Scores from other English language proficiency exams may be considered in lieu of the TOEFL. They must also take the SAT or ACT.

ADMISSIONS: 78% of the 2016-2017 applicants were accepted. The SAT scores for the 2016-2017 freshman class were: Critical Reading-- 19% below 500, 43% between 500 and 599, 32% between 600 and 699, and 6% between 700 and 800. Math-- 18% below 500, 43% between 500 and 599, 33% between 600 and 699, and 6% between 700 and 800. The ACT scores were 1% between 12 and 17, 34% between 18 and 23, 51% between 24 and 29, and 14% above 30. 39% of the current freshmen were in the top fifth of their class; 71% were in the top two fifths. There were 6 National Merit finalists. 65 freshmen graduated first in their class. **Admissions Contact:** Melissa Trifiletti, Director of Admissions. Email: *admissions@colostate.edu* Web: *www.colostate.edu*

FINANCIAL AID: In 2016-2017, 67% of all full-time freshmen and 58% of continuing full-time students received some form of financial aid. 50% of all full-time freshmen and 45% of continuing full-time students received need-based aid. The average freshman award was $10,664. Need-based scholarships or need-based grants averaged $8,107; need-based self-help aid (loans and jobs) averaged $5,396; non-need-based athletic scholarships averaged $22,190; and other non-need-based awards and non-need-based scholarships averaged $5,142. 31% of undergraduate students work part-time. Average annual earnings from campus work are $3314. The average financial indebtedness of the 2016 graduate was $25,155. The FAFSA code is 001350. The priority date for freshman financial aid applications for fall entry is March 1.

COLORADO STATE UNIVERSITY-PUEBLO D-3

www.csupueblo.edu

Pueblo, CO 81001 (719) 549-2462 (719) 549-2100
Fax: (719) 549-2419 **Email: chrissy.holiday@csupueblo.edu**

Full-time: 1774 men, 1968 women	**Faculty:** n/av
Part-time: 540 men, 925 women	**Ph.D.s:** 70%
Graduate: 374 men, 1508 women	**Student/Faculty:** n/av
Year: semesters, summer session	**Tuition:** $9378 ($21,512)
Room & Board: $8856	**Freshman Class:** n/av
SAT: required **ACT:** 21	**CEEB CODE:** 4611
Application Deadline: August 1	**COMPETITIVE**

Colorado State University-Pueblo, founded in 1933, is part of the Colorado State University System. The public institution offers undergraduate programs in humanities and social sciences, fine arts, business administration, nursing, the natural sciences, technology, engineering, and education. There are 4 undergraduate schools and 1 graduate school. In addition to regional accreditation, CSU-Pueblo has baccalaureate program accreditation with AACSB, ABET, CSWE, NASM, NLN, TEAC, ACS, and CAATE. The 275-acre campus is in an urban area 100 miles south of Denver, 50 miles south of Colorado Springs, 100 miles north of New Mexico. Including any residence halls, there are 23 buildings.

STUDENT LIFE: 87% of undergraduates are from Colorado. Others are from 41 states, 40 foreign countries, and Canada. 51% are White; 30% Hispanic; 7% African American; 3% Foreign; 3% two or more races; 3% race unknown; 2% Asian American; 1% American Indian/Alaska Native. **Female To Male Ratio:** 1.6:1. The average age of freshmen is 19; all undergraduates, 26. 39% do not continue beyond their first year; 27% remain to graduate. **Housing:** 652 students can be accommodated in college housing, which includes coed dorms and on-campus apartments. On-campus housing is guaranteed for the freshman year only, and is available on a first-come, and first-served basis. 81% of students commute. Alcohol is not permitted. All students may keep cars.

FACULTY/CLASSROOMS: 57% of faculty are male; 43% are female. 99% teach undergraduates, 10% do research, and 4% do both. No introductory courses are taught by graduate students. The average class size in an introductory lecture is 70; in a laboratory is 24; and in a regular course is 22.

PROGRAMS OF STUDY: CSU-Pueblo confers B.A., B.S., B.S.B.A., B.F.A., B.S.C.E.T., B.S.I.En., B.S.N. and B.S.W. degrees. Master's degrees are also awarded. Bachelor's degrees are awarded in BIOLOGICAL SCIENCE (biochemistry, biology/biological science, and biotechnology), BUSINESS (accounting, business administration and management, and recreation and leisure services), COMMUNICATIONS AND THE ARTS (art, broadcasting, communications, English, journalism, music performance, music theory and composition, and Spanish), COMPUTER AND PHYSICAL SCIENCE (chemistry, information sciences and systems, mathematics, and physics), EDUCATION (music education), ENGINEERING AND ENVIRONMENTAL DESIGN (automotive technology, civil engineering technology, electrical/electronics engineering technology, industrial administration/management, industrial engineering, mechanical engineering technology, and preengineering), HEALTH PROFESSIONS (chiropractic, environmental health science, exercise science, medical technology, nursing, occupational therapy, physician's assistant, predentistry, premedicine, preoptometry, preosteopathy, prepharmacy, prepodiatry, preveterinary science, and speech pathology/audiology), SOCIAL SCIENCE (criminology, economics, history, political science/government, prelaw, psychology, social science, social work, and sociology). Business, engineering, and nursing are the strongest academically. Business, nursing, and biology have the largest enrollments.

ACTIVITIES: 1% of men belong to 2 national fraternities; 1% of women belong to 1 local sorority. There are 68 groups on campus, including art, cheerleading, choir, chorale, computers, drama, ethnic, forensics, honors, international, jazz band, LGBT, literary magazine, marching band, newspaper, pep band, political, professional, radio and TV, religious, social, social service, student government, and symphony. Popular campus events include Distinguished Lecture Series and Departmental Lecture Series, Pueblo Symphony, Career Fair, and Homecoming. **Sports:** There are 7 intercollegiate sports for men and 8 for women, and 7 intramural sports for men and 7 for women. Facilities include an arena with an indoor swimming pool, a weight room, rock-climbing wall, racquetball, basketball, and volleyball courts, a sports complex with tennis courts, baseball, softball, football and soccer fields, bike trails, and a rope course. **Graduates:** From July 1, 2015 to June 30, 2016, 889 bachelor's degrees were awarded. In an average class, 18% graduate in 4 years or less, 28% graduate in 5 years or less, and 33% graduate in 6 years or less.

SERVICES: Counseling and information services are available, as is tutoring in most subjects. **Library/Resources:** The library contains 350,000 volumes, 10,000 microform items, and 16,862 audio/video tapes/CDs/DVDs, and subscribes to 1,327 periodicals including electronic. Computerized library services include interlibrary loans and database searching. Special learning facilities include an art gallery, radio station, TV station, and observatory at nature center. **Physically Challenged Students:** All of the campus is accessible. Facilities include wheelchair ramps, elevators, special parking, specially equipped restrooms, special class scheduling, lowered drinking fountains, and lowered telephones. **Special:** CSU-Pueblo offers co-op programs, internships, study abroad in 8 countries, and on-campus work-study programs. Also available are 5-year combined B.S.B.A./M.B.A. degrees, a 3-2 engineering degree with Colorado State University, dual majors, nondegree study, and preprofessional programs in forestry, physical therapy, and wildlife management. CSU-Pueblo is a member of the National Student Exchange. There are 10 national honor societies, a freshman honors program, and 10 departmental honors programs. **Visiting:** There are regularly scheduled orientations for prospective students, including a tour, lunch, and mini-sessions on financial aid, athletics, scholarships, and student services. There are guides for informal visits and visitors may sit in on classes. To schedule a visit, contact Tiffany Kingrey at tiffany.kingrey@colostate-pueblo.edu. **Campus Safety and Security:** Measures include 24-hour foot and vehicle patrol, self-defense education, and security escort services. There are emergency telephones and lighted pathways/sidewalks.

REQUIREMENTS: The SAT or ACT is required. Applicants must be graduates of an accredited secondary school or have a GED certificate with a minimum score of 45. CSU-Pueblo computes a CCHE admission index comprised of the high school GPA and SAT or ACT scores. Students scoring below the minimum will still be considered by an admissions committee. Academic preparation should consist of 4 years of English, 3 of math including algebra and geometry, 2 of natural science including physical science, 3 years of social studies including American government, and 1 year of a foreign language. A GPA of 2.0 is required. AP and CLEP credits are accepted. Important factors in the admissions decision are advanced placement or honors courses, leadership record, and recommendations by school officials. To graduate, all students must complete at least 120 semester hours, including 40 in upper-division courses and 30 to 48 in the major, with a minimum GPA of 2.0. General education requirements include a 14-credit skills component of courses in communication, computer literacy, and quantitative skills, as well as a 19-credit knowledge component of courses in humanities, social sciences, and science and technology. Other requirements vary with the major. **Procedure:** Freshmen are admitted to all sessions. Entrance exams should be taken during spring of the junior year or fall of the senior year. There is a rolling admissions plan. Applications should be filed by August 1 for fall entry. The fall 2016 application fee was $25. Notification is sent on a rolling basis. **Transfer Students:** A minimum GPA of 2.0 and official transcripts of previous college work are required. Applicants with fewer than 30 credit hours must submit ACT or SAT scores and high school transcripts. 30 of 120 credits required for the bachelor's degree must be completed at CSU-Pueblo. **International Students:** The school actively recruits these students. They must take the TOEFL or MELAB.

Admissions Contact: Christin Holliday, Director of Admissions. Email: *chrissy.holiday@csupueblo.edu* Web: *www.csupueblo.edu*

FINANCIAL AID: 54% of all full-time freshmen received need-based aid. The average freshman award was $8,637. Need-based scholarships or need-based grants averaged $6,610; need-based self-help aid (loans and jobs) averaged $3,336; non-need-based athletic scholarships averaged $3,688; and other non-need-based awards and non-need-based scholarships averaged $3,483. The FAFSA code is 001365. Check with the school for current application deadlines.

COLORADO TECHNICAL UNIVERSITY *(The complete profile is made available exclusively on our website, www.barronspac.com)*

FORT LEWIS COLLEGE — B-4

www.fortlewis.edu

Durango, CO 81301	(970) 247-7180
Fax: (970) 247-7179	Email: admission@fortlewis.edu
Full-time: 1633 men, 1705 women	**Faculty:** 174; IIB, av$
Part-time: 130 men, 102 women	**Ph.D.s:** 87%
Graduate: 4 men, 9 women	**Student/Faculty:** 17 to 1
Year: varies, summer session	**Tuition:** $9850 ($19,562)
Room & Board: $9130	**Freshman Class:** 3105 applied, 2669 accepted, 814 enrolled
SAT CR/M/W: 505/518/465 **ACT:** 22	**CEEB CODE:** 4310
Application Deadline: August 1	**COMPETITIVE**

Fort Lewis College, founded in 1911, is a public institution with undergraduate programs in arts and sciences, business, and education. The figures in the above capsule and in this profile are approximate. There are 2 undergraduate schools and 1 graduate school. In addition to regional accreditation, FLC has baccalaureate program accreditation with AACSB, ABET, NASM, and TEAC. The 362-acre campus is in a small town in Durango, Colorado, the southwestern corner of Colorado, about 330 southwest of Denver. Including any residence halls, there are 58 buildings.

STUDENT LIFE: 50% of undergraduates are from out of state, mostly the Southwest. Students are from 50 states, 20 foreign countries, and Canada. 85% are from public schools. 72% are White; 5% Asian American; 5% Foreign; 4% two or more races; 2% African American; 10% Hispanic; 1% race unknown. **Female To Male Ratio:** 1.0:1. The average age of freshmen is 18; all undergraduates, 21. 35% do not continue beyond their first year; 38% remain to graduate. **Housing:** 1572 students can be accommodated in college housing, which includes coed dorms, on-campus apartments, and married student housing. There is also living learning and theme housing. On-campus housing is guaranteed for the freshman year only, and is available on a first-come, and first-served basis. 60% of students commute. Alcohol is not permitted. All students may keep cars.

FACULTY/CLASSROOMS: 50% of faculty are male; 50% are female. All teach undergraduates. No introductory courses are taught by graduate students. The average class size in an introductory lecture is 21; in a laboratory is 20; and in a regular course is 21.

PROGRAMS OF STUDY: FLC confers B.A. and B.S. degrees. Master's degrees are also awarded. Bachelor's degrees are awarded in AGRICULTURE (environmental studies), BIOLOGICAL SCIENCE (biochemistry and biology/biological science), BUSINESS (accounting, business administration and management, business economics, and marketing and distribution), COMMUNICATIONS AND THE ARTS (art, dramatic arts, English, music, and Spanish), COMPUTER AND PHYSICAL SCIENCE (chemistry, geology, mathematics, and physics), EDUCATION (athletic training), HEALTH PROFESSIONS (exercise science and public health), SOCIAL SCIENCE (American Indian studies, anthropology, economics, gender studies, history, humanities, interdisciplinary studies, philosophy, political science/government, psychology, sociology, and Southwest American studies). Business, psychology, and biology have the largest enrollments.

ACTIVITIES: There are no fraternities or sororities. There are 65 groups on campus, including art, band, cheerleading, choir, chorale, chorus, computers, dance, drama, environmental, ethnic, honors, jazz band, LGBT, literary magazine, newspaper, pep band, political, professional, radio station, religious, social, social service, and student government. Popular campus events include Fiesta on the Mesa, Fall Blaze, Homecoming and Hozhoni Days. **Sports:** There are 5 intercollegiate sports for men and 6 for women, and 16 intramural sports for men and 16 for women. Facilities include a field house, an outdoor sports complex, an indoor swimming pool, and a student life center, which includes a 3-court gym, racquetball court, aerobic/dance studio, track, climbing wall, and cardio/weight area. **Graduates:** From July 1, 2015 to June 30, 2016, 649 bachelor's degrees were awarded. The most popular majors were business/marketing (17%), social sciences (13%), and parks and recreation (10%). 140 companies recruited on campus in 2015-2016. In an average class, 40% graduate in 6 years or less. Of the 2015 graduating class, 17% were enrolled in graduate school within 6 months of graduation.

SERVICES: Counseling and information services are available, as is

tutoring in most subjects. There is a reader service for the blind, and remedial math, reading, and writing. **Library/Resources:** The library contains 257,653 volumes, 344,803 microform items, and 10,300 audio/video tapes/CDs/DVDs, and subscribes to 26,820 periodicals including electronic. Computerized library services include interlibrary loans, database searching, Internet access, and Wi-Fi capability. Special learning facilities include an art gallery, and a center for Southwest studies. **Physically Challenged Students:** All of the campus is accessible. Facilities include wheelchair ramps, elevators, special parking, specially equipped restrooms, special class scheduling, lowered drinking fountains, lowered telephones, and special housing. There are also workstations modified for individual needs. **Special:** The college offers cooperative programs in most majors, numerous internships, a Washington semester for political science majors, study abroad in 32 countries, student-designed majors, a general studies degree, nondegree study, pass/fail option, and B.A.-B.S. degrees. There are 3-2 engineering degrees with 4 universities and a preforestry degree with Colorado State and Northern Arizona Universities. There are 5 national honor societies and a freshman honors program. **Visiting:** There are regularly scheduled orientations for prospective students. There are guides for informal visits, visitors may sit in on classes, and stay overnight. To schedule a visit, contact the Office of Admission. **Campus Safety and Security:** Measures include 24-hour foot and vehicle patrol, emergency notification system, self-defense education, and security escort services. There are shuttle buses, emergency telephones, lighted pathways/sidewalks, and controlled access to dorms/residences.

REQUIREMENTS: The SAT or ACT is required. Applicants must be graduates of an accredited secondary school or have a GED certificate. An interview is recommended. 17 units required are 4 units in English, and math, 3 units in science, of those, 2 must be lab, 2 units in social studies, and academic electives, and 1 each in foreign language, and history. AP and CLEP credits are accepted. Important factors in the admissions decision are leadership record, advanced placement or honors courses, parents or siblings attended your school, evidence of special talent, personality/intangible qualities, recommendations by alumni, and recommendations by school officials. To graduate, students must complete 120 semester hours with 30 to 40 hours in the major, 50 credits outside the major, and a minimum GPA of 2.0 overall and in the major. A total of 32 to 44 hours in general distribution courses is required. **Procedure:** Freshmen are admitted to all sessions. Entrance exams should be taken in spring of the junior year. There are deferred admissions and rolling admissions plans. Applications should be filed by August 1 for fall entry. The fall 2016 application fee was $40. Notifications are sent October 18. Applications are accepted on-line. **Transfer Students:** 354 transfer students enrolled in 2015-2016. Applicants for transfer should have completed a minimum of 12 credit hours and have a GPA of 2.40. Courses completed with a grade of C- or better may transfer. An interview is recommended. Student may enroll in the fall, spring, and summer. 30 credits required for the bachelor's degree must be completed at FLC. **International Students:** There are 61 international students enrolled. They must take the TOEFL with a minimum score of 500 on the paper-based TOEFL (PBT) or 61 on the Internet-based version (iBT).

ADMISSIONS: 86% of the 2016-2017 applicants were accepted. The SAT scores for the 2016-2017 freshman class were: Critical Reading-- 43% below 500, 46% between 500 and 599, 10% between 600 and 699, and 2% between 700 and 800. Math-- 44% below 500, 38% between 500 and 599, and 16% between 600 and 699. Writing-- 60% below 500, 31% between 500 and 599, and 8% between 600 and 699. The ACT scores were 11% between 12 and 17, 56% between 18 and 23, 30% between 24 and 29, and 4% above 30. 32% of the current freshmen were in the top fifth of their class; 65% were in the top two fifths. **Admissions Contact:** Andy Burns, Director of Admissions. Email: *admission@fortlewis.edu* Web: *www.fortlewis.edu*

FINANCIAL AID: In 2016-2017, 62% of all full-time freshmen and 60% of continuing full-time students received some form of financial aid. 62% of all full-time freshmen and 60% of continuing full-time students received need-based aid. The average freshman award was $14,517. Need-based scholarships or need-based grants averaged $4,902; need-based self-help aid (loans and jobs) averaged $3,493; non-need-based athletic scholarships averaged $5,562; other non-need-based awards and non-need-based scholarships averaged $3,362; and $3,325 from other forms of aid. The average financial indebtedness of the 2016 graduate was $15,973. FLC is a member of CSS. The EAFSA code is 001353. The priority date for freshman financial aid applications for fall entry is January 15.

JOHNSON & WALES UNIVERSITY/ DENVER CAMPUS C-2

www.jwu.edu/denver

Denver, CO 80220 (303) 256-9300
(877) 598-3368

Fax: (303) 256-9333 Email: den@admissions.jwu.edu

Full-time: 496 men, 731 women	**Faculty:** 48
Part-time: 56 men, 73 women	**Ph.D.s:** n/av
Graduate: 13 men, 19 women	**Student/Faculty:** 17 to 1
Year: quarters, summer session	**Tuition:** $30,746
Room & Board: $11,961	**Freshman Class:** 2319 applied, 1883 accepted, 339 enrolled
	CEEB CODE: 3567
Application Deadline: n/av	**COMPETITIVE**

Johnson & Wales University/Denver Campus, founded in 2000, offers degree programs in its college of business, college of culinary arts, hospitality college, and school of education. The figures given in the above capsule and in this profile are approximate. There are 5 undergraduate schools and 1 graduate school. In addition to regional accreditation, JWU has baccalaureate program accreditation with NEASC. The 26-acre campus is in a suburban area in Park Hill. Including any residence halls, there are 19 buildings.

STUDENT LIFE: 63% of undergraduates are from out of state, mostly the West. Students are from 50 states, 11 foreign countries, and Canada. 48% are White; 4% African American; 3% Asian American; 2% Foreign; 11% Hispanic; 1% American Indian/Alaska Native. **Female To Male Ratio:** 1.5:1. The average age of freshmen is 18; all undergraduates, 22. 67% remain to graduate. **Housing:** College-sponsored housing includes coed dorms, and on-campus apartments, and wellness housing. On-campus housing is available on a lottery system for upperclassmen. 53% of students commute. Alcohol is not permitted. All students may keep cars.

FACULTY/CLASSROOMS: No introductory courses are taught by graduate students.

PROGRAMS OF STUDY: JWU confers B.S. degrees. Associate degrees are also awarded. Bachelor's degrees are awarded in BIOLOGICAL SCIENCE (nutrition), BUSINESS (apparel and accessories marketing, business administration and management, entrepreneurial studies, hospitality management services, hotel/motel and restaurant management, marketing/retailing/merchandising, meeting / special event mgmt, organizational behavior, retailing, small business management, and tourism), COMMUNICATIONS AND THE ARTS (applied communication, communications, English, English literature, English Writing, and English and Professional Communication), HEALTH PROFESSIONS (applied nutrition, health, health administration and policy, health communication, health care administration, health promotion, health science, and pre-health studies), SOCIAL SCIENCE (counseling/psychology, criminal justice, criminology, food production/management/services, industrial and organizational psychology, law enforcement and corrections, liberal arts/general studies, liberal arts, sciences, general studies, humanities, psychology, and sociology). Culinary, sports entertainment event management, and food service management have the largest enrollments.

ACTIVITIES: There are no fraternities; 1% of women belong to 1 national sorority. There are 26 groups on campus, including leadership academy, campus activities board, cheerleading, dance, drama, international, LGBT, literary magazine, musical theater, newspaper, professional, social, student government, and yearbook. Popular campus events include Winter Week, Love Fest, and Spring Fling. **Sports:** There are 5 intercollegiate sports for men and 6 for women, and 5 intramural sports for men and 6 for women. Facilities include a gym, weight room, cardio room, a sand volleyball pit, and an outdoor basketball court. **Graduates:** From July 1, 2015 to June 30, 2016, 238 bachelor's degrees were awarded. The most popular majors were family and consumer sciences (35%), business/marketing (29%), and personal and culinary services (17%). 120 companies recruited on campus in 2015-2016. In an average class, 53% graduate in 6 years or less.

SERVICES: Counseling and information services are available, as is tutoring in every subject. **Library/Resources:** The library contains 29,000 volumes, and 1,200 audio/video tapes/CDs/DVDs, and subscribes to 215 periodicals including electronic. Computerized library services include interlibrary loans, database searching, Internet access, and Wi-Fi capability. **Physically Challenged Students:** All of the campus is accessible. Facilities include wheelchair ramps, elevators, special parking, specially equipped restrooms, special class scheduling, lowered drinking fountains, and lowered telephones. **Special:** The university offers co-op programs, accelerated degree programs, dual majors, study abroad, and worldwide work-study opportunities in business, hospitality, technology, and culinary arts. Most majors require 11-week internships. There are a freshman honors program. **Visiting:** There are guides for informal visits, visitors may sit in on classes, and stay overnight. To schedule a visit, contact the Admissions Office. **Campus Safety and Security:** Measures include 24-hour foot and vehicle patrol, emergency notification system, self-defense education, and security escort services. There are emergency telephones, lighted pathways/sidewalks, and controlled access to dorms/residences.

REQUIREMENTS: Although SAT and ACT scores are required only for students applying for honors admissions, students who have taken these tests are encouraged to submit their scores. High school diploma is required, and the GED is accepted. Requirements are 4 years of English, 3 years each of mathematics, and science, and 2 years of social studies. A GPA of 2.0 is required. AP and CLEP credits are accepted. Important factors in the admissions decision are advanced placement or honors courses, extracurricular activities record, parents or siblings attended your school, and recommendations by school officials. To graduate, students must complete 180 quarter credit hours, including at least 36 in the major, with a minimum GPA of 2.0. Required classes include English, math, history, psychology, sociology, economics, science, and professional development. **Procedure:** Freshmen are admitted to all sessions. There are early admissions, deferred admissions, and rolling admissions plans. Application deadlines are open. Applications are accepted on-line. **Transfer Students:** 96 transfer students enrolled in 2015-2016. Applicants are required to submit official high school and college transcripts and must have earned a minimum college GPA of 2.0. Student may enroll in the fall, winter, spring and summer. 45 of 180 credits required for the bachelor's degree must be completed at JWU. **International Students:** There are 18 international students enrolled. The school actively recruits these students. They must take the TOEFL with a minimum score of 550 on the paper-based TOEFL (PBT) or 80 on the Internet-based version (iBT) and the Comprehensive English Language Test.

ADMISSIONS: 81% of the 2016-2017 applicants were accepted. **Admissions Contact:** Michael Rusk, Assistant Director of Admissions. Email: *den@admissions.jwu.edu* Web: *www.jwu.edu/denver*

FINANCIAL AID: In 2016-2017, 95% of all full-time freshmen received some form of financial aid. The average freshman award was $25,367. Need-based scholarships or need-based grants averaged $9,346; need-based self-help aid (loans and jobs) averaged $4,393; other non-need-based awards and non-need-based scholarships averaged $3,390; and $11,224 from other forms of aid. JWU is a member of CSS. The FAFSA code is 003404. The priority date for freshman financial aid applications for fall entry is March 1.

METROPOLITAN STATE UNIVERSITY OF DENVER *(The complete profile is made available exclusively on our website, www.barronspac.com)*

NAROPA UNIVERSITY *(The complete profile is made available exclusively on our website, www.barronspac.com)*

REGIS UNIVERSITY C-2

www.regis.edu

Denver, CO 80221	**(303) 458-4900** **(800) 388-2366**
Fax: (303) 964-5534	
Full-time: 853 men, 1467 women	**Faculty:** n/av
Part-time: 758 men, 992 women	**Ph.D.s:** n/av
Graduate: 1530 men, 2768 women	**Student/Faculty:** n/av
Year: varies, summer session	**Tuition:** $34,100
Room & Board: $10,420	**Freshman Class:** 6761 applied, 3827 accepted, 553 enrolled
SAT or ACT: required	**CEEB CODE:** 4656
Application Deadline: August 1	**COMPETITIVE**

Regis University, founded in 1877, is a private, Roman Catholic, liberal arts institution operated by the Society of Jesus, the Jesuits. There are 5 undergraduate schools and 5 graduate schools. In addition to regional accreditation, Regis has baccalaureate program accreditation with ABET, ACPE, TEAC, CACREP, CAPTE, GAC, CAHIIM, COAMFTE, CCNE, and CPT. The 90-acre campus is in a suburban area in North Denver. Including any residence halls, there are 17 buildings.

STUDENT LIFE: 64% of undergraduates are from Colorado. Others are from 50 states, 17 foreign countries, and Canada. 7% are race unknown; 58% White; 5% African American; 5% Asian American; 4% two or more races; 20% Hispanic; 1% Foreign. 32% are Catholic; 17% Buddhist, Latter-Day Saints, Islamic, Agnostic, and unknown denomination. **Female To Male Ratio:** 1.7:1. The average age of freshmen is 18; all undergraduates, 28. **Housing:** College-sponsored housing includes coed dorms and on-campus apartments. In addition, there are honors houses and special-interest houses. On-campus housing is guaranteed for all 4 years. All students may keep cars.

FACULTY/CLASSROOMS: No introductory courses are taught by graduate students.

PROGRAMS OF STUDY: Regis confers B.A., B.S., B.S.N., B.A.S., B.A.S.C. degrees. Master's and doctoral degrees are also awarded. Bachelor's degrees are awarded in AGRICULTURE (environmental studies), BIOLOGICAL SCIENCE (biochemistry, biology/biological science, and neurosciences), BUSINESS (accounting, accounting (finance), business administration and management, business economics, business and technology, finance, international business management, and marketing/retailing/merchandising), COMMUNICATIONS AND THE ARTS (art history, communications, English, French, information technology, music, music performance, Spanish, and visual and performing arts), COMPUTER AND PHYSICAL SCIENCE (chemistry, computer networks & systems, computer science, mathematics, and physics), EDUCATION (education and health information management), ENGINEERING AND ENVIRONMENTAL DESIGN (environmental science and preengineering), HEALTH PROFESSIONS (biology, health care administration, health science, nursing, pharmacy, physical therapy, and premedicine), SOCIAL SCIENCE (applied psychology, criminology, economics, history, liberal arts/general studies, peace studies, philosophy, political science/government, prelaw, psychology, public administration, religion, sociology, and women's studies). Nursing is the strongest academically. Nursing, business, and computer science have the largest enrollments.

ACTIVITIES: There are no fraternities or sororities. There are 26 groups on campus, including art, cheerleading, chess, choir, chorus, dance, debate, environmental, ethnic, forensics, honors, international, jazz band, Leadership Club , LGBT, literary magazine, musical theater, newspaper, orchestra, photography, political, professional, radio and TV, religious, social, social service, student government, and yearbook. Popular campus events include Mistletoe Madness, Ranger Week, Hall Olympics, Snow Week, Best of Colorado, Senior Life Last Call, Thursday Thrills, and Twelve Programs. **Sports:** There are 5 intercollegiate sports for men and 7 for women, and 8 intramural sports for men and 8 for women. Facilities include a fieldhouse that sits 1,800 spectators, a baseball field, a soccer/lacrosse pitch, a fitness center, and an indoor golf facility. **Graduates:** From July 1, 2015 to June 30, 2016, 1331 bachelor's degrees were awarded. The most popular majors were nursing (29%), business administration (10%), and accounting (7%). In an average class, 49% graduate in 4 years or less, 62% graduate in 5 years or less, and 64% graduate in 6 years or less.

SERVICES: Counseling and information services are available, as is tutoring in every subject. There is a reader service for the blind. **Library/Resources:** The library contains 393,000 volumes, 118,000 microform items, and 13,000 audio/video tapes/CDs/DVDs. Computerized library services include interlibrary loans, database searching, Internet access, and Wi-Fi capability. Special learning facilities include an art gallery, radio station, nursing labs, physical therapy labs, a cadaver lab, music labs, classrooms in residence halls, and arboretum. **Physically Challenged Students:** 80% of the campus is accessible. Facilities include wheelchair ramps, elevators, special parking, specially equipped restrooms, special class scheduling, lowered drinking fountains, and lowered telephones. **Special:** Cross-registration is possible with Denver University and Metropolitan State. Internships, study abroad, and work-study programs with Regis are available. The college offers B.A.-B.S. degrees, dual majors, student-designed majors, a 3-2 engineering degree with Washington University, and pass/fail options. An accelerated degree program in nursing is also offered. There are 7 national honor societies and a freshman honors program. **Visiting:** There are guides for informal visits, visitors may sit in on classes, and stay overnight. To schedule a visit, contact Regis University Admissions. **Campus Safety and Security:** Measures include 24-hour foot and vehicle patrol, emergency notification system, self-defense education, and security escort services. There are shuttle buses, emergency telephones, lighted pathways/sidewalks, and controlled access to dorms/residences.

REQUIREMENTS: The SAT or ACT is required. Applicants should be graduates of an accredited secondary school. The GED is accepted. A recommendation from the high school counselor and an essay are required. An interview is recommended. AP and CLEP credits are accepted. Important factors in the admissions decision are advanced placement or honors courses, leadership record, and recommendations by school officials. Students must complete 128 credit hours with a minimum GPA of 2.0. Required courses include 58 credit hours in the core curriculum, of which 12 are seminars, 7 to 8 are math and natural science, 6 are in literature/humanities, social science, religious studies, and philosophy, and 3 each are in economics, communication arts, and fine arts. **Procedure:** Freshmen are admitted fall and spring. Entrance exams should be taken in the fall. There are deferred admissions and rolling admissions plans. Application deadlines are open. Application fee is $40. Notification is sent on a rolling basis. Applications are accepted on-line. **Transfer Students:** 65 transfer students enrolled in 2015-2016. Applicants must have a GPA of 2.5. All previous college work is considered. The university reviews each applicant individually. 30 of 128 credits required for the bachelor's degree must be completed at Regis. **International Students:** There are 48 international students enrolled. The school actively recruits these students. They must take the TOEFL with a minimum score of 550 on the paper-based TOEFL (PBT) or 82 on the Internet-based version (iBT) or take the MELAB, and the ELS.

ADMISSIONS: 57% of the 2016-2017 applicants were accepted. The SAT scores for the 2016-2017 freshman class were: Critical Reading-- 25% below 500, 47% between 500 and 599, 24% between 600 and 699, and 4% between 700 and 800. Math-- 37% below 500, 43% between 500 and 599, 18% between 600 and 699, and 2% between 700 and 800. Writing-- 38% below 500, 43% between 500 and 599, and 19% between 600 and 699. The ACT scores were 6% between 12 and 17, 35% between 18 and 23, 29% between 24 and 29, and 28% above 30. 47% of the current freshmen were in the top fifth of their class; 77% were in the top two fifths. 30 freshmen graduated first in their class. **Admissions Contact:** Regis University Web: *www.regis.edu*

FINANCIAL AID: In 2016-2017, 99% of all full-time freshmen and 92% of continuing full-time students received some form of financial aid. The average freshman award was $28,628. The college's own financial statement is required. The FAFSA code is 001363. The priority date for freshman financial aid applications for fall entry is April 15.

ROCKY MOUNTAIN COLLEGE OF ART AND DESIGN *(The complete profile is made available exclusively on our website, www.barronspac.com)*

UNITED STATES AIR FORCE ACADEMY D-3

www.usafa.af.mil

Colorado Springs, CO 80840 — **(719) 333-2520**, **(800) 443-9266**

Fax: (719) 333-3012 — **Email: alo_webmail@usafa.edu**

Full-time: 3635 men, 835 women	**Faculty:** n/av
Part-time: n/av	**Ph.D.s:** 49%
Graduate: n/av	**Student/Faculty:** n/av
Year: semesters, summer session	**Tuition:** see profile
Room & Board: see profile	**Freshman Class:** n/av
SAT or ACT: required	**CEEB CODE:** 4830
Application Deadline: n/av	**COMPETITIVE**

The United States Air Force Academy, was founded in 1954 and is a public institution. Graduates receive the B.S. degree and a second lieutenant's commission in the regular Air Force. All graduates are obligated to serve at least 5 years of active duty military service. Tuition, room and board, medical, and dental expenses are paid by the U.S. government. Each cadet receives a monthly salary from which they pay for uniforms, supplies, and personal expenses. Entering freshmen are required to deposit $2,500 to defray the initial costs of uniforms and personal expenses incurred upon entry. Students who are unable to submit the full deposit will receive a reduced monthly cash allotment until prescribed levels are reached. The figures in the above capsule and in this profile are approximate. There is 1 undergraduate school. In addition to regional accreditation, USAFA has baccalaureate program accreditation with ABET and CSAB. The 18,000-acre campus is in a suburban area 70 miles south of downtown Denver and 8 miles north of downtown Colorado Springs. Including any residence halls, there are 13 buildings.

STUDENT LIFE: 95% of undergraduates are from out of state, mostly the South. Students are from 30 foreign countries. 8% are Asian American; 77% White; 7% Hispanic; 5% African American; 2% American Indian/Alaska Native; 1% Foreign. 58% are Protestant; 30% Catholic. **Male To Female Ratio:** 4.4:1. The average age of freshmen is 18; all undergraduates, 20. 15% do not continue beyond their first year; 85% remain to graduate. **Housing:** 4550 students can be accommodated in college housing, which includes coed dorms. On-campus housing is guaranteed for all 4 years. Alcohol is not permitted. Upperclassmen may keep cars.

FACULTY/CLASSROOMS: 85% of faculty are male; 15% are female. All teach undergraduates, and 10% do research. No introductory courses are taught by graduate students. The average class size in an introductory lecture is 17; in a laboratory is 17; and in a regular course is 17.

PROGRAMS OF STUDY: USAFA confers B.S. degrees. Bachelor's degrees are awarded in BIOLOGICAL SCIENCE (biology/biological science), BUSINESS (management science and operations research), COMMUNICATIONS AND THE ARTS (English), COMPUTER AND PHYSICAL SCIENCE (atmospheric sciences and meteorology, chemistry, computer science, mathematics, physics, and science), ENGINEERING AND ENVIRONMENTAL DESIGN (aeronautical engineering, aerospace studies, civil engineering, computer engineering, electrical/electronics engineering, engineering, engineering and applied science, engineering mechanics, environmental engineering, mechanical engineering, and military science), SOCIAL SCIENCE (behavioral science, economics, geography, history, humanities, international studies, law, political science/government, psychology, and social science). Engineering and basic sciences are the strongest academically. Engineering, management, and social sciences have the largest enrollments.

ACTIVITIES: There are no fraternities or sororities. There are 87 groups on campus, including band, chamber music, cheerleading, chess, choir, chorale, chorus, computers, drama, drill team, drum and bugle corps, ethnic, film, forensics, honors, marching band, musical theater, pep band, photography, professional, radio and TV, religious, show choir, social, social service, and student government. Popular campus events include Acceptance Parade and Christmas events. **Sports:** There are 17 intercollegiate sports for men and 10 for women, and 14 intramural sports for men and 13 for women. Facilities include a 47,000-seat stadium, a cadet gym, a field house, 143 acres of athletic facilities and recreational areas, 3 basketball gyms, 4 indoor tennis courts, an Olympic-size swimming pool, a water polo pool, 3 squash and 19 racquetball/handball courts, 3 weight-training rooms, and 2 18-hole golf courses. **Graduates:** From July 1, 2015 to June 30, 2016, 986 bachelor's degrees were awarded. The most popular majors were social sciences (36%), engineering (35%), and basic sciences (15%). In an average class, 71% graduate in 4 years or less and 77% graduate in 5 years or less. Of the 2015 graduating class, 3% were enrolled in graduate school within 6 months of graduation, and 97% were employed.

SERVICES: Counseling and information services are available, as is tutoring in every subject. There is remedial math, reading, and writing. **Library/Resources:** The 2 libraries contain 551,476 volumes, 729,880 microform items, and 3,643 audio/video tapes/CDs/DVDs, and subscribe to 36,252 periodicals including electronic. Computerized library services include interlibrary loans, database searching, Internet access, and Wi-Fi capability. Special learning facilities include an art gallery, planetarium, radio station, TV station, a field engineering and readiness lab, and an aeronautics lab/aeronautical research center. **Physically Challenged Students:** All of the campus is accessible. Facilities include wheelchair ramps, elevators, special parking, specially equipped restrooms, and lowered drinking fountains. **Special:** All cadets receive orientation flights in Air Force aircraft and take aviation science courses. A semester exchange program is available with the French Air Force Academy and U.S. Army, Naval, and Coast Guard academies. Freshman classes start in June, and basic cadet training must be completed before academics begin in August. Work-study programs are available, and dual majors are possible in all areas. There is an interdisciplinary space operations major. There are 2 national honor societies and a freshman honors program. **Visiting:** There are regularly scheduled orientations for prospective students, consisting of a 2-day orientation held in March and April. Students are given briefings by the superintendent, the commandant of cadets, the dean of cadets, and the director of athletics. Students stay overnight in the dormitories and shadow their escort cadets the second day, attending classes, training, and meals. There is also a daily tour. There are guides for informal visits. To schedule a visit, contact the Director of Admissions. **Campus Safety and Security:** Measures include 24-hour foot and vehicle patrol, self-defense education, and security escort services. There are emergency telephones and lighted pathways/sidewalks.

REQUIREMENTS: The SAT or ACT is required. Candidates must be U.S. citizens between 17 and 22 years of age, unmarried and with no dependents, and nominated from a legal source. Students should have completed 4 years each of English, math, and lab sciences and 2 years each of social sciences and foreign languages. A computer course is recommended. A personal interview is required, as is an essay and a drug and alcohol abuse certificate. AP credits are accepted. Important factors in the admissions decision are advanced placement or honors courses, leadership record, and personality/intangible qualities. Cadets must complete the requirements for the core curriculum and for an academic major. They must be proficient in phys ed and military training and demonstrate an aptitude for commissioned service and leadership. A total of 145 to 161 semester hours is required, with a minimum GPA of 2.0, to graduate. The required curriculum includes 9 hours of military arts and sciences, 6 hours of phys ed, and 1 hour of aviation. **Procedure:** Freshmen are admitted summer. Entrance exams should be taken in the spring of the junior year. Check with the school for current application deadlines. Applications are accepted on-line. **Transfer Students:** All students must enter as freshmen and attend 4 years. 145 of 145 credits required for the bachelor's degree must be completed at USAFA. **International Students:** There are 52 international students enrolled. They must also take the SAT or ACT.

ADMISSIONS: 45 freshmen graduated first in their class. **Admissions Contact:** Maj. Andrew L Mattson, Associate Director, Admissions/Selections. Email: *alo_webmail@usafa.edu* Web: *www.usafa.af.mill*

FINANCIAL AID: Check with the school for current application deadlines.

UNIVERSITY OF COLORADO BOULDER C-2

www.colorado.edu

Boulder, CO 80309	(303) 492-6301
Fax: (303) 492-7115	**Email:** apply@colorado.edu
Full-time: 13,613 men, 11,195 women	**Faculty:** 1455; I, av$
	Ph.D.s: 92%
Part-time: 1067 men, 616 women	**Student/Faculty:** 17 to 1
Graduate: 3186 men, 2291 women	**Tuition:** $11,091 ($34,125)
Year: semesters, summer session	**Freshman Class:** 31326 applied, 24941 accepted, 6208 enrolled
Room & Board: $13,194	
SAT CR/M: 590/600 **ACT:** 27	**CEEB CODE:** 4841
Application Deadline: January 15	**VERY COMPETITIVE+**

The University of Colorado Boulder, established in 1876, is a public institution offering undergraduate and graduate programs in arts and sciences, business, engineering, environmental design, music, education, journalism and mass communication, and law. There are 6 undergraduate schools and 3 graduate schools. In addition to regional accreditation, CU-Boulder has baccalaureate program accreditation with AACSB, ABET, ACEJMC, NASM, and NCATE. The 600-acre campus is in a suburban area 30 miles northwest of Denver. Including any residence halls, there are 200 buildings.

STUDENT LIFE: 60% of undergraduates are from Colorado. Others are from 50 states, 113 foreign countries, and Canada. 90% are from public schools. 71% are White; 6% Foreign; 5% Asian American; 5% two or more races; 2% African American; 11% Hispanic; 1% race unknown. **Male To Female Ratio:** 1.3:1. The average age of freshmen is 18; all undergraduates, 20. 14% do not continue beyond their first year; 70% remain to graduate. **Housing:** 8027 students can be accommodated in college housing, which includes coed dorms, on-campus apartments, and married student housing. In addition, there are honors houses, and special-interest houses, including theme housing. On-campus housing is guaranteed for the freshman year only, and is available on a first-come, and first-served basis. 71% of students commute. All students may keep cars.

FACULTY/CLASSROOMS: 60% of faculty are male; 40% are female. 89% teach undergraduates, and 89% do research. Graduate students teach 12% of introductory courses. The average class size in an introductory lecture is 38; in a laboratory is 20; and in a regular course is 24.

PROGRAMS OF STUDY: CU-Boulder confers B.A., B.Envd., B.F.A., B.A.Mus., B.Mus., B.Mus.Ed., B.S. and I.B.A. degrees. Master's and doctoral degrees are also awarded. Bachelor's degrees are awarded in BIOLOGICAL SCIENCE (biochemistry, ecology, evolutionary biology, molecular biology, neurosciences, and physiology), BUSINESS (accounting, business administration and management, finance, management science, and marketing management), COMMUNICATIONS AND THE ARTS (advertising, art history, Chinese, classics, communications, dance, English, film arts, fine arts, French, German studies, Italian, Japanese, journalism, linguistics, music, music performance, Russian languages and literature, Spanish, studio art, and theatre arts), COMPUTER AND PHYSICAL SCIENCE (applied mathematics, astronomy, chemistry, computer science, geology, information science, mathematics, and physics), EDUCATION (Asian studies and music education), ENGINEERING AND ENVIRONMENTAL DESIGN (aeronautical engineering, architectural engineering, bioengineering, chemical engineering, civil engineering, computer engineering, electrical/electronics engineering, engineering physics, environmental design, environmental engineering, environmental science, and mechanical engineering), HEALTH PROFESSIONS (speech pathology/audiology), SOCIAL SCIENCE (anthropology, economics, ethnic studies, geography, history, humanities, international relations, Judaic studies, philosophy, political science/government, psychology, religious studies, sociology, and women & gender studies). Integrative physiology, psychology, and economics have the largest enrollments.

ACTIVITIES: 10% of men belong to 18 national fraternities; 19% of women belong to 14 national sororities. There are 430 groups on campus, including art, band, cheerleading, chess, choir, chorale, chorus, communications, computers, dance, debate, drama, drill team, environmental, ethnic, film, honors, international, jazz band, LGBT, literary magazine, marching band, musical theater, newspaper, opera, orchestra, pep band, photography, political, professional, radio and TV, religious, social, social service, student government, and symphony. Popular campus events include Conference on World Affairs, Colorado Shakespeare Festival, Holiday Festival (orchestra, choir, & other musical group performances), Football Games, International Festival, and Global Jam. **Sports:** There are 6 intercollegiate sports for men and 9 for women, and 13 intramural sports for men and 13 for women. Facilities include a 50,000-seat stadium, an 11,000-seat events center, 4 outdoor lighted basketball courts, and 5 outdoor recreational fields to accommodate rugby, ultimate frisbee, and soccer. The student recreation center facilities include an 8-lane swimming pool, diving pool, 2 large general purpose gyms, 3 indoor basketball courts, a 1/10th-mile indoor running track; courts for handball, racquetball, and squash, aerobics studio, extensive weight training and cardio space, a wellness suite, massage studio, private area for health screenings, five fitness studios including mind body, indoor cycling, and functional training, a new ice rink with cutting edge 200X85 sheet and stadium seating, 3 outdoor tennis courts on the roof of the ice rink (in addition to five other courts on campus), a buffalo-shaped, 2-yard, 2-lane outdoor leisure pool, state-of-the-art climbing wall, and locker rooms with dry heat saunas. Additionally, four program areas are offered instruction, outdoor program, intramurals, and club sports that provide organized sports and classes. **Graduates:** From July 1, 2015 to June 30, 2016, 5289 bachelor's degrees were awarded. The most popular majors were psychology (8%), integrative physiology (6%), and communication (6%). 436 companies recruited on campus in 2015-2016. In an average class, 47% graduate in 4 years or less, 67% graduate in 5 years or less, and 71% graduate in 6 years or less. Of the 2015 graduating class, 20% were enrolled in graduate school within 6 months of graduation, and 74% were employed.

SERVICES: Counseling and information services are available, as is tutoring in most subjects. Disability Services Academic Skills Kit (ASK) service to assist students in improving study habits, organizing their workload, and developing strategies to prepare for exams. **Library/Resources:** The 7 libraries contain 7.6 million volumes. Computerized library services include interlibrary loans, database searching, Internet access, and Wi-Fi capability. Special learning facilities include an art gallery, natural history museum, planetarium, radio station, an interactive foreign language video center, a mountain research station, integrated teaching and learning lab in engineering, and multidisciplinary information technology center. **Physically Challenged Students:** 85% of the campus is accessible. Facilities include wheelchair ramps, elevators, special parking, specially equipped restrooms, special class scheduling, lowered drinking fountains, lowered telephones, and special housing. **Special:** Fourteen residential programs for freshmen and sophomores offer a small liberal arts college atmosphere while taking advantage of the resources of a major university. Student-designed and dual majors, internships, 5-year B.A.-M.A. degrees, and cooperative programs in engineering and computer science are available. Study abroad in 65 countries, work-study programs in federal labs, internships, and cross-registration with other University of Colorado campuses are also offered. There are 28 national honor societies, Phi Beta Kappa, a freshman honors program, and 78 departmental honors programs. **Visiting:** There are regularly scheduled orientations for prospective students, consisting of a 1-hour information session hosted by an admission representative, followed by a student-led, 90-minute walking tour of campus. CU-Boulder also offers all-day visit programs. There are guides for informal visits and visitors may sit in on classes. To schedule a visit, contact the Admissions Office at (303) 493-6301. **Campus Safety and Security:** Measures include 24-hour foot and vehicle patrol, emergency notification system, self-defense education, and security escort services. There are shuttle buses, emergency telephones, lighted pathways/sidewalks, controlled access to dorms/residences, and campus police that are academy-trained and commissioned officers of the Boulder police force.

REQUIREMENTS: Applicants must send an official score report for either the SAT or the ACT and either an official high school transcript or an official copy of certificate of high school equivalency and official GED scores. They are expected to have completed 17 credits of high school work as identified by the CU-Boulder Minimum Academic Preparation Standards. High school diploma is required and GED is accepted. Required application materials include 2 short-answer essay questions and one academic letter of recommendation. Interviews are not used in the decision-making process. Auditions are required for consideration to the College of Music. Portfolios are discouraged. A GPA of 2.0 is required. AP and CLEP credits are accepted. Undergraduate degree and graduation requirements (e.g., number of credits overall and in the major, minimum GPA, core curriculum requirements) vary by degree program (e.g., B.A., B.F.A) and by undergraduate college and program. **Procedure:** Freshmen are admitted fall, spring, and summer. Entrance exams should be taken no later than December of the senior year. There are early admissions and deferred admissions plans. Early decision applications should be filed by November 15; regular applications, by January 15 for fall entry; October 1 for spring entry; and January 15 for summer entry, along with a $50 fee. Notification of early decision is sent February 1; regular decision, April 1. 1062 applicants were on the 2016 waiting list; 218 were admitted. Applications are accepted on-line. **Transfer Students:** 1237 transfer students enrolled in 2015-2016. Transfer applicants must submit official high school and college transcripts. Students who have completed fewer than 24 semester hours of transferable college work must also submit SAT or ACT results. Required application materials include 2 short-answer essay questions and one academic letter of recommendation. College of Music applicants must also complete a College of Music application after their admission application has been submitted, provide a letter of reference, and schedule an audition. 45 of 120 credits required for the bachelor's degree must be completed at CU-Boulder. **International Students:** There are 1497 international students enrolled. The school actively recruits these students. They must take the TOEFL with a minimum score of 75 on the Internet-based version (iBT), or IELTS required.

ADMISSIONS: 80% of the 2016-2017 applicants were accepted. The SAT scores for the 2016-2017 freshman class were: Critical Reading-- 14% below 500, 41% between 500 and 599, 36% between 600 and 699, and 9% between 700 and 800. Math-- 8% below 500, 38% between 500 and 599, 40% between 600 and 699, and 14% between 700 and 800. The ACT scores were 17% between 18 and 23, 54% between 24 and 29, and 29% above 30. 47% of the current freshmen were in the top fifth of their class; 78% were in the top two fifths. 120 freshmen graduated first in their class. **Admissions Contact:** Kevin MacLennan, Director of Admissions. Email: *apply@colorado.edu* Web: *www.colorado.edu*

FINANCIAL AID: In 2016-2017, 73% of all full-time freshmen and 58% of continuing full-time students received some form of financial aid. 41% of all full-time freshmen and 33% of continuing full-time students received need-based aid. The average freshman award was $12,650. Need-based scholarships or need-based grants averaged $10,233 ($45,604 maximum); need-based self-help aid (loans and jobs) averaged $5,599 ($16,800 maximum); non-need-based athletic scholarships averaged $28,476 ($59,230 maximum); and other non-need-based awards and non-need-based scholarships averaged $8,380 ($55,118 maximum). 17% of undergraduate students work part-time. Average annual earnings from campus work are $2459. The average financial indebtedness of the 2016 graduate was $25,605. The FAFSA code is 001370. The priority date for freshman financial aid applications for fall entry is March 1.

UNIVERSITY OF COLORADO COLORADO SPRINGS D-3

www.uccs.edu

Colorado Springs, CO 80918 (719) 255-3640

Email: cbeiswan@uccs.edu

Full-time: 3910 men, 4010 women
Part-time: 973 men, 1294 women
Graduate: 818 men, 990 women
Year: semesters, summer session
Room & Board: $9800
Faculty: 406
Ph.D.s: 67%
Student/Faculty: 19 to 1
Tuition: $9863 ($23,273)
Freshman Class: 12158 applied, 8970 accepted, 2056 enrolled
SAT CR/M/W: 531/533/502 **ACT:** 23
Application Deadline: May 1
CEEB CODE: 4874
COMPETITIVE

University of Colorado Colorado Springs is a public institution offering 45 baccalaureate, 22 master's, and 5 doctorate programs in a broad range of disciplines including engineering, education, nursing & health sciences, business, public affairs, and arts & sciences. There are 6 undergraduate schools and 6 graduate schools. In addition to regional accreditation, UCCS has baccalaureate program accreditation with AACSB, ABET, ADA, NCATE, NLN, ACS, APA, Council for the Accreditation of Educator Preparat, and NASPAA. The 548-acre campus is in a suburban area in the heart of Colorado Springs, CO. Including any residence halls, there are 58 buildings.

STUDENT LIFE: 88% of undergraduates are from Colorado. Others are from 50 states, 71 foreign countries, and Canada. 65% are White; 17% Hispanic; 7% two or more races; 4% African American; 3% Asian American; 2% race unknown; 1% American Indian/Alaska Native; 1% Foreign. **Female To Male Ratio:** 1.1:1. The average age of freshmen is 19; all undergraduates, 23. 33% do not continue beyond their first year; 47% remain to graduate. **Housing:** 1684 students can be accommodated in college housing, which includes single-sex and coed dorms and on-campus apartments. In addition, there are honors houses, theme floors, and special interest housing. On-campus housing is available on a first-come and first-served basis. All students may keep cars.

FACULTY/CLASSROOMS: 46% of faculty are male; 54% are female. All teach undergraduates. No introductory courses are taught by graduate students. The average class size in an introductory lecture is 29; in a laboratory is 18; and in a regular course is 27.

PROGRAMS OF STUDY: UCCS confers B.A., B.S. and B.I. degrees. Master's and doctoral degrees are also awarded. Bachelor's degrees are awarded in BIOLOGICAL SCIENCE (biochemistry and biology/biological science), BUSINESS (business administration and management), COMMUNICATIONS AND THE ARTS (communications, English, Spanish, and visual and performing arts), COMPUTER AND PHYSICAL SCIENCE (chemistry, computer game design/development, computer science, mathematics, and physics), EDUCATION (education), ENGINEERING AND ENVIRONMENTAL DESIGN (computer engineering, electrical/electronics engineering, and mechanical engineering), HEALTH PROFESSIONS (health science and nursing), SOCIAL SCIENCE (anthropology, criminal justice, economics, ethnic studies, geography, history, philosophy, political science/government, psychology, sociology, and women's studies). Engineering, and nursing are the strongest academically. Business, nursing, and biology have the largest enrollments.

ACTIVITIES: 1% of men belong to 2 national fraternities; 2% of women belong to 2 national sororities. There are 207 groups on campus, including cheerleading, communications, computers, dance, drama, environmental, ethnic, film, honors, international, LGBT, literary magazine, musical theater, newspaper, pep band, political, professional, radio and

TV, religious, social, and student government. Popular campus events include Clyde's Kickoff, DisOrientation Week, Homecoming Week, Annual Leadership Conference, Roar Daze, Annual Concerts, and Annual Significant Speaker Events. **Sports:** There are 6 intercollegiate sports for men and 8 for women, and 19 intramural sports for men and 19 for women. Facilities include an aquatic center, a fitness center, gymnasium, indoor track, bouldering wall, multipurpose studio, locker rooms, track and field, basketball, cross-country, soccer, golf, softball, and outdoor trails. There is also an recreation and wellness center. **Graduates:** From July 1, 2015 to June 30, 2016, 1531 bachelor's degrees were awarded. The most popular majors were business (16%), nursing (10%), and communication (10%). In an average class, 23% graduate in 4 years or less, 40% graduate in 5 years or less, and 44% graduate in 6 years or less.

SERVICES: Counseling and information services are available, as is tutoring in most subjects. The Office of First Year Experience and the five centers for Academic Excellence (communication, language, science, math, and writing), are also available for students. There is a reader service for the blind, and remedial math, reading, and writing. **Library/Resources:** The library contains 407,599 volumes, 451,929 microform items, and 8,910 audio/video tapes/CDs/DVDs, and subscribes to 3,079 periodicals including electronic. Computerized library services include interlibrary loans, database searching, Internet access, and Wi-Fi capability. Special learning facilities include an art gallery, radio station, TV station, communication center, languages & social sciences center, mathematics center, science center, and the writing center. **Physically Challenged Students:** Facilities include wheelchair ramps, elevators, special parking, specially equipped restrooms, special class scheduling, lowered drinking fountains, lowered telephones, and special housing. **Special:** UCCS offers a distributed studies option that allows students to design their course of study. Additionally, we offer 7 undergraduate online completion programs in health care sciences, nursing, business, sociology, philosophy, criminal justice, and communication. There are 9 national honor societies, Phi Beta Kappa, a freshman honors program, and 8 departmental honors programs. **Visiting:** There are regularly scheduled orientations for prospective students. There are guides for informal visits and visitors may sit in on classes. To schedule a visit, contact Chris Beiswanger at go@uccs.edu. **Campus Safety and Security:** Measures include 24-hour foot and vehicle patrol, emergency notification system, self-defense education, and security escort services. There are shuttle buses, emergency telephones, lighted pathways/sidewalks, and controlled access to dorms/residences. UCCS employs highly-trained officers within the Department of Public Safety. While having the authority via Colorado Revised Statutes and the CU Board of Regents to enforce campus, municipal, county, and state laws, the Department also provides numerous classes and training for personal and public safety on campus.

REQUIREMENTS: AP and CLEP credits are accepted. To earn a baccalaureate degree, students must complete at least 120 credit hours (with at least 30 hours earned in the major) and a minimum GPA of 2.0. Additional requirements vary by academic program. **Procedure:** Freshmen are admitted to all sessions. There are deferred admissions and rolling admissions plans. Applications should be filed by May 1 for fall entry; December 1 for spring entry, along with a $50 fee. Applications are accepted on-line. **Transfer Students:** 1499 transfer students enrolled in 2015-2016. GPA of 2.0 and 13 or more transferable credit hours 30 of 120 credits required for the bachelor's degree must be completed at UCCS. **International Students:** There are 112 international students enrolled. The school actively recruits these students. They must take the TOEFL with a minimum score of 550 on the paper-based TOEFL (PBT) or 85 on the Internet-based version (iBT). They must also take the SAT or ACT.

ADMISSIONS: 23% of the current freshmen were in the top fifth of their class; 46% were in the top two fifths. 11 freshmen graduated first in their class. **Admissions Contact:** Chris Beiswanger, Director of Admissions. Email: *cbeiswan@uccs.edu* Web: *www.uccs.edu*

FINANCIAL AID: The FAFSA code is 004509. The priority date for freshman financial aid applications for fall entry is March 1.

UNIVERSITY OF COLORADO DENVER C-2

www.ucdenver.edu

Denver, CO 80204 **(303) 556-3287**

Fax: (303) 556-4838 **Email: admissions@cudenver.edu**

Full-time: 3686 men, 4371 women	**Faculty:** 3520; I, av$
Part-time: 1308 men, 1383 women	**Ph.D.s:** 72%
Graduate: 1887 men, 2374 women	**Student/Faculty:** 16 to 1
Year: semesters, summer session	**Tuition:** $10,250 ($30,200)
Room & Board: $12,980	**Freshman Class:** 8615 applied, 5808 accepted, 1372 enrolled
SAT CR/M: 555/540 **ACT:** 23	**CEEB CODE:** 4875
Application Deadline: July 22	**COMPETITIVE**

University of Colorado at Denver is a public institution that was established in 1912. The University has two campuses. The downtown Denver campus is a commuter school with programs in the liberal arts and sciences, business, engineering and applied sciences, music, architecture and planning, and education. The Anschutz Medical Campus is a commuter school with programs in medicine, nursing, pharmacy, and dentistry. There are 7 undergraduate schools and 8 graduate schools. In addition to regional accreditation, CU Denver has baccalaureate program accreditation with AACSB, ABET, NAAB, NASM, NCATE, ACS, and CACREP. The 151-acre campus is in an urban area in downtown Denver.

STUDENT LIFE: 86% of undergraduates are from Colorado. Others are from 48 states, 66 foreign countries, and Canada. 50% are White; 5% African American; 5% Foreign; 5% two or more races; 21% Hispanic; 2% race unknown; 10% Asian American. **Female To Male Ratio:** 1.2:1. The average age of freshmen is 18; all undergraduates, 23. 32% do not continue beyond their first year; 45% remain to graduate. **Housing:** 685 students can be accommodated in college housing, which includes coed dorms and off-campus apartments. On-campus housing is guaranteed for the freshman year only. 95% of students commute. Alcohol is not permitted. All students may keep cars.

FACULTY/CLASSROOMS: 48% of faculty are male; 52% are female. No introductory courses are taught by graduate students. The average class size in an introductory lecture is 27; in a laboratory is 20; and in a regular course is 27.

PROGRAMS OF STUDY: CU Denver confers B.A., B.S. and B.F.A degrees. Master's and doctoral degrees are also awarded. Bachelor's degrees are awarded in BIOLOGICAL SCIENCE (biology/biological science), BUSINESS (business administration and management), COMMUNICATIONS AND THE ARTS (communications, English, English Writing, fine arts, French, music, Spanish, and visual and performing arts), COMPUTER AND PHYSICAL SCIENCE (chemistry, computer science, mathematics, and physics), EDUCATION (education), ENGINEERING AND ENVIRONMENTAL DESIGN (architecture, bioengineering, civil engineering, electrical/electronics engineering, and mechanical engineering), HEALTH PROFESSIONS (medical science, nursing, and public health), SOCIAL SCIENCE (anthropology, criminal justice, economics, ethnic studies, geography, history, interdisciplinary studies, international studies, philosophy, political science/government, psychology, and sociology). Biology, psychology, and music have the largest enrollments.

ACTIVITIES: There are no fraternities or sororities. There are 228 groups on campus, including art, cheerleading, chorale, computers, dance, drama, environmental, ethnic, film, honors, international, jazz band, LGBT, men's hockey club, musical theater, newspaper, political, professional, radio and TV, religious, social, social service, and student government. Popular campus events include Fall Festival. **Sports:** There are 10 intramural sports for men and 12 for women. Facilities include a diving well, weight room, squash, racquetball/handball, and tennis courts, a basketball half-court, dance studio, 3 gym arenas, a fitness center & green room, a 400-meter track, a field for football, rugby, and lacrosse, softball fields, a baseball field, soccer field, sand volleyball court, ice hockey for men, utlimate frisbee, and Taekwondo. **Graduates:** From July 1, 2015 to June 30, 2016, 1892 bachelor's degrees were awarded. The most popular majors were business/marketing (16%), health professions and related programs, and social sciences (14%), and biological/life sciences (10%). In an average class, 23% graduate in 4 years or less and 46% graduate in 6 years or less.

SERVICES: Counseling and information services are available, as is

tutoring in most subjects. There is a reader service for the blind. There are ESL classes and study skills courses. **Library/Resources:** The library contains 1.3 million volumes, 37,425 microform items, and 14,534 audio/video tapes/CDs/DVDs, and subscribes to 177,659 periodicals including electronic. Computerized library services include interlibrary loans, database searching, Internet access, and Wi-Fi capability. Special learning facilities include an art gallery, radio station, and a writing center. **Physically Challenged Students:** All of the campus is accessible. Facilities include wheelchair ramps, elevators, special parking, specially equipped restrooms, special class scheduling, lowered drinking fountains, and lowered telephones. Transit system, and an adaptive computer lab are available. **Special:** Students can cross-register with Metropolitan State College, Community College of Denver, and Red Rocks Community College. Concurrent enrollment with any University of Colorado campus is possible. Cooperative programs, 1-semester internships, study abroad in 12 countries, work-study programs, an accelerated degree program in Liberal Arts and Arts and Media, and B.A.-B.S. degrees are available. The university offers dual majors, a general studies degree, nondegree study, and pass/fail options. There are small, individualized classes, peer advocates, and workshops.There is also an international college in Beijing, China. There are 10 national honor societies and a freshman honors program. **Visiting:** There are regularly scheduled orientations for prospective students. Student visits include a minilecture, campus tour, and financial aid and academic advising. There are guides for informal visits and visitors may sit in on classes. To schedule a visit, contact the Office of Admissions. **Campus Safety and Security:** Measures include 24-hour foot and vehicle patrol, emergency notification system, self-defense education, and security escort services. There are shuttle buses, emergency telephones, lighted pathways/sidewalks, and crime prevention programs.

REQUIREMENTS: The SAT or ACT is required. Preference for admission is given to applicants who rank in the top 30% of their high school graduating class and present a composite score of 21 or higher on the ACT, or a combined score of 950 or higher on the SAT. 18 academic units are required: 4 each in English, and math, 3 each in science, with those 2 must be lab, and social studies, and 1 each in foreign language and history, and 2 in academic electives. CU Denver requires applicants to be in the upper 30% of their class. A GPA of 2.5 is required. AP and CLEP credits are accepted. Important factors in the admissions decision are advanced placement or honors courses, evidence of special talent, and extracurricular activities record. To graduate, students must complete 120 credit hours with a minimum GPA of 2.0. All students must complete the core curriculum courses in addition to the requirements for the major. **Procedure:** Freshmen are admitted fall, spring, and summer. Entrance exams should be taken in the junior or senior year of high school. There are deferred admissions and rolling admissions plans. Applications should be filed by July 22 for fall entry; December 1 for spring entry; and May 3 for summer entry, along with a $50 fee. Notification is sent on a rolling basis. Applications are accepted on-line. **Transfer Students:** 1520 transfer students enrolled in 2015-2016. Students transferring less than 30 approved college credits are required to submit standardized test scores and high school GPA and rank. Students transferring 30 approved credits or more from an accredited college only need to submit their current college transcript and proof of good standing. Students may enroll in the fall, spring and summer. 60 of 120 credits required for the bachelor's degree must be completed at CU Denver. **International Students:** There are 1052 international students enrolled. The school actively recruits these students. They must take the TOEFL with a minimum score of 537 on the paper-based TOEFL (PBT) or 75 on the Internet-based version (iBT). They must also take the SAT or ACT.

ADMISSIONS: 67% of the 2016-2017 applicants were accepted. The SAT scores for the 2016-2017 freshman class were: Critical Reading-- 26% below 500, 42% between 500 and 599, 27% between 600 and 699, and 5% between 700 and 800. Math-- 26% below 500, 47% between 500 and 599, 25% between 600 and 699, and 2% between 700 and 800. 47% of the current freshmen were in the top fifth of their class; 75% were in the top two fifths. **Admissions Contact:** Chris Dowen, Director of Admissions. Email: *admissions@cudenver.edu* Web: *www.ucdenver.edu*

FINANCIAL AID: In 2016-2017, 60% of all full-time freshmen and 58% of continuing full-time students received some form of financial aid. 51% of all full-time freshmen and 45% of continuing full-time students received need-based aid. The average freshman award was $8,730. Need-based scholarships or need-based grants averaged $6,033; need-based self-help aid (loans and jobs) averaged $3,983; other non-need-based awards and non-need-based scholarships averaged $3,413; and $3,254 from other forms of aid. The average financial indebtedness of the 2016 graduate was $21,190. The the college's own financial statement, and and tax returns is required. The FAFSA code is 004508. The priority date for freshman financial aid applications for fall entry is April 1.

UNIVERSITY OF DENVER — C-2

www.du.edu

Denver, CO 80208 — **(303) 871-2036**

Fax: (303) 871-3301 — **Email:** admission@du.edu

Full-time: 2496 men, 2801 women	**Faculty:** I, -$
Part-time: 118 men, 214 women	**Ph.D.s:** 90%
Graduate: 2473 men, 3519 women	**Student/Faculty:** 11 to 1
Year: quarters, summer session	**Tuition:** $46,422
Room & Board: $12,021	**Freshman Class:** 13670 applied, 10456 accepted, 1424 enrolled
SAT CR/M/W: 595/610/565 **ACT:** 28	**CEEB CODE:** 4852
Application Deadline: January 15	**VERY COMPETITIVE+**

University of Denver, established in 1864, is a private institution offering degrees in arts and sciences, fine arts, music, business, engineering, and education. The figures in the above capsule and in this profile are approximate. There are 8 undergraduate schools and 10 graduate schools. In addition to regional accreditation, DU has baccalaureate program accreditation with AACSB, ABET, NASAD, NASM, and ACS. The 125-acre campus is in an urban area 8 miles south of downtown Denver. Including any residence halls, there are 74 buildings.

STUDENT LIFE: 59% of undergraduates are from out of state, mostly the Midwest. Students are from 50 states, 47 foreign countries, and Canada. 68% are White; 4% Asian American; 3% African American. **Female To Male Ratio:** 1.3:1. The average age of freshmen is 18; all undergraduates, 21. 14% do not continue beyond their first year; 85% remain to graduate. **Housing:** College-sponsored housing includes single-sex and coed dorms, on-campus apartments, off-campus apartments, and married student housing. In addition, there are honors houses, special-interest houses, fraternity houses, sorority houses, 5 living and learning communities, and a pioneer leadership program floor. On-campus housing is guaranteed for the freshman year only and is available on a lottery system for upperclassmen. 53% of students commute. All students may keep cars.

FACULTY/CLASSROOMS: 50% of faculty are male; 50% are female. 71% teach undergraduates, 70% do research, and 53% do both. Graduate students teach 5% of introductory courses. The average class size in an introductory lecture is 23; in a laboratory is 18; and in a regular course is 19.

PROGRAMS OF STUDY: DU confers B.A., B.S., B.B.A., B.F.A., B.M., B.S.ACC., B.S.B.A., B.S.CH., B.S.CPE., B.S.EE. and B.S.ME. degrees. Master's and doctoral degrees are also awarded. Bachelor's degrees are awarded in BIOLOGICAL SCIENCE (biochemistry, bioinformatics, biology/biological science, ecology, and molecular biology), BUSINESS (accounting, banking and finance, business administration and management, business economics, business statistics, finance, hospitality management services, international business management, marketing/retailing/merchandising, and real estate), COMMUNICATIONS AND THE ARTS (animation, art history, art, art/art studies, art history and appreciation, communication studies, dramatic arts, English, film arts, French, German, Italian, jazz, journalism, languages, media arts, music, music production/recording technology, music performance, Russian, Spanish, strategic communication, and theatre studies), COMPUTER AND PHYSICAL SCIENCE (chemistry, computer game design/development, computer science, digital arts/technology, environmental chemistry, information sciences and systems, mathematics, physics, science, and statistics), ENGINEERING AND ENVIRONMENTAL DESIGN (bioengineering, computer engineering, construction management, electrical and computer engineering, electrical/electronics engineering, environmental science, materials science, mechanical engineering, and mechatronics engineering), HEALTH PROFESSIONS (biology), SOCIAL SCIENCE (anthropology, Asian/American studies, cognitive science, criminology, economics, geography, history, interdisciplinary studies, international studies, Judaic studies, philosophy, political science/government, psychology, public affairs, religion, social science, sociology, and women's studies). Information technology studies, real estate and construction management, and accounting are the strongest academically. Management, biology, and general business have the largest enrollments.

ACTIVITIES: 24% of men belong to 9 national fraternities; 32% of women belong to 5 national sororities. There are 160 groups on campus, including art, band, cheerleading, chess, choir, chorale, chorus, communications, computers, dance, debate, drama, drum and bugle corps, environmental, ethnic, film, forensics, honors, international, jazz band, LGBT, literary magazine, musical theater, newspaper, opera, orchestra, pep band, photography, political, professional, radio and TV, religious, social, social service, student government, and symphony. Popular campus events include Winter Carnival, May Days, and Festival of Nations Celebration. **Sports:** There are 8 intercollegiate sports for men and 9 for women. Facilities include a sports and wellness center housing 2 ice arenas, a gym, a multipurpose field house, an Olympic-size swimming pool, a fitness center, racquetball courts, studios for yoga, dance, cycling, and karate, a 25-foot climbing wall, a health clinic, a soccer field, a lacrosse stadium, and a tennis pavilion. **Graduates:** From July 1, 2015 to June 30, 2016, 1239 bachelor's degrees were awarded. The most popular majors were business/marketing (28%), social sciences (18%), and visual and performing arts (10%). 200 companies recruited on campus in 2015-2016. In an average class, 2% graduate in 3 years or less, 66% graduate in 4 years or less, 76% graduate in 5 years or less, and 78% graduate in 6 years or less.

SERVICES: Counseling and information services are available, as is tutoring in most subjects. There is a reader service for the blind. **Library/Resources:** The 2 libraries contain 2.3 million volumes, 1.1 million microform items, and 24,425 audio/video tapes/CDs/DVDs, and subscribe to 282,209 periodicals including electronic. Computerized library services include interlibrary loans, database searching, Internet access, and Wi-Fi capability. Special learning facilities include an art gallery, radio station, a high-altitude lab, an observatory, and an elementary and early learning center. **Physically Challenged Students:** 85% of the campus is accessible. Facilities include wheelchair ramps, elevators, special parking, specially equipped restrooms, special class scheduling, lowered drinking fountains, lowered telephones, and special housing. **Special:** DU offers co-op programs, study abroad through more than 59 programs, internships across the country and internationally, a Washington quarter, work-study programs, accelerated degree programs, and dual majors. Non-degree study and pass/fail options are also available. There are 19 national honor societies, Phi Beta Kappa, and a freshman honors program. **Visiting:** There are regularly scheduled orientations for prospective students, including tours and information sessions throughout the year, and 2 day-long open houses in the fall. Visitors may sit in on classes and stay overnight. To schedule a visit, contact the Office of Undergraduate Admission. **Campus Safety and Security:** Measures include 24-hour foot and vehicle patrol, emergency notification system, self-defense education, and security escort services. There are shuttle buses, emergency telephones, lighted pathways/sidewalks, controlled access to dorms/residences, and in-room safes.

REQUIREMENTS: The SAT or ACT is required. Applicants must be graduates of an accredited secondary school. The GED is accepted. DU recommends that applicants have 4 years in English, 3 to 4 each in math, social studies, 3 to 4 in science (of those, 2 must be lab), and 2 to 4 in foreign language. An essay and a counselor recommendation are required, and a Hyde interview is strongly encouraged. AP and CLEP credits are accepted. Important factors in the admissions decision are leadership record, advanced placement or honors courses, personality/intangible qualities, extracurricular activities record, recommendations by school officials, parents or siblings attended your school, evidence of special talent, recommendations by alumni, and geographical diversity. For graduation, students must complete 183 to 194 quarter hours, including 40 to 135 in the major, with a minimum GPA of 2.0. They must fulfill foundational requirements in the freshman and sophomore years, and with junior standing take core courses in communities and environments, self and identities, and change and continuity, and must complete a writing-intensive course. Distribution requirements include 12 quarter hours each of English, natural sciences, arts and humanities, and social sciences, 8 of math and computer science, and 4 of oral communication. **Procedure:** Freshmen are admitted to all sessions. Entrance exams should be taken by January of the senior year. There are early admissions and deferred admissions plans. Early decision applications should be filed by November 1; regular applications, by January 15 for fall entry; December 1 for winter entry; February 15 for spring entry; and May 1 for summer entry, along with a $60 fee. Notification of early decision is sent January 15; regular decision, March 15. 1659 applicants were on the 2016 waiting list; 108 were admitted. Applications are accepted on-line. **Transfer Students:** 194 transfer students enrolled in 2015-2016. Applicants must submit an official transcript from all colleges attended. Those students with fewer than 30 semester hours of college credit must submit a high school transcript and test scores. A minimum GPA of 2.0 is required, but a GPA of 3.0 is recommended. 45 of 138 credits required for the bachelor's degree must be completed at DU. **International Students:** There are 475 international students enrolled. The school actively recruits these students. They must take the TOEFL with a minimum score of 550 on the paper-based TOEFL (PBT) or 80 on the Internet-based version (iBT). Students must take the IELTS. They must also take the SAT or ACT.

ADMISSIONS: 76% of the 2016-2017 applicants were accepted. The SAT scores for the 2016-2017 freshman class were: Critical Reading-- 10% below 500, 37% between 500 and 599, 44% between 600 and 699, and 9% between 700 and 800. Math-- 5% below 500, 37% between 500 and 599, 46% between 600 and 699, and 12% between 700 and 800. Writing-- 19% below 500, 45% between 500 and 599, 31% between 600 and 699, and 4% between 700 and 800. 70% of the current freshmen were in the top fifth of their class; 92% were in the top two fifths. 22 freshmen graduated first in their class. **Admissions Contact:** Hannah Stone, Director of Admissins. Email: *admission@du.edu* Web: *www.du.edu*

FINANCIAL AID: In 2016-2017, 86% of all full-time freshmen received some form of financial aid. The average freshman award was $34,455. Need-based scholarships or need-based grants averaged $28,597; need-based self-help aid (loans and jobs) averaged $5,018; non-need-based athletic scholarships averaged $36,371; other non-need-based awards and non-need-based scholarships averaged $4,181; and $14,724 from other forms of aid. The average financial indebtedness of the 2016 graduate was $29,050. DU is a member of CSS. The CSS/Profile is required. The FAFSA code is 001371. The priority date for freshman financial aid applications for fall entry is February 15. The deadline for filing freshman financial aid applications for fall entry is May 1.

UNIVERSITY OF NORTHERN COLORADO D-1
www.unco.edu

Greeley, CO 80634	**(970) 351-2881** **(888) 700-4UNC**
Fax: (970) 351-2984	**Email: admissions@unco.edu**
Full-time: 3035 men, 5219 women	**Faculty:** 428; I, --$
Part-time: 272 men, 582 women	**Ph.D.s:** n/av
Graduate: 601 men, 1521 women	**Student/Faculty:** 22 to 1
Year: semesters, summer session	**Tuition:** $9365 ($19,277)
Room & Board: $11,486	**Freshman Class:** 7831 applied, 5551 accepted, 1969 enrolled
SAT CR/M: 525/530 **ACT:** 22	**CEEB CODE:** 4074
Application Deadline: August 1	**COMPETITIVE**

University of Northern Colorado, founded in 1890, is a state-supported public institution offering undergraduate and graduate programs in liberal arts and sciences, business, education, health and human sciences, and performing and visual arts. The figures in the above capsule and in this profile are approximate. There are 6 undergraduate schools and 1 graduate school. In addition to regional accreditation, UNC has baccalaureate program accreditation with AACSB, ADA, NASM, NCATE, and NLN. The 260-acre campus is in a suburban area 50 miles north of Denver. Including any residence halls, there are 86 buildings.

STUDENT LIFE: 87% of undergraduates are from Colorado. Others are from 50 states, 23 foreign countries, and Canada. 55% are White; 4% African American; 2% Asian American; 2% American Indian/Alaska Native; 13% Hispanic. **Female To Male Ratio:** 1.9:1. The average age of freshmen is 18; all undergraduates, 21. **Housing:** 3176 students can be accommodated in college housing, which includes single-sex and coed dorms, on-campus apartments, off-campus apartments, and married student housing. In addition, there are special-interest houses, fraternity houses, sorority houses, graduate women's houses, and wellness housing. On-campus housing is guaranteed for the freshman year only, and is available on a first-come, first-served basis, and is available on a lottery system for upperclassmen. 64% of students commute. All students may keep cars.

FACULTY/CLASSROOMS: 50% of faculty are male; 50% are female. All teach undergraduates, and all do research. Graduate students teach 17% of introductory courses. The average class size in an introductory lecture is 46; in a laboratory is 27; and in a regular course is 28.

PROGRAMS OF STUDY: UNC confers B.A., B.M., B.M.E. and B.S. degrees. Master's and doctoral degrees are also awarded. Bachelor's degrees are awarded in AGRICULTURE (natural resource management), BIOLOGICAL SCIENCE (biology/biological science and nutrition), BUSINESS (business administration and management, management science, marketing/retailing/merchandising, and recreation and leisure services), COMMUNICATIONS AND THE ARTS (American Sign Language, art, communications, English, fine arts, French, German, graphic design, journalism, music, musical theater, Spanish, telecommunications, and visual and performing arts), COMPUTER AND PHYSICAL SCIENCE (chemistry, earth science, geology, information sciences and systems, mathematics, physics, and statistics), EDUCATION (athletic training, education, music education, physical education, science education, social science education, and special education), HEALTH PROFESSIONS (exercise science, nursing, rehabilitation therapy, and speech pathology/audiology), SOCIAL SCIENCE (African American studies, anthropology, Asian/American studies, criminal justice, dietetics, economics, ethics, politics, social policy, geography, gerontology, history, human services, interdisciplinary studies, international relations, Mexican-American/Chicano studies, philosophy, physical fitness/movement, political science/government, psychology, social science, and sociology). Business, music, and nursing are the strongest academically. Business, interdisciplinary studies, and sport & exercise science have the largest enrollments.

ACTIVITIES: 6% of men belong to 11 national fraternities; 6% of women belong to 9 national sororities. There are 138 groups on campus, including art, band, cheerleading, chess, choir, chorale, chorus, computers, dance, drama, drill team, ethnic, film, honors, international, jazz band, LGBT, literary magazine, marching band, musical theater, newspaper, opera, orchestra, pep band, photography, political, professional, radio and TV, religious, social, social service, student government, and symphony. Popular campus events include Hawaiian Luau, Academic Excellence Week, and International Dinner. **Sports:** There are 8 intercollegiate sports for men and 9 for women, and 16 intramural sports for men and 16 for women. Facilities include a rock climbing wall, full high-ropes course and bouldering cave, fitness center, treadmills, spin cycles, ellipticals, strength equipment and free weights, gymnasium, hockey rink, Olympic-size swimming pool with a diving well, field house, complete with indoor track, basketball, volleyball and indoor lacrosse courts, racquetball courts, squash courts, dance studio, physical therapy/training room, courts for tennis and basketball and a quarter-mile track. There is also a field for softball, soccer, lacrosse, and intramural competition. **Graduates:** From July 1, 2015 to June 30, 2016, 2167 bachelor's degrees were awarded. The most popular majors were interdisciplinary studies (16%), health professions and related programs (16%), and business/marketing and parks and recreation (8%). 469 companies recruited on campus in 2015-2016. In an average class, 87% graduate in 4 years or less, 92% graduate in 5 years or less, and 94% graduate in 6 years or less.

SERVICES: Counseling and information services are available, as is tutoring in most subjects. There is a reader service for the blind, and remedial math, reading, and writing. **Library/Resources:** The 2 libraries contain 1.1 million volumes, 2.1 million microform items, and 36,009 audio/video tapes/CDs/DVDs, and subscribe to 40,304 periodicals including electronic. Computerized library services include interlibrary loans, database searching, Internet access, and Wi-Fi capability. Special learning facilities include an art gallery and radio station. **Physically Challenged Students:** All of the campus is accessible. Facilities include wheelchair ramps, elevators, special parking, specially equipped restrooms, special class scheduling, lowered drinking fountains, lowered telephones, and special housing. Academic support services such as note taking, transportation, interpreters, adaptive computer instruction, and library assistance are available. **Special:** UNC offers internships and co-op programs in many majors and study abroad in England, Australia, Spain, France, and Germany or through the International Student Exchange Program. Dual majors, student-designed majors, credit by exam, and pass/fail options are also available. There are 7 national honor societies and a freshman honors program. **Visiting:** There are regularly scheduled orientations for prospective students, including academic advising, registration, tours, and special activities. There are guides for informal visits and visitors may sit in on classes. To schedule a visit, contact the UNC Visitors Center at visitors.center@unco.edu. **Campus Safety and Security:** Measures include 24-hour foot and vehicle patrol, emergency notification system, and security escort services. There are shuttle buses, emergency telephones, and lighted pathways/sidewalks.

REQUIREMENTS: The SAT or ACT is required. Admission standards are set by the Colorado Commission on Higher Education, but each applicant is evaluated on an individual basis. In general, an ACT score of 22, or an SAT composite score of 1000, and a cumulative GPA of 2.9 are required. Graduation from an accredited high school is required. AP and CLEP credits are accepted. Important factors in the admissions decision are leadership record, recommendations by school officials, evidence of special talent, advanced placement or honors courses, parents or siblings attended your school, personality/intangible qualities, extracurricular activities record, and geographical diversity. Students must earn a minimum of 120 semester hours (some majors require additional hours) with a minimum GPA of 2.0. All students must complete 40 semester hours in required general education courses and meet all degree requirements in the major. **Procedure:** Freshmen are admitted fall, spring, and summer. Entrance exams should be taken as early as possible. There are deferred admissions and rolling admissions plans. Applications should be filed by August 1 for fall entry; December 20 for spring entry; and May 1 for summer entry, along with a $45 fee. Applications are accepted on-line. **Transfer Students:** 670 transfer students enrolled in 2015-2016. Transfer students who have completed 12 or fewer hours of college must meet the same criteria for admission as entering freshmen. Transfers with 13 or more semester hours must have a minimum 2.4 GPA. 30 of 120 credits required for the bachelor's degree must be completed at UNC. **International Students:** There are 130 international students enrolled. They must take the TOEFL with a minimum score of 520 on the paper-based TOEFL (PBT) or 70 on the Internet-based version (iBT) or take the MELAB. They must also take the SAT or ACT.

ADMISSIONS: 71% of the 2016-2017 applicants were accepted. The SAT scores for the 2016-2017 freshman class were: Critical Reading-- 38% below 500, 47% between 500 and 599, 12% between 600 and 699, and 3% between 700 and 800. Math-- 37% below 500, 40% between 500 and 599, 20% between 600 and 699, and 3% between 700 and 800. 29 freshmen graduated first in their class. **Admissions Contact:** Sean Broghammer, Director of Admissions. Email: *admissions@unco.edu* Web: *www.unco.edu*

FINANCIAL AID: In 2016-2017, 56% of all full-time freshmen and 72% of continuing full-time students received some form of financial aid. 36% of all full-time freshmen and 50% of continuing full-time students received need-based aid. The average freshman award was $7,114. Need-based scholarships or need-based grants averaged $5,175; need-based self-help aid (loans and jobs) averaged $3,164; non-need-based athletic scholarships averaged $192; other non-need-based awards and non-need-based scholarships averaged $2,986; and $301 from other forms of aid. The average financial indebtedness of the 2016 graduate was $24,446. The FAFSA code is 001349. The deadline for filing freshman financial aid applications for fall entry is March 1.

WESTERN STATE COLORADO UNIVERSITY — B-3

www.western.edu

Gunnison, CO 81231 — **(970) 943-2119**, **(800) 876-5309**

Fax: (970) 943-2212 — **Email: admissions@western.edu**

Full-time: 1159 men, 780 women	**Faculty:** 114
Part-time: 280 men, 271 women	**Ph.D.s:** 76%
Graduate: 127 men, 285 women	**Student/Faculty:** 15 to 1
Year: semesters, summer session	**Tuition:** $9193 ($20,497)
Room & Board: $9446	**Freshman Class:** n/av
	CEEB CODE: 4946
Application Deadline: June 1	**COMPETITIVE**

Western State Colorado University, founded in 1901, is a public institution offering undergraduate programs in liberal arts and sciences, business, recreation, and education. There are 8 undergraduate schools and 2 graduate schools. In addition to regional accreditation, Western has baccalaureate program accreditation with NASM. The 228-acre campus is in a rural area 210 miles southwest of Denver. Including any residence halls, there are 31 buildings.

STUDENT LIFE: 75% of undergraduates are from Colorado. Others are from 50 states, 8 foreign countries, and Canada. 85% are from public schools. 73% are White; 7% race unknown; 4% two or more races; 3% African American; 11% Hispanic; 1% Asian American; 1% American Indian/Alaska Native. **Male To Female Ratio:** 1.2:1. The average age of freshmen is 18; all undergraduates, 21. 32% do not continue beyond their first year; 68% remain to graduate. **Housing:** 1234 students can be accommodated in college housing, which includes single-sex and coed dorms, on-campus apartments, and married student housing. In addition, there are special interest houses, theme floors on art, science, and outdoor pursuits. On-campus housing is guaranteed for the freshman year only, and is available on a first-come, and first-served basis. 55% of students commute. All students may keep cars.

FACULTY/CLASSROOMS: 53% of faculty are male; 47% are female. 97% teach undergraduates, and 97% do research. No introductory courses are taught by graduate students. The average class size in an introductory lecture is 22; in a laboratory is 15; and in a regular course is 19.

PROGRAMS OF STUDY: Western confers B.A., B.S. and B.F.A. degrees. Master's degrees are also awarded. Bachelor's degrees are awarded in AGRICULTURE (environmental studies), BIOLOGICAL SCIENCE (biology/biological science), BUSINESS (accounting, business administration and management, and recreation and leisure services), COMMUNICATIONS AND THE ARTS (art, communications, dramatic arts, English, fine arts, music, and Spanish), COMPUTER AND PHYSICAL SCIENCE (chemistry, computer science, geology, and mathematics), EDUCATION (art education, elementary education, foreign languages education, music education, science education, and secondary education), ENGINEERING AND ENVIRONMENTAL DESIGN (preengineering), HEALTH PROFESSIONS (predentistry), SOCIAL SCIENCE (anthropology, economics, history, physical fitness/movement, political science/government, prelaw, psychology, and sociology). Business, biological sciences, and communications are the strongest academically. Business, exercise & sports science, and recreation & outdoor education have the largest enrollments.

ACTIVITIES: There are no fraternities or sororities. There are 60 groups on campus, including adventure race team, alpine ski, baseball, climbing, English performance poetry club, hockey, men's and women's rugby, men's and women's soccer, mountain bike/road cycling, art, band, cheerleading, choir, chorale, chorus, dance, drama, environmental, ethnic, honors, international, jazz band, LGBT, literary magazine, marching band, musical theater, newspaper, nordic, opera, orchestra, pep band, photography, political, professional, radio and TV, religious, social, social service, student government, symphony, and wilderness pursuits. Popular campus events include Family Weekend, Spring Carnival, and Winter Fest. **Sports:** There are 15 intercollegiate sports for men and 14 for women, and 9 intramural sports for men and 9 for women. Facilities include a fitness center, 2 gyms, a 5000-seat football stadium, an all-weather track, a number of playing fields, a weight room, an indoor swimming pool, a games/pool area, and tennis and volleyball courts. **Graduates:** From July 1, 2015 to June 30, 2016, 339 bachelor's degrees were awarded. The most popular majors were business (26%), exercise, sports science (15%), and biology (10%). 45 companies recruited on campus in 2015-2016. In an average class, 1% graduate in 3 years or less, 18% graduate in 4 years or less, 20% graduate in 5 years or less, and 45% graduate in 6 years or less.

SERVICES: Counseling and information services are available, as is tutoring in most subjects. There is a reader service for the blind, and remedial math and writing. **Library/Resources:** The library contains 252,757 volumes, 105,363 microform items, and 10,268 audio/video tapes/CDs/DVDs, and subscribes to 211 periodicals including electronic. Computerized library services include interlibrary loans and database searching. Special learning facilities include an art gallery, radio station, TV station, a greenhouse, Westen mountain archeological site, and media production studio. **Physically Challenged Students:** 90% of the campus is accessible. Facilities include wheelchair ramps, elevators, special parking, specially equipped restrooms, special class scheduling, lowered drinking fountains, lowered telephones, and special housing. There are screen reader programs available on all student lab computers, ADA compliant rooms in residence halls, and an audio device that increases telephone volume. **Special:** The Department of business and accounting offers a co-op program. Study abroad, internships, work-study programs, an accelerated degree program in teacher education, dual and student-designed majors, and credit for military and work experience are available. There are 9 national honor societies and a freshman honors program. **Visiting:** There are regularly scheduled orientations for prospective students, consisting of campus tours, and meetings with faculty, coaches, and admissions counselors are available. There are guides for informal visits and visitors may sit in on classes. To schedule a visit, contact the Admissions Office. **Campus Safety and Security:** Measures include 24-hour foot and vehicle patrol and security escort services. There are emergency telephones, lighted pathways/sidewalks, and special event van shuttle service.

REQUIREMENTS: The SAT or ACT is required. An essay is required and interview is recommended. Applicants must be graduates of an accredited secondary school. Western recommends that in high school students complete 4 units of English, 4 units of math, 3 units of laboratory science, 3 units of social science, and at least 1 unit of foreign language. A GPA of 2.5 is required. AP and CLEP credits are accepted. Important factors in the admissions decision are advanced placement or honors courses, leadership record, and extracurricular activities record. To be eligible to graduate, students must complete 120 credit hours and attain a minimum GPA of 2.0. Students must complete 35 core curriculum credits, 26 of which must be fulfilled through liberal arts credits in human relationships, natural sciences, and creative arts, as well as completing competencies in written expression, oral communication, and math. **Procedure:** Freshmen are admitted to all sessions. Entrance exams should be taken during spring of junior year or fall of senior year. There are deferred admissions and rolling admissions plans. Applications should be filed by June 1 for fall entry; November 1 for spring entry, along with a $30 fee. Notification is sent on a rolling basis. Applications are accepted on-line. **Transfer Students:** 153 transfer students enrolled in 2015-2016. Transfer applicants must have a minimum GPA of 2.0, and may be asked to submit SAT or ACT test scores. 30 of 120 credits required for the bachelor's degree must be completed at Western. **International Students:** There are 10 international students enrolled. They must take the TOEFL with a minimum score of 550 on the paper-based TOEFL (PBT) or 96 on the Internet-based version (iBT).

ADMISSIONS: The SAT scores for the 2016-2017 freshman class were: Math-- 45% below 500, 40% between 500 and 599, 14% between 600 and 699, and 1% between 700 and 800. The ACT scores were 11% between 12 and 17, 53% between 18 and 23, 30% between 24 and 29, and 4% above 30. **Admissions Contact:** Admissions Officer Email: *admissions@western.edu* Web: *www.western.edu*

FINANCIAL AID: In 2016-2017, 93% of all full-time freshmen and 80% of continuing full-time students received some form of financial aid. 53% of all full-time freshmen and 50% of continuing full-time students received need-based aid. 30% of undergraduate students work part-time. Average annual earnings from campus work are $1400. The average financial indebtedness of the 2016 graduate was $25,589. The FAFSA code is 001372. The priority date for freshman financial aid applications for fall entry is March 1.

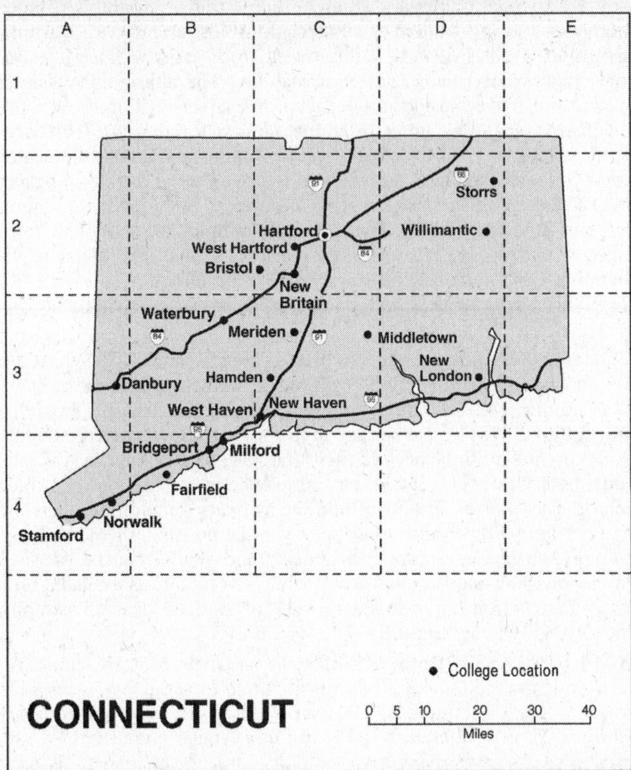

ALBERTUS MAGNUS COLLEGE *(The complete profile is made available exclusively on our website, www.barronspac.com)*

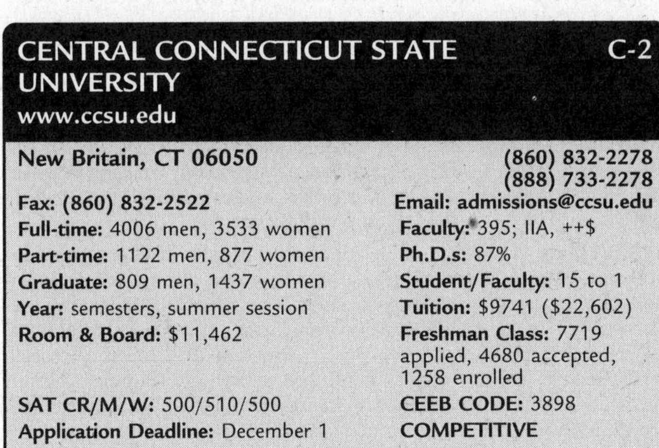

CENTRAL CONNECTICUT STATE UNIVERSITY C-2

www.ccsu.edu

New Britain, CT 06050 (860) 832-2278
(888) 733-2278

Fax: (860) 832-2522 Email: admissions@ccsu.edu

Full-time: 4006 men, 3533 women
Part-time: 1122 men, 877 women
Graduate: 809 men, 1437 women
Year: semesters, summer session
Room & Board: $11,462

SAT CR/M/W: 500/510/500
Application Deadline: December 1

Faculty: 395; IIA, ++$
Ph.D.s: 87%
Student/Faculty: 15 to 1
Tuition: $9741 ($22,602)
Freshman Class: 7719 applied, 4680 accepted, 1258 enrolled
CEEB CODE: 3898
COMPETITIVE

Central Connecticut State University is a regional, comprehensive master's level public university dedicated to learning in the liberal arts and sciences and to education for the professions. CCSU comprises five schools the Carol A. Ammon School of Arts & Sciences, Business, Education & Professional Studies, Engineering, Science & Technology, and Graduate Studies. CCSU offers over 130 undergraduate and graduate programs through the Master's and sixth-year levels and the Ed.D. in Educational Leadership. There are 4 undergraduate schools and 1 graduate school. In addition to regional accreditation, CCSU has baccalaureate program accreditation with AACSB, ABET, CSAB, CSWE, NCATE, NLN, NAIT, and ACS. The 314-acre campus is in a suburban area in the northern edge of New Britain, 15 minutes from the state capital of Hartford and about 2 hours from New York City and Boston. Including any residence halls, there are 70 buildings.

STUDENT LIFE: 95% of undergraduates are from Connecticut. Others are from 37 states, 27 foreign countries, and Canada. 63% are White; 4% Asian American; 3% two or more races; 3% race unknown; 2% Foreign; 14% Hispanic; 12% African American. **Male To Female Ratio:** 1.0:1. The average age of freshmen is 18; all undergraduates, 23. 24% do not continue beyond their first year; 53% remain to graduate. **Housing:** 2247 students can be accommodated in college housing, which includes single-sex and coed dorms. On-campus housing is guaranteed for all 4 years, and is available on a first-come, and first-served basis. 76% of students commute. All students may keep cars.

FACULTY/CLASSROOMS: 58% of faculty are male; 42% are female. 90% teach undergraduates. No introductory courses are taught by graduate students.

PROGRAMS OF STUDY: CCSU confers B.A., B.S., B.F.A. and B.S.N. degrees. Master's and doctoral degrees are also awarded. Bachelor's degrees are awarded in BIOLOGICAL SCIENCE (biochemistry and biology/biological science), BUSINESS (accounting, business administration and management, finance, hospitality management services, management information systems, management, marketing management, and office supervision and management), COMMUNICATIONS AND THE ARTS (art, digital media technologies, English, French, German, graphic design, Italian, journalism, film and media studies, music, Spanish, strategic communication, and theatre arts), COMPUTER AND PHYSICAL SCIENCE (chemistry, computer engineering technology, computer science, earth science, mathematics, physical sciences, and physics), EDUCATION (art education, athletic training, dance education, elementary education, music education, physical education, and technical education), ENGINEERING AND ENVIRONMENTAL DESIGN (civil engineering, civil engineering technology, construction management, electrical/electronics engineering technology, industrial engineering technology, manufacturing technology, mechanical engineering, mechanical engineering technology, and mechatronics engineering), HEALTH PROFESSIONS (exercise science and nursing), SOCIAL SCIENCE (anthropology, criminology, economics, geography, history, international studies, philosophy, political science/government, psychology, social science, social work, and sociology). Psychology, criminology, and accounting have the largest enrollments.

ACTIVITIES: 1% of men belong to 2 national fraternities; 1% of women belong to 1 national sorority. There are 100 groups on campus, including art, band, cheerleading, choir, chorale, chorus, computers, dance, drama, ethnic, honors, international, jazz band, LGBT, literary magazine, marching band, newspaper, orchestra, pep band, photography, political, professional, radio and TV, religious, social, social service, student government, and symphony. Popular campus events include Winter and Spring Weekends, First Week and Vance Lectures. **Sports:** There are 7 intercollegiate sports for men and 8 for women. Facilities include a 3,800-seat gym, 8 tennis courts, a 6,000-seat football stadium, a 37,000-square-foot air-supported recreation facility, a natatorium, weight training rooms, and softball, baseball, touch football, and soccer fields. **Graduates:** From July 1, 2015 to June 30, 2016, 1902 bachelor's degrees were awarded. The most popular majors were business/marketing/management (23%), social sciences (14%), and psychology (8%). In an average class, 21% graduate in 4 years or less, 47% graduate in 5 years or less, and 53% graduate in 6 years or less.

SERVICES: Counseling and information services are available, as is tutoring in some subjects. There is a reader service for the blind, and remedial math, reading, and writing. **Library/Resources:** The library contains 572,464 volumes, 84,580 microform items, and 11,959 audio/video tapes/CDs/DVDs, and subscribes to 5,436 periodicals including electronic. Computerized library services include interlibrary loans, database searching, Internet access, and Wi-Fi capability. Special learning facilities include an art gallery, planetarium, radio station, TV station, the Elihu Burritt collection, Connecticut Polish American Archive, the Equity Archive Collection, and the John Woodcock collection. **Physically Challenged Students:** 90% of the campus is accessible. Facilities include wheelchair ramps, elevators, special parking, specially equipped restrooms, special class scheduling, lowered drinking fountains, and lowered telephones. Personal care attendants serve as roommates for physically disabled resident students. **Special:** The university offers co-op programs and cross-registration with several other Connecticut educational institutions, study abroad in more than 45 countries, internships in most departments, work-study programs, dual majors, and student-designed majors. There are 7 national honor societies, a freshman honors program, and 1 departmental honors program. **Visiting:** There are regularly scheduled orientations for prospective students, including a fall open house in October and daily and select Saturday visits throughout the fall and spring. There are guides for informal visits and visitors may sit in on classes. To schedule a visit, contact the Admissions Office.

Campus Safety and Security: Measures include 24-hour foot and vehicle patrol, emergency notification system, self-defense education, and security escort services. There are shuttle buses, emergency telephones, lighted pathways/sidewalks, and controlled access to dorms/residences.

REQUIREMENTS: The SAT is required. The ACT Optional Writing test is also required. Applicants must be graduates of an accredited secondary school or have earned a GED. An interview is recommended. CCSU also recommends that applicants have 14 academic credits: 4 in English, 3 each in math and a foreign language, and 2 each in science and social sciences, including 1 in U.S. history. AP and CLEP credits are accepted. Important factors in the admissions decision are extracurricular activities record, recommendations by school officials, and advanced placement or honors courses. Requirements depend on the major. To graduate all students need a minimum GPA of 2.0, and must complete at least 120 credit hours depending on the major. General education requirements total 44 to 46 credits in arts and humanities, sciences, math, communications, and fitness/wellness studies. Students must also demonstrate foreign language proficiency, complete 6 credits in courses with a global context, and satisfy a First-Year Experience requirement. **Procedure:** Freshmen are admitted fall and spring. Entrance exams should be taken in May of the junior year or November of the senior year. There are deferred admissions and rolling admissions plans. Applications should be filed by December 1 for fall entry, along with a $50 fee. Notifications are sent April 1. 95 applicants were on the 2016 waiting list; 79 were admitted. Applications are accepted on-line. **Transfer Students:** 1067 transfer students enrolled in 2015-2016. Applicants must have a minimum of 12 transferable credits and a GPA of 2.0, and must submit official transcripts from previous schools attended. 30 of 120 credits required for the bachelor's degree must be completed at CCSU. **International Students:** There are 69 international students enrolled. They must take the TOEFL with a minimum score of 500 on the paper-based TOEFL (PBT).

ADMISSIONS: 61% of the 2016-2017 applicants were accepted. The SAT scores for the 2016-2017 freshman class were: Critical Reading-- 46% below 500, 44% between 500 and 599, 9% between 600 and 699, and 1% between 700 and 800. Math-- 43% below 500, 44% between 500 and 599, 12% between 600 and 699, and 1% between 700 and 800. Writing-- 49% below 500, 42% between 500 and 599, 9% between 600 and 699, and 1% between 700 and 800. The ACT scores were 7% between 12 and 17, 62% between 18 and 23, 27% between 24 and 29, and 4% above 30. **Admissions Contact:** Larry Hall, Director of Recruitment and Admissions. Email: *admissions@ccsu.edu* Web: *www.ccsu.edu*

FINANCIAL AID: In 2016-2017, 85% of all full-time freshmen and 74% of continuing full-time students received some form of financial aid. 81% of all full-time freshmen and 72% of continuing full-time students received need-based aid. The average freshman award was $10,006. Need-based scholarships or need-based grants averaged $6,178 ($7,500 maximum); need-based self-help aid (loans and jobs) averaged $4,200 ($5,500 maximum); non-need-based athletic scholarships averaged $14,000 ($23,000 maximum); and other non-need-based awards and non-need-based scholarships averaged $3,200 ($4,800 maximum). 80% of undergraduate students work part-time. Average annual earnings from campus work are $2500. The average financial indebtedness of the 2016 graduate was $28,016. CCSU is a member of CSS. The FAFSA code is 001378. The priority date for freshman financial aid applications for fall entry is March 1.

CHARTER OAK STATE COLLEGE *(The complete profile is made available exclusively on our website, www.barronspac.com)*

CONNECTICUT COLLEGE D-3

www.conncoll.edu

New London, CT 06320 **(860) 439-2200**

Fax: (860) 439-4301	**Email:** info@conncoll.edu
Full-time: 694 men, 1158 women	**Faculty:** 180; IIB, +$
Part-time: 1 men, 1 women	**Ph.D.s:** 91%
Graduate: 1 men, 3 women	**Student/Faculty:** 9 to 1
Year: semesters	**Tuition:** $65,000
Room & Board: n/app	**Freshman Class:** 5182 applied, 2071 accepted, 482 enrolled
SAT CR/M/W: required **ACT:** required	**CEEB CODE:** 3284
Application Deadline: January 1	**MOST COMPETITIVE**

Connecticut College is a highly selective residential liberal arts college known for interdisciplinary studies, international programs, funded internships, strong student-faculty relationships, and service learning. Institutional values include commitment to diversity, academic excellence, shared governance, and sustainability. The approximate figures given in the above capsule and in this profile covers tuition, fee's, room and board depending upon programs chosen for the 2016/2017 academic school year. The College operates under a student-adjudicated honor code, has no Greek system, and is a member of the New England Small College Athletic Conference. There are 2 undergraduate schools and one graduate school. The 750-acre campus is in a small town midway between Boston and New York City, just off Interstate 95. Including any residence halls, there are 103 buildings.

STUDENT LIFE: 82% of undergraduates are from out of state, mostly the Northeast. Students are from 42 states, 46 foreign countries, and Canada. 50% are from public schools. 8% are Hispanic; 74% White; 4% African American; 4% Foreign; 3% Asian American. 27% are Protestant; 26% Catholic; 17% claim no religious affiliation; 14% Jewish. **Female To Male Ratio:** 1.7:1. The average age of freshmen is 19; all undergraduates, 20. 8% do not continue beyond their first year; 85% remain to graduate. **Housing:** 1790 students can be accommodated in college housing, which includes coed dorms and on-campus apartments. In addition, there are language houses, special-interest houses, quiet housing, theme housing, wellness housing, substance-free housing and gender-neutral housing. On-campus housing is guaranteed for all 4 years and is available on a lottery system for upperclassmen. 99% of students live on campus. Upperclassmen may keep cars.

FACULTY/CLASSROOMS: 49% of faculty are male; 51% are female. All teach undergraduates, and all do research. No introductory courses are taught by graduate students. The average class size in an introductory lecture is 25; in a laboratory is 13; and in a regular course is 19.

PROGRAMS OF STUDY: Connecticut College confers B.A. degrees. Master's degrees are also awarded. Bachelor's degrees are awarded in BIOLOGICAL SCIENCE (biochemistry, biology/biological science, botany, and neurosciences), COMMUNICATIONS AND THE ARTS (art, art history and appreciation, Chinese, classics, dance, dramatic arts, English, film arts, French, German, Japanese, music, and music technology), COMPUTER AND PHYSICAL SCIENCE (chemistry, mathematics, and physics), ENGINEERING AND ENVIRONMENTAL DESIGN (architecture and environmental science), SOCIAL SCIENCE (African studies, American studies, anthropology, East Asian studies, economics, gender studies, Hispanic American studies, history, human development, international relations, Italian studies, Latin American studies, philosophy, political science/government, psychology, religion, Russian and Slavic studies, sociology, and urban studies). Economics, English, and government have the largest enrollments.

ACTIVITIES: There are no fraternities or sororities. There are 55 groups on campus, including art, band, a capella choir, chorus, communications, computers, dance, drama, environmental, ethnic, film, international, jazz band, LGBT, literary magazine, newspaper, orchestra, photography, political, professional, radio and TV, religious, social, social service, student government, and symphony. Popular campus events include Eclipse Weekend, Harvestfest, and Floralia. **Sports:** There are 12 intercollegiate sports for men and 14 for women, and 12 intramural sports for men and 10 for women. Facilities include an athletics complex includes the Charles B. Luce Field House, Dayton Arena, a 10,000-square-foot fitness/wellness center, Lott Natatorium, a lighted artificial-turf field, an eight-lane all-weather track, tennis courts, and playing fields on Tempel Green at the center of campus. **Graduates:** From July 1, 2015 to June 30, 2016, 444 bachelor's degrees were awarded. The most popular majors were social sciences (32%), biological/life science (16%), and viual and performing arts (10%). In an average class, 83% graduate in 6 years or less. Of the 2015 graduating class, 25% were enrolled in graduate school within 6 months of graduation, and 75% were employed.

SERVICES: Counseling and information services are available, as is tutoring in some subjects, such as math, writing, and biological sciences. **Library/Resources:** Computerized library services include interlibrary loans, database searching, Internet access, and Wi-Fi capability. Special learning facilities include an art gallery, radio station, 750-acre arboretum, greenhouse, ion accelerator, refracting telescope and observatory, scanning and transmission electron microscopes, nuclear magnetic resonance spectrometer, tunable diode laser spectroscopy laboratory, center for electronic and digital sound, neuroscience and animal behavior laboratories, and clinical and social psychology research observation suites.

Physically Challenged Students: Facilities include wheelchair ramps, elevators, special parking, specially equipped restrooms, special class scheduling, lowered drinking fountains, lowered telephones, and special housing. Case-by-case accommodations are made for housing. **Special:** Cross-registration with 12 area colleges, internships in government, human services, and other fields, a Washington semester at American University, dual majors, student-designed majors, a 3-2 engineering degree with Washington University in St. Louis and Boston University, non-degree study, and satisfactory/unsatisfactory options are available. About half of the junior class studies abroad. Students may supplement their majors by earning certificates from one of our four interdisciplinary centers (focused on international studies, arts and technology, community action and public policy, or the environment. Students can also earn a certificate in museum studies or earn Connecticut teacher certification. There are 5 national honor societies and a chapter of Phi Beta Kappa. **Visiting:** There are regularly scheduled orientations for prospective students. Student visits include an introduction to the college, student perspectives, academic programs, a luncheon for parents and students, tours, and a reception. There are guides for informal visits, visitors may sit in on classes, and stay overnight. To schedule a visit, contact the Office of Admission. **Campus Safety and Security:** Measures include 24-hour foot and vehicle patrol, emergency notification system, and security escort services. There are shuttle buses, emergency telephones, lighted pathways/sidewalks, controlled access to dorms/residences, and a campus-wide emergency communications system.

REQUIREMENTS: The submission of standardized test scores is optional, although students whose primary language is not English are required to submit the TOEFL or its equivalent. In addition, applicants must be graduates of an accredited secondary school. An essay is required and an interview is recommended. AP credits are accepted. Important factors in the admissions decision are personality/intangible qualities, evidence of special talent, extracurricular activities record, and recommendations by school officials. To graduate, students must complete at least 128 credit hours with a minimum GPA of 2.0. The number of courses required for our majors varies somewhat. Our General Education distribution requirements cover 7 courses from 7 academic areas, plus a foreign language and 2 writing-intensive courses. **Procedure:** Freshmen are admitted fall and spring. Entrance exams should be taken by January of the senior year. There are early decision and deferred admissions plans. Early decision applications should be filed by November 15; regular applications, by January 1 for fall entry; and December 1 for spring entry, along with a $60 fee. Notification of early decision is sent December 15; regular decision, February 15. 268 early decision candidates were accepted for the 2016-2017 class. 637 applicants were on the 2016 waiting list; 61 were admitted. Applications are accepted online. **Transfer Students:** 24 transfer students enrolled in 2015-2016. Applicants must have a minimum college GPA of 3.0 and be in good standing at the previous school attended. SAT or ACT scores are required and an interview is recommended. Students may enroll in the fall and spring. 64 of 128 credits required for the bachelor's degree must be completed at Connecticut College. **International Students:** There are 90 international students enrolled. The school actively recruits these students. They must take the TOEFL with a minimum score of 600 on the paper-based TOEFL (PBT) or 100 on the Internet-based version (iBT), or take any one of these tests: APIEL, IELTS, MELAB, ELPT or equivalent.

ADMISSIONS: 40% of the 2016-2017 applicants were accepted. **Admissions Contact:** Benjamin Brown, Assistant Director of Admissions. Email: *info@conncoll.edu* Web: *www.conncoll.edu*

FINANCIAL AID: In 2016-2017, 48% of all full-time freshmen and 48% of continuing full-time students received some form of financial aid. 48% of all full-time freshmen and 48% of continuing full-time students received need-based aid. The average freshman award was $40,019. Need-based scholarships or need-based grants averaged $37,224; need-based self-help aid (loans and jobs) averaged $4,759; and other non-need-based awards and non-need-based scholarships averaged $3,314. Connecticut College is a member of CSS. The CSS/Profile and parent and student tax forms, including noncustodial parent's statement are required. The FAFSA code is 001379. The priority date for freshman financial aid applications for fall entry is February 1.

EASTERN CONNECTICUT STATE UNIVERSITY — D-2

www.easternct.edu

Willimantic, CT 06226 — **(860) 465-4398**

Email: admissions@easternct.edu

Full-time: 1903 men, 2389 women
Part-time: 372 men, 507 women
Graduate: 62 men, 129 women
Year: semesters, summer session
Room & Board: $12,559
SAT CR/M/W: 520/510/510 **ACT:** 22
Application Deadline: May 1

Faculty: 199; IIA, +$
Ph.D.s: 95%
Student/Faculty: 22 to 1
Tuition: $10,500 ($23,361)
Freshman Class: 5863 applied, 3395 accepted, 1013 enrolled
CEEB CODE: 3966
COMPETITIVE

Eastern Connecticut State University, founded in 1889, is the state's public liberal arts university. There are 3 undergraduate schools and one graduate school. In addition to regional accreditation, Eastern has baccalaureate program accreditation with CSWE, NCATE, and NAEYC. The 182-acre campus is in a small town 29 miles east of Hartford and 90 miles southwest of Boston. Including any residence halls, there are 45 buildings.

STUDENT LIFE: 95% of undergraduates are from Connecticut. Others are from 29 states, 74 foreign countries, and Canada. 95% are from public schools. 67% are White; 11% Hispanic; 8% African American; 8% race unknown; 3% Asian American; 3% two or more races; 1% Foreign. **Female To Male Ratio:** 1.3:1. The average age of freshmen is 18; all undergraduates, 22. 24% do not continue beyond their first year; 54% remain to graduate. **Housing:** 2650 students can be accommodated in college housing, which includes coed dorms and on-campus apartments. In addition, there are honors houses and special-interest houses. 52% of students live on campus; of those, 60% remain on campus on weekends. Alcohol is not permitted. Upperclassmen may keep cars.

FACULTY/CLASSROOMS: 54% of faculty are male; 46% are female. All teach undergraduates. No introductory courses are taught by graduate students. The average class size in an introductory lecture is 26; in a laboratory is 17; and in a regular course is 23.

PROGRAMS OF STUDY: Eastern confers B.A., B.S. and B.G.S. degrees. Associate and master's degrees are also awarded. Bachelor's degrees are awarded in BIOLOGICAL SCIENCE (biochemistry and biology/biological science), BUSINESS (accounting, business administration and management, business information systems, finance, industrial and labor relations, and sports management), COMMUNICATIONS AND THE ARTS (communications, digital media, English, music, Spanish, theatre acting, and visual and performing arts), COMPUTER AND PHYSICAL SCIENCE (computer science and mathematics), EDUCATION (early childhood education, elementary education, and physical education), ENGINEERING AND ENVIRONMENTAL DESIGN (environmental science), HEALTH PROFESSIONS (health science), SOCIAL SCIENCE (criminology, economics, history, liberal arts/general studies, philosophy, political science/government, psychology, social science, social work, sociology, and women & gender studies). Business administration, psychology, and social sciences have the largest enrollments.

ACTIVITIES: There are no fraternities or sororities. There are 95 groups on campus, including art, cheerleading, chorale, club sports include cheerleading, computers, dance, drama, environmental, ethnic, film, honors, international, jazz band, LGBT, literary magazine, musical theater, newspaper, photography, political, professional, radio and TV, religious, social, social service, student government, and yearbook. Popular campus events include Jazzin' It Up at Eastern, Day of Giving, University Hour, and Shackathon. **Sports:** There are 5 intercollegiate sports for men and 8 for women, and 15 intramural sports for men and 15 for women. Facilities include a student center with theaters, café, billiards, fitness center, a 2800-seat field house, a 6-lane swimming pool, soccer field, baseball complex, softball stadium, 400 meter 8-lane track, field hockey field, intramural field, tennis, basketball, racquetball, and squash courts, weight room, matted rooms for yoga and martial arts, and trails in an arboretum. **Graduates:** From July 1, 2015 to June 30, 2016, 1102 bachelor's degrees were awarded. The most popular majors were business administration (11%), psychology (10%), and general studies (10%). In an average class, 1% graduate in 3 years or less, 47% graduate in 4 years or less, 51% graduate in 5 years or less, and 54% graduate in 6 years or less.

SERVICES: Counseling and information services are available, as is tutoring in every subject. **Library/Resources:** The library contains 2.0 million volumes, 965,946 microform items, and 7,910 audio/video tapes/CDs/DVDs, and subscribes to 55,085 periodicals including electronic. Computerized library services include interlibrary loans, database searching, Internet access, and Wi-Fi capability. Special learning facilities include an art gallery, planetarium, radio station, TV station, an arboretum, child and family development resource center, and the Church Farm Center for the Arts and Sciences. **Physically Challenged Students:** Facilities include wheelchair ramps, elevators, special parking, specially equipped restrooms, special class scheduling, and lowered drinking fountains. **Special:** The University Honors Program promotes undergraduate scholarship by providing academically talented students with opportunities to participate in specially designed courses that prepare them to conduct independent research and/or scholarly activity under the oversight of a faculty mentor. The Individualized Major Plan is a student's self-designed interdisciplinary plan of study, which consists of courses from two or more disciplines and results in a B.A. or B.S. degree. The self-designed plan of study allows the student to take courses in areas that naturally complement each other in today's workplace and to develop a strong educational base in at least one subject to facilitate entrance into a graduate program. There are 9 national honor societies and a freshman honors program. **Visiting:** There are regularly scheduled orientations for prospective students, including small group discussions, a tour of the campus, and a personal interview. There are guides for informal visits and visitors may sit in on classes. To schedule a visit, contact the Office of Admissions. **Campus Safety and Security:** Measures include 24-hour foot and vehicle patrol, emergency notification system, and security escort services. There are shuttle buses, emergency telephones, lighted pathways/sidewalks, and controlled access to dorms/residences.

REQUIREMENTS: Applicants must be graduates of an accredited secondary school or have a GED. They should have completed 15 high school academic credits, including 4 years of English, 4 of math, and 2 each of foreign language, social studies, and science (including 1 of lab science). While interviews are not generally required of students applying for admission, the Admission staff may request an interview with certain applicants to obtain additional information or clarify information. AP and CLEP credits are accepted. Important factors in the admissions decision are advanced placement or honors courses, personality/intangible qualities, and extracurricular activities record. To graduate, students must complete 120 credit hours, including the requirements of an academic major, with a GPA of 2.0. Liberal Arts Core Curriculum requirements include 26 credits in Methods and Concepts, 15 in Synthesis and Application, and 3 credits in Independent Inquiry. **Procedure:** Freshmen are admitted fall and spring. Entrance exams should be taken in November or December of the senior year. There are deferred admissions and rolling admissions plans. Applications should be filed by May 1 for fall entry, along with a $50 fee. Notification is sent on a rolling basis. Applications are accepted on-line. **Transfer Students:** Official college and high school transcripts are required. 30 of 120 credits required for the bachelor's degree must be completed at Eastern. **International Students:** There are 43 international students enrolled. The school actively recruits these students. They must take the TOEFL. They must also take the SAT or ACT.

ADMISSIONS: 58% of the 2016-2017 applicants were accepted. The SAT scores for the 2016-2017 freshman class were: Critical Reading-- 38% below 500, 46% between 500 and 599, 14% between 600 and 699, and 1% between 700 and 800. Math-- 40% below 500, 46% between 500 and 599, 13% between 600 and 699, and 1% between 700 and 800. Writing-- 39% below 500, 48% between 500 and 599, 11% between 600 and 699, and 1% between 700 and 800. The ACT scores were 8% between 12 and 17, 53% between 18 and 23, 37% between 24 and 29, and 3% above 30. 28% of the current freshmen were in the top fifth of their class; 63% were in the top two fifths. **Admissions Contact:** Christopher Dorsey, Director of Admissions. Email: *admissions@easternct.edu* Web: *www.easternct.edu*

FINANCIAL AID: Eastern is a member of CSS. The FAFSA code is 001425. The deadline for filing freshman financial aid applications for fall entry is March 15.

FAIRFIELD UNIVERSITY — B-4

www.fairfield.edu

Fairfield, CT 06824	(203) 254-4100
Fax: (203) 254-4199	Email: admis@fairfield.edu
Full-time: 1495 men, 2308 women	**Faculty:** 249; IIA, ++$
Part-time: 91 men, 138 women	**Ph.D.s:** 93%
Graduate: 350 men, 755 women	**Student/Faculty:** 15 to 1
Year: semesters, summer session	**Tuition:** $46,000
Room & Board: $13,860	**Freshman Class:** 11055 applied, 6795 accepted, 1056 enrolled
SAT CR/M/W: 590/610/600 **ACT:** 27	**CEEB CODE:** 3390
Application Deadline: January 15	**VERY COMPETITIVE+**

Fairfield University was founded by the Society of Jesus (the Jesuits) in 1942 and is rooted in one of the world's oldest intellectual and spiritual traditions. There are 4 undergraduate schools and 5 graduate schools. In addition to regional accreditation, Fairfield has baccalaureate program accreditation with AACSB, ABET, NCATE, NLN, ACS, CCNE, and IACS. The 200-acre campus is in a suburban area 60 miles northeast of New York City and 1 mile from Long Island Sound. Including any residence halls, there are 49 buildings.

STUDENT LIFE: 72% of undergraduates are from out of state, mostly the Northeast. Students are from 34 states, 49 foreign countries, and Canada. 60% are from public schools. 8% are Hispanic; 77% White; 6% race unknown; 3% Foreign; 2% African American; 2% Asian American; 1% two or more races. 66% are Catholic; 25% claim no religious affiliation. **Female To Male Ratio:** 1.7:1. The average age of freshmen is 18; all undergraduates, 20. 11% do not continue beyond their first year; 89% remain to graduate. **Housing:** 2935 students can be accommodated in college housing, which includes single-sex and coed dorms and on-campus apartments. In addition, there are special-interest houses, and a substance-free floor. In addition to Healthy Living (now Health and Wellness), we have Man 2 Man, Women in Science Technology, Engineering and Mathematics (WiSTEM), Sisters Inspiring Sisters, and Leadership Through Service, for our first-year students. For our sophomores we have 3 residential colleges, Creative Life, Service for Justice, and Ignatian. On-campus housing is guaranteed for all 4 years and is available on a lottery system for upperclassmen. 70% of students live on campus. Upperclassmen may keep cars.

FACULTY/CLASSROOMS: 48% of faculty are male; 52% are female. 86% teach undergraduates. No introductory courses are taught by graduate students. The average class size in an introductory lecture is 19 and in a laboratory is 14.

PROGRAMS OF STUDY: Fairfield confers B.A., B.S. and B.S.N. degrees. Master's and doctoral degrees are also awarded. Bachelor's degrees are awarded in AGRICULTURE (environmental studies), BIOLOGICAL SCIENCE (biochemistry and biology/biological science), BUSINESS (accounting, finance, international business management, management science, and marketing), COMMUNICATIONS AND THE ARTS (art history, communications, English, film, television and digital media, French, German, Italian, journalism & technical communications, music, public relations, Spanish, studio art, and theatre arts), COMPUTER AND PHYSICAL SCIENCE (chemistry, information sciences and systems, mathematics, physics, and software engineering), ENGINEERING AND ENVIRONMENTAL DESIGN (bioengineering, computational sciences, computer engineering, electrical/electronics engineering, and mechanical engineering), HEALTH PROFESSIONS (nursing), SOCIAL SCIENCE (American studies, economics, history, international studies, liberal arts/general studies, philosophy, political science/government, psychology, religious studies, and sociology). Accounting, finance, and nursing are the strongest academically. Nursing, finance, and marketing have the largest enrollments.

ACTIVITIES: There are no fraternities or sororities. There are 90 groups on campus, including art, band, cheerleading, chess, choir, chorale, chorus, communications, computers, dance, debate, drama, environmental, ethnic, film, honors, including equestrian and sailing clubs, international, jazz band, LGBT, literary magazine, musical theater, newspaper, orchestra, pep band, photography, political, professional, radio and TV, religious, social, social service, student government, and yearbook. Popular campus events include Presidential Ball, Dogwoods Dance, Midnight Breakfast, Senior Week, FUSA Concert, Relay for Life,

Wit 'n Grit, Glee Club Pops Concert, Clam Jam, Noche Client, Remixx Showcase, Late Night @ Barone, South Side Café, BINGO, La Gala, and Flavors of Asia. **Sports:** There are 9 intercollegiate sports for men and 11 for women, and 23 intramural sports for men and 16 for women. The Leslie C Quick Jr. Recreation Complex houses three levels of recreational space. The "recplex" lower level consists of five multi-use exercise/fitness rooms, an eight lane 25 meter pool and racquetball court. The ground floor boasts a strength and conditioning space, with designated areas for Selectorized equipment and free weight training stations. Also on the ground level is The James W. Birkenstock Fieldhouse, which features three multipurpose regulation basketball courts and an elevated indoor track. The mezzanine level incorporates more than 75 pieces of cardio equipment. **Graduates:** From July 1, 2015 to June 30, 2016, 939 bachelor's degrees were awarded. The most popular majors were nursing (12%), finance (12%), and marketing (11%). 218 companies recruited on campus in 2015-2016. In an average class, 78% graduate in 4 years or less, 81% graduate in 5 years or less, and 82% graduate in 6 years or less. Of the 2015 graduating class, 22% were enrolled in graduate school within 6 months of graduation, and 73% were employed.

SERVICES: Counseling and information services are available, as is group-based peer tutoring, which is offered in the following courses: chemistry, biology, engineering, finance, physics, psychology, and nursing as well as Modern Languages courses in French, Italian, Japanese, and Spanish. There is a reader service for the blind. Additional tutoring is offered in accounting and economics. Fairfield University also offers tutoring at both the writing and math center. **Library/Resources:** The library contains 1.3 million volumes, 945,373 microform items, and 154,029 audio/video tapes/CDs/DVDs, and subscribes to 38,926 periodicals including electronic. Computerized library services include interlibrary loans, database searching, Internet access, and Wi-Fi capability. Special learning facilities include an art gallery, radio station, TV station, a media center, 750-seat concert hall/theater, a rehearsal and improvisation theater, a black box 150-seat theater, language learning lab, business education simulation training (BEST) classroom, SIM/simulated hospital environment and human patient simulators in the nursing facility, an art gallery and an art museum, model interactive high technology classrooms, and resource center for core science. **Physically Challenged Students:** 95% of the campus is accessible. Facilities include wheelchair ramps, elevators, special parking, specially equipped restrooms, special class scheduling, and special housing. Accommodations for assistance animals and services animals and a library computer station for physically challenged and learning disabled students are also available. **Special:** Fairfield administers its own study abroad centers in Madrid, Managua, Florence, Aix-en-Provence, Brisbane, and Galway. In addition, Fairfield students may choose from a list of over 60 different study abroad programs in five continents and engage in research, internships, and service learning at most of these sites. Fairfield has available to students a federal work-study program, B.A.-B.S. degrees in economics, international studies, and psychology, individually-designed majors, and dual majors in all subjects. The University offers fifth year graduate degree programs in education, psychology, and engineering. Fairfield University offers a four-year Honors Program across the University open, by special admission, to all undergraduates regardless of the school in which they are enrolled. A bachelor of Arts/Sciences in Liberal Studies is offered for part-time students through the College of Arts and Sciences. Internships, both credit and noncredit, are offered at area corporations, publications, banks, and other organizations nationally and internationally. Interdisciplinary minors include humanitarian action, women's studies, entrepreneurship, marine science, Black studies, environmental studies, jazz, classical performance, Italian studies, Russian and Eastern European studies, Catholic studies and Judaic studies, applied ethics, Asian studies, Irish studies, Latin American and Caribbean studies, and peace and justice. There are 21 national honor societies, including Phi Beta Kappa, and a freshman honors program. **Visiting:** There are regularly scheduled orientations for prospective students. Seasonal information sessions and tours are offered weekdays and some weekends. Individualized class visits are available. There are guides for informal visits and visitors may sit in on classes. To schedule a visit, contact the Office of Undergraduate Admission at (203) 254-4100. **Campus Safety and Security:** Measures include 24-hour foot and vehicle patrol, emergency notification system, self-defense education, and security escort services. There are shuttle buses, emergency telephones, lighted pathways/sidewalks, controlled access to dorms/residences, EMT public safety officers, bike patrol, closed circuit television system, crime prevention seminars, and information via campus television network.

REQUIREMENTS: Fairfield has test-optional admission. There is no additional information required if students choose not to submit test scores. There is no required grade point average, although most admitted students have a B+ average or better in a solid college preparatory program, which should include advanced and/or honors classes. Students should have completed 15 academic credits, including 4 credits of English, 3 to 4 credits each of history, math, and lab science, and 2 to 4 credits of a foreign language. AP and CLEP credits are accepted. Important factors in the admissions decision are advanced placement or honors courses, extracurricular activities record, and recommendations by school officials. To graduate, students must complete a minimum of 120 credits and completed at least 38 three or four credit courses with a minimum GPA of 2.0 both overall and in the major. 60 of the 120 credits are in general education core requirements. Distribution requirements include 15 credits in philosophy, religious studies, and ethics, 15 credits in English and fine arts, 12 credits in math and natural sciences, 12 credits in history and social sciences, and 6 credits in foreign languages. Students are also required to take courses in US and world diversity. **Procedure:** Freshmen are admitted fall. Entrance exams should be taken in the spring of the junior year or fall of the senior year. There are early decision, early admissions, and deferred admissions plans. Early decision applications should be filed by November 15; regular applications, by January 15 for fall entry, along with a $60 fee. Notification of early decision is sent December 15; regular decision, April 1. 144 early decision candidates were accepted for the 2016-2017 class. 931 applicants were on the 2016 waiting list; 12 were admitted. Applications are accepted on-line. Application fees are waived if application is completed on-line. **Transfer Students:** 35 transfer students enrolled in 2015-2016. The following are needed to complete the transfer application: common application for transfer students, application fee, personal statement/essay addressing why you are seeking transfer, official high school transcript, official college transcript from all universities attended (whether or not credit was earned, mid-term grade progress report, Dean of Students Certification Form from all colleges attended, and course catalog descriptions of all classes taken. Additionally required are SAT or ACT results, if you choose to submit them. Refer to our Standardized Test Optional Policy for more details. 60 of 120 credits required for the bachelor's degree must be completed at Fairfield. **International Students:** There are 106 international students enrolled. The school actively recruits these students. They must take the TOEFL with a minimum score of 550 on the paper-based TOEFL (PBT) or 80 on the Internet-based version (iBT), and take the IELTS.

ADMISSIONS: 61% of the 2016-2017 applicants were accepted. The SAT scores for the 2016-2017 freshman class were: Critical Reading-- 5% below 500, 48% between 500 and 599, 43% between 600 and 699, and 4% between 700 and 800. Math-- 4% below 500, 41% between 500 and 599, 50% between 600 and 699, and 5% between 700 and 800. Writing-- 4% below 500, 44% between 500 and 599, 46% between 600 and 699, and 6% between 700 and 800. The ACT scores were 8% between 18 and 23, 76% between 24 and 29, and 15% above 30. 55% of the current freshmen were in the top fifth of their class; 88% were in the top two fifths. **Admissions Contact:** Karen Pellegrino, Associate VP & Dean of Enrollment. Email: *admis@fairfield.edu* Web: *www.fairfield.edu*

FINANCIAL AID: In 2016-2017, 94% of all full-time freshmen and 88% of continuing full-time students received some form of financial aid. 60% of all full-time freshmen and 52% of continuing full-time students received need-based aid. The average freshman award was $27,928. Need-based scholarships or need-based grants averaged $35,513 ($63,000 maximum); need-based self-help aid (loans and jobs) averaged $4,769 ($7,500 maximum); non-need-based athletic scholarships averaged $24,319 ($62,535 maximum); and other non-need-based awards and non-need-based scholarships averaged $13,181 ($45,350 maximum). 83% of undergraduate students work part-time. Average annual earnings from campus work are $1004. The average financial indebtedness of the 2016 graduate was $24,937. Fairfield is a member of CSS. The CSS/Profile is required. The FAFSA code is 001385. The deadline for filing freshman financial aid applications for fall entry is January 15.

GOODWIN COLLEGE *(The complete profile is made available exclusively on our website, www.barronspac.com)*

MITCHELL COLLEGE D-3
www.mitchell.edu

New London, CT 06320	(800) 443-2811 (800) 443-2811
Fax: (860) 444-1209	Email: admissions@mitchell.edu
Full-time: 395 men, 336 women	Faculty: 35
Part-time: 59 men, 68 women	Ph.D.s: 74%
Graduate: n/av	Student/Faculty: 14 to 1
Year: semesters, summer session	Tuition: $30,780
Room & Board: $12,500	Freshman Class: n/av CEEB CODE: 3582
Application Deadline: rolling	COMPETITIVE

Mitchell College, founded in 1938, is a private institution offering associate and bachelors degree programs in the liberal arts and professional areas. The figures in the above capsule and in this profile are approximate. There is 1 undergraduate school. In addition to regional accreditation, has baccalaureate program accreditation with NEASCE-CIHE. The 68-acre campus is in a suburban area in Southeastern Connecticut on the shore of the Thames River where it meets Long Island Sound. Including any residence halls, there are 26 buildings.

STUDENT LIFE: 54% of undergraduates are from Connecticut. Others are from 26 states, and 5 foreign countries. 50% are from public schools. 66% are White; 2% Asian American; 12% Hispanic; 10% African American; 1% American Indian/Alaska Native; 1% Foreign. 61% claim no religious affiliation; 18% Catholic; 12% Protestant. **Male To Female Ratio:** 1.1:1. The average age of freshmen is 19; all undergraduates, 20. 43% do not continue beyond their first year; 47% remain to graduate. **Housing:** 598 students can be accommodated in college housing, which includes single-sex and coed dorms and on-campus apartments. On-campus housing is guaranteed for all 4 years. 80% of students live on campus; of those, 60% remain on campus on weekends. All students may keep cars.

FACULTY/CLASSROOMS: 49% of faculty are male; 51% are female. All teach undergraduates. No introductory courses are taught by graduate students. The average class size in an introductory lecture is 14; in a laboratory is 10; and in a regular course is 14.

PROGRAMS OF STUDY: Mitchell confers B.A. and B.S. degrees. Associate degrees are also awarded. Bachelor's degrees are awarded in AGRICULTURE (environmental studies), BUSINESS (business administration and management, hospitality management services, and sports management), COMMUNICATIONS AND THE ARTS (communications), EDUCATION (early childhood education), SOCIAL SCIENCE (criminal justice, homeland security, human development, liberal arts/general studies, and psychology). Early childhood education is the strongest academically. Business administration, criminal justice, and sport & fitness management have the largest enrollments.

ACTIVITIES: There are no fraternities or sororities. There are 35 groups on campus, including academic club, art, cheerleading, choir, chorus, computers, dance, drama, ethnic, honors, international, LGBT, professional, radio and TV, religious, social, social service, and student government. **Sports:** There are 8 intercollegiate sports for men and 7 for women, and 4 intramural sports for men and 4 for women. Facilities include a basketball court, a fitness center, tennis courts, and athletic fields for all varsity teams. There are also natural and groomed trails. **Graduates:** From July 1, 2015 to June 30, 2016, 190 bachelor's degrees were awarded. The most popular majors were liberal and professional studies (23%), business administration (22%), and criminal justice (18%).

SERVICES: Counseling and information services are available, as is tutoring in most subjects. There is a reader service for the blind. **Library/Resources:** The library contains 94,542 volumes, and 1,658 audio/video tapes/CDs/DVDs, and subscribes to 90 periodicals including electronic. Computerized library services include interlibrary loans, database searching, Internet access, and Wi-Fi capability. Special learning facilities include a radio station. **Physically Challenged Students:** 50% of the campus is accessible. Facilities include wheelchair ramps, elevators, special parking, specially equipped restrooms, and special class scheduling. **Special:** Internships are available through academic department chairs. Liberal & Professional Studies offers an Individualized (student-designed) option. Work study jobs are available. Bachelor degrees (BA or BS) offered. There are 8 national honor societies, Phi Beta Kappa, and 1 departmental honors program. **Visiting:** There are regularly scheduled orientations for prospective students, including a student-guided tour and an interview with an admissions counselor. There are guides for informal visits and visitors may sit in on classes. To schedule a visit, contact the Visit Coordinator, Admissions Office. **Campus Safety and Security:** Measures include 24-hour foot and vehicle patrol, emergency notification system, and security escort services. There are shuttle buses, emergency telephones, lighted pathways/sidewalks, and controlled access to dorms/residences.

REQUIREMENTS: The GED is accepted. A recommendation and a personal statement are required. A personal interview is recommended but not required. A GPA of 2.0 is required. AP and CLEP credits are accepted. Important factors in the admissions decision are personality/intangible qualities, recommendations by school officials, and extracurricular activities record. To graduate, bachelor-degree-seeking students must complete 120 credits (associate-degree-seeking 60 credits) with a minimum GPA of 2.0 (2.67 for early childhood education). Required general education curriculum. Several majors contain a cumulating experience (a capstone, senior project, or internship). **Procedure:** Freshmen are admitted fall and spring. Entrance exams should be taken during summer orientation. There are early decision, deferred admissions, and rolling admissions plans. Early decision applications should be filed by November 15, along with a $30 fee. Notification of early decision is sent December 15; regular decision, on a rolling basis. Applications are accepted on-line. **Transfer Students:** 74 transfer students enrolled in 2015-2016. In addition to fulfilling regular application requirements, transfer applicants must submit official college transcripts from all colleges/universities attended. 30 of 120 credits required for the bachelor's degree must be completed at Mitchell. **International Students:** There are 7 international students enrolled. The school actively recruits these students. They must take the TOEFL with a minimum score of 500 on the paper-based TOEFL (PBT), or take the APIEL.

Admissions Contact: Gregg Gorneault, Director of Admissions. Email: *admissions@mitchell.edu* Web: *www.mitchell.edu*

FINANCIAL AID: In 2016-2017, 83% of all full-time freshmen and 73% of continuing full-time students received some form of financial aid. 83% of all full-time freshmen and 73% of continuing full-time students received need-based aid. The average freshman award was $20,235. Need-based scholarships or need-based grants averaged $16,739; need-based self-help aid (loans and jobs) averaged $7,281; and other non-need-based awards and non-need-based scholarships averaged $7,636. The FAFSA code is 001393. The priority date for freshman financial aid applications for fall entry is April 1.

POST UNIVERSITY B-3
www.post.edu

Waterbury, CT 06723	(203) 596-4520 (800) 345-2562
Fax: (203) 756-5810	Email: admissions@post.edu
Full-time: 325 men, 400 women	Faculty: n/av
Part-time: 200 men, 350 women	Ph.D.s: 61%
Graduate: n/av	Student/Faculty: n/av
Year: semesters, summer session	Tuition: $29,550
Room & Board: $11,600	Freshman Class: n/av
SAT or ACT: required	CEEB CODE: 3698
Application Deadline: open	COMPETITIVE

Post University, founded in 1890, is a private institution offering liberal arts and business programs. The figures in the above capsule and in this profile are approximate. There are 2 undergraduate schools. In addition to regional accreditation, TPU has baccalaureate program accreditation with NEASC. The 70-acre campus is in an urban area 1 mile west of Waterbury. Including any residence halls, there are 13 buildings.

STUDENT LIFE: 83% of undergraduates are from Connecticut. Others are from 12 states, 20 foreign countries, and Canada. 75% are from public schools. 8% are Hispanic; 63% White; 5% Foreign; 2% Asian American; 17% African American. **Female To Male Ratio:** 1.4:1. The average age of freshmen is 19; all undergraduates, 26. 23% do not continue beyond their first year; 39% remain to graduate. **Housing:** 424 students can be accommodated in college housing, which includes coed dorms and off-campus apartments. On-campus housing is guaranteed for all 4 years. 58% of students live on campus; of those, 60% remain on campus on weekends. All students may keep cars.

FACULTY/CLASSROOMS: 57% of faculty are male; 43% are female. All

teach undergraduates. No introductory courses are taught by graduate students. The average class size in an introductory lecture is 20; in a laboratory is 15; and in a regular course is 35.

PROGRAMS OF STUDY: TPU confers B.A., and B.S. degrees. Associate degrees are also awarded. Bachelor's degrees are awarded in BUSINESS (accounting, banking and finance, business administration and management, management science, and marketing/retailing/merchandising), COMMUNICATIONS AND THE ARTS (English), SOCIAL SCIENCE (criminal justice, history, liberal arts/general studies, psychology, and sociology). Biology is the strongest academically. Management and general studies have the largest enrollments.

ACTIVITIES: There are no fraternities or sororities. There are 30 groups on campus, including cheerleading, chorale, chorus, computers, drama, ethnic, honors, international, LGBT, literary magazine, musical theater, social, social service, student government, and yearbook. Popular campus events include Dances, Concerts, and International Food Festivals. **Sports:** There are 5 intercollegiate sports for men and 5 for women, and 4 intramural sports for men and 4 for women. Facilities include a soccer field, fitness center, weight room, racquetball court, a swimming pool, and tennis courts.

SERVICES: Counseling and information services are available, as is tutoring in most subjects. There is a reader service for the blind, and remedial math, reading, and writing. **Library/Resources:** The library contains 85,000 volumes, 75,158 microform items, and 1,027 audio/video tapes/CDs/DVDs, and subscribes to 427 periodicals including electronic. Computerized library services include interlibrary loans and database searching. **Physically Challenged Students:** 70% of the campus is accessible. Facilities include wheelchair ramps, elevators, special parking, specially equipped restrooms, and special class scheduling. **Special:** Co-op programs in all majors, cross-registration with Naugatuck Valley Community College, study abroad in England, the Netherlands, and Japan are offered. There are also internships with area businesses, general studies degrees, accelerated degree programs, B.A.-B.S. degrees, and credit for life experience available. There are 2 national honor societies and 1 departmental honors program. **Visiting:** There are regularly scheduled orientations for prospective students, including tours, interviews with admissions counselors, and meetings with faculty and students. There are guides for informal visits, visitors may sit in on classes, and stay overnight. To schedule a visit, contact the Admissions Office. **Campus Safety and Security:** Measures include 24-hour foot and vehicle patrol, self-defense education, and security escort services. There are shuttle buses and lighted pathways/sidewalks.

REQUIREMENTS: The SAT or ACT is required. Applicants must be graduates of an accredited secondary school, with 4 years of English and at least 16 total academic credits. The GED is accepted. A GPA of 2.0 is required. AP and CLEP credits are accepted. Important factors in the admissions decision are personality/intangible qualities, extracurricular activities record, and recommendations by school officials. To graduate, all students must maintain a minimum GPA of 2.0, earn a total of 120 credits, including at least 33 in the major, and take a computer course. **Procedure:** Freshmen are admitted to all sessions. There are early admissions, deferred admissions, and rolling admissions plans. Check with the school for current application deadlines. The fall 2016 application fee was $40. Notification is sent on a rolling basis. Applications are accepted on-line. **Transfer Students:** Applicants must have a minimum college GPA of 2.0, submit an official college transcript, and have an interview. The SAT is recommended. 30 of 120 credits required for the bachelor's degree must be completed at TPU. **International Students:** There are 48 international students enrolled. The school actively recruits these students. They must take the TOEFL with a minimum score of 500 on the paper-based TOEFL (PBT) or 79 on the Internet-based version (iBT).

Admissions Contact: Aline Rossiter, Dean of Admissions. Email: *admissions@post.edu* Web: *www.post.edu*

FINANCIAL AID: In 2016-2017, 100% of all full-time freshmen received some form of financial aid. The college's own financial statement, and parent and student federal tax returns, are required. The FAFSA code is 001401. Check with the school for current application deadlines.

QUINNIPIAC UNIVERSITY — C-3

www.qu.edu

Hamden, CT 06518	**(203) 582-8600** **(800) 462-1944**
Fax: (203) 582-8906	**Email: admissions@qu.edu**
Full-time: 2669 men, 4111 women	**Faculty:** 351
Part-time: 128 men, 194 women	**Ph.D.s:** 89%
Graduate: 1003 men, 1795 women	**Student/Faculty:** 19 to 1
Year: semesters, summer session	**Tuition:** $43,940
Room & Board: $15,170	**Freshman Class:** 23492 applied, 17957 accepted, 1908 enrolled
SAT CR/M: 530/550 **ACT:** 25	**CEEB CODE:** 3712
Application Deadline: February 1	**COMPETITIVE**

Quinnipiac University, founded in 1929, is a private institution offering 58-plus undergraduate majors and 22 graduate programs through the schools of health sciences, nursing, business, engineering, communications, education, the college of arts and sciences, the school of law and the Frank H. Netter MD school of medicine. There are 6 undergraduate schools and 9 graduate schools. In addition to regional accreditation, Quinnipiac has baccalaureate program accreditation with AACSB, ABET, APTA, CAHEA, NCATE, NLN, ABA, ACOTE, ARC-PA, NAACLS, CAATE, CAPTE, CCNE, and COA. The 600-acre campus is in a suburban area in Hamden and North Haven CT, just 8 miles north of New Haven, CT, and 80 miles Northeast of NYC. Including any residence halls, there are 80 buildings.

STUDENT LIFE: 75% of undergraduates are from out of state, mostly the Middle Atlantic. Students are from 42 states, 30 foreign countries, and Canada. 76% are from public schools. 8% are Hispanic; 76% White; 5% African American; 3% Asian American; 3% Foreign; 3% race unknown; 2% two or more races. 51% are Catholic; 26% Protestant. **Female To Male Ratio:** 1.6:1. The average age of freshmen is 19; all undergraduates, 21. 10% do not continue beyond their first year; 78% remain to graduate. **Housing:** 5020 students can be accommodated in college housing, which includes coed dorms, on-campus apartments, and off-campus apartments. In addition, there are honors houses, special-interest houses, wellness housing, nursing cohort, advanced (3+1 BS/MBA) business and advanced (3+1 BA/MA) communications cohort housing. On-campus housing is guaranteed for all 4 years. 80% of students live on campus; of those, 75% remain on campus on weekends. Upperclassmen may keep cars.

FACULTY/CLASSROOMS: 44% of faculty are male; 56% are female. 94% teach undergraduates, 40% do research, and 40% do both. No introductory courses are taught by graduate students. The average class size in an introductory lecture is 35; in a laboratory is 18; and in a regular course is 26.

PROGRAMS OF STUDY: Quinnipiac confers B.A., B.S. and B.F.A. degrees. Master's and doctoral degrees are also awarded. Bachelor's degrees are awarded in BIOLOGICAL SCIENCE (biochemistry, biology/biological science, biotechnology, microbiology, and neurosciences), BUSINESS (accounting, banking and finance, business administration and management, entrepreneurial studies, finance, international business management, management science, marketing management, and marketing/retailing/merchandising), COMMUNICATIONS AND THE ARTS (advertising, communications, dramatic arts, English, journalism, public relations, Spanish, and theatre arts), COMPUTER AND PHYSICAL SCIENCE (chemistry, computer science, digital arts/technology, mathematics, software engineering, and web technology), EDUCATION (athletic training, elementary education, and secondary education), ENGINEERING AND ENVIRONMENTAL DESIGN (civil engineering, engineering, industrial engineering, and mechanical engineering), HEALTH PROFESSIONS (biomedical science, health science, nursing, occupational therapy, physical therapy, physician's assistant, predentistry, premedicine, and radiological science), SOCIAL SCIENCE (criminal justice, economics, gerontology, history, liberal arts/general studies, paralegal studies, philosophy, political science/government, prelaw, psychobiology, psychology, social science, and sociology). Physician assistant, physical therapy, nursing, and business are the strongest academically. Nursing, physical therapy, and management have the largest enrollments.

ACTIVITIES: 20% of men belong to 9 national fraternities; 30% of women belong to 10 national sororities. There are 142 groups on campus, including cheerleading, chorale, chorus, communications, dance, drama, environmental, ethnic, film, honors, international, jazz band, LGBT, literary magazine, newspaper, pep band, political, professional, radio and TV, religious, social, social service, student government, and yearbook. Popular campus events include The BIG Event, Parents Weekend, Relay for Life, Holiday Party, and Fall and Spring Concerts. **Sports:** There are 7 intercollegiate sports for men and 14 for women, and 6 intramural sports for men and 6 for women. Facilities include TD Bank Sports Center with twin arenas, each seating more than 3000 for ice hockey and basketball, more than 20 acres of playing fields, and a recreation center with a weight training room, a steam room, a large multipurpose room for indoor tennis, basketball, volleyball, and aerobics, and a suspended indoor track. Weight room and 'spinning' room on the York Hill campus plus exercise and yoga space on the North Haven Campus. **Graduates:** From July 1, 2015 to June 30, 2016, 1676 bachelor's degrees were awarded. The most popular majors were health professions (35%), business (21%), and communications (14%). 275 companies recruited on campus in 2015-2016. In an average class, 4% graduate in 3 years or less, 72% graduate in 4 years or less, and 76% graduate in 5 years or less. Of the 2015 graduating class, 35% were enrolled in graduate school within 6 months of graduation, and 59% were employed.

SERVICES: Counseling and information services are available, as is tutoring in most subjects, such as all freshman-level courses and others by request. Special workshops on work study skills, library resources, and time management are available. **Library/Resources:** The 3 libraries contain 311,000 volumes, 592,900 microform items, and 6,000 audio/video tapes/CDs/DVDs, and subscribe to 44,700 periodicals including electronic. Computerized library services include interlibrary loans, database searching, Internet access, and Wi-Fi capability. Special learning facilities include an art gallery, radio station, TV station, Exhibits on the Irish famine, part of Quinnipiac's Ireland's Great Hunger Museum which is located on Whitney Avenue, and the Albert Schweitzer Institute. **Physically Challenged Students:** All of the campus is accessible. Facilities include wheelchair ramps, elevators, special parking, specially equipped restrooms, special class scheduling, and lowered drinking fountains. **Special:** Internships or clinical placements are available in all majors. Students can choose to study abroad in more than 25 countries most popular being Australia, Italy, Ireland, Spain, France, and England. A 6-or 7-year freshman entry-level doctorate (BS/DPT) in physical therapy and a 5 1/2 year freshman entry-level master's (BS/MOT) in occupational therapy are offered, as well as a 6-year BS in Health Sciences/MHS in a physician assistant master's program. For those interested in teaching elementary or secondary education, a 5-year BA in an academic major plus a master of arts in teaching (MAT) which includes student teaching is offered. An innovative BS/MBA is offered to academically talented business students in a 4-year (3+1) format to complete both degrees in 4 years. A similar program is offered for talented communications students to complete their BA/MA in 4 years. In addition, a 3+3 BA or BS/JD degree with the School of Law invites academically talented students who wish to complete both degrees in 6 rather than 7 years. There are 11 national honor societies, a freshman honors program, and 20 departmental honors programs. **Visiting:** There are regularly scheduled orientations for prospective students, Visit options include interviews, group information sessions, student-guided tours. During open houses an opportunity to speak with faculty and various offices and student life groups. There are guides for informal visits and visitors may sit in on classes. To schedule a visit, contact The Admissions Office. **Campus Safety and Security:** Measures include 24-hour foot and vehicle patrol, emergency notification system, self-defense education, and security escort services. There are shuttle buses, emergency telephones, lighted pathways/sidewalks, controlled access to dorms/residences, perimeter security staffed by Public Safety Officers at all entrances, and vehicle and occupant check-in identification.

REQUIREMENTS: A minimum composite score of 1140 on the SAT or 23 composite on the ACT is recommended. All students must have completed 16 academic credits, including 4 in English, 3 in math, 2 each in science and social studies, and 5 in electives. The GED is accepted. An interview is recommended, and an essay and at least one letter of recommendation are required. For majors in the health sciences, 4 years each of math and science are required. Physics is highly recommended for those applying to the physical therapy and physician assistant programs. Test Optional Policy: Test scores (either SAT or ACT) are required for all students applying to the School of Health Sciences and Nursing. All other majors do not require test scores to be submitted for an admissions decision, but test scores will be considered if submitted. Quinnipiac requires applicants to be in the upper 50% of their class. A GPA of 2.9 is required. AP and CLEP credits are accepted. Important factors in the admissions decision are advanced placement or honors courses, extracurricular activities record, and personality/intangible qualities. All students must complete the University Curriculum, including the first-year seminar, English, math, fine arts, social sciences, humanities, and sciences, plus the specific course standards and requirements of a student's chosen major and a University Curriculum Capstone course or experience. To graduate, students must maintain a GPA of 2.0 over 120 total semester hours. **Procedure:** Freshmen are admitted fall and spring. Entrance exams should be taken in the junior year and early in the senior year. There are early decision, deferred admissions, and rolling admissions plans. Early decision applications should be filed by November 1; regular applications, by February 1 for fall entry; and December 15 for spring entry, along with a $65 fee. Notification of early decision is sent November 30; regular decision, December 15. 248 early decision candidates were accepted for the 2016-2017 class. 2850 applicants were on the 2016 waiting list; 297 were admitted. Applications are accepted on-line. Application fees are waived if application is completed on-line. **Transfer Students:** 247 transfer students enrolled in 2015-2016. Transfer students must have a minimum college GPA of 2.5 (some programs require a minimum of 3.0) and must submit SAT scores and high school or college transcripts if they have not received an associate degree prior to enrollment. An interview is recommended. 45 of 120 credits required for the bachelor's degree must be completed at Quinnipiac. **International Students:** There are 158 international students enrolled. The school actively recruits these students. They must take the TOEFL with a minimum score of 550 on the paper-based TOEFL (PBT) or 80 on the Internet-based version (iBT), or take the IELTS. They must also take the SAT or ACT only if the language of instruction is in English.

ADMISSIONS: 76% of the 2016-2017 applicants were accepted. The SAT scores for the 2016-2017 freshman class were: Critical Reading-- 31% below 500, 47% between 500 and 599, 20% between 600 and 699, and 2% between 700 and 800. Math-- 25% below 500, 46% between 500 and 599, 26% between 600 and 699, and 3% between 700 and 800. The ACT scores were 3% between 12 and 17, 34% between 18 and 23, 55% between 24 and 29, and 8% above 30. 54% of the current freshmen were in the top fifth of their class; 86% were in the top two fifths. 16 freshmen graduated first in their class. **Admissions Contact:** Joan Isaac Mohr, VP for Admissions/Financial Aid. Email: *admissions@qu.edu* Web: *www.qu.edu*

FINANCIAL AID: In 2016-2017, 90% of all full-time freshmen and 85% of continuing full-time students received some form of financial aid. 69% of all full-time freshmen and 61% of continuing full-time students received need-based aid. The average freshman award was $27,621. Need-based scholarships or need-based grants averaged $22,466 ($55,780 maximum); need-based self-help aid (loans and jobs) averaged $4,213 ($11,000 maximum); non-need-based athletic scholarships averaged $30,055 ($57,734 maximum); and other non-need-based awards and non-need-based scholarships averaged $17,609 ($38,000 maximum). 28% of undergraduate students work part-time. Average annual earnings from campus work are $2171. The average financial indebtedness of the 2016 graduate was $47,217. The FAFSA code is 001402. The priority date for freshman financial aid applications for fall entry is March 1. The deadline for filing freshman financial aid applications for fall entry is April 1.

SACRED HEART UNIVERSITY B-4

www.sacredheart.edu

Fairfield, CT 06825	**(203) 371-7881**
Fax: (203) 365-7607	**Email: osullivank6@sacredheart.edu**
Full-time: 1769 men, 3025 women	**Faculty:** 220
Part-time: 183 men, 451 women	**Ph.D.s:** 79%
Graduate: 891 men, 2213 women	**Student/Faculty:** 22 to 1
Year: semesters, summer session	**Tuition:** $38,300
Room & Board: $14,450	**Freshman Class:** 10017 applied, 5731 accepted, 1322 enrolled
SAT or ACT: required	**CEEB CODE:** 3780
Application Deadline: rolling	**COMPETITIVE**

As one of the fastest-growing Catholic institutions in the country, Sacred

Heart University (SHU) offers more than 70 undergraduate, graduate and doctoral programs in business, communications, engineering, sciences, performing and visual arts, education, technology, health professions, and nursing. SHU also offers an expansive Division I varsity athletics program, club sports, Greek Life, performing arts, media groups, and community service programs. There are 7 undergraduate schools and 7 graduate schools. In addition to regional accreditation, SHU has baccalaureate program accreditation with AACSB, APTA, NCATE, NLN, AOTA, and CAATE. The 300-acre campus is in a suburban area 90 minutes from Manhattan and 150 minutes from Boston. Including any residence halls, there are 31 buildings.

STUDENT LIFE: 63% of undergraduates are from out of state, mostly the Northeast. Students are from 50 states, 34 foreign countries, and Canada. 77% are from public schools. 9% are Hispanic; 7% race unknown; 69% White; 6% Foreign; 5% African American; 2% Asian American; 2% two or more races. 61% are Catholic; 24% claim no religious affiliation; 13% Protestant. **Female To Male Ratio:** 2.0:1. The average age of freshmen is 18; all undergraduates, 20. 19% do not continue beyond their first year; 81% remain to graduate. **Housing:** 2784 students can be accommodated in college housing, which includes coed dorms, on-campus apartments, and off-campus apartments. In addition, there are honors houses, special-interest houses, and living and learning communities with themes such as honors, business, wellness, and community service. On-campus housing is guaranteed for all 4 years, is available on a first-come, first-served basis, and is available on a lottery system for upperclassmen. 51% of students live on campus. Upperclassmen may keep cars.

FACULTY/CLASSROOMS: 46% of faculty are male; 54% are female. 67% teach undergraduates. No introductory courses are taught by graduate students. The average class size in an introductory lecture is 25; in a laboratory is 15; and in a regular course is 22.

PROGRAMS OF STUDY: SHU confers B.A., and B.S. degrees. Associate, master's, and doctoral degrees are also awarded. Bachelor's degrees are awarded in BIOLOGICAL SCIENCE (biology/biological science), BUSINESS (accounting, business administration and management, business economics, marketing management, and sports management), COMMUNICATIONS AND THE ARTS (communications, English, media arts, and Spanish), COMPUTER AND PHYSICAL SCIENCE (chemistry, computer science, information sciences and systems, and mathematics), EDUCATION (athletic training), HEALTH PROFESSIONS (exercise science and health science), SOCIAL SCIENCE (criminal justice, history, liberal arts/general studies, psychology, social work, and sociology). Physical therapy, nursing, and business management are the strongest academically. Nursing, exercise science, and psychology have the largest enrollments.

ACTIVITIES: 15% of men belong to 1 local and 6 national fraternities; 36% of women belong to 8 national sororities. There are 150 groups on campus, including student events team, Habitat for Humanity, academic clubs, art, bagpipe, band, cheerleading, chess, choir, chorale, chorus, communications, computers, dance, debate, drama, drill team, environmental, ethnic, film, honors, international, jazz band, LGBT, literary magazine, marching band, musical theater, newspaper, orchestra, pep band, photography, political, professional, radio and TV, religious, social, social service, student government, and yearbook. Popular campus events include Spring Concert, Family Weekend, Pack the Pitt, SHU Hoops Madness, President's Gala, and Just SHU it!. **Sports:** There are 33 intercollegiate sports for men and 35 for women, and 9 intramural sports for men and 6 for women. The William H. Pitt Health and Recreation Center features a 2,062-seat arena, four basketball courts, weight training/fitness center, aerobics, and fencing room, and a varsity wrestling room. Facilities also include Pioneer Park softball stadium, a Spinturf athletic field with state-of-the-art Daktronics scoreboard, eight-lane outdoor running track and six superior Deco II tennis courts.**Graduates:** From July 1, 2015 to June 30, 2016, 925 bachelor's degrees were awarded. The most popular majors were business/marketing (33%), health professions (27%), and psychology (10%). 162 companies recruited on campus in 2015-2016. In an average class, 1% graduate in 3 years or less, 54% graduate in 4 years or less, and 60% graduate in 5 years or less.

SERVICES: Counseling and information services are available, as is tutoring in every subject. There is a reader service for the blind, and remedial math, reading, and writing. **Library/Resources:** The 2 libraries contain 122,977 volumes, 223,098 microform items, and 1,264 audio/video tapes/CDs/DVDs.. Computerized library services include interlibrary loans, database searching, Internet access, and Wi-Fi capability. Special learning facilities include an art gallery, radio station, TV station, and Edgerton Center for Performing Arts. The Martire Business, and Communications Center facilities include an active trading floor with 30 work stations, 13 Bloomberg terminals, wallboard ticker tapes and real time data from NASDAQ and NYSE. There are also screening venues; smart classrooms with multi-media technology; interactive labs; a motion capture lab; and two large television studios for TV, video and film production. Healthcare Education includes a medical gym, audiology suite, motion analysis and human performance labs, an immersive acute care simulation lab with video and data capture capability, a simulated outpatient suite, high-fidelity mannequin, roles, a homecare suite, an expanded human anatomy lab, and many more learning resources featuring the latest technology. Facilities supporting the School of Computing include a Gaming Lab (which also supports the intercollegiate Gaming team), state-of-the-art computing labs, a closed LAN laboratory and the motion lab. Other facilities include a fashion design studio, art studios, 3D Printing Lab and cadaver lab. The Jandrisevits Learning Center and the Student Success Center include spaces and technologies to provide academic support to students, including those with disabilities. **Physically Challenged Students:** Facilities include wheelchair ramps, elevators, special parking, specially equipped restrooms, special class scheduling, lowered drinking fountains, and lowered telephones. Special housing rooms are equipped with special audible alarms for students with hearing disabilities and other special accommodations can be made through Res Life. **Special:** SHU offers paid and unpaid internships at local, regional, and national organizations, including Fortune 500 and 1000 companies, hospitals, media outlets, social service agencies, and schools. Study abroad opportunities exist worldwide and year-round, and on-campus employment is available through the University's work-study program. SHU also has campuses in Dingle, Ireland, Luxembourg, and Stamford, CT. A new engineering degree allows SHU to partner with other colleges we also offer accelerated masters programs. There are 2 national honor societies, a freshman honors program, and 1 departmental honors program. **Visiting:** There are regularly scheduled orientations for prospective students, including Monday-Friday tours and interviews, weekend tours, information sessions, and open house programs during the academic year and summer. There are guides for informal visits, visitors may sit in on classes, and stay overnight. To schedule a visit, contact Robert Gilmore at (203) 365-7880. **Campus Safety and Security:** Measures include 24-hour foot and vehicle patrol, emergency notification system, self-defense education, and security escort services. There are shuttle buses, emergency telephones, lighted pathways/sidewalks, controlled access to dorms/residences. The SHU-Safe safety app allows students to make medical information instantly available, link to emergency services, pinpoint their location for emergency personnel, and set up safety checks. SHU Safety Week, sponsored by the student government, includes programs on self-defense, social media safety, bystander intervention and more. Other programs and services include the personal safety escort program, silent witness program and blue light call boxes. All campus residence halls have sprinklers and alarms and are designated nonsmoking.

REQUIREMENTS: A completed application, essay, and 1 letter of recommendation are required. An interview is required for early decision candidates and recommended for all other candidates. Required are 4 years of English and 3 years of math, science, history, and language, with 4 years preferred. AP and CLEP credits are accepted. Important factors in the admissions decision are advanced placement or honors courses, recommendations by school officials, and leadership record. At the undergraduate level, Sacred Heart University offers two baccalaureate degrees: Bachelor of Arts or Bachelor of Science depending upon the nature of the discipline of the major. The University offers more than 60 degree programs. The University also offers Associate in Arts and Associate in Science degrees. A central component of undergraduate study is the University's Core Curriculum, the Human Journey, which embodies the University's commitment to academic excellence, social responsibility, and ethical awareness. All candidates for the baccalaureate degree must complete at least 120 credits, with a minimum of 30 credits taken at Sacred Heart University. A minimum cumulative GPA 2.0 is required. **Procedure:** Freshmen are admitted fall and spring. Entrance exams should be taken in May of the junior year through November of the senior year. There are early decision, early admissions, deferred admissions, and rolling admissions plans. Early decision applications should be filed by December 1, along with a $50 fee. Notification of early decision is sent December 15; regular decision, April 1. 182 early decision candidates were accepted for the 2016-2017 class. Applications are accepted on-line. **Transfer Students:** 132 transfer students enrolled in 2015-2016. A minimum college GPA of 2.5 is required. 30 of 120 credits required for the bachelor's degree must be completed at SHU. **International Students:** There are 70 international students enrolled. The school actively recruits these students. They must take the TOEFL with a minimum score of 550 on the paper-based TOEFL (PBT) or 80 on the Internet-based version (iBT). SHU offers a test-optional admissions policy.

ADMISSIONS: 57% of the 2016-2017 applicants were accepted. 23% of the current freshmen were in the top fifth of their class. **Admissions Contact:** Kevin O'Sullivan, Executive Director Admissions. Email: *osullivank6@sacredheart.edu* Web: *www.sacredheart.edu*

FINANCIAL AID: In 2016-2017, 71% of all full-time freshmen and 67% of continuing full-time students received some form of financial aid. 71% of all full-time freshmen and 66% of continuing full-time students received need-based aid. The average freshman award was $19,822. Need-based scholarships or need-based grants averaged $15,890; need-based self-help aid (loans and jobs) averaged $4,933; non-need-based athletic scholarships averaged $16,129; other non-need-based awards and non-need-based scholarships averaged $12,778; and $4,121 from other forms of aid. 23% of undergraduate students work part-time. Average annual earnings from campus work are $1322. The average financial indebtedness of the 2016 graduate was $23,813. SHU is a member of CSS. The CSS/Profile is required. The FAFSA code is 001403. The priority date for freshman financial aid applications for fall entry is March 1.

SOUTHERN CONNECTICUT STATE UNIVERSITY *(The complete profile is made available exclusively on our website, www.barronspac.com)*

TRINITY COLLEGE — C-2

www.trincoll.edu

Hartford, CT 06106 — (860) 297-2180

Fax: (860) 297-2287 — Email: admissions.office@trincoll.edu

Full-time: 1115 men, 984 women	Faculty: 193
Part-time: 67 men, 57 women	Ph.D.s: 93%
Graduate: 49 men, 59 women	Student/Faculty: 10 to 1
Year: 4-1-4	Tuition: $50,776
Room & Board: $13,144	Freshman Class: 7570 applied, 2530 accepted, 559 enrolled
SAT CR/M/W: 610/650/630 ACT: 28	CEEB CODE: 3899
Application Deadline: January 1	HIGHLY COMPETITIVE+

Trinity College, founded in 1823, is an independent, nonsectarian liberal arts college. Figures in the above capsule and in this profile are approximate. There is 1 undergraduate school and 1 graduate school. In addition to regional accreditation, Trinity has baccalaureate program accreditation with ABET. The 100-acre campus is in an urban area southwest of downtown Hartford. Including any residence halls, there are 78 buildings.

STUDENT LIFE: 84% of undergraduates are from out of state, mostly the Northeast. Students are from 44 states, 63 foreign countries, and Canada. 43% are from public schools. 7% are Hispanic; 65% White; 6% African American; 5% race unknown; 4% Asian American; 3% two or more races; 10% Foreign. 30% claim no religious affiliation; 28% Protestant; 27% Catholic. **Male To Female Ratio:** 1.1:1. The average age of freshmen is 18; all undergraduates, 20. 12% do not continue beyond their first year; 86% remain to graduate. **Housing:** 2000 students can be accommodated in college housing, which includes coed dorms, on-campus apartments, and off-campus apartments. In addition, there are special-interest houses. On-campus housing is guaranteed for all 4 years. 90% of students live on campus; of those, 70% remain on campus on weekends. Upperclassmen may keep cars.

FACULTY/CLASSROOMS: 52% of faculty are male; 48% are female. All teach undergraduates, and all do research. No introductory courses are taught by graduate students. The average class size in an introductory lecture is 20; in a laboratory is 16; and in a regular course is 13.

PROGRAMS OF STUDY: Trinity confers B.A., and B.S. degrees. Master's degrees are also awarded. Bachelor's degrees are awarded in BIOLOGICAL SCIENCE (biochemistry, biology/biological science, and neurosciences), COMMUNICATIONS AND THE ARTS (art history and appreciation, classics, comparative literature, dance, dramatic arts, English, fine arts, French, German, Italian, modern language, music, Russian, Spanish, studio art, and theater management), COMPUTER AND PHYSICAL SCIENCE (chemistry, computer science, mathematics, and physics), EDUCATION (education), ENGINEERING AND ENVIRONMENTAL DESIGN (engineering and environmental science), SOCIAL SCIENCE (American studies, anthropology, classical/ancient civilization, economics, history, interdisciplinary studies, international studies, Judaic studies, philosophy, political science/government, psychology, public affairs, religion, sociology, and women's studies). Political science, economics, and psychology have the largest enrollments.

ACTIVITIES: 20% of men belong to 7 national fraternities; 16% of women belong to 1 local and 2 national sororities. There are 120 groups on campus, including art, bagpipe, band, cheerleading, chess, choir, chorale, chorus, dance, debate, drama, ethnic, film, honors, international, jazz band, LGBT, literary magazine, musical theater, newspaper, pep band, photography, political, professional, radio and TV, religious, social, social service, student government, and yearbook. Popular campus events include Human Rights Lecture Series, Black History Month and Latino Heritage Week. **Sports:** There are 15 intercollegiate sports for men and 13 for women, and 14 intramural sports for men and 14 for women. Facilities include a pool, outdoor and indoor tracks, playing fields, a weight room, a fitness center, tennis, squash, and basketball courts. **Graduates:** From July 1, 2015 to June 30, 2016, 523 bachelor's degrees were awarded. The most popular majors were political science (13%), economics (13%), and psychology (7%). 200 companies recruited on campus in 2015-2016. In an average class, 1% graduate in 3 years or less, 77% graduate in 4 years or less, 84% graduate in 5 years or less, and 86% graduate in 6 years or less.

SERVICES: Counseling and information services are available, as is tutoring in every subject. There is a reader service for the blind. The writing center offers instruction in all forms of writing, and the math center provides individual tutoring on topics related to math and other courses involving quantitative reasoning. **Library/Resources:** The library contains 992,817 volumes, 399,394 microform items, and 225,477 audio/video tapes/CDs/DVDs, and subscribes to 2,438 periodicals including electronic. Computerized library services include interlibrary loans, database searching, Internet access, and Wi-Fi capability. Special learning facilities include an art gallery, radio station, and TV station. **Physically Challenged Students:** 60% of the campus is accessible. Facilities include wheelchair ramps, elevators, special parking, specially equipped restrooms, special class scheduling, lowered drinking fountains, and lowered telephones. **Special:** Trinity offers special freshman programs for exceptional students, including interdisciplinary programs in the sciences and the humanities. There is an intensive study program under which students can devote a semester to 1 subject. Cross-registration through such programs as the Hartford Consortium and the Twelve-College Exchange Program, hundreds of internships (some with Connecticut Public Radio and TV on campus), study abroad virtually worldwide, including Rome, South Africa, Trinidad, Russia, and Nepal, a Washington semester, dual majors in all disciplines, student-designed majors, nondegree study, and pass/fail options also are offered. A 5-year advanced degree in electrical or mechanical engineering with Rensselaer Polytechnic Institute is available. There are 4 national honor societies and a chapter of Phi Beta Kappa. **Visiting:** There are regularly scheduled orientations for prospective students. There are guides for informal visits, visitors may sit in on classes, and stay overnight. To schedule a visit, contact the Admissions Office. **Campus Safety and Security:** Measures include 24-hour foot and vehicle patrol, emergency notification system, self-defense education, and security escort services. There are shuttle buses, emergency telephones, lighted pathways/sidewalks, and controlled access to dorms/residences.

REQUIREMENTS: Trinity strongly emphasizes individual character and personal qualities in admission. Consequently, an interview and essay are recommended. The college requires 4 years of English, 2 years each in foreign language and algebra, and 1 year each in geometry, history, and lab science. AP credits are accepted. Important factors in the admissions decision are advanced placement or honors courses, extracurricular activities record, and evidence of special talent. All students must complete 36 course credits, including 10 to 15 in the major and 1 from each of 5 distribution areas: arts, humanities, natural sciences, numerical and symbolic reasoning, and social sciences. Students must maintain at least a C average overall. **Procedure:** Freshmen are admitted fall. Entrance exams should be taken in the fall of the senior year. There are early decision and deferred admissions plans. Early decision applications should be filed by November 15; regular applications, by January 1 for fall entry, along with a $60 fee. Notification of early decision is sent December 15;

regular decision, April 1. 300 early decision candidates were accepted for the 2016-2017 class. 574 applicants were on the 2016 waiting list; 83 were admitted. Applications are accepted on-line. **Transfer Students:** 17 transfer students enrolled in 2015-2016. Transfer applicants must take the SAT or ACT. A minimum college GPA of 3.0 is recommended. 18 of 36 credits required for the bachelor's degree must be completed at Trinity. **International Students:** There are 214 international students enrolled. The school actively recruits these students. They must take the TOEFL.

ADMISSIONS: 33% of the 2016-2017 applicants were accepted. The SAT scores for the 2016-2017 freshman class were: Critical Reading-- 7% below 500, 30% between 500 and 599, 49% between 600 and 699, and 15% between 700 and 800. Math-- 2% below 500, 30% between 500 and 599, 51% between 600 and 699, and 17% between 700 and 800. Writing-- 5% below 500, 29% between 500 and 599, 53% between 600 and 699, and 13% between 700 and 800. The ACT scores were 4% between 18 and 23, 61% between 24 and 29, and 35% above 30. **Admissions Contact:** Angel Perez, Dean of Admissions/Financial Aid. Email: *admissions.office@trincoll.edu* Web: *www.trincoll.edu*

FINANCIAL AID: In 2016-2017, 48% of all full-time freshmen and 45% of continuing full-time students received some form of financial aid. 46% of all full-time freshmen and 43% of continuing full-time students received need-based aid. The average freshman award was $45,859. Need-based scholarships or need-based grants averaged $42,969 ($67,658 maximum); need-based self-help aid (loans and jobs) averaged $5,508 ($11,000 maximum); and other non-need-based awards and non-need-based scholarships averaged $26,799 ($65,650 maximum). 29% of undergraduate students work part-time. Average annual earnings from campus work are $2500. The average financial indebtedness of the 2016 graduate was $12,447. Trinity is a member of CSS. The CSS/Profile is required. The FAFSA code is 001414. The priority date for freshman financial aid applications for fall entry is February 1. The deadline for filing freshman financial aid applications for fall entry is March 1.

UNITED STATES COAST GUARD ACADEMY D-3

www.cga.edu

New London, CT 06320 (860) 444-8500 (800) 883-8724

Fax: (860) 701-6700 **Email:** uscga.admissions@uscga.edu

Full-time: 585 men, 313 women	**Faculty:** 147
Part-time: n/av	**Ph.D.s:** 36%
Graduate: n/av	**Student/Faculty:** 6 to 1
Year: semesters, summer session	**Tuition:** $942
Room & Board: see profile	**Freshman Class:** 1948 applied, 388 accepted, 267 enrolled
SAT CR/M/W: 610/650/605 **ACT:** 28	**CEEB CODE:** 5807
Application Deadline: February 1	**MOST COMPETITIVE**

The U.S. Coast Guard Academy, founded in 1876, is an Armed Forces Service Academy for men and women. Appointments are made solely on the basis of an annual nationwide competition. The federal government provides a yearly allowance of $12,192 to help cover cadet expenses. The figure in the above capsule is for required fees. There is 1 undergraduate school. In addition to regional accreditation, USCGA has baccalaureate program accreditation with AACSB and ABET. The 103-acre campus is in a suburban area next to New London, 2 hours south of Boston, and 2 hours north of New York City. Including any residence halls, there are 28 buildings.

STUDENT LIFE: 94% of undergraduates are from out of state, mostly the Northeast. Students are from 50 states, and 13 foreign countries. 76% are from public schools. 8% are two or more races; 7% Asian American; 67% White; 4% African American; 10% Hispanic. **Male To Female Ratio:** 1.9:1. The average age of freshmen is 18; all undergraduates, 20. 2% do not continue beyond their first year; 87% remain to graduate. **Housing:** College-sponsored housing includes coed dorms. On-campus housing is guaranteed for all 4 years. Alcohol is not permitted. Upperclassmen may keep cars.

FACULTY/CLASSROOMS: 70% of faculty are male; 30% are female. All teach undergraduates, 50% do research, and 50% do both. No introductory courses are taught by graduate students. The average class size in an introductory lecture is 25; in a laboratory is 14; and in a regular course is 18.

PROGRAMS OF STUDY: USCGA confers B.S. degrees. Bachelor's degrees are awarded in BIOLOGICAL SCIENCE (marine science), BUSINESS (management science and operations research), ENGINEERING AND ENVIRONMENTAL DESIGN (civil engineering, electrical/electronics engineering, mechanical engineering, and naval architecture and marine engineering), SOCIAL SCIENCE (political science/government). Engineering, marine science, and government have the largest enrollments.

ACTIVITIES: There are no fraternities or sororities. There are 51 groups on campus, including art, band, cheerleading, choir, chorale, chorus, computers, dance, debate, drama, drill team, drum and bugle corps, environmental, ethnic, honors, international, jazz band, LGBT, marching band, musical theater, newspaper, pep band, political, professional, religious, social, social service, student government, and yearbook. Popular campus events include Parents' weekend, Coast Guard Day, Homecoming, Graduation, Cultural History, Heritage Events, and Sporting Events. **Sports:** There are 15 intercollegiate sports for men and 13 for women, and 22 intramural sports for men and 22 for women. Facilities include a field house with 3 basketball courts, a 6-lane swimming pool, 5 racquetball courts, and facilities for track meets, tennis matches, baseball and softball games, an additional athletic facility with wrestling and weight rooms, basketball courts, gymnastics areas, swimming pool, saunas, a 4500-seat stadium, practice and playing fields, outdoor tennis courts, rowing and seamanship-sailing centers. **Graduates:** From July 1, 2015 to June 30, 2016, 219 bachelor's degrees were awarded. The most popular majors were management (20%), government (19%), and marine & environmental sciences (17%). In an average class, 78% graduate in 4 years or less, 77% graduate in 5 years or less, and 86% graduate in 6 years or less. Of the 2015 graduating class, 100% were employed within 6 months of graduation.

SERVICES: Counseling and information services are available, as is tutoring in every subject. There is remedial math, reading, and writing. **Library/Resources:** The library contains 247,000 volumes, 410,000 microform items, and 2,400 audio/video tapes/CDs/DVDs, and subscribes to 74,000 periodicals including electronic. Computerized library services include interlibrary loans, database searching, Internet access, and Wi-Fi capability. **Physically Challenged Students:** 24% of the campus is accessible. Facilities include wheelchair ramps, elevators, special parking, and specially equipped restrooms. **Special:** Cross-registration with Connecticut College, summer cruises to foreign ports, 6-week internships with various government agencies and some engineering and science organizations, and 1-semester exchange program with the 3 other military academies are available. All U.S. citizen graduates are commissioned in the U.S. Coast Guard (foreign nationals are not commissioned in the U.S. Coast Guard). There are 2 national honor societies, a freshman honors program, and 3 departmental honors programs. **Visiting:** There are regularly scheduled orientations for prospective students, including an admissions briefing and tour of the academy every Monday, Wednesday, and Friday at 1 p.m. To schedule a visit, contact the Admissions Receptionist at www.uscga.edu. **Campus Safety and Security:** Measures include 24-hour foot and vehicle patrol, emergency notification system, self-defense education, and security escort services. There are lighted pathways/sidewalks and controlled access to dorms/residences.

REQUIREMENTS: The SAT or ACT is required. The ACT Optional Writing test is also required. Applicants must have reached the age of 17 but not the age of 23 by July 1 of the year of admission, be citizens of the United States, and be single at the time of appointment and remain single while attending the academy. Required secondary school courses include 4 years each of English and math. International non-US Citizens must apply through their consulate. These requirements for the degree of Bachelor of Science and a commission as an Ensign in the United States Coast Guard are as follows: a. Pass or validate every course in the core curriculum, b. Pass at least 37 courses of 3.00 credits or greater, c. Attain an average of at least a 2.00 in all required "upper-division" courses in the major, as specified in the official catalog of courses. For repeated courses, all grades earned are included in the average. Satisfy the academic requirements for one of the majors as specified in the official catalog of courses. Attain a cumulative grade point average of at least a 2.00. Be in residence at the Academy for at least four academic years. Successfully complete all required portions of the physical education program, including meeting minimum swimming and physical fitness standards. Meet all military performance standards, demonstrating all aspects of personal and professional development necessary to serve as ensigns in the United States Coast Guard, unless a commission will not be offered due to a medical disqualification. International cadets must meet the same standards of personal and professional development as all other graduates, notwithstanding that they are not entitled to appointment in the U.S. Coast Guard. **Procedure:** Freshmen are admitted fall. Entrance exams should be taken must receive by March 1, 2015. There are early admissions, deferred admissions, and rolling admissions plans. Applications should be filed by February 1 for fall entry. Notification is sent on a rolling basis. 148 applicants were on the 2016 waiting list; 36 were admitted. Applications are accepted on-line. **Transfer Students:** All transfer students must meet the same standards as incoming freshmen and must begin as freshmen no matter how many semesters or years of college they have completed. 126 of 126 credits required for the bachelor's degree must be completed at USCGA. **International Students:** There are 22 international students enrolled. They must take the TOEFL with a minimum score of 560 on the paper-based TOEFL (PBT). They must also take the SAT or ACT.

ADMISSIONS: 20% of the 2016-2017 applicants were accepted. The SAT scores for the 2016-2017 freshman class were: Critical Reading-- 5% below 500, 35% between 500 and 599, 50% between 600 and 699, and 10% between 700 and 800. Math-- 10% below 500, 17% between 500 and 599, 59% between 600 and 699, and 24% between 700 and 800. Writing-- 7% below 500, 39% between 500 and 599, 45% between 600 and 699, and 9% between 700 and 800. The ACT scores were 1% between 12 and 17, 7% between 18 and 23, 60% between 24 and 29, and 33% above 30. 72% of the current freshmen were in the top fifth of their class; 92% were in the top two fifths. 9 freshmen graduated first in their class. **Admissions Contact:** Captain McKenna, Director of Admissions. Email: *uscga.admissions@uscga.edu* Web: *www.cga.edu*

FINANCIAL AID: Check with the school for current application deadlines.

UNIVERSITY OF BRIDGEPORT *(The complete profile is made available exclusively on our website, www.barronspac.com)*

UNIVERSITY OF CONNECTICUT — D-2

www.uconn.edu

Storrs, CT 06269	(860) 486-3137
Fax: (860) 486-1476	**Email:** beahusky@uconn.edu
Full-time: 8851 men, 8826 women	**Faculty:** I, +$
Part-time: 428 men, 290 women	**Ph.D.s:** 94%
Graduate: 3903 men, 4243 women	**Student/Faculty:** 16 to 1
Year: semesters, summer session	**Tuition:** $13,364 ($34,908)
Room & Board: $12,174	**Freshman Class:** n/av
SAT or ACT: required	**CEEB CODE:** 3915
Application Deadline: December 1	**HIGHLY COMPETITIVE**

University of Connecticut, founded in 1881, is a public, land-grant, sea-grant, multicampus research institution offering degree programs in liberal arts & sciences and professional studies. There are 9 undergraduate schools and 5 graduate schools. In addition to regional accreditation, UConn has baccalaureate program accreditation with AACSB, ABET, ASLA, NASAD, NASM, NCATE, ACEND, ACS, CAATE, CAPTE, CCNE, LAAB, NAACLS, ABET EAC, and ABET CAC. The 4099-acre campus is in a rural area 25 miles east of Hartford. Including any residence halls, there are 350 buildings.

STUDENT LIFE: 75% of undergraduates are from Connecticut. Others are from 41 states, 113 foreign countries, and Canada. 8% are Hispanic; 8% race unknown; 61% White; 5% African American; 5% Foreign; 3% two or more races; 10% Asian American. **Female To Male Ratio:** 1.0:1. The average age of freshmen is 18; all undergraduates, 20. 7% do not continue beyond their first year; 81% remain to graduate. **Housing:** 12668 students can be accommodated in college housing, which includes single-sex and coed dorms, on-campus apartments, off-campus apartments, and married student housing. In addition, there are honors houses, language houses, special-interest houses, fraternity houses, sorority houses, living and learning communities, Eco-house, global house, humanities house, and a public health house. On-campus housing is guaranteed for the freshman year only. 71% of students live on campus; of those, 70% remain on campus on weekends. Upperclassmen may keep cars.

FACULTY/CLASSROOMS: 59% of faculty are male; 42% are female. No introductory courses are taught by graduate students.

PROGRAMS OF STUDY: UConn confers B.A., B.S., B.F.A., B.G.S., B.Mus., B.S.E., B.S.N. and B.S.Pharm. degrees. Associate, master's, and doctoral degrees are also awarded. Bachelor's degrees are awarded in AGRICULTURE (agricultural economics, agriculture, agronomy, animal science, horticulture, and natural resource management), BIOLOGICAL SCIENCE (biology/biological science, biophysics, evolutionary biology, genetics, marine science, molecular biology, nutrition, and physiology), BUSINESS (accounting, banking and finance, business administration and management, insurance and risk management, management information systems, marketing/retailing/merchandising, and real estate), COMMUNICATIONS AND THE ARTS (art, art history and appreciation, classics, communications, dramatic arts, English, French, German, journalism, linguistics, music, Spanish, theater design, and visual and performing arts), COMPUTER AND PHYSICAL SCIENCE (actuarial mathematics, chemistry, computer science, geology, mathematics, physics, and statistics), EDUCATION (agricultural education, athletic training, education, elementary education, English education, foreign languages education, mathematics education, music education, recreation education, science education, social studies education, and special education), ENGINEERING AND ENVIRONMENTAL DESIGN (biomedical engineering, chemical engineering, civil engineering, computer engineering, electrical/electronics engineering, environmental engineering, environmental science, landscape architecture/design, manufacturing engineering, materials engineering, and mechanical engineering), HEALTH PROFESSIONS (cytotechnology, exercise science, health care administration, medical laboratory technology, nursing, pharmacy, and physical therapy), SOCIAL SCIENCE (anthropology, dietetics, economics, geography, history, human development, Italian studies, Latin American studies, Middle Eastern studies, philosophy, political science/government, psychology, sociology, urban studies, and women's studies). Biological sciences, psychology, and political science have the largest enrollments.

ACTIVITIES: There are 400 groups on campus, including art, band, cheerleading, chess, choir, chorale, chorus, communications, computers, dance, debate, drama, drill team, environmental, ethnic, film, honors, international, jazz band, LGBT, literary magazine, marching band, musical theater, newspaper, opera, orchestra, pep band, photography, political, professional, radio and TV, religious, social, social service, student government, symphony, and yearbook. Popular campus events include Husky WOW (Week of Welcome), Homecoming, Winter Weekend/One Ton Sundae, Lipsync, Oozeball, Huskymania/Midnight Madness, Family Weekend, UConn Late Night, and Midnight Breakfast. **Sports:** There are 11 intercollegiate sports for men and 13 for women, and 29 intramural sports for men and 28 for women. Facilities include a sports center, field house, a 16,000-seat football stadium, a 10,000-seat basketball stadium, and a workout center. **Graduates:** From July 1, 2015 to June 30, 2016, 5200 bachelor's degrees were awarded. The most popular majors were psychology (7%), nursing (5%), and economics (5%). In an average class, 70% graduate in 4 years or less and 81% graduate in 6 years or less.

SERVICES: Counseling and information services are available, as is tutoring in most subjects. There is a reader service for the blind, a Braille printer, a Kurzweil reading machine and Mac computer with voice synthesizer, a machine to enlarge printed material, a talking calculator, and a TDD. **Library/Resources:** The library contains 3.2 million volumes, and computerized library services include interlibrary loans, database searching, and Internet access. Special learning facilities include an art gallery, natural history museum, planetarium, radio station, and TV station. **Physically Challenged Students:** 90% of the campus is accessible. Facilities include wheelchair ramps, elevators, special parking, specially equipped restrooms, special class scheduling, lowered drinking fountains, lowered telephones, special housing, a tactile map, and 4 specially equipped transportation vans. **Special:** UConn offers co-op programs in most majors, internships, more than 200 study-abroad programs in 65 countries, dual majors, general studies degrees, student-designed majors, work-study programs, nondegree study, and pass/fail options. There are 31 national honor societies, Phi Beta Kappa, a freshman honors program, and 8 departmental honors programs. **Visiting:** There are regularly scheduled orientations for prospective students, including daily tours and information sessions. Visitors may sit in on classes. To schedule a visit, contact Lodewick Visitors Center at (860) 486-4900. **Campus Safety and Security:** Measures include 24-hour foot and vehicle patrol, emergency notification system, self-defense education, and security escort services. There are shuttle buses, emergency telephones, and lighted pathways/sidewalks.

REQUIREMENTS: The SAT or ACT is required. Applicants must be graduates of an approved secondary school and should rank in the upper range of their class. The GED is accepted. Students must complete 16 high school academic units, including 4 years of English, 3 of math, 2 each of foreign language, science, and social studies, and 3 of electives. An essay is required. An audition is required for music and theater students and a portfolio for art students. AP credits are accepted. To graduate, students must complete 120 credits with a GPA of 2.0. There are general education requirements in foreign language, expository writing, math, literature and the arts, culture and modern society, philosophical and ethical analysis, social scientific and comparative analysis, and science and technology. Students must complete a course that provides hands-on experience in a major computer application. **Procedure:** Freshmen are admitted fall and spring. Entrance exams should be taken in the spring of the junior year or fall of the senior year. There are deferred admissions and rolling admissions plans. Applications should be filed by December 1 for fall entry, along with a $70 fee. Notifications are sent March 1. 4107 applicants were on the 2016 waiting list; 1409 were admitted. Applications are accepted on-line. **Transfer Students:** 805 transfer students enrolled in 2015-2016. Applicants should have a minimum GPA of 2.7 and submit official transcripts from all colleges previously attended, the high school transcript, and SAT or ACT scores as needed. An associate degree or a minimum of 54 credit hours is recommended. 30 of 120 credits required for the bachelor's degree must be completed at UConn. **International Students:** There are 875 international students enrolled. The school actively recruits these students. They must take the TOEFL with a minimum score of 91 on the Internet-based version (iBT) and the college's own test. They must also take the SAT or ACT.

Admissions Contact: Nathan Fuerst, Director of Admissions. Email: *beahusky@uconn.edu* Web: *www.uconn.edu*

FINANCIAL AID: In 2016-2017, 56% of all full-time freshmen and 57% of continuing full-time students received some form of financial aid. 39% of all full-time freshmen and 20% of continuing full-time students received need-based aid. The average freshman award was $14,256. Need-based scholarships or need-based grants averaged $9,827; need-based self-help aid (loans and jobs) averaged $3,683; non-need-based athletic scholarships averaged $27,764; and other non-need-based awards and non-need-based scholarships averaged $7,535. Average annual earnings from campus work are $2025. The average financial indebtedness of the 2016 graduate was $24,999. The priority date for freshman financial aid applications for fall entry is March 1.

UNIVERSITY OF HARTFORD — C-2

www.hartford.edu

West Hartford, CT 06117	**(860) 243-4296** **(800) 947-4303**
Fax: (860) 768-4961	**Email: admission@hartford.edu**
Full-time: 2281 men, 2222 women	**Faculty:** 347; IIA, av$
Part-time: 315 men, 466 women	**Ph.D.s:** 86%
Graduate: 651 men, 959 women	**Student/Faculty:** 12 to 1
Year: semesters, summer session	**Tuition:** $37,790
Room & Board: $11,986	**Freshman Class:** 14683 applied, 9086 accepted, 1289 enrolled
SAT CR/M: 521/530 **ACT:** 22	**CEEB CODE:** 3436
Application Deadline: open	**COMPETITIVE**

University of Hartford, founded in 1877, is an independent, nonsectarian institution offering extensive undergraduate and graduate programs ranging from liberal arts to business. Figures in the above capsule and in this profile are approximate. There are 7 undergraduate schools and 6 graduate schools. In addition to regional accreditation, Hartford has baccalaureate program accreditation with AACSB, ABET, APTA, CAHEA, NASAD, NASM, NCATE, and NLN. The 320-acre campus is in a suburban area 4 miles northwest of Hartford. Including any residence halls, there are 32 buildings.

STUDENT LIFE: 58% of undergraduates are from out of state, mostly the Northeast. Students are from 45 states, 37 foreign countries, and Canada. 80% are from public schools. 7% are Hispanic; 7% Foreign; 61% White; 3% Asian American; 14% African American. 91% claim no religious affiliation. **Female To Male Ratio:** 1.1:1. The average age of freshmen is 18; all undergraduates, 22. 27% do not continue beyond their first year; 57% remain to graduate. **Housing:** 3530 students can be accommodated in college housing, which includes coed dorms, and on-campus apartments. In addition, there are honors houses, and special-interest houses. There is a residential college for the arts, and for international. On-campus housing is guaranteed for all 4 years. 61% of students live on campus; of those, 85% remain on campus on weekends. All students may keep cars.

FACULTY/CLASSROOMS: 61% of faculty are male; 39% are female. All teach undergraduates, and 97% do research. No introductory courses are taught by graduate students. The average class size in an introductory lecture is 43; in a laboratory is 21; and in a regular course is 24.

PROGRAMS OF STUDY: Hartford confers B.A., B.F.A., B.Mus., B.S., B.S.A.E.T., B.S.B.A., B.S.C.E., B.S.Comp.E., B.S.Ed., B.S.E.E. and B.S.M.E. degrees. Associate, master's, and doctoral degrees are also awarded. Bachelor's degrees are awarded in BIOLOGICAL SCIENCE (biology/biological science), BUSINESS (accounting, banking and finance, business administration and management, entrepreneurial studies, insurance, management information systems, management science, and marketing/retailing/merchandising), COMMUNICATIONS AND THE ARTS (art history and appreciation, audio technology, ceramic art and design, communications, dance, design, dramatic arts, drawing, English, film arts, illustration, jazz, languages, media arts, music, music business management, music history and appreciation, music performance, music technology, music theory and composition, musical theater, painting, performing arts, photography, printmaking, sculpture, technical and business writing, theater management, video, and visual and performing arts), COMPUTER AND PHYSICAL SCIENCE (chemistry, computer science, information sciences and systems, mathematics, physics, and radiological technology), EDUCATION (early childhood education, elementary education, music education, secondary education, and special education), ENGINEERING AND ENVIRONMENTAL DESIGN (architectural engineering, biomedical engineering, chemical engineering technology, civil engineering, computer engineering, electrical/electronics engineering, electrical/electronics engineering technology, engineering, engineering technology, mechanical engineering, and mechanical engineering technology), HEALTH PROFESSIONS (health science, nursing, physical therapy, predentistry, premedicine, and preoptometry), SOCIAL SCIENCE (criminal justice, economics, history, interdisciplinary studies, international studies, Judaic studies, law, philosophy, political science/government, psychology, and sociology). Physical therapy, radiologic technology, acoustical engineering and music are the strongest academically. Communication, architectural engineering technology, and psychology have the largest enrollments.

ACTIVITIES: 17% of men belong to 7 national fraternities; 21% of women belong to 7 national sororities. There are 100 groups on campus, including art, band, cheerleading, choir, chorale, chorus, communications, computers, drama, ethnic, film, honors, international, jazz band, LGBT, literary magazine, musical theater, newspaper, opera, orchestra, pep band, political, professional, radio and TV, religious, social, social service, student government, and symphony. Popular campus events include Spring Fling, and Hawktober Weekend. **Sports:** There are 7 intercollegiate sports for men and 8 for women, and 15 intramural sports for men and 15 for women. Facilities include playing fields, a 25-meter outdoor pool, tennis courts, golf practice cages, a fitness trail, and a sports center with a 4,600-seat multipurpose court, an 8-lane swimming pool, a weight room, racquetball courts, a squash court, and saunas. **Graduates:** From July 1, 2015 to June 30, 2016, 955 bachelor's degrees were awarded. The most popular majors were communications (7%), psychology (4%), and architectural engineering tech. (4%). 182 companies recruited on campus in 2015-2016. In an average class, 53% graduate in 4 years or less, 58% graduate in 5 years or less, and 59% graduate in 6 years or less. Of the 2015 graduating class, 35% were enrolled in graduate school within 6 months of graduation, and 75% were employed.

SERVICES: Counseling and information services are available, as is tutoring in most subjects. There is a reader service for the blind, and remedial math, reading, and writing. The health education office offers peer counseling and workshops on health-related topics. Professional counseling is available. **Library/Resources:** The 2 libraries contain 590,724 volumes, 383,386 microform items, and 5,921 audio/video tapes/CDs/DVDs, and subscribe to 49,600 periodicals including electronic. Computerized library services include interlibrary loans, database searching, Internet access, and Wi-Fi capability. Special learning facilities include an art gallery, radio station, TV station, and the Museum of

American Political Life. **Physically Challenged Students:** Facilities include wheelchair ramps, elevators, special parking, specially equipped restrooms, lowered drinking fountains, lowered telephones, and special housing. **Special:** Cross-registration with the Greater Hartford Consortium, internships in all majors, study abroad, a Washington semester, work-study programs, credit for life experience, non-degree study, and pass/fail options are available. In addition, students may pursue accelerated degrees, B.A.-B.S. degrees, dual majors, or their own individually designed majors. There are interdisciplinary majors in acoustics and music and in experimental studio combining performing, literary, and visual arts. Also available are preprofessional programs in biology/preoptometry with the New England College of Optometry, predentistry with the New York University School of Dentistry, prechiropractic with the New York Chiropractic College, preosteopathic with the University of New England College of Osteopathic Medicine, and prepodiatry with the New York College of Podiatric Medicine. There are 19 national honor societies, a freshman honors program, and 7 departmental honors programs. **Visiting:** There are regularly scheduled orientations for prospective students. There are guides for informal visits, visitors may sit in on classes, and stay overnight. To schedule a visit, contact the Office of Admissions. **Campus Safety and Security:** Measures include 24-hour foot and vehicle patrol, emergency notification system, self-defense education, and security escort services. There are shuttle buses, emergency telephones, lighted pathways/sidewalks, controlled access to dorms/residences, including a bicycle patrol.

REQUIREMENTS: The SAT is required. Applicants should have 16 academic high school credits and 16 Carnegie units, including 4 units in English, 3 in math (3.5 for B.S. candidates), and 2 each in foreign language, science, and social studies. A portfolio and an audition are required for B.F.A. and B.Mus. candidates, respectively. A personal statement is required, and an interview is recommended for all students. AP and CLEP credits are accepted. Important factors in the admissions decision are advanced placement or honors courses, recommendations by school officials, and leadership record. To graduate, students must complete at least 120 credit hours, fulfill the university's core curriculum requirements, and maintain an overall GPA of 2.0. Specific core and course requirements vary with the major. **Procedure:** Freshmen are admitted fall and spring. Entrance exams should be taken in the spring of the junior year or the fall of the senior year. There are deferred admissions and rolling admissions plans. Application deadlines are open. The fall 2016 application fee was $40. Notification is sent on a rolling basis. Applications are accepted on-line. **Transfer Students:** 232 transfer students enrolled in 2015-2016. Transfer students must have a minimum college GPA of 2.25, with 2.5 recommended, and must submit SAT or ACT scores if they have fewer than 30 transferable college-level credits. An interview is also recommended. 30 of 120 credits required for the bachelor's degree must be completed at Hartford. **International Students:** There are 195 international students enrolled. The school actively recruits these students. They must take the TOEFL with a minimum score of 550 on the paper-based TOEFL (PBT). The SAT or the ACT is recommended.

ADMISSIONS: 62% of the 2016-2017 applicants were accepted. The SAT scores for the 2016-2017 freshman class were: Critical Reading-- 46% below 500, 39% between 500 and 599, 14% between 600 and 699, and 1% between 700 and 800. Math-- 44% below 500, 37% between 500 and 599, 17% between 600 and 699, and 2% between 700 and 800. The ACT scores were 38% below 12, 28% between 12 and 17, 20% between 18 and 23, 6% between 24 and 29, and 8% above 30. 12% of the current freshmen were in the top fifth of their class; 27% were in the top two fifths. **Admissions Contact:** Richard A. Zeiser, Dean of Admissions. Email: *admission@hartford.edu* Web: *www.hartford.edu*

FINANCIAL AID: In 2016-2017, 94% of all full-time freshmen and 97% of continuing full-time students received some form of financial aid. 80% of all full-time freshmen and 78% of continuing full-time students received need-based aid. 22% of undergraduate students work part-time. Average annual earnings from campus work are $3200. The FAFSA code is 001422. The priority date for freshman financial aid applications for fall entry is February 1. The deadline for filing freshman financial aid applications for fall entry is March 1.

UNIVERSITY OF NEW HAVEN — C-3

www.newhaven.edu

West Haven, CT 06516	**(203) 932-7319** **(800) 342-5864 ext. 7319**
Fax: (203) 931-6093	**Email: admissions@newhaven.edu**
Full-time: 2220 men, 2332 women	**Faculty:** IIA, +$
Part-time: 232 men, 152 women	**Ph.D.s:** 82%
Graduate: 1010 men, 889 women	**Student/Faculty:** n/av
Year: 4-1-4, summer session	**Tuition:** $37,060
Room & Board: $15,130	**Freshman Class:** 10720 applied, 8633 accepted, 1128 enrolled
SAT CR/M: 520/530 **ACT:** required	**CEEB CODE:** 3663
Application Deadline: open	**COMPETITIVE**

University of New Haven is a private, top-tier comprehensive institution recognized as a national leader in experiential education. Founded in 1920, the University provides its students with a unique combination of a liberal arts education and real-world, hands-on career and research opportunities. There are 5 undergraduate schools and 4 graduate schools. In addition to regional accreditation, UNH has baccalaureate program accreditation with ABET, ADA, NCATE, FEPAC, and ACEND. The 82-acre campus is in a suburban area 90 minutes from New York City and approximately 2 1/2 hours from Boston.

STUDENT LIFE: 56% of undergraduates are from out of state, mostly the Northeast. Students are from 36 states, 31 foreign countries, and Canada. 7% are Foreign; 61% White; 6% race unknown; 3% Asian American; 2% two or more races; 11% African American; 10% Hispanic. **Male To Female Ratio:** 1.0:1. The average age of freshmen is 18; all undergraduates, 21. 20% do not continue beyond their first year; 56% remain to graduate. **Housing:** 2836 students can be accommodated in college housing, which includes coed dorms, on-campus apartments, off-campus apartments, and living learning communities. On-campus housing is guaranteed for all 4 years, is available on a first-come, first-served basis, and is available on a lottery system for upperclassmen. 52% of students live on campus. Upperclassmen may keep cars.

FACULTY/CLASSROOMS: 65% of faculty are male; 35% are female. No introductory courses are taught by graduate students.

PROGRAMS OF STUDY: UNH confers B.A., B.S., and B.F.A. degrees. Associate, master's, and doctoral degrees are also awarded. Bachelor's degrees are awarded in BIOLOGICAL SCIENCE (biology/biological science, biotechnology, marine biology, and nutrition), BUSINESS (accounting, banking and finance, business administration and management, hospitality management services, hotel/motel and restaurant management, marketing/retailing/merchandising, sports management, and tourism), COMMUNICATIONS AND THE ARTS (art, audio technology, communications, communications technology, creative writing, design, English, fine arts, fine/studio arts, general, graphic design, literature, music, music business management, music performance, music technology, theatre arts, visual and performing arts, and visual design), COMPUTER AND PHYSICAL SCIENCE (applied mathematics, chemistry, computer management, computer mathematics, computer programming, computer science, cyber operations, mathematics, and natural sciences), EDUCATION (global studies and mathematics education), ENGINEERING AND ENVIRONMENTAL DESIGN (chemical engineering, civil engineering, computer engineering, electrical/electronics engineering, engineering, environmental science, fire protection engineering, interior design, mechanical engineering, and systems engineering), HEALTH PROFESSIONS (dental hygiene), SOCIAL SCIENCE (clinical psychology, community psychology, corrections, counseling/psychology, criminal justice, criminology, dietetics, economics, family/juvenile justice, fire control and safety technology, fire protection, fire science, fire services administration, forensic studies, history, law enforcement and corrections, legal studies, liberal arts/general studies, political science/government, and psychology). Criminal justice, forensic science, and mechanical engineering have the largest enrollments.

ACTIVITIES: There are 140 groups on campus, including art, cheerleading, communications, computers, dance, debate, ethnic, film, forensics, honors, international, jazz band, LGBT, literary magazine, marching band, newspaper, pep band, photography, political, professional, radio and TV, religious, social, social service, student government, and yearbook. **Sports:** There are 7 intercollegiate sports for men and 9 for women, and 11 intramural sports for men and 11 for women. Facilities include baseball, softball, intramural playing fields, tennis courts, a gym with basketball courts, weight training room, racquetball court, a recreation center, and an outdoor stadium for football, soccer, and lacrosse. **Graduates:** From July 1, 2015 to June 30, 2016, 1152 bachelor's degrees were awarded. The most popular majors were criminal justice (26%), forensic science (8%), and psychology (5%). In an average class, 56% graduate in 6 years or less.

SERVICES: Counseling and information services are available, as is tutoring in every subject. There is a reader service for the blind, and remedial math, reading, and writing. There are also campus access services, and centers for academic success and advising. **Library/Resources:** The library contains 387,910 volumes, 410,677 microform items, and 1,565 audio/video tapes/CDs/DVDs, and subscribes to 38,888 periodicals including electronic. Computerized library services include interlibrary loans, database searching, Internet access, and Wi-Fi capability. Special learning facilities include an art gallery, radio station, TV station, institute of forensic science, crime scene training & technology center, dental hygiene center, finance and technology center, communication studios, and music and sound recording facilities. **Physically Challenged Students:** Facilities include wheelchair ramps, elevators, special parking, specially equipped restrooms, special class scheduling, lowered drinking fountains, lowered telephones, and special housing. **Special:** UNH offers co-op programs in some majors, internships in all majors, work-study programs, interdisciplinary majors, fast-track business programs leading to bachelor's degrees in 3 years, 5-year B.S.-M.S. programs in education and in environmental science, and nondegree study programs. Study-abroad programs are also available. There is a freshman honors program. **Visiting:** There are regularly scheduled orientations for prospective students, including daily information sessions, open houses, accepted student days, charger days, and summer preview days. There are guides for informal visits, visitors may sit in on classes, and stay overnight. To schedule a visit, contact Office of Undergraduate Admissions. **Campus Safety and Security:** Measures include 24-hour foot and vehicle patrol, emergency notification system, self-defense education, and security escort services. There are shuttle buses, emergency telephones, lighted pathways/sidewalks, controlled access to dorms/residencesrequired programs during orientation for new students as well as crime prevention program.

REQUIREMENTS: The SAT or ACT is required. Applicants should be graduates of an accredited secondary school. The GED is accepted. An interview is recommended. A letter of recommendation is required along with a personal essay. AP and CLEP credits are accepted. Important factors in the admissions decision are advanced placement or honors courses, extracurricular activities record, and recommendations by school officials. To graduate, all students must maintain a GPA of 2.0, pass a writing proficiency exam, and complete a total of 120 to 132 credits, depending on the major. Students must complete at least 40 credits from the university core curriculum, including a total of 28 credits in lab science, social sciences, history, literature or philosophy, art, music, or theater, 9 credits in communication skills, and 3 credits each in quantitative skills, computers, and scientific methodology. **Procedure:** Freshmen are admitted fall and spring. Entrance exams should be taken in the fall or winter of the senior year. There are early decision, early admissions, and rolling admissions plans. Application deadlines are open. The fall 2016 application fee was $50. Applications are accepted on-line. Application fees are waived if application is completed on-line. **Transfer Students:** 217 transfer students enrolled in 2015-2016. Applicants should have a minimum college GPA of 2.3 and should submit all official transcripts. An interview is recommended, and the SAT is required for students with fewer than 24 college credits. 30 of 120 credits required for the bachelor's degree must be completed at UNH. **International Students:** There are 349 international students enrolled. The school actively recruits these students. They must take the TOEFL with a minimum score of 75 on the Internet-based version (iBT). They must also take the SAT or ACT. English-speaking students may submit the SAT or ACT scores instead.

ADMISSIONS: 81% of the 2016-2017 applicants were accepted. The SAT scores for the 2016-2017 freshman class were: Critical Reading-- 41% below 500, 42% between 500 and 599, 15% between 600 and 699, and 2% between 700 and 800. Math-- 38% below 500, 44% between 500 and 599, 16% between 600 and 699, and 2% between 700 and 800. **Admissions Contact:** Kevin J. Phillips, Associate Vice President for Enrollment. Email: *admissions@newhaven.edu* Web: *www.newhaven.edu*

FINANCIAL AID: UNH is a member of CSS. The FAFSA code is 001397. Check with the school for current application deadlines.

UNIVERSITY OF SAINT JOSEPH C-2

www.usj.edu

West Hartford, CT 06117

(860) 231-5223
(866) 442-8752
Email: admissions@usj.edu

Full-time: 10 men, 757 women	**Faculty:** IIA, av$
Part-time: 15 men, 178 women	**Ph.D.s:** 88%
Graduate: 277 men, 1316 women	**Student/Faculty:** n/av
Year: semesters, summer session	**Tuition:** $36,140
Room & Board: $13,410	**Freshman Class:** 751 applied, 697 accepted, 213 enrolled
	CEEB CODE: 3754
Application Deadline: n/av	**COMPETITIVE**

University of Saint Joseph, is a private institution consisting of an undergraduate women's program, a coed bachelor's degree completion program for adults, a coed graduate program, and a coed School of Pharmacy. There is 1 undergraduate school. In addition to regional accreditation, USJ has baccalaureate program accreditation with NEASC. The 90-acre campus is in a suburban area 3 miles from Hartford, CT. approximately two hours to Boston, MA. and approximately 2.5 hours to New York, NY. Including any residence halls, there are 17 buildings.

STUDENT LIFE: 95% of undergraduates are from Connecticut. 51% are White; 17% Hispanic; 16% African American; 10% race unknown; 2% two or more races; 1% Asian American; 1% American Indian/Alaska Native; 1% Foreign. **Female To Male Ratio:** 7.5:1. The average age of freshmen is 18; all undergraduates, 24. 22% do not continue beyond their first year; 55% remain to graduate. **Housing:** 403 students can be accommodated in college housing, which includes single-sex dorms. In addition, there are special-interest houses. On-campus housing is available on a first-come, first-served basis, and is available on a lottery system for upperclassmen. 71% of students commute. All students may keep cars.

FACULTY/CLASSROOMS: No introductory courses are taught by graduate students.

PROGRAMS OF STUDY: USJ confers B.A., and B.S. degrees. Master's and doctoral degrees are also awarded. Bachelor's degrees are awarded in BIOLOGICAL SCIENCE (biochemistry, biology/biological science, and nutrition), BUSINESS (accounting and management science), COMMUNICATIONS AND THE ARTS (art history and appreciation, English, and Spanish), COMPUTER AND PHYSICAL SCIENCE (chemistry and mathematics), EDUCATION (special education), HEALTH PROFESSIONS (nursing and public health), SOCIAL SCIENCE (child psychology/development, criminal justice, family/consumer studies, history, international studies, philosophy, psychology, religion, social work, and women's studies). Nursing, and education are the strongest academically. Nursing, psychology, and biology have the largest enrollments.

ACTIVITIES: There are no fraternities or sororities. Groups on campus include choir, dance, drama, ethnic, honors, international, LGBT, literary magazine, political, professional, religious, social, social service, and student government. **Sports:** There are 8 intercollegiate sports for women. Facilities include fitness center, a pool, indoor and outdoor tracks, tennis courts, basketball court, softball field, soccer field, and dance studio. **Graduates:** From July 1, 2015 to June 30, 2016, 236 bachelor's degrees were awarded. The most popular majors were nursing (31%), social work (15%), and psychology (9%).

SERVICES: Counseling and information services are available, as is tutoring in most subjects. **Library/Resources:** The 2 libraries contain 80,003 volumes, and 31 microform items, and subscribe to 57,146 periodicals including electronic. Computerized library services include interlibrary loans, database searching, Internet access, and Wi-Fi capability. Special learning facilities include an art gallery, and two lab schools: (1) School for Young Children and (2) the Gengras Center. **Physically Challenged Students:** Facilities include wheelchair ramps, elevators, special parking, specially equipped restrooms, special class scheduling, and special housing. **Special:** USJ offers cross-registration at member colleges through the Hartford Consortium for Higher Education. Internship opportunities, study abroad, double majors, and student-designed majors are also available. There is a freshman honors program. **Visiting:** There are regularly scheduled orientations for prospective students. There are guides for informal visits, visitors may sit in on classes, and stay overnight.. **Campus Safety and Security:** Measures include 24-hour foot and vehicle patrol, emergency notification system, and security escort services. There are shuttle buses, emergency telephones, lighted pathways/sidewalks, and controlled access to dorms/residences.

REQUIREMENTS: SAT/ACT scores are optional except for a few programs that require it. High school transcripts should show a minimum of 16 units (18 units if the SAT/ACT is not submitted). Full requirements are posted at www.usj.edu/admissions-financial-aid/. AP and CLEP credits are accepted. To earn a bachelor's degree: students must have a minimum 2.0 GPA and 120 earned credits that meet requirements in the general education curriculum and the major area of study. **Procedure:** Freshmen are admitted fall and spring. There are deferred admissions and rolling admissions plans. Application deadlines are open. Application fee is $50. Applications are accepted on-line. **Transfer Students:** 96 transfer students enrolled in 2015-2016. 45 of 120 credits required for the bachelor's degree must be completed at USJ. **International Students:** There are 4 international students enrolled. They must take the TOEFL. They must also take the SAT or ACT.

ADMISSIONS: 93% of the 2016-2017 applicants were accepted. **Admissions Contact:** Director of Admissions Email: *admissions@usj.edu* Web: *www.usj.edu*

FINANCIAL AID: In 2016-2017, 90% of all full-time freshmen and 90% of continuing full-time students received some form of financial aid. 90% of all full-time freshmen and 90% of continuing full-time students received need-based aid. The average freshman award was $28,228. Need-based scholarships or need-based grants averaged $23,958; and need-based self-help aid (loans and jobs) averaged $4,653. USJ is a member of CSS. The FAFSA code is 001409. The priority date for freshman financial aid applications for fall entry is March 1.

WESLEYAN UNIVERSITY C-3

www.wesleyan.edu

Middletown, CT 06459 **(860) 685-3000**

Fax: (860) 685-3001	**Email:** admission@wesleyan.edu
Full-time: 1342 men, 1576 women	**Faculty:** 372; IIA, ++$
Part-time: 25 men, 28 women	**Ph.D.s:** 92%
Graduate: 106 men, 129 women	**Student/Faculty:** 8 to 1
Year: semesters, summer session	**Tuition:** $50,612
Room & Board: $14,904	**Freshman Class:** 11928 applied, 2127 accepted, 774 enrolled
SAT CR/M/W: 690/680/690 **ACT:** 32	**CEEB CODE:** 3959
Application Deadline: January 1	**MOST COMPETITIVE**

Wesleyan University, founded in 1831, is a private institution offering programs in the liberal arts and sciences. There is 1 undergraduate school and 1 graduate school. In addition to regional accreditation, Wesleyan has baccalaureate program accreditation with NEASE-CIHE. The 316-acre campus is in a suburban area 15 miles south of Hartford, and 2 hours from both Boston and New York City. Including any residence halls, there are 301 buildings.

STUDENT LIFE: 92% of undergraduates are from out of state, mostly the Northeast. Students are from 48 states, 47 foreign countries, and Canada. 50% are from public schools. 7% are African American; 7% Asian American; 55% White; 5% two or more races; 5% race unknown; 10% Hispanic; 10% Foreign. **Female To Male Ratio:** 1.2:1. The average age of freshmen is 18; all undergraduates, 20. 5% do not continue beyond their first year; 94% remain to graduate. **Housing:** 2915 students can be accommodated in college housing, which includes single-sex and coed dorms and on-campus apartments. In addition, there are language houses, special-interest houses, and fraternity houses. On-campus housing is guaranteed for all 4 years. All students may keep cars.

FACULTY/CLASSROOMS: 53% of faculty are male; 47% are female. All teach undergraduates, and all do research. No introductory courses are taught by graduate students. The average class size in an introductory lecture is 21; in a laboratory is 35; and in a regular course is 17.

PROGRAMS OF STUDY: Wesleyan confers B.A. degrees. Master's and doctoral degrees are also awarded. Bachelor's degrees are awarded in AGRICULTURE (environmental studies), BIOLOGICAL SCIENCE (biology/biological science, molecular biology, and neurosciences), COMMUNICATIONS AND THE ARTS (art history and appreciation, classics, dance, dramatic arts, English, English literature, film arts, music, romance languages and literature, and studio art), COMPUTER AND PHYSICAL SCIENCE (astronomy, chemistry, computer science, earth science, mathematics, and physics), SOCIAL SCIENCE (African American studies, American studies, anthropology, archeology, classical/ancient civilization, East Asian studies, economics, French studies, gender studies, German area studies, Hispanic American studies, history, Italian studies, Latin American studies, medieval studies, philosophy, political science/government, psychology, religion, Russian and Slavic studies, science and society, social studies, and sociology). Sciences, economics, and history are the strongest academically. Psychology, chemistry, and music have the largest enrollments.

ACTIVITIES: 4% of men belong to 4 local and 3 national fraternities; 1% of women belong to 1 local sorority. There are 238 groups on campus, including art, band, cheerleading, chess, choir, chorale, chorus, communications, computers, dance, debate, drama, environmental, ethnic, film, honors, international, jazz band, LGBT, literary magazine, musical theater, newspaper, opera, orchestra, pep band, photography, political, professional, radio and TV, religious, social, social service, student government, symphony, and yearbook. Popular campus events include Cultural Shows, and Spring Fling. **Sports:** There are 15 intercollegiate sports for men and 14 for women, and 5 intramural sports for men and 5 for women. Facilities include a 5000-seat stadium, a 1200-seat gym, 50-meter Olympic-size pool, 400-meter outdoor track, cross-country trail, hockey arena, strength and fitness center, 12 outdoor tennis courts, eight squash courts, three soccer fields, two football practice fields, rugby pitch, boathouse, baseball diamond, softball diamond, and two artificial turf fields. The field house contains a 200-meter indoor track, four indoor tennis courts, three recreational basketball courts, three volleyball courts, and three badminton courts. **Graduates:** From July 1, 2015 to June 30, 2016, 732 bachelor's degrees were awarded. The most popular majors were economics (14%), psychology (12%), and government (11%). 658 companies recruited on campus in 2015-2016. In an average class, 87% graduate in 4 years or less, 91% graduate in 5 years or less, and 91% graduate in 6 years or less. Of the 2015 graduating class, 10% were enrolled in graduate school within 6 months of graduation, and 67% were employed.

SERVICES: Counseling and information services are available, as is tutoring in most subjects. Peer advisor assistance in time management and academic skills development, writing tutors, math tutoring, quantitative skills and quantitative analysis, as well as supplemental instruction in biology and chemistry are available for students. **Library/Resources:** The 2 libraries contain 1.6 million volumes, 295,898 microform items, and 77,705 audio/video tapes/CDs/DVDs, and subscribe to 75,956 periodicals including electronic. Computerized library services include interlibrary loans, database searching, Internet access, and Wi-Fi capability. Special learning facilities include an art gallery, radio station, and observatory. **Physically Challenged Students:** 53% of the campus is accessible. Facilities include wheelchair ramps, elevators, special parking, specially equipped restrooms, special class scheduling, lowered drinking fountains, lowered telephones, and special housing. **Special:** Wesleyan offers exchange programs with 11 northeastern colleges, cross-registration with 2 area colleges, study abroad in 45 countries on 6 continents, internships, dual and student-designed majors, and pass/fail options. 3-2 engineering programs with Cal Tech, Columbia University, and Dartmouth College are also available. There are 2 national honor societies, Phi Beta Kappa, and 48 departmental honors programs. **Visiting:** There are regularly scheduled orientations for prospective students, consisting of hour-long campus tours and group information sessions. There are guides for informal visits, visitors may sit in on classes, and stay overnight. To schedule a visit, contact the Office of Admissions. **Campus Safety and Security:** Measures include 24-hour foot and vehicle patrol, emergency notification system, self-defense education, and security escort services. There are shuttle buses, emergency telephones, lighted pathways/sidewalks, and controlled access to dorms/residences.

REQUIREMENTS: Applicants must submit the common application, transcript, and recommendations. Standardized tests are optional. Students should have a minimum of 20 academic credits, including 4 years each of English, foreign language, math, science, and social studies. AP credits are accepted. Important factors in the admissions decision are advanced placement or honors courses, recommendations by school officials, and personality/intangible qualities. To graduate, all students must complete 128 credit hours. All students are expected, but not required, to take courses each in humanities and arts, social and behavioral sciences, and natural science and math. A minimum academic average of 74 must be maintained, with at least 6 semesters of full-time residency. **Procedure:** Freshmen are admitted fall. Entrance exams should be taken in the spring of the junior year or the fall of the senior year. There are early decision, early admissions, and deferred admissions plans. Early decision applications should be filed by November 15; regular applications, by January 1 for fall entry, along with a $55 fee. Notification of early decision is sent December 15; regular decision, April 1. 427 early decision candidates were accepted for the 2016-2017 class. 1134 applicants were on the 2016 waiting list; 55 were admitted. Applications are accepted on-line. **Transfer Students:** 65 transfer students enrolled in 2015-2016. Applicants need a strong academic record. Standardized tests are optional. An interview is recommended. 64 of 128 credits required for the bachelor's degree must be completed at Wesleyan. **International Students:** There are 297 international students enrolled. The school actively recruits these students. They must take the TOEFL with a minimum score of 600 on the paper-based TOEFL (PBT) or 100 on the Internet-based version (iBT), or take the IELTS.

ADMISSIONS: 18% of the 2016-2017 applicants were accepted. The SAT scores for the 2016-2017 freshman class were: Critical Reading-- 3% below 500, 14% between 500 and 599, 34% between 600 and 699, and 49% between 700 and 800. Math-- 14% between 500 and 599, 43% between 600 and 699, and 43% between 700 and 800. Writing-- 3% below 500, 10% between 500 and 599, 39% between 600 and 699, and 49% between 700 and 800. The ACT scores were 2% between 18 and 23, 21% between 24 and 29, and 77% above 30. 69% of the current freshmen were in the top fifth of their class; 95% were in the top two fifths. **Admissions Contact:** Nancy Hargrave-Meislahn, Dean of Admissions and Financial Aid. Email: *admission@wesleyan.edu* Web: *www.wesleyan.edu*

FINANCIAL AID: In 2016-2017, 48% of all full-time freshmen and 47% of continuing full-time students received some form of financial aid. 44% of all full-time freshmen and 44% of continuing full-time students received need-based aid. The average freshman award was $44,344. Need-based scholarships or need-based grants averaged $41,149; and need-based self-help aid (loans and jobs) averaged $4,593. 60% of undergraduate students work part-time. Average annual earnings from campus work are $1285. The average financial indebtedness of the 2016 graduate was $17,509. Wesleyan is a member of CSS. The CSS/Profile, parent and student 1040 forms, W-2s, business tax returns are required. The FAFSA code is 001424. The priority date for freshman financial aid applications for fall entry is February 15.

WESTERN CONNECTICUT STATE UNIVERSITY *(The complete profile is made available exclusively on our website, www.barronspac.com)*

YALE UNIVERSITY — C-3

www.yale.edu

New Haven, CT 06511 — **(203) 432-9316**

Fax: (203) 432-9370
Email: apply.questions@yale.edu
Full-time: 2812 men, 2696 women
Faculty: 1159; I, ++$
Part-time: 16 men, 4 women
Ph.D.s: 92%
Graduate: 3455 men, 3398 women
Student/Faculty: 6 to 1
Year: semesters, summer session
Tuition: $49,480
Room & Board: $15,170
Freshman Class: 30236 applied, 2034 accepted, 1364 enrolled
SAT CR/M/W: 760/755/750 **ACT:** 33
CEEB CODE: 3987
Application Deadline: January 1
MOST COMPETITIVE

Yale University, founded in 1701, is a private liberal arts institution. The figures in the above capsule and in this profile are approximate. There is 1 undergraduate school and 13 graduate schools. In addition to regional accreditation, Yale has baccalaureate program accreditation with AACSB, ABET, CAHEA, NAAB, NASM, NLN, SAF, ABA, APA, ATS, AMA, CAAHEP, CCNE, LCME, and NEASC. The 342-acre campus is in an urban area 75 miles northeast of New York City. Including any residence halls, there are 440 buildings.

STUDENT LIFE: 93% of undergraduates are from out of state, mostly the West. Students are from 49 states, 74 foreign countries, and Canada. 57% are from public schools. 7% are African American; 53% White; 17% Asian American; 11% Hispanic; 10% Foreign; 1% American Indian/Alaska Native. **Male To Female Ratio:** 1.0:1. The average age of freshmen is 18; all undergraduates, 20. 1% do not continue beyond their first year; 96% remain to graduate. **Housing:** College-sponsored housing includes coed dorms. Students are ramdomly assigned to one of 12 residential colleges where they live, eat, socialize, and pursue varius academic and extracurricular activities. On-campus housing is guaranteed for the freshman year only and is available on a lottery system for upperclassmen. 84% of students live on campus. All students may keep cars.

FACULTY/CLASSROOMS: 64% of faculty are male; 36% are female. All teach undergraduates. No introductory courses are taught by graduate students.

PROGRAMS OF STUDY: Yale confers B.A., and B.S. degrees. Master's and doctoral degrees are also awarded. Bachelor's degrees are awarded in AGRICULTURE (environmental studies), BIOLOGICAL SCIENCE (biochemistry, biology/biological science, biophysics, evolutionary biology, and molecular biology), COMMUNICATIONS AND THE ARTS (art history, art, Chinese, classics, dramatic arts, East Asian languages and literature, English, film arts, French, Germanic languages and literature, Italian, Japanese, linguistics, literature, music, Portuguese, Russian, Russian languages and literature, Slavic languages, and Spanish), COMPUTER AND PHYSICAL SCIENCE (applied mathematics, applied physics, astronomy, chemistry, computer science, geology, mathematics, mathematics/economics, mathematics/philosophy, physics, and statistics), ENGINEERING AND ENVIRONMENTAL DESIGN (architecture, biomedical engineering, chemical engineering, electrical/electronics engineering, engineering, engineering and applied science, environmental engineering, and mechanical engineering), SOCIAL SCIENCE (African studies, African American studies, American studies, anthropology, archeology, classical/ancient civilization, cognitive science, East Asian studies, Eastern European studies, economics, ethics, politics, and social policy, ethnic studies, German area studies, history, history of science, humanities, international studies, Judaic studies, Latin American studies, Middle Eastern studies, Near Eastern studies, philosophy, political science/government, psychology, religion, Russian and Slavic studies, sociology, South Asian studies, and women's studies). History, political science, and economics have the largest enrollments.

ACTIVITIES: There are 400 groups on campus, including art, band, cheerleading, chess, choir, chorale, chorus, communications, computers, dance, debate, drama, environmental, ethnic, film, honors, international, jazz band, LGBT, literary magazine, marching band, musical theater, newspaper, opera, orchestra, pep band, photography, political, professional, radio and TV, religious, social, social service, student government, symphony, and yearbook. Popular campus events include Freshman Dinner, Spring Fling Concert, Fall Show, Yale Symphony Orchestra Halloween Show, Yale Top Chef Competition, Yale-Harvard Football Game and special cultural dinners in the residential colleges. **Sports:** There are 16 intercollegiate sports for men and 18 for women, and 25 intramural sports for men and 21 for women. Facilities include an 71,000-seat Yale Bowl for football, a sports complex, 1 gym, 2 swimming pools, a fitness center, an ice rink, squash center, tennis center, golf course, a sailing center, and boathouse. **Graduates:** From July 1, 2015 to June 30, 2016, 1327 bachelor's degrees were awarded. The most popular majors were social sciences (29%), biological/life sciences (10%), area, ethnic, and gender studies, history, and interdisciplinary studies (7%). In an average class, 97% graduate in 6 years or less. Of the 2015 graduating class, 21% were enrolled in graduate school within 6 months of graduation, and 75% were employed.

SERVICES: Counseling and information services are available, as is tutoring in every subject. There is a reader service for the blind. **Library/Resources:** The 15 libraries contain 15.0 million volumes, 10.0 million microform items, and 400,000 audio/video tapes/CDs/DVDs, and subscribe to 450,000 periodicals including electronic. Computerized library services include interlibrary loans, database searching, Internet access, and Wi-Fi capability. Special learning facilities include an art gallery, natural history museum, planetarium, radio station, Yale Center for British Art, Beinecke Rare Book and Manuscript Library, Film Study Center, Center for Engineering Innovation and Design, Marsh Botanical Gardens and Yale Natural Preserves, and numerous research centers. **Physically Challenged Students:** Facilities include wheelchair ramps, elevators, special parking, specially equipped restrooms, special class scheduling, lowered drinking fountains, lowered telephones, special housing, and a door-to-door lift-van service. **Special:** The university runs a study abroad program in England and offers opportunities for term-time or summer study in many other countries. It also offers an accelerated degree program, B.A.-B.S. degrees, dual majors, and student-designed majors. Directed Studies, a special freshman program in the humanities, affords outstanding students the opportunity to survey the

Western cultural tradition. Perspectives on Science is a special freshmen program for students who are especially strong in science and mathematics. Freshmen Seminars offer the opportunity for first-year students to enroll in small classes with some of Yale's most distinguished faculty members. The STARS (Science, Technology and Research Scholars) program offers research opportunities, mentoring, and support to students historically under-represented in fields of natural science and quantitative reasoning. There is a chapter of Phi Beta Kappa. **Visiting:** There are regularly scheduled orientations for prospective students, flexible: admissions information sessions, campus tours, and in summer, Student Forums. There are guides for informal visits and visitors may sit in on classes. To schedule a visit, contact the Receptionist Office at (203) 432-9300. **Campus Safety and Security:** Measures include 24-hour foot and vehicle patrol, emergency notification system, self-defense education, and security escort services. There are shuttle buses, emergency telephones, lighted pathways/sidewalks, and controlled access to dorms/residences.

REQUIREMENTS: Only those applicants submitting SAT scores must also take any 2 SAT Subject tests. ACT submitters must take the ACT with Writing. Most successful applicants rank in the top 10% of their high school class. All students must have completed a rigorous high school program encompassing all academic disciplines. 2 essays, 2 teacher recommendations and a counselor letter are required, and an interview is recommended. Yale offers a non-binding Single Choice Early Action option (not Early Decision). AP credits are accepted. Important factors in the admissions decision are leadership record, parents or siblings attended your school, recommendations by alumni, geographical diversity, advanced placement or honors courses, evidence of special talent, personality/intangible qualities, extracurricular activities record, and recommendations by school officials. To graduate, students must complete at least 36 semester courses, including 2 course credits in the humanities, 2 in the social sciences and 2 in the sciences, 2 writing courses, 2 in quantitative reasoning, and courses to further proficiency in a foreign language. All students complete requirements for an academic major. Yale does not have a minor program but students may have two majors. **Procedure:** Freshmen are admitted fall. Entrance exams should be taken at any time up to and including the January test date in the year of application. There is a deferred admissions plan. Applications should be filed by January 1 for fall entry, along with a $80 fee. Notifications are sent April 1. 1098 applicants were on the 2016 waiting list; 713 were admitted. Applications are accepted on-line. **Transfer Students:** 24 transfer students enrolled in 2015-2016. Applicants must take either the SAT or ACT and have 1 full year of credit. An essay and 3 letters of recommendation are required. Student may transfer in the fall, closing date is March 1, notification date is mid-May, students must reply by late May. 18 of 36 credits required for the bachelor's degree must be completed at Yale. **International Students:** There are 555 international students enrolled. The school actively recruits these students. They must take the TOEFL with a minimum score of 600 on the paper-based TOEFL (PBT) or 100 on the Internet-based version (iBT), or take the ELTS or Pearson Test of English. Students must also take the SAT and 2 SAT Subject tests, or the ACT with Writing.

ADMISSIONS: 7% of the 2016-2017 applicants were accepted. The SAT scores for the 2016-2017 freshman class were: Critical Reading-- 3% between 500 and 599, 17% between 600 and 699, and 80% between 700 and 800. Math-- 1% between 500 and 599, 17% between 600 and 699, and 82% between 700 and 800. Writing-- 2% between 500 and 599, 17% between 600 and 699, and 81% between 700 and 800. **Admissions Contact:** Margit A. Dahl, Director of Undergraduate Admissions. Email: *apply.questions@yale.edu* Web: *www.yale.edu*

FINANCIAL AID: 100% of all full-time freshmen received need-based aid. The average freshman award was $52,016. Need-based scholarships or need-based grants averaged $50,359; need-based self-help aid (loans and jobs) averaged $2,266; and other non-need-based awards and non-need-based scholarships averaged $2,272. 56% of undergraduate students work part-time. Average annual earnings from campus work are $1433. The average financial indebtedness of the 2016 graduate was $15,521. Yale is a member of CSS. The CSS/Profile, student and parent tax returns, CSS divorced/separated parents statement, and business/farm supplement if appropriate are required. The FAFSA code is 001426. The deadline for filing freshman financial aid applications for fall entry is March 1.

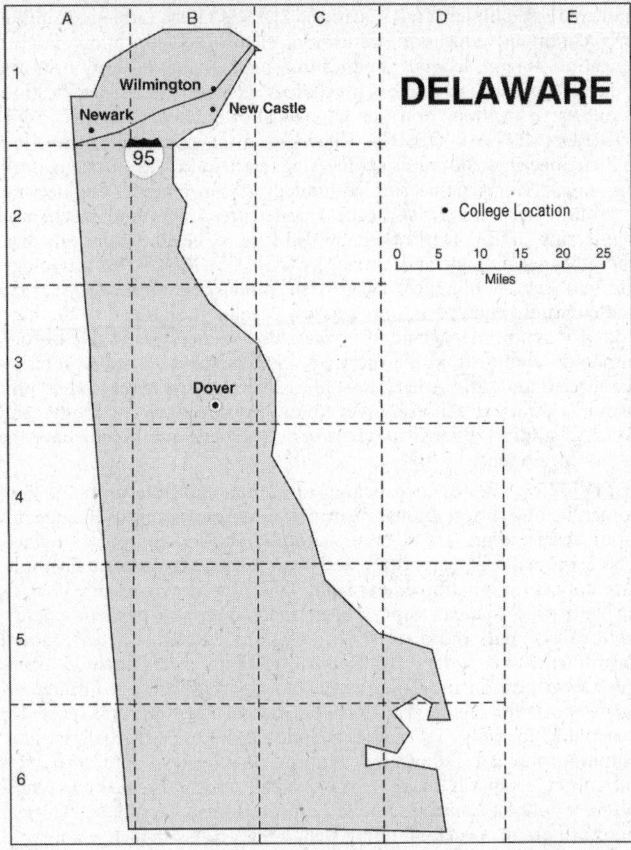

DELAWARE STATE UNIVERSITY *(The complete profile is made available exclusively on our website, www.barronspac.com)*

GOLDEY-BEACOM COLLEGE B-1

www.gbc.edu

Wilmington, DE 19808	**(302) 225-6248** **(800) 833-4877**
Fax: (302) 996-5408	**Email: admissions@gbc.edu**
Full-time: 208 men, 254 women	**Faculty:** 18
Part-time: 70 men, 93 women	**Ph.D.s:** 100%
Graduate: 458 men, 269 women	**Student/Faculty:** 24 to 1
Year: semesters, summer session	**Tuition:** $19,800
Room & Board: $11,950	**Freshman Class:** 717 applied, 385 accepted, 128 enrolled
SAT: required	**CEEB CODE:** 5255
Application Deadline: August 15	**COMPETITIVE**

Goldey-Beacom College, founded in 1886, is a private coeducational college offering programs in psychology, criminal justice, English, economics, and other areas of business. The figures in the above capsule and in this profile are approximate, which is based on 30 undergraduate credit hours. There is 1 undergraduate school and 1 graduate school. In addition to regional accreditation, The college has baccalaureate program accreditation with ACBSP. The 24-acre campus is in a suburban area in the Pike Creek Valley suburb of Wilmington, Delaware. Including any residence halls, there are 6 buildings.

STUDENT LIFE: 67% of undergraduates are from Delaware. Others are from 19 states, 60 foreign countries, and Canada. 75% are from public schools. 5% are Asian American; 41% White; 4% Hispanic; 28% Foreign; 15% African American. **Male To Female Ratio:** 1.2:1. The average age of freshmen is 19; all undergraduates, 21. 24% do not continue beyond their first year; 62% remain to graduate. **Housing:** 271 students can be accommodated in college housing, which includes coed on-campus apartments. In addition, there are special-interest houses. On-campus housing is guaranteed for all 4 years, and is available on a first-come, and first-served basis. 64% of students commute. All students may keep cars.

FACULTY/CLASSROOMS: 59% of faculty are male; 41% are female. 89% teach undergraduates. No introductory courses are taught by graduate students. The average class size in an introductory lecture is 28 and in a regular course is 21.

PROGRAMS OF STUDY: Goldey-Beacom confers B.A., and B.S. degrees. Associate and master's degrees are also awarded. Bachelor's degrees are awarded in BUSINESS (accounting, banking and finance, business administration and management, human resources, international business management, management information systems, marketing management, and sports management), COMPUTER AND PHYSICAL SCIENCE (information sciences and systems), SOCIAL SCIENCE (economics and psychology). Accounting, economics, and finance are the strongest academically. Accounting, management, and business administration have the largest enrollments.

ACTIVITIES: There are no fraternities or sororities. There are 14 groups on campus, including computers, drama, ethnic, honors, international, newspaper, professional, religious, social service, and student government. Popular campus events include Spring Fest, Karaoke Night, Casino Night, and Homecoming. **Sports:** There are 4 intercollegiate sports for men and 6 for women. Facilities include soccer and softball fields, tennis and handball courts, a gym with basketball and volleyball courts, and a fitness center available to all students and staff. When there is a student interest, an intermural sports team is established. **Graduates:** From July 1, 2015 to June 30, 2016, 119 bachelor's degrees were awarded. The most popular majors were business administration (63%), accounting (26%), and psychology (5%). 81 companies recruited on campus in 2015-2016. In an average class, 41% graduate in 6 years or less. Of the 2015 graduating class, 45% were enrolled in graduate school within 6 months of graduation, and 90% were employed.

SERVICES: Counseling and information services are available, as is tutoring in most subjects. There is a reader service for the blind, and remedial math, reading, and writing. **Library/Resources:** The library contains 191,268 volumes, and 3,793 audio/video tapes/CDs/DVDs, and subscribes to 17,434 periodicals including electronic. Computerized library services include interlibrary loans, database searching, Internet access, and Wi-Fi capability. **Physically Challenged Students:** All of the campus is accessible. Facilities include wheelchair ramps, elevators, special parking, specially equipped restrooms, lowered drinking fountains, and lowered telephones. **Special:** A 5-year B.S/M.B.A degree, dual majors, internships, and work-study programs are available. There is 1 national honor society, a freshman honors program, and 1 departmental honors program. **Visiting:** There are regularly scheduled orientations for prospective students, consisting of a meeting with an admissions representative which includes a campus tour. There are guides for informal visits, visitors may sit in on classes, and stay overnight. To schedule a visit, contact the College's Admissions Office. **Campus Safety and Security:** Measures include 24-hour foot and vehicle patrol, emergency notification system, self-defense education, and security escort services. There are lighted pathways/sidewalks and controlled access to dorms/residences.

REQUIREMENTS: Applicants must be high school graduates or have a GED and submit their official high school transcripts and SAT scores. A GPA of 2.0 is required. AP and CLEP credits are accepted. Important factors in the admissions decision are advanced placement or honors courses, extracurricular activities record, and recommendations by school officials. To graduate, students must complete a minimum of 136 credit hours with an overall GPA of 2.0. Students must also fulfill the College's degree requirements. **Procedure:** Freshmen are admitted to all sessions. There are early admissions, deferred admissions, and rolling admissions plans. Applications should be filed by August 15 for fall entry. Applications are accepted on-line. **Transfer Students:** 77 transfer students enrolled in 2015-2016. Transfer applicants must submit high school and college transcripts. 65 of 136 credits required for the bachelor's degree must be completed at Golden-Beacom. **International Students:** There are 55 international students enrolled. The school actively recruits these students. They must take the TOEFL with a minimum score of 500 on the paper-based TOEFL (PBT) or 60 on the Internet-based version (iBT), or take the IELTS. They must also take the SAT or ACT.

ADMISSIONS: 54% of the 2016-2017 applicants were accepted. **Admis-**

sions Contact: Larry Eby, Director of Admissions. Email: *admissions@gbc.edu* Web: *www.gbc.edu*

FINANCIAL AID: In 2016-2017, 100% of all full-time freshmen and 80% of continuing full-time students received some form of financial aid. 99% of all full-time freshmen received need-based aid. 90% of undergraduate students work part-time. Average annual earnings from campus work are $1200. Goldey-Beacom is a member of CSS. The FAFSA code is 001429. The priority date for freshman financial aid applications for fall entry is April 15. The deadline for filing freshman financial aid applications for fall entry is July 15.

UNIVERSITY OF DELAWARE — A-1

www.udel.edu

Newark, DE 19716	**(302) 831-2021**
Fax: (302) 831-8530	**Email: admissions@udel.edu**
Full-time: 7087 men, 9702 women	**Faculty:** 1165; I, +$
Part-time: 351 men, 435 women	**Ph.D.s:** 86%
Graduate: 1783 men, 1911 women	**Student/Faculty:** 13 to 1
Year: 4-1-4, summer session	**Tuition:** $12,830 ($34,830)
Room & Board: $12,146	**Freshman Class:** 24657 applied, 15621 accepted, 3806 enrolled
SAT CR/M/W: 600/610/600 **ACT:** 27	**CEEB CODE:** 5811
Application Deadline: January 15	**VERY COMPETITIVE+**

University of Delaware, founded in 1743 and chartered in 1833, is a state-assisted, land-grant, sea-grant, space-grant, Carnegie Research University offering programs in agriculture and natural resources, arts and sciences, business and economics, engineering, health sciences, and education and public policy. The figures in the above capsule and in this profile are approximate. There are 7 undergraduate schools and 7 graduate schools. In addition to regional accreditation, Delaware has baccalaureate program accreditation with AACSB, ABET, ADA, APTA, CAHEA, NASM, NCATE, and NLN. The 969-acre campus is in a small town 12 miles southwest of Wilmington. Including any residence halls, there are 347 buildings.

STUDENT LIFE: 61% of undergraduates are from out of state, mostly the Middle Atlantic. Students are from 47 states, 77 foreign countries, and Canada. 77% are White; 6% Hispanic; 5% African American; 4% Asian American; 4% Foreign; 2% two or more races. 36% are Catholic; 26% claim no religious affiliation. **Female To Male Ratio:** 1.3:1. The average age of freshmen is 18; all undergraduates, 20. 10% do not continue beyond their first year; 80% remain to graduate. **Housing:** College-sponsored housing includes single-sex and coed dorms, on-campus apartments, and married student housing. In addition, there are honors houses, special-interest houses, fraternity houses, sorority houses, alcohol/smoke-free residence halls, women's dorms, gender-neutral, executive apartments in traditional residence halls, and living learning communities. On-campus housing is guaranteed for all 4 years. 57% of students commute. All students may keep cars.

FACULTY/CLASSROOMS: 61% of faculty are male; 39% are female. All teach undergraduates. No introductory courses are taught by graduate students. The average class size in a laboratory is 18 and in a regular course is 35.

PROGRAMS OF STUDY: Delaware confers B.A., B.S., B.A.E.S., B.A. Liberal Studies, B.C.E., B.Ch.E., B.C.P.E., B.E.E., B.En.E., B.F.A., B.M.E., B.Mus., B.R.N., B.S.Ed. and B.S.N. degrees. Associate, master's, and doctoral degrees are also awarded. Bachelor's degrees are awarded in AGRICULTURE (agricultural business management, agricultural economics, agriculture, animal science, natural resource management, plant science, soil science, and wildlife management), BIOLOGICAL SCIENCE (biochemistry, biology/biological science, biotechnology, entomology, nutrition, and plant pathology), BUSINESS (accounting, banking and finance, business administration and management, hotel/motel and restaurant management, management information systems, management science, marketing/retailing/merchandising, operations management, organizational leadership and management, and sports management), COMMUNICATIONS AND THE ARTS (apparel design, applied music, art, art history and appreciation, communications, comparative literature, English, fine arts, historic preservation, Italian, journalism, languages, music, music theory and composition, theater management, and visual design), COMPUTER AND PHYSICAL SCIENCE (astronomy, chemistry, computer science, geology, information sciences and systems, mathematics, physics, and statistics), EDUCATION (athletic training, early childhood education, education, elementary education, English education, foreign languages education, mathematics education, music education, physical education, psychology education, science education, secondary education, and special education), ENGINEERING AND ENVIRONMENTAL DESIGN (bioengineering, chemical engineering, civil engineering, computer engineering, electrical/electronics engineering, engineering, engineering technology, environmental engineering, environmental science, landscape architecture/design, and mechanical engineering), HEALTH PROFESSIONS (health, health science, medical laboratory technology, and nursing), SOCIAL SCIENCE (anthropology, criminal justice, dietetics, East Asian studies, economics, European studies, family and community services, fashion design and technology, food production/management/services, food science, geography, history, human development, human services, interdisciplinary studies, international relations, Latin American studies, liberal arts/general studies, philosophy, political science/government, psychology, sociology, and women's studies). Biological sciences, psychology, and nursing have the largest enrollments.

ACTIVITIES: 19% of men belong to 20 national fraternities; 23% of women belong to 15 national sororities. Groups on campus include art, band, cheerleading, chess, choir, chorale, chorus, computers, dance, debate, drama, drill team, drum and bugle corps, environmental, ethnic, film, honors, international, jazz band, LGBT, literary magazine, marching band, musical theater, newspaper, opera, orchestra, pep band, political, professional, radio and TV, religious, social service, student government, and symphony. Popular campus events include Greek Week, Convocation and Commencement. **Sports:** There are 11 intercollegiate sports for men and 12 for women, and 32 intramural sports for men and 32 for women. Facilities include a 23,000-seat football stadium, 3 multipurpose gyms, 6 outdoor multipurpose fields, 8 outdoor basketball courts, 1 squash court, 15 racquetball courts, 21 outdoor tennis courts, indoor and outdoor pools, a universal weight room, a 5,000-seat basketball arena, a rock-climbing wall, a high-ropes challenge course, 4 student fitness centers, a strength and conditioning room with free weights, outdoor and indoor tracks, softball, baseball, lacrosse and soccer fields, 2 ice arenas, and an outdoor hockey rink. **Graduates:** From July 1, 2015 to June 30, 2016, 3830 bachelor's degrees were awarded. The most popular majors were business/marketing (20%), social sciences (12%), and health professions and related programs (10%). 491 companies recruited on campus in 2015-2016. In an average class, 79% graduate in 4 years or less, 67% graduate in 5 years or less, and 82% graduate in 6 years or less. Of the 2015 graduating class, 15% were enrolled in graduate school within 6 months of graduation, and 75% were employed.

SERVICES: Counseling and information services are available, as is tutoring in every subject. There is a reader service for the blind, and remedial math, reading, and writing. There is also a writing center, a math center, an academic services center for assistance with academic self-management development, critical thinking, and problem solving, as well as individual assistance for learning-disabled students. **Library/Resources:** The 5 libraries contain 2.8 million volumes, 3.4 million microform items, and 600,000 audio/video tapes/CDs/DVDs, and subscribe to 30,000 periodicals including electronic. Computerized library services include interlibrary loans, database searching, Internet access, and Wi-Fi capability. Special learning facilities include an art gallery, radio station, TV station, a preschool lab, development ice skating science center, computer-controlled greenhouse, nursing practice labs, physical therapy clinic, agricultural research complex, exercise physiology biomechanics labs, foreign language media center, and composite materials center. **Physically Challenged Students:** 95% of the campus is accessible. Facilities include wheelchair ramps, elevators, special parking, specially equipped restrooms, special class scheduling, lowered drinking fountains, lowered telephones, and special housing. **Special:** Students may participate in cooperative programs, internships, study abroad in 55 countries, a Washington semester, and work-study programs. The university offers accelerated degree programs, B.A.and B.S. degrees, dual majors, minors, student-designed majors (Bachelor of Arts in Liberal Studies), and pass/fail options. There are 4-1 degree programs in engineering, and hotel and restaurant management. Non-degree study is available through the Division of Continuing Education. There is an extensive undergraduate research program. Students may earn an enriched degree through the University Honors Program. There are 35 national honor societies, Phi Beta Kappa, and a freshman honors program. **Visiting:** There are regularly scheduled orientations for prospective students, student visits consist of a 40-minute admissions information session and a 90-minute walking tour of campus. There are guides for informal visits and visitors may sit in on classes. To schedule a visit, contact the Admissions Office. **Campus Safety and Security:** Measures include 24-hour foot and vehicle patrol, emergency notification system, self-defense education, and security escort services. There are shuttle buses, emergency telephones, lighted pathways/sidewalks, controlled access to dorms/residences, ongoing student-awareness programs in the residence halls, community policing, and keycard access to residence halls.

REQUIREMENTS: The SAT or ACT is required. The ACT Optional Writing test is also required. Applicants should be graduates of an accredited secondary school. The GED is accepted. Students should have completed a minimum of 18 high school academic units, including 4 units of English, 3 units of math, 3 units of science with 2 lab units, 2 units each of foreign language, history, and social studies, and 2 units of academic course electives. SAT Subject Tests are recommended, especially for honors program applicants. A writing sample and at least 1 letter of recommendation are required. AP credits are accepted. Important factors in the admissions decision are advanced placement or honors courses, leadership record, evidence of special talent, personality/intangible qualities, extracurricular activities record, recommendations by alumni, recommendations by school officials, parents or siblings attended your school, and geographical diversity. For graduation, students must complete at least 120 credits with a minimum GPA of 2.0. All students must take freshman English and 3 credits of coursework with multicultural, ethnic, and/or gender-related content. Most majors require more than 120 credits. Most degree programs require that half of the courses be in the major field of study. Students must also have 1 incoming semester of First Year Experience (FYE) and 3 credits of Discovery Learning Experience (DLE). **Procedure:** Freshmen are admitted fall and spring. Entrance exams should be taken by junior year or the beginning of the senior year. There are early admissions and deferred admissions plans. Applications should be filed by January 15 for fall entry; December 15 for spring entry, along with a $75 fee. Notifications are sent November 1. Applications are accepted on-line. **Transfer Students:** 366 transfer students enrolled in 2015-2016. Applicants for transfer should have completed at least 24 credits with a minimum GPA of 2.5 for most majors. Some majors require a GPA of 3.0 or better and/or specific coursework. All transfer students must submit high school and college transcripts, an essay, and a statement of good standing from their prior institution. In some cases, an interview and standardized test scores are required. Application priority date for fall is May 1 (rolling after April 1), spring is Nov. 1 (rolling mid-November). 30 of 120 credits required for the bachelor's degree must be completed at Delaware. **International Students:** There are 716 international students enrolled. The school actively recruits these students. They must take the TOEFL with a minimum score of 550 on the paper-based TOEFL (PBT) or 80 on the Internet-based version (iBT). Students must take the IELTS. The SAT is recommended.

ADMISSIONS: 63% of the 2016-2017 applicants were accepted. The SAT scores for the 2016-2017 freshman class were: Critical Reading-- 41% between 500 and 599, 39% between 600 and 699, and 14% between 700 and 800. Math-- 6% below 500, 33% between 500 and 599, 48% between 600 and 699, and 13% between 700 and 800. Writing-- 8% below 500, 41% between 500 and 599, 43% between 600 and 699, and 8% between 700 and 800. The ACT scores were 1% between 12 and 17, 15% between 18 and 23, 64% between 24 and 29, and 20% above 30. 97 freshmen graduated first in their class. **Admissions Contact:** Dr. Heather Kelly, Director of Institutional Research. Email: *admissions@udel.edu* Web: *www.udel.edu*

FINANCIAL AID: In 2016-2017, 62% of all full-time freshmen received some form of financial aid. 62% of all full-time freshmen received need-based aid. The average freshman award was $13,608. Need-based scholarships or need-based grants averaged $10,072; need-based self-help aid (loans and jobs) averaged $3,499; other non-need-based awards and non-need-based scholarships averaged $9,715; and $7,512 from other forms of aid. The average financial indebtedness of the 2016 graduate was $34,101. The FAFSA code is 001431. The priority date for freshman financial aid applications for fall entry is February 1. The deadline for filing freshman financial aid applications for fall entry is March 15.

WESLEY COLLEGE *(The complete profile is made available exclusively on our website, www.barronspac.com)*

WILMINGTON UNIVERSITY *(The complete profile is made available exclusively on our website, www.barronspac.com)*

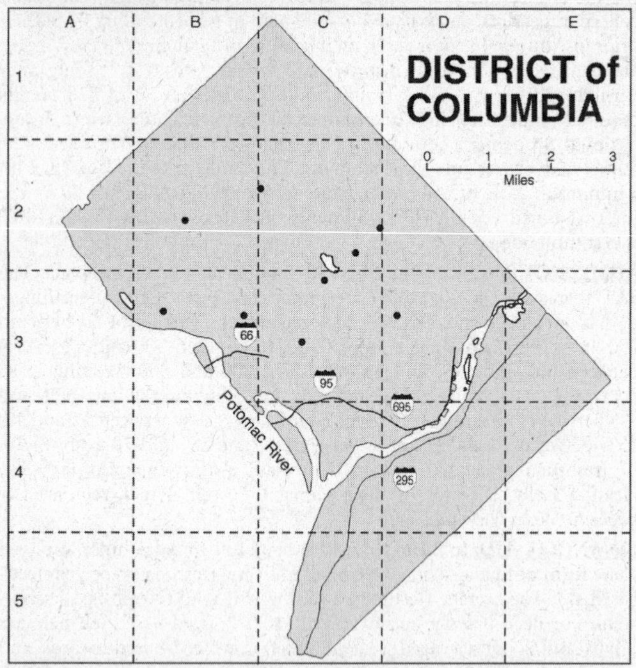

AMERICAN UNIVERSITY A-2

www.american.edu

Washington, DC 20016 (202) 885-6000

Fax: (202) 885-1025	**Email:** admissions@american.edu
Full-time: 2533 men, 4449 women	**Faculty:** I, av$
Part-time: 138 men, 157 women	**Ph.D.s:** n/av
Graduate: 3113 men, 2333 women	**Student/Faculty:** n/av
Year: semesters, summer session	**Tuition:** $44,853
Room & Board: $14,526	**Freshman Class:** 19325 applied, 5008 accepted, 1679 enrolled
SAT CR/M/W: 640/610/620 **ACT:** 28	**CEEB CODE:** 5007
Application Deadline: January 10	**HIGHLY COMPETITIVE+**

American University offers five schools for degree-seeking undergraduate study: School of Public Affairs, School of International Service, Kogod School of Business, School of Communication, and the College of Arts and Sciences, the university's liberal arts core and home to distinguished artists and writers, scientists, and presidential and judicial historians. Students may elect to double major, pursue an interdisciplinary program or one of three 3-year bachelor programs, participate in living learning communities, and take advantage of AU's extensive study abroad opportunities. There are 5 undergraduate schools and 7 graduate schools. In addition to regional accreditation, AU has baccalaureate program accreditation with AACSB, ACEJMC, NASDTEC, NASM, CAEP, NASPAA, and APA. The 84-acre campus is in a suburban area 5 miles northwest of downtown Washington, D.C. Including any residence halls, there are 57 buildings.

STUDENT LIFE: 82% of undergraduates are from out of state, mostly the Middle Atlantic. Students are from 51 states, 122 foreign countries, and Canada. 7% are African American; 6% Asian American; 56% White; 4% two or more races; 4% race unknown; 12% Hispanic; 10% Foreign. **Female To Male Ratio:** 1.6:1. The average age of freshmen is 18; all undergraduates, 20. 10% do not continue beyond their first year; 81% remain to graduate. **Housing:** 4000 students can be accommodated in college housing, which includes coed dorms and off-campus apartments. In addition, there are honors houses, special-interest houses, living learning communities, and community service housing. On-campus housing is guaranteed for the freshman year only, and is available on a first-come, and first-served basis. Alcohol is not permitted. Upperclassmen may keep cars.

FACULTY/CLASSROOMS: No introductory courses are taught by graduate students.

PROGRAMS OF STUDY: AU confers B.A., B.F.A., B.S. and B.S.B.A. degrees. Associate, master's, and doctoral degrees are also awarded. Bachelor's degrees are awarded in AGRICULTURE (environmental studies), BIOLOGICAL SCIENCE (biochemistry, biology/biological science, and neurosciences), BUSINESS (business administration and management and international business management), COMMUNICATIONS AND THE ARTS (American literature, Arabic, art, art history and appreciation, audio technology, Chinese, communication studies, communications, creative writing, dramatic arts, film arts, fine arts, French, German, graphic design, Hebrew, Italian, Japanese, journalism, Korean, literature, multimedia, music, musical theater, performing arts, public relations, Russian, Spanish, strategic communication, and studio art), COMPUTER AND PHYSICAL SCIENCE (applied mathematics, chemistry, computer science, mathematics, physics, and statistics), EDUCATION (elementary education, foreign languages education, health education, and secondary education), ENGINEERING AND ENVIRONMENTAL DESIGN (computational sciences and environmental science), HEALTH PROFESSIONS (health promotion and public health), SOCIAL SCIENCE (American studies, anthropology, area studies, criminal justice, economics, government, French studies, gender studies, German area studies, history, interdisciplinary studies, international studies, Judaic studies, Latin American studies, philosophy, political science/government, psychology, religious studies, Russian and Slavic studies, sociology, Spanish studies, and women's studies). International studies, business administration, and political science have the largest enrollments.

ACTIVITIES: There are 200 groups on campus, including art, band, cheerleading, chess, choir, chorale, chorus, computers, dance, debate, drama, environmental, ethnic, film, honors, international, jazz band, LGBT, literary magazine, musical theater, newspaper, opera, orchestra, pep band, photography, political, professional, radio and TV, religious, social, social service, student government, symphony, various athletic clubs, and yearbook. Popular campus events include Family Weekend, Founders Day Ball, and Campus Beautification Day. **Sports:** There are 6 intercollegiate sports for men and 8 for women. Facilities include a 6,000-seat sports arena, a main fitness center, 2 swimming pools, hockey and soccer fields, a softball diamond, an all-purpose field, cardiovascular and strength training equipment, weight rooms, courts for tennis, basketball, and volleyball, an aerobics studio, an indoor jogging track, an outdoor 6-lane tartan track, and fitness centers within residence halls. **Graduates:** From July 1, 2015 to June 30, 2016, 1743 bachelor's degrees were awarded. The most popular majors were international studies (25%), business administration (14%), and political science (8%). In an average class, 6% graduate in 3 years or less, 76% graduate in 4 years or less, 80% graduate in 5 years or less, and 81% graduate in 6 years or less.

SERVICES: Counseling and information services are available, as is tutoring in every subject. There is a reader service for the blind, and remedial math, reading, and writing. Academic Support and Access Center is available to help students develop the tools needed for college success. In addition, a math and statistics tutoring lab, a writing center, and a foreign language resource center are available. **Library/Resources:** The library contains 1,000,000 volumes, 1.1 million microform items, and 66,000 audio/video tapes/CDs/DVDs, and subscribes to 125,650 periodicals including electronic. Computerized library services include interlibrary loans, database searching, Internet access, and Wi-Fi capability. Special learning facilities include an art gallery, radio station, TV station, American University's Washington College of Law library, a music library, a language resource center, multimedia design and development labs, science and computer science labs, well-equipped buildings for art and the performing arts, and a National Public Radio station (WAMU 88.5FM). The American University Game Lab serves as a hub for experiential education, persuasive play research, and innovative production in the fields of games for change and rhetorical play. Part of a university-wide commitment to high-impact research, this multidisciplinary initiative combines the expertise of the School of Communication and the College of Arts and Sciences. AU's Kreeger Building is the site of the Audio Technology Program recording studios. **Physically Challenged Students:** 95% of the campus is accessible. Facilities include wheelchair ramps, elevators, special parking, specially equipped restrooms, special class scheduling, lowered drinking fountains, lowered telephones, and special housing. The Academic Support and Access Center is committed to providing access for individuals with disabilities within the university's diverse community. Also, university shuttles are equipped to accommodate students in wheelchairs. **Special:** AU offers co-op programs and internships in all majors, over 100 distinct study abroad programs in more than 45 countries, and the Washington Semester and Gateway programs. Work-study is available on campus and with local community service agencies. Dual majors, interdisciplinary programs, student-designed majors, 3-year B.A. degree programs, 3-2 engineering degrees, and B.A./B.S.degrees are also available. Combined bachelor's/master's programs are available in most majors. Cross-registration may be arranged through the Consortium of Universities of the Washington Metropolitan Area. Credit for life experience, nondegree study, and pass/fail options are available. There are preprofessional programs in engineering, law, and medicine (the medical program is aimed at strengthening credentials for applying to programs in medicine, dentistry, optometry, podiatry, oral survey, veterinary medicine, and public health). There are 12 national honor societies, Phi Beta Kappa, and a freshman honors program. **Visiting:** There are regularly scheduled orientations for prospective students, including student-led daily tours and information sessions, open houses, and overnight programs. There are guides for informal visits, visitors may sit in on classes, and stay overnight. To schedule a visit, contact the Admissions Office Tours and Infromation Program at admissions@american.edu. **Campus Safety and Security:** Measures include 24-hour foot and vehicle patrol, emergency notification system, self-defense education, and security escort services. There are shuttle buses, emergency telephones, lighted pathways/sidewalks, controlled access to dorms/residences, crime prevention programs, building alarms, video surveillance, posted crime alerts, on-line annual crime reports, escorts, laptop security protocols, RAD courses, and emergency preparedness protocols and alerting system.

REQUIREMENTS: Prospective students may apply to American University through our Early or Regular Decision Plan without submitting standardized test scores. Students graduating from a secondary school located outside the United States, please note that neither the SAT or ACT is required for admission. Students must have graduated from an accredited secondary school with at least 16 Carnegie units, including at least 4 units in English, 3 units in college preparatory math (including the equivalent of 2 units in algebra), 3 units in science, 2 units each in social sciences, and foreign language(s). Applicants who have satisfactory scores on the GED may also apply. All students must submit an essay and 2 letters of recommendation. American University's test-optional plan is open to all students graduating from a secondary school within the United States. AP and CLEP credits are accepted. Important factors in the admissions decision are advanced placement or honors courses, recommendations by school officials, and extracurricular activities record. To graduate, students must complete 120 credit hours with a minimum GPA of 2.0. In addition, students must complete 31 credit hours of general education requirements in 5 curricular areas and fulfill the school's competency requirements in English composition and mathematics by either passing an exam or taking a course in each area. Please see program-specific websites for additional requirements. **Procedure:** Freshmen are admitted to all sessions. Entrance exams should be taken in the spring of the junior year or the fall of the senior year. There are early decision and deferred admissions plans. Early decision applications should be filed by November 10; regular applications, by January 10 for fall entry; and October 1 for spring entry, along with a $70 fee. Notification of early decision is sent December 31; regular decision, April 1. Applications are accepted on-line. **Transfer Students:** 199 transfer students enrolled in 2015-2016. Transfer applicants who wish to be considered competitive candidates should have a cumulative GPA of at least 2.5 from all schools attended. All applicants with a cumulative GPA of 2.0 or above will be considered. 45 of 120 credits required for the bachelor's degree must be completed at AU. **International Students:** There are 797 international students enrolled. The school actively recruits these students. They must take the TOEFL with a minimum score of 550 on the paper-based TOEFL (PBT) or 80 on the Internet-based version (iBT) and the college's own test. Students may also take the IELTS Composite with a score 6.5 or higher, or the Pearson Test of English with score 53 or higher.

ADMISSIONS: 26% of the 2016-2017 applicants were accepted. The SAT scores for the 2016-2017 freshman class were: Critical Reading-- 3% below 500, 25% between 500 and 599, 48% between 600 and 699, and 24% between 700 and 800. Math-- 5% below 500, 38% between 500 and 599, 48% between 600 and 699, and 9% between 700 and 800. Writing-- 3% below 500, 32% between 500 and 599, 50% between 600 and 699, and 15% between 700 and 800. The ACT scores were 6% between 18 and 23, 56% between 24 and 29, and 38% above 30. **Admissions Contact:** Jeremy Lowe, Acting Asst Vice Provost UG Admissions. Email: *admissions@american.edu* Web: *www.american.edu*

FINANCIAL AID: The CSS/Profile is required. The FAFSA code is 001434. The priority date for freshman financial aid applications for fall entry is November 10. The deadline for filing freshman financial aid applications for fall entry is January 10.

GALLAUDET UNIVERSITY *(The complete profile is made available exclusively on our website, www.barronspac.com)*

GEORGE WASHINGTON UNIVERSITY B-3

www.gwu.edu

Washington, DC 20052	(202) 994-6040 (800) 447-3765
Fax: (202) 994-0325	Email: gwadm@gwu.edu
Full-time: 4215 men, 5533 women	**Faculty:** I, +$
Part-time: 343 men, 352 women	**Ph.D.s:** n/av
Graduate: 6521 men, 8296 women	**Student/Faculty:** 13 to 1
Year: semesters, summer session	**Tuition:** $50,785
Room & Board: $12,050	**Freshman Class:** n/av
SAT or ACT: required	**CEEB CODE:** 5246
Application Deadline: n/av	**MOST COMPETITIVE**

George Washington University, founded in 1821, is a private institution providing degree programs in arts and sciences, business, engineering, international affairs, health sciences, education, law, and public health. The tuition cost varies by programs chosen. The figures in the above capsule and in this profile are approximate. There are 7 undergraduate schools and 10 graduate schools. In addition to regional accreditation, GW has baccalaureate program accreditation with AACSB, ABET, CAHEA, CSAB, NASAD, NASM, and NCATE. The 37-acre campus is in an urban area 3 blocks west of the White House. Including any residence halls, there are 123 buildings.

STUDENT LIFE: 98% of undergraduates are from out of state, mostly the Middle Atlantic. Students are from 50 states, 137 foreign countries, and Canada. 70% are from public schools. 9% are Asian American; 65% White; 6% African American; 5% Hispanic; 4% Foreign. **Female To Male Ratio:** 1.3:1. The average age of freshmen is 18; all undergraduates, 20. 7% do not continue beyond their first year; 81% remain to graduate. **Housing:** 8245 students can be accommodated in college housing, which includes coed dorms and on-campus apartments. In addition, there are special-interest houses, fraternity houses, sorority houses, and sorority floors. On-campus housing is available on a lottery system for upperclassmen. 70% of students live on campus. All students may keep cars.

FACULTY/CLASSROOMS: 61% of faculty are male; 39% are female. No introductory courses are taught by graduate students.

PROGRAMS OF STUDY: GW confers B.A., B.S., B.Accy., B.B.A., B.Mus., B.S.C.E., B.S.C.Eng., B.S.C.S., B.S.E.E., B.S.H.S., B.S.M.E. and B.S.S.A. degrees. Associate, master's, and doctoral degrees are also awarded. Bachelor's degrees are awarded in BIOLOGICAL SCIENCE (biology/biological science), BUSINESS (accounting, banking and finance, business administration and management, business economics, human resources, international business management, marketing management, and tourism), COMMUNICATIONS AND THE ARTS (art history and appreciation, broadcasting, Chinese, classics, communications, dance, dramatic arts, English, fine arts, French, German, Japanese, journalism, literature, multimedia, music, music performance, public relations, Russian, and Spanish), COMPUTER AND PHYSICAL SCIENCE (applied mathematics, chemistry, computer science, geology, information sciences and systems, mathematics, physics, statistics, and systems analysis), ENGINEERING AND ENVIRONMENTAL DESIGN (civil engineering, computer engineering, electrical/electronics engineering, engineering, environmental science, and mechanical engineering), HEALTH PROFESSIONS (clinical science, emergency medical technologies, medical laboratory technology, nuclear medical technology, physician's assistant, premedicine, radiological science, and speech pathology/audiology), SOCIAL SCIENCE (American studies, anthropology, archeology, criminal justice, East Asian studies, economics, European studies, geography, history, human services, humanities, interdisciplinary studies, international relations, Judaic studies, Latin American studies, liberal arts/general studies, Middle Eastern studies, philosophy, physical fitness/movement, political science/government, psychology, religion, and sociology). Political communication, international affairs, and biological sciences are the strongest academically. Psychology, and political science have the largest enrollments.

ACTIVITIES: 23% of men belong to 11 national fraternities; 23% of women belong to 7 national sororities. There are 257 groups on campus, including art, band, cheerleading, chess, choir, chorale, chorus, computers, dance, debate, drama, ethnic, film, folk life, forensics, geology, honors, international, jazz band, LGBT, literary magazine, marching band, musical theater, newspaper, opera, orchestra, pep band, photography, political, professional, radio and TV, religious, social, social service, and student government. Popular campus events include Spring Fling, Fall Fest and a yearly Benefit Auction. **Sports:** There are 9 intercollegiate sports for men and 8 for women, and 16 intramural sports for men and 16 for women. Facilities include a 5000-seat gym with 2 auxiliary gyms, an AAU swimming pool, weight rooms, a jogging track, squash and racquetball courts, and soccer and baseball fields.

SERVICES: Counseling and information services are available, as is tutoring in every subject. There is a reader service for the blind. **Library/Resources:** Computerized library services include interlibrary loans and database searching. Special learning facilities include an art gallery, radio station, and TV station. **Physically Challenged Students:** 95% of the campus is accessible. Facilities include wheelchair ramps, elevators, special parking, specially equipped restrooms, special class scheduling, lowered drinking fountains, and lowered telephones. **Special:** Cross-registration is available through the Consortium of Colleges and Universities. There are co-op programs in education, business, engineering, arts and sciences, and international affairs and internships in the Washington metropolitan area. Study abroad in locations throughout the world, work-study programs, dual majors, student-designed majors, and a 3-2 engineering degree program with 8 colleges are also available. Nondegree study, a general studies degree, credit by exam, and pass/fail options are possible. There are 12 national honor societies, Phi Beta Kappa, a freshman honors program, and 21 departmental honors programs. **Visiting:** There are regularly scheduled orientations for prospective students, including group information sessions and campus tours. Class visitation, lunch with current students, and other activities can be arranged, if requested in advance. There are guides for informal visits, visitors may sit in on classes, and stay overnight. To schedule a visit, contact the University Visitor Center at (202) 994-6602. **Campus Safety and Security:** Measures include 24-hour foot and vehicle patrol, self-defense education, and security escort services. There are emergency telephones, lighted pathways/sidewalks, a bike patrol.

REQUIREMENTS: The SAT or ACT is required. Students must have successfully completed a strong academic program in high school. SAT: Subject tests are strongly recommended. An essay, 1 teacher recommendation, and 1 counselor recommendation are required. An interview is encouraged. AP and CLEP credits are accepted. Important factors in the admissions decision are advanced placement or honors courses, recommendations by school officials, and leadership record. Students must complete 120 semester hours with a minimum GPA of 2.0 for most majors. Arts and sciences majors must meet general curriculum requirements that include literacy, quantitative and logical reasoning, natural sciences, social and behavioral sciences, creative and performing arts, literature, Western civilization, and foreign languages or culture. Other specific course requirements vary with the different divisions of the university. **Procedure:** Freshmen are admitted to all sessions. Entrance exams should be taken in the junior year and the fall semester of the senior year. There are early decision and deferred admissions plans. Check with the school for current application deadlines. The fall 2016 application fee was $60. Applications are accepted on-line. **Transfer Students:** In addition to a record of high grades and exam scores, applicants must submit official transcripts of all postsecondary work. Minimum GPA requirements vary from 2.5 to 3.0, depending on the major. The SAT or ACT is required, and an interview is encouraged. 30 of 120 credits required for the bachelor's degree must be completed at GW. **International Students:** The school actively recruits these students. They must take the TOEFL and the college's own test. They must also take the SAT or ACT.

Admissions Contact: Dr. Kathryn M. Napper, Executive Dean for Undergraduate Admissions. Email: *gwadm@gwu.edu* Web: *www.gwu.edu*

FINANCIAL AID: GW is a member of CSS. The CSS/Profile is required. The FAFSA code is 001444. Check with the school for current application deadlines.

GEORGETOWN UNIVERSITY — B-3

www.georgetown.edu

Washington, DC 20057 — **(202) 687-3600**

Fax: (202) 687-5084	**Email:** guadmiss@georgetown.edu
Full-time: 3212 men, 4030 women	**Faculty:** I, ++$
Part-time: 142 men, 168 women	**Ph.D.s:** 74%
Graduate: 4798 men, 5007 women	**Student/Faculty:** 12 to 1
Year: semesters, summer session	**Tuition:** $50,964
Room & Board: $14,962	**Freshman Class:** 20115 applied, 3413 accepted, 1570 enrolled
SAT or ACT: required	**CEEB CODE:** 5422
Application Deadline: January 10	**MOST COMPETITIVE**

Georgetown University, founded in 1789, is a private institution affiliated with the Roman Catholic Church and offers programs in arts and sciences, business administration, foreign service, languages and linguistics, and nursing. The tuition figures in the above capsule are for the Georgetown Undergraduate COL, MSB, and SFS schools. Tuition cost varies for undergraduate NHS and BALS schools. There are 4 undergraduate schools and 3 graduate schools. In addition to regional accreditation, Georgetown has baccalaureate program accreditation with AACSB and CCNE. The 104-acre campus is in an urban area 1.5 miles northwest of downtown Washington, D.C. Including any residence halls, there are 64 buildings.

STUDENT LIFE: 96% of undergraduates are from out of state, mostly the Middle Atlantic. Students are from 50 states, 91 foreign countries, and Canada. 46% are from public schools. 9% are Asian American; 8% Hispanic; 60% White; 6% African American; 11% Foreign. 42% are Catholic; 21% Protestant. **Female To Male Ratio:** 1.1:1. The average age of freshmen is 18; all undergraduates, 21. 4% do not continue beyond their first year; 94% remain to graduate. **Housing:** 5053 students can be accommodated in college housing, which includes coed dorms and on-campus apartments. Special interest floors are available in some residence halls. On-campus housing is available on a lottery system for upperclassmen. 63% of students live on campus. No one may keep cars.

FACULTY/CLASSROOMS: 62% of faculty are male; 38% are female. All teach undergraduates, and all do research. No introductory courses are taught by graduate students.

PROGRAMS OF STUDY: Georgetown confers A.B., B.S., B.A.L.S., B.S.B.A., B.S.F.S. and B.S.N. degrees. Master's and doctoral degrees are also awarded. Bachelor's degrees are awarded in BIOLOGICAL SCIENCE (biochemistry, biology/biological science, and environmental biology), BUSINESS (accounting, banking and finance, business administration and management, finance, international business management, and marketing/retailing/merchandising), COMMUNICATIONS AND THE ARTS (Arabic, art history, art, Chinese, classics, comparative literature, English, fine arts, French, German, Italian, Japanese, linguistics, Portuguese, Russian, and Spanish), COMPUTER AND PHYSICAL SCIENCE (chemistry, computer science, mathematics, and physics), HEALTH PROFESSIONS (health and nursing), SOCIAL SCIENCE (American studies, anthropology, economics, history, interdisciplinary studies, international relations, philosophy, political science/government, psychology, religion, and sociology). International politics, and government, have the largest enrollments.

ACTIVITIES: There are no fraternities or sororities. There are 171 groups on campus, including art, band, cheerleading, chess, choir, chorale, chorus, computers, dance, debate, drama, ethnic, film, honors, international, jazz band, LGBT, literary magazine, musical theater, newspaper, orchestra, pep band, photography, political, professional, radio and TV, religious, social, social service, student government, and symphony. Popular campus events include GU Day, Career Week, and Senior Salute. **Sports:** There are 11 intercollegiate sports for men and 12 for women. Facilities include a 5,000-seat gym for basketball and volleyball, along with sports medicine and training room facilities, a 2,500-seat multi-sport field for football and lacrosse, and a 4-level sports and recreation facility that houses a swimming pool, basketball courts, aerobics rooms, a weight area, cardiovascular equipment, a wellness center, locker rooms, and racquetball courts. **Graduates:** From July 1, 2015 to June 30, 2016, 1871 bachelor's degrees were awarded. The most popular majors were government (11%), international politics (9%), and nursing (9%). In an average class, 91% graduate in 4 years or less, 93% graduate in 5 years or less, and 94% graduate in 6 years or less.

SERVICES: Counseling and information services are available, as is tutoring in some subjects, such as accounting, finance, biological sciences, math, Spanish, French and Arabic. There is a reader service for the blind. **Library/Resources:** The 6 libraries contain 3.0 million volumes, 4.0 million microform items, and 54,513 audio/video tapes/CDs/DVDs, and subscribe to 61,257 periodicals including electronic. Computerized library services include interlibrary loans, database searching, Internet access, and Wi-Fi capability. Special learning facilities include an art gallery, planetarium, radio station, and TV station. **Physically Challenged Students:** 94% of the campus is accessible. Facilities include wheelchair ramps, elevators, special parking, specially equipped restrooms, special class scheduling, lowered drinking fountains, lowered telephones, and special housing. A special map of the campus with accessibility routes, a tactile map of the campus for visually disabled students, and a paratransit vehicle for mobility on the main campus are available. **Special:** Cross-registration is available with a consortium of universities in the Washington metropolitan area. Opportunities are provided for internships, study abroad in 30 countries, work-study programs, student-designed majors, and dual majors. A liberal studies degree, B.A. and B.S. degrees, non-degree study, credit by examination, and pass/fail options are also offered. There is a chapter of Phi Beta Kappa and a freshman honors program. **Visiting:** There are regularly scheduled orientations for prospective students, throughout the year, including a question and answer period led by an admissions officer, followed by a campus tour led by a student guide. There are guides for informal visits and visitors may sit in on classes. To schedule a visit, contact the Office of Undergraduate Admissions. **Campus Safety and Security:** Measures include 24-hour foot and vehicle patrol, emergency notification system, and security escort services. There are shuttle buses, emergency telephones, lighted pathways/sidewalks, controlled access to dorms/residences, laptop computer registration, bicycle registration, and off-campus security assesments.

REQUIREMENTS: The SAT or ACT is required. Graduation from an accredited secondary school is required, including 4 years of English, a minimum of 2 each of a foreign language, math, and social studies, and 1 of natural science. An additional 2 years each of math and science is required for students intending to major in math, science, nursing, or business. SAT subject tests are strongly recommended. AP credits are accepted. Important factors in the admissions decision are recommendations by school officials, leadership record, and advanced placement or honors courses. Students must complete 120 credits and maintain a minimum GPA of 2.0. A core of liberal arts courses is required, consisting of 2 courses each in philosophy and theology. Additional requirements are specific to undergraduate school as well as major concentration. **Procedure:** Freshmen are admitted fall. Entrance exams should be taken in the junior year and again at the beginning of the senior year. There is a deferred admissions plan. Early decision applications should be filed by November 1; regular applications, by January 10 for fall entry, along with a $70 fee. Notification of early decision is sent December 15; regular decision, April 1. Applications are accepted on-line. **Transfer Students:** 168 transfer students enrolled in 2015-2016. Transfer students must have successfully completed a minimum of 12 credit hours with a minimum GPA of 3.0. Either the SAT or the ACT is required. An interview is recommended. Transfers must complete their last 2 years at Georgetown. 60 of 120 credits required for the bachelor's degree must be completed at Georgetown. **International Students:** There are 781 international students enrolled. The school actively recruits these students. They must take the TOEFL. They must also take the SAT or ACT.

ADMISSIONS: 17% of the 2016-2017 applicants were accepted. **Admissions Contact:** Charles A. Deacon, Dean of Admissions. Email: *guadmiss@georgetown.edu* Web: *www.georgetown.edu*

FINANCIAL AID: Georgetown is a member of CSS. The CSS/Profile, non-custodial profile, business/farm supplement, and tax returns are required. The FAFSA code is 001445. The deadline for filing freshman financial aid applications for fall entry is February 1.

HOWARD UNIVERSITY — C-3

www.howard.edu

Washington, DC 20059	**(202) 806-2864** **(800) 822-6363**
Fax: (202) 806-2818	**Email: dkindle@howard.edu**
Full-time: 2071 men, 4341 women	**Faculty:** 746; I, --$
Part-time: 171 men, 300 women	**Ph.D.s:** 73%
Graduate: 1230 men, 1889 women	**Student/Faculty:** 8 to 1
Year: semesters, summer session	**Tuition:** $23,970
Room & Board: $13,646	**Freshman Class:** n/av
SAT CR/M/W: required **ACT:** required	**CEEB CODE:** 5297
Application Deadline: February 15	**COMPETITIVE+**

Howard University, founded in 1867, is the largest predominantly Black university in the United States. As a culturally diverse, comprehensive, nonsectarian, research intensive, and historically Black private university, Howard University provides an educational experience of exceptional quality at the undergraduate, graduate, and professional levels to students of high academic standing and potential, with particular emphasis upon educational opportunities for Black students. Moreover, the University is dedicated to attracting and sustaining a cadre of faculty who are, through their teaching, research, and service, committed to the development of distinguished, historically aware, and compassionate graduates and to the discovery of solutions to human problems in the United States and throughout the world. With an abiding interest in both domestic and international affairs, the University is committed to continuing to produce leaders for America and the global community. There are 6 undergraduate schools and 12 graduate schools. In addition to regional accreditation, Howard has baccalaureate program accreditation with AACSB, ABET, ACEJMC, ACPE, ADA, APTA, CSWE, NAAB, NASAD, NASDTEC, NASM, NCATE, ABA, ATS, APA, CCNE, ARL, NAEYC, NCSS LCME JRCERT, NAACLS, MLA, AALL, ASLHA, ACEI, NASP, ACOTE, CADE, AAHPERD, ACS, NAST, NASPE, CEC, AALS, ARCPA, and AUPHA. The 258-acre campus is in an urban area in Northwest Washington, D.C. Including any residence halls, there are 127 buildings.

STUDENT LIFE: 96% of undergraduates are from out of state, mostly the Middle Atlantic. Students are from 45 states, 38 foreign countries, and Canada. 87% are African American; 5% Foreign; 3% White; 2% Asian American; 2% Hispanic; 1% American Indian/Alaska Native. **Female To Male Ratio:** 1.9:1. The average age of freshmen is 18; all undergraduates, 21. 17% do not continue beyond their first year; 83% remain to graduate. **Housing:** 5748 students can be accommodated in college housing, which includes single-sex and coed dorms, on-campus apartments, and off-campus apartments. In addition, there are honors houses and special-interest houses. On-campus housing is guaranteed for the freshman year only, and is available on a first-come, first-served basis, and is available on a lottery system for upperclassmen. 56% of students live on campus; of those, 40% remain on campus on weekends. Alcohol is not permitted. All students may keep cars.

FACULTY/CLASSROOMS: 55% of faculty are male; 45% are female. 65% teach undergraduates, 35% do research, and 40% do both. No introductory courses are taught by graduate students. The average class size in an introductory lecture is 35; in a laboratory is 20; and in a regular course is 20.

PROGRAMS OF STUDY: Howard confers B.B.A., B.A., B.S. and B.F.A. degrees. Master's and doctoral degrees are also awarded. Bachelor's degrees are awarded in BIOLOGICAL SCIENCE (anatomy, biochemistry, biology/biological science, genetics, microbiology, nutrition, and physiology), BUSINESS (accounting, banking and finance, business administration and management, fashion merchandising, international business management, labor studies, marketing/retailing/merchandising, sports management, and supply chain management), COMMUNICATIONS AND THE ARTS (acting, advertising, art history and appreciation, broadcasting, ceramic art and design, communications, communication science, dance, design, dramatic arts, English, film arts, French, graphic design, jazz, journalism, media arts, music, music business management, music history and appreciation, musical theater, painting, photography, playwriting/screenwriting, printmaking, public relations, sculpture, Spanish, telecommunications, and theatre arts), COMPUTER AND PHYSICAL SCIENCE (atmospheric sciences and meteorology, chemistry, computer engineering technology, computer science, mathematics, physics, and radiological technology), EDUCA-

TION (art education, early childhood education, education, education administration, elementary education, health education, music education, physical education, reading education, school psychology, and secondary education), ENGINEERING AND ENVIRONMENTAL DESIGN (architecture, chemical engineering, civil engineering, computer engineering, electrical/electronics engineering, environmental science, interior design, and mechanical engineering), HEALTH PROFESSIONS (allied health, clinical science, community health work, dental hygiene, health care administration, health science, music therapy, nursing, occupational therapy, pharmaceutical science, pharmacology, pharmacy, physical therapy, physician's assistant, predentistry, premedicine, public health, radiation therapy, radiograph medical technology, speech pathology/audiology, and sports medicine), SOCIAL SCIENCE (administration of justice , African studies, African American studies, anthropology, child psychology/development, classical/ancient civilization, counseling/psychology, criminal justice, economics, fashion design and technology, geography, history, human development, interdisciplinary studies, law, legal studies, philosophy, political science/government, psychology, public administration, public affairs, religion, social work, sociology, Spanish studies, textiles and clothing, urban studies, and women's studies). Chemical engineering, computer engineering, and physics are the strongest academically. Biology, psychology, and political science have the largest enrollments.

ACTIVITIES: 3% of men belong to 10 local fraternities; 5% of women belong to 8 local sororities. There are 155 groups on campus, including programming boards (residence halls and activities), step teams, entertainment industry clubs, art, band, cheerleading, chess, choir, chorus, communications, community service, youth/peer mentorship, residence hall councils, computers, dance, debate, drama, drill team, drum and bugle corps, environmental, ethnic, film, honors, international, jazz band, LGBT, marching band, musical theater, newspaper, opera, orchestra, pep band, photography, political, professional, radio and TV, religious, social, social service, student government, symphony, and yearbook. Popular campus events include Orientation, Freshman Welcome Pep Rally and Pinning Ceremony, Opening Convocation, Charter Day Dinner, Global Community Week, Howard Homecoming, Spring Black Arts Festival (Springfest), MLK Day of Service, and Student Leadership Conference. **Sports:** There are 8 intercollegiate sports for men and 10 for women, and 6 intramural sports for men and 5 for women. Greene Stadium has an outdoor track, and football/soccer/lacrosse field, Burr Gymnasium has basketball courts, a swimming pool, indoor track, classrooms, weight room, and cardio fitness center. Blackburn Recreational Center has a bowling alley and a pool hall, and several practice fields. **Graduates:** From July 1, 2015 to June 30, 2016, 2045 bachelor's degrees were awarded. The most popular majors were biology, health professions, and related programs (22%), business, management, marketing, and related support services (18%), communication, journalism, and and related programs (16%). 211 companies recruited on campus in 2015-2016. In an average class, 49% graduate in 4 years or less, and 62% graduate in 5 years or less. Of the 2015 graduating class, 54% were enrolled in graduate school within 6 months of graduation, and 65% were employed.

SERVICES: Counseling and information services are available, as is tutoring in most subjects. There is a reader service for the blind, and remedial math, reading, and writing. Tutoring is also available for the following subjects: humanities, research, mathematics, foreign languages, English, science, psychology, and statistics. **Library/Resources:** The 8 libraries contain 2.5 million volumes, 4.2 million microform items, and 194,000 audio/video tapes/CDs/DVDs, and subscribe to 82,758 periodicals including electronic. Computerized library services include interlibrary loans, database searching, Internet access, and Wi-Fi capability. Special learning facilities include an art gallery, radio station, TV station, history and culture research centers (e.g. Moorland-Spingarn Research Center (MSRC), Ralph Bunche International Center, and the E. Frankin Frazier Reading Room). **Physically Challenged Students:** All of the campus is accessible. Facilities include wheelchair ramps, elevators, special parking, specially equipped restrooms, special class scheduling, lowered drinking fountains, lowered telephones, and special housing. **Special:** Cross-registration is available with the Consortium of Universities in the Washington Metropolitan Area. Opportunities are also provided for internships, work-study, co-op programs, study abroad in 5 countries including those in Europe and Africa, B.A.-B.S. degrees in engineering and business, student-designed majors, pass/fail options, and accelerated degree programs in medicine and dentistry. There are 20 national honor societies, Phi Beta Kappa, and a freshman honors program. **Visiting:** There are regularly scheduled orientations for prospective students, consisting of a verbal presentation by an admission staff member, followed by a walking guided tour. There are guides for informal visits and visitors may sit in on classes. To schedule a visit, contact the Office of Admissions. **Campus Safety and Security:** Measures include 24-hour foot and vehicle patrol, emergency notification system, self-defense education, and security escort services. There are shuttle buses, emergency telephones, lighted pathways/sidewalks, controlled access to dorms/residences, biweekly checks of calls for service and response time, blue light emergency system, fingerprinting services, town-hall meetings, and crime prevention program.

REQUIREMENTS: Evaluation of an applicant's qualifications for admission is based on high school course work, grade point average, class rank, test scores, extracurricular activities, and letters of recommendation. An essay, audition, portfolio, or interview also may be required. Academic Eligibility, we consider the applicant's secondary school academic record, standardized college entrance exams (SAT or ACT), leadership in school and community activities, unique talents and skills, and educational objectives. For admission consideration, an applicant should have a well-balanced college preparatory program that includes the following coursework; 4 years English, 3 years mathematics, 2 years social science, 2 years science (with lab), 2 years foreign language. Admission Requirements Package; A complete application package includes the following credentials; Application for Admission, official high school transcript or GED certificate, score results from the Scholastic Aptitude Test (SAT) or the American College Test (ACT), one letter of recommendation from a high school counselor, Guidance Counselor Recommendation Form; one letter of recommendation from a high school teacher, Teacher Recommendation Form, an Admission essay, and a resume (optional). A GPA of 3.0 is required. AP and CLEP credits are accepted. Important factors in the admissions decision are leadership record, advanced placement or honors courses, and extracurricular activities record. To graduate, students must complete a total of 120 semester hours, exclusive of courses taken through the Center for Academic Reinforcement (CAR), maintain grades of C or better in all courses used to satisfy the minimum credit-hour requirement for departmental majors, maintain grades higher than C for courses used to satisfy requirements for departmental majors in any department stipulating this requirement, and maintain a cumulative grade point average of 2.0 or better in departmental majors, as well as in the minor fields of concentration. **Procedure:** Freshmen are admitted fall, spring, and summer. Entrance exams should be taken by January of Senior Year. There are early decision, deferred admissions, and rolling admissions plans. Early decision applications should be filed by November 1; regular applications, by February 15 for fall entry; November 1 for spring entry; and April 1 for summer entry, along with a $45 fee. Notification of early decision is sent December 20; regular decision, January 15. 636 early decision candidates were accepted for the 2016-2017 class. Applications are accepted on-line. **Transfer Students:** 317 transfer students enrolled in 2015-2016. Admission criteria vary among Howard University's schools and colleges. As a transfer applicant, you must meet the following minimum requirements for admission consideration: 15 transferrable credit hours (30 credit hours for the School of Business) from a regionally accredited postsecondary institution, earned a 2.5 cumulative GPA (3.0 GPA for the School of Business), and received a passing grade of C or better in both a college-level English and college-level math course. Additional credentials such as a high school transcript and SAT scores may be requested for admission. 30 of 120 credits required for the bachelor's degree must be completed at Howard. **International Students:** There are 292 international students enrolled. The school actively recruits these students. They must take the TOEFL with a minimum score of 550 on the paper-based TOEFL (PBT) or 79 on the Internet-based version (iBT). If TOEFL is not offered in your country, applicants may submit results from IELTS. They must also take the SAT or ACT.

ADMISSIONS: 55% of the current freshmen were in the top fifth of their class; 81% were in the top two fifths. **Admissions Contact:** Derek Kindle, Director of Student Financial Services. Email: *dkindle@howard.edu* Web: *www.howard.edu*

FINANCIAL AID: In 2016-2017, 93% of all full-time freshmen and 90% of continuing full-time students received some form of financial aid. 50% of all full-time freshmen and 53% of continuing full-time students received need-based aid. The average freshman award was $17,752. Need-based scholarships or need-based grants averaged $5,729 ($15,188 maximum); need-based self-help aid (loans and jobs) averaged $3,699 ($5,000 maximum); non-need-based athletic scholarships averaged $23,128 ($23,970 maximum); and other non-need-based awards and non-need-based scholarships averaged $27,266 ($41,983 maximum). 10% of undergraduate students work part-time. Average annual earnings from campus work are $4900. The average financial indebtedness of the 2016 graduate was $32,071. The FAFSA code is 001448. The priority date for freshman financial aid applications for fall entry is February 1.

THE CATHOLIC UNIVERSITY OF AMERICA C-2

www.cua.edu

Washington, DC 20064 (202) 319-5305 (800) 673-2772

Fax: (202) 319-6533 **Email:** cua-admissions@cua.edu

Full-time: 1601 men, 1972 women	**Faculty:** 270
Part-time: 102 men, 124 women	**Ph.D.s:** 98%
Graduate: n/av	**Student/Faculty:** 10 to 1
Year: semesters, summer session	**Tuition:** $42,536
Room & Board: $13,820	**Freshman Class:** n/av
SAT or ACT: required	**CEEB CODE:** 5104
Application Deadline: February 15	**VERY COMPETITIVE**

The Catholic University of America, founded in 1887 and affiliated with the Roman Catholic Church, offers undergraduate programs in arts and sciences, engineering, architecture, nursing, philosophy, social service, and music. CUA's location provides a unique college experience and a wide spectrum of internship opportunities. A student's academic program determines the rate at which tuition is assessed. The figures in the above capsule and in this profile are approximate. There are 8 undergraduate schools and 12 graduate schools. In addition to regional accreditation, CUA has baccalaureate program accreditation with AACSB, ABET, ACPE, CSWE, NAAB, NASM, NCATE, NLN, and APA. The 180-acre campus is in an urban area in the heart of the nation's capital, Washington, DC. Including any residence halls, there are 52 buildings.

STUDENT LIFE: 96% of undergraduates are from out of state, mostly the Middle Atlantic. Students are from 50 states, 86 foreign countries, and Canada. 56% are from public schools. 8% are Hispanic; 62% White; 6% African American; 4% Foreign; 3% Asian American. 80% are Catholic. **Female To Male Ratio:** 1.2:1. The average age of freshmen is 18; all undergraduates, 20. 20% do not continue beyond their first year; 73% remain to graduate. **Housing:** College-sponsored housing includes single-sex dorms and on-campus apartments. In addition, there are honors houses, special-interest houses, a freshman residential college, and a residential college for upperclassmen, and living and learning communities based on common interest. On-campus housing is available on a first-come, first-served basis, and is available on a lottery system for upperclassmen. 62% of students live on campus. Upperclassmen may keep cars.

FACULTY/CLASSROOMS: 70% teach undergraduates, and 70% do research. No introductory courses are taught by graduate students. The average class size in an introductory lecture is 21; in a laboratory is 20; and in a regular course is 19.

PROGRAMS OF STUDY: CUA confers B.A., B.S., B.A.G.S., B.Arch., B.B.E., B.C.E., B.E.E., B.M., B.M.E., B.S.Arch., B.S.N. and B.S.B.A. degrees. Master's and doctoral degrees are also awarded. Bachelor's degrees are awarded in BIOLOGICAL SCIENCE (biochemistry, biology/biological science, and biotechnology), BUSINESS (accounting, banking and finance, business administration and management, finance, international economics, management science, and marketing and distribution), COMMUNICATIONS AND THE ARTS (art history, art, art history and appreciation, ceramic art and design, classics, communications, dramatic arts, English, English literature, French, German, Greek (classical), Italian, Latin, music, music history and appreciation, music performance, music theory and composition, musical theater, painting, piano/organ, Spanish, studio art, and voice), COMPUTER AND PHYSICAL SCIENCE (chemical physics, chemistry, computer science, elementary particle physics, mathematics, and physics), EDUCATION (art education, drama education, early childhood education, education, elementary education, English education, mathematics education, music education, and secondary education), ENGINEERING AND ENVIRONMENTAL DESIGN (architecture, biomedical engineering, civil engineering, computer engineering, construction engineering, electrical/electronics engineering, engineering, environmental engineering, environmental science, and mechanical engineering), HEALTH PROFESSIONS (medical laboratory technology, medical technology, nursing, predentistry, premedicine, and preveterinary science), SOCIAL SCIENCE (anthropology, economics, French studies, history, liberal arts/general studies, medieval studies, philosophy, political science/government, prelaw, psychology, religion, social science, social work, sociology, Spanish studies, and theological studies). Politics is the strongest academically. Architecture has the largest enrollment.

ACTIVITIES: 1% of men belong to 2 national fraternities. There are 90 groups on campus, including art, cheerleading, choir, chorale, chorus, computers, dance, debate, drama, ethnic, film, honors, international, jazz band, literary magazine, musical theater, newspaper, opera, orchestra, pep band, political, professional, radio and TV, religious, social, social service, student government, symphony, and yearbook. Popular campus events include Luaupalooza, Movies on the Mall, Fall Fiesta, Beaux Arts Ball, and Mistletoe Ball. **Sports:** There are 10 intercollegiate sports for men and 11 for women, and 9 intramural sports for men and 9 for women. The DuFour Athletic Center houses 4 basketball and 5 handball/racquetball courts, a 6-lane, 25-meter swimming pool, a weight training room, an aerobics room, men's and women's saunas, 2 dance studios, an indoor jogging track, and 3 volleyball courts. Outdoor facilities include Cardinal Stadium, made with state-of-the-art FieldTurf, adjoining grass playing fields, baseball and softball facilities, and 6 tennis courts. **Graduates:** The most popular majors were architecture, nursing, and politics. In an average class, 62% graduate in 4 years or less and 68% graduate in 6 years or less. Of the 2015 graduating class, 36% were enrolled in graduate school within 6 months of graduation.

SERVICES: Counseling and information services are available, as is tutoring in most subjects. There is a Center for Academic Success: drop-in tutoring, individual tutoring, smart-thinking online service, and a writing center. There is a reader service for the blind, and remedial math, reading, and writing. Taped books/scanned books, assistive technology, including reading software and screen readers, test accommodations, and sign language interpreters are available. **Library/Resources:** The 3 libraries contain 1.6 million volumes, 1.2 million microform items, and 40,697 audio/video tapes/CDs/DVDs, and subscribe to 10,448 periodicals including electronic. Computerized library services include interlibrary loans, database searching, Internet access, and Wi-Fi capability. Special learning facilities include an art gallery and radio station. **Physically Challenged Students:** 78% of the campus is accessible. Facilities include wheelchair ramps, elevators, special parking, specially equipped restrooms, special class scheduling, lowered drinking fountains, lowered telephones, and special housing. **Special:** Cross-registration is available with the Consortium of Universities of the Washington Metropolitan Area. Opportunities are also provided for internships, accelerated degree programs, dual majors, B.A.-B.S. degrees, work study, pass/fail options, and study abroad in 13 countries. There are 15 national honor societies, Phi Beta Kappa, and a freshman honors program. **Visiting:** There are regularly scheduled orientations for prospective students, visits include an information session with an admissions counselor and a guided campus tour. There are guides for informal visits, visitors may sit in on classes, and stay overnight. To schedule a visit, contact the Admissions Office. **Campus Safety and Security:** Measures include 24-hour foot and vehicle patrol, emergency notification system, self-defense education, and security escort services. There are shuttle buses, emergency telephones, lighted pathways/sidewalks, controlled access to dorms/residences, fixed security posts, emergency whistles, watch captains in every building, and an access control system.

REQUIREMENTS: The SAT or ACT is required. Applicants must be graduates of an accredited secondary school. Students should present 17 academic credits, including 4 each in English and social studies, 3 each in math and science, 2 in foreign languages, and 1 in fine arts or humanities. An essay is required, along with one letter of recommendation, official high school transcripts, and either an SAT or ACT score. An audition is required for music applicants, and a portfolio for architecture applicants is recommended. A GPA of 3.0 is required. AP credits are accepted. Important factors in the admissions decision are extracurricular activities record, leadership record, and advanced placement or honors courses. To graduate, students must complete 120 credit hours, including 36 to 42 hours in the major, with a minimum GPA of 2.0. Courses must meet distribution requirements in theology and religious studies, philosophy, English composition, humanities, language and literature, math and natural sciences, and social and behavioral sciences. A comprehensive exam is required in most majors. **Procedure:** Freshmen are admitted fall and spring. Entrance exams should be taken by February of the senior year of high school. There are early admissions and deferred admissions plans. Early decision applications should be filed by November 15; regular applications, by February 15 for fall entry. The fall 2016 application fee was $55. Notification of early decision is sent December 20; regular decision, March 15. Applications are accepted on-line. **Transfer Students:** Applicants must submit a high school transcript, SAT or ACT scores, and a college transcript. A letter of recommendation and an essay are required. Terms of admission are finalized by the dean of the appropriate school. 60 of 120 credits required for the bachelor's degree must be completed at CUA. **International Students:** There are 66 international students enrolled. The school actively recruits these students. They must take the TOEFL. They must also take the SAT or ACT.

Admissions Contact: Christine Mica, Dean of University Admissions. Email: *cua-admissions@cua.edu* Web: *www.cua.edu*

FINANCIAL AID: In 2016-2017, 90% of all full-time freshmen received some form of financial aid. CUA is a member of CSS. The FAFSA code is 001437. The priority date for freshman financial aid applications for fall entry is February 15.

TRINITY WASHINGTON UNIVERSITY C-2

www.trinitydc.edu

Washington, DC 20017	**(202) 884-9400** **(800) 492-6882**
Fax: (202) 884-9403	**Email: admissions@trinitydc.edu**
Full-time: 17 men, 841 women	**Faculty:** 48; IIB, av$
Part-time: 45 men, 488 women	**Ph.D.s:** 98%
Graduate: 107 men, 515 women	**Student/Faculty:** 12 to 1
Year: semesters	**Tuition:** $23,730
Room & Board: $10,096	**Freshman Class:** n/av
SAT or ACT: recommended	**CEEB CODE:** 5796
Application Deadline: July 31	**COMPETITIVE+**

Trinity Washington University, founded in 1897, is a private, women's liberal arts college in the nation's capital. The school year consists of traditional semesters for its College of Arts and Sciences plus accelerated 8-week terms for its graduate and professional programs. The School of Business and Graduate Studies, School of Professional Studies, School of Education, and School of Nursing and Health Professions offer co-educational options for adult students seeking an associate's, bachelor's, and master's degree with evening, weekend, and hybrid class options. A student's academic program determines the rate at which tuition is assessed. Figures in the above capsule and in this profile are approximate. There are 4 undergraduate schools and 3 graduate schools. In addition to regional accreditation, Trinity has baccalaureate program accreditation with NCATE and CCNE. The 26-acre campus is in an urban area 2 1/2 miles north of the U.S. Capitol. Including any residence halls, there are 8 buildings.

STUDENT LIFE: 51% of undergraduates are from out of state, mostly the Middle Atlantic. Students are from 21 states, and 2 foreign countries. 90% are from public schools. 7% are Hispanic; 68% African American; 6% White; 4% Foreign; 1% Asian American. 52% claim no religious affiliation; 35% Protestant; 12% Catholic. **Female To Male Ratio:** 10.9:1. The average age of freshmen is 18; all undergraduates, 22. 30% do not continue beyond their first year; 50% remain to graduate. **Housing:** 275 students can be accommodated in college housing, which includes single-sex dorms. On-campus housing is available on a first-come, first-served basis, and is available on a lottery system for upperclassmen. Priority is given to out-of-town students. 75% of students commute. Alcohol is not permitted. All students may keep cars.

FACULTY/CLASSROOMS: 35% of faculty are male; 65% are female. 72% teach undergraduates. No introductory courses are taught by graduate students. The average class size in an introductory lecture is 16; in a laboratory is 16; and in a regular course is 13.

PROGRAMS OF STUDY: Trinity confers B.A., and B.S. degrees. Associate and master's degrees are also awarded. Bachelor's degrees are awarded in BIOLOGICAL SCIENCE (biochemistry and biology/biological science), BUSINESS (business administration and management), COMMUNICATIONS AND THE ARTS (communications and English), COMPUTER AND PHYSICAL SCIENCE (chemistry and mathematics), EDUCATION (early childhood education, education, and elementary education), HEALTH PROFESSIONS (exercise science and nursing), SOCIAL SCIENCE (criminal justice, economics, history, human services, international studies, political science/government, psychology, and sociology). Nursing, exercise science, and biology are the strongest academically. Psychology, business administration, and nursing have the largest enrollments.

ACTIVITIES: There are no fraternities or sororities. There are 23 groups on campus, including choir, computers, dance, debate, drama, ethnic, honors, international, literary magazine, newspaper, political, professional, religious, social, social service, student government, and yearbook. Popular campus events include Founders Day, Class Days, Junior Ring Day, and Cap & Gown. **Sports:** There are 5 intercollegiate sports for women and 2 intramural sports for women. Facilities include 2 athletic fields for soccer and lacrosse, a fitness center, 6 tennis courts, and a state-of-the-art sports center with pool, weight room, basketball court and volleyball court. **Graduates:** From July 1, 2015 to June 30, 2016, 130 bachelor's degrees were awarded. The most popular majors were psychology (36%), business administration (15%), and English (10%).

SERVICES: Counseling and information services are available, as is tutoring in every subject. There is a reader service for the blind. There is also signing for hearing-impaired students. **Library/Resources:** The library contains 215,338 volumes, 6,826 microform items, and 13,797 audio/video tapes/CDs/DVDs, and subscribes to 509 periodicals including electronic. Computerized library services include interlibrary loans, database searching, Internet access, and Wi-Fi capability. Special learning facilities include an art gallery. **Physically Challenged Students:** 85% of the campus is accessible. Facilities include wheelchair ramps, elevators, special parking, and specially equipped restrooms. **Special:** Cross-registration is offered through the Consortium of Universities of the Washington Metropolitan Area. Trinity offers internships in all majors and minors, as well as work-study programs. Students may study in France, Italy, and various other countries by arrangement with their faculty adviser. B.A.-B.S. degrees, a 5-year accelerated degree in teaching, dual and student-designed majors, a general studies degree, credit for life experience, nondegree study, and pass/fail options are also available. There are 7 national honor societies, Phi Beta Kappa, and a freshman honors program. **Visiting:** There are regularly scheduled orientations for prospective students, consisting of a half-day program, including an overview of the college, the curriculum, and financing. There are guides for informal visits, visitors may sit in on classes, and stay overnight. To schedule a visit, contact the Office of Admissions. **Campus Safety and Security:** Measures include 24-hour foot and vehicle patrol, self-defense education, and security escort services. There are shuttle buses, emergency telephones, lighted pathways/sidewalks, and controlled access to dorms/residences.

REQUIREMENTS: The SAT or ACT is recommended. Graduation from an accredited secondary school or satisfactory scores on the GED are required for admission. A total of 16 academic credits is required, including 4 years of English and 3 to 4 years each of a foreign language, history, math, and science. An essay or graded writing sample is required, as are two letters of recommendation from faculty/guidance counselor. An interview is optional, but may be required of some applicants. Standardized tests are not required, but are recommended. A GPA of 2.0 is required. AP and CLEP credits are accepted. Important factors in the admissions decision are leadership record, extracurricular activities record, and recommendations by school officials. To graduate, students must complete a total of 128 credit hours with a minimum GPA of 2.0. Between 42 and 60 hours are required in the major. All students must take the courses required in the general education curriculum and must complete a senior seminar, **Procedure:** Freshmen are admitted fall and spring. Entrance exams should be taken by the junior year is preferred. There are deferred admissions and rolling admissions plans. Applications should be filed by July 31 for fall entry, along with a $40 fee. Applications are accepted on-line. **Transfer Students:** 130 transfer students enrolled in 2015-2016. Transfer applicants must have a GPA of 2.5. An interview is recommended, and an essay and recommendation are required. 45 of 128 credits required for the bachelor's degree must be completed at Trinity. **International Students:** There are 2 international students enrolled. They must take the TOEFL with a minimum score of 543 on the paper-based TOEFL (PBT) or 76 on the Internet-based version (iBT).

ADMISSIONS: 2 freshmen graduated first in their class. **Admissions Contact:** Kelly Gosnell, Vice President of Admissions. Email: *admissions@trinitydc.edu* Web: *www.trinitydc.edu*

FINANCIAL AID: In 2016-2017, 98% of all full-time freshmen received some form of financial aid. 98% of all full-time freshmen received need-based aid. Trinity is a member of CSS. The FAFSA code is 001460. Check with the school for current application deadlines.

UNIVERSITY OF THE DISTRICT OF COLUMBIA *(The complete profile is made available exclusively on our website, www.barronspac.com)*

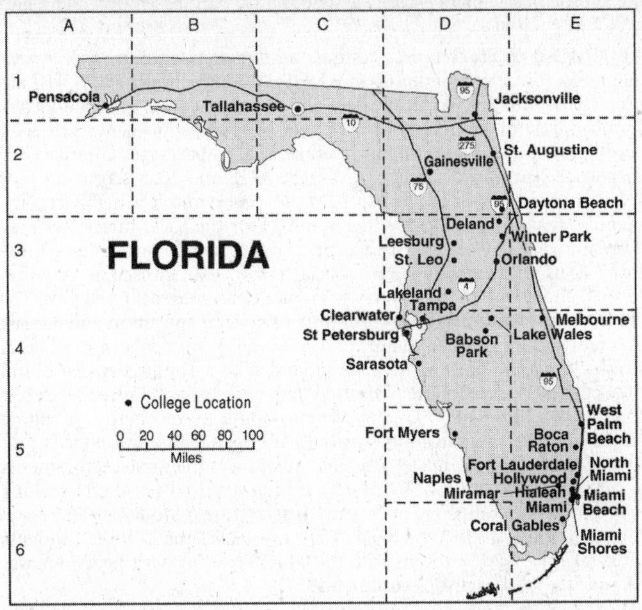

ADVENTIST UNIVERSITY OF HEALTH SCIENCES *(The complete profile is made available exclusively on our website, www.barronspac.com)*

BARRY UNIVERSITY E-5

www.barry.edu

Miami Shores, FL 33161	(305) 899-3134 (800) 695-2279
Fax: (305) 899-2971	Email: admissions@barry.edu
Full-time: 1270 men, 2900 women	**Faculty:** n/av
Part-time: 350 men, 630 women	**Ph.D.s:** 80%
Graduate: 1270 men, 2400 women	**Student/Faculty:** n/av
Year: semesters, summer session	**Tuition:** $28,800
Room & Board: $9030	**Freshman Class:** n/av
SAT or ACT: required	**CEEB CODE:** 5053
Application Deadline: open	**COMPETITIVE**

Barry University, founded by the Dominican Sisters of Adrian, is an independent Roman Catholic institution of liberal arts and professional studies. There are 6 undergraduate schools and 8 graduate schools. In addition to regional accreditation, Barry has baccalaureate program accreditation with CAHEA, NLN, and SACSCOC. The 122-acre campus is in a suburban area 14 miles from Fort Lauderdale and 7 miles north of downtown Miami. Including any residence halls, there are 26 buildings.

STUDENT LIFE: 62% of undergraduates are from Florida. Others are from 47 states, 81 foreign countries, and Canada. 80% are from public schools. 4% are Foreign; 31% Hispanic; 26% White; 24% African American; 1% Asian American. 24% are Catholic. **Female To Male Ratio:** 2.1:1. The average age of freshmen is 18; all undergraduates, 21. **Housing:** 750 students can be accommodated in college housing, which includes single-sex and coed dorms and off-campus apartments. In addition, there are special-interest houses. On-campus housing is guaranteed for the freshman year only, and is available on a first-come, first-served basis, and is available on a lottery system for upperclassmen. Priority is given to out-of-town students. 65% of students commute. All students may keep cars.

FACULTY/CLASSROOMS: 49% of faculty are male; 51% are female. 72% teach undergraduates. No introductory courses are taught by graduate students. The average class size in an introductory lecture is 17; in a laboratory is 14; and in a regular course is 17.

PROGRAMS OF STUDY: Barry confers B.A., B.S., B.F.A., B.L.S., B.P.A., B.P.S., B.S.L.S., B.S.N., B.S.T. and B.S.W. degrees. Master's and doctoral degrees are also awarded. Bachelor's degrees are awarded in BIOLOGICAL SCIENCE (biology/biological science and marine biology), BUSINESS (accounting, international business management, management information systems, management science, marketing/retailing/merchandising, and sports management), COMMUNICATIONS AND THE ARTS (advertising, art, broadcasting, communications, dramatic arts, English, French, music performance, photography, public relations, Spanish, and theater management), COMPUTER AND PHYSICAL SCIENCE (chemistry, computer science, and mathematics), EDUCATION (early childhood education and physical education), ENGINEERING AND ENVIRONMENTAL DESIGN (preengineering), HEALTH PROFESSIONS (cytotechnology, medical technology, nuclear medical technology, nursing, occupational therapy, predentistry, premedicine, prepharmacy, and ultrasound technology), SOCIAL SCIENCE (criminology, economics, history, international studies, liberal arts/general studies, philosophy, political science/government, prelaw, psychology, sociology, and theological studies). Biology, chemistry, and elementary & early childhood education are the strongest academically. Nursing, elementary & early childhood education, and biology have the largest enrollments.

ACTIVITIES: 11% of men belong to 3 national fraternities; 6% of women belong to 2 national sororities. There are 85 groups on campus, including cheerleading, chorale, computers, dance, drama, ethnic, honors, international, literary magazine, musical theater, newspaper, photography, political, professional, radio and TV, religious, social, social service, and student government. Popular campus events include Halloween Dance, Festival of Nations, and World AIDS Day. **Sports:** There are 5 intercollegiate sports for men and 7 for women. Facilities include baseball, softball, and soccer fields, a health and sports center with an indoor gym, outdoor basketball courts, and racquetball and tennis courts, an outdoor swimming pool, a strength and conditioning center, an athletic training room, a human performance lab, and a biomechanics lab.

SERVICES: Counseling and information services are available, as is tutoring in most subjects. There is remedial math, reading, and writing. **Library/Resources:** The library contains 322,079 volumes, 617,792 microform items, and 7,706 audio/video tapes/CDs/DVDs, and subscribes to 1,851 periodicals including electronic. Computerized library services include interlibrary loans and database searching. Special learning facilities include an art gallery, radio station, a human performance lab, biotechnology lab, photography studios, TV studio, theater, biomechanics lab, computer simulation lab, and multimedia business classrooms. **Physically Challenged Students:** 85% of the campus is accessible. Facilities include wheelchair ramps, elevators, special parking, specially equipped restrooms, special class scheduling, lowered drinking fountains, and lowered telephones. **Special:** Barry offers junior- or senior-year internships, a Washington semester for prelaw/political science students, on-campus work-study programs in all departments, dual majors, a liberal studies degree, an accelerated degree program in nursing, nondegree study, and pass/fail options. Students may study in 25 European countries. Barry is a member of the College Consortium for International Studies, students can participate in more than 50 programs offered by members. There are 15 national honor societies and a freshman honors program. **Visiting:** There are guides for informal visits and visitors may sit in on classes. To schedule a visit, contact the Undergraduate Admissions. **Campus Safety and Security:** Measures include 24-hour foot and vehicle patrol, self-defense education, and security escort services. There are shuttle buses, emergency telephones, and lighted pathways/sidewalks.

REQUIREMENTS: The SAT or ACT is required. Graduation from an accredited secondary school or satisfactory scores on the GED are required for admission. A GPA of 2.0 is required. AP and CLEP credits are accepted. To graduate, students must complete 120 credit hours, including at least 48 in upper-division courses, 40 to 60 in the major, and 45 distributed in these curricular divisions: theology and philosophy, written and oral communication, physical or natural science and math, social and behavior sciences, and humanities and the arts. A minimum GPA of 2.0 must be maintained. **Procedure:** Freshmen are admitted to all sessions. Entrance exams should be taken as early as possible. There is a rolling admissions plan. Application deadlines are open. The fall 2016 application fee was $30. Applications are accepted on-line. **Transfer Students:** Applicants must have earned at least 12 acceptable credit hours with a minimum GPA of 2.0. 30 of 120 credits required for the bachelor's degree must be completed at Barry. **International Students:** The school actively recruits these students. They must take the TOEFL with a minimum score of 550 on the paper-based TOEFL (PBT) or 79 on the Internet-based version (iBT).

Admissions Contact: Daniel A Diaz, Director of Admissions. Email: *admissions@barry.edu* Web: *www.barry.edu*

FINANCIAL AID: In 2016-2017, 97% of all full-time freshmen received some form of financial aid. The average freshman award was $20,048. Barry is a member of CSS. The FAFSA code is 001466. Check with the school for current application deadlines.

BEACON COLLEGE D-3

www.beaconcollege.edu

Leesburg, FL 34748	(352) 787-7249
Fax: (352) 787-0721	**Email:** admissions@beaconcollege.edu
Full-time: 120 men, 103 women	**Faculty:** n/av
Part-time: n/av	**Ph.D.s:** 100%
Graduate: n/av	**Student/Faculty:** 12 to 1
Year: semesters, summer session	**Tuition:** $36,172
Room & Board: $10,690	**Freshman Class:** n/av
	CEEB CODE: 3611
Application Deadline: August 20	**COMPETITIVE**

Beacon College, founded in 1989, is a private institution that offers undergraduate degrees in liberal studies, human services, and computer information systems exclusively for students with language-based learning disabilities and/or ADHD. The figures in the above capsule and in this profile are approximate. There is 1 undergraduate school. In addition to regional accreditation, Beacon has baccalaureate program accreditation with SACSCOC. The 2-acre campus is in a small town in the historic downtown Leesburg, approximately 50 miles northwest of Orlando. Including any residence halls, there are 11 buildings.

STUDENT LIFE: 84% of undergraduates are from out of state, mostly the South. Students are from 35 states, and 10 foreign countries. 48% are from public schools. 81% are White; 3% Asian American; 3% Hispanic; 14% African American; 1% Foreign. **Male To Female Ratio:** 1.2:1. The average age of freshmen is 21. 23% do not continue beyond their first year; 76% remain to graduate. **Housing:** College-sponsored housing includes coed on-campus apartments and off-campus apartments. On-campus housing is guaranteed for all 4 years. Alcohol is not permitted. All students may keep cars.

FACULTY/CLASSROOMS: All teach undergraduates. No introductory courses are taught by graduate students. The average class size in an introductory lecture is 8; in a laboratory is 10; and in a regular course is 8.

PROGRAMS OF STUDY: Beacon confers B.A., and B.S. degrees. Associate degrees are also awarded. Bachelor's degrees are awarded in COMPUTER AND PHYSICAL SCIENCE (information sciences and systems), SOCIAL SCIENCE (human services and liberal arts/general studies). Information sciences & systems and liberal studies have the largest enrollments.

ACTIVITIES: There are 15 groups on campus, including performance club, camping club, graphic novel club, theatre goers club, art, beach goers club, choir, computers, drama, literary magazine, musical theater, newspaper, religious, social, social service, student government, and yearbook. **Sports:** There is no sports program at Beacon.

SERVICES: Counseling and information services are available, as is tutoring in every subject. There is remedial math, reading, and writing. There is an academic mentoring program. **Library/Resources:** The library contains 20,075 volumes, and 554 audio/video tapes/CDs/DVDs, and subscribes to 182 periodicals including electronic. Computerized library services include interlibrary loans, database searching, and Internet access. Special learning facilities include an art gallery, center for student success, the writing center, a math lab, supplemental instruction and the Kristin Michelle Mason Art Gallery. **Physically Challenged Students:** 90% of the campus is accessible. Facilities include wheelchair ramps, special parking, specially equipped restrooms, special class scheduling, and special housing. **Special:** Internships, B.A.-B.S. degrees, dual majors, and study abroad are possible. **Visiting:** There are regularly scheduled orientations for prospective students. There are guides for informal visits. To schedule a visit, contact the Admissions Office. **Campus Safety and Security:** Measures include 24-hour foot and vehicle patrol, emergency notification system, and security escort services. There are shuttle buses, lighted pathways/sidewalks, parking enforcement, and safety inspections.

REQUIREMENTS: Required testing and documentation include a clear diagnosis of learning disability or ADHD; Wechsler scales (WAIS-III are preferred) with full scale, cluster, and subtest scores; and Woodcock Johnson Test of Achievement with age- or grade-equivalency scores in reading, writing, and math, and average or above average IQ range with diagnosed learning disability. Although ACT and SAT scores are not required, the information is usual for placement and it is highly recommended that students take either the ACT or the SAT. Interviews may be required. CLEP credits are accepted. Important factors in the admissions decision are evidence of special talent, extracurricular activities record, and geographical diversity. To graduate, students must have 120 credit hours, including 33 credit hours of general education and at least 63 credit hours in their major, and a 2.0 GPA. Students in the liberal studies program must write a thesis and take a comprehensive exam. **Procedure:** Freshmen are admitted fall and spring. Entrance exams should be taken within 3 years prior to application. There is a rolling admissions plan. Application deadlines are open. Application fee is $50. **Transfer Students:** Transfer students must meet the same requirements as all incoming students. 60 of 120 credits required for the bachelor's degree must be completed at Beacon. **International Students:** There was 1 international student enrolled. They must take the TOEFL. Students must take the WAIS subtests with the GLE in reading, writing, and math. SATand/or ACT is also recommended.

Admissions Contact: Stephanie Knight, Director of Admissions. Email: *admissions@beaconcollege.edu* Web: *www.beaconcollege.edu*

FINANCIAL AID: The college's own financial statement is required. The FAFSA code is 033733. Check with the school for current application deadlines.

BETHUNE-COOKMAN UNIVERSITY D-2

www.cookman.edu

Daytona Beach, FL 32114	(386) 481-2600 (800) 448-0228
Fax: (386) 481-2601	**Email:** admissions@cookman.edu
Full-time: 1305 men, 2013 women	**Faculty:** 183; IIB, --$
Part-time: 101 men, 108 women	**Ph.D.s:** 58%
Graduate: 28 men, 23 women	**Student/Faculty:** 16 to 1
Year: semesters, summer session	**Tuition:** $14,410
Room & Board: $8560	**Freshman Class:** 4707 applied, 3152 accepted, 886 enrolled
SAT or ACT: required	**CEEB CODE:** 5061
Application Deadline: July 30	**COMPETITIVE**

Bethune-Cookman University, founded in 1904, is a private liberal arts institution affiliated with the United Methodist Church. The figures in the above capsule and in this profile are approximate. There are 6 undergraduate schools and 2 graduate schools. In addition to regional accreditation, B-CU has baccalaureate program accreditation with NCATE, SACS, and NCATE. The 84-acre campus is in a small town 65 miles east of Orlando. Including any residence halls, there are 63 buildings.

STUDENT LIFE: 67% of undergraduates are from Florida. Others are from 39 states, 21 foreign countries, and Canada. 90% are from public schools. 92% are African American; 3% Foreign; 2% Hispanic; 1% White; 1% Asian American; 1% American Indian/Alaska Native. 56% are Protestant; 28% Seventh Day Adventist, Muslim, and Jehovah Witness. **Female To Male Ratio:** 1.5:1. The average age of freshmen is 18; all undergraduates, 21. 31% do not continue beyond their first year; 69% remain to graduate. **Housing:** 1961 students can be accommodated in college housing, which includes single-sex and coed dorms. In addition, there are honors houses, and leadership house. On-campus housing is guaranteed for the freshman year only, and is available on a first-come, and first-served basis. Priority is given to out-of-town students. 53% of students commute. Alcohol is not permitted. Upperclassmen may keep cars.

FACULTY/CLASSROOMS: 46% of faculty are male; 54% are female. No introductory courses are taught by graduate students. The average class size in an introductory lecture is 20; in a laboratory is 20; and in a regular course is 25.

PROGRAMS OF STUDY: B-CU confers B.A., and B.S. degrees. Master's degrees are also awarded. Bachelor's degrees are awarded in BIOLOGICAL SCIENCE (biology/biological science), BUSINESS (accounting, business administration and management, hotel/motel and restaurant management, and international business management), COMMUNICATIONS AND THE ARTS (communications, dramatic arts, English, modern language, and music), COMPUTER AND PHYSICAL SCIENCE (chemistry, computer science, information sciences and systems, and mathematics), EDUCATION (business education, education, education of the exceptional child, elementary education, English education, music education, physical education, science education, and social science education), ENGINEERING AND ENVIRONMENTAL DESIGN (computer engineering), HEALTH PROFESSIONS (clinical science and nursing), SOCIAL SCIENCE (criminal justice, gerontology, history, international studies, liberal arts/general studies, political science/government, psychology, religion, and sociology). Business administration, education, and nursing are the strongest academically. Criminal justice has the largest enrollment.

ACTIVITIES: 25% of men belong to 5 national fraternities; 35% of women belong to 4 national sororities. There are 60 groups on campus, including band, cheerleading, choir, chorale, computers, dance, drama, drill team, honors, international, jazz band, literary magazine, marching band, newspaper, pep band, political, professional, radio and TV, religious, social, social service, student government, symphony, and yearbook. Popular campus events include Religious Outreach, Career Day, and Founders Day. **Sports:** There are 8 intercollegiate sports for men and 9 for women, and 6 intramural sports for men and 8 for women. Facilities include a gym, weight-rooms, and practice fields. **Graduates:** From July 1, 2015 to June 30, 2016, 561 bachelor's degrees were awarded. The most popular majors were education (15%), criminal justice (14%), and business administration (12%). 240 companies recruited on campus in 2015-2016. In an average class, 2% graduate in 3 years or less, 15% graduate in 4 years or less, 31% graduate in 5 years or less, and 37% graduate in 6 years or less. Of the 2015 graduating class, 20% were enrolled in graduate school within 6 months of graduation, and 17% were employed.

SERVICES: Counseling and information services are available, as is tutoring in most subjects. There is remedial math, reading, and writing. **Library/Resources:** The library contains 162,911 volumes, 45,000 microform items, and 6,345 audio/video tapes/CDs/DVDs, and subscribes to 32,767 periodicals including electronic. Computerized library services include interlibrary loans, database searching, Internet access, and Wi-Fi capability. Special learning facilities include an art gallery, radio station, TV station, an observatory and founders' home and gravesite. **Physically Challenged Students:** 35% of the campus is accessible. Facilities include wheelchair ramps, elevators, special parking, specially equipped restrooms, special class scheduling, lowered drinking fountains, and lowered telephones. **Special:** Students may take courses at other institutions with the approval of the area adviser or registrar. B-CU offers cooperative courses in all divisions, internships related to the student's major, work-study programs, an accelerated degree program in business administration, non-degree-study, and 3-2 engineering degrees. Study abroad is available in South Africa, Ghana, Cuba, Brazil and Zimbabwe. There are 11 national honor societies, a freshman honors program, and 1 departmental honors program. **Visiting:** There are guides for informal visits and visitors may sit in on classes. To schedule a visit, contact the Office of Admissions. **Campus Safety and Security:** Measures include 24-hour foot and vehicle patrol and security escort services. There are lighted pathways/sidewalks, controlled access to dorms/residences, and surveillance cameras and auto-lock door.

REQUIREMENTS: The SAT or ACT is required. Graduation from an accredited secondary school or satisfactory scores on the GED are required for admission. High school courses must include 24 credits with 4 of English, 3 each of math and science, 3 of social science and history, and 6 electives, 2 years of a modern language and 1 year of computer literacy are strongly recommended. Students must submit an essay and a letter of recommendation. A GPA of 2.3 is required. AP and CLEP credits are accepted. Important factors in the admissions decision are recommendations by school officials, leadership record, and geographical diversity. To graduate, students must have a minimum of 120 credit hours with a minimum GPA of 2.0. All students must complete a total of 39 hours in general education requirements, and pass at a specified level a senior exit exam that may include a standardized exam and/or senior area comprehensive exam. They must also complete a senior seminar and senior research paper, and must have 1 year residency, especially the last semester of study at B-CU. **Procedure:** Freshmen are admitted to all sessions. Entrance exams should be taken during the fall prior to application. There are deferred admissions and rolling admissions plans. Applications should be filed by July 30 for fall entry; November 30 for spring entry; and April 30 for summer entry, along with a $25 fee. Notification is sent on a rolling basis. **Transfer Students:** 108 transfer students enrolled in 2015-2016. Applicants must submit transcripts from previous institutions attended and a statement of good standing and eligibility to return. A minimum GPA of 2.25 is required. Students having fewer than 24 credit hours must meet the requirements for entering freshmen. 30 of 120 credits required for the bachelor's degree must be completed at B-CU. **International Students:** There are 70 international students enrolled. The school actively recruits these students. They must take the TOEFL with a minimum score of 550 on the paper-based TOEFL (PBT) or 73 on the Internet-based version (iBT). They must also take the SAT or ACT.

ADMISSIONS: 67% of the 2016-2017 applicants were accepted. **Admissions Contact:** Manicia Finch, Director of Admissions. Email: *admissions@cookman.edu* Web: *www.cookman.edu*

FINANCIAL AID: In 2016-2017, 82% of all full-time freshmen and 92% of continuing full-time students received some form of financial aid. 80% of all full-time freshmen and 89% of continuing full-time students received need-based aid. The average freshman award was $13,190. Need-based scholarships or need-based grants averaged $9,903 ($19,000 maximum); need-based self-help aid (loans and jobs) averaged $3,796 ($5,500 maximum); non-need-based athletic scholarships averaged $10,338 ($22,300 maximum); and other non-need-based awards and non-need-based scholarships averaged $8,380 ($20,000 maximum). 23% of undergraduate students work part-time. Average annual earnings from campus work are $2100. The average financial indebtedness of the 2016 graduate was $21,435. The FAFSA code is 001467. The priority date for freshman financial aid applications for fall entry is April 1.

CARLOS ALBIZU UNIVERSITY *(The complete profile is made available exclusively on our website, www.barronspac.com)*

ECKERD COLLEGE — D-4

www.eckerd.edu

St. Petersburg, FL 33711	(727) 864-8331 (800) 456-9009
Fax: (727) 866-2304	**Email:** admissions@eckerd.edu
Full-time: 638 men, 1170 women	**Faculty:** 122
Part-time: 15 men, 21 women	**Ph.D.s:** 89%
Graduate: n/av	**Student/Faculty:** 13 to 1
Year: 4-1-4, summer session	**Tuition:** $41,538
Room & Board: $11,336	**Freshman Class:** 4603 applied, 3320 accepted, 577 enrolled
SAT CR/M: 550/540 **ACT:** required	**CEEB CODE:** 5223
Application Deadline: April 1	**COMPETITIVE**

Eckerd College, founded in 1958, is a private liberal arts institution affiliated with the Presbyterian Church. Interdisciplinary programs are an important part of the school's curriculum, thus faculty are organized into collegia, rather than into traditional departments. Figures in the above capsule and in this profile are approximate. There is 1 undergraduate school. In addition to regional accreditation, Eckerd has baccalaureate program accreditation with SACSCOC. The 188-acre campus is in a suburban area 1 1/4 miles of Waterfront, 5 miles south of St. Petersburg. Including any residence halls, there are 87 buildings.

STUDENT LIFE: 79% of undergraduates are from out of state, mostly the Middle Atlantic. Students are from 45 states, 40 foreign countries, and Canada. 8% are Hispanic; 78% White; 5% Foreign; 3% African American; 3% two or more races; 2% Asian American; 1% race unknown. **Female To Male Ratio:** 1.8:1. The average age of freshmen is 18; all undergraduates, 20. 19% do not continue beyond their first year; 66% remain to graduate. **Housing:** 1678 students can be accommodated in college housing, which includes single-sex and coed dorms and on-campus apartments. In addition, there are language houses, community service, pet dorms, and substance-free houses. On-campus housing is guaranteed for the freshman year only, and is available on a first-come, first-served basis, and is available on a lottery system for upperclassmen. 88% of students live on campus. All students may keep cars.

FACULTY/CLASSROOMS: 53% of faculty are male; 47% are female. All

teach undergraduates, and all do research. No introductory courses are taught by graduate students. The average class size in a regular course is 19.

PROGRAMS OF STUDY: Eckerd confers B.A., and B.S. degrees. Bachelor's degrees are awarded in AGRICULTURE (environmental studies), BIOLOGICAL SCIENCE (biochemistry, biology/biological science, and marine science), BUSINESS (business administration and management, international business management, and management science), COMMUNICATIONS AND THE ARTS (communications, comparative literature, creative writing, dramatic arts, French, literature, music, Spanish, and visual and performing arts), COMPUTER AND PHYSICAL SCIENCE (chemistry, computer science, geoscience, mathematics, and physics), HEALTH PROFESSIONS (predentistry and premedicine), SOCIAL SCIENCE (American studies, anthropology, classical/ancient civilization, East Asian studies, economics, history, human development, humanities, international relations, philosophy, political science/government, prelaw, psychology, religion, sociology, and women's studies). Marine science, biology, and environmental science have the largest enrollments.

ACTIVITIES: There are no fraternities or sororities. There are 90 groups on campus, including art, band, cheerleading, chess, choir, chorale, chorus, communications, computers, dance, drama, environmental, ethnic, film, honors, international, LGBT, literary magazine, newspaper, photography, political, professional, religious, social, social service, student government, and water search and rescue group. Popular campus events include Festival of Hope, EC Surreal-fest in partnership with the Dali Museum, Festival of Cultures, and Earth Fest. **Sports:** There are 6 intercollegiate sports for men and 8 for women, and 13 intramural sports for men and 13 for women. Facilities include a gym, baseball and softball complex, soccer fields, tennis courts, an open-air multi-purpose sports pavilion, a weight room, fitness room, swimming pool, and waterfront facilities. **Graduates:** From July 1, 2015 to June 30, 2016, 380 bachelor's degrees were awarded. The most popular majors were environmental science (14%), marine science (14%), and psychology (11%). 150 companies recruited on campus in 2015-2016. In an average class, 61% graduate in 4 years or less, 65% graduate in 5 years or less, and 66% graduate in 6 years or less.

SERVICES: Counseling and information services are available, as is tutoring in some subjects, such as math, sciences, and foreign languages. **Library/Resources:** Computerized library services include interlibrary loans, database searching, and Internet access. Special learning facilities include an art gallery. **Physically Challenged Students:** 95% of the campus is accessible. Facilities include wheelchair ramps, elevators, special parking, specially equipped restrooms, special class scheduling, lowered drinking fountains, lowered telephones, and special housing. **Special:** Eckerd offers internships, study abroad, work-study programs, and dual majors in all subjects, interdisciplinary majors in international relations and environmental studies, student-designed majors, nondegree study, and pass/fail options. Students may earn B.A.-B.S. degrees in biology, chemistry, and marine science. A 3-2 engineering degree is offered with Washington and Columbia Universities, a 3-3 Juris Doctorate degree is offered with Florida State University. There are 8 national honor societies, Phi Beta Kappa, and a freshman honors program. **Visiting:** There are regularly scheduled orientations for prospective students, consisting of an interview and a tour. There are guides for informal visits, visitors may sit in on classes, and stay overnight. To schedule a visit, contact the Admissions Office. **Campus Safety and Security:** Measures include 24-hour foot and vehicle patrol, emergency notification system, and security escort services. There are emergency telephones and lighted pathways/sidewalks.

REQUIREMENTS: The SAT or ACT is required. Graduation from an accredited secondary school or satisfactory scores on the GED is required. High school courses must include 4 years of English, 3 years each of math and science, with 2 units of lab, 2 years each of a foreign language and social studies, 1 year of history, and 3 academic electives. SAT: Subject tests in writing, literature, and math are recommended. An essay is required and an interview is recommended. A GPA of 2.0 is required. AP and CLEP credits are accepted. Important factors in the admissions decision are advanced placement or honors courses, leadership record, parents or siblings attended your school, evidence of special talent, personality/intangible qualities, and extracurricular activities record. To graduate, students must complete a total of 36 courses or 126 semester hours with a minimum GPA of 2.0. Required courses include 1 each in the arts, humanities, natural and social sciences, and environmental and global perspectives. Students must also demonstrate competencies in writing, speaking, foreign language, computation, and technology and must take a comprehensive exam or submit a thesis or project in the senior year. **Procedure:** Freshmen are admitted fall, winter, and spring. Entrance exams should be taken in October, November or December. There are early admissions, deferred admissions, and rolling admissions plans. Applications should be filed by April 1 for fall entry; December 1 for winter entry; and December 1 for spring entry, along with a $40 fee. 51 applicants were on the 2016 waiting list; 8 were admitted. Applications are accepted on-line. **Transfer Students:** 62 transfer students enrolled in 2015-2016. Applicants must have a minimum GPA of 2.5. The SAT or ACT is required. An interview is recommended. A faculty recommendation is required. Students may enroll in the fall, winter, spring, and summer. 63 of 126 credits required for the bachelor's degree must be completed at Eckerd. **International Students:** There are 85 international students enrolled. The school actively recruits these students. They must take the TOEFL with a minimum score of 550 on the paper-based TOEFL (PBT) or 79 on the Internet-based version (iBT). They must also take the SAT or ACT.

ADMISSIONS: 72% of the 2016-2017 applicants were accepted. The SAT scores for the 2016-2017 freshman class were: Critical Reading-- 24% below 500, 45% between 500 and 599, 25% between 600 and 699, and 6% between 700 and 800. Math-- 26% below 500, 50% between 500 and 599, 21% between 600 and 699, and 3% between 700 and 800. The ACT scores were 1% between 12 and 17, 32% between 18 and 23, 50% between 24 and 29, and 17% above 30. **Admissions Contact:** John Sullivan, Vice President Enrollment Management. Email: *admissions@eckerd.edu* Web: *www.eckerd.edu*

FINANCIAL AID: The average freshman award was $31,285. Need-based scholarships or need-based grants averaged $23,934; need-based self-help aid (loans and jobs) averaged $4,684; non-need-based athletic scholarships averaged $20,085; other non-need-based awards and non-need-based scholarships averaged $15,937; and $3,265 from other forms of aid. The average financial indebtedness of the 2016 graduate was $36,546. The FAFSA code is 001487. The priority date for freshman financial aid applications for fall entry is March 1.

EDWARD WATERS COLLEGE *(The complete profile is made available exclusively on our website, www.barronspac.com)*

EMBRY-RIDDLE AERONAUTICAL UNIVERSITY - DAYTONA BEACH D-2

www.erau.edu

Daytona Beach, FL 32114

(386) 226-6100
(800) 862-2416
Email: dbadmit@db.erau.edu

Full-time: 4004 men, 1013 women	**Faculty:** IIA, +$
Part-time: 354 men, 76 women	**Ph.D.s:** 78%
Graduate: 405 men, 159 women	**Student/Faculty:** n/av
Year: semesters, summer session	**Tuition:** $33,886
Room & Board: $10,826	**Freshman Class:** 4908 applied, 3469 accepted, 1273 enrolled
SAT CR/M/W: 550/580/530 **ACT:** 25	**CEEB CODE:** 5190
Application Deadline: July 1	**VERY COMPETITIVE**

Embry-Riddle is dedicated to providing applied research solutions to the challenges facing our nation's aerospace, aviation, and related industries. While rooted in aviation, research at our Daytona Beach Campus has expanded to include a diverse range of areas, including engineering, cyber and homeland security, human factors, modeling and simulation, and business. There are 4 undergraduate schools and 4 graduate schools. In addition to regional accreditation, ERAU has baccalaureate program accreditation with ABET, ACBSP, and AABI. The 185-acre campus is in an urban area 48 miles northeast of Orlando. Including any residence halls, there are 45 buildings.

STUDENT LIFE: 64% of undergraduates are from out of state, mostly the South. Students are from 54 states, 105 foreign countries, and Canada. 9% are two or more races; 8% race unknown; 6% African American; 54% White; 5% Asian American; 4% Hispanic; 13% Foreign. **Male To Female Ratio:** 3.8:1. The average age of freshmen is 18; all undergraduates, 21. 28% do not continue beyond their first year; 55% remain to graduate. **Housing:** 2104 students can be accommodated in college housing, which includes coed dorms, on-campus apartments, and off-campus apartments. In addition, there are honors houses. On-campus housing is guaranteed for the freshman year only, and is available on a first-come, first-served basis, and is available on a lottery system for upperclassmen. 64% of students commute. All students may keep cars.

FACULTY/CLASSROOMS: 73% of faculty are male; 27% are female. No introductory courses are taught by graduate students.

PROGRAMS OF STUDY: ERAU confers B.S. degrees. Associate, master's, and doctoral degrees are also awarded. Bachelor's degrees are awarded in BUSINESS (business administration/aviation), COMMUNICATIONS AND THE ARTS (communications), COMPUTER AND PHYSICAL SCIENCE (astronomy and physics, computer science, cyber intelligence/security studies, mathematics/computational, space physics, and software engineering), EDUCATION (global studies), ENGINEERING AND ENVIRONMENTAL DESIGN (aeronautical science, aerospace engineering, aerospace studies, air traffic management, aircraft mechanics, aviation business administration, aviation maintenance technology, civil engineering, computer engineering, electrical and computer engineering, engineering physics, mechanical engineering, and systems engineering), HEALTH PROFESSIONS (electrical engineering and multidisciplinary studies), SOCIAL SCIENCE (homeland security, interdisciplinary studies, and safety science). Aviation, aerospace, and engineering are the strongest academically. Aerospace engineering, aeronautical science, and mechanical engineering have the largest enrollments.

ACTIVITIES: There are 167 groups on campus, including cheerleading, chorale, computers, dance, debate, drama, environmental, ethnic, film, honors, international, LGBT, literary magazine, musical theater, newspaper, pep band, photography, political, professional, radio and TV, religious, social, social service, and student government. Popular campus events include Homecoming, Touch-n-Go events, Bands, Comedians, Magicians, Movies every Thursday night, Student Activities Fair, and Annual Arts & Letters Shakespeare Production. **Sports:** There are 9 intercollegiate sports for men and 10 for women, and 15 intramural sports for men and 15 for women. Facilities include campus recreation, athletics, fitness center, strength-training, a cardio deck, group fitness classes, and an outdoor pool, tennis teams & basketball courts, racquetball & martial arts complex, softball, volleyball, soccer, and playing fields. **Graduates:** From July 1, 2015 to June 30, 2016, 936 bachelor's degrees were awarded. The most popular majors were aerospace engineering (23%), aeronautical science (17%), and aeronautics (12%). In an average class, 2% graduate in 3 years or less, 30% graduate in 4 years or less, 51% graduate in 5 years or less, and 55% graduate in 6 years or less.

SERVICES: Counseling and information services are available, as is tutoring in some subjects, such as first year math, physics, chemistry and writing (composition). There is remedial math, reading, and writing. **Library/Resources:** The library contains 77,356 volumes, 39,380 microform items, and 3,931 audio/video tapes/CDs/DVDs, and subscribes to 1,566 periodicals including electronic. Computerized library services include interlibrary loans, database searching, Internet access, and Wi-Fi capability. Special learning facilities include a radio station, state-of-the-art Advanced Flight Simulation Center, Advanced Vehicles Green Garage, Aerospace Forensics Lab, Air Traffic Control Labs, Applied Aviation Simulation Lab, Aquaponics Lab, Clean Energy Systems Lab, Creekside Observatory, Eagle Flight Research Center, Emil Buehler Aviation Maintenance Science building, Laser Darkroom, Flight Operations Center, Hagedorn Aviation Complex, High-Performance Vehicle Laboratory, Homeland Security Situation Room, Next-Generation ERAU Advanced Research (NEAR) Center, Scanning Electron Microscope, Teaching Airport Kiosk, 1-meter Ritchey-Chretien reflecting telescope (largest university-based research telescope in Florida), Titus Engine Repair Station, Weather Broadcasting and Weather Center Labs, and Wind Tunnel Lab. These are just a few of ERAU's multitude of high-tech labs. **Physically Challenged Students:** 95% of the campus is accessible. Facilities include wheelchair ramps, elevators, special parking, specially equipped restrooms, lowered drinking fountains, and lowered telephones. **Special:** ERAU offers co-op programs and internships in all majors, study abroad in 21 countries, work-study programs, accelerated degree programs in aerospace engineering and engineering physics, credit for life experience, and non-degree study. There are 3 national honor societies and a freshman honors program. **Visiting:** There are regularly scheduled orientations for prospective students. Tours are available weekdays at 9:00 a.m., 11:00 a.m., and 2:00 p.m. All visitors are encouraged to allocate three hours or more for an admission presentation and in-depth tour. There are guides for informal visits and visitors may sit in on classes. To schedule a visit, contact the Admissions Office. **Campus Safety and Security:** Measures include 24-hour foot and vehicle patrol, emergency notification system, self-defense education, and security escort services. There are emergency telephones, lighted pathways/sidewalks, controlled access to dorms/residences, and in-room safes.

REQUIREMENTS: The SAT or ACT is recommended. Students should complete a competitive academic program in high school, including 16 Carnegie units with at least 3 years of math. Admissions decisions are based on the strength of the academic record, rank in class, standardized test scores, recommendations, and the written statement. High school transcript/diploma preferred, GED accepted. A GPA of 2.0 is required. AP and CLEP credits are accepted. To graduate, students must complete a total of 120 to 136 credit hours, including 60 in the major, with a minimum GPA of 2.0. All students must complete 36 credits of general education requirements, including courses in communication skills, technical report writing, humanities/social sciences, math, physical science, economics, and computer science. **Procedure:** Freshmen are admitted fall, spring, and summer. Entrance exams should be taken during spring of the junior year or fall of the senior year. There are deferred admissions and rolling admissions plans. Early decision applications should be filed by December 1; regular applications, by July 1 for fall entry; November 1 for spring entry; and April 1 for summer entry, along with a $50 fee. Notification is sent on a rolling basis. Applications are accepted on-line. **Transfer Students:** 391 transfer students enrolled in 2015-2016. A GPA of 2.5 is preferred. 30 of 120 credits required for the bachelor's degree must be completed at ERAU. **International Students:** There are 640 international students enrolled. The school actively recruits these students. They must take the TOEFL with a minimum score of 550 on the paper-based TOEFL (PBT) or 79 on the Internet-based version (iBT). Applicants whose native language is not English are required to submit official TOEFL or IELTS scores. SAT 1 reasoning test or ACT is strongly recommended for admission for U.S. citizens and permanent residents.

ADMISSIONS: 71% of the 2016-2017 applicants were accepted. The SAT scores for the 2016-2017 freshman class were: Critical Reading-- 27% below 500, 43% between 500 and 599, 26% between 600 and 699, and 4% between 700 and 800. Math-- 18% below 500, 39% between 500 and 599, 35% between 600 and 699, and 8% between 700 and 800. Writing-- 36% below 500, 44% between 500 and 599, 18% between 600 and 699, and 2% between 700 and 800. The ACT scores were 5% between 12 and 17, 30% between 18 and 23, 47% between 24 and 29, and 18% above 30. 42% of the current freshmen were in the top fifth of their class; 69% were in the top two fifths. 21 freshmen graduated first in their class. **Admissions Contact:** Pablo Alvarez, Director of Undergraduate Admissions. Email: *dbadmit@db.erau.edu* Web: *www.erau.edu*

FINANCIAL AID: In 2016-2017, 95% of all full-time freshmen and 84% of continuing full-time students received some form of financial aid. 93% of all full-time freshmen and 82% of continuing full-time students received need-based aid. The average freshman award was $20,560. Need-based scholarships or need-based grants averaged $17,105; need-based self-help aid (loans and jobs) averaged $3,744; and non-need-based athletic scholarships averaged $18,224. 20% of undergraduate students work part-time. Average annual earnings from campus work are $2126. The FAFSA code is 001479. The priority date for freshman financial aid applications for fall entry is March 1.

EMBRY-RIDDLE AERONAUTICAL UNIVERSITY - WORLDWIDE

http://worldwide.erau.edu

Daytona Beach, FL 32114 — **(800) 522-6787**

Fax: (386) 226-6984
Full-time: 2507 men, 376 women
Part-time: 7278 men, 976 women
Graduate: 3367 men, 953 women
Year: other, summer session
Room & Board: $8644
SAT or ACT: recommended
Application Deadline: n/av

Email: worldwide@erau.edu
Faculty: n/av
Ph.D.s: 81%
Student/Faculty: n/av
Tuition: $8836
Freshman Class: n/av

COMPETITIVE

Embry-Riddle Worldwide's programs are designed specifically to suit demanding schedules. We offer the ultimate experience in flexibility with more than 125 campuses across the globe more than 90 of which are located on military bases, 12 enrollment dates per year, five modes of learning, and coursework that can be completed as it fits into your busy life. There are 3 undergraduate schools and 3 graduate schools. In addition to regional accreditation, ERAU - Worldwide has baccalaureate program accreditation with ACBSP, AABI, and Project Management Institute Global Accreditation. The campus is in a suburban area Embry-Riddle Aeronautical University's Worldwide Campus is made up of over 125 locations in the United States, Europe, the Middle East, and Asia.

STUDENT LIFE: 9% are African American; 6% Hispanic; 6% two or more races; 55% White; 4% Foreign; 3% Asian American; 15% race unknown. **Male To Female Ratio:** 5.7:1. The average age of freshmen is 27; all undergraduates, 32. 28% remain to graduate.

FACULTY/CLASSROOMS: 72% of faculty are male; 28% are female. No introductory courses are taught by graduate students.

PROGRAMS OF STUDY: ERAU - Worldwide confers B.S. degrees. Associate, master's, and doctoral degrees are also awarded. Bachelor's degrees are awarded in BIOLOGICAL SCIENCE (industrial/organizational psychology), BUSINESS (logistics, management information systems, management, management & strategic leadership, and transportation management), COMMUNICATIONS AND THE ARTS (communications and information technology), ENGINEERING AND ENVIRONMENTAL DESIGN (aerospace engineering, aviation business administration, aviation maintenance management, emergency/disaster science, engineering management, engineering science, engineering technology, occupational safety and health, systems engineering, technical operations management, and transportation engineering), SOCIAL SCIENCE (interdisciplinary studies, psychology, safety and security technology, and safety management). Aeronautics, aeronautical science, and technical management are the strongest academically. Aeronautics, technical management, and master of aeronautical science have the largest enrollments.

ACTIVITIES: There are no fraternities or sororities. **Sports:** There is no sports program at ERAU - Worldwide. **Graduates:** From July 1, 2015 to June 30, 2016, 1637 bachelor's degrees were awarded. The most popular majors were aeronautics (64%), technical management (25%), and aviation maintenance (7%). In an average class, 16% graduate in 3 years or less, 22% graduate in 4 years or less, 26% graduate in 5 years or less, and 28% graduate in 6 years or less.

SERVICES: **Library/Resources:** The library contains 77,356 volumes, 39,380 microform items, and 3,931 audio/video tapes/CDs/DVDs, and subscribes to 1,566 periodicals including electronic. Computerized library services include interlibrary loans, database searching, Internet access, and Wi-Fi capability. **Special:** Embry-Riddle Aeronautical University is the world's oldest and largest fully accredited university specializing in aviation and aerospace. With more than 150 campuses, Embry-Riddle Worldwide's online and web-based EagleVision Home courses provide you the flexibility you need to complete your studies no matter where you are, day or night. Members of the military don't have to worry about getting transferred and starting over – they can take their studies with them.

REQUIREMENTS: The SAT or ACT is recommended. Embry-Riddle considers all aspects of a student's qualifications and offers admission to the most competitive applicants, building a talented and diverse population of students motivated toward careers in aviation and aerospace. Applications for admission are valid for one year from date received. Admitted students must enroll and maintain enrollment beyond the add/drop period within one year of admission or must reapply. The following documentation is required for consideration of admission for all applicants under the age of 20 that are not active members of the United States military and not a transfer student. An Official High School transcript or equivalent (GED). Rigor of high school academic program and academic performance will be assessed 2.0 GPA or higher on a 4.0 scale, SAT with a minimum score of 1000 -OR- ACT with a minimum score of 21, 300-500 word essay, 2 letters of recommendation from a school counselor or teacher, an official transcripts from all post-secondary accredited degree-granting institutions with less than 12 college credits earned, if applicable. The university expects all applicants, at a minimum, to have completed by high school graduation the following course work: 4 years of English, 3 years of mathematics, including algebra I or applied math I & II, formal logic or geometry, 2 years of history or social science, 2 years of science in at least two different areas, with at least one lab experience. Applicants age 20 and over that are not classified as a transfer student or have not served in the military must provide the following documentation: Official High School transcript or equivalent (GED) 2.0 GPA or higher on a 4.0 scale, official transcripts from all post-secondary accredited degree-granting institutions attended, and a resume. A GPA of 2.0 is required. AP and CLEP credits are accepted. Graduate students are required to complete all graduate coursework with ERAU with a maximum of 12 credit hours of transfer work permitted. For undergraduate degree completion, at least 25 percent of semester credit hours must be earned through ERAU instruction. Students pursuing any undergraduate degree must earn a minimum cumulative grade point average (CGPA) of 2.0 for all work completed within the degree program at the University. Students pursuing any graduate degree must earn a minimum cumulative grade point average (CGPA) of 3.0 for all work completed within the degree program at the University. Students must complete the general graduation requirements as prescribed by the University, as well as all degree requirements specified in the degree program being pursued. Graduation requirements are not subject to petition or waiver. Students must initiate an application for graduation through the student information system, and follow up by completing a Graduation Information Sheet in ERNIE. A qualified student will not be graduated by ERAU until a graduation application and information sheet have been received and processed by the University, and the graduation fee has been remitted. **Procedure:** Freshmen are admitted to all sessions. There are deferred admissions and rolling admissions plans. Application deadlines are open. Application fee is $50. Notification is sent on a rolling basis. Applications are accepted on-line. **Transfer Students:** Applicants who graduated from high school and subsequently completed a minimum of 12 semester hours of college level credit from an accredited degree granting institution are considered transfer students. Embry-Riddle considers each application for transfer admission individually, reviewing the student's academic record, grades received in all college-level courses, completion of fundamental studies in English and Mathematics, and the rigor of the student's academic program. To be considered for admission a transfer applicant must have a minimum of a 2.0 cumulative grade point average (CGPA) on a 4.0 scale from an accredited degree granting institution. When an applicant has attended more than one institution, a cumulative average for all previous college work attempted will be calculated to determine the overall CGPA, official transcripts from all colleges and universities (postsecondary) accredited degree-granting institutions attended, military documents, if applicable. 30 of 120 credits required for the bachelor's degree must be completed at ERAU - Worldwide. **International Students:** The school actively recruits these students. They must take the TOEFL with a minimum score of 550 on the paper-based TOEFL (PBT) or 79 on the Internet-based version (iBT).

Admissions Contact: Admissions Office Email: *worldwide@erau.edu* Web: *http:/worldwide.erau.edu*

FINANCIAL AID: In 2016-2017, 51% of all full-time freshmen and 50% of continuing full-time students received some form of financial aid. 48% of all full-time freshmen and 47% of continuing full-time students received need-based aid. The average freshman award was $8,635. Need-based scholarships or need-based grants averaged $3,926; and need-based self-help aid (loans and jobs) averaged $3,650. The FAFSA code is 001479. The priority date for freshman financial aid applications for fall entry is March 1.

FLAGLER COLLEGE D-2
www.flagler.edu

St. Augustine, FL 32084 (904) 829-6481
(800) 304-4208

Fax: (904) 819-6466
Email: admissions@flagler.edu

Full-time: 1017 men, 1585 women	**Faculty:** 112; IIB, -$
Part-time: 42 men, 58 women	**Ph.D.s:** 69%
Graduate: n/av	**Student/Faculty:** 22 to 1
Year: semesters, summer session	**Tuition:** $16,830
Room & Board: $9630	**Freshman Class:** 3589 applied, 2617 accepted, 620 enrolled
SAT CR/M/W: 540/510/520 **ACT:** 24	**CEEB CODE:** 5235
Application Deadline: March 1	**COMPETITIVE**

Flagler College, founded in 1968, is an independent liberal arts college that emphasizes undergraduate education in select liberal studies and preprofessional studies. There is 1 undergraduate school. The 49-acre campus is in a small town 35 miles south of Jacksonville and 45 miles north of Daytona Beach. Including any residence halls, there are 36 buildings.

STUDENT LIFE: 58% of undergraduates are from Florida. Others are from 43 states, 44 foreign countries, and Canada. 77% are White. **Female To Male Ratio:** 1.6:1. The average age of freshmen is 18; all undergraduates, 21. 28% do not continue beyond their first year; 65% remain to graduate. **Housing:** 1025 students can be accommodated in college housing, which includes single-sex dorms. On-campus housing is guaranteed for the freshman year only, and is available on a first-come, first-served basis. 63% of students commute. Alcohol is not permitted. All students may keep cars.

FACULTY/CLASSROOMS: 49% of faculty are male; 51% are female. All teach undergraduates. No introductory courses are taught by graduate students. The average class size in an introductory lecture is 19; in a laboratory is 20; and in a regular course is 18.

PROGRAMS OF STUDY: Flagler confers B.A., and B.F.A. degrees. Bachelor's degrees are awarded in BUSINESS (accounting, business administration and management, and sports management), COMMUNICATIONS AND THE ARTS (art history, communications, dramatic arts, English, fine arts, graphic design, journalism, film and media studies, public relations, Spanish, strategic communication, and theatre arts), EDUCATION (art education, education of the deaf and hearing impaired, education of the exceptional child, elementary education, English education, and social studies secondary school education), ENGINEERING AND ENVIRONMENTAL DESIGN (environmental science), SOCIAL SCIENCE (criminology, economics, history, international studies, Latin American studies, liberal arts/general studies, philosophy and religion, political science/government, psychology, public administration, public history/archives, and sociology). Business, education, communication, and coastal environmental science are the strongest academically. Psychology, communication, and business administration have the largest enrollments.

ACTIVITIES: There are no fraternities or sororities. There are 45 groups on campus, including art, cheerleading, choir, chorus, dance, dive club, deaf awareness club, drama, environmental, ethnic, film, honors, international, LGBT, literary magazine, musical theater, newspaper, photography, political, professional, radio and TV, religious, social, social service, and student government. Popular campus events include De-Stress Day, Bachelor Bids, Harry Potter Month, Halloween Midnight Breakfast, and Flagler Follies. **Sports:** There are 7 intercollegiate sports for men and 8 for women, and 12 intramural sports for men and 12 for women. Facilities include an athletic complex which includes baseball, softball and soccer fields, with locker rooms, a 6-court tennis facility and on-site gymnasium that houses the weight room facility and locker rooms for men's & women's basketball and volleyball. **Graduates:** From July 1, 2014 to June 30, 2015, 562 bachelor's degrees were awarded. The most popular majors were business administration (15%), communication (11%), and psychology (11%). 230 companies recruited on campus in 2014-2015. In an average class, 3% graduate in 3 years or less, 45% graduate in 4 years or less, 58% graduate in 5 years or less, and 61% graduate in 6 years or less. Of the 2014 graduating class, 16% were enrolled in graduate school within 6 months of graduation, and 51% were employed.

SERVICES: Counseling and information services are available, as is tutoring in most subjects, such as business, finance, accounting, higher math, natural sciences, study skills, and Spanish. There is a reader service for the blind, remedial math, reading, and writing. **Library/Resources:** The library contains 100,454 volumes, 3,893 audio/video tapes/CDs/DVDs, and subscribes to 639 periodicals including electronic. Computerized library services include interlibrary loans, database searching, Internet access, and Wi-Fi capability. Special learning facilities include an art gallery, radio station, Learning Resource Center for assistance in writing, mathematics, and study skills. **Physically Challenged Students:** 90% of the campus is accessible. Facilities include wheelchair ramps, elevators, special parking, specially equipped restrooms, special class scheduling, lowered drinking fountains, lowered telephones, and special housing. **Special:** The school offers internships, work-study, and dual majors. Students may participate in study-abroad programs in almost any country. Students majoring in deaf education can work directly with students at the Florida State School for the Deaf and Blind. There are 11 national honor societies and 7 departmental honors programs. **Visiting:** There are regularly scheduled orientations for prospective students, Prospective Student Information Sessions, and tours Monday-Friday (30 minute presentation by an Admissions Representative and tour of campus by a Student Ambassador); Each fall and spring, we offer a day-long Campus Visit Day on a Saturday. There are guides for informal visits and visitors may sit in on classes. To schedule a visit, contact Philadelphia Shoop at pshoop@flagler.edu. **Campus Safety and Security:** Measures include 24-hour foot and vehicle patrol, emergency notification system, self-defense education, and security escort services. There are shuttle buses, emergency telephones, lighted pathways/sidewalks, controlled access to dorms/residences, and uniformed police officer from 6 pm to 6 am.

REQUIREMENTS: The SAT or ACT is required. The ACT Optional Writing test is also required. Student must have graduated from an accredited secondary school or have a satisfactory score on the GED. Students must have a total of 19 academic credits. High school courses must include 4 credits of English, 3 credits each of math and science, and 2 credits of a foreign language. An essay is required, and an interview is recommended. AP and CLEP credits are accepted. Important factors in the admissions decision are advanced placement or honors courses, leadership record, and extracurricular activities record. To graduate a student must complete 120 semester hours with at least a 2.0 grade point average. Completion of at least one major required in accordance with the requirements set forth by the academic department. Completion of 39 hours in General Education. Students are required to take a minimum of five courses designated Writing Intensive within the General Education curriculum. Students must earn a grade of "C-" or better in ENG 152 or ENG 172. The final 30 credit hours required for the degree must be earned at Flagler College. **Procedure:** Freshmen are admitted fall and spring. Entrance exams should be taken during the fall of the senior year at the latest. There are early decision, early admissions, and deferred admissions plans. Early decision applications should be filed by November 1; regular applications, by March 1 for fall entry; and December 15 for spring entry, along with a $50 fee. Notification of early decision is sent December 15; regular decision, March 31. 279 early decision candidates were accepted for the 2015-2016 class. 59 applicants were on the 2015 waiting list; 21 were admitted. Applications are accepted on-line. **Transfer Students:** 315 transfer students enrolled in 2014-2015. Applicants transferring from another institution must be in good standing with a satisfactory grade point average for all work attempted and must be eligible to return to the institution last attended. Transfer applicants from four-year institutions may receive a maximum of 75 semester hours of credit awarded. Applicants who transfer from junior or community colleges will be allowed no more than 64 semester hours of credit toward the completion of degree requirements at Flagler. The College imposes a minimum testing requirement for students planning to major in Education. All Education majors must have a combined score (Critical Reading plus Mathematics) of at least 1010 on a single administration of the SAT or a composite score of at least 21 on the ACT. 45 of 120 credits required for the bachelor's degree must be completed at Flagler. **International Students:** There are 76 international students enrolled. The school actively recruits these students. They must take the TOEFL with a minimum score of 550 on the paper-based TOEFL (PBT) or 75 on the Internet-based version (iBT). They must also take the SAT or ACT.

ADMISSIONS: 73% of the 2015-2016 applicants were accepted. The SAT scores for the 2015-2016 freshman class were: Critical Reading--28% below 500, 50% between 500 and 599, 21% between 600 and 699, and 1% between 700 and 800. Math-- 40% below 500, 49% between 500 and 599, and 12% between 600 and 699. Writing-- 33% below 500, 48% between 500 and 599, 19% between 600 and 699, and 1% between 700 and 800. The ACT scores were 1% between 12 and 17, 48% between 18 and 23, 45% between 24 and 29, and 6% above 30. **Admissions Contact:** Deborah Thompson, Vice President of Enrollment Management. Email: *admissions@flagler.edu* Web: *www.flagler.edu*

FINANCIAL AID: In 2015-2016, 91% of all full-time freshmen and 90% of continuing full-time students received some form of financial aid. 58% of all full-time freshmen and 60% of continuing full-time students received need-based aid. The average freshman award was $15,452. Need-based scholarships or need-based grants averaged $5,729; need-based self-help aid (loans and jobs) averaged $3,405; non-need-based athletic scholarships averaged $7,304; and other non-need-based awards and non-need-based scholarships averaged $9,639. 64% of undergraduate students work part-time. Average annual earnings from campus work are $1400. The average financial indebtedness of the 2015 graduate was $26,048. The FAFSA, and Florida resident affidavit if applying for the Florida Resident Access Grant, is required. The priority date for freshman financial aid applications for fall entry is April 1.

FLORIDA AGRICULTURAL AND MECHANICAL UNIVERSITY C-1

www.famu.edu

Tallahassee, FL 32307 (850) 599-3796

Fax: (850) 599-3069 Email: ugradadmissions@famu.edu

Full-time: 2306 men, 4311 women
Part-time: 472 men, 721 women
Graduate: 644 men, 1165 women
Year: semesters, summer session
Room & Board: $10,100

SAT CR/M/W: 515/503/494 **ACT:** 23
Application Deadline: May 15

Faculty: 415; IIA, av$
Ph.D.s: 74%
Student/Faculty: 15 to 1
Tuition: $5785 ($17,725)
Freshman Class: 5198 applied, 1755 accepted, 855 enrolled
CEEB CODE: 5215
COMPETITIVE

Florida Agricultural and Mechanical University, founded in 1887, is a public institution within the state university system of Florida, offers undergraduate programs in agriculture, allied health science, architecture, the arts and sciences, business and industry, education, engineering, journalism, pharmacy and pharmaceutical sciences, upper-level nursing, and technology. There are 12 undergraduate schools and 1 graduate school. In addition to regional accreditation, FAMU has baccalaureate program accreditation with AACSB, ABET, ACEJMC, ACPE, APTA, CSWE, NAAB, NCATE, and NLN. The 422-acre campus is in an urban area 169 miles west of Jacksonville, Florida. Including any residence halls, there are 211 buildings.

STUDENT LIFE: 87% of undergraduates are from Florida. Others are from 45 states, 59 foreign countries, and Canada. 84% are African American; 3% Hispanic; 2% Foreign; 10% White; 1% Asian American. **Female To Male Ratio:** 1.8:1. The average age of freshmen is 19; all undergraduates, 21. 20% do not continue beyond their first year; 40% remain to graduate. **Housing:** 2394 students can be accommodated in college housing, which includes single-sex dorms, on-campus apartments, and married student housing. On-campus housing is guaranteed for the freshman year only, and is available on a first-come, first-served basis. Priority is given to out-of-town students. 73% of students commute. Alcohol is not permitted. Upperclassmen may keep cars.

FACULTY/CLASSROOMS: 54% of faculty are male; 46% are female. 72% teach undergraduates, 72% do research, and 72% do both. No introductory courses are taught by graduate students.

PROGRAMS OF STUDY: FAMU confers B.A., B.Arch., B.C.J., B.S., B.S.Arch. and Constr.E.T., B.S.Arch.E.T., B.S.Studies., B.S.C.E., B.S.C.E.T., B.S.Ch.E., B.S.Constr.E.T., B.S.E.E., B.S.Elect.E.T., B.S.H.C.M., B.S.I.E., B.S.J., B.S.M.E., B.S.M.R.A., B.S.N., B.S.Pharm., B.S.P.T., B.S.R.T., B.S.T. and B.S.W. degrees. Associate, master's, and doctoral degrees are also awarded. Bachelor's degrees are awarded in AGRICULTURE (animal science and horticulture), BIOLOGICAL SCIENCE (biology/biological science), BUSINESS (accounting, banking and finance, business administration and management, and business economics), COMMUNICATIONS AND THE ARTS (dramatic arts, English, fine arts, journalism, and music), COMPUTER AND PHYSICAL SCIENCE (actuarial science, chemistry, computer science, mathematics, and physics), EDUCATION (art education, business education, early childhood education, elementary education, industrial arts education, music education, and science education), ENGINEERING AND ENVIRONMENTAL DESIGN (chemical engineering, civil engineering, electrical/electronics engineering, engineering technology, industrial engineering, and mechanical engineering), HEALTH PROFESSIONS (nursing, occupational therapy, pharmacy, physical therapy, predentistry, and premedicine), SOCIAL SCIENCE (criminal justice, economics, history, political science/government, psychology, public administration, social science, social work, and sociology). Business, engineering, and pharmacy are the strongest academically. Business administration, management, and biology/bological sciences have the largest enrollments.

ACTIVITIES: 2% of men belong to 4 national fraternities; 3% of women belong to 4 national sororities. There are 135 groups on campus, including cheerleading, choir, chorus, dance, drama, drill team, ethnic, honors, international, jazz band, marching band, newspaper, orchestra, pep band, political, professional, radio and TV, religious, social, social service, student government, and symphony. Popular campus events include FAMU Essen-Theater, FAMU Orchesis Dance Theater and Ebony Fashion Fair. **Sports:** There are 8 intercollegiate sports for men and 8 for women. Facilities include a 3,300-seat gym, a 1,600-seat auditorium, a 25,559-seat football stadium, swimming pools, baseball diamonds, softball and track fields, tennis courts, a bowling alley, pool hall, a student activities center, and a fitness center. **Graduates:** From July 1, 2015 to June 30, 2016, 1653 bachelor's degrees were awarded. The most popular majors were health (17%), business administration and management (9%), and criminal justice (7%). 76 companies recruited on campus in 2015-2016. In an average class, 13% graduate in 4 years or less, 29% graduate in 5 years or less, and 38% graduate in 6 years or less. Of the 2015 graduating class, 33% were enrolled in graduate school within 6 months of graduation.

SERVICES: Counseling and information services are available, as is tutoring in some subjects, such as math, English, and reading. There is remedial math, reading, and writing. **Library/Resources:** The 4 libraries contain 1.5 million volumes, 515,136 microform items, and 63,067 audio/video tapes/CDs/DVDs, and subscribe to 302,781 periodicals including electronic. Computerized library services include interlibrary loans, database searching, Internet access, and Wi-Fi capability. Special learning facilities include an art gallery, radio station, TV station, an Black Archives, and a observatory. **Physically Challenged Students:** 90% of the campus is accessible. Facilities include wheelchair ramps, elevators, special parking, and specially equipped restrooms. **Special:** Cooperative programs and cross-registration are offered in conjunction with Florida State University. Internships are available either on or off campus. Florida A&M also offers a Washington semester for architecture majors, a B.A.-B.S. degree, credit for life experience, and pass/fail options. Nondegree study is possible. There is a freshman honors program. **Visiting:** There are regularly scheduled orientations for prospective students. There are guides for informal visits and visitors may sit in on classes. To schedule a visit, contact the Admissions Office. **Campus Safety and Security:** Measures include 24-hour foot and vehicle patrol, emergency notification system, self-defense education, and security escort services. There are shuttle buses, emergency telephones, and lighted pathways/sidewalks.

REQUIREMENTS: The SAT or ACT is required, with a satisfactory score on the SAT, or 19 on the ACT. Applicants must be graduates of accredited secondary schools or have earned a GED. The university requires 19 academic credits, including 4 each in English and academic electives, 3 each in math, science, and social studies, and 2 in foreign language. A GPA of 2.5 is required. AP and CLEP credits are accepted. Important factors in the admissions decision are recommendations by school officials, extracurricular activities record, and evidence of special talent. General education requirements include 36 credit hours in English, humanities, social science, natural science, American history, foreign language, and math at the college algebra level or above. In order to graduate, students must complete at least 120 credit hours, including 30 in a major field, with a minimum GPA of 2.0. **Procedure:** Freshmen are admitted to all sessions. Entrance exams should be taken by the fall of the senior year. There are deferred admissions and rolling admissions plans. Applications should be filed by May 15 for fall entry; November 15 for spring entry; and April 1 for summer entry, along with a $30 fee. Applications are accepted on-line. **Transfer Students:** 496 transfer students enrolled in 2015-2016. Applicants must present a minimum GPA of 2.0 in at least 60 semester hours or 90 quarter hours earned. 30 of 120 credits required for the bachelor's degree must be completed at FAMU. **International Students:** There are 80 international students enrolled. They must take the TOEFL with a minimum score of 500 on the paper-based TOEFL (PBT) or 61 on the Internet-based version (iBT). They must also take the SAT or ACT.

ADMISSIONS: 34% of the 2016-2017 applicants were accepted. The SAT scores for the 2016-2017 freshman class were: Critical Reading-- 61% below 500, 27% between 500 and 599, 11% between 600 and 699, and 2% between 700 and 800. Math-- 63% below 500, 28% between 500 and 599, and 9% between 600 and 699. Writing-- 68% below 500, 23% between 500 and 599, and 8% between 600 and 699. The ACT scores were 18% between 12 and 17, 61% between 18 and 23, 19% between 24 and 29, and 2% above 30. **Admissions Contact:** Barbara Cox, Director. Email: *ugradadmissions@famu.edu* Web: *www.famu.edu*

FINANCIAL AID: The FAFSA code is 001480. The priority date for freshman financial aid applications for fall entry is March 1.

FLORIDA ATLANTIC UNIVERSITY E-5
www.fau.edu

Boca Raton, FL 33431	**(561) 297-3040** **(800) 299-4FAU**
Fax: (561) 297-2758	**Email: admissions@fau.edu**
Full-time: 7085 men, 8508 women	**Faculty:** 875; I, --$
Part-time: 3843 men, 5387 women	**Ph.D.s:** 90%
Graduate: 1991 men, 3224 women	**Student/Faculty:** 22 to 1
Year: semesters, summer session	**Tuition:** $5986 ($21,543)
Room & Board: $11,353	**Freshman Class:** 27888 applied, 10876 accepted, 3237 enrolled
SAT CR/M/W: required **ACT:** required	**CEEB CODE:** 5529
Application Deadline: May 1	**COMPETITIVE**

Florida Atlantic University, founded in 1964, FAU was one of the few universities in the country to offer only upper-division and graduate-level work on the theory that freshmen and sophomores could be served by the community college system. Today, with its well-developed system of distributed campuses and sites that offer students high-quality degree programs at seven locations, FAU serves as a model for America's urban, regional universities. Figures in the above capsule and in this profile are approximate. There are 9 undergraduate schools and 8 graduate schools. In addition to regional accreditation, FAU has baccalaureate program accreditation with AACSB, ABET, CSAB, CSWE, NAAB, NASM, NCATE, NLN, ACS, ASLHA, NAACLS, and NASPAA. The 850-acre campus is in a suburban area 17 miles north of Ft. Lauderdale, 45 miles north of Miami, and 22 miles south of Palm Beach. Including any residence halls, there are 160 buildings.

STUDENT LIFE: 95% of undergraduates are from Florida. Others are from 49 states, 135 foreign countries, and Canada. 73% are from public schools. 50% are White; 4% Asian American; 22% Hispanic; 2% Foreign; 18% African American; 1% American Indian/Alaska Native. **Female To Male Ratio:** 1.3:1. The average age of freshmen is 18; all undergraduates, 24. 22% do not continue beyond their first year; 43% remain to graduate. **Housing:** 3750 students can be accommodated in college housing, which includes single-sex and coed dorms and on-campus apartments. In addition, there are honors houses, special-interest houses, living learning communities, and theme housing. On-campus housing is guaranteed for the freshman year only, and is available on a first-come, first-served basis. 94% of students commute. All students may keep cars.

FACULTY/CLASSROOMS: 54% of faculty are male; 46% are female. All teach undergraduates, and do research. No introductory courses are taught by graduate students. The average class size in an introductory lecture is 38; in a laboratory is 21; and in a regular course is 29.

PROGRAMS OF STUDY: FAU confers B.A., B.S., B.A.E., B.Arch., B.B.A., B.E.C.E. B.F.A., B.H.S., B.I.E.T., B.Mus., B.P.M., B.S.C.E., B.S.C.V., B.S.E., B.S.E.E., B.S.G.E., B.S.H.S., B.S.M.E., B.S.M.T., B.S.N., B.S.O.E., B.S.W. and B.U.R.P. degrees. Associate, master's, and doctoral degrees are also awarded. Bachelor's degrees are awarded in BIOLOGICAL SCIENCE (biology/biological science and marine biology), BUSINESS (accounting, banking and finance, business administration and management, business economics, hospitality management services, human resources, international business management, management information systems, marketing/retailing/merchandising, real estate, and small business management), COMMUNICATIONS AND THE ARTS (art, communications, dramatic arts, English, fine arts, French, German, graphic design, Italian, jazz, journalism, linguistics, media arts, multimedia, music, Spanish, and visual and performing arts), COMPUTER AND PHYSICAL SCIENCE (chemistry, computer science, computer security and information assurance, geology, information sciences and systems, mathematics, and physics), EDUCATION (education of the exceptional child, elementary education, English education, foreign languages education, physical education, and special education), ENGINEERING AND ENVIRONMENTAL DESIGN (architecture, civil engineering, computer engineering, electrical/electronics engineering, engineering, mechanical engineering, ocean engineering, and urban planning technology), HEALTH PROFESSIONS (health care administration, health science, medical laboratory technology, and nursing), SOCIAL SCIENCE (anthropology, criminal justice, economics, geography, history, interdisciplinary studies, Judaic studies, liberal arts/general studies, philosophy, political science/government, psychobiology, psychology, public administration, social psychology, social science, social work, and sociology). Engineering, education, and business are the strongest academically. Biological science, psychology, and elementary education have the largest enrollments.

ACTIVITIES: 1% of men belong to 11 national fraternities; 1% of women belong to 8 national sororities. There are 250 groups on campus, including art, band, cheerleading, chess, choir, chorale, chorus, computers, dance, debate, drama, drill team, environmental, ethnic, film, forensics, honors, international, jazz band, LGBT, literary magazine, marching band, musical theater, newspaper, opera, orchestra, pep band, photography, political, professional, radio and TV, religious, social, social service, student government, and symphony. Popular campus events include Luau, African American Festival, Festival of Nations, and Homecoming. **Sports:** There are 8 intercollegiate sports for men and 9 for women, and 10 intramural sports for men and 10 for women. Facilities include weight rooms, training rooms, lighted baseball, softball, and soccer stadiums, arena for volleyball and basketball, cross country and track field complex, football practice field, aquatic center tennis courts, fitness center with cardio, outdoor basketball courts, practice fields, and a football stadium. **Graduates:** From July 1, 2015 to June 30, 2016, 4892 bachelor's degrees were awarded. The most popular majors were business/marketing (23%), education (10%), and social sciences (9%). 200 companies recruited on campus in 2015-2016. In an average class, 17% graduate in 4 years or less, 35% graduate in 5 years or less, and 43% graduate in 6 years or less.

SERVICES: Counseling and information services are available, as is tutoring in most subjects. There is a reader service for the blind. Remedial work must be taken at the community college level. **Library/Resources:** The 4 libraries contain 206,615 volumes, 2.1 million microform items, and 22,414 audio/video tapes/CDs/DVDs, and subscribe to 12,549 periodicals including electronic. Computerized library services include interlibrary loans, database searching, Internet access, and Wi-Fi capability. Special learning facilities include an art gallery, planetarium, radio station, TV station, engineering research labs, a marine sciences research center, a K-12 developmental research school, a nonnative fish research lab, an environmental sciences center, and medical school. **Physically Challenged Students:** All of the campus is accessible. Facilities include wheelchair ramps, elevators, special parking, specially equipped restrooms, lowered drinking fountains, and lowered telephones. **Special:** FAU offers cooperative programs and internships in most majors. Work-study programs, dual and student-designed majors, a general studies degree, credit for military experience, nondegree study, and pass/fail options are available. The school offers a Washington semester, study abroad through all state university system of Florida programs. There are 21 national honor societies, a freshman honors program, and 9 departmental honors programs. **Visiting:** There are regularly scheduled orientations for prospective students, consisting of a group tour. There are guides for informal visits. To schedule a visit, contact the Admissions Office. **Campus Safety and Security:** Measures include 24-hour foot and vehicle patrol, emergency notification system, self-defense education, and security escort services. There are shuttle buses, emergency telephones, lighted pathways/sidewalks, and controlled access to dorms/residences.

REQUIREMENTS: The SAT or ACT is required, with a satisfactory score on the SAT Critical Reading and Math sections or on the ACT. In addition, graduation from an accredited secondary school or satisfactory scores on the GED are required. Students must have 19 academic credits, including 4 units of English, 3 each of math (algebra I and higher), science (including 2 with substantial lab work), and social studies, and 2 of a foreign language, plus 4 of electives in computer science, fine arts, or humanities. A portfolio or an audition may be requested by individual departments. An essay and an interview are required. A GPA of 2.0 is required. AP and CLEP credits are accepted. Important factors in the admissions decision are advanced placement or honors courses, evidence of special talent, and recommendations by school officials. All students must take the College Level Academic Skills Test (CLAST) required by the state. To graduate, students must complete a total of 120 credit hours, with a minimum GPA of 2.0. All students must take the required courses in the core curriculum, including 9 credits each of humanities and social sciences, and 6 each of math, communication, and natural sciences, and must demonstrate proficiency in a foreign language. **Procedure:** Freshmen are admitted fall, spring, and summer. There are early decision, early admissions, deferred admissions, and rolling admissions plans. Applications should be filed by May 1 for fall entry; October 15 for spring entry; and March 15 for summer entry, along with a $30 fee. Applications are accepted on-line. **Transfer Students:** 3678 transfer students enrolled in 2015-2016. Students must have a minimum GPA of 2.0, submit official transcripts from the previous schools attended, and be in good standing at those institutions. Applicants from a community or junior college in Florida with an associate degree are automatically admitted. Students with fewer than 60 transferable hours must meet the same criteria as entering freshmen. 30 credits required for the bachelor's degree must be completed at FAU. **International Students:** There are 268 international students enrolled. The school actively recruits these students. They must take the TOEFL with a minimum score of 550 on the paper-based TOEFL (PBT). They must also take the SAT or ACT.

ADMISSIONS: 39% of the 2016-2017 applicants were accepted. 51% of the current freshmen were in the top fifth of their class; 80% were in the top two fifths. There were 2 National Merit finalists. **Admissions Contact:** Barbar Pletcher, Director of Admissions. Email: *admissions@fau.edu* Web: *www.fau.edu*

FINANCIAL AID: The average freshman award was $10,684. Need-based scholarships or need-based grants averaged $5,871; need-based self-help aid (loans and jobs) averaged $6,849; non-need-based athletic scholarships averaged $9,892; other non-need-based awards and non-need-based scholarships averaged $6,777; and $2,275 from other forms of aid. The average financial indebtedness of the 2016 graduate was $13,229. FAU is a member of CSS. The FAFSA code is 001481. The priority date for freshman financial aid applications for fall entry is March 1.

FLORIDA GULF COAST UNIVERSITY D-5

www.fgcu.edu

Fort Myers, FL 33965	**(239) 590-7891** **(888) 889-1095**
Fax: (239) 590-7894	**Email: admissions@fgcu.edu**
Full-time: 4429 men, 5709 women	**Faculty:** IIA, -$
Part-time: 1291 men, 1432 women	**Ph.D.s:** 72%
Graduate: 401 men, 836 women	**Student/Faculty:** 23 to 1
Year: semesters, summer session	**Tuition:** $7341
Room & Board: $3364	**Freshman Class:** 10804 applied, 7108 accepted, 2761 enrolled
SAT: required	**CEEB CODE:** 5221
Application Deadline: May 1	**COMPETITIVE**

Florida Gulf Coast University, founded in 1991, is part of the State University System of Florida. Figures in the above capsule and in this profile are approximate. There are 5 undergraduate schools. In addition to regional accreditation, FGCU has baccalaureate program accreditation with AACSB, APTA, CSWE, NLN, and CAPTE. The 760-acre campus is in a suburban area in southwest Florida in southern Lee County. Including any residence halls, there are 112 buildings.

STUDENT LIFE: 93% of undergraduates are from Florida. Others are from 46 states, 87 foreign countries, and Canada. 67% are White; 19% Hispanic; 10% American Indian/Alaska Native; 7% African American; 2% Asian American; 2% Foreign; 2% two or more races; 1% race unknown. **Female To Male Ratio:** 1.3:1. The average age of freshmen is 18; all undergraduates, 22. **Housing:** 4200 students can be accommodated in college housing, which includes coed dorms, on-campus apartments, and off-campus apartments. On-campus housing is available on a first-come and first-served basis. 67% of students commute. Alcohol is not permitted. Some may keep cars.

FACULTY/CLASSROOMS: 55% of faculty are male; 45% are female. All teach undergraduates, and all do research. No introductory courses are taught by graduate students. The average class size in a regular course is 25.

PROGRAMS OF STUDY: FGCU confers B.A., and B.S. degrees. Associate, master's, and doctoral degrees are also awarded. Bachelor's degrees are awarded in AGRICULTURE (environmental studies), BIOLOGICAL SCIENCE (biology/biological science, biotechnology, and marine science), BUSINESS (accounting, banking and finance, marketing and distribution, and recreational facilities management), COMMUNICATIONS AND THE ARTS (art, communications, English, music, and Spanish), COMPUTER AND PHYSICAL SCIENCE (applied science, chemistry, computer science, and mathematics), EDUCATION (athletic training, early childhood education, elementary education, mathematics education, music education, secondary education, social science education, and special education), ENGINEERING AND ENVIRONMENTAL DESIGN (civil engineering and environmental engineering), HEALTH PROFESSIONS (clinical science, community health work, exercise science, health science, nursing, and occupational therapy), SOCIAL SCIENCE (anthropology, child psychology/development, counseling/psychology, criminal justice, criminology, economics, forensic studies, history, law, liberal arts/general studies, philosophy, political science/government, psychology, social work, and sociology). Management, communication, and psychology have the largest enrollments.

ACTIVITIES: 1% of men and 3% of women belong to 7 national fraternities; 7% of women belong to 5 national sororities. There are 125 groups on campus, including art, cheerleading, chess, computers, dance, debate, drama, environmental, ethnic, film, honors, international, LGBT, literary magazine, musical theater, newspaper, political, professional, religious, social, social service, and student government. Popular campus events include Eagle Expo and President's Lecture Series. **Sports:** There are 6 intercollegiate sports for men and 8 for women, and 9 intramural sports for men and 9 for women. Facilities include a fitness center, a lakefront, a 4500-seat teaching gym, 2 playing fields, 12 tennis courts, softball complex seating 2500, baseball field, Swanson Stadium seating 2500, and Aquatics Center with a 50-meter Olympic sized pool and 25 yard recreational pool. **Graduates:** From July 1, 2015 to June 30, 2016, 1873 bachelor's degrees were awarded. The most popular majors were communication/journalism (10%), management (8%), and psychology (6%). In an average class, 47% graduate in 6 years or less.

SERVICES: Counseling and information services are available, as is tutoring in most subjects. **Library/Resources:** The library contains 276,638 volumes, 843,772 microform items, and 319,258 audio/video tapes/CDs/DVDs, and subscribes to 409,967 periodicals including electronic. Computerized library services include interlibrary loans, database searching, Internet access, and Wi-Fi capability. Special learning facilities include an art gallery, TV station, chickee huts, computer labs, and a family resource center. **Physically Challenged Students:** All of the campus is accessible. Facilities include wheelchair ramps, elevators, special parking, specially equipped restrooms, special class scheduling, lowered drinking fountains, lowered telephones, and special housing. **Special:** The university offers cross-registration with the University of Central Florida, study abroad in China, a Washington semester, accelerated degree in biology, and work-study programs. There is 1 national honor society, a chapter of Phi Beta Kappa, a freshman honors program, and 1 departmental honors program. **Visiting:** There are regularly scheduled orientations for prospective students. There are guides for informal visits and visitors may sit in on classes. To schedule a visit, contact the Admissions Office. **Campus Safety and Security:** Measures include 24-hour foot and vehicle patrol, self-defense education, and security escort services. There are shuttle buses, emergency telephones, and lighted pathways/sidewalks.

REQUIREMENTS: The SAT is required. The ACT Optional Writing test is also required. A GPA of 2.0 is required. AP and CLEP credits are accepted. To graduate, students must have a 2.0 minimum GPA and 120 credit hours that include courses in phys ed, computer science, general education, service learning, and university colloquium. **Procedure:** Freshmen are admitted fall, spring, and summer. Entrance exams should be taken in the junior year. There is a deferred admissions plan. Applications should be filed by May 1 for fall entry; November 9 for spring entry; and February 1 for summer entry, along with a $30 fee. Applications are accepted on-line. **Transfer Students:** 1058 transfer students enrolled in 2015-2016. Lower level transfers must meet the same requirements as regular admissions. Upper level transfers must have a 2.0 GPA and 60 hours of transferable credit, and be in good standing at their last institution. 30 of 120 credits required for the bachelor's degree must be completed at FGCU. **International Students:** There are 206 international students enrolled. The school actively recruits these students. They must take the TOEFL with a minimum score of 550 on the paper-based TOEFL (PBT) or 79 on the Internet-based version (iBT). They must also take the SAT or ACT.

ADMISSIONS: 66% of the 2016-2017 applicants were accepted. The SAT scores for the 2016-2017 freshman class were: Critical Reading-- 43% below 500, 46% between 500 and 599, 10% between 600 and 699, and 1% between 700 and 800. Math-- 41% below 500, 46% between 500 and 599, 12% between 600 and 699, and 1% between 700 and 800. Writing-- 52% below 500, 40% between 500 and 599, 7% between 600 and 699, and 1% between 700 and 800. The ACT scores were 5% below 12, 70% between 12 and 17, 23% between 24 and 29, and 2% above 30. 27% of the current freshmen were in the top fifth of their class; 61% were in the top two fifths. 4 freshmen graduated first in their class. **Admissions**

Contact: Marc Maviolette, Director of Admissions. Email: *admissions@fgcu.edu* Web: *www.fgcu.edu*

FINANCIAL AID: In 2016-2017, 57% of all full-time freshmen received some form of financial aid. 36% of all full-time freshmen received need-based aid. The average freshman award was $9,135. Need-based scholarships or need-based grants averaged $5,080; need-based self-help aid (loans and jobs) averaged $6,887; and non-need-based athletic scholarships averaged $6,774. The average financial indebtedness of the 2016 graduate was $23,863. FGCU is a member of CSS. The FAFSA code is 032553. The deadline for filing freshman financial aid applications for fall entry is March 1.

FLORIDA INSTITUTE OF TECHNOLOGY E-4

www.fit.edu

Melbourne, FL 32901	**(321) 674-8030** **(800) 888-4348**
Fax: (321) 674-8004	**Email: admission@fit.edu**
Full-time: 2306 men, 980 women	**Faculty:** 231
Part-time: 230 men, 113 women	**Ph.D.s:** 91%
Graduate: 1714 men, 1108 women	**Student/Faculty:** 11 to 1
Year: semesters, summer session	**Tuition:** $39,696
Room & Board: $13,610	**Freshman Class:** 7428 applied, 4386 accepted, 756 enrolled
SAT CR/M: 550/590 **ACT:** 25	**CEEB CODE:** 5080
Application Deadline: n/av	**VERY COMPETITIVE**

Florida Institute of Technology, founded in 1958, offers undergraduate degrees in engineering, science, business, psychology, liberal arts, and aeronautics. There are 6 undergraduate schools and 7 graduate schools. In addition to regional accreditation, Florida Tech has baccalaureate program accreditation with ABET, CSAB, ACS, APA, and CAA. The 130-acre campus is in a suburban area 65 miles east of Orlando. Including any residence halls, there are 86 buildings.

STUDENT LIFE: 28% of undergraduates are from out of state, mostly the Middle Atlantic. Students are from 48 states, 113 foreign countries, and Canada. 49% are from public schools. 6% are Hispanic; 5% African American; 45% White; 24% Foreign; 2% Asian American. **Male To Female Ratio:** 1.9:1. The average age of freshmen is 18; all undergraduates, 21. 21% do not continue beyond their first year; 55% remain to graduate. **Housing:** 2127 students can be accommodated in college housing, which includes single-sex and coed dorms and on-campus apartments. In addition, there are fraternity houses and sorority houses. On-campus housing is guaranteed for the freshman year only, and is available on a first-come, and first-served basis. 56% of students commute. All students may keep cars.

FACULTY/CLASSROOMS: 75% of faculty are male; 25% are female. 7% teach undergraduates, and 5% do research. Graduate students teach 4% of introductory courses. The average class size in an introductory lecture is 22; in a laboratory is 20; and in a regular course is 21.

PROGRAMS OF STUDY: Florida Tech confers B.A., and B.S. degrees. Master's and doctoral degrees are also awarded. Bachelor's degrees are awarded in AGRICULTURE (conservation and regulation and environmental studies), BIOLOGICAL SCIENCE (biochemistry, biology/biological science, biomathematics, ecology, marine biology, and molecular biology), BUSINESS (accounting, business administration and management, electronic business, international business management, management information systems, marketing management, and sports management), COMMUNICATIONS AND THE ARTS (communications), COMPUTER AND PHYSICAL SCIENCE (applied mathematics, astronomy, astrophysics, atmospheric sciences and meteorology, chemistry, computer science, information sciences and systems, mathematics, oceanography, physics, planetary and space science, and software engineering), EDUCATION (mathematics education, middle school education, and science education), ENGINEERING AND ENVIRONMENTAL DESIGN (aeronautical engineering, aeronautical science, aviation administration/management, aviation computer technology, biomedical engineering, chemical engineering, civil engineering, computer engineering, construction engineering, construction management, electrical/electronics engineering, environmental science, mechanical engineering, military science, and ocean engineering), HEALTH PROFESSIONS (premedicine), SOCIAL SCIENCE (forensic studies, humanities, interdisciplinary studies, prelaw, and psychology). Engineering, science, and aeronautics are the strongest academically. Aerospace engineering, mechanical engineering, and computer science have the largest enrollments.

ACTIVITIES: 14% of men belong to 8 national fraternities; 11% of women belong to 3 national sororities. There are 147 groups on campus, including cheerleading, chess, chorus, computers, dance, drama, drill team, ethnic, film, honors, international, jazz band, LGBT, literary magazine, newspaper, pep band, photography, political, professional, radio and TV, religious, social, social service, and student government. Popular campus events include International Festival, Homecoming, Campus Cleanup, Relay for Life, Engineering Week, and Greek Week. **Sports:** There are 11 intercollegiate sports for men and 11 for women, and 15 intramural sports for men and 15 for women. The Charles and Ruth Clemente Center for Sports and Recreation is equipped with 2 basketball courts, a racquetball court, group fitness rooms, volleyball and badminton courts, and a 5000-square-foot weight and fitness area with cardiovascular machines, free weights, and specialized weight equipment. The Panther Aquatic Center is a 32,000-sq.-ft. facility that features a competition pool and a recreation pool. The competition pool includes nine 25-yard lanes complete with one- and three-meter diving boards. The depth ranges from 5.5 to 13 feet. The recreation pool varies in depth from three to six feet and includes three 25-yard lanes, stair entry and wading benches. Both pools are equipped with geothermal heating and cooling systems. **Graduates:** From July 1, 2015 to June 30, 2016, 521 bachelor's degrees were awarded. The most popular majors were aerospace engineering (12%), electrical engineering (8%), and mechanical engineering (8%). 154 companies recruited on campus in 2015-2016. In an average class, 2% graduate in 3 years or less, 37% graduate in 4 years or less, 52% graduate in 5 years or less, and 55% graduate in 6 years or less. Of the 2015 graduating class, 42% were enrolled in graduate school within 6 months of graduation, and 49% were employed.

SERVICES: Counseling and information services are available, as is tutoring in every subject. There is a reader service for the blind, and remedial math, reading, and writing. **Library/Resources:** The library contains 541,305 volumes, 310,471 microform items, and 10,319 audio/video tapes/CDs/DVDs, and subscribes to 68,007 periodicals including electronic. Computerized library services include interlibrary loans, database searching, Internet access, and Wi-Fi capability. Special learning facilities include an art gallery, radio station, TV station, and the Ruth Funk Center for Textile Arts, and the only textiles gallery in the state of Florida. **Physically Challenged Students:** 90% of the campus is accessible. Facilities include wheelchair ramps, elevators, special parking, specially equipped restrooms, special class scheduling, lowered drinking fountains, and lowered telephones. **Special:** The ProTrack cooperative education program allows students in the College of Engineering to complete three semester-long (amounting to one year) paid work experiences within the four years it takes to earn a bachelor's degree. Students graduate with their employers' names on their final transcripts. The Fast-Track accelerated master's degree program allows students to take graduate coursework as undergraduates, so students can complete a master's degree in as little as one additional year of study. Earned scholarships carry over to the fifth year. Florida Tech offers co-op programs in all majors. Students may choose to pursue more than 1 degree by completing degree requirements for each major. Internships are available in the senior year for many majors, including psychology, engineering, and aeronautics. Study abroad and work-study programs are available. There are 8 national honor societies and 1 departmental honors program. **Visiting:** There are regularly scheduled orientations for prospective students, including tours and interviews with admissions staff, faculty, or department heads upon request. There are guides for informal visits and visitors may sit in on classes. To schedule a visit, contact the Office of Undergraduate Admissions at admission@fit.edu. **Campus Safety and Security:** Measures include 24-hour foot and vehicle patrol, emergency notification system, self-defense education, and security escort services. There are shuttle buses, emergency telephones, lighted pathways/sidewalks, and controlled access to dorms/residences.

REQUIREMENTS: The SAT or ACT is required. Applicants must be graduates of an accredited secondary school or have a GED certificate. At least 18 academic credits or Carnegie units are required, including 4 years each of English, math, and science. An experiential essay is required and an interview is recommended. A GPA of 2.8 is required. AP and CLEP credits are accepted. Important factors in the admissions decision are advanced placement or honors courses, recommendations by school officials, and extracurricular activities record. To graduate, students must have a minimum 2.0 GPA and 120 to 135 credit hours. The required number of hours in the major varies. All students must take 9 hours in communication and humanities and 3 in English composition. The core curriculum also requires 6 credit hours each in physical or life sciences and math and 3 hours in computer science and social sciences. **Procedure:** Freshmen are admitted fall and spring. Entrance exams should be taken during the junior year or the beginning of the senior year of high school. There are deferred admissions and rolling admissions plans. Application deadlines are open. Applications are accepted on-line. **Transfer Students:** 207 transfer students enrolled in 2015-2016. Applicants must have a minimum 2.5 GPA. If transfer students have fewer than 30 semester hours, high school transcripts and SAT or ACT scores are required. A personal statement is recommended. 25 of 120 credits required for the bachelor's degree must be completed at Florida Tech. **International Students:** There are 791 international students enrolled. The school actively recruits these students. They must take the TOEFL with a minimum score of 550 on the paper-based TOEFL (PBT) or 79 on the Internet-based version (iBT), and a math entrance qualifying exam. If students score below the minimum, they take language courses on campus.

ADMISSIONS: 59% of the 2016-2017 applicants were accepted. The SAT scores for the 2016-2017 freshman class were: Critical Reading-- 24% below 500, 44% between 500 and 599, 25% between 600 and 699, and 7% between 700 and 800. Math-- 12% below 500, 40% between 500 and 599, 36% between 600 and 699, and 12% between 700 and 800. The ACT scores were 12% below 12, 23% between 12 and 17, 25% between 18 and 23, 17% between 24 and 29, and 23% above 30. 52% of the current freshmen were in the top fifth of their class; 74% were in the top two fifths. 17 freshmen graduated first in their class. **Admissions Contact:** Michael J. Perry, Director, Undergraduate Admissions. Email: *admission@fit.edu* Web: *www.fit.edu*

FINANCIAL AID: In 2016-2017, 63% of all full-time freshmen and 58% of continuing full-time students received some form of financial aid. 63% of all full-time freshmen and 58% of continuing full-time students received need-based aid. The average freshman award was $32,855. Need-based scholarships or need-based grants averaged $21,560 ($48,297 maximum); need-based self-help aid (loans and jobs) averaged $4,419 ($11,000 maximum); non-need-based athletic scholarships averaged $16,636 ($48,650 maximum); and other non-need-based awards and non-need-based scholarships averaged $13,696 ($49,927 maximum). 21% of undergraduate students work part-time. Average annual earnings from campus work are $8300. The average financial indebtedness of the 2016 graduate was $22,161. The FAFSA code is 001469. The priority date for freshman financial aid applications for fall entry is March 1.

FLORIDA INTERNATIONAL UNIVERSITY E-5

www.fiu.edu

Miami, FL 33199	(305) 348-2363
Fax: (305) 348-3648	Email: admiss@fiu.edu
Full-time: 11,315 men, 14,340 women	Faculty: n/av
	Ph.D.s: 86%
Part-time: 6921 men, 8462 women	Student/Faculty: n/av
Graduate: 3679 men, 5175 women	Tuition: $8038 ($20,437)
Year: semesters, summer session	Freshman Class: 15863 applied, 7874 accepted, 2555 enrolled
Room & Board: $11,836	
SAT CR/M/W: 560/550/540 ACT: 24	CEEB CODE: 5206
Application Deadline: January 18	COMPETITIVE+

Florida International University (FIU) is a multi-campus public research university offering a broad array of undergraduate, graduate, and professional programs. FIU offers more than 180 baccalaureate, masters, professional, and research doctorate programs and conducts basic and applied research. Interdisciplinary centers and institutes conduct collaborative research to seek innovative solutions to economic, technological, and social problems. FIU is dynamic. We have a can-do spirit that you will feel on our campuses. This vibrancy is reflected in the campus through modern architecture and the energy of our students. Figures in the above capsule and in this profile are approximate. There are 11 undergraduate schools. In addition to regional accreditation, FIU has baccalaureate program accreditation with AACSB, ABET, ACCE, ACEJMC, APTA, ASLA, CSWE, NAAB, NASAD, NASM, NCATE, NLN, AANA, ACS, ABA, ACOTE, NLNAC, CORPA, NASPAA, CEPH, ASHA, NAST, CIDA, CAPTE, CCNE, CACREP, and CORE. The 582-acre campus is in an urban area. Modesto A. Maidique campus is in western Miami-Dade County, and the Biscayne Bay Campus is in northeast Miami-Dade County. Including any residence halls, there are 189 buildings.

STUDENT LIFE: 92% of undergraduates are from Florida. Others are from 51 states, 155 foreign countries, and Canada. 7% are Foreign; 63% Hispanic; 3% Asian American; 2% two or more races; 12% African American; 11% White; 1% race unknown. **Female To Male Ratio:** 1.3:1. The average age of freshmen is 18; all undergraduates, 23. **Housing:** 3259 students can be accommodated in college housing, which includes coed dorms, on-campus apartments, and married student housing. In addition, there are fraternity houses. On-campus housing is available on a first-come and first-served basis. 92% of students commute. All students may keep cars.

FACULTY/CLASSROOMS: 55% of faculty are male; 45% are female. No introductory courses are taught by graduate students.

PROGRAMS OF STUDY: FIU confers B.A., B.S., B.Ac., B.B.A., B.F.A., B.H.S.A., B.M., B.P.A. and B.S.N. degrees. Master's and doctoral degrees are also awarded. Bachelor's degrees are awarded in BIOLOGICAL SCIENCE (biology/biological science and marine biology), BUSINESS (accounting, banking and finance, business administration and management, hospitality management services, international business management, management information systems, marketing/retailing/merchandising, and real estate), COMMUNICATIONS AND THE ARTS (art, art history and appreciation, dramatic arts, English, fine arts, French, Italian, music, Portuguese, and Spanish), COMPUTER AND PHYSICAL SCIENCE (chemistry, computer science, geology, mathematics, physics, and statistics), EDUCATION (art education, early childhood education, education, elementary education, physical education, science education, special education, and specific learning disabilities), ENGINEERING AND ENVIRONMENTAL DESIGN (architecture, biomedical engineering, civil engineering, computer engineering, construction engineering, construction technology, electrical/electronics engineering, environmental engineering, environmental science, interior design, landscape architecture/design, and mechanical engineering), HEALTH PROFESSIONS (exercise science and health care administration), SOCIAL SCIENCE (Asian/Oriental studies, criminal justice, dietetics, economics, geography, history, international relations, liberal arts/general studies, parks and recreation management, philosophy, political science/government, psychology, public administration, religion, social work, sociology, and women's studies).

ACTIVITIES: There are 556 groups on campus, including band, cheerleading, chorus, drama, environmental, ethnic, honors, international, jazz band, LGBT, marching band, newspaper, opera, political, professional, radio and TV, religious, social, social service, student government, and symphony. Popular campus events include Welcome Week, Homecoming, and Dance Marathon. **Sports:** There are 10 intercollegiate sports for men and 10 for women, and 9 intramural sports for men and 9 for women. Facilities include a 20,000 seat football stadium, a 5000-seat arena with basketball and racquetball courts, an aquatic center, baseball and soccer fields, a fitness center with Nautilus machines, and a racquet sports center with lighted tennis and racquetball courts. **Graduates:** From July 1, 2015 to June 30, 2016, 9061 bachelor's degrees were awarded. The most popular majors were business administration (29%), social sciences (12%), and psychology (9%).

SERVICES: Counseling and information services are available, as is tutoring in most subjects. There is a reader service for the blind, and remedial math, reading, and writing. Note taking, adapted testing, and special registration may be arranged for disabled students. **Library/Resources:** The 5 libraries contain 2.0 million volumes, 4.4 million microform items, and 381,598 audio/video tapes/CDs/DVDs, and subscribe to 106,622 periodicals including electronic. Computerized library services include interlibrary loans, database searching, Internet access, and Wi-Fi capability. Special learning facilities include an art gallery, radio station, art museums, nature preserve, and the Biscayne Bay preserve. **Physically Challenged Students:** All of the campus is accessible. Facilities include wheelchair ramps, elevators, special parking, specially equipped restrooms, special class scheduling, lowered drinking fountains, and lowered telephones. There is also accessible computer equipment for visually impaired students, including talking and large-print computers. **Special:** FIU offers co-op and work-study programs and study abroad in 30 countries. Accelerated degree programs, nondegree study, dual majors, and several combined bachelor's-master's programs. There are 40 national honor societies, Phi Beta Kappa, and a freshman honors program. **Visiting:** There are regularly scheduled orientations for prospective students, tours are available on both the Modesto Maidique campus and Biscayne Bay campuses. There are guides for informal visits and visitors may sit in on classes. To schedule a visit, contact Undgergraduate Admissions at (305) 348-2363. **Campus Safety and Security:** Measures include 24-hour foot and vehicle patrol, emergency notification system, and security escort services. There are emergency telephones and lighted pathways/sidewalks.

REQUIREMENTS: The SAT or ACT is required. In addition to the application, the following credentials are required: Official secondary school transcripts and appropriate test scores: Scholastic Aptitude Test (SAT) or the American College Test (ACT with writing). Proof of graduation from an accredited secondary school must be submitted before enrolling. High school diplomas accepted for undergraduate degree-seeking admission to FIU must be completed at a secondary institution accredited by a regional accrediting body or at an institution accredited by a national accrediting agency recognized by the United States Department of Education. Eighteen academic units in college preparatory courses are required as follows: 4 each in English, and mathematics, 3 each in natural science, and social science, 2 each in foreign languages, and academic electives (see notes). Freshman admission decisions are made based on the student's strong academic preparation. Competition for placement in the freshman class includes a review of all academic credentials and a completed file. Applicants are encouraged to complete the MyMajorMatch assessment to match their interest with FIU majors, find an appropriate major, and explore possible careers. Students who apply to majors in Theatre and Music must meet University academic standards and receive the approval of the respective department through an audition. Students should contact the specific department for audition dates. Notes: (1) Two units in the same foreign language are required, (2) Academic Electives are from the fields of mathematics, English, natural science, social science, and a foreign language. The academic grade point average will be computed only on the units listed above. Grades in honors courses, International Baccalaureate (IB), and advanced placement (AP) courses will be given additional weight. Admission to the University is a selective process and satisfying the general requirements does not guarantee acceptance. A GPA of 2.0 is required. AP and CLEP credits are accepted. Important factors in the admissions decision are advanced placement or honors courses, evidence of special talent, and recommendations by school officials. To graduate, students must complete between 120 and 152 hours with a 2.0 GPA. There are also general education and writing requirements. **Procedure:** Freshmen are admitted fall, spring, and summer. Entrance exams should be taken during the spring of the junior year. There is a rolling admissions plan. Application deadlines are open. Application fee is $30. Applications are accepted on-line. **Transfer Students:** 5135 transfer students enrolled in 2015-2016. Degree-seeking applicants with fewer than 60 semester hours of transfer credits must meet the same requirements as beginning freshmen students. In addition, they must demonstrate satisfactory performance in their college work. Applicants who receive an Associate in Arts (A.A.) degree from a Florida Public Community College or State University in Florida will be considered for admission without restriction except for published limited access programs within the University. Students transferring from independent Florida and out-of-state colleges into the University's upper division must have maintained a minimum 2.0 grade point average using a 4.0 scale (with the exception of some limited access programs). All applicants must meet the criteria published for limited access programs and should consult the specific college and major for requirements. Applicants who meet the above admissions requirements, but have not completed the University's core curriculum requirements, or the prerequisites of their proposed major, may complete this college work at FIU, or at any other accredited institution. Students may also fulfill general education requirements through the College Level Examination Program (CLEP). Official transcripts from all previous post secondary institutions must be forwarded to the institution. All students seeking admission to the University regardless of whether the student holds an A.A., should have completed two years of credit in one foreign language at the high school level or 8-10 credits in one foreign language at the college level (American Sign Language is acceptable). If a student is admitted to the University without this requirement, the credits must be completed prior to graduation. Students who can demonstrate continuous enrollment in a degree program at an SUS institution or Florida Community College since Fall Term 1989 (continuous enrollment is defined by the state to be the completion of at least one course per academic year) can be exempt from this requirement. Students holding an A.A. degree from a Florida Community College or SUS institution prior to Fall Term 1989 will also be exempt. Students, who are applying to majors in Theatre and Music, in addition to meeting university academic standards, must meet the approval of the respective department through an audition. Students should contact the department for audition dates. Admission to the University is a selective process and satisfying the general requirements does not guarantee acceptance. 30 of 120 credits required for the bachelor's degree must be completed at FIU. **International Students:** There are 1912 international students enrolled. The school actively recruits these students. They must take the TOEFL with a minimum score of 550 on the paper-based TOEFL (PBT) or 80 on the Internet-based version (iBT). They must also take the SAT or ACT.

ADMISSIONS: 50% of the 2016-2017 applicants were accepted. The SAT scores for the 2016-2017 freshman class were: Critical Reading-- 10% below 500, 61% between 500 and 599, 27% between 600 and 699, and 2% between 700 and 800. Math-- 16% below 500, 58% between 500 and 599, 24% between 600 and 699, and 2% between 700 and 800. Writing-- 19% below 500, 59% between 500 and 599, 20% between 600 and 699, and 2% between 700 and 800. The ACT scores were 38% between 18 and 23, 55% between 24 and 29, and 7% above 30. **Admissions Contact:** Jody Glassman, Admissions Director. Email: *admiss@fiu.edu* Web: *www.fiu.edu*

FINANCIAL AID: FIU is a member of CSS. The FAFSA code is 009635. The deadline for filing freshman financial aid applications for fall entry is March 1.

FLORIDA MEMORIAL UNIVERSITY *(The complete profile is made available exclusively on our website, www.barronspac.com)*

FLORIDA SOUTHERN COLLEGE D-3

www.flsouthern.edu

Lakeland, FL 33801	(863) 680-4131 (800) 274-4131
Fax: (863) 680-4120	**Email:** fscadm@flsouthern.edu
Full-time: 847 men, 1472 women	**Faculty:** 153; IIB, -$
Part-time: 27 men, 39 women	**Ph.D.s:** 79%
Graduate: 89 men, 290 women	**Student/Faculty:** 14 to 1
Year: semesters, summer session	**Tuition:** $33,100
Room & Board: $10,680	**Freshman Class:** 6192 applied, 2820 accepted, 648 enrolled
SAT CR/M/W: 560/560/530 **ACT:** 26	**CEEB CODE:** 5218
Application Deadline: May 1	**COMPETITIVE+**

Florida Southern College, founded in 1885, is a private, comprehensive college that maintains its commitment to academic excellence through 52 undergraduate programs and distinctive graduate programs in business administration, accounting, education, and nursing. Florida Southern is a national leader in engaged learning, and boasts 27 NCAA Division II National Championships. Figures in the above capsule and in this profile are approximate. There are 4 undergraduate schools and 3 graduate schools. In addition to regional accreditation, Florida Southern has baccalaureate program accreditation with AACSB, NASM, CCNE, and CAATE. The 113-acre campus is in a suburban area is 30 miles east of Tampa, and 40 miles west of Orlando. Including any residence halls, there are 121 buildings.

STUDENT LIFE: 64% of undergraduates are from Florida. Others are from 46 states, 52 foreign countries, and Canada. 82% are from public schools. 72% are White; 11% Hispanic; 6% African American; 4% Foreign; 2% Asian American; 2% two or more races; 1% American Indian/Alaska Native; 1% race unknown. 40% are Protestant; 28% claim no religious affiliation; 21% Catholic. **Female To Male Ratio:** 1.9:1. The average age of freshmen is 18; all undergraduates, 21. 19% do not continue beyond their first year; 81% remain to graduate. **Housing:** 2085 students can be accommodated in college housing, which includes single-sex and coed dorms and off-campus apartments. In addition, there are honors houses, special-interest houses, fraternity houses, and sorority houses. On-campus housing is guaranteed for all 4 years. 87% of students live on campus; of those, 90% remain on campus on weekends. Alcohol is not permitted. All students may keep cars.

FACULTY/CLASSROOMS: 51% of faculty are male; 49% are female. All

teach undergraduates, 75% do research, and 75% do both. No introductory courses are taught by graduate students. The average class size in an introductory lecture is 18; in a laboratory is 17; and in a regular course is 18.

PROGRAMS OF STUDY: Florida Southern confers B.A., B.S., B.F.A., B.M., B.M.E. and B.S.N. degrees. Master's and doctoral degrees are also awarded. Bachelor's degrees are awarded in AGRICULTURE (agricultural business management, agriculture, environmental studies, and horticulture), BIOLOGICAL SCIENCE (biochemistry, biology/biological science, marine biology, and molecular biology), BUSINESS (accounting and business administration and management), COMMUNICATIONS AND THE ARTS (advertising, art history and appreciation, broadcasting, communications, communication rhetoric/communication, creative writing, dance, digital communications, dramatic arts, English, graphic design, journalism, music, music business management, music performance, musical theater, public relations, Spanish, studio art, theatre acting, theatre arts, and theater design), COMPUTER AND PHYSICAL SCIENCE (chemistry, computer mathematics, computer science, and mathematics), EDUCATION (art education, athletic training, elementary education, music education, and secondary education), ENGINEERING AND ENVIRONMENTAL DESIGN (landscape architecture/design), HEALTH PROFESSIONS (exercise science, nursing, predentistry, premedicine, prepharmacy, and prephysical therapy), SOCIAL SCIENCE (criminology, economics, history, humanities, philosophy, political science/government, psychology, religion, and youth ministry). Biological sciences, nursing, business, and communication are the strongest academically. Business administration, biology, and nursing have the largest enrollments.

ACTIVITIES: 29% of men belong to 7 national fraternities; 35% of women belong to 7 national sororities. There are 102 groups on campus, including art, band, cheerleading, chess, choir, chorale, chorus, community service and shared interest groups, dance, drama, environmental, ethnic, film, forensics, honors, international, jazz band, LGBT, literary magazine, musical theater, newspaper, opera, orchestra, pep band, photography, political, professional, radio and TV, religious, social, social service, student government, symphony, and yearbook. Popular campus events include Graduating Class Water Dome Splash, Greek Week, Flick 'n' Float movies in the pool, FSC's Got Talent, Flap Jack Fling, annual Winter Carnival and Farewell Festival, Homecoming, Festival of Fine Arts, and Founders Day. **Sports:** There are 10 intercollegiate sports for men and 11 for women, and 25 intramural sports for men and 25 for women. Facilities include a variety of outdoor recreational areas, including intramural fields for softball, soccer, lacrosse, flag football, frisbee golf, water-skiing, canoeing, kayaking, and a 3-mile walk/run. The Hollis Wellness Center provides a fully-equipped weight room with personal trainers, an aerobics, Pilates, and yoga studio, a large gymnasium for basketball and volleyball and other intramural sports, and a heated competition-size swimming pool. The College's 1,800-seat Jenkins Field House is used for intercollegiate basketball and volleyball, and features locker rooms, weight rooms, and athletic training facilities. Facilities for baseball, lacrosse, and golf are conveniently located near campus. The Warden Tennis Center with a grandstand, two championship courts and eight tournament courts, and there is a 2.3-acre central open space ideal for recreational and social events. **Graduates:** From July 1, 2015 to June 30, 2016, 643 bachelor's degrees were awarded. The most popular majors were business/marketing (25%), health professions and related programs (13%), and nursing (12%). In an average class, 57% graduate in 4 years or less, 63% graduate in 5 years or less, and 60% graduate in 6 years or less. Of the 2015 graduating class, 24% were enrolled in graduate school within 6 months of graduation, and 70% were employed.

SERVICES: The Student Solutions Center provides tutoring in various subjects Monday through Friday as well as peer-assisted study sessions in select areas. The center also offers support for navigating financial aid, academic advising, student life, and billing. Additional resources include the Center for English Proficiency and Academic Success to assist international students. **Library/Resources:** The 2 libraries contain 162,938 volumes, 357 microform items, and 8,077 audio/video tapes/CDs/DVDs, and subscribe to 97,791 periodicals including electronic. Computerized library services include interlibrary loans, database searching, Internet access, and Wi-Fi capability. Special learning facilities include an art gallery, planetarium, radio station, TV station, the Rinker Technology Center, computer labs across campus, including the popular TuTu's Cyber Café, the Christoverson Humanities Building with a film studies theater and modern language lab, the state-of-the-art Blanton Nursing Building with high-tech classrooms and a learning lab featuring a full complement of patient simulators, the McKay Archives Center, which houses the College's original Frank Lloyd Wright drawings and documents, the Florida Citrus Hall of Fame, the Center for Florida History, and the Davis Performing Arts Center, including the nationally renowned Branscomb Auditorium, modern Buckner Theatre, and Melvin Art Gallery. The campus also is home to The Roberts Center for Learning and Literacy and The Roberts Academy, a transitional school for gifted elementary-age students with dyslexia that also serves as a learning lab for education students, the Wynee Warden Dance Studio, and the Barney Barnett School of Business and Free Enterprise. **Physically Challenged Students:** 68% of the campus is accessible. Facilities include wheelchair ramps, elevators, special parking, specially equipped restrooms, special class scheduling, lowered drinking fountains, lowered telephones, and special housing. **Special:** Florida Southern College offers a dynamic, transformational curriculum complemented by a variety of exciting experiential opportunities, including guaranteed internships for all students, numerous travel-study programs, student-faculty research, service learning, and music/theater performances. FSC is the only private college in the state affiliated with the prestigious Washington Center, a D.C.-based internship provider supporting students to study and work in the nation's capital, as well as other major cities around the world. The Honors Program offers innovative curriculum options to talented students seeking extraordinary inter-disciplinary learning opportunities. Honors students receive priority registration and are able to take course overloads without paying additional fees. An agreement with the University of South Florida's School of Medicine guarantees admission to all Honors students who complete the undergraduate requirements. A self-designed major provides motivated students with the option to create a degree program to suit a unique interest or career path, such as art therapy, politics and justice, technology management, and more. All FSC students are encouraged to participate in an international or domestic travel-study experience at little to no additional cost as part of their educational journey. Month- and semester-long internships have taken FSC students to England, France, Italy, Spain, China, the Bahamas, Peru, Greece, and Turkey. The College also offers yearlong study through Regent's College in London and a popular modern language school in Spain. In fall 2013, the College launched the Hollingsworth Scholars program, a full-tuition scholarship offered to select students of extraordinary academic talent and vision. There are 27 national honor societies, a freshman honors program, and 9 departmental honors programs. **Visiting:** There are regularly scheduled orientations for prospective students, including a meeting with faculty, a campus tour, and class visits, as well as special programming for parents with a brief history of Frank Lloyd Wright, the architect of FSC's West Campus. There are guides for informal visits, visitors may sit in on classes, and stay overnight. To schedule a visit, contact the Admissions Office. **Campus Safety and Security:** Measures include 24-hour foot and vehicle patrol, emergency notification system, self-defense education, and security escort services. There are shuttle buses, emergency telephones, lighted pathways/sidewalks, controlled access to dorms/residences, and a safety key that students can use in emergency.

REQUIREMENTS: Applicants are expected to have earned credit in at least 18 units of college preparatory courses and graduated from an accredited secondary school. It is recommended that students have a 3.0 GPA. An essay is required, and an interview is recommended. Applicants must submit either the SAT or ACT. A GPA of 2.0 is required. AP and CLEP credits are accepted. Important factors in the admissions decision are leadership record, geographical diversity, and recommendations by school officials. To gradate, a student needs a minimum of 124 semester credit hours from Florida Southern College and other regionally accredited colleges or universities. A maximum 62 of the required semester credit hours may have been earned at a junior/community college. After completing 96 hours, a student must finish the remaining credits at Florida Southern College. Some degree programs require more than 124 semester hours. **Procedure:** Freshmen are admitted to all sessions. Entrance exams should be taken starting in the junior year of high school. There are early decision, early admissions, deferred admissions, and rolling admissions plans. Early decision applications should be filed by December 1; regular applications, by May 1 for fall entry; and December 1 for spring entry, along with a $30 fee. Notification of early decision is sent December 15; regular decision, on a rolling basis. 70 early decision candidates were accepted for the 2016-2017 class. Applications are accepted on-line. **Transfer Students:** 111 transfer students enrolled in 2015-2016. Students who have successfully completed work at a regionally accredited college or university may apply for admission to Florida Southern College. Applicants should submit SAT or ACT scores, if available, along with a personal statement indicating the reason for the transfer. Official transcripts are required from each postsecondary institution attended. Transfer students must have a minimum 2.5 GPA in all college work attempted. An associate degree and an interview are recommended. 32 of 124 credits required for the bachelor's degree must be completed at Florida Southern. **International Students:** There are 95 international students enrolled. The school actively recruits these students. They must take the TOEFL with a minimum score of 550 on the paper-based TOEFL (PBT) or 79 on the Internet-based version (iBT). They must also take the SAT or ACT.

ADMISSIONS: 46% of the 2016-2017 applicants were accepted. The SAT scores for the 2016-2017 freshman class were: Critical Reading-- 18% below 500, 32% between 500 and 599, 25% between 600 and 699, and 5% between 700 and 800. Math-- 11% below 500, 57% between 500 and 599, 28% between 600 and 699, and 4% between 700 and 800. Writing-- 33% below 500, 50% between 500 and 599, 15% between 600 and 699, and 3% between 700 and 800. The ACT scores were 1% between 12 and 17, 28% between 18 and 23, 59% between 24 and 29, and 12% above 30. 53% of the current freshmen were in the top fifth of their class; 80% were in the top two fifths. 8 freshmen graduated first in their class. **Admissions Contact:** Arden Mitchell, Director of Admissions. Email: *fscadm@flsouthern.edu* Web: *www.flsouthern.edu*

FINANCIAL AID: In 2016-2017, 99% of all full-time freshmen and 99% of continuing full-time students received some form of financial aid. 75% of all full-time freshmen and 67% of continuing full-time students received need-based aid. The average freshman award was $32,813. Need-based scholarships or need-based grants averaged $23,569 ($49,505 maximum); need-based self-help aid (loans and jobs) averaged $1,572 ($3,058 maximum); non-need-based athletic scholarships averaged $11,519 ($44,630 maximum); and other non-need-based awards and non-need-based scholarships averaged $20,580 ($45,150 maximum). 64% of undergraduate students work part-time. Average annual earnings from campus work are $2228. The average financial indebtedness of the 2016 graduate was $26,637. The college's own financial statement, and parents' and student's tax returns are required. The FAFSA code is 001488. The priority date for freshman financial aid applications for fall entry is March 1. The deadline for filing freshman financial aid applications for fall entry is July 1.

FLORIDA STATE UNIVERSITY C-1

www.fsu.edu

Tallahassee, FL 32306 **(850) 644-6200**

Fax: (850) 644-0197	**Email:** admissions@fsu.edu
Full-time: 12,778 men, 16,407 women	**Faculty:** 1382; I, -$
	Ph.D.s: 92%
Part-time: 1932 men, 1589 women	**Student/Faculty:** 25 to 1
Graduate: 3660 men, 4464 women	**Tuition:** $6507 ($21,673)
Year: semesters, summer session	**Freshman Class:** 29828 applied, 16674 accepted, 6100 enrolled
Room & Board: $10,264	
SAT CR/M/W: 623/618/615 **ACT:** 28	**CEEB CODE:** 5219
Application Deadline: January 25	**HIGHLY COMPETITIVE**

Florida State University, a public institution founded in 1851, is a residential university designated as a Doctoral Research (Extensive) University by the Carnegie Foundation for the Advancement of Teaching. Figures in the above capsule and in this profile are approximate. There are 15 undergraduate schools and 16 graduate schools. In addition to regional accreditation, FSU has baccalaureate program accreditation with AACSB, ABET, ADA, AHEA, ASLA, CSWE, FIDER, NASAD, NASM, NCATE, NLN, NRPA, NASM, PRSA, and ACS. The 475-acre campus is in a suburban area 163 miles west of Jacksonville. Including any residence halls, there are 260 buildings.

STUDENT LIFE: 93% of undergraduates are from Florida. Others are from 50 states, 143 foreign countries, and Canada. 82% are from public schools. 8% are African American; 64% White; 3% two or more races; 2% Asian American; 19% Hispanic; 1% Foreign; 1% race unknown. **Female To Male Ratio:** 1.2:1. The average age of freshmen is 18; all undergraduates, 21. 8% do not continue beyond their first year; 92% remain to graduate. **Housing:** 6280 students can be accommodated in college housing, which includes single-sex and coed dorms, on-campus apartments, and married student housing. In addition, there are honors houses, special-interest houses, fraternity houses, sorority houses, living and learning centers, music residence, scholarship houses, academic discipline houses, wellness housing, cooperative living through the southern scholarship foundation and several private residence halls. On-campus housing is available on a first-come and first-served basis. 81% of students commute. All students may keep cars.

FACULTY/CLASSROOMS: 58% of faculty are male; 42% are female. Graduate students teach 49% of introductory courses. The average class size in an introductory lecture is 40; in a laboratory is 18; and in a regular course is 36.

PROGRAMS OF STUDY: FSU confers B.A., B.S., B.S.N., B.F.A, B.M. and B.M.Ed. degrees. Associate, master's, and doctoral degrees are also awarded. Bachelor's degrees are awarded in AGRICULTURE (environmental studies and plant science), BIOLOGICAL SCIENCE (biochemistry, biology/biological science, cell biology, ecology, evolutionary biology, genetics, marine biology, molecular biology, nutrition, physiology, and zoology), BUSINESS (accounting, banking and finance, business administration and management, entrepreneurial studies, fashion merchandising, hotel/motel and restaurant management, insurance and risk management, international business management, management science, marketing/retailing/merchandising, personnel management, recreation and leisure services, recreational facilities management, small business management, and sports management), COMMUNICATIONS AND THE ARTS (advertising, American literature, apparel design, art history and appreciation, broadcasting, classics, communications, creative writing, dance, dramatic arts, English, fiber/textiles/weaving, film arts, French, German, Greek, Italian, jazz, Latin, linguistics, music, music history and appreciation, music performance, music theory and composition, musical theater, piano/organ, public relations, Russian, Spanish, speech/debate/rhetoric, strings, studio art, theater design, voice, and winds), COMPUTER AND PHYSICAL SCIENCE (actuarial science, applied mathematics, atmospheric sciences and meteorology, chemical technology, chemistry, computer science, geology, information sciences and systems, mathematics, physics, and statistics), EDUCATION (art education, athletic training, early childhood education, education of the emotionally handicapped, education of the mentally handicapped, education of the visually handicapped, elementary education, English education, foreign languages education, health education, home economics education, mathematics education, music education, physical education, reading education, science education, social science education, and specific learning disabilities), ENGINEERING AND ENVIRONMENTAL DESIGN (bioengineering, biomedical engineering, chemical engineering, civil engineering, computer engineering, electrical/electronics engineering, environmental engineering, environmental science, graphic arts technology, industrial engineering, interior design, materials engineering, and mechanical engineering), HEALTH PROFESSIONS (community health work, music therapy, nursing, predentistry, premedicine, preoptometry, prepharmacy, preveterinary science, rehabilitation therapy, speech pathology/audiology, and sports medicine), SOCIAL SCIENCE (American studies, anthropology, Asian/Oriental studies, Caribbean studies, child care/child and family studies, classical/ancient civilization, clothing and textiles management/production/services, criminology, dietetics, Eastern European studies, economics, family/consumer studies, fashion design and technology, food science, geography, history, home economics, humanities, international relations, Latin American studies, philosophy, political science/government, prelaw, psychology, religion, Russian and Slavic studies, social science, social work, sociology, and women's studies). Biology, meteorology, and physics are the strongest academically. Psychology, political science, and business have the largest enrollments.

ACTIVITIES: 19% of men belong to 29 national fraternities; 25% of women belong to 26 national sororities. There are 723 groups on campus, including art, band, cheerleading, chess, choir, chorale, chorus, computers, dance, debate, drama, drill team, ethnic, forensics, honors, international, jazz band, LGBT, literary magazine, marching band, musical theater, newspaper, opera, orchestra, pep band, political, professional, radio and TV, religious, social, social service, student government, and symphony. Popular campus events include Twelve Days of Dance, Parents Weekend, and Seven Days of Opening Nights. **Sports:** There are 9 intercollegiate sports for men and 10 for women, and 27 intramural sports for men and 27 for women. Facilities include a 80,000-seat stadium, an aquatic center with a heated outdoor swimming pool, golf course, track, courts for basketball, tennis, racquetball, and handball, a student recreation center with an indoor Olympic-size swimming pool, 2 Jacuzzis, a steam room, sauna, 10 racquetball courts, a squash court, multipurpose gym, 3-lane jogging track, aerobic rooms, aerobic exercise machines, free and fixed weights, and a lakefront recreation area for outdoor water sports. **Graduates:** From July 1, 2015 to June 30, 2016, 8421 bachelor's degrees were awarded. The most popular majors were criminal justice/safety studies (6%), psychology, general (6%), English language and literature, and general (5%). 173 companies recruited on campus in 2015-2016. In an average class, 62% graduate in 4 years or less, 77% graduate in 5 years or less, and 79% graduate in 6 years or less. Of the 2015 graduating class, 53% were enrolled in graduate school within 6 months of graduation, and 72% were employed.

SERVICES: Counseling and information services are available, as is tutoring in most subjects. There is a reader service for the blind, and remedial math, reading, and writing. **Library/Resources:** The 8 libraries contain 2.8 million volumes, 9.8 million microform items, and 257,419 audio/video tapes/CDs/DVDs, and subscribe to 119,385 periodicals including electronic. Computerized library services include interlibrary loans, database searching, and Internet access. Special learning facilities include an art gallery, planetarium, radio station, TV station, nuclear accelerator, x-ray emission lab, marine lab, supercomputers, and the National High Magnetic Field Laboratory. **Physically Challenged Students:** 99% of the campus is accessible. Facilities include wheelchair ramps, elevators, special parking, specially equipped restrooms, special class scheduling, lowered drinking fountains, and lowered telephones. **Special:** Cross-registration with Florida Agricultural and Mechanical University and Tallahassee Community College is possible, as is study at FSU centers in London or Florence, and in programs in Costa Rica, France, Russia, Spain, Switzerland, and Vietnam, among other countries. FSU offers cooperative programs in engineering, computer science, business, and communication, work-study programs, general studies and combined B.A.-B.S. degrees, dual majors, and accelerated degree programs. Internships are required in criminology, human science, education, nursing, business (PMG), and social work. There are preprofessional programs in health and law. There are 35 national honor societies, Phi Beta Kappa, a freshman honors program, and 60 departmental honors programs. **Visiting:** There are regularly scheduled orientations for prospective students, including campus tours several times daily on weekdays. Walking and riding tours are available, and tours are coordinated around an 11:00 admissions information session. There are guides for informal visits and visitors may sit in on classes. To schedule a visit, contact the Visitor Services at visitorservices@admin.fsu.edu. **Campus Safety and Security:** Measures include 24-hour foot and vehicle patrol, emergency notification system, self-defense education, and security escort services. There are shuttle buses, emergency telephones, lighted pathways/sidewalks, a full-time police force, a bicycle identification program, a valuables identification program, and a victim advocate program.

REQUIREMENTS: The SAT or ACT is required. It is recommended that in-state students have at least an A-/B+ weighted average and a satisfactory SAT or ACT score. Out-of-state students must meet higher standards. Applicants should have at least the following high school units; 4 units in English and math, 3 units in natural science, and social science, and 2 units in a foreign language. Other factors include the number of honors, AP, and IB classes, strength of academic curriculum, and class rank, among other requirements. A GPA of 3.9 is required. AP and CLEP credits are accepted. Important factors in the admissions decision are advanced placement or honors courses, evidence of special talent, and recommendations by school officials. Students must satisfy the Florida College-Level Academic Skills (CLAS) requirement or an approved alternative. The required core curriculum includes 6 semester hours in mathematics, 6 semester hours in English composition, 6 to 12 semester hours in history/social science, 5 to 11 semester hours in humanities/fine arts, and 7 in natural sciences. Students must satisfy major requirements of their chosen degree program, including additional requirements set by the college offering the degree. All academic areas require at least 120 semester hours for graduation. Additional information is available in the General Bulletin. **Procedure:** Freshmen are admitted fall, spring, and summer. Entrance exams should be taken beginning in the second semester of the junior year. There is a rolling admissions plan. Applications should be filed by January 25 for fall entry; November 1 for spring entry; and February 13 for summer entry, along with a $30 fee. Applications are accepted on-line. **Transfer Students:** 1883 transfer students enrolled in 2015-2016. Transfer applicants should present at least a 3.0 cumulative college GPA unless transferring from a Florida public community college with an associate in arts degree, in which case the minimum college GPA needed varies according to major. Applicants with less than 60 semester hours of transferable credit must also meet freshman admission requirements. All transfers must have completed 2 years of the same foreign language in high school or have 8 semester hours at the college level. Students must pass the Floridá CLAST. 30 of 120 credits required for the bachelor's degree must be completed at FSU. **International Students:** There are 589 international students enrolled. They must take the TOEFL with a minimum score of 550 on the paper-based TOEFL (PBT) or 80 on the Internet-based version (iBT). They must also take the SAT or ACT.

ADMISSIONS: 56% of the 2016-2017 applicants were accepted. The SAT scores for the 2016-2017 freshman class were: Critical Reading-- 2% below 500, 44% between 500 and 599, 46% between 600 and 699, and 8% between 700 and 800. Math-- 3% below 500, 42% between 500 and 599, 48% between 600 and 699, and 6% between 700 and 800. Writing-- 3% below 500, 45% between 500 and 599, 45% between 600 and 699, and 6% between 700 and 800. The ACT scores were 1% between 12 and 17, 19% between 18 and 23, 69% between 24 and 29, and 11% above 30. 76% of the current freshmen were in the top fifth of their class. There were 22 National Merit finalists. **Admissions Contact:** Admissions Office Email: *admissions@fsu.edu* Web: *www.fsu.edu*

FINANCIAL AID: In 2016-2017, 85% of all full-time freshmen and 87% of continuing full-time students received some form of financial aid. 43% of all full-time freshmen and 48% of continuing full-time students received need-based aid. The average freshman award was $8,745. Need-based scholarships or need-based grants averaged $5,078; need-based self-help aid (loans and jobs) averaged $3,607; non-need-based athletic scholarships averaged $6,911; and other non-need-based awards and non-need-based scholarships averaged $3,257. 2% of undergraduate students work part-time. Average annual earnings from campus work are $2120. The average financial indebtedness of the 2016 graduate was $24,347. The college's own financial statement is required. The FAFSA code is 001489. The priority date for freshman financial aid applications for fall entry is January 15.

HODGES UNIVERSITY *(The complete profile is made available exclusively on our website, www.barronspac.com)*

JACKSONVILLE UNIVERSITY D-1

www.ju.edu

Jacksonville, FL 32211	(904) 256-7000 (800) 225-2027
Fax: (904) 256-7012	Email: admissions@ju.edu
Full-time: 958 men, 1133 women	**Faculty:** IIA, av$
Part-time: 187 men, 132 women	**Ph.D.s:** 78%
Graduate: 228 men, 1429 women	**Student/Faculty:** n/av
Year: semesters, summer session	**Tuition:** $33,930
Room & Board: $12,300	**Freshman Class:** 2939 applied, 1648 accepted, 400 enrolled
SAT CR/M: 505/505 **ACT:** 22	**CEEB CODE:** 5331
Application Deadline: open	**COMPETITIVE**

Jacksonville University, founded in 1934, is a private institution offering undergraduate and graduate degree programs in the arts and sciences, fine arts, and business. The figures in the above capsule and in this profile are approximate. There are 3 undergraduate schools and 4 graduate schools. In addition to regional accreditation, JU has baccalaureate program accreditation with NASAD, NASM, NLN, and CCNE. The 198-acre campus is in a suburban area 10 minutes from downtown Jacksonville, near the St. Johns River. Including any residence halls, there are 48 buildings.

STUDENT LIFE: 60% of undergraduates are from Florida. Others are from 48 states, 55 foreign countries, and Canada. 7% are Hispanic; 52% White; 3% Asian American; 2% Foreign; 19% two or more races; 16% African American. 35% claim no religious affiliation; 18% Protestant; 16% Catholic. **Female To Male Ratio:** 2.0:1. The average age of freshmen is 19; all undergraduates, 22. 35% do not continue beyond their first year; 49% remain to graduate. **Housing:** 1342 students can be accommodated in college housing, which includes single-sex dorms and on-campus apartments. On-campus housing is guaranteed for the freshman year only, is available on a first-come, first-served basis, and is available on a lottery system for upperclassmen. 59% of students live on campus;

of those, 60% remain on campus on weekends. All students may keep cars.

FACULTY/CLASSROOMS: 53% of faculty are male; 47% are female. No introductory courses are taught by graduate students. The average class size in an introductory lecture is 18; in a laboratory is 16; and in a regular course is 14.

PROGRAMS OF STUDY: JU confers B.A., B.S., B.B.A., B.F.A., B.G.S., B.Mus., B.Mus.Ed. and B.S.N. degrees. Master's degrees are also awarded. Bachelor's degrees are awarded in BIOLOGICAL SCIENCE (biology/biological science and marine science), BUSINESS (accounting, banking and finance, business administration and management, international business management, and marketing/retailing/merchandising), COMMUNICATIONS AND THE ARTS (art history and appreciation, communications, dance, dramatic arts, English, French, music, music performance, music theory and composition, Spanish, and studio art), COMPUTER AND PHYSICAL SCIENCE (chemistry, computer science, information sciences and systems, mathematics, and physics), EDUCATION (art education, dance education, education of the exceptional child, elementary education, music education, and physical education), ENGINEERING AND ENVIRONMENTAL DESIGN (aviation administration/management, computer graphics, electrical/electronics engineering, engineering physics, environmental science, and mechanical engineering), HEALTH PROFESSIONS (nursing), SOCIAL SCIENCE (economics, geography, history, humanities, international studies, philosophy, political science/government, psychology, and sociology). Business administration, nursing, and biology have the largest enrollments.

ACTIVITIES: 20% of men belong to 8 national fraternities; 15% of women belong to 7 national sororities. There are 100 groups on campus, including art, band, cheerleading, choir, chorale, chorus, computers, dance, debate, drama, drill team, environmental, ethnic, film, honors, international, jazz band, LGBT, literary magazine, musical theater, newspaper, orchestra, pep band, photography, political, professional, radio and TV, religious, social, social service, student government, and symphony. Popular campus events include FIN Fest and Campus Movie Fest. **Sports:** There are 8 intercollegiate sports for men and 9 for women. Facilities include a 1500-seat stadium, a gym, swimming pool, a boathouse, baseball and softball diamonds, soccer and football fields, and an archery range. There are tennis, basketball, handball/racquetball, volleyball, and shuffleboard courts, an all-purpose playing field, a 440-yard track, a 540-seat auditorium, a 220-seat recital hall, and a dance pavilion.

SERVICES: Counseling and information services are available, as is tutoring in most subjects. There is a reader service for the blind, and remedial math, reading, and writing. There also is a writer service for note taking in class. **Library/Resources:** The library contains 385,016 volumes, 253,284 microform items, and 24,919 audio/video tapes/CDs/DVDs, and subscribes to 19,740 periodicals including electronic. Computerized library services include interlibrary loans, database searching, and Internet access. Special learning facilities include an art gallery, planetarium, radio station, TV station, a chemistry research lab, and a marine science center. **Physically Challenged Students:** Facilities include wheelchair ramps, elevators, special parking, specially equipped restrooms, special class scheduling, and lowered drinking fountains. Accommodation for all students regardless of disability. **Special:** Internships and work-study are available, as are student-designed majors and a dual major in music and business. There is a co-op program in art, and a 3-2 engineering degree is available with 7 other universities and technological institutes. There is a Washington semester and study abroad in 12 countries. Credit is granted for military experience. There are 16 national honor societies, Phi Beta Kappa, and a freshman honors program. **Visiting:** There are regularly scheduled orientations for prospective students, consisting of an interview, a campus tour, advisement, area presentations, registration, a parents program, and mock classes. There are guides for informal visits, visitors may sit in on classes, and stay overnight. To schedule a visit, contact the Admissions Office. **Campus Safety and Security:** Measures include 24-hour foot and vehicle patrol, self-defense education, and security escort services. There are emergency telephones and lighted pathways/sidewalks.

REQUIREMENTS: The SAT or ACT is required. Applicants must be graduates of an accredited secondary school and provide an official copy of their secondary school transcripts or have a GED. At least 18 academic credits are required, including 4 in English, 3 each in math, natural science, and social sciences, and 2 of the same foreign language. Art students must submit a portfolio. Music, theater, and dance students must audition. A GPA of 2.0 is required. AP and CLEP credits are accepted. Important factors in the admissions decision are advanced placement or honors courses, extracurricular activities record, and leadership record. All students must complete a core curriculum, which provides the liberal arts foundation for all bachelor's degrees. The core includes 4 hours of lab science and 3 hours each of English composition, world literature, economics, fine arts, global studies, humanities, modern world history, math, philosophy, social science, and technology. The B.A. degree requires completion of a foreign language component in place of 3 hours of global studies. A minimum of 120 credit hours, with a minimum GPA of 2.0, is needed to graduate. **Procedure:** Freshmen are admitted to all sessions. Entrance exams should be taken in the spring of the junior year or the fall or spring of the senior year. There are early admissions, deferred admissions, and rolling admissions plans. Application deadlines are open. The fall 2016 application fee was $30. Applications are accepted on-line. **Transfer Students:** Transfer students must submit official transcripts from all colleges attended. Art students must submit a portfolio; music and dance students must audition. Transfer applicants must have completed at least 1 semester at an accredited college or university, be in good standing at the last institution attended, and have a minimum GPA of 2.0. 30 of 120 credits required for the bachelor's degree must be completed at JU. **International Students:** The school actively recruits these students. They must take the TOEFL with a minimum score of 540 on the paper-based TOEFL (PBT) or 76 on the Internet-based version (iBT). They must also take the SAT or ACT.

Admissions Contact: Lisa Hannasch, Director of Admissions. Email: *admissions@ju.edu* Web: *www.ju.edu*

FINANCIAL AID: JU is a member of CSS. The college's own financial statement, a federal tax return and W-2 are required. The FAFSA code is 001495. Check with the school for current application deadlines.

JOHNSON & WALES UNIVERSITY/NORTH MIAMI CAMPUS E-5
www.jwu.edu/miami

North Miami, FL 33181	(866) 598-3567
Fax: (305) 892-7020	**Email:** mia@admissions.jwu.edu
Full-time: 583 men, 993 women	**Faculty:** 57
Part-time: 70 men, 106 women	**Ph.D.s:** n/av
Graduate: n/av	**Student/Faculty:** 25 to 1
Year: trimesters	**Tuition:** $30,746
Room & Board: $11,961	**Freshman Class:** n/av **CEEB CODE:** 3441
Application Deadline: n/av	**COMPETITIVE**

Johnson & Wales University/North Miami Campus, founded in 1992, offers degree programs in its college of culinary arts, college of business, and hospitality college. Figures in the above capsule and in this profile are approximate. There are 3 undergraduate schools. In addition to regional accreditation, JWU has baccalaureate program accreditation with NEASCE-CIHE. The campus is in a small town in the heart of North Miami, between Miami and Fort Lauderdale. Including any residence halls, there are 13 buildings.

STUDENT LIFE: 53% of undergraduates are from out of state, mostly the South. Students are from 44 states, 54 foreign countries, and Canada. 9% are Foreign; 24% African American; 23% White; 21% Hispanic; 1% Asian American; 1% American Indian/Alaska Native. **Female To Male Ratio:** 1.7:1. The average age of freshmen is 18; all undergraduates, 21. **Housing:** 1184 students can be accommodated in college housing, which includes coed dorms and on-campus apartments. apartments for single students, wellness housing, and theme housing. On-campus housing is available on a lottery system for upperclassmen. 55% of students live on campus. All students may keep cars.

FACULTY/CLASSROOMS: 61% of faculty are male; 37% are female. No introductory courses are taught by graduate students.

PROGRAMS OF STUDY: JWU confers B.S. degrees. Associate degrees are also awarded. Bachelor's degrees are awarded in BUSINESS (accounting, business administration and management, entrepreneurial studies, hospitality management services, hotel/motel and restaurant management, marketing management, marketing/retailing/merchandising, recreation and leisure services, sports management, and tourism), ENGINEERING AND ENVIRONMENTAL DESIGN (electrical/electronics engineering and food services technology),

SOCIAL SCIENCE (clothing and textiles management/production/services, criminal justice, food production/management/services, paralegal studies, and parks & recreation management).

ACTIVITIES: Groups on campus include campus ministries, cheerleading, dance, ethnic, honors, international, LGBT, music ensembles, newspaper, pep band, professional, religious, social, and student government. **Sports:** There are 4 intercollegiate sports for men and 4 for women, and 5 intramural sports for men and 5 for women. Facilities include a fitness center equipped with cardio machines, free weights, universal machines, and treadmills. **Graduates:** From July 1, 2015 to June 30, 2016, 357 bachelor's degrees were awarded. The most popular majors were English (41%), family and consumer sciences (38%), and law/legal studies (12%). In an average class, 37% graduate in 6 years or less.

SERVICES: Counseling and information services are available, as is tutoring in every subject. **Library/Resources:** The library contains 12,525 volumes, and 2,301 audio/video tapes/CDs/DVDs, and subscribes to 232 periodicals including electronic. Computerized library services include interlibrary loans, database searching, Internet access, and Wi-Fi capability. **Physically Challenged Students:** Facilities include wheelchair ramps, elevators, special parking, specially equipped restrooms, special class scheduling, lowered drinking fountains, lowered telephones, and special housing. **Special:** The university offers co-op programs, accelerated degree programs, dual majors, study abroad, and worldwide work-study opportunities in business, hospitality, technology, and culinary arts. Most majors require 11-week internships, **Visiting:** There are regularly scheduled orientations for prospective students, including an introduction to the academic and social aspects of the campus experience through interactive sessions. There are guides for informal visits, visitors may sit in on classes, and stay overnight. To schedule a visit, contact Admissions. **Campus Safety and Security:** Measures include 24-hour foot and vehicle patrol and security escort services. There are shuttle buses and emergency telephones.

REQUIREMENTS: Although SAT and ACT scores are required only for students applying for honors admissions, students who have taken these test are encouraged to submit their scores. High school diploma is required; the GED is accepted. Student requirements are 4 years of English, 3 years each of mathematics and science, and 2 years of social studies. A GPA of 2.0 is required. AP and CLEP credits are accepted. Important factors in the admissions decision are leadership record, advanced placement or honors courses, extracurricular activities record, evidence of special talent, personality/intangible qualities, and recommendations by school officials. To graduate, students must complete 180 quarter credit hours, including at least 36 in the major, with a minimum GPA of 2.0. Required classes include English, math history, economics, science, psychology, sociology, and professional development. **Procedure:** Freshmen are admitted to all sessions. There are deferred admissions and rolling admissions plans. Application deadlines are open. **Transfer Students:** 103 transfer students enrolled in 2015-2016. Applicants are required to submit official high school and college transcripts and must have earned a minimum college GPA of 2.0. Students may enroll in the fall, winter, spring and summer. **International Students:** There are 192 international students enrolled. The school actively recruits these students. They must take the TOEFL.

ADMISSIONS: 76% of the 2016-2017 applicants were accepted. **Admissions Contact:** George J. Rezendes, Director of Admissions. Email: *mia@admissions.jwu.edu* Web: *www.jwu.edu/miami*

FINANCIAL AID: The average freshman award was $25,819. Need-based scholarships or need-based grants averaged $10,213; need-based self-help aid (loans and jobs) averaged $4,709; other non-need-based awards and non-need-based scholarships averaged $3,371; and $9,280 from other forms of aid. JWU is a member of CSS. Check with the school for current application deadlines.

KEISER UNIVERSITY *(The complete profile is made available exclusively on our website, www.barronspac.com)*

LYNN UNIVERSITY *(The complete profile is made available exclusively on our website, www.barronspac.com)*

NEW COLLEGE OF FLORIDA — D-4

www.ncf.edu

Sarasota, FL 34243	**(941) 487-5000**
Fax: (941) 487-5001	**Email: admissions@ncf.edu**
Full-time: 336 men, 525 women	**Faculty:** 78; IIB, av$
Part-time: n/av	**Ph.D.s:** 95%
Graduate: n/av	**Student/Faculty:** 10 to 1
Year: 4-1-4, summer session	**Tuition:** $6916 ($29,944)
Room & Board: $8932	**Freshman Class:** 1655 applied, 1009 accepted, 261 enrolled
SAT CR/M/W: 670/610/620 **ACT:** 29	**CEEB CODE:** 5506
Application Deadline: February 15	**MOST COMPETITIVE**

New College of Florida, established in 1960, is the honors college for the liberal arts and sciences of the State University System of Florida. There is 1 undergraduate school. The 119-acre campus is in a suburban area 50 miles south of Tampa, Florida, on Sarasota Bay. Including any residence halls, there are 61 buildings.

STUDENT LIFE: 85% of undergraduates are from Florida. Others are from 38 states, 23 foreign countries, and Canada. 79% are from public schools. 69% are White; 4% two or more races; 3% African American; 3% Asian American; 3% race unknown; 2% Foreign; 16% Hispanic. **Female To Male Ratio:** 1.6:1. The average age of freshmen is 18; all undergraduates, 20. 19% do not continue beyond their first year; 71% remain to graduate. **Housing:** 636 students can be accommodated in college housing, which includes coed dorms and on-campus apartments. Specialized housing options may be arranged in response to student interest. On-campus housing is guaranteed for all 4 years and is available on a lottery system for upperclassmen. 77% of students live on campus. All students may keep cars.

FACULTY/CLASSROOMS: 45% of faculty are male; 55% are female. All teach undergraduates. No introductory courses are taught by graduate students. The average class size in an introductory lecture is 16; in a laboratory is 13; and in a regular course is 16.

PROGRAMS OF STUDY: New College confers B.A. degrees. Bachelor's degrees are awarded in AGRICULTURE (environmental studies), BIOLOGICAL SCIENCE (biochemistry, biology/biological science, marine biology, and neurosciences), COMMUNICATIONS AND THE ARTS (art, art history and appreciation, Chinese, classics, English, French, Germanic languages and literature, literature, music, Russian languages and literature, and Spanish), COMPUTER AND PHYSICAL SCIENCE (applied mathematics, chemistry, mathematics, natural sciences, and physics), ENGINEERING AND ENVIRONMENTAL DESIGN (computational sciences), SOCIAL SCIENCE (anthropology, economics, French studies, gender studies, German area studies, history, humanities, international studies, Latin American studies, medieval studies, philosophy, political science/government, psychology, public affairs, religion, social science, sociology, Spanish studies, and urban studies). Biology, psychology, and economics have the largest enrollments.

ACTIVITIES: There are no fraternities or sororities. Groups on campus include art, chess, chorale, chorus, computers, dance, debate, drama, environmental, ethnic, film, international, jazz band, LGBT, literary magazine, newspaper, photography, political, radio and TV, religious, social, social service, and student government. Popular campus events include Halloween and Graduation Parties, Diversity Discussion Service, and a Kickball Tournament. **Sports:** There is 1 intercollegiate sports for men and 1 for women, and 20 intramural sports for men and 20 for women. Facilities include a soccer field, softball diamond, fitness path, outdoor tennis and basketball courts, a volleyball pit, playground equipment, swimming pool, and a fitness center with Cybex equipment and indoor facilities for racquetball, aerobics, dance, and yoga. **Graduates:** From July 1, 2015 to June 30, 2016, 177 bachelor's degrees were awarded. The most popular majors were psychology (13%), anthropology (10%), and biology (9%). In an average class, 1% graduate in 3 years or less, 63% graduate in 4 years or less, 69% graduate in 5 years or less, and 71% graduate in 6 years or less. Of the 2015 graduating class, 19% were enrolled in graduate school within 6 months of graduation, and 35% were employed.

SERVICES: There is a reader service for the blind. A writing resource center provides assistance in developing writing skills and strategies. A quantitative resource center provides assistance in math and statistics as well as the technology needed in these fields. **Library/Resources:** The library contains 258,314 volumes, 198,287 microform items, and 1,864 audio/video tapes/CDs/DVDs, and subscribes to 915 periodicals including electronic. Computerized library services include interlibrary loans, database searching, Internet access, and Wi-Fi capability. Special learning facilities include an art gallery, radio station, a media and educational technology center, public archaeology lab, writing resource center, quantitative resource center, language resource center, marine biology research center, black box theater, fine arts complex, and a living ecosystem teaching and research aquarium. **Physically Challenged Students:** 80% of the campus is accessible. Facilities include wheelchair ramps, elevators, special parking, specially equipped restrooms, special class scheduling, lowered drinking fountains, lowered telephones, and special housing. **Special:** Domestic and international internships, study abroad, accelerated degree programs, student-designed interdisciplinary and dual majors, and independent study are available. There is a freshman honors program. **Visiting:** There are regularly scheduled orientations for prospective students, including a campus tour, admissions information session, and/or class visits, which must be scheduled individually by the student through Admissions. Visitors may sit in on classes. To schedule a visit, contact Carley Ray at admissions@ncf.edu. **Campus Safety and Security:** Measures include 24-hour foot and vehicle patrol, emergency notification system, self-defense education, and security escort services. There are emergency telephones, lighted pathways/sidewalks, controlled access to dorms/residences, 24-hour dispatch/information services, and fire/smoke alarm systems in all dorms.

REQUIREMENTS: The SAT or ACT is required. The ACT Optional Writing test is also required. Graduation from an accredited secondary school (preferred) or the GED. High school students should pursue at least 5 academic courses each year, at the most rigorous level available, with a minimum distribution of 4 years of English and mathematics, 3 years each of sciences and social sciences, 2 consecutive years of the same foreign language, and 3 other academic courses. Application essays must be submitted. AP credits are accepted. Important factors in the admissions decision are advanced placement or honors courses, extracurricular activities record, and personality/intangible qualities. An academic credit system is not used. To qualify for graduation, students must complete 7 semester contracts, which are designed by the student in consultation with faculty, 3 independent study projects completed during January each year, between the fall and spring semesters, a senior thesis, that involves original research or creative work and includes working closely with a faculty committee of the student's choice, and an oral baccalaureate exam, which is primarily a defense of the senior thesis. To fulfill the liberal arts curriculum requirements, students must complete 8 LAC-designated courses, including 1 each in humanities, natural sciences, and social sciences. Exemptions from the LAC requirements are possible through AP exam scores of 3 or above, IB exam scores of 5 to 7, and transferable college course work at the general education level. Students also must use on-line training to sign up for a college e-mail account and complete the College Level Academic Skills Test or be exempted by appropriate college course work or SAT or ACT scores. **Procedure:** Freshmen are admitted fall and spring. Entrance exams should be taken fall of the senior year. There is a deferred admissions plan. Applications should be filed by February 15 for fall entry; December 1 for spring entry, along with a $30 fee. Notifications are sent April 1. Applications are accepted on-line. **Transfer Students:** 24 transfer students enrolled in 2015-2016. Transfers must be in good academic and financial standing with their previous college(s). Transfers with less than 60 semester hours must submit SAT or ACT scores. 72 of 124 credits required for the bachelor's degree must be completed at New College. **International Students:** There are 33 international students enrolled. The school actively recruits these students. They must take the TOEFL with a minimum score of 560 on the paper-based TOEFL (PBT) or 83 on the Internet-based version (iBT). They must also take the SAT or ACT.

ADMISSIONS: 61% of the 2016-2017 applicants were accepted. The SAT scores for the 2016-2017 freshman class were: Critical Reading-- 1% below 500, 18% between 500 and 599, 45% between 600 and 699, and 35% between 700 and 800. Math-- 3% below 500, 40% between 500 and 599, 44% between 600 and 699, and 13% between 700 and 800. Writing-- 3% below 500, 29% between 500 and 599, 51% between 600 and 699, and 17% between 700 and 800. The ACT scores were 4% between 18 and 23, 51% between 24 and 29, and 45% above 30. 73% of the current freshmen were in the top fifth of their class; 94% were in the top two fifths. 3 freshmen graduated first in their class. **Admissions Contact:** Kathleen M. Killion, Dean of Enrollment Services. Email: *admissions@ncf.edu* Web: *www.ncf.edu*

FINANCIAL AID: In 2016-2017, 100% of all full-time freshmen and 96% of continuing full-time students received some form of financial aid. 47% of all full-time freshmen and 43% of continuing full-time students received need-based aid. The average freshman award was $14,517. Need-based scholarships or need-based grants averaged $7,186; need-based self-help aid (loans and jobs) averaged $3,056; and other non-need-based awards and non-need-based scholarships averaged $9,917. The average financial indebtedness of the 2016 graduate was $15,777. The FAFSA code is 039574. The priority date for freshman financial aid applications for fall entry is February 15.

NOVA SOUTHEASTERN UNIVERSITY E-5

www.nova.edu

Fort Lauderdale, FL 33314 (954) 262-8000
(800) 338-4723
Email: admissions@nova.edu

Full-time: 1062 men, 2132 women
Part-time: 413 men, 1034 women
Graduate: 5699 men, 12,896 women
Year: trimesters, summer session
Room & Board: $10,874

Faculty: n/av
Ph.D.s: 79%
Student/Faculty: 16 to 1
Tuition: $27,760
Freshman Class: 4333 applied, 2567 accepted, 657 enrolled

SAT CR/M: 550/550 **ACT:** 25
Application Deadline: August 1
CEEB CODE: 5514
COMPETITIVE+

Nova Southeastern University, founded in 1964, is an independent institution offering degree programs in liberal arts, sciences, business, health sciences, education, and preprofessional studies. The university also offers graduate and first-professional programs. Figures in the above capsule and in this profile are approximate. There are 8 undergraduate schools and 14 graduate schools. In addition to regional accreditation, NSU has baccalaureate program accreditation with APTA, CAHEA, NCATE, CCNE, COATE, and IACBE. The 314-acre campus is in a suburban area 10 miles west of downtown Fort Lauderdale. Including any residence halls, there are 39 buildings.

STUDENT LIFE: 83% of undergraduates are from Florida. Others are from 48 states, 68 foreign countries, and Canada. 9% are Asian American; 5% Foreign; 32% Hispanic; 31% White; 3% race unknown; 2% two or more races; 17% African American. **Female To Male Ratio:** 2.2:1. The average age of freshmen is 19; all undergraduates, 25. 20% do not continue beyond their first year; 44% remain to graduate. **Housing:** 1472 students can be accommodated in college housing, which includes coed dorms, on-campus apartments, and married student housing. In addition, there are fraternity houses, sorority houses, theme housing, leadership, CoED Greek, quiet, international, and disabled housing. On-campus housing is guaranteed for all 4 years. 77% of students commute. All students may keep cars.

FACULTY/CLASSROOMS: 44% of faculty are male; 56% are female. No introductory courses are taught by graduate students. The average class size in an introductory lecture is 15.

PROGRAMS OF STUDY: NSU confers B.A., B.H.Sc., B.S., and B.S.N. degrees. Associate, master's, and doctoral degrees are also awarded. Bachelor's degrees are awarded in BIOLOGICAL SCIENCE (biological sciences, marine biology, marine science, and neurosciences), BUSINESS (accounting, business administration and management, finance, and marketing), COMMUNICATIONS AND THE ARTS (art, arts administration/management, communication studies, dance, dramatic arts, fine arts, information technology, music, and theatre acting), COMPUTER AND PHYSICAL SCIENCE (chemistry, computer engineering technology, computer information systems, computer science, mathematics, and software engineering), EDUCATION (athletic training, early childhood education, education, education administration, education of the exceptional child, elementary education, English education, general studies, middle school education, physical education, science education, secondary education, and sports and wellness studies), ENGINEERING AND ENVIRONMENTAL DESIGN (computer engineering and environmental science), HEALTH PROFESSIONS (biology, diagnostic medical sonography, exercise science, health promotion, kinesiology, nursing, recreation therapy, respiratory therapy, and speech pathology/audiology), SOCIAL SCIENCE (anthropology, behavioral science, criminal justice, human development, human services, international relations, legal studies, paralegal studies, philosophy, philosophy and religion, political science/government, psychology, public administration, and sociology). Biology, nursing, and business have the largest enrollments.

ACTIVITIES: 8% of men belong to 6 national fraternities; 7% of women belong to 6 national sororities. There are 316 groups on campus, including band, cheerleading, chorale, chorus, computers, dance, drama, environmental, ethnic, honors, international, LGBT, musical theater, newspaper, orchestra, political, professional, radio and TV, religious, social, social service, and student government. Popular campus events include Homecoming, Sharkapalooza, Student Life Achievement Awards, Cinema Tuesday, and Superbowl Party. **Sports:** There are 7 intercollegiate sports for men and 10 for women, and 7 intramural sports for men and 7 for women. Facilities include baseball and soccer fields and a recreational complex with a swimming pool and basketball and tennis courts. **Graduates:** From July 1, 2015 to June 30, 2016, 1412 bachelor's degrees were awarded. The most popular majors were nursing (17%), biology (premedical) (16%), and business administration (9%). In an average class, 4% graduate in 3 years or less, 31% graduate in 4 years or less, 40% graduate in 5 years or less, and 44% graduate in 6 years or less.

SERVICES: Counseling and information services are available, as is tutoring in some subjects, such as science, math, and writing. **Library/Resources:** The 5 libraries contain 827,004 volumes, 2.3 million microform items, and 65,295 audio/video tapes/CDs/DVDs, and subscribe to 50,033 periodicals including electronic. Computerized library services include interlibrary loans, database searching, Internet access, and Wi-Fi capability. Special learning facilities include an art gallery, radio station, a center of excellence for coral reef ecosystems science, and dryland training. Palm Beach student educational center, nursing simulation labs, the Huizenga Sales Institute, a neuro immune medicine clinic, health professions division museum, hall of fame, performing arts center, oceanographic center, law center, family village center, and a preschool. **Physically Challenged Students:** All of the campus is accessible. Facilities include wheelchair ramps, elevators, special parking, specially equipped restrooms, special class scheduling, lowered drinking fountains, and special housing. **Special:** NSU offers internships, study abroad, work-study, accelerated degree programs, nondegree study, Washington semester, undergraduate honors program, and undergraduate research experience. Combined bachelor-professional degree programs and a dual admission program are also available. There are 9 national honor societies and a freshman honors program. **Visiting:** There are regularly scheduled orientations for prospective students. There are guides for informal visits and visitors may sit in on classes. **Campus Safety and Security:** Measures include 24-hour foot and vehicle patrol, emergency notification system, and security escort services. There are shuttle buses, emergency telephones, lighted pathways/sidewalks, and controlled access to dorms/residences.

REQUIREMENTS: The SAT or ACT is required. Applicants must be graduates of an accredited secondary school or have a GED certificate. An interview is recommended. AP and CLEP credits are accepted. Important factors in the admissions decision are advanced placement or honors courses, leadership record, evidence of special talent, and extracurricular activities record. To graduate, all students must complete at least 120 credit hours, at least 30 of the credits must be earned at NSU, and at least 50% of the credits in the major area must be earned at NSU. A minimum 2.25 GPA is needed for courses in the major, and a 2.0 for all other courses. **Procedure:** Freshmen are admitted to all sessions. Entrance exams must be received by July for the fall term. There are deferred admissions and rolling admissions plans. Applications should be filed by August 1 for fall entry, along with a $50 fee. Notification is sent on a rolling basis. Applications are accepted on-line. **Transfer Students:** 760 transfer students enrolled in 2015-2016. Students transfering in good standing with AA or 60 credits from SACS accredited college are accepted and guaranteed junior standing. 30 of 120 credits required for the bachelor's degree must be completed at NSU. **International Students:** There are 286 international students enrolled. The school actively recruits these students. They must take the TOEFL with a minimum score of 550 on the paper-based TOEFL (PBT) or 79 on the Internet-based version (iBT), or take the MELAB, the Comprehensive English Language Test, and the college's own test, or take the IELTS, or the PTE-Academic.

ADMISSIONS: 59% of the 2016-2017 applicants were accepted. The SAT scores for the 2016-2017 freshman class were: Critical Reading-- 26% below 500, 45% between 500 and 599, 25% between 600 and 699, and 4% between 700 and 800. Math-- 27% below 500, 39% between 500 and 599, 29% between 600 and 699, and 5% between 700 and 800. The ACT scores were 1% between 12 and 17, 39% between 18 and 23, 40% between 24 and 29, and 20% above 30. 51% of the current freshmen were in the top fifth of their class; 79% were in the top two fifths. 4 freshmen graduated first in their class. **Admissions Contact:** Deanna Voss, Dean of Undergraduate Admissions. Email: *admissions@nova.edu* Web: *www.nova.edu*

FINANCIAL AID: The FAFSA code is 001509. Check with the school for current application deadlines.

PALM BEACH ATLANTIC UNIVERSITY — E-5

www.pba.edu

West Palm Beach, FL 33416	(561) 803-2100 (888) GO TO PBA
Fax: (561) 803-2115	**Email:** admit@pba.edu
Full-time: 775 men, 1520 women	**Faculty:** 207; IIB, -$
Part-time: 69 men, 110 women	**Ph.D.s:** 80%
Graduate: 266 men, 572 women	**Student/Faculty:** 12 to 1
Year: semesters, summer session	**Tuition:** $29,950
Room & Board: $9770	**Freshman Class:** 1449 applied, 1353 accepted, 505 enrolled
SAT CR/M/W: 535/515/516 **ACT:** 24	**CEEB CODE:** 5553
Application Deadline: n/av	**COMPETITIVE**

Palm Beach Atlantic University, founded in 1968, is an interdenominational Christian university with some 48 undergraduate majors (including nursing). Graduate degrees in business, leadership, counseling psychology, divinity, pharmacy, and nursing practice are offered. PBA is an ideal place to grow and explore your faith with young people of many races, nationalities, and creeds. There are 9 undergraduate schools and 4 graduate schools. In addition to regional accreditation, PBA has baccalaureate program accreditation with ACPE, NASM, IACBE, CCNE, NSCA, CAATE, ACSI, and NSCA. The 106-acre campus is in an urban area 60 miles north of Miami, 180 miles south of Orlando. Including any residence halls, there are 48 buildings.

STUDENT LIFE: 68% of undergraduates are from Florida. Others are from 44 states, 44 foreign countries, and Canada. 61% are White; 4% Foreign; 3% two or more races; 2% Asian American; 15% Hispanic; 11% African American; 1% race unknown. **Female To Male Ratio:** 2.0:1. The average age of freshmen is 18; all undergraduates, 23. 26% do not continue beyond their first year; 55% remain to graduate. **Housing:** 1237 students can be accommodated in college housing, which includes single-sex and coed on-campus apartments. In addition, there are honors houses, special-interest houses, apartments for single students, theme housing, all women's dorm, men's dorm, and coed dorms. On-campus housing is available on a first-come and first-served basis. 52% of students commute. Alcohol is not permitted. All students may keep cars.

FACULTY/CLASSROOMS: 49% of faculty are male; 42% are female. 85% teach undergraduates. No introductory courses are taught by graduate students. The average class size in an introductory lecture is 19; in a laboratory is 17; and in a regular course is 18.

PROGRAMS OF STUDY: PBA confers B.A., B.S., B.G.S., B.Mus. and B.S.N. degrees. Associate, master's, and doctoral degrees are also awarded. Bachelor's degrees are awarded in BIOLOGICAL SCIENCE (biology/biological science), BUSINESS (banking and finance, business administration and management, international business management, management science, marketing management, and organizational leadership and management), COMMUNICATIONS AND THE ARTS (art, communications, dance, English, film arts, graphic design, journalism, music, music performance, music theory and composition, musical theater, piano/organ, theater design, and voice), COMPUTER AND PHYSICAL SCIENCE (chemistry, computer science, and mathematics), EDUCATION (art education, athletic training, elementary education, English education, mathematics education, music education, physical education, science education, and secondary education), HEALTH PROFESSIONS (exercise science and nursing), SOCIAL SCIENCE (biblical studies, crosscultural studies, history, interdisciplinary studies, liberal arts/general studies, ministries, philosophy, political science/government, prelaw, and psychology). English, biology, and medicinal & biological chemistry are the strongest academically. Business, phamacy, and psychology have the largest enrollments.

ACTIVITIES: There are no fraternities or sororities. There are 39 groups on campus, including art, choir, chorale, chorus, communications, computers, dance, drama, environmental, ethnic, film, honors, jazz band, literary magazine, musical theater, newspaper, orchestra, pep band, photography, political, professional, social, social service, student government, and symphony. Popular campus events include American Free Enterprise Day and Christival. **Sports:** There are 5 intercollegiate sports for men and 7 for women, and 8 intramural sports for men and 8 for women. Facilities include 65,000 square foot facility known as the Greene Complex for Sports and Recreation. The Greene complex houses the Rubin Arena, locker rooms, athletic training facility, fitness center, and recreational space for both its varsity and club level sports programs. Rinker Athletic Complex which will house all of PBA's outside sports including baseball, softball, tennis and soccer. **Graduates:** From July 1, 2015 to June 30, 2016, 506 bachelor's degrees were awarded. The most popular majors were business/marketing (27%), health professions and related programs (12%), and theology and religious vocations (10%). In an average class, 51% graduate in 6 years or less.

SERVICES: Counseling and information services are available, as is tutoring in most subjects. There is a reader service for the blind, and remedial math and writing. **Library/Resources:** The library contains 265,143 volumes, 79,094 microform items, and 6,254 audio/video tapes/CDs/DVDs, and subscribes to 32,000 periodicals including electronic. Computerized library services include interlibrary loans, database searching, Internet access, and Wi-Fi capability. Special learning facilities include an art gallery, center for writing excellence (writing assistance); student success center, peer tutoring, first year experience, and ADA accomodations. **Physically Challenged Students:** 60% of the campus is accessible. Facilities include wheelchair ramps, elevators, special parking, specially equipped restrooms, and special class scheduling. **Special:** PBA offers work-study, internships, a student-designed interdisciplinary major, accelerated degree programs in organizational management (evening program only) and ministry, a London semester, study abroad through the Coalition of Christian Colleges and Universities, and teacher certification. There are 13 national honor societies, a freshman honors program, and 1 departmental honors program. **Visiting:** There are regularly scheduled orientations for prospective students, including a general open house and a school-specific open house. There are guides for informal visits, visitors may sit in on classes, and stay overnight. To schedule a visit, contact the Admissions Office. **Campus Safety and Security:** Measures include 24-hour foot and vehicle patrol, emergency notification system, self-defense education, and security escort services. There are emergency telephones, lighted pathways/sidewalks, controlled access to dorms/residences, and closed circuit television system.

REQUIREMENTS: The SAT or ACT is required. Applicants must be graduates of an accredited secondary school or have a GED certificate, and have completed 18 academic credits: 4 in English, 3 each in math, and science with lab, 2 recommended in a foreign language, and 5 in electives. An essay and an interview are required. A portfolio is recommended for art students. A GPA of 3.6 is required. AP and CLEP credits are accepted. Important factors in the admissions decision are leadership record, advanced placement or honors courses, personality/intangible qualities, evidence of special talent, extracurricular activities record, recommendations by school officials, and recommendations by alumni. Students must complete general education requirements and a minimum of 120 credit hours. Students must complete 42 credit hours in courses numbered 3000 or above (Bachelor of Music students, 33 hours). The last 32 credit hours must be completed at PBA and a minimum 2.0 GPA is required. **Procedure:** Freshmen are admitted to all sessions. Entrance exams should be taken in the junior year of high school. There are deferred admissions and rolling admissions plans. Application deadlines are open. Application fee is $50. Notifications are sent September 1. Applications are accepted on-line. **Transfer Students:** 251 transfer students enrolled in 2015-2016. Transfer students must have a minimum 2.5 GPA on at least 12 semester hours, 300-500 word essay, and 2 letters of recommendation. An interview is required. Application for Admission is in the fall, spring and summer. 32 of 120 credits required for the bachelor's degree must be completed at PBA. **International Students:** There are 112 international students enrolled. The school actively recruits these students. They must take the TOEFL with a minimum score of 79 on the Internet-based version (iBT). They must also take the SAT or ACT.

ADMISSIONS: 93% of the 2016-2017 applicants were accepted. The SAT scores for the 2016-2017 freshman class were: Critical Reading-- 34% below 500, 38% between 500 and 599, 22% between 600 and 699, and 5% between 700 and 800. Math-- 45% below 500, 37% between 500 and 599, 14% between 600 and 699, and 4% between 700 and 800. Writing-- 44% below 500, 37% between 500 and 599, 16% between 600 and 699, and 3% between 700 and 800. The ACT scores were 5% between 12 and 17, 40% between 18 and 23, 40% between 24 and 29, and 14% above 30. **Admissions Contact:** Jamie Zugelder, Director of Admissions. Email: *admit@pba.edu* Web: *www.pba.edu*

FINANCIAL AID: In 2016-2017, 100% of all full-time freshmen and 100% of continuing full-time students received some form of financial aid. 73% of all full-time freshmen and 74% of continuing full-time students received need-based aid. The average freshman award was $21,274. Need-based scholarships or need-based grants averaged $19,109; need-based self-help aid (loans and jobs) averaged $3,552; non-need-based athletic scholarships averaged $10,085; and other non-need-based awards and non-need-based scholarships averaged $13,696. 13% of undergraduate students work part-time. Average annual earnings from campus work are $2600. The average financial indebtedness of the 2016 graduate was $28,639. The state aid form is required. The priority date for freshman financial aid applications for fall entry is May 1.

RINGLING COLLEGE OF ART AND DESIGN *(The complete profile is made available exclusively on our website, www.barronspac.com)*

ROLLINS COLLEGE — D-3

www.rollins.edu

Winter Park, FL 32789 — (407) 646-2161

Email: admission@rollins.edu

Full-time: 804 men, 1144 women	**Faculty:** 196; IIA, av$
Part-time: n/av	**Ph.D.s:** 92%
Graduate: 249 men, 324 women	**Student/Faculty:** 10 to 1
Year: semesters	**Tuition:** $44,760
Room & Board: $13,910	**Freshman Class:** 4922 applied, 2972 accepted, 493 enrolled
	CEEB CODE: 5572
Application Deadline: February 15	**HIGHLY COMPETITIVE**

Rollins College, founded in 1885, is a nonsectarian institution focused on excellence, and fueled by dedication to pragmatic liberal arts. Students experience small classes led by faculty nationally recognized for innovative teaching and scholarship. Figures in the above capsule and in this profile are approximate. There are 2 undergraduate schools and 2 graduate schools. In addition to regional accreditation, Rollins has baccalaureate program accreditation with AACSB, NASM, ACS, AAM, and CACREP. The 80-acre campus is in a suburban area in Winter Park, Florida, adjacent to the city of Orlando.

STUDENT LIFE: 50% of undergraduates are from out of state, mostly the Middle Atlantic. Students are from 41 states, 60 foreign countries, and Canada. 8% are Foreign; 60% White; 6% African American; 4% race unknown; 3% Asian American; 3% two or more races; 16% Hispanic. **Female To Male Ratio:** 1.4:1. The average age of freshmen is 18; all undergraduates, 20. 16% do not continue beyond their first year; 62% remain to graduate. **Housing:** 1320 students can be accommodated in college housing, which includes single-sex and coed dorms and on-campus apartments. In addition, there are honors houses, special-interest houses, fraternity houses, and sorority houses. On-campus housing is guaranteed for the freshman year only. 60% of students live on campus. Upperclassmen may keep cars.

FACULTY/CLASSROOMS: 56% of faculty are male; 44% are female. No introductory courses are taught by graduate students.

PROGRAMS OF STUDY: Rollins confers A.B. degrees. Master's degrees are also awarded. Bachelor's degrees are awarded in BIOLOGICAL SCIENCE (biochemistry, biology/biological science, and marine biology), BUSINESS (international business management and organizational behavior), COMMUNICATIONS AND THE ARTS (art history and appreciation, communications, dramatic arts, English, French, media arts, music, music performance, Spanish, studio art, and theatre arts), COMPUTER AND PHYSICAL SCIENCE (chemistry, computer science, mathematics, and physics), EDUCATION (elementary education), ENGINEERING AND ENVIRONMENTAL DESIGN (environmental science), SOCIAL SCIENCE (anthropology, Asian/Oriental studies, classical/ancient civilization, crosscultural studies, economics, history, humanities, international relations, Latin American studies, philosophy, political science/government, psychology, religion, and sociology). International business, psychology, and communication studies have the largest enrollments.

ACTIVITIES: 38% of men belong to 1 local and 5 national fraternities; 42% of women belong to 1 local and 6 national sororities. There are 110 groups on campus, including art, band, cheerleading, chess, choir, chorale, chorus, computers, dance, debate, drama, drum and bugle corps, environmental, ethnic, film, honors, international, jazz band, LGBT, literary magazine, musical theater, newspaper, orchestra, pep band, photography, political, professional, radio and TV, religious, social, social service, student government, symphony, and yearbook. Popular campus events include Greek Week, Lip Sync, R-Big Event, and Fox Day. **Sports:** There are 11 intercollegiate sports for men and 12 for women, and 9 intramural sports for men and 10 for women. Facilities include a 2500-seat auditorium, a 600-seat stadium, tennis courts, baseball and soccer fields, a field house with a gym that seats 2500, a weight room, a boat house, and a swimming pool. **Graduates:** From July 1, 2015 to June 30, 2016, 623 bachelor's degrees were awarded. The most popular majors were international business (12%), communication studies (11%), and economics (10%). In an average class, 64% graduate in 4 years or less, 69% graduate in 5 years or less, and 71% graduate in 6 years or less.

SERVICES: Counseling and information services are available, as is tutoring in every subject. There is a reader service for the blind, and remedial math, reading, and writing. **Library/Resources:** The library contains 259,302 volumes, and 112 microform items. Computerized library services include interlibrary loans, database searching, Internet access, and Wi-Fi capability. Special learning facilities include an art gallery, radio station, TV station, art museum, theaters, writing center, and student resource center. **Physically Challenged Students:** 80% of the campus is accessible. Facilities include wheelchair ramps, elevators, special parking, specially equipped restrooms, special class scheduling, lowered drinking fountains, lowered telephones, and special housing. **Special:** Rollins offers cross-registration with the evening studies division, co-op programs with American University in Washington, D.C. and Duke University School of Forestry and Environmental Studies. Departmental and professional internships, study abroad in 9 countries, and a Washington semester are also options. Also available are an accelerated (3-2) MBA program, a B.A.-B.S. degree in preengineering with Washington University (St. Louis), Auburn, and Columbia Universities, an interdepartmental biochemistry/molecular biology major, dual majors in any combination, and student-designed majors. Nondegree study and pass/fail options are possible. There are 5 national honor societies, a freshman honors program, and 30 departmental honors programs. **Visiting:** There are regularly scheduled orientations for prospective students. There are guides for informal visits and visitors may sit in on classes. To schedule a visit, contact The Office of Admissions. **Campus Safety and Security:** Measures include 24-hour foot and vehicle patrol, emergency notification system, self-defense education, and security escort services. There are shuttle buses, emergency telephones, lighted pathways/sidewalks, controlled access to dorms/residences, and 24-hour locked residential units.

REQUIREMENTS: Applicants must be graduates of an accredited secondary school or have a GED certificate and have completed 4 years of English, 3 years of math, and 2 years each of foreign language, science, and social studies. An essay is required. SAT Subject tests in writing, math, and foreign language and an interview are recommended. AP and CLEP credits are accepted. Important factors in the admissions decision are advanced placement or honors courses, evidence of special talent, and extracurricular activities record. Students must complete a minimum of 140 semester hours of academic work, of which at least sixty-four semester hours must be outside a single departmental prefix. All students must complete a minimum of sixteen semester hours that are not used to meet either a general education curriculum or major requirement. Students must earn a minimum academic average of a 2.00 (C) for all courses taken at Rollins. **Procedure:** Freshmen are admitted fall and spring. Entrance exams should be taken by the first semester of the senior year. There are early decision and deferred admissions plans. Early decision applications should be filed by November 15; regular applications, by February 15 for fall entry; and November 1 for spring entry. The fall 2016 application fee was $40. Notification of early decision is sent December 15; regular decision, April 1. 102 applicants were on the 2016 waiting list; 10 were admitted. Applications are accepted on-line. **Transfer Students:** 69 transfer students enrolled in 2015-2016. Transfer students must satisfy all regular admission requirements and submit official transcripts of college and high school work and SAT or ACT scores. A recommended 3.0 GPA and a year's worth of credit hours earned are required. An interview is recommended. 64 of 140 credits required for the bachelor's degree must be completed at Rollins. **International Students:** There are 173 international students enrolled. The school actively recruits these students. They must take the TOEFL with a minimum score of 550 on the paper-based TOEFL (PBT) or 80 on the Internet-based version (iBT). They must also take the SAT or ACT.

ADMISSIONS: 60% of the 2016-2017 applicants were accepted. The SAT scores for the 2016-2017 freshman class were: Critical Reading-- 4% below 500, 41% between 500 and 599, 45% between 600 and 699, and 10% between 700 and 800. Math-- 5% below 500, 43% between 500 and 599, 40% between 600 and 699, and 13% between 700 and 800. Writing-- 8% below 500, 44% between 500 and 599, 39% between 600 and 699, and 10% between 700 and 800. **Admissions Contact:** Office of Admission Email: *admission@rollins.edu* Web: *www.rollins.edu*

FINANCIAL AID: 27% of undergraduate students work part-time. Average annual earnings from campus work are $1289. Rollins is a member of CSS. The college's own financial statement is required. The FAFSA code is 001515. The priority date for freshman financial aid applications for fall entry is March 1.

SAINT LEO UNIVERSITY — D-3

www.saintleo.edu

Saint Leo, FL 33574 — (352) 588-8283, (800) 334-5532

Fax: (352) 588-8257 — Email: admissions@saintleo.edu

Full-time: 930 men, 1262 women	**Faculty:** 129
Part-time: 42 men, 30 women	**Ph.D.s:** 84%
Graduate: 1373 men, 2261 women	**Student/Faculty:** 17 to 1
Year: semesters, summer session	**Tuition:** $21,440
Room & Board: $10,210	**Freshman Class:** 4501 applied, 3139 accepted, 610 enrolled
SAT CR/M/W: 490/500/470 **ACT:** 22	**CEEB CODE:** 5638
Application Deadline: rolling	**COMPETITIVE**

Saint Leo University was founded in 1889. Undergraduate students benefit from a rewarding, values-based education that integrates caring faculty, state-of-the-art technology and active learning as they choose from more than 50 outstanding academic programs and endorsements. There are 3 undergraduate schools and 7 graduate schools. In addition to regional accreditation, Saint Leo has baccalaureate program accreditation with ACBSP, CSWE, IACBE, and COSMA. The 280-acre campus is in a rural area just 40 miles north of Tampa. Including any residence halls, there are 32 buildings.

STUDENT LIFE: 70% of undergraduates are from Florida. Others are from 47 states, 63 foreign countries, and Canada. 71% are from public schools. 7% are race unknown; 43% White; 3% two or more races; 2% Asian American; 19% Hispanic; 14% African American; 12% Foreign. 45% claim no religious affiliation; 28% Catholic; 23% Protestant. **Female To Male Ratio:** 1.5:1. The average age of freshmen is 18; all undergraduates, 21. 28% do not continue beyond their first year; 40% remain to graduate. **Housing:** 1583 students can be accommodated in college housing, which includes single-sex and coed dorms, on-campus apartments, and off-campus apartments. In addition, there are honors houses, theme housing, and wellness housing. On-campus housing is guaranteed for all 4 years. 67% of students live on campus; of those, 85% remain on campus on weekends. All students may keep cars.

FACULTY/CLASSROOMS: 49% of faculty are male; 51% are female. All teach undergraduates. No introductory courses are taught by graduate students. The average class size in a laboratory is 15 and in a regular course is 17.

PROGRAMS OF STUDY: Saint Leo confers B.A., B.S., and B.S.W. degrees. Associate, master's, and doctoral degrees are also awarded. Bachelor's degrees are awarded in BIOLOGICAL SCIENCE (biology ecology and field biology and biology/biological science), BUSINESS (accounting, business communications, hospitality management services, management information systems, management science, marketing management, and sports management), COMMUNICATIONS AND THE ARTS (English, English literature, English Writing, and multimedia), COMPUTER AND PHYSICAL SCIENCE (computer information systems, computer security, information sciences and systems, and mathematics), EDUCATION (elementary education, English secondary education, global studies, middle school education, and secondary education), HEALTH PROFESSIONS (biomedical science and health care administration), SOCIAL SCIENCE (criminal justice, developmental psychology, economics, experimental psychology, history, homeland security, political science/government, psychology, religion, social work, and sociology). Cybersecurity, biology, and criminal justice are the strongest academically. Criminal justice, biology, and psychology have the largest enrollments.

ACTIVITIES: 9% of men belong to 1 local and 3 national fraternities; 16% of women belong to 1 local and 5 national sororities. There are 80 groups on campus, including Caribbean Student Association, The Quest, campus activities board, cheerleading, chorus, computers, drama, environmental, ethnic, honors, international, literary magazine, musical theater, newspaper, political, professional, religious, social, social service, student government, and yearbook. Popular campus events include Spring Fling, Winter Formal, Family Fall Festival, and Halloween Horror Nights Trip. **Sports:** There are 9 intercollegiate sports for men and 10 for women, and 14 intramural sports for men and 10 for women. Facilities include a 1400-seat indoor gym, a fitness center, an outdoor swimming pool, golf course, soccer, softball, baseball, and practice fields, basketball, volleyball, racquetball, and lighted tennis courts, a turf field, sailing, and canoeing. **Graduates:** From July 1, 2015 to June 30, 2016, 436 bachelor's degrees were awarded. The most popular majors were computer information systems/information assurance (11%), sport business (9%), and management (8%). 67 companies recruited on campus in 2015-2016. In an average class, 31% graduate in 4 years or less, 39% graduate in 5 years or less, and 40% graduate in 6 years or less.

SERVICES: Counseling and information services are available, as is tutoring in most subjects. There is a reader service for the blind, and remedial math and writing. **Library/Resources:** The library contains 500,538 volumes, 21,293 microform items, and 813 audio/video tapes/CDs/DVDs, and subscribes to 179,835 periodicals including electronic. Computerized library services include interlibrary loans, database searching, Internet access, and Wi-Fi capability. Special learning facilities include an art gallery and TV station. **Physically Challenged Students:** 95% of the campus is accessible. Facilities include wheelchair ramps, elevators, special parking, specially equipped restrooms, lowered drinking fountains, and special housing. Students with disability needs are assessed on a case-by-case basis with proper documentation. **Special:** Saint Leo offers internships in most majors, study abroad in 11 countries, work-study programs on campus, dual majors, and credit for military experience. There is a prelaw program, preprofessional programs in medicine, dentistry, and veterinary science, and Air Force and Army ROTC programs. Saint Leo also has an ambassador program with the University of St. Augustine for Health Sciences (occupational and physical therapy). There are 20 national honor societies, a freshman honors program, and 1 departmental honors program. **Visiting:** There are regularly scheduled orientations for prospective students, consisting of overnight campus visitation programs. There are guides for informal visits, visitors may sit in on classes, and stay overnight. To schedule a visit, contact the Office of Admission. **Campus Safety and Security:** Measures include 24-hour foot and vehicle patrol, emergency notification system, and security escort services. There are shuttle buses, emergency telephones, lighted pathways/sidewalks, and controlled access to dorms/residences.

REQUIREMENTS: Applicants for regular admission status are recommended to have successfully completed the following high school courses by the time they enroll at Saint Leo University: English (4 years), mathematics and history/social science (3 years each), science, foreign language, and electives (2 years each). Students must submit an application, official high school transcript, letter of recommendation from a high school guidance counselor or teacher and standardized test scores if not applying as test optional. AP and CLEP credits are accepted. Important factors in the admissions decision are advanced placement or honors courses, leadership record, and recommendations by school officials. To graduate, all students must complete a minimum of 120 academic credits with 30 to 60 hours in the major, all the requirements of their division and major, and 42 hours in the University Explorations program. The honors program may be substituted for general education requirements. A minimum 2.0 GPA and capstone course are required, and there is a 30-hour residency requirement. **Procedure:** Freshmen are admitted fall and spring. Entrance exams should be taken March 1. There are deferred admissions and rolling admissions plans. Application deadlines are open. Application fee is $40. Notification is sent on a rolling basis. Applications are accepted on-line. Application fees are waived if application is completed on-line. **Transfer Students:** 126 transfer students enrolled in 2015-2016. Entering transfers are classified according to the number of credits earned at their previous institution(s): Freshman (fewer than 30 credits), Sophomore (at least 30 and fewer than 60 credits), Junior (at least 60 and fewer than 90 credits), and Senior (at least 90 credits). Transfer applicants must submit an application along with an official college transcript from each institution attended and a recommendation from the Dean of Students or equivalent. High school transcripts and standardized test scores are required for students transferring with fewer than 24 academic credits. Student must be in good standing at the institution most recently attended. 30 of 120 credits required for the bachelor's degree must be completed at Saint Leo. **International Students:** There are 261 international students enrolled. The school actively recruits these students. They must take the TOEFL with a minimum score of 550 on the paper-based TOEFL (PBT) or 78 on the Internet-based version (iBT), SAT Verbal (minimum score 450 required) or IELTS (minimum score 6 required) may be substituted for TOEFL.

ADMISSIONS: 70% of the 2016-2017 applicants were accepted. The SAT scores for the 2016-2017 freshman class were: Critical Reading-- 52% below 500, 35% between 500 and 599, and 13% between 600 and 699. Math-- 46% below 500, 43% between 500 and 599, 10% between 600 and 699, and 1% between 700 and 800. Writing-- 64% below 500, 28% between 500 and 599, 7% between 600 and 699, and 1% between 700 and 800. The ACT scores were 3% between 12 and 17, 59% between 18 and 23, 31% between 24 and 29, and 7% above 30. 24% of the current freshmen were in the top fifth of their class; 59% were in the top two fifths. 3 freshmen graduated first in their class. **Admissions Contact:** Michael Halligan, Associate Director of Admissions. Email: *admissions@saintleo.edu* Web: *www.saintleo.edu*

FINANCIAL AID: In 2016-2017, 100% of all full-time freshmen and 97% of continuing full-time students received some form of financial aid. 90% of all full-time freshmen and 84% of continuing full-time students received need-based aid. The average freshman award was $23,748. Need-based scholarships or need-based grants averaged $9,379 ($26,132 maximum); need-based self-help aid (loans and jobs) averaged $10,232 ($33,892 maximum); non-need-based athletic scholarships averaged $12,021 ($33,650 maximum); and other non-need-based awards and non-need-based scholarships averaged $6,224 ($27,760 maximum). 21% of undergraduate students work part-time. Average annual earnings from campus work are $4830. The average financial indebtedness of the 2016 graduate was $18,590. Saint Leo is a member of CSS. The FAFSA code is 001526. The priority date for freshman financial aid applications for fall entry is March 1.

SOUTHEASTERN UNIVERSITY D-3

www.seu.edu

Lakeland, FL 33801	**(863) 667-5018** **(800) 500-8760**
Fax: (863) 667-5200	**Email: admissions@seu.edu**
Full-time: 896 men, 1210 women	**Faculty:** 93; IIB, -$
Part-time: 184 men, 158 women	**Ph.D.s:** 67%
Graduate: 106 men, 149 women	**Student/Faculty:** 22 to 1
Year: semesters, summer session	**Tuition:** $23,160
Room & Board: $8605	**Freshman Class:** 1442 applied, 707 accepted, 592 enrolled
SAT CR/M/W: 509/487/494 **ACT:** 21	**CEEB CODE:** 5621
Application Deadline: n/av	**COMPETITIVE**

Southeastern University, founded in 1935, is a Christian liberal arts institution offering over 60 degree programs that equip students to serve in both professional careers and ministry-related fields. The figures in the above capsule and in this profile are approximate. There are 5 undergraduate schools and 4 graduate schools. In addition to regional accreditation, Southeastern has baccalaureate program accreditation with SACS. The 88-acre campus is in a suburban area 30 miles east of Tampa and 45 miles west of Orlando. Including any residence halls, there are 30 buildings.

STUDENT LIFE: 65% of undergraduates are from Florida. Others are from 47 states, 21 foreign countries, and Canada. 67% are White; 13% Hispanic; 10% African American; 1% Asian American; 1% Foreign. 99% are Protestant. **Female To Male Ratio:** 1.3:1. The average age of freshmen is 20; all undergraduates, 23. 36% do not continue beyond their first year; 39% remain to graduate. **Housing:** 1355 students can be accommodated in college housing, which includes single-sex dorms and on-campus apartments. On-campus housing is available on a first-come and first-served basis. 51% of students live on campus; of those, 60% remain on campus on weekends. Alcohol is not permitted. All students may keep cars.

FACULTY/CLASSROOMS: 66% of faculty are male; 34% are female. All teach undergraduates, and all do research. No introductory courses are taught by graduate students. The average class size in an introductory lecture is 60; in a laboratory is 20; and in a regular course is 32.

PROGRAMS OF STUDY: Southeastern confers B.A., B.S., B.M. and B.S.W. degrees. Associate, master's, and doctoral degrees are also awarded. Bachelor's degrees are awarded in BIOLOGICAL SCIENCE (biology/biological science), BUSINESS (accounting, banking and finance, business administration and management, management information systems, marketing/retailing/merchandising, and sports management), COMMUNICATIONS AND THE ARTS (broadcasting, communications, dramatic arts, English, journalism, music, and public relations), COMPUTER AND PHYSICAL SCIENCE (mathematics), EDUCATION (education of the exceptional child, elementary education, middle school education, music education, and secondary education), SOCIAL SCIENCE (biblical studies, criminal justice, history, interdisciplinary studies, ministries, pastoral studies, psychology, public administration, religion, religious music, and social work). Religion, education, and business are the strongest academically. Religion and business have the largest enrollment.

ACTIVITIES: There are no fraternities or sororities. There are 30 groups on campus, including band, cheerleading, choir, chorale, chorus, communications, computers, drama, ethnic, honors, international, jazz band, musical theater, newspaper, opera, orchestra, political, professional, radio and TV, religious, social, social service, student government, symphony, and yearbook. **Sports:** There are 6 intercollegiate sports for men and 7 for women, and 8 intramural sports for men and 8 for women. Facilities include a gym, baseball and soccer fields, softball, flag football, tennis, racquetball, and beach volleyball courts, a weight room, and intramural fields.

SERVICES: Counseling and information services are available, as is tutoring in most subjects, such as English, science, math, religion, history, music, and communication. There is remedial math, reading, and writing. There is also a career service counselor available. **Library/Resources:** The 2 libraries contain 131,072 volumes, 2,163 microform items, and 8,046 audio/video tapes/CDs/DVDs, and subscribe to 1,223 periodicals including electronic. Computerized library services include interlibrary loans, database searching, Internet access, and Wi-Fi capability. Special learning facilities include an art gallery, radio station, TV station, and a Pentecostal Research Library. **Physically Challenged Students:** 90% of the campus is accessible. Facilities include wheelchair ramps, elevators, special parking, specially equipped restrooms, special class scheduling, and lowered drinking fountains. **Special:** Internships are available in communications, education, ministry, psychology, pastoral studies, Christian education, and business. There are accelerated degree programs in church leadership and in business and professional leadership, study abroad in 7 countries, and a Washington semester. There are 2 national honor societies, a freshman honors program, and 2 departmental honors programs. **Visiting:** There are regularly scheduled orientations for prospective students, and Preview Days (fall and spring), which consist of a 24-hour overview of campus life with class visits, faculty reception, admission/financial aid workshops, student panel discussion, and a worship service. There are guides for informal visits, visitors may sit in on classes, and stay overnight. To schedule a visit, contact the Admission Office. **Campus Safety and Security:** Measures include 24-hour foot and vehicle patrol, emergency notification system, and security escort services. There are emergency telephones, lighted pathways/sidewalks, controlled access to dorms/residences, a main entrance security booth attendant text alert system, and closed circuit security cameras.

REQUIREMENTS: The SAT or ACT is required. The GED is accepted. A GPA of 1.5 is required. AP and CLEP credits are accepted. Important factors in the admissions decision are extracurricular activities record, recommendations by school officials, and personality/intangible qualities. Every degree student must complete 125 to 130 hours, including 36 hours of general education and up to 20 hours of religion (transfer students may have fewer required, based on transfer hours). Distribution requirements include 6 to 12 hours each in arts and communications, human adjustment, science and math, social sciences, and humanities and fine arts. A minimum GPA of 2.0 must be maintained. **Procedure:** Freshmen are admitted to all sessions. Entrance exams should be taken prior to enrollment. There is a rolling admissions plan. Check with the school for current application deadlines. The application fee is $40. Applications are accepted on-line. **Transfer Students:** 257 transfer students enrolled in 2015-2016. Admission requirements for transfer applicants are the same as for first-time students. 30 of 124 credits required for the bachelor's degree must be completed at Southeastern. **International Students:** The school actively recruits these students. They must take the TOEFL. They must also take the SAT or ACT.

ADMISSIONS: 49% of the 2016-2017 applicants were accepted. The SAT scores for the 2016-2017 freshman class were: Critical Reading-- 45% below 500, 39% between 500 and 599, 15% between 600 and 699, and 2% between 700 and 800. Math-- 53% below 500, 35% between 500 and 599, 12% between 600 and 699, and 1% between 700 and 800. Writing-- 52% below 500, 35% between 500 and 599, 12% between 600 and 699, and 2% between 700 and 800. The ACT scores were 50% below 12, 22% between 12 and 17, 18% between 18 and 23, 6% between 24 and 29, and 4% above 30. **Admissions Contact:** Omar Rashed, Director of Admissions. Email: *admissions@seu.edu* Web: *www.seu.edu*

FINANCIAL AID: The college's own financial statement is required. The FAFSA code is 001521. The deadline for filing freshman financial aid applications for fall entry is April 15.

ST. THOMAS UNIVERSITY *(The complete profile is made available exclusively on our website, www.barronspac.com)*

STETSON UNIVERSITY — D-3

www.stetson.edu

DeLand, FL 32723	**(386) 822-7100** **(800) 688-0101**
Fax: (386) 822-7112	**Email: admissions@stetson.edu**
Full-time: 1279 men, 1769 women	**Faculty:** 216; IIA, ++$
Part-time: 19 men, 22 women	**Ph.D.s:** 95%
Graduate: 547 men, 721 women	**Student/Faculty:** 13 to 1
Year: semesters, summer session	**Tuition:** $43,240
Room & Board: $12,326	**Freshman Class:** 12130 applied, 7957 accepted, 813 enrolled
SAT CR/M/W: 590/570/560 **ACT:** 26	**CEEB CODE:** 5630
Application Deadline: March 15	**VERY COMPETITIVE**

Stetson University is the oldest private university in the State of Florida. Founded in 1883 by Henry A. DeLand as the DeLand Academy and later renamed Stetson University to honor its benefactor, John B. Stetson, the university has a storied history of leadership, values, and significance. The university is home to many Florida firsts, including the first collegiate newspaper, the first chapter of Phi Beta Kappa (the nation's oldest and most prestigious undergraduate honor society), the oldest schools of business administration and music and the first college of law. Stetson also was Florida's first private university to integrate. Stetson is about more than the buildings and those who helped build them; it's really about a vibrant, growing institution where students are prepared to lead lives of significance. The university is led by its ninth president, Wendy B. Libby, and is home to 73 undergraduate academic programs in law, music, arts and sciences, and business with graduate studies offered in business and education. The university is accredited by numerous agencies, including the Southern Association of Colleges and Schools Commission on Colleges, and curriculum is closely aligned with the marketplace to prepare students for life after Stetson. Undergraduate leadership, research, social justice, advocacy and volunteer service, and participatory activities flourish at all four of the university's locations. There are 3 undergraduate schools and 2 graduate schools. In addition to regional accreditation, Stetson has baccalaureate program accreditation with AACSB, NASM, and NCATE. The 159-acre campus is in a small town in DeLand, 35 miles north of Orlando and 25 miles west of Dayton, Beach, with a second campus in Gulfport and two satellite campuses, one in Celebration and the other in Tampa. Including any residence halls, there are 98 buildings.

STUDENT LIFE: 68% of undergraduates are from Florida. Others are from 45 states, 59 foreign countries, and Canada. 77% are from public schools. 63% are White; 15% Hispanic; 8% African American; 6% Foreign; 4% two or more races; 2% Asian American; 1% American Indian/Alaska Native; 1% race unknown. 40% claim no religious affiliation; 36% Protestant; 16% Catholic. **Female To Male Ratio:** 1.4:1. The average age of freshmen is 18; all undergraduates, 20. 21% do not continue beyond their first year; 64% remain to graduate. **Housing:** 2057 students can be accommodated in college housing, which includes single-sex and coed dorms and on-campus apartments. In addition, there are honors houses, language houses, special-interest houses, fraternity houses, sorority houses, family & partnered housing, gender-neutral housing, animal-friendly options, and themed-housing options: First-Year Experience, Women's Leadership, Wellness, and Honors Houses. On-campus housing is guaranteed for all 4 years. 65% of students live on campus; of those, 80% remain on campus on weekends. All students may keep cars.

FACULTY/CLASSROOMS: 56% of faculty are male; 44% are female. All teach undergraduates. No introductory courses are taught by graduate students. The average class size in an introductory lecture is 20; in a laboratory is 20; and in a regular course is 18.

PROGRAMS OF STUDY: Stetson confers B.A., B.S., B.B.A., B.M. and B.M.E. degrees. Master's and doctoral degrees are also awarded. Bachelor's degrees are awarded in BIOLOGICAL SCIENCE (biochemistry, biology/biological science, marine biology, and molecular biology), BUSINESS (accounting, banking and finance, business administration and management, business economics, business information systems, business intelligence and analytics, international business management, marketing/retailing/merchandising, small business management, and sports management), COMMUNICATIONS AND THE ARTS (art history, communications, dramatic arts, English, French, German, guitar, music, music composition, music performance, music technology, music theory and composition, piano/organ, Spanish, studio art, voice, and winds), COMPUTER AND PHYSICAL SCIENCE (applied physics, chemistry, computer science, digital arts/technology, mathematics, and physics), EDUCATION (elementary education, music education, and social science education), ENGINEERING AND ENVIRONMENTAL DESIGN (environmental science), HEALTH PROFESSIONS (health science), SOCIAL SCIENCE (American studies, economics, geography, history, international studies, philosophy, political science/government, prelaw, psychology, religion, Russian and Slavic studies, and sociology). Biology, environmental science, and finance are the strongest academically. Psychology, business administration, finance, and health science have the largest enrollments.

ACTIVITIES: 30% of men belong to 7 national fraternities; 35% of women belong to 7 national sororities. There are 100 groups on campus, including art, band, cheerleading, chess, choir, chorale, chorus, computers, dance, debate, drama, environmental, ethnic, film, honors, international, jazz band, LGBT, literary magazine, musical theater, newspaper, opera, orchestra, pep band, political, professional, radio and TV, religious, social, social service, student government, and symphony. Popular campus events include Homecoming, Greenfeather (a community fundraising event coinciding with Homecoming), Hatterpalooza (a live music festival) and Winter Wonderland (snow in Florida). **Sports:** There are 8 intercollegiate sports for men and 10 for women, and 15 intramural sports for men and 17 for women. Facilities include weightroom and exercise facilities, fieldhouse, basketball courts, volleyball courts, tennis courts, handball courts, softball fields, soccer fields, baseball fields, running trail, and swimming pool. **Graduates:** From July 1, 2015 to June 30, 2016, 606 bachelor's degrees were awarded. The most popular majors were psychology (12%), finance (9%), and integrative health science (7%). 121 companies recruited on campus in 2015-2016. In an average class, 4% graduate in 3 years or less, 56% graduate in 4 years or less, 63% graduate in 5 years or less, and 64% graduate in 6 years or less. Of the 2015 graduating class, 25% were enrolled in graduate school within 6 months of graduation, and 51% were employed.

SERVICES: Counseling and information services are available, as is tutoring in most subjects. There is a reader service for the blind, and remedial writing. **Library/Resources:** The 3 libraries contain 406,238 volumes, 269,447 microform items, and 16,034 audio/video tapes/CDs/DVDs, and subscribe to 106,140 periodicals including electronic. Computerized library services include interlibrary loans, database searching, Internet access, and Wi-Fi capability. Special learning facilities include an art gallery, radio station, and a museum of minerals. **Physically Challenged Students:** 80% of the campus is accessible. Facilities include wheelchair ramps, elevators, special parking, specially equipped restrooms, special class scheduling, lowered drinking fountains, and lowered telephones. **Special:** Stetson's curriculum is designed to provide students with a high quality education that includes high-impact practices such as experiential learning, internships that are available to all students, and community engagement throughout the curriculum. Stetson offers interdisciplinary programs, including environmental studies, entrepreneurship, music education, and others. The 3+3 BA/JD program offers accelerated admission to the College of Law. In finance, the Roland George Investments Program gives students the experience of managing over $3.4 million in stocks and bonds. Through the David and Leighan Rinker Center for International Learning, students study throughout the world, including Argentina, Australia, Austria, Belgium, Botswana, Brazil, Cambodia, Cayman Islands, Chile, China, Colombia, Costa Rica, Cuba, Czech Republic, Denmark, Dominican Republic, Ecuador, England, Finland, France, Germany, Ghana, Greece, Guatemala, Hong Kong, Hungary, Ireland, Italy, Japan, Jordan, Mexico, Morocco, Netherlands, Nicaragua, Peru, Poland, Russia, Scotland, Serbia, Senegal, South Africa, South Korea, Spain, Switzerland, Taiwan, Tanzania, Thailand, and Vietnam. Students in Stetson University's Honors Program take a uniquely integrated curriculum, receive special funding for personal research and travel, may design their major and some courses, and work closely with their advisor to be especially competitive for national scholarships and fellowships. There are 27 national honor societies, Phi Beta Kappa, and a freshman honors program. **Visiting:** There are regularly scheduled orientations for prospective students, consisting of a campus tour and orientation, interviews, class visits, and presentations. There are guides for informal visits, visitors may sit in on classes, and stay overnight. To schedule a visit, contact the Admissions Office. **Campus Safety and Security:** Measures include 24-hour foot and vehicle patrol, emergency notification system, self-defense education, and security escort services. There are emergency telephones, lighted pathways/sidewalks, and controlled access to dorms/residences.

REQUIREMENTS: Applicants must be graduates of an accredited secondary school or have a GED, and have completed 4 years of English, 3 years of math and science, and 2 years each of foreign language, social sciences, and electives. Auditions are required for music students. AP credits are accepted. Important factors in the admissions decision are advanced placement or honors courses, leadership record, and evidence of special talent. Stetson University provides an integrated, comprehensive learning experience for all students through a combination of courses in the major and general education. General education requirements are based on a set of highly desirable learning outcomes that enable students to succeed academically and in future endeavors. These learning outcomes include communication skills, quantitative reasoning skills, critical thinking, personal and social responsibility, and specific knowledge areas such as the physical world and creative arts. All students at Stetson University accomplish this learning through our First Year Seminars, courses in quantitative reasoning, writing, and personal and social responsibility, a selection of knowledge-area courses, the interdisciplinary junior seminar, and senior research capstone courses. Students have a wide range of options from which to select these and other general education courses. To graduate, all students must complete 32 units/courses, equivalent to 128 credits. **Procedure:** Freshmen are admitted fall, spring, and summer. Entrance exams should be taken spring of the junior year or the fall of the senior year. There are deferred admissions and rolling admissions plans. Application deadlines are open. Application fee is $50. Notification is sent on a rolling basis. Applications are accepted on-line. **Transfer Students:** 90 transfer students enrolled in 2015-2016. Transfer students must have completed a semester of academic work in good standing at an accredited college with a minimum 2.0 GPA. A 2.75 GPA and an interview (in person or remotely) are encouraged but not required. They must submit college transcripts and also an essay or personal statement at the time of application. High school transcripts may be requested as part of the application process if less than 30 college credits have been earned prior to the time of application. 64 of 128 credits required for the bachelor's degree must be completed at Stetson. **International Students:** There are 180 international students enrolled. The school actively recruits these students.

ADMISSIONS: 66% of the 2016-2017 applicants were accepted. The SAT scores for the 2016-2017 freshman class were: Critical Reading-- 14% below 500, 49% between 500 and 599, 29% between 600 and 699, and 8% between 700 and 800. Math-- 20% below 500, 46% between 500 and 599, 28% between 600 and 699, and 5% between 700 and 800. Writing-- 23% below 500, 52% between 500 and 599, 23% between 600 and 699, and 3% between 700 and 800. The ACT scores were 1% between

12 and 17, 26% between 18 and 23, 55% between 24 and 29, and 19% above 30. 50% of the current freshmen were in the top fifth of their class; 77% were in the top two fifths. 138 freshmen graduated first in their class. **Admissions Contact:** Admissions, Director of Admissions. Email: *admissions@stetson.edu* Web: *www.stetson.edu*

FINANCIAL AID: In 2016-2017, 100% of all full-time freshmen and 99% of continuing full-time students received some form of financial aid. 69% of all full-time freshmen and 63% of continuing full-time students received need-based aid. The average freshman award was $37,783. Need-based scholarships or need-based grants averaged $28,933 ($58,266 maximum); need-based self-help aid (loans and jobs) averaged $5,086 ($11,500 maximum); non-need-based athletic scholarships averaged $24,915 ($55,570 maximum); and other non-need-based awards and non-need-based scholarships averaged $24,027 ($42,000 maximum). 20% of undergraduate students work part-time. Average annual earnings from campus work are $2644. The average financial indebtedness of the 2016 graduate was $31,457. Stetson is a member of CSS. The FAFSA code is 001531. The priority date for freshman financial aid applications for fall entry is March 15.

UNIVERSITY OF CENTRAL FLORIDA D-3

www.ucf.edu

Orlando, FL 32816 **(407) 823-3000**

Fax: (407) 823-5625
Full-time: 17,511 men, 20,943 women
Part-time: 7861 men, 9461 women
Graduate: 3658 men, 4887 women
Year: semesters, summer session
Room & Board: $9554
SAT CR/M/W: 588/593/558 **ACT:** 26
Application Deadline: May 1

Email: admission@ucf.edu
Faculty: I, --$
Ph.D.s: 81%
Student/Faculty: 30 to 1
Tuition: $6368 ($22,467)
Freshman Class: 34886 applied, 17441 accepted, 6403 enrolled
CEEB CODE: 5233
VERY COMPETITIVE

University of Central Florida, founded in 1963, is the one of the nation's largest universities and offers 181 bachelor's and master's degrees and 31 doctoral programs. The Carnegie Foundation for the Advancement of Teaching named UCF a university with "highest research activity." There are 11 undergraduate schools and 11 graduate schools. In addition to regional accreditation, UCF has baccalaureate program accreditation with AACSB, ABET, CAHEA, CSWE, NASM, NCATE, NAACLS, CCNE, and CAATE. The 1415-acre campus is in a suburban area 13 miles northeast of downtown Orlando. Including any residence halls, there are 173 buildings.

STUDENT LIFE: 95% of undergraduates are from Florida. Others are from 50 states, 152 foreign countries, and Canada. 6% are Asian American; 51% White; 4% two or more races; 25% Hispanic; 2% Foreign; 11% African American; 1% race unknown. **Female To Male Ratio:** 1.2:1. The average age of freshmen is 18; all undergraduates, 22. 11% do not continue beyond their first year; 69% remain to graduate. **Housing:** 11641 students can be accommodated in college housing, which includes single-sex and coed dorms, on-campus apartments, and off-campus apartments. In addition, there are honors houses, special-interest houses, fraternity houses, and sorority houses. On-campus housing is available on a first-come, and first-served basis. 83% of students commute. All students may keep cars.

FACULTY/CLASSROOMS: 54% of faculty are male; 46% are female. 70% teach undergraduates, 67% do research, and 41% do both. Graduate students teach 8% of introductory courses. The average class size in an introductory lecture is 43; in a laboratory is 14; and in a regular course is 43.

PROGRAMS OF STUDY: UCF confers B.A., B.S., B.A.B.A., B.A.S., B.F.A., B.M., B.M.E., B.S.A.E., B.S.B.A., B.S.C.E., B.S.Con.E., B.S.Cp.E., B.S.E.E., B.S.E.E.T., B.S.Env.E., B.S.E.T., B.S.I.E., B.S.M.E., B.S.N., B.Des., B.S.P.S.E., and B.S.W. degrees. Associate, master's, and doctoral degrees are also awarded. Bachelor's degrees are awarded in BIOLOGICAL SCIENCE (biology/biological science, biotechnology, and forensic science), BUSINESS (accounting, banking and finance, business administration and management, business economics, hospitality management services, management science, marketing/retailing/merchandising, and real estate), COMMUNICATIONS AND THE ARTS (advertising, art, broadcasting, communications, dramatic arts, English, film arts, fine arts, French, information technology, journalism, languages, music, music performance, photography, public relations, radio/television technology, Spanish, theatre arts, theatre studies, and writing), COMPUTER AND PHYSICAL SCIENCE (applied science, chemistry, computer science, digital arts/technology, information sciences and systems, mathematics, optics, physics, and statistics), EDUCATION (art education, athletic training, business education, early childhood education, education of the exceptional child, elementary education, English education, foreign languages education, global studies, health information management, mathematics education, music education, science education, social science education, and technical education), ENGINEERING AND ENVIRONMENTAL DESIGN (aeronautical engineering, aerospace studies, architecture, civil engineering, computer engineering, construction engineering, electrical/electronics engineering, environmental engineering, food services technology, industrial engineering, and mechanical engineering), HEALTH PROFESSIONS (biomedical science, exercise science, health care administration, health science, medical laboratory technology, nursing, and speech pathology/audiology), SOCIAL SCIENCE (anthropology, criminal justice, economics, food production/management/services, forensic studies, history, humanities, interdisciplinary studies, international studies, Latin American studies, legal studies, liberal arts/general studies, philosophy, political science/government, psychology, public administration, religion, social science, social work, and sociology). Engineering, business administration, and computer science are the strongest academically. Psychology, biomedical sciences, and healthrelated fields have the largest enrollments.

ACTIVITIES: 7% of men belong to 27 national fraternities; 7% of women belong to 22 national sororities. There are 654 groups on campus, including pre-professional medical society club, art, band, cheerleading, chess, choir, chorus, communications, computers, dance, debate, drama, drill team, environmental, ethnic, film, forensics, honors, international, jazz band, LGBT, literary magazine, marching band, musical theater, newspaper, opera, orchestra, pep band, photography, political, professional, radio and TV, religious, social, social service, student government, symphony, and volunteer UCF. Popular campus events include Homecoming Events, Spirit Splash, Pegasuspalloza, Symphony Under the Stars, Concerts, Comedians, and Movies on the Plaza. **Sports:** There are 6 intercollegiate sports for men and 10 for women, and 54 intramural sports for men and 54 for women. Facilities include football, men's and women's basketball, volleyball, baseball, locker rooms, a weight room, training room and equipment room with complete laundry facilities, 3 batting cages and 2 pitching mounds, softball complex, game day ticketing, retail, marketing and concessions, a lighted indoor batting cage, bullpen area, and roomy home dugout, soccer, track complex, rowing facility, tennis complex, and a golf facility; climbing tower, group exercise studio, lap pool, outdoor adventure center, disc golf course, and leisure pool. **Graduates:** From July 1, 2015 to June 30, 2016, 13003 bachelor's degrees were awarded. The most popular majors were business (21%), health professions (16%), and psychology (9%). 1184 companies recruited on campus in 2015-2016. In an average class, 3% graduate in 3 years or less, 40% graduate in 4 years or less, 63% graduate in 5 years or less, and 69% graduate in 6 years or less. Of the 2015 graduating class, 9% were enrolled in graduate school within 6 months of graduation, and 75% were employed.

SERVICES: Counseling and information services are available, as is tutoring in some subjects, such as Bio & Microbio, Chem (Organic & Biochem), Genetics, Human Anat & Physio, Astronomy, Accountting, Finance, Stats, C Programming, Object-oriented Prog, Comp Eng Statics & Dynamics, Thermodynamics, Physics, Quant Bus Tools, Elec Networks, Phy Sci, and Comp Sci. **Library/Resources:** The library contains 2.0 million volumes, 3.3 million microform items, and 58,583 audio/video tapes/CDs/DVDs, and subscribes to 53,544 periodicals including electronic. Computerized library services include interlibrary loans, database searching, Internet access, and Wi-Fi capability. Special learning facilities include an art gallery, radio station, TV station, the University Writing Center, Robinson Observatory, UCF Arboretum, Townes Laser Institute, Siemens Energy Center, Morgridge International Reading Center, Center for Research and Education in Optics and Lasers, Toni Jennings Exceptional Education Institute, Communication Disorders Clinic, Institute for Simulation and Training, Florida Solar Energy Center, Biomolecular Science Center, fine art research facility and nonprofit publisher, Florida Space Institute, Community Counseling and Research Center, Florida Photonics Center of Excellence, Institute for Diversity and Ethics in Sport, Blackstone LaunchPad, Business Incubation Program, Center for Entrepreneurship and Innovation, Small Business Development Center, Center for Advanced Turbomachinery and Energy Research, Center for Computer Vision, Interactive Systems and User Experience Research Cluster of Excellence, Dick Pope Sr. Institute for Tourism Studies, Lou Frey Institute of Politics and Government, NanoScience Technology Center, Advanced Materials Processing and Analysis Center, and a partnership with the Central Florida Research Park. **Physically Challenged Students:** 97% of the campus is accessible. Facilities include wheelchair ramps, elevators, special parking, specially equipped restrooms, special class scheduling, lowered drinking fountains, and lowered telephones. **Special:** Internships are available in most majors through UCF's extensive partnerships with area businesses and industries such as NASA, Disney, Universal Studios, and AT&T. Students may participate in study abroad and co-op and work-study programs, earn B.A.-B.S. degrees or a liberal studies degree, or pursue dual majors. Nondegree study and pass/fail options are available. There are 22 national honor societies, a freshman honors program, and 59 departmental honors programs. **Visiting:** There are regularly scheduled orientations for prospective students, including tours offered twice a day, Monday through Friday, followed by a group information session or personal interview. There are guides for informal visits and visitors may sit in on classes. To schedule a visit, contact the Undergraduate Admissions Office. **Campus Safety and Security:** Measures include 24-hour foot and vehicle patrol, emergency notification system, self-defense education, and security escort services. There are shuttle buses, emergency telephones, lighted pathways/sidewalks, controlled access to dorms/residences, including a college-sponsored transportation system that buses students to and from apartment complexes within a 2- or 3-mile radius of the school.

REQUIREMENTS: The SAT or ACT is required. The ACT Optional Writing test is also required. GPA and standardized test scores are rated on a sliding scale. A high school diploma or GED is required. Applicants should have completed 4 units of English, 4 each of math, 3 units of science (2 with labs) and social studies, and 2 of a foreign language, plus 2 of academic electives. A GPA of 2.0 is required. AP and CLEP credits are accepted. Important factors in the admissions decision are advanced placement or honors courses, evidence of special talent, and leadership record. To graduate, students must complete at least 120 semester hours, with 36 hours in general education program courses, including 9 each in communication foundations and cultural and historical foundations and 6 each in math foundations, science foundations, and social foundations. Students must maintain a minimum GPA of 2.0. There is a 30-hour residency requirement, and the last semester is required in residence. **Procedure:** Freshmen are admitted fall, spring, and summer. Entrance exams should be taken during the junior year or the first semester of the senior year. There is a rolling admissions plan. Applications should be filed by May 1 for fall entry; November 1 for spring entry; and March 1 for summer entry, along with a $30 fee. Notification is sent on a rolling basis. 1880 applicants were on the 2016 waiting list; 71 were admitted. Applications are accepted on-line. **Transfer Students:** 11428 transfer students enrolled in 2015-2016. A minimum GPA of 2.0 is required. Either the SAT or the ACT is required of applicants with fewer than 30 credit hours. Other transfer requirements vary widely. 30 of 120 credits required for the bachelor's degree must be completed at UCF. **International Students:** There are 985 international students enrolled. The school actively recruits these students. They must take the TOEFL with a minimum score of 550 on the paper-based TOEFL (PBT) or 80 on the Internet-based version (iBT). Students with fewer than 30 semester hours of college credit must take either the SAT or the ACT.

ADMISSIONS: 50% of the 2016-2017 applicants were accepted. The SAT scores for the 2016-2017 freshman class were: Critical Reading-- 8% below 500, 48% between 500 and 599, 36% between 600 and 699, and 8% between 700 and 800. Math-- 8% below 500, 45% between 500 and 599, 39% between 600 and 699, and 8% between 700 and 800. Writing-- 18% below 500, 53% between 500 and 599, 25% between 600 and 699, and 4% between 700 and 800. The ACT scores were 1% between 12 and 17, 21% between 18 and 23, 61% between 24 and 29, and 17% above 30. 61% of the current freshmen were in the top fifth of their class; 93% were in the top two fifths. There were 77 National Merit finalists. 56 freshmen graduated first in their class. **Admissions Contact:** Undergraduate Admissions Email: *admission@ucf.edu* Web: *www.ucf.edu*

FINANCIAL AID: In 2016-2017, 81% of all full-time freshmen and 76% of continuing full-time students received some form of financial aid. 50% of all full-time freshmen and 58% of continuing full-time students received need-based aid. The average freshman award was $9,510. Need-based scholarships or need-based grants averaged $5,824 ($13,825 maximum); need-based self-help aid (loans and jobs) averaged $3,585 ($12,946 maximum); non-need-based athletic scholarships averaged $9,394 ($24,008 maximum); and other non-need-based awards and non-need-based scholarships averaged $4,023 ($41,858 maximum). Average annual earnings from campus work are $6000. The average financial indebtedness of the 2016 graduate was $21,911. The FAFSA code is 003954. The priority date for freshman financial aid applications for fall entry is March 1. The deadline for filing freshman financial aid applications for fall entry is June 30.

UNIVERSITY OF FLORIDA D-2

www.ufl.edu

Gainesville, FL 32611 **(352) 294-3683**

Email: webrequest@admissions.ufl.edu

Full-time: 13,513 men, 17,413 women	**Faculty:** I, -$
	Ph.D.s: 80%
Part-time: 1854 men, 1684 women	**Student/Faculty:** n/av
Graduate: 8496 men, 9317 women	**Tuition:** $6381 ($28,658)
Year: semesters, summer session	**Freshman Class:** 30144 applied, 13861 accepted, 6842 enrolled
Room & Board: $9910	
SAT CR/M/W: 631/644/628 **ACT:** 29	**CEEB CODE:** 5812
Application Deadline: November 1	**HIGHLY COMPETITIVE+**

University of Florida, founded in 1853, is a public liberal arts institution that is part of the state university system of Florida. The figures in the above capsule and in this profile are approximate. There are 16 undergraduate schools. In addition to regional accreditation, UF has baccalaureate program accreditation with AACSB, ABET, ACCE, ACEJMC, ACPE, ADA, APTA, ASLA, FIDER, NAAB, NASAD, NASM, NCATE, SAF, CEPH, CAATE, and CCNE. The 1955-acre campus is in a suburban area 75 miles from Jacksonville, FL. Including any residence halls, there are 887 buildings.

STUDENT LIFE: 92% of undergraduates are from Florida. Others are from 50 states, 157 foreign countries, and Canada. 9% are Foreign; 7% Asian American; 6% African American; 55% White; 3% race unknown; 2% two or more races; 17% Hispanic. **Female To Male Ratio:** 1.2:1. The average age of freshmen is 18; all undergraduates, 21. **Housing:** 9706 students can be accommodated in college housing, which includes coed dorms, on-campus apartments, off-campus apartments, and married student housing. In addition, there are honors houses, special-interest houses, fraternity houses, sorority houses, honors residential college, career exploration community, wellness community, faculty in residence, and entrepreneurial living learning community. On-campus housing is available on a first-come, first-served basis. All students may keep cars.

FACULTY/CLASSROOMS: 63% of faculty are male; 37% are female. No introductory courses are taught by graduate students.

PROGRAMS OF STUDY: UF confers B.A., and B.S., degrees. Associate, master's, and doctoral degrees are also awarded. Bachelor's degrees are awarded in AGRICULTURE (agricultural business management, agronomy, animal science, dairy science, forestry and related sciences, horticulture, natural resource management, plant science, and soil science), BIOLOGICAL SCIENCE (botany, entomology, microbiology, wildlife biology, and zoology), BUSINESS (accounting, banking and finance, business administration and management, human resources, insurance, management science, marketing/retailing/merchandising, and recreation and leisure services), COMMUNICATIONS AND THE ARTS (advertising, art, art history and appreciation, creative writing, dance, East Asian languages and literature, English, French, German, graphic design, journalism, linguistics, music, performing arts, photography, Portuguese, public relations, Russian, Spanish, speech/debate/rhetoric, telecommunications, theater design, and visual and performing arts), COMPUTER AND PHYSICAL SCIENCE (astronomy, chemistry, computer science, earth science, geology, information sciences and systems, mathematics, physics, and statistics), EDUCATION (agricultural education, art education, elementary education, health education, and music education), ENGINEERING AND ENVIRONMENTAL DESIGN (aeronautical engineering, agricultural engineering, architecture, chemical engineering, civil engineering, computer engineering, construction engineering, electrical/electronics engineering, emergency/disaster science, engineering and applied science, environmental engineering, industrial engineering technology, interior design, landscape architecture/design, materials engineering, mechanical engineering, nuclear engineering, and nuclear engineering technology), HEALTH PROFESSIONS (allied health, exercise science, health science, nursing, occupational therapy, physical therapy, prepharmacy, rehabilitation therapy, and speech pathology/audiology), SOCIAL SCIENCE (American studies, anthropology, Asian/Oriental studies, classical/ancient civilization, criminology, economics, food science, geography, history, home economics, interdisciplinary studies, Judaic studies, philosophy, physical fitness/movement, political science/government, psychology, religion, and sociology). Biology, finance, and psychology have the largest enrollments.

ACTIVITIES: 22% of men belong to 37 national fraternities; 22% of women belong to 27 national sororities. There are 1149 groups on campus, including art, band, cheerleading, chess, choir, chorale, chorus, computers, dance, debate, drama, environmental, ethnic, film, forensics, honors, international, jazz band, LGBT, literary magazine, marching band, newspaper, opera, orchestra, pep band, photography, political, professional, radio and TV, religious, social, social service, student government, and symphony. Popular campus events include Homecoming Parade, Annual Dance Marathon, Soulfest, Gator Growl Student Run Pep Rally, and Florida Invitational Step Show. **Sports:** There are 9 intercollegiate sports for men and 12 for women, and 42 intramural sports for men and 42 for women. Facilities include a football stadium with locker rooms, a weight room, multipurpose facility which houses basketball, volleyball, gymnastics, a practice court, weight rooms, an indoor track, Olympic pool, a private gymnastics arena, dance studio, martial arts studio, baseball, softball, soccer, lacrosse, tennis, golf, football, basketball, and tennis. **Graduates:** From July 1, 2015 to June 30, 2016, 8451 bachelor's degrees were awarded. The most popular majors were psychology (6%), biology (5%), and finance (5%). 920 companies recruited on campus in 2015-2016. In an average class, 5% graduate in 3 years or less, 66% graduate in 4 years or less, 84% graduate in 5 years or less, and 86% graduate in 6 years or less.

SERVICES: Counseling and information services are available, as is tutoring in every subject. There is a reader service for the blind. In addition to a free centralized tutoring service, UF provides subject-specific tutoring including a writing center, math tutoring lab, a sciences tutoring lab, and others. **Library/Resources:** The 7 libraries contain 5.3 million volumes, 6.5 million microform items, and 87,369 audio/video tapes/CDs/DVDs, and subscribe to 148,034 periodicals including electronic. Computerized library services include interlibrary loans, database searching, Internet access, and Wi-Fi capability. Special learning facilities include an art gallery, natural history museum, radio station, TV station, performing arts center, and a teaching hospital. **Physically Challenged Students:** 95% of the campus is accessible. Facilities include wheelchair ramps, elevators, special parking, specially equipped restrooms, special class scheduling, lowered drinking fountains, lowered telephones, and special housing. **Special:** Numerous internships, study abroad, and research opportunities are available to students through the top-ranked UF Career Resource Center, UF International Center, UF Center for Undergraduate Research, and individual colleges and departments. Students can pursue accelerated degree programs and dual majors, which vary in eligibility and requirements by college and program. Students can pursue Interdisciplinary Studies in the College of Liberal Arts and Sciences. Innovation Academy at UF is a groundbreaking living/learning community that offers a minor in Innovation, a flexible spring-summer cohort, enlightening guest speakers, diverse internship opportunities, and a co-curricular environment that emphasizes creativity and making. UF offers the Washington semester and work study programs. The Herbert Wertheim College of Engineering administers a 3-2 mathematics-engineering degree program for students from the University of the Virgin Islands. UF enjoys a strong partnership with local Santa Fe College through its support of transfer students and unique academic programs, such as those administered by the Colleges of Engineering and Design, Construction, and Planning, that provide an additional pathway to UF for first-time-in-college students. The International Scholars Program has a graduation medallion program that offers students both a means of organizing and recognition for their international engagement while a student at the University of Florida. Students must accomplish the following: complete 12 credits of academic coursework with an international focus; participate in an approved study abroad program, other approved international learning experiences, or at least one year of language learning beyond their specific college requirement; attend at least four internationally focused campus life events; complete an e-portfolio in which the student reflects on the role of the international in their broader UF experience. UF Online provides an array of fully online, 4-year undergraduate degree programs. Whether as a transfer or first-time in college student, UF Online students earn the same degree with the same faculty as our residential students. Pathway to Campus Enrollment (PaCE) is a hybrid admissions program for select majors which allows first- time-in-college students to complete the first 60 hours of their degree online. Once they have completed their lower division requirements, these students complete the remainder of their degree on campus just like any other residential student. There are 100 national honor societies, Phi Beta Kappa, a freshman honors program, and 100 departmental honors programs. **Visiting:** There are regularly scheduled orientations for prospective students. Refer to Welcome Center calendar for tour time as tours are based on the time of the year. There are guides for informal visits, visitors may sit in on classes, and stay overnight. To schedule a visit, contact the UF Welcome Center. **Campus Safety and Security:** Measures include 24-hour foot and vehicle patrol, emergency notification system, self-defense education, and security escort services. There are shuttle buses, emergency telephones, lighted pathways/sidewalks, and controlled access to dorms/residences.

REQUIREMENTS: A satisfactory score on the SAT and a minimum score of 19 on the ACT are required. Candidates should have graduated from an accredited secondary school or have a GED, and have completed 4 years each of English, and math, 3 years each of science, and social studies, 2 years of a foreign language, and 4 units of academic electives. A GPA of 2.5 is required. AP and CLEP credits are accepted. Important factors in the admissions decision are advanced placement or honors courses, extracurricular activities record, and evidence of special talent. Requirements for Undergraduate graduation vary depending on the major elected, but all students are required to complete a minimum of 120 credits and maintain a minimum 2.0 GPA, including 36 credits of general education courses. **Procedure:** Freshmen are admitted to all sessions. Entrance exams should be taken in the junior year. Applications should be filed by November 1 for fall entry along with a $30 fee. Notifications are sent February 10. Applications are accepted on-line. **Transfer Students:** 3414 transfer students enrolled in 2015-2016. Admission requirements for transfer students vary by college. Students must have 60 hours or AA degree. 30 of 120 credits required for the bachelor's degree must be completed at UF. **International Students:** There are 465 international students enrolled. The school actively recruits these students. They must take the TOEFL with a minimum score of 550 on the paper-based TOEFL (PBT) or 80 on the Internet-based version (iBT) or take the MELAB, or take the IELTS. They must also take the SAT or ACT, with same scoring requirements as any FTIC applicant.

ADMISSIONS: 47% of the 2016-2017 applicants were accepted. The SAT scores for the 2016-2017 freshman class were: Critical Reading-- 5% below 500, 29% between 500 and 599, 48% between 600 and 699, and 18% between 700 and 800. Math-- 4% below 500, 24% between 500 and 599, 49% between 600 and 699, and 23% between 700 and 800. Writing-- 5% below 500, 30% between 500 and 599, 49% between 600 and 699, and 16% between 700 and 800. The ACT scores were 7% between 18 and 23, 48% between 24 and 29, and 45% above 30. There were 157 National Merit finalists. **Admissions Contact:** Zina Evans, Vice President for Enrollment Management. Email: *webrequest@admissions.ufl.edu* Web: *www.ufl.edu*

FINANCIAL AID: In 2016-2017, 98% of all full-time freshmen and 98% of continuing full-time students received some form of financial aid. 36% of all full-time freshmen and 40% of continuing full-time students received need-based aid. The average freshman award was $11,000. Need-based scholarships or need-based grants averaged $7,939; need-based self-help aid (loans and jobs) averaged $3,705; non-need-based athletic scholarships averaged $15,404; and other non-need-based awards and non-need-based scholarships averaged $6,641. 14% of undergraduate students work part-time. Average annual earnings from campus work are $1617. The FAFSA code is 001535. The priority date for freshman financial aid applications for fall entry is March 15.

UNIVERSITY OF MIAMI E-6
www.miami.edu

Coral Gables, FL 33124 (305) 284-2211

Fax: (305) 284-2507
Email: admission@miami.edu
Full-time: 4854 men, 5296 women
Faculty: 1108; I, av$
Part-time: 212 men, 253 women
Ph.D.s: 90%
Graduate: 2921 men, 3031 women
Student/Faculty: 12 to 1
Year: semesters, summer session
Tuition: $47,004
Room & Board: $16,490
Freshman Class: 32525 applied, 12266 accepted, 2065 enrolled
SAT CR/M/W: 640/660/635 **ACT:** 30
CEEB CODE: 5815
Application Deadline: April 1
MOST COMPETITIVE

At the University of Miami, we transform lives through teaching, research, and service. Through our core values of diversity, integrity, responsibility, excellence, compassion, creativity, and teamwork, the University of Miami creates a learning environment where contributions are recognized and valued. We educate leaders, problem-solvers, and agents of change who are passionate about learning, eager to contribute to their community, and free to color outside the lines. As a student, you are admitted directly to your major, none of that waiting two years to get down to business. Whether you seek to make your mark in science, service, or the arts, we nurture that passion through a curriculum that integrates academic rigor and theory with real-world experience. With the flexibility to choose from more than 180 majors and programs across nine schools and colleges, you are encouraged to design a curriculum that crosses disciplines and is distinctly you. Our unique Cognates Program lets you complete your general education requirements in a way that reflects your individual interests and goals. Cognates allow, you to combine all of your passions by taking three related classes from our various departments, schools, and colleges for an education that is both broad and deep. Our students translate knowledge, experiences, and connections into successful and fulfilling achievements. With access to an international metropolitan city, the experiential learning opportunities are endless. Here, you are doing something in labs and internships, in Miami, and in countries half way around the world. If you are looking for a chance to travel and to immerse yourself in another culture, UM on Location Programs bring study abroad within reach. With programs taught by UM faculty and coordinated by staff, you do not have to worry about transferring credits, and your financial assistance goes with you. The vibrant, diverse city of Miami offers a broad range of internship opportunities in your own backyard, from nonprofit organizations to multinational corporations, and everything in between, you can connect with faculty on projects ranging from volunteer experiences to cutting-edge research, explore topics, such as genomics, the humanities, climate change, and more, and make major contributions to new knowledge as early as your freshman year. Our faculty members lead by example and will instill in you the importance of using your skills to advance your community, at both a local and a global level. The diversity of academics, resources, and students at UM make it the perfect place to gain a truly global education. There are 9 undergraduate schools and 3 graduate schools. In addition to regional accreditation, UM has baccalaureate program accreditation with AACSB, ABET, ADA, APTA, NAAB, NASM, COA-NA, CAHME, and CCNE. The 230-acre campus is in a suburban area 7 miles from Miami International Airport. Including any residence halls, there are 200 buildings.

STUDENT LIFE: 58% of undergraduates are from out of state, mostly the Middle Atlantic. Students are from 50 states, 104 foreign countries, and Canada. 8% are African American; 5% Asian American; 43% White; 4% race unknown; 3% two or more races; 23% Hispanic; 14% Foreign. 36% are Catholic; 30% Protestant; 18% Buddhist, Hindu, Islamic, Jehovah's Witness, Latter Day Saints, E. Orthodox Christian, Christian Science, and Unitarian.; 15% Jewish. **Female To Male Ratio:** 1.1:1. The average age of freshmen is 18; all undergraduates, 21. 8% do not continue beyond their first year; 92% remain to graduate. **Housing:** 4330 students can be accommodated in college housing, which includes coed dorms and on-campus apartments. In addition, there are special-interest houses, fraternity houses, freshmen-only housing, and theme housing. On-campus housing is guaranteed for the freshman year only, is available on a first-come, first-served basis, and is available on a lottery system for upperclassmen. 71% of students commute. Some may keep cars.

FACULTY/CLASSROOMS: 55% of faculty are male; 45% are female. No introductory courses are taught by graduate students.

PROGRAMS OF STUDY: UM confers A.B., B.A., B.S., B.A.M., B.A.M.A., B.Arch., B.B.A., B.F.A., B.G.S., B.L.A., B.M., B.S.A.E., B.S.A.S.E., B.S.B.A., B.S.B.E., B.S.C., B.S.C.E., B.S.Cp.E., B.S.Ed., B.S.E.E., B.S.E.S., B.S.En.E., B.S.H.S., B.S.I.E., B.S.M.A.S., B.S.M.E., B.S.N. and B.S.P.H. degrees. Master's and doctoral degrees are also awarded. Bachelor's degrees are awarded in BIOLOGICAL SCIENCE (biochemistry, marine affairs, marine biology, marine science, microbiology, and neurosciences), BUSINESS (accounting, business and technology, entrepreneurial studies, finance, human resources/organizational mgmt, international finance, international marketing, management science, marketing, marketing management, real estate, and sports management), COMMUNICATIONS AND THE ARTS (advertising, Africana studies, art history, art, ceramic art and design, classics, communication studies, communications, English, film arts, fine arts, French, German, graphic design, instrumental performance, jazz, journalism, media management, music, music business management, music composition, music performance, music technology, musical theater, painting, photography, printmaking, public relations, sculpture, Spanish, studio art, theatre acting, theatre arts, theater design, theater management, and vocal performance), COMPUTER AND PHYSICAL SCIENCE (atmospheric sciences and meteorology, chemistry, computer science, geology, geoscience, mathematics, physics, and statistics), EDUCATION (athletic training, elementary education, and music education), ENGINEERING AND ENVIRONMENTAL DESIGN (aerospace studies, architectural engineering, architecture, biomedical engineering, civil engineering, computer engineering, computer graphics, electrical/electronics engineering, engineering science, environmental engineering, environmental science, industrial engineering, and mechanical engineering), HEALTH PROFESSIONS (biology, exercise science, health administration and policy, health care administration, health science, music therapy, nursing, pre-health studies, predentistry, premedicine, prepharmacy, prephysical therapy, preveterinary science, and public health), SOCIAL SCIENCE (American studies, anthropology, criminology, economics, gender studies, geography, history, human development, interdisciplinary studies, international studies, Judaic studies, Latin American studies, legal studies, liberal arts/general studies, philosophy, political science/government, prelaw, psychology, religion, religious studies, sociology, and women's studies). Business/marketing, biological/life sciences, and social sciences have the largest enrollments.

ACTIVITIES: 19% of men belong to 17 national fraternities; 19% of women belong to 14 national sororities. There are 285 groups on campus, including art, athletic organization clubs, band, cheerleading, chess, choir, chorale, chorus, computers, dance, debate, drama, environmental, ethnic, film, honors, international, jazz band, LGBT, literary magazine, marching band, musical theater, newspaper, opera, orchestra, pep band, political, professional, radio and TV, religious, social, social service, student government, symphony, and yearbook. Popular campus events include SportsFest, International Week, Homecoming Week (Various Activities), Fun Day, National Gandhi Day of Service, Miami International Film Festival, Black Awareness Month Day of Service, Canefest, Festival Miami, Alumni Weekend, and Hug the Lake. **Sports:** There are 7 intercollegiate sports for men and 10 for women, and 18 intramural sports for men and 18 for women. Facilities include a stadium, soccer, track & field, basketball, athletic training facility, equipped with diagnostic and rehabilitative equipment, baseball stadium, a tennis center, swimming pool, football, a recreation and wellness facility that includes a fitness room, aerobic classes, indoor track, gymnasium, basketball, volleyball and badminton courts, racquetball and squash courts, and tennis. **Graduates:** From July 1, 2015 to June 30, 2016, 2601 bachelor's degrees were awarded. The most popular majors were business/marketing (20%), social science (12%), and health professions and related programs (10%). 387 companies recruited on campus in 2015-2016. In an average class, 2% graduate in 3 years or less, 68% graduate in 4 years or less, 79% graduate in 5 years or less, and 82% graduate in 6 years or less. Of the 2015 graduating class, 19% were enrolled in graduate school within 6 months of graduation, and 31% were employed.

SERVICES: Counseling and information services are available, as is tutoring in some subjects. There is a reader service for the blind. **Library/Resources:** The 9 libraries contain 3.7 million volumes, 4.2 million microform items, and 118,548 audio/video tapes/CDs/DVDs, and subscribe to 99,060 periodicals including electronic. Computerized library services include interlibrary loans, database searching, Internet access, and Wi-Fi capability. Special learning facilities include an art gallery, radio station, TV station, a cinema, an observatory, palmetum, marine science research vessels, broadcasting studios, concert hall, arboretum, performing arts theater, film studios, sound stage, a museum, wave machine, wellness center, and state-of-the-art student activities center. **Physically Challenged Students:** Facilities include wheelchair ramps, elevators, special parking, specially equipped restrooms, special class scheduling, lowered drinking fountains, lowered telephones, and special housing. **Special:** Our internships, work-study programs, and study-abroad programs provide the opportunity for UM students to acquire an expansive perspective in their academic career. Opportunities to learn and grow flourish through our special programs, such as our accelerated degree programs as well as our dual-degree programs. There are 41 national honor societies, Phi Beta Kappa, and a freshman honors program. **Visiting:** There are regularly scheduled orientations for prospective students, and several open house programs. Daily information sessions are offered on campus as well as walking tours. There are guides for informal visits and visitors may sit in on classes. **Campus Safety and Security:** Measures include 24-hour foot and vehicle patrol, emergency notification system, self-defense education, and security escort services. There are shuttle buses, emergency telephones, lighted pathways/sidewalks, controlled access to dorms/residences. There has been a comprehensive crime prevention program since 1981.

REQUIREMENTS: SAT or ACT is required. ACT with Writing is required. SAT with Essay component is required. It is recommended that applicants have completed 4 units each of English, and mathematics, 3 units of science, with 2 of being in lab, and social studies, and 2 units each of foreign language and history, and 2 units of academic electives with 1 unit being in computer science and 1 unit being in visual/performing arts. Applicants are based on the strength of their high school curriculum and grades earned, standardized test scores, letters of recommendation, essay, extracurricular activities, and awards/achievements. The GED is accepted. Portfolios are required for the arts and architecture programs. Auditions are required for the music and theatre programs. Supplemental applications are required for the Frost School of Music, BFA Theatre, BFA Art, Architecture, and Dual Degree Programs. AP and CLEP credits are accepted. Important factors in the admissions decision are evidence of special talent, advanced placement or honors courses, personality/intangible qualities, extracurricular activities record, and recommendations by school officials. To receive a Bachelor's degree from the University, the student must earn at least 120 semester hours of credit, more in some schools, with a C average or better as well as a C average for all work done at the University of Miami. Students must also meet all of the degree requirements of their respective schools and should not expect requirements in composition, mathematics, foreign languages, or other subject areas to be waived for any reason. A student transferring credit hours from a 2-year community or junior college (this being the last school attended) must complete a minimum of 56 credit hours in residence at the University of Miami to earn an undergraduate degree. A student transferring credit hours from a 4-year college or university (this being the last school attended) must complete a minimum of 45 credit hours in residence at the University of Miami to earn an undergraduate degree. In addition, each student must complete at least half of the credit hours specified for his or her major in residence at the University of Miami. Not more than 30 credit hours of correspondence work and extension work combined will be accepted toward a degree, and neither correspondence nor extension work may be credited as a part of the last 45/56 credit hours of the student's program. Not more than 30 credit hours based on military experience will be awarded toward the degree. Credit hours earned in a manner other than by course registration, i.e., proficiency examination, CLEP, placement tests, etc., may not be used to meet the final 45/56 credit hour residency requirement, however such credit by examination may be earned while the student is enrolled in the courses needed to meet the final 45/56 credit-hour residency requirement. Once a degree has been awarded, no changes will be made to the academic record. **Procedure:** Freshmen are admitted fall and spring. Entrance exams should be taken The summer before the senior year in high school. There are early decision, early admissions, and deferred admissions plans. Early decision applications should be filed by November 1; regular applications, by April 1 for fall entry; and November 1 for spring entry, along with a $70 fee. Notification of early decision is sent December 20; regular decision, April 15. 252 early decision candidates were accepted for the 2016-2017 class. 1440 applicants were on the 2016 waiting list; 215 were admitted. Applications are accepted on-line. **Transfer Students:** 517 transfer students enrolled in 2015-2016. Only credits from a regionally accredited institution are transferable to the University of Miami. The average admitted transfer student has a 3.3 GPA. Courses with a grade lower than a C will not transfer; however, these grades will still be used to compute an admission GPA. If the student has fewer than 30 college credits when submitting the application, official high school transcripts, the Common Application Final Report, and official SAT/ACT test scores must be submitted in addition to the core application documents. If a student is applying to a special program (Bachelor of Architecture, Art B.F.A., Theatre Arts B.F.A., or Frost School of Music), a supplemental application, a portfolio, and/or an audition may be required. 45 of 120 credits required for the bachelor's degree must be completed at UM. **International Students:** There are 1555 international students enrolled. The school actively recruits these students. They must take the TOEFL with a minimum score of 550 on the paper-based TOEFL (PBT) or 80 on the Internet-based version (iBT). All students whose native language is not English are required to submit official results of the TOEFL or IELTS. SAT/ACT not required and shouldn't be submitted for admission consideration from applicants attending school outside US.

ADMISSIONS: 38% of the 2016-2017 applicants were accepted. The SAT scores for the 2016-2017 freshman class were: Critical Reading-- 4% below 500, 21% between 500 and 599, 53% between 600 and 699, and 22% between 700 and 800. Math-- 2% below 500, 18% between 500 and 599, 49% between 600 and 699, and 30% between 700 and 800. Writing-- 4% below 500, 26% between 500 and 599, 53% between 600 and 699, and 18% between 700 and 800. The ACT scores were 1% between 12 and 17, 2% between 18 and 23, 39% between 24 and 29, and 58% above 30. 90% of the current freshmen were in the top fifth of their class; 97% were in the top two fifths. There were 8 National Merit finalists. 38 freshmen graduated first in their class. **Admissions Contact:** John Haller, Vice President of Enrollment Management. Email: *admission@miami.edu* Web: *www.miami.edu*

FINANCIAL AID: In 2016-2017, 84% of all full-time freshmen and 99% of continuing full-time students received some form of financial aid. 84% of all full-time freshmen and 99% of continuing full-time students received need-based aid. The average freshman award was $42,187. Need-based scholarships or need-based grants averaged $8,925; need-based self-help aid (loans and jobs) averaged $5,047; non-need-based athletic scholarships averaged $27,263; other non-need-based awards and non-need-based scholarships averaged $19,877; and $3,425 from other forms of aid. 56% of undergraduate students work part-time. Average annual earnings from campus work are $2500. The average financial indebtedness of the 2016 graduate was $31,000. UM is a member of CSS. The CSS/Profile, Noncustodial Profile, Business/Farm Supplement, all student/parent W-2's, and individual and corporate income tax returns are required. The priority date for freshman financial aid applications for fall entry is January 1. The deadline for filing freshman financial aid applications for fall entry is April 15.

UNIVERSITY OF NORTH FLORIDA — D-1

www.unf.edu

Jacksonville, FL 32224	**(904) 620-2624** **(866) 808-0626**
Fax: (904) 620-2414	**Email: Admissions@unf.edu**
Full-time: 4237 men, 5465 women	**Faculty:** 454; IIA, av$
Part-time: 1873 men, 2271 women	**Ph.D.s:** 92%
Graduate: 687 men, 1229 women	**Student/Faculty:** 19 to 1
Year: semesters, summer session	**Tuition:** $6394 ($20,798)
Room & Board: $9602	**Freshman Class:** 6799 applied, 3397 accepted, 809 enrolled
SAT CR/M: 612/597 **ACT:** 26	**CEEB CODE:** 5490
Application Deadline: August 1	**VERY COMPETITIVE**

University of North Florida, founded in 1965, is a public university that is part of the state university system. There are 5 undergraduate schools and 5 graduate schools. In addition to regional accreditation, UNF has baccalaureate program accreditation with AACSB, ABET, ACCE, APTA, NASM, NCATE, NLN, ACS, CAAHEP, CAATE, CAHME, CoA-NA, FBN, CCNE, CACREP, CADE, CAPTE, COSMA, CED, FDE, ACEND, NASPAA, NASM, NAACLS, ACS, EAC, CAC, and AUPHA. The 1300-acre campus is in an urban area 12 miles southeast of downtown Jacksonville. Including any residence halls, there are 94 buildings.

STUDENT LIFE: 94% of undergraduates are from Florida. Others are from 46 states, 105 foreign countries, and Canada. 67% are White; 5% Asian American; 5% two or more races; 2% Foreign; 10% African American; 10% Hispanic; 1% race unknown. 99% claim no religious affiliation. **Female To Male Ratio:** 1.3:1. The average age of freshmen is 18; all undergraduates, 23. 20% do not continue beyond their first year; 53% remain to graduate. **Housing:** 3500 students can be accommodated in college housing, which includes coed dorms, on-campus apartments, and off-campus apartments. In addition, there are honors houses, and special interest houses are the living learning communities. On-campus housing is guaranteed for the freshman year only, and is available on a first-come, first-served basis. 79% of students commute. All students may keep cars.

FACULTY/CLASSROOMS: 51% of faculty are male; 49% are female. 93% teach undergraduates, 81% do research, and 75% do both. No introductory courses are taught by graduate students. The average class size in an introductory lecture is 35; in a laboratory is 20; and in a regular course is 33.

PROGRAMS OF STUDY: UNF confers B.A., B.S., B.A.E., B.B.A., B.F.A., B.H.A., B.M., B.M.E., B.S.A.T., B.S.E.E., B.S.H., B.S.N. and B.S.W. degrees. Associate, master's, and doctoral degrees are also awarded. Bachelor's degrees are awarded in BIOLOGICAL SCIENCE (biology/biological science and nutrition), BUSINESS (accounting, banking and finance, business administration and management, business economics, finance, global/general management, international business management, marketing management, sports management, and transportation management), COMMUNICATIONS AND THE ARTS (American Sign Language, art, communications, English, English literature, fine arts, jazz, music, music performance, and Spanish), COMPUTER AND PHYSICAL SCIENCE (applied mathematics, chemistry, computer science, information sciences and systems, mathematics, physics, and statistics), EDUCATION (art education, athletic training, elementary education, English education, mathematics education, middle school education, music education, physical education, science education, secondary education, social studies education, and special education), ENGINEERING AND ENVIRONMENTAL DESIGN (civil engineering, construction engineering, construction management, electrical/electronics engineering, and mechanical engineering), HEALTH PROFESSIONS (health care administration, health science, mental health/human services, nursing, and physical therapy), SOCIAL SCIENCE (anthropology, counseling/psychology, criminal justice, dietetics, economics, ethnic studies, French studies, history, interdisciplinary studies, philosophy, political science/government, psychology, public administration, religion, and sociology). Nursing, fine arts, and elementary education are the strongest academically. Psychology, communication, and business management have the largest enrollments.

ACTIVITIES: 3% of men belong to 10 national fraternities; 4% of women belong to 9 national sororities. There are 233 groups on campus, including art, band, cheerleading, choir, chorale, chorus, computers, dance, drama, drum and bugle corps, environmental, ethnic, film, honors, international, jazz band, LGBT, literary magazine, newspaper, photography, political, professional, radio and TV, religious, social, social service, and student government. Popular campus events include Clubfest, Spring Bash and Earth Music Fest. **Sports:** There are 7 intercollegiate sports for men and 10 for women, and 11 intramural sports for men and 11 for women. Facilities include a baseball stadium, softball, soccer, and multipurpose fields, a soccer stadium, an aquatic center, fitness center, jogging trails, racquetball, basketball, volleyball, tennis courts, a multipurpose arena, climbing wall, indoor 3-lane rubber track, fitness rooms, and weight machines. **Graduates:** From July 1, 2015 to June 30, 2016, 3255 bachelor's degrees were awarded. The most popular majors were psychology (10%), communications (8%), and nursing (6%). 281 companies recruited on campus in 2015-2016. In an average class, 2% graduate in 3 years or less, 26% graduate in 4 years or less, 47% graduate in 5 years or less, and 53% graduate in 6 years or less.

SERVICES: Counseling and information services are available, as is tutoring in some subjects, such as accounting, biology, chemistry, computer science, economics, history, mathematics, physics, psychology, statistics, and world languages. Writing tutoring is available by appointment through the Writing Center. **Library/Resources:** The library contains 860,144 volumes, 1.5 million microform items, and 32,755 audio/video tapes/CDs/DVDs, and subscribes to 38,246 periodicals including electronic. Computerized library services include interlibrary loans, database searching, Internet access, and Wi-Fi capability. Special learning facilities include an art gallery, radio station, TV station, a theater, an auditorium, a nature preserve, and the Museum of Science and History (MOSH). **Physically Challenged Students:** Facilities include wheelchair ramps, elevators, special parking, specially equipped restrooms, special class scheduling, lowered drinking fountains, lowered telephones, and special housing. The Disability Resource Center provides specialized assistance and equipment, including priority registration, interpreters for the hearing impaired, and proctored testing. **Special:** There are cooperative programs and internships in most majors and work-study programs with several Jacksonville businesses. Study abroad, an accelerated degree program in nursing, B.A.-B.S. degrees in math, statistics, and psychology, dual majors, and student-designed majors also are available. Credit is given for military experience. There are 6 national honor societies, a freshman honors program, and 14 departmental honors programs. **Visiting:** There are regularly scheduled orientations for prospective students, consisting of open houses, which include tours of the campus and housing, a general information session, financial aid sessions, academic advising, and personal interviews by request. There are guides for informal visits. To schedule a visit, contact the Admissions Office. **Campus Safety and Security:** Measures include 24-hour foot and vehicle patrol, emergency notification system, self-defense education, and security escort services. There are shuttle buses, emergency telephones, lighted pathways/sidewalks, and university police presentations at new student orientation.

REQUIREMENTS: The Office of Admissions will recalculate a grade point average (GPA) based on eighteen (18) academic units in college preparatory courses. Additional weight is given to grades of "C" or higher earned in honors, Dual Enrollment, Advanced Placement, IB, or AICE courses. While students may not have completed all the required courses at the time an application is submitted, they are required to complete them prior to high school graduation and entrance into UNF. The State of Florida has implemented new minimum admission standards for freshmen applicants to all state universities. In order to be considered, students must have a minimum 2.5 recalculated GPA, on a 4.0 scale, and meet minimum test score requirements (460 SAT Critical Reading, 460 SAT Math, 440 SAT Writing; or 19 ACT Reading, 19 ACT Math, 18 ACT English/Writing). Please keep in mind that these standards only outline potential eligibility for admission to a state university. UNF's admission criteria depend on the applicant pool and will be higher than these minimums. A GPA of 2.5 is required. AP and CLEP credits are accepted. Important factors in the admissions decision are advanced placement or honors courses, recommendations by school officials, and evidence of special talent. Students are required to take general education distribution requirements, including 9 hours of composition and humanities and 6 each of natural science, math, and social science. There is a core curriculum in Western civilization and cultural diversity. A minimum 2.0 GPA and 120 credit hours, with a minimum of 60 hours in the major, are needed for graduation. **Procedure:** Freshmen are admitted to all sessions. Entrance exams should be taken during the spring of the junior year or the fall of the senior year. There are deferred admissions and rolling admissions plans. Application deadlines are open. Application fee is $30. Notification is sent on a rolling basis. Applications are accepted online. **Transfer Students:** 2671 transfer students enrolled in 2015-2016. Upper-level transfer students are defined as those with at least 60 transferable credit hours or an Associate of Arts degree from a Florida public or postsecondary institution. Admission requirements will vary by major, term, and space-availability. In order to be considered, applicants must meet or exceed a cumulative college GPA of 2.0 or higher, including a "C" or higher average and "good standing" status at the most recent college attended. Additional requirements will exist for students applying to limited access/selective admission programs or as international students. 30 of 120 credits required for the bachelor's degree must be completed at UNF. **International Students:** There are 233 international students enrolled. The school actively recruits these students. They must take the TOEFL. They must also take the SAT or ACT.

ADMISSIONS: 50% of the 2016-2017 applicants were accepted. The SAT scores for the 2016-2017 freshman class were: Critical Reading-- 3% below 500, 37% between 500 and 599, 52% between 600 and 699, and 8% between 700 and 800. Math-- 2% below 500, 48% between 500 and 599, 47% between 600 and 699, and 3% between 700 and 800. Writing-- 13% below 500, 52% between 500 and 599, 33% between 600 and 699, and 2% between 700 and 800. The ACT scores were 80% between 24 and 29, and 20% above 30. 55% of the current freshmen were in the top fifth of their class; 78% were in the top two fifths. **Admissions Contact:** Karen Lucas, Director of Admissions. Email: *Admissions@unf.edu* Web: *www.unf.edu*

FINANCIAL AID: In 2016-2017, 74% of all full-time freshmen and 70% of continuing full-time students received some form of financial aid. 43% of all full-time freshmen and 43% of continuing full-time students received need-based aid. The average freshman award was $9,649. Need-based scholarships or need-based grants averaged $6,212 ($17,843 maximum); need-based self-help aid (loans and jobs) averaged $2,444 ($13,681 maximum); non-need-based athletic scholarships averaged $11,239 ($25,723 maximum); and other non-need-based awards and non-need-based scholarships averaged $6,229 ($35,806 maximum). 7% of undergraduate students work part-time. The average financial indebtedness of the 2016 graduate was $17,452. The deadline for filing freshman financial aid applications for fall entry is April 1.

UNIVERSITY OF SOUTH FLORIDA/ST. PETERSBURG — D-4

www.usfsp.edu

St. Petersburg, FL 33701 — 727-873-4142

Fax: 727-873-4525	Email: admissions@usf.edu
Full-time: 1134 men, 1654 women	**Faculty:** 107; I, --$
Part-time: 462 men, 756 women	**Ph.D.s:** n/av
Graduate: 155 men, 303 women	**Student/Faculty:** 24 to 1
Year: semesters, summer session	**Tuition:** $8412 ($16,736)
Room & Board: $7568	**Freshman Class:** 1996 applied, 914 accepted, 474 enrolled
SAT CR/M/W: 530/530/510 **ACT:** 23	**CEEB CODE:** 5828
Application Deadline: March 15	**COMPETITIVE**

University of South Florida, St. Petersburg, offers master's level and undergraduate programs in the arts and sciences, business, and education within a student-centered environment. The first regional institution in the USF System with separate accreditation, USFSP retains its separate identity and mission while contributing to and benefiting from the associations, cooperation, and shared resources of a premier national research university. The figures in the above capsule and in this profile are approximate. There are 3 undergraduate schools and 1 graduate school. In addition to regional accreditation, USF St. Petersburg has baccalaureate program accreditation with AACSB, ACEJMC, and NCATE. The 50-acre campus is in an urban area on Bayboro Harbor in downtown St. Petersburg.

STUDENT LIFE: 97% of undergraduates are from Florida. 8% are African American; 74% White; 4% Asian American; 13% Hispanic. **Female To Male Ratio:** 1.5:1. **Housing:** 600 students can be accommodated in college housing, which includes coed dorms. On-campus housing is guaranteed for the freshman year only. Priority is given to out-of-town students. 85% of students commute. Alcohol is not permitted. All students may keep cars.

FACULTY/CLASSROOMS: 48% of faculty are male; 52% are female. No introductory courses are taught by graduate students. The average class size in an introductory lecture is 36 and in a laboratory is 23.

PROGRAMS OF STUDY: USF St. Petersburg confers B.A., B.S. and B.F.A. degrees. Master's degrees are also awarded. Bachelor's degrees are awarded in BIOLOGICAL SCIENCE (biology/biological science), BUSINESS (accounting, business administration and management, entrepreneurial studies, finance, global/general management, management science, and marketing and distribution), COMMUNICATIONS AND THE ARTS (communications, English, and graphic design), COMPUTER AND PHYSICAL SCIENCE (information sciences and systems), EDUCATION (education), ENGINEERING AND ENVIRONMENTAL DESIGN (environmental science), HEALTH PROFESSIONS (health science), SOCIAL SCIENCE (anthropology, criminology, economics, history, political science/government, psychology, and social science).

ACTIVITIES: There are no fraternities or sororities. There are 100 groups on campus, including debate, environmental, ethnic, LGBT, newspaper, professional, religious, social service, and student government. Popular campus events include Welcome Week, Homecoming Week, Spring Fling, and Leadership Retreats. **Sports:** There are 5 intramural sports for men and 5 for women. Facilities include recreation center, aquatics center, and waterfront activities such as sailing, kayaking and paddle boarding. **Graduates:** From July 1, 2015 to June 30, 2016, 705 bachelor's degrees were awarded. The most popular majors were accounting (15%), psychology (10%), and general business (10%). In an average class, 11% graduate in 4 years or less, 26% graduate in 5 years or less, and 33% graduate in 6 years or less.

SERVICES: Counseling and information services are available, as is tutoring in some subjects. There is remedial math and writing. **Library/Resources:** The library contains 236,793 volumes, 899,329 microform items, and 10,329 audio/video tapes/CDs/DVDs, and subscribes to 52,812 periodicals including electronic. Computerized library services include interlibrary loans, database searching, Internet access, and Wi-Fi capability. **Physically Challenged Students:** Facilities include wheelchair ramps, elevators, special parking, specially equipped restrooms, special class scheduling, lowered drinking fountains, lowered telephones, and special housing. **Special:** There are 7 national honor societies, a freshman honors program, and 3 departmental honors programs. **Visiting:** There are regularly scheduled orientations for prospective students. There are guides for informal visits. To schedule a visit, contact Prospective Student Outreach at (727) USF-4802. **Campus Safety and Security:** Measures include 24-hour foot and vehicle patrol, emergency notification system, and security escort services. There are emergency telephones, lighted pathways/sidewalks, and controlled access to dorms/residences.

REQUIREMENTS: The SAT or ACT is required. The ACT Optional Writing test is also required. AP and CLEP credits are accepted. **Procedure:** Freshmen are admitted fall and spring. Entrance exams should be taken junior year in high school. There are deferred admissions and rolling admissions plans. Applications should be filed by March 15 for fall entry; November 15 for spring entry, along with a $30 fee. Applications are accepted on-line. **Transfer Students:** 582 transfer students enrolled in 2015-2016. Courses taken at a regionally accredited school, minimum GPA of 2.5 (or a GPA of 2.0 if holding an AA degree). **International Students:** They must take the TOEFL.

ADMISSIONS: 46% of the 2016-2017 applicants were accepted. 6% of the current freshmen were in the top fifth of their class. **Admissions Contact:** Holly Kickliter, Director, Admissions and Marketing. Email: *admissions@usf.edu* Web: *www.usfsp.edu*

FINANCIAL AID: In 2016-2017, 73% of all full-time freshmen and 70% of continuing full-time students received some form of financial aid. 38% of all full-time freshmen and 43% of continuing full-time students received need-based aid. The FAFSA code is 009016. Check with the school for current application deadlines.

UNIVERSITY OF SOUTH FLORIDA/TAMPA — D-4

www.usf.edu

Tampa, FL 33620 — (813) 974-4150

	Email: dlhenry@usf.edu
Full-time: 10,666 men, 12,937 women	**Faculty:** 1244; I, -$
	Ph.D.s: n/av
Part-time: 3349 men, 3601 women	**Student/Faculty:** 24 to 1
Graduate: 5016 men, 6384 women	**Tuition:** $6410 ($17,324)
Year: semesters, summer session	**Freshman Class:** 28623 applied, 13349 accepted, 4049 enrolled
Room & Board: $9700	
SAT CR/M/W: 575/585/555 **ACT:** 26	**CEEB CODE:** 5828
Application Deadline: March 15	**VERY COMPETITIVE+**

University of South Florida/Tampa, founded in 1956, is a comprehensive public institution and part of the Florida Division of Colleges and Universities, offer programs in liberal and fine arts, business, engineering, health science, and education. USF also maintains campuses at Lakeland, Sarasota, and St. Petersburg. There are 6 undergraduate schools and 12 graduate schools. In addition to regional accreditation, USF/Tampa has baccalaureate program accreditation with AACSB, ABET, ACEJMC, ASLA, CSAB, CSWE, NAAB, NASAD, NASM, NCATE, and NLN. The 1657-acre campus is in an urban area in Tampa, Florida. Including any residence halls, there are 434 buildings.

STUDENT LIFE: 91% of undergraduates are from Florida. Others are from 50 states, 154 foreign countries, and Canada. 7% are Asian American; 6% Foreign; 50% White; 4% two or more races; 21% Hispanic; 2% race unknown; 10% African American. **Female To Male Ratio:** 1.2:1. The average age of freshmen is 18; all undergraduates, 22. 12% do not continue beyond their first year; 88% remain to graduate. **Housing:** 9297 students can be accommodated in college housing, which includes single-sex and coed dorms, on-campus apartments, and married student housing. In addition, there are honors houses, special-interest houses, fraternity houses, sorority houses, wellness housing, cooperative housing, and living learning communities. On-campus housing is available on a first-come and first-served basis. 78% of students live on campus. All students may keep cars.

FACULTY/CLASSROOMS: 56% of faculty are male; 44% are female. 61% teach undergraduates, and 18% do research. No introductory courses are taught by graduate students. The average class size in an introductory lecture is 39; in a laboratory is 21; and in a regular course is 26.

PROGRAMS OF STUDY: USF/Tampa confers B.A., B.S., B.F.A., B.I.S., B.M. and B.S.W. degrees. Associate, master's, and doctoral degrees are also awarded. Bachelor's degrees are awarded in BIOLOGICAL SCIENCE (biology/biological science and microbiology), BUSINESS (accounting, banking and finance, business administration and management, business economics, management information systems, management science, and marketing/retailing/merchandising), COMMUNICATIONS AND THE ARTS (classics, communications, dance, dramatic arts, English literature, French, German, Italian, music, Russian, Spanish, and speech/debate/rhetoric), COMPUTER AND PHYSICAL SCIENCE (chemistry, geology, mathematics, physical sciences, and physics), EDUCATION (art education, business education, education, education of the emotionally handicapped, education of the mentally handicapped, elementary education, English education, foreign languages education, mathematics education, music education, physical education, science education, social studies education, special education, and specific learning disabilities), ENGINEERING AND ENVIRONMENTAL DESIGN (chemical engineering, civil engineering, computer engineering, electrical/electronics engineering, engineering, environmental science, industrial engineering, and mechanical engineering), HEALTH PROFESSIONS (medical technology and nursing), SOCIAL SCIENCE (African American studies, American studies, anthropology, criminology, economics, geography, gerontology, history, humanities, international relations, liberal arts/general studies, philosophy, political science/government, psychology, religion, social science, social work, and sociology). Medicine, engineering, and business are the strongest academically. Business, education, and engineering have the largest enrollments.

ACTIVITIES: 10% of men belong to 26 national fraternities; 15% of women belong to 23 national sororities. Groups on campus include art, band, cheerleading, chess, choir, chorale, chorus, computers, dance, drama, drill team, ethnic, film, honors, international, jazz band, LGBT, literary magazine, marching band, musical theater, newspaper, opera, orchestra, pep band, photography, political, professional, radio and TV, religious, social, social service, student government, and symphony. Popular campus events include Minority and International events, and the University Lecture Series. **Sports:** There are 9 intercollegiate sports for men and 10 for women, and 19 intramural sports for men and 20 for women. Facilities include a multipurpose arena, pools, tennis and indoor racquetball courts, a track, jogging course, an indoor recreation center with weight training and aerobics rooms, a soccer stadium, softball complex, baseball stadium, tennis complex, sailing facility, and an 18-hole golf course. The Lee Roy Selmon Athletics Center provides modern locker room facilities for cross country, indoor and outdoor track, soccer, softball, baseball, tennis, and basketball. The women's and men's golf programs are in their Golf Training Center which houses each team's locker and meeting space as well as coaches offices and specialty training areas. Women's volleyball utilizes a newly renovated locker and meeting space just below their venue. Competition facilities include the Sun Dome Corral for women's volleyball; a soccer specific stadium for the men's and women's soccer teams; women's and men's basketball share the 10,000 seat USF Sun Dome located within the Athletics District; women's and men's track and field and cross country compete in a track facility featuring the same track surface used in the 2008 Summer Olympics. Softball and baseball have their own state-of-the-art facilities for competition on campus. The golf teams share the campus-owned golf course. The sailing program has a facility on the USF-St. Pete Campus.**Graduates:** From July 1, 2015 to June 30, 2016, 8171 bachelor's degrees were awarded. The most popular majors were health professions and related programs (20%), business/marketing (16%), and social sciences (12%). In an average class, 68% graduate in 6 years or less.

SERVICES: Counseling and information services are available, as is tutoring in most subjects. There is a reader service for the blind. **Library/Resources:** The 4 libraries contain 2.6 million volumes. Computerized library services include interlibrary loans, database searching, and Internet access. Special learning facilities include an art gallery, radio station, TV station, an anthropology museum and a botanical garden. **Physically Challenged Students:** All of the campus is accessible. Facilities include wheelchair ramps, elevators, special parking, specially equipped restrooms, special class scheduling, lowered drinking fountains, and lowered telephones. **Special:** USF offers co-op programs in business and engineering, study abroad, cross-registration, work-study programs, accelerated degree programs in public health and medicine, internships, a Washington semester, dual and student-designed majors, a liberal arts degree, nondegree study, and pass/fail options for some courses. There are 26 national honor societies, a freshman honors program, and 18 departmental honors programs. **Visiting:** There are regularly scheduled orientations for prospective students, including a 2-day program. There are guides for informal visits and visitors may sit in on classes. To schedule a visit, contact the Admissions Office/New Student Orientation. **Campus Safety and Security:** Measures include 24-hour foot and vehicle patrol, self-defense education, and security escort services. There are shuttle buses, emergency telephones, and lighted pathways/sidewalks.

REQUIREMENTS: The SAT or ACT is required. Candidates for admission should have completed 19 units, 4 units each of English and math, 3 units of science, of those, 2 units must be lab, 3 units each of social studies, 2 each of academic electives, and foreign language. The GED is accepted. Applicants who do not meet minimum requirements but have important attributes, special talents, or unique circumstances are considered for admission by an academic faculty committee. A GPA of 2.0 is required. AP and CLEP credits are accepted. Important factors in the admissions decision are advanced placement or honors courses, parents or siblings attended your school, evidence of special talent, personality/intangible qualities, extracurricular activities record, geographical diversity, and recommendations by school officials. To graduate, all students are required to complete at least 120 credit hours, including 36 distributed among English, math, science, social science, historical perspectives, fine arts, and humanities and 9 of exit requirements in major works/major issues and literature/writing. The number of hours required for each major varies. Students must maintain a minimum GPA of 2.0. **Procedure:** Freshmen are admitted to all sessions. Entrance exams should be taken at the end of the junior year or the beginning of the senior year. Applications should be filed by March 15 for fall entry. The fall 2016 application fee was $30. Notification of early decision is sent October 1; regular decision, April 15. Applications are accepted on-line. **Transfer Students:** 3575 transfer students enrolled in 2015-2016. Transfer apps with less than 24 transfer hours are required to submit a personal statement and reviewed by committee. Transfers with 25-59 hours must have a transfer GPA of 3.0. Florida College System AA degree transfers must have a minimum GPA of 2.0; other transfers with 60+ hours must have a minimum GPA of 2.5. Transfers to limited, access majors must meet the minimum GPA stated or the GPA for the specified major, whichever is higher. All transfer apps must be in good standing at their previous institution. 30 of 120 credits required for the bachelor's degree must be completed at USF. **International Students:** There are 1484 international students enrolled. The school actively recruits these students. They must take the TOEFL, or the IELTS is required. They must also take the SAT or ACT.

ADMISSIONS: There were 10 National Merit finalists. **Admissions Contact:** David Lee Henry, Director : Admissions. Email: *dlhenry@usf.edu* Web: *www.usf.edu*

FINANCIAL AID: In 2016-2017, 92% of all full-time freshmen and 84% of continuing full-time students received some form of financial aid. 53% of all full-time freshmen and 57% of continuing full-time students received need-based aid. The average freshman award was $12,007. Need-based scholarships or need-based grants averaged $9,183; need-based self-help aid (loans and jobs) averaged $5,110; non-need-based athletic scholarships averaged $10,046; other non-need-based awards and non-need-based scholarships averaged $3,074; and $4,717 from other forms of aid. The priority date for freshman financial aid applications for fall entry is March 1.

UNIVERSITY OF TAMPA D-4

www.ut.edu

Tampa, FL 33606	**(813) 257-1808** **(888) 646-2738**
Fax: (813) 258-7398	**Email: admissions@ut.edu**
Full-time: 2967 men, 4157 women	**Faculty:** 311; IIA, av$
Part-time: 103 men, 136 women	**Ph.D.s:** 93%
Graduate: 389 men, 464 women	**Student/Faculty:** 17 to 1
Year: semesters, summer session	**Tuition:** $27,740
Room & Board: $10,196	**Freshman Class:** 19947 applied, 9634 accepted, 1906 enrolled
SAT CR/M/W: 540/550/520 **ACT:** 20	**CEEB CODE:** 5819
Application Deadline: January 15	**COMPETITIVE**

University of Tampa, founded in 1931, is a comprehensive, independent institution that offers degree programs in more than 200 undergraduate and preprofessional areas of study and graduate and evening programs. The figures in the above capsule and in this profile are approximate. There are 4 undergraduate schools and one graduate school. In addition to regional accreditation, UT has baccalaureate program accreditation with AACSB, ABET, NASM, and NLN. The 105-acre campus is in an urban area in Tampa, Florida. Including any residence halls, there are 60 buildings.

STUDENT LIFE: 66% of undergraduates are from out of state, mostly the Middle Atlantic. Students are from 50 states, 140 foreign countries, and Canada. 8% are race unknown; 59% White; 5% African American; 3% two or more races; 2% Asian American; 12% Hispanic; 11% Foreign. 55% claim no religious affiliation; 21% Catholic; 21% Christian, Baptist, Presbyterian, Muslim, Methodist, and Episcopal. **Female To Male Ratio:** 1.4:1. The average age of freshmen is 18; all undergraduates, 21. 25% do not continue beyond their first year; 56% remain to graduate. **Housing:** 3890 students can be accommodated in college housing, which includes single-sex and coed dorms, on-campus apartments, 3 honors floors, 1 leadership themed floor, and 1 entrepreneurial themed floor. 58% of students live on campus; of those, 75% remain on campus on weekends. All students may keep cars.

FACULTY/CLASSROOMS: 49% of faculty are male; 51% are female. All teach undergraduates. No introductory courses are taught by graduate students. The average class size in an introductory lecture is 25; in a laboratory is 16; and in a regular course is 25.

PROGRAMS OF STUDY: UT confers B.A., B.S., B.F.A., B.L.S., B.M., B.S.A.T. and B.S.N. degrees. Master's degrees are also awarded. Bachelor's degrees are awarded in BIOLOGICAL SCIENCE (biochemistry, biology/biological science, and marine science), BUSINESS (accounting, banking and finance, business administration and management, business economics, entrepreneurial studies, finance enterprise systems, information & communication technology, international business management, management information systems, management, marketing/retailing/merchandising, mathematical programming, and sports management), COMMUNICATIONS AND THE ARTS (advertising, art, communications, creative writing, dance, dramatic arts, English, film arts, graphic design, human performance, journalism, music, music performance, musical theater, new media production, performing arts, Spanish, theatre acting, and writing), COMPUTER AND PHYSICAL SCIENCE (chemistry, computer security, digital arts/technology, mathematics, and physics), EDUCATION (athletic training, elementary education, music education, physical education, and secondary education), ENGINEERING AND ENVIRONMENTAL DESIGN (computer graphics and environmental science), HEALTH PROFESSIONS (allied health, exercise science, nursing, and public health), SOCIAL SCIENCE (criminology, economics, forensic studies, history, international studies, liberal arts/general studies, philosophy, political science/government, psychology, and sociology). Secondary Education (math, English, social studies), performing arts, and elementary education are the strongest academically. Nursing, finance, and biology have the largest enrollments.

ACTIVITIES: 15% of men belong to 14 national fraternities; 27% of women belong to 13 national sororities. There are 180 groups on campus, including leadership, media and special interest, academic, art, band, cheerleading, chess, chorale, chorus, computers, dance, debate, drama, environmental, ethnic, film, honors, international, jazz band, LGBT, literary magazine, musical theater, newspaper, orchestra, pep band, photography, political, professional, radio and TV, religious, social, social service, student government, symphony, and yearbook. Popular campus events include Into the Street (volunteer program), Campus Movie Fest, Leadership Awards Night, Greek Variety Show, and Spring Concert. **Sports:** There are 8 intercollegiate sports for men and 11 for women, and 22 intramural sports for men and 22 for women. Facilities include an Olympic-size swimming pool, tennis courts, a track, basketball, sand volleyball courts, crew training facility, a fitness center with exercise rooms, a main gymnasium with 3 full, size courts, training room, weight room, soccer, baseball, softball, and tennis. **Graduates:** From July 1, 2015 to June 30, 2016, 1412 bachelor's degrees were awarded. The most popular majors were business/marketing (29%), communications (12%), and social sciences (11%). 330 companies recruited on campus in 2015-2016. In an average class, 2% graduate in 3 years or less, 51% graduate in 4 years or less, 60% graduate in 5 years or less, and 61% graduate in 6 years or less. Of the 2015 graduating class, 23% were enrolled in graduate school within 6 months of graduation, and 85% were employed.

SERVICES: Counseling and information services are available, as is tutoring in most subjects, such as financial accounting, managerial accounting, chemistry & society, general chemistry I & II, organic chemistry, principles of microeconomis & macroeconomics, financial management, human anatomy & physiology I & II, physics, psychology, and statistics. There is a reader service for the blind, and remedial math, reading, and writing. Students can get assistance with any writing assignment at the Writing Center and with presentations in the Center for Public Speaking. **Library/Resources:** The library contains 275,000 volumes, 83,413 microform items, and 8,175 audio/video tapes/CDs/DVDs, and subscribes to 97,927 periodicals including electronic. Computerized library services include interlibrary loans, database searching, Internet access, and Wi-Fi capability. Special learning facilities include an art gallery, radio station, TV station, an entrepreneurship center, a fully equipped research vessel for marine science studies, a music facility, writing and language labs, an academic center for excellence, a graphic design studio, a marine science lab, and art studios. **Physically Challenged Students:** All of the campus is accessible. Facilities include wheelchair ramps, elevators, special parking, specially equipped restrooms, lowered drinking fountains, lowered telephones, and special housing. **Special:** Students may participate in internships, independent studies, work-study programs on campus, study abroad in 14 countries, a Washington Center internship, and an Oxford semester program. UT also offers summer marine science courses at the Gulf Coast Research Laboratory, nondegree study, pass/fail options, dual majors, accelerated degree programs, and credit for life, military, and work experience. There are 7 national honor societies and a freshman honors program. **Visiting:** There are regularly scheduled orientations for prospective students, including a campus tour and an interview with an admissions counselor, faculty, and others as requested. There are guides for informal visits, visitors may sit in on classes, and stay overnight. To schedule a visit, contact the Admissions Office at admissions@ut.edu. **Campus Safety and Security:** Measures include 24-hour foot and vehicle patrol, emergency notification system, self-defense education, and security escort services. There are shuttle buses, emergency telephones, lighted pathways/sidewalks, controlled access to dorms/residences, and on-campus security office. There are partnership with local law enforcement and the Tampa police department.

REQUIREMENTS: The SAT or ACT is required. Candidates for admission should have completed 4 credits in English, 3 credits each in math, science, and social studies, and 3 credits in college-preparatory electives. Of the science units, 2 must be labs. The GED is accepted. A portfolio or an audition is required for specific art and music programs. A GPA of 2.5 is required. AP and CLEP credits are accepted. Important factors in the admissions decision are recommendations by school officials, evidence of special talent, and extracurricular activities record. To graduate, students must maintain a minimum GPA of 2.0 in at least 124 credit hours, including the 2-year learning community, 11 hours each in humanities/fine arts and social science, 6 in natural science, global issues, non-Western studies, and art/aesthetics as well as writing-intensive course-work. The requirements for individual majors vary. **Procedure:** Freshmen are admitted fall, spring, and summer. Entrance exams should be taken by the end of the junior year or early in the senior year. There are deferred admissions and rolling admissions plans. Application deadlines are open. Application fee is $40. Notifications are sent April 1. 1556 applicants were on the 2016 waiting list; 124 were admitted. Applications are accepted on-line. Application fees are waived if application is completed on-line. **Transfer Students:** 450 transfer students enrolled in 2015-2016. Applicants should have earned 17 or more college credits with a minimum GPA of 2.0. 31 of 124 credits required for the bachelor's degree must be completed at UT. **International Students:** There are 770 international students enrolled. The school actively recruits these students. They must take the TOEFL with a minimum score of 550 on the paper-based TOEFL (PBT) or 79 on the Internet-based version (iBT).

ADMISSIONS: 48% of the 2016-2017 applicants were accepted. The SAT scores for the 2016-2017 freshman class were: Critical Reading-- 26% below 500, 56% between 500 and 599, 16% between 600 and 699, and 1% between 700 and 800. Math-- 22% below 500, 57% between 500 and 599, 19% between 600 and 699, and 2% between 700 and 800. Writing-- 31% below 500, 53% between 500 and 599, 15% between 600 and 699, and 1% between 700 and 800. The ACT scores were 38% between 18 and 23, 53% between 24 and 29, and 9% above 30. 36% of the current freshmen were in the top fifth of their class; 72% were in the top two fifths. **Admissions Contact:** Dennis Nostrand, Vice President for Enrollment. Email: *admissions@ut.edu* Web: *www.ut.edu*

FINANCIAL AID: In 2016-2017, 95% of all full-time freshmen and 90%

of continuing full-time students received some form of financial aid. 65% of all full-time freshmen and 60% of continuing full-time students received need-based aid. The average freshman award was $16,000. Need-based scholarships or need-based grants averaged $18,113 ($59,575 maximum); need-based self-help aid (loans and jobs) averaged $7,560 ($31,978 maximum); non-need-based athletic scholarships averaged $8,500 ($34,125 maximum); and other non-need-based awards and non-need-based scholarships averaged $6,885 ($40,753 maximum). 20% of undergraduate students work part-time. Average annual earnings from campus work are $1750. The average financial indebtedness of the 2016 graduate was $25,500. The FAFSA code is 001538. The priority date for freshman financial aid applications for fall entry is February 1.

UNIVERSITY OF WEST FLORIDA — A-1

www.uwf.edu

Pensacola, FL 32514	**(850) 474-2230** **(800) 263-1074**
Fax: (850) 474-3360	**Email: admissions@uwf.edu**
Full-time: 3227 men, 4332 women	**Faculty:** IIA, -$
Part-time: 1164 men, 1609 women	**Ph.D.s:** n/av
Graduate: 836 men, 1483 women	**Student/Faculty:** 24 to 1
Year: semesters, summer session	**Tuition:** $6360 ($19,260)
Room & Board: $9488	**Freshman Class:** 13623 applied, 8284 accepted, 1797 enrolled
SAT or ACT: required	**CEEB CODE:** 5833
Application Deadline: June 30	**COMPETITIVE**

University of West Florida, founded in 1967, is a public, regional, comprehensive institution that is part of the State University System of Florida. The figures in the above capsule and in this profile are approximate. There are 3 undergraduate schools and 3 graduate schools. In addition to regional accreditation, UWF has baccalaureate program accreditation with AACSB, ABET, CSWE, NASM, NCATE, NLN, ACS, NAACLS, and MPAC. The 1600-acre campus is in a suburban area 10 miles north of downtown Pensacola. Including any residence halls, there are 205 buildings.

STUDENT LIFE: 95% of undergraduates are from Florida. Others are from 48 states, 70 foreign countries, and Canada. 8% are Hispanic; 70% White; 3% Asian American; 12% African American; 1% American Indian/Alaska Native; 1% Foreign. **Female To Male Ratio:** 1.4:1. The average age of freshmen is 19; all undergraduates, 24. 16% do not continue beyond their first year; 74% remain to graduate. **Housing:** 1800 students can be accommodated in college housing, which includes coed dorms and on-campus apartments. In addition, there are honors houses. On-campus housing is available on a first-come, first-served basis. 82% of students commute. All students may keep cars.

FACULTY/CLASSROOMS: 53% of faculty are male; 47% are female. No introductory courses are taught by graduate students. The average class size in an introductory lecture is 34; in a laboratory is 21; and in a regular course is 26.

PROGRAMS OF STUDY: UWF confers B.A., B.S., B.F.A., B.S.B.A., B.S.C.E., B.S.E.E. and B.S.N degrees. Associate, master's, and doctoral degrees are also awarded. Bachelor's degrees are awarded in BIOLOGICAL SCIENCE (biology/biological science and marine biology), BUSINESS (accounting, banking and finance, business administration and management, business economics, and marketing/retailing/merchandising), COMMUNICATIONS AND THE ARTS (communications, English, music, and studio art), COMPUTER AND PHYSICAL SCIENCE (chemistry, computer science, mathematics, physics, and statistics), EDUCATION (art education, early childhood education, elementary education, health education, middle school education, music education, and secondary education), ENGINEERING AND ENVIRONMENTAL DESIGN (computer engineering and electrical/electronics engineering), HEALTH PROFESSIONS (medical laboratory technology, nursing, predentistry, and premedicine), SOCIAL SCIENCE (criminal justice, history, philosophy, political science/government, prelaw, psychology, religion, social science, and social work). Accounting, communication arts, and management are the strongest academically. Communication arts, psychology, and business have the largest enrollments.

ACTIVITIES: There are 158 groups on campus, including art, band, cheerleading, chess, choir, chorale, chorus, communications, computers, dance, debate, drama, environmental, ethnic, film, forensics, honors, international, jazz band, LGBT, literary magazine, musical theater, newspaper, orchestra, political, professional, radio and TV, religious, social, social service, student government, and symphony. **Sports:** There are 6 intercollegiate sports for men and 8 for women, and 12 intramural sports for men and 12 for women. Facilities include baseball, a track, tennis, racquetball, handball, softball, soccer, swimming, diving, weight lifting, and aerobics. **Graduates:** From July 1, 2015 to June 30, 2016, 2082 bachelor's degrees were awarded. The most popular majors were psychology (8%), nursing (5%), and criminal justice (5%).

SERVICES: Counseling and information services are available, as is tutoring in most subjects. There is remedial math. Remedial courses are offered on campus by the local community college. **Library/Resources:** The library contains 767,633 volumes, 1.2 million microform items, and 5,224 audio/video tapes/CDs/DVDs, and subscribes to 5,056 periodicals including electronic. Computerized library services include interlibrary loans and database searching. Special learning facilities include an art gallery, radio station, TV station, and an archeology museum. **Physically Challenged Students:** 80% of the campus is accessible. Facilities include wheelchair ramps, elevators, special parking, specially equipped restrooms, special class scheduling, lowered drinking fountains, and special housing. **Special:** Internships are arranged on an individual basis through a student's major department. The college offers pass/fail options and credit for military experience. A 3-2 engineering degree is also offered. There are 5 national honor societies and a freshman honors program. **Visiting:** There are regularly scheduled orientations for prospective students, including 5 Open House programs per year. There are guides for informal visits and visitors may sit in on classes. To schedule a visit, contact the Admissions Office. **Campus Safety and Security:** Measures include 24-hour foot and vehicle patrol, emergency notification system, self-defense education, and security escort services. There are emergency telephones, lighted pathways/sidewalks, a trolley system.

REQUIREMENTS: The SAT or ACT is required. Students must have completed 4 years of English, 3 each of math (algebra 1 and higher), science, and social studies, and 2 of a foreign language. A GPA of 2.0 is required. AP and CLEP credits are accepted. Important factors in the admissions decision are advanced placement or honors courses, evidence of special talent, and geographical diversity. To graduate, students must maintain a 2.0 GPA and complete 120 semester hours with a minimum of 24 hours in the major and 24 hours in upper-division courses. **Procedure:** Freshmen are admitted to all sessions. Entrance exams should be taken by the fall of the senior year. There are early admissions and rolling admissions plans. Early decision applications should be filed by June 30; regular applications, along with a $30 fee. Applications are accepted online. **Transfer Students:** Applicants must have a 2.0 GPA and a 2.0 at their last institution. Transfer students with fewer than 60 semester hours of transferable credit must meet freshman admission requirements. 30 of 120 credits required for the bachelor's degree must be completed at UWF. **International Students:** There are 228 international students enrolled. They must take the TOEFL with a minimum score of 525 on the paper-based TOEFL (PBT) or 69 on the Internet-based version (iBT) or take the MELAB. They must also take the SAT or ACT.

ADMISSIONS: 61% of the 2016-2017 applicants were accepted. The SAT scores for the 2016-2017 freshman class were: Critical Reading-- 44% below 500, 44% between 500 and 599, 10% between 600 and 699, and 1% between 700 and 800. Math-- 49% below 500, 41% between 500 and 599, 9% between 600 and 699, and 1% between 700 and 800. Writing-- 60% below 500, 34% between 500 and 599, 5% between 600 and 699, and 1% between 700 and 800. The ACT scores were 8% below 12, 56% between 12 and 17, 32% between 18 and 23, 2% between 24 and 29, and 2% above 30. 4 freshmen graduated first in their class. **Admissions Contact:** Katie Condon, Interim Director of Admissions. Email: *admissions@uwf.edu* Web: *www.uwf.edu*

FINANCIAL AID: In 2016-2017, 23% of all full-time freshmen and 54% of continuing full-time students received some form of financial aid. 15% of all full-time freshmen and 57% of continuing full-time students received need-based aid. The average freshman award was $2,034. Need-based scholarships or need-based grants averaged $1,735 ($4,000 maximum); need-based self-help aid (loans and jobs) averaged $2,352 ($3,500 maximum); non-need-based athletic scholarships averaged $626 ($1,500 maximum); and other non-need-based awards and non-need-based scholarships averaged $2,276 ($10,900 maximum). The college's own financial statement is required. The FAFSA code is 003955. Check with the school for current application deadlines.

WARNER UNIVERSITY D-4
www.warner.edu

Lake Wales, FL 33859	**(863) 638-7212** **(800) 309-9563**
Fax: (863) 638-7290	**Email: admissions@warner.edu**
Full-time: 340 men, 450 women	**Faculty:** 52
Part-time: 65 men, 235 women	**Ph.D.s:** 42%
Graduate: 40 men, 20 women	**Student/Faculty:** 17 to 1
Year: semesters, summer session	**Tuition:** $20,112
Room & Board: $8104	**Freshman Class:** n/av
SAT or ACT: required	**CEEB CODE:** 5883
Application Deadline: open	**COMPETITIVE**

Warner University is a Christian university in the liberal arts tradition committed to the search for truth in the context of Christian faith and academic excellence. The figures in the above capsule and in this profile are approximate. There are 2 undergraduate schools and 1 graduate school. In addition to regional accreditation, Warner has baccalaureate program accreditation with SACS. The 300-acre campus is in a rural area 5 miles south of Lake Wales, in Polk County, Florida. Including any residence halls, there are 20 buildings.

STUDENT LIFE: 88% of undergraduates are from Florida. Others are from 29 states, 22 foreign countries, and Canada. 8% are Hispanic; 40% African American; 39% White; 2% race unknown; 1% Asian American; 1% American Indian/Alaska Native. 61% are Protestant; 29% claim no religious affiliation. **Female To Male Ratio:** 1.6:1. The average age of freshmen is 19; all undergraduates, 22. 62% do not continue beyond their first year; 50% remain to graduate. **Housing:** 235 students can be accommodated in college housing, which includes single-sex dorms and off-campus apartments. On-campus housing is guaranteed for all 4 years. 58% of students commute. Alcohol is not permitted. All students may keep cars.

FACULTY/CLASSROOMS: 52% of faculty are male; 48% are female. All teach undergraduates, 20% do research, and 20% do both. No introductory courses are taught by graduate students. The average class size in an introductory lecture is 28; in a laboratory is 20; and in a regular course is 18.

PROGRAMS OF STUDY: Warner confers B.A. degrees. Associate and master's degrees are also awarded. Bachelor's degrees are awarded in BIOLOGICAL SCIENCE (biology/biological science), BUSINESS (accounting, banking and finance, business administration and management, business law, institutional management, marketing management, and sports management), COMMUNICATIONS AND THE ARTS (communications and English), COMPUTER AND PHYSICAL SCIENCE (information sciences and systems), EDUCATION (business education, education of the exceptional child, elementary education, English education, music education, physical education, science education, and social science education), HEALTH PROFESSIONS (exercise science), SOCIAL SCIENCE (biblical studies, history, pastoral studies, psychology, religious music, and social work). Biblical studies, social work, and teacher education are the strongest academically. Organizational management, church ministry, and teacher education have the largest enrollments.

ACTIVITIES: There are no fraternities or sororities. There are 14 groups on campus, including band, cheerleading, choir, chorale, chorus, computers, honors, newspaper, pep band, photography, religious, social, social service, and student government. Popular campus events include Christmas Banquet, Barn Party, and Spring Banquet. **Sports:** There are 7 intercollegiate sports for men and 8 for women, and 4 intramural sports for men and 3 for women. Facilities include baseball, basketball, cross-country, football, golf, softball, soccer, tennis, track & field, volleyball, and sand volleyball. **Graduates:** From July 1, 2015 to June 30, 2016, 368 bachelor's degrees were awarded. The most popular majors were organizational management (63%), elementary education (6%), and business administration (3%). In an average class, 25% graduate in 4 years or less, 32% graduate in 5 years or less, and 35% graduate in 6 years or less.

SERVICES: Counseling and information services are available, as is tutoring in most subjects. There is remedial math, reading, and writing. **Library/Resources:** The library contains 74,000 volumes, 7,267 microform items, and 15,200 audio/video tapes/CDs/DVDs, and subscribes to 178 periodicals including electronic. Computerized library services include interlibrary loans, database searching, and Internet access. **Physically Challenged Students:** 90% of the campus is accessible. Facilities include wheelchair ramps, special parking, specially equipped restrooms, lowered drinking fountains, and lowered telephones. **Special:** Internships are required in many majors, including teacher education, social work, sports management, and church ministry. An accelerated degree program is available in organizational management. HEART (Hunger Education and Resource Training) is a missionary training program designed to equip students to serve in missions, community development work, or crosscultural assignments in developing countries. There are 5 national honor societies and 1 departmental honors program. **Visiting:** There are regularly scheduled orientations for prospective students, consisiting of Warner Weekend held in the spring. There are guides for informal visits, visitors may sit in on classes, and stay overnight. To schedule a visit, contact the Admissions Office. **Campus Safety and Security:** Measures include 24-hour foot and vehicle patrol and security escort services. There are shuttle buses, emergency telephones, lighted pathways/sidewalks, special training in CPR/First Aid and emergency response.

REQUIREMENTS: The SAT or ACT is required. A GPA of 2.3 is required. AP and CLEP credits are accepted. To graduate, students must complete 128 credit hours with a GPA of 2.0 to 2.5, depending on the major. 30 to 80 hours are required in the major. 48 hours of upper-division courses are required, as is a computer application course in the major. **Procedure:** Freshmen are admitted fall and spring. Entrance exams should be taken in the junior or senior year. There are early admissions, deferred admissions, and rolling admissions plans. Application deadlines are open. Application fee is $20. Applications are accepted on-line. **Transfer Students:** 39 transfer students enrolled in 2015-2016. Applicants may transfer 24 or more hours from a regionally accredited school and must present a GPA of 2.0 or higher. 36 of 128 credits required for the bachelor's degree must be completed at Warner. **International Students:** There are 31 international students enrolled. The school actively recruits these students. They must take the TOEFL. They must also take the SAT or ACT.

ADMISSIONS: There was 1 National Merit finalist. 2 freshmen graduated first in their class. **Admissions Contact:** Jason Roe, Director of Admissions. Email: *admissions@warner.edu* Web: *www.warner.edu*

FINANCIAL AID: In 2016-2017, 98% of all full-time freshmen and 93% of continuing full-time students received some form of financial aid. 98% of all full-time freshmen and 93% of continuing full-time students received need-based aid. 47% of undergraduate students work part-time. Average annual earnings from campus work are $1528. The state aid form is required. The FAFSA code is 008848. The priority date for freshman financial aid applications for fall entry is May 10. The deadline for filing freshman financial aid applications for fall entry is October 1.

WEBBER INTERNATIONAL UNIVERSITY D-4
www.webber.edu

Babson Park, FL 33827	**(863) 638-2927** **(800) 741-1844**
Fax: (863) 638-1591	**Email: admissions@webber.edu**
Full-time: 426 men, 202 women	**Faculty:** 20
Part-time: 16 men, 11 women	**Ph.D.s:** 60%
Graduate: 28 men, 34 women	**Student/Faculty:** 27 to 1
Year: semesters, summer session	**Tuition:** $23,210
Room & Board: $8694	**Freshman Class:** 521 applied, 380 accepted, 263 enrolled
SAT or ACT: required	**CEEB CODE:** 5893
Application Deadline: August 1	**COMPETITIVE**

Webber International University, founded in 1927, is a privately endowed institution offering undergraduate and graduate degrees in business. There is 1 undergraduate school and 1 graduate school. In addition to regional accreditation, Webber has baccalaureate program accreditation with IACBE. The 110-acre campus is in a small town 50 miles east of Tampa and 50 miles south of Orlando. Including any residence halls, there are 12 buildings.

STUDENT LIFE: 69% of undergraduates are from Florida. Others are from 24 states, 41 foreign countries, and Canada. 9% are Hispanic; 41% White; 24% African American; 23% Foreign; 1% Asian American; 1% American Indian/Alaska Native. **Male To Female Ratio:** 1.9:1. The average age of freshmen is 19; all undergraduates, 22. 14% do not continue beyond their first year; 86% remain to graduate. **Housing:** 419 students can be accommodated in college housing, which includes single-sex and coed dorms and off-campus apartments. On-campus housing is guaranteed for all 4 years, is guaranteed for the freshman year only, and is available on a first-come, first-served basis. 53% of students live on campus. All students may keep cars.

FACULTY/CLASSROOMS: 56% of faculty are male; 44% are female. All teach undergraduates. No introductory courses are taught by graduate students. The average class size in a regular course is 21.

PROGRAMS OF STUDY: Webber confers B.S. degrees. Associate and master's degrees are also awarded. Bachelor's degrees are awarded in BUSINESS (accounting, banking and finance, business administration and management, business communications, hospitality management services, management science, marketing management, and sports management), COMPUTER AND PHYSICAL SCIENCE (computer security and information assurance and information sciences and systems), SOCIAL SCIENCE (prelaw). General business studies is the strongest academically and has the largest enrollment.

ACTIVITIES: There are no fraternities or sororities. There are 11 groups on campus, including band, cheerleading, debate, honors, international, marching band, newspaper, pep band, photography, political, professional, religious, social, social service, and student government. Popular campus events include Webber Weekend, International Day, and End-of-the-Year Beach Party. **Sports:** There are 9 intercollegiate sports for men and 9 for women, and 6 intramural sports for men and 6 for women. Facilities include a gym, 2 weight rooms, 6 tennis courts, a football practice field, swimming pool, softball, baseball, and soccer fields, 4 beach volleyball courts, and a pier for fishing on the lake. **Graduates:** From July 1, 2015 to June 30, 2016, 131 bachelor's degrees were awarded. The most popular majors were general business (73%), sport management (18%), and communications (1%). 40 companies recruited on campus in 2015-2016. In an average class, 1% graduate in 3 years or less, 48% graduate in 4 years or less, 50% graduate in 5 years or less, and 54% graduate in 6 years or less.

SERVICES: Counseling and information services are available, as is tutoring in most subjects. There is remedial math, reading, and writing. **Library/Resources:** The library contains 15,000 volumes, and 200 audio/video tapes/CDs/DVDs, and subscribes to 2 periodicals including electronic. Computerized library services include interlibrary loans, database searching, Internet access, and Wi-Fi capability. **Physically Challenged Students:** 90% of the campus is accessible. Facilities include wheelchair ramps, special parking, specially equipped restrooms, special class scheduling, and special housing. **Special:** Internships, study abroad in 5 countries, work study, and B.S. degrees are offered. Any combination of majors requires an additional 30 credit hours for a total of 150 to graduate. There is a freshman honors program. **Visiting:** There are regularly scheduled orientations for prospective students, including a campus tour and individual attention from admission counselors and other office representatives, such as financial aid, coaches, and professors. There are guides for informal visits, visitors may sit in on classes, and stay overnight. To schedule a visit, contact Vice President of Enrollment Management at PicardRP@webber.edu. **Campus Safety and Security:** Measures include 24-hour foot and vehicle patrol, emergency notification system, self-defense education, and security escort services. There are lighted pathways/sidewalks, and security patrol at night and weekend.

REQUIREMENTS: The SAT or ACT is required. Applicants should be graduates of accredited secondary schools and have completed 3 years each of English, math, and science and 2 years of social studies. An essay is also required. The GED is accepted. A GPA of 2.0 is required. AP and CLEP credits are accepted. To graduate, all students must complete 120 credit hours, including courses in their major, a 36-credit general curriculum, a 36-credit business core, 18-credit tailored electives, and 30-credit area of concentration. A GPA of 2.0 or better must be maintained. Students must pass the college's required English courses and meet its writing requirements. All students must take at least 3 computer courses. **Procedure:** Freshmen are admitted to all sessions. Entrance exams should be taken during the senior year. There are deferred admissions and rolling admissions plans. Applications should be filed by August 1 for fall entry; December 1 for spring entry; and April 1 for summer entry, along with a $35 fee. Applications are accepted on-line. **Transfer Students:** 42 transfer students enrolled in 2015-2016. Applicants must have a minimum GPA of 2.0 with 15 credit hours and leave their previous institution in good academic standing. Students with fewer than 15 credits must meet freshman requirements. 30 of 120 credits required for the bachelor's degree must be completed at Webber. **International Students:** There are 170 international students enrolled. The school actively recruits these students. They must take the TOEFL. Webber considers each application on a case by case basis.

ADMISSIONS: 73% of the 2016-2017 applicants were accepted. The SAT scores for the 2016-2017 freshman class were: Critical Reading-- 68% below 500, 29% between 500 and 599, and 3% between 600 and 699. Math-- 63% below 500, 32% between 500 and 599, 4% between 600 and 699, and 1% between 700 and 800. The ACT scores were 70% below 12, 20% between 12 and 17, and 1% between 24 and 29. **Admissions Contact:** Ryan P Picard, Director of Admissions. Email: *admissions@webber.edu* Web: *www.webber.edu*

FINANCIAL AID: In 2016-2017, 98% of all full-time freshmen and 99% of continuing full-time students received some form of financial aid. 62% of all full-time freshmen and 60% of continuing full-time students received need-based aid. The average freshman award was $18,697. Need-based scholarships or need-based grants averaged $15,812 ($24,550 maximum); need-based self-help aid (loans and jobs) averaged $3,139 ($11,000 maximum); non-need-based athletic scholarships averaged $3,755 ($12,000 maximum); and other non-need-based awards and non-need-based scholarships averaged $12,973 ($16,000 maximum). 40% of undergraduate students work part-time. Average annual earnings from campus work are $1300. The average financial indebtedness of the 2016 graduate was $26,676. Webber is a member of CSS. The FAFSA code is 001540. The priority date for freshman financial aid applications for fall entry is April 1. The deadline for filing freshman financial aid applications for fall entry is August 1.

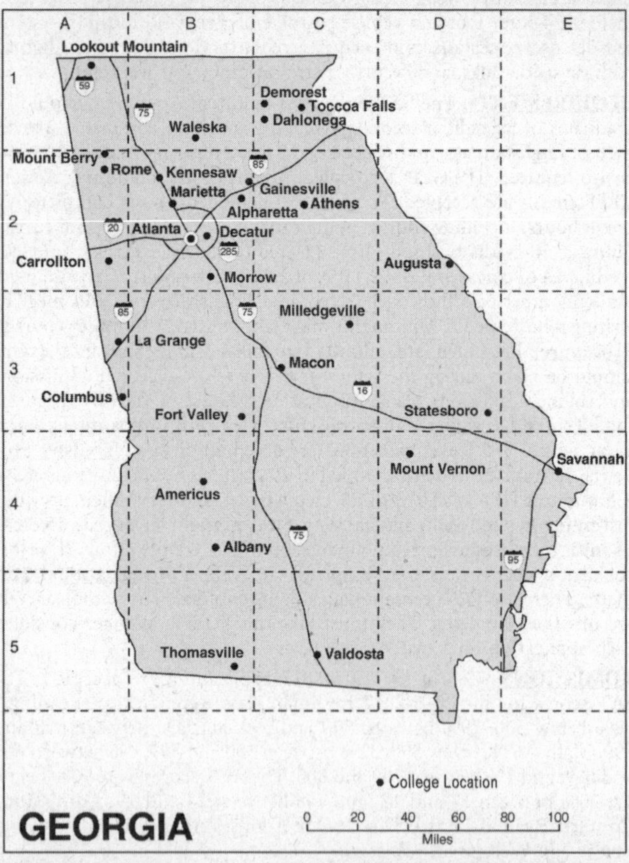

AGNES SCOTT COLLEGE — B-2
www.agnesscott.edu

Decatur, GA 30030	**40404.471.6423**
	(800) 868-8602
	Email: admissions@agnesscott.edu
Full-time: 4 men, 913 women	**Faculty:** 73; IIB, +$
Part-time: 4 men, 6 women	**Ph.D.s:** 100%
Graduate: n/av	**Student/Faculty:** 10 to 1
Year: semesters, summer session	**Tuition:** $39,960
Room & Board: $11,970	**Freshman Class:** 1399 applied, 905 accepted, 272 enrolled
SAT CR/M: 610/580 **ACT:** 27	**CEEB CODE:** 5002
Application Deadline: March 15	**VERY COMPETITIVE+**

Agnes Scott College, founded in 1889, is an independent liberal arts college for women and is affiliated with the Presbyterian Church. There is 1 undergraduate school. In addition to regional accreditation, Agnes Scott has baccalaureate program accreditation with SACSCoC. The 100-acre campus is in an urban area 6 miles from downtown Atlanta. Including any residence halls, there are 27 buildings.

STUDENT LIFE: 52% of undergraduates are from out of state, mostly the South. Students are from 44 states, 26 foreign countries, and Canada. 75% are from public schools. 8% are Asian American; 6% two or more races; 35% White; 29% African American; 2% race unknown; 11% Foreign; 10% Hispanic. 35% are Protestant. **Female To Male Ratio:** 114.9:1. The average age of freshmen is 18; all undergraduates, 20. 16% do not continue beyond their first year; 70% remain to graduate. **Housing:** College-sponsored housing includes single-sex dorms and on-campus apartments. In addition, there are special-interest houses and theme housing. On-campus housing is guaranteed for all 4 years. 86% of students live on campus. All students may keep cars.

FACULTY/CLASSROOMS: 36% of faculty are male; 64% are female. All teach undergraduates, and all do research. No introductory courses are taught by graduate students. The average class size in a regular course is 16.

PROGRAMS OF STUDY: Agnes Scott confers B.A. and B.S. degrees. Bachelor's degrees are awarded in BIOLOGICAL SCIENCE (biochemistry, biology/biological science, and neurosciences), BUSINESS (business administration and management), COMMUNICATIONS AND THE ARTS (art history and appreciation, classical languages, creative writing, dance, dramatic arts, English literature, French, German, music, Spanish, and studio art), COMPUTER AND PHYSICAL SCIENCE (astrophysics, chemistry, computer science, mathematics, and physics), ENGINEERING AND ENVIRONMENTAL DESIGN (engineering), HEALTH PROFESSIONS (nursing and public health), SOCIAL SCIENCE (African studies, anthropology, classical/ancient civilization, economics, history, international relations, philosophy, political science/government, psychology, religion, sociology, and women's studies). Psychology, public health, and English literature-creative writing have the largest enrollments.

ACTIVITIES: There are no fraternities or sororities. There are 65 groups on campus, including art, cheerleading, choir, chorale, chorus, communications, dance, drama, environmental, ethnic, honors, international, LGBT, literary magazine, musical theater, newspaper, orchestra, pep band, photography, political, professional, radio and TV, religious, social, social service, student government, symphony, and yearbook. Popular campus events include Black Cat, Spring Fling, Sophomore Ring Ceremony, Opening Convocation, and Senior Investiture. **Sports:** There are 6 intercollegiate sports for women and 7 intramural sports for women. Facilities include 2 fitness centers, a gym with a regulation basketball court, an 8-lane indoor pool, soccer field, tennis facility, weight room, track, aerobics room, and dance studios. **Graduates:** From July 1, 2015 to June 30, 2016, 217 bachelor's degrees were awarded. The most popular majors were psychology (12%), English lit - creative writing (12%), and public health (11%). In an average class, 2% graduate in 3 years or less, 64% graduate in 4 years or less, 69% graduate in 5 years or less, and 70% graduate in 6 years or less.

SERVICES: Counseling and information services are available, as is tutoring in some subjects, such as classical languages, English, math, physics, biology, psychology, chemistry, economics and foreign languages. There is a reader service for the blind, center for writing and speaking, and a resource center for math and science. **Library/Resources:** The library contains 238,754 volumes, and 27,101 audio/video tapes/CDs/DVDs, and subscribes to 94,565 periodicals including electronic. Computerized library services include interlibrary loans, database searching, Internet access, and Wi-Fi capability. Special learning facilities include an art gallery, planetarium, and radio station. There is also available a Center for Writing and Speaking, Economics Learning Center, Sociology and Anthropology Research Lab, and Science Center for Women. **Physically Challenged Students:** 90% of the campus is accessible. Facilities include wheelchair ramps, elevators, special parking, specially equipped restrooms, special class scheduling, lowered drinking fountains, lowered telephones, special housing, and lifts. **Special:** All first-year students will be required to participate in first-year travel and leadership immersion experiences. There is cross-registration through ARCHE (a 19-member consortium), and more than 300 credit and non-credit internships are available. There is a 3-2 engineering program with the Georgia Institute of Technology, a Computer Science dual-degree program with Emory University, a 3-2 nursing program with Emory University, and the college also offers student-designed interdisciplinary majors. Pass/fail options are also available. Also offered are a Washington semester, the PLEN Public Policy Semester, the Mills College Exchange, and work-study programs. B.A. degree requirements may be completed in 3 years. There are 9 national honor societies, Phi Beta Kappa, and 19 departmental honors programs. **Visiting:** There are regularly scheduled orientations for prospective students, campus tours, interviews, residence hall experiences, and informational sessions. There are guides for informal visits, and visitors may sit in on classes and stay overnight. To schedule a visit, contact the Admissions Office. **Campus Safety and Security:** Measures include 24-hour foot and vehicle patrol, emergency notification system, self-defense education, and security escort services. There are emergency telephones, lighted pathways/sidewalks, and controlled access to dorms/residences.

REQUIREMENTS: US citizens must submit at least one of the following: SAT/ACT scores; an interview with an Agnes Scott College representative; a graded writing sample. Non-US citizens must submit SAT/ACT scores or complete a video interview. All home-schooled students must submit SAT I or ACT scores and SAT II Subject tests. AP credits are accepted. Important factors in the admissions decision are leadership record, advanced placement or honors courses, and recommendations by school officials. To qualify for a degree, each student must successfully complete 128 hours of credit, including no more than 10 semester hours of internship credit, with a cumulative grade point average of 2.0 (C average), satisfy the Global Learning, Leadership Development, Intellectual Breadth, SUMMIT Portfolio, and depth standards; satisfy the residency requirement. Students must have a cumulative GPA of 2.0 in the major to receive the degree. A student must complete and submit an application for graduation by the first day of course selection in the semester prior to the one in which she intends to graduate. **Procedure:** Freshmen are admitted fall. Entrance exams should be taken late in the junior year or by January of the senior year. There are early decision, early admissions, and deferred admissions plans. Early decision applications should be filed by November 1; regular applications, by March 15 for fall entry. Notification of early decision is sent December 1; regular decision, April 15. Applications are accepted on-line. Application fees are waived if application is completed on-line. **Transfer Students:** 11 transfer students enrolled in 2015-2016. A minimum college GPA of 3.0 is required, as is an interview and a letter of recommendation from a professor. 64 of 128 credits required for the bachelor's degree must be completed at Agnes Scott. **International Students:** There are 98 international students enrolled. The school actively recruits these students. They must take the TOEFL, with a score of 600 recommended. They must also take the SAT or ACT.

ADMISSIONS: 65% of the 2016-2017 applicants were accepted. The SAT scores for the 2016-2017 freshman class were: Critical Reading-- 8% below 500, 33% between 500 and 599, 41% between 600 and 699, and 18% between 700 and 800. Math-- 13% below 500, 48% between 500 and 599, 29% between 600 and 699, and 9% between 700 and 800. Writing-- 8% below 500, 39% between 500 and 599, 44% between 600 and 699, and 9% between 700 and 800. The ACT scores were 19% between 18 and 23, 55% between 24 and 29, and 26% above 30. 60% of the current freshmen were in the top fifth of their class; 90% were in the top two fifths. **Admissions Contact:** Alexa Gaeta, Associate Vice President for Enrollment. Email: *admissions@agnesscott.edu* Web: *www.agnesscott .edu*

FINANCIAL AID: In 2016-2017, 100% of all full-time freshmen and 100% of continuing full-time students received some form of financial aid. 81% of all full-time freshmen and 77% of continuing full-time students received need-based aid. The average freshman award was $35,471.. The average financial indebtedness of the 2016 graduate was $34,022. Agnes Scott is a member of CSS. The college's own financial statement and previous year's tax return are required. The FAFSA code is 001542. The priority date for freshman financial aid applications for fall entry is February 15. The deadline for filing freshman financial aid applications for fall entry is May 1.

ALBANY STATE UNIVERSITY — B-4

www.asurams.edu

Albany, GA 31705	**(229) 430-4646** **(800) 822-RAMS**
Fax: (229) 430-4105	**Email: frank.archer@asurams.edu**
Full-time: 855 men, 1610 women	**Faculty:** n/av
Part-time: 150 men, 410 women	**Ph.D.s:** 52%
Graduate: 115 men, 330 women	**Student/Faculty:** n/av
Year: semesters, summer session	**Tuition:** $6470 ($21,550)
Room & Board: $12,992	**Freshman Class:** n/av
SAT or ACT: required	**CEEB CODE:** 5004
Application Deadline: June 1	**COMPETITIVE**

Albany State University, founded in 1903, is a state-supported institution within the University System of Georgia offering programs in liberal arts, business, health fields, and teacher education. The figures in the above capsule and in this profile are approximate. There are 4 undergraduate schools and 1 graduate school. In addition to regional accreditation, Albany State has baccalaureate program accreditation with ACBSP, NCATE, and NLN. The 144-acre campus is in an urban area 175 miles south of Atlanta. Including any residence halls, there are 28 buildings.

STUDENT LIFE: 98% of undergraduates are from Georgia. 91% are African American; 8% White; 1% Hispanic. **Female To Male Ratio:** 2.1:1. The average age of all undergraduates is 24. **Housing:** College-sponsored housing includes single-sex dorms. On-campus housing is available on a first-come, first-served basis, and is available on a lottery system for upperclassmen. Alcohol is not permitted. All students may keep cars.

FACULTY/CLASSROOMS: 56% of faculty are male; 44% are female. No introductory courses are taught by graduate students.

PROGRAMS OF STUDY: Associate and master's degrees are also awarded. Bachelor's degrees are awarded in BIOLOGICAL SCIENCE (biology/biological science), BUSINESS (accounting, marketing/retailing/merchandising, and office supervision and management), COMMUNICATIONS AND THE ARTS (art, dramatic arts, English, fine arts, French, music, Spanish, and speech/debate/rhetoric), COMPUTER AND PHYSICAL SCIENCE (chemistry, computer science, information sciences and systems, and mathematics), EDUCATION (early childhood education, health education, middle school education, music education, physical education, science education, and special education), HEALTH PROFESSIONS (allied health and nursing), SOCIAL SCIENCE (criminal justice, forensic studies, history, political science/government, psychology, social work, and sociology).

ACTIVITIES: Groups on campus include art, band, cheerleading, choir, chorale, computers, dance, debate, drama, drill team, honors, jazz band, marching band, musical theater, pep band, political, professional, religious, social, social service, student government, and yearbook. Popular campus events include Honors Day and Founders Day. **Sports:** There are 5 intercollegiate sports for men and 6 for women, and 2 intramural sports for men and 1 for women. Facilities include tennis courts, baseball and softball fields, an Olympic-size pool, a recreation room, and an all-weather track. **Graduates:** From July 1, 2015 to June 30, 2016, 485 bachelor's degrees were awarded. The most popular majors were criminal justice (9%), sociology (7%), and allied health science (6%).

SERVICES: There is remedial math, reading, and writing. **Library/Resources:** The library contains 351,467 volumes, 743,621 microform items, and 3,431 audio/video tapes/CDs/DVDs, and subscribes to 169,097 periodicals including electronic. Computerized library services include interlibrary loans and database searching. **Physically Challenged Students:** 90% of the campus is accessible. Facilities include wheelchair ramps, elevators, special parking, specially equipped restrooms, lowered drinking fountains, and lowered telephones. **Special:** The university offers co-op programs in all majors, 2+2 programs with Darton College, dual majors in social sciences, and 3-2 engineering degrees with the Georgia Institute of Technology. Several work-study programs and a gerontology training program are available. Albany State participates in the Georgian Intern Programs. All language majors are eligible to study abroad. There are 5 national honor societies, a freshman honors program, and 4 departmental honors programs. **Visiting:** There are regularly scheduled orientations for prospective students, consisting of summer and fall orientations and planned campus visitations. There are guides for informal visits, and visitors may sit in on classes. To schedule a visit, contact the Office of Student Affairs. **Campus Safety and Security:** Measures include 24-hour foot and vehicle patrol and security escort services. There are emergency telephones and lighted pathways/sidewalks.

REQUIREMENTS: The SAT or ACT is required. Applicants must be graduates of an accredited secondary school and have completed 4 years each of English and math, 3 each of science and social sciences, and 2 of a foreign language. A GED is accepted; however, GED students must take and pass SAT: Subject tests in areas where college-preparatory courses are deficient. A GPA of 2.0 is required. AP and CLEP credits are accepted. To graduate, all students must complete 120 semester hours, including 30 in the major. The core curriculum includes 12 hours of social science, 10 to 11 of science, math and technology, 9 of essential composition and math skills, 6 of humanities and fine arts, 5 of leadership and global awareness, and 3 of phys ed. Most majors require a minimum GPA of 2.25. Students must take a Regents exam to assess English language skills competency, pass a comprehensive exam in their major, and/or score satisfactorily on the aptitude section of the GRE. **Procedure:** Freshmen are admitted to all sessions. Entrance exams should be taken by December of the senior year. There is an early admissions plan. Applications should be filed by June 1 for fall entry; November 1 for spring entry; and April 1 for summer entry. The fall 2016 application fee was $20. **Transfer Students:** Students must provide official transcripts of all previous college work. Students with fewer than 30 transferable semester hours must meet freshman requirements. 30 of 120 credits required for the bachelor's degree must be completed at Albany State. **International Students:** They must take the TOEFL. They must also take the SAT or ACT and the college's own entrance exam.

Admissions Contact: Fred Archer lll, Director of Institutional Research. Email: *frank.archer@asurams.edu* Web: *www.asurams.edu*

FINANCIAL AID: The FAFSA code is 001544. Check with the school for current application deadlines.

ARMSTRONG STATE UNIVERSITY E-4

www.armstrong.edu

Savannah, GA 31419 (912) 344-2503 (800) 633-2349

Fax: (912) 344-3417 Email: admissions.info@armstrong.edu

Full-time: 1627 men, 3110 women	**Faculty:** 247
Part-time: 559 men, 1101 women	**Ph.D.s:** n/av
Graduate: 188 men, 572 women	**Student/Faculty:** 17 to 1
Year: semesters, summer session	**Tuition:** $6332 ($19,152)
Room & Board: $10,630	**Freshman Class:** 2168 applied, 1702 accepted, 863 enrolled
SAT CR/M/W: 506/488/475 **ACT:** 21	**CEEB CODE:** 5012
Application Deadline: July 1	**COMPETITIVE**

Armstrong State University is teaching-centered and student-focused, providing diverse learning experiences and professional programs grounded in the liberal arts. Armstrong is governed by the Board of Regents of the University System of Georgia. Armstrong offers more than 100 academic programs and majors. The university grants more than 60 academic credentials including undergraduate and graduate certificates, as well as associate, bachelor, and master's degrees. Armstrong offers an Doctor of Physical Therapy degree. There are 4 undergraduate schools and 4 graduate schools. In addition to regional accreditation, Armstrong has baccalaureate program accreditation with ABET, NASM, NCATE, ACS, NAACLS, CAPTE, CoARC, CAHME, CAA, JRCERT, JRCNMT, CEPH, and CCNE. The 267-acre campus is in a suburban area 250 miles from Atlanta and 150 miles from Jacksonville, FL. Including any residence halls, there are 59 buildings.

STUDENT LIFE: 86% of undergraduates are from Georgia. Others are from 42 states, 71 foreign countries, and Canada. 8% are Hispanic; 56% White; 5% two or more races; 4% Asian American; 25% African American; 2% Foreign. **Female To Male Ratio:** 2.0:1. The average age of freshmen is 19; all undergraduates, 24. 28% do not continue beyond their first year; 33% remain to graduate. **Housing:** 1411 students can be accommodated in college housing, which includes coed dorms and on-campus apartments. On-campus housing is guaranteed for the freshman year only, and is available on a first-come, first-served basis, and is available on a lottery system for upperclassmen. 79% of students commute. Alcohol is not permitted. All students may keep cars.

FACULTY/CLASSROOMS: 41% of faculty are male; 59% are female. No introductory courses are taught by graduate students. The average class size in an introductory lecture is 25; in a laboratory is 20; and in a regular course is 24.

PROGRAMS OF STUDY: Armstrong confers B.A., B.S., B.F.A., B.H.S., B.I.T., B.L.S., B.M.E., B.S.B.E., B.S.Ed., B.S.M.L.S., B.S.N., B.S.N.C., B.S.P. and B.S.R.S. degrees. Associate, master's, and doctoral degrees are also awarded. Bachelor's degrees are awarded in BIOLOGICAL SCIENCE (biochemistry and biology/biological science), BUSINESS (business economics), COMMUNICATIONS AND THE ARTS (art, English, French, music, music performance, Spanish, theatre arts, and visual and performing arts), COMPUTER AND PHYSICAL SCIENCE (applied mathematics, applied physics, chemistry, computer science, cyber intelligence/security studies, inform, science, systms & tech, and mathematics), EDUCATION (art education, early childhood education, English education, health education, health information management, mathematics education, middle school education, music education, physical education, secondary education, and special education), HEALTH PROFESSIONS (health services administration, health science, medical laboratory science, medical technology, nursing, public health, radiological science, rehabilitation therapy, and respiratory therapy), SOCIAL SCIENCE (child care/child and family studies, communication sciences & disorders, criminal justice, economics, history, liberal arts/general studies, political science/government, psychology, and women & gender studies). Biology, nursing, and rehabilitation sciences have the largest enrollments.

ACTIVITIES: There are 115 groups on campus, including band, cheerleading, choir, chorus, computers, dance, debate, drama, ethnic, honors, international, jazz band, LGBT, literary magazine, musical theater, newspaper, political, professional, religious, social, social service, and student government. Popular campus events include Celebrate Armstrong, International Week and HOLA (Hispanic Outreach and Leadership), and Treasure Savannah. **Sports:** There are 5 intercollegiate sports for men and 6 for women, and 11 intramural sports for men and 8 for women. Facilities include the ARC which houses the volleyball program where our volleyball team practices and competes, a student recreation center, 2 basketball courts, a multipurpose room, a weight room area, and 2 locker rooms. The outdoor field has a 4 acre lighted area, 3 flag football fields or 2 softball fields, baseball and soccer. **Graduates:** From July 1, 2015 to June 30, 2016, 1053 bachelor's degrees were awarded. The most popular majors were nursing (15%), liberal studies (8%), and biology (5%). In an average class, 2% graduate in 3 years or less, 15% graduate in 4 years or less, 27% graduate in 5 years or less, and 31% graduate in 6 years or less.

SERVICES: Counseling and information services are available, as is tutoring in most subjects. There is a reader service for the blind, and remedial math, reading, and writing. **Library/Resources:** The 2 libraries contain 207,421 volumes, 535,080 microform items, and 1,435 audio/video tapes/CDs/DVDs. Computerized library services include interlibrary loans, database searching, Internet access, and Wi-Fi capability. Special learning facilities include an art gallery. **Physically Challenged Students:** Facilities include wheelchair ramps, elevators, special parking, specially equipped restrooms, special class scheduling, lowered drinking fountains, and special housing. **Special:** There are 3 national honor societies and a freshman honors program. **Visiting:** There are regularly scheduled orientations for prospective students, including a tour of the campus and departments. There are guides for informal visits. To schedule a visit, contact Danielle Debien at (912) 344-2503. **Campus Safety and Security:** Measures include 24-hour foot and vehicle patrol, emergency notification system, self-defense education, and security escort services. There are emergency telephones, lighted pathways/sidewalks, and controlled access to dorms/residences.

REQUIREMENTS: The SAT or ACT is required. Applicants should graduate from an accredited secondary school. A GED may be accepted. College preparatory work should include 4 units of English and science, 3 units of math, and social studies, and 2 of foreign language. Art students must submit a portfolio. A GPA of 2.5 is required. AP and CLEP credits are accepted. The core curriculum consists of 60 hours in humanities, math, natural sciences, and social sciences and 3 in phys ed. A minimum GPA of 2.0 overall and a grade of C or better in each major course is required. Each student must complete 123 hours, with 29 hours in the major, and must take a comprehensive exam. **Procedure:** Freshmen are admitted to all sessions. There are deferred admissions and rolling admissions plans. Applications should be filed by July 1 for fall entry; December 1 for spring entry; and April 15 for summer entry, along with a $25 fee. Applications are accepted on-line. **Transfer Students:** 631 transfer students enrolled in 2015-2016. Transfer applicants must submit all transcripts and must be in good standing at the last college attended. 30 of 124 credits required for the bachelor's degree must be completed at Armstrong. **International Students:** There are 186 international students enrolled. The school actively recruits these students. They must take the TOEFL with a minimum score of 523 on the paper-based TOEFL (PBT) or 70 on the Internet-based version (iBT). They must also take the SAT or ACT.

ADMISSIONS: 79% of the 2016-2017 applicants were accepted. The SAT scores for the 2016-2017 freshman class were: Critical Reading-- 50% below 500, 38% between 500 and 599, 11% between 600 and 699, and 2% between 700 and 800. Math-- 58% below 500, 36% between 500 and 599, and 6% between 600 and 699. Writing-- 64% below 500, 30% between 500 and 599, 5% between 600 and 699, and 1% between 700 and 800. The ACT scores were 10% between 12 and 17, 66% between 18 and 23, 23% between 24 and 29, and 1% above 30. **Admissions Contact:** Tobe Frierson, Director of Admissions. Email: *admissions.info@armstrong.edu* Web: *www.armstrong.edu*

FINANCIAL AID: In 2016-2017, 60% of all full-time freshmen and 62% of continuing full-time students received some form of financial aid. 89% of all full-time freshmen and 82% of continuing full-time students received need-based aid. The average freshman award was $10,538. Need-based scholarships or need-based grants averaged $1,000 ($2,500 maximum); need-based self-help aid (loans and jobs) averaged $5,500 ($8,500 maximum); non-need-based athletic scholarships averaged $1,500; other non-need-based awards and non-need-based scholarships averaged $1,500; and $2,130 from other forms of aid. Average annual earnings from campus work are $559. The average financial indebtedness of the 2016 graduate was $25,809. The FAFSA code is 001546. The priority date for freshman financial aid applications for fall entry is March 15. The deadline for filing freshman financial aid applications for fall entry is April 20.

AUGUSTA UNIVERSITY D-2

Georgia Regents University
www.augusta.edu

Augusta, GA 30912 **(706) 667-4095**

Fax: (706) 721-7279 **Email:** admissions@augusta.edu
Full-time: 1431 men, 2646 women
Part-time: 449 men, 698 women
Graduate: 1129 men, 1624 women
Year: semesters, summer session
Room & Board: n/app
SAT or ACT: required
Application Deadline: November 15
Faculty: n/av
Ph.D.s: 88%
Student/Faculty: n/av
Tuition: $4632 ($16,248)
Freshman Class: n/av
CEEB CODE: 5406
COMPETITIVE

Augusta Univesity, formerly Georgia Regents University, is a public comprehensive research institution as well as an academic health center. The figures in the above capsule is for the tuition and fees only. There are 6 undergraduate schools and 3 graduate schools. In addition to regional accreditation, AU has baccalaureate program accreditation with AACSB, CSWE, NASAD, NASM, NCATE, NLN, CODA, CAEP, and CCNE. The campus is in an urban area 140 miles east of Atlanta on the Georgia-South Carolina border. Augusta, is situated on the southern banks of the storied Savannah River which serves as a halfway point between the Appalachian Mountains to the north and the Atlantic Ocean to the south. Including any residence halls, there are 145 buildings.

STUDENT LIFE: 89% of undergraduates are from Georgia. Others are from 45 states, 40 foreign countries, and Canada. 7% are race unknown; 58% White; 5% Hispanic; 4% Asian American; 3% two or more races; 20% African American; 1% Foreign. **Female To Male Ratio:** 1.7:1. The average age of freshmen is 18; all undergraduates, 24. 69% do not continue beyond their first year; 32% remain to graduate. **Housing:** 825 students can be accommodated in college housing, which includes coed dorms, on-campus apartments, and married student housing. On-campus housing is available on a first-come and first-served basis. 85% of students commute. Alcohol is not permitted. All students may keep cars.

FACULTY/CLASSROOMS: 57% of faculty are male; 43% are female. No introductory courses are taught by graduate students.

PROGRAMS OF STUDY: AU confers B.A., B.A.F.L., B.S., B.B.A., B.F.A., B.M., B.S.A.I.T., B.S.Ed., B.S.W., B.S.N., B.S.C.L.S, B.S.D.H., B.S.H.I.A., B.S.R.P.T., B.S.R.S., and B.S.K. degrees. Associate, master's, and doctoral degrees are also awarded. Bachelor's degrees are awarded in BIOLOGICAL SCIENCE (biology/biological science, cell biology, and ecology), BUSINESS (accounting, banking and finance, business administration and management, management information systems, and marketing/retailing/merchandising), COMMUNICATIONS AND THE ARTS (art, communications, English, music, and music performance), COMPUTER AND PHYSICAL SCIENCE (chemistry, computer science, information sciences and systems, mathematics, and physics), EDUCATION (elementary education, foreign languages education, health education, health information management, middle school education, music education, and special education), HEALTH PROFESSIONS (dental hygiene, kinesiology, medical laboratory science, medical technology, nuclear medical technology, nursing, radiation therapy, and respiratory therapy), SOCIAL SCIENCE (anthropology, criminal justice, history, political science/government, psychology, social work, and sociology). Chemistry, nursing, and psychology have the largest enrollments.

ACTIVITIES: 1% of men belong to 6 national fraternities; 1% of women belong to 5 national sororities. There are 160 groups on campus, including art, band, cheerleading, choir, chorus, drama, ethnic, film, honors, international, jazz band, LGBT, literary magazine, musical theater, newspaper, orchestra, pep band, photography, political, professional, radio and TV, religious, social, social service, student government, and symphony. Popular campus events include Week of Welcome, and Homecoming, Lyceum Series, Family Fun Days, and Pig Out (Student Appreciation Day). **Sports:** There are 6 intercollegiate sports for men and 7 for women. Facilities include a 2000-seat gym and fitness center, baseball, soccer, softball fields, a tennis center, an 18-hole golf course with club house, golf house, and a fitness center in the student activites center. **Graduates:** From July 1, 2015 to June 30, 2016, 996 bachelor's degrees were awarded. The most popular majors were nursing (17%), communications (6%), and psychology (5%). In an average class, 32% graduate in 6 years or less.

SERVICES: Counseling and information services are available, as is tutoring in most subjects. There is a reader service for the blind, and remedial math. **Library/Resources:** The 2 libraries contain 619,931 volumes, and 9,888 audio/video tapes/CDs/DVDs, and subscribe to 37,383 periodicals including electronic. Computerized library services include interlibrary loans, database searching, Internet access, and Wi-Fi capability. Special learning facilities include an art gallery, radio station, a history walk and guardhouse museum. **Physically Challenged Students:** 95% of the campus is accessible. Facilities include wheelchair ramps, elevators, special parking, specially equipped restrooms, special class scheduling, lowered drinking fountains, and lowered telephones. **Special:** The school offers co-op programs and internships with area companies, work-study programs, dual majors, nondegree study, and cross-registration with Paine College. There is a freshman honors program. **Visiting:** There are regularly scheduled orientations for prospective students, including a meal, campus tour, discussion of schedules, deadlines, and registration. There are guides for informal visits, and visitors may sit in on classes. To schedule a visit, contact Erin Smith at emsith35@gru.edu. **Campus Safety and Security:** Measures include 24-hour foot and vehicle patrol, emergency notification system, self-defense education, and security escort services. There are shuttle buses, emergency telephones, lighted pathways/sidewalks, controlled access to dorms/residences, and controlled access to labs after hours.

REQUIREMENTS: Applicants must have at least a 2.0 GPA, with a verbal score of 430 and math score of 400 on the SAT or a comparable score on the ACT. Applicants must be graduates of an accredited secondary school. The GED is accepted. Secondary school courses must include 4 units each of English and math, 3 each of science and social science, and 2 of a foreign language. AP and CLEP credits are accepted. Students must complete 125 hours with a minimum GPA of 2.0. All students are required to take 6 courses in phys ed, pass the Regents test in reading and composition, and demonstrate, through course completion or exam, a knowledge of U.S. and Georgia history and their constitutions. **Procedure:** Freshmen are admitted fall, spring, and summer. There are deferred admissions and rolling admissions plans. Applications should be filed by November 15 for fall entry. Applications are accepted on-line. **International Students:** The school actively recruits these students. They must take the TOEFL. They must also take the SAT or ACT.

Admissions Contact: Scott Argo, Interim Director of Admissions. Email: *admissions@gruedu* Web: *www.gru.edu*

FINANCIAL AID: In 2016-2017, 86% of all full-time freshmen and 86% of continuing full-time students received some form of financial aid. 53% of all full-time freshmen and 59% of continuing full-time students received need-based aid. The average freshman award was $5,692. Need-based scholarships or need-based grants averaged $2,964 ($2,908 maximum); need-based self-help aid (loans and jobs) averaged $1,732 ($2,190 maximum); non-need-based athletic scholarships averaged $3,688 ($4,250 maximum); and other non-need-based awards and non-need-based scholarships averaged $4,069 ($20,000 maximum). 2% of undergraduate students work part-time. The average financial indebtedness of the 2016 graduate was $20,914. The priority date for freshman financial aid applications for fall entry is April 1.

BERRY COLLEGE A-2

www.berry.edu

Mount Berry, GA 30149 **(706) 236-2215**
(800) BERRYGA

Fax: (706) 290-2178 **Email:** admissions@berry.edu
Full-time: 813 men, 1237 women
Part-time: 8 men, 15 women
Graduate: 34 men, 67 women
Year: semesters, summer session
Room & Board: $11,730
SAT CR/M/W: 570/570/550 **ACT:** 26
Application Deadline: July 25
Faculty: 167; IIA, -$
Ph.D.s: 95%
Student/Faculty: 12 to 1
Tuition: $33,556
Freshman Class: 4347 applied, 2407 accepted, 575 enrolled
CEEB CODE: 5059
COMPETITIVE+

Berry College, founded in 1902, is a private nonsectarian college offering programs in fine and liberal arts and preprofessional programs in education and business. Figures in the above capsule and in this profile are approximate. There are 4 undergraduate schools and 2 graduate schools. In addition to regional accreditation, Berry has baccalaureate program accreditation with AACSB, NASM, ACS, and SACSCOC. The 27000-acre campus is in a suburban area north of Rome on U.S. 27 in northwest Georgia, 72 miles northwest of Atlanta and 75 miles from Chattanooga, TN. Including any residence halls, there are 47 buildings.

STUDENT LIFE: 66% of undergraduates are from Georgia. Others are from 42 states, 11 foreign countries, and Canada. 66% are from public schools. 81% are White; 6% Hispanic; 4% African American; 3% two or more races; 3% race unknown; 1% Asian American; 1% Foreign. **Female To Male Ratio:** 1.5:1. The average age of freshmen is 19; all undergraduates, 21. 17% do not continue beyond their first year; 65% remain to graduate. **Housing:** 1895 students can be accommodated in college housing, which includes single-sex and coed dorms and on-campus apartments. On-campus housing is guaranteed for all 4 years. 86% of students live on campus; of those, 60% remain on campus on weekends. Alcohol is not permitted. All students may keep cars.

FACULTY/CLASSROOMS: 57% of faculty are male; 43% are female. 99% teach undergraduates, and 99% do research. No introductory courses are taught by graduate students. The average class size in an introductory lecture is 18 and in a laboratory is 16.

PROGRAMS OF STUDY: Berry confers B.A., B.S., B.Mus., and B.S.N. degrees. Master's degrees are also awarded. Bachelor's degrees are awarded in AGRICULTURE (animal science), BIOLOGICAL SCIENCE (biochemistry and biology/biological science), BUSINESS (accounting, business administration and management, finance, international business management, and marketing management), COMMUNICATIONS AND THE ARTS (art, art history and appreciation, communications, creative writing, English, French, German, music, music business management, Spanish, studio art, and theatre arts), COMPUTER AND PHYSICAL SCIENCE (chemistry, mathematics, and physics), EDUCATION (art education, early childhood education, mathematics education, middle school education, and music education), ENGINEERING AND ENVIRONMENTAL DESIGN (environmental science), HEALTH PROFESSIONS (exercise science and nursing), SOCIAL SCIENCE (anthropology, economics, history, interdisciplinary studies, international studies, philosophy, political science/government, psychology, religion, and sociology). Animal science, psychology, and exercise science have the largest enrollments.

ACTIVITIES: There are no fraternities or sororities. There are 79 groups on campus, including art, cheerleading, chess, choir, chorus, communications, computers, dance, drama, environmental, ethnic, forensics, honors, international, jazz band, literary magazine, musical theater, newspaper, orchestra, pep band, political, professional, religious, social, social service, student government, symphony, and yearbook. Popular campus events include Mountain Day, Conson Wilson Lecture Series, and BCTC Theatre Season. **Sports:** There are 11 intercollegiate sports for men and 12 for women, and 15 intramural sports for men and 15 for women. Facilities include new stadium for football, lacrosse, and track and field, athletic and recreational facility with six-lane 25-yard competitive swimming/diving, multipurpose athletic court, basketball court, racquetball courts, a performance gym, equine center, baseball, softball, and soccer/lacrosse fields, numerous running and biking trails, 6 camping pads, including 1 ADA pad, an 18-hole disc golf course, and 10 tennis courts. **Graduates:** From July 1, 2015 to June 30, 2016, 419 bachelor's degrees were awarded. The most popular majors were animal science, general (12%), psychology, general (8%), and biology/biological sciences and general (7%). 90 companies recruited on campus in 2015-2016. In an average class, 2% graduate in 3 years or less, 57% graduate in 4 years or less, and 65% graduate in 5 years or less.

SERVICES: Counseling and information services are available, as is tutoring in most subjects. There is a reader service for the blind and remedial writing. **Library/Resources:** The library contains 748,279 volumes, 19,020 microform items, and 6,019 audio/video tapes/CDs/DVDs, and subscribes to 56,093 periodicals including electronic. Computerized library services include interlibrary loans, database searching, Internet access, and Wi-Fi capability. Special learning facilities include an art gallery, an observatory, an equine center, a forestry center, beef-and-dairy-cattle operations, BOLD (Berry Outdoor Leadership Development), wildlife management area, and the Longleaf Pine Project. **Physically Challenged Students:** 80% of the campus is accessible. Facilities include wheelchair ramps, elevators, special parking, specially equipped restrooms, lowered drinking fountains, and special housing. **Special:** The college offers internships, study abroad in more than 20 countries, work-study programs, student-designed majors, co-op programs, cross-registration with Shorter College, dual majors, credit by exam, and non-degree study. There are 3-2 engineering degrees and dual-degree programs in several fields with the Georgia Institute of Technology and Kennesaw State University. There is also a dual-degree program in nursing with Emory University. There are 12 national honor societies, a freshman honors program, and 21 departmental honors programs. **Visiting:** There are regularly scheduled orientations for prospective students, including weekdays and Saturday mornings. Students should schedule campus visits in advance. There are guides for informal visits, visitors may sit in on classes and stay overnight. To schedule a visit, contact the Office of Admissions. **Campus Safety and Security:** Measures include 24-hour foot and vehicle patrol and emergency notification system. There are emergency telephones, lighted pathways/sidewalks, controlled access to dorms/residences, a gated campus, mobile police patrols, and limited access to campus.

REQUIREMENTS: The SAT or ACT is required. Applicants should be graduates of an accredited high school or have a GED. 20 academic credits are required, including 4 units each of English and math (to include algebra I, algebra II, and either geometry or trigonometry), 3 each of science and social studies, and 2 of a foreign language. Either SAT or ACT is required. AP credits are accepted. Important factors in the admissions decision are advanced placement or honors courses, leadership record, and recommendations by school officials. General education requirements include 5 courses in the humanities and fine arts, 3 each in behavioral science, math and natural sciences, communication, and health and phys ed, and 2 in electives. A 2.0 GPA and a total of 124 credits, including at least 30 hours in the major, are required for graduation. All students are also required to attend at least 3 approved cultural events per semester and pass a comprehensive exam or other senior assessment in the major. **Procedure:** Freshmen are admitted to all sessions. Entrance exams should be taken by the fall of the senior year. There is a rolling admissions plan. Applications should be filed by July 25 for fall entry. Notifications are sent November 1. 20 applicants were on the 2016 waiting list; 6 were admitted. Applications are accepted on-line. **Transfer Students:** 39 transfer students enrolled in 2015-2016. Applicants must submit official transcripts from all colleges previously attended, have a minimum GPA of 2.5, and be in good standing at the last school attended. 62 of 124 credits required for the bachelor's degree must be completed at Berry. **International Students:** There are 16 international students enrolled. The school actively recruits these students. They must take the TOEFL with a minimum score of 550 on the paper-based TOEFL (PBT) or 80 on the Internet-based version (iBT), or take the IELTS. They must also take the SAT or ACT if the student is from an English-speaking country.

ADMISSIONS: 55% of the 2016-2017 applicants were accepted. The SAT scores for the 2016-2017 freshman class were: Critical Reading-- 12% below 500, 47% between 500 and 599, 33% between 600 and 699, and 8% between 700 and 800. Math-- 13% below 500, 55% between 500 and 599, 28% between 600 and 699, and 4% between 700 and 800. Writing-- 20% below 500, 49% between 500 and 599, 27% between 600 and 699, and 4% between 700 and 800. The ACT scores were 1% between 12 and 17, 22% between 18 and 23, 46% between 24 and 29, and 32% above 30. 33% of the current freshmen were in the top fifth of their class; 51% were in the top two fifths. 16 freshmen graduated first in their class. **Admissions Contact:** Brett Kennedy, Assistant Vice President of Admissions. Email: *admissions@berry.edu* Web: *www.berry.edu*

FINANCIAL AID: In 2016-2017, 100% of all full-time freshmen and 99% of continuing full-time students received some form of financial aid. 71% of all full-time freshmen and 70% of continuing full-time students received need-based aid. The average freshman award was $28,103. Need-based scholarships or need-based grants averaged $15,355; need-based self-help aid (loans and jobs) averaged $4,267; and other non-need-based awards and non-need-based scholarships averaged $5,718. 84% of undergraduate students work part-time. Average annual earnings from campus work are $2206. The average financial indebtedness of the 2016 graduate was $24,383. The FAFSA code is 001554. The priority date for freshman financial aid applications for fall entry is March 1.

BRENAU UNIVERSITY - WOMEN'S COLLEGE *(The complete profile is made available exclusively on our website, www.barronspac.com)*

BREWTON-PARKER COLLEGE D-4

www.bpc.edu

Mt. Vernon, GA 30445	(912) 583-3247 (800) 342-1087
Fax: (912) 583-4498	**Email:** admissions@bpc.edu
Full-time: 237 men, 231 women	**Faculty:** 31
Part-time: 79 men, 82 women	**Ph.D.s:** 45%
Graduate: n/av	**Student/Faculty:** 9 to 1
Year: semesters, summer session	**Tuition:** $16,140
Room & Board: $7350	**Freshman Class:** n/av
SAT: required	**CEEB CODE:** 5068
Application Deadline: n/av	**COMPETITIVE**

Brewton-Parker College is a four-year Christian college. Affiliated with the Georgia Baptist Convention, the College offers four baccalaureate degrees in a caring, Christian environment that nurtures the whole student. Students enjoy challenging academic programs in an unapologetically Christian setting. Residential students participate in a comprehensive campus life program involving student organizations, intramural sports, campus ministry opportunities, and weekend activities. There is 1 undergraduate school. In addition to regional accreditation, BPC has baccalaureate program accreditation with NCATE. The 270-acre campus is in a rural area on Hwy 280 in the adjoining towns of Mt. Vernon and Ailey. Including any residence halls, there are 36 buildings.

STUDENT LIFE: 95% of undergraduates are from Georgia. **Male To Female Ratio:** 1.0:1. The average age of freshmen is 20; all undergraduates, 26. **Housing:** 500 students can be accommodated in college housing, which includes single-sex dorms. On-campus housing is guaranteed for all 4 years. 50% of students commute. Alcohol is not permitted. All students may keep cars.

FACULTY/CLASSROOMS: 54% of faculty are male; 46% are female. No introductory courses are taught by graduate students. The average class size in an introductory lecture is 20; in a laboratory is 24; and in a regular course is 17.

PROGRAMS OF STUDY: BPC confers B.A., B.S., and B.Min. degrees. Associate degrees are also awarded. Bachelor's degrees are awarded in BIOLOGICAL SCIENCE (biology/biological science), BUSINESS (accounting, business administration and management, and management information systems), COMMUNICATIONS AND THE ARTS (communications, dramatic arts, and English), COMPUTER AND PHYSICAL SCIENCE (information sciences and systems), EDUCATION (early childhood education, physical education, and sports studies), ENGINEERING AND ENVIRONMENTAL DESIGN (technological management), SOCIAL SCIENCE (Christian studies, history, human services, liberal arts/general studies, political science/government, psychology, social science, and sociology). Business, education, and psychology have the largest enrollments.

ACTIVITIES: There are 22 groups on campus, including band, cheerleading, choir, chorus, Circle K, honors, international, professional, religious, social, social service, and student government. Popular campus events include Homecoming, Alumni Weekend, and Fall Festival. **Sports:** There are 4 intercollegiate sports for men and 5 for women, and 8 intramural sports for men and 8 for women. Facilities include softball, baseball, and soccer fields, tennis courts, a swimming pool, a gym, a track, an intramural field, an outdoor volleyball court, a physical fitness building, a game room, and a campus lake. **Graduates:** From July 1, 2015 to June 30, 2016, 124 bachelor's degrees were awarded. The most popular majors were early childhood education (10%), business (9%), and psychology (8%).

SERVICES: Counseling and information services are available, as is tutoring in most subjects. There is remedial math, reading, and writing. Tutoring in Spanish is available. **Library/Resources:** The library contains 98,045 volumes, 1,562 microform items, and 6,941 audio/video tapes/CDs/DVDs, and subscribes to 132 periodicals including electronic. Computerized library services include interlibrary loans, database searching, Internet access, and Wi-Fi capability. **Physically Challenged Students:** 80% of the campus is accessible. Facilities include wheelchair ramps, special parking, specially equipped restrooms, and special housing. **Special:** The college offers internships, a general studies degree, B.A.-B.S. degrees, B.Min. degree, and nondegree study. There are 3 national honor societies. **Visiting:** There are regularly scheduled orientations for prospective students, consisting of a campus tour and academic and financial aid sessions. There are guides for informal visits, visitors may sit in on classes, and stay overnight. To schedule a visit, contact the Office of Admissions. **Campus Safety and Security:** There are lighted pathways/sidewalks, controlled access to dorms/residences, and an evening security guard on campus.

REQUIREMENTS: The SAT is required. The ACT and ACT Writing Test are recommended. The GED is accepted. Students should prepare with 4 years of English, 3 of social studies, and 2 each of foreign language, math, and science. A GPA of 2.0 is required. AP and CLEP credits are accepted. Important factors in the admissions decision are personality/intangible qualities, leadership record, and advanced placement or honors courses. The required core curriculum consists of humanities, math, natural science, social science, phys ed, and computer science. Students must maintain a minimum 2.0 GPA with half of the major taken at Brewton Parker. **Procedure:** Freshmen are admitted to all sessions. Entrance exams should be taken during the senior year of high school. There is a deferred admissions plan. Application deadlines are open. Application fee is $25. Applications are accepted on-line. **Transfer Students:** 81 transfer students enrolled in 2015-2016. Applicants must submit transcripts from previously attended institutions, along with high school transcripts, if they have completed fewer than 30 semester hours. **International Students:** There are 13 international students enrolled. They must also take the SAT.

ADMISSIONS: The SAT scores for the 2016-2017 freshman class were: Critical Reading-- 65% below 500, 29% between 500 and 599, 5% between 600 and 699, and 1% between 700 and 800. Math-- 65% below 500, 29% between 500 and 599, and 6% between 600 and 699. Writing-- 65% below 500, 29% between 500 and 599, and 6% between 600 and 699. The ACT scores were 87% between 12 and 17, 11% between 24 and 29, and 2% above 30. **Admissions Contact:** Sandra Clay, Director of Admissions. Email: *admissions@bpc.edu* Web: *www.bpc.edu*

FINANCIAL AID: In 2016-2017, 95% of all full-time freshmen and 95% of continuing full-time students received some form of financial aid. BPC is a member of CSS. The college's own financial statement is required. The FAFSA code is 001557. Check with the school for current application deadlines.

CLARK ATLANTA UNIVERSITY *(The complete profile is made available exclusively on our website, www.barronspac.com)*

CLAYTON STATE UNIVERSITY B-2

www.clayton.edu

Morrow, GA 30260	(678) 466-4115
Fax: (678) 66-4149	**Email:** stephenjenkins@clayton.edu
Full-time: n/av	**Faculty:** IIB, -$
Part-time: n/av	**Ph.D.s:** 51%
Graduate: n/av	**Student/Faculty:** n/av
Year: semesters, summer session	**Tuition:** $10,251 ($17,678)
Room & Board: $9484	**Freshman Class:** 840 applied, 600 accepted, 483 enrolled
SAT CR/M: 500/458 **ACT:** required	**CEEB CODE:** 5145
Application Deadline: n/av	**COMPETITIVE**

Clayton State University, founded in 1969 as a public junior college, has been a 4-year undergraduate college in the University System of Georgia since 1985. The figures in the above capsule and in this profile are approximate. There are 4 undergraduate schools and one graduate school. In addition to regional accreditation, Clayton State has baccalaureate program accreditation with ADA, NCATE, and NLN. The 160-acre campus is in a suburban area 17 miles south of downtown Atlanta near Hartsfield International Airport. Including any residence halls, there are 16 buildings.

STUDENT LIFE: 92% of undergraduates are from Georgia. Others are from 28 states, 60 foreign countries, and Canada. The average age of freshmen is 18; all undergraduates, 28. 30% do not continue beyond their first year. **Housing:** 1200 students can be accommodated in college housing, which includes single-sex and coed dorms and on-campus apartments. On-campus housing is guaranteed for the freshman year only, and is available on a first-come, first-served basis. Priority is given to out-of-town students. 65% of students commute. Alcohol is not permitted. All students may keep cars.

FACULTY/CLASSROOMS: 51% of faculty are male; 49% are female. All teach undergraduates. No introductory courses are taught by graduate students.

PROGRAMS OF STUDY: Clayton State confers B.A., B.S., B.A.S., B.B.A., B.M., and B.S.N. degrees. Associate and master's degrees are also awarded. Bachelor's degrees are awarded in BUSINESS (accounting, accounting (finance), business administration and management, business (dual major program), business administration - international, business administration, management, operations, business administration marketing, business economics, finance, business management, management, marketing, and marketing and distribution), COMMUNICATIONS AND THE ARTS (film arts, film, television and digital media, film and media studies, music, music performance, music theory and composition, and musical theater), COMPUTER AND PHYSICAL SCIENCE (chemistry, computer information technology, information sciences and systems, and mathematics), EDUCATION (art education, childhood education, computer education, education, and middle school education), ENGINEERING AND ENVIRONMENTAL DESIGN (preengineering and technological management), HEALTH PROFESSIONS (allied health, biology, dental hygiene, exercise science, health care administration, nursing, pre-health studies, and predentistry), SOCIAL SCIENCE (African studies, architectural studies, criminal justice, economics, history, interdisciplinary studies, and psychology). Nursing, middle school education, and music performance are the strongest academically. Management has the largest enrollment.

ACTIVITIES: There are 35 groups on campus, including art, band, cheerleading, choir, chorale, chorus, computers, drama, ethnic, film, honors, international, jazz band, LGBT, musical theater, newspaper, professional, radio and TV, religious, social, social service, and student government. Popular campus events include Freshman Preview Day, Majors Monday, and Nontrad Tuesday. **Sports:** There are 6 intercollegiate sports for men and 6 for women. Facilities include a gym, jogging trails, a circuit training facility, a weight room, soccer fields, and tennis, badminton, volleyball, and basketball courts.

SERVICES: Counseling and information services are available, as is tutoring in most subjects. There is remedial math, reading, and writing. **Library/Resources:** The library contains 97,835 volumes, 254,014 microform items, and 5,113 audio/video tapes/CDs/DVDs, and subscribes to 750 periodicals including electronic. Computerized library services include interlibrary loans, database searching, Internet access, and Wi-Fi capability. Special learning facilities include a radio station, and a concert facility. **Physically Challenged Students:** All of the campus is accessible. Facilities include wheelchair ramps, elevators, special parking, specially equipped restrooms, special class scheduling, lowered drinking fountains, and lowered telephones. **Special:** Co-op programs and internships can be arranged in all majors except middle school education. The B.A.S. career program enables associate degree holders to complete the baccalaureate degree. Cross-registration is offered through the University Center Consortium. Dual majors, B.A.-B.S. degrees, study abroad, student-designed majors, and work-study programs are offered. Distance learning opportunities are possible. There are 2 national honor societies and a freshman honors program. **Visiting:** There are regularly scheduled orientations for prospective students, including tours of the campus and the opportunity to meet faculty and staff and learn about the athletic programs, the notebook computers, and campus life. There are guides for informal visits, and visitors may sit in on classes. To schedule a visit, contact Admissions Welcome Center. **Campus Safety and Security:** Measures include 24-hour foot and vehicle patrol, emergency notification system, self-defense education, and security escort services. There are emergency telephones, lighted pathways/sidewalks, and controlled access to dorms/residences.

REQUIREMENTS: The SAT or ACT is required. Applicants should be graduates of accredited secondary schools. High school preparation should include 4 courses each in English and math, 3 each in science, history, and social studies, and 2 in a foreign language. Students may also be admitted on the strength of their high school academic records. A GPA of 2.0 is required. AP and CLEP credits are accepted. Students in the baccalaureate program must complete 120 to 126 semester hours, including a 60-hour core curriculum in English and humanities, math or sciences, and social sciences. A 2.0 minimum GPA is required for graduation. **Procedure:** Freshmen are admitted to all sessions. Entrance exams should be taken before registration. There are early admissions, deferred admissions, and rolling admissions plans. Check with the school for current application deadlines. The fall 2016 application fee was $40. Notification is sent on a rolling basis. Applications are accepted on-line. **Transfer Students:** Applicants with fewer than 30 semester hours or 45 quarter credits must meet the same criteria as entering freshmen. 30 of 120 credits required for the bachelor's degree must be completed at Clayton State. **International Students:** The school actively recruits these students. They must take the TOEFL, and Georgia State Test for English Proficiency (G-STEP). They must also take the SAT or ACT.

ADMISSIONS: 71% of the 2016-2017 applicants were accepted. **Admissions Contact:** Stephen Jenkins, Director of Undergraduate Admissions. Email: *stephenjenkins@clayton.edu* Web: *www.clayton.edu*

FINANCIAL AID: Clayton State is a member of CSS. The college's own financial statement is required. The FAFSA code is 008976. Check with the school for current application deadlines.

COLUMBUS STATE UNIVERSITY *(The complete profile is made available exclusively on our website, www.barronspac.com)*

COVENANT COLLEGE — A-1

www.covenant.edu

Lookout Mountain, GA 30750	**(706) 820-2398** **(888) 451-2683**
Fax: (706) 820-0893	**Email: admissions@covenant.edu**
Full-time: 440 men, 609 women	**Faculty:** 62; IIB, av$
Part-time: 11 men, 6 women	**Ph.D.s:** 90%
Graduate: 17 men, 51 women	**Student/Faculty:** 14 to 1
Year: semesters, summer session	**Tuition:** $30,160
Room & Board: $8830	**Freshman Class:** 655 applied, 633 accepted, 265 enrolled
SAT CR/M/W: 610/570/590 **ACT:** 26	**CEEB CODE:** 6124
Application Deadline: May 1	**VERY COMPETITIVE**

Covenant College, founded in 1955, is a private liberal arts college affiliated with the Presbyterian Church in America. At Covenant, we seek to inspire and equip our students to be faithful stewards of their God-given abilities-all of our programs are designed with this in mind. There is 1 undergraduate school and 1 graduate school. In addition to regional accreditation, Covenant has baccalaureate program accreditation with SACS-COC. The 350-acre campus is in a suburban area 12 miles southwest of Chattanooga, Tennessee. Including any residence halls, there are 15 buildings.

STUDENT LIFE: 78% of undergraduates are from out of state, mostly the South. Students are from 48 states, 23 foreign countries, and Canada. 90% are White; 3% African American; 2% Asian American; 2% Hispanic; 2% Foreign; 1% American Indian/Alaska Native. 49% are Protestant. **Female To Male Ratio:** 1.4:1. The average age of freshmen is 18; all undergraduates, 20. 15% do not continue beyond their first year; 58% remain to graduate. **Housing:** 917 students can be accommodated in college housing, which includes single-sex dorms, coed dorms, and on-campus apartments. On-campus housing is guaranteed for all 4 years. 98% of students live on campus. Alcohol is not permitted. All students may keep cars.

FACULTY/CLASSROOMS: 75% of faculty are male; 26% are female. All teach undergraduates. No introductory courses are taught by graduate students. The average class size in an introductory lecture is 19; in a laboratory is 16; and in a regular course is 18.

PROGRAMS OF STUDY: Covenant confers B.A. and B.S. degrees. Master's degrees are also awarded. Bachelor's degrees are awarded in BIOLOGICAL SCIENCE (biology/biological science), BUSINESS (business administration and management), COMMUNICATIONS AND THE ARTS (art, dramatic arts, English, French, music, music performance, and Spanish), COMPUTER AND PHYSICAL SCIENCE (chemistry, computer science, mathematics, and physics), EDUCATION (elementary education, English education, mathematics education, and science education), SOCIAL SCIENCE (biblical studies, economics, history, interdisciplinary studies, philosophy, philosophy and religion, psychology, social science, and sociology). English, history, and sociology have the largest enrollments.

ACTIVITIES: There are no fraternities or sororities. There are 43 groups on campus, including campus ministries, music ensembles and student-run film society, radio station, bagpipe, choir, chorale, concert band, dance, debate, drama, film, honors, international, jazz band, literary magazine, musical theater, newspaper, photography, professional, religious, social, social service, student government, and yearbook. Popular campus events include Madrigal Dinner, Spring Banquet, and Kilter Night. **Sports:** There are 6 intercollegiate sports for men and 7 for women, and 9 intramural sports for men and 9 for women. Facilities include a gym, weight room, swimming pool, tennis courts, 3 soccer fields, running trails, an aerobics room, and a wellness room equipped with a variety of fitness machines. **Graduates:** From July 1, 2015 to June 30, 2016, 243 bachelor's degrees were awarded. The most popular majors were social sciences (14%), English (13%), and education (10%).

SERVICES: Counseling and information services are available, as is tutoring in some subjects. There is remedial math, reading, and writing. **Library/Resources:** The library contains 89,449 volumes, 121,159 microform items, and 4,500 audio/video tapes/CDs/DVDs, and subscribes to 525 periodicals including electronic. Computerized library services include interlibrary loans, database searching, Internet access, and Wi-Fi capability. Special learning facilities include an art gallery. **Physically Challenged Students:** All of the campus is accessible. Facilities include wheelchair ramps, elevators, special parking, specially equipped restrooms, lowered drinking fountains, and lowered telephones. **Special:** Cross-registration is possible with the Council for Christian Colleges and Universities (CCCU). Students may study abroad in 9 countries or spend a semester in Washington. There is a 3-2 engineering program with Georgia Tech, a cooperative nursing program with Emory, and a Bridge program for MSN with Vanderbilt. Juniors and seniors may take classes on a pass/fail basis. There are 5 national honor societies and 5 departmental honors programs. **Visiting:** There are regularly scheduled orientations for prospective students, consisting of a campus preview weekend during which high school students stay in dormitories and attend classes, seminars, and other college activities. There are guides for informal visits, visitors may sit in on classes, and stay overnight. **Campus Safety and Security:** Measures include 24-hour foot and vehicle patrol, emergency notification system, and security escort services. There are lighted pathways/sidewalks, and a watchman who maintains campus security at night.

REQUIREMENTS: The SAT or ACT is required. Students must submit the following: application for admission, application fee, Christian testimony, official high school transcript, minimum GPA of 2.5, a combined SAT score of at least 1000 (sum of critical reading and math section scores) or composite ACT score of at least 21, academic references, and a church reference. Applicants must graduate from an accredited high school or have a GED. Applicants should have 14 total units, including 4 years of high school English, 3 years of math, and 2 years each of science, and social studies, and academic electives. An essay and an interview are required. AP and CLEP credits are accepted. Important factors in the admissions decision are advanced placement or honors courses, personality/intangible qualities, recommendations by school officials, leadership record, parents or siblings attended your school, extracurricular activities record, and recommendations by alumni. All students must complete 55 to 63 hours of core and distribution requirements, including course-work in Bible studies, interdisciplinary studies, English composition, cross-cultural experience, language, phys ed, lab science, social science, and history. A minimum total of 126 credits and a GPA of 2.0 are required for graduation. All students must also complete an oral interview and a senior integration project, in which they explore a problem in their major field in light of Christian philosophy. **Procedure:** Freshmen are admitted fall and spring. Entrance exams should be taken by January of the senior year. There is a rolling admissions plan. Applications should be filed by May 1 for fall entry; November 1 for spring entry, along with a $35 fee. Notification of early decision is sent August 15; regular decision, in rolling . Applications are accepted on-line. Application fees are waived if application is completed on-line. **Transfer Students:** 39 transfer students enrolled in 2015-2016. Transfer applicants must take either the SAT, with a minimum satisfactory score, or the ACT, with a minimum composite of 21. Courses with a grade of C or better that apply toward the selected Covenant program will receive transfer credit. 32 of 126 credits required for the bachelor's degree must be completed at Covenant. **International Students:** There are 23 international students enrolled. The school actively recruits these students. They must take the TOEFL with a minimum score of 540 on the paper-based TOEFL (PBT) or 76 on the Internet-based version (iBT). Applicants are encouraged to take the SAT or ACT if it is available in their country.

ADMISSIONS: 97% of the 2016-2017 applicants were accepted. The SAT scores for the 2016-2017 freshman class were: Critical Reading-- 10% below 500, 38% between 500 and 599, 35% between 600 and 699, and 17% between 700 and 800. Math-- 17% below 500, 45% between 500 and 599, 32% between 600 and 699, and 6% between 700 and 800. Writing-- 19% below 500, 35% between 500 and 599, 37% between 600 and 699, and 9% between 700 and 800. The ACT scores were 7% below 12, 18% between 12 and 17, 25% between 18 and 23, 21% between 24 and 29, and 28% above 30. 46% of the current freshmen were in the top fifth of their class; 65% were in the top two fifths. **Admissions Contact:** Scott Schindler, Assoc. Director of Admissions. Email: *admissions@covenant.edu* Web: *www.covenant.edu*

FINANCIAL AID: In 2016-2017, 100% of all full-time freshmen and 100% of continuing full-time students received some form of financial aid. 70% of all full-time freshmen and 68% of continuing full-time students received need-based aid. The average freshman award was $21,771. Need-based scholarships or need-based grants averaged $17,722 ($30,430 maximum); need-based self-help aid (loans and jobs) averaged $5,450 ($33,522 maximum); and other non-need-based awards and non-need-based scholarships averaged $12,131 ($27,850 maximum). 56% of undergraduate students work part-time. Average annual earnings from campus work are $2427. The average financial indebtedness of the 2016 graduate was $22,208. The state aid form and the college's own financial statement are required. The FAFSA code is 003484. The priority date for freshman financial aid applications for fall entry is March 1. The deadline for filing freshman financial aid applications for fall entry is March 31.

EMORY UNIVERSITY — B-2

www.emory.edu

Atlanta, GA 30322 — (404) 727-6036

Email: admission@emory.edu

Full-time: 3321 men, 4355 women	**Faculty:** 780
Part-time: 72 men, 88 women	**Ph.D.s:** 100%
Graduate: 2935 men, 3742 women	**Student/Faculty:** 8 to 1
Year: semesters, summer session	**Tuition:** $47,300
Room & Board: $13,486	**Freshman Class:** 17681 applied, 4685 accepted, 1354 enrolled
SAT CR/M/W: 660/700/690 **ACT:** 31	**CEEB CODE:** 5187
Application Deadline: January 1	**MOST COMPETITIVE**

Emory University, founded in 1836, is a private institution affiliated with the United Methodist Church. There are 5 undergraduate schools and 8 graduate schools. In addition to regional accreditation, Emory has baccalaureate program accreditation with SACS. The 634-acre campus is in a suburban area 5 miles northeast of downtown Atlanta. Including any residence halls, there are 150 buildings.

STUDENT LIFE: 73% of undergraduates are from out of state, mostly the South. Students are from 50 states, 48 foreign countries, and Canada. 60% are from public schools. 9% are African American; 6% Hispanic; 41% White; 4% race unknown; 3% two or more races; 22% Asian American; 15% Foreign. 43% claim no religious affiliation; 18% Protestant; 13% Muslim, Hindu, and Buddhist.; 12% Catholic; 11% Jewish. **Female To Male Ratio:** 1.3:1. The average age of freshmen is 18; all undergraduates, 20. 6% do not continue beyond their first year; 89% remain to graduate. **Housing:** 4425 students can be accommodated in college housing, which includes single-sex and coed dorms, on-campus apartments, and married student housing. In addition, there are honors houses, language houses, special-interest houses, fraternity houses, sorority houses, and theme housing. On-campus housing is guaranteed for all 4 years. 67% of students live on campus; of those, 95% remain on campus on weekends. Upperclassmen may keep cars.

FACULTY/CLASSROOMS: 59% of faculty are male; 41% are female. No introductory courses are taught by graduate students.

PROGRAMS OF STUDY: Emory confers B.A., B.S., B.B.A., and B.S.N. degrees. Associate, master's, and doctoral degrees are also awarded. Bachelor's degrees are awarded in AGRICULTURE (environmental studies), BIOLOGICAL SCIENCE (biology/biological science and neurosciences), BUSINESS (accounting, banking and finance, business administration and management, business economics, and marketing/retailing/merchandising), COMMUNICATIONS AND THE ARTS (art, art history and appreciation, Chinese, classics, comparative literature, creative writing, dance, dramatic arts, English, film arts, fine arts, French, Greek, Italian, Japanese, journalism, Latin, linguistics, music, Russian languages and literature, and Spanish), COMPUTER AND PHYSICAL SCIENCE (chemistry, computer science, mathematics, and physics), EDUCATION (educational statistics and research), HEALTH PROFESSIONS (nursing), SOCIAL SCIENCE (African studies, African American studies, American studies, anthropology, Asian/American studies, Asian/Oriental studies, Caribbean studies, classical/ancient civilization, economics, French studies, German area studies, history, interdisciplinary studies, international studies, Italian studies, Judaic studies, Latin American studies, medieval studies, Middle Eastern studies, philosophy, political science/government, psychology, religion, Russian and Slavic studies, sociology, and women's studies). Business administration, biology, and neuroscience & behavioral biology have the largest enrollments.

ACTIVITIES: 30% of men belong to 12 national fraternities; 31% of women belong to 13 national sororities. There are 220 groups on campus, including art, bagpipe, band, cheerleading, chess, choir, chorale, chorus, computers, dance, debate, drama, ethnic, film, honors, international, jazz band, LGBT, literary magazine, musical theater, newspaper, orchestra, pep band, photography, political, professional, radio and TV, religious, social, social service, student government, symphony, and yearbook. Popular campus events include Heritage Ball, Dooley's Week, and Festival of Nine Lessons. **Sports:** There are 8 intercollegiate sports for men and 8 for women, and 20 intramural sports for men and 20 for women. Facilities include a recreation center, which contains a 3000-seat gym with 4 basketball courts, 5 volleyball courts, an Olympic-size swimming pool, indoor track, 2 Nautilus weight rooms, a sheer rock wall, and tennis, racquetball, and squash courts. In addition, there is a soccer field and a 400-meter track with seating for 2000 spectators. **Graduates:** The most popular majors were business administration and management, general (14%), biology/biological sciences, general (9%), economics, general (9%). Of the 2015 graduating class, 43% were enrolled in graduate school within 6 months of graduation, and 31% were employed.

SERVICES: Counseling and information services are available, as is tutoring in most subjects. There is a reader service for the blind. **Library/Resources:** The 9 libraries contain 3.9 million volumes, 6.3 million microform items, and 117,143 audio/video tapes/CDs/DVDs. Computerized library services include interlibrary loans, database searching, Internet access, and Wi-Fi capability. Special learning facilities include an art gallery, planetarium, radio station, TV station, the Michael C. Carlos museum, and the Carter enter. **Physically Challenged Students:** 90% of the campus is accessible. Facilities include wheelchair ramps, elevators, special parking, specially equipped restrooms, special class scheduling, lowered drinking fountains, lowered telephones, and special housing. **Special:** Special academic programs include cross-registration with Atlanta-area colleges and universities, departmental internships, work-study programs, dual majors, 3-2 and 4-2 engineering degrees with Georgia Tech, and pass/fail options. A Washington semester and B.A.-B.S. degrees are available, and students may study abroad in many countries. There are accelerated degree programs offered in chemistry, math, math and computer science, English, history, philosophy, political science, and sociology. There are 30 national honor societies and Phi Beta Kappa. **Visiting:** There are regularly scheduled orientations for prospective students, including a student-led campus tour and an informational focus session led by a member of our Admission staff. Prospective students may also arrange to sit in on classes, as well as meet with faculty or athletic coaches. There are guides for informal visits. To schedule a visit, contact the Office of Undergraduate Admission. **Campus Safety and Security:** Measures include 24-hour foot and vehicle patrol, self-defense education, and security escort services. There are shuttle buses, emergency telephones, and lighted pathways/sidewalks, and the campus patrol is a fully accredited police department.

REQUIREMENTS: The SAT or ACT is required. In addition, students must submit a high school transcript. Students may submit SAT results, but they are not required unless a student is home-schooled. A recommendation from a high school counselor and up to 2 additional letters of recommendation are required. The student must have acquired 16 academic credits in secondary school, including 4 years of English, 3 years of math, and 2 years each of history, science, and foreign language. AP credits are accepted. Important factors in the admissions decision are advanced placement or honors courses, recommendations by school officials, and extracurricular activities record. To graduate, students must complete 127 semester hours, including courses during the first 2 years in English, science, math, history, the social sciences, health, and phys ed. Students must maintain at least a C (2.0) average in any major or minor they complete. The number of hours required for the major varies by department. A thesis is required for students in honors or dual B.A.-M.A. or B.S.-M.S. programs. **Procedure:** Freshmen are admitted fall. Entrance exams should be taken prior to applying. There are early decision, early admissions, and deferred admissions plans. Early decision applications should be filed by November 1; regular applications, by January 1 for fall entry, along with a $75 fee. Notification of early decision is sent December 15; regular decision, April 1. Applications are accepted on-line. **Transfer Students:** 164 transfer students enrolled in 2015-2016. Applicants must have taken the SAT or ACT and completed at least 1 year of college, with a GPA of 3.0. 64 of 127 credits required for the bachelor's degree must be completed at Emory. **International Students:** The school actively recruits these students. They must take the TOEFL. They must also take the SAT or ACT.

ADMISSIONS: 26% of the 2016-2017 applicants were accepted. The SAT scores for the 2016-2017 freshman class were: Critical Reading-- 1% below 500, 19% between 500 and 599, 47% between 600 and 699, and 33% between 700 and 800. Math-- 10% between 500 and 599, 36% between 600 and 699, and 54% between 700 and 800. Writing-- 1% below 500, 10% between 500 and 599, 44% between 600 and 699, and 45% between 700 and 800. The ACT scores were 2% between 18 and 23, 32% between 24 and 29, and 66% above 30. There were 43 National Merit finalists. **Admissions Contact:** Dr. Tran, Dean of Admissions. Email: *admission@emory.edu* Web: *www.emory.edu*

FINANCIAL AID: In 2016-2017, 45% of all full-time freshmen and 49% of continuing full-time students received some form of financial aid. 43% of all full-time freshmen and 44% of continuing full-time students received need-based aid. 17% of undergraduate students work part-time. Average annual earnings from campus work are $1090. The average financial indebtedness of the 2016 graduate was $19,397. Emory is a member of CSS. The CSS/Profile is required. The FAFSA code is 001564. Check with the school for current application deadlines.

FORT VALLEY STATE UNIVERSITY — B-3

www.fvsu.edu

Fort Valley, GA 31030 — **(478) 825-6307**

Fax: (478) 825-6169	**Email:** admissions@fvsu.edu
Full-time: 1313 men, 1688 women	**Faculty:** 153
Part-time: 175 men, 245 women	**Ph.D.s:** 64%
Graduate: 64 men, 86 women	**Student/Faculty:** 20 to 1
Year: semesters, summer session	**Tuition:** $9480 ($18,954)
Room & Board: $8508	**Freshman Class:** 5343 applied, 2161 accepted, 960 enrolled
SAT or ACT: required	**CEEB CODE:** 5220
Application Deadline: June 15	**VERY COMPETITIVE**

Fort Valley State University, founded in 1895, is a public land-grant member of the University System of Georgia. The university offers undergraduate programs in the arts and sciences, business, education, agriculture, engineering, and other vocational and technical fields. Graduate programs are offered in early childhood, middle grades education, mental health and rehabilitation counseling, and guidance counseling. The figures in the above capsule and in this profile are approximate. There are 3 undergraduate schools and 1 graduate school. In addition to regional accreditation, FVSU has baccalaureate program accreditation with NCATE. The 1375-acre campus is in a rural area 30 miles southwest of Macon. Including any residence halls, there are 35 buildings.

STUDENT LIFE: 96% of undergraduates are from Georgia. Others are from 29 states and 5 foreign countries. 92% are African American; 6% White; 1% Asian American; 1% Hispanic. **Female To Male Ratio:** 1.3:1. The average age of freshmen is 19; all undergraduates, 21. 27% do not continue beyond their first year; 39% remain to graduate. **Housing:** 1450 students can be accommodated in college housing, which includes single-sex and coed dorms and on-campus apartments. On-campus housing is guaranteed for the freshman year only, and is available on a first-come, first-served basis. 62% of students live on campus. Alcohol is not permitted. All students may keep cars.

FACULTY/CLASSROOMS: 50% of faculty are male; 50% are female. No introductory courses are taught by graduate students. The average class size in a regular course is 25.

PROGRAMS OF STUDY: FVSU confers B.A., B.S., B.B.A., and B.S.W.

degrees. Associate and master's degrees are also awarded. Bachelor's degrees are awarded in AGRICULTURE (agricultural economics, animal science, horticulture, and plant science), BIOLOGICAL SCIENCE (biology/biological science, nutrition, and zoology), BUSINESS (accounting, business administration and management, marketing/retailing/merchandising, and office supervision and management), COMMUNICATIONS AND THE ARTS (communications and English), COMPUTER AND PHYSICAL SCIENCE (chemistry, computer science, information sciences and systems, and mathematics), EDUCATION (agricultural education, early childhood education, home economics education, mathematics education, middle school education, physical education, and secondary education), ENGINEERING AND ENVIRONMENTAL DESIGN (agricultural engineering technology, commercial art, and electrical/electronics engineering technology), HEALTH PROFESSIONS (veterinary science), SOCIAL SCIENCE (child psychology/development, criminal justice, economics, political science/government, psychology, social work, and sociology).

ACTIVITIES: 5% of men belong to 4 national fraternities; 2% of women belong to 5 national sororities. There are 73 groups on campus, including band, cheerleading, choir, chorus, dance, drama, honors, international, jazz band, marching band, newspaper, opera, orchestra, political, religious, social service, and student government. Popular campus events include Black History month. **Sports:** There are 5 intercollegiate sports for men and 6 for women, and 3 intramural sports for men and 3 for women. Facilities include a stadium, a gym, a baseball field, lighted tennis courts, an indoor swimming pool, indoor and outdoor tracks, and shuffleboard courts. **Graduates:** From July 1, 2015 to June 30, 2016, 230 bachelor's degrees were awarded. The most popular majors were mathmatics (43%), visual/performing arts (17%), and psychology (10%). In an average class, 13% graduate in 4 years or less, 33% graduate in 5 years or less, and 39% graduate in 6 years or less.

SERVICES: Counseling and information services are available, as is tutoring in most subjects. There is remedial math, reading, and writing. **Library/Resources:** The library contains 250,000 volumes, 172,000 microform items, and subscribes to 1,168 periodicals including electronic. Computerized library services include interlibrary loans and database searching. Special learning facilities include a radio station, TV station, experimental agricultural plots, animal research centers, and a greenhouse complex. **Physically Challenged Students:** All of the campus is accessible. Facilities include wheelchair ramps, elevators, special parking, specially equipped restrooms, and special housing. **Special:** Students may participate in cooperative work-study programs with local industries, cross-register for courses at Robins Residence Center, and study abroad. Fort Valley also offers a 3-2 dual degree program in chemistry, geosciences with University of Oklahoma, in engineering or other technical fields with Georgia Institute of Technology, and a 3-2 engineering degree with University of Nevada, Las Vegas. There are 5 national honor societies and a freshman honors program. **Visiting:** There are regularly scheduled orientations for prospective students, including an overview, an introduction of administration and faculty, and a tour. There are guides for informal visits and visitors may sit in on classes. To schedule a visit, contact the Office of Enrollment Management. **Campus Safety and Security:** Measures include 24-hour foot and vehicle patrol. There are emergency telephones.

REQUIREMENTS: The SAT or ACT is required. Applicants must be graduates of an accredited secondary school or have earned a GED. The university requires at least 17 academic units of study, including 4 in English, 3 in social science, 3 each in math and science, and 2 of foreign language. A GPA of 2.7 is required. AP and CLEP credits are accepted. Students must complete a minimum of 120 credit hours, plus 5 additional hours to satisfy requirements for freshmen orientation and for military science or phys ed. General education requirements include courses in humanities, social science, math, science, and courses in the major. The bachelor's degree requires a minimum GPA of 2.0 and no grade below C in the major. **Procedure:** Freshmen are admitted to all sessions. There are early admissions, deferred admissions, and rolling admissions plans. Applications should be filed by June 15 for fall entry; November 1 for spring entry; and April 1 for summer entry, along with a $30 fee. Applications are accepted on-line. **Transfer Students:** 135 transfer students enrolled in 2015-2016. In addition to meeting standard admission requirements, transfers must submit transcripts from all colleges previously attended. Transfer credit is accepted based on a 2.0 minimum GPA, and only courses with a C or better will be accepted. 45 of 125 credits required for the bachelor's degree must be completed at FVSU. **International Students:** There are 23 international students enrolled. They must take the TOEFL and the college's own test. They must also take the SAT or ACT.

ADMISSIONS: 40% of the 2016-2017 applicants were accepted. **Admissions Contact:** Calandra Wright, Director of Admissions. Email: *admissions@fvsu.edu* Web: *www.fvsu.edu*

FINANCIAL AID: In 2016-2017, 94% of all full-time freshmen received some form of financial aid. 8% of all full-time freshmen received need-based aid. The average freshman award was $2,300. Need-based scholarships or need-based grants averaged $2,300; need-based self-help aid (loans and jobs) averaged $2,425; and other non-need-based awards and non-need-based scholarships averaged $1,850. The FAFSA code is 001566. The deadline for filing freshman financial aid applications for fall entry is March 1.

GEORGIA COLLEGE & STATE UNIVERSITY C-3
www.gcsu.edu

Milledgeville, GA 31061 **(478) 445-1283**

Fax: (478) 445-1914
Full-time: 2120 men, 3435 women
Part-time: 211 men, 281 women
Graduate: 285 men, 583 women
Year: semesters, summer session
Room & Board: $11,946
SAT or ACT: required
Application Deadline: April 1

Email: admissions@gcsu.edu
Faculty: IIA, -$
Ph.D.s: n/av
Student/Faculty: n/av
Tuition: $9202 ($27,550)
Freshman Class: 3980 applied, 3364 accepted, 1381 enrolled
CEEB CODE: 5252
COMPETITIVE+

Georgia College and State University, founded in 1889, is the public liberal arts university of Georgia. There are 4 undergraduate schools and 1 graduate school. In addition to regional accreditation, Georgia College has baccalaureate program accreditation with AACSB, NASM, NCATE, NMSA, AMTA, and AEE. The 602-acre campus is in a small town 30 miles from Macon. Including any residence halls, there are 93 buildings.

STUDENT LIFE: 98% of undergraduates are from Georgia. Others are from 26 states, 39 foreign countries, and Canada. 83% are White; 5% African American; 5% Hispanic; 3% two or more races; 2% Asian American; 1% Foreign. **Female To Male Ratio:** 1.6:1. **Housing:** 2237 students can be accommodated in college housing, which includes single-sex and coed dorms and off-campus apartments. In addition, there are honors houses and special-interest houses. On-campus housing is guaranteed for the freshman year only, and is available on a first-come, first-served basis. 67% of students commute. All students may keep cars.

FACULTY/CLASSROOMS: No introductory courses are taught by graduate students.

PROGRAMS OF STUDY: Georgia College confers B.A., B.S., B.B.A., B.M.E., B.M.T. and B.S.N. degrees. Master's and doctoral degrees are also awarded. Bachelor's degrees are awarded in BIOLOGICAL SCIENCE (biology/biological science), BUSINESS (accounting, business administration and management, management information systems, marketing and distribution, and recreation and leisure services), COMMUNICATIONS AND THE ARTS (art, English, journalism, music, speech/debate/rhetoric, and theatre arts), COMPUTER AND PHYSICAL SCIENCE (chemistry, computer science, mathematics, and physics), EDUCATION (athletic training, early childhood education, middle school education, music education, and special education), ENGINEERING AND ENVIRONMENTAL DESIGN (environmental science), HEALTH PROFESSIONS (community health work, exercise science, music therapy, and nursing), SOCIAL SCIENCE (criminal justice, economics, geography, history, liberal arts/general studies, philosophy, political science/government, psychology, sociology, and world cultural studies). Biology, nursing, and marketing have the largest enrollments.

ACTIVITIES: 22% of men belong to 10 national fraternities; 40% of women belong to 12 national sororities. There are 204 groups on campus, including art, band, cheerleading, choir, chorale, chorus, computers, dance, drama, environmental, ethnic, honors, international, jazz band, LGBT, literary magazine, musical theater, newspaper, photography, political, professional, radio and TV, religious, social, social service, student government, and symphony. Popular campus events include Week of Welcome, Progressive Dinner, and International Week. **Sports:** There are 5 intercollegiate sports for men and 6 for women, and 13 intramural sports for men and 13 for women. The wellness and recreation center is LEED Silver certified and encompasses 101,000 square feet. Reflecting the university's commitment to a holistic approach to health and wellness, the center combines fitness and recreation activities, health education programs and formal wellness courses with health services and counseling services. Also available is the 95,000 square foot, over 4,000 capacity centennial center home of the basketball and volleyball teams. **Graduates:** From July 1, 2015 to June 30, 2016, 1163 bachelor's degrees were awarded. The most popular majors were nursing (9%), management (9%), and mass communications (7%). In an average class, 42% graduate in 4 years or less, 58% graduate in 5 years or less, and 59% graduate in 6 years or less.

SERVICES: Counseling and information services are available, as is tutoring in some subjects, such as math, biology, chemistry, physics, kinesiology, economics, accounting, env science, geology, astronomy, computer science, French, Spanish, and psychology stats. **Library/Resources:** The library contains 210,500 volumes, 24,465 microform items, and 12,065 audio/video tapes/CDs/DVDs, and subscribes to 56,543 periodicals including electronic. Computerized library services include interlibrary loans, database searching, Internet access, and Wi-Fi capability. Special learning facilities include an art gallery, natural history museum, planetarium, radio station, TV station, a campus theatre, and an art deco theatre adjacent to the campus that serves as a performance space and bookstore for both the college and the community. **Physically Challenged Students:** 90% of the campus is accessible. Facilities include wheelchair ramps, elevators, special parking, specially equipped restrooms, special class scheduling, lowered drinking fountains, lowered telephones, and special housing. **Special:** GCSU has study-abroad agreements with institutions worldwide, a Washington semester, co-op programs, internships, work-study programs, dual majors, independent study, and student-designed majors. There is a 3-2 engineering degree program with the Georgia Institute of Technology. There are 3 national honor societies. **Visiting:** There are regularly scheduled orientations for prospective students, including receptions, tours, school meetings, information sessions, academic and cocurricular advising, and registration. There are guides for informal visits, and visitors may sit in on classes. To schedule a visit, contact the Office of Admissions at admissions@gcsu.edu. **Campus Safety and Security:** Measures include 24-hour foot and vehicle patrol, emergency notification system, self-defense education, and security escort services. There are shuttle buses, emergency telephones, lighted pathways/sidewalks, and controlled access to dorms/residences.

REQUIREMENTS: The SAT or ACT is required. The ACT Optional Writing test is also required. Applicants must be graduates of an accredited or recognized secondary school and must complete the Georgia college preparatory curriculum requirements, including 4 units each of English and math (with math I or algebra I being the minimum level for consideration), 4 units of science, (including 2 lab sciences), 2 units of the same foreign language, and 3 units of social science. AP and CLEP credits are accepted. Important factors in the admissions decision are advanced placement or honors courses, extracurricular activities record, and evidence of special talent. To graduate, students must complete at least 120 semester hours, of which 40 must be completed in residence. That must complete 21 of the last 30 credit hours at the upper level. All B.A. candidates and some B.S. candidates must demonstrate a foreign language proficiency. All students must pass an exam on the history and Constitution of both the United States and Georgia, and a senior exit exam in the major. They must also earn a C or better in English 1101. **Procedure:** Freshmen are admitted to all sessions. Entrance exams should be taken ACT in February and SAT in March. There are early admissions, deferred admissions, and rolling admissions plans. Applications should be filed by April 1 for fall entry; November 1 for spring entry; and May 1 for summer entry, along with a $40 fee. Notification is sent on a rolling basis. 29 applicants were on the 2016 waiting list. Applications are accepted on-line. **Transfer Students:** 277 transfer students enrolled in 2015-2016. To transfer applicants must submit official transcripts from all colleges attended and be eligible to return to their previous institution. Those who have completed fewer than 30 semester hours must meet all freshman admissions requirements. 40 of 120 credits required for the bachelor's degree must be completed at Georgia College. **International Students:** There are 60 international students enrolled. The school actively recruits these students. They must take the TOEFL with a minimum score of 500 on the paper-based TOEFL (PBT) or 61 on the Internet-based version (iBT), SAT Verbal score of 440, ACT English score of 17, or IELTS score of 6.0. To comply with NCAA regulations, international students who will compete in intercollegiate athletics must take either the SAT or ACT.

ADMISSIONS: 85% of the 2016-2017 applicants were accepted. The SAT scores for the 2016-2017 freshman class were: Critical Reading-- 16% below 500, 51% between 500 and 599, 30% between 600 and 699, and 3% between 700 and 800. Math-- 17% below 500, 50% between 500 and 599, 31% between 600 and 699, and 2% between 700 and 800. Writing-- 24% below 500, 51% between 500 and 599, 21% between 600 and 699, and 3% between 700 and 800. The ACT scores were 1% between 12 and 17, 38% between 18 and 23, 56% between 24 and 29, and 5% above 30. **Admissions Contact:** Ramon Blakley, Director of Admissions. Email: *admissions@gcsu.edu* Web: *www.gcsu.edu*

FINANCIAL AID: In 2016-2017, 60% of all full-time freshmen received some form of financial aid. 20% of all full-time freshmen received need-based aid. The average freshman award was $9,835. Need-based scholarships or need-based grants averaged $4,544 ($10,230 maximum); need-based self-help aid (loans and jobs) averaged $3,320 ($8,454 maximum); non-need-based athletic scholarships averaged $4,002 ($17,914 maximum); and other non-need-based awards and non-need-based scholarships averaged $1,683 ($6,000 maximum). 16% of undergraduate students work part-time. Average annual earnings from campus work are $7909. The average financial indebtedness of the 2016 graduate was $22,950. The FAFSA code is 001602. The priority date for freshman financial aid applications for fall entry is March 1. The deadline for filing freshman financial aid applications for fall entry is July 1.

GEORGIA INSTITUTE OF TECHNOLOGY B-2

www.gatech.edu

Atlanta, GA 30332	(404) 894-4154
Fax: (404) 894-9511	Email: admission@gatech.edu
Full-time: 8670 men, 5145 women	**Faculty:** I, +$
Part-time: 1157 men, 517 women	**Ph.D.s:** 80%
Graduate: 8729 men, 2621 women	**Student/Faculty:** 20 to 1
Year: semesters, summer session	**Tuition:** $12,212 ($32,404)
Room & Board: $11,148	**Freshman Class:** 30528 applied, 7868 accepted, 2877 enrolled
SAT CR/M/W: 680/730/690 **ACT:** 32	**CEEB CODE:** 5248
Application Deadline: January 1	**MOST COMPETITIVE**

Georgia Institute of Technology, founded in 1885, is a public technological institution offering programs in architecture, management, policy, international affairs, engineering, computing, and science. There are 6 undergraduate schools and 6 graduate schools. In addition to regional accreditation, Georgia Tech has baccalaureate program accreditation with AACSB, ABET, ACCE, NASAD, ACS, and RICS. The 400-acre campus is in an urban area in Atlanta, GA. Including any residence halls, there are 244 buildings.

STUDENT LIFE: 60% of undergraduates are from Georgia. Others are from 50 states, 108 foreign countries, and Canada. 7% are African American; 7% Hispanic; 49% White; 4% two or more races; 3% race unknown; 20% Asian American; 10% Foreign. **Male To Female Ratio:** 2.2:1. The average age of freshmen is 18; all undergraduates, 20. 3% do not continue beyond their first year; 86% remain to graduate. **Housing:** 10005 students can be accommodated in college housing, which includes single-sex and coed dorms, off-campus apartments, and married student housing. In addition, there are honors houses, language houses, special-interest houses, fraternity houses, sorority houses, and freshman experience floors. On-campus housing is guaranteed for the freshman year only, and is available on a first-come, first-served basis. 53% of students live on campus; of those, 80% remain on campus on weekends. All students may keep cars.

FACULTY/CLASSROOMS: 72% of faculty are male; 28% are female. No introductory courses are taught by graduate students. The average class size in an introductory lecture is 36; in a laboratory is 19; and in a regular course is 32.

PROGRAMS OF STUDY: Georgia Tech confers B.S. degrees. Master's and doctoral degrees are also awarded. Bachelor's degrees are awarded in BIOLOGICAL SCIENCE (biochemistry and biology/biological science), BUSINESS (business administration and management and international economics), COMMUNICATIONS AND THE ARTS (digital communications, digital media, and industrial design), COMPUTER AND PHYSICAL SCIENCE (applied mathematics, chemistry, computer science, earth science, mathematics, physics, and science and technology studies), EDUCATION (foreign languages education), ENGINEERING AND ENVIRONMENTAL DESIGN (aerospace engineering, architecture, bioengineering, biomedical engineering, chemical engineering, civil engineering, computer engineering, electrical/electronics engineering, environmental engineering, industrial engineering, materials engineering, materials science, materials science and engineering, mechanical engineering, and nuclear engineering), SOCIAL SCIENCE (economics, history of science, international relations, international studies, psychology, and public affairs). Engineering, computer science, and business administration are the strongest academically. Mechanical engineering, computer science, and industrial engineering have the largest enrollments.

ACTIVITIES: 25% of men belong to 40 national fraternities; 30% of women belong to 16 national sororities. There are 573 groups on campus, including art, band, cheerleading, chess, choir, chorale, chorus, communications, computers, dance, debate, departmental, drama, drill team, environmental, ethnic, film, honors, international, jazz band, LGBT, literary magazine, marching band, musical theater, newspaper, orchestra, pep band, photography, political, professional, radio and TV, religious, social, social service, student government, symphony, and yearbook. Popular campus events include Team Buzz, Tech Beautification Day, and Dance Marathon. **Sports:** There are 10 intercollegiate sports for men and 9 for women, and 8 intramural sports for men and 4 for women. Facilities include a 4,000-seat baseball stadium, a 55,000-seat football stadium, softball fields, an 8,600-seat basketball arena, a golf practice facility, an 88,000-square-foot football practice facility, a basketball practice center with a 2,000-square-foot weight room, an Olympic aquatic center for swimming and diving, an eight-lane outdoor track with a state-of-the-art Mondo surface and 1,500-seat grandstand, a state-of-the-art 6-court indoor tennis complex that seats 232 spectators, outdoor tennis courts, an outdoor turf field featuring flag football fields, 4 recreational fields including one with 2 outdoor sand volleyball courts, and a 300,659 square foot recreation center with 6 multipurpose indoor courts, 4 racquetball/wallyball/squash courts, a running track, an auxiliary court, a climbing wall, co-ed sauna, a fitness center with weights and cardio machines, and 3 studios for aerobic fitness programs. **Graduates:** From July 1, 2015 to June 30, 2016, 3419 bachelor's degrees were awarded. The most popular majors were mechanical engineering (15%), industrial engineering (11%), and computer science (11%). 396 companies recruited on campus in 2015-2016. In an average class, 41% graduate in 4 years or less, 80% graduate in 5 years or less, and 86% graduate in 6 years or less. Of the 2015 graduating class, 78% were employed within 6 months of graduation.

SERVICES: Counseling and information services are available, as is tutoring in most subjects. There is a reader service for the blind, and remedial math, reading, and writing. The Learning Assistance Program, drop-in tutoring sessions for calculus, chemistry, physics, accounting, linear algebra, and computer science. One-to-One Tutoring is offered in addition to success workshops, Peer Led Undergraduate Study (PLUS), walk-in tutoring and academic coaching. **Library/Resources:** The library contains 1.7 million volumes, 2.2 million microform items, and 40,565 audio/video tapes/CDs/DVDs, and subscribes to 27,533 periodicals including electronic. Computerized library services include interlibrary loans, database searching, Internet access, and Wi-Fi capability. Special learning facilities include an art gallery, radio station, TV station, G. Wayne Clough Undergraduate Learning Commons, Center for Academic Enrichment, Center for Academic Success, Center for the Enhancement of Teaching and Learning, Communication Center, and Center for Career Discovery and Development. **Physically Challenged Students:** 75% of the campus is accessible. Facilities include wheelchair ramps, elevators, special parking, specially equipped restrooms, special class scheduling, lowered drinking fountains, and special housing. **Special:** Extensive co-op programs, cross-registration with other Atlanta-area colleges, internships, and undergraduate research opportunities are available. Numerous study abroad opportunities are available. An engineering transfer program is offered within the university system, and a liberal arts-engineering dual degree program serves area colleges and institutions nationwide. Students have access to multidisciplinary and certificate programs outside their major field of study. The College of Engineering offers the opportunity to transfer to Georgia Tech via the Dual Degree Engineering Program (DDEP) and the Regional Engineering Transfer Program (RETP). There are 13 national honor societies, a freshman honors program, and 11 departmental honors programs. **Visiting:** There are regularly scheduled orientations for prospective students. The session is conducted by a counselor from the Office of Undergraduate Admission who discusses the admission process, majors, opportunities outside of the classroom, campus activities, and student life. There are guides for informal visits, and visitors may sit in on classes, and stay overnight. To schedule a visit, contact the Office of Undergraduate Admissions. **Campus Safety and Security:** Measures include 24-hour foot and vehicle patrol, emergency notification system, self-defense education, and security escort services. There are shuttle buses, emergency telephones, lighted pathways/sidewalks, controlled access to dorms/residences, foot patrol, bike patrol, limited access to dorms, mobile security patrol, video cameras, and a K-9 force, bike and laptop registration is offered.

REQUIREMENTS: The SAT or ACT is required. The ACT Optional Writing test is also required. Candidates for admission must have completed 4 units each of English and math, 3 units of social studies, 4 units of science, including 2 units of lab sciences, and 2 units of a foreign language. An essay is required. AP credits are accepted. All students must fulfill the core curriculum requirements and maintain a 2.0 GPA for their entire academic program. Core curriculum requirements include 12 hours of science, math, and technology, 12 hours of social sciences, 13 hours of essential skills courses (English composition, calculus, and computing), 6 hours of humanities, and 5 or more hours of electives depending on the major. Other course requirements include an ethics course and a wellness course. **Procedure:** Freshmen are admitted fall and summer. Entrance exams should be taken by the end of the junior year. There are early admissions and deferred admissions plans. Applications should be filed by January 1 for fall entry. The fall 2016 application fee was $75. Notifications are sent March 14. 2267 applicants were on the 2016 waiting list; 470 were admitted. Applications are accepted on-line. **Transfer Students:** 816 transfer students enrolled in 2015-2016. Transfer applicants must have completed a minimum of 30 credit hours, not including AP/IB/DE, of coursework and have a minimum 3.0 cumulative GPA and a 3.0 math and science combined GPA. All of the specifically required courses on the course requirements chart for the prospective major must be completed. Grades and academic standing must be satisfactory for the last term of enrollment at the prior college. 36 of 122 credits required for the bachelor's degree must be completed at Georgia Tech. **International Students:** There are 1506 international students enrolled. They must also take the SAT or ACT.

ADMISSIONS: 26% of the 2016-2017 applicants were accepted. The SAT scores for the 2016-2017 freshman class were: Critical Reading-- 1% below 500, 9% between 500 and 599, 45% between 600 and 699, and 45% between 700 and 800. Math-- 1% below 500, 4% between 500 and 599, 29% between 600 and 699, and 66% between 700 and 800. Writing-- 2% below 500, 9% between 500 and 599, 43% between 600 and 699, and 46% between 700 and 800. The ACT scores were 1% between 18 and 23, 16% between 24 and 29, and 83% above 30. There were 59 National Merit finalists. **Admissions Contact:** Rick Clark, Director of Undergraduate Admissions. Email: *admission@gatech.edu* Web: *www.gatech.edu*

FINANCIAL AID: The average financial indebtedness of the 2016 graduate was $25,603. Georgia Tech is a member of CSS. The CSS/Profile and the college's own financial statement are required. The FAFSA code is 001569. The priority date for freshman financial aid applications for fall entry is January 31.

GEORGIA SOUTHERN UNIVERSITY — D-3

www.georgiasouthern.edu

Statesboro, GA 30458 — **(912) 478-5391**

Fax: (912) 478-7240 — **Email:** admissions@georgiasouthern.edu

Full-time: 7866 men, 8110 women	**Faculty:** 709; IIA, --$
Part-time: 1013 men, 1016 women	**Ph.D.s:** 84%
Graduate: 874 men, 1794 women	**Student/Faculty:** 21 to 1
Year: semesters, summer session	**Tuition:** $6796 ($18,692)
Room & Board: $9800	**Freshman Class:** 9834 applied, 6348 accepted, 3600 enrolled
SAT CR/M/W: 550/550/520 **ACT:** 23	**CEEB CODE:** 5253
Application Deadline: May 1	**COMPETITIVE**

Georgia Southern University is the state's largest and most comprehensive center of higher education south of Atlanta. With 120-plus degree programs at the baccalaureate, master's and doctoral levels, Georgia Southern has been designated a Carnegie Doctoral-Research university and provides the classic residential campus experience and online learning options. Since 1906, the University's hallmark has been a culture of engagement that bridges theory with practice, extends the learning environment beyond the classroom, and promotes student growth and life success. Central to the University's mission is the faculty's dedication to excellence in teaching and the development of a fertile learning environment exemplified by a free exchange of ideas, high academic expectations, and individual responsibility for academic achievement. There are 7 undergraduate schools and 1 graduate school. In addition to regional accreditation, Georgia Southern has baccalaureate program accreditation with AACSB, ABET, ACCE, NASAD, NASM, NCATE, NRPA, NCAA, IACS, AAM, ACCE, NASP, NCACE, CIDA, GPSC, NAEYC, CACREP, CADE, CAATE, CEPH, CCNE, GBN, NASPAA, NAST, ACS, and AALRCA. The 900-acre campus is in a small town 1 hour from Savannah, 2 hours from Florida, and about 3 hours from metropolitan Atlanta. Including any residence halls, there are 210 buildings.

STUDENT LIFE: 94% of undergraduates are from Georgia. Others are from 50 states, 76 foreign countries, and Canada. 62% are White; 5% Hispanic; 25% African American; 2% Asian American; 2% Foreign; 2% two or more races; 1% race unknown. 98% claim no religious affiliation. **Female To Male Ratio:** 1.1:1. The average age of freshmen is 18; all undergraduates, 21. 19% do not continue beyond their first year; 51% remain to graduate. **Housing:** 4935 students can be accommodated in college housing, which includes coed dorms, on-campus apartments, and off-campus apartments. In addition, there are honors houses and special-interest houses. On-campus housing is guaranteed for the freshman year only, and is available on a first-come, first-served basis, is available on a lottery system for upperclassmen. 73% of students commute. All students may keep cars.

FACULTY/CLASSROOMS: 51% of faculty are male; 49% are female. 84% teach undergraduates, 72% do research, and 70% do both. Graduate students teach 6% of introductory courses. The average class size in an introductory lecture is 23; in a laboratory is 20; and in a regular course is 35.

PROGRAMS OF STUDY: Georgia Southern confers B.A., B.B.A., B.F.A, B.G.S., B.M., B.S.A.T., B.S., B.S.B., B.S.C.E., B.S.Chem., B.S.Cons., B.S.Ed., B.S.E.E., B.S.GraphCom., B.S.P.H., B.S.I.T., B.S.J.S., B.S.K., B.S.Mat., B.S.M.E., B.S.N. B.S.M.A.N.E., B.S.F.C.S., and B.S.P. degrees. Master's and doctoral degrees are also awarded. Bachelor's degrees are awarded in BIOLOGICAL SCIENCE (biology/biological science and nutrition), BUSINESS (accounting, finance, logistics, management science, marketing management, and sports management), COMMUNICATIONS AND THE ARTS (art, communications, English, graphic communications, journalism, linguistics, multimedia, music, public relations, and writing), COMPUTER AND PHYSICAL SCIENCE (chemistry, chemistry education, computer science, geology, information science, and physics), EDUCATION (athletic training, early childhood education, health education, health and physical education, mathematics education, middle school education, nursing education, recreation education, and special education), ENGINEERING AND ENVIRONMENTAL DESIGN (civil engineering, construction management, electrical/electronics engineering, and mechanical engineering), HEALTH PROFESSIONS (exercise science), SOCIAL SCIENCE (anthropology, child care/child and family studies, economics, geography, history, international studies, philosophy, political science/government, and psychology). Family nurse practitioner, geology, and geography are the strongest academically. Mechanical engineering, biology, and exercise science have the largest enrollments.

ACTIVITIES: 19% of women belong to 12 national sororities. There are 280 groups on campus, including art, band, cheerleading, choir, chorale, chorus, communications, computers, dance, drama, environmental, ethnic, film, honors, international, jazz band, LGBT, literary magazine, marching band, musical theater, newspaper, opera, orchestra, political, professional, radio and TV, religious, social, social service, student government, and symphony. Popular campus events include Homecoming, Concerts, and Final Feast. **Sports:** There are 6 intercollegiate sports for men and 9 for women, and 23 intramural sports for men and 23 for women. Facilities include baseball, football, and softball stadiums, volleyball and basketball field house, natatorium, tennis courts, track/soccer stadium and golf practice facility, and a rifle shooting range. **Graduates:** From July 1, 2015 to June 30, 2016, 3200 bachelor's degrees were awarded. The most popular majors were business/marketing (19%), parks and recreation (10%), and liberal arts/general studies (8%). 120 companies recruited on campus in 2015-2016. In an average class, 1% graduate in 3 years or less, 26% graduate in 4 years or less, 47% graduate in 5 years or less, and 51% graduate in 6 years or less.

SERVICES: Counseling and information services are available, as is tutoring in most subjects. There is a reader service for the blind, and remedial math and writing. **Library/Resources:** The library contains 667,972 volumes, 900,843 microform items, and 92,501 audio/video tapes/CDs/DVDs, and subscribes to 86,323 periodicals including electronic. Computerized library services include interlibrary loans, database searching, Internet access, and Wi-Fi capability. Special learning facilities include an art gallery, natural history museum, planetarium, radio station, Bureau of Business Research and Economic Development, Center for Addiction Recovery, The Center for Africana Studies, Karl E. Peace Center for Bio-statistics and Survey, Center for Education Leadership, Center for Entrepreneurial Learning and Leadership, Center for Forensic Studies in Accounting, Center for International Schooling, Center for International Studies, Center for Irish Studies, Center for Retail Studies, Center for Sustainability, Center for Wildlife Education, Center for Women's and Gender Studies, Child Development Center, Graduate Academic Services Center (GASC), Instructional Resources Center (IRC), Institute for Coastal Plain Science, Magnolia Coastlands AHEC, National Youth-At-Risk Center (NYAR), Small Business Development Center, Student Success Center (SSC), Black Box Theatre, Performing Arts Center, and Garden of the Coastal Plain. **Physically Challenged Students:** 97% of the campus is accessible. Facilities include wheelchair ramps, elevators, special parking, specially equipped restrooms, special class scheduling, lowered drinking fountains, and special housing. **Special:** Co-op programs in: Accounting, finance, construction management, biology, geology, engineering technology (civil, electrical, and mechanical), information technology, industrial management, engineering (electrical, civil, and mechanical), and logistics. Internships: A number of academic degree programs require internships as part of the program requirements and offer academic credit for internship experiences. Non-academic internships are offered for all majors through the Office of career Services. We do offer a Washington Semester. Accelerate degree program Move On When Ready (MOWR) is state-funded program for public and private high school students that provide dual enrollment tuition assistance in Georgia. The program offers the opportunity to earn dual credit, satisfying high school and college core curriculum requirements. Admissions requirements for MOWR are: 1. Have earned an academic GPA of 3.0 as recalculated by the Office of Admissions; 2. Submit SAT scores of at least 1010 (math and critical reading only) or ACT 21 composite; 3. Gain permission from their high school guidance counselor and parents by completing the MOWR student participation agreement; 4. Meet all other (non provisional) admissions requirements. Dual majors; students may be granted a second baccalaureate degree if the following conditions are met: 1. If the first degree is earned at GSU, a student may seek a second degree if it is different from the first degree. 2. The student must satisfy all major requirements; 3. The student must complete the history and constitution requirements; 4. Take 32-34 additional credit hours at GSU; 5. The student must earn at least 50% of the credits toward the major at GSU; 6. The student may work on two degrees at the same time. Regents Engineering Pathway Program (REPP). The Regents Engineering Pathway Program (REPP) – formerly the Regents Engineering Transfer Program – allows students at colleges and universities in the University System of Georgia to study for two years at their home institution, then transfer to Georgia Southern, Georgia Tech, Kennesaw State, Mercer University, or the University of Georgia to complete their engineering degrees. The purpose of the REP Program at Georgia Southern University is to: Increase the accessibility to an engineering education in the State of Georgia. Develop study habits and engineering problem-solving capability for students to be successful in their junior and senior engineering courses as well as in their professional careers. Provide the coursework required. Georgia Southern has cross-registration available with East Georgia and GOML (Georgia OnMyLine) programs. Study abroad in Argentina, Australia, Austria, Belgium, Bolivia, Botswana, Brazil, Bulgaria, Canada, Chile, China, Colombia, Costa Rica, Czech Republic, Denmark, Ecuador, England, Estonia, Fiji, Finland, France, Germany, Ghana, Greece, Honduras, Hungary, India, Indonesia, Ireland, Italy, Japan, Latvia, Lithuania, Malaysia, Malta, Mexico, Morocco, Netherlands, New Zealand, Nicaragua, Norway, Panama, Poland, Portugal, Romania, Russia, Scotland, Senegal, South Africa, South Korea, Spain, Sweden, Switzerland, Thailand, Turkey, United Arab Emirates, Uruguay, and Vietnam. Work-study programs: Career Services assists students in relevant work experience through several different formats. Through our Experiential

Education program, students can participate in job shadowing, nonacademic internships, and cooperative education assignments. The student's assignments vary based on their majors and interests. Some of the companies that students are currently participating with are The Southern Company, Bell South, BMW, the United States Army Corps, Target, and Coca-Cola. B.A. degrees include: Modern Languages, English, Writing and Linguistics, Biology, Philosophy, Chemistry, Geology, Physics, Anthropology, Economics, Geography, International Studies, Political Science, Theatre, Art, Music, and History. B.S. degrees include: Journalism, Multimedia Communication, Public Relations and Organizational Communications, Computer Science, Nutrition and Food Science, Child and Family Development, Fashion Merchandising and Apparel Design, Communication Studies, Mathematics. Recreation, Sport Management, Geology, Psychology, Geography, Political Science, Sociology, Interior Design, and International Trade. Student-Designed Majors are offered. There are 17 national honor societies, a freshman honors program, and 32 departmental honors programs. **Visiting:** There are regularly scheduled orientations for prospective students. There are guides for informal visits, and visitors may sit in on classes. To schedule a visit, contact Sean Cleary at (912) 478-5851. **Campus Safety and Security:** Measures include 24-hour foot and vehicle patrol, emergency notification system, self-defense education, and security escort services. There are shuttle buses, emergency telephones, lighted pathways/sidewalks, controlled access to dorms/residences, and panic button alarms in all residence hall rooms.

REQUIREMENTS: The SAT or ACT is required. Applicants must have a high school diploma or the equivalent. A minimum of 17 credits in college preparatory courses should include 4 each in English and math, 3 in social studies, 4 in science, and 2 in a foreign language. A GPA of 2.0 is required. AP and CLEP credits are accepted. All students must complete a total of 126-135 semester credit hours, including at least 32-34 semester credit hours in the major, with a minimum GPA of 2.0. Students must complete specific courses in English, math, humanities, science, and social sciences, a healthful living class, two physical activity courses, orientation course and interdisciplinary studies class. **Procedure:** Freshmen are admitted fall, spring, and summer. Entrance exams should be taken during the junior year. There are deferred admissions and rolling admissions plans. Applications should be filed by May 1 for fall entry; December 1 for spring entry; and April 1 for summer entry, along with a $30 fee. Notification is sent on a rolling basis. Applications are accepted on-line. **Transfer Students:** 1114 transfer students enrolled in 2015-2016. Applicants must have completed at least 30 semester credit hours of college courses with a minimum GPA of 2.0. Those with fewer than 30 hours must meet freshman requirements. Students transferring with an associate degree must have a minimum GPA of 2.0 in a school with a parallel curriculum. 30 of 126 credits required for the bachelor's degree must be completed at Georgia Southern. **International Students:** There are 297 international students enrolled. The school actively recruits these students. They must take the TOEFL with a minimum score of 69 on the Internet-based version (iBT), or take the IELTS. They must also take the SAT or ACT, scoring 1090. International students whose native language is not English, must submit TOEFL or SAT/ACT.

ADMISSIONS: 65% of the 2016-2017 applicants were accepted. The SAT scores for the 2016-2017 freshman class were: Critical Reading-- 13% below 500, 63% between 500 and 599, 23% between 600 and 699, and 2% between 700 and 800. Math-- 15% below 500, 59% between 500 and 599, 25% between 600 and 699, and 2% between 700 and 800. Writing-- 33% below 500, 51% between 500 and 599, 16% between 600 and 699, and 1% between 700 and 800. The ACT scores were 1% below 12, 54% between 12 and 17, 27% between 18 and 23, 10% between 24 and 29, and 7% above 30. 39% of the current freshmen were in the top fifth of their class; 69% were in the top two fifths. **Admissions Contact:** Amy Smith, Director. Email: *admissions@georgiasouthern.edu* Web: *www.georgiasouthern.edu*

FINANCIAL AID: In 2016-2017, 91% of all full-time freshmen and 88% of continuing full-time students received some form of financial aid. 59% of all full-time freshmen and 55% of continuing full-time students received need-based aid. The average freshman award was $9,952. Need-based scholarships or need-based grants averaged $7,559 ($40,145 maximum); need-based self-help aid (loans and jobs) averaged $4,297 ($33,916 maximum); non-need-based athletic scholarships averaged $11,618 ($31,440 maximum); and other non-need-based awards and non-need-based scholarships averaged $1,652 ($8,215 maximum). Average annual earnings from campus work are $2160. The average financial indebtedness of the 2016 graduate was $28,098. Georgia Southern is a member of CSS. The FAFSA code is 001572. The priority date for freshman financial aid applications for fall entry is April 20.

GEORGIA SOUTHWESTERN STATE UNIVERSITY B-4

www.gsw.edu

Americus, GA 31709 **(229) 928-1273** **(800) 338-0082**

Fax: (229) 931-2983 **Email: Admissions@gsw.edu**

Full-time: 673 men, 1096 women
Part-time: 303 men, 486 women
Graduate: 61 men, 335 women
Year: semesters, summer session
Room & Board: $7672
SAT CR/M: 490/470 **ACT:** 21
Application Deadline: July 21

Faculty: 107
Ph.D.s: 73%
Student/Faculty: 17 to 1
Tuition: $6198 ($19,018)
Freshman Class: 1397 applied, 948 accepted, 485 enrolled
CEEB CODE: 5250
COMPETITIVE

Georgia Southwestern State University, founded in 1906, is a comprehensive state university within the University System of Georgia. GSW offers a full range of bachelor degree programs, along with selected master's degree programs in English, computer science, business, education, and nursing. There are 5 undergraduate schools and 5 graduate schools. In addition to regional accreditation, GSW has baccalaureate program accreditation with AACSB, NCATE, and CCNE. The 250-acre campus is in a small town 38 miles north of Albany, Georgia, and 135 miles south of Atlanta, Georgia. Including any residence halls, there are 33 buildings.

STUDENT LIFE: 93% of undergraduates are from Georgia. Others are from 23 states, 30 foreign countries, and Canada. 82% are from public schools. 63% are White; 4% Hispanic; 27% African American; 2% Foreign; 2% two or more races; 1% Asian American. **Female To Male Ratio:** 1.8:1. The average age of freshmen is 18; all undergraduates, 24. 31% do not continue beyond their first year; 32% remain to graduate. **Housing:** 950 students can be accommodated in college housing, which includes coed dorms and on-campus apartments. 68% of students commute. All students may keep cars.

FACULTY/CLASSROOMS: 44% of faculty are male; 56% are female. All teach undergraduates. No introductory courses are taught by graduate students.

PROGRAMS OF STUDY: GSW confers B.A., B.S., B.B.A., B.F.A., B.S.Ed., and B.S.N. degrees. Master's degrees are also awarded. Bachelor's degrees are awarded in BIOLOGICAL SCIENCE (biology/biological science), BUSINESS (accounting, business administration and management, human resources/organizational mgmt, and marketing), COMMUNICATIONS AND THE ARTS (art, dramatic arts, English, fine arts, and music), COMPUTER AND PHYSICAL SCIENCE (chemistry, computer information technology, computer science, geology, and mathematics), EDUCATION (early childhood education, health and physical education, middle school education, and special education), HEALTH PROFESSIONS (exercise science and nursing), SOCIAL SCIENCE (criminal justice, history, political science/government, psychology, and sociology). Business, nursing, and education are the strongest academically, and nursing have the largest enrollments.

ACTIVITIES: There are 60 groups on campus, including art, cheerleading, choir, dance, drama, ethnic, honors, international, LGBT, literary magazine, musical theater, newspaper, political, professional, radio and TV, religious, social, social service, and student government. Popular campus events include Welcome Week, FallFest, Student Appreciation Day, Taste of the World, and Convocation Series. **Sports:** There are 4 intercollegiate sports for men and 4 for women. Facilities include 2 gyms, tennis courts, indoor climbing wall, fitness center, group exercise room, racquetball courts, game room, lake for canoeing, and playing fields for baseball, softball, flag football, and soccer. **Graduates:** From July 1, 2015 to June 30, 2016, 432 bachelor's degrees were awarded. The most popular majors were management (18%), nursing (17%), and accounting (13%). In an average class, 14% graduate in 4 years or less, 27% graduate in 5 years or less, and 32% graduate in 6 years or less.

SERVICES: Counseling and information services are available, as is tutoring in most subjects. There is a reader service for the blind, and remedial math and writing. **Library/Resources:** The library contains

181,241 volumes, 905,573 microform items, and 7,205 audio/video tapes/CDs/DVDs, and subscribes to 6,703 periodicals including electronic. Computerized library services include interlibrary loans, database searching, Internet access, and Wi-Fi capability. Special learning facilities include an art gallery, radio station, TV station, a glass-blowing facility and state of the art simulation technology labs for the nursing program. **Physically Challenged Students:** 95% of the campus is accessible. Facilities include wheelchair ramps, elevators, special parking, specially equipped restrooms, special class scheduling, and lowered drinking fountains. **Special:** There are 6 national honor societies and a freshman honors program. **Visiting:** There are regularly scheduled orientations for prospective students. There are guides for informal visits. **Campus Safety and Security:** Measures include 24-hour foot and vehicle patrol, emergency notification system, self-defense education, and security escort services. There are emergency telephones, lighted pathways/sidewalks, and controlled access to dorms/residences.

REQUIREMENTS: Freshmen applicants must submit official results of ACT or SAT and transcripts of his/her high school record. 17 high school curriculum courses, based on 4 units of English, 4 of science and 4 of math, 3 units of social science (including one focusing on world studies) and 2 units in the same foreign language are required of students who graduated from high school spring 2012 or later. Non-traditional, transfer, international students, and beginning freshmen applicants from home schools or graduates of non-accredited high schools should contact Admissions for additional requirements. All new students are required to submit proof of required immunizations and health history on the forms provided by GSW prior to enrollment. A GPA of 2.0 is required. AP and CLEP credits are accepted. To graduate, students must complete a minimum of 120 semester credit hours consisting of 60 hours in the General Core Curriculum and 60 hour in upper division courses with a minimum GPA of 2.0. The Core curriculum requires 42 hours in general education courses (English, math, humanities, social sciences, sciences, institutional options) and 18 hours in a major area of study. Students are also required to complete 3 courses in physical education. **Procedure:** Freshmen are admitted fall, spring, and summer. Entrance exams should be taken before the end of the senior year. There are early admissions, deferred admissions, and rolling admissions plans. Applications should be filed by July 21 for fall entry; December 10 for spring entry; and May 15 for summer entry. The fall 2016 application fee was $25. Applications are accepted on-line. **Transfer Students:** 490 transfer students enrolled in 2015-2016. Applicants should be in good standing at their former institutions, with a cumulative GPA of 2.0 or higher on a 4.0 scale. Students with fewer than 30 hours of transfer credit must meet freshman requirements. 30 of 120 credits required for the bachelor's degree must be completed at GSW. **International Students:** There are 37 international students enrolled. The school actively recruits these students. They must take the TOEFL with a minimum score of 523 on the paper-based TOEFL (PBT) or 69 on the Internet-based version (iBT), or take the IELTS.

ADMISSIONS: 68% of the 2016-2017 applicants were accepted. The SAT scores for the 2016-2017 freshman class were: Critical Reading-- 56% below 500, 36% between 500 and 599, and 7% between 600 and 699. Math-- 63% below 500, 31% between 500 and 599, and 6% between 600 and 699. The ACT scores were 10% between 12 and 17, 67% between 18 and 23, 21% between 24 and 29, and 2% above 30. 32% of the current freshmen were in the top fifth of their class; 67% were in the top two fifths. **Admissions Contact:** David Jenkins, Assistant Director of Admissions. Email: *Admissions@gsw.edu* Web: *www.gsw.edu*

FINANCIAL AID: In 2016-2017, 97% of all full-time freshmen and 90% of continuing full-time students received some form of financial aid. 66% of all full-time freshmen and 63% of continuing full-time students received need-based aid. The average freshman award was $9,984. Need-based scholarships or need-based grants averaged $5,098 ($6,615 maximum); need-based self-help aid (loans and jobs) averaged $3,495 ($9,725 maximum); non-need-based athletic scholarships averaged $2,281 ($9,000 maximum); and other non-need-based awards and non-need-based scholarships averaged $4,738 ($14,260 maximum). The FAFSA code is 001573. The priority date for freshman financial aid applications for fall entry is April 15. The deadline for filing freshman financial aid applications for fall entry is June 15.

GEORGIA STATE UNIVERSITY — B-2

www.gsu.edu

Atlanta, GA 30302 — **(404) 413-2000**

Fax: (404) 413-2002	**Email:** admissions@gsu.edu
Full-time: 7713 men, 11,251 women	**Faculty:** n/av
Part-time: 2603 men, 3593 women	**Ph.D.s:** 90%
Graduate: 2705 men, 4215 women	**Student/Faculty:** 22 to 1
Year: semesters, summer session	**Tuition:** $10,686 ($28,896)
Room & Board: $13,646	**Freshman Class:** 13568 applied, 7831 accepted, 3682 enrolled
SAT or ACT: required	**CEEB CODE:** 5251
Application Deadline: July 1	**VERY COMPETITIVE**

Georgia State University, founded in 1913 and a part of the University System of Georgia, is a public research university offering programs in liberal arts and sciences, business administration, education, law, health sciences, and public policy. There are 6 undergraduate schools and 7 graduate schools. In addition to regional accreditation, Georgia State has baccalaureate program accreditation with AACSB, ADA, APTA, CAHEA, CSWE, NASAD, NASM, NCATE, NLN, ABA, ACS, APA, CADE, CACREP, and CAPTE. The 72-acre campus is in an urban area in downtown Atlanta. Including any residence halls, there are 63 buildings.

STUDENT LIFE: 96% of undergraduates are from Georgia. Others are from 49 states, 118 foreign countries, and Canada. 5% are two or more races; 42% African American; 3% race unknown; 26% White; 2% Foreign; 12% Asian American; 10% Hispanic. **Female To Male Ratio:** 1.5:1. The average age of freshmen is 19; all undergraduates, 22. 18% do not continue beyond their first year; 54% remain to graduate. **Housing:** 4163 students can be accommodated in college housing, which includes coed dorms, on-campus apartments, and married student housing. In addition, there are special-interest houses, fraternity houses, and sorority houses. On-campus housing is available on a first-come, and first-served basis. 82% of students commute. All students may keep cars.

FACULTY/CLASSROOMS: 52% of faculty are male; 48% are female. No introductory courses are taught by graduate students.

PROGRAMS OF STUDY: Georgia State confers B.A., B.S., B.B.A., B.F.A., B.I.S., B.M., B.S.Ed., B.M.U., and B.S.W. degrees. Master's and doctoral degrees are also awarded. Bachelor's degrees are awarded in BIOLOGICAL SCIENCE (biology/biological science and nutrition), BUSINESS (accounting, banking and finance, business administration and management, business economics, hospitality management services, insurance and risk management, management information systems, marketing/retailing/merchandising, office supervision and management, and real estate), COMMUNICATIONS AND THE ARTS (art, art history and appreciation, classics, English, film arts, fine arts, French, German, journalism, music, music business management, Spanish, speech/debate/rhetoric, and studio art), COMPUTER AND PHYSICAL SCIENCE (actuarial science, chemistry, computer science, geology, mathematics, physics, and statistics), EDUCATION (art education, early childhood education, and physical education), HEALTH PROFESSIONS (exercise science, nursing, and respiratory therapy), SOCIAL SCIENCE (African American studies, anthropology, criminal justice, economics, geography, history, interdisciplinary studies, philosophy, political science/government, psychology, religious education, social work, sociology, urban studies, and women's studies). Business is the strongest academically. Biological sciences, computer science, and psychology have the largest enrollments.

ACTIVITIES: 3% of men belong to 10 national fraternities; 4% of women belong to 11 national sororities. There are 456 groups on campus, including art, band, cheerleading, chess, chorale, chorus, computers, dance, debate, drama, environmental, ethnic, film, honors, an outdoor club, international, jazz band, LGBT, literary magazine, musical theater, newspaper, opera, orchestra, pep band, photography, political, professional, radio and TV, religious, social, social service, and student government. Popular campus events include Welcome Week, Panther Prowl, and Homecoming. **Sports:** There are 6 intercollegiate sports for men and 9 for women, and 19 intramural sports for men and 19 for women. Facilities include a phys ed complex with 3 gyms, a pool, a diving well, a weight room, indoor and outdoor tennis courts, a climbing wall, a jogging track, exercise rooms, a dance studio, and racquetball courts. In addition, the Indian Creek recreation area has a pool, 3 tennis courts, picnic facilities, regular and sand volleyball, basketball courts, and a rope challenge course. There are also athletic fields. **Graduates:** From July 1, 2015 to June 30, 2016, 4788 bachelor's degrees were awarded. The most popular majors were biological science (6%), psychology (6%), and accounting (5%). In an average class, 24% graduate in 4 years or less, 46% graduate in 5 years or less, and 54% graduate in 6 years or less.

SERVICES: Counseling and information services are available, as is tutoring in most subjects. There is a reader service for the blind. Programs are available in effective studying, reading comprehension, speed reading, test and note taking, test anxiety, fear of public speaking, and organization and planning. **Library/Resources:** The 2 libraries contain 1.7 million volumes, 2.3 million microform items, and 7.9 million audio/video tapes/CDs/DVDs, and subscribe to 13,194 periodicals including electronic. Computerized library services include interlibrary loans, database searching, Internet access, and Wi-Fi capability. Special learning facilities include an art gallery, radio station, TV station, a digital arts lab, an observatory, an instructional technology center, and distance learning classrooms. **Physically Challenged Students:** All of the campus is accessible. Facilities include wheelchair ramps, elevators, special parking, specially equipped restrooms, special class scheduling, lowered drinking fountains, and lowered telephones. **Special:** There is cross-registration with the Atlanta Regional Consortium for Higher Education (ARCHE). Internships with numerous employers and government agencies can be arranged. Study abroad is available in various countries. Work-study, an accelerated degree program in nursing, and dual majors are available. There are 8 national honor societies and a freshman honors program. **Visiting:** There are regularly scheduled orientations for prospective students, 45 minute informations session followed by a 90 minute campus Atlanta tour. There are guides for informal visits and visitors may sit in on classes. To schedule a visit, contact Welcome Center at (404) 651-3900. **Campus Safety and Security:** Measures include 24-hour foot and vehicle patrol, emergency notification system, self-defense education, and security escort services. There are shuttle buses, emergency telephones, lighted pathways/sidewalks, controlled access to dorms/residences, and bicycle patrol.

REQUIREMENTS: The SAT or ACT is required. The ACT Optional Writing test is also required. A high school diploma is required. A total of 17 academic units is required, with 4 units in English, mathematics, and science (2 units must be lab), 2 units in foreign language, and 3 units in social studies. A GPA of 2.8 is required. AP and CLEP credits are accepted. Students must complete core curriculum requirements, including courses in written communication, mathematics, institutional foundations, humanities and fine arts, natural and computational sciences, social science, and lower division major requirements. A minimum of 120 hours must be completed for graduation. **Procedure:** Freshmen are admitted fall, spring, and summer. There are early admissions and deferred admissions plans. Applications should be filed by July 1 for fall entry; December 1 for spring entry; and April 1 for summer entry. The fall 2016 application fee was $60. Applications are accepted on-line. **Transfer Students:** 2327 transfer students enrolled in 2015-2016. Transfer applicants must submit official transcripts of all college-level work, have a minimum GPA of 2.5, have earned 30 semester hours, and be in good academic standing. Those with fewer than 30 semester hours earned must meet freshman requirements. 39 of 120 credits required for the bachelor's degree must be completed at Georgia State. **International Students:** There are 693 international students enrolled. The school actively recruits these students. They must take the TOEFL with a minimum score of 550 on the paper-based TOEFL (PBT) or 80 on the Internet-based version (iBT). They must also take the SAT or ACT.

ADMISSIONS: 58% of the 2016-2017 applicants were accepted. The SAT scores for the 2016-2017 freshman class were: Critical Reading-- 33% below 500, 48% between 500 and 599, 17% between 600 and 699, and 2% between 700 and 800. Math-- 37% below 500, 43% between 500 and 599, 18% between 600 and 699, and 3% between 700 and 800. **Admissions Contact:** Scott Burke, Assistant VP for Undergraduates. Email: *admissions@gsu.edu* Web: *www.gsu.edu*

FINANCIAL AID: 59% of all full-time freshmen and 49% of continuing full-time students received need-based aid. The average freshman award was $12,444. Need-based scholarships or need-based grants averaged $5,089; and need-based self-help aid (loans and jobs) averaged $3,477. Average annual earnings from campus work are $9178. The deadline for filing freshman financial aid applications for fall entry is April 1.

KENNESAW STATE UNIVERSITY B-2

www.kennesaw.edu

Kennesaw, GA 30144 (770) 423-6300

Fax: (470) 578-9169	**Email:** ksuadmit@kennesaw.edu
Full-time: 12,498 men, 11,914 women	**Faculty:** IIA, --$
	Ph.D.s: 78%
Part-time: 4187 men, 3567 women	**Student/Faculty:** n/av
Graduate: 1160 men, 1692 women	**Tuition:** $8125 ($21,581)
Year: semesters, summer session	**Freshman Class:** 15122 applied, 8847 accepted, 5347 enrolled
Room & Board: $11,467	
SAT CR/M/W: 540/540/520 **ACT:** 23	**CEEB CODE:** 5359
Application Deadline: May 5	**VERY COMPETITIVE**

For more than 50 years, Kennesaw State University has been known for its entrepreneurial spirit and sense of community, offering campuses in Marietta and Kennesaw. As Georgia's third-largest university, Kennesaw State offers more than 150 undergraduate and graduate degrees, including a growing doctoral program. Designated by the Board of Regents of the University System of Georgia as a comprehensive university, Kennesaw State is committed to becoming a world-class academic institution positioned to broaden its academic and research missions and expand its scope on a local, regional, and national level. On January 6, 2015, the Board of Regents of the University System of Georgia approved the consolidation of Kennesaw State and Southern Polytechnic State University. This represents the USG's fifth and largest consolidation in its continuing commitment to increase efficiencies and effectiveness to better serve students and the state. The new Kennesaw State University combines the best from two of Georgia's most respected institutions in higher education. A comprehensive university, Kennesaw State is a destination campus offering students a broad spectrum of quality academics, a growing and vibrant campus life, award-winning dining facilities, and a wide array of athletic offerings. With nationally ranked degrees in business, engineering, and first-year programs, as well as premier teaching, nursing, architecture, science, and math programs, the new Kennesaw State University is poised to become Georgia's next world-class institution. There are 12 undergraduate schools and 10 graduate schools. In addition to regional accreditation, Kennesaw State or KSU has baccalaureate program accreditation with AACSB, ABET, ACCE, CSWE, NAAB, NASAD, NASM, NCATE, NLN, ACTFL, ACEI, ACTFL, AMLE, CCNE, CAEP, CEC, IFMA, MACTE, NAACLS, NAST, NASPE, NCSS, NSTA, NASPAA-CORPA, SHAPE America - PETE, and TESOL. The 602-acre campus is in a suburban area is approximately 27 miles north of Atlanta. The Marietta campus is located approximately 20 miles north of Atlanta. Including any residence halls, there are 158 buildings.

STUDENT LIFE: 90% of undergraduates are from Georgia. Others are from 51 states, 131 foreign countries, and Canada. 9% are Hispanic; 57% White; 5% Asian American; 4% two or more races; 21% African American; 2% Foreign; 2% race unknown. **Male To Female Ratio:** 1.0:1. The average age of freshmen is 18; all undergraduates, 23. 23% do not continue beyond their first year; 42% remain to graduate. **Housing:** 5202 students can be accommodated in college housing, which includes coed on-campus apartments. On-campus housing is available on a first-come and first-served basis. 85% of students commute. Alcohol is not permitted. All students may keep cars.

FACULTY/CLASSROOMS: 47% of faculty are male; 53% are female. No introductory courses are taught by graduate students. The average class size in an introductory lecture is 37; in a laboratory is 23; and in a regular course is 37.

PROGRAMS OF STUDY: KSU confers B.A., B.A.R.C.H., B.S., B.B.A., B.F.A., B.M., B.S.N., B.A.S., B.A.T., B.S.C.E., B.S.C.G.D.D., B.S.C.V.E., B.S.E.E., B.S.E.S., B.S.I.T., B.S.M.E., B.S.S.E.N.G., B.S.S.W.E., and B.S.T.E.T. degrees. Master's and doctoral degrees are also awarded. Bachelor's degrees are awarded in BIOLOGICAL SCIENCE (biochemistry, biology/biological science, and biotechnology), BUSINESS (accounting, apparel and textiles, business administration and management, finance, integrative studies, international business management, management science, and marketing/retailing/merchandising), COMMUNICATIONS AND THE ARTS (art history, art, communications, dance, English, modern language, music, music performance, public relations, telecommunications engineering technology, and theatre arts), COMPUTER AND PHYSICAL SCIENCE (chemistry, computer engineering technology, computer game design/development, computer science, computer security and information assurance, information sciences and systems, mathematics, physics, and software engineering), EDUCATION (art education, childhood education, early childhood education, English education, health education, mathematics education, middle school education, music education, and physical education), ENGINEERING AND ENVIRONMENTAL DESIGN (agricultural engineering technology, civil engineering, civil engineering technology, construction engineering, electrical/electronics engineering, electrical/electronics engineering technology, environmental engineering technology, environmental science, industrial engineering technology, mechanical engineering, mechanical engineering technology, survey and mapping technology, and systems engineering), HEALTH PROFESSIONS (exercise science and nursing), SOCIAL SCIENCE (African studies, anthropology, architectural studies, criminal justice, culinary arts, economics, geography, history, human services, international studies, philosophy, political science/government, psychology, and sociology). Nursing, biology, and psychology have the largest enrollments.

ACTIVITIES: 5% of men belong to 18 national fraternities; 10% of women belong to 13 national sororities. There are 367 groups on campus, including special interest, competition teams, military, applied academic, art, band, cheerleading, chess, choir, chorale, chorus, communications, computers, dance, drama, ethnic, honors, international, jazz band, LGBT, literary magazine, marching band, musical theater, newspaper, opera, orchestra, pep band, political, professional, radio and TV, religious, social, social service, student government, and symphony. Popular campus events include KSU Day, Year of Program, Greek Week, First Year Convocation, and International Student Association International Bazaar. **Sports:** There are 7 intercollegiate sports for men and 9 for women, and 17 intramural sports for men and 17 for women. Facilities include Bobbie Bailey Athletic Complex for softball and baseball, a softball stadium, stadium for football, soccer, and lacrosse, Dr. Betty L. Siegel student recreation and activities center, men's and women's basketball and volleyball teams, golf indoor practice facility, indoor practice facility for men's and women's basketball and volleyball teams, outdoor track and field facility, athletics rehabilitation center, Stillwell baseball stadium, sports performance facility, student-athlete success services, and the Pinetree country club for men's and women's golf. **Graduates:** From July 1, 2015 to June 30, 2016, 4687 bachelor's degrees were awarded. The most popular majors were management (20%), computer and information sciences (9%), and communication (8%). In an average class, 14% graduate in 4 years or less, 33% graduate in 5 years or less, and 42% graduate in 6 years or less.

SERVICES: Counseling and information services are available, as is tutoring in some subjects, such as math, foreign languages, and English. There is academic coaching for writing and research skills There is a reader service for the blind, and remedial math, reading, and writing. **Library/Resources:** The 2 libraries contain 416,838 volumes, 500,000 microform items, and 5,862 audio/video tapes/CDs/DVDs, and subscribe to 103,549 periodicals including electronic. Computerized library services include interlibrary loans, database searching, Internet access, and Wi-Fi capability. Special learning facilities include an art gallery, radio station, Museum of History and Holocaust Education, Bentley Rare Book Gallery; Zuckerman Museum of Art; The 3D Center; Alternative Energy Innovation Center; Center for Advanced Materials Research and Education; Center for African and African Diaspora Studies; Center for Georgia Aggregates Research (CGAR); Center for Information Security Education; Center for Literacy and Learning; Center for Machine Vision and Security Research; Center for Professional Selling; Center for Student Leadership; The Entrepreneurship Center; The ESL Center; Georgia Pavement and Traffic Research Center (GPTRC); The Intensive English Program; The Internal Audit Center; Mobile Application Development Center; Student Development Center; Visualization and Simulation Research Center, and a Writing Center, and KSU Challenge Corner. **Physically Challenged Students:** All of the campus is accessible. Facilities include wheelchair ramps, elevators, special parking, specially equipped restrooms, special class scheduling, lowered drinking fountains, and lowered telephones. **Special:** Students may register for courses with any of the colleges in the University System of Georgia. Students can participate in study abroad, directed study, cooperative study, internship, directed study, federal work-study, dual majors, online programs, and non-degree programs. Additionally, the Division of Global Affairs offers a wide range of programs for students, such as: The Annual Country Study Program; Center for African and African Diaspora Studies; and the Confucius Institute. The Honors College at Kennesaw State University houses the Undergraduate Honors Program, including the Great Books cohort. In addition, the Honors College is home to the Dual Enrollment Honors Program, which allows academically talented high school students to take classes at KSU. There are 21 national honor societies and a freshman honors program. **Visiting:** There are regularly scheduled orientations for prospective students. Kennesaw Campus: Monday through Friday 9 a.m., 11 a.m., and 2 p.m. Marietta Campus: Monday through Friday 10 a.m. and 2 p.m. There are guides for informal visits. To schedule a visit, contact the Office of Undergraduate Admissions. **Campus Safety and Security:** Measures include 24-hour foot and vehicle patrol, emergency notification system, self-defense education, and security escort services. There are shuttle buses, emergency telephones, lighted pathways/sidewalks, full-service police department, siren system with messages, pop-up computer notification on the KSU network, telephone emergency message system, email emergency notification, security badges, intrusion alarms and video surveillance.

REQUIREMENTS: Applications for admission and all required credentials (such as transcripts and test scores) must be submitted by established deadlines. New applications received after the deadline dates will be processed for the following term. The Required High School Curriculum (RHSC) is a key factor considered in freshman admissions decisions. Completion of the University System of Georgia's RHSC requirements at a regionally accredited or USG-recognized high school is expected of most successful traditional freshman applicants. The Required Course Emphasis is 4 years each of English and mathematics, 3 years each of science and social science, and 2 years of foreign language. Freshmen are recent high school graduates who will be attending college for the first time. KSU's minimum requirements for admission as a freshman include the following: Graduation from one of the following: A regionally accredited high school, a high school accredited by the Georgia Accreditation Commission, a high school accredited by an approved University System of Georgia agency, a public school under the authority of the State Department of Education, Completion of the 17 required RHSC units. High School academic GPA of at least a 2.5; All minimum SAT or ACT scores as follow: SAT I Critical Reading and Math Combined-950 (1000 for the Architecture Program), SAT I Critical Reading-No lower than 450, SAT I Math- No lower than 450 Or, SAT taken March 2016 or later: Redesigned SAT Total Score (on 1600 scale) - 1030 (1080 for the Architecture Program); Redesigned Reading Test Score - No lower than 25; Redesigned Math Test Score - No lower than 490, or ACT-Composite Score-20 (21 for the Architecture Program), ACT-English- No lower than 18, ACT-Math- No lower than 18. Honors Opportunities are available for students who have recently graduated from high school, are entering Kennesaw State as first-year students, have a high school grade point average of 3.5 or better in their academic courses, and have made a composite score of 1150 or better on the Critical Reading and Math sections of the Scholastic Aptitude Test (SAT) taken prior to March 2016, or 1220 on the SAT Total Score on the Redesigned SAT taken March 2016 or later. (The equivalent composite ACT score of 25 or higher is also accepted.) Rising high school juniors and seniors who are at least fifteen years of age at the time of enrollment are eligible for the Dual Enrollment Honors Program if they earn: Cumulative grade point average of 3.0 or better in their core academic course work (not electives) and are on track to complete the Required High School Curriculum, a composite score of 1100 on the old SAT taken prior to March 2016, with minimum subparts of 530 critical reading and 530 math; or SAT Total Score of 1170 on a 1600 scale on the new/redesigned SAT (taken March 2016 or later) with minimums of SAT Reading Test Score of 29 and Math Section Score of 560, or an ACT composite score minimum of 24 with subpart minimums of 23 English and 22 math. Kennesaw State University welcomes students who have pursued accelerated academic course work while in high school or through recognized national standardized programs. Such programs include College Board's Advanced Placement (AP), International Baccalaureate (IB), College Level Subject Examination Program (CLEP), and Defense Activity for Nontraditional Educational Support (DANTES). Kennesaw State recognizes the choice and rights of a family to home educate their children. However, some home-educated applicants bear the burden of demonstrating through proper documentation that they meet all of the standard requirements for regular or limited freshman admission. Home school applicants are defined as completing a high school program of study that is not from a regionally accredited or University System-recognized high school and those who have not satisfactorily completed the prescribed Carnegie units of the Required High School Curriculum in a manner acceptable to the University System. Nevertheless, the University System of Georgia permits home- educated applicants to be considered if they demonstrate sufficient Required High

School Curriculum preparedness on appropriate standardized subject matter tests. The portfolio review approach for handling exceptions for home school students waives the high school graduation requirement, the academic HSGPA requirement, and the Carnegie unit requirements of the Required High School Curriculum. These waivers are in exchange for satisfactory performance on additional standardized testing, which validates college preparedness and demonstrates a satisfactory comprehensive high school academic experience. The applicant must meet or exceed the required minimum freshmen average scores on the SAT I or ACT of the prior fall semester freshman class at KSU. Prospective home school applicants are encouraged to contact the Office of Undergraduate Admissions at least six months prior to the planned date of entry to obtain information and direction as to how to pursue these alternatives and exceptions for admission. A GPA of 2.5 is required. AP and CLEP credits are accepted. Undergraduate students should submit a formal petition for the degree through the online petition process no later than the published deadline and pay the graduation fee. The student must pay all required fees, fines, and other financial obligations to KSU prior to receiving his/her diploma and/or other services. Students with a balance may have a HOLD placed on their account until balance is paid. Student must satisfy BOR Core Overlay requirements regarding Critical Thinking, United States Perspectives and Global Perspectives. In all instances, meeting the requirements for graduation is the responsibility of the student. Each student must have a minimum institutional Grade Point Average (GPA) of 2.0 for graduation. Specific degree programs may have higher requirements. Complete all required General Education courses; ENGL 1101 AND ENGL 102 require a grade of "C" or higher (or equivalents, if a transfer student). Complete a minimum of 123 semester hours. Specific degree programs may require additional hours. A minimum institutional grade point average of 2.0 on all coursework attempted at KSU is required. No course may be counted more than one time in meeting the total credit hours required for the degree. Have at least a 2.0 institutional grade point average with at least 30 hours of credit for KSU coursework not excluded because of repeated courses or "fresh start" status. If the student has fewer than 30 earned hours of credit for non-excluded KSU coursework, he/she must have a 2.0 cumulative grade point average. Baccalaureate degrees consist of a minimum of 120 semester hours, exclusive of the university-wide requirements (WELL 1000 and the first-year seminar/learning community). Exceptions to the maximum degree-length requirements have been made with the approval of the Board of Regents. A baccalaureate degree program requires at least 21 semester hours of upper division courses in the major field to be completed at KSU, and at least 39 semester hours of upper division work overall are required for the degree. All students entering Kennesaw State University are required to take the Foundations for Healthy Living (WELL 1000) course. Students who previously completed HPS 1000 - Fitness for Living have met the Foundations for Healthy Living requirement. This requirement is WAIVED for majors in the following three colleges: 1) College of Architecture and Construction Management, 2) College of Computing and Software Engineering, and 3) College of Engineering and Engineering Technology. Complete at least 30 semester hours in residence at Kennesaw State (Coles College of Business requires 33 hours). "In residence" is defined as courses for which a student has registered at KSU. Note: Individual departments may have higher requirements. Courses for which the student registers at KSU, including cross-registration, are considered to be "in residence". Coursework completed as a transient student at another institution, transfer credit, credit by examination (including CLEP, AP, IB, etc. are not considered to be in residence. **Procedure:** Freshmen are admitted fall, spring, and summer. Entrance exams should be taken before June 1. There is a rolling admissions plan. Early decision applications should be filed by October 28; regular applications, by May 5 for fall entry; November 4 for spring entry; and March 31 for summer entry. The fall 2016 application fee was $40. Applications are accepted on-line. **Transfer Students:** 2786 transfer students enrolled in 2015-2016. Transfer students must make arrangements with each college previously attended, whether credit was completed or not, to have a complete official transcript forwarded to the Office of Undergraduate Admissions at Kennesaw State University. Official transcripts are required, regardless of the applicant's wishes concerning transfer credit or financial holds, and must be mailed directly from the sending institution to the Office of Undergraduate Admissions. Transcripts must be issued within one year of the application submission. Transfer students' records will be evaluated in the same manner as Kennesaw State University resident students. Transfer students must have completed 30 semester hours of transferable credit with a 2.0 cumulative GPA or above and be in good academic standing at their most recent college. Transfer applicants who have been academically dismissed from their previous institution may not enter Kennesaw State until they are fully eligible to return to their former institution, have attained good academic standing, and have a cumulative grade point average of at least 2.0. Students transferring from another institution in the University System of Georgia must have satisfied any and all learning support requirements before being admitted to KSU. Transferring students who took physical education hours at one institution will not be required to duplicate those hours at KSU. However, students who took an orientation course at another institution may be required to take the KSU 1101 orientation course. All admission application deadlines cited earlier apply to transfer applicants. All of the required documents cited earlier for a complete application file apply to transfer applicants with the following exceptions: •High school transcripts are not required for applicants with 30 or more earned semester hours of acceptable transfer credit. (However, all college and university transcripts are required) •SAT or ACT scores are not required for applicants with 30 or more earned semester hours of acceptable transfer credit. Transfer credit will be awarded from official AARTS, SMART, or Coast Guard transcripts utilizing ACE Guidelines. Military training and experience with a credit recommendation at the lower-division and upper-division baccalaureate degree category level is evaluated. For further details regarding Military Transfer Credits, visit the Transfer Evaluation Services website. 30 of 123 credits required for the bachelor's degree must be completed at Kennesaw State or KSU. **International Students:** There are 461 international students enrolled. The school actively recruits these students. They must take the TOEFL with a minimum score of 550 on the paper-based TOEFL (PBT) or 79 on the Internet-based version (iBT), IELTS test score of 6.5. They must also take the SAT or ACT, scoring ACT-Composite Score, 20 (21 for Architect Program) or SAT I Critical Reading and Math Combined, 950 (1000 for the Architecture Program).

ADMISSIONS: 59% of the 2016-2017 applicants were accepted. The SAT scores for the 2016-2017 freshman class were: Critical Reading-- 22% below 500, 54% between 500 and 599, 22% between 600 and 699, and 2% between 700 and 800. Math-- 21% below 500, 54% between 500 and 599, 22% between 600 and 699, and 3% between 700 and 800. Writing-- 36% below 500, 49% between 500 and 599, 14% between 600 and 699, and 1% between 700 and 800. The ACT scores were 1% between 12 and 17, 56% between 18 and 23, 38% between 24 and 29, and 5% above 30. **Admissions Contact:** Angela Evans, Director of Admissions. Email: *ksuadmit@kennesaw.edu* Web: *www.kennesaw.edu*

FINANCIAL AID: Kennesaw State is a member of CSS. Check with the school for current application deadlines.

LAGRANGE COLLEGE — A-3

www.lagrange.edu

LaGrange, GA 30240	(706) 880-8005 (800) 593-2885
Fax: (706) 880-8010	**Email:** admissions@lagrange.edu
Full-time: 444 men, 410 women	**Faculty:** 72
Part-time: 15 men, 33 women	**Ph.D.s:** 80%
Graduate: 30 men, 90 women	**Student/Faculty:** 12 to 1
Year: 4-1-4, summer session	**Tuition:** $28,490
Room & Board: $11,440	**Freshman Class:** 1568 applied, 905 accepted, 236 enrolled
SAT CR/M: 500/490 **ACT:** 22	**CEEB CODE:** 5362
Application Deadline: n/av	**COMPETITIVE**

LaGrange College, founded in 1831, is a private liberal arts institution affiliated with the United Methodist Church. Major undergraduate programs include business, visual and performing arts, education, biology, psychology, and exercise science. Figures in the above capsule and in this profile are approximate. There is 1 undergraduate school and 1 graduate school. In addition to regional accreditation, LaGrange has baccalaureate program accreditation with ACBSP, NLN, and GPSC. The 120-acre campus is in a small town 70 miles southwest of Atlanta. Including any residence halls, there are 27 buildings.

STUDENT LIFE: 83% of undergraduates are from Georgia. Others are from 18 states and 7 foreign countries. 75% are from public schools. 71% are White; 23% African American; 2% two or more races; 1% Asian American; 1% Hispanic; 1% Foreign. 76% are Protestant; 19% unknown religious affiliation. **Female To Male Ratio:** 1.1:1. The average age of freshmen is 18; all undergraduates, 21. 34% do not continue beyond their first year; 47% remain to graduate. **Housing:** 654 students can be accommodated in college housing, which includes single-sex and coed dorms, on-campus apartments, and married student housing. In addition, there are special-interest houses, fraternity houses, and sorority houses. On-campus housing is guaranteed for all 4 years. 62% of students live on campus; of those, 63% remain on campus on weekends. Alcohol is not permitted. All students may keep cars.

FACULTY/CLASSROOMS: 49% of faculty are male; 51% are female. 98% teach undergraduates. No introductory courses are taught by graduate students. The average class size in an introductory lecture is 18 and in a laboratory is 17.

PROGRAMS OF STUDY: LaGrange confers B.A, B.S., B.S.N., B.B.A., and B.M. degrees. Master's degrees are also awarded. Bachelor's degrees are awarded in BIOLOGICAL SCIENCE (biochemistry and biology/biological science), BUSINESS (accounting and business administration and management), COMMUNICATIONS AND THE ARTS (art, English, music, Spanish, and theatre arts), COMPUTER AND PHYSICAL SCIENCE (chemistry, computer science, and mathematics), EDUCATION (early childhood education and education), HEALTH PROFESSIONS (exercise science and nursing), SOCIAL SCIENCE (history, interdisciplinary studies, political science/government, psychology, religion, and sociology). Nursing, business, and exercise science have the largest enrollments.

ACTIVITIES: 23% of men belong to 3 national fraternities; 40% of women belong to 3 national sororities. There are 25 groups on campus, including art, cheerleading, choir, chorale, chorus, drama, environmental, ethnic, honors, international, LGBT, literary magazine, marching band, musical theater, newspaper, orchestra, pep band, political, professional, religious, social, social service, and student government. Popular campus events include Spirit and Traditions Kickoff, First-week Hypnotist, Christmas on the Hill, Homecoming, May Day, Vegas on the Hill, and Quadrangle Formal. **Sports:** There are 8 intercollegiate sports for men and 8 for women, and 10 intramural sports for men and 10 for women. Facilities include a fitness center, West Point Lake, an auditorium, indoor and outdoor pools, 2 gyms, 10 lighted tennis courts, lighted softball, baseball stadium, soccer fields, a football practice field, and a football stadium. **Graduates:** From July 1, 2015 to June 30, 2016, 182 bachelor's degrees were awarded. The most popular majors were nursing (19%), business (9%), and exercise science (8%). 7 companies recruited on campus in 2015-2016. In an average class, 43% graduate in 4 years or less, 47% graduate in 5 years or less, and 47% graduate in 6 years or less. Of the 2015 graduating class, 15% were enrolled in graduate school within 6 months of graduation, and 63% were employed.

SERVICES: Counseling and information services are available, as is tutoring in most subjects, such as French, Religion, Spanish, chemistry, nursing, political science, American experience, psychology, art history, statistics, problem solving, biology, economics, and history. There is remedial math, reading, and writing center. **Library/Resources:** The library contains 399,318 volumes, 268,299 microform items, and 31,260 audio/video tapes/CDs/DVDs, and subscribes to 132 periodicals including electronic. Computerized library services include interlibrary loans, database searching, Internet access, and Wi-Fi capability. Special learning facilities include an art gallery, 2 music technology labs, an exercise science lab, and a performing arts theater and auditorium. **Physically Challenged Students:** 85% of the campus is accessible. Facilities include wheelchair ramps, elevators, special parking, specially equipped restrooms, special class scheduling, lowered drinking fountains, and special housing. **Special:** Students may participate in an international study tour progam currently offered through the Interim Program in January. A 3-2 engineering degree is offered with Georgia Institute of Technology and Auburn University. A self-designed B.A. in Interdisciplinary Studies is also available to qualifying students. Internships and work-study programs are offered in numerous disciplines. The CHIP program allows students to work and study in Washington, D.C. Cross-registration relationships have been established with postsecondary institutions in Japan. There are 13 national honor societies. **Visiting:** There are regularly scheduled orientations for prospective students, Preview Day consists of a welcome and introduction to the college, guided campus tour, showcase sessions (including major departments and financial aid). There are guides for informal visits, visitors may sit in on classes, and stay overnight. To schedule a visit, contact Holly Phillips at (760) 880-8005. **Campus Safety and Security:** Measures include 24-hour foot and vehicle patrol, emergency notification system, and security escort services. There are emergency telephones, lighted pathways/sidewalks, and controlled access to dorms/residences.

REQUIREMENTS: The SAT or ACT is required. Applicants should be graduates of accredited secondary schools or have a GED certificate. They should have completed a minimum of 4 units of English and math, 3 of social studies, 3 of science (2 with labs), and 2 units of a foreign language. A GPA of 2.5 is required. AP and CLEP credits are accepted. Important factors in the admissions decision are leadership record, evidence of special talent, personality/intangible qualities, recommendations by alumni, recommendations by school officials, parents or siblings attended your school, and extracurricular activities record. To graduate, all students must complete 120 semester hours. The core curriculum includes First-Year Cornerstone, rhetoric and compostion, math, world languages and culture, laboratory science, problem solving, computer applications, humanities, fine arts, religion, and the American experience. All students must have a minimum GPA of 2.0. **Procedure:** Freshmen are admitted to all sessions. There are early admissions, deferred admissions, and rolling admissions plans. Application deadlines are open. Applications are accepted on-line. Application fees are waived if application is completed on-line. **Transfer Students:** 89 transfer students enrolled in 2015-2016. Transfer students must have a minimum 2.0 College GPA and be in good standing with the previous college. Transfer students must also have a minimum high school GPA of 3.0 if less than 30 hours of college credit is transferred. 39 of 120 credits required for the bachelor's degree must be completed at LaGrange. **International Students:** There are 7 international students enrolled. They must take the TOEFL with a minimum score of 500 on the paper-based TOEFL (PBT) or 61 on the Internet-based version (iBT). They must also take the SAT or ACT, scoring 450.

ADMISSIONS: 58% of the 2016-2017 applicants were accepted. The SAT scores for the 2016-2017 freshman class were: Critical Reading-- 47% below 500, 37% between 500 and 599, 12% between 600 and 699, and 3% between 700 and 800. Math-- 55% below 500, 37% between 500 and 599, and 9% between 600 and 699. The ACT scores were 17, 70% between 18 and 23, 28% between 24 and 29, and 1% above 30. 31% of the current freshmen were in the top fifth of their class; 57% were in the top two fifths. 2 freshmen graduated first in their class. **Admissions Contact:** Holly Phillips, Admissions Services Coordinator. Email: *admissions@lagrange.edu* Web: *www.lagrange.edu*

FINANCIAL AID: In 2016-2017, 99% of all full-time freshmen and 99% of continuing full-time students received some form of financial aid. 85% of all full-time freshmen and 80% of continuing full-time students received need-based aid. The average freshman award was $31,234. Need-based scholarships or need-based grants averaged $5,282 ($21,315 maximum); need-based self-help aid (loans and jobs) averaged $4,478 ($7,950 maximum); other non-need-based awards and non-need-based scholarships averaged $13,833 ($38,700 maximum); and $4,662 from other forms of aid. 38% of undergraduate students work part-time. Average annual earnings from campus work are $1750. The average financial indebtedness of the 2016 graduate was $37,318. The college's own financial statement is required. The FAFSA code is 001578. The priority date for freshman financial aid applications for fall entry is March 1.

MERCER UNIVERSITY C-3
www.mercer.edu

Macon, GA 31207	(478) 301-2650 (800) 840-8577
Fax: (478) 301-2828	Email: admissions@mercer.edu
Full-time: 1258 men, 1214 women	**Faculty:** IIA, av$
Part-time: 35 men, 31 women	**Ph.D.s:** 94%
Graduate: 1410 men, 2522 women	**Student/Faculty:** 12 to 1
Year: semesters, summer session	**Tuition:** $34,450
Room & Board: $10,898	**Freshman Class:** 3864 applied, 2666 accepted, 727 enrolled
SAT CR/M/W: 580/590/560 **ACT:** 26	**CEEB CODE:** 5025
Application Deadline: April 1	**VERY COMPETITIVE**

Mercer University, founded in 1833, is a private institution of higher learning that seeks to achieve excellence and scholarly discipline in the fields of liberal learning and professional knowledge. The university offers degree programs in liberal arts, music, business and economics, education, engineering, nursing, and professional studies. Mercer also offers a Great Books program as an alternative to the traditional core curriculum. Figures in the above capsule and in this profile are approximate. There are 5 undergraduate schools and 11 graduate schools. In addition to regional accreditation, Mercer has baccalaureate program accreditation with AACSB, ABET, NASM, NCATE, ACS, CCNE, and NCAA. The 130-acre campus is in a suburban area 85 miles south of Atlanta.

STUDENT LIFE: 83% of undergraduates are from Georgia. Others are from 37 states, 42 foreign countries, and Canada. 7% are Asian American; 59% White; 4% Hispanic; 4% Foreign; 3% two or more races; 3% race unknown; 19% African American. 50% are Protestant; 23% claim no religious affiliation; 11% Catholic. **Female To Male Ratio:** 1.4:1. The average age of freshmen is 18; all undergraduates, 20. 18% do not continue beyond their first year; 61% remain to graduate. **Housing:** 1647 students can be accommodated in college housing, which includes single-sex and coed dorms, on-campus apartments, off-campus apartments, and married student housing. In addition, there are special-interest houses and fraternity houses. On-campus housing is available on a first-come, first-served basis, and is available on a lottery system for upperclassmen. Priority is given to out-of-town students. 65% of students live on campus. Alcohol is not permitted. All students may keep cars.

FACULTY/CLASSROOMS: 50% of faculty are male; 50% are female. No introductory courses are taught by graduate students. The average class size in a laboratory is 20 and in a regular course is 20.

PROGRAMS OF STUDY: Mercer confers B.A., B.S., B.B.A., B.M., B.M.E., B.S.E., B.S.ED., B.S.M., and B.S.N. degrees. Master's and doctoral degrees are also awarded. Bachelor's degrees are awarded in AGRICULTURE (environmental studies), BIOLOGICAL SCIENCE (biochemistry, biology/biological science, and environmental biology), BUSINESS (accounting, business administration and management, finance, international business management, and marketing management), COMMUNICATIONS AND THE ARTS (art, communications, communication rhetoric/communication, creative writing, dramatic arts, English literature, French, German, journalism, Latin, media arts, music, Spanish, and technical communication), COMPUTER AND PHYSICAL SCIENCE (chemistry, computer science, earth science, information sciences and systems, mathematics, natural sciences, and physics), EDUCATION (early childhood education, education, elementary education, music education, secondary education, and special education), ENGINEERING AND ENVIRONMENTAL DESIGN (computational sciences, engineering, and industrial administration/management), HEALTH PROFESSIONS (predentistry, premedicine, and prepharmacy), SOCIAL SCIENCE (African studies, anthropology, area studies, Christian studies, criminal justice, economics, gender studies, history, philosophy, political science/government, prelaw, psychology, religion, social science, sociology, and women's studies). Engineering, business, and biology have the largest enrollments.

ACTIVITIES: 22% of men belong to 8 national fraternities; 24% of women belong to 7 national sororities. There are 115 groups on campus, including bagpipe, band, cheerleading, choir, chorale, chorus, computers, dance, debate, drama, environmental, ethnic, film, honors, international, jazz band, LGBT, literary magazine, marching band, musical theater, newspaper, opera, orchestra, pep band, photography, political, professional, radio and TV, religious, social, social service, student government, and symphony. Popular campus events include Bearstock (outdoor concert), Pilgrimage to Penfield, Homecoming, and Mercer Madness. **Sports:** There are 8 intercollegiate sports for men and 10 for women, and 10 intramural sports for men and 10 for women. Facilities include 2 gyms, 3 playing fields, a student center, a swimming pool, a lighted intramural complex, and tennis, volleyball, and racquetball courts. **Graduates:** From July 1, 2015 to June 30, 2016, 446 bachelor's degrees were awarded. The most popular majors were business (18%), biology (12%), and engineering (10%). In an average class, 45% graduate in 4 years or less, 59% graduate in 5 years or less, and 61% graduate in 6 years or less.

SERVICES: Counseling and information services are available, as is tutoring in most subjects. There is a reader service for the blind, and remedial math. **Library/Resources:** The 2 libraries contain 864,793 volumes, 3.4 million microform items, and 70,477 audio/video tapes/CDs/DVDs, and subscribe to 14,491 periodicals including electronic. Computerized library services include interlibrary loans, database searching, and Internet access. Special learning facilities include a radio station, TV station, and a music building. **Physically Challenged Students:** 85% of the campus is accessible. Facilities include wheelchair ramps, elevators, special parking, specially equipped restrooms, special class scheduling, lowered drinking fountains, and lowered telephones. Assistance with registration. **Special:** Mercer offers co-op programs in all majors, cross-registration with Wesleyan and Macon State Colleges, B.A.-B.S. degrees in various science and math fields, internships, student-designed majors, work-study programs, and satisfactory-unsatisfactory options for elective courses. Mercer offers a wide variety of study-abroad opportunities, including independent semester or year-long programs, faculty-led programs, or Mercer on Mission. There are 2 national honor societies, a freshman honors program, and 20 departmental honors programs. **Visiting:** There are regularly scheduled orientations for prospective students. There are guides for informal visits, visitors may sit in on classes, and stay overnight. To schedule a visit, contact the Office of Admissions. **Campus Safety and Security:** Measures include 24-hour foot and vehicle patrol, emergency notification system, self-defense education, and security escort services. There are shuttle buses, emergency telephones, lighted pathways/sidewalks, controlled access to dorms/residences, and External CCTV cameras monitored by the police department.

REQUIREMENTS: The SAT or ACT is required. Applicants must be graduates of an accredited secondary school and have completed 16 academic units. Students should submit their transcript and class rank, a recommendation from a guidance counselor, and a list of extracurricular activities, including employment. AP and CLEP credits are accepted. To graduate, all students must complete at least 120 semester hours with a minimum GPA of 2.0. **Procedure:** Freshmen are admitted fall, spring, and summer. Entrance exams should be taken in the spring of the junior year or fall of the senior year. There are deferred admissions and rolling admissions plans. Applications should be filed by April 1 for fall entry. The fall 2016 application fee was $50. Notification is sent on a rolling basis. Applications are accepted on-line. **Transfer Students:** A minimum GPA of 2.0 is required for all transfer students. Applicants with fewer than 9 semester hours must meet freshman entrance requirements. Those with fewer than 20 semester hours must submit a high school transcript and SAT or ACT scores, and those with more than 20 semester hours must submit transcripts from all colleges attended and be in good academic standing at their present school, or present evidence of satisfactory work in a previously attended college. 30 of 120 credits required for the bachelor's degree must be completed at Mercer. **International Students:** There are 103 international students enrolled. The school actively recruits these students. They must take the TOEFL or Mercer's ELI exit examination. They must also take the SAT or ACT, scoring 1000.

ADMISSIONS: 69% of the 2016-2017 applicants were accepted. The SAT scores for the 2016-2017 freshman class were: Critical Reading-- 9% below 500, 47% between 500 and 599, 35% between 600 and 699, and 9% between 700 and 800. Math-- 7% below 500, 48% between 500 and 599, 37% between 600 and 699, and 8% between 700 and 800. Writing-- 19% below 500, 46% between 500 and 599, 29% between 600 and 699, and 6% between 700 and 800. **Admissions Contact:** Lael Whiteside, Director of Admissions. Email: *admissions@mercer.edu* Web: *www.mercer.edu*

FINANCIAL AID: In 2016-2017, 99% of all full-time freshmen and 97% of continuing full-time students received some form of financial aid. 81% of all full-time freshmen and 73% of continuing full-time students received need-based aid. The average financial indebtedness of the 2016 graduate was $29,101. The college's own financial statement is required. The FAFSA code is 001580. The deadline for filing freshman financial aid applications for fall entry is April 1.

MOREHOUSE COLLEGE — B-2

www.morehouse.edu

Atlanta, GA 30314 — **(404) 215-2632**, **(800) 851-1254**

Fax: (404) 572-3668 — **Email: admissions@morehouse.edu**

Full-time: 2016 men, no women	**Faculty:** 158; IIB, -$
Part-time: 88 men, no women	**Ph.D.s:** 87%
Graduate: none	**Student/Faculty:** 13 to 1
Year: semesters, summer session	**Tuition:** $26,722
Room & Board: $13,322	**Freshman Class:** 3168 applied, 2105 accepted, 611 enrolled
SAT: required **ACT:** 21	**CEEB CODE:** 5415
Application Deadline: February 15	**COMPETITIVE**

Morehouse is the nation's historically black college for men of exceptional ambition and promise. Our students engage with renowned faculty members in an intensive liberal arts and sciences program that inspires intellectual growth, character development, and the pursuit of social justice. Supported and enriched by a close-knit, diverse brotherhood like none other, Morehouse students build their skills and networks through extensive internship opportunities, push their boundaries through a residential experience that spurs lively debate and constant interaction, and hone their leadership capabilities through a wide variety of student-run organizations, formal and informal discussions with nationally known speakers and scholars, and boundless international travel opportunities. There is 1 undergraduate school. In addition to regional accreditation, Morehouse has baccalaureate program accreditation with AACSB, NASM, and ACS. The 66-acre campus is in an urban area in Atlanta, Georgia. Including any residence halls, there are 42 buildings.

STUDENT LIFE: 71% of undergraduates are from out of state, mostly the South. Students are from 42 states, and 17 foreign countries. 81% are from public schools. 95% are African American; 2% Foreign; 2% race unknown; 1% Hispanic. The student base is all male. The average age of freshmen is 18; all undergraduates, 20. 24% do not continue beyond their first year; 50% remain to graduate. **Housing:** 1580 students can be accommodated in college housing, which includes single-sex dorms and on-campus apartments. In addition, there are special-interest houses. On-campus housing is available on a first-come, and first-served basis. 74% of students live on campus. Alcohol is not permitted. All students may keep cars.

FACULTY/CLASSROOMS: 64% of faculty are male; 36% are female. All teach undergraduates, and all do research. No introductory courses are taught by graduate students. The average class size in an introductory lecture is 20 and in a laboratory is 15.

PROGRAMS OF STUDY: Morehouse confers B.A., B.S., and B.S.G.S. degrees. Bachelor's degrees are awarded in BIOLOGICAL SCIENCE (biology/biological science), BUSINESS (business administration and management), COMMUNICATIONS AND THE ARTS (art, dramatic arts, English, film, television and digital media, French, music, and Spanish), COMPUTER AND PHYSICAL SCIENCE (chemistry, computer science, mathematics, and physics), EDUCATION (early childhood education, health and physical education, and physical education), ENGINEERING AND ENVIRONMENTAL DESIGN (engineering physics and engineering science), SOCIAL SCIENCE (African American studies, economics, history, international studies, philosophy, political science/government, psychology, religion, sociology, and urban studies). Business administration, biology, political science, and dual degree engineering are the strongest academically. Business administration, biology, and dual-degree engineering have the largest enrollments.

ACTIVITIES: 3% of men belong to 7 national fraternities. There are 42 groups on campus, including campus alliance for student activities, debate team, a glee club, band, cheerleading, chess, choir, chorus, communications, computers, dance, debate, drama, drill team, environmental, ethnic, film, forensics, honors, international, jazz band, LGBT, literary magazine, marching band, newspaper, orchestra, pep band, photography, political, professional, religious, social, social service, student government, symphony, and yearbook. Popular campus events include New Student Orientation, Homecoming, Founder's Day, Parent's Weekend, Admitted Students Day, Martin Luther King Jr. Commemoration, and Spring Fest. **Sports:** There are 7 intercollegiate sports for men, and 10 intramural sports for men. Samuel H. Archer Hall is a 54,000 square foot facility that houses a swimming pool, television lounge, a game room, weight room, cardio room, locker rooms, gymnasium/basketball courts, conference rooms, and a multipurpose room. Forbes Arena, the home of the Maroon Tigers basketball team, is a 6000-seat, 3-level facility with four locker rooms, a first-aid station, a training room, a weight room, and four concession stands. Other facilities include the 9000-seat B.T. Harvey football stadium, the Edwin Moses track, and the tennis center. **Graduates:** From July 1, 2015 to June 30, 2016, 345 bachelor's degrees were awarded. The most popular majors were business administration (22%), biology (14%), and economics (8%). In an average class, 1% graduate in 3 years or less, 39% graduate in 4 years or less, 49% graduate in 5 years or less, and 50% graduate in 6 years or less.

SERVICES: Counseling and information services are available, as is tutoring in most subjects. There is a reader service for the blind, and remedial math, reading, and writing. **Library/Resources:** The library contains 364,010 volumes, 841,341 microform items, and 8,277 audio/video tapes/CDs/DVDs, and subscribes to 10,860 periodicals including electronic. Computerized library services include interlibrary loans, database searching, Internet access, and Wi-Fi capability. **Physically Challenged Students:** All of the campus is accessible. Facilities include wheelchair ramps, elevators, special parking, specially equipped restrooms, lowered drinking fountains, lowered telephones, and special housing. **Special:** Morehouse is a member of the Atlanta University Center, and Morehouse students may register for courses at any of other member institutions (i.e., Clark Atlanta University, Spelman College, and Morehouse School of Medicine). Morehouse students can complete a major (art, drama or early childhood education) at Spelman College. Moreover, through the Atlanta Regional Consortium for Higher Education (ARCHE), students can take courses at Atlanta-area colleges, and universities such as Agnes Scott College, Kennesaw State University, Emory University, Georgia Institute of Technology, Georgia State University, and many others. In addition, students may elect to participate in a wide range of study abroad and domestic exchange programs. Morehouse also offers students the option to study engineering through the Dual Degree Engineering Program (DDEP); participating engineering institutions include the University of Michigan, Columbia University, Dartmouth College, Georgia Institute of Technology, Rensselaer Polytechnic Institute, and nine other institutions. Other opportunities that Morehouse students engage include summer internships, work study, and undergraduate research programs. There are 15 national honor societies, Phi Beta Kappa, a freshman honors program, and 14 departmental honors programs. **Visiting:** There are regularly scheduled orientations for prospective students. There are guides for informal visits and visitors may sit in on classes. To schedule a visit, contact Erica S. Johnson at (404) 653-7736. **Campus Safety and Security:** Measures include 24-hour foot and vehicle patrol, emergency notification system, self-defense education, and security escort services. There are shuttle buses, emergency telephones, lighted pathways/sidewalks, and controlled access to dorms/residences.

REQUIREMENTS: The SAT or ACT is required. Students must have a high school diploma or GED. A general college-preparatory high school curriculum is recommended, including 4 units in English, 3 units in math, 2 units each in natural and social sciences, and foreign language.. Applicants must write an application essay and are urged to seek an interview. AP and CLEP credits are accepted. Important factors in the admissions decision are advanced placement or honors courses, leadership record, and recommendations by school officials. Student must complete a minimum of 120 semester hours, including 53 hours in general education core curriculum, plus 8 noncredit hours in Freshman Orientation and Crown Forum. An approved major concentration sequence and at least two years of coursework (a minimum of 60 semester hours) in residence at Morehouse College are required as well. **Procedure:** Freshmen are admitted fall and spring. Entrance exams should be taken by the fall of the senior year. There are early decision, early admissions, and deferred admissions plans. Early decision applications should be filed by November 1; regular applications, by February 15 for fall entry; and November 1 for spring entry, along with a $50 fee. Notification of early decision is sent December 15; regular decision, March 15. 499 early decision candidates were accepted for the 2016-2017 class. 117 applicants were on the 2016 waiting list; 76 were admitted. Applications are accepted on-line. **Transfer Students:** 63 transfer students enrolled in 2015-2016. Transfer applicants must have at least a 2.5 GPA and a minimum of 26 semester hours of credit. Students may enroll in the fall and spring. 60 of 120 credits required for the bachelor's degree must be completed at Morehouse. **International Students:** There are 34 international students enrolled. The school actively recruits these students. They must take the TOEFL with a minimum score of 78 on the Internet-based version (iBT). They must also take the SAT or ACT.

ADMISSIONS: 66% of the 2016-2017 applicants were accepted. The SAT scores for the 2016-2017 freshman class were: Critical Reading-- 55% below 500, 35% between 500 and 599, 9% between 600 and 699, and 2% between 700 and 800. Math-- 55% below 500, 34% between 500 and 599, 10% between 600 and 699, and 1% between 700 and 800. Writing-- 63% below 500, 30% between 500 and 599, and 7% between 600 and 699. The ACT scores were 19% between 12 and 17, 51% between 18 and 23, 24% between 24 and 29, and 6% above 30. 29% of the current freshmen were in the top fifth of their class; 58% were in the top two fifths. 1 freshman graduated first in the class. **Admissions Contact:** Darryl Isom, Director of Admissions and Recruitment. Email: *admissions@morehouse.edu* Web: *www.morehouse.edu*

FINANCIAL AID: In 2016-2017, 97% of all full-time freshmen and 91% of continuing full-time students received some form of financial aid.

90% of all full-time freshmen and 84% of continuing full-time students received need-based aid. The average freshman award was $21,078. Need-based scholarships or need-based grants averaged $13,233 ($47,952 maximum); need-based self-help aid (loans and jobs) averaged $3,379 ($13,000 maximum); non-need-based athletic scholarships averaged $897 ($41,647 maximum); and other non-need-based awards and non-need-based scholarships averaged $3,569 ($44,806 maximum). The average financial indebtedness of the 2016 graduate was $24,818. Morehouse is a member of CSS. The college's own financial statement is required. The FAFSA code is 001582. The priority date for freshman financial aid applications for fall entry is Febuary 15.

OGLETHORPE UNIVERSITY B-2
www.oglethorpe.edu

Atlanta, GA 30319 **(404) 364-8307** **(800) 428-8491**

Fax: (404) 364-8500 **Email: admission@oglethorpe.edu**

Full-time: 455 men, 612 women	**Faculty:** 60
Part-time: 57 men, 60 women	**Ph.D.s:** n/av
Graduate: n/av	**Student/Faculty:** n/av
Year: semesters, summer session	**Tuition:** $32,500
Room & Board: $11,700	**Freshman Class:** 2768 applied, 2172 accepted, 277 enrolled
SAT CR/M/W: 570/550/550 **ACT:** 24	**CEEB CODE:** 5521
Application Deadline: open	**COMPETITIVE+**

Oglethorpe University, founded in 1835, is an independent institution offering programs in the liberal arts and science, business, and preprofessional studies. The figures in the above capsule and in this profile are approximate. There are 2 undergraduate schools. The 102-acre campus is in a suburban area 10 miles northeast of downtown Atlanta. Including any residence halls, there are 25 buildings.

STUDENT LIFE: 74% of undergraduates are from Georgia. Others are from 33 states, 36 foreign countries, and Canada. 74% are from public schools. 6% are Foreign; 4% Asian American; 34% White; 3% two or more races; 25% race unknown; 18% African American; 10% Hispanic. **Female To Male Ratio:** 1.3:1. The average age of freshmen is 18; all undergraduates, 21. 28% do not continue beyond their first year; 55% remain to graduate. **Housing:** 803 students can be accommodated in college housing, which includes single-sex and coed dorms. In addition, there are fraternity houses and sorority houses. On-campus housing is guaranteed for the freshman year only, and is available on a first-come, first-served basis. Priority is given to out-of-town students. 65% of students live on campus; of those, 75% remain on campus on weekends. All students may keep cars.

FACULTY/CLASSROOMS: 58% of faculty are male; 42% are female. No introductory courses are taught by graduate students. The average class size in an introductory lecture is 20; in a laboratory is 18; and in a regular course is 15.

PROGRAMS OF STUDY: Oglethorpe confers B.A., B.S., B.A.L.S. and B.B.A. degrees. Bachelor's degrees are awarded in BIOLOGICAL SCIENCE (biology/biological science), BUSINESS (accounting and business administration and management), COMMUNICATIONS AND THE ARTS (art, art history and appreciation, communications, English, French, and Spanish), COMPUTER AND PHYSICAL SCIENCE (chemistry, mathematics, and physics), SOCIAL SCIENCE (American studies, behavioral science, biopsychology, economics, history, international studies, philosophy, political science/government, psychology, social work, and sociology). Biology, business, and pyschology are the strongest academically. Business administration, biology, communications, and rhetoric have the largest enrollments.

ACTIVITIES: 26% of men belong to 5 national fraternities; 22% of women belong to 1 local and 4 national sororities. There are 51 groups on campus, including art, cheerleading, choir, chorale, chorus, computers, dance, drama, ethnic, honors, international, LGBT, literary magazine, newspaper, orchestra, pep band, photography, political, professional, radio and TV, religious, social, social service, student government, and yearbook. Popular campus events include Oglethorpe Day, and Liberal Arts Symposium. **Sports:** There are 8 intercollegiate sports for men and 8 for women, and 6 intramural sports for men and 6 for women. Facilities include a field house and recreation center housing basketball and volleyball courts, a running track, handball courts, and a weight room. Outdoor facilities include 6 tennis courts, an all-weather track, a sand volleyball court, and soccer, baseball, and intramural fields. **Graduates:** From July 1, 2015 to June 30, 2016, 154 bachelor's degrees were awarded. The most popular majors were business and accounting (18%), English and communications (14%), and social sciences (14%).

SERVICES: Counseling and information services are available, as is tutoring in most subjects, including all core (general education) courses, English, writing, accounting, and math. **Library/Resources:** The library contains 157,000 volumes, 4,189 microform items, and 6,786 audio/video tapes/CDs/DVDs, and subscribes to 775 periodicals including electronic. Computerized library services include interlibrary loans, database searching, Internet access, and Wi-Fi capability. Special learning facilities include an art gallery, radio station, Atlanta Laboratory for Learning, which includes the Center for Civic Engagement, Global Education Opportunities, and Professional Development. Additionally, Oglethorpe has an in-residence, professional theatre program. **Physically Challenged Students:** 80% of the campus is accessible. Facilities include wheelchair ramps, elevators, special parking, specially equipped restrooms, special class scheduling, lowered drinking fountains, and special housing. **Special:** Oglethorpe offers co-op programs in all majors, cross-registration through the Atlanta Regional Consortium for Higher Education, international exchange agreements with several universities in Europe, Asia, and South America, and other study-abroad options. Internships are available in all areas of study for up to 15 credit hours for upperclassmen with a minimum 2.8 GPA, and a Washington semester offers internships with Georgia senators and others. There is a 3-2 engineering program with Georgia Institute of Technology, the Universities of Florida and Southern California, and Auburn University. Accelerated degrees, dual majors, student-designed majors, federal work-study programs, and nondegree study are offered. There are 7 national honor societies, a freshman honors program, and 99 departmental honors programs. **Visiting:** There are regularly scheduled orientations for prospective students, including placement tests, class registration, an activities fair, and group activities. There are guides for informal visits, visitors may sit in on classes, and stay overnight. To schedule a visit, contact the Admissions Office at admissions@oglethorpe.edu. **Campus Safety and Security:** Measures include 24-hour foot and vehicle patrol, emergency notification system, self-defense education, and security escort services. There are lighted pathways/sidewalks, and controlled access to dorms/residences, and an ID card-swipe system.

REQUIREMENTS: The SAT or ACT is required. Students should graduate from an accredited high school or have a GED certificate. They should have completed 4 courses in English, 3 each in science and social studies, and a math sequence of algebra I and II and geometry. A counselor's or teacher's recommendation is required, and an essay is required for a scholarship. An interview is recommended. AP and CLEP credits are accepted. Important factors in the admissions decision are recommendations by school officials, extracurricular activities record, and advanced placement or honors courses. To graduate with a B.A. or B.S., all students must complete at least 128 credit hours (120 for B.B.A. and B.A.L.S.). They must fulfill a major as well as complete the core curriculum and achieve a minimum GPA of 2.0. The core curriculum is a unique 4-year sequence of related interdisciplinary courses, 1 per semester. All freshman must complete the first-year experience program. **Procedure:** Freshmen are admitted to all sessions. Entrance exams should be taken late in the junior year or early in the senior year. There are early decision, early admissions, deferred admissions, and rolling admissions plans. Check with the school for current application deadlines. The application fee is $50. Notification is sent on a rolling basis. Applications are accepted on-line. **Transfer Students:** 42 transfer students enrolled in 2015-2016. Applicants who have completed less than a full year of college work must take the SAT or ACT. All transfers must be in good academic standing with a minimum GPA of 2.5. An interview is recommended. 64 of 128 credits required for the bachelor's degree must be completed at Oglethorpe. **International Students:** There are 66 international students enrolled. The school actively recruits these students. They must take the TOEFL with a minimum score of 550 on the paper-based TOEFL (PBT), or demonstrate proficiency in English by other means. They must also take the SAT or ACT.

ADMISSIONS: 78% of the 2016-2017 applicants were accepted. The SAT scores for the 2016-2017 freshman class were: Critical Reading-- 8% below 500, 51% between 500 and 599, 35% between 600 and 699, and 6% between 700 and 800. Math-- 20% below 500, 52% between 500 and 599, 23% between 600 and 699, and 4% between 700 and 800. Writing--

24% below 500, 49% between 500 and 599, 24% between 600 and 699, and 3% between 700 and 800. The ACT scores were 12% below 12, 30% between 12 and 17, 25% between 18 and 23, 14% between 24 and 29, and 19% above 30. 45% of the current freshmen were in the top fifth of their class; 78% were in the top two fifths. **Admissions Contact:** Lucy Leusch, Vice President for Enrollment. Email: *admission@oglethorpe.edu* Web: *www.oglethorpe.edu*

FINANCIAL AID: In 2016-2017, 98% of all full-time freshmen and 97% of continuing full-time students received some form of financial aid. 73% of all full-time freshmen and 71% of continuing full-time students received need-based aid. The average freshman award was $33,046. Need-based scholarships or need-based grants averaged $7,062; need-based self-help aid (loans and jobs) averaged $3,062; other non-need-based awards and non-need-based scholarships averaged $20,887; and $2,034 from other forms of aid. 12% of undergraduate students work part-time. Average annual earnings from campus work are $1750. The average financial indebtedness of the 2016 graduate was $27,650. Oglethorpe is a member of CSS. The FAFSA code is 001586. The priority date for freshman financial aid applications for fall entry is February 15.

PAINE COLLEGE *(The complete profile is made available exclusively on our website, www.barronspac.com)*

PIEDMONT COLLEGE — C-1

www.piedmont.edu

Demorest, GA 30535	**(706) 778-3000** **(800) 277-7020**
Fax: (706) 776-6635	**Email: bboonstra@piedmont.edu**
Full-time: 438 men, 739 women	**Faculty:** n/av
Part-time: 33 men, 85 women	**Ph.D.s:** 74%
Graduate: 210 men, 761 women	**Student/Faculty:** 11 to 1
Year: semesters, summer session	**Tuition:** $23,112
Room & Board: $9400	**Freshman Class:** 1337 applied, 647 accepted, 274 enrolled
SAT CR/M: required **ACT:** required	**CEEB CODE:** 5537
Application Deadline: August 1	**COMPETITIVE**

Piedmont College is an independent, comprehensive, co-educational liberal arts college that offers bachelors, masters and doctoral degrees. With campuses in Demorest and Athens, GA, students are challenged to immerse themselves in discovery, analysis, and communication. The college maintains affiliation with the National Association of Congregational Christian Churches and United Church of Christ. There are 4 undergraduate schools and 2 graduate schools. In addition to regional accreditation, Piedmont College has baccalaureate program accreditation with ACBSP and NLN. The 186-acre campus is in a small town 75 miles northeast of Atlanta. Including any residence halls, there are 35 buildings.

STUDENT LIFE: 92% of undergraduates are from Georgia. Others are from 21 states, and 4 foreign countries. 9% are African American; 7% Hispanic; 69% White; 3% two or more races; 2% Asian American; 10% race unknown. **Female To Male Ratio:** 2.3:1. The average age of freshmen is 18; all undergraduates, 23. 32% do not continue beyond their first year; 50% remain to graduate. **Housing:** 705 students can be accommodated in college housing, which includes single-sex and coed dorms and on-campus apartments. On-campus housing is guaranteed for all 4 years, and is available on a first-come, and first-served basis. 69% of students live on campus; of those, 40% remain on campus on weekends. Alcohol is not permitted. All students may keep cars.

FACULTY/CLASSROOMS: 46% of faculty are male; 54% are female. No introductory courses are taught by graduate students. The average class size in a regular course is 12.

PROGRAMS OF STUDY: Piedmont College confers B.A., B.S., B.F.A., and B.S.N. degrees. Master's and doctoral degrees are also awarded. Bachelor's degrees are awarded in AGRICULTURE (environmental studies), BIOLOGICAL SCIENCE (biology/biological science, forensic science, and nutritional sciences), BUSINESS (business administration and management), COMMUNICATIONS AND THE ARTS (art, arts administration/management, communications, dramatic arts, English, fine arts, music, musical theater, performing arts, Spanish, theatre arts, and theater design), COMPUTER AND PHYSICAL SCIENCE (applied mathematics, applied physics, chemistry, mathematics, physics, and science), EDUCATION (art education, athletic training, early childhood education, education, English education, mathematics education, middle school education, music education, science education, secondary education, social science education, social studies education, and special education), ENGINEERING AND ENVIRONMENTAL DESIGN (environmental science), HEALTH PROFESSIONS (cardiac sonography, exercise science, nursing, and nutrition and wellness), SOCIAL SCIENCE (criminal justice, history, interdisciplinary studies, philosophy, political science/government, psychology, religion, social science, and sociology). Nursing, education, and social sciences are the strongest academically. Education, nursing, and business administration have the largest enrollments.

ACTIVITIES: There are no fraternities or sororities. There are 32 groups on campus, including art, cheerleading, choir, chorale, chorus, dance, debate, drama, environmental, film, honors, jazz band, literary magazine, musical theater, newspaper, pep band, photography, professional, radio and TV, religious, social, social service, student government, and yearbook. Popular campus events include Arrendale Amphitheatre Festivals, Bands, Athletic events, Music Recitals & Performances, and Art Museum Receptions. **Sports:** There are 9 intercollegiate sports for men and 10 for women, and 5 intramural sports for men and 5 for women. Facilities include an athletic center, 8 tennis courts, beach volleyball courts, regulation baseball, softball, soccer and lacrosse fields, indoor training facility for baseball and softball, fitness center, indoor walking track & intramural basketball court, and a climbing wall. **Graduates:** From July 1, 2015 to June 30, 2016, 277 bachelor's degrees were awarded. The most popular majors were nursing (31%), education (14%), and business (13%). In an average class, 2% graduate in 3 years or less, 45% graduate in 4 years or less, 49% graduate in 5 years or less, and 50% graduate in 6 years or less.

SERVICES: Counseling and information services are available, as is tutoring in most subjects. The Learning Center offers academic support, including accounting, foreign languages, math, science, and writing. **Library/Resources:** The 2 libraries contain 516,373 volumes, and 73,670 audio/video tapes/CDs/DVDs, and subscribe to 24,272 periodicals including electronic. Computerized library services include interlibrary loans, database searching, Internet access, and Wi-Fi capability. Special learning facilities include an art gallery, radio station, and TV station. **Physically Challenged Students:** 85% of the campus is accessible. Facilities include wheelchair ramps, elevators, special parking, specially equipped restrooms, special class scheduling, and special housing. **Special:** Piedmont College assists students with internships in business, psychology, education, art management, criminal justice, sociology, political science and other areas. Study abroad and interdisciplinary majors are available. There are 4 national honor societies and 1 departmental honors program. **Visiting:** There are regularly scheduled orientations for prospective students, which include a campus tour, introduction to student activities, academic overview, admissions counseling, resident orientation, and a financial aid presentation. There are guides for informal visits, visitors may sit in on classes, and stay overnight. To schedule a visit, contact the Undergraduate Admissions Office. **Campus Safety and Security:** Measures include 24-hour foot and vehicle patrol, emergency notification system, self-defense education, and security escort services. There are shuttle buses, emergency telephones, lighted pathways/sidewalks, controlled access to dorms/residences, and patrolls by the local police department. There are student security hosts in each residence hall.

REQUIREMENTS: The SAT is required. Applicants must be graduates of an accredited secondary school or have a GED certificate. Students must have completed a minimum of 23 academic units. A portfolio is required for art scholarship applicants and an audition for music scholarship applicants. An interview is recommended for all students. AP and CLEP credits are accepted. To graduate with a bachelor's degree a minimum of 120 credit hours is required. Students must complete credit hours for their major, including general education coursework in the humanities, fine arts, math, natural sciences, social sciences, and computer science. **Procedure:** Freshmen are admitted to all sessions. There are deferred admissions and rolling admissions plans. Applications should be filed by August 1 for fall entry; January 1 for spring entry; and May 1 for summer entry. Applications are accepted on-line. **Transfer Students:** 112 transfer students enrolled in 2015-2016. Applicants must have a GPA of 2.0 at each institution attended. An interview is recommended. 30 of 120 credits required for the bachelor's degree must be completed at Piedmont College. **International Students:** There are 12 international students enrolled. They must take the TOEFL with a minimum score of 550 on the paper-based TOEFL (PBT) or 80 on the Internet-based version (iBT). They must also take the SAT or ACT.

Admissions Contact: Brenda Boonstra, Director of Undergraduate Admissions. Email: *bboonstra@piedmont.edu* Web: *www.piedmont.edu*

FINANCIAL AID: In 2016-2017, 100% of all full-time freshmen and 98% of continuing full-time students received some form of financial aid. 66% of all full-time freshmen and 73% of continuing full-time students received need-based aid. The average freshman award was $24,080. Need-based scholarships or need-based grants averaged $5,462 ($17,207 maximum); need-based self-help aid (loans and jobs) averaged $3,281 ($5,256 maximum); other non-need-based awards and non-need-based scholarships averaged $14,429 ($29,836 maximum); and $6,960 from other forms of aid. 32% of undergraduate students work part-time. Average annual earnings from campus work are $2052. The average financial indebtedness of the 2016 graduate was $24,651. The state aid form is required. The FAFSA code is 001588. Check with the school for current application deadlines.

REINHARDT UNIVERSITY — B-1

www.reinhardt.edu

Waleska, GA 30183	**(770) 720-5526** **1-87REINHARDT**
Fax: (770) 720-5899	**Email: admissions@reinhardt.edu**
Full-time: 390 men, 575 women	**Faculty:** n/av
Part-time: 65 men, 90 women	**Ph.D.s:** n/av
Graduate: n/av	**Student/Faculty:** n/av
Year: semesters, summer session	**Tuition:** $21,544
Room & Board: $7948	**Freshman Class:** n/av
SAT or ACT: required	**CEEB CODE:** 5568
Application Deadline: August 15	**COMPETITIVE**

Reinhardt University, founded in 1883, is a private institution affiliated with the Methodist Church and offering undergraduate degrees. The figures in the above capsule and in this profile are approximate. There are 4 undergraduate schools. In addition to regional accreditation, Reinhardt has baccalaureate program accreditation with SACS. The 600-acre campus is in a small town 40 miles north of Atlanta. Including any residence halls, there are 31 buildings.

STUDENT LIFE: 98% of undergraduates are from Georgia. Others are from 4 states, 6 foreign countries, and Canada. 90% are from public schools. 82% are White; 8% African American; 2% Hispanic; 2% Foreign; 1% Asian American; 1% American Indian/Alaska Native. 70% are Protestant; 23% claim no religious affiliation. **Female To Male Ratio:** 1.5:1. The average age of freshmen is 18; all undergraduates, 23. 36% do not continue beyond their first year; 50% remain to graduate. **Housing:** 404 students can be accommodated in college housing, which includes single-sex dorms. On-campus housing is guaranteed for all 4 years. 64% of students commute. Alcohol is not permitted. All students may keep cars.

FACULTY/CLASSROOMS: 45% of faculty are male; 55% are female. All teach undergraduates. No introductory courses are taught by graduate students. The average class size in an introductory lecture is 17; in a laboratory is 17; and in a regular course is 17.

PROGRAMS OF STUDY: Reinhardt confers B.A., B.S., B.F.A., and B.S.B.A. degrees. Associate degrees are also awarded. Bachelor's degrees are awarded in BIOLOGICAL SCIENCE (biology/biological science), BUSINESS (business administration and management), COMMUNICATIONS AND THE ARTS (communications), SOCIAL SCIENCE (liberal arts/general studies). Business and liberal studies have the largest enrollments.

ACTIVITIES: There are no fraternities or sororities. There are 14 groups on campus, including cheerleading, honors, newspaper, professional, radio and TV, religious, social, social service, student government, and yearbook. Popular campus events include Spring Day, Spring Formal and Diversity Days. **Sports:** There are 5 intercollegiate sports for men and 4 for women, and 4 intramural sports for men and 4 for women. Facilities include jogging trails, outdoor volleyball, golf, cross-country, tennis and basketball courts, soccer and softball fields, a pool, weight room, bowling alley, and racquetball courts.

SERVICES: Counseling and information services are available, as is tutoring in every subject. **Library/Resources:** The library contains 48,000 volumes, 1,983 microform items, and 3,598 audio/video tapes/CDs/DVDs, and subscribes to 315 periodicals including electronic. Computerized library services include interlibrary loans, database searching, and Internet access. Special learning facilities include an art gallery, natural history museum, radio station, and TV station. **Physically Challenged Students:** 90% of the campus is accessible. Facilities include wheelchair ramps, elevators, special parking, specially equipped restrooms, special class scheduling, and lowered drinking fountains. **Special:** Internships, study abroad, and work-study programs are available. There is an accelerated degree program in organizational leadership. There is 1 national honor society and a freshman honors program. **Visiting:** There are regularly scheduled orientations for prospective students. There are guides for informal visits and visitors may sit in on classes. To schedule a visit, contact the Admissions Office. **Campus Safety and Security:** Measures include 24-hour foot and vehicle patrol and self-defense education. There are lighted pathways/sidewalks.

REQUIREMENTS: The SAT or ACT is required. The GED is accepted, and a placement test may be required. AP and CLEP credits are accepted. Important factors in the admissions decision are recommendations by alumni, recommendations by school officials, and parents or siblings attended your school. To graduate, students must have a core curriculum in the humanities, math and science, social science, language, phys ed, and wellness. A total of 120 semester hours is required, including 65 in the major. A 2.0 GPA must be maintained. **Procedure:** Freshmen are admitted to all sessions. Entrance exams should be taken before acceptance. There are early admissions and rolling admissions plans. Application deadlines are open. Application fee is $25. Applications are accepted on-line. **Transfer Students:** A GPA of 2.0 or better may be considered for transfer applicants. 40 of 120 credits required for the bachelor's degree must be completed at Reinhardt. **International Students:** They must take the TOEFL.

Admissions Contact: Lacy Satterfield, Director of Admissions. Email: *admissions@reinhardt.edu* Web: *www.reinhardt.edu*

FINANCIAL AID: Reinhardt is a member of CSS. The FAFSA code is 001589. Check with the school for current application deadlines.

SAVANNAH COLLEGE OF ART AND DESIGN — E-4

www.scad.edu

Savannah, GA 31401	**(912) 525-5100** **(800) 869-7223**
Fax: (912) 525-5986	**Email: admission@scad.edu**
Full-time: 2886 men, 5939 women	**Faculty:** 532
Part-time: 636 men, 1112 women	**Ph.D.s:** 80%
Graduate: 864 men, 1514 women	**Student/Faculty:** 16 to 1
Year: quarters, summer session	**Tuition:** $35,690
Room & Board: $13,905	**Freshman Class:** n/av
SAT CR/M/W: required **ACT:** required	**CEEB CODE:** 5631
Application Deadline: open	**COMPETITIVE**

The Savannah College of Art and Design is a private, nonprofit, accredited institution conferring bachelor's and master's degrees at distinctive locations and online to prepare talented students for professional careers. SCAD offers degrees in over 40 majors, as well as minors in more than 60 disciplines across its locations in Savannah and Atlanta, Georgia, Hong Kong, Lacoste, France, and online through SCAD eLearning. SCAD demonstrates an exceptional education and unparalleled career preparation. Each student is nurtured and motivated by a faculty of nearly 700 professors with extraordinary academic credentials and valuable professional experience. These professors emphasize learning through individual attention in an inspiring university environment. The innovative SCAD curriculum is enhanced by advanced, professional-level technology, equipment, and learning resources, and has garnered acclaim from respected organizations and publications. There are 9 undergraduate schools and 8 graduate schools. In addition to regional accreditation, SCAD has baccalaureate program accreditation with NAAB and CIDA. The campus is in an urban area in Savannah, Georgia, on the southeast coast of Georgia, midway between Charleston, SC, and Jacksonville, FL.

STUDENT LIFE: 79% of undergraduates are from out of state, mostly the South. Students are from 50 states, 105 foreign countries, and

Canada. 52% are White; 21% Foreign; 10% African American; 8% Hispanic; 5% Asian American; 3% race unknown; 1% American Indian/Alaska Native; 1% two or more races. **Female To Male Ratio:** 2.0:1. The average age of freshmen is 18; all undergraduates, 21. **Housing:** College-sponsored housing includes single-sex, coed dorms, on-campus apartments, and freshmen-only buildings. On-campus housing is available on a first-come, first-served basis, and is available on a lottery system for upperclassmen. 58% of students commute. Alcohol is not permitted. Some may keep cars.

FACULTY/CLASSROOMS: 57% of faculty are male; 43% are female. All teach undergraduates. No introductory courses are taught by graduate students.

PROGRAMS OF STUDY: SCAD confers B.A. and B.F.A. degrees. Master's degrees are also awarded. Bachelor's degrees are awarded in AGRICULTURE (equine science), BUSINESS (fashion merchandising), COMMUNICATIONS AND THE ARTS (advertising, animation, art, art history and appreciation, audio technology, broadcasting, communications, design, fiber/textiles/weaving, film arts, graphic design, historic preservation, illustration, industrial design, media arts, metal/jewelry, painting, performing arts, photography, printmaking, sculpture, visual effects, and writing), COMPUTER AND PHYSICAL SCIENCE (digital arts/technology), ENGINEERING AND ENVIRONMENTAL DESIGN (architectural history, architecture, computer graphics, furniture design, and interior design), SOCIAL SCIENCE (fashion design and technology). Animation, graphic design, and fashion have the largest enrollments.

ACTIVITIES: There are no fraternities or sororities. Groups on campus include art, communications, computers, dance, drama, environmental, ethnic, film, honors, international, LGBT, literary magazine, musical theater, newspaper, photography, professional, radio and TV, religious, and social service. Popular campus events include Savannah Film Festival, Fashion Show, deFINE ART, SCAD Style, Sidewalk Arts Festival, Sand Arts Festival, and Alumni Concert. **Sports:** There are 11 intercollegiate sports for men and 11 for women, and 11 intramural sports for men and 11 for women. Facilities include Club SCAD, Turner fitness center, Atlanta fitness center, SCAD Studio, Waranch Equestrian center and athletic fields. **Graduates:** From July 1, 2015 to June 30, 2016, 1867 bachelor's degrees were awarded. The most popular majors were animation (10%), graphic design (9%), and fashion marketing and design (7%). 588 companies recruited on campus in 2015-2016. In an average class, 48% graduate in 4 years or less, 64% graduate in 5 years or less, and 67% graduate in 6 years or less.

SERVICES: Counseling and information services are available, as is tutoring in most subjects. There is a sign language interpreter for hearing-impaired students, a coordinator of disability services, writing center, drawing center, and learning resource hive. **Library/Resources:** The 4 libraries contain 260,652 volumes, 6,988 microform items, and 632,567 audio/video tapes/CDs/DVDs, and subscribe to 52,780 periodicals including electronic. Computerized library services include interlibrary loans, database searching, Internet access, and Wi-Fi capability. Special learning facilities include an art gallery, radio station, TV station, an international student center, writing center, SCAD Museum of Art, and SCAD FASH Museum of Fashion and Film. **Physically Challenged Students:** Facilities include wheelchair ramps, elevators, special parking, specially equipped restrooms, special class scheduling, lowered drinking fountains, and lowered telephones. Facilities vary by building and location. Individual situations are accommodated. **Special:** The college offers study abroad in France and Hong Kong, cross-registration with Atlanta Regional Council of Higher Education, on-campus work-study programs, dual majors in all disciplines, and internships with artists, designers, museums, agencies, and architectural firms in the United States and abroad. **Visiting:** There are regularly scheduled orientations for prospective students consisting of tours, visits with faculty from areas of interest, portfolio reviews, financial aid counseling, admissions counseling, and workshops. There are guides for informal visits and visitors may sit in on classes. To schedule a visit, contact the Admission Office. **Campus Safety and Security:** Measures include 24-hour foot and vehicle patrol, emergency notification system, self-defense education, and security escort services. There are shuttle buses, emergency telephones, lighted pathways/sidewalks, controlled access to dorms/residences, and video surveillance cameras.

REQUIREMENTS: The SAT or ACT is required. Students must submit a completed application and high school transcript indicating successful completion. Preference is given to students with a 3.0 GPA or above and to students whose SAT or ACT scores are above the national average (B.F.A. Architecture candidates with math scores below 540 or 23, respectively, may be admitted to architecture on a conditional basis); 3 letters of recommendation and a statement of purpose are required. An interview is recommended, and a portfolio is encouraged. AP and CLEP credits are accepted. Important factors in the admissions decision are recommendations by school officials, evidence of special talent, and leadership record. Students must earn 180 quarter hours of appropriate credit in an approved program of study. The final 45 hours of any degree program must be completed at SCAD (may include eLearning and study abroad). In order to graduate, students must have a cumulative grade point average of 2.0 or higher, as well as a 3.0 or higher in their major or concentration. **Procedure:** Freshmen are admitted to all sessions. Entrance exams should be taken by January of the senior year. There are deferred admissions and rolling admissions plans. Application deadlines are open. Application fee is $40. Notification is sent on a rolling basis. Applications are accepted on-line. **Transfer Students:** 647 transfer students enrolled in 2015-2016. Transfer students must submit a completed application and college transcripts. (High school transcripts may be required if the number of college credits is insufficient for evaluating performance.) An official report of SAT or ACT scores (architecture majors only) and 3 recommendations are required. A portfolio and an interview are encouraged but not required. 45 of 180 credits required for the bachelor's degree must be completed at SCAD. **International Students:** There are 1854 international students enrolled. The school actively recruits these students. They must take the TOEFL with a minimum score of 550 on the paper-based TOEFL (PBT) or 85 on the Internet-based version (iBT). They must also take the SAT or ACT.

Admissions Contact: Jenny Jaquillard, Exec Director of Admission, Recruitment. Email: *admission@scad.edu* Web: *www.scad.edu*

FINANCIAL AID: SCAD is a member of CSS. The state aid form and the college's own financial statement are required. The FAFSA code is 015022. The deadline for filing freshman financial aid applications for fall entry is August 31.

SAVANNAH STATE UNIVERSITY — E-4

www.savannahstate.edu

Savannah, GA 31404	**(912) 358-4338** **(800) 788-0478**
Fax: (912) 358-3171	**Email: admissions@savannahstate.edu**
Full-time: 1727 men, 2077 women	**Faculty:** n/av
Part-time: 277 men, 332 women	**Ph.D.s:** n/av
Graduate: 38 men, 131 women	**Student/Faculty:** 23 to 1
Year: semesters, summer session	**Tuition:** $8381
Room & Board: $7250	**Freshman Class:** 3374 applied, 2134 accepted, 1104 enrolled
SAT or ACT: required	**CEEB CODE:** 5609
Application Deadline: July 15	**COMPETITIVE**

Savannah State University, founded in 1890, is a liberal arts institution that is part of the University System of Georgia. Undergraduate and graduate degrees are offered through the colleges of business, liberal arts and social sciences, and sciences and technology. Preprofessional programs are available. The figures in the above capsule and in this profile are approximate. There are 3 undergraduate schools and 5 graduate schools. In addition to regional accreditation, Savannah State has baccalaureate program accreditation with ABET, CSWE, and NCATE. The 165-acre campus is in a suburban area 265 miles southeast of Atlanta. Including any residence halls, there are 45 buildings.

STUDENT LIFE: Students are from 38 states, 33 foreign countries, and Canada. 87% are African American; 6% White; 2% Hispanic; 1% Foreign. **Female To Male Ratio:** 1.2:1. The average age of freshmen is 19; all undergraduates, 21. 28% do not continue beyond their first year; 32% remain to graduate. **Housing:** 2745 students can be accommodated in college housing, which includes single-sex dorms, on-campus apartments, and married student housing. On-campus housing is available on a first-come, and first-served basis. Alcohol is not permitted. All students may keep cars.

FACULTY/CLASSROOMS: 54% of faculty are male; 46% are female. No introductory courses are taught by graduate students.

PROGRAMS OF STUDY: Savannah State confers B.A., B.S., B.B.A. and B.S.W. degrees. Associate and master's degrees are also awarded. Bachelor's degrees are awarded in BIOLOGICAL SCIENCE (biology/biological science and marine biology), BUSINESS (accounting, business administration and management, management information systems, and marketing/retailing/merchandising), COMMUNICATIONS AND THE ARTS (communications, English, and visual and performing arts), COMPUTER AND PHYSICAL SCIENCE (chemistry, computer science, and mathematics), ENGINEERING AND ENVIRONMENTAL DESIGN (civil engineering, electrical/electronics engineering technology, and environmental science), SOCIAL SCIENCE (African studies, behavioral science, criminal justice, history, homeland security, political science/government, social work, and sociology). Marine science, social work, and computer information systems are the strongest academically. Biology, mass communications, and management have the largest enrollments.

ACTIVITIES: 2% of men belong to 7 national fraternities; 3% of women belong to 6 national sororities. Groups on campus include art, band, cheerleading, choir, chorale, computers, dance, debate, drama, drill team, ethnic, international, jazz band, literary magazine, marching band, newspaper, political, professional, radio and TV, religious, and student government. Popular campus events include Drama Presentations, a Fine Arts Festival, Christmas Concert, and Spring Concerts. **Sports:** There are 5 intercollegiate sports for men and 4 for women, and 1 intramural sports for men. Facilities include a student center, a gym complex, a swimming pool, a stadium, a field house, a tennis court, a track, and a field. **Graduates:** From July 1, 2015 to June 30, 2016, 395 bachelor's degrees were awarded. The most popular majors were mass communications (10%), business management (10%), and criminal justice (8%). In an average class, 32% graduate in 6 years or less.

SERVICES: Counseling and information services are available, as is tutoring in every subject. There is remedial math, reading, and writing. **Library/Resources:** The library contains 209,714 volumes, 586,633 microform items, and 3,725 audio/video tapes/CDs/DVDs, and subscribes to 360 periodicals including electronic. Computerized library services include interlibrary loans, database searching, and Internet access. Special learning facilities include a radio station, an arts center, and marine science lab. **Physically Challenged Students:** Facilities include wheelchair ramps, elevators, special parking, specially equipped restrooms, lowered drinking fountains, and special housing. **Special:** The college offers co-op programs, cross-registration with Armstrong Atlantic State University, study abroad, a dual-degree program with Georgia Institute of Technology, the Georgia Legislative Internship Program, and a variety of other internship programs across the curriculum, on- and off-campus work-study programs, correspondence study, credit for military experience, and non-degree study. There is a freshman honors program. **Visiting:** There are guides for informal visits and visitors may sit in on classes. To schedule a visit, contact the Office of Admissions. **Campus Safety and Security:** Measures include 24-hour foot and vehicle patrol, and emergency notification system. There are shuttle buses, emergency telephones, lighted pathways/sidewalks, and the campus police department is staffed with public safety officers, building attendants, security guards, safety inspectors, and telephone operators.

REQUIREMENTS: A minimum composite score of 830 on the SAT or 17 on the ACT is required. In addition, applicants must be graduates of an accredited secondary school. Students should have completed 4 units each of English, math, and science, 3 units of social science, and 2 units of 1 foreign language. A GPA of 2.0 is required. AP and CLEP credits are accepted. To graduate, all students must complete a minimum of 120 credit hours with satisfactory completion of the core curriculum requirements. Students must maintain a minimum 2.0 GPA. Exit competency exams and other requirements may be required. **Procedure:** Freshmen are admitted fall, spring, and summer. Entrance exams should be taken early in the senior year. There are early admissions and deferred admissions plans. Applications should be filed by July 15 for fall entry; November 15 for spring entry; and May 1 for summer entry, along with a $20 fee. Notification is sent on a rolling basis. Applications are accepted online. **Transfer Students:** Applicants with at least 45 quarter hours or 30 semester hours of core curriculum credit do not need to submit high school transcripts, but must have a 2.0 average. All transfers must submit college transcripts, standardized test scores, and proof of good standing at the previous institution. 30 of 120 credits required for the bachelor's degree must be completed at Savannah State. **International Students:** There are 50 international students enrolled. The school actively recruits these students. They must take the TOEFL with a minimum score of 530 on the paper-based TOEFL (PBT). They must also take the SAT or ACT and the college's own entrance exam or the Collegiate Placement Exams.

ADMISSIONS: 63% of the 2016-2017 applicants were accepted. **Admissions Contact:** Brian Dawsey, Director of Admissions. Email: *admissions@savannahstate.edu* Web: *www.savannahstate.edu*

FINANCIAL AID: The CSS/Profile, the college's own financial statement, and the Scholarship Application Form are required. The FAFSA code is 001590. The deadline for filing freshman financial aid applications for fall entry is July 15.

SHORTER UNIVERSITY *(The complete profile is made available exclusively on our website, www.barronspac.com)*

SOUTH UNIVERSITY *(The complete profile is made available exclusively on our website, www.barronspac.com)*

SPELMAN COLLEGE — B-2

www.spelman.edu

Atlanta, GA 30314	**(404) 681-3643** **(800) 982-2411**
Fax: (404) 215-7788	**Email: admiss@spelman.edu**
Full-time: 2203 women	**Faculty:** n/av
Part-time: 97 women	**Ph.D.s:** n/av
Graduate: n/av	**Student/Faculty:** 14 to 1
Year: semesters	**Tuition:** $26,388
Room & Board: $12,363	**Freshman Class:** 4534 applied, 1771 accepted, 531 enrolled
SAT: required **ACT:** 23	**CEEB CODE:** 5628
Application Deadline: February 1	**COMPETITIVE**

Spelman College, founded in 1881, is a private, nonsectarian, liberal arts college for black women. The figures in the above capsule and in this profile are approximate. There is 1 undergraduate school. In addition to regional accreditation, Spelman has baccalaureate program accreditation with NASM and NCATE. The 32-acre campus is in an urban area 3 miles southwest of downtown Atlanta. Including any residence halls, there are 24 buildings.

STUDENT LIFE: 71% of undergraduates are from out of state, mostly the South. Students are from 46 states, 21 foreign countries, and Canada. 86% are from public schools. 96% are African American. **Female To Male Ratio:** 127.8:1. The average age of freshmen is 18; all undergraduates, 20. 10% do not continue beyond their first year; 72% remain to graduate. **Housing:** 1169 students can be accommodated in college housing, which includes dorms. In addition, there are honors houses. On-campus housing is guaranteed for the freshman year only, is available on a first-come, first-served basis, and is available on a lottery system for upperclassmen. Priority is given to out-of-town students. 60% of students live on campus; of those, 67% remain on campus on weekends. Alcohol is not permitted. Upperclassmen may keep cars.

FACULTY/CLASSROOMS: 36% of faculty are male; 64% are female. No introductory courses are taught by graduate students.

PROGRAMS OF STUDY: Spelman confers B.A. and B.S. degrees. Bachelor's degrees are awarded in BIOLOGICAL SCIENCE (biochemistry and biology/biological science), COMMUNICATIONS AND THE ARTS (art, dramatic arts, English, fine arts, French, music, and Spanish), COMPUTER AND PHYSICAL SCIENCE (chemistry, computer science, mathematics, natural sciences, and physics), EDUCATION (art education), ENGINEERING AND ENVIRONMENTAL DESIGN (engineering), SOCIAL SCIENCE (anthropology, child psychology/development, economics, history, philosophy, political science/government, psychology, religion, sociology, and women's studies). Biology and engineering are the strongest academically. Psychology, biology, and English have the largest enrollments.

ACTIVITIES: There are no fraternities; 8% of women belong to 4 local and 4 national sororities. There are 60 groups on campus, including art, band, cheerleading, choir, chorus, communications, dance, drama, honors, international, jazz band, LGBT, literary magazine, musical theater, newspaper, political, religious, social, student government, and yearbook. Popular campus events include Founders Day, and Martin Luther King Jr.'s Birthday. **Sports:** There are 4 intercollegiate sports for women, and 6 intramural sports for women. Facilities include a gym, tennis courts, swimming pool, weight room, dance studios, and bowling lanes.

SERVICES: Counseling and information services are available, as is

tutoring in every subject. **Library/Resources:** The library contains 500,000 volumes, 385,538 microform items, and subscribes to 1,439 periodicals including electronic. Special learning facilities include an art gallery, a language lab, a media center, and music and art studios. **Physically Challenged Students:** 25% of the campus is accessible. Facilities include wheelchair ramps, elevators, special parking, and specially equipped restrooms. **Special:** Students may cross-register with Atlanta University Center member institutions. Spelman offers internships, study abroad in several countries, student-designed majors, work-study programs at the school, B.A.-B.S. degrees, and dual majors, as well as a 3-2 engineering degree with Georgia Tech, Rochester Institute of Technology, University of Alabama at Huntsville, Auburn and Boston Universities, and North Carolina Agricultural and Technical State University. The college grants credit for life experience and permits nondegree study. There are 9 national honor societies, Phi Beta Kappa, and a freshman honors program. **Visiting:** There are regularly scheduled orientations for prospective students, including a general information session and a campus tour. There are also high school senior days and junior days. There are guides for informal visits. To schedule a visit, contact the Admissions Office. **Campus Safety and Security:** Measures include 24-hour foot and vehicle patrol, self-defense education, and security escort services. There are shuttle buses, emergency telephones, and lighted pathways/sidewalks.

REQUIREMENTS: The SAT or ACT is required. Applicants should be high school graduates or have a GED certificate. Students should have earned at least 12 academic credits, including 4 in English, 2 each in foreign language, math (algebra and geometry), social studies, and science (including a lab science). Students with additional years in math, science, and language and with AP and honors courses are considered more competitive. An essay is required. An audition or portfolio is recommended for art majors. A GPA of 2.0 is required. AP and CLEP credits are accepted. Important factors in the admissions decision are advanced placement or honors courses, leadership record, and recommendations by school officials. To graduate, students must complete 120 semester hours, including at least 30 or more in the major, and maintain a GPA of 2.0. Core requirements include 8 credits of African studies, up to 8 of foreign language, 4 of international or women's studies, up to 4 each of English composition, computer literacy, and math, and 2 to 3 of phys ed, plus freshman orientation and sophmore assembly. Students also must complete 4 credits each of divisional requirements in social science, humanities, natural science, and fine arts. A reading course may be required based on the placement test scores. **Procedure:** Freshmen are admitted fall. Entrance exams should be taken by December of the senior year. There are early decision, early admissions, and deferred admissions plans. Early decision applications should be filed by November 15; regular applications, by February 1 for fall entry, along with a $35 fee. Notification of early decision is sent December 31; regular decision, April 1. 297 early decision candidates were accepted for the 2016-2017 class. **Transfer Students:** 47 transfer students enrolled in 2015-2016. A 3.0 GPA is recommended, with a minimum 2.0 required. Applicants must submit high school and college transcripts, as well as 2 recommendations from instructors at the last school attended. Students with fewer than 30 semester hours of credit must also submit SAT or ACT scores. 30 of 120 credits required for the bachelor's degree must be completed at Spelman. **International Students:** The school actively recruits these students. They must take the TOEFL. They must also take the SAT or ACT.

ADMISSIONS: 39% of the 2016-2017 applicants were accepted. 71% of the current freshmen were in the top fifth of their class; 91% were in the top two fifths. **Admissions Contact:** Tiffany Nelson, Director of Admissions. Email: *admiss@spelman.edu* Web: *www.spelman.edu*

FINANCIAL AID: In 2016-2017, 82% of all full-time freshmen received some form of financial aid. 82% of all full-time freshmen received need-based aid. 20% of undergraduate students work part-time. Average annual earnings from campus work are $900. The average financial indebtedness of the 2016 graduate was $18,000. Spelman is a member of CSS. The college's own financial statement is required. The FAFSA code is 001594. The deadline for filing freshman financial aid applications for fall entry is April 1.

THE ART INSTITUTE OF ATLANTA *(The complete profile is made available exclusively on our website, www.barronspac.com)*

THOMAS UNIVERSITY *(The complete profile is made available exclusively on our website, www.barronspac.com)*

TOCCOA FALLS COLLEGE C-1
www.tfc.edu

Toccoa Falls, GA 30598 **(706) 886-6831**

Fax: (706) 282-6012
Email: admission@tfc.edu
Full-time: 384 men, 392 women
Faculty: 49; IIB
Part-time: 51 men, 47 women
Ph.D.s: 55%
Graduate: n/av
Student/Faculty: 16 to 1
Year: 4-1-4, summer session
Tuition: $20,510
Room & Board: $7410
Freshman Class: 1008 applied, 556 accepted, 258 enrolled
SAT CR/M: 505/500 **ACT:** required
CEEB CODE: 5799
Application Deadline: August 1
COMPETITIVE

Toccoa Falls College is a private, interdenominational Christian college founded in 1907 that offers programs in Biblical studies, biology, business administration, counseling, Christian education, communication, education, history, theology, music, philosophy, science, youth ministries, and general studies. The figures in the above capsule and in this profile are approximate. There are 3 undergraduate schools. In addition to regional accreditation, TFC has baccalaureate program accreditation with NASM and ABHE. The 1100-acre campus is in a small town 90 miles northeast of Atlanta. Including any residence halls, there are 45 buildings.

STUDENT LIFE: 55% of undergraduates are from Georgia. Others are from 42 states, 27 foreign countries, and Canada. 61% are from public schools. 9% are Asian American; 83% White; 5% African American; 2% Hispanic; 1% Foreign. 100% are Protestant. **Female To Male Ratio:** 1.0:1. The average age of freshmen is 19; all undergraduates, 22. 32% do not continue beyond their first year; 47% remain to graduate. **Housing:** 616 students can be accommodated in college housing, which includes single-sex dorms, on-campus apartments, and married student housing. On-campus housing is guaranteed for all 4 years. 64% of students live on campus; of those, 50% remain on campus on weekends. Alcohol is not permitted. All students may keep cars.

FACULTY/CLASSROOMS: 75% of faculty are male; 25% are female. 94% teach undergraduates. No introductory courses are taught by graduate students. The average class size in an introductory lecture is 23; in a laboratory is 12; and in a regular course is 12.

PROGRAMS OF STUDY: TFC confers B.A., B.S., and B.M. degrees. Associate degrees are also awarded. Bachelor's degrees are awarded in BIOLOGICAL SCIENCE (biology/biological science), BUSINESS (business administration and management), COMMUNICATIONS AND THE ARTS (choral music, communications, English, music, and music performance), EDUCATION (early childhood education, middle school education, music education, recreation education, and science education), SOCIAL SCIENCE (biblical studies, Christian studies, counseling/psychology, crosscultural studies, history, ministries, pastoral studies, philosophy, and youth ministry). Counseling /psychology, cross-cultural studies, and early childhood education are the strongest academically.

ACTIVITIES: There are no fraternities or sororities. There are 11 groups on campus, including band, choir, chorus, drama, ethnic, international, jazz band, newspaper, orchestra, outdoor club, photography, radio and TV, religious, social, social service, and student government. Popular campus events include Spiritual Emphasis Week, Lecture Series, and World Outreach Conference. **Sports:** There are 5 intercollegiate sports for men and 5 for women, and 5 intramural sports for men and 5 for women. Facilities include a gymnasium with racquetball courts and a weight room, tennis courts, and soccer and baseball fields. **Graduates:** From July 1, 2015 to June 30, 2016, 185 bachelor's degrees were awarded. The most popular majors were counseling/psychology (18%), cross-cultural studies (13%), and early childhood education (8%). 75 companies recruited on campus in 2015-2016. In an average class, 1% graduate in 3 years or less, 43% graduate in 4 years or less, 47% graduate in 5 years or less.

SERVICES: Counseling and information services are available, as is tutoring in most subjects. **Library/Resources:** The library contains 151,427 volumes, 6,471 microform items, and 3,008 audio/video tapes/CDs/DVDs, and subscribes to 20,310 periodicals including electronic. Computerized library services include interlibrary loans, database searching, Internet access, and Wi-Fi capability. Special learning facilities include a natural history museum and radio station. **Physically Chal-**

lenged Students: 70% of the campus is accessible. Facilities include wheelchair ramps, elevators, special parking, specially equipped restrooms, special class scheduling, lowered drinking fountains, and special housing. **Special:** The college offers dual majors, and B.A.-B.S. degrees are available. An on-campus work-study program and internships for many majors are also provided. There are 2 national honor societies. **Visiting:** There are regularly scheduled orientations for prospective students, which include visits to the admissions counselor, school directors, and the financial aid office arranged 2 weeks in advance. There are guides for informal visits, visitors may sit in on classes, and stay overnight. To schedule a visit, contact the Office of Admissions. **Campus Safety and Security:** Measures include 24-hour foot and vehicle patrol, emergency notification system, and security escort services. There are emergency telephones, and lighted pathways/sidewalks, and the campus is closed at night, with a guard at the entrance.

REQUIREMENTS: The SAT or ACT is required. A high school education or GED certificate is required. A personal reference from the student's pastor and an essay submitted with the student's application are also required. Admission is based on an index found by multiplying high school GPA by the best total standardized test score. AP and CLEP credits are accepted. Important factors in the admissions decision are personality/intangible qualities, extracurricular activities record, and leadership record. Students must successfully complete at least 126 semester hours, with an average of 42 hours in the major, maintaining a C- or better, to earn a bachelor's degree. All students must also complete a core curriculum of 69 hours, which includes 30 hours of Bible and doctrine. A GPA of at least 2.0 must be maintained. Additional requirements for graduation include 4 semesters of student ministry and a senior oral comprehensive exam or a thesis in some majors. **Procedure:** Freshmen are admitted to all sessions. Entrance exams should be taken early in the senior year. There are deferred admissions and rolling admissions plans. Applications should be filed by August 1 for fall entry; January 1 for spring entry; and May 15 for summer entry, along with a $25 fee. Notification is sent on a rolling basis. Applications are accepted online. **Transfer Students:** 66 transfer students enrolled in 2015-2016. Transfer students must have successfully completed 12 semester hours of college credit courses and have maintained a minimum GPA of 2.0. Students must also provide 3 references and write an essay. **International Students:** There are 18 international students enrolled. They must take the TOEFL. They must also take the SAT or ACT.

ADMISSIONS: 55% of the 2016-2017 applicants were accepted. The SAT scores for the 2016-2017 freshman class were: Critical Reading-- 44% below 500, 36% between 500 and 599, and 20% between 600 and 699. Math-- 49% below 500, 41% between 500 and 599, 9% between 600 and 699, and 1% between 700 and 800. The ACT scores were 69% below 12, 18% between 12 and 17, 9% between 18 and 23, 3% between 24 and 29, and 1% above 30. **Admissions Contact:** Ken Gassiot, Director of Admissions. Email: *admission@tfc.edu* Web: *www.tfc.edu*

FINANCIAL AID: In 2016-2017, 99% of all full-time freshmen and 98% of continuing full-time students received some form of financial aid. 66% of all full-time freshmen and 67% of continuing full-time students received need-based aid. The average freshman award was $12,728. Need-based scholarships or need-based grants averaged $2,871; need-based self-help aid (loans and jobs) averaged $3,340; and other non-need-based awards and non-need-based scholarships averaged $9,399. 31% of undergraduate students work part-time. Average annual earnings from campus work are $1855. The average financial indebtedness of the 2016 graduate was $17,341. The state aid form and the college's own financial statement are required. The FAFSA code is 001596. The priority date for freshman financial aid applications for fall entry is May 1. The deadline for filing freshman financial aid applications for fall entry is July 15.

UNIVERSITY OF GEORGIA C-2

www.uga.edu

Athens, GA 30602 **(706) 542-2112**

Email: adm-info@uga.edu

Full-time: 11,017 men, 14,789 women
Part-time: 847 men, 779 women
Graduate: 3474 men, 5075 women
Year: semesters, summer session
Room & Board: $9450

SAT or ACT: required
Application Deadline: January 15

Faculty: I, av$
Ph.D.s: 88%
Student/Faculty: n/av
Tuition: $11,622 ($29,832)
Freshman Class: 21945 applied, 11604 accepted, 5262 enrolled
CEEB CODE: 5813
HIGHLY COMPETITIVE

University of Georgia, chartered in 1785 and part of the University System of Georgia, offers degree programs in agricultural and environmental sciences, arts and sciences, business, ecology, education, engineering, environment and design, family and consumer sciences, forestry and natural resources, journalism and mass communication, law, pharmacy, public health, public and international affairs, social work, and veterinary medicine. There are 17 undergraduate schools and 1 graduate school. In addition to regional accreditation, UGA has baccalaureate program accreditation with AACSB, ABET, ACEJMC, ACPE, ADA, ASLA, CSWE, NASAD, NASM, NCATE, NRPA, SAF, ALA/CoA, APA/CoA, ASHA, AVMA, AAMFT/COAMFTE, CFA, CADE-ADA, CACREP, CIDA, NASD, NASPAA-COPRA, and NAST. The 762-acre campus is in a small town 60 miles northeast of downtown Atlanta. Including any residence halls, there are 460 buildings.

STUDENT LIFE: 90% of undergraduates are from Georgia. Others are from 50 states, 125 foreign countries, and Canada. 8% are African American; 8% Asian American; 69% White; 5% Hispanic; 5% Foreign; 3% two or more races; 1% race unknown. 17% are Protestant. **Female To Male Ratio:** 1.3:1. The average age of freshmen is 18; all undergraduates, 20. 5% do not continue beyond their first year; 85% remain to graduate. **Housing:** 9973 students can be accommodated in college housing, which includes single-sex and coed dorms, on-campus apartments, and married student housing. In addition, there are honors houses, language houses, fraternity houses, sorority houses, theme housing and learning communities within residence halls. On-campus housing is guaranteed for the freshman year only, and is available on a first-come, and first-served basis. 67% of students commute. Alcohol is not permitted. All students may keep cars.

FACULTY/CLASSROOMS: 65% of faculty are male; 35% are female. No introductory courses are taught by graduate students.

PROGRAMS OF STUDY: UGA confers A.B., A.B.J., B.B.A., B.F.A., B.L.A., B.Mus., B.S., B.S.A., B.S.A.B., B.S.A.E., B.S.Bch.E., B.S.B.E., B.S.C.E., B.S.Chem., B.S.C.S.E., B.S.Ed., B.S.Env.E., B.S.E.H., B.S.Env., B.S.E.S., B.S.F.C.S., B.S.F.R., B.S.H.P., B.S.M.E., and B.S.W. degrees. Master's and doctoral degrees are also awarded. Bachelor's degrees are awarded in AGRICULTURE (agricultural communications, agricultural economics, animal science, dairy science, fishing and fisheries, forestry and related sciences, horticulture, natural resource/environmental economics, natural resources, plant science, poultry science, soil science, and turfgrass and landscape management), BIOLOGICAL SCIENCE (biochemistry, bioinformatics, biology/biological science, biotechnology, ecology, entomology, genetics, marine science, microbiology, neurosciences, nutritional sciences, plant pathology, and toxicology), BUSINESS (accounting, business administration and management, business administration, management, operations, fashion merchandising, finance, human resources, international business, management information systems, management science, marketing, nonprofit/public organization management, real estate, recreation and leisure services, and sports management), COMMUNICATIONS AND THE ARTS (advertising, Arabic, art history, art, art history and appreciation, broadcasting, Chinese, classical languages, communication studies, communication science, comparative literature, dance, English, French, German, Germanic languages and literature, Greek, historic preservation, Italian, Japanese, journalism, Latin, linguistics, media arts, music, music composition, music performance, music theory and composition, public relations, romance languages and literature, Russian, Spanish, studio art, and theatre arts), COMPUTER AND PHYSICAL SCIENCE (astronomy and physics, chemistry, computer science, environmental chemistry, geology, mathematics, physics, and statistics), EDUCATION (agricultural education, art education, athletic training, early childhood education, education administration, elementary education, English education, health education, mathematics education, middle school education, music education, reading education, school psychology, science education, social studies education, special education, and teaching English as a second/foreign language (TESOL/TEFOL)), ENGINEERING AND ENVIRONMENTAL DESIGN (agricultural engineering, civil engineering, electrical/electronics engineering, engineering, environmental engineering, landscape architecture, and mechanical engineering), HEALTH PROFESSIONS (biology, biomedical science, environmental health science, exercise science, health promotion, kinesiology, music therapy, pharmaceutical science, pharmacy, public health, and veterinary science), SOCIAL SCIENCE (African American studies, anthropology, communication sciences & disorders, cognitive science, counseling/psychology, criminal justice, dietetics, economics, food production/management/services, food science, geography, history, home economics, human development, industrial and organizational psychology, interdisciplinary studies, Latin American studies, law, philosophy, political science/government, psychology, public administration, religion, social work, sociology, water resources, and women's studies). Biology, psychology, and finance have the largest enrollments.

ACTIVITIES: 22% of men belong to 35 national fraternities; 31% of women belong to 27 national sororities. There are 762 groups on campus, including art, band, cheerleading, chess, choir, chorale, chorus, computers, dance, debate, drama, drill team, environmental, ethnic, film, forensics, honors, international, jazz band, LGBT, literary magazine, marching band, musical theater, newspaper, orchestra, pep band, photography, political, professional, radio and TV, religious, social, social service, student government, symphony, and yearbook. Popular campus events include Dance Marathon, Relay for Life, and Dawgs after Dark. **Sports:** There are 8 intercollegiate sports for men and 11 for women, and 24 intramural sports for men and 24 for women. Facilities include a 92,746-seat stadium, 12,000-seat basketball arena, 4,500-seat tennis stadium, 4 indoor tennis courts, 3,200-seat baseball field, complete football-training facilities, and a sports complex with a lake, a beach, playing fields, and trails. There is also the Ramsey Student Center with 5 gyms, 3 swimming pools, a strength/conditioning room, 10 racquetball courts, an indoor track, and a climbing wall. The Women's Athletic Complex hosts women's soccer and softball programs with 3,000-spectator capacity. **Graduates:** From July 1, 2015 to June 30, 2016, 7427 bachelor's degrees were awarded. The most popular majors were finance (6%), psychology (5%), and biology (5%). In an average class, 4% graduate in 3 years or less, 63% graduate in 4 years or less, 82% graduate in 5 years or less, and 85% graduate in 6 years or less. Of the 2015 graduating class, 15% were enrolled in graduate school within 6 months of graduation, and 63% were employed.

SERVICES: Counseling and information services are available, as is tutoring in every subject. There is a reader service for the blind, and remedial math, reading, and writing. Alternate format textbooks and class materials, note takers, modifications for tests and assignments, and counseling and advisement from learning disability specialists are available. There are also sign language interpreters, text type machines, FM/assistive listening devices, and a pilot closed-captioning program. **Library/Resources:** The 3 libraries contain 5.1 million volumes. Computerized library services include interlibrary loans, database searching, Internet access, and Wi-Fi capability. Special learning facilities include an art gallery, natural history museum, radio station, TV station, Bioscience Learning Center, Rare Book and Manuscript Library, Performing Arts Center, Broadcast Newsroom, State Botanical Garden of Georgia, Peabody Awards Archives, Cox Institute for Newspaper Management Studies, and Georgia Museum of Art. **Physically Challenged Students:** 90% of the campus is accessible. Facilities include wheelchair ramps, elevators, special parking, specially equipped restrooms, special class scheduling, lowered drinking fountains, lowered telephones, and special housing. Wheelchair vans, auxiliary aides, residence hall accommodations, and an adaptive technology lab are available. **Special:** UGA offers cross-registration with University Center institutions in urban Atlanta. With the Governor's Intern Program, students may serve a full-time 10-week internship in a state government agency; many other internships are available within the departments, as well as work-study programs within the university and with many area businesses. A Washington semester, an accelerated degree program in business, a general studies degree, student-designed majors, dual degrees and double majors, and nondegree study are also available. There are 25 national honor societies, Phi Beta Kappa, and a freshman honors program. **Visiting:** There are regularly scheduled orientations for prospective students, including walking and driving tours of the campus and meetings with faculty, staff, and students. There are guides for informal visits, visitors may sit in on classes, and stay overnight. To schedule a visit, contact the Visitor Center at (706) 542-0842. **Campus Safety and Security:** Measures include 24-hour foot and vehicle patrol, emergency notification system, self-defense education, and security escort services. There are shuttle buses, emergency telephones, lighted pathways/sidewalks, and controlled access to dorms/residences.

REQUIREMENTS: The SAT or ACT is required. UGA admits freshmen primarily on the basis of high school curriculum, grades earned, and college admissions test scores. The university may consider qualitative information to determine a student's potential for success. Applicants should be high school graduates or present a GED certificate. Students should have taken 4 years each of English, math, and science (of these 2 must be lab), 3 of social studies, and 2 of a foreign language. Satisfactory scores are required on the SAT or ACT. An audition is required for music majors. AP and CLEP credits are accepted. Students must have a 2.0 GPA graduate, and must complete a minimum of 120 semester hours. A baccalaureate degree program must require at least 21 semester hours of upper division courses in the major field and at least 39 semester hours of upper division work overall. The core curriculum includes 9 credit hours of Foundation courses, 7-8 hours of Sciences, 3-4 hours of Quantitative Reasoning, 12 hours of World Languages and Culture, Humanities and the Arts, 9 hours of Social Sciences. Required specific disciplines are grammar, composition, literature, math, biological sciences, history, American government, and environmental literacy. Specific courses include basic phys ed and English 1101 and 1102. UGA also requires all students to pass the Regents Exit Exam, as well as exams on the federal and state constitutions. **Procedure:** Freshmen are admitted fall, spring, and summer. Entrance exams should be taken by January of the senior year. There is a deferred admissions plan. Early decision applications should be filed by October 15; regular applications, by January 15 for fall entry; October 1 for spring entry; and January 15 for summer entry, along with a $60 fee. Notification of early decision is sent December 1; regular decision, April 1. 954 applicants were on the 2016 waiting list; 34 were admitted. Applications are accepted on-line. **Transfer Students:** 1293 transfer students enrolled in 2015-2016. A transfer GPA of 3.2 is required of all sophomores (30-59 hrs) and 2.8 required with 60 hrs or more. These students are admitted based on space availability, and there is no minimum GPA that guarantees admission. Students with fewer than 30 transferable hours are not eligible for transfer admission. 45 of 120 credits required for the bachelor's degree must be completed at UGA. **International Students:** There are 1290 international students enrolled. They must take the TOEFL with a minimum score of 550 on the paper-based TOEFL (PBT) or 80 on the Internet-based version (iBT). They must also take the SAT or ACT.

ADMISSIONS: 53% of the 2016-2017 applicants were accepted. The SAT scores for the 2016-2017 freshman class were: Critical Reading-- 4% below 500, 33% between 500 and 599, 49% between 600 and 699, and 14% between 700 and 800. Math-- 4% below 500, 29% between 500 and 599, 52% between 600 and 699, and 15% between 700 and 800. Writing-- 6% below 500, 32% between 500 and 599, 49% between 600 and 699, and 13% between 700 and 800. The ACT scores were 8% between 18 and 23, 58% between 24 and 29, and 33% above 30. There were 28 National Merit finalists. **Admissions Contact:** Nancy G. McDuff, VP of Admissions and Enrollment Management. Email: *adm-info@uga.edu* Web: *www.uga.edu*

FINANCIAL AID: In 2016-2017, 44% of all full-time freshmen received some form of financial aid. 43% of all full-time freshmen received need-based aid. The average freshman award was $13,142. Need-based scholarships or need-based grants averaged $10,210; need-based self-help aid (loans and jobs) averaged $3,502; non-need-based athletic scholarships averaged $18,346; and other non-need-based awards and non-need-based scholarships averaged $3,118. The average financial indebtedness of the 2016 graduate was $22,087. UGA is a member of CSS. The FAFSA code is 001598. The priority date for freshman financial aid applications for fall entry is March 1.

UNIVERSITY OF NORTH GEORGIA C-1

www.ung.edu

Dahlonega, GA 30597	**(706) 864-2886** **(800) 498-9581**
Fax: (706) 864-1478	**Email: admissions-dah@ung.edu**
Full-time: 5650 men, 6917 women	**Faculty:** 584; IIA
Part-time: 2208 men, 2929 women	**Ph.D.s:** n/av
Graduate: 165 men, 350 women	**Student/Faculty:** 23 to 1
Year: semesters, summer session	**Tuition:** $7178 ($20,720)
Room & Board: $10,138	**Freshman Class:** 10558 applied, 7694 accepted, 4063 enrolled
SAT CR/M/W: 530/530/500 **ACT:** 23	**CEEB CODE:** 5497
Application Deadline: February 15	**COMPETITIVE**

University of North Georgia, formed from the consolidation of North Georgia College and State University and Gainesville State College, is a liberal arts college within the University System of Georgia. UNG is 1 of 6 colleges in the United States classified as a military colleges by the Department of the Army. There are 6 undergraduate schools and 1 graduate school. In addition to regional accreditation, UNG has baccalaureate program accreditation with AACSB, ACBSP, APTA, NASAD, NCATE, NLN, ACEN, ABA, and ACS. The 212-acre campus is in a small town 60 miles north of Atlanta. Including any residence halls, there are 25 buildings.

STUDENT LIFE: 95% of undergraduates are from Georgia. Others are from 47 states, 94 foreign countries, and Canada. 90% are from public schools. 78% are White; 4% African American; 4% Foreign; 3% Asian American; 3% two or more races; 10% Hispanic; 1% race unknown. **Female To Male Ratio:** 1.3:1. The average age of freshmen is 18; all undergraduates, 22. **Housing:** 2685 students can be accommodated in college housing, which includes single-sex and coed dorms and on-campus apartments. On-campus housing is available on a first-come and first-served basis. 85% of students commute. Alcohol is not permitted. All students may keep cars.

FACULTY/CLASSROOMS: 47% of faculty are male; 51% are female. No introductory courses are taught by graduate students. The average class size in an introductory lecture is 23; in a laboratory is 19; and in a regular course is 19.

PROGRAMS OF STUDY: UNG confers B.A., B.A.S., B.S., B.B.A., B.F.A., and B.S.N. degrees. Associate, master's, and doctoral degrees are also awarded. Bachelor's degrees are awarded in BIOLOGICAL SCIENCE (biology/biological science), BUSINESS (accounting, banking and finance, business administration and management, business economics, finance, management, marketing/retailing/merchandising, and recreation and leisure services), COMMUNICATIONS AND THE ARTS (art, arts administration/management, communication studies, English, fine arts, French, modern language, music, and Spanish), COMPUTER AND PHYSICAL SCIENCE (chemistry, computer science, mathematics, and physics), EDUCATION (art education, early childhood education, elementary education, foreign languages education, health education, mathematics education, middle school education, music education, physical education, science education, secondary education, social science education, and special education), ENGINEERING AND ENVIRONMENTAL DESIGN (preengineering and technological management), HEALTH PROFESSIONS (nursing, predentistry, premedicine, prepharmacy, and preveterinary science), SOCIAL SCIENCE (criminal justice, history, human services, international political science, paralegal studies, political science/government, prelaw, psychology, social science, and sociology). Education and premedicine are the strongest academically. Biology, nursing, and psychology have the largest enrollments.

ACTIVITIES: 2% of men belong to 2 local and 6 national fraternities; 4% of women belong to 6 national sororities. There are 364 groups on campus, including art, band, chess, choir, chorale, chorus, communications, computers, dance, debate, drama, drill team, environmental, ethnic, forensics, honors, international, jazz band, LGBT, literary magazine, marching band, musical theater, newspaper, pep band, political, professional, radio and TV, religious, social, social service, student government, and yearbook. Popular campus events include Fall/Spring Jam, Frisbee Golf, and military reviews. **Sports:** There are 6 intercollegiate sports for men and 8 for women, and 19 intramural sports for men and 19 for women. Facilities include a student recreation center, a swimming pool, a track, a fully equipped exercise room, a rappeling tower, a confidence course, a picnic area, a 2000-seat gym, and a 250-seat arena. **Graduates:** From July 1, 2015 to June 30, 2016, 1796 bachelor's degrees were awarded. The most popular majors were registered nursing (10%), business administration and management (9%), and biology (7%). 222 companies recruited on campus in 2015-2016.

SERVICES: Counseling and information services are available, as is tutoring in most subjects. There is a reader service for the blind, and remedial math, reading, and writing. **Library/Resources:** The 2 libraries contain 270,623 volumes, 774,482 microform items, and 9,889 audio/video tapes/CDs/DVDs, and subscribe to 2,546 periodicals including electronic. Computerized library services include interlibrary loans, database searching, and Internet access. Special learning facilities include an art gallery, planetarium, radio station, a math lab, language lab, and writing center. **Physically Challenged Students:** 50% of the campus is accessible. Facilities include wheelchair ramps, elevators, special parking, specially equipped restrooms, and lowered drinking fountains. **Special:** Special academic programs include a co-op program in business, internships, a 3-2 engineering degree with Georgia Institute of Technology, a joint Engineering degree program with Clemson University, study abroad in Europe, South America, and Canada, dual majors, and credit for life, military, or work experience. There are 9 national honor societies, a freshman honors program, and 23 departmental honors programs. **Visiting:** There are regularly scheduled orientations for prospective students, including an admissions video, college overview, tour, and a meeting with an admissions counselor. There are guides for informal visits and visitors may stay overnight. To schedule a visit, contact Admissions Office. **Campus Safety and Security:** Measures include 24-hour foot and vehicle patrol, emergency notification system, and security escort services. There are shuttle buses, emergency telephones, lighted pathways/sidewalks, and controlled access to dorms/residences.

REQUIREMENTS: The SAT or ACT is required. Students must have graduated from a secondary school with 4 years of English, 3 each of math, science, and social science, and 2 of a foreign language. The GED is accepted if granted at least 5 years later than expected high school graduation date. SAT II: Subject tests are required of home-schooled students. AP and CLEP credits are accepted. Important factors in the admissions decision are leadership record, advanced placement or honors courses, and evidence of special talent. To graduate, students must complete 120 semester credit hours with a minimum GPA of 2.0. English, math, lab sciences, and social sciences are required. **Procedure:** Freshmen are admitted fall, spring, and summer. Entrance exams should be taken in the junior year. There are deferred admissions and rolling admissions plans. Applications should be filed by February 15 for fall entry; December 15 for spring entry; and April 15 for summer entry, along with a $30 fee. Applications are accepted on-line. **Transfer Students:** Transfer students must have maintained a C average and a clear conduct record and be in good academic standing. Those who have not completed 90 semester hours of transferable credit must have completed the approved precollege curriculum and must submit high school transcripts and the SAT or ACT results. 30 of 120 credits required for the bachelor's degree must be completed at UNG. **International Students:** There are 139 international students enrolled. The school actively recruits these students. They must take the TOEFL with a minimum score of 550 on the paper-based TOEFL (PBT) or 79 on the Internet-based version (iBT). They must also take the SAT or ACT.

ADMISSIONS: 73% of the 2016-2017 applicants were accepted. The SAT scores for the 2016-2017 freshman class were: Critical Reading-- 33% below 500, 47% between 500 and 599, 18% between 600 and 699, and 2% between 700 and 800. Math-- 30% below 500, 47% between 500 and 599, 21% between 600 and 699, and 2% between 700 and 800. Writing-- 45% below 500, 41% between 500 and 599, 12% between 600 and 699, and 1% between 700 and 800. The ACT scores were 7% between 12 and 17, 50% between 18 and 23, 39% between 24 and 29, and 3% above 30. 18% of the current freshmen were in the top fifth of their class; 40% were in the top two fifths. **Admissions Contact:** Molly Potts, Director of Undergraduate Admissions. Email: *admissions-dah@ung.edu* Web: *www.ung.edu*

FINANCIAL AID: In 2016-2017, 95% of all full-time freshmen and 83% of continuing full-time students received some form of financial aid. 28% of all full-time freshmen and 34% of continuing full-time students received need-based aid. The average freshman award was $1,973. The college's own financial statement is required. The FAFSA code is 001585. Check with the school for current application deadlines.

UNIVERSITY OF WEST GEORGIA *(The complete profile is made available exclusively on our website, www.barronspac.com)*

VALDOSTA STATE UNIVERSITY — C-5

www.valdosta.edu

Valdosta, GA 31698	**(229) 333-5791 (800) 618-1878**
Fax: (229) 333-5482	**Email: admissions@valdosta.edu**
Full-time: 3739 men, 5280 women	**Faculty:** 416
Part-time: 557 men, 792 women	**Ph.D.s:** 75%
Graduate: 518 men, 1545 women	**Student/Faculty:** 20 to 1
Year: semesters, summer session	**Tuition:** $7162 ($20,058)
Room & Board: $7864	**Freshman Class:** 6703 applied, 4744 accepted, 2467 enrolled
SAT CR/M/W: 503/492/482 **ACT:** 21	**CEEB CODE:** 5855
Application Deadline: July 1	**COMPETITIVE**

Valdosta State University, founded in 1906 and a unit of the University

System of Georgia, is a public liberal arts institution offering degrees in arts and sciences, education, business administration, nursing, fine arts, social work, and library. The figures in the above capsule and in this profile are approximate. There are 5 undergraduate schools and 1 graduate school. In addition to regional accreditation, VSU has baccalaureate program accreditation with AACSB, NASAD, NASM, NCATE, CCNE, and NAST. The 172-acre campus is in a suburban area in southern Georgia, 3 1/2 hours from Atlanta and from Orlando, Florida. Including any residence halls, there are 94 buildings.

STUDENT LIFE: 96% of undergraduates are from Georgia. Others are from 45 states, 70 foreign countries, and Canada. 64% are White; 28% African American; 1% Asian American; 1% Hispanic; 1% Foreign. **Female To Male Ratio:** 1.6:1. The average age of freshmen is 18; all undergraduates, 22. **Housing:** 2896 students can be accommodated in college housing, which includes coed dorms and on-campus apartments. In addition, there are honors houses, language houses, special-interest houses, honors, wellness, living learning communities, and 24-hour quiet wings in the dorms. On-campus housing is available on a first-come and first-served basis. 72% of students commute. All students may keep cars.

FACULTY/CLASSROOMS: 48% of faculty are male; 52% are female. 91% teach undergraduates. No introductory courses are taught by graduate students. The average class size in an introductory lecture is 30; in a laboratory is 23; and in a regular course is 18.

PROGRAMS OF STUDY: VSU confers B.A., B.S., B.B.A., B.G.S., B.M., B.S.Ed., B.S.E.P., and B.S.N. degrees. Associate degrees are also awarded. Biology, early childhood education, and nursing have the largest enrollments.

ACTIVITIES: There are 163 groups on campus, including art, band, cheerleading, chess, chorale, chorus, computers, dance, debate, drama, drum and bugle corps, environmental, ethnic, film, honors, international, jazz band, LGBT, literary magazine, marching band, musical theater, newspaper, orchestra, outdoor/recreation, pep band, political, professional, radio and TV, religious, social, social service, student government, and symphony. Popular campus events include Family Day, and the Happening. **Sports:** There are 6 intercollegiate sports for men and 5 for women, and 12 intramural sports for men and 12 for women. Facilities include a phys ed complex with a 5500-seat basketball arena, a health fitness center, weight traning room, a human performance lab, a gym with a weight room, dance studio, auxiliary gym, outdoor pool, climbing wall, racketball courts, and a indoor track. **Graduates:** From July 1, 2015 to June 30, 2016, 1631 bachelor's degrees were awarded. The most popular majors were childhood education (11%), communication arts (6%), and nursing (6%). 110 companies recruited on campus in 2015-2016. In an average class, 16% graduate in 4 years or less, 37% graduate in 5 years or less, and 43% graduate in 6 years or less.

SERVICES: Counseling and information services are available, as is tutoring in some subjects, such as biology, chemistry, physics, math computer science, foreign languages, social science, and writing. There is a reader service for the blind. **Library/Resources:** The library contains 539,557 volumes, 1.1 million microform items, and 27,582 audio/video tapes/CDs/DVDs, and subscribes to 2,732 periodicals including electronic. Computerized library services include interlibrary loans, database searching, Internet access, and Wi-Fi capability. Special learning facilities include an art gallery, planetarium, radio station, TV station, and herbarium. **Physically Challenged Students:** All of the campus is accessible. Facilities include wheelchair ramps, elevators, special parking, specially equipped restrooms, special class scheduling, lowered drinking fountains, lowered telephones, and special housing. Students registered with the Access Office are able to register for classes on the first day of registration regardless of classification. Also all campus transportation is accessible. **Special:** Valdosta offers co-op programs, internships, study abrod, accelerated degree program in RN to BSN/MSN Nursing program and 3-2 engineering degree with Georgia Institute of Technology. There are 28 national honor societies, Phi Beta Kappa, and a freshman honors program. **Visiting:** There are regularly scheduled orientations for prospective students, including a tour of the campus, information sessions, advising, meal plan selection, fee payment. There are guides for informal visits and visitors may sit in on classes. To schedule a visit, contact the Admissions Office. **Campus Safety and Security:** Measures include 24-hour foot and vehicle patrol, emergency notification system, self-defense education, and security escort services. There are shuttle buses, emergency telephones, lighted pathways/sidewalks, bicycle patrol, security cameras, and electronic key card access to residence halls.

REQUIREMENTS: The SAT or ACT is required. AP and CLEP credits are accepted. To graduate, all students must complete a minimum of 120 semester hours, including 60 in the core curriculm and 21 in a major, with a GPA of 2.0. Reseasonable proficiency in written and spoken English is also required. **Procedure:** There are deferred admissions and rolling admissions plans. Applications should be filed by July 1 for fall entry; December 1 for spring entry; and May 1 for summer entry. Notification is sent on a rolling basis. **Transfer Students:** 2094 transfer students enrolled in 2015-2016. 30 of 120 credits required for the bachelor's degree must be completed at VSU. **International Students:** There are 200 international students enrolled. They must take the TOEFL with a minimum score of 523 on the paper-based TOEFL (PBT) or 69 on the Internet-based version (iBT). TOEFL can be subsituted with SAT.

ADMISSIONS: 71% of the 2016-2017 applicants were accepted. The SAT scores for the 2016-2017 freshman class were: Critical Reading--51% below 500, 40% between 500 and 599, and 8% between 600 and 699. Math-- 58% below 500, 35% between 500 and 599, and 7% between 600 and 699. Writing-- 59% below 500, 35% between 500 and 599, and 6% between 600 and 699. **Admissions Contact:** Ryan Hogan, Director of Admissions. Email: *admissions@valdosta.edu* Web: *www.valdosta.edu*

FINANCIAL AID: In 2016-2017, 89% of all full-time freshmen and 83% of continuing full-time students received some form of financial aid. 56% of all full-time freshmen and 53% of continuing full-time students received need-based aid. The average freshman award was $14,351. Need-based scholarships or need-based grants averaged $4,044 ($6,700 maximum); need-based self-help aid (loans and jobs) averaged $2,840 ($7,000 maximum); non-need-based athletic scholarships averaged $3,339 ($12,176 maximum); and other non-need-based awards and non-need-based scholarships averaged $9,895 ($26,226 maximum). 6% of undergraduate students work part-time. Average annual earnings from campus work are $2150. The average financial indebtedness of the 2016 graduate was $21,117. VSU is a member of CSS. The FAFSA code is 001599. The priority date for freshman financial aid applications for fall entry is May 1. The deadline for filing freshman financial aid applications for fall entry is June 1.

WESLEYAN COLLEGE — C-3

www.wesleyancollege.edu

Macon, GA 31210	**(912) 757-5206** **(800) 447-6610**
Fax: (912) 757-4030	**Email: admissions@wesleyancollege.edu**
Full-time: 379 women	**Faculty:** 50; IIB, --$
Part-time: 3 men, 210 women	**Ph.D.s:** 94%
Graduate: 13 men, 86 women	**Student/Faculty:** 11 to 1
Year: semesters, summer session	**Tuition:** $20,140
Room & Board: $9554	**Freshman Class:** 617 applied, 302 accepted, 135 enrolled
SAT: required **ACT:** 22	**CEEB CODE:** 5895
Application Deadline: August 1	**COMPETITIVE+**

Wesleyan College, founded in 1836, is a private liberal arts college for women affiliated with the United Methodist Church. It is the world's first college chartered to grant degrees to women. Figures in the above capsule and in this profile are approximate. There are 2 undergraduate schools. In addition to regional accreditation, Wesleyan has baccalaureate program accreditation with NASM. The 200-acre campus is in a suburban area 90 miles south of Atlanta. Including any residence halls, there are 19 buildings.

STUDENT LIFE: 74% of undergraduates are from Georgia. Others are from 25 states, and 20 foreign countries. 90% are from public schools. 48% are White; 3% Asian American; 23% Foreign; 22% African American; 2% Hispanic. 53% are Protestant; 34% claim no religious affiliation. **Female To Male Ratio:** 42.2:1. The average age of freshmen is 18; all undergraduates, 22. 32% do not continue beyond their first year; 56% remain to graduate. **Housing:** 600 students can be accommodated in college housing, which includes single-sex dorms and on-campus apartments. On-campus housing is guaranteed for all 4 years. 76% of students live on campus; of those, 60% remain on campus on weekends. Alcohol is not permitted. All students may keep cars.

FACULTY/CLASSROOMS: 42% of faculty are male; 58% are female. All teach undergraduates, and 75% do research. No introductory courses are taught by graduate students. The average class size in an introductory lecture is 13; in a laboratory is 12; and in a regular course is 10.

PROGRAMS OF STUDY: Wesleyan confers A.B. and B.S.B.A. degrees. Master's degrees are also awarded. Bachelor's degrees are awarded in BIOLOGICAL SCIENCE (biology/biological science), BUSINESS (business administration and management and international business management), COMMUNICATIONS AND THE ARTS (advertising, art history and appreciation, communications, dramatic arts, English, French, music, Spanish, and studio art), COMPUTER AND PHYSICAL SCIENCE (chemistry, information sciences and systems, mathematics, physical sciences, and physics), EDUCATION (early childhood education and middle school education), ENGINEERING AND ENVIRONMENTAL DESIGN (environmental science), SOCIAL SCIENCE (American studies, economics, history, humanities, interdisciplinary studies, international relations, philosophy, political science/government, psychology, religion, and social science). Chemistry, biology, and philosophy are the strongest academically. Business, education, and psychology have the largest enrollments.

ACTIVITIES: There are no fraternities or sororities. There are 51 groups on campus, including art, choir, chorus, computers, dance, debate, drama, ethnic, forensics, honors, international, LGBT, literary magazine, musical theater, newspaper, photography, political, professional, recreation, religious, social, social service, and student government. Popular campus events include Casino Night, Benefit Ball, and STUNT. **Sports:** There are 6 intercollegiate sports for women. Facilities include an equestrian arena, softball and soccer fields, an indoor pool, a gym, dance studio, weight room, a lake, and fitness trail & center. **Graduates:** From July 1, 2015 to June 30, 2016, 92 bachelor's degrees were awarded. The most popular majors were business administration (28%), education (12%), and psychology (11%). In an average class, 41% graduate in 4 years or less, 44% graduate in 5 years or less, and 45% graduate in 6 years or less. Of the 2015 graduating class, 22% were enrolled in graduate school within 6 months of graduation, and 36% were employed.

SERVICES: Counseling and information services are available, as is tutoring in some subjects. There is remedial math and reading. Free tutors are available upon request. The Academic Center is available for all students. **Library/Resources:** The library contains 143,071 volumes, 33,438 microform items, and 4,267 audio/video tapes/CDs/DVDs, and subscribes to 615 periodicals including electronic. Computerized library services include interlibrary loans, database searching, and Internet access. Special learning facilities include an art gallery, a computerized teaching classroom, language and math labs, collaborative research science labs, and arboretum. **Physically Challenged Students:** 65% of the campus is accessible. Facilities include wheelchair ramps, elevators, special parking, specially equipped restrooms, special class scheduling, lowered drinking fountains, and lowered telephones. **Special:** Wesleyan offers cross-registration with Mercer University and a 3-2 engineering degree with Georgia Institute of Technology and Auburn and Mercer Universities. More than 150 internships are available, as are interdisciplinary, student-designed, and dual majors, study abroad in 10 countries, a Washington semester, work-study programs, credit for life experience, nondegree study, and pass/fail options. There are 10 national honor societies and a freshman honors program. **Visiting:** There are regularly scheduled orientations for prospective students, including a campus tour, parent/student panels, class visits, admission and financial aid sessions, and meals in the dining hall. There are guides for informal visits, visitors may sit in on classes, and stay overnight. To schedule a visit, contact the Admissions Office. **Campus Safety and Security:** Measures include 24-hour foot and vehicle patrol, self-defense education, and security escort services. There are emergency telephones, lighted pathways/sidewalks, and dorm entrances are locked 24 hours a day, 7 days a week.

REQUIREMENTS: The SAT or ACT is required. The ACT Optional Writing test is also required. Each applicant for admission is reviewed on the following: performance in and quality of a college preparatory curriculum, standardized test score, counselor and teacher recommendation, writing ability, and cocurricular involvement. A minimum of 15 Carnegie units is required, including 4 units of English, 3 each of math, natural sciences, and social sciences, and 2 of foreign language. Admitted students must graduate from an accredited secondary school or have a GED certificate. The admission staff does not require but welcomes the opportunity to interview prospective students. Students who wish to be considered for a performance arts scholarship must submit a portfolio or audition. AP and CLEP credits are accepted. Important factors in the admissions decision are advanced placement or honors courses, evidence of special talent, and leadership record. To graduate, students must complete 120 credit hours with a minimum GPA of 2.0. Requirements include proficiency in writing, math, and modern foreign language, 10 courses distributed with 2 but no more than 3 from fine arts, humanities, science and math, and social sciences. A first-year seminar, a speech-intensive course, cross-cultural and workplace experience, and integrative experience in the major are also required. All classes are seminar based. **Procedure:** Freshmen are admitted fall and spring. Entrance exams should be taken by the fall of the senior year. There are early decision, early admissions, deferred admissions, and rolling admissions plans. Early decision applications should be filed by November 15; regular applications, by August 1 for fall entry; and December 1 for spring entry, along with a $30 fee. Notification of early decision is sent December 15. 40 early decision candidates were accepted for the 2016-2017 class. Applications are accepted on-line. **Transfer Students:** 5 transfer students enrolled in 2015-2016. Applicants with fewer than 24 transferable semester hours must submit a final high school transcript and record of standardized test scores in addition to their college transcripts. 30 of 120 credits required for the bachelor's degree must be completed at Wesleyan. **International Students:** There are 79 international students enrolled. The school actively recruits these students. They must take the TOEFL. They must also take the SAT or ACT.

ADMISSIONS: 49% of the 2016-2017 applicants were accepted. The ACT scores were 36% below 12, 27% between 12 and 17, 25% between 18 and 23, 7% between 24 and 29, and 7% above 30. 49% of the current freshmen were in the top fifth of their class; 72% were in the top two fifths. 3 freshmen graduated first in their class. **Admissions Contact:** Julie Jones, Director of Institutional Advancement. Email: *admissions@wesleyancollege.edu* Web: *www.wesleyancollege.edu*

FINANCIAL AID: In 2016-2017, 99% of all full-time freshmen and 96% of continuing full-time students received some form of financial aid. 71% of all full-time freshmen and 58% of continuing full-time students received need-based aid. The average freshman award was $13,842. Need-based scholarships or need-based grants averaged $10,116; need-based self-help aid (loans and jobs) averaged $3,064; and other non-need-based awards and non-need-based scholarships averaged $12,230. 40% of undergraduate students work part-time. Average annual earnings from campus work are $1000. The average financial indebtedness of the 2016 graduate was $21,872. The college's own financial statement is required. The FAFSA code is 001600. The priority date for freshman financial aid applications for fall entry is March 1. The deadline for filing freshman financial aid applications for fall entry is May 1.

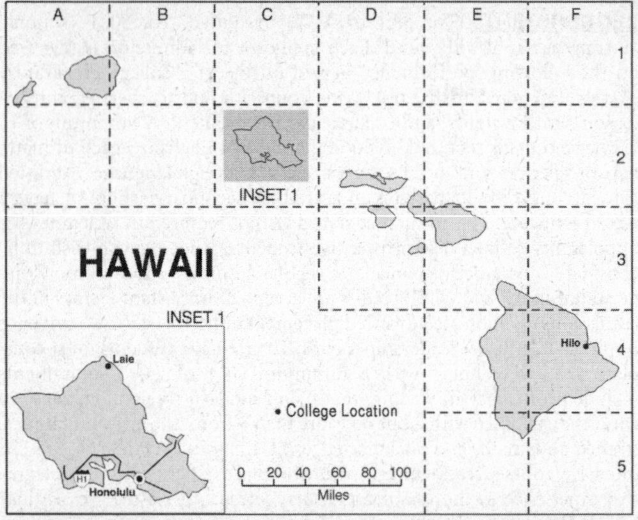

BRIGHAM YOUNG UNIVERSITY/HAWAII C-2

www.byuh.edu

Laie, HI 96762 **(808) 675-3738**

Fax: (808) 675-3211	**Email:** admissions@byuh.edu
Full-time: 945 men, 1200 women	**Faculty:** 120
Part-time: 99 men, 153 women	**Ph.D.s:** 60%
Graduate: n/av	**Student/Faculty:** 18 to 1
Year: semesters, summer session	**Tuition:** $5240
Room & Board: $6050	**Freshman Class:** 1265 applied, 603 accepted, 297 enrolled
SAT: recommended **ACT:** 23	**CEEB CODE:** 4106
Application Deadline: February 15	**COMPETITIVE**

BYU-Hawaii is a private, comprehensive undergraduate institution. The figures in the above capsule and in this profile are approximate. There are 4 undergraduate schools. In addition to regional accreditation, BYU-Hawaii has baccalaureate program accreditation with NCATE and CSWE. The 200-acre campus is in a rural area 38 miles from Honolulu. Including any residence halls, there are 42 buildings.

STUDENT LIFE: 83% of undergraduates are from out of state, mostly the West. Students are from 41 states, 75 foreign countries, and Canada. 44% are Foreign; 29% White; 22% Asian American; 2% Hispanic; 1% African American; 1% American Indian/Alaska Native. **Female To Male Ratio:** 1.3:1. The average age of freshmen is 21; all undergraduates, 23. 35% do not continue beyond their first year; 47% remain to graduate. **Housing:** 1635 students can be accommodated in college housing, which includes single-sex dorms, on-campus apartments, and married student housing. On-campus housing is guaranteed for the freshman year only, and is available on a first-come, and first-served basis. 62% of students live on campus. All students may keep cars. Alcohol is not permitted.

FACULTY/CLASSROOMS: 80% of faculty are male; 20% are female. All teach undergraduates. No introductory courses are taught by graduate students. The average class size in an introductory lecture is 21; in a laboratory is 17; and in a regular course is 19.

PROGRAMS OF STUDY: BYU-Hawaii confers B.A., B.S., B.F.A. and B.S.W. degrees. Bachelor's degrees are awarded in BIOLOGICAL SCIENCE (biology/biological science), BUSINESS (accounting, hospitality management services, international business management, and tourism), COMMUNICATIONS AND THE ARTS (art, English, fine arts, and music), COMPUTER AND PHYSICAL SCIENCE (computer science, information sciences and systems, and mathematics), EDUCATION (art education, business education, elementary education, English education, mathematics education, science education, social science education, special education, and teaching English as a second/foreign language (TESOL/TEFOL)), HEALTH PROFESSIONS (predentistry and premedicine), SOCIAL SCIENCE (Hawaiian studies, history, interdisciplinary studies, international studies, Pacific area studies, physical fitness/movement, political science/government, psychology, and social work). International business management, accounting, hospitality and tourism management have the largest enrollments.

ACTIVITIES: There are no fraternities or sororities. There are 41 groups on campus, including art, band, cheerleading, chess, choir, chorale, communications, computers, dance, drama, ethnic, film, honors, international, jazz band, literary magazine, musical theater, newspaper, pep band, political, professional, religious, social, social service, and student government. Popular campus events include International Food Fest, International Cultural Night, and Talent Show. **Sports:** There are 5 intercollegiate sports for men and 6 for women, and 10 intramural sports for men and 10 for women. Facilities include softball fields, soccer fields, a rugby field, tennis, racquetball courts, swimming pool, weight room, bowling alley, dance studio, pool tables, and 2 gyms. **Graduates:** From July 1, 2015 to June 30, 2016, 557 bachelor's degrees were awarded. The most popular majors were international business management (15%), information system (8%), and social work (6%). In an average class, 47% graduate in 6 years or less. Of the 2015 graduating class, 44% were enrolled in graduate school within 6 months of graduation, and 61% were employed.

SERVICES: Counseling and information services are available, as is tutoring in most subjects. There is remedial math, reading, and writing. **Library/Resources:** The library contains 21,004 volumes, 450,000 microform items, 9,538 audio/video tapes/CDs/DVDs, and subscribes to 17,000 periodicals including electronic. Computerized library services include interlibrary loans, database searching, Internet access, and Wi-Fi capability. Special learning facilities include an art gallery, natural history museum, the nearby Polynesian Cultural Center, that houses an art collection, and an artifact collection, and provides valuable research opportunities for students in related programs. **Physically Challenged Students:** 95% of the campus is accessible. Facilities include wheelchair ramps, elevators, special parking, specially equipped restrooms, lowered drinking fountains, and lowered telephones. **Special:** BYUH offers work-study programs with the Polynesian Cultural Center, internships, cooperative programs in most majors, non-degree study, student-designed majors in interdisciplinary studies, and pass/fail options. There are 5 national honor societies and a freshman honors program. **Visiting:** There are guides for informal visits. To schedule a visit, contact the University Advancement Office. **Campus Safety and Security:** Measures include 24-hour foot and vehicle patrol and security escort services. There are emergency telephones and lighted pathways/sidewalks.

REQUIREMENTS: The ACT is required, and SAT recommended. Applicants should be high school graduates. Homeschooled and other nontraditional students should call the school for more information. A GPA of 2.0 is required. AP and CLEP credits are accepted. Important factors in the admissions decision are geographical diversity, recommendations by alumni, and personality/intangible qualities. Students must complete the 31 to 43 credits in general education curriculum, as well as meet English proficiency, religious education, and exercise science requirements. A total of 120 credit hours, including 40 in the major, must be earned with a minimum GPA of 2.0 for graduation. A thesis is required in certain areas. **Procedure:** Freshmen are admitted to all sessions. Entrance exams should be taken prior to the application deadline. There is a deferred admissions plan. Applications should be filed by February 15 for fall entry; October 1 for winter entry; February 15 for spring entry; and February 15 for summer entry, along with a $35 fee. Notifications are sent April 1. Applications are accepted online. **Transfer Students:** 209 transfer students enrolled in 2015-2016. Applicants must have 30 hours of college credit, with a minimum GPA of 2.5. 30 of 120 credits required for the bachelor's degree must be completed at BYU-Hawaii. **International Students:** There are 942 international students enrolled. The school actively recruits these students. They must take the TOEFL with a minimum score of 500 on the paper-based TOEFL (PBT), and also take the ACT.

ADMISSIONS: 48% of the 2016-2017 applicants were accepted. The ACT scores were 26% below 12, 22% between 12 and 17, 24% between 18 and 23, 16% between 24 and 29, and 12% above 30. **Admissions Contact:** Arapata Meha, Dean of Admissions and Records. Email: *admissions@byuh.edu* Web: *www.byuh.edu*

FINANCIAL AID: The FAFSA code is 001606. Check with the school for current application deadlines.

CHAMINADE UNIVERSITY OF HONOLULU C-2

www.chaminade.edu

Honolulu, HI 96816 (808) 735-4711
(800) 735-3733

Fax: (808) 739-4647 Email: admissions@chaminade.edu

Full-time: 326 men, 824 women	**Faculty:** IIB, av$
Part-time: 12 men, 21 women	**Ph.D.s:** n/av
Graduate: 176 men, 418 women	**Student/Faculty:** 12 to 1
Year: semesters, summer session	**Tuition:** $23,310
Room & Board: $12,690	**Freshman Class:** n/av
SAT: CR/M required **ACT:** required	**CEEB CODE:** 4105
Application Deadline: n/av	**COMPETITIVE**

Chaminade University, is a private Catholic college offering a rich educational environment with a dedicated, involved faculty, and small class sizes. Figures in the above capsule and in this profile are approximate. There are 6 undergraduate schools and 4 graduate schools. In addition to regional accreditation, Chaminade has baccalaureate program accreditation with WASC. The 65-acre campus is in an urban area 4 miles east of downtown Honolulu. Including any residence halls, there are 16 buildings.

STUDENT LIFE: 69% of undergraduates are from Hawaii. Others are from 33 states, and 14 foreign countries. 38% are Asian American; 14% White; 13% two or more races; 5% Hispanic; 4% race unknown; 3% African American; 2% Foreign; 1% American Indian/Alaska Native. 44% are Catholic; 14% claim no religious affiliation. **Female To Male Ratio:** 2.5:1. The average age of freshmen is 18; all undergraduates, 22. 26% do not continue beyond their first year; 56% remain to graduate. **Housing:** 328 students can be accommodated in college housing, which includes single-sex and coed dorms, on-campus apartments, and off-campus apartments. On-campus housing is available on a first-come and first-served basis. 76% of students commute. All students may keep cars.

FACULTY/CLASSROOMS: 56% of faculty are male; 44% are female. All teach undergraduates. No introductory courses are taught by graduate students. The average class size in an introductory lecture is 19; in a laboratory is 18; and in a regular course is 19.

PROGRAMS OF STUDY: Chaminade confers B.A., B.S., B.S.N., and B.F.A. degrees. Associate and master's degrees are also awarded. Bachelor's degrees are awarded in AGRICULTURE (environmental studies), BIOLOGICAL SCIENCE (biochemistry and biology/biological science), BUSINESS (accounting, business administration and management, and management science), COMMUNICATIONS AND THE ARTS (communications and English), COMPUTER AND PHYSICAL SCIENCE (computer science), EDUCATION (early childhood education, elementary education, and secondary education), ENGINEERING AND ENVIRONMENTAL DESIGN (interior design), HEALTH PROFESSIONS (nursing), SOCIAL SCIENCE (behavioral science, criminal justice, forensic studies, history, humanities, international relations, liberal arts/general studies, psychology, religion, and social studies). Forsensic sciences, nursing, and biology are the strongest academically. Nursing, criminal justice, and forensic sciences have the largest enrollments.

ACTIVITIES: There are no fraternities or sororities. There are 38 groups on campus, including art, cheerleading, chorale, computers, dance, drama, ethnic, forensics, honors, international, musical theater, newspaper, orchestra, political, professional, radio and TV, religious, social, social service, and student government. Popular campus events include Spring Serendipity, International Extravaganza, and Club Fest. **Sports:** There are 4 intercollegiate sports for men and 6 for women. Facilities include volleyball, tennis, and basketball courts, fitness and weight-training facilities, and a student center. **Graduates:** From July 1, 2015 to June 30, 2016, 255 bachelor's degrees were awarded. The most popular majors were nursing (22%), criminal justice (19%), and psychology (10%). 92 companies recruited on campus in 2015-2016. In an average class, 35% graduate in 4 years or less, 52% graduate in 5 years or less, and 54% graduate in 6 years or less.

SERVICES: Counseling and information services are available, as is tutoring in most subjects, and mremedial math, reading, and writing. **Library/Resources:** The library contains 53,239 volumes, 134,000 microform items, and 4,771 audio/video tapes/CDs/DVDs, and subscribes to 273 periodicals including electronic. Computerized library services include interlibrary loans, database searching, Internet access, and Wi-Fi capability. Special learning facilities include a radio station, an observatory, and theater. **Physically Challenged Students:** 95% of the campus is accessible. Facilities include wheelchair ramps, elevators, special parking, specially equipped restrooms, special class scheduling, lowered drinking fountains, lowered telephones, and special housing. **Special:** Internships are available with local companies through the Career Development office. Students may design majors toward a B.A. in humanities. There is a sister university exchange program with the University of Dayton and St. Mary's University. Students may take independent study courses with instructor approval. Accelerated degree programs are available for business administration, management, criminal justice, early childhood education, elementary education, secondary education, English, historical and political studies, psychology, religious studies, and social studies. Distance Learning is also available for business, criminal justice, early childhood education, English, elementary education, historical and political studies, psychology, secondary education, management, and religious studies. There are 11 national honor societies. **Visiting:** There are guides for informal visits and visitors may sit in on classes. To schedule a visit, contact the Admissions Office at admissions@chaminade.edu. **Campus Safety and Security:** Measures include 24-hour foot and vehicle patrol, emergency notification system, self-defense education, and security escort services, emergency telephones, and lighted pathways/sidewalks.

REQUIREMENTS: General Requirements include: GPA 2.5, old SAT 920, new SAT 1000, or ACT 19, and high school diploma or equivalent. Recommendations: 4 years each of English, and college preparatory electives, 3 years of social studies, 3 years of mathematics, and 2 years of science. Nursing Requirements: GPA of 2.75, old SAT 950, new SAT 1030, or ACT 20. One year of high school chemistry or equivalent, completion of algebra II, 1-page personal statement, and at least 2 letters of recommendation. AP and CLEP credits are accepted. Important factors in the admissions decision are leadership record, personality/intangible qualities, and extracurricular activities record. To graduate, students must complete 120 credit hours, including 61 in general education courses and at least 24 in the major at the upper-division level. A 2.0 GPA is required in all majors except criminal justice (2.5), communications (2.5), and education (2.75). Students must complete courses in art, English, history, humanities, mathematics, philosophy, sciences, social studies, and communications. **Procedure:** Freshmen are admitted in the fall and spring. Entrance exams should be taken during the first semester of the senior year. There are deferred admissions and rolling admissions plans. Application deadlines are open. Application fee is $50. Notification is sent on a rolling basis. Applications are accepted online. **Transfer Students:** 148 transfer students enrolled in 2015-2016. Applicants must have a minimum GPA of 2.0. If fewer than 24 college credits, applicants must meet requirements for first-year students. Nursing applicants must have aminimum GPA of 2.75, completed Chemistry and College Algebra, and meet the same requirements of first-year nursing applicants. 30 of 120 credits required for the bachelor's degree must be completed at Chaminade. **International Students:** There are 16 international students enrolled. They must take the TOEFL with a minimum score of 550 on the paper-based TOEFL (PBT) or 79 on the Internet-based version (iBT). They must also take the SAT or ACT.

ADMISSIONS: 41% of the current freshmen were in the top fifth of their class; 72% were in the top two fifths. **Admissions Contact:** Shauna Pimentel-Motooka, Director of Admissions. Email: *admissions@chaminade.edu* Web: *www.chaminade.edu*

FINANCIAL AID: In 2016-2017, 100% of all full-time freshmen and 97% of continuing full-time students received some form of financial aid. 74% of all full-time freshmen and 70% of continuing full-time students received need-based aid. The average freshman award was $20,956. Need-based scholarships or need-based grants averaged $4,944 ($20,099 maximum); need-based self-help aid (loans and jobs) averaged $5,402 ($12,369 maximum); non-need-based athletic scholarships averaged $9,842 ($35,782 maximum); and other non-need-based awards and non-need-based scholarships averaged $9,290 ($53,970 maximum). Chaminade is a member of CSS. The FAFSA code is 001605. The priority date for freshman financial aid applications for fall entry is March 1.

HAWAII PACIFIC UNIVERSITY C-2

www.hpu.edu

Honolulu, HI 96813	(808) 543-8088 (866) 225-5478
Fax: (808) 543-8065	**Email:** admissions@hpu.edu
Full-time: 1566 men, 2378 women	**Faculty:** 235
Part-time: 1197 men, 1027 women	**Ph.D.s:** 64%
Graduate: 578 men, 717 women	**Student/Faculty:** 17 to 1
Year: semesters, summer session	**Tuition:** $22,440
Room & Board: $10,980	**Freshman Class:** 4129 applied, 2980 accepted, 492 enrolled
SAT: required **ACT:** 21	**CEEB CODE:** 4352
Application Deadline: August 15	**COMPETITIVE**

Hawaii Pacific University, founded in 1965, is a private, coeducational institution offering 50 undergraduate and 14 graduate programs in liberal arts, business, natural sciences, nursing, international studies, and communication. Figures in the above capsule and in this profile are approximate. There is 1 undergraduate school. In addition to regional accreditation, HPU has baccalaureate program accreditation with CSWE, NLN, SATE, and WASC. The 135-acre campus is in an urban area in downtown Honolulu and suburban Kaneohe on the island of Oahu. Including any residence halls, there are 16 buildings.

STUDENT LIFE: 64% of undergraduates are from Hawaii. Others are from 50 states, 80 foreign countries, and Canada. 67% are from public schools. 5% are African American; 29% White; 19% Asian American; 13% Hispanic; 13% Foreign; 1% American Indian/Alaska Native. **Female To Male Ratio:** 1.2:1. The average age of freshmen is 19; all undergraduates, 26. 34% do not continue beyond their first year; 39% remain to graduate. **Housing:** 200 students can be accommodated in college housing, which includes single-sex and coed dorms and off-campus apartments. There is also a Homestay program available. The housing office assists students in finding apartments and other living arrangements in Honolulu. On-campus housing is available on a first-come and first-served basis. Priority is given to out-of-town students. 97% of students commute. All students may keep cars. Alcohol is not permitted.

FACULTY/CLASSROOMS: 54% of faculty are male; 46% are female. 91% teach undergraduates, 42% do research, and 42% do both. No introductory courses are taught by graduate students. The average class size in an introductory lecture is 18; in a laboratory is 10; and in a regular course is 18.

PROGRAMS OF STUDY: HPU confers B.A., B.S., B.S.B.A., B.S.N., B.S.W., B.Ed., and B.S.H.S. degrees. Associate and master's degrees are also awarded. Bachelor's degrees are awarded in AGRICULTURE (environmental studies), BIOLOGICAL SCIENCE (biochemistry, biology/biological science, marine biology, and marine science), BUSINESS (accounting, banking and finance, business administration and management, business economics, entrepreneurial studies, finance, human resources, international business management, management information systems, management science, marketing management, personnel management, small business management, and tourism), COMMUNICATIONS AND THE ARTS (advertising, communications, English, journalism, multimedia, and public relations), COMPUTER AND PHYSICAL SCIENCE (applied mathematics, chemistry, computer programming, computer science, mathematics, oceanography, and science), EDUCATION (elementary education and teaching English as a second/foreign language (TESOL/TEFOL)), ENGINEERING AND ENVIRONMENTAL DESIGN (environmental science and military science), HEALTH PROFESSIONS (nursing, premedicine, and public health), SOCIAL SCIENCE (anthropology, classical/ancient civilization, criminal justice, economics, history, human services, humanities, international relations, international studies, Pacific area studies, political science/government, psychology, public administration, social science, social work, and sociology). Marine biology, nursing, and computer science are the strongest academically. Nursing, computer science, and management have the largest enrollments.

ACTIVITIES: There are no fraternities or sororities. There are 93 groups on campus, including art, band, cheerleading, chorale, computers, dance, debate, drama, environmental, ethnic, film, honors, international, LGBT, literary magazine, musical theater, newspaper, orchestra, pep band, political, professional, religious, social, social service, and student government. Popular campus events include Intercultural Day, Honors Banquet and Club Carnival. **Sports:** There are 6 intercollegiate sports for men and 6 for women, and 6 intramural sports for men and 6 for women. Facilities include a soccer field, softball fields, tennis courts, basketball courts, and women's softball team. **Graduates:** From July 1, 2015 to June 30, 2016, 926 bachelor's degrees were awarded. The most popular majors were business administration (33%), nursing (28%), and psychology (7%). 133 companies recruited on campus in 2015-2016. In an average class, 4% graduate in 3 years or less, 23% graduate in 4 years or less, 36% graduate in 5 years or less, and 39% graduate in 6 years or less. Of the 2015 graduating class, 40% were enrolled in graduate school within 6 months of graduation, and 69% were employed.

SERVICES: Counseling and information services are available, as is tutoring in most subjects, and remedial math, reading, and writing. **Library/Resources:** The 2 libraries contain 175,000 volumes, 415,000 microform items, and 6,300 audio/video tapes/CDs/DVDs, and subscribe to 45,000 periodicals including electronic. Computerized library services include interlibrary loans, database searching, Internet access, and Wi-Fi capability. Special learning facilities include an art gallery, and a research vessel. **Physically Challenged Students:** 75% of the campus is accessible. Facilities include wheelchair ramps, elevators, special parking, specially equipped restrooms, special class scheduling, lowered drinking fountains, and lowered telephones. **Special:** Upperclassmen may participate in internships and work-study programs with numerous companies and study abroad in 16 countries. HPU also offers accelerated degree and co-op programs in all majors, B.A.-B.S. degrees in most majors, student-designed majors, dual majors in all business subjects, a 3-2 engineering degree with Washington University in St. Louis, and the University of Southern California, credit for military experience, nondegree study, and pass/fail options. There are 18 national honor societies, a freshman honors program, and 7 departmental honors programs. **Visiting:** There are regularly scheduled orientations for prospective students, 9 am daily with an appointment. There are also guides for informal visits and visitors may sit in on classes. To schedule a visit, contact the Admissions Office. **Campus Safety and Security:** Measures include 24-hour foot and vehicle patrol, emergency notification system, and security escort services. There are also shuttle buses, emergency telephones, and lighted pathways/sidewalks.

REQUIREMENTS: The SAT or ACT is required. Hawaii Pacific University prefers completion of 20 credits based on 4 years of English, 2 each of math, and social studies, and 2 each of history, and science. An essay and an interview are recommended. Certain programs, for example, marine science and nursing, have more specific admission requirements. A GPA of 2.5 is required. AP and CLEP credits are accepted. Important factors in the admissions decision are recommendations by school officials, extracurricular activities record, and evidence of special talent. Seniors who have completed a minimum of 100 semester hours of credit toward their undergraduate degree program and have a cumulative GPA of at least 3.0 may enroll concurrently in certain graduate degree programs. Students enrolled in this program may earn a maximum of 12 semester hours of dual graduate and undergraduate credit while pursuing both degrees. (MA-TESL allows only 6 AL concurrent credits). **Procedure:** Freshmen are admitted to all sessions. Entrance exams should be taken during the spring or summer of the junior year, and fall of the senior year. There are early admissions, deferred admissions, and rolling admissions plans. Applications should be filed by August 15 for fall entry; October 15 for spring entry, along with a $50 fee. Applications are accepted online. **Transfer Students:** 890 transfer students enrolled in 2015-2016. Applicants must have a GPA of 2.0 in a minimum of 24 credit hours. The SAT or ACT and an interview are recommended. 30 of 124 credits required for the bachelor's degree must be completed at HPU. **International Students:** There are 632 international students enrolled. The school actively recruits these students. They must take the TOEFL with a minimum score of 550 on the paper-based TOEFL (PBT) or 80 on the Internet-based version (iBT), and the college's own test, or take the IELTS, scoring a minimum of 6, or the APIEL, scoring a minimum of 3.

ADMISSIONS: 72% of the 2016-2017 applicants were accepted. The SAT scores for the 2016-2017 freshman class were: Critical Reading-- 57% below 500, 35% between 500 and 599, 8% between 600 and 699, and 1% between 700 and 800. Math-- 52% below 500, 38% between 500 and 599, 9% between 600 and 699, and 1% between 700 and 800. Writing-- 63% below 500, 32% between 500 and 599, and 5% between 600 and 699. The ACT scores were 47% below 12, 30% between 12 and 17,

14% between 18 and 23, 5% between 24 and 29, and 5% above 30. 44% of the current freshmen were in the top fifth of their class; 76% were in the top two fifths. 18 freshmen graduated first in their class. **Admissions Contact:** Sara Sato, Asst. V.P. Enrollment Management. Email: *admissions@hpu.edu* Web: *www.hpu.edu*

FINANCIAL AID: 36% of all full-time freshmen received need-based aid. The FAFSA code is 007279. The priority date for freshman financial aid applications for fall entry is March 1.

UNIVERSITY OF HAWAII AT HILO F-4
www.uhh.hawaii.edu

Hilo, HI 96720	**(808) 974-7414** **(800) 897-4456**
Fax: (808) 933-0861	**Email: uhhadm@hawaii.edu**
Full-time: 880 men, 1335 women	**Faculty:** 162; IIB, +$
Part-time: 235 men, 400 women	**Ph.D.s:** 80%
Graduate: 30 men, 75 women	**Student/Faculty:** 14 to 1
Year: semesters, summer session	**Tuition:** $7620 ($20,580)
Room & Board: $10,418	**Freshman Class:** n/av
SAT or ACT: required	**CEEB CODE:** 4869
Application Deadline: July 1	**COMPETITIVE**

The University of Hawaii at Hilo, founded in 1970, is part of the public University of Hawaii and offers degree programs through its Colleges of Agriculture, Arts and Sciences, and Hawaiian language. The college also has a branch campus at Kealakekua, West Hawaii. Major programs include marine science, volcanology, and astronomy. The figures in the above capsule and in this profile are approximate. There are 3 undergraduate schools and 2 graduate schools. In addition to regional accreditation, UH-Hilo has baccalaureate program accreditation with NLN. The 115-acre campus is in a small town 200 miles southeast of Honolulu. Including any residence halls, there are 54 buildings.

STUDENT LIFE: 69% of undergraduates are from Hawaii. Others are from 46 states, 32 foreign countries, and Canada. 76% are from public schools. 9% are Foreign; 31% White; 27% Asian American; 2% Hispanic; 18% American Indian/Alaska Native; 1% African American. **Female To Male Ratio:** 1.6:1. The average age of all undergraduates is 27. 29% do not continue beyond their first year; 31% remain to graduate. **Housing:** 800 students can be accommodated in college housing, which includes coed dorms, on-campus apartments, off-campus apartments, and married student housing. In addition, there are honors houses, and special-interest houses. There is an educational/recreational enrichment hall. On-campus housing is available on a first-come and first-served basis. Priority is given to out-of-town students. 79% of students commute. All students may keep cars. Alcohol is not permitted.

FACULTY/CLASSROOMS: 60% of faculty are male; 40% are female. All teach undergraduates and do research. No introductory courses are taught by graduate students. The average class size in an introductory lecture is 25; in a laboratory is 25; and in a regular course is 17.

PROGRAMS OF STUDY: UH-Hilo confers B.A., B.S., B.B.A., and B.S.N. degrees. Master's degrees are also awarded. Bachelor's degrees are awarded in AGRICULTURE (agriculture and environmental studies), BIOLOGICAL SCIENCE (biology/biological science and marine science), BUSINESS (business administration and management), COMMUNICATIONS AND THE ARTS (art, art/art studies, communications, English, Hawaiian, Japanese, linguistics, and music), COMPUTER AND PHYSICAL SCIENCE (astronomy, chemistry, computer science, geology, mathematics, natural sciences, and physics), ENGINEERING AND ENVIRONMENTAL DESIGN (environmental science), HEALTH PROFESSIONS (nursing), SOCIAL SCIENCE (administration of justice , anthropology, criminal justice, economics, geography, Hawaiian studies, history, Japanese studies, liberal arts/general studies, philosophy, political science/government, psychology, and sociology). Business, computer science, and biology are the strongest academically. Business, psychology, and marine science have the largest enrollments.

ACTIVITIES: There are no fraternities or sororities. There are 40 groups on campus, including art, band, cheerleading, chess, choir, chorale, chorus, computers, dance, drama, ethnic, honors, international, jazz band, LGBT, literary magazine, musical theater, newspaper, pep band, political, professional, religious, social, social service, and student government. Popular campus events include International Night, May Day, and Dances. **Sports:** There are 5 intercollegiate sports for men and 4 for women, and 10 intramural sports for men and 10 for women. Facilities include a student activities center with billiards and a game room, an athletic complex with basketball courts, a weight room, tennis courts, baseball, softball, and soccer fields. **Graduates:** From July 1, 2015 to June 30, 2016, 419 bachelor's degrees were awarded. The most popular majors were psychology (15%), business administration (11%), and marine science (8%). 36 companies recruited on campus in 2015-2016. In an average class, 1% graduate in 3 years or less, 10% graduate in 4 years or less, 25% graduate in 5 years or less, and 31% graduate in 6 years or less.

SERVICES: Counseling and information services are available, as is tutoring in most subjects, and remedial math, reading, and writing. **Library/Resources:** The library contains 240,000 volumes, 11,000 microform items, and subscribes to 1,200 periodicals including electronic. Computerized library services include interlibrary loans and database searching. Special learning facilities include an art gallery, a space science center, and marine education center. **Physically Challenged Students:** 95% of the campus is accessible. Facilities include wheelchair ramps, elevators, special parking, specially equipped restrooms, special class scheduling, lowered drinking fountains, and lowered telephones. **Special:** UH-Hilo offers cross-registration with Hawaii Community College, a political science legislative internship and other internships in business, and psychology, including many work-study programs. Students may study abroad through a variety of programs and other internships in business and psychology. The school permits a student-designed liberal studies major, dual degrees, a 3-2 engineering degree with the University of Hawaii at Manoa, nondegree study, pass/fail options, and credit for military experience. There is a freshman honors program and 1 departmental honors program. **Visiting:** There are regularly scheduled orientations for prospective students, including a campus tour and a meeting with an admissions counselor. There are guides for informal visits and visitors may sit in on classes. To schedule a visit, contact the Admissions Office. **Campus Safety and Security:** Measures include 24-hour foot, vehicle patrol, and self-defense education, emergency telephones, and lighted pathways/sidewalks.

REQUIREMENTS: The SAT or ACT is required. Applicants should be high school graduates or present a GED certificate. Students should have earned 22 academic credits, including 4 units of English, 3 of math, 3 of life and physical sciences, and 7 of electives. A GPA of 2.5 is required. AP and CLEP credits are accepted. Important factors in the admissions decision are advanced placement or honors courses, recommendations by school officials, and evidence of special talent. To graduate, students must earn a minimum of 120 semester hours, including at least 30 in the college from which a degree is sought, with a 2.0 GPA overall and in the major. Students also must complete general education requirements, including 10 semester hours of natural sciences with 1 hour of lab, 9 each of humanitites and social sciences, 6 of world cultures, and 3 each of English composition and quantitative reasoning. 3 writing-intensive sourses and 1 Hawaiian/Asian/Pacific course are also required. **Procedure:** Freshmen are admitted in the fall and spring. Entrance exams should be taken by November of the senior year. There are early admissions and rolling admissions plans. Applications should be filed by July 1 for fall entry; December 1 for spring entry, along with a $25 fee. Applications are accepted online. **Transfer Students:** 577 transfer students enrolled in 2015-2016. Applicants must have a GPA of 2.0; those with fewer than 24 college credits must submit their high school transcript and SAT I or ACT results. 30 of 120 credits required for the bachelor's degree must be completed at UH-Hilo. **International Students:** There are 311 international students enrolled. The school actively recruits these students. They must take the TOEFL and the college's own test. The SAT I or ACT is not required, but is recommended.

ADMISSIONS: 4 freshmen graduated first in their class. **Admissions Contact:** Admissions Office Email: *uhhadm@hawaii.edu* Web: *www.uhh.hawaii.edu*

FINANCIAL AID: In 2016-2017, 55% of all full-time freshmen and 41% of continuing full-time students received some form of financial aid. 55% of all full-time freshmen received need-based aid. The average freshman award was $3,853. 70% of undergraduate students work part-time. Average annual earnings from campus work are $2600. The average financial indebtedness of the 2016 graduate was $10,698. UH-Hilo is a member of CSS. The college's own financial statement is required. The FAFSA code is 001611. The deadline for filing freshman financial aid applications for fall entry is March 1.

UNIVERSITY OF HAWAII AT MANOA C-2

www.hawaii.edu

Honolulu, HI 96822 **(808) 956-8111** **(800) 823-9771**

Fax: (808) 956-4148 **Email: uhmanoa.admissions@hawaii.edu**

Full-time: 5388 men, 6246 women	**Faculty:** 1209; I, av$
Part-time: 1261 men, 1507 women	**Ph.D.s:** 87%
Graduate: 2473 men, 3554 women	**Student/Faculty:** 13 to 1
Year: semesters, summer session	**Tuition:** $10,622 ($29,414)
Room & Board: $13,284	**Freshman Class:** 6541 applied, 5130 accepted, 2010 enrolled
SAT CR/M/W: 530/560/520 **ACT:** 23	**CEEB CODE:** 4867
Application Deadline: May 1	**COMPETITIVE**

The University of Hawaii at Manoa, founded in 1907, is a public research institution in the University of Hawaii system. The undergraduate programs offered include liberal arts and sciences, business, education, engineering, nursing, tropical agriculture, architecture, travel industry management, physical science, technology, Hawaiian, Asian-Pacific studies, social work, and medicine. Figures in the above capsule and in this profile are approximate. There are 14 undergraduate schools and 15 graduate schools. In addition to regional accreditation, UHM has baccalaureate program accreditation with AACSB, ABET, ADA, CSWE, NAAB, NASM, NCATE, NLN, CODA, and NLNAC. The 320-acre campus is in a small town in Manoa, Valley, just outside downtown Honolulu.

STUDENT LIFE: 66% of undergraduates are from Hawaii. Others are from 50 states, 126 foreign countries, and Canada. 68% are from public schools. 36% are Asian American; 23% White; 19% two or more races. **Female To Male Ratio:** 1.2:1. The average age of freshmen is 18; all undergraduates, 22. 23% do not continue beyond their first year; 55% remain to graduate. **Housing:** 3696 students can be accommodated in college housing, which includes single-sex and coed dorms, on-campus apartments, and married student housing. In addition, there are honors houses, language houses, special-interest houses, substance free/wellness, first-year experience, technology, and 24-hour quiet halls. On-campus housing is guaranteed for the freshman year only and is available on a lottery system for upperclassmen. Priority is given to out-of-town students. 81% of students commute. All students may keep cars.

FACULTY/CLASSROOMS: 56% of faculty are male; 44% are female. 81% teach undergraduates. Graduate students teach 20% of introductory courses. The average class size in an introductory lecture is 38; in a laboratory is 15; and in a regular course is 22.

PROGRAMS OF STUDY: UHM confers B.A., B.S., B.B.A., B.Ed., B.F.A., B.Mus., and B.S.W. degrees. Master's and doctoral degrees are also awarded. Bachelor's degrees are awarded in AGRICULTURE (animal science, natural resource management, plant protection (pest management), plant science, and soil science), BIOLOGICAL SCIENCE (biology/biological science, botany, marine biology, microbiology, and zoology), BUSINESS (accounting, banking and finance, business administration and management, human resources, international business management, management information systems, management science, marketing/retailing/merchandising, recreation and leisure services, and tourism), COMMUNICATIONS AND THE ARTS (apparel design, art, Chinese, classics, communications, dance, dramatic arts, English, English as a second/foreign language, French, German, Hawaiian, Japanese, journalism, Korean, linguistics, music, Russian, Spanish, and speech/debate/rhetoric), COMPUTER AND PHYSICAL SCIENCE (atmospheric sciences and meteorology, chemistry, computer science, geology, geophysics and seismology, information sciences and systems, mathematics, and physics), EDUCATION (elementary education, physical education, and secondary education), ENGINEERING AND ENVIRONMENTAL DESIGN (bioengineering, civil engineering, electrical/electronics engineering, environmental science, and mechanical engineering), HEALTH PROFESSIONS (dental hygiene, exercise science, medical laboratory technology, medical technology, nursing, and speech pathology/audiology), SOCIAL SCIENCE (American studies, anthropology, Asian/Oriental studies, economics, ethnic studies, family/consumer resource management, food science, geography, Hawaiian studies, history, interdisciplinary studies, Pacific area studies, peace studies, philosophy, political science/government, psychology, religion, social work, sociology, and women's studies). Biology, art, and business have the largest enrollments.

ACTIVITIES: 1% of men belong to 1 local and 2 national fraternities; 1% of women belong to 1 local and 1 national sororities. There are 100 groups on campus, including art, band, cheerleading, chess, choir, chorale, chorus, dance, drama, drill team, ethnic, film, honors, international, LGBT, literary magazine, marching band, musical theater, newspaper, opera, pep band, photography, political, professional, radio and TV, religious, social, social service, student government, and symphony. Popular campus events include Live Band at Bale, Movie Nights, Sustainable UH, and Recreational Sports Events. **Sports:** There are 9 intercollegiate sports for men and 13 for women, and 24 intramural sports for men and 21 for women. Facilities include a arena for basketball, volleyball, as well as gymnasiums, with a weight training and conditioning center, baseball stadium, swimming facilities, a turf field and rubberized track, softball field, tennis courts, golf, sailing, water polo, cross country, football, and women's soccer. **Graduates:** From July 1, 2014 to June 30, 2015, 2957 bachelor's degrees were awarded. The most popular majors were buisness/marketing (21%), social sciences (11%), and education (7%). 100 companies recruited on campus in 2014-2015. In an average class, 15% graduate in 4 years or less, 40% graduate in 5 years or less, and 51% graduate in 6 years or less.

SERVICES: Counseling and information services are available, as is tutoring in some subjects, and a reader service for the blind. **Library/Resources:** The 5 libraries contain 3.4 million volumes, 2.4 million microform items, 73,000 audio/video tapes/CDs/DVDs, and subscribe to 59,000 periodicals including electronic. Computerized library services include interlibrary loans, database searching, Internet access, and Wi-Fi capability. Special learning facilities include an art gallery, radio station, and TV station, as well as research collections in humanities, social sciences and technology, Asia, Hawaii and the Pacific, and also archived manuscripts and other special collections. **Physically Challenged Students:** 40% of the campus is accessible. Facilities include wheelchair ramps, elevators, special parking, specially equipped restrooms, special class scheduling, lowered drinking fountains, and lowered telephones. Disability access information is available on request, and auxiliary aids and program adjustments can be arranged on an individual basis. **Special:** Internships are available with a variety of employers, including the state legislature, and through 55 different offices as well as academic departments via career services. Co-op and work-study programs, internships, dual majors, non-degree study, and pass/fail options are also available. The liberal studies program offers student-designed majors. Students may study abroad in any one of 20 countries for a summer, a semester, or a year. There are 9 national honor societies, Phi Beta Kappa, a freshman honors program, and 45 departmental honors programs. **Visiting:** There are regularly scheduled orientations for prospective students, and visiting students can meet with an admissions representative and tour the campus with a current UH Manoa Student. To schedule a visit, contact the Admissions Office at manoa.admissions@hawaii.edu. **Campus Safety and Security:** Measures include 24-hour foot and vehicle patrol, emergency notification system, and security escort services. There are also shuttle buses, emergency telephones, lighted pathways/sidewalks, crime alerts via campuswide e-mail, and a campus security web site.

REQUIREMENTS: The ACT Optional Writing test is required. Applicants must be graduates of an accredited secondary school, and have the minimum required score of 510 for each SAT section, or 22 on the ACT composite. The GED is also accepted. UHM requires 22 Carnegie units or 17 academic credits, including 4 units of English, and 3 units each of math, science, and social studies, as well as 4 additional units of college preparatory courses and 5 electives. UHM requires applicants to be in the upper 40% of their class. A GPA of 2.8 is required. AP and CLEP credits are accepted. Important factors in the admissions decision are advanced placement or honors courses, recommendations by school officials, and leadership record. In most disciplines, a minimum GPA of 2.0 and a total of 124 credit hours are required for graduation. The total number of hours required in the major varies according to discipline. All students must fulfill general education core requirements. **Procedure:** Freshmen are admitted in fall and spring. Entrance exams should be taken by December of the senior year for fall admission. There is a rolling admissions plan. Applications should be filed by May 1 for fall entry; October 1 for spring entry, along with a $70 fee. Notification is sent on a rolling basis. Applications are accepted online. **Transfer Students:** 1855 transfer students enrolled in 2014-2015. Applicants must have a total of 24 semester credits with a minimum GPA of 2.5. 30 of 124 credits required for the bachelor's degree must be completed at UHM. **International Students:** There are 628 international students enrolled. The school actively recruits these students. They must take the TOEFL with a minimum score of 500 on the paper-based TOEFL (PBT) or 100 on the Internet-based version (iBT). They must also take the SAT or ACT, scoring 510.

ADMISSIONS: 78% of the 2015-2016 applicants were accepted. The SAT scores for the 2015-2016 freshman class were: Critical Reading-- 34% below 500, 46% between 500 and 599, 18% between 600 and 699, and 2% between 700 and 800. Math-- 24% below 500, 47% between 500 and 599, 25% between 600 and 699, and 4% between 700 and 800. Writing-- 36% below 500, 49% between 500 and 599, 14% between 600 and 699, and 1% between 700 and 800. The ACT scores were 25% below 12, 32% between 12 and 17, 26% between 18 and 23, 10% between 24 and 29, and 7% above 30. 60% of the current freshmen were in the top fifth of their class; 82% were in the top two fifths. 24 freshmen graduated first in their class. **Admissions Contact:** Dr. Alan Yang, Interim Director of Admissions and Records. E-Mail: *uhmanoa.admissions@hawaii.edu* Web: *www.hawaii.edu*

FINANCIAL AID: In 2015-2016, 66% of all full-time freshmen and 59% of continuing full-time students received some form of financial aid. 38% of all full-time freshmen and 42% of continuing full-time students received need-based aid. The average freshman award was $11,914. Need-based scholarships or need-based grants averaged $9,133 ($14,050 maximum); need-based self-help aid (loans and jobs) averaged $3,246 ($7,700 maximum); non-need-based athletic scholarships averaged $10,460 ($16,900 maximum); and other non-need-based awards and non-need-based scholarships averaged $8,863 ($28,019 maximum). 27% of undergraduate students work part-time. Average annual earnings from campus work are $3211. The average financial indebtedness of the 2015 graduate was $17,447. The FAFSA and the college's own financial statement are required. The deadline for filing freshman financial aid applications for fall entry is March 1.

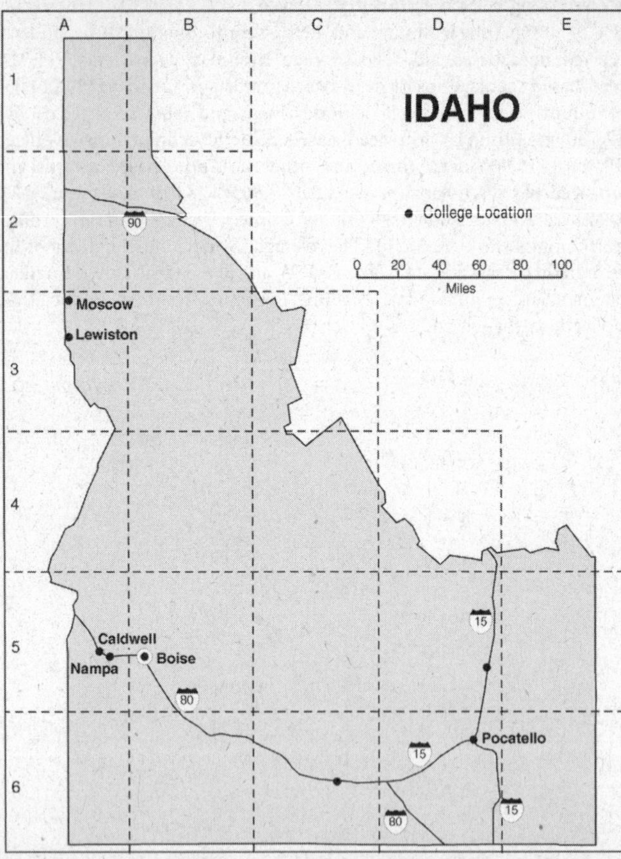

BOISE STATE UNIVERSITY B-5

www.boisestate.edu

Boise, ID 83725 (208) 426-1156
(800) 824-7017

Fax: (208) 426-3765 Email: bsuinfo@boisestate.edu

Full-time: 5868 men, 6507 women
Part-time: 3383 men, 4451 women
Graduate: 1364 men, 2313 women
Year: semesters, summer session
Room & Board: $7780

SAT CR/M: required **ACT:** required
Application Deadline: May 15

Faculty: 530; IIA, -$
Ph.D.s: 67%
Student/Faculty: 24 to 1
Tuition: $7080 ($21,530)
Freshman Class: 8330 applied, 6808 accepted, 2570 enrolled
CEEB CODE: 4018
COMPETITIVE

Boise State University, founded in 1932, is a public, metropolitan research university offering an array of undergraduate and graduate degrees in the arts and sciences, business, education, engineering, health science, public affairs, and technology. There are 7 undergraduate schools and 1 graduate school. In addition to regional accreditation, Boise State has baccalaureate program accreditation with AACSB, ABET, ACCE, CAHEA, CSWE, NASAD, NASM, NCATE, NLN, JCERT, EHAC, and CoARC. The 285-acre campus is in an urban area in Boise, Idaho. Including any residence halls, there are 207 buildings.

STUDENT LIFE: 72% of undergraduates are from Idaho. Others are from 50 states, 58 foreign countries, and Canada. 74% are White; 11% Hispanic; 5% Foreign; 4% two or more races; 2% African American; 2% Asian American; 2% race unknown; 1% American Indian/Alaska Native. **Female To Male Ratio:** 1.3:1. The average age of freshmen is 18; all undergraduates, 24. 24% do not continue beyond their first year; 38% remain to graduate. **Housing:** 2692 students can be accommodated in college housing, which includes coed dorms, on-campus apartments, married student housing, honors houses, special-interest houses, fraternity houses, and sorority houses. On-campus housing is guaranteed for the freshman year only, and is available on a first-come, and first-served basis. All students may keep cars.

FACULTY/CLASSROOMS: 49% of faculty are male; 51% are female. No introductory courses are taught by graduate students. The average class size in an introductory lecture is 42 and in a laboratory is 20.

PROGRAMS OF STUDY: Boise State confers B.A., B.A.S., B.G.S., B.B.A., B.F.A., B.S. and B.Mus. degrees. Associate, master's, and doctoral degrees are also awarded. Bachelor's degrees are awarded in AGRICULTURE (environmental studies), BIOLOGICAL SCIENCE (biology/biological science), BUSINESS (accounting, business administration and management, economics – statistics, finance, international business management, marketing/retailing/merchandising, and supply chain management), COMMUNICATIONS AND THE ARTS (art, communications, dramatic arts, English, English literature, English writing, fine arts, French, German, music, Spanish, and theatre arts), COMPUTER AND PHYSICAL SCIENCE (chemistry, computer science, geology, geophysics and seismology, geoscience, information sciences and systems, mathematics, physics, and radiological technology), EDUCATION (art education, education, elementary education, English education, music education, physical education, secondary education, social science education, and special education), ENGINEERING AND ENVIRONMENTAL DESIGN (civil engineering, construction management, electrical/electronics engineering, materials science, and mechanical engineering), HEALTH PROFESSIONS (environmental health science, health science, nursing, predentistry, premedicine, prepharmacy, prephysical therapy, preveterinary science, and respiratory therapy), SOCIAL SCIENCE (anthropology, criminal justice, early childhood studies, economics, history, interdisciplinary studies, philosophy, political science/government, psychology, social science, social work, and sociology). Health science studies & nursing, management, and marketing & finance have the largest enrollments.

ACTIVITIES: There are 461 groups on campus, including the residence life club, art, band, cheerleading, choir, chorale, communications, computers, dance, debate, drama, drill team, environmental, ethnic, film, health & ability club, honors, international, jazz band, LGBT, literary magazine, marching band, newspaper, orchestra, pep band, political, professional, radio and TV, religious, social, social service, and student government. Popular campus events include Bronco Welcome, Annual Seven Arrows Contest Pow Wow, Homecoming, Annual Spring Fling, Tunnel of Oppression, and Undergraduate Research & Scholarship Conference. **Sports:** There are 6 intercollegiate sports for men and 9 for women, and 10 intramural sports for men and 10 for women. Facilities include a student recreation center, stadium, indoor arena, aquatic complex, racquetball courts, indoor and outdoor tennis courts, and indoor and outdoor tracks. **Graduates:** From July 1, 2015 to June 30, 2016, 2998 bachelor's degrees were awarded. The most popular majors were registered nursing (10%), communication studies (7%), and general psychology (6%). In an average class, 15% graduate in 4 years or less, 30% graduate in 5 years or less, and 38% graduate in 6 years or less.

SERVICES: Counseling and information services are available, as is tutoring in some subjects, such as accounting, biology, foreign language, algebra, physics, economics, finance, chemistry, and engineering. There is also a reader service for the blind, and remedial math, reading, and writing. **Library/Resources:** The library contains 800,205 volumes, 14,842 audio/video tapes/CDs/DVDs, and subscribes to 2,058 periodicals including electronic. Computerized library services include interlibrary loans, database searching, Internet access, and Wi-Fi capability. Special learning facilities include an art gallery, radio station, and a technology center. **Physically Challenged Students:** 97% of the campus is accessible. Facilities include wheelchair ramps, elevators, special parking, specially equipped restrooms, special class scheduling, lowered drinking fountains, lowered telephones, and special housing. **Special:** Boise State offers internships, work-study programs, dual majors, a general studies degree, nondegree study, pass/fail options, and study abroad. There are 7 national honor societies, Phi Beta Kappa, a freshman honors program, and 5 departmental honors programs. **Visiting:** There are regularly scheduled orientations for prospective students, information sessions, campus tour, workshops, housing, and stadium tour. There are guides for informal visits and visitors may sit in on classes. To schedule a visit, contact Admissions Office. **Campus Safety and Security:** Measures include 24-hour foot and vehicle patrol, emergency notification system, and security escort services. There are also shuttle buses, emergency telephones, lighted pathways/sidewalks, and controlled access to dorms/residences.

REQUIREMENTS: Students must graduate from an accredited high school and have an appropriate GPA and ACT or SAT test score (as rated by the school's admission index). Students must have completed 4 years of English, 3 each of math (algebra I and higher) and natural science, 2 1/2 of social science, 1 of humanities or foreign language, and 1 1/2 in other college-preparatory classes. Students who have not completed all the above classes but meet the other admission requirements will be considered for provisional admission status. AP and CLEP credits are accepted. To graduate, students must complete the number of credits specified for their degree with a minimum GPA of 2.0. Requirements include 6 semester hours in English composition and 12 each in arts and humanities, social sciences, math, and natural sciences. Students must fulfill all Foundation Studies Program requirements. A minimum grade of C is required in all major courses and courses used to meet the core requirements. **Procedure:** Freshmen are admitted in the fall, spring, and summer. Entrance exams should be taken and scores received by May 15. There is a rolling admissions plan. Applications should be filed by May 15 for fall entry; November 15 for spring entry; and May 15 for summer entry, along with a $50 fee. Notification is sent on a rolling basis. Application fees are waived if application is completed on-line. **Transfer Students:** 1485 transfer students enrolled in 2015-2016. A minimum GPA of 2.0 is required for students with at least 14 college credits. Those students with fewer credits must submit SAT or ACT scores and a high school transcript. 30 of 120 credits required for the bachelor's degree must be completed at Boise State. **International Students:** There are 730 international students enrolled. The school actively recruits these students. They must take the TOEFL with a minimum score of 520 on the paper-based TOEFL (PBT) or 68 on the Internet-based version (iBT). They must also take the SAT or ACT.

ADMISSIONS: 37% of the current freshmen were in the top fifth of their class; 73% were in the top two fifths. **Admissions Contact:** Kelly Talbert, Director of Admission. Email: *bsuinfo@boisestate.edu* Web: *www.boisestate.edu*

FINANCIAL AID: The average freshman award was $10,747. Need-based scholarships or need-based grants averaged $5,457; and need-based self-help aid (loans and jobs) averaged $3,593. Boise State is a member of CSS. The FAFSA code is 001616. The priority date for freshman financial aid applications for fall entry is February 15. The filing deadline for fall entry is May 15.

IDAHO STATE UNIVERSITY *(The complete profile is made available exclusively on our website, www.barronspac.com)*

LEWIS-CLARK STATE COLLEGE — A-3

www.lcsc.edu

Lewiston, ID 83501	**(208) 792-2210** **(800) 933-LCSC**
Fax: (208) 792-2876	**Email: admissions@lcsc.edu**
Full-time: 960 men, 1315 women	**Faculty:** 134; IIB
Part-time: 415 men, 805 women	**Ph.D.s:** 71%
Graduate: n/av	**Student/Faculty:** 17 to 1
Year: semesters, summer session	**Tuition:** $6000 ($17,000)
Room & Board: $8202	**Freshman Class:** n/av
SAT or ACT: required	**CEEB CODE:** 4385
Application Deadline: August 8	**COMPETITIVE**

Lewis-Clark State College, founded in 1893 and part of the Idaho Higher Education System, offers programs in the arts and sciences, business, education, nursing, and preprofessional and technical training. Figures in the above capsule and in this profile are approximate. There are 8 undergraduate schools. In addition to regional accreditation, Lewis-Clark has baccalaureate program accreditation with AACSB, NASDTEC, NCATE, and NLN. The 44-acre campus is in an urban area 100 miles southeast of Spokane. Including any residence halls, there are 29 buildings.

STUDENT LIFE: 86% of undergraduates are from Idaho. Others are from 20 states, 30 foreign countries, and Canada. 82% are White; 5% American Indian/Alaska Native; 3% Hispanic; 3% Foreign; 1% African American; 1% Asian American. **Female To Male Ratio:** 1.5:1. The average age of freshmen is 21; all undergraduates, 25. 46% do not continue beyond their first year; 28% remain to graduate. **Housing:** 300 students can be accommodated in college housing, which includes single-sex and coed dorms, off-campus apartments, married student housing, honors houses and language houses. On-campus housing is available on a first-come and first-served basis. 91% of students commute. All students may keep cars. Alcohol is not permitted.

FACULTY/CLASSROOMS: 58% of faculty are male; 42% are female. All teach undergraduates. No introductory courses are taught by graduate students. The average class size in an introductory lecture is 33 and in a laboratory is 25.

PROGRAMS OF STUDY: Lewis-Clark confers B.A., B.S., B. Applied Sc., B. Applied Tech., B.S.N. and B.S.W. degrees. Associate degrees are also awarded. Bachelor's degrees are awarded in BIOLOGICAL SCIENCE (biology/biological science), BUSINESS (business administration and management), COMMUNICATIONS AND THE ARTS (communications, English, and sports administration), COMPUTER AND PHYSICAL SCIENCE (chemistry, computer science, geoscience, mathematics, and natural sciences), EDUCATION (early childhood education, education, elementary education, and secondary education), ENGINEERING AND ENVIRONMENTAL DESIGN (automotive technology and welding engineering), HEALTH PROFESSIONS (nursing and radiograph medical technology), SOCIAL SCIENCE (addiction studies, criminal justice, history, interdisciplinary studies, liberal arts/general studies, physical fitness/movement, psychology, social science, social work, and sociology). Education, business, and nursing are the strongest academically, and have the largest enrollments.

ACTIVITIES: There are no fraternities or sororities. There are 46 groups on campus, including art, chess, choir, chorale, chorus, computers, dance, debate, drama, ethnic, honors, international, jazz band, literary magazine, musical theater, newspaper, orchestra, political, professional, radio and TV, religious, social, and student government. Popular campus events include Artists Series and Dogwood Festival. **Sports:** There are 5 intercollegiate sports for men and 5 for women, and 8 intramural sports for men and 7 for women. Facilities include a gym, indoor tennis courts, and a baseball field. **Graduates:** From July 1, 2015 to June 30, 2016, 299 bachelor's degrees were awarded. The most popular majors were business (25%), justice studies (15%), and nursing (14%). Of the 2015 graduating class, 8% were enrolled in graduate school within 6 months of graduation.

SERVICES: Counseling and information services are available, as is tutoring in every subject. There is a reader service for the blind, and remedial math, reading, and writing. **Library/Resources:** The library contains 253,000 volumes, 53,000 microform items, 7,000 audio/video tapes/CDs/DVDs, and subscribes to 4,000 periodicals including electronic. Computerized library services include interlibrary loans and database searching. Special learning facilities include an art gallery, planetarium, radio station, TV station, and an educational technology center. **Physically Challenged Students:** 99% of the campus is accessible. Facilities include wheelchair ramps, elevators, special parking, specially equipped restrooms, and special class scheduling. **Special:** Lewis-Clark offers cooperative programs and cross-registration with 3 Idaho universities, on-campus internships, work-study programs, student-designed majors, nondegree study, and pass/fail options. The college grants credit for military experience. There are also between-semester and weekend academic programs, and flexible scheduling in a variety of programs. A 3-2 engineering degree is available at Boise or Idaho State Universities. There is 1 national honor society and a freshman honors program. **Visiting:** There are regularly scheduled orientations for prospective students, including STAR (Student Advising and Registration), and Warrior Discovery Day. There are guides for informal visits, visitors may sit in on classes, and stay overnight. To schedule a visit, contact the Office of Recruitment and Retention at (208) 792-2378. **Campus Safety and Security:** Measures include 24-hour foot and vehicle patrol, emergency notification system, self-defense education, and security escort services. There are also shuttle buses and lighted pathways/sidewalks.

REQUIREMENTS: The SAT or ACT is required. Lewis-Clark has a liberal admissions policy, but students must be high school graduates or present a GED certificate. They must have fulfilled requirements in English, math, social and natural sciences, fine arts, and speech, with a minimum GPA of 2.0. A GPA of 2.0 is required. AP and CLEP credits are accepted. Students must earn between 120 and 128 credit hours depending on program, including 38 to 40 in the core curriculum and 48 in their major, with a minimum GPA of 2.0 to graduate. **Procedure:** Freshmen are admitted to all sessions. Entrance exams should be taken before registration. There are early admissions, deferred admissions, and rolling admissions plans. Application deadlines are open. Application fee is $35. Applications are accepted on-line. **Transfer Students:** 389 transfer students enrolled in 2015-2016. Applicants who do not have a minimum GPA of 2.0 must submit standardized test scores. 32 of 128 credits required for the bachelor's degree must be completed at Lewis-Clark. **International Students:** There are 94 international students enrolled. The school actively recruits these students. They must take the TOEFL.

ADMISSIONS: 5 freshmen graduated first in their class. **Admissions Contact:** Steven J. Bussolini, Director of Admission and Market Development. Email: *admissions@lcsc.edu* Web: *www.lcsc.edu*

FINANCIAL AID: In 2016-2017, 68% of all full-time freshmen and 62% of continuing full-time students received some form of financial aid. 52% of all full-time freshmen and 50% of continuing full-time students received need-based aid. The average freshman award was $4,033. Need-based scholarships or need-based grants averaged $2,781; need-based self-help aid (loans and jobs) averaged $2,652; non-need-based athletic scholarships averaged $4,485; and other non-need-based awards and non-need-based scholarships averaged $2,873. 10% of undergraduate students work part-time. Lewis-Clark is a member of CSS. The FAFSA code is 001621. The deadline for filing freshman financial aid applications for fall entry is March 1.

NORTHWEST NAZARENE UNIVERSITY A-5

www.nnu.edu

Nampa, ID 83686	**(208) 467-8950** **(877) NNU-4-YOU**
Fax: (208) 467-8645	**Email: admissions@nnu.edu**
Full-time: 633 men, 691 women	**Faculty:** 106
Part-time: 62 men, 95 women	**Ph.D.s:** 72%
Graduate: 273 men, 451 women	**Student/Faculty:** 16 to 1
Year: semesters, summer session	**Tuition:** $29,000
Room & Board: $7000	**Freshman Class:** 1099 applied, 1150 accepted, 271 enrolled
SAT CR/M/W: 525/515/510 **ACT:** 24	**CEEB CODE:** 4544
Application Deadline: August 15	**COMPETITIVE**

Northwest Nazarene University, founded in 1913, is a comprehensive Christian university offering over 60 areas of study, 19 master's degrees in seven different disciplines, and one doctoral degree. The University also offers programs online as well as in Boise, Idaho Falls, McCall, Twin Falls and in cooperation with programs in 10 countries. The approximate figures in the above capsule are for tuition, room and board. There is 1 undergraduate school and 1 graduate school. In addition to regional accreditation, NNU has baccalaureate program accreditation with ABET, ACBSP, CSWE, NASM, NCATE, CACREP, CCNE, and NACEP. The 90-acre campus is in a small town 20 miles west of Boise. Including any residence halls, there are 34 buildings.

STUDENT LIFE: 43% of undergraduates are from out of state, mostly the Northwest. Students are from 41 states, 21 foreign countries, and Canada. 73% are White; 7% Hispanic; 7% race unknown; 4% two or more races; 2% African American; 2% Asian American; 1% American Indian/Alaska Native; 1% Foreign. 66% are Protestant; 12% claim no religious affiliation. **Female To Male Ratio:** 1.3:1. The average age of freshmen is 18; all undergraduates, 23. 28% do not continue beyond their first year; 48% remain to graduate. **Housing:** 788 students can be accommodated in college housing, which includes single-sex dorms, on-campus apartments, and married student housing. On-campus housing is guaranteed for all 4 years. 76% of students live on campus. All students may keep cars. Alcohol is not permitted.

FACULTY/CLASSROOMS: 57% of faculty are male; 43% are female. No introductory courses are taught by graduate students.

PROGRAMS OF STUDY: NNU confers B.A., and B.S., degrees. Associate, master's, and doctoral degrees are also awarded. Bachelor's degrees are awarded in BIOLOGICAL SCIENCE (biochemistry and biology/biological science), BUSINESS (accounting, business administration and management, business administration, management, operations, and recreation and leisure services), COMMUNICATIONS AND THE ARTS (art, communications, English, graphic design, music, and Spanish), COMPUTER AND PHYSICAL SCIENCE (chemistry, computer information systems, computer science, mathematics, and physics), EDUCATION (art education, Christian education, education of the exceptional child, elementary education, English education, mathematics education, music education, physical education, recreation education, and secondary education), ENGINEERING AND ENVIRONMENTAL DESIGN (computer graphics, engineering, and engineering physics), HEALTH PROFESSIONS (nursing), SOCIAL SCIENCE (biblical studies, criminal justice, cultural studies/critical theory & analysis, history, international studies, liberal arts/general studies, ministries, philosophy and religion, political science/government, psychology, social work, and youth ministry). Nursing, engineering, and teaching are the strongest academically. Nursing, engineering, and biology/chemistry have the largest enrollments.

ACTIVITIES: There are no fraternities or sororities. There are 50 groups on campus, including art, band, cheerleading, choir, chorale, chorus, computers, debate, drama, environmental, ethnic, film, forensics, honors, international, jazz band, literary magazine, musical theater, newspaper, orchestra, pep band, photography, political, professional, radio and TV, religious, social, social service, student government, symphony, and yearbook. Popular campus events include Welcome Week, Week One, and Spiritual Emphasis Week. **Sports:** There are 6 intercollegiate sports for men and 6 for women, and 7 intramural sports for men and 7 for women. Facilities include a baseball field, soccer fields, outdoor basketball, tennis, sand volleyball courts, track-and-field facility, golf, cross country, field house, park, and a softball field. **Graduates:** From July 1, 2015 to June 30, 2016, 332 bachelor's degrees were awarded. The most popular majors were business/marketing (27%), education (12%), health professions, and and related programs (10%). 105 companies recruited on campus in 2015-2016. In an average class, 49% graduate in 6 years or less.

SERVICES: Counseling and information services are available, as is tutoring in every subject, and remedial math, reading, and writing. **Library/Resources:** Computerized library services include interlibrary loans, database searching, Internet access, and Wi-Fi capability. Special learning facilities include an art gallery, radio station, an educational media center. **Physically Challenged Students:** Facilities include wheelchair ramps, elevators, special parking, specially equipped restrooms, special class scheduling, lowered drinking fountains, lowered telephones, and special housing. **Special:** NNU offers cross-registration with other Nazarene schools and study abroad in 14 countries. The university also offers internships, which are required in many majors, a work-study program, a general studies degree, dual and student-designed majors, and credit for military experience (Army ROTC program). Adult and Professional programs are offered in business, education and religion. There are 4 national honor societies, a freshman honors program, and 3 departmental honors programs. **Visiting:** There are regularly scheduled orientations for prospective students, including an overnight stay in a dorm, a campus tour, class attendance, financial and admission counseling, meetings with professor and coaches, and music and athletic tryouts. There are guides for informal visits, visitors may sit in on classes, and stay overnight. To schedule a visit, contact the Campus Visit Coordinator at (208) 467-8000. **Campus Safety and Security:** Measures include 24-hour foot and vehicle patrol, emergency notification system, and security escort services. There are also emergency telephones, lighted pathways/sidewalks, controlled access to dorms/residences, a professional security company, student lock-up-unlock and walk-around-campus teams, and a city police substation.

REQUIREMENTS: Applicants should be graduates of an accredited secondary school; the GED may also be accepted. For standard admission, students must fulfill 2 of the 3 following requirements: graduate with a 2.5 (or higher) GPA on a 4.0 scale, rank in the top 50% of their graduating class, or have an ACT composite score of 18 or a combined score of 870 on the math and critical reasoning sections of the SAT. Provisional admission may be available for students who do not meet the above requirements. Applicants should prepare with recommended units of 4 years of English, 3 each of math, science, and 2 of foreign language, 1.5 each if social studies and history. NNU requires applicants to be in the upper 50% of their class. A GPA of 2.5 is required. AP and CLEP credits are accepted. All students must complete 124 semester credits, of which 43 must be upper division. Students must show competency in communication and language skills, have a 2.0 GPA, demonstrate math proficiency, complete a major field of study, and take a comprehensive exam. In addition, each student must complete general education requirements, which are divided into three categories: abilities (17 credits of English, communications, kinesiology, math, and humanities courses), contextual disciplines (15 credits of bible, theology, philosophy, and history courses as well as a cross-cultural experience), and explorations (23 credits of upper-division bible literature or theology, humanities, science, and social sciences electives). The number of hours required varies per major, as do senior internships and projects. **Procedure:** Freshmen are admitted in the fall, spring, and summer. Entrance exams should be taken early in the senior year. There are early admissions and rolling admissions plans. Early decision applications should be filed by December 15; regular applications, by August 15 for fall entry; and December 15 for winter entry, along with a $40 fee. Notification is sent on a rolling basis. Applications are accepted on-line. **Transfer Students:** 91 transfer students enrolled in 2015-2016. Students wishing to transfer to NNU must have completed 28 college or university semester credits and have a cumulative GPA of at least 2.0 and be in good academic standing at their previous institution. Students below the required GPA may be accepted provisionally at the discretion of the Admissions Committee. Students who have earned the equivalent of 12 semester credits may be admitted as transfer students. Official transcripts from all colleges previously attended must be submitted. 24 of 124 credits required for the bachelor's degree must be completed at NNU. **International Students:** There are 30 international students enrolled. The school actively recruits these students. They must take the TOEFL with a minimum score of 500 on the paper-based TOEFL (PBT) or 61 on the Internet-based version (iBT). They must also take the SAT or ACT, scoring 18.

ADMISSIONS: 15% of the 2016-2017 applicants were accepted. The SAT scores for the 2016-2017 freshman class were: Critical Reading-- 32% below 500, 46% between 500 and 599, 16% between 600 and 699, and 6% between 700 and 800. Math-- 38% below 500, 42% between 500 and 599, 16% between 600 and 699, and 4% between 700 and 800. Writing-- 53% below 500, 25% between 500 and 599, 19% between 600 and 699, and 3% between 700 and 800. The ACT scores were 8% between 12 and 17, 39% between 18 and 23, 40% between 24 and 29, and 13% above 30. There were 43 National Merit finalists. 10 freshmen graduated first in their class. **Admissions Contact:** Shawn Blenker, Director of Admissions. Email: *admissions@nnu.edu* Web: *www.nnu.edu*

FINANCIAL AID: In 2016-2017, 99% of all full-time freshmen received some form of financial aid. 99% of all full-time freshmen received need-based aid. The average freshman award was $23,814. Need-based scholarships or need-based grants averaged $19,358; need-based self-help aid (loans and jobs) averaged $7,554; non-need-based athletic scholarships averaged $12,170; other non-need-based awards and non-need-based scholarships averaged $7,554; and $13,992 from other forms of aid. 66% of undergraduate students work part-time. The average financial indebtedness of the 2016 graduate was $23,672. The FAFSA code is 001624. The priority date for freshman financial aid applications for fall entry is January 15.

THE COLLEGE OF IDAHO — A-5

www.collegeofidaho.edu

Caldwell, ID 83605 — (208) 459-5834, (800) 224-3246

Fax: (208) 459-5849 — **Email:** admission@collegeofidaho.edu

Full-time: 499 men, 508 women	**Faculty:** 84
Part-time: 11 men, 21 women	**Ph.D.s:** 83%
Graduate: 9 men, 22 women	**Student/Faculty:** 12 to 1
Year: other	**Tuition:** $27,425
Room & Board: $8990	**Freshman Class:** 955 applied, 863 accepted, 201 enrolled
SAT CR/M/W: 510/505/490 **ACT:** 23	**CEEB CODE:** 4060
Application Deadline: July 15	**COMPETITIVE**

The College of Idaho, founded in 1891, is a private institution offering degree programs in liberal arts education and the sciences. The college runs on a 13-4-13 calendar, with a 6-week intercession. Figures in the above capsule and in this profile are approximate. There is 1 undergraduate school. In addition to regional accreditation, C of I has baccalaureate program accreditation with NASDTEC. The 50-acre campus is in a small town 25 miles west of Boise. Including any residence halls, there are 21 buildings.

STUDENT LIFE: 70% of undergraduates are from Idaho. Others are from 26 states, 54 foreign countries, and Canada. 66% are White; 14% Hispanic; 7% Foreign; 5% race unknown; 3% two or more races; 2% African American; 2% Asian American; 1% American Indian/Alaska Native. **Female To Male Ratio:** 1.1:1. The average age of freshmen is 18; all undergraduates, 20. 15% do not continue beyond their first year; 68% remain to graduate. **Housing:** 683 students can be accommodated in college housing, which includes single-sex and coed dorms, on-campus apartments, off-campus apartments, honors houses, and special-interest houses. On-campus housing is guaranteed for the freshman year only, and is available on a first-come, first-served basis, and on a lottery system for upperclassmen. 57% of students live on campus; of those, 100% remain on campus on weekends. All students may keep cars.

FACULTY/CLASSROOMS: 53% of faculty are male; 47% are female. All teach undergraduates. No introductory courses are taught by graduate students.

PROGRAMS OF STUDY: C of I confers B.A., and B.S., degrees. Master's degrees are also awarded. Bachelor's degrees are awarded in AGRICULTURE (environmental studies), BIOLOGICAL SCIENCE (biology/biological science), BUSINESS (accounting, business administration and management, and international economics), COMMUNICATIONS AND THE ARTS (art, creative writing, literature, music, music theory and composition, Spanish, and theatre arts), COMPUTER AND PHYSICAL SCIENCE (chemistry and mathematics), EDUCATION (education, elementary education, and physical education), ENGINEERING AND ENVIRONMENTAL DESIGN (preengineering), HEALTH PROFESSIONS (clinical science, exercise science, health, nursing, pharmacy, and speech pathology/audiology), SOCIAL SCIENCE (anthropology, history, philosophy, political science/government, psychology, and religion). Biology, business, and psychology have the largest enrollments.

ACTIVITIES: 15% of men belong to 3 national fraternities; 22% of women belong to 1 local and 3 national sororities. There are 33 groups on campus, including art, band, cheerleading, chess, choir, chorale, chorus, Coyote cinemas, dance, debate, drama, environmental, ethnic, forensics, honors, international, jazz band, LGBT, literary magazine, musical theater, newspaper, pep band, political, professional, religious, social, social service, student government, and yearbook. Popular campus events include Spring Fling, coyote Connection, Taste of Harvest, and Winterfest. **Sports:** There are 8 intercollegiate sports for men and 10 for women, and 7 intramural sports for men and 7 for women. Facilities available to students include basketball, volleyball, weight room, athletic training, a pool, dance, rock climbing wall, football, soccer, and a synthetic turf baseball field, tennis matches, and softball games. **Graduates:** From July 1, 2015 to June 30, 2016, 191 bachelor's degrees were awarded. The most popular majors were business (15%), social sciences (13%), and psychology (12%). 10 companies recruited on campus in 2015-2016. In an average class, 55% graduate in 4 years or less, 64% graduate in 5 years or less, and 68% graduate in 6 years or less.

SERVICES: Counseling and information services are available, as is tutoring in most subjects. **Library/Resources:** Computerized library services include interlibrary loans, database searching, Internet access, and Wi-Fi capability. Special learning facilities include an art gallery, natural history museum, planetarium, a rock and mineral collection, and the Robert E. Smylie Archives. **Physically Challenged Students:** 95% of the campus is accessible. Facilities include wheelchair ramps, elevators, special parking, specially equipped restrooms, lowered drinking fountains, special housing, a pool lift, and van service. **Special:** Co-op Programs: There are Dual Degree Doctoral Program in Pharmacy (BS/Pharm.D.), Nursing (BS/BS), Medical Laboratory Science (BS/BS), Speech-Language Pathology and Audiology (BS/BS), and Juris Doctor (BA or BS/JD). Faculty are leading month-long study abroad courses in Australia, London, and Idaho's Sawtooth Mountains. The College of Idaho offers two types of off-campus study opportunities: study programs led by faculty for our students, and foreign study opportunities for individual students offered by partner, institutions, study tours to such places as Australia, China, Florida, France, Greece, Italy, London, Mexico, and Peru. C of I students also can study for a semester or more in more than 57 countries through our partner institutions. Approved Partner Programs for Study Abroad: Arcadia University-Center for Education Abroad, Brethren Colleges Abroad (BCA), Council Study Centers (CIEE), International Studies Abroad, Schiller International University, School for International Training (SIT), University Studies Abroad Consortium, and University of Idaho **Visiting:** There are regularly scheduled orientations for prospective students, student visits include an overnight stay with student hosts, class visitations, personal appointments with financial aid counselors, professors, and coaches, social events, and a campus tour. Individual tours can also be arranged. There are guides for informal visits, visitors may sit in on classes, and stay overnight. To schedule a visit, contact the Visit and Event Coordinator at visitcenter@collegeofidaho.com. **Campus Safety and Security:** Measures include 24-hour foot and vehicle patrol, emergency notification system, self-defense education, and security escort services. There are also emergency telephones, lighted pathways/

sidewalks, controlled access to dorms/residences, electronic identification cards to all dorms and certain buildings throughout the campus.

REQUIREMENTS: Freshmen applicants who have graduated from high school, presented acceptable GED scores in lieu of a high school record, or met the college's home school policy (see section on home school applicants), and transfer applicants whose college record is of sufficient quality, may be admitted to the college in clear standing. Students not meeting the minimum standard for regular or conditional admission may be admitted to the college on a probational basis. Students may begin the application process any time after the last semester of their junior year in high school. In order to be considered for admission, students should submit the following materials to the Admission Office; an application for admission, official high school transcript, transcript of any college work attempted. If you are considered for the Boone Program, you will need an on-campus interview with the Dean of Students and Dean of Enrollment. Official ACT or SAT test scores (Optional). Applicants are encouraged to consider test optional and will be prompted to follow an alternate application process. While there is no required pattern of high school study necessary for admission, the following combination is strongly recommended: 4 years each of English, math, history and social studies, 3 each of language, and laboratory science. AP credits are accepted. Important factors in the admissions decision are leadership record, advanced placement or honors courses, evidence of special talent, recommendations by school officials, personality/intangible qualities, extracurricular activities record, recommendations by alumni, geographical diversity, ability to finance college education, and parents or siblings attended your school. In order to earn the BA or BS degree, students must complete 124 credits, to include at least one major and three minors, covering all four PEAKs: Humanities and Fine Arts, Natural Sciences and Mathematics, Social Sciences and History, Professional Studies and Enhancement. Beyond the majors and minors chosen from the four PEAKs above, students must complete the following: The First-Year Seminar- this requirement covers the essential elements of academic inquiry: analytical reading, critical thinking, and well-reasoned writing pre-modern Civilization- this requirement provides students with exposure to pre-1800 historical developments that form the foundation of modern systems of thought and ideals of education, thus conveying essential knowledge of the basic dimensions of Western or World intellectual cultures. Liberal Arts Expectations- students are expected to engage in each of the areas listed below as part of their academic program in writing, history, mathematics, natural science, foreign language, social science, literature, philosophy/religion, fine arts, and cultural diversity. GPA Requirements-A grade-point average of at least 2.0 (a) in The College of Idaho record and (b) in the entire undergraduate record. A grade-point average of at least 2.0 in the major field (a) in The College of Idaho record and (b) in the entire undergraduate record. A grade-point average of at least 2.0 in all minors. **Procedure:** Freshmen are admitted in the fall and spring. Entrance exams should be taken by the fall of the senior year. There are early admissions, deferred admissions, and rolling admissions plans. Early decision applications should be filed by November 15; regular applications, by July 15 for fall entry; December 1 for winter entry; and January 15 for spring entry. Notification of early decision is sent December 15; regular decision, March 15. Applications are accepted online. **Transfer Students:** 56 transfer students enrolled in 2015-2016. Students who have already completed at least 28 semester credits or 42 quarter credits of continuous enrollment at accredited colleges or universities will be considered for admission on the basis of that academic record (rather than the secondary school record) provided they have a cumulative GPA of 2.0 or better. Transfer applicants should submit an application for admission and an official high school transcript, as well as official transcripts from all post-secondary institutions attended. A one to two page essay/personal statement and faculty evaluation is required. The transfer application deadline is August 1. Any applications submitted after this date will be considered by petition only. 30 of 124 credits required for the bachelor's degree must be completed at C of I. **International Students:** There are 74 international students enrolled. The school actively recruits these students. They must take the TOEFL with a minimum score of 550 on the paper-based TOEFL (PBT) or 79 on the Internet-based version (iBT), or take the IELTS language proficiency. They must also take the SAT or ACT.

ADMISSIONS: 90% of the 2016-2017 applicants were accepted. The SAT scores for the 2016-2017 freshman class were: Critical Reading-- 40% below 500, 42% between 500 and 599, 16% between 600 and 699, and 2% between 700 and 800. Math-- 41% below 500, 40% between 500 and 599, 16% between 600 and 699, and 3% between 700 and 800. Writing-- 51% below 500, 35% between 500 and 599, 13% between 600 and 699, and 1% between 700 and 800. The ACT scores were 2% between 12 and 17, 53% between 18 and 23, 37% between 24 and 29, and 8% above 30. **Admissions Contact:** Lorna Hunter, Vice President of Enrollment Management. Email: *admission@collegeofidaho.edu* Web: *www.collegeofidaho.edu*

FINANCIAL AID: In 2016-2017, 98% of all full-time freshmen and 96% of continuing full-time students received some form of financial aid. 76% of all full-time freshmen and 71% of continuing full-time students received need-based aid. The average freshman award was $22,793. Need-based scholarships or need-based grants averaged $3,831; need-based self-help aid (loans and jobs) averaged $3,465; and other non-need-based awards and non-need-based scholarships averaged $15,497. The average financial indebtedness of the 2016 graduate was $30,865. The college's own financial statement is required. The FAFSA code is 001617. The priority date for freshman financial aid applications for fall entry is February 15.

UNIVERSITY OF IDAHO — A-3

www.uidaho.edu

Moscow, ID 83844	(208) 885-6326 (888) 884-3246
Fax: (208) 885-9119	**Email:** admissions@uidaho.edu
Full-time: 3943 men, 3457 women	**Faculty:** n/av
Part-time: 795 men, 921 women	**Ph.D.s:** 78%
Graduate: 1257 men, 999 women	**Student/Faculty:** 16 to 1
Year: semesters, summer session	**Tuition:** $7020 ($21,024)
Room & Board: $8328	**Freshman Class:** 8515 applied, 5746 accepted, 1590 enrolled
SAT CR/M/W: 523/528/506 **ACT:** 24	**CEEB CODE:** 4843
Application Deadline: August 1	**COMPETITIVE**

University of Idaho, founded in 1889 as a public institution, offers programs in art, architecture, agriculture, business and economics, education, engineering, letters and social sciences, natural resources, forestry, wildlife, and range sciences. Figures in this profile are approximate. There are 8 undergraduate schools and 1 graduate school. In addition to regional accreditation, U Idaho has baccalaureate program accreditation with AACSB, ABET, ADA, ASLA, CSAB, FIDER, NAAB, NASAD, NASM, NCATE, NRPA, SAF, and NWCCU. The 1450-acre campus is in a small town 90 miles southeast of Spokane, Washington. Including any residence halls, there are 146 buildings.

STUDENT LIFE: 74% of undergraduates are from Idaho. Others are from 50 states, 56 foreign countries, and Canada. 98% are from public schools. 73% are White; 9% Hispanic; 7% Foreign; 4% race unknown; 3% two or more races; 1% African American; 1% Asian American; 1% American Indian/Alaska Native. **Male To Female Ratio:** 1.1:1. The average age of freshmen is 18; all undergraduates, 21. 23% do not continue beyond their first year; 57% remain to graduate. **Housing:** 2020 students can be accommodated in college housing, which includes single-sex and coed dorms, on-campus apartments, and married student housing. In addition, there are honors houses, special-interest houses, fraternity houses, sorority houses, alcohol-free, smoke-free, and living-learning communities. On-campus housing is guaranteed for all 4 years. 77% of students commute. All students may keep cars. Alcohol is not permitted.

FACULTY/CLASSROOMS: 62% of faculty are male; 38% are female. 90% teach undergraduates, and 75% do research. No introductory courses are taught by graduate students. The average class size in an introductory lecture is 30; in a laboratory is 17; and in a regular course is 24.

PROGRAMS OF STUDY: U Idaho confers B.A., B.F.A., B.G.S., B.I.D., B.Mus., B.S., B.S.A.V.S., B.S.Ag.Econ., B.S.Ag.Ed., B.S.Ag.L.S., B.S.Arch., B.S.Biochem., B.S.Bus., B.S.C.E., B.S.C.S., B.S.Ch.E., B.S.Comp.E., B.S.Dan.,B.S.E.E., B.S.E.S.H., B.S.Ecol.Cons.Biol., B.S.Ed., B.S.Env.S., B.S.Early.Chdhd.Dev.Ed., B.S.F.C.S., B.S.F.S., B.S.Fire.Ecol.Mgmt., B.S.Fish.Res., B.S.For.Res.,B.S.I.S., B.S.L.A., B.S.M.B.B., B.S.M.E., B.S.M.S.E., B.S.Microbiol., B.S.Nat.Resc.Consv., B.S.Rangeland Ecol.-Mgt., B.S.Rec., B.S.Renew.Mat., B.S.Tech. and B.S.Wildl.Res. degrees. Master's and doctoral degrees are also awarded. Bachelor's degrees are awarded in AGRICULTURE (agricultural business management, agricultural communications, agricultural economics, agricultural mechanics, agricultural sciences, agriculture, animal science, dairy science, fish and game management, fishing and fisheries, forestry production and processing, forestry and related sciences, horticulture, natural resource management, plant science, range/farm management, soil science, and wildlife management), BIOLOGICAL SCIENCE (biochemistry, biology/biological science, microbiology, and molecular biology), BUSINESS (accounting, business administration and management, business economics, finance, human resources, management information systems, marketing management, marketing/retailing/merchandising, operations management, recreation and leisure services, and professional golf management), COMMUNICATIONS AND THE ARTS (advertising, animation, apparel design, applied art, applied music, art, broadcasting, creative writing, dance, design, digital communications, dramatic arts, English, English writing, fine arts, French, journalism, modern language, music, music history and appreciation, music performance, music theory and composition, public relations, Spanish, studio art, and telecommunications), COMPUTER AND PHYSICAL SCIENCE (applied mathematics, chemistry, computer science, digital arts/technology, geology, information sciences and systems, mathematics, and physics), EDUCATION (agricultural education, art education, career, technical education & training, education, elementary education, foreign languages education, general studies, mathematics education, music education, physical education, science education, secondary education, and technical education), ENGINEERING AND ENVIRONMENTAL DESIGN (architecture, bioengineering, biomedical engineering, chemical engineering, civil engineering, computer engineering, electrical and computer engineering, electrical/electronics engineering, engineering, environmental engineering, environmental science, geological engineering, interior design, landscape architecture/design, materials engineering, and mechanical engineering), HEALTH PROFESSIONS (exercise science, movement science, and veterinary science), SOCIAL SCIENCE (anthropology, child care/child and family studies, counseling/psychology, economics, family/consumer studies, fire science, food science, geography, history, interdisciplinary studies, international relations, international studies, Latin American studies, parks and recreation management, philosophy, political science/government, psychology, rural economics, sociology, and textiles and clothing). engineering, natural resources, and business are the strongest academically. Business, engineering, and psychology have the largest enrollments.

ACTIVITIES: 14% of men belong to 17 national fraternities; 14% of women belong to 10 national sororities. There are 191 groups on campus, including art, band, cheerleading, choir, chorale, chorus, computers, dance, drama, drill team, environmental, ethnic, film, honors, international, jazz band, LGBT, literary magazine, marching band, musical theater, newspaper, opera, orchestra, pep band, photography, political, professional, radio and TV, religious, social, social service, student government, and symphony. Popular campus events include Lionel Hampton Jazz Festival, the Borah Symposium, and Palouse fest, Homecoming, Mom's Weekend, and Dad's Weekend. **Sports:** There are 6 intercollegiate sports for men and 8 for women, and 15 intramural sports for men and 16 for women. Facilities include an activity center, domed stadium for basketball and football games, indoor and outdoor tracks, pool swim center, gyms, auditorium, golf course, tennis, racquetball and handball courts, and a student recreation center with a climbing wall. **Graduates:** From July 1, 2015 to June 30, 2016, 2861 bachelor's degrees were awarded. The most popular majors were business/marketing (16%), engineering (8%), and psychology (8%). In an average class, 1% graduate in 3 years or less, 29% graduate in 4 years or less, 54% graduate in 5 years or less, and 57% graduate in 6 years or less.

SERVICES: Counseling and information services are available, as is tutoring in most subjects. There is also a reader service for the blind, and remedial math and writing. **Library/Resources:** The 2 libraries contain 1.4 million volumes, 2.6 million microform items, and 14,204 audio/video tapes/CDs/DVDs, subscribe to 25,189 periodicals including electronic. Computerized library services include interlibrary loans, database searching, Internet access, and Wi-Fi capability. Special learning facilities include an art gallery, radio station, TV station, an electron microscopy center, IQ-station, lab animal facility, research institutes for water resources, geospatial lab, microelectronics, aquaculture, university farms, experimental forests, arboretum and botanical garden. **Physically Challenged Students:** 87% of the campus is accessible. Facilities include wheelchair ramps, elevators, special parking, specially equipped restrooms, special class scheduling, lowered drinking fountains, lowered telephones, and special housing. 2 motorized wheelchairs, readers, note takers, sign language interpreters, alternate text, assistive devices, assistive technology computers, priority registration, real-time capturing, enlarged print classroom materials, advocacy, specialized classroom furniture, testing accommodations, and on-campus transportation. **Special:** UIdaho offers cooperative programs and cross-registration with Washington State and Idaho State Universities, internships, extensive study-abroad programs, work-study programs, B.A.-B.S. degrees, dual and student-designed majors, a general studies degree, credit for life and work experience, non-degree study, and pass/fail options. There are 11 national honor societies and a freshman honors program. **Visiting:** There are regularly scheduled orientations for prospective students, scheduled visits include a visit with faculty and financial aid personnel, a tour of campus, and an overnight stay in the dorms or Greek houses and a visit to the recreation center. There are guides for informal visits and visitors may sit in on classes. To schedule a visit, contact the Office of Admissions and Campus Visits. **Campus Safety and Security:** Measures include 24-hour foot and vehicle patrol, emergency notification system, and self-defense education. There are shuttle buses, emergency telephones, lighted pathways/sidewalks, and controlled access to dorms/residences. There is also a violence prevention programs office.

REQUIREMENTS: The SAT or ACT is required. Students from accredited high schools must have graduated and completed 15 academic units: 4 units in English, 3 units in math, 3 units in science (of those, 1 unit must be lab), 2.5 units in social studies, and 1.5 units in academic electives, 1 unit in humanities and foreign language. Home-schooled students and non-accredited high school students, including GED students, will have their application for admission referred to a committee for a decision. A GPA of 2.2 is required. AP and CLEP credits are accepted. To graduate, students must complete at least 120 credit hours (128 for some majors), including 36 in upper-division courses and 40 in the major, with a minimum GPA of 2.0. The core curriculum requires a total of 33 to 36 credits in the following categories: communication, natural and applied sciences, mathematics, statistics or computer science, humanities, social sciences, one American diversity course, one international course, one lower-division seminar, one upper-division seminar. **Procedure:** Freshmen are admitted to all sessions. Entrance exams should be taken during the junior or senior year of high school. There are deferred admissions and rolling admissions plans. Applications should be filed by August 1 for fall entry; December 15 for spring entry; and May 1 for summer entry, along with a $60 fee. Notification is sent on a rolling basis. Applications are accepted online. **Transfer Students:** 601 transfer students enrolled in 2015-2016. Transfer applicants must have completed at least 14 credit hours with a cumulative GPA of at least 2.0. Students transferring from out-of-state schools into the College of Engineering must have a minimum cumulative GPA of 2.8. 32 of 120 credits required for the bachelor's degree must be completed at U Idaho. **International Students:** There are 522 international students enrolled. The school actively recruits these students. They must take the TOEFL with a minimum score of 550 on the paper-based TOEFL (PBT) or 79 on the Internet-based version (iBT). They must also take the SAT or ACT.

ADMISSIONS: 67% of the 2016-2017 applicants were accepted. The SAT scores for the 2016-2017 freshman class were: Critical Reading-- 41% below 500, 37% between 500 and 599, 17% between 600 and 699, and 5% between 700 and 800. Math-- 38% below 500, 38% between 500 and 599, 18% between 600 and 699, and 6% between 700 and 800. Writing-- 47% below 500, 36% between 500 and 599, 14% between 600 and 699, and 3% between 700 and 800. The ACT scores were 9% between 12 and 17, 40% between 18 and 23, 40% between 24 and 29, and 11% above 30. 34% of the current freshmen were in the top fifth of their class; 61% were in the top two fifths. There were 23 National Merit finalists. 62 freshmen graduated first in their class. **Admissions Contact:** Cezar Mesquita, Director, Admissions. Email: *admissions@uidaho.edu* Web: *www.uidaho.edu*

FINANCIAL AID: In 2016-2017, 86% of all full-time freshmen and 64% of continuing full-time students received some form of financial aid. 64% of all full-time freshmen and continuing full-time students received need-based aid. The average freshman award was $13,279. Need-based scholarships or need-based grants averaged $4,660 ($9,780 maximum); need-based self-help aid (loans and jobs) averaged $5,878 ($15,392 maximum); non-need-based athletic scholarships averaged $18,967 ($34,321 maximum); and other non-need-based awards and non-need-based scholarships averaged $5,337 ($7,284 maximum). 91% of undergraduate students work part-time. Average annual earnings from campus work are $2000. The average financial indebtedness of the 2016 graduate was $26,741. U Idaho is a member of CSS. The FAFSA code is 001626. The deadline for filing freshman financial aid applications for fall entry is February 15.

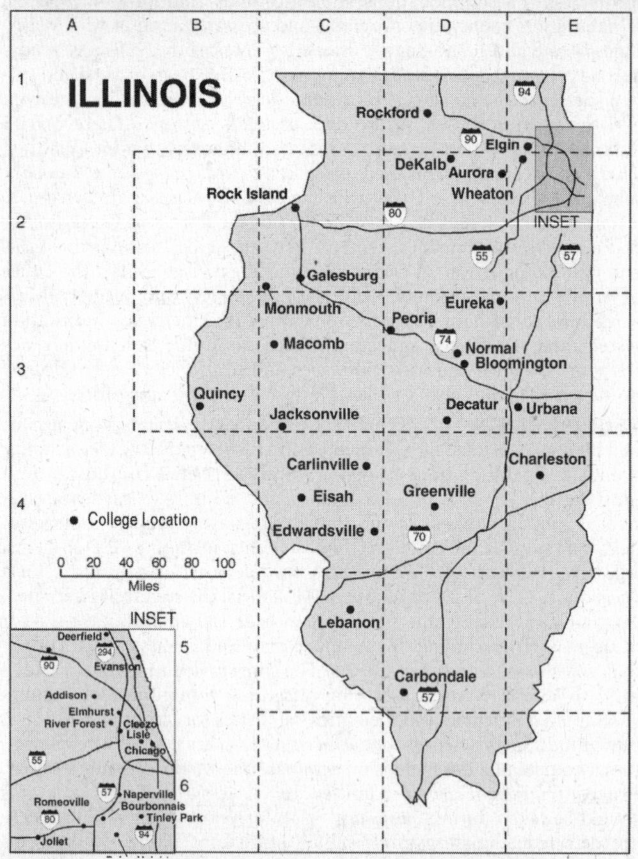

AUGUSTANA COLLEGE C-2

www.augustana.edu

Rock Island, IL 61201 **(309) 794-7341** **(800) 798-8100**

Fax: (309) 794-7422 **Email: admissions@augustana.edu**

Full-time: 1080 men, 1443 women
Part-time: 7 men, 7 women
Graduate: n/av
Year: quarters, summer session
Room & Board: $10,037
SAT CR/M/W: 570/570/550 **ACT:** 25
Application Deadline: open
Faculty: 191; IIB, av$
Ph.D.s: 93%
Student/Faculty: 12 to 1
Tuition: $39,621
Freshman Class: 6712 applied, 3312 accepted, 678 enrolled
CEEB CODE: 1025
VERY COMPETITIVE

Augustana College is a private, selective liberal arts college. Augustana's focus on creating a well-rounded experience for students has generated an environment of learning that goes beyond the classroom. From the moment students set foot on campus, the college provides them with tools that will help them be successful now and in the future. In addition to working closely with their professors on special projects and research, students benefit from visiting scholars and lecturers as well as from international study opportunities. There is 1 undergraduate school. In addition to regional accreditation, Augustana has baccalaureate program accreditation with NASM and NCATE. The 115-acre campus is in a suburban area near the Mississippi River in Rock Island, and is 165 miles west of Chicago. Including any residence halls, there are 99 buildings.

STUDENT LIFE: 85% of undergraduates are from Illinois. Others are from 32 states, 43 foreign countries, and Canada. 75% are White; 5% Foreign; 4% African American; 3% two or more races; 2% Asian American; 10% Hispanic; 1% race unknown. 31% are Catholic; 29% other unknown denominations ; 21% Protestant; 18% claim no religious affiliation. **Female To Male Ratio:** 1.3:1. The average age of freshmen is 18; all undergraduates, 20. 11% do not continue beyond their first year; 77% remain to graduate. **Housing:** 1853 students can be accommodated in college housing, which includes single-sex and coed dorms, on-campus apartments, and off-campus apartments. In addition, there are special-interest houses, and wellness housing. On-campus housing is guaranteed for the freshman year only. 70% of students live on campus; of those, 75% remain on campus on weekends. Alcohol is not permitted. All students may keep cars.

FACULTY/CLASSROOMS: 50% of faculty are male; 50% are female. All teach undergraduates, 65% do research, and 65% do both. No introductory courses are taught by graduate students.

PROGRAMS OF STUDY: Augustana confers B.A. degrees. Bachelor's degrees are awarded in AGRICULTURE (environmental studies), BIOLOGICAL SCIENCE (biochemistry, biology/adolescence education, biology/biological science, and neurosciences), BUSINESS (accounting, business administration and management, and international business management), COMMUNICATIONS AND THE ARTS (Africana studies, art, art history and appreciation, classics, communication studies, creative writing, English, English writing, French, German, graphic design, multimedia, music, music performance, Scandinavian languages, Spanish, and theatre arts), COMPUTER AND PHYSICAL SCIENCE (applied mathematics, chemistry, chemistry/adolescence education, computer science, earth science / adolescence education, geology, mathematics, physics secondary education, and physics), EDUCATION (art education, elementary education, English education, French studies K-12 education, history education, mathematics education, music education, secondary education, and Spanish adolescense education), ENGINEERING AND ENVIRONMENTAL DESIGN (engineering physics), HEALTH PROFESSIONS (premedicine and public health), SOCIAL SCIENCE (anthropology, Asian/Oriental studies, communication sciences & disorders, economics, geography, history, philosophy, political science/government, psychology, religion, social work, sociology, and women's studies). Education, pre-medicine, and neuroscience are the strongest academically. Business/accounting, biology, and psychology have the largest enrollments.

ACTIVITIES: 25% of men belong to 7 local fraternities; 37% of women belong to 7 local sororities. There are 110 groups on campus, including art, band, cheerleading, choir, chorale, chorus, communications, computers, dance, debate, drama, environmental, ethnic, film, honors, international, jazz band, LGBT, literary magazine, musical theater, newspaper, opera, orchestra, pep band, photography, political, professional, religious, social, social service, student government, and symphony. Popular campus events include Symposium Day, and Slough Fest. **Sports:** There are 12 intercollegiate sports for men and 11 for women, and 28 intramural sports for men and 27 for women. The PepsiCo Recreation Center has a 6-lane, 200-meter track, courts for basketball, volleyball, badminton, and tennis, and a cardio and weight room facility. A primary athletic building has courts for basketball, volleyball, badminton, weight and physical conditioning rooms, golf practice area, wrestling facilities, and a swimming pool. There is a lighted synthetic turf field and an all-weather track for football, track and field, and a field for lacrosse and soccer, a baseball field, outdoor tennis courts, and a dance studio. **Graduates:** From July 1, 2015 to June 30, 2016, 573 bachelor's degrees were awarded. The most popular majors were biology/life science (19%), business/marketing (19%), and pre-medicine (10%). In an average class, 71% graduate in 4 years or less, 76% graduate in 5 years or less, and 77% graduate in 6 years or less.

SERVICES: There is a reader service for the blind. **Library/Resources:** The 2 libraries contain 151,734 volumes, 2,392 microform items, and 13,256 audio/video tapes/CDs/DVDs, and subscribe to 27,659 periodicals including electronic. Computerized library services include interlibrary loans, database searching, Internet access, and Wi-Fi capability. Special learning facilities include an art gallery, natural history museum, planetarium, a center for communicative disorders, a geology museum, a planetarium and observatory, a U.S. geological survey map repository, a Swedish immigration research center, 3 outdoor environmental labs, a 3D printer, and a spectrometer. **Physically Challenged Students:** 75% of the campus is accessible. Facilities include wheelchair ramps, elevators, special parking, specially equipped restrooms, lowered drinking fountains, lowered telephones, and special housing. **Special:** Coordinated degree programs (3-2, 3-3, 3-4) are offered in Accounting (Wake Forest University), Engineering (Northern Illinois University, Washington University, and Columbia), Environmental Management & Forestry (Duke University), Landscape Architecture (University of Illinois), Occupational Therapy (Washington University), Optometry (Illinois College of Optometry), Pre-Law (Capital University Law School), Nursing (Trinity College of Nursing and Health Sciences), Physical Therapy (Washington University), and Veterinary Medicine (University of Illinois). Domestic and international internships are offered in London, New York, Syndney, Denver, Washington D.C, and New Zealand. Study abroad programs travel to France, Ecuador, Germany, Nicaragua, Brazil, England, Norway, Guatemala, Greece, Botswana, Hong Kong, Japan, Sweden, India, Italy, Spain, China, Australia, Switzerland, Austria, Ghana, Senegal, and Jamaica. There are 16 national honor societies, Phi Beta Kappa, a freshman honors program, and 1 departmental honors program. **Visiting:** There are regularly scheduled orientations for prospective students, including information sessions with speakers, exhibits, campus tours, meetings with faculty, counselors, and students, and social activities. There are guides for informal visits, visitors may sit in on classes, and stay overnight. To schedule a visit, contact W. Kent Barnds at wkentbarnds@augustana.edu. **Campus Safety and Security:** Measures include 24-hour foot and vehicle patrol, emergency notification system, self-defense education, and security escort services. There are shuttle buses, emergency telephones, lighted pathways/sidewalks, and controlled access to dorms/residences.

REQUIREMENTS: The SAT or ACT is recommended. Applicants should be graduates of an accredited secondary school with 16 academic credits, including 3-4 each in English, math, science with 2 lab, and 1 each in social studies, foreign language, and history, plus 4 recommended in academic electives. An audition for music majors and an interview are recommended. The GED is accepted. Students who choose not to submit ACT or SAT scores must interview and submit a photocopy of a graded high school paper. AP credits are accepted. Important factors in the admissions decision are advanced placement or honors courses, evidence of special talent, and recommendations by school officials. A total of 123 credits with a minimum GPA of 2.0 is required to graduate. Courses in foreign language, religion, writing, phys ed, fine arts, humanities, literature, and the sciences must be completed. **Procedure:** Freshmen are admitted fall, winter, and spring. Entrance exams should be taken by fall of the senior year. There are early decision, early admissions, deferred admissions, and rolling admissions plans. Application deadlines are open. The fall 2016 application fee was $35. Notification of early decision is sent November 15; regular decision, on a rolling basis. 36 early decision candidates were accepted for the 2016-2017 class. Applications are accepted on-line. Application fees are waived if application is completed on-line. **Transfer Students:** 60 transfer students enrolled in 2015-2016. A minimum GPA of 2.0 is required. SAT or ACT scores and an interview are recommended. Students may enroll fall, winter, and spring. 60 of 123 credits required for the bachelor's degree must be completed at Augustana. **International Students:** There are 129 international students enrolled. The school actively recruits these students. They must take the TOEFL with a minimum score of 550 on the paper-based TOEFL (PBT) or 80 on the Internet-based version (iBT).

ADMISSIONS: 49% of the 2016-2017 applicants were accepted. The ACT scores were 1% between 12 and 17, 30% between 18 and 23, 54% between 24 and 29, and 14% above 30. 58% of the current freshmen were in the top fifth of their class; 83% were in the top two fifths. 9 freshmen graduated first in their class. **Admissions Contact:** Kent Barnds, Vice President of Enrollment. Email: *admissions@augustana.edu* Web: *www.augustana.edu*

FINANCIAL AID: Augustana is a member of CSS. The college's own financial statement is required. The FAFSA code is 001633. The priority date for freshman financial aid applications for fall entry is February 1.

AURORA UNIVERSITY — D-2
www.aurora.edu

Aurora, IL 60506 — (630) 844-5533, (800) 742-5281

Fax: (630) 844-5535	**Email:** admission@aurora.edu
Full-time: 1218 men, 2084 women	**Faculty:** IIA
Part-time: 121 men, 373 women	**Ph.D.s:** n/av
Graduate: 426 men, 1421 women	**Student/Faculty:** 20 to 1
Year: semesters, summer session	**Tuition:** $22,830
Room & Board: $11,140	**Freshman Class:** 3007 applied, 2295 accepted, 654 enrolled
SAT CR/M: required **ACT:** 22	**CEEB CODE:** 1027
Application Deadline: n/av	**COMPETITIVE**

Aurora University, founded in 1893, is a private, independent institution that offers graduate and undergraduate degrees in arts and sciences, education, accounting, business, information technology, communication, criminal justice, nursing, health sciences, physical education, athletic training, recreation, special education, and social work. There are 6 undergraduate schools and 5 graduate schools. In addition to regional accreditation, AU has baccalaureate program accreditation with CSWE, CCNE, CAATE, and CAEP. The 35-acre campus is in a suburban area 40 miles from downtown Chicago. Including any residence halls, there are 28 buildings.

STUDENT LIFE: 88% of undergraduates are from Illinois. Others are from 38 states, 4 foreign countries, and Canada. 8% are African American; 54% White; 5% race unknown; 3% two or more races; 27% Hispanic; 2% Asian American. 81% claim no religious affiliation. **Female To Male Ratio:** 2.2:1. The average age of freshmen is 18; all undergraduates, 23. 32% do not continue beyond their first year; 58% remain to graduate. **Housing:** 746 students can be accommodated in college housing, which includes single-sex and coed dorms. On-campus housing is available on a first-come and first-served basis. 75% of students commute. Alcohol is not permitted. All students may keep cars.

FACULTY/CLASSROOMS: 36% of faculty are male; 64% are female. 96% teach undergraduates. No introductory courses are taught by graduate students. The average class size in an introductory lecture is 19; in a laboratory is 12; and in a regular course is 16.

PROGRAMS OF STUDY: AU confers B.A., B.S., B.S.N., and B.S.W. degrees. Master's and doctoral degrees are also awarded. Bachelor's degrees are awarded in BIOLOGICAL SCIENCE (biology/biological science), BUSINESS (accounting, business administration and management, finance, management information systems, management science, marketing, organizational leadership and management, recreation and leisure services, and sustainable management), COMMUNICATIONS AND THE ARTS (art, communications, English, music, musical theater, Spanish, and theatre studies), COMPUTER AND PHYSICAL SCIENCE (actuarial science, computer science, and mathematics), EDUCATION (athletic training, bilingual/bicultural education, elementary education, physical education, secondary education, and special education), HEALTH PROFESSIONS (biology, disabilities studies, exercise science, health science, and nursing), SOCIAL SCIENCE (criminal justice, history, liberal arts/general studies, parks and recreation management, philosophy, political science/government, psychology, religion, social work, and sociology). Nursing, health sciences, and education are the strongest academically. Social work, nursing, and education have the largest enrollments.

ACTIVITIES: 1% of men belong to 1 national fraternity; 1% of women belong to 1 local and 4 national sororities. There are 55 groups on campus, including art, cheerleading, choir, chorale, computers, dance, debate, drama, environmental, ethnic, forensics, honors, jazz band, LGBT, literary magazine, musical theater, newspaper, pep band, photography, political, professional, radio and TV, religious, social, social service, and student government. Popular campus events include Spring Fling, Homecoming Week, Arts and Ideas Series, and Student Organization Events. **Sports:** There are 11 intercollegiate sports for men and 11 for women, and 22 intramural sports for men and 22 for women. Facilities include a fitness center, a weight room, a 1,250-seat gym, football and soccer fields, a theater, and voice and chorale facilities. **Graduates:** From July 1, 2015 to June 30, 2016, 820 bachelor's degrees were awarded. The most popular majors were health professions and related services (23%), business (22%), and social work (13%). In an average class, 2% graduate in 3 years or less, 47% graduate in 4 years or less, 56% graduate in 5 years or less, and 58% graduate in 6 years or less.

SERVICES: Counseling and information services are available, as is tutoring in most subjects. There are professional and peer tutors, workshops, and computer-based tutorials. **Library/Resources:** The 2 libraries contain 38,404 volumes, and 6,162 audio/video tapes/CDs/DVDs, and subscribe to 46,506 periodicals including electronic. Computerized library services include interlibrary loans, database searching, Internet access, and Wi-Fi capability. Special learning facilities include a natural history museum, radio station, a Native American museum. The Jenks Memorial collection of Adventual Materials, and the Doris K. Colby Memorial Archives. **Physically Challenged Students:** 98% of the campus is accessible. Facilities include wheelchair ramps, elevators, special parking, specially equipped restrooms, special class scheduling, lowered drinking fountains, and special housing. **Special:** AU offers cross-registration with North Central College and Benedictine University, field-related job experience, work-study programs, study abroad in a number of countries, and travel programs during the Summer-May term. Internships, accelerated degree programs in Accounting and Marketing, and an MBA/MSW dual major are available. There are 2 national honor societies and 7 departmental honors programs. **Visiting:** There are regularly scheduled orientations for prospective students, including meeting with an admission representative, a campus tour with students, and classroom and/or faculty visits if set up. There are guides for informal visits, visitors may sit in on classes, and stay overnight. To schedule a visit, contact Melody Ulin at mulin@aurora.edu. **Campus Safety and Security:** Measures include 24-hour foot and vehicle patrol, emergency notification system, self-defense education, and security escort services. There are emergency telephones and lighted pathways/sidewalks.

REQUIREMENTS: The ACT is required. Applicants must be graduates of an accredited secondary school or have earned the GED. Secondary school academic units must include a minimum of 4 years of English and 3 years each of mathematics, social studies, science, and electives. An interview is recommended but not required. A GPA of 2.0 is required. AP and CLEP credits are accepted. Important factors in the admissions decision are advanced placement or honors courses, extracurricular activities record, and leadership record. To graduate, students must complete a minimum of 120 semester hours with a GPA of at least 2.0 on a 4.0 scale, including at least 52 semester hours at a senior college. Completion at Aurora University of at least 30 semester hours required, including the last 24 semester hours in the degree, and including at least 18 semester hours in the major. A minimum of 30 semester hours numbered 3000 or above required of which 15 semester hours must lie within the major and 15 semester hours must be completed at AU. Completion of the major requirements (with no grades lower than C) for an approved major, including the senior capstone. **Procedure:** Freshmen are admitted fall and spring. Entrance exams should be taken by late in the junior year or early in the senior year. There is a rolling admissions plan. Application deadlines are open. Notifications are sent September 1. Applications are accepted on-line. **Transfer Students:** 462 transfer students enrolled in 2015-2016. Applicants are required to have a minimum GPA of 2.0 and must have completed at least 15 semester hours at the post-secondary level. 30 of 120 credits required for the bachelor's degree must be completed at AU. **International Students:** There are 8 international students enrolled. They must take the TOEFL with a minimum score of 550 on the paper-based TOEFL (PBT) or 79 on the Internet-based version (iBT).

ADMISSIONS: 76% of the 2016-2017 applicants were accepted. The SAT scores for the 2016-2017 freshman class were: Critical Reading-- 24% below 500, 13% between 500 and 599, and 7% between 600 and 699. Math-- 24% below 500, 13% between 500 and 599, and 7% between 600 and 699. The ACT scores were 7% between 12 and 17, 68% between 18 and 23, 24% between 24 and 29, and 1% above 30. **Admissions Contact:** Tracy Phillippe, Director of Enrollment Systems. Email: *admission@aurora.edu* Web: *www.aurora.edu*

FINANCIAL AID: In 2016-2017, 100% of all full-time freshmen and 99% of continuing full-time students received some form of financial aid. 86% of all full-time freshmen and 79% of continuing full-time students received need-based aid. The average freshman award was $21,566. Need-based scholarships or need-based grants averaged $17,131 ($28,035 maximum); need-based self-help aid (loans and jobs) averaged $4,551 ($15,558 maximum); and other non-need-based awards and non-need-based scholarships averaged $11,637 ($15,750 maximum). The average financial indebtedness of the 2016 graduate was $27,578. The FAFSA code is 001634. The priority date for freshman financial aid applications for fall entry is October 1.

BENEDICTINE UNIVERSITY — E-2

www.ben.edu

Lisle, IL 60532	(630) 829-6300
Fax: (630) 829-6301	**Email:** admissions@ben.edu
Full-time: 1046 men, 1358 women	**Faculty:** IIA, av$
Part-time: 243 men, 293 women	**Ph.D.s:** 89%
Graduate: 655 men, 1711 women	**Student/Faculty:** 18 to 1
Year: semesters, summer session	**Tuition:** $29,700
Room & Board: $8600	**Freshman Class:** 2558 applied, 1974 accepted, 486 enrolled
ACT: 23	**CEEB CODE:** 1707
Application Deadline: March 30	**COMPETITIVE**

Benedictine University, founded in 1887, is a private, Roman Catholic liberal arts and sciences institution. There are 4 undergraduate schools and 4 graduate schools. In addition to regional accreditation, Benedictine has baccalaureate program accreditation with ADA and CCLN. The 108-acre campus is in a suburban area 25 miles west of Chicago. Including any residence halls, there are 11 buildings.

STUDENT LIFE: 94% of undergraduates are from Illinois. Others are from 50 states, 10 foreign countries, and Canada. 7% are Hispanic; 45% White; 21% Asian American; 2% Foreign; 12% African American; 12% race unknown; 1% American Indian/Alaska Native. **Female To Male Ratio:** 1.7:1. The average age of freshmen is 18; all undergraduates, 25. 27% do not continue beyond their first year; 52% remain to graduate. **Housing:** 756 students can be accommodated in college housing, which includes single-sex and coed dorms and on-campus apartments. On-campus housing is available on a first-come and first-served basis. All students may keep cars.

FACULTY/CLASSROOMS: 49% of faculty are male; 51% are female. All teach undergraduates, and all do research. No introductory courses are taught by graduate students. The average class size in an introductory lecture is 21; in a laboratory is 17; and in a regular course is 19.

PROGRAMS OF STUDY: Benedictine confers B.A., B.S., B.B.A., and B.S.N. degrees. Associate, master's, and doctoral degrees are also awarded. Bachelor's degrees are awarded in BIOLOGICAL SCIENCE (biochemistry, biology/biological science, molecular biology, and nutrition), BUSINESS (accounting, banking and finance, business administration and management, business economics, international business management, management information systems, marketing management, marketing/retailing/merchandising, and organizational behavior), COMMUNICATIONS AND THE ARTS (arts administration/management, communications, creative writing, fine arts, literature, music, publishing, Spanish, and studio art), COMPUTER AND PHYSICAL SCIENCE (chemistry, computer science, mathematics, and physics), EDUCATION (elementary education and special education), ENGINEERING AND ENVIRONMENTAL DESIGN (engineering and applied science and environmental science), HEALTH PROFESSIONS (clinical science, health care administration, health science, nuclear medical technology, nursing, and radiation therapy), SOCIAL SCIENCE (economics, history, international studies, philosophy, political science/government, psychology, social science, sociology, and theological studies). Management, health science, and psychology have the largest enrollments.

ACTIVITIES: There are no fraternities or sororities. There are 46 groups on campus, including art, band, cheerleading, choir, chorus, computers, dance, debate, ethnic, honors, international, jazz band, literary magazine, musical theater, newspaper, pep band, political, professional, radio and TV, religious, social, social service, and student government. Popular campus events include Relay for Life, Quad Day, and Spring Ball. **Sports:** There are 8 intercollegiate sports for men and 9 for women, and 11 intramural sports for men and 11 for women. Facilities include a recreation center housing the main arena, a weight room, a dance room, racquetball and tennis courts, and a sports complex that includes a football/soccer/track stadium, a baseball stadium, and a softball stadium. **Graduates:** From July 1, 2015 to June 30, 2016, 723 bachelor's degrees were awarded. The most popular majors were health science (12%), accounting (7%), and management (7%).

SERVICES: Counseling and information services are available, as is tutoring in most subjects. There is a reader service for the blind, and remedial math, reading, and writing. **Library/Resources:** The 4 libraries contain 274,635 volumes, 23,377 microform items, and 51,032 audio/video tapes/CDs/DVDs, and subscribe to 66,295 periodicals including electronic. Computerized library services include interlibrary loans, database searching, Internet access, and Wi-Fi capability. Special learning facilities include an art gallery, natural history museum, radio station, and TV station. **Physically Challenged Students:** All of the campus is accessible. Facilities include wheelchair ramps, elevators, special parking, specially equipped restrooms, and lowered drinking fountains. **Special:** There is cross-registration with North Central College, Aurora University, and the Illinois Institute of Technology. Benedictine offers study abroad in 9 countries, and exchange programs can be arranged through other colleges. There are 3-2 pre-engineering degrees with Marquette University and the Universities of Illinois, Detroit, and Notre Dame, and an engineering degree with the Illinois Institute of Technology. Pre-professional programs including pre-podiatry, pre-physical therapy, and pre-nursing, are offered. Work-study programs with a number of surrounding firms, internships, an accelerated degree program in management, credit for work and life experience, and dual majors are also offered. There are 11 national honor societies and a freshman honors program. **Visiting:** There are regularly scheduled orientations for prospective students. Student visits include a regularly scheduled visit day and open houses each semester. There are guides for informal visits, visitors may sit in on classes, and stay overnight. To schedule a visit, contact the Enrollment Center. **Campus Safety and Security:** Measures include 24-hour foot and vehicle patrol, self-defense education, and security escort services. There are emergency telephones and lighted pathways/sidewalks.

REQUIREMENTS: The ACT is required. Students must complete 4 years of English, 3 years each of social studies, math, and lab science, and 2 years of foreign language. The GED is accepted. Benedictine requires applicants to be in the upper 50% of their class. AP and CLEP credits are accepted. To graduate, students must complete 120 semester hours, including 36 in their majors, and maintain a minimum GPA of 2.0. They must complete 12 hours in the arts and humanities, 9 each in social sciences, natural sciences, and cultural heritage, 6 in rhetoric, and 3 each in speech, math, and freshman seminar. A thesis, capstone course or project, or comprehensive exam is required in specific departments. **Procedure:** Freshmen are admitted fall and spring. There is a rolling admissions plan. Application deadlines are open. Application fee is $40. Applications are accepted on-line. **Transfer Students:** 449 transfer students enrolled in 2015-2016. Applicants must have a C average. A minimum GPA of 2.0 is necessary, and an interview is required in some cases. Students who have completed fewer than 20 semester hours must submit ACT or SAT scores. 30 of 120 credits required for the bachelor's degree must be completed at Benedictine. **International Students:** There are 50 international students enrolled. The school actively recruits these students. They must take the TOEFL with a minimum score of 550 on the paper-based TOEFL (PBT) or 79 on the Internet-based version (iBT).

ADMISSIONS: 77% of the 2016-2017 applicants were accepted. The ACT scores were 30% below 12, 27% between 12 and 17, 26% between 18 and 23, 9% between 24 and 29, and 8% above 30. 28% of the current freshmen were in the top fifth of their class; 59% were in the top two fifths. 3 freshmen graduated first in their class. **Admissions Contact:** Robert A. Stanley, Ed. D., Vice President Office of the Provost. Email: *admissions@ben.edu* Web: *www.ben.edu*

FINANCIAL AID: In 2016-2017, 98% of all full-time freshmen and 89% of continuing full-time students received some form of financial aid. 70% of all full-time freshmen and 62% of continuing full-time students received need-based aid. The average freshman award was $24,046. Need-based scholarships or need-based grants averaged $7,689 ($14,450 maximum); need-based self-help aid (loans and jobs) averaged $5,542 ($8,500 maximum); and other non-need-based awards and non-need-based scholarships averaged $16,585 ($36,600 maximum). 13% of undergraduate students work part-time. Average annual earnings from campus work are $1905. The average financial indebtedness of the 2016 graduate was $27,110. The FAFSA code is 001767. The priority date for freshman financial aid applications for fall entry is March 1.

BLACKBURN COLLEGE *(The complete profile is made available exclusively on our website, www.barronspac.com)*

BRADLEY UNIVERSITY D-3

www.bradley.edu

Peoria, IL 61625 **(309) 677-1000**

Fax: (309) 677-2797	**Email:** admissions@bradley.edu
Full-time: 2102 men, 2176 women	**Faculty:** IIA, av$
Part-time: 107 men, 88 women	**Ph.D.s:** 83%
Graduate: 463 men, 662 women	**Student/Faculty:** 12 to 1
Year: varies, summer session	**Tuition:** $32,120
Room & Board: $10,010	**Freshman Class:** 9786 applied, 6832 accepted, 1093 enrolled
SAT CR/M/W: 547/555/526 **ACT:** 25	**CEEB CODE:** 1070
Application Deadline: February 1	**VERY COMPETITIVE**

Bradley University is a private university that offers more opportunities than small colleges and more personalized experiences than large universities. More than 185 academic programs are available in business, communications, education, engineering, fine and performing arts, health sciences, the liberal arts, science, and technology. Distinctive programs include entrepreneurship, game design, hospitality leadership, internal auditing, music and entertainment industry, sports communication and physical therapy. There are 5 undergraduate schools and 1 graduate school. In addition to regional accreditation, Bradley has baccalaureate program accreditation with AACSB, ABET, ACCE, CSWE, NASAD, NASM, NCATE, CCNE, NAEYC, and NAST. The 85-acre campus is in a suburban area in Peoria, Illinois, in the historic West Bluff residential neighborhood, three hours from Chicago, Indianapolis, and St. Louis. Including any residence halls, there are 77 buildings.

STUDENT LIFE: 83% of undergraduates are from Illinois. Others are from 39 states, 30 foreign countries, and Canada. 57% are White; 25% race unknown; 7% Hispanic; 5% African American; 3% Asian American; 1% American Indian/Alaska Native; 1% Foreign; 1% two or more races. **Female To Male Ratio:** 1.1:1. The average age of freshmen is 18; all undergraduates, 20. 13% do not continue beyond their first year; 74% remain to graduate. **Housing:** 3290 students can be accommodated in college housing, which includes coed dorms and on-campus apartments. In addition, there are fraternity houses, sorority houses, and honors floor in a residence hall. On-campus housing is guaranteed for all 4 years. 62% of students live on campus; of those, 75% remain on campus on weekends. All students may keep cars.

FACULTY/CLASSROOMS: 54% of faculty are male; 46% are female. No introductory courses are taught by graduate students.

PROGRAMS OF STUDY: Bradley confers B.A., B.F.A., B.Mus., B.S., B.S.Civil Eng., B.S.Constr., B.S.E.E., B.S.I.E., B.S.M.E., B.S.Mfg.E., B.S.Mfg.E.Tech., and B.S.N. degrees. Master's and doctoral degrees are also awarded. Bachelor's degrees are awarded in BIOLOGICAL SCIENCE (biology ecology and field biology, biochemistry, biology/biological science, and cell & molecular biology), BUSINESS (accounting, business administration and management, business economics, business information systems, entrepreneurial studies, finance, hospitality management services, human resources/organizational mgmt, international business, management information systems, marketing, management & strategic leadership, organizational leadership and management, retailing, and supply chain management), COMMUNICATIONS AND THE ARTS (advertising, animation, art, art history and appreciation, communications, drawing, English, game design and development, journalism, music, music business management, music composition, music industry, music performance, Spanish, sports communication, studio art graphic design, television & digital media production, theatre arts, and visual effects), COMPUTER AND PHYSICAL SCIENCE (actuarial science, chemistry, computer information systems, computer security, computer science, mathematics, physics, statistics, and web technology), EDUCATION (art education, early childhood education, education, education of the emotionally handicapped, education of the exceptional child, education of the mentally handicapped, education of the physically handicapped, elementary education, middle school education, music education, and secondary education), ENGINEERING AND ENVIRONMENTAL DESIGN (civil engineering, construction, electrical and computer engineering, electrical/electronics engineering, engineering physics, environmental science, industrial engineering, manufacturing engineering, manufacturing technology, and mechanical engineering), HEALTH PROFESSIONS (community health work, health science, medical laboratory science, medical technology, nursing, nutrition and dietetics, and premedicine), SOCIAL SCIENCE (criminal justice, economics, family/consumer studies, French studies, history, international studies, legal studies, liberal arts, sciences, general studies, humanities, philosophy, political science/government, prelaw, psychology, religious studies, social work, and sociology). Business, engineering, and health have the largest enrollments.

ACTIVITIES: 30% of men belong to 17 national fraternities; 29% of women belong to 12 national sororities. There are 240 groups on campus, including art, band, cheerleading, chess, choir, chorale, chorus, communications, computers, dance, drama, drill team, environmental, ethnic, forensics, honors, international, jazz band, LGBT, literary magazine, musical theater, newspaper, orchestra, pep band, photography, political, professional, radio and TV, religious, social, social service, student government, and symphony. Popular campus events include Late Night BU, Student Activities Fair, and Taste of Bradley. **Sports:** There are 6 intercollegiate sports for men and 7 for women, and 14 intramural sports for men and 14 for women. Facilities include tennis courts, basketball arena at local civic center, intramural playing fields, softball field, baseball field at local minor league ball park, hockey rink at local skating center, outdoor lighted basketball courts, and a 130,000-square-foot student recreation center with a pool, indoor track, weights, cardio machines, spinning room, practice courts, and a climbing wall. **Graduates:** From July 1, 2015 to June 30, 2016, 1156 bachelor's degrees were awarded. The most popular majors were business, management, marketing and related support services (19%), engineering (19%), and health professions and related programs (13%). 367 companies recruited on campus in 2015-2016. In an average class, 54% graduate in 4 years or less.

SERVICES: Counseling and information services are available, as is tutoring in most subjects, such as introductory subjects and selected higher-level classes. There is remedial math and writing. **Library/Resources:** The library contains 446,041 volumes, 84,300 microform items, and 18,438 audio/video tapes/CDs/DVDs, and subscribes to 58,243 periodicals including electronic. Computerized library services include interlibrary loans, database searching, Internet access, and Wi-Fi capability. Special learning facilities include an art gallery, radio station, and TV station. **Physically Challenged Students:** 75% of the campus is accessible. Facilities include wheelchair ramps, elevators, special parking, specially equipped restrooms, special class scheduling, and lowered drinking fountains. **Special:** Special academic programs include an honors program, co-op programs, internships, a Washington semester, a Hollywood semester, work-study programs, study abroad in 30 countries, B.A.-B.S. degrees in most majors, dual and student-designed majors, independent study, distance learning, certificate programs, four 3-2 programs and two 4-1 programs, and leadership fellowships. There are 15 national honor societies, a freshman honors program, and 16 departmental honors programs. **Visiting:** There are regularly scheduled orientations for prospective students, class visits, campus tours, admissions information, financial assistance seminars, lunch, and student and parent meetings. There are guides for informal visits, visitors may sit in on classes, and stay overnight. To schedule a visit, contact Office of Undergraduate Admission. **Campus Safety and Security:** Measures include 24-hour foot and vehicle patrol, emergency notification system, self-defense education, and security escort services. There are shuttle buses, emergency telephones, lighted pathways/sidewalks, and controlled access to dorms/residences.

REQUIREMENTS: Must have a high school diploma or GED; require either the SAT or ACT; require 16 academic credits: 4 English, 3 Mathematics, 2 Science (2 lab), 2 Social Studies; recommend 22 academic credits: 5 English, 4 Mathematics, 3 Science (3 lab), 2 Foreign Language, 3 Social Studies, 2 History; audition required for music and theatre programs; test scores waived for any person who has not attended high school in 365 days. AP and CLEP credits are accepted. To graduate, the student must complete the school's basic skills and core curriculum. Overall, the college requires 124 total credit hours, with 32 hours in the student's major and a minimum of 40 semester hours in junior and senior courses (those numbered 300 or above). A minimum of 30 semester hours must be earned in residence, and 24 of the last 30 semester hours must be earned in residence. Additionally, students must have a minimum GPA of 2.0. **Procedure:** Freshmen are admitted fall, spring, and summer. Entrance exams should be taken in the spring of the junior year or the fall of the senior year. There are deferred admissions and rolling admissions plans. Application deadlines are open. Application fee is $35. Notifications are sent October 15. Applications are accepted online. Application fees are waived if application is completed on-line. **Transfer Students:** 210 transfer students enrolled in 2015-2016. Transfer students must have a minimum GPA of 2.0. Those with fewer than 15 hours of college credit must submit their ACT or SAT scores and a high school transcript. Additionally, college transcripts and a statement of good standing from prior institution(s) required of all, interview recommended and essay or personal statement required for some. 30 of 124 credits required for the bachelor's degree must be completed at Bradley. **International Students:** There are 66 international students enrolled. The school actively recruits these students. They must take the TOEFL with a minimum score of 550 on the paper-based TOEFL (PBT) or 79 on the Internet-based version (iBT). The SAT or ACT is recommended.

ADMISSIONS: 70% of the 2016-2017 applicants were accepted. The SAT scores for the 2016-2017 freshman class were: Critical Reading-- 38% below 500, 30% between 500 and 599, 26% between 600 and 699, and 6% between 700 and 800. Math-- 29% below 500, 38% between 500 and 599, 26% between 600 and 699, and 7% between 700 and 800. Writing-- 35% below 500, 46% between 500 and 599, 18% between 600 and 699, and 1% between 700 and 800. The ACT scores were 1% between 12 and 17, 36% between 18 and 23, 48% between 24 and 29, and 15% above 30. 21% of the current freshmen were in the top fifth of their class; 36% were in the top two fifths. There were 2 National Merit finalists. 23 freshmen graduated first in their class. **Admissions Contact:** Dr. Justin Ball, Associate Vice President for Enrollment. Email: *admissions@bradley.edu* Web: *www.bradley.edu*

FINANCIAL AID: Bradley is a member of CSS. The FAFSA code is 001641. The priority date for freshman financial aid applications for fall entry is March 1.

CHICAGO STATE UNIVERSITY E-2

www.csu.edu

Chicago, IL 60628 (773) 995-2513 (800) 278-3011

Fax: (773) 995-3820 **Email:** ug-admissions@csu.edu

Full-time: 917 men, 2092 women	**Faculty:** IIA, -$
Part-time: 392 men, 1211 women	**Ph.D.s:** 62%
Graduate: 467 men, 1022 women	**Student/Faculty:** n/av
Year: other, summer session	**Tuition:** $7500 ($13,880)
Room & Board: $12,644	**Freshman Class:** n/av
ACT: required	**CEEB CODE:** 1118
Application Deadline: July 15	**COMPETITIVE**

Chicago State University, founded in 1867, is a public commuter and residential institution controlled by the State of Illinois. It offers day and evening undergraduate programs through the Colleges of Arts and Sciences, Health Sciences, Business Administration, Education, and nontraditional programs. The figures in the above capsule and in this profile are approximate. There are 5 undergraduate schools and 2 graduate schools. In addition to regional accreditation, Chicago State has baccalaureate program accreditation with AACSB, ACPE, ADA, CAHEA, NCATE, and NLN. The 161-acre campus is in an urban area, on the Southside of Chicago, 12 miles south of downtown Chicago. Including any residence halls, there are 13 buildings.

STUDENT LIFE: 98% of undergraduates are from Illinois. Others are from 24 states, 21 foreign countries, and Canada. 80% are African American; 7% Hispanic; 10% White; 1% Asian American. **Female To Male Ratio:** 2.4:1. The average age of freshmen is 21; all undergraduates, 29. **Housing:** 360 students can be accommodated in college housing, which includes coed dorms. On-campus housing is available on a first-come and first-served basis. 97% of students commute. Alcohol is not permitted. All students may keep cars.

FACULTY/CLASSROOMS: 99% teach undergraduates. No introductory courses are taught by graduate students. The average class size in an introductory lecture is 60; in a laboratory is 26; and in a regular course is 35.

PROGRAMS OF STUDY: Chicago State confers B.A., B.S., B.M.E., and B.S.Ed. degrees. Master's and doctoral degrees are also awarded. Bachelor's degrees are awarded in BIOLOGICAL SCIENCE (biochemistry and biology/biological science), BUSINESS (accounting, banking and finance, business administration and management, management science, marketing/retailing/merchandising, and recreation and leisure services), COMMUNICATIONS AND THE ARTS (art, broadcasting, English, music, Spanish, and speech/debate/rhetoric), COMPUTER AND PHYSICAL SCIENCE (chemistry, computer science, information sciences and systems, mathematics, and physics), EDUCATION (art education, bilingual/bicultural education, business education, early childhood education, elementary education, industrial arts education, music education, physical education, secondary education, and vocational education), HEALTH PROFESSIONS (health, health care administration, health science, nursing, predentistry, and premedicine), SOCIAL SCIENCE (African American studies, criminal justice, economics, geography, history, political science/government, prelaw, psychology, and sociology). Business administration, and computer science are the strongest academically. Elementary education, and nursing have the largest enrollments.

ACTIVITIES: There are 72 groups on campus, including cheerleading, chess, choir, dance, honors, international, jazz band, literary magazine, newspaper, political, professional, radio and TV, religious, social, social service, and student government. Popular campus events include Welcome Week activities, Black Writers Conference, and Hispanic Heritage Month. **Sports:** There are 6 intercollegiate sports for men and 6 for women, and 4 intramural sports for men and 2 for women. Facilities include tennis courts, indoor/outdoor tracks, an Olympic-size swimming pool, weight rooms, basketball courts, a fitness center, dance studio, a baseball field, and Convocation Center with 6300 seating capacity. **Graduates:** From July 1, 2015 to June 30, 2016, 839 bachelor's degrees were awarded. The most popular majors were general studies (26%), business administration (13%), and criminal justice (6%). In an average class, 7% graduate in 4 years or less and 22% graduate in 6 years or less.

SERVICES: Counseling and information services are available, as is tutoring in some subjects. There is remedial math, reading, and writing. Math, science, and accounting are also available. **Library/Resources:** The library contains 26,000 volumes, 388,028 microform items, and subscribes to 1,734 periodicals including electronic. Computerized library services include interlibrary loans, database searching, and Internet access. Special learning facilities include an art gallery, radio station, and a TV studio. **Physically Challenged Students:** All of the campus is accessible. Facilities include wheelchair ramps, elevators, special parking, specially equipped restrooms, lowered drinking fountains, and lowered telephones. **Special:** Chicago State offers a combined B.A.-B.S. degree, a board of governors degree program, a University Without Walls Program, and an individualized curriculum program. Study abroad in Liberia and life experience credits are also provided. There is a freshman honors program. **Visiting:** There are regularly scheduled orientations for prospective students, including a tour of campus, admissions overview, and financial aid information. To schedule a visit, contact the Office of Admissions. **Campus Safety and Security:** Measures include 24-hour foot and vehicle patrol and security escort services. There are emergency telephones and lighted pathways/sidewalks.

REQUIREMENTS: The ACT is required, but scores need not be submitted if the applicant is over 25 years of age. Graduation from an accredited secondary school is required; a GED will be accepted. Minimum credits submitted should include 4 units of English, 3 of math, 3 of science, and 3 of social sciences. A GPA of 2.5 is required. AP and CLEP credits are accepted. All students must complete 120 credit hours, including 40 hours in the major, maintain a 2.0 GPA, and fulfill foreign language requirement. They must complete a 39-hour core curriculum as well as examinations in English, math, reading, and the U.S. Constitution. **Procedure:** Freshmen are admitted to all sessions. There is a rolling admissions plan. Applications should be filed by July 15 for fall entry; November 15 for spring entry; and May 1 for summer entry, along with a $25 fee. Notification is sent on a rolling basis. Applications are accepted on-line. **Transfer Students:** Transfer students must have a minimum GPA of 2.0, and those with fewer than 24 hours must also meet freshman admission requirements. 30 of 120 credits required for the bachelor's degree must be completed at Chicago State. **International Students:** There are 26 international students enrolled. The school actively recruits these students. They must take the TOEFL with a minimum score of 525 on the paper-based TOEFL (PBT) or 69 on the Internet-based version (iBT) and the college's own test, or take the IETLS with a score of 7 and minimum. They must also take the SAT or ACT.

Admissions Contact: Matt Harrison, Director of Admissions. Email: *ug-admissions@csu.edu* Web: *www.csu.edu*

FINANCIAL AID: In 2016-2017, 97% of all full-time freshmen and 97% of continuing full-time students received some form of financial aid. 97% of all full-time freshmen and 97% of continuing full-time students received need-based aid. The average freshman award was $16,154. Need-based scholarships or need-based grants averaged $7,263 ($9,540 maximum); need-based self-help aid (loans and jobs) averaged $3,473 ($7,000 maximum); non-need-based athletic scholarships averaged $10,575 ($17,010 maximum); and other non-need-based awards and non-need-based scholarships averaged $6,898 ($19,522 maximum). 5% of undergraduate students work part-time. Average annual earnings from campus work are $1918. The average financial indebtedness of the 2016 graduate was $28,955. The FAFSA code is 001694. The priority date for freshman financial aid applications for fall entry is February 1. The deadline for filing freshman financial aid applications for fall entry is April 15.

COLUMBIA COLLEGE CHICAGO E-2

www.colum.edu

Chicago, IL 60605 **(312) 369-7130**

Email: admissions@colum.edu

Full-time: 2990 men, 4152 women	**Faculty:** 267
Part-time: 318 men, 349 women	**Ph.D.s:** 16%
Graduate: 112 men, 199 women	**Student/Faculty:** 27 to 1
Year: semesters, summer session	**Tuition:** $25,334
Room & Board: $13,298	**Freshman Class:** 8327 applied, 7333 accepted, 1555 enrolled
ACT: 23	**CEEB CODE:** 1135
Application Deadline: n/av	**COMPETITIVE**

Columbia College Chicago educates students for the real world through hands-on training in the arts, media, and communications. Surrounding and infusing this practical career preparation is a strong framework of required courses in the liberal arts and sciences. A Columbia education combines the pragmatic and the theoretical, the entrepreneurial and the academic. Thanks to our faculty members' immersion in the working world and our location in the heart of downtown Chicago, Columbia students and graduates are surrounded by exceptional internship and career opportunities. There are 3 undergraduate schools and 3 graduate schools. The campus is in an urban area in Chicago, IL. Including any residence halls, there are 23 buildings.

STUDENT LIFE: 56% of undergraduates are from Illinois. Others are from 50 states, 26 foreign countries, and Canada. 55% are White; 14% African American; 13% Hispanic; 6% race unknown; 4% Asian American; 4% two or more races; 1% American Indian/Alaska Native; 1% Foreign. **Female To Male Ratio:** 1.4:1. 30% do not continue beyond their first year; 44% remain to graduate. **Housing:** 3000 students can be accommodated in college housing, which includes coed dorms. In addition, there are special-interest houses. On-campus housing is available on a first-come and first-served basis. Priority is given to out-of-town students. 67% of students commute. Alcohol is not permitted. All students may keep cars.

FACULTY/CLASSROOMS: 55% of faculty are male; 45% are female. No introductory courses are taught by graduate students.

PROGRAMS OF STUDY: Columbia confers B.A., B.F.A., B.S., and B.Mus degrees. Master's degrees are also awarded. Bachelor's degrees are awarded in BUSINESS (marketing and marketing management), COMMUNICATIONS AND THE ARTS (acting, advertising, American Sign Language, art history, art, arts administration/management, audio technology, creative writing, dance, dramatic arts, fashion studies, film arts, game design and development, game programming, graphic design, illustration, journalism, multimedia, music, music business management, photography, public relations, radio/TV, radio/television technology, theatre arts, and writing), COMPUTER AND PHYSICAL SCIENCE (computer game design/development), EDUCATION (early childhood education), ENGINEERING AND ENVIRONMENTAL DESIGN (computer graphics), SOCIAL SCIENCE (crosscultural studies, cultural studies/critical theory & analysis, and interpreter for the deaf). Film, game design, comedy writing, and performance are the strongest academically. Cinema art and science, theatre, and business and entrepreneurship have the largest enrollments.

ACTIVITIES: There are no fraternities or sororities. There are 85 groups on campus, including art, chorale, chorus, computers, dance, drama, ethnic, film, international, jazz band, LGBT, literary magazine, musical theater, newspaper, orchestra, photography, political, professional, radio and TV, religious, social, social service, student government, symphony, and yearbook. Popular campus events include African Heritage, Dr. Martin Luther King Jr.'s Birthday, and Women in the Arts. **Graduates:** From July 1, 2015 to June 30, 2016, 1908 bachelor's degrees were awarded. The most popular majors were cinema art & science (14%), graphic design (6%), and fashion business (5%). In an average class, 33% graduate in 4 years or less, 43% graduate in 5 years or less, and 45% graduate in 6 years or less.

SERVICES: Counseling and information services are available, as is tutoring in most subjects. There is a reader service for the blind, and remedial math, reading, and writing. **Library/Resources:** Computerized library services include interlibrary loans, database searching, Internet access, and Wi-Fi capability. Special learning facilities include an art gallery, radio station, TV station, museum of contemporary photography, a center for black music research, ShopColumbia, Big Mouth open mic, Averill and Bernard Leviton Gallery, C33 Gallery, center for book, paper and print, Fashion Studies Exhibition Windows, Fashion Study Collection, Glass Curtain Gallery, Hokin Project, Project Rm, The Arcade, Efroymson Art + Design Resource Center, Anchor Graphics, Fashion Lab, Media Production Center, Digital Music Lab, Music MFA Lab, Digital Photography Lab, Papermaker's Garden, and The Loft. **Physically Challenged Students:** Facilities include wheelchair ramps, elevators, specially equipped restrooms, special class scheduling, lowered drinking fountains, and lowered telephones. **Special:** Columbia offers study abroad in many countries, independent study, internships, work-study programs, student-designed majors, and a general studies degree. There is a freshman honors program. **Visiting:** There are regularly scheduled orientations for prospective students. There are guides for informal visits and visitors may sit in on classes. To schedule a visit, contact the Undergraduate Admissions Office. **Campus Safety and Security:** Measures include 24-hour foot and vehicle patrol, emergency notification system, self-defense education, and security escort services. There are emergency telephones and lighted pathways/sidewalks.

REQUIREMENTS: Applicants should be graduates of accredited secondary schools. The GED is also accepted. An interview is recommended. AP and CLEP credits are accepted. To graduate, all students must complete 124 semester hours of study with a minimum 2.0 GPA. General studies distribution consists of 9 hours each of literature/humanities and science/math, 6 each of English, history, and social science, and 3 each of computer applications, oral communications, senior seminar, and electives, and 1 intensive writing course. **Procedure:** Freshmen are admitted to all sessions. There are deferred admissions and rolling admissions plans. Check with the school for current application deadlines. The application fee is $35. Applications are accepted on-line. **Transfer Students:** Up to 88 credit hours are accepted with a grade of C or better; up to 62 credit hours from 2-year colleges with a grade of C or better are accepted. 36 of 124 credits required for the bachelor's degree must be completed at Columbia. **International Students:** There are 278 international students enrolled. The school actively recruits these students.

ADMISSIONS: 88% of the 2016-2017 applicants were accepted. The ACT scores were 13% between 12 and 17, 45% between 18 and 23, 34% between 24 and 29, and 8% above 30. **Admissions Contact:** Jill Huntsberger, Interim Director of Admissions & Recruit. Email: *admissions@colum.edu* Web: *www.colum.edu*

FINANCIAL AID: In 2016-2017, 91% of all full-time freshmen received some form of financial aid. The average freshman award was $18,214. The FAFSA code is 001665. Check with the school for current application deadlines.

CONCORDIA UNIVERSITY, CHICAGO — E-2

www.curf.edu

River Forest, IL 60305 — **(708) 209-3101** **(866) GO-2-CURF**

Fax: (708) 209-3473 — **Email: admission@cuchicago.edu**

Full-time: 351 men, 610 women	**Faculty:** 74
Part-time: 21 men, 50 women	**Ph.D.s:** 65%
Graduate: 428 men, 1323 women	**Student/Faculty:** 13 to 1
Year: semesters, summer session	**Tuition:** $30,522
Room & Board: $9172	**Freshman Class:** 680 applied, 628 accepted, 210 enrolled
ACT: required	**CEEB CODE:** 1140
Application Deadline: n/av	**COMPETITIVE**

Concordia University Chicago, founded in 1864, is a private liberal arts institution affiliated with the Lutheran Church, Missouri Synod. The figures in the above capsule, and in this profile are approximate. The figures are traditional undergraduate cost. There are 4 undergraduate schools and 1 graduate school. In addition to regional accreditation, Concordia University has baccalaureate program accreditation with NCATE and NLN. The 40-acre campus is in a suburban area 10 miles west of downtown Chicago. Including any residence halls, there are 24 buildings.

STUDENT LIFE: 65% of undergraduates are from Illinois. Others are from 21 states, 1 foreign country, and Canada. 66% are from public schools. 51% are White; 5% Hispanic; 10% African American; 1% Asian American. 59% are Undeclared denomination; 31% Protestant; 13% Catholic. **Female To Male Ratio:** 2.5:1. The average age of freshmen is 18; all undergraduates, 22. 27% do not continue beyond their first year; 53% remain to graduate. **Housing:** 775 students can be accommodated in college housing, which includes single-sex and coed dorms and married student housing. On-campus housing is guaranteed for all 4 years. 65% of students live on campus; of those, 75% remain on campus on weekends. Alcohol is not permitted. All students may keep cars.

FACULTY/CLASSROOMS: 50% of faculty are male; 50% are female. 82% teach undergraduates, and 82% do research. No introductory courses are taught by graduate students. The average class size in an introductory lecture is 20; in a laboratory is 18; and in a regular course is 25.

PROGRAMS OF STUDY: Concordia University confers B.A., B.Mus., and B.Mus.Ed. degrees. Master's and doctoral degrees are also awarded. Bachelor's degrees are awarded in BIOLOGICAL SCIENCE (biology/biological science), BUSINESS (accounting and business administration and management), COMMUNICATIONS AND THE ARTS (art, communications, English, and music), COMPUTER AND PHYSICAL SCIENCE (chemistry, computer programming, computer science, mathematics, natural sciences, and physical sciences), EDUCATION (computer education, early childhood education, elementary education, middle school education, music education, physical education, science education, and secondary education), HEALTH PROFESSIONS (premedicine), SOCIAL SCIENCE (geography, history, physical fitness/movement, political science/government, prelaw, psychology, religion, social science, social work, sociology, and theological studies). Elementary education, exercise science, and theology are the strongest academically. Elementary education, business, and psychology have the largest enrollments.

ACTIVITIES: There are no fraternities or sororities. There are 43 groups on campus, including band, cheerleading, choir, chorale, chorus, communications, dance, drama, ethnic, honors, jazz band, literary magazine, musical theater, newspaper, pep band, professional, religious, social, social service, student government, symphony, and yearbook. Popular campus events include Orientation Week, Campus Awareness Day, and Family Weekend. **Sports:** There are 7 intercollegiate sports for men and 7 for women, and 12 intramural sports for men and 12 for women. Facilities include 2 gyms, an indoor swimming pool, a weight training room, human performance lab, football and soccer fields, tennis courts, baseball and softball fields, track, first aid training room, table tennis, and billiards. **Graduates:** From July 1, 2015 to June 30, 2016, 216 bachelor's degrees were awarded. The most popular majors were education (34%), business (8%), and sociology/social work (4%). In an average class, 36% graduate in 4 years or less, and 41% graduate in 5 years or less. Of the 2015 graduating class, 23% were enrolled in graduate school within 6 months of graduation, and 98% were employed.

SERVICES: Counseling and information services are available, as is tutoring in every subject. There is remedial math, reading, and writing. **Library/Resources:** The library contains 140,000 volumes, 480,000 microform items, and 2,250 audio/video tapes/CDs/DVDs, and subscribes to 235 periodicals including electronic. Computerized library services include interlibrary loans, database searching, Internet access, and Wi-Fi capability. Special learning facilities include an art gallery, natural history museum, TV station, an early childhood resource center, human performance lab, a language lab, computer center, and weather station. **Physically Challenged Students:** 74% of the campus is accessible. Facilities include wheelchair ramps, elevators, special parking, specially equipped restrooms, special class scheduling, lowered drinking fountains, and lowered telephones. **Special:** Cross-registration is possible with Dominican University and the Chicago Consortium of Colleges. Concordia also offers internships for liberal arts majors in the Chicago area, which provides numerous opportunities, study abroad in England, and pass/fail options. Work-study is possible, as is an accelerated degreee program in organizational management. There are 3 national honor societies, Phi Beta Kappa, and a freshman honors program. **Visiting:** There are regularly scheduled orientations for prospective students, consisting of daily planned activities during orientation in the first week of the fall semester. There are guides for informal visits, visitors may sit in on classes, and stay overnight. To schedule a visit, contact the Office of Admission. **Campus Safety and Security:** Measures include 24-hour foot and vehicle patrol, self-defense education, and security escort services. There are shuttle buses, emergency telephones, and lighted pathways/sidewalks.

REQUIREMENTS: The ACT is required. Applicants should have 15 units of credit, with 11 units in college preparatory courses, including English, math, lab science, and social studies. A letter of recommendation is required, as is a minimum GPA of 2.0 in the college preparatory subjects and a ranking in the top half of their graduating class. Concordia University requires applicants to be in the upper 50% of their class. A GPA of 2.0 is required. AP and CLEP credits are accepted. Important factors in the admissions decision are advanced placement or honors courses, recommendations by school officials, and leadership record. All students are required to take 2 years of liberal arts, including humanities, English, science, religion, and social science, and 5 quarter hours of phys ed. A 2.0 to 2.25 GPA and a total of 128 to 150 quarter hours are required. The number of hours required for the major varies by program. **Procedure:** Freshmen are admitted to all sessions. Entrance exams should be taken in the spring of the junior year or fall of the senior year. There is a rolling admissions plan. Application deadlines are open. Applications are accepted on-line. **Transfer Students:** 90 transfer students enrolled in 2015-2016. A cumulative GPA of 2.0 or higher at all previous colleges plus a letter of recommendation are required. 48 of 128 credits required for the bachelor's degree must be completed at Concordia University. **International Students:** There are 5 international students enrolled. They must take the TOEFL or MELAB, or successfully complete Level 109 at an ELS language center.

ADMISSIONS: 92% of the 2016-2017 applicants were accepted. The ACT scores were 36% below 12, 23% between 12 and 17, 20% between 18 and 23, 9% between 24 and 29, and 12% above 30. 30% of the current freshmen were in the top fifth of their class; 41% were in the top two fifths. **Admissions Contact:** James P. Malley, Director of Admissions. Email: *admission@cuchicago.edu* Web: *www.curf.edu*

FINANCIAL AID: In 2016-2017, 93% of all full-time freshmen and 87% of continuing full-time students received some form of financial aid. 85% of all full-time freshmen and 67% of continuing full-time students received need-based aid. The average freshman award was $12,000. The average financial indebtedness of the 2016 graduate was $12,000. The college's own financial statement and student and parent 1040 U.S. tax forms are required. Check with the school for current application deadlines.

DEPAUL UNIVERSITY — E-2

www.depaul.edu

Chicago, IL 60604	**(312) 362-8300** **(800) 4-DEPAUL**
Fax: (312) 362-5749	**Email: admission@depaul.edu**
Full-time: 6396 men, 7247 women	**Faculty:** 799; I, av$
Part-time: 1169 men, 1341 women	**Ph.D.s:** 86%
Graduate: 3584 men, 4062 women	**Student/Faculty:** n/av
Year: quarters, summer session	**Tuition:** $34,390
Room & Board: $12,552	**Freshman Class:** 19533 applied, 13649 accepted, 2544 enrolled
SAT CR/M: 586/569 **ACT:** 25	**CEEB CODE:** 1165
Application Deadline: February 1	**VERY COMPETITIVE**

DePaul University is the nation's largest Catholic university. Its partnerships throughout Chicago enable DePaul to provide an exceptional educational experience that is vibrant, pragmatic, and socially engaged. Classes are small and taught by knowledgeable and experienced faculty members who take full advantage of Chicago's resources. DePaul's mission to provide a quality education to students from a broad range of backgrounds has resulted in one of the nation's most diverse student bodies. There are 9 undergraduate schools and 10 graduate schools. In addition to regional accreditation, DePaul has baccalaureate program accreditation with AACSB and NASM. The 38-acre campus is in an urban area. Including any residence halls, there are 48 buildings.

STUDENT LIFE: 79% of undergraduates are from Illinois. Others are from 50 states, 86 foreign countries, and Canada. 78% are from public schools. 8% are African American; 8% Asian American; 55% White; 4% two or more races; 4% race unknown; 3% Foreign; 17% Hispanic. 34% are Catholic. **Female To Male Ratio:** 1.1:1. The average age of freshmen is 18; all undergraduates, 23. 13% do not continue beyond their first year; 71% remain to graduate. **Housing:** 2644 students can be accommodated in college housing, which includes coed dorms, on-campus apartments, and off-campus apartments. In addition, there are special-interest houses, private studios and apartments, and traditional residence-style units. On-campus housing is available on a first-come, first-served basis, and is available on a lottery system for upperclassmen. Priority is given to out-of-town students. 84% of students commute. All students may keep cars.

FACULTY/CLASSROOMS: 53% of faculty are male; 47% are female. 80% teach undergraduates, and 80% do research. Graduate students teach 2% of introductory courses. The average class size in an introductory lecture is 25; in a laboratory is 19; and in a regular course is 29.

PROGRAMS OF STUDY: DePaul confers B.A., B.S., B.F.A., B.M., B.S.B. and B.S.P.E. degrees. Master's and doctoral degrees are also awarded. Bachelor's degrees are awarded in BIOLOGICAL SCIENCE (biology/biological science), BUSINESS (accounting, banking and finance, business administration and management, business economics, finance, hospitality management services, human resources, management information systems, management science, marketing management, organizational behavior, and real estate), COMMUNICATIONS AND THE ARTS (animation, Arabic, art history, art, Chinese, communications, creative writing, dramatic arts, English, fine arts, French, German, graphic design, information technology, Italian, jazz, journalism, media arts, music, music business management, music performance, music theory and composition, performing arts, playwriting/screenwriting, public relations, Spanish, speech/debate/rhetoric, theatre arts, theater design, and theater management), COMPUTER AND PHYSICAL SCIENCE (applied mathematics, chemistry, computer programming, computer game design/development, computer science, computer security and information assurance, digital arts/technology, information sciences and systems, mathematics, physical sciences, and physics), EDUCATION (art education, early childhood education, education, education administration, elementary education, foreign languages education, health education, music education, physical education, secondary education, and special education), ENGINEERING AND ENVIRONMENTAL DESIGN (architectural history, computational sciences, computer graphics, computer technology, and environmental science), HEALTH PROFESSIONS (art therapy, clinical science, health science, and nursing), SOCIAL SCIENCE (African studies, American studies, anthropology, community services, East Asian studies, economics, geography, history, humanities, international studies, Islamic studies, Judaic studies, Latin American studies, peace studies, philosophy, political science/government, psychology, public administration, public affairs, religion, social science, social studies, sociology, urban studies, and women's studies). Accounting, finance, and psychology have the largest enrollments.

ACTIVITIES: 3% of men belong to 11 national fraternities; 8% of women belong to 16 national sororities. There are 317 groups on campus, including art, cheerleading, chess, choir, chorale, chorus, communications, computers, dance, debate, drama, environmental, ethnic, film, honors, international, LGBT, literary magazine, newspaper, pep band, photography, political, professional, radio and TV, religious, social, social service, and student government. Popular campus events include FEST (University Festival), Blue Demon Week, Blue Demon Dance, Welcome Week, Vincentian Service Day, New Student Service Day, and DemonTHON (DePaul's Dance Marathon). **Sports:** There are 6 intercollegiate sports for men and 7 for women, and 34 intramural sports for men and 34 for women. The Ray Meyer Fitness and Recreation Center is located on DePaul University's Lincoln Park Campus location. This facility offers: strength and conditioning area with a free weight area, swimming pool, gymnasium for basketball, volleyball, and badminton, racquetball courts, an 1/8 mile banked jogging track, aquatics, yoga, dance, Pilates, marital arts, fitness training, and safety training. There are also Outdoor Adventure trips for students, faculty, and staff, and team challenge. **Graduates:** From July 1, 2015 to June 30, 2016, 3748 bachelor's degrees were awarded. The most popular majors were accountancy (7%), public relations and advertising (7%), and psychology (7%). 504 companies recruited on campus in 2015-2016. In an average class, 2% graduate in 3 years or less, 56% graduate in 4 years or less, 69% graduate in 5 years or less, and 71% graduate in 6 years or less.

SERVICES: There is a reader service for the blind, and remedial reading and writing. The Center for Students with Disabilities offers clinician services, which include remediation of skills for time management, organizational skills, reading strategies, and writing skills. The University provides free tutoring services across a range of departments and subjects area: University Writing Center, Quantitative Reasoning Lab, Math Department, College of Science/Health, computer software (Word, Excel, etc.), Computer Programming, and Accounting, amongst others.

Library/Resources: The 6 libraries contain 1.1 million volumes, 241,432 microform items, and 31,989 audio/video tapes/CDs/DVDs, and subscribe to 70,452 periodicals including electronic. Computerized library services include interlibrary loans, database searching, Internet access, and Wi-Fi capability. Special learning facilities include an art gallery, radio station, LEED-certified environmental science, and chemistry building with greenhouse & green roof, digital cinema laboratory with motion-capture system, green-screen studio, converged newsroom, 10 specialized computer research labs including artificial intelligence, biomedics informatics & mobile e-commerce, 1,300-seat theatre, art museum, and a fitness and recreational center with pool. **Physically Challenged Students:** Facilities include wheelchair ramps, elevators, special parking, specially equipped restrooms, special class scheduling, lowered drinking fountains, lowered telephones, and special housing. The Center for Students with Disabilities coordinates DePaul University's provision of accommodations and other services to students with documented disabilities in accordance with the Americans with Disabilities Act and Section 504 of the Rehabilitation Act. All CSD programs and services are free of charge with the exception of a modest fee for students requesting weekly clinician services for academic support strategies. CSD works with the range of all documented disabilities, e.g., LD, AD/HD, medical conditions, chronic illness, psychiatric, physical/visual/hearing impaired, etc. Students may be full time, part-time, and undergraduate or graduate. CSD students are enrolled in university-wide colleges and schools such as Education, Business, Science and Health, Cinema Digital Media (CDM), Communication, Law, Music, Theatre, Liberal Arts and Social Sciences, and the School for New Learning (SNL) with declared majors across a wide spectrum of career tracks. **Special:** DePaul University is known and respected for its nearly 300 graduate and undergraduate programs and concentrations. The Irwin W. Steans Center for Community-based Service Learning (CbSL) and Community Service Studies provides opportunities and experiences for students to develop social agency through CbSL courses, community internships, research, scholarships, placements, and community-based student employment. The University Internship Program assists students in finding an internship that fits their course of study and career goals. With several locations and programs available, the study abroad office is available to students who are looking for a variety of study abroad opportunities and programs. DePaul also offers accelerated degree programs, dual majors, certificate programs, pass/fail options, and concentrations within the theater major, including acting, costume design, general theater studies, lighting design, playwriting, production theater management, and theater technology. The School for New Learning provides evening and weekend degree programs for adult learners, with credit given for life and work experience. There are 19 national honor societies and a freshman honors program. **Visiting:** There are regularly scheduled orientations for prospective students, Freshmen orientation, DePaul Premiere, and Transfer and Adult student orientation. Transition DePaul provides academic advising, assessment testing, course registration, and information on social activities and residence life. There are guides for informal visits, visitors may sit in on classes, and stay overnight. To schedule a visit, contact the Office of Admission. **Campus Safety and Security:** Measures include 24-hour foot and vehicle patrol, emergency notification system, self-defense education, and security escort services. There are emergency telephones, lighted pathways/sidewalks, and controlled access to dorms/residences.

REQUIREMENTS: The SAT or ACT is recommended. Based on research and DePaul's student-centered approach to education, DePaul has adopted a test-optional alternative for freshman admission. Students applying for freshman admission can choose whether or not to submit ACT or SAT scores as part of the application. Students who do not submit test scores will be required to send responses to several short essay questions. Music School applicants and applicants for the Acting Program in the Theatre School are required to schedule an audition. An interview or portfolio review is required for Design, Technical, or Theatre Studies program applicants. A GPA of 2.0 is required. AP and CLEP credits are accepted. Important factors in the admissions decision are advanced placement or honors courses, leadership record, and personality/intangible qualities. At DePaul, our core curriculum-the Liberal Studies Program-consists of two primary components: the Common Core and six distinct learning domains. All students (except School for New Learning) must complete general education requirements, including 4 courses in arts and literature, philosophical inquiry, religious dimensions, scientific inquiry self, society and the modern world, and understanding the past. These liberal studies vary by college. A total of 192 quarter hour credits, and a minimum GPA of 2.0 are required to graduate. **Procedure:** Freshmen are admitted to all sessions. Scores need to be submitted by February 1. There are early admissions, deferred admissions, and rolling admissions plans. Early decision applications should be filed by November 15; regular applications, by February 1 for fall entry; November 1 for winter entry; March 1 for spring entry; and May 1 for summer entry, along with a $25 fee. Notification of early decision is sent January 15; regular decision, March 15. Applications are accepted on-line. **Transfer Students:** 2574 transfer students enrolled in 2015-2016. A 2.0 GPA is required for most programs; a 2.5 for Driehaus College of Business, College of Education, and School of Music. Applicants with fewer than 30 semester hours or 44 quarter hours should submit high school transcripts and SAT or ACT scores. An audition is required for music and theater majors. 60 of 192 credits required for the bachelor's degree must be completed at DePaul. **International Students:** There are 466 international students enrolled. The school actively recruits these students. They must take the TOEFL with a minimum score of 550 on the paper-based TOEFL (PBT) or 80 on the Internet-based version (iBT), or take the International English Testing Systems, based on research and DePaul's student-centered approach to education.

ADMISSIONS: 70% of the 2016-2017 applicants were accepted. The SAT scores for the 2016-2017 freshman class were: Critical Reading-- 13% below 500, 41% between 500 and 599, 37% between 600 and 699, and 8% between 700 and 800. Math-- 18% below 500, 43% between 500 and 599, 32% between 600 and 699, and 6% between 700 and 800. The ACT scores were 10% below 12, 22% between 12 and 17, 29% between 18 and 23, 17% between 24 and 29, and 22% above 30. 45% of the current freshmen were in the top fifth of their class; 75% were in the top two fifths. 8 freshmen graduated first in their class. **Admissions Contact:** Carlene Klaas-Kennelly, Dean of Undergraduate Admission. Email: *admission@depaul.edu* Web: *www.depaul.edu*

FINANCIAL AID: In 2016-2017, 73% of all full-time freshmen and 69% of continuing full-time students received some form of financial aid. 63% of all full-time freshmen and 59% of continuing full-time students received need-based aid. The average freshman award was $23,440. Need-based scholarships or need-based grants averaged $11,204; need-based self-help aid (loans and jobs) averaged $3,663; non-need-based athletic scholarships averaged $19,759; and other non-need-based awards and non-need-based scholarships averaged $10,941. 17% of undergraduate students work part-time. The average financial indebtedness of the 2016 graduate was $24,292. The FAFSA code is 001671. The priority date for freshman financial aid applications for fall entry is January 1. The deadline for filing freshman financial aid applications for fall entry is March 1.

DOMINICAN UNIVERSITY — E-2

www.dom.edu

River Forest, IL 60305	**(708) 524-6795** **(800) 828-8475**
Fax: (708) 524-6864	**Email: domadmis@dom.edu**
Full-time: 712 men, 1361 women	**Faculty:** 139; IIA, -$
Part-time: 59 men, 137 women	**Ph.D.s:** 87%
Graduate: 310 men, 1114 women	**Student/Faculty:** 11 to 1
Year: semesters, summer session	**Tuition:** $31,570
Room & Board: $9652	**Freshman Class:** 4568 applied, 2911 accepted, 495 enrolled
SAT CR/M/W: 550/534/515 **ACT:** 23	**CEEB CODE:** 1667
Application Deadline: July 1	**COMPETITIVE**

Dominican University, founded in 1901, is an independent liberal arts institution affiliated with the Roman Catholic Church and sponsored by the Sinsinawa Dominicans. The figures in the above capsule and in this profile are approximate. There are 6 undergraduate schools and 6 graduate schools. In addition to regional accreditation, Dominican University has baccalaureate program accreditation with AACSB, ADA, CSWE, NCATE, ALA, and ARC-PA. The 37-acre campus is in a suburban area 10 miles west of downtown Chicago. Including any residence halls, there are 13 buildings.

STUDENT LIFE: 93% of undergraduates are from Illinois. Others are from 29 states, 19 foreign countries, and Canada. 8% are African American; 8% race unknown; 43% White; 34% Hispanic; 3% Asian American; 3% Foreign; 1% two or more races. 28% are Catholic; 28% claim no religious affiliation. **Female To Male Ratio:** 2.4:1. The average age of freshmen is 19; all undergraduates, 22. 28% do not continue beyond their first year; 59% remain to graduate. **Housing:** 610 students can be accommodated in college housing, which includes single-sex and coed dorms, off-campus apartments, and married student housing. On-campus housing is available on a first-come and first-served basis. Priority is given to out-of-town students. 74% of students commute. All students may keep cars.

FACULTY/CLASSROOMS: 37% of faculty are male; 63% are female. 79% teach undergraduates. No introductory courses are taught by graduate students. The average class size in an introductory lecture is 17 and in a regular course is 17.

PROGRAMS OF STUDY: Dominican University confers B.A., B.S., B.S.N, B.L.S., B.H.S., and B.M.S. degrees. Master's and doctoral degrees are also awarded. Bachelor's degrees are awarded in BIOLOGICAL SCIENCE (biochemistry, biology/biological science, neurosciences, and nutrition), BUSINESS (accounting, apparel and accessories marketing, business administration and management, fashion merchandising, finance, information & communication technology, international business management, and marketing management), COMMUNICATIONS AND THE ARTS (apparel design, art history, communications, dramatic arts, English, film arts, fine arts, French, graphic design, Italian, journalism, music, painting, performing arts, photography, Spanish, and theatre arts), COMPUTER AND PHYSICAL SCIENCE (chemistry, computer science, digital arts/technology, mathematics, and natural sciences), EDUCATION (early childhood education, education, elementary education, and secondary education), ENGINEERING AND ENVIRONMENTAL DESIGN (engineering and environmental science), HEALTH PROFESSIONS (nursing, predentistry, premedicine, and prepharmacy), SOCIAL SCIENCE (American studies, criminal justice, dietetics, economics, fashion design and technology, food production/management/services, food science, gender studies, history, international relations, legal studies, ministries, philosophy, political science/government, prelaw, psychology, religion, social science, sociology, theological studies, and women's studies). Business administration, health professions, and psychology are the strongest academically. Business administration, psychology, and biology have the largest enrollments.

ACTIVITIES: There are no fraternities or sororities. There are 55 groups on campus, including art, band, choir, chorus, communications, computers, dance, drama, environmental, ethnic, honors, international, LGBT, literary magazine, musical theater, newspaper, photography, political, professional, religious, social, social service, student government, and students for Peace and Justice. Popular campus events include Caritas Veritas Symposium. **Sports:** There are 7 intercollegiate sports for men and 6 for women, and 6 intramural sports for men and 6 for women. Facilities include a gym, an indoor running track, a weight room, a training room, a fitness center, a dance room, racquetball courts, and soccer fields. **Graduates:** From July 1, 2015 to June 30, 2016, 420 bachelor's degrees were awarded. The most popular majors were business administration/marketing (20%), health professions (16%), and social sciences (15%). 40 companies recruited on campus in 2015-2016. In an average class, 51% graduate in 4 years or less, 60% graduate in 5 years or less, and 62% graduate in 6 years or less. Of the 2015 graduating class, 28% were enrolled in graduate school within 6 months of graduation, and 81% were employed.

SERVICES: Counseling and information services are available, as is tutoring in most subjects. There is remedial math and writing. **Library/Resources:** The library contains 250,000 volumes, 50,000 microform items, and 5,000 audio/video tapes/CDs/DVDs, and subscribes to 35,000 periodicals including electronic. Computerized library services include interlibrary loans, database searching, Internet access, and Wi-Fi capability. Special learning facilities include an art gallery, a language lab, and a writing center. **Physically Challenged Students:** All of the campus is accessible. Facilities include wheelchair ramps, elevators, special parking, specially equipped restrooms, special class scheduling, lowered drinking fountains, and special housing. **Special:** Co-op programs in nursing with Rush University, cross-registration with Concordia University, internships, study abroad in 11 countries, and a Washington semester are offered. Student-designed majors and interdisciplinary majors, including computer information systems, math and computer science, and environmental science, credit for prior learning, and pass/fail options are possible. There is an accelerated degree program in organizational leadership, a joint B.A.-B.S. in engineering with the Illinois Institute of Technology, and a dual admission program with Midwestern University for pharmacy. There are 18 national honor societies, a freshman honors program, and 1 departmental honors program. **Visiting:** There are regularly scheduled orientations for prospective students, including visiting day and open house programs, which consist of faculty and student presentations, tours, and an academic and co-curricular fair. Special events are also held during the summer. There are guides for informal visits, visitors may sit in on classes, and stay overnight. To schedule a visit, contact the Office of Undergraduate Admissions. **Campus Safety and Security:** Measures include 24-hour foot and vehicle patrol, emergency notification system, self-defense education, and security escort services. There are shuttle buses, emergency telephones, lighted pathways/sidewalks, controlled access to dorms/residences, and door alarms.

REQUIREMENTS: The ACT is required. Graduation from an accredited secondary school or satisfactory scores on the GED are required for admission. The school requires 14 academic credits or 16 Carnegie units. High school courses should include English, math, foreign language, social science, and lab science. An essay is required and an interview is recommended. A GPA of 2.5 is required. AP and CLEP credits are accepted. Important factors in the admissions decision are advanced placement or honors courses, recommendations by school officials, and leadership record. To graduate, students must complete 124 credit hours with a minimum GPA of 2.0. A total of 30 to 56 hours is required in the major. All students must demonstrate proficiency, through a placement exam or the completion of specified courses, in English composition, math, computer competency, and library skills. In addition, students must take 1 interdisciplinary seminar at each academic level and 1 course each in natural sciences, history, fine arts and literature, social sciences, theology, and philosophy. 1 course must meet the multicultural requirement. **Procedure:** Freshmen are admitted fall and spring. Entrance exams should be taken in the junior year. There are deferred admissions and rolling admissions plans. Application deadlines are open. Application fee is $25. Notification is sent on a rolling basis. Applications are accepted on-line. **Transfer Students:** 166 transfer students enrolled in 2015-2016. A college transcript is required. Applicants must have a minimum of 12 credit hours with a GPA of 2.5. An interview is recommended. The high school record will be evaluated if GPA is below 2.5 at the previous college. 34 of 124 credits required for the bachelor's degree must be completed at Dominican University. **International Students:** There are 70 international students enrolled. The school actively recruits these students. They must take the TOEFL with a minimum score of 550 on the paper-based TOEFL (PBT) or 79 on the Internet-based version (iBT). They must also take the SAT or ACT.

ADMISSIONS: 64% of the 2016-2017 applicants were accepted. The SAT scores for the 2016-2017 freshman class were: Critical Reading-- 33% below 500, 42% between 500 and 599, 17% between 600 and 699, and 8% between 700 and 800. Math-- 42% below 500, 25% between 500 and 599, 25% between 600 and 699, and 8% between 700 and 800. Writing-- 58% below 500, 25% between 500 and 599, 8% between 600 and 699, and 8% between 700 and 800. The ACT scores were 3% between 12 and 17, 60% between 18 and 23, 34% between 24 and 29, and 2% above 30. 51% of the current freshmen were in the top fifth of their class; 83% were in the top two fifths. **Admissions Contact:** Glenn Hamilton, Assistant Vice President for Enrollment. Email: *domadmis@dom.edu* Web: *www.dom.edu*

FINANCIAL AID: In 2016-2017, 100% of all full-time freshmen and 90% of continuing full-time students received some form of financial aid. 90% of all full-time freshmen and 88% of continuing full-time students received need-based aid. The average freshman award was $24,562. Need-based scholarships or need-based grants averaged $20,870; need-based self-help aid (loans and jobs) averaged $4,038; and other non-need-based awards and non-need-based scholarships averaged $9,404. 21% of undergraduate students work part-time. Average annual earnings from campus work are $2500. The average financial indebtedness of the 2016 graduate was $28,533. Dominican University is a member of CSS. The FAFSA code is 001750. The priority date for freshman financial aid applications for fall entry is November 15.

EASTERN ILLINOIS UNIVERSITY E-4
www.eiu.edu

Charleston, IL 61920 **(217) 581-2223**

Fax: (217) 581-7060	**Email:** admissions@eiu.edu
Full-time: 2050 men, 3083 women	**Faculty:** IIA, av$
Part-time: 285 men, 539 women	**Ph.D.s:** n/av
Graduate: 598 men, 860 women	**Student/Faculty:** n/av
Year: semesters, summer session	**Tuition:** $11,580 ($13,740)
Room & Board: $9546	**Freshman Class:** 8420 applied, 3947 accepted, 739 enrolled
ACT: 21	**CEEB CODE:** 1199
Application Deadline: August 15	**COMPETITIVE**

Eastern Illinois University is a public comprehensive university that offers superior, accessible undergraduate and graduate education. Students learn the methods and results of free and rigorous inquiry in the arts, humanities, sciences, and professions, guided by a faculty known for its excellence in teaching, research, creative activity, and service. The University community is committed to diversity and inclusion and fosters opportunities for student-faculty scholarship and applied learning experiences within a student-centered campus culture. Throughout their education, students refine their abilities to reason and to communicate clearly so as to become responsible citizens and leaders. There are 5 undergraduate schools and one graduate school. In addition to regional accreditation, EIU has baccalaureate program accreditation with AACSB, ACEJMC, NASAD, NASM, NCATE, NRPA, AAFCS, ACS, ACTFL, NASPE, NCTM, NASP, CTTE, SABPAC, NAST, CAA-ASHA, ELCC, ACEI, NCTE, AAHE, NSTA, NAEYC, CACREP, ATMAE, CCNE, NCSS, CEC, HLC, and CAATE. The 320-acre campus is in a small town 110 miles from Indianapolis, Indiana, and 147 miles from St. Louis, Missouri. Including any residence halls, there are 80 buildings.

STUDENT LIFE: 94% of undergraduates are from Illinois. Others are from 35 states, 42 foreign countries, and Canada. 66% are White; 6% Hispanic; 6% Foreign; 2% two or more races; 2% race unknown; 17% African American; 1% Asian American. **Female To Male Ratio:** 1.5:1. The average age of freshmen is 18; all undergraduates, 22. 29% do not continue beyond their first year; 57% remain to graduate. **Housing:** 5425 students can be accommodated in college housing, which includes single-sex and coed dorms, on-campus apartments, and married student housing. In addition, there are honors houses, special-interest houses, fraternity houses, and sorority houses. On-campus housing is guaranteed for the freshman year only, is available on a first-come, and first-served basis. 62% of students commute. All students may keep cars.

FACULTY/CLASSROOMS: No introductory courses are taught by graduate students. The average class size in a regular course is 16.

PROGRAMS OF STUDY: EIU confers B.A., B.F.A., B.Mus., B.S., B.S.Bus., and B.S.Ed. degrees. Master's degrees are also awarded. Bachelor's degrees are awarded in BIOLOGICAL SCIENCE (biology/biological science), BUSINESS (accounting, business administration and management, finance, management information systems, marketing, and organizational leadership and management), COMMUNICATIONS AND THE ARTS (Africana studies, art, communication studies, English, foreign language, journalism, music, recreation administration, and theatre arts), COMPUTER AND PHYSICAL SCIENCE (chemistry, clinical laboratory science, computer science, geology, mathematics, and physics), EDUCATION (athletic training, early childhood education, elementary education, general studies, middle school education, science education, social science education, special education, and technical education), ENGINEERING AND ENVIRONMENTAL DESIGN (engineering and industrial engineering technology), HEALTH PROFESSIONS (health, kinesiology, and nursing), SOCIAL SCIENCE (communication sciences & disorders, economics, family/consumer studies, geography, history, philosophy, political science/government, psychology, and sociology). Communication disorders science is the strongest academically. Kinesiology & sports studies, general studies and psychology have the largest enrollments.

ACTIVITIES: 16% of men belong to 13 national fraternities; 20% of women belong to 12 national sororities. There are 171 groups on campus, including art, band, cheerleading, chess, choir, chorale, chorus, communications, dance, drama, drill team, environmental, ethnic, film, honors, international, jazz band, LGBT, literary magazine, marching band, musical theater, newspaper, orchestra, pep band, political, professional, radio and TV, religious, social, social service, student government, symphony, and yearbook. Popular campus events include Homecoming, Family Weekend, Greek Week, PantherPalooza, Panther Service Day, Prowl, and Prowlin with the Prez. **Sports:** There are 10 intercollegiate sports for men and 10 for women, and 31 intramural sports for men and 31 for women. Facilities include a swimming pool, gym, student recreation center, track, tennis courts, racquetball courts, jogging trail, baseball field, softball field, football field, basketball court, soccer field, and a rugby field. **Graduates:** From July 1, 2015 to June 30, 2016, 1812 bachelor's degrees were awarded. The most popular majors were kinesiology & sports studies (10%), general studies (9%), and communication studies (8%). 265 companies recruited on campus in 2015-2016. In an average class, 34% graduate in 4 years or less, 53% graduate in 5 years or less, and 57% graduate in 6 years or less.

SERVICES: Counseling and information services are available, as is tutoring in most subjects, such as biology, business, chemistry, writing (all subjects), economics, foreign language, geology/geography, history, mathematics, physics, and psychology. There is remedial math, reading, and writing. Student success center for help on study skills, test-taking, and time management. **Library/Resources:** The library contains 1.8 million volumes, 578,049 microform items, and 76,151 audio/video tapes/CDs/DVDs, and subscribes to 39,134 periodicals including electronic. Computerized library services include interlibrary loans, database searching, Internet access, and Wi-Fi capability. Special learning facilities include an art gallery, radio station, TV station, an observatory, scanning electron microscope, and a Thut greenhouse. **Physically Challenged Students:** 80% of the campus is accessible. Facilities include wheelchair ramps, elevators, special parking, specially equipped restrooms, lowered drinking fountains, and special housing. **Special:** EIU offers a B.S. in Engineering Cooperative with the University of Illinois at Champaign-Urbana or Southern Illinois University at Carbondale. Internships, study abroad, and double major options are available. Credit for life experience may be granted through the general studies program and the organizational and professional development program. There are 44 national honor societies, a freshman honors program, and 24 departmental honors programs. **Visiting:** There are regularly scheduled orientations for prospective students, including a tour of the campus and residence halls, sessions on financial aid, housing, admission process, tips for academic success, steps to take after admission, transfer admission, academic and student services fair. There are guides for informal visits and visitors may sit in on classes. To schedule a visit, contact Libby Warner at (217) 581-2223. **Campus Safety and Security:** Measures include 24-hour foot and vehicle patrol, emergency notification system, and self-defense education. There are shuttle buses, emergency telephones, lighted pathways/sidewalks, controlled access to dorms/residences, student patrols, alert EIU, and warning sirens.

REQUIREMENTS: All applicants must submit ACT or SAT scores and meet one of the following: rank in the top quarter of their high school class based on 6 or more semesters or have a GPA of 3.0 and have an ACT composite of at least 18 (SAT 860); rank in the top one half of their high school class based on 6 or more semesters or have a GPA of 2.5 and have an ACT composite score of at least 19 (SAT 910); rank in the top three quarters of their high school class based on 6 or more semesters or have a GPA of 2.25 and an ACT composite score of at least 22 (SAT 1020). Applicants must be graduates of an accredited secondary school or have passed the GED. 15 academic credits are required and should include 4 years of English and 3 years each of math, science, and social studies, and 2 years of electives. 2 years foreign language are recommended. EIU requires applicants to be in the upper 75% of their class. A GPA of 2.3 is required. AP and CLEP credits are accepted. A total of 120 credit hours, with a minimum of 40 hours in upper-division courses, must be completed for graduation. The minimum GPA required for graduation is 2.0 (2.65 in education). A core curriculum of 40 hours includes courses in language, humanities and fine arts, math, and social and behavioral science, scientific awareness, and senior seminar. **Procedure:** Freshmen are admitted fall, spring, and summer. EIU does not require entrance exams. There are deferred admissions and rolling admissions plans. Applications should be filed by August 15 for fall entry; January 8 for spring entry; and June 10 for summer entry, along with a $30 fee. Notification is sent on a rolling basis. Applications are accepted on-line. Application fees are waived if application is completed on-line. **Transfer Students:** 536 transfer students enrolled in 2015-2016. Applicants with 30 or more college-level semester hours must have a cumulative grade point average of 2.0 on a 4.0 grading scale based on all college-level work attempted and a 2.0 cumulative grade point average on a 4.0 scale from the last institution attended. Applicants with 24 or more college-level semester hours must have a cumulative grade point average of 2.5 on a 4.0 grading scale based on all college-level work attempted and a 2.0 cumulative grade point average on a 4.0 scale from the last institution attended. Applicants with fewer than the required number of hours of earned credit must have at least a 2.0 grade point average on a 4.0 scale based on all college-level work attempted, a 2.0 grade point average on a 4.0 scale from the last institution attended and meet the freshman admission criteria. 42 of 120 credits required for the bachelor's degree must be completed at EIU. **International Students:** There are 109 international students enrolled. The school actively recruits these students. They must take the TOEFL with a minimum score of 500 on the paper-based TOEFL (PBT) or 61 on the Internet-based version (iBT). Students must take the MELAB, or take the IELTS.

ADMISSIONS: 47% of the 2016-2017 applicants were accepted. The ACT scores were 15% between 12 and 17, 58% between 18 and 23, 23% between 24 and 29, and 4% above 30. 25% of the current freshmen were in the top fifth of their class; 54% were in the top two fifths. **Admissions Contact:** Kelly Miller, Director of Admissions. Email: *admissions@eiu.edu* Web: *www.eiu.edu*

FINANCIAL AID: In 2016-2017, 76% of all full-time freshmen and 67% of continuing full-time students received some form of financial aid. 57% of all full-time freshmen and 51% of continuing full-time students received need-based aid. The average freshman award was $10,546. Need-based scholarships or need-based grants averaged $8,743; need-based self-help aid (loans and jobs) averaged $3,884; non-need-based athletic scholarships averaged $7,599; and other non-need-based awards and non-need-based scholarships averaged $3,222. 26% of undergraduate students work part-time. Average annual earnings from campus work are $1417. The average financial indebtedness of the 2016 graduate was $31,382. The FAFSA code is 001674. The priority date for freshman financial aid applications for fall entry is March 1.

ELMHURST COLLEGE — E-2

www.elmhurst.edu

Elmhurst, IL 60126	(630) 617-3400 (800) 697-1871
Fax: (630) 617-5501	Email: admit@elmhurst.edu
Full-time: 1116 men, 1596 women	Faculty: 136; IIB, av$
Part-time: 52 men, 92 women	Ph.D.s: 79%
Graduate: 190 men, 357 women	Student/Faculty: 20 to 1
Year: 4-1-4, summer session	Tuition: $35,500
Room & Board: $9928	Freshman Class: 3528 applied, 2486 accepted, 477 enrolled
SAT CR/M/W: 530/550/520 ACT: 23	CEEB CODE: 1204
Application Deadline: n/av	COMPETITIVE

Elmhurst College is a premier, private, liberal arts college. Among Elmhurst's specialties is its synergy of two indispensable elements of a quality college experience: professional preparation and liberal learning. For 143 years, Elmhurst College has sought to prepare students superbly, both for their first jobs and for fulfilling lives. Elmhurst offers students of many backgrounds purposeful learning for the whole of life. There are 2 undergraduate schools and 1 graduate school. In addition to regional accreditation, Elmhurst has baccalaureate program accreditation with CCNE. The 48-acre campus is in a suburban area 15 miles west of Chicago. Including any residence halls, there are 23 buildings.

STUDENT LIFE: 91% of undergraduates are from Illinois. Others are from 34 states, 30 foreign countries, and Canada. 89% are from public schools. 64% are White; 6% African American; 6% Asian American; 3% two or more races; 2% race unknown; 19% Hispanic. 31% are Catholic; 30% claim no religious affiliation; 11% Protestant. **Female To Male Ratio:** 1.5:1. The average age of freshmen is 18; all undergraduates, 22. 16% do not continue beyond their first year; 69% remain to graduate. **Housing:** 974 students can be accommodated in college housing, which includes coed dorms, on-campus apartments, and off-campus apartments. 70% of students commute. Some may keep cars.

FACULTY/CLASSROOMS: 40% of faculty are male; 60% are female. 91% teach undergraduates, all do research, and 91% do both. No introductory courses are taught by graduate students. The average class size in an introductory lecture is 19; in a laboratory is 15; and in a regular course is 18.

PROGRAMS OF STUDY: Elmhurst confers B.A., B.F.A, B.S., B.L.S., and B.Mus. degrees. Master's degrees are also awarded. Bachelor's degrees are awarded in BIOLOGICAL SCIENCE (biology/biological science), BUSINESS (accounting, business administration and management, finance, international business management, management science, marketing/retailing/merchandising, sports management, and supply chain management), COMMUNICATIONS AND THE ARTS (art, arts administration/management, communications, communication science, English, French, German, graphic design, information technology, jazz, music, music business management, music performance, music theory and composition, Spanish, and theatre arts), COMPUTER AND PHYSICAL SCIENCE (actuarial science, chemistry, computer game design/development, computer science, information sciences and systems, mathematics, and physics), EDUCATION (art education, early childhood education, elementary education, mathematics education, music education, physical education, secondary education, and special education), ENGINEERING AND ENVIRONMENTAL DESIGN (environmental science and preengineering), HEALTH PROFESSIONS (exercise science, nursing, pre-health studies, pre-health biological studies, premedicine, prephysical therapy, preveterinary science, and speech pathology/audiology), SOCIAL SCIENCE (American studies, communication sciences & disorders, criminal justice, economics, geography, geography information science, history, liberal arts/general studies, philosophy, political science/government, psychology, religion, sociology, theological studies, and urban studies). Biology, English, nursing, and education are the strongest academically. Business, health professions, and education-related programs have the largest enrollments.

ACTIVITIES: 9% of men belong to 3 national fraternities; 14% of women belong to 4 national sororities. There are 92 groups on campus, including art, band, cheerleading, chess, choir, chorale, chorus, communications, computers, dance, drama, environmental, ethnic, film, honors, international, jazz band, LGBT, literary magazine, musical theater, newspaper, orchestra, pep band, political, professional, radio and TV, religious, social, social service, student government, symphony, and yearbook. Popular campus events include Elmhurst College Jazz Festival, Lecture Series, Theater Performances, Summer Extravaganza, and the Performances by Elmhurst College Ensembles. **Sports:** There are 10 intercollegiate sports for men and 10 for women, and 7 intramural sports for men and 7 for women. Facilities include a phys ed center, weight rooms, and courts for tennis, racquetball, and handball. Langhorst Athletic Field is home to the college's football, soccer, and track and field teams. **Graduates:** From July 1, 2015 to June 30, 2016, 751 bachelor's degrees were awarded. The most popular majors were business (24%), health sciences (13%), and psychology (9%). 30 companies recruited on campus in 2015-2016. In an average class, 56% graduate in 4 years or less, 66% graduate in 5 years or less, and 69% graduate in 6 years or less. Of the 2015 graduating class, 15% were enrolled in graduate school within 6 months of graduation, and 83% were employed.

SERVICES: Counseling and information services are available, as is tutoring in most subjects. There is remedial math, reading, and writing. **Library/Resources:** The library contains 237,539 volumes, 49,798 microform items, and 49,413 audio/video tapes/CDs/DVDs, and subscribes to 24,245 periodicals including electronic. Computerized library services include interlibrary loans, database searching, Internet access, and Wi-Fi capability. Special learning facilities include an art gallery, radio station, a recording studio that offers recording and control room spaces with grand piano and isolation booth and a digital 24-track hard drive Otari Radar system with automated status console; the SimBaby, a life-size, robotic model of an infant and SimMan, an adult patient simulator, an electron microscopy lab, and an accelerator lab. **Physically Challenged Students:** 95% of the campus is accessible. Facilities include wheelchair ramps, elevators, special parking, specially equipped restrooms, lowered drinking fountains, and lowered telephones. **Special:** There are cooperative programs in all majors. In keeping with the hallmarks of the Elmhurst Experience, of self-formation and early professional preparation, Career Education starts early-on in most students' academic experience. The Center for Professional Excellence provides experiential opportunities for career exploration of majors in 23 academic departments, e.g., internships, informational interviews, career shadowing, and connections to professional mentors. Internships varying from 1 month to one term are available in approximately 20 major fields. Students may study abroad in over 40 countries. Elmhurst also offers a Washington and Chicago Semester and a 3-2 engineering degree with the Illinois Institute of Technology, Washington University, and the Universities of Illinois and Southern California. There are accelerated degree programs in business administration, organizational leadership & communication, information technology, and pre-clinical psychology. Credit for life, military, and work experience, nondegree study and pass/fail options are possible. There are 23 national honor societies, a freshman honors program, and 25 departmental honors programs. **Visiting:** There are regularly scheduled orientations for prospective students, including an admissions interview, a campus tour, and faculty meetings if desired. There are guides for informal visits, visitors may sit in on classes, and stay overnight. To schedule a visit, contact Francesca Garza at (630) 617-3400. **Campus Safety and Security:** Measures include 24-hour foot and vehicle patrol, emergency notification system, and security escort services. There are shuttle buses, emergency telephones, lighted pathways/sidewalks, and controlled access to dorms/residences.

REQUIREMENTS: The SAT is required, with the ACT preferred. Candidates for admission must have completed 16 academic units of credit including at least 3 units in English and 2 units each of math, social science, and natural science lab courses. 2 years of a foreign language are recommended. AP and CLEP credits are accepted. Important factors in the admissions decision are advanced placement or honors courses, leadership record, and extracurricular activities record. Complete all aspects of the Integrated Curriculum or General Education program, complete all the requirements for a major, earn a minimum of 32.00 course credits, complete at least 10.00 course credits at the 300/400 level at a four-year institution, achieve a minimum combined and institutional GPA of 2.0 (some majors require a higher GPA), and earn one's final 8.00 course credits at Elmhurst College (residency requirement). **Procedure:** Freshmen are admitted fall and spring. Entrance exams should be taken by the spring of the senior year. There are early admissions, deferred admissions, and rolling admissions plans. Applications should be filed by January 15 for spring entry. Notification is sent on a rolling basis. Applications are accepted on-line. **Transfer Students:** 371 transfer students enrolled in 2015-2016. Qualified applicants should show evidence of their ability to successfully complete college-level work, based on their good standing at the last college or university attended. 32 of 128 credits required for the bachelor's degree must be completed at Elmhurst. **International Students:** There are 43 international students enrolled. The school actively recruits these students. They must take the TOEFL with a minimum score of 550 on the paper-based TOEFL (PBT) or 79 on the Internet-based version (iBT) or take the MELAB.

ADMISSIONS: 70% of the 2016-2017 applicants were accepted. The SAT scores for the 2016-2017 freshman class were: Critical Reading-- 28% below 500, 45% between 500 and 599, 21% between 600 and 699, and 7% between 700 and 800. Math-- 31% below 500, 34% between 500 and 599, 31% between 600 and 699, and 3% between 700 and 800. Writing-- 34% below 500, 48% between 500 and 599, 14% between 600 and 699, and 3% between 700 and 800. The ACT scores were 7% between 12 and 17, 44% between 18 and 23, 41% between 24 and 29, and 7% above 30. 44% of the current freshmen were in the top fifth of their class; 73% were in the top two fifths. **Admissions Contact:** Stephanie Levenson, Director of Admissions. Email: *admit@elmhurst.edu* Web: *www.elmhurst.edu*

FINANCIAL AID: The FAFSA code is 001676. The priority date for freshman financial aid applications for fall entry is Februray 1.

EUREKA COLLEGE D-3

www.eureka.edu

Eureka, IL 61530	(309) 467-6350 (888) 4-EUREKA
Fax: (309) 467-6576	**Email:** admissions@eureka.edu
Full-time: 340 men, 350 women	**Faculty:** 44
Part-time: 10 women	**Ph.D.s:** 85%
Graduate: n/av	**Student/Faculty:** 13 to 1
Year: semesters, summer session	**Tuition:** $21,120
Room & Board: $9100	**Freshman Class:** 900 applied, 600 accepted, 140 enrolled
SAT: required **ACT:** 23	**CEEB CODE:** 1206
Application Deadline: August 1	**COMPETITIVE**

Eureka College, founded in 1855, is a small, private, liberal arts college affiliated with the Christian Church (Disciples of Christ) and welcoming students of all backgrounds and faiths. The figures in the above capsule and in this profile are approximate. There is 1 undergraduate school. In addition to regional accreditation, E.C. has baccalaureate program accreditation with NCATE. The 100-acre campus is in a small town 20 minutes east of Peoria, 20 minutes west of Bloomington, and 2 hours south of Chicago. Including any residence halls, there are 24 buildings.

STUDENT LIFE: 90% of undergraduates are from Illinois. Others are from 17 states, and 3 foreign countries. 80% are from public schools. 87% are White; 6% African American; 2% Hispanic; 2% Foreign; 1% Asian American. 37% claim no religious affiliation; 31% Protestant; 28% Catholic. **Female To Male Ratio:** 1.1:1. The average age of freshmen is 18; all undergraduates, 21. 25% do not continue beyond their first year; 65% remain to graduate. **Housing:** 550 students can be accommodated in college housing, which includes single-sex and coed dorms. In addition, there are fraternity houses and sorority houses. On-campus housing is guaranteed for all 4 years. 80% of students live on campus; of those, 70% remain on campus on weekends. All students may keep cars.

FACULTY/CLASSROOMS: 64% of faculty are male; 36% are female. All teach undergraduates. No introductory courses are taught by graduate students. The average class size in an introductory lecture is 15; in a laboratory is 10; and in a regular course is 15.

PROGRAMS OF STUDY: Eureka confers B.A. and B.S. degrees. Bachelor's degrees are awarded in BIOLOGICAL SCIENCE (biology/biological science), BUSINESS (accounting, business administration and management, business economics, and management information systems), COMMUNICATIONS AND THE ARTS (communications, dramatic arts, English, fine arts, and music), COMPUTER AND PHYSICAL SCIENCE (chemistry, computer science, mathematics, and physical sciences), EDUCATION (athletic training, education, elementary education, music education, physical education, science education, and secondary education), HEALTH PROFESSIONS (medical laboratory technology), SOCIAL SCIENCE (child care/child and family studies, history, liberal arts/general studies, philosophy, physical fitness/movement, political science/government, psychology, religion, social science, and sociology). Chemistry, biology, and business administration are the strongest academically. Business administration, education, and psychology have the largest enrollments.

ACTIVITIES: 35% of men belong to 3 national fraternities; 35% of women belong to 1 local and 2 national sororities. There are 41 groups on campus, including art, band, cheerleading, choir, chorale, chorus, communications, computers, dance, drama, ethnic, honors, international, literary magazine, musical theater, newspaper, pep band, photography, political, professional, religious, social, social service, student government, and yearbook. Popular campus events include Pride Day, Tree Lighting Ceremony, and Ivy Ceremony. **Sports:** There are 8 intercollegiate sports for men and 8 for women, and 6 intramural sports for men and 6 for women. Facilities include a gym, pool, weight room, tennis courts, basketball, cross country, soccer, swimming and diving, track and field, football, softball, and baseball fields, and a wellness center. **Graduates:** From July 1, 2015 to June 30, 2016, 131 bachelor's degrees were awarded. The most popular majors were education (24%), business (23%), and psychology (15%). In an average class, 2% graduate in 3 years or less, 58% graduate in 4 years or less, and 65% graduate in 5 years or less. Of the 2015 graduating class, 20% were enrolled in graduate school within 6 months of graduation, and 75% were employed.

SERVICES: Counseling and information services are available, as is tutoring in most subjects. There is remedial reading and writing. In the Learning Center there is a writing center, and math lab available for students. **Library/Resources:** The library contains 85,000 volumes, 4,989 microform items, and 977 audio/video tapes/CDs/DVDs, and subscribes to 343 periodicals including electronic. Computerized library services include interlibrary loans, database searching, and Internet access. Special learning facilities include an art gallery, and the Ronald Reagan Museum. **Physically Challenged Students:** 50% of the campus is accessible. Facilities include wheelchair ramps, elevators, special parking, and specially equipped restrooms. **Special:** Cooperative programs include a 3-2 engineering degree with Washington University in St. Louis and Illinois Institute of Technology, a 2-2 B.S.N. with Mennonite College of Nursing or St. Francis College of Nursing, and a 3-1 clinical lab science degree with St. Francis or St. John's School of Clinical Laboratory Science. Students may study abroad in most countries. Professional programs in arts management, art therapy, communications, prelaw, premedicine, preministry, and teacher education are offered. An interdisciplinary major in arts and letters combines visual, performing, and literary arts. internships and student-designed and dual majors are offered in various areas. A Washington semester is available. There are 7 national honor societies, a freshman honors program, and 100 departmental honors programs. **Visiting:** There are regularly scheduled orientations for prospective students, including visits with admissions and financial aid advisers, observing student panels, meetings with faculty and coaches, and campus tours. There are guides for informal visits, visitors may sit in on classes, and stay overnight. To schedule a visit, contact the Office of Admissions. **Campus Safety and Security:** There are lighted pathways/sidewalks, and a city officer provides campus security in the evenings and on weekends.

REQUIREMENTS: The SAT or ACT is required. Applicants should be graduates of accredited secondary schools or have the GED. E.C. requires applicants to be in the upper 50% of their class. A GPA of 2.3 is required. AP and CLEP credits are accepted. Important factors in the admissions decision are recommendations by school officials, extracurricular activities record, and leadership record. All students must take English composition, biological and physical sciences, general studies, math, phys ed, Western civilization, 3 humanities courses, 3 social science courses, and a global awareness component. A total of at least 124 hours is required for graduation, including 32 hours in the major. A minimum GPA of 2.0 is required. **Procedure:** Freshmen are admitted to all sessions. Entrance exams should be taken by December of the senior year. There are deferred admissions and rolling admissions plans. Applications should be filed by August 1 for fall entry. Notification is sent on a rolling basis. Applications are accepted on-line. **Transfer Students:** 90 transfer students enrolled in 2015-2016. Applicants must have at least a 2.0 GPA in previous college work. Those with fewer than 30 hours of transferable credit must submit high school transcripts and ACT scores. Courses with grades below C are not accepted. 30 of 124 credits required for the bachelor's degree must be completed at Eureka. **International Students:** There are 12 international students enrolled. The school actively recruits these students. They must take the TOEFL.

ADMISSIONS: 67% of the 2016-2017 applicants were accepted. 35% of the current freshmen were in the top fifth of their class; 65% were in the top two fifths. **Admissions Contact:** Dr. Brian Sajko, Dean of Admissions and Financial Aid. Email: *admissions@eureka.edu* Web: *www.eureka.edu*

FINANCIAL AID: In 2016-2017, 98% of all full-time freshmen and 98% of continuing full-time students received some form of financial aid. 30% of all full-time freshmen and 30% of continuing full-time students received need-based aid. The average freshman award was $4,000. 49% of undergraduate students work part-time. Average annual earnings from campus work are $1000. The average financial indebtedness of the 2016 graduate was $8,500. Eureka is a member of CSS. The FAFSA code is 001678. The priority date for freshman financial aid applications for fall entry is April 1.

GREENVILLE COLLEGE D-4

www.greenville.edu

Greenville, IL 62246	**(618) 664-7100** **(800) 345-4440**
Fax: (618) 664-9841	**Email: admissions@greenville.edu**
Full-time: 606 men, 724 women	**Faculty:** 63; IIB, --$
Part-time: 21 men, 31 women	**Ph.D.s:** 66%
Graduate: 52 men, 142 women	**Student/Faculty:** 21 to 1
Year: 4-1-4, summer session	**Tuition:** $20,216
Room & Board: $6796	**Freshman Class:** 932 applied, 727 accepted, 252 enrolled
SAT CR/M/W: required **ACT:** 23	**CEEB CODE:** 1256
Application Deadline: August 1	**COMPETITIVE**

Greenville College, founded in 1892, is a private liberal arts institution affiliated with the Free Methodist Church. Greenville College seeks to transform students for lives of character and service through a Christ-centered education in the liberal arts and sciences. The figures in the above capsule and in this profile are approximate. There are 3 undergraduate schools. The 25-acre campus is in a small town 50 miles east of St. Louis. Including any residence halls, there are 48 buildings.

STUDENT LIFE: 72% of undergraduates are from Illinois. Others are from 42 states, 12 foreign countries, and Canada. 87% are White; 8% African American; 2% Hispanic; 1% Asian American; 1% American Indian/Alaska Native; 1% Foreign. 72% are Protestant; 21% claim no religious affiliation. **Female To Male Ratio:** 1.3:1. The average age of freshmen is 18; all undergraduates, 24. 27% do not continue beyond their first year; 48% remain to graduate. **Housing:** 792 students can be accommodated in college housing, which includes single-sex dorms and on-campus apartments. On-campus housing is guaranteed for all 4 years. 54% of students live on campus; of those, 60% remain on campus on weekends. Alcohol is not permitted. All students may keep cars.

FACULTY/CLASSROOMS: 67% of faculty are male; 33% are female. 95% teach undergraduates. No introductory courses are taught by graduate students. The average class size in an introductory lecture is 20; in a laboratory is 16; and in a regular course is 19.

PROGRAMS OF STUDY: Greenville confers B.A., B.Mus.Ed., and B.S. degrees. Master's degrees are also awarded. Bachelor's degrees are awarded in BIOLOGICAL SCIENCE (biology/biological science and environmental biology), BUSINESS (accounting, business administration and management, management information systems, marketing/retailing/merchandising, organizational leadership and management, and recreation and leisure services), COMMUNICATIONS AND THE ARTS (art, communications, contemporary Christian music, dramatic arts, English, media arts, music, music business management, public relations, Spanish, and speech/debate/rhetoric), COMPUTER AND PHYSICAL SCIENCE (chemistry, computer science, digital arts/technology, mathematics, and physics), EDUCATION (early childhood education, elementary education, English education, mathematics education, music education, physical education, science education, and special education), SOCIAL SCIENCE (criminal justice, history, international studies, liberal arts/general studies, ministries, pastoral studies, philosophy, psychology, religion, social work, sociology, and youth ministry). Biology, chemistry, and physics are the strongest academically. Education, music, and biology have the largest enrollments.

ACTIVITIES: There are no fraternities or sororities. There are 20 groups on campus, including art, band, cheerleading, choir, chorale, chorus, drama, ethnic, honors, jazz band, musical theater, newspaper, orchestra, pep band, professional, radio club, religious, social, social service, and student government. Popular campus events include Agape Music Festival, All College Hike, and Back to School Bash. **Sports:** There are 7 intercollegiate sports for men and 7 for women, and 6 intramural sports for men and 6 for women. Facilities include a gym, a sports training annex, a recreational center, 6 tennis courts, a fitness pool, an all-weather track, and softball, baseball, football, soccer, and practice fields. **Graduates:** From July 1, 2015 to June 30, 2016, 357 bachelor's degrees were awarded. The most popular majors were education (19%), biology (7%), and music (6%). In an average class, 1% graduate in 3 years or less, 39% graduate in 4 years or less, 49% graduate in 5 years or less, and 50% graduate in 6 years or less.

SERVICES: Counseling and information services are available, as is tutoring in some subjects, such as in lower-division general education courses. There is remedial math, reading, and writing. There is a program for at-risk freshmen. **Library/Resources:** The library contains 135,210 volumes, 17,384 microform items, and 3,873 audio/video tapes/CDs/DVDs, and subscribes to 8,543 periodicals including electronic. Computerized library services include interlibrary loans, database searching, and Internet access. Special learning facilities include an art gallery, and the Bock Sulpture Museum. **Physically Challenged Students:** 25% of the campus is accessible. Facilities include wheelchair ramps, elevators, special parking, specially equipped restrooms, special class scheduling, and lowered drinking fountains. **Special:** The college provides opportunities for dual majors in such areas as psychology/religion, B.A.-B.S. degrees, student-designed programs in work-study programs, study abroad, credit by exam, internships, a general studies degree, pass/fail options, and nondegree study. A 3-2 engineering degree with the University of Illinois and Washington University, a 2-2 degree with St. John's College of Nursing, a 3-3 degree with Logan College of Chiropractic; an early acceptance program with Kirksville College of Osteopathic Medicine of A.T. Still University; and an American Studies program in Washington, D.C. are also available. Cross-registration is offered within the Wesleyan Urban Coalition, the Christian College Consortium, and the Council of Christian Colleges and Universities. There are 6 national honor societies and a freshman honors program. **Visiting:** There are regularly scheduled orientations for prospective students, including campus visits during scheduled preview days. There are guides for informal visits, visitors may sit in on classes, and stay overnight. To schedule a visit, contact the Admissions Office. **Campus Safety and Security:** Measures include self-defense education and security escort services. There are emergency telephones, lighted pathways/sidewalks, controlled access to dorms/residences, and alarm systems in some buildings.

REQUIREMENTS: The SAT or ACT is required. The college recommends that applicants have 4 years of English, 2 years of foreign language, and 1 year each of algebra and geometry, laboratory science, and American history. Personal and academic references may also be considered in the application process. An essay is required. A GED certificate will be accepted. Greenville requires applicants to be in the upper 50% of their class. A GPA of 2.0 is required. AP and CLEP credits are accepted. Important factors in the admissions decision are leadership record, advanced placement or honors courses, and personality/intangible qualities. A minimum of 126 credits and a 2.0 GPA are required for graduation. All students must successfully complete the core requirements in addition to specific courses in communication, English, history, phys ed, and foreign language (B.A. only). Other degree requirements are fulfilled by in-depth study in biblical studies, cross-cultural experience, physical fitness activities, lab science, math, literature, philosophy, fine arts, psychology or sociology, and a writing-intensive course. **Procedure:** Freshmen are admitted to all sessions. Entrance exams should be taken in the spring of the junior year. There is a rolling admissions plan. Applications should be filed by August 1 for fall entry; December 1 for winter entry; December 1 for spring entry; and April 1 for summer entry, along with a $25 fee. Notification is sent on a rolling basis. Applications are accepted on-line. **Transfer Students:** 170 transfer students enrolled in 2015-2016. A minimum average grade of C or better is required. An associate degree will be accepted for transfer. 40 of 126 credits required for the bachelor's degree must be completed at Greenville. **International Students:** There are 26 international students enrolled. The school actively recruits these students. They must take the TOEFL with a minimum score of 500 on the paper-based TOEFL (PBT).

ADMISSIONS: 78% of the 2016-2017 applicants were accepted. The SAT scores for the 2016-2017 freshman class were: Critical Reading-- 56% below 500, 26% between 500 and 599, 17% between 600 and 699, and 1% between 700 and 800. Math-- 51% below 500, 36% between 500 and 599, and 13% between 600 and 699. Writing-- 60% below 500, 21% between 500 and 599, and 19% between 600 and 699. The ACT scores were 32% below 12, 20% between 12 and 17, 21% between 18 and 23, 13% between 24 and 29, and 14% above 30. 33% of the current freshmen were in the top fifth of their class; 62% were in the top two fifths. 7 freshmen graduated first in their class. **Admissions Contact:** Karl Hatton, Dean of Admissions. Email: *admissions@greenville.edu* Web: *www.greenville.edu*

FINANCIAL AID: In 2016-2017, 92% of all full-time freshmen and 95% of continuing full-time students received some form of financial aid. 87% of all full-time freshmen and 66% of continuing full-time students received need-based aid. The average freshman award was $18,738. Need-based scholarships or need-based grants averaged $4,817; need-based self-help aid (loans and jobs) averaged $7,362; and other non-need-based awards and non-need-based scholarships averaged $6,971. 30% of undergraduate students work part-time. Average annual earnings from campus work are $996. The average financial indebtedness of the 2016 graduate was $25,000. Greenville is a member of CSS. The FAFSA code is 001684. The priority date for freshman financial aid applications for fall entry is April 1. The deadline for filing freshman financial aid applications for fall entry is July 1.

ILLINOIS COLLEGE C-3

www.ic.edu

Jacksonville, IL 62650	**(217) 245-3030** **(866) 464-5265**
Fax: (217) 245-3034	**Email: info@mail.ic.edu**
Full-time: 487 men, 474 women	**Faculty:** 71; IIB, -$
Part-time: 5 men, 4 women	**Ph.D.s:** 80%
Graduate: 1 men, 16 women	**Student/Faculty:** 14 to 1
Year: semesters	**Tuition:** $31,660
Room & Board: $9190	**Freshman Class:** 2357 applied, 1370 accepted, 285 enrolled
SAT or ACT: required	**CEEB CODE:** 1315
Application Deadline: August 15	**VERY COMPETITIVE**

Illinois College, founded in 1829, is a private liberal arts institution with historical ties to the Presbyterian Church and the United Church of Christ. The figures in the above capsule are approximate. There are no undergraduate schools. The 62-acre campus is in a small town 30 miles west of Springfield. Including any residence halls, there are 36 buildings.

STUDENT LIFE: 89% of undergraduates are from Illinois. Others are from 22 states, and 15 foreign countries. 91% are White; 3% African American; 2% Hispanic; 2% Foreign; 1% Asian American; 1% American Indian/Alaska Native. 62% are Protestant; 25% Catholic; 12% claim no religious affiliation. **Female To Male Ratio:** 1.0:1. The average age of freshmen is 18; all undergraduates, 20. 20% do not continue beyond their first year; 60% remain to graduate. **Housing:** 742 students can be accommodated in college housing, which includes single-sex and coed dorms and on-campus apartments. In addition, there are honors houses, language houses, and special-interest houses. On-campus housing is guaranteed for all 4 years. 67% of students live on campus; of those, 65% remain on campus on weekends. All students may keep cars.

FACULTY/CLASSROOMS: 57% of faculty are male; 43% are female. All teach undergraduates. No introductory courses are taught by graduate students. The average class size in an introductory lecture is 40; in a laboratory is 20; and in a regular course is 16.

PROGRAMS OF STUDY: IC confers B.A. and B.S. degrees. Bachelor's degrees are awarded in BIOLOGICAL SCIENCE (biochemistry and biology/biological science), BUSINESS (accounting and business administration and management), COMMUNICATIONS AND THE ARTS (communications, dramatic arts, English, fine arts, French, German, music, Spanish, and speech/debate/rhetoric), COMPUTER AND PHYSICAL SCIENCE (chemistry, computer science, information sciences and systems, mathematics, and physics), EDUCATION (elementary education, foreign languages education, science education, and secondary education), ENGINEERING AND ENVIRONMENTAL DESIGN (environmental science), HEALTH PROFESSIONS (exercise science and medical laboratory technology), SOCIAL SCIENCE (American studies, economics, history, international relations, philosophy, political science/government, prelaw, psychology, religion, and sociology). Life sciences is the strongest academically. Business management, education, and biology have the largest enrollments.

ACTIVITIES: There are no fraternities or sororities. There are 72 groups on campus, including art, band, cheerleading, chess, choir, chorale, communications, computers, dance, debate, drama, ethnic, forensics, honors, international, LGBT, literary magazine, music ensembles, newspaper, photography, political, professional, radio and TV, religious, social, social service, student government, and symphony. Popular campus events include Osage Orange Picnic, Honors Retreat and McGaw Fine Arts Series. **Sports:** There are 10 intercollegiate sports for men and 10 for women, and 7 intramural sports for men and 7 for women. Facilities include a fitness center with an olympic sized swimming pool, several gyms, weight and exercise room, an aerobics room, basketball courts, volleyball courts, an indoor track, an outdoor track, and playing fields for soccer and football, a baseball field, an all-weather track, and tennis courts. **Graduates:** From July 1, 2015 to June 30, 2016, 168 bachelor's degrees were awarded. The most popular majors were biological/life sciences (18%), interdisciplinary studies (16%), and education (13%). 6 companies recruited on campus in 2015-2016. In an average class, 1% graduate in 3 years or less, 50% graduate in 4 years or less, 62% graduate in 5 years or less, and 62% graduate in 6 years or less. Of the 2015 graduating class, 20% were enrolled in graduate school within 6 months of graduation, and 80% were employed.

SERVICES: Counseling and information services are available, as is tutoring in every subject. There is a reader service for the blind. Note takers, scribes, and test readers are also available. **Library/Resources:** The library contains 183,172 volumes, 8,049 microform items, and 4,041 audio/video tapes/CDs/DVDs, and subscribes to 631 periodicals including electronic. Computerized library services include interlibrary loans, database searching, Internet access, and Wi-Fi capability. Special learning facilities include an art gallery, radio station, a theater, and an observatory. **Physically Challenged Students:** 35% of the campus is accessible. Facilities include wheelchair ramps, elevators, special parking, specially equipped restrooms, special class scheduling, lowered drinking fountains, lowered telephones, and special housing. **Special:** The college offers study abroad in various countries, on- and off-campus work-study programs, and internships through the departments of communication, computer science and information systems, economics and business administration, English and political science, and sociology. Also available are student-designed and dual majors, B.A.-B.S. degrees, a 3-2 engineering degree with the University of Illinois, Washington University, or Southern Illinois University-Edwardsville, and a 3-2 occupational therapy program with Washington University. A 3-1 cytotechnology program with Mayo School of Health-related Sciences, a 3-1 program in Medical Technology with St. John's Hospital in Springfield, an Intercultural Exchange Program with Ritsumeikan University in Kyoto, Japan, Model United Nations simulations, and the Urban Studies Program of Associated Colleges of the Midwest in Chicago are offered. The College also offers opportunities for collaborative student/faculty research. There are 12 national honor societies, Phi Beta Kappa, and 12 departmental honors programs. **Visiting:** There are regularly scheduled orientations for prospective students, including general information sessions with a member of the admissions staff, meeting with faculty, a campus tour, and lunch. There are guides for informal visits and visitors may sit in on classes. To schedule a visit, contact the Admissions Office. **Campus Safety and Security:** Measures include 24-hour foot and vehicle patrol, self-defense education, and security escort services. There are shuttle buses, emergency telephones, and lighted pathways/sidewalks.

REQUIREMENTS: The SAT or ACT is required. The ACT Optional

Writing test is also required. Applicants must be graduates of an accredited secondary school or have a GED certificate. Students should have completed at least 15 academic credits, including 3 in English and 7 from the following: English, foreign language, history, lab science, math, and social studies. 1 recommendation and 1 essay or 2 letters recommendations are required. A GPA of 2.5 is required. AP and CLEP credits are accepted. Important factors in the admissions decision are advanced placement or honors courses, evidence of special talent, and ability to finance college education. To graduate, all students must fulfill general graduation and convocation requirements and complete at least 120 semester hours, including 24 hours of electives outside of the major discipline. Other requirements include 1 unit in public speaking, 1 unit in writing, 1 unit of library research methods, and a first-year seminar. To meet the Convocation requirement, students must attend 30 cultural, artistic, or public affairs events. A 2.0 GPA is required. **Procedure:** Freshmen are admitted to all sessions. Entrance exams should be taken in the spring of the junior year or fall of the senior year of high school. There is a rolling admissions plan. Application deadlines are open. Notification is sent on a rolling basis. Applications are accepted on-line. **Transfer Students:** 44 transfer students enrolled in 2015-2016. Transfer students must have graduated from an accredited four-year high school. A minimum of 2.0 for their most recent full-time semester of college level work and a minimum cumulative 2.0 GPA for all college work attempted. If 24 credits have not been completed, these student's high school record will be reviewed. 36 of 120 credits required for the bachelor's degree must be completed at IC. **International Students:** There are 24 international students enrolled. They must take the TOEFL.

ADMISSIONS: 58% of the 2016-2017 applicants were accepted. 13 freshmen graduated first in their class. **Admissions Contact:** Barbara J. Lundberg, Vice President for Enrollment. Email: *info@mail.ic.edu* Web: *www.ic.edu*

FINANCIAL AID: In 2016-2017, 99% of all full-time freshmen and 98% of continuing full-time students received some form of financial aid. 73% of all full-time freshmen and 67% of continuing full-time students received need-based aid. 55% of undergraduate students work part-time. Average annual earnings from campus work are $999. The average financial indebtedness of the 2016 graduate was $23,156. The FAFSA code is 001688. The priority date for freshman financial aid applications for fall entry is March 1. The deadline for filing freshman financial aid applications for fall entry is May 1.

ILLINOIS INSTITUTE OF TECHNOLOGY E-2

www.iit.edu

Chicago, IL 60616	**(312) 567-3000** **(800) 448-2329**
Fax: (312) 567-6939	**Email: admission@iit.edu**
Full-time: 2013 men, 907 women	**Faculty:** I, +$
Part-time: 101 men, 25 women	**Ph.D.s:** 88%
Graduate: 2831 men, 1819 women	**Student/Faculty:** 13 to 1
Year: semesters, summer session	**Tuition:** $45,214
Room & Board: $11,612	**Freshman Class:** 3559 applied, 1801 accepted, 440 enrolled
SAT CR/M/W: 580/690/580 **ACT:** 28	**CEEB CODE:** 1318
Application Deadline: open	**HIGHLY COMPETITIVE+**

Illinois Institute of Technology, founded in 1890, is a Ph.D.-granting university in engineering, sciences, architecture, psychology, design, humanities, business, and law. IIT's interprofessional, technology-focused curriculum is designed to advance knowledge through research and scholarship, to cultivate invention improving the human condition, and to prepare students from throughout the world for a life of professional achievement, service to society, and individual fulfillment. There are 6 undergraduate schools and 8 graduate schools. In addition to regional accreditation, IIT has baccalaureate program accreditation with ABET and NAAB. The 120-acre campus is in an urban area 3 miles south of downtown Chicago. Including any residence halls, there are 33 buildings.

STUDENT LIFE: 57% of undergraduates are from Illinois. Others are from 47 states, 83 foreign countries, and Canada. 83% are from public schools. 7% are Hispanic; 50% White; 4% African American; 16% Foreign; 14% Asian American. **Male To Female Ratio:** 1.8:1. The average age of freshmen is 18; all undergraduates, 22. 15% do not continue beyond their first year. **Housing:** 1184 students can be accommodated in college housing, which includes single-sex and coed dorms, on-campus apartments, and married student housing. In addition, there are fraternity houses and sorority houses. On-campus housing is guaranteed for all 4 years. 62% of students live on campus. All students may keep cars.

FACULTY/CLASSROOMS: No introductory courses are taught by graduate students. The average class size in an introductory lecture is 24; in a laboratory is 22; and in a regular course is 15.

PROGRAMS OF STUDY: IIT confers B.A. and B.S. degrees. Master's and doctoral degrees are also awarded. Bachelor's degrees are awarded in BIOLOGICAL SCIENCE (biochemistry, biology/biological science, biophysics, and molecular biology), COMMUNICATIONS AND THE ARTS (technical and business writing), COMPUTER AND PHYSICAL SCIENCE (applied mathematics, chemistry, computer science, information sciences and systems, physics, and web technology), ENGINEERING AND ENVIRONMENTAL DESIGN (aeronautical engineering, architectural engineering, architecture, chemical engineering, civil engineering, computer engineering, electrical/electronics engineering, engineering management, industrial administration/management, manufacturing technology, materials science, mechanical engineering, and metallurgical engineering), SOCIAL SCIENCE (humanities, political science/government, and psychology). Architecture, engineering, and science & letters have the largest enrollments.

ACTIVITIES: 13% of men belong to 7 national fraternities; 15% of women belong to 2 local and 1 national sororities. There are 100 groups on campus, including a union club, art, chess, choir, chorus, commuter club, computers, dance, drama, environmental, ethnic, film, honors, international, LGBT, musical theater, newspaper, photography, professional, radio and TV, religious, social, social service, student government, and yearbook. Popular campus events include International Fest, Greek Week, and Spring Formal. **Sports:** There are 5 intercollegiate sports for men and 5 for women, and 10 intramural sports for men and 10 for women. Facilities include tennis, basketball, volleyball, racquetball, and squash courts, soccer and softball fields, a swimming pool, exercise room, weight room, bowling alley, and a game room. **Graduates:** From July 1, 2015 to June 30, 2016, 587 bachelor's degrees were awarded. The most popular majors were engineering (51%), natural resources and conservation (17%), and computer and information sciences (10%). In an average class, 3% graduate in 3 years or less, 38% graduate in 4 years or less, 62% graduate in 5 years or less, and 67% graduate in 6 years or less.

SERVICES: Counseling and information services are available, as is tutoring in some subjects, such as math, electrical and computer engineering, chemistry, biology, mechanical, materials and aerospace engineering, physics, computer science and writing courses. There is a reader service for the blind. **Library/Resources:** The 3 libraries contain 1.3 million volumes, and 4,256 audio/video tapes/CDs/DVDs, and subscribe to 24,596 periodicals including electronic. Computerized library services include interlibrary loans, database searching, Internet access, and Wi-Fi capability. Special learning facilities include an art gallery and radio station. **Physically Challenged Students:** 90% of the campus is accessible. Facilities include wheelchair ramps, elevators, special parking, specially equipped restrooms, lowered drinking fountains, and special housing. **Special:** Co-op programs and internships are available to all majors. All countries are eligible for study abroad. Dual majors may include a variety of majors. Cross-registration available. There are 3 national honor societies. **Visiting:** There are regularly scheduled orientations for prospective students, including special events and open houses. Open houses include a brief welcome, tours of Main Campus, academic exploration sessions with faculty members, discussion panels with current students, and staff from numerous student service departments on hand to answer questions. There are guides for informal visits, visitors may sit in on classes, and stay overnight. To schedule a visit, contact the Office of Undergraduate Admission at admission@iit.edu. **Campus Safety and Security:** Measures include 24-hour foot and vehicle patrol, emergency notification system, and security escort services. There are shuttle buses, emergency telephones, lighted pathways/sidewalks, and controlled access to dorms/residences.

REQUIREMENTS: Graduation from an accredited secondary school is required for admission. 17 academic credits are required for admission. 4 units each of English and math, 3 units of science, of those; 2 units must be laboratory science, 2 units of social studies, and 2 units of history (recommended). In addition, 2 units of foreign language and 1 unit of computer science are also recommended. Visual/performing arts 1 unit. AP credits are accepted. Important factors in the admissions decision are leadership record, parents or siblings attended your school, evidence of special talent, recommendations by school officials, advanced placement or honors courses, personality/intangible qualities, extracurricular activities record, and recommendations by alumni. To graduate, all degree-seeking undergraduate students must complete departmental curriculum, credit hour requirements as appropriate to the various curricula (a minimum of 126 hours total, a minimum of 45 hours taken at IIT), general education requirements and a minimum major GPA of 2.0. General education requirements include 5 credit hours of mathematics, 2 credit hours in computer science, 21 credit hours in humanities and social or behavioral sciences, 11 credit hours in natural science or engineering, 2 credit hours of Introduction to the Profession and 6 credit hours of Interprofessional Projects (IPRO). **Procedure:** Freshmen are admitted fall, spring, and summer. There are deferred admissions and rolling admissions plans. Application deadlines are open. Notification is sent on a rolling basis. Applications are accepted on-line. **Transfer Students:** 232 transfer students enrolled in 2015-2016. Good academic standing at previous postsecondary institution, and a minimum 3.0 cumulative GPA required. 45 credits required for the bachelor's degree must be completed at IIT. **International Students:** There are 388 international students enrolled. The school actively recruits these students. They must take the TOEFL with a minimum score of 550 on the paper-based TOEFL (PBT) or 80 on the Internet-based version (iBT).

ADMISSIONS: 51% of the 2016-2017 applicants were accepted. The SAT scores for the 2016-2017 freshman class were: Critical Reading-- 13% below 500, 44% between 500 and 599, 32% between 600 and 699, and 11% between 700 and 800. Math-- 8% between 500 and 599, 44% between 600 and 699, and 48% between 700 and 800. Writing-- 12% below 500, 40% between 500 and 599, 41% between 600 and 699, and 7% between 700 and 800. The ACT scores were 11% below 12, 53% between 18 and 23, and 37% above 30. 61% of the current freshmen were in the top fifth of their class; 87% were in the top two fifths. 2 freshmen graduated first in their class. **Admissions Contact:** Gerald Doyle, Associate Vice President, Undergraduate Admissions. Email: *admission@iit.edu* Web: *www.iit.edu*

FINANCIAL AID: In 2016-2017, 58% of all full-time freshmen received some form of financial aid. 56% of all full-time freshmen received need-based aid. The average freshman award was $35,649. Need-based scholarships or need-based grants averaged $28,262; need-based self-help aid (loans and jobs) averaged $5,870; other non-need-based awards and non-need-based scholarships averaged $4,918; and $19,854 from other forms of aid. The average financial indebtedness of the 2016 graduate was $31,907. IIT is a member of CSS. The FAFSA code is 001691. The priority date for freshman financial aid applications for fall entry is February 1.

ILLINOIS STATE UNIVERSITY D-3

www.illinoisstate.edu

Normal, IL 61761	(309) 438-2181 (800) 366-2478
Fax: (309) 438-3932	Email: Admissions@IllinoisState.edu
Full-time: 7689 men, 9465 women	Faculty: 877; I
Part-time: 623 men, 650 women	Ph.D.s: 65%
Graduate: 845 men, 1535 women	Student/Faculty: 20 to 1
Year: semesters, summer session	Tuition: $13,664 ($21,480)
Room & Board: $9754	Freshman Class: n/av
ACT: 24	CEEB CODE: 1319
Application Deadline: April 1	VERY COMPETITIVE

Illinois State University, founded in 1857, is a public institution offering instruction through schools of applied science and technology, arts and sciences, business, education, fine arts, and nursing. There are 6 undergraduate schools and 1 graduate school. In addition to regional accreditation, ISU has baccalaureate program accreditation with AACSB, ABET, ACCE, CSWE, NASAD, NASM, NCATE, and NRPA. The 1100-acre campus is in an urban area 137 miles southwest of Chicago and 164 miles northeast of St. Louis. Including any residence halls, there are 191 buildings.

STUDENT LIFE: 97% of undergraduates are from Illinois. Others are from 43 states, 67 foreign countries, and Canada. 9% are Hispanic; 77% White; 7% African American; 3% two or more races; 2% Asian American; 2% Foreign. **Female To Male Ratio:** 1.3:1. The average age of freshmen is 19; all undergraduates, 21. 18% do not continue beyond their first year; 73% remain to graduate. **Housing:** 6046 students can be accommodated in college housing, which includes single-sex and coed dorms, on-campus apartments, and married student housing. In addition, there are honors houses and special-interest houses. On-campus housing is available on a first-come, first-served basis. 67% of students commute. Alcohol is not permitted. All students may keep cars.

FACULTY/CLASSROOMS: 45% of faculty are male; 55% are female. All teach undergraduates. Graduate students teach 33% of introductory courses. The average class size in an introductory lecture is 51 and in a laboratory is 22.

PROGRAMS OF STUDY: ISU confers B.S., B.A., B.S. Ed., B.S.W., B.S./M.P.A., B.F.A, B.M.E., B.M., and B.S.N. degrees. Master's and doctoral degrees are also awarded. Bachelor's degrees are awarded in AGRICULTURE (agricultural business management and agriculture), BIOLOGICAL SCIENCE (biochemistry, biology/biological science, and molecular biology), BUSINESS (accounting, business administration and management, business information systems, finance, insurance, international business, and marketing), COMMUNICATIONS AND THE ARTS (art, communication studies, dramatic arts, English, French, German, graphic communications, journalism, media arts, music, music performance, public relations, Spanish, speech/debate/rhetoric, telecommunications, and theatre acting), COMPUTER AND PHYSICAL SCIENCE (chemistry, computer science, digital arts/technology, geology, information sciences and systems, mathematics, and physics), EDUCATION (business education, early childhood education, elementary education, health education, health information management, middle school education, music education, social science education, special education, and technical education), ENGINEERING AND ENVIRONMENTAL DESIGN (construction management, energy management technology, and industrial engineering technology), HEALTH PROFESSIONS (environmental health science, exercise science, health care administration, medical laboratory technology, nursing, and speech pathology/audiology), SOCIAL SCIENCE (anthropology, criminal justice, economics, family/consumer studies, fashion design and technology, geography, history, home economics, interdisciplinary studies, legal studies, parks and recreation management, philosophy, political science/government, psychology, safety management, social science, social work, and sociology). Elementary education, special education, and business administration have the largest enrollments.

ACTIVITIES: 9% of men belong to 18 national fraternities; 16% of women belong to 18 national sororities. There are 380 groups on campus, including art, band, cheerleading, chess, choir, chorale, chorus, communications, computers, dance, debate, drama, drill team, ethnic, film, forensics, honors, international, jazz band, LGBT, literary magazine, marching band, musical theater, newspaper, opera, orchestra, pep band, photography, political, professional, radio and TV, religious, social, social service, student government, and symphony. Popular campus events include Festival ISU, International Fair, Madrigal Dinners, Family Weekend, and Homecoming. **Sports:** There are 7 intercollegiate sports for men and 10 for women, and 29 intramural sports for men and 29 for women. Facilities include a student recreational building, a basketball arena, a football stadium, a field house, baseball diamonds, tennis courts, olympic-size pools, an 18-hole golf course, a soccer and softball field, 18 acre field area that is devoted to intramurals and sport clubs, and a bowling and billiards center. **Graduates:** From July 1, 2015 to June 30, 2016, 4322 bachelor's degrees were awarded. The most popular majors were elementary education (5%), marketing (4%), and nursing (4%). In an average class, 48% graduate in 4 years or less, 70% graduate in 5 years or less, and 73% graduate in 6 years or less.

SERVICES: Counseling and information services are available, as is tutoring in most subjects. There is a reader service for the blind, and remedial math. Tutoring available for most 100 level courses. Course materials are provided in an alternate format. **Library/Resources:** The library contains 1.6 million volumes, 84,905 microform items, and 38,797 audio/video tapes/CDs/DVDs, and subscribes to 52,249 periodicals including electronic. Computerized library services include interlibrary loans, database searching, Internet access, and Wi-Fi capability. Special learning facilities include an art gallery, planetarium, radio station, TV station, distance-learning classrooms, a farm, and Jgardens. **Physically Challenged Students:** All of the campus is accessible. Facilities include wheelchair ramps, elevators, special parking, specially equipped restrooms, special class scheduling, lowered drinking fountains, lowered telephones, and special housing. **Special:** There are numerous cooperative programs and internships, dual majors, student-designed majors, and work-study programs both on campus and with nonprofit organizations. There is also a general studies degree, a 3-2 engineering program with the University of Illinois or Bradley University, a BS/MPA, and study abroad in 32 countries. Pass/fail options are available. Credit is given for military experience. ISU is part of the National Student Exchange, enabling qualifying juniors and seniors to study for up to 1 year at one of several hundred colleges around the country. There are 24 national honor societies, a freshman honors program, and 1 departmental honors program. **Visiting:** There are regularly scheduled orientations for prospective students. While attending Preview, students will have the opportunity to meet with their academic advisor, register for classes, meet current Illinois State students and their future classmates, and interact with faculty and staff from various academic departments. There are guides for informal visits, visitors may sit in on classes, and stay overnight. To schedule a visit, contact the Admissions Office. **Campus Safety and Security:** Measures include 24-hour foot and vehicle patrol, emergency notification system, self-defense education, and security escort services. There are shuttle buses, emergency telephones, lighted pathways/sidewalks, and controlled access to dorms/residences.

REQUIREMENTS: The ACT is required. Admission is based on a combination of factors including rigor of secondary school record, academic GPA, standardized test scores, and application essay. AP and CLEP credits are accepted. Students must complete 39 hours of General Education and a total of 120 credit hours with a minimum GPA of 2.0. In addition, the senior college hours must total at least 42 hours. Every student must have successfully completed a course designated as a course in the cultures and traditions of societies or peoples from Asia, the Middle East, Africa, Latin America, or Indigenous Peoples of the World. **Procedure:** Freshmen are admitted fall, spring, and summer. Entrance exams should be taken in the spring of junior year. There are deferred admissions and rolling admissions plans. Applications should be filed by April 1 for fall entry, along with a $50 fee. Notifications are sent September 1. 139 applicants were on the 2016 waiting list; 11 were admitted. Applications are accepted on-line. **Transfer Students:** 1882 transfer students enrolled in 2015-2016. Illinois State University requires transfer students to provide official transcripts from all colleges and universities attended. Transfer students must be in good academic standing at the last institution attended. Many programs have required courses and minimum GPA requirements. Transfer students with a minimum 2.4 cumulative transfer GPA may be admitted to the University as undeclared if program prerequisites were not met or if space is not available in the preferred major. Students with 75 or more semester hours completed will not be admitted as undeclared. Transfer requirements by program can be found at http:/admissions.illinoisstate.edu/transfer/apply/transfer_requirements/. 30 of 120 credits required for the bachelor's degree must be completed at ISU. **International Students:** There are 117 international students enrolled. The school actively recruits these students. They must take the TOEFL with a minimum score of 550 on the paper-based TOEFL (PBT) or 79 on the Internet-based version (iBT). They must also take the SAT or ACT.

ADMISSIONS: The ACT scores were 1% between 12 and 17, 54% between 18 and 23, 37% between 24 and 29, and 4% above 30. **Admissions Contact:** Ryan Smith, Director of Institutional Research. Email: *Admissions@IllinoisState.edu* Web: *www.illinoisstate.edu*

FINANCIAL AID: The CCS/Profile, FAFSA, FFS, or SFS is required. The FAFSA code is 001692. The deadline for filing freshman financial aid applications for fall entry is March 1.

ILLINOIS WESLEYAN UNIVERSITY D-3

www.iwu.edu

Bloomington, IL 61702	(309) 556-3031 (800) 332-2498 Email: iwuadmit@iwu.edu
Full-time: 817 men, 943 women	**Faculty:** 148; IIB, av$
Part-time: 1 men, 2 women	**Ph.D.s:** 95%
Graduate: n/av	**Student/Faculty:** 10 to 1
Year: other	**Tuition:** $45,856
Room & Board: $10,574	**Freshman Class:** 3841 applied, 2236 accepted, 425 enrolled
SAT: required **ACT:** 27	**CEEB CODE:** 1320
Application Deadline: March 1	**VERY COMPETITIVE+**

Illinois Wesleyan University, founded in 1850, is a private institution offering major programs in liberal arts, fine arts, and nursing. The figures in the above capsule and in this profile are approximate. There are 5 undergraduate schools. In addition to regional accreditation, Illinois Wesleyan has baccalaureate program accreditation with NASM and CCNE. The 80-acre campus is in a suburban area 130 miles from Chicago and 160 miles from St. Louis, Missouri. Including any residence halls, there are 54 buildings.

STUDENT LIFE: 79% of undergraduates are from Illinois. Others are from 32 states, and 24 foreign countries. 80% are from public schools. 9% are Foreign; 71% White; 7% Hispanic; 4% African American; 4% Asian American; 3% two or more races; 2% race unknown. **Female To Male Ratio:** 1.2:1. The average age of freshmen is 18; all undergraduates, 20. 7% do not continue beyond their first year; 83% remain to graduate. **Housing:** 1229 students can be accommodated in college housing, which includes coed dorms and on-campus apartments. In addition, there are honors houses, language houses, special-interest houses, fraternity houses, sorority houses, Internationalism, environmentalism, art and interfaith learning housing areas, and theme housing. On-campus housing is guaranteed for all 4 years. 72% of students live on campus; of those, 75% remain on campus on weekends. All students may keep cars.

FACULTY/CLASSROOMS: 57% of faculty are male; 43% are female. All teach undergraduates, and do research. No introductory courses are taught by graduate students. The average class size in a laboratory is 13 and in a regular course is 17.

PROGRAMS OF STUDY: Illinois Wesleyan confers B.A., B.S., B.F.A., B.Mus., B.Mus.Ed., and B.S.N. degrees. Bachelor's degrees are awarded in AGRICULTURE (environmental studies), BIOLOGICAL SCIENCE (biology/biological science), BUSINESS (accounting, business administration and management, insurance and risk management, and international business management), COMMUNICATIONS AND THE ARTS (art, classics, English, French, German, guitar, music, music performance, music theory and composition, musical theater, performing arts, piano/organ, theater design, theater management, and voice), COMPUTER AND PHYSICAL SCIENCE (chemistry, computer science, and physics), EDUCATION (education and music education), HEALTH PROFESSIONS (nursing), SOCIAL SCIENCE (American studies, anthropology, economics, history, interdisciplinary studies, international studies, philosophy, political science/government, psychology, religion, sociology, and women & gender studies). Business administration/accounting, biology, and psychology have the largest enrollments.

ACTIVITIES: 33% of men belong to 6 national fraternities; 30% of women belong to 1 local and 4 national sororities. There are 185 groups on campus, including art, band, cheerleading, choir, chorale, chorus, computers, dance, drama, ethnic, film, honors, international, jazz band, LGBT, literary magazine, musical theater, newspaper, opera, orchestra, pep band, political, professional, radio and TV, religious, social, social service, student government, symphony, and yearbook. Popular campus events include Family Days, Comedy Clubs and International Festivals. **Sports:** There are 9 intercollegiate sports for men and 9 for women, and 15 intramural sports for men and 13 for women. Facilities include a fitness center with weight/exercise equipment and racquetball courts, swimming pool with 1- and 3-meter diving boards, an activity center with a 200-meter, 6-lane indoor track and courts for tennis, recreational basketball, and volleyball, a separate gym for intercollegiate and other activities, an outdoor track, and softball, baseball, and soccer fields. **Graduates:** From July 1, 2015 to June 30, 2016, 439 bachelor's degrees were awarded. The most popular majors were business/marketing (22%), biological/life sciences (10%), and social sciences and visual and performing arts (10%). 49 companies recruited on campus in 2015-2016. In an average class, 78% graduate in 4 years or less, 82% graduate in 5 years or less, and 83% graduate in 6 years or less. Of the 2015 graduating class, 21% were enrolled in graduate school within 6 months of graduation, and 72% were employed.

SERVICES: Counseling and information services are available, as is tutoring in every subject. There is a reader service for the blind, and assistance in writing and study skills is also available but not at the remedial level. **Library/Resources:** The library contains 315,166 volumes, and 20,239 audio/video tapes/CDs/DVDs. Computerized library services include interlibrary loans, database searching, Internet access, and Wi-Fi capability. Special learning facilities include an art gallery, radio station, TV station, an observatory, multicultural center, action research center, a center for human rights, a peace garden and a 20-acre tract of virgin timberland. **Physically Challenged Students:** 90% of the campus is accessible. Facilities include wheelchair ramps, elevators, special parking, specially equipped restrooms, special class scheduling, lowered drinking fountains, lowered telephones, and special housing. **Special:** There are several combined degree programs, including a 3-2 degree in forestry and environmental studies with Duke University and a 2-2 engineering degree with the University of Illinois. Students may study abroad in many locations throughout the world through the Institute for the International Education of Students (IES), Pembroke College, Keio University, University of Oxford, Arcadia University Center for Study Abroad, and other programs. Illinois Wesleyan also offers its own semester-long programs in London and Barcelona. The university also offers on-campus work-study, both credit and noncredit internships, Washington and United Nations semesters, B.A.-B.S. degrees, dual and student-designed majors, pass/fail options, and an honors research program for upperclass students. There are 25 national honor societies, Phi Beta Kappa, and 44 departmental honors programs. **Visiting:** There are regularly scheduled orientations for prospective students, including a 1 to 1-1/2 hour guided tour in small groups, and with advance scheduling, interviews with an admissions counselor and faculty members in the fields of the student interest. Accepted applicants may visit classes or stay overnight. There are guides for informal visits, visitors may sit in on classes, and stay overnight. To schedule a visit, contact the Admissions Office. **Campus Safety and Security:** Measures include 24-hour foot and vehicle patrol, emergency notification system, self-defense education, and security escort services. There are shuttle buses, emergency telephones, lighted pathways/sidewalks, controlled access to dorms/residences, and an emergency response team of key executives and staff members has developed policies and procedures for natural disasters.

REQUIREMENTS: The SAT or ACT is required. Applicants should graduate from an accredited secondary school; a GED may be accepted. 15 academic credits are recommended. It is strongly recommended that these units include 4 units of English, 3 each of natural science, math, and a foreign language, and 2 units of social studies. An audition is required for theater and music majors and a portfolio for art majors. A GPA of 3.0 is required. AP credits are accepted. Important factors in the admissions decision are advanced placement or honors courses, evidence of special talent, and personality/intangible qualities. For B.A., B.S., B.S.N., and B.F.A. degrees, a total of 32 course units (128 semester hours) is required for the bachelor's degree with a 2.0 GPA. General education requirements include 2 course units in natural sciences and 1 each in literature, English, intellectual traditions, formal reasoning, cultural and historical change, contemporary social institutions, the arts, history, humanities, math, and social science, analysis of values, and Gateway Colloquium, plus demonstrated proficiency in a foreign language. 2 additional writing-intensive courses are required, as is coursework focusing on U.S. and global diversity issues. 2 degree programs (B.M.Ed. and B.M.) require more than 32 course units due to additional requirements in the major. Phys. ed. is a noncredit graduation requirement. **Procedure:** Freshmen are admitted fall and spring. Entrance exams should be taken in the spring of the junior year. There are early admissions, deferred admissions, and rolling admissions plans. Early decision applications should be filed by November 1; regular applications, by March 1 for fall entry; and November 1 for spring entry. Notifications are sent January 15. 193 applicants were on the 2016 waiting list; 21 were admitted. Applications are accepted on-line. **Transfer Students:** 36 transfer students enrolled in 2015-2016. Applicants must submit all high school and college transcripts. A GPA of at least 2.5 is required. An essay or personal statement is required. 16 of 32 credits required for the bachelor's degree must be completed at Illinois Wesleyan. **International Students:** There are 170 international students enrolled. The school actively recruits these students. They must take the TOEFL with a minimum score of 550 on the paper-based TOEFL (PBT) or 80 on the Internet-based version (iBT). They must also take the SAT or ACT.

ADMISSIONS: 58% of the 2016-2017 applicants were accepted. The ACT scores were 13% between 18 and 23, 63% between 24 and 29, and 24% above 30. **Admissions Contact:** Bob Geraty, Interim Dean of Admissions. Email: *iwuadmit@iwu.edu* Web: *www.iwu.edu*

FINANCIAL AID: In 2016-2017, 71% of all full-time freshmen and 67% of continuing full-time students received some form of financial aid. 71% of all full-time freshmen and 67% of continuing full-time students received need-based aid. The average freshman award was $34,845. Need-based scholarships or need-based grants averaged $28,592; need-based self-help aid (loans and jobs) averaged $6,505; other non-need-based awards and non-need-based scholarships averaged $21,219; and $4,620 from other forms of aid. The average financial indebtedness of the 2016 graduate was $37,841. Illinois Wesleyan is a member of CSS. The college's own financial statement is required. The FAFSA code is 001696. The priority date for freshman financial aid applications for fall entry is March 1.

JUDSON UNIVERSITY — E-1

www.judsonu.edu

Elgin, IL 60123	(847) 628-2521 (800) 879-5376
Fax: (847) 695-0216	**Email:** admissions@judsonu.edu
Full-time: 394 men, 521 women	**Faculty:** 54
Part-time: 106 men, 174 women	**Ph.D.s:** 86%
Graduate: 27 men, 23 women	**Student/Faculty:** 10 to 1
Year: semesters	**Tuition:** $28,250
Room & Board: $9450	**Freshman Class:** 626 applied, 484 accepted, 221 enrolled
SAT or ACT: required	**CEEB CODE:** 1351
Application Deadline: open	**COMPETITIVE**

Judson University formerly Judson College, is an evangelical Christian college of the liberal arts, sciences, and professions. The figures in the above capsule and in this profile are approximate. There are 2 undergraduate schools and 1 graduate school. In addition to regional accreditation, Judson has baccalaureate program accreditation with NAAB. The 90-acre campus is in a suburban area 45 miles northwest of Chicago. Including any residence halls, there are 15 buildings.

STUDENT LIFE: 65% of undergraduates are from Illinois. Others are from 30 states, 25 foreign countries, and Canada. 71% are White; 5% Hispanic; 4% African American; 4% Foreign; 1% Asian American. 80% are Protestant. **Female To Male Ratio:** 1.4:1. The average age of freshmen is 18; all undergraduates, 20. 22% do not continue beyond their first year; 50% remain to graduate. **Housing:** 670 students can be accommodated in college housing, which includes single-sex dorms, on-campus apartments, and married student housing. On-campus housing is guaranteed for all 4 years. 65% of students live on campus. Alcohol is not permitted. All students may keep cars.

FACULTY/CLASSROOMS: 66% of faculty are male; 34% are female. 80% teach undergraduates, 20% do research, and 20% do both. No introductory courses are taught by graduate students. The average class size in an introductory lecture is 28; in a laboratory is 9; and in a regular course is 16.

PROGRAMS OF STUDY: Judson confers B.A. degrees. Master's degrees are also awarded. Bachelor's degrees are awarded in BIOLOGICAL SCIENCE (biology/biological science), BUSINESS (accounting, business administration and management, international business management, and sports management), COMMUNICATIONS AND THE ARTS (art and design, communications, dramatic arts, English, fine arts, media arts, and music), COMPUTER AND PHYSICAL SCIENCE (chemistry, computer science, and mathematics), EDUCATION (early childhood education, education, elementary education, mathematics education, music education, physical education, science education, and secondary education), ENGINEERING AND ENVIRONMENTAL DESIGN (architecture and preengineering), HEALTH PROFESSIONS (medical laboratory technology, nursing, predentistry, and premedicine), SOCIAL SCIENCE (anthropology, biblical studies, history, political science/government, prelaw, psychology, sociology, and youth ministry). Architecture, visual communications/graphic design, and education are the strongest academically. Business, youth ministry, and worship arts have the largest enrollments.

ACTIVITIES: There are no fraternities or sororities. There are 23 groups on campus, including a business club, art, band, cheerleading, choir, chorale, chorus, computers, drama, ethnic, honors, international, literary magazine, newspaper, orchestra, photography, political, radio and TV, religious, social, social service, and student government. Popular campus events include Spiritual Enrichment Week, Fall Orientation, and Christmas by Candlelight. **Sports:** There are 3 intercollegiate sports for men and 4 for women, and 9 intramural sports for men and 8 for women. Facilities include a fitness center, gym, soccer field, baseball and softball, tennis courts, racquetball and handball courts, indoor and outdoor running tracks, Nautilus, and free-weight room. **Graduates:** From July 1, 2015 to June 30, 2016, 339 bachelor's degrees were awarded. In an average class, 46% graduate in 4 years or less and 48% graduate in 5 years or less.

SERVICES: Counseling and information services are available, as is tutoring in some subjects. There is remedial math, reading, and writing. **Library/Resources:** The library contains 92,000 volumes, 27,000 microform items, and 17,000 audio/video tapes/CDs/DVDs, and subscribes to 470 periodicals including electronic. Computerized library services include interlibrary loans, database searching, and Internet access. Special learning facilities include an art gallery and radio station. **Physically Challenged Students:** 80% of the campus is accessible. Facilities include wheelchair ramps, elevators, special parking, specially equipped restrooms, special class scheduling, lowered drinking fountains, lowered telephones, and special housing. **Special:** The college has co-op programs with North Park College, Rush University, and the Mennonite College of Nursing, cross-registration with the Christian College Coalition, and work-study programs with many businesses. Students may serve internships in art and business, take a Washington semester, a film studies semester in Hollywood, an ecology studies semester at Sable Institute in Michigan, or study abroad in numerous external programs recognized by Judson College. The college allows dual majors, student-designed majors, and accelerated degrees in business leadership and management, human services, human resource management, and criminal justice management. There is 1 national honor society, a freshman honors program, and 2 departmental honors programs. **Visiting:** There are regularly scheduled orientations for prospective students, including a tour, class visits, individual meetings with professors, coaches, choir and/or band director, and other select campus administrators if requested. In addition, there is lunch or dinner in the cafeteria and the opportunity to meet with current students and the opportunity to stay a night in the dorms. There are guides for informal visits. To schedule a visit, contact the Enrollment Services Office/Admissions. **Campus Safety and Security:** Measures include 24-hour foot and vehicle patrol and security escort services. There are emergency telephones and lighted pathways/sidewalks.

REQUIREMENTS: Minimum ACT score of 18 or SAT score of 840 is required. Judson requires applicants to be in the upper 50% of their class. A GPA of 2.0 is required. AP and CLEP credits are accepted. Most students must have a GPA of 2.0; education majors must have a 2.5. Students must complete at least 126 credit hours, including 45 to 66 in the major, and take the college's core courses of Bible study, writing, speech, literature, math, science, history, fine arts, human relations, and phys ed, as well as a course in either psychology or sociology. **Procedure:** Freshmen are admitted to all sessions. Entrance exams should be taken in the spring of the junior year or the fall of the senior year. There are deferred admissions and rolling admissions plans. Application deadlines are open. Application fee is $35. Notification is sent on a rolling basis. Applications are accepted on-line. **Transfer Students:** 86 transfer students enrolled in 2015-2016. Students with fewer than 28 hours of college credit must submit high school transcripts showing a GPA of at least 2.0, as well as ACT results with a composite score of at least 18 or 840 on the SAT. Transfer students with more than 28 hours must have a GPA of at least 2.0. 30 of 126 credits required for the bachelor's degree must be completed at Judson. **International Students:** There are 44 international students enrolled. The school actively recruits these students. They must take the TOEFL or MELAB. They must also take the SAT or ACT.

ADMISSIONS: 77% of the 2016-2017 applicants were accepted. **Admissions Contact:** Nate McNeely, Director of Admissions. Email: *admissions@judsonu.edu* Web: *www.judsonu.edu*

FINANCIAL AID: In 2016-2017, 90% of all full-time freshmen and continuing full-time students received some form of financial aid. 90% of all full-time freshmen and continuing full-time students received need-based aid. The college's own financial statement is required. The FAFSA code is 001700. Check with the school for current application deadlines.

KENDALL COLLEGE E-2
www.kendall.edu

Chicago, IL 60642	(312) 752-2240 (877) 588-8860
Fax: (312) 752-2241	Email: info@kendall.edu
Full-time: 498 men, 982 women	**Faculty:** 41
Part-time: 162 men, 903 women	**Ph.D.s:** 11%
Graduate: n/av	**Student/Faculty:** 35 to 1
Year: quarters, summer session	**Tuition:** $22,125
Room & Board: $10,485	**Freshman Class:** n/av **CEEB CODE:** 1366
Application Deadline: rolling	**COMPETITIVE**

Kendall College, part of Laureate International Universities, was founded in 1934 and is a private institution committed to cultivating extraordinary talent for the global business, hospitality, culinary, and education fields. Kendall offers 4 schools of study: Culinary Arts, Business, Hospitality Management, and Education. Figures in the above capsule and in this profile are approximate. Tuition figures are different for each academic program. There are 4 undergraduate schools. The campus is in an urban area in Chicago. Including any residence halls, there is 1 building.

STUDENT LIFE: 73% of undergraduates are from Illinois. Others are from 35 states, 62 foreign countries, and Canada. 6% are Foreign; 51% White; 4% Asian American; 20% African American; 12% Hispanic. **Female To Male Ratio:** 2.9:1. The average age of freshmen is 21; all undergraduates, 31. 46% do not continue beyond their first year; 37% remain to graduate. **Housing:** 180 students can be accommodated in college housing, which includes single-sex and coed off-campus apartments. On-campus housing is available on a first-come, first-served basis. 89% of students commute. Alcohol is not permitted. No one may keep cars.

FACULTY/CLASSROOMS: 50% of faculty are male; 50% are female. 91% teach undergraduates. No introductory courses are taught by graduate students. The average class size in an introductory lecture is 25; in a laboratory is 18; and in a regular course is 20.

PROGRAMS OF STUDY: Kendall confers B.A. degrees. Associate degrees are also awarded. Bachelor's degrees are awarded in BUSINESS (business administration and management, hospitality management services, and hotel/motel and restaurant management), EDUCATION (early childhood education), SOCIAL SCIENCE (culinary arts). Culinary arts and education have the largest enrollments.

ACTIVITIES: There are no fraternities or sororities. There are 10 groups on campus, including chorus, computers, dance, environmental, ethnic, honors, international, LGBT, professional, social, social service, and student government. Popular campus events include Fright Fest, African American History Community Dinner, and Monthly Birthday Celebrations. **Sports:** There is no sports program at Kendall. **Graduates:** From July 1, 2015 to June 30, 2016, 185 bachelor's degrees were awarded. The most popular majors were hospitality management (89%) and early childhood education (75%). 41 companies recruited on campus in 2015-2016. In an average class, 2% graduate in 3 years or less, 33% graduate in 4 years or less, and 43% graduate in 5 years or less. Of the 2015 graduating class, 92% were employed within 6 months of graduation.

SERVICES: Counseling and information services are available, as is tutoring in every subject. There is remedial math, reading, and writing. **Library/Resources:** The library contains 36,293 volumes, and 453 audio/video tapes/CDs/DVDs, and subscribes to 187 periodicals including electronic. Computerized library services include interlibrary loans, database searching, and Internet access. **Physically Challenged Students:** All of the campus is accessible. Facilities include wheelchair ramps, elevators, special parking, specially equipped restrooms, special class scheduling, lowered drinking fountains, and lowered telephones. **Special:** All majors require internships. Study abroad in 8 countries and work-study programs are available. An accelerated degree in culinary arts and B.A.-B.S. degrees are also possible. There are 2 national honor societies. **Visiting:** There are regularly scheduled orientations for prospective students, including program overviews, financial aid information and campus tours. There are guides for informal visits and visitors may sit in on classes. To schedule a visit, contact the Admissions Office. **Campus Safety and Security:** Measures include 24-hour foot and vehicle patrol and emergency notification system. There are lighted pathways/sidewalks and controlled access to dorms/residences.

REQUIREMENTS: Applicants need to submit a high school transcript with a minimum 2.0 GPA or a GED and a personal statement. The ACT or SAT scores are required for all applicants who have graduated within 5 years of intended start date and have a GPA below 2.5. An interview with an Enrollment Advisor is required, and a campus tour is recommended. AP and CLEP credits are accepted. Students must complete 180 credit hours and meet all major requirements as well as the residency requirement. A 2.0 GPA is required to graduate. **Procedure:** Freshmen are admitted to all sessions. There are deferred admissions and rolling admissions plans. Application deadlines are open. Application fee is $50. Applications are accepted on-line. **Transfer Students:** 217 transfer students enrolled in 2015-2016. Students must submit an official college transcript with at least 12 earned semester credits (or 18 quarter credits) with a cumulative GPA of at least 2.0. An interview and a personal statement are required. A campus tour is recommended. 45 of 180 credits required for the bachelor's degree must be completed at Kendall. **International Students:** There are 180 international students enrolled. The school actively recruits these students. They must take the TOEFL with a minimum score of 525 on the paper-based TOEFL (PBT) or 71 on the Internet-based version (iBT), or take the IELTS.

Admissions Contact: Richard Kriofsky, Director of Admissions. Email: *info@kendall.edu* Web: *www.kendall.edu*

FINANCIAL AID: In 2016-2017, 84% of all full-time freshmen and 73% of continuing full-time students received some form of financial aid. 71% of all full-time freshmen and 64% of continuing full-time students received need-based aid. The average freshman award was $6,659. Need-based scholarships or need-based grants averaged $1,136 ($10,990 maximum); need-based self-help aid (loans and jobs) averaged $1,927 ($4,000 maximum); and other non-need-based awards and non-need-based scholarships averaged $3,596 ($32,000 maximum). 8% of undergraduate students work part-time. Average annual earnings from campus work are $3825. The average financial indebtedness of the 2016 graduate was $11,801. The college's own financial statement is required. The FAFSA code is 001703. Check with the school for current application deadlines.

KNOX COLLEGE — C-2
www.knox.edu

Galesburg, IL 61401	**(309) 341-7100** **(800) 678-KNOX**
Fax: (309) 341-7070	**Email: admission@knox.edu**
Full-time: 540 men, 787 women	**Faculty:** 112; IIB, -$
Part-time: 16 men, 14 women	**Ph.D.s:** 96%
Graduate: n/av	**Student/Faculty:** 12 to 1
Year: trimesters	**Tuition:** $43,285
Room & Board: $9330	**Freshman Class:** 3514 applied, 2292 accepted, 347 enrolled
SAT CR/M/W: 635/580/565 **ACT:** 27	**CEEB CODE:** 1372
Application Deadline: January 15	**VERY COMPETITIVE+**

Knox College, founded in 1837, is a nationally ranked, private, residential liberal arts college. There is 1 undergraduate school. The 82-acre campus is in a small town, just a convenient drive from most Midwestern states. Including any residence halls, there are 55 buildings.

STUDENT LIFE: 56% of undergraduates are from Illinois. Others are from 42 states, and 45 foreign countries. 70% are from public schools. 8% are African American; 6% Asian American; 5% two or more races; 49% White; 3% race unknown; 14% Hispanic; 14% Foreign. **Female To Male Ratio:** 1.4:1. The average age of freshmen is 18; all undergraduates, 20. 13% do not continue beyond their first year; 77% remain to graduate. **Housing:** 1225 students can be accommodated in college housing, which includes single-sex and coed dorms and on-campus apartments. In addition, there are language houses, special-interest houses, fraternity houses, cultural centers, international house, Casa Latina, and ABLE (Allied Blacks for Liberty and Equality) House. On-campus housing is guaranteed for all 4 years and is available on a lottery system for upperclassmen. 87% of students live on campus; of those, 75% remain on campus on weekends. All students may keep cars.

FACULTY/CLASSROOMS: 58% of faculty are male; 42% are female. All teach undergraduates, and all do research. No introductory courses are taught by graduate students. The average class size in an introductory lecture is 27; in a laboratory is 14; and in a regular course is 17.

PROGRAMS OF STUDY: Knox confers B.A. degrees. Bachelor's degrees are awarded in AGRICULTURE (environmental studies), BIOLOGICAL SCIENCE (biochemistry, biology/biological science, and neurosciences), COMMUNICATIONS AND THE ARTS (Africana studies, art history and appreciation, classics, creative writing, dramatic arts, English literature, French, German, Greek (classical), Latin, modern language, music, Spanish, studio art, and theatre arts), COMPUTER AND PHYSICAL SCIENCE (chemistry, computer science, mathematics, and physics), EDUCATION (elementary education, secondary education, and social science education), SOCIAL SCIENCE (American studies, anthropology, Asian/Oriental studies, economics, history, international relations, international studies, Latin American studies, philosophy, political science/government, psychology, sociology, and women & gender studies). Creative writing, computer science, psychology, theatre, biology, and economics are the strongest academically. Creative writing, psychology, and economics have the largest enrollments.

ACTIVITIES: 32% of men belong to 1 local and 5 national fraternities; 18% of women belong to 4 national sororities. There are 90 groups on campus, including band, chess, choir, communications, computers, dance, drama, drill team, environmental, ethnic, film, international, jazz band, LGBT, literary magazine, newspaper, orchestra, photography, political, professional, radio and TV, religious, social, social service, student government, and symphony. Popular campus events include International Fair, Rootabaga Jazz Festival, Lincoln Fest (local band all-day festival), and Pause for Paws (finals stress relief program with visiting canines). **Sports:** There are 10 intercollegiate sports for men and 10 for women, and 3 intramural sports for men and 3 for women. Facilities include a fitness center with cardio and selectorized equipment, a fitness studio, free weight area, track and court space for various activities, a gymnasium, natatorium, football, softball, baseball, outdoor track, tennis, and a soccer field. **Graduates:** From July 1, 2015 to June 30, 2016, 311 bachelor's degrees were awarded. The most popular majors were creative writing (10%), psychology (7%), and biology (7%). 96 companies recruited on campus in 2015-2016. In an average class, 3% graduate in 3 years or less, 68% graduate in 4 years or less, 75% graduate in 5 years or less, and 77% graduate in 6 years or less. Of the 2015 graduating class, 21% were enrolled in graduate school within 6 months of graduation, and 30% were employed.

SERVICES: Counseling and information services are available, as is tutoring in most subjects. The Center for Teaching and Learning provides academic support to students in most subjects, particularly in development of writing skills. **Library/Resources:** The 2 libraries contain 342,308 volumes, 98,713 microform items, and 14,901 audio/video tapes/CDs/DVDs, and subscribe to 14,950 periodicals including electronic. Computerized library services include interlibrary loans, database searching, Internet access, and Wi-Fi capability. Special learning facilities include a radio station, Green Oaks Biological Field Station Green Oaks, a biological field station, is both a research and recreation area, consisting of tallgrass prairie, forest, and aquatic habitat. Every other year, 12 Knox students have the opportunity to participate in Green Oaks Term, a 10-week immersive term during which students take interdisciplinary courses in ecology, anthropology, nature writing, nature and art, utopian societies, regional natural history, and sustainability and live at the field station. The Knox Farm consisting of an acre of outdoor growing area and two season-extending "high tunnel" structures, produces food for on-campus use and for sharing with the greater community. Old Main, an academic and administrative building at the heart of the Knox campus, is the only remaining building from the 1858 Lincoln-Douglas Debates and has been designated a National Historic Landmark by the U.S. Department of the Interior. The Dr. Douglas L. Wilson Gallery on the first floor of the building focuses on the history of Old Main and feature dozens of documents, maps, and photographs drawn from the College's 178-year history. Old Main is also an official stop on the statewide Looking for Lincoln Heritage Coalition, which is noted by a wayside marker to the east of the building. The Whitcomb Heritage CenterŸ features exhibits that vividly illustrate the historical context local, regional, and national for the Lincoln-Douglas Debate at Knox in 1858. **Physically Challenged Students:** 85% of the campus is accessible. Facilities include wheelchair ramps, elevators, special parking, specially equipped restrooms, lowered drinking fountains, lowered telephones, and special housing. **Special:** One hundred percent of Knox students pursue experiential learning opportunities, including independent research or creative work, immersive learning, internships, community service, or off-campus study. Knox offers six immersive terms Clinical Psychology Term, Green Oaks Term, Japan Term, Open Studio, Repertory Theatre Term, and StartUp Term that provide students with a focused, hands-on exploration of a single field of study over the course of an entire term. Cooperative programs are offered with Washington University in St. Louis in architecture and engineering; Columbia University in engineering and law; University of Illinois at Urbana-Champaign and Rensselaer Polytechnic Institute in engineering; Rush University in nursing and medical technology; Duke University in forestry and environmental management; and University of Chicago in law and social work. A cooperative program with The George Washington University School of Medicine and Health Sciences means guaranteed admission for selected sophomores. A Direct Admission Program with University of Rochester Simon School of Business allows highly qualified Knox juniors and seniors to apply for an M.B.A. with this graduate program. The Knox College Law Scholars Program helps Knox graduates pursue an affordable legal education at Indiana University Maurer School of Law. Individuals who are selected for the program will receive a scholarship that reduces the cost of tuition at the Maurer School of Law by about 50%. Students also will participate in a mentorship program and other opportunities through the law school. Knox is the first college or university in the country to have an official Peace Corps Preparatory Program, designed to prepare students for the Peace Corps or other international service programs. Study abroad is available in more than 30 countries. Other off-campus study programs include a Washington semester, an urban studies semester, science and library research programs, work-study programs, and numerous internships. Knox participates in the Kemper Scholars Program, which provides students with scholarships, practical experience, and opportunities to explore careers. Self-designed majors and minors may be pursued by students when they have an interest in an intellectual issue that is best studied through an integrative approach based in multiple academic disciplines. A self-designed major/minor has the same characteristics of an established major/minor. There are 8 national honor societies, Phi Beta Kappa, and 39 departmental honors programs. **Visiting:** There are regularly scheduled orientations for prospective students, Open houses for prospective students are offered in July, October, November, January and May, and offer campus tours, class visits, lunch with students and professors, and informational sessions. Interviews are available on request. There are guides for informal visits, visitors may sit in on classes, and stay overnight. To schedule a visit, contact Sarah Bainter at (800) 678-KNOX. **Campus Safety and Security:** Measures include 24-hour foot and vehicle patrol, emergency notification system, self-defense education, and security escort services. There are emergency telephones, lighted pathways/sidewalks, and controlled access to dorms/residences.

REQUIREMENTS: Successful applicants have excelled in a challenging college preparatory course of study, including at least 4 years of English, 3-4 years each of mathematics, science, and social studies, and 2-3 years of a second language. An essay is required and interview strongly recommended. Submission of ACT or SAT scores is optional for most applicants; scores will be considered if submitted. Auditions or portfolio presentations are required for scholarship consideration only. AP credits are accepted. Important factors in the admissions decision are advanced placement or honors courses, personality/intangible qualities, and recommendations by school officials. Knox works on a 3-3 academic schedule 3 terms per year, 3 courses per term. The academic program is structured by four goals, or guideposts: an understanding of five broad areas of human inquiry (Foundations), developing expertise in a field of study (Specialization), acquiring competencies in key areas required for personal and professional success in the new century (Key Competencies); and applying classroom learning through hands-on experience (Experiential Learning). The advising system engages students in a four-year dialogue with faculty through which they a develop a personalized Educational Plan addressing these four goals, but tailored to their own unique aspirations, values, and talents. Breadth requirements include 1 course each in the 5 areas of arts, humanities, quantitative reasoning, natural & physical sciences, and social sciences. An additional minor or major, not in the department of the first major, and a 2.0 GPA, overall and in each major and minor, are required. **Procedure:** Freshmen are admitted fall. Entrance exams should be taken by December. There are early admissions and deferred admissions plans. Early decision applications should be filed by November 1; regular applications, by January 15 for fall entry, along with a $50 fee. Notification of early decision is sent November 15; regular decision, March 15. 139 applicants were on the 2016 waiting list; 2 were admitted. Applications are accepted on-line. **Transfer Students:** 23 transfer students enrolled in 2015-2016. A 3.0 college GPA is expected. An interview is recommended. 14 of 36 credits required for the bachelor's degree must be completed at Knox. **International Students:** There are 195 international students enrolled. The school actively recruits these students. They must take the TOEFL with a minimum score of 550 on the paper-based TOEFL (PBT) or 80 on the Internet-based version (iBT), or the IELTS is also acceptable.

ADMISSIONS: 65% of the 2016-2017 applicants were accepted. The SAT scores for the 2016-2017 freshman class were: Critical Reading-- 17% below 500, 26% between 500 and 599, 41% between 600 and 699, and 17% between 700 and 800. Math-- 26% below 500, 26% between 500 and 599, 38% between 600 and 699, and 10% between 700 and 800. Writing-- 10% below 500, 57% between 500 and 599, 24% between 600 and 699, and 10% between 700 and 800. The ACT scores were 21% between 18 and 23, 48% between 24 and 29, and 30% above 30. 63% of the current freshmen were in the top fifth of their class; 87% were in the top two fifths. There were 2 National Merit finalists. 10 freshmen graduated first in their class. **Admissions Contact:** Paul Steenis, Dean of Admission. Email: *admission@knox.edu* Web: *www.knox.edu*

FINANCIAL AID: In 2016-2017, 100% of all full-time freshmen and 99% of continuing full-time students received some form of financial aid. 83% of all full-time freshmen and 76% of continuing full-time students received need-based aid. The average freshman award was $37,100. Need-based scholarships or need-based grants averaged $30,609; and need-based self-help aid (loans and jobs) averaged $6,511. 65% of undergraduate students work part-time. Average annual earnings from campus work are $1465. The average financial indebtedness of the 2016 graduate was $26,968. Knox is a member of CSS. The college's own financial statement is required. The FAFSA code is 001704. The priority date for freshman financial aid applications for fall entry is November 1.

LAKE FOREST COLLEGE — E-1

www.lakeforest.edu

Lake Forest, IL 60045 — (847) 735-5000, (800) 828-4751

Fax: (847) 735-6271 — **Email: admissions@lakeforest.edu**

Full-time: 676 men, 913 women	**Faculty:** 101; IIB, +$
Part-time: 12 men, 6 women	**Ph.D.s:** 98%
Graduate: 4 men, 15 women	**Student/Faculty:** 15 to 1
Year: semesters, summer session	**Tuition:** $41,172
Room & Board: $9480	**Freshman Class:** 3451 applied, 1905 accepted, 416 enrolled
	CEEB CODE: 1392
Application Deadline: February 15	**VERY COMPETITIVE**

Lake Forest College, founded in 1857, is a private liberal arts institution. There is 1 undergraduate school. In addition to regional accreditation, Lake Forest has baccalaureate program accreditation with HLC. The 107-acre campus is in a suburban area 30 miles north of Chicago. Including any residence halls, there are 43 buildings.

STUDENT LIFE: 54% of undergraduates are from Illinois. Others are from 43 states, 73 foreign countries, and Canada. 73% are from public schools. 9% are Foreign; 7% African American; 57% White; 5% Asian American; 4% two or more races; 3% race unknown; 15% Hispanic. **Female To Male Ratio:** 1.3:1. The average age of freshmen is 18; all undergraduates, 20. 15% do not continue beyond their first year; 85% remain to graduate. **Housing:** 1270 students can be accommodated in college housing, which includes coed dorms and on-campus apartments. In addition, there are special-interest houses, an international house, and themed/special interest suites within residence halls. On-campus housing is guaranteed for the freshman year only and is available on a lottery system for upperclassmen. Priority is given to out-of-town students. 75% of students live on campus; of those, 80% remain on campus on weekends. Upperclassmen may keep cars.

FACULTY/CLASSROOMS: 52% of faculty are male; 48% are female. All teach undergraduates, and all do research. No introductory courses are taught by graduate students.

PROGRAMS OF STUDY: Lake Forest confers B.A. degrees. Master's degrees are also awarded. Bachelor's degrees are awarded in BIOLOGICAL SCIENCE (biology/biological science and neurosciences), BUSINESS (business economics and finance), COMMUNICATIONS AND THE ARTS (art, communications, English, French, music, Spanish, and theatre arts), COMPUTER AND PHYSICAL SCIENCE (chemistry, computer science, mathematics, and physics), EDUCATION (education and music education), ENGINEERING AND ENVIRONMENTAL DESIGN (environmental science), SOCIAL SCIENCE (American studies, anthropology, area studies, Asian/Oriental studies, economics, history, international relations, Latin American studies, philosophy, political science/government, psychology, religion, and sociology). Business, communication, and biology have the largest enrollments.

ACTIVITIES: 12% of men belong to 3 national fraternities; 16% of women belong to 4 national sororities. There are 66 groups on campus, including art, band, cheerleading, chess, choir, chorus, computers, dance, debate, drama, environmental, ethnic, film, honors, international, jazz band, LGBT, literary magazine, musical theater, newspaper, orchestra, pep band, photography, political, professional, radio and TV, religious, social, social service, and student government. Popular campus events include Homecoming, Global Fest, Gates Day of Service, and Spring Concert. **Sports:** There are 9 intercollegiate sports for men and 10 for women, and 16 intramural sports for men and 16 for women. The

Sports and Recreation Center houses a gymnasium, 1,200-square-foot training room, 9,600-square-foot weight room, 2,500-square-foot cardio suite, dance studio, basketball courts, racquetball and handball courts, three playing surfaces (wood court, tartan-surface, and artificial turf), batting/golf cages, suspended track, a pool, separate varsity locker rooms, and a cafe. Adjacent is an indoor hockey rink, outdoor sand volleyball courts, tennis courts, and baseball, football, soccer, and intramural fields. **Graduates:** From July 1, 2015 to June 30, 2016, 348 bachelor's degrees were awarded. The most popular majors were communication (15%), economics (9%), and psychology (8%). 850 companies recruited on campus in 2015-2016. In an average class, 64% graduate in 4 years or less, 72% graduate in 5 years or less, and 73% graduate in 6 years or less. Of the 2015 graduating class, 77% were employed within 6 months of graduation.

SERVICES: Counseling and information services are available, as is tutoring in most subjects. **Library/Resources:** The library contains 360,848 volumes, 111,460 microform items, and 10,324 audio/video tapes/CDs/DVDs, and subscribes to 16,980 periodicals including electronic. Computerized library services include interlibrary loans, database searching, Internet access, and Wi-Fi capability. Special learning facilities include an art gallery, radio station, a multimedia language lab, an electronic music studio with practice rooms, a technology resource center equipped with high-end computing hardware and software, and a rhetoric and production room. **Physically Challenged Students:** 75% of the campus is accessible. Facilities include wheelchair ramps, elevators, special parking, specially equipped restrooms, special class scheduling, lowered drinking fountains, lowered telephones, and special housing. **Special:** Lake Forest offers cross-registration with Associated Colleges of the Midwest, an extensive internship program, a student-designed Independent Scholar major, extensive off-campus study opportunities in 15 + countries with international internships available. Lake Forest has a number of accelerated and dual-degree programs including a 3-3 program in cooperation with a number of law schools whereby a student can earn a BA and JD in six years instead of seven. Students at Lake Forest can choose to earn a BA degree in communication or philosophy in just three years. The College also offers accelerated and dual-degree programs in engineering, international studies, pharmacy, and nursing. There are 14 national honor societies, Phi Beta Kappa, a freshman honors program, and 14 departmental honors programs. **Visiting:** There are regularly scheduled orientations for prospective students, visits include class visitation, panel presentations, tours, and individual appointments with faculty, coaches, and/or admission officers. There are guides for informal visits and visitors may sit in on classes. To schedule a visit, contact the Admissions Office. **Campus Safety and Security:** Measures include 24-hour foot and vehicle patrol, emergency notification system, self-defense education, and security escort services. There are shuttle buses, emergency telephones, lighted pathways/sidewalks, and controlled access to dorms/residences.

REQUIREMENTS: Applicants are advised to complete a minimum of 16 academic credits, including 4 in English, 3 in math, 2 to 4 each in social and natural sciences, and study in 1 or more foreign languages. A GED is accepted. An interview is encouraged. AP credits are accepted. Important factors in the admissions decision are personality/intangible qualities, advanced placement or honors courses, and extracurricular activities record. All students are required to complete 32 courses with a minimum GPA of 2.0. General education requirements include 2 courses in natural science or math, 2 cultural diversity courses, and 1 course each in freshman studies, freshman writing, humanities, social science, and senior studies. **Procedure:** Freshmen are admitted fall and spring. Entrance exams should be taken in the junior or senior year. There are early decision and deferred admissions plans. Early decision applications should be filed by November 15; regular applications, by February 15 for fall entry; and December 1 for spring entry. Notification of early decision is sent December 15; regular decision, March 20. 70 early decision candidates were accepted for the 2016-2017 class. Applications are accepted on-line. **Transfer Students:** 74 transfer students enrolled in 2015-2016. Transfer applicants should have a minimum C average in all college work and should be in good standing with their previous institution. High school and college transcripts and a letter of recommendation from the academic dean or a teacher at the most recent college attended are required. 16 of 32 credits required for the bachelor's degree must be completed at Lake Forest. **International Students:** There are 242 international students enrolled. The school actively recruits these students. They must take the TOEFL with a minimum score of 550 on the paper-based TOEFL (PBT) or 83 on the Internet-based version (iBT). They must also take the SAT or ACT.

ADMISSIONS: 55% of the 2016-2017 applicants were accepted. **Admissions Contact:** Irene Rarliff, Director of Communications. Email: *admissions@lakeforest.edu* Web: *www.lakeforest.edu*

FINANCIAL AID: 14% of undergraduate students work part-time. Average annual earnings from campus work are $2000. Lake Forest is a member of CSS. The FAFSA code is 001706. The priority date for freshman financial aid applications for fall entry is February 15. The deadline for filing freshman financial aid applications for fall entry is May 1.

LEWIS UNIVERSITY — E-2

www.lewisu.edu

Romeoville, IL 60446 — (815) 838-0500, (800) 897-9000

Fax: (815) 836-5002 — **Email:** admissions@lewisu.edu

Full-time: 1734 men, 2010 women	**Faculty:** n/av
Part-time: 385 men, 424 women	**Ph.D.s:** 78%
Graduate: 690 men, 1301 women	**Student/Faculty:** 13 to 1
Year: semesters, summer session	**Tuition:** $30,050
Room & Board: $10,320	**Freshman Class:** 6199 applied, 3669 accepted, 642 enrolled
SAT CR/M: 530/555 **ACT:** 23	**CEEB CODE:** 1404
Application Deadline: open	**COMPETITIVE**

Lewis University is a Catholic university offering distinctive undergraduate and graduate programs. Lewis offers multiple campus locations, online degree programs, and a variety of formats that provide accessibility and convenience to a growing student population. Sponsored by the De La Salle Christian Brothers, Lewis prepares intellectually engaged, ethically grounded, globally aware, and socially responsible graduates. Lewis provides a well-rounded liberal and professional education in fields including business, education, nursing, criminal/social justice, and aviation. There are 5 undergraduate schools and 11 graduate schools. In addition to regional accreditation, Lewis has baccalaureate program accreditation with ACBSP, CSWE, NCATE, CCNE, FAA, and CAATE. The 410-acre campus is in a suburban area 30 miles southwest of downtown Chicago. Including any residence halls, there are 38 buildings.

STUDENT LIFE: 90% of undergraduates are from Illinois. Others are from 33 states, 24 foreign countries, and Canada. 61% are White; 6% African American; 5% race unknown; 4% Asian American; 3% two or more races; 19% Hispanic; 1% Foreign. 52% are Catholic; 42% Other Christian Religions, and 17% did not report religious preference. **Female To Male Ratio:** 1.3:1. The average age of freshmen is 18; all undergraduates, 23. 17% do not continue beyond their first year; 66% remain to graduate. **Housing:** 1400 students can be accommodated in college housing, which includes coed dorms. In addition, there are special-interest houses, learning communities, and suite style accommodations available. On-campus housing is available on a first-come and first-served basis. 76% of students commute. All students may keep cars.

FACULTY/CLASSROOMS: 51% of faculty are male; 49% are female. All teach undergraduates. No introductory courses are taught by graduate students.

PROGRAMS OF STUDY: Lewis confers B.A., B.S., B.E.S., and B.S.N. degrees. Associate, master's, and doctoral degrees are also awarded. Bachelor's degrees are awarded in BIOLOGICAL SCIENCE (biochemistry, bioinformatics, biology/biological science, biology (pre-physician assistant), biological sciences, biology/ gen science secondary education, and forensic science), BUSINESS (accounting, business administration and management, business administration/international, business administration, operations, business administration marketing, business administration/aviation, business economics, business information systems, finance, human resources, international business, international business management, business management, management information systems, management, management science, marketing, marketing management, organizational leadership and management, sports management, and professional studies), COMMUNICATIONS AND THE ARTS (art, art/art studies, art and design, broadcasting, communication studies, communications, communication rhetoric/communication, communications technology, creative writing, drawing, English, English as a second/foreign language, English literature, English writing, graphic design, graphic design & media, illustration, information technology, intermedia/multimedia, journalism, media management, multimedia, music, music business management, music performance, painting, public relations, radio/TV, Spanish, speech/debate/rhetoric, sport & lifestyle studies, theatre arts, and theatre studies), COMPUTER AND PHYSICAL SCIENCE (chemical physics, chemistry, chemistry/forensic chemistry, chemistry/gen science second education, chemistry secondary education, computer networks & systems, computer information technology, computer information systems, computer security, computer science, computer science & informatics, computer security and information assurance, cyber intelligence/security studies, information sciences and systems, mathematics, physics/general science secondary education, and physics), EDUCATION (athletic training, early childhood education, education, education administration, elementary education, English secondary education, global studies, mathematics education, secondary education, Spanish education K-12, special education, spec education/early child dual program, special education/middle level, and sports and wellness studies), ENGINEERING AND ENVIRONMENTAL DESIGN (air traffic control, air traffic management, aircraft mechanics, airline piloting and navigation, aviation administration/management, aviation flight technology, aviation maintenance management, aviation maintenance technology, computer engineering, computer technology, environmental science, nuclear medicine technology, and preengineering), HEALTH PROFESSIONS (biology, dental hygiene, diagnostic medical sonography, exercise science, health care administration, medical laboratory science, nursing, preallied health, pre-health studies, pre-health biological studies, predentistry, premedicine, preoptometry, pre-occupational therapy, prepharmacy, pre-physician assistant, prephysical therapy, prepodiatry, preveterinary science, radiation therapy, radiograph medical technology, respiratory therapy, ultrasound technology, and vascular sonography), SOCIAL SCIENCE (counseling/psychology, criminal justice, economics, fire science, fire services administration, forensic studies, history, law enforcement and corrections, liberal arts/general studies, liberal arts, sciences, general studies, humanities, paralegal studies, philosophy, political science/government, prelaw, psychology, public administration, social work, sociology, theology, and theological studies). Aviation transportation, nursing, and education are the strongest academically. Nursing, aviation transportation, and justice law & public safety programs have the largest enrollments.

ACTIVITIES: There are 100 groups on campus, including art, band, cheerleading, choir, chorale, chorus, computers, dance, debate, drama, environmental, ethnic, film, Flight Team, forensics, honors, international, LGBT, literary magazine, mock trial, musical theater, newspaper, orchestra, pep band, photography, political, professional, radio and TV, religious, social, social service, student government, student nurses association, symphony, and teachers of tomorrow. Popular campus events include Fall and Spring Formals, Homecoming, Founders Week events, and International Student Food Festival. **Sports:** There are 9 intercollegiate sports for men and 9 for women, and 20 intramural sports for men and 20 for women. The Student Recreation and Fitness Center contains a field house with multipurpose courts, weight room, aerobics studio, 8-lane swimming pool, and indoor track. The Neil Carey Arena hosts basketball & volleyball competition. Lewis Stadium hosts soccer and track & field activities. Powerhouse Flex and Fitness Center is for individual and group activities. Outdoor facilities include baseball and softball fields, tennis courts, disc golf course, nature trail, sand volleyball, and intramural/rugby fields. **Graduates:** From July 1, 2015 to June 30, 2016, 1205 bachelor's degrees were awarded. The most popular majors were criminal social justice (9%), nursing (8%), and psychology (6%). In an average class, 41% graduate in 4 years or less, 58% graduate in 5 years or less, and 61% graduate in 6 years or less.

SERVICES: Counseling and information services are available, as is tutoring in most subjects. There is remedial reading and writing. University Success Program provides assistance to those students who do not meet the outright scholastic requirements. **Library/Resources:** The library contains 141,150 volumes and 13,419 audio/video tapes/CDs/DVDs. Computerized library services include interlibrary loans, database searching, Internet access, and Wi-Fi capability. Special learning facilities include an art gallery, radio station, TV station, Lewis University Airport and Harold E. White Aviation Center, Oremus Fine Arts Center with theatre, art and music facilities, Brother Paul French FSC Learning Resource Center, James A. LaGrippe Pastoral Center, Sancta Alberta Chapel, Academic Building for College of Arts & Sciences, Science Center, St. Charles Borromeo Center for College of Business programs, De La Salle Hall for College of Education programs, South Hall for College of Nursing and Health Professions programs, Leckrone Academic Resource Center/Career Services. **Physically Challenged Students:** 95% of the campus is accessible. Facilities include wheelchair ramps, elevators, special parking, specially equipped restrooms, special class scheduling, lowered drinking fountains, lowered telephones, and special housing. **Special:** Lewis offers an honors program, undergraduate research opportunities, study abroad options in a number of locations, work-study programs, service members opportunities, student-designed majors, continuing education, distance learning, evening courses, and weekend courses. There are joint programs with a number of colleges in the Allied Health areas, including Midwest University for pharmacy and Logan Chiropractic College. There are accelerated-degree programs for adults that include business administration, information security and risk management, information technology management, management, social media marketing, aviation maintenance management, computer science, criminal social justice, human resource management, organizational leadership, paralegal studies, psychology, healthcare leadership, RN-BSN completion, BAC to BSN, and professional studies. The aviation program permits graduates to qualify for the FAA Airframe and Powerplant certificate, air traffic control, and flight certifications. There is a freshman honors program. **Visiting:** There are regularly scheduled orientations for prospective students consisting of 1-day sessions (parent orientation included) followed by welcome week activities before the first class day in the fall. There are guides for informal visits, visitors may sit in on classes, and stay overnight. To schedule a visit, contact the Admission Office. **Campus Safety and Security:** Measures include 24-hour foot and vehicle patrol, emergency notification system, self-defense education, and security escort services. There are shuttle buses, emergency telephones, lighted pathways/sidewalks, and controlled access to dorms/residences.

REQUIREMENTS: The SAT or ACT is required. Applicants must have graduated from an approved high school with a combination of grade point average, class rank, and test scores that indicates a strong likelihood of success in university studies. Students should have completed 18 units consisting of 3 in English and 15 in other college preparatory subjects. The GED is accepted. A GPA of 2.0 is required. AP and CLEP credits are accepted. Important factors in the admissions decision are advanced placement or honors courses, leadership record, and extracurricular activities record. All students must earn 128 credit hours in courses acceptable for graduation, with about one-third of these courses in the core curriculum, such as science, mathematics, fine arts, writing, human communications, literature, western civilization, philosophy, ethics, theology, economics, and social sciences. Students must maintain a minimum cumulative GPA that varies depending upon the academic program selected. At least 4 upper-division courses must be taken in the major, and the final 32 hours must be completed at Lewis. Requirement for practicums, capstone courses, internships, major field tests, and student portfolios vary depending on academic program selected. **Procedure:** Freshmen are admitted fall and spring. Entrance exams should be taken prior to enrollment. There are deferred admissions and rolling admissions plans. Application deadlines are open. Application fee is $40. Notification is sent on a rolling basis. Applications are accepted on-line. **Transfer Students:** 481 transfer students enrolled in 2015-2016. Biology, chemistry, education and nursing programs require a minimum 2.75 cumulative transfer GPA. Air traffic control, allied health and computer engineering programs require a minimum 3.0 cumulative transfer GPA. Pre-professional biology programs require a 3.25 minimum biology course and cumulative transfer GPA (based on a 4.0 grading scale), 2.0 GPA in transferable course work of at least 12 semester hours for admission to other programs. Transfer students should submit official transcripts from all colleges attended, and be in good standing at the previous institution. 32 of 128 credits required for the bachelor's degree must be completed at Lewis. **International Students:** There are 57 international students enrolled. The school actively recruits these students. They must take the TOEFL with a minimum score of 79 on the Internet-based version (iBT). They must also take the SAT or ACT.

ADMISSIONS: 59% of the 2016-2017 applicants were accepted. The SAT scores for the 2016-2017 freshman class were: Critical Reading--41% below 500, 35% between 500 and 599, 21% between 600 and 699, and 3% between 700 and 800. Math-- 21% below 500, 47% between 500 and 599, 26% between 600 and 699, and 6% between 700 and 800. The ACT scores were 4% between 12 and 17, 54% between 18 and 23, 36% between 24 and 29, and 6% above 30. 39% of the current freshmen were in the top fifth of their class; 69% were in the top two fifths. 4 freshmen graduated first in their class. **Admissions Contact:** Ryan Cockerill, Director of Admission. Email: *admissions@lewisu.edu* Web: *www.lewisu.edu*

FINANCIAL AID: In 2016-2017, 99% of all full-time freshmen and 93% of continuing full-time students received some form of financial aid.

86% of all full-time freshmen and 76% of continuing full-time students received need-based aid. Average annual earnings from campus work are $4200. Lewis is a member of CSS. The FAFSA code is 001707. The priority date for freshman financial aid applications for fall entry is October 31. The deadline for filing freshman financial aid applications for fall entry is May 1.

LOYOLA UNIVERSITY CHICAGO E-2

www.luc.edu

Chicago, IL 60660	(773) 508-3075 (800) 262-2373
Fax: (773) 508-8926	Email: admission@luc.edu
Full-time: 3503 men, 6859 women	**Faculty:** I, av$
Part-time: 261 men, 506 women	**Ph.D.s:** 93%
Graduate: 1823 men, 3470 women	**Student/Faculty:** 14 to 1
Year: semesters, summer session	**Tuition:** $40,426
Room & Board: $13,310	**Freshman Class:** 21555 applied, 15360 accepted, 2194 enrolled
SAT CR/M/W: 580/580/570 **ACT:** 26	**CEEB CODE:** 1412
Application Deadline: May 1	**VERY COMPETITIVE**

Loyola University of Chicago, founded in 1870, is a private Roman Catholic (Jesuit) university offering undergraduate curricula in the arts and sciences, business, communication, nursing, social work, and education. There are 8 undergraduate schools and 7 graduate schools. In addition to regional accreditation, Loyola has baccalaureate program accreditation with AACSB, ACPE, CSWE, NCATE, NLN, ACS, NAST, CCNE, and NCA-HLC. The 105-acre campus is in an urban area in Chicago. Including any residence halls, there are 74 buildings.

STUDENT LIFE: 65% of undergraduates are from Illinois. Others are from 49 states, 64 foreign countries, and Canada. 64% are from public schools. 56% are White; 5% Foreign; 5% two or more races; 5% race unknown; 4% African American; 14% Hispanic; 11% Asian American. 59% are Catholic; 22% Orthodox Hindu, Buddhist and Islam; 17% Protestant. **Female To Male Ratio:** 1.9:1. The average age of freshmen is 18; all undergraduates, 21. 14% do not continue beyond their first year; 74% remain to graduate. **Housing:** 4544 students can be accommodated in college housing, which includes single-sex and coed dorms, on-campus apartments, and off-campus apartments. In addition, there are honors houses, fraternity houses, sorority houses, and living-learning community floors. On-campus housing is available on a lottery system for upperclassmen. 59% of students commute. All students may keep cars.

FACULTY/CLASSROOMS: 50% of faculty are male; 50% are female. 92% teach undergraduates, and 92% do research. No introductory courses are taught by graduate students.

PROGRAMS OF STUDY: Loyola confers B.A., B.S., B.A.Classics, B.B.A., B.F.A., B.G., B.S.Ed., B.S.N., and B.S.W. degrees. Master's and doctoral degrees are also awarded. Bachelor's degrees are awarded in BIOLOGICAL SCIENCE (biochemistry, bioinformatics, biology/biological science, and biophysics), BUSINESS (accounting, business administration and management, business economics, entrepreneurial studies, finance, human resources, international business management, management information systems, marketing/retailing/merchandising, organizational leadership and management, and sports management), COMMUNICATIONS AND THE ARTS (advertising, art history, communications, dance, digital communications, English, fine arts, French, Greek, Greek (classical), Italian, journalism, Latin, media arts, music, Spanish, studio art, theatre arts, and visual design), COMPUTER AND PHYSICAL SCIENCE (chemistry, clinical laboratory science, computer science, computer security and information assurance, information sciences and systems, mathematics, mathematics/computational, physics, software engineering, and statistics), EDUCATION (bilingual/bicultural education, early childhood education, elementary education, health information management, mathematics education, science education, secondary education, and special education), ENGINEERING AND ENVIRONMENTAL DESIGN (engineering science, environmental engineering technology, and environmental science), HEALTH PROFESSIONS (clinical science, exercise science, and nursing), SOCIAL SCIENCE (African studies, African American studies, anthropology, applied psychology, classical/ancient civilization, criminal justice, criminology, economics, forensic studies, history, human services, international studies, pastoral studies, philosophy, political science/government, psychology, religious education, social work, sociology, theological studies, and women's studies). Biology, psychology, and nursing have the largest enrollments.

ACTIVITIES: 8% of men belong to 6 national fraternities; 14% of women belong to 9 national sororities. There are 250 groups on campus, including fencing, ice hockey, lacrosse, quidditch, rugby, running club, soccer, softball, swim club, tennis, ultimate frisbee, volleyball, art, band, chess, choir, chorus, dance, debate, drama, environmental, ethnic, film, honors, international, jazz band, LGBT, literary magazine, newspaper, photography, political, professional, radio and TV, religious, social, social service, student government, and waterpolo. Popular campus events include New Year's Festival, President's Ball and Department of Programming Concert and Mainstage Events. **Sports:** There are 7 intercollegiate sports for men and 8 for women, and 20 intramural sports for men and 20 for women. Facilities include a soccer park with press box. Norville Center athletics complex includes a student-athlete academic center, a sports medicine facility, strength and conditioning equipment, and athletics Wall of Fame. **Graduates:** From July 1, 2015 to June 30, 2016, 2212 bachelor's degrees were awarded. The most popular majors were biology (15%), nursing (12%), and psychology (11%). In an average class, 1% graduate in 3 years or less, 69% graduate in 4 years or less, and 74% graduate in 5 years or less.

SERVICES: Counseling and information services are available, as is tutoring in some subjects, such as in general education courses. A writing center for small-group tutoring, tutor-led study halls, academic skills workshop, and language learning center are available. **Library/Resources:** Computerized library services include interlibrary loans, database searching, Internet access, and Wi-Fi capability. Special learning facilities include an art gallery, radio station, theaters, art museums, digital media labs, convergence media studio, language learning resource center, neuroscience labs, clean energy lab, mock trial room, performance and specialized fine arts rooms, clinical simulation nursing laboratory, histology lab, geothermal system, ecodome greenhouse, aquaponics system showcase, artificial stream research facility, and retreat and ecology campus. **Physically Challenged Students:** 90% of the campus is accessible. Facilities include wheelchair ramps, elevators, specially equipped restrooms, special class scheduling, lowered drinking fountains, lowered telephones. Selected dorms are wheelchair accessible. **Special:** There are study abroad service, and learning opportunities in Vietnam, Peru, El Salvador, South Africa, Chile, Spain, and India. Dual majors in math education/secondary education and physics/engineering, nondegree study, and pass/fail options are available. The school also offers a B.A.-B.S. degree in chemistry and a 3-2 engineering degree with Columbia and Washington Universities. There are 5-year programs and combination bachelor's/master's available. Loyola also offers Engineering majors: Bioengineering, Computer Engineering, and Environmental Health Engineering. There are 9 national honor societies, Phi Beta Kappa, and a freshman honors program. **Visiting:** There are regularly scheduled orientations for prospective students, including interviews and tours, and students may attend classes if previous arrangements have been made. There are guides for informal visits and visitors may stay overnight. To schedule a visit, contact the Undergraduate Admissions Office. **Campus Safety and Security:** Measures include 24-hour foot and vehicle patrol, emergency notification system, self-defense education, and security escort services. There are shuttle buses, emergency telephones, lighted pathways/sidewalks, hot spot tours, and bicycle safety U-lock program.

REQUIREMENTS: The SAT or ACT is required. Graduation from an accredited secondary school or satisfactory scores on the GED are required for admission. 15 academic credits are required. Secondary school courses should include 4 credits of English and 3 each of math, science, and social studies. AP and CLEP credits are accepted. Important factors in the admissions decision are advanced placement or honors courses, leadership record, and extracurricular activities record. To graduate, students must have a total of 120 credit hours with a minimum GPA of 2.0. There is a core requirement. The Core includes a total of 15 courses (45 credit hours of coursework), primarily from the arts and sciences, which develop important college-level skills and integrate an understanding of values through 10 required areas of knowledge. Important skills on which the Core focuses are communication, critical thinking, ethical awareness, information literacy, quantitativeand qualitative analysis, research methods, and technological literacy. The 10 required areas of knowledge include a college writing seminar, artistic knowledge and experience, historical knowledge, literary knowledge, quantitative analysis, scientific literacy, societal and cultural knowledge, philosophical knowledge, theological and religious studies, and ethics. For the core requirement, all students must take 9 hours each of theology, philosophy, and social sciences and 6 hours each of English composition and humanities. **Procedure:** Freshmen are admitted to all sessions. Entrance exams should be taken as early as possible, normally in the spring of the junior year. There is a rolling admissions plan. Applications should be filed by May 1 for fall entry. Applications are accepted on-line. Application fees are waived if application is completed on-line. **Transfer Students:** 519 transfer students enrolled in 2015-2016. Transfer students must have 20 transferable semester hours of credit, with a minimum GPA of 2.0 for the schools of arts and sciences and education. A minimum GPA of 2.5 is required for the schools of nursing and business administration. If transfers have fewer then 20 hours, students must meet the same requirements as entering freshmen. 45 of 120 credits required for the bachelor's degree must be completed at Loyola. **International Students:** There are 579 international students enrolled. The school actively recruits these students. They must take the TOEFL with a minimum score of 550 on the paper-based TOEFL (PBT) or 79 on the Internet-based version (iBT). They must also take the SAT or ACT.

ADMISSIONS: 71% of the 2016-2017 applicants were accepted. The SAT scores for the 2016-2017 freshman class were: Critical Reading-- 18% below 500, 42% between 500 and 599, 35% between 600 and 699, and 5% between 700 and 800. Math-- 17% below 500, 42% between 500 and 599, 34% between 600 and 699, and 7% between 700 and 800. Writing-- 17% below 500, 44% between 500 and 599, 32% between 600 and 699, and 7% between 700 and 800. The ACT scores were 22% between 18 and 23, 58% between 24 and 29, and 20% above 30. 60% of the current freshmen were in the top fifth of their class; 88% were in the top two fifths. 19 freshmen graduated first in their class. **Admissions Contact:** Erin Moriarty, Director for Undergraduate Admissions. Email: *admission@luc.edu* Web: *www.luc.edu*

FINANCIAL AID: In 2016-2017, 97% of all full-time freshmen and 92% of continuing full-time students received some form of financial aid. 59% of all full-time freshmen and 60% of continuing full-time students received need-based aid. The average freshman award was $24,879. Need-based scholarships or need-based grants averaged $9,335 ($56,390 maximum); need-based self-help aid (loans and jobs) averaged $5,131 ($9,500 maximum); non-need-based athletic scholarships averaged $27,214 ($58,467 maximum); and other non-need-based awards and non-need-based scholarships averaged $16,828 ($58,717 maximum). 30% of undergraduate students work part-time. Average annual earnings from campus work are $2348. The average financial indebtedness of the 2016 graduate was $31,750. The FAFSA code is 001710. The deadline for filing freshman financial aid applications for fall entry is March 1.

MACMURRAY COLLEGE — C-3

www.mac.edu

Jacksonville, IL 62650	(217) 479-7056 (800) 252-7485
Fax: (217) 291-0702	Email: admiss@mac.edu
Full-time: 267 men, 375 women	**Faculty:** 45; IIB
Part-time: 15 men, 44 women	**Ph.D.s:** 62%
Graduate: n/av	**Student/Faculty:** 13 to 1
Year: semesters, summer session	**Tuition:** $25,110
Room & Board: $8510	**Freshman Class:** 1421 applied, 806 accepted, 186 enrolled
SAT: required **ACT:** 21	**CEEB CODE:** 1435
Application Deadline: rolling	**COMPETITIVE**

MacMurray College, founded in 1846, is a private, liberal arts, general education institution affiliated with the United Methodist Church. The figures in the above capsule and in this profile are approximate. There are 2 undergraduate schools. In addition to regional accreditation, MacMurray has baccalaureate program accreditation with CSWE, CCNE, and NCACS. The 60-acre campus is in a small town in Jacksonville, Illinois, easy driving distance of St. Louis and Chicago.

STUDENT LIFE: 88% of undergraduates are from Illinois. Others are from 17 states, 3 foreign countries, and Canada. 90% are from public schools. 79% are White; 3% Hispanic; 11% African American; 1% American Indian/Alaska Native; 1% Foreign. 78% are Protestant; 18% Catholic. **Female To Male Ratio:** 1.5:1. The average age of freshmen is 19; all undergraduates, 22. 40% do not continue beyond their first year; 56% remain to graduate. **Housing:** 725 students can be accommodated in college housing, which includes single-sex and coed dorms. On-campus housing is guaranteed for all 4 years. 54% of students live on campus; of those, 70% remain on campus on weekends. All students may keep cars.

FACULTY/CLASSROOMS: 42% of faculty are male; 58% are female. All teach undergraduates. No introductory courses are taught by graduate students. The average class size in an introductory lecture is 41; in a laboratory is 14; and in a regular course is 17.

PROGRAMS OF STUDY: MacMurray confers B.A., B.S., B.S.N., and B.S.W. degrees. Associate degrees are also awarded. Bachelor's degrees are awarded in BIOLOGICAL SCIENCE (biology/biological science), BUSINESS (accounting, business administration and management, management information systems, marketing/retailing/merchandising, and sports management), COMMUNICATIONS AND THE ARTS (art, dramatic arts, English, music, and Spanish), COMPUTER AND PHYSICAL SCIENCE (chemistry, computer science, mathematics, and physics), EDUCATION (education of the deaf and hearing impaired, elementary education, music education, physical education, science education, secondary education, and special education), ENGINEERING AND ENVIRONMENTAL DESIGN (preengineering), HEALTH PROFESSIONS (nursing, predentistry, premedicine, and preveterinary science), SOCIAL SCIENCE (criminal justice, history, interpreter for the deaf, liberal arts/general studies, philosophy, political science/government, prelaw, psychology, religion, social work, and youth ministry). Nursing, criminal justice, and homeland security are the strongest academically.

ACTIVITIES: 9% of men belong to 1 local and 2 national fraternities; 15% of women belong to 3 local sororities. There are 31 groups on campus, including art, bagpipe, band, cheerleading, choir, chorale, chorus, dance, drama, ethnic, international, LGBT, literary magazine, musical theater, newspaper, orchestra, pep band, photography, professional, religious, social, social service, student government, and yearbook. Popular campus events include Spring Formal, Sigma Tau Gamma Day, and Midnight Breakfasts. **Sports:** There are 9 intercollegiate sports for men and 8 for women, and 15 intramural sports for men and 15 for women. Facilities include a gym, basketball courts, football, volleyball, soccer, golf, tennis and outdoor basketball courts, a swimming pool, weight room, wrestling room, dance studios, a game room, and TV lounge. **Graduates:** From July 1, 2015 to June 30, 2016, 115 bachelor's degrees were awarded. The most popular majors were social work (12%), nursing (10%), and psychology (10%). 75 companies recruited on campus in 2015-2016. In an average class, 36% graduate in 4 years or less, 45% graduate in 5 years or less, and 52% graduate in 6 years or less. Of the 2015 graduating class, 15% were enrolled in graduate school within 6 months of graduation, and 90% were employed.

SERVICES: Counseling and information services are available, as is tutoring in every subject. There is remedial math, reading, and writing. The college provides services to visually and hearing impaired students through interpreters, readers, and note takers. **Library/Resources:** The library contains 1.8 million volumes, 28,093 microform items, and 1,085 audio/video tapes/CDs/DVDs, and subscribes to 130 periodicals including electronic. Computerized library services include interlibrary loans, database searching, Internet access, and Wi-Fi capability. Special learning facilities include an art gallery. **Physically Challenged Students:** 90% of the campus is accessible. Facilities include wheelchair ramps, elevators, special parking, specially equipped restrooms, special class scheduling, and special housing. **Special:** The school has co-op programs in modern languages and international studies and cross-registration with 5 colleges through the West Central Illinois Foreign Language Consortium. A 3-2 engineering degree with Washington and Columbia Universities a Washington semester, internships in all majors, work-study programs, dual majors, and pass/fail options are available. Students may study abroad in England, Germany, Japan, or Russia. There are 4 national honor societies, a freshman honors program, and 5 departmental honors programs. **Visiting:** There are regularly scheduled orientations for prospective students, including a financial aid conference, a tour, and faculty appointments. There are guides for informal visits, visitors may sit in on classes, and stay overnight. To schedule a visit, contact the Office of Admissions. **Campus Safety and Security:** Measures include security escort services. There are emergency telephones, lighted pathways/sidewalks, evening patrols, and evening sign-in at dorms.

REQUIREMENTS: The SAT or ACT is required. Applicants must be graduates of an accredited secondary school. The GED is accepted. Secondary school courses should include 4 years of English, 3 years of math, and 2 years each of science, foreign language, and social studies. MacMurray requires applicants to be in the upper 50% of their class. A GPA of 2.5 is required. AP and CLEP credits are accepted. Important factors in the admissions decision are advanced placement or honors courses, extracurricular activities record, and leadership record. To graduate, students must complete 120 semester hours with a minimum GPA of 2.0. All students must take 3 courses in rhetorical skills and a 3-course sequence on major ideas in Western civilization, a course in Diversity and the American Experience, and satisfy the requirements of the breadth component, a 16-hour distribution of non-major courses. They also must pass a proficiency exam in writing, given when students attain junior standing. **Procedure:** Freshmen are admitted to all sessions. Entrance exams should be taken in the spring of the junior year. There are deferred admissions and rolling admissions plans. Application deadlines are open. Notification is sent on a rolling basis. Applications are accepted on-line. **Transfer Students:** 101 transfer students enrolled in 2015-2016. Transfer students must have a minimum GPA of 2.0 in at least 28 transferable semester credits. Nursing applicants must have a GPA of 2.75 and a minimum score of 20 on the ACT. 30 of 120 credits required for the bachelor's degree must be completed at MacMurray. **International Students:** There are 8 international students enrolled. They must take the TOEFL. Some may be required to take the SAT with a minimum score of 950, or 20 on the ACT.

ADMISSIONS: 57% of the 2016-2017 applicants were accepted. The ACT scores were 50% below 12, 28% between 12 and 17, 15% between 18 and 23, 4% between 24 and 29, and 3% above 30. 28% of the current freshmen were in the top fifth of their class; 50% were in the top two fifths. 3 freshmen graduated first in their class. **Admissions Contact:** Kathryn Hall, Director of Admissions. Email: *admiss@mac.edu* Web: *www.mac.edu*

FINANCIAL AID: In 2016-2017, 98% of all full-time freshmen received some form of financial aid. 98% of all full-time freshmen received need-based aid. MacMurray is a member of CSS. The FAFSA code is 001717. The deadline for filing freshman financial aid applications for fall entry is open.

MCKENDREE UNIVERSITY — C-5

www.mckendree.edu

Lebanon, IL 62254	**(618) 537-6833** **(800) BEARCAT**
Fax: (618) 537-6496	**Email: inquiry@mckendree.edu**
Full-time: 883 men, 937 women	**Faculty:** IIA, --$
Part-time: 195 men, 327 women	**Ph.D.s:** 90%
Graduate: 208 men, 445 women	**Student/Faculty:** 14 to 1
Year: semesters, summer session	**Tuition:** $28,740
Room & Board: $9200	**Freshman Class:** 1097 applied
ACT: 24	**CEEB CODE:** 1456
Application Deadline: n/av	**COMPETITIVE+**

McKendree University, formerly McKendree College, founded in 1828, is the oldest college in Illinois. It is a private liberal arts institution affiliated with the United Methodist Church, offering 54 majors, 46 minors, 6 graduate programs, and 2 doctorate programs. The figures in the above capsule and in this profile are approximate. There are 4 undergraduate schools and 4 graduate schools. In addition to regional accreditation, McKendree has baccalaureate program accreditation with NCATE, NLN, IACBE, and CAAHEP. The 235-acre campus is in a suburban area in Lebanon, Illinois, 23 miles east of St. Louis.

STUDENT LIFE: Students are from 41 states, 24 foreign countries, and Canada. 71% are White; 13% African American; 6% race unknown; 4% Hispanic; 2% Foreign; 2% two or more races; 1% Asian American; 1% American Indian/Alaska Native. **Female To Male Ratio:** 1.3:1. The average age of freshmen is 18; all undergraduates, 23. 29% do not continue beyond their first year; 71% remain to graduate. **Housing:** 1200 students can be accommodated in college housing, which includes coed dorms and on-campus apartments. In addition, there are special interest houses, 6 residence halls, and 2 apartment-style living halls. On-campus housing is guaranteed for all 4 years. Alcohol is not permitted. All students may keep cars.

FACULTY/CLASSROOMS: All teach undergraduates, and all do research. No introductory courses are taught by graduate students. The average class size in an introductory lecture is 20; in a laboratory is 17; and in a regular course is 14.

PROGRAMS OF STUDY: McKendree confers B.A., B.S., B.B.A., B.F.A., B.M.E., B.S.Ed., and B.S.N. degrees. Master's and doctoral degrees are also awarded. Bachelor's degrees are awarded in AGRICULTURE (environmental studies), BIOLOGICAL SCIENCE (biology/biological science), BUSINESS (accounting, banking and finance, business administration and management, and marketing/retailing/merchandising), COMMUNICATIONS AND THE ARTS (art, dramatic arts, English, music, music business management, music history and appreciation, music performance, public relations, and speech/debate/rhetoric), COMPUTER AND PHYSICAL SCIENCE (chemistry, computer information systems, computer science, information sciences and systems, and mathematics), EDUCATION (art education, athletic training, business education, elementary education, global studies, middle school education, music education, physical education, and special education), HEALTH PROFESSIONS (health, medical laboratory technology, nursing, and occupational therapy), SOCIAL SCIENCE (biopsychology, criminal justice, economics, gerontology, history, international relations, international studies, philosophy, political science/government, psychology, religion, religious studies, religious music, social science, social work, and sociology). Business, math, and computer science are the strongest academically. Business, education, and nursing have the largest enrollments.

ACTIVITIES: There are 86 groups on campus, including art, band, cheerleading, choir, chorale, chorus, communications, computers, dance, debate, drama, environmental, ethnic, film, forensics, honors, international, jazz band, LGBT, literary magazine, marching band, musical theater, newspaper, pep band, photography, political, professional, religious, social, social service, and student government. Popular campus events include Model United Nations, Family Festival, and Midnight Breakfast. **Sports:** There are 17 intercollegiate sports for men and 16 for women. Facilities include a gym, an intramural gym, a fitness center, tennis courts, a student center with table tennis and billiards, an all-weather track, a football stadium, and playing fields for baseball, softball, basketball, bowling, cross country, fencing, golf, hockey, powerlifting, soccer, volleyball, wrestling, lacrosse, and co-ed bass fishing. **Graduates:** From July 1, 2015 to June 30, 2016, 786 bachelor's degrees were awarded. The most popular majors were business (37%), education (20%), and nursing (20%). 150 companies recruited on campus in 2015-2016. In an average class, 48% graduate in 4 years or less, 66% graduate in 5 years or less, and 70% graduate in 6 years or less. Of the 2015 graduating class, 29% were enrolled in graduate school within 6 months of graduation, and 90% were employed.

SERVICES: Counseling and information services are available, as is tutoring in every subject. There is a reader service for the blind, and remedial reading and writing. **Library/Resources:** The library contains 140,000 volumes, 43,234 microform items, and 30,000 audio/video tapes/CDs/DVDs, and subscribes to 9,000 periodicals including electronic. Computerized library services include interlibrary loans, database searching, Internet access, and Wi-Fi capability. **Physically Challenged Students:** Facilities include wheelchair ramps, elevators, special parking, specially equipped restrooms, special class scheduling, and lowered drinking fountains. **Special:** McKendree offers internships, work-study programs, study abroad in over 120 different locations across the globe, dual and student-designed majors, and nondegree study, as well as a 3-2 program in occupational therapy with Washington University in St. Louis. There are 12 national honor societies, a freshman honors program, and 1 departmental honors program. **Visiting:** There are regularly scheduled orientations for prospective students, and consisting of Preview Days, where faculty members and personnel from several departments answer questions. Student-led tours of the campus and various other events are also available. There are guides for informal visits, visitors may sit in on classes, and stay overnight. To schedule a visit, contact the Admissions Office. **Campus Safety and Security:** Measures include 24-hour foot and vehicle patrol, emergency notification system, and security escort services. There are shuttle buses, emergency telephones, and lighted pathways/sidewalks.

REQUIREMENTS: The ACT is required. Students must be high school graduates or submit the GED certificate. Completion of at least 15 units of high school work is recommended. A recommendation from the secondary school counselor is recommended. McKendree requires applicants to be in the upper 50% of their class. A GPA of 2.5 is required. AP and CLEP credits are accepted. Important factors in the admissions decision are advanced placement or honors courses, leadership record, and evidence of special talent. To graduate, students must complete 120 semester hours, with a minimum GPA of 2.0. The 51-credit-hour core curriculum includes 9 credits of social science, 7 of science, 6 of freshman English, 3 each of speech, math, ethics, philosophy or religion, history, cross-cultural studies, literature, fine or performing arts, and computer competency, and 1 to 2 of phys ed. In addition, 2 writing-intensive courses and a writing proficiency exam must be taken. A thesis is required for biology majors seeking a B.S. degree. **Procedure:** Freshmen are admitted to all sessions. Entrance exams should be taken in the junior year. There is a rolling admissions plan. Application deadlines are open. Applications are accepted on-line. **Transfer Students:** Applicants must have a minimum 2.0 GPA from all colleges previously attended. 30 of 120 credits required for the bachelor's degree must be completed at McKendree. **International Students:** There are 30 international students enrolled. The school actively recruits these students. They must take the TOEFL with a minimum score of 520 on the paper-based TOEFL (PBT) or 70 on the Internet-based version (iBT). They must also take the SAT or ACT.

ADMISSIONS: The SAT scores for the 2016-2017 freshman class were: Critical Reading-- 56% below 500 and 44% between 500 and 599. Math-- 41% below 500, 54% between 500 and 599, and 5% between 600 and 699. Writing-- 79% below 500, 15% between 500 and 599, and 5% between 600 and 699. The ACT scores were 27% below 12, 34% between 12 and 17, 27% between 18 and 23, 4% between 24 and 29, and 7% above 30. There were 96 National Merit finalists. 97 freshmen graduated first in their class. **Admissions Contact:** Chris Hall, Vice President for Admission and Financial Aid. Email: *inquiry@mckendree.edu* Web: *www.mckendree.edu*

FINANCIAL AID: In 2016-2017, 100% of all full-time freshmen and 96% of continuing full-time students received some form of financial aid. 94% of all full-time freshmen and 89% of continuing full-time students received need-based aid. The average freshman award was $20,472. Need-based scholarships or need-based grants averaged $17,039 ($29,920 maximum); need-based self-help aid (loans and jobs) averaged $4,093 ($11,500 maximum); and non-need-based athletic scholarships averaged $7,956 ($29,920 maximum). 22% of undergraduate students work part-time. Average annual earnings from campus work are $972. The average financial indebtedness of the 2016 graduate was $17,839. The FAFSA code is 001722. Check with the school for current application deadlines.

MILLIKIN UNIVERSITY — D-3

www.millikin.edu

Decatur, IL 62522-2084	**(217) 424-6210** **(800) 373-7733**
Fax: (217) 425-4669	**Email: admis@millikin.edu**
Full-time: 786 men, 1039 women	**Faculty:** 141; IIB, --$
Part-time: 39 men, 107 women	**Ph.D.s:** 80%
Graduate: 32 men, 53 women	**Student/Faculty:** 13 to 1
Year: semesters, summer session	**Tuition:** $31,824
Room & Board: $10,334	**Freshman Class:** 3608 applied, 2302 accepted, 448 enrolled
SAT CR/M/W: 528/477/496 **ACT:** 23	**CEEB CODE:** 1470
Application Deadline: rolling	**COMPETITIVE**

Millikin is an independent, four-year university with undergraduate programs. The signature of a Millikin University education is a unique experience called Performance Learning. When James Millikin founded the university in 1901, he did so based upon the idea of combining theory and practice. While this was a radical idea at the time, today, we know that practice is not enough. Today's students must perform their knowledge in order to be truly prepared for life after college. Millikin's students can participate in various classes, programs, projects, and performances to gain experience and the confidence to succeed. Millikin offers undergraduate programs in arts and sciences, fine arts, professional studies, and business; graduate studies in business administration, and nursing; and accelerated adult learning programs. There are 4 undergraduate schools and 2 graduate schools. In addition to regional accreditation, Millikin has baccalaureate program accreditation with ACBSP, NASM, CANAEP, CCNE, and CAATE. The 75-acre campus is in a suburban area 180 miles southwest of Chicago and 130 miles northeast of St. Louis. Including any residence halls, there are 31 buildings.

STUDENT LIFE: 84% of undergraduates are from Illinois. Others are from 33 states, 24 foreign countries, and Canada. 91% are from public schools. 71% are White; 14% African American; 6% Hispanic; 4% two or more races; 3% Foreign; 1% Asian American; 1% race unknown. **Female To Male Ratio:** 1.4:1. The average age of freshmen is 18; all undergraduates, 21. 28% do not continue beyond their first year; 61% remain to graduate. **Housing:** 1083 students can be accommodated in college housing, which includes single-sex and coed dorms, on-campus apartments, and married student housing. In addition, there are special-interest houses, fraternity houses, sorority houses, living-learning communities, and single-gender floors. On-campus housing is available on a first-come and first-served basis. 58% of students live on campus; of those, 75% remain on campus on weekends. Upperclassmen may keep cars.

FACULTY/CLASSROOMS: 46% of faculty are male; 54% are female. All teach undergraduates. No introductory courses are taught by graduate students. The average class size in an introductory lecture is 21; in a laboratory is 13; and in a regular course is 17.

PROGRAMS OF STUDY: Millikin confers B.A., B.S., B.F.A., B.M. and B.S.N. degrees. Master's and doctoral degrees are also awarded. Bachelor's degrees are awarded in AGRICULTURE (environmental studies), BIOLOGICAL SCIENCE (biochemistry, biology/adolescence education, biology/biological science, and molecular biology), BUSINESS (accounting, business administration and management, entrepreneurial studies, international business management, management science, marketing/retailing/merchandising, organizational leadership and management, recreational facilities management, and sports management), COMMUNICATIONS AND THE ARTS (acting, art, communications, digital media, dramatic arts, English, journalism, music, music business management, music performance, musical theater, performing arts, piano/organ, public relations, Spanish, sports communication, studio art, theatre arts, theater design, theatre production, theater management, visual and performing arts, and voice), COMPUTER AND PHYSICAL SCIENCE (actuarial mathematics, chemistry, chemistry/adolescence education, information sciences and systems, mathematics, and physics), EDUCATION (art education, athletic training, early childhood education, education, elementary education, English education, foreign languages education, mathematics education, music education, physical education, secondary education, and social science education), ENGINEERING AND ENVIRONMENTAL DESIGN (commercial art, computer graphics, and preengineering), HEALTH PROFESSIONS (allied health, art therapy, health and physical activity, nursing, predentistry, premedicine, preoptometry, prepharmacy, pre-physician assistant, pre-physical therapy, and preveterinary science), SOCIAL SCIENCE (ethics, politics, and social policy, history, human services, interdisciplinary studies, philosophy, political science/government, prelaw, psychology, and sociology). Music and theater are the strongest academically. Nursing, music, and theater have the largest enrollments.

ACTIVITIES: 23% of men belong to 5 national fraternities; 27% of women belong to 6 national sororities. There are 90 groups on campus, including art, band, cheerleading, chess, choir, chorale, chorus, computers, dance, debate, drama, drill team, environmental, ethnic, film, honors, international, jazz band, LGBT, literary magazine, musical theater, newspaper, opera, orchestra, pep band, photography, political, professional, radio and TV, religious, social, social service, student government, and symphony. Popular campus events include Homecoming, Fall Family Weekend, Millipalooza, University Event (big name entertainment), Halloween in the Halls, and Cookie Party. **Sports:** There are 10 intercollegiate sports for men and 9 for women, and 8 intramural sports for men and 8 for women. Facilities include 87,000-square feet indoor sports center with a 4-lane, 200-meter competitive-grade track, indoor soccer, 5 basketball/volleyball courts, batting cages, golf practice area, a climbing wall, aerobic and dance areas, and a fitness/wellness center; physical education center with a 6-lane, 25-yard pool, a 3000-seat field house with 3 regulation-sized basketball courts, a 4000-seat, recently refurbished football field encircled by 8-lane all-weather track, 2 outdoor soccer fields, additional practice fields, and tennis courts. **Graduates:** From July 1, 2015 to June 30, 2016, 453 bachelor's degrees were awarded. The most popular majors were business/marketing (24%), visual and performing arts (17%), and health professions (12%). 50 companies recruited on campus in 2015-2016. In an average class, 49% graduate in 4 years or less, 59% graduate in 5 years or less, and 60% graduate in 6 years or less. Of the 2015 graduating class, 19% were enrolled in graduate school within 6 months of graduation, and 79% were employed.

SERVICES: Counseling and information services are available, as is

tutoring in most subjects. There is a reader service for the blind. Math and writing centers, and workshops on various topics are available. **Library/Resources:** The library contains 167,802 volumes, 9,000 microform items, and 11,690 audio/video tapes/CDs/DVDs, and subscribes to 53,000 periodicals including electronic. Computerized library services include interlibrary loans, database searching, Internet access, and Wi-Fi capability. Special learning facilities include an art gallery, radio station, 32-track recording studio, computer imaging center, art museum and galleries, observatory with 20" reflecting telescope, 280-seat proscenium theater, 90-seat experimental space for student-directed productions, 3D arts building; student-owned and operated art gallery (Blue Connection), business incubator (The Hub), printing press (Carriage House Press), record label and music publishing company (First Step Records), publishing company (Bronze Man Books), and theatre company (Pipe Dreams Studio Theatre). **Physically Challenged Students:** 66% of the campus is accessible. Facilities include wheelchair ramps, elevators, special parking, specially equipped restrooms, special class scheduling, lowered drinking fountains, and special housing. **Special:** Millikin offers internships, a Washington semester through American University, study abroad in 28 countries, student-designed majors, 3-2 engineering dual degrees with Washington University and University of Missouri-Kansas City, credit by exam, and pass/fail options. Students may study multiple majors of their choice; Millikin also offers dual-degree programs. There are preprofessional programs in engineering, law, optometry, dentistry, medicine, veterinary science, occupational therapy, medical technology, physical therapy, chiropractic, physician's assistant, and pharmacy. Students are also offered a United Nations semester at Drew University and can benefit from affiliate agreements with programs such as the Institute for the International Education of Students (IES), Paris School of Business (PSB), International Teacher-Scholars Program (ITSP), Tunghai University and the Chicago Center for Urban Life and Culture semester. There are 13 national honor societies, a freshman honors program, and 20 departmental honors programs. **Visiting:** There are regularly scheduled orientations for prospective students go to. Meet with students, faculty, coaches, and staff; tour the campus facilities; and curriculum, honors, housing, and financial aid discussions/presentations. There is also an opportunity for students to audition or have portfolios reviewed. There are guides for informal visits, visitors may sit in on classes, and stay overnight. To schedule a visit, contact Office of Admission. **Campus Safety and Security:** Measures include 24-hour foot and vehicle patrol, emergency notification system, and security escort services. There are shuttle buses, emergency telephones, lighted pathways/sidewalks, and controlled access to dorms/residences.

REQUIREMENTS: The SAT or ACT is required. Applicants should be graduates of an accredited secondary school or have a GED. They should prepare with 4 units of English, 3 each of math and science, and 2 each of foreign language, social studies, and history. An audition is required for music-theater, music, or theater majors. A portfolio is required for art majors. Millikin requires applicants to be in the upper 50% of their class. A GPA of 2.5 is required. AP and CLEP credits are accepted. Important factors in the admissions decision are recommendations by school officials, advanced placement or honors courses, and leadership record. Requirements for graduation include courses in writing, math, fine arts, natural sciences, and oral communication. Sequential interdisciplinary requirements include first-year seminar, critical writing, reading, and research 1 and 2, U.S. culture studies, U.S. social structures, and global issues. Nonsequential requirements include quantitative reasoning, natural science with a lab, oral communication, creative arts, and 2 courses in international cultures and structures. The minimum GPA is 2.0 (higher for some programs); additional requirements for specific programs must be met. Students must complete a minimum of 124 credits (or more for some programs) with a minimum of 39 credits earned in courses numbered 300 or above; at least 12 credits must be in the major department or area. **Procedure:** Freshmen are admitted fall, spring, and summer. Entrance exams should be taken by May 1. There are deferred admissions and rolling admissions plans. Application deadlines are open. Notification is sent on a rolling basis. Applications are accepted on-line. **Transfer Students:** 122 transfer students enrolled in 2015-2016. Applicants are required to provide official transcripts from previous institutions and are asked to submit ACT/SAT scores. Applicants who are in good standing at the previous institution and who have earned at least a C average in all college study previously attempted will be favorably considered for admission (additional requirements for specific programs). 33 of 124 credits required for the bachelor's degree must be completed at Millikin. **International Students:** There are 52 international students enrolled. The school actively recruits these students. They must take the TOEFL with a minimum score of 550 on the paper-based TOEFL (PBT) or 79 on the Internet-based version (iBT).

ADMISSIONS: 64% of the 2016-2017 applicants were accepted. The SAT scores for the 2016-2017 freshman class were: Critical Reading-- 34% below 500, 47% between 500 and 599, and 19% between 600 and 699. Math-- 71% below 500, 19% between 500 and 599, and 10% between 600 and 699. Writing-- 52% below 500, 32% between 500 and 599, and 16% between 600 and 699. The ACT scores were 8% between 12 and 17, 52% between 18 and 23, 32% between 24 and 29, and 8% above 30. 30% of the current freshmen were in the top fifth of their class; 57% were in the top two fifths. 9 freshmen graduated first in their class. **Admissions Contact:** Kevin McIntyre, Dean of Admission. Email: *admis@millikin.edu* Web: *www.millikin.edu*

FINANCIAL AID: In 2016-2017, 100% of all full-time freshmen and 98% of continuing full-time students received some form of financial aid. 88% of all full-time freshmen and 84% of continuing full-time students received need-based aid. The average freshman award was $24,230. Need-based scholarships or need-based grants averaged $9,192; need-based self-help aid (loans and jobs) averaged $4,533; and other non-need-based awards and non-need-based scholarships averaged $13,705. 48% of undergraduate students work part-time. Average annual earnings from campus work are $615. The average financial indebtedness of the 2016 graduate was $34,225. The FAFSA code is 001724. The priority date for freshman financial aid applications for fall entry is January 6.

MONMOUTH COLLEGE C-2

www.monmouthcollege.edu

Monmouth, IL 61462	(309) 457-2210 (800) 747-2687
Fax: (309) 457-2141	**Email:** admissions@monmouthcollege.edu
Full-time: 561 men, 618 women	**Faculty:** 92; IIB, -$
Part-time: 6 men, 13 women	**Ph.D.s:** 88%
Graduate: n/av	**Student/Faculty:** 11 to 1
Year: semesters	**Tuition:** $34,200
Room & Board: $8060	**Freshman Class:** 2657 applied, 1658 accepted, 272 enrolled
SAT: required **ACT:** 23	**CEEB CODE:** 1484
Application Deadline: rolling	**COMPETITIVE**

Monmouth College, founded in 1853, is a selective, residential, private liberal arts and sciences college. There is 1 undergraduate school. In addition to regional accreditation, Monmouth College has baccalaureate program accreditation with ACS. The 112-acre campus is in a small town in west-central Illinois, 20 miles east of the Mississippi River, and 45 miles south of Rock Island and Moline. Including any residence halls, there are 39 buildings.

STUDENT LIFE: 89% of undergraduates are from Illinois. Others are from 26 states, 22 foreign countries, and Canada. 61% are White; 13% Hispanic; 9% African American; 7% Foreign; 5% race unknown; 2% Asian American; 2% two or more races; 1% American Indian/Alaska Native. 53% claim no religious affiliation; 30% Protestant; 17% Catholic. **Female To Male Ratio:** 1.1:1. The average age of freshmen is 18; all undergraduates, 20. 26% do not continue beyond their first year; 56% remain to graduate. **Housing:** 1435 students can be accommodated in college housing, which includes single-sex and coed dorms and on-campus apartments. In addition, there are honors houses, special-interest houses, fraternity houses, and sorority houses. On-campus housing is guaranteed for all 4 years. 92% of students live on campus; of those, 75% remain on campus on weekends. All students may keep cars.

FACULTY/CLASSROOMS: 56% of faculty are male; 44% are female. All teach undergraduates, and all do research. No introductory courses are taught by graduate students. The average class size in an introductory lecture is 22; in a laboratory is 12; and in a regular course is 15.

PROGRAMS OF STUDY: Monmouth College confers B.A. degrees. Bachelor's degrees are awarded in BIOLOGICAL SCIENCE (biochemistry and biology/biological science), BUSINESS (accounting, business administration and management, and international business management), COMMUNICATIONS AND THE ARTS (art, classics, communications, dramatic arts, English, French, Greek, Latin, music, and Spanish), COMPUTER AND PHYSICAL SCIENCE (chemistry, computer programming, computer science, mathematics, and physics),

EDUCATION (elementary education, physical education, and secondary education), ENGINEERING AND ENVIRONMENTAL DESIGN (environmental science), HEALTH PROFESSIONS (exercise science), SOCIAL SCIENCE (anthropology, biopsychology, economics, history, international studies, philosophy, political science/government, psychology, religion, and sociology). English, classics (Greek and Latin), history, and chemistry are the strongest academically. Business, communications, and psychology have the largest enrollments.

ACTIVITIES: 18% of men belong to 4 national fraternities; 34% of women belong to 3 national sororities. There are 70 groups on campus, including art, bagpipe, band, cheerleading, chess, choir, chorale, chorus, computers, dance, debate, drama, environmental, ethnic, film, forensics, honors, international, jazz band, LGBT, literary magazine, marching band, musical theater, newspaper, orchestra, pep band, photography, political, professional, radio and TV, religious, social, social service, and student government. Popular campus events include Homecoming, Scots Day (Founders Day) and Parents Weekend. **Sports:** There are 11 intercollegiate sports for men and 11 for women, and 14 intramural sports for men and 14 for women. The Huff Athletic Center includes gym, indoor and outdoor track, all-purpose indoor courts, indoor batting cages, natatorium, 6-court tennis stadium, weight room, fitness/wellness center, dance studio, football, baseball, soccer, and softball fields, sand volleyball court, climbing wall, sauna, and steam room. **Graduates:** From July 1, 2015 to June 30, 2016, 269 bachelor's degrees were awarded. The most popular majors were business management (20%), communication/journalism (14%), and social sciences (10%). In an average class, 48% graduate in 4 years or less, 55% graduate in 5 years or less, and 56% graduate in 6 years or less. Of the 2015 graduating class, 26% were enrolled in graduate school within 6 months of graduation, and 74% were employed.

SERVICES: Counseling and information services are available, as is tutoring in most subjects, such as accounting, biology, chemistry, education, math/statistics, Spanish, French, business/economics, psychology, and sociolgy/anthropology. There is a reader service for the blind, and remedial math, reading, and writing. Individualized academic-support services available to students who seek assistance including one-on-one tutoring and small-group and group tutoring. **Library/Resources:** The library contains 356,564 volumes, 237,283 microform items, and 12,511 audio/video tapes/CDs/DVDs, and subscribes to 28,190 periodicals including electronic. Computerized library services include interlibrary loans, database searching, Internet access, and Wi-Fi capability. Special learning facilities include an art gallery, planetarium, radio station, and TV station. Monmouth College has a prairie-habitat biology field station, Spring Grove Prairie, a freshwater pond for field research on amphibians and reptiles, an educational garden (and a farm under development), the Le Suer Nature Preserve, the James Christie Shields Collection of Art and Antiquities housed in the Len G. Everett Galleries, the Lewis L. Gould U.S. First Ladies letter collection, and the region's largest collection of Western Illinois Native American artifacts, and archeology lab. Hewes Library is a federal government documents repository. **Physically Challenged Students:** 98% of the campus is accessible. Facilities include wheelchair ramps, elevators, special parking, specially equipped restrooms, special class scheduling, lowered drinking fountains, lowered telephones, and special housing. **Special:** Monmouth has agreements with Rush University, Chicago, for nursing, occupational therapy, and medical technology; and 5- and 6-year coordinated degree partnerships (Masters) with Case Western Reserve (engineering), the University of Southern California (engineering), and Creighton University (atmospheric science). Students have the opportunity to study in more than 25 countries in Europe, Asia, Central and South America, and Africa, as well as in programs within the United States. All Associated Colleges of the Midwest (ACM) programs, as well as internships, a Washington semester, and dual and student-designed majors are available. There are 13 national honor societies, a freshman honors program, and 20 departmental honors programs. **Visiting:** There are regularly scheduled orientations for prospective students, including tours, admissions and financial aid discussions, faculty appointments, lunch and entertainment, and a talk with the president. There are guides for informal visits, visitors may sit in on classes, and stay overnight. To schedule a visit, contact Maria Godina at admissions@monmouthcollege.edu. **Campus Safety and Security:** Measures include 24-hour foot and vehicle patrol, emergency notification system, self-defense education, and security escort services. There are shuttle buses, emergency telephones, lighted pathways/sidewalks, controlled access to dorms/residences, and key cards that are required for entrance to all residence halls.

REQUIREMENTS: The SAT or ACT is required. A score of at least 22 on the ACT is highly recommended. Applicants must be graduates of accredited high schools with a GPA of 2.5. We strongly recommend that applicants have completed 4 years of English, 2 years each of math, social studies, and science, including 1 year of lab, 2 years of foreign language, and at least 1 year of history. We accept the GED. A GPA of 2.5 is required. AP credits are accepted. Important factors in the admissions decision are advanced placement or honors courses, evidence of special talent, and extracurricular activities record. To graduate, all students must complete 32 course credits (equivalent to 128 credit hours) with a minimum GPA of 2.0. A major program must be completed with a minimum of C in all courses. Students must also fulfill 9 courses within the general education program, including an art course, science course with lab and language course(s). Students must successfully complete the integrated studies curriculum (one course per year) within the general education program. A topical major (of the student's design) is also possible. **Procedure:** Freshmen are admitted fall and spring. Entrance exams should be taken by the spring of the junior year. There are early admissions, deferred admissions, and rolling admissions plans. Application deadlines are open. Notification is sent on a rolling basis. Applications are accepted on-line. **Transfer Students:** Students must have a minimum GPA of 2.5. A satisfactory score of at least 19 on the ACT is recommended. 64 of 128 credits required for the bachelor's degree must be completed at Monmouth College. **International Students:** There are 54 international students enrolled. The school actively recruits these students. They must also take the SAT or ACT.

ADMISSIONS: 62% of the 2016-2017 applicants were accepted. The ACT scores were 5% between 12 and 17, 55% between 18 and 23, 33% between 24 and 29, and 7% above 30. 27% of the current freshmen were in the top fifth of their class; 56% were in the top two fifths. **Admissions Contact:** Trent Gilbert, VP Enrollment Management. Email: *admissions@monmouthcollege.edu* Web: *www.monmouthcollege.edu*

FINANCIAL AID: In 2016-2017, 100% of all full-time freshmen and 100% of continuing full-time students received some form of financial aid. 94% of all full-time freshmen and 91% of continuing full-time students received need-based aid. The average freshman award was $34,600. Need-based scholarships or need-based grants averaged $26,884; need-based self-help aid (loans and jobs) averaged $4,777; other non-need-based awards and non-need-based scholarships averaged $3,241; and $2,485 from other forms of aid. 51% of undergraduate students work part-time. Average annual earnings from campus work are $1400. The average financial indebtedness of the 2016 graduate was $29,238. The FAFSA code is 001725. The priority date for freshman financial aid applications for fall entry is February 1. The deadline for filing freshman financial aid applications for fall entry is May 1.

NATIONAL LOUIS UNIVERSITY *(The complete profile is made available exclusively on our website, www.barronspac.com)*

NORTH CENTRAL COLLEGE — E-2

www.northcentralcollege.edu

Naperville, IL 60540	**(630) 637-5800** **(800) 411-1861**
Fax: (630) 637-5819	**Email: admissions@noctrl.edu**
Full-time: 1091 men, 1469 women	**Faculty:** 130; IIA, av$
Part-time: 90 men, 105 women	**Ph.D.s:** 89%
Graduate: 140 men, 147 women	**Student/Faculty:** 20 to 1
Year: quarters, summer session	**Tuition:** $37,054
Room & Board: $11,658	**Freshman Class:** 3987 applied, 2401 accepted, 552 enrolled
ACT: 24	**CEEB CODE:** 1555
Application Deadline: February 20	**VERY COMPETITIVE**

North Central College, founded in 1861, is a private comprehensive liberal arts institution affiliated with the United Methodist Church. The college is highly selective, primarily residential, and primarily full-time undergraduate. There is 1 undergraduate school and 1 graduate school. In addition to regional accreditation, North Central has baccalaureate program accreditation with CAATE and ACS. The 64-acre campus is in a suburban area 30 miles west of Chicago. Including any residence halls, there are 42 buildings.

STUDENT LIFE: 93% of undergraduates are from Illinois. Others are from 30 states, 22 foreign countries, and Canada. 90% are from public schools. 8% are Hispanic; 79% White; 4% African American; 2% Asian American; 1% Foreign. 56% are Protestant; 34% Catholic. **Female To Male Ratio:** 1.3:1. The average age of freshmen is 18; all undergraduates, 21. 20% do not continue beyond their first year; 66% remain to graduate. **Housing:** 1537 students can be accommodated in college housing, which includes single-sex and coed dorms, on-campus apartments, and off-campus apartments, and substance free housing. On-campus housing is available on a lottery system for upperclassmen. 54% of students live on campus; of those, 90% remain on campus on weekends. All students may keep cars.

FACULTY/CLASSROOMS: 53% of faculty are male; 47% are female. All teach undergraduates. No introductory courses are taught by graduate students. The average class size in an introductory lecture is 24; in a laboratory is 20; and in a regular course is 22.

PROGRAMS OF STUDY: North Central confers B.A. and B.S. degrees. Master's degrees are also awarded. Bachelor's degrees are awarded in BIOLOGICAL SCIENCE (biochemistry and biology/biological science), BUSINESS (accounting, business administration and management, finance, human resources, international business management, marketing/retailing/merchandising, and sports management), COMMUNICATIONS AND THE ARTS (art history, art, broadcasting, Chinese, communications, English, English literature, English Writing, French, German, Japanese, jazz, journalism, music, Spanish, speech/debate/rhetoric, studio art, and theatre arts), COMPUTER AND PHYSICAL SCIENCE (actuarial science, applied mathematics, chemistry, computer science, mathematics, and physics), EDUCATION (art education, athletic training, elementary education, music education, and secondary education), ENGINEERING AND ENVIRONMENTAL DESIGN (graphic arts technology and preengineering), HEALTH PROFESSIONS (exercise science, nuclear medical technology, predentistry, premedicine, preveterinary science, and radiation therapy), SOCIAL SCIENCE (anthropology, classical/ancient civilization, East Asian studies, economics, history, philosophy, political science/government, prelaw, psychology, religion, social science, and sociology). Business and education have the largest enrollment.

ACTIVITIES: There are no fraternities or sororities. There are 60 groups on campus, including art, band, cheerleading, choir, chorale, chorus, dance, drama, environmental, ethnic, forensics, honors, international, jazz band, LGBT, literary magazine, musical theater, newspaper, pep band, photography, political, professional, radio and TV, religious, social, social service, and student government. Popular campus events include Springfest, Winter Comedy Series, and Honors Day. **Sports:** There are 10 intercollegiate sports for men and 10 for women, and 12 intramural sports for men and 12 for women. Facilities include indoor and outdoor tracks, recreation center, weight room, football and baseball stadiums, soccer fields, swimming pool, tennis courts, athletic training facility, and a human performance lab. **Graduates:** From July 1, 2015 to June 30, 2016, 582 bachelor's degrees were awarded. The most popular majors were psychology (7%), marketing (6%), and elementary education (6%). In an average class, 1% graduate in 3 years or less, 57% graduate in 4 years or less, 66% graduate in 5 years or less, and 68% graduate in 6 years or less.

SERVICES: Counseling and information services are available, as is tutoring in most subjects. There is a reader service for the blind, and remedial math. There is limited technology for students with disabilities. **Library/Resources:** The library contains 138,968 volumes, 105,494 microform items, and 4,405 audio/video tapes/CDs/DVDs, and subscribes to 11,821 periodicals including electronic. Computerized library services include interlibrary loans, database searching, and Internet access. Special learning facilities include an art gallery, radio station, a foreign language lab, academic support services center, and a writing center. **Physically Challenged Students:** 90% of the campus is accessible. Facilities include wheelchair ramps, elevators, special parking, specially equipped restrooms, special class scheduling, lowered drinking fountains, lowered telephones, and special housing. **Special:** North Central offers co-op programs in radiation therapy, nuclear medicine technology, and chemical microscopy; cross-registration with Benedictine University and Aurora University, a Washington semester, and study abroad. Internships in most subject areas, a 3-2 engineering degree with the Universities of Minnesota and Illinois at Urbana-Champaign, experiential credit, and nondegree study are available. Dual majors, student-designed majors, and 5-year integrated Bachelor's/Master's degree programs are available. There are 18 national honor societies, a freshman honors program, and 14 departmental honors programs. **Visiting:** There are regularly scheduled orientations for prospective students, including the opportunity to hear a presentation about academic programs, student life, admission guidelines, and financial aid. Campus tours, faculty presentations, and coaches are also available. There are guides for informal visits, visitors may sit in on classes, and stay overnight. To schedule a visit, contact the Office of Admissions at admissions@noctrl.edu. **Campus Safety and Security:** Measures include 24-hour foot and vehicle patrol, emergency notification system, self-defense education, and security escort services. There are emergency telephones, lighted pathways/sidewalks, and controlled access to dorms/residences.

REQUIREMENTS: The ACT is required, with a minimum of 20 on the ACT or 940 on the SAT. Minimum requirements also include a GPA of at least 2.5 and involvement in school and/or community. An admission essay and/or admission interview may be recommended. The GED is accepted. The recommended secondary school courses are 4 years of English and 3 years each of math, science, social science, and foreign language. A GPA of 2.5 is required. AP and CLEP credits are accepted. All students must complete a general education core, including 9 hours in humanities and fine arts, 9 hours in social sciences, 6.5 hours in life and physical sciences, 3 to 6 hours in composition, and 3 hours each in speech communication and math. All freshmen must complete an interdisciplinary course. In addition, all students take an intercultural seminar, a leadership, ethics, and values seminar, and a course in religion and ethics. A GPA of 2.0 and a total of 120 credit hours are required for graduation, with 27 to 51 credits taken in the major. Students in the College Scholars program must complete an Honor Thesis. **Procedure:** Freshmen are admitted to all sessions. Entrance exams should be taken in the spring of the junior year or the fall of the senior year. There are deferred admissions and rolling admissions plans. Application deadlines are open. Application fee is $25. Applications are accepted on-line. **Transfer Students:** 360 transfer students enrolled in 2015-2016. Applicants need a minimum 2.5 transferrable GPA or better and 27 transferrable semester hours. If they have not earned 27 transferrable hours, their high school transcripts and ACT/SAT scores are also considered. Students can be considered for admission with a college grade point average of 2.25 or above. 30 of 120 credits required for the bachelor's degree must be completed at North Central. **International Students:** There are 28 international students enrolled. The school actively recruits these students. They must take the TOEFL with a minimum score of 520 on the paper-based TOEFL (PBT) or 68 on the Internet-based version (iBT), or take the IELTS.

ADMISSIONS: 60% of the 2016-2017 applicants were accepted. The ACT scores were 11% below 12, 30% between 12 and 17, 31% between 18 and 23, 15% between 24 and 29, and 13% above 30. 47% of the current freshmen were in the top fifth of their class; 78% were in the top two fifths. 5 freshmen graduated first in their class. **Admissions Contact:** Marty Sauer, Dean of Admission and Financial Aid. Email: *admissions@noctrl.edu* Web: *www.northcentralcollege.edu*

FINANCIAL AID: In 2016-2017, 99% of all full-time freshmen and 98% of continuing full-time students received some form of financial aid. 80% of all full-time freshmen and 76% of continuing full-time students received need-based aid. The average freshman award was $28,066. Need-based scholarships or need-based grants averaged $6,140; need-based self-help aid (loans and jobs) averaged $2,418; other non-need-based awards and non-need-based scholarships averaged $12,966; and $6,542 from other forms of aid. The average financial indebtedness of the 2016 graduate was $25,644. The college's own financial statement is required. The FAFSA code is 001734. Check with the school for current application deadlines.

NORTH PARK UNIVERSITY — E-2

www.northpark.edu

Chicago, IL 60625

(773) 244-5500
(800) 888-6728
Email: admissions@northpark.edu

Full-time: 699 men, 1070 women
Part-time: 158 men, 297 women
Graduate: 322 men, 683 women
Year: semesters, summer session
Room & Board: $8770

SAT CR/M: 530/500 **ACT:** 22
Application Deadline: April 1

Faculty: 108
Ph.D.s: 90%
Student/Faculty: 18 to 1
Tuition: $27,090
Freshman Class: 1864 applied, 1618 accepted, 425 enrolled
CEEB CODE: 1556
COMPETITIVE

North Park University, founded in 1891, is a private comprehensive university affiliated with the Evangelical Covenant Church offering undergraduate and graduate education liberal arts, professional, and theological programs. The figures in the above capsule and in this profile are approximate. There are 6 undergraduate schools and 5 graduate schools. In addition to regional accreditation, North Park has baccalaureate program accreditation with NLN, ATS, CCNE, IACBE, and NASM. The 30-acre campus is in an urban area 10 miles northwest of downtown Chicago. Including any residence halls, there are 30 buildings.

STUDENT LIFE: 66% of undergraduates are from Illinois. Others are from 40 states, 28 foreign countries, and Canada. 8% are African American; 6% Asian American; 6% Foreign; 58% White; 11% Hispanic. 33% are Protestant; 20% Catholic; 20% claim no religious affiliation. **Female To Male Ratio:** 1.7:1. The average age of freshmen is 18; all undergraduates, 21. 23% do not continue beyond their first year; 58% remain to graduate. **Housing:** 1130 students can be accommodated in college housing, which includes single-sex dorms, on-campus apartments, and off-campus apartments. In addition, there are special-interest houses. On-campus housing is guaranteed for all 4 years. Priority is given to out-of-town students. 50% of students commute. Alcohol is not permitted. Upperclassmen may keep cars.

FACULTY/CLASSROOMS: 47% of faculty are male; 53% are female. All teach undergraduates. No introductory courses are taught by graduate students. The average class size in an introductory lecture is 25; in a laboratory is 25; and in a regular course is 18.

PROGRAMS OF STUDY: North Park confers B.A., B.S., B.Mus., B.S.N., B.G.S., and B.M.E. degrees. Master's and doctoral degrees are also awarded. Bachelor's degrees are awarded in BIOLOGICAL SCIENCE (biology/biological science), BUSINESS (accounting, banking and finance, business administration and management, international business management, and marketing/retailing/merchandising), COMMUNICATIONS AND THE ARTS (advertising, communications, English, French, music, music theory and composition, Scandinavian languages, and Spanish), COMPUTER AND PHYSICAL SCIENCE (chemistry, mathematics, and physics), EDUCATION (athletic training, early childhood education, elementary education, and secondary education), ENGINEERING AND ENVIRONMENTAL DESIGN (environmental science), HEALTH PROFESSIONS (exercise science, medical laboratory technology, nursing, physical therapy, predentistry, and premedicine), SOCIAL SCIENCE (African studies, anthropology, biblical studies, criminal justice, economics, French studies, history, international relations, philosophy, political science/government, prelaw, psychology, sociology, and youth ministry). Sciences, nursing, education, and liberal arts are the strongest academically. Business has the largest enrollment.

ACTIVITIES: There are no fraternities or sororities. There are 25 groups on campus, including art, band, cheerleading, choir, chorale, chorus, communications, computers, drama, environmental, ethnic, honors, international, jazz band, literary magazine, musical theater, newspaper, opera, orchestra, pep band, photography, political, professional, religious, social, social service, student government, symphony, and yearbook. Popular campus events include Dances, Concerts, and Film Festivals. **Sports:** There are 7 intercollegiate sports for men and 8 for women, and 5 intramural sports for men and 5 for women. Facilities include football, baseball, track, and soccer fields, tennis courts, a weight room, a gym, and a fitness center. **Graduates:** From July 1, 2015 to June 30, 2016, 481 bachelor's degrees were awarded. The most popular majors were business and marketing (23%), health and related programs (22%), and communication (8%). In an average class, 39% graduate in 4 years or less, 52% graduate in 5 years or less, and 58% graduate in 6 years or less.

SERVICES: Counseling and information services are available, as is tutoring in every subject. There is a reader service for the blind, and remedial math, reading, and writing. An extended orientation program is available. **Library/Resources:** The library contains 225,000 volumes, 93,000 microform items, and 6,500 audio/video tapes/CDs/DVDs, and subscribes to 995 periodicals including electronic. Computerized library services include interlibrary loans, database searching, Internet access, and Wi-Fi capability. Special learning facilities include an art gallery. **Physically Challenged Students:** 90% of the campus is accessible. Facilities include wheelchair ramps, elevators, special parking, specially equipped restrooms, lowered drinking fountains, lowered telephones, and special housing. **Special:** Opportunities are provided for a co-op program in occupational therapy, internships, work-study, a Washington semester, 3-2 engineering degrees, accelerated degree programs in organization management and nursing, credit by examination, dual majors, student-designed majors, B.A.-B.S. degrees, pass/fail options, and study abroad. There are 6 national honor societies, a freshman honors program, and 5 departmental honors programs. **Visiting:** There are regularly scheduled orientations for prospective students. There are guides for informal visits, visitors may sit in on classes, and stay overnight. To schedule a visit, contact the Campus Visit Counselor at (773) 244-5511. **Campus Safety and Security:** Measures include 24-hour foot and vehicle patrol, emergency notification system, self-defense education, and security escort services. There are emergency telephones, lighted pathways/sidewalks, and controlled access to dorms/residences.

REQUIREMENTS: The SAT or ACT and ACT Writing Test are recommended. Graduation from an accredited secondary school is required; a GED will be accepted. Students should have completed course-work in a foreign language, 4 years of English, and 3 years each of math, science, and social studies. A recommendation from a teacher is required. An essay is required. An interview is recommended and sometimes required. A GPA of 2.8 is required. AP and CLEP credits are accepted. Important factors in the admissions decision are evidence of special talent, personality/intangible qualities, and extracurricular activities record. Students must successfully complete 120 semester hours with a minimum 2.0 GPA. The required number of hours in the major varies. Students must meet a general education requirement of 46 semester hours. **Procedure:** Freshmen are admitted fall and winter. Entrance exams should be taken during spring of the junior year or fall of the senior year. There is a rolling admissions plan. Applications should be filed by April 1 for fall entry; December 15 for winter entry, along with a $40 fee. Applications are accepted on-line. **Transfer Students:** 300 transfer students enrolled in 2015-2016. To be eligible for transfer admission, students must submit 1 letter of recommendation and official transcripts from the previous college and must have maintained a minimum GPA of 2.5. An interview is also recommended. 30 of 120 credits required for the bachelor's degree must be completed at North Park. **International Students:** There are 100 international students enrolled. The school actively recruits these students. They must take the TOEFL with a minimum score of 550 on the paper-based TOEFL (PBT) or 80 on the Internet-based version (iBT) and the college's own test.

ADMISSIONS: 87% of the 2016-2017 applicants were accepted. The SAT scores for the 2016-2017 freshman class were: Critical Reading-- 33% below 500, 49% between 500 and 599, 17% between 600 and 699, and 1% between 700 and 800. Math-- 40% below 500, 43% between 500 and 599, 14% between 600 and 699, and 3% between 700 and 800. The ACT scores were 41% below 12, 25% between 12 and 17, 16% between 18 and 23, 9% between 24 and 29, and 9% above 30. 32% of the current freshmen were in the top fifth of their class; 61% were in the top two fifths. **Admissions Contact:** Mark Olson, Acting Director Undergraduate Admission. Email: *admissions@northpark.edu* Web: *www.northpark.edu*

FINANCIAL AID: In 2016-2017, 98% of all full-time freshmen and 95% of continuing full-time students received some form of financial aid. 79% of all full-time freshmen received need-based aid. 20% of undergraduate students work part-time. Average annual earnings from campus work are $2000. The average financial indebtedness of the 2016 graduate was $28,467. The FAFSA code is 001735. The priority date for freshman financial aid applications for fall entry is March 1. The deadline for filing freshman financial aid applications for fall entry is August 15.

NORTHEASTERN ILLINOIS UNIVERSITY *(The complete profile is made available exclusively on our website, www.barronspac.com)*

NORTHERN ILLINOIS UNIVERSITY D-2

www.niu.edu

DeKalb, IL 60115	(815) 753-0446
Fax: (815) 753-1783	**Email:** admissions@niu.edu
Full-time: 8044 men, 8308 women	**Faculty:** 922; I
Part-time: 900 men, 1025 women	**Ph.D.s:** 83%
Graduate: 2635 men, 3512 women	**Student/Faculty:** 18 to 1
Year: semesters, summer session	**Tuition:** $10,588 ($17,440)
Room & Board: $9588	**Freshman Class:** 17787 applied, 10409 accepted, 3033 enrolled
ACT: 22	**CEEB CODE:** 1559
Application Deadline: August 1	**COMPETITIVE**

Northern Illinois University, founded in 1895, is a publicly funded institution offering undergraduate and graduate programs in a comprehensive range of disciplines. There are 6 undergraduate schools and 2 graduate schools. The figures in the above capsule and in this profile are approximate. In addition to regional accreditation, NIU has baccalaureate program accreditation with AACSB, ABET, ACEJMC, APTA, ASLA, CAHEA, NASAD, NASM, NCATE, and NLN. The 755-acre campus is in a small town 65 miles west of Chicago. Including any residence halls, there are 55 buildings.

STUDENT LIFE: 95% of undergraduates are from Illinois. Others are from 50 states, 95 foreign countries, and Canada. 84% are from public schools. 73% are White; 7% Hispanic; 6% Asian American; 13% African American; 1% Foreign. **Female To Male Ratio:** 1.1:1. The average age of freshmen is 18; all undergraduates, 22. 22% do not continue beyond their first year; 78% remain to graduate. **Housing:** 5800 students can be accommodated in college housing, which includes single-sex and coed dorms, on-campus apartments, and married student housing. In addition, there are honors houses, language houses, and special-interest houses, such as computer science, law, music, political science, and health professions. On-campus housing is guaranteed for the freshman year only, and is available on a first-come, first-served basis. 67% of students live on campus; of those, 60% remain on campus on weekends. All students may keep cars.

FACULTY/CLASSROOMS: 54% of faculty are male; 46% are female. Graduate students teach 20% of introductory courses. The average class size in an introductory lecture is 37; in a laboratory is 17; and in a regular course is 30.

PROGRAMS OF STUDY: NIU confers B.A., B.S., B.F.A., B.G.S., B.M., and B.S.Ed. degrees. Master's and doctoral degrees are also awarded. Bachelor's degrees are awarded in BIOLOGICAL SCIENCE (biology/biological science and nutrition), BUSINESS (accounting, banking and finance, business administration and management, and marketing/retailing/merchandising), COMMUNICATIONS AND THE ARTS (art, art history and appreciation, communications, dramatic arts, English, French, German, journalism, music, Russian, Spanish, and studio art), COMPUTER AND PHYSICAL SCIENCE (atmospheric sciences and meteorology, chemistry, computer science, geology, geoscience, information sciences and systems, mathematics, and physics), EDUCATION (art education, early childhood education, elementary education, health education, music education, physical education, and special education), ENGINEERING AND ENVIRONMENTAL DESIGN (electrical/electronics engineering, industrial engineering, mechanical engineering, and technological management), HEALTH PROFESSIONS (clinical science, community health work, health science, nursing, and speech pathology/audiology), SOCIAL SCIENCE (anthropology, child care/child and family studies, dietetics, early childhood studies, economics, geography, history, liberal arts/general studies, philosophy, physical fitness/movement, political science/government, psychology, sociology, and textiles and clothing). Business, engineering, and sciences are the strongest academically. Business, education, and communications have the largest enrollments.

ACTIVITIES: 15% of men belong to 22 national fraternities; 11% of women belong to 15 national sororities. There are 200 groups on campus, including art, band, cheerleading, chess, choir, chorale, chorus, computers, dance, drama, drill team, ethnic, film, honors, international, jazz band, LGBT, literary magazine, marching band, musical theater, newspaper, orchestra, pep band, photography, political, professional, radio and TV, religious, social, social service, student government, and symphony. Popular campus events include Unity in Diversity Week, Greek Week, and Springfest. **Sports:** There are 8 intercollegiate sports for men and 8 for women, and 15 intramural sports for men and 15 for women. Facilities include a sports stadium, a recreation center, a field house with facilities for basketball, volleyball, badminton, table tennis, tennis, racquetball/handball, and weight training, and swimming pools. **Graduates:** From July 1, 2015 to June 30, 2016, 4027 bachelor's degrees were awarded. The most popular majors were teacher education (7%), communication studies (6%), and accountancy (6%). 800 companies recruited on campus in 2015-2016. In an average class, 47% graduate in 5 years or less and 48% graduate in 6 years or less. Of the 2015 graduating class, 19% were enrolled in graduate school within 6 months of graduation.

SERVICES: Formal tutoring is provided for eligible students. **Library/Resources:** The 4 libraries contain 2.2 million volumes, 3.6 million microform items, and 59,076 audio/video tapes/CDs/DVDs, and subscribe to 32,722 periodicals including electronic. Computerized library services include interlibrary loans and database searching. Special learning facilities include an art gallery, radio station, TV station, and anthropology museum. **Physically Challenged Students:** 85% of the campus is accessible. Facilities include wheelchair ramps, elevators, special parking, specially equipped restrooms, special class scheduling, lowered drinking fountains, lowered telephones, and special housing. **Special:** NIU offers internships in several areas. Students may study abroad in 30 countries. A physics/engineering degree is offered in cooperation with the University of Illinois. Either a B.A. or a B.S. may be obtained in the social science programs. Work-study programs, a general studies degree, co-op programs, pass/fail options, and student-designed majors are available. There are 5 national honor societies, a freshman honors program, and 18 departmental honors programs. **Visiting:** There are regularly scheduled orientations for prospective students, including open house programs, bus tours, faculty meetings, residence hall tours, and department receptions. There are guides for informal visits, visitors may sit in on classes, and stay overnight. To schedule a visit, contact the Office of Orientation and Student Assistance at (815) 753-1535. **Campus Safety and Security:** Measures include 24-hour foot and vehicle patrol, self-defense education, and security escort services. There are shuttle buses, emergency telephones, lighted pathways/sidewalks, and a bicycle patrol.

REQUIREMENTS: Students must have a minimum score of 19 on the ACT, and be in the top half of their class, or have an ACT score of 23 and be in the upper two-thirds of their class. Graduation from an accredited secondary school or satisfactory scores on the GED are required for admission. Secondary school courses must include 4 years of English and 2 to 3 years each of math, science, and social studies. In addition, students must have completed 1 to 2 years of art, film, foreign language, music, or theater. NIU requires applicants to be in the upper 50% of their class. AP and CLEP credits are accepted. To graduate, students must have a minimum of 124 credit hours and a minimum GPA of 2.0. All students must take English 103 and 104 and Communication Studies 100. In addition, they must take Math 101 or obtain at least a C in Math 155, 201, 206, 210, 211, or 229. The school also requires that students complete 29 hours in distributive studies areas, consisting of 9 to 12 hours in the humanities and arts, 7 to 11 hours in science and math, 6 to 9 hours in social science, and 3 to 6 hours in interdisciplinary studies. **Procedure:** Freshmen are admitted to all sessions. Entrance exams should be taken during the junior year. There is a rolling admissions plan. Applications should be filed by August 1 for fall entry. The fall 2016 application fee was $30. Applications are accepted on-line. **Transfer Students:** 2248 transfer students enrolled in 2015-2016. Transfer students with 24 or more credit hours must have a minimum GPA of 2.0. The core competency requirement in English, math, and speech must be satisfied by all transfer students. 30 of 124 credits required for the bachelor's degree must be completed at NIU. **International Students:** They must take the TOEFL with a minimum score of 527 on the paper-based TOEFL (PBT) or 71 on the Internet-based version (iBT).

ADMISSIONS: 59% of the 2016-2017 applicants were accepted. The ACT scores were 37% below 12, 30% between 12 and 17, 21% between 18 and 23, 7% between 24 and 29, and 5% above 30. 23% of the current freshmen were in the top fifth of their class; 54% were in the top two fifths. **Admissions Contact:** Brandon Lagana, Director of Admissions. Email: *admissions@niu.edu* Web: *www.niu.edu*

FINANCIAL AID: In 2016-2017, 85% of all full-time freshmen and 75% of continuing full-time students received some form of financial aid. 67% of all full-time freshmen and 58% of continuing full-time students received need-based aid. 12% of undergraduate students work part-time. Average annual earnings from campus work are $1722. The average financial indebtedness of the 2016 graduate was $16,838. The college's own financial statement is required. The FAFSA code is 001737. The priority date for freshman financial aid applications for fall entry is March 1.

NORTHWESTERN UNIVERSITY — E-2

www.northwestern.edu

Evanston, IL 60208 — **(847) 491-7271**

Email: ug-admission@northwestern.edu

Full-time: 4100 men, 4058 women	**Faculty:** I, ++$
Part-time: 78 men, 78 women	**Ph.D.s:** 100%
Graduate: 6935 men, 5706 women	**Student/Faculty:** 7 to 1
Year: quarters, summer session	**Tuition:** $50,855
Room & Board: $15,489	**Freshman Class:** n/av
SAT or ACT: required	**CEEB CODE:** 1565
Application Deadline: January 1	**MOST COMPETITIVE**

Northwestern University combines innovative teaching and pioneering research in a highly collaborative environment that transcends traditional academic boundaries. It provides students and faculty with exceptional opportunities for intellectual, personal and professional growth in three richly unique settings: Chicago, Evanston and Doha, Qatar. Northwestern is committed to excellent teaching, innovative research, and the personal and intellectual growth of its students in a diverse academic community. There are 6 undergraduate schools and 7 graduate schools. In addition to regional accreditation, Northwestern has baccalaureate program accreditation with AACSB, ABET, ACEJMC, APTA, and NASM. The 240-acre campus is in a suburban area 12 miles north of Chicago on the shores of Lake Michigan. Including any residence halls, there are 180 buildings.

STUDENT LIFE: 72% of undergraduates are from out of state, mostly the Midwest. Students are from 50 states, 78 foreign countries, and Canada. 68% are from public schools. 50% are White; 17% Asian American; 11% Hispanic; 9% Foreign; 6% African American; 5% two or more races; 1% American Indian/Alaska Native; 1% race unknown. **Male To Female Ratio:** 1.1:1. The average age of freshmen is 18; all undergraduates, 20. 3% do not continue beyond their first year; 93% remain to graduate. **Housing:** College-sponsored housing includes single-sex and coed dorms and off-campus apartments. In addition, there are special-interest houses, fraternity houses, and sorority houses. On-campus housing is guaranteed for the freshman year only. Alcohol is not permitted. Upperclassmen may keep cars.

FACULTY/CLASSROOMS: 63% of faculty are male; 37% are female. All teach undergraduates, and all do research. No introductory courses are taught by graduate students.

PROGRAMS OF STUDY: Northwestern confers B.A., B.S., B.A.C.M.N., B.A.Mus., B.M.E., B.Mus., B.Ph., B.P.H.C., B.S.A.M., B.S.B.M., B.S.C.H., B.S.C.I., B.S.C.M.N., B.S.C.O., B.S.C.S., B.S.Ed., B.S.E.E., B.S.E.N., B.S.E.S., B.S.G.E., B.S.G.S., B.S.I.E., B.S.J., B.S.M., B.S.M.D., B.S.M.E., B.S.M.F., B.S.M.T., B.S.S.E., and B.S.S.P. degrees. Master's and doctoral degrees are also awarded. Bachelor's degrees are awarded in BIOLOGICAL SCIENCE (biology/biological science, ecology, molecular biology, and neurosciences), BUSINESS (organizational behavior), COMMUNICATIONS AND THE ARTS (art, art history and appreciation, classics, communications, communications technology, comparative literature, dance, dramatic arts, English, fine arts, French, German, Italian, jazz, journalism, linguistics, music, music performance, music technology, music theory and composition, percussion, performing arts, piano/organ, radio/television technology, Slavic languages, Spanish, strings, voice, and winds), COMPUTER AND PHYSICAL SCIENCE (applied mathematics, astronomy, chemistry, computer science, geology, information sciences and systems, mathematics, physics, and statistics), EDUCATION (education, mathematics education, music education, and secondary education), ENGINEERING AND ENVIRONMENTAL DESIGN (biomedical engineering, chemical engineering, civil engineering, computer engineering, electrical/electronics engineering, engineering, environmental engineering, environmental science, industrial engineering, manufacturing engineering, materials engineering, materials science, and mechanical engineering), HEALTH PROFESSIONS (premedicine and speech pathology/audiology), SOCIAL SCIENCE (African American studies, American studies, anthropology, cognitive science, economics, ethics, politics, and social policy, European studies, gender studies, geography, history, human development, international studies, philosophy, political science/government, psychology, religion, science and society, sociology, and urban studies). Economics, political science, and engineering have the largest enrollments.

ACTIVITIES: 29% of men belong to 17 local fraternities; 32% of women belong to 12 local sororities. There are 400 groups on campus, including art, band, cheerleading, chess, choir, chorale, chorus, communications, dance, debate, drama, ethnic, film, honors, international, jazz band, LGBT, literary magazine, marching band, musical theater, newspaper, opera, orchestra, pep band, photography, political, professional, radio and TV, religious, social, social service, student government, symphony, and yearbook. Popular campus events include Dillo Day Music Festival, Dance Marathon, Wildcat Welcome, Family Weekend, and Homecoming. **Sports:** There are 8 intercollegiate sports for men and 11 for women, and 21 intramural sports for men and 19 for women. Facilities include a sailing center, sports pavilion, aquatics center, tennis center, and gymnasium. **Graduates:** From July 1, 2015 to June 30, 2016, 2694 bachelor's degrees were awarded. The most popular majors were economics, journalism, and psychology. In an average class, 86% graduate in 4 years or less, 93% graduate in 5 years or less, and 94% graduate in 6 years or less.

SERVICES: Counseling and information services are available, as is tutoring in most subjects. One-on-one tutoring, peer mentoring, and study groups are also available. **Library/Resources:** The 5 libraries contain 6.0 million volumes. Computerized library services include interlibrary loans, database searching, Internet access, and Wi-Fi capability. Special learning facilities include an art gallery, planetarium, radio station, TV station, and observatory. **Physically Challenged Students:** All of the campus is accessible. Facilities include wheelchair ramps, elevators, special parking, specially equipped restrooms, special class scheduling, lowered drinking fountains, lowered telephones, and special housing. **Special:** The university offers cooperative engineering programs throughout the country, many off-campus field studies and research opportunities, internships in the arts, journalism, and teaching, study abroad in 50 countries, a Washington semester, and numerous work-study programs both on and off campus. There is an accelerated degree program in medical education, and B.A.-B.S. degrees in liberal arts and engineering, liberal arts and music, and music and engineering. An integrated science program, an interdisciplinary study in mathematical methods in social sciences and numerous other interdisciplinary majors, a variety of dual and student-designed majors, and pass/fail options are available. Teaching media programs are also available. There are 23 national honor societies, Phi Beta Kappa, a freshman honors program, and 40 departmental honors programs. **Visiting:** There are regularly scheduled orientations for prospective students, daily information sessions and campus tours Monday through Friday. There are guides for informal visits, visitors may sit in on classes, and stay overnight. To schedule a visit, contact Justin Clarke at justin.clarke@northwestern.edu. **Campus Safety and Security:** Measures include 24-hour foot and vehicle patrol, emergency notification system, self-defense education, and security escort services. There are shuttle buses, emergency telephones, lighted pathways/sidewalks, controlled access to dorms/residences, and security keycard system in residence halls.

REQUIREMENTS: The SAT or ACT is required. Applicants must be graduates of an accredited secondary school or have a GED certificate, and have completed a minimum of 16 units, including 4 units of English, 3 units of math, 2 or 3 units each of a foreign language and history, and 2 units of lab sciences. SAT II: Subject tests are required for the accelerated honors program in medical education and the integrated science program. Auditions are required for applicants to the Bienen School of Music. AP credits are accepted. Important factors in the admissions decision are leadership record, advanced placement or honors courses, evidence of special talent, personality/intangible qualities, recommendations by school officials, ability to finance college education, parents or siblings attended your school, extracurricular activities record, recommendations by alumni, and geographical diversity. Requirements for graduation vary by school and degree program. Students must maintain a minimum 2.0 GPA and complete a total of 45 to 48 quarter units (courses). **Procedure:** Freshmen are admitted in the fall. Entrance exams should be taken by December of the senior year. There are early decision and deferred admissions plans. Early decision applications should be filed by November 1; regular applications, by January 1 for fall entry, along with a $75 fee. Notification of early decision is sent December 15; regular decision, April 1. 1068 early decision candidates were accepted for the 2016-2017 class. 2614 applicants were on the 2016 waiting list; 43 were admitted. Applications are accepted on-line. **Transfer Students:** 111 transfer students enrolled in 2015-2016. We require a minimum of one full year of college coursework for a student to be eligible to transfer. This is usually equivalent to 24 semester hours or 36 quarter hours. Our minimum GPA requirement is a 3.0, but most successful applicants have at least a 3.5. We do not have any course prerequisites for transfer applicants. 24 of 45 credits required for the bachelor's degree must be completed at Northwestern. **International Students:** There are 724 international students enrolled. The school actively recruits these students. They must take the TOEFL. They must also take the SAT or ACT.

ADMISSIONS: The SAT scores for the 2016-2017 freshman class were: Critical Reading-- 4% between 500 and 599, 25% between 600 and 699, and 72% between 700 and 800. Math-- 3% between 500 and 599, 16% between 600 and 699, and 81% between 700 and 800. The ACT scores were 1% between 18 and 23, 24% between 24 and 29, and 75% above 30. **Admissions Contact:** Christopher Watson, Dean of Undergraduate Admission. Email: *ug-admission@northwestern.edu* Web: *www.northwestern.edu*

FINANCIAL AID: In 2016-2017, 46% of all full-time freshmen and 47% of continuing full-time students received some form of financial aid. 44% of all full-time freshmen and 46% of continuing full-time students

received need-based aid. The average freshman award was $43,971. Need-based scholarships or need-based grants averaged $42,088; need-based self-help aid (loans and jobs) averaged $4,618; and non-need-based athletic scholarships averaged $3,961. Northwestern is a member of CSS. The CSS/Profile, noncustodial profile, and parent and student tax forms are required. The FAFSA code is 001739. The priority date for freshman financial aid applications for fall entry is March 5.

OLIVET NAZARENE UNIVERSITY E-2

www.olivet.edu

Bourbonnais, IL 60914	**(815) 939-5203** **(800) 648-1463**
Fax: (815) 935-4998	**Email: admissions@olivet.edu**
Full-time: 1253 men, 1766 women	**Faculty:** 137
Part-time: 98 men, 241 women	**Ph.D.s:** 70%
Graduate: 304 men, 1245 women	**Student/Faculty:** 16 to 1
Year: semesters, summer session	**Tuition:** $33,940
Room & Board: $7900	**Freshman Class:** 4132 applied, 3047 accepted, 704 enrolled
ACT: 24	**CEEB CODE:** 1596
Application Deadline: August 1	**COMPETITIVE**

Olivet Nazarene University is a private, Christian, liberal arts university with a strong emphasis on academic excellence and Christ-centered living. The campus atmosphere and world-class facilities support the University's mission to provide high-quality academic instruction for the purpose of personal development, career and professional readiness, and the preparation of individuals for lives of service to God and humanity. There are 7 undergraduate schools and 1 graduate school. In addition to regional accreditation, Olivet has baccalaureate program accreditation with ABET, ADA, CSWE, NASM, NCATE, CCNE, CAATE, and IACBE. The 275-acre campus is in a suburban area 50 miles south of Chicago, IL. Including any residence halls, there are 53 buildings.

STUDENT LIFE: 64% of undergraduates are from Illinois. Others are from 43 states, 23 foreign countries, and Canada. 80% are White; 7% African American; 7% Hispanic; 3% two or more races; 2% Asian American; 1% Foreign. 56% are Protestant. **Female To Male Ratio:** 2.0:1. The average age of freshmen is 18; all undergraduates, 20. 22% do not continue beyond their first year; 61% remain to graduate. **Housing:** 2400 students can be accommodated in college housing, which includes single-sex dorms, on-campus apartments, and married student housing. In addition, there are honors houses. On-campus housing is guaranteed for all 4 years. 80% of students live on campus; of those, 80% remain on campus on weekends. Alcohol is not permitted. All students may keep cars.

FACULTY/CLASSROOMS: 56% of faculty are male; 44% are female. All teach undergraduates. No introductory courses are taught by graduate students. The average class size in an introductory lecture is 30 and in a laboratory is 22.

PROGRAMS OF STUDY: Olivet confers B.A., B.B.A., B.M., B.S., B.S.N., and B.S.W. degrees. Associate, master's, and doctoral degrees are also awarded. Bachelor's degrees are awarded in BIOLOGICAL SCIENCE (biology/biological science and zoology), BUSINESS (accounting, business administration and management, business communications, fashion merchandising, international business management, marketing/retailing/merchandising, recreation and leisure services, and sports management), COMMUNICATIONS AND THE ARTS (art, communications, digital communications, dramatic arts, drawing, English, journalism, media arts, music, music performance, music theory and composition, and Spanish), COMPUTER AND PHYSICAL SCIENCE (actuarial science, chemistry, computer science, digital arts/technology, geoscience, information sciences and systems, mathematics, and physical sciences), EDUCATION (art education, athletic training, Christian education, early childhood education, elementary education, English education, mathematics education, music education, physical education, science education, and social science education), ENGINEERING AND ENVIRONMENTAL DESIGN (computer engineering, engineering, environmental design, environmental science, and geological engineering), HEALTH PROFESSIONS (exercise science and nursing), SOCIAL SCIENCE (biblical studies, child psychology/development, criminal justice, crosscultural studies, dietetics, economics, family/consumer studies, geography, history, ministries, missions, pastoral studies, philosophy, political science/government, psychology, public affairs, religion, religious music, social science, social work, sociology, Spanish studies, and youth ministry). Engineering, nursing, pre-medicine, dietetics and business are the strongest academically. Engineering, nursing, and business have the largest enrollments.

ACTIVITIES: There are no fraternities or sororities. There are 90 groups on campus, including art, band, cheerleading, choir, chorale, chorus, communications, computers, debate, drama, environmental, ethnic, film, honors, international, jazz band, literary magazine, marching band, musical theater, newspaper, orchestra, pep band, photography, political, professional, radio and TV, religious, social, social service, student government, symphony, and yearbook. Popular campus events include Concerts, Revival Services, Chapel, and Ollies Follies (Class Olympics). **Sports:** There are 9 intercollegiate sports for men and 9 for women, and 19 intramural sports for men and 19 for women. Facilities include basketball, volleyball, and racquetball courts, a gymnasium, a weight-lifting room, a turf football field, athletic park with softball, baseball, and soccer fields, a jogging track, track and field facilities, and tennis courts. The Student Life and Recreation Center boasts pools, basketball courts, an 8-lane indoor track, work-out facilities, gaming area, and a four-story rock climbing wall. **Graduates:** From July 1, 2015 to June 30, 2016, 796 bachelor's degrees were awarded. The most popular majors were nursing (31%), business administration (8%), and psychology (4%). 65 companies recruited on campus in 2015-2016. In an average class, 4% graduate in 3 years or less, 51% graduate in 4 years or less, 59% graduate in 5 years or less, and 61% graduate in 6 years or less.

SERVICES: Counseling and information services are available, as is tutoring in every subject. There is a reader service for the blind, and remedial math, reading, and writing. **Library/Resources:** The library contains 529,092 volumes, 312,729 microform items, and 7,703 audio/video tapes/CDs/DVDs, and subscribes to 12,100 periodicals including electronic. Computerized library services include interlibrary loans, database searching, Internet access, and Wi-Fi capability. Special learning facilities include an art gallery, radio station, TV station, Strickler Planetarium, one of only three planetariums in the state of Illinois with digital projection capabilities; Reed Hall of Science Engineering wing, featuring state-of-the-art equipment and lab space, including a tech shop and additive manufacturing lab, Greer Botanical Greenhouse, solar telescope, television studio, Shine FM radio station, ROTC training facility, wireless campus, Mac labs for design students, and music labs, including a lab where students are able to compose, arrange, and transcribe music. **Physically Challenged Students:** 99% of the campus is accessible. Facilities include wheelchair ramps, elevators, special parking, specially equipped restrooms, special class scheduling, lowered drinking fountains, lowered telephones, and special housing. **Special:** Special academic programs include a work-study program, which can be arranged with other institutions, and a general studies degree. A 4-year engineering program (ABET) is available. There are 6 national honor societies, a freshman honors program, and 5 departmental honors programs. **Visiting:** There are regularly scheduled orientations for prospective students, class/faculty/athletic visits, financial aid appointments, campus tour, lunch, entrance interview. There are guides for informal visits, visitors may sit in on classes, and stay overnight. To schedule a visit, contact Admissions Office, Jean Milton at admissions@olivet.edu. **Campus Safety and Security:** Measures include 24-hour foot and vehicle patrol, emergency notification system, self-defense education, and security escort services. There are shuttle buses, emergency telephones, lighted pathways/sidewalks, and controlled access to dorms/residences.

REQUIREMENTS: SAT or ACT test scores are required. The minimum ACT score required is 18. Olivet requires graduation from an accredited secondary school. Olivet does not have any specific high school course requirements, but there are some suggestions for high school courses. College preparatory courses completed with a C or above are recommended. In general, you should have 3 years of English and 2 years each of math, foreign language, and natural or social science. To enroll in the nursing program, you need a year of biology and a year of chemistry. In choosing high school courses, you should also take into consideration the career/major you intend to pursue. The GED is accepted. A GPA of 2.0 is required. AP and CLEP credits are accepted. To graduate, students must complete 128 semester hours of credit, with 32 to 70 in a major and a minimum of 40 hours of credit in upper-division courses, and maintain a minimum GPA of 2.0. The required general education studies, 50 to 61 hours, include 12 credit hours of Christianity, 9 to 10 of communication, 9 of natural science and math, 6 of social sciences,

6 to 8 of international culture, 6 of literature and the arts, and 3 of wellness/nutrition. **Procedure:** Freshmen are admitted to all sessions. Entrance exams should be taken spring of junior year, or fall of senior year. There are deferred admissions and rolling admissions plans. Applications should be filed by August 1 for fall entry; December 1 for spring entry, along with a $25 fee. Notification is sent on a rolling basis. Applications are accepted on-line. Application fees are waived if application is completed on-line. **Transfer Students:** 268 transfer students enrolled in 2015-2016. Application and transcripts of all college work must be submitted. 30 of 128 credits required for the bachelor's degree must be completed at Olivet. **International Students:** There are 26 international students enrolled. They must take the TOEFL with a minimum score of 500 on the paper-based TOEFL (PBT) or 61 on the Internet-based version (iBT). They must also take the ACT.

ADMISSIONS: 74% of the 2016-2017 applicants were accepted. The ACT scores were 3% between 12 and 17, 46% between 18 and 23, 41% between 24 and 29, and 10% above 30. **Admissions Contact:** Susan Wolff, Dean of Undergraduate Admissions. Email: *admissions@olivet.edu* Web: *www.olivet.edu*

FINANCIAL AID: In 2016-2017, 99% of all full-time freshmen and continuing full-time students received some form of financial aid. 83% of all full-time freshmen and 80% of continuing full-time students received need-based aid. The average freshman award was $30,000. 36% of undergraduate students work part-time. Average annual earnings from campus work are $1300. The FAFSA code is 001741. The priority date for freshman financial aid applications for fall entry is November 15. The deadline for filing freshman financial aid applications for fall entry is August 1.

PRINCIPIA COLLEGE — C-4
www.principiacollege.edu

Elsah, IL 62028	**(618) 374-5181** **(800) 277-4648**
Fax: (618) 374-4000	**Email: enroll@principia.edu**
Full-time: 224 men, 228 women	**Faculty:** 61
Part-time: 4 men, 4 women	**Ph.D.s:** 67%
Graduate: n/av	**Student/Faculty:** 8 to 1
Year: semesters	**Tuition:** $27,980
Room & Board: $11,030	**Freshman Class:** n/av
SAT CR/M/W: 560/550/540 **ACT:** 25	**CEEB CODE:** 1630
Application Deadline: March 1	**COMPETITIVE+**

Principia College, founded in 1910, is a private liberal arts and sciences college for Christian Scientists. It is the only college in the world strictly for Christian Scientists. There is 1 undergraduate school. In addition to regional accreditation, Prin has baccalaureate program accreditation with NCATE. The 2600-acre campus is in a rural area 30 miles northeast of St. Louis. Including any residence halls, there are 33 buildings.

STUDENT LIFE: 91% of undergraduates are from out of state, mostly the Midwest. Students are from 35 states, 27 foreign countries, and Canada. 44% are from public schools. 71% are White; 3% two or more races; 20% Foreign; 2% African American; 2% race unknown; 1% Asian American. 100% are Christian Scientist. **Female To Male Ratio:** 1.0:1. The average age of freshmen is 19; all undergraduates, 22. 12% do not continue beyond their first year; 79% remain to graduate. **Housing:** 555 students can be accommodated in college housing, which includes single-sex and coed dorms, on-campus apartments, and married student housing. In addition, there are special-interest houses. On-campus housing is guaranteed for all 4 years. 98% of students live on campus; of those, 100% remain on campus on weekends. Alcohol is not permitted. All students may keep cars.

FACULTY/CLASSROOMS: 51% of faculty are male; 49% are female. All teach undergraduates. No introductory courses are taught by graduate students. The average class size in an introductory lecture is 14; in a laboratory is 13; and in a regular course is 14.

PROGRAMS OF STUDY: Prin confers B.A., and B.S. degrees. Bachelor's degrees are awarded in BIOLOGICAL SCIENCE (biology/biological science), BUSINESS (business administration and management and sports management), COMMUNICATIONS AND THE ARTS (communications, dramatic arts, English, fine arts, French, languages, music, Spanish, and studio art), COMPUTER AND PHYSICAL SCIENCE (chemistry, computer science, mathematics, and physics), EDUCATION (elementary education), ENGINEERING AND ENVIRONMENTAL DESIGN (environmental science), SOCIAL SCIENCE (economics, history, international relations, philosophy, political science/government, religion, and sociology). Business, biology, art, computer science, mass communication are the strongest academically. Business administration, mass communication, and education studies have the largest enrollments.

ACTIVITIES: There are no fraternities or sororities. There are 45 groups on campus, including art, cheerleading, choir, chorus, computers, dance, debate, drama, environmental, ethnic, film, honors, international, jazz band, literary magazine, musical theater, newspaper, orchestra, photography, political, radio and TV, religious, social, social service, student government, and yearbook. Popular campus events include Athletic Events, Dances, and Drama and Dance Performances. **Sports:** There are 7 intercollegiate sports for men and 8 for women, and 3 intramural sports for men and 3 for women. Facilities include gyms, a pool, indoor and outdoor tennis courts, a racquetball court, basketball/volleyball courts, a dance studio, a weight room, baseball, football, soccer, and practice fields, and a 6-lane track. **Graduates:** From July 1, 2015 to June 30, 2016, 109 bachelor's degrees were awarded. The most popular majors were business administration (19%), mass communication (14%), and education studies (10%). 20 companies recruited on campus in 2015-2016. In an average class, 83% graduate in 4 years or less, 98% graduate in 5 years or less, and 98% graduate in 6 years or less.

SERVICES: Counseling and information services are available, as is tutoring in most subjects. There is remedial reading and writing. Assistance in study skills is available. **Library/Resources:** The library contains 180,352 volumes, 19 microform items, and 5,818 audio/video tapes/CDs/DVDs, and subscribes to 58,000 periodicals including electronic. Computerized library services include interlibrary loans, database searching, Internet access, and Wi-Fi capability. Special learning facilities include an art gallery, planetarium, radio station, and TV station. **Physically Challenged Students:** 85% of the campus is accessible. Facilities include wheelchair ramps, elevators, special parking, specially equipped restrooms, and lowered drinking fountains. **Special:** Students may design their own majors, study abroad, or pursue a B.A.-B.S. degree. Internships, student-planned with a professor, independent study, work-study, and an interdisciplinary major, global studies, are available. An accredited engineering degree is offered as part of a dual-degree program with a few other institutions. **Visiting:** There are regularly scheduled orientations for prospective students, including a visit to classes, meeting professors, living in a dorm, and meeting students (3-day weekend). There are guides for informal visits. To schedule a visit, contact Amber McCartt at (618) 374-5175. **Campus Safety and Security:** Measures include 24-hour foot and vehicle patrol and emergency notification system. There are emergency telephones, lighted pathways/sidewalks, and controlled access to dorms/residences.

REQUIREMENTS: SAT or ACT is required. An essay is required. SAT Subject Tests in foreign language and math are recommended. High school preparation should include 4 years of English, 3 years of math (including algebra II), 2 to 3 years of a foreign language, and 2 to 3 years of natural sciences, history, or social sciences, including electives. A GPA of 2.3 is required. AP and CLEP credits are accepted. Important factors in the admissions decision are advanced placement or honors courses, recommendations by school officials, and leadership record. All students must complete a minimum of 120 semester hours, with 30 to 71 semester hours in the major (10 to 19 courses) and at least a 2.0 overall GPA. Courses in Arts, Humanities, Math, Natural Sciences, Social Sciences, and Bible are required. In addition, students must be certified as proficient in written English, a second (foreign) language, pass a moral reasoning seminar, and earn 2 credits in individual or team phys ed activities. **Procedure:** Freshmen are admitted fall and spring. Entrance exams should be taken in the spring of the junior year and again in the fall of the senior year. There are deferred admissions and rolling admissions plans. Applications should be filed by March 1 for fall entry; November 1 for winter entry. Notification of early decision is sent December 1; regular decision, March 15. Applications are accepted on-line. **Transfer Students:** 15 transfer students enrolled in 2015-2016. Applicants must be in good standing at their previous college or university and have a 2.3 GPA. 45 of 180 credits required for the bachelor's degree must be completed at Prin. **International Students:** There are 76 international students enrolled. The school actively recruits these students. They must take the TOEFL with a minimum score of 79 on the Internet-based version (iBT). They must also take the SAT or ACT, scoring 1010 - SAT, 19 - ACT.

ADMISSIONS: The SAT scores for the 2016-2017 freshman class were:

Critical Reading-- 20% below 500, 41% between 500 and 599, 30% between 600 and 699, and 9% between 700 and 800. Math-- 28% below 500, 43% between 500 and 599, 25% between 600 and 699, and 4% between 700 and 800. Writing-- 33% below 500, 42% between 500 and 599, 24% between 600 and 699, and 1% between 700 and 800. The ACT scores were 2% between 12 and 17, 27% between 18 and 23, 55% between 24 and 29, and 16% above 30. 29% of the current freshmen were in the top fifth of their class; 57% were in the top two fifths. 1 freshman graduated first in the class. **Admissions Contact:** Tami Gavaletz, Director of Admissions and Financial Aid. Email: *enroll@principia.edu* Web: *www.principiacollege.edu*

FINANCIAL AID: In 2016-2017, 100% of all full-time freshmen and 97% of continuing full-time students received some form of financial aid. 68% of all full-time freshmen and 73% of continuing full-time students received need-based aid. The average freshman award was $31,608. Need-based scholarships or need-based grants averaged $27,264 ($37,510 maximum); need-based self-help aid (loans and jobs) averaged $5,835 ($6,000 maximum); and other non-need-based awards and non-need-based scholarships averaged $21,155 ($38,510 maximum). 63% of undergraduate students work part-time. Average annual earnings from campus work are $1815. The average financial indebtedness of the 2016 graduate was $20,949. Prin is a member of CSS. The CSS/Profile is required. The deadline for filing freshman financial aid applications for fall entry is March 1.

QUINCY UNIVERSITY — B-3
www.quincy.edu

Quincy, IL 62301	(217) 228-5210 (800) 688-4295
Fax: (217) 228-5479	Email: admissions@quincy.edu
Full-time: 486 men, 608 women	**Faculty:** 50
Part-time: 61 men, 86 women	**Ph.D.s:** 77%
Graduate: 185 men, 419 women	**Student/Faculty:** 14 to 1
Year: semesters, summer session	**Tuition:** $26,998
Room & Board: $10,000	**Freshman Class:** 986 applied, 892 accepted, 249 enrolled
SAT CR/M: required **ACT:** 21	**CEEB CODE:** 1645
Application Deadline: n/av	**COMPETITIVE**

Founded in 1860 by Franciscan friars, Quincy University is a Catholic, residential university offering undergraduate, graduate, and adult education programs that integrate liberal arts, active learning, practical experience, and Franciscan values. There are 3 undergraduate schools and 3 graduate schools. The figures in the above capsule and in this profile are approximate. In addition to regional accreditation, QU has baccalaureate program accreditation with CCNE. The 70-acre campus is in a small town 120 miles from St. Louis, and 250 miles from Kansas City, 275 miles from Indianapolis. Including any residence halls, there are 55 buildings.

STUDENT LIFE: 75% of undergraduates are from Illinois. Others are from 25 states, 4 foreign countries, and Canada. 48% are from public schools. 75% are White; 4% Hispanic; 10% African American; 1% Asian American; 1% Foreign. 46% are Catholic; 28% Protestant; 21% claim no religious affiliation. **Female To Male Ratio:** 1.5:1. The average age of freshmen is 19; all undergraduates, 23. 31% do not continue beyond their first year; 42% remain to graduate. **Housing:** 690 students can be accommodated in college housing, which includes single-sex and coed dorms, on-campus apartments, and married student housing. In addition, there are honors houses, special-interest houses, fraternity houses, and sorority houses. On-campus housing is guaranteed for all 4 years. 58% of students live on campus; of those, 85% remain on campus on weekends. All students may keep cars.

FACULTY/CLASSROOMS: 46% of faculty are male; 54% are female. 94% teach undergraduates. No introductory courses are taught by graduate students. The average class size in an introductory lecture is 35; in a laboratory is 20; and in a regular course is 20.

PROGRAMS OF STUDY: QU confers B.A., B.F.A., B.S., and B.S.N. degrees. Associate and master's degrees are also awarded. Bachelor's degrees are awarded in BIOLOGICAL SCIENCE (biology/biological science), BUSINESS (accounting, banking and finance, business administration and management, marketing/retailing/merchandising, and sports management), COMMUNICATIONS AND THE ARTS (communications, English, graphic design, and music), COMPUTER AND PHYSICAL SCIENCE (chemistry, computer science, information sciences and systems, and mathematics), EDUCATION (education, elementary education, music education, physical education, and special education), ENGINEERING AND ENVIRONMENTAL DESIGN (aviation administration/management), HEALTH PROFESSIONS (clinical science, exercise science, and nursing), SOCIAL SCIENCE (criminal justice, history, human services, humanities, interpreter for the deaf, political science/government, psychology, social work, and theological studies). Business, education, and science are the strongest academically. Elementary education, nursing, and management have the largest enrollments.

ACTIVITIES: 3% of men belong to 1 national fraternity; 13% of women belong to 2 national sororities. There are 40 groups on campus, including band, cheerleading, choir, chorale, chorus, communications, computers, dance, drama, environmental, ethnic, honors, international, jazz band, literary magazine, musical theater, newspaper, opera, orchestra, pep band, political, professional, radio and TV, religious, social, social service, student government, and symphony. Popular campus events include Hawk Wild Weekend, Hawk Back Weekend, and Family Weekend. **Sports:** There are 7 intercollegiate sports for men and 6 for women, and 18 intramural sports for men and 17 for women. Facilities include the Health and Fitness Center, which features 3 multipurpose gym courts, a 3,600-square-foot fitness room, 17 cardio machines, an aerobics room, an indoor walking/running track, 2 racquetball courts, and a 6-lane intercollegiate pool with whirlpool. QU also has a 2,000-seat basketball/volleyball arena, a large campus recreation field, as well as a softball complex, a football/baseball stadium, and a 3-field soccer complex with support building. **Graduates:** From July 1, 2015 to June 30, 2016, 208 bachelor's degrees were awarded. The most popular majors were nursing (12%), elementary education (9%), and marketing (9%). 43 companies recruited on campus in 2015-2016. In an average class, 31% graduate in 4 years or less, 41% graduate in 5 years or less, and 42% graduate in 6 years or less. Of the 2015 graduating class, 23% were enrolled in graduate school within 6 months of graduation, and 59% were employed.

SERVICES: Counseling and information services are available, as is tutoring in every subject. There is a reader service for the blind, and remedial math and writing. Academic Success workshops and courses are available. **Library/Resources:** The library contains 212,930 volumes, 193,810 microform items, and 9,334 audio/video tapes/CDs/DVDs, and subscribes to 324 periodicals including electronic. Computerized library services include interlibrary loans, database searching, Internet access, and Wi-Fi capability. Special learning facilities include an art gallery, radio station, TV station, a 200-seat theater, center for music, multimedia and graphic design labs, an environmental studies institute, a temperature-controlled rare books library archive, a hospital simulation lab, an aviation facility, and University Chapel and a nondenominational praise/worship chapel. **Physically Challenged Students:** 95% of the campus is accessible. Facilities include wheelchair ramps, elevators, special parking, specially equipped restrooms, special class scheduling, and lowered drinking fountains. **Special:** Dual majors, study abroad in 31 countries, credit by exam, and upper-class and early exploratory internships are available. Pass/fail options, credit for life experience, student-designed majors, adult accelerated degree programs, and a 3-2 degree with Washington University in St. Louis are also offered. An interdisciplinary major in communication and music production is available. Study abroad in Assisi, London, Rome, or other programs available in 29 countries. There are 8 national honor societies, a freshman honors program, and 1 departmental honors program. **Visiting:** There are regularly scheduled orientations for prospective students, including advising and registration programs throughout the summer. There are guides for informal visits, visitors may sit in on classes, and stay overnight. To schedule a visit, contact the Admissions Office. **Campus Safety and Security:** Measures include 24-hour foot and vehicle patrol, emergency notification system, self-defense education, and security escort services. There are shuttle buses, emergency telephones, lighted pathways/sidewalks, and controlled access to dorms/residences.

REQUIREMENTS: The SAT or ACT is required. The GED is accepted. The recommended high school curriculum includes 4 years of English and 3 each in math, sciences, and social studies. Courses in another language, computers, and the arts are helpful. Art students must submit a portfolio, and music students must audition. QU requires applicants to be in the upper 50% of their class. A GPA of 2.0 is required. AP and CLEP credits are accepted. Important factors in the admissions decision are leadership record, evidence of special talent, and recommendations by school officials. Each student is required to complete a minimum of 124 credit hours, with at least 33 in the major and a minimum of 39 in upper-level courses. In addition, students must complete required courses in rhetoric, science, math, social sciences, humanities, fine arts, theology, and phys ed; complete a senior comprehensive seminar or practicum; maintain a minimum GPA of 2.0; earn at least 30 semester hours in residency at QU, including 21 hours in the major; and earn a minimum of 56 semester hours from a 4-year college/university. **Procedure:** Freshmen are admitted fall and spring. Entrance exams should be taken in October of the senior year. There are deferred admissions and rolling admissions plans. Application deadlines are open. Application fee is $25. Notification is sent on a rolling basis. Applications are accepted on-line. **Transfer Students:** 200 transfer students enrolled in 2015-2016. Applicants must have a minimum GPA of 2.0. Grades of C or better in college-level courses normally transfer for credit. 30 of 124 credits required for the bachelor's degree must be completed at QU. **International Students:** There are 7 international students enrolled. The school actively recruits these students. They must take the TOEFL with a minimum score of 500 on the paper-based TOEFL (PBT) or 61 on the Internet-based version (iBT). They must also take the SAT or ACT.

ADMISSIONS: 90% of the 2016-2017 applicants were accepted. The SAT scores for the 2016-2017 freshman class were: Critical Reading-- 79% below 500 and 21% between 500 and 599. Math-- 53% below 500, 32% between 500 and 599, 10% between 600 and 699, and 5% between 700 and 800. The ACT scores were 44% below 12, 30% between 12 and 17, 15% between 18 and 23, 8% between 24 and 29, and 3% above 30. 27% of the current freshmen were in the top fifth of their class; 55% were in the top two fifths. 3 freshmen graduated first in their class. **Admissions Contact:** Syndi Peck, Director of Admissions. Email: *admissions@quincy.edu* Web: *www.quincy.edu*

FINANCIAL AID: In 2016-2017, 99% of all full-time freshmen and 91% of continuing full-time students received some form of financial aid. 76% of all full-time freshmen and 71% of continuing full-time students received need-based aid. The average freshman award was $26,877. Need-based scholarships or need-based grants averaged $10,727 ($22,331 maximum); need-based self-help aid (loans and jobs) averaged $3,907 ($4,500 maximum); non-need-based athletic scholarships averaged $10,800 ($30,410 maximum); and other non-need-based awards and non-need-based scholarships averaged $11,281 ($29,900 maximum). 26% of undergraduate students work part-time. Average annual earnings from campus work are $2000. The average financial indebtedness of the 2016 graduate was $19,935. QU is a member of CSS. The FAFSA code is 001745. The priority date for freshman financial aid applications for fall entry is March 1.

ROCKFORD UNIVERSITY D-1

www.rockford.edu

Rockford, IL 61108 (815) 226-3383
(800) 892-2984

Fax: (815) 226-2822 **Email:** admissions@rockford.edu

Full-time: 299 men, 454 women	**Faculty:** 69
Part-time: 46 men, 70 women	**Ph.D.s:** 71%
Graduate: 176 men, 295 women	**Student/Faculty:** 11 to 1
Year: semesters, summer session	**Tuition:** $29,280
Room & Board: $6750	**Freshman Class:** n/av
ACT: 22	**CEEB CODE:** 1665
Application Deadline: August 15	**COMPETITIVE**

Rockford College, founded in 1847, is a private coeducational institution offering undergraduate and graduate instruction in liberal arts and professional programs. There is 1 undergraduate school and 2 graduate schools. In addition to regional accreditation, Rockford has baccalaureate program accreditation with NLN, ACS, and IACBE. The 135-acre campus is in a suburban area 90 miles west of Chicago. Including any residence halls, there are 27 buildings.

STUDENT LIFE: 91% of undergraduates are from Illinois. Others are from 26 states and 2 foreign countries. 73% are White; 7% African American; 6% Hispanic; 2% Asian American. **Female To Male Ratio:** 1.6:1. The average age of freshmen is 18; all undergraduates, 24. **Housing:** 356 students can be accommodated in college housing, which includes single-sex and coed dorms. In addition, there are special-interest houses, first-year student housing, substance-free, and 24- hour quiet housing, and health and science major housing. On-campus housing is guaranteed for all 4 years. 65% of students commute. All students may keep cars.

FACULTY/CLASSROOMS: 56% of faculty are male; 44% are female. All teach undergraduates. No introductory courses are taught by graduate students. The average class size in an introductory lecture is 18; in a laboratory is 11; and in a regular course is 15.

PROGRAMS OF STUDY: Rockford confers B.A., B.S., B.F.A., and B.S.N. degrees. Master's degrees are also awarded. Bachelor's degrees are awarded in BIOLOGICAL SCIENCE (biochemistry and biology/biological science), BUSINESS (accounting, business administration and management, and management information systems), COMMUNICATIONS AND THE ARTS (art, art history and appreciation, classics, dramatic arts, English, French, German, Latin, music, music performance, romance languages and literature, and Spanish), COMPUTER AND PHYSICAL SCIENCE (chemistry, computer science, mathematics, and science), EDUCATION (elementary education, physical education, and special education), HEALTH PROFESSIONS (nursing), SOCIAL SCIENCE (anthropology, economics, history, humanities, international studies, philosophy, political science/government, psychology, social science, and sociology). Business, education, and nursing have the largest enrollments.

ACTIVITIES: There are no fraternities or sororities. There are 21 groups on campus, including senior club, Anime, Black Student Union, bowling, muli-cultural, nursing, poker, RAGE, Rockford Paranormal Society, Alpha Helix, art, band, cheerleading, chess, choir, chorale, dance, drama, environmental, ethnic, honors, international, LGBT, literary magazine, musical theater, opera, orchestra, pep band, political, professional, religious, social, social service, and student government. Popular campus events include Snowball Dance, International Food Fair, and Black History Month Events. **Sports:** There are 9 intercollegiate sports for men and 8 for women, and 7 intramural sports for men and 7 for women. Facilities include a swimming pool, athletic fields, tennis courts, and a fitness center. **Graduates:** From July 1, 2015 to June 30, 2016, 224 bachelor's degrees were awarded. The most popular majors were education (28%), business (22%), and nursing (10%). In an average class, and 44% graduate in 5 years or less.

SERVICES: Counseling and information services are available, as is tutoring in most subjects. There is a reader service for the blind, and remedial math and reading. Diagnostic testing is available. **Library/Resources:** The library contains 146,829 volumes, 8,430 microform items, and 2,819 audio/video tapes/CDs/DVDs, and subscribes to 389 periodicals including electronic. Computerized library services include interlibrary loans, database searching, and Internet access. Special learning facilities include an art gallery. **Physically Challenged Students:** Facilities include wheelchair ramps, elevators, special parking, specially equipped restrooms, special class scheduling, lowered drinking fountains, lowered telephones, and special housing. **Special:** Rockford College offers a variety of special academic opportunities including community-based learning, liberal arts honors program, internships, study abroad, and Washington semester. In addition to our traditional undergraduate programs, we offer English as a second language and an accelerated bachelor's degree in management studies. There are 6 national honor societies and a chapter of Phi Beta Kappa. **Visiting:** There are regularly scheduled orientations for prospective students consisting of an acedemic fair, opportunity to meet with social/athletic programs, and administrative offices, admission presentation, meal, tour, and meet with current students. There are guides for informal visits, visitors may sit in on classes, and stay overnight. To schedule a visit, contact the Admissions Office. **Campus Safety and Security:** Measures include 24-hour foot and vehicle patrol, emergency notification system, and security escort services. There are emergency telephones and lighted pathways/sidewalks.

REQUIREMENTS: The ACT is required. Admission to Rockford College is based primarily on high school GPA and test scores (GED also accepted). Prospective students are expected to have completed a college preparatory program of 15 units including, 4 years of English; 3 years of mathematics (introductory through advanced algebra, geometry, and trigonometry), 3 years of social sciences (emphasizing history and government), 3 years of laboratory science, and 2 years of electives chosen from music, art, and/or foreign language at an accredited secondary school. Home schooled students also should meet the unit requirements. Auditions are required for performing arts students. Rockford requires applicants to be in the upper 50% of their class. A GPA of 2.7 is required.

AP and CLEP credits are accepted. To graduate, students must have a total of at least 124 credit hours and a minimum GPA of 2.0 (nursing 2.75). The required hours for each major varies. Students are required to take 12 hours of social sciences, 8 to 12 of science, mathematics, and computer science, 8 of language and literature, 11 of rhetoric, 6 of art, and 2 hours of physical education. All students must complete a senior seminar or project. **Procedure:** Freshmen are admitted to all sessions. There are early admissions, deferred admissions, and rolling admissions plans. Application deadlines are open. Application fee is $35. Notifications are sent September 15. Applications are accepted on-line. **Transfer Students:** 164 transfer students enrolled in 2015-2016. In order to be considered for transfer admission, prospective students must have completed at least 12 credit hours of college-level work (at the 100-level or higher). Students transferring from other colleges must be in good academic standing in order to be considered for standard admission. High school transcripts and standardized test scores (ACT/SAT) also may be requested. 30 of 124 credits required for the bachelor's degree must be completed at Rockford. **International Students:** There are 4 international students enrolled. The school actively recruits these students. They must take the TOEFL with a minimum score of 550 on the paper-based TOEFL (PBT) or 79 on the Internet-based version (iBT). Rockford College will also accept the IELTS test. They must also take the SAT or ACT.

ADMISSIONS: The ACT scores were 43% below 12, 26% between 12 and 17, 24% between 18 and 23, and 3% between 24 and 29. 28% of the current freshmen were in the top fifth of their class; 55% were in the top two fifths. **Admissions Contact:** Jennifer Nordstrom, Associate Vice President for Undergraduate Admissions and Strategy. Email: *admissions@rockford.edu* Web: *www.rockford.edu*

FINANCIAL AID: In 2016-2017, 100% of all full-time freshmen and 100% of continuing full-time students received some form of financial aid. 81% of all full-time freshmen and 95% of continuing full-time students received need-based aid. The average freshman award was $24,895. Need-based scholarships or need-based grants averaged $8,332 ($13,468 maximum); need-based self-help aid (loans and jobs) averaged $3,768 ($11,600 maximum); and other non-need-based awards and non-need-based scholarships averaged $14,970 ($35,660 maximum). 24% of undergraduate students work part-time. Average annual earnings from campus work are $1355. The average financial indebtedness of the 2016 graduate was $26,000. The FAFSA code is 001748. The priority date for freshman financial aid applications for fall entry is March 15.

ROOSEVELT UNIVERSITY E-2

www.roosevelt.edu

Chicago, IL 60605	(847) 619-8620 (877) APPLYRU
Fax: (847) 619-8636	Email: admission@roosevelt.edu
Full-time: 680 men, 1180 women	Faculty: 190
Part-time: 745 men, 1695 women	Ph.D.s: 85%
Graduate: 1035 men, 2205 women	Student/Faculty: 10 to 1
Year: semesters, summer session	Tuition: $28,119
Room & Board: $12,532	Freshman Class: n/av
SAT or ACT: required	CEEB CODE: 1666
Application Deadline: rolling	VERY COMPETITIVE

Roosevelt University, founded in 1945, is an independent, comprehensive university. The figures in the above capsule and in this profile are approximate. There are 5 undergraduate schools and 5 graduate schools. In addition to regional accreditation, Roosevelt has baccalaureate program accreditation with AACSB, NASM, and NCATE. The campus is in an urban area in downtown Chicago. Including any residence halls, there are 2 buildings.

STUDENT LIFE: 90% of undergraduates are from Illinois. Others are from 24 states, 70 foreign countries, and Canada. 44% are White; 4% Asian American; 27% African American; 12% Hispanic; 10% Foreign; 1% American Indian/Alaska Native. **Female To Male Ratio:** 2.1:1. The average age of freshmen is 21; all undergraduates, 27. **Housing:** 300 students can be accommodated in college housing, which includes coed dorms. On-campus housing is available on a first-come, first-served basis. 94% of students commute.

FACULTY/CLASSROOMS: All teach undergraduates. No introductory courses are taught by graduate students.

PROGRAMS OF STUDY: Roosevelt confers B.A., B.S., B.A.Comp.Sci., B.A.Ed., B.F.A.Mus.Theater, B.G.S., B.M., B.S.B.A., B.S. in Hospitality Mgt. and B.S.Telecomm. degrees. Master's and doctoral degrees are also awarded. Bachelor's degrees are awarded in BIOLOGICAL SCIENCE (biology/biological science), BUSINESS (accounting, banking and finance, business administration and management, hotel/motel and restaurant management, insurance, insurance and risk management, management science, marketing/retailing/merchandising, and personnel management), COMMUNICATIONS AND THE ARTS (advertising, art history and appreciation, broadcasting, communications, dramatic arts, English, French, guitar, jazz, journalism, languages, literature, media arts, music, music history and appreciation, music performance, music theory and composition, musical theater, percussion, performing arts, piano/organ, public relations, Spanish, strings, telecommunications, theater design, theater management, voice, and winds), COMPUTER AND PHYSICAL SCIENCE (actuarial science, chemistry, computer science, information sciences and systems, mathematics, and statistics), EDUCATION (early childhood education, elementary education, music education, and secondary education), ENGINEERING AND ENVIRONMENTAL DESIGN (electrical/electronics engineering technology and environmental science), HEALTH PROFESSIONS (allied health, medical technology, nuclear medical technology, predentistry, premedicine, prepharmacy, and preveterinary science), SOCIAL SCIENCE (African American studies, American studies, economics, history, international studies, liberal arts/general studies, philosophy, political science/government, prelaw, psychology, public administration, social science, sociology, urban studies, and women's studies). Journalism, accounting, and psychology are the strongest academically.

ACTIVITIES: 1% of men belong to 1 local fraternity; 1% of women belong to 1 local sorority. There are 45 groups on campus, including model United Nations, band, choir, chorale, chorus, computers, cultural, drama, ethnic, honors, international, jazz band, literary magazine, musical theater, newspaper, opera, orchestra, political, professional, radio and TV, religious, social service, student government, and symphony. **Sports:** There is 1 intramural sports for men and 1 for women. Facilities include a fitness center and a recreational gym for basketball, volleyball, soccer, and intramural activities.

SERVICES: Counseling and information services are available, as is tutoring in most subjects. There is remedial math, reading, and writing. Arranged counseling and testing are available. Emphasis is placed on individual program planning. **Library/Resources:** The 2 libraries contain 405,022 volumes, 130,233 microform items, and 10,000 audio/video tapes/CDs/DVDs, and subscribe to 1,601 periodicals including electronic. Computerized library services include interlibrary loans and database searching. Special learning facilities include a radio station. **Physically Challenged Students:** All of the campus is accessible. Facilities include wheelchair ramps, elevators, specially equipped restrooms, special class scheduling, and lowered telephones. **Special:** Roosevelt offers internships in approximately 20 subject areas, on-campus work-study, study abroad in 4 countries, dual and student-designed majors, pass/fail options, and noncredit courses. Adults older than 25 years of age may earn a Bachelor of General Studies through an accelerated degree program. Credit for life, military, and work experience is available in some majors through continuing education. The Roosevelt Scholars Program is offered. There are 4 national honor societies, a freshman honors program, and 20 departmental honors programs. **Visiting:** There are regularly scheduled orientations for prospective students, including open houses and transfer days. There are guides for informal visits and visitors may sit in on classes. To schedule a visit, contact the Undergraduate Admissions Office. **Campus Safety and Security:** There are shuttle buses and lighted pathways/sidewalks.

REQUIREMENTS: The SAT or ACT is required. Students must have completed 15 academic units, including 4 of English, 3 of math, 2 each of science, social studies, and foreign language, and 1 each of history and electives. An interview is recommended for all applicants, and an audition is required for music and theater candidates. A GPA of 2.3 is required. AP and CLEP credits are accepted. Important factors in the admissions decision are advanced placement or honors courses, evidence of special talent, and extracurricular activities record. For graduation, students must complete 120 credit hours, including 54 in the major, with a minimum GPA of 2.0, or 2.5 in the College of Education. The core curriculum consists of courses in the social sciences, natural sciences, and humanities, including English 101 and 102. The last 54 hours must be from a 4-year school. **Procedure:** Freshmen are admitted to all sessions. There are early decision, early admissions, deferred admissions, and rolling admissions plans. Application deadlines are open. The fall 2016 application fee was $25. Notification is sent on a rolling basis. Applications are accepted on-line. **Transfer Students:** 732 transfer students enrolled in 2015-2016. Applicants must have earned a minimum GPA of 2.0 in all accredited college course-work. Offical transcripts must be received from each college where course-work was attempted. 30 of 120 credits required for the bachelor's degree must be completed at Roosevelt. **International Students:** The school actively recruits these students. They must take the college's own test.

Admissions Contact: Gwen Kanelos, Assistant Vice President for Enrollment Services. Email: *admission@roosevelt.edu* Web: *www.roosevelt.edu*

FINANCIAL AID: In 2016-2017, 85% of all full-time freshmen and 65% of continuing full-time students received some form of financial aid. 75% of all full-time freshmen and 65% of continuing full-time students received need-based aid. The average freshman award was $10,500. Need-based scholarships or need-based grants averaged $7,725; need-based self-help aid (loans and jobs) averaged $7,170; and other non-need-based awards and non-need-based scholarships averaged $5,220. The college's own financial statement is required. The FAFSA code is 001749. Check with the school for current application deadlines.

SAINT XAVIER UNIVERSITY E-2

www.sxu.edu

Chicago, IL 60655 (773) 298-3050 (800) 462-9288

Fax: (773) 298-3076	**Email:** admissions@sxu.edu
Full-time: 705 men, 1630 women	**Faculty:** IIA, --$
Part-time: 170 men, 565 women	**Ph.D.s:** 86%
Graduate: 510 men, 1995 women	**Student/Faculty:** n/av
Year: semesters, summer session	**Tuition:** $32,250
Room & Board: $11,060	**Freshman Class:** n/av
ACT: required	**CEEB CODE:** 1708
Application Deadline: May 1	**COMPETITIVE**

Saint Xavier University is a private institution founded by the Sisters of Mercy in 1846 and is affiliated with the Roman Catholic Church. The figures in the above capsule and in this profile are approximate. There are 4 undergraduate schools and 4 graduate schools. In addition to regional accreditation, SXU has baccalaureate program accreditation with AACSB, ACBSP, NASM, NLN, CAEP, and CCNE. The 70-acre campus is in an urban area 15 miles southwest of Chicago's Loop. Including any residence halls, there are 16 buildings.

STUDENT LIFE: 96% of undergraduates are from Illinois. Others are from 21 states, and 4 foreign countries. 50% are from public schools. 49% are White; 3% Asian American; 15% African American; 11% Hispanic. 80% are Catholic; 16% Protestant. **Female To Male Ratio:** 3.0:1. The average age of freshmen is 18; all undergraduates, 23. 24% do not continue beyond their first year. **Housing:** 630 students can be accommodated in college housing, which includes single-sex and coed dorms. On-campus housing is guaranteed for all 4 years. 81% of students commute. Alcohol is not permitted. All students may keep cars.

FACULTY/CLASSROOMS: 44% of faculty are male; 56% are female. All teach undergraduates. No introductory courses are taught by graduate students. The average class size in an introductory lecture is 20; in a laboratory is 15; and in a regular course is 16.

PROGRAMS OF STUDY: SXU confers B.A., B.S., and B.M. degrees. Master's degrees are also awarded. Bachelor's degrees are awarded in BIOLOGICAL SCIENCE (biology/biological science), BUSINESS (accounting, banking and finance, business administration and management, international business management, and marketing/retailing/merchandising), COMMUNICATIONS AND THE ARTS (communications, English, French, music, and Spanish), COMPUTER AND PHYSICAL SCIENCE (chemistry, computer science, and mathematics), EDUCATION (art education, early childhood education, elementary education, foreign languages education, middle school education, music education, science education, and secondary education), HEALTH PROFESSIONS (nursing, predentistry, premedicine, prepharmacy, and speech pathology/audiology), SOCIAL SCIENCE (criminal justice, history, philosophy, political science/government, prelaw, psychology, religion, social science, and sociology). Business, nursing, and education are the strongest academically and have the largest enrollments.

ACTIVITIES: There are no fraternities or sororities. There are 37 groups on campus, including art, band, cheerleading, choir, chorus, computers, drama, ethnic, honors, international, jazz band, literary magazine, marching band, musical theater, newspaper, pep band, political, professional, radio and TV, religious, social service, student government, and yearbook. Popular campus events include Xavierfest, Boat Bash, and Octoberfest. **Sports:** There are 4 intercollegiate sports for men and 5 for women, and 4 intramural sports for men and 4 for women. Facilities include baseball, softball, an outdoor sports facility, and football field. The convocation and athletic center seats 2200 in the main arena with 4 additional competition courts, racquetball courts, an indoor running track, training rooms, and a health and fitness center.

SERVICES: Counseling and information services are available, as is tutoring in every subject. There are reading and language clinics and a center for learning disabilities. **Library/Resources:** The library contains 172,104 volumes, 10,519 microform items, and 2,282 audio/video tapes/CDs/DVDs, and subscribes to 798 periodicals including electronic. Computerized library services include interlibrary loans, database searching, and Internet access. Special learning facilities include an art gallery and radio station. **Physically Challenged Students:** 98% of the campus is accessible. Facilities include wheelchair ramps, elevators, special parking, specially equipped restrooms, special class scheduling, lowered drinking fountains, and lowered telephones. **Special:** The university offers internships and study abroad in England, Ireland, and Italy. There is a freshman honors program. **Visiting:** There are regularly scheduled orientations for prospective students. There are guides for informal visits, visitors may sit in on classes, and stay overnight. To schedule a visit, contact the Director of Admissions. **Campus Safety and Security:** Measures include 24-hour foot and vehicle patrol, self-defense education, and security escort services. There are shuttle buses, emergency telephones, and lighted pathways/sidewalks.

REQUIREMENTS: The ACT is required. Students must be graduates of an accredited secondary school and have earned 16 specific academic credits, including 4 years each of English and the natural and social sciences, 3 each of math and academic electives, and 2 years of a foreign language. The GED is accepted. AP and CLEP credits are accepted. To graduate, the student must complete 120 credit hours, including the school's 57-semester-hour core curriculum, and earn a GPA of 2.0. The credit hours required in the student's major vary by subject. **Procedure:** Freshmen are admitted fall and spring. Entrance exams should be taken during the spring of the junior year. There are deferred admissions and rolling admissions plans. Applications should be filed by May 1 for fall entry, along with a $35 fee. Notification is sent on a rolling basis. Applications are accepted on-line. **Transfer Students:** 471 transfer students enrolled in 2015-2016. Applicants must have completed 12 semester hours with a GPA of 2.25. An interview is recommended. 30 of 120 credits required for the bachelor's degree must be completed at SXU. **International Students:** The school actively recruits these students. They must take the TOEFL.

Admissions Contact: Beth Gierach, Director of Enrollment Services. Email: *admissions@sxu.edu* Web: *www.sxu.edu*

FINANCIAL AID: In 2016-2017, 96% of all full-time freshmen received some form of financial aid. 96% of all full-time freshmen received need-based aid. Check with the school for current application deadlines.

SCHOOL OF THE ART INSTITUTE OF CHICAGO *(The complete profile is made available exclusively on our website, www.barronspac.com)*

SHIMER COLLEGE C-1

www.shimer.edu

Chicago, IL 60616 (312) 235-3504

Fax: (312) 235-3501	**Email:** admission@shimer.edu
Full-time: 36 men, 31 women	**Faculty:** 11
Part-time: 3 men, 4 women	**Ph.D.s:** 100%
Graduate: n/av	**Student/Faculty:** 7 to 1
Year: semesters, summer session	**Tuition:** $31,326
Room & Board: $10,804	**Freshman Class:** 31 applied, 26 accepted, 12 enrolled
SAT CR/M/W: 690/570/560	**CEEB CODE:** 1717
Application Deadline: August 1	**VERY COMPETITIVE+**

Shimer College, founded in 1853, is a private liberal arts institution that shares space on the campus of the Illinois Institute of Technology. Figures in the above capsule and in this profile are approximate. There is 1 undergraduate school. The 120-acre campus is in an urban area in Chicago, IL. Including any residence halls, there are 40 buildings.

STUDENT LIFE: 52% of undergraduates are from out of state. 77% are White; 4% Asian American; 4% Hispanic; 2% African American. **Male To Female Ratio:** 1.1:1. The average age of freshmen is 19; all undergraduates, 23. 16% do not continue beyond their first year; 63% remain to graduate. **Housing:** 76 students can be accommodated in college housing, which includes single-sex and coed dorms, on-campus apartments, and married student housing. Coed dorms, single students apartments, and theme housing available. On-campus housing is guaranteed for all 4 years. 95% of students commute. All students may keep cars.

FACULTY/CLASSROOMS: 67% of faculty are male; 33% are female. All teach undergraduates. No introductory courses are taught by graduate students. The average class size in a regular course is 9.

PROGRAMS OF STUDY: Shimer confers B.A. and B.S. degrees. Bachelor's degrees are awarded in COMPUTER AND PHYSICAL SCIENCE (natural sciences), SOCIAL SCIENCE (humanities, liberal arts/general studies, and social science). Humanities and social science are the strongest academically. Humanities has the largest enrollment.

ACTIVITIES: There are no fraternities or sororities. There are 62 groups on campus, including art, band, chess, computers, dance, drama, ethnic, film, international, jazz band, LGBT, literary magazine, newspaper, orchestra, photography, political, radio and TV, religious, social, social service, and student government. Popular campus events include Community Lunch, Poetry Readings, and a Talent Show. **Sports:** There is no sports program at Shimer. Students have use of a full service athletic facility and access to intramural sports. **Graduates:** From July 1, 2015 to June 30, 2016, 33 bachelor's degrees were awarded. The most popular majors were liberal arts/general studies (78%) and social sciences (22%). In an average class, 7% graduate in 3 years or less, 50% graduate in 4 years or less, 53% graduate in 5 years or less, and 58% graduate in 6 years or less. Of the 2015 graduating class, 20% were enrolled in graduate school within 6 months of graduation, and 70% were employed.

SERVICES: Counseling and information services are available, as is tutoring in every subject. **Library/Resources:** The 3 libraries contain 20,500 volumes, and 100 microform items. Computerized library services include interlibrary loans, database searching, and Internet access. Special learning facilities include a radio station. **Physically Challenged Students:** All of the campus is accessible. Facilities include wheelchair ramps, elevators, special parking, specially equipped restrooms, and special housing. **Special:** Shimer offers internships in all areas of study and study abroad at Oxford in England. There is an accelerated degree program, a B.A.-B.S. degree, dual majors in all areas, and a general studies degree. Nondegree study and pass/fail options are possible. **Visiting:** There are regularly scheduled orientations for prospective students, consisting of class visits, lunch, a tour, and an admission interview. There are guides for informal visits and visitors may sit in on classes. To schedule a visit, contact the Admissions Office. **Campus Safety and Security:** Measures include 24-hour foot and vehicle patrol, emergency notification system, and security escort services. There are shuttle buses, emergency telephones, lighted pathways/sidewalks, and controlled access to dorms/residences.

REQUIREMENTS: Applicants must submit essays, letters of recommendation, and an interview. The SAT or ACT required only of students who are applying for our Early Entrance program, a 55-year old program that offers full admission to high school age students - those who would be enrolling in their junior or senior years of high school, but prefer to matriculate early. Important factors in the admissions decision are evidence of special talent, personality/intangible qualities, and recommendations by school officials. To graduate, students must earn 125 credit hours with a GPA of at least 2.0, complete 2 comprehensive exams, and submit a thesis. The school requires 60 credit hours in the major for the B.S. degree, 40 for the B.A.; 65 in the core curriculum for the B.S., 85 for the B.A. **Procedure:** Freshmen are admitted fall, spring, and summer. There are deferred admissions and rolling admissions plans. Applications should be filed by August 1 for fall entry, along with a $25 fee. Applications are accepted on-line. **Transfer Students:** 7 transfer students enrolled in 2015-2016. Same as for all other applicants plus all post-secondary transcripts. 65 of 125 credits required for the bachelor's degree must be completed at Shimer. **International Students:** The school actively recruits these students. They must take the TOEFL with a minimum score of 590 on the paper-based TOEFL (PBT) or 97 on the Internet-based version (iBT).

ADMISSIONS: The SAT scores for the 2016-2017 freshman class were: Critical Reading-- 34% between 600 and 699 and 67% between 700 and 800. Math-- 67% between 500 and 599 and 34% between 600 and 699. **Admissions Contact:** Elaine Vincent, Director of Admissions. Email: *admission@shimer.edu* Web: *www.shimer.edu*

FINANCIAL AID: In 2016-2017, 74% of all full-time freshmen and 84% of continuing full-time students received some form of financial aid. 74% of all full-time freshmen and 84% of continuing full-time students received need-based aid. The average freshman award was $17,741. Need-based scholarships or need-based grants averaged $13,902; need-based self-help aid (loans and jobs) averaged $13,789; other non-need-based awards and non-need-based scholarships averaged $5,120; and $3,150 from other forms of aid. 52% of undergraduate students work part-time. Average annual earnings from campus work are $1800. The average financial indebtedness of the 2016 graduate was $25,125. Shimer is a member of CSS. The college's own financial statement is required. The FAFSA code is 001756. The priority date for freshman financial aid applications for fall entry is April 15. The deadline for filing freshman financial aid applications for fall entry is July 30.

SOUTHERN ILLINOIS UNIVERSITY CARBONDALE — D-5

www.siu.edu

Carbondale, IL 62901	(618) 536-4405
	Email: admissions@siu.edu
Full-time: 5652 men, 4857 women	**Faculty:** 762
Part-time: 919 men, 628 women	**Ph.D.s:** 80%
Graduate: 1937 men, 1868 women	**Student/Faculty:** 14 to 1
Year: semesters, summer session	**Tuition:** $13,481 ($27,130)
Room & Board: $10,186	**Freshman Class:** 9106 applied, 6980 accepted, 1611 enrolled
SAT CR/M: 505/500 **ACT:** 22	**CEEB CODE:** 1726
Application Deadline: May 1	**COMPETITIVE**

Southern Illinois University Carbondale, is a public institution founded in 1869. The multi-campus research university offer undergraduate and graduate programs. There are 8 undergraduate schools and 3 graduate schools. In addition to regional accreditation, SIU Carbondale has baccalaureate program accreditation with AACSB, ABET, ABFSE, ACEJMC, ADA, APTA, CSWE, NAAB, NASAD, NASM, NCATE, SAF, AAAHC, ACPHA, ACEND, ARC-PA, AAM, ABA, ACAIL, ACS, APA, AAALAC, AALS, LCME, AMA, AAMC, ATMAE, AABI, COLA, NAST, NATEF, NAEYC, NASPAA, CAAHEP, CARF, CEA, and CIDA. The 1136-acre campus is in a small town 100 miles southeast of St. Louis, MO. Including any residence halls, there are 243 buildings.

STUDENT LIFE: 83% of undergraduates are from Illinois. Others are from 48 states, 56 foreign countries, and Canada. 9% are Hispanic; 65% White; 4% Foreign; 3% two or more races; 2% Asian American; 17% African American. **Male To Female Ratio:** 1.2:1. The average age of freshmen is 18; all undergraduates, 23. 32% do not continue beyond their first year; 45% remain to graduate. **Housing:** 4610 students can be accommodated in college housing, which includes single-sex and coed dorms, on-campus apartments, and married student housing. In addition, there are honors houses, special-interest houses, theme and wellness housing, and living learning communities. On-campus housing is guaranteed for the freshman year only, and is available on a first-come, first-served basis. 74% of students commute. All students may keep cars.

FACULTY/CLASSROOMS: 62% of faculty are male; 38% are female. 83% teach undergraduates, 56% do research, and 49% do both. Graduate students teach 28% of introductory courses. The average class size in an introductory lecture is 26.

PROGRAMS OF STUDY: SIU Carbondale confers B.A., B.S., B.F.A., and B.Mus. degrees. Associate, master's, and doctoral degrees are also awarded. Bachelor's degrees are awarded in AGRICULTURE (agricultural economics, agriculture, animal science, forestry and related sciences, horticulture, plant science, and soil science), BIOLOGICAL SCIENCE (biology/biological science, botany, microbiology, physiology, and zoology), BUSINESS (accounting, banking and finance, business administration and management, business economics, fashion merchandising, funeral home services, hospitality management services, management science, marketing/retailing/merchandising, and recreation and leisure services), COMMUNICATIONS AND THE ARTS (Africana studies, art, broadcasting, design, dramatic arts, English, English literature, film arts, fine arts, foreign language, information technology, journalism, linguistics, music, musical theater, photography, radio/tv, speech/debate/rhetoric, and sports administration), COMPUTER AND PHYSICAL SCIENCE (chemistry, computer science, geology, information sciences and systems, mathematics, physics, and radiological technology), EDUCATION (early childhood education, elementary education, health education, health information management, physical education, physical science secondary school education, special education, and vocational education), ENGINEERING AND ENVIRONMENTAL DESIGN (architecture, automotive technology, aviation administration/management, aviation computer technology, civil engineering, computer engineering, electrical/electronics engineering, electrical/electronics engineering technology, engineering technology, industrial engineering technology, interior design, mechanical engineering, mining and mineral engineering, and technological management), HEALTH PROFESSIONS (dental hygiene, health care administration, kinesiology, and rehabilitation therapy), SOCIAL SCIENCE (anthropology, architectural studies, clothing and textiles management/production/services, communication sciences & disorders, criminal justice, dietetics, economics, fire protection, geography, history, liberal arts/general studies, paralegal studies, philosophy, political science/government, psychology, social science, social work, and sociology). Accounting, biological sciences, and psychology have the largest enrollments.

ACTIVITIES: 9% of men belong to 23 national fraternities; 8% of women belong to 12 national sororities. There are 400 groups on campus, including art, band, cheerleading, chess, choir, chorale, communications, computers, dance, debate, drama, drill team, environmental, ethnic, film, forensics, honors, international, jazz band, LGBT, literary magazine, marching band, musical theater, newspaper, opera, pep band, photography, political, professional, radio and TV, religious, social, social service, student government, symphony, and yearbook. Popular campus events include Cardboard Boat Regatta, International Festival, Heritage Celebration Months, and Homecoming. **Sports:** There are 9 intercollegiate sports for men and 9 for women, and 27 intramural sports for men and 27 for women. Facilities include a football stadium, basketball arena, softball stadium, a gym, volleyball, a track & field complex, swimming & diving, tennis, baseball, and a student-athlete academic center & weight room. **Graduates:** From July 1, 2015 to June 30, 2016, 3171 bachelor's degrees were awarded. The most popular majors were education (12%), business/marketing (9%), and engineering technologies (8%). 282 companies recruited on campus in 2015-2016. In an average class, 1% graduate in 3 years or less, 26% graduate in 4 years or less, and 45% graduate in 6 years or less.

SERVICES: Counseling and information services are available, as is tutoring in most subjects, such as 100- and 200- level general education courses, and there is a reader service for the blind. Through the Center for Learning Support Services, students can receive one-on-one tutoring, group study sessions, peer mentoring, and academic coaching. **Library/Resources:** The library contains 3.0 million volumes, 1.4 million microform items, 19,506 audio/video tapes/CDs/DVDs, and subscribes to 49,990 periodicals including electronic. Computerized library services include interlibrary loans, database searching, Internet access, and Wi-Fi capability. Special learning facilities include an art gallery, student-run newspaper and broadcast programs, farms and timberlands, greenhouses, livestock facilities, archeological center, aviation program, a crime study center, wildlife lab, engineering and science labs, simulated commodity and financial trading floor, child development laboratories, international programs and services, broadcasting division that operates public television and radio stations, a dental lab, a craft shop, and museum. **Physically Challenged Students:** 98% of the campus is accessible. Facilities include wheelchair ramps, elevators, special parking, specially equipped restrooms, special class scheduling, lowered drinking fountains, lowered telephones, special housing. classroom accommodations, and disability support services. **Special:** If you want to learn, we'll help take you as far as you want to go. Our academic offerings extend from the classroom to the lab room, as well as your residence hall and overseas. There i an honors program that will produce high-achieving students. The university honors program is an enriching, rewarding experience much like that of a private college. The UHP courses are more exclusive than others you will take at SIU small, limited to UHP students, and taught by our best faculty. There are scholarship, leadership, mentorship, hands-on research, and other opportunities. REACH (Research-Enriched Academic Challenge) is just one program that offers undergraduates small grants and other opportunities to gain research expertise by working alongside faculty mentors. We offer a variety of university-level, international study abroad experiences through semester or year-abroad programs, short-term travel/study programs, and educational exchanges. There are Living/Learning Communities for those who want to live with like-minded students. You'll get to know professors and classmates better, have greater access to academic resources, and find specialized programs right in your residence hall. Students who participate in a Living/Learning Community often have higher GPAs more positive campus experiences, and are more likely to graduate. At SIU, you also have access to The Saluki First Year, internships/co-ops, service learning, and writing in the disciplines. There are 8 national honor societies, a freshman honors program, and 11 departmental honors programs. **Visiting:** There are regularly scheduled orientations for prospective students, including new Student Orientation a one-day program for new SIU students and their families. There are guides for informal visits, visitors may sit in on classes, and stay overnight. To schedule a visit, contact the Undergraduate Admissions Office. **Campus Safety and Security:** Measures include 24-hour foot and vehicle patrol, emergency notification system, self-defense education, and security escort services. There are shuttle buses, emergency telephones, lighted pathways/sidewalks, controlled access to dorms/residences, a student patrol program, and campus police officers.

REQUIREMENTS: First-time students will be admitted to SIU if they have earned: 23 on the ACT and 2.0 GPA or an 18 ACT and 3.0 high school GPA. All other students' applications are holistically reviewed. We also consider class rank, ACT composite scores and sub-scores, absences, a personal statement (optional), activities, extracurricular participation, and other features of the application. SIU does not require a foreign language in high school. However, SIU does require 2 years of electives whether that be music, P.E., or art. In addition to the 2 years of electives, SIU requires 4 years of English, 3 years of math (4 years strongly suggested), 3 years of science with lab, and 3 years of social studies/science. AP and CLEP credits are accepted. Important factors in the admissions decision are extracurricular activities record, and evidence of special talent. All students must complete the University Core Curriculum. The University Core Curriculum is a carefully structured and deliberately sequenced program of study required of all SIU Carbondale undergraduate students. The program's objectives are to develop students' abilities to communicate orally and in writing, to think mathematically, and to analyze and conceptualize effectively. The Core is grounded in the traditional arts and sciences and fosters a life of inquiry, creativity, and civic participation. **Procedure:** Freshmen are admitted fall, spring, and summer. Entrance exams should be taken during spring of the junior year. There are deferred admissions and rolling admissions plans. Applications should be filed by May 1 for fall entry, along with a $40 fee. Notification is sent on a rolling basis. Applications are accepted on-line. **Transfer Students:** 1520 transfer students enrolled in 2015-2016. Transfer students must have 26 transferable semester hours or 39 quarter hours and a GPA of 2.0 on a 4.0 scale (as calculated by SIUC grading policies). If less than 26 transferable hours are acquired, transfer students must have a 2.0 GPA on a 4.0 scale (as calculated by SIUC grading policies) and also meet Freshman Admission Requirements. 30 of 120 credits required for the bachelor's degree must be completed at SIU-C. **International Students:** There are 448 international students enrolled. The school actively recruits these students. They must take the TOEFL with a minimum score of 520 on the paper-based TOEFL (PBT) or 68 on the Internet-based version (iBT), or IELTS with a score of 6 and iTEP with a score of 4. They must also take the SAT or ACT.

ADMISSIONS: 77% of the 2016-2017 applicants were accepted. The SAT scores for the 2016-2017 freshman class were: Critical Reading--45% below 500, 36% between 500 and 599, and 19% between 600 and 699. Math-- 42% below 500, 41% between 500 and 599, 15% between 600 and 699, and 2% between 700 and 800. The ACT scores were 7% between 12 and 17, 54% between 18 and 23, 32% between 24 and 29, and 7% above 30. 17% of the current freshmen were in the top fifth of their class; 36% were in the top two fifths. 30 freshmen graduated first in their class. **Admissions Contact:** Terri Harfst, Interim Director of Undergrad Admissions. Email: *admissions@siu.edu* Web: *www.siu.edu*

FINANCIAL AID: The average freshman award was $16,329. Need-based scholarships or need-based grants averaged $8,605; need-based self-help aid (loans and jobs) averaged $5,201; non-need-based athletic scholarships averaged $19,840; other non-need-based awards and non-need-based scholarships averaged $7,224; and $3,373 from other forms of aid. The average financial indebtedness of the 2016 graduate was

$27,819. The FAFSA code is 001758. The priority date for freshman financial aid applications for fall entry is March 1. The deadline for filing freshman financial aid applications for fall entry is rolling.

SOUTHERN ILLINOIS UNIVERSITY EDWARDSVILLE C-4

www.siue.edu

Edwardsville, IL 62026
(618) 650-3705
(800) 447-SIUE
Fax: (618) 650-5013
Email: admissions@siue.edu

Full-time: 4496 men, 5152 women
Part-time: 810 men, 883 women
Graduate: 1089 men, 1625 women
Year: semesters, summer session
Room & Board: $9051
ACT: 23
Application Deadline: May 1
Faculty: 556; IIA, -$
Ph.D.s: 79%
Student/Faculty: 15 to 1
Tuition: $13,592 ($26,120)
Freshman Class: 7660 applied, 6272 accepted, 2075 enrolled
CEEB CODE: 1759
COMPETITIVE

Southern Illinois University Edwardsville, founded in 1957, is part of the Southern Illinois University system and offers undergraduate programs in business, education, engineering, arts and sciences, and nursing. Graduate programs also are offered in 34 subject areas, including professional programs in pharmacy and dental medicine. There are 5 undergraduate schools and 1 graduate school. In addition to regional accreditation, SIUE has baccalaureate program accreditation with AACSB, ABET, ACCE, ACEJMC, CSWE, NASM, NCATE, CCNE, ASHA, and NAST. The 2660-acre campus is in a suburban area 18 miles northeast of downtown St. Louis, Missouri. Including any residence halls, there are 25 buildings.

STUDENT LIFE: 90% of undergraduates are from Illinois. Others are from 36 states, 40 foreign countries, and Canada. 74% are White; 3% Hispanic; 2% Asian American; 2% Foreign; 13% African American. **Female To Male Ratio:** 1.2:1. The average age of all undergraduates is 21. 27% do not continue beyond their first year; 52% remain to graduate. **Housing:** 3524 students can be accommodated in college housing, which includes coed dorms, on-campus apartments, and married student housing. In addition, there are fraternity houses, Honors wings, and special-interest wings. On-campus housing is available on a first-come, first-served basis. Priority is given to out-of-town students. 71% of students commute. All students may keep cars.

FACULTY/CLASSROOMS: 51% of faculty are male; 49% are female. 84% teach undergraduates. Graduate students teach 4% of introductory courses.

PROGRAMS OF STUDY: SIUE confers B.A., B.S., B.F.A., B.L.S., B.M., B.S.A., and B.S.W. degrees. Master's degrees are also awarded. Bachelor's degrees are awarded in BIOLOGICAL SCIENCE (biochemistry, biology/biological science, ecology, and genetics), BUSINESS (accounting, business administration and management, business economics, entrepreneurial studies, human resources, international business management, management information systems, and marketing and distribution), COMMUNICATIONS AND THE ARTS (American literature, art, art history and appreciation, communications, dance, dramatic arts, English, French, German, journalism, languages, media arts, music, music business management, music history and appreciation, music performance, music theory and composition, musical theater, public relations, radio/television technology, Spanish, speech/debate/rhetoric, studio art, and theater design), COMPUTER AND PHYSICAL SCIENCE (actuarial science, applied mathematics, chemistry, computer management, computer science, earth science, mathematics, physics, and statistics), EDUCATION (art education, early childhood education, elementary education, health education, health information management, mathematics education, music education, physical education, science education, social science education, and special education), ENGINEERING AND ENVIRONMENTAL DESIGN (civil engineering, computer engineering, construction management, electrical/electronics engineering, industrial engineering, manufacturing engineering, and mechanical engineering), HEALTH PROFESSIONS (community health work, exercise science, medical technology, medical science, nursing, and speech pathology/audiology), SOCIAL SCIENCE (anthropology, criminal justice, economics, forensic studies, geography, gerontology, history, liberal arts/general studies, philosophy, political science/government, psychology, social work, and sociology). Nursing, biological sciences, and business administration have the largest enrollments.

ACTIVITIES: 7% of men belong to 9 national fraternities; 5% of women belong to 7 national sororities. There are 170 groups on campus, including academic and recreational, art, band, cheerleading, choir, chorale, chorus, dance, drama, environmental, ethnic, honors, international, jazz band, LGBT, literary magazine, musical theater, newspaper, opera, orchestra, pep band, photography, political, professional, radio and TV, religious, social, social service, student government, and symphony. Popular campus events include Welcome Week, Arts and Issues Series, International Week, and Homecoming. **Sports:** There are 9 intercollegiate sports for men and 9 for women, and 17 intramural sports for men and 17 for women. Facilities include the Vadalabene Center and Student Fitness Center, which offer racquetball, basketball, aquatics, volleyball, indoor track, exercise, and weight training. The University Center, features restaurants, a recreation center, billiards, and a bowling alley. There is also an outdoor pool, canoeing and sailing, an outdoor track-and-field and soccer stadium, baseball, softball, and soccer fields, walking and biking trail, and a frisbee course. **Graduates:** From July 1, 2015 to June 30, 2016, 2223 bachelor's degrees were awarded. The most popular majors were business administration (20%), education (19%), and engineering (10%). 550 companies recruited on campus in 2015-2016. In an average class, 1% graduate in 3 years or less, 28% graduate in 4 years or less, 45% graduate in 5 years or less, and 50% graduate in 6 years or less.

SERVICES: Counseling and information services are available, as is tutoring in most subjects. There is a reader service for the blind, and remedial math, reading, and writing. **Library/Resources:** The library contains 810,537 volumes, 1.7 million microform items, and 33,438 audio/video tapes/CDs/DVDs, and subscribes to 32,858 periodicals including electronic. Computerized library services include interlibrary loans, database searching, and Internet access. Special learning facilities include an art gallery, radio station, TV station, a recording studio, engineering labs, an anthropology museum, a greenhouse, an arboretum, and a nursing psychomotor skills lab. **Physically Challenged Students:** All of the campus is accessible. Facilities include wheelchair ramps, elevators, special parking, specially equipped restrooms, special class scheduling, lowered drinking fountains, and lowered telephones. **Special:** SIUE offers cross-registration with the University of Missouri at St. Louis, co-op programs, internships, which are required by several majors, including mass communications and sociology, work-study programs, dual majors, B.A.-B.S. degrees, student-designed majors (available to specific honors students only), study abroad in 5 countries (England, France, Germany, the Netherlands, and Mexico), a liberal studies degree, and a 5-year (3+2) program in dental medicine. There are 20 national honor societies, a freshman honors program, and 15 departmental honors programs. **Visiting:** There are regularly scheduled orientations for prospective students, including visits before the semester starts. There are guides for informal visits and visitors may sit in on classes. To schedule a visit, contact the Office of Admissions. **Campus Safety and Security:** Measures include 24-hour foot and vehicle patrol, emergency notification system, self-defense education, and security escort services. There are shuttle buses, emergency telephones, lighted pathways/sidewalks, and emergency blue lights located throughout campus.

REQUIREMENTS: The ACT is required. Applicants must be graduates of an accredited secondary school or have a GED certificate. They must have completed 15 academic credits, based on 4 years of English, 3 each of math and lab science, 2 years of any combination of art, foreign language, music, and vocational education, at least 2 years of government and/or history, plus 1 more year of social studies. A GPA of 2.5 is required. AP and CLEP credits are accepted. To graduate, students must complete a total of 124 semester hours with a minimum GPA of 2.0. Students must fulfill general education requirements, including 9 hours of math/science, and complete a senior project. **Procedure:** Freshmen are admitted to all sessions. Entrance exams should be taken before high school graduation. There is a rolling admissions plan. Applications should be filed by May 1 for fall entry; December 15 for spring entry; and May 3 for summer entry, along with a $30 fee. Notification is sent on a rolling basis. Applications are accepted on-line. **Transfer Students:** 1242 transfer students enrolled in 2015-2016. Applicants must have a minimum 2.0 GPA in at least 30 semester hours earned. 30 of 124 credits required for the bachelor's degree must be completed at SIUE. **International Students:** There are 320 international students enrolled. The school actively recruits these students. They must take the TOEFL with a minimum score of 550 on the paper-based TOEFL (PBT) or 80 on the Internet-based version (iBT).

ADMISSIONS: 82% of the 2016-2017 applicants were accepted. The ACT scores were 31% below 12, 30% between 12 and 17, 22% between 18 and 23, 9% between 24 and 29, and 8% above 30. 33% of the current freshmen were in the top fifth of their class; 64% were in the top two fifths. **Admissions Contact:** Office of Admissions Email: *admissions@siue.edu* Web: *www.siue.edu*

FINANCIAL AID: In 2016-2017, 75% of all full-time freshmen and 65% of continuing full-time students received some form of financial aid. 70% of all full-time freshmen and 65% of continuing full-time students received need-based aid. The average freshman award was $11,620. Need-based scholarships or need-based grants averaged $8,827; need-based self-help aid (loans and jobs) averaged $8,130; and non-need-based athletic scholarships averaged $10,660. 27% of undergraduate students work part-time. The average financial indebtedness of the 2016 graduate was $25,998. The FAFSA code is 001759. The deadline for filing freshman financial aid applications for fall entry is March 1.

TRINITY CHRISTIAN COLLEGE E-2

www.trnty.edu

Palos Heights, IL 60463	**(708) 597-3000** **(800) 748-0085**
Fax: (708) 385-5665	**Email: admissions@trnty.edu**
Full-time: 365 men, 716 women	**Faculty:** 79; IIB, --$
Part-time: 112 men, 257 women	**Ph.D.s:** 67%
Graduate: n/av	**Student/Faculty:** 11 to 1
Year: semesters, summer session	**Tuition:** $26,190
Room & Board: $9390	**Freshman Class:** 625 applied, 536 accepted, 201 enrolled
SAT CR/M: 543/552 **ACT:** 23	**CEEB CODE:** 1820
Application Deadline: August 15	**COMPETITIVE**

Trinity Christian College, founded in 1959, is a private college offering programs in arts and sciences, business, health science, liberal arts, music, religion, and teacher preparation. There is 1 undergraduate school and one graduate school. In addition to regional accreditation, Trinity has baccalaureate program accreditation with AACSB, CSWE, and CCNE. The 170-acre campus is in a suburban area 20 miles southwest of the Chicago Loop. Including any residence halls, there are 22 buildings.

STUDENT LIFE: 71% of undergraduates are from Illinois. Others are from 34 states, 3 foreign countries, and Canada. 52% are from public schools. 9% are African American; 80% White; 7% Hispanic; 2% Asian American; 2% Foreign. 86% are Protestant; 14% Catholic. **Female To Male Ratio:** 2.0:1. The average age of freshmen is 18; all undergraduates, 21. 27% do not continue beyond their first year; 58% remain to graduate. **Housing:** 726 students can be accommodated in college housing, which includes coed dorms and off-campus apartments. On-campus housing is guaranteed for all 4 years. 61% of students live on campus; of those, 45% remain on campus on weekends. Alcohol is not permitted. All students may keep cars.

FACULTY/CLASSROOMS: 60% of faculty are male; 40% are female. All teach undergraduates, and all do research. No introductory courses are taught by graduate students. The average class size in an introductory lecture is 25; in a laboratory is 18; and in a regular course is 18.

PROGRAMS OF STUDY: Trinity confers B.A., B.S., B.S.N., B.F.A., and B.S.W. degrees. Master's degrees are also awarded. Bachelor's degrees are awarded in BIOLOGICAL SCIENCE (biochemistry, bioinformatics, and biology/biological science), BUSINESS (accounting and business administration and management), COMMUNICATIONS AND THE ARTS (applied music, art, communications, English, music, music production/recording technology, music performance, Spanish, and studio art), COMPUTER AND PHYSICAL SCIENCE (chemistry, computer science, digital arts/technology, information sciences and systems, and mathematics), EDUCATION (art education, education, elementary education, music education, special education, and sports studies), HEALTH PROFESSIONS (nursing, predentistry, premedicine, and preoptometry), SOCIAL SCIENCE (biblical studies, criminal justice, history, ministries, philosophy, prelaw, psychology, social work, sociology, and theological studies). Business, education, and nursing are the strongest academically and have the largest enrollments.

ACTIVITIES: There are no fraternities or sororities. There are 18 groups on campus, including art, band, cheerleading, choir, chorale, chorus, dance, drama, ethnic, honors, jazz band, literary magazine, newspaper, pep band, photography, political, professional, religious, social, social service, student government, and yearbook. Popular campus events include the Opus Fine Arts Festival and the Trollstock Concert. **Sports:** There are 6 intercollegiate sports for men and 6 for women, and 7 intramural sports for men and 7 for women. Facilities include a gym, track, stadium, baseball diamond, and softball and soccer fields. **Graduates:** From July 1, 2015 to June 30, 2016, 303 bachelor's degrees were awarded. The most popular majors were elementary education (38%), business (17%), and nursing (13%). 10 companies recruited on campus in 2015-2016. In an average class, 54% graduate in 4 years or less, 58% graduate in 5 years or less, and 59% graduate in 6 years or less. Of the 2015 graduating class, 10% were enrolled in graduate school within 6 months of graduation, and 82% were employed.

SERVICES: Counseling and information services are available, as is tutoring in every subject. **Library/Resources:** The library contains 75,298 volumes, 54,158 microform items, and 1,841 audio/video tapes/CDs/DVDs, and subscribes to 16,711 periodicals including electronic. Computerized library services include interlibrary loans, database searching, Internet access, and Wi-Fi capability. Special learning facilities include an art gallery, a Dutch heritage collection. **Physically Challenged Students:** 95% of the campus is accessible. Facilities include wheelchair ramps, elevators, special parking, specially equipped restrooms, and lowered drinking fountains. **Special:** Students may have various part-time or full-time internships in their major field. There are study abroad programs in Spain, Nicaragua, Ecuador, and South Korea. Pass/fail options exist. Dual majors are offered. There is 1 national honor society and a freshman honors program. **Visiting:** There are regularly scheduled orientations for prospective students, including a tour, an interview, a seminar, and class visits. There are guides for informal visits, visitors may sit in on classes, and stay overnight. To schedule a visit, contact the Admissions Office. **Campus Safety and Security:** Measures include 24-hour foot and vehicle patrol, self-defense education, and security escort services. There are emergency telephones and lighted pathways/sidewalks.

REQUIREMENTS: The ACT is recommended. Applicants should graduate from an accredited high school or have a GED. They should prepare with 3 or 4 years of high school English, 3 years of math, science, and social studies, or 2 years each of a combination of 2 subject areas chosen among foreign language, math, science, or social studies. An interview is required. AP and CLEP credits are accepted. Important factors in the admissions decision are advanced placement or honors courses, leadership record, and recommendations by school officials. All students must take 9 credits in English, 6 each in philosophy, history, and theology, as well as distribution requirements in cross-cultural studies, natural sciences, social sciences, fine arts, math, and phys ed. Students must complete 125 credit hours and maintain a minimum GPA of 2.0 to graduate. **Procedure:** Freshmen are admitted fall and spring. Entrance exams should be taken during the last semester of the junior year. There is a rolling admissions plan. Applications should be filed by August 15 for fall entry; January 15 for spring entry. The fall 2016 application fee was $20. Notification is sent on a rolling basis. **Transfer Students:** 218 transfer students enrolled in 2015-2016. Applicants must have 24 hours of acceptable credits and a minimum 2.3 GPA. Associate degrees are recognized for transfer. 45 of 125 credits required for the bachelor's degree must be completed at Trinity. **International Students:** There are 36 international students enrolled. They must take the TOEFL. They must also take the SAT or ACT.

ADMISSIONS: 86% of the 2016-2017 applicants were accepted. The SAT scores for the 2016-2017 freshman class were: Critical Reading-- 32% below 500, 52% between 500 and 599, 11% between 600 and 699, and 5% between 700 and 800. Math-- 37% below 500, 47% between 500 and 599, and 16% between 600 and 699. The ACT scores were 35% below 12, 22% between 12 and 17, 14% between 18 and 23, 13% between 24 and 29, and 16% above 30. 36% of the current freshmen were in the top fifth of their class; 60% were in the top two fifths. 3 freshmen graduated first in their class. **Admissions Contact:** Pete Hamstra, Vice President for Admissions. Email: *admissions@trnty.edu* Web: *www.trnty.edu*

FINANCIAL AID: In 2016-2017, 98% of all full-time freshmen received some form of financial aid. 98% of all full-time freshmen received need-based aid. Average annual earnings from campus work are $1500. The FAFSA code is 001771. The deadline for filing freshman financial aid applications for fall entry is February 15.

TRINITY COLLEGE OF NURSING AND HEALTH SCIENCES *(The complete profile is made available exclusively on our website, www.barronspac.com)*

TRINITY INTERNATIONAL UNIVERSITY E-2
www.tiu.edu/college

Deerfield, IL 60015	(847) 317-7000 (800) 822-3225
Fax: (847) 317-7081	**Email:** admissions@tiu.edu
Full-time: 445 men, 590 women	**Faculty:** IIA, --$
Part-time: 45 men, 185 women	**Ph.D.s:** 85%
Graduate: 1080 men, 550 women	**Student/Faculty:** n/av
Year: semesters, summer session	**Tuition:** $23,370
Room & Board: $7700	**Freshman Class:** n/av **CEEB CODE:** 1810
Application Deadline: open	**VERY COMPETITIVE**

Trinity International University, established in 1897 by the Evangelical Free Church, is a Christian liberal arts institution offering undergraduate, graduate, and doctoral programs. There are 8 undergraduate schools and 3 graduate schools. In addition to regional accreditation, Trinity has baccalaureate program accreditation with ATS and CAAHEP. The 111-acre campus is in a suburban area 25 miles north of Chicago. Including any residence halls, there are 34 buildings.

STUDENT LIFE: 52% of undergraduates are from Illinois. Others are from 48 states, 46 foreign countries, and Canada. 69% are from public schools. 8% are African American; 77% White; 4% Asian American; 4% Hispanic; 2% Foreign. 96% are Protestant. **Male To Female Ratio:** 1.2:1. The average age of freshmen is 18; all undergraduates, 21. 22% do not continue beyond their first year; 47% remain to graduate. **Housing:** 700 students can be accommodated in college housing, which includes single-sex dorms, on-campus apartments, and married student housing. On-campus housing is guaranteed for all 4 years. 58% of students live on campus; of those, 75% remain on campus on weekends. Alcohol is not permitted. All students may keep cars.

FACULTY/CLASSROOMS: 68% of faculty are male; 32% are female. 56% teach undergraduates. No introductory courses are taught by graduate students. The average class size in an introductory lecture is 40; in a laboratory is 20; and in a regular course is 15.

PROGRAMS OF STUDY: Trinity confers B.A. degrees. Master's and doctoral degrees are also awarded. Bachelor's degrees are awarded in BIOLOGICAL SCIENCE (biology/biological science), BUSINESS (accounting, business administration and management, human resources, international business management, marketing/retailing/merchandising, and sports management), COMMUNICATIONS AND THE ARTS (communications, digital communications, digital media, English, graphic design, graphic design & media, media arts, and music), COMPUTER AND PHYSICAL SCIENCE (chemistry and mathematics), EDUCATION (athletic training, elementary education, music education, physical education, and secondary education), HEALTH PROFESSIONS (physical therapy, premedicine, prephysical therapy, and sports medicine), SOCIAL SCIENCE (biblical studies, Christian studies, criminal justice, family and community services, history, human services, humanities, liberal arts/general studies, philosophy, psychology, social science, and youth ministry). Music, education, and Biblical studies are the strongest academically. Business, Christian ministries, and education have the largest enrollments.

ACTIVITIES: There are no fraternities or sororities. There are 36 groups on campus, including art, band, cheerleading, choir, chorale, computers, debate, drama, ethnic, handbell choir and gospel choir, honors, international, jazz band, literary magazine, newspaper, orchestra, pep band, political, religious, social service, student government, symphony, and yearbook. Popular campus events include Santa Lucia Festival, Fine Arts Series and Day of Prayer. **Sports:** There are 5 intercollegiate sports for men and 5 for women, and 6 intramural sports for men and 6 for women. Facilities include a student center, sports complex, and football and soccer fields. Students have access to a nearby indoor tennis and racquetball club. **Graduates:** From July 1, 2015 to June 30, 2016, 168 bachelor's degrees were awarded. The most popular majors were business (21%), Christian ministries (16%), and elementary education (12%). 24 companies recruited on campus in 2015-2016. In an average class, 33% graduate in 4 years or less. Of the 2015 graduating class, 21% were enrolled in graduate school within 6 months of graduation, and 55% were employed.

SERVICES: Counseling and information services are available, as is tutoring in every subject. There is a reader service for the blind, and remedial math, reading, and writing. **Library/Resources:** The library contains 247,650 volumes, 110,503 microform items, and 6,741 audio/video tapes/CDs/DVDs, and subscribes to 1,091 periodicals including electronic. Computerized library services include interlibrary loans, database searching, Internet access, and Wi-Fi capability. **Physically Challenged Students:** 75% of the campus is accessible. Facilities include wheelchair ramps, elevators, special parking, specially equipped restrooms, and special class scheduling. **Special:** Students can cross-register with the Christian College Consortium and at Trinity Evangelical Divinity School. Trinity offers 3 levels of internships, study abroad in 7 countries, and an opportunity through the American Studies Program to spend a semester in Washington. Dual majors, a general studies degree, and nondegree study are offered. There are 2 national honor societies, a freshman honors program, and 15 departmental honors programs. **Visiting:** There are regularly scheduled orientations for prospective students, including class visits, meetings with professors, and admission counselors, and a dorm visit. There are guides for informal visits, visitors may sit in on classes, and stay overnight. To schedule a visit, contact the Campus Visit Coordinator at visits@tiu.edu. **Campus Safety and Security:** Measures include 24-hour foot and vehicle patrol, self-defense education, and security escort services. There are emergency telephones and lighted pathways/sidewalks.

REQUIREMENTS: The ACT is preferred. A satisfactory score on the SAT is required. Applicants should be graduates of an accredited high school and have completed 15 academic credits in art, a foreign language, math, music, science, social studies, and English. A GED is accepted. Recommendations from a pastor must be submitted. A GPA of 2.5 is required. AP and CLEP credits are accepted. Important factors in the admissions decision are personality/intangible qualities, leadership record, and advanced placement or honors courses. To graduate, all students must complete 126 semester hours, including 58 general education hours and a variable 36 to 54 hours in the major. A GPA of 2.0 is required. Chapel attendance, Christian service, Bible study, and science are also required. **Procedure:** Freshmen are admitted fall and spring. Entrance exams should be taken during spring of the junior year or fall of the senior year. There is a rolling admissions plan. Application deadlines are open. The fall 2016 application fee was $25. Applications are accepted on-line. **Transfer Students:** 90 transfer students enrolled in 2015-2016. Applicants must submit college transcripts and have a cumulative college GPA of 2.0 or higher. 30 of 126 credits required for the bachelor's degree must be completed at Trinity. **International Students:** They must take the TOEFL with a minimum score of 580 on the paper-based TOEFL (PBT). They must also take the SAT or ACT, scoring 19.

ADMISSIONS: 6 freshmen graduated first in their class. **Admissions Contact:** Jordan Bryant, Director of Undergraduate Admissions. Email: *admissions@tiu.edu* Web: *www.tiu.edu/college*

FINANCIAL AID: In 2016-2017, 90% of all full-time freshmen and 86% of continuing full-time students received some form of financial aid. 63% of all full-time freshmen and 60% of continuing full-time students received need-based aid. The average freshman award was $17,895. Need-based scholarships or need-based grants averaged $8,442 ($12,000 maximum); need-based self-help aid (loans and jobs) averaged $5,513 ($5,625 maximum); and non-need-based athletic scholarships averaged $9,389 ($22,980 maximum). 53% of undergraduate students work part-time. Average annual earnings from campus work are $875. The average financial indebtedness of the 2016 graduate was $20,621. Trinity is a member of CSS. The FAFSA code is 001772. Check with the school for current application deadlines.

UNIVERSITY OF CHICAGO E-2
www.uchicago.edu

Chicago, IL 60637	(773) 702-8655
Fax: (773) 702-4199	**Email:** collegeadmissions@uchicago.edu
Full-time: 3043 men, 2752 women	**Faculty:** I, ++$
Part-time: 31 men, 18 women	**Ph.D.s:** 100%
Graduate: 4324 men, 2794 women	**Student/Faculty:** 5 to 1
Year: quarters, summer session	**Tuition:** $50,193
Room & Board: $14,777	**Freshman Class:** 30,069 applied, 2521 accepted, 1537 enrolled
SAT CR/M/W: 760/760/740 **ACT:** 34	**CEEB CODE:** 1832
Application Deadline: January 1	**MOST COMPETITIVE**

University of Chicago, founded in 1890, is a private liberal arts institution offering undergraduate and graduate programs with an emphasis on interdisciplinary studies, and rigorous theoretical inquiry, performed through open discussions between faculty and students. There is 1 undergraduate school and 12 graduate schools. In addition to regional accreditation, Chicago has baccalaureate program accreditation with NCATE. The 217-acre campus is in an urban area in Chicago. Including any residence halls, there are 163 buildings.

STUDENT LIFE: 85% of undergraduates are from out of state, mostly the Midwest. Students are from 50 states, 76 foreign countries, and Canada. 9% are Hispanic; 5% African American; 44% White; 4% two or more races; 17% Asian American; 11% Foreign. **Male To Female Ratio:** 1.3:1. The average age of freshmen is 19; all undergraduates, 20. 92% remain to graduate. **Housing:** 3000 students can be accommodated in college housing, which includes single-sex and coed dorms, on-campus apartments, and married student housing. On-campus housing is guaranteed for all 4 years, is available on a first-come, first-served basis, and is available on a lottery system for upperclassmen. 52% of students live on campus. Upperclassmen may keep cars.

FACULTY/CLASSROOMS: 69% of faculty are male; 31% are female. No introductory courses are taught by graduate students.

PROGRAMS OF STUDY: Chicago confers B.A. and B.S. degrees. Master's and doctoral degrees are also awarded. Bachelor's degrees are awarded in BIOLOGICAL SCIENCE (biochemistry and biology/biological science), COMMUNICATIONS AND THE ARTS (art history and appreciation, classics, comparative literature, East Asian languages and literature, English, film arts, German, linguistics, media arts, music, romance languages and literature, Russian, Slavic languages, theatre studies, and visual and performing arts), COMPUTER AND PHYSICAL SCIENCE (applied mathematics, chemistry, computer science, geoscience, mathematics, physics, and statistics), ENGINEERING AND ENVIRONMENTAL DESIGN (environmental science), HEALTH PROFESSIONS (medical science), SOCIAL SCIENCE (African American studies, anthropology, classical/ancient civilization, economics, gender studies, geography, history, human development, humanities, interdisciplinary studies, international studies, Judaic studies, Latin American studies, law, medieval studies, Near Eastern studies, philosophy, political science/government, psychology, public affairs, religion, social science, sociology, South Asian studies, and theological studies). Economics, biological sciences, and mathematics have the largest enrollments.

ACTIVITIES: 8% of men belong to 13 national fraternities; 12% of women belong to 8 national sororities. There are 400 groups on campus, including art, band, cheerleading, chess, choir, chorale, chorus, college bowl, computers, dance, debate, drama, ethnic, film, honors, improv group, international, jazz band, LGBT, literary magazine, Model UN, musical theater, newspaper, orchestra, photography, political, professional, radio and TV, religious, social, social service, student government, and symphony. Popular campus events include Scavenger Hunt, Summer Breeze Festival, Kuviasungnerk Winter Festival, and Festival of the Arts. **Sports:** There are 10 intercollegiate sports for men and 9 for women, and 13 intramural sports for men and 13 for women. Facilities include a field house, a stadium, an outdoor 400m track, baseball and softball fields, an arena, indoor basketball and squash courts, an indoor 200m track, weight and wrestling rooms, aerobic machines, and an indoor Olympic-sized pool, and a student activities center. **Graduates:** From July 1, 2015 to June 30, 2016, 1326 bachelor's degrees were awarded. The most popular majors were economics (25%), biological sciences (11%), and mathematics (9%). In an average class, 86% graduate in 4 years or less and 92% graduate in 6 years or less.

SERVICES: Counseling and information services are available, as is tutoring in some subjects such as biology, computer science, economics, general chemistry, organic chemistry, math, physics, statistics, and writing. There is a reader service for the blind. **Library/Resources:** The 5 libraries contain 1.3 million volumes, 3.2 million microform items, and 88,092 audio/video tapes/CDs/DVDs, and subscribe to 124,682 periodicals including electronic. Computerized library services include interlibrary loans, database searching, Internet access, and Wi-Fi capability. Special learning facilities include an art gallery, radio station, accessible high-quality computer labs, sate of the art research laboratories, multiple buildings dedicated to fine arts and performance (practice rooms, performance halls, studio space, etc.), on-campus museums (Oriental Institute, Renaissance Society), and daily tutor/mentor services. **Physically Challenged Students:** Facilities include wheelchair ramps, elevators, special parking, specially equipped restrooms, lowered drinking fountains, lowered telephones, and special housing. **Special:** Special academic programs include "Careers In" programs that emphasize pre-professional skills, and study abroad programs in 18 countries, as well as many on-campus research and internship opportunities. B.A.-B.S. and general studies degrees are offered, as are student-designed majors. Bachelors, Masters joint programs are offered in many fields. Professional options in Public Policy Studies, Social Service Administration, and early admission to the University of Chicago Pritzker School of Medicine are available. Non-degree study and pass/fail options are also possible. There are 5 national honor societies and a chapter of Phi Beta Kappa. **Visiting:** There are regularly scheduled orientations for prospective students, There are daily tours and information sessions with admissions counselors during the week, and prospective students can sit in on classes, meet faculty, and current students. Interviews and overnight visits are available upon appointment. There are guides for informal visits. To schedule a visit, contact the Office of Admissions. **Campus Safety and Security:** Measures include 24-hour foot and vehicle patrol, emergency notification system, self-defense education, and security escort services. There are shuttle buses, emergency telephones, lighted pathways/sidewalks, and controlled access to dorms/residences.

REQUIREMENTS: The SAT or ACT is required. Admissions criteria include a recommended secondary school curriculum of 4 years each of English, mathematics, and science, 3 years of foreign language, and 2 years each of history and social studies. GED is accepted. Complete applications consist of test scores, a high school transcript, a school report, letters of recommendation, and essays. Interviews are optional. AP credits are accepted. To graduate, students must complete 42 quarter courses, including 9 to 13 courses in the major, with an overall GPA of at least 1.75 and at least 2.0 in the major. The core curriculum includes diverse sequences in humanities, social sciences, biological and physical sciences, civilization studies, and foreign languages. These sequences vary in length and content depending on the student's requests. Also required are 2 quarters of math and 1 of art, music, or drama. Students are free to shape and schedule this curriculum according to their interests. **Procedure:** Freshmen are admitted fall. Entrance exams should be taken during the junior or senior year. There are early admissions and deferred admissions plans. Early decision applications should be filed by November 1; regular applications, by January 1 for fall entry, along with a $75 fee. Notification of early decision is sent December 15; regular decision, March 15. Applications are accepted on-line. **Transfer Students:** 29 transfer students enrolled in 2015-2016. Proven ability and interest in liberal arts education is considered. Essay, broad course-work, and solid performance at the home institution is considered critical. A recommendation is required from a secondary school, instructors, and dean of previous institution. A 2-year residency is a requirement. 42 of 42 credits required for the bachelor's degree must be completed at Chicago. **International Students:** There are 633 international students enrolled. The school actively recruits these students. They must take the TOEFL with a minimum score of 104 on the Internet-based version (iBT), or take the IELTS, with a minimum overall score of 7. They must also take the SAT or ACT.

ADMISSIONS: 8% of the 2016-2017 applicants were accepted. The SAT scores for the 2016-2017 freshman class were: Critical Reading-- 1% between 500 and 599, 17% between 600 and 699, and 82% between 700 and 800. Math-- 1% between 500 and 599, 15% between 600 and 699, and 85% between 700 and 800. Writing-- 1% between 500 and 599, 21% between 600 and 699, and 78% between 700 and 800. The ACT scores were 5% between 24 and 29, and 95% above 30. 99% of the current freshmen were in the top fifth of their class. **Admissions Contact:** Tina Baskin, Director. Email: *collegeadmissions@uchicago.edu* Web: *www.uchicago.edu*

FINANCIAL AID: In 2016-2017, 64% of all full-time freshmen and 62% of continuing full-time students received some form of financial aid. The average freshman award was $51,043. Need-based scholarships or need-based grants averaged $46,854; and need-based self-help aid (loans and jobs) averaged $2,200. The average financial indebtedness of the 2016 graduate was $21,291. Chicago is a member of CSS. The college's own financial statement, and federal tax return are required. The FAFSA code is 001774. The priority date for freshman financial aid applications for fall entry is February 15.

UNIVERSITY OF ILLINOIS AT CHICAGO E-2

www.uic.edu

Chicago, IL 60607	(312) 996-4366
Fax: (312) 413-7628	Email: uicadmit@uic.edu
Full-time: 8154 men, 8363 women	**Faculty:** I, av$
Part-time: 780 men, 662 women	**Ph.D.s:** n/av
Graduate: 4785 men, 6376 women	**Student/Faculty:** n/av
Year: semesters, summer session	**Tuition:** $13,664 ($26,520)
Room & Board: $11,342	**Freshman Class:** 17931 applied, 13196 accepted, 3307 enrolled
SAT CR/M/W: 550/575/530 **ACT:** 24	**CEEB CODE:** 1851
Application Deadline: January 15	**VERY COMPETITIVE**

University of Illinois at Chicago, provides undergraduate and graduate programs in liberal arts, fine arts, business, engineering, architecture, health sciences, music, teacher preparation, and social work and professional training in dentistry, medicine, and pharmacy. There are 9 undergraduate schools and 14 graduate schools. In addition to regional accreditation, UIC has baccalaureate program accreditation with AACSB, ABET, ACPE, APTA, CAHEA, CSAB, CSWE, NAAB, APA, AOTA, and ACME. The 244-acre campus is in an urban area just west of downtown Chicago. Including any residence halls, there are 180 buildings.

STUDENT LIFE: 94% of undergraduates are from Illinois. Others are from 43 states, 65 foreign countries, and Canada. 95% are from public schools. 8% are African American; 32% White; 31% Hispanic; 3% Foreign; 3% two or more races; 22% Asian American; 1% race unknown. **Female To Male Ratio:** 1.1:1. The average age of freshmen is 18; all undergraduates, 21. **Housing:** 3718 students can be accommodated in college housing, which includes coed dorms and on-campus apartments. In addition, there are honors houses, special-interest houses, The President's Award House, and special-interest floors. On-campus housing is available on a first-come, first-served basis. 83% of students commute. All students may keep cars.

FACULTY/CLASSROOMS: 54% of faculty are male; 46% are female. 56% teach undergraduates. Graduate students teach 35% of introductory courses. The average class size in an introductory lecture is 104; in a laboratory is 107; and in a regular course is 111.

PROGRAMS OF STUDY: UIC confers B.A., B.B.A., B.Des., B.Mus., B.S.N., B.S., and B.F.A. degrees. Master's and doctoral degrees are also awarded. Bachelor's degrees are awarded in AGRICULTURE (environmental studies), BIOLOGICAL SCIENCE (biochemistry, biology/biological science, biophysics, forensic science, neurosciences, nutrition, and nutritional sciences), BUSINESS (accounting, banking and finance, business administration and management, business economics, business information systems, entrepreneurial studies, finance, management science, marketing/retailing/merchandising, and real estate), COMMUNICATIONS AND THE ARTS (applied music, art history, art/art studies, art history and appreciation, communications, dramatic arts, English, English literature, film arts, film, television and digital media, fine arts, French, French and Francophone studies, German, Germanic languages and literature, graphic design, graphic design & media, industrial design, Italian, jazz, music, music performance, painting, photography, Polish, Russian, Russian languages and literature, sculpture, Slavic languages, Spanish, studio art, theatre acting, theatre arts, theater design, theatre production, theatre studies, and visual and performing arts), COMPUTER AND PHYSICAL SCIENCE (chemistry, computer mathematics, computer science, digital arts/technology, earth science, environmental geology, geoenvironmental studies, information sciences and systems, mathematics, mathematics/computational, physics, science of earth systems, and statistics), EDUCATION (art education, early childhood education, elementary education, English education, health education, health information management, learner designed area of study, mathematics education, museum studies, nutrition education, physical education, secondary education, and sports and wellness studies), ENGINEERING AND ENVIRONMENTAL DESIGN (architecture, bioengineering, chemical engineering, civil engineering, computer engineering, electrical/electronics engineering, energy systems technology, engineering, engineering physics, history of architecture / urban development, industrial engineering technology, materials engineering, and mechanical engineering), HEALTH PROFESSIONS (allied health, exercise science, nursing, occupational therapy, pharmacology, pharmacy, physical therapy, pre-health studies, predentistry, premedicine, prepharmacy, and public health), SOCIAL SCIENCE (African American studies, anthropology, applied psychology, architectural studies, classical/ancient civilization, criminal justice, criminology, economics, ethnic studies, forensic studies, French studies, gender studies, German area studies, history, humanities, Italian studies, Latin American studies, law enforcement and corrections, philosophy, physical fitness/movement, political science/government, psychology, public administration, public affairs, Russian and Slavic studies, sociology, Spanish studies, urban studies, and women & gender studies). Math, history, and fine arts are the strongest academically. Psychology, biological science, and accounting have the largest enrollments.

ACTIVITIES: 5% of men belong to 18 national fraternities; 4% of women belong to 15 national sororities. There are 285 groups on campus, including The American Medical Student Association and the American Student Dental Association, Indian Graduate Student Association, Muslim Student Association, accounting club, art, band, cheerleading, chess, choir, chorus, communications, computers, dance, drama, environmental, ethnic, honors, international, jazz band, LGBT, literary magazine, musical theater, newspaper, orchestra, pep band, political, professional, radio and TV, religious, social, social service, student government, and symphony. Popular campus events include Fun Fair, Meet the Greeks, New Student Convocation and Spark in the Park, and LOL @ UIC. **Sports:** There are 9 intercollegiate sports for men and 10 for women, and 52 intramural sports for men and 42 for women. Facilities include The Curtis Granderson Stadium, a 12,000-seat sports pavilion, 2 sports and fitness centers, a recreation center, 1000-seat gym, 3 pools, racquetball and tennis courts, baseball, softball, and soccer fields, a bowling alley, indoor and outdoor tracks, and weight rooms. **Graduates:** From July 1, 2015 to June 30, 2016, 3912 bachelor's degrees were awarded. The most popular majors were business/marketing (15%), biological sciences (14%), and psychology (13%). 300 companies recruited on campus in 2015-2016. In an average class, 34% graduate in 4 years or less, 55% graduate in 5 years or less, and 58% graduate in 6 years or less.

SERVICES: Counseling and information services are available, as is tutoring in most subjects. There is a reader service for the blind, remedial math, reading, and writing, a writing center, and academic skills classes are also available. **Library/Resources:** The 2 libraries contain 17.9 million volumes, 440,000 microform items, and 27,000 audio/video tapes/CDs/DVDs, and subscribe to 61,000 periodicals including electronic. Computerized library services include interlibrary loans, database searching, Internet access, and Wi-Fi capability. Special learning facilities include an art gallery, radio station, Jane Addams Hull House, which is a restored settlement house, and the James Woodworth Prairie Reserve. **Physically Challenged Students:** 80% of the campus is accessible. Facilities include wheelchair ramps, elevators, special parking, specially equipped restrooms, special class scheduling, lowered drinking fountains, and lowered telephones. **Special:** Special academic programs include a wide variety of co-op and program internships, work-study with some 70 on- and off-campus employers, and study abroad opportunities at accredited foreign universities, as well as special programs in France, Italy, Canada, Austria, Spain, and Mexico. Interdisciplinary majors are offered in architectural studies, communications and theater, math and computer science, bioengineering, and information and decision sciences. Up to 4 semester hours of credit may be granted for military experience. Dual and student-designed majors, nondegree study, and pass/fail options are available. There are 4 national honor societies, Phi Beta Kappa, a freshman honors program, and 90 departmental honors programs. **Visiting:** There are regularly scheduled orientations for prospective students, consisting of a general meeting, a college meeting, and campus tours. There are guides for informal visits, visitors may sit in on classes, and stay overnight. To schedule a visit, contact Robert M. Moranetz at (312) 413-7628. **Campus Safety and Security:** Measures include 24-hour foot and vehicle patrol, emergency notification system, self-defense education, and security escort services. There are shuttle buses, emergency telephones, lighted pathways/sidewalks, controlled access to dorms/residences, and emergency call buttons across campus.

REQUIREMENTS: Either the ACT, SAT or SAT-I are required. Applicants should be graduates of an accredited secondary school the GED is accepted. The recommended secondary school curriculum varies according to the college program chosen, but 15 high school credits are required as follows: 4 in English, 3 in math, science, and foreign language, and 2 in social studies. AP and CLEP credits are accepted. Students must demonstrate proficiency in written English through either course-work or testing and complete 24 hours of general education, including at least 1 course in each of the general education categories: Analyzing the Natural World, Understanding the Individual and Society, Understanding the Past, Understanding the Creative Arts, Exploring the World Cultures, and Understanding U.S. Society. A minimum overall GPA of 2.0 is required. Total number of hours to graduate varies by major but is always at least 120. **Procedure:** Freshmen are admitted fall. Entrance exams should be taken in the spring of the junior year or the fall of the senior year. There is a rolling admissions plan. Applications should be filed by January 15 for fall entry, along with a $50 fee. Notification is sent on a rolling basis. Applications are accepted on-line. **Transfer Students:** 1958 transfer students enrolled in 2015-2016. Transferable hours and minimum GPA vary according to program. 30 of 120 credits required for the bachelor's degree must be completed at UIC. **International Students:** There are 566 international students enrolled. The school actively recruits these students. They must take the TOEFL with a minimum score of 550 on the paper-based TOEFL (PBT) or 80 on the Internet-based version (iBT). They must also take the SAT or ACT. Freshmen minimum required scores depend on the specific college.

ADMISSIONS: 74% of the 2016-2017 applicants were accepted. The SAT scores for the 2016-2017 freshman class were: Critical Reading-- 25% below 500, 44% between 500 and 599, 23% between 600 and 699, and 8% between 700 and 800. Math-- 27% below 500, 31% between 500 and 599, 29% between 600 and 699, and 13% between 700 and 800. Writing-- 36% below 500, 43% between 500 and 599, 15% between 600 and 699, and 6% between 700 and 800. The ACT scores were 3% between 12 and 17, 45% between 18 and 23, 43% between 24 and 29, and 10% above 30. 51% of the current freshmen were in the top fifth of their class; 81% were in the top two fifths. **Admissions Contact:** Malinda Lorkovich, Managing Director of Admissions. Email: *uicadmit@uic.edu* Web: *www.uic.edu*

FINANCIAL AID: In 2016-2017, 62% of all full-time freshmen and 65% of continuing full-time students received some form of financial aid. 62% of all full-time freshmen and 61% of continuing full-time students received need-based aid. The average freshman award was $14,869. Need-based scholarships or need-based grants averaged $13,899; need-based self-help aid (loans and jobs) averaged $3,589; non-need-based athletic scholarships averaged $22,030; and other non-need-based awards and non-need-based scholarships averaged $5,926. 18% of undergraduate students work part-time. Average annual earnings from campus work are $4881. The average financial indebtedness of the 2016 graduate was $23,669. UIC is a member of CSS. The FAFSA code is 001776. The deadline for filing freshman financial aid applications for fall entry is March 1.

UNIVERSITY OF ILLINOIS AT URBANA-CHAMPAIGN E-3

www.illinois.edu

Urbana, IL 61801	(217) 333-0302
	Email: admissions@illinois.edu
Full-time: 17,685 men, 13,831 women	**Faculty:** I, +$
	Ph.D.s: 92%
Part-time: 770 men, 409 women	**Student/Faculty:** 19 to 1
Graduate: 6343 men, 5904 women	**Tuition:** $15,698 ($30,796)
Year: semesters, summer session	**Freshman Class:** n/av
Room & Board: $11,308	
SAT or ACT: required	**CEEB CODE:** 1836
Application Deadline: December 1	**HIGHLY COMPETITIVE**

The University of Illinois at Urbana-Champaign, founded in 1867, is the oldest and largest campus in the University of Illinois system, offering some 150 undergraduate, and more than 100 graduate degree programs. There are 18 undergraduate schools. In addition to regional accreditation, Illinois has baccalaureate program accreditation with AACSB, AALE, ABET, ACEJMC, ADA, ASLA, CSAB, CSWE, NAAB, NASAD, NASM, NCATE, NRPA, SAF, ABA, ACS, APA, CAAHEP, CADE, NASD, and NAST. The 4938-acre campus is in a small town 140 miles south of Chicago, 125 miles west of Indianapolis, and 180 miles northeast of St. Louis. Including any residence halls, there are 705 buildings.

STUDENT LIFE: 76% of undergraduates are from Illinois. Others are from 50 states, 115 foreign countries, and Canada. 7% are African American; 7% Hispanic; 66% White; 6% Foreign; 13% Asian American; 1% American Indian/Alaska Native. **Male To Female Ratio:** 1.2:1. The average age of freshmen is 18; all undergraduates, 20. 7% do not continue beyond their first year; 83% remain to graduate. **Housing:** 11034 students can be accommodated in college housing, which includes single-sex and coed dorms, on-campus apartments, and married student housing. In addition, there are language houses, special-interest houses, and privately owned university-approved residence halls, fraternity and sorority houses. On-campus housing is guaranteed for all 4 years. 50% of students commute. All students may keep cars.

FACULTY/CLASSROOMS: 67% of faculty are male; 33% are female. 95% teach undergraduates, and 95% do research. Graduate students teach 38% of introductory courses. The average class size in an introductory lecture is 19; in a laboratory is 22; and in a regular course is 29.

PROGRAMS OF STUDY: Illinois confers A.B., B.S., B.A.U.P., B.F.A., B.Land.Arch., B.Mus., B.S.Ed., B.S.J., B.S.W., and B.V.M. degrees. Master's and doctoral degrees are also awarded. Bachelor's degrees are awarded in AGRICULTURE (agricultural business management, agricultural communications, agricultural economics, agricultural mechanics, agronomy, animal science, forestry and related sciences, horticulture, natural resource management, range/farm management, and wildlife management), BIOLOGICAL SCIENCE (biology/biological science, biophysics, biotechnology, botany, cell biology, entomology, microbiology, molecular biology, nutrition, physiology, plant physiology, and wildlife biology), BUSINESS (accounting, banking and finance, entrepreneurial studies, hospitality management services, human resources, insurance, labor studies, logistics, management information systems, management science, marketing and distribution, marketing management, marketing/retailing/merchandising, operations research, organizational behavior, personnel management, purchasing/inventory management, real estate, and recreation and leisure services), COMMUNICATIONS AND THE ARTS (advertising, art history and appreciation, broadcasting, classics, communications, comparative literature, crafts, dance, dramatic arts, East Asian languages and literature, English, English literature, film arts, fine arts, French, Germanic languages and literature, graphic design, Hebrew, industrial design, Italian, journalism, linguistics, media arts, music, music history and appreciation, music performance, music theory and composition, painting, photography, Portuguese, Russian languages and literature, sculpture, Spanish, speech/debate/rhetoric, and voice), COMPUTER AND PHYSICAL SCIENCE (actuarial science, astronomy, chemistry, computer management, computer mathematics, computer programming, geology, mathematics, physics, and statistics), EDUCATION (agricultural education, art education, athletic training, computer education, early childhood education, education, education of the multiply handicapped, elementary education, English education, foreign languages education, mathematics education, music education, physical education, science education, secondary education, and vocational education), ENGINEERING AND ENVIRONMENTAL DESIGN (aeronautical engineering, agricultural engineering, airline piloting and navigation, architectural engineering, architecture, aviation administration/management, bioengineering, ceramic engineering, chemical engineering, city/community/regional planning, civil engineering, computational sciences, computer engineering, computer technology, electrical/electronics engineering, engineering, engineering mechanics, engineering physics, geological engineering, industrial administration/management, industrial engineering, landscape architecture/design, materials engineering, materials science, mechanical engineering, metallurgical engineering, nuclear engineering, and plastics engineering), HEALTH PROFESSIONS (biomedical science, community health work, exercise science, health care administration, preveterinary science, public health, and rehabilitation therapy), SOCIAL SCIENCE (anthropology, child psychology/development, dietetics, East Asian studies, economics, family/consumer studies, food production/management/services, food science, geography, history, human development, humanities, international studies, Latin American studies, liberal arts/general studies, parks and recreation management, philosophy, political science/government, prelaw, psychology, religion, Russian and Slavic studies, sociology, textiles and clothing, and women's studies). Engineering, computer science, and business are the strongest academically. Psychology, biology, and electrical & computer engineering have the largest enrollments.

ACTIVITIES: 21% of men belong to 3 local and 59 national fraternities; 21% of women belong to 2 local and 34 national sororities. There are 1000 groups on campus, including art, band, cheerleading, chess, choir, chorale, chorus, computers, dance, debate, drama, drill team, environmental, ethnic, film, forensics, honors, international, jazz band, LGBT, literary magazine, marching band, musical theater, newspaper, opera, orchestra, pep band, photography, political, professional, radio and TV, religious, social, social service, student government, symphony, and yearbook. Popular campus events include Quad Day to introduce Campus Organizations, Homecoming, Dad's Weekend, and Mom's Weekend. **Sports:** There are 10 intercollegiate sports for men and 12 for women, and 21 intramural sports for men and 21 for women. Facilities include an indoor recreation space, an outdoor recreation space for students' fitness, and wellness needs, all major varsity sport facilities, and numerous student union facilities from bowling to exercise facilities. **Graduates:** The most popular majors were business, engineering, and social sciences/engineering technology. 6500 companies recruited on campus in 2015-2016.

SERVICES: Counseling and information services are available, as is tutoring in every subject. There is a reader service for the blind, and remedial math, reading, and writing. Transportation and rehabilitation services are offered, as well as interpreters, note taking, taped lectures, and priority registration. **Library/Resources:** The 27 libraries contain 11.0 million volumes, and 1,000,000 audio/video tapes/CDs/DVDs. Computerized library services include interlibrary loans, database searching, Internet access, and Wi-Fi capability. Special learning facilities include an art gallery, natural history museum, planetarium, radio station, TV station, a language learning lab, performing arts center, a graphic technologies lab, world history and cultural museum, rehabilitation-education center, center for American music, a Japannse house and gardens, and rare books and special collections libraries. **Physically Challenged Students:** All of the campus is accessible. Facilities include wheelchair ramps, elevators, special parking, specially equipped restrooms, special class scheduling, lowered drinking fountains, lowered telephones, and special housing. **Special:** Illinois offers numerous academic opportunities students outside of the classroom. Participate in research with a faculty member, work in Research Park, take a trip on one of our 400 study abroad programs taking you to every continent except Antarctica, and engage in a flexible curriculum that prepares you for life after Illinois. There are 89 national honor societies, a chapter of Phi Beta Kappa, a freshman honors program, and 99 departmental honors programs. **Visiting:** There are regularly scheduled orientations for prospective students, consisting of a university overview and admission presentation followed by student-led campus tour. There are guides for informal visits and visitors may sit in on classes. To schedule a visit, contact Campus Visits at (217) 333-0824. **Campus Safety and Security:** Measures include 24-hour foot and vehicle patrol, emergency notification system, self-defense education, and security escort services. There are shuttle buses, emergency telephones, lighted pathways/sidewalks, controlled access to dorms/residences, Saferides program, safety presentations, and evaluations by campus police.

REQUIREMENTS: The SAT or ACT is required. The ACT Optional Writing test is also required. Applicants should be graduates of accredited secondary schools or have the GED. Advanced placement tests are encouraged and accepted. High school preparation must include 4 years of English, 3 or more of math, 2 each of lab science, and social studies, 2 of the same foreign language, and 2 of flexible academic units. A personal and professional essay is required. Visual arts applicants must submit a portfolio; performing arts applicants are required to audition. AP credits are accepted. Important factors in the admissions decision are advanced placement or honors courses, evidence of special talent, and geographical diversity. All students must demonstrate satisfactory proficiency in the use of English and 6 hours each in approved composition classes, Western/non-Western cultural studies, arts and humanities, social sciences/behavior, natural sciences/technology, and quantitative reasoning. Successful completion of either the third or fourth year (depending on college) of a language other than the student's primary language is required. Students must maintain a minimum GPA of 2.0 while completing 120 to 132 credit hours (depending on the major) in order to graduate. **Procedure:** Freshmen are admitted fall. Applications should be filed by December 1 for fall entry. The fall 2016 application fee was $50. Notifications are sent February 13. Applications are accepted on-line. **Transfer Students:** 1343 transfer students enrolled in 2015-2016. Transfer application requirements differ by degree program. Transfer requirements by program can be viewed in the Transfer Handbook on the Admissions website. Admission is also subject to the number of places available. 30 of 132 credits required for the bachelor's degree must be completed at Illinois. **International Students:** There are 5031 international students enrolled. The school actively recruits these students. They must take the TOEFL with a minimum score of 550 on the paper-based TOEFL (PBT) or 79 on the Internet-based version (iBT), or take the IELTS. They must also take the SAT and ACT if the student has attended a U.S. institution for 2 or more years.

ADMISSIONS: There were 54 National Merit finalists. 9 freshmen graduated first in their class. **Admissions Contact:** Mike Drish, Director of Undergraduate Admissions. Email: *admissions@illinois.edu* Web: *www.illinois.edu*

FINANCIAL AID: The FAFSA code is 001775. Check with the school for current application deadlines.

UNIVERSITY OF ST. FRANCIS — E-2

www.stfrancis.edu

Joliet, IL 60435	**(815) 740-3400** **(800) 735-7500**
Fax: (815) 740-5032	**Email: admissions@stfrancis.edu**
Full-time: 493 men, 808 women	**Faculty:** 81; IIA, av$
Part-time: 21 men, 40 women	**Ph.D.s:** 69%
Graduate: 272 men, 944 women	**Student/Faculty:** 12 to 1
Year: semesters, summer session	**Tuition:** $30,840
Room & Board: $9084	**Freshman Class:** 1560 applied, 768 accepted, 215 enrolled
ACT: 23	**CEEB CODE:** 1130
Application Deadline: August 1	**COMPETITIVE**

The University of St. Francis, founded as a college in 1920, is a private liberal arts, and professional institution affiliated with the Roman Catholic Church. There are 4 undergraduate schools and 4 graduate schools. In addition to regional accreditation, USF has baccalaureate program accreditation with ACBSP, CSWE, NCATE, NRPA, ARCPA, and CCNE. The 34-acre campus is in a suburban area 35 miles southwest of Chicago. Including any residence halls, there are 7 buildings.

STUDENT LIFE: 95% of undergraduates are from Illinois. Others are from 20 states, and 14 foreign countries. 84% are from public schools. 8% are African American; 63% White; 3% Foreign; 3% two or more races; 20% Hispanic; 2% Asian American; 1% race unknown. 50% are Catholic; 25% Protestant. **Female To Male Ratio:** 2.3:1. The average age of freshmen is 18; all undergraduates, 22. 18% do not continue beyond their first year; 63% remain to graduate. **Housing:** 422 students can be accommodated in college housing, which includes coed dorms and on-campus apartments. On-campus housing is guaranteed for the freshman year only, and is available on a first-come, first-served basis, and is available on a lottery system for upperclassmen. 72% of students commute. All students may keep cars.

FACULTY/CLASSROOMS: 38% of faculty are male; 59% are female. 66% teach undergraduates. No introductory courses are taught by graduate students. The average class size in a laboratory is 12 and in a regular course is 17.

PROGRAMS OF STUDY: USF confers B.A., B.S., B.B.A., B.S.N., and B.S.W. degrees. Master's and doctoral degrees are also awarded. Bachelor's degrees are awarded in BIOLOGICAL SCIENCE (biology/biological science), BUSINESS (accounting, banking and finance, business administration and management, entrepreneurial studies, international business management, logistics, management science, marketing/retailing/merchandising, organizational leadership and management, and recreational facilities management), COMMUNICATIONS AND THE ARTS (art and design, communications, English, journalism, music, music performance, and visual and performing arts), COMPUTER AND PHYSICAL SCIENCE (computer programming, computer science, information sciences and systems, mathematics, and web technology), EDUCATION (art education, elementary education, music education, secondary education, and special education), ENGINEERING AND ENVIRONMENTAL DESIGN (computer technology and environmental science), HEALTH PROFESSIONS (allied health, health administration and policy, health care administration, medical technology, nuclear medical technology, nursing, predentistry, premedicine, preoptometry, prepharmacy, prephysical therapy, preveterinary science, radiation therapy, and radiograph medical technology), SOCIAL SCIENCE (addiction studies, counseling/psychology, criminal justice, history, liberal arts/general studies, political science/government, psychology, social work, and theological studies). Biology, education, and nursing are the strongest academically. Business, nursing, and biology have the largest enrollments.

ACTIVITIES: There are no fraternities; 2% of women belong to 1 national sorority. There are 64 groups on campus, including saints ambassador corps, business, nursing, education, art, cheerleading, choir, chorale, chorus, communications, computers, dance, drama, environmental, ethnic, honors, international, LGBT, literary magazine, musical theater, newspaper, opera, orchestra, pep band, political, professional, radio and TV, religious, social, social service, student government, and symphony. Popular campus events include Hypnotist, Homecoming Dance, and Comedians. **Sports:** There are 9 intercollegiate sports for men and 9 for women, and 10 intramural sports for men and 10 for women. Facilities include a football/soccer stadium, a track a baseball stadium are among the many off-campus facilities, a lighted softball complex, golf courses, soccer fields, and an indoor/outdoor tennis complex. On campus, a recreation center houses a gymnasium, racquetball court, a golf hitting studio, and a fitness center. **Graduates:** From July 1, 2015 to June 30, 2016, 322 bachelor's degrees were awarded. The most popular majors were nursing (28%), business/marketing (13%), and biology (9%). 76 companies recruited on campus in 2015-2016. In an average class, 44% graduate in 4 years or less, 62% graduate in 5 years or less, and 63% graduate in 6 years or less. Of the 2015 graduating class, 15% were enrolled in graduate school within 6 months of graduation, and 90% were employed.

SERVICES: Counseling and information services are available, as is tutoring in most subjects. There is a reader service for the blind. **Library/Resources:** The library contains 143,887 volumes, 1,767 microform items, and 9,573 audio/video tapes/CDs/DVDs, and subscribes to 21,237 periodicals including electronic. Computerized library services include interlibrary loans, database searching, Internet access, and Wi-Fi capability. Special learning facilities include an art gallery, radio station, TV station, wireless and multimedia classrooms, private music practice and instruction rooms, digital audio, and recording arts studio with state-of-the-art recording capabilities, 2D/3D design labs, medical, and skills simulation labs, a cadaver lab, a mock trial courtroom, a business incubator, an art & design complex with studio spaces for senior students, an international student center, a greenhouse, numerous multi-purpose spaces, on-campus beehives, and an outdoor challenge course. **Physically Challenged Students:** All of the campus is accessible. Facilities include wheelchair ramps, elevators, special parking, specially equipped restrooms, special class scheduling, lowered drinking fountains, and special housing. **Special:** Internships, on- and off-campus, paid and unpaid, are available in most majors. USF is the only school in Illinois that offers a B.A. in Substance Abuse Counseling. Dual and interdisciplinary majors, a pass/fail option, a Washington semester, study abroad, cross-registration with OCICU (Online Consortium of Independent Colleges and Universities), CIC (The Council of Independent Colleges) and credit for life, military, and work experience are available. Individualized major. Study abroad in France, Italy, England, Austria, Sweden, Bolivia, China, Finland, Costa Rica and Iceland. There are 19 national honor societies and a freshman honors program. **Visiting:** There are regularly scheduled orientations for prospective students, visiting students can participate in an orientation, meet faculty, a tour, and student presentations. There are guides for informal visits, visitors may sit in on classes, and stay overnight. To schedule a visit, contact USF Welcome Center Emily Ellis at (815) 740-2270. **Campus Safety and Security:** Measures include 24-hour foot and vehicle patrol, emergency notification system, and security escort services. There are shuttle buses, emergency telephones, lighted pathways/sidewalks, controlled access to dorms/residences, and routine fire inspection.

REQUIREMENTS: The ACT is required. Applicants must take 4 years of English, 3 of either art, music, foreign language, or computer science, 3 math, including geometry, 2 science (1 lab), 2 social studies, and 3 electives. USF requires applicants to be in the upper 50% of their class. A GPA of 2.5 is required. AP and CLEP credits are accepted. Important factors in the admissions decision are leadership record, advanced placement or honors courses, and personality/intangible qualities. Candidates for the bachelor's degree must complete the following: the Application for Graduation available in the Registrar's Office or through the MyUSF portal (Consult the Academic Calendar for specific deadlines). Earn a minimum of 128 semester hours of college credit. Complete the residency requirement of a minimum of 32 semester hours of approved undergraduate credit at USF. All students must complete a minimum of 15 hours of upper division (300-400) course-work, in the major, in residence at USF. In addition, 30 of the last 36 hours taken before graduation must be USF courses. (Note: individual colleges may have additional residency requirements). Complete all requirements with respect to the major program, support courses, liberal education, and electives. Complete the writing intensive (WI) course requirements as listed, achieve a cumulative grade point average of 2.0 or higher at USF, earn grades of C or higher in all courses required by the major and any minor programs, satisfy all financial requirements with the Business and Financial Aid Offices. It is the responsibility of the student to see that all graduation requirements are met. If a student withdraws for more than 1 semester, the catalog and regulations in effect at the time of their return will apply. Students completing a double major must select which degree they wish to receive since the University only awards one degree at graduation (however, the second major will appear on the transcript). If a student returns to complete a second major, they may apply for a second degree only if the new major leads to a different degree and they have met the current general education requirements in place at the time of awarding. **Procedure:** Freshmen are admitted fall and spring. Entrance exams should be taken in the spring of the junior year or the fall of the senior year. There are deferred admissions and rolling admissions plans. Applications should be filed by August 1 for fall entry. Notifications are sent September 15. Applications are accepted on-line. **Transfer Students:** 172 transfer students enrolled in 2015-2016. Transfer students must have a GPA of 2.5 and must submit transcripts from colleges previously attended. Applicants with fewer than 30 semester hours must also submit high school transcripts. Applicants must have taken English at the college level, and math at the intermediate algebra level. 32 of 128 credits required for the bachelor's degree must be completed at USF. **International Students:** There are 29 international students enrolled. The school actively recruits these students. They must take the TOEFL with a minimum score of 550 on the paper-based TOEFL (PBT) or 79 on the Internet-based version (iBT). They must also take the SAT or ACT.

ADMISSIONS: 49% of the 2016-2017 applicants were accepted. The SAT scores for the 2016-2017 freshman class were: Critical Reading-- 50% below 500 and 50% between 500 and 599. Math-- 38% below 500, 50% between 500 and 599, and 12% between 600 and 699. Writing-- 63% below 500, 25% between 500 and 599, and 12% between 600 and 699. The ACT scores were 3% between 12 and 17, 54% between 18 and 23, 40% between 24 and 29, and 3% above 30. 33% of the current freshmen were in the top fifth of their class; 63% were in the top two fifths. **Admissions Contact:** Eric Ruiz, Director of Undergraduate Admissions. Email: *admissions@stfrancis.edu* Web: *www.stfrancis.edu*

FINANCIAL AID: In 2016-2017, 100% of all full-time freshmen and continuing full-time students received some form of financial aid. 71% of all full-time freshmen and 77% of continuing full-time students received need-based aid. The average freshman award was $24,374. Need-based scholarships or need-based grants averaged $20,660; need-based self-help aid (loans and jobs) averaged $5,250; non-need-based athletic scholarships averaged $19,731; and other non-need-based awards and non-need-based scholarships averaged $12,745. 20% of undergraduate students work part-time. Average annual earnings from campus work are $2176. The average financial indebtedness of the 2016 graduate was $31,506. The college's own financial statement is required. The FAFSA code is 001664. The priority date for freshman financial aid applications for fall entry is February 15.

VANDERCOOK COLLEGE OF MUSIC *(The complete profile is made available exclusively on our website, www.barronspac.com)*

WESTERN ILLINOIS UNIVERSITY C-3

www.wiu.edu

Macomb, IL 61455	**(309) 298-3157** **(877) PICK WIU**
Fax: (309) 298-3111	**Email: admissions@wiu.edu**
Full-time: 4011 men, 4095 women	**Faculty:** 570; IIA, av$
Part-time: 531 men, 504 women	**Ph.D.s:** 72%
Graduate: 796 men, 1157 women	**Student/Faculty:** 14 to 1
Year: semesters, summer session	**Tuition:** $11,509 ($15,911)
Room & Board: $9580	**Freshman Class:** 10877 applied, 6534 accepted, 1535 enrolled
SAT: required **ACT:** 21	**CEEB CODE:** 1900
Application Deadline: May 15	**COMPETITIVE**

WIU-Macomb, a traditional, residential four-year campus, opened its doors in September 1902. WIU-Quad Cities, an urban, non-residential campus and the only public university in the Quad Cities, has been providing educational opportunities to the region for more than 50 years. There are 5 undergraduate schools and 1 graduate school. In addition to regional accreditation, WIU has baccalaureate program accreditation with AACSB, ABET, ADA, ASLA, CSWE, NASAD, NASM, NCATE, NRPA, ATMAE, ACCGC, and NAST. The 1050-acre campus is in a rural area 76 miles from Peoria, IL, 83 miles from Springfield, IL and 151 miles from St. Louis, MO. Including any residence halls, there are 64 buildings.

STUDENT LIFE: 89% of undergraduates are from Illinois. Others are from 41 states, 51 foreign countries, and Canada. 91% are from public schools. 65% are White; 18% African American. **Female To Male Ratio:** 1.1:1. The average age of freshmen is 18; all undergraduates, 22. 33% do not continue beyond their first year; 68% remain to graduate. **Housing:** 4400 students can be accommodated in college housing, which includes single-sex and coed dorms, on-campus apartments, and married student housing. In addition, there are honors houses, special-interest houses, academic majors, honors, and wellness floors in residence halls. On-campus housing is guaranteed for all 4 years. 56% of students commute. Alcohol is not permitted. All students may keep cars.

FACULTY/CLASSROOMS: 54% of faculty are male; 46% are female. 80% teach undergraduates, 60% do research, and 58% do both. No introductory courses are taught by graduate students. The average class size in an introductory lecture is 27; in a laboratory is 21; and in a regular course is 18.

PROGRAMS OF STUDY: WIU confers B.A., B.B., B.F.A, B.M., B.S., B.S.Ed., and B.S.W degrees. Master's and doctoral degrees are also awarded. Bachelor's degrees are awarded in AGRICULTURE (agriculture and animal science), BIOLOGICAL SCIENCE (forensic science), BUSINESS (accounting, business administration and management, business administration marketing, finance, human resources/organizational mgmt, marketing, and supply chain management), COMMUNICATIONS AND THE ARTS (art, broadcasting, communication, English, foreign language, graphic communications, information technology, journalism, music, musical theater, Spanish, and theatre arts), COMPUTER AND PHYSICAL SCIENCE (chemistry, clinical laboratory science, computer science, geology, mathematics, and physics), EDUCATION (agricultural education, art education, bilingual/bicultural education, elementary education, museum studies, physical education, and special education), ENGINEERING AND ENVIRONMENTAL DESIGN (construction management, emergency/disaster science, engineering, engineering technology, and instructional design), HEALTH PROFESSIONS (biology, exercise science, health administration and policy, health science, nursing, and public health), SOCIAL SCIENCE (African American studies, anthropology, communication sciences & disorders, criminal justice, economics, family/consumer studies, fire protection, geography, history, history and political science, interdisciplinary studies, law enforcement and corrections, liberal arts, sciences, general studies, humanities, parks and recreation management, philosophy, psychology, religious studies, social work, sociology, and women's studies). Law enforcement & justice administration, biology, agriculture, and elementary education are the strongest academically. Law enforcement & justice administration, biology, and psychology have the largest enrollments.

ACTIVITIES: 6% of men belong to 17 national fraternities; 6% of women belong to 11 national sororities. There are 259 groups on campus, including art, band, cheerleading, chess, choir, chorale, chorus, communications, computers, dance, drama, drill team, environmental, ethnic, film, honors, international, jazz band, LGBT, literary magazine, marching band, musical theater, newspaper, opera, orchestra, pep band, photography, political, professional, radio and TV, religious, social, social service, student government, and symphony. Popular campus events include Family Weekend, Homecoming Weekend, and International Bazaar. **Sports:** There are 10 intercollegiate sports for men and 10 for women, and 40 intramural sports for men and 40 for women. Facilities include an 18-hole golf course, tennis courts, basketball court, swimming pool, recreation center, softball, soccer, and football fields. **Graduates:** From July 1, 2014 to June 30, 2015, 2218 bachelor's degrees were awarded. The most popular majors were law enforcement and justice (17%), bachelor of general studies (11%), and agriculture (5%). 241 companies recruited on campus in 2014-2015. In an average class, 32% graduate in 4 years or less, 48% graduate in 5 years or less, and 53% graduate in 6 years or less.

SERVICES: Counseling and information services are available, as is tutoring in some subjects, such as business, art, English, math, computer science, science, social sciences, and humanities. There is a reader service for the blind, and remedial math and writing. **Library/Resources:** The 5 libraries contain 1.0 million volumes, 112,081 microform items, and 23,110 audio/video tapes/CDs/DVDs, and subscribe to 5,000 periodicals including electronic. Computerized library services include interlibrary loans, database searching, Internet access, and Wi-Fi capability. Special learning facilities include an art gallery, natural history museum, radio station, TV station, and international studies center. **Physically Challenged Students:** 95% of the campus is accessible. Facilities include wheelchair ramps, elevators, special parking, specially equipped restrooms, special class scheduling, lowered drinking fountains, and lowered telephones. **Special:** WIU offers internships in business, law enforcement, and physical training to name a few; study abroad group and exchange programs; and dual programs in engineering and clinical laboratory science. Student-designed majors and independent study are available through the General Studies and Interdisciplinary Studies programs. The General Studies degree program offers credit for work experience. Also available are a field campus and a life science station on the Mississippi River. There are 21 national honor societies, a freshman honors program, and 51 departmental honors programs. **Visiting:** There are regularly scheduled orientations for prospective students, consisting of registration, continental breakfast, university fair, question and answer program, campus tour, meet with an advisor, lunch and residence hall tour, and financial aid session. There are guides for informal visits, visitors may sit in on classes, and stay overnight. To schedule a visit, contact the Admissions Office at admissions@wiu.edu. **Campus Safety and Security:** Measures include 24-hour foot and vehicle patrol, emergency notification system, self-defense education, and security escort services. There are shuttle buses, emergency telephones, lighted pathways/sidewalks, a beacon/call box system, and student patrols.

REQUIREMENTS: The SAT or ACT is required. Students must have 4 years of English, 3 years each of math, science, and social studies, and 2 years in electives, art, film, foreign language, music, speech, theater, journalism, religion, philosophy, or vocational education. Academic Services is a program for selected students who do not meet regular admission requirements. A GPA of 2.2 is required. AP and CLEP credits are accepted. To graduate, all students must complete at least 120 credit hours, with at least 32 hours in the major, and have a minimum 2.0 GPA. Students must take 43 hours in the fields of basic skills, well-being, natural science, and math, historical and social foundations, and humanities. **Procedure:** Freshmen are admitted fall, spring, and summer. Entrance exams should be taken by April of the senior year. There are deferred admissions and rolling admissions plans. Applications should be filed by May 15 for fall entry, along with a $30 fee. Applications are accepted online. **Transfer Students:** 1213 transfer students enrolled in 2014-2015. Students transferring fewer than 24 semester credits or 36 quarter credits must meet freshman admissions standards, have a combined C average for all hours attempted, and be in good standing at their previous college. 30 of 120 credits required for the bachelor's degree must be completed at WIU. **International Students:** There are 128 international students enrolled. The school actively recruits these students. They must take the TOEFL with a minimum score of 550 on the paper-based TOEFL (PBT) or 79 on the Internet-based version (iBT), or successfully complete WIU's ESL program.

ADMISSIONS: 60% of the 2015-2016 applicants were accepted. The ACT scores were 51% below 12, 27% between 12 and 17, 13% between 18 and 23, 4% between 24 and 29, and 5% above 30. 21% of the current freshmen were in the top fifth of their class; 49% were in the top two fifths. **Admissions Contact:** Office of Admissions E-Mail: *admissions@wiu.edu* Web: *www.wiu.edu*

FINANCIAL AID: In 2015-2016, 91% of all full-time freshmen and 89% of continuing full-time students received some form of financial aid. 70% of all full-time freshmen and 66% of continuing full-time students received need-based aid. The average freshman award was $14,820. Need-based scholarships or need-based grants averaged $5,667; need-based self-help aid (loans and jobs) averaged $2,680; non-need-based athletic scholarships averaged $269; other non-need-based awards and non-need-based scholarships averaged $2,372; and $3,832 from other forms of aid. 18% of undergraduate students work part-time. Average annual earnings from campus work are $2164. The average financial indebtedness of the 2015 graduate was $25,900. The priority date for freshman financial aid applications for fall entry is February 15. The deadline for filing freshman financial aid applications for fall entry is open.

WHEATON COLLEGE E-2
www.wheaton.edu

Wheaton, IL 60187 (630) 752-5005
(800) 222-2419
Fax: (630) 752-5285 Email: admissions@wheaton.edu

Full-time: 1117 men, 1283 women	**Faculty:** IIB, +$
Part-time: 32 men, 24 women	**Ph.D.s:** 95%
Graduate: 177 men, 268 women	**Student/Faculty:** n/av
Year: semesters, summer session	**Tuition:** $34,050
Room & Board: $9560	**Freshman Class:** 1850 applied, 1455 accepted, 588 enrolled
SAT CR/M/W: 660/640/630 **ACT:** 30	**CEEB CODE:** 1905
Application Deadline: January 10	**MOST COMPETITIVE**

Wheaton College, founded in 1860, is a private nondenominational institution committed to providing students with a Christian education. Wheaton is a liberal arts school, offering undergraduate programs in the sciences, business, arts and fine arts, music, teacher preparation, religious and Biblical studies. There is 1 undergraduate school and 1 graduate school. In addition to regional accreditation, Wheaton has baccalaureate program accreditation with NASM and NCATE. The 80-acre campus is in a suburban area 25 miles west of Chicago. Including any residence halls, there are 69 buildings.

STUDENT LIFE: 74% of undergraduates are from out of state, mostly the Midwest. Students are from 50 states, 39 foreign countries, and Canada. 45% are from public schools. 74% are White; 9% Asian American; 6% Hispanic; 4% two or more races; 3% African American; 3% Foreign; 1% race unknown. 99% are Protestant. **Female To Male Ratio:** 1.2:1. The average age of freshmen is 18; all undergraduates, 20. 5% do not continue beyond their first year; 91% remain to graduate. **Housing:** 2167 students can be accommodated in college housing, which includes single-sex and coed dorms, on-campus apartments, off-campus apartments, and married student housing. In addition, the college owns and rents houses to groups of students. On-campus housing is guaranteed for all 4 years, is available on a first-come, first-served basis, and is available on a lottery system for upperclassmen. 88% of students live on campus; of those, 95% remain on campus on weekends. Alcohol is not permitted. Upperclassmen may keep cars.

FACULTY/CLASSROOMS: 61% of faculty are male; 39% are female. All teach and do research. No introductory courses are taught by graduate students. The average class size in an introductory lecture is 24; in a laboratory is 21; and in a regular course is 20.

PROGRAMS OF STUDY: Wheaton confers B.A., B.S., B.M., and B.M.E. degrees. Master's and doctoral degrees are also awarded. Bachelor's degrees are awarded in BIOLOGICAL SCIENCE (biology/biological science), BUSINESS (business economics), COMMUNICATIONS AND THE ARTS (art, classical languages, communications, English, French, German, music, and Spanish), COMPUTER AND PHYSICAL SCIENCE (applied mathematics, chemistry, computer science, geology, mathematics, and physics), EDUCATION (Christian education, elementary education, music education, and secondary education), ENGINEERING AND ENVIRONMENTAL DESIGN (engineering and environmental science), HEALTH PROFESSIONS (health science and nursing), SOCIAL SCIENCE (anthropology, archeology, biblical studies, economics, history, interdisciplinary studies, international relations, philosophy, political science/government, psychology, social science, sociology, and urban studies). Business/economics, English, and applied health science have the largest enrollments.

ACTIVITIES: There are no fraternities or sororities. There are 91 groups on campus, including art, band, cheerleading, chess, choir, chorale, chorus, communications, computers, dance, debate, drama, environmental, ethnic, film, international, jazz band, literary magazine, musical theater, newspaper, opera, orchestra, pep band, political, professional, religious, social, social service, student government, and symphony. Popular campus events include New Student Orientation, College Union Concerts, and a Talent Show. **Sports:** There are 11 intercollegiate sports for men and 10 for women, and 11 intramural sports for men and 10 for women. Facilities include a sports and recreation complex that features a weight room, student recreational gyms, an elevated jogging track, a climbing wall, natatorium, and the King Arena. **Graduates:** From July 1, 2015 to June 30, 2016, 607 bachelor's degrees were awarded. The most popular majors were business economics (12%), biology (9%), and English (8%). In an average class, 82% graduate in 4 years or less, 90% graduate in 5 years or less, and 91% graduate in 6 years or less.

SERVICES: Counseling and information services are available, as is tutoring in most subjects. There is a reader service for the blind, and a writing center. **Library/Resources:** The library contains 603,517 volumes, 130,371 microform items, and 70,606 audio/video tapes/CDs/DVDs, and subscribes to 6,577 periodicals including electronic. Computerized library services include interlibrary loans, database searching, Internet access, and Wi-Fi capability. Special learning facilities include an art gallery, a special collection of British authors' books and papers, an evangelical museum with document archives, and the Center for Applied Christian Ethics. The Science Building includes a unique, interactive atrium museum featuring the Perry Mastodon, a geology exhibit, a natural history exhibit, and the Foucault Pendulum. **Physically Challenged Students:** 97% of the campus is accessible. Facilities include wheelchair ramps, elevators, special parking, specially equipped restrooms, lowered drinking fountains, lowered telephones, and special housing. **Special:** Pre-Professional Programs - Health Professions and Pre-Law, Liberal Arts/Nursing 3-2 program (Emory University, Vanderbilt University) Liberal Arts/Engineering 3-2 program (Illinois Institute of Technology). There are 12 national honor societies and 15 departmental honors programs. **Visiting:** There are regularly scheduled orientations for prospective students consisting of presentations by faculty, administrators, students, financial aid, and admissions staff, as well as social activities. There are guides for informal visits, visitors may sit in on classes, and stay overnight. **Campus Safety and Security:** Measures include 24-hour foot and vehicle patrol, emergency notification system, self-defense education, and security escort services. There are shuttle buses, emergency telephones, lighted pathways/sidewalks, and controlled access to dorms/residences.

REQUIREMENTS: The SAT or ACT is required. A high school diploma is required and the GED is accepted. Wheaton requires a general college preparatory program of 15 units, including 4 units of English, 3 to 4 units of math, science, and social studies, and 2 to 3 units of a foreign language. AP credits are accepted. Important factors in the admissions decision are recommendations by school officials, advanced placement or honors courses, and personality/intangible qualities. To graduate, students must complete 124 semester hours, with 36 in upper-division courses and a minimum of 32 in a major, and maintain at least a 2.0 GPA. Students must satisfactorily meet all general education requirements in the areas of competency, a shared core requiring Bible & Theology and Integrative Studies courses, and a Thematic core requiring 10 areas of study, including the arts, humanities, social science and science courses. A senior capstone is also required. **Procedure:** Freshmen are admitted fall and spring. Entrance exams should be taken in October of senior year (early action) and December. There are early admissions and deferred admissions plans. Applications should be filed by January 10 for fall entry, along with a $50 fee. Notifications are sent April 1. 74 applicants were on the 2016 waiting list; 55 were admitted. Applications are accepted on-line. **Transfer Students:** 72 transfer students enrolled in 2015-2016. Applicants must have completed 15 semester hours with a 3.0 average and present a high school transcript, college transcript, and an essay or personal statement. 48 of 124 credits required for the bachelor's degree must be completed at Wheaton. **International Students:** There are 77 international students enrolled. The school actively recruits these students. They must take the TOEFL with a minimum score of 587 on the paper-based TOEFL (PBT) or 95 on the Internet-based version (iBT), or take the TSE and TWE. They must also take the SAT or ACT.

ADMISSIONS: 79% of the 2016-2017 applicants were accepted. The SAT scores for the 2016-2017 freshman class were: Critical Reading-- 4% below 500, 23% between 500 and 599, 42% between 600 and 699, and 32% between 700 and 800. Math-- 6% below 500, 24% between 500 and 599, 47% between 600 and 699, and 23% between 700 and 800. Writing-- 5% below 500, 26% between 500 and 599, 48% between 600 and 699, and 21% between 700 and 800. The ACT scores were 7% between 18 and 23, 42% between 24 and 29, and 51% above 30. 69% of the current freshmen were in the top fifth of their class; 90% were in the top two fifths. There were 17 National Merit finalists. **Admissions Contact:** Shawn Wynne, Director of Admissions. Email: *admissions@wheaton.edu* Web: *www.wheaton.edu*

FINANCIAL AID: In 2016-2017, 90% of all full-time freshmen and 79% of continuing full-time students received some form of financial aid. 58% of all full-time freshmen and 53% of continuing full-time students received need-based aid. The average freshman award was $24,703. Need-based scholarships or need-based grants averaged $20,671

($43,540 maximum); need-based self-help aid (loans and jobs) averaged $4,438 ($7,900 maximum); and other non-need-based awards and non-need-based scholarships averaged $6,247 ($48,098 maximum). 45% of undergraduate students work part-time. Average annual earnings from campus work are $1200. The average financial indebtedness of the 2016 graduate was $27,354. Wheaton is a member of CSS. The college's own financial statement is required. The FAFSA code is 001781. The priority date for freshman financial aid applications for fall entry is December 1.

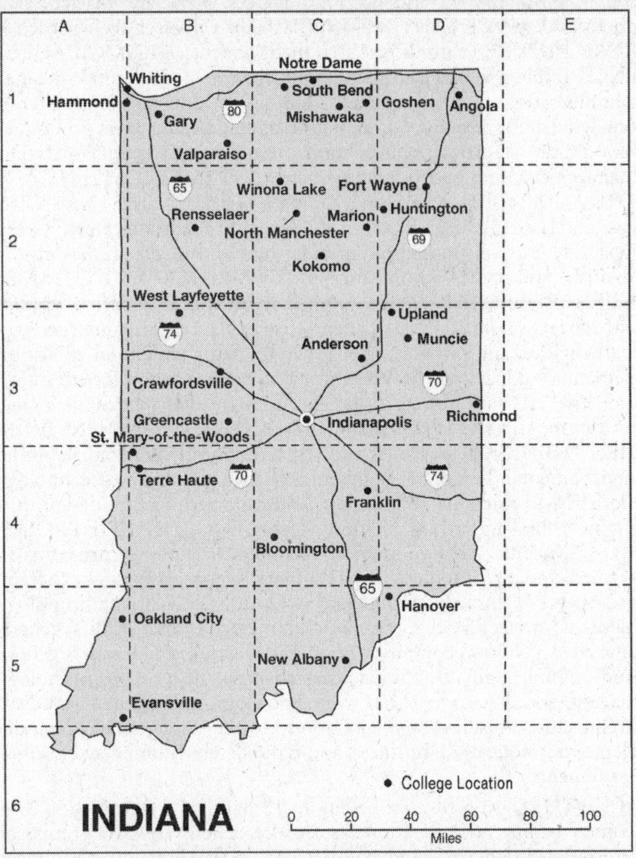

ANDERSON UNIVERSITY C-3

www.anderson.edu

Anderson, IN 46012	**(765) 641-4080** **(800) 428-6414**
Fax: (765) 641-4091	**Email: info@anderson.edu**
Full-time: 661 men, 930 women	**Faculty:** 112
Part-time: 93 men, 199 women	**Ph.D.s:** 85%
Graduate: 193 men, 156 women	**Student/Faculty:** 11 to 1
Year: semesters, summer session	**Tuition:** $28,650
Room & Board: $9550	**Freshman Class:** 2650 applied, 1760 accepted, 426 enrolled
SAT CR/M: 501/509 **ACT:** 22	**CEEB CODE:** 1016
Application Deadline: open	**COMPETITIVE**

Anderson University, founded in 1917, is a private liberal arts institution affiliated with the Church of God. The university offers programs in theoretical, and applied science, social and professional studies, the arts, culture, and religion. There are 6 undergraduate schools and 4 graduate schools. In addition to regional accreditation, Anderson has baccalaureate program accreditation with ACBSP, CSWE, NASM, NCATE, and NLN. The 163-acre campus is in a suburban area 40 miles northeast of Indianapolis. Including any residence halls, there are 36 buildings.

STUDENT LIFE: 76% of undergraduates are from Indiana. Others are from 40 states, 19 foreign countries, and Canada. 90% are from public schools. 76% are White; 13% African American; 3% race unknown; 2% Asian American; 2% Hispanic; 2% Foreign; 1% American Indian/Alaska Native; 1% two or more races. 43% claim no religious affiliation; 40% Protestant. **Female To Male Ratio:** 1.4:1. The average age of freshmen is 18; all undergraduates, 22. 22% do not continue beyond their first year; 59% remain to graduate. **Housing:** 1161 students can be accommodated in college housing, which includes single-sex dorms, on-campus apartments, off-campus apartments, and married student housing. On-campus housing is guaranteed for all 4 years. 63% of students live on campus; of those, 50% remain on campus on weekends. Alcohol is not permitted. All students may keep cars.

FACULTY/CLASSROOMS: 56% of faculty are male; 44% are female. 94% teach undergraduates. No introductory courses are taught by graduate students. The average class size in an introductory lecture is 19; in a laboratory is 17; and in a regular course is 17.

PROGRAMS OF STUDY: Anderson confers B.A., B.S., B.Mus., and B.S.N. degrees. Associate, master's, and doctoral degrees are also awarded. Bachelor's degrees are awarded in BIOLOGICAL SCIENCE (biology/biological science), BUSINESS (accounting, banking and finance, business administration and management, management science, marketing/retailing/merchandising, and sports management), COMMUNICATIONS AND THE ARTS (communications, dramatic arts, English, fine arts, French, graphic design, music business management, music performance, and Spanish), COMPUTER AND PHYSICAL SCIENCE (chemistry, computer science, mathematics, and physics), EDUCATION (art education, Christian education, elementary education, foreign languages education, health education, music education, physical education, science education, and social studies education), HEALTH PROFESSIONS (medical laboratory technology and nursing), SOCIAL SCIENCE (criminal justice, economics, family/consumer studies, history, philosophy, political science/government, psychology, religion, social work, and sociology). Physical sciences is the strongest academically. Business, education, and nursing have the largest enrollments.

ACTIVITIES: There are no fraternities or sororities. There are 41 groups on campus, including art, band, cheerleading, choir, chorale, dance, debate, drama, ethnic, film, honors, international, jazz band, literary magazine, musical theater, newspaper, opera, orchestra, photography, political, professional, radio and TV, religious, social, social service, student government, and symphony. Popular campus events include Heritage Week, Spiritual Emphasis Week, Candles, and Carols Christmas Performance. **Sports:** There are 9 intercollegiate sports for men and 9 for women, and 7 intramural sports for men and 7 for women. Facilities include gyms, football, baseball/softball, and soccer fields, an 8-lane all-weather track, tennis courts, bowling alley, and a game room. The campus stadium seats 4200 and the indoor gym seats 2400. **Graduates:** From July 1, 2015 to June 30, 2016, 393 bachelor's degrees were awarded. The most popular majors were business/marketing (19%), health professions and related programs (15%), and education (12%). 35 companies recruited on campus in 2015-2016. In an average class, 44% graduate in 4 years or less, 52% graduate in 5 years or less, and 54% graduate in 6 years or less.

SERVICES: Counseling and information services are available, as is tutoring in most subjects. There is a reader service for the blind, and remedial math, reading, and writing. **Library/Resources:** The library contains 2.6 million volumes, 38,706 microform items, and 83,285 audio/video tapes/CDs/DVDs, and subscribes to 457 periodicals including electronic. Computerized library services include interlibrary loans and database searching. Special learning facilities include an art gallery, radio station, and Museum of the Bible and the Ancient Near East. **Physically Challenged Students:** 97% of the campus is accessible. Facilities include wheelchair ramps, elevators, special parking, specially equipped restrooms, special class scheduling, lowered drinking fountains, and lowered telephones. **Special:** Anderson offers co-op programs with Purdue University, internships, study abroad in 25 countries through the International Studies Program, and a Washington semester. Also available are credit for military experience and pass/fail options. Courses in electronic engineering may be taken through the Purdue Anderson campus. Preprofessional programs are offered in medical, podiatry, dentistry, law, engineering, seminary, and several allied health fields. There are 16 national honor societies, a freshman honors program, and 10 departmental honors programs. **Visiting:** There are regularly scheduled orientations for prospective students, including a campus tour, an academic overview, a financial aid and athletics overview, and appointments with professors and departmental chairs. There are guides for informal visits, visitors may sit in on classes, and stay overnight. To schedule a visit, contact the Admissions Office. **Campus Safety and Security:** Measures include 24-hour foot and vehicle patrol, emergency notification system, self-defense education, and security escort services. There are emergency telephones, lighted pathways/sidewalks, and Indiana state police academy graduates as security officers.

REQUIREMENTS: The SAT or ACT is required. Applicants must be graduates of an accredited secondary school or have a GED certificate and submit a photograph, references, and a health form. AP and CLEP credits are accepted. Important factors in the admissions decision are leadership record, recommendations by alumni, and personality/intangible qualities. Requirements for graduation include 120 credit hours with 40 to 58 hours in the general education core and at least 36 hours in the major. A minimum 2.0 GPA overall and in the major is required. All students must complete a liberal arts seminar. The last 24 credit hours must be taken in residence. **Procedure:** Freshmen are admitted fall and spring. Entrance exams should be taken in the fall of the junior year. There is a rolling admissions plan. Application deadlines are open. Application fee is $25. Applications are accepted on-line. **Transfer Students:** 82 transfer students enrolled in 2015-2016. Applicants must have a minimum 2.0 GPA, satisfactory SAT or ACT scores, and transcripts for all previously attended colleges. 24 of 120 credits required for the bachelor's degree must be completed at Anderson. **International Students:** There are 38 international students enrolled. They must take the TOEFL with a minimum score of 547 on the paper-based TOEFL (PBT) or 78 on the Internet-based version (iBT). They must also take the SAT, scoring 900.

ADMISSIONS: 66% of the 2016-2017 applicants were accepted. The SAT scores for the 2016-2017 freshman class were: Critical Reading-- 44% below 500, 37% between 500 and 599, 13% between 600 and 699, and 2% between 700 and 800. Math-- 43% below 500, 44% between 500 and 599, 12% between 600 and 699, and 1% between 700 and 800. The ACT scores were 17% between 12 and 17, 42% between 18 and 23, 38% between 24 and 29, and 3% above 30. 41% of the current freshmen were in the top fifth of their class; 64% were in the top two fifths. 10 freshmen graduated first in their class. **Admissions Contact:** Admissions Counselor Email: *info@anderson.edu* Web: *www.anderson.edu*

FINANCIAL AID: Anderson is a member of CSS. The FAFSA code is 001785. Check with the school for current application deadlines.

BALL STATE UNIVERSITY — D-3

www.bsu.edu

Muncie, IN 47306	**(765) 285-8287** **(800) 482-4BSU**
Fax: (765) 285-1632	**Email: askus@bsu.edu**
Full-time: 6170 men, 8940 women	**Faculty:** I
Part-time: 715 men, 1186 women	**Ph.D.s:** 75%
Graduate: 1860 men, 3127 women	**Student/Faculty:** n/av
Year: semesters, summer session	**Tuition:** $9654 ($25,428)
Room & Board: $9936	**Freshman Class:** 24735 applied, 15398 accepted, 3877 enrolled
SAT CR/M/W: 546/538/527 **ACT:** 22	**CEEB CODE:** 1051
Application Deadline: August 10	**COMPETITIVE**

Ball State University, founded in 1918, is a public university offering undergraduate and graduate programs through 8 academic colleges in applied sciences and technology, architecture and planning, business, communication, information, and media, fine arts, sciences and humanities, health science, and teacher education. There are 8 undergraduate schools and 1 graduate school. In addition to regional accreditation, Ball State has baccalaureate program accreditation with AACSB, ABET, ACBSP, ACEJMC, ADA, AHEA, ASLA, CAHEA, CSAB, CSWE, NAAB, NASAD, NASM, NCATE, NLN, and TEAC. The 1140-acre campus is in a suburban area 56 miles northwest of Indianapolis. Including any residence halls, there are 106 buildings.

STUDENT LIFE: 86% of undergraduates are from Indiana. Others are from 50 states, and Canada. 80% are White; 8% African American; 4% Hispanic; 3% two or more races; 2% Foreign; 2% race unknown; 1% Asian American. **Female To Male Ratio:** 1.5:1. The average age of freshmen is 18; all undergraduates, 22. 18% do not continue beyond their first year; 62% remain to graduate. **Housing:** 6695 students can be accommodated in college housing, which includes single-sex and coed dorms, on-campus apartments, and married student housing. In addition, there are honors houses, special-interest houses, and sorority houses. On-campus housing is guaranteed for the freshman year only. 57% of students commute. Alcohol is not permitted. All students may keep cars.

FACULTY/CLASSROOMS: 50% of faculty are male; 50% are female. No introductory courses are taught by graduate students.

PROGRAMS OF STUDY: Ball State confers B.A., B.A.T., B.F.A., B.G.S., B.L.A., B.M., B.S.W., and B.U.P.D. degrees. Associate, master's, and doctoral degrees are also awarded. Bachelor's degrees are awarded in AGRICULTURE (natural resource management), BIOLOGICAL SCIENCE (biology/biological science), BUSINESS (accounting, business administration and management, business administration - international, business administration, mgmt, operations, business economics, economics – statistics, finance, human resources, marketing, operations management, and sports management), COMMUNICATIONS AND THE ARTS (acting, advertising, animation, art, Chinese, classical languages, classics, dance, digital media, English, French, German, Greek, Japanese, journalism, Latin, literature, film and media studies, music, Spanish, and sports administration), COMPUTER AND PHYSICAL SCIENCE (actuarial science, applied mathematics, applied physics, astronomy, chemistry, computer science, data processing, geology, mathematics, and physics), EDUCATION (early childhood education, elementary education, health education, home economics education, industrial arts education, physical education, reading education, science education, and special education), ENGINEERING AND ENVIRONMENTAL DESIGN (architecture, city/community/regional planning, environmental design, environmental science, graphic arts technology, industrial engineering technology, landscape architecture/design, pre-engineering, and urban planning technology), HEALTH PROFESSIONS (health science, medical technology, nursing, predentistry, premedicine, preoptometry, preveterinary science, respiratory therapy, and speech pathology/audiology), SOCIAL SCIENCE (anthropology, criminal justice, dietetics, economics, family/consumer studies, geography, history, home economics, international studies, liberal arts/general studies, philosophy, political science/government, prelaw, psychology, religion, social science, social work, sociology, and women's studies). Architecture, business, and education are the strongest academically. Elementary education, business, and radio & television have the largest enrollments.

ACTIVITIES: 15% of men belong to 18 national fraternities; 17% of women belong to 15 national sororities. There are 390 groups on campus, including art, band, cheerleading, chess, choir, chorale, chorus, computers, dance, debate, drama, drill team, ethnic, film, forensics, honors, international, jazz band, LGBT, literary magazine, marching band, musical theater, newspaper, opera, orchestra, pep band, photography, political, professional, radio and TV, religious, social, social service, student government, and symphony. Popular campus events include Late Night Carnival, Unity Week, and Family Weekend. **Sports:** The student recreation/wellness facility, which holds a 13,000-sq-ft fitness center with elevated jogging track, a 5-court basketball/volleyball gym, a 33-ft climbing wall, indoor turf field including 2 batting cages, an auxiliary gym, a game room, 9 racquetball/handball and 2 wallyball courts, a 6-lane, 25-yd competitive pool, and a field sports building. There is also a fitness center, an 11,500-seat arena and a 22,500-seat stadium. **Graduates:** From July 1, 2015 to June 30, 2016, 3454 bachelor's degrees were awarded. The most popular majors were business/marketing (17%), communication/journalism (14%), and health professions and related programs (10%).

SERVICES: Counseling and information services are available, as is tutoring in most subjects. There is a reader service for the blind. **Library/Resources:** The 3 libraries contain 1.1 million volumes, 1.1 million microform items, and 77,472 audio/video tapes/CDs/DVDs, and subscribe to 72,065 periodicals including electronic. Computerized library services include interlibrary loans, database searching, Internet access, and Wi-Fi capability. Special learning facilities include an art gallery, planetarium, radio station, TV station, research centers in solar energy, a human performance lab, and international programs. **Physically Challenged Students:** 95% of the campus is accessible. Facilities include wheelchair ramps, elevators, special parking, specially equipped restrooms, special class scheduling, lowered drinking fountains, lowered telephones, and special housing. A special resource guide, an accessibility map (including tactile), and text telephones (TDD) in all key offices are also available. **Special:** Nearly all undergraduate disciplines offer internships, and work study is available. Study abroad is possible at the university's London center and in 20 other programs; students may also spend a semester in Washington, D.C. Most disciplines offer dual majors, and accelerated degrees are available. There is a B.A.-B.S. degree in elementary/special education, 3-2 program in engineering, an award-winning program in entrepreneurship, a general studies degree, nondegree study, and pass/fail options. There are 35 national honor societies and a freshman honors program. **Visiting:** There are regularly scheduled orientations for prospective students, consisting of twice-a-day presentations and tours. There are guides for informal visits and visitors may sit in on classes. To schedule a visit, contact Welcome Center at (765) 285-5683. **Campus Safety and Security:** Measures include 24-hour foot and vehicle patrol, emergency notification system, self-defense education, and security escort services. There are shuttle buses, emergency telephones, lighted pathways/sidewalks, and controlled access to dorms/residences.

REQUIREMENTS: Admission is a holistic review based on strength of applicants' curriculum, grades in English, math, lab sciences, social sciences, and foreign language, curricula patterns and grade trends, and the SAT or ACT scores. AP and CLEP credits are accepted. All students must take at least 120 credits and maintain a 2.0 GPA for graduation, and required hours in the major vary by program. Required courses are in English composition, math, speech, history, personal finance, physical sciences, social or behavioral sciences, humanities or fine arts, global studies, and 2 hours of phys ed. In addition, all juniors must pass a writing proficiency exam. **Procedure:** Freshmen are admitted fall, spring, and summer. Entrance exams should be taken during the spring of the junior year or early in the senior year. There are deferred admissions and rolling admissions plans. Applications should be filed by August 10 for fall entry, along with a $55 fee. Notification is sent on a rolling basis. 3085 applicants were on the 2016 waiting list; 1124 were admitted. Applications are accepted on-line. Application fees are waived if application is completed on-line. **Transfer Students:** 882 transfer students enrolled in 2015-2016. We'll consider you for transfer admission if you've earned a minimum cumulative grade point average (GPA) of 2.0 on a 4.0 scale for all transferable course-work attempted. Courses from remedial programs, vocational and technical schools, and colleges and universities that are not regionally accredited cannot be transferred. Accrediting associations include: Middle States Commission on Higher Education, Higher Learning Commission, New England Association, Northwest Commission on Colleges and Universities, Southern Association, and Western Association. Admissions decisions will be based upon your academic records at all educational institutions you've attended. You must be in good academic standing and eligible to return immediately to the last institution you attended. If you apply for transfer admission to Ball State while you're enrolled at another college or university, you may be considered for admission on the basis of your current college or university cumulative GPA. If you're admitted to Ball State while enrolled at another college or university (referred to as "admit with conditions"), your cumulative GPA must remain above 2.0. Admission granted under such circumstances may be withdrawn if your cumulative GPA falls below 2.0. 30 of 120 credits required for the bachelor's degree must be completed at Ball State. **International Students:** There are 196 international students enrolled. The school actively recruits these students. They must take the TOEFL with a minimum score of 550 on the paper-based TOEFL (PBT) or 79 on the Internet-based version (iBT). The SAT or ACT is recommended.

ADMISSIONS: 62% of the 2016-2017 applicants were accepted. The SAT scores for the 2016-2017 freshman class were: Critical Reading-- 37% below 500, 46% between 500 and 599, 15% between 600 and 699, and 2% between 700 and 800. Math-- 38% below 500, 48% between 500 and 599, 13% between 600 and 699, and 1% between 700 and 800. Writing-- 46% below 500, 44% between 500 and 599, 9% between 600 and 699, and 1% between 700 and 800. The ACT scores were 3% between 12 and 17, 59% between 18 and 23, 33% between 24 and 29, and 5% above 30. 54% of the current freshmen were in the top fifth of their class; 67% were in the top two fifths. 26 freshmen graduated first in their class. **Admissions Contact:** Chris Munchel, Assoc. VP of Enrollment and Director of Admissions. Email: *askus@bsu.edu* Web: *www.bsu.edu*

FINANCIAL AID: Ball State is a member of CSS. The FAFSA code is 001786. The priority date for freshman financial aid applications for fall entry is March 15.

BETHEL COLLEGE — C-1

www.bethelcollege.edu

Mishawaka, IN 46545 — (574) 807-7600, (800) 422-4101

Fax: (574) 807-7650 — **Email:** admissions@BethelCollege.edu

Full-time: 431 men, 697 women	**Faculty:** 71; IIB
Part-time: 64 men, 196 women	**Ph.D.s:** 58%
Graduate: 94 men, 157 women	**Student/Faculty:** 12 to 1
Year: semesters, summer session	**Tuition:** $27,390
Room & Board: $8470	**Freshman Class:** 1157 applied, 1140 accepted, 241 enrolled
SAT CR/M/W: 500/520/490 **ACT:** 23	**CEEB CODE:** 1079
Application Deadline: n/av	**COMPETITIVE**

Bethel College, founded in 1947, is a private institution affiliated with the Missionary Church, offering undergraduate and master's degree programs with a Christian perspective. There is 1 undergraduate school and 1 graduate school. In addition to regional accreditation, Bethel has baccalaureate program accreditation with NASM, NCATE, and ACEN. The 80-acre campus is in a suburban area in Northern Indiana, adjacent to South Bend, 90 miles east of Chicago. Including any residence halls, there are 52 buildings.

STUDENT LIFE: 72% of undergraduates are from Indiana. Others are from 27 states, and 11 foreign countries. 82% are from public schools. 74% are White; 7% Hispanic; 4% two or more races; 2% Asian American; 2% Foreign; 11% African American; 1% race unknown. 72% are Protestant; 22% claim no religious affiliation. **Female To Male Ratio:** 1.8:1. The average age of freshmen is 19; all undergraduates, 24. 24% do not continue beyond their first year; 63% remain to graduate. **Housing:** 814 students can be accommodated in college housing, which includes single-sex dorms, on-campus apartments, off-campus apartments, and married student housing. In addition, there are special-interest houses, cultural awareness house, missions house, and urban ministries house. On-campus housing is guaranteed for all 4 years. 52% of students live on campus; of those, 40% remain on campus on weekends. Alcohol is not permitted. Upperclassmen may keep cars.

FACULTY/CLASSROOMS: 55% of faculty are male; 45% are female. All teach undergraduates. No introductory courses are taught by graduate students. The average class size in an introductory lecture is 35; in a laboratory is 15; and in a regular course is 19.

PROGRAMS OF STUDY: Bethel confers B.A., B.S., and B.S.N. degrees. Associate and master's degrees are also awarded. Bachelor's degrees are awarded in BIOLOGICAL SCIENCE (biochemistry and biology/biological science), BUSINESS (accounting, business administration and management, business economics, financial services, and sports management), COMMUNICATIONS AND THE ARTS (American Sign Language, communications, dramatic arts, English Writing, graphic design, music, music performance, studio art, and theatre arts), COMPUTER AND PHYSICAL SCIENCE (chemistry, mathematics, and physical sciences), EDUCATION (art education, childhood education, early childhood education, education, elementary education, English secondary education, mathematics education, music education, physical education, science education, secondary education, social studies education, and sports studies), ENGINEERING AND ENVIRONMENTAL DESIGN (engineering management, engineering physics, and preengineering), HEALTH PROFESSIONS (exercise science and nursing), SOCIAL SCIENCE (behavioral science, biblical studies, Christian studies, criminal justice, economics, history, human services, interdisciplinary studies, international studies, interpreter for the deaf, liberal arts/general studies, ministries, missions, pastoral studies, philosophy, philosophy and religion, political science/government, psychology, religion, and sociology). Psychology, religion/philosophy, and nursing are the strongest academically. Business, nursing, and elementary education have the largest enrollments.

ACTIVITIES: There are no fraternities or sororities. There are 15 groups on campus, including American Sign Language Club, art, band, cheerleading, choir, chorale, chorus, drama, ethnic, honors, international, jazz band, musical theater, newspaper, pep band, political, professional, psychology club, radio and TV, religious, social, student government, and yearbook. Popular campus events include All-Campus Christmas Party, BABE and Dude Week, Spiritual Emphasis Week, Service Day, Midnight Breakfast, Leadership Weekend, and World Christian Action Conference. **Sports:** There are 9 intercollegiate sports for men and 10 for women, and 7 intramural sports for men and 5 for women. Facilities include two gyms, two weight rooms, two exercise rooms, indoor baseball training facilities, baseball, softball, and soccer fields, tennis courts, and a practice track. **Graduates:** From July 1, 2015 to June 30, 2016, 387 bachelor's degrees were awarded. The most popular majors were nursing (18%), business (16%), and interdisciplinary studies/liberal studies (13%). 160 companies recruited on campus in 2015-2016. In an average class, 1% graduate in 3 years or less, 61% graduate in 4 years or less, 63% graduate in 5 years or less, and 66% graduate in 6 years or less.

SERVICES: Counseling and information services are available, as is tutoring in most subjects. There is remedial math, reading, and writing. **Library/Resources:** The library contains 288,422 volumes, 4,577 microform items, and 1,676 audio/video tapes/CDs/DVDs, and subscribes to 1,938 periodicals including electronic. Computerized library services include interlibrary loans, database searching, Internet access, and Wi-Fi capability. Special learning facilities include an art gallery and radio station. **Physically Challenged Students:** 80% of the campus is accessible. Facilities include wheelchair ramps, elevators, special parking, specially equipped restrooms, lowered drinking fountains, and special housing. **Special:** Students may cross-register for courses at various local colleges including Northern Indiana Consortium for Education (NICE). Also available are a 3-2 engineering degree with the University of Notre Dame and Trine University (Angola), a liberal arts degree, degree programs for nontraditional students, and online degree programs. Bethel also offers a pass/fail course option, student teaching, internships, and study abroad in several countries. Army and Air Force ROTC programs are available. There is 1 national honor society and a freshman honors program. **Visiting:** There are regularly scheduled orientations for prospective students, including an interview, chapel visit, tour, lunch, and a class or professor visit as requested. There are guides for informal visits, visitors may sit in on classes, and stay overnight. To schedule a visit, contact the Office of Admission. **Campus Safety and Security:** Measures include 24-hour foot and vehicle patrol, emergency notification system, self-defense education, and security escort services. There are emergency telephones, lighted pathways/sidewalks, and controlled access to dorms/residences.

REQUIREMENTS: The SAT or ACT is required. Applicants should be graduates of a secondary school program or have the GED. Recommended that 17 academic units in secondary school include 4 in English, 3 in math, 2 in history, 1 in lab science, 1 in social science, and 2 in a foreign language. An audition is required of music program applicants. AP and CLEP credits are accepted. To graduate, students must complete 120 credits, including 24 to 52 in the major, with a minimum 2.0 GPA. Also are required 9 credits in Bible and religion, courses in communication, social science, history, fine arts, humanities, natural sciences, mathematics, fitness, and physical activity. The last 30 hours of a bachelor's degree must be completed at Bethel. **Procedure:** Freshmen are admitted to all sessions. Entrance exams should be taken as early as possible in the junior or senior year. There are early admissions, deferred admissions, and rolling admissions plans. Application deadlines are open. Applications are accepted on-line. Application fees are waived if application is completed on-line. **Transfer Students:** 128 transfer students enrolled in 2015-2016. Grades of C or better are eligible for transfer; students without a minimum GPA of 2.0 may be admitted on probation. Other admission requirements are the same as for entering freshmen. 30 of 120 credits required for the bachelor's degree must be completed at Bethel. **International Students:** There are 13 international students enrolled. They must take the TOEFL with a minimum score of 540 on the paper-based TOEFL (PBT) or 76 on the Internet-based version (iBT), or take the IELTS. They must also take the SAT or ACT.

ADMISSIONS: 99% of the 2016-2017 applicants were accepted. The SAT scores for the 2016-2017 freshman class were: Critical Reading-- 48% below 500, 40% between 500 and 599, 9% between 600 and 699, and 3% between 700 and 800. Math-- 44% below 500, 34% between 500 and 599, 20% between 600 and 699, and 2% between 700 and 800. Writing-- 54% below 500, 37% between 500 and 599, 9% between 600 and 699, and 1% between 700 and 800. The ACT scores were 8% between 12 and 17, 49% between 18 and 23, 39% between 24 and 29, and 4% above 30. 38% of the current freshmen were in the top fifth of their class; 66% were in the top two fifths. 6 freshmen graduated first in their class. **Admissions Contact:** Toni Pauls, Vice President for Enrollment. Email: *admissions@BethelCollege.edu* Web: *www.bethelcollege.edu*

FINANCIAL AID: In 2016-2017, 99% of all full-time freshmen and 97% of continuing full-time students received some form of financial aid. 81% of all full-time freshmen and 74% of continuing full-time students received need-based aid. The average freshman award was $27,940. Need-based scholarships or need-based grants averaged $9,988; need-based self-help aid (loans and jobs) averaged $3,586; non-need-based athletic scholarships averaged $4,034; and other non-need-based awards and non-need-based scholarships averaged $11,544. 30% of undergraduate students work part-time. Average annual earnings from campus work are $1500. The average financial indebtedness of the 2016 graduate was $29,482. Bethel is a member of CSS. The FAFSA code is 001787. The priority date for freshman financial aid applications for fall entry is March 1. The deadline for filing freshman financial aid applications for fall entry is March 1.

BUTLER UNIVERSITY — C-3

www.butler.edu

Indianapolis, IN 46208 — (317) 940-8100, (888) 940-8100

Fax: (317) 940-8150 — **Email:** admission@butler.edu

Full-time: 1777 men, 2680 women	**Faculty:** IIA, av$
Part-time: 39 men, 53 women	**Ph.D.s:** 79%
Graduate: 231 men, 315 women	**Student/Faculty:** 12 to 1
Year: semesters, summer session	**Tuition:** $38,405
Room & Board: $12,947	**Freshman Class:** 11042 applied, 9411 accepted, 1256 enrolled
SAT CR/M/W: 580/580/560 **ACT:** 27	**CEEB CODE:** 1073
Application Deadline: February 1	**VERY COMPETITIVE**

Butler University, founded in 1855, is an independent, private institution offering programs in liberal arts and sciences, business, communications, fine and performing arts, pharmacy and health sciences, and education. Butler emphasizes experiential learning (including internships, service learning, and research) and job placement outcomes. There are 6 undergraduate schools and 5 graduate schools. In addition to regional accreditation, Butler has baccalaureate program accreditation with AACSB, ACPE, NASAD, NASM, NCATE, ARCPA, ACS, CACREP, IDOE, NASD, and NAST. The 295-acre campus is in a suburban area in the city of Indianapolis, approximately five miles north of downtown, near the Broad Ripple cultural district. Including any residence halls, there are 39 buildings.

STUDENT LIFE: 55% of undergraduates are from out of state, mostly the Midwest. Students are from 50 states, 22 foreign countries, and Canada. 83% are White; 4% African American; 4% Hispanic; 3% Asian American; 3% two or more races; 3% race unknown; 1% Foreign. 45% are Protestant; 28% Catholic; 17% claim no religious affiliation. **Female To Male Ratio:** 1.5:1. The average age of freshmen is 18; all undergraduates, 20. 8% do not continue beyond their first year; 74% remain to graduate. **Housing:** 2319 students can be accommodated in college housing, which includes single-sex and coed dorms, on-campus apartments, and off-campus apartments. In addition, there are fraternity houses and sorority houses. On-campus housing is guaranteed for all 4 years and is available on a lottery system for upperclassmen. 68% of students live on campus. Alcohol is not permitted. All students may keep cars.

FACULTY/CLASSROOMS: 50% of faculty are male; 50% are female. No introductory courses are taught by graduate students. The average class size in an introductory lecture is 23; in a laboratory is 19; and in a regular course is 22.

PROGRAMS OF STUDY: Butler confers B.A., B.S., B.F.A., B.M., B.S.H.S., and B.S.E. degrees. Associate, master's, and doctoral degrees are also awarded. Bachelor's degrees are awarded in BIOLOGICAL SCIENCE (biochemistry and biology/biological science), BUSINESS (accounting, banking and finance, international business management, management information systems, and marketing/retailing/merchandising), COMMUNICATIONS AND THE ARTS (advertising, art, arts administration/management, communications, dance, dramatic arts, English, French, German, Greek (classical), jazz, journalism, Latin, media arts, music, music performance, music theory and composition, performing arts, public relations, Spanish, speech/debate/rhetoric, strategic communication, theatre arts, and voice), COMPUTER AND PHYSICAL SCIENCE (actuarial science, chemistry, computer science, mathematics, physics, and software engineering), EDUCATION (elementary education, middle school education, music education, secondary education, and special education), ENGINEERING AND ENVIRONMENTAL DESIGN (biomedical engineering and engineering), HEALTH PROFESSIONS (health science, pharmacy, and speech pathology/audiology), SOCIAL SCIENCE (anthropology, criminal justice, economics, gender studies, history, international studies, philosophy, political science/government, psychology, religion, science and society, and sociology). Pharmacy, dance, and business are the strongest academically. Marketing, pharmacy, and biology have the largest enrollments.

ACTIVITIES: 24% of men belong to 5 national fraternities; 36% of women belong to 9 national sororities. There are 155 groups on campus, including Alpha Phi Omega, Alternative Breaks, College Mentors for Kids, mentoring, philantropic, strategic games club, veterans, art, band, cheerleading, chess, choir, chorale, chorus, computers, dance, debate, drama, drill team, emerging leaders, environmental, ethnic, film, honors, international, jazz band, LGBT, literary magazine, marching band, musical theater, newspaper, opera, orchestra, pep band, photography, political, professional, radio and TV, religious, social, social service, student government, symphony, and yearbook. Popular campus events include Bulldogs Into the Streets, Homecoming, Dance Marathon, ButlerPalooza, and Spring Sports Spectacular. **Sports:** There are 9 intercollegiate sports for men and 11 for women, and 16 intramural sports for men and 16 for women. Facilities include a field house, football stadium, tennis courts, indoor and outdoor tracks, a weight-training room, an aerobics/exercise room, intramural fields, and baseball, softball, and soccer fields. Butler University's Health and Recreation Complex offers many new services to students, faculty, and staff, while expanding others presently available. In addition to being the main stomping ground for Butler's Department of Recreation, the HRC also houses Counseling and Consultation Services, Health Education, and Health Services, making it a true wellness center on campus. **Graduates:** From July 1, 2015 to June 30, 2016, 838 bachelor's degrees were awarded. The most popular majors were marketing (11%), finance (8%), and health sciences (6%). 665 companies recruited on campus in 2015-2016. In an average class, 51% graduate in 4 years or less, 65% graduate in 5 years or less, and 74% graduate in 6 years or less. Of the 2015 graduating class, 20% were enrolled in graduate school within 6 months of graduation, and 55% were employed.

SERVICES: Counseling and information services are available, as is tutoring in every subject, such as math, most sciences, and the Core curriculum. There is a reader service for the blind. A writer's studio offers assistance in all areas of the writing process. **Library/Resources:** The 2 libraries contain 262,824 volumes, 12,260 microform items, and 20,132 audio/video tapes/CDs/DVDs, and subscribe to 45,274 periodicals including electronic. Computerized library services include interlibrary loans, database searching, Internet access, and Wi-Fi capability. Special learning facilities include a planetarium, radio station, TV station, and The Holcomb Observatory & Planetarium. **Physically Challenged Students:** All of the campus is accessible. Facilities include wheelchair ramps, elevators, special parking, specially equipped restrooms, special class scheduling, and lowered drinking fountains. **Special:** Butler offers co-op programs in business administration, internships in most academic programs, extensive study abroad programs, a Washington learning semester, and work study-programs. Also available is a 3-2 degree program in engineering with Indiana University, Purdue University in Indianapolis, as well as cross-registration with the 6 other members of the Consortium for Urban Education, which includes Franklin College, University of Indianapolis, Indiana University, Purdue University in Indianapolis, Indiana Vocational Technical College, Marian University, and Martin University. In addition to numerous majors offered for a Bachelor of Arts or Bachelor of Science degree, Butler offers several dual majors, including a sociology major combined with criminology, majors in philosophy, anthropology, criminology, sociology, and political science combined with psychology, a history major combined with anthropology or political science, and a religion major combined with anthropology or philosophy. Other offerings include student-designed majors, a general studies associate degree, pass/fail options, and non-degree study. Also offered are graduate non-degree certificate programs in college and career readiness, wellness and sport leadership, International Baccalaureate teaching and learning, licensed mental health counselor, and teachers of the visually impaired, and an alternative graduate initial licensure program, as well as an accelerated alternative certificate for licensure in Mild Interventions. There are 9 national honor societies, Phi Beta Kappa, and a freshman honors program. **Visiting:** There are regularly scheduled orientations for prospective students. Traditional prospective student visits include an admission and financial aid presentation followed by a campus tour. There are guides for informal visits and visitors may sit in on classes. To schedule a visit, contact the Office of Admission. **Campus Safety and Security:** Measures include 24-hour foot and vehicle patrol, emergency notification system, self-defense education, and security escort services. There are shuttle buses, emergency telephones, lighted pathways/sidewalks, and controlled access to dorms/residences.

REQUIREMENTS: The SAT or ACT is required. Applicants must be slated to graduate from an accredited secondary school and/or have demonstrated successful completion of all required academic units. Applicants must be on track to earn at least 17 core academic units, including 4 years of English, 3 each of math and lab science, 2 each of the same foreign language, and 2 each of history/social science; the balance of coursework may include electives or advanced coursework in core academic courses. In addition to submitting the Common Application or Butler University Application, a separate application and audition or interview is required for all candidates applying for admission to the Jordan College of the Arts. AP and CLEP credits are accepted. Important factors in the admissions decision are advanced placement or honors courses, extracurricular activities record, and recommendations by school officials. Complementing students' majors, the Butler University Core Curriculum emphasizes the development of key skills that transfer directly into careers post-graduation. Employers are seeking flexible, creative, and critical thinkers who can demonstrate competencies in strong written and oral communication, information fluency, intercultural awareness, and analytical and ethical reasoning skills. Through direct experience working in the Indianapolis community, study abroad opportunities, and rich cultural experiences in the Core Curriculum, Butler students also engage central issues of our increasingly globalized world, including diversity, personal and social responsibility, and social justice. In these varied ways, the Core Curriculum prepares Butler students to enter the workforce as successful professionals and well-rounded individuals. **Procedure:** Freshmen are admitted to all sessions. Entrance exams should be taken during the junior year or early the senior year. There are early admissions and deferred admissions plans. Early decision applications should be filed by November 1; regular applications, by February 1 for fall entry; and November 1 for spring entry. Notification of early decision is sent December 15; regular decision, February 15. 46 applicants were on the 2016 waiting list; 15 were admitted. Applications are accepted on-line. **Transfer Students:** 88 transfer students enrolled in 2015-2016. Applicants who have completed more than 11 hours of college work following graduation from an accredited secondary school must present transcripts from all previous college attended, indicating good standing and a minimum GPA of 2.5, and an official high school transcript showing a posted date of graduation. Those students with fewer than 20 hours must also, submit SAT or ACT scores. Students wishing to transfer into pharmacy must apply through PharmCAS; Students applying to the professional phase of physician assistant program must apply through CASPA. Transfer credits for classes taken online may be restricted. 45 of 120 credits required for the bachelor's degree must be completed at Butler. **International Students:** There are 148 international students enrolled. The school actively recruits these students. They must take the TOEFL with a minimum score of 550 on the paper-based TOEFL (PBT) or 79 on the Internet-based version (iBT), or complete level 5 at the American Language Academy on Butler's campus.

ADMISSIONS: 85% of the 2016-2017 applicants were accepted. The SAT scores for the 2016-2017 freshman class were: Critical Reading-- 12% below 500, 49% between 500 and 599, 33% between 600 and 699, and 5% between 700 and 800. Math-- 12% below 500, 46% between 500 and 599, 36% between 600 and 699, and 6% between 700 and 800. Writing-- 17% below 500, 52% between 500 and 599, 29% between 600 and 699, and 3% between 700 and 800. The ACT scores were 15% between 18 and 23, 59% between 24 and 29, and 26% above 30. 69% of the current freshmen were in the top fifth of their class; 91% were in the top two fifths. 39 freshmen graduated first in their class. **Admissions Contact:** Delorean Menifee, Director of Admissions. Email: *admission@butler.edu* Web: *www.butler.edu*

FINANCIAL AID: In 2016-2017, 97% of all full-time freshmen and 90% of continuing full-time students received some form of financial aid. 61% of all full-time freshmen and 59% of continuing full-time students received need-based aid. The average freshman award was

$23,481. Need-based scholarships or need-based grants averaged $19,085; need-based self-help aid (loans and jobs) averaged $4,228; non-need-based athletic scholarships averaged $27,386; and other non-need-based awards and non-need-based scholarships averaged $14,998. 25% of undergraduate students work part-time. Average annual earnings from campus work are $1200. The average financial indebtedness of the 2016 graduate was $35,730. Butler is a member of CSS. The FAFSA code is 001788. The deadline for filing freshman financial aid applications for fall entry is March 1.

CALUMET COLLEGE OF ST. JOSEPH — B-1

www.ccsj.edu

Whiting, IN 46394	(219) 473-4739 (877) 700-9100
Fax: (219) 473-4259	**Email:** admissions@ccsj.edu
Full-time: 160 men, 310 women	**Faculty:** IIA
Part-time: 345 men, 385 women	**Ph.D.s:** 50%
Graduate: 100 men, 40 women	**Student/Faculty:** n/av
Year: semesters, summer session	**Tuition:** $17,135
Room & Board: $5600	**Freshman Class:** n/av
SAT or ACT: recommended	**CEEB CODE:** 1776
Application Deadline: open	**COMPETITIVE**

Calumet College of St. Joseph, founded in 1951, is a private Catholic institution offering commuting students a liberal arts education in a Christian environment. The figures in the above capsule and in this profile are approximate. There are 2 undergraduate schools. The 256-acre campus is in a small town 15 miles southeast of Chicago in northwest Indiana. Including any residence halls, there is 1 building.

STUDENT LIFE: 70% of undergraduates are from Indiana. Others are from 2 states. 65% are from public schools. 46% are White; 33% African American; 19% Hispanic. 45% are Catholic. **Female To Male Ratio:** 1.2:1. The average age of freshmen is 21; all undergraduates, 35. 42% do not continue beyond their first year; 58% remain to graduate. **Housing:** Alcohol is not permitted. All students commute. All students may keep cars.

FACULTY/CLASSROOMS: 75% of faculty are male; 25% are female. All teach undergraduates. No introductory courses are taught by graduate students. The average class size in an introductory lecture is 25; in a laboratory is 20; and in a regular course is 20.

PROGRAMS OF STUDY: CCSJ confers B.A., B.S., B.S.Ed. and B.S.M.T. degrees. Associate and master's degrees are also awarded. Bachelor's degrees are awarded in BUSINESS (accounting, business administration and management, and institutional management), COMMUNICATIONS AND THE ARTS (English and media arts), COMPUTER AND PHYSICAL SCIENCE (information sciences and systems), EDUCATION (elementary education and secondary education), HEALTH PROFESSIONS (health care administration), SOCIAL SCIENCE (criminal justice, human services, law enforcement and corrections, liberal arts/general studies, paralegal studies, psychology, religion, theological studies, and urban studies). Management, accounting, and criminal justice are the strongest academically. Management, human services, and education have the largest enrollments.

ACTIVITIES: There are no fraternities or sororities. There are 15 groups on campus, including cheerleading, drama, ethnic, literary magazine, musical theater, newspaper, photography, professional, religious, social, social service, and student government. Popular campus events include Thanksgiving Ethnicfest and Student Appreciation Week. **Sports:** There is 1 intramural sport for men.

SERVICES: Counseling and information services are available, as is tutoring in most subjects. There is remedial math, reading, and writing. **Library/Resources:** The library contains 93,055 volumes, 3,035 microform items, and 6,412 audio/video tapes/CDs/DVDs, and subscribes to 354 periodicals including electronic. Computerized library services include interlibrary loans and database searching. Special learning facilities include an art gallery. **Physically Challenged Students:** All of the campus is accessible. Facilities include wheelchair ramps, elevators, special parking, and specially equipped restrooms. **Special:** The college offers a cooperative 3-1 baccalaureate degree in medical technology with the schools of St. Margaret-Mercy Hospital in Indiana, where students complete their study and a clinical internship. Accelerated degree programs in organizational management, health-care management, and law enforcement management are possible. The LEAP program offers credit for life experience. Study abroad, internships, work-study programs, a general studies degree, pass/fail options, and nondegree study are possible. **Visiting:** There are regularly scheduled orientations for prospective students. There are guides for informal visits and visitors may sit in on classes. To schedule a visit, contact the Director of Admissions. **Campus Safety and Security:** There are emergency telephones and lighted pathways/sidewalks.

REQUIREMENTS: The SAT or ACT is recommended. Applicants should have completed 4 years of high school English, 3 to 4 of math, 2 to 3 of science, and 2 of social studies. The GED is accepted. An essay and an interview are recommended. The Vocabulary and Reading Assessment Test is required. AP and CLEP credits are accepted. Important factors in the admissions decision are extracurricular activities record, leadership record, and evidence of special talent. All students must complete 42 semester hours of general education courses, including English composition, economics, speech, theology, philosophy, communication and fine arts, science and math, and social and behavioral science. A total of 124 semester hours with a minimum GPA of 2.0 is required to graduate. **Procedure:** Freshmen are admitted to all sessions. There are deferred admissions and rolling admissions plans. Application deadlines are open. Applications are accepted on-line. **Transfer Students:** A 2.0 GPA is required. An interview is recommended. The Vocabulary and Reading Assessment Test is required. 30 of 124 credits required for the bachelor's degree must be completed at CCSJ. **International Students:** They must take the TOEFL.

Admissions Contact: Carl Cutton, Director of Admissions and Financial Aid. Email: *admissions@ccsj.edu* Web: *www.ccsj.edu*

FINANCIAL AID: CCSJ is a member of CSS. The college's own financial statement is required. The FAFSA code is 001834. Check with the school for current application deadlines.

DEPAUW UNIVERSITY — B-3

www.depauw.edu

Greencastle, IN 46135	(765) 658-4006 (800) 447-2495
Fax: (765) 658-4007	**Email:** admission@depauw.edu
Full-time: 1046 men, 1179 women	**Faculty:** 224; IIB, +$
Part-time: n/av	**Ph.D.s:** 91%
Graduate: n/av	**Student/Faculty:** 10 to 1
Year: 4-1-4	**Tuition:** $46,448
Room & Board: $12,240	**Freshman Class:** 4913 applied, 3023 accepted, 578 enrolled
SAT CR/M/W: 580/600/580 **ACT:** 27	**CEEB CODE:** 1166
Application Deadline: March 1	**HIGHLY COMPETITIVE+**

DePauw University, founded in 1837, is a private institution offering programs in the fields of liberal arts and music. Figures in the above capsule and in this profile are approximate. There are 2 undergraduate schools. In addition to regional accreditation, DePauw has baccalaureate program accreditation with NASM, NCATE, ACS, and CAAHEP. The 695-acre campus is in a rural area 45 miles west of Indianapolis. Including any residence halls, there are 81 buildings.

STUDENT LIFE: 64% of undergraduates are from out of state, mostly the Midwest. Students are from 49 states, and 30 foreign countries. 88% are from public schools. 75% are White; 7% Foreign; 6% African American; 4% Hispanic; 3% Asian American. 45% are Protestant; 20% Catholic. **Female To Male Ratio:** 1.1:1. The average age of freshmen is 19; all undergraduates, 20. 10% do not continue beyond their first year; 83% remain to graduate. **Housing:** 1490 students can be accommodated in college housing, which includes coed dorms, on-campus apartments, and off-campus apartments. In addition, there are special-interest houses, fraternity houses, sorority houses, and international student housing. On-campus housing is guaranteed for all 4 years. 99% of students live on campus. All students may keep cars.

FACULTY/CLASSROOMS: 55% of faculty are male; 45% are female. All teach undergraduates, and 82% do research. No introductory courses are taught by graduate students. The average class size in an introductory lecture is 20; in a laboratory is 14; and in a regular course is 18.

PROGRAMS OF STUDY: DePauw confers B.A., B.M.A., B.M.E., and B.Mu. degrees. Bachelor's degrees are awarded in AGRICULTURE (natural resource management), BIOLOGICAL SCIENCE (biochemistry and biology/biological science), COMMUNICATIONS AND THE ARTS (art history and appreciation, classical languages, communications, English, English literature, French, German, Greek, Latin, linguistics, literature, music, music business management, music performance, music theory and composition, romance languages and literature, Spanish, and studio art), COMPUTER AND PHYSICAL SCIENCE (chemistry, computer science, earth science, geology, mathematics, and physics), EDUCATION (elementary education, foreign languages education, and music education), ENGINEERING AND ENVIRONMENTAL DESIGN (environmental science and preengineering), HEALTH PROFESSIONS (health), SOCIAL SCIENCE (African American studies, anthropology, classical/ancient civilization, East Asian studies, economics, gender studies, geography, history, interdisciplinary studies, peace studies, philosophy, physical fitness/movement, political science/government, psychology, religion, Russian and Slavic studies, sociology, and women's studies). English, economics, and communications have the largest enrollments.

ACTIVITIES: 78% of men belong to 12 national fraternities; 64% of women belong to 10 national sororities. There are 80 groups on campus, including art, band, cheerleading, chess, choir, chorale, chorus, computers, dance, debate, drama, ethnic, film, forensics, honors, international, jazz band, LGBT, literary magazine, musical theater, newspaper, opera, orchestra, pep band, political, professional, radio and TV, religious, social, social service, student government, and symphony. Popular campus events include Little 5 Track Meet, Monon Bell Football Game, and Old Gold Day. **Sports:** There are 17 intercollegiate sports for men and 16 for women, and 14 intramural sports for men and 12 for women. Facilities include a recreation center, a 4000-seat stadium, baseball, soccer, and field hockey fields, 3 basketball courts, indoor/outdoor tennis courts and tracks, a pool, a fitness center, volleyball and badminton courts, and a 3200-seat indoor gym. **Graduates:** From July 1, 2015 to June 30, 2016, 499 bachelor's degrees were awarded. The most popular majors were English, communication/theatre, and music. In an average class, 79% graduate in 4 years or less and 81% graduate in 5 years or less.

SERVICES: Counseling and information services are available, as is tutoring in most subjects. There is a reader service for the blind. **Library/Resources:** The 3 libraries contain 818,618 volumes, 381,066 microform items, and 34,325 audio/video tapes/CDs/DVDs, and subscribe to 29,188 periodicals including electronic. Computerized library services include interlibrary loans, database searching, and Internet access. Special learning facilities include an art gallery, natural history museum, radio station, TV station, nature park, an observatory, an arboretum, a digital video studio, institute for ethics, and a digital media lab. **Physically Challenged Students:** 85% of the campus is accessible. Facilities include wheelchair ramps, elevators, special parking, specially equipped restrooms, special class scheduling, lowered drinking fountains, and lowered telephones. **Special:** DePauw offers dual majors in any 2 disciplines, student-designed majors, internships for honors programs and winter-term projects, unlimited study-abroad options through cooperative arrangements with other universities, a Washington semester, pass/fail options, and credit by departmental examination. Also available are 3-2 engineering degrees with Case Western Reserve, Columbia, and Washington Universities and a 3-2 nursing program with Rush University Hospital in Chicago. The Media Fellows, Management Fellows, and Science Research Fellows programs offer majors in any discipline, plus a semester-long internship. There are 13 national honor societies, Phi Beta Kappa, a freshman honors program, and 12 departmental honors programs. **Visiting:** There are regularly scheduled orientations for prospective students, consisting of day-long student/parent programs that include campus tours, faculty viewpoints, conversations with students, admissions information, financial aid and career planning sessions, and a meal in a residence hall. There are guides for informal visits, visitors may sit in on classes, and stay overnight. To schedule a visit, contact the Admission Program and Visit Coordinator. **Campus Safety and Security:** Measures include 24-hour foot and vehicle patrol, emergency notification system, self-defense education, and security escort services. There are shuttle buses, emergency telephones, and lighted pathways/sidewalks.

REQUIREMENTS: The SAT or ACT is required. Graduation from an accredited secondary school or a GED is required for admission. Course distribution should include 4 each in English and math, 3 to 4 each in social studies and science (2 or more with lab), and 2 to 4 in a foreign language. An essay is required, and an interview is strongly recommended. Applicants for the School of Music must audition. AP credits are accepted. Important factors in the admissions decision are advanced placement or honors courses, recommendations by school officials, and personality/intangible qualities. Students must demonstrate competence in oral communications, quantitative reasoning, and writing. Successful completion of 124 semester hours, including 32 to 40 in the major, is required for graduation. In addition, students must fulfill distribution requirements in natural sciences, social and behavioral sciences, literature and the arts, historical and philosophical understanding, foreign language, and self-expression. A comprehensive exam, thesis, or seminar is required for each major. **Procedure:** Freshmen are admitted fall and spring. Entrance exams should be taken as early as possible. There are early decision, early admissions, and deferred admissions plans. Early decision applications should be filed by November 1; regular applications, by March 1 for fall entry; and December 1 for spring entry, along with a $40 fee. Notification of early decision is sent January 1; regular decision, April 1. 50 early decision candidates were accepted for the 2016-2017 class. 216 applicants were on the 2016 waiting list; 112 were admitted. Applications are accepted on-line. **Transfer Students:** 21 transfer students enrolled in 2015-2016. Applicants must submit either SAT or ACT scores. High school and college transcripts are required, and a minimum GPA on previous college work of 3.0 is preferred. 60 of 124 credits required for the bachelor's degree must be completed at DePauw. **International Students:** There are 185 international students enrolled. The school actively recruits these students. They must take the TOEFL with a minimum score of 560 on the paper-based TOEFL (PBT) or 83 on the Internet-based version (iBT), or take the IELTS. They must also take the SAT or ACT.

ADMISSIONS: 62% of the 2016-2017 applicants were accepted. The SAT scores for the 2016-2017 freshman class were: Critical Reading-- 14% below 500, 40% between 500 and 599, 35% between 600 and 699, and 10% between 700 and 800. Math-- 8% below 500, 36% between 500 and 599, 41% between 600 and 699, and 14% between 700 and 800. Writing-- 13% below 500, 42% between 500 and 599, 37% between 600 and 699, and 7% between 700 and 800. **Admissions Contact:** Becca Moore, Senior Assoc. of Admissions. Email: *admission@depauw.edu* Web: *www.depauw.edu*

FINANCIAL AID: DePauw is a member of CSS. The CSS/Profile and the college's own financial statement are required. The FAFSA code is 001792. The priority date for freshman financial aid applications for fall entry is February 15.

EARLHAM COLLEGE D-3

www.earlham.edu

Richmond, IN 47374	**(765) 983-1600** **(800) 327-5426**
Fax: (765) 983-1560	**Email: admission@earlham.edu**
Full-time: 454 men, 570 women	**Faculty:** 103; IIB, -$
Part-time: 2 men, 5 women	**Ph.D.s:** 97%
Graduate: 26 men, 43 women	**Student/Faculty:** 10 to 1
Year: semesters	**Tuition:** $45,300
Room & Board: $9570	**Freshman Class:** 2917 applied, 1681 accepted, 355 enrolled
SAT CR/M/W: 620/610/600 **ACT:** 28	**CEEB CODE:** 1195
Application Deadline: February 15	**HIGHLY COMPETITIVE**

Recognized as one of the nation's finest liberal arts colleges, Earlham College is distinguished by a global mindset shaped through a challenging academic program, community-building, and immersive experiences. Our students gain a rich, intellectual framework and inspiration to explore global issues, whether cultural, economic, environmental, political, or science-related through a wide array of undergraduate research, study abroad, and internship opportunities. Earlham graduates are prepared for success and committed to making a positive difference in the world There is 1 undergraduate school and 2 graduate schools. In addition to regional accreditation, Earlham has baccalaureate program accreditation with ACS and ATS. The 800-acre campus is in a small town 70 miles east of Indianapolis and 40 miles west of Dayton, OH. Including any residence halls, there are 64 buildings.

STUDENT LIFE: 83% of undergraduates are from out of state, mostly the Midwest. Students are from 45 states, 59 foreign countries, and Canada. 65% are from public schools. 49% are White; 23% Foreign; 12% African American; 7% Hispanic; 5% Asian American; 2% race unknown; 1% American Indian/Alaska Native; 1% two or more races. 41% claim no religious affiliation; 40% Quaker, Christian, Buddhist, Hindu and Muslim; 11% Protestant. **Female To Male Ratio:** 1.3:1. The average age of freshmen is 18; all undergraduates, 20. 17% do not continue beyond their first year; 70% remain to graduate. **Housing:** 1010 students can be accommodated in college housing, which includes single-sex and coed dorms. In addition, there are language houses, special-interest houses, service learning house, Jewish cultural center, an African American cultural center, international cultural center, and LBGTQ housing. On-campus housing is guaranteed for all 4 years. 96% of students live on campus; of those, 84% remain on campus on weekends. All students may keep cars.

FACULTY/CLASSROOMS: 49% of faculty are male; 51% are female. All teach undergraduates. No introductory courses are taught by graduate students. The average class size in an introductory lecture is 48; in a laboratory is 15; and in a regular course is 12.

PROGRAMS OF STUDY: Earlham confers B.A. degrees. Master's degrees are also awarded. Bachelor's degrees are awarded in AGRICULTURE (environmental studies), BIOLOGICAL SCIENCE (biochemistry, biology/biological science, and neurosciences), BUSINESS (business administration and management), COMMUNICATIONS AND THE ARTS (art, dramatic arts, English, French, German, languages, linguistics, music, and Spanish), COMPUTER AND PHYSICAL SCIENCE (chemistry, computer science, geology, mathematics, and physics), ENGINEERING AND ENVIRONMENTAL DESIGN (environmental science), HEALTH PROFESSIONS (premedicine), SOCIAL SCIENCE (African American studies, anthropology, classical/ancient civilization, economics, history, human development, international studies, Japanese studies, Latin American studies, peace studies, philosophy, political science/government, psychology, religion, sociology, and women's studies). Life sciences (pre-medical) and psychology are the strongest academically. Biology, psychology, and business non-profit management have the largest enrollments.

ACTIVITIES: There are no fraternities or sororities. There are 63 groups on campus, including art, cheerleading, choir, chorale, chorus, computers, dance, drama, environmental, ethnic, film, honors, international, jazz band, LGBT, literary magazine, newspaper, orchestra, photography, political, professional, radio and TV, religious, social, social service, student government, and symphony. Popular campus events include Student Research Conference, International Festival, Dance Alloy student performance, and Homecoming Dance. **Sports:** There are 9 intercollegiate sports for men and 9 for women, and 8 intramural sports for men and 8 for women. Facilities include fitness center with classes and cardiovascular equipment and weights, dance, tennis, volleyball, basketball, racquetball courts, golf, climbing wall, running track, pool, and a performance gym. The Randal R. Sadler baseball stadium features a turf playing surface, a stadium for football, field hockey, lacrosse, an equestrian center (with indoor and outdoor riding areas), tennis courts, basketball courts, and outdoor areas (for cross-country running, skiing or hiking). **Graduates:** From July 1, 2015 to June 30, 2016, 177 bachelor's degrees were awarded. The most popular majors were social sciences (21%), biology/life sciences (18%), and interdisciplinary studies (16%). In an average class, 1% graduate in 3 years or less, 61% graduate in 4 years or less, 68% graduate in 5 years or less, and 70% graduate in 6 years or less. Of the 2015 graduating class, 24% were enrolled in graduate school within 6 months of graduation, and 65% were employed.

SERVICES: Counseling and information services are available, as is tutoring in most subjects, such as most 100- and 200-level courses and some 300-level courses. A writing center is available. There is a reader service for the blind. **Library/Resources:** The 2 libraries contain 380,360 volumes, 151,115 microform items, and 9,670 audio/video tapes/CDs/DVDs, and subscribe to 74,422 periodicals including electronic. Computerized library services include interlibrary loans, database searching, Internet access, and Wi-Fi capability. Special learning facilities include an art gallery, natural history museum, planetarium, and radio station. There is a center for science and technology (CST) and a center for the visual and performing arts. Other notable facilities include the Landrum Bolling Center; which features the Center for Career and Community Engagement; and the Center for Global Education; the CoLab (dedicated to collaborative learning) theme residential houses an observatory; herbarium; and a greenhouse. **Physically Challenged Students:** 80% of the campus is accessible. Facilities include wheelchair ramps, elevators, special parking, specially equipped restrooms, lowered drinking fountains, lowered telephones, and special housing. **Special:** The Earlham Plan for Integrative Collaboration (EPIC) is the College's distinctive approach to the liberal arts, collaborative academic inquiry, and integrative learning. In order to offer the richest possible undergraduate experience, EPIC purposefully links the College's academic program with exceptional experiential learning opportunities through the Center for Career and Community Engagement and the Center for Global Education as well as research and study opportunities through Earlham's three Interdisciplinary Academic Centers: Global Health, Entrepreneurship and Innovation, and Social Justice. There are 2 national honor societies and a chapter of Phi Beta Kappa. **Visiting:** There are regularly scheduled orientations for prospective students, including class visitation, an admissions interview, a tour, and special appointments with faculty. There are guides for informal visits, visitors may sit in on classes, and stay overnight. To schedule a visit, contact the Admissions Office at (765) 983-1600. **Campus Safety and Security:** Measures include 24-hour foot and vehicle patrol, emergency notification system, self-defense education, and security escort services. There are shuttle buses, emergency telephones, lighted pathways/sidewalks, and controlled access to dorms/residences.

REQUIREMENTS: In most cases, graduation from an accredited secondary school is required; a GED will be accepted. Students must have completed at least 15 academic credits, including 4 years of English, 3 of math, and 2 each of science, history or social studies, and a foreign language. Students are required to submit an essay and letters of recommendation from a teacher and guidance counselor. An interview is recommended. A GPA of 2.5 is required. AP credits are accepted. Important factors in the admissions decision are advanced placement or honors courses, evidence of special talent, and extracurricular activities record. To graduate, all students must complete core requirements, featuring a global seminar, courses in cultural diversity, and an integrated pathway tailored to students' academic passions and pre-professional interests. Every student also has multiple immersive learning opportunities, such as a research experience, internship, or off-campus study. Students must also maintain a minimum GPA of 2.0 and complete a total of 122 semester hours, including 32 semester hours in the major and at least 36-upper level semester hours and 40 outside the major division. A senior capstone experience is required. **Procedure:** Freshmen are admitted fall and spring. Entrance exams should be taken during the spring of the junior year or early fall of the senior year. There are early decision, early admissions, and deferred admissions plans. Early decision applications should be filed by November 1; regular applications, by February 15 for fall entry; November 1 for winter entry; and spring entry. Notification of early decision is sent December 1; regular decision, February 15. 10 early decision candidates were accepted for the 2016-2017 class. 336 applicants were on the 2016 waiting list; 60 were admitted. Applications are accepted on-line. **Transfer Students:** 14 transfer students enrolled in 2015-2016. Applicants must have a minimum GPA of 2.5 in college-course work. An interview is recommended. High school and college transcripts, an essay, and a statement of good standing from the prior institution are required. 62 of 122 credits required for the bachelor's degree must be completed at Earlham. **International Students:** There are 233 international students enrolled. The school actively recruits these students. They must take the TOEFL with a minimum score of 550 on the paper-based TOEFL (PBT) or 80 on the Internet-based version (iBT).

ADMISSIONS: 58% of the 2016-2017 applicants were accepted. The SAT scores for the 2016-2017 freshman class were: Critical Reading-- 4% below 500, 32% between 500 and 599, 44% between 600 and 699, and 20% between 700 and 800. Math-- 9% below 500, 32% between 500 and 599, 35% between 600 and 699, and 24% between 700 and 800. Writing-- 10% below 500, 38% between 500 and 599, 34% between 600 and 699, and 18% between 700 and 800. The ACT scores were 13% between 18 and 23, 52% between 24 and 29, and 35% above 30. 65% of the current freshmen were in the top fifth of their class; 87% were in the top two fifths. 7 freshmen graduated first in their class. **Admissions Contact:** Jonathan Stroud, VP for Enrollment and Communications. Email: *admission@earlham.edu* Web: *www.earlham.edu*

FINANCIAL AID: In 2016-2017, 97% of all full-time freshmen and 90% of continuing full-time students received some form of financial aid. 85% of all full-time freshmen and 45% of continuing full-time students received need-based aid. The average freshman award was $41,876. Need-based scholarships or need-based grants averaged $36,206; need-based self-help aid (loans and jobs) averaged $3,225; and other non-need-based awards and non-need-based scholarships averaged $17,500. 65% of undergraduate students work part-time. Average annual earnings from campus work are $2200. The average financial indebtedness of the 2016 graduate was $25,784. Earlham is a member of CSS. The FAFSA code is 001793. The priority date for freshman financial aid applications for fall entry is March 1.

FRANKLIN COLLEGE C-4

www.franklincollege.edu

Franklin, IN 46131	**(317) 738-8758** **(800) 852-0232**
Fax: (317) 738-8274	**Email: admissions@franklincollege.edu**
Full-time: 468 men, 493 women	**Faculty:** 79; IIB, -$
Part-time: 24 men, 31 women	**Ph.D.s:** 83%
Graduate: 1 men, 6 women	**Student/Faculty:** 11 to 1
Year: 4-1-4, summer session	**Tuition:** $30,025
Room & Board: $9355	**Freshman Class:** 1404 applied, 1224 accepted, 237 enrolled
SAT CR/M/W: 480/500/480 **ACT:** 22	**CEEB CODE:** 1228
Application Deadline: open	**COMPETITIVE**

Founded in 1834, Franklin College provides a liberal arts and sciences education that fosters independent thinking, innovation, leadership, and action for ever-changing professions and a globally connected world. With an emphasis on engaged learning opportunities, Franklin offers a Bachelor of Arts degree in more than 50 majors and a Master of Science degree in athletic training. A vibrant part of the Indianapolis metropolitan area, the college values collaboration and upholds common values that benefit communities and inspire students. Franklin College is historically related to the American Baptist Churches. There is 1 undergraduate school and 1 graduate school. In addition to regional accreditation, Franklin College has baccalaureate program accreditation with NCATE and CAATE. The 207-acre campus is in a small town 25 miles south of downtown Indianapolis. Including any residence halls, there are 23 buildings.

STUDENT LIFE: 92% of undergraduates are from Indiana. Others are from 17 states, and 9 foreign countries. 84% are White; 4% African American; 4% two or more races; 3% Hispanic; 2% race unknown; 1% Asian American; 1% American Indian/Alaska Native; 1% Foreign. 53% are Protestant; 29% claim no religious affiliation; 13% Catholic. **Female To Male Ratio:** 1.1:1. The average age of freshmen is 19; all undergraduates, 21. 26% do not continue beyond their first year; 61% remain to graduate. **Housing:** 730 students can be accommodated in college housing, which includes single-sex and coed dorms. In addition, there are language houses, special-interest houses, fraternity houses, and a substance/alcohol-free residence hall living area. On-campus housing is available on a first-come, first-served basis, and is available on a lottery system for upperclassmen. 72% of students live on campus. All students may keep cars.

FACULTY/CLASSROOMS: 55% of faculty are male; 45% are female. All teach undergraduates. No introductory courses are taught by graduate students. The average class size in an introductory lecture is 18; in a laboratory is 15; and in a regular course is 14.

PROGRAMS OF STUDY: Franklin College confers B.A. degrees. Master's degrees are also awarded. Bachelor's degrees are awarded in BIOLOGICAL SCIENCE (biology ecology and field biology, biology/biological science, and life science secondary school education), BUSINESS (accounting, business administration and management, business administration - international, and business administration marketing), COMMUNICATIONS AND THE ARTS (art history, creative writing, English, French, journalism, multimedia, music, public relations, Spanish, studio art, studio art graphic design, studio art painting, and theatre arts), COMPUTER AND PHYSICAL SCIENCE (applied mathematics, chemistry, computer programming, computer science, and mathematics), EDUCATION (athletic training, elementary education, English education, mathematics education, physical education, science education, secondary education, and social studies education), HEALTH PROFESSIONS (biology and exercise science), SOCIAL SCIENCE (economics, history, philosophy, political science/government, psychology, religion, and sociology). Biology, business, and psychology are the strongest academically. Biology, business, and education have the largest enrollments.

ACTIVITIES: 25% of men belong to 5 national fraternities; 46% of women belong to 3 national sororities. There are 55 groups on campus, including art, band, cheerleading, choir, chorus, drama, drum and bugle corps, environmental, ethnic, film, honors, international, LGBT, literary magazine, newspaper, pep band, photography, political, professional, radio and TV, religious, social, social service, and student government. Popular campus events include Grizzly Grand Prix and Greek Week. **Sports:** There are 9 intercollegiate sports for men and 10 for women, and 6 intramural sports for men and 6 for women. Facilities include athletic and soccer fields, track, tennis courts, athletic center including basketball, fitness, and racquetball, and a fitness center including indoor athletic practice facilities. **Graduates:** From July 1, 2015 to June 30, 2016, 214 bachelor's degrees were awarded. The most popular majors were biology (12%), business (11%), and education (10%). 49 companies recruited on campus in 2015-2016. In an average class, 55% graduate in 4 years or less, 60% graduate in 5 years or less, and 61% graduate in 6 years or less. Of the 2015 graduating class, 18% were enrolled in graduate school within 6 months of graduation.

SERVICES: Counseling and information services are available, as is tutoring in most subjects. There is a reader service for the blind, and remedial math, reading, and writing. **Library/Resources:** The library contains 111,154 volumes, 310,676 microform items, and 5,261 audio/video tapes/CDs/DVDs, and subscribes to 33,498 periodicals including electronic. Computerized library services include interlibrary loans, database searching, Internet access, and Wi-Fi capability. Special learning facilities include a radio station. **Physically Challenged Students:** All of the campus is accessible. Facilities include wheelchair ramps, elevators, special parking, specially equipped restrooms, special class scheduling, lowered drinking fountains, lowered telephones, and special housing. **Special:** Cooperative programs are available in Biology and Chemistry (health-related professions). A 3-2 Accelerated Masters in Public Health, and a 3-2 engineering degree with Indiana University-Purdue University in Indianapolis are available. Also available are fall, winter, spring, and summer internships. Study abroad in various countries and cross-registration with 7 Indiana universities and colleges (Consortium for Urban Education) are available. There are 10 national honor societies and a chapter of Phi Beta Kappa. **Visiting:** There are guides for informal visits, visitors may sit in on classes, and stay overnight. To schedule a visit, contact Visit Coordinator at visits@franklincollege.edu. **Campus Safety and Security:** Measures include 24-hour foot and vehicle patrol, emergency notification system, and security escort services. There are emergency telephones, lighted pathways/sidewalks, and controlled access to dorms/residences.

REQUIREMENTS: A complete application file includes a submitted Franklin College application and an official transcript submitted by the guidance office or via parchment. For Guidance Offices that use PrepHQ, Franklin College is able to accept transcripts through the ConnectEDU system. Official SAT Code: 1228, ACT Code: 1194. Other items we take into consideration for admission include: Academic achievements: grade point average, official high school transcript, the student's course load and class rank. Standardized test scores (SAT or ACT); remember that the writing section of either test is required. Personal Statement/Essay (optional), Extracurricular involvement and leadership experience: athletic, literary, artistic, social service, church, and community involvement and employment. The quality of a student's high school. If a school no longer ranks students, our admission team may call to ask for an estimated class rank for scholarship purposes. Students must receive at least an Indiana Core 40 degree to be considered for admission to Franklin College. AP credits are accepted. Important factors in the admissions decision are advanced placement or honors courses, leadership record, and recommendations by school officials. Requirements for graduation include 80 hours outside the major, including general education, a minimum of 40 hours in the major, and 120 total credit hours. Students must demonstrate proficiency in a foreign language at the 111 level. Each student must maintain a minimum GPA of 2.0 and must pass the Senior Competency Test, which is administered by the department in which the student completes a major. **Procedure:** Freshmen are admitted to all sessions. Entrance exams should be taken in spring of the junior year or fall of the senior year. There is a rolling admissions plan. Application deadlines are open. Application fee is $40. Notification is sent on a rolling basis.

Applications are accepted on-line. Application fees are waived if application is completed on-line. **Transfer Students:** 33 transfer students enrolled in 2015-2016. Transfer students must have at least a 2.0 cumulative GPA. Required materials: Official high school transcript or GED certificatefranklin_0410_-2007, official college transcripts from all previously attended institutions. Transfer student recommendation form is required for all applicants who have attended another institution since completing high school. Also required are SAT or ACT score and a written personal statement of one or two pages, typed that addresses why you have chosen to transfer to Franklin College. Your personal statement may be submitted online via the Transfer Student Application or via email to admissions@franklincollege.edu. Students who have been removed from high school for more than five years are not required to submit a transcript or SAT/ACT scores. 48 of 120 credits required for the bachelor's degree must be completed at Franklin College. **International Students:** There are 7 international students enrolled. They must take the TOEFL with a minimum score of 550 on the paper-based TOEFL (PBT). Completion of level 109 in an English language service (ELS) center is necessary. They must also take the SAT or ACT.

ADMISSIONS: 87% of the 2016-2017 applicants were accepted. The SAT scores for the 2016-2017 freshman class were: Critical Reading-- 57% below 500, 30% between 500 and 599, 12% between 600 and 699, and 1% between 700 and 800. Math-- 50% below 500, 38% between 500 and 599, 11% between 600 and 699, and 1% between 700 and 800. Writing-- 60% below 500, 31% between 500 and 599, and 9% between 600 and 699. The ACT scores were 18% between 12 and 17, 50% between 18 and 23, 27% between 24 and 29, and 5% above 30. 45% of the current freshmen were in the top fifth of their class; 73% were in the top two fifths. 3 freshmen graduated first in their class. **Admissions Contact:** Jennifer Bostrom, Director of Admissions. Email: *admissions@franklincollege.edu* Web: *www.franklincollege.edu*

FINANCIAL AID: In 2016-2017, 85% of all full-time freshmen and 83% of continuing full-time students received some form of financial aid. 85% of all full-time freshmen and 85% of continuing full-time students received need-based aid. The average freshman award was $20,900. Need-based scholarships or need-based grants averaged $17,782; need-based self-help aid (loans and jobs) averaged $3,530; and other non-need-based awards and non-need-based scholarships averaged $14,397. 28% of undergraduate students work part-time. Average annual earnings from campus work are $1583. The average financial indebtedness of the 2016 graduate was $34,515. The college's own financial statement is required. The FAFSA code is 001798. The priority date for freshman financial aid applications for fall entry is March 10.

GOSHEN COLLEGE C-1
www.goshen.edu

Goshen, IN 46526	(574) 535-7535 (800) 348-7422
Fax: (574) 535-7609	Email: admissions@goshen.edu
Full-time: 293 men, 448 women	Faculty: 68; IIB, --$
Part-time: 24 men, 35 women	Ph.D.s: 69%
Graduate: 9 men, 61 women	Student/Faculty: 11 to 1
Year: 4-1-4, summer session	Tuition: $32,200
Room & Board: $10,300	Freshman Class: 975 applied, 623 accepted, 185 enrolled
SAT CR/M/W: 510/500/490 ACT: 25	CEEB CODE: 1251
Application Deadline: August 1	COMPETITIVE

Goshen College, founded in 1894, is a private, Christian, liberal arts institution affiliated with the Mennonite Church offering bachelor's and master's degrees in a variety of fields. The figures in the above capsule and in this profile are approximate. There are 3 undergraduate schools and 1 graduate school. In addition to regional accreditation, Goshen College has baccalaureate program accreditation with CSWE and NCATE. The 135-acre campus is in a small town approximately 120 miles east of Chicago and 30 miles southeast of South Bend, IN. Including any residence halls, there are 25 buildings.

STUDENT LIFE: 60% of undergraduates are from Indiana. Others are from 34 states, 25 foreign countries, and Canada. 79% are from public schools. 8% are Foreign; 66% White; 4% African American; 2% Asian American; 2% two or more races; 17% Hispanic. 65% are Protestant; 13% Catholic. **Female To Male Ratio:** 1.7:1. The average age of freshmen is 18; all undergraduates, 22. 19% do not continue beyond their first year; 67% remain to graduate. **Housing:** 700 students can be accommodated in college housing, which includes single-sex and coed dorms, on-campus apartments, off-campus apartments, and married student housing. In addition, there are special-interest houses. On-campus housing is guaranteed for all 4 years. 53% of students live on campus; of those, 85% remain on campus on weekends. Alcohol is not permitted. All students may keep cars.

FACULTY/CLASSROOMS: 43% of faculty are male; 57% are female. 98% teach undergraduates. No introductory courses are taught by graduate students. The average class size in an introductory lecture is 27; in a laboratory is 20; and in a regular course is 22.

PROGRAMS OF STUDY: Goshen College confers B.A., B.S., and B.S.N. degrees. Master's degrees are also awarded. Bachelor's degrees are awarded in AGRICULTURE (environmental studies), BIOLOGICAL SCIENCE (biochemistry, biology/biological science, ecology, and molecular biology), BUSINESS (accounting, business administration and management, institutional management, information & communication technology, and marketing management), COMMUNICATIONS AND THE ARTS (American Sign Language, art, broadcasting, communications, creative writing, dramatic arts, English, English Writing, film, television and digital media, journalism, music, public relations, Spanish, theatre arts, and writing), COMPUTER AND PHYSICAL SCIENCE (chemistry, computer science, information sciences and systems, mathematics, and physics), EDUCATION (art education, business education, early childhood education, elementary education, English education, environmental education, foreign languages education, health education, mathematics education, middle school education, music education, physical education, science education, secondary education, and teaching English as a second/foreign language (TESOL/TEFOL)), ENGINEERING AND ENVIRONMENTAL DESIGN (environmental science and preengineering), HEALTH PROFESSIONS (nursing, predentistry, premedicine, prepharmacy, and preveterinary science), SOCIAL SCIENCE (biblical studies, economics, history, interdisciplinary studies, peace studies, psychology, religion, social work, and sociology). Nursing, elementary education, and biology have the largest enrollments.

ACTIVITIES: There are no fraternities or sororities. There are 24 groups on campus, including art, choir, chorale, chorus, drama, environmental, ethnic, international, jazz band, literary magazine, musical theater, newspaper, opera, orchestra, photography, professional, radio and TV, religious, social, social service, student government, and yearbook. Popular campus events include Kick Off (student talent show), Martin Luther King Jr Day, and Homecoming. **Sports:** There are 8 intercollegiate sports for men and 8 for women, and 3 intramural sports for men and 3 for women. Facilities include a fitness center with an indoor track, weight room, 3 basketball courts, 3 racquetball courts, and workout equipment. Athletic facilities include a soccer field, tennis courts, a sand volleyball court, a 400-meter all-weather track, and baseball and softball diamonds. **Graduates:** From July 1, 2015 to June 30, 2016, 193 bachelor's degrees were awarded. The most popular majors were nursing (20%), biology (11%), and social work (7%). In an average class, 1% graduate in 3 years or less, 55% graduate in 4 years or less, 66% graduate in 5 years or less, and 67% graduate in 6 years or less. Of the 2015 graduating class, 12% were enrolled in graduate school within 6 months of graduation, and 76% were employed.

SERVICES: Counseling and information services are available, as is tutoring in every subject. There is a reader service for the blind, and remedial math, reading, and writing. **Library/Resources:** The library contains 106,765 volumes, 140,000 microform items, and 2,261 audio/video tapes/CDs/DVDs, and subscribes to 212 periodicals including electronic. Computerized library services include interlibrary loans, database searching, Internet access, and Wi-Fi capability. Special learning facilities include an art gallery, radio station, and TV station. **Physically Challenged Students:** All of the campus is accessible. Facilities include wheelchair ramps, elevators, special parking, specially equipped restrooms, special class scheduling, lowered drinking fountains, and lowered telephones. **Special:** A semester abroad in the required Study Service Term is possible in Cambodia, Morocco, Peru, Tanzania, Nicaragua, China and Senegal. **Visiting:** There are regularly scheduled orientations for prospective students, campus tour, a parents session, talks with professors, a financial aid session, visiting classes, an overnight stay in residence halls, a student panel, and a campus interview. There are guides for informal visits, visitors may sit in on classes. To schedule a visit, contact the Admission Office. **Campus Safety and Security:** Measures include 24-hour foot and vehicle patrol, emergency notification system, and security escort services. There are lighted pathways/sidewalks and controlled access to dorms/residences.

REQUIREMENTS: The SAT or ACT is required. Applicants should be graduates of an accredited secondary school or have a GED equivalent, with 4 years of high school English, 2 to 4 years of math, and 2 years each of foreign language, science, history, and social studies. AP and CLEP credits are accepted. Important factors in the admissions decision are advanced placement or honors courses, leadership record, and recommendations by school officials. All students must complete the general education program, including courses in literature and communication, fine arts, Bible, religion, philosophy, natural science, math, social science, and history, and 12 hours of international education in the study service term and 1 hour of phys ed. A total of 120 credit hours with a minimum GPA of 2.0 is required to graduate. **Procedure:** Freshmen are admitted to all sessions. Entrance exams should be taken by fall of the senior year. There are deferred admissions and rolling admissions plans. Applications should be filed by August 1 for fall entry, along with a $25 fee. Notification is sent on a rolling basis. Applications are accepted on-line. **Transfer Students:** 48 transfer students enrolled in 2015-2016. A GPA of 2.0 or higher is required on previous college work. 30 of 120 credits required for the bachelor's degree must be completed at Goshen College. **International Students:** There are 66 international students enrolled. The school actively recruits these students. They must take the TOEFL with a minimum score of 550 on the paper-based TOEFL (PBT) or 79 on the Internet-based version (iBT). They must also take the SAT or ACT.

ADMISSIONS: 64% of the 2016-2017 applicants were accepted. The SAT scores for the 2016-2017 freshman class were: Critical Reading-- 48% below 500, 23% between 500 and 599, 23% between 600 and 699, and 7% between 700 and 800. Math-- 49% below 500, 29% between 500 and 599, 16% between 600 and 699, and 7% between 700 and 800. Writing-- 55% below 500, 19% between 500 and 599, 20% between 600 and 699, and 7% between 700 and 800. The ACT scores were 8% between 12 and 17, 27% between 18 and 23, 44% between 24 and 29, and 21% above 30. 32% of the current freshmen were in the top fifth of their class; 60% were in the top two fifths. 5 freshmen graduated first in their class. **Admissions Contact:** Adela Hufford, Dean of Admissions. Email: *admissions@goshen.edu* Web: *www.goshen.edu*

FINANCIAL AID: In 2016-2017, 100% of all full-time freshmen and 99% of continuing full-time students received some form of financial aid. 80% of all full-time freshmen and 74% of continuing full-time students received need-based aid. The average freshman award was $31,947. Need-based scholarships or need-based grants averaged $8,172 ($23,035 maximum); need-based self-help aid (loans and jobs) averaged $3,204 ($26,000 maximum); non-need-based athletic scholarships averaged $1,437 ($20,000 maximum); and other non-need-based awards and non-need-based scholarships averaged $19,133 ($46,070 maximum). 115% of undergraduate students work part-time. Average annual earnings from campus work are $2000. The average financial indebtedness of the 2016 graduate was $21,512. Goshen College is a member of CSS. The FAFSA code is 001799. The deadline for filing freshman financial aid applications for fall entry is March 10.

GRACE COLLEGE AND SEMINARY — C-2

www.grace.edu

Winona Lake, IN 46590	(574) 372-5100 (800) 54-GRACE
Fax: (574) 372-5120	**Email:** enroll@grace.edu
Full-time: 633 men, 888 women	**Faculty:** 49
Part-time: 217 men, 196 women	**Ph.D.s:** 63%
Graduate: 217 men, 182 women	**Student/Faculty:** 20 to 1
Year: semesters, summer session	**Tuition:** $23,120
Room & Board: $8404	**Freshman Class:** 4199 applied, 3298 accepted, 454 enrolled
SAT CR/M: 519/512 **ACT:** 24	**CEEB CODE:** 1252
Application Deadline: March 1	**COMPETITIVE**

Grace College, founded in 1948, is a Christian liberal arts institution affiliated with the Fellowship of Grace Brethren Churches. There are 5 undergraduate schools and 2 graduate schools. In addition to regional accreditation, Grace has baccalaureate program accreditation with NCATE, ATS, and CACREP. The 150-acre campus is in a small town 40 miles west of Fort Wayne. Including any residence halls, there are 25 buildings.

STUDENT LIFE: 74% of undergraduates are from Indiana. Others are from 32 states, 12 foreign countries, and Canada. 74% are from public schools. 79% are White; 7% race unknown; 6% Hispanic; 5% African American; 2% two or more races; 1% Asian American. **Female To Male Ratio:** 1.2:1. The average age of freshmen is 18; all undergraduates, 21. 17% do not continue beyond their first year; 67% remain to graduate. **Housing:** 850 students can be accommodated in college housing, which includes single-sex dorms and on-campus apartments. On-campus housing is guaranteed for all 4 years, is guaranteed for the freshman year only, and is available on a first-come, first-served basis, and is available on a lottery system for upperclassmen. Priority is given to out-of-town students. 75% of students live on campus; of those, 80% remain on campus on weekends. Alcohol is not permitted. All students may keep cars.

FACULTY/CLASSROOMS: 57% of faculty are male; 43% are female. All teach undergraduates, 10% do research, and 10% do both. No introductory courses are taught by graduate students. The average class size in an introductory lecture is 48; in a laboratory is 14; and in a regular course is 17.

PROGRAMS OF STUDY: Grace confers B.A. and B.S. degrees. Associate, master's, and doctoral degrees are also awarded. Bachelor's degrees are awarded in BIOLOGICAL SCIENCE (biology/biological science), BUSINESS (accounting, business administration and management, and management information systems), COMMUNICATIONS AND THE ARTS (art, communications, English, French, German, graphic design, journalism, music, and Spanish), COMPUTER AND PHYSICAL SCIENCE (mathematics and science), EDUCATION (art education, business education, elementary education, English education, foreign languages education, journalism education, mathematics education, music education, physical education, science education, and special education), HEALTH PROFESSIONS (predentistry and premedicine), SOCIAL SCIENCE (biblical studies, counseling/psychology, criminal justice, prelaw, psychology, religion, social work, sociology, and youth ministry). Biology, psychology, and business are the strongest academically. Psychology, elementary education, and business have the largest enrollments.

ACTIVITIES: There are no fraternities or sororities. There are 14 groups on campus, including band, cheerleading, choir, chorale, communications, drama, honors, international, musical theater, newspaper, orchestra, pep band, religious, social, student government, and yearbook. Popular campus events include Fall Fest, Heart of the Holidays, Missionary Conference, Day of Prayer, MLK. **Sports:** There are 7 intercollegiate sports for men and 8 for women, and 3 intramural sports for men and 3 for women. Facilities include gym, soccer fields, tennis courts, softball and baseball diamonds, and a recreation center with basketball courts, indoor & outdoor track, and weight and exercise rooms. **Graduates:** From July 1, 2015 to June 30, 2016, 362 bachelor's degrees were awarded. The most popular majors were business/marketing (30%), psychology (20%), and education (13%). In an average class, 28% graduate in 3 years or less, 66% graduate in 4 years or less, 66% graduate in 5 years or less.

SERVICES: Counseling and information services are available, as is tutoring in most subjects. There is a reader service for the blind, and remedial math, reading, and writing. **Library/Resources:** The library contains 150,843 volumes, 26,000 microform items, and 3,714 audio/video tapes/CDs/DVDs, and subscribes to 19,360 periodicals including electronic. Computerized library services include interlibrary loans, database searching, Internet access, and Wi-Fi capability. Special learning facilities include an art gallery, and the Winona History Center. **Physically Challenged Students:** 80% of the campus is accessible. Facilities include wheelchair ramps, elevators, special parking, specially equipped restrooms, and special class scheduling. **Special:** Students may study abroad in 5 countries. A B.A.-B.S. degree is available in all majors except languages, English, and biblical studies. Dual majors are offered in psychology, sociology, communication, business, accounting, youth ministries, and management information technology. There is 1 national honor society and a freshman honors program. **Visiting:** There are regularly scheduled orientations for prospective students, including tours, class visits, and meetings with professors. There are guides for informal visits, visitors may sit in on classes, and stay overnight. To schedule a visit, contact the Admissions/Visitors Center. **Campus Safety and Security:** Measures include 24-hour foot and vehicle patrol, emergency notification system, and security escort services. There are emergency telephones, lighted pathways/sidewalks, and controlled access to dorms/residences.

REQUIREMENTS: The SAT or ACT is recommended. Applicants must have completed 15 Carnegie units, including 4 of English, 3 each of math and science, 2 each of a foreign language and social studies, and 1 of history. A GED is accepted. Grace requires applicants to be in the upper 50% of their class. A GPA of 2.3 is required. AP and CLEP credits are accepted. Important factors in the admissions decision are advanced placement or honors courses, leadership record, and personality/intangible qualities. **Procedure:** Freshmen are admitted to all sessions. Entrance exams should be taken in October, December, or February. There are deferred admissions and rolling admissions plans. Applications should be filed by March 1 for fall entry, along with a $30 fee. Notification is sent on a rolling basis. Applications are accepted on-line. **Transfer Students:** Transfer applicants should have a minimum 2.0 GPA in addition to fulfilling freshman entrance requirements. 60 of 124 credits required for the bachelor's degree must be completed at Grace. **International Students:** There are 9 international students enrolled. They must take the TOEFL. They must also take the SAT or ACT.

ADMISSIONS: 79% of the 2016-2017 applicants were accepted. The SAT scores for the 2016-2017 freshman class were: Critical Reading-- 40% below 500, 41% between 500 and 599, 17% between 600 and 699, and 2% between 700 and 800. Math-- 40% below 500, 39% between 500 and 599, 19% between 600 and 699, and 2% between 700 and 800. The ACT scores were 6% between 12 and 17, 34% between 18 and 23, 50% between 24 and 29, and 10% above 30. 2% of the current freshmen were in the top fifth of their class; 10% were in the top two fifths. **Admissions Contact:** Cynthia Sisson, VP of Enrollment Management and Marketin. Email: *enroll@grace.edu* Web: *www.grace.edu*

FINANCIAL AID: The FAFSA code is 001800. The deadline for filing freshman financial aid applications for fall entry is March 1.

HANOVER COLLEGE D-5

www.hanover.edu

Hanover, IN 47243	(812) 866-7021 (800) 213-2178
Fax: (812) 866-7098	Email: admission@hanover.edu
Full-time: 463 men, 621 women	**Faculty:** 87; IIB, av$
Part-time: 4 men, 2 women	**Ph.D.s:** 94%
Graduate: n/av	**Student/Faculty:** 12 to 1
Year: 4-1-4	**Tuition:** $35,514
Room & Board: $10,850	**Freshman Class:** n/av
SAT or ACT: required	**CEEB CODE:** 1290
Application Deadline: March 1	**COMPETITIVE+**

Hanover College, founded in 1827 and the oldest private college in Indiana, is a liberal arts school affiliated with the United Presbyterian Church. There is 1 undergraduate school. In addition to regional accreditation, Hanover has baccalaureate program accreditation with NCATE. The 650-acre campus is in a rural area 45 miles northeast of Louisville, Kentucky, 70 miles southwest of Cincinnati, OH, and 90 miles south of Indianapolis. Including any residence halls, there are 36 buildings.

STUDENT LIFE: 67% of undergraduates are from Indiana. Others are from 28 states, and 26 foreign countries. 81% are from public schools. 80% are White; 5% African American; 5% race unknown; 4% Foreign; 3% Hispanic; 1% Asian American; 1% American Indian/Alaska Native; 1% two or more races. **Female To Male Ratio:** 1.3:1. The average age of freshmen is 18; all undergraduates, 19. 18% do not continue beyond their first year; 69% remain to graduate. **Housing:** 1150 students can be accommodated in college housing, which includes single-sex and coed dorms and on-campus apartments. In addition, there are honors houses, special-interest houses, fraternity houses, sorority houses, and a multicultural center. On-campus housing is guaranteed for all 4 years. 93% of students live on campus. All students may keep cars.

FACULTY/CLASSROOMS: 59% of faculty are male; 41% are female. All teach undergraduates. No introductory courses are taught by graduate students. The average class size in an introductory lecture is 16; in a laboratory is 15; and in a regular course is 16.

PROGRAMS OF STUDY: Hanover confers B.A. and B.S. degrees. Bachelor's degrees are awarded in BIOLOGICAL SCIENCE (biochemistry, biology/biological science, and environmental biology), COMMUNICATIONS AND THE ARTS (art, art history and appreciation, classics, communications, dramatic arts, English, French, music, and Spanish), COMPUTER AND PHYSICAL SCIENCE (chemistry, computer science, environmental geology, geology, mathematics, and physics), EDUCATION (elementary education), ENGINEERING AND ENVIRONMENTAL DESIGN (environmental science), HEALTH PROFESSIONS (health and physical activity and kinesiology), SOCIAL SCIENCE (anthropology, economics, gender studies, history, international studies, medieval studies, philosophy, political science/government, psychology, sociology, and theological studies). Arts & sciences, and interdisciplinary studies are the strongest academically. Psychology, kinesiology, integrative physiology, and biology have the largest enrollments.

ACTIVITIES: 42% of men belong to 4 national fraternities; 32% of women belong to 4 national sororities. There are 60 groups on campus, including art, band, cheerleading, choir, chorus, communications, computers, dance, debate, drama, environmental, ethnic, film, honors, international, jazz band, LGBT, literary magazine, marching band, musical theater, newspaper, orchestra, pep band, photography, political, professional, radio and TV, religious, social, social service, student government, and yearbook. Popular campus events include Hanover Enrichment Series, Wiffleball Tournament, and MLK Marade. **Sports:** There are 9 intercollegiate sports for men and 9 for women, and 10 intramural sports for men and 10 for women. Facilities include a health and recreation center consisting of a 2000-seat performance gym, a multisports forum, a suspended running track, racquetball and squash courts, a weight room, a training room, and a physiology lab. There also is an outdoor athletic complex consisting of a 5000-seat football/track stadium, baseball, softball and soccer facilities, tennis courts, and a lacrosse field. **Graduates:** From July 1, 2015 to June 30, 2016, 276 bachelor's degrees were awarded. The most popular majors were psychology (9%), economics (7%), and communication (7%). 35 companies recruited on campus in 2015-2016. In an average class, 67% graduate in 4 years or less, 70% graduate in 5 years or less, and 71% graduate in 6 years or less.

SERVICES: Counseling and information services are available, as is tutoring in most subjects. There is remedial writing. **Library/Resources:** The library contains 299,841 volumes, 53,006 microform items, and 7,501 audio/video tapes/CDs/DVDs, and subscribes to 45,968 periodicals including electronic. Computerized library services include interlibrary loans, database searching, Internet access, and Wi-Fi capability. Special learning facilities include an art gallery, planetarium, radio station, TV station, and a geology museum. **Physically Challenged Students:** 75% of the campus is accessible. Facilities include wheelchair ramps, elevators, special parking, specially equipped restrooms, special class scheduling, lowered drinking fountains, lowered telephones, and special housing. **Special:** B.S. and B.A. degrees; Internships; study abroad in Australia, Belgium, France, Turkey, City Semester programs in Philadelphia, Washington, D.C., and Chicago; and self-designed majors including 2 or more disciplines are offered. The Business Scholars Program provides preparation for a career in business, built on a liberal arts foundation, where everyone in the program completes a paid internship. There are 8 national honor societies and 8 departmental honors programs. **Visiting:** There are regularly scheduled orientations for prospective students. There are guides for informal visits, visitors may sit in on classes, and stay overnight. To schedule a visit, contact Lyn Lyon at (800) 213-2178. **Campus Safety and Security:** Measures include 24-hour foot and vehicle patrol, emergency notification system, self-defense education, and security escort services. There are shuttle buses, emergency telephones, lighted pathways/sidewalks, and controlled access to dorms/residences.

REQUIREMENTS: The SAT or ACT is required. Admission is competitive, based on the applicant pool. The college requires 18 academic credits, including 4 years of English and 2 each of a foreign language, math, science, and either history or social studies. The GED is accepted. The college also requires a foreign language achievement test for those who wish to meet their world language requirement in the language they studied in high school, as well as an essay; an interview is recommended.

AP credits are accepted. Important factors in the admissions decision are recommendations by school officials, advanced placement or honors courses, and extracurricular activities record. To graduate, students must complete 36 units of credit, including 8 to 12 in the major, LADRs or CCRs/ACEs (12 to 13 units of general degree requirements), maintain a GPA of 2.0 overall and in the major, pass a comprehensive exam, and participate in a culminating experience in the major. **Procedure:** Freshmen are admitted fall and winter. Entrance exams should be taken late in the spring of the junior year. There are deferred admissions and rolling admissions plans. Early decision applications should be filed by December 1; regular applications, by March 1 for fall entry. Applications are accepted on-line. Application fees are waived if application is completed on-line. **Transfer Students:** 19 transfer students enrolled in 2015-2016. Transfer students must submit transcripts from all colleges attended and must have performed successfully. SAT or ACT scores and high school record may also be taken into consideration. 17 of 36 credits required for the bachelor's degree must be completed at Hanover. **International Students:** There are 45 international students enrolled. The school actively recruits these students. They must take the TOEFL with a minimum score of 550 on the paper-based TOEFL (PBT) or 80 on the Internet-based version (iBT). They must also take the SAT or ACT.

ADMISSIONS: 45% of the current freshmen were in the top fifth of their class; 81% were in the top two fifths. 8 freshmen graduated first in their class. **Admissions Contact:** Victoria Hidalgo, Director of Admission. Email: *admission@hanover.edu* Web: *www.hanover.edu*

FINANCIAL AID: In 2016-2017, 99% of all full-time freshmen and 97% of continuing full-time students received some form of financial aid. 63% of all full-time freshmen and 89% of continuing full-time students received need-based aid. The average freshman award was $25,651. Hanover is a member of CSS. The FAFSA code is 001801. The deadline for filing freshman financial aid applications for fall entry is March 1.

HUNTINGTON UNIVERSITY D-2

www.huntington.edu

Huntington, IN 46750	**(260) 358-4016** **(800) 642-6493**
Fax: (260) 358-3699	**Email: admissions@huntington.edu**
Full-time: 389 men, 487 women	**Faculty:** 63; IIB, --$
Part-time: 60 men, 65 women	**Ph.D.s:** 87%
Graduate: 90 men, 209 women	**Student/Faculty:** 13 to 1
Year: 4-1-4, summer session	**Tuition:** $25,540
Room & Board: $8456	**Freshman Class:** 799 applied, 713 accepted, 196 enrolled
SAT or ACT: required	**CEEB CODE:** 1304
Application Deadline: open	**COMPETITIVE**

Huntington University, is a comprehensive Christian college of the liberal arts offering graduate and undergraduate programs in more than 70 academic concentrations. Founded in 1897, by the Church of the United Brethren in Christ, the university is a member of the Council for Christian Colleges and Universities (CCCU). Figures in the above capsule and in this profile are approximate. There are 2 undergraduate schools and 1 graduate school. In addition to regional accreditation, Huntington has baccalaureate program accreditation with CSWE, NASM, NCATE, NCA-HLC, CCNE, and NCATE. The 170-acre campus is in a small town 20 miles southwest of Fort Wayne. Including any residence halls, there are 25 buildings.

STUDENT LIFE: 66% of undergraduates are from Indiana. Others are from 37 states, 24 foreign countries, and Canada. 84% are White; 5% Hispanic; 5% Foreign; 4% two or more races; 2% African American. 76% are Protestant; 20% Non-denominational. **Female To Male Ratio:** 1.4:1. The average age of freshmen is 18; all undergraduates, 20. 24% do not continue beyond their first year; 68% remain to graduate. **Housing:** 831 students can be accommodated in college housing, which includes single-sex dorms, on-campus apartments, off-campus apartments, and married student housing. In addition, there are special-interest houses, and an international student house. On-campus housing is guaranteed for all 4 years. 75% of students live on campus; of those, 50% remain on campus on weekends. Alcohol is not permitted. All students may keep cars.

FACULTY/CLASSROOMS: 52% of faculty are male; 48% are female. 88% teach undergraduates. No introductory courses are taught by graduate students. The average class size in an introductory lecture is 25; in a laboratory is 15; and in a regular course is 20.

PROGRAMS OF STUDY: Huntington confers B.A., B.S., B.Mus., B.S.Sc., and B.S.N. degrees. Associate, master's, and doctoral degrees are also awarded. Bachelor's degrees are awarded in AGRICULTURE (agricultural business management, agricultural sciences, and agriculture), BIOLOGICAL SCIENCE (biology/biological science and biological sciences), BUSINESS (accounting, accounting (finance), accounting (information systems), business administration and management, business administration, management, operations, business administration marketing, entrepreneurial studies, marketing management, nonprofit/public organization management, organizational behavior, small business management, and sports management), COMMUNICATIONS AND THE ARTS (acting, animation, art, broadcasting, communications, creative writing, digital communications, digital media, dramatic arts, English, English as a second/foreign language, English literature, film arts, fine arts, graphic design, journalism, media arts, music business management, music performance, music theory and composition, performing arts, public relations, studio art, theatre arts, and theater design), COMPUTER AND PHYSICAL SCIENCE (actuarial science, actuarial mathematics, chemistry, chemistry / chemical biology, computer science, information sciences and systems, mathematics, and physics), EDUCATION (agricultural education, art education, education, elementary education, English education, mathematics education, music education, physical education, science education, secondary education, social studies education, sports studies, and teaching English as a second/foreign language (TESOL/TEFOL)), ENGINEERING AND ENVIRONMENTAL DESIGN (computational sciences), HEALTH PROFESSIONS (biology, exercise science, nursing, premedicine, prepharmacy, prephysical therapy, and recreation therapy), SOCIAL SCIENCE (area studies, biblical studies, counseling/psychology, criminal justice, economics, history, ministries, parks and recreation management, philosophy, prelaw, psychology, religion, religious music, social work, sociology, and youth ministry). Film, animation, and nursing are the strongest academically. Business, animation, and psychology have the largest enrollments.

ACTIVITIES: There are no fraternities or sororities. There are 35 groups on campus, including art, band, cheerleading, choir, chorale, chorus, communications, computers, dance, drama, environmental, ethnic, film, Friesen Center for Volunteer Service, honors, international, jazz band, literary magazine, musical theater, newspaper, orchestra, pep band, political, professional, radio and TV, religious, social, social service, student government, and symphony. Popular campus events include Olympiad, Forester Night, Chapel Series and Hoe Down. **Sports:** There are 8 intercollegiate sports for men and 8 for women, and 9 intramural sports for men and 9 for women. Facilities include a fieldhouse with an indoor running track, 3 basketball courts, 1 outdoor basketball court, indoor and outdoor tennis courts, softball and baseball diamonds, an outdoor track, soccer and intramural fields, weight room and aerobic facility, and a gym. **Graduates:** From July 1, 2015 to June 30, 2016, 210 bachelor's degrees were awarded. The most popular majors were business (9%), nursing (9%), and elementary and special education (5%). In an average class, 55% graduate in 4 years or less and 68% graduate in 6 years or less.

SERVICES: Counseling and information services are available, as is tutoring in most subjects. There is a reader service for the blind, and remedial math and writing. **Library/Resources:** The library contains 236,659 volumes, 11,803 microform items, and 7,718 audio/video tapes/CDs/DVDs, and subscribes to 52,798 periodicals including electronic. Computerized library services include interlibrary loans, database searching, Internet access, and Wi-Fi capability. Special learning facilities include an art gallery, radio station, TV station, a writing center and an Enterprise Resource Center, which helps students with internships, resumes, job training and practicum, herbarium, nature preserve (Thornhill Nature Preserve), arboretum, greenhouse, studio theatre, exercise science training facilities (including a BODPOD), and historical archives (United Brethren Historical Center). **Physically Challenged Students:** 64% of the campus is accessible. Facilities include wheelchair ramps, elevators, special parking, specially equipped restrooms, lowered drinking fountains, and special housing. **Special:** Companies in the area offer a number of internships to students in concentrations such as business, sociology, social work, ministry and missions, education, graphic design, digital media arts, music business, and sport and recreation management. Students may study abroad in a number of countries. A

Washington semester, a Hollywood semester, dual majors, correspondence courses with other schools, and accelerated degree program, in organizational management, business administration, accounting, nursing, marketing, human resource management, and organizational management are available. There are 11 national honor societies, a freshman honors program, and 6 departmental honors programs. **Visiting:** There are regularly scheduled orientations for prospective students, available on 3 days notice. There are guides for informal visits, visitors may sit in on classes, and stay overnight. To schedule a visit, contact Carlene Peters at (260) 359-4020. **Campus Safety and Security:** Measures include emergency notification system and security escort services. There are emergency telephones, lighted pathways/sidewalks, controlled access to dorms/residences, and security on duty from 6 p.m. to 6 a.m.

REQUIREMENTS: The SAT or ACT is required. Applicants must have 4 years of English, 2 years of college-preparatory math, and 3years of social studies. AP and CLEP credits are accepted. Important factors in the admissions decision are recommendations by school officials, recommendations by alumni, and personality/intangible qualities. Students must complete a minimum of 128 credit hours including 36 in the major, and maintain a GPA of 2.0 overall and a major GPA of at least 2.0 (higher for some programs). Students must complete a program in general education and take 36 hours in upper-division courses numbered 300 or above, 3 hours of math or computer science, and religion courses. **Procedure:** Freshmen are admitted to all sessions. Entrance exams should be taken before or during the fall semester of the senior year. There are deferred admissions and rolling admissions plans. Application deadlines are open. Application fee is $20. Applications are accepted on-line. Application fees are waived if application is completed on-line. **Transfer Students:** 46 transfer students enrolled in 2015-2016. Transfer applicants should be in good standing at the college previously attended and have maintained a GPA of 2.0. Courses with a grade of C or better transfer. All transcripts and an essay are required. 30 of 128 credits required for the bachelor's degree must be completed at Huntington. **International Students:** There are 49 international students enrolled. The school actively recruits these students. They must take the TOEFL with a minimum score of 525 on the paper-based TOEFL (PBT) or 65 on the Internet-based version (iBT). They must also take the SAT or ACT, scoring 800.

ADMISSIONS: 89% of the 2016-2017 applicants were accepted. The SAT scores for the 2016-2017 freshman class were: Critical Reading-- 48% below 500, 34% between 500 and 599, 15% between 600 and 699, and 3% between 700 and 800. Math-- 45% below 500, 36% between 500 and 599, 17% between 600 and 699, and 2% between 700 and 800. Writing-- 57% below 500, 29% between 500 and 599, 13% between 600 and 699, and 1% between 700 and 800. The ACT scores were 16% between 12 and 17, 45% between 18 and 23, 35% between 24 and 29, and 4% above 30. 2 freshmen graduated first in their class. **Admissions Contact:** Daniel Solms, VP for Enrollment Management. Email: *admissions@huntington.edu* Web: *www.huntington.edu*

FINANCIAL AID: In 2016-2017, 100% of all full-time freshmen and 90% of continuing full-time students received some form of financial aid. 51% of all full-time freshmen and 45% of continuing full-time students received need-based aid. The average freshman award was $22,983. Need-based scholarships or need-based grants averaged $13,992; need-based self-help aid (loans and jobs) averaged $7,009; and non-need-based athletic scholarships averaged $4,764. 10% of undergraduate students work part-time. Average annual earnings from campus work are $1953. The average financial indebtedness of the 2016 graduate was $34,625. The college's own financial statement is required. The FAFSA code is 001803. The priority date for freshman financial aid applications for fall entry is March 10.

INDIANA INSTITUTE OF TECHNOLOGY *(The complete profile is made available exclusively on our website, www.barronspac.com)*

INDIANA STATE UNIVERSITY *(The complete profile is made available exclusively on our website, www.barronspac.com)*

INDIANA UNIVERSITY BLOOMINGTON C-4

www.iub.edu

Bloomington, IN 47405 **(812) 855-0661**

Fax: (812) 855-5102
Full-time: 16,131 men, 15,874 women
Part-time: 3069 men, 4110 women
Graduate: 5720 men, 4791 women
Year: semesters, summer session
Room & Board: $10,041

SAT CR/M/W: 573/598/565 **ACT:** 27
Application Deadline: February 1

Email: iuadmit@indiana.edu
Faculty: I, av$
Ph.D.s: 82%
Student/Faculty: 17 to 1
Tuition: $10,388 ($34,246)
Freshman Class: 34646 applied, 27272 accepted, 7673 enrolled
CEEB CODE: 1324
VERY COMPETITIVE

Bloomington is the flagship residential, doctoral-extensive campus of Indiana University. Its mission is to create, disseminate, preserve, and apply knowledge. It does so through its commitments to cutting-edge research, scholarship, arts, and creative activity; to challenging and inspired undergraduate, graduate, professional, and lifelong education; to culturally diverse and international educational programs and communities; to first-rate library and museum collections; to economic development in the state and region and to meaningful experiences outside the classroom. The Bloomington campus is committed to full diversity, academic freedom, and meeting the changing educational and research needs of the state, the nation, and the world. There are 17 undergraduate schools. In addition to regional accreditation, IU has baccalaureate program accreditation with AACSB, ACEJMC, CSWE, NASAD, NASM, NCATE, COAPRT, CCNE, and CAA. The 1936-acre campus is in a small town 50 miles southwest of Indianapolis. Including any residence halls, there are 562 buildings.

STUDENT LIFE: 65% of undergraduates are from Indiana. Others are from 50 states, 153 foreign countries, and Canada. 67% are White; 5% Asian American; 5% Hispanic; 4% African American; 3% two or more races; 2% race unknown; 13% Foreign. **Male To Female Ratio:** 1.0:1. The average age of freshmen is 18; all undergraduates, 20. 9% do not continue beyond their first year. **Housing:** 12559 students can be accommodated in college housing, which includes single-sex and coed dorms, on-campus apartments, off-campus apartments, and married student housing. In addition, there are honors houses, language houses, special-interest houses, living-learning centers, an international center, a center for women, a wellness center, freshman interest groups (FIGs), and thematic communities. On-campus housing is guaranteed for the freshman year only, is available on a first-come, and first-served basis. 65% of students commute. Alcohol is not permitted. All students may keep cars.

FACULTY/CLASSROOMS: 60% of faculty are male; 40% are female. No introductory courses are taught by graduate students.

PROGRAMS OF STUDY: IU-Bloomington confers B.A., B.A.J., B.F.A., B.G.S., B.M., B.M.E., B.M.Ed., B.S., B.S.Ed., B.S.M., B.S.N., B.S.P.A., B.S.P.H., and B.S.W. degrees. Associate, master's, and doctoral degrees are also awarded. Bachelor's degrees are awarded in AGRICULTURE (animal science and environmental studies), BIOLOGICAL SCIENCE (biochemistry, biology/adolescence education, biotechnology, human biology, health, and society, microbiology, and neurosciences), BUSINESS (accounting, apparel and accessories marketing, business administration and management, entrepreneurial studies, finance, human resources/organizational management, labor studies, management, marketing, real estate, recreation and leisure services, sports marketing, and tourism), COMMUNICATIONS AND THE ARTS (art history, arts administration/management, ballet, communication studies, comparative literature, dance, East Asian languages and literature, English, fine arts, folklore and mythology, French, game design and development, German studies, Greek (classical), guitar, Italian, jazz, journalism, linguistics, media arts, music, music production/recording technology, music performance, musical theater, organ performance, percussion, piano/organ, Portuguese, Russian, sculpture, Slavic languages, Spanish, sports communication, studio art, telecommunications, theatre arts, visual and performing arts, and voice), COMPUTER AND PHYSICAL SCIENCE (astronomy, astrophysics, chemistry, chemistry/adolescence education, computer science, earth science/adolescence education, geology, informatics and computer science, mathematics, physics secondary education, physics, and statistics), EDUCATION (Asian studies, athletic training, early childhood education, elementary education, English education, general studies, health education, journalism education, mathematics education, music education, physical education/exercise science, secondary education, social studies education, special education, and world language education), ENGINEERING AND ENVIRONMENTAL DESIGN (computational sciences, environmental science, interior design, and systems engineering), HEALTH PROFESSIONS (allied health, biology, community health work, environmental health science, exercise science, health administration and policy, health care administration, health science, human biology, kinesiology, nursing, optometry, public health, recreation therapy, and speech pathology/audiology), SOCIAL SCIENCE (African American studies, American studies, anthropology, Asian/American studies, classical/ancient civilization, classical and near eastern civilization, cognitive science, criminal justice, cultural studies/critical theory & analysis, dietetics, East Asian studies, Eastern European studies, economics, fashion design and technology, gender studies, geography, history, human development & family studies, international studies, Judaic studies, legal studies, liberal arts/general studies, Near Eastern studies, philosophy, political science/government, psychology, public affairs, religious studies, Russian and Slavic studies, safety science, social work, sociology, and South Asian studies). Business, music, law, public health, and education are the strongest academically. Business, informatics, and biology have the largest enrollments.

ACTIVITIES: 25% of men belong to 38 national fraternities; 21% of women belong to 32 national sororities. There are 766 groups on campus, including art, band, cheerleading, chess, choir, chorale, chorus, communications, computers, dance, debate, drama, drill team, drum and bugle corps, environmental, ethnic, film, honors, international, jazz band, LGBT, literary magazine, marching band, musical theater, newspaper, opera, orchestra, pep band, photography, political, professional, radio and TV, religious, social, social service, student government, and symphony. Popular campus events include Little 500, Founder's Day, Homecoming Parade, IU Dance Marathon, and Welcome Week. **Sports:** There are 10 intercollegiate sports for men and 12 for women, and 20 intramural sports for men and 20 for women. The 204,000 square foot Student Recreational Sports Center features three multi-sport gyms, a spacious strength & conditioning area with more than 400 pieces of cardiovascular and weight-training equipment, the Counsilman/Billingsley Aquatic Center, and an elevated running track. The historic, Wildermuth Intramural Center features 10 basketball/volleyball courts, a track, squash courts, strength & conditioning areas, and pool. Woodlawn Field is for soccer, flag football, and numerous tennis courts. IUB also has the Harry Gladstein Fieldhouse for track & field, the Andy Mohr softball field, the Bart Kaufman baseball complex with indoor and outdoor hitting cages, Bill Armstrong Stadium for soccer, the Memorial Stadium for football, Assembly Hall for basketball, the IU Field Hockey Complex, the IU Championship Golf Course, a cross-country course and the Dale England rowing center. **Graduates:** From July 1, 2015 to June 30, 2016, 7316 bachelor's degrees were awarded. The most popular majors were business/marketing (19%), communication/journalism (9%), and biological/life sciences (9%). In an average class, 60% graduate in 4 years or less, 73% graduate in 5 years or less, and 77% graduate in 6 years or less.

SERVICES: Counseling and information services are available, as is tutoring in most subjects. There is a reader service for the blind, and remedial math, reading, and writing. Skills workshops are also offered. **Library/Resources:** The 24 libraries contain 10.4 million volumes. Computerized library services include interlibrary loans, database searching, Internet access, and Wi-Fi capability. Special learning facilities include an art gallery, natural history museum, radio station, TV station, an observatory, arboretum, museum of world cultures, garden and nature center, musical arts center, and more than 70 research centers. **Physically Challenged Students:** 95% of the campus is accessible. Facilities include wheelchair ramps, elevators, special parking, specially equipped restrooms, special class scheduling, lowered drinking fountains, and lowered telephones. Scheduled transportation is available. **Special:** IU offers cooperative programs with universities in many countries, a variety of internships, and study abroad. A Washington semester, work-study programs, B.A.-B.S. degrees in the sciences and liberal arts, dual majors, online degrees, and general studies degree are available. Student-designed majors through the Individualized Major Program, credit for military experience, nondegree study and pass/fail options are also available. There are 18 national honor societies, Phi Beta Kappa, and a freshman honors program. **Visiting:** There are regularly scheduled orientations for prospective students, including admissions counseling and answers to students' questions about the school. There are guides for informal visits, visitors may sit in on classes, and stay overnight. To schedule a visit, contact the Office of Admissions. **Campus Safety and Security:** Measures include 24-hour foot and vehicle patrol, emergency notification system, self-defense education, and security escort services. There are shuttle buses, emergency telephones, lighted pathways/sidewalks, controlled access to dorms/residences, and safety awareness education.

REQUIREMENTS: The SAT or ACT is required. Applicants must be graduates of an accredited secondary high school or have a GED certificate. Indiana residents must be on track to complete Core 40 curriculum, Core 40 academic curriculum, or the equivalent as a condition of offered admission. SAT: Subject tests are recommended for credit and placement. Auditions for music majors are required. An interview is recommended for information purposes. AP and CLEP credits are accepted. Important factors in the admissions decision are advanced placement or honors courses, parents or siblings attended your school, and recommendations by school officials. The general requirements for graduation include courses in English and writing, math, foreign language, arts and humanities, social and behavioral sciences, natural sciences, and culture studies. Students must complete 120 credit hours, with approximately 36 hours in the major. Many degrees have intensive writing requirements, and the minimum GPA requirement varies by department. Liberal arts requirements are common throughout all degree programs. **Procedure:** Freshmen are admitted to all sessions. Entrance exams should be taken late in the junior year or early in the senior year. There are deferred admissions and rolling admissions plans. Applications should be filed by February 1 for fall entry; November 1 for spring entry, along with a $60 fee. Applications are accepted on-line. **Transfer Students:** 898 transfer students enrolled in 2015-2016. Admission for transfers is selective. Decisions based on high school background, college curriculum, grade trends, are choice of major, overall performance. If transferring with fewer than 26 credit hours, must also meet freshman guidelines. 2,3 GPA required for residents; 2.5 GPA for non-residents for consideration. 30 of 120 credits required for the bachelor's degree must be completed at IU. **International Students:** There are 3648 international students enrolled. The school actively recruits these students. They must take the TOEFL with a minimum score of 550 on the paper-based TOEFL (PBT) or 79 on the Internet-based version (iBT). They must also take the SAT or ACT.

ADMISSIONS: 79% of the 2016-2017 applicants were accepted. The SAT scores for the 2016-2017 freshman class were: Critical Reading--16% below 500, 45% between 500 and 599, 30% between 600 and 699, and 8% between 700 and 800. Math-- 11% below 500, 40% between 500 and 599, 35% between 600 and 699, and 15% between 700 and 800. Writing-- 19% below 500, 47% between 500 and 599, 28% between 600 and 699, and 6% between 700 and 800. The ACT scores were 1% between 12 and 17, 17% between 18 and 23, 51% between 24 and 29, and 31% above 30. 72% of the current freshmen were in the top fifth of their class; 96% were in the top two fifths. **Admissions Contact:** Sacha Thieme, Executive Director of Admissions. Email: *iuadmit@indiana.edu* Web: *www.iub.edu*

FINANCIAL AID: In 2016-2017, 77% of all full-time freshmen and 76% of continuing full-time students received some form of financial aid. 44% of all full-time freshmen and 40% of continuing full-time students received need-based aid. The average freshman award was $13,416. Need-based scholarships or need-based grants averaged $12,488 ($47,890 maximum); need-based self-help aid (loans and jobs) averaged $5,622 ($42,122 maximum); non-need-based athletic scholarships averaged $20,098 ($51,219 maximum); and other non-need-based awards and non-need-based scholarships averaged $8,013 ($53,815 maximum). 21% of undergraduate students work part-time. Average annual earnings from campus work are $1941. The average financial indebtedness of the 2016 graduate was $28,039. IU is a member of CSS. The FAFSA code is 001809. The priority date for freshman financial aid applications for fall entry is March 1. The deadline for filing freshman financial aid applications for fall entry is March 10.

INDIANA UNIVERSITY EAST D-3

www.iue.edu

Richmond, IN 47374 (765) 973-8208
(800) 959-4485
Fax: (765) 973-8209 Email: applyiue@indiana.edu

Full-time: 607 men, 1261 women
Part-time: 937 men, 1482 women
Graduate: 46 men, 146 women
Year: semesters, summer session
Room & Board: n/app
SAT CR/M/W: required **ACT:** 20
Application Deadline: open
Faculty: IIB, -$
Ph.D.s: 75%
Student/Faculty: 14 to 1
Tuition: $7072 ($18,683)
Freshman Class: 1226 applied, 739 accepted, 365 enrolled
CEEB CODE: 1194
COMPETITIVE

Indiana University East, a regional campus of Indiana University, offers residents of eastern Indiana, western Ohio, and beyond a broad range of bachelor's degrees and selected master's degrees and certificates through its traditional main campus in Richmond, off-campus sites, and online program options. IU East challenges students to grow intellectually and personally in a supportive and scholarly environment where faculty teaching skills and participation in the creation and dissemination of new knowledge and artistic work enhance learning opportunities for all. IU East values a diversity of backgrounds, experiences, and intellectual perspectives among its faculty, staff, and students and in its contributions to the cultural and economic development of the communities it serves. There are 8 undergraduate schools. In addition to regional accreditation, IU East has baccalaureate program accreditation with ACBSP, CSWE, NCATE, ACEN, and CAEP. The 182-acre campus is in a small town 45 miles west of Dayton, Ohio. Including any residence halls, there are 11 buildings.

STUDENT LIFE: 77% of undergraduates are from Indiana. Others are from 45 states, 46 foreign countries, and Canada. 84% are White; 4% African American; 4% race unknown; 3% Hispanic; 3% two or more races; 1% Asian American; 1% Foreign. **Female To Male Ratio:** 1.8:1. The average age of freshmen is 18; all undergraduates, 27. 33% do not continue beyond their first year. Alcohol is not permitted. All students commute. All students may keep cars.

FACULTY/CLASSROOMS: 39% of faculty are male; 61% are female. No introductory courses are taught by graduate students.

PROGRAMS OF STUDY: IU East confers B.A., B.A.S., B.F.A., B.G.S., B.S., B.S.Ed., B.S.N, and B.S.W. degrees. Associate and master's degrees are also awarded. Bachelor's degrees are awarded in BIOLOGICAL SCIENCE (biochemistry, biotechnology, and life science), BUSINESS (business administration and management), COMMUNICATIONS AND THE ARTS (communication studies, English, fine arts, and Spanish), COMPUTER AND PHYSICAL SCIENCE (applied science, informatics and computer science, mathematics, and natural sciences/mathematics), EDUCATION (elementary education, general studies, and secondary education), HEALTH PROFESSIONS (biology, health science, and nursing), SOCIAL SCIENCE (criminal justice, history, humanities, international studies, political science/government, psychology, social work, and sociology). Business, nursing, and psychology have the largest enrollments.

ACTIVITIES: There are 41 groups on campus, including art, cheerleading, communications, computers, dance, drama, environmental, ethnic, honors, international, LGBT, newspaper, pep band, political, professional, radio and TV, religious, social, social service, and student government. Popular campus events include Homecoming and Spirit of Philanthropy. **Sports:** There are 6 intercollegiate sports for men and 7 for women. Facilities include Graf Recreation/Fitness Center, a softball field, tennis, sand volleyball courts, and a field house. **Graduates:** From July 1, 2015 to June 30, 2016, 741 bachelor's degrees were awarded. The most popular majors were business, management, marketing (26%), health professions and related programs (19%), and psychology (11%). In an average class, 14% graduate in 4 years or less, 28% graduate in 5 years or less, and 32% graduate in 6 years or less.

SERVICES: Counseling and information services are available, as is tutoring in some subjects, as in several freshman-level courses. There is a reader service for the blind, and remedial math, reading, and writing. **Library/Resources:** The library contains 82,500 volumes. Computerized library services include interlibrary loans, database searching, Internet access, and Wi-Fi capability. Special learning facilities include an art gallery and radio station. **Physically Challenged Students:** 98% of the campus is accessible. Facilities include wheelchair ramps, elevators, special parking, lowered drinking fountains, and lowered telephones. Special testing accommodations and note taking offered. **Special:** IU East offers a cooperative program in criminal justice with Indiana University-Purdue University and an organizational leadership program through Purdue's Statewide Technology program. IU East also offers online degrees, cross-registration with Earlham College, dual majors, independent study, an internship in social work, pass/fail options, study abroad through Indiana University Bloomington, and credit for life experience. Nondegree study is possible. There are 7 national honor societies and a freshman honors program. **Visiting:** There are regularly scheduled orientations for prospective students, Visits include tours, counseling, registration, and financial aid sessions. There are guides for informal visits and visitors may sit in on classes. To schedule a visit, contact the Admissions Office. **Campus Safety and Security:** Measures include emergency notification system and security escort services. There are emergency telephones, lighted pathways/sidewalks, and 14-hour foot and vehicle patrol.

REQUIREMENTS: The SAT is required. The ACT is recommended. Recent high school graduates from Indiana are expected to complete the Core 40 curriculum. Out-of-state students are expected to complete a minimum of 28 semester hours of college prep courses. The four units of academic electives include additional math, lab science, social science, computer science, foreign language, or other college-prep courses. Recent high school graduates should rank in the upper half of their graduating class. AP and CLEP credits are accepted. To graduate, students must satisfactorily complete the General Education Curriculum (30 credit hours) (applies to all IU East students admitted effective Summer), 2 Written Communication Competency 6 cr/hrs, Speaking and Listening Competency 3 cr/hrs, Quantitative Reasoning Competency 3 cr/hrs., Natural Sciences Competency 5-6 cr/hrs, must include at least one course with laboratory, Humanistic Artistic Competency 6 cr/hrs, must include at least two different disciplines, Social-Behavioral Competency 6 cr/hrs, must include at least 2 different disciplines. Students must complete a minimum of 120 semester hours (30 hours taken at IU East) with a GPA of at least 2.0. **Procedure:** Freshmen are admitted to all sessions. Entrance exams should be taken during the junior or senior year. There are early admissions, deferred admissions, and rolling admissions plans. Application deadlines are open. Application fee is $35. Applications are accepted on-line. **Transfer Students:** 401 transfer students enrolled in 2015-2016. High school graduation, or equivalent. Completion of 12 or more semester hours at an accredited university or college (including junior and community colleges), with a GPA of 2.0 (2.5 for out-of-state transfer applicants) and submit college transcripts. Grades of C or better transfer for credit. 30 of 120 credits required for the bachelor's degree must be completed at IU East. **International Students:** There are 39 international students enrolled. They must take the TOEFL with a minimum score of 550 on the paper-based TOEFL (PBT) or 79 on the Internet-based version (iBT).

ADMISSIONS: 60% of the 2016-2017 applicants were accepted. The SAT scores for the 2016-2017 freshman class were: Critical Reading-- 67% below 500, 28% between 500 and 599, 5% between 600 and 699, and 1% between 700 and 800. Math-- 67% below 500, 26% between 500 and 599, and 7% between 600 and 699. Writing-- 73% below 500, 24% between 500 and 599, and 3% between 600 and 699. The ACT scores were 24% between 12 and 17, 53% between 18 and 23, 21% between 24 and 29, and 1% above 30. 27% of the current freshmen were in the top fifth of their class; 67% were in the top two fifths. **Admissions Contact:** Molly Vanderpool, Director of Admissions. Email: *applyiue@indiana.edu* Web: *www.iue.edu*

FINANCIAL AID: In 2016-2017, 94% of all full-time freshmen and 89% of continuing full-time students received some form of financial aid. 80% of all full-time freshmen and 77% of continuing full-time students received need-based aid. The average freshman award was $8,771. Need-based scholarships or need-based grants averaged $7,500 ($29,706 maximum); need-based self-help aid (loans and jobs) averaged $3,526 ($11,500 maximum); non-need-based athletic scholarships averaged $1,141 ($4,709 maximum); and other non-need-based awards and non-need-based scholarships averaged $3,963 ($14,139 maximum). 5% of undergraduate students work part-time. Average annual earnings from campus work are $2763. The average financial indebtedness of the 2016 graduate was $27,379. The college's own financial statement is required. The FAFSA code is 001811. The priority date for freshman financial aid applications for fall entry is March 1. The deadline for filing freshman financial aid applications for fall entry is March 10.

INDIANA UNIVERSITY KOKOMO C-2

www.iuk.edu

Kokomo, IN 46902	(765) 455-9217 (888) 875-4485
Fax: (765) 455-9537	**Email:** iuadmis@iuk.edu
Full-time: 703 men, 1386 women	**Faculty:** IIB, -$
Part-time: 669 men, 1219 women	**Ph.D.s:** 63%
Graduate: 50 men, 79 women	**Student/Faculty:** 15 to 1
Year: semesters, summer session	**Tuition:** $7073 ($18,683)
Room & Board: n/app	**Freshman Class:** 1513 applied, 1046 accepted, 507 enrolled
SAT CR/M/W: required **ACT:** 21	**CEEB CODE:** 1337
Application Deadline: August 24	**COMPETITIVE**

The mission of Indiana University Kokomo, a regional campus of Indiana University, is to enhance the educational and professional attainment of the residents of north central Indiana by providing a wide range of bachelor's degrees and a limited number of master's and associate degrees. IU Kokomo is further dedicated to enhancing research, creative work, and other scholarly activity and to strengthening the economic and cultural vitality of the region through a variety of partnerships and programs. There are 7 undergraduate schools. In addition to regional accreditation, IUK has baccalaureate program accreditation with AACSB, NCATE, CCNE, JRCERT, and ACEN. The 52-acre campus is in a small town 53 miles north of Indianapolis. Including any residence halls, there are 13 buildings.

STUDENT LIFE: 99% of undergraduates are from Indiana. Others are from 13 states and 28 foreign countries. 82% are White; 5% Hispanic; 5% race unknown; 4% African American; 2% two or more races; 1% Asian American; 1% Foreign. **Female To Male Ratio:** 1.9:1. The average age of freshmen is 19; all undergraduates, 24. 37% do not continue beyond their first year. **Housing:** Alcohol is not permitted. All students commute. All students may keep cars.

FACULTY/CLASSROOMS: 38% of faculty are male; 62% are female. No introductory courses are taught by graduate students.

PROGRAMS OF STUDY: IU Kokomo confers B.A., B.A.S., B.S., B.F.A., B.G.S., B.S.B., B.S.Ed. and B.S.N. degrees. Associate and master's degrees are also awarded. Bachelor's degrees are awarded in BIOLOGICAL SCIENCE (biochemistry and biology/biological science), BUSINESS (business administration and management, labor studies, and tourism), COMMUNICATIONS AND THE ARTS (communications, English, fine arts, media arts, and communication arts - speech), COMPUTER AND PHYSICAL SCIENCE (applied science, chemistry, chemistry/ chemical biology, clinical laboratory science, combined science, information sciences and systems, informatics and computer science, mathematics, and physical sciences), EDUCATION (elementary education, general studies, health information management, and secondary education), HEALTH PROFESSIONS (biology, cytotechnology, dental hygiene, health science, medical imaging, medical technology, nursing, radiation therapy, and respiratory therapy), SOCIAL SCIENCE (criminal justice, history and political science, humanities, psychology, public administration, and sociology). Nursing, business, and health sciences have the largest enrollments.

ACTIVITIES: 3% of men belong to 1 national fraternity; 1% of women belong to 1 national sorority. There are 40 groups on campus, including cheerleading, choir, chorale, communications, computers, dance, drama, environmental, ethnic, honors, international, LGBT, literary magazine, newspaper, political, professional, radio and TV, religious, social, social service, and student government. Popular campus events include Campus Fall Kick-off BBQ, Campus Beautification Day, Dance-a-Thon and Take Back the Night. **Sports:** There are 3 intercollegiate sports for men and 4 for women. **Graduates:** From July 1, 2015 to June 30, 2016, 518 bachelor's degrees were awarded. The most popular majors were health professions (39%), liberal arts and sciences, general studies and humanities (12%), business, management, marketing, and related support services (10%). In an average class, 17% graduate in 4 years or less, 35% graduate in 5 years or less, and 39% graduate in 6 years or less.

SERVICES: Counseling and information services are available, as is tutoring in most subjects. There is remedial math, reading, and writing. Students who do not meet regular admissions standards can be admitted under the Guided Study Program, which includes courses in basic skills as needed, counseling and tutoring, and a seminar on studying. **Library/ Resources:** The library contains 116,036 volumes. Computerized library services include interlibrary loans, database searching, and Internet access. Special learning facilities include an art gallery, radio station, an observatory, and art gallery downtown. **Physically Challenged Students:** All of the campus is accessible. Facilities include wheelchair ramps, elevators, special parking, specially equipped restrooms, special class scheduling, lowered drinking fountains, and lowered telephones. **Special:** Student-designed majors, a general studies degree, internships, study abroad, joint programs with other Indiana University campuses and with Purdue University, pass/fail options, nondegree study, credit for military experience and by exam, and online degrees are available. There are 2 national honor societies and a freshman honors program. **Visiting:** There are regularly scheduled orientations for prospective students. There are guides for informal visits and visitors may sit in on classes. To schedule a visit, contact the Admissions Office. **Campus Safety and Security:** Measures include emergency notification system and security escort services. There are emergency telephones, lighted pathways/sidewalks, and campus police on duty from 7 a.m. to 10 p.m.

REQUIREMENTS: The SAT or ACT is required. If you have not earned an Academic Honors or Core 40 high school diploma, your high school preparation should include a minimum of at least the 40 college preparatory courses. The academic electives include foreign language, additional mathematics, laboratory science, social science, computer science, or other college preparatory courses. AP and CLEP credits are accepted. Important factors in the admissions decision are recommendations by school officials and advanced placement or honors courses. All students must maintain a minimum GPA of 2.0 while taking 120 credit hours. The following general education curriculum is required of each student who is granted a baccalaureate degree at the Kokomo campus. Total credit hours will typically number 42 or 44. If a student takes more than the required number of courses within a section, the course(s) with the highest grade(s) will be used in the GPA calculation. Additional departments and/or schools may have specific general education requirements rather than the general ones listed here. Students should consult with their advisor for more information. General education curriculum: Communication Skills Requirement – three required courses (total of 9 hours); Information Literacy; Quantitative Literacy (total of 4 – 8 hours); Critical Thinking (total of 3 hours); Cultural Diversity (total of 3 hours); Ethics and Civic Engagement (total of 3 hours); Social and Behavioral Sciences - two 3 credit hour courses, each from a different area (total of 6 hours); Humanities and Arts - two 3 credit hour courses, each from a different area (total of 6 hours); Physical and Life Sciences - one 5 credit hour course with a lab and one 3 credit hour course from a different area (total of 8 hours). All students must complete course work in English, computer, and math. **Procedure:** Freshmen are admitted to all sessions. Entrance exams should be taken prior to registration. There are deferred admissions and rolling admissions plans. Applications should be filed by August 24 for fall entry; January 12 for spring entry; and May 18 for summer entry, along with a $35 fee. Applications are accepted on-line. **Transfer Students:** 277 transfer students enrolled in 2015-2016. Transfer applicants must have at least 13 credits with a minimum GPA of 2.0 and clear records of conduct from previously attended colleges. Transcripts are required. Transfers are considered on a case-by-case basis. 30 of 120 credits required for the bachelor's degree must be completed at IUK. **International Students:** There are 18 international students enrolled. They must take the TOEFL with a minimum score of 530 on the paper-based TOEFL (PBT) or 61 on the Internet-based version (iBT).

ADMISSIONS: 69% of the 2016-2017 applicants were accepted. The SAT scores for the 2016-2017 freshman class were: Critical Reading-- 64% below 500, 31% between 500 and 599, and 5% between 600 and 699. Math-- 67% below 500, 28% between 500 and 599, and 5% between 600 and 699. Writing-- 77% below 500, 19% between 500 and 599, and 4% between 600 and 699. The ACT scores were 1% below 12, 19% between 12 and 17, 64% between 18 and 23, 16% between 24 and 29, and 1% above 30. 25% of the current freshmen were in the top fifth of their class; 63% were in the top two fifths. **Admissions Contact:** Angie Siders, Director of Admissions. Email: *iuadmis@iuk.edu* Web: *www.iuk.edu*

FINANCIAL AID: In 2016-2017, 91% of all full-time freshmen and

86% of continuing full-time students received some form of financial aid. 74% of all full-time freshmen and 70% of continuing full-time students received need-based aid. The average freshman award was $8,317. Need-based scholarships or need-based grants averaged $7,526 ($19,782 maximum); need-based self-help aid (loans and jobs) averaged $3,520 ($9,500 maximum); non-need-based athletic scholarships averaged $367 ($400 maximum); and other non-need-based awards and non-need-based scholarships averaged $4,211 ($16,143 maximum). 9% of undergraduate students work part-time. Average annual earnings from campus work are $1685. The average financial indebtedness of the 2016 graduate was $25,675. The FAFSA code is 001814. The priority date for freshman financial aid applications for fall entry is March 1. The deadline for filing freshman financial aid applications for fall entry is March 10.

INDIANA UNIVERSITY NORTHWEST B-1

www.iun.edu

Gary, IN 46408	(219) 980-6991 (888) 968-7486
Fax: (219) 981-4219	Email: admit@iun.edu
Full-time: 898 men, 1878 women	**Faculty:** IIA, --$
Part-time: 894 men, 1574 women	**Ph.D.s:** 74%
Graduate: 113 men, 234 women	**Student/Faculty:** 14 to 1
Year: semesters, summer session	**Tuition:** $7072 ($18,683)
Room & Board: n/app	**Freshman Class:** 1723 applied, 1306 accepted, 600 enrolled
SAT CR/M/W: required **ACT:** 21	**CEEB CODE:** 1338
Application Deadline: July 1	**COMPETITIVE**

The mission of Indiana University Northwest, a regional campus of Indiana University, is to provide a high-quality and relevant education to the citizens of northwest Indiana, the most diverse and industrialized area of the state. The institution strives to create a community dedicated to the pursuit of knowledge and intellectual development, leading to undergraduate and selected graduate degrees in the liberal arts, sciences, and professional disciplines. The campus is strongly dedicated to the value of education, lifelong learning, diversity, celebration of cultures, and opportunity for all, as well as to participating in the sustainable economic development of the region and of the state. Indiana University Northwest is committed to the health and well-being of the communities it serves. There are 4 undergraduate schools. In addition to regional accreditation, IUN has baccalaureate program accreditation with AACSB, CSWE, NCATE, JRCERT, CAHIIM, and CODA. The 43-acre campus is in an urban area 35 miles southeast of Chicago. Including any residence halls, there are 18 buildings.

STUDENT LIFE: 97% of undergraduates are from Indiana. Others are from 9 states, 31 foreign countries, and Canada. 47% are White; 2% Asian American; 2% two or more races; 18% Hispanic; 16% race unknown; 14% African American. **Female To Male Ratio:** 1.9:1. The average age of freshmen is 19; all undergraduates, 24. 35% do not continue beyond their first year. **Housing:** 100% of students commute. Alcohol is not permitted. All students may keep cars.

FACULTY/CLASSROOMS: 42% of faculty are male; 58% are female. No introductory courses are taught by graduate students.

PROGRAMS OF STUDY: IU Northwest confers B.A., B.S., B.A.S., B.F.A., B.G.S., B.S.Ed., B.S.H.S.M., B.S.N., B.S.P.A., and B.S.W. degrees. Associate and master's degrees are also awarded. Bachelor's degrees are awarded in BIOLOGICAL SCIENCE (biochemistry and biology/adolescence education), BUSINESS (accounting, business administration and management, and labor studies), COMMUNICATIONS AND THE ARTS (communications, English, fine arts, French, Spanish, and theatre arts), COMPUTER AND PHYSICAL SCIENCE (actuarial science, applied science, chemistry, chemistry/adolescence education, computer information systems, geology, informatics and computer science, and mathematics), EDUCATION (elementary education, English education, general studies, health information management, mathematics education, secondary education, and social studies education), HEALTH PROFESSIONS (biology, dental hygiene, health science, medical imaging, nursing, and radiological science), SOCIAL SCIENCE (African American studies, anthropology, criminal justice, economics, history, philosophy, political science/government, psychology, public affairs, social work, and sociology). General studies, business, and nursing have the largest enrollments.

ACTIVITIES: There are 45 groups on campus, including art, cheerleading, communications, computers, dance, drama, environmental, ethnic, film, honors, international, LGBT, literary magazine, musical theater, newspaper, political, professional, radio and TV, religious, social, social service, and student government. Popular campus events include Back2School Week, Table Tennis Tournament, Communications Week, and Health Fair. **Sports:** There are 3 intercollegiate sports for men and 4 for women, and 2 intramural sports for men and 2 for women. The Savannah Fitness and Recreation Center is open to students, staff, faculty, and the public. The center has a full work-out room with Cybex equipment, a suspended 1/12th mile walking/running track, and a 3-court gymnasium where the IU Northwest RedHawk Basketball and Volleyball teams play in NAIA competitions. **Graduates:** From July 1, 2015 to June 30, 2016, 604 bachelor's degrees were awarded. The most popular majors were health professions (26%), liberal arts and sciences, general studies, and humanities (14%), business, management, and marketing (11%). In an average class, 7% graduate in 4 years or less, 17% graduate in 5 years or less, and 23% graduate in 6 years or less.

SERVICES: Counseling and information services are available, as is tutoring in some subjects. There is a reader service for the blind, and remedial math, reading, and writing. **Library/Resources:** The library contains 228,500 volumes. Computerized library services include interlibrary loans, database searching, Internet access, and Wi-Fi capability. Special learning facilities include an art gallery and radio station. **Physically Challenged Students:** 90% of the campus is accessible. Facilities include wheelchair ramps, elevators, special parking, specially equipped restrooms, special class scheduling, lowered drinking fountains, and lowered telephones. **Special:** IUN offers cross-registration with Purdue University, work-study, dual majors, independent study, internships, study abroad, credit for life, military, work experience, nondegree study, accelerated degree programs, student-designed majors, pass/fail options and online degrees. There are 10 national honor societies. **Visiting:** There are regularly scheduled orientations for prospective students. There are guides for informal visits and visitors may sit in on classes. To schedule a visit, contact the Admissions Office. **Campus Safety and Security:** Measures include 24-hour foot and vehicle patrol, emergency notification system, and security escort services. There are emergency telephones and lighted pathways/sidewalks.

REQUIREMENTS: The SAT or ACT is required. Freshman applicants should be on track to graduate, or should have graduated, from a commissioned Indiana high school, comparable out-of-state institution, or an approved homeschool, successfully completing a college prep curriculum. The Indiana Core 40 Diploma is a minimum requirement for admission. Students not achieving a Core 40 should apply to Ivy Tech Community College and complete 12 general education credit hours (100 level or higher) then apply to transfer to IU Northwest. In addition, applicants should have a minimum cumulative grade point average of 2.0 on a 4.0 scale; rank in the upper half of the high school graduating class; score above the median established by northwest Indiana students on the SAT or ACT. (If you have been out of school for more than one year, these scores are not required); GED recipients must have a total score that is above the average for Indiana residents. IU Northwest may accept students who are deficient in the standards listed above after additional testing. AP and CLEP credits are accepted. Important factors in the admissions decision are advanced placement or honors courses, leadership record, and recommendations by school officials. Each division sets its own degree requirements. All students must maintain a minimum GPA of 2.0 and complete at least 120 credit hours to graduate. Students must fulfill general education requirements for graduation. The courses required to fulfill the general education requirements vary depending upon the specific major that the student chooses. Each academic division has incorporated specific general education courses into the degree requirements to ensure that the following five principles and their learning outcomes are achieved. Principle 1: Foundations for Effective Learning and Communication - Fluency in reading, writing, and oral communication, mastery of the basic principles of logical, mathematical, and scientific reasoning, and literacy in information resources and learning technologies. Principle 2: Breadth of Learning - Mastery of the core concepts, principles, and methods in arts and humanities, cultural and historical studies, the social and behavioral sciences, and the mathematical, physical, and life sciences. Principle 3: Critical Thinking, Integration, and Application of Knowledge - Logical analysis and synthesis of information and ideas from multiple perspectives, critical acquisition, integration, and application of knowledge in students' intellectual, personal, professional, and community lives. Principle 4: Diversity - Valuing the diversity of human experience, as exemplified in race, ethnicity, social class, language, religion, gender, sexual orientation, age, or disabilities, understanding how these categories are often used to create injustice, recognizing our common human heritage and the interconnectedness of communities in the region, the nation, and the world. Principle 5: Ethics and Citizenship - The application of the principles of ethics and governance to the larger society, one's immediate community, and to individual conduct on campus and in society. **Procedure:** Freshmen are admitted to all sessions. Entrance exams should be taken as early as possible. There are deferred admissions and rolling admissions plans. Applications should be filed by July 1 for fall entry; December 1 for spring entry; and April 1 for summer entry, along with a $35 fee. Notification is sent on a rolling basis. Applications are accepted on-line. **Transfer Students:** 279 transfer students enrolled in 2015-2016. Transfer students requirements are; an official high school transcript (unless 26 semester hours of 100-level or above work has been completed at the time of the application); an official college or university transcript showing average or above average achievement (at least a 2.0 on a 4.0 scale), and an IU Intercampus Transfer Application if transferring from another IU campus, and a criminal activity disclosure policy, if applicable. A list of courses that will transfer among all Indiana public college and university campuses can be found at Indiana Core Transfer Library. A grade of "C" or better is required for credit. 30 of 120 credits required for the bachelor's degree must be completed at IUN. **International Students:** There are 13 international students enrolled.

ADMISSIONS: 76% of the 2016-2017 applicants were accepted. The SAT scores for the 2016-2017 freshman class were: Critical Reading--70% below 500, 26% between 500 and 599, 3% between 600 and 699, and 1% between 700 and 800. Math-- 71% below 500, 24% between 500 and 599, and 6% between 600 and 699. Writing-- 74% below 500, 23% between 500 and 599, and 3% between 600 and 699. The ACT scores were 24% between 12 and 17, 52% between 18 and 23, 20% between 24 and 29, and 4% above 30. 32% of the current freshmen were in the top fifth of their class; 72% were in the top two fifths. **Admissions Contact:** Dorothy Frink, Director of Admissions. Email: *admit@iun.edu* Web: *www.iun.edu*

FINANCIAL AID: In 2016-2017, 86% of all full-time freshmen and 83% of continuing full-time students received some form of financial aid. 65% of all full-time freshmen and 66% of continuing full-time students received need-based aid. The average freshman award was $7,636. Need-based scholarships or need-based grants averaged $6,480 ($15,312 maximum); need-based self-help aid (loans and jobs) averaged $4,420 ($12,000 maximum); non-need-based athletic scholarships averaged $1,333 ($2,000 maximum); and other non-need-based awards and non-need-based scholarships averaged $4,498 ($21,344 maximum). 5% of undergraduate students work part-time. Average annual earnings from campus work are $2073. The average financial indebtedness of the 2016 graduate was $29,701. The FAFSA code is 001815. The priority date for freshman financial aid applications for fall entry is March 1. The deadline for filing freshman financial aid applications for fall entry is March 10.

INDIANA UNIVERSITY SOUTH BEND C-1

www.iusb.edu

South Bend, IN 46615	**(574) 520-4839** **(877) GO-2-IUSB**
Fax: (574) 520-4834	**Email: admissions@iusb.edu**
Full-time: 1495 men, 2320 women	**Faculty:** IIA, --$
Part-time: 1131 men, 1707 women	**Ph.D.s:** 76%
Graduate: 177 men, 355 women	**Student/Faculty:** 14 to 1
Year: semesters, summer session	**Tuition:** $7072 ($18,683)
Room & Board: $7170	**Freshman Class:** 2451 applied, 1888 accepted, 913 enrolled
SAT CR/M/W: required **ACT:** 21	**CEEB CODE:** 1339
Application Deadline: August 1	**COMPETITIVE**

Indiana University South Bend is the comprehensive undergraduate and graduate regional campus of Indiana University that is committed to serving north central Indiana and southwestern Michigan. Its mission is to create, disseminate, preserve, and apply knowledge. The campus is committed to excellence in teaching, learning, research, and creative activity; to strong liberal arts and sciences programs and professional disciplines; to acclaimed programs in the arts and nursing/health professions; to diversity, civic engagement, and a global perspective. IU South Bend supports student learning, access, and success for a diverse residential and nonresidential student body that includes underrepresented and international students. The campus fosters student-faculty collaboration in research and learning. Committed to the economic development of its region and state, Indiana University South Bend meets the changing educational and research needs of the community and serves as a vibrant cultural resource. There are 7 undergraduate schools. In addition to regional accreditation, IUSB has baccalaureate program accreditation with AACSB, CSWE, NASM, CCNE, CODA, and CAEP. The 104-acre campus is in a suburban area 95 miles east of Chicago. Including any residence halls, there are 30 buildings.

STUDENT LIFE: 95% of undergraduates are from Indiana. Others are from 20 states, 66 foreign countries, and Canada. 73% are White; 7% African American; 3% Foreign; 3% two or more races; 3% race unknown; 2% Asian American; 10% Hispanic. **Female To Male Ratio:** 1.6:1. The average age of freshmen is 18; all undergraduates, 24. 36% do not continue beyond their first year. **Housing:** 388 students can be accommodated in college housing, which includes single-sex and coed on-campus apartments and off-campus apartments. Special housing available for international students. On-campus housing is available on a first-come, first-served basis. 92% of students commute. Alcohol is not permitted. All students may keep cars.

FACULTY/CLASSROOMS: 48% of faculty are male; 52% are female. No introductory courses are taught by graduate students.

PROGRAMS OF STUDY: IU South Bend confers B.A., B.S., B.F.A, B.G.S., B.M., B.S.Ed., B.S.M.I.T., B.S.N., and B.S.W. degrees. Associate and master's degrees are also awarded. Bachelor's degrees are awarded in BIOLOGICAL SCIENCE (biochemistry, biology/adolescence education, and biology/biological science), BUSINESS (business administration and management and labor studies), COMMUNICATIONS AND THE ARTS (communication studies, English, fine arts, French, German, music, Spanish, and theatre arts), COMPUTER AND PHYSICAL SCIENCE (actuarial science, applied science, chemistry, chemistry/adolescence education, clinical laboratory science, computer science, informatics and computer science, mathematics, and physics), EDUCATION (art education, elementary education, English education, general studies, French studies K-12 education, mathematics education, music education, secondary education, social studies education, Spanish education K-12, and special education), HEALTH PROFESSIONS (dental hygiene, health care administration, health science, medical imaging, and nursing), SOCIAL SCIENCE (anthropology, criminal justice, economics, history, philosophy, political science/government, psychology, social work, sociology, and women & gender studies). Business, nursing, and elementary education have the largest enrollments.

ACTIVITIES: There are 108 groups on campus, including art, cheerleading, choir, communications, dance, debate, drama, environmental, ethnic, film, honors, international, jazz band, LGBT, literary magazine, musical theater, newspaper, opera, pep band, photography, political, professional, religious, social, social service, and student government. Popular campus events include Titan Fest, Red & White Dance, Mini University Welcome Week, and Alternative Spring Break Trips. **Sports:** There are 4 intercollegiate sports for men and 4 for women, and 11 intramural sports for men and 11 for women. Student Activities Center features: Courtside Café, basketball and volleyball courts, 3 racquetball/vallyball courts, 3 indoor running tracks (1/8 mile), group exercise/aerobic room, table tennis, billiards tables, locker rooms, athletic offices and a wellness center. The fitness center features Life Fitness (plate-loaded) equipment and Hampton Strength free-weight equipment, along with 23 pieces of cardiovascular machines and weight training machines. **Graduates:** From July 1, 2015 to June 30, 2016, 768 bachelor's degrees were awarded. The most popular majors were business, management, marketing (20%), health professions (17%), liberal arts and sciences, and general studies and humanities (14%). In an average class, 7% graduate in 4 years or less, 21% graduate in 5 years or less, and 28% graduate in 6 years or less.

SERVICES: Counseling and information services are available, as is tutoring in most subjects. There is remedial math, reading, and writing. Taped texts, note takers, and interpreters or transcription services are available. **Library/Resources:** The library contains 334,989 volumes.

Computerized library services include interlibrary loans, database searching, Internet access, and Wi-Fi capability. Special learning facilities include an art gallery, science labs, studios for fine and performing arts, instructional media services, and an academic resource center. **Physically Challenged Students:** 95% of the campus is accessible. Facilities include wheelchair ramps, elevators, special parking, specially equipped restrooms, special class scheduling, lowered drinking fountains, and lowered telephones. **Special:** Cross-registration with Northern Indiana Consortium for education (NICE), internships, study abroad, accelerated degree programs, online degrees and dual majors are possible. There are 2 national honor societies and a freshman honors program. **Visiting:** There are regularly scheduled orientations for prospective students, including a visit to the admissions office, a campus tour, professor meetings, and information on financial aid. There are guides for informal visits, visitors may sit in on classes, and stay overnight. To schedule a visit, contact the Admissions Office. **Campus Safety and Security:** Measures include 24-hour foot and vehicle patrol, emergency notification system, and security escort services. There are emergency telephones and lighted pathways/sidewalks.

REQUIREMENTS: The SAT or ACT is required. Indiana high school graduates are expected to complete the Core 40 curriculum and are strongly encouraged to earn the Academic Honors Diploma. Out-of-state students are expected to complete a comparable college-prep curriculum. CLEP credits are accepted. Important factors in the admissions decision are advanced placement or honors courses, extracurricular activities record, and leadership record. All students must complete the campus-wide general education curriculum which is composed of three elements and requires a total of between 33 and 39 credit hours of course-work. I. Fundamental Literacies Courses (13-19 cr.) -Writing, Critical Thinking, Oral Communication, Visual Literacy, Quantitative Reasoning, Information Literacy and Computer Literacy. II. Common Core Courses (12 cr.) -The Natural World, Human Behavior and Social Institutions, Literary and Intellectual Traditions, Art, Aesthetics, and Creativity. III. Contemporary Social Values Courses (8 cr.) -Non-Western Cultures, Diversity in U.S. Society, Health and Wellness. A total of 120 semester hours, with a minimum GPA of 2.0, is required to graduate. **Procedure:** Freshmen are admitted to all sessions. Entrance exams should be taken 1 year to 6 months before entering the university. There are deferred admissions and rolling admissions plans. Application deadlines are open. Application fee is $35. Applications are accepted on-line. **Transfer Students:** 407 transfer students enrolled in 2015-2016. A 2.0 GPA is required. College transcripts must be submitted. 30 of 120 credits required for the bachelor's degree must be completed at IU South Bend. **International Students:** There are 154 international students enrolled. The school actively recruits these students. They must take the TOEFL with a minimum score of 530 on the paper-based TOEFL (PBT) or 71 on the Internet-based version (iBT).

ADMISSIONS: 77% of the 2016-2017 applicants were accepted. The SAT scores for the 2016-2017 freshman class were: Critical Reading-- 64% below 500, 27% between 500 and 599, 8% between 600 and 699, and 1% between 700 and 800. Math-- 61% below 500, 30% between 500 and 599, 8% between 600 and 699, and 1% between 700 and 800. Writing-- 72% below 500, 23% between 500 and 599, and 5% between 600 and 699. The ACT scores were 22% between 12 and 17, 55% between 18 and 23, 22% between 24 and 29, and 1% above 30. 29% of the current freshmen were in the top fifth of their class; 65% were in the top two fifths. **Admissions Contact:** Constance Peterson-Miller, Director of Admissions. Email: *admissions@iusb.edu* Web: *www.iusb.edu*

FINANCIAL AID: In 2016-2017, 88% of all full-time freshmen and 86% of continuing full-time students received some form of financial aid. 70% of all full-time freshmen and 72% of continuing full-time students received need-based aid. The average freshman award was $8,228. Need-based scholarships or need-based grants averaged $7,042 ($20,946 maximum); need-based self-help aid (loans and jobs) averaged $4,011 ($12,551 maximum); non-need-based athletic scholarships averaged $739 ($12,700 maximum); and other non-need-based awards and non-need-based scholarships averaged $3,979 ($16,371 maximum). 8% of undergraduate students work part-time. Average annual earnings from campus work are $2047. The average financial indebtedness of the 2016 graduate was $27,306. The FAFSA code is 001816. The priority date for freshman financial aid applications for fall entry is March 1. The deadline for filing freshman financial aid applications for fall entry is March 10.

INDIANA UNIVERSITY SOUTHEAST *(The complete profile is made available exclusively on our website, www.barronspac.com)*

INDIANA UNIVERSITY-PURDUE UNIVERSITY FORT WAYNE — D-2
www.ipfw.edu

Fort Wayne, IN 46805	**(260) 481-6812** **(866) 597-0010**
Fax: (260) 481-5450	**Email: ASK@ipfw.edu**
Full-time: 2828 men, 3556 women	**Faculty:** 397; IIA, -$
Part-time: 2198 men, 2871 women	**Ph.D.s:** 85%
Graduate: 229 men, 328 women	**Student/Faculty:** 17 to 1
Year: semesters, summer session	**Tuition:** $8213 ($19,727)
Room & Board: $9340	**Freshman Class:** 3240 applied, 3191 accepted, 1600 enrolled
SAT: required **ACT:** 22	**CEEB CODE:** 1336
Application Deadline: August 1	**COMPETITIVE**

Indiana University, founded in 1917, joined Purdue University at Fort Wayne, founded in 1944. The combined school, a state-controlled institution, offers programs in liberal arts, science, business, education, health sciences, engineering, technology, public affairs, and visual and performing arts. There are 8 undergraduate schools and 5 graduate schools. In addition to regional accreditation, IPFW has baccalaureate program accreditation with AACSB, ABET, ADA, NASAD, NASM, NCATE, NLN, ACS, AMTA, CAC, CODA, EAC, NASPAA, TAC, and NAST. The 688-acre campus is in a suburban area 113 miles north of Indianapolis. Including any residence halls, there are 51 buildings.

STUDENT LIFE: 94% of undergraduates are from Indiana. Others are from 41 states, 44 foreign countries, and Canada. 81% are White; 6% Hispanic; 4% African American; 3% Asian American; 3% two or more races; 2% Foreign; 1% race unknown. **Female To Male Ratio:** 1.3:1. The average age of freshmen is 20; all undergraduates, 23. 37% do not continue beyond their first year; 25% remain to graduate. **Housing:** 1204 students can be accommodated in college housing, which includes coed on-campus apartments. On-campus housing is available on a first-come, first-served basis. 93% of students commute. Alcohol is not permitted. All students may keep cars.

FACULTY/CLASSROOMS: 55% of faculty are male; 45% are female. All teach undergraduates, and 92% do research. Graduate students teach 3% of introductory courses. The average class size in an introductory lecture is 20; in a laboratory is 19; and in a regular course is 20.

PROGRAMS OF STUDY: IPFW confers B.A., B.S., B.F.A., B.G.S, B.Mus., B.Mus.Ed., B.S.B., B.S.C., B.S.C.E., B.S.Cp.E., B.S.Ed., B.S.E.E., B.S.G., B.S.M.E., B.S.P.A., B.S.L.S., and B.S.M.T. degrees. Associate, master's, and doctoral degrees are also awarded. Bachelor's degrees are awarded in BIOLOGICAL SCIENCE (biochemistry and biology/biological science), BUSINESS (accounting, banking and finance, business administration and management, business economics, hospitality management services, labor studies, management science, marketing/retailing/merchandising, and organizational leadership and management), COMMUNICATIONS AND THE ARTS (communications, crafts, dramatic arts, drawing, English, English literature, fine arts, French, German, graphic design, music, music performance, painting, percussion, photography, piano/organ, printmaking, sculpture, Spanish, speech/debate/rhetoric, strings, technical and business writing, telecommunications, visual design, and voice), COMPUTER AND PHYSICAL SCIENCE (actuarial science, chemistry, computer programming, computer science, earth science, geology, information sciences and systems, mathematics, physical sciences, physics, and statistics), EDUCATION (art education, computer education, early childhood education, elementary education, English education, foreign languages education, mathematics education, middle school education, music education, science education, and secondary education), ENGINEERING AND ENVIRONMENTAL DESIGN (civil engineering, computer engineering, computer graphics, electrical/electronics engineering, electrical/electronics engineering technology, engineering, engineering technology, industrial engineering technology, interior design, mechanical engineering, and mechanical engineering technology), HEALTH PROFESSIONS (health care administration, medical technology, music therapy, nursing, predentistry, premedicine, preoptometry, prepharmacy, preveterinary science, and speech pathology/audiology), SOCIAL SCIENCE (anthropology, criminal justice, economics, history, human services, liberal arts/general studies, philosophy, political science/

government, prelaw, psychology, public administration, public affairs, social science, sociology, and women's studies). Engineering and biology are the strongest academically. Business, education, and engineering have the largest enrollments.

ACTIVITIES: There are 120 groups on campus, including art, band, cheerleading, chess, choir, chorus, dance, debate, drama, ethnic, film, forensics, honors, international, jazz band, LGBT, literary magazine, musical theater, newspaper, opera, orchestra, pep band, political, professional, radio and TV, religious, social, social service, student government, and symphony. Popular campus events include Mastodon Roast, and Freshmen Fest. **Sports:** There are 6 intercollegiate sports for men and 7 for women, and 18 intramural sports for men and 18 for women. Facilities include a physical fitness center with a gym, 3 basketball courts, an indoor track, a weight room, 4 racquetball courts, 1 wallyball court, a fencing and dance room, baseball and soccer fields, and an indoor soccer facility. **Graduates:** From July 1, 2015 to June 30, 2016, 1384 bachelor's degrees were awarded. The most popular majors were general studies (12%), nursing (7%), and psychology (5%). 180 companies recruited on campus in 2015-2016. In an average class, 7% graduate in 4 years or less, 19% graduate in 5 years or less, and 25% graduate in 6 years or less.

SERVICES: Counseling and information services are available, as is tutoring in most subjects. There is a reader service for the blind, and remedial math, reading, and writing. **Library/Resources:** The library contains 332,018 volumes, 285,185 microform items, and 7,972 audio/video tapes/CDs/DVDs, and subscribes to 90,000 periodicals including electronic. Computerized library services include interlibrary loans, database searching, Internet access, and Wi-Fi capability. Special learning facilities include an art gallery, radio station, and TV station. **Physically Challenged Students:** All of the campus is accessible. Facilities include wheelchair ramps, elevators, special parking, specially equipped restrooms, special class scheduling, lowered drinking fountains, lowered telephones, and special housing. **Special:** There are continuing education, co-op, and work-study programs, as well as study abroad in 5 countries. An accelerated general studies degree, cross-registration with other Fort Wayne colleges, B.A.-B.S. degrees, dual majors, a Washington semester for public affairs students, internships, and credit for military experience are available. Nondegree study and pass/fail options are possible. An accelerated MBA degree is also offered. There are 16 national honor societies and a freshman honors program. **Visiting:** There are regularly scheduled orientations for prospective students. There are guides for informal visits, and visitors may sit in on classes. To schedule a visit, contact the Admissions Office. **Campus Safety and Security:** Measures include 24-hour foot and vehicle patrol, emergency notification system, self-defense education, and security escort services. There are shuttle buses, emergency telephones, lighted pathways/sidewalks, and controlled access to dorms/residences.

REQUIREMENTS: The SAT or ACT is required, with a minimum composite score of 1420 on the SAT or a minimum composite score of 20 on the ACT. Indiana Core 40, Academic Honors, or Technical Honors Diploma required. Out-of-state students must complete a college prep curriculum IPFW requires applicants to be in the upper 50% of their class. A GPA of 2.8 is required. AP and CLEP credits are accepted. Important factors in the admissions decision are recommendations by school officials, evidence of special talent, and advanced placement or honors courses. All bachelor's degree students must complete 120 credits, including 33 general education hours, with a GPA of 2.0, and take English composition, speech communication, and math to graduate. Students must take 32 credit hours at the 200 level or above (including 15 credit hours at the 300 level or above) in their major. **Procedure:** Freshmen are admitted fall, spring, and summer. Entrance exams should be taken in the senior year of high school. There are deferred admissions and rolling admissions plans. Applications should be filed by August 1 for fall entry; December 15 for spring entry; and May 1 for summer entry, along with a $50 fee. Notification is sent on a rolling basis. Applications are accepted on-line. **Transfer Students:** 532 transfer students enrolled in 2015-2016. Transfer applicants must have a minimum GPA of 2.0. Grades of C or better transfer for credit. 32 of 120 credits required for the bachelor's degree must be completed at IPFW. **International Students:** There are 141 international students enrolled. The school actively recruits these students. They must take the TOEFL with a minimum score of 550 on the paper-based TOEFL (PBT) or 77 on the Internet-based version (iBT), or pass level 112 of an ESL program. They may also take the ACT or SAT.

ADMISSIONS: 98% of the 2016-2017 applicants were accepted. The SAT scores for the 2016-2017 freshman class were: Critical Reading-- 57% below 500, 33% between 500 and 599, 9% between 600 and 699, and 1% between 700 and 800. Math-- 55% below 500, 34% between 500 and 599, 9% between 600 and 699, and 2% between 700 and 800. Writing-- 66% below 500, 29% between 500 and 599, 5% between 600 and 699, and 1% between 700 and 800. The ACT scores were 18% between 12 and 17, 52% between 18 and 23, 24% between 24 and 29, and 6% above 30. 21% of the current freshmen were in the top fifth of their class; 47% were in the top two fifths. 7 freshmen graduated first in their class. **Admissions Contact:** Kenneth Christmon, Director of Admissions. Email: *ASK@ipfw.edu* Web: *www.ipfw.edu*

FINANCIAL AID: In 2016-2017, 75% of all full-time freshmen and 70% of continuing full-time students received some form of financial aid. 47% of all full-time freshmen received need-based aid. The average freshman award was $8,500. Need-based scholarships or need-based grants averaged $5,600 ($13,000 maximum); need-based self-help aid (loans and jobs) averaged $3,170 ($26,400 maximum); non-need-based athletic scholarships averaged $12,770 ($39,800 maximum); and other non-need-based awards and non-need-based scholarships averaged $4,000 ($24,900 maximum). 1% of undergraduate students work part-time. Average annual earnings from campus work are $2000. The average financial indebtedness of the 2016 graduate was $30,000. IPFW is a member of CSS. The FAFSA code is 001828. The priority date for freshman financial aid applications for fall entry is March 10.

INDIANA UNIVERSITY-PURDUE UNIVERSITY INDIANAPOLIS C-3

www.iupui.edu

Indianapolis, IN 46202 (317) 274-4591

Fax: (317) 278-1862	**Email:** apply@iupui.edu
Full-time: 7523 men, 9866 women	**Faculty:** n/av
Part-time: 1980 men, 2379 women	**Ph.D.s:** 85%
Graduate: 3611 men, 4445 women	**Student/Faculty:** 17 to 1
Year: semesters, summer session	**Tuition:** $9205 ($29,792)
Room & Board: $9430	**Freshman Class:** 13301 applied, 9839 accepted, 4003 enrolled
SAT CR/M/W: 504/510/485 **ACT:** 23	**CEEB CODE:** 1325
Application Deadline: May 1	**COMPETITIVE**

Indiana University–Purdue University Indianapolis (IUPUI), a partnership between Indiana and Purdue Universities, is Indiana's urban research and academic health sciences campus. IUPUI's mission is to advance the State of Indiana and the intellectual growth of its citizens to the highest levels nationally and internationally through research and creative activity, teaching and learning, and civic engagement. By offering a distinctive range of bachelor's, master's, professional, and Ph.D. degrees, IUPUI promotes the educational, cultural, and economic development of central Indiana and beyond through innovative collaborations, external partnerships, and a strong commitment to diversity. There are 20 undergraduate schools. In addition to regional accreditation, IUPUI has baccalaureate program accreditation with AACSB, ABET, CSWE, NASAD, NASM, NCATE, FEPAC, CAAHEP, and CODA. The 534-acre campus is in an urban area near downtown Indianapolis. Including any residence halls, there are 138 buildings.

STUDENT LIFE: 93% of undergraduates are from Indiana. Others are from 50 states, 145 foreign countries, and Canada. 9% are African American; 7% Foreign; 68% White; 6% Hispanic; 5% Asian American; 3% two or more races; 1% race unknown. **Female To Male Ratio:** 1.3:1. The average age of freshmen is 18; all undergraduates, 23. 26% do not continue beyond their first year. **Housing:** 2595 students can be accommodated in college housing, which includes coed dorms, on-campus apartments, off-campus apartments, and married student housing. In addition, there are honors houses, special-interest houses, international house, women in science house, and sustainability house. On-campus housing is available on a first-come, first-served basis. 88% of students commute. Alcohol is not permitted. All students may keep cars.

FACULTY/CLASSROOMS: 55% of faculty are male; 45% are female. No introductory courses are taught by graduate students.

PROGRAMS OF STUDY: IUPUI confers B.A., B.S., B.S.B., B.A.E.D.,

B.F.A., B.G.S., B.S.CE., B.S. Ch., B.S.CJ., B.S.E., B.S.ED., B.S.EE., B.S.HSM., B.S.ME., B.S.MT., B.S.N., B.S.PA., B.S.PH., and B.SW. degrees. Associate, master's, and doctoral degrees are also awarded. Bachelor's degrees are awarded in BIOLOGICAL SCIENCE (biotechnology, forensic science, and neurosciences), BUSINESS (business administration and management, labor studies, organizational leadership and management, and tourism), COMMUNICATIONS AND THE ARTS (Africana studies, American Sign Language, art history, communication studies, English, fine arts, French, German, journalism, media arts, music technology, Spanish, and technical communication), COMPUTER AND PHYSICAL SCIENCE (chemistry, clinical laboratory science, computer engineering technology, computer information technology, computer science, energy science, geology, informatics and computer science, mathematics, and physics), EDUCATION (art education, elementary education, English education, general studies, health information management, social studies education, and Spanish education K-12), ENGINEERING AND ENVIRONMENTAL DESIGN (biomedical engineering, computer engineering, computer graphics, construction engineering, electrical/electronics engineering, electrical/electronics engineering technology, engineering technology, environmental science, interior design, mechanical engineering, mechanical engineering technology, and nuclear medicine technology), HEALTH PROFESSIONS (biology, cytotechnology, dental hygiene, health care administration, health science, medical imaging, kinesiology, mental health/human services, nursing, premedicine, pre-occupational therapy, prepharmacy, pre-physician assistant, prephysical therapy, preveterinary science, public health, radiation therapy, and respiratory therapy), SOCIAL SCIENCE (anthropology, criminal justice, economics, geography, history, interdisciplinary studies, international studies, law, philosophy, political science/government, prelaw, psychology, public affairs, religious studies, social work, and sociology). Engineering and medicine are the strongest academically. Nursing, elementary education, and general studies have the largest enrollments.

ACTIVITIES: 3% of men belong to 9 national fraternities; 5% of women belong to 12 national sororities. There are 480 groups on campus, including art, band, cheerleading, chess, choir, communications, computers, dance, debate, drama, environmental, ethnic, film, forensics, honors, international, LGBT, literary magazine, newspaper, pep band, photography, political, professional, radio and TV, religious, social, social service, and student government. Popular campus events include Weeks of Welcome, Spring Dance, InternationalFest, Jag-A-Palooza, Cultural Heritage Months, IUPUI Regatta and FountainFest. **Sports:** There are 7 intercollegiate sports for men and 9 for women, and 11 intramural sports for men and 11 for women. Facilities include a gymnasium that features basketball and volleyball courts. Michael A. Carroll Soccer Stadium features two FIFA regulated game fields. The Natatorium features a competition pool, instructional pool and diving well. Softball Complex has 3 fields, 12,000-seat track and field stadium, and the National Institute for Fitness and Sport features a 117,000-square foot facility with a 200-meter indoor track, free weights, Cybex and cardio equipment, pilates studio, indoor batting nets, and half-size basketball courts. **Graduates:** From July 1, 2015 to June 30, 2016, 4026 bachelor's degrees were awarded. The most popular majors were health professions (19%), business, management and marketing (17%), liberal arts and sciences, and general studies and humanities (8%). In an average class, 19% graduate in 4 years or less, 39% graduate in 5 years or less, and 47% graduate in 6 years or less.

SERVICES: Counseling and information services are available, as is tutoring in most subjects. There is a reader service for the blind, and remedial math, reading, and writing. **Library/Resources:** The 5 libraries contain 1.9 million volumes. Computerized library services include interlibrary loans, database searching, Internet access, and Wi-Fi capability. Special learning facilities include an art gallery, radio station, an 85-acre medical center, 100 research centers, 27 signature centers, the IU Research and Technology Corporation. **Physically Challenged Students:** All of the campus is accessible. Facilities include wheelchair ramps, elevators, special parking, specially equipped restrooms, special class scheduling, lowered drinking fountains, and lowered telephones. Classroom aids and sign language interpreters available. **Special:** There is a metropolitan studies program for career work in the city and cross-registration with the Consortium for Urban Education. IUPUI also offers study abroad, combined B.A.-B.S. degree programs, internships, work-study programs, dual and student-designed majors, online degrees, nondegree study, nontraditional programs for adult learners, and interdisciplinary majors such as business economics and public policy, health occupations education, and interdisciplinary engineering. There are 12 national honor societies and a freshman honors program. **Visiting:** There are regularly scheduled orientations for prospective students, consisting of a campus tour and talks with students. There are guides for informal visits and visitors may sit in on classes. To schedule a visit, contact Office of Admissions. **Campus Safety and Security:** Measures include 24-hour foot and vehicle patrol, emergency notification system, self-defense education, and security escort services. There are shuttle buses, emergency telephones, and lighted pathways/sidewalks.

REQUIREMENTS: The SAT or ACT is required. Indiana high school graduates are expected to complete the Core 40 curriculum and are strongly encouraged to earn the Academic Honors Diploma. Out-of-state students are expected to complete the required core of classes to be considered for admission. The units of academic electives can be a combination of additional mathematics, laboratory science, social science, computer science, foreign language, or other courses of college preparatory nature. Some IUPUI schools require additional courses. Rank in upper half of high school class or show above average on the GED. SAT or ACT scores for Indiana residents should be at or above the Indiana median. Student who have been out of high school for more than 1 year are not required to submit. AP and CLEP credits are accepted. All students must complete 120 to 126 credits required for the bachelor's degree. Most schools also require grades of C or higher in major courses. All beginning first-year students at Indiana University–Purdue University Indianapolis (IUPUI) will complete 30 hours of general education course work (the IUPUI General Education Core) prior to graduation with either an associate degree a baccalaureate degree. Course-work is divided into the broad domains of Foundational Intellectual Skills (core communication, analytical reasoning, and cultural understanding) and course-work that promotes Intellectual Breadth and Adaptiveness (life and physical sciences, and arts, humanities, and social sciences). **Procedure:** Freshmen are admitted to all sessions. Entrance exams should be taken by the end of junior year or fall of senior year. There are deferred admissions and rolling admissions plans. Application deadlines are open. Application fee is $55. Notification is sent on a rolling basis. Applications are accepted on-line. **Transfer Students:** 1373 transfer students enrolled in 2015-2016. Transfers who are Indiana residents must present a minimum GPA of 2.0 in all previous college work; out-of-state residents need a minimum 2.5. All applicants must be in good standing at their former schools. 30 of 120 credits required for the bachelor's degree must be completed at IUPUI. **International Students:** There are 909 international students enrolled. The school actively recruits these students. They must take the TOEFL with a minimum score of 550 on the paper-based TOEFL (PBT) or 61 on the Internet-based version (iBT).

ADMISSIONS: 74% of the 2016-2017 applicants were accepted. The SAT scores for the 2016-2017 freshman class were: Critical Reading-- 49% below 500, 37% between 500 and 599, 13% between 600 and 699, and 2% between 700 and 800. Math-- 45% below 500, 38% between 500 and 599, 15% between 600 and 699, and 2% between 700 and 800. Writing-- 58% below 500, 33% between 500 and 599, 9% between 600 and 699, and 1% between 700 and 800. The ACT scores were 13% between 12 and 17, 47% between 18 and 23, 33% between 24 and 29, and 7% above 30. 45% of the current freshmen were in the top fifth of their class; 87% were in the top two fifths. **Admissions Contact:** Yohlunda Mosley, Director of Undergraduate Admissions. Email: *apply@iupui.edu* Web: *www.iupui.edu*

FINANCIAL AID: In 2016-2017, 89% of all full-time freshmen and 87% of continuing full-time students received some form of financial aid. 68% of all full-time freshmen and 66% of continuing full-time students received need-based aid. The average freshman award was $11,403. Need-based scholarships or need-based grants averaged $9,558 ($41,553 maximum); need-based self-help aid (loans and jobs) averaged $4,788 ($32,475 maximum); non-need-based athletic scholarships averaged $9,649 ($31,681 maximum); and other non-need-based awards and non-need-based scholarships averaged $6,400 ($40,500 maximum). 10% of undergraduate students work part-time. Average annual earnings from campus work are $2790. The average financial indebtedness of the 2016 graduate was $28,951. The FAFSA code is 001813. The priority date for freshman financial aid applications for fall entry is March 1. The deadline for filing freshman financial aid applications for fall entry is March 10.

INDIANA WESLEYAN UNIVERSITY C-2

www.indwes.edu

Marion, IN 46953 (765) 677-1677
(866) GO-TO-IWU

Fax: (765) 677-2333 Email: admissions@indwes.edu

Full-time: 887 men, 1731 women	**Faculty:** IIB, -$
Part-time: 69 men, 95 women	**Ph.D.s:** 67%
Graduate: 73 men, 185 women	**Student/Faculty:** 14 to 1
Year: semesters, summer session	**Tuition:** $25,526
Room & Board: $8148	**Freshman Class:** 3323 applied, 2455 accepted, 683 enrolled
SAT CR/M/W: 525/535/515 **ACT:** 24	**CEEB CODE:** 1446
Application Deadline: n/av	**COMPETITIVE**

Indiana Wesleyan University, founded in 1920, is a private, Evangelical Christian, liberal arts institution, and is a Christ-centered academic community committed to changing the world by developing students in character, scholarship, and leadership. There are 6 undergraduate schools and 3 graduate schools. In addition to regional accreditation, IWU has baccalaureate program accreditation with CSWE, NASM, NCATE, CCNE, CACREP, and CAATE. The 320-acre campus is in a small town in north-central Indiana, 70 miles north of Indianapolis, 50 miles south of Fort Wayne. Including any residence halls, there are 64 buildings.

STUDENT LIFE: 53% of undergraduates are from Indiana. Others are from 46 states, 7 foreign countries, and Canada. 91% are White; 3% Hispanic; 2% African American; 1% Asian American; 1% American Indian/Alaska Native; 1% Foreign; 1% two or more races. 92% are Protestant. **Female To Male Ratio:** 2.0:1. The average age of freshmen is 18; all undergraduates, 20. 26% do not continue beyond their first year; 70% remain to graduate. **Housing:** 2801 students can be accommodated in college housing, which includes single-sex dorms, on-campus apartments, and married student housing. In addition, there are special-interest houses. On-campus housing is guaranteed for all 4 years, and is available on a first-come, first-served basis. 82% of students live on campus; of those, 75% remain on campus on weekends. Alcohol is not permitted. All students may keep cars.

FACULTY/CLASSROOMS: 60% of faculty are male; 40% are female. 98% teach undergraduates, 20% do research, and 20% do both. No introductory courses are taught by graduate students. The average class size in an introductory lecture is 50; in a laboratory is 15; and in a regular course is 18.

PROGRAMS OF STUDY: IWU confers A.B., B.A., B.S.N., B.S.M., and M.A. degrees. Associate, master's, and doctoral degrees are also awarded. Bachelor's degrees are awarded in BIOLOGICAL SCIENCE (biology/biological science), BUSINESS (accounting, banking and finance, business administration and management, management science, marketing/retailing/merchandising, and recreational facilities management), COMMUNICATIONS AND THE ARTS (applied music, art, ceramic art and design, communications, creative writing, English, illustration, music, music theory and composition, painting, photography, printmaking, Spanish, and studio art), COMPUTER AND PHYSICAL SCIENCE (chemistry, computer science, information sciences and systems, mathematics, and science), EDUCATION (art education, athletic training, elementary education, English education, mathematics education, music education, nursing education, physical education, science education, secondary education, social studies education, and special education), ENGINEERING AND ENVIRONMENTAL DESIGN (computer graphics and interior design), HEALTH PROFESSIONS (health, medical laboratory technology, nursing, and premedicine), SOCIAL SCIENCE (addiction studies, biblical studies, criminal justice, economics, history, law enforcement and corrections, liberal arts/general studies, ministries, political science/government, prelaw, psychology, religion, religious education, religious music, social studies, social work, and sociology). Nursing, education, and pre-medicine are the strongest academically. Nursing, education, and business have the largest enrollments.

ACTIVITIES: There are no fraternities or sororities. There are 35 groups on campus, including art, band, cheerleading, choir, chorale, chorus, computers, drama, environmental, ethnic, film, honors, international, jazz band, literary magazine, musical theater, newspaper, opera, orchestra, pep band, photography, political, professional, radio and TV, religious, social, social service, student government, symphony, and yearbook. Popular campus events include Spotted Cow Music Festival, Friday Night Live and Taste of Marion. **Sports:** There are 9 intercollegiate sports for men and 9 for women, and 21 intramural sports for men and 21 for women. Facilities include recreation and wellness center: fitness rooms, weight rooms, swimming pool, athletic training center, indoor track, practice/intramural gym, basketball gymnasium, soccer, baseball, softball, track and field, tennis courts, long/triple jump pits, pole vault area, indoor weight throw, 8-lane 200-meter track, and a competition area. **Graduates:** From July 1, 2015 to June 30, 2016, 635 bachelor's degrees were awarded. The most popular majors were nursing (18%), elementary education (8%), and psychology (6%). In an average class, 56% graduate in 4 years or less, 68% graduate in 5 years or less, and 70% graduate in 6 years or less.

SERVICES: Counseling and information services are available, as is tutoring in most subjects. There is a reader service for the blind, and remedial math, reading, and writing. External testing, a note-taker service, and advocacy are available. **Library/Resources:** The library contains 276,070 volumes, 315,162 microform items, and 11,479 audio/video tapes/CDs/DVDs, and subscribes to 106,118 periodicals including electronic. Computerized library services include interlibrary loans, database searching, Internet access, and Wi-Fi capability. Special learning facilities include an art gallery, radio station, TV station, a globe theatre, and the Daily Planet. **Physically Challenged Students:** 95% of the campus is accessible. Facilities include wheelchair ramps, elevators, special parking, specially equipped restrooms, special class scheduling, lowered drinking fountains, lowered telephones, and special housing. **Special:** Students may study abroad in 20 countries. IWU also offers business, pastoral, nursing, and social work internships, cross-registration with CCCU, a Washington semester, work-study programs with the Economic Growth Council, pass/fail options, and nondegree study. Accelerated degree programs are available in accounting, business administration, business information, management, and nursing. Students may earn a B.A.-B.S. degree in management, business, and education. Dual majors and student-designed majors are available. Adult learners may earn credit for life experience toward bachelor's degrees in business. There are 6 national honor societies, a freshman honors program, and 12 departmental honors programs. **Visiting:** There are regularly scheduled orientations for prospective students, including appointments with admissions counselors and professors, campus tours, classroom visits, and meals. There are guides for informal visits, visitors may sit in on classes, and stay overnight. To schedule a visit, contact the Admissions Office. **Campus Safety and Security:** Measures include 24-hour foot and vehicle patrol, emergency notification system, self-defense education, and security escort services. There are emergency telephones, lighted pathways/sidewalks, and controlled access to dorms/residences.

REQUIREMENTS: The SAT or ACT is required. The completed application, high school transcript, test scores including an essay (SAT or ACT), recommendation, and a community values contract are necessary for an admission decision. A tuition deposit is required before registration and is fully refundable until May 1. The admission decision may be made with a high school transcript at the end of the junior year. It is to be followed later by the full four-year record and certification of graduation. A student should have a minimum of each of the following: 8 credits in language arts (equivalent to 4 years); 6-8 credits in mathematics (equivalent to 3-4 years); 6 credits in science (equivalent to 3 years); 6 credits in social studies (equivalent to 3 years); 4 credits in foreign language (equivalent to 2 years); 2 credits in health, physical education, safety (equivalent to 1 year); and 4-6 credits from other courses offered (equivalent to 2-3 years). Regular admission requires that applicants have at least a 2.6 cumulative high school GPA on a 4.0 scale and a 880 SAT (Math and Critical Reading) or 18 ACT score. Applicants who do not meet the requirements for regular admission may request special consideration. A GPA of 2.6 is required. AP and CLEP credits are accepted. Important factors in the admissions decision are ability to finance college education, advanced placement or honors courses, parents or siblings attended your school, evidence of special talent, personality/intangible qualities, extracurricular activities record, recommendations by alumni, recommendations by school officials, leadership record, and geographical diversity. A 52-credit general education core includes 12 credit hours of humanities, 10 of math and science, 9 each of English and history or social studies, 6 of biblical literature, and 3 each of intercultural experience and phys ed. Foreign language courses are required for the B.A., computer literacy courses for the B.S. To graduate, students must complete at least 124 semester hours, including 40 to 60 in a major field of study, with a minimum GPA of 2.0 overall and 2.25 in the major. A thesis is required for the honors college. **Procedure:** Freshmen are admitted to all sessions. Entrance exams should be taken durning junior year, or early in their senior year. There are early decision, deferred admissions, and rolling admissions plans. Application deadlines are open. Applications are accepted on-line. **Transfer Students:** 106 transfer students enrolled in 2015-2016. In addition to standard admissions requirements, transfers must submit transcripts of all previous college work and be in good standing at their former school. 30 credits required for the bachelor's degree must be completed at IWU. **International Students:** There are 111 international students enrolled. The school actively recruits these students. They must take the TOEFL with a minimum score of 550 on the paper-based TOEFL (PBT) or 79 on the Internet-based version (iBT). They must also take the SAT or ACT, scoring 18.

ADMISSIONS: 74% of the 2016-2017 applicants were accepted. The SAT scores for the 2016-2017 freshman class were: Critical Reading-- 36% below 500, 40% between 500 and 599, 20% between 600 and 699, and 4% between 700 and 800. Math-- 36% below 500, 42% between 500 and 599, 19% between 600 and 699, and 3% between 700 and 800. Writing-- 44% below 500, 37% between 500 and 599, 17% between 600 and 699, and 2% between 700 and 800. The ACT scores were 7% between 12 and 17, 37% between 18 and 23, 45% between 24 and 29, and 11% above 30. 57% of the current freshmen were in the top fifth of their class; 85% were in the top two fifths. **Admissions Contact:** Tracy Curfman, Admissions Admistrative Assistant. Email: *admissions@indwes.edu* Web: *www.indwes.edu*

FINANCIAL AID: In 2016-2017, 99% of all full-time freshmen and 94% of continuing full-time students received some form of financial aid. 73% of all full-time freshmen and 63% of continuing full-time students received need-based aid. The average freshman award was $21,377. Need-based scholarships or need-based grants averaged $13,847; need-based self-help aid (loans and jobs) averaged $7,446; non-need-based athletic scholarships averaged $6,994; and other non-need-based awards and non-need-based scholarships averaged $5,185. 51% of undergraduate students work part-time. The average financial indebtedness of the 2016 graduate was $31,482. The college's own financial statement is required. The FAFSA code is 001822. The deadline for filing freshman financial aid applications for fall entry is March 1.

MANCHESTER UNIVERSITY C-2

www.manchester.edu

North Manchester, IN 46962	(260) 982-5055 (800) 852-3648
Fax: (260) 982-5239	Email: admitinfo@manchester.edu
Full-time: 600 men, 600 women	**Faculty:** IIB, +$
Part-time: 5 men, 10 women	**Ph.D.s:** n/av
Graduate: n/av	**Student/Faculty:** n/av
Year: 4-1-4, summer session	**Tuition:** $30,802
Room & Board: $9620	**Freshman Class:** n/av
SAT or ACT: required	**CEEB CODE:** 1440
Application Deadline: open	**COMPETITIVE**

Manchester University, formerly Manchester College, established in 1889, is a private liberal arts college affiliated with the Church of the Brethren offering undergraduate programs in accounting, business and economics, premedicine, education, psychology, the social sciences, and the humanities. The figures in the above capsule and in this profile are approximate. There are 3 undergraduate schools and 1 graduate school. In addition to regional accreditation, Manchester has baccalaureate program accreditation with CSWE and NCATE. The 124-acre campus is in a small town 35 miles west of Fort Wayne, Indiana. Including any residence halls, there are 44 buildings.

STUDENT LIFE: 90% of undergraduates are from Indiana. Others are from 21 states, 20 foreign countries, and Canada. 99% are from public schools. 89% are White; 4% Foreign; 3% African American; 3% Hispanic; 1% Asian American. 36% are Protestant; 15% Catholic. **Female To Male Ratio:** 1.0:1. The average age of freshmen is 18; all undergraduates, 20. 30% do not continue beyond their first year; 55% remain to graduate. **Housing:** 995 students can be accommodated in college housing, which includes single-sex and coed dorms, on-campus apartments, off-campus apartments, and married student housing. In addition, there are special-interest houses. The Intercultural Center is a special interest facility providing social, cultural, and educational opportunities to students. Theme units for students interested in science, health, and international issues are located within the residence hall system. On-campus housing is guaranteed for all 4 years. 79% of students live on campus; of those, 50% remain on campus on weekends. Alcohol is not permitted. All students may keep cars.

FACULTY/CLASSROOMS: 53% of faculty are male; 47% are female. All teach undergraduates, 20% do research, and 20% do both. No introductory courses are taught by graduate students. The average class size in an introductory lecture is 30; in a laboratory is 15; and in a regular course is 20.

PROGRAMS OF STUDY: Manchester confers B.A. and B.S. degrees. Associate degrees are also awarded. Bachelor's degrees are awarded in AGRICULTURE (environmental studies), BIOLOGICAL SCIENCE (biochemistry and biology/biological science), BUSINESS (accounting, banking and finance, and business administration and management), COMMUNICATIONS AND THE ARTS (art, communications, English, French, German, music, and Spanish), COMPUTER AND PHYSICAL SCIENCE (chemistry, computer science, mathematics, and physics), EDUCATION (art education, elementary education, health education, middle school education, and secondary education), ENGINEERING AND ENVIRONMENTAL DESIGN (engineering), HEALTH PROFESSIONS (medical laboratory technology), SOCIAL SCIENCE (economics, history, interdisciplinary studies, peace studies, philosophy, political science/government, prelaw, psychology, religion, social work, and sociology). Education, accounting, and biology-chemistry are the strongest academically. Education, accounting, and communication studies have the largest enrollments.

ACTIVITIES: There are no fraternities or sororities. There are 53 groups on campus, including band, cheerleading, choir, chorale, chorus, computers, dance, drama, environmental, ethnic, honors, international, jazz band, LGBT, literary magazine, musical theater, newspaper, opera, orchestra, pep band, photography, political, professional, radio and TV, religious, social, social service, student government, symphony, and yearbook. Popular campus events include Parents Weekend, Sibling Weekend, International Fair, and May Day Weekend. **Sports:** There are 9 intercollegiate sports for men and 8 for women, and 13 intramural sports for men and 12 for women. Facilities include an 1800-seat gym, racquetball courts, a fitness center, tennis courts, cross-country and an all-weather track, and athletic fields for baseball, softball, soccer, and football. **Graduates:** From July 1, 2015 to June 30, 2016, 198 bachelor's degrees were awarded. The most popular majors were business (27%), education (17%), and health sciences (12%). 25 companies recruited on campus in 2015-2016. In an average class, 42% graduate in 4 years or less, 52% graduate in 5 years or less, and 52% graduate in 6 years or less. Of the 2015 graduating class, 18% were enrolled in graduate school within 6 months of graduation, and 75% were employed.

SERVICES: Counseling and information services are available, as is tutoring in every subject. There is a reader service for the blind. There is also a learning center with an academic assistance program, a seminar to enhance study and learning skills, and time project management. **Library/Resources:** The library contains 174,078 volumes, 23,014 microform items, and 5,258 audio/video tapes/CDs/DVDs, and subscribes to 973 periodicals including electronic. Computerized library services include interlibrary loans, database searching, and Internet access. Special learning facilities include an art gallery, planetarium, radio station, and 100-acre nature preserve. **Physically Challenged Students:** 50% of the campus is accessible. Facilities include wheelchair ramps, elevators, special parking, specially equipped restrooms, special class scheduling, lowered drinking fountains, lowered telephones, and special housing. **Special:** The college offers cooperative programs in nursing and engineering science. The Brethren Colleges Abroad program allows study abroad in 13 countries, including Ecuador, China, England, France, Germany, Ireland, Japan, Mexico, and Spain. Manchester also offers B.A.-B.S. degrees, internships, work-study programs, dual majors, student-designed majors, a 3-2 engineering program, pass/fail options, and nondegree study. Other special academic features include independent study, required study in non-Western culture, and interdisciplinary programs in both peace studies and environmental studies. A January interterm permits internships, travel abroad, and concentrated classes on campus. There are 6 national honor societies, a freshman honors program, and 5 departmental honors programs. **Visiting:** There are regularly scheduled orientations for prospective students, include meetings about financial aid, meetings with faculty and admissions, and campus tours. Visitors may also eat meals on campus, sit in on classes, and meet with current students. There are guides for informal visits, visitors may sit in on classes, and stay overnight. To schedule a visit, contact the Campus Visit Coordinator. **Campus Safety and Security:** Measures include 24-hour foot and vehicle patrol, emergency notification system, and security escort services. There are emergency telephones and lighted pathways/sidewalks.

REQUIREMENTS: The SAT or ACT is required. Applicants must have a minimum SAT I composite of 900, with 450 on each part, or an ACT composite of 18. Each application is reviewed on an individual basis. The GED is accepted. For high school students, the college recommends completion of 28 academic credits, based on 4 years each of English, math, and science, and 2 years each of foreign language, history, and social studies. A GPA of 2.3 is required. AP and CLEP credits are accepted. Important factors in the admissions decision are advanced placement or honors courses, leadership record, and recommendations by school officials. Students must complete a core curriculum, including requirements in humanities, social sciences, and natural sciences, as well as specific courses in English composition, public communication, Western civilization, and physical fitness. In order to graduate, students must complete a minimum of 128 semester hours, including 26 to 52 hours in a major field, with a GPA of at least 2,0 (2.5 for the education and athletic training majors). A comprehensive exam in the major is also required. A thesis for honors students is optional. **Procedure:** Freshmen are admitted to all sessions. Entrance exams should be taken by November of the senior year. There are deferred admissions and rolling admissions plans. Application deadlines are open. Application fee is $20. Notification is sent on a rolling basis. Applications are accepted on-line. **Transfer Students:** 29 transfer students enrolled in 2015-2016. Transfer students must present a minimum GPA of 2.0 in all previous college work. 96 of 128 credits required for the bachelor's degree must be completed at Manchester. **International Students:** There are 41 international students enrolled. The school actively recruits these students. They must take the TOEFL with a minimum score of 550 on the paper-based TOEFL (PBT).

Admissions Contact: Adam Hohman, Associate Director of Admissions. Email: *admitinfo@manchester.edu* Web: *www.manchester.edu*

FINANCIAL AID: In 2016-2017, 100% of all full-time freshmen and 96% of continuing full-time students received some form of financial aid. The average freshman award was $18,110.. 40% of undergraduate students work part-time. The average financial indebtedness of the 2016 graduate was $16,333. The FAFSA code is 001820. The deadline for filing freshman financial aid applications for fall entry is rolling.

MARIAN UNIVERSITY C-3

www.marian.edu

Indianapolis, IN 46222	**(317) 955-6306** **(800) 772-7264**
Fax: (317) 955-6401	**Email: lbrames@marian.edu**
Full-time: 735 men, 1029 women	**Faculty:** 112
Part-time: 103 men, 280 women	**Ph.D.s:** 66%
Graduate: 462 men, 556 women	**Student/Faculty:** 16 to 1
Year: semesters, summer session	**Tuition:** $31,500
Room & Board: $9720	**Freshman Class:** 2072 applied, 1148 accepted, 293 enrolled
SAT CR/M/W: 530/520/520 **ACT:** 22	**CEEB CODE:** 1442
Application Deadline: August 1	**COMPETITIVE**

Marian University is a private institution founded in 1851 by the Sisters of St. Francis and is affiliated with the Roman Catholic Church. The college offers undergraduate programs and graduate programs, as well as a doctorate in osteopathic medicine. There are 4 undergraduate schools and 5 graduate schools. In addition to regional accreditation, Marian has baccalaureate program accreditation with AHEA, NCATE, NLN, CCNE, IACBE, and COCA. The 114-acre campus is in a suburban area 6 miles from downtown Indianapolis. Including any residence halls, there are 21 buildings.

STUDENT LIFE: 79% of undergraduates are from Indiana. Others are from 34 states, 18 foreign countries, and Canada. 82% are from public schools. 72% are White; 5% Hispanic; 5% race unknown; 3% two or more races; 2% Asian American; 12% African American; 1% Foreign. 50% are Buddhism, Islam, Hinduism, Eastern Orthodox, and unknown; 38% Catholic; 11% Protestant. **Female To Male Ratio:** 1.4:1. The average age of freshmen is 19; all undergraduates, 24. 23% do not continue beyond their first year; 69% remain to graduate. **Housing:** 878 students can be accommodated in college housing, which includes coed dorms and on-campus apartments. In addition, there are special-interest houses, The Dorothy Day House for Peace and Justice is a special-interest house for those interested in living in community working for peace and justice. On-campus housing is guaranteed for all 4 years. 63% of students commute. Alcohol is not permitted. All students may keep cars.

FACULTY/CLASSROOMS: 42% of faculty are male; 58% are female. 74% teach undergraduates. No introductory courses are taught by graduate students. The average class size in an introductory lecture is 19; in a laboratory is 15; and in a regular course is 18.

PROGRAMS OF STUDY: Marian confers B.A., B.S., and B.S.N. degrees. Associate, master's, and doctoral degrees are also awarded. Bachelor's degrees are awarded in BIOLOGICAL SCIENCE (biology/biological science), BUSINESS (accounting, business administration and management, business intelligence and analytics, finance, management science, marketing, and sports management), COMMUNICATIONS AND THE ARTS (communications, English, instrumental performance, instrumental music education, music, music ministry, Spanish, studio art, vocal performance, and vocal music education), COMPUTER AND PHYSICAL SCIENCE (chemistry, clinical laboratory science, and mathematics), EDUCATION (education, educational studies, elementary education, health and physical education, secondary education, and special education), HEALTH PROFESSIONS (exercise science, health services administration, nursing, and public health), SOCIAL SCIENCE (history, pastoral studies, philosophy, political science/government, psychology, religious education, religious studies, sociology, and theology). Accounting, nursing, and education are the strongest academically. Nursing, management, and biology have the largest enrollments.

ACTIVITIES: There are no fraternities or sororities. There are 46 groups on campus, including art, band, cheerleading, choir, chorale, chorus, computers, dance, debate, departmental clubs, drama, drill team, ethnic, forensics, honors, international, jazz band, literary magazine, marching band, musical theater, newspaper, pep band, photography, political, professional, religious, social, social service, student government, and yearbook. Popular campus events include Homecoming, Fall and Spring Formals, and monthly Coffeehouse and Open Mic Series. **Sports:** There are 12 intercollegiate sports for men and 12 for women, and 6 intramural sports for men and 6 for women. Facilities include varsity and intramural gyms, a stadium, Velodrome and cycling center, racquetball courts, a fitness center, a weight-training room, and a phys ed assessment lab. **Graduates:** From July 1, 2015 to June 30, 2016, 520 bachelor's degrees were awarded. The most popular majors were nursing (50%), business/management/marketing/accounting/finance (24%), and biology (5%). 68 companies recruited on campus in 2015-2016. In an average class, 1% graduate in 3 years or less, 28% graduate in 4 years or less, 52% graduate in 5 years or less, and 53% graduate in 6 years or less. Of the 2015 graduating class, 17% were enrolled in graduate school within 6 months of graduation, and 69% were employed.

SERVICES: Counseling and information services are available, as is tutoring in most subjects. There is a reader service for the blind, and remedial math, reading, and writing. Study skills training and peer tutoring are available. **Library/Resources:** The library contains 79,801 volumes, 150 microform items, 3,860 audio/video tapes/CDs/DVDs, and subscribes to 250,000 periodicals including electronic. Computerized library services include interlibrary loans, database searching, Internet access, and Wi-Fi capability. Special learning facilities include an art gallery, and the 55-acre Wetlands Ecology Laboratory. **Physically Challenged Students:** 95% of the campus is accessible. Facilities include wheelchair ramps, elevators, special parking, specially equipped restrooms, special class scheduling, and lowered drinking fountains. **Special:** Co-op programs in accounting, finance, business administration, chemistry, management information systems, and sociology and cross-registration through the Consortium for Urban Education are offered. A dual-degree program in math and computer science, a 3-2 engineering degree, and accelerated degrees in nursing and business administration are also offered. Internships, study abroad, work-study, independent study, dual and student-designed majors, and pass/fail options are available. There are 11 national honor societies and a freshman honors program. **Visiting:** There are regularly scheduled orientations for prospective students, including a campus tour, visits with faculty and coaches, and financial aid information. There are guides for informal visits, visitors may sit in on classes, and stay overnight. To schedule a visit, contact Matt Cramer at (317 955-6300. **Campus Safety and Security:** Measures include 24-hour foot and vehicle patrol, emergency notification system, self-defense education, and security escort services. There are shuttle buses, emergency telephones, lighted pathways/sidewalks, and controlled access to dorms/residences.

REQUIREMENTS: The SAT or ACT is required. The ACT Optional Writing test is also required. Applicants must be graduates of an accredited secondary school or have a GED. Marian requires 20 academic units, including 4 units in English, 2 units in math, of which algebra and geometry are recommended, and 2 units each in a lab science and social studies. AP and CLEP credits are accepted. Important factors in the admissions decision are recommendations by school officials, recommendations by alumni, and leadership record. To graduate, students must complete 128 semester hours, including 30 to 40 in the major, with a minimum GPA of 2.0 overall and in the major. General education requirements include 14 semester hours in cultural awareness, 10 to 12 in scientific and quantitative reasoning, 9 to 17 in written and oral communication and foreign language, 9 in philosophical and theological reasoning, and 9 to 15 in individual and social understanding. **Procedure:** Freshmen are admitted to all sessions. Entrance exams should be taken at the end of the junior year or the beginning of the senior year. There are deferred admissions and rolling admissions plans. Applications should be filed by August 1 for fall entry; December 10 for spring entry; and April 15 for summer entry, along with a $35 fee. Notification is sent on a rolling basis. Applications are accepted on-line. Application fees are waived if application is completed on-line. **Transfer Students:** 94 transfer students enrolled in 2015-2016. In addition to meeting standard admissions requirements, applicants must submit transcripts of all college work and be in good standing at their former school. Students transferring must have a 2.0 GPA. 30 of 128 credits required for the bachelor's degree must be completed at Marian. **International Students:** There are 24 international students enrolled. The school actively recruits these students. They must take the TOEFL with a minimum score of 550 on the paper-based TOEFL (PBT) or 80 on the Internet-based version (iBT). They must also take the SAT or ACT.

ADMISSIONS: 55% of the 2016-2017 applicants were accepted. The SAT scores for the 2016-2017 freshman class were: Critical Reading-- 46% below 500, 39% between 500 and 599, 12% between 600 and 699, and 3% between 700 and 800. Math-- 40% below 500, 46% between 500 and 599, 13% between 600 and 699, and 1% between 700 and 800. Writing-- 59% below 500, 33% between 500 and 599, 7% between 600 and 699, and 1% between 700 and 800. The ACT scores were 10% between 12 and 17, 49% between 18 and 23, 34% between 24 and 29, and 7% above 30. 34% of the current freshmen were in the top fifth of their class; 65% were in the top two fifths. 5 freshmen graduated first in their class. **Admissions Contact:** Luann Brames, Director of Freshman Admissions. Email: *lbrames@marian.edu* Web: *www.marian.edu*

FINANCIAL AID: 11% of undergraduate students work part-time. Average annual earnings from campus work are $1300. The college's own financial statement is required. The FAFSA code is 001821. The priority date for freshman financial aid applications for fall entry is March 10.

MARTIN UNIVERSITY *(The complete profile is made available exclusively on our website, www.barronspac.com)*

OAKLAND CITY UNIVERSITY *(The complete profile is made available exclusively on our website, www.barronspac.com)*

PURDUE UNIVERSITY/NORTHWEST B-1

Purdue University Calumet & Purdue University North Central
www.pnw.edu

Hammond, IN 46323	**(219) 989-2213** **(800) HI PURDUE**
Fax: (219) 989-2775	**Email: admissions@pnw.edu**
Full-time: 3236 men, 3384 women	**Faculty:** n/av
Part-time: 2635 men, 5130 women	**Ph.D.s:** n/av
Graduate: 369 men, 532 women	**Student/Faculty:** n/av
Year: semesters, summer session	**Tuition:** $7478 ($16,895)
Room & Board: $7560	**Freshman Class:** n/av
SAT: required **ACT:** 21	**CEEB CODE:** 1638
Application Deadline: August 1	**COMPETITIVE**

Part of the internationally respected Purdue University system, Purdue University Northwest offers world-class educational opportunities at an excellent value on two culturally diverse, student-centered campuses located in Northwest Indiana and in easy driving distance of Chicago, Illinois. Purdue Northwest is the fifth-largest public university in Indiana, offering nearly 70 programs at the baccalaureate, master's, and doctoral levels. The institution is distinguished by opportunities for experiential learning, undergraduate research, and one-to-one relationships between students and faculty members. There are 6 undergraduate schools and 2 graduate schools. In addition to regional accreditation, PUN has baccalaureate program accreditation with AACSB, ABET, NCATE, NLN, ACEN, ATMAE, and COAMFTE. The 441-acre campus is in an urban area. Hammond campus is 29 miles southeast of Chicago. Westville campus is 12 miles south of Michigan City. Including any residence halls, there are 29 buildings.

STUDENT LIFE: 82% of undergraduates are from Indiana. Others are from 30 states, 49 foreign countries, and Canada. 60% are White; 15% Hispanic; 8% African American; 6% race unknown; 5% Foreign; 2% Asian American; 2% two or more races; 1% American Indian/Alaska Native. **Female To Male Ratio:** 1.4:1. The average age of freshmen is 21; all undergraduates, 26. **Housing:** 749 students can be accommodated in college housing, which includes coed on-campus apartments. On-campus housing is guaranteed for all 4 years and is available on a first-come, first-served basis. Alcohol is not permitted. All students may keep cars.

FACULTY/CLASSROOMS: 46% of faculty are male; 54% are female. No introductory courses are taught by graduate students.

PROGRAMS OF STUDY: PUN confers B.A., B.A.B., B.L.S., B.S., B.S.A., B.S.B., B.S.C.E., B.S.CH., B.S.CMP.E., B.S.E., B.S.E.E., B.S.M.E. and B.S.N. degrees. Associate, master's, and doctoral degrees are also awarded. Bachelor's degrees are awarded in BIOLOGICAL SCIENCE (biology ecology and field biology, biology/biological science, biotechnology, ecology, forensic science, and microbiology), BUSINESS (accounting, banking and finance, business economics, finance, hotel/motel and restaurant management, human resources, human resources/organizational mgmt, leadership, management, marketing/retailing/merchandising, and organizational leadership and management), COMMUNICATIONS AND THE ARTS (advertising, broadcasting, communications, English, English literature, English Writing, French, German, journalism, public relations, Spanish, and visual communication), COMPUTER AND PHYSICAL SCIENCE (chemistry, computer programming, computer science, information sciences and systems, mathematics, and physics), EDUCATION (early childhood education, elementary education, English education, foreign languages education, mathematics education, science education, secondary education, and social studies education), ENGINEERING AND ENVIRONMENTAL DESIGN (civil engineering, computer engineering, computer graphics, computer technology, construction technology, electrical/electronics engineering, electrical/electronics engineering technology, engineering, engineering mechanics, engineering physics, engineering technology, environmental science, industrial engineering technology, materials science, mechanical engineering, mechanical engineering technology, mechatronics engineering, and survey and mapping technology), HEALTH PROFESSIONS (environmental health science, health science, medical laboratory technology, nursing, and physical therapy), SOCIAL SCIENCE (behavioral science, criminal justice, early childhood studies, history, liberal arts/general studies, philosophy, political science/

government, psychology, social work, and sociology). Nursing and engineering are the strongest academically. Nursing, business, and psychology have the largest enrollments.

ACTIVITIES: 1% of women belong to 1 local sorority. There are 102 groups on campus, including cheerleading, environmental, honors, international, LGBT, newspaper, pep band, professional, radio and TV, religious, social, social service, and student government. Popular campus events include Welcome Week (Fall & Spring), Haunted Hall - Halloween Event, Homecoming, and Alternative Spring Break Program. **Sports:** There are 6 intercollegiate sports for men and 7 for women, and 42 intramural sports for men and 42 for women. Facilities include a 1500-seat gym, racquetball courts, an outdoor volleyball court, a running track, a weight room, and a total fitness center. **Graduates:** From July 1, 2015 to June 30, 2016, 1444 bachelor's degrees were awarded. The most popular majors were nursing (41%), managment (6%), and communication (4%).

SERVICES: Counseling and information services are available, as is tutoring in some subjects. **Library/Resources:** The 2 libraries contain 269,648 volumes, 764,621 microform items, and 998 audio/video tapes/CDs/DVDs, and subscribe to 228 periodicals including electronic. Computerized library services include interlibrary loans, database searching, and Internet access. Special learning facilities include an art gallery, radio station, a computer education building, and an educational media laboratory. **Physically Challenged Students:** All of the campus is accessible. Facilities include wheelchair ramps, elevators, special parking, specially equipped restrooms, special class scheduling, lowered drinking fountains, and lowered telephones. **Special:** Purdue Northwest offers cross-registration in philosophy, programs that include trips to Cuba, South Korea, Canada, and Spain among other countries, credit for military experience, as well as nondegree study and pass/fail options. Some cooperative programs, internships, and work-study programs are also available. There are 2 national honor societies and a freshman honors program. **Visiting:** There are regularly scheduled orientations for prospective students. There are guides for informal visits and visitors may sit in on classes. To schedule a visit, contact the Office of Admissions and Recruitment. **Campus Safety and Security:** Measures include 24-hour foot and vehicle patrol, emergency notification system, self-defense education, and security escort services. There are shuttle buses, emergency telephones, lighted pathways/sidewalks, and controlled access to dorms/residences.

REQUIREMENTS: The SAT or ACT test is required. Applicants must be graduates of an accredited secondary school. The GED is accepted. 33 Carnegie units are required for admission. Required courses vary, depending on the curriculum, and include 3 or 4 years of English, 2 or 3 years of math, 2 years of foreign language (for some majors), and 1 year of history or social studies. AP and CLEP credits are accepted. Graduation requirements vary depending on the program. The total number of credit hours required for a degree varies from 126 to 136, with 24 to 73 in the major. All students must take English composition and 36 hours of general education courses and maintain a C average. **Procedure:** Freshmen are admitted fall, spring, and summer. Entrance exams should be taken during their Junior and/or Senior year, as early as possible. There is a rolling admissions plan. Applications should be filed by August 1 for fall entry; December 20 for spring entry; and June 1 for summer entry, along with a $25 fee. Applications are accepted online. Application fees are waived if application is completed on-line. **Transfer Students:** Must have completed at least 12 college-level credits with a minimum cumulative GPA of 2.0 for admission to university. Some programs have higher requirements. 32 of 120 credits required for the bachelor's degree must be completed at PUN. **International Students:** There are 426 international students enrolled. The school actively recruits these students. They must take the TOEFL with a minimum score of 550 on the paper-based TOEFL (PBT) or 79 on the Internet-based version (iBT). International students can take the SAT in place of the TOEFL.

ADMISSIONS: The SAT scores for the 2016-2017 freshman class were: Critical Reading-- 61% below 500, 32% between 500 and 599, and 7% between 600 and 699. Math-- 63% below 500, 30% between 500 and 599, 6% between 600 and 699, and 1% between 700 and 800. Writing-- 71% below 500, 24% between 500 and 599, and 4% between 600 and 699. The ACT scores were 24% between 12 and 17, 50% between 18 and 23, 23% between 24 and 29, and 2% above 30. 22% of the current freshmen were in the top fifth of their class; 32% were in the top two fifths. **Admissions Contact:** Jeffrey J Lochowicz, Executive Director, Undergrad Admissions. Email: *admissions@pnw.edu* Web: *http:/www.pnw.edu/admissions/*

FINANCIAL AID: PUN is a member of CSS. The FAFSA code is 001827. The priority date for freshman financial aid applications for fall entry is March 10. The deadline for filing freshman financial aid applications for fall entry is June 30.

PURDUE UNIVERSITY/WEST LAFAYETTE B-3

www.purdue.edu

West Lafayette, IN 47907 **(765) 494-1776**

Fax: (765) 494-0544
Full-time: 16,558 men, 12,168 women
Part-time: 755 men, 562 women
Graduate: 5903 men, 4505 women
Year: semesters, summer session
Room & Board: $10,030

SAT CR/M/W: 570/680/570 **ACT:** 29
Application Deadline: February 1

Email: admissions@purdue.edu
Faculty: n/av
Ph.D.s: 97%
Student/Faculty: 12 to 1
Tuition: $10,002 ($28,804)
Freshman Class: 48776 applied, 27227 accepted, 7243 enrolled
CEEB CODE: 1631
MOST COMPETITIVE

Purdue University/West Lafayette, founded in 1869, is a publicly supported institution offering degree programs with an emphasis on engineering, business, communications, arts, social sciences, allied health, and technology. There are 12 undergraduate schools and 1 graduate school. In addition to regional accreditation, Purdue University has baccalaureate program accreditation with AACSB, ABET, ACCE, ACPE, ADA, ASLA, FIDER, NASM, NCATE, NLN, SAF, ACS, APA, AVMA, CACREP, and CCNE. The 2595-acre campus is in a suburban area 65 miles northwest of Indianapolis. Including any residence halls, there are 376 buildings.

STUDENT LIFE: 53% of undergraduates are from Indiana. Others are from 50 states, 122 foreign countries, and Canada. 7% are Asian American; 63% White; 5% Hispanic; 3% African American; 3% race unknown; 2% two or more races; 17% Foreign. **Male To Female Ratio:** 1.3:1. The average age of freshmen is 18; all undergraduates, 20. 8% do not continue beyond their first year; 77% remain to graduate. **Housing:** 11284 students can be accommodated in college housing, which includes single-sex and coed dorms, on-campus apartments, and married student housing. In addition, there are honors houses, fraternity houses, sorority houses, and living learning communities. On-campus housing is guaranteed for all 4 years. 62% of students commute. Alcohol is not permitted. Upperclassmen may keep cars.

FACULTY/CLASSROOMS: 65% of faculty are male; 35% are female. No introductory courses are taught by graduate students. The average class size in an introductory lecture is 45; in a laboratory is 24; and in a regular course is 39.

PROGRAMS OF STUDY: Purdue University confers B.A., B.F.A., B.S., B.S.A.A.E., B.S.A.G.E., B.S.B.E., B.S.B.M.E., B.S.C.E., B.S.C.H., B.S.C.H.E., B.S.C.M.P.E., B.S.C.N.E., B.S.E., B.S.E.E., B.S.E.E.E., B.S.E.H., B.S.F.O.R., B.S.I.E., B.S.I.M., B.S.L.A., B.S.M.E., B.S.M.S.E., B.S.N., and B.S.N.E., degrees. Associate, master's, and doctoral degrees are also awarded. Bachelor's degrees are awarded in AGRICULTURE (agricultural business management, agricultural communications, agricultural economics, agriculture, agronomy, animal science, fishing and fisheries, forestry and related sciences, horticulture, natural resource management, plant protection (pest management), plant science, soil science, and wood science), BIOLOGICAL SCIENCE (biochemistry, biology/biological science, cell biology, ecology, entomology, genetics, microbiology, molecular biology, nutrition, plant genetics, plant physiology, and wildlife biology), BUSINESS (accounting, banking and finance, entrepreneurial studies, fashion merchandising, hospitality management services, human resources, marketing management, marketing/retailing/merchandising, organizational leadership and management, retailing, and tourism), COMMUNICATIONS AND THE ARTS (advertising, apparel design, art history and appreciation, audio technology, broadcasting, classics, communications, comparative literature, creative writing, dramatic arts, English, film arts, fine arts, French, German, graphic design, industrial design, Japanese, journalism, Latin, Latin, linguistics, photography, public relations, Russian, Spanish, and visual and performing arts), COMPUTER AND PHYSICAL SCIENCE (actuarial science, applied mathematics, applied physics, atmospheric sciences and meteorology, chemistry, computer science, earth science, geology, information sciences and systems, mathematics, physics, radiological technology, science, software engineering, and statistics), EDUCATION (agricultural education, art education, athletic training, early childhood education, education, elementary education, English education, foreign languages education, health education, mathematics education, science education, secondary education, social studies education, special education, and technical education), ENGINEERING AND ENVIRONMENTAL DESIGN (aeronautical engineering, aeronautical technology, agricultural engineering, air traffic control, airline piloting and navigation, aviation administration/management, aviation computer technology, bioengineering, biomedical engineering, chemical engineering, chemical engineering technology, civil engineering, computational sciences, computer engineering, computer graphics, computer technology, construction engineering, construction management, construction technology, electrical/electronics engineering, electrical/electronics engineering technology, engineering management, environmental science, food services technology, industrial administration/management, industrial engineering, industrial engineering technology, interior design, landscape architecture/design, manufacturing engineering, manufacturing technology, materials science, mechanical engineering, mechanical engineering technology, nuclear engineering, occupational safety and health, and surveying engineering), HEALTH PROFESSIONS (clinical science, environmental health science, exercise science, health science, medical laboratory technology, nursing, pharmaceutical science, radiological science, and speech pathology/audiology), SOCIAL SCIENCE (African American studies, anthropology, Asian/American studies, Asian/Oriental studies, behavioral science, criminal justice, dietetics, economics, family and community services, family/consumer studies, fashion design and technology, food production/management/services, food science, French studies, history, Italian studies, Japanese studies, Judaic studies, liberal arts/general studies, medieval studies, philosophy, physical fitness/movement, political science/government, psychology, religion, Russian and Slavic studies, social studies, social work, sociology, Spanish studies, and women's studies). Engineering, actuarial science, and industrial management are the strongest academically. Management, preengineering, and mechanical engineering have the largest enrollments.

ACTIVITIES: 24% of men belong to 5 local and 50 national fraternities; 26% of women belong to 7 local and 33 national sororities. There are 983 groups on campus, including band, cheerleading, chess, choir, chorale, chorus, computers, dance, debate, drama, ethnic, film, forensics, honors, international, jazz band, LGBT, literary magazine, marching band, newspaper, orchestra, pep band, photography, political, professional, radio and TV, religious, social, social service, student government, and symphony. Popular campus events include Grand Prix Race, Old Masters, Gala week, Mortar Board Leadership Conference, Purdue University Dance Marathon, Martin Luther King Day of Service, Industrial Round Table, Big Man on Campus, Diwali, Relay for Life, B-Involved Fair, and Starry Night. **Sports:** There are 10 intercollegiate sports for men and 10 for women, and 40 intramural sports for men and 40 for women. Facilities include Athletic - A 56,000-seat football stadium, 14,000-seat basketball arena, 2,300-seat volleyball and wrestling gymnasium, indoor football practice facility, a field house, track & field complex, two Pete Dye-designed golf courses, Olympic-size competition pool and diving well, baseball, softball and soccer stadiums. Recreational- recreational sports gymnasiums, recreational turf facility, fitness and recreational pools, weight rooms/cardio equipment rooms, outdoor intramural playing fields, 6 outdoor tennis courts, 4 outdoor sand volleyball courts, 2 outdoor basketball courts, 18-hole disc golf, climbing areas, trap and skeet range, and crew boathouse. **Graduates:** From July 1, 2015 to June 30, 2016, 6834 bachelor's degrees were awarded. The most popular majors were management (6%), mechanical engineering (5%), and accounting (3%). 1345 companies recruited on campus in 2015-2016. In an average class, 1% graduate in 3 years or less, 49% graduate in 4 years or less, 71% graduate in 5 years or less, and 74% graduate in 6 years or less. Of the 2015 graduating class, 63% were employed within 6 months of graduation.

SERVICES: Counseling and information services are available, as is tutoring in every subject. There is a reader service for the blind, and remedial math, reading, and writing. **Library/Resources:** The 13 libraries contain 3.8 million volumes, 2.7 million microform items, and 10,182 audio/video tapes/CDs/DVDs, and subscribe to 59,223 periodicals including electronic. Computerized library services include interlibrary loans, database searching, Internet access, and Wi-Fi capability. Special learning facilities include an art gallery and radio station. **Physically Challenged Students:** 90% of the campus is accessible. Facilities include wheelchair ramps, elevators, special parking, specially equipped restrooms, special class scheduling, lowered drinking fountains, lowered telephones, and special housing. Lab with assistive technology and special computers available. **Special:** Cooperative programs are available in engineering, technology, agriculture, science, and health and human sciences. Cross-registration with Purdue's regional campuses, numerous internships, study abroad in 60+ countries, dual majors, student-designed majors, nondegree study, and pass/fail options are also offered. There are 33 national honor societies, Phi Beta Kappa, a freshman honors program, and 10 departmental honors programs. **Visiting:** There are regularly scheduled orientations for prospective students, including fall and spring preview days, which consist of admission, financial aid, housing, and school sessions, a campus tour, and dormitory visits. The Summer Visit Program consists of a counselors' orientation and campus and residence hall visits. There are guides for informal visits and visitors may sit in on classes. To schedule a visit, contact the Office of Admissions. **Campus Safety and Security:** Measures include 24-hour foot and vehicle patrol, emergency notification system, self-defense education, and security escort services. There are shuttle buses, emergency telephones, lighted pathways/sidewalks, and public transportation routes throughout campus.

REQUIREMENTS: The SAT or ACT is required. The ACT Optional Writing test is also required. Purdue requires that most students have 8 semesters of English, 8 semesters of math, 6 semesters of lab sciences-(for engineering, nursing, pharmacy, and veterinary technology, 2 semesters must be chemistry; nursing also requires 2 semesters of biology), 6 semesters of social studies, and 4 semesters of foreign language. The GED is also accepted. AP and CLEP credits are accepted. Important factors in the admissions decision are advanced placement or honors courses, extracurricular activities record, and geographical diversity. To graduate, students must be enrolled for at least 2 semesters and complete 32 semester hours of course- work, complete approximately 128 hours, and earn a minimum GPA of 2.0. In most majors, students must take courses in English, math, science, computer science, and social sciences. **Procedure:** Freshmen are admitted to all sessions. Entrance exams should be taken at the end of the junior year. There is a rolling admissions plan. Applications should be filed by February 1 for fall entry, along with a $60 fee. Applications are accepted on-line. **Transfer Students:** 676 transfer students enrolled in 2015-2016. Requirements for transfer students vary greatly depending on each students unique situation, including academic background and intended major. For this reason, we encourage prospective students to visit our website and read in depth about the requirements that pertain to your specific situation. 32 of 120 credits required for the bachelor's degree must be completed at Purdue University. **International Students:** There are 4904 international students enrolled. The school actively recruits these students. They must take the TOEFL with a minimum score of 570 on the paper-based TOEFL (PBT) or 88 on the Internet-based version (iBT), or take the IELTS, SAT, or the ACT.

ADMISSIONS: 56% of the 2016-2017 applicants were accepted. The SAT scores for the 2016-2017 freshman class were: Critical Reading-- 16% below 500, 44% between 500 and 599, 32% between 600 and 699, and 9% between 700 and 800. Math-- 7% below 500, 27% between 500 and 599, 37% between 600 and 699, and 28% between 700 and 800. Writing-- 16% below 500, 43% between 500 and 599, 33% between 600 and 699, and 7% between 700 and 800. The ACT scores were 8% below 12, 16% between 12 and 17, 23% between 18 and 23, 13% between 24 and 29, and 41% above 30. 70% of the current freshmen were in the top fifth of their class; 94% were in the top two fifths. 101 freshmen graduated first in their class. **Admissions Contact:** Pamela Horne, Dean of Admissions/Assistant VP for Enrollment. Email: *admissions@purdue.edu* Web: *www.purdue.edu*

FINANCIAL AID: In 2016-2017, 73% of all full-time freshmen and 74% of continuing full-time students received some form of financial aid. 48% of all full-time freshmen and 45% of continuing full-time students received need-based aid. The average freshman award was $10,723. Need-based scholarships or need-based grants averaged $4,145; need-based self-help aid (loans and jobs) averaged $2,651; non-need-based athletic scholarships averaged $303; and other non-need-based awards and non-need-based scholarships averaged $3,624. 31% of undergraduate students work part-time. Average annual earnings from campus work are $1989. The average financial indebtedness of the 2016 graduate was $27,530. The priority date for freshman financial aid applications for fall entry is March 1. The deadline for filing freshman financial aid applications for fall entry is March 1.

ROSE-HULMAN INSTITUTE OF TECHNOLOGY B-4

www.rose-hulman.edu

Terre Haute, IN 47803 (812) 877-8892
(800) 248-7448
Fax: (812) 877-8941 Email: admissions@rose-hulman.edu

Full-time: 1633 men, 548 women	**Faculty:** 184; IIB, +$
Part-time: 14 men, 7 women	**Ph.D.s:** 99%
Graduate: 61 men, 15 women	**Student/Faculty:** 12 to 1
Year: quarters, summer session	**Tuition:** $44,010
Room & Board: $13,293	**Freshman Class:** 4241 applied, 2590 accepted, 543 enrolled
SAT CR/M/W: 620/680/600 **ACT:** 30	**CEEB CODE:** 1668
Application Deadline: February 1	**MOST COMPETITIVE**

Rose-Hulman Institute of Technology, founded in 1874, is a private college emphasizing engineering, science, and math. The figures given in the above capsule and in this profile are approximate. There is 1 undergraduate school. In addition to regional accreditation, Rose-Hulman has baccalaureate program accreditation with ABET. The 200-acre campus is in a suburban area on the east side of Terre Haute. Including any residence halls, there are 37 buildings.

STUDENT LIFE: 68% of undergraduates are from out of state, mostly the Midwest. Students are from 46 states, and 12 foreign countries. 71% are White; 5% Asian American; 4% Hispanic; 4% two or more races; 2% African American; 13% Foreign. **Male To Female Ratio:** 3.0:1. The average age of freshmen is 18; all undergraduates, 20. 6% do not continue beyond their first year; 94% remain to graduate. **Housing:** 1267 students can be accommodated in college housing, which includes single-sex and coed dorms and on-campus apartments. In addition, there are fraternity houses, sorority houses, and sophomore residence hall. On-campus housing is guaranteed for the freshman year only and is available on a first-come, first-served basis. 60% of students live on campus; of those, 60% remain on campus on weekends. All students may keep cars.

FACULTY/CLASSROOMS: 74% of faculty are male; 26% are female. All teach undergraduates, and 20% do research. No introductory courses are taught by graduate students. The average class size in an introductory lecture is 20; in a laboratory is 22; and in a regular course is 20.

PROGRAMS OF STUDY: Rose-Hulman confers B.S. degrees. Master's degrees are also awarded. Bachelor's degrees are awarded in BIOLOGICAL SCIENCE (biochemistry and biology/biological science), COMPUTER AND PHYSICAL SCIENCE (chemistry, computer science, mathematics, physics, and software engineering), ENGINEERING AND ENVIRONMENTAL DESIGN (biomedical engineering, chemical engineering, civil engineering, computer engineering, electrical/electronics engineering, engineering physics, mechanical engineering, and optical engineering), SOCIAL SCIENCE (economics). Engineering, science, and mathematics are the strongest academically. Mechanical engineering, chemical engineering, and computer science have the largest enrollments.

ACTIVITIES: 35% of men belong to 8 national fraternities; 35% of women belong to 3 national sororities. There are 100 groups on campus, including art, band, cheerleading, chess, chorale, chorus, computers, dance, debate, drama, drill team, environmental, ethnic, film, honors, international, jazz band, LGBT, literary magazine, musical theater, newspaper, pep band, photography, political, professional, radio and TV, religious, social, social service, and student government. Popular campus events include art shows, concerts and plays. **Sports:** There are 11 intercollegiate sports for men and 11 for women, and 22 intramural sports for men and 22 for women. Facilities include a field house, recreational center, swimming pool, tennis courts, and intramural fields. **Graduates:** From July 1, 2015 to June 30, 2016, 519 bachelor's degrees were awarded. The most popular majors were mechanical engineering (35%), chemical engineering (12%), and electrical engineering (10%). 382 companies recruited on campus in 2015-2016. In an average class, 1% graduate in 3 years or less, 69% graduate in 4 years or less, 80% graduate in 5 years or less, and 82% graduate in 6 years or less. Of the 2015 graduating class, 19% were enrolled in graduate school within 6 months of graduation, and 74% were employed.

SERVICES: Counseling and information services are available, as is tutoring in most subjects. **Library/Resources:** The library contains 396,640 volumes, and 1,387 audio/video tapes/CDs/DVDs, and subscribes to 76,374 periodicals including electronic. Computerized library services include interlibrary loans, database searching, and Internet access. Special learning facilities include an art gallery, planetarium, and radio station. **Physically Challenged Students:** 95% of the campus is accessible. Facilities include wheelchair ramps, elevators, special parking, specially equipped restrooms, special class scheduling, and lowered drinking fountains. **Special:** The institute offers co-op programs, independent study, cross-registration with Indiana State University and Saint Mary-of-the-Woods College, summer industrial internships, study abroad, and dual majors. Pass/fail options also are available. There are 7 national honor societies and 3 departmental honors programs. **Visiting:** There are regularly scheduled orientations for prospective students, including interviews, campus tours, and academic meetings. There are guides for informal visits, visitors may sit in on classes, and stay overnight. To schedule a visit, contact Kelli Lloyd at (800) 248-7448. **Campus Safety and Security:** Measures include 24-hour foot and vehicle patrol, emergency notification system, and security escort services. There are emergency telephones, lighted pathways/sidewalks, medical transports, and free traffic assistance.

REQUIREMENTS: The SAT or ACT is required. Candidates should have at least 16 units of credit, including 4 units in English, 2 units in social sciences, and 1 unit each in math, chemistry, physics, and electives. An essay and interview are recommended. Rose-Hulman requires applicants to be in the upper 25% of their class. AP credits are accepted. Important factors in the admissions decision are advanced placement or honors courses, recommendations by school officials, and extracurricular activities record. All students must complete at least 192 to 195 quarter hours with a minimum GPA of 2.0 and 36 hours in the humanities and social sciences. Freshmen are required to take math, biology, chemistry, or physics. The total number of hours required in the major varies. **Procedure:** Freshmen are admitted fall. Entrance exams should be taken in the fall of the senior year or spring of the junior year. There is a deferred admissions plan. Early decision applications should be filed by February 1; regular applications, by February 1 for fall entry, along with a $40 fee. Notification of early decision is sent December 15; regular decision, March 15. 416 applicants were on the 2016 waiting list; 41 were admitted. Applications are accepted on-line. Application fees are waived if application is completed on-line. **Transfer Students:** 19 transfer students enrolled in 2015-2016. Applicants need 1 year each of calculus, physics, and chemistry and a minimum GPA of 3.0. An interview is recommended. **International Students:** There are 282 international students enrolled. The school actively recruits these students. They must take the TOEFL with a minimum score of 550 on the paper-based TOEFL (PBT) or 80 on the Internet-based version (iBT). They must also take the SAT or ACT.

ADMISSIONS: 61% of the 2016-2017 applicants were accepted. The SAT scores for the 2016-2017 freshman class were: Critical Reading-- 3% below 500, 35% between 500 and 599, 50% between 600 and 699, and 13% between 700 and 800. Math-- 11% between 500 and 599, 55% between 600 and 699, and 35% between 700 and 800. Writing-- 8% below 500, 40% between 500 and 599, 44% between 600 and 699, and 9% between 700 and 800. The ACT scores were 4% between 18 and 23, 41% between 24 and 29, and 55% above 30. 88% of the current freshmen were in the top fifth of their class; 99% were in the top two fifths. There were 14 National Merit finalists. 27 freshmen graduated first in their class. **Admissions Contact:** Lisa Norton, Dean of Admissions. Email: *admissions@rose-hulman.edu* Web: *www.rose-hulman.edu*

FINANCIAL AID: In 2016-2017, 98% of all full-time freshmen and 98% of continuing full-time students received some form of financial aid. 63% of all full-time freshmen and 59% of continuing full-time students received need-based aid. The average freshman award was $29,690. Need-based scholarships or need-based grants averaged $27,896 ($60,768 maximum); need-based self-help aid (loans and jobs) averaged $10,237 ($48,563 maximum); and other non-need-based awards and non-need-based scholarships averaged $13,597 ($59,478 maximum). 39% of undergraduate students work part-time. Average annual earnings from campus work are $1280. The average financial indebtedness of the 2016 graduate was $41,384. Rose-Hulman is a member of CSS. The FAFSA code is 001830. The priority date for freshman financial aid applications for fall entry is March 1.

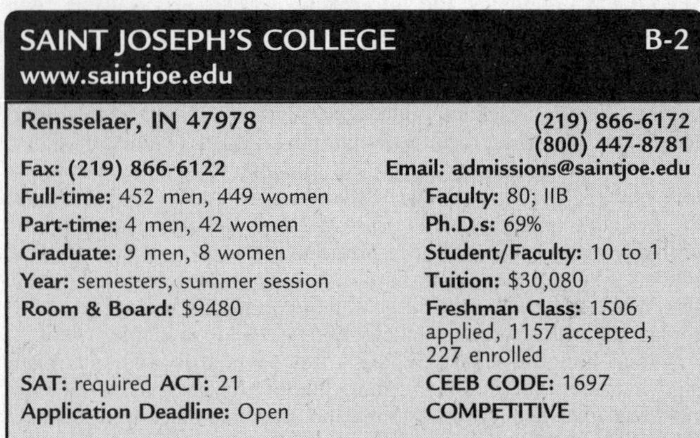

SAINT JOSEPH'S COLLEGE B-2

www.saintjoe.edu

Rensselaer, IN 47978	**(219) 866-6172** **(800) 447-8781**
Fax: (219) 866-6122	**Email: admissions@saintjoe.edu**
Full-time: 452 men, 449 women	**Faculty:** 80; IIB
Part-time: 4 men, 42 women	**Ph.D.s:** 69%
Graduate: 9 men, 8 women	**Student/Faculty:** 10 to 1
Year: semesters, summer session	**Tuition:** $30,080
Room & Board: $9480	**Freshman Class:** 1506 applied, 1157 accepted, 227 enrolled
SAT: required **ACT:** 21	**CEEB CODE:** 1697
Application Deadline: Open	**COMPETITIVE**

Saint Joseph's College, founded in 1889, is a private Catholic institution providing a liberal arts core curriculum with an interdisciplinary approach and practical, career-oriented experiences. There is one undergraduate school and one graduate school. In addition to regional accreditation, Saint Joseph College has baccalaureate program accreditation with NCATE, IACBE, CCNE, and NCATE. The 180-acre campus is in a small town 80 miles south of Chicago, IL, and 90 miles north of Indianapolis. Including any residence halls, there are 26 buildings.

STUDENT LIFE: 76% of undergraduates are from Indiana. Others are from 25 states, 14 foreign countries, and Canada. 85% are from public schools. 76% are White; 6% Hispanic; 4% two or more races; 3% Foreign; 10% African American; 1% race unknown. 60% are Protestant; 38% Catholic; 19% claim no religious affiliation. **Female To Male Ratio:** 1.1:1. The average age of freshmen is 19; all undergraduates, 21. 30% do not continue beyond their first year; 46% remain to graduate. **Housing:** 755 students can be accommodated in college housing, which includes single-sex and coed dorms and on-campus apartments. There is housing for nontraditional or adult students and special-interest floors. On-campus housing is guaranteed for all 4 years. 69% of students live on campus; of those, 69% remain on campus on weekends. All students may keep cars.

FACULTY/CLASSROOMS: 51% of faculty are male; 49% are female. 98% teach undergraduates. No introductory courses are taught by graduate students. The average class size in an introductory lecture is 14; in a laboratory is 14; and in a regular course is 17.

PROGRAMS OF STUDY: Saint Joseph College confers B.A., B.S., and B.S.N. degrees. Associate and master's degrees are also awarded. Bachelor's degrees are awarded in BIOLOGICAL SCIENCE (biology/biological science), BUSINESS (accounting, business administration and management, and sports management), COMMUNICATIONS AND THE ARTS (art, communications, creative writing, dramatic arts, English, music, music business management, and theatre arts), COMPUTER AND PHYSICAL SCIENCE (chemistry, computer science, and mathematics), EDUCATION (athletic training, elementary education, middle school education, physical education, and secondary education), HEALTH PROFESSIONS (medical technology, nursing, predentistry, and premedicine), SOCIAL SCIENCE (criminal justice, economics, history, international studies, ministries, philosophy, political science/government, prelaw, psychology, religion, and sociology). Accounting, biology-chemistry, and education are the strongest academically. Business administration, biological sciences, and nursing have the largest enrollments.

ACTIVITIES: There are no fraternities or sororities. There are 50 groups on campus, including art, band, cheerleading, chess, choir, chorale, chorus, computers, dance, debate, drama, environmental, ethnic, film, forensics, honors, jazz band, literary magazine, marching band, musical theater, newspaper, orchestra, pep band, photography, political, professional, radio and TV, religious, social, social service, and student government. Popular campus events include Little 500 Go-Kart Race, Homecoming Weekend, and Kairos Retreats. **Sports:** There are 9 intercollegiate sports for men and 9 for women, and 7 intramural sports for men and 7 for women. Facilities include a field house, 2500-seat gym, recreation center, baseball complex, softball complex, lighted soccer field, football facility, and outdoor track and field facility. **Graduates:** From July 1, 2015 to June 30, 2016, 211 bachelor's degrees were awarded. The most popular majors were nursing (26%), business administration (12%), and biology (12%). 6 companies recruited on campus in 2015-2016. In an average class, 1% graduate in 3 years or less, 42% graduate in 4 years or less, 48% graduate in 5 years or less, and 49% graduate in 6 years or less. Of the 2015 graduating class, 16% were enrolled in graduate school within 6 months of graduation, and 83% were employed.

SERVICES: Counseling and information services are available, as is tutoring in most subjects. There is remedial math. **Library/Resources:** The library contains 131,216 volumes, 67,764 microform items, and 1,902 audio/video tapes/CDs/DVDs, and subscribes to 77 periodicals including electronic. Computerized library services include interlibrary loans, database searching, Internet access, and Wi-Fi capability. Special learning facilities include a radio station and TV station. **Physically Challenged Students:** 74% of the campus is accessible. Facilities include wheelchair ramps, elevators, special parking, specially equipped restrooms, special class scheduling, lowered drinking fountains, and lowered telephones. **Special:** Cross-registration with Saint Elizabeth's School of Nursing is offered. Internships in all fields, a Washington semester, accelerated degree programs, and study abroad throughout Europe and Latin America are available. Dual majors are offered in biology/chemistry and music/business administration. Credit for life, military, and work experience, nondegree study, student-designed majors, and pass/fail options are offered. The Core program consists of lectures and discussions over a 4-year period. There are 4 national honor societies and a freshman honors program. **Visiting:** There are regularly scheduled orientations for prospective students, consisting of discover days, special interest days, early registration, and freshman orientation. There are guides for informal visits, visitors may sit in on classes, and stay overnight. To schedule a visit, contact Admissions Office. **Campus Safety and Security:** Measures include 24-hour foot and vehicle patrol, emergency notification system, and security escort services. There are emergency telephones, lighted pathways/sidewalks, and controlled access to dorms/residences.

REQUIREMENTS: The SAT or ACT is required. Applicants should be graduates of an accredited secondary school or have earned the GED. They should have completed 15 academic credits, 10 of which must be from the following academic fields: English, foreign language, social studies, math, science, and history. Acceptance is based on high school GPA and SAT or ACT scores. A GPA of 2.0 is required. AP and CLEP credits are accepted. Important factors in the admissions decision are advanced placement or honors courses, extracurricular activities record, and leadership record. Students must complete 45 hours in the general education program and 36 hours in the major. A total of 120 credit hours with a minimum GPA of 2.0 is required to graduate. **Procedure:** Freshmen are admitted fall and spring. Entrance exams should be taken by January of the senior year. There are deferred admissions and rolling admissions plans. Application deadlines are open. Application fee is $25. Notifications are sent December 15. Applications are accepted on-line. Application fees are waived if application is completed on-line. **Transfer Students:** 24 transfer students enrolled in 2015-2016. Applicants must have a GPA of 2.0. Grades of C or better transfer for credit. 30 of 120 credits required for the bachelor's degree must be completed at SJC. **International Students:** There are 30 international students enrolled. They must take the TOEFL with a minimum score of 550 on the paper-based TOEFL (PBT) or 80 on the Internet-based version (iBT).

ADMISSIONS: 77% of the 2016-2017 applicants were accepted. 22% of the current freshmen were in the top fifth of their class; 61% were in the top two fifths. **Admissions Contact:** Brian Studebaker, Director of Admissions. Email: *admissions@saintjoe.edu* Web: *www.saintjoe.edu*

FINANCIAL AID: In 2016-2017, 84% of all full-time freshmen and 85% of continuing full-time students received some form of financial aid. 83% of all full-time freshmen and 84% of continuing full-time students received need-based aid. The average freshman award was $29,143. Need-based scholarships or need-based grants averaged $11,849 ($39,330 maximum); need-based self-help aid (loans and jobs) averaged $2,172 ($39,330 maximum); non-need-based athletic scholarships averaged $6,094 ($35,410 maximum); and other non-need-based awards and non-need-based scholarships averaged $9,704 ($39,330 maximum). 26% of undergraduate students work part-time. Average annual earnings from campus work are $1500. The average financial indebtedness of the 2016 graduate was $28,526. Saint Joseph College is a member of CSS. The FAFSA code is 001833. The deadline for filing freshman financial aid applications for fall entry is March 1.

SAINT MARY-OF-THE-WOODS COLLEGE *(The complete profile is made available exclusively on our website, www.barronspac.com)*

SAINT MARY'S COLLEGE C-1

www.saintmarys.edu

Notre Dame, IN 46556	**(574) 284-4587** **(800) 551-7621**
Fax: (574) 284-4841	**Email: admission@saintmarys.edu**
Full-time: 1581 women	**Faculty:** 133; IIB, -$
Part-time: 13 women	**Ph.D.s:** 87%
Graduate: 10 men, 66 women	**Student/Faculty:** 10 to 1
Year: semesters, summer session	**Tuition:** $38,880
Room & Board: $11,720	**Freshman Class:** 1771 applied, 1446 accepted, 432 enrolled
SAT CR/M/W: 545/529/543 **ACT:** 25	**CEEB CODE:** 1702
Application Deadline: February 15	**COMPETITIVE**

Saint Mary's College, established in 1844, was founded and sponsored by the Congregation of the Sisters of the Holy Cross. It continues to be a Catholic comprehensive college for women in the liberal arts tradition. Figures in the above capsule and in this profile are approximate. There is 1 undergraduate school and 1 graduate school. In addition to regional accreditation, Saint Mary's has baccalaureate program accreditation with CSWE, NASAD, NASM, NCATE, and CCNE. The 100-acre campus is in a suburban area in South Bend, IN and 90 miles east of Chicago, IL. Including any residence halls, there are 20 buildings.

STUDENT LIFE: 73% of undergraduates are from out of state, mostly the Midwest. Students are from 43 states, 10 foreign countries, and Canada. 51% are from public schools. 77% are White; 3% two or more races; 3% race unknown; 2% African American; 2% Asian American; 2% Foreign; 11% Hispanic. 76% are Catholic; 11% Protestant. **Female To Male Ratio:** 166.0:1. The average age of freshmen is 18; all undergraduates, 20. 13% do not continue beyond their first year; 73% remain to graduate. **Housing:** 1350 students can be accommodated in college housing, which includes single-sex dorms and on-campus apartments. On-campus housing is guaranteed for all 4 years, and is available on a first-come, first-served basis. 86% of students live on campus; of those, 75% remain on campus on weekends. All students may keep cars.

FACULTY/CLASSROOMS: 31% of faculty are male; 69% are female. All teach undergraduates, and all do research. No introductory courses are taught by graduate students. The average class size in an introductory lecture is 20; in a laboratory is 15; and in a regular course is 15.

PROGRAMS OF STUDY: Saint Mary's confers B.A., B.S., B.S.W., B.B.A., B.F.A., and B.Mus. degrees. Master's and doctoral degrees are also awarded. Bachelor's degrees are awarded in BIOLOGICAL SCIENCE (biology/biological science), BUSINESS (accounting, business administration and management, and management information systems), COMMUNICATIONS AND THE ARTS (art, communications, creative writing, English literature, English Writing, fine arts, music, Spanish, and visual and performing arts), COMPUTER AND PHYSICAL SCIENCE (actuarial mathematics, applied mathematics, chemistry, mathematics, mathematics/computational, physics, and statistics), EDUCATION (elementary education and global studies), HEALTH PROFESSIONS (nursing and speech pathology/audiology), SOCIAL SCIENCE (communication sciences & disorders, economics, history, humanities, international studies, philosophy, political science/government, psychology, religion, social work, sociology, and women & gender studies). Nursing, psychology and business administration have the largest enrollments.

ACTIVITIES: There are no fraternities or sororities. There are 75 groups on campus, including art, band, cheerleading, choir, chorale, chorus, dance, drama, environmental, ethnic, honors, international, LGBT, literary magazine, marching band, musical theater, newspaper, opera, orchestra, pep band, photography, political, professional, radio and TV, religious, social, social service, student government, and yearbook. Popular campus events include Back to School Dance, School Formal and Dance Marathon. **Sports:** There are 8 intercollegiate sports for women, and 8 intramural sports for women. Facilities include an athletic facility, outdoor tennis and volleyball courts, and soccer, lacrosse and softball fields. **Graduates:** From July 1, 2015 to June 30, 2016, 359 bachelor's degrees were awarded. The most popular majors were nursing (14%), business administration (9%), and biology (9%). 306 companies recruited on campus in 2015-2016. In an average class, 71% graduate in 4 years or less, 76% graduate in 5 years or less, and 77% graduate in 6 years or less. Of the 2015 graduating class, 29% were enrolled in graduate school within 6 months of graduation, and 74% were employed.

SERVICES: Counseling and information services are available, as is tutoring in most subjects. **Library/Resources:** The library contains 244,651 volumes, 18,729 microform items, and 3,539 audio/video tapes/CDs/DVDs, and subscribes to 30,704 periodicals including electronic. Computerized library services include interlibrary loans, database searching, Internet access, and Wi-Fi capability. Special learning facilities include an art gallery, radio station, and TV station. **Physically Challenged Students:** All of the campus is accessible. Facilities include wheelchair ramps, elevators, special parking, specially equipped restrooms, lowered drinking fountains, and special housing. **Special:** Cross-registration is permitted with the University of Notre Dame and a consortium of 6 northern Indiana colleges. Opportunities are provided for internships, a Washington semester, dual and student-designed majors, a 3-2 engineering degree with the University of Notre Dame, non-degree study, pass/fail options, and study abroad in more than 20 countries. All students must complete a senior comprehensive project or exam and demonstrate proficiency in writing before graduating. There are 14 national honor societies. **Visiting:** There are regularly scheduled orientations for prospective students, including campus tours and visits with admissions and financial aid counselors and faculty and athletic staff. There are guides for informal visits, visitors may sit in on classes, and stay overnight. To schedule a visit, contact Campus Visit Coordinator at (800) 551-7621. **Campus Safety and Security:** Measures include 24-hour foot and vehicle patrol, emergency notification system, self-defense education, and security escort services. There are shuttle buses, emergency telephones, lighted pathways/sidewalks, controlled access to dorms/residences, and key cards for controlled residence hall entry.

REQUIREMENTS: The SAT or ACT is required. Graduation from an accredited secondary school is required; a GED will be accepted. Applicants must have completed 16 academic credits, including 4 in English, 3 in math, and 2 each in a foreign language, history or social studies, and lab science with the remainder from college preparatory electives in the above areas. An essay is required. AP and CLEP credits are accepted. Important factors in the admissions decision are extracurricular activities record, advanced placement or honors courses, and recommendations by school officials. Students must successfully complete 128 credits, with at least 24 in the major, and must maintain a minimum GPA of 2.0. Students must complete the Sophia Program, a learning outcomesbased general education curriculum promoting integration with majors and minors. Advanced proficiency in composition within the student's major must also be demonstrated, and a comprehensive exam in the major area is required by the end of the senior year. **Procedure:** Freshmen are admitted fall and spring. Entrance exams should be taken between March of the junior year and December of senior year. There are early decision, deferred admissions, and rolling admissions plans. Early decision applications should be filed by November 15; regular applications, by February 15 for fall entry; and November 15 for spring entry. Notification of early decision is sent December 15; regular decision, January 15. 56 early decision candidates were accepted for the 2016-2017 class. Applications are accepted on-line. Application fees are waived if application is completed on-line. **Transfer Students:** 32 transfer students enrolled in 2015-2016. Students must submit a transcript from high school and each previous college attended, along with an essay, a recommendation from a college adviser, and SAT or ACT test scores if the student has fewer than 24 semester hours of transferable credit. All transfer applicants must have maintained a minimum GPA of 2.75. An informational meeting with a counselor is recommended. Syllabi or course description required for credit evaluation. 60 of 128 credits required for the bachelor's degree must be completed at Saint Mary's. **International Students:** There are 25 international students enrolled. The school actively recruits these students. They must take the TOEFL with a minimum score of 500 on the paper-based TOEFL (PBT) or 80 on the Internet-based version (iBT), or take the IELTS. They must also take the SAT or ACT.

ADMISSIONS: 82% of the 2016-2017 applicants were accepted. The SAT scores for the 2016-2017 freshman class were: Critical Reading-- 25% below 500, 51% between 500 and 599, 22% between 600 and 699, and 3% between 700 and 800. Math-- 33% below 500, 47% between 500 and 599, 17% between 600 and 699, and 3% between 700 and 800. Writing-- 28% below 500, 46% between 500 and 599, 24% between 600 and 699, and 1% between 700 and 800. The ACT scores were 1% between 12 and 17, 35% between 18 and 23, 52% between 24 and 29, and 11% above 30. 48% of the current freshmen were in the top fifth of their class; 82% were in the top two fifths. 6 freshmen graduated first in their class. **Admissions Contact:** Sarah Gallagher Dvorak, Director of Admissions. Email: *admission@saintmarys.edu* Web: *www.saintmarys.edu*

FINANCIAL AID: In 2016-2017, 100% of all full-time freshmen and 98% of continuing full-time students received some form of financial aid. 75% of all full-time freshmen and 66% of continuing full-time students received need-based aid. The average freshman award was $29,550. Need-based scholarships or need-based grants averaged $24,872; need-based self-help aid (loans and jobs) averaged $4,457; and other non-need-based awards and non-need-based scholarships averaged $13,429. 83% of undergraduate students work part-time. Average annual earnings from campus work are $1800. The average financial indebtedness of the 2016 graduate was $31,986. Saint Mary's is a member of CSS. The FAFSA code is 001836. The priority date for freshman financial aid applications for fall entry is March 1.

TAYLOR UNIVERSITY — D-3

www.taylor.edu

Upland, IN 46989	**(765) 998-5565** **(800) 882-3456**
Fax: (765) 998-4925	**Email: admissions@taylor.edu**
Full-time: 792 men, 1034 women	**Faculty:** 129; IIB, --$
Part-time: 128 men, 179 women	**Ph.D.s:** 88%
Graduate: 16 men, 23 women	**Student/Faculty:** 14 to 1
Year: 4-1-4, summer session	**Tuition:** $31,472
Room & Board: $8845	**Freshman Class:** 1775 applied, 1413 accepted, 472 enrolled
SAT CR/M/W: 560/550/540 **ACT:** 25	**CEEB CODE:** 1802
Application Deadline: December 1	**COMPETITIVE+**

Taylor University, founded in 1846, is a private Christian interdenominational liberal arts institution that integrates faith, living, and learning. There are 3 undergraduate schools and 1 graduate school. In addition to regional accreditation, Taylor has baccalaureate program accreditation with ABET, CSWE, NASM, NCATE, CSWE, and CELP. The 952-acre campus is in a rural area 70 miles north of Indianapolis and 45 miles south of Fort Wayne. Including any residence halls, there are 43 buildings.

STUDENT LIFE: 62% of undergraduates are from out of state, mostly the Midwest. Students are from 43 states, 30 foreign countries, and Canada. 82% are White; 7% Foreign; 4% Hispanic; 3% African American; 3% Asian American; 1% American Indian/Alaska Native. 98% are Protestant. **Female To Male Ratio:** 1.3:1. The average age of freshmen is 19; all undergraduates, 21. 14% do not continue beyond their first year; 76% remain to graduate. **Housing:** 1752 students can be accommodated in college housing, which includes single-sex and coed dorms, on-campus apartments, off-campus apartments, and married student housing. On-campus housing is guaranteed for all 4 years. 83% of students live on campus; of those, 82% remain on campus on weekends. Alcohol is not permitted. Upperclassmen may keep cars.

FACULTY/CLASSROOMS: 73% of faculty are male; 27% are female. 98% teach undergraduates. No introductory courses are taught by graduate students. The average class size in an introductory lecture is 20; in a laboratory is 10; and in a regular course is 20.

PROGRAMS OF STUDY: Taylor confers B.A., B.B.A., B.Mus., B.F.A., and B.S. degrees. Associate and master's degrees are also awarded. Bachelor's degrees are awarded in AGRICULTURE (environmental studies), BIOLOGICAL SCIENCE (biochemistry and biology/biological science), BUSINESS (accounting, banking and finance, business administration and management, business administration marketing, finance, international business, international business management, marketing, sports management, and sustainable management), COMMUNICATIONS AND THE ARTS (art, art and design, communications, communications technology, digital media, dramatic arts, English, English as a second/foreign language, English literature, English Writing, film arts, film, television and digital media, fine arts, journalism, media arts, English and Professional Communication, music, music performance, music theory and composition, musical theater, public relations, Spanish, studio art, technical and business writing, theatre arts, visual and performing arts, vocal performance, and writing), COMPUTER AND PHYSICAL SCIENCE (chemistry, computer engineering technology, computer science, mathematics, natural sciences, physics, and web services), EDUCATION (art education, childhood education, Christian education, early childhood education, education, elementary education, English education, foreign languages education, health education, mathematics education, music education, physical education, science education, secondary education, social studies education, social studies secondary school education, and teaching English as a second/foreign language (TESOL/TEFOL)), ENGINEERING AND ENVIRONMENTAL DESIGN (computer engineering, computer graphics, engineering physics, environmental engineering, environmental science, and systems engineering), HEALTH PROFESSIONS (biology, exercise science, health science, kinesiology, music therapy, premedicine, and public health), SOCIAL SCIENCE (biblical studies, Christian studies, development economics, economics, geography, history, humanities, interdisciplinary studies, international relations, international studies, liberal arts/general studies, liberal arts, sciences, general studies, humanities, ministries, philosophy, philosophy and religion, political science/government, psychology, social work, and sociology). Engineering, physics, and biology are the strongest academically. Business, education, and kinesiology have the largest enrollments.

ACTIVITIES: There are no fraternities or sororities. There are 65 groups on campus, including art, band, choir, chorale, chorus, communications, computers, debate, drama, ethnic, film, honors, international, jazz band, literary magazine, musical theater, newspaper, opera, orchestra, pep band, photography, political, professional, radio and TV, religious, social, social service, student government, and symphony. Popular campus events include Taylathon, AirBand, Silent Night and Spiritual Renewal, and Emphasis Weeks. **Sports:** There are 8 intercollegiate sports for men and 8 for women, and 9 intramural sports for men and 9 for women. Facilities include Odle Arena and Kesler Student Activities Center which house an indoor track, multi-purpose athletic courts and fitness center with swimming/lap pool. There is a field house, Wheeler football stadium, and practice fields with artificial turf, tennis and racquetball courts, outdoor track, multiple baseball and softball fields, soccer field and a lake for swimming and ice skating. **Graduates:** From July 1, 2015 to June 30, 2016, 485 bachelor's degrees were awarded. The most popular majors were business management (16%), education (12%), and art (11%). 100 companies recruited on campus in 2015-2016. In an average class, 4% graduate in 3 years or less, 66% graduate in 4 years or less, 74% graduate in 5 years or less, and 76% graduate in 6 years or less. Of the 2015 graduating class, 15% were enrolled in graduate school within 6 months of graduation, and 76% were employed.

SERVICES: Counseling and information services are available, as is tutoring in most subjects. There is a reader service for the blind, and remedial math, reading, and writing. **Library/Resources:** The library contains 207,722 volumes, 14,661 microform items, and 15,841 audio/video tapes/CDs/DVDs, and subscribes to 41,429 periodicals including electronic. Computerized library services include interlibrary loans, database searching, Internet access, and Wi-Fi capability. Special learning facilities include an art gallery, radio station, TV station, environmental study laboratory, NASA-approved clean room, particle accelerator, NASA project space research equipment, 65-acre arboretum, C. S. Lewis Collection, observatory room, 10 kW Photo-Voltaic Solar Array, and two 50 kW Wind Turbines available for student data collection. **Physically Challenged Students:** 95% of the campus is accessible. Facilities include wheelchair ramps, elevators, special parking, specially equipped restrooms, special class scheduling, lowered drinking fountains, and lowered telephones. **Special:** Opportunities are provided for internships, cooperative programs, a Washington semester, very active study abroad program in over 35 countries, work-study programs, dual majors, student-designed majors, and B.A., B.S., B.M., and B.F.A. degrees. There is cross-registration with the other members of the

Council for Christian Colleges and Universities, and the Christian College Consortium. There are 7 national honor societies, Phi Beta Kappa, a freshman honors program, and 23 departmental honors programs. **Visiting:** There are regularly scheduled orientations for prospective students, including a campus tour, lunch, class meetings, faculty meetings, a financial aid session, and an admissions interview. There are guides for informal visits, visitors may sit in on classes, and stay overnight. To schedule a visit, contact Amy Barnett at (765) 998-5134. **Campus Safety and Security:** Measures include 24-hour foot and vehicle patrol, emergency notification system, self-defense education, and security escort services. There are lighted pathways/sidewalks.

REQUIREMENTS: The SAT or ACT and ACT Writing Test are recommended. Graduation from an accredited secondary school is required; a GED will be accepted. It is recommended that applicants complete 4 years of English, 3 to 4 each of math and lab science, 2 each of social studies and a foreign language, and course-work in computing, typing/keyboarding, and the arts. The applications includes 1 essay. Either ACT or SAT scores are required in most cases. High school transcripts and recommendation forms from a guidance counselor and pastor are also required. An interview is recommended for all students, and an audition is required for music majors. A GPA of 2.5 is required. AP and CLEP credits are accepted. Important factors in the admissions decision are recommendations by school officials, extracurricular activities record, and leadership record. Students must complete at least 128 total hours of which at least 42 must be upper division (300/400). To graduate, students must have a minimum cumulative GPA of 2.0 and a 2.3 GPA (2.5 in social work) in all majors and minors and demonstrate proficiency in writing, math, science, and reading. Students must also complete a senior paper, exam, or project in their major(s). General education requirements include courses in spiritual formation, speech, expository writing, fine arts, computer science, literature, science, history, math, social science, and a course designated as cross-cultural. The B.A. degree requires the equivalency of 2 years of 1 foreign language. Most B.S. degrees must be combined with systems analysis curriculum. **Procedure:** Freshmen are admitted fall, winter, and spring. Entrance exams should be taken during the spring of the junior year or fall of the senior year. There are early admissions and deferred admissions plans. Early decision applications should be filed by November 1; regular applications, by December 1 for fall entry; February 1 for winter entry; and April 1 for spring entry, along with a $25 fee. Notification of early decision is sent November 20. Applications are accepted on-line. **Transfer Students:** 50 transfer students enrolled in 2015-2016. Applicants must have maintained a minimum GPA of 2.5 and have completed at least 12 credit hours at the previous college. An interview is recommended. 64 of 128 credits required for the bachelor's degree must be completed at Taylor. **International Students:** There are 122 international students enrolled. The school actively recruits these students. They must take the TOEFL with a minimum score of 550 on the paper-based TOEFL (PBT). Taylor will accept the TOEFL in lieu of the SAT or the ACT.

ADMISSIONS: 80% of the 2016-2017 applicants were accepted. The SAT scores for the 2016-2017 freshman class were: Critical Reading-- 31% below 500, 35% between 500 and 599, 23% between 600 and 699, and 10% between 700 and 800. Math-- 30% below 500, 35% between 500 and 599, 29% between 600 and 699, and 6% between 700 and 800. Writing-- 30% below 500, 41% between 500 and 599, 23% between 600 and 699, and 5% between 700 and 800. The ACT scores were 3% between 12 and 17, 30% between 18 and 23, 48% between 24 and 29, and 18% above 30. 58% of the current freshmen were in the top fifth of their class; 83% were in the top two fifths. **Admissions Contact:** Amy Barnett, Executive Director of Admissions. Email: *admissions@taylor.edu* Web: *www.taylor.edu*

FINANCIAL AID: In 2016-2017, 99% of all full-time freshmen and 99% of continuing full-time students received some form of financial aid. 60% of all full-time freshmen and 58% of continuing full-time students received need-based aid. The average freshman award was $21,698. Need-based scholarships or need-based grants averaged $3,323 ($16,000 maximum); need-based self-help aid (loans and jobs) averaged $3,168 ($7,400 maximum); non-need-based athletic scholarships averaged $1,500 ($31,232 maximum); and other non-need-based awards and non-need-based scholarships averaged $13,707 ($31,232 maximum). 64% of undergraduate students work part-time. Average annual earnings from campus work are $1326. The average financial indebtedness of the 2016 graduate was $29,263. Taylor is a member of CSS. The FAFSA code is 001838. The deadline for filing freshman financial aid applications for fall entry is March 10.

TRINE UNIVERSITY D-1

www.trine.edu

Angola, IN 46703	(260) 665-4149 (800) 347-4878
Fax: (260) 665-4578	**Email:** admit@trine.edu
Full-time: 1240 men, 475 women	**Faculty:** 116
Part-time: 47 men, 18 women	**Ph.D.s:** 64%
Graduate: 283 men, 75 women	**Student/Faculty:** 13 to 1
Year: semesters, summer session	**Tuition:** $30,960
Room & Board: $10,350	**Freshman Class:** n/av
SAT CR/M: 510/540 **ACT:** 23	**CEEB CODE:** 1811
Application Deadline: August 1	**COMPETITIVE**

Trine University, founded in 1884, is a private, independent university. Figures in the above capsule and in this profile are approximate. There are 5 undergraduate schools and 1 graduate school. In addition to regional accreditation, Trine has baccalaureate program accreditation with ABET, ACBSP, and NCATE. The 400-acre campus is in a small town 40 miles north of Ft. Wayne. Including any residence halls, there are 22 buildings.

STUDENT LIFE: 71% of undergraduates are from Indiana. Others are from 31 states, 20 foreign countries, and Canada. 80% are from public schools. 84% are White; 4% Foreign; 4% race unknown; 3% Hispanic; 2% African American; 2% two or more races. **Male To Female Ratio:** 2.8:1. The average age of freshmen is 18; all undergraduates, 21. 24% do not continue beyond their first year; 51% remain to graduate. **Housing:** 1241 students can be accommodated in college housing, which includes single-sex and coed dorms and on-campus apartments. In addition, there are honors houses. On-campus housing is guaranteed for all 4 years. 90% of students live on campus; of those, 65% remain on campus on weekends. Alcohol is not permitted. All students may keep cars.

FACULTY/CLASSROOMS: 62% of faculty are male; 38% are female. All teach undergraduates, 10% do research, and 10% do both. No introductory courses are taught by graduate students. The average class size in an introductory lecture is 25; in a laboratory is 16; and in a regular course is 18.

PROGRAMS OF STUDY: Trine confers B.A. and B.S. degrees. Associate, master's, and doctoral degrees are also awarded. Bachelor's degrees are awarded in BIOLOGICAL SCIENCE (biology/biological science), BUSINESS (accounting, banking and finance, business administration and management, management information systems, management science, marketing/retailing/merchandising, recreation and leisure services, recreational facilities management, and sports management), COMMUNICATIONS AND THE ARTS (communications), COMPUTER AND PHYSICAL SCIENCE (chemistry, computer science, cyber intelligence/security studies, information sciences and systems, mathematics, and physical sciences), EDUCATION (elementary education, English education, mathematics education, physical education, science education, secondary education, and social science education), ENGINEERING AND ENVIRONMENTAL DESIGN (chemical engineering, civil engineering, computer engineering, drafting and design technology, electrical/electronics engineering, engineering management, environmental science, industrial administration/management, and mechanical engineering), HEALTH PROFESSIONS (physical therapy and premedicine), SOCIAL SCIENCE (criminal justice, forensic studies, psychology, and social science). Engineering, math/computer science, and science are the strongest academically. Engineering, psychology, and business have the largest enrollments.

ACTIVITIES: 26% of men belong to 8 national fraternities; 20% of women belong to 5 local and 2 national sororities. There are 35 groups on campus, including band, cheerleading, choir, chorus, communications, computers, dance, drama, environmental, ethnic, forensics, honors, international, jazz band, marching band, newspaper, pep band, professional, radio and TV, religious, social, social service, student government, and yearbook. Popular campus events include Homecoming, Bingo for Bucks, and Moonlight Breakfast. **Sports:** There are 10 intercollegiate sports for men and 9 for women, and 6 intramural sports for men and 5 for women. Facilities include Fred Zollner Athletic Stadium, a micro–stadium for football, lacrosse, and soccer. With a capacity of more than 5,000 fans, the stadium is complete with four suites, press box, control room, a spacious hospitality box for supporters, and its open–air Thunder deck. The stadium provides a tremendous facility for both day and night games and practice for Thunder teams. The stadium also houses football offices, a weight room, sports medicine area, and a large scoreboard. The Keith E. Busse/Steel Dynamics Athletic and Recreation Center is a multi-purpose sports complex with an indoor 200-meter track, tennis courts, volleyball, baseball/softball cages, basketball, indoor soccer, lacrosse, and is also open to the public for recreational activities at designated times. Trine athletes also utilize a gym, basketball and racquetball courts, an 18-hole championship golf course, tennis courts, and practice and playing fields for soccer, lacrosse, baseball, and softball. A brand new softball field was recently built with stadium seating, a brick press box, and concessions. **Graduates:** From July 1, 2015 to June 30, 2016, 264 bachelor's degrees were awarded. The most popular majors were engineering (33%), business (19%), and education (9%). 80 companies recruited on campus in 2015-2016. In an average class, 35% graduate in 4 years or less, 50% graduate in 5 years or less, and 51% graduate in 6 years or less. Of the 2015 graduating class, 25% were enrolled in graduate school within 6 months of graduation, and 97% were employed.

SERVICES: Counseling and information services are available, as is tutoring in some subjects, such as math, business, engineering, accounting, science, and English. There is remedial math. **Library/Resources:** The library contains 154,527 volumes, 668 microform items, and 19,216 audio/video tapes/CDs/DVDs, and subscribes to 31,993 periodicals including electronic. Computerized library services include interlibrary loans, database searching, Internet access, and Wi-Fi capability. Special learning facilities include a radio station. **Physically Challenged Students:** 98% of the campus is accessible. Facilities include wheelchair ramps, elevators, special parking, specially equipped restrooms, special class scheduling, lowered drinking fountains, lowered telephones, and special housing. **Special:** Cooperative education programs are available in engineering and business. Opportunities exist for internships and work-study programs with the university and many companies. Study abroad is offered in more than 31 countries. There are 12 national honor societies and a freshman honors program. **Visiting:** There are regularly scheduled orientations for prospective students, including meetings with faculty, administrators, financial aid personnel, and a coach (if the student is an athlete), and a campus tour. There are guides for informal visits, visitors may sit in on classes, and stay overnight. To schedule a visit, contact the Admissions Office. **Campus Safety and Security:** Measures include 24-hour foot and vehicle patrol, emergency notification system, self-defense education, and security escort services. There are emergency telephones and lighted pathways/sidewalks.

REQUIREMENTS: The SAT or ACT is required. Candidates for admission should be graduates of accredited secondary schools. The GED is accepted. Most students should have 4 years of English and 3 years each of science, social studies, and math. AP and CLEP credits are accepted. Important factors in the admissions decision are advanced placement or honors courses, recommendations by school officials, and leadership record. Candidates for graduation must complete 120 to 132 semester hours, satisfying the general education program and major requirements and maintaining a minimum overall GPA of 2.0. Required courses vary by degree sought. All students must complete a general education curriculum including science, math, American studies, social science, global studies, English composition, humanistics, computer literacy, and oral communication course-work. Some majors have senior design projects. The number of hours in the major varies from 40 to 60. **Procedure:** Freshmen are admitted to all sessions. Entrance exams should be taken in the junior or senior year. There are deferred admissions and rolling admissions plans. Applications should be filed by August 1 for fall entry. Notifications are sent August 15. Applications are accepted on-line. **Transfer Students:** 27 transfer students enrolled in 2015-2016. In addition to meeting the university's requirements for freshmen, applicants must have satisfactory records from previous institutions. 30 of 120 credits required for the bachelor's degree must be completed at Trine. **International Students:** There are 179 international students enrolled. The school actively recruits these students. They must take the TOEFL with a minimum score of 550 on the paper-based TOEFL (PBT) or 79 on the Internet-based version (iBT). Applicants not transferring credits in math or English must be tested in those subjects.

ADMISSIONS: The SAT scores for the 2016-2017 freshman class were: Critical Reading-- 42% below 500, 38% between 500 and 599, 17% between 600 and 699, and 3% between 700 and 800. Math-- 27% below 500, 40% between 500 and 599, 29% between 600 and 699, and 4% between 700 and 800. The ACT scores were 8% between 12 and 17, 45% between 18 and 23, 38% between 24 and 29, and 9% above 30. 37% of the current freshmen were in the top fifth of their class; 73% were in the top two fifths. 8 freshmen graduated first in their class. **Admissions Contact:** Scott Goplin, Vice President, Enrollment Management. Email: *admit@trine.edu* Web: *www.trine.edu*

FINANCIAL AID: In 2016-2017, 84% of all full-time freshmen and 78% of continuing full-time students received some form of financial aid. 84% of all full-time freshmen and 78% of continuing full-time students received need-based aid. The average freshman award was $27,189. Need-based scholarships or need-based grants averaged $5,796 ($7,000 maximum); need-based self-help aid (loans and jobs) averaged $5,721 ($5,500 maximum); and other non-need-based awards and non-need-based scholarships averaged $11,230 ($17,000 maximum). 56% of undergraduate students work part-time. Average annual earnings from campus work are $774. The average financial indebtedness of the 2016 graduate was $32,641. The FAFSA code is 001839. The priority date for freshman financial aid applications for fall entry is March 1.

UNIVERSITY OF EVANSVILLE — A-5

www.evansville.edu

Evansville, IN 47722	(812) 488-2468 (800) 423-8633
Fax: (812) 488-4076	Email: admission@evansville.edu
Full-time: 960 men, 1122 women	**Faculty:** 169
Part-time: 63 men, 89 women	**Ph.D.s:** 85%
Graduate: 43 men, 121 women	**Student/Faculty:** 13 to 1
Year: semesters, summer session	**Tuition:** $32,946
Room & Board: $11,240	**Freshman Class:** 3916 applied, 2765 accepted, 515 enrolled
SAT CR/M/W: 560/570/535 **ACT:** 27	**CEEB CODE:** 1208
Application Deadline: n/av	**VERY COMPETITIVE+**

University of Evansville, founded in 1854, is a private institution affiliated with the United Methodist Church. Evansville offers undergraduate degree programs in arts and sciences, business administration, education and health sciences, and engineering and computer science. There are 4 undergraduate schools and 4 graduate schools. In addition to regional accreditation, UE has baccalaureate program accreditation with AACSB, ABET, APTA, NASM, NCATE, NLN, and CAATE. The 75-acre campus is in an urban area 180 miles southwest of Indianapolis, 170 miles east of St. Louis, and 120 miles west of Louisville. Including any residence halls, there are 54 buildings.

STUDENT LIFE: 60% of undergraduates are from Indiana. Others are from 41 states, 47 foreign countries, and Canada. 72% are White; 3% African American; 3% Hispanic; 3% race unknown; 2% Asian American; 2% two or more races; 15% Foreign. 57% are Protestant; 33% Catholic. **Female To Male Ratio:** 1.2:1. The average age of freshmen is 18; all undergraduates, 20. 19% do not continue beyond their first year; 69% remain to graduate. **Housing:** 1919 students can be accommodated in college housing, which includes single-sex and coed dorms and on-campus apartments. In addition, there are honors houses, fraternity houses, International connection house, and housing for students in math and sciences. On-campus housing is guaranteed for the freshman year only, is available on a first-come, first-served basis, and is available on a lottery system for upperclassmen. Priority is given to out-of-town students. 63% of students live on campus; of those, 85% remain on campus on weekends. Alcohol is not permitted. All students may keep cars.

FACULTY/CLASSROOMS: 52% of faculty are male; 48% are female. All teach undergraduates. No introductory courses are taught by graduate students.

PROGRAMS OF STUDY: UE confers B.A., B.S., B.F.A., and B.M. degrees. Associate, master's, and doctoral degrees are also awarded. Bachelor's degrees are awarded in AGRICULTURE (environmental studies), BIOLOGICAL SCIENCE (biochemistry, biology/biological science, and neurosciences), BUSINESS (accounting, business administration and management, finance, international business, marketing, and sports management), COMMUNICATIONS AND THE ARTS (art history, art, communications, creative writing, dramatic arts, French, German, graphic design, literature, music, music business management, music performance, Spanish, and theater management), COMPUTER AND PHYSICAL SCIENCE (chemistry, clinical laboratory science, computer science, mathematics, and physics), EDUCATION (art education, athletic training, drama education, elementary education, English education, foreign languages education, mathematics education, music education, science education, social studies education, and special education), ENGINEERING AND ENVIRONMENTAL DESIGN (civil engineering, computer engineering, electrical/electronics engineering, environmental science, and mechanical engineering), HEALTH PROFESSIONS (exercise science, health care administration, music therapy, nursing, predentistry, premedicine, preoptometry, prepharmacy, preveterinary science, and public health), SOCIAL SCIENCE (archeology, biblical studies, classical/ancient civilization, cognitive science, criminal justice, economics, history, interdisciplinary studies, international studies, liberal arts/general studies, philosophy, political science/government, prelaw, psychology, sociology, and theological studies). Theater, engineering, and physical therapy are the strongest academically. Exercise science, mechanical engineering, and theatre have the largest enrollments.

ACTIVITIES: 30% of men belong to 6 national fraternities; 29% of women belong to 1 local and 4 national sororities. There are 144 groups on campus, including art, band, cheerleading, choir, chorale, chorus, computers, dance, drama, drill team, environmental, ethnic, film, honors, international, jazz band, LGBT, literary magazine, musical theater, newspaper, opera, orchestra, pep band, political, professional, radio and TV, religious, social, social service, student government, symphony, and yearbook. Popular campus events include Labor Day Picnic and Student Organization Fair, Bike Race, and Sunset Concert. **Sports:** There are 6 intercollegiate sports for men and 8 for women, and 17 intramural sports for men and 17 for women. Facilities include a 2500-seat soccer stadium, 650-seat softball stadium, 1200-seat baseball stadium, a 25-yard pool, a conditioning room, an aerobics room, three free- weight rooms, an indoor track, eight outdoor tennis courts, a 1/2-mile security, lighted jogging trail, basketball, racquetball, and volleyball courts. **Graduates:** From July 1, 2015 to June 30, 2016, 562 bachelor's degrees were awarded. The most popular majors were health professions and related programs (14%), business/marketing (13%), and parks and recreation (10%). In an average class, 58% graduate in 4 years or less, 67% graduate in 5 years or less, and 69% graduate in 6 years or less.

SERVICES: Counseling and information services are available, as is tutoring in some subjects, such as science, math, and foreign language; special requests in most subjects are accommodated. There is remedial writing. **Library/Resources:** The library contains 282,262 volumes, 474,391 microform items, and 14,597 audio/video tapes/CDs/DVDs, and subscribes to 50 periodicals including electronic. Computerized library services include interlibrary loans, database searching, Internet access, and Wi-Fi capability. Special learning facilities include an art gallery and radio station. **Physically Challenged Students:** 87% of the campus is accessible. Facilities include wheelchair ramps, elevators, special parking, specially equipped restrooms, special class scheduling, lowered drinking fountains, and special housing. **Special:** Students may study abroad at the University of Evansville British campus, Harlaxton College, and many places throughout the world. There is also an Israeli archeological excavation program, an accelerated bachelor of science in global leadership degree, combined bachelor's/graduate degrees, cooperative education (business administration, chemistry, engineering, environmental studies), dual enrollment of high school students, ESL, and teacher certification, as well as honors, independent study programs, internships, and student-designed majors. There are 15 national honor societies and a freshman honors program. **Visiting:** There are regularly scheduled orientations for prospective students, including a campus tour, faculty academic sessions, financial aid and admission appointments, and study abroad and honors program sessions. There are guides for informal visits, visitors may sit in on classes, and stay overnight. To schedule a visit, contact Carla Hachem at (800) 423-8633. **Campus Safety and Security:** Measures include 24-hour foot and vehicle patrol, emergency notification system, self-defense education, and security escort services. There are emergency telephones and lighted pathways/sidewalks.

REQUIREMENTS: The ACT Optional Writing test is required. To be competitive for admission, students should submit a minimum SAT composite score of 1500 (math, critical reading, and writing) or ACT composite of 21. Applicants must be graduates of accredited secondary schools; applicants who have been homeschooled are also considered. The University requires completion of 4 years of college preparatory English, 3 years of math, 3 years of science, and 3 years of social studies. Two years of a foreign language are recommended. An interview is recommended but not required. AP and CLEP credits are accepted. Important factors in the admissions decision are extracurricular activities record, personality/intangible qualities, and advanced placement or honors courses. To graduate, students must complete at least 120 semester hours with a minimum GPA of 2.0 cumulative and in their major. All students must complete a 41-hour general education program. A demonstration of writing proficiency, a capstone course in the major, and a demonstration of foreign language proficiency are required for graduation. Students must complete at least 39 credit hours in courses numbered 300 or above, at least 48 credit hours in residence at UE, and at least 51 percent of course-work in their major at UE. **Procedure:** Freshmen are admitted fall and spring. Entrance exams should be taken by fall of senior year. There is a deferred admissions plan. Early decision applications should be filed by December 1. Notification of early decision is sent December 15. Applications are accepted on-line. Application fees are waived if application is completed on-line. **Transfer Students:** 75 transfer students enrolled in 2015-2016. Applicants must submit official transcripts from each college from which they earned credit and must have a minimum GPA of 2.5 in all previous college work. High school transcripts, standardized test scores, and comments from the Dean of Students Recommendation Form are optional but considered if submitted with the application. 48 of 120 credits required for the bachelor's degree must be completed at UE. **International Students:** There are 296 international students enrolled. The school actively recruits these students. They must take the TOEFL with a minimum score of 61 on the Internet-based version (iBT).

ADMISSIONS: 71% of the 2016-2017 applicants were accepted. The SAT scores for the 2016-2017 freshman class were: Critical Reading-- 21% below 500, 46% between 500 and 599, 25% between 600 and 699, and 8% between 700 and 800. Math-- 20% below 500, 43% between 500 and 599, 31% between 600 and 699, and 6% between 700 and 800. Writing-- 29% below 500, 46% between 500 and 599, 21% between 600 and 699, and 4% between 700 and 800. The ACT scores were 2% between 12 and 17, 27% between 18 and 23, 49% between 24 and 29, and 22% above 30. 57% of the current freshmen were in the top fifth of their class; 85% were in the top two fifths. There were 7 National Merit finalists. 23 freshmen graduated first in their class. **Admissions Contact:** Scott Henne, Dean of Admission. Email: *admission@evansville.edu* Web: *www.evansville.edu*

FINANCIAL AID: In 2016-2017, 93% of all full-time freshmen and 93% of continuing full-time students received some form of financial aid. 71% of all full-time freshmen and 70% of continuing full-time students received need-based aid. The average freshman award was $29,342. Need-based scholarships or need-based grants averaged $24,275 ($31,900 maximum); need-based self-help aid (loans and jobs) averaged $8,217 ($25,025 maximum); and non-need-based athletic scholarships averaged $18,943 ($49,760 maximum). 18% of undergraduate students work part-time. Average annual earnings from campus work are $1525. The average financial indebtedness of the 2016 graduate was $31,013. UE is a member of CSS. The FAFSA code is 001795. The deadline for filing freshman financial aid applications for fall entry is March 10.

UNIVERSITY OF INDIANAPOLIS C-3

www.uindy.edu

Indianapolis, IN 46227	**(317) 788-3216** **(800) 232-8634**
Fax: (317) 788-3300	**Email: admissions@uindy.edu**
Full-time: 1319 men, 2131 women	**Faculty:** IIA, --$
Part-time: 168 men, 507 women	**Ph.D.s:** 77%
Graduate: 300 men, 967 women	**Student/Faculty:** 11 to 1
Year: semesters, summer session	**Tuition:** $26,550
Room & Board: $9930	**Freshman Class:** 7216 applied, 5297 accepted, 961 enrolled
SAT or ACT: required	**CEEB CODE:** 1321
Application Deadline: open	**COMPETITIVE**

University of Indianapolis, established in 1902, is a private liberal arts school affiliated with the United Methodist Church. It provides undergraduate and graduate studies with an emphasis on education, business, nursing, and arts and sciences. The figures in the above capsule and in this profile are approximate. There are 8 undergraduate schools and 8 graduate schools. In addition to regional accreditation, UIndy has baccalaureate program accreditation with ACBSP, ACEJMC, CSWE, NASAD, NASM, NCATE, NLN, and APA. The 65-acre campus is in a suburban area on the south side of Indianapolis. Including any residence halls, there are 32 buildings.

STUDENT LIFE: 93% of undergraduates are from Indiana. Others are from 44 states, and Canada. 9% are Foreign; 8% African American; 71% White; 4% Hispanic; 4% race unknown; 3% two or more races; 2% Asian American. 43% claim no religious affiliation; 42% Protestant. **Female To Male Ratio:** 2.0:1. The average age of freshmen is 20; all undergraduates, 23. 23% do not continue beyond their first year; 50% remain to graduate. **Housing:** 1432 students can be accommodated in college housing, which includes single-sex and coed dorms, on-campus apartments, off-campus apartments, and married student housing. In addition, there are honors houses. On-campus housing is guaranteed for all 4 years. 63% of students commute. Alcohol is not permitted. All students may keep cars.

FACULTY/CLASSROOMS: 42% of faculty are male; 58% are female. No introductory courses are taught by graduate students. The average class size in a regular course is 18.

PROGRAMS OF STUDY: UIndy confers B.A., B.S., B.S.N., B.S.W., B.S.A.T., B.M., B.L.S., and B.F.A. degrees. Associate, master's, and doctoral degrees are also awarded. Bachelor's degrees are awarded in BIOLOGICAL SCIENCE (biology/biological science), BUSINESS (accounting, banking and finance, business administration and management, business communications, business economics, entrepreneurial studies, international business management, management information systems, marketing/retailing/merchandising, and sports management), COMMUNICATIONS AND THE ARTS (art, broadcasting, communications, digital communications, digital media, dramatic arts, English, French, German, journalism, music, music performance, musical theater, public relations, Spanish, studio art, and theatre studies), COMPUTER AND PHYSICAL SCIENCE (actuarial science, chemistry, computer information systems, computer science, earth science, mathematics, and physics), EDUCATION (art education, athletic training, drama education, elementary education, English education, foreign languages education, mathematics education, middle school education, music education, physical education, science education, secondary education, and social studies education), ENGINEERING AND ENVIRONMENTAL DESIGN (commercial art, electrical/electronics engineering, environmental science, and mechanical engineering), HEALTH PROFESSIONS (art therapy, exercise science, medical laboratory technology, nursing, and respiratory therapy), SOCIAL SCIENCE (anthropology, archeology, criminal justice, economics, history, international relations, philosophy, political science/government, psychology, religion, social science, social work, and sociology). Nursing, science (biology/chemistry), exercise science, and psychology are the strongest academically. Business, nursing, and health sciences have the largest enrollments.

ACTIVITIES: There are no fraternities or sororities. There are 45 groups on campus, including academic clubs, art, cheerleading, chess, choir, chorale, chorus, computers, dance, debate, drama, ethnic, forensics, honors, international, jazz band, LGBT, literary magazine, musical theater, newspaper, orchestra, pep band, photography, political, professional, radio and TV, religious, social, social service, and student government. Popular campus events include Winter and Spring Formals, Ceremony of Flags, and Midnight Breakfast. **Sports:** There are 12 intercollegiate sports for men and 11 for women, and 8 intramural sports for men and 7 for women. Facilities include a health and fitness center which has a 3500-seat gym, an Olympic-size swimming pool, racquetball courts, a weight room, and a dance studio. **Graduates:** From July 1, 2015 to June 30, 2016, 771 bachelor's degrees were awarded. 180 companies recruited on campus in 2015-2016. In an average class, 1% graduate in 3 years or less, 41% graduate in 4 years or less, 53% graduate in 5 years or less, and 54% graduate in 6 years or less.

SERVICES: Counseling and information services are available, as is tutoring in every subject. There is remedial math and writing. There is a special learning disabled program (BUILD). **Library/Resources:** The library contains 197,419 volumes, 19,841 microform items, and 6,775 audio/video tapes/CDs/DVDs, and subscribes to 401 periodicals including electronic. Computerized library services include interlibrary loans, database searching, Internet access, and Wi-Fi capability. Special learning facilities include an art gallery, planetarium, radio station, TV station, and archeology and forensics lab. **Physically Challenged Students:** 95% of the campus is accessible. Facilities include wheelchair ramps, elevators, special parking, specially equipped restrooms, special class scheduling, lowered drinking fountains, and lowered telephones. **Special:** Cross-registration is offered in conjunction with 6 area colleges. Cooperative programs, internships, various work-study programs, study abroad, dual and student-designed majors, accelerated programs in liberal studies and organizational leadership, pass/fail options, and a 3-2 engineering degree with Indiana University-Purdue University Indianapolis are available. A fleximester, which is a 3-week spring term, is also offered. There are 14 national honor societies and a freshman honors program. **Visiting:** There are regularly scheduled orientations for prospective students, including campus visits and tours. There are guides for informal visits, visitors may sit in on classes, and stay overnight. To schedule a visit, contact the Admissions Office. **Campus Safety and Security:** Measures include 24-hour foot and vehicle patrol, emergency notification system, self-defense education, and security escort services. There are emergency telephones, lighted pathways/sidewalks, and controlled access to dorms/residences.

REQUIREMENTS: The SAT or ACT is required. Each applicant should complete a college preparatory curriculum with 15 to 20 academic credits from English/language arts, social studies, science, math, and world languages. The GED is accepted. An interview is recommended. UIndy requires applicants to be in the upper 50% of their class. AP and CLEP credits are accepted. Important factors in the admissions decision are leadership record, recommendations by school officials, and advanced placement or honors courses. All undergraduates must complete at least 120 hours, including 24 hours or more in the major with a GPA of 2.0 or better. Requirements include a core curriculum in which 4 learning goals must be met. Students must also take a health and phys ed course and 1 spring term, and attend lecture/performance events. Specific courses include math, history, modern language, science, global/local, writing and speaking, communication, philosophy/ethics, religion, and English composition and literature. **Procedure:** Freshmen are admitted to all sessions. There are deferred admissions and rolling admissions plans. Application deadlines are open. 63 applicants were on the 2016 waiting list; 39 were admitted. Applications are accepted on-line. Application fees are waived if application is completed on-line. **Transfer Students:** 212 transfer students enrolled in 2015-2016. ACT or SAT is not needed if applicants have a GPA of C and 20 semester hours of credit. 30 of 120 credits required for the bachelor's degree must be completed at UIndy. **International Students:** The school actively recruits these students. They must take the TOEFL with a minimum score of 500 on the paper-based TOEFL (PBT) or 61 on the Internet-based version (iBT) or take the MELAB, or Cambridge Examinations IELTS, CPE, or CAE. They must also take the SAT or ACT.

ADMISSIONS: 73% of the 2016-2017 applicants were accepted. 48% of the current freshmen were in the top fifth of their class; 73% were in the top two fifths. **Admissions Contact:** Ron Wilks, Director of Admissions. Email: *admissions@uindy.edu* Web: *www.uindy.edu*

FINANCIAL AID: In 2016-2017, 93% of all full-time freshmen and 85% of continuing full-time students received some form of financial aid. 50% of all full-time freshmen and 44% of continuing full-time students received need-based aid. The average freshman award was $23,460. Need-based scholarships or need-based grants averaged $8,500; need-based self-help aid (loans and jobs) averaged $3,250; non-need-based athletic scholarships averaged $1,510 ($39,530 maximum); and other non-need-based awards and non-need-based scholarships averaged $10,000. 16% of undergraduate students work part-time. Average annual earnings from campus work are $2600. The average financial indebtedness of the 2016 graduate was $35,480. UIndy is a member of CSS. The college's own financial statement is required. The FAFSA code is 001804. The priority date for freshman financial aid applications for fall entry is March 10.

UNIVERSITY OF NOTRE DAME C-1

www.nd.edu

Notre Dame, IN 46556 **(574) 631-7505**

Fax: (574) 631-8865
Email: admissions@nd.edu
Full-time: 4491 men, 4023 women
Faculty: I, +$
Part-time: 13 men, 3 women
Ph.D.s: 91%
Graduate: 2285 men, 1578 women
Student/Faculty: 10 to 1
Year: semesters, summer session
Tuition: $49,685
Room & Board: $14,358
Freshman Class: 19505 applied, 3654 accepted, 2046 enrolled
SAT CR/M/W: 710/730/700 **ACT:** 34
CEEB CODE: 1841
Application Deadline: January 1
MOST COMPETITIVE

University of Notre Dame, founded in 1842, is a comprehensive Catholic research university. Programs are offered through the Colleges of Arts and Letters, Engineering, Science, Mendoza College of Business, and the School of Architecture. There are 5 undergraduate schools and 6 graduate schools. In addition to regional accreditation, Notre Dame has baccalaureate program accreditation with AACSB, ABET, and NAAB. The 1250-acre campus is in a suburban area 90 miles east of Chicago. Including any residence halls, there are 159 buildings.

STUDENT LIFE: 92% of undergraduates are from out of state, mostly the Midwest. Students are from 50 states, 68 foreign countries, and Canada. 44% are from public schools. 68% are White; 6% Foreign; 5% African American; 5% Asian American; 5% two or more races; 11% Hispanic. **Male To Female Ratio:** 1.2:1. The average age of freshmen is 18; all undergraduates, 20. 2% do not continue beyond their first year; 98% remain to graduate. **Housing:** 6929 students can be accommodated in college housing, which includes single-sex dorms. On-campus housing is guaranteed for the freshman year only is available on a first-come, first-served basis. 79% of students live on campus; of those, 95% remain on campus on weekends. Upperclassmen may keep cars.

FACULTY/CLASSROOMS: 68% of faculty are male; 32% are female. No introductory courses are taught by graduate students.

PROGRAMS OF STUDY: Notre Dame confers B.A., B.S., B.Arch., B.B.A., and B.F.A. degrees. Master's and doctoral degrees are also awarded. Bachelor's degrees are awarded in BIOLOGICAL SCIENCE (biochemistry, biological sciences, environmental earth resources, and neurosciences), BUSINESS (accounting, finance, international economics, management, and marketing), COMMUNICATIONS AND THE ARTS (Africana studies, Arabic, art history, Chinese, design, English, film, television and digital media, French, German, Greek, information technology, Italian, Japanese, music, romance languages and literature, Russian, Spanish, and studio art), COMPUTER AND PHYSICAL SCIENCE (applied mathematics, chemistry, computer science, environmental geology, mathematics, physics, science, and statistics), EDUCATION (classical studies and science education), ENGINEERING AND ENVIRONMENTAL DESIGN (aerospace engineering, architecture, chemical engineering, civil engineering, computer engineering, electrical/electronics engineering, environmental engineering, environmental science, and mechanical engineering), SOCIAL SCIENCE (American studies, anthropology, economics, gender studies, history, liberal arts/general studies, medieval studies, philosophy, philosophy and religion, political science/government, psychology, sociology, and theology). Engineering, theology, and business are the strongest academically. Finance, psychology, and economics have the largest enrollments.

ACTIVITIES: There are no fraternities or sororities. There are 465 groups on campus, including art, bagpipe, band, cheerleading, chess, choir, chorale, chorus, computers, dance, debate, drama, drill team, ethnic, film, forensics, honors, international, jazz band, literary magazine, marching band, musical theater, newspaper, orchestra, pep band, photography, political, professional, radio club, religious, social, social service, student government, symphony, and yearbook. Popular campus events include Spring Festival, Home Football Weekends, and Collegiate Jazz Festival. **Sports:** There are 13 intercollegiate sports for men and 13 for women, and 16 intramural sports for men and 13 for women. Facilities include indoor and outdoor tennis, swimming pools, golf courses, several outdoor general use recreational fields, indoor 100-yard general use facility with track, 2 full-service fitness and rec centers, varsity softball/baseball stadiums, football stadium, basketball/volleyball arena, a track, soccer stadium, lacrosse stadium, hockey arena, fencing gym, volleyball practice area, varsity rowing, a gym, and varsity football practice fields. **Graduates:** From July 1, 2015 to June 30, 2016, 2135 bachelor's degrees were awarded. The most popular majors were finance (13%), accountancy (7%), and finance (7%). In an average class, 90% graduate in 4 years or less, and 95% graduate in 5 years or less.

SERVICES: There is a reader service for the blind. **Library/Resources:** Computerized library services include interlibrary loans, database searching, Internet access, and Wi-Fi capability. Special learning facilities include an art gallery, an art museum, and a performing arts center. **Physically Challenged Students:** 95% of the campus is accessible. Facilities include wheelchair ramps, elevators, special parking, specially equipped restrooms, special class scheduling, lowered drinking fountains, lowered telephones, and special housing. **Special:** Cross-registration is offered with Saint Mary's College. Study abroad is possible in 20 countries. A 5-year arts and letters/engineering B.A.-B.S. degree is offered. There is a program of liberal studies centered on the discussion of great books. Internships, an accelerated degree program, a Washington semester, dual majors, 3-2 engineering degrees, and pass/fail options are available. There are 16 national honor societies, Phi Beta Kappa, and 24 departmental honors programs. **Visiting:** There are regularly scheduled orientations for prospective students, including small group sessions for students, larger sessions for parents, and tours for all. Visitors may sit in on classes and stay overnight. To schedule a visit, contact the Admissions Office. **Campus Safety and Security:** Measures include 24-hour foot and vehicle patrol, emergency notification system, self-defense education, and security escort services. There are shuttle buses, emergency telephones, lighted pathways/sidewalks, controlled access to dorms/residences, controlled, open vehicle access pedestrian access, property registration, lost and found, and monthly electronic safety newsletter.

REQUIREMENTS: The SAT or ACT is required. Applicants should be graduates of an accredited secondary school with 16 Carnegie credits completed, including 4 years of English, 3 years of math, and 2 years each of science, foreign language, and history. The SAT subject test in a foreign language is recommended. An essay is required. An audition or a portfolio is recommended for some majors. AP credits are accepted. All students must complete courses in English, philosophy, science, history, theology, math, social science, and phys ed. A total of 125 semester hours with a minimum GPA of 2.0 is required to graduate. **Procedure:** Freshmen are admitted fall. Entrance exams should be taken by fall of the senior year. There is a deferred admissions plan. Applications should be filed by January 1 for fall entry, along with a $75 fee. Notification of early decision is sent December 21; regular decision, April 10. Applications are accepted on-line. **Transfer Students:** 125 transfer students enrolled in 2015-2016. Applicants should have completed at least 27 semester hours of transferable credit and maintained a 3.3 GPA in all courses. Admission depends on openings in each undergraduate college. 60 of 125 credits required for the bachelor's degree must be completed at Notre Dame. **International Students:** There are 526 international students enrolled. The school actively recruits these students. They must take the TOEFL with a minimum score of 560 on the paper-based TOEFL (PBT) or 100 on the Internet-based version (iBT). They must also take the SAT or ACT.

ADMISSIONS: 19% of the 2016-2017 applicants were accepted. The SAT scores for the 2016-2017 freshman class were: Critical Reading-- 1% below 500, 7% between 500 and 599, 30% between 600 and 699, and 62% between 700 and 800. Math-- 4% between 500 and 599, 28% between 600 and 699, and 68% between 700 and 800. Writing-- 1% below 500, 9% between 500 and 599, 38% between 600 and 699, and 52% between 700 and 800. The ACT scores were 1% between 18 and 23, 9% between 24 and 29, and 90% above 30. **Admissions Contact:** Donald Bishop, AVP for Undergraduate Enrollment. Email: *admissions@nd.edu* Web: *www.nd.edu*

FINANCIAL AID: In 2016-2017, 66% of all full-time freshmen and 77% of continuing full-time students received some form of financial aid. 93% of all full-time freshmen and 95% of continuing full-time students received need-based aid. The average freshman award was $42,499. Need-based scholarships or need-based grants averaged $35,998; need-based self-help aid (loans and jobs) averaged $5,256; non-need-based athletic scholarships averaged $40,822; and other non-need-based awards and non-need-based scholarships averaged $21,979. The average financial indebtedness of the 2016 graduate was $26,674. Notre

Dame is a member of CSS. The CSS/Profile, Federal Tax form(s), and W-2 forms are required. The FAFSA code is 001840. The priority date for freshman financial aid applications for fall entry is February 15.

UNIVERSITY OF SAINT FRANCIS D-2

www.sf.edu

Fort Wayne, IN 46808	260-399-8000 800-729-4732 Email: admis@sf.edu
Full-time: 461 men, 1014 women	**Faculty:** 119
Part-time: 48 men, 287 women	**Ph.D.s:** 50%
Graduate: 133 men, 269 women	**Student/Faculty:** 12 to 1
Year: semesters, summer session	**Tuition:** $28,310
Room & Board: $9090	**Freshman Class:** 977 applied, 945 accepted, 343 enrolled
SAT CR/M/W: 500/490/480 **ACT:** 22	**CEEB CODE:** 1693
Application Deadline: n/av	**COMPETITIVE**

University of Saint Francis is a private, Catholic university enrolling students in majors ranging from the liberal arts to the creative arts to the health sciences with small class sizes, personal attention, and the freedom to explore your options a USF education has a lot to offer. There are 4 undergraduate schools and 1 graduate school. In addition to regional accreditation, USF has baccalaureate program accreditation with ACBSP, CAHEA, CSWE, NASAD, NCATE, NLN, ACEN, ACEND, and ARC-PA. The 100-acre campus is in an urban area in Fort Wayne, Indiana, 125 miles north of Indianapolis and 150 miles east of Chicago, IL. Including any residence halls, there are 30 buildings.

STUDENT LIFE: 91% of undergraduates are from Indiana. Others are from 17 states, 6 foreign countries, and Canada. 83% are from public schools. 80% are White; 8% Hispanic; 7% African American; 2% two or more races; 1% Asian American; 1% race unknown. 47% are Protestant; 28% Catholic. **Female To Male Ratio:** 2.4:1. The average age of freshmen is 18; all undergraduates, 23. 29% do not continue beyond their first year; 71% remain to graduate. **Housing:** 409 students can be accommodated in college housing, which includes coed dorms and on-campus apartments. On-campus housing is guaranteed for the freshman year only and is available on a first-come, first-served basis. 80% of students commute. Alcohol is not permitted. All students may keep cars.

FACULTY/CLASSROOMS: 34% of faculty are male; 66% are female. 95% teach undergraduates. No introductory courses are taught by graduate students. The average class size in an introductory lecture is 19; in a laboratory is 15; and in a regular course is 16.

PROGRAMS OF STUDY: USF confers B.A., B.F.A., B.S., B.S.Ed., B.S.N., and B.S.W. degrees. Associate and master's degrees are also awarded. Bachelor's degrees are awarded in BIOLOGICAL SCIENCE (biology/biological science, biology (pre-physician assistant), and nutrition), BUSINESS (accounting, business administration and management, finance, insurance and risk management, management, and marketing), COMMUNICATIONS AND THE ARTS (animation, art history, communications, dance, English, graphic design, music technology, and studio art), COMPUTER AND PHYSICAL SCIENCE (chemistry, clinical laboratory science, chemistry/forensic chemistry, computer game design/development, computer information systems, computer security, mathematics, and science and management), EDUCATION (art education, educational studies, elementary education, museum studies, and special education), ENGINEERING AND ENVIRONMENTAL DESIGN (environmental science), HEALTH PROFESSIONS (art therapy, exercise science, health services administration, nursing, predentistry, premedicine, and preveterinary science), SOCIAL SCIENCE (criminal justice, history, liberal arts/general studies, ministries, philosophy, political science/government, psychology, social work, sociology, and theology). Nursing is the strongest academically. Nursing, exercise science, and business administration have the largest enrollments.

ACTIVITIES: There are no fraternities or sororities. There are 45 groups on campus, including art, cheerleading, chorale, communications, dance, drama, environmental, ethnic, film, gaming club, TRIO navigators, honors, jazz band, literary magazine, marching band, musical theater, newspaper, pep band, photography, professional, religious, social, social service, and student government. Popular campus events include Homecoming Week, Casino Night, Ultimate Road Trip, SOCA Art Openings, Legacy Seasonal Conferences, Spring Fling Week, and Football and Basketball Games. **Sports:** There are 8 intercollegiate sports for men and 8 for women, and 7 intramural sports for men and 7 for women. Facilities include athletic center, gym with 2 basketball courts or 3 volleyball courts, fitness center, exercise studio, baseball diamond, football stadium, football training center, and soccer, baseball, and softball fields. **Graduates:** From July 1, 2015 to June 30, 2016, 317 bachelor's degrees were awarded. The most popular majors were nursing (41%), health & exercise science (8%), and business administration (8%). 129 companies recruited on campus in 2015-2016. In an average class, 1% graduate in 3 years or less, 40% graduate in 4 years or less, 54% graduate in 5 years or less, and 56% graduate in 6 years or less. Of the 2015 graduating class, 10% were enrolled in graduate school within 6 months of graduation, and 79% were employed.

SERVICES: Counseling and information services are available, as is tutoring in every subject. There is a reader service for the blind, and remedial math, reading, and writing. **Library/Resources:** The library contains 216,145 volumes, 14,250 microform items, and 29,271 audio/video tapes/CDs/DVDs, and subscribes to 35,178 periodicals including electronic. Computerized library services include interlibrary loans, database searching, Internet access, and Wi-Fi capability. Special learning facilities include an art gallery, simulation lab, performing arts center, creative art studios, and specialized facilities. **Physically Challenged Students:** Facilities include wheelchair ramps, elevators, special parking, specially equipped restrooms, and lowered drinking fountains. **Special:** Cross-registration available with the Fort Wayne Higher Education Consortium; dual majors available with A.S. in Physical Therapist Assistant and B.S. in Exercise Science, A.S. in Radiologic Technology and B.S. in Health Services, A.S. in Surgical Technology and B.S. in Health Services; internships available in many academic programs; co-operative education program available to business majors; Media Entrepreneurship Training in the Arts; student-designed major. There are 6 national honor societies, a freshman honors program, and 1 departmental honors programs. **Visiting:** There are regularly scheduled orientations for prospective students, student tours and meetings with faculty and staff. There are guides for informal visits and visitors may sit in on classes. To schedule a visit, contact Aaron West at (260) 434-3279. **Campus Safety and Security:** Measures include 24-hour foot and vehicle patrol, emergency notification system, and security escort services. There are shuttle buses, emergency telephones, lighted pathways/sidewalks, and controlled access to dorms/residences.

REQUIREMENTS: The SAT or ACT is required. Incoming students should meet the following requirements: graduate from an accredited high school; rank in the upper half of the high school graduation class; have a 2.3 grade point average on a 4.0 scale; earn a Scholastic Aptitude Test (SAT) score of 1000 or above (Verbal/Critical Reading and Math combined) or an American College Test (ACT) composite score of 21 or above. USF requires applicants to be in the upper 50% of their class. A GPA of 2.3 is required. AP and CLEP credits are accepted. To complete a bachelor's degree at the University of Saint Francis, the student must meet the following criteria: Completion of the general education requirements; a minimum of 120 semester hours of credit earned as required by the academic program curriculum; a major of at least 30 hours, with no fewer than 12 hours earned from the University of Saint Francis; a year's residence-that is, at least 30 semester hours of credit earned at the University of Saint Francis; a cumulative GPA of at least 2.0 on a 4.0 scale; satisfactory and completion of a comprehensive examination or senior project as specified by the department; completion of the academic advising file audit with a representative of Academic Affairs. **Procedure:** Freshmen are admitted fall, spring, and summer. Entrance exams should be taken spring of the junior year or fall of the senior year. There are deferred admissions and rolling admissions plans. Application deadlines are open. Notification is sent on a rolling basis. Applications are accepted on-line. Application fees are waived if application is completed on-line. **Transfer Students:** 287 transfer students enrolled in 2015-2016. To be considered for admission to the University of Saint Francis, a transfer student must: request that an official copy of the final high school transcript (must include date of graduation) and/or GED score be sent directly to the Office of Admissions, and request that official transcripts from all colleges and universities attended be sent directly to the Office of Admissions, students who have earned a cumulative grade point average of 2.3 or better will be considered for admission. 30 of 120 credits required for the bachelor's degree must be completed at USF. **International Students:** There are 9 international students enrolled. They must take the TOEFL with a minimum score of 550 on the paper-based TOEFL (PBT) or 80 on the Internet-based version (iBT). They must also take the SAT or ACT, scoring 21 ACT.

ADMISSIONS: 97% of the 2016-2017 applicants were accepted. The SAT scores for the 2016-2017 freshman class were: Critical Reading-- 50% below 500, 41% between 500 and 599, and 9% between 600 and 699. Math-- 51% below 500, 40% between 500 and 599, 8% between 600 and 699, and 1% between 700 and 800. Writing-- 56% below 500, 36% between 500 and 599, 7% between 600 and 699, and 1% between 700 and 800. The ACT scores were 15% between 12 and 17, 55% between 18 and 23, 28% between 24 and 29, and 1% above 30. 32% of the current freshmen were in the top fifth of their class; 67% were in the top two fifths. 4 freshmen graduated first in their class. **Admissions Contact:** Maria Gerber, Director of Undergraduate Admissions. Email: *admis@sf.edu* Web: *www.sf.edu*

FINANCIAL AID: In 2016-2017, 100% of all full-time freshmen and 98% of continuing full-time students received some form of financial aid. 89% of all full-time freshmen and 87% of continuing full-time students received need-based aid. 11% of undergraduate students work part-time. Average annual earnings from campus work are $2350. The average financial indebtedness of the 2016 graduate was $37,167. The FAFSA code is 001832. The priority date for freshman financial aid applications for fall entry is March 10. The deadline for filing freshman financial aid applications for fall entry is rolling.

UNIVERSITY OF SOUTHERN INDIANA A-5

www.usi.edu

Evansville, IN 47712	**(812) 464-1765** **(800) 467-1965**
Fax: (812) 465-7154	**Email: enroll@usi.edu**
Full-time: 2629 men, 4064 women	**Faculty:** 355; IIA, --$
Part-time: 418 men, 833 women	**Ph.D.s:** 72%
Graduate: 276 men, 792 women	**Student/Faculty:** 17 to 1
Year: semesters, summer session	**Tuition:** $7605 ($17,847)
Room & Board: $8896	**Freshman Class:** 4552 applied, 4183 accepted, 1685 enrolled
SAT CR/M/W: 490/500/470 **ACT:** 22	**CEEB CODE:** 1335
Application Deadline: August 15	**COMPETITIVE**

University of Southern Indiana, founded in 1965, enrolls over 10,000 dual credit, undergraduate, and graduate students students in 80 majors. USI offers programs through the College of Liberal Arts, College of Nursing and Health Professions, Romain College of Business, and the Pott College of Science, Engineering, and Education. There are 6 undergraduate schools and one graduate school. In addition to regional accreditation, USI has baccalaureate program accreditation with AACSB, ABET, CSWE, NASAD, NCATE, ACS, ACEND, ACOTE, CCNE, CDA/ADA, CARC, JRCERT, NACEP, NAEYC, and NCTE. The 1400-acre campus is in a suburban area in Evansville, Indiana, and is within 150 miles of Indianapolis, IN, St. Louis, MO. and Nashville, TN. Including any residence halls, there are 89 buildings.

STUDENT LIFE: 88% of undergraduates are from Indiana. Others are from 40 states, 55 foreign countries, and Canada. 87% are White; 4% African American; 3% Hispanic; 2% Foreign; 2% two or more races; 1% Asian American; 1% American Indian/Alaska Native. **Female To Male Ratio:** 1.7:1. The average age of freshmen is 19; all undergraduates, 23. 30% do not continue beyond their first year; 26% remain to graduate. **Housing:** 2800 students can be accommodated in college housing, which includes coed dorms and on-campus apartments. In addition, there are honors houses, special-interest houses, fraternity houses, sorority houses, and international student housing. On-campus housing is available on a first-come, first-served basis. Priority is given to out-of-town students. 69% of students commute. Alcohol is not permitted. All students may keep cars.

FACULTY/CLASSROOMS: 40% of faculty are male; 60% are female. All teach undergraduates. No introductory courses are taught by graduate students. The average class size in an introductory lecture is 26; in a laboratory is 24; and in a regular course is 24.

PROGRAMS OF STUDY: USI confers B.A., B.S., B.P.S., B.S.E., B.S.N., B.G.S., and B.S.W. degrees. Associate, master's, and doctoral degrees are also awarded. Bachelor's degrees are awarded in BIOLOGICAL SCIENCE (biochemistry, biology/biological science, biophysics, and nutrition), BUSINESS (accounting, business administration and management, electronic business, finance, management information systems, marketing/retailing/merchandising, nonprofit/public organization management, and sports management), COMMUNICATIONS AND THE ARTS (advertising, art, broadcasting, communications, English, English as a second/foreign language, French, German, journalism, performing arts, public relations, radio/television technology, Spanish, speech/debate/rhetoric, and theatre arts), COMPUTER AND PHYSICAL SCIENCE (chemistry, computer science, geology, mathematics, and physics), EDUCATION (art education, early childhood education, elementary education, English education, health information management, mathematics education, middle school education, physical education, science education, secondary education, social science education, and special education), ENGINEERING AND ENVIRONMENTAL DESIGN (civil engineering technology, electrical/electronics engineering technology, engineering, environmental science, industrial administration/management, manufacturing technology, mechanical engineering technology, and mining and mineral engineering), HEALTH PROFESSIONS (dental hygiene, dental laboratory technology, exercise science, health care administration, nursing, occupational therapy, radiological science, and respiratory therapy), SOCIAL SCIENCE (anthropology, criminal justice, economics, history, international studies, philosophy, political science/government, psychology, public administration, social science, social work, and sociology). Nursing is the strongest academically. Nursing, general studies, and teachers education have the largest enrollments.

ACTIVITIES: 9% of men belong to 7 national fraternities; 10% of women belong to 7 national sororities. There are 137 groups on campus, including art, cheerleading, chess, choir, chorale, chorus, communications, computers, dance, drama, environmental, ethnic, film, honors, international, jazz band, LGBT, literary magazine, musical theater, newspaper, pep band, photography, political, professional, radio and TV, religious, social, social service, and student government. Popular campus events include Welcome Week, Welcome Fun Fest, Midnight Madness, and International Food Festival. **Sports:** There are 7 intercollegiate sports for men and 8 for women, and 8 intramural sports for men and 8 for women. Facilities include 100,000 square feet of recreational space, cardio and weight machine area, treadmills, elliptical machines, stationary bikes, Nu-step, 16 pieces with personal entertainment monitors, 12 large screen plasma TVs, stretching and ab area, free-weight room, 3 multipurpose courts, men's and women's locker rooms with showers, indoor track, a climbing center, equipment checkout, group exercise rooms, wireless access, a game room, lactation room, and computer lab. **Graduates:** From July 1, 2015 to June 30, 2016, 1536 bachelor's degrees were awarded. The most popular majors were nursing (13%), health services (10%), and psychology (6%). 170 companies recruited on campus in 2015-2016. In an average class, 19% graduate in 4 years or less, 34% graduate in 5 years or less, and 37% graduate in 6 years or less. Of the 2015 graduating class, 15% were enrolled in graduate school within 6 months of graduation, and 88% were employed.

SERVICES: Counseling and information services are available, as is tutoring in most subjects. There is a reader service for the blind, and remedial math, reading, and writing. **Library/Resources:** The library contains 546,128 volumes, 536,385 microform items, and 6,603 audio/video tapes/CDs/DVDs, and subscribes to 52,440 periodicals including electronic. Computerized library services include interlibrary loans, database searching, Internet access, and Wi-Fi capability. Special learning facilities include an art gallery, radio station, and TV station. **Physically Challenged Students:** 95% of the campus is accessible. Facilities include wheelchair ramps, elevators, special parking, specially equipped restrooms, special class scheduling, lowered drinking fountains, and lowered telephones. **Special:** Students may participate in cooperative programs, internships, and work-study programs. Study abroad, dual majors, pass/fail options, accelerated degree programs, and B.A.-B.S. degrees are possible. There are 9 national honor societies and a freshman honors program. **Visiting:** There are regularly scheduled orientations for prospective students. Tour campus and housing and hear about the USI experience and admission process. Meetings with faculty members can be arranged upon request. There are guides for informal visits, visitors may sit in on classes, and stay overnight. To schedule a visit, contact Cindy Braker at (800) 467-1965. **Campus Safety and Security:** Measures include 24-hour foot and vehicle patrol, emergency notification system, self-defense education, and security escort services. There are shuttle buses, emergency telephones, and lighted pathways/sidewalks.

REQUIREMENTS: The SAT or ACT is required. Applicants must be graduates of an accredited secondary school, with a minimum GPA of 2.0. The GED is accepted. An interview is recommended if the student is below admissions standards. AP and CLEP credits are accepted. Important factors in the admissions decision are advanced placement or honors courses, evidence of special talent, and leadership record. A student must have a 2.0 (C) minimum grade-point average on all University courses counted for graduation requirements. Some curricula, such a teacher education programs, require a higher grade point average. Effective summer 2013, a student must have a minimum of 120 semester hours of credit for a baccalaureate degree (124 hours required for students following a spring 2013 or earlier bulletin). If all specified requirements are completed with fewer than 120 semester hours, a student must elect sufficient work to total at least 120 hours. Some curricula or combination of fields require more. Students must have a minimum of 60 semester hours of credit for an associate degree (64 hours required for students following a spring 2013 or earlier bulletin). If all specified requirements are completed with fewer than 60 semester hours, a student must elect sufficient work to total at least 60 hours. Some curricula or combination of fields requires more. A student must earn a minimum of 30 semester hours of credit toward a baccalaureate, and 18 semester hours of credit toward an associate degree from the University. All students who began seeking a degree in the 1996 fall semester or after must complete a minimum of 39 semester hours at the 300- and 400-level to complete a baccalaureate degree. A student must complete the minimum University Core Curriculum program. Specific requirements for the University Core Curriculum component of each degree program are noted in the sections of the bulletin describing each of the academic programs. Incomplete grades should be resolved at least six weeks before the end of the term of graduation. Course requirements for graduation in the student's degree program(s) may be those in effect at the time of matriculation into the program or at graduation, but not a combination of both. **Procedure:** Freshmen are admitted fall, spring, and summer. There are deferred admissions and rolling admissions plans. Applications should be filed by August 15 for fall entry, along with a $40 fee. Applications are accepted on-line. Application fees are waived if application is completed on-line. **Transfer Students:** 525 transfer students enrolled in 2015-2016. Grades of C and above will transfer for credit. 30 of 120 credits required for the bachelor's degree must be completed at USI. **International Students:** There are 210 international students enrolled. The school actively recruits these students. They must take the TOEFL with a minimum score of 525 on the paper-based TOEFL (PBT) or 71 on the Internet-based version (iBT). They must also take the SAT or ACT.

ADMISSIONS: 92% of the 2016-2017 applicants were accepted. The SAT scores for the 2016-2017 freshman class were: Critical Reading-- 51% below 500, 40% between 500 and 599, 8% between 600 and 699, and 1% between 700 and 800. Math-- 50% below 500, 39% between 500 and 599, and 11% between 600 and 699. Writing-- 63% below 500, 32% between 500 and 599, and 5% between 600 and 699. The ACT scores were 13% between 12 and 17, 55% between 18 and 23, 29% between 24 and 29, and 3% above 30. 30% of the current freshmen were in the top fifth of their class; 63% were in the top two fifths. 39 freshmen graduated first in their class. **Admissions Contact:** Rashad Smith, Director of Undergraduate Admissions. Email: *enroll@usi.edu* Web: *www.usi.edu*

FINANCIAL AID: In 2016-2017, 67% of all full-time freshmen and 61% of continuing full-time students received some form of financial aid. 60% of all full-time freshmen and 50% of continuing full-time students received need-based aid. The average freshman award was $9,908. Need-based scholarships or need-based grants averaged $7,997; need-based self-help aid (loans and jobs) averaged $3,267; non-need-based athletic scholarships averaged $4,627; and other non-need-based awards and non-need-based scholarships averaged $3,847. 15% of undergraduate students work part-time. Average annual earnings from campus work are $1789. The average financial indebtedness of the 2016 graduate was $22,262. The college's own financial statement is required. The FAFSA code is 001808. The deadline for filing freshman financial aid applications for fall entry is March 10.

VALPARAISO UNIVERSITY — B-1

www.valpo.edu

Valparaiso, IN 46383 — **(219) 464-5011**, **(888) GO-VALPO**

Fax: (219) 464-6898 — **Email: undergrad.admission@valpo.edu**

Full-time: 1497 men, 1745 women	**Faculty:** n/av
Part-time: 25 men, 32 women	**Ph.D.s:** n/av
Graduate: 568 men, 572 women	**Student/Faculty:** n/av
Year: semesters, summer session	**Tuition:** $37,450
Room & Board: $10,920	**Freshman Class:** 7484 applied, 6205 accepted, 862 enrolled
SAT or ACT: required	**CEEB CODE:** 1874
Application Deadline: rolling	**COMPETITIVE+**

Valparaiso University, founded in 1859, is an independent institution affiliated with the Lutheran Church and offering degree programs in arts and sciences, business, engineering, nursing and health professions, and law. Figures in the above capsule and in this profile are approximate. There are 5 undergraduate schools and 4 graduate schools. In addition to regional accreditation, Valpo has baccalaureate program accreditation with AACSB, ABET, CSWE, NASM, NCATE, ABA, AALS, ACS, CCNE, and CACREP. The 350-acre campus is in a small town 55 miles southeast of Chicago, IL. Including any residence halls, there are 60 buildings.

STUDENT LIFE: 58% of undergraduates are from out of state, mostly the Midwest. Students are from 47 states, 32 foreign countries, and Canada. 9% are Hispanic; 71% White; 6% African American; 6% Foreign; 3% two or more races; 3% race unknown; 2% Asian American. 57% are Protestant; 26% Catholic. **Female To Male Ratio:** 1.1:1. The average age of freshmen is 18; all undergraduates, 20. 14% do not continue beyond their first year; 66% remain to graduate. **Housing:** 2175 students can be accommodated in college housing, which includes single-sex and coed dorms and on-campus apartments. In addition, there are language houses, fraternity houses, and sorority houses. On-campus housing is guaranteed for all 4 years. 61% of students live on campus. Alcohol is not permitted. Upperclassmen may keep cars.

FACULTY/CLASSROOMS: 90% teach undergraduates. No introductory courses are taught by graduate students. The average class size in an introductory lecture is 23; in a laboratory is 24; and in a regular course is 23.

PROGRAMS OF STUDY: Valpo confers B.A., B.L.P.S., B.Mus., B.Mus.Ed., B.S., B.S.Acc., B.S.Bus.Adm., B.S.C.E., B.S.Comp.Eng., B.S.Ed., B.S.E.E., B.S.H.C.L., B.S.M.E., B.S.N., B.S.P.E., and B.S.W. degrees. Associate, master's, and doctoral degrees are also awarded. Bachelor's degrees are awarded in BIOLOGICAL SCIENCE (biochemistry and biology/biological science), BUSINESS (accounting, banking and finance, business administration and management, business intelligence and analytics, finance, international economics, management science, marketing/retailing/merchandising, and sports management), COMMUNICATIONS AND THE ARTS (art, classics, communications, creative writing, digital communications, dramatic arts, English, English Writing, French, German, music, music performance, music theory and composition, Spanish, technical and business writing, theatre arts, and voice), COMPUTER AND PHYSICAL SCIENCE (actuarial science, astronomy, atmospheric sciences and meteorology, chemistry, computer science, geology, mathematics, and physics), EDUCATION (art education, elementary education, English education, foreign languages education, global studies, mathematics education, music education, physical education, psychology education, science education, secondary education, social science education, and social studies education), ENGINEERING AND ENVIRONMENTAL DESIGN (civil engineering, computer engineering, computer technology, electrical/electronics engineering, environmental science, and mechanical engineering), HEALTH PROFESSIONS (exercise science, health care administration, health science, nursing, pre-health studies, premedicine, and public health), SOCIAL SCIENCE (American studies, criminology, East Asian studies, economics, geography, history, humanities, interdisciplinary studies, international public service, international relations, ministries, philosophy, political science/government, prelaw, psychology, religion, religious music, social science, social work, sociology, and theological studies). Nursing, business, and engineering have the largest enrollments.

ACTIVITIES: 26% of men belong to 9 national fraternities; 25% of

women belong to 6 national sororities. There are 94 groups on campus, including art, band, cheerleading, choir, chorale, chorus, dance, debate, drama, environmental, ethnic, film, honors, international, jazz band, LGBT, literary magazine, musical theater, newspaper, orchestra, pep band, photography, political, professional, radio and TV, religious, social, social service, student government, symphony, and yearbook. Popular campus events include Christmas Concert, Martin Luther King Day Celebration, and Jazz Festival. **Sports:** There are 9 intercollegiate sports for men and 10 for women, and 20 intramural sports for men and 20 for women. Facilities include a 5,100-seat arena, swimming pool, 7 additional playing floors, a track and field facility, racquetball/handball courts, a fitness center, a football stadium, a tennis complex, soccer, softball, and baseball fields, and indoor batting facilities. **Graduates:** From July 1, 2015 to June 30, 2016, 738 bachelor's degrees were awarded. The most popular majors were nursing (16%), mechanical engineering (6%), and biology (5%). 250 companies recruited on campus in 2015-2016. In an average class, 1% graduate in 3 years or less, 63% graduate in 4 years or less, and 71% graduate in 5 years or less. Of the 2015 graduating class, 18% were enrolled in graduate school within 6 months of graduation, and 74% were employed.

SERVICES: Counseling and information services are available, as is tutoring in most subjects. There is a reader service for the blind. A writing center provides assistance. The Academic Success Center coordinates all academic support services and resources, including tutoring, advising, and support groups. **Library/Resources:** Computerized library services include interlibrary loans, database searching, Internet access, and Wi-Fi capability. Special learning facilities include an art gallery, planetarium, radio station, TV station, observatory, weather station, center for visual and performing arts, virtual nursing learning center, solar energy research facility, and scientific visualization laboratory. **Physically Challenged Students:** 59% of the campus is accessible. Facilities include wheelchair ramps, elevators, special parking, specially equipped restrooms, lowered drinking fountains, and special housing. **Special:** There is cross-registration with Indiana University Northwest at the undergraduate level in geology. Off-campus study programs in the United States include a Washington semester programs, a Chicago urban semester, a Chicago arts semester, and a Chicago business, entrepreneurship, and society program. Students may also study abroad in 26 countries including Greece, England, Spain, China, Japan, Namibia, France, Germany, Mexico, India, Thailand, Costa Rica, Chile, Israel, Ireland, Hungary, Nicaragua, Italy, New Zealand, Australia, Argentina, Czech Republic, Ecuador, Oman, Peru, and South Africa. Co-op programs, internships, the B.A.-B.S. degree, work-study programs, dual and student-designed majors, an accelerated degree program in numerous majors, pass/fail options, and non-degree study are also available. Other special academic features include Christ College, which is the honors college. There are 8 national honor societies, a chapter of Phi Beta Kappa, a freshman honors program, and 27 departmental honors programs. **Visiting:** There are regularly scheduled orientations for prospective students, which include a campus tour conducted by a current student, an interview with a counselor, the option to meet with professors, attend a class, and meet with a coach. There are guides for informal visits, visitors may sit in on classes, and stay overnight. To schedule a visit, contact the Office of Admission at (219) 464-5011. **Campus Safety and Security:** Measures include 24-hour foot and vehicle patrol, emergency notification system, and security escort services. There are shuttle buses, emergency telephones, lighted pathways/sidewalks, and controlled access to dorms/residences.

REQUIREMENTS: The SAT or ACT is required. In addition, Valparaiso University requires completion of 4 years of English, 3 to 4 years of math, 2 to 3 years of lab science, 2 years each of history and foreign language, and 3 years of additional academic courses. An application essay is required and an interview is recommended for all applicants; an audition is required for music majors. AP and CLEP credits are accepted. Important factors in the admissions decision are advanced placement or honors courses, extracurricular activities record, and evidence of special talent. General education requirements include the 10-credit Valpo core plus 2 courses in theology, courses in natural sciences, humanities, cultural diversity, and social sciences, 1 course in quantitative analysis, and 1 credit hour in physical education. Requirements may vary by degree program, particularly in the professional colleges. To graduate, students must complete at least 124 credit hours, including a minimum of 27 in the major, with a GPA of at least 2.0. **Procedure:** Freshmen are admitted fall, spring, and summer. Entrance exams should be taken prior to the senior year. There are deferred admissions and rolling admissions plans. Application deadlines are open. Notifications are sent October 1. Applications are accepted on-line. **Transfer Students:** 195 transfer students enrolled in 2015-2016. Applicants must submit official transcripts from all colleges attended. To be considered for admission, a minimum 2.0 cumulative grade point average in college coursework is required for most programs. However, some programs require a minimum 3.0 grade point average for transfer students. If the applicant has completed fewer than 24 credit hours, entrance exam scores and a high school transcript are required. A completed transfer evaluation form from the Dean of Students of the current institution must also be submitted. An interview is recommended. 30 of 124 credits required for the bachelor's degree must be completed at Valpo. **International Students:** There are 192 international students enrolled. The school actively recruits these students. They must take the TOEFL with a minimum score of 550 on the paper-based TOEFL (PBT) or 80 on the Internet-based version (iBT), IELTS, GCE, or GCSE English Exam, and IB Higher Level English Exam. They must also take the SAT or ACT.

ADMISSIONS: 54% of the current freshmen were in the top fifth of their class; 83% were in the top two fifths. There were 6 National Merit finalists. 18 freshmen graduated first in their class. **Admissions Contact:** David Fevig, Assistant Vice President, Enrollment Management. Email: *undergrad.admission@valpo.edu* Web: *www.valpo.edu*

FINANCIAL AID: In 2016-2017, 98% of all full-time freshmen and 94% of continuing full-time students received some form of financial aid. 83% of all full-time freshmen and 74% of continuing full-time students received need-based aid. The average freshman award was $31,818. Need-based scholarships or need-based grants averaged $28,306; need-based self-help aid (loans and jobs) averaged $4,692; non-need-based athletic scholarships averaged $12,053; and other non-need-based awards and non-need-based scholarships averaged $20,585. 37% of undergraduate students work part-time. Average annual earnings from campus work are $2037. The average financial indebtedness of the 2016 graduate was $37,294. Valpo is a member of CSS. The FAFSA code is 001842. The priority date for freshman financial aid applications for fall entry is March 1.

WABASH COLLEGE — B-3

www.wabash.edu

Crawfordsville, IN 47933	**(765) 361-6225** **(800) 345-5385**
Fax: (765) 361-6437	**Email: admissions@wabash.edu**
Full-time: 843 men	**Faculty:** 86; IIB, +$
Part-time: n/av	**Ph.D.s:** 100%
Graduate: n/av	**Student/Faculty:** 10 to 1
Year: semesters	**Tuition:** $41,050
Room & Board: $9600	**Freshman Class:** 1284 applied, 804 accepted, 215 enrolled
SAT CR/M/W: 546/580/510 **ACT:** 25	**CEEB CODE:** 1895
Application Deadline: January 15	**VERY COMPETITIVE**

Wabash College, founded in 1832, is a private liberal arts college that educates men to think critically, act responsibly, lead effectively, and live humanely. There is 1 undergraduate school. The 94-acre campus is in a small town 45 miles northwest of Indianapolis. Including any residence halls, there are 65 buildings.

STUDENT LIFE: 77% of undergraduates are from Indiana. Others are from 30 states, and 13 foreign countries. 90% are from public schools. 8% are Hispanic; 72% White; 7% Foreign; 6% African American; 3% race unknown; 2% two or more races; 1% Asian American. The student base is all male. The average age of freshmen is 19; all undergraduates, 20. 8% do not continue beyond their first year; 72% remain to graduate. **Housing:** 940 students can be accommodated in college housing, which includes single-sex dorms and on-campus apartments. In addition, there are fraternity houses. On-campus housing is guaranteed for the freshman year only and is available on a first-come, first-served basis. 91% of students live on campus. All students may keep cars.

FACULTY/CLASSROOMS: 63% of faculty are male; 37% are female. All teach undergraduates, 75% do research, and 75% do both. No introductory courses are taught by graduate students.

PROGRAMS OF STUDY: Wabash confers A.B. degrees. Bachelor's degrees are awarded in BIOLOGICAL SCIENCE (biochemistry and biology/biological science), BUSINESS (finance), COMMUNICATIONS AND THE ARTS (art, classics, dramatic arts, English, French, German, Greek, Latin, music, Spanish, and speech/debate/rhetoric), COMPUTER AND PHYSICAL SCIENCE (chemistry, mathematics, and physics), SOCIAL SCIENCE (economics, Hispanic American studies, history, philosophy, political science/government, psychology, and religion). Chemistry, financial economics, and theater are the strongest academically. Biology, mathematics, and economics have the largest enrollments.

ACTIVITIES: 66% of men belong to 9 national fraternities. There are no sororities. There are 60 groups on campus, including art, band, chess, choir, chorale, chorus, communications, computers, dance, debate, drama, environmental, ethnic, film, forensics, honors, international, jazz band, LGBT, literary magazine, musical theater, newspaper, orchestra, pep band, photography, political, professional, radio and TV, religious, social, social service, student government, symphony, and yearbook. Popular campus events include Homecoming, Pan-Hel Weekend, Monon Bell, Scarlet Honors Weekend, National Act, Oktoberfest, and Chapel Sing. **Sports:** There are 12 intercollegiate sports for men, and 24 intramural sports for men. Facilities include a 4500-seat football stadium with FieldTurf Dura-spine Pro surface, indoor and outdoor tennis courts, baseball stadium, soccer stadium, natatorium, indoor track, all-weather outdoor track, wrestling practice facility, 1800-seat basketball arena, racquetball courts, aerobics room, and wellness center. **Graduates:** From July 1, 2015 to June 30, 2016, 195 bachelor's degrees were awarded. The most popular majors were political science (12%), history (11%), and mathematics (10%). 45 companies recruited on campus in 2015-2016. In an average class, 66% graduate in 4 years or less and 72% graduate in 6 years or less. Of the 2015 graduating class, 23% were enrolled in graduate school within 6 months of graduation, and 51% were employed.

SERVICES: Counseling and information services are available, as is tutoring in some subjects, such as economics, math, physics, biology, chemistry, and Spanish. There is a reader service for the blind. There is a quantitative skills center as well as a writing center where, under professional supervision, students help each other. **Library/Resources:** The library contains 198,775 volumes, 18,420 microform items, and 19,985 audio/video tapes/CDs/DVDs, and subscribes to 225,732 periodicals including electronic. Computerized library services include interlibrary loans, database searching, Internet access, and Wi-Fi capability. Special learning facilities include an art gallery, radio station, an archival center, Wabash Center for the Teaching of Theology and Religion, Center of Inquiry in the Liberal Arts, and two biological field stations. **Physically Challenged Students:** 60% of the campus is accessible. Facilities include wheelchair ramps, elevators, special parking, specially equipped restrooms, special class scheduling, lowered drinking fountains, and special housing. There is Braille signage in some buildings. Theater is equipped for hearing-impared patrons. Some laboratory rooms have lowered work stations. **Special:** Wabash offers internships with off-campus organizations, study abroad in approximately 40 countries, a Washington semester with American University, dual majors, and a 3-2 engineering program with Purdue University, Columbia University, and Washington University in St. Louis. A tuition-free Ninth Semester Teacher Education Program is also available. Wabash also has a pipeline program that will guide students through the prerequisites for admission to the Master of Science in Accounting (MSA) degree program and give privileged access to Wabash students so that they may enroll at IU immediately upon graduation. Wabash has a new major in financial economics and interdisciplinary minors in Hispanic studies, Asian studies, Multicultural American studies, international studies, and gender studies. There are 9 national honor societies and a chapter of Phi Beta Kappa. **Visiting:** There are regularly scheduled orientations for prospective students, consisting of a tour, lunch, opportunity to meet faculty, coaches, and alumni, and panel discussions on academics, extracurricular activities, and financial aid. There are guides for informal visits, visitors may sit in on classes, and stay overnight. To schedule a visit, contact Mary Towell at (800) 345-5385. **Campus Safety and Security:** Measures include 24-hour foot and vehicle patrol, emergency notification system, and security escort services. There are lighted pathways/sidewalks and controlled access to dorms/residences.

REQUIREMENTS: The SAT or ACT is required. Wabash recommends applicants have 4 high school courses in English, 3 to 4 in math, and 2 each in foreign language, lab science, and social studies. An essay is required, and an interview is recommended. AP credits are accepted. Important factors in the admissions decision are advanced placement or honors courses, leadership record, and extracurricular activities record. All students must complete at least 3 courses each in literature/fine arts, behavioral science, and natural science/math, 2 in history, philosophy, or religion, and 1 in quantitative skills. To graduate, students must maintain a minimum 2.0 GPA for 136 credit hours (34 courses), which include a freshman tutorial and the all-freshmen course Enduring Questions. The student must pass a written comprehensive exam in the major as well as a senior oral exam and must demonstrate proficiency in English and proficiency in a foreign language at a level equivalent to 2 college courses. **Procedure:** Freshmen are admitted fall and spring. Entrance exams should be taken by the spring of the junior year or fall of the senior year. There are early decision, early admissions, deferred admissions, and rolling admissions plans. Early decision applications should be filed by October 15; regular applications, by January 15 for fall entry; and January 15 for spring entry, along with a $40 fee. Notification of early decision is sent November 16; regular decision, on a rolling basis. 42 early decision candidates were accepted for the 2016-2017 class. 32 applicants were on the 2016 waiting list; 5 were admitted. Applications are accepted on-line. **Transfer Students:** 8 transfer students enrolled in 2015-2016. Applicants must submit official transcripts of all college courses attended. Wabash strongly considers the overall high school and college background of applicants. Courses must be liberal arts in nature with a minimum GPA of 2.0 to transfer. Recommendations from the college adviser and dean of students at the previous college attended and a personal written statement are required, with an interview strongly recommended. 24 of 34 credits required for the bachelor's degree must be completed at Wabash. **International Students:** There are 57 international students enrolled. The school actively recruits these students. They must take the TOEFL with a minimum score of 550 on the paper-based TOEFL (PBT) or 80 on the Internet-based version (iBT). They must also take the SAT or ACT.

ADMISSIONS: 63% of the 2016-2017 applicants were accepted. The SAT scores for the 2016-2017 freshman class were: Critical Reading-- 26% below 500, 48% between 500 and 599, 23% between 600 and 699, and 3% between 700 and 800. Math-- 14% below 500, 44% between 500 and 599, 37% between 600 and 699, and 5% between 700 and 800. Writing-- 39% below 500, 38% between 500 and 599, 21% between 600 and 699, and 2% between 700 and 800. The ACT scores were 35% between 18 and 23, 47% between 24 and 29, and 18% above 30. 56% of the current freshmen were in the top fifth of their class; 85% were in the top two fifths. 4 freshmen graduated first in their class. **Admissions Contact:** Michael Thorp, Dean for Enrollment Management. Email: *admissions@wabash.edu* Web: *www.wabash.edu*

FINANCIAL AID: In 2016-2017, 99% of all full-time freshmen and 98% of continuing full-time students received some form of financial aid. 77% of all full-time freshmen and 73% of continuing full-time students received need-based aid. The average freshman award was $39,469. Need-based scholarships or need-based grants averaged $28,590; need-based self-help aid (loans and jobs) averaged $5,217; and other non-need-based awards and non-need-based scholarships averaged $5,662. 52% of undergraduate students work part-time. Average annual earnings from campus work are $2650. The average financial indebtedness of the 2016 graduate was $32,916. Wabash is a member of CSS. The CSS/Profile and federal tax transcript with W-2 statements are required. The FAFSA code is 001844. The priority date for freshman financial aid applications for fall entry is February 15. The deadline for filing freshman financial aid applications for fall entry is March 1.

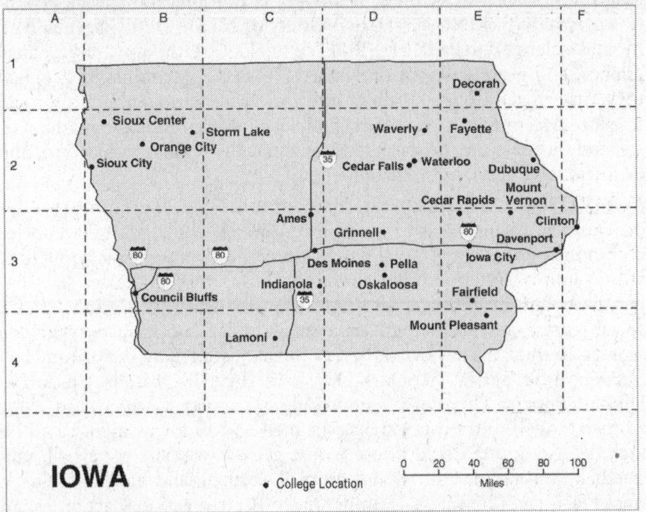

ALLEN COLLEGE *(The complete profile is made available exclusively on our website, www.barronspac.com)*

BRIAR CLIFF UNIVERSITY — B-2
www.briarcliff.edu

Sioux City, IA 51104 — **(712) 279-5200**, **(800) 662-3303**
Fax: (712) 279-1632 — **Email: admissions@briarcliff.edu**

Full-time: 417 men, 476 women
Part-time: 54 men, 132 women
Graduate: 13 men, 66 women
Year: trimesters, summer session
Room & Board: $8348
ACT: 21
Application Deadline: open
Faculty: 61
Ph.D.s: 75%
Student/Faculty: 13 to 1
Tuition: $28,608
Freshman Class: 1774 applied, 1035 accepted, 237 enrolled
CEEB CODE: 6046
COMPETITIVE

Briar Cliff University, founded in 1930, is a private Roman Catholic-Franciscan liberal arts institution. Figures in the above capsule and in this profile are approximate. There are 2 undergraduate schools and 1 graduate school. In addition to regional accreditation, Briar Cliff University has baccalaureate program accreditation with AACSB, CSWE, and NLN. The 70-acre campus is in a suburban area minutes from downtown Sioux City. Including any residence halls, there are 13 buildings.

STUDENT LIFE: 65% of undergraduates are from Iowa. Others are from 26 states, 2 foreign countries, and Canada. 82% are from public schools. 82% are White; 7% Hispanic; 6% African American; 2% Asian American; 2% American Indian/Alaska Native. 55% are Catholic; 26% claim no religious affiliation; 23% Protestant. **Female To Male Ratio:** 1.4:1. The average age of freshmen is 18; all undergraduates, 23. 34% do not continue beyond their first year; 41% remain to graduate. **Housing:** 577 students can be accommodated in college housing, which includes coed dorms. In addition, there are special-interest houses. On-campus housing is guaranteed for the freshman year only. 63% of students live on campus. All students may keep cars.

FACULTY/CLASSROOMS: 48% of faculty are male; 52% are female. All teach undergraduates. No introductory courses are taught by graduate students. The average class size in an introductory lecture is 20; in a laboratory is 18; and in a regular course is 20.

PROGRAMS OF STUDY: Briar Cliff confers B.A., B.S., B.S.N., and B.S.W. degrees. Associate and master's degrees are also awarded. Bachelor's degrees are awarded in BIOLOGICAL SCIENCE (biology/biological science), BUSINESS (accounting, business administration and management, and human resources), COMMUNICATIONS AND THE ARTS (art, communications, dramatic arts, English, graphic design, journalism, media arts, music, and Spanish), COMPUTER AND PHYSICAL SCIENCE (chemistry, computer science, information sciences and systems, mathematics, and radiological technology), EDUCATION (elementary education, health education, and secondary education), ENGINEERING AND ENVIRONMENTAL DESIGN (environmental science), HEALTH PROFESSIONS (medical technology, nursing, and sports medicine), SOCIAL SCIENCE (criminal justice, history, political science/government, psychology, social work, sociology, and theological studies). Biology, business administration, and education are the strongest academically. Nursing has the largest enrollment.

ACTIVITIES: There are no fraternities or sororities. There are 44 groups on campus, including art, cheerleading, choir, chorale, chorus, computers, dance, drama, ethnic, film, honors, jazz band, literary magazine, musical theater, newspaper, pep band, photography, professional, radio and TV, religious, social, social service, and student government. Popular campus events include Texas Hold 'em Tournaments, Welcome Week, and Theater Productions. **Sports:** There are 9 intercollegiate sports for men and 10 for women, and 9 intramural sports for men and 9 for women. Facilities include baseball, softball, and soccer fields, and a recreation center with racquetball courts, a running track, tennis courts, basketball/volleyball courts, and weight-lifting facilities. **Graduates:** From July 1, 2015 to June 30, 2016, 204 bachelor's degrees were awarded. The most popular majors were business/ marketing (33%), health professions and related sciences (11%), and biological/ life sciences (8%). 46 companies recruited on campus in 2015-2016. In an average class, 43% graduate in 4 years or less, 53% graduate in 5 years or less, and 55% graduate in 6 years or less. Of the 2015 graduating class, 37% were enrolled in graduate school within 6 months of graduation.

SERVICES: Counseling and information services are available, as is tutoring in most subjects, and remedial math, reading, and writing. **Library/Resources:** The library contains 82,007 volumes, 21,664 microform items, and 1,244 audio/video tapes/CDs/DVDs. Computerized library services include interlibrary loans, database searching, Internet access, and Wi-Fi capability. Special learning facilities include an art gallery, radio station, TV station, an integrated multimedia center, a nursing simulation lab, a human anatomy/cadaver lab, and an entrepreneurship lab. **Physically Challenged Students:** 90% of the campus is accessible. Facilities include wheelchair ramps, elevators, special parking, specially equipped restrooms, lowered drinking fountains, and lowered telephones. **Special:** Internships, study abroad, dual majors, work-study programs, accelerated degree programs in business administration, human resource management, and professional studies, student-designed interdisciplinary majors, and pass/fail options are available. Students may earn a 3-2 engineering degree with Iowa State University. There are 4 national honor societies, a freshman honors program, and 3 departmental honors programs. **Visiting:** There are regularly scheduled orientations for prospective students, including a presidential welcome, a meeting with faculty and student panels, a luncheon, campus tours, a slide show, and financial aid information. There are guides for informal visits, visitors may sit in on classes, and stay overnight. To schedule a visit, contact the Admissions Office. **Campus Safety and Security:** Measures include 24-hour foot and vehicle patrol, emergency notification system, security escort services, and emergency telephones, lighted pathways/sidewalks, and controlled access to dorms/residences.

REQUIREMENTS: SAT is accepted but the ACT is preferred, and a score of 18 qualifies for automatic acceptance review. Applicants need not be graduates of an accredited secondary school. The GED is accepted. Admission to freshman standing requires 4 years each of English and math, 3 of science, 2 of history, and 1 of social studies, and 2 years of foreign language is recommended. AP and CLEP credits are accepted. Important factors in the admissions decision are leadership record, extracurricular activities record, and advanced placement or honors courses. To graduate, students must complete a minimum of 124 semester hours, maintain a GPA of 2.0 with no more than 1 D in the major, complete the three components of Briar Cliff's general educational program, and complete a major field of concentration. **Procedure:** Freshmen are admitted to all sessions. Entrance exams should be taken by October for scholarship consideration, and by April for admission. There is a rolling admissions plan. Application deadlines are open. Application fee is $20. Notification is sent on a rolling basis. Applications are accepted online. **Transfer Students:** 37 transfer students enrolled in 2015-2016. Applicants must have a minimum GPA of 2.0 with at least 10 credit hours earned and satisfactory dismissal from the previous institution. Grades of D or better transfer for credit. 31 of 124 credits required for the bachelor's degree must be completed at Briar Cliff University. **International Students:** There are 6 international students enrolled. They must take the TOEFL or MELAB. Students may be required to have a telephone interview with an ESL advisor.

ADMISSIONS: 58% of the 2016-2017 applicants were accepted. The ACT scores were 40% below 12, 28% between 12 and 17, 20% between 18 and 23, 9% between 24 and 29, and 3% above 30. 25% of the current freshmen were in the top fifth of their class; 50% were in the top two fifths. 2 freshmen graduated first in their class. **Admissions Contact:** Adam Cory, Assistant Director of Admissions. Email: *admissions@briarcliff.edu* Web: *www.briarcliff.edu*

FINANCIAL AID: In 2016-2017, 100% of all full-time freshmen and 98% of continuing full-time students received some form of financial aid. 73% of all full-time freshmen and 64% of continuing full-time students received need-based aid. The average freshman award was $12,250. Need-based scholarships or need-based grants averaged $3,900; need-based self-help aid (loans and jobs) averaged $7,255; and non-need-based athletic scholarships averaged $5,109. 23% of undergraduate students work part-time. Average annual earnings from campus work are $750. The average financial indebtedness of the 2016 graduate was $30,100. The FAFSA code is 001846. The priority date for freshman financial aid applications for fall entry is March 1.

BUENA VISTA UNIVERSITY — B-2

www.bvu.edu

Storm Lake, IA 50588	(712) 749-2078 (800) 383-9600
Fax: (712) 749-2035	**Email:** admissions@bvu.edu
Full-time: 385 men, 399 women	**Faculty:** 82; IIB, av$
Part-time: 5 men, 6 women	**Ph.D.s:** 77%
Graduate: 5 men, 29 women	**Student/Faculty:** 10 to 1
Year: 4-1-4, summer session	**Tuition:** $32,210
Room & Board: $9304	**Freshman Class:** 1256 applied, 800 accepted, 183 enrolled
ACT: 22	**CEEB CODE:** 6047
Application Deadline: open	**COMPETITIVE**

Buena Vista University, founded in 1891, is a private institution affiliated with the Presbyterian Church. The university offers undergraduate degree programs in business, education, communication and arts, science, social science, philosophy, and religion, and an accredited master's program in education. Programs emphasize career education with a liberal arts foundation. There are 5 undergraduate schools and 1 graduate school. In addition to regional accreditation, Buena Vista has baccalaureate program accreditation with CSWE and CAATE. The 60-acre campus is in a small town 65 miles east of Sioux City. Including any residence halls, there are 16 buildings.

STUDENT LIFE: 79% of undergraduates are from Iowa. Others are from 27 states, and 15 foreign countries. 90% are from public schools. 74% are White; 7% Hispanic; 6% Foreign; 4% two or more races; 4% race unknown; 3% African American; 2% Asian American. **Female To Male Ratio:** 1.1:1. The average age of freshmen is 18; all undergraduates, 20. 27% do not continue beyond their first year; 53% remain to graduate. **Housing:** 1012 students can be accommodated in college housing, which includes coed dorms, and special-interest houses. On-campus housing is guaranteed for all 4 years. 90% of students live on campus. All students may keep cars.

FACULTY/CLASSROOMS: 45% of faculty are male; 55% are female. All teach undergraduates. No introductory courses are taught by graduate students. The average class size in an introductory lecture is 25; in a laboratory is 20; and in a regular course is 14.

PROGRAMS OF STUDY: Buena Vista confers B.A., B.S., B.A.S., and B.A.Sc. degrees. Master's degrees are also awarded. Bachelor's degrees are awarded in BIOLOGICAL SCIENCE (biochemistry and biology/biological science), BUSINESS (accounting, banking and finance, business administration and management, business economics, marketing/retailing/merchandising, and sports management), COMMUNICATIONS AND THE ARTS (animation, art, arts administration/management, communications, digital media, English, graphic design, music, music production/recording technology, Spanish, and theatre arts), COMPUTER AND PHYSICAL SCIENCE (chemistry, computer science, mathematics, physics, and science), EDUCATION (art education, athletic training, business education, elementary education, music education, science education, secondary education, and special education), ENGINEERING AND ENVIRONMENTAL DESIGN (environmental science), HEALTH PROFESSIONS (art therapy, biomedical science, and exercise science), SOCIAL SCIENCE (criminal justice, history, interdisciplinary studies, physical fitness/movement, political science/government, psychology, and social work). Biology, mathematics, and business are the strongest academically. Biology, education, and business have the largest enrollments.

ACTIVITIES: There are no fraternities or sororities. There are 60 groups on campus, including art, band, cheerleading, choir, chorale, chorus, communications, computers, dance, drama, drill team, environmental, ethnic, honors, international, jazz band, LGBT, musical theater, newspaper, photography, political, professional, radio and TV, religious, social, social service, and student government. Popular campus events include Academic and Cultural Events Series, Buenafication Day, American Heritage Lecture Series, Scholars Day, and the All-Campus Christmas Dinner. **Sports:** There are 9 intercollegiate sports for men and 8 for women, and 10 intramural sports for men and 10 for women. Facilities include a stadium, a field house with a gym, basketball, volleyball, racquetball, and tennis courts, and football, softball, and baseball fields, a track, facilities for weight training and other recreational activities, an indoor pool, and a game room. **Graduates:** From July 1, 2015 to June 30, 2016, 173 bachelor's degrees were awarded. The most popular majors were business (14%), biology (13%), and exercise science (8%).

SERVICES: Counseling and information services are available, as is tutoring in most subjects, a reader service for the blind, and remedial math, reading, and writing. **Library/Resources:** The library contains 5,000 volumes, 41,372 microform items, 6,000 audio/video tapes/CDs/DVDs, and subscribes to 639 periodicals including electronic. Computerized library services include interlibrary loans, database searching, Internet access, and Wi-Fi capability. Special learning facilities include an art gallery, radio station, TV station, a student newspaper desktop production lab. **Physically Challenged Students:** Facilities include wheelchair ramps, elevators, special parking, specially equipped restrooms, special class scheduling, lowered drinking fountains, and lowered telephones. **Special:** Special academic offerings include a 3-2 engineering degree program with Washington University School of Engineering and Applied Science in St. Louis. Buena Vista has also partnered with the University of Iowa College of Law and the Creighton University School of Law in a 3+3 Accelerated Law School Entry Program. Students may study abroad in Japan, Taiwan, Australia, and Europe. Buena Vista offers dual and student-designed majors, credit for life experience, and pass/fail options in courses outside the major field. Nondegree study is possible. Internships are required in many majors and encouraged in most. The J. Leslie Rollins Fellowship allows 1 or 2 students each year to design an internship anywhere in the world. There are 6 national honor societies and a freshman honors program. **Visiting:** There are regularly scheduled orientations for prospective students, campus tour and meetings with an admissions counselor, faculty representatives, coaches, and activity representatives in the student's areas of interest. There are guides for informal visits, visitors may sit in on classes, and stay overnight. To schedule a visit, contact Deb Willer at (712) 749-2078. **Campus Safety and Security:** Measures include 24-hour foot and vehicle patrol, emergency notification system, self-defense education, and security escort services. There are also shuttle buses, emergency telephones, lighted pathways/sidewalks, controlled access to dorms/residences, and an enhanced 911 system on campus.

REQUIREMENTS: The ACT is required. The SAT scores may be submitted. Applicants must be graduates of an accredited secondary school or have earned a GED. The college requires 13 academic credits, including 4 of English and 3 each of math, social studies, and science. Campus visits and an interview are recommended. AP and CLEP credits are accepted. Important factors in the admissions decision are advanced placement or honors courses, leadership record, and recommendations by school officials. All students must complete 12 semester hours of humanities, 9 semester hours each of natural sciences and social sciences, and 3 semester hours of fine arts. In addition, students must successfully complete requirements in intellectual foundation courses in mathematics and communication. Students must also participate in the Academic and Cultural Events Series, through which they attend lectures and performances by national and world leaders. The bachelor's degree requires a minimum of 128 semester hours, including 32 to 64 hours in the major, with a GPA of at least 2.0, or higher for some majors. **Procedure:** Freshmen are admitted in the fall, winter, and spring. Entrance exams should be taken during the spring of the junior year or October of the senior year. There are deferred admissions and rolling admissions plans. Application deadlines are open. Notification is sent on a rolling basis. Application fees are waived if application is completed on-line. **Transfer Students:** 33 transfer students enrolled in 2015-2016. A high school diploma and a minimum GPA of 2.5 from the applicant's college are required. 30 of 128 credits required for the bachelor's degree must be completed at Buena Vista. **International Students:** There are 44 international students enrolled. The school actively recruits these students. They must take the TOEFL with a minimum score of 500 on the paper-based TOEFL (PBT) or 59 on the Internet-based version (iBT), and the college's own test.

ADMISSIONS: 64% of the 2016-2017 applicants were accepted. The ACT scores were 12% between 12 and 17, 49% between 18 and 23, 34% between 24 and 29, and 5% above 30. 31% of the current freshmen were in the top fifth of their class; 63% were in the top two fifths. 7 freshmen graduated first in their class. **Admissions Contact:** Michael Fox, Director of Admissions. Email: *admissions@bvu.edu* Web: *www.bvu.edu*

FINANCIAL AID: In 2016-2017, 99% of all full-time freshmen and 98% of continuing full-time students received some form of financial aid. The college's own financial statement is required. The FAFSA code is 001847. The deadline for filing freshman financial aid applications for fall entry is June 1.

CENTRAL COLLEGE — D-3

www.central.edu

Pella, IA 50219	**(641) 628-7637** **(877) 462-3687**
Fax: (641) 628-5316	**Email: admission@central.edu**
Full-time: 580 men, 624 women	**Faculty:** 97; IIB, -$
Part-time: 13 men, 31 women	**Ph.D.s:** 94%
Graduate: n/av	**Student/Faculty:** 12 to 1
Year: semesters, summer session	**Tuition:** $34,612
Room & Board: $9980	**Freshman Class:** 3899 applied, 2863 accepted, 323 enrolled
SAT M/W: 530/540	**CEEB CODE:** 6087
Application Deadline: August 15	**COMPETITIVE**

Central College, founded in 1853, is a private, residential four-year liberal arts college known for its academic rigor and strength in global experiential learning, STEM (science, technology, engineering and math), sustainability education, athletics success and tradition, and leadership and service. Central continues to value its long-standing relationship with the Reformed Church in America. The college participates in NCAA Division III athletics and is a member of the Iowa Conference. There is 1 undergraduate school. In addition to regional accreditation, Central College has baccalaureate program accreditation with NASM, NCATE, ACS, and CAATE. The 169-acre campus is in a small town 45 miles southeast of Des Moines. Including any residence halls, there are 58 buildings.

STUDENT LIFE: 75% of undergraduates are from Iowa. Others are from 26 states, and 7 foreign countries. 95% are from public schools. 89% are White; 5% race unknown; 4% Hispanic; 2% African American; 2% Asian American; 2% two or more races; 1% Foreign. 62% are Protestant; 22% claim no religious affiliation; 16% Catholic. **Female To Male Ratio:** 1.1:1. The average age of freshmen is 18; all undergraduates, 20. 21% do not continue beyond their first year; 65% remain to graduate. **Housing:** 1405 students can be accommodated in college housing, which includes single-sex and coed dorms and on-campus apartments, language houses, special-interest houses, fraternity houses, and sorority houses. On-campus housing is guaranteed for all 4 years. 94% of students live on campus. All students may keep cars. Alcohol is not permitted.

FACULTY/CLASSROOMS: 51% of faculty are male; 49% are female. All teach and do research. No introductory courses are taught by graduate students. The average class size in an introductory lecture is 19; in a laboratory is 19; and in a regular course is 16.

PROGRAMS OF STUDY: Central College confers B.A. and B.S. degrees. Bachelor's degrees are awarded in BIOLOGICAL SCIENCE (biochemistry and biology/biological science), BUSINESS (accounting and business administration and management), COMMUNICATIONS AND THE ARTS (art, communications, dramatic arts, English, French, German, linguistics, music, Spanish, and theatre arts), COMPUTER AND PHYSICAL SCIENCE (actuarial science, chemistry, computer science, mathematics, natural sciences, and physics), EDUCATION (athletic training, elementary education, and music education), ENGINEERING AND ENVIRONMENTAL DESIGN (engineering and environmental science), HEALTH PROFESSIONS (exercise science), SOCIAL SCIENCE (anthropology, economics, history, international studies, philosophy, political science/government, psychology, religion, and sociology). Exercise science, business management, and biology have the largest enrollments.

ACTIVITIES: 4% of men belong to 5 local fraternities; 3% of women belong to 2 local sororities. There are 100 groups on campus, including mock trial, entrepreneurship, art, band, cheerleading, choir, chorale, chorus, communications, dance, drama, environmental, ethnic, honors, international, jazz band, LGBT, literary magazine, musical theater, orchestra, pep band, political, professional, religious, social, social service, student government, and sustainability. Popular campus events include Lemming Race, Breakfast of Champions, and Candlelight Christmas Concert and Charity Ball. **Sports:** There are 9 intercollegiate sports for men and 9 for women, and 8 intramural sports for men and 8 for women. Facilities include a gymnasium and fieldhouse with indoor track, tennis, fitness center for strength/conditioning, football/track stadium, competition and practice soccer fields, golf practice facility, cross country course, baseball and softball fields, and a fitness center for general student use. **Graduates:** From July 1, 2015 to June 30, 2016, 280 bachelor's degrees were awarded. The most popular majors were biology (11%), elementary education (11%), and business management (10%). 93 companies recruited on campus in 2015-2016. In an average class, 58% graduate in 4 years or less, 64% graduate in 5 years or less, and 65% graduate in 6 years or less. Of the 2015 graduating class, 20% were enrolled in graduate school within 6 months of graduation, and 75% were employed.

SERVICES: Counseling and information services are available, as is tutoring in every subject. **Library/Resources:** The library contains 150,877 volumes, 2,085 microform items, 4,143 audio/video tapes/CDs/DVDs, and subscribes to 204 periodicals including electronic. Computerized library services include interlibrary loans, database searching, Internet access, and Wi-Fi capability. Special learning facilities include an art gallery. **Physically Challenged Students:** 90% of the campus is accessible. Facilities include wheelchair ramps, elevators, special parking, specially equipped restrooms, special class scheduling, lowered drinking fountains, lowered telephones, and special housing. **Special:** Central College offers a B.S. in engineering degree and a partnership program with Allen College whereby students receive a B.A. from Central and a BSN from Allen College. About 50% of Central students participate in study abroad in Vienna, London, Granada, Merida, Bangor, and Budapest. 76% of students complete at least one internship, including the Washington semester and the Chicago semester as well as opportunities abroad. 30% of students participate in music ensembles. There is a freshman honors program and 10 departmental honors programs. **Visiting:** There are regularly scheduled orientations for prospective students, consisting of registration session with academic advisor, and presentations by the academic dean, student life dean, financial aid director, registrar and admission staff. There are guides for informal visits, visitors may sit in on classes, and stay overnight. To schedule a visit, contact Sue Cerwinske at admission@central.edu. **Campus Safety and Security:** Measures include 24-hour foot and vehicle patrol, emergency notification system, self-defense education, security escort services, emergency telephones, lighted pathways/sidewalks, and controlled access to dorms/residences.

REQUIREMENTS: The ACT is required. All applicants must be graduates of an accredited secondary school or have earned a GED. Candidates who have an ACT composite score of 20 or above (940-970 SAT critical reading and mathematics combined), have a 2.70 cumulative high school GPA, rank in the top half of their secondary school graduating class and have met the recommended college-preparatory curriculum are typically admitted. Central College requires applicants to be in the upper 50% of their class. A GPA of 2.7 is required. AP and CLEP credits are accepted. Important factors in the admissions decision are advanced placement or honors courses, extracurricular activities record, and leadership record. Students are required to complete 120 semester hours, including at least 20 hours of 300-level or above, with a minimum 2.0 cumulative and major GPA. Core requirements include courses in integrative studies, disciplinary studies, global sustainability, global perspective, and writing intensive. **Procedure:** Freshmen are admitted in the fall, spring, and summer. Entrance exams should be taken spring of your junior year of high school. There are deferred admissions and rolling admissions plans. Applications should be filed by August 15 for fall entry; January 1 for spring entry; and May 1 for summer entry, along with a $25 fee. Notification is sent on a rolling basis. Application fees are waived if application is completed online. **Transfer Students:** 31 transfer students enrolled in 2015-2016. Each transfer student is considered individually. Interviews are encouraged. 45 of 120 credits required for the bachelor's degree must be completed at Central College. **International Students:** There are 10 international students enrolled. The school actively recruits these students. They must take the TOEFL with a minimum score of 530 on the paper-based TOEFL (PBT) or 71 on the Internet-based version (iBT). They must also take the SAT or ACT.

ADMISSIONS: 17% of the current freshmen were in the top fifth of their class; 80% were in the top two fifths. **Admissions Contact:** Chevy Frieburger, Director of Admission. Email: *admission@central.edu* Web: *www.central.edu*

FINANCIAL AID: In 2016-2017, 100% of all full-time freshmen and 99% of continuing full-time students received some form of financial aid. 86% of all full-time freshmen and 78% of continuing full-time students received need-based aid. The average freshman award was $32,165. Need-based scholarships or need-based grants averaged $21,485 ($34,612 maximum); need-based self-help aid (loans and jobs) averaged $3,144 ($7,500 maximum); other non-need-based awards and non-need-based scholarships averaged $4,787 ($34,612 maximum); and $2,749 from other forms of aid. 57% of undergraduate students work part-time. Average annual earnings from campus work are $128. The average financial indebtedness of the 2016 graduate was $29,590. Central College is a member of CSS. The FAFSA code is 001850. The priority date for freshman financial aid applications for fall entry is January 15.

CLARKE UNIVERSITY — E-2

www.clarke.edu

Dubuque, IA 52001	**(563) 588-6436** **(800) 383-2345**
Fax: (563) 588-6789	**Email: admissions@clarke.edu**
Full-time: 264 men, 528 women	**Faculty:** 83; IIB, --$
Part-time: 27 men, 49 women	**Ph.D.s:** 84%
Graduate: 40 men, 167 women	**Student/Faculty:** 10 to 1
Year: semesters, summer session	**Tuition:** $29,940
Room & Board: $9000	**Freshman Class:** 1257 applied, 904 accepted, 180 enrolled
SAT CR/M: 507/520 **ACT:** 23	**CEEB CODE:** 6099
Application Deadline: open	**COMPETITIVE**

Clarke University, established in 1843, is a private Catholic institution. A strong liberal arts core integrated into all majors and pre-professional programs. There is 1 undergraduate school and 1 graduate school. In addition to regional accreditation, Clarke has baccalaureate program accreditation with APTA, CSWE, NASM, NCATE, NLN, CAPTE, COSW, CCNE, CAATE, Iowa Department of Education, and National Association of Schools of Music. The 55-acre campus is in a small town 150 miles west of Chicago. Including any residence halls, there are 14 buildings.

STUDENT LIFE: 56% of undergraduates are from Iowa. Others are from 28 states, and 6 foreign countries. 80% are from public schools. 85% are White; 7% Hispanic; 4% African American; 2% two or more races; 1% Asian American; 1% Foreign; 1% race unknown. 45% claim no religious affiliation; 41% Catholic; 13% Protestant. **Female To Male Ratio:** 2.2:1. The average age of freshmen is 19; all undergraduates, 23. 23% do not continue beyond their first year; 65% remain to graduate. **Housing:** 577 students can be accommodated in college housing, which includes single-sex and coed dorms, on-campus apartments, honors houses. A residence hall is reserved for upperclassmen, and an apartment is residence building reserved for juniors and seniors. On-campus housing is guaranteed for all 4 years. 60% of students commute. All students may keep cars.

FACULTY/CLASSROOMS: 33% of faculty are male; 67% are female. 91% teach undergraduates and do research. No introductory courses are taught by graduate students. The average class size in an introductory lecture is 24; in a laboratory is 11; and in a regular course is 14.

PROGRAMS OF STUDY: Clarke confers B.A., B.S., B.A.S., B.F.A., B.S.W., and B.S.N. degrees. Associate, master's, and doctoral degrees are also awarded. Bachelor's degrees are awarded in AGRICULTURE (environmental studies), BIOLOGICAL SCIENCE (biochemistry and biology/biological science), BUSINESS (accounting, business administration and management, and sports management), COMMUNICATIONS AND THE ARTS (art history and appreciation, communications, dramatic arts, English, graphic design, musical theater, Spanish, and studio art), COMPUTER AND PHYSICAL SCIENCE (chemistry, computer information systems, computer science, and mathematics), EDUCATION (art education, athletic training, elementary education, music education, secondary education, and special education), ENGINEERING AND ENVIRONMENTAL DESIGN (environmental science), HEALTH PROFESSIONS (nursing and physical therapy), SOCIAL SCIENCE (food science, history, liberal arts/general studies, philosophy, psychology, religion, and social work). Physical therapy, biology, and chemistry are the strongest academically. Business administration, nursing, and psychology have the largest enrollments.

ACTIVITIES: There are no fraternities or sororities. There are 26 groups on campus, including art, cheerleading, choir, chorale, chorus, computers, dance, drama, environmental, ethnic, honors, international, jazz band, LGBT, literary magazine, musical theater, newspaper, pep band, photography, political, professional, religious, social, social service, and student government. Popular campus events include Family Weekend, New Year's Dance, Homecoming Activities, Christmas Dinner, and Midnight Pancake Breakfast. **Sports:** There are 9 intercollegiate sports for men and 10 for women, and 7 intramural sports for men and 7 for women. Facilities include a gym, an arena, indoor track, soccer field, basketball, volleyball, tennis, racquetball courts, fitness trail, weight and aerobics rooms, an indoor batting cage/pitching mound area, baseball/softball fields and alpine ski courses nearby, plus a municipal golf course. **Graduates:** From July 1, 2015 to June 30, 2016, 203 bachelor's degrees were awarded. The most popular majors were nursing (30%), philosophy (14%), and education (9%). 50 companies recruited on campus in 2015-2016. In an average class, 49% graduate in 4 years or less, 66% graduate in 5 years or less, and 68% graduate in 6 years or less. Of the 2015 graduating class, 31% were enrolled in graduate school within 6 months of graduation, and 69% were employed.

SERVICES: Counseling and information services are available, as is tutoring in most subjects, a reader service for the blind, and remedial math, reading, and writing. **Library/Resources:** The library contains 98,480 volumes, 6,700 microform items, 1,500 audio/video tapes/CDs/DVDs, and subscribes to 68,000 periodicals including electronic. Computerized library services include interlibrary loans, database searching, Internet access, and Wi-Fi capability. Special learning facilities include an art gallery, planetarium, an art slide library, electronic music studio, and several computer-integrated specialized departmental labs. **Physically Challenged Students:** 90% of the campus is accessible. Facilities include wheelchair ramps, elevators, special parking, specially equipped restrooms, special class scheduling, lowered drinking fountains, and lowered telephones. **Special:** There are 4 national honor societies, a freshman honors program, and 3 departmental honors programs. **Visiting:** There are regularly scheduled orientations for prospective students, Admissions presentation, tour, faculty appointments, and lunch. There are guides for informal visits, visitors may sit in on classes, and stay overnight. To schedule a visit, contact Julie Cirks at julie.cirks@clarke.edu. **Campus Safety and Security:** Measures include 24-hour foot and vehicle patrol, emergency notification system, and security escort services, emergency telephones, lighted pathways/sidewalks, and controlled access to dorms/residences.

REQUIREMENTS: The SAT or ACT is required. The high school transcript should include 4 years of English, 3 each of math, history/social science, and science (4 for human biology and physical therapy majors), 2 of the same foreign language, and 5 of electives. AP and CLEP credits are accepted. To graduate, all students must complete 124 semester hours, with 30 to 70 in the major, and maintain a GPA of 2.0 (2.5 for education majors or 3.25 for physical therapy majors). Students must complete Cornerstone I and II, a Capstone course, and 6 hours each in religious studies, philosophy, fine arts, humanities, math, and natural sciences, and social sciences **Procedure:** Freshmen are admitted to all sessions. Entrance exams should be taken in the spring of the junior year or the fall of the senior year. There are deferred admissions and rolling admissions plans. Application deadlines are open. Application fee is $25. Application fees are waived if application is completed online. **Transfer Students:** 55 transfer students enrolled in 2015-2016. Applicants must submit a transcript and a recommendation from the dean of students for each college attended. Students with fewer than 24 completed semester hours must also submit a high school transcript and SAT or ACT scores. 30 of 124 credits required for the bachelor's degree must be completed at Clarke. **International Students:** There are 7 international students enrolled. The school actively recruits these students. They must take the TOEFL with a minimum score of 527 on the paper-based TOEFL (PBT) or 71 on the Internet-based version (iBT). They must also take the SAT or ACT.

ADMISSIONS: 72% of the 2016-2017 applicants were accepted. The SAT scores for the 2016-2017 freshman class were: Critical Reading-- 43% below 500, 43% between 500 and 599, and 14% between 600 and 699. Math-- 48% below 500, 33% between 500 and 599, 14% between 600 and 699, and 5% between 700 and 800. The ACT scores were 4% between 12 and 17, 56% between 18 and 23, 37% between 24 and 29, and 3% above 30. 40% of the current freshmen were in the top fifth of their class; 70% were in the top two fifths. **Admissions Contact:** Julie Cirks, Associate Director of Admissions. Email: *admissions@clarke.edu* Web: *www.clarke.edu*

FINANCIAL AID: In 2016-2017, 100% of all full-time freshmen and continuing full-time students received some form of financial aid. 87% of all full-time freshmen and continuing full-time students received need-based aid. The average freshman award was $27,301. Need-based scholarships or need-based grants averaged $6,157; need-based self-help aid (loans and jobs) averaged $3,648; non-need-based athletic scholarships averaged $2,513; and other non-need-based awards and non-need-based scholarships averaged $12,582. 35% of undergraduate students work part-time. Average annual earnings from campus work are $964. The average financial indebtedness of the 2016 graduate was $30,594. The FAFSA code is 001852. The priority date for freshman financial aid applications for fall entry is April 15. The filing deadline for fall entry is rolling.

COE COLLEGE — E-3

www.coe.edu

Cedar Rapids, IA 52402 — (319) 399-8046, (877) CALL-COE

Fax: (319) 399-8816	**Email:** admission@coe.edu
Full-time: 563 men, 780 women	**Faculty:** 96; IIB, -$
Part-time: 39 men, 26 women	**Ph.D.s:** 91%
Graduate: n/av	**Student/Faculty:** 8 to 1
Year: semesters, summer session	**Tuition:** $42,430
Room & Board: $9140	**Freshman Class:** 6173 applied, 3249 accepted, 362 enrolled
SAT CR/M/W: 580/570/545 **ACT:** 25	**CEEB CODE:** 6101
Application Deadline: March 1	**VERY COMPETITIVE**

Coe College offers superb academics and exciting social opportunities in a thriving urban setting that allows students to grow and succeed. With a residential campus established in 1851, Coe has a distinctive reputation for quality. There is 1 undergraduate school. In addition to regional accreditation, Coe has baccalaureate program accreditation with NASM, CAAHEP, CCNE, CAATE, and ACS. The 53-acre campus is in an urban area in the heart of the Cedar Rapids community, close to a major interstate and a regional airport, 225 miles west of Chicago. Including any residence halls, there are 32 buildings.

STUDENT LIFE: 55% of undergraduates are from out of state, mostly the Midwest. Students are from 38 states, 18 foreign countries, and Canada. 9% are Hispanic; 70% White; 6% African American; 6% Foreign; 4% race unknown; 3% two or more races; 2% Asian American. **Female To Male Ratio:** 1.3:1. The average age of freshmen is 18; all undergraduates, 20. 25% do not continue beyond their first year; 67% remain to graduate. **Housing:** 1150 students can be accommodated in college housing, which includes single-sex and coed dorms, on-campus apartments, honors houses, special-interest houses, and living learning community. On-campus housing is guaranteed for all 4 years. 86% of students live on campus; of those, 75% remain on campus on weekends. All students may keep cars.

FACULTY/CLASSROOMS: 48% of faculty are male; 50% are female. All teach undergraduates, and 95% do research. No introductory courses are taught by graduate students. The average class size in an introductory lecture is 17; in a laboratory is 12; and in a regular course is 11.

PROGRAMS OF STUDY: Coe confers B.A., B.M., and B.S.N. degrees. Bachelor's degrees are awarded in AGRICULTURE (environmental studies), BIOLOGICAL SCIENCE (biochemistry, biology/biological science, molecular biology, and neurosciences), BUSINESS (accounting, business administration and management, and organizational behavior), COMMUNICATIONS AND THE ARTS (art, art history and appreciation, communications, creative writing, English, film arts, French, German, literature, music, public relations, Spanish, theatre arts, and writing), COMPUTER AND PHYSICAL SCIENCE (chemistry, computer science, mathematics, physics, and science), EDUCATION (athletic training, elementary education, music education, physical education, and secondary education), ENGINEERING AND ENVIRONMENTAL DESIGN (environmental science and preengineering), HEALTH PROFESSIONS (nursing, physical therapy, predentistry, premedicine, prephysical therapy, and preveterinary science), SOCIAL SCIENCE (African American studies, American studies, Asian/Oriental studies, economics, French studies, gender studies, German area studies, history, industrial and organizational psychology, interdisciplinary studies, philosophy, political science/government, prelaw, psychology, religion, sociology, Spanish studies, and women's studies). Biology, physics, and psychology are the strongest academically. Business administration, psychology, and biology have the largest enrollments.

ACTIVITIES: 24% of men belong to 5 national fraternities; 26% of women belong to 3 national sororities. There are 80 groups on campus, including art, band, cheerleading, choir, chorale, chorus, communications, computers, dance, drama, environmental, ethnic, film, honors, international, jazz band, LGBT, literary magazine, musical theater, newspaper, orchestra, pep band, photography, political, professional, radio and TV, religious, social, social service, student government, student senate, and symphony. Popular campus events include Coe Olympics, International Student Banquet and Cultural Show, Flunk Day, and Prez Ball. **Sports:** There are 11 intercollegiate sports for men and 10 for women, and 8 intramural sports for men and 6 for women. Facilities include a racquet center with indoor and outdoor tennis courts, racquetball courts, squash courts, and indoor track, a field house with an indoor natatorium, wrestling room, fitness center, rock-climbing wall, courts for basketball and volleyball, and batting cages for baseball and softball. There is also an outdoor track, softball diamond, football/soccer stadium, baseball field, and soccer practice field. **Graduates:** From July 1, 2015 to June 30, 2016, 286 bachelor's degrees were awarded. The most popular majors were business administration (18%), psychology (16%), and physical education (8%). In an average class, 60% graduate in 4 years or less, 66% graduate in 5 years or less, and 67% graduate in 6 years or less.

SERVICES: Counseling and information services are available, as is tutoring in most subjects, such as sciences, math, business, and foreign languages. There is also a reader service for the blind, and remedial math, reading, and writing. In addition a writing center, speaking center, and an academic achievement program are available. **Library/Resources:** The 2 libraries contain 550,116 volumes, 5,979 microform items, 12,664 audio/video tapes/CDs/DVDs, and subscribe to 4,031 periodicals including electronic. Computerized library services include interlibrary loans, database searching, Internet access, and Wi-Fi capability. Special learning facilities include an art gallery, radio station, an ornithological wing. **Physically Challenged Students:** 80% of the campus is accessible. Facilities include wheelchair ramps, elevators, special parking, specially equipped restrooms, special class scheduling, lowered drinking fountains, lowered telephones, and special housing. **Special:** Coe offers cross-registration with nearby Mount Mercy University and the University of Iowa. 31 Off-campus programs are offered; 8 domestic and 23 international in 19 countries. Nondegree study, dual majors and student-designed majors also are possible. Practicum experience is required for graduation. Core course instructors serve as students' academic advisors. There are 8 national honor societies, Phi Beta Kappa, and a freshman honors program. **Visiting:** There are regularly scheduled orientations for prospective students, consisting of tours, a luncheon, and informational sessions on admission, financial aid, and student life. There are guides for informal visits, visitors may sit in on classes, and stay overnight. To schedule a visit, contact Larimer Porter or Maggie St. Clair at (319) 399-8500. **Campus Safety and Security:** Measures include 24-hour foot and vehicle patrol, emergency notification system, security escort services, emergency telephones, lighted pathways/sidewalks, and controlled access to dorms/residences.

REQUIREMENTS: The SAT or ACT is required. Coe recommends that applicants have 4 years in English, 3 each in math, history, science, and social studies, and 2 in foreign language. All students must submit an essay. The GED is accepted. A GPA of 3.0 is required. AP credits are accepted. Important factors in the admissions decision are advanced placement or honors courses, recommendations by school officials, and extracurricular activities record. All students must take 5 writing-emphasis courses, a first-year seminar, and a distribution of courses in fine arts, humanities, natural sciences and mathematics, social sciences, and diverse cultural perspectives. A minimum of 32 course credits, including 9 to 12 in the major, and a 2.0 GPA are required for graduation. All students are required to do a practicum experience including an internship, independent research project, or off-campus study program. Students in the honors program must submit a thesis. **Procedure:** Freshmen are admitted fall and spring. Entrance exams should be taken in the spring of the junior year or the fall of the senior year. There are deferred admissions and rolling admissions plans. Applications should be filed by March 1 for fall entry, along with a $30 fee. Notification is sent on a rolling basis. Applications are accepted on-line. Application fees are waived if application is completed on-line. **Transfer Students:** 42 transfer students enrolled in 2015-2016. Applicants must be high school graduates, have a minimum GPA of 2.5, and submit either SAT or ACT scores. An associate degree and an interview also are recommended. 8 of 32 credits required for the bachelor's degree must be completed at Coe. **International Students:** There are 79 international students enrolled. The school actively recruits these students. They must take the TOEFL with a minimum score of 520 on the paper-based TOEFL (PBT) or 68 on the Internet-based version (iBT), or take the IELTS. They must also take the SAT or ACT.

ADMISSIONS: 53% of the 2016-2017 applicants were accepted. The SAT scores for the 2016-2017 freshman class were: Critical Reading-- 13% below 500, 48% between 500 and 599, 23% between 600 and 699, and 16% between 700 and 800. Math-- 16% below 500, 42% between 500 and 599, 29% between 600 and 699, and 13% between 700 and 800. Writing-- 40% below 500, 25% between 500 and 599, 30% between 600 and 699, and 5% between 700 and 800. The ACT scores were 1% between 12 and 17, 37% between 18 and 23, 46% between 24 and 29, and 16% above 30. 53% of the current freshmen were in the top fifth of their class; 79% were in the top two fifths. 9 freshmen graduated first in their class. **Admissions Contact:** Julie Staker, Dean of Admission. Email: *admission@coe.edu* Web: *www.coe.edu*

FINANCIAL AID: In 2016-2017, 99% of all full-time freshmen and 99% of continuing full-time students received some form of financial aid. 87% of all full-time freshmen and 84% of continuing full-time students received need-based aid. The average freshman award was $38,065. Need-based scholarships or need-based grants averaged $8,650 ($31,000 maximum); need-based self-help aid (loans and jobs) averaged $6,950 ($8,800 maximum); and other non-need-based awards and non-need-based scholarships averaged $26,200 ($40,670 maximum). 51% of undergraduate students work part-time. Average annual earnings from campus work are $1200. The average financial indebtedness of the 2016 graduate was $35,008. The FAFSA code is 001854. The priority date for freshman financial aid applications for fall entry is March 1.

CORNELL COLLEGE — E-4

www.cornellcollege.edu

Mount Vernon, IA 52314	**(319) 895-4215** **(800) 747-1112**
Fax: (319) 895-4451	**Email: admission@cornellcollege.edu**
Full-time: 489 men, 484 women	**Faculty:** 95; IIB, -$
Part-time: 1 women	**Ph.D.s:** 98%
Graduate: 2 men, 2 women	**Student/Faculty:** 10 to 1
Year: other	**Tuition:** $39,900
Room & Board: $8900	**Freshman Class:** 1973 applied, 1396 accepted, 287 enrolled
SAT CR/M/W: 560/580/540 **ACT:** 26	**CEEB CODE:** 6119
Application Deadline: March 1	**VERY COMPETITIVE**

Cornell College, founded in 1853, and is private college affiliated with the United Methodist Church that emphases on the liberal arts, and on student service and leadership. Cornell has a one-course-at-a-time calendar in which the year is divided into eight 3 1/2 week terms. There is 1 undergraduate school. In addition to regional accreditation, Cornell has baccalaureate program accreditation with ACS. The 130-acre campus is in a small town 15 miles east of Cedar Rapids and 3 hours west of Chicago. Including any residence halls, there are 60 buildings.

STUDENT LIFE: 83% of undergraduates are from out of state, mostly the Midwest. Students are from 45 states, and 22 foreign countries. 65% are White; 12% Hispanic; 5% African American; 5% Foreign; 5% race unknown; 3% Asian American; 3% two or more races; 1% American Indian/Alaska Native. **Male To Female Ratio:** 1.0:1. The average age of freshmen is 18; all undergraduates, 20. 22% do not continue beyond their first year; 68% remain to graduate. **Housing:** 1052 students can be accommodated in college housing, which includes single-sex, coed dorms and on-campus apartments, special-interest houses, living and learning communities, and connect floors. On-campus housing is guaranteed for all 4 years, is available on a first-come, first-served basis, and on a lottery system for upperclassmen. 93% of students live on campus; of those, 66% remain on campus on weekends. All students may keep cars.

FACULTY/CLASSROOMS: 56% of faculty are male; 54% are female. All teach undergraduates and do research. No introductory courses are taught by graduate students. The average class size in an introductory lecture is 18; in a laboratory is 18; and in a regular course is 16.

PROGRAMS OF STUDY: Cornell confers B.A., B.Mus., and B.S.S. degrees. Bachelor's degrees are awarded in BIOLOGICAL SCIENCE (biochemistry and biology/biological science), BUSINESS (business economics, business intelligence and analytics, and business systems analysis), COMMUNICATIONS AND THE ARTS (art history and appreciation, English, English literature, English Writing, French, German, music, Russian, Spanish, studio art, and theatre studies), COMPUTER AND PHYSICAL SCIENCE (chemistry, computer science, geology, mathematics, and physics), EDUCATION (elementary education, foreign languages education, music education, and secondary education), ENGINEERING AND ENVIRONMENTAL DESIGN (engineering science and environmental science), SOCIAL SCIENCE (classical/ancient civilization, economics, ethnic studies, gender studies, history, international relations, Latin American studies, philosophy, political science/government, psychology, religion, Russian and Slavic studies, sociology, and women & gender studies). Biochemistry and molecular biology, psychology, economics and business, and theatre are the strongest academically. Psychology, kinesiology, and biochemistry & molecular biology have the largest enrollments.

ACTIVITIES: 21% of men belong to 8 local fraternities; 39% of women belong to 8 local sororities. There are 78 groups on campus, including and leadership development, steel drum band, art, band, cheerleading, chess, choir, chorale, chorus, communications, computers, dance, debate, drama, environmental, ethnic, honors, international, jazz band, LGBT, literary magazine, Mock trial, musical theater, newspaper, opera, orchestra, photography, political, professional, radio and TV, religious, social, social service, student government, and yearbook. Popular campus events include Music Mondays. **Sports:** There are 10 intercollegiate sports for men and 9 for women, and 15 intramural sports for men and 15 for women. Facilities include multisport center, basketball and volleyball arena, sports fitness and training facilities, indoor track, a wrestling room, multipurpose courts for tennis, basketball, and volleyball, batting cages, golf hitting nets, football and track stadium, baseball, soccer, softball, football practice fields, outdoor tennis courts, and ultimate frisbee. **Graduates:** From July 1, 2015 to June 30, 2016, 275 bachelor's degrees were awarded. The most popular majors were psychology (14%), biochemistry and molecular biology (13%), and art/art history (10%). 15 companies recruited on campus in 2015-2016. In an average class, 69% graduate in 3 years or less, 70% graduate in 4 years or less, 70% graduate in 5 years or less, and 68% graduate in 6 years or less. Of the 2015 graduating class, 12% were enrolled in graduate school within 6 months of graduation, and 82% were employed.

SERVICES: Counseling and information services are available, as is tutoring in most subjects, quantitative reasoning studio, and a center for teaching and learning for writing, research, academic technology, and careers. **Library/Resources:** The library contains 232,914 volumes, 69,348 microform items, and 9,467 audio/video tapes/CDs/DVDs, and subscribes to 491 periodicals including electronic. Computerized library services include interlibrary loans, database searching, Internet access, and Wi-Fi capability. Special learning facilities include an art gallery, natural history museum, and radio station. **Physically Challenged Students:** 25% of the campus is accessible. Facilities include wheelchair ramps, elevators, special parking, specially equipped restrooms, special class scheduling, lowered drinking fountains, lowered telephones, and special housing. **Special:** Special academic programs include study abroad in 25 to 30 countries, internships including a Washington semester, student-designed majors, and interdisciplinary majors. Degree programs in combination with professional schools in environmental management, forestry, law, medical technology, and dentistry. Preprofessional advising programs in architecture, education, engineering, law, medicine, physical therapy, social work/human services, and theology. There are 16 national honor societies, Phi Beta Kappa, and 22 departmental honors programs. **Visiting:** There are regularly scheduled orientations for prospective students, including campus tours and meetings with an informational panel, a student panel, financial aid staff, and faculty and coaches as requested. There are guides for informal visits, visitors may sit in on classes, and stay overnight. To schedule a visit, contact Visit Coordinator at (800) 747-1112. **Campus Safety and Security:** Measures include 24-hour foot and vehicle patrol, emergency notification system, self-defense education, security escort services, emergency telephones, lighted pathways/sidewalks, and controlled access to dorms/residences.

REQUIREMENTS: Applicants are required to submit a ACT, SAT or personal portfolio with responses to two short answer questions. Applicants should be graduates of an accredited secondary school, with a recommended 4 years each of English, 3 or more years of math and science, and social studies, 2 or more years of a foreign language. An essay and a secondary school report are required, and an interview is advised. The GED is accepted. AP credits are accepted. Important factors in the admissions decision are advanced placement or honors courses, evidence of special talent, and leadership record. Students choosing the BA degree must complete 31 course credits (124 semester hours), with at least a 2.0 cumulative GPA. B.A. candidates must complete the requirements of a faculty approved major usually 8 to 15 courses in the major and distribution requirements including: a first year seminar, a first year writing course, 2 courses in humanities, 1 course each in the natural sciences, social sciences, fine arts and math, and 1 to 4 courses in a foreign language. **Procedure:** Freshmen are admitted in the fall. There are early decision, early admissions, and deferred admissions plans. Early decision applications should be filed by November 1; regular applications, by March 1 for fall entry, along with a $30 fee. Notification of early decision is sent December 15; regular decision, April 1. 17 early decision candidates were accepted for the 2016-2017 class. 4 applicants were on the 2016 waiting list; 3 were admitted. Applications are accepted online. **Transfer Students:** 30 transfer students enrolled in 2015-2016. Applicants must provide all items required of traditional students; in addition, they must submit official college transcripts from all other institutions they have attended. 15 of 31 credits required for the bachelor's degree must be completed at Cornell. **International Students:** There are 64 international students enrolled. The school actively recruits these students. They must take the TOEFL with a minimum score of 550 on the paper-based TOEFL (PBT) or 79 on the Internet-based version (iBT), or take the IELTS, STEP or SAT or ACT exams may also be submitted.

ADMISSIONS: 71% of the 2016-2017 applicants were accepted. The SAT scores for the 2016-2017 freshman class were: Critical Reading-- 30% below 500, 26% between 500 and 599, 30% between 600 and 699, and 15% between 700 and 800. Math-- 25% below 500, 41% between 500 and 599, 26% between 600 and 699, and 8% between 700 and 800. Writing-- 39% below 500, 36% between 500 and 599, 20% between 600 and 699, and 5% between 700 and 800. The ACT scores were 1% between 12 and 17, 27% between 18 and 23, 53% between 24 and 29, and 19% above 30. 32% of the current freshmen were in the top fifth of their class; 65% were in the top two fifths. 7 freshmen graduated first in their class. **Admissions Contact:** Marie Schofer, Director of Admissions. Email: *admission@cornellcollege.edu* Web: *www.cornellcollege.edu*

FINANCIAL AID: In 2016-2017, 100% of all full-time freshmen and 98% of continuing full-time students received some form of financial aid. 72% of all full-time freshmen and continuing full-time students received need-based aid. The average freshman award was $33,026. Need-based scholarships or need-based grants averaged $29,444 ($48,800 maximum); need-based self-help aid (loans and jobs) averaged $4,340 ($7,500 maximum); and other non-need-based awards and non-need-based scholarships averaged $11,482 ($33,134 maximum). 50% of undergraduate students work part-time. Average annual earnings from campus work are $981. The average financial indebtedness of the 2016 graduate was $30,761. Cornell is a member of CSS. The FAFSA code is 001856. The priority date for freshman financial aid applications for fall entry is March 1.

DORDT COLLEGE B-2
www.dordt.edu

Sioux Center, IA 51250 (712) 722-6080
(800) 34-DORDT

Fax: (712) 722-1967
Email: admissions@dordt.edu

Full-time: 728 men, 658 women	**Faculty:** 80; IIB, -$
Part-time: 44 men, 41 women	**Ph.D.s:** 85%
Graduate: 25 men, 29 women	**Student/Faculty:** 15 to 1
Year: semesters	**Tuition:** $29,130
Room & Board: $8730	**Freshman Class:** 1355 applied, 1022 accepted, 381 enrolled
SAT: required **ACT:** 25	**CEEB CODE:** 6171
Application Deadline: August 1	**COMPETITIVE+**

Dordt College, founded in 1955, is a private institution affiliated with the Christian Reformed Church. The curriculum, which is designed to reflect the principles of the Christian faith, leads to degrees in liberal arts, agriculture, art, music, business, engineering, and teaching preparation. The figures in the above capsule and in this profile are approximate. There are 4 undergraduate schools. In addition to regional accreditation, Dordt has baccalaureate program accreditation with ABET and CSWE. The 120-acre campus is in a rural area 42 miles north of Sioux City. Including any residence halls, there are 25 buildings.

STUDENT LIFE: 60% of undergraduates are from out of state, mostly the Midwest. Students are from 34 states, 26 foreign countries, and Canada. 40% are from public schools. 88% are White; 3% African American; 3% Asian American; 3% Hispanic; 3% Foreign. 99% are Protestant. **Male To Female Ratio:** 1.1:1. The average age of freshmen is 18; all undergraduates, 21. 15% do not continue beyond their first year; 68% remain to graduate. **Housing:** 1300 students can be accommodated in college housing, which includes single-sex dorms, on-campus apartments, and off-campus apartments. On-campus housing is guaranteed for all 4 years. 90% of students live on campus; of those, 80% remain on campus on weekends. All students may keep cars. Alcohol is not permitted.

FACULTY/CLASSROOMS: 85% of faculty are male; 15% are female. All teach undergraduates. No introductory courses are taught by graduate students. The average class size in an introductory lecture is 30; in a laboratory is 20; and in a regular course is 25.

PROGRAMS OF STUDY: Dordt confers B.A., B.S., B.S.N., and B.S.W. degrees. Associate and master's degrees are also awarded. Bachelor's degrees are awarded in AGRICULTURE (agricultural business management, agriculture, and animal science), BIOLOGICAL SCIENCE (biology/biological science), BUSINESS (accounting, banking and finance, business administration and management, business economics, management information systems, marketing management, recreational facilities management, secretarial studies/office management, and sports management), COMMUNICATIONS AND THE ARTS (advertising, art history, art, broadcasting, church music, communications, dramatic arts, Dutch, English, English as a second/foreign language, film, television and digital media, fine arts, German, graphic design, journalism, languages, literature, music, music performance, music theory and composition, Spanish, speech/debate/rhetoric, theatre acting, theatre arts, visual and performing arts, and vocal music education), COMPUTER AND PHYSICAL SCIENCE (actuarial science, chemistry, computer programming, computer science, information sciences and systems, mathematics, physical sciences, and physics), EDUCATION (agricultural education, art education, athletic training, business education, childhood education, early childhood education, education, elementary education, English education, foreign languages education, mathematics education, middle school education, music education, physical education, physical science secondary school education, science education, secondary education, social science education, and special education), ENGINEERING AND ENVIRONMENTAL DESIGN (architectural engineering, bioengineering, chemical engineering, civil engineering, computer engineering, construction management, electrical/electronics engineering, engineering, environmental science, and mechanical engineering), HEALTH PROFESSIONS (exercise science, health science, medical laboratory technology, nursing, predentistry, premedicine, preoptometry, prepharmacy, prephysical therapy, and preveterinary science), SOCIAL SCIENCE (criminal justice, economics, history, ministries, missions, philosophy, philosophy and religion, political science/government, prelaw, psychology, public administration, religion, religious studies, social science, social work, sociology, and youth ministry). Engineering, business administration, and social work are the strongest academically. Education has the largest enrollment.

ACTIVITIES: There are no fraternities or sororities. There are 25 groups on campus, including band, choir, chorale, chorus, computers, dance, debate, drama, drill team, environmental, film, forensics, international, jazz band, literary magazine, newspaper, opera, orchestra, pep band, photography, PLIA (Putting Love into Action), political, professional, radio and TV, religious, social, social service, student government, symphony, and yearbook. Popular campus events include Parents Day in October. **Sports:** There are 7 intercollegiate sports for men and 7 for women, and 10 intramural sports for men and 10 for women. Facilities include a gym with courts, recreation center with an indoor track, basketball, volleyball, tennis, and racquetball courts, weight-lifting and exercise equipment rooms, and a golf simulation room, an outdoor track, soccer, softball, and baseball fields, an indoor pool, and ice arena adjacent to the campus. **Graduates:** From July 1, 2015 to June 30, 2016, 290 bachelor's degrees were awarded. The most popular majors were business, education, and engineering. 40 companies recruited on campus in 2015-2016. In an average class, 68% graduate in 4 years or less. Of the 2015 graduating class, 15% were enrolled in graduate school within 6 months of graduation, and 96% were employed.

SERVICES: Counseling and information services are available, as is tutoring in every subject. There is a reader service for the blind, and remedial math, reading, and writing. **Library/Resources:** The library contains 185,000 volumes, 14,819 microform items, 5,000 audio/video tapes/CDs/DVDs, and subscribes to 700 periodicals including electronic. Computerized library services include interlibrary loans. Special learning facilities include a planetarium, radio station, 2 observatories, as well as a agriculture stewardship center just north of the campus. **Physically Challenged Students:** All of the campus is accessible. Facilities include wheelchair ramps, elevators, special parking, specially equipped restrooms, special class scheduling, lowered drinking fountains, lowered telephones, and special housing. **Special:** Students may study abroad in 10 countries. Dordt also offers a Washington semester, a Chicago Metro semester, a joint nursing degree program with St. Luke's School of Nursing, a B.S.N. with Briar Cliff University, B.A.-B.S. degrees in engineering and agriculture, and numerous internships in all majors. Dual majors, student-designed majors, and pass/fail options are available. There is a freshman honors program. **Visiting:** There are regularly scheduled orientations for prospective students, including tours, class visits, personal visits with professors and coaches, and a financial aid session. There are guides for informal visits, visitors may sit in on classes, and stay overnight. To schedule a visit, contact the Admissions Office. **Campus Safety and Security:** Measures include a 24-hour foot and vehicle patrol, and lighted pathways/sidewalks.

REQUIREMENTS: The SAT or ACT is required. Applicants must be graduates of accredited secondary schools or have earned a GED. The college requires 18 academic credits, including 4 in English and 2 each in foreign language, math, science, and social studies. A GPA of 2.3 is required. AP and CLEP credits are accepted. Important factors in the admissions decision are advanced placement or honors courses, evidence of special talent, and leadership record. All students must complete a college introductory course and a distribution of 14 other courses in the various academic disciplines, including General Education 300. Proficiency requirements must be met in English, math, and phys ed. To graduate, students must complete a minimum of 126 credits with a 2.0 GPA. **Procedure:** Freshmen are admitted in the fall and spring. Entrance exams should be taken by October of the senior year and no later than April. There is a rolling admissions plan. Applications should be filed by August 1 for fall entry; December 1 for spring entry. Applications are accepted online. **Transfer Students:** 60 transfer students enrolled in 2015-2016. Transfer students must have a GPA of 2.0. 62 of 126 credits required for the bachelor's degree must be completed at Dordt. **International Students:** There are 60 international students enrolled. The school actively recruits these students. They must take the TOEFL with a minimum score of 72 on the Internet-based version (iBT). They must also take the SAT or ACT.

ADMISSIONS: 75% of the 2016-2017 applicants were accepted. The SAT scores for the 2016-2017 freshman class were: Critical Reading-- 47% below 500, 29% between 500 and 599, 21% between 600 and 699, and 3% between 700 and 800. Math-- 22% below 500, 45% between 500 and 599, 30% between 600 and 699, and 3% between 700 and 800. Writing-- 43% below 500, 40% between 500 and 599, and 17% between 600 and 699. The ACT scores were 15% below 12, 25% between 12 and 17, 36% between 18 and 23, 20% between 24 and 29, and 15% above 30. 62% of the current freshmen were in the top fifth of their class; 75% were in the top two fifths. **Admissions Contact:** Greg Van Dyke, Director of Admissions. Email: *admissions@dordt.edu* Web: *www.dordt.edu*

FINANCIAL AID: In 2016-2017, 98% of all full-time freshmen and 95% of continuing full-time students received some form of financial aid. 85% of all full-time freshmen and continuing full-time students received need-based aid. The average freshman award was $21,900. Need-based scholarships or need-based grants averaged $4,000 ($6,000 maximum); need-based self-help aid (loans and jobs) averaged $8,000 ($12,000 maximum); non-need-based athletic scholarships averaged $6,000 ($9,000 maximum); and other non-need-based awards and non-need-based scholarships averaged $7,000 ($12,500 maximum). 70% of undergraduate students work part-time. Average annual earnings from campus work are $1500. The average financial indebtedness of the 2016 graduate was $22,400. Dordt is a member of CSS. The college's own financial statement is required. The FAFSA code is 001859. Check with the school for current application deadlines.

DRAKE UNIVERSITY — C-3

www.drake.edu

Des Moines, IA 50311	**(515) 271-3181** **(800) 44-DRAKE**
Fax: (515) 271-2831	**Email: admission@drake.edu**
Full-time: 1315 men, 1787 women	**Faculty:** IIA, +$
Part-time: 83 men, 82 women	**Ph.D.s:** 92%
Graduate: 592 men, 1142 women	**Student/Faculty:** 12 to 1
Year: semesters, summer session	**Tuition:** $35,206
Room & Board: $9850	**Freshman Class:** 4959 applied, 3419 accepted, 767 enrolled
ACT: 27	**CEEB CODE:** 6168
Application Deadline: March 1	**HIGHLY COMPETITIVE**

Drake University, founded in 1881, is a private institution offering undergraduate and graduate programs in arts and sciences, business and public administration, pharmacy and health sciences, journalism and mass communication, education, fine arts, and law. There are 5 undergraduate schools and 4 graduate schools. In addition to regional accreditation, Drake has baccalaureate program accreditation with ACEJMC, ACPE, NASAD, and NASM. The 120-acre campus is in an urban area in Des Moines. Including any residence halls, there are 49 buildings.

STUDENT LIFE: 72% of undergraduates are from out of state, mostly the Midwest. Students are from 49 states, 41 foreign countries, and Canada. 81% are White; 5% Foreign; 4% Hispanic; 3% African American; 3% Asian American; 2% two or more races; 1% race unknown. **Female To Male Ratio:** 1.5:1. The average age of freshmen is 18; all undergraduates, 20. 12% do not continue beyond their first year; 78% remain to graduate. **Housing:** 1787 students can be accommodated in college housing, which includes coed dorms, off-campus apartments, fraternity houses and sorority houses. On-campus housing is guaranteed for the freshman year only, and is available on a first-come, first-served basis, and is available on a lottery system for upperclassmen. 70% of students live on campus; of those, 70% remain on campus on weekends. All students may keep cars.

FACULTY/CLASSROOMS: 49% of faculty are male; 51% are female. No introductory courses are taught by graduate students. The average class size in an introductory lecture is 29; in a laboratory is 14; and in a regular course is 27.

PROGRAMS OF STUDY: Drake confers B.A., B.S., B.A.Journ., and Mass Comm., B.F.A., B.Mus., B.Mus.Ed., B.S.B.A., and B.S.Ed. degrees. Master's and doctoral degrees are also awarded. Bachelor's degrees are awarded in BIOLOGICAL SCIENCE (biology/biological science and neurosciences), BUSINESS (accounting, banking and finance, business administration and management, international business management, management science, and marketing management), COMMUNICATIONS AND THE ARTS (advertising, art history and appreciation, broadcasting, communications, dramatic arts, English, graphic design, journalism, music, music business management, music performance, printmaking, public relations, speech/debate/rhetoric, and studio art), COMPUTER AND PHYSICAL SCIENCE (actuarial science, chemistry, computer science, information sciences and systems, mathematics, and physics), EDUCATION (elementary education, mathematics education, music education, and secondary education), ENGINEERING AND ENVIRONMENTAL DESIGN (environmental science), HEALTH PROFESSIONS (pharmacy), SOCIAL SCIENCE (economics, ethics, politics, and social policy, history, international relations, philosophy, political science/government, psychology, religion, and sociology). Actuarial science, pharmacy, and physics/astronomy are the strongest academically. Pharmacy, marketing, and actuarial science have the largest enrollments.

ACTIVITIES: 36% of men belong to 9 national fraternities; 29% of women belong to 5 national sororities. There are 160 groups on campus, including art, band, cheerleading, chess, choir, chorale, chorus, computers, dance, drama, drill team, ethnic, film, honors, international, jazz band, LGBT, literary magazine, marching band, musical theater, newspaper, opera, orchestra, pep band, photography, political, professional, radio and TV, religious, social, social service, student government, and symphony. Popular campus events include Drake Relays, Supreme Court Days and Iowa Caucuses. **Sports:** There are 8 intercollegiate sports for men and 10 for women, and 24 intramural sports for men and 24 for women. Facilities include a football stadium, indoor swimming pool, aerobics room, weight rooms, basketball, volleyball, and badminton courts, indoor tracks and outdoor track, racquetball courts, and indoor and outdoor tennis courts, and a recreation and sports facility. **Graduates:** From July 1, 2015 to June 30, 2016, 783 bachelor's degrees were awarded. The most popular majors were business/marketing (31%), communication/journalism (11%), and education (8%). In an average class, 70% graduate in 4 years or less, 77% graduate in 5 years or less, and 78% graduate in 6 years or less.

SERVICES: There is a reader service for the blind, and a student disability service works with recordings for blind dyslexic students. **Library/Resources:** The 2 libraries contain 558,044 volumes, 936,863 microform items, 3,609 audio/video tapes/CDs/DVDs, and subscribe to 74,473 periodicals including electronic. Computerized library services include interlibrary loans, database searching, Internet access, and Wi-Fi capability. Special learning facilities include an art gallery, radio station, TV station, an observatory, and the Henry G. Harmon Fine Arts Center. **Physically Challenged Students:** 90% of the campus is accessible. Facilities include wheelchair ramps, elevators, special parking, specially equipped restrooms, special class scheduling, lowered drinking fountains, lowered telephones, an IBM-compatible computer and scanner that includes a voice and screen enlargement program, closed-caption television, and TDD at multiple locations. **Special:** Study abroad is available in 60 countries and at sea. The university offers cross-registration with Des Moines area colleges, including Grand View, internships, a Washington semester, cooperative programs in computer science, and work-study programs. Dual majors, B.A.-B.S. degrees, a 3-2 engineering degree with Washington University, student-designed majors, credit for military experience, and nondegree study are possible. Students may take a maximum of 12 hours of course work on a credit/no credit basis. There are 25 national honor societies, Phi Beta Kappa, a freshman honors program, and 19 departmental honors programs. **Visiting:** There are regularly scheduled orientations for prospective students, including an opportunity for students and parents to confer with professors, meet with current students, and attend information sessions on academic programs, financial aid, housing, and the Drake campus. Also included are a walking tour and lunch. There are guides for informal visits, visitors may sit in on classes, and stay overnight. To schedule a visit, contact the Office of Admission. **Campus Safety and Security:** Measures include 24-hour foot and vehicle patrol, emergency notification system, self-defense education, and security escort services. There are also shuttle buses, emergency telephones, and lighted pathways/sidewalks.

REQUIREMENTS: Applicants must be graduates of an accredited secondary school. The GED is accepted. Students should have completed 4 years of English, 3 years of math, and 9 other units to be selected from English, foreign languages, social studies, math, lab sciences, and others. A portfolio is required for art majors and for those seeking scholarship consideration. An audition is necessary for admission to the music and theatre programs. Tapes are accepted. A GPA of 3.3 is required. AP and CLEP credits are accepted. Important factors in the admissions decision are advanced placement or honors courses, recommendations by school officials, and extracurricular activities record. Undergraduates must take a first-year seminar and general education courses and satisfy 11 areas of inquiry requirements that include writing, critical thinking, artistic experience, historical consciousness, information and technical literacy, multicultural experience, scientific and quantitative literacy, values and ethics, and the engaged citizen. A capstone demonstration is required. For graduation, 124 credit hours are required with 27 to 36 hours in the major. The minimum GPA is 2.0. **Procedure:** Freshmen are admitted to all sessions. Entrance exams should be taken during the spring of the junior year or early fall of the senior year. There are deferred admissions and rolling admissions plans. Applications should be filed by March 1 for fall entry, along with a $25 fee. Application fees are waived if application is completed online. **Transfer Students:** Applicants must have a minimum GPA of 2.0 and have completed 24 credit hours for evaluation. Grades of C or better transfer for credit. There is no assurance that all courses transferred will apply toward the major requirement. The final 30 hours must be completed in residence. Transfer students are admitted in the fall, spring, and summer. 30 of 124 credits required for the bachelor's degree must be completed at Drake. **International Students:** There are 248 international students enrolled. The school actively recruits these students. They must take the TOEFL with a minimum score of 550 on the paper-based TOEFL (PBT) or 79 on the Internet-based version (iBT). They must also take the SAT or ACT.

ADMISSIONS: 69% of the 2016-2017 applicants were accepted. The SAT scores for the 2016-2017 freshman class were: Critical Reading-- 18% below 500, 33% between 500 and 599, 38% between 600 and 699, and 10% between 700 and 800. Math-- 10% below 500, 40% between 500 and 599, 32% between 600 and 699, and 18% between 700 and 800. The ACT scores were 13% between 18 and 23, 58% between 24 and 29, and 29% above 30. **Admissions Contact:** Anne Kremer, Dean of Admissions. Email: *admission@drake.edu* Web: *www.drake.edu*

FINANCIAL AID: 76% of all full-time freshmen and continuing full-time students received need-based aid. The average freshman award was $26,153. Need-based scholarships or need-based grants averaged $20,124; need-based self-help aid (loans and jobs) averaged $4,887; non-need-based athletic scholarships averaged $21,525; and other non-need-based awards and non-need-based scholarships averaged $16,178. Drake is a member of CSS. The FAFSA code is 001860. Check with the school for current application deadlines.

GRACELAND UNIVERSITY C-4

www.graceland.edu

Lamoni, IA 50140	(641) 784-5211 (866) 893-6882
Fax: (641) 784-5058	**Email:** admissions@graceland.edu
Full-time: 579 men, 664 women	**Faculty:** IIB
Part-time: 104 men, 209 women	**Ph.D.s:** 47%
Graduate: 105 men, 631 women	**Student/Faculty:** 15 to 1
Year: trimesters, summer session	**Tuition:** $27,010
Room & Board: $8280	**Freshman Class:** 1031 accepted, 290 enrolled
SAT or ACT: required	**CEEB CODE:** 6249
Application Deadline: n/av	**COMPETITIVE**

Graceland University, established in 1895, is a private liberal arts college sponsored by the Community of Christ. Graceland also maintains a campus in Independence, Missouri. There are 4 undergraduate schools and 4 graduate schools. In addition to regional accreditation, Graceland has baccalaureate program accreditation with NCATE, NLN, CCNE, and CAATE. The 170-acre campus is in a small town 80 miles south of Des Moines. Including any residence halls, there are 28 buildings.

STUDENT LIFE: Undergraduate are from out of state, mostly the Midwest. **Female To Male Ratio:** 1.9:1. The average age of freshmen is 18; all undergraduates, 20. **Housing:** 815 students can be accommodated in college housing, which includes single-sex and coed dorms, on-campus apartments, and married student housing. On-campus housing is guaranteed for all 4 years. 70% of students live on campus. All students may keep cars. Alcohol is not permitted.

FACULTY/CLASSROOMS: 47% of faculty are male; 53% are female. 93% teach undergraduates, and 10% do research. No introductory courses are taught by graduate students. The average class size in an introductory lecture is 24; in a laboratory is 24; and in a regular course is 11.

PROGRAMS OF STUDY: Graceland confers B.A., B.S., and B.S.N. degrees. Master's and doctoral degrees are also awarded. Bachelor's degrees are awarded in BIOLOGICAL SCIENCE (biology/biological science), BUSINESS (accounting, business administration and management, international business management, recreation and leisure services, and recreational facilities management), COMMUNICATIONS AND THE ARTS (communications, dramatic arts, English, German, graphic design, literature, modern language, music, Spanish, speech/debate/rhetoric, and studio art), COMPUTER AND PHYSICAL SCIENCE (chemistry, computer science, information sciences and systems, mathematics, and science), EDUCATION (athletic training, elementary education, music education, and physical education), ENGINEERING AND ENVIRONMENTAL DESIGN (commercial art), HEALTH PROFESSIONS (health, medical laboratory technology, nursing, predentistry, premedicine, and preveterinary science), SOCIAL SCIENCE (addiction studies, criminal justice, economics, history, human services, international studies, liberal arts/general studies, philosophy, psychology, religion, social science, and sociology). Business administration, education, and nursing have the largest enrollments.

ACTIVITIES: There are no fraternities or sororities. There are 54 groups on campus, including art, band, cheerleading, chess, choir, chorale, chorus, computers, dance, drama, drill team, entrepreneurial, ethnic, environmental, honors, international, jazz band, LGBT, literary magazine, musical theater, newspaper, orchestra, pep band, political, professional, radio and TV, religious, social, social service, student government, symphony, and yearbook. Popular campus events include Renaissance Week, Multicultural Week, and New Year's in November. **Sports:** There are 9 intercollegiate sports for men and 8 for women, and 17 intramural sports for men and 17 for women. Facilities include a sports complex with an all-weather track, soccer and football fields, a phys ed center with an indoor pool, a gym, an indoor track, a weight room, and courts for racquetball, basketball, volleyball, and tennis. An intramural sports complex has tennis courts, and golf course. **Graduates:** The most popular majors were health professons and related programs (23%), education (21%), and business (16%).

SERVICES: Counseling and information services are available, as is tutoring in most subjects, and a reader service for the blind, and remedial math, reading, and writing. **Library/Resources:** The library contains 199,447 volumes, 914 microform items, and 3,658 audio/video tapes/CDs/DVDs, and subscribes to 624 periodicals including electronic. Computerized library services include interlibrary loans, database searching, Internet access, and Wi-Fi capability. Special learning facilities include an art gallery and a radio station. **Physically Challenged Students:** 86% of the campus is accessible. Facilities include wheelchair ramps, elevators, special parking, specially equipped restrooms, special class scheduling, lowered drinking fountains, and lowered telephones. **Special:** Internships are required in business, education, recreation, communications, and publication design. Graceland offers study abroad, cross-registration, B.A.-B.S. degrees, work-study, dual and student-designed majors, and a general studies degree. Credit for life, military, or work experience is possible. A pass/fail option is available for 2 courses each semester. The university also offers nondegree study, home study in addiction studies and nursing, a program for students with learning disabilities, an accelerated degree program in nursing, and a 3-2 engineering degree with the University of Iowa and the University of Missouri-Rolla. There is a freshman honors program. **Visiting:** There are regularly scheduled orientations for prospective students, including a campus tour and opportunities to meet students, faculty, and campus personnel. There are guides for informal visits, visitors may sit in on classes, and stay overnight. To schedule a visit, contact the Admissions Office. **Campus Safety and Security:** Measures include 24-hour foot and vehicle patrol, emergency notification system, and security escort services, emergency telephones, lighted pathways/sidewalks, controlled access to dorms/residences, and night security personnel.

REQUIREMENTS: The SAT or ACT is required. Graceland requires applicants to meet 2 of the following 3 criteria: rank in the upper 50% of their class, a GPA of 2.5, or a minimum score on the SAT or ACT. Applicants must be graduates of an accredited secondary school. The GED is accepted. A GPA of 2.5 is required. AP and CLEP credits are accepted. Important factors in the admissions decision are advanced placement or honors courses, evidence of special talent, and leadership record. To graduate, students must complete 128 credit hours, including 39 in upper-division courses and an average of 40 in the major, and maintain a minimum GPA of 2.0 overall and in the major. General education requirements include studies in humanities, social sciences, natural sciences, behavioral sciences, ethics, math, computer science, leadership, thinking skills, human diversity, and the arts. **Procedure:** Freshmen are admitted to all sessions. Entrance exams should be taken in the junior or senior year. There is a rolling admissions plan. Check with the school for current application deadlines. The application fee is $50. Applications are accepted online. **Transfer Students:** 191 transfer students enrolled in 2015-2016. Applicants must submit official transcripts from all colleges attended and from high school. The required GPA varies by the number of hours of college study completed. Transfer students are admitted every term. 32 of 128 credits required for the bachelor's degree must be completed at Graceland. **International Students:** The school actively recruits these students. They must take the TOEFL.

ADMISSIONS: The SAT scores for the 2016-2017 freshman class were: Critical Reading-- 87% below 500, 11% between 500 and 599, and 2% between 600 and 699. Math-- 78% below 500, 16% between 500 and 599, 5% between 600 and 699, and 1% between 700 and 800. The ACT scores were 18% between 12 and 17, 55% between 18 and 23, 24% between 24 and 29, and 3% above 30. **Admissions Contact:** Jim Uhlenkamp, Director of Institutional Research. Email: *admissions@graceland.edu* Web: *www.graceland.edu*

FINANCIAL AID: The FAFSA code is 001866. Check with the school for current application deadlines.

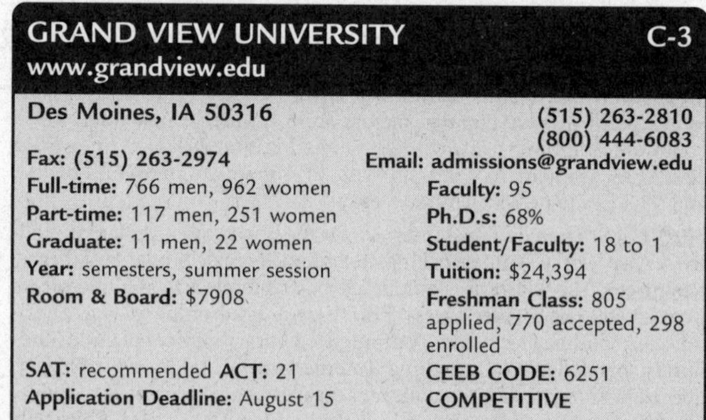

GRAND VIEW UNIVERSITY C-3
www.grandview.edu

Des Moines, IA 50316	**(515) 263-2810** **(800) 444-6083**
Fax: (515) 263-2974	**Email: admissions@grandview.edu**
Full-time: 766 men, 962 women	**Faculty:** 95
Part-time: 117 men, 251 women	**Ph.D.s:** 68%
Graduate: 11 men, 22 women	**Student/Faculty:** 18 to 1
Year: semesters, summer session	**Tuition:** $24,394
Room & Board: $7908	**Freshman Class:** 805 applied, 770 accepted, 298 enrolled
SAT: recommended **ACT:** 21	**CEEB CODE:** 6251
Application Deadline: August 15	**COMPETITIVE**

Grand View University, founded in 1896, is a private liberal arts college affiliated with the Evangelical Lutheran Church in America, that focuses on connecting liberal arts with career preparation. There are 2 undergraduate schools and 1 graduate school. In addition to regional accreditation, Grand View has baccalaureate program accreditation with NLN. The 25-acre campus is in an urban area in a residential area of Des Moines. Including any residence halls, there are 27 buildings.

STUDENT LIFE: 87% of undergraduates are from Iowa. Others are from 34 states, 16 foreign countries, and Canada. 80% are White; 8% African American; 4% two or more races; 3% Hispanic; 2% Asian American; 1% American Indian/Alaska Native; 1% Foreign. 15% are Catholic; 13% Protestant. **Female To Male Ratio:** 1.4:1. The average age of freshmen is 18; all undergraduates, 22. 31% do not continue beyond their first year; 49% remain to graduate. **Housing:** 900 students can be accommodated in college housing, which includes coed dorms, on-campus apartments, and special-interest houses. On-campus housing is available on a first-come, first-served basis, and is available on a lottery system for upperclassmen. Priority is given to out-of-town students. 63% of students commute. All students may keep cars.

FACULTY/CLASSROOMS: 39% of faculty are male; 61% are female. All teach undergraduates. No introductory courses are taught by graduate students. The average class size in an introductory lecture is 20; in a laboratory is 10; and in a regular course is 15.

PROGRAMS OF STUDY: Grand View confers B.A., and B.S.N. degrees. Master's degrees are also awarded. Bachelor's degrees are awarded in BIOLOGICAL SCIENCE (biochemistry, biology/biological science, and biotechnology), BUSINESS (accounting, business administration and management, management information systems, and sports management), COMMUNICATIONS AND THE ARTS (broadcasting, communications, English, graphic design, journalism, music, and visual and performing arts), COMPUTER AND PHYSICAL SCIENCE (computer science and mathematics), EDUCATION (art education, elementary education, music education, physical education, and secondary education), HEALTH PROFESSIONS (nursing), SOCIAL SCIENCE (criminal justice, human services, political science/government, and psychology). Art, nursing, and education are the strongest academically. Business, nursing, and biology have the largest enrollments.

ACTIVITIES: There are no fraternities or sororities. There are 43 groups

on campus, including art, band, cheerleading, choir, chorale, chorus, computers, dance, departmental, drama, drill team, ethnic, honors, international, jazz band, LGBT, literary magazine, newspaper, pep band, political, professional, radio and TV, religious, social service, student government, and yearbook. **Sports:** There are 12 intercollegiate sports for men and 12 for women, and 8 intramural sports for men and 8 for women. Facilities include a wellness with facilities for varsity athletics, and recreation programs, and an athletic field. **Graduates:** From July 1, 2015 to June 30, 2016, 460 bachelor's degrees were awarded. The most popular majors were business administration (23%), nursing (14%), and education (10%). 70 companies recruited on campus in 2015-2016. In an average class, 39% graduate in 4 years or less, 47% graduate in 5 years or less, and 49% graduate in 6 years or less. Of the 2015 graduating class, 8% were enrolled in graduate school within 6 months of graduation, and 90% were employed.

SERVICES: Counseling and information services are available, as is tutoring in every subject, and a reader service for the blind, and remedial math, reading, and writing. **Library/Resources:** The library contains 135,448 volumes, 11,386 microform items, and 3,875 audio/video tapes/CDs/DVDs, and subscribes to 27,077 periodicals including electronic. Computerized library services include interlibrary loans, database searching, and Internet access. Special learning facilities include an art gallery, radio station, and TV station. **Physically Challenged Students:** 90% of the campus is accessible. Facilities include wheelchair ramps, elevators, special parking, specially equipped restrooms, special class scheduling, lowered drinking fountains, and lowered telephones. There is also a support service for the disabled. **Special:** Co-op programs, cross-registration with Drake University and Des Moines Area Community College, student-designed majors, study abroad, and internships for most majors are available. Dual majors, a B.A.-B.S. degree, a Washington semester, work-study programs, and an accelerated degree program in business administration are offered. Nondegree study, a liberal arts degree, a certificate in art therapy, and pass/fail options are possible. There are 10 national honor societies, a freshman honors program, and 1 departmental honors programs. **Visiting:** There are regularly scheduled orientations for prospective students, including placement tests, a financial aid session, lunch, advisor meetings, and a registration session. There are guides for informal visits, visitors may sit in on classes, and stay overnight. To schedule a visit, contact the Admissions Office. **Campus Safety and Security:** Measures include 24-hour foot and vehicle patrol, emergency notification system, and security escort services. There are emergency telephones, lighted pathways/sidewalks, and controlled access to dorms/residences.

REQUIREMENTS: The ACT is required. The SAT and ACT Writing Test are recommended. Students must be graduates of an accredited secondary school. The GED is also accepted. Grand View recommends that students should have completed 4 courses in English, 3 courses each in math, science, and social science, and 2 courses in a foreign language. A GPA of 2.0 is required. AP and CLEP credits are accepted. Students must complete core requirements, including courses in English, public speaking, liberal arts, integrating seminar, other culture encounter, religion or philosophy, history or other humanities, lab science, and social science. Students must complete at least 124 hours of work, including 60 hours in courses other than the major and 24 hours in the major. Students must maintain an overall GPA of 2.0 and a 2.2 GPA in the major. Students must also demonstrate computer proficiency. **Procedure:** Freshmen are admitted in the fall, spring, and summer. Entrance exams should be taken during the second semester of the junior year. There are deferred admissions and rolling admissions plans. Applications should be filed by August 15 for fall entry. Applications are accepted online. **Transfer Students:** 303 transfer students enrolled in 2015-2016. Applicants must submit transcripts from each college attended. Students who are not transferring in with an associate or bachelor's degree must submit a high school transcript. Those with less than 24 college credits must also submit ACT or SAT test results. 30 of 124 credits required for the bachelor's degree must be completed at Grand View. **International Students:** There are 35 international students enrolled. They must take the TOEFL with a minimum score of 550 on the paper-based TOEFL (PBT) or 77 on the Internet-based version (iBT). They must also take the SAT or ACT.

ADMISSIONS: 8 freshmen graduated first in their class. **Admissions Contact:** Diane Schafer Johnson, Director of Admissions. Email: *admissions@grandview.edu* Web: *www.grandview.edu*

FINANCIAL AID: In 2016-2017, 99% of all full-time freshmen and 98% of continuing full-time students received some form of financial aid. 90% of all full-time freshmen and 86% of continuing full-time students received need-based aid. Average annual earnings from campus work are $1500. The average financial indebtedness of the 2016 graduate was $36,794. The FAFSA code is 001867. The deadline for filing freshman financial aid applications for fall entry is April 15.

GRINNELL COLLEGE — D-3
www.grinnell.edu

Grinnell, IA 50112	**(641) 269-3600** **(800) 247-0113**
Fax: (641) 269-4800	**Email: admission@grinnell.edu**
Full-time: 744 men, 914 women	**Faculty:** 160; IIB, +$
Part-time: 26 men, 15 women	**Ph.D.s:** 100%
Graduate: n/av	**Student/Faculty:** 9 to 1
Year: semesters	**Tuition:** $48,758
Room & Board: $11,980	**Freshman Class:** 3979 applied, 1395 accepted, 423 enrolled
SAT CR/M: 685/710 **ACT:** 32	**CEEB CODE:** 6252
Application Deadline: January 15	**MOST COMPETITIVE**

Grinnell College, founded in 1846, is a private institution that offers undergraduate degree programs in the arts and sciences. There is 1 undergraduate school. The 120-acre campus is in a small town 55 miles east of Des Moines. Including any residence halls, there are 64 buildings.

STUDENT LIFE: 77% of undergraduates are from out of state, mostly the Midwest. Students are from 49 states, 42 foreign countries, and Canada. 70% are from public schools. 8% are Asian American; 8% Hispanic; 6% African American; 52% White; 5% two or more races; 5% race unknown; 18% Foreign. 41% claim no religious affiliation; 21% Protestant; 18% Muslim, Hindu and Buddhist; 14% Catholic. **Female To Male Ratio:** 1.2:1. The average age of freshmen is 18; all undergraduates, 20. 8% do not continue beyond their first year; 86% remain to graduate. **Housing:** 1340 students can be accommodated in college housing, which includes single-sex, coed dorms and on-campus apartments, language houses, special-interest houses, theme housing, wellness housing, and cooperative housing. On-campus housing is guaranteed for all 4 years. 88% of students live on campus; of those, 95% remain on campus on weekends. All students may keep cars.

FACULTY/CLASSROOMS: 54% of faculty are male; 46% are female. All teach undergraduates and do research. No introductory courses are taught by graduate students. The average class size in an introductory lecture is 20; in a laboratory is 13; and in a regular course is 17.

PROGRAMS OF STUDY: Grinnell confers B.A. degrees. Bachelor's degrees are awarded in BIOLOGICAL SCIENCE (biochemistry and biology/biological science), COMMUNICATIONS AND THE ARTS (art history and appreciation, Chinese, classics, English, French, German, music, Russian, Spanish, studio art, and theatre arts), COMPUTER AND PHYSICAL SCIENCE (chemistry, computer science, mathematics, physics, and science), SOCIAL SCIENCE (anthropology, economics, gender studies, history, philosophy, political science/government, psychology, religion, and sociology). Economics, psychology, and political science have the largest enrollments.

ACTIVITIES: There are no fraternities or sororities. There are 250 groups on campus, including art, chess, choir, chorale, chorus, computers, dance, debate, drama, environmental, ethnic, film, forensics, honors, international, jazz band, LGBT, literary magazine, musical theater, newspaper, orchestra, photography, political, radio and TV, religious, social, social service, student government, and yearbook. Popular campus events include the Titular Head Student Film Festival and Grinnell Relays. **Sports:** There are 10 intercollegiate sports for men and 10 for women, and 16 intramural sports for men and 16 for women. Facilities include a recreation and athletic complex with a gymnasium, fieldhouse, natatorium, fitness center, auxillary practice gymnasium, climbing and bouldering walls, racquetball courts, sports fields, an outdoor track, and intramural fields. **Graduates:** From July 1, 2015 to June 30, 2016, 334 bachelor's degrees were awarded. The most popular majors were economics (9%), political science (8%), and history (8%). 19 companies recruited on campus in 2015-2016. In an average class, 81% graduate in 4 years or less, 86% graduate in 5 years or less, and 86% graduate in 6 years or less. Of the 2015 graduating class, 33% were enrolled in graduate school within 6 months of graduation, and 50% were employed.

SERVICES: Counseling and information services are available, as is

tutoring in every subject, a reader service for the blind, reading, writing, math, and science labs. **Library/Resources:** The 3 libraries contain 768,671 volumes, 416,593 microform items, and 34,144 audio/video tapes/CDs/DVDs, and subscribe to 22,059 periodicals including electronic. Computerized library services include interlibrary loans, database searching, Internet access, and Wi-Fi capability. Special learning facilities include an art gallery, radio station, an observatory, physics museum, a print and drawing study room. **Physically Challenged Students:** 80% of the campus is accessible. Facilities include wheelchair ramps, elevators, special parking, specially equipped restrooms, special class scheduling, lowered drinking fountains, lowered telephones, and special housing. **Special:** Students may participate in 63 study-abroad programs in 33 countries or in off-campus study at selected locations in the United States. Grinnell offers cooperative programs in architecture with Washington University in St. Louis and a 3-2 engineering program with California Institute of Technology, Columbia University, Washington University, and Rensselaer Polytechnic Institute. There is also an extensive internship program, a Washington semester, a general studies degree in science, student-designed majors, and S/D/F grading options in selected courses. Grinnell's special "plus-2" option permits students to add 2 credits to a regular course through independent study. Students may pursue one of 11 interdisciplinary concentrations in addition to their major. Accelerated degree programs of 6 to 7 semesters may be approved on an individual basis. There are 2 national honor societies and a chapter of Phi Beta Kappa. **Visiting:** There are regularly scheduled orientations for prospective students, including a campus tour, and interview with a member of the admissions staff, as well as an opportunity to attend classes, presentations/discussions with students and faculty from a number of academic departments, and complimentary meals. There are guides for informal visits, visitors may sit in on classes, and stay overnight. To schedule a visit, contact the Admissions Office. **Campus Safety and Security:** Measures include 24-hour foot and vehicle patrol, emergency notification system, self-defense education, and security escort services. There are emergency telephones, lighted pathways/sidewalks, controlled access to dorms/residences, fire drills, and a committee on personal safety education.

REQUIREMENTS: The SAT or ACT is required. Applicants must be graduates of accredited secondary schools. The college recommends 20 Carnegie units, 4 each in English and math, 3/4 years each in lab science, social studies or history, and a foreign language. An essay is required and an interview is recommended. AP credits are accepted. Important factors in the admissions decision are advanced placement or honors courses, extracurricular activities record, and leadership record. All students are required to take a tutorial in the first semester focusing on writing. All students must also complete a major field, which includes between 32 and 48 credits in most departments. Of the total 124 credits needed for the bachelor's degree, no more than 48 may be earned in any one department or 92 in any one division, and a minimum 2.0 GPA must be maintained. **Procedure:** Freshmen are admitted in the fall. Entrance exams should be taken during the second semester of the junior year or early in the fall semester of the senior year. There are early decision, early admissions, and deferred admissions plans. Early decision applications should be filed by November 15; regular applications, by January 15 for fall entry; and November 1 for spring entry, along with a $30 fee. Notification of early decision is sent December 15; regular decision, April 1. 137 early decision candidates were accepted for the 2016-2017 class. 1266 applicants were on the 2016 waiting list; 8 were admitted. Applications are accepted on-line. **Transfer Students:** 14 transfer students enrolled in 2015-2016. Students must have a 3.0 GPA and submit all high school transcripts, college transcripts, an essay or personal statement, standardized test scores, and a statement of good standing from prior institutions. Students may enroll in the fall, and spring. 62 of 124 credits required for the bachelor's degree must be completed at Grinnell. **International Students:** There are 257 international students enrolled. The school actively recruits these students. They must take the TOEFL with a minimum score of 550 on the paper-based TOEFL (PBT) or 80 on the Internet-based version (iBT). They must also take the SAT or ACT.

ADMISSIONS: 35% of the 2016-2017 applicants were accepted. The SAT scores for the 2016-2017 freshman class were: Critical Reading-- 12% between 500 and 599, 44% between 600 and 699, and 43% between 700 and 800. Math-- 1% between 500 and 599, 9% between 600 and 699, and 37% between 700 and 800. 70% of the current freshmen were in the top fifth of their class; 92% were in the top two fifths. **Admissions Contact:** Joseph P. Bagnoli Jr., Vice President for Enrollment, Dean of Admissions. Email: *admission@grinnell.edu* Web: *www.grinnell.edu*

FINANCIAL AID: In 2016-2017, 89% of all full-time freshmen and 87% of continuing full-time students received some form of financial aid. 73% of all full-time freshmen and 71% of continuing full-time students received need-based aid. The average freshman award was $42,392. Need-based scholarships or need-based grants averaged $36,762; need-based self-help aid (loans and jobs) averaged $4,974; and other non-need-based awards and non-need-based scholarships averaged $656. The average financial indebtedness of the 2016 graduate was $16,570. Grinnell is a member of CSS. The CSS/Profile, and a noncustodial profile are required. The FAFSA code is 001868. The deadline for filing freshman financial aid applications for fall entry is February 8.

IOWA STATE UNIVERSITY C-3

www.iastate.edu

Ames, IA 50011 — **(515) 294-5836**, **(800) 262-3810**

Fax: (515) 294-2592 — **Email: admissions@iastate.edu**

Full-time: 17,584 men, 13,087 women
Faculty: I, -$
Ph.D.s: 88%
Part-time: n/av
Student/Faculty: n/av
Graduate: 2994 men, 2102 women
Tuition: $8219 ($21,583)
Year: semesters, summer session
Freshman Class: n/av
Room & Board: $8356
SAT or ACT: required
CEEB CODE: 6306
Application Deadline: rolling
COMPETITIVE

Iowa State University, established in 1858, is a public land-grant institution offering undergraduate and graduate programs in agriculture, business, design, engineering, human sciences, liberal arts and sciences, and veterinary medicine. There are 7 undergraduate schools and 1 graduate school. In addition to regional accreditation, Iowa State has baccalaureate program accreditation with AACSB, ABET, ACEJMC, ADA, AHEA, ASLA, CSAB, FIDER, NAAB, NASM, SAF, ACS, and APA. The 1813-acre campus is in an urban area I 30 minutes north of Des Moines. Including any residence halls, there are 284 buildings.

STUDENT LIFE: 62% of undergraduates are from Iowa. Others are from 50 states, 121 foreign countries, and Canada. 11% are Foreign. **Male To Female Ratio:** 1.4:1. The average age of freshmen is 18; all undergraduates, 21. 12% do not continue beyond their first year. **Housing:** 12000 students can be accommodated in college housing, which includes single-sex and coed dorms, on-campus apartments, off-campus apartments, and married student housing. In addition, there are honors houses, special-interest houses, fraternity houses, sorority houses, nonalcoholic houses, cross-cultural houses, nonsmoking houses, quiet houses, academic learning communities, and adult undergraduate housing. On-campus housing is guaranteed for all 4 years. All students may keep cars.

FACULTY/CLASSROOMS: 60% of faculty are male; 40% are female. 85% teach undergraduates, and 85% do research. Graduate students teach 15% of introductory courses. The average class size in a laboratory is 18 and in a regular course is 33.

PROGRAMS OF STUDY: Iowa State confers B.A, B.S., B.Arch., B.B.A., B.F.A., B.L.A., B.L.S., and B.Mus. degrees. Master's and doctoral degrees are also awarded. Bachelor's degrees are awarded in AGRICULTURE (agricultural business management, agriculture, agronomy, animal science, dairy science, forestry and related sciences, horticulture, international agriculture, plant protection (pest management), and plant science), BIOLOGICAL SCIENCE (biochemistry, biology/biological science, biophysics, entomology, genetics, microbiology, nutrition, and plant pathology), BUSINESS (accounting, banking and finance, business administration and management, fashion merchandising, hotel/motel and restaurant management, international business management, management science, marketing/retailing/merchandising, and transportation management), COMMUNICATIONS AND THE ARTS (advertising, communications, creative writing, design, English, fine arts, French, German, graphic design, journalism, linguistics, music, Russian, Spanish, and speech/debate/rhetoric), COMPUTER AND PHYSICAL SCIENCE (atmospheric sciences and meteorology, chemistry, computer science, earth science, geology, mathematics, physics, and statistics), EDUCATION (agricultural education, early childhood education, elementary education, health education, industrial arts education, music education, physical education, and secondary education), ENGINEERING AND ENVIRONMENTAL DESIGN (aeronautical engineering, agricultural engineering, architecture, chemical engineering, city/

community/regional planning, civil engineering, computer engineering, construction engineering, electrical/electronics engineering, engineering, engineering technology, environmental science, industrial engineering technology, interior design, landscape architecture/design, materials engineering, and mechanical engineering), SOCIAL SCIENCE (anthropology, child care/child and family studies, child psychology/development, dietetics, economics, family/consumer resource management, family/consumer studies, fashion design and technology, food science, history, international relations, liberal arts/general studies, philosophy, political science/government, psychology, religion, sociology, and textiles and clothing). Engineering, agriculture, and statistics are the strongest academically. Engineering, business, and agriculture have the largest enrollments.

ACTIVITIES: 13% of men belong to 1 local and 29 national fraternities; 12% of women belong to 1 local and 17 national sororities. There are 800 groups on campus, including special interest, recreation/sports, art, band, cheerleading, chess, choir, chorale, chorus, computers, dance, debate, drama, drum and bugle corps, ethnic, film, forensics, honoraries, honors, international, jazz band, LGBT, literary magazine, marching band, musical theater, newspaper, opera, orchestra, pep band, photography, political, professional, radio and TV, religious, social, social service, student government, and symphony. Popular campus events include Homecoming. **Sports:** There are 7 intercollegiate sports for men and 11 for women, and 43 intramural sports for men and 43 for women. Facilities include a coliseum, a stadium/field, baseball and softball complex, a track complex, tennis complex, multipurpose gyms, swimming pools, an ice center, a phys ed building, recreation centers, multipurpose intramural-recreation fields, and a competitive soccer site.

SERVICES: Counseling and information services are available, as is tutoring in most subjects, a reader service for the blind, and remedial math and writing. A Kurzweil and Arkanstone reader, enlargement services, talking and braille text from the Iowa Commission for the blind, a braille printer, loaner computers, steno-captioning service, a TTY telecommunications device, FM listeners, and sign interpreters are also available. **Library/Resources:** The library contains 2.9 million volumes, 3.5 million microform items, 64,524 audio/video tapes/CDs/DVDs, and subscribes to 112,491 periodicals including electronic. Computerized library services include interlibrary loans, database searching, Internet access, and Wi-Fi capability. Special learning facilities include an art gallery, natural history museum, planetarium, radio station, and a TV station. **Physically Challenged Students:** 95% of the campus is accessible. Facilities include wheelchair ramps, elevators, special parking, specially equipped restrooms, special class scheduling, lowered drinking fountains, lowered telephones, and special housing. **Special:** Iowa State offers cooperative programs in engineering, forestry, agronomy, chemistry, computer science, economics, agricultural systems technology, business administration, industrial technology, and performing arts and cross-registration with the Universities of Iowa and Northern Iowa. Internships, study abroad in 38 countries, dual majors, the B.A.-B.S. degree, student-designed majors, and accelerated degree programs are available. Interdisciplinary studies include agricultural biochemistry, agricultural systems technology, animal ecology, public service and administration in agriculture, and engineering operations. There are work-study programs, a Washington semester, nondegree study, and pass/no pass options. There are 16 national honor societies, Phi Beta Kappa, and a freshman honors program. **Visiting:** There are regularly scheduled orientations for prospective students, including presentations on academics, admissions, residence hall living, fraternity and sorority life, and financial aid. There is also a group session with an adviser and a tour of the campus. There are guides for informal visits, visitors may sit in on classes, and stay overnight. To schedule a visit, contact Office of Admissions. **Campus Safety and Security:** Measures include 24-hour foot and vehicle patrol, self-defense education, and security escort services. There are also shuttle buses, emergency telephones, lighted pathways/sidewalks, controlled access to dorms/residences, and SafeRide ISU app.

REQUIREMENTS: The SAT or ACT is required. Students who wish to enter Iowa State University directly from high school will be admitted based upon their Regent Admission Index (RAI) score. There are two mathematical formulas for computing student's RAI scores, the primary RAI formula (for students whose high school provides class rank) and the Alternative RAI formula (for students whose high school does not provide class rank). Students who wish to enter Iowa State University directly from high school must also meet the minimum high school course requirements for admission, 4 years of English/Language arts, and mathematics, 3 years of science, 2 years of social studies. Iowa State requires applicants to be in the upper 50% of their class. AP and CLEP credits are accepted. A minimum of 120 1/2 to 169 1/2 credit hours, depending on the major, and a GPA of 2.0 are required for graduation. The total number of credits required in the major varies. All students must take freshman English, library instruction, 3 credits in U.S. diversity, and 3 credits in internationalization. **Procedure:** Freshmen are admitted to all sessions. Entrance exams should be taken during the spring of the junior year or the fall of the senior year. There are deferred admissions and rolling admissions plans. Check with the school for current application deadlines. The fall 2016 application fee was $40. Applications are accepted online. **Transfer Students:** Applicants must have a minimum GPA of 2.0 and at least 24 semester credits of acceptable transfer course work. They must also submit standardized test scores and provide a statement of good standing from prior institutions. 32 of 125 credits required for the bachelor's degree must be completed at Iowa State. **International Students:** There are 4131 international students enrolled. The school actively recruits these students. They must take the TOEFL and the college's own test.

Admissions Contact: Phil Caffrey, Associate Director of Admissions. Email: *admissions@iastate.edu* Web: *www.iastate.edu*

FINANCIAL AID: The FAFSA code is 001869. Check with the school for current application deadlines.

IOWA WESLEYAN UNIVERSITY — E-4

Iowa Wesleyan College
www.iw.edu

Mount Pleasant, IA 52641 — (319) 385-6230, (800) 582-2383

Fax: (319) 385-6240	**Email:** admit@iw.edu
Full-time: 250 men, 273 women	**Faculty:** n/av
Part-time: n/av	**Ph.D.s:** 85%
Graduate: n/av	**Student/Faculty:** 10 to 1
Year: semesters, summer session	**Tuition:** $29,146
Room & Board: $10,054	**Freshman Class:** 5449 applied, 2773 accepted, 169 enrolled
SAT: required **ACT:** 22	**CEEB CODE:** 0608
Application Deadline: open	**COMPETITIVE**

Iowa Wesleyan University, founded in 1842 is a coeducational liberal arts university it has a rich history of innovation in education, pioneering in the sciences, with opportunities for women and service-learning. Seven female Iowa Wesleyan students founded the P.E.O. Sisterhood on campus in 1869. The academic program at Iowa Wesleyan combines a liberal arts foundation with education in a specific career fields, including art, business, English, music, nursing, psychology, teacher education, among others. Service-learning is integrated into the curriculum, ensuring that all students connect classroom learning with service to others. Internships and other field experience opportunities are part of every major, giving students hands-on professional experience before graduation. There are 2 undergraduate schools. In addition to regional accreditation, IW has baccalaureate program accreditation with Iowa Department of Education, ACEN, and University Senate of the United Methodist Church. The 60-acre campus is in a small town 45 miles south of Iowa City in the Southeastern region of Iowa. Including any residence halls, there are 15 buildings.

STUDENT LIFE: 60% of undergraduates are from out of state, mostly the Midwest. Students are from 25 states, 22 foreign countries, and Canada. 90% are from public schools. 6% are Foreign; 45% White; 36% African American; 2% Asian American; 13% Hispanic. 46% claim no religious affiliation. **Female To Male Ratio:** 1.1:1. The average age of freshmen is 18; all undergraduates, 21. 47% do not continue beyond their first year; 38% remain to graduate. **Housing:** 493 students can be accommodated in college housing, which includes single-sex and coed dorms. On-campus housing is guaranteed for all 4 years. 75% of students live on campus; of those, 70% remain on campus on weekends. All students may keep cars.

FACULTY/CLASSROOMS: 59% of faculty are male; 41% are female. All teach undergraduates. No introductory courses are taught by graduate students. The average class size in an introductory lecture is 22; in a laboratory is 24; and in a regular course is 11.

PROGRAMS OF STUDY: IW confers B.A., B.S., B.M.E., and B.S.N.

degrees. Bachelor's degrees are awarded in BIOLOGICAL SCIENCE (biology ecology and field biology and biology/biological science), BUSINESS (accounting, business administration and management, business administration marketing, management & strategic leadership, and sports management), COMMUNICATIONS AND THE ARTS (digital media, fine arts, music, stage management, and visual communication), COMPUTER AND PHYSICAL SCIENCE (chemistry), EDUCATION (early childhood education, elementary education, music education, physical education, physical ed teacher education, and secondary education), HEALTH PROFESSIONS (biology, environmental health science, nursing, predentistry, premedicine, preoptometry, prephysical therapy, and preveterinary science), SOCIAL SCIENCE (Christian studies, criminal justice, prelaw, psychology, religion, and sociology). Nursing, and education are the strongest academically. Business, elementary education, and nursing have the largest enrollments.

ACTIVITIES: 6% of men belong to 1 national fraternity; 12% of women belong to 2 local and 1 national sororities. There are 35 groups on campus, including art, band, cheerleading, choir, chorus, dance, ethnic, film, international, jazz band, literary magazine, newspaper, orchestra, pep band, photography, political, professional, religious, social, social service, student government, symphony, and yearbook. Popular campus events include Forum, Winterfest, and Spring Thing. **Sports:** There are 5 intercollegiate sports for men and 5 for women, and 6 intramural sports for men and 6 for women. Facilities include a complex with baseball, softball, football fields, and an all-weather track. There is also a basketball/volleyball courts, an athletic training room, a walking/jogging track, and a fitness/wellness center.

SERVICES: Counseling and information services are available, as is tutoring in every subject. There is remedial math, reading, and writing. **Library/Resources:** The library contains 83,244 volumes, 25,305 microform items, 27,259 audio/video tapes/CDs/DVDs, and subscribes to 11,460 periodicals including electronic. Computerized library services include interlibrary loans, database searching, Internet access, and Wi-Fi capability. Special learning facilities include an art gallery. **Physically Challenged Students:** 77% of the campus is accessible. Facilities include wheelchair ramps, elevators, special parking, and special class scheduling. **Special:** The Office of Internships at Iowa Wesleyan University supports the mission of the institution by combining the values of a liberal education with those of professional preparation. Internships are a key component of how our programs provide opportunities to acquire the necessary theoretical and applied knowledge, which permits students to function effectively in professional life and a changing global community. Working with practicing professionals provides students the opportunity to integrate theory with practical learning. As part of a student's participation in the internship process, they will be evaluated in the workplace regarding the Institutional Learning Outcomes of Communication, Critical Reasoning, and Civic Engagement. While participating in experiential learning programs, students will face challenges and issues which they will continue to encounter throughout their professional careers There are 5 national honor societies and 2 departmental honors programs. **Visiting:** There are regularly scheduled orientations for prospective students, including meetings with admissions, financial aid, and academic staff, as well as social activities. There are guides for informal visits, visitors may sit in on classes, and stay overnight. To schedule a visit, contact The Admissions Office. **Campus Safety and Security:** Measures include 24-hour foot and vehicle patrol, emergency notification system, self-defense education, security escort services, emergency telephones, lighted pathways/sidewalks, and controlled access to dorms/residences.

REQUIREMENTS: The SAT or ACT and ACT Writing Test are recommended. Applicants must be graduates of accredited secondary schools or have earned a GED. A GPA of 2.5 is required. AP and CLEP credits are accepted. Important factors in the admissions decision are geographical diversity, extracurricular activities record, and evidence of special talent. General education requirements of 35 to 40 hours include 6 of English, 4 of science, and 3 each of computer science, math, communication, civic issues, fine arts, religion, English literature, and global issues. Students must complete English 102 with a minimum of C-, satisfy a safety and survival requirement, and complete 6 semester hours of service learning and 6 to 14 semester hours of a field experience in the major. A minimum of 124 semester hours is required for the bachelor's degree, 28 or more must be in the major. **Procedure:** Freshmen are admitted in the fall and spring. Entrance exams should be taken in April of the junior year or in June, October, or December of the senior year. There are deferred admissions and rolling admissions plans. Application deadlines are open. Applications are accepted online. **Transfer Students:** 51 transfer students enrolled in 2015-2016. A minimum cumulative college GPA of 2.0 is required. 30 of 124 credits required for the bachelor's degree must be completed at IW. **International Students:** There are 70 international students enrolled. The school actively recruits these students. They must take the TOEFL with a minimum score of 500 on the paper-based TOEFL (PBT).

ADMISSIONS: 51% of the 2016-2017 applicants were accepted. The ACT scores were 2% between 12 and 17, 75% between 18 and 23, 22% between 24 and 29, and 1% above 30. **Admissions Contact:** Jeremy Hommowun, Associate Director of Admissions. Email: *admit@iw.edu* Web: *www.iw.edu*

FINANCIAL AID: In 2016-2017, 100% of all full-time freshmen and continuing full-time students received some form of financial aid. 100% of all full-time freshmen and continuing full-time students received need-based aid. The average freshman award was $24,000. Other non-need-based awards and non-need-based scholarships averaged $14,000 ($20,000 maximum). IW is a member of CSS. The college's own financial statement is required. The FAFSA code is 001871. The priority date for freshman financial aid applications for fall entry is April. The deadline for filing freshman financial aid applications for fall entry is Open.

LORAS COLLEGE E-2
www.loras.edu

Dubuque, IA 52004	**(563) 588-7236** **(800) 245-6727**
Fax: (563) 588-7119	**Email: admission@loras.edu**
Full-time: 731 men, 669 women	**Faculty:** 100
Part-time: 38 men, 25 women	**Ph.D.s:** 97%
Graduate: 26 men, 35 women	**Student/Faculty:** 14 to 1
Year: semesters, summer session	**Tuition:** $31,525
Room & Board: $7697	**Freshman Class:** 1269 applied, 1172 accepted, 328 enrolled
SAT: required **ACT:** 23	**CEEB CODE:** 0670
Application Deadline: open	**COMPETITIVE**

Loras College enables students to thrive and discover paths they're excited to follow through in their challenging academic programs, co-curricular offerings, and faith tradition that inspires responsibility, excellence, service and respect. Relating the rich liberal arts tradition to a changing world, Loras strives to develop active learners, reflective thinkers, ethical decision makers, and responsible contributors in their diverse professional, social, and religious roles. There is 1 undergraduate school and 1 graduate school. In addition to regional accreditation, Loras has baccalaureate program accreditation with ABET, ACS, and CAATE. The 64-acre campus is in a small town 180 miles west of Chicago and 250 miles south of Minneapolis. Including any residence halls, there are 23 buildings.

STUDENT LIFE: 60% of undergraduates are from out of state, mostly the Midwest. Students are from 26 states, 9 foreign countries, and Canada. 63% are from public schools. 81% are White; 7% Hispanic; 5% race unknown; 2% African American; 2% two or more races; 1% Asian American; 1% Foreign. 65% are Catholic; 18% Protestant. **Male To Female Ratio:** 1.1:1. The average age of freshmen is 18; all undergraduates, 20. 20% do not continue beyond their first year; 71% remain to graduate. **Housing:** 1061 students can be accommodated in college housing, which includes single-sex and coed dorms, on-campus apartments, and off-campus apartments. On-campus housing is guaranteed for all 4 years and is available on a lottery system for upperclassmen. 65% of students live on campus; of those, 75% remain on campus on weekends. All students may keep cars.

FACULTY/CLASSROOMS: 54% of faculty are male; 46% are female. All teach undergraduates. No introductory courses are taught by graduate students. The average class size in an introductory lecture is 21; in a laboratory is 16; and in a regular course is 18.

PROGRAMS OF STUDY: Loras confers B.A. and B.S. degrees. Associate and master's degrees are also awarded. Bachelor's degrees are awarded in BIOLOGICAL SCIENCE (biochemistry and neurosciences), BUSINESS (accounting, business administration and management, finance, management information systems, management science, marketing, and sports management), COMMUNICATIONS AND THE ARTS (communication studies, creative writing, English literature, music, public relations, and Spanish), COMPUTER AND PHYSICAL SCIENCE (chemistry, computer science, and mathematics), EDUCATION (athletic training, elementary education, and music education), ENGINEERING AND ENVIRONMENTAL DESIGN (engineering physics), HEALTH PROFESSIONS (biology and exercise science), SOCIAL SCIENCE (criminal justice, economics, history, international relations, philosophy, political science/government, psychology, religion, social work, and sociology). Business/marketing, communication/journalism, and education have the largest enrollments.

ACTIVITIES: 5% of men belong to 1 national fraternity; 4% of women belong to 1 national sorority. There are 66 groups on campus, including a drumline club, band, cheerleading, choir, chorus, computers, dance, debate, drama, ethnic, film, forensics, honors, international, jazz band, LGBT, literary magazine, musical theater, newspaper, photography, political, professional, programming board, radio and TV, religious, social, social service, student government, and yearbook. Popular campus events include Campus Fest, Homecoming, and Family Weekend. **Sports:** There are 12 intercollegiate sports for men and 11 for women, and 7 intramural sports for men and 6 for women. Facilities include an athletic wellness facility, sports center with gym floors, swimming pool, racquetball courts, indoor/outdoor track. There are also outdoor tennis courts, a field house for basketball games, football field, soccer field, and a softball field. **Graduates:** From July 1, 2015 to June 30, 2016, 314 bachelor's degrees were awarded. The most popular majors were business/marketing (23%), sports management and kinesiology (11%), and communication/journalism (8%). 119 companies recruited on campus in 2015-2016. In an average class, 61% graduate in 4 years or less, 70% graduate in 5 years or less, and 71% graduate in 6 years or less.

SERVICES: Counseling and information services are available, as is tutoring in every subject, a reader service for the blind, and remedial math and writing. **Library/Resources:** The library contains 444,493 volumes, 77,688 microform items, 3,271 audio/video tapes/CDs/DVDs, and subscribes to 170 periodicals including electronic. Computerized library services include interlibrary loans, database searching, Internet access, and Wi-Fi capability. Special learning facilities include a planetarium, radio station, TV station, Center for Dubuque History, and an observatory. **Physically Challenged Students:** 63% of the campus is accessible. Facilities include wheelchair ramps, elevators, special parking, specially equipped restrooms, special class scheduling, lowered drinking fountains, lowered telephones, and special housing. **Special:** The college offers 3+2 programs in athletic training and business analytics, paid internships for needy students, and a first generation scholars program. We offer study abroad through both Loras College and affiliate programs, along with internships, work-study programs, a Washington semester, and pre-professional programs. There are 4 national honor societies and a freshman honors program. **Visiting:** There are regularly scheduled orientations for prospective students. Meetings with faculty, and admission representative, and coach, and tour of the campus. There are guides for informal visits, visitors may sit in on classes, and stay overnight. To schedule a visit, contact Kristie Arthofer at kristie.arthofer@loras.edu. **Campus Safety and Security:** Measures include 24-hour foot and vehicle patrol, emergency notification system, security escort services, emergency telephones, and lighted pathways/sidewalks.

REQUIREMENTS: The SAT or ACT is required. Applicants must be graduates of an accredited secondary school or have a GED certificate and have completed 4 units each of English and math, 3 units of science with 2 units of lab, 3 units of social studies, and 2 units of academic electives. AP and CLEP credits are accepted. To earn any degree students must complete a total of 120 hours with a minimum GPA of 2.0 and 35 to 36 hours of general education. All students must complete and present a student portfolio for review. A thesis and/or comprehensive exam is required for some majors. **Procedure:** Freshmen are admitted in the fall and spring. Entrance exams should be taken in April or June before the senior year or October of the senior year. There are deferred admissions and rolling admissions plans. Application deadlines are open. Application fee is $25. Notification is sent on a rolling basis. Application fees are waived if application is completed online. **Transfer Students:** 62 transfer students enrolled in 2015-2016. Transfer students must have a minimum 2.5 GPA and submit transcripts from all previous educational institutions as well as ACT or SAT scores. Students may apply in the fall, winter, spring and summer. 30 of 120 credits required for the bachelor's degree must be completed at Loras. **International Students:** There are 18 international students enrolled. They must take the TOEFL with a minimum score of 550 on the paper-based TOEFL (PBT) or 79 on the Internet-based version (iBT).

ADMISSIONS: 92% of the 2016-2017 applicants were accepted. The ACT scores were 3% between 12 and 17, 57% between 18 and 23, 36% between 24 and 29, and 4% above 30. 30% of the current freshmen were in the top fifth of their class; 59% were in the top two fifths. **Admissions Contact:** Kyle Klapatauskas, Admission Director. Email: *admission@loras.edu* Web: *www.loras.edu*

FINANCIAL AID: In 2016-2017, 100% of all full-time freshmen and continuing full-time students received some form of financial aid. 78% of all full-time freshmen and 72% of continuing full-time students received need-based aid. 39% of undergraduate students work part-time. The FAFSA code is 001873. The priority date for freshman financial aid applications for fall entry is March 1.

LUTHER COLLEGE — E-1

www.luther.edu

Decorah, IA 52101	**(563) 387-1287** **(800) 458-8437**
Fax: (563) 387-2159	**Email: admissions@luther.edu**
Full-time: 952 men, 1179 women	**Faculty:** 177
Part-time: 18 men, 20 women	**Ph.D.s:** 95%
Graduate: n/av	**Student/Faculty:** 12 to 1
Year: 4-1-4, summer session	**Tuition:** $40,040
Room & Board: $8500	**Freshman Class:** 3856 applied, 2608 accepted, 520 enrolled
SAT CR/M/W: 500/550/490 **ACT:** 26	**CEEB CODE:** 6375
Application Deadline: n/av	**COMPETITIVE+**

Luther College, founded in 1891 is a residential, liberal arts institution affiliated with the Evangelical Lutheran Church. Luther offers more than 60 majors, minors, pre-professional and special programs leading to the bachelor of arts degree. There is 1 undergraduate school. In addition to regional accreditation, Luther has baccalaureate program accreditation with CSWE, NASM, NCATE, and NLN. The 200-acre campus is in a small town in Northeast Iowa at the intersection of State Highway 9 and U.S. Route 52, and is 70 miles southeast of Rochester, Minnesota, and 56 miles southwest of La Crosse, Wisconsin. Including any residence halls, there are 35 buildings.

STUDENT LIFE: 71% of undergraduates are from out of state, mostly the Midwest. Students are from 38 states, 68 foreign countries, and Canada. 90% are from public schools. 82% are White; 7% Foreign; 5% Hispanic; 2% African American; 2% Asian American; 2% two or more races. 53% are Protestant; 17% Catholic. **Female To Male Ratio:** 1.2:1. The average age of freshmen is 18; all undergraduates, 20. 15% do not continue beyond their first year; 79% remain to graduate. **Housing:** 2017 students can be accommodated in college housing, which includes single-sex and coed dorms, on-campus apartments, off-campus apartments, married student housing, special-interest houses, sustainability house, dialogue floors, and wellness floors. On-campus housing is guaranteed for all 4 years and is available on a lottery system for upperclassmen. 89% of students live on campus; of those, 90% remain on campus on weekends. All students may keep cars.

FACULTY/CLASSROOMS: 48% of faculty are male; 52% are female. All teach undergraduates. No introductory courses are taught by graduate students. The average class size in an introductory lecture is 17; in a laboratory is 11; and in a regular course is 17.

PROGRAMS OF STUDY: Luther confers B.A. degrees. Bachelor's degrees are awarded in AGRICULTURE (environmental studies), BIOLOGICAL SCIENCE (biology/biological science and neurosciences), BUSINESS (accounting and management science), COMMUNICATIONS AND THE ARTS (art, classical languages, communications, dance, English, French, German, music, Russian, Spanish, and theatre arts), COMPUTER AND PHYSICAL SCIENCE (chemistry, computer science, computer science & informatics, mathematics, physics, and statistics), EDUCATION (athletic training, elementary education, and physical education), HEALTH PROFESSIONS (health and nursing), SOCIAL SCIENCE (African American studies, anthropology, biblical languages, economics, history, international studies, philosophy, political science/government, psychology, religion, social work, sociology, and women's studies). Biology, music, and English are the strongest academically. Biology, management, and music have the largest enrollments.

ACTIVITIES: 1% of men belong to 3 local fraternities; 2% of women belong to 3 local sororities. There are 99 groups on campus, including art, band, cheerleading, choir, chorale, chorus, communications, computers, dance, debate, drama, drill team, environmental, ethnic, forensics, honors, international, jazz band, LGBT, literary magazine, musical theater, newspaper, opera, orchestra, pep band, photography, political, professional, radio and TV, religious, social, social service, student government, and symphony. Popular campus events include Christmas at Luther, Ethnic Arts Fair, Dance Marathon, and Family Weekend. **Sports:** There are 10 intercollegiate sports for men and 9 for women, and 45 intramural sports for men and 45 for women. Facilities include basketball courts, aquatic center, batting cages, a fitness center, climbing wall, soccer fields, golf driving range, dance studio, stadium, gym, indoor tennis courts, racquetball courts, an indoor track, outdoor track, and outdoor tennis courts. **Graduates:** From July 1, 2015 to June 30, 2016, 562 bachelor's degrees were awarded. The most popular majors were biology (17%), management (13%), and music (9%). 227 companies recruited on campus in 2015-2016. In an average class, 72% graduate in 4 years or less, 78% graduate in 5 years or less, and 79% graduate in 6 years or less. Of the 2015 graduating class, 15% were enrolled in graduate school within 6 months of graduation, and 68% were employed.

SERVICES: Counseling and information services are available, as is tutoring in every subject, a reader service for the blind, and remedial math, reading, and writing. Drop in tutoring is available in mathematics, writing, speech/debate, accounting, chemistry, music theory, modern languages, and physics. Reading machines, tape recorders, note taking, and a learning center are also available. **Library/Resources:** The library contains 565,593 volumes, 24,839 microform items, 69,881 audio/video tapes/CDs/DVDs, and subscribes to 30,000 periodicals including electronic. Computerized library services include interlibrary loans, database searching, and Internet access. Special learning facilities include an art gallery, natural history museum, planetarium, and radio station. **Physically Challenged Students:** 95% of the campus is accessible. Facilities include wheelchair ramps, elevators, special parking, specially equipped restrooms, special class scheduling, lowered drinking fountains, lowered telephones, and special housing. **Special:** Internships in most disciplines, study away opportunities both domestically and in many countries (e.g. Malta, Germany, England, France, Ireland, Italy, South Africa, Tanzania, China, Ecuador, Switzerland, Austria, Ireland, Norway, Netherlands, Belgium, Denmark, Sweden, Jamaica, Chile, Cambodia, Czech Republic, Poland, Japan, Belize, Peru, Dominican Republic, Ukraine, Vietnam, Cuba, Spain), a Washington semester, student-designed and dual majors, and 3-2 engineering degrees with Washington University in St. Louis and the University of Minnesota are available, on-campus work-study programs. There are 17 national honor societies, Phi Beta Kappa, and a freshman honors program. **Visiting:** There are regularly scheduled orientations for prospective students. There are guides for informal visits, visitors may sit in on classes, and stay overnight. To schedule a visit, contact the Admissions Office. **Campus Safety and Security:** Measures include 24-hour foot and vehicle patrol, emergency notification system, self-defense education, and security escort services. There are also shuttle buses, emergency telephones, lighted pathways/sidewalks, controlled access to dorms/residences, personal safety education, safety alerts, security cameras, and shelter areas in residence halls known as SHIP (Shelter Here Inside Phone).

REQUIREMENTS: The SAT or ACT is required. In order to be considered for admission, the applicant should be within 2 semesters of graduation from an accredited high school and complete the following college preparatory coursework: 4 years of English, which may include 1 year of speech, communications, or journalism, 3 years each of math, and social science, 2 years of natural science, including 1 year of lab science, and 2 years of a foreign language study are recommended. Applicants who do not meet these standards will be considered for admission if they submit above-average ACT or SAT scores. A GPA of 2.5 is required. AP and CLEP credits are accepted. Important factors in the admissions decision are advanced placement or honors courses, evidence of special talent, and extracurricular activities record. Students must complete 128 credit hours for a B.A. with a cumulative grade-point average of 2.0 (C) or higher. The 128 hours must include the following: 30 fall/spring full courses or their equivalents. A full course is equivalent to 4 credit hours; other courses offered are equivalent to 2 credit hours or 1 credit hour. Including 2 January terms, these 2 month-long terms must include a first-year seminar, and one of the following types of experiences: study away, directed readings, student-initiated project. At least 20 course equivalents outside the student's major discipline. 64 credit hours completed in residence. All-college requirements: common ground; fields of inquiry; integrative understanding; perspectives and skills. **Procedure:** Freshmen are admitted in the fall, winter, and spring. Entrance exams should be taken by the fall of the senior year. There are deferred admissions and rolling admissions plans. Application deadlines are open. Notifications are sent September 1. Application fees are waived if application is completed online. **Transfer Students:** 27 transfer students enrolled in 2015-2016. Applicants must meet the same high school standards and the SAT or ACT requirements as entering freshmen, with a minimum GPA of 2.5 in parallel college course work. 64 of 128 credits required for the bachelor's degree must be completed at Luther. **International Students:** There are 146 international students enrolled. The school actively recruits these students. They must take the TOEFL with a minimum score of 550 on the paper-based TOEFL (PBT) or 80 on the Internet-based version (iBT), or the IELTS.

ADMISSIONS: 68% of the 2016-2017 applicants were accepted. The SAT scores for the 2016-2017 freshman class were: Critical Reading-- 47% below 500, 32% between 500 and 599, 13% between 600 and 699, and 8% between 700 and 800. Math-- 27% below 500, 39% between 500 and 599, 13% between 600 and 699, and 21% between 700 and 800. Writing-- 55% below 500, 26% between 500 and 599, 11% between 600 and 699, and 8% between 700 and 800. The ACT scores were 28% between 18 and 23, 51% between 24 and 29, and 21% above 30. 45% of the current freshmen were in the top fifth of their class; 75% were in the top two fifths. There were 2 National Merit finalists. 24 freshmen graduated first in their class. **Admissions Contact:** Scot Schaeffer, Vice President for Enrollment Management. Email: *admissions@luther.edu* Web: *www.luther.edu*

FINANCIAL AID: In 2016-2017, 100% of all full-time freshmen and continuing full-time students received some form of financial aid. 83% of all full-time freshmen and 77% of continuing full-time students received need-based aid. The average freshman award was $37,684. Need-based scholarships or need-based grants averaged $26,547; and need-based self-help aid (loans and jobs) averaged $7,030. The average financial indebtedness of the 2016 graduate was $26,476. Luther is a member of CSS. The college's own financial statement, and a family tax return is required. The FAFSA code is 001874. The priority date for freshman financial aid applications for fall entry is March 1.

MAHARISHI UNIVERSITY OF MANAGEMENT E-3

www.mum.edu

Fairfield, IA 52557	**(641) 472-1110** **(800) 369-6480**
Fax: (641) 472-1179	**Email: admissions@mum.edu**
Full-time: 120 men, 80 women	**Faculty:** n/av
Part-time: 10 men, 10 women	**Ph.D.s:** 100%
Graduate: 610 men, 145 women	**Student/Faculty:** n/av
Year: semesters	**Tuition:** $27,530
Room & Board: $7400	**Freshman Class:** n/av CEEB CODE: 4497
Application Deadline: open	**VERY COMPETITIVE**

Maharishi University of Management, established in 1971, is a private institution offering undergraduate and graduate programs in a broad range of disciplines. The University provides consciousness-based education and incorporates the group practice of the Maharishi Transcendental Meditation technique into a traditional academic program. There are 5 undergraduate schools and 5 graduate schools. The 272-acre campus is in a small town 114 miles southeast of Des Moines and 60 miles southwest of Iowa City. Including any residence halls, there are 50 buildings.

STUDENT LIFE: 61% of undergraduates are from out of state, mostly the Midwest. Students are from 21 states, 29 foreign countries, and Canada. 74% are White; 5% Asian American; 2% African American; 2% Hispanic; 17% Foreign. **Male To Female Ratio:** 3.1:1. 39% do not continue beyond their first year; 46% remain to graduate. **Housing:** 350 students can be accommodated in college housing, which includes single-sex dorms, on-campus apartments, married student housing, special-interest houses, and privately owned, on-campus family housing for students with families. On-campus housing is guaranteed for all 4 years. 70% of students live on campus; of those, 90% remain on campus on weekends. All students may keep cars. Alcohol is not permitted.

FACULTY/CLASSROOMS: 80% of faculty are male; 20% are female. All

teach undergraduates, 20% do research, and 20% do both. No introductory courses are taught by graduate students. The average class size in an introductory lecture is 35 and in a regular course is 10.

PROGRAMS OF STUDY: MUM confers B.A., B.S., and B.F.A. degrees. Master's and doctoral degrees are also awarded. Bachelor's degrees are awarded in BUSINESS (management science), COMMUNICATIONS AND THE ARTS (dramatic arts, fine arts, and literature), COMPUTER AND PHYSICAL SCIENCE (computer science and mathematics), EDUCATION (education). Sustainable living, Maharishi Vedic science, and business have the largest enrollments.

ACTIVITIES: There are no fraternities or sororities. There are 15 groups on campus, including permaculture, entrepreneurial, international, art, chess, chorale, chorus, dance, drama, ecology, environmental, ethnic, international, musical theater, newspaper, photography, political, professional, radio and TV, religious, social, social service, student government, and yearbook. Popular campus events include Sports Festivals, Seasonal Celebrations, and International Cultural Exchange Festival. **Sports:** There are 2 intercollegiate sports for men and 1 for women, and 5 intramural sports for men and 5 for women. Facilities include outdoor and indoor tennis, basketball, and volleyball courts, a gym, a weight-training room, a field house, swimming pool, table tennis room, batting and golf driving cages, a golf putting range, an indoor jogging track, dance studio, and a rock-climbing wall.

SERVICES: Counseling and information services are available, as is tutoring in every subject, and remedial math, reading, and writing. **Library/Resources:** The library contains 150,294 volumes, 59,851 microform items, 21,291 audio/video tapes/CDs/DVDs, and subscribes to 23,345 periodicals including electronic. Computerized library services include interlibrary loans, database searching, and Internet access. Special learning facilities include an art gallery, radio station, a psychophysiology, electronic engineering, visual technology, and physics labs, a scanning electron microscope, and domes for practicing the Transcendental Meditation Sidhi program. **Physically Challenged Students:** 95% of the campus is accessible. Facilities include wheelchair ramps, special parking, specially equipped restrooms, and lowered telephones. **Special:** Opportunities are provided for internships, study abroad, and nondegree study. Systematic programs are offered in the Science of Creative Intelligence, by which students apply knowledge to practical professional values. There are several 1-month blocks a year during which students may study, art in Italy, literature in Switzerland, or business in China. There is a freshman honors program. **Visiting:** There are regularly scheduled orientations for prospective students, including campus tours, visits to classes, interviews, student panels, and informal dinners. There are guides for informal visits, visitors may sit in on classes, and stay overnight. To schedule a visit, contact the Admissions Office. **Campus Safety and Security:** Measures include 24-hour foot and vehicle patrol, security escort services, emergency telephones and lighted pathways/sidewalks.

REQUIREMENTS: Applicants must graduate from an accredited secondary school or have a GED. An essay and 2 personal recommendations are required. An interview is recommended. A GPA of 2.5 is required. AP and CLEP credits are accepted. Important factors in the admissions decision are personality/intangible qualities, recommendations by school officials, and leadership record. Students must complete 166 credit units with a minimum of 60 credits in the major and must also complete the core curriculum of 18 units as well as 20 units in a distribution of academic fields. All students must maintain a minimum GPA of 2.0. Requirements include health and fitness courses, the Science of Creative Intelligence course with its applied aspect, the Transcendental Meditation program, and courses in math and writing. The 42-week school year and block scheduling system allow students to take 1 course at a time. **Procedure:** Freshmen are admitted in the fall and spring. Entrance exams should be taken in the fall of the senior year or spring of the junior year. There are early admissions, deferred admissions, and rolling admissions plans. Application deadlines are open. Application fee is $15. Applications are accepted online. **Transfer Students:** Students must have a 2.5 GPA and acceptable recommendations as well as meet all standards set by the university. 66 of 166 credits required for the bachelor's degree must be completed at MUM. **International Students:** The school actively recruits these students. They must take the TOEFL and the college's own test.

ADMISSIONS: There is 1 National Merit finalist. **Admissions Contact:** Barbara Rainbow, Associate Dean of Admissions. Email: *admissions@mum.edu* Web: *www.mum.edu*

FINANCIAL AID: The FAFSA code is 011113. Check with the school for current application deadlines.

MERCY COLLEGE OF HEALTH SCIENCES C-3

www.mchs.edu

Des Moines, IA 50309 (515) 643-6604 (800) 637-2994

Fax: (515) 643-6698	**Email:** admissions@mchs.edu
Full-time: 68 men, 404 women	**Faculty:** 46
Part-time: 30 men, 269 women	**Ph.D.s:** n/av
Graduate: n/av	**Student/Faculty:** 17 to 1
Year: semesters, summer session	**Tuition:** $16,920
Room & Board: n/app	**Freshman Class:** 886 applied, 446 accepted, 231 enrolled
ACT: 21	**CEEB CODE:** 2803
Application Deadline: June 15	**COMPETITIVE**

Mercy College of Health Sciences is on the forefront of health science education. It's our focus and what we do. Our students major in subjects that lead to high-demand careers in healthcare. While you're studying here, you'll be challenged to get involved and make a difference on campus and throughout the community. Health science graduates make a difference in lives every day, while in school and once they translate their knowledge into a career of service. As healthcare undergoes dramatic change the demand for the skills you acquire at Mercy College will only grow. There are 3 undergraduate schools. In addition to regional accreditation, Mercy College has baccalaureate program accreditation with CCNE. The 5-acre campus is in an urban area in downtown, Des Moines, Iowa. Including any residence halls, there are 5 buildings.

STUDENT LIFE: 98% of undergraduates are from Iowa. Others are from 4 states. 82% are White; 7% African American; 4% Hispanic; 3% Asian American; 2% two or more races; 2% race unknown. **Female To Male Ratio:** 6.9:1. The average age of freshmen is 22.9; all undergraduates, 26.6. All students commute. Alcohol is not permitted.

FACULTY/CLASSROOMS: 20% of faculty are male; 80% are female. All teach undergraduates. No introductory courses are taught by graduate students.

PROGRAMS OF STUDY: Mercy College confers B.S. degrees. Associate degrees are also awarded. Bachelor's degrees are awarded in HEALTH PROFESSIONS (health care administration, health science, nursing, and premedicine). Nursing has the largest enrollment.

ACTIVITIES: There are no fraternities or sororities. Groups on campus include association of nursing students, Sigma Theta Tau International Honor Society of Nursing, professional, science club, and student government. Popular campus events include Cultural Fair, Student Academic Showcase, Research Symposium, Mitten Tree Project, Alumni Christmas Luncheon, Blessing of the Brains, Faith & Healing Speaker Series, and Lenten Stations of the Cross. **Sports:** There is no sports program at Mercy College. **Graduates:** From July 1, 2015 to June 30, 2016, 88 bachelor's degrees were awarded. The most popular majors were nursing (RN) (34%), nursing (RN to BSN) (29%), and health sciences/Pre-Med (5%).

SERVICES: Counseling and information services are available, as is tutoring in most subjects. **Library/Resources:** The library contains 13,000 volumes, 825 audio/video tapes/CDs/DVDs, and subscribes to 18,845 periodicals including electronic. Computerized library services include interlibrary loans, database searching, Internet access, and Wi-Fi capability. **Physically Challenged Students:** All of the campus is accessible. Facilities include wheelchair ramps, elevators, special parking, specially equipped restrooms, and lowered drinking fountains. **Special:** There are 2 national honor societies and 2 departmental honors programs. **Visiting:** There are regularly scheduled orientations for prospective students, and guides for informal visits. To schedule a visit, contact Heather Gaumer at (515) 643-6715. **Campus Safety and Security:** Measures include emergency notification system and security escort services. There are shuttle buses and lighted pathways/sidewalks.

REQUIREMENTS: The ACT is required. A GPA of 2.3 is required. AP and CLEP credits are accepted. Graduation requirements: service learning, critical thinking, speaking competency, writing competency, and a minimum GPA. **Procedure:** Freshmen are admitted fall, spring, and summer. There is a rolling admissions plan. Applications should be filed by June 15 for fall entry; October 15 for spring entry; and March 15 for summer entry. Applications are accepted online. **Transfer Students:** Requirements vary by program. 30 credits required for the bachelor's degree must be completed at Mercy College.

ADMISSIONS: 50% of the 2016-2017 applicants were accepted. The

ACT scores were 15% between 12 and 17, 60% between 18 and 23, and 25% between 24 and 29. **Admissions Contact:** Heather Gaumer, Director of Admissions. Email: *admissions@mchs.edu* Web: *www.mchs.edu*

FINANCIAL AID: The FAFSA code is 006273. The priority date for freshman financial aid applications for fall entry is April 1. The filing deadline for fall entry is July 1.

MORNINGSIDE COLLEGE — B-2

www.morningside.edu

Sioux City, IA 51106	(712) 274-5111 (800) 831-0806
Fax: (712) 274-5101	Email: mscadm@morningside.edu
Full-time: 647 men, 648 women	Faculty: 80; IIB, --$
Part-time: 13 men, 13 women	Ph.D.s: 75%
Graduate: 780 men, 801 women	Student/Faculty: 16 to 1
Year: semesters, summer session	Tuition: $28,155 ($29,094)
Room & Board: $9210	Freshman Class: 4562 applied, 2597 accepted, 340 enrolled
ACT: 23	CEEB CODE: 6415
Application Deadline: open	COMPETITIVE

Morningside College, founded in 1894, is a private college affiliated with the United Methodist Church. Its curriculum includes the liberal arts, and pre-professional and professional programs of study. There is 1 undergraduate school and 1 graduate school. In addition to regional accreditation, Morningside has baccalaureate program accreditation with NASM, NCATE, and HLC. The 69-acre campus is in a suburban area 100 miles north of Omaha at the convergence of the states of South Dakota, Iowa, and Nebraska. Including any residence halls, there are 25 buildings.

STUDENT LIFE: 57% of undergraduates are from Iowa. Others are from 30 states, and 16 foreign countries. 78% are White; 6% Hispanic; 5% Foreign; 4% race unknown; 3% two or more races; 2% African American; 1% Asian American; 1% American Indian/Alaska Native. 62% claim no religious affiliation; 27% Protestant. **Female To Male Ratio:** 1.0:1. The average age of freshmen is 18; all undergraduates, 21. 31% do not continue beyond their first year; 45% remain to graduate. **Housing:** 912 students can be accommodated in college housing, which includes coed dorms, on-campus apartments, and married student housing. In addition, there are fraternity houses, sorority houses, including freshman halls, upperclassman leadership-themed, and apartment-style residence hall. On-campus housing is guaranteed for all 4 years. 60% of students live on campus; of those, 75% remain on campus on weekends. All students may keep cars.

FACULTY/CLASSROOMS: 51% of faculty are male; 49% are female. 55% teach undergraduates. No introductory courses are taught by graduate students. The average class size in an introductory lecture is 27; in a laboratory is 16; and in a regular course is 20.

PROGRAMS OF STUDY: Morningside confers B.A., B.S., B.Mus., B.Mus.Ed., and B.S.N. degrees. Master's degrees are also awarded. Bachelor's degrees are awarded in AGRICULTURE (agricultural business management and agricultural sciences), BIOLOGICAL SCIENCE (biology/biological science), BUSINESS (business administration and management and management information systems), COMMUNICATIONS AND THE ARTS (advertising, art, communications, dramatic arts, English, graphic design, music, photography, and Spanish), COMPUTER AND PHYSICAL SCIENCE (chemistry, computer science, mathematics, and physics), EDUCATION (art education, education, elementary education, English education, mathematics education, music education, science education, social studies education, and special education), HEALTH PROFESSIONS (medical technology and nursing), SOCIAL SCIENCE (history, international relations, philosophy, political science/government, psychology, and religion). Business administration, biology, and nursing have the largest enrollments.

ACTIVITIES: 4% of men belong to 2 national fraternities; 2% of women belong to 1 national sorority. There are 41 groups on campus, including art, band, cheerleading, choir, chorale, chorus, computers, dance, drama, drill team, environmental, ethnic, honors, international, jazz band, literary magazine, marching band, newspaper, orchestra, pep band, photography, political, professional, radio and TV, religious, social, and student government. Popular campus events include Friday is Writing Day, Campus Event Series, and Christmas at Morningside. **Sports:** There are 11 intercollegiate sports for men and 10 for women, and 13 intramural sports for men and 13 for women. Facilities include a stadium, football field, a campus recreation center with basketball, volleyball, racquetball/handball courts, an elevated track, a weight room, and a pool. **Graduates:** From July 1, 2015 to June 30, 2016, 225 bachelor's degrees were awarded. The most popular majors were business (23%), biology (22%), and nursing (10%). 30 companies recruited on campus in 2015-2016. In an average class, 8% graduate in 3 years or less, 45% graduate in 4 years or less, 55% graduate in 5 years or less, and 54% graduate in 6 years or less. Of the 2015 graduating class, 17% were enrolled in graduate school within 6 months of graduation.

SERVICES: Counseling and information services are available, as is tutoring in most subjects, a reader service for the blind, and remedial math, reading, and writing. **Library/Resources:** The library contains 47,802 volumes, 285,794 microform items, and 1,455 audio/video tapes/CDs/DVDs, and subscribes to 170 periodicals including electronic. Computerized library services include interlibrary loans, database searching, and Internet access. Special learning facilities include an art gallery, radio station, TV station, and a theater. **Physically Challenged Students:** 80% of the campus is accessible. Facilities include wheelchair ramps, elevators, special parking, specially equipped restrooms, special class scheduling, lowered drinking fountains, and lowered telephones. **Special:** There is a co-op program in medical technology. Internships are available in all departments. Study abroad in 11 countries, a Washington semester, work-study programs, both on campus and with 20 nonprofit agencies, and student-designed majors are available. There are 15 national honor societies and a freshman honors program. **Visiting:** There are regularly scheduled orientations for prospective students, consists of a campus tour, appointments with faculty and financial aid, and an interview with an admissions counselor. There are guides for informal visits, visitors may sit in on classes, and stay overnight. To schedule a visit, contact the Office of Admissions at mscadm@morningside.edu. **Campus Safety and Security:** Measures include emergency notification system, self-defense education, security escort services, emergency telephones, lighted pathways/sidewalks, and controlled access to dorms/residences.

REQUIREMENTS: The ACT is required. Applicants must be graduates of an accredited secondary school. The GED is accepted. A portfolio is required for all studio art majors and an audition for performing music majors. Applicants graduating from high school 5 years or more prior to entering college are exempted from submitting the ACT scores. Those entering from a home-schooled environment must submit a completed Home School Credit Evaluation form, which may be obtained in the Office of Admissions. Morningside requires applicants to be in the upper 50% of their class. A GPA of 2.5 is required. AP and CLEP credits are accepted. Important factors in the admissions decision are recommendations by school officials, evidence of special talent, and advanced placement or honors courses. The total number of credit hours required for graduation is 124 with 44 hours of core curriculum in liberal arts and 30 hours minimum in the major. Students must have a minimum GPA of 2.0 to graduate. **Procedure:** Freshmen are admitted to all sessions. Entrance exams should be taken in the junior year. There is a rolling admissions plan. Application deadlines are open. Applications are accepted on-line. **Transfer Students:** 52 transfer students enrolled in 2015-2016. Transfer applicants must take the ACT and have an interview. They must have 24 semester hours with a 2.25 or above cumulative GPA. They must present official transcripts of previous collegiate records. 30 of 124 credits required for the bachelor's degree must be completed at Morningside. **International Students:** There are 50 international students enrolled. The school actively recruits these students. They must take the TOEFL with a minimum score of 500 on the paper-based TOEFL (PBT) or 61 on the Internet-based version (iBT). They must also take the ACT.

ADMISSIONS: 57% of the 2016-2017 applicants were accepted. The ACT scores were 7% between 12 and 17, 52% between 18 and 23, 32% between 24 and 29, and 9% above 30. 29% of the current freshmen were in the top fifth of their class; 54% were in the top two fifths. 3 freshmen graduated first in their class. **Admissions Contact:** Terri Curry, VP Admissions. Email: *mscadm@morningside.edu* Web: *www.morningside.edu*

FINANCIAL AID: In 2016-2017, 100% of all full-time freshmen and continuing full-time students received some form of financial aid. 69% of all full-time freshmen and 78% of continuing full-time students received need-based aid. The average freshman award was $31,778. Need-based scholarships or need-based grants averaged $6,716 ($15,465 maximum); need-based self-help aid (loans and jobs) averaged $5,162 ($10,700 maximum); non-need-based athletic scholarships averaged $4,411 ($10,000 maximum); other non-need-based awards and non-need-based scholarships averaged $15,928 ($46,309 maximum); and $8,622 from other forms of aid. 66% of undergraduate students work part-time. Average annual earnings from campus work are $1575. The average financial indebtedness of the 2016 graduate was $36,233. The FAFSA code is 001879. The priority date for freshman financial aid applications for fall entry is March 1.

MOUNT MERCY UNIVERSITY E-3

www.mtmercy.edu

Cedar Rapids, IA 52402	(319) 368-6460 (800) 248-4504
Fax: (319) 363-5270	**Email:** admission@.mtmercy.edu
Full-time: 290 men, 667 women	**Faculty:** 76
Part-time: 157 men, 429 women	**Ph.D.s:** 64%
Graduate: 98 men, 236 women	**Student/Faculty:** 14 to 1
Year: 4-1-4, summer session	**Tuition:** $28,226
Room & Board: $8600	**Freshman Class:** 1308 applied, 672 accepted, 232 enrolled
SAT: recommended **ACT:** 22	**CEEB CODE:** 6417
Application Deadline: August 14	**COMPETITIVE**

The men and women who make up the Mount Mercy University student body come from all over Iowa and the world. They choose Mount Mercy for our small, hands-on classes, meaningful faculty interaction, vibrant student life and our commitment to leadership and compassionate service. There are 5 undergraduate schools and 5 graduate schools. In addition to regional accreditation, Mount Mercy has baccalaureate program accreditation with CSWE and NLN. The 40-acre campus is in an urban area in Cedar Rapids in eastern Iowa. Including any residence halls, there are 19 buildings.

STUDENT LIFE: 88% of undergraduates are from Iowa. Others are from 24 states, 28 foreign countries, and Canada. 80% are White; 7% African American; 4% race unknown; 3% Foreign; 2% Asian American; 2% two or more races; 1% American Indian/Alaska Native; 1% Hispanic. 68% are Protestant; 23% Catholic. **Female To Male Ratio:** 2.4:1. The average age of freshmen is 18; all undergraduates, 26. 22% do not continue beyond their first year; 65% remain to graduate. **Housing:** 480 students can be accommodated in college housing, which includes single-sex, coed dorms and on-campus apartments, special-interest houses, and themed living learning communities. On-campus housing is guaranteed for all 4 years. 59% of students commute. All students may keep cars.

FACULTY/CLASSROOMS: 36% of faculty are male; 64% are female. 94% teach undergraduates, 2% do research, and 2% do both. No introductory courses are taught by graduate students. The average class size in an introductory lecture is 25; in a laboratory is 14; and in a regular course is 25.

PROGRAMS OF STUDY: Mount Mercy confers B.A., B.A.A., B.A.S., B.B.A., B.S. and B.S.N. degrees. Master's degrees are also awarded. Bachelor's degrees are awarded in AGRICULTURE (conservation and regulation), BIOLOGICAL SCIENCE (biology/biological science), BUSINESS (accounting, business administration and management, finance, human resources, management information systems, and marketing/retailing/merchandising), COMMUNICATIONS AND THE ARTS (art, communications, English, graphic design, journalism, and music), COMPUTER AND PHYSICAL SCIENCE (actuarial science, computer science, and mathematics), EDUCATION (early childhood education, elementary education, middle school education, and secondary education), HEALTH PROFESSIONS (health care administration, medical laboratory technology, and nursing), SOCIAL SCIENCE (criminal justice, history, international studies, philosophy, political science/government, psychology, religion, social work, and sociology). Business, nursing, and education have the largest enrollments.

ACTIVITIES: There are no fraternities or sororities. There are 34 groups on campus, including academic club, art, cheerleading, choir, chorale, chorus, computers, dance, drama, drill team, environmental, ethnic, film, honors, international, jazz band, literary magazine, musical theater, newspaper, political, professional, religious, social, social service, and student government. Popular campus events include Octoberfest, Bingo Nights, and Vegas Night. **Sports:** There are 7 intercollegiate sports for men and 8 for women, and 17 intramural sports for men and 17 for women. The recreation center offers practice facilities, weight room, training room, a cardio area, plus large group exercise rooms. .**Graduates:** From July 1, 2015 to June 30, 2016, 407 bachelor's degrees were awarded. The most popular majors were nursing (29%), business (10%), and criminal justice (7%). 47 companies recruited on campus in 2015-2016. In an average class, 1% graduate in 3 years or less, 58% graduate in 4 years or less, 64% graduate in 5 years or less, and 65% graduate in 6 years or less. Of the 2015 graduating class, 12% were enrolled in graduate school within 6 months of graduation, and 96% were employed.

SERVICES: Counseling and information services are available, as is tutoring in most subjects, such as all communication skills. There is also a reader service for the blind, and remedial math, reading, and writing. **Library/Resources:** The library contains 126,903 volumes, 54,940 microform items, 8,999 audio/video tapes/CDs/DVDs, and subscribes to 3,531 periodicals including electronic. Computerized library services include interlibrary loans, database searching, Internet access, and Wi-Fi capability. Special learning facilities include an art gallery, all of the classrooms are "smart" technology classrooms. **Physically Challenged Students:** 95% of the campus is accessible. Facilities include wheelchair ramps, elevators, special parking, specially equipped restrooms, special class scheduling, and lowered drinking fountains. **Special:** Mount Mercy offers internships in most majors, study abroad opportunities, work-study programs on campus, several adult accelerated business majors, an accelerated degree completion program for RNs, and student-designed, interdisciplinary majors. Credit for prior experiential learning may be granted, and pass/fail options are available. There are 3 national honor societies, a freshman honors program, and 10 departmental honors programs. **Visiting:** There are regularly scheduled orientations for prospective students, consisting of a presidential welcome, campus tour, student panel, faculty academic fair, presentations on college selection and admission requirements, and student evaluation. There are guides for informal visits, visitors may sit in on classes, and stay overnight. To schedule a visit, contact the Admissions Office. **Campus Safety and Security:** Measures include 24-hour foot and vehicle patrol, emergency notification system, self-defense education, security escort services, emergency telephones, lighted pathways/sidewalks, and controlled access to dorms/residences. In addition, safety personnel are on duty 24-hours-a-day, 365-days-a-year, with regularly scheduled patrols, extensive video monitoring of building entrances building exits, and most parking facilities. Surveillance is monitored and recorded. After hours, use of residence elevators and entry to student room corridors require a resident-only passkey.

REQUIREMENTS: The SAT or ACT is recommended. The Admissions Committee evaluates all applications on an individual basis. Strong consideration will be given to applicants with the following: Cumulative grade point average of 2.75 (on a 4.0 scale), Composite ACT score of 20 (940 SAT) with sub-scores of 17 or higher, class rank in the top half of their graduating class. While specific courses are not required for admission, students applying to Mount Mercy are encouraged to complete the following high school coursework: 4 years of English, 3 years each of mathematics, social studies, and science. AP and CLEP credits are accepted. Important factors in the admissions decision are leadership record, extracurricular activities record, and geographical diversity. To graduate, students must complete 123 semester hours, have a minimum cumulative GPA of at least 2.00, a minimum cumulative GPA in all credits taken at MMU, completion of the core curriculum requirements, completions of a major program of study, at least 12 semester hours, above course number 200, completed in the major at MMU, a minimum of 30 semester hours completed at MMU, a minimum of 30 consecutive semester hours completed at MMU immediately preceding graduation. **Procedure:** Freshmen are admitted to all sessions. Entrance exams should be taken in the junior year or the fall of the senior year. There are deferred admissions and rolling admissions plans. Applications should be filed by August 14 for fall entry. Notification is sent on a rolling basis. Application fees are waived if application is completed online. **Transfer Students:** 161 transfer students enrolled in 2015-2016. Mount Mercy evaluates all files on an individual basis. While specific courses are not required for admission, the transcripts will be evaluated to ensure that strong college curriculum has been successfully completed. Strong consideration will be given to applicants who have the following: Cumulative transfer grade point average of 2.50 (on a 4.0 scale). Students looking to transfer with two semesters or less will be reviewed by the Admission Committee. A complete admission file includes: Application for admission, official high school transcripts. For applicants who have not earned an associates degree or higher from an accredited college or university official transcripts from all previous colleges attended are required. For applicants who have earned an associates degree or higher from an accredited college or university, updated copies of college transcripts will need to be sent prior to enrollment for students who apply for admission while enrolled at another college. 30 of 123 credits required for the bachelor's degree must be completed at Mount Mercy. **International Students:** There are 52 international students enrolled. The school actively recruits these students. They must take the TOEFL with a minimum score of 550 on the paper-based TOEFL (PBT) or 79 on the Internet-based version (iBT), ICHS 6.5; Step EIKEN Grade 1; IELTS (6.5); ACT (20); SAT (940). They must also take the SAT or ACT.

ADMISSIONS: 51% of the 2016-2017 applicants were accepted. The ACT scores were 2% below 12, 10% between 12 and 17, 66% between 18 and 23, 21% between 24 and 29, and 3% above 30. 28% of the current freshmen were in the top fifth of their class; 61% were in the top two fifths. 2 freshmen graduated first in their class. **Admissions Contact:** Terri Crumley, Dean of Admissions. Email: *admission@.mtmercy.edu* Web: *www.mtmercy.edu*

FINANCIAL AID: In 2016-2017, 100% of all full-time freshmen and 97% of continuing full-time students received some form of financial aid. 81% of all full-time freshmen and 90% of continuing full-time students received need-based aid. The average freshman award was $17,878. 41% of undergraduate students work part-time. Average annual earnings from campus work are $1570. The average financial indebtedness of the 2016 graduate was $26,603. The FAFSA code is 001880. The priority date for freshman financial aid applications for fall entry is March 1.

NORTHWESTERN COLLEGE OF IOWA — B-2

www.nwciowa.edu

Orange City, IA 51041 — (712) 707-7114, (800) 747-4757

Fax: (712) 707-7164 — Email: admissions@nwciowa.edu

Full-time: 457 men, 588 women	**Faculty:** 82; IIB, --$
Part-time: 26 men, 28 women	**Ph.D.s:** 83%
Graduate: 12 men, 149 women	**Student/Faculty:** 13 to 1
Year: semesters, summer session	**Tuition:** $29,500
Room & Board: $8900	**Freshman Class:** 2199 applied, 1441 accepted, 282 enrolled
SAT CR/M/W: 500/540/580 **ACT:** 24	**CEEB CODE:** 6490
Application Deadline: August 15	**COMPETITIVE+**

Northwestern College, is a Christian academic community engaging students in courageous and faithful learning and living that empowers them to follow Christ and pursue God's redeeming work in the world. There is 1 undergraduate school and 1 graduate school. In addition to regional accreditation, Northwestern has baccalaureate program accreditation with CSWE, NCATE, CAATE, IACBE, and CCNE. The 100-acre campus is in a small town 40 miles northeast of Sioux City, and 75 miles southeast of Sioux Falls, South Dakota. Including any residence halls, there are 32 buildings.

STUDENT LIFE: 53% of undergraduates are from Iowa. Others are from 31 states, 25 foreign countries, and Canada. 75% are from public schools. 83% are White; 4% Hispanic; 4% race unknown; 3% Foreign; 2% African American; 2% two or more races; 1% Asian American; 1% American Indian/Alaska Native. 75% are Protestant; 19% claim no religious affiliation. **Female To Male Ratio:** 1.5:1. The average age of freshmen is 18; all undergraduates, 20. 19% do not continue beyond their first year; 64% remain to graduate. **Housing:** 1045 students can be accommodated in college housing, which includes single-sex dorms and on-campus apartments. On-campus housing is guaranteed for all 4 years. 87% of students live on campus; of those, 75% remain on campus on weekends. All students may keep cars. Alcohol is not permitted.

FACULTY/CLASSROOMS: 58% of faculty are male; 42% are female. All teach undergraduates and 80% do research. No introductory courses are taught by graduate students. The average class size in an introductory lecture is 22; in a laboratory is 15; and in a regular course is 16.

PROGRAMS OF STUDY: Northwestern confers B.A., B.A.A.T., and B.S.N. degrees. Master's degrees are also awarded. Bachelor's degrees are awarded in AGRICULTURE (agricultural business management), BIOLOGICAL SCIENCE (biochemistry, biology/biological science, and genetics), BUSINESS (accounting, business administration and management, and business economics), COMMUNICATIONS AND THE ARTS (dramatic arts, graphic design, journalism, literature, music, public relations, and Spanish), COMPUTER AND PHYSICAL SCIENCE (actuarial science, chemistry, computer science, information sciences and systems, and mathematics), EDUCATION (art education, athletic training, business education, Christian education, early childhood education, elementary education, foreign languages education, middle school education, music education, physical education, science education, secondary education, and special education), HEALTH PROFESSIONS (medical laboratory technology, nursing, predentistry, and premedicine), SOCIAL SCIENCE (criminal justice, economics, history, philosophy, physical fitness/movement, political science/government, prelaw, psychology, religion, religious music, social work, sociology, and youth ministry). Biology, education, and religion are the strongest academically. Business, education, and kinesiology have the largest enrollments.

ACTIVITIES: There are no fraternities or sororities. There are 50 groups on campus, including art, band, cheerleading, choir, chorus, communications, computers, dance, drama, drill team, environmental, ethnic, honors, international, jazz band, literary magazine, musical theater, newspaper, orchestra, photography, political, professional, religious, social, social service, student government, symphony, and yearbook. Popular campus events include Clash of the Classes competition, Airband competition, Coly Christmas Bash, Raider Days Homecoming, NC/DC singing competition, RUSH Student Dance Exhibition, and Winter Formal. **Sports:** There are 8 intercollegiate sports for men and 8 for women, and 21 intramural sports for men and 21 for women. Facilities include a gymnasium for intercollegiate basketball and volleyball, outdoor turf football field, practice football fields, soccer fields, an indoor practice facility for intercollegiate baseball, softball, football, and track, weight room and training facilities dedicated to intercollegiate athletes, wrestling room, a one-tenth-mile/six-lane indoor track, handball/racquetball courts, basketball and volleyball courts for recreational use, indoor tennis courts, a student and community fitness center with free weights and fitness equipment. **Graduates:** From July 1, 2015 to June 30, 2016, 252 bachelor's degrees were awarded. The most popular majors were elementary education (16%), business administration (12%), and nursing (9%). In an average class, 1% graduate in 3 years or less, 56% graduate in 4 years or less, 64% graduate in 5 years or less, and 65% graduate in 6 years or less. Of the 2015 graduating class, 16% were enrolled in graduate school within 6 months of graduation, and 83% were employed.

SERVICES: Counseling and information services are available, as is tutoring in most subjects, and remedial math, reading, and writing. **Library/Resources:** The library contains 80,000 volumes, 6,000 audio/video tapes/CDs/DVDs, and subscribes to 650 periodicals including electronic. Computerized library services include interlibrary loans, database searching, Internet access, and Wi-Fi capability. Special learning facilities include an art gallery. **Physically Challenged Students:** 90% of the campus is accessible. Facilities include wheelchair ramps, elevators, special parking, specially equipped restrooms, lowered drinking fountains, and special housing. **Special:** Northwestern offers cross-registration with Dordt College, student-designed majors, numerous internships, off-campus semester programs in Chicago, Washington, D.C., and Denver, and study abroad in over 20 countries, including China, Oman, Romania, Egypt, Spain, France, and the Netherlands. There are 2 national honor societies, a freshman honors program, and 23 departmental honors programs. **Visiting:** There are regularly scheduled orientations for prospective students, campus tour, meet with financial aid and admissions personnel, attend chapel, meet with a faculty member and attend a class in the student's area of interest. There are guides for informal visits, visitors may sit in on classes, and stay overnight. To schedule a visit, contact Laura De Boer at (712) 707-7142. **Campus Safety and Security:** Measures include emergency notification system, emergency telephones, lighted pathways/sidewalks, and controlled access to dorms/residences.

REQUIREMENTS: The ACT is required. Applicants with a minimum ACT composite of 19, in the top half of their high school class, and with a 2.4 GPA are generally accepted. Applicants should be graduates of an accredited secondary school. The suggested distribution of high school courses is 4 years of English, 3 years each of math, foreign language, and social studies, and 2 of natural science. The GED is accepted. AP and CLEP credits are accepted. All students are required to take an integrated general education core curriculum, including a first-year seminar, eight credits of Christian story and tradition courses, between 31 and 44 credits in a variety of disciplines, and a senior seminar. Students must maintain a 2.0 GPA for 124 total credits and pass both writing and math competency levels. **Procedure:** Freshmen are admitted to all sessions. Entrance exams should be taken Spring semester of the junior year of high school. There is a rolling admissions plan. Application deadlines are open. Notifications are sent November 1. Application fees are waived if application is completed online. **Transfer Students:** 53 transfer students enrolled in 2015-2016. Transfer applicants must submit a transcript and letter of recommendation. A minimum college GPA of 2.0 is required. 30 of 124 credits required for the bachelor's degree must be completed at Northwestern. **International Students:** There are 40 international students enrolled. The school actively recruits these students. They must take the TOEFL with a minimum score of 475 on the paper-based TOEFL (PBT) or 53 on the Internet-based version (iBT).

ADMISSIONS: 66% of the 2016-2017 applicants were accepted. The SAT scores for the 2016-2017 freshman class were: Critical Reading-- 47% below 500, 35% between 500 and 599, 7% between 600 and 699, and 11% between 700 and 800. Math-- 33% below 500, 35% between 500 and 599, 24% between 600 and 699, and 8% between 700 and 800. Writing-- 56% below 500, 33% between 500 and 599, and 11% between 700 and 800. The ACT scores were 4% between 12 and 17, 39% between 18 and 23, 40% between 24 and 29, and 17% above 30. 39% of the current freshmen were in the top fifth of their class; 63% were in the top two fifths. There were 2 National Merit finalists. 25 freshmen graduated first in their class. **Admissions Contact:** Jackie Davis, Director of Admissions. Email: *admissions@nwciowa.edu* Web: *www.nwciowa.edu*

FINANCIAL AID: In 2016-2017, 100% of all full-time freshmen and 99% of continuing full-time students received some form of financial aid. 83% of all full-time freshmen and 95% of continuing full-time students received need-based aid. The average freshman award was $28,351. Need-based scholarships or need-based grants averaged $6,618 ($24,265 maximum); need-based self-help aid (loans and jobs) averaged $4,725 ($11,380 maximum); non-need-based athletic scholarships averaged $5,847 ($19,000 maximum); and other non-need-based awards and non-need-based scholarships averaged $16,198 ($40,000 maximum). 85% of undergraduate students work part-time. Average annual earnings from campus work are $1200. The average financial indebtedness of the 2016 graduate was $28,373. The FAFSA code is 001883. The priority date for freshman financial aid applications for fall entry is April 1. The filing deadline for fall entry is June 30.

SIMPSON COLLEGE — C-3

www.simpson.edu

Indianola, IA 50125	**(515) 961-1624**
Fax: (515) 961-1870	**Email: admiss@simpson.edu**
Full-time: 605 men, 774 women	**Faculty:** 105
Part-time: 80 men, 84 women	**Ph.D.s:** 82%
Graduate: 24 men, 41 women	**Student/Faculty:** 14 to 1
Year: other, summer session	**Tuition:** $35,876
Room & Board: $7963	**Freshman Class:** 1265 applied, 1081 accepted, 348 enrolled
ACT: 24	**CEEB CODE:** 6650
Application Deadline: rolling	**VERY COMPETITIVE**

Simpson College, founded in 1860, is a private liberal arts college affiliated with the United Methodist Church. Simpson combines the best of a liberal arts education with outstanding career preparation and extracurricular programs. More than 80 majors, minors, and pre-professional programs are offered. Extra-curricular activities at Simpson are designed to supplement and reinforce the academic program and contribute toward a total learning experience. Activities range from award-winning fine arts programs to nationally recognized NCAA Division III teams. There are 3 undergraduate schools and one graduate school. In addition to regional accreditation, Simpson has baccalaureate program accreditation with NASM and CAATE. The 80-acre campus is in a small town 12 miles south of Des Moines, Iowa's capital city. Including any residence halls, there are 45 buildings.

STUDENT LIFE: 82% of undergraduates are from Iowa. Others are from 28 states, and 5 foreign countries. 84% are White; 6% race unknown; 4% Hispanic; 2% African American; 2% two or more races; 1% Asian American. 33% are Protestant; 18% unknown, Agnostic, and Atheist; 17% Catholic. **Female To Male Ratio:** 1.3:1. The average age of freshmen is 18; all undergraduates, 22. 22% do not continue beyond their first year; 63% remain to graduate. **Housing:** 1268 students can be accommodated in college housing, which includes single-sex and coed dorms and on-campus apartments, special-interest houses, fraternity houses, sorority houses, and theme houses. On-campus housing is guaranteed for all 4 years. 86% of students live on campus; of those, 75% remain on campus on weekends. All students may keep cars.

FACULTY/CLASSROOMS: 52% of faculty are male; 48% are female. All teach undergraduates. No introductory courses are taught by graduate students. The average class size in an introductory lecture is 25; in a laboratory is 22; and in a regular course is 17.

PROGRAMS OF STUDY: Simpson confers B.A. and B.Mus. degrees. Master's degrees are also awarded. Bachelor's degrees are awarded in BIOLOGICAL SCIENCE (biochemistry, biology/biological science, and neurosciences), BUSINESS (accounting, business administration and management, international business management, management information systems, marketing management, and sports management), COMMUNICATIONS AND THE ARTS (art, communications, dramatic arts, English, French, German, graphic design, journalism, multimedia, music, music performance, public relations, and Spanish), COMPUTER AND PHYSICAL SCIENCE (actuarial science, chemistry, computer science, information sciences and systems, mathematics, and physics), EDUCATION (athletic training, elementary education, music education, physical education, and secondary education), ENGINEERING AND ENVIRONMENTAL DESIGN (environmental science and preengineering), HEALTH PROFESSIONS (exercise science, predentistry, premedicine, preoptometry, prepharmacy, prephysical therapy, and preveterinary science), SOCIAL SCIENCE (criminal justice, economics, forensic studies, history, interdisciplinary studies, international relations, philosophy, political science/government, prelaw, psychology, religion, and sociology). Education, sciences, and music are the strongest academically. Management, communication studies, and education have the largest enrollments.

ACTIVITIES: 25% of men belong to 1 local and 3 national fraternities; 21% of women belong to 3 national sororities. There are 75 groups on campus, including art, band, campus activities board, cheerleading, choir, chorale, computers, drama, drill team, environmental, ethnic, honors, international, jazz band, LGBT, literary magazine, musical theater, newspaper, opera, pep band, political, professional, radio and TV, religious, social, social service, student government, and yearbook. Popular campus events include Back to School Stand-Around, Homecoming Yell Like Hell Pep Rally, Campus Day, Lessons and Carols Christmas Concert. **Sports:** There are 10 intercollegiate sports for men and 9 for women, and 50 intramural sports for men and 50 for women. Facilities include a gym, wrestling practice room, weight room/workout facility, training facility, racquetball courts, field house for volleyball, basketball, and wrestling, football and soccer stadium with track, tennis courts, baseball field, softball complex, practice and intramural fields, outdoor basketball, and sand volleyball courts. **Graduates:** From July 1, 2015 to June 30, 2016, 413 bachelor's degrees were awarded. The most popular majors were business, management (13%), criminal justice (8%), and psychology (7%). 50 companies recruited on campus in 2015-2016. In an average class, 1% graduate in 3 years or less, 53% graduate in 4 years or less, 61% graduate in 5 years or less, and 63% graduate in 6 years or less. Of the 2015 graduating class, 22% were enrolled in graduate school within 6 months of graduation, and 75% were employed.

SERVICES: Counseling and information services are available, as is tutoring in every subject, and a reader service for the blind. **Library/Resources:** The library contains 134,098 volumes, 8,539 microform items, 4,621 audio/video tapes/CDs/DVDs, and subscribes to 87,887 periodicals including electronic. Computerized library services include interlibrary loans, database searching, Internet access, and Wi-Fi capability. Special learning facilities include an art gallery, radio station, Avery O. Craven antebellum period collection, the George Washington Carver papers, the Iowa History Center, the John C. Culver Center for Public Policy Studies, an education lab, and a cadaver lab. **Physically Challenged Students:** All of the campus is accessible. Facilities include wheelchair ramps, elevators, special parking, specially equipped restrooms, special class scheduling, lowered drinking fountains, and special housing. **Special:** Internships, study abroad, a Washington semester, and work-study are all available. Dual and student-designed majors are possible. There are several preprofessional programs in health related areas, and

3-2 engineering degrees are offered with Washington University at St. Louis, Iowa State University, and Institute of Technology (University of Minnesota). We also offer a 3 + 3 Law program with Drake University, and a 3 + 2 Nursing program in conjunction with Allen College of Nursing. There are 15 national honor societies, a freshman honors program, and 5 departmental honors programs. **Visiting:** There are orientations scheduled 4 times throughout the summer to allow incoming students to meet with an academic advisor, register for classes, and participate in activity information sessions. Parents are encouraged to attend. There are guides for informal visits, visitors may sit in on classes, and stay overnight. To schedule a visit, contact the Visit Coordinator at admiss@simpson.edu. **Campus Safety and Security:** Measures include 24-hour foot and vehicle patrol, emergency notification system, security escort services, emergency telephones, lighted pathways/sidewalks, and controlled access to dorms/residences.

REQUIREMENTS: Applicants must be graduates of an accredited secondary school; however, the GED is accepted. ACT or SAT test scores, counselor recommendations, GPA, college prep course grades, and class rank are all considered in a selective admissions process. The college strongly recommends that applicants complete 4 years of English, 3 each of math, lab science, social science, and a foreign language. A visit to campus to speak with an admissions representative is also recommended. AP and CLEP credits are accepted. Students must satisfactorily complete the Engaged Citizenship curriculum including a first-year colloquium, a senior capstone course, complete two May term courses, and complete a major course load. **Procedure:** Freshmen are admitted to all sessions. Entrance exams should be taken during the junior or senior year. There are deferred admissions and rolling admissions plans. Application deadlines are open. Notification is sent on a rolling basis. Applications are accepted on-line. **Transfer Students:** 69 transfer students enrolled in 2015-2016. In addition to freshman requirements, transfer applicants are considered on the basis of college work taken and grades received. It is recommended that applicants take either the SAT or ACT. The recommended GPA is 2.5, and grades of 2.0 and above transfer for credit. 32 of 128 credits required for the bachelor's degree must be completed at Simpson. **International Students:** There are 7 international students enrolled. The school actively recruits these students. They must take the TOEFL with a minimum score of 550 on the paper-based TOEFL (PBT) or 79 on the Internet-based version (iBT), SAT or ACT scores are also recommended. They must also take the SAT and ACT. or take the TOEFL.

ADMISSIONS: 85% of the 2016-2017 applicants were accepted. The SAT scores for the 2016-2017 freshman class were: The ACT scores were % below 12, 2% between 12 and 17, 41% between 18 and 23, 45% between 24 and 29, and 12% above 30. **Admissions Contact:** Deborah Tierney, Vice President for Enrollment. Email: *admiss@simpson.edu* Web: *www.simpson.edu*

FINANCIAL AID: In 2016-2017, 100% of all full-time freshmen and continuing full-time students received some form of financial aid. 84% of all full-time freshmen and 82% of continuing full-time students received need-based aid. The average freshman award was $32,435. Need-based scholarships or need-based grants averaged $26,776; need-based self-help aid (loans and jobs) averaged $5,286; and other non-need-based awards and non-need-based scholarships averaged $22,431. 43% of undergraduate students work part-time. Average annual earnings from campus work are $1250. The average financial indebtedness of the 2016 graduate was $24,748. The FAFSA code is 001887. The priority date for freshman financial aid applications for fall entry is February 1. The filing deadline for fall entry is July 1.

ST. AMBROSE UNIVERSITY — E-3

www.sau.edu

Davenport, IA 52803

(563) 333-6306
(800) 383-2627
Email: admit@sau.edu

Full-time: 951 men, 1237 women
Part-time: 74 men, 136 women
Graduate: 258 men, 522 women
Year: semesters, summer session
Room & Board: $9869

ACT: 23
Application Deadline: n/av

Faculty: n/av
Ph.D.s: n/av
Student/Faculty: 11 to 1
Tuition: $29,150
Freshman Class: 4436 applied, 2821 accepted, 454 enrolled
CEEB CODE: 6617
COMPETITIVE

St. Ambrose University, founded in 1882, is Catholic independent, coeducational institution affiliated with the Diocese of Davenport. It is recognized as a leading Midwestern university, consistently rated among the top universities in the region by major national ranking publications. The University offers more than 60 areas of study leading to bachelor's degrees, as well as graduate programs granting master's and doctoral degrees. Robust academic and co-curricular programs are offered in the liberal arts and sciences, education, business, the health sciences, and increasingly in STEM fields. There are 3 undergraduate schools and 3 graduate schools. In addition to regional accreditation, St. Ambrose has baccalaureate program accreditation with ABET, ACBSP, APTA, CSWE, TEAC, ACOTE, AOTA, CAPTE, ARC-PA, NAEYC, CCNE, and ASHA. The 123-acre campus is in an urban area St. Ambrose University is located 180 miles west of Chicago in Davenport, Iowa. Including any residence halls, there are 35 buildings.

STUDENT LIFE: 60% of undergraduates are from out of state, mostly the Midwest. Students are from 27 states, 18 foreign countries, and Canada. 70% are from public schools. 79% are White; 6% Hispanic; 4% African American; 4% race unknown; 3% Foreign; 2% two or more races; 1% Asian American; 1% American Indian/Alaska Native. 49% are Protestant; 38% Catholic; 34% claim no religious affiliation; 12% Musim, Hindu, and Unitarian. **Female To Male Ratio:** 1.5:1. The average age of freshmen is 18; all undergraduates, 22. 77% do not continue beyond their first year; 63% remain to graduate. **Housing:** 1700 students can be accommodated in college housing, which includes single-sex and coed dorms, on-campus apartments, and off-campus apartments, honors houses, special-interest houses, and townhouse residences for upper-division students. On-campus housing is guaranteed for all 4 years. 63% of students live on campus. All students may keep cars.

FACULTY/CLASSROOMS: No introductory courses are taught by graduate students. The average class size in an introductory lecture is 18; in a laboratory is 15; and in a regular course is 16.

PROGRAMS OF STUDY: St. Ambrose confers B.A., B.S., B.A.M.T., B.B.A., B.M.E., B.S.I.E., B.S.N., B.A.IS., and B.S.S., B.Ed degrees. Master's and doctoral degrees are also awarded. Bachelor's degrees are awarded in BIOLOGICAL SCIENCE (biology/gen science secondary education, and forensic psychology), BUSINESS (accounting (finance), business administration - international, business administration, management, operations, business administration marketing, business economics, economics – statistics, finance, international business, integrative studies, leadership, marketing, organizational leadership and management, sports management, sports marketing), COMMUNICATIONS AND THE ARTS (art history, English, English as a second/foreign language, English writing, French, graphic design, music, painting, printmaking, radio/TV, Spanish, speech and theatre education, stage management, theatre acting, voice, vocal music education), COMPUTER AND PHYSICAL SCIENCE (chemistry, chemistry education, computer networks & systems, computer security, computer science, mathematics, and mathematics), EDUCATION (art education, business education, childhood education, early childhood education, education, education administration, elementary education, English secondary education, foreign languages education, mathematics education, music education, secondary education, Spanish education K-12, and special education), ENGINEERING AND ENVIRONMENTAL DESIGN (engineering, industrial engineering, and mechanical engineering), HEALTH PROFESSIONS (biology, exercise science, kinesiology, nursing, occupational therapy, physical therapy, physician's assistant, speech pathology/audiology, and speech therapy), SOCIAL SCIENCE (area studies, criminal justice, early childhood studies, economics, feminist, gender, sexuality studies, gender studies, history, international studies, pastoral studies, philosophy, political science/government, prelaw, psychology, social work, sociology, theological studies, and women & gender studies). Nursing, biology, chemistry, exercise science, and engineering are the strongest academically. Nursing, business, and psychology have the largest enrollments.

ACTIVITIES: There are no fraternities or sororities. There are 60 groups on campus, including art, band, cheerleading, choir, chorale, chorus, computers, dance, Dance Marathon, Ambrosians for Peace and Justice, debate, drama, environmental, ethnic, honors, international, jazz band, LGBT, literary magazine, marching band, musical theater, newspaper, pep band, photography, political, professional, radio and TV, religious, social, social service, and student government. Popular campus events include Homecoming, Dance Marathon, Multicultural Week, Mission Week, and Brother/Sister Weekend. **Sports:** There are 11 intercollegiate sports for men and 11 for women, and 13 intramural sports for men and

13 for women. Facilities include SAU which will open it's new Wellness and Recreation Center in the fall of 2017. The facilities will provide exercise and activity space, lab space for some of the University's health and wellness-related academic programs including Kinesiology, for student-athletes who participate in the University's 23 varsity sports. **Graduates:** From July 1, 2015 to June 30, 2016, 641 bachelor's degrees were awarded. The most popular majors were nursing (15%), psychology (11%), and exercise science (7%). 185 companies recruited on campus in 2015-2016. In an average class, 51% graduate in 4 years or less, 62% graduate in 5 years or less, and 63% graduate in 6 years or less. Of the 2015 graduating class, 8% were enrolled in graduate school within 6 months of graduation, and 79% were employed.

SERVICES: Counseling and information services are available, as is tutoring in most subjects, such as biology, psychology, and chemisty. There is a reader service for the blind, and remedial math, reading, and writing. **Library/Resources:** The library contains 172,838 volumes, 7,185 microform items, 4,390 audio/video tapes/CDs/DVDs, and subscribes to 165,241 periodicals including electronic. Computerized library services include interlibrary loans, database searching, Internet access, and Wi-Fi capability. Special learning facilities include an art gallery, radio station, TV station, an observatory. **Physically Challenged Students:** 96% of the campus is accessible. Facilities include wheelchair ramps, elevators, special parking, specially equipped restrooms, special class scheduling, lowered drinking fountains, and special housing. **Special:** The university offers credit for life, military, and work experience, nondegree study, and pass/fail options also are available. Students can design their own integrative major. Six bacbachelor's degree are offered at an accelerated pace that is both convenient and affordable. There are over 400 workstudy positions available to students through the University, as well as the opportunity to study abroad in over 20 countries including: Australia, Belize, China, Czech Republic, Ecuador, England, France, Germany, India, Ireland, Italy, Morocco, the Netherlands, South Africa, Greece, Spain, Israel and Palestine. With the support of both faculty and the Career Center, students can earn academic credit for internships both locally and afar. Transfer students may earn an associate's degree at their community college and then continue to St. Ambrose to finish their bachelor's degree with the seamless transition of the Dual Admissions Program. Students currently enrolled at community colleges not only save money by attending a community college for their first two years, but are granted academic advising, scholarship funds, a student ID, access to the library and other student faciliies at SAU prior to enrolling. There are 16 national honor societies and a freshman honors program. **Visiting:** There are regularly scheduled orientations for prospective students, Institutional welcome and overview, advising and registration, financial aid counseling, campus tour, presentations from student service offices, and overnight stay. There are guides for informal visits, visitors may sit in on classes, and stay overnight. To schedule a visit, contact the Admissions Office at admit@sau.edu. **Campus Safety and Security:** Measures include 24-hour foot and vehicle patrol, emergency notification system, self-defense education, security escort services, emergency telephones, lighted pathways/sidewalks, and controlled access to dorms/residences.

REQUIREMENTS: Individuals are eligible for admission to St. Ambrose University as a First Year student if they meet the following requirements: Have a cumulative grade point average of 2.5 or above (on a 4.0 scale) from an accredited high school and either have a composite score of 20 or above on the American College Testing Program (ACT) or a 950 or above on the Scholastic Aptitude Test (SAT) of the College Board. Students who graduated from high school five or more years ago do not need to supply ACT or SAT scores. The writing portion of the ACT is optional for admission to St. Ambrose University. Student may also have an ACT composite score of 18 or 19 (or an SAT score between 870 and 950) AND graduate in the upper half of their senior class. Prospective students who do not have a high school diploma (home school student) are required to receive a passing score on the General Education Development Test (GED) and to have earned an ACT composite score of 18 or an SAT score of 870. Students who have been out of high school (or equivalent) at least five years do not need SAT or ACT scores. Students who are ineligible for full admission because they do not meet the above standards may be admitted on a provisional basis. The academic progress of provisional students is monitored each semester by the Board of Studies. Minimum requirements for the provisional status include a 2.0 cumulative GPA (on a 4.0 non-weighted scale) and a score of 18 on the ACT or 870 on the SAT. Applicants who don't meet the minimum criteria for either category above may petition the Admissions Standards Committee. More information on this process is available from the Admissions Office. All undergraduate students are required to have on file in the Health Services Office a properly completed health form. This information is confidential and available only to the Director of Health Services. Release of any health information requires the student's signature. This form is available on the Health Services website. St. Ambrose requires applicants to be in the upper 50% of their class. A GPA of 2.5 is required. AP and CLEP credits are accepted. To graduate, all students must complete at least 120 credit hours, including 45 outside the major and 30 in upper-level courses. A minimum GPA of 2.0 is required. Students must also demonstrate proficiency in English composition, math, public speaking, and library skills, among other requirements. Selections of courses must include those that provide an opportunity to develop specific skills, content knowledge, and exposure to attitude and value development. **Procedure:** Freshmen are admitted to all sessions. Entrance exams should be taken Spring of the junior year of high school. There is a rolling admissions plan. Application deadlines are open. Application fees are waived if application is completed online. **Transfer Students:** 192 transfer students enrolled in 2015-2016. Transfer students are eligible for admission to St. Ambrose University if they meet the following requirements: Have completed 12 college transferable credits of academic work from a fully accredited institution of higher education. Maintained a 2.0 grade point average or above (on a 4.0 scale). Students must submit transcripts of all prior work at higher education levels. With less than 12 transferable semester credits of college work, admission will be based on high school GPA and test scores. 30 of 120 credits required for the bachelor's degree must be completed at St. Ambrose. **International Students:** There are 83 international students enrolled. The school actively recruits these students. They must take the TOEFL with a minimum score of 550 on the paper-based TOEFL (PBT) or 79 on the Internet-based version (iBT).

ADMISSIONS: 64% of the 2016-2017 applicants were accepted. The ACT scores were 2% between 12 and 17, 59% between 18 and 23, 35% between 24 and 29, and 4% above 30. 35% of the current freshmen were in the top fifth of their class; 61% were in the top two fifths. 6 freshmen graduated first in their class. **Admissions Contact:** Allie Conklin, Director of First Year Admissions. Email: *admit@sau.edu* Web: *www.sau.edu*

FINANCIAL AID: In 2016-2017, 99% of all full-time freshmen and 84% of continuing full-time students received some form of financial aid. 69% of all full-time freshmen and 42% of continuing full-time students received need-based aid. The average freshman award was $25,643. Need-based scholarships or need-based grants averaged $3,328 ($10,106 maximum); need-based self-help aid (loans and jobs) averaged $5,405 ($28,000 maximum); non-need-based athletic scholarships averaged $3,450 ($18,870 maximum); other non-need-based awards and non-need-based scholarships averaged $7,782 ($29,300 maximum); and $5,678 from other forms of aid. 24% of undergraduate students work part-time. Average annual earnings from campus work are $1850. The average financial indebtedness of the 2016 graduate was $39,973. St. Ambrose is a member of CSS. The FAFSA code is 001889. The priority date for freshman financial aid applications for fall entry is March 15.

UNIVERSITY OF DUBUQUE — E-2

www.dbq.edu

Dubuque, IA 52001	**(563) 589-3214** **(800) 722-5583**
Fax: (563) 589-3690	**Email: admssns@dbq.edu**
Full-time: 710 men, 410 women	**Faculty:** n/av
Part-time: 30 men, 35 women	**Ph.D.s:** 80%
Graduate: 170 men, 110 women	**Student/Faculty:** n/av
Year: semesters, summer session	**Tuition:** $28,700
Room & Board: $9124	**Freshman Class:** n/av
SAT or ACT: required	**CEEB CODE:** 6869
Application Deadline: August 15	**COMPETITIVE**

University of Dubuque, established in 1852, is a private, liberal arts institution affiliated with the Presbyterian Church. Strengths in the undergraduate curriculum include environmental science, business, aviation, education, and computer graphics/interactive media. There are 3 undergraduate schools and 2 graduate schools. The 56-acre campus is in a suburban area 180 miles northwest of Chicago. Including any residence halls, there are 24 buildings.

STUDENT LIFE: 60% of undergraduates are from out of state, mostly

the Midwest. Students are from 35 states, and 21 foreign countries. 90% are from public schools. 79% are White; 4% Hispanic; 2% American Indian/Alaska Native; 12% African American; 1% Asian American; 1% Foreign. 50% are Catholic; 40% Protestant; 35% claim no religious affiliation. **Male To Female Ratio:** 1.6:1. The average age of freshmen is 18; all undergraduates, 22. 12% do not continue beyond their first year; 59% remain to graduate. **Housing:** 600 students can be accommodated in college housing, which includes coed dorms, on-campus apartments, married student housing, and special-interest houses. On-campus housing is guaranteed for all 4 years. 30% of students commute. All students may keep cars. Alcohol is not permitted.

FACULTY/CLASSROOMS: 55% of faculty are male; 45% are female. All teach undergraduates. No introductory courses are taught by graduate students. The average class size in an introductory lecture is 25; in a laboratory is 16; and in a regular course is 17.

PROGRAMS OF STUDY: UD confers B.A., B.S. and B.B.A. degrees. Associate, master's, and doctoral degrees are also awarded. Bachelor's degrees are awarded in BIOLOGICAL SCIENCE (biology/biological science), BUSINESS (accounting and business administration and management), COMMUNICATIONS AND THE ARTS (English and speech/debate/rhetoric), COMPUTER AND PHYSICAL SCIENCE (computer science), EDUCATION (education and physical education), ENGINEERING AND ENVIRONMENTAL DESIGN (aviation administration/management, computer graphics, and environmental science), HEALTH PROFESSIONS (nursing), SOCIAL SCIENCE (philosophy, psychology, religion, and sociology). Nursing, computer graphics, and business are the strongest academically. Business, aviation management/flight operations, and computer graphics have the largest enrollments.

ACTIVITIES: 11% of men belong to 5 local fraternities; 10% of women belong to 3 local sororities. There are 50 groups on campus, including art, cheerleading, choir, chorale, chorus, computers, dance, drama, ecology club, ethnic, honors, international, musical theater, newspaper, pep band, political, professional, religious, social, social service, and student government. Popular campus events include Founder's Day Ball, Annual Gala, and Family Weekend. **Sports:** There are 10 intercollegiate sports for men and 9 for women, and 13 intramural sports for men and 13 for women. Facilities include a sports center with basketball and volleyball courts, racquetball courts, wrestling room, athletic training room, football field and track, baseball and softball fields, practice football/intramural field, and a cardiovascular workout center.

SERVICES: Counseling and information services are available, as is tutoring in some subjects, such as English, math, economics, accounting, and computer literacy. There is also remedial math, reading, and writing. **Library/Resources:** The library contains 164,859 volumes, 20,739 microform items, 2,180 audio/video tapes/CDs/DVDs, and subscribes to 801 periodicals including electronic. Computerized library services include interlibrary loans, database searching, and Internet access. Special learning facilities include an art gallery and planetarium. **Physically Challenged Students:** 50% of the campus is accessible. Facilities include wheelchair ramps, elevators, special parking, specially equipped restrooms, special class scheduling, and lowered drinking fountains. **Special:** UD offers cross-registration with Loras and Clarke Colleges, internships, study abroad through the Maastricht Center for Transatlantic Studies, work-study programs, accelerated degree programs, B.A.-B.S. degrees, dual and student-designed majors, credit for life, military, and work experience, nondegree study, and pass/fail options. B.A.-M.A. programs are offered in conjunction with the university's theological seminary. Adult degree programs and an environmental field trip to Colorado and New Mexico are available. There are 8 national honor societies and 2 departmental honors programs. **Visiting:** There are regularly scheduled orientations for prospective students, including a campus tour and visits with coaches, faculty, admissions, and financial aid advisers. There are guides for informal visits, visitors may sit in on classes, and stay overnight. To schedule a visit, contact the Admission Director. **Campus Safety and Security:** Measures include 24-hour foot and vehicle patrol, self-defense education, and security escort services. There are also shuttle buses, emergency telephones, lighted pathways/sidewalks, and security-locked residence halls.

REQUIREMENTS: The SAT or ACT is required. Applicants must graduate from an accredited secondary school with a minimum of 4 years in English and 3 each in math, social sciences, and natural sciences. Other academic areas, such as foreign languages, business courses, computer programming, and the fine and performing arts, are also considered. The GED is accepted. Essays and recommendations are required. Auditions are required for music scholarship candidates. A GPA of 2.5 is required. AP and CLEP credits are accepted. Important factors in the admissions decision are leadership record, recommendations by school officials, and extracurricular activities record. As part of our mission, the University aims to prepare students for successful, professional careers and fulfilling lives by providing them with an education that encourages their growth as whole persons. A total of 120 credits must be earned, with a minimum GPA of 2.0 (2.5 for education majors) for graduation. At UD, we combine professional preparation and the liberal arts to create programs that serve our students. **Procedure:** Freshmen are admitted in the fall and spring. Entrance exams should be taken before the senior year. There are deferred admissions and rolling admissions plans. Applications should be filed by August 15 for fall entry; December 1 for spring entry. The fall 2016 application fee was $25. Applications are accepted online. **Transfer Students:** A minimum GPA of 2.0 is required. The applicant must be in good standing at all previously attended institutions. 30 of 120 credits required for the bachelor's degree must be completed at UD. **International Students:** The school actively recruits these students. They must take the TOEFL and the college's own test.

ADMISSIONS: 10 freshmen graduated first in their class. **Admissions Contact:** Jesse L. James, Admission Director. Email: *admssns@dbq.edu* Web: *www.dbq.edu*

FINANCIAL AID: The FAFSA code is 001891. Check with the school for current application deadlines.

UNIVERSITY OF IOWA — E-3

www.uiowa.edu

Iowa City, IA 52242	**(319) 335-3847**
Fax: (319) 335-1535	**Email:** admissions@uiowa.edu
Full-time: 9906 men, 10,962 women	**Faculty:** I, av$
Part-time: 1718 men, 1890 women	**Ph.D.s:** 96%
Graduate: 4476 men, 4382 women	**Student/Faculty:** 15 to 1
Year: semesters, summer session	**Tuition:** $8575 ($28,813)
Room & Board: $10,108	**Freshman Class:** 28525 applied, 23996 accepted, 5643 enrolled
SAT CR/M: 570/610 **ACT:** 26	**CEEB CODE:** 6681
Application Deadline: April 1	**VERY COMPETITIVE+**

University of Iowa is one of the nation's top public research universities, a member of the Big Ten conference since 1899, and an Association of American Universities member since 1909. Iowa is known around the world for its balanced commitment to the arts, sciences, and humanities. It's home to one of the nation's largest academic medical centers, the pioneering Iowa Writers' Workshop, and hundreds of options for affordable, accessible education. The University delivers the energy and opportunity of a leading university, but remains one of the smallest and most affordable universities among its peer institutions. There are 5 undergraduate schools and 11 graduate schools. In addition to regional accreditation, Iowa has baccalaureate program accreditation with AACSB, ABET, ACEJMC, ACPE, ADA, APTA, CSWE, NASM, NRPA, CACREP, ISBE, and ACEJ. The 1700-acre campus is in a small town 110 miles east of Des Moines and 220 miles west of Chicago. Including any residence halls, there are 500 buildings.

STUDENT LIFE: 54% of undergraduates are from Iowa. Others are from 50 states, 64 foreign countries, and Canada. 91% are from public schools. 69% are White; 10% Foreign; 7% Hispanic; 4% Asian American; 3% African American; 3% two or more races; 3% race unknown; 1% American Indian/Alaska Native. **Female To Male Ratio:** 1.1:1. The average age of freshmen is 18; all undergraduates, 21. 14% do not continue beyond their first year; 72% remain to graduate. **Housing:** 6818 students can be accommodated in college housing, which includes coed dorms, on-campus apartments, off-campus apartments, married student housing, honors houses, and special-interest houses. In addition there are Living-Learning Communities: Arts, Business, Education, Global Village, Healthy Living, Chemistry, Journalism, Leadership, Engineering, Pre-Med, Sustainability, and Iowa Writers. On-campus housing is available on a first-come and first-served basis. 71% of students commute. All students may keep cars. Alcohol is not permitted.

FACULTY/CLASSROOMS: 60% of faculty are male; 40% are female.

Graduate students teach 13% of introductory courses. The average class size in an introductory lecture is 105; in a laboratory is 16; and in a regular course is 18.

PROGRAMS OF STUDY: Iowa confers B.A., B.S., B.A.S., B.B.A., B.F.A., B.L.S., B.M., B.S.E., and B.S.N. degrees. Master's and doctoral degrees are also awarded. Bachelor's degrees are awarded in BIOLOGICAL SCIENCE (biochemistry, biology/biological science, and microbiology), BUSINESS (accounting, banking and finance, business administration and management, business economics, management science, marketing management, recreation and leisure services, and recreational facilities management), COMMUNICATIONS AND THE ARTS (art, art history and appreciation, ceramic art and design, Chinese, classics, communications, comparative literature, dance, dramatic arts, drawing, English, film arts, fine arts, French, German, graphic design, Greek, Italian, Japanese, jazz, journalism, Latin, linguistics, metal/jewelry, music, painting, percussion, performing arts, photography, piano/organ, Portuguese, printmaking, Russian, sculpture, Spanish, speech/debate/rhetoric, strings, theatre arts, and voice), COMPUTER AND PHYSICAL SCIENCE (actuarial science, applied physics, astronomy, chemistry, computer science, geology, information sciences and systems, mathematics, physics, and statistics), EDUCATION (art education, athletic training, elementary education, foreign languages education, health education, mathematics education, middle school education, music education, science education, secondary education, and sports studies), ENGINEERING AND ENVIRONMENTAL DESIGN (biomedical engineering, chemical engineering, civil engineering, electrical/electronics engineering, engineering, environmental science, industrial administration/management, industrial engineering, and mechanical engineering), HEALTH PROFESSIONS (medical laboratory science, medical laboratory technology, music therapy, nuclear medical technology, nursing, pharmacy, predentistry, premedicine, preoptometry, prepharmacy, prephysical therapy, prepodiatry, preveterinary science, radiological science, recreation therapy, and speech pathology/audiology), SOCIAL SCIENCE (African American studies, American studies, anthropology, Asian/Oriental studies, classical/ancient civilization, economics, gender studies, geography, history, international studies, liberal arts/general studies, parks and recreation management, philosophy, political science/government, prelaw, psychology, religion, Russian and Slavic studies, Sanskrit and Indian studies, social science, social work, sociology, and women's studies). Business, engineering, and creative writing are the strongest academically. Business, engineering, and nursing have the largest enrollments.

ACTIVITIES: 14% of men belong to 27 national fraternities; 19% of women belong to 23 national sororities. There are 500 groups on campus, including art, bagpipe, band, cheerleading, chess, choir, chorale, chorus, communications, computers, dance, debate, drama, drill team, environmental, ethnic, film, forensics, honors, international, jazz band, LGBT, literary magazine, marching band, musical theater, newspaper, opera, orchestra, pep band, photography, political, professional, radio and TV, religious, social, social service, student government, and symphony. Popular campus events include Dance Marathon, Riverfest, RiverRun and Cultural Diversity Festivals. **Sports:** There are 10 intercollegiate sports for men and 12 for women, and 36 intramural sports for men and 32 for women. Facilities include a campus recreation and wellness center, which has a climbing wall, swimming pool, lazy river, deep diving well, leisure pool, jogging track, basketball/volleyball courts, a multi-activity gym, fitness rooms. Iowa also has a stadium for football, an arena, softball and baseball stadiums, golf course, racquetball, handball courts, outdoor and indoor tennis courts, running tracks, weight and fitness rooms, a field hockey stadium, a field campus for hiking (Lake Macbride), cross-country skiing, canoeing, and a soccer field. **Graduates:** From July 1, 2015 to June 30, 2016, 5367 bachelor's degrees were awarded. The most popular majors were finance (8%), psychology (6%), and communication studies (5%). 679 companies recruited on campus in 2015-2016. In an average class, 2% graduate in 3 years or less, 51% graduate in 4 years or less, 69% graduate in 5 years or less, and 72% graduate in 6 years or less. Of the 2015 graduating class, 18% were enrolled in graduate school within 6 months of graduation, and 72% were employed.

SERVICES: Counseling and information services are available, as is tutoring in most subjects, a reader service for the blind, and remedial math, reading, and writing. **Library/Resources:** The 8 libraries contain 7.8 million volumes. Computerized library services include interlibrary loans, database searching, Internet access, and Wi-Fi capability. Special learning facilities include an art gallery, natural history museum, radio station, TV station, UI hospitals and clinics, the Iowa Center for the Arts, Oakdale Research Center, Iowa Raptor Project, Iowa Lakeside lab, and a driving simulator. **Physically Challenged Students:** 98% of the campus is accessible. Facilities include wheelchair ramps, elevators, special parking, specially equipped restrooms, special class scheduling, lowered drinking fountains, lowered telephones, and special housing. Transportation service when needed. **Special:** The University offers a wide array of internships and experience-based learning opportunities, combined degree programs, 3+3 program with College of Law, joint bachelors/master programs, 3+2 program with College of Public Health, 22 certificate programs including Aging Studies, American Indian and Native Studies, American Sign Language and Deaf Studies, Critical Cultural Competence, Disability Studies, Entrepreneurial Management, Fundraising and Philanthropy Communication, Global Health Studies, Human Rights, International Business, Latin American Studies, Leadership Studies, Medieval Studies, Museum Studies, Nonprofit Management, Performing Arts Entrepreneurship, Public Health, Risk Management and Insurance, Sustainability, Technological Entrepreneurship, Writing, and Wind Energy. Iowa's Study Abroad Program includes studies in 75 countries worldwide. There are 18 national honor societies, Phi Beta Kappa, a freshman honors program, and 52 departmental honors programs. **Visiting:** There are regularly scheduled orientations for prospective students, including information sessions, campus tours, lunch, and visits to departments and residence halls. There are guides for informal visits and visitors may sit in on classes. To schedule a visit, contact Admission Visitors Center at (319) 335-1569. **Campus Safety and Security:** Measures include 24-hour foot and vehicle patrol, emergency notification system, self-defense education, and security escort services. There are also shuttle buses, emergency telephones, lighted pathways/sidewalks, controlled access to dorms/residences, code blue phones, defense courses, and WhistleSAFE program.

REQUIREMENTS: The SAT or ACT is required. All applicants must have completed 4 years of high school English, 3 years each of social studies, science, and math (including 2 years of algebra and 1 of geometry), and 2 years of a single world language. Music and dance students must audition. AP and CLEP credits are accepted. To graduate, students must complete at least 120 semester hours, with a GPA of 2.0. The general education program includes rhetoric, historical perspectives, world language, quantitative and formal reasoning, international and global issues, values, society and diversity, and natural and social sciences. **Procedure:** Freshmen are admitted to all sessions. Entrance exams should be taken in the junior year. There are deferred admissions and rolling admissions plans. Applications should be filed by April 1 for fall entry; November 15 for spring entry; and April 1 for summer entry, along with a $40 fee. Notification is sent on a rolling basis. Applications are accepted on-line. **Transfer Students:** 1265 transfer students enrolled in 2015-2016. For the College of Liberal Arts, a GPA of at least 2.5 is required for applicants with 24 or more semester hours of credit. Those with fewer credits are considered on the same criteria as freshmen. Other colleges have different requirements. 30 of 120 credits required for the bachelor's degree must be completed at Iowa. **International Students:** There are 2522 international students enrolled. The school actively recruits these students.

ADMISSIONS: 84% of the 2016-2017 applicants were accepted. The SAT scores for the 2016-2017 freshman class were: Critical Reading--30% below 500, 29% between 500 and 599, 28% between 600 and 699, and 13% between 700 and 800. Math-- 14% below 500, 29% between 500 and 599, 39% between 600 and 699, and 18% between 700 and 800. The ACT scores were 1% between 12 and 17, 30% between 18 and 23, 50% between 24 and 29, and 19% above 30. 49% of the current freshmen were in the top fifth of their class; 81% were in the top two fifths. There were 26 National Merit finalists. 141 freshmen graduated first in their class. **Admissions Contact:** Brent Gage, Associate VP for Enrollment Management. Email: *admissions@uiowa.edu* Web: *www.uiowa.edu*

FINANCIAL AID: In 2016-2017, 84% of all full-time freshmen and 78% of continuing full-time students received some form of financial aid. 59% of all full-time freshmen and 57% of continuing full-time students received need-based aid. The average freshman award was $13,439. Need-based scholarships or need-based grants averaged $8,087; need-based self-help aid (loans and jobs) averaged $6,339; non-need-based athletic scholarships averaged $12,545; and other non-need-based awards and non-need-based scholarships averaged $4,972. 44% of undergraduate students work part-time. Average annual earnings from campus work are $2950. The average financial indebtedness of the 2016 graduate was $23,316. The FAFSA code is 001892. The priority date for freshman financial aid applications for fall entry is March 1.

UNIVERSITY OF NORTHERN IOWA D-2

www.uni.edu

Cedar Falls, IA 50614 (319) 273-2281
(800) 772-2037
Fax: (319) 273-2885 Email: admissions@uni.edu

Full-time: 3867 men, 5279 women
Part-time: 485 men, 473 women
Graduate: 510 men, 927 women
Year: semesters, summer session
Room & Board: $8320
ACT: 23
Application Deadline: August 15
Faculty: 491; IIA, av$
Ph.D.s: 79%
Student/Faculty: 19 to 1
Tuition: $7817 ($18,005)
Freshman Class: 5287 applied, 4346 accepted, 1962 enrolled
CEEB CODE: 6307
COMPETITIVE

University of Northern Iowa, established in 1876, is a public institution offering degree programs in business administration, education, humanities, arts, sciences, and social and behavioral sciences. There are 4 undergraduate schools and 1 graduate school. In addition to regional accreditation, UNI has baccalaureate program accreditation with AACSB, ABET, CSWE, NASM, NRPA, ACS, ASHA, ATMAE, CAATE, CACREP, CEA, NCFR, NASP, and NAST. The 908-acre campus is in a small town in Cedar Falls, Iowa, about 60 miles northwest of Cedar Rapids. Including any residence halls, there are 106 buildings.

STUDENT LIFE: 88% of undergraduates are from Iowa. Others are from 36 states, 68 foreign countries, and Canada. 93% are from public schools. 82% are White; 5% Foreign; 4% Hispanic; 4% race unknown; 3% African American; 2% two or more races; 1% Asian American. **Female To Male Ratio:** 1.4:1. The average age of freshmen is 18; all undergraduates, 21. 15% do not continue beyond their first year; 68% remain to graduate. **Housing:** 4766 students can be accommodated in college housing, which includes single-sex, coed dorms, on-campus apartments, married student housing, honors houses and special-interest houses. On-campus housing is guaranteed for all 4 years, is available on a first-come, first-served basis, and on a lottery system for upperclassmen. 60% of students commute. All students may keep cars.

FACULTY/CLASSROOMS: 50% of faculty are male; 50% are female. 85% teach undergraduates and do research. Graduate students teach 4% of introductory courses. The average class size in an introductory lecture is 29; in a laboratory is 23; and in a regular course is 33.

PROGRAMS OF STUDY: UNI confers B.A., B.A.S., B.S., B.F.A., B.L.S., and B.Mus. degrees. Master's and doctoral degrees are also awarded. Bachelor's degrees are awarded in BIOLOGICAL SCIENCE (biochemistry, bioinformatics, biology/biological science, biotechnology, microbiology, and nutrition), BUSINESS (accounting, banking and finance, management information systems, management science, marketing/retailing/merchandising, real estate, recreation and leisure services, and supply chain management), COMMUNICATIONS AND THE ARTS (art history, communications, digital media, dramatic arts, English, fine arts, graphic design, music, music performance, music theory and composition, public relations, Spanish, speech/debate/rhetoric, studio art, and theatre arts), COMPUTER AND PHYSICAL SCIENCE (actuarial science, chemistry, computer management, computer science, earth science, geology, information sciences and systems, mathematics, physics, and science), EDUCATION (art education, athletic training, business education, early childhood education, elementary education, foreign languages education, health education, middle school education, music education, physical education, science education, social science education, special education, teaching English as a second/foreign language (TESOL/TEFOL), and technical education), ENGINEERING AND ENVIRONMENTAL DESIGN (computer technology, construction management, electrical/electronics engineering technology, energy management technology, environmental science, industrial engineering technology, and manufacturing technology), HEALTH PROFESSIONS (communicative disorders, exercise science, health promotion, and speech pathology/audiology), SOCIAL SCIENCE (anthropology, clothing and textiles management/production/services, criminal justice, criminology, economics, family and community services, geography, geography information science, gerontology, history, humanities, liberal arts/general studies, philosophy, political science/government, psychology, public administration, religion, social work, sociology, and world cultural studies). Teaching majors, biology, communication, and accounting are the strongest academically. Elementary education, management, and accounting have the largest enrollments.

ACTIVITIES: 3% of men belong to 5 national fraternities; 6% of women belong to 5 national sororities. There are 260 groups on campus, including alumni tomorrow, student admissions ambassadors club, connecting alumni to students, art, band, cheerleading, chess, choir, chorale, chorus, communications, computers, dance, debate, drama, drill team, environmental, ethnic, film, forensics, honors, international, jazz band, LGBT, literary magazine, marching band, musical theater, newspaper, opera, orchestra, pep band, political, professional, radio and TV, religious, social, social service, student government, students today, and symphony. Popular campus events include UNI NOW! Welcome Week, Relay for Life, Dance Marathon, and Homecoming. **Sports:** There are 7 intercollegiate sports for men and 10 for women, and 41 intramural sports for men and 37 for women. Facilities include a domed stadium, field house, basketball arena, tennis courts, multi purpose play fields, track, wellness/recreation center with swimming pool, leisure pool, handball/racquetball courts, climbing wall, weight rooms, and basketball courts, fitness center, and exercise rooms. **Graduates:** From July 1, 2015 to June 30, 2016, 2166 bachelor's degrees were awarded. The most popular majors were elementary education (11%), communication (7%), and management (6%). 462 companies recruited on campus in 2015-2016. In an average class, 2% graduate in 3 years or less, 39% graduate in 4 years or less, 62% graduate in 5 years or less, and 65% graduate in 6 years or less. Of the 2015 graduating class, 12% were enrolled in graduate school within 6 months of graduation, and 82% were employed.

SERVICES: Counseling and information services are available, as is tutoring in some subjects, such as liberal arts core (general educationand major courses in science, math, humanities, biology, chemistry, physics, earth science, economics, calculus, statistics, research methods, music, mangement, finance, accounting, writing, and reading assistance. There is a reader service for the blind, and remedial math, reading, and writing. Supplemental instruction in calculus I &II, humanities, statistics, anatomy & physiology I, organic chemistry, college success workshops, and supportive seminars in Humanities are also available. **Library/Resources:** The library contains 949,093 volumes, 1.1 million microform items, 29,733 audio/video tapes/CDs/DVDs, and subscribes to 78,638 periodicals including electronic. Computerized library services include interlibrary loans, database searching, Internet access, and Wi-Fi capability. Special learning facilities include an art gallery, natural history museum, planetarium, radio station, The university sponsors the Native Roadside Vegetation Center, the Iowa Center for Immigrant Leadership and Integration, a waste reduction center, a performing arts center, and several research institutes. **Physically Challenged Students:** 95% of the campus is accessible. Facilities include wheelchair ramps, elevators, special parking, specially equipped restrooms, special class scheduling, lowered drinking fountains, lowered telephones, and special housing. **Special:** Internships and co-op programs are offered through all colleges of the university. Students may study abroad in 28 countries and may participate in a Washington semester. Interdisciplinary majors include safety education, chemistry/marketing, design/human environment, and natural history interpretation. Cross-registration, work-study programs, a general studies degree, dual and student-designed majors, nondegree study, and pass/fail options are also available. There are 25 national honor societies and a freshman honors program. **Visiting:** There are regularly scheduled orientations for prospective students, including a student panel, lunch, a campus tour, and presentations by admissions, financial aid, housing, and academic departments. There are guides for informal visits and visitors may sit in on classes. To schedule a visit, contact Jenny Connolly at admissions@uni.edu. **Campus Safety and Security:** Measures include 24-hour foot and vehicle patrol, emergency notification system, self-defense education, and security escort services. There are also shuttle buses, emergency telephones, lighted pathways/sidewalks, and controlled access to dorms/residences.

REQUIREMENTS: The ACT is required. A Regents Admissions Index (RAI) score of 245 guarantees admission. High school requirements include 4 years of English, 3 years each of math, social studies, and science, and 2 years or more of electives, which may include foreign language and fine arts. The GED with a minimum standard score average of 57, and no single score below 500, is accepted. The HiSET is also accepted. AP and CLEP credits are accepted. Important factors in the admissions decision are advanced placement or honors courses, evidence of special talent, and recommendations by school officials. Degree requirements include completion of 120 to 130 credits, with 30 to 60 in the major. Liberal arts majors must maintain a minimum GPA of 2.0 (2.5 for business, communication, and education majors). Liberal arts core requirements include 11 hours of civilizations and cultures, 9 each of natural science/technology, social science, and communication, 6 of arts/literature/philosophy/religion, and 3 of personal wellness. Students must meet requirements in foreign language and complete a capstone course. Education students must complete a 32-credit professional sequence. **Procedure:** Freshmen are admitted to all sessions. Entrance exams should be taken By October of the senior year. There is a rolling admissions plan. Applications should be filed by August 15 for fall entry; December 31 for spring entry; and May 15 for summer entry, along with a $40 fee. Applications are accepted on-line. **Transfer Students:** 919 transfer students enrolled in 2015-2016. Applicants must have a minimum GPA of 2.0 to 2.5, depending on the number of credits they wish to transfer. A small number of applicants may be admitted on academic probation. 32 of 120 credits required for the bachelor's degree must be completed at UNI. **International Students:** There are 404 international students enrolled. The school actively recruits these students. They must take the TOEFL with a minimum score of 550 on the paper-based TOEFL (PBT) or 79 on the Internet-based version (iBT) or take the MELAB, the Comprehensive English Language Test, and the college's own test.

ADMISSIONS: 82% of the 2016-2017 applicants were accepted. The ACT scores were 6% between 12 and 17, 53% between 18 and 23, 35% between 24 and 29, and 6% above 30. 37% of the current freshmen were in the top fifth of their class; 69% were in the top two fifths. 63 freshmen graduated first in their class. **Admissions Contact:** Kara M. Hadley-Shakya, Director of Admissions. Email: *admissions@uni.edu* Web: *http:/uni.edu/admissions/*

FINANCIAL AID: In 2016-2017, 94% of all full-time freshmen and 92% of continuing full-time students received some form of financial aid. 53% of all full-time freshmen and 43% of continuing full-time students received need-based aid. The average freshman award was $12,008. Need-based scholarships or need-based grants averaged $4,908 ($18,297 maximum); need-based self-help aid (loans and jobs) averaged $2,604 ($5,500 maximum); non-need-based athletic scholarships averaged $7,024 ($28,326 maximum); and other non-need-based awards and non-need-based scholarships averaged $3,254 ($11,463 maximum). 35% of undergraduate students work part-time. Average annual earnings from campus work are $2377. The average financial indebtedness of the 2016 graduate was $22,923. The FAFSA code is 001890. The deadline for filing freshman financial aid applications for fall entry is open.

UPPER IOWA UNIVERSITY *(The complete profile is made available exclusively on our website, www.barronspac.com)*

WARTBURG COLLEGE — D-2

www.wartburg.edu

Waverly, IA 50677	**(319) 352-8264** **(800) 772-2085**
Fax: (319) 352-8579	**Email: admissions@wartburg.edu**
Full-time: 687 men, 747 women	**Faculty:** IIB, -$
Part-time: 24 men, 24 women	**Ph.D.s:** 97%
Graduate: n/av	**Student/Faculty:** 11 to 1
Year: other, summer session	**Tuition:** $38,380
Room & Board: $9460	**Freshman Class:** 2949 applied, 2749 accepted, 445 enrolled
SAT CR/M/W: 490/500/480 **ACT:** 24	**CEEB CODE:** 6926
Application Deadline: May 1	**COMPETITIVE**

Wartburg College is a selective liberal arts college of the ELCA, internationally recognized for community engagement. Wartburg is dedicated to challenging and nurturing students for lifes of leadership and service as a spirited expression of their faith and learning. Opportunities for service-learning, leadership, undergraduate research, global and multicultural studies, and participation in co-curricular activities enrich the academic experience. Wartburg helps students discover their life's purpose through meaning and vocal discernment. There are 3 undergraduate schools. In addition to regional accreditation, Wartburg has baccalaureate program accreditation with CSWE, NASM, and NCATE. The 118-acre campus is in a small town 15 miles north of Waterloo/Cedar Falls, Iowa. Including any residence halls, there are 37 buildings.

STUDENT LIFE: 65% of undergraduates are from Iowa. Others are from 28 states, and 58 foreign countries. 9% are Foreign; 8% African American; 76% White; 5% Hispanic; 4% Asian American; 4% race unknown; 3% two or more races. 62% are Protestant; 28% Catholic. **Female To Male Ratio:** 1.1:1. The average age of freshmen is 18; all undergraduates, 20. 20% do not continue beyond their first year; 69% remain to graduate. **Housing:** 1380 students can be accommodated in college housing, which includes single-sex and coed dorms, on-campus apartments, honors houses, language houses, and special-interest houses. On-campus housing is guaranteed for all 4 years. 85% of students live on campus; of those, 75% remain on campus on weekends. All students may keep cars.

FACULTY/CLASSROOMS: 50% of faculty are male; 50% are female. All teach undergraduates, and 45% do research. No introductory courses are taught by graduate students. The average class size in a laboratory is 18 and in a regular course is 18.

PROGRAMS OF STUDY: Wartburg confers B.A., B.A.A., B.A.S., B.M. and B.M.E. degrees. Bachelor's degrees are awarded in BIOLOGICAL SCIENCE (biochemistry and biology/biological science), BUSINESS (accounting, banking and finance, business administration and management, international business management, marketing/retailing/merchandising, and recreation and leisure services), COMMUNICATIONS AND THE ARTS (applied music, art, arts administration/management, broadcasting, communications, creative writing, dramatic arts, English, French, German, graphic design, journalism, music, music performance, music theory and composition, public relations, and Spanish), COMPUTER AND PHYSICAL SCIENCE (chemistry, computer science, information sciences and systems, mathematics, and physics), EDUCATION (art education, elementary education, English education, foreign languages education, journalism education, mathematics education, music education, physical education, science education, secondary education, and social studies education), ENGINEERING AND ENVIRONMENTAL DESIGN (engineering and applied science), HEALTH PROFESSIONS (medical laboratory technology, music therapy, and occupational therapy), SOCIAL SCIENCE (economics, French studies, German area studies, history, international relations, peace studies, philosophy, political science/government, psychology, religion, religious music, social work, and sociology). Biology, music education, business, journalism/communications, elementary education, leadership are the strongest academically. Business, biology, and journalism/communications have the largest enrollments.

ACTIVITIES: There are no fraternities or sororities. There are 100 groups on campus, including art, band, cheerleading, chess, choir, chorale, chorus, communications, computers, dance, debate, drama, drum and bugle corps, environmental, ethnic, forensics, honors, international, jazz band, LGBT, literary magazine, musical theater, newspaper, opera, orchestra, pep band, political, professional, radio and TV, religious, social, social service, student government, and symphony. Popular campus events include Artist Series, Convocations, Family Weekend, Homecoming, Culture Week, Martin Luther King Week and Outfly. **Sports:** There are 10 intercollegiate sports for men and 10 for women, and 4 intramural sports for men and 4 for women. Facilities include a sports and wellness center that has an indoor pool, track, racquetball courts, batting cages, golf hitting area, tennis/badminton/volleyball courts, weight rooms, a fitness area, an aerobics and wrestling room, a stadium with a football field and track, gym, baseball park, football, soccer, softball, lacrosse field, and outdoor tennis courts. **Graduates:** From July 1, 2015 to June 30, 2016, 392 bachelor's degrees were awarded. The most popular majors were biology (20%), business administration (18%), and communication arts (8%). In an average class, 3% graduate in 3 years or less, 63% graduate in 4 years or less, 65% graduate in 5 years or less, and 69% graduate in 6 years or less. Of the 2015 graduating class, 23% were enrolled in graduate school within 6 months of graduation, and 69% were employed.

SERVICES: Counseling and information services are available, as is tutoring in most subjects, and remedial math. There is a comprehensive academic support center, a supplemental instruction program, and assistance with mathematics, and speech writing and delivery. A writing and reading center is also available. Academic support services are also delivered in the residence halls. **Library/Resources:** The library contains 485,092 volumes, 375 microform items, 7,880 audio/video tapes/CDs/DVDs, and subscribes to 122,508 periodicals including electronic. Computerized library services include interlibrary loans, database searching, Internet access, and Wi-Fi capability. Special learning facilities include an art gallery, radio station, TV station, a business center, classroom technology center, fine arts center, journalism lab, symbolic computation lab, music computer lab, Center for Community Engagement, Institute for Leadership Education, 6 acres of native grasses and prairie plants, and more than 100 acres of native timber used for field trips and research. **Physically Challenged Students:** 85% of the campus is accessible. Facilities include wheelchair ramps, elevators, special parking, specially equipped restrooms, special class scheduling, lowered drinking fountains, lowered telephones, and special housing. **Special:** Special academic programs at Wartburg include those in leadership education and global and multicultural studies. Internships are available in all majors and there are internship programs in Denver, Washington, D.C., and abroad. Study abroad in 65 countries, on and off campus work-study, dual majors in any combination, and individualized majors are possible. 3-1 degrees are possible in clinical laboratory science and occupational therapy, as well as 3-1 and 2-2 degrees in nursing. A deferred admit program with the University of Iowa College of Dentistry is offered, as is an array of experiential learning opportunities. There are 15 national honor societies, a freshman honors program, and 1 departmental honors program. **Visiting:** There are regularly scheduled orientations for prospective students, including an introduction to academic and student life conducted by administrators, faculty, and students. There are guides for informal visits, visitors may sit in on classes, and stay overnight. To schedule a visit, contact the Admissions Office. **Campus Safety and Security:** Measures include 24-hour foot and vehicle patrol, emergency notification system, security escort services, emergency telephones, lighted pathways/sidewalks, controlled access to dorms/residences, 24-hour patrol, and student escort service.

REQUIREMENTS: The SAT or ACT is required, with a minimum score of 910 on the SAT or 19 on the ACT expected. Candidates for admission must be graduates of an accredited secondary school, having completed 4 years of English, 3 each of math and science, 2 each of social studies and foreign language, and 1 of introduction to computers. The GED is accepted, with an average of 50 or above. AP and CLEP credits are accepted. Important factors in the admissions decision are advanced placement or honors courses, recommendations by school officials, and leadership record. Degree requirements include a minimum cumulative and major GPA of 2.0 and completion of 36 course credits (128 semester hours), including 4 May term course credits. All students must complete the Wartburg Plan of Essential Education, an integrative and interdisciplinary program of study, based on course work in thinking strategies, reasoning skills, faith and reflection, health and wellness, and literacy in writing, diversity, and a foreign lanaguage. Students must also demonstrate proficiency in information systems and in oral communication and must complete a Capstone course. Inquiry Studies 101/201 are required of all students. **Procedure:** Freshmen are admitted in the fall and winter. Entrance exams should be taken before the senior year. There are early admissions and rolling admissions plans. Applications should be filed by May 1 for fall entry. Notification is sent on a rolling basis. Applications are accepted online. **Transfer Students:** Applicants must have earned an associate degree or have maintained a minimum GPA of 2.0 in previous college work for 1 year. The ACT or the SAT must be taken; the minimum acceptable ACT score is 19. Students must submit official transcripts from all colleges attended. 7 of 36 credits required for the bachelor's degree must be completed at Wartburg. **International Students:** There are 131 international students enrolled. The school actively recruits these students. They must take the TOEFL with a minimum score of 480 on the paper-based TOEFL (PBT) or 55 on the Internet-based version (iBT). SAT or ACT scores are not required but are useful in admissions decisions, and for placement.

ADMISSIONS: 93% of the 2016-2017 applicants were accepted. The SAT scores for the 2016-2017 freshman class were: Critical Reading-- 43% below 500, 36% between 500 and 599, 14% between 600 and 699, and 7% between 700 and 800. Math-- 36% below 500, 43% between 500 and 599, 14% between 600 and 699, and 7% between 700 and 800. Writing-- 36% below 500, 43% between 500 and 599, and 21% between 600 and 699. The ACT scores were 5% between 12 and 17, 43% between 18 and 23, 42% between 24 and 29, and 10% above 30. 43% of the current freshmen were in the top fifth of their class; 72% were in the top two fifths. 22 freshmen graduated first in their class. **Admissions Contact:** Todd Coleman, Assistant Vice President for Admissions. Email: *admissions@wartburg.edu* Web: *www.wartburg.edu*

FINANCIAL AID: In 2016-2017, 99% of all full-time freshmen and continuing full-time students received some form of financial aid. 69% of all full-time freshmen and 78% of continuing full-time students received need-based aid. The average freshman award was $36,671. Need-based scholarships or need-based grants averaged $12,936 ($35,115 maximum); need-based self-help aid (loans and jobs) averaged $5,835 ($9,876 maximum); and other non-need-based awards and non-need-based scholarships averaged $26,935 ($51,279 maximum). 74% of undergraduate students work part-time. Average annual earnings from campus work are $1380. The average financial indebtedness of the 2016 graduate was $29,650. The FAFSA code is 001896. The priority date for freshman financial aid applications for fall entry is March 1.

WILLIAM PENN UNIVERSITY D-3

www.wmpenn.edu

Oskaloosa, IA 52577	**(641) 673-1012** **(800) 779-7366**
Fax: (641) 673-2113	**Email: admissions@wmpenn.edu**
Full-time: 900 men, 750 women	**Faculty:** n/av
Part-time: 70 men, 115 women	**Ph.D.s:** n/av
Graduate: 40 men, 45 women	**Student/Faculty:** n/av
Year: varies, summer session	**Tuition:** $20,000
Room & Board: $6000	**Freshman Class:** n/av
ACT: required	**CEEB CODE:** 6943
Application Deadline: open	**COMPETITIVE**

William Penn University, founded in 1873, is a private liberal arts institution affiliated with the Society of Friends (Quakers). There are 2 undergraduate schools and 1 graduate school. In addition to regional accreditation, William Penn has baccalaureate program accreditation with NCATE and CCNE. The 53-acre campus is in a rural area 58 miles southeast of Des Moines. Including any residence halls, there are 14 buildings.

STUDENT LIFE: 73% of undergraduates are from Iowa. Others are from 40 states, 10 foreign countries, and Canada. 90% are from public schools. 83% are White; 3% Hispanic; 10% African American; 1% Asian American; 1% American Indian/Alaska Native; 1% Foreign. 44% are Protestant; 39% claim no religious affiliation; 13% Catholic. **Male To Female Ratio:** 1.1:1. The average age of freshmen is 19; all undergraduates, 25. 35% do not continue beyond their first year; 35% remain to graduate. **Housing:** 500 students can be accommodated in college housing, which includes single-sex and coed dorms, on-campus apartments, and married student housing. On-campus housing is guaranteed for all 4 years. 55% of students commute. All students may keep cars. Alcohol is not permitted.

FACULTY/CLASSROOMS: 57% of faculty are male; 43% are female. All teach undergraduates. No introductory courses are taught by graduate students. The average class size in an introductory lecture is 25.

PROGRAMS OF STUDY: William Penn confers B.A., B.S., and B.S.N. degrees. Associate and master's degrees are also awarded. Bachelor's degrees are awarded in BIOLOGICAL SCIENCE (biology/biological science and biotechnology), BUSINESS (accounting, business administration and management, recreation and leisure services, and sports management), COMMUNICATIONS AND THE ARTS (communications, digital communications, English, fine arts, journalism, and public relations), COMPUTER AND PHYSICAL SCIENCE (computer science), EDUCATION (elementary education, health education, physical education, science education, secondary education, and special education), ENGINEERING AND ENVIRONMENTAL DESIGN (environmental science, industrial administration/management, and industrial engineering technology), SOCIAL SCIENCE (criminology, history, human services, political science/government, psychology, and sociology). Elementary & secondary education, industrial technology, and business are the strongest academically. Education, and business have the largest enrollments.

ACTIVITIES: 5% of men belong to 2 local fraternities; 5% of women belong to 2 local and 1 national sororities. There are 25 groups on campus, including art, band, cheerleading, choir, chorale, chorus, computers, dance, drama, drum and bugle corps, ethnic, honors, international, jazz band, literary magazine, marching band, musical theater, newspaper, pep band, photography, political, professional, radio and TV, religious, social, social service, student government, and yearbook. Popular campus events include Multicultural Day, and Campus Beautification Day. **Sports:** There are 8 intercollegiate sports for men and 7 for women, and 6 intramural sports for men and 6 for women. Facilities include include a gym with basketball courts, wrestling and weight training rooms, baseball and softball fields, tennis courts, football, and soccer practice fields, walking/jogging track, basketball/volleyball courts, and an aerobic fitness area. **Graduates:** From July 1, 2015 to June 30, 2016, 220 bachelor's degrees were awarded. The most popular majors were business management (61%), elementary education (9%), and psychology (5%). 160 companies recruited on campus in 2015-2016. In an average class, 56% graduate in 4 years or less, 90% graduate in 5 years or less, and 98% graduate in 6 years or less. Of the 2015 graduating class, 15% were enrolled in graduate school within 6 months of graduation, and 75% were employed.

SERVICES: Counseling and information services are available, as is tutoring in most subjects, and remedial math, reading, and writing. **Library/Resources:** The library contains 64,974 volumes, and 1,733 audio/video tapes/CDs/DVDs, and subscribes to 31,974 periodicals including electronic. Computerized library services include interlibrary loans, database searching, Internet access, and Wi-Fi capability. Special learning facilities include an art gallery, radio station, and Mideast collection. **Physically Challenged Students:** 70% of the campus is accessible. Facilities include wheelchair ramps, elevators, special parking, specially equipped restrooms, special class scheduling, and lowered drinking fountains. **Special:** William Penn offers internships, work-study programs with local businesses, dual majors, nondegree study, pass/fail options, and 3-2 engineering degree programs with Iowa State and Washington Universities. Preprofessional studies, driver and safety education, and endorsements in numerous secondary education subjects are also offered. There are 2 national honor societies and a chapter of Phi Beta Kappa. **Visiting:** There are regularly scheduled orientations for prospective students, including a 1-day visit comprised of meetings with faculty, student services, financial aid, personnel, and people who share students' interests. There are guides for informal visits, visitors may sit in on classes, and stay overnight. To schedule a visit, contact the Visitor Coordinater. **Campus Safety and Security:** Measures include 24-hour foot and vehicle patrol, emergency notification system, self-defense education, emergency telephones, lighted pathways/sidewalks, and controlled access to dorms/residences.

REQUIREMENTS: Applicants must be graduates of an accredited secondary and should have completed 15 high school units. The GED is accepted. The ACT is required of traditional undergraduates only. Our college for working adults does not require ACT scores. AP and CLEP credits are accepted. Important factors in the admissions decision are evidence of special talent, extracurricular activities record, and leadership record. To graduate, students must complete 124 hours, with 30 to 75 hours in the major. A GPA of 2.0 overall and in major and minor courses is required. Leadership core requirements total 47 hours in English/communications, math, natural science, social science, religion, fine arts, and philosophy. **Procedure:** Freshmen are admitted to all sessions. Entrance exams should be taken late in the junior year or early in the senior year. There are early admissions, deferred admissions, and rolling admissions plans. Application deadlines are open. Application fee is $20. Applications are accepted online. **Transfer Students:** 189 transfer students enrolled in 2015-2016. Applicants must be in good standing at their previous institution and submit official transcripts from previously attended schools. 30 of 124 credits required for the bachelor's degree must be completed at William Penn. **International Students:** There are 20 international students enrolled. The school actively recruits these students. They must take the TOEFL with a minimum score of 500 on the paper-based TOEFL (PBT) exam.

ADMISSIONS: 2 freshmen graduated first in their class. **Admissions Contact:** Kerra Strong, Director of Admissions. Email: *admissions@wmpenn.edu* Web: *www.wmpenn.edu*

FINANCIAL AID: In 2016-2017, 99% of all full-time freshmen and continuing full-time students received some form of financial aid. 96% of all full-time freshmen and continuing full-time students received need-based aid. The average freshman award was $18,373.. 70% of undergraduate students work part-time. Average annual earnings from campus work are $1600. The average financial indebtedness of the 2016 graduate was $18,600. The FAFSA code is 001900. Check with the school for current application deadlines.

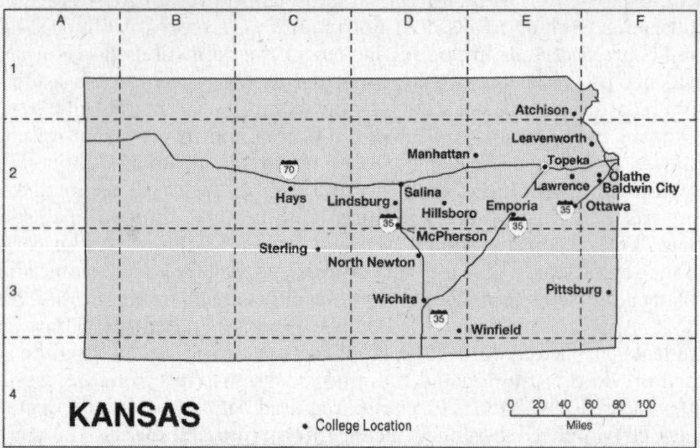

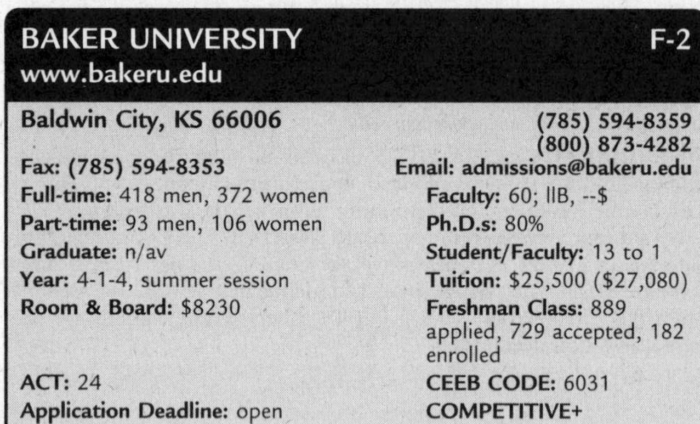

BAKER UNIVERSITY F-2

www.bakeru.edu

Baldwin City, KS 66006	**(785) 594-8359** **(800) 873-4282**
Fax: (785) 594-8353	**Email: admissions@bakeru.edu**
Full-time: 418 men, 372 women	**Faculty:** 60; IIB, --$
Part-time: 93 men, 106 women	**Ph.D.s:** 80%
Graduate: n/av	**Student/Faculty:** 13 to 1
Year: 4-1-4, summer session	**Tuition:** $25,500 ($27,080)
Room & Board: $8230	**Freshman Class:** 889 applied, 729 accepted, 182 enrolled
ACT: 24	**CEEB CODE:** 6031
Application Deadline: open	**COMPETITIVE+**

Baker University, founded in 1858, is a private liberal arts institution affiliated with the United Methodist Church. There are 3 undergraduate schools and 2 graduate schools. In addition to regional accreditation, Baker has baccalaureate program accreditation with ACBSP, NASM, NCATE, and CCNE. The 26-acre campus is in a rural area 50 miles southwest of Kansas City and 15 miles south of Lawrence. Including any residence halls, there are 26 buildings.

STUDENT LIFE: 73% of undergraduates are from Kansas. Others are from 28 states, 16 foreign countries, and Canada. 95% are from public schools. 74% are White; 8% African American; 6% Hispanic; 3% American Indian/Alaska Native; 3% race unknown; 2% Foreign; 1% Asian American; 1% two or more races. **Male To Female Ratio:** 1.1:1. The average age of freshmen is 18; all undergraduates, 20. 24% do not continue beyond their first year; 58% remain to graduate. **Housing:** 588 students can be accommodated in college housing, which includes single-sex, coed dorms, and on-campus apartments, fraternity houses, and sorority houses. On-campus housing is guaranteed for all 4 years. 82% of students live on campus; of those, 50% remain on campus on weekends. All students may keep cars. Alcohol is not permitted.

FACULTY/CLASSROOMS: 46% of faculty are male; 52% are female. All teach undergraduates. No introductory courses are taught by graduate students. The average class size in an introductory lecture is 17; in a laboratory is 11; and in a regular course is 16.

PROGRAMS OF STUDY: Baker confers B.A., B.M.E., and B.S. degrees. Bachelor's degrees are awarded in BIOLOGICAL SCIENCE (biology/biological science), BUSINESS (accounting, business administration and management, international business management, and sports management), COMMUNICATIONS AND THE ARTS (art history and appreciation, communications, English, French, German, media arts, music, Spanish, studio art, and theatre studies), COMPUTER AND PHYSICAL SCIENCE (chemistry, computer science, mathematics, and physics), EDUCATION (elementary education, mathematics education, music education, physical education, and secondary education), HEALTH PROFESSIONS (exercise science and nursing), SOCIAL SCIENCE (economics, history, international studies, philosophy, psychology, religion, and sociology). Business, exercise science, and elementary education have the largest enrollments.

ACTIVITIES: 31% of men belong to 1 local and 3 national fraternities; 44% of women belong to 4 national sororities. There are 55 groups on campus, including art, band, cheerleading, choir, chorale, chorus, communications, computers, dance, drama, environmental, ethnic, honors, international, jazz band, LGBT, literary magazine, newspaper, orchestra, pep band, photography, professional, radio and TV, religious, social, social service, and student government. Popular campus events include Maple Leaf Festival, International Education Week and Springfest Week. **Sports:** There are 10 intercollegiate sports for men and 10 for women, and 5 intramural sports for men and 5 for women. Facilities include a 3,500-seat football/track stadium, a gym, baseball stadium, practice and varsity fields for football, track, soccer, softball and baseball, basketball courts, racquetball courts, tennis courts, a jogging track, a wellness facility, and a weight room. **Graduates:** From July 1, 2015 to June 30, 2016, 169 bachelor's degrees were awarded. The most popular majors were business (20%), exercise science (14%), and elemenatry education (8%). In an average class, 2% graduate in 3 years or less, 40% graduate in 4 years or less, 56% graduate in 5 years or less, and 58% graduate in 6 years or less.

SERVICES: Counseling and information services are available, as is tutoring in most subjects, and a reader service for the blind, and remedial math, reading, and writing. **Library/Resources:** Computerized library services include interlibrary loans, database searching, Internet access, and Wi-Fi capability. Special learning facilities include an art gallery, radio station, TV station, a greenhouse, and wetlands. **Physically Challenged Students:** 90% of the campus is accessible. Facilities include wheelchair ramps, elevators, special parking, specially equipped restrooms, special class scheduling, lowered drinking fountains, lowered telephones, and special housing. **Special:** Internships are encouraged for students in most majors. Baker also offers study abroad, work-study, B.A.-B.S. degrees, accelerated degrees, and dual and student-designed majors. A 3-2 engineering degree may be earned in conjunction with Washington University in St. Louis, the University of Kansas, and University of Missouri in Kansas City. There are 13 national honor societies, a freshman honors program, and 7 departmental honors programs. **Visiting:** There are regularly scheduled orientations for prospective students, including Preview Days scheduled for both freshman and transfers in spring and fall. Individual visits are scheduled daily. There are guides for informal visits, visitors may sit in on classes, and stay overnight. To schedule a visit, contact the Admissions Office. **Campus Safety and Security:** Measures include 24-hour foot and vehicle patrol, emergency notification system, and security escort services. There are also lighted pathways/sidewalks and controlled access to dorms/residences.

REQUIREMENTS: The ACT is required. Candidates for admission must graduate from an accredited secondary school or earn a GED. High school course work in English, a foreign language, social studies, math, and natural science is recommended. Applications of students not meeting these requirements will be reviewed, and students may be invited for an on-campus interview, as necessary. AP and CLEP credits are accepted. To graduate, all students must complete 128 credit hours, including 24 to 36 hours in the major, a cornerstone liberal arts core, 6 core liberal studies courses, 4 exploratory courses in disciplines, and a minimal level of proficiency in written and oral communication and math. A minimum GPA of 2.0 is required. **Procedure:** Freshmen are admitted to all sessions. Entrance exams should be taken in the fall of the senior year. There is a rolling admissions plan. Application deadlines are open. Applications are accepted online. **Transfer Students:** 46 transfer students enrolled in 2015-2016. Transfer applicants must supply a recommendation form, available from the Baker Admissions Office. The ACT or the SAT score, official high school transcript, and official transcripts of all college courses are required. The minimum GPA is 2.3. 31 of 128 credits required for the bachelor's degree must be completed at Baker. **International Students:** There are 22 international students enrolled. The school actively recruits these students. They must take the TOEFL with a minimum score of 525 on the paper-based TOEFL (PBT) or 69 on the Internet-based version (iBT). They must also take the SAT or ACT.

ADMISSIONS: 82% of the 2016-2017 applicants were accepted. The ACT scores were 6% between 12 and 17, 54% between 18 and 23, 37% between 24 and 29, and 3% above 30. 34% of the current freshmen were in the top fifth of their class; 67% were in the top two fifths. 8 freshmen graduated first in their class. **Admissions Contact:** Kevin Kropf, Director of Enrollment Management. Email: *admissions@bakeru.edu* Web: *www.bakeru.edu*

FINANCIAL AID: The college's own financial statement is required. The

FAFSA code is 001903. The priority date for freshman financial aid applications for fall entry is March 1. The filing deadline for fall entry is rolling.

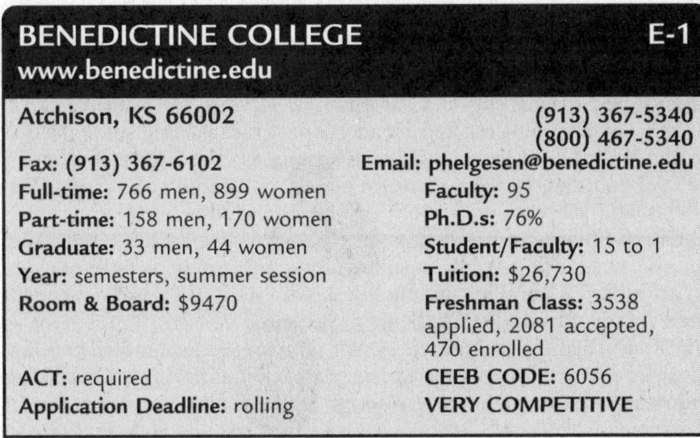

BENEDICTINE COLLEGE E-1

www.benedictine.edu

Atchison, KS 66002 (913) 367-5340
(800) 467-5340

Fax: (913) 367-6102 Email: phelgesen@benedictine.edu

Full-time: 766 men, 899 women	**Faculty:** 95
Part-time: 158 men, 170 women	**Ph.D.s:** 76%
Graduate: 33 men, 44 women	**Student/Faculty:** 15 to 1
Year: semesters, summer session	**Tuition:** $26,730
Room & Board: $9470	**Freshman Class:** 3538 applied, 2081 accepted, 470 enrolled
ACT: required	**CEEB CODE:** 6056
Application Deadline: rolling	**VERY COMPETITIVE**

Benedictine College, established in 1971 by a merger of St. Benedict's College and Mount Saint Scholastics College, is a liberal arts, Catholic, Benedictine institution. Figures in the above capsule and in this profile are approximate. There is 1 undergraduate school and 2 graduate schools. In addition to regional accreditation, Benedictine has baccalaureate program accreditation with NASM, NCATE, CAATE, and CCNE. The 225-acre campus is in a small town 45 miles north of Kansas City. Including any residence halls, there are 27 buildings.

STUDENT LIFE: 75% of undergraduates are from out of state, mostly the Midwest. Students are from 48 states, 12 foreign countries, and Canada. 55% are from public schools. 84% are White; 5% Hispanic; 3% African American; 1% Asian American; 1% American Indian/Alaska Native; 1% Foreign. 89% are Catholic. **Female To Male Ratio:** 1.2:1. The average age of freshmen is 18; all undergraduates, 20. 20% do not continue beyond their first year; 55% remain to graduate. **Housing:** 1240 students can be accommodated in college housing, which includes single-sex and coed dorms. On-campus housing is guaranteed for all 4 years. 77% of students live on campus; of those, 70% remain on campus on weekends. All students may keep cars.

FACULTY/CLASSROOMS: 66% of faculty are male; 34% are female. All teach undergraduates, 40% do research, and 40% do both. No introductory courses are taught by graduate students. The average class size in an introductory lecture is 25; in a laboratory is 20; and in a regular course is 20.

PROGRAMS OF STUDY: Benedictine confers B.A., B.S. and B.Mus.Ed degrees. Associate and master's degrees are also awarded. Bachelor's degrees are awarded in BIOLOGICAL SCIENCE (biochemistry and biology/biological science), BUSINESS (accounting and business administration and management), COMMUNICATIONS AND THE ARTS (art, dramatic arts, English, French, journalism, music, Spanish, and theater management), COMPUTER AND PHYSICAL SCIENCE (astronomy, chemistry, computer science, mathematics, natural sciences, and physics), EDUCATION (athletic training, elementary education, music education, physical education, secondary education, and special education), ENGINEERING AND ENVIRONMENTAL DESIGN (engineering), HEALTH PROFESSIONS (nursing), SOCIAL SCIENCE (economics, history, liberal arts/general studies, philosophy, political science/government, psychology, religion, social science, sociology, and youth ministry). Biology, engineering, and education are the strongest academically. Business, and theology have the largest enrollments.

ACTIVITIES: There are no fraternities or sororities. There are 35 groups on campus, including band, cheerleading, choir, chorale, computers, dance, drama, drill team, ethnic, honors, international, jazz band, literary magazine, musical theater, newspaper, orchestra, pep band, photography, political, professional, religious, social, social service, student government, and symphony. Popular campus events include Discovery Week, Parents Weekend, and All School Mass. **Sports:** There are 7 intercollegiate sports for men and 8 for women, and 7 intramural sports for men and 7 for women. Facilities include a gym, weight rooms, a football and track stadium, baseball, softball, track fields, lacrosse, rugby, wrestling, volleyball, cheer and dance, and an isometrics training room. **Graduates:** From July 1, 2015 to June 30, 2016, 336 bachelor's degrees were awarded. The most popular majors were business (20%), education (10%), and theology/youth ministry (6%). 26 companies recruited on campus in 2015-2016. In an average class, 42% graduate in 4 years or less, 46% graduate in 5 years or less, and 53% graduate in 6 years or less. Of the 2015 graduating class, 15% were enrolled in graduate school within 6 months of graduation, and 75% were employed.

SERVICES: Counseling and information services are available, as is tutoring in most subjects, and remedial math, reading, and writing. **Library/Resources:** The library contains 231,796 volumes, 10,803 microform items, and 52,593 audio/video tapes/CDs/DVDs, and subscribes to 425 periodicals including electronic. Computerized library services include interlibrary loans, database searching, and Internet access. **Physically Challenged Students:** 80% of the campus is accessible. Facilities include wheelchair ramps, elevators, special parking, specially equipped restrooms, special class scheduling, and lowered drinking fountains. **Special:** Benedictine offers cross-registration with the 14 other members of the Kansas City Regional Council for Higher Education and study abroad in several countries. The school also offers a 3-2 occupational therapy program with Washington University of St. Louis and a 3-2 engineering degree. Internships, work-study programs, dual majors, B.A.-B.S. degrees in chemistry and biology, an interdisciplinary music marketing major, student-designed majors, pass/fail options, and nondegree study are also available. There are 4 national honor societies, a freshman honors program, and 4 departmental honors programs. **Visiting:** There are regularly scheduled orientations for prospective students, consisting of an advanced placement exam, preregistration, meetings with the dean, student affairs, and business office and financial aid representatives, and campus tours. The orientations are scheduled for April, June, and July. There are guides for informal visits, visitors may sit in on classes, and stay overnight. To schedule a visit, contact the Admissions Office. **Campus Safety and Security:** Measures include 24-hour foot and vehicle patrol, emergency notification system, and security escort services. There are also lighted pathways/sidewalks and controlled access to dorms/residences.

REQUIREMENTS: The ACT is required. Applicants should graduate in the upper 50% of their class at an accredited secondary school. Students should have 16 academic units, including 4 in English, 3 to 4 in math, 2 to 4 in foreign language and science, 2 in social science, and 1 in history. An interview is recommended. Counselor recommendations are required. A GPA of 2.0 is required. AP and CLEP credits are accepted. Important factors in the admissions decision are advanced placement or honors courses, and recommendations by school officials, and by alumni. To graduate, students must complete 128 semester hours, pass a comprehensive exam in their major, and earn a minimum GPA of 2.0 overall and in the major. Curriculum requirements include 9 hours each in philosophy and religious studies, 8 hours each in English, natural science, and foreign language, 6 each in Western civilization and social science, 4 in math, 3 in fine arts, and 2 each in speech communication and phys ed. A dean's colloquium and a comprehensive exam are also required. **Procedure:** Freshmen are admitted to all sessions. Entrance exams should be taken before the July following graduation from high school. There are deferred admissions and rolling admissions plans. Application deadlines are open. Application fee is $25. Notification is sent on a rolling basis. Applications are accepted online. **Transfer Students:** 78 transfer students enrolled in 2015-2016. Applicants must submit transcripts from all colleges attended, a statement of courses in progress, and, if transferring with less than 60 hours, a high school transcript and ACT score. A minimum GPA of 2.0 is required. 30 of 128 credits required for the bachelor's degree must be completed at Benedictine. **International Students:** There are 21 international students enrolled. The school actively recruits these students. They must take the TOEFL with a minimum score of 533 on the paper-based TOEFL (PBT) or 72 on the Internet-based version (iBT), or take the MELAB. They must also take the SAT or ACT.

ADMISSIONS: 59% of the 2016-2017 applicants were accepted. 47% of the current freshmen were in the top fifth of their class; 70% were in the top two fifths. **Admissions Contact:** Pete Helgesen, Dean of Enrollment Management. Email: *phelgesen@benedictine.edu* Web: *www.benedictine.edu*

FINANCIAL AID: In 2016-2017, 100% of all full-time freshmen and 99% of continuing full-time students received some form of financial aid. 64% of all full-time freshmen and continuing full-time students received need-based aid. The average freshman award was $21,132. Need-based scholarships or need-based grants averaged $4,015 ($8,550 maximum); need-based self-help aid (loans and jobs) averaged $3,880 ($5,234 maximum); non-need-based athletic scholarships averaged

$14,444 ($28,900 maximum); other non-need-based awards and non-need-based scholarships averaged $12,426 ($20,000 maximum); and $2,828 from other forms of aid. 28% of undergraduate students work part-time. Average annual earnings from campus work are $778. The average financial indebtedness of the 2016 graduate was $27,303. Benedictine is a member of CSS. The college's own financial statement is required. The FAFSA code is 010256. The priority date for freshman financial aid applications for fall entry is April 1. The filing deadline for fall entry is August 1.

BETHANY COLLEGE *(The complete profile is made available exclusively on our website, www.barronspac.com)*

BETHEL COLLEGE D-3
www.bethel-college.edu

North Newton, KS 67117	(316) 284-5230 (800) 522-1887
Fax: (316) 284-5870	Email: admissions@bethelks.edu
Full-time: 220 men, 221 women	**Faculty:** 38
Part-time: 9 men, 10 women	**Ph.D.s:** 66%
Graduate: n/av	**Student/Faculty:** 10 to 1
Year: 4-1-4	**Tuition:** $26,920
Room & Board: $8450	**Freshman Class:** 99 applied, 349 accepted, 99 enrolled
SAT: required **ACT:** 22	**CEEB CODE:** 6037
Application Deadline: rolling	**COMPETITIVE**

Bethel College, established in 1887, is a private liberal arts institution affiliated with the Mennonite Church. The figures in the above capsule and in this profile are approximate. There is 1 undergraduate school. In addition to regional accreditation, Bethel College has baccalaureate program accreditation with CSWE, NCATE, CCNE, and CAATE. The 90-acre campus is in a suburban area 25 miles north of Wichita. Including any residence halls, there are 21 buildings.

STUDENT LIFE: 65% of undergraduates are from Kansas. Others are from 27 states, 2 foreign countries, and Canada. 8% are Hispanic; 71% White; 5% two or more races; 14% African American; 1% Asian American; 1% American Indian/Alaska Native. **Female To Male Ratio:** 1.0:1. The average age of freshmen is 18; all undergraduates, 22. 23% do not continue beyond their first year; 53% remain to graduate. **Housing:** 434 students can be accommodated in college housing, which includes coed dorms. coed dorms, and special housing for international students and disabled students. On-campus housing is guaranteed for all 4 years. 68% of students live on campus; of those, 88% remain on campus on weekends. All students may keep cars. Alcohol is not permitted.

FACULTY/CLASSROOMS: 42% of faculty are male; 58% are female. All teach undergraduates, 50% do research, and 50% do both. No introductory courses are taught by graduate students. The average class size in an introductory lecture is 21; in a laboratory is 11; and in a regular course is 18.

PROGRAMS OF STUDY: Bethel College confers B.A., B.S., and B.S.N. degrees. Bachelor's degrees are awarded in BIOLOGICAL SCIENCE (biology/biological science), BUSINESS (business administration and management), COMMUNICATIONS AND THE ARTS (art, communications, English, graphic design, and music), COMPUTER AND PHYSICAL SCIENCE (chemistry, mathematics, and natural sciences), EDUCATION (athletic training, elementary education, and health and physical education), HEALTH PROFESSIONS (nursing), SOCIAL SCIENCE (history, psychology, religion, and social work). Business, biology, and psychology are the strongest academically. Nursing, and elementary education have the largest enrollments.

ACTIVITIES: There are no fraternities or sororities. There are 30 groups on campus, including choral groups, theater and music ensembles, band, campus ministries, cheerleading, chess, choir, chorale, chorus, computers, debate, drama, environmental, ethnic, forensics, international, jazz band, LGBT, literary magazine, newspaper, orchestra, political, professional, radio and TV, religious, social, social service, student government, symphony, and yearbook. Popular campus events include Fall Festival, Christmas Gala, and Spring Fling. **Sports:** There are 7 intercollegiate sports for men and 7 for women, and 18 intramural sports for men and 18 for women. Facilities include indoor gyms, weight rooms, cardio-exercise room, tennis courts, soccer practice fields, all-weather track, outdoor stadium complex for football, soccer, track, artificial turf field, football practice field, outdoor basketball court, and an outdoor sand volleyball court. **Graduates:** From July 1, 2015 to June 30, 2016, 137 bachelor's degrees were awarded. The most popular majors were health professions/related programs (20%), business/marketing and visual and performing arts (18%), and elementary education (9%). In an average class, 35% graduate in 4 years or less and 15% graduate in 5 years or less.

SERVICES: Counseling and information services are available, as is tutoring in most subjects, and a reader service for the blind, and remedial math, reading, and writing. **Library/Resources:** The 2 libraries contain 147,965 volumes, 14,377 microform items, 7,113 audio/video tapes/CDs/DVDs, and subscribe to 32,765 periodicals including electronic. Computerized library services include interlibrary loans, database searching, Internet access, and Wi-Fi capability. Special learning facilities include an art gallery, natural history museum, radio station, TV station, and an observatory. **Physically Challenged Students:** 75% of the campus is accessible. Facilities include wheelchair ramps, elevators, special parking, specially equipped restrooms, special class scheduling, lowered drinking fountains, and special housing. **Special:** Students may cross-register with Associated Colleges of Central Kansas institutions and Hesston College. Internships are required in many majors. Work-study programs, study abroad, dual majors, and a Washington semester are available. The college offers a 3-2 engineering degree with University of Kansas, Kansas State University, and Wichita State University. **Visiting:** There are regularly scheduled orientations for prospective students, including a campus tour, classroom observations, visits with faculty, an interview with an admissions counselor, and lunch, and overnight residence hall lodging. There are guides for informal visits, visitors may sit in on classes, and stay overnight. To schedule a visit, contact the Admissions Office. **Campus Safety and Security:** There are emergency telephones and lighted pathways/sidewalks.

REQUIREMENTS: Applicants should present a satisfactory score for SAT and ACT, with a minimum GPA of 2.5 for automatic admission. The GED is accepted. Auditions are required of candidates applying for some scholarships, and interviews are recommended for all applicants. Specific departmental requirements may vary. CLEP, AP, and International Baccalaureate credit may be awarded. A GPA of 2.0 is required. AP and CLEP credits are accepted. Important factors in the admissions decision are evidence of special talent, recommendations by alumni, and parents or siblings have attended the school. To graduate, students must earn a total of 124 credits, including 24 to 50 in the major, 12 to 50 of those in upper-level courses, with a GPA of 2.0. Students must also meet general education requirements that include demonstrating competency in writing, math, speech, and foreign language. Additional core requirements include convocation, religious studies, cross-cultural learning, and peace, justice, and conflict studies. Distribution requirements include at least six hours in each division: arts and humanities, science and mathematics, and social sciences. **Procedure:** Freshmen are admitted to all sessions. Entrance exams should be taken by the fall of the senior year. There is a rolling admissions plan. Application deadlines are open. Application fee is $20. Notification is sent on a rolling basis. Applications are accepted online. **Transfer Students:** 61 transfer students enrolled in 2015-2016. A high school transcript (or GED), or official college transcript (minimum 2.0 GPA), ACT or SAT scores (waived if the student has more than 24 hours accepted in transfer to Bethel College), and a transfer recommendation are required. Automatic admission requires a cumulative GPA of 2.0 and satisfactory ACT or SAT scores. 30 of 30 credits required for the bachelor's degree must be completed at Bethel College. **International Students:** There are 3 international students enrolled. They must take the TOEFL with a minimum score of 540 on the paper-based TOEFL (PBT) or 76 on the Internet-based version (iBT). They must also take the SAT or ACT.

ADMISSIONS: 33% of the 2016-2017 applicants were accepted. The ACT scores were 2% between 12 and 17, 68% between 18 and 23, 28% between 24 and 29, and 2% above 30. **Admissions Contact:** Todd H. Moore, Vice President for Admissions. Email: *admissions@bethelks.edu* Web: *www.bethel-college.edu*

FINANCIAL AID: In 2016-2017, 100% of all full-time freshmen and 80% of continuing full-time students received some form of financial aid. 87% of all full-time freshmen and 78% of continuing full-time students received need-based aid. The average freshman award was $26,000. Need-based scholarships or need-based grants averaged $4,910; need-based self-help aid (loans and jobs) averaged $7,083; non-need-based athletic scholarships averaged $5,125; other non-need-based awards and non-need-based scholarships averaged $5,933; and $9,631 from other forms of aid. 45% of undergraduate students work part-time. Average annual earnings from campus work are $1384. The average financial indebtedness of the 2016 graduate was $24,132. The FAFSA code is 001905. The priority date for freshman financial aid applications for fall entry is August 15.

EMPORIA STATE UNIVERSITY E-2

www.emporia.edu

Emporia, KS 66801	(620) 341-5465
Fax: (620) 341-5599	**Email:** go2esu@emporia.edu
Full-time: 1305 men, 2126 women	**Faculty:** 245; IIA, --$
Part-time: 115 men, 156 women	**Ph.D.s:** 50%
Graduate: 685 men, 1500 women	**Student/Faculty:** 18 to 1
Year: semesters, summer session	**Tuition:** $6179 ($19,392)
Room & Board: $8391	**Freshman Class:** 1702 applied, 1488 accepted, 665 enrolled
ACT: required	**CEEB CODE:** 6335
Application Deadline: open	**COMPETITIVE**

Emporia State University, founded in 1863, is a comprehensive university focused on academic excellence, student success, leadership, and community and global engagement. Emporia State University is a dynamic and progressive student-centered learning community that fosters student success through engagement in academic excellence, community and global involvement, and the pursuit of personal and professional fulfillment. Figures in the above capsule and in this profile are approximate. There are 3 undergraduate schools and 1 graduate school. In addition to regional accreditation, ESU has baccalaureate program accreditation with AACSB, NASAD, NASM, NCATE, NLN, CAAHEP, and ACS. The 207-acre campus is in a small town 110 miles from Kansas City. Including any residence halls, there are 20 buildings.

STUDENT LIFE: 92% of undergraduates are from Kansas. Others are from 49 states, and 50 foreign countries. 8% are Foreign; 64% White; 5% Hispanic; 5% two or more races; 4% African American; 12% race unknown; 1% Asian American. **Female To Male Ratio:** 1.8:1. The average age of freshmen is 18; all undergraduates, 22. 29% do not continue beyond their first year; 44% remain to graduate. **Housing:** 890 students can be accommodated in college housing, which includes single-sex and coed dorms, on-campus apartments, honors houses, special-interest houses, fraternity houses, and sorority houses. On-campus housing is guaranteed for the freshman year only, is available on a first-come, and first-served basis. Priority is given to out-of-town students. 74% of students commute. All students may keep cars.

FACULTY/CLASSROOMS: 54% of faculty are male; 43% are female. 96% teach undergraduates. Graduate students teach 9% of introductory courses. The average class size in an introductory lecture is 20; in a laboratory is 10; and in a regular course is 23.

PROGRAMS OF STUDY: ESU confers B.A., B.S., B.F.A., B.I.S., B Mus., B.Mus.Ed., B.S.Bus., B.S.Ed. and B.S.N. degrees. Master's and doctoral degrees are also awarded. Bachelor's degrees are awarded in BIOLOGICAL SCIENCE (biochemistry and biology/biological science), BUSINESS (accounting, business administration and management, marketing/retailing/merchandising, and recreation and leisure services), COMMUNICATIONS AND THE ARTS (art, communications, dramatic arts, English, modern language, music, and theatre arts), COMPUTER AND PHYSICAL SCIENCE (chemistry, computer science, earth science, information sciences and systems, mathematics, physical sciences, and physics), EDUCATION (art education, athletic training, business education, elementary education, foreign languages education, health education, music education, physical education, and secondary education), HEALTH PROFESSIONS (health care administration, health science, nursing, and rehabilitation therapy), SOCIAL SCIENCE (criminal justice, economics, history, liberal arts/general studies, political science/government, psychology, social science, and sociology). Teacher education elementary and secondary is the strongest academically. Elementary education, business administration, and biology have the largest enrollments.

ACTIVITIES: 16% of men belong to 8 national fraternities; 12% of women belong to 6 national sororities. There are 130 groups on campus, including art, band, cheerleading, choir, chorale, chorus, computers, debate, drama, drill team, environmental, ethnic, film, honors, international, jazz band, LGBT, literary magazine, marching band, musical theater, newspaper, opera, orchestra, pep band, political, professional, religious, social, social service, student government, symphony, and yearbook. Popular campus events include Family Day, International Student Festival, and Homecoming. **Sports:** There are 7 intercollegiate sports for men and 8 for women, and 12 intramural sports for men and 12 for women. Facilities include a stadium student recreation center, pool, gyms, handball courts, dance rooms, a sports complex with softball fields and baseball diamond, and an all-weather track. **Graduates:** From July 1, 2015 to June 30, 2016, 757 bachelor's degrees were awarded. The most popular majors were education (22%), business administration (15%), and health fields (10%). 185 companies recruited on campus in 2015-2016. In an average class, 23% graduate in 4 years or less, 40% graduate in 5 years or less, and 44% graduate in 6 years or less. Of the 2015 graduating class, 20% were enrolled in graduate school within 6 months of graduation, and 22% were employed.

SERVICES: There is a reader service for the blind, and remedial math, reading, and writing. **Library/Resources:** The library contains 527,389 volumes. Computerized library services include interlibrary loans, database searching, Internet access, and Wi-Fi capability. Special learning facilities include an art gallery, natural history museum, planetarium, theaters, geology museum, and Great Plains study center. **Physically Challenged Students:** All of the campus is accessible. Facilities include wheelchair ramps, elevators, special parking, specially equipped restrooms, special class scheduling, lowered drinking fountains, lowered telephones, and special housing. **Special:** ESU offers internships in many majors, study abroad in 34 countries, work-study programs, on-campus and on-line general studies degrees, B.A.-B.S. degrees, dual and student-designed majors, 3-2 engineering degrees with Kansas State University, Wichita State University, and the University of Kansas, credit for military experience, non-degree study, independent study, evening and Saturday classes, and pass/no credit options. There are 22 national honor societies and a freshman honors program. **Visiting:** There are regularly scheduled orientations for prospective students, visits include campus and residence hall tours, meetings with admissions and financial aid personnel, and appointments with academic and extracurricular personnel. There are guides for informal visits and visitors may sit in on classes. To schedule a visit, contact the Admissions Office. **Campus Safety and Security:** Measures include a 24-hour foot and vehicle patrol, emergency notification system, self-defense education, and security escort services. There are also emergency telephones, lighted pathways/sidewalks, motorist-assist programs, safety and self-awareness programs for students and parents, 24-hour residence hall monitoring, and smoke detectors in residence halls.

REQUIREMENTS: Applicants must meet 1 of these 3 criteria: an ACT score of 21 or above, class rank in the top third, or a 2.0 GPA in the Kansas core curriculum in-state and a 2.5 for out-of-state applicants. Students should have completed 4 units of English, 3 each of natural science, math, and social science, and 1 of computer technology. Applicants may also be admitted through an exceptions window and are encouraged to apply. AP and CLEP credits are accepted. To graduate, all students must complete at least 124 credit hours, including 40 in upper-division courses, with a minimum GPA of 2.0. Students must complete the general education program for their field of study, which includes courses in math, physical and applied science, humanities, history, speech, cultural diversity, and fitness and phys ed. **Procedure:** Freshmen are admitted to all sessions. Entrance exams should be taken during October or December of the senior year. There are deferred admissions and rolling admissions plans. Application deadlines are open. Application fee is $30. Applications are accepted online. **Transfer Students:** 350 transfer students enrolled in 2015-2016. Applicants must submit official transcripts of all previous college work. The minimum GPA depends on the number of semester hours earned. Physical activity requirements must be met. 30 of 124 credits required for the bachelor's degree must be completed at ESU. **International Students:** There are 477 international students enrolled. The school actively recruits these students. They must take the TOEFL with a minimum score of 520 on the paper-based TOEFL (PBT) or 68 on the Internet-based version (iBT). They must also take the ACT.

ADMISSIONS: 33% of the current freshmen were in the top fifth of their class; 69% were in the top two fifths. 3 freshmen graduated first in their class. **Admissions Contact:** Dr. Shelly Gehrke, Assistant Provost Enrollment Management. Email: *go2esu@emporia.edu* Web: *www.emporia.edu*

FINANCIAL AID: In 2016-2017, 95% of all full-time freshmen and 88%

of continuing full-time students received some form of financial aid. 67% of all full-time freshmen and 66% of continuing full-time students received need-based aid. The average freshman award was $8,900. Need-based scholarships or need-based grants averaged $5,755 ($34,378 maximum); need-based self-help aid (loans and jobs) averaged $2,131 ($6,250 maximum); non-need-based athletic scholarships averaged $3,890 ($28,261 maximum); and other non-need-based awards and non-need-based scholarships averaged $8,106 ($30,968 maximum). 15% of undergraduate students work part-time. Average annual earnings from campus work are $3300. The average financial indebtedness of the 2016 graduate was $20,433. The state aid form is required. The FAFSA code is 001927. The priority date for freshman financial aid applications for fall entry is February 2.

FORT HAYS STATE UNIVERSITY C-2

www.fhsu.edu

Hays, KS 67601	(785) 628-5666 (800) 628-FHSU
Fax: (785) 628-4014	Email: tigers@fhsu.edu
Full-time: 2270 men, 3248 women	**Faculty:** IIA, --$
Part-time: 2205 men, 3575 women	**Ph.D.s:** 77%
Graduate: 746 men, 1176 women	**Student/Faculty:** n/av
Year: semesters, summer session	**Tuition:** $4654 ($13,656)
Room & Board: $7477	**Freshman Class:** 3199 applied, 2887 accepted, 2185 enrolled
ACT: 21	**CEEB CODE:** 6218
Application Deadline: open	**COMPETITIVE**

Fort Hays State University, established in 1902, is a public liberal arts institution offering programs in arts and sciences, business and entrepreneurship, education, health and life sciences, and pre-professional study. The figures in the above capsule and in this profile are approximate. There are 4 undergraduate schools and 1 graduate school. In addition to regional accreditation, FHSU has baccalaureate program accreditation with AACSB, NASM, NCATE, and NLN. The 200-acre campus is in a small town 180 miles northwest of Wichita. Including any residence halls, there are 44 buildings.

STUDENT LIFE: 93% of undergraduates are from Kansas. Others are from 36 states, 32 foreign countries, and Canada. 95% are from public schools. 87% are White; 2% Asian American; 2% Hispanic; 1% African American; 1% American Indian/Alaska Native. **Female To Male Ratio:** 1.5:1. The average age of freshmen is 18; all undergraduates, 23. 61% do not continue beyond their first year; 40% remain to graduate. **Housing:** 1000 students can be accommodated in college housing, which includes single-sex and coed dorms, on-campus apartments, and married student housing. In addition, there are fraternity houses, sorority houses, apartments for students with families, and apartments for nontraditional-age students. 82% of students commute. All students may keep cars.

FACULTY/CLASSROOMS: 59% of faculty are male; 41% are female. All teach undergraduates. No introductory courses are taught by graduate students. The average class size in an introductory lecture is 17; in a laboratory is 17; and in a regular course is 18.

PROGRAMS OF STUDY: FHSU confers B.A., B.S., B.B.A., B.F.A., B.G.S., B.M., and B.S.W. degrees. Associate and master's degrees are also awarded. Bachelor's degrees are awarded in AGRICULTURE (agricultural business management and agriculture), BIOLOGICAL SCIENCE (biology/biological science), BUSINESS (accounting, banking and finance, business administration and management, management information systems, marketing/retailing/merchandising, and office supervision and management), COMMUNICATIONS AND THE ARTS (art, communications, English, fine arts, French, German, modern language, music, music performance, music theory and composition, Spanish, and telecommunications), COMPUTER AND PHYSICAL SCIENCE (chemistry, computer science, geology, information sciences and systems, mathematics, physical sciences, physics, radiological technology, and science), EDUCATION (art education, elementary education, music education, physical education, and technical education), HEALTH PROFESSIONS (nursing and speech pathology/audiology), SOCIAL SCIENCE (criminal justice, economics, history, liberal arts/general studies, philosophy, political science/government, psychology, social work, and sociology). Speech pathology is the strongest academically. Interdisciplinary studies, teacher education, and business administration have the largest enrollments.

ACTIVITIES: 1% of men belong to 3 national fraternities; 1% of women belong to 3 national sororities. There are 85 groups on campus, including art, band, cheerleading, choir, chorale, chorus, computers, dance, debate, drama, drill team, ethnic, film, honors, international, jazz band, LGBT, literary magazine, marching band, musical theater, newspaper, opera, orchestra, pep band, photography, political, professional, radio and TV, religious, social, social service, student government, symphony, and yearbook. Popular campus events include Octoberfest and Parents Day. **Sports:** There are 8 intercollegiate sports for men and 7 for women, and 40 intramural sports for men and 40 for women. Facilities include a stadium, tennis courts, and a coliseum containing a basketball arena, a track, and wrestling and training rooms. **Graduates:** From July 1, 2015 to June 30, 2016, 2572 bachelor's degrees were awarded. The most popular majors were business/marketing (49%), liberal arts/general studies (13%), and education (11%).

SERVICES: Counseling and information services are available, as is tutoring in most subjects, and remedial math and reading. **Library/Resources:** The library contains 300,000 volumes, 500,000 microform items, 1,480 audio/video tapes/CDs/DVDs, and subscribes to 3,100 periodicals including electronic. Computerized library services include interlibrary loans, database searching, Internet access, and Wi-Fi capability. Special learning facilities include an art gallery, radio station, TV station, and an English lab. **Physically Challenged Students:** 95% of the campus is accessible. Facilities include wheelchair ramps, elevators, special parking, specially equipped restrooms, special class scheduling, lowered drinking fountains, and lowered telephones. **Special:** Students may, with approval, earn their degrees through a cooperative program with FHSU and another accredited institution, or a correspondence or extension school. Cross-registration with several community colleges, internships, study abroad, work-study programs, a 3-2 engineering degree with Kansas State University, B.A.-B.S. degrees, a general studies degree, and pass/fail options are available. There are 21 national honor societies and a freshman honors program. **Visiting:** There are regularly scheduled orientations for prospective students. There are guides for informal visits, visitors may sit in on classes, and stay overnight. To schedule a visit, contact the Campus Tour Coordinator. **Campus Safety and Security:** Measures include 24-hour foot and vehicle patrol, security escort services, emergency telephones and lighted pathways/sidewalks.

REQUIREMENTS: The ACT is recommended. 14 total high school units are recommended 4 in English, 3 in math and science, 2 in social studies, and 1 in history and computer science A GPA of 2.0 is required. AP and CLEP credits are accepted. To graduate, students must earn an overall minimum GPA of 2.0 or higher in some departments for 124 credit hours, including 40 hours in upper-level study, and 30 hours minimum in the major. The 55-hour liberal arts general education curriculum includes courses addressing personal wellness, analysis and communication, international studies, humanities, math, and natural, social, and behavioral sciences. **Procedure:** Freshmen are admitted fall, spring, and summer. Entrance exams should be taken in the senior year. There is a rolling admissions plan. Application deadlines are open. Application fee is $30. Applications are accepted online. **Transfer Students:** Applicants must have a minimum college GPA of 2.0 and submit official college transcripts from all institutions previously attended. 30 of 124 credits required for the bachelor's degree must be completed at FHSU. **International Students:** The school actively recruits these students. They must take the TOEFL.

ADMISSIONS: 90% of the 2016-2017 applicants were accepted. **Admissions Contact:** Tricia Cline, Director of Admissions. Email: *tigers@fhsu.edu* Web: *www.fhsu.edu*

FINANCIAL AID: The average freshman award was $7,207. Need-based scholarships or need-based grants averaged $5,074; need-based self-help aid (loans and jobs) averaged $3,154; non-need-based athletic scholarships averaged $3,716; other non-need-based awards and non-need-based scholarships averaged $1,406; and $2,953 from other forms of aid. The FFS and the college's own financial statement are required. The FAFSA code is 001915. Check with the school for current application deadlines.

FRIENDS UNIVERSITY D-3
www.friends.edu

Wichita, KS 67213 (316) 295-5100
(800) 794-6945
Fax: (316) 295-5101 Email: admissions@friends.edu

Full-time: 434 men, 486 women
Part-time: 120 men, 152 women
Graduate: 192 men, 378 women
Year: semesters, summer session
Room & Board: $7590
Application Deadline: open
Faculty: n/av
Ph.D.s: n/av
Student/Faculty: n/av
Tuition: $26,865
Freshman Class: 737 applied, 399 accepted, 159 enrolled
CEEB CODE: 6224
COMPETITIVE

Friends University, established in 1898, is a nondenominational, independent Christian University that incorporates liberal arts instruction and professional studies into a high-quality undergraduate and graduate education. Figures in the above capsule and in this profile are approximate. There are 2 undergraduate schools and 1 graduate school. In addition to regional accreditation, Friends has baccalaureate program accreditation with NASM and NCATE. The 54-acre campus is in an urban area in the heart of Wichita, Kansas adjacent to highway 54, approximately 200 miles southwest of Kansas City. Including any residence halls, there are 19 buildings.

STUDENT LIFE: 70% of undergraduates are from Kansas. Others are from 39 states, 11 foreign countries, and Canada. 81% are from public schools. 70% are White; 2% Asian American; 2% American Indian/ Alaska Native; 11% African American; 11% Hispanic; 1% Foreign. 66% are Protestant; 37% claim no religious affiliation; 12% Catholic. **Female To Male Ratio:** 1.4:1. The average age of freshmen is 18; all undergraduates, 21. 40% do not continue beyond their first year; 60% remain to graduate. **Housing:** 423 students can be accommodated in college housing, which includes coed dorms, on-campus apartments, off-campus apartments, and university owned housing. On-campus housing is available on a first-come and first-served basis. 56% of students commute. All students may keep cars. Alcohol is not permitted.

FACULTY/CLASSROOMS: 92% teach undergraduates. No introductory courses are taught by graduate students. The average class size in an introductory lecture is 35; in a laboratory is 18; and in a regular course is 25.

PROGRAMS OF STUDY: Friends confers B.A., B.S., B.B.A., B.F.A., and B.Mus. degrees. Associate and master's degrees are also awarded. Bachelor's degrees are awarded in BIOLOGICAL SCIENCE (biology/biological science, wildlife biology, and zoology), BUSINESS (accounting, banking and finance, business administration and management, business economics, human resources, international business management, and management information systems), COMMUNICATIONS AND THE ARTS (art, ballet, communications, English, fine arts, music, music performance, musical theater, performing arts, and Spanish), COMPUTER AND PHYSICAL SCIENCE (chemistry, computer science, information sciences and systems, mathematics, and radiological technology), EDUCATION (art education, business education, drama education, education, elementary education, English education, foreign languages education, health education, music education, recreation education, science education, secondary education, and social science education), ENGINEERING AND ENVIRONMENTAL DESIGN (environmental science), HEALTH PROFESSIONS (health science, premedicine, and radiological science), SOCIAL SCIENCE (Christian studies, counseling/ psychology, criminal justice, forensic studies, history, human services, liberal arts/general studies, philosophy and religion, political science/ government, psychology, and religion). Science is the strongest academically. Business, and education have the largest enrollments.

ACTIVITIES: There are no fraternities or sororities. There are 24 groups on campus, including art, band, cheerleading, choir, chorale, chorus, communications, computers, dance, drama, ethnic, honors, international, jazz band, literary magazine, musical theater, newspaper, orchestra, pep band, photography, political, professional, psychology club, religious, Singing Quakers, social, social service, student government, Spanish club, symphony, zoo science and yearbook. Popular campus events include Homecoming Week, Cherry Carnival and Chili Cookoff. **Sports:** There are 8 intercollegiate sports for men and 10 for women, and 8 intramural sports for men and 8 for women. Facilities include a stadium with turf for football and soccer, tennis courts, and gymnasium for basketball, volleyball, indoor practice facility for baseball, softball, track programs, racquetball courts, weight rooms, and the athletic training and sports medicine facilities. **Graduates:** The most popular majors were business/marketing (51%), computer and information sciences (9%), and psychology (7%).

SERVICES: Counseling and information services are available, as is tutoring in most subjects, and a reader service for the blind. **Library/ Resources:** Computerized library services include interlibrary loans, database searching, Internet access, and Wi-Fi capability. Special learning facilities include an art gallery, and an observatory. **Physically Challenged Students:** 95% of the campus is accessible. Facilities include wheelchair ramps, elevators, special parking, specially equipped restrooms, special class scheduling, lowered drinking fountains, and lowered telephones. **Special:** Students may cross-register with Newman University at no additional charge. Oportunity to participate in a long-standing study-abroad program is available in Cancun, Mexico; several other study-abroad programs of both shorter and longer duration have occurred in London, Paris, Italy, Cuba, Germany, Scotland,to name a few. Friends University offers several accelerated degree completion programs for the adult student in the College of Adult and Professional Studies. Friends also offers credit for life, military, and work experience. There is 1 national honor society, a freshman honors program, and 1 departmental honors program. **Visiting:** There are regularly scheduled orientations for prospective students, including half-day classroom visits, individual instructor visits, discussion with current students, a tour, lunch, and a financial aid session. There are guides for informal visits, visitors may sit in on classes, and stay overnight. To schedule a visit, contact the Admissions Office. **Campus Safety and Security:** Measures include 24-hour foot and vehicle patrol, emergency notification system, and security escort services, lighted pathways/sidewalks, and controlled access to dorms/residences.

REQUIREMENTS: Candidates for admission must graduate from an accredited secondary school or earn a GED, having completed 4 courses in English, 2 each in history and math, and 1 each in science and social studies. The composite ACT score or converted SAT score is multiplied by the high school GPA. A result of 45 is the minimum for full admission, students scoring lower may be admitted provisionally. Transfer students with at least 15 transferrable hours and adult students aged 23 or older are not required to submit test scores. A GPA of 2.0 is required. AP and CLEP credits are accepted. To graduate, students must complete 124 credit hours, including 33 to 54 in general education (varies by degree sought) and 24 to 45 in the major, with a minimum GPA of 2.0. Distribution requirements include course work in humanities, fine arts, religion and philosophy, behavioral science, and natural science. **Procedure:** Freshmen are admitted in the fall and spring. Entrance exams should be taken in the spring of the junior year or fall of the senior year. There is a rolling admissions plan. Application deadlines are open. Notification is sent on a rolling basis. Application fees are waived if application is completed online. **Transfer Students:** 121 transfer students enrolled in 2015-2016. Applicants with fewer than 15 semester hours must submit ACT or SAT I scores and high school and college transcripts. 30 of 124 credits required for the bachelor's degree must be completed at Friends. **International Students:** There are 12 international students enrolled. The school actively recruits these students. They must take the TOEFL with a minimum score of 52 on the Internet-based version (iBT), unless they are either native speakers of English or non-native speakers who attended an English-speaking high school. SAT or ACT scores may be submited in place of TOEFL scores.

ADMISSIONS: 54% of the 2016-2017 applicants were accepted. The ACT scores were 6% between 12 and 17, 57% between 18 and 23, 30% between 24 and 29, and 7% above 30. 24% of the current freshmen were in the top fifth of their class; 50% were in the top two fifths. 7 freshmen graduated first in their class. **Admissions Contact:** Brandon Pierce, Senior Director of Admissions. Web: *www.friends.edu*

FINANCIAL AID: In 2016-2017, 100% of all full-time freshmen and continuing full-time students received some form of financial aid. 52% of all full-time freshmen and 50% of continuing full-time students received need-based aid. The average freshman award was $24,142. Need-based scholarships or need-based grants averaged $2,190; need-based self-help aid (loans and jobs) averaged $3,438; non-need-based athletic scholarships averaged $4,784; other non-need-based awards and non-need-based scholarships averaged $11,086; and $2,644 from other forms of aid. The average financial indebtedness of the 2016 graduate was $13,418. The FAFSA code is 001918. The priority date for freshman financial aid applications for fall entry is March 15.

KANSAS STATE UNIVERSITY E-2

www.k-state.edu

Manhattan, KS 66506	**(785) 532-6250**
Fax: (785) 532-6393	**Email:** k-state@k-state.edu
Full-time: 9388 men, 8547 women	**Faculty:** I, av$
Part-time: 960 men, 964 women	**Ph.D.s:** 84%
Graduate: 1917 men, 2370 women	**Student/Faculty:** 19 to 1
Year: semesters, summer session	**Tuition:** $9350 ($23,429)
Room & Board: $8430	**Freshman Class:** 9178 applied, 8712 accepted, 3624 enrolled
ACT: 25	**CEEB CODE:** 6334
Application Deadline: open	**VERY COMPETITIVE**

Kansas State University, established in 1863, is a land-grant institution offering degree programs in agriculture, arts and sciences, business, engineering, human ecology, architecture, education, veterinary medicine, technology, and aviation. There are 9 undergraduate schools and 1 graduate school. In addition to regional accreditation, K-State has baccalaureate program accreditation with AACSB, ABET, ACCE, ACEJMC, AHEA, CSWE, FIDER, NAAB, NASAD, NASM, NCATE, NRPA, LAAB, CEA, CIDA, CAATE, CAA, CADE, NASPAA, CADE, NAEYC, ACPHA, AVMA, AABI, and NAST. The 668-acre campus is in a suburban area in Manhattan, Kansas, 125 miles west of Kansas City. Including any residence halls, there are 96 buildings.

STUDENT LIFE: 77% of undergraduates are from Kansas. Others are from 50 states, 110 foreign countries, and Canada. 75% are White; 8% Foreign; 6% Hispanic; 3% African American; 3% two or more races; 2% Asian American; 2% race unknown; 1% American Indian/Alaska Native. **Male To Female Ratio:** 1.0:1. The average age of freshmen is 18; all undergraduates, 21. 16% do not continue beyond their first year; 63% remain to graduate. **Housing:** 4319 students can be accommodated in college housing, which includes single-sex and coed dorms, on-campus apartments, married student housing, honors houses, and special-interest houses. On-campus housing is available on a first-come and first-served basis. 77% of students commute. All students may keep cars.

FACULTY/CLASSROOMS: 56% of faculty are male; 44% are female. No introductory courses are taught by graduate students. The average class size in a regular course is 30.

PROGRAMS OF STUDY: K-State confers B.A., B.S., B.F.A., B.M. and B.M.E. degrees. Associate, master's, and doctoral degrees are also awarded. Bachelor's degrees are awarded in AGRICULTURE (agricultural business management, agricultural communications, agricultural economics, agronomy, animal science, animal feed science, bakery science, fish and game management, horticulture, milling science, and wildlife management), BIOLOGICAL SCIENCE (biochemistry, biology/biological science, life science, microbiology, nutrition, and wildlife biology), BUSINESS (accounting, apparel and accessories marketing, banking and finance, business administration and management, entrepreneurial studies, hotel/motel and restaurant management, management information systems, marketing/retailing/merchandising, and personal financial planning), COMMUNICATIONS AND THE ARTS (apparel design, applied music, art, communications, dramatic arts, English, journalism, modern language, and music), COMPUTER AND PHYSICAL SCIENCE (chemistry, computer science, geology, information sciences and systems, mathematics, physical sciences, physics, and statistics), EDUCATION (agricultural education, art education, athletic training, early childhood education, elementary education, music education, and secondary education), ENGINEERING AND ENVIRONMENTAL DESIGN (aeronautical technology, agricultural engineering, agricultural engineering technology, airline piloting and navigation, architectural engineering, architecture, chemical engineering, civil engineering, computer engineering, construction management, electrical/electronics engineering, electrical/electronics engineering technology, engineering management, engineering technology, industrial engineering, interior design, landscape architecture/design, manufacturing engineering, and mechanical engineering), HEALTH PROFESSIONS (exercise science, medical technology, preveterinary science, and speech pathology/audiology), SOCIAL SCIENCE (anthropology, child care/child and family studies, dietetics, economics, ethnic studies, family and community services, family/consumer studies, food science, geography, history, human ecology, humanities, parks and recreation management, philosophy, physical fitness/movement, political science/government, psychology, social science, social work, sociology, textiles and clothing, and women's studies). Architecture, engineering, and accounting are the strongest academically. Business administration, mechanical engineering, and animal sciences have the largest enrollments.

ACTIVITIES: There are 478 groups on campus, including American Society of Civil Engineers, Public Relations Student Society of America, band, cheerleading, chess, choir, chorale, chorus, computers, dance, debate, drama, drill team, environmental, ethnic, honors, international, jazz band, LGBT, literary magazine, marching band, musical theater, newspaper, orchestra, pep band, photography, political, pre-nursing club, professional, radio and TV, religious, social, social service, student government, symphony, and yearbook. Popular campus events include Family Weekend, K-State Open House, and the Festival of Nations. **Sports:** There are 6 intercollegiate sports for men and 8 for women, and 49 intramural sports for men and 49 for women. Facilities include indoor and outdoor tracks, baseball fields, tennis courts, basketball courts, swimming pools, a football stadium, and an indoor practice field. A multipurpose recreation facility is open 16 hours a day. **Graduates:** From July 1, 2015 to June 30, 2016, 3887 bachelor's degrees were awarded. The most popular majors were business and marketing (17%), agriculture and engineering (13%), and social sciences (7%). In an average class, 31% graduate in 4 years or less, 56% graduate in 5 years or less, and 62% graduate in 6 years or less. Of the 2015 graduating class, 21% were enrolled in graduate school within 6 months of graduation, and 73% were employed.

SERVICES: Counseling and information services are available, as is tutoring in every subject, and a reader service for the blind, and remedial math, reading, and writing. **Library/Resources:** The 5 libraries contain 3.2 million volumes, 1.6 million microform items, 209,055 audio/video tapes/CDs/DVDs, and subscribe to 107,980 periodicals including electronic. Computerized library services include interlibrary loans, database searching, and Internet access. Special learning facilities include an art gallery, planetarium, radio station, TV station, a nuclear reactor, laser center, a cancer research center, and telecommunications satellite teaching. **Physically Challenged Students:** 90% of the campus is accessible. Facilities include wheelchair ramps, elevators, special parking, specially equipped restrooms, special class scheduling, lowered drinking fountains, lowered telephones, and special housing. **Special:** K-State offers co-op programs, internships, and dual degrees and majors through most of its colleges. Study abroad is available in more than 100 countries. Concurrent bachelor's/master's degree programs are available in 11 major areas. There are 78 national honor societies, Phi Beta Kappa, a freshman honors program, and 7 departmental honors programs. **Visiting:** There are regularly scheduled orientations for prospective students, including campus tours and visits with academic advisers and admissions representatives. There are guides for informal visits, visitors may sit in on classes, and stay overnight. To schedule a visit, contact the Office of Admissions. **Campus Safety and Security:** Measures include 24-hour foot and vehicle patrol, emergency notification system, self-defense education, and security escort services. There are shuttle buses, emergency telephones, lighted pathways/sidewalks, controlled access to dorms/residences, televised monitors in parking lots, CPR classes, and vehicle assistance devices.

REQUIREMENTS: Applicants must have earned a 2.0 GPA in the Kansas high school core curriculum or equivalent. It is recommended that students complete 4 units of English, 3 each of natural science, math, and social studies, and 1.5 of history, and 1 of computer technology. The GED is accepted. In addition, applicants must meet 1 of these 2 criteria: an ACT score of 21 or above OR class rank in the top third of their high school graduating class. AP and CLEP credits are accepted. Bachelor's degree programs require a minimum of 120 or more semester credit hours for completion. All undergraduates must complete 6 credit hours of expository writing and 2 credit hours of public speaking. Other requirements vary by college and program. **Procedure:** Freshmen are admitted to all sessions. Entrance exams should be taken in the junior and senior years. There is a rolling admissions plan. Application deadlines are open. The fall 2016 application fee was $30. Notification is sent on a rolling basis. Applications are accepted oline. **Transfer Students:** 1474 transfer students enrolled in 2015-2016. Applicants must have a minimum of 24 transfer credit hours and a college GPA of 2.0 or otherwise must meet freshman requirements. Students must submit official transcripts from previous colleges attended. 30 of 120 credits required for the bachelor's degree must be completed at K-State. **International Students:** There are 1269 international students enrolled. The school actively recruits these students. They must take the TOEFL with a minimum score of 550 on the paper-based TOEFL (PBT) or 79 on the Internet-based version (iBT), or present acceptable scores on the SAT or the ACT. Students must also take an English proficiency test given at the university.

ADMISSIONS: 95% of the 2016-2017 applicants were accepted. The ACT scores were 3% between 12 and 17, 37% between 18 and 23, 44% between 24 and 29, and 16% above 30. **Admissions Contact:** Larry Moeder, Assistant VP for Student Life/Director of Admissions & Financial Aid. Email: *k-state@k-state.edu* Web: *www.k-state.edu*

FINANCIAL AID: In 2016-2017, 84% of all full-time freshmen and 72% of continuing full-time students received some form of financial aid. 40% of all full-time freshmen and 42% of continuing full-time students received need-based aid. The average freshman award was $13,462. Need-based scholarships or need-based grants averaged $4,623 ($9,925 maximum); need-based self-help aid (loans and jobs) averaged $3,839 ($11,000 maximum); non-need-based athletic scholarships averaged $18,890 ($36,210 maximum); and other non-need-based awards and non-need-based scholarships averaged $6,869 ($40,154 maximum). The average financial indebtedness of the 2016 graduate was $24,993. K-State is a member of CSS. The FAFSA code is 001928. The priority date for freshman financial aid applications for fall entry is March 1.

KANSAS WESLEYAN UNIVERSITY D-2

www.kwu.edu

Salina, KS 67401	**(785) 827-5541** **(800) 874-1154**
Fax: (785) 827-0927	**Email: admissions@kwu.edu**
Full-time: 310 men, 380 women	**Faculty:** n/av
Part-time: 40 men, 70 women	**Ph.D.s:** n/av
Graduate: 45 men, 30 women	**Student/Faculty:** 14 to 1
Year: semesters, summer session	**Tuition:** $28,000
Room & Board: $8600	**Freshman Class:** n/av
SAT or ACT: required	**CEEB CODE:** 6337
Application Deadline: open	**COMPETITIVE**

Kansas Wesleyan University, founded in 1886, is affiliated with the United Methodist Church, and offers undergraduate programs in the arts and sciences, business, and education. The figures in the above capsule and in this profile are approximate. There are 3 undergraduate schools and 1 graduate school. In addition to regional accreditation, Kansas Wesleyan has baccalaureate program accreditation with NCATE and NLN. The 28-acre campus is in an urban area 85 miles north of Wichita. Including any residence halls, there are 12 buildings.

STUDENT LIFE: 61% of undergraduates are from Kansas. Others are from 14 states, 12 foreign countries, and Canada. 92% are from public schools. 85% are White; 7% African American; 3% Hispanic; 2% Asian American; 1% American Indian/Alaska Native. 48% are Protestant; 39% claim no religious affiliation; 13% Catholic. **Female To Male Ratio:** 1.2:1. The average age of freshmen is 20; all undergraduates, 24. 33% do not continue beyond their first year. **Housing:** 450 students can be accommodated in college housing, which includes single-sex dorms, on-campus apartments, and married student housing. On-campus housing is guaranteed for all 4 years. 65% of students live on campus; of those, 45% remain on campus on weekends. All students may keep cars. Alcohol is not permitted.

FACULTY/CLASSROOMS: All teach undergraduates, 65% do research, and 65% do both. No introductory courses are taught by graduate students. The average class size in an introductory lecture is 24; in a laboratory is 7; and in a regular course is 13.

PROGRAMS OF STUDY: Kansas Wesleyan confers B.A., B.S., and B.S.N. degrees. Associate and master's degrees are also awarded. Bachelor's degrees are awarded in BIOLOGICAL SCIENCE (biology/biological science), BUSINESS (accounting and business economics), COMMUNICATIONS AND THE ARTS (communications, dramatic arts, English, music, Spanish, speech/debate/rhetoric, and studio art), COMPUTER AND PHYSICAL SCIENCE (chemistry, computer science, mathematics, and physics), EDUCATION (art education, music education, physical education, secondary education, and special education), HEALTH PROFESSIONS (nursing), SOCIAL SCIENCE (addiction studies, criminal justice, history, prelaw, psychology, religion, religious education, and sociology). Premedicine, nursing, and preengineering are the strongest academically. Education, nursing, and business have the largest enrollments.

ACTIVITIES: There are no fraternities or sororities. There are 38 groups on campus, including art, band, cheerleading, choir, chorale, chorus, computers, dance, departmental clubs, drama, ethnic, film, honors, international, literary magazine, musical theater, newspaper, pep band, photography, professional, radio and TV, religious, social, social service, student government, and yearbook. Popular campus events include Lilac Fete, Sweetheart Dance, and Family Weekend. **Sports:** There are 7 intercollegiate sports for men and 7 for women, and 8 intramural sports for men and 6 for women. Facilities include a student activities center, a gym, a sand volleyball court, football practice and game fields, a multipurpose courtyard, a track and a weight room. **Graduates:** In an average class, 24% graduate in 4 years or less.

SERVICES: Counseling and information services are available, as is tutoring in most subjects. There is remedial reading and writing. **Library/Resources:** The library contains 76,621 volumes, 33,505 microform items, and 984 audio/video tapes/CDs/DVDs, and subscribes to 421 periodicals including electronic. Computerized library services include interlibrary loans, database searching, and Internet access. Special learning facilities include an art gallery, planetarium, radio station, and TV station. **Physically Challenged Students:** 90% of the campus is accessible. Facilities include wheelchair ramps, elevators, special parking, specially equipped restrooms, special class scheduling, lowered drinking fountains, and lowered telephones. **Special:** Cross-registration is available with other members of the Associated Colleges of Central Kansas and the Salina College Consortium. Cooperative degree programs are offered in agriculture, cytotechnology, engineering, environmental studies, and medical technology. Kansas Wesleyan also offers January interterm study trips throughout the United States and abroad, Washington, D.C., and UN semesters, internships, dual majors, student designed majors, credit for life experience, and nondegree study. A 3-2 engineering degree is offered with Columbia University and Washington University at St. Louis. There are 4 national honor societies and a freshman honors program. **Visiting:** There are regularly scheduled orientations for prospective students. There are guides for informal visits, visitors may sit in on classes, and stay overnight. To schedule a visit, contact the Admissions Office. **Campus Safety and Security:** Measures include self-defense education and security escort services, and lighted pathways/sidewalks, random security checks, and private service security guards.

REQUIREMENTS: The SAT or ACT is required. Applicants must be graduates of accredited secondary schools or have earned a GED. An interview is recommended. A GPA of 2.5 is required. AP and CLEP credits are accepted. Students must demonstrate proficiency in English and math and must fulfill distribution requirements in 15 liberal arts components, including environmental awareness, biblical heritage, and lifetime recreation. Courses in phys ed and computers are required. To graduate, students must complete at least 126 credit hours, including 30 to 40 in a major field of study, with a minimum GPA of 2.0. **Procedure:** Freshmen are admitted to all sessions. Entrance exams should be taken as early as possible. There are deferred admissions and rolling admissions plans. Application deadlines are open. The fall 2016 application fee was $20. Notification is sent on a rolling basis. **Transfer Students:** Transfers must submit transcripts from all colleges previously attended. Those students transferring fewer than 15 credit hours must submit ACT scores and a high school transcript. A minimum GPA of 2.0 is recommended. 63 of 126 credits required for the bachelor's degree must be completed at Kansas Wesleyan. **International Students:** The school actively recruits these students. They must take the TOEFL.

Admissions Contact: Esteban Paredes, Admissions Office. Email: *admissions@kwu.edu* Web: *www.kwu.edu*

FINANCIAL AID: In 2016-2017, 99% of all full-time freshmen received some form of financial aid. 99% of all full-time freshmen received need-based aid. The FAFSA code is 001929. Check with the school for current application deadlines.

MCPHERSON COLLEGE D-2

www.mcpherson.edu

McPherson, KS 67460	**(620) 241-0731** **(800) 365-7402**
Fax: (620) 241-8443	**Email: admiss@mcpherson.edu**
Full-time: 365 men, 234 women	**Faculty:** IIA
Part-time: 18 men, 15 women	**Ph.D.s:** 72%
Graduate: 5 men, 7 women	**Student/Faculty:** 14 to 1
Year: 4-1-4, summer session	**Tuition:** $26,498
Room & Board: $8411	**Freshman Class:** n/av
SAT or ACT: required	**CEEB CODE:** 6404
Application Deadline: August 1	**COMPETITIVE**

McPherson College, founded in 1887 and affiliated with the Church of the Brethren, is a private, institution offering undergraduate programs in the arts and sciences, business, and education. The figures in the above capsule and in this profile are approximate. There is 1 undergraduate school and 1 graduate school. In addition to regional accreditation, McPherson has baccalaureate program accreditation with NCATE. The 27-acre campus is in a small town in central Kansas, 50 miles north of Wichita. Including any residence halls, there are 16 buildings.

STUDENT LIFE: 53% of undergraduates are from Kansas. Others are from 29 states, and 2 foreign countries. 99% are from public schools. 80% are White; 6% Hispanic; 2% American Indian/Alaska Native; 13% African American; 1% Asian American; 1% Foreign. 43% claim no religious affiliation; 13% Catholic. **Male To Female Ratio:** 1.5:1. The average age of freshmen is 18; all undergraduates, 23. **Housing:** 392 students can be accommodated in college housing, which includes single-sex and coed dorms and on-campus apartments. On-campus housing is guaranteed for all 4 years. 79% of students live on campus; of those, 65% remain on campus on weekends. All students may keep cars. Alcohol is not permitted.

FACULTY/CLASSROOMS: 72% of faculty are male; 28% are female. All teach undergraduates. No introductory courses are taught by graduate students. The average class size in an introductory lecture is 30; in a laboratory is 12; and in a regular course is 15.

PROGRAMS OF STUDY: McPherson confers B.A., and B.S., degrees. Master's degrees are also awarded. Bachelor's degrees are awarded in BIOLOGICAL SCIENCE (biology/biological science), BUSINESS (business administration and management), COMMUNICATIONS AND THE ARTS (art, communications, dramatic arts, English, music, Spanish, and speech/debate/rhetoric), COMPUTER AND PHYSICAL SCIENCE (chemistry and mathematics), EDUCATION (elementary education, physical education, secondary education, and special education), SOCIAL SCIENCE (history, philosophy, psychology, religion, and sociology). Business, education, and technology have the largest enrollments.

ACTIVITIES: There are no fraternities or sororities. There are 18 groups on campus, including art, band, cheerleading, choir, chorus, computers, drama, ethnic, honors, international, LGBT, musical theater, newspaper, orchestra, pep band, professional, religious, social service, and student government. Popular campus events include Family Weekend. **Sports:** There are 5 intercollegiate sports for men and 6 for women, and 6 intramural sports for men and 6 for women. Facilities include a sports center with basketball/volleyball courts, a racquetball court, and a fitness center with weight-training room, football/track stadium, practice fields, and tennis courts. **Graduates:** From July 1, 2015 to June 30, 2016, 105 bachelor's degrees were awarded.

SERVICES: Counseling and information services are available, as is tutoring in most subjects, and remedial reading and writing. **Library/Resources:** The library contains 98,214 volumes, 60,799 microform items, 4,626 audio/video tapes/CDs/DVDs, and subscribes to 26,828 periodicals including electronic. Computerized library services include interlibrary loans, database searching, Internet access, and Wi-Fi capability. Special learning facilities include an art gallery, natural history museum, and an automobile restoration center. **Physically Challenged Students:** 95% of the campus is accessible. Facilities include wheelchair ramps, elevators, special parking, specially equipped restrooms, special class scheduling, lowered drinking fountains, and special housing. **Special:** Cross-registration with other colleges is available through the Associated Colleges of Central Kansas. McPherson also offers internships, study abroad in 10 countries, co-op programs, credit by exam, a general studies degree, student-designed majors, and pass/fail options. There are preprofessional programs in health, engineering, law, forestry, veterinary medicine, nursing and medicine, optometry, and dentistry. There are 3 national honor societies, Phi Beta Kappa, and 3 departmental honors programs. **Visiting:** There are regularly scheduled orientations for prospective students, consisting of campus tours, meetings with admissions personnel, and class attendance. There are guides for informal visits, visitors may sit in on classes, and stay overnight. To schedule a visit, contact the Admissions Office. **Campus Safety and Security:** Measures include an emergency notification system, emergency telephones and lighted pathways/sidewalks.

REQUIREMENTS: The SAT or ACT is required. The GED is accepted. A GPA of 2.0 is required. AP and CLEP credits are accepted. Important factors in the admissions decision are recommendations by school officials, evidence of special talent, and parents or siblings have attended the school. To graduate, students must complete 124 credits, including 32 in the major, with a GPA of 2.0. All students must fulfill general education requirements in the following areas: written and oral communication, aesthetics, history, society, natural sciences, technology and culture, and religion/beliefs/values. Students must also participate in an integrative seminar and a service experience, and must complete a global/intercultural experience, which may include intercultural studies courses or modern language courses. **Procedure:** Freshmen are admitted in the fall, winter, and spring. Entrance exams should be taken in the junior year of high school. There are deferred admissions and rolling admissions plans. Applications should be filed by August 1 for fall entry, along with a $25 fee. Notification is sent on a rolling basis. Applications are accepted online. **Transfer Students:** 288 transfer students enrolled in 2015-2016. Applicants must have satisfactorily completed 12 credit hours of college course work covering 3 academic areas with a 2.0 GPA. 32 of 124 credits required for the bachelor's degree must be completed at McPherson. **International Students:** There are 12 international students enrolled. They must take the TOEFL, as well as take the ACT.

Admissions Contact: Carol Williams, Director of Admissions and Financial Aid. Email: *admiss@mcpherson.edu* Web: *www.mcpherson.edu*

FINANCIAL AID: In 2016-2017, 99% of all full-time freshmen received some form of financial aid. 99% of all full-time freshmen received need-based aid. The FAFSA code is 001933. Check with the school for current application deadlines.

MIDAMERICA NAZARENE UNIVERSITY F-2

www.mnu.edu

Olathe, KS 66062	**(913) 791-3380** **(800) 800-8887**
Fax: (913) 791-3487	**Email: admissions@mnu.edu**
Full-time: 448 men, 553 women	**Faculty:** 67
Part-time: 107 men, 201 women	**Ph.D.s:** 64%
Graduate: 111 men, 456 women	**Student/Faculty:** 12 to 1
Year: semesters, summer session	**Tuition:** $27,650
Room & Board: $7900	**Freshman Class:** 1077 applied, 588 accepted, 176 enrolled
	CEEB CODE: 6437
Application Deadline: August 1	**COMPETITIVE**

MidAmerica Nazarene University, founded in 1966 as is a private liberal arts institution affiliated with the Church of the Nazarene. The figures in the above capsule and in this profile are approximate. Tuition cost varies by program chosen by student. There are 5 undergraduate schools and 4 graduate schools. In addition to regional accreditation, MNU has baccalaureate program accreditation with ACBSP, NASM, NCATE, NLN, HLC, CAATE, KSBE, CACREP, and CCNE. The 105-acre campus is in a suburban area 19 miles southwest of downtown Kansas City, Missouri. Including any residence halls, there are 22 buildings.

STUDENT LIFE: 58% of undergraduates are from Kansas. Others are from 42 states, 15 foreign countries, and Canada. 63% are White; 2% Asian American; 2% Hispanic; 2% two or more races; 16% race unknown; 13% African American; 1% American Indian/Alaska Native. 74% are Protestant; 19% Buddist, Islamic, and unknown. **Female To Male Ratio:** 1.8:1. The average age of freshmen is 18; all undergraduates, 18. 32% do not continue beyond their first year. **Housing:** 695 students can be accommodated in college housing, which includes single-sex dorms. On-campus housing is guaranteed for all 4 years. 59% of students live on campus; of those, 80% remain on campus on weekends. All students may keep cars. Alcohol is not permitted.

FACULTY/CLASSROOMS: 53% of faculty are male; 47% are female. No introductory courses are taught by graduate students.

PROGRAMS OF STUDY: MNU confers B.A., B.S., B.M.Ed., and B.S.N. degrees. Associate and master's degrees are also awarded. Bachelor's degrees are awarded in BIOLOGICAL SCIENCE (biology/gen sci/envir sci second ed), BUSINESS (accounting, business administration and management, international business management, marketing/retailing/merchandising, organizational leadership and management, recreation/leisure (community recreation), and sports management), COMMUNICATIONS AND THE ARTS (communications, English, graphic design, music, and speech and theatre education), COMPUTER AND PHYSICAL SCIENCE (chemistry, mathematics, and physics), EDUCATION (athletic training, elementary education, English education, health education, mathematics education, music education, physical education, science education, and social studies education), HEALTH PROFESSIONS (biology, kinesiology, and nursing), SOCIAL SCIENCE (criminal justice, cultural studies/critical theory & analysis, history, interdisciplinary studies, ministries, psychology, religious studies, sociology, and youth ministry). Nursing, and business are the strongest academically. Nursing, business administration, and behavioral science have the largest enrollments.

ACTIVITIES: There are no fraternities or sororities. There are 43 groups on campus, including cheerleading, choir, chorus, computers, drama, ethnic, honors, improv, international, jazz band, newspaper, orchestra, pep band, political, professional, psychology, radio and TV, religious, student government, writers, and yearbook. Popular campus events include White Light Event, Root Beer Fest, Homecoming Hoe Down, and Welcome Week. **Sports:** There are 7 intercollegiate sports for men and 7 for women, and 7 intramural sports for men and 7 for women. Facilities include a weight room, basketball/volleyball arena, a gym, track, tennis, sand volleyball courts, softball, baseball, and soccer fields. **Graduates:** From July 1, 2015 to June 30, 2016, 444 bachelor's degrees were awarded. The most popular majors were applied organizational leadership (52%), nursing (41%), and management and human relations (3%). In an average class, 43% graduate in 4 years or less, 53% graduate in 5 years or less, and 54% graduate in 6 years or less.

SERVICES: Counseling and information services are available, as is tutoring in most subjects, such as nursing, business, psychology, sociology, history, music, chemistry, biology, and physics. There is a reader service for the blind, and remedial math, reading, and writing. There are also test-taking accommodations, interpreters for the hearing impaired, and note takers for the blind, hearing impaired, and learning disabled. **Library/Resources:** The library contains 75,972 volumes, 1,315 audio/video tapes/CDs/DVDs, and subscribes to 228 periodicals including electronic. Computerized library services include interlibrary loans, database searching, Internet access, and Wi-Fi capability. Special learning facilities include a radio station and TV station. **Physically Challenged Students:** Facilities include wheelchair ramps, elevators, special parking, specially equipped restrooms, special class scheduling, and lowered drinking fountains. **Special:** Mid-America Nazarene University, offers nondegree study, cross-registration with the Christian College Coalition, study abroad in 4 countries, internships, and a Washington semester. There are accelerated degree programs in management and human relations and in nursing. There are 4 national honor societies, a freshman honors program, and 4 departmental honors programs. **Visiting:** There are regularly scheduled orientations for prospective students, including an academic fair, advising, class visitation, informational meetings, social activities, and experiencing residential life. There are guides for informal visits, visitors may sit in on classes, and stay overnight. To schedule a visit, contact The Office of Admissions. **Campus Safety and Security:** Measures include 24-hour foot and vehicle patrol, emergency notification system, self-defense education, and security escort services. There are emergency telephones, lighted pathways/sidewalks, and controlled access to dorms/residences.

REQUIREMENTS: Recommended composite score of 18 on the ACT or a satisfactory score on the SAT. Candidates for admission should be graduates of an accredited secondary school. The GED is accepted. Students should have completed 15 units of study, including 4 units of English and 3 each of natural science, social studies, and math. An essay is optional. AP and CLEP credits are accepted. All students must meet core curriculum requirements in humanities-communications, natural sciences-math, social sciences, religion-philosophy, and phys ed. Students must maintain a minimum GPA of 2.0 and complete 126 semester hours to graduate. **Procedure:** Freshmen are admitted to all sessions. Entrance exams should be taken during the senior year. There is a rolling admissions plan. Applications should be filed by August 1 for fall entry; January 1 for spring entry, along with a $25 fee. Applications are accepted online. **Transfer Students:** 116 transfer students enrolled in 2015-2016. Transfer applicants should have earned 24 or more hours at an accredited institution and not be on academic or disciplinary probation. ACT or SAT scores are required. 30 of 126 credits required for the bachelor's degree must be completed at MNU. **International Students:** There are 26 international students enrolled. The school actively recruits these students. They must take the TOEFL with a minimum score of 76 on the Internet-based version (iBT). The ACT and/or SAT must be taken where English is the official first language, as well as placement tests for incoming freshmen.

ADMISSIONS: 55% of the 2016-2017 applicants were accepted. The ACT scores were 1% below 12, 17% between 12 and 17, 48% between 18 and 23, 29% between 24 and 29, and 5% above 30. **Admissions Contact:** Derry Ebert, Vice President and Dean. Email: *admissions@mnu.edu* Web: *www.mnu.edu*

FINANCIAL AID: In 2016-2017, 98% of all full-time freshmen and 97% of continuing full-time students received some form of financial aid. 71% of all full-time freshmen and 73% of continuing full-time students received need-based aid. The average freshman award was $30,914. Need-based scholarships or need-based grants averaged $4,046 ($9,158 maximum); need-based self-help aid (loans and jobs) averaged $1,724 ($3,232 maximum); non-need-based athletic scholarships averaged $3,494 ($13,275 maximum); other non-need-based awards and non-need-based scholarships averaged $6,086 ($16,125 maximum); and $7,437 from other forms of aid. 11% of undergraduate students work part-time. Average annual earnings from campus work are $1296. The average financial indebtedness of the 2016 graduate was $29,569. The FAFSA code is 007032. The priority date for freshman financial aid applications for fall entry is March 1.

NEWMAN UNIVERSITY — D-3

www.newmanu.edu

Wichita, KS 67213	(316) 942-4291 (877) NEWMANU
Fax: (316) 942-4483	Email: admissions@newmanu.edu
Full-time: 394 men, 727 women	**Faculty:** 74
Part-time: 668 men, 1006 women	**Ph.D.s:** 61%
Graduate: 219 men, 722 women	**Student/Faculty:** 17 to 1
Year: semesters, summer session	**Tuition:** $27,716
Room & Board: $7674	**Freshman Class:** 2378 applied, 1050 accepted, 165 enrolled
SAT CR/M/W: 509/548/487 **ACT:** 24	**CEEB CODE:** 6615
Application Deadline: open	**COMPETITIVE**

Newman University, founded in 1933, is a private, liberal arts institution affiliated with the Roman Catholic Church, named for John Henry Cardinal Newman and founded by the Adorers of the Blood of Christ for the purpose of empowering graduates to transform society. Figures in the above capsule and in this profile are approximate. Tuition is based on 16 credit hours. There are 3 undergraduate schools and 3 graduate schools. In addition to regional accreditation, NU has baccalaureate program accreditation with CSWE, NCATE, ACOTE, CoARC, ARRT, KS Dept of Ed, CCNE, and COA. The 61-acre campus is in an urban area in Wichita west of downtown. Including any residence halls, there are 12 buildings.

STUDENT LIFE: 91% of undergraduates are from Kansas. Others are from 28 states, 30 foreign countries, and Canada. 54% are from public schools. 74% are White; 10% Hispanic; 5% Asian American; 4% African American; 2% American Indian/Alaska Native; 2% foreign; 2% two or more races; 1% race unknown. 59% are Catholic. **Female To Male Ratio:** 1.9:1. The average age of freshmen is 18; all undergraduates, 21. 24% do not continue beyond their first year; 52% remain to graduate. **Housing:** 406 students can be accommodated in college housing, which includes single-sex and coed dorms, on-campus apartments, married student housing, and special-interest houses. On-campus housing is guaranteed for the freshman year only, and is available on a first-come, and first-served basis. 75% of students commute. All students may keep cars. Alcohol is not permitted.

FACULTY/CLASSROOMS: 33% of faculty are male; 67% are female. 94% teach undergraduates, 25% do research, and 25% do both. No introductory courses are taught by graduate students. The average class size in an introductory lecture is 22; in a laboratory is 16; and in a regular course is 19.

PROGRAMS OF STUDY: NU confers B.A., B.B.A., B.S., and B.S.N. degrees. Associate and master's degrees are also awarded. Bachelor's degrees are awarded in BIOLOGICAL SCIENCE (biochemistry and biology/biological science), BUSINESS (accounting, business administration and management, and management information systems), COMMUNICATIONS AND THE ARTS (art, communications, English, and sports media), COMPUTER AND PHYSICAL SCIENCE (chemistry, information sciences and systems, and mathematics), EDUCATION (early childhood education, elementary education, and secondary education), HEALTH PROFESSIONS (health science, nursing, and ultrasound technology), SOCIAL SCIENCE (counseling/psychology, criminal justice, forensic studies, history, interdisciplinary studies, liberal arts/general studies, pastoral studies, philosophy, psychology, sociology, and theological studies). Nursing, allied health & pre-med, and biology are the strongest academically. Nursing, biology, and education have the largest enrollments.

ACTIVITIES: There are no fraternities or sororities. There are 26 groups on campus, including art, cheerleading, choir, chorale, chorus, communications, computers, dance, drama, environmental, ethnic, honors, international, literary magazine, musical theater, newspaper, pep band, photography, political, professional, religious, social, social service, and student government. Popular campus events include Family Weekend, Newman Week, Homecoming, Weeks of Welcome/Welcome Back Bash, and Gerber Institute Activities. **Sports:** There are 8 intercollegiate sports for men and 9 for women, and 10 intramural sports for men and 9 for women. Facilities include baseball and softball fields, soccer fields, a gym with a main basketball court, weight room, aerobics room, and wrestling room. **Graduates:** From July 1, 2015 to June 30, 2016, 266 bachelor's degrees were awarded. The most popular majors were nursing (18%), education (14%), and biology (11%). 48 companies recruited on campus in 2015-2016. In an average class, 36% graduate in 4 years or less and 52% graduate in 6 years or less. Of the 2015 graduating class, 17% were enrolled in graduate school within 6 months of graduation, and 76% were employed.

SERVICES: Counseling and information services are available, as is tutoring in most subjects, and a reader service for the blind, and remedial math and writing. **Library/Resources:** The library contains 90,129 volumes, 143,723 microform items, 2,300 audio/video tapes/CDs/DVDs, and subscribes to 7,015 periodicals including electronic. Computerized library services include interlibrary loans, database searching, Internet access, and Wi-Fi capability. Special learning facilities include an art gallery, an allied health and nursing labs, and ITV studio facilities. **Physically Challenged Students:** All of the campus is accessible. Facilities include wheelchair ramps, elevators, special parking, specially equipped restrooms, special class scheduling, and lowered drinking fountains. **Special:** Newman University offers co-op placements in most majors, internships, dual majors, and study abroad in England, Europe, and Latin America. Majors in counseling, business studies, education, RN to BSN, and interdisciplinary studies can be satisfied through evening, weekend and online classes. There are 11 national honor societies and a freshman honors program. **Visiting:** There are regularly scheduled orientations for prospective students, include meetings with faculty, athletic coaches, co-curricular sponsors, financial aid counselors, admissions counselors, and a tour of the campus. There are guides for informal visits, which visitors may sit in on classes, and stay overnight. To schedule a visit, contact Jann Reusser at (316) 942-4291 ext. 2144. **Campus Safety and Security:** Measures include 24-hour foot and vehicle patrol, emergency notification system, self-defense education, and security escort services, as well as emergency telephones, lighted pathways/sidewalks, and controlled access to dorms/residences.

REQUIREMENTS: Requirements needed are a cumulative grade point average of at least 2.0 on a 4.0 scale or an average GED score of 450 with no individual score below 410, ACT composite score of 18 or a combined verbal, math and writing SAT score of 1290. The recommended high school curriculum is 4 units English, 3 unit math, 3 units science and 3 units social science. A GPA of 2.0 is required. AP and CLEP credits are accepted. Important factors in the admissions decision are leadership record, advanced placement or honors courses, evidence of special talent, personality/intangible qualities, recommendations by alumni, recommendations by school officials, ability to finance college education, parents or siblings attended your school, extracurricular activities record, and geographical diversity. Degree requirements include completion of 124 credit hours, 40 of which must be upper division and 30 resident. The number of credits required in the major varies. A minimum GPA of 2.0 is required for graduation, and students must fulfill the university's Newman Studies Program requirements which include skills, general education and core courses. **Procedure:** Freshmen are admitted fall, spring, and summer. Entrance exams should be taken during the spring of the junior year or fall of the senior year. There are deferred admissions and rolling admissions plans. Application deadlines are open. Application fee is $20. Notification is sent on a rolling basis. Applications are accepted on-line. Application fees are waived if application is completed on-line. **Transfer Students:** 309 transfer students enrolled in 2015-2016. A minimum GPA of 2.0 is required. 30 of 124 credits required for the bachelor's degree must be completed at NU. **International Students:** There are 73 international students enrolled. They must take the TOEFL with a minimum score of 530 on the paper-based TOEFL (PBT) or 74 on the Internet-based version (iBT).

ADMISSIONS: 45% of the current freshmen were in the top fifth of their class; 68% were in the top two fifths. 10 freshmen graduated first in their class. **Admissions Contact:** Kristen English, Director of Undergraduate Admissions. Email: *admissions@newmanu.edu* Web: *www.newmanu.edu*

FINANCIAL AID: In 2016-2017, 99% of all full-time freshmen and 94% of continuing full-time students received some form of financial aid. 68% of all full-time freshmen and continuing full-time students received need-based aid. The average freshman award was $11,344. Need-based scholarships or need-based grants averaged $2,777 ($6,448 maximum); need-based self-help aid (loans and jobs) averaged $1,574 ($2,750 maximum); non-need-based athletic scholarships averaged $3,870 ($10,714 maximum); and other non-need-based awards and non-need-based scholarships averaged $9,641 ($17,863 maximum). 10% of undergraduate students work part-time. Average annual earnings from campus work are $1748. The average financial indebtedness of the 2016 graduate was $25,936. The FAFSA code is 001939. The priority date for freshman financial aid applications for fall entry is March 1.

OTTAWA UNIVERSITY — E-2

www.ottawa.edu

Ottawa, KS 66067	(785) 242-5200, ext. 5555 (800) 755-5200
Fax: (785) 229-1008	Email: admiss@ottawa.edu
Full-time: 350 men, 200 women	**Faculty:** IIB, -$
Part-time: 15 men, 20 women	**Ph.D.s:** n/av
Graduate: n/av	**Student/Faculty:** n/av
Year: semesters, summer session	**Tuition:** $26,724
Room & Board: $9350	**Freshman Class:** n/av
ACT: required	**CEEB CODE:** 6547
Application Deadline: open	**VERY COMPETITIVE**

Ottawa University, founded in 1865 and affiliated with the American Baptist Churches, is a private institution offering programs through the divisions of arts and humanities, natural sciences, and social and behavioral sciences. The figures in the above capsule and in this profile are approximate. There is 1 undergraduate school. The 64-acre campus is in a small town 45 miles southwest of Kansas City. Including any residence halls, there are 15 buildings.

STUDENT LIFE: 55% of undergraduates are from Kansas. Others are from 18 states, 5 foreign countries, and Canada. 99% are from public schools. 77% are White; 7% foreign; 4% Hispanic; 2% American Indian/Alaska Native; 11% African American; 1% Asian American. 64% are Protestant; 20% claim no religious affiliation; 13% Catholic. **Male To Female Ratio:** 1.7:1. The average age of freshmen is 19; all undergraduates, 22. 25% do not continue beyond their first year; 30% remain to graduate. **Housing:** 428 students can be accommodated in college housing, which includes single-sex dorms, on-campus apartments, and married student housing. On-campus housing is guaranteed for all 4 years. 58% of students live on campus; of those, 65% remain on campus on weekends. All students may keep cars. Alcohol is not permitted.

FACULTY/CLASSROOMS: 60% of faculty are male; 40% are female. All teach undergraduates. No introductory courses are taught by graduate students. The average class size in a laboratory is 12.

PROGRAMS OF STUDY: OU confers B.A. degrees. Bachelor's degrees are awarded in BIOLOGICAL SCIENCE (biology/biological science), BUSINESS (accounting, business administration and management, and management information systems), COMMUNICATIONS AND THE ARTS (art, communications, dramatic arts, English, and music), COMPUTER AND PHYSICAL SCIENCE (chemistry, information sciences and systems, and mathematics), EDUCATION (elementary education and physical education), SOCIAL SCIENCE (history, human services, political science/government, psychology, religion, and sociology). English, business, and math are the strongest academically. Business, teacher education, and human services have the largest enrollments.

ACTIVITIES: There are no fraternities or sororities. There are 35 groups on campus, including cheerleading, choir, chorale, chorus, computers, dance, debate, drama, ethnic, forensics, honors, international, jazz band, musical theater, newspaper, orchestra, pep band, photography, professional, radio and TV, religious, social, social service, student government, and yearbook. Popular campus events include Family Day, Charter Day, and Christmas Feast. **Sports:** There are 7 intercollegiate sports for men and 7 for women, and 12 intramural sports for men and 12 for women. Facilities include a field, a sports complex, an athletic center, and a gym with a wellness center. Men's sports include baseball, basketball, cross country, football, golf, lacrosse, soccer, tennis, track & field, volleyball, and wrestling. Women's sports include basketball, cross-country, golf, lacrosse, soccer, softball, tennis, track & field, volleyball, and wrestling.

SERVICES: Counseling and information services are available, as is tutoring in most subjects, and remedial math, reading, and writing. **Library/Resources:** The library contains 90,000 volumes, and subscribes to 400 periodicals including electronic. Computerized library services include interlibrary loans and database searching. Special learning facilities include an art gallery, and radio station. **Physically Challenged Students:** 50% of the campus is accessible. Facilities include wheelchair ramps, elevators, special parking, specially equipped restrooms, and special class scheduling. **Special:** Internships are available, especially in business, human services, and teacher education. Student-designed majors are an option. 3/2 engineering degrees with Kansas state and the University of Kansas, 3 +1 degree in medical technology, and preprofessional programs in premedicine, predentistry, prelaw, and preministry are available. Work-study programs are also offered. There are 2 national honor societies. **Visiting:** There are regularly scheduled orientations for prospective students, including Discovery Day in the early spring, which gives prospective students a chance to meet faculty, students, and staff and to learn more about Ottawa University, the admissions process, and financial aid. There are guides for informal visits, visitors may sit in on classes, and stay overnight. To schedule a visit, contact the Admissions Office. **Campus Safety and Security:** Measures include self-defense education, security escort services, and lighted pathways/sidewalks, controlled access to dorms/residences, and a nighttime security guard.

REQUIREMENTS: The ACT is required. The GED is accepted. There are no specific high school courses required, but a sound college preparatory curriculum is highly recommended. A GPA of 2.5 is required. AP and CLEP credits are accepted. Important factors in the admissions decision are parents or siblings attended your school, recommendations by alumni, and recommendations by school officials. To graduate, students must complete 9 courses in 8 academic areas with a minimum GPA of 2.0. The university requires students to complete 124 semester hours, with 24 to 40 in the major. Three interdisciplinary general education seminars must be completed. In addition, students must attend 10 University Program events each semester for 6 semesters. **Procedure:** Freshmen are admitted to all sessions. Entrance exams should be taken as early as possible. There is a rolling admissions plan. Application deadlines are open. The fall 2016 application fee was $15. **Transfer Students:** Transfer applicants must submit transcripts from all colleges attended and must have a 2.0 GPA and 12 hours of college credit, or else they must meet freshman requirements. 30 of 124 credits required for the bachelor's degree must be completed at OU. **International Students:** The school actively recruits these students. They must take the TOEFL or MELAB.

Admissions Contact: Tim Albers, Director of Admissions. Email: *admiss@ottawa.edu* Web: *www.ottawa.edu*

FINANCIAL AID: The college's own financial statement is required. The FAFSA code is 001937. Check with the school for current application deadlines.

PITTSBURG STATE UNIVERSITY *(The complete profile is made available exclusively on our website, www.barronspac.com)*

SOUTHWESTERN COLLEGE — D-3
www.sckans.edu

Winfield, KS 67156	(620) 229-6364 (800) 846-1543 x 6236
Fax: (620) 229-6344	**Email:** scadmit@sckans.edu
Full-time: 247 men, 256 women	**Faculty:** 45; IIB, --$
Part-time: 13 men, 6 women	**Ph.D.s:** 71%
Graduate: 25 men, 35 women	**Student/Faculty:** 12 to 1
Year: semesters, summer session	**Tuition:** $24,685
Room & Board: $6846	**Freshman Class:** 339 applied, 298 accepted, 148 enrolled
SAT CR/M/W: required **ACT:** 22	**CEEB CODE:** 6670
Application Deadline: August 1	**COMPETITIVE**

Southwestern College, established in 1885, is a private institution affiliated with the Kansas West Conference of the United Methodist Church. Figures in the above capsule and in this profile are approximate. There are 2 undergraduate schools. In addition to regional accreditation, Southwestern has baccalaureate program accreditation with CSWE, NASM, NCATE, CAATE, CCNE, and NAEYC. The 82-acre campus is in a small town in Winfield, Kansas, 40 miles from Wichita. Including any residence halls, there are 20 buildings.

STUDENT LIFE: 59% of undergraduates are from Kansas. Others are from 25 states, and 10 foreign countries. 9% are African American; 8% Hispanic; 7% Foreign; 66% White; 3% American Indian/Alaska Native; 1% Asian American. 36% claim no religious affiliation; 31% Protestant; 11% Catholic. **Female To Male Ratio:** 1.0:1. The average age of freshmen is 19; all undergraduates, 21. 40% do not continue beyond their first year; 51% remain to graduate. **Housing:** 625 students can be accommodated in college housing, which includes single-sex and coed dorms, on-campus apartments, married student housing, and honors houses. On-campus housing is guaranteed for the freshman year only, and is available on a first-come, and first-served basis. 71% of students live on campus; of those, 42% remain on campus on weekends. All students may keep cars. Alcohol is not permitted.

FACULTY/CLASSROOMS: 51% of faculty are male; 49% are female. All teach undergraduates. No introductory courses are taught by graduate students. The average class size in an introductory lecture is 16; in a laboratory is 10; and in a regular course is 7.

PROGRAMS OF STUDY: Southwestern confers B.A., B.S., B.G.S., B.Mus., and B.Ph. degrees. Master's and doctoral degrees are also awarded. Bachelor's degrees are awarded in BIOLOGICAL SCIENCE (biochemistry, biology/biological science, and marine biology), BUSINESS (accounting, business administration and management, business communications, and sports management), COMMUNICATIONS AND THE ARTS (communications, dramatic arts, English, music, music performance, speech and theatre education, speech and theatre education, and theatre arts), COMPUTER AND PHYSICAL SCIENCE (chemistry, computer science, digital arts/technology, and mathematics), EDUCATION (athletic training, drama education, early childhood education, elementary education, mathematics education, music education, physical education, secondary education, secondary education, and sports and wellness studies), ENGINEERING AND ENVIRONMENTAL DESIGN (chemical engineering and engineering physics), SOCIAL SCIENCE (history, interdisciplinary studies, liberal arts/general studies, philosophy and religion, and psychology). Biology, business administration, and education have the largest enrollments.

ACTIVITIES: There are 33 groups on campus, including band, cheerleading, choir, chorus, computers, dance, discipleship club, drama, environmental, ethnic, film, honors, green team, international, jazz band, leadership, literary magazine, musical theater, newspaper, orchestra, pep band, photography, political, professional, radio and TV, religious, social, student government, symphony, and yearbook. Popular campus events include Movie Nights, Spring Formal, and Stau Bau. **Sports:** There are 7 intercollegiate sports for men and 8 for women, and 4 intramural sports for men and 4 for women. Facilities include a stadium, tennis and basketball courts, volleyball, softball, playing floors, exercise rooms, a gym, indoor swimming pool, track and field, cross country, soccer field, a weight room, and frisbee golf course. **Graduates:** From July 1, 2015 to June 30, 2016, 137 bachelor's degrees were awarded. The most popular majors were nursing (10%), biology (8%), and psychology (7%). In an average class, 1% graduate in 3 years or less, 41% graduate in 4 years or less, 50% graduate in 5 years or less, and 51% graduate in 6 years or less. Of the 2015 graduating class, 39% were enrolled in graduate school within 6 months of graduation, and 39% were employed.

SERVICES: Counseling and information services are available, as is tutoring in every subject, and remedial math, reading, and writing. A reader service is available for dyslexic students. **Library/Resources:** The library contains 68,081 volumes, 192 microform items, 9,758 audio/video tapes/CDs/DVDs, and subscribes to 26,372 periodicals including electronic. Computerized library services include interlibrary loans, database searching, Internet access, and Wi-Fi capability. Special learning facilities include an art gallery, radio station, TV station, and biological field station. **Physically Challenged Students:** 80% of the campus is accessible. Facilities include wheelchair ramps, elevators, special parking, specially equipped restrooms, special class scheduling, lowered drinking fountains, and lowered telephones. **Special:** Southwestern offers internships in industry and social and civic agencies and a Washington semester through The Institute for Experiential Learning. Exchange programs are available. Combinations or degrees are possible with approval from the Academic Affairs Committee. Work-study programs, nondegree study, and pass/fail options are also available. There are 3 national honor societies, a freshman honors program, and 2 departmental honors programs. **Visiting:** There are regularly scheduled orientations for prospective students, including 4 Explore More events. There are also guides for informal visits, visitors may sit in on classes, and stay overnight. To schedule a visit, contact the Admissions Office. **Campus Safety and Security:** Measures include 24-hour foot and vehicle patrol, emergency notification system, self-defense education, and security escort services, lighted pathways/sidewalks, and controlled access to dorms/residences.

REQUIREMENTS: The ACT is required. The SAT is recommended. All candidates for admission must graduate from an accredited secondary school with a specified college-bound curriculum. The GED is accepted and an essay is required. Interviews are recommended. A GPA of 2.5 is required. AP and CLEP credits are accepted. To graduate, students must earn 124 credits, fulfill all requirements of the major, and maintain a GPA of 2.0. Students must complete the general education requirements. **Procedure:** Freshmen are admitted in the fall, spring, and summer. There is a rolling admissions plan. Applications should be filed by August 1 for fall entry; January 1 for spring entry, along with a $25 fee. Applications are accepted online. **Transfer Students:** 79 transfer students enrolled in 2015-2016. Applicants must have a college GPA of 2.0 and must submit an essay. 30 of 124 credits required for the bachelor's degree must be completed at Southwestern. **International Students:** There are 31 international students enrolled. The school actively recruits these students. They must take the TOEFL with a minimum score of 550 on the paper-based TOEFL (PBT) or 80 on the Internet-based version (iBT).

ADMISSIONS: 88% of the 2016-2017 applicants were accepted. The SAT scores for the 2016-2017 freshman class were: Critical Reading-- 69% below 500, 25% between 500 and 599, 3% between 600 and 699, and 3% between 700 and 800. Math-- 61% below 500, 29% between 500 and 599, 7% between 600 and 699, and 3% between 700 and 800. Writing-- 75% below 500, 22% between 500 and 599, and 3% between 600 and 699. The ACT scores were 31% below 12, 29% between 12 and 17, 27% between 18 and 23, 9% between 24 and 29, and 4% above 30. 34% of the current freshmen were in the top fifth of their class; 70% were in the top two fifths. 8 freshmen graduated first in their class. **Admissions Contact:** Marla Sexson, Vice President for Enrollment Management. Email: *marla.sexson@sckans.edu* Web: *www.sckans.edu*

FINANCIAL AID: In 2016-2017, 100% of all full-time freshmen received some form of financial aid, and need-based aid. The average freshman award was $25,059. Need-based scholarships or need-based grants averaged $5,809 ($9,550 maximum); need-based self-help aid (loans and jobs) averaged $4,894 ($9,000 maximum); non-need-based athletic scholarships averaged $4,000 ($4,000 maximum); and other non-need-based awards and non-need-based scholarships averaged $8,124 ($13,500 maximum). Average annual earnings from campus work are $1400. The average financial indebtedness of the 2016 graduate was $34,056. The college's own financial statement is required. The FAFSA code is 001940. Check with the school for current application deadlines.

STERLING COLLEGE — C-3

www.sterling.edu

Sterling, KS 67579 — (620) 278-4275, (800) 346-1017

Fax: (620) 278-4416 — Email: admissions@sterling.edu

Full-time: 297 men, 249 women	**Faculty:** 38
Part-time: 45 men, 51 women	**Ph.D.s:** 53%
Graduate: n/av	**Student/Faculty:** 14 to 1
Year: 4-1-4, summer session	**Tuition:** $24,250
Room & Board: $8580	**Freshman Class:** 821 applied, 414 accepted, 149 enrolled
SAT CR/M/W: required **ACT:** 21	**CEEB CODE:** 6684
Application Deadline: April 1	**COMPETITIVE**

Sterling College, established in 1887, is a private liberal arts institution with a historical affiliation with the Presbyterian Church, offering undergraduate curricula in over 90 programs including teacher preparation. There is 1 undergraduate school. In addition to regional accreditation, Sterling has baccalaureate program accreditation with NCATE, CAATE, and NCATE. The 43-acre campus is in a rural area 70 miles northwest of Wichita. Including any residence halls, there are 19 buildings.

STUDENT LIFE: 51% of undergraduates are from out of state, mostly the Midwest. Students are from 32 states, 9 foreign countries, and Canada. 85% are from public schools. 71% are White; 3% American Indian/Alaska Native; 12% African American; 12% Hispanic; 1% Asian American; 1% Foreign. 46% are Protestant; 43% claim no religious affiliation; 11% Catholic. **Male To Female Ratio:** 1.1:1. The average age of freshmen is 18; all undergraduates, 20. 35% do not continue beyond their first year; 46% remain to graduate. **Housing:** 589 students can be accommodated in college housing, which includes single-sex dorms. On-campus housing is guaranteed for all 4 years. All students may keep cars. Alcohol is not permitted.

FACULTY/CLASSROOMS: 71% of faculty are male; 29% are female. All teach undergraduates, 30% do research, and 30% do both. No introductory courses are taught by graduate students. The average class size in an introductory lecture is 40; in a laboratory is 25; and in a regular course is 20.

PROGRAMS OF STUDY: Sterling confers B.A., and B.S. degrees. Bachelor's degrees are awarded in BIOLOGICAL SCIENCE (biology/biological science), BUSINESS (business administration and management and sports management), COMMUNICATIONS AND THE ARTS (art, art and design, communications, creative writing, dramatic arts, English, media arts, music, and theatre arts), COMPUTER AND PHYSICAL SCIENCE (chemistry and mathematics), EDUCATION (athletic training, elementary education, and music education), HEALTH PROFESSIONS (exercise science and health science), SOCIAL SCIENCE (behavioral science, biblical studies, Christian studies, criminal justice, history, interdisciplinary studies, psychology, religious education, and theological studies). Business administration, education, and exercise science have the largest enrollments.

ACTIVITIES: There are no fraternities or sororities. There are 23 groups on campus, including art, band, cheerleading, chess, choir, chorale, dance, debate, drama, ethnic, forensics, honors, jazz band, literary magazine, musical theater, newspaper, pep band, photography, political, professional, radio and TV, religious, social, social service, student government, and yearbook. Popular campus events include Mission Trips, Last Blast (end of year party), and Fall Musical and Theater Productions. **Sports:** There are 6 intercollegiate sports for men and 6 for women, and 6 intramural sports for men and 6 for women. Facilities include a weight-training facility, exercise deck, swimming pool, track, football field and stadium, baseball diamond, soccer field, practice fields, basketball and tennis courts, sand volleyball, outdoor basketball, and horseshoe pits. **Graduates:** From July 1, 2015 to June 30, 2016, 131 bachelor's degrees were awarded. In an average class, 42% graduate in 4 years or less, 48% graduate in 5 years or less, and 49% graduate in 6 years or less.

SERVICES: Counseling and information services are available, as is tutoring in most subjects, and remedial writing. Special accommodations are provided to students on an as-needed basis. **Library/Resources:** The library contains 61,430 volumes, 2,120 microform items, and 2,125 audio/video tapes/CDs/DVDs, and subscribes to 846 periodicals including electronic. Computerized library services include interlibrary loans, database searching, and Internet access. Special learning facilities include an art gallery, radio station, a museum, and a theater. **Physically Challenged Students:** 88% of the campus is accessible. Facilities include wheelchair ramps, elevators, special parking, specially equipped restrooms, and special class scheduling. **Special:** Sterling offers cross-registration with the Associated Colleges of Central Kansas and the Council of Christian Colleges and Universities. Internships are available in most majors, as is study abroad in 7 countries. A Washington semester and work-study programs are offered. Student-designed majors and a dual degree program in biology and medical technology with Wichita State University are possible. There are 3 national honor societies. **Visiting:** There are regularly scheduled orientations for prospective students, including visits with admissions, financial aid, current students, and faculty and campus and housing tours. There are guides for informal visits, visitors may sit in on classes, and stay overnight. To schedule a visit, contact the Admissions Office. **Campus Safety and Security:** Measures include emergency notification system. There are lighted pathways/sidewalks, controlled access to dorms/residences, evening foot and vehicle patrol.

REQUIREMENTS: The SAT or ACT is required. Applicants must graduate from an accredited secondary school or have a GED. An interview is recommended. AP and CLEP credits are accepted. Important factors in the admissions decision are personality/intangible qualities, extracurricular activities record, and leadership record. To graduate, students must complete 52 to 57 credits in a general education curriculum, including writing, math, science, social science, philosophy, fine arts, and religion. They must have an overall GPA of 2.0, with 2.5 in the major. (Higher for Education Licensure students.) A total of 124 credits must be earned, with 45 to 60 in the major. Chapel/convocation requirements must also be met. **Procedure:** Freshmen are admitted in the fall and spring. Entrance exams should be taken in the spring of the junior year. There are early admissions, deferred admissions, and rolling admissions plans. Application deadlines are open. Application fee is $25. Notification of early decision is sent December 1; regular decision, on a rolling basis. Applications are accepted online. **Transfer Students:** 57 transfer students enrolled in 2015-2016. Transfer students must have a minimum composite ACT score of 18 or a satisfactory SAT score if they have fewer than 12 hours of college credit; and a 2.2 GPA. 24 of 124 credits required for the bachelor's degree must be completed at Sterling. **International Students:** There are 11 international students enrolled. They must take the TOEFL with a minimum score of 525 on the paper-based TOEFL (PBT) or 70 on the Internet-based version (iBT). They must also take the SAT or ACT.

ADMISSIONS: 50% of the 2016-2017 applicants were accepted. The SAT scores for the 2016-2017 freshman class were: Critical Reading-- 73% below 500, 23% between 500 and 599, and 4% between 600 and 699. Math-- 65% below 500, 31% between 500 and 599, and 4% between 600 and 699. Writing-- 77% below 500, 15% between 500 and 599, and 8% between 600 and 699. The ACT scores were 37% below 12, 31% between 12 and 17, 20% between 18 and 23, 5% between 24 and 29, and 7% above 30. 19% of the current freshmen were in the top fifth of their class; 49% were in the top two fifths. 4 freshmen graduated first in their class. **Admissions Contact:** Dennis Dutton, VP for Enrollment Services. Email: *admissions@sterling.edu* Web: *www.sterling.edu*

FINANCIAL AID: Average annual earnings from campus work are $1200. The FAFSA code is 001945. The deadline for filing freshman financial aid applications for fall entry is April 1.

TABOR COLLEGE — D-2
www.tabor.edu

Hillsboro, KS 67063	(620) 947-3121 (800) TABOR-99
Fax: (620) 947-6276	Email: admissions@tabor.edu
Full-time: 307 men, 216 women	Faculty: 36
Part-time: 52 men, 95 women	Ph.D.s: 21%
Graduate: 28 men, 29 women	Student/Faculty: 12 to 1
Year: 4-1-4	Tuition: $26,590
Room & Board: $9280	Freshman Class: 836 applied, 442 accepted, 203 enrolled
ACT: 21	CEEB CODE: 6815
Application Deadline: August 1	COMPETITIVE

Tabor College, established in 1908, is a private liberal arts facility affiliated with the Mennonite Brethren Church. The mission of Tabor College is to prepare people for a life of learning, work and service for Christ and His Kingdom. The vision of Tabor College is to be the college of choice for students who seek a life-transforming, academically excellent, globally relevant, and decidedly Christian education. There is 1 undergraduate school and 1 graduate school. In addition to regional accreditation, Tabor has baccalaureate program accreditation with CSWE, NASM, NCATE, CCNE, and CAATE. The 86-acre campus is in a small town is located in Hillsboro, Kansas, about 50 miles north of Wichita. Including any residence halls, there are 43 buildings.

STUDENT LIFE: 55% of undergraduates are from out of state, mostly the West. Students are from 32 states, 14 foreign countries, and Canada. 9% are African American; 67% White; 4% foreign; 4% two or more races; 3% race unknown; 12% Hispanic; 1% American Indian/Alaska Native. 64% are Protestant; 24% claim no religious affiliation. **Male To Female Ratio:** 1.1:1. The average age of freshmen is 18; all undergraduates, 23. 38% do not continue beyond their first year; 48% remain to graduate. **Housing:** 590 students can be accommodated in college housing, which includes single-sex dorms and off-campus apartments, and theme housing. On-campus housing is guaranteed for all 4 years. 86% of students live on campus; of those, 90% remain on campus on weekends. All students may keep cars. Alcohol is not permitted.

FACULTY/CLASSROOMS: 47% of faculty are male; 53% are female. 87% teach undergraduates. No introductory courses are taught by graduate students. The average class size in an introductory lecture is 22; in a laboratory is 14; and in a regular course is 13.

PROGRAMS OF STUDY: Tabor confers B.A., B.S., and B.S.N degrees. Associate and master's degrees are also awarded. Bachelor's degrees are awarded in BIOLOGICAL SCIENCE (biochemistry and biology/biological science), BUSINESS (accounting and business administration and management), COMMUNICATIONS AND THE ARTS (applied art, communications, English, graphic design, music, studio art, and theatre arts), COMPUTER AND PHYSICAL SCIENCE (chemistry and mathematics), EDUCATION (athletic training, educational studies, elementary education, general studies, health education, music education, physical education, physical education/exercise science, physical ed teacher education, and secondary education), HEALTH PROFESSIONS (nursing), SOCIAL SCIENCE (behavioral science, biblical studies, Christian studies, criminal justice, history, international studies, liberal arts/general studies, ministries, psychology, religion, and social work). Science, business, and education are the strongest academically. Elementary education, psychology, and business have the largest enrollments.

ACTIVITIES: There are no fraternities or sororities. There are 18 groups on campus, including art, band, campus ministries, science, cheerleading, choir, chorale, chorus, computers, drama, drill team, ethnic, honors, international, jazz band, math and business clubs, musical theater, newspaper, pep band, photography, religious, social, social service, student government, and yearbook. Popular campus events include Service Emphasis Week, Mission Emphasis Week, Taborstock, Sadie Hawkins Event, and Winter Banquet. **Sports:** There are 9 intercollegiate sports for men and 9 for women, and 8 intramural sports for men and 8 for women. Facilities include a campus recreation center and an athletic stadium, lighted tennis courts, racquetball courts, lighted football and baseball fields, several practice fields, soccer field, curbed metric all-weather track, a gym with playing floors, practice/intramural gym, indoor soccer court, aerobic exercise, athletic training, and weight rooms. **Graduates:** The most popular majors were business (13%), psychology (9%), and elementary education (8%). 10 companies recruited on campus in 2015-2016. In an average class, 80% graduate in 4 years or less, 11% graduate in 5 years or less, and 9% graduate in 6 years or less.

SERVICES: Counseling and information services are available, as is tutoring in most subjects. Tutoring in writing is available for all students through the campus writing center. Student Support Services serves students who need additional academic support. Life-skills courses and individualized help sessions are also available. **Library/Resources:** The library contains 61,171 volumes, 435 microform items, and 1,640 audio/video tapes/CDs/DVDs, and subscribes to 21 periodicals including electronic. Computerized library services include interlibrary loans, database searching, Internet access, and Wi-Fi capability. **Physically Challenged Students:** 75% of the campus is accessible. Facilities include wheelchair ramps, elevators, special parking, and specially equipped restrooms. **Special:** Cross-registration is offered within the Associated Colleges of Central Kansas. Dual majors, student-designed majors, internships, and semester-long study-abroad opportunities are available. There is a freshman honors program and 1 departmental honors program. **Visiting:** There are regularly scheduled orientations for prospective students, visits include a campus tour, admissions interview, and faculty, class, and financial aid visits. If requested, an audition or tryout will be scheduled. There are guides for informal visits, visitors may sit in on classes, and stay overnight. To schedule a visit, contact Brenda Hamm at brendah@tabor.edu. **Campus Safety and Security:** Measures include an emergency notification system, and lighted pathways/sidewalks. Active-Shooter Training is also provided to all students and staff.

REQUIREMENTS: Applicants with an ACT/GPA product of 45 or above and a minimum ACT composite score of 18 (SAT score of 860 if taken before March 2016, or 940 if taken March 2016 or later, based on Evidence-Based Reading/Writing and Mathematics Composite scores) will be considered for Admission to Tabor College. AP and CLEP credits are accepted. Tabor College has Core Curriculum requirements which include Tabor Distinctives, courses which must be taken at Tabor College. Students must complete 124 degree-applicable credit hours to graduate, of which the last 33 hours must be completed through Tabor. Credit-hours per major must be met as well as a minimum GPA of 2.0

in all required courses; individual majors may require a higher GPA in content-specific coursework. For more detailed information visit www.tabor.edu **Procedure:** Freshmen are admitted to all sessions. Entrance exams should be taken early in senior year of high school. There is a rolling admissions plan. Applications should be filed by August 1 for fall entry, along with a $50 fee. Application fees are waived if application is completed online. **Transfer Students:** 119 transfer students enrolled in 2015-2016. A minimum 2.0 GPA is required and an interview is recommended. 33 of 124 credits required for the bachelor's degree must be completed at Tabor. **International Students:** There are 29 international students enrolled. They must take the TOEFL with a minimum score of 525 on the paper-based TOEFL (PBT) or 70 on the Internet-based version (iBT). They must also take the SAT or ACT.

Admissions Contact: Kelly Dugger, Interim Director of Admissions. Email: *admissions@tabor.edu* Web: *www.tabor.edu*

FINANCIAL AID: The FAFSA code is 001946. Check with the school for current application deadlines.

UNIVERSITY OF KANSAS — E-2

www.ku.edu

Lawrence, KS 66045	(785) 864-3911
Fax: (785) 864-5017	Email: adm@ku.edu
Full-time: 8468 men, 8673 women	**Faculty:** 1404; I, -$
Part-time: 987 men, 1134 women	**Ph.D.s:** 90%
Graduate: 3577 men, 4726 women	**Student/Faculty:** 13 to 1
Year: semesters, summer session	**Tuition:** $10,549 ($25,932)
Room & Board: $9586	**Freshman Class:** 15015 applied, 13965 accepted, 4233 enrolled
ACT: 26	**CEEB CODE:** 6871
Application Deadline: n/av	**COMPETITIVE+**

University of Kansas, founded in 1865, is a public, comprehensive research institution. Its undergraduate and graduate programs emphasize the liberal arts, architecture, business, engineering, fine arts, health professions, journalism, law, medicine, music, nursing, pharmacy, social welfare, and teacher preparation. KU is a member of the highly prestigious Association of American Universities and has a national cancer institute designation. There are 11 undergraduate schools and 3 graduate schools. In addition to regional accreditation, KU has baccalaureate program accreditation with AACSB, ABET, ACEJMC, ACPE, CSWE, NAAB, NASAD, NASM, NCATE, CAAHEP, CAHIIM, CoARC, CCNE, NAACLS, ACOTE, AMTA, caATe, and CEA. The 1000-acre campus is in a suburban area 30 miles west of Kansas City. Including any residence halls, there are 220 buildings.

STUDENT LIFE: 67% of undergraduates are from Kansas. Others are from 50 states, 76 foreign countries, and Canada. 71% are White; 8% Hispanic; 6% Foreign; 5% Asian American; 5% two or more races; 4% African American; 1% race unknown. **Female To Male Ratio:** 1.1:1. The average age of freshmen is 18; all undergraduates, 21. 19% do not continue beyond their first year; 63% remain to graduate. **Housing:** 4910 students can be accommodated in college housing, which includes single-sex and coed dorms, on-campus apartments, honors houses, special-interest floors, and 1 residence hall with a fine arts. On-campus housing is available on a first-come and first-served basis. 75% of students commute. All students may keep cars. Alcohol is not permitted.

FACULTY/CLASSROOMS: 58% of faculty are male; 42% are female. 98% teach undergraduates and do research. Graduate students teach 18% of introductory courses. The average class size in a laboratory is 15 and in a regular course is 25.

PROGRAMS OF STUDY: KU confers B.A., B.S., B.A.E., B.A.S., B.B.A., B.F.A., B.G.S., B.M., B.M.E., B.S.B., B.S.E., B.S.J., B.S.N., B.S.P.S., and B.S.W. degrees. Master's and doctoral degrees are also awarded. Bachelor's degrees are awarded in AGRICULTURE (environmental studies), BIOLOGICAL SCIENCE (biochemistry, biology/biological science, biotechnology, microbiology, and molecular biology), BUSINESS (accounting, business administration and management, business information systems, entrepreneurial studies, finance, management information systems, marketing/retailing/merchandising, sports management, and supply chain management), COMMUNICATIONS AND THE ARTS (art history, art, ceramic art and design, choral music, classical languages, communication studies, dance, design, dramatic arts, East Asian languages and literature, English, fiber/textiles/weaving, film, television and digital media, fine arts, French, German, Germanic languages and literature, graphic design, illustration, industrial design, information technology, journalism, linguistics, film and media studies, metal/jewelry, music, music composition, music history and appreciation, music performance, music theory and composition, musicology/ethnomusicology, painting, percussion, piano/organ, printmaking, sculpture, Slavic languages, Spanish, speech/debate/rhetoric, strings, theatre arts, theater design, voice, and winds), COMPUTER AND PHYSICAL SCIENCE (astronomy, atmospheric sciences and meteorology, chemistry, computer science, geology, information sciences and systems, mathematics, and physics), EDUCATION (art education, athletic training, early childhood education, elementary education, global studies, health education, health information management, middle school education, music education, physical ed teacher education, and secondary education), ENGINEERING AND ENVIRONMENTAL DESIGN (aerospace engineering, architectural engineering, architecture, chemical engineering, civil engineering, computer engineering, electrical and computer engineering, electrical/electronics engineering, engineering physics, interior design, mechanical engineering, and petroleum/natural gas engineering), HEALTH PROFESSIONS (communicative disorders, community health work, exercise science, human biology, medical laboratory technology, music therapy, nursing, occupational therapy, pharmacy, respiratory therapy, and sports medicine), SOCIAL SCIENCE (African studies, African American studies, American studies, anthropology, archeology, architectural studies, behavioral science, classical/ancient civilization, economics, European studies, gender studies, geography, history, humanities, international studies, Judaic studies, Latin American studies, liberal arts/general studies, philosophy, political science/government, psychology, public administration, religion, Russian and Slavic studies, social work, sociology, women & gender studies, and women's studies). Pharmacy, and engineering are the strongest academically. Engineering, business/accounting, and psychology have the largest enrollments.

ACTIVITIES: 18% of men belong to 30 national fraternities; 25% of women belong to 17 national sororities. There are 470 groups on campus, including art, band, cheerleading, chess, choir, chorale, chorus, communications, computers, dance, debate, drama, environmental, ethnic, film, honors, international, jazz band, LGBT, literary magazine, marching band, musical theater, newspaper, opera, orchestra, pep band, photography, political, professional, radio and TV, religious, social, social service, student government, and symphony. Popular campus events include Late Night in the Phog (basketball season kickoff), Homecoming, Rock Chalk Revue, Hawk Week, Basketball, and Football Games. **Sports:** There are 7 intercollegiate sports for men and 11 for women, and 30 intramural sports for men and 30 for women. Facilities include a basketball arena, football stadium, sports pavilion with an indoor football field and indoor track, health and phys ed center with indoor pools, handball and racquetball courts, and gyms, lacrosse, cricket, rugby fields, a tennis center, a student recreation center containing an indoor climbing wall, a suspended jogging track, racquetball courts, a free weight/cardiovascular area, aerobic and martial arts studios, multipurpose courts, golf simulator, a rowing boathouse, an athletic center with volleyball and basketball courts, a football complex, softball stadium, a baseball park with clubhouse, soccer stadium, track and field stadium, strength center, golf training center, and an outdoor education center/challenge course. **Graduates:** From July 1, 2015 to June 30, 2016, 4158 bachelor's degrees were awarded. The most popular majors were business (16%), engineering (10%), and Journalism (6%). 550 companies recruited on campus in 2015-2016. In an average class, 2% graduate in 3 years or less, 47% graduate in 4 years or less, 60% graduate in 5 years or less, and 63% graduate in 6 years or less. Of the 2015 graduating class, 29% were enrolled in graduate school within 6 months of graduation, and 67% were employed.

SERVICES: Counseling and information services are available, as is tutoring in most subjects. There is a how-to sessions on study and organizational skills and a workshop. There is a reader service for the blind, and remedial math, as well as a writing center available to all students. **Library/Resources:** The 12 libraries contain 4.7 million volumes. Computerized library services include interlibrary loans, database searching, Internet access, and Wi-Fi capability. Special learning facilities include a natural history museum, radio station, TV station, art museum, classics museum, entomology museum, invertebrate paleontology collection, film studio, space technology center, performing arts center, organ recital hall, institute of politics, and a Hall Center for the Humanities. **Physically Challenged Students:** 95% of the campus is accessible. Facilities include wheelchair ramps, elevators, special parking, specially equipped restrooms, special class scheduling, lowered drinking fountains, and lowered telephones. **Special:** Special academic programs include honors program, internships, study abroad has over 130 programs in over 70 countries, a Washington semester, and work-study programs with the university. A cooperative program in engineering is offered, as are B.A.-B.S. degrees in many combinations, interdisciplinary majors, and dual majors in any approved combination. General studies degrees are available in many areas, and student-designed majors are possible. Nondegree study and pass/fail options are offered. There are 16 national honor societies, Phi Beta Kappa, and a freshman honors program. **Visiting:** There are regularly scheduled orientations for prospective students, consisting of a summer orientation program that includes a 1-day campus visit. There are guides for informal visits, visitors may sit in on classes, and stay overnight. To schedule a visit, contact the KU Visitor Center at (785) 864-3911. **Campus Safety and Security:** Measures include 24-hour foot and vehicle patrol, emergency notification system, and security escort services. There are also shuttle buses, emergency telephones, lighted pathways/sidewalks, and controlled access to dorms/residences.

REQUIREMENTS: Kansas Qualified Admissions Curriculum includes 4 units of English, 3 of college preparatory math with students meeting the ACT/SAT college readiness math benchmark (22+ ACT/550+ SAT on math section) or complete 4 math units, with one taken in the graduating year, 3 of natural science (1 must be chemistry or physics), 3 of social sciences (includes history), and 3 electives. Since fall 2016, Kansas residents must complete the Kansas Qualified Admissions Curriculum with 2.0+ GPA, have an overall 3.0 GPA and 24+ ACT (1160+ SAT), or 3.25 overall GPA and 21+ ACT (1060+ SAT). Nonresidents must meet the above criteria with a 2.5+ GPA, have an overall 3.0+ GPA and 24+ ACT (1160+ SAT), or 3.25+ overall GPA and 21+ ACT (1060+ SAT). Students who don't meet these criteria will be asked to answer two to four short answer questions on the application. Their application will be individually reviewed on these factors: cumulative high school GPA, ACT or SAT scores, GPA in the core curriculum, and strength of classes. A GPA of 2.0 is required. AP and CLEP credits are accepted. To graduate with a B.A., B.S., or B.G.S. degree, all students must complete at least 120 credit hours, including 30 to 50 credit hours in the major, and maintain a GPA of at least 2.0. These, as well as curricula and distribution requirements, vary according to the school and the major. **Procedure:** Freshmen are admitted to all sessions. Entrance exams should be taken by the end of the junior year. There is a rolling admissions plan. Application deadlines are open. Application fee is $40. Applications are accepted on-line. **Transfer Students:** 1136 transfer students enrolled in 2015-2016. Entrance to the College of Liberal Arts and Sciences, and transfer students must meet minimum GPA of 2.0 in-state or 2.5 out-of-state and freshman admissions requirements, if the student is transferring with less than 24 credit hours. The criteria vary widely within the other KU schools, some of which may also consider the ACT score and course work. 30 of 120 credits required for the bachelor's degree must be completed at KU. **International Students:** There are 1097 international students enrolled. The school actively recruits these students. They must take the TOEFL, or take the IELTS.

ADMISSIONS: 93% of the 2016-2017 applicants were accepted. The ACT scores were 1% between 12 and 17, 39% between 18 and 23, 41% between 24 and 29, and 19% above 30. There were 18 National Merit finalists. **Admissions Contact:** Lisa Pinamonti Kress, Director of Admissions. Email: *adm@ku.edu* Web: *www.admissions.ku.edu*

FINANCIAL AID: In 2016-2017, 76% of all full-time freshmen and 67% of continuing full-time students received some form of financial aid. 44% of all full-time freshmen and 36% of continuing full-time students received need-based aid. The average freshman award was $15,269. Need-based scholarships or need-based grants averaged $7,545; need-based self-help aid (loans and jobs) averaged $3,340; non-need-based athletic scholarships averaged $18,548; and other non-need-based awards and non-need-based scholarships averaged $5,444. 15% of undergraduate students work part-time. Average annual earnings from campus work are $4896. The average financial indebtedness of the 2016 graduate was $27,479. The FAFSA code is 001948. The priority date for freshman financial aid applications for fall entry is November 1. The filing deadline for fall entry is March 1.

UNIVERSITY OF SAINT MARY — F-2

www.stmary.edu

Leavenworth, KS 66048	**(913) 682-5151** **(800) 752-7043**
Fax: (913) 758-6140	**Email: admiss@stmary.edu**
Full-time: 310 men, 338 women	**Faculty:** 53
Part-time: 49 men, 140 women	**Ph.D.s:** 72%
Graduate: 207 men, 365 women	**Student/Faculty:** 12 to 1
Year: semesters, summer session	**Tuition:** $26,750
Room & Board: $7940	**Freshman Class:** 134 applied, 440 accepted, 130 enrolled
SAT: required **ACT:** 22	**CEEB CODE:** 6630
Application Deadline: n/av	**COMPETITIVE**

University of Saint Mary, founded in 1923, is a private liberal arts institution affiliated with the Roman Catholic Church and sponsored by the Sisters of Charity of Leavenworth. There is 1 undergraduate school and 1 graduate school. In addition to regional accreditation, USM has baccalaureate program accreditation with NCATE, IACBE, CCNE, and CAPTE. The 240-acre campus is in a small town 25 miles northwest of Kansas City, Missouri. Including any residence halls, there are 13 buildings.

STUDENT LIFE: 55% of undergraduates are from Kansas. Others are from 42 states, 4 foreign countries, and Canada. 59% are White; 18% Hispanic; 9% African American; 6% race unknown; 4% two or more races; 1% Asian American; 1% Foreign. 30% are Catholic; 26% claim no religious affiliation. **Female To Male Ratio:** 1.5:1. The average age of freshmen is 18; all undergraduates, 24. 29% do not continue beyond their first year; 34% remain to graduate. **Housing:** 320 students can be accommodated in college housing, which includes coed dorms. On-campus housing is guaranteed for all 4 years. 68% of students commute. All students may keep cars.

FACULTY/CLASSROOMS: 36% of faculty are male; 64% are female. All teach undergraduates. No introductory courses are taught by graduate students. The average class size in an introductory lecture is 25 and in a laboratory is 12.

PROGRAMS OF STUDY: USM confers B.A., and B.S. degrees. Associate, master's, and doctoral degrees are also awarded. Bachelor's degrees are awarded in BIOLOGICAL SCIENCE (biology/biological science), BUSINESS (accounting, business administration and management, and sports management), COMMUNICATIONS AND THE ARTS (art, dramatic arts, English, music, and theatre arts), COMPUTER AND PHYSICAL SCIENCE (chemistry, information sciences and systems, and mathematics), EDUCATION (education and elementary education), HEALTH PROFESSIONS (biology, biomedical science, clinical science, health, health care administration, and nursing), SOCIAL SCIENCE (applied psychology, behavioral science, child psychology/development, criminology, history, interdisciplinary studies, international studies, liberal arts/general studies, pastoral studies, political science/government, psychology, sociology, and theological studies). Elementry education, business administration, and psychology are the strongest academically. Nursing, biology, and business have the largest enrollments.

ACTIVITIES: There are no fraternities or sororities. There are 25 groups on campus, including art, band, cheerleading, choir, chorale, chorus, computers, dance, drama, honors, literary magazine, musical theater, newspaper, opera, political, professional, religious, social, social service, and student government. Popular campus events include Fall Convocation, Founders Day, and Family Weekend. **Sports:** There are 9 intercollegiate sports for men and 9 for women, and 8 intramural sports for men and 8 for women. Facilities include an athletic stadium, a sports center, soccer and softball fields, multipurpose field, a sandlot volleyball court, racquetball courts, a weight and exercise room, a swimming pool, a dance and aerobics space, a walking trail, and an indoor jogging track. **Graduates:** From July 1, 2015 to June 30, 2016, 191 bachelor's degrees were awarded. The most popular majors were nursing (53%), biology (8%), and psychology (6%). In an average class, 28% graduate in 4 years or less and 34% graduate in 6 years or less.

SERVICES: Counseling and information services are available, as is tutoring in most subjects. **Library/Resources:** The library contains 115,000 volumes, 1,675 microform items, and subscribes to 301 periodicals including electronic. Computerized library services include interlibrary loans, database searching, and Internet access. Special learning facilities include an art gallery, and several special library collections. **Physically Challenged Students:** 90% of the campus is accessible. Facilities include wheelchair ramps, elevators, special parking, and specially equipped restrooms. **Special:** The university offers study abroad at various locations in Europe, Latin America, or Australia. CLEP and credit for life experience, internships in most major programs, evening and weekend study programs, pass/fail option, and dual majors are also available. There are 2 national honor societies, a freshman honors program, and 2 departmental honors programs. **Visiting:** There are regularly scheduled orientations for prospective students, visits include interviews with faculty and financial aid representatives, and touring the campus. There are guides for informal visits, visitors may sit in on classes, and stay overnight. To schedule a visit, contact Wendi Fugitt at admiss@stmary.edu. **Campus Safety and Security:** Measures include 24-hour foot and vehicle patrol, emergency notification system, self-defense education, and security escort services, lighted pathways/sidewalks, and controlled access to dorms/residences.

REQUIREMENTS: The SAT or ACT is required. Applicants should be graduates of an accredited secondary school. The GED is accepted. A GPA of 2.5 is required. AP and CLEP credits are accepted. Important factors in the admissions decision are parents or siblings attended your school, recommendations by alumni, and recommendations by school officials. To graduate, students must complete all general education requirements and earn at least 128 credits, including 30 to 60 in the major, with a minimum GPA of 2.0. The core curriculum includes freshman humanities and a senior integration project. Distribution requirements include courses in English, math, natural science, social and behavioral sciences, philosophy, history, and foreign language, plus an additional literature course, a fine arts course, and 2 courses in theology. Students must also fulfill cultural literacy and lifetime physical wellness requirements. **Procedure:** Freshmen are admitted in the fall and spring. Entrance exams should be taken in the spring of the junior year and fall of the senior year. There are early decision, early admissions, and rolling admissions plans. Application deadlines are open. Application fee is $25. Notification is sent on a rolling basis. Application fees are waived if application is completed online. **Transfer Students:** 251 transfer students enrolled in 2015-2016. A college GPA of 2.0 is required. 30 of 128 credits required for the bachelor's degree must be completed at USM. **International Students:** There are 6 international students enrolled. The school actively recruits these students. They must take the TOEFL with a minimum score of 500 on the paper-based TOEFL (PBT) or 61 on the Internet-based version (iBT).

ADMISSIONS: 28% of the 2016-2017 applicants were accepted. **Admissions Contact:** John Shultz, VP for Admissions and Marketing. Email: *admiss@stmary.edu* Web: *www.stmary.edu*

FINANCIAL AID: In 2016-2017, 100% of all full-time freshmen received some form of financial aid. 100% of all full-time freshmen received need-based aid. Average annual earnings from campus work is $700. USM is a member of CSS. The FAFSA code is 001943. Check with the school for current application deadlines.

WASHBURN UNIVERSITY — E-2

www.washburn.edu

Topeka, KS 66621 — **(785) 670-1030**, **(877) 281-2637**

Fax: (785) 670-1113 — **Email: admissions@washburn.edu**

Full-time: 1610 men, 2256 women	**Faculty:** 260; IIA, -$
Part-time: 723 men, 1191 women	**Ph.D.s:** 84%
Graduate: 333 men, 523 women	**Student/Faculty:** 13 to 1
Year: semesters, summer session	**Tuition:** $8300 ($18,620)
Room & Board: $7527	**Freshman Class:** 1678 applied, 1671 accepted, 908 enrolled
ACT: 22	**CEEB CODE:** 6928
Application Deadline: August 1	**COMPETITIVE**

Washburn University, is a publicly funded, independently governed, state-coordinated university, established in 1865, offering more than 200 programs leading to certification, associate, bachelor, master, professional, and juris doctor degrees through the college of arts and sciences, the schools of law, business, nursing, and applied studies. There are 4 undergraduate schools and 5 graduate schools. In addition to regional accreditation, Washburn has baccalaureate program accreditation with AACSB, CAHEA, CSWE, NASAD, NASM, NCATE, ACS, CAAHEP, and CAATE. The 160-acre campus is in an urban area 60 miles west of Kansas City. Including any residence halls, there are 30 buildings.

STUDENT LIFE: 89% of undergraduates are from Kansas. Others are from 39 states, 28 foreign countries, and Canada. 91% are from public schools. **Female To Male Ratio:** 1.5:1. The average age of freshmen is 19; all undergraduates, 24. 28% do not continue beyond their first year; 36% remain to graduate. **Housing:** 986 students can be accommodated in college housing, which includes coed dorms and on-campus apartments. On-campus housing is available on a first-come and first-served basis. Priority is given to out-of-town students. All students may keep cars. Alcohol is not permitted.

FACULTY/CLASSROOMS: 41% of faculty are male; 59% are female. 91% teach undergraduates. No introductory courses are taught by graduate students.

PROGRAMS OF STUDY: Washburn confers B.A., B.A.S., B.B.A., B.Ed., B.F.A., B.H.S., B.I.S., B.L.S., B.M., B.P.A., B.S., B.S.C.J., B.S.N. and B.S.W. degrees. Associate, master's, and doctoral degrees are also awarded. Bachelor's degrees are awarded in BIOLOGICAL SCIENCE (biochemistry, biology/biological science, and molecular biology), BUSINESS (accounting, banking and finance, business administration and management, business economics, entrepreneurial studies, finance, international business management, and marketing/retailing/merchandising), COMMUNICATIONS AND THE ARTS (art, art history and appreciation, communications, dramatic arts, English, French, German, media arts, music, music performance, Spanish, speech/debate/rhetoric, and theater design), COMPUTER AND PHYSICAL SCIENCE (chemistry, computer science, mathematics, physics, and science), EDUCATION (art education, athletic training, early childhood education, education, elementary education, music education, physical education, physical ed teacher education, and secondary education), ENGINEERING AND ENVIRONMENTAL DESIGN (technological management), HEALTH PROFESSIONS (clinical science, health care administration, kinesiology, nursing, prepharmacy, and ultrasound technology), SOCIAL SCIENCE (anthropology, corrections, criminal justice, economics, forensic studies, history, human services, interdisciplinary studies, law enforcement and corrections, liberal arts/general studies, paralegal studies, philosophy, political science/government, psychology, public administration, religion, social work, and sociology). Business administration, criminal justice, and nursing have the largest enrollments.

ACTIVITIES: There are 78 groups on campus, including art, band, campus activities board and peer educators., cheerleading, chess, choir, chorus, computers, dance, debate, drama, drill team, drum and bugle corps, environmental, ethnic, forensics, honors, international, jazz band, LGBT, literary magazine, marching band, musical theater, newspaper, orchestra, pep band, political, professional, radio and TV, religious, social, social service, student government, symphony, and yearbook. Popular campus events include Greek Week, Student Activities Fair, and the Annual Sunflower Music Festival. **Sports:** There are 7 intercollegiate sports for men and 7 for women, and 15 intramural sports for men and 15 for women. Facilities include a recreation and wellness center with rock-climbing wall, indoor track, gym, cardiovascular and resistance training area, and wellness suite, a field house for indoor sports, a stadium for intercollegiate football, and a health center with a 6-lane swimming pool. **Graduates:** From July 1, 2015 to June 30, 2016, 841 bachelor's degrees were awarded. The most popular majors were nursing/health professions (26%), business (18%), and education (7%). 200 companies recruited on campus in 2015-2016. In an average class, 36% graduate in 6 years or less.

SERVICES: Counseling and information services are available, as is tutoring in most subjects. There is a reader service for the blind, and remedial math and writing. **Library/Resources:** The 2 libraries contain 451,534 volumes, 88,198 microform items, 4,612 audio/video tapes/CDs/DVDs, and subscribe to 87,358 periodicals including electronic. Computerized library services include interlibrary loans, database searching, Internet access, and Wi-Fi capability. Special learning facilities include an art gallery, planetarium, radio station, and TV station. **Physically Challenged Students:** 95% of the campus is accessible. Facilities include wheelchair ramps, elevators, special parking, specially equipped restrooms, special class scheduling, lowered drinking fountains, lowered telephones, and special housing. **Special:** Washburn offers a co-op program in computer information science, engineering, social/behavioral science, education, and health profession; internships in numerous departments; and study abroad in 20 countries. Dual and student-designed majors, B.A.-B.S. degrees, an integrated studies degree, credit by examination, nondegree study, and pass/fail options are also available. A 3-2 engineering degree is possible in conjunction with the University of Kansas and Kansas State University. There are 11 national honor societies and a freshman honors program. **Visiting:** There are regularly scheduled orientations for prospective students, Students will get to learn expectations of the classroom environment, meet with current students over our free lunch, register for their first semester courses, explore the MyWashburn online portal, attend meetings about activities and organizations. There are guides for informal visits, visitors may sit in on classes, and stay overnight. To schedule a visit, contact Office of Admissions at (877) 281-2637. **Campus Safety and Security:** Measures include 24-hour foot and vehicle patrol, emergency notification system, self-defense education, security escort services, emergency telephones, lighted pathways/sidewalks, sexual assault reduction program & bystander skill building intervention,bicycle patrol, and fire safety programs for residential living facilities.

REQUIREMENTS: The ACT is required. Applicants should be graduates of an accredited secondary school or have the GED. AP and CLEP credits are accepted. **Procedure:** Freshmen are admitted to all sessions. Entrance exams should be taken during the junior year. There is a rolling admissions plan. Applications should be filed by August 1 for fall entry; January 2 for spring entry; and May 12 for summer entry. The fall 2016 application fee was $20. Application fees are waived if application is completed online. **Transfer Students:** 611 transfer students enrolled in 2015-2016. Applicants must meet the same requirements as incoming freshmen. 30 of 120 credits required for the bachelor's degree must be completed at Washburn. **International Students:** There are 226 international students enrolled. The school actively recruits these students. They must take the TOEFL with a minimum score of 72 on the Internet-based version (iBT).

ADMISSIONS: 100% of the 2016-2017 applicants were accepted. The ACT scores were 15% between 12 and 17, 51% between 18 and 23, 32% between 24 and 29, and 2% above 30. 27% of the current freshmen were in the top fifth of their class; 54% were in the top two fifths. 29 freshmen graduated first in their class. **Admissions Contact:** Kris Klima, Director, Admissions. Email: *admissions@washburn.edu* Web: *www.washburn.edu*

FINANCIAL AID: In 2016-2017, 60% of all full-time freshmen and 59% of continuing full-time students received some form of financial aid. 36% of all full-time freshmen and 38% of continuing full-time students received need-based aid. The average freshman award was $9,616. Need-based scholarships or need-based grants averaged $4,850; need-based self-help aid (loans and jobs) averaged $4,081; non-need-based athletic scholarships averaged $5,670; and other non-need-based awards and non-need-based scholarships averaged $3,611. The average financial indebtedness of the 2016 graduate was $27,328. Washburn is a member of CSS. The FAFSA code is 001949. The priority date for freshman financial aid applications for fall entry is February 15.

WICHITA STATE UNIVERSITY — D-3

www.wichita.edu

Wichita, KS 67260	(316) 978-3085 (800) 362-2594
Fax: (316) 978-3174	**Email:** admissions@wichita.edu
Full-time: 4208 men, 4482 women	**Faculty:** I
Part-time: 1184 men, 1425 women	**Ph.D.s:** 80%
Graduate: 1484 men, 1540 women	**Student/Faculty:** 18 to 1
Year: semesters, summer session	**Tuition:** $8789 ($18,777)
Room & Board: $12,854	**Freshman Class:** 4517 applied, 4315 accepted, 1584 enrolled
SAT or ACT: required	**CEEB CODE:** 6884
Application Deadline: n/av	**COMPETITIVE**

Wichita State University, established in 1895, is a public institution offering programs in the liberal arts and sciences, business, engineering, education, and health professions. Figures in the above capsule and in this profile are approximate. There are 6 undergraduate schools and 1 graduate school. In addition to regional accreditation, WSU has baccalaureate program accreditation with AACSB, ABET, ADA, APTA, CAHEA, CSWE, NASM, NCATE, and NLN. The 330-acre campus is in an urban area in the metropolitan Wichita area. Including any residence halls, there are 61 buildings.

STUDENT LIFE: 94% of undergraduates are from Kansas. Others are from 49 states, 88 foreign countries, and Canada. 9% are Foreign; 7% African American; 7% Hispanic; 64% White; 6% Asian American; 1% American Indian/Alaska Native. **Female To Male Ratio:** 1.1:1. The average age of freshmen is 19; all undergraduates, 24. 27% do not continue beyond their first year; 43% remain to graduate. **Housing:** 1453 students can be accommodated in college housing, which includes coed dorms, on-campus apartments, married student housing, honors houses, fraternity houses, sorority houses, and theme housing. On-campus housing is available on a first-come and first-served basis. 91% of students commute. All students may keep cars.

FACULTY/CLASSROOMS: 51% of faculty are male; 49% are female. No introductory courses are taught by graduate students. The average class size in an introductory lecture is 23; in a laboratory is 20; and in a regular course is 15.

PROGRAMS OF STUDY: WSU confers A.A.,B.A., B.A.Ed., BAES., BASM., B.B.A, B.F.A., B.G.S., B.M., B.M.E., B.S., BSASE., B.S.CPE., B.S.E.E., B.S.H.S., B.S.I.E., B.S.M.E., B.S.M.F.E. and B.S.N. degrees. Associate, master's, and doctoral degrees are also awarded. Bachelor's degrees are awarded in BIOLOGICAL SCIENCE (biology/biological science), BUSINESS (accounting, banking and finance, business administration and management, economics – statistics, entrepreneurial studies, finance, human resources, international business management, management science, marketing/retailing/merchandising, and sports management), COMMUNICATIONS AND THE ARTS (art, art history and appreciation, audio technology, communications, creative writing, dance, English, French, graphic design, Latin, music, music business management, music composition, music history and appreciation, Spanish, studio art, theatre arts, and visual and performing arts), COMPUTER AND PHYSICAL SCIENCE (chemistry, computer science, earth science / adolescence education, geology, mathematics, and physics), EDUCATION (art education, elementary education, general studies, music education, physical education, secondary education, and special education), ENGINEERING AND ENVIRONMENTAL DESIGN (aeronautical engineering, computer engineering, electrical/electronics engineering, industrial engineering, manufacturing engineering, and mechanical engineering), HEALTH PROFESSIONS (dental education, health, health care administration, health services technology, medical laboratory technology, nursing, physician's assistant, and speech pathology/audiology), SOCIAL SCIENCE (anthropology, criminal justice, economics, ethnic studies, gerontology, history, liberal arts/general studies, philosophy, political science/government, psychology, social work, sociology, women & gender studies, and women's studies). Engineering programs, and physics & chemistry are the strongest academically. Psychology, nursing, and elementary education have the largest enrollments.

ACTIVITIES: 4% of men belong to 10 national fraternities; 5% of women belong to 8 national sororities. There are 200 groups on campus, including TV station, art, band, cheerleading, chess, choir, chorus, computers, dance, debate, drama, environmental, ethnic, film, honors, international, jazz band, LGBT, literary magazine, Model UN, musical theater, newspaper, opera, orchestra, pep band, photography, political, professional, religious, social, social service, student government, and symphony. Popular campus events include Hippodrome, International Week, and ShocktoberFest. **Sports:** There are 14 intercollegiate sports for men and 12 for women, and 30 intramural sports for men and 30 for women. Facilities include an arena, stadiums, golf course, baseball field, tennis complex, and a recreation and sports center. **Graduates:** From July 1, 2015 to June 30, 2016, 2124 bachelor's degrees were awarded. The most popular majors were buisness/marketing and Health Professionals (17%), engineering (11%), and education (9%). 75 companies recruited on campus in 2015-2016. In an average class, 44% graduate in 6 years or less.

SERVICES: Counseling and information services are available, as is tutoring in most subjects. There is also a reader service for the blind, and remedial math, reading, and writing. Group and individual psychological services are available for students and their families. **Library/ Resources:** The library contains 1.9 million volumes, 1.2 million microform items, 200,973 audio/video tapes/CDs/DVDs, and subscribes to 61,010 periodicals including electronic. Computerized library services include interlibrary loans, database searching, Internet access, and Wi-Fi capability. Special learning facilities include an art gallery, natural history museum, TV station, an electronic classroom, telecourses, the National

Institute for Aviation Research, museum of art, and a public observatory. **Physically Challenged Students:** 98% of the campus is accessible. Facilities include wheelchair ramps, elevators, special parking, specially equipped restrooms, special class scheduling, lowered drinking fountains, lowered telephones, wheelchairs, and braille typewriters. Interpreters for the hearing impaired, note taking, and typing services are also offered. **Special:** WSU offers accelerated programs, co-op programs, cross registration, internships, study abroad, work-study programs, and a Washington semester. Dual and student-designed majors, a general studies degree, credit by exam, nondegree study, and pass/fail options are also available. There are 14 national honor societies and a freshman honors program. **Visiting:** There are regularly scheduled orientations for prospective students. There are guides for informal visits, visitors may sit in on classes, and stay overnight. To schedule a visit, contact the Admissions Office. **Campus Safety and Security:** Measures include 24-hour foot and vehicle patrol, self-defense education, and security escort services, as well as shuttle buses, emergency telephones, lighted pathways/sidewalks, and a bicycle patrol.

REQUIREMENTS: Applicants must submit a minimum composite ACT score of 21 or a satisfactory SAT score, rank in the top one third of their high school graduating class, and have a 2.0 GPA (nonresidents, 2.5). Requirements needed are 4 years of English, 3 each of math, natural and social sciences, (one of these units must be lab), social studies, and academic electives. Recommended units are 3 years of foreign language, and computer science. AP and CLEP credits are accepted. Important factors in the admissions decision are leadership record, evidence of special talent, and extracurricular activities record. To graduate, students need at least 124 credit hours, with a GPA of 2.0 to 2.5, depending on the major. Specific distribution requirements, as well as department requirements, must also be met. The core curriculum consists of 14 courses (42 hours) in general education. Students must have a minimum of 45 credit hours in courses numbered 300 or above. **Procedure:** Freshmen are admitted to all sessions. There are deferred admissions and rolling admissions plans. Application deadlines are open. Application fee is $30. Applications are accepted online. **Transfer Students:** 1478 transfer students enrolled in 2015-2016. Applicants must have a minimum GPA of 2.0 to 2.5, depending on the WSU college they wish to enter. Including all college transcripts. 30 of 60 credits required for the bachelor's degree must be completed at WSU. **International Students:** The school actively recruits these students. They must take the TOEFL with a minimum score of 530 on the paper-based TOEFL (PBT) or 72 on the Internet-based version (iBT).

ADMISSIONS: 20% of the current freshmen were in the top fifth of their class; 80% were in the top two fifths. **Admissions Contact:** Bobby Gandu, Director of Admissions. Email: *admissions@wichita.edu* Web: *www.wichita.edu*

FINANCIAL AID: In 2016-2017, 68% of all full-time freshmen received some form of financial aid. 58% of all full-time freshmen received need-based aid. The average freshman award was $5,812. Need-based scholarships or need-based grants averaged $4,400; need-based self-help aid (loans and jobs) averaged $3,332; non-need-based athletic scholarships averaged $7,618; other non-need-based awards and non-need-based scholarships averaged $3,267; and $2,430 from other forms of aid. The average financial indebtedness of the 2016 graduate was $23,534. The FAFSA code is 001950. The deadline for filing freshman financial aid applications for fall entry is March 15.

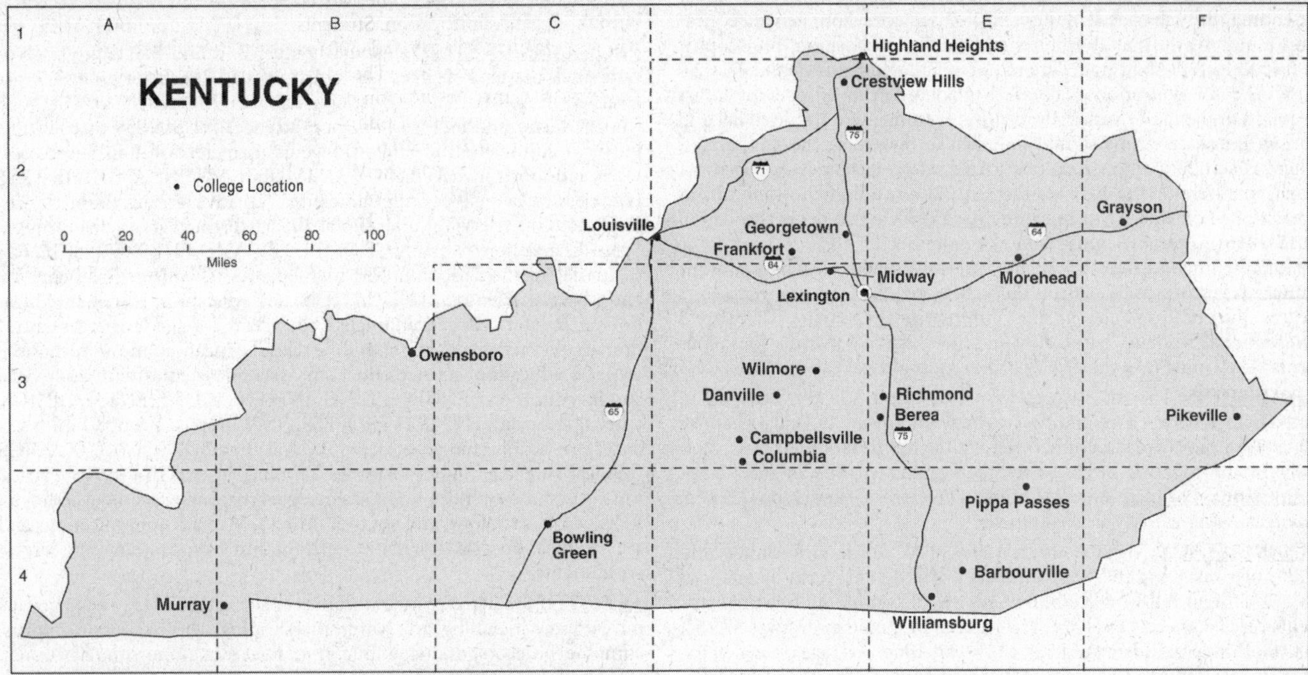

ALICE LLOYD COLLEGE E-4

www.alc.edu

Pippa Passes, KY 41844	**(606) 368-2101** **(888) 280-4252**
Fax: (606) 368-6215	**Email:** admissions@alc.edu
Full-time: 281 men, 308 women	**Faculty:** 27
Part-time: 11 men, 12 women	**Ph.D.s:** 65%
Graduate: n/av	**Student/Faculty:** 22 to 1
Year: semesters	**Tuition:** n/av
Room & Board: $8190	**Freshman Class:** n/av
SAT: required **ACT:** 20	**CEEB CODE:** 1098
Application Deadline: n/av	**COMPETITIVE**

Alice Lloyd College, founded in 1923, is a private liberal arts facility emphasizing Christian values and serving the Appalachian community. Qualified students from ALC's 108-county service area are awarded the Appalachian Leaders College Scholarship, which covers the cost of up to 10 semesters. The figures in the above capsule and in this profile are approximate. There is 1 undergraduate school. In addition to regional accreditation, ALC has baccalaureate program accreditation with NCATE. The 225-acre campus is in a rural area. Including any residence halls, there are 38 buildings.

STUDENT LIFE: 85% of undergraduates are from Kentucky. Others are from 7 states, and 2 foreign countries. 90% are from public schools. 97% are White; 2% African American; 1% Hispanic. **Female To Male Ratio:** 1.1:1. The average age of freshmen is 18; all undergraduates, 20. 37% do not continue beyond their first year. **Housing:** 451 students can be accommodated in college housing, which includes single-sex dorms. The Caney cottage scholarship program, provides housing for students to continue their education after the undergraduate level. On-campus housing is guaranteed for all 4 years. 78% of students live on campus; of those, 35% remain on campus on weekends. Alcohol is not permitted. All students may keep cars.

FACULTY/CLASSROOMS: 74% of faculty are male; 26% are female. All teach undergraduates, and 10% do research. No introductory courses are taught by graduate students. The average class size in an introductory lecture is 25; in a laboratory is 12; and in a regular course is 17.

PROGRAMS OF STUDY: ALC confers B.A. and B.S. degrees. Bachelor's degrees are awarded in BIOLOGICAL SCIENCE (biology/biological science), BUSINESS (business administration and management), COMMUNICATIONS AND THE ARTS (English), EDUCATION (elementary education, middle school education, physical education, secondary education, and social studies education), ENGINEERING AND ENVIRONMENTAL DESIGN (preengineering), HEALTH PROFESSIONS (prepharmacy), SOCIAL SCIENCE (history). Biology, education, and business administration are the strongest academically. Biology has the largest enrollment.

ACTIVITIES: There are no fraternities or sororities. There are 16 groups on campus, including art, cheerleading, choir, chorus, computers, drama, honors, newspaper, pep band, photography, professional, religious, social, student government, and yearbook. Popular campus events include Religious Emphasis Week, Alcohol Awareness Week, and Appalachia Day. **Sports:** There are 5 intercollegiate sports for men and 5 for women, and 11 intramural sports for men and 11 for women. Facilities include an indoor pool, weight rooms, a 1500-seat gym, recreation areas, 2 tennis courts, a baseball/athletic field, and 2 racquetball courts. **Graduates:** From July 1, 2015 to June 30, 2016, 107 bachelor's degrees were awarded. The most popular majors were biology, business, and elementary education. 30 companies recruited on campus in 2015-2016. In an average class, 20% graduate in 4 years or less, 21% graduate in 5 years or less, and 22% graduate in 6 years or less. Of the 2015 graduating class, 96% were employed within 6 months of graduation.

SERVICES: Counseling and information services are available, as is tutoring in every subject. There is remedial math, reading, and writing. **Library/Resources:** The library contains 62,000 volumes, 1,500 microform items, and 300 audio/video tapes/CDs/DVDs, and subscribes to 300 periodicals including electronic. Computerized library services include interlibrary loans, database searching, and Internet access. Special learning facilities include an art gallery, radio station, TV station, and performing arts center. **Physically Challenged Students:** 95% of the campus is accessible. Facilities include wheelchair ramps, elevators, special parking, specially equipped restrooms, and special class scheduling. **Special:** Special arrangements include a 2-2 engineering degree with the Universities of Kentucky, Louisville, and West Virginia. Credit by exam is possible. There is 1 national honor society and a chapter of Phi Beta Kappa. **Visiting:** There are regularly scheduled orientations for prospective students, consisting of summer and fall orientations. There are guides for informal visits, visitors may sit in on classes, and stay overnight. To schedule a visit, contact the Admissions Assistant. **Campus Safety and Security:** Measures include 24-hour foot and vehicle patrol, self-defense education, and security escort services. There are emergency telephones and lighted pathways/sidewalks.

REQUIREMENTS: The SAT or ACT is required. Applicants must be graduates of an accredited secondary school or have a GED, having successfully completed 12 academic credits, including 4 in English, 3 each in math and science, and 2 in social studies. AP and CLEP credits are accepted. Important factors in the admissions decision are leadership record, recommendations by alumni, and recommendations by school officials. To graduate, students must complete a work-study requirement extending through each semester and a 49-semester-hour general education requirement, including phys ed, health, composition, philosophy, and speech. 128 credit hours are required. Students must maintain a 2.0 GPA (2.5 for education majors) to graduate. The number of hours required in the major varies. **Procedure:** Freshmen are admitted fall and spring. Entrance exams should be taken in the fall of the senior year. There is a rolling admissions plan. Application deadlines are open. 31 applicants were on the 2016 waiting list; 22 were admitted. Applications are accepted on-line. **Transfer Students:** 35 transfer students enrolled in 2015-2016. Applicants must have a minimum 2.0 GPA, 2.5 for some majors, be in good standing at their previous school, and have a minimum ACT score of 17. 30 of 128 credits required for the bachelor's degree must be completed at ALC. **International Students:** There are 3 international students enrolled. The school actively recruits these students. They must take the TOEFL. They must also take the SAT or ACT.

ADMISSIONS: The ACT scores were 48% below 12, 35% between 12 and 17, 13% between 18 and 23, 3% between 24 and 29, and 1% above 30. 50% of the current freshmen were in the top fifth of their class; 82% were in the top two fifths. 6 freshmen graduated first in their class. **Admissions Contact:** Angela Phipps, Director of Admissions. Email: *admissions@alc.edu* Web: *www.alc.edu*

FINANCIAL AID: In 2016-2017, 100% of all full-time freshmen and 100% of continuing full-time students received some form of financial aid. 52% of all full-time freshmen and 4% of continuing full-time students received need-based aid. The average freshman award was $7,783. 100% of undergraduate students work part-time. Average annual earnings from campus work are $1648. The average financial indebtedness of the 2016 graduate was $1,060. The FAFSA code is 001951. The priority date for freshman financial aid applications for fall entry is February 15. The deadline for filing freshman financial aid applications for fall entry is March 15.

ASBURY UNIVERSITY — D-3
www.asbury.edu

Wilmore, KY 40390	(859) 858-3511 (800) 888-1818
Fax: (859) 858-3921	Email: admissions@asbury.edu
Full-time: 517 men, 809 women	Faculty: 87
Part-time: 90 men, 116 women	Ph.D.s: 74%
Graduate: 54 men, 196 women	Student/Faculty: 12 to 1
Year: semesters, summer session	Tuition: $28,432
Room & Board: $6748	Freshman Class: 1211 applied, 796 accepted, 322 enrolled
SAT CR/M: 568/558 ACT: 24	CEEB CODE: 1019
Application Deadline: open	COMPETITIVE+

Asbury University is an independent liberal arts university providing undergraduate and graduate educational programs guided by the classical tradition of orthodox Christian thought. Figures in the above capsule and in this profile are approximate. There are 3 undergraduate schools and 3 graduate schools. In addition to regional accreditation, Asbury has baccalaureate program accreditation with CSWE, NASM, and NCATE. The 65-acre campus is in a small town 20 minutes south of Lexington, KY. Including any residence halls, there are 30 buildings.

STUDENT LIFE: 52% of undergraduates are from Kentucky. Others are from 44 states, 17 foreign countries, and Canada. 67% are from public schools. 85% are White; 5% two or more races; 2% African American; 2% Hispanic; 2% Foreign; 2% race unknown; 1% Asian American. 83% are Protestant; 15% unknown denominations. **Female To Male Ratio:** 1.7:1. The average age of freshmen is 18; all undergraduates, 20. 17% do not continue beyond their first year; 68% remain to graduate. **Housing:** 1168 students can be accommodated in college housing, which includes single-sex dorms, on-campus apartments, off-campus apartments, and married student housing. In addition, there are language houses. On-campus housing is guaranteed for all 4 years. 85% of students live on campus; of those, 70% remain on campus on weekends. Alcohol is not permitted. Upperclassmen may keep cars.

FACULTY/CLASSROOMS: 51% of faculty are male; 49% are female. 94% teach undergraduates, and 1% do research. No introductory courses are taught by graduate students. The average class size in an introductory lecture is 20; in a laboratory is 16; and in a regular course is 18.

PROGRAMS OF STUDY: Asbury confers B.A. and B.S. degrees. Associate and master's degrees are also awarded. Bachelor's degrees are awarded in AGRICULTURE (equine science), BIOLOGICAL SCIENCE (biochemistry and biology/biological science), BUSINESS (accounting, business administration and management, recreation and leisure services, and sports management), COMMUNICATIONS AND THE ARTS (art, classical languages, communications, creative writing, dramatic arts, English, film, television and digital media, French, journalism, music, Spanish, and theatre acting), COMPUTER AND PHYSICAL SCIENCE (actuarial mathematics, applied mathematics, chemistry, mathematics, and physical sciences), EDUCATION (art education, Christian education, elementary education, English education, foreign languages education, mathematics education, middle school education, music education, physical education, science education, secondary education, and social studies education), ENGINEERING AND ENVIRONMENTAL DESIGN (preengineering), HEALTH PROFESSIONS (exercise science, health science, pre-health studies, and prephysical therapy), SOCIAL SCIENCE (biblical languages, biblical studies, criminal justice, history, ministries, missions, philosophy, political science/government, psychology, religion, social work, sociology, and youth ministry). Media communications and communication arts, teacher education, and business have the largest enrollments.

ACTIVITIES: There are no fraternities or sororities. There are 45 groups on campus, including art, band, cheerleading, choir, chorale, chorus, computers, debate, drama, ethnic, film, forensics, honors, international, jazz band, literary magazine, musical theater, newspaper, opera, orchestra, photography, political, professional, radio and TV, religious, social service, student government, and yearbook. Popular campus events include High Bridge Film Festival, Homecoming, Fall Revival, and Missions Conference. **Sports:** There are 8 intercollegiate sports for men and 9 for women, and 7 intramural sports for men and 7 for women. Facilities include a 1,500-seat gym, athletic fields, lacrosse, volleyball, golf, cross-country, tennis courts, an indoor swimming pool, indoor/outdoor basketball courts, indoor horseback riding arena, and student center. **Graduates:** From July 1, 2015 to June 30, 2016, 323 bachelor's degrees were awarded. The most popular majors were media communication (16%), education (13%), and business management (9%). In an average class, 2% graduate in 3 years or less, 56% graduate in 4 years or less, 63% graduate in 5 years or less, and 64% graduate in 6 years or less.

SERVICES: Counseling and information services are available, as is tutoring in most subjects. There is remedial writing. For students on academic probation, there are special classes and mentors who provide help in areas such as time management and test-taking skills. There is some help available for the visually impaired, such as tapes and agencies that offer aid. **Library/Resources:** The library contains 184,084 volumes, 13,238 microform items, and 7,188 audio/video tapes/CDs/DVDs, and subscribes to 299 periodicals including electronic. Computerized library services include interlibrary loans, database searching, Internet access, and Wi-Fi capability. Special learning facilities include an art gallery, radio station, TV station, Miller Center for Communication Arts which features a television studio, and a blackbox theatre. Equine Center houses classrooms, stables, and a riding arena. **Physically Challenged Students:** 80% of the campus is accessible. Facilities include wheelchair ramps, elevators, special parking, specially equipped restrooms, special class scheduling, lowered drinking fountains, and lowered telephones. **Special:** For-credit internships are available in several academic areas, as are opportunities for study abroad in 14 countries. 3-2 engineering degrees are offered with the University of Kentucky. There are 6 national honor societies. **Visiting:** There are regularly scheduled orientations for prospective students, including visits, scheduled individually or during planned visitation weekends, in which students stay overnight in dorms, visit classes, attend departmental open houses and financial aid sessions, and participate in chapel and campus events. There are guides for informal visits. To schedule a visit, contact the Admissions Visit Coordinators at visit@asbury.edu. **Campus Safety and Security:** Measures include 24-hour foot and vehicle patrol, emergency notification system, and security escort services. There are lighted pathways/sidewalks, planning forums, and a student parking and safety committee.

REQUIREMENTS: Either the SAT or ACT is required. An official high school transcript or the GED is required for all new students and for transfer students with fewer than 30 college credit hours. Applicants should have completed 15 high school academic credits, including 4 units of English, 3 of math, and 2 each of lab science, social studies, and a foreign language. AP and CLEP credits are accepted. To graduate with a bachelor's degree, students must complete a minimum of 124 cumulative semester hours, fulfill any liberal arts core requirements, and meet all requirements for at least one chosen major (50% of which must be completed at Asbury University), plus maintain a minimum GPA of 2.0. Traditional undergraduates earning a Bachelor of Arts degree must demonstrate proficiency in foreign language through the third semester college level. Students must complete 12 of their final 21 credit hours with Asbury University. **Procedure:** Freshmen are admitted to all sessions. Entrance exams should be taken in the junior year or in the first semester of the senior year. There are early admissions, deferred admissions, and rolling admissions plans. Application deadlines are open. Notification is sent on a rolling basis. Applications are accepted on-line. **Transfer Students:** 52 transfer students enrolled in 2015-2016. Applicants with 18 quarter hours or 12 semester hours of college work or more are considered transfers. They must have an overall minimum GPA of 2.5 and be in good standing at each previous institution attended. Transfers with fewer than 30 semester hours of college work must submit a high school transcript. 49 of 124 credits required for the bachelor's degree must be completed at Asbury. **International Students:** There are 25 international students enrolled. They must take the TOEFL with a minimum score of 550 on the paper-based TOEFL (PBT) or 80 on the Internet-based version (iBT).

ADMISSIONS: 66% of the 2016-2017 applicants were accepted. The SAT scores for the 2016-2017 freshman class were: Critical Reading--21% below 500, 41% between 500 and 599, 33% between 600 and 699, and 5% between 700 and 800. Math-- 24% below 500, 40% between 500 and 599, 32% between 600 and 699, and 4% between 700 and 800. The ACT scores were 17% below 12, 27% between 12 and 17, 26% between 18 and 23, 11% between 24 and 29, and 19% above 30. 47% of the current freshmen were in the top fifth of their class; 75% were in the top two fifths. 9 freshmen graduated first in their class. **Admissions Contact:** Brandon Combs, Director of Undergraduate Admissions. Email: *admissions@asbury.edu* Web: *www.asbury.edu*

FINANCIAL AID: In 2016-2017, 79% of all full-time freshmen and 79% of continuing full-time students received some form of financial aid. 79% of all full-time freshmen and 77% of continuing full-time students received need-based aid. The average freshman award was $19,835. Need-based scholarships or need-based grants averaged $14,781; need-based self-help aid (loans and jobs) averaged $4,117; non-need-based athletic scholarships averaged $5,261; and other non-need-based awards and non-need-based scholarships averaged $13,764. The average financial indebtedness of the 2016 graduate was $27,916. The college's own financial statement is required. The priority date for freshman financial aid applications for fall entry is February 1.

BELLARMINE UNIVERSITY — D-2

www.bellarmine.edu

Louisville, KY 40205	**(502) 272-8131** **(800) 274-4723**
Fax: (502) 272-8002	**Email: admissions@bellarmine.edu**
Full-time: 869 men, 1475 women	**Faculty:** 129; IIA, av$
Part-time: 90 men, 296 women	**Ph.D.s:** 82%
Graduate: 275 men, 597 women	**Student/Faculty:** 17 to 1
Year: semesters, summer session	**Tuition:** $39,750
Room & Board: $11,470	**Freshman Class:** 4317 applied, 3716 accepted, 607 enrolled
SAT CR/M: 546/551 **ACT:** 24	**CEEB CODE:** 1056
Application Deadline: August 15	**COMPETITIVE**

Bellarmine University, founded in 1950, is an independent Catholic university offering undergraduate and graduate programs in the liberal arts and professional studies. Figures in the above capsule and in this profile are approximate. There are 6 undergraduate schools and 6 graduate schools. In addition to regional accreditation, Bellarmine has baccalaureate program accreditation with AACSB, NCATE, CAAHEP, CAPTE, CCNE, CoARC, and NAACLS. The 144-acre campus is in a suburban area in Louisville, Kentucky. Including any residence halls, there are 42 buildings.

STUDENT LIFE: 68% of undergraduates are from Kentucky. Others are from 29 states, 20 foreign countries, and Canada. 63% are from public schools. 81% are White; 4% African American; 3% Asian American; 2% Hispanic; 2% Foreign. 49% are Catholic; 25% Protestant. **Female To Male Ratio:** 1.9:1. The average age of freshmen is 18; all undergraduates, 21. 22% do not continue beyond their first year; 63% remain to graduate. **Housing:** 1127 students can be accommodated in college housing, which includes single-sex and coed dorms and on-campus apartments. In addition, there are honors houses and special-interest houses. On-campus housing is available on a first-come, first-served basis, and is available on a lottery system for upperclassmen. Priority is given to out-of-town students. 53% of students commute. Alcohol is not permitted. All students may keep cars.

FACULTY/CLASSROOMS: 48% of faculty are male; 52% are female. 85% teach undergraduates, 75% do research, and 75% do both. No introductory courses are taught by graduate students. The average class size in an introductory lecture is 21; in a laboratory is 17; and in a regular course is 21.

PROGRAMS OF STUDY: Bellarmine confers B.A., B.S., B.S.H.S. and B.S.N. degrees. Master's and doctoral degrees are also awarded. Bachelor's degrees are awarded in BIOLOGICAL SCIENCE (biochemistry, biology/biological science, biophysics, and molecular biology), BUSINESS (accounting, banking and finance, and business administration and management), COMMUNICATIONS AND THE ARTS (arts administration/management, communications, English, fine arts, languages, music, music technology, Spanish, speech/debate/rhetoric, and studio art), COMPUTER AND PHYSICAL SCIENCE (actuarial science, chemistry, computer science, mathematics, and physics), EDUCATION (elementary education, middle school education, and special education), ENGINEERING AND ENVIRONMENTAL DESIGN (computer engineering, computer technology, and preengineering), HEALTH PROFESSIONS (clinical science, exercise science, medical technology, nursing, predentistry, premedicine, prephysical therapy, preveterinary science, and respiratory therapy), SOCIAL SCIENCE (criminal justice, economics, history, interdisciplinary studies, international studies, liberal arts/general studies, philosophy, political science/government, psychology, sociology, and theological studies). Preprofessional programs, nursing, and accounting are the strongest academically.

ACTIVITIES: 1% of women belong to 1 national sorority. There are 50 groups on campus, including wind ensemble, art, band, cheerleading, chess, choir, chorale, chorus, computers, dance, debate, drama, ethnic, honors, international, jazz band, LGBT, literary magazine, mock trial team, musical theater, newspaper, opera, pep band, photography, political, professional, radio and TV, religious, social, social service, and student government. Popular campus events include Hillside Concerts, Midnight Breakfast, and Ball on the Belle (Halloween Cruise). **Sports:** There are 9 intercollegiate sports for men and 10 for women, and 8 intramural sports for men and 8 for women. Facilities include a 3000-seat basketball and volleyball arena, 2000-seat soccer, field hockey, lacrosse, and track stadium with an artificial turf field and an 8-lane dual-durometer polyurethane poured surface. **Graduates:** From July 1, 2015 to June 30, 2016, 607 bachelor's degrees were awarded. The most popular majors were health professions and related sciences (32%), business/marketing (16%), and psychology (9%). In an average class, 1% graduate in 3 years or less, 51% graduate in 4 years or less, 65% graduate in 5 years or less, and 66% graduate in 6 years or less. Of the 2015 graduating class, 23% were enrolled in graduate school within 6 months of graduation, and 90% were employed.

SERVICES: Counseling and information services are available, as is tutoring in every subject. The Academic Resource Center provides one-on-one or group tutoring for all 100- and 200-level courses. Disability Services provides note takers, distraction-reduced testing environments, extended time, books on tape, and scribe services. **Library/Resources:** The library contains 128,772 volumes, 316,810 microform items, and 4,964 audio/video tapes/CDs/DVDs, and subscribes to 105,441 periodicals including electronic. Computerized library services include interlibrary loans, database searching, Internet access, and Wi-Fi capability. Special learning facilities include an art gallery and radio station. The Thomas Merton Center is the official repository of the collection of materials by and about Thomas Merton (1915-1968 writer and Trappist Monk at Our Lady of Gethsemani Abbey in Kentucky). **Physically Challenged Students:** 85% of the campus is accessible. Facilities include wheelchair ramps, elevators, special parking, specially equipped restrooms, special class scheduling, lowered drinking fountains, lowered telephones, and special housing. **Special:** Cross-registration may be arranged through Kentuckiana Metroversity, a consortium of colleges in

Kentucky and southern Indiana. Bellarmine also offers study abroad in more than 50 countries, internships in most majors, a Washington semester, a liberal studies degree, dual majors, accelerated degree programs, credit for life experience, pass/fail options during the junior and senior years, and a marine biology program in the Bahamas. There is also an honors program and the Brown Leadership Program. There are 5 national honor societies and a freshman honors program. **Visiting:** There are regularly scheduled orientations for prospective students, including an admissions and financial aid session, a campus tour, interviews with faculty, and participation in a student panel. There are guides for informal visits, visitors may sit in on classes, and stay overnight. To schedule a visit, contact the Office of Admission. **Campus Safety and Security:** Measures include 24-hour foot and vehicle patrol, self-defense education, and security escort services. There are shuttle buses, emergency telephones, lighted pathways/sidewalks, controlled access to dorms/residences, security alert bulletins, CPR-certified security, and security cameras in residence halls and in the parking lot.

REQUIREMENTS: The SAT or ACT is required. High school courses should include 4 years of English, 3 years of math, and 2 years each of science and social studies, and 2 years of foreign language is recommended. The GED is accepted. An essay may be requested. A GPA of 2.5 is required. AP and CLEP credits are accepted. Important factors in the admissions decision are recommendations by school officials, advanced placement or honors courses, and extracurricular activities record. In order to graduate, students must complete a minimum of 126 credit hours with a minimum GPA of 2.0. Between 24 and 52 hours are required in the major. All students must fulfill 49 credit hours of core requirements, including English, philosophy, theology, math, social sciences, natural sciences, fine arts, and Western civilization. Required freshman, sophomore, junior, and senior seminars focus on the American experience, transcultural experience, and Catholic social justice. Students in the honors program must complete a senior honors thesis. **Procedure:** Freshmen are admitted fall, spring, and summer. Entrance exams should be taken by December of the senior year. There is a deferred admissions plan. Applications should be filed by August 15 for fall entry, along with a $25 fee. Applications are accepted on-line. **Transfer Students:** 78 transfer students enrolled in 2015-2016. Applicants should have a minimum college GPA of 2.0 and submit transcripts from all postsecondary schools attended. 36 of 126 credits required for the bachelor's degree must be completed at Bellarmine. **International Students:** There are 51 international students enrolled. The school actively recruits these students. They must take the TOEFL with a minimum score of 550 on the paper-based TOEFL (PBT) or 80 on the Internet-based version (iBT), or take the MELAB. The SAT or ACT be used in lieu of the TOEFL.

ADMISSIONS: 86% of the 2016-2017 applicants were accepted. The SAT scores for the 2016-2017 freshman class were: Critical Reading-- 28% below 500, 46% between 500 and 599, 25% between 600 and 699, and 1% between 700 and 800. Math-- 24% below 500, 48% between 500 and 599, 24% between 600 and 699, and 4% between 700 and 800. The ACT scores were 12% below 12, 33% between 12 and 17, 30% between 18 and 23, 12% between 24 and 29, and 11% above 30. 50% of the current freshmen were in the top fifth of their class; 80% were in the top two fifths. 10 freshmen graduated first in their class. **Admissions Contact:** Timothy Sturgeon, Dean of Admissions. Email: *admissions@bellarmine.edu* Web: *www.bellarmine.edu*

FINANCIAL AID: In 2016-2017, 100% of all full-time freshmen and 97% of continuing full-time students received some form of financial aid. 77% of all full-time freshmen and 71% of continuing full-time students received need-based aid. The average freshman award was $27,350. Need-based scholarships or need-based grants averaged $20,704; need-based self-help aid (loans and jobs) averaged $5,923; non-need-based athletic scholarships averaged $6,000; other non-need-based awards and non-need-based scholarships averaged $20,404; and $3,391 from other forms of aid. 65% of undergraduate students work part-time. Average annual earnings from campus work are $1000. The average financial indebtedness of the 2016 graduate was $23,925. The FAFSA code is 001954. The priority date for freshman financial aid applications for fall entry is March 1. The deadline for filing freshman financial aid applications for fall entry is May 1.

BEREA COLLEGE — E-3

www.berea.edu

Berea, KY 40404 — (859) 985-3500, (800) 326-5948

Fax: (859) 985-3512 — **Email:** hodsonl@berea.edu

Full-time: 699 men, 917 women	**Faculty:** 137
Part-time: 26 men, 23 women	**Ph.D.s:** 91%
Graduate: n/av	**Student/Faculty:** 11 to 1
Year: semesters, summer session	**Tuition:** see profile
Room & Board: $6472	**Freshman Class:** 1744 applied, 572 accepted, 418 enrolled
SAT CR/M/W: 530/560/550 **ACT:** 24	**CEEB CODE:** 1060
Application Deadline: April 30	**COMPETITIVE**

Berea College, founded in 1855, is a private liberal arts institution. All students admitted to Berea College receive our Tuition Promise Scholarship. This scholarship is combined with financial aid you may receive as well as any other scholarship you may be awarded by outside parties or organizations to cover 100% of tuition costs. For most Berea students, the Tuition Promise Scholarship amounts to nearly $100,000 over four years. There is 1 undergraduate school. In addition to regional accreditation, Berea has baccalaureate program accreditation with NCATE and CCNE. The 140-acre campus is in a suburban area 40 miles south of Lexington, KY. Including any residence halls, there are 48 buildings.

STUDENT LIFE: 56% of undergraduates are from out of state, mostly the South. Students are from 40 states, and 70 foreign countries. 9% are Hispanic; 8% Foreign; 6% two or more races; 59% White; 2% Asian American; 15% African American; 1% race unknown. **Female To Male Ratio:** 1.3:1. The average age of freshmen is 18; all undergraduates, 20. 16% do not continue beyond their first year; 84% remain to graduate. **Housing:** 1500 students can be accommodated in college housing, which includes single-sex dorms, on-campus apartments, and married student housing. In addition, there are special-interest houses, Ecovillage and Deep Green Residence Hall (sustainable living). On-campus housing is guaranteed for all 4 years. 97% of students live on campus. Alcohol is not permitted. Some may keep cars.

FACULTY/CLASSROOMS: 53% of faculty are male; 47% are female. All teach undergraduates. No introductory courses are taught by graduate students. The average class size in a laboratory is 20 and in a regular course is 20.

PROGRAMS OF STUDY: Berea confers B.A. and B.S. degrees. Bachelor's degrees are awarded in AGRICULTURE (agriculture and environmental studies), BIOLOGICAL SCIENCE (biology/biological science), BUSINESS (business administration and management), COMMUNICATIONS AND THE ARTS (art, communications, dramatic arts, English, French, German, music, Spanish, and theatre arts), COMPUTER AND PHYSICAL SCIENCE (applied mathematics, chemistry, computer science, mathematics, and physics), EDUCATION (education, elementary education, and physical education), ENGINEERING AND ENVIRONMENTAL DESIGN (industrial engineering technology), HEALTH PROFESSIONS (nursing), SOCIAL SCIENCE (African studies, African American studies, Asian/Oriental studies, child care/child and family studies, economics, history, peace studies, philosophy, political science/government, psychology, religion, sociology, and women's studies). Business administration, technology & applied design, and child & family studies have the largest enrollments.

ACTIVITIES: There are no fraternities or sororities. There are 75 groups on campus, including art, band, cheerleading, chess, choir, chorus, communications, dance, debate, drama, environmental, ethnic, honors, international, jazz band, LGBT, literary magazine, newspaper, orchestra, pep band, photography, political, professional, religious, social, social service, student government, and yearbook. Popular campus events include Mountain Day and Labor Day. **Sports:** There are 7 intercollegiate sports for men and 7 for women, and 9 intramural sports for men and 9 for women. Facilities include an indoor swimming pool, 5 racquetball courts, 15 tennis courts, playing fields, dance studio, 3-lane indoor walking track, an 8-lane all-weather track, and weight training and cardiovascular exercise rooms. **Graduates:** From July 1, 2015 to June 30, 2016, 312 bachelor's degrees were awarded. The most popular majors were business administration (10%), English (7%), and child and family studies (7%). 110 companies recruited on campus in 2015-2016. In an average class, 47% graduate in 4 years or less, 65% graduate in 5 years or less, and 63% graduate in 6 years or less.

SERVICES: Counseling and information services are available, as is tutoring in some subjects. There is a reader service for the blind, and remedial math, reading, and writing. The Center for Transformative Learning supports research, writing, and public speaking across the curriculum, valuing writing in all disciplines that include the spoken and written word. **Library/Resources:** The library contains 346,053 volumes, 149,822 microform items, and 15,959 audio/video tapes/CDs/DVDs, and subscribes to 68,520 periodicals including electronic. Computerized library services include interlibrary loans, database searching, Internet access, and Wi-Fi capability. Special learning facilities include an art gallery, planetarium, and a geology museum. **Physically Challenged Students:** 53% of the campus is accessible. Facilities include wheelchair ramps, elevators, special parking, specially equipped restrooms, special class scheduling, lowered drinking fountains, lowered telephones, electronic doors, and a lift chair for the indoor pool. **Special:** Students may study abroad in many countries. They can also participate in internships independent and team-initiated studies. Student-designed majors are available. A 3-2 engineering degree is offered with the University of Kentucky. All students must participate in an on-campus work program 10 to 15 hours per week. There are 19 national honor societies. **Visiting:** There are regularly scheduled orientations for prospective students. Student visits consist of an introductory session and a tour of campus and residence halls. For applicants, the visit includes a private interview and/or conversation with an admissions representative. There are guides for informal visits, visitors may sit in on classes, and stay overnight. To schedule a visit, contact Denessa McPherson at (800) 326-5948 or (859) 985-3500. **Campus Safety and Security:** Measures include 24-hour foot and vehicle patrol, emergency notification system, self-defense education, and security escort services. There are emergency telephones, lighted pathways/sidewalks, and ongoing programs on campus safety, theft prevention, assault and rape prevention, fire prevention, defensive driving, and occupational safety, including work with hazardous materials.

REQUIREMENTS: Either the ACT or SAT is required. Applicants should be graduates of an accredited secondary school. The GED is accepted. Home-schooled students are also encouraged to apply. Financial need is a requirement for admission. Berea recommends 4 units in English, 3 in math, and 2 each in foreign language, science, and social studies. AP and CLEP credits are accepted. Important factors in the admissions decision are ability to finance college education, geographical diversity, and advanced placement or honors courses. Berea's curriculum offers the advantage of interdisciplinary general study coupled with intensive study in 31 major fields (some of which have multiple concentrations) and 32 minor fields of study. In all academic disciplines, students acquire knowledge and deepen their understanding of the subject area while gaining competency in applying the content and methods of inquiry to daily life. A degree is conferred upon the completion of both the General Education curriculum and the curriculum of a selected major, provided the student has earned the minimum number of credits (including 20 outside the major), and has earned a cumulative grade point average (GPA) of 2.0 or higher in all courses, as well as in the major course-work. (Please be aware that some academic programs require a GPA higher than the College requirement of 2.0). To calculate the minimum GPA requirement for a major, the College combines all grades earned in both the discipline (requirements and electives in the major rubric and concentration, if any) and in collateral courses, unless otherwise indicated by a particular program for its major requirements. A minimum of 32 earned course credits (typically 34 in Nursing) is required for graduation, with at least 20 courses taken outside the major discipline. **Procedure:** Freshmen are admitted fall. Entrance exams should be taken during the junior year or early in the senior year. There is a rolling admissions plan. Application deadlines are open. Notifications are sent November 1. Applications are accepted on-line. **Transfer Students:** 48 transfer students enrolled in 2015-2016. Applicants must be in good standing at the last college attended and have a minimum GPA of 2.0. 8 of 32 credits required for the bachelor's degree must be completed at Berea. **International Students:** There are 122 international students enrolled. They must take the TOEFL with a minimum score of 500 on the paper-based TOEFL (PBT) or 61 on the Internet-based version (iBT). They must also take the IELTS, scoring 5 overall and 5 in each exam area; SAT, scoring 1210 (430 Critical Reading); or ACT, scoring 17.

ADMISSIONS: 33% of the 2016-2017 applicants were accepted. The SAT scores for the 2016-2017 freshman class were: Critical Reading-- 29% below 500, 44% between 500 and 599, and 27% between 600 and 699. Math-- 12% below 500, 56% between 500 and 599, 29% between 600 and 699, and 2% between 700 and 800. Writing-- 22% below 500, 46% between 500 and 599, 29% between 600 and 699, and 2% between 700 and 800. The ACT scores were 43% between 18 and 23, 48% between 24 and 29, and 9% above 30. 51% of the current freshmen were in the top fifth of their class; 89% were in the top two fifths. 7 freshmen graduated first in their class. **Admissions Contact:** Luke Hodson, Director of Admissions. Email: *hodsonl@berea.edu* Web: *www.berea.edu*

FINANCIAL AID: In 2016-2017, 100% of all full-time freshmen and 100% of continuing full-time students received some form of financial aid. 100% of all full-time freshmen and 100% of continuing full-time students received need-based aid. The average freshman award was $34,366. Need-based scholarships or need-based grants averaged $31,803; and need-based self-help aid (loans and jobs) averaged $1,825. 100% of undergraduate students work part-time. Average annual earnings from campus work are $2383. The average financial indebtedness of the 2016 graduate was $7,891. The FAFSA code is 001955. The priority date for freshman financial aid applications for fall entry is February 1. The deadline for filing freshman financial aid applications for fall entry is May 1.

BRESCIA UNIVERSITY — B-3

www.brescia.edu

Owensboro, KY 42301	(270) 685-3131 (877) BRESCIA Email: admissions@brescia.edu
Full-time: 199 men, 443 women	**Faculty:** 38
Part-time: 23 men, 136 women	**Ph.D.s:** 70%
Graduate: 6 men, 11 women	**Student/Faculty:** 13 to 1
Year: semesters, summer session	**Tuition:** $20,390
Room & Board: $9500	**Freshman Class:** 5798 applied, 1189 accepted, 163 enrolled
SAT or ACT: required	**CEEB CODE:** 1071
Application Deadline: open	**VERY COMPETITIVE+**

Brescia University, founded in 1925 as a women's junior college, became a 4-year, coeducational liberal arts institution in 1950. It is a private school affiliated with the Roman Catholic Church. The university offers certificates, associate, baccalaureate, and master's degrees through on-ground and online classes. Figures in the above capsule and in this profile are approximate. There are 6 undergraduate schools and 2 graduate schools. In addition to regional accreditation, Brescia has baccalaureate program accreditation with CSWE and NCATE. The 6-acre campus is in an urban area Downtown Owensboro, KY, 32 miles southeast of Evansville, Indiana, and 125 miles from both Louisville and Nashville. Including any residence halls, there are 20 buildings.

STUDENT LIFE: 78% of undergraduates are from Kentucky. Others are from 42 states, 8 foreign countries, and Canada. 89% are White; 4% African American; 4% Foreign; 1% American Indian/Alaska Native; 1% Hispanic. 39% are Catholic; 32% Protestant; 27% claim no religious affiliation. **Female To Male Ratio:** 2.6:1. The average age of freshmen is 19; all undergraduates, 26. 33% do not continue beyond their first year. **Housing:** 224 students can be accommodated in college housing, which includes single-sex and coed dorms and on-campus apartments. In addition, there are honors houses and special-interest houses. On-campus housing is available on a first-come, first-served basis and is available on a lottery system for upperclassmen. 60% of students commute. Alcohol is not permitted. All students may keep cars.

FACULTY/CLASSROOMS: 47% of faculty are male; 53% are female. All teach undergraduates. No introductory courses are taught by graduate students. The average class size in an introductory lecture is 14; in a laboratory is 10; and in a regular course is 12.

PROGRAMS OF STUDY: Brescia confers B.A., B.S., and B.S.W. degrees. Associate and master's degrees are also awarded. Bachelor's degrees are awarded in BIOLOGICAL SCIENCE (biochemistry and biology/biological science), BUSINESS (accounting, banking and finance, business administration and management, business economics, and human resources), COMMUNICATIONS AND THE ARTS (art, English, graphic design, Spanish, and theatre arts), COMPUTER AND PHYSICAL SCIENCE (chemistry, computer science, mathematics, and physical sciences), EDUCATION (art education, early childhood education, education of the mentally handicapped, elementary education, and special education), HEALTH PROFESSIONS (medical laboratory technology, medical technology, and speech pathology/audiology), SOCIAL SCIENCE (addiction studies, history, liberal arts/general studies, pastoral studies, psychology, religion, social studies, and social work). Education, business, and English are the strongest academically. Business, social work, and education have the largest enrollments.

ACTIVITIES: There are no fraternities or sororities. There are 25 groups on campus, including Z.E.S.T. (Zombie Emergency Survival Team), black student union, clay club, Habitat for Humanity, philosophy club, art, choir, chorus, communications, computers, creative writing, drama, honors, international, literary magazine, musical theater, newspaper, pep band, political, professional, religious, social, social service, and student government. Popular campus events include Homecoming, Opening Year Mass, Founders Convocation, and Inaugural Ball. **Sports:** There are 7 intercollegiate sports for men and 8 for women, and 5 intramural sports for men and 5 for women. Facilities include a gym, 2 tennis courts, a weight room, a game room, a cardiovascular workout room, a racquetball court, a batting cage, a baseball field, and soccer field. **Graduates:** From July 1, 2015 to June 30, 2016, 87 bachelor's degrees were awarded. The most popular majors were social work (25%), business (16%), and communication sciences and disorders (10%). In an average class, 17% graduate in 4 years or less, 26% graduate in 5 years or less, and 32% graduate in 6 years or less.

SERVICES: Counseling and information services are available, as is tutoring in most subjects. There is remedial math, reading, and writing. **Library/Resources:** The library contains 156,380 volumes, 55,283 microform items, and 3,709 audio/video tapes/CDs/DVDs, and subscribes to 27,527 periodicals including electronic. Computerized library services include interlibrary loans, database searching, Internet access, and Wi-Fi capability. Special learning facilities include an art gallery. **Physically Challenged Students:** 95% of the campus is accessible. Facilities include wheelchair ramps, elevators, special parking, specially equipped restrooms, lowered drinking fountains, and lowered telephones. **Special:** Brescia offers a combined engineering degree with the University of Kentucky and the University of Louisville. Work-study programs, student-designed majors, nondegree study, dual majors, study abroad in Mexico, an internship in professional writing, pass/fail options, and cross-registration with Kentucky Wesleyan are available. The Weekend College offers four 9-week modules of study. There are 2 national honor societies and a freshman honors program. **Visiting:** There are regularly scheduled orientations for prospective students, including spring and fall open houses for freshmen and a spring transfer open house. There are guides for informal visits, visitors may sit in on classes, and stay overnight. To schedule a visit, contact the Office of Admissions at 1-877-BRESCIA. **Campus Safety and Security:** Measures include emergency notification system and security escort services. There are emergency telephones, lighted pathways/sidewalks, including night security.

REQUIREMENTS: The SAT or ACT is required. Essays and recommendations are helpful. High school units should include 4 of English, 3 of math, and 2 each in social studies, science, foreign language, fine arts, and computer science. Applications are accepted on-line at the university's web-site. A GPA of 2.5 is required. AP and CLEP credits are accepted. Important factors in the admissions decision are advanced placement or honors courses and recommendations by school officials. All students must earn 128 credit hours, including 42 upper-division hours, and 30 or more hours in the major, while maintaining an overall GPA of 2.0 and 2.5 in the major. Distribution requirements include 18 hours in aesthetics, language, and literature, 12 in social science, 9 each in fine arts, science, and math, 6 in religious studies, and 3 in philosophy. Students must also demonstrate computer competency. **Procedure:** Freshmen are admitted to all sessions. Entrance exams should be taken at the end of the junior year. There is a rolling admissions plan. Application deadlines are open. The fall 2016 application fee was $25. Applications are accepted on-line. **Transfer Students:** 120 transfer students enrolled in 2015-2016. Transfer students must have a minimum GPA of 2.0. 42 of 128 credits required for the bachelor's degree must be completed at Brescia. **International Students:** The school actively recruits these students. They must take the TOEFL. They must also take the SAT or ACT.

ADMISSIONS: 21% of the 2016-2017 applicants were accepted. The SAT scores for the 2016-2017 freshman class were: Math-- 53% below 500 and 47% between 500 and 599. The ACT scores were 20% below 12, 45% between 12 and 17, 17% between 18 and 23, 15% between 24 and 29, and 3% above 30. **Admissions Contact:** Christy Rohner, Director of Admissions. Email: *admissions@brescia.edu* Web: *www.brescia.edu*

FINANCIAL AID: 100% of undergraduate students work part-time. Brescia is a member of CSS. The FAFSA code is 001958. The deadline for filing freshman financial aid applications for fall entry is March 1.

CAMPBELLSVILLE UNIVERSITY — D-3

www.campbellsville.edu

Campbellsville, KY 42718	**(270) 789-5220** **(800) 264-6014**
Fax: (270) 789-5071	**Email: admissions@campbellsville.edu**
Full-time: 895 men, 1103 women	**Faculty:** 146
Part-time: 505 men, 846 women	**Ph.D.s:** 67%
Graduate: 449 men, 507 women	**Student/Faculty:** 14 to 1
Year: semesters, summer session	**Tuition:** $24,596
Room & Board: $7896	**Freshman Class:** 2966 applied, 2072 accepted, 599 enrolled
ACT: 21	**CEEB CODE:** 1097
Application Deadline: August 1	**COMPETITIVE**

Campbellsville University is a comprehensive Christian institution that offers pre-professional, undergraduate, and graduate programs. The university is dedicated to academic excellence solidly grounded in the liberal arts that fosters personal growth, integrity, and professional preparation within a caring environment. The university prepares students as Christian servant leaders for life-long learning, continued scholarship, and active participation in a diverse, global society. There are 7 undergraduate schools and 6 graduate schools. In addition to regional accreditation, Campbellsville has baccalaureate program accreditation with CSWE, NASM, NCATE, and IACBE. The 90-acre campus is in a small town 85 miles southwest of Lexington and 85 miles southeast of Louisville. Including any residence halls, there are 56 buildings.

STUDENT LIFE: 85% of undergraduates are from Kentucky. Others are from 41 states, 56 foreign countries, and Canada. 9% are African American; 76% White; 7% Foreign; 3% race unknown; 2% Hispanic; 1% Asian American; 1% two or more races. 60% are Protestant; 12% claim no religious affiliation. **Female To Male Ratio:** 1.3:1. The average age of freshmen is 19; all undergraduates, 25. 30% do not continue beyond their first year; 42% remain to graduate. **Housing:** 1044 students can be accommodated in college housing, which includes single-sex dorms, on-campus apartments, off-campus apartments, and married student housing. On-campus housing is guaranteed for all 4 years. 54% of students commute. Alcohol is not permitted. All students may keep cars.

FACULTY/CLASSROOMS: 51% of faculty are male; 49% are female. All teach undergraduates. No introductory courses are taught by graduate students. The average class size in an introductory lecture is 24; in a laboratory is 12; and in a regular course is 17.

PROGRAMS OF STUDY: Campbellsville confers B.A., B.S., B.M., B.S.B.A., and B.S.W. degrees. Associate and master's degrees are also awarded. Bachelor's degrees are awarded in BIOLOGICAL SCIENCE (biology/biological science), BUSINESS (accounting, business administration and management, business economics, marketing management, office supervision and management, and sports management), COMMUNICATIONS AND THE ARTS (art, communications, English, music, music performance, theatre arts, and voice), COMPUTER AND PHYSICAL SCIENCE (chemistry, computer science, information sciences and systems, and mathematics), EDUCATION (early childhood education, elementary education, health education, middle school education, music education, physical education, recreation education, social science education, and teaching English as a second/foreign language (TESOL/TEFOL)), ENGINEERING AND ENVIRONMENTAL DESIGN (preengineering), HEALTH PROFESSIONS (exercise science, medical laboratory technology, nursing, predentistry, premedicine, prepharmacy, and sports medicine), SOCIAL SCIENCE (biblical studies, Christian studies, criminal justice, economics, history, political science/government, prelaw, psychology, religious education, religious music, social work, sociology, and youth ministry). Biology, social work, business, and music are the strongest academically. Elementary education, business administration, and social work have the largest enrollments.

ACTIVITIES: There are no fraternities or sororities. There are 45 groups on campus, including art, band, cheerleading, choir, chorale, chorus, computers, dance, drama, environmental, ethnic, honors, international, jazz band, literary magazine, marching band, musical theater, newspaper, opera, orchestra, pep band, photography, political, professional, radio and TV, religious, social, social service, student government, and symphony. Popular campus events include Valentine Banquet, a Christmas Celebration, and Heritage Day. **Sports:** There are 13 intercollegiate sports for men and 12 for women, and 10 intramural sports for men and 10 for women. Facilities include a swimming pool, gym, football stadium, baseball field, an intramural activities center with skating facilities, and large game rooms. There are also softball and soccer fields, and an indoor practice field. **Graduates:** From July 1, 2015 to June 30, 2016, 325 bachelor's degrees were awarded. The most popular majors were education (18%), business (16%), and religion (16%). In an average class, 42% graduate in 6 years or less.

SERVICES: Counseling and information services are available, as is tutoring in every subject. There is remedial math, reading, and writing. There is also an AIDS education program and a study skills program. **Library/Resources:** The library contains 404,600 volumes, 12,000 microform items, and 689 audio/video tapes/CDs/DVDs, and subscribes to 78 periodicals including electronic. Computerized library services include interlibrary loans, database searching, and Internet access. Special learning facilities include an art gallery, radio station, TV station, a teacher resource center, the Kentuckiana Collection, Clay Hill Memorial Forest, and the American Civil War Institute. **Physically Challenged Students:** 85% of the campus is accessible. Facilities include wheelchair ramps, elevators, special parking, specially equipped restrooms, special class scheduling, lowered drinking fountains, and lowered telephones. **Special:** Legislative and public administration internships, a Washington semester, and federal work-study programs are available. The university also offers a semester in London program, a 3-2 engineering degree with the University of Kentucky, dual majors, credit by exam, credit for life, military, and work experience, non-degree study, and pass/fail options. There is a freshman honors program. **Visiting:** There are regularly scheduled orientations for prospective students, consisting of visitation days held in October, February, and April. There are guides for informal visits, visitors may sit in on classes, and stay overnight. To schedule a visit, contact the Admissions Office. **Campus Safety and Security:** Measures include 24-hour foot and vehicle patrol, emergency notification system, self-defense education, and security escort services. There are emergency telephones, lighted pathways/sidewalks, and controlled access to dorms/residences.

REQUIREMENTS: The SAT may be substituted for the ACT. Applicants must be graduates of an accredited secondary school with a GPA of 2.0. The GED is accepted. An interview is recommended. AP and CLEP credits are accepted. Important factors in the admissions decision are evidence of special talent, leadership record, and advanced placement or honors courses. All candidates must be of good moral character. All students must complete a minimum of 128 semester hours, including 30 in the major, 21 in the minor, and 51 in general education courses. The minimum GPA is 2.5 for education majors, 2.1 for all others. All students must fulfill an English composition requirement. **Procedure:** Freshmen are admitted fall and spring. Entrance exams should be taken no later than February of the senior year. There are deferred admissions and rolling admissions plans. Application deadlines are open. Application fee is $20. Applications are accepted on-line. Application fees are waived if application is completed on-line. **Transfer Students:** 280 transfer students enrolled in 2015-2016. Of the 128 credits needed to graduate, all students must complete one third of the credits required for the major and the minor at the university. The last year must be completed in residence. 30 of 120 credits required for the bachelor's degree must be completed at Campbellsville. **International Students:** There are 159 international students enrolled. The school actively recruits these students. They must take the TOEFL. They must also take the SAT or ACT.

ADMISSIONS:70% of the 2016-2017 applicants were accepted. The SAT scores for the 2016-2017 freshman class were: Critical Reading-- 65% below 500, 24% between 500 and 599, 9% between 600 and 699, and 3% between 700 and 800. Math-- 42% below 500, 39% between 500 and 599, 13% between 600 and 699, and 5% between 700 and 800. Writing-- 71% below 500, 26% between 500 and 599, and 3% between 600 and 699. The ACT scores were 15% between 12 and 17, 56% between 18 and 23, 25% between 24 and 29, and 4% above 30. 32% of the current freshmen were in the top fifth of their class; 60% were in the top two fifths. 12 freshmen graduated first in their class. **Admissions Contact:** Rita Creason, Director of Admissions. Email: *admissions@campbellsville.edu* Web: *www.campbellsville.edu*

FINANCIAL AID: In 2016-2017, 95% of all full-time freshmen and 94% of continuing full-time students received some form of financial aid. 87% of all full-time freshmen and 83% of continuing full-time students received need-based aid. 44% of undergraduate students work part-time. Average annual earnings from campus work are $1700. The average financial indebtedness of the 2016 graduate was $18,132. The FAFSA code is 001959. The priority date for freshman financial aid applications for fall entry is February 20. The deadline for filing freshman financial aid applications for fall entry is July 31.

CENTRE COLLEGE D-3
www.centre.edu

Danville, KY 40422	(859) 238-5350 (800) 423-6236
Fax: (859) 238-5373	Email: admission@centre.edu
Full-time: 700 men, 728 women	**Faculty:** 129; IIB, av$
Part-time: 1 men, 1 women	**Ph.D.s:** 98%
Graduate: n/av	**Student/Faculty:** 10 to 1
Year: 4-1-4	**Tuition:** $39,300
Room & Board: $9950	**Freshman Class:** 2603 applied, 1935 accepted, 400 enrolled
SAT CR/M/W: 590/630/600 **ACT:** 29	**CEEB CODE:** 1109
Application Deadline: January 15	**HIGHLY COMPETITIVE**

Centre College is a small, independent, and selective educational community dedicated to study in the liberal arts as the means to develop the intellectual, personal, and moral potential of its students. Centre nurtures in its students the ability to think logically and critically, to work creatively, to analyze and compare values, and to write and speak with clarity and grace. It acquaints students with the range of accomplishments of the human mind and spirit in a variety of arts and theoretical disciplines. It enables students to choose and fulfill significant responsibilities in society. In short, Centre's highest priority is to prepare its students for lives of learning, leadership, and service. The Centre Commitment guarantees students who meet the College's academic and social expectations an internship or (beginning with the class of 2017) a research opportunity, study abroad, and graduation in four years. If a student is unable to secure the components of the Centre Commitment within four consecutive years of enrollment, the College will provide up to an additional year of study tuition-free. There is 1 undergraduate school. In addition to regional accreditation, Centre has baccalaureate program accreditation with NASDTEC and NCATE. The 160-acre campus is in a small town 35 miles southwest of Lexington and 80 miles southeast of Louisville. Including any residence halls, there are 83 buildings.

STUDENT LIFE: 57% of undergraduates are from Kentucky. Others are from 45 states, 11 foreign countries, and Canada. 64% are from public schools. 75% are White; 7% Foreign; 5% African American; 4% Asian American; 4% Hispanic; 3% two or more races; 1% race unknown. 45% are Protestant; 26% claim no religious affiliation; 21% Catholic. **Female To Male Ratio:** 1.0:1. The average age of freshmen is 18; all undergraduates, 20. 10% do not continue beyond their first year; 80% remain to graduate. **Housing:** 1461 students can be accommodated in college housing, which includes single-sex and coed dorms and on-campus apartments. In addition, there are special-interest houses, fraternity houses, sorority houses, and theme housing. On-campus housing is guaranteed for all 4 years. 98% of students live on campus; of those, 90% remain on campus on weekends. All students may keep cars.

FACULTY/CLASSROOMS: 57% of faculty are male; 43% are female. All teach undergraduates, and all do research. No introductory courses are taught by graduate students. The average class size in an introductory lecture is 25; in a laboratory is 15; and in a regular course is 19.

PROGRAMS OF STUDY: Centre confers B.A. and B.S. degrees. Bachelor's degrees are awarded in AGRICULTURE (environmental studies), BIOLOGICAL SCIENCE (biochemistry, biology/biological science, and molecular biology), BUSINESS (finance), COMMUNICATIONS AND THE ARTS (art history and appreciation, dramatic arts, English, fine arts, French, German, music, and Spanish), COMPUTER AND PHYSICAL SCIENCE (chemical physics, chemistry, computer science, mathematics, physical chemistry, and physics), SOCIAL SCIENCE (anthropology, classical/ancient civilization, economics, history, international relations, philosophy, political science/government, psychobiology, psychology, religion, and sociology). Biochemistry & molecular biology, chemistry, and economics & finance are the strongest academically. Biology, economics & finance, and history have the largest enrollments.

ACTIVITIES: 40% of men belong to 6 national fraternities; 43% of women belong to 5 national sororities. There are 70 groups on campus, including art, band, cheerleading, choir, chorale, chorus, communications, computers, dance, debate, drama, environmental, ethnic, film, honors, international, jazz band, LGBT, literary magazine, musical theater, newspaper, orchestra, pep band, photography, political, professional, radio and TV, religious, social, social service, and student government. Popular campus events include Carnival, Homecoming, Homelessness and Poverty Week, International Dinner, Green Week, CARE Trick or Treat, the Honors Convocation, and the Honor Walk. **Sports:** There are 10 intercollegiate sports for men and 11 for women, and 8 intramural sports for men and 8 for women. Facilities include a complex with a 1500-seat gym, 3 basketball courts, 2 volleyball courts, training room, game room, sauna, weight room, fitness center, and racquetball/handball courts. There is also a 2500-seat stadium, tennis courts, and playing fields for football, track, baseball, softball, soccer, field hockey, and other sports. The natatorium has a 25-yard, 6-lane swimming pool. Golf teams compete at the local country club. Two outdoor turf fields support lacrosse, football, and field hockey. **Graduates:** From July 1, 2015 to June 30, 2016, 298 bachelor's degrees were awarded. The most popular majors were social sciences (30%), psychology (11%), and biological/life sciences (10%). 35 companies recruited on campus in 2015-2016. In an average class, 86% graduate in 4 years or less. Of the 2015 graduating class, 27% were enrolled in graduate school within 6 months of graduation, and 68% were employed.

SERVICES: Counseling and information services are available, as is tutoring in most subjects. There is a reader service for the blind, and remedial writing. **Library/Resources:** The library contains 267,580 volumes, 31,034 microform items, and 7,694 audio/video tapes/CDs/DVDs, and subscribes to 119,283 periodicals including electronic. Computerized library services include interlibrary loans, database searching, Internet access, and Wi-Fi capability. Special learning facilities include an art gallery, natural history museum, and radio station. There is the Center for Teaching and Learning, a hot glass studio, digital media editing lab, and a performing arts center. **Physically Challenged Students:** 70% of the campus is accessible. Facilities include wheelchair ramps, elevators, special parking, specially equipped restrooms, special class scheduling, lowered drinking fountains, lowered telephones, and special housing. **Special:** Centre offers internships, study abroad in 12 countries, a Washington semester through American University, work-study, and a 3-2 engineering degree with Vanderbilt University, Washington University at St. Louis, Columbia University, and the University of Kentucky. Student-designed majors, interdisciplinary majors including chemical physics, secondary education certification, and pre-law, pre-business, and pre-medicine programs are available. Pass/fail options also are available. There are 8 national honor societies and a chapter of Phi Beta Kappa. **Visiting:** There are regularly scheduled orientations for prospective students, including a campus tour, an interview, pre-tour, and faculty appointments. There are guides for informal visits, visitors may sit in on classes, and stay overnight. To schedule a visit, contact Bob Nesmith at bob.nesmith@centre.edu. **Campus Safety and Security:** Measures include 24-hour foot and vehicle patrol, emergency notification system, self-defense education, and security escort services. There are emergency telephones, lighted pathways/sidewalks, controlled access to dorms/residences, and a working relationship with outside agencies.

REQUIREMENTS: The SAT or ACT and ACT Writing Test are recommended. No minimum test scores are required. Students should have completed 13 academic credits, 20 recommended, including 4 years in English, 3-4 years of math, 2-4 years each in science, with 2 years of lab, 2-4 years in foreign language, 2 years recommended of social studies, 2 years of history, and 1 year in an art, or music-related course. An essay is required, and an interview is strongly recommended. AP credits are accepted. Important factors in the admissions decision are leadership record, advanced placement or honors courses, recommendations by school officials, parents or siblings attended your school, evidence of special talent, personality/intangible qualities, extracurricular activities record, recommendations by alumni, and geographical diversity. All students must earn an overall GPA of 2.0 and complete a minimum of 110 credit hours. Students also must demonstrate competency in writing, foreign language, and mathematics plus 1 course beyond basic skills in mathematics, foreign language, or computer science. A first-year humanities program and a freshman seminar must be completed. Core curriculum requirements include 2 courses each in the humanities or art from the aesthetic context, the scientific/technological context, the social context, and the fundamental questions context. **Procedure:** Freshmen are admitted fall. Entrance exams should be taken by January of the senior year. There are early decision, early admissions, and deferred admissions plans. Early decision applications should be filed by November 15; regular applications, by January 15 for fall entry. Notification of early decision is sent December 15; regular decision, March 15. 62 early decision candidates were accepted for the 2016-2017 class. 198 applicants were on the 2016 waiting list; 22 were admitted. Applications are accepted on-line. Application fees are waived if application is completed on-line. **Transfer Students:** 4 transfer students enrolled in 2015-2016. Applicants for transfer must have all previous college transcripts on file and a recommendation from the dean of the most recent college attended. If the student has completed fewer than 2 years of college work, high school records must also be submitted. Students may enroll in the fall, winter, and spring. An interview is recommended. 45 of 111 credits required for the bachelor's degree must be completed at Centre. **International Students:** There are 101 international students enrolled. The school actively recruits these students. They must take the TOEFL with a minimum score of 90 on the Internet-based version (iBT), or may submit SAT or ACT scores.

ADMISSIONS: 74% of the 2016-2017 applicants were accepted. The SAT scores for the 2016-2017 freshman class were: Critical Reading-- 14% below 500, 41% between 500 and 599, 32% between 600 and 699, and 13% between 700 and 800. Math-- 8% below 500, 28% between 500 and 599, 40% between 600 and 699, and 24% between 700 and 800. Writing-- 9% below 500, 40% between 500 and 599, 39% between 600 and 699, and 12% between 700 and 800. The ACT scores were 7% between 18 and 23, 50% between 24 and 29, and 43% above 30. 76% of the current freshmen were in the top fifth of their class; 94% were in the top two fifths. There was 1 National Merit finalist. 24 freshmen graduated first in their class. **Admissions Contact:** Bob Nesmith, Dean of Admission and Financial Aid. Email: *admission@centre.edu* Web: *www.centre.edu*

FINANCIAL AID: In 2016-2017, 97% of all full-time freshmen and 96% of continuing full-time students received some form of financial aid. 61% of all full-time freshmen and 56% of continuing full-time students received need-based aid. The average freshman award was $34,106. Need-based scholarships or need-based grants averaged $31,508 ($52,500 maximum); need-based self-help aid (loans and jobs) averaged $4,420 ($7,300 maximum); other non-need-based awards and non-need-based scholarships averaged $21,980 ($49,250 maximum); and $3,368 from other forms of aid. 31% of undergraduate students work part-time. Average annual earnings from campus work are $1000. The average financial indebtedness of the 2016 graduate was $22,607. The the college's own financial statement is required. The FAFSA code is 001961. The priority date for freshman financial aid applications for fall entry is January 31.

EASTERN KENTUCKY UNIVERSITY — E-3

www.eku.edu

Richmond, KY 40475	(859) 622-2106 (800) 465-9191
Fax: (859) 622-3024	**Email:** admissions@eku.edu
Full-time: n/av	**Faculty:** 687; IIA, --$
Part-time: n/av	**Ph.D.s:** 66%
Graduate: n/av	**Student/Faculty:** 17 to 1
Year: semesters, summer session	**Tuition:** $8568 ($17,880)
Room & Board: $8340	**Freshman Class:** n/av
ACT: required	**CEEB CODE:** 1200
Application Deadline: August 1	**COMPETITIVE**

Eastern Kentucky University, established in 1906, is a public, state-supported institution offering degree programs in the arts and sciences, business, environmental studies, health fields, education, and public service occupations. The figures in the above capsule and in this profile are approximate. There are 6 undergraduate schools and 1 graduate school. In addition to regional accreditation, EKU has baccalaureate program accreditation with AACSB, ACCE, ADA, AHEA, CSWE, FIDER, NASM, NCATE, NLN, NRPA, ACEN ACEND, ACOTE, ACS, CAHIIM, CACREP, CAEP, CCNE, CCIE, CAATE, and CAEP. The 628-acre campus is in a small town 20 miles south of Lexington. Including any residence halls, there are 98 buildings.

STUDENT LIFE: 87% of undergraduates are from Kentucky. Others are from 50 states, 46 foreign countries, and Canada. 90% are from public schools. 82% are White; 5% African American; 3% race unknown; 2% Hispanic; 2% two or more races; 1% Asian American; 1% Foreign. The average age of freshmen is 19; all undergraduates, 23. 35% do not continue beyond their first year; 37% remain to graduate. **Housing:** 5260 students can be accommodated in college housing, which includes single-sex and coed dorms, on-campus apartments, and married student housing. In addition, there are honors houses, special-interest houses, and special accommodations for senior home economics students. On-campus housing is guaranteed for all 4 years. 71% of students commute. Alcohol is not permitted. All students may keep cars.

FACULTY/CLASSROOMS: 49% of faculty are male; 51% are female. 98% teach undergraduates, 25% do research, and 25% do both. No introductory courses are taught by graduate students. The average class size in an introductory lecture is 30; in a laboratory is 15; and in a regular course is 25.

PROGRAMS OF STUDY: EKU confers B.A., B.S., B.B.A., B.F.A., B.I.S., B.M., B.M.Ed., B.S.N., and B.S.W. degrees. Associate, master's, and doctoral degrees are also awarded. Bachelor's degrees are awarded in AGRICULTURE (agriculture, horticulture, and wildlife management), BIOLOGICAL SCIENCE (biology/biological science and microbiology), BUSINESS (accounting, banking and finance, business administration and management, and marketing/retailing/merchandising), COMMUNICATIONS AND THE ARTS (apparel design, art, broadcasting, dramatic arts, English, French, journalism, music, performing arts, public relations, Spanish, and speech/debate/rhetoric), COMPUTER AND PHYSICAL SCIENCE (chemistry, computer programming, computer science, geology, mathematics, and statistics), EDUCATION (art education, business education, education of the deaf and hearing impaired, elementary education, foreign languages education, health education, home economics education, industrial arts education, middle school education, music education, physical education, secondary education, special education, and technical education), ENGINEERING AND ENVIRONMENTAL DESIGN (airline piloting and navigation, construction technology, environmental science, interior design, and manufacturing technology), HEALTH PROFESSIONS (environmental health science, health care administration, nursing, and occupational therapy), SOCIAL SCIENCE (anthropology, child care/child and family studies, corrections, dietetics, economics, fire protection, forensic studies, geography, history, paralegal studies, philosophy, political science/government, psychology, social work, and sociology). Occupational therapy, psychology, and nursing are the strongest academically. Education, nursing, and law enforcement have the largest enrollments.

ACTIVITIES: There are 230 groups on campus, including art, band, cheerleading, choir, chorale, chorus, computers, dance, debate, drama, drill team, ethnic, film, honors, international, jazz band, LGBT, marching band, musical theater, newspaper, orchestra, pep band, photography, political, professional, radio and TV, religious, social service, student government, and symphony. Popular campus events include Hanging of the Greens at Christmas, International Month, and Fraternity/Sorority Competitions. **Sports:** There are 8 intercollegiate sports for men and 8 for women, and 12 intramural sports for men and 12 for women. Facilities include a dance studio, 5 gyms, 1 outdoor and 2 indoor swimming pools, 19 outdoor hard-courts and 4 indoor tennis courts, handball and racquetball courts, training rooms, a martial arts room, a wellness center, a 7000-seat basketball arena, a 20,000-seat stadium, an 8-lane outdoor track, a field hockey area, an 18-hole golf course, fields for baseball, softball, soccer, weight facilities, and a conditioning center. **Graduates:** From July 1, 2015 to June 30, 2016, 2532 bachelor's degrees were awarded. The most popular majors were criminal justice and police studies (9%), nursing (9%), and curriculum and instruction (9%).

SERVICES: Counseling and information services are available, as is tutoring in some subjects, such as math, English, and reading. There is a reader service for the blind, and remedial math, reading, and writing. **Library/Resources:** The 3 libraries contain 764,662 volumes, 1.3 million microform items, and 12,209 audio/video tapes/CDs/DVDs, and subscribe to 19,033 periodicals including electronic. Computerized library services include interlibrary loans, database searching, and Internet access. Special learning facilities include an art gallery, natural history museum, planetarium, radio station, TV station, and law enforcement complex that includes a training tank for underwater rescue and recovery. **Physically Challenged Students:** 85% of the campus is accessible. Facilities include wheelchair ramps, elevators, special parking, specially equipped restrooms, special class scheduling, lowered drinking fountains, and lowered telephones. **Special:** EKU offers cooperative programs with all academic colleges, internships, study abroad in various European countries, and a 3-2 engineering degree with the University of Kentucky or Auburn University. Students may opt for credit by exam, non-degree study, pass/fail options, student-designed and dual majors, and a general studies degree. There are 23 national honor societies, Phi Beta Kappa, a freshman honors program, and 1 departmental honors program. **Visiting:** There are regularly scheduled orientations for prospective students, consisting of a 1-day program during the summer prior to fall enrollment. There are guides for informal visits, visitors may sit in on classes, and stay overnight. To schedule a visit, contact the Admissions Office. **Campus Safety and Security:** Measures include 24-hour foot and vehicle patrol, emergency notification system, self-defense education, and security escort services. There are shuttle buses, emergency telephones, lighted pathways/sidewalks, and 16 crime-prevention programs.

REQUIREMENTS: The ACT is required. AP and CLEP credits are accepted. Important factors in the admissions decision are evidence of special talent, extracurricular activities record, and leadership record. All students must complete 51 credit hours of general education requirements, including courses in phys ed, health, English, natural science, social science, math, and the humanities. Students must complete a total of 128 credit hours, including 45 to 60 credits in the major, with a minimum GPA of 2.0. **Procedure:** Freshmen are admitted to all sessions. Entrance exams should be taken prior to enrollment. There is a rolling admissions plan. Applications should be filed by August 1 for fall entry, along with a $35 fee. Applications are accepted on-line. **Transfer Students:** 1075 transfer students enrolled in 2015-2016. Applicants must have a 2.0 cumulative GPA from all accredited institutions previously attended and must not have been dismissed. 30 of 120 credits required for the bachelor's degree must be completed at EKU. **International Students:** There are 159 international students enrolled. The school actively recruits these students. They must take the TOEFL with a minimum score of 530 on the paper-based TOEFL (PBT) or 71 on the Internet-based version (iBT). They must also take the ACT, scoring 21, or the SAT for those applicants from states where the SAT is dominant.

Admissions Contact: Stephanie L. Whaley, Director of Admissions. Email: *admissions@eku.edu* Web: *www.eku.edu*

FINANCIAL AID: EKU is a member of CSS. The CSS/Profile and the college's own financial statement are required. The FAFSA code is 001963. The deadline for filing freshman financial aid applications for fall entry is April 15.

GEORGETOWN COLLEGE D-2

www.georgetowncollege.edu

Georgetown, KY 40324 (502) 863-8204 (800) 788-9985

Fax: (502) 868-7733 **Email:** admissions@georgetowncollege.edu

Full-time: 438 men, 469 women	**Faculty:** 76; IIB, --$
Part-time: 26 men, 51 women	**Ph.D.s:** 96%
Graduate: 87 men, 293 women	**Student/Faculty:** 10 to 1
Year: semesters, summer session	**Tuition:** $32,960
Room & Board: $8480	**Freshman Class:** 2145 applied, 1452 accepted, 282 enrolled
SAT CR/M: 494/511 **ACT:** 23	**CEEB CODE:** 1249
Application Deadline: August 1	**COMPETITIVE**

Georgetown College, dating back to 1787 and chartered in 1829, is a small residential liberal arts college distinguished by a combination of respected, rigorous undergraduate and graduate programs, an array of opportunities for involvement and leadership, a commitment to Christian values and its distinctive heritage. There is 1 undergraduate school and 1 graduate school. In addition to regional accreditation, Georgetown has baccalaureate program accreditation with NCATE, ACS, and CAATE. The 104-acre campus is in a suburban area 12 miles north of Lexington just off I-75, and about an hour from Louisville, KY and Cincinnati, OH. Including any residence halls, there are 42 buildings.

STUDENT LIFE: 74% of undergraduates are from Kentucky. Others are from 30 states, and 11 foreign countries. 85% are from public schools. 79% are White; 3% Hispanic; 3% race unknown; 2% Foreign; 2% two or more races; 10% African American; 1% Asian American. 81% are Protestant; 11% Catholic. **Female To Male Ratio:** 1.5:1. The average age of freshmen is 18; all undergraduates, 20. 28% do not continue beyond their first year; 57% remain to graduate. **Housing:** 1325 students can be accommodated in college housing, which includes single-sex dorms, on-campus apartments, and married student housing. In addition, there are fraternity houses and sorority houses. On-campus housing is guaranteed for all 4 years. 91% of students live on campus; of those, 50% remain on campus on weekends. Alcohol is not permitted. All students may keep cars.

FACULTY/CLASSROOMS: 50% of faculty are male; 50% are female. 92% teach undergraduates, 20% do research, and 20% do both. No introductory courses are taught by graduate students. The average class size in an introductory lecture is 14 and in a regular course is 12.

PROGRAMS OF STUDY: Georgetown confers B.A. and B.S. degrees. Master's degrees are also awarded. Bachelor's degrees are awarded in BIOLOGICAL SCIENCE (biochemistry and biology/biological science), BUSINESS (accounting, banking and finance, business administration and management, business economics, international business management, management information systems, marketing/retailing/merchandising, and sports management), COMMUNICATIONS AND THE ARTS (art, communications, creative writing, dramatic arts, English, fine/studio arts, general, French, music, performing arts, and Spanish), COMPUTER AND PHYSICAL SCIENCE (chemistry, mathematics, and physics), EDUCATION (athletic training, elementary education, English education, foreign languages education, history education, mathematics education, middle school education, secondary education, and social studies secondary school education), ENGINEERING AND ENVIRONMENTAL DESIGN (environmental science and preengineering), HEALTH PROFESSIONS (exercise science, predentistry, premedicine, prepharmacy, and prephysical therapy), SOCIAL SCIENCE (American studies, economics, European studies, family/juvenile justice, history, interdisciplinary studies, justice and society, liberal arts/general studies, philosophy, political science/government, prelaw, psychology, religion, safety and security technology, and sociology). Biology, chemistry, and psychology are the strongest academically. Kinesiology, psychology, and education have the largest enrollments.

ACTIVITIES: 27% of men belong to 1 local and 4 national fraternities; 35% of women belong to 5 national sororities. There are 98 groups on campus, including equine scholars, Christian leadership scholars, art, band, cheerleading, choir, chorale, chorus, communications, computers, dance, dance team, drama, environmental, ethnic, forensics, honors, international, jazz band, literary magazine, musical theater, newspaper, pep band, photography, political, professional, radio and TV, religious, social, social service, and student government. Popular campus events include Songfest, Chapel Day/Bid Day, Belle of the Blue, Midnight Brunch, Grubfest, Family Weekend, and Hanging of the Green. **Sports:** There are 8 intercollegiate sports for men and 11 for women, and 11 intramural sports for men and 11 for women. Facilities include a 3000-seat stadium, 8 tennis courts, soccer, baseball, football, softball, and intramural fields, a 1550-seat gym, racquetball courts, a training room, and a fitness center housing a Nautilus area, a weight lifting area, basketball courts, recreation room, and dressing rooms. **Graduates:** From July 1, 2015 to June 30, 2016, 224 bachelor's degrees were awarded. The most popular majors were business/marketing (13%), biological/life sciences (12%), and communication and media studies (12%). 65 companies recruited on campus in 2015-2016. In an average class, 51% graduate in 4 years or less, 60% graduate in 5 years or less, and 67% graduate in 6 years or less.

SERVICES: Counseling and information services are available, as is tutoring in every subject. **Library/Resources:** The library contains 150,279 volumes, 238,214 microform items, and 11,204 audio/video tapes/CDs/DVDs, and subscribes to 43,132 periodicals including electronic. Computerized library services include interlibrary loans, database searching, Internet access, and Wi-Fi capability. Special learning facilities include an art gallery, planetarium, radio station, center for civic engagement, center for solids an alaysis and a writing lab. **Physically Challenged Students:** 70% of the campus is accessible. Facilities include wheelchair ramps, elevators, special parking, specially equipped restrooms, special class scheduling, and lowered drinking fountains. **Special:** Georgetown offers an innovative Spanish Immersion program, and cross-registration with the University of Kentucky for Army and Air Force ROTC for aerospace studies. A 3-2 engineering degree and nursing degree are available with the University of Kentucky. Internships, co-op programs in math, political science and other areas; study abroad in 28 countries, including a dual degree at Oxford University are available. Work-study programs, student-designed majors, and pass/fail options are available. Interdisciplinary majors of all kinds, frequently including business administration, communication arts, psychology, and religion combinations among others are designed by students. A dual BA/BTh degree is offered in religion with Regents Park College of Oxford University. There are 20 national honor societies and a freshman honors program. **Visiting:** There are regularly scheduled orientations for prospective students, consisting of campus tours and information on admissions, financial assistance, student life, academic programs, and meetings with faculty. There are guides for informal visits, visitors may sit in on classes, and stay overnight. To schedule a visit, contact Terri Hulette at (800) 788-9985. **Campus Safety and Security:** Measures include 24-hour foot and vehicle patrol, emergency notification system, self-defense education, and security escort services. There are shuttle buses, emergency telephones, lighted pathways/sidewalks, and controlled access to dorms/residences.

REQUIREMENTS: ACT or SAT required. Applicants should have completed 4 high school credits in English, 3 each in math and science, 2 in a foreign language, and 1 each in social studies and history, with additional credits in electives strongly encouraged. A student essay is required; Kentucky high school applicants may substitute a writing portfolio entry. AP and CLEP credits are accepted. Important factors in the admissions decision are advanced placement or honors courses, evidence of special talent, extracurricular activities record, and leadership record. All students are required to complete the Foundations and Core curriculum, a general education program including courses from several disciplines across campus emphasizing writing, quantitative skills, world languages, wellness, science and inquiry, religion, and culture. A minimum of 120 semester hours, including 24 to 42 in the major, with a minimum GPA of 2.0, is required to graduate, as is successful completion of a comprehensive exam in the major. **Procedure:** Freshmen are admitted to all sessions. Entrance exams should be taken between December of the junior year through October of the senior year. There are early decision and rolling admissions plans. Early decision applications should be filed by October 15; regular applications, by August 1 for fall entry. Notification is sent on a rolling basis. Applications are accepted on-line. Application fees are waived if application is completed on-line. **Transfer Students:** 46 transfer students enrolled in 2015-2016. Applicants must be in good standing at the school most recently attended and must submit official college and sometimes high school transcripts. 30 of 120 credits required for the bachelor's degree must be completed at Georgetown. **International Students:** There are 14 international students enrolled. The school actively recruits these students. They must take the TOEFL with a minimum score of 520 on the paper-based TOEFL (PBT) or 68 on the Internet-based version (iBT).

ADMISSIONS: 68% of the 2016-2017 applicants were accepted. The SAT scores for the 2016-2017 freshman class were: Critical Reading--57% below 500, 29% between 500 and 599, and 14% between 600 and 699. Math-- 43% below 500, 46% between 500 and 599, and 11% between 600 and 699. The ACT scores were 4% between 12 and 17, 50% between 18 and 23, 39% between 24 and 29, and 7% above 30. 40% of the current freshmen were in the top fifth of their class; 69% were in the top two fifths. 10 freshmen graduated first in their class. **Admissions Contact:** Jonathan Sands Wise, V.P. for Enrollment Management. Email: *admissions@georgetowncollege.edu* Web: *www.georgetowncollege.edu*

FINANCIAL AID: In 2016-2017, 100% of all full-time freshmen and 96% of continuing full-time students received some form of financial aid. 86% of all full-time freshmen and 85% of continuing full-time students received need-based aid. The average freshman award was $29,516. Need-based scholarships or need-based grants averaged $26,011 ($41,290 maximum); need-based self-help aid (loans and jobs) averaged $2,799 ($8,500 maximum); non-need-based athletic scholarships averaged $7,089 ($29,147 maximum); and other non-need-based awards and non-need-based scholarships averaged $13,174 ($38,690 maximum). 61% of undergraduate students work part-time. Average annual earnings from campus work are $937. The average financial indebtedness of the 2016 graduate was $31,267. The FAFSA code is 001964. The priority date for freshman financial aid applications for fall entry is February 1. The deadline for filing freshman financial aid applications for fall entry is March 1.

KENTUCKY CHRISTIAN UNIVERSITY *(The complete profile is made available exclusively on our website, www.barronspac.com)*

KENTUCKY STATE UNIVERSITY *(The complete profile is made available exclusively on our website, www.barronspac.com)*

KENTUCKY WESLEYAN COLLEGE B-3

www.kwc.edu

Owensboro, KY 42301	**(270) 852-3120** **(800) 999-0592**
Fax: (270) 852-3133	**Email: admissions@kwc.edu**
Full-time: 326 men, 315 women	**Faculty:** 48
Part-time: 19 men, 18 women	**Ph.D.s:** 84%
Graduate: n/av	**Student/Faculty:** 12 to 1
Year: semesters, summer session	**Tuition:** $23,600
Room & Board: $8480	**Freshman Class:** 910 applied, 193 accepted, 158 enrolled
SAT CR/M/W: required **ACT:** 22	**CEEB CODE:** 1369
Application Deadline: open	**COMPETITIVE**

Kentucky Wesleyan College, founded in 1858, is a private liberal arts institution affiliated with the United Methodist Church. KWC offers undergraduate programs in natural sciences, humanities and fine arts, and social sciences. Cost is based upon 12-18 credit hours. Figures in the above capsule and in this profile are approximate. There are 4 undergraduate schools. In addition to regional accreditation, KWC has baccalaureate program accreditation with IACBE. The 52-acre campus is in a suburban area 40 minutes east of Evansville, IN, and 2 hours north of Nashville, TN. Including any residence halls, there are 15 buildings.

STUDENT LIFE: 72% of undergraduates are from Kentucky. Others are from 22 states, 6 foreign countries, and Canada. 90% are from public schools. 74% are White; 10% African American; 1% Asian American; 1% American Indian/Alaska Native; 1% Hispanic; 1% Foreign. 60% are Protestant; 25% claim no religious affiliation; 12% Catholic. **Male To Female Ratio:** 1.0:1. The average age of freshmen is 18; all undergraduates, 22. 30% do not continue beyond their first year; 44% remain to graduate. **Housing:** 520 students can be accommodated in college housing, which includes single-sex and coed dorms, on-campus apartments, and off-campus apartments. On-campus housing is guaranteed for all 4 years. 55% of students commute. Alcohol is not permitted. All students may keep cars.

FACULTY/CLASSROOMS: 50% of faculty are male; 50% are female. All teach undergraduates. No introductory courses are taught by graduate students. The average class size in an introductory lecture is 20; in a laboratory is 15; and in a regular course is 15.

PROGRAMS OF STUDY: KWC confers B.A., B.S., B.M., and B.M.E. degrees. Bachelor's degrees are awarded in BIOLOGICAL SCIENCE (biology/biological science and zoology), BUSINESS (accounting, business administration and management, business economics, human resources, and sports management), COMMUNICATIONS AND THE ARTS (art, communications, English, fine arts, music, music business management, and Spanish), COMPUTER AND PHYSICAL SCIENCE (chemistry, computer science, and physics), EDUCATION (art education, elementary education, middle school education, music education, physical education, and secondary education), ENGINEERING AND ENVIRONMENTAL DESIGN (preengineering), HEALTH PROFESSIONS (health, predentistry, and premedicine), SOCIAL SCIENCE (criminal justice, history, political science/government, prelaw, psychology, and sociology). Natural sciences, education, and business are the strongest academically. Business administration, biology, and education have the largest enrollments.

ACTIVITIES: 11% of men belong to 3 national fraternities; 11% of women belong to 2 national sororities. There are 48 groups on campus, including art, band, cheerleading, choir, chorale, chorus, computers, dance, drama, ethnic, literary magazine, marching band, musical theater, newspaper, pep band, photography, political, professional, radio and TV, religious, social, social service, student government, symphony, and yearbook. Popular campus events include Family Weekend, Theater Productions and Lessons in Carols. **Sports:** There are 6 intercollegiate sports for men and 7 for women, and 7 intramural sports for men and 7 for women. Facilities include a health and recreation center, which houses an 800-seat gym, a fully equipped weight training center, racquetball courts, indoor batting and pitching facilities for softball and baseball, and a multipurpose auxiliary gym. Outdoor facilities include a baseball park, a softball park, a soccer field, a football field, and additional practice fields for football and soccer. Varsity basketball games are played in the 5,000-seat Owensboro Sports Center. **Graduates:** From July 1, 2015 to June 30, 2016, 155 bachelor's degrees were awarded. The most popular majors were business (22%), education (12%), and biology (9%). 20 companies recruited on campus in 2015-2016. In an average class, 30% graduate in 4 years or less, 40% graduate in 5 years or less, and 44% graduate in 6 years or less. Of the 2015 graduating class, 21% were enrolled in graduate school within 6 months of graduation, and 21% were employed.

SERVICES: Counseling and information services are available, as is tutoring in most subjects. There is a reader service for the blind, and remedial math, reading, and writing. **Library/Resources:** The library contains 99,795 volumes, 144,661 microform items, and 2,027 audio/video tapes/CDs/DVDs, and subscribes to 145 periodicals including electronic. Computerized library services include interlibrary loans, database searching, Internet access, and Wi-Fi capability. Special learning facilities include an art gallery and radio station. **Physically Challenged Students:** 95% of the campus is accessible. Facilities include wheelchair ramps, elevators, special parking, specially equipped restrooms, special class scheduling, and lowered drinking fountains. **Special:** Internships, dual majors, and student-designed majors are available in many programs and are established on an individual basis. A 3-2 degree in engineering is offered with Auburn University and the University of Kentucky. A Washington semester and study abroad in 5 countries are also available. There are 8 national honor societies and 7 departmental honors programs. **Visiting:** There are regularly scheduled orientations for prospective students, including a campus tour, meetings with faculty and students, and dining on campus. There are guides for informal visits, visitors may sit in on classes, and stay overnight. To schedule a visit, contact the Admissions Office. **Campus Safety and Security:** Measures include 24-hour foot and vehicle patrol, emergency notification system, and security escort services. There are lighted pathways/sidewalks and controlled access to dorms/residences.

REQUIREMENTS: The SAT or ACT is required. Applicants should have completed 13 high school units in college preparatory English, math, science, social studies, and a foreign language, or the GED equivalent. Applicants are considered individually. AP and CLEP credits are accepted. All students are required to complete the following general education program of skills and content requirements: 9 hours each in humanities, 6 hours each in aesthetics and social sciences, 3 hours each in math, religion, multicultural studies, communication skills, and 7 in natural science. Students must demonstrate proficiency in math, computing, and oral and written communication. To graduate, students must complete a total of 128 credit hours, including 36 in the major, with a 2.0 GPA. **Procedure:** Freshmen are admitted to all sessions. Entrance exams should be taken during the spring of the junior year or the fall of the senior year. There are deferred admissions and rolling admissions plans. Application deadlines are open. Notification is sent on a rolling basis. Applications are accepted on-line. **Transfer Students:** 95 transfer students enrolled in 2015-2016. Transfer applicants should have a minimum GPA of 2.0 in all course-work and be in good standing at the previously attended institution. 30 of 120 credits required for the bachelor's degree must be completed at KWC. **International Students:** There are 10 international students enrolled. The school actively recruits these students. They must take the TOEFL with a minimum score of 500 on the paper-based TOEFL (PBT) or 70 on the Internet-based version (iBT). SAT or ACT scores are required of international students who do not have a TOEFL score or who want to play NCAA sports.

ADMISSIONS: 21% of the 2016-2017 applicants were accepted. The SAT scores for the 2016-2017 freshman class were: Critical Reading-- 58% below 500, 36% between 500 and 599, and 6% between 600 and 699. Math-- 55% below 500, 36% between 500 and 599, and 9% between 600 and 699. Writing-- 61% below 500, 36% between 500 and 599, and 3% between 600 and 699. The ACT scores were 38% below 12, 29% between 12 and 17, 16% between 18 and 23, 7% between 24 and 29, and 10% above 30. 1 freshman graduated first in the class. **Admissions Contact:** Rahad Smith, Director of Admissions. Email: *admissions@kwc.edu* Web: *www.kwc.edu*

FINANCIAL AID: In 2016-2017, 100% of all full-time freshmen and 95% of continuing full-time students received some form of financial aid. 100% of all full-time freshmen and 95% of continuing full-time students received need-based aid. 50% of undergraduate students work part-time. The FAFSA code is 001969. The priority date for freshman financial aid applications for fall entry is March 15. The deadline for filing freshman financial aid applications for fall entry is August 1.

LINDSEY WILSON COLLEGE D-3
www.lindsey.edu

Columbia, KY 42728	(270) 384-8100 (800) 264-0138
Fax: (270) 384-8591	Email: admissions@lindsey.edu
Full-time: 797 men, 1208 women	**Faculty:** 98
Part-time: 54 men, 85 women	**Ph.D.s:** 55%
Graduate: 88 men, 358 women	**Student/Faculty:** 20 to 1
Year: semesters, summer session	**Tuition:** $23,762
Room & Board: $9120	**Freshman Class:** n/av
SAT CR/M/W: 480/500/395 **ACT:** 21	**CEEB CODE:** 1409
Application Deadline: open	**COMPETITIVE**

Lindsey Wilson College, founded in 1903, is a private liberal arts college affiliated with the United Methodist Church offering undergraduate programs in arts and sciences, business administration, education, human services, and pre-health. There are 3 undergraduate schools and 1 graduate school. In addition to regional accreditation, Lindsey has baccalaureate program accreditation with NCATE. The 45-acre campus is in a small town 100 miles southeast of Louisville. Including any residence halls, there are 45 buildings.

STUDENT LIFE: 78% of undergraduates are from Kentucky. Others are from 31 states, 35 foreign countries, and Canada. 67% are White; 18% race unknown; 9% African American; 2% two or more races; 1% Asian American; 1% American Indian/Alaska Native; 1% Hispanic; 1% Foreign. 52% are Protestant; 33% claim no religious affiliation. **Female To Male Ratio:** 1.8:1. The average age of freshmen is 19; all undergraduates, 23. 37% do not continue beyond their first year; 32% remain to graduate. **Housing:** 1150 students can be accommodated in college housing, which includes single-sex dorms and on-campus apartments. In addition, there are honors houses. On-campus housing is guaranteed for all 4 years, is available on a first-come, first-served basis, and is available on a lottery system for upperclassmen. 50% of students commute. Alcohol is not permitted. All students may keep cars.

FACULTY/CLASSROOMS: 41% of faculty are male; 59% are female. All teach undergraduates. No introductory courses are taught by graduate students. The average class size in an introductory lecture is 20; in a laboratory is 20; and in a regular course is 20.

PROGRAMS OF STUDY: Lindsey confers B.A., B.S.N., and B.S. degrees. Associate, master's, and doctoral degrees are also awarded. Bachelor's degrees are awarded in BIOLOGICAL SCIENCE (biology/biological science), BUSINESS (accounting, business administration and management, and recreation and leisure services), COMMUNICATIONS AND THE ARTS (art, communications, English, media arts, and theatre studies), COMPUTER AND PHYSICAL SCIENCE (mathematics), EDUCATION (art education, elementary education, music education, and secondary education), HEALTH PROFESSIONS (nursing), SOCIAL SCIENCE (American studies, criminal justice, history, human services, liberal arts/general studies, ministries, psychobiology, psychology, and social science). Human services and biology are the strongest academically. Human services, business, and education have the largest enrollments.

ACTIVITIES: There are no fraternities or sororities. There are 40 groups on campus, including art, band, cheerleading, choir, chorale, chorus, computers, dance, drama, environmental, film, honors, international, jazz band, literary magazine, marching band, musical theater, newspaper, pep band, photography, political, professional, religious, social, social service, and student government. Popular campus events include Founders Day and Malvina Farkle Day (community service). **Sports:** There are 10 intercollegiate sports for men and 13 for women, and 10 intramural sports for men and 10 for women. Facilities include a sports center with a 1000-seat gym and a 72000 sq ft health and wellness center with a weight-training room, competition swimming pool and many other amenities, a sand volleyball court, and the student union building. **Graduates:** From July 1, 2015 to June 30, 2016, 449 bachelor's degrees were awarded. The most popular majors were human services and counseling (49%), business administration (12%), and criminal justice (5%). In an average class, 3% graduate in 3 years or less, 27% graduate in 4 years or less, 32% graduate in 5 years or less, and 32% graduate in 6 years or less.

SERVICES: Counseling and information services are available, as is tutoring in every subject. There is remedial math, reading, and writing. **Library/Resources:** The library contains 105,000 volumes, 16,000 microform items, and 5,250 audio/video tapes/CDs/DVDs, and subscribes to 16,000 periodicals including electronic. Computerized library services include interlibrary loans, database searching, Internet access, and Wi-Fi capability. Special learning facilities include an art gallery. **Physically Challenged Students:** 95% of the campus is accessible. Facilities include wheelchair ramps, elevators, special parking, specially equipped restrooms, special class scheduling, lowered drinking fountains, and special housing. **Special:** Human services majors are offered a social services practicum in their field of study. Internships, work-study programs, a Washington semester, a general studies degree, student-designed majors, and pass/fail options in some courses are available. Study abroad is possible through Lindsey in London and the Northern Ireland Exchange. There are 3 national honor societies and a freshman honors program. **Visiting:** There are regularly scheduled orientations for prospective students. There are guides for informal visits, visitors may sit in on classes, and stay overnight. To schedule a visit, contact the Admissions Office at admissions@lindsey.edu. **Campus Safety and Security:** Measures include 24-hour foot and vehicle patrol, emergency notification system, and security escort services. There are lighted pathways/sidewalks and controlled access to dorms/residences.

REQUIREMENTS: The ACT is required. Applicants should have completed 20 academic high school credits or the GED equivalent. A GPA of 2.5 is required. AP and CLEP credits are accepted. Important factors in the admissions decision are geographical diversity, recommendations by alumni, and recommendations by school officials. All students must complete 45 hours of general education core requirements, including courses in communication of ideas, math, natural science, religion, humanities, fine arts, social behavioral science, and phys ed, as well as a 1-hour personal development career seminar. A total of 120 semester hours, with a minimum GPA of 2.0, is required to graduate. **Procedure:** Freshmen are admitted to all sessions. Entrance exams should be taken during the junior year. There is a rolling admissions plan. Application deadlines are open. Applications are accepted on-line. **Transfer Students:** 68 transfer students enrolled in 2015-2016. Transfer applicants are required to submit an official transcript from schools previously attended. An interview is recommended. 120 of 120 credits required for the bachelor's degree must be completed at Lindsey. **International Students:** There are 93 international students enrolled. The school actively recruits these students. They must take the TOEFL with a minimum score of 450 on the paper-based TOEFL (PBT) or 45 on the Internet-based version (iBT). They must also take the SAT or ACT.

ADMISSIONS: The SAT scores for the 2016-2017 freshman class were: Critical Reading-- 62% below 500, 30% between 500 and 599, and 8% between 600 and 699. Math-- 46% below 500 and 54% between 500 and 599. Writing-- 100% below 500. The ACT scores were 46% below 12, 28% between 12 and 17, 18% between 18 and 23, 5% between 24 and 29, and 3% above 30. 29% of the current freshmen were in the top fifth of their class; 55% were in the top two fifths. 10 freshmen graduated first in their class. **Admissions Contact:** Charity Fergurson, Director of Admissions. Email: *admissions@lindsey.edu* Web: *www.lindsey.edu*

FINANCIAL AID: In 2016-2017, 100% of all full-time freshmen and 100% of continuing full-time students received some form of financial aid. 100% of all full-time freshmen and 100% of continuing full-time students received need-based aid. The average freshman award was $26,790. Need-based scholarships or need-based grants averaged $220,071 ($34,544 maximum); and need-based self-help aid (loans and jobs) averaged $6,989 ($28,910 maximum). Lindsey is a member of CSS. The FAFSA code is 001972. The priority date for freshman financial aid applications for fall entry is November 1.

MIDWAY UNIVERSITY *(The complete profile is made available exclusively on our website, www.barronspac.com)*

MOREHEAD STATE UNIVERSITY E-2
www.moreheadstate.edu

Morehead, KY 40351	(606) 783-2000 (800) 585-6781
Fax: (606) 783-5038	Email: admissions@moreheadstate.edu
Full-time: 2456 men, 3507 women	**Faculty:** 349; IIA, --$
Part-time: 1406 men, 2385 women	**Ph.D.s:** 72%
Graduate: 374 men, 620 women	**Student/Faculty:** 18 to 1
Year: semesters, summer session	**Tuition:** $8530 ($12,796)
Room & Board: $8892	**Freshman Class:** 4451 applied, 3812 accepted, 1272 enrolled
ACT: 23	**CEEB CODE:** 1487
Application Deadline: open	**COMPETITIVE**

Morehead State University, founded in 1887, is a public institution offering degree programs in applied science and technology, humanities, educational and behavioral sciences, and business. The figures in the above capsule and in this profile are approximate. There are 4 undergraduate schools and 1 graduate school. In addition to regional accreditation, MSU has baccalaureate program accreditation with AACSB, ACBSP, CSWE, NASAD, NASM, NCATE, and NLN. The 1187-acre campus is in a small town 60 miles east of Lexington. Including any residence halls, there are 120 buildings.

STUDENT LIFE: 86% of undergraduates are from Kentucky. Others are from 45 states, 23 foreign countries, and Canada. 95% are from public schools. 89% are White; 4% African American; 2% Hispanic; 2% Foreign; 2% two or more races; 1% race unknown. **Female To Male Ratio:** 1.5:1. The average age of freshmen is 18; all undergraduates, 23. 34% do not continue beyond their first year. **Housing:** 3198 students can be accommodated in college housing, which includes coed dorms, on-campus apartments, and married student housing. In addition, there are honors houses, language houses, cross-cultural house, and limited housing for agricultural students at the University Farm. On-campus housing is guaranteed for all 4 years. 60% of students commute. Alcohol is not permitted. All students may keep cars.

FACULTY/CLASSROOMS: 55% of faculty are male; 45% are female. All teach undergraduates. No introductory courses are taught by graduate students. The average class size in a regular course is 19.

PROGRAMS OF STUDY: MSU confers A.B., B.S., B.B.A., B.M., B.M.Ed., B.S.N., B.S.W. and B.U.S. degrees. Associate, master's, and doctoral degrees are also awarded. Bachelor's degrees are awarded in AGRICULTURE (agriculture), BIOLOGICAL SCIENCE (biology/biological science and neurosciences), BUSINESS (accounting, banking and finance, business economics, management information systems, management science, marketing management, and real estate), COMMUNICATIONS AND THE ARTS (communications, dramatic arts, English, and music), COMPUTER AND PHYSICAL SCIENCE (chemistry, computer science, earth science, geology, mathematics, and physics), EDUCATION (agricultural education, business education, elementary education, health education, middle school education, physical education, and special education), ENGINEERING AND ENVIRONMENTAL DESIGN (industrial engineering technology), HEALTH PROFESSIONS (medical technology and nursing), SOCIAL SCIENCE (history, liberal arts/general studies, paralegal studies, philosophy, political science/government, psychology, social science, social work, and sociology). Biology, medical radiologic technology, and nursing are the strongest academically. Nursing, biomedical science, and social work have the largest enrollments.

ACTIVITIES: 6% of men belong to 12 national fraternities; 7% of women belong to 9 national sororities. There are 153 groups on campus, including art, band, cheerleading, choir, chorale, chorus, computers, dance, drama, drill team, drum and bugle corps, environmental, ethnic, honors, international, jazz band, LGBT, marching band, musical theater, newspaper, opera, orchestra, pep band, photography, political, professional, radio and TV, religious, social, social service, student government, symphony, and yearbook. Popular campus events include Greek Week, Black History Month, Welcome Week, Women's History Month, Leadership Dev Series, and LGBTQ+. **Sports:** There are 7 intercollegiate sports for men and 9 for women, and 15 intramural sports for men and 15 for women. Facilities include an athletic complex, a gym, a stadium, a pool, bowling lanes, and a wellness/fitness center. **Graduates:** From July 1, 2015 to June 30, 2016, 1306 bachelor's degrees were awarded. The most popular majors were business/marketing (13%), education (11%), and liberal arts and general studies (10%). 70 companies recruited on campus in 2015-2016. In an average class, 40% graduate in 6 years or less.

SERVICES: Counseling and information services are available, as is tutoring in most subjects. There is a reader service for the blind, and remedial math, reading, and writing. **Library/Resources:** The library contains 307,571 volumes, 48,201 microform items, and 19,314 audio/video tapes/CDs/DVDs, and subscribes to 3,046 periodicals including electronic. Computerized library services include interlibrary loans, database searching, Internet access, and Wi-Fi capability. Special learning facilities include an art gallery, planetarium, radio station, TV station, a 320-acre farm complex, Space Science Center, Browning Apple Orchard and robotics lab. **Physically Challenged Students:** 85% of the campus is accessible. Facilities include wheelchair ramps, elevators, special parking, specially equipped restrooms, special class scheduling, lowered drinking fountains, lowered telephones, and special housing. **Special:** Cross-registration is offered with the University of Kentucky. Students may earn specialist certification in education. Co-op programs, internships, study abroad in 3 countries, a Washington semester, a 3-2 engineering degree, dual and student-designed majors, a general studies degree, credit for life experience, pass/fail options, and non-degree study are available. There are 12 national honor societies and a freshman honors program. **Visiting:** There are regularly scheduled orientations for prospective students, consisting of registration for classes, advisement, and an overview of MSU. There are guides for informal visits and visitors may sit in on classes. To schedule a visit, contact Enrollment Services at admissions@moreheadstate.edu. **Campus Safety and Security:** Measures include 24-hour foot and vehicle patrol, emergency notification system, self-defense education, and security escort services. There are shuttle buses, emergency telephones, lighted pathways/sidewalks, and controlled access to dorms/residences.

REQUIREMENTS: The SAT or ACT is required. Applicants should have completed the Kentucky Pre-College Curriculum requirement. An interview is recommended. 24 High School units required, using Carnegie units: 4 in English, 3 each in math, science, and social studies, 2 in foreign language, 7 in academic electives, 1 in computer science (recommended), 1 in visual/performing arts, and 1 in health and physical education. A GPA of 2.0 is required. AP and CLEP credits are accepted. Important factors in the admissions decision are advanced placement or honors courses and recommendations by school officials. All students must complete 42 semester hours (45 for teacher certification) of general education courses, including 15 hours in communications and humanities, 12 in natural and mathematical sciences, 12 in social and behavioral sciences, and 3 in health or phys ed. A total of 128 semester hours, with a minimum GPA of 2.0, is required to graduate. **Procedure:** Freshmen are admitted fall, winter, spring, and summer. Entrance exams should be taken in the spring of the junior year. There is a rolling admissions plan. Application deadlines are open. Application fee is $30. Notification is sent on a rolling basis. Applications are accepted on-line. **Transfer Students:** 456 transfer students enrolled in 2015-2016. Applicants should have a minimum GPA of 2.0 with at least 12 credit hours earned and be in good standing at their previous institution. They must have completed a pre-college curriculum or meet any deficiencies. Transfers may be admitted on probation. Applicants with 24 or more hours in credit do not need to submit test scores. 32 of 120 credits required for the bachelor's degree must be completed at MSU. **International Students:** There are 184 international students enrolled. The school actively recruits these students. They must take the TOEFL with a minimum score of 500 on the paper-based TOEFL (PBT) or 61 on the Internet-based version (iBT). They must also take the SAT or ACT.

ADMISSIONS: 86% of the 2016-2017 applicants were accepted. The ACT scores were 8% between 12 and 17, 52% between 18 and 23, 35% between 24 and 29, and 5% above 30. 38% of the current freshmen were in the top fifth of their class; 71% were in the top two fifths. **Admissions Contact:** Tim Rhodes, Vice President Enrollment Services. Email: *admissions@moreheadstate.edu* Web: *www.moreheadstate.edu*

FINANCIAL AID: In 2016-2017, 96% of all full-time freshmen received some form of financial aid. 65% of all full-time freshmen received need-based aid. The average freshman award was $14,547. Need-based scholarships or need-based grants averaged $6,425 ($10,930 maximum); need-based self-help aid (loans and jobs) averaged $3,656 ($9,254 maximum); non-need-based athletic scholarships averaged $8,855 ($25,936 maximum); and other non-need-based awards and non-need-based scholarships averaged $5,923 ($28,939 maximum). Average annual earnings from campus work are $2572. The college's own financial statement is required. The FAFSA code is 001976. The deadline for filing freshman financial aid applications for fall entry is April 1.

MURRAY STATE UNIVERSITY — B-4

www.murraystate.edu

Murray, KY 42071 — (270) 809-3750, (800) 272-4678

Fax: (270) 809-3780 — Email: msu.admissions@murraystate.edu

Full-time: 2982 men, 3998 women	**Faculty:** 436; IIA, --$
Part-time: 706 men, 1200 women	**Ph.D.s:** 79%
Graduate: 653 men, 956 women	**Student/Faculty:** 16 to 1
Year: semesters, summer session	**Tuition:** $8400 ($22,680)
Room & Board: $8598	**Freshman Class:** n/av
SAT CR/M: 540/525 **ACT:** 24	**CEEB CODE:** 1494
Application Deadline: August 15	**COMPETITIVE**

Murray State University, founded in 1922, is a public institution offering degree programs in business, education, health professions, human services, humanities, fine arts, engineering, technology, science, nursing, and agriculture. There are 6 undergraduate schools and 6 graduate schools. In addition to regional accreditation, MSU has baccalaureate program accreditation with AACSB, ABET, ACEJMC, CSWE, NASAD, NASM, NCATE, ACEND, ACS, AVMA, CAATE, CAEP, CCNE, CACREP, COA, MPAC, NAST, and NKBA. The 253-acre campus is in a small town 115 miles northwest of Nashville in Murray, Kentucky. Including any residence halls, there are 90 buildings.

STUDENT LIFE: 68% of undergraduates are from Kentucky. Others are from 44 states, 42 foreign countries, and Canada. 81% are White; 6% African American; 4% Foreign; 3% race unknown; 2% Hispanic; 2% two or more races; 1% Asian American. **Female To Male Ratio:** 1.4:1. The average age of freshmen is 18; all undergraduates, 23. 26% do not continue beyond their first year; 49% remain to graduate. **Housing:** 3106 students can be accommodated in college housing, which includes single-sex and coed dorms, on-campus apartments, and married student housing. In addition, there are honors houses. We have a residential college system, with a faculty member serving as a college head in each building. On-campus housing is guaranteed for all 4 years, is available on a first-come, first-served basis. 67% of students commute. Alcohol is not permitted. All students may keep cars.

FACULTY/CLASSROOMS: 54% of faculty are male; 46% are female. 98% teach undergraduates. No introductory courses are taught by graduate students.

PROGRAMS OF STUDY: MSU confers B.A., B.S., B.A.B., B.S.B., B.F.A., B.I.S., B.M., B.S.A., B.S.N., B.S.E., and B.S.W. degrees. Associate, master's, and doctoral degrees are also awarded. Bachelor's degrees are awarded in AGRICULTURE (agricultural business management, agricultural mechanics, agricultural sciences, agronomy, equine science, and horticulture), BIOLOGICAL SCIENCE (biology/adolescence education, biology/biological science, biology (pre-physician assistant), forensic science, marine biology, molecular biology, nutrition, and wildlife biology), BUSINESS (accounting, accounting (finance), accounting (information systems), business administration and management, business communications, business intelligence and analytics, entrepreneurial studies, finance, finance (financial planning), human resources/organizational mgmt, international business, integrative studies, management science, marketing, nonprofit/public organization management, recreation and leisure services, recreation/leisure (adventure leadership), recreation/leisure (community recreation), and supply chain management), COMMUNICATIONS AND THE ARTS (advertising, art history, creative writing, English literature, French, German, graphic design & media, instrumental music education, Japanese, journalism, keyboard - piano concentration, music, music business management, music composition, music performance, public relations, radio/television technology, Spanish, studio art, telecommunications systems mgmt, theatre arts, and vocal music education), COMPUTER AND PHYSICAL SCIENCE (applied mathematics, applied physics, applied physics (pre-MBA), chemistry, chemistry/adolescence education, chemistry / chemical biology, chemistry (pre-MBA), computer information systems, computer science, earth science, earth science / adolescence education, environmental geology, mathematics, mathematics - actuarial concentration, physics, and polymer science), EDUCATION (agricultural education, art education, athletic training, early childhood education, elementary education, English education, foreign languages education, health information management, health and physical education, history education, home economics education, industrial arts education, marketing and distribution education, mathematics education, middle school education, physical science secondary school education, social studies secondary school education, Spanish education K-12, specific learning disabilities, teaching English as a second/foreign language (TESOL/TEFOL), and technical education), ENGINEERING AND ENVIRONMENTAL DESIGN (agricultural engineering technology, architectural technology, civil engineering technology, construction technology, electrical/electronics engineering technology, engineering graphics & design, engineering physics, environmental engineering technology, interior design, manufacturing technology, and occupational safety and health), HEALTH PROFESSIONS (biomedical science, community health work, exercise science, nursing, nutrition and dietetics, pre-health studies, predentistry, premedicine, preoptometry, pre-occupational therapy, prepharmacy, pre-physician assistant, prephysical therapy, preveterinary science, speech pathology/audiology, and veterinary technology), SOCIAL SCIENCE (archeology, criminal justice, economics, food production/management/services, geography information science, history, international studies, liberal arts, sciences, general studies, humanities, philosophy, philosophy (aesthetics/media writing), philosophy (history/contemporary thought), philosophy (political thought), philosophy and religion, political science/government, psychology, public administration, social work, and sociology). Telecommunications systems management, occupational safety & health, and accounting are the strongest academically. Nursing, animal health technology, and agriculture have the largest enrollments.

ACTIVITIES: 17% of men belong to 12 national fraternities; 19% of women belong to 9 national sororities. There are 184 groups on campus, including art, band, cheerleading, chess, choir, chorale, chorus, communications, computers, dance, debate, drama, drill team, environmental, ethnic, film, forensics, honors, international, jazz band, LGBT, literary magazine, marching band, musical theater, newspaper, opera, orchestra, pep band, photography, political, professional, radio and TV, religious, social, social service, student government, symphony, and Veteran Student Organization. Popular campus events include Presidential Lecture Series, All-Campus Sing, Campus Lights, Alpha Phi Alpha Step-Off, Mr. MSU, Miss MSU, Homecoming and Related Festivities, Take Back the Night, Alliance Drag Show, and NPHC Step Show. **Sports:** There are 6 intercollegiate sports for men and 9 for women, and 10 intramural sports for men and 10 for women. Facilities include a recreation and wellness center with 2 pools, 3 gyms, racquetball courts, indoor track, cardio and weight areas, an Internet lounge, aerobic studios, and a fitness assessment center. An additional gym with swimming pool, basketball court, dance/aerobic studio, and racquetball courts is also available for student use. Athletic and recreation sports facilities include a stadium, a sports arena and special events center, golf course, soccer fields, baseball fields, rifle range, volleyball courts, basketball courts, tennis courts, and a fitness trail. **Graduates:** From July 1, 2015 to June 30, 2016, 1696 bachelor's degrees were awarded. The most popular majors were integrated studies (8%), nursing (7%), and agriculture (7%). 280 companies recruited on campus in 2015-2016. In an average class, 25% graduate in 4 years or less, 43% graduate in 5 years or less, and 49% graduate in 6 years or less.

SERVICES: Counseling and information services are available, as is tutoring in most subjects. There is a reader service for the blind, and remedial math, reading, and writing. **Library/Resources:** The 4 libraries contain 556,745 volumes, 1,112 microform items, and 11,399 audio/video tapes/CDs/DVDs, and subscribe to 956 periodicals including electronic. Computerized library services include interlibrary loans, database searching, Internet access, and Wi-Fi capability. Special learning facilities include an art gallery, radio station, TV station, writing center, oral communications center, Ross Mathematics Studies and Career Center, speech and hearing clinic, voice and swallowing clinic, arboretum, biological research station, Watershed Studies Institute, Mid-America Remote Sensing center, Wrather Museum (history museum and cultural events center), Lovett Auditorium and CFSB Center (used for musical and theater productions, concerts, and lectures), Price Doyle Fine Arts Center (for performances and exhibitions), State Farm Financial Services Center (applied learning for students in finance and economics), 4 agricultural research farms, Breathitt Veterinary Center (veterinary research center), and Cherry Agricultural Exposition Center. **Physically Challenged Students:** Facilities include wheelchair ramps, elevators, special parking, specially equipped restrooms, special class scheduling, lowered drinking fountains, lowered telephones, and special housing. Accommodations and services for students are provided by the Office of Student Disability Services. Accommodations for faculty, staff, and students are facilitated by the Office of Institutional Diversity, Equity, and Access. **Special:** Students can pursue double majors in any bachelor's degree programs. Students can design interdisciplinary majors in the Liberal Arts and Integrated Studies programs. MSU emphasizes experiential learning opportunities, including internships, co-ops, service learning, student teaching, and other experience-rich activities, in all majors. MSU offers study abroad courses in several countries. Cross-registration is available through the National Student Exchange. Work-study opportunities are also available. There are 16 national honor societies and a freshman honors program. **Visiting:** There are regularly scheduled orientations for prospective students, Students are invited to attend sessions planned before all academic terms for which they are first enrolling. These sessions contain both academic and social orientation. There are guides for informal visits and visitors may sit in on classes. To schedule a visit, contact Shawn Smee at ssmee@murraystate.edu. **Campus Safety and Security:** Measures include 24-hour foot and vehicle patrol, emergency notification system, self-defense education, and security escort services. There are shuttle buses, emergency telephones, lighted pathways/

sidewalks, controlled access to dorms/residences, and LiveSafe app (a mobile app that allows students to contact campus police to report crimes, request an escort, or report emergencies).

REQUIREMENTS: For unconditional admission to a baccalaureate program, students must meet the following criteria: scored at least 18 on the ACT or at least 870 on the SAT; completed pre-college high school curriculum requirements; ranked in top half of high school class or earned a GPA of 3.0 or greater; and requires no developmental courses. Students who need to take one developmental course, but meet all other admission criteria, may be admitted conditionally to a baccalaureate program. High school curriculum must include 22 high school academic credits, including 4 units in English, 3 each in math, science, social studies (including US history and world history), 2 in foreign languages, 1 in visual/performing arts, and 5 electives. MSU requires applicants to be in the upper 50% of their class. A GPA of 3.0 is required. AP and CLEP credits are accepted. All students must complete University Studies (general education) requirements, including courses in communications, science, math, humanities, history, social sciences, and, for the BA degree, foreign languages. Programs require at least 120 semester hours, with a minimum of 40 hours earned in residence. 42 of the 120 hours must be earned in courses at the 300-level or above. **Procedure:** Freshmen are admitted to all sessions. Entrance exams should be taken before January of the enrollment year. There is a rolling admissions plan. Applications should be filed by August 15 for fall entry; January 10 for spring entry, along with a $40 fee. Applications are accepted on-line. Application fees are waived if application is completed on-line. **Transfer Students:** 1078 transfer students enrolled in 2015-2016. A student who has 24 semester hours or more of transferable degree credit, with a minimum of a 2.0 cumulative grade point average on all previous courses, is eligible for admission. Applicants must be in good standing academically and financially at all previous schools attended. Students who have less than 24 hours of credit must present official copies of high school transcript and either ACT or SAT scores. 40 of 120 credits required for the bachelor's degree must be completed at MSU. **International Students:** There are 358 international students enrolled. The school actively recruits these students. They must take the TOEFL with a minimum score of 527 on the paper-based TOEFL (PBT) or 71 on the Internet-based version (iBT). Students must take the TOEFL or IELTS.

ADMISSIONS: The SAT scores for the 2016-2017 freshman class were: Critical Reading-- 38% below 500, 31% between 500 and 599, 27% between 600 and 699, and 4% between 700 and 800. Math-- 35% below 500, 51% between 500 and 599, 12% between 600 and 699, and 2% between 700 and 800. The ACT scores were 1% between 12 and 17, 43% between 18 and 23, 46% between 24 and 29, and 10% above 30. 41% of the current freshmen were in the top fifth of their class; 66% were in the top two fifths. 54 freshmen graduated first in their class. **Admissions Contact:** Lesa Harris, Director of Undergraduate Admissions. Email: *msu.admissions@murraystate.edu* Web: *www.murraystate.edu*

FINANCIAL AID: In 2016-2017, 93% of all full-time freshmen and 85% of continuing full-time students received some form of financial aid. 68% of all full-time freshmen and 64% of continuing full-time students received need-based aid. The average freshman award was $14,923. Need-based scholarships or need-based grants averaged $13,219 ($39,475 maximum); need-based self-help aid (loans and jobs) averaged $5,461 ($21,722 maximum); non-need-based athletic scholarships averaged $12,495 ($33,908 maximum); and other non-need-based awards and non-need-based scholarships averaged $14,069 ($36,076 maximum). 24% of undergraduate students work part-time. Average annual earnings from campus work are $2283. The average financial indebtedness of the 2016 graduate was $27,564. The college's own financial statement, and International Student's Certification of Finances are required. The FAFSA code is 001977. The priority date for freshman financial aid applications for fall entry is February 1. The deadline for filing freshman financial aid applications for fall entry is September 1.

NORTHERN KENTUCKY UNIVERSITY D-1

www.nku.edu

Highland Heights, KY 41099	**(859) 572-5220** **(800) 637-9948**
Fax: (859) 572-6665	**Email: admitnku@nku.edu**
Full-time: 4332 men, 5064 women	**Faculty:** IIA, --$
Part-time: 1034 men, 1221 women	**Ph.D.s:** 72%
Graduate: 797 men, 1398 women	**Student/Faculty:** 19 to 1
Year: semesters, summer session	**Tuition:** $8736 ($17,472)
Room & Board: $7750	**Freshman Class:** 6957 applied, 6489 accepted, 2193 enrolled
SAT CR/M/W: 505/505/480 **ACT:** 23	**CEEB CODE:** 1574
Application Deadline: August 18	**COMPETITIVE**

Northern Kentucky University, founded in 1968, is a publicly controlled institution offering undergraduate and graduate programs in arts and sciences, business, health professions, informatics, and education and human services. The figures in the above capsule and in this profile are approximate. There are 5 undergraduate schools and 6 graduate schools. In addition to regional accreditation, NKU has baccalaureate program accreditation with AACSB, ABET, ACCE, CSWE, NASM, NCATE, NLN, NASPAA, CAATE, and JRCERT. The 424-acre campus is in a suburban area in Highland Heights, Kentucky, 7 miles southeast of Cincinnati, Ohio. Including any residence halls, there are 41 buildings.

STUDENT LIFE: 69% of undergraduates are from Kentucky. Others are from 45 states, 59 foreign countries, and Canada. 82% are White; 7% African American; 4% Foreign; 2% Hispanic; 2% two or more races; 2% race unknown; 1% Asian American. **Female To Male Ratio:** 1.2:1. The average age of freshmen is 19; all undergraduates, 13. 33% do not continue beyond their first year. **Housing:** 1820 students can be accommodated in college housing, which includes single-sex and coed dorms and on-campus apartments. In addition, there are honors houses, including theme housing. On-campus housing is available on a first-come and first-served basis. Priority is given to out-of-town students. 84% of students commute. Alcohol is not permitted. All students may keep cars.

FACULTY/CLASSROOMS: 54% of faculty are male; 46% are female. No introductory courses are taught by graduate students.

PROGRAMS OF STUDY: NKU confers B.A., B.S., B.M., B.S.N., B.F.A , B.H.S. and B.S.W. degrees. Associate, master's, and doctoral degrees are also awarded. Bachelor's degrees are awarded in BIOLOGICAL SCIENCE (biology/adolescence education and biology/biological science), BUSINESS (accounting, business administration and management, business information systems, entrepreneurial studies, finance, human resources, labor studies, marketing and distribution, organizational leadership and management, and sports management), COMMUNICATIONS AND THE ARTS (communications, dramatic arts, English, fine arts, French, German, Japanese, journalism, music, music composition, music performance, public relations, radio/television technology, Spanish, speech/debate/rhetoric, studio art, and theatre arts), COMPUTER AND PHYSICAL SCIENCE (chemistry, chemistry/adolescence education, computer engineering technology, computer information technology, computer science, geology, information sciences and systems, mathematics, physics, radiological technology, science, and statistics), EDUCATION (athletic training, business education, early childhood education, elementary education, English education, industrial arts education, mathematics education, middle school education, music education, physical education, secondary education, Spanish adolescense education, and special education), ENGINEERING AND ENVIRONMENTAL DESIGN (architectural engineering, construction management, construction technology, electrical/electronics engineering technology, environmental science, manufacturing engineering, manufacturing technology, and mechanical engineering technology), HEALTH PROFESSIONS (exercise science, health science, medical technology, mental health/human services, nursing, predentistry, premedicine, preoptometry, prepharmacy, prephysical therapy, and preveterinary science), SOCIAL SCIENCE (anthropology, criminal justice, economics, forensic studies, geography, history, liberal arts/general studies, philosophy, political science/government, prelaw, psychology, public administration, public history/archives, social science, social studies, social work, sociology, and women's studies). Organizational leadership, computer information technology, and nursing have the largest enrollments.

ACTIVITIES: 7% of men belong to 7 national fraternities; 10% of women belong to 7 national sororities. There are 221 groups on campus, including and mock trial club, leadership, recreational, special interest, art, cheerleading, choir, chorale, chorus, computers, cultural, dance, drama, drill team, environmental, ethnic, film, honors, international, jazz band, LGBT, literary magazine, musical theater, newspaper, pep band, photography, political, professional, radio and TV, religious, social, social service, and student government. Popular campus events include Welcome Week, Freshfusion, Pumpkin Bust, Feast4Finals and Homecoming. **Sports:** There are 8 intercollegiate sports for men and 9 for women, and 12 intramural sports for men and 13 for women. Facilities include a 2000-seat gym, baseball and soccer fields, tennis and racquetball courts, a track, weight room, and swimming pool. **Graduates:** From July 1, 2015 to June 30, 2016, 2143 bachelor's degrees were awarded. The most popular majors were business/marketing (26%), health professions and related programs (12%), communication/journalism, and and education (9%). 225 companies recruited on campus in 2015-2016. In an average class, 14% graduate in 4 years or less, 31% graduate in 5 years or less, and 38% graduate in 6 years or less.

SERVICES: Counseling and information services are available, as is tutoring in most subjects. There is a reader service for the blind, and remedial math, reading, and writing. There are also developmental education courses. **Library/Resources:** The 2 libraries contain 925,652 volumes, 620,179 microform items, and 20,088 audio/video tapes/CDs/DVDs, and subscribe to 51,986 periodicals including electronic. Computerized library services include interlibrary loans, database searching, Internet access, and Wi-Fi capability. Special learning facilities include an art gallery, planetarium, radio station, TV station, a digitorium, herbarium, and the anthropology museum. **Physically Challenged Students:** All of the campus is accessible. Facilities include wheelchair ramps, elevators, special parking, specially equipped restrooms, special class scheduling, lowered drinking fountains, lowered telephones, and special housing. **Special:** A 3-2 engineering degree is offered with the University of Kentucky. Cross-registration is possible through the Greater Cincinnati Area Consortium of colleges and universities. Study abroad in 34 countries, a Washington semester, on-campus work-study programs, an accelerated degree program, an interdisciplinary honors program, B.A.-B.S. degrees, dual majors, and pass/fail options are offered. There are co-op programs in most majors. Student-designed majors and credit for work experience are available. Non-degree study is possible. There are 14 national honor societies, a freshman honors program, and 9 departmental honors programs. **Visiting:** There are regularly scheduled orientations for prospective students, consisting of a 1-day program with sessions on student services and financial aid, activities, a campus tour, and academic information, advising, and registration. There are guides for informal visits, visitors may sit in on classes, and stay overnight. To schedule a visit, contact the Office of Admissions at (859) 572-5220. **Campus Safety and Security:** Measures include 24-hour foot and vehicle patrol, emergency notification system, and security escort services. There are shuttle buses, emergency telephones, lighted pathways/sidewalks, controlled access to dorms/residences, and ALICE training.

REQUIREMENTS: The SAT or ACT is required. 16 academic units are required, 24 is recommended, 4 in English, 3 each in math science, of those 1 unit must be a lab, and social studies, 2 in foreign language, recommended units are 1 in history 5 in academic electives, 1 in computer science, and 1 in visual/performing arts. A GPA of 2.0 is required. AP and CLEP credits are accepted. Important factors in the admissions decision are leadership record, advanced placement or honors courses, recommendations by alumni, and recommendations by school officials. All students must complete 37 semester hours of general studies, including communication--written and oral, mathematics/statistics, natural sciences, culture, self & society, and global viewpoints, along with major and minor requirements. A total of 120 semester hours, with a minimum GPA of 2.0, is required to graduate. **Procedure:** Freshmen are admitted fall, spring, and summer. Entrance exams should be taken prior to enrollment. There are deferred admissions and rolling admissions plans. Early decision applications should be filed by February 1; regular applications, by August 18 for fall entry; December 1 for winter entry; December 1 for spring entry; and May 1 for summer entry, along with a $40 fee. Applications are accepted on-line. **Transfer Students:** 671 transfer students enrolled in 2015-2016. Students must be eligible to return to their previous institution. College transcripts from previous institutions are required. 30 of 120 credits required for the bachelor's degree must be completed at NKU. **International Students:** There are 504 international students enrolled. The school actively recruits these students. They must take the TOEFL with a minimum score of 86 on the Internet-based version (iBT).

ADMISSIONS: 93% of the 2016-2017 applicants were accepted. The SAT scores for the 2016-2017 freshman class were: Critical Reading-- 47% below 500, 38% between 500 and 599, 12% between 600 and 699, and 4% between 700 and 800. Math-- 46% below 500, 36% between 500 and 599, 14% between 600 and 699, and 3% between 700 and 800. Writing-- 55% below 500, 34% between 500 and 599, 7% between 600 and 699, and 4% between 700 and 800. **Admissions Contact:** Melissa Gorbrandt, Director of Admissions. Email: *admitnku@nku.edu* Web: *www.nku.edu*

FINANCIAL AID: In 2016-2017, 71% of all full-time freshmen and 70% of continuing full-time students received some form of financial aid. 71% of all full-time freshmen and 70% of continuing full-time students received need-based aid. The average freshman award was $11,120. Need-based scholarships or need-based grants averaged $5,869; need-based self-help aid (loans and jobs) averaged $4,139; non-need-based athletic scholarships averaged $12,510; other non-need-based awards and non-need-based scholarships averaged $5,334; and $3,388 from other forms of aid. The average financial indebtedness of the 2016 graduate was $27,594. The college's own financial statement is required. The FAFSA code is 009275. The priority date for freshman financial aid applications for fall entry is March 1. The deadline for filing freshman financial aid applications for fall entry is April 1.

SPALDING UNIVERSITY — D-2

www.spalding.edu

Louisville, KY 40203	**(502) 873-4177** **(800) 896-8941**
Fax: (502) 992-2418	**Email: admissions@spalding.edu**
Full-time: 254 men, 666 women	**Faculty:** n/av
Part-time: 130 men, 266 women	**Ph.D.s:** n/av
Graduate: 201 men, 805 women	**Student/Faculty:** n/av
Year: other, summer session	**Tuition:** $24,338
Room & Board: $7600	**Freshman Class:** 1469 applied, 736 accepted, 196 enrolled
SAT or ACT: required	**CEEB CODE:** 1552
Application Deadline: n/av	**sCOMPETITIVE**

Spalding University, established in 1814, is a private institution affiliated with the Roman Catholic Church. Today this urban, co-educational institution offers over 24 degree programs at the bachelor's, master's and doctoral level, providing quality, real-world learning in liberal and professional studies. There are 11 undergraduate schools and 9 graduate schools. In addition to regional accreditation, Spalding has baccalaureate program accreditation with ACBSP, CSWE, NCATE, NLN, APA, AACD, and CCNE. The 24-acre campus is in an urban area in downtown Louisville, KY. Including any residence halls, there are 14 buildings.

STUDENT LIFE: 80% of undergraduates are from Kentucky. Others are from 41 states, 3 foreign countries, and Canada. 60% are White; 3% Hispanic; 3% two or more races; 17% African American; 16% race unknown; 1% Asian American. **Female To Male Ratio:** 3.0:1. The average age of freshmen is 21; all undergraduates, 25. 27% do not continue beyond their first year; 47% remain to graduate. **Housing:** 340 students can be accommodated in college housing, which includes coed dorms. On-campus housing is available on a first-come, first-served basis. 88% of students commute. Alcohol is not permitted. All students may keep cars.

FACULTY/CLASSROOMS: No introductory courses are taught by graduate students.

PROGRAMS OF STUDY: Spalding confers B.A., B.S., B.S.N., and B.F.A. degrees. Associate, master's, and doctoral degrees are also awarded. Bachelor's degrees are awarded in BUSINESS (accounting, business administration and management, human resources, and marketing), COMMUNICATIONS AND THE ARTS (communication rhetoric/communication, creative writing, media arts, and studio art), COMPUTER AND PHYSICAL SCIENCE (natural sciences), EDUCATION (education, elementary education, middle school education, and secondary education), HEALTH PROFESSIONS (health science, nursing, and occupational therapy), SOCIAL SCIENCE (humanities and social science, liberal arts/general studies, psychology, social science, and social work). Nursing, art, and business have the largest enrollments.

ACTIVITIES: There are 25 groups on campus, including art, chorale, dance, ethnic, honors, LGBT, literary magazine, professional, religious, social, social service, and student government. Popular campus events include Annual Running of the Rodents, Scholarship and Learning Day, HOOPLA, Pelican Ball, and UAM Halloween Party. **Sports:** There are 7 intercollegiate sports for men and 9 for women. Facilities include a gym and an exercise room. **Graduates:** From July 1, 2015 to June 30, 2016, 221 bachelor's degrees were awarded. The most popular majors were nursing (7%), art (6%), and business (6%).

SERVICES: Counseling and information services are available, as is tutoring in every subject. There is remedial math, reading, and writing. **Library/Resources:** The library contains 473,838 volumes, and 76,469 audio/video tapes/CDs/DVDs, and subscribes to 19,300 periodicals including electronic. Computerized library services include interlibrary loans, database searching, Internet access, and Wi-Fi capability. Special learning facilities include an art gallery, a writing center, and mathematics lab. **Physically Challenged Students:** 90% of the campus is accessible. Facilities include wheelchair ramps, elevators, special parking, specially equipped restrooms, special class scheduling, and lowered drinking fountains. **Special:** Internships, study abroad, B.A. - B.S. degrees, dual majors, work-study programs, and accelerated degree programs in business, psychology, and nursing are available. The Adult Accelerated Program enables students to earn a bachelor's degree by attending classes on weekends and evenings. Credit is given for military experience and pass/fail options are available. Cross-registration is offered with the Kentuckiana Metroversity Consortium. There are 8 national honor societies. **Visiting:** There are regularly scheduled orientations for prospective students, New Student Orientation, AAP Orientation, and Graduate Program Specific Orientation. There are guides for informal visits, visitors may sit in on classes, and stay overnight. To schedule a visit, contact the Office of University Admission. **Campus Safety and Security:** Measures include 24-hour foot and vehicle patrol, emergency notification system, and security escort services. There are emergency telephones, lighted pathways/sidewalks, controlled access to dorms/residences, emergency call boxes, camera surveillance, in campus buildings and parking lots, and direct access to campus security from campus phones.

REQUIREMENTS: The SAT or ACT is required. Applicants must be graduates of an accredited secondary school and should have completed 4 years of high school English and 2 years each of a foreign language, math, science, and social studies. A GED may be substituted for the high school degree. A GPA of 2.5 is required. AP and CLEP credits are accepted. Important factors in the admissions decision are advanced placement or honors courses, recommendations by school officials, and extracurricular activities record. To graduate, students must earn 120 credits and a minimum overall GPA of 2.0. All students must complete a university studies requirement (average 51 credits) in humanities, social sciences, communication, natural sciences and math, credits in religious studies, and one general introduction course to the college. **Procedure:** Freshmen are admitted to all sessions. Entrance exams should be taken entrance exams are on a rolling basis. There are early admissions, deferred admissions, and rolling admissions plans. Application deadlines are open. Application fee is $20. Notification is sent on a rolling basis. Applications are accepted on-line. **Transfer Students:** 110 transfer students enrolled in 2015-2016. It is preferred that applicants have a 2.5 GPA. Anyone wishing to transfer to Spalding University from another college or university must submit the following documents to the Admissions Office: the completed application with the nonrefundable $20 application fee; proof of high school graduation (or official GED test score report); an official transcript from each college and/or university previously attended; a scan or photocopy of the applicant's state-issued driver's license or state-issued identification card. 30 of 120 credits required for the bachelor's degree must be completed at Spalding. **International Students:** There are 3 international students enrolled. The school actively recruits these students. They must take the TOEFL with a minimum score of 535 on the paper-based TOEFL (PBT) or 75 on the Internet-based version (iBT). They must also take the SAT or ACT, scoring 20.

ADMISSIONS: 50% of the 2016-2017 applicants were accepted. **Admissions Contact:** Matthew Elder, Director of Undergraduate Admissions. Email: *admissions@spalding.edu* Web: *www.spalding.edu*

FINANCIAL AID: The FAFSA code is 001960. The deadline for filing freshman financial aid applications for fall entry is January 1.

THOMAS MORE COLLEGE D-2

www.thomasmore.edu

Crestview Hills, KY 41017 (859) 344-3514 (800) 825-4557

Fax: (859) 344-3444 **Email: admissions@thomasmore.edu**

Full-time: 579 men, 561 women	**Faculty:** 72
Part-time: 223 men, 139 women	**Ph.D.s:** 75%
Graduate: 56 men, 42 women	**Student/Faculty:** 16 to 1
Year: semesters, summer session	**Tuition:** $28,750
Room & Board: $7970	**Freshman Class:** 1053 applied, 924 accepted, 264 enrolled
SAT: required **ACT:** 22	**CEEB CODE:** 1876
Application Deadline: August 1	**COMPETITIVE**

Thomas More College, founded in 1921 as Villa Madonna College, is a private Catholic institution offering undergraduate programs in liberal arts and sciences, plus graduate degrees in business administration and education. Figures in the above capsule and in this profile are approximate. There is 1 undergraduate school and 2 graduate schools. In addition to regional accreditation, Thomas More has baccalaureate program accreditation with NLN. The 100-acre campus is in a suburban area 8 miles south of Cincinnati, OH. Including any residence halls, there are 10 buildings.

STUDENT LIFE: 53% of undergraduates are from out of state, mostly the Midwest. Students are from 17 states, and 3 foreign countries. 65% are from public schools. 78% are White; 6% African American; 2% Hispanic; 2% two or more races; 10% race unknown; 1% Asian American; 1% Foreign. 46% claim no religious affiliation; 28% Catholic; 22% Protestant. **Male To Female Ratio:** 1.2:1. The average age of freshmen is 18; all undergraduates, 23. 39% do not continue beyond their first year; 50% remain to graduate. **Housing:** 400 students can be accommodated in college housing, which includes single-sex and coed dorms. On-campus housing is available on a first-come, first-served basis. Priority is given to out-of-town students. 68% of students commute. All students may keep cars.

FACULTY/CLASSROOMS: 59% of faculty are male; 41% are female. All teach undergraduates. No introductory courses are taught by graduate students. The average class size in an introductory lecture is 14; in a laboratory is 11; and in a regular course is 14.

PROGRAMS OF STUDY: Thomas More confers B.A., B.S., B.B.A., B.E.S. and B.S.N. degrees. Associate and master's degrees are also awarded. Bachelor's degrees are awarded in BIOLOGICAL SCIENCE (biology/biological science), BUSINESS (accounting, business administration and management, and sports marketing), COMMUNICATIONS AND THE ARTS (art, communications, dramatic arts, English, and Spanish), COMPUTER AND PHYSICAL SCIENCE (chemistry, computer science, mathematics, and physics), EDUCATION (art education, business education, elementary education, middle school education, secondary education, and social studies education), ENGINEERING AND ENVIRONMENTAL DESIGN (environmental science), HEALTH PROFESSIONS (health care administration, medical laboratory technology, and nursing), SOCIAL SCIENCE (criminal justice, economics, forensic studies, history, humanities, international studies, liberal arts/general studies, philosophy, political science/government, psychology, sociology, and theological studies). Business, biology, and nursing have the largest enrollments.

ACTIVITIES: 2% of men belong to 1 national fraternity; 2% of women belong to 1 national sorority. There are 35 groups on campus, including art, cheerleading, chorus, computers, drama, environmental, ethnic, honors, international, literary magazine, marching band, political, professional, religious, social, social service, student government, and yearbook. Popular campus events include Spring Pig Roast, Welcome Carnival, and Presidential Inauguration Ball. **Sports:** There are 8 intercollegiate sports for men and 8 for women, and 5 intramural sports for men and 5 for women. Facilities include an athletic/convocation center with a 1500-seat indoor gym, a football/soccer complex plus baseball and softball fields, 16 tennis courts (8 indoor), 4 racquetball courts, an indoor pool, a track, and weight and exercise rooms. **Graduates:** From July 1, 2015 to June 30, 2016, 254 bachelor's degrees were awarded. The most popular majors were business (42%), nursing (10%), and education (8%). 46 companies recruited on campus in 2015-2016. In an average class, 35% graduate in 4 years or less, 46% graduate in 5 years or less, and 49% graduate in 6 years or less. Of the 2015 graduating class, 27% were enrolled in graduate school within 6 months of graduation, and 95% were employed.

SERVICES: Counseling and information services are available, as is tutoring in every subject. There is a reader service for the blind, and remedial math, reading, and writing. Signing for the hearing impaired is available. **Library/Resources:** The library contains 114,230 volumes, 28,429 microform items, and 2,386 audio/video tapes/CDs/DVDs, and subscribes to 368 periodicals including electronic. Computerized library services include interlibrary loans, database searching, and Internet access. Special learning facilities include an art gallery, observatory on campus, and biology field station on the Ohio River. **Physically Challenged Students:** 90% of the campus is accessible. Facilities include wheelchair ramps, elevators, special parking, and specially equipped restrooms. **Special:** There are co-op programs in all majors except nursing. The 3-2 engineering degree is available from the accredited engineering school of the student's choice. Cross-registration is possible through the

Greater Cincinnati Consortium. There are also internships, study abroad in many countries, many B.A. & B.S. degrees, student-designed majors, work-study programs, credit for life experience, and pass/fail options. The Bachelor of Elected Studies and Bachelor of Arts-Student Initiated degrees provide students with an individualized program. Nondegree study is possible. There are 9 national honor societies and 9 departmental honors programs. **Visiting:** There are regularly scheduled orientations for prospective students, including a campus tour and meetings with an admissions counselor, a professor in one's major field (if decided), and financial aid staff. There are guides for informal visits, visitors may sit in on classes, and stay overnight. To schedule a visit, contact the Admissions Office. **Campus Safety and Security:** Measures include 24-hour foot and vehicle patrol, emergency notification system, self-defense education, and security escort services. There are lighted pathways/sidewalks and controlled access to dorms/residences.

REQUIREMENTS: The SAT or ACT is required, with a minimum composite score of 20 on the ACT (20 on the English section) or 1010 on the SAT (480 on the verbal section). Applicants should have completed 17 high school academic units, including 4 of English, 3 each of math, science, and social studies, 2 of non-native language, and 1 each of arts appreciation and computer literacy. Thomas More requires applicants to be in the upper 50% of their class. AP and CLEP credits are accepted. Important factors in the admissions decision are advanced placement or honors courses, leadership record, and personality/intangible qualities. All students must complete 56 to 61 hours of core requirements, including 9 credits in theology, 6 each in English, social sciences, global history, fine arts, foreign language, philosophy, and natural sciences, and 3 each in communication and math. A total of 128 credit hours, including 36 to 76 in the major, with a minimum GPA of 2.0 is required to graduate. **Procedure:** Freshmen are admitted to all sessions. Entrance exams should be taken in the spring of the junior year or in the fall of the senior year. There are deferred admissions and rolling admissions plans. Applications should be filed by August 1 for fall entry; January 2 for spring entry, along with a $25 fee. Applications are accepted on-line. **Transfer Students:** 65 transfer students enrolled in 2015-2016. Applicants should be in good academic standing and have a minimum GPA of 2.0 in 24 semester hours earned. 38 of 128 credits required for the bachelor's degree must be completed at Thomas More. **International Students:** There are 8 international students enrolled. The school actively recruits these students. They must take the TOEFL with a minimum score of 515 on the paper-based TOEFL (PBT) or 66 on the Internet-based version (iBT). They must also take the SAT or ACT.

ADMISSIONS: The SAT scores for the 2016-2017 freshman class were: Critical Reading-- 55% below 500, 36% between 500 and 599, and 9% between 600 and 699. Math-- 51% below 500, 31% between 500 and 599, 13% between 600 and 699, and 5% between 700 and 800. The ACT scores were 28% below 12, 35% between 12 and 17, 24% between 18 and 23, 5% between 24 and 29, and 8% above 30. 23% of the current freshmen were in the top fifth of their class; 52% were in the top two fifths. **Admissions Contact:** Dr. Christopher Powers, Associate VP Enrollment Management. Email: *admissions@thomasmore.edu* Web: *www.thomasmore.edu*

FINANCIAL AID: In 2016-2017, 100% of all full-time freshmen and 86% of continuing full-time students received some form of financial aid. 82% of all full-time freshmen and 63% of continuing full-time students received need-based aid. The average freshman award was $21,063. Need-based scholarships or need-based grants averaged $16,356; need-based self-help aid (loans and jobs) averaged $4,458; and other non-need-based awards and non-need-based scholarships averaged $15,861. Average annual earnings from campus work are $2100. The average financial indebtedness of the 2016 graduate was $32,601. Thomas More is a member of CSS. The college's own financial statement is required. The FAFSA code is 002001. The deadline for filing freshman financial aid applications for fall entry is January 15.

TRANSYLVANIA UNIVERSITY D-3

www.transy.edu

Lexington, KY 40508	**(859) 233-8242** **(800) 872-6798**
Fax: (859) 233-8797	**Email: admissions@transy.edu**
Full-time: 395 men, 558 women	**Faculty:** 84; IIB, av$
Part-time: 3 men, 4 women	**Ph.D.s:** 96%
Graduate: n/av	**Student/Faculty:** 11 to 1
Year: 4-1-4, summer session	**Tuition:** $35,830
Room & Board: $9860	**Freshman Class:** 1216 applied, 1153 accepted, 242 enrolled
SAT CR/M: 560/560 **ACT:** 27	**CEEB CODE:** 1808
Application Deadline: February 1	**VERY COMPETITIVE+**

Transylvania University, founded in 1780, is an independent liberal arts institution affiliated with the Christian Church (Disciples of Christ). Through an engagement with the liberal arts, Transylvania prepares its students for a humane and fulfilling personal and public life by cultivating independent thinking, open-mindedness, creative expression, and commitment to lifelong learning and social responsibility in a diverse world. There is 1 undergraduate school. In addition to regional accreditation, Transy has baccalaureate program accreditation with NCATE. The 70-acre campus is in an urban area in historic district of downtown Lexington. Including any residence halls, there are 33 buildings.

STUDENT LIFE: 74% of undergraduates are from Kentucky. Others are from 29 states, and 7 foreign countries. 85% are from public schools. 79% are White; 6% Hispanic; 4% African American; 4% Foreign; 3% two or more races; 2% race unknown; 1% Asian American. 39% are Mormon, Muslim, Orthodox and Buddhist; 27% Protestant; 17% Catholic; 16% claim no religious affiliation. **Female To Male Ratio:** 1.4:1. The average age of freshmen is 18; all undergraduates, 20. 14% do not continue beyond their first year; 75% remain to graduate. **Housing:** 900 students can be accommodated in college housing, which includes single-sex and coed dorms and on-campus apartments. On-campus housing is guaranteed for all 4 years. 76% of students live on campus; of those, 80% remain on campus on weekends. All students may keep cars.

FACULTY/CLASSROOMS: 55% of faculty are male; 45% are female. All teach undergraduates. No introductory courses are taught by graduate students. The average class size in an introductory lecture is 18; in a laboratory is 14; and in a regular course is 18.

PROGRAMS OF STUDY: Transy confers B.A. degrees. Bachelor's degrees are awarded in BIOLOGICAL SCIENCE (biochemistry, biology/biological science, and neurosciences), BUSINESS (accounting and business administration and management), COMMUNICATIONS AND THE ARTS (art history, art, classics, dramatic arts, English, French, Germanic languages and literature, music, music technology, Spanish, studio art, and theatre arts), COMPUTER AND PHYSICAL SCIENCE (chemistry, computer science, mathematics, and physics), EDUCATION (education, elementary education, and middle school education), HEALTH PROFESSIONS (exercise science), SOCIAL SCIENCE (anthropology, economics, history, philosophy, political science/government, psychology, religion, and sociology). Accounting, business, and biology have the largest enrollments.

ACTIVITIES: 50% of men belong to 4 national fraternities; 54% of women belong to 4 national sororities. There are 60 groups on campus, including art, band, cheerleading, choir, chorale, chorus, computers, dance, debate, drama, environmental, ethnic, forensics, honors, international, jazz band, LGBT, literary magazine, musical theater, newspaper, opera, orchestra, pep band, political, professional, radio and TV, religious, social, social service, student government, and yearbook. **Sports:** There are 10 intercollegiate sports for men and 12 for women, and 18 intramural sports for men and 18 for women. Facilities include a 1300-seat performance gym, a fitness center with an indoor jogging track, a swimming pool, basketball courts, tennis courts, and athletic fields for baseball, field hockey, lacrosse, soccer, softball, and track/field. **Graduates:** From July 1, 2015 to June 30, 2016, 254 bachelor's degrees were awarded. The most popular majors were business (12%) and accounting and biology (10%). 13 companies recruited on campus in 2015-2016. In an average class, 1% graduate in 3 years or less, 71% graduate in 4 years or less, 74% graduate in 5 years or less, and 75% graduate in 6 years or less. Of the 2015 graduating class, 40% were enrolled in graduate school within 6 months of graduation, and 41% were employed.

SERVICES: Counseling and information services are available, as is tutoring in every subject. There is an Academic Center for Excellence (ACE) that provides additional help. **Library/Resources:** The library contains 334,492 volumes, 59 microform items, and 3,976 audio/video tapes/CDs/DVDs, and subscribes to 19,000 periodicals including electronic. Computerized library services include interlibrary loans, database searching, Internet access, and Wi-Fi capability. Special learning facilities include an art gallery, natural history museum, and radio station. **Physically Challenged Students:** 90% of the campus is accessible. Facilities include wheelchair ramps, elevators, special parking, specially equipped restrooms, special class scheduling, and lowered drinking fountains. Arrangements are made according to individual needs. **Special:** 3-2 engineering degrees with the University of Kentucky and Vanderbilt University are offered, along with a pre-engineering partnership with the University of Kentucky. Internships, study abroad, work-study programs, a Washington semester, dual majors, and student-designed majors are available. There are 9 national honor societies. **Visiting:**

There are regularly scheduled orientations for prospective students, consisting of campus open houses in fall and winter for high school juniors and seniors, which include a welcome program, an academic information fair, campus tours, a luncheon, a financial aid session, and a faculty session. There are guides for informal visits, visitors may sit in on classes, and stay overnight. To schedule a visit, contact Office of Admissions. **Campus Safety and Security:** Measures include 24-hour foot and vehicle patrol, emergency notification system, self-defense education, and security escort services. There are shuttle buses, emergency telephones, lighted pathways/sidewalks, and controlled access to dorms/residences.

REQUIREMENTS: Transylvania is Test Optional. Transy requires applicants to be in the upper 50% of their class. A GPA of 2.0 is required. AP credits are accepted. Important factors in the admissions decision are advanced placement or honors courses, recommendations by school officials, and extracurricular activities record. The college believes that all students, no matter what career or vocation they choose, benefit from liberal education; and so the college encourages the free search for knowledge and understanding drawn from the natural and social sciences, the humanities, and the arts. By so doing, the college strives to empower students to develop lifelong habits of learning and intelligent, respectful discussion. Therefore, students must fulfill requirements in five general areas: Area I Introduction to Critical Skills, Area II Approaches to Learning, Area III Cultural Traditions, Area IV Upper-level Liberal Arts (2+2), and Area V Writing Intensive Courses **Procedure:** Freshmen are admitted fall and winter. Entrance exams should be taken during the junior year and no later than December of the senior year for scholarship consideration or February for general admission. There are early admissions and deferred admissions plans. Early decision applications should be filed by October 15; regular applications, by February 1 for fall entry; and December 1 for winter entry. Notification of early decision is sent December 1; regular decision, March 15. Applications are accepted on-line. Application fees are waived if application is completed on-line. **Transfer Students:** 13 transfer students enrolled in 2015-2016. Applicants must have a minimum college GPA of 2.75 and should submit official copies of all college transcripts, 2 recommendations, and 1 essay. A high school transcript or GED is required. 18 of 36 credits required for the bachelor's degree must be completed at Transy. **International Students:** There are 36 international students enrolled. The school actively recruits these students. They must take the TOEFL. They must also take the SAT or ACT.

ADMISSIONS: 95% of the 2016-2017 applicants were accepted. The SAT scores for the 2016-2017 freshman class were: Critical Reading-- 17% below 500, 48% between 500 and 599, 31% between 600 and 699, and 3% between 700 and 800. Math-- 34% below 500, 24% between 500 and 599, 14% between 600 and 699, and 28% between 700 and 800. The ACT scores were 14% between 18 and 23, 58% between 24 and 29, and 28% above 30. 70% of the current freshmen were in the top fifth of their class; 89% were in the top two fifths. **Admissions Contact:** Holly Sheilley, VP for Enrollment & Student Affairs. Email: *admissions@transy.edu* Web: *www.transy.edu*

FINANCIAL AID: In 2016-2017, 99% of all full-time freshmen and 98% of continuing full-time students received some form of financial aid. 72% of all full-time freshmen and 66% of continuing full-time students received need-based aid. The average freshman award was $27,139. Need-based scholarships or need-based grants averaged $24,019 ($45,690 maximum); need-based self-help aid (loans and jobs) averaged $4,113 ($9,500 maximum); and other non-need-based awards and non-need-based scholarships averaged $15,197 ($45,690 maximum). 51% of undergraduate students work part-time. Average annual earnings from campus work are $1568. The average financial indebtedness of the 2016 graduate was $27,256. Transy is a member of CSS. The FAFSA code is 001987. The priority date for freshman financial aid applications for fall entry is October 1. The deadline for filing freshman financial aid applications for fall entry is February 1.

UNION COLLEGE E-4

www.unionky.edu

Barbourville, KY 40906	(606) 546-1612 (800) 489-8646
Fax: (606) 546-1667	Email: enrollme@unionky.edu
Full-time: 455 men, 398 women	Faculty: 52; IIB
Part-time: 18 men, 41 women	Ph.D.s: 52%
Graduate: 76 men, 147 women	Student/Faculty: 13 to 1
Year: semesters, summer session	Tuition: $25,060
Room & Board: $7250	Freshman Class: 1385 applied, 1042 accepted, 240 enrolled
SAT CR/M: 469/506 ACT: 22	CEEB CODE: 1825
Application Deadline: open	COMPETITIVE

Union College, founded in 1879, is a private liberal arts institution affiliated with the United Methodist Church. Figures in the above capsule and in this profile are approximate. There are 4 undergraduate schools and 1 graduate school. The 100-acre campus is in a small town 95 miles south of Lexington, Kentucky, and 85 miles north of Knoxville, Tennessee. Including any residence halls, there are 20 buildings.

STUDENT LIFE: 66% of undergraduates are from Kentucky. Others are from 35 states, 17 foreign countries, and Canada. 70% are White; 6% Foreign; 4% two or more races; 3% Hispanic; 15% African American; 1% race unknown. **Female To Male Ratio:** 1.1:1. The average age of freshmen is 20; all undergraduates, 22. 36% do not continue beyond their first year; 32% remain to graduate. **Housing:** 472 students can be accommodated in college housing, which includes single-sex dorms, on-campus apartments, off-campus apartments, and married student housing. On-campus housing is guaranteed for all 4 years, and is available on a first-come, first-served basis. 52% of students live on campus. Alcohol is not permitted. All students may keep cars.

FACULTY/CLASSROOMS: 52% of faculty are male; 48% are female. 84% teach undergraduates. No introductory courses are taught by graduate students. The average class size in an introductory lecture is 25 and in a regular course is 20.

PROGRAMS OF STUDY: Union confers B.A. and B.S. degrees. Master's degrees are also awarded. Bachelor's degrees are awarded in BIOLOGICAL SCIENCE (biology/biological science), BUSINESS (accounting, business administration and management, international business management, marketing management, organizational leadership and management, recreational facilities management, and sports management), COMMUNICATIONS AND THE ARTS (communications, dramatic arts, English, and fine arts), COMPUTER AND PHYSICAL SCIENCE (chemistry and mathematics), EDUCATION (athletic training, education, elementary education, middle school education, physical education, science education, secondary education, social studies education, and special education), ENGINEERING AND ENVIRONMENTAL DESIGN (computer technology), HEALTH PROFESSIONS (exercise science, health, and nursing), SOCIAL SCIENCE (criminal justice, history, Latin American studies, ministries, psychology, religion, social work, and sociology). Education, business, and nursing are the strongest academically, and have the largest enrollments.

ACTIVITIES: There are no fraternities or sororities. There are 31 groups on campus, including cheerleading, choir, chorale, chorus, computers, drama, ethnic, honors, international, LGBT, literary magazine, pep band, professional, radio and TV, religious, social, social service, student government, and yearbook. Popular campus events include Springfest, Student Holiday Dinner, and CIRCLES Ceremony. **Sports:** There are 14 intercollegiate sports for men and 13 for women, and 5 intramural sports for men and 3 for women. Facilities include a 3,000-seat campus stadium, an 1,800-seat gym, an indoor pool with bleachers for 300, 6 tennis courts, a weight-training center, an athletic training center, a 500-seat baseball stadium with 3 batting cages and a practice infield, a soccer field with stands for 250, a softball field with stands for 150, and practice fields for football and soccer. **Graduates:** From July 1, 2015 to June 30, 2016, 112 bachelor's degrees were awarded. The most popular majors were education (21%), business/marketing (19%), and health professions/related programs (10%). In an average class, 17% graduate in 4 years or less, 30% graduate in 5 years or less, and 32% graduate in 6 years or less.

SERVICES: Counseling and information services are available, as is tutoring in most subjects. There is a reader service for the blind, and remedial math, reading, and writing. There is a tutoring lab with computer support. **Library/Resources:** The library contains 108,583 volumes, 123,928 microform items, and 3,432 audio/video tapes/CDs/DVDs, and subscribes to 365,525 periodicals including electronic. Computerized library services include interlibrary loans, database searching, Internet access, and Wi-Fi capability. Special learning facilities include a radio station. **Physically Challenged Students:** 85% of the campus is accessible. Facilities include wheelchair ramps, elevators, special parking, specially equipped restrooms, special class scheduling, and lowered drinking fountains. **Special:** Work-study programs, study abroad in 7 countries, an accelerated business degree completion program, and internships in business, sociology, psychology, recreational management, and mass communications are available. There are 2 national honor societies and a freshman honors program. **Visiting:** There are regularly scheduled orientations for prospective students consisting of advising and registration, parent sessions, and break-out sessions. There are guides for informal visits, visitors may sit in on classes, and stay overnight. To schedule a visit, contact Sam Lee at slee@unionky.edu. **Campus**

Safety and Security: Measures include 24-hour foot and vehicle patrol, emergency notification system, self-defense education, and security escort services. There are emergency telephones, lighted pathways/ sidewalks, and controlled access to dorms/residences. The campus web site has a notification system (alert system) that provides information about recent crimes on campus.

REQUIREMENTS: The SAT or ACT is required. Standardized test scores are not required for students 25 or older. All first-year students should have completed a pre-college high school curriculum that includes 4 units of English, 3 of math, 2 each of lab science and social science, and the study of a foreign language. An official, sealed high school transcript or an official GED score report is also required. A GPA of 2.0 is required. AP and CLEP credits are accepted. Important factors in the admissions decision are evidence of special talent, geographical diversity, and advanced placement or honors courses. All students are required to complete 43 credits in a liberal education core, including 21 hours in humanities, 7 to 8 of general science, 6 of social science, and 3 each of wellness, math, and cultural studies. **Procedure:** Freshmen are admitted to all sessions. Entrance exams should be taken by January of the senior year. There are deferred admissions and rolling admissions plans. Application deadlines are open. Application fee is $10. Notification is sent on a rolling basis. Applications are accepted on-line. **Transfer Students:** 75 transfer students enrolled in 2015-2016. Applicants should have a minimum GPA of 2.0. 32 of 120 credits required for the bachelor's degree must be completed at Union. **International Students:** There are 51 international students enrolled. The school actively recruits these students. They must take the TOEFL with a minimum score of 550 on the paper-based TOEFL (PBT) and the college's own test, and also complete an ELS program at level 109. They must also take the SAT or ACT.

ADMISSIONS: 75% of the 2016-2017 applicants were accepted. The ACT scores were 50% below 12, 29% between 12 and 17, 14% between 18 and 23, 6% between 24 and 29, and 1% above 30. **Admissions Contact:** Sam Lee, Director: Undergraduate Enrollment. Email: *enrollme@unionky.edu* Web: *www.unionky.edu*

FINANCIAL AID: In 2016-2017, 100% of all full-time freshmen and 100% of continuing full-time students received some form of financial aid. 83% of all full-time freshmen and 78% of continuing full-time students received need-based aid. The average freshman award was $24,687. Need-based scholarships or need-based grants averaged $18,482; need-based self-help aid (loans and jobs) averaged $3,552; and other non-need-based awards and non-need-based scholarships averaged $6,687. Average annual earnings from campus work are $1500. The average financial indebtedness of the 2016 graduate was $24,948. Union is a member of CSS. The CSS/Profile is required. The FAFSA code is 001988. The priority date for freshman financial aid applications for fall entry is February 15. The deadline for filing freshman financial aid applications for fall entry is February 15.

UNIVERSITY OF KENTUCKY — D-3

www.uky.edu

Lexington, KY 40506	(859) 257-2000
Fax: (859) 257-3823	**Email:** admissions@uky.edu
Full-time: 9445 men, 9733 women	**Faculty:** 1207; I, -$
Part-time: 878 men, 771 women	**Ph.D.s:** 93%
Graduate: 3152 men, 4055 women	**Student/Faculty:** n/av
Year: semesters, summer session	**Tuition:** $21,872 ($24,268)
Room & Board: $11,434	**Freshman Class:** n/av
SAT or ACT: required	**CEEB CODE:** 1837
Application Deadline: February 15	**COMPETITIVE**

The University of Kentucky, founded in 1865, is a public land-grant institution offering undergraduate and graduate programs in a variety of areas. Figures in the above capsule and in this profile are approximate. There are 13 undergraduate schools and 1 graduate school. In addition to regional accreditation, UK has baccalaureate program accreditation with AACSB, ABET, ACEJMC, ACPE, ADA, AHEA, APTA, ASLA, CAHEA, CSWE, FIDER, NAAB, NASAD, NASM, NCATE, NLN, NRPA, and SAF. The 764-acre campus is in a suburban area 75 miles south of Cincinnati. Including any residence halls, there are 335 buildings.

STUDENT LIFE: 79% of undergraduates are from Kentucky. Others are from 49 states, 114 foreign countries, and Canada. 8% are African American; 79% White; 3% Hispanic; 3% race unknown; 2% Asian American; 2% Foreign; 2% two or more races. **Female To Male Ratio:** 1.1:1. The average age of freshmen is 18; all undergraduates, 21. 19% do not continue beyond their first year; 58% remain to graduate. **Housing:** 6166 students can be accommodated in college housing, which includes single-sex and coed dorms, on-campus apartments, and married student housing. In addition, there are honors houses, language houses, special-interest houses, fraternity houses, and sorority houses. On-campus housing is available on a first-come, first-served basis. 74% of students commute. Alcohol is not permitted. All students may keep cars.

FACULTY/CLASSROOMS: 64% of faculty are male; 36% are female. No introductory courses are taught by graduate students.

PROGRAMS OF STUDY: UK confers B.A., B.S., B.Arch., B.B.A., B.F.A., B.H.S., and B.M. degrees. Master's and doctoral degrees are also awarded. Bachelor's degrees are awarded in AGRICULTURE (agricultural economics, agriculture, animal science, and forestry and related sciences), BIOLOGICAL SCIENCE (biology/biological science, botany, and zoology), BUSINESS (accounting, banking and finance, business economics, hotel/motel and restaurant management, and marketing/ retailing/merchandising), COMMUNICATIONS AND THE ARTS (advertising, art history and appreciation, arts administration/ management, communications, dramatic arts, English, French, German, Italian, journalism, linguistics, music, music performance, Russian, Spanish, and telecommunications), COMPUTER AND PHYSICAL SCIENCE (chemistry, computer science, geology, mathematics, and physics), EDUCATION (agricultural education, art education, business education, early childhood education, elementary education, foreign languages education, health education, mathematics education, middle school education, music education, physical education, science education, secondary education, social studies education, and special education), ENGINEERING AND ENVIRONMENTAL DESIGN (chemical engineering, civil engineering, electrical/electronics engineering, landscape architecture/design, materials engineering, mechanical engineering, and mining and mineral engineering), HEALTH PROFESSIONS (nursing, physical therapy, and physician's assistant), SOCIAL SCIENCE (anthropology, economics, food science, geography, history, Latin American studies, philosophy, political science/government, psychology, social work, sociology, and textiles and clothing). Pharmacy, architecture, and allied health are the strongest academically. Finance, accounting, and marketing have the largest enrollments.

ACTIVITIES: 16% of men belong to 24 national fraternities; 25% of women belong to 19 national sororities. There are 272 groups on campus, including band, cheerleading, chess, choir, chorale, chorus, computers, dance, debate, drama, drill team, environmental, ethnic, honors, international, jazz band, LGBT, literary magazine, marching band, musical theater, newspaper, orchestra, pep band, photography, political, professional, radio and TV, religious, social, social service, student government, symphony, and yearbook. Popular campus events include Little Kentucky Derby, Cultural Diversity Week, and Spotlight Jazz Series. **Sports:** There are 11 intercollegiate sports for men and 12 for women, and 22 intramural sports for men and 22 for women. Facilities include a football stadium, an arena for basketball and other activities, an aquatic center and swimming pool, baseball fields, a training center, indoor tennis courts, and a field house. **Graduates:** From July 1, 2015 to June 30, 2016, 3285 bachelor's degrees were awarded. The most popular majors were business (20%), engineering (10%), and health professions (9%). In an average class, 21% graduate in 4 years or less, 43% graduate in 5 years or less, and 51% graduate in 6 years or less.

SERVICES: There is a reader service for the blind, and remedial math. **Library/Resources:** The 13 libraries contain 2.8 million volumes, 5.9 million microform items, and 73,600 audio/video tapes/CDs/DVDs, and subscribe to 26,539 periodicals including electronic. Computerized library services include database searching. Special learning facilities include an art gallery, natural history museum, radio station, and TV station. **Physically Challenged Students:** 90% of the campus is accessible. Facilities include wheelchair ramps, elevators, special parking, specially equipped restrooms, special class scheduling, lowered drinking fountains, and lowered telephones. **Special:** Co-op programs are offered in engineering, business, computer science, math, and agriculture. The Academic Common Market allows students in 14 southern states to study outside the university. Internships in a variety of fields, study abroad in 36 countries, work-study programs with the university and local businesses, and credit for life experience are also available. An accelerated degree program, B.A.-B.S. degrees, dual and double majors, a general studies degree, student-designed majors, a 3-2 engineering degree with several smaller schools in Kentucky, non-degree study, and pass/fail options are also offered. There are 12 national honor societies, Phi Beta Kappa, and a freshman honors program. **Visiting:** There are regularly scheduled orientations for prospective students, including a campus tour and information on admissions, housing, financial aid, and campus activities. There are guides for informal visits and visitors may sit in on classes. **Campus Safety and Security:** Measures include 24-hour foot and vehicle patrol, emergency notification system, self-defense education, and security escort services. There are shuttle buses, emergency telephones, lighted pathways/sidewalks, and controlled access to dorms/residences.

REQUIREMENTS: The SAT or ACT is required. Minimum scores vary with the GPA. Applicants must complete 20 Carnegie units, including 4 years of English, 3 of math, and 2 each of science and social studies. A fourth year of math, 2 years of foreign language, and 1 year of fine arts also are recommended. A portfolio is required for art studio courses, and an audition is required for music performance. A GPA of 2.0 is required. AP and CLEP credits are accepted. All students must maintain a minimum 2.0 GPA and complete at least 120 credit hours. Students must demonstrate competency in math, foreign language, writing, and oral communications. Required studies include courses in basic skills, inference, and communicative skills, along with disciplinary and cross-disciplinary studies. **Procedure:** Freshmen are admitted to all sessions. Entrance exams should be taken before Christmas of the senior year. There is a rolling admissions plan. Early decision applications should be filed by December 1; regular applications, by February 15 for fall entry; October 15 for spring entry; and February 15 for summer entry, along with a $20 fee. **Transfer Students:** 1443 transfer students enrolled in 2015-2016. Transfer students need a minimum GPA of 2.0. If they have fewer than 24 credit hours, they must meet freshmen admission standards. With 24 credits or more, the SAT I or ACT is not required. 30 of 120 credits required for the bachelor's degree must be completed at UK. **International Students:** There are 366 international students enrolled. The school actively recruits these students. They must take the TOEFL.

Admissions Contact: Steven Barnett, Associate Director for Admissions. Email: *admissions@uky.edu* Web: *www.uky.edu*

FINANCIAL AID: 32% of all full-time freshmen and 34% of continuing full-time students received need-based aid. The average freshman award was $6,007. UK is a member of CSS. The FAFSA code is 001989. The deadline for filing freshman financial aid applications for fall entry is February 15.

UNIVERSITY OF LOUISVILLE — D-2

www.louisville.edu

Louisville, KY 40292	**(502) 852-6531** **(800) 334-8635**
Fax: (502) 852-4476	**Email: admitme@louisville.edu**
Full-time: 5985 men, 6449 women	**Faculty:** I, -$
Part-time: 1808 men, 1585 women	**Ph.D.s:** 86%
Graduate: 2746 men, 3006 women	**Student/Faculty:** 16 to 1
Year: semesters, summer session	**Tuition:** $11,068 ($26,090)
Room & Board: $8560	**Freshman Class:** 10834 applied, 7949 accepted, 2765 enrolled
SAT CR/M/W: 540/540/550 **ACT:** 24	**CEEB CODE:** 1838
Application Deadline: n/av	**COMPETITIVE**

University of Louisville, founded in 1798, is a public institution offering a wide range of undergraduate and graduate academic programs. There are 9 undergraduate schools and 12 graduate schools. In addition to regional accreditation, U of L has baccalaureate program accreditation with AACSB, ABET, ACCE, ADA, CSWE, NASM, NCATE, ABA, CCNE, CEPH, CIDA, COAES, COSMA, NAST, CAEP, and ACS. The 1180-acre campus is in an urban area in Louisville, KY. Including any residence halls, there are 207 buildings.

STUDENT LIFE: 80% of undergraduates are from Kentucky. Others are from 50 states, 83 foreign countries, and Canada. 73% are White; 4% Asian American; 4% Hispanic; 4% Foreign; 4% two or more races; 10% African American. **Female To Male Ratio:** 1.0:1. The average age of freshmen is 17; all undergraduates, 22. 20% do not continue beyond their first year; 53% remain to graduate. **Housing:** 7044 students can be accommodated in college housing, which includes single-sex dorms, on-campus apartments, off-campus apartments, and married student housing. In addition, there are honors houses, special-interest houses, living-learning communities, and themed communities. On-campus housing is guaranteed for the freshman year only. 69% of students commute. All students may keep cars.

FACULTY/CLASSROOMS: 56% of faculty are male; 44% are female. No introductory courses are taught by graduate students.

PROGRAMS OF STUDY: U of L confers B.A., B.A.L., B.A.M., B.A.R., B.A.S., B.B.E., B.C.C., B.C.E., B.C.H., B.C.S., B.D.P., B.E.E., B.E.S., B.F.A., B.H.A., B.H.C, B.H.L, B.H.N., B.H.P, B.H.S., B.H.T., B.I.E., B.L.S., B.M., B.M.C., B.M.E., B.S., B.S.B., B.S.C., B.S.E., B.S.G., B.S.H., B.S.I., B.S.L., B.S.M., B.S.N., B.S.P., B.S.R., and B.S.W degrees. Associate, master's, and doctoral degrees are also awarded. Bachelor's degrees are awarded in AGRICULTURE (equine science), BIOLOGICAL SCIENCE (biology/biological science), BUSINESS (accounting, banking and finance, business administration and management, business economics, entrepreneurial studies, management science, marketing/retailing/merchandising, and sports management), COMMUNICATIONS AND THE ARTS (American Sign Language, art history, art, art history and appreciation, communications, dramatic arts, English, French, linguistics, music, Spanish, and theatre arts), COMPUTER AND PHYSICAL SCIENCE (atmospheric sciences and meteorology, chemistry, computer science, information sciences and systems, mathematics, and physics), EDUCATION (art education, Asian studies, business education, early childhood education, elementary education, foreign languages education, middle school education, music education, physical education, science education, secondary education, and teaching English as a second/foreign language (TESOL/TEFOL)), ENGINEERING AND ENVIRONMENTAL DESIGN (bioengineering, chemical engineering, civil engineering, computer engineering, electrical/electronics engineering, engineering, engineering management, industrial engineering, and mechanical engineering), HEALTH PROFESSIONS (dental hygiene, health, medical laboratory technology, medical science, music therapy, nursing, and public health), SOCIAL SCIENCE (administration of justice, anthropology, clinical psychology, criminal justice, geography, history, humanities, liberal arts/general studies, paralegal studies, philosophy, political science/government, psychology, public administration, social work, sociology, and women's studies). Engineering, health professional, and business management are the strongest academically. Arts & sciences, education and human development, and engineering have the largest enrollments.

ACTIVITIES: 11% of men belong to 19 national fraternities; 11% of women belong to 14 national sororities. There are 458 groups on campus, including art, band, cheerleading, chess, choir, chorale, chorus, computers, dance, debate, ethnic, honors, international, jazz band, LGBT, literary magazine, marching band, newspaper, opera, orchestra, pep band, photography, political, professional, radio and TV, religious, social, social service, student government, and symphony. Popular campus events include Homecoming, Welcome Week, International Fashion Show, and Fryberger Greek Sing. **Sports:** There are 10 intercollegiate sports for men and 13 for women, and 37 intramural sports for men and 37 for women. Facilities include KFC Yum center, a football stadium, soccer, volleyball, women's basketball practice, Trager Center Fieldhouse, Marshall Center (multi-sport weight training facility), indoor practice courts for basketball and volleyball, Ralph R. Wright Natatorium, Bass-Rudd Tennis Center, University of Louisville Golf Club, track & field stadium, softball, baseball, Garvin Brown II Rowing Center, Thorntons Academic Center of Excellence, lacrosse stadium, and a Student Recreation Center (exercise and weight facility, six basketball courts, a multi-activity court, jogging track, aerobics studio, fitness labs, boathouse for rowing, a gaming area, and classrooms). **Graduates:** From July 1, 2015 to June 30, 2016, 2705 bachelor's degrees were awarded. The most popular majors were psychology (7%), communication (7%), and health and human performance (6%). In an average class, 27% graduate in 4 years or less, 48% graduate in 5 years or less, and 53% graduate in 6 years or less.

SERVICES: Counseling and information services are available, as is tutoring in most subjects. There is a reader service for the blind. **Library/Resources:** The 6 libraries contain 2.2 million volumes, 2.3 million microform items, and 62,146 audio/video tapes/CDs/DVDs, and subscribe to 92,972 periodicals including electronic. Computerized library services include interlibrary loans, database searching, Internet access, and Wi-Fi capability. Special learning facilities include an art gallery, planetarium, and radio station. **Physically Challenged Students:** 90% of the campus is accessible. Facilities include wheelchair ramps, elevators, special parking, specially equipped restrooms, special class scheduling, lowered drinking fountains, lowered telephones, and special housing. **Special:** U of L offers cross-registration with other schools, study abroad in 5 countries (China, Panama, Portugal, Trinidad, Canada), work-study programs, and B.A.-B.S. degrees. A general studies degree, nondegree study, and pass/fail options are available. Co-op programs in engineering and business and internships are also possible. There are 16 national honor societies, a freshman honors program, and 4 departmental honors programs. **Visiting:** There are regularly scheduled orientations for prospective students, and admissions presentation, campus tour, and optional faculty appointments. There are guides for informal visits. To schedule a visit, contact Kristen Ellis at kristen.ellis@louisville.edu **Campus Safety and Security:** Measures include 24-hour foot and vehicle patrol, emergency notification system, self-defense education, and security escort services. There are shuttle buses, emergency telephones, lighted pathways/sidewalks, and controlled access to dorms/residences.

REQUIREMENTS: The SAT or ACT is required. Applicants must be graduates of an accredited high school or have received a GED, must have completed a precollege curriculum with a GPA of 2.5, and must have at least 1 of the following: a composite ACT score of 20 or a satisfactory SAT score; completion of the U of L enhanced precollege curriculum (PCC) with a minimum GPA of 2.5; or a rank in the top 15% of the high school graduating class. AP and CLEP credits are accepted. Requirements include at least 6 hours each in social sciences, natural sciences, the history of world civilizations, and humanities. Freshmen are required to take college writing or advanced composition and 2 phys ed courses. A total of 123 semester hours, including 46 to 60 hours in the major, with a minimum GPA of 2.5, 2.0 in education, 2.75 in engineering. **Procedure:** Freshmen are admitted to all sessions. Entrance exams should be taken no later than December of the senior year. There is a rolling admissions plan. Application deadlines are open. Application fee is $50. Applications are accepted on-line. Application fees are waived if application is completed on-line. **Transfer Students:** 1218 transfer students enrolled in 2015-2016. Transfer students must have a minimum GPA of 2.0. 30 of 123 credits required for the bachelor's degree must be completed at U of L. **International Students:** There are 202 international students enrolled. They must take the TOEFL with a minimum score of 550 on the paper-based TOEFL (PBT) or 79 on the Internet-based version (iBT), or take the IELTS. Some programs may require proof of calculus readiness.

ADMISSIONS: 73% of the 2016-2017 applicants were accepted. The SAT scores for the 2016-2017 freshman class were: Critical Reading-- 37% below 500, 31% between 500 and 599, 26% between 600 and 699, and 5% between 700 and 800. Math-- 26% below 500, 53% between 500 and 599, and 21% between 600 and 699. The ACT scores were 3% between 12 and 17, 38% between 18 and 23, 45% between 24 and 29, and 13% above 30. There were 19 National Merit finalists. **Admissions Contact:** Jenny Sawyer, Executive Director of Admissions. Email: *admitme@louisville.edu* Web: *www.louisville.edu*

FINANCIAL AID: In 2016-2017, 97% of all full-time freshmen and 79% of continuing full-time students received some form of financial aid. 45% of all full-time freshmen and 41% of continuing full-time students received need-based aid. The average freshman award was $7,511. Need-based scholarships or need-based grants averaged $1,420 ($8,229 maximum); need-based self-help aid (loans and jobs) averaged $1,671 ($2,250 maximum); non-need-based athletic scholarships averaged $2,164 ($15,131 maximum); other non-need-based awards and non-need-based scholarships averaged $2,075 ($13,045 maximum); and $2,944 from other forms of aid. The average financial indebtedness of the 2016 graduate was $27,210. The FAFSA code is 001999. The priority date for freshman financial aid applications for fall entry is February 15.

UNIVERSITY OF PIKEVILLE *(The complete profile is made available exclusively on our website, www.barronspac.com)*

UNIVERSITY OF THE CUMBERLANDS E-4

www.ucumberlands.edu

Williamsburg, KY 40769 (606) 539-4241 (800) 343-1609

Fax: (606) 539-4303 **Email:** admiss@ucumberlands.edu

Full-time: 814 men, 966 women	**Faculty:** 113
Part-time: 555 men, 747 women	**Ph.D.s:** 72%
Graduate: 1833 men, 2778 women	**Student/Faculty:** 16 to 1
Year: semesters, summer session	**Tuition:** $23,000
Room & Board: $9000	**Freshman Class:** 1676 applied, 1629 accepted, 399 enrolled
SAT: required **ACT:** 22	**CEEB CODE:** 1145
Application Deadline: August 31	**COMPETITIVE**

University of the Cumberlands, founded in 1888, is a private liberal arts institution affiliated with the Kentucky Baptist Convention. The school is committed to challenging students with an innovative education while remaining keenly aware of the importance of a traditional liberal arts education. Our commitment to traditional values is reflected by our undergraduate curriculum which provides the foundation for a deeper understanding of advanced studies. The figures in the above capsule and in this profile are approximate. There is 1 undergraduate school and 9 graduate schools. In addition to regional accreditation, University of the Cumberlands has baccalaureate program accreditation with NCATE and SACSCOC. The 150-acre campus is in a small town 100 miles south of Lexington and 65 miles north of Knoxville, TN. Including any residence halls, there are 49 buildings.

STUDENT LIFE: 66% of undergraduates are from Kentucky. Others are from 39 states, 35 foreign countries, and Canada. 95% are from public schools. 73% are White; 13% race unknown; 6% African American; 4% Hispanic; 2% Foreign; 1% Asian American; 1% two or more races. 42% are Protestant; 11% claim no religious affiliation. **Female To Male Ratio:** 1.4:1. The average age of freshmen is 18; all undergraduates, 20. 35% do not continue beyond their first year; 40% remain to graduate. **Housing:** 1258 students can be accommodated in college housing, which includes single-sex dorms, on-campus apartments, and married student housing. On-campus housing is guaranteed for all 4 years. 80% of students live on campus; of those, 55% remain on campus on weekends. Alcohol is not permitted. All students may keep cars.

FACULTY/CLASSROOMS: 46% of faculty are male; 54% are female. 56% teach undergraduates. No introductory courses are taught by graduate students. The average class size in an introductory lecture is 23; in a laboratory is 15; and in a regular course is 22.

PROGRAMS OF STUDY: University of the Cumberlands confers B.A., B.S., B.G.S. and B.M. degrees. Associate, master's, and doctoral degrees are also awarded. Bachelor's degrees are awarded in BIOLOGICAL SCIENCE (biology/biological science), BUSINESS (accounting, business administration and management, office supervision and management, and sports management), COMMUNICATIONS AND THE ARTS (art, church music, communications, dramatic arts, English, journalism, music, and Spanish), COMPUTER AND PHYSICAL SCIENCE (chemistry, information sciences and systems, mathematics, and physics), EDUCATION (art education, elementary education, English education, health education, mathematics education, middle school education, music education, physical education, science education, social studies education, Spanish education K-12, and special education), ENGINEERING AND ENVIRONMENTAL DESIGN (preengineering), HEALTH PROFESSIONS (exercise science, health, nursing, predentistry, premedicine, prepharmacy, prephysical therapy, preveterinary science, and public health), SOCIAL SCIENCE (criminal justice, history, missions, political science/government, prelaw, psychology, religion, religious music, and social work). Biology, business administration, and education are the strongest academically and have the largest enrollments.

ACTIVITIES: There are no fraternities or sororities. There are 39 groups on campus, including art, band, cheerleading, choir, chorale, chorus, communications, dance, debate, drama, drill team, environmental, forensics, honors, international, jazz band, literary magazine, marching band, musical theater, newspaper, outdoor adventure club, pep band, political, professional, radio and TV, religious, social, social service, and student government. Popular campus events include Madrigal Dinner, Hanging of the Greens, and Homecoming. **Sports:** There are 13 intercollegiate sports for men and 13 for women, and 18 intramural sports for men and 18 for women. UC has some of the top athletic and recreation facilities in their athletic conference, including an athletic complex for men's and women's basketball, volleyball and swimming, an intramural gym for intramurals and recreation weight room, a baseball facility and football and track facility, softball and lacrosse complexes, a health & wellness fitness facility, and a tennis program. There is also a fully furnished gym for the wrestling program. **Graduates:** From July 1, 2015 to June 30, 2016, 347 bachelor's degrees were awarded. The most popular majors were business administration (23%), psychology (13%), and criminal justice (10%). In an average class, 1% graduate in 3 years or less, 24% graduate in 4 years or less, 40% graduate in 5 years or less, and 43% graduate in 6 years or less.

SERVICES: Counseling and information services are available, as is tutoring in every subject. **Library/Resources:** The library contains 456,451 volumes, 806,000 microform items, and 5,195 audio/video tapes/CDs/DVDs, and subscribes to 63,808 periodicals including electronic. Computerized library services include interlibrary loans, database searching, Internet access, and Wi-Fi capability. Special learning facilities include an art gallery, natural history museum, radio station, and TV station. **Physically Challenged Students:** 75% of the campus is accessible. Facilities include wheelchair ramps, elevators, special parking, specially equipped restrooms, special class scheduling, lowered drinking fountains, and lowered telephones. **Special:** Internships, study abroad in England, China, Spain, France, and Thailand, and work-study programs with the university, local businesses, and other educational institutions are available. The university offers B.A.-B.S. degrees in all majors except music, dual majors in all major fields, a General Studies degree, nondegree study, and a 3-2 engineering degree with University of Kentucky. There are 13 national honor societies, a freshman honors program, and 13 departmental honors programs. **Visiting:** There are regularly scheduled orientations for prospective students. Each visit consists of an admissions presentation and a campus tour that shows both academic and residence buildings. Attending a class and/or meeting professors is encouraged. Visitors have the option to also eat a meal and/or stay the night. There are guides for informal visits. To schedule a visit, contact Shelleigh Moses at shelleigh.moses@ucumberlands.edu. **Campus Safety and Security:** Measures include 24-hour foot and vehicle patrol, emergency notification system, self-defense education, and security escort services. There are lighted pathways/sidewalks and controlled access to dorms/residences.

REQUIREMENTS: Admission requires a composite score of better than 17 for the ACT or 780 for the SAT. Consideration is given to those with ACT scores of 16 and 17, provided the high school GPA is 2.5 or above in college prep classes. Although each application is considered individually, students must have fulfilled general high school requirements of 4 years of English, 3 each of math and science, and 2 of social studies. A GPA of 2.0 is required. AP and CLEP credits are accepted. Important factors in the admissions decision are advanced placement or honors courses, leadership record, and recommendations by school officials. All students must complete 128 semester hours, including 40 hours of liberal arts courses and an average of 36 hours in a major, while maintaining an overall GPA of 2.0 (2.5 for those seeking teacher certification). General education requirements include 37 credit hours to be chosen from the areas of Christian Faith, Writing Competence, Mathematical & Science Reasoning, Historical & Cultural Understanding, Aesthetic Appreciation, and Social & Professional Awareness. A comprehensive exam may be required. Programs presented for graduation must include 2 majors, 1 major and 1 minor, 1 major with 15 hours of restricted electives, or 3 minors, or 1 concentration. **Procedure:** Freshmen are admitted to all sessions. Entrance exams should be taken prior to admission consideration. There is a rolling admissions plan. Applications should be filed by August 31 for fall entry. Applications are accepted on-line. Application fees are waived if application is completed on-line. **Transfer Students:** 64 transfer students enrolled in 2015-2016. Applicants must have verification from their previous school that they are eligible to return. Students with fewer than 30 semester or 45 quarter hours must meet freshman admissions requirements. 30 of 128 credits required for the bachelor's degree must be completed at UC. **International Students:** There are 75 international students enrolled. The school actively recruits these students. They must also take the SAT or ACT, scoring 17-ACT; 920-SAT.

ADMISSIONS: 97% of the 2016-2017 applicants were accepted. The SAT scores for the 2016-2017 freshman class were: Critical Reading--64% below 500, 33% between 500 and 599, and 3% between 600 and 699. Math-- 64% below 500, 28% between 500 and 599, 5% between 600 and 699, and 3% between 700 and 800. The ACT scores were 8% between 12 and 17, 57% between 18 and 23, 27% between 24 and 29, and 8% above 30. 33% of the current freshmen were in the top fifth of their class; 62% were in the top two fifths. 8 freshmen graduated first in their class. **Admissions Contact:** Erica Harris, Director of Admissions. Email: *admiss@ucumberlands.edu* Web: *www.ucumberlands.edu*

FINANCIAL AID: The FAFSA code is 001962. The priority date for freshman financial aid applications for fall entry is February 1.

WESTERN KENTUCKY UNIVERSITY C-4

www.wku.edu

Bowling Green, KY 42101	**(270) 745-2551** **(800) 495-8463**
Fax: (270) 745-6133	**Email: admission@wku.edu**
Full-time: 7583 men, 9876 women	**Faculty:** IIA, --$
Part-time: n/av	**Ph.D.s:** 75%
Graduate: 881 men, 1838 women	**Student/Faculty:** 18 to 1
Year: semesters, summer session	**Tuition:** $9482 ($24,132)
Room & Board: $7368	**Freshman Class:** 8957 applied, 8303 accepted, 3121 enrolled
SAT CR/M: 520/510 **ACT:** 23	**CEEB CODE:** 1901
Application Deadline: August 1	**COMPETITIVE**

Western Kentucky University, founded in 1906, is a public institution that provides students with rigorous academic programs in the liberal arts and sciences and traditional and emerging professional programs, with emphasis at the baccalaureate level, complemented by relevant associate-and graduate-level programs. The figures in the above capsule and in this profile are approximate. There are 6 undergraduate schools and 1 graduate school. In addition to regional accreditation, WKU has baccalaureate program accreditation with AACSB, ABET, ACCE, ACEJMC, ADA, CSAB, CSWE, NASAD, NASM, NCATE, NLN, NRPA, ACEN, ACEND, ACS, AMA, AHIMA, AUPHA, CAHIM, CODA, ASHLA, CCNE, NAIT, CAA, CACREP, COAPRT, CEPH, EAC, NLN, EPSB, NAB, NASD, NAST, NASPAA, and ATMAE. The 200-acre campus is in a suburban area 65 miles north of Nashville, Tennessee, and 110 miles south of Louisville. Including any residence halls, there are 87 buildings.

STUDENT LIFE: 79% of undergraduates are from Kentucky. Others are from 48 states, 55 foreign countries, and Canada. 9% are African American; 75% White; 2% Hispanic; 2% two or more races; 1% Asian American; 1% race unknown. **Female To Male Ratio:** 1.4:1. The average age of freshmen is 18; all undergraduates, 22. 27% do not continue beyond their first year; 50% remain to graduate. **Housing:** 5083 students can be accommodated in college housing, which includes single-sex and coed dorms and on-campus apartments. In addition, there are honors houses, special-interest houses, and special housing for Gatton Academy students. On-campus housing is available on a first-come, first-served basis. Alcohol is not permitted. All students may keep cars.

FACULTY/CLASSROOMS: 47% of faculty are male; 53% are female. No introductory courses are taught by graduate students.

PROGRAMS OF STUDY: WKU confers A.B., B.S., B.F.A., B.G.S., B.M. and B.S.N. degrees. Associate, master's, and doctoral degrees are also awarded. Bachelor's degrees are awarded in AGRICULTURE (agricultural mechanics, agriculture, agronomy, dairy science, environmental studies, and horticulture), BIOLOGICAL SCIENCE (biochemistry, biology/biological science, biophysics, and genetics), BUSINESS (accounting, banking and finance, business administration and management, business (dual major program), business administration - international, business administration, management operations, business administration marketing, business communications, business economics, entrepreneurial studies, environment & natnl resource economics, hospitality management services, hotel and restaurant administration, management engineering, management information systems, management science, marketing, marketing and distribution, nonprofit/public organization management, and recreation and leisure services), COMMUNICATIONS AND THE ARTS (acting, advertising, Arabic, art history, broadcasting, Chinese, classics, communication studies, communications, communications technology, dance, design, dramatic arts, English, English as a second/foreign language, film arts, fine arts, French, German, graphic design & media, journalism, language arts, literature, film and media studies, music, performing arts, public relations,

Spanish, and visual and performing arts), COMPUTER AND PHYSICAL SCIENCE (actuarial science, astronomy, astronomy and physics, atmospheric sciences and meteorology, chemistry, computer science, geology, industrial technology, mathematics, and physics), EDUCATION (agricultural education, art education, Asian studies, athletic training, business education, childhood education, early childhood education, education of the exceptional child, elementary education, English secondary education, general studies, home economics education, marketing and distribution education, middle school education, physical education, physical education / exercise science, technical education, and vocational education), ENGINEERING AND ENVIRONMENTAL DESIGN (aerospace studies, agricultural engineering technology, chemical engineering, city/community/regional planning, civil engineering, civil engineering technology, computational sciences, construction management, construction management/commercial/industrial, electrical/electronics engineering, electromechanical technology, industrial engineering technology, manufacturing technology, mechanical engineering, occupational safety and health, and technology and public affairs), HEALTH PROFESSIONS (allied health, biology, communicative disorders, dental hygiene, environmental health science, exercise science, health care administration, medical technology, nursing, public health, and speech pathology/audiology), SOCIAL SCIENCE (African American studies, anthropology, archeology, clinical psychology, communication sciences & disorders, criminology, crosscultural studies, cultural anthropology, economics, family and community services, family/consumer studies, geography, history, human development & family studies, liberal arts/general studies, Middle Eastern studies, paralegal studies, philosophy, political science/government, psychology, religion, social studies, social work, sociology, and textiles and clothing). Education, nursing, and business have the largest enrollments.

ACTIVITIES: There are 350 groups on campus, including art, band, cheerleading, chess, choir, chorale, chorus, communications, computers, dance, debate, drama, drill team, environmental, ethnic, film, forensics, forensics club, honors, international, jazz band, LGBT, literary magazine, marching band, musical theater, newspaper, opera, orchestra, pep band, photography, political, professional, radio and TV, religious, social, social service, student government, symphony, and yearbook. Popular campus events include Homecoming and Cultural Enhancement Series. **Sports:** There are 6 intercollegiate sports for men and 9 for women, and 13 intramural sports for men and 13 for women. Facilities include a 17,500-seat football stadium, a basketball arena, baseball fields, softball fields, a soccer complex, and tennis courts. The Preston Center adds a weight room, a fitness room, a gym, a dance studio, racquetball courts, a swimming pool, a pro shop, an outdoor recreation and adventure center, and a health and fitness lab. **Graduates:** From July 1, 2015 to June 30, 2016, 2751 bachelor's degrees were awarded. The most popular majors were business/marketing (14%), health professions and related programs, and education (11%), social sciences, and communication/journalism (11%). 202 companies recruited on campus in 2015-2016. In an average class, 27% graduate in 4 years or less, 41% graduate in 5 years or less, and 45% graduate in 6 years or less.

SERVICES: Counseling and information services are available, as is tutoring in every subject. The Student Support Services Center ensures each student has the opportunity to succeed in the classroom with the help of a tutor. There is a reader service for the blind, and remedial math, reading, and writing. **Library/Resources:** The 2 libraries contain 656,517 volumes, 2.0 million microform items, and 19,805 audio/video tapes/CDs/DVDs, and subscribe to 13,912 periodicals including electronic. Computerized library services include interlibrary loans, database searching, Internet access, and Wi-Fi capability. Special learning facilities include an art gallery, planetarium, radio station, TV station, and a Kentucky Museum. **Physically Challenged Students:** 75% of the campus is accessible. Facilities include wheelchair ramps, elevators, special parking, specially equipped restrooms, special class scheduling, lowered drinking fountains, lowered telephones, and special housing. **Special:** Internships in many areas, study abroad in 34 countries, work-study programs, and cooperative programs are available. Accelerated degree programs are available in some majors. There are 36 national honor societies and a freshman honors program. **Visiting:** There are regularly scheduled orientations for prospective students, campus tours, informational sessions, presentations, departmental visits, residence hall visits, and a video. There are guides for informal visits and visitors may sit in on classes. To schedule a visit, contact the Admissions Office at tours@wku.edu. **Campus Safety and Security:** Measures include 24-hour foot and vehicle patrol, emergency notification system, self-defense education, and security escort services. There are shuttle buses, emergency telephones, lighted pathways/sidewalks, and controlled access to dorms/residences.

REQUIREMENTS: Students must meet ONE of the following requirements for admission: ACT composite of 20 or greater, or SAT (math + critical reading) of 940 or higher, or unweighted high school GPA of 2.50 or higher, or Achieve the required Composite Admission Index (CAI) score. AP and CLEP credits are accepted. To graduate, all students must complete at least 128 semester hours, with a varying number of hours in the major, and maintain a minimum GPA of 2.0. Curricula must include 44 semester hours of general education requirements and 42 semester hours in upper-division courses, and include 6 semester hours of English composition and 3 semester hours each of Western civilization, foreign language, speech, and literature. **Procedure:** Freshmen are admitted to all sessions. Entrance exams should be taken by fall of the senior year. There are early admissions, deferred admissions, and rolling admissions plans. Applications should be filed by August 1 for fall entry; January 1 for spring entry; and May 1 for summer entry, along with a $45 fee. Notification is sent on a rolling basis. Applications are accepted on-line. **Transfer Students:** 963 transfer students enrolled in 2015-2016. Transfer students must have a minimum GPA 2.0 for the last semester or term of full-time work, a cumulative GPA of 2.0, and be in good standing at the institution from which they are transferring. Students with fewer than 24 hours earned are required to have completed the pre-college curriculum. **International Students:** There are 201 international students enrolled. They must take the TOEFL or MELAB. They must also take the SAT or ACT.

ADMISSIONS: 93% of the 2016-2017 applicants were accepted. The SAT scores for the 2016-2017 freshman class were: Critical Reading-- 39% below 500, 38% between 500 and 599, 20% between 600 and 699, and 2% between 700 and 800. Math-- 45% below 500, 36% between 500 and 599, 16% between 600 and 699, and 3% between 700 and 800. The ACT scores were 7% between 12 and 17, 48% between 18 and 23, 35% between 24 and 29, and 10% above 30. 40% of the current freshmen were in the top fifth of their class; 66% were in the top two fifths. There were 4 National Merit finalists. 73 freshmen graduated first in their class. **Admissions Contact:** Dr. Jace Lux, Director of Recruitment and Admissions. Email: *admission@wku.edu* Web: *www.wku.edu*

FINANCIAL AID: In 2016-2017, 62% of all full-time freshmen received some form of financial aid. 62% of all full-time freshmen received need-based aid. The average freshman award was $13,488. Need-based scholarships or need-based grants averaged $5,174; need-based self-help aid (loans and jobs) averaged $3,112; non-need-based athletic scholarships averaged $13,093; other non-need-based awards and non-need-based scholarships averaged $3,061; and $6,483 from other forms of aid. 8% of undergraduate students work part-time. Average annual earnings from campus work are $2098. WKU is a member of CSS. The FAFSA code is 002002. The deadline for filing freshman financial aid applications for fall entry is April 1.

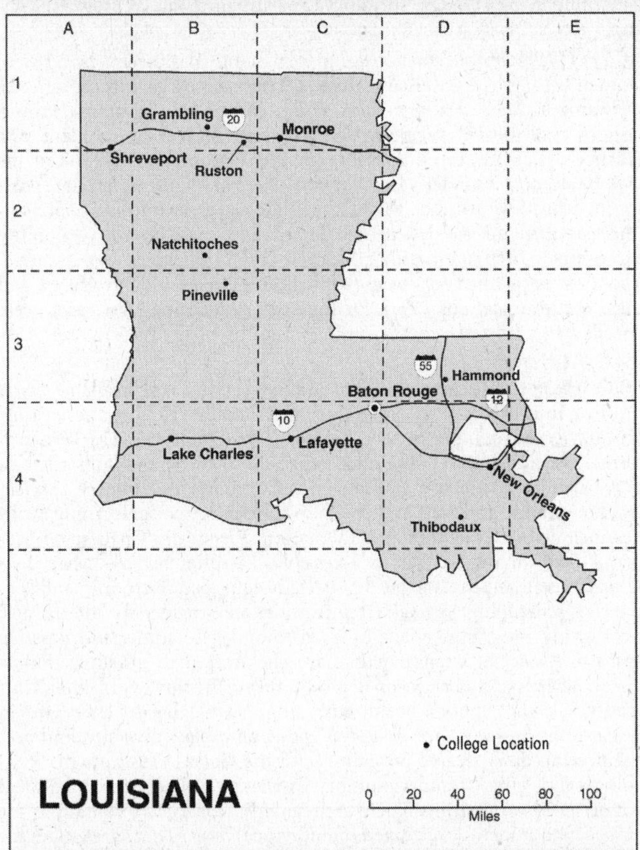

CENTENARY COLLEGE OF LOUISIANA A-1

www.centenary.edu

Shreveport, LA 71104 (318) 869-5131
(800) 234-4448

Fax: (318) 869-5005 **Email:** admission@centenary.edu
Full-time: 248 men, 323 women **Faculty:** 54; IIB, -$
Part-time: 10 men, 5 women **Ph.D.s:** 100%
Graduate: 29 men, 46 women **Student/Faculty:** 9 to 1
Year: semesters, summer session **Tuition:** $33,500
Room & Board: $12,150 **Freshman Class:** 670 applied, 442 accepted, 128 enrolled
SAT CR/M: required **ACT:** required **CEEB CODE:** 6082
Application Deadline: August 1 **COMPETITIVE+**

Centenary College of Louisiana is a private, four-year arts and sciences college affiliated with the United Methodist Church. Founded in 1825, it is the oldest chartered liberal arts college west of the Mississippi River. There are 5 undergraduate schools and 2 graduate schools. In addition to regional accreditation, Centenary College has baccalaureate program accreditation with NASM and ACS. The 65-acre campus is in an urban area in the Shreveport/Bossier City area located in the northwest corner of Louisiana near the Texas and Arkansas borders. Including any residence halls, there are 23 buildings.

STUDENT LIFE: 64% of undergraduates are from Louisiana. Others are from 28 states, and 7 foreign countries. **Female To Male Ratio:** 1.3:1. The average age of freshmen is 18; all undergraduates, 20. **Housing:** College-sponsored housing includes single-sex and coed dorms. In addition, there are fraternity houses, sorority houses, and theme housing. On-campus housing is guaranteed for all 4 years, and is available on a first-come, and first-served basis. 60% of students live on campus. Alcohol is not permitted. All students may keep cars.

FACULTY/CLASSROOMS: 61% of faculty are male; 39% are female. No introductory courses are taught by graduate students. The average class size in an introductory lecture is 12 and in a laboratory is 11.

PROGRAMS OF STUDY: Centenary College confers B.A. and B.S. degrees. Master's degrees are also awarded. Bachelor's degrees are awarded in BIOLOGICAL SCIENCE (biochemistry, biology/biological science, biophysics, and neurosciences), BUSINESS (business administration and management and business economics), COMMUNICATIONS AND THE ARTS (art, communications, dance, dramatic arts, English, French, German, Latin, music, music performance, Spanish, and studio art), COMPUTER AND PHYSICAL SCIENCE (chemistry, geology, mathematics, and physics), ENGINEERING AND ENVIRONMENTAL DESIGN (environmental science), SOCIAL SCIENCE (economics, history, interdisciplinary studies, liberal arts/general studies, philosophy, political science/government, psychology, religion, religious music, and sociology). Biological/life sciences, business & marketing, and visual & performing arts have the largest enrollments.

ACTIVITIES: There are 60 groups on campus, including cheerleading, choir, chorale, communications, dance, drama, environmental club, film, honors, international, jazz band, LGBT, musical theater, newspaper, opera, photography, political, professional, radio and TV, religious, social, social service, student government, symphony, and yearbook. Popular campus events include Spring Fling, President's Convocation and Freak Week. **Sports:** There are 8 intercollegiate sports for men and 9 for women. Facilities include a 3000-seat gym, 2 weight rooms, basketball, racquetball, volleyball, and tennis courts, baseball, soccer, and softball fields, a fitness center with aerobic exercise and strengthening equipment, and a natatorium. **Graduates:** From July 1, 2015 to June 30, 2016, 198 bachelor's degrees were awarded. The most popular majors were biological/life sciences (18%), business and marketing (17%), and visual and performing arts (16%). In an average class, 1% graduate in 3 years or less and 59% graduate in 4 years or less.

SERVICES: Counseling and information services are available, as is tutoring in most subjects. **Library/Resources:** The 2 libraries contain 180,000 volumes, 310,671 microform items, and 425 audio/video tapes/CDs/DVDs, and subscribe to 942 periodicals including electronic. Computerized library services include interlibrary loans, database searching, and Internet access. Special learning facilities include an art gallery, radio station, a theater, and an art museum. **Physically Challenged Students:** 95% of the campus is accessible. Facilities include wheelchair ramps, elevators, special parking, specially equipped restrooms, special class scheduling, lowered drinking fountains, and lowered telephones. **Special:** Centenary offers study abroad in 7 countries, cross-registration with Associated Colleges of the South, internships in all majors, a Washington semester, and a work-study program within the college. A 3-1 communications disorders degree with Louisiana State University Medical Center is possible, as is a 3-2 engineering degree with Washington University in St. Louis, University of Southern California, and Columbia University, Texas A&M University, and Case Western Reserve Universities. A 3-2 applied science pre-professional degree combines with health administration or medical school. Pre-veterinary studies, general studies and interdisciplinary degrees, and student-designed majors are available. There are 7 national honor societies and 15 departmental honors programs. **Visiting:** There are regularly scheduled orientations for prospective students, consisting of information sessions with a counselor, tour of the campus, visit to a class or with faculty, and lunch. There are guides for informal visits, visitors may sit in on classes, and stay overnight. To schedule a visit, contact Nora Fradin at nfradin@centenary.edu. **Campus Safety and Security:** Measures include 24-hour foot and vehicle patrol and security escort services. There are emergency telephones and lighted pathways/sidewalks.

REQUIREMENTS: Applicants should be high school graduates with a minimum composite score of 950 on the SAT or 20 on the ACT, although accepted students average 1145 and 26 respectively. Secondary school preparation should include 15 academic credits, including 4 of English, 3 each of math and science, 2 each of a foreign language and history, 1 of social studies, and electives. Music students must audition; art students are advised to present a portfolio. A GPA of 2.0 is required. AP credits are accepted. Important factors in the admissions decision are advanced placement or honors courses, extracurricular activities record, and personality/intangible qualities. To graduate, all students must complete 124 semester hours, with a maximum of 45 in a non-interdisciplinary major and a minimum of 30 at the upper-division level, including a writing and speaking class in the major at the junior level, and maintain a minimum GPA of 2.0. There are 48 to 52 hours of distribution requirements. Core curriculum requirements include courses in the humanities, social sciences, hard sciences, and math. In addition, freshmen must take a first-year experience course. All students must complete a Trek component, study or live in a different culture, or study abroad, and fulfill career explorations. **Procedure:** Freshmen are admitted fall, spring, and summer. Entrance exams should be taken by the fall of the senior year. There are early decision, early admissions, and rolling admissions plans. Early decision applications should be filed by December 15; regular applications, by August 1 for fall entry, along with a $30 fee. Notifications are sent September 1. Applications are accepted on-line. **Transfer Students:** 19 transfer students enrolled in 2015-2016. Transfer applicants must have a minimum GPA of 2.0 and demonstrate good performance in a liberal arts curriculum. 45 credits required for the bachelor's degree must be completed at Centenary College. **International Students:** There are 16 international students enrolled. The school actively recruits these students. They must take the TOEFL with a minimum score of 550 on the paper-based TOEFL (PBT) or 79 on the Internet-based version (iBT).

ADMISSIONS: 66% of the 2016-2017 applicants were accepted. **Admissions Contact:** Thomas Newton, Director of Admissions. Email: *admission@centenary.edu* Web: *www.centenary.edu*

FINANCIAL AID: In 2016-2017, 99% of all full-time freshmen and continuing full-time students received some form of financial aid. 77% of all full-time freshmen and 75% of continuing full-time students received need-based aid. The average freshman award was $27,911. Need-based scholarships or need-based grants averaged $25,646 ($35,740 maximum); need-based self-help aid (loans and jobs) averaged $6,723 ($14,200 maximum); and other non-need-based awards and non-need-based scholarships averaged $14,369 ($36,126 maximum). 32% of undergraduate students work part-time. The average financial indebtedness of the 2016 graduate was $23,760. The FAFSA code is 002003. The priority date for freshman financial aid applications for fall entry is February 15.

DILLARD UNIVERSITY D-4

www.dillard.edu

New Orleans, LA 70122	**(504) 816-4632** **(800) 216-6637**
Fax: 504-816-4895	**Email: dpage@dillard.edu**
Full-time: 624 men, 625 women	**Faculty:** 82
Part-time: n/av	**Ph.D.s:** 56%
Graduate: n/av	**Student/Faculty:** n/av
Year: semesters, summer session	**Tuition:** $15,250
Room & Board: $5690	**Freshman Class:** n/av
SAT or ACT: recommended	**CEEB CODE:** 6164
Application Deadline: n/av	**VERY COMPETITIVE**

Dillard University, established in 1869, is an independent, nonsectarian, liberal arts institution affiliated with the United Church of Christ and the United Methodist Church. It offers undergraduate programs and 19 baccalaureate degrees in the colleges of arts of sciences, professional studies, and general studies. There are 2 undergraduate schools. In addition to regional accreditation, Dillard has baccalaureate program accreditation with NLN. The 55-acre campus is in an urban area in New Orleans. Including any residence halls, there are 21 buildings.

STUDENT LIFE: 67% of undergraduates are from Louisiana. Others are from 29 states, 12 foreign countries, and Canada. 98% are African American. **Female To Male Ratio:** 1.0:1. 28% do not continue beyond their first year. **Housing:** College-sponsored housing includes single-sex dorms, on-campus apartments, and off-campus apartments. On-campus housing is guaranteed for the freshman year only, and is available on a first-come, first-served basis, is available on a lottery system for upperclassmen. Priority is given to out-of-town students. 30% of students commute. Alcohol is not permitted. All students may keep cars.

FACULTY/CLASSROOMS: 43% of faculty are male; 57% are female. All teach undergraduates. No introductory courses are taught by graduate students. The average class size in an introductory lecture is 30.

PROGRAMS OF STUDY: Dillard confers B.A., B.S., and B.S.N. degrees. Bachelor's degrees are awarded in BIOLOGICAL SCIENCE (biology/biological science), BUSINESS (accounting and business administration and management), COMMUNICATIONS AND THE ARTS (art, communications, English, music, music business management, and music performance), COMPUTER AND PHYSICAL SCIENCE (chemistry, computer science, and physics), HEALTH PROFESSIONS (nursing and public health), SOCIAL SCIENCE (economics, history, political science/government, psychology, sociology, and urban studies). Biological sciences has the largest enrollment.

ACTIVITIES: 4% of men belong to 5 national fraternities; 11% of women belong to 4 national sororities. There are 64 groups on campus, including art, cheerleading, chess, choir, chorus, dance, drama, ethnic, honors, professional, religious, social service, student government, and yearbook. Popular campus events include Coronation, Avenue of the Oaks Gala, and Founder's Day. **Sports:** There are 3 intercollegiate sports for men and 3 for women. Facilities include a gym, swimming pool, nautilus room, tennis courts, dance facility, and game room. **Graduates:** From July 1, 2015 to June 30, 2016, 278 bachelor's degrees were awarded. The most popular majors were public health (16%), biology (13%), and mass communications (9%). Of the 2015 graduating class, 45% were enrolled in graduate school within 6 months of graduation, and 45% were employed.

SERVICES: Counseling and information services are available, as is tutoring in every subject. There is remedial math, reading, and writing. **Library/Resources:** The library contains 104,615 volumes, 21,638 microform items, and 426 audio/video tapes/CDs/DVDs, and subscribes to 295 periodicals including electronic. Computerized library services include interlibrary loans and database searching. Special learning facilities include an art gallery and TV station. **Physically Challenged Students:** 70% of the campus is accessible. Facilities include wheelchair ramps, elevators, special parking, specially equipped restrooms, and special class scheduling. **Special:** Opportunities are provided for internships, work-study programs, credit by exam, nondegree study, and pass/fail options. All social science majors are encouraged to pursue a double major. There is a 4-year co-op degree in music therapy with Loyola University, a clinical public health curriculum with Howard University, a 5-year joint degree in urban studies with Columbia University, and pre-engineering dual- degree programs with the Georgia Institute of Technology and Auburn and Columbia Universities. There are 3 national honor societies. **Visiting:** There are regularly scheduled orientations for prospective students, scheduled on individual basis. There are guides for informal visits, visitors may sit in on classes, and stay overnight. To schedule a visit, contact Office of Admissions. **Campus Safety and Security:** Measures include 24-hour foot and vehicle patrol and emergency notification system. There are shuttle buses and lighted pathways/sidewalks.

REQUIREMENTS: The SAT or ACT is recommended. Graduation from an accredited secondary school is required; a GED will be accepted. Applicants must submit an academic record of 20 units, distributed as follows: 4 units in English, 3 each in math and natural sciences, 2 in social studies, and 8 in other academic electives. Recommendations from a high school teacher and the principal or a student counselor are required. AP credits are accepted. Important factors in the admissions decision are recommendations by school officials, leadership record, and personality/intangible qualities. Students must successfully complete 125 semester hours and maintain a minimum overall GPA of 2.0 and a GPA of 2.0 or better in all courses in the major. In addition, all students must complete 35 semester hours in the core curriculum, which includes courses in English composition, world literature, English literature, math, natural sciences, world history, political science, economics, university assembly, phys ed, and academic orientation. Additionally, each student must engage in a minimum of 120 clock hours of volunteer service in the community. **Procedure:** Freshmen are admitted spring. Entrance exams should be taken between April of the junior year and December of the senior year. There are early admissions, deferred admissions, and rolling admissions plans. Applications should be filed by December 1 for spring entry, along with a $36 fee. Notification is sent on a rolling basis. Applications are accepted on-line. **Transfer Students:** 46 transfer students enrolled in 2015-2016. Applicants for transfer must submit a secondary school record or equivalent, transcripts from previous colleges showing an average grade of C, and personal recommendations. No more than 60 semester hours may be submitted for transfer credit. 65 of 125 credits required for the bachelor's degree must be completed at Dillard. **International Students:** There are 12 international students enrolled. They must take the TOEFL with a minimum score of 550 on the paper-based TOEFL (PBT). They must also take the SAT or ACT.

Admissions Contact: David Page, VP for Enrollment Management. Email: *dpage@dillard.edu* Web: *www.dillard.edu*

FINANCIAL AID: In 2016-2017, 99% of all full-time freshmen received some form of financial aid. 93% of all full-time freshmen received need-based aid. 25% of undergraduate students work part-time. Average annual earnings from campus work are $2000. The average financial indebtedness of the 2016 graduate was $26,250. Dillard is a member of CSS. The college's own financial statement is required. The FAFSA code is 002004. The deadline for filing freshman financial aid applications for fall entry is March 1.

GRAMBLING STATE UNIVERSITY B-1

www.gram.edu

Grambling, LA 71245	(318) 274-6423 (888) 863-3655
Fax: (318) 274-3292	**Email:** admissions@gram.edu
Full-time: 1529 men, 2069 women	**Faculty:** n/av
Part-time: 122 men, 163 women	**Ph.D.s:** n/av
Graduate: 264 men, 716 women	**Student/Faculty:** n/av
Year: semesters, summer session	**Tuition:** $7063 ($16,086)
Room & Board: $8638	**Freshman Class:** 6366 applied, 1372 accepted, 865 enrolled
SAT or ACT: required	**CEEB CODE:** 6250
Application Deadline: July 1	**COMPETITIVE**

Grambling State University, founded in 1901, is a constituent member of the University of Louisiana System, and is a historically and predominantly black comprehensive university offering degrees ranging from associate to doctorate. There are 4 undergraduate schools and one graduate school. In addition to regional accreditation, GSU has baccalaureate program accreditation with AACSB, ABET, ACEJMC, CSAB, CSWE, NASAD, NASM, NCATE, NLN, NRPA, NASPAA, ACS, and NAST. The 590-acre campus is in a small town 60 miles from Shreveport. Including any residence halls, there are 147 buildings.

STUDENT LIFE: 69% of undergraduates are from Louisiana. Others are from 41 states, 27 foreign countries, and Canada. 91% are African American; 4% Foreign; 1% White; 1% Hispanic; 1% two or more races; 1% race unknown. **Female To Male Ratio:** 1.5:1. The average age of freshmen is 20; all undergraduates, 22. **Housing:** 2581 students can be accommodated in college housing, which includes single-sex and coed dorms. On-campus housing is guaranteed for all 4 years. Alcohol is not permitted. All students may keep cars.

FACULTY/CLASSROOMS: No introductory courses are taught by graduate students.

PROGRAMS OF STUDY: GSU confers B.A., B.S., B.S.W., and B.P.A. degrees. Associate, master's, and doctoral degrees are also awarded. Bachelor's degrees are awarded in BIOLOGICAL SCIENCE (biology/biological science), BUSINESS (accounting, business administration and management, business economics, hotel/motel and restaurant management, marketing/retailing/merchandising, and recreation and leisure services), COMMUNICATIONS AND THE ARTS (communications, English, music, and visual and performing arts), COMPUTER AND PHYSICAL SCIENCE (chemistry, computer science, information sciences and systems, mathematics, and physics), EDUCATION (early childhood education, elementary education, English education, mathematics education, physical education, secondary education, social studies education, and special education), ENGINEERING AND ENVIRONMENTAL DESIGN (engineering technology), HEALTH PROFESSIONS (nursing), SOCIAL SCIENCE (criminal justice, economics, history, political science/government, psychology, public administration, social work, and sociology). Criminal justice and biology are the strongest academically. Criminal justice has the largest enrollment.

ACTIVITIES: 2% of men belong to 3 national fraternities; 2% of women belong to 4 national sororities. There are 62 groups on campus, including art, band, cheerleading, choir, chorus, communications, computers, dance, drama, honors, international, jazz band, marching band, newspaper, orchestra, political, professional, radio and TV, religious, social, social service, student government, symphony, and yearbook. Popular campus events include Candlelight and Pinning Ceremony, Founder's Day/Week, Black History Month, and Springfest. **Sports:** There are 5 intercollegiate sports for men and 8 for women, and 4 intramural sports for men and 4 for women. Facilities include a men's memorial gymnasium, a stadium, an assembly center, stadium support building, intramural center, park and field, baseball complex, softball field, and tennis courts. **Graduates:** From July 1, 2015 to June 30, 2016, 686 bachelor's degrees were awarded. The most popular majors were criminal justice (17%), social work (10%), and nursing (8%).

SERVICES: Counseling and information services are available, as is tutoring in some subjects, such as biology, English, chemistry, history, math, and physics. There is remedial math, reading, and writing. **Library/Resources:** The library contains 1.6 million volumes, 122,298 microform items, and 6,394 audio/video tapes/CDs/DVDs, and subscribes to 109,517 periodicals including electronic. Computerized library services include interlibrary loans, database searching, Internet access, and Wi-Fi capability. Special learning facilities include an art gallery, radio station, TV station, and student technology labs. **Physically Challenged Students:** Facilities include wheelchair ramps, elevators, special parking, specially equipped restrooms, special class scheduling, lowered drinking fountains, and lowered telephones. **Special:** Special training programs available in the Department of Biological Sciences are designed to encourage and assist biology majors interested in medicine, dentistry, or allied health professions to apply for summer programs conducted by medical/dental schools at major universities throughout the nation; prepare students for graduate schools to earn Ph.D. or MD/Ph.D. degrees and pursue research careers in biomedical sciences; and increase the number and quality of students earning baccalaureate and doctoral degrees in the areas of science, engineering, and mathematic. The College of Business faculty members have partnered with various organizations and/or economic programs to provide students with economic development activities. Industry-based internships are available in accounting and finance, housekeeping, recreation, banquet/catering, front office, restaurants, culinary and pastry arts, human resources, and sales. Through an agreement with Southern University at Shreveport their students are enabled to engage in a military science curriculum at Grambling State University. The university-wide Honors College provides unique intellectual and educational experiences for academically talented students to extend their academic, personal, and social development while completing requirements in their chosen majors. There are 5 national honor societies and a freshman honors program. **Visiting:** There are guides for informal visits. To schedule a visit, contact the Office of Admissions and Recruitment. **Campus Safety and Security:** Measures include 24-hour foot and vehicle patrol and emergency notification system. There are shuttle buses, emergency telephones, and lighted pathways/sidewalks.

REQUIREMENTS: All applicants must submit the general admissions documents, complete 19 units from Core 4 Curriculum, have a minimum 2.0 overall GPA (on 4.0 scale), need no more than one developmental course, and either have a minimum 2.0 GPA on Core 4 Curriculum or ACT Composite 20 or SAT 940 (reading & math combined). Admission to the university is conditional until evidence of graduation from high school and completion of required core units are received. Applicants with Certificate of Achievement diplomas and General Equivalency Diplomas (GED) are not eligible for admission to Grambling; however, assistance is provided with a referral to the BPCC at GSU Program where requirements for admission to Grambling State University can be completed. AP and CLEP credits are accepted. In order to graduate and be awarded a bachelor's degree from Grambling State University, students must complete all course requirements in an academic major, with no grades lower than C; complete all academic requirements in the General Education Program; complete at least 125 credit hours of course-work, pass examinations required for the chosen major; pass the Rising Junior Examination, have a minimum grade point average of 2.0. Earn at least 25 percent of the required credit hours for graduation in residence. **Procedure:** Freshmen are admitted fall, spring, and summer. There is a rolling admissions plan. Applications should be filed by July 1 for fall entry; December 1 for spring entry; and May 1 for summer entry, along with a $20 fee. Notifications are sent in daily. Applications are accepted on-line. **Transfer Students:** 262 transfer students enrolled in 2015-2016. Transfer applicants must submit an application fee (check with the school for fee), submit proof of immunization, submit official transcript from EACH regionally accredited institution attended, regardless if credits appear on another transcript, have earned at least 18 semester hours of college-level course work (excluding developmental courses). Students must have completed a college-level English and math course designed to fulfill general education requirement, have earned a cumulative GPA of at least 2.0 on college-level courses, and be in good standing and eligible to return to the last college or university of attendance. 30 of 120 credits required for the bachelor's degree must be completed at GSU. **International Students:** There are 173 international students enrolled. The school actively recruits these students. They must take the TOEFL with a minimum score of 500 on the paper-based TOEFL (PBT) or 62 on the Internet-based version (iBT). They must also take the SAT or ACT.

ADMISSIONS: 22% of the 2016-2017 applicants were accepted. The

SAT scores for the 2016-2017 freshman class were: Critical Reading-- 86% below 500 and 14% between 500 and 599. Math-- 80% below 500, 19% between 500 and 599, and 1% between 600 and 699. Writing-- 91% below 500 and 10% between 500 and 599. The ACT scores were 41% between 12 and 17, 54% between 18 and 23, and 14% between 24 and 29. **Admissions Contact:** Chemia Herron, Assis Director of Admissions/ Recruitment. Email: *admissions@gram.edu* Web: *www.gram.edu*

FINANCIAL AID: In 2016-2017, 98% of all full-time freshmen and 98% of continuing full-time students received some form of financial aid. 94% of all full-time freshmen and 94% of continuing full-time students received need-based aid. The average freshman award was $18,031. Need-based scholarships or need-based grants averaged $6,027 ($4,357,523 maximum); need-based self-help aid (loans and jobs) averaged $3,898 ($3,047,976 maximum); non-need-based athletic scholarships averaged $11,063 ($531,002 maximum); and other non-need-based awards and non-need-based scholarships averaged $9,137 ($7,263,502 maximum). 24% of undergraduate students work part-time. Average annual earnings from campus work are $1450. The college's own financial statement is required. The FAFSA code is 002006. The priority date for freshman financial aid applications for fall entry is April 1. The deadline for filing freshman financial aid applications for fall entry is June 1.

LOUISIANA COLLEGE B-3

www.lacollege.edu

Pineville, LA 71359	**(318) 487-7259** **(800) 487-1906**
Fax: (318) 487-7550	**Email: admissions@lacollege.edu**
Full-time: 436 men, 420 women	**Faculty:** 60
Part-time: 67 men, 133 women	**Ph.D.s:** 60%
Graduate: n/av	**Student/Faculty:** 14 to 1
Year: semesters, summer session	**Tuition:** $17,630
Room & Board: $4256	**Freshman Class:** 549 applied, 429 accepted, 246 enrolled
SAT: required **ACT:** 22	**CEEB CODE:** 6371
Application Deadline: August 15	**COMPETITIVE**

Louisiana College, founded in 1906, is a private liberal arts college affiliated with the Southern Baptist Churches of Louisiana. LC offers more than 80 majors, minors, and pre-professional programs of study. The college is one of the most recognized colleges in the South. Figures in the above capsule and in this profile are approximate. There are 5 undergraduate schools. In addition to regional accreditation, LC has baccalaureate program accreditation with AACSB, ACBSP, CSWE, NASM, and NLN. The 81-acre campus is in a small town in the heart of Louisiana, 1 mile northeast of Alexandria, VA. Including any residence halls, there are 25 buildings.

STUDENT LIFE: 92% of undergraduates are from Louisiana. Others are from 16 states, 5 foreign countries, and Canada. 88% are White; 8% African American; 1% Asian American; 1% American Indian/Alaska Native; 1% Hispanic; 1% Foreign. 66% are Protestant; 18% claim no religious affiliation; 13% Catholic. **Female To Male Ratio:** 1.1:1. The average age of freshmen is 18; all undergraduates, 22. 36% do not continue beyond their first year; 43% remain to graduate. **Housing:** 726 students can be accommodated in college housing, which includes single-sex dorms, on-campus apartments, and married student housing. On-campus housing is guaranteed for all 4 years. 54% of students live on campus. Alcohol is not permitted. All students may keep cars.

FACULTY/CLASSROOMS: 57% of faculty are male; 43% are female. All teach undergraduates. No introductory courses are taught by graduate students. The average class size in an introductory lecture is 30; in a laboratory is 20; and in a regular course is 18.

PROGRAMS OF STUDY: LC confers B.A., B.S., B.G.S., B.M., B.S.N. and B.S.W. degrees. Associate degrees are also awarded. Bachelor's degrees are awarded in BIOLOGICAL SCIENCE (biology/biological science), BUSINESS (business administration and management), COMMUNICATIONS AND THE ARTS (communications, dramatic arts, English, French, graphic design, journalism, languages, multimedia, music, speech/debate/rhetoric, and studio art), COMPUTER AND PHYSICAL SCIENCE (chemistry and mathematics), EDUCATION (art education, athletic training, business education, elementary education, English education, health education, mathematics education, music education, science education, secondary education, social studies education, and special education), HEALTH PROFESSIONS (exercise science, medical laboratory technology, music therapy, nursing, predentistry, premedicine, preoptometry, and preveterinary science), SOCIAL SCIENCE (criminal justice, economics, history, philosophy, prelaw, psychology, public administration, religion, religious education, religious music, social work, and sociology). Education, biology, and business have the largest enrollments.

ACTIVITIES: 5% of men belong to 4 local fraternities; 15% of women belong to 4 local sororities. There are 57 groups on campus, including and Union Board (campus programming), art, band, Breaking All Barriers (Diversity), cheerleading, choir, chorale, chorus, communications, debate, drama, honors, international, jazz band, literary magazine, marching band, musical theater, newspaper, opera, pep band, political, professional, radio and TV, religious, social, social service, student government, symphony, and yearbook. Popular campus events include Gala Christmas, Sanders Lecture Series, and Miss LC Pageant. **Sports:** There are 5 intercollegiate sports for men and 5 for women, and 11 intramural sports for men and 11 for women. Facilities include a field house for basketball, a baseball field, a fitness/wellness center, a jogging trail, tennis courts, an intramural/soccer/football field, an outdoor beach volleyball court, softball field, and a practice football field. **Graduates:** From July 1, 2015 to June 30, 2016, 159 bachelor's degrees were awarded. The most popular majors were nursing (9%), biology (9%), and social work (8%). 65 companies recruited on campus in 2015-2016. In an average class, 24% graduate in 4 years or less, 41% graduate in 5 years or less, and 45% graduate in 6 years or less.

SERVICES: Counseling and information services are available, as is tutoring in most subjects. There is a reader service for the blind, and remedial math and writing. PASS (Program to Assist Student Success) offers services for students with documented learning disabilities. **Library/Resources:** The library contains 138,985 volumes, 126,266 microform items, and 2,500 audio/video tapes/CDs/DVDs, and subscribes to 19,993 periodicals including electronic. Computerized library services include interlibrary loans, database searching, and Internet access. Special learning facilities include an art gallery, radio station, and a performing arts center. **Physically Challenged Students:** 95% of the campus is accessible. Facilities include wheelchair ramps, elevators, special parking, specially equipped restrooms, and lowered telephones. **Special:** Study abroad in London and Hong Kong, interdisciplinary studies, work-study programs, non-degree study, internships, dual majors, and pass/fail options are offered. There are 13 national honor societies and a freshman honors program. **Visiting:** There are regularly scheduled orientations for prospective students, consisting of spring and fall campus preview days and a 2-day orientation and pre-registration in June. There are guides for informal visits, visitors may sit in on classes, and stay overnight. To schedule a visit, contact the Office of Admissions at admissions@lacollege.edu. **Campus Safety and Security:** Measures include 24-hour foot and vehicle patrol, self-defense education, and security escort services. There are lighted pathways/sidewalks.

REQUIREMENTS: Candidates for admission must have completed 17 units, which must include 4 of English, 3 of math (algebra I, II, and geometry), 3 of social studies, and 3 of science (2 with lab). Graduates of accredited high school's must meet one of the following requirements for unconditional admission: (1) Score at least 20 composite on ACT or satisfactorily on the SAT and possess a GPA of 2.0 on a 4.0 scale; or (2) Possess an academic GPA of 2.0 on a 4.0 scale and rank in the upper 50% of their graduating class with an acceptable ACT or SAT score. A GPA of 2.0 is required. AP and CLEP credits are accepted. Important factors in the admissions decision are extracurricular activities record, leadership record, and advanced placement or honors courses. To graduate, students must complete 127 total credit hours, 42 of which must be junior-senior level, including a central core of 56 hours in all degree programs, and maintain a minimum GPA of 2.0, and a 2.25 in the major. They must also complete Cultural/Intellectual and Spiritual Enrichment requirements and earn at least 25% of credit applied toward degree through instruction offered by LC. They must complete the last 30 hours of course work at LC, and take 3 hours each of phys ed and computer applications. **Procedure:** Freshmen are admitted fall, spring, and summer. Entrance exams should be taken during the junior or senior year. There is a rolling admissions plan. Application deadlines are open. Application fee is $25. Notification is sent on a rolling basis. Applications are accepted on-line. **Transfer Students:** Applicants must have an overall minimum GPA of 2.0 and finish all remedial course work prior to transfer. 30 of 127 credits required for the bachelor's degree must be completed at LC. **International Students:** They must take the TOEFL, the TOEFL, is waived for students taking the SAT who earn 480 on the verbal section. They must also take the SAT or ACT.

ADMISSIONS: 78% of the 2016-2017 applicants were accepted. The ACT scores were 38% below 12, 29% between 12 and 17, 16% between 18 and 23, 9% between 24 and 29, and 8% above 30. **Admissions Contact:** Renee Melder, Director of Admissions. Email: *admissions@lacollege.edu* Web: *www.lacollege.edu*

FINANCIAL AID: 19% of undergraduate students work part-time. The FFS and the college's own financial statement are required. The FAFSA code is 002007. The priority date for freshman financial aid applications for fall entry is March 15. The deadline for filing freshman financial aid applications for fall entry is October 1.

LOUISIANA STATE UNIVERSITY AND A&M COLLEGE C-4

www.lsu.edu

Baton Rouge, LA 70803 (225) 578-1175

Fax: (225) 578-4433	**Email:** admissions@lsu.edu
Full-time: 10979 men, 11832 women	**Faculty:** 1053; I, -$
	Ph.D.s: 89%
Part-time: 1101 men, 1011 women	**Student/Faculty:** 22 to 1
Graduate: 2713 men, 2842 women	**Tuition:** $7873 ($25,790)
Year: semesters, summer session	**Freshman Class:** 16,005 applied, 12,002 accepted, 5501 enrolled
Room & Board: $10,804	
SAT CR/M: 559/577 **ACT:** 26	**CEEB CODE:** 6373
Application Deadline: April 15	**VERY COMPETITIVE**

Louisiana State University and A&M College, a public institution founded in 1860 and part of the Louisiana State University System, offers programs in the colleges of agriculture, humanities and social sciences, business administration, coast and environment, art and design, human sciences and education, engineering, music and dramatic arts, mass communication, and science. Figures in the above capsule and in this profile are approximate. There are 11 undergraduate schools and 2 graduate schools. In addition to regional accreditation, LSU has baccalaureate program accreditation with AACSB, ABET, ACCE, ACEJMC, ASLA, CSWE, FIDER, NAAB, NASAD, NASM, NCATE, SAF, and ADA. The 2000-acre campus is in an urban area in Baton Rouge, Louisiana. Including any residence halls, there are 250 buildings.

STUDENT LIFE: 80% of undergraduates are from Louisiana. Others are from 49 states, 81 foreign countries, and Canada. 52% are from public schools. 76% are White; 5% Hispanic; 3% Asian American; 2% Foreign; 2% two or more races; 11% African American. 40% are Catholic; 33% Protestant; 23% claim no religious affiliation. **Female To Male Ratio:** 1.1:1. The average age of freshmen is 19; all undergraduates, 21. 18% do not continue beyond their first year; 69% remain to graduate. **Housing:** 7450 students can be accommodated in college housing, which includes single-sex and coed dorms, on-campus apartments, and married student housing. In addition, there are honors houses, special-interest houses, fraternity houses, and sorority houses. 75% of students commute. All students may keep cars.

FACULTY/CLASSROOMS: 64% of faculty are male; 36% are female. 89% teach undergraduates. Graduate students teach 17% of introductory courses. The average class size in an introductory lecture is 52; in a laboratory is 25; and in a regular course is 38.

PROGRAMS OF STUDY: LSU confers B.A., B.S., B.A.M.C., B.Arch., B.F.A., B.I.S., B.I.D., B.L.A., B.M., B.M.Ed., B.S.B.E., B.S.C.E., B.S.Ch.E., B.S.E.E., B.S.Env.E., B.S.C.M., B.S.F., B.S.I.E., B.S. in Coastal Environmental Science, B.S. in Geol., B.S.M.E., and B.S.P.E. degrees. Master's and doctoral degrees are also awarded. Bachelor's degrees are awarded in AGRICULTURE (agricultural business management, animal science, environmental studies, forestry and related sciences, natural resource management, and plant science), BIOLOGICAL SCIENCE (biochemistry, biology/biological science, microbiology, and nutrition), BUSINESS (accounting, banking and finance, business administration and management, human resources, international economics, management science, marketing/retailing/merchandising, and sports management), COMMUNICATIONS AND THE ARTS (communications, dramatic arts, English, French, journalism, music, Spanish, and studio art), COMPUTER AND PHYSICAL SCIENCE (chemistry, computer science, geology, information sciences and systems, mathematics, and physics), EDUCATION (agricultural education, athletic training, early childhood education, elementary education, music education, and special education), ENGINEERING AND ENVIRONMENTAL DESIGN (architecture, bioengineering, chemical engineering, civil engineering, computer engineering, construction management, electrical/electronics engineering, environmental engineering, environmental science, industrial engineering, interior design, landscape architecture/design, mechanical engineering, and petroleum/natural gas engineering), HEALTH PROFESSIONS (speech pathology/audiology), SOCIAL SCIENCE (anthropology, child care/child and family studies, economics, geography, history, interdisciplinary studies, international studies, liberal arts/general studies, philosophy, physical fitness/movement, political science/government, psychology, sociology, and textiles and clothing). Biological sciences, chemistry, and civil & environmental engineering are the strongest academically. Biological sciences, mass communication, and kinesiology have the largest enrollments.

ACTIVITIES: 17% of men belong to 23 national fraternities; 26% of women belong to 16 national sororities. There are 300 groups on campus, including art, band, cheerleading, choir, chorus, communications, computers, dance, debate, drama, environmental, ethnic, film, honors, international, jazz band, LGBT, literary magazine, marching band, musical theater, newspaper, opera, orchestra, pep band, political, professional, radio and TV, religious, social, social service, student government, symphony, and yearbook. Popular campus events include Fall Fest, Home Football Games, and Groovin on the Grounds. **Sports:** There are 9 intercollegiate sports for men and 11 for women, and 23 intramural sports for men and 23 for women. Facilities include a 92,300-seat football stadium, a 13,500-seat domed sports center, a 9,200-seat baseball stadium, a 400-meter track with seating for 5,600, a natatorium with an 8-lane Olympic pool and diving well, an indoor track, and courts for handball, badminton, volleyball, and tennis. The campus recreation facility provides a multifaceted program that includes aquatics, sports clubs, informal recreation, fitness classes, instructional sports, personal training, intramural sports, outdoor recreation, challenge course, climbing wall, and special-events activities. There is also an indoor practice facility for football, a soccer field that seats 1,200, and a softball stadium that seats 1,200. **Graduates:** From July 1, 2015 to June 30, 2016, 4529 bachelor's degrees were awarded. The most popular majors were biological sciences (7%), kinesiology (6%), and mass communication (6%). 527 companies recruited on campus in 2015-2016. In an average class, 40% graduate in 4 years or less, 65% graduate in 5 years or less, and 69% graduate in 6 years or less. Of the 2015 graduating class, 22% were enrolled in graduate school within 6 months of graduation, and 58% were employed.

SERVICES: Counseling and information services are available, as is tutoring in some subjects, such as English, math, foreign languages, and sciences. There is remedial reading and writing. **Library/Resources:** The 5 libraries contain 3.8 million volumes, 2.3 million microform items, and 26,938 audio/video tapes/CDs/DVDs, and subscribe to 337,837 periodicals including electronic. Computerized library services include interlibrary loans, database searching, Internet access, and Wi-Fi capability. Special learning facilities include an art gallery, natural history museum, radio station, TV station, 3 herbaria, and museums of natural science, natural history, geoscience, rural life, and art. **Physically Challenged Students:** 85% of the campus is accessible. Facilities include wheelchair ramps, elevators, special parking, specially equipped restrooms, special class scheduling, lowered drinking fountains, lowered telephones, and special housing. **Special:** Co-op programs in all areas of engineering and landscape architecture, cross-registration with Southern University and Baton Rouge Community College, study abroad, and work-study programs are offered. B.A.-B.S. degrees, dual majors, a general studies degree, non-degree study, an evening school, a program of study for adult learners, and pass/fail options are available. There are 23 national honor societies, Phi Beta Kappa, and a freshman honors program. **Visiting:** There are regularly scheduled orientations for prospective students, including an information session and a tour of campus. Department appointments can be arranged. There are guides for informal visits. To schedule a visit, contact the Office of Enrollment Management. **Campus Safety and Security:** Measures include 24-hour foot and vehicle patrol, emergency notification system, self-defense education, and security escort services. There are shuttle buses, emergency telephones, lighted pathways/sidewalks, controlled access to dorms/residences, and specialized crime prevention programs.

REQUIREMENTS: The SAT or ACT is required. Applicants must be graduates of an accredited secondary school. GED certificates may be accepted in unusual circumstances. Students must have completed 19 units, including 4 credits in English, 4 each in specific math, science, and social studies courses, 2 credits in a foreign language, and one additional credit from certain courses in the visual and performing arts. A GPA of 3.0 is required. AP and CLEP credits are accepted. Important factors in the admissions decision are advanced placement or honors courses, extracurricular activities record, and evidence of special talent. To graduate, all students must have a minimum overall 2.0 GPA in 120 to 162 credit hours. They must complete a general education component of 39 semester hours in approved courses in 6 major areas, including humanities, natural sciences, English composition, analytical reasoning, social sciences, and the arts. Students must earn at least 25% of required hours for their degree at LSU and meet college residency requirements. **Procedure:** Freshmen are admitted to all sessions. Entrance exams should be taken in spring of the junior year or fall of the senior year. There are early admissions, deferred admissions, and rolling admissions plans. Applications should be filed by April 15 for fall entry; December 1 for spring entry; and April 15 for summer entry, along with a $40 fee. Notification is sent on a rolling basis. Applications are accepted on-line. **Transfer Students:** 866 transfer students enrolled in 2015-2016. Transfer students must submit an official transcript from each previously attended school. Requirements are 30 or more semester hours with a minimum 2.5 GPA, and college level English and math courses. 30 of 120 credits required for the bachelor's degree must be completed at LSU. **International Students:** There are 442 international students enrolled. The school actively recruits these students. They must take the TOEFL with a minimum score of 550 on the paper-based TOEFL (PBT) or 79 on the Internet-based version (iBT), or take the IELTS (minimum score of 6.5). They must also take the SAT or ACT.

ADMISSIONS: 75% of the 2016-2017 applicants were accepted. The SAT scores for the 2016-2017 freshman class were: Critical Reading--22% below 500, 51% between 500 and 599, 24% between 600 and 699, and 4% between 700 and 800. Math-- 15% below 500, 44% between 500 and 599, 35% between 600 and 699, and 6% between 700 and 800. The ACT scores were 5% below 12, 27% between 12 and 17, 31% between 18 and 23, 17% between 24 and 29, and 21% above 30. 44% of the current freshmen were in the top fifth of their class; 73% were in the top two fifths. There were 43 National Merit finalists. 355 freshmen graduated first in their class. **Admissions Contact:** David Kurpius, Associate VC Enrollment Management. Email: *admissions@lsu.edu* Web: *www.lsu.edu*

FINANCIAL AID: In 2016-2017, 93% of all full-time freshmen and 84% of continuing full-time students received some form of financial aid. 38% of all full-time freshmen and 35% of continuing full-time students received need-based aid. The average freshman award was $12,800. Need-based scholarships or need-based grants averaged $7,300; need-based self-help aid (loans and jobs) averaged $3,400; non-need-based athletic scholarships averaged $19,500; and other non-need-based awards and non-need-based scholarships averaged $6,600. 27% of undergraduate students work part-time. Average annual earnings from campus work are $2500. The average financial indebtedness of the 2016 graduate was $21,613. The college's own financial statement is required. The priority date for freshman financial aid applications for fall entry is April 1.

LOUISIANA STATE UNIVERSITY IN SHREVEPORT — A-1

www.lsus.edu

Shreveport, LA 71115	(318) 797-5061
Fax: (318) 797-5286	**Email:** admissions@isus.edu
Full-time: 722 men, 1128 women	**Faculty:** 127
Part-time: 390 men, 579 women	**Ph.D.s:** 79%
Graduate: 570 men, 994 women	**Student/Faculty:** 20 to 1
Year: semesters, summer session	**Tuition:** $6902 ($20,057)
Room & Board: n/app	**Freshman Class:** 695 applied, 621 accepted, 345 enrolled
SAT CR/M: 500/530 **ACT:** 22	**CEEB CODE:** 6355
Application Deadline: July 15	**COMPETITIVE**

Louisiana State University in Shreveport, established in 1965, is a state-supported, primarily commuter institution offering undergraduate and graduate programs through the colleges of liberal arts, business, education, and sciences. Figures in the above capsule and in this profile are approximate. There are 4 undergraduate schools and 4 graduate schools. In addition to regional accreditation, LSUS has baccalaureate program accreditation with AACSB, ABET, NCATE, and ACS. The 258-acre campus is in an urban area 7 miles south of downtown Shreveport. Including any residence halls, there are 18 buildings.

STUDENT LIFE: 92% of undergraduates are from Louisiana. Others are from 47 states, 25 foreign countries, and Canada. 95% are from public schools. 53% are White; 23% African American; 13% race unknown; 4% Hispanic; 3% Asian American; 3% two or more races; 2% Foreign; 1% American Indian/Alaska Native. **Female To Male Ratio:** 1.6:1. The average age of freshmen is 18; all undergraduates, 23. 35% do not continue beyond their first year; 30% remain to graduate. **Housing:** 480 students can be accommodated in college housing, which includes single-sex and coed On-campus housing is available on a first-come and first-served basis. All students may keep cars.

FACULTY/CLASSROOMS: 59% of faculty are male; 41% are female. 80% teach undergraduates, 70% do research, and 70% do both. No introductory courses are taught by graduate students. The average class size in an introductory lecture is 30; in a laboratory is 18; and in a regular course is 19.

PROGRAMS OF STUDY: LSUS confers B.A., B.S., B.C.J. and B.G.S. degrees. Master's and doctoral degrees are also awarded. Bachelor's degrees are awarded in BIOLOGICAL SCIENCE (biochemistry and biology/biological science), BUSINESS (accounting, banking and finance, business administration and management, management science, and marketing/retailing/merchandising), COMMUNICATIONS AND THE ARTS (communications, English, and fine arts), COMPUTER AND PHYSICAL SCIENCE (chemistry, computer science, mathematics, and physics), EDUCATION (elementary education and secondary education), HEALTH PROFESSIONS (community health work), SOCIAL SCIENCE (history, liberal arts/general studies, psychology, and sociology). Biology, computer science, and chemistry are the strongest academically. Psychology, and biology have the largest enrollments.

ACTIVITIES: 5% of men belong to 6 national fraternities; 2% of women belong to 4 national sororities. There are 70 groups on campus, including computers, dance, debate, drama, ethnic, film, forensics, honors, international, literary magazine, photography, political, professional, religious, social, social service, student activities board, student government, and yearbook. Popular campus events include Fall Fest, Spring Fling and Welcome Back Bash. **Sports:** There are 3 intercollegiate sports for men and 3 for women. Facilities include tennis and racquetball courts, sand or volleyball courts, a swimming pool, gym, weight room, dance studio, football fields, softball diamonds, and a soccer field. **Graduates:** From July 1, 2015 to June 30, 2016, 639 bachelor's degrees were awarded. The most popular majors were business/marketing (23%), general studies (14%), and biology (11%). In an average class, 30% graduate in 6 years or less.

SERVICES: Counseling and information services are available, as is tutoring in some subjects. There is remedial math and writing. **Library/Resources:** The library contains 915,751 volumes, 396,114 microform items, and 4,508 audio/video tapes/CDs/DVDs, and subscribes to 2,000 periodicals including electronic. Computerized library services include interlibrary loans, database searching, and Internet access. Special learning facilities include an art gallery, natural history museum, a pioneer heritage center, and a museum of life sciences. **Physically Challenged Students:** All of the campus is accessible. Facilities include wheelchair ramps, elevators, special parking, specially equipped restrooms, special class scheduling, lowered drinking fountains, lowered telephones, special housing. **Special:** Opportunities are provided internships, a Washington semester, a general studies degree, credit for military service schools, non-degree study, and pass/fail options. There are 12 national honor societies and a freshman honors program. **Visiting:** There are regularly scheduled orientations for prospective students, including a preview program during the spring semester for high school juniors and seniors, students may stay overnight for this scheduled visit. There are guides for informal visits. **Campus Safety and Security:** Measures include 24-hour foot and vehicle patrol, self-defense education, and security escort services. There are emergency telephones, lighted pathways/sidewalks, and commissioned university police officers.

REQUIREMENTS: The ACT is required. Students must have a minimum composite score of 20. Graduation from an accredited secondary school is required with the 19 State approved core courses. AP and CLEP credits are accepted. A minimum of 120 semester hours, with a minimum GPA of 2.0, is required for the bachelor's degree. **Procedure:** Freshmen are admitted to all sessions. Entrance exams should be taken at least 2 months before start of the current semester. There is a rolling admissions plan. Applications should be filed by July 15 for fall entry; December 1 for spring entry; and May 1 for summer entry, along with a $20 fee. Notification is sent on a rolling basis. **Transfer Students:** Transfers must be in good academic standing, with 18 transferable hours and a GPA of 2.0. They must be eligible to continue at the last institution attended. 30 of 120 credits required for the bachelor's degree must be completed at LSUS. **International Students:** There are 43 international students enrolled. They must take the TOEFL with a minimum score of 173 on the paper-based TOEFL (PBT) or 61 on the Internet-based version (iBT). They must also take the SAT or ACT.

ADMISSIONS: 89% of the 2016-2017 applicants were accepted. The SAT scores for the 2016-2017 freshman class were: Critical Reading-- 40% below 500 and 60% between 500 and 599. Math-- 17% below 500 and 83% between 500 and 599. The ACT scores were 30% below 12, 32% between 12 and 17, 24% between 18 and 23, 6% between 24 and 29, and 5% above 30. **Admissions Contact:** Lauren M Wood, Assistant Director of Admissions. Email: *admissions@lsus.edu* Web: *www.lsus.edu*

FINANCIAL AID: 90% of undergraduate students work part-time. Average annual earnings from campus work are $3200. The FAFSA code is 002013. The deadline for filing freshman financial aid applications for fall entry is June 1.

LOUISIANA TECH UNIVERSITY — B-1

www.latech.edu

Ruston, LA 71272	**(318) 257-3036** **(800) LATECH-1**
Fax: (318) 257-2499	**Email: bulldog@latech.edu**
Full-time: n/av	**Faculty:** 397; I
Part-time: 800 men, 1000 women	**Ph.D.s:** 80%
Graduate: 820 men, 1410 women	**Student/Faculty:** 23 to 1
Year: trimesters, summer session	**Tuition:** $7302 ($18,411)
Room & Board: $4120	**Freshman Class:** n/av
ACT: 24	**CEEB CODE:** 4633
Application Deadline: September 1	**VERY COMPETITIVE**

Louisiana Tech University, founded in 1894, is a public institution offering programs in arts and sciences, business, agriculture, engineering, health science, education, fine and liberal arts, and human ecology. There are 5 undergraduate schools and 5 graduate schools. In addition to regional accreditation, Tech has baccalaureate program accreditation with AACSB, ABET, ADA, AHEA, ASLA, CAHEA, FIDER, NAAB, NASAD, NASM, NCATE, NLN, SAF, CIDA, CAA, CAHIIM, and NAEYC. The 260-acre campus is in a small town 30 miles west of Monroe and 90 miles east of Shreveport, Louisiana. Including any residence halls, there are 146 buildings.

STUDENT LIFE: 85% of undergraduates are from Louisiana. Others are from 44 states, 65 foreign countries, and Canada. 70% are White; 6% Foreign; 16% African American; 1% Asian American; 1% American Indian/Alaska Native; 1% Hispanic. 51% are Protestant; 12% Catholic. **Female To Male Ratio:** 1.5:1. The average age of freshmen is 19; all undergraduates, 20. 22% do not continue beyond their first year; 49% remain to graduate. **Housing:** 3067 students can be accommodated in college housing, which includes single-sex and coed dorms and married student housing. In addition, there are honors houses. On-campus housing is guaranteed for all 4 years. 74% of students commute. Alcohol is not permitted. All students may keep cars.

FACULTY/CLASSROOMS: 65% of faculty are male; 35% are female. 95% teach undergraduates, 75% do research, and 75% do both. Graduate students teach 2% of introductory courses. The average class size in an introductory lecture is 40; in a laboratory is 20; and in a regular course is 26.

PROGRAMS OF STUDY: Tech confers B.A., B.S., B. Arch., B.F.A., and B.G.S. degrees. Associate, master's, and doctoral degrees are also awarded. Bachelor's degrees are awarded in AGRICULTURE (agricultural business management, animal science, forestry and related sciences, and wildlife management), BIOLOGICAL SCIENCE (biology/biological science), BUSINESS (accounting, banking and finance, business administration and management, business economics, business systems analysis, management science, marketing/retailing/merchandising, and personnel management), COMMUNICATIONS AND THE ARTS (English, fine arts, French, journalism, music, music performance, Spanish, and speech/debate/rhetoric), COMPUTER AND PHYSICAL SCIENCE (chemistry, computer science, geology, mathematics, and physics), EDUCATION (art education, early childhood education, elementary education, foreign languages education, music education, physical education, secondary education, and special education), ENGINEERING AND ENVIRONMENTAL DESIGN (airline piloting and navigation, architecture, aviation administration/management, biomedical engineering, chemical engineering, civil engineering, construction engineering, electrical/electronics engineering technology, environmental science, industrial engineering, and mechanical engineering), HEALTH PROFESSIONS (medical laboratory technology, medical records administration/services, and speech pathology/audiology), SOCIAL SCIENCE (dietetics, geography, history, liberal arts/general studies, political science/government, psychology, and sociology). Business and engineering are the strongest academically and have the largest enrollments.

ACTIVITIES: 7% of men belong to 9 national fraternities; 11% of women belong to 5 national sororities. There are 121 groups on campus, including art, band, cheerleading, choir, chorale, chorus, computers, dance, debate, drama, drill team, drum and bugle corps, ethnic, film, honors, international, jazz band, marching band, musical theater, newspaper, opera, orchestra, pep band, photography, political, professional, radio and TV, religious, social, social service, student government, symphony, and yearbook. Popular campus events include International Student Festival, Spring Fling, and Little Theater Concerts. **Sports:** There are 5 intercollegiate sports for men and 5 for women, and 10 intramural sports for men and 10 for women. Facilities include a football stadium, a coliseum, an intramural complex, natatorium, 9-hole golf course, and 10 lighted tennis courts. **Graduates:** From July 1, 2015 to June 30, 2016, 1401 bachelor's degrees were awarded. The most popular majors were business (22%), engineering (17%), and education (11%). 632 companies recruited on campus in 2015-2016. In an average class, 29% graduate in 4 years or less, 49% graduate in 5 years or less, and 55% graduate in 6 years or less.

SERVICES: Counseling and information services are available, as is tutoring in some subjects. There is a reader service for the blind, and remedial math, reading, and writing. **Library/Resources:** The library contains 1.1 million volumes, 2.1 million microform items, and 511 audio/video tapes/CDs/DVDs, and subscribes to 2,932 periodicals including electronic. Computerized library services include interlibrary loans and database searching. Special learning facilities include an art gallery, natural history museum, planetarium, and radio station. **Physically Challenged Students:** 95% of the campus is accessible. Facilities include wheelchair ramps, elevators, special parking, specially equipped restrooms, lowered drinking fountains, and lowered telephones. **Special:** Co-op programs are available in engineering and applied and natural sciences, and cross-registration with Grambling State University is offered. Internships in agriculture, engineering, dietetics, and human ecology are offered. Study abroad, work-study programs, dual majors, a general studies degree, non-degree study, and pass/fail options are available. There is a chapter of Phi Beta Kappa, a freshman honors program, and 20 departmental honors programs. **Visiting:** There are regularly scheduled orientations for prospective students. There are guides for informal visits and visitors may stay overnight. To schedule a visit, contact the Admissions Office. **Campus Safety and Security:** Measures include 24-hour foot and vehicle patrol, self-defense education, and security escort services. There are emergency telephones and lighted pathways/sidewalks.

REQUIREMENTS: The ACT is required. Applicants must be graduates of an accredited secondary school or have a GED. Students must have graduated in the upper half of their class. AP credits are accepted. All students must complete 45 quarter hours of general education courses, including 12 hours in humanities, 9 each in natural and social sciences, 6 each in English and math, and 3 in arts or computer literacy. A total of 120 to 142 quarter hours, with a minimum GPA of 2.0, is required to graduate. **Procedure:** Freshmen are admitted to all sessions. There is a rolling admissions plan. Applications should be filed by September 1 for fall entry; November 1 for winter entry; February 1 for spring entry; and May 1 for summer entry. The fall 2016 application fee was $20. **Transfer Students:** 526 transfer students enrolled in 2015-2016. Transfer applicants should have a 2.0 GPA and be eligible to enroll in the school from which they are transferring. 30 of 120 credits required for the bachelor's degree must be completed at Tech. **International Students:** There are 139 international students enrolled. The school actively recruits these students. They must take the TOEFL.

ADMISSIONS: There were 5 National Merit finalists. **Admissions Contact:** Jan Albritton, Admissions Office. Email: *bulldog@latech.edu* Web: *www.latech.edu*

FINANCIAL AID: In 2016-2017, 71% of all full-time freshmen received some form of financial aid. 71% of all full-time freshmen received need-based aid. 27% of undergraduate students work part-time. The FAFSA code is 002008. The deadline for filing freshman financial aid applications for fall entry is July 16.

LOYOLA UNIVERSITY NEW ORLEANS D-4
www.loyno.edu

New Orleans, LA 70118	(504) 865-3240 (800) 4-LOYOLA
Fax: (504) 865-3383	**Email:** admit@loyno.edu
Full-time: 918 men, 1420 women	**Faculty:** 186; IIA, av$
Part-time: 61 men, 84 women	**Ph.D.s:** 91%
Graduate: 364 men, 832 women	**Student/Faculty:** 12 to 1
Year: semesters, summer session	**Tuition:** $38,504
Room & Board: $13,204	**Freshman Class:** 5160 applied, 3496 accepted, 615 enrolled
SAT or ACT: required	**CEEB CODE:** 6374
Application Deadline: February 20	**VERY COMPETITIVE+**

Loyola University New Orleans, founded in 1912, is a private, Catholic, Jesuit university that serves undergraduate, graduate, professional, and continuing education students. There are 4 undergraduate schools and 3 graduate schools. In addition to regional accreditation, Loyola has baccalaureate program accreditation with AACSB, ACEJMC, NASM, NLN, AALS, ABA, APT, ACS, CACREP, CCNE, LSBN, NASM, NLNAC, and CEPR. The 26-acre campus is in a suburban area in the Uptown university district of New Orleans. Including any residence halls, there are 29 buildings.

STUDENT LIFE: 57% of undergraduates are from out of state, mostly the South. Students are from 48 states, 39 foreign countries, and Canada. 56% are from public schools. 51% are White; 17% Hispanic; 15% African American; 5% two or more races; 4% Foreign; 4% race unknown; 3% Asian American; 1% American Indian/Alaska Native. 37% are Catholic; 33% Baptist, Buddhist, Episcopalian, Hindu, Lutheran, Methodist, Muslim, Presbyterian, and other; 21% claim no religious affiliation. **Female To Male Ratio:** 1.7:1. The average age of freshmen is 18; all undergraduates, 21. 21% do not continue beyond their first year; 79% remain to graduate. **Housing:** 1332 students can be accommodated in college housing, which includes single-sex and coed dorms and on-campus apartments. In addition, there are honors houses, special-interest houses, theme housing and wellness housing, including LEAD community, honors, and SPARK community. On-campus housing is guaranteed for the freshman year only, and is available on a first-come, first-served basis. Priority is given to out-of-town students. 51% of students commute. All students may keep cars.

FACULTY/CLASSROOMS: 55% of faculty are male; 45% are female. 77% teach undergraduates, and 90% do research. No introductory courses are taught by graduate students. The average class size in an introductory lecture is 24; in a laboratory is 13; and in a regular course is 16.

PROGRAMS OF STUDY: Loyola confers B.A., B.S., B.Acc., B.B.A., B.C.J., B.F.A., B.L.S., B.Mus., B.Mus.Ed., B.Mus. Therapy, B.S.N., B.A. Music, B.S. Mus. Industry, and B.Design degrees. Master's and doctoral degrees are also awarded. Bachelor's degrees are awarded in AGRICULTURE (environmental studies), BIOLOGICAL SCIENCE (biology/biological science), BUSINESS (accounting, banking and finance, business administration and management, business intelligence and analytics, international business management, management science, and marketing/retailing/merchandising), COMMUNICATIONS AND THE ARTS (advertising, communications, creative writing, design, dramatic arts, English literature, film, television and digital media, fine arts, fine/studio arts, general, French, game programming, graphic design, Greek (classical), guitar, jazz, journalism, languages, music, music business management, music composition, music industry, music performance, music theory and composition, piano/organ, Spanish, studio art, visual and performing arts, and voice), COMPUTER AND PHYSICAL SCIENCE (chemistry, computer information systems, mathematics, mathematics/computational, and physics), EDUCATION (music education), ENGINEERING AND ENVIRONMENTAL DESIGN (environmental science and preengineering), HEALTH PROFESSIONS (music therapy, nursing, predentistry, premedicine, and preveterinary science), SOCIAL SCIENCE (classical/ancient civilization, criminal justice, economics, food production/management/services, forensic studies, history, humanities, Latin American studies, liberal arts/general studies, philosophy, political science/government, psychology, religion, religious education, social science, and sociology). Music industry studies, psychology, and biological sciences are the strongest academically and have the largest enrollments.

ACTIVITIES: 11% of men belong to 4 national fraternities; 20% of women belong to 7 national sororities. There are 129 groups on campus, including art, band, cheerleading, chess, choir, chorale, chorus, communications, computers, dance, debate, drama, environmental, ethnic, film, forensics, honors, international, jazz band, LGBT, literary magazine, musical theater, newspaper, opera, orchestra, pep band, photography, political, professional, radio and TV, religious, social, social service, student government, symphony, Ultimate Frisbee, and yearbook. Popular campus events include Take Back the Night, Maroon and Gold, Senior Crawfish Boil, Sneaux, Family Weekend, Mass & Pancakes, Get to NOLA Excursions, and New Student Convocation. **Sports:** There are 8 intercollegiate sports for men and 8 for women, and 8 intramural sports for men and 8 for women. Facilities include a sports complex with an arena, 6 multipurpose courts for basketball, tennis, volleyball, badminton, and floor hockey, 2 racquetball courts, an Olympic-style natatorium, a jogging track, and a weight lifting and conditioning area. Off- campus facilities for baseball, tennis, cross country, and track/field and golf. **Graduates:** From July 1, 2015 to June 30, 2016, 473 bachelor's degrees were awarded. The most popular majors were music industry (12%), psychology (9%), and mass communication (8%). 275 companies recruited on campus in 2015-2016. In an average class, 50% graduate in 4 years or less, 55% graduate in 5 years or less, and 55% graduate in 6 years or less. Of the 2015 graduating class, 25% were enrolled in graduate school within 6 months of graduation, and 70% were employed.

SERVICES: Counseling and information services are available, as is tutoring in most subjects. There is remedial math and writing. Peer tutoring is available in all introductory common curriculum courses. A reader service for the blind is provided for all exams and for course-work if books on tape are not sufficient. **Library/Resources:** The 2 libraries contain 584,939 volumes, 1.4 million microform items, and 17,352 audio/video tapes/CDs/DVDs, and subscribe to 169,032 periodicals including electronic. Computerized library services include interlibrary loans, database searching, Internet access, and Wi-Fi capability. Special learning facilities include an art gallery, radio station, TV station, art gallery, humanities lab with Perseus Project and TLG TV, multimedia classrooms graphic lab, visual arts lab, ad club communications lab, business computer lab, multimedia training center, live stock tracking floor, and center for non-profit communication. **Physically Challenged Students:** 99% of the campus is accessible. Facilities include wheelchair ramps, elevators, special parking, specially equipped restrooms, lowered drinking fountains, lowered telephones, special housing, and special class relocation to provide accessibility. **Special:** Cross-registration is available with, Our Lady of Holy Cross, Xavier University, Notre Dame Seminary, the University of New Orleans, Tulane University, and Southern University of New Orleans. Internships with the New Orleans business community are also available. Study abroad in 40 countries, dual and student-designed majors, nondegree studies, an accelerated B.S.N. to D.N.P nursing program, and a general studies degree are offered. A Washington semester through American University and a 3-2 engineering degree with Tulane University and the University of New Orleans are also available. There are 12 national honor societies, a freshman honors program, and 8 departmental honors programs. **Visiting:** There are regularly scheduled orientations for prospective students, including class and department visits, a student panel, a tour, a financial aid session, a campus support panel, and meetings with faculty members. There are guides for informal visits, visitors may sit in on classes, and stay overnight. To schedule a visit, contact the Admissions Office. **Campus Safety and Security:** Measures include 24-hour foot and vehicle patrol, emergency notification system, self-defense education, and security escort services. There are shuttle buses, emergency telephones, lighted pathways/sidewalks, controlled access to dorms/residences, CCTV coverage, card access control, ID cards issued, intrusion alarm monitoring, first aid medical assistance, motorist vehicle assistance, bicycle registration, fingerprinting service, crime prevention services, multiple vehicle patrols (including a Segway, electric scooter, electric golf carts, international certified police bike patrols and other patrol vehicles). There are off-campus police patrols, Silent Witness program (which allows students to anonymously report criminal activity via the internet); RAVE Guardian Campus Safety App (Panic Button, Tip Texting and Personal Guardian); direct radio communication with city police (NOPD), adjoining Tulane University police and other police departments during a local area or in-state emergencies; officers are trained in active shooter response and a SERT (Special Emergency Response Team) is in place and Active Shooter education for all community members. All officers are trained in First-Aid/CPR/AED. LUPD serves on several university committees as well as off-campus organizations: Emergency Management Team, Threat Assessment Team, Care & Concern Committee, Tobacco Free Committee, Loyola/Tulane Transportation Advisory Board, Maple St. Quality of Life Committee, Women Resource Center Advisory Committee, Advocate Training Committee, Sexual Assault Committee, Bias-Incident Related Committee, New Orleans Anti-Terrorism Advisory Council (ATAC), and NOPD Compstat and NONPAC organizations.

REQUIREMENTS: The SAT or ACT is required. Candidates for admission must be graduates of an accredited secondary school or have a GED. They should have completed 4 units in English, 3 each in math, science (1 must be a lab), 2 each in foreign language, history, and social studies, and an academic elective. A portfolio is required for fine arts students, an audition for music majors. An interview is recommended for scholarship consideration. Home schooled students require proof of high school graduation or its equivalent. AP and CLEP credits are accepted. Important factors in the admissions decision are advanced placement or honors courses, evidence of special talent, extracurricular activities record, recommendations by school officials, personality/intangible qualities, recommendations by alumni, and geographical diversity. All students must complete a core curriculum that includes courses in English composition and literature, math, philosophy, science, global history, social science, and religious studies; the number of credit hours varies by college. At least 120 credit hours, with at least 30 in the major, and a minimum GPA of 2.0 are required to graduate. **Procedure:** Freshmen are admitted fall, spring, and summer. Entrance exams should be taken during the junior or senior year. There are early admissions, deferred admissions, and rolling admissions plans. Application deadlines are open. Applications are accepted on-line. Application fees are waived if application is completed on-line. **Transfer Students:** 93 transfer students enrolled in 2015-2016. Transfers must submit the application for admission, an essay, a letter of recommendation, a resume, and two official transcripts from each institution previously attended. Students attempting less than 12 semester hours of credit should also submit the high school transcript and the results of the ACT or SAT. 30 of 120 credits required for the bachelor's degree must be completed at Loyola. **International Students:** There are 85 international students enrolled. The school actively recruits these students. They must take the TOEFL with a minimum score of 550 on the paper-based TOEFL (PBT) or 79 on the Internet-based version (iBT) and the college's own test. Scores are a minimum score for a student to be admitted through the LIEP Pilot Program. They must also take the SAT or ACT.

ADMISSIONS: 68% of the 2016-2017 applicants were accepted. 47% of the current freshmen were in the top fifth of their class; 77% were in the top two fifths. 10 freshmen graduated first in their class. **Admissions Contact:** Ms. Susan O. Oakes, Director of Admissions. Email: *admit@loyno.edu* Web: *www.loyno.edu*

FINANCIAL AID: In 2016-2017, 85% of all full-time freshmen and 89% of continuing full-time students received some form of financial aid. 85% of all full-time freshmen and 89% of continuing full-time students received need-based aid. The average freshman award was $34,087. Need-based scholarships or need-based grants averaged $30,311; need-based self-help aid (loans and jobs) averaged $4,426; non-need-based athletic scholarships averaged $8,599; other non-need-based awards and non-need-based scholarships averaged $17,357; and $3,308 from other forms of aid. 25% of undergraduate students work part-time. Average annual earnings from campus work are $1600. The FAFSA code is 002016. The priority date for freshman financial aid applications for fall entry is March 1.

MCNEESE STATE UNIVERSITY B-4

www.mcneese.edu

Lake Charles, LA 70609	**(337) 475-5504** **(800) 622-3352**
Fax: (337) 475-5151	**Email: admissions@mcneese.edu**
Full-time: 2300 men, 3659 women	**Faculty:** IIA, --$
Part-time: 582 men, 960 women	**Ph.D.s:** 66%
Graduate: 270 men, 578 women	**Student/Faculty:** 21 to 1
Year: semesters, summer session	**Tuition:** $7838 ($11,075)
Room & Board: n/app	**Freshman Class:** n/av **CEEB CODE:** 6403
Application Deadline: August 18	**COMPETITIVE**

McNeese State University, founded in 1939 and part of the University of Louisiana System, is a public institution offering programs in business, engineering, education, science, liberal arts, and nursing. Figures in the above capsule and in this profile are approximate. There are 7 undergraduate schools and 1 graduate school. In addition to regional accreditation, MSU has baccalaureate program accreditation with AACSB, ADA, CAHEA, CSAB, NASAD, NASM, NCATE, AAFCS, ACS, EAC/ABET, CAATE, CADE, CCNE, CAC/ABET, NAACLS, NLNAC, JRCET, and TAC/ABET. The 121-acre campus is in a suburban area 130 miles west of Baton Rouge and 150 miles east of Houston, Texas. Including any residence halls, there are 88 buildings.

STUDENT LIFE: 90% of undergraduates are from Louisiana. Others are from 34 states, 49 foreign countries, and Canada. 73% are White; 4% Foreign; 2% Hispanic; 2% two or more races; 18% African American; 1% Asian American; 1% American Indian/Alaska Native. **Female To Male Ratio:** 1.6:1. The average age of freshmen is 20; all undergraduates, 23. 31% do not continue beyond their first year. **Housing:** 975 students can be accommodated in college housing, which includes coed dorms and on-campus apartments. On-campus housing is guaranteed for all 4 years, and is available on a first-come, first-served basis. Alcohol is not permitted. All students may keep cars.

FACULTY/CLASSROOMS: 48% of faculty are male; 52% are female. No introductory courses are taught by graduate students.

PROGRAMS OF STUDY: MSU confers B.A., B.S., B.S.N., and B.G.S. degrees. Associate and master's degrees are also awarded. Bachelor's degrees are awarded in AGRICULTURE (agriculture and natural resource management), BIOLOGICAL SCIENCE (biology/biological science and nutritional sciences), BUSINESS (accounting, business administration and management, marketing, and organizational leadership and management), COMMUNICATIONS AND THE ARTS (art, communications, English, languages, and music), COMPUTER AND PHYSICAL SCIENCE (chemistry, computer science, mathematics, and radiological technology), EDUCATION (athletic training, early childhood education, elementary education, and health education), ENGINEERING AND ENVIRONMENTAL DESIGN (engineering and engineering technology), HEALTH PROFESSIONS (clinical science and nursing), SOCIAL SCIENCE (criminal justice, gender studies, history, liberal arts/general studies, political science/government, psychology, and sociology). Nursing, engineering, and education have the largest enrollments.

ACTIVITIES: Groups on campus include art, band, cheerleading, choir, chorale, chorus, computers, dance, debate, drama, drill team, ethnic, honors, international, jazz band, marching band, musical theater, newspaper, orchestra, pep band, political, professional, religious, social, social service, student government, symphony, and yearbook. Popular campus events include Homecoming and Spring Fling. **Sports:** Facilities include a football stadium, softball and intramural fields, an indoor/outdoor track, a 50-meter pool, baseball complex, outdoor tennis courts, weight room, racquetball courts, and 3 regulation basketball courts, golf, cross country, volleyball, and soccer. **Graduates:** From July 1, 2015 to June 30, 2016, 1177 bachelor's degrees were awarded. The most popular majors were general studies (15%), nursing (14%), and engineering (6%).

SERVICES: Counseling and information services are available, as is tutoring in some subjects. **Library/Resources:** Computerized library services include interlibrary loans, database searching, Internet access, and Wi-Fi capability. Special learning facilities include an art gallery, planetarium, a 503-acre farm, a vertebrate museum, a community health care clinic, a meat processing plant, and the Southwest Louisiana Entrepreneurial and Economic Development Center. **Physically Challenged Students:** Facilities include wheelchair ramps, elevators, special parking, specially equipped restrooms, lowered drinking fountains, academic planning and registration assistance, and classroom and testing accommodations. **Special:** MSU offers co-op programs in engineering, internships in clinical lab sciences, radiologic science, business, and education, dual majors, a general studies degree, nondegree study, and credit for military experience. Innovation program available. There is a freshman honors program. **Visiting:** There are regularly scheduled orientations for prospective students. There are guides for informal visits, visitors may sit in on classes, and stay overnight. To schedule a visit, contact the Admissions Office. **Campus Safety and Security:** Measures include 24-hour foot and vehicle patrol, emergency notification system, and security escort services. There are emergency telephones and lighted pathways/sidewalks.

REQUIREMENTS: First-time freshmen who are graduates of state-approved Louisiana high schools must meet the following admission criteria: Completion of the Regents' High School Core 4 Curriculum; need no developmental courses; and have a minimum high school overall GPA of 2.35; and ONE of the following: Minimum high school core GPA of 2.0 on a 4.0 scale as reported by the Department of Education OR ACT composite score of 20 or greater (SAT combined mathematics and critical reading score of 940). AP and CLEP credits are accepted. McNeese State University's general education curriculum consists of coursework from six broad disciplinary areas: 6 hours each in writing, mathematics, natural sciences, and fine arts; 9 hours in humanities, and social and behavioral sciences, and 3 hours in fine arts. The mission of this core curriculum is to provide students with a foundation of knowledge, skills, and methods of inquiry that support advanced study in their chosen degree program and constitute the characteristics of an informed, college-educated citizen. **Procedure:** Freshmen are admitted to all sessions. There are early admissions and rolling admissions plans. Applications should be filed by August 18 for fall entry, along with a $20 fee. Applications are accepted on-line. **Transfer Students:** Transfer students who have earned 18 or more college-level academic credit hours must either have earned a transferable associate degree or higher from a regionally accredited institution OR meet the following admission standards: Cumulative GPA of at least 2.0 on all college-level academic courses; be eligible to return to the institution from which they are transferring, and have completed a college-level English and mathematics course designed to fulfill general education requirements. Transfer students who have a cumulative GPA of at least 2.0 on all college-level academic courses, but who have earned less than 18 college-level academic hours, must meet first-time freshman admission standards. 30 of 120 credits required for the bachelor's degree must be completed at MSU. **International Students:** There are 292 international students enrolled. The school actively recruits these students. They must take the TOEFL with a minimum score of 500 on the paper-based TOEFL (PBT). They must also take the SAT or ACT.

ADMISSIONS: The ACT scores were 36% below 12, 37% between 12 and 17, 17% between 18 and 23, 5% between 24 and 29, and 5% above 30. **Admissions Contact:** Kara Smith, Director of Admissions and Recruiting. Email: *admissions@mcneese.edu* Web: *www.mcneese.edu*

FINANCIAL AID: The FFS and the college's own financial statement are required. The FAFSA code is 002017. Check with the school for current application deadlines.

NICHOLLS STATE UNIVERSITY D-4
www.nicholls.edu

Thibodaux, LA 70310	**(985) 448-4507** **(877) 642-4655**
Fax: (985) 448-4929	**Email: nicholls@nicholls.edu**
Full-time: 1815 men, 2929 women	**Faculty:** 283
Part-time: 297 men, 474 women	**Ph.D.s:** 56%
Graduate: 125 men, 414 women	**Student/Faculty:** 20 to 1
Year: semesters, summer session	**Tuition:** $7234 ($17,480)
Room & Board: $3300	**Freshman Class:** 2424 applied, 2142 accepted, 1210 enrolled
ACT: 21	**CEEB CODE:** 6221
Application Deadline: August 15	**COMPETITIVE**

Nicholls State University, established in 1948 and part of the University of Louisiana System, is a public liberal arts institution offering instruction in health sciences, fine arts, business, teacher preparation, and agricultural and technical disciplines. Figures in the above capsule and in this profile are approximate. There are 6 undergraduate schools and 4 graduate schools. In addition to regional accreditation, Nicholls has baccalaureate program accreditation with AACSB, ACEJMC, ADA, CSAB, NASAD, NASM, NCATE, NLN, AAFCS, CAAHEP, and CCNE. The 210-acre campus is in a small town 50 miles southwest of New Orleans and 60 miles southeast of Baton Rouge. Including any residence halls, there are 48 buildings.

STUDENT LIFE: 96% of undergraduates are from Louisiana. Others are from 32 states, 45 foreign countries, and Canada. 69% are from public schools. 75% are White; 2% American Indian/Alaska Native; 2% Hispanic; 18% African American; 1% Asian American. 37% are Catholic; 18% Protestant. **Female To Male Ratio:** 1.7:1. The average age of freshmen is 18; all undergraduates, 23. 34% do not continue beyond their first year; 26% remain to graduate. **Housing:** 1503 students can be accommodated in college housing, which includes single-sex and coed dorms, on-campus apartments, and married student housing. On-campus housing is guaranteed for the freshman year only and is available on a first-come, first-served basis. 53% of students commute. Alcohol is not permitted. All students may keep cars.

FACULTY/CLASSROOMS: 51% of faculty are male; 49% are female. Graduate students teach 1% of introductory courses.

PROGRAMS OF STUDY: Nicholls confers B.A., B.S., B.G.S., B.M.E., and B.S.N. degrees. Associate and master's degrees are also awarded. Bachelor's degrees are awarded in AGRICULTURE (agricultural business management), BIOLOGICAL SCIENCE (biology/biological science), BUSINESS (accounting, banking and finance, business administration and management, marketing/retailing/merchandising, and personnel management), COMMUNICATIONS AND THE ARTS (art, communications, English, French, journalism, and music), COMPUTER AND PHYSICAL SCIENCE (chemistry, computer science, information sciences and systems, and mathematics), EDUCATION (business education, elementary education, music education, secondary education, and special education), ENGINEERING AND ENVIRONMENTAL DESIGN (manufacturing technology and petroleum/natural gas engineering), HEALTH PROFESSIONS (health science, nursing, and speech pathology/audiology), SOCIAL SCIENCE (dietetics, family/consumer studies, food production/management/services, history, political science/government, psychology, and sociology). Languages, literature, and biological sciences are the strongest academically. Nursing, general studies, and teacher education have the largest enrollments.

ACTIVITIES: 8% of men belong to 7 national fraternities; 8% of women belong to 7 national sororities. Groups on campus include art, band, cheerleading, choir, chorale, chorus, computers, dance, debate, drama, drill team, ethnic, honors, international, jazz band, LGBT, literary magazine, marching band, musical theater, newspaper, pep band, photography, political, professional, radio and TV, religious, social, social service, student government, symphony, and yearbook. Popular campus events include Midterm Exam Week Breakfast, Family Day, and Crawfish Boil. **Sports:** There are 6 intercollegiate sports for men and 8 for women, and 4 intramural sports for men and 4 for women. Facilities include a stadium, 2 gyms, tennis and racquetball courts, a soccer field, a swimming pool, baseball and softball fields, and a weight room. **Graduates:** From July 1, 2015 to June 30, 2016, 967 bachelor's degrees were awarded. The most popular majors were business/marketing (24%), health professions and related programs (17%), and liberal arts/general studies (14%). 196 companies recruited on campus in 2015-2016. In an average class, 9% graduate in 4 years or less, 20% graduate in 5 years or less, and 26% graduate in 6 years or less.

SERVICES: Counseling and information services are available, as is tutoring in most subjects. There is a reader service for the blind, and remedial math and writing. Tutoring is available in math, English, computer science, biology, chemistry, physics, and foreign languages. **Library/Resources:** Computerized library services include interlibrary loans, database searching, and Internet access. Special learning facilities include an art gallery, radio station, TV station, a culinary institute, a rural development institute, and centers for the study of dyslexia, women and government, and economic education. **Physically Challenged Students:** Facilities include wheelchair ramps, elevators, special parking, specially equipped restrooms, special class scheduling, lowered drinking fountains, and lowered telephones. **Special:** Internships are offered in business areas, government, home economics, computer science, and psychology. A Washington semester congressional internship and dual majors in education are available. Cross-registration with Fletcher Community College and River Parishes Community College and study abroad in 5 countries are offered. There are 12 national honor societies, a freshman honors program, and 1 departmental honors program. **Visiting:** There are regularly scheduled orientations for prospective students, consisting of general information, advising, and registration. There are guides for informal visits, visitors may sit in on classes, and stay overnight. To schedule a visit, contact the Admissions Office. **Campus Safety and Security:** Measures include 24-hour foot and vehicle patrol, emergency notification system, self-defense education, and security escort services. There are emergency telephones and lighted pathways/sidewalks.

REQUIREMENTS: The ACT is recommended. Applicants must be graduates of an accredited secondary school or have the GED. 19 High school units required: 4 each in English, math, and science, 2 each in foreign language, social studies, and history, and 1 in visual/performing arts Nicholls requires applicants to be in the upper 50% of their class. AP and CLEP credits are accepted. Important factors in the admissions decision are leadership record and extracurricular activities record. All students must complete general education requirements, including 9 hours each in English, natural sciences, and humanities, 6 hours each in social sciences and math, 3 hours in the arts, and student development, freshman, and computer science courses. At least 120 total credit hours, plus a minimum of 24 hours in the major, with a minimum GPA of 2.0, are required to graduate. Students also take a general education competency test before graduation. **Procedure:** Freshmen are admitted to all sessions. Entrance exams should be taken as early as possible. There are deferred admissions and rolling admissions plans. Application deadlines are open. The fall 2016 application fee was $20. Notification is sent on a rolling basis. Applications are accepted on-line. **Transfer Students:** 267 transfer students enrolled in 2015-2016. Transfer applicants must be eligible to return to the institution from which they are transferring, must have earned a minimum of 12 college-level hours, have a GPA of 2.0 on college-level courses, and require not more than 1 developmental course. 30 of 120 credits required for the bachelor's degree must be completed at Nicholls. **International Students:** There are 42 international students enrolled. The school actively recruits these students. They must take the TOEFL with a minimum score of 500 on the paper-based TOEFL (PBT) or 61 on the Internet-based version (iBT).

ADMISSIONS: 88% of the 2016-2017 applicants were accepted. 31% of the current freshmen were in the top fifth of their class; 58% were in the top two fifths. 43 freshmen graduated first in their class. **Admissions Contact:** Becky L. Durocher, Director of Admissions. Email: *nicholls@nicholls.edu* Web: *www.nicholls.edu*

FINANCIAL AID: In 2016-2017, 84% of all full-time freshmen and 74% of continuing full-time students received some form of financial aid. 46% of all full-time freshmen and 48% of continuing full-time students received need-based aid. The average freshman award was $9,919. Need-based scholarships or need-based grants averaged $7,751 ($7,257 maximum); need-based self-help aid (loans and jobs) averaged $2,640 ($5,797 maximum); non-need-based athletic scholarships averaged $9,589 ($7,751 maximum); other non-need-based awards and non-need-based scholarships averaged $2,550 ($6,039 maximum); and $3,934 from other forms of aid. 9% of undergraduate students work part-time. Average annual earnings from campus work are $1696. The average financial indebtedness of the 2016 graduate was $16,710. The FAFSA code is 002005. The priority date for freshman financial aid applications for fall entry is April 15. The deadline for filing freshman financial aid applications for fall entry is November 1.

NORTHWESTERN STATE UNIVERSITY OF LOUISIANA B-2

www.nsula.edu

Natchitoches, LA 71497	(318) 357-4503 (800) 327-1903
Fax: (318) 357-5567	**Email:** applications@nsula.edu
Full-time: 1752 men, 3472 women	**Faculty:** n/av
Part-time: 961 men, 2515 women	**Ph.D.s:** 59%
Graduate: 237 men, 882 women	**Student/Faculty:** n/av
Year: semesters, summer session	**Tuition:** $7620 ($18,408)
Room & Board: $8914	**Freshman Class:** n/av
SAT CR/M/W: required **ACT:** 22	**CEEB CODE:** 6492
Application Deadline: n/av	**COMPETITIVE**

Northwestern State University is a responsive, student-oriented institution that is committted to the creation, dissemination, and acquisition of knowledge through teaching, research, and service. The University maintains as its highest priority excellence in teaching in graduate and undergraduate programs. Northwestern State University will prepare its students to become productive members of society and will promote economic development and improvements in the quality of life of the citizens in its region. There are 4 undergraduate schools and 1 graduate school. In addition to regional accreditation, NSU has baccalaureate program accreditation with AACSB, ABET, CSWE, NASAD, NASM, NCATE, NLN, AAFCS, AVMA, CCNE, JRCERT, NAST, CAEP, and CACREP. The 916-acre campus is in a small town in central Louisiana, 60 miles south of Shreveport and 50 miles north of Alexandria. Including any residence halls, there are 56 buildings.

STUDENT LIFE: 81% of undergraduates are from Louisiana. Others are from 50 states, and 10 foreign countries. 59% are White; 26% African American; 5% Hispanic; 4% two or more races; 2% American Indian/Alaska Native; 2% race unknown; 1% Asian American; 1% Foreign. **Female To Male Ratio:** 2.3:1. The average age of freshmen is 19; all undergraduates, 23. 40% remain to graduate. **Housing:** 1298 students can be accommodated in college housing, which includes coed dorms and on-campus apartments. In addition, there are honors houses and special-interest houses. On-campus housing is available on a first-come, first-served basis. 81% of students commute. Alcohol is not permitted. All students may keep cars.

FACULTY/CLASSROOMS: 40% of faculty are male; 60% are female. Graduate students teach 1% of introductory courses.

PROGRAMS OF STUDY: NSU confers B.A., B.A.S, B.S., B.F.A., B.G.S., B.M., B.M.Ed., B.S.N. and B.S.W. degrees. Associate, master's, and doctoral degrees are also awarded. Bachelor's degrees are awarded in BIOLOGICAL SCIENCE (biology/biological science and biological sciences), BUSINESS (accounting, business administration and management, business communications, hospitality management services, organizational leadership and management, and tourism), COMMUNICATIONS AND THE ARTS (communications, dramatic arts, English, fine arts, foreign language, music, music business management, and musical theater), COMPUTER AND PHYSICAL SCIENCE (computer information systems, information sciences and systems, mathematics, and physical sciences), EDUCATION (early childhood education, elementary education, health education, music education, and secondary education), ENGINEERING AND ENVIRONMENTAL DESIGN (electrical/electronics engineering technology, engineering technology, industrial engineering, and industrial engineering technology), HEALTH PROFESSIONS (allied health, biology, exercise science, hospital administration, nursing, and radiological science), SOCIAL SCIENCE (addiction studies, criminal justice, developmental psychology, European studies, family/consumer studies, geography, history, humanities, humanities and social science, international relations, liberal arts/general studies, psychology, public administration, and social work). Liberal arts (scholars' college), creative & performing arts, computer information systems, and nursing are the strongest academically. Nursing, liberal arts/general studies, and business administration have the largest enrollments.

ACTIVITIES: 10% of men belong to 7 national fraternities; 6% of women belong to 8 national sororities. There are 103 groups on campus, including art, band, cheerleading, choir, chorale, chorus, communications, computers, dance, debate, drama, drill team, ethnic, film, honors, international, jazz band, LGBT, literary magazine, marching band, musical theater, newspaper, opera, orchestra, pep band, photography, political, professional, radio and TV, religious, social, social service, student government, symphony, and yearbook. Popular campus events include Spring Fling Weeks, Greek Week, and Welcome Week. **Sports:** There are 5 intercollegiate sports for men and 5 for women, and 18 intramural sports for men and 18 for women. The Wellness, Recreation, and Activities Center offers comprehensive, quality programs and services that enhance and promote healthy lifestyles, competition, and leisurely activities with 2 gyms, 4 basketball courts, a 3000-square foot free weights area, a 2800-square foot strength machine weight area, a 2800-square foot cardio-equipment area, a group exercise studio, a spin cycle class studio, a fitness assessment lab, 2 game rooms, 3 racquetball courts, men's and women's locker areas, steam rooms, a massage room, an equipment service center, a student café, meeting rooms, and an indoor track. NSU also boasts a 16,000-seat football stadium, a 5000-seat indoor gym, sports training and basketball centers, a track, and a coliseum. The largest auditorium/arena seats 1500.The Northwestern State University Robert W. Wilson Recreation Complex is a unique facility that provides students with a "country club" atmosphere focused entirely on fun and relaxation. **Graduates:** From July 1, 2015 to June 30, 2016, 1176 bachelor's degrees were awarded. The most popular majors were health professions and related programs (25%), liberal arts and sciences, general studies, and humanities (23%), and education (13%). In an average class, 2% graduate in 3 years or less, 23% graduate in 4 years or less, 35% graduate in 5 years or less, and 40% graduate in 6 years or less.

SERVICES: Counseling and information services are available, as is tutoring in most subjects. There is a reader service for the blind, and remedial math. **Library/Resources:** The library contains 333,427 volumes, 632,044 microform items, and 5,009 audio/video tapes/CDs/DVDs, and subscribes to 751 periodicals including electronic. Computerized library services include interlibrary loans, database searching, Internet access, and Wi-Fi capability. Special learning facilities include an art gallery, natural history museum, radio station, TV station, Cammie G. Henry Research Center - collection of Louisiana books, rare books and documents, Creole Heritage Center - center related to the promotion, fostering, and engagement of activities and endeavors related to Louisiana Creoles and their culture. **Physically Challenged Students:** 96% of the campus is accessible. Facilities include wheelchair ramps, elevators, special parking, specially equipped restrooms, special class scheduling, lowered drinking fountains, lowered telephones, and special housing. **Special:** NSU offers cooperative programs with local businesses, internships, an exchange program in education with South Korea, and work-study programs. A general studies degree, credit for experience, nondegree study, dual majors, and pass/fail options are available. There are 9 national honor societies, a freshman honors program, and 5 departmental honors programs. **Visiting:** There are regularly scheduled orientations for prospective students, consisting of a campus tour, with special focus on financial aid, housing and board, academic requirements, selecting a major, registration, campus organizations, and adapting to the college. There are guides for informal visits and visitors may sit in on classes. To schedule a visit, contact Jana Lucky at (318) 357-4503. **Campus Safety and Security:** Measures include 24-hour foot and vehicle patrol, emergency notification system, self-defense education, and security escort services. There are shuttle buses, emergency telephones, and lighted pathways/sidewalks.

REQUIREMENTS: First Time Freshman Admission: Louisiana High School Graduates must meet the following criteria for regular admission: Complete Regents' Core Curriculum (19 units), earn a minimum 2.35 Cumulative High School GPA, and 18 or Higher ACT English Subscore (450 SAT, 68 COMPASS Writing), or 19 or Higher ACT Math Subscore (460 SAT, 40 COMPASS Algebra), and High School Core GPA 2.0 or 20 ACT (940 SAT). Students should meet the following criteria for conditional admission to the NSU Co-requisite program: The Louisiana Board of Regents approved a pilot program at NSU effective with the fall 2014 semester. Students admitted through the Co-requisite program are admitted conditionally and must complete the required English or math lab within three consecutive semesters to continue at NSU. They must also: 1. Complete Regents' Core Curriculum (19 units). 2. Earn a minimum of 2.35 Cumulative High School GPA, and achieve one of the following criteria: 18 or higher ACT English sub score (450 SAT, 68 COMPASS Writing) and 17 or higher ACT Math sub score (420 SAT, 31 COMPASS Algebra), or 19 or higher ACT Math sub score (460 SAT, 40 COMPASS Algebra), and 16 or higher ACT English sub score (400 SAT, 61 COMPASS Writing), and High School Core GPA 2.0 or 20 ACT (940 SAT), and conditional admission to the NSU/NSTCC Concurrent Enrollment Program (Math only). Northwestern State University and Northshore Technical Community College have entered into an agreement to deliver developmental course requirements to those students who need more than one developmental course. The course is taught at NSU by an NSTCC instructor. Students will transfer the grade from NSTCC to NSU at the end of the semester. Students admitted through the NSU/NSTCC Concurrent Enrollment Program are admitted conditionally until competition of the required math lab within three consecutive semesters to continue at NSU. Students must also complete Regents' Core Curriculum (19 units), earn a minimum 2.35 Cumulative High School GPA, and achieve one of the following criteria: 18 or higher ACT English sub score (450 SAT, 68 COMPASS Writing), and 16 or lower ACT Math sub score (400 or lower SAT, 30 or lower COMPASS Algebra). High School Core GPA 2.00 or 20 ACT (940 SAT) Out of State High Schools, Non-State Approved High Schools, or Home School Programs: Meet one of the In-State criteria above or one of the criteria below: Less than 19 units, but at least 17 units of the Regents' Core Curriculum, and Minimum 2.35 Cumulative High School GPA, and 18 or higher ACT English subscore (450 SAT) or 19 or higher ACT Math subscore (420 SAT) or ACT 23+ (1050 SAT), and 18 or higher ACT English subscore (450 SAT, 68 COMPASS Writing) or 19 or higher ACT Math subscore (460 SAT, 40 COMPASS Algebra). A GPA of 2.0 is required. AP and CLEP credits are accepted. To graduate, all students must complete their senior year in residence, plus an approved 39-hour core curriculum, the university education requirement, and a minimum of 120 semester hours, with at least 30 semester hours in the major field. Distribution requirements include 9 credits each of humanities and natural sciences; 6 each of English, mathematics, and social/behavioral sciences; as well as 3 in fine arts. A minimum 2.0 GPA is needed for all hours taken at NSU. **Procedure:** Freshmen are admitted fall, spring, and summer. Entrance exams should be taken before the semester begins. There are deferred admissions and rolling admissions plans. Check with the school for current application deadlines. The application fee is $20. Applications are accepted on-line. **Transfer Students:** 931 transfer students enrolled in 2015-2016. Students applying for transfer admission must: Have a transferable Associate Degree (AA or AS) or higher from a regionally accredited institution. or 18 college-level hours earned with a 2.0 college level GPA on those hours (this GPA does not include remedial/developmental coursework). Student must have completed a college-level English and a college-level mathematics course (with a grade of "C" in both) designated to fulfill general education requirements (Examples: English Composition I and College Algebra or equivalents). Transfer students who are ages 25 or older can be admitted needing one developmental course. *No transfer student will be admitted, even by exception, if he/she needs any remedial course work. *30 of 120 credits required for the bachelor's degree must be completed at NSU. **International Students:** There are 104 international students enrolled. The school actively recruits these students. They must take the TOEFL with a minimum score of 500 on the paper-based TOEFL (PBT) or 61 on the Internet-based version (iBT). They must also take the SAT or ACT.

ADMISSIONS: The SAT scores for the 2016-2017 freshman class were: Math-- 47% below 500, 42% between 500 and 599, 9% between 600 and 699, and 2% between 700 and 800. Writing-- 73% below 500, 20% between 500 and 599, and 1% between 600 and 699. The ACT scores were 11% between 12 and 17, 60% between 18 and 23, 26% between 24 and 29, and 3% above 30. 50% of the current freshmen were in the top fifth of their class; 15% were in the top two fifths. **Admissions Contact:** Jana Lucky, Director of University Recruiting. Email: *applications@nsula.edu* Web: *www.nsula.edu*

FINANCIAL AID: In 2016-2017, 92% of all full-time freshmen and 88% of continuing full-time students received some form of financial aid. The average freshman award was $11,525. 5% of undergraduate students work part-time. The average financial indebtedness of the 2016 graduate was $26,442. The college's own financial statement is required. The FAFSA code is 002021. Check with the school for current application deadlines.

SOUTHEASTERN LOUISIANA UNIVERSITY D-3

www.southeastern.edu

Hammond, LA 70402 — **(985) 549-5910** / **(800) 222-7358**

Fax: (985) 549-5632 — **Email: admissions@southeastern.edu**

Full-time: 3465 men, 5555 women	**Faculty:** 423; IIA
Part-time: 1669 men, 2870 women	**Ph.D.s:** 65%
Graduate: 251 men, 689 women	**Student/Faculty:** 21 to 1
Year: semesters, summer session	**Tuition:** $7773 ($20,251)
Room & Board: $8464	**Freshman Class:** 3949 applied, 3534 accepted, 2474 enrolled
ACT: 22	**CEEB CODE:** 6656
Application Deadline: August 1	**COMPETITIVE**

Southeastern Louisiana University, founded in 1925, is a public university offering more than 60 undergraduate and graduate degree programs. There are 5 undergraduate schools. In addition to regional accreditation, Southeastern has baccalaureate program accreditation with AACSB, ABET, CSWE, NASAD, NASM, ACS, CCNE, AAFCS, CACREP, ATMAE, CAATE, CAAASLP, and CAEP. The 365-acre campus is in a small town 60 miles northwest of New Orleans and 50 miles east of Baton Rouge. Including any residence halls, there are 101 buildings.

STUDENT LIFE: 95% of undergraduates are from Louisiana. Others are from 38 states, 51 foreign countries, and Canada. 7% are Hispanic; 7%

race unknown; 61% White; 5% two or more races; 2% Asian American; 2% Foreign; 18% African American. **Female To Male Ratio:** 1.7:1. The average age of freshmen is 18; all undergraduates, 21. 37% do not continue beyond their first year; 39% remain to graduate. **Housing:** 2387 students can be accommodated in college housing, which includes single-sex and coed dorms and on-campus apartments. In addition, there are honors houses, fraternity houses, and sorority houses. On-campus housing is available on a first-come, first-served basis. Priority is given to out-of-town students. 82% of students commute. All students may keep cars.

FACULTY/CLASSROOMS: 42% of faculty are male; 58% are female. 92% teach undergraduates, 41% do research, and 41% do both. No introductory courses are taught by graduate students. The average class size in an introductory lecture is 32; in a laboratory is 18; and in a regular course is 18.

PROGRAMS OF STUDY: Southeastern confers B.A., B.S., B.B.A., B.G.S., B.S.N., and B.M. degrees. Associate, master's, and doctoral degrees are also awarded. Bachelor's degrees are awarded in BIOLOGICAL SCIENCE (biology/biological science), BUSINESS (accounting, business administration and management, finance, management, marketing, sports management, and supply chain management), COMMUNICATIONS AND THE ARTS (art, communications, English, information technology, music, and Spanish), COMPUTER AND PHYSICAL SCIENCE (chemistry, computer science, mathematics, and physics), EDUCATION (athletic training, early childhood education, elementary education, English education, health education, middle school education, physical education, social science education, and special education), ENGINEERING AND ENVIRONMENTAL DESIGN (engineering technology, industrial engineering technology, and occupational safety and health), HEALTH PROFESSIONS (health, kinesiology, nursing, and occupational hygiene & safety), SOCIAL SCIENCE (communication sciences & disorders, criminal justice, family/consumer resource management, history, liberal arts/general studies, political science/government, psychology, and social work, and sociology). Nursing, biology, and kinesiology have the largest enrollments.

ACTIVITIES: 2% of men belong to 11 national fraternities; 4% of women belong to 9 national sororities. There are 94 groups on campus, including art, band, cheerleading, choir, computers, dance, environmental, ethnic, film, honors, international, jazz band, LGBT, marching band, musical theater, newspaper, orchestra, photography, political, professional, radio and TV, religious, social, social service, student government, and yearbook. Popular campus events include Fanfare (cultural events monthly), Strawberry Jubilee, and Gumbo Ya Ya. **Sports:** There are 6 intercollegiate sports for men and 7 for women, and 20 intramural sports for men and 20 for women. Facilities include a weight, fitness, and aerobics rooms, an indoor elevated track, basketball, volleyball, badminton, tennis, and racquetball courts, multipurpose fields, a pool, gym, a football stadium, and baseball and soccer fields. **Graduates:** From July 1, 2015 to June 30, 2016, 1760 bachelor's degrees were awarded. The most popular majors were general studies (12%), nursing (8%), and management (8%). In an average class, 18% graduate in 4 years or less, 35% graduate in 5 years or less, and 39% graduate in 6 years or less.

SERVICES: Counseling and information services are available, as is tutoring in some subjects, math, such as English, biology, physics, chemistry, foreign languages, accounting, economics, and computer science. There is remedial math and reading. **Library/Resources:** The library contains 366,589 volumes, 682,166 microform items, and 43,921 audio/video tapes/CDs/DVDs, and subscribes to 1,579 periodicals including electronic. Computerized library services include interlibrary loans, database searching, Internet access, and Wi-Fi capability. Special learning facilities include an art gallery, radio station, and TV station. **Physically Challenged Students:** 90% of the campus is accessible. Facilities include wheelchair ramps, elevators, special parking, specially equipped restrooms, special class scheduling, and special housing. **Special:** Through a special adult learning initiative known as CALL (Center for Adult Learning in Louisiana), Southeastern is now offering registered nurses who are graduates of associate or diploma programs the opportunity to earn their bachelor of science degree in nursing completely online. The Turtle Cove Environmental Research Station is the environmental research, education, outreach, and restoration facility for Southeastern Louisiana University. The Institute for Biodiversity and Interdisciplinary Studies (IBIS) the mission to increase our understanding of the ecosystems of the Gulf Coast and the Lake Pontchartrain drainage basin in particular with an emphasis on fostering interdisciplinary understanding for students and other participants that will allow a generation to address environmental and biodiversity issues in a more comprehensive and inclusive manner. The University also offers summer abroad programs. There are 16 national honor societies, a freshman honors program, and 18 departmental honors programs. **Visiting:** There are regularly scheduled orientations for prospective students, includes a 1-day program of academic advising, class registration, social programs, and session presentations. There are guides for informal visits, visitors may sit in on classes, and stay overnight. To schedule a visit, contact the Admissions Office at admissions@selu.edu. **Campus Safety and Security:** Measures include 24-hour foot and vehicle patrol, emergency notification system, self-defense education, and security escort services. There are shuttle buses, emergency telephones, lighted pathways/sidewalks, controlled access to dorms/residences, community policing, bicycle patrols, and video cameras.

REQUIREMENTS: The ACT is required. Applicants should have completed the Louisiana Regents High School core curriculum, no developmental course requirement, have a minimum high school GPA of 2.35 (ACT 21 or a core GPA of 2.0). AP and CLEP credits are accepted. To graduate, students must complete one of the curricula, including demonstrated profiency in English and math, and have a cumulative degree GPA of 2.0 (2.5 in some majors). **Procedure:** Freshmen are admitted fall, spring, and summer. Entrance exams should be taken prior to registering for classes. There are deferred admissions and rolling admissions plans. Applications should be filed by August 1 for fall entry; December 1 for spring entry; and May 1 for summer entry, along with a $20 fee. Applications are accepted on-line. **Transfer Students:** 599 transfer students enrolled in 2015-2016. Option 1 - Transferrable associate's degree or higher from regionally accredited institution & cumulative GPA of 2.0 or higher. Option 2 - Cumulative GPA of 2.0 or higher on all college work, college-level English and Math credits earned, must be eligible to return to last institution attended. 30 of 120 credits required for the bachelor's degree must be completed at Southeastern. **International Students:** There are 174 international students enrolled. They must take the TOEFL with a minimum score of 500 on the paper-based TOEFL (PBT) or 61 on the Internet-based version (iBT). They must also take the ACT, scoring 21.

ADMISSIONS: 89% of the 2016-2017 applicants were accepted. The ACT scores were 4% between 12 and 17, 64% between 18 and 23, 30% between 24 and 29, and 2% above 30. 28% of the current freshmen were in the top fifth of their class; 59% were in the top two fifths. 42 freshmen graduated first in their class. **Admissions Contact:** Mike Rivault, Interim Director of Admissions. Email: *admissions@southeastern.edu* Web: *www.southeastern.edu*

FINANCIAL AID: The average financial indebtedness of the 2016 graduate was $23,536. Southeastern is a member of CSS. The FAFSA code is 002024. The priority date for freshman financial aid applications for fall entry is May 1.

SOUTHERN UNIVERSITY AND A&M COLLEGE *(The complete profile is made available exclusively on our website, www.barronspac.com)*

SOUTHERN UNIVERSITY AT NEW ORLEANS *(The complete profile is made available exclusively on our website, www.barronspac.com)*

TULANE UNIVERSITY — D-4
www.tulane.edu

New Orleans, LA 70118	**(504) 865-5731** **(800) 873-9283**
Fax: (504) 862-8715	**Email: undergrad.admission@tulane.edu**
Full-time: 2782 men, 3970 women	**Faculty:** 506; I, av$
Part-time: 670 men, 917 women	**Ph.D.s:** 96%
Graduate: 2374 men, 2736 women	**Student/Faculty:** 13 to 1
Year: semesters, summer session	**Tuition:** $49,638
Room & Board: $13,758	**Freshman Class:** 26257 applied, 8008 accepted, 1719 enrolled
SAT CR/M/W: 670/670/680 **ACT:** 31	**CEEB CODE:** 6832
Application Deadline: January 15	**HIGHLY COMPETITIVE+**

Tulane University is one of the country's most respected universities. With top-ranked programs in the academic and professional schools, research and educational partnerships that span the globe. Tulane University offers an unparalleled educational experience. Founded in 1834, Tulane is home to schools and colleges offering undergraduate, graduate, and professional degrees in architecture, business, science and engineering, law, liberal arts, medicine, public health and tropical medicine, and social work. There are 6 undergraduate schools and 8 graduate schools. In addition to regional accreditation, Tulane University has baccalaureate program accreditation with AACSB, ABET, CSAB, CSWE, NAAB, TEAC, and ACS. The 110-acre campus is in an urban area in Uptown New Orleans. Including any residence halls, there are 92 buildings.

STUDENT LIFE: 76% of undergraduates are from out of state, mostly the Northeast. Students are from 50 states, 100 foreign countries, and Canada. 9% are African American; 73% White; 6% Hispanic; 3% Asian American; 3% Foreign; 3% two or more races. **Female To Male Ratio:** 1.3:1. The average age of freshmen is 18; all undergraduates, 22. **Housing:** 4056 students can be accommodated in college housing, which includes single-sex and coed dorms, on-campus apartments, and married student housing. In addition, there are honors houses, special-interest houses, fraternity houses, sorority houses, and special-interest floors. On-campus housing is available on a lottery system for upperclassmen. 55% of students commute. Upperclassmen may keep cars.

FACULTY/CLASSROOMS: 58% of faculty are male; 42% are female. 13% teach undergraduates. No introductory courses are taught by graduate students.

PROGRAMS OF STUDY: Tulane University confers B.A., B.A.R., B.B.S., B.F.A., B.G.S., B.M.T., B.P.A., B.P.E., B.P.H., B.S., B.S.E., B.S.M., B.S.W. and M.Arch degrees. Associate, master's, and doctoral degrees are also awarded. Bachelor's degrees are awarded in BIOLOGICAL SCIENCE (biochemistry, cell biology, ecology, environmental biology, evolutionary biology, molecular biology, and neurosciences), BUSINESS (accounting, banking and finance, business administration and management, entrepreneurial studies, finance, management science, and marketing management), COMMUNICATIONS AND THE ARTS (art history and appreciation, classics, communications, dance, dramatic arts, English, film arts, French, German, Greek (modern), Italian, jazz, journalism, linguistics, media arts, music, music composition, Portuguese, Russian, Spanish, studio art, and theater design), COMPUTER AND PHYSICAL SCIENCE (chemistry, digital arts/technology, earth science, geology, information sciences and systems, mathematics, physics, science, and web technology), EDUCATION (early childhood education, global studies, health education, and psychology education), ENGINEERING AND ENVIRONMENTAL DESIGN (architecture, biomedical engineering, chemical engineering, computer technology, engineering physics, and environmental science), HEALTH PROFESSIONS (community health work and public health), SOCIAL SCIENCE (African studies, American studies, anthropology, Asian/Oriental studies, cognitive science, economics, gender studies, history, homeland security/emergency preparedness, humanities, Judaic studies, Latin American studies, legal studies, liberal arts/general studies, medieval studies, paralegal studies, philosophy, political science/government, psychology, religion, Russian and Slavic studies, social science, social studies, social work, sociology, and women's studies). Environmental sciences, political economy, and preprofessional programs are the strongest academically. Liberal arts, business, and science have the largest enrollments.

ACTIVITIES: 31% of men belong to 12 national fraternities; 51% of women belong to 12 national sororities. There are 344 groups on campus, including art, band, cheerleading, chess, choir, chorale, chorus, communications, computers, dance, debate, drama, drill team, drum and bugle corps, environmental, ethnic, film, honors, international, jazz band, LGBT, literary magazine, marching band, musical theater, newspaper, orchestra, pep band, photography, political, professional, radio and TV, religious, social, social service, student government, symphony, and yearbook. Popular campus events include Crawfest, Wave Good-Bye, Technology Expo, and Homecoming. **Sports:** There are 6 intercollegiate sports for men and 7 for women, and 24 intramural sports for men and 24 for women. Facilities include a baseball diamond, a track complex, tennis facility, a recreation center with indoor and outdoor pools, indoor track, squash and racquetball courts, gymnastics area, weight room, exercise rooms and equipment, and basketball and volleyball facilities. Yulman Stadium is the on-campus venue for football. **Graduates:** From July 1, 2015 to June 30, 2016, 1740 bachelor's degrees were awarded. The most popular majors were business (25%), social science (16%), and biological/life science (10%). 141 companies recruited on campus in 2015-2016.

SERVICES: Counseling and information services are available, as is tutoring in most subjects. There is a reader service for the blind. **Library/Resources:** The 8 libraries contain 4.5 million volumes, 2.5 million microform items, and 156,920 audio/video tapes/CDs/DVDs, and subscribe to 137,773 periodicals including electronic. Computerized library services include interlibrary loans, database searching, Internet access, and Wi-Fi capability. Special learning facilities include an art gallery, natural history museum, radio station, TV station, an observatory, Middle American Research Institute, Amistad Research Center, Tulane Jazz Archives, Latin American Library, Tulane Center for Research on Women, Koch Herbarium, Tulane Museum of Natural History, and Newcomb Art Gallery. **Physically Challenged Students:** 60% of the campus is accessible. Facilities include wheelchair ramps, elevators, special parking, specially equipped restrooms, lowered drinking fountains, lowered telephones, and special housing. **Special:** Students may pursue cross-registration with Loyola and Xavier Universities, numerous internships, study abroad in 23 countries, work-study programs, a Washington semester, and B.A.-B.S. degrees in liberal arts, engineering, and architecture. Tulane also offers accelerated joint degrees with its schools of medicine, law, business, and public health; student-designed, dual, and interdisciplinary majors, including art and biology, Greek and Latin, mathematical economics, political economy, and cognitive studies; a 3-2 engineering degree with Xavier University of Louisiana, joint graduate/professional programs, and 4+1 programs. There are 37 national honor societies, Phi Beta Kappa, a freshman honors program, and 37 departmental honors programs. **Visiting:** There are regularly scheduled orientations for prospective students, including 3 on-campus Saturday programs in the fall, daily information sessions, and tours Monday through Friday and Saturday mornings during the academic year. Also, selected classes are open to visitors. In the spring semester, more structured programs are available daily. There are guides for informal visits, visitors may stay overnight. To schedule a visit, contact the Office of Undergraduate Admissions at undergrad.admission@tulane.edu. **Campus Safety and Security:** Measures include 24-hour foot and vehicle patrol, emergency notification system, self-defense education, and security escort services. There are shuttle buses, emergency telephones, lighted pathways/sidewalks, controlled access to dorms/residences, including trained student patrols, and programs about living safely off campus. Victim resources include academic assistance, legal counseling, emergency housing, and security review of home and personal security habits. In addition, there are bike patrols, limited dorm access, smoke detectors in dorms, and surveillance cameras.

REQUIREMENTS: The SAT or ACT is required. AP credits are accepted. Important factors in the admissions decision are advanced placement or honors courses, recommendations by school officials, and extracurricular activities record. All students in the liberal arts and sciences must meet proficiency requirements in English, foreign language, and math. They must take a distribution component including courses in humanities and fine arts, social sciences, and sciences and math. A total of 120 credits, including at least 24 in the major, with a minimum cumulative GPA of 2.0, is required to graduate. **Procedure:** Freshmen are admitted fall and spring. Entrance exams should be taken during spring of the junior year or fall of the senior year. There is a deferred admissions plan. Applications should be filed by January 15 for fall entry; November 1 for spring entry. Notifications are sent April 1. 3413 applicants were on the 2016 waiting list. Applications are accepted on-line. **Transfer Students:** 132 transfer students enrolled in 2015-2016. Applicants must submit SAT or ACT scores, high school transcripts, proof of good standing at previously attended institutions, and transcripts (with course descriptions) from all colleges or universities attended. A minimum 3.0 GPA is recommended. 60 of 120 credits required for the bachelor's degree must be completed at Tulane University. **International Students:** There are 257 international students enrolled. The school actively recruits these students. They must take the TOEFL with a minimum score of 550 on the paper-based TOEFL (PBT) or 88 on the Internet-based version (iBT). They must also take the SAT or ACT.

ADMISSIONS: 30% of the 2016-2017 applicants were accepted. The SAT scores for the 2016-2017 freshman class were: Critical Reading-- 2% below 500, 12% between 500 and 599, 56% between 600 and 699, and 30% between 700 and 800. Math-- 1% below 500, 12% between 500 and 599, 58% between 600 and 699, and 29% between 700 and 800. Writing-- 1% below 500, 6% between 500 and 599, 53% between 600 and 699, and 39% between 700 and 800. **Admissions Contact:** Earl Retif, VP for Enrollment Management. Email: *undergrad.admission@tulane.edu* Web: *www.tulane.edu*

FINANCIAL AID: In 2016-2017, 42% of all full-time freshmen received some form of financial aid. 42% of all full-time freshmen received need-based aid. 55% of undergraduate students work part-time. Average annual earnings from campus work are $2500. The average financial indebtedness of the 2016 graduate was $32,040. Tulane University is a member of CSS. The CSS/Profile, the Noncustodial Profile, and the Business/Farm Supplement (as applicable) are required. The FAFSA code is 002029. The priority date for freshman financial aid applications for fall entry is February 15.

UNIVERSITY OF HOLY CROSS D-4

Our Lady of Holy Cross College
www.olhcc.edu

New Orleans, LA 70131 **(504) 394-7744**

Fax: (504) 391-2421	**Email:** admissions@olhcc.edu
Full-time: 85 men, 411 women	**Faculty:** n/av
Part-time: 30 men, 243 women	**Ph.D.s:** n/av
Graduate: 84 men, 318 women	**Student/Faculty:** n/av
Year: semesters, summer session	**Tuition:** $12,450
Room & Board: $9073	**Freshman Class:** n/av
	CEEB CODE: 6002
Application Deadline: n/av	**COMPETITIVE**

The University of Holy Cross, founded in 1916, is a private, coed university. UHC prepares our students for life. The University was founded in 1916 as Our Lady of Holy Cross College, a Ministry of the Marianites of Holy Cross, and was created to educate and prepare teachers for work in the many schools the Marianites were opening across South Louisiana. The University's continued unwavering connection to the beliefs of the Marianite Sisters and its roots in educating those who would eventually teach others are both part of the foundation that makes the UHC experience so special. For our students, this means smaller classes, a faith-based atmosphere and more personal attention from a generous, responsive team of professionals. It means collaborating in an exciting, entrepreneurial environment where the focus is always excellence. It means the support of a compassionate, caring faculty and staff all dedicated to making sure you get the most out of your educational experience. There are 4 undergraduate schools. In addition to regional accreditation, UHC has baccalaureate program accreditation with NLN, CACREP, JRCERT, and IACBE. The 16-acre campus is in a suburban area in a residential neighborhood of the Algiers area of New Orleans, Louisiana. Including any residence halls, there are 2 buildings.

STUDENT LIFE: 99% of undergraduates are from Louisiana. Others are from 6 states. 6% are Hispanic; 39% race unknown; 33% White; 3% Asian American; 19% African American; 1% American Indian/Alaska Native. **Female To Male Ratio:** 4.9:1. The average age of freshmen is 18; all undergraduates, 25. 10% do not continue beyond their first year; 70% remain to graduate. **Housing:** College-sponsored housing includes Alcohol is not permitted. All students commute. Some may keep cars.

FACULTY/CLASSROOMS: 20% of faculty are male; 80% are female. 98% teach undergraduates, and 2% do research. No introductory courses are taught by graduate students. The average class size in an introductory lecture is 25; in a laboratory is 24; and in a regular course is 20.

PROGRAMS OF STUDY: UHC confers B.A. and B.S. degrees. Associate, master's, and doctoral degrees are also awarded. Bachelor's degrees are awarded in BIOLOGICAL SCIENCE (biology/biological science), BUSINESS (accounting and business administration and management), COMMUNICATIONS AND THE ARTS (English), EDUCATION (elementary education and secondary education), HEALTH PROFESSIONS (health science and nursing), SOCIAL SCIENCE (behavioral science, history, liberal arts/general studies, social psychology, and social science). Nursing is the strongest academically. Nursing, business, and education have the largest enrollments.

ACTIVITIES: There are no fraternities or sororities. There are 11 groups on campus, including environmental, ethnic, honors, international, professional, social, social service, and student government. Popular campus events include Crawfish Boil and Christmas dances. **Sports:** There are 5 intramural sports for men and 4 for women. Facilities include Frisbee-golf course.

SERVICES: There is remedial math, reading, and writing. **Library/Resources:** The library contains 56,700 volumes, 136,015 microform items, and 13,598 audio/video tapes/CDs/DVDs, and subscribes to 601 periodicals including electronic. Computerized library services include interlibrary loans and database searching. **Physically Challenged Students:** 99% of the campus is accessible. Facilities include wheelchair ramps, elevators, special parking, specially equipped restrooms, lowered drinking fountains, and lowered telephones. **Visiting:** There are regularly scheduled orientations for prospective students. There are guides for informal visits and visitors may sit in on classes. **Campus Safety and Security:** Measures include security escort services. There are lighted pathways/sidewalks, There is a foot patrol inside and outside of the building from 7:30 a.m. to 10 p.m.

REQUIREMENTS: AP and CLEP credits are accepted. Important factors in the admissions decision are leadership record, recommendations by school officials, and recommendations by alumni. A total of 120 credit hours, with 33 to 36 hours in the major, and a minimum GPA of 2.0 are required to graduate. All students must take courses in theology, philosophy, literature, English composition, math, natural sciences, library orientation, social sciences, speech, fine arts, and computer science. **Procedure:** Freshmen are admitted to all sessions. Check with the school for current application deadlines. **International Students:** They must take the TOEFL.

Admissions Contact: Dr. Fawn Ukpolo, Director of Admissions. Email: *admissions@olhcc.edu* Web: *www.olhcc.edu*

FINANCIAL AID: The the college's own financial statement is required. Check with the school for current application deadlines.

UNIVERSITY OF LOUISIANA AT LAFAYETTE C-4

www.louisiana.edu

Lafayette, LA 70504 **(337) 482-6473**

Fax: (337) 482-6195	**Email:** admissions@louisiana.edu
Full-time: 5000 men, 7000 women	**Faculty:** 666
Part-time: 920 men, 1640 women	**Ph.D.s:** 79%
Graduate: 700 men, 930 women	**Student/Faculty:** 18 to 1
Year: semesters, summer session	**Tuition:** $8256 ($19,364)
Room & Board: $6260	**Freshman Class:** n/av
SAT or ACT: required	**CEEB CODE:** 6672
Application Deadline: open	**COMPETITIVE**

University of Louisiana at Lafayette, founded in 1898, is a public institution offering degree programs in liberal arts, fine arts, business, agriculture, technical disciplines, health science, engineering, and teacher preparation. Figures in the above capsule and in this profile are approximate. There are 9 undergraduate schools and one graduate school. In addition to regional accreditation, UL Lafayette has baccalaureate program accreditation with AACSB, ABET, ACEJMC, ADA, AHEA, ASLA, CAHEA, CSAB, FIDER, NAAB, NASM, NCATE, and NLN. The 1375-acre campus is in an urban area 129 miles west of New Orleans. Including any residence halls, there are 239 buildings.

STUDENT LIFE: 95% of undergraduates are from Louisiana. Others are from 48 states, 102 foreign countries, and Canada. 74% are White; 4% Foreign; 2% Asian American; 17% African American; 1% American Indian/Alaska Native; 1% Hispanic. 50% are Catholic; 31% claim no religious affiliation; 12% Protestant. **Female To Male Ratio:** 1.4:1. The average age of freshmen is 19; all undergraduates, 24. 28% do not continue beyond their first year; 30% remain to graduate. **Housing:** 1860 students can be accommodated in college housing, which includes single-sex dorms, on-campus apartments, and married student housing. Residence halls for athletes and for Pan-Hellenic groups available. On-campus housing is guaranteed for all 4 years. 89% of students commute. All students may keep cars.

FACULTY/CLASSROOMS: 59% of faculty are male; 41% are female. No introductory courses are taught by graduate students.

PROGRAMS OF STUDY: UL Lafayette confers B.A., B.S., B.A.M., B.F.A., B.G.S., B.M.E., B.M.P., B.M.P.P., B.S.A., B.S.A.E., B.S.B.A., B.S.C.E., B.S.C.I.E., B.S.E.E., B.S.I.T., B.S.M.E., B.S.N., and B.S.P.E. degrees. Master's and doctoral degrees are also awarded. Bachelor's degrees are awarded in BUSINESS (accounting, banking and finance, business administration and management, fashion merchandising, hotel/motel and restaurant management, management science, marketing/

retailing/merchandising, and personnel management), COMMUNICATIONS AND THE ARTS (advertising, broadcasting, communications, dance, dramatic arts, English, fine arts, French, music, public relations, Spanish, and telecommunications), COMPUTER AND PHYSICAL SCIENCE (chemistry, computer science, geology, mathematics, physics, and statistics), EDUCATION (agricultural education, art education, elementary education, English education, foreign languages education, health education, home economics education, industrial arts education, mathematics education, music education, science education, secondary education, social studies education, and special education), ENGINEERING AND ENVIRONMENTAL DESIGN (chemical engineering, civil engineering, computer engineering, electrical/electronics engineering, industrial engineering, interior design, land use management and reclamation, mechanical engineering, and petroleum/natural gas engineering), HEALTH PROFESSIONS (nursing and speech pathology/audiology), SOCIAL SCIENCE (anthropology, criminal justice, dietetics, economics, history, philosophy, political science/government, psychology, and sociology). Computer science, engineering, and math are the strongest academically. Nursing, elementary education, and business administration have the largest enrollments.

ACTIVITIES: 5% of women belong to 8 national sororities. There are 200 groups on campus, including wakeboard club, camping club, band, cheerleading, choir, chorus, computers, dance, debate, drama, drum and bugle corps, ethnic, forensics, honors, international, jazz band, LGBT, marching band, musical theater, newspaper, opera, orchestra, photography, political, powerlifting club, professional, radio and TV, religious, social, social service, student government, and yearbook. Popular campus events include Rajun Roar, Welcome Week, Homecoming Week, Mardi Gras Parade and Celebration, and Freshman First Down. **Sports:** There are 8 intercollegiate sports for men and 7 for women, and 16 intramural sports for men and 16 for women. Facilities include a stadium, basketball arena, gym, track, a softball park, tennis courts, various playing fields, and a health and phys ed complex. Recreation such as fishing, ice hockey, lacrosse, soccer, bowling, sport shooting, and volleyball offered. **Graduates:** From July 1, 2015 to June 30, 2016, 2494 bachelor's degrees were awarded. The most popular majors were business (20%), general studies (14%), and education (14%). 114 companies recruited on campus in 2015-2016. In an average class, 7% graduate in 4 years or less, 21% graduate in 5 years or less, and 29% graduate in 6 years or less.

SERVICES: Counseling and information services are available, as is tutoring in most subjects. There is remedial math, reading, and writing. Entering freshman can only be in 1 remedial course. **Library/Resources:** The library contains 873,173 volumes, 1.8 million microform items, and 255,992 audio/video tapes/CDs/DVDs, and subscribes to 4,965 periodicals including electronic. Computerized library services include interlibrary loans and database searching. Special learning facilities include an art gallery, radio station, and numerous research centers for environmental, business, science, computer, and business studies. **Physically Challenged Students:** 90% of the campus is accessible. Facilities include wheelchair ramps, elevators, special parking, specially equipped restrooms, and special class scheduling. **Special:** Various internships are available, including a Washington semester. Students may study in France, Canada, Belgium, Japan, and Mexico. UL Lafayette also offers an accelerated degree program in nursing, B.A.-B.S. degrees, and dual majors. There are 6 national honor societies and a freshman honors program. **Visiting:** There are regularly scheduled orientations for prospective students, including campus tours. There are guides for informal visits. To schedule a visit, contact the Admissions Office. **Campus Safety and Security:** Measures include 24-hour foot and vehicle patrol and security escort services. There are shuttle buses, emergency telephones, and lighted pathways/sidewalks.

REQUIREMENTS: The SAT or ACT is required. Admissions criteria are based on a sliding scale of standardized test scores and GPA. Students should be graduates of accredited secondary schools or have the GED. UL Lafayette requires that students have at least 4 units in English, 3 each in math, science, and social studies, and 4 1/2 in electives, recommended to include 2 in foreign language, 1 each in fine arts and speech, and 1/2 in computer studies. A GPA of 2.0 is required. AP and CLEP credits are accepted. Students are required to complete 42 semester hours of general education courses in the arts, literature, history, math, sciences, behavioral sciences, and composition. Phys ed is required in all but engineering and nursing programs. A minimum of 124 semester hours, with at least 33 in the major, is required for graduation. A minimum GPA of 2.0 is needed; some majors require higher GPAs. **Procedure:** Freshmen are admitted to all sessions. There are early admissions, deferred admissions, and rolling admissions plans. Application deadlines are open. Application fee is $20. **Transfer Students:** 740 transfer students enrolled in 2015-2016. A cumulative GPA of 2.0 is required. 30 of 124 credits required for the bachelor's degree must be completed at UL Lafayette. **International Students:** There are 259 international students enrolled. The school actively recruits these students. They must take the TOEFL. They must also take the SAT or ACT.

Admissions Contact: Leroy Broussard, Director of Admissions. Email: *admissions@louisiana.edu* Web: *www.louisiana.edu*

FINANCIAL AID: 30% of undergraduate students work part-time. Average annual earnings from campus work are $1250. UL Lafayette is a member of CSS. The FAFSA code is 002031. The deadline for filing freshman financial aid applications for fall entry is March 1.

UNIVERSITY OF LOUISIANA AT MONROE C-1

www.ulm.edu

Monroe, LA 71209 (318) 342-5259

Email: schmeer@ulm.edu

Full-time: 1856 men, 3352 women	**Faculty:** IIA, --$
Part-time: 985 men, 1585 women	**Ph.D.s:** n/av
Graduate: 413 men, 847 women	**Student/Faculty:** n/av
Year: semesters, summer session	**Tuition:** $8282 ($20,382)
Room & Board: $7688	**Freshman Class:** 3944 applied, 3551 accepted, 1430 enrolled
SAT CR/M: 500/570 **ACT:** 22	**CEEB CODE:** 6482
Application Deadline: open	**COMPETITIVE**

University of Louisiana at Monroe, founded in 1931, is a public institution offering programs in business, education, liberal arts, pharmacy and health sciences, and pure and applied science. There are 3 undergraduate schools and 1 graduate school. In addition to regional accreditation, ULM has baccalaureate program accreditation with AACSB, ABET, ACCE, ACPE, CSWE, NASM, NCATE, ACOTE, CNNE, CODA, CAEP, JRCERT, and NAACLS. The 238-acre campus is in an urban area in Northeast Louisiana, 90 miles east of Shreveport on I-20. Including any residence halls, there are 97 buildings.

STUDENT LIFE: 88% of undergraduates are from Louisiana. Others are from 48 states, 55 foreign countries, and Canada. 65% are White; 4% Foreign; 22% African American; 2% Asian American; 2% Hispanic; 2% two or more races; 2% race unknown. **Female To Male Ratio:** 1.8:1. The average age of freshmen is 18; all undergraduates, 21. **Housing:** 1862 students can be accommodated in college housing, which includes single-sex and coed dorms and on-campus apartments, and a scholastic residence hall. On-campus housing is available on a first-come, first-served basis. 76% of students commute. Alcohol is not permitted. All students may keep cars.

FACULTY/CLASSROOMS: No introductory courses are taught by graduate students.

PROGRAMS OF STUDY: ULM confers B.A., B.S., B.B.A., B.F.A., B.G.S., B.M., and B.S.N. degrees. Associate, master's, and doctoral degrees are also awarded. Bachelor's degrees are awarded in AGRICULTURE (agricultural business management), BIOLOGICAL SCIENCE (biological sciences and toxicology), BUSINESS (accounting, business administration and management, finance, insurance, marketing, management & strategic leadership, and organizational leadership and management), COMMUNICATIONS AND THE ARTS (art, communications, English, foreign language, modern language, and music), COMPUTER AND PHYSICAL SCIENCE (atmospheric science, computer information systems, computer science, mathematics, and radiological technology), EDUCATION (education, elementary education, secondary education, and special education), ENGINEERING AND ENVIRONMENTAL DESIGN (aviation business administration and construction management), HEALTH PROFESSIONS (dental hygiene, exercise science, health science, kinesiology, medical laboratory science, nursing, occupational therapy, pharmaceutical science, pharmacy, and speech pathology/audiology), SOCIAL SCIENCE (criminal justice, history, political science/government, psychology, and social work). Pharmacy, nursing, and health sciences are the strongest academically. Pharmacy, nursing, and kinesiology have the largest enrollments.

ACTIVITIES: 9% of men belong to 7 national fraternities; 11% of

women belong to 8 national sororities. There are 108 groups on campus, including art, band, cheerleading, choir, chorale, chorus, computers, dance, debate, drama, drill team, drum and bugle corps, ethnic, film, forensics, honors, international, jazz band, literary magazine, marching band, musical theater, newspaper, opera, orchestra, pep band, political, professional, radio and TV, religious, social, social service, student government, symphony, and yearbook. Popular campus events include Week of Welcome, Lyceum Series, Spring Fever, and Casino Night. **Sports:** There are 7 intercollegiate sports for men and 10 for women, and 28 intramural sports for men and 28 for women. Facilities include a coliseum, 2 stadiums, tennis courts, a softball complex, an activity center, a baseball complex, outdoor volleyball courts, and a bayou. **Graduates:** From July 1, 2015 to June 30, 2016, 1023 bachelor's degrees were awarded. The most popular majors were political science (9%), general studies (8%), and kinesiology (7%).

SERVICES: Counseling and information services are available, as is tutoring in most subjects. There is remedial math, reading, and writing. **Library/Resources:** The library contains 1.1 million volumes, 578,611 microform items, and subscribes to 83,979 periodicals including electronic. Computerized library services include interlibrary loans, database searching, Internet access, and Wi-Fi capability. Special learning facilities include an art gallery, natural history museum, planetarium, radio station, a herbarium, state poison control center, and state tumor registry. **Physically Challenged Students:** 98% of the campus is accessible. Facilities include wheelchair ramps, elevators, special parking, specially equipped restrooms, special class scheduling, lowered drinking fountains, and specially equipped dorm rooms. **Special:** ULM offers cross registration with selected other institutions as well as internships across a wide variety of academic disciplines. There are 30 national honor societies, a freshman honors program, and 23 departmental honors programs. **Visiting:** There are regularly scheduled orientations for prospective students. Visiting students may participate in the mandatory PREP program, which includes campus tours, meetings with deans/advisers, class registration, and placement examinations. There are guides for informal visits and visitors may sit in on classes. To schedule a visit, contact the Office of Recruitment and Admissions. **Campus Safety and Security:** Measures include 24-hour foot and vehicle patrol, emergency notification system, self-defense education, and security escort services. There are emergency telephones, lighted pathways/sidewalks, and controlled access to dorms/residences.

REQUIREMENTS: The ACT is required. Applicants must be graduates of an accredited high school or have a GED. CLEP credits are accepted. 1 hour university seminar, 6 hours English composition, 6 hours mathematics, 9 hours natural/physical sciences, 9 hours humanities, 3 hours fine arts, 6 hours social/behavioral sciences required. Overall minimum GPA of 2.0 required for graduation, plus variable total hours earned dependent upon program. **Procedure:** Freshmen are admitted to all sessions. Entrance exams should be taken by April 1. There is a rolling admissions plan. Application deadlines are open. The fall 2016 application fee was $20. Applications are accepted on-line. **Transfer Students:** Applicants must have a minimum overall GPA of 2.0 from a regionally accredited institution and at least 12 semester hours of college-level credit above the remedial level, including a math and an English course. Students who have completed fewer than 12 semester hours of college credit must meet ULM freshman admission requirements. 30 credits required for the bachelor's degree must be completed at ULM. **International Students:** There are 282 international students enrolled. The school actively recruits these students. They must take the TOEFL with a minimum score of 61 on the Internet-based version (iBT). They must also take the SAT or ACT.

ADMISSIONS: 90% of the 2016-2017 applicants were accepted. The SAT scores for the 2016-2017 freshman class were: Critical Reading--50% below 500, 34% between 500 and 599, 14% between 600 and 699, and 2% between 700 and 800. Math-- 32% below 500, 27% between 500 and 599, 27% between 600 and 699, and 14% between 700 and 800. The ACT scores were 6% between 12 and 17, 58% between 18 and 23, 54% between 24 and 29, and 5% above 30. **Admissions Contact:** Mary Schmeer, Director of Enrollment and Scholarships. Email: *schmeer@ulm.edu* Web: *www.ulm.edu*

FINANCIAL AID: The FAFSA code is 002020. Check with the school for current application deadlines.

UNIVERSITY OF NEW ORLEANS D-4

www.uno.edu

New Orleans, LA 70148 **(504) 280-6595**

Fax: (504) 280-5522	**Email:** admissions@uno.edu
Full-time: 3104 men, 3400 women	**Faculty:** 326; I
Part-time: 974 men, 1175 women	**Ph.D.s:** 67%
Graduate: 1116 men, 1594 women	**Student/Faculty:** 20 to 1
Year: semesters, summer session	**Tuition:** $7600 ($11,175)
Room & Board: $5240	**Freshman Class:** 1767 applied, 1430 accepted, 1119 enrolled
SAT CR/M/W: 550/550/540 **ACT:** 21	**CEEB CODE:** 6379
Application Deadline: July 25	**COMPETITIVE**

University of New Orleans, founded in 1958, is a public liberal arts institution. Figures in the above capsule and in this profile are approxiate. There are 6 undergraduate schools. In addition to regional accreditation, UNO has baccalaureate program accreditation with AACSB, ABET, NASM, NCATE, NAST, CACREP, and NLN. The 195-acre campus is in an urban area on the southern shore of Lake Pontchartrain, 15 minutes from the French Quarter. Including any residence halls, there are 34 buildings.

STUDENT LIFE: 70% of undergraduates are from Louisiana. Others are from 42 states, 74 foreign countries, and Canada. 62% are from public schools. 7% are Hispanic; 60% White; 6% Asian American; 6% Foreign; 19% African American; 1% American Indian/Alaska Native. 67% claim no religious affiliation; 19% Catholic. **Female To Male Ratio:** 1.2:1. The average age of freshmen is 19; all undergraduates, 24. 31% do not continue beyond their first year. **Housing:** 1426 students can be accommodated in college housing, which includes coed dorms and married student housing. On-campus housing is available on a first-come, first-served basis. 95% of students commute. All students may keep cars.

FACULTY/CLASSROOMS: 59% of faculty are male; 41% are female. No introductory courses are taught by graduate students.

PROGRAMS OF STUDY: UNO confers B.A., B.S. and B.G.S. degrees. Master's and doctoral degrees are also awarded. Bachelor's degrees are awarded in BIOLOGICAL SCIENCE (biology/biological science), BUSINESS (accounting, banking and finance, business administration and management, hotel/motel and restaurant management, marketing/retailing/merchandising, and tourism), COMMUNICATIONS AND THE ARTS (art, art history and appreciation, communications, dramatic arts, English, fine arts, French, music, Spanish, and studio art), COMPUTER AND PHYSICAL SCIENCE (chemistry, computer science, earth science, geology, geophysics and seismology, mathematics, and physics), EDUCATION (early childhood education, elementary education, English education, foreign languages education, mathematics education, music education, physical education, and secondary education), ENGINEERING AND ENVIRONMENTAL DESIGN (civil engineering, electrical/electronics engineering, environmental science, marine engineering, mechanical engineering, and naval architecture and marine engineering), HEALTH PROFESSIONS (health, medical technology, premedicine, and preveterinary science), SOCIAL SCIENCE (anthropology, economics, geography, history, international studies, philosophy, political science/government, psychology, sociology, and urban studies). Business administration, general studies, and film have the largest enrollments.

ACTIVITIES: 1% of men belong to 8 national fraternities; 1% of women belong to 8 national sororities. There are 108 groups on campus, including art, band, choir, chorale, chorus, computers, dance, drama, ethnic, film, honors, international, jazz band, LGBT, literary magazine, newspaper, opera, orchestra, pep band, political, professional, radio and TV, religious, social, social service, and student government. Popular campus events include International Night, Privateer Plunge for New Students, Homecoming, Holi a Hindu Celebration, Krewe of UNO Parade, Swampball, Behind the Scenes, and Commencement Celebration. **Sports:** There are 3 intercollegiate sports for men and 3 for women, and 10 intramural sports for men and 10 for women. Facilities include a lakefront arena, a Privateer Park, 1/10 mile indoor jogging/walking track, various group exercise classes such as indoor cycling, yoga and step aerobics, 2 dry saunas, 2 racquetball courts, 3 basketball courts, snack bar, outdoor deck adjacent to pool, and natatorium (25-yard/4-lane lap pool) for water group exercise and lap/recreational swimming. **Graduates:** From

July 1, 2015 to June 30, 2016, 1368 bachelor's degrees were awarded. The most popular majors were business (16%), psychology (5%), and film, theater, and communication arts (5%). 284 companies recruited on campus in 2015-2016. In an average class, 47% graduate in 4 years or less, 64% graduate in 5 years or less, and 88% graduate in 6 years or less.

SERVICES: Counseling and information services are available, as is tutoring in most subjects. There is a reader service for the blind, and remedial math, reading, and writing. **Library/Resources:** The library contains 896,000 volumes, 12.4 million microform items, and 22,775 audio/video tapes/CDs/DVDs, and subscribes to 4,950 periodicals including electronic. Computerized library services include interlibrary loans, database searching, and Internet access. Special learning facilities include an art gallery and radio station. **Physically Challenged Students:** 80% of the campus is accessible. Facilities include wheelchair ramps, elevators, special parking, specially equipped restrooms, lowered drinking fountains, lowered telephones, and special housing. **Special:** Students may participate in co-op programs and may cross-register with Southern University in New Orleans, Elaine P. Nunez Community College, and Delgado Community College. Internships are available, and work-study programs are available with various federal agencies and private companies. Students may study abroad in 14 countries or participate in a Washington semester. UNO also offers dual majors, B.A.-B.S. and degrees, pre-professional programs in cardiopulmonary science, dental hygiene, dentistry, medical technology, medicine, nursing, occupational therapy, opthhalmic medical technology, pharmacy, physical therapy, physician's assistant, rehabilitation counseling, and veterinary medicine. 3-2 engineering degrees with Xavier University, Southern University in New Orleans, Loyola University New Orleans, and Dillard University are offered. There are 12 national honor societies, a freshman honors program, and 29 departmental honors programs. **Visiting:** There are guides for informal visits. To schedule a visit, contact Privateer Enrollment Center at leverink@uno.edu. **Campus Safety and Security:** Measures include 24-hour foot and vehicle patrol, emergency notification system, self-defense education, and security escort services. There are emergency telephones, lighted pathways/sidewalks, and monitored parking.

REQUIREMENTS: Students who graduate from state-approved high schools must complete the Louisiana Board of Regents Core Curriculum and require no more than one developmental/remedial course and meet one of the following criteria: ACT composite score of 23 or greater (SAT 1060) or high school cumulative GPA of 2.5 or greater with an ACT (SAT equivalent) of 18 or greater on the English and or Math sub scores OR, high school graduation rank top 25% of class. UNO requires applicants to be in the upper 25% of their class. A GPA of 2.5 is required. AP and CLEP credits are accepted. Important factors in the admissions decision are advanced placement or honors courses, recommendations by school officials, and evidence of special talent. Requirements for graduation include completion of courses in English, literature, math, humanities and art, science, social science, and computer literacy. Students must complete 120 hours with a minimum GPA of 2.0. **Procedure:** Freshmen are admitted to all sessions. Entrance exams should be taken at least 6 months prior to enrollment. There are early admissions, deferred admissions, and rolling admissions plans. Applications should be filed by July 25 for fall entry; November 15 for spring entry; and May 1 for summer entry, along with a $40 fee. Applications are accepted on-line. **Transfer Students:** A student must have completed at least 18 hours of non-remedial course-work, have a 2.25 GPA from an accredited college or university, and completed all developmental course-work before transferring. Students who have not earned at least 18 hours of non-remedial course work, are required to submit an official high school transcript and official ACT or SAT test scores. 30 of 120 credits required for the bachelor's degree must be completed at UNO. **International Students:** There are 267 international students enrolled. The school actively recruits these students. They must take the TOEFL with a minimum score of 525 on the paper-based TOEFL (PBT) or 71 on the Internet-based version (iBT). If they do not have the TOEFL, they must submit the ACT or SAT.

ADMISSIONS: 81% of the 2016-2017 applicants were accepted. The SAT scores for the 2016-2017 freshman class were: Critical Reading-- 35% below 500, 31% between 500 and 599, 30% between 600 and 699, and 4% between 700 and 800. Math-- 32% below 500, 34% between 500 and 599, 29% between 600 and 699, and 5% between 700 and 800. Writing-- 35% below 500, 40% between 500 and 599, 22% between 600 and 699, and 3% between 700 and 800. The ACT scores were 37% below 12, 35% between 12 and 17, 18% between 18 and 23, 6% between 24 and 29, and 4% above 30. **Admissions Contact:** Office of Admissions Email: *admissions@uno.edu* Web: *www.uno.edu*

FINANCIAL AID: In 2016-2017, 71% of all full-time freshmen and 67% of continuing full-time students received some form of financial aid. 46% of all full-time freshmen and 45% of continuing full-time students received need-based aid. The average freshman award was $6,830. UNO is a member of CSS. The deadline for filing freshman financial aid applications for fall entry is May 15.

XAVIER UNIVERSITY OF LOUISIANA D-4

www.xula.edu

New Orleans, LA 70125	**(504) 520-7388** **(877) XAVIERU**
Fax: (504) 520-7941	**Email: apply@xula.edu**
Full-time: 577 men, 1620 women	**Faculty:** 221
Part-time: 34 men, 62 women	**Ph.D.s:** 96%
Graduate: 191 men, 479 women	**Student/Faculty:** 14 to 1
Year: semesters, summer session	**Tuition:** $23,166
Room & Board: $8523	**Freshman Class:** 6640 applied, 4084 accepted, 764 enrolled
SAT CR/M/W: 509/494/476 **ACT:** 24	**CEEB CODE:** 6975
Application Deadline: July 1	**COMPETITIVE+**

Xavier University of Louisiana, founded by Saint Katharine Drexel and the Sisters of the Blessed Sacrament, is Catholic and historically Black. The ultimate purpose of the University is to contribute to the promotion of a more just and humane society by preparing its students to assume roles of leadership and service in a global society. This preparation takes place in a diverse learning and teaching environment that incorporates all relevant educational means, including research and community service. There is 1 undergraduate school and 1 graduate school. In addition to regional accreditation, Xavier has baccalaureate program accreditation with ACBSP, ACPE, NASM, and NCATE. The 29-acre campus is in an urban area 2 miles from downtown New Orleans. Including any residence halls, there are 65 buildings.

STUDENT LIFE: 60% of undergraduates are from Louisiana. Others are from 40 states, and 12 foreign countries. 20% are from public schools. 9% are Asian American; 78% African American; 3% White; 3% Hispanic; 3% two or more races. 30% are Baptist; 25% Catholic. **Female To Male Ratio:** 2.7:1. The average age of freshmen is 18; all undergraduates, 20. 28% do not continue beyond their first year; 41% remain to graduate. **Housing:** 1433 students can be accommodated in college housing, which includes single-sex and coed dorms and on-campus apartments. In addition, there are honors houses, and wellness housing. On-campus housing is available on a first-come and first-served basis. Priority is given to out-of-town students. 52% of students commute. Alcohol is not permitted. All students may keep cars.

FACULTY/CLASSROOMS: 52% of faculty are male; 48% are female. No introductory courses are taught by graduate students. The average class size in an introductory lecture is 25; in a laboratory is 21; and in a regular course is 21.

PROGRAMS OF STUDY: Xavier confers B.A., B.S., and B.M. degrees. Master's and doctoral degrees are also awarded. Bachelor's degrees are awarded in BIOLOGICAL SCIENCE (biochemistry and biology/biological science), BUSINESS (accounting, business administration and management, and business economics), COMMUNICATIONS AND THE ARTS (communications, English, fine arts, French, languages, music, music performance, and Spanish), COMPUTER AND PHYSICAL SCIENCE (chemistry, computer science, mathematics, physics, and statistics), EDUCATION (art education, elementary education, English education, mathematics education, middle school education, music education, science education, and social studies education), HEALTH PROFESSIONS (premedicine and speech pathology/audiology), SOCIAL SCIENCE (history, philosophy, political science/government, psychology, sociology, and theological studies). Science, education, and English are the strongest academically. Pharmacy, biology, and business have the largest enrollments.

ACTIVITIES: 1% of men belong to 4 national fraternities; 2% of women belong to 4 national sororities. There are 80 groups on campus, including art, band, cheerleading, chess, choir, chorus, communications, computers, dance, debate, drill team, ethnic, honors, international, jazz band, literary magazine, newspaper, opera, pep band, political, professional, radio and TV, religious, social, social service, student government, symphony, and yearbook. Popular campus events include Wellness Week, Octoberfest, Homecoming, Neophyte Show, and Culturefest. **Sports:** There are 4 intercollegiate sports for men and 3 for women, and 12 intramural sports for men and 12 for women. Facilities include a health and fitness center. **Graduates:** From July 1, 2015 to June 30, 2016, 353 bachelor's degrees were awarded. The most popular majors were biological/life sciences (37%), physical sciences (14%), and psychology (11%). 25 companies recruited on campus in 2015-2016. In an average class, 29% graduate in 4 years or less, 40% graduate in 5 years or less, and 43% graduate in 6 years or less. Of the 2015 graduating class, 31% were enrolled in graduate school within 6 months of graduation, and 14% were employed.

SERVICES: Counseling and information services are available, as is tutoring in every subject. There is a reader service for the blind, and remedial math, reading, and writing. **Library/Resources:** The library contains 261,000 volumes, 779,654 microform items, and 6,074 audio/video tapes/CDs/DVDs, and subscribes to 1,624 periodicals including electronic. Computerized library services include interlibrary loans, database searching, Internet access, and Wi-Fi capability. Special learning facilities include an art gallery, radio station, TV station, Confucius Institute, and Xavier University of Louisiana Confucius Institute, in partnering with Hebei University in China, is the first Confucius Institute among the nation's HBCUs and in the State of Louisiana. The Confucius Institute helps prepare students to become global leaders, and to teach Chinese language, culture, and economic development courses to Xavier students and the surrounding communities, including local groups, government agencies, and businesses. It also aims to facilitate research activities in the above areas and promote increased understanding between the United States and China. **Physically Challenged Students:** 99% of the campus is accessible. Facilities include wheelchair ramps, elevators, special parking, specially equipped restrooms, special class scheduling, lowered drinking fountains, lowered telephones, and special housing. **Special:** The university offers cooperative programs in any major and 3-2 engineering degrees with Tulane, Louisiana State, Morgan State, and Southern Universities as well as the Universities of Wisconsin, Maryland, New Orleans, and Detroit, and Georgia Institute of Technology. In addition, students may cross-register at colleges of the New Orleans Consortium. Internships are available in legal, political, and pharmaceutical areas. Students may earn an accelerated degree in biology, chemistry, psychology, or political science, pursue dual majors in engineering and biostatistics, opt for non-degree study, and earn a B.A.-B.S. degree in almost any combination. Students may study abroad in 6 countries or participate in an exchange program with Notre Dame University. There are 7 national honor societies, a freshman honors program, and 7 departmental honors programs. **Visiting:** There are guides for informal visits, visitors may sit in on classes, and stay overnight. To schedule a visit, contact the Admissions Office. **Campus Safety and Security:** Measures include 24-hour foot and vehicle patrol, emergency notification system, and security escort services. There are shuttle buses, emergency telephones, and lighted pathways/sidewalks.

REQUIREMENTS: The SAT or ACT is required. Applicants must have earned a high school diploma or the GED. Candidates must also have completed 16 academic units; 4 units of English, 2-4 of math, and 2-3 science, 1 unit of social studies, and 7 of academic electives, and recommended 1 each of foreign language and history. A GPA of 2.0 is required. AP and CLEP credits are accepted. Important factors in the admissions decision are advanced placement or honors courses and recommendations by school officials. Requirements for graduation include 9 semester hours in English, 6 each in history, social science, language, theology, philosophy, and natural sciences, 3 each in speech, math, and the arts, and 1 in health and phys ed. Students must complete 128 to 132 total credit hours, including 24 to 54 total hours in the major. Students must maintain a minimum GPA of 2.0, take Introduction to African American History/Culture, pass a comprehensive exam, and by the beginning of the junior year declare a minor in an academic discipline other than the major. **Procedure:** Freshmen are admitted fall, spring, and summer. Entrance exams should be taken in the spring of the junior year or the fall of the senior year. Early decision applications should be filed by March 1; regular applications, by July 1 for fall entry. Notification of early decision is sent October 15; regular decision, April 15. 100 applicants were on the 2016 waiting list. Applications are accepted on-line. **Transfer Students:** 128 transfer students enrolled in 2015-2016. Applicants must submit college transcripts. High school transcripts are required of applicants with fewer than 30 transferable credits. Enrollment for Admissions are in the fall and spring. 30 of 128 credits required for the bachelor's degree must be completed at Xavier. **International Students:** There are 33 international students enrolled. They must take the TOEFL. They must also take the SAT or ACT.

ADMISSIONS: 29% of the current freshmen were in the top fifth of their class; 55% were in the top two fifths. **Admissions Contact:** Winston D. Brown, Dean of Admissions. Email: *apply@xula.edu* Web: *www.xula.edu*

FINANCIAL AID: In 2016-2017, 93% of all full-time freshmen and 90% of continuing full-time students received some form of financial aid. 86% of all full-time freshmen and 82% of continuing full-time students received need-based aid. The average freshman award was $22,835. Need-based scholarships or need-based grants averaged $5,773; need-based self-help aid (loans and jobs) averaged $5,417; non-need-based athletic scholarships averaged $14,963; other non-need-based awards and non-need-based scholarships averaged $12,833; and $4,698 from other forms of aid. The average financial indebtedness of the 2016 graduate was $26,106. Xavier is a member of CSS. The FAFSA code is 002032. The priority date for freshman financial aid applications for fall entry is January 1. The deadline for filing freshman financial aid applications for fall entry is rolling.

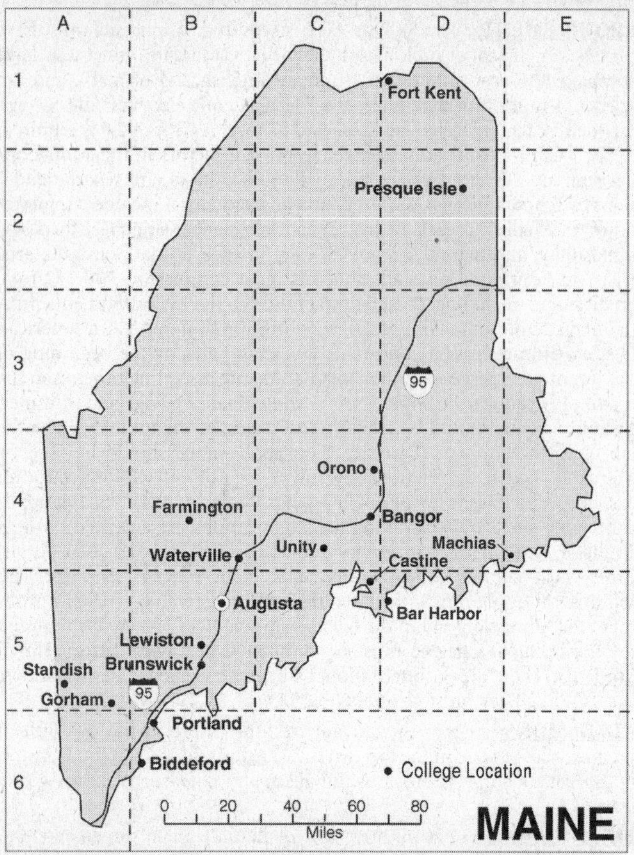

BATES COLLEGE B-5
www.bates.edu

Lewiston, ME 04240	(207) 786-6000 1-855-228-3755
Fax: (207) 786-6025	Email: admission@bates.edu
Full-time: 881 men, 899 women	**Faculty:** 163; IIB, ++$
Part-time: n/av	**Ph.D.s:** 93%
Graduate: n/av	**Student/Faculty:** 10 to 1
Year: other	**Tuition:** $50,310
Room & Board: $14,190	**Freshman Class:** 5356 applied, 1213 accepted, 484 enrolled
SAT CR/M/W: 630/640/630 **ACT:** 30	**CEEB CODE:** 3076
Application Deadline: January 1	**MOST COMPETITIVE**

Bates College is a private, highly selective, residential college devoted to undergraduate study in the liberal arts. Bates has always stood firmly for the ideals of academic rigor, intellectual curiosity, egalitarianism, social justice, and freedom. Bates is recognized for its inclusive social character and progressive tradition, and is rightly celebrated as one of the first U.S. institutions of higher learning to admit women and people of color. A Bates education fosters intellectual inquiry and reflection, personal growth, and a commitment to the world beyond oneself. There is one undergraduate school. In addition to regional accreditation, Bates has baccalaureate program accreditation with CFAT and ACS. The 133-acre campus is in a small town 35 miles north of Portland. Including any residence halls, there are 170 buildings.

STUDENT LIFE: 90% of undergraduates are from out of state, mostly the Northeast. Students are from 43 states, 60 foreign countries, and Canada. 55% are from public schools. 9% are Hispanic; 70% White; 7% Foreign; 6% African American; 4% Asian American; 4% two or more races. **Female To Male Ratio:** 1.0:1. The average age of freshmen is 19; all undergraduates, 20. 5% do not continue beyond their first year; 88% remain to graduate. **Housing:** 1715 students can be accommodated in college housing, which includes single-sex and coed dorms. In addition, there are special-interest houses, chemical-free housing, quiet/study housing, and themed-based housing (by application; ex. sustainability, arts). On-campus housing is guaranteed for all 4 years. 90% of students live on campus; of those, 100% remain on campus on weekends. All students may keep cars.

FACULTY/CLASSROOMS: 49% of faculty are male; 51% are female. All teach undergraduates, and all do research. No introductory courses are taught by graduate students.

PROGRAMS OF STUDY: Bates confers B.A. and B.S. degrees. Bachelor's degrees are awarded in AGRICULTURE (environmental studies), BIOLOGICAL SCIENCE (biochemistry, biology/biological science, and neurosciences), COMMUNICATIONS AND THE ARTS (art/visual culture, Chinese, English, French and Francophone studies, German, Japanese, music, Russian, Spanish, speech/debate/rhetoric, and theatre acting), COMPUTER AND PHYSICAL SCIENCE (chemistry, geology, mathematics, and physics), EDUCATION (Asian studies), SOCIAL SCIENCE (African American studies, American studies, anthropology, classical/ancient civilization, East Asian studies, economics, European studies, history, interdisciplinary studies, Latin American studies, medieval studies, philosophy, political science/government, psychology, religious studies, sociology, and women & gender studies). Economics, politics, and psychology have the largest enrollments.

ACTIVITIES: There are no fraternities or sororities. There are 110 groups on campus, including art, chess, choir, chorale, chorus, computers, dance, debate, drama, environmental, ethnic, film, honors, international, jazz band, LGBT, literary magazine, musical theater, newspaper, orchestra, pep band, photography, political, professional, radio and TV, religious, social, social service, student government, symphony, and yearbook. Popular campus events include Parents and Family Weekend, Homecoming, Mount David Summit, Winter Carnival, Reunion Weekend, International Dinners, and Ocean Clambakes. **Sports:** There are 21 intercollegiate sports for men and 22 for women, and 12 intramural sports for men and 12 for women. Bates offers a pool, a field house, indoor and outdoor tracks, indoor and outdoor tennis courts, 3 basketball courts, 3 volleyball courts, dance and fencing space, squash and racquetball courts, training rooms, a rock-climbing wall, a boat house, a winter sports arena, a weight room and football, soccer, baseball, softball, and lacrosse fields. **Graduates:** From July 1, 2015 to June 30, 2016, 462 bachelor's degrees were awarded. The most popular majors were economics (13%), politics (13%), and psychology (11%). In an average class, 84% graduate in 4 years or less, 87% graduate in 5 years or less, and 88% graduate in 6 years or less.

SERVICES: Counseling and information services are available, as is tutoring in every subject. There is a reader service for the blind, and remedial math and writing. **Library/Resources:** The library contains 550,000 volumes, 183,300 microform items, and 35,783 audio/video tapes/CDs/DVDs, and subscribes to 73,000 periodicals including electronic. Computerized library services include interlibrary loans, database searching, Internet access, and Wi-Fi capability. Special learning facilities include an art gallery, planetarium, radio station, TV station, a learning research center, art gallery, planetarium, radio station, television studio, a 654-acre mountain conservation area, an observatory, a language resource center, and the Edmund S. Muskie archives. **Physically Challenged Students:** 80% of the campus is accessible. Facilities include wheelchair ramps, elevators, special parking, specially equipped restrooms, special class scheduling, lowered drinking fountains, and lowered telephones. **Special:** Bates College offers co-op programs in engineering, internships, research apprenticeships, work-study programs, study abroad, and a Washington semester. Student-designed, and interdisciplinary majors, and a dual-degree 3-2 engineering degree with Columbia University, Dartmouth College, Case Western Reserve University, Rensselaer Polytechnic Institute, and Washington University in St. Louis are available. Students in any major may graduate in 3 years. Students may also participate in the Williams-Mystic Seaport program in marine biology and maritime history, and exchanges with Spelman College, Morehouse College, Washington and Lee University, and McGill University are possible. There are 3 national honor societies, Phi Beta Kappa, and 32 departmental honors programs. **Visiting:** There are guides for informal visits, visitors may sit in on classes, and stay overnight. To schedule a visit, contact the Office of Admission at (855) 228-3755. **Campus Safety and Security:** Measures include 24-hour foot and vehicle patrol, emergency notification system, self-defense education, and security escort services. There are shuttle buses, emergency telephones, lighted pathways/sidewalks, controlled access to dorms/residences, electronic access control in residence halls and all major buildings on campus, automated 911 telephone system, and emergency public address system.

REQUIREMENTS: Candidates for admission should have completed at least 4 years of English, 3 each of math, social science, and a foreign language, and 2 of lab science. Essays are required and an interview on or off campus is strongly recommended. The submission of test scores is optional. AP credits are accepted. Important factors in the admissions decision are advanced placement or honors courses, evidence of special talent, and leadership record. Requirements for graduation include one major plus two general education concentrations (which comprise four courses and may alternatively be satisfied by another major(s) or minor(s) or a combination thereof); three writing attentive courses; and three courses focused on scientific reasoning, laboratory experience, and quantitative literacy. The total number of hours in the major varies by department, but students should take at least 32 courses, plus 2 short terms, and maintain a minimum GPA of 2.0. All majors require a senior thesis or capstone project. **Procedure:** Freshmen are admitted fall and winter. There are early decision and deferred admissions plans. Early decision applications should be filed by November 15; regular applications, by January 1 for fall entry; and November 1 for winter entry, along with a $60 fee. Notification of early decision is sent December 20; regular decision, April 1. 273 early decision candidates were accepted for the 2016-2017 class. 1536 applicants were on the 2016 waiting list; 11 were admitted. Applications are accepted on-line. Application fees are waived if application is completed on-line. **Transfer Students:** 5 transfer students enrolled in 2015-2016. More weight is given to the student's college record than to high school credentials. Applicants must submit official college and final high school transcripts, a statement of good standing, 3 letters of recommendation, and an essay. An interview is strongly recommended. 16 of 32 credits required for the bachelor's degree must be completed at Bates. **International Students:** There are 122 international students enrolled. The school actively recruits these students. They must take the TOEFL.

ADMISSIONS: 23% of the 2016-2017 applicants were accepted. The SAT scores for the 2016-2017 freshman class were: Critical Reading-- 5% below 500, 28% between 500 and 599, 45% between 600 and 699, and 22% between 700 and 800. Math-- 5% below 500, 27% between 500 and 599, 42% between 600 and 699, and 26% between 700 and 800. Writing-- 6% below 500, 24% between 500 and 599, 47% between 600 and 699, and 23% between 700 and 800. The ACT scores were 1% between 12 and 17, 9% between 18 and 23, 36% between 24 and 29, and 54% above 30. 79% of the current freshmen were in the top fifth of their class; 92% were in the top two fifths. **Admissions Contact:** Leigh Weisenburger, Dean of Admission and Financial Aid. Email: *admission@bates.edu* Web: *www.bates.edu*

FINANCIAL AID: In 2016-2017, 47% of all full-time freshmen and 46% of continuing full-time students received some form of financial aid. 42% of all full-time freshmen and 43% of continuing full-time students received need-based aid. The average freshman award was $43,523. Bates is a member of CSS. The CSS/Profile, FAFSA, and parent and student tax returns and W-2 forms are required. The FAFSA code is 002036. The deadline for filing freshman financial aid applications for fall entry is February 15.

BOWDOIN COLLEGE B-5

www.bowdoin.edu

Brunswick, ME 04011 **(207) 725-3100**

Fax: (207) 725-3101	**Email:** admissions@bowdoin.edu
Full-time: 901 men, 900 women	**Faculty:** 195; IIB, ++$
Part-time: 1 men, 4 women	**Ph.D.s:** 99%
Graduate: n/av	**Student/Faculty:** 9 to 1
Year: semesters	**Tuition:** $49,900
Room & Board: $13,600	**Freshman Class:** 6799 applied, 1009 accepted, 503 enrolled
SAT CR/M/W: 710/710/710 **ACT:** 32	**CEEB CODE:** 3089
Application Deadline: January 1	**MOST COMPETITIVE**

Bowdoin College, established in 1794, is a private liberal arts institution. In addition to regional accreditation, Bowdoin has baccalaureate program accreditation with ACS. The 207-acre campus is in a small town 25 miles northeast of Portland. Including any residence halls, there are 120 buildings.

STUDENT LIFE: 90% of undergraduates are from out of state, mostly the Northeast. Students are from 48 states, 32 foreign countries, and Canada. 50% are from public schools. 7% are two or more races; 64% White; 6% African American; 6% Asian American; 5% Foreign; 11% Hispanic; 1% race unknown. 42% claim no religious affiliation; 23% Catholic; 21% Protestant. **Female To Male Ratio:** 1.0:1. The average age of freshmen is 18; all undergraduates, 20. 6% do not continue beyond their first year; 94% remain to graduate. **Housing:** 1756 students can be accommodated in college housing, which includes coed dorms, on-campus apartments, and off-campus apartments. All first-year students participate in the College House System; their residence floor is affiliated with one of eight College Houses. All upperclass students are also eligible to participate. Housing is guaranteed for first-year and sophomore students; historically, Bowdoin has also accommodated any junior or senior who desired on-campus housing. On-campus housing is available on a lottery system for upperclassmen. 88% of students live on campus; of those, 95% remain on campus on weekends. Upperclassmen may keep cars.

FACULTY/CLASSROOMS: 49% of faculty are male; 51% are female. All teach undergraduates, and all do research. No introductory courses are taught by graduate students. The average class size in an introductory lecture is 28; in a laboratory is 12; and in a regular course is 16.

PROGRAMS OF STUDY: Bowdoin confers A.B. degrees. Bachelor's degrees are awarded in AGRICULTURE (environmental studies), BIOLOGICAL SCIENCE (biochemistry, biology/biological science, and neurosciences), COMMUNICATIONS AND THE ARTS (Africana studies, art history, classics, English, French, German, music, romance languages and literature, Russian, Spanish, studio art, and theatre arts), COMPUTER AND PHYSICAL SCIENCE (chemical physics, chemistry, computer mathematics, computer science, earth science, mathematics, mathematics – economics, oceanography, and physics), EDUCATION (Asian studies, education, and mathematics education), SOCIAL SCIENCE (anthropology, archeology, classical/ancient civilization, Eastern European studies, economics, gender studies, history, interdisciplinary studies, Latin American studies, philosophy, political science/government, psychology, religion, sociology, and women's studies). Biology, economics, and government and legal studies are the strongest academically. Government and legal studies, economics, and mathematics have the largest enrollments.

ACTIVITIES: There are no fraternities or sororities. There are 120 groups on campus, including Students for Justice in Palestine, equestrian club, cultural clubs, curling club, environmental awareness groups, fencing club, literary society, mock trial, organic garden club, outing club, peer counseling and advising, science clubs, ski and ride, slam poets society, art, cheerleading, chess, choir, chorus, communications, dance, drama, environmental, ethnic, film, honors, improvisational comedy, international, jazz band, LGBT, literary magazine, musical theater, newspaper, political, professional, radio and TV, religious, social, social service, and student government. Popular campus events include Common Good Day, Ivies Weekend, Winter Weekend, Asia Week, Student Night at the Museum of Art, Student Night at the Arctic Museum, Junior/Senior Ball, First-Year/Sophomore Semi Formal, Common Hour, Spring Gala, and Bowdoin-Colby Ice Hockey Games. **Sports:** There are 15 intercollegiate sports for men and 17 for women, and 6 intramural sports for men and 6 for women. Facilities include ice arena, field house, swimming pool, two gyms, indoor and outdoor track facilities, tennis and squash courts, climbing wall, crew boathouse, outdoor leadership center, and cross-country ski trails. The fitness center offers cardiovascular fitness equipment, weight machines, free weights, and rowing machines along with a variety of fitness classes. There are sixty acres of playing fields for football, baseball, softball, lacrosse, field hockey, soccer, rugby, and ultimate frisbee. **Graduates:** From July 1, 2015 to June 30, 2016, 461 bachelor's degrees were awarded. The most popular majors were government and legal studies (19%), economics (13%), and biology (8%). 140 companies recruited on campus in 2015-2016. In an average class, 89% graduate in 4 years or less, 94% and graduate in 5 years or less. Of the 2015 graduating class, 9% were enrolled in graduate school within 6 months of graduation.

SERVICES: Counseling and information services are available, as is tutoring in most subjects. There is a reader service for the blind. A counselor is available to assist students with accommodations as needed. Tutoring is available through the Quantitative Reasoning Program and the Writing Project. **Library/Resources:** The 4 libraries contain 1.5 million volumes, 33,052 microform items, and 29,736 audio/video tapes/CDs/DVDs, and subscribe to 64,688 periodicals including electronic. Computerized library services include interlibrary loans, database searching, Internet access, and Wi-Fi capability. Special learning facilities include an art gallery, radio station, TV station, Museum of Art, Arctic Museum, language media center, women's resource center, electronic classroom, coastal studies center and marine laboratory, individual and group screening rooms, production studios, multimedia lab, African American center, crafts center, ceramics studio, photography darkroom, printmaking studio, woodworking studio, sculpture studio, dance studio, scientific station located in the Bay of Fundy, educational research and development program, theaters, music halls, recording studio, community service resource center, environmental studies center, and visual arts center. **Physically Challenged Students:** 72% of the campus is accessible. Facilities include wheelchair ramps, elevators, special parking, specially equipped restrooms, special class scheduling, lowered drinking fountains, lowered telephones, and special housing. All buildings are built to ADA compliance standards. **Special:** A.B. degrees in 43 majors (including nine interdisciplinary majors), with single, coordinate, double, and self-designed major options. Plus (+) and minus (-) grading system, with credit/D/fail option. Dean's list, Latin Honors, and departmental honors awarded. First-year seminars, intermediate, and advanced independent study, student research, and close work with faculty advisors strongly emphasized. Study abroad during the junior year encouraged. Washington semester. Academic support programs include the Baldwin Program for Academic Development, Quantitative Reasoning Program, Writing Project, Office of Student Fellowships and Research, and Health Professions Advising. Dual-degree programs offered in Engineering (3-2 with California Institute of Tech., Columbia University, Dartmouth College, and University of Maine, Orono) and Law (3-3 with Columbia University). Teacher Certification program. There is 1 national honor society and a chapter of Phi Beta Kappa. **Visiting:** There are regularly scheduled orientations for prospective students, The Admissions Office offers student-led campus tours, one-hour information sessions with an Admissions representative, and personal interviews. There are guides for informal visits, visitors may sit in on classes, and stay overnight. To schedule a visit, contact the Admissions Office. **Campus Safety and Security:** Measures include 24-hour foot and vehicle patrol, emergency notification system, self-defense education, and security escort services. There are shuttle buses, emergency telephones, lighted pathways/sidewalks, and controlled access to dorms/residences; residences are locked 24 hours a day, and a staffed communications center is available around the clock.

REQUIREMENTS: Applicants for admission will have had 4 years each of English, social studies, foreign language, and math, 3 to 4 years of laboratory sciences, and 1 course each in art, music, and history. A high school record, two teacher recommendations, an advisor's estimate of the applicant's character and accomplishments, and an essay are required. Applicants must submit the Common Application as well as the Bowdoin Supplement to be considered for admission. AP credits are accepted. Important factors in the admissions decision are advanced placement or honors courses, recommendations by school officials, and extracurricular activities record. To qualify for the bachelor of arts degree, a student must have successfully passed thirty-two full-credit courses (or the equivalent), completed a first-year seminar, completed at least one full-credit course (or the equivalent) in each of the following five distribution areas   mathematical, computational, or statistical reasoning; inquiry in the natural sciences; exploring social differences; international perspectives; and visual & performing arts; completed at least one full-credit course (or the equivalent) in natural sciences and mathematics, social & behavioral sciences, and humanities (in addition to the required course in the visual and performing arts), and completed an approved major. **Procedure:** Freshmen are admitted fall. Entrance exams should be taken by the late summer before the freshman year. There are early decision and deferred admissions plans. Early decision applications should be filed by November 15; regular applications, by January 1 for fall entry, along with a $65 fee. Notification of early decision is sent December 15; regular decision, March 20. 237 early decision candidates were accepted for the 2016-2017 class. Applications are accepted on-line. Application fees are waived if application is completed on-line. **Transfer Students:** One transfer student enrolled in 2015-2016. College grades of "B" or better are required to transfer. Applicants should submit high school and college transcripts, a dean's or advisor's statement from the most recent college attended, and two recommendations from recent professors. Transfer applicants must submit the Common Application, transfer essay, and Bowdoin Supplement to be considered for admission. 16 of 32 credits required for the bachelor's degree must be completed at Bowdoin. **International Students:** There are 87 international students enrolled. The school actively recruits these students. They must take the TOEFL with a minimum score of 600 on the paper-based TOEFL (PBT) or 100 on the Internet-based version (iBT). SAT scores are not required for admission but must be submitted at matriculation for counseling and placement.

ADMISSIONS: 15% of the 2016-2017 applicants were accepted. The SAT scores for the 2016-2017 freshman class were: Critical Reading-- 2% below 500, 9% between 500 and 599, 30% between 600 and 699, and 59% between 700 and 800. Math-- 3% below 500, 10% between 500 and 599, 33% between 600 and 699, and 54% between 700 and 800. Writing-- 3% below 500, 7% between 500 and 599, 34% between 600 and 699, and 56% between 700 and 800. The ACT scores were 3% between 18 and 23, 17% between 24 and 29, and 80% above 30. 93% of the current freshmen were in the top fifth of their class; 99% were in the top two fifths. There were 30 National Merit finalists. 22 freshmen graduated first in their class. **Admissions Contact:** Whitney W. Soule, Dean of Admissions and Financial Aid. Email: *admissions@bowdoin.edu* Web: *www.bowdoin.edu*

FINANCIAL AID: In 2016-2017, 48% of all full-time freshmen and 47% of continuing full-time students received some form of financial aid. 47% of all full-time freshmen and 45% of continuing full-time students received need-based aid. The average freshman award was $43,895. Need-based scholarships or need-based grants averaged $42,165 ($61,540 maximum); need-based self-help aid (loans and jobs) averaged $1,819 ($1,900 maximum); and other non-need-based awards and non-need-based scholarships averaged $1,000 ($1,000 maximum). 63% of undergraduate students work part-time. Average annual earnings from campus work are $1363. The average financial indebtedness of the 2016 graduate was $23,120. Bowdoin is a member of CSS. The CSS/Profile, Noncustodial Profile, and Business/Farm Supplement are required. The FAFSA code is 002038. The deadline for filing freshman financial aid applications for fall entry is February 15.

COLBY COLLEGE — B-4

www.colby.edu

Waterville, ME 04901	**(207) 859-4818** **(800) 723-3032**
Fax: (207) 859-4828	**Email: admissions@colby.edu**
Full-time: 887 men, 970 women	**Faculty:** 180; IIB, ++$
Part-time: n/av	**Ph.D.s:** 98%
Graduate: n/av	**Student/Faculty:** 9 to 1
Year: 4-1-4	**Tuition:** $50,960
Room & Board: $13,100	**Freshman Class:** 7593 applied, 1710 accepted, 508 enrolled
SAT CR/M/W: 675/690/680 **ACT:** 31	**CEEB CODE:** 3280
Application Deadline: January 1	**MOST COMPETITIVE**

Colby College, founded in 1813, is a private liberal arts college. Figures in the above capsule and in this profile are approximate. There is 1 undergraduate school. In addition to regional accreditation, Colby has baccalaureate program accreditation with ACS. The 714-acre campus is in a small town 75 miles north of Portland. Including any residence halls, there are 60 buildings.

STUDENT LIFE: 87% of undergraduates are from out of state, mostly the Northeast. Students are from 42 states, 76 foreign countries, and Canada. 51% are from public schools. 9% are Foreign; 60% White; 6% Asian American; 6% Hispanic; 5% two or more races; 3% African American; 11% race unknown. **Female To Male Ratio:** 1.1:1. The average age of freshmen is 18; all undergraduates, 20. 7% do not continue beyond their first year; 90% remain to graduate. **Housing:** 1779 students can be accommodated in college housing, which includes coed dorms and on-campus apartments. In addition, there are special-interest houses, substance-free halls, theme housing, wellness housing, green, chem-free, quiet housing, and residence halls and apartments for seniors. On-campus housing is guaranteed for all 4 years. 94% of students live on campus; of those, 95% remain on campus on weekends. All students may keep cars.

FACULTY/CLASSROOMS: 58% of faculty are male; 42% are female. All teach undergraduates, and all do research. No introductory courses are taught by graduate students. The average class size in an introductory lecture is 27; in a laboratory is 16; and in a regular course is 16.

PROGRAMS OF STUDY: Colby confers B.A. degrees. Bachelor's degrees are awarded in AGRICULTURE (environmental studies), BIOLOGICAL SCIENCE (biochemistry, biology/biological science, environmental biology, and neurosciences), COMMUNICATIONS AND THE ARTS (art history, classics, creative writing, English, Germanic languages and literature, music, Russian languages and literature, Spanish, studio art, and theatre arts), COMPUTER AND PHYSICAL SCIENCE (applied mathematics, chemistry, computer science, geology, geoscience, mathematics, physics, and science technology), EDUCATION (global studies), SOCIAL SCIENCE (African American studies, American studies, anthropology, classical/ancient civilization, East Asian studies, economics, French studies, history, Latin American studies, philosophy, political science/government, psychology, religion, sociology, and women's studies). Economics, biology, and global studies have the largest enrollments.

ACTIVITIES: There are no fraternities or sororities. There are 107 groups on campus, including coed woodsmen's team, outdoor, art, band, choir, chorale, chorus, communications, computers, dance, debate, drama, environmental, ethnic, film, honors, human rights, international, jazz band, LGBT, literary magazine, musical theater, newspaper, orchestra, photography, political, professional, religious, social, social service, student government, symphony, and yearbook. Popular campus events include Winter Carnival, Foss Arts Festival, and International Extravaganza. **Sports:** There are 16 intercollegiate sports for men and 17 for women, and 8 intramural sports for men and 8 for women. Facilities include an athletic center with fitness, weight training, yoga, and exercise areas, a gym with badminton, volleyball, and basketball courts, a hockey and skating rink, a field house for track and field, climbing wall, soccer, baseball, softball, tennis, lacrosse, golf, a swimming pool and saunas, physical therapy and athletic training center, and squash and handball courts. Outdoor playing fields include two artificial-turf fields, tennis courts, an all-weather track, cross-country skiing and running trails, and an FIS-certified Nordic ski race course adjacent to campus. There is a woodsmen's area for lumberjack events and competition. **Graduates:** From July 1, 2015 to June 30, 2016, 491 bachelor's degrees were awarded. The most popular majors were social sciences (25%), interdisciplinary studies (11%), and biology/life sciences (10%). 46 companies recruited on campus in 2015-2016. In an average class, 94% graduate in 6 years or less. Of the 2015 graduating class, 24% were enrolled in graduate school within 6 months of graduation, and 87% were employed.

SERVICES: Counseling and information services are available, as is tutoring in every subject. There is a reader service for the blind. There is also a writing center and a support program. **Library/Resources:** The 3 libraries contain 1.6 million volumes, 300,500 microform items, and 26,052 audio/video tapes/CDs/DVDs, and subscribe to 19,877 periodicals including electronic. Computerized library services include interlibrary loans, database searching, Internet access, and Wi-Fi capability. Special learning facilities include an art gallery, an astronomy observatory and classroom, 128-acre arboretum, electronic-research classroom, MIDI studio/electronic-music lab, language resource center, proscenium-style theater, research greenhouses, and a world-class collection in Maine's largest art museum. **Physically Challenged Students:** 93% of the campus is accessible. Facilities include wheelchair ramps, elevators, special parking, specially equipped restrooms, special class scheduling, lowered drinking fountains, and lowered telephones. **Special:** Colby incorporates research in majors across the curriculum and showcases research results at its annual Colby Liberal Arts Symposium. Study abroad is accessible through more than 200 programs in more than 60 countries, and two thirds of students participate during their time at Colby. Colby offers opportunities to study or intern in Washington, D.C. on-campus work-study, exchange programs with the Claremont Colleges and Howard University, 3-2 engineering degree programs with Dartmouth College and Columbia University, and a semester-in-residence program working with research scientists at the Bigelow Laboratory for Ocean Sciences. Students, with approval, may pursue independent majors. Colby offers combined and interdisciplinary majors including four that combine interdisciplinary computation with biology, environmental studies, music, and theater and dance. The Jan Plan offers a month-long term for internships or focused study on or off campus. There are 9 national honor societies, Phi Beta Kappa, and 26 departmental honors programs. **Visiting:** There are regularly scheduled orientations for prospective students, including panel discussions, tours, class visits, complimentary meals, interviews, and information sessions. There are guides for informal visits, visitors may sit in on classes, and stay overnight. To schedule a visit, contact the Admissions Office at (800) 723-3032. **Campus Safety and Security:** Measures include 24-hour foot and vehicle patrol, emergency notification system, self-defense education, and security escort services. There are shuttle buses, emergency telephones, lighted pathways/sidewalks, controlled access to dorms/residences, radical attack defense classes for women, fire safety with drills and inspections, ID program for bikes, and computers, party checks, and alcohol education programs.

REQUIREMENTS: Student must submit either SAT, ACT, or three SAT Subject Tests. Candidates should be high school graduates with a recommended academic program of 16 units in 4 years of English, 3 each of foreign language and math, and 2 each of science, (of those, 2 units must be lab work) 2 units of social studies, and other college-preparatory courses. AP credits are accepted. Important factors in the admissions decision are personality/intangible qualities, advanced placement or honors courses, evidence of special talent, extracurricular activities record, leadership record, parents or siblings attended your school, recommendations by alumni, geographical diversity, and recommendations by school officials. To graduate, all students must take English composition and fulfill a three-semester foreign language requirement. They must also take 2 courses in the natural sciences and 1 course each in the arts, historical studies, literature, quantitative reasoning, the social sciences, and human or cultural diversity, and meet Colby's wellness requirement by attending 8 lectures. Students must complete a total of 128 credit hours, including 3 January term courses, and maintain a GPA of 2.0. **Procedure:** Freshmen are admitted fall and spring. Entrance exams should be taken by January of the senior year. There are early decision and deferred admissions plans. Early decision applications should be filed by November 15; regular applications, by January 1 for fall and winter entry. Notification of early decision is sent December 15; regular decision, February 15. 259 early decision candidates were accepted for the 2016-2017 class. 634 applicants were on the 2016 waiting list; 42 were admitted. Applications are accepted on-line. Application fees are waived if application is completed on-line. **Transfer Students:** 8 transfer students enrolled in 2015-2016. Applicants must have a minimum GPA of 3.0 and, as a rule, have earned enough credit hours to qualify for at least sophomore standing. They must be in good academic and social standing and should submit references from a faculty member and a dean of their current school. If the SAT or ACT has been taken, the results may be submitted as well. Students may enroll in the fall and spring. 64 of 128 credits required for the bachelor's degree must be completed at Colby. **International Students:** There are 153 international students enrolled. The school actively recruits these students. They must take the TOEFL, or IELTS if English is neither their first language nor their current language of instruction. They must take the SAT or ACT or three SAT Subject Tests of their choice, sent by the testing agency.

ADMISSIONS: 23% of the 2016-2017 applicants were accepted. The SAT scores for the 2016-2017 freshman class were: Critical Reading-- 1% below 500, 13% between 500 and 599, 53% between 600 and 699, and 34% between 700 and 800. Math-- 1% below 500, 7% between 500 and 599, 48% between 600 and 699, and 44% between 700 and 800. Writing-- 11% between 500 and 599, 43% between 600 and 699, and 45% between 700 and 800. The ACT scores were 2% between 18 and 23, 36% between 24 and 29, and 62% above 30. 84% of the current freshmen were in the top fifth of their class; 98% were in the top two fifths. There were 2 National Merit finalists. 4 freshmen graduated first in their class. **Admissions Contact:** Steve Thomas, Director of Admissions. Email: *admissions@colby.edu* Web: *www.colby.edu*

FINANCIAL AID: In 2016-2017, 33% of all full-time freshmen received some form of financial aid. 32% of all full-time freshmen received need-based aid. The average freshman award was $42,991. Need-based scholarships or need-based grants averaged $43,762; need-based self-help aid (loans and jobs) averaged $2,357; and $2,925 from other forms of aid. 67% of undergraduate students work part-time. Average annual earnings from campus work are $1325. The average financial indebtedness of the 2016 graduate was $21,958. Colby is a member of CSS. The CSS/Profile, the college's own financial statement, current tax returns to finalize aid awards, and business or farm supplement are required. The FAFSA code is 002039. The deadline for filing freshman financial aid applications for fall entry is February 1.

COLLEGE OF THE ATLANTIC D-5

www.coa.edu

Bar Harbor, ME 04609	(207) 288-5015 (800) 528-0025
Fax: (207) 288-4126	Email: inquiry@coa.edu
Full-time: 81 men, 231 women	**Faculty:** 25
Part-time: 10 men, 15 women	**Ph.D.s:** 96%
Graduate: 1 men, 6 women	**Student/Faculty:** 12 to 1
Year: trimesters	**Tuition:** $43,542
Room & Board: $9747	**Freshman Class:** 485 applied, 314 accepted, 79 enrolled
SAT CR/M/W: 650/550/600 **ACT:** 28	**CEEB CODE:** 3305
Application Deadline: February 15	**HIGHLY COMPETITIVE+**

College of the Atlantic was founded in 1969 on the premise that education should go beyond understanding the world as it is, to enabling students to actively shape its future. A leader in experiential education and environmental stewardship, COA has pioneered a distinctive interdisciplinary approach to learning human ecology that develops the kinds of creative thinkers and doers needed by all sectors of society to address the compelling and growing needs of our world. Figures in the above capsule and in this profile are approximate. There is 1 undergraduate school and 1 graduate school. In addition to regional accreditation, COA has baccalaureate program accreditation with NEASC. The 35-acre campus is in a small town 45 miles southeast of Bangor, along the Atlantic Ocean shoreline. Including any residence halls, there are 20 buildings.

STUDENT LIFE: 75% of undergraduates are from out of state, mostly the Northeast. Students are from 36 states, 46 foreign countries, and Canada. 51% are from public schools. 66% are White; 5% Hispanic; 3% Asian American; 3% race unknown; 21% Foreign; 1% African American; 1% two or more races. **Female To Male Ratio:** 2.7:1. The average age of freshmen is 19; all undergraduates, 21. 16% do not continue beyond their first year; 65% remain to graduate. **Housing:** 153 students can be accommodated in college housing, which includes coed dorms. There are also theme and wellness housing, substance-free housing, and green housing. On-campus housing is guaranteed for the freshman year only, and is available on a first-come, first-served basis, is available on a lottery system for upperclassmen. Priority is given to out-of-town students. 50% of students commute. Alcohol is not permitted. All students may keep cars.

FACULTY/CLASSROOMS: 54% of faculty are male; 46% are female. All teach undergraduates, 80% do research, and 80% do both. No introductory courses are taught by graduate students. The average class size in an introductory lecture is 12; in a laboratory is 12; and in a regular course is 12.

PROGRAMS OF STUDY: COA confers B.A. degrees. Master's degrees are also awarded. Bachelor's degrees are awarded in SOCIAL SCIENCE (human ecology). Human ecology is the strongest academically, and has the largest enrollment.

ACTIVITIES: There are no fraternities or sororities. There are 20 groups on campus, including botany club, fiber club, taxidermy club and gentleman's club, art, campus committee on sustainability, chess, chorus, computers, dance, drama, environmental, film, international, jazz band, LGBT, literary magazine, newspaper, orchestra, photography, political, social, social service, student government, and yearbook. Popular campus events include Bar Island Swim, Fandango Talent Show, Earth Day, and Aurora Ball-ealis (winter dance), Spanish Festival, Human Ecology Forums, and Fall Community Show. **Sports:** There is no sports program at COA. All students are members of the local YMCA and may use its pool, Nautilus equipment, and volleyball and basketball facilities, as well as nearby tennis courts. Acadia National Park offers seasonal outdoor activities for hiking, biking, and cross-country skiing. The college has an active outdoor program, with camping and outdoor equipment and canoes, sea kayaks, sailboats and lessons, sea kayaking, and wilderness first responder class. There are yoga and martial arts classes, as well as a bouldering wall, and an ice-skating rink in winter. SCUBA instruction is offered using the Y facilities. Dance instruction is also available. **Graduates:** From July 1, 2015 to June 30, 2016, 80 bachelor's degrees were awarded. The most popular majors were human ecology (100%). 15 companies recruited on campus in 2015-2016. In an average class, 59% graduate in 4 years or less, 68% graduate in 5 years or less, and 69% graduate in 6 years or less. Of the 2015 graduating class, 3% were enrolled in graduate school within 6 months of graduation, and 80% were employed.

SERVICES: Counseling and information services are available, as is tutoring in some subjects, such as writing, math, language, photography, and computer use. There is remedial math and writing. **Library/ Resources:** The library contains 60,000 volumes, 37,000 microform items, and 3,300 audio/video tapes/CDs/DVDs, and subscribes to 30,000 periodicals including electronic. Computerized library services include interlibrary loans, database searching, Internet access, and Wi-Fi capability. Special learning facilities include an art gallery, natural history museum, writing center, taxidermy lab, sculpture, painting, animation and ceramics studios, marine mammal research center, 2 greenhouses, community garden on campus, 2 organic farms (a few miles off campus), sustainable enterprise hatchery, ocean-going vessels, and 2 offshore island research centers. **Physically Challenged Students:** 80% of the campus is accessible. Facilities include wheelchair ramps, elevators, special parking, specially equipped restrooms, lowered drinking fountains, and lowered telephones. **Special:** Students may cross-register with the University of Maine; Eco League exchanges are available with Alaska Pacific University, and Green Mountain, Northland, and Prescott colleges. COA offers study abroad programs in Mexico, Guatemala, and France, and supports other study abroad programs as well as independent residencies abroad. A 10-week internship is a requirement of graduationl; students are assisted in finding internships in the US and abroad in an area of interest. All students design their own path to completion of their B.A. in human ecology. **Visiting:** There are regularly scheduled orientations for prospective students, there is an annual fall tour for high school seniors on Columbus Day. Students attend classes, stay in student housing, and are invited to join outings at Acadia National Park. There is also a weekend for transfer students. There are guides for informal visits, visitors may sit in on classes, and stay overnight. To schedule a visit, contact Donna McFarland at (207) 288-5015. **Campus Safety and Security:** Measures include 24-hour foot and vehicle patrol and security escort services. There are shuttle buses, emergency telephones, and lighted pathways/sidewalks.

REQUIREMENTS: Candidates for admission must be high school graduates who have completed 4 years of English, 3-4 years of math, 2-3 years of science, with 2 units of lab, 2 years recommended of a foreign language, and history, and 2 years of social studies, and 1 academic elective. AP credits are accepted. Important factors in the admissions decision are personality/intangible qualities, extracurricular activities record, and recommendations by school officials. All students major in human ecology, which serves as a focus for a self-designed pathway to understanding the relationships between humans and our environment. Students complete a total of 36 COA credits, including an interdisciplinary core course, two courses each in environmental science, human studies, and arts and design, along with a history, writing, and quantitative reasoning course. Also required are a 3-credit internship (taking students off-campus either for a term, or during the summer), a human ecology essay, community service, and a culminating 3-credit senior, or capstone, project, which can be accomplished either in one term or spread out throughout the senior year. **Procedure:** Freshmen are admitted fall, winter, and spring. Entrance exams should be taken in the junior or senior year. There are early decision and deferred admissions plans. Early decision applications should be filed by December 1; regular applications, by February 15 for fall entry; and November 15 for winter entry, along with a $50 fee. Notification of early decision is sent December 15; regular decision, April 1. 30 early decision candidates were accepted for the 2016-2017 class. Applications are accepted on-line. **Transfer Students:** 29 transfer students enrolled in 2015-2016. Only coursework for which the student has received a grade of "C" (2.0) or better will be accepted for transfer credit. Students need to apply and send a transcript. COA credits refer to one COA course (one trimester course). Student may enroll in the fall, winter, and spring. 18 of 36 credits required for the bachelor's degree must be completed at COA. **International Students:** There are 56 international students enrolled. The school actively recruits these students. They must take the TOEFL or submit SAT scores or the IB English exam score.

ADMISSIONS: 65% of the 2016-2017 applicants were accepted. The SAT scores for the 2016-2017 freshman class were: Critical Reading-- 6% below 500, 24% between 500 and 599, 49% between 600 and 699, and 21% between 700 and 800. Math-- 15% below 500, 58% between 500 and 599, and 27% between 600 and 699. Writing-- 3% below 500, 42% between 500 and 599, 46% between 600 and 699, and 9% between 700 and 800. The ACT scores were 6% between 18 and 23, 63% between 24 and 29, and 31% above 30. 60% of the current freshmen were in the top fifth of their class; 90% were in the top two fifths. **Admissions Contact:** Heather Albert-Knopp, Dean of Admissions. Email: *inquiry@coa.edu* Web: *www.coa.edu*

FINANCIAL AID: In 2016-2017, 97% of all full-time freshmen and 93% of continuing full-time students received some form of financial aid. 90% of all full-time freshmen and 81% of continuing full-time students received need-based aid. The average freshman award was $42,118. Need-based scholarships or need-based grants averaged $36,362; need-based self-help aid (loans and jobs) averaged $5,762; other non-need-based awards and non-need-based scholarships averaged $4,043; and $11,786 from other forms of aid. 74% of undergraduate students work part-time. Average annual earnings from campus work are $2500. The average financial indebtedness of the 2016 graduate was $26,114. COA is a member of CSS. The college's own financial statement is required. The FAFSA code is 011385. The priority date for freshman financial aid applications for fall entry is February 15.

HUSSON UNIVERSITY *(The complete profile is made available exclusively on our website, www.barronspac.com)*

MAINE COLLEGE OF ART *(The complete profile is made available exclusively on our website, www.barronspac.com)*

MAINE MARITIME ACADEMY C-5

www.mainemaritime.edu

Castine, ME 04420	**(207) 326-2215** **(800) 227-8465**
Fax: (207) 326-2515	**Email: jeff.wright@mma.edu**
Full-time: 750 men, 175 women	**Faculty:** n/av
Part-time: 5 men, 5 women	**Ph.D.s:** n/av
Graduate: 10 men, 10 women	**Student/Faculty:** n/av
Year: semesters	**Tuition:** $12,988 ($25,572)
Room & Board: $9548	**Freshman Class:** n/av
SAT or ACT: required	**CEEB CODE:** 3505
Application Deadline: May 1	**COMPETITIVE**

Maine Maritime Academy, founded in 1941, is a public institution offering 18 degree programs in ocean- and marine-oriented studies, with emphasis on engineering, transportation, business management, and ocean sciences, to prepare graduates for private-and-public sector careers and the uniformed services of the United States. The academic calendar consists of 2 semesters plus a 2- to 3- month annual training cruise for the USCG Unlimited license majors and summer internships for others. The figures given in the above capsule and in this profile are approximate. There are 4 undergraduate schools and 1 graduate school. In addition to regional accreditation, MMA has baccalaureate program accreditation with ABET, NEASC, USCG, and STCW. The 50-acre campus is in a small town 38 miles south of Bangor on the east coast of Penobscot Bay. Including any residence halls, there are 14 buildings.

STUDENT LIFE: 69% of undergraduates are from Maine. Others are from 40 states, 7 foreign countries, and Canada. 90% are from public schools. 98% are White; 1% Asian American; 1% Hispanic. **Male To Female Ratio:** 4.0:1. The average age of freshmen is 19; all undergraduates, 24. 12% do not continue beyond their first year; 75% remain to graduate. **Housing:** 625 students can be accommodated in college housing, which includes single-sex and coed dorms, on-campus apartments, and graduate housing. On-campus housing is guaranteed for all 4 years. 85% of students live on campus; of those, 40% remain on campus on weekends. Alcohol is not permitted. All students may keep cars.

FACULTY/CLASSROOMS: 75% of faculty are male; 25% are female. All teach undergraduates. No introductory courses are taught by graduate students. The average class size in an introductory lecture is 30; in a laboratory is 15; and in a regular course is 25.

PROGRAMS OF STUDY: MMA confers B.S. degrees. Associate and master's degrees are also awarded. Bachelor's degrees are awarded in BUSINESS (international business management), COMPUTER AND PHYSICAL SCIENCE (oceanography), ENGINEERING AND ENVIRONMENTAL DESIGN (engineering, engineering technology, marine engineering, maritime science, and transportation technology). Marine systems engineering is the strongest academically. Marine transportation and marine engineering degree programs have the largest enrollments.

ACTIVITIES: There are 30 groups on campus, including martial arts, billiards, chess, engineering, hockey, outing, rugby, sailing, scuba, social, amateur radio, bagpipe, band, chess, chorale, drama, drill team, drum and bugle corps, environmental, ethnic, international, newspaper, pep band, photography, professional, social, social service, student government, and yearbook. Popular campus events include GSA Weekend, BSA Klondike Derby, and Veterans Day. **Sports:** There are 6 intercollegiate sports for men and 6 for women, and 10 intramural sports for men and 10 for women. Facilities include Olympic pool, 2 weight rooms, field house with 3 climbing walls, a gym, racquetball/squash courts, aerobics room, a weight/workout room on the training ship, and synthetic multi-sport athletic field. **Graduates:** From July 1, 2015 to June 30, 2016, 160 bachelor's degrees were awarded. The most popular majors were marine engineering (30%), marine transportation (30%), and power engineering (15%).

SERVICES: Counseling and information services are available, as is tutoring in most subjects. There is a reader service for the blind, and remedial math, reading, and writing. **Library/Resources:** The library contains 88,490 volumes, 5,000 microform items, and 808 audio/video tapes/CDs/DVDs, and subscribes to 1,311 periodicals including electronic. Computerized library services include interlibrary loans, database searching, Internet access, and Wi-Fi capability. Special learning facilities include a natural history museum, planetarium, more than 60 vessels, a bridge simulator, radar sims, power plant sims, a cargo system simulators, and multiple sophisticated training vessels. **Physically Challenged Students:** All of the campus is accessible. Facilities include wheelchair ramps, elevators, special parking, specially equipped restrooms, and special housing. **Special:** The 2-month freshman and junior year training cruises give students practical experience aboard the academy's 500-foot ship. Cadet shipping co-ops on assigned merchant ships for 65 to 90 days. Co-op programs and internships for all programs are offered, as is study abroad through special agreements with other maritime colleges worldwide. Dual and student-designed majors are possible. **Visiting:** There are regularly scheduled orientations for prospective students, consisting of 3 open houses per year; campus visits are available weekdays throughout the year. Visitors may sit in on classes and stay overnight. To schedule a visit, contact admissions office at admissions@mma.edu. **Campus Safety and Security:** Measures include 24-hour foot and vehicle patrol and self-defense education. There are emergency telephones, lighted pathways/sidewalks, controlled access to dorms/residences, on-campus medical and counseling services, and locked dorms.

REQUIREMENTS: The SAT or ACT is required. Candidates for admission must have completed 4 years of English, 3 years of math, and 2 years of lab science. Courses must include algebra I, algebra II, trigonometry, geometry, and either chemistry or physics with a lab. AP and CLEP credits are accepted. Important factors in the admissions decision are advanced placement or honors courses, evidence of special talent, and leadership record. A minimum GPA of 2.0 in an average of 140 total credit hours is required for graduation. GPA in the major must be at least 2.25. A senior thesis is required for some majors, and a comprehensive exam is required for USCG license candidates. **Procedure:** Freshmen are admitted fall and spring. Entrance exams should be taken as early as possible in the senior year. There are early decision, deferred admissions, and rolling admissions plans. Early decision applications should be filed by December 31; regular applications, by May 1 for fall entry; and November 1 for spring entry. The fall 2016 application fee was $15. Applications are accepted on-line. **Transfer Students:** 16 transfer students enrolled in 2015-2016. Applicants must have a minimum 2.0 GPA in previous college work and meet the same prerequisites as entering freshmen. **International Students:** They must take the TOEFL.

Admissions Contact: Jeff Wright, Director of Admissions. Email: *jeff.wright@mma.edu* Web: *www.mainemaritime.edu*

FINANCIAL AID: The FAFSA code is 002044. Check with the school for current application deadlines.

SAINT JOSEPH'S COLLEGE OF MAINE A-5

www.sjcme.edu

Standish, ME 04084	**(207) 893-7746** **(800) 338-7057**
Fax: (207) 893-7862	**Email: admission@sjcme.edu**
Full-time: 300 men, 600 women	**Faculty:** 63
Part-time: 9 men, 21 women	**Ph.D.s:** 98%
Graduate: n/av	**Student/Faculty:** 15 to 1
Year: semesters, summer session	**Tuition:** $33,600
Room & Board: $12,885	**Freshman Class:** n/av
SAT: required **ACT:** 21	**CEEB CODE:** 3755
Application Deadline: August 1	**COMPETITIVE**

Saint Joseph's College of Maine, founded in 1912, is a private, Roman Catholic institution offering liberal arts and pre-professional programs. Figures in the above capsule and in this profile are approximate. There are 5 undergraduate schools. In addition to regional accreditation, Saint Joseph's College of Maine has baccalaureate program accreditation with CCNE. The 350-acre campus is in a rural area 18 miles west of Portland. Including any residence halls, there are 20 buildings.

STUDENT LIFE: 60% of undergraduates are from Maine. Others are from 15 states, 3 foreign countries, and Canada. 82% are White; 1% African American; 1% Asian American; 1% American Indian/Alaska Native; 1% Hispanic; 1% Foreign. **Female To Male Ratio:** 2.0:1. The average age of freshmen is 18; all undergraduates, 20. 18% do not continue beyond their first year; 59% remain to graduate. **Housing:** 829 students can be accommodated in college housing, which includes single-sex and coed dorms and substance free housing. On-campus housing is guaranteed for all 4 years. 83% of students live on campus; of those, 65% remain on campus on weekends. All students may keep cars.

FACULTY/CLASSROOMS: 48% of faculty are male; 52% are female. All teach undergraduates. No introductory courses are taught by graduate students. The average class size in an introductory lecture is 25; in a laboratory is 12; and in a regular course is 18.

PROGRAMS OF STUDY: Saint Joseph's College of Maine confers B.A., B.S., B.S.B.A., and B.S.N. degrees. Associate degrees are also awarded. Bachelor's degrees are awarded in BIOLOGICAL SCIENCE (biology/biological science), BUSINESS (business administration and management), COMMUNICATIONS AND THE ARTS (communications and English), COMPUTER AND PHYSICAL SCIENCE (chemistry and mathematics), EDUCATION (elementary education and physical education), ENGINEERING AND ENVIRONMENTAL DESIGN (environmental science), HEALTH PROFESSIONS (nursing and prepharmacy), SOCIAL SCIENCE (criminal justice, history, philosophy, psychology, sociology, and theological studies). Business, nursing, and biology are the strongest academically. Elementary education, business, and nursing have the largest enrollments.

ACTIVITIES: There are no fraternities or sororities. There are 28 groups on campus, including campus activities board, campus ministry, high adventure club, SuperKids, cheerleading, choir, chorale, computers, dance, drama, ethnic, Habitat for Humanity, honors, international, literary magazine, musical theater, newspaper, pep band, photography, political, professional, radio and TV, religious, social, social service, student government, and yearbook. Popular campus events include Family Weekend, Christmas Benefit Concert, and Spring Fling. **Sports:** There are 5 intercollegiate sports for men and 6 for women, and 12 intramural sports for men and 12 for women. Facilities include a gym, workout room with free weights, Nautilus and other weight-training equipment, a cardiovascular workout room, dance aerobics rooms, climbing wall, 25-meter pool, saunas, and an elevated jogging track. There are also soccer and field hockey fields, a private beach on a lake, lighted athletic fields for baseball and softball, cross-country running and ski trails, and a low ropes course. **Graduates:** From July 1, 2015 to June 30, 2016, 213 bachelor's degrees were awarded. The most popular majors were education (20%), business (20%), and nursing (12%). 43 companies recruited on campus in 2015-2016. In an average class, 54% graduate in 4 years or less, 60% graduate in 5 years or less, and 61% graduate in 6 years or less. Of the 2015 graduating class, 15% were enrolled in graduate school within 6 months of graduation, and 89% were employed.

SERVICES: Counseling and information services are available, as is tutoring in every subject. There is a reader service for the blind. **Library/Resources:** The library contains 98,626 volumes, 29,010 microform items, and 1,000 audio/video tapes/CDs/DVDs, and subscribes to 11,461 periodicals including electronic. Computerized library services include interlibrary loans, database searching, and Internet access. Special learning facilities include a radio station and a telescope observatory. **Physically Challenged Students:** 75% of the campus is accessible. Facilities include wheelchair ramps, elevators, special parking, specially equipped restrooms, special class scheduling, and lowered drinking fountains. **Special:** Saint Joseph's offers internships, cross-registration with 4 southern Maine colleges, study abroad in 5 countries, a semester at sea, dual majors, work-study programs, and non-degree study. There are 2 national honor societies, a freshman honors program, and 6 departmental honors programs. **Visiting:** There are regularly scheduled orientations for prospective students, including Application and Acceptance Day programs, visits on Saturdays, and during the summer. There are guides for informal visits, visitors may sit in on classes, and stay overnight. **Campus Safety and Security:** Measures include 24-hour foot and vehicle patrol, self-defense education, and security escort services. There are emergency telephones, lighted pathways/sidewalks, and around-the-clock security officers.

REQUIREMENTS: The SAT or ACT is required. Candidates for admission must be high school graduates who have completed a college preparatory curriculum with a recommended 4 units in English, 3 to 4 in math, 2 in foreign language, and 1 to 3 each in history, science, and social studies. AP and CLEP credits are accepted. Important factors in the admissions decision are advanced placement or honors courses, recommendations by school officials, and extracurricular activities record. To graduate, students must complete 128 credit hours with a minimum GPA of 2.0, including 8 hours of English, history, theology, and a foreign language, 4 each of science and math, and 8 of electives. **Procedure:** Freshmen are admitted fall and spring. Entrance exams should be taken by January of the senior year. There are early admissions, deferred admissions, and rolling admissions plans. Applications should be filed by August 1 for fall entry. The fall 2016 application fee was $40. Notifications are sent December 18. 45 applicants were on the 2016 waiting list; 25 were admitted. Applications are accepted on-line. **Transfer Students:** 40 transfer students enrolled in 2015-2016. Transfer students should have a minimum GPA of 2.0. 32 of 128 credits required for the bachelor's degree must be completed at Saint Joseph's College of Maine. **International Students:** There are 3 international students enrolled. For non-English speaking students we require TOEFL exam. Students may also include SAT or ACT.

ADMISSIONS: 2 freshmen graduated first in their class. **Admissions Contact:** Vincent Kloskowski, Dean of Admissions. Email: *admission@sjcme.edu* Web: *www.sjcme.edu*

FINANCIAL AID: In 2016-2017, 99% of all full-time freshmen and 99% of continuing full-time students received some form of financial aid. 80% of all full-time freshmen and 81% of continuing full-time students received need-based aid. The average freshman award was $17,086. Need-based scholarships or need-based grants averaged $12,302 ($25,700 maximum); need-based self-help aid (loans and jobs) averaged $5,772 ($6,625 maximum); and other non-need-based awards and non-need-based scholarships averaged $13,398 ($20,390 maximum). 35% of undergraduate students work part-time. Average annual earnings from campus work are $896. The average financial indebtedness of the 2016 graduate was $16,020. Saint Joseph's College of Maine is a member of CSS. The college's own financial statement is required. The FAFSA code is 002051. The priority date for freshman financial aid applications for fall entry is March 1.

THOMAS COLLEGE *(The complete profile is made available exclusively on our website, www.barronspac.com)*

UNITY COLLEGE — C-4
www.unity.edu

Unity, ME 04988	**800-624-1024** **800-624-1024**
Fax: 207-948-9205	**Email: admissions@unity.edu**
Full-time: 356 men, 354 women	**Faculty:** 38
Part-time: 6 men, 19 women	**Ph.D.s:** 80%
Graduate: 2 men, 8 women	**Student/Faculty:** 12 to 1
Year: semesters, summer session	**Tuition:** $27,570
Room & Board: $10,100	**Freshman Class:** 407 applied, 350 accepted, 120 enrolled
SAT or ACT: recommended	**CEEB CODE:** 3925
Application Deadline: February 15	**COMPETITIVE**

Unity College is a small, private college in rural Maine that provides dedicated, engaged students with a liberal arts education that emphasizes the environment and natural resources. Unity College graduates are prepared to be environmental stewards, effective leaders, and responsible citizens through active learning experiences within a supportive community. There is 1 undergraduate school and 1 graduate school. The 225-acre campus is in a small town in mid-coast Maine. Including any residence halls, there are 30 buildings.

STUDENT LIFE: 70% of undergraduates are from out of state, mostly the Northeast. Students are from 32 states, and 1 foreign country. 97% are from public schools. 89% are White; 3% Hispanic; 3% two or more races; 2% Asian American; 1% African American; 1% American Indian/Alaska Native; 1% Foreign. **Female To Male Ratio:** 1.0:1. The average age of freshmen is 19; all undergraduates, 20. 28% do not continue beyond their first year; 53% remain to graduate. **Housing:** 570 students can be accommodated in college housing, which includes single-sex and coed dorms and on-campus apartments. On-campus housing is guaranteed for all 4 years and is available on a lottery system for upperclassmen. 71% of students live on campus; of those, 89% remain on campus on weekends. All students may keep cars.

FACULTY/CLASSROOMS: 54% of faculty are male; 46% are female. All teach undergraduates, and all do research. No introductory courses are taught by graduate students. The average class size in an introductory lecture is 19; in a laboratory is 14; and in a regular course is 18.

PROGRAMS OF STUDY: Unity confers B.A. and B.S. degrees. Associate and master's degrees are also awarded. Bachelor's degrees are awarded in AGRICULTURE (agriculture, animal science, conservation and regulation, environmental studies, natural resource management, range/farm management, and wildlife management), BIOLOGICAL SCIENCE (biology/biological science, ecology, marine biology, and wildlife biology), BUSINESS (recreation and leisure services), COMMUNICATIONS AND THE ARTS (art), COMPUTER AND PHYSICAL SCIENCE (natural sciences), EDUCATION (education and secondary education), ENGINEERING AND ENVIRONMENTAL DESIGN (environmental science and land use management and reclamation), HEALTH PROFESSIONS (recreation therapy), SOCIAL SCIENCE (ethics, politics, and social policy, law enforcement and corrections, and parks and recreation management). Biology, earth & environmental science, and sustainablee agriculture are the strongest academically. Conservation law enforcement, captive wildlife care & education, and wildlife biology have the largest enrollments.

ACTIVITIES: There are no fraternities or sororities. There are 36 groups on campus, including art, band, chorus, drama, environmental, honors, LGBT, literary magazine, outdoor and environmental clubs, photography, and student government. Popular campus events include Community Weekend in late September, Regional Woodsman's Meet in October, and Earth Day Activities. **Sports:** There are 3 intercollegiate sports for men and 4 for women, and 10 intramural sports for men and 10 for women. Facilities include a gym, weight training room, playing fields, indoor climbing wall, nature trails, and game rooms. **Graduates:** From July 1, 2015 to June 30, 2016, 138 bachelor's degrees were awarded. The most popular majors were conservation law enforcement (20%), captive wildlife care and education (17%), and wildlife biology/management (16%). 76 companies recruited on campus in 2015-2016. In an average class, 10% graduate in 3 years or less, 45% graduate in 4 years or less, and 53% graduate in 5 years or less. Of the 2015 graduating class, 13% were enrolled in graduate school within 6 months of graduation, and 90% were employed.

SERVICES: Counseling and information services are available, as is tutoring in most subjects. There is a reader service for the blind, and remedial math, reading, and writing. A full-time learning disability specialist is on staff. **Library/Resources:** The library contains 53,340 volumes, and 2,649 audio/video tapes/CDs/DVDs, and subscribes to 1,932 periodicals including electronic. Computerized library services include interlibrary loans, database searching, Internet access, and Wi-Fi capability. Special learning facilities include an art gallery, farm research station, organic gardens, greenhouses, and performing art center. **Physically Challenged Students:** Facilities include wheelchair ramps, special parking, specially equipped restrooms, and special housing. **Special:** The college offers credit-bearing internships, study abroad, a partnership with the Washington Semester, work-study programs, accelerated degree programs, dual majors, and an honors program. **Visiting:** There are regularly scheduled orientations for prospective students. There are guides for informal visits, visitors may sit in on classes, and stay overnight. To schedule a visit, contact the Admissions Office. **Campus Safety and Security:** Measures include 24-hour foot and vehicle patrol and emergency notification system. There are emergency telephones, lighted pathways/sidewalks, and controlled access to dorms/residences.

REQUIREMENTS: The SAT or ACT and ACT Writing Test are recommended. Applicants must be graduates of an accredited secondary school with a minimum GPA of 2.3. The GED is accepted. SAT or ACT scores, though not required, should be submitted, if available, for placement purposes. Five-short answer essays are required, and an interview is recommended. AP and CLEP credits are accepted. Important factors in the admissions decision are extracurricular activities record, advanced placement or honors courses, and leadership record. General education requirements include 38 credits. Included are composition and communication, math, computer science proficiency, life science, physical science, humanities, art, community-based learning, and environmental studies. Students must complete 120 credit hours with a minimum GPA of 2.0. A capstone course is required in all bachelor's degree programs. A minimum of 30 credits must be earned at the junior and senior level. **Procedure:** Freshmen are admitted fall and spring. Entrance exams should be taken in the junior or senior year. There are early decision, early admissions, and deferred admissions plans. Early decision applications should be filed by December 15; regular applications, by February 15 for fall entry; and November 1 for spring entry, along with a $25 fee. Notification of early decision is sent January 2; regular decision, March 1. Applications are accepted on-line. **Transfer Students:** 34 transfer students enrolled in 2015-2016. Applicants must present a minimum college GPA of 2.4 and are encouraged to submit SAT scores. 30 of 120 credits required for the bachelor's degree must be completed at Unity. **International Students:** The school actively recruits these students. They must take the TOEFL.

ADMISSIONS: 86% of the 2016-2017 applicants were accepted. The SAT scores for the 2016-2017 freshman class were: 20% of the current freshmen were in the top fifth of their class; 55% were in the top two fifths. **Admissions Contact:** Joe Saltalamachia, Director of Admission. Email: *admissions@unity.edu* Web: *www.unity.edu*

FINANCIAL AID: In 2016-2017, 99% of all full-time freshmen and 97% of continuing full-time students received some form of financial aid. 91% of all full-time freshmen and 86% of continuing full-time students received need-based aid. The average freshman award was $27,943. Need-based scholarships or need-based grants averaged $15,799 ($24,405 maximum); need-based self-help aid (loans and jobs) averaged $5,390 ($6,700 maximum); and other non-need-based awards and non-need-based scholarships averaged $6,754 ($22,659 maximum). 59% of undergraduate students work part-time. Average annual earnings from campus work are $1062. The average financial indebtedness of the 2016 graduate was $40,320. The FAFSA code is 006858. The priority date for freshman financial aid applications for fall entry is March.

UNIVERSITY OF MAINE — C-4

www.umaine.edu

Orono, ME 04469 — (207) 581-1622, (877) 486-2364

Fax: (207) 581-1213 — **Email:** umaineadmissions@maine.edu

Full-time: 4309 men, 3816 women	**Faculty:** I, --$
Part-time: 613 men, 585 women	**Ph.D.s:** 85%
Graduate: 699 men, 1197 women	**Student/Faculty:** n/av
Year: semesters, summer session	**Tuition:** $10,628 ($29,498)
Room & Board: $10,164	**Freshman Class:** 12952 applied, 11625 accepted, 2230 enrolled
SAT CR/M/W: 530/540/510 **ACT:** 23	**CEEB CODE:** 3916
Application Deadline: February 1	**COMPETITIVE**

The University of Maine, established in 1865, is the publicly funded land grant and sea grant institution in the University of Maine System. The university offers degree programs in the arts and sciences, business, public policy, health fields, engineering, education, forestry and agriculture. There are 6 undergraduate schools and 1 graduate school. In addition to regional accreditation, UMaine has baccalaureate program accreditation with AACSB, ABET, ADA, CSAB, CSWE, NASAD, NASM, NCATE, SAF, ACS, APA, SAF, ASHA, SWST, CCNE, and NAEYC. The 660-acre campus is in a small town 5 miles north of Bangor. Including any residence halls, there are 202 buildings.

STUDENT LIFE: 69% of undergraduates are from Maine. Others are from 50 states, 39 foreign countries, and Canada. 81% are White; 6% race unknown; 3% Hispanic; 3% Foreign; 3% two or more races; 2% African American; 1% Asian American; 1% American Indian/Alaska Native. **Male To Female Ratio:** 1.0:1. The average age of freshmen is 18; all undergraduates, 21. 24% do not continue beyond their first year; 76% remain to graduate. **Housing:** 3650 students can be accommodated in college housing, which includes coed dorms, on-campus apartments, off-campus apartments, and married student housing. In addition, there are honors houses, language houses, special-interest houses, living learning communities such as engineering and technology; first-generation;

education; natural sciences, forestry and agriculture; substance-free; and green living. Also offered: first-year residential experience and graduate family housing. On-campus housing is guaranteed for the freshman year only, and is available on a first-come, first-served basis. 63% of students commute. All students may keep cars.

FACULTY/CLASSROOMS: 56% of faculty are male; 44% are female. Graduate students teach 11% of introductory courses. The average class size in an introductory lecture is 49; in a laboratory is 19; and in a regular course is 41.

PROGRAMS OF STUDY: UMaine confers B.A., B.S., B.F.A., and B.M.E. degrees. Master's and doctoral degrees are also awarded. Bachelor's degrees are awarded in AGRICULTURE (agriculture, animal science, forest engineering, forestry and related sciences, horticulture, wildlife management, and wood science), BIOLOGICAL SCIENCE (biochemistry, biology/biological science, botany, marine science, microbiology, molecular biology, nutrition, and zoology), BUSINESS (accounting, business administration and management, business administration marketing, business economics, and finance), COMMUNICATIONS AND THE ARTS (art history, communications, dramatic arts, English, French, journalism, media arts, modern language, music, music performance, Spanish, and studio art), COMPUTER AND PHYSICAL SCIENCE (chemistry, computer science, earth science, mathematics, and physics), EDUCATION (art education, athletic training, elementary education, music education, physical education, secondary education, and university studies), ENGINEERING AND ENVIRONMENTAL DESIGN (bioengineering, chemical engineering, civil engineering, computer engineering, construction technology, electrical/electronics engineering, electrical/electronics engineering technology, engineering physics, environmental science, mechanical engineering, mechanical engineering technology, paper and pulp science, and surveying engineering), HEALTH PROFESSIONS (kinesiology, medical laboratory technology, nursing, speech pathology/audiology, and veterinary science), SOCIAL SCIENCE (anthropology, child care/child and family studies, economics, food science, history, interdisciplinary studies, international studies, parks and recreation management, philosophy, political science/government, psychology, social work, sociology, and women & gender studies). Engineering, forest resources, marine sciences, climate and earth sciences, wildlife ecology, ecology and environmental sciences are the strongest academically. Psychology, nursing, and mechanical engineering have the largest enrollments.

ACTIVITIES: There are 218 groups on campus, including art, band, cheerleading, chess, choir, chorale, chorus, computers, dance, debate, drama, drill team, environmental, ethnic, film, forensics, honors, international, jazz band, LGBT, literary magazine, marching band, musical theater, newspaper, opera, orchestra, pep band, photography, political, professional, radio and TV, religious, social, social service, student government, symphony, and yearbook. Popular campus events include Maine Day, Homecoming, Family and Friends Weekend, Culturefest, and International Dance Festival. **Sports:** There are 8 intercollegiate sports for men and 9 for women, and 26 intramural sports for men and 26 for women. Facilities include on- and off-campus sports arenas for hockey and basketball, field house, swimming and diving center, indoor climbing center, a student recreation center featuring a recreational swimming pool, weight room, indoor track, dance studio, basketball, volleyball, badminton, squash, tennis, racquetball courts; baseball, softball, soccer, field hockey, football fields, sports dome, and a year-round maintained forest trail system. **Graduates:** From July 1, 2015 to June 30, 2016, 1660 bachelor's degrees were awarded. The most popular majors were management (5%), nursing (5%), and psychology (5%). 212 companies recruited on campus in 2015-2016. In an average class, 36% graduate in 4 years or less, 55% graduate in 5 years or less, and 59% graduate in 6 years or less.

SERVICES: Counseling and information services are available, as is tutoring in some subjects, such as in 100- and 200-level courses. There is a reader service for the blind. **Library/Resources:** The library contains 3.6 million volumes, 1.7 million microform items, and 154,948 audio/video tapes/CDs/DVDs, and subscribes to 104,000 periodicals including electronic. Computerized library services include interlibrary loans, database searching, Internet access, and Wi-Fi capability. Special learning facilities include an art gallery, planetarium, radio station, a concert hall and other performance and art spaces, music facilities, new media production and prototyping facilities, anthropology museum, laboratory for surface science and technology, advanced structures and composites center, virtual reality lab, astronomy center, and advanced manufacturing center. **Physically Challenged Students:** 90% of the campus is accessible. Facilities include wheelchair ramps, elevators, special parking, specially equipped restrooms, special class scheduling, lowered drinking fountains, lowered telephones, and a transport van. **Special:** Cross-registration at other University of Maine campuses, internships at the upper level, a Washington semester, work-study programs both on- and off-campus, dual majors, a general studies degree, and pass/fail options are available. Students may study abroad in 78 countries. Cooperative programs are available in most majors, and accelerated degrees may be arranged. Innovate for Maine Fellows program connects the best and brightest Maine college students with Maine's most exciting, growing companies and business leaders in an effort to help grow and create jobs across the state of Maine. There are 20 national honor societies, Phi Beta Kappa, and a freshman honors program. **Visiting:** There are regularly scheduled orientations for prospective students, which include an opening welcome, campus tours, registration, department tours, a student panel, admissions, financial aid and student life sessions, a performing arts presentation, and music auditions. There are guides for informal visits and visitors may sit in on classes. To schedule a visit, contact Silverio Barrera at silverio.barrerajr@maine.edu. **Campus Safety and Security:** Measures include 24-hour foot and vehicle patrol, emergency notification system, self-defense education, and security escort services. There are emergency telephones, lighted pathways/sidewalks, controlled access to dorms/residences, and text and email emergency communication system.

REQUIREMENTS: The SAT or ACT is required. The GED is accepted. The number of academic or Carnegie credits required varies according to the program. The required secondary school courses also vary with each program but should include 4 credits of English, 3 of math, 2 of lab science, 2 of social studies, 2 in a foreign language, and 3 of electives. Guidance counselor recommendation is required for high school students. An audition is required for music majors. An essay is also required. AP and CLEP credits are accepted. Important factors in the admissions decision are advanced placement or honors courses, recommendations by school officials, leadership record, and extracurricular activities record. To graduate, students must complete a minimum of 120 credit hours, including at least 48 in the major, with a GPA of 2.0 or higher. 40 credits in approved courses must be taken. General education requirements include 18 credits in human values and social context, 6 credits in math/statistics/computer science, 2 courses in science, and at least 1 course in ethics. English composition is required. Students must demonstrate writing competency and complete a capstone. **Procedure:** Freshmen are admitted fall and spring. Entrance exams should be taken by October of the senior year. There are early admissions and deferred admissions plans. Applications should be filed by February 1 for fall entry. The fall 2016 application fee was $40. Notifications are sent February 1. 152 applicants were on the 2016 waiting list; 16 were admitted. Applications are accepted on-line. Application fees are waived if application is completed on-line. **Transfer Students:** 633 transfer students enrolled in 2015-2016. Applicants must submit transcripts of all college and high school records. A minimum GPA of 2.0 is required. Some majors specify a higher cumulative GPA. 30 of 120 credits required for the bachelor's degree must be completed at UMaine. **International Students:** There are 199 international students enrolled. The school actively recruits these students. They must take the TOEFL with a minimum score of 550 on the paper-based TOEFL (PBT) or 79 on the Internet-based version (iBT).

ADMISSIONS: 90% of the 2016-2017 applicants were accepted. The SAT scores for the 2016-2017 freshman class were: Critical Reading-- 34% below 500, 45% between 500 and 599, 18% between 600 and 699, and 3% between 700 and 800. Math-- 32% below 500, 42% between 500 and 599, 22% between 600 and 699, and 4% between 700 and 800. Writing-- 40% below 500, 44% between 500 and 599, 14% between 600 and 699, and 2% between 700 and 800. The ACT scores were 7% between 12 and 17, 45% between 18 and 23, 41% between 24 and 29, and 7% above 30. 34% of the current freshmen were in the top fifth of their class; 64% were in the top two fifths. There were 6 National Merit finalists. 16 freshmen graduated first in their class. **Admissions Contact:** Whitney Yorston, Director of Communications. Email: *umaineadmissions@maine.edu* Web: *www.umaine.edu*

FINANCIAL AID: In 2016-2017, 99% of all full-time freshmen and 92% of continuing full-time students received some form of financial aid. 70% of all full-time freshmen and 68% of continuing full-time students received need-based aid. The average freshman award was $19,525. Need-based scholarships or need-based grants averaged $7,125; need-based self-help aid (loans and jobs) averaged $4,866; non-need-based athletic scholarships averaged $227; and other non-need-based awards and non-need-based scholarships averaged $7,533. 31% of undergraduate students work part-time. Average annual earnings from campus work are $1920. The average financial indebtedness of the 2016 graduate was $34,920. The FAFSA code is 002053. The priority date for freshman financial aid applications for fall entry is March 1.

UNIVERSITY OF MAINE AT AUGUSTA B-5

www.uma.edu

Augusta, ME 04430	(207) 621-3465
Fax: (207) 621-3333	Email: umaadm@maine.edu
Full-time: 639 men, 1260 women	Faculty: 104; IIB, -$
Part-time: 772 men, 2319 women	Ph.D.s: 54%
Graduate: n/av	Student/Faculty: 15 to 1
Year: semesters, summer session	Tuition: $7812 ($19,332)
Room & Board: n/app	Freshman Class: 875 applied, 817 accepted, 512 enrolled
	CEEB CODE: 3929
Application Deadline: August 15	COMPETITIVE

University of Maine at Augusta, founded in 1965, offers both associate and baccalaureate degrees and is part of the University of Maine System. Figures in the above capsule and in this profile are approximate. There are 3 undergraduate schools. In addition to regional accreditation, UMA has baccalaureate program accreditation with ADA, NLN, and NEASC. The 159-acre campus is in a small town 50 miles north of Portland. Including any residence halls, there are 15 buildings.

STUDENT LIFE: 97% of undergraduates are from Maine. Others are from 35 states, 3 foreign countries, and Canada. 99% are from public schools. 73% are White; 3% American Indian/Alaska Native; 1% African American; 1% Asian American; 1% Hispanic. **Female To Male Ratio:** 2.5:1. The average age of freshmen is 27; all undergraduates, 32. 46% do not continue beyond their first year; 30% remain to graduate. **Housing:** Alcohol is not permitted. All students commute. All students may keep cars.

FACULTY/CLASSROOMS: 43% of faculty are male; 47% are female. All teach undergraduates. No introductory courses are taught by graduate students. The average class size in an introductory lecture is 20; in a laboratory is 16; and in a regular course is 18.

PROGRAMS OF STUDY: UMA confers B.A., B.A.S., B. Mus., and B.S. degrees. Associate degrees are also awarded. Bachelor's degrees are awarded in BIOLOGICAL SCIENCE (biology/biological science), BUSINESS (accounting and business administration and management), COMMUNICATIONS AND THE ARTS (art, English, and jazz), COMPUTER AND PHYSICAL SCIENCE (applied science and information sciences and systems), EDUCATION (library science), ENGINEERING AND ENVIRONMENTAL DESIGN (architecture), HEALTH PROFESSIONS (dental hygiene, mental health/human services, and nursing), SOCIAL SCIENCE (interdisciplinary studies, law enforcement and corrections, liberal arts/general studies, public administration, and social science). Mental health and human services have the largest enrollments.

ACTIVITIES: There are no fraternities or sororities. There are 17 groups on campus, including music ensembles, art, drama, honors, international, jazz band, LGBT, literary magazine, newspaper, pep band, professional, religious, social, social service, student government, and theater. Popular campus events include Mile of Art, Jazz Week, and Plunkett Poetry Festival. **Sports:** There are 2 intercollegiate sports for men and 3 for women, and 4 intramural sports for men and 4 for women. Facilities include the UMA Community Outdoor Leisure Center, which provides for seasonal activities and feature a running and cross-country skiing trail, tennis courts, a soccer field, and a softball field. Indoor facilities include a gym, a racquetball court, and a fitness center. **Graduates:** From July 1, 2015 to June 30, 2016, 362 bachelor's degrees were awarded. The most popular majors were health professions (29%), liberal arts/general studies (20%), and business/marketing (17%). 10 companies recruited on campus in 2015-2016.

SERVICES: Counseling and information services are available, as is tutoring in some subjects. There is remedial math and writing. There are workshops on a variety of student success skills, such as effective learning and reducing test anxiety. **Library/Resources:** The 2 libraries contain 93,897 volumes, 4,676 microform items, and 4,783 audio/video tapes/CDs/DVDs, and subscribe to 493 periodicals including electronic. Computerized library services include interlibrary loans, database searching, Internet access, and Wi-Fi capability. Special learning facilities include an art gallery, an interactive television system. **Physically Challenged Students:** 95% of the campus is accessible. Facilities include wheelchair ramps, elevators, special parking, specially equipped restrooms, special class scheduling, lowered drinking fountains, and lowered telephones. **Special:** Work-study and internship programs with local employers, study abroad in Germany, and a student-designed interdisciplinary studies major are available. Cross-registration is offered with University of Maine System campuses. There is 1 national honor society. **Visiting:** There are regularly scheduled orientations for prospective students, during the month before the beginning of a semester. There are guides for informal visits and visitors may sit in on classes. To schedule a visit, contact the Admissions Office. **Campus Safety and Security:** Measures include emergency notification system and security escort services. There are emergency telephones and lighted pathways/sidewalks.

REQUIREMENTS: Students are encouraged to submit SAT scores for placement only. Applicants should have a high school diploma or the GED. Recommended secondary preparation varies according to the degree program. Applicants for the B.M. program must audition. UMA requires applicants to be in the upper 25% of their class. A GPA of 2.0 is required. AP and CLEP credits are accepted. All students must complete at least 120 hours, including 30 to 40 in the major, with a minimum GPA of 2.0. All degree programs require courses in communications, humanities, college writing, and fine arts. 6 credits of writing-intensive course-work is required. **Procedure:** Freshmen are admitted fall, spring, and summer. There are deferred admissions and rolling admissions plans. Applications should be filed by August 15 for fall entry; October 15 for spring entry, along with a $40 fee. Notification is sent on a rolling basis. Applications are accepted on-line. **Transfer Students:** 625 transfer students enrolled in 2015-2016. High school/college transcripts and a statement of good standing from prior institutions are required. Standardized test scores are required for some students, and an interview is recommended. 30 of 120 credits required for the bachelor's degree must be completed at UMA. **International Students:** There are 42 international students enrolled. They must take the TOEFL with a minimum score of 500 on the paper-based TOEFL (PBT).

ADMISSIONS: 93% of the 2016-2017 applicants were accepted. 12% of the current freshmen were in the top fifth of their class; 63% were in the top two fifths. **Admissions Contact:** Kathy Trask, Associate Director of Admissions. Email: *umaadm@maine.edu* Web: *www.uma.edu*

FINANCIAL AID: In 2016-2017, 90% of all full-time freshmen and 99% of continuing full-time students received some form of financial aid. 84% of all full-time freshmen and 90% of continuing full-time students received need-based aid. The average freshman award was $8,026. Need-based scholarships or need-based grants averaged $5,816 ($6,640 maximum); need-based self-help aid (loans and jobs) averaged $6,164 ($7,500 maximum); non-need-based athletic scholarships averaged $2,850; and other non-need-based awards and non-need-based scholarships averaged $6,156 ($2,600 maximum). 5% of undergraduate students work part-time. Average annual earnings from campus work are $1757. The average financial indebtedness of the 2016 graduate was $24,353. The FAFSA code is 006760. The priority date for freshman financial aid applications for fall entry is March 1.

UNIVERSITY OF MAINE AT FARMINGTON B-4

www.umf.maine.edu

Farmington, ME 04938	(207) 778-7050
Fax: (207) 778-8182	Email: umfadmit@maine.edu
Full-time: 576 men, 1086 women	Faculty: 110; IIB, -$
Part-time: 37 men, 83 women	Ph.D.s: 88%
Graduate: 37 men, 181 women	Student/Faculty: 14 to 1
Year: semesters, summer session	Tuition: $9217 ($18,305)
Room & Board: $8970	Freshman Class: 1881 applied, 1512 accepted, 435 enrolled
SAT CR/M/W: 510/490/500	CEEB CODE: 3506
Application Deadline: rolling	COMPETITIVE

University of Maine at Farmington, founded in 1863 and part of the University of Maine System, is a public liberal arts institution offering programs in arts and sciences, teacher education, and human services. There is 1 undergraduate school and 1 graduate school. In addition to regional accreditation, UMF has baccalaureate program accreditation with NCATE. The 55-acre campus is in a small town 38 miles northwest of Augusta, and 80 miles north of Portland. Including any residence halls, there are 43 buildings.

STUDENT LIFE: 83% of undergraduates are from Maine. Others are from 19 states, and 7 foreign countries. 88% are from public schools. 87% are White; 5% race unknown; 2% African American; 2% Hispanic; 2% two or more races; 1% Asian American; 1% Foreign. **Female To Male Ratio:** 2.1:1. The average age of freshmen is 18; all undergraduates, 21. 24% do not continue beyond their first year; 55% remain to graduate. **Housing:** 1034 students can be accommodated in college housing, which includes single-sex and coed dorms. Interest-based themes floors available in residence halls. On-campus housing is guaranteed for all 4 years. 53% of students live on campus; of those, 70% remain on campus on weekends. All students may keep cars.

FACULTY/CLASSROOMS: 37% of faculty are male; 63% are female. All teach undergraduates, 80% do research, and 80% do both. No introductory courses are taught by graduate students. The average class size in an introductory lecture is 38; in a laboratory is 18; and in a regular course is 17.

PROGRAMS OF STUDY: UMF confers B.A., B.S., B.F.A., and B.G.S. degrees. Master's degrees are also awarded. Bachelor's degrees are awarded in AGRICULTURE (environmental studies), BIOLOGICAL SCIENCE (biology/biological science), BUSINESS (business administration and management, business economics, and recreation and leisure services), COMMUNICATIONS AND THE ARTS (art, creative writing, English, media arts, and visual and performing arts), COMPUTER AND PHYSICAL SCIENCE (actuarial science, computer science, geology, and mathematics), EDUCATION (early childhood education, elementary education, health education, health information management, secondary education, and special education), ENGINEERING AND ENVIRONMENTAL DESIGN (environmental science), HEALTH PROFESSIONS (community health work and rehabilitation therapy), SOCIAL SCIENCE (anthropology, geography, history, interdisciplinary studies, international studies, liberal arts/general studies, philosophy and religion, political science/government, psychology, and sociology). Creative writing, actuarial science, secondary education, and biology are the strongest academically. Education, psychology, and community health education have the largest enrollments.

ACTIVITIES: There are no fraternities or sororities. There are 65 groups on campus, including animee, improvisation, poetry, table gaming, art, band, cheerleading, choir, chorus, communications, computers, dance, drama, environmental, ethnic, film, honors, international, jazz band, LGBT, literary magazine, musical theater, newspaper, orchestra, political, professional, radio and TV, religious, social, social service, Student Education Association of Maine, and student government. Popular campus events include Parents and Alumni weekends, excursions to Boston & other destinations, outdoor recreation excursions, Michael D. Wilson Symposium Day, Spring Fling, Sustainability Carnival & Sledding Event, Skating Under the Stars, and Days of Service. **Sports:** There are 12 intercollegiate sports for men and 12 for women, and 10 intramural sports for men and 10 for women. Facilities include a gymnasium, with comprehensive training room, baseball field with grandstand seating, a skinned softball field with dugouts, practice and game field hockey, lacrosse, and soccer fields as well as a rugby pitch, ultimate Frisbee and intramural field, a field house with an indoor jogging track, 4 multipurpose courts (one of which is split for use as a group fitness area and a cardio and strength area, plus a freeweight area and a 25-yard swimming pool. The track and field teams have access to the local high school's track and field facility. The golf team utilizes a nearby comprehensive 18-hole facility for practice. The student ski team and recreational skiers and boarders have free access to an in-town ski co-op run Alpine and Nordic venue. **Graduates:** From July 1, 2015 to June 30, 2016, 368 bachelor's degrees were awarded. The most popular majors were education (27%), psychology (12%), and community health (8%). 50 companies recruited on campus in 2015-2016. In an average class, 36% graduate in 4 years or less, 51% graduate in 5 years or less, and 54% graduate in 6 years or less.

SERVICES: Counseling and information services are available, as is tutoring in every subject. There is a reader service for the blind, and remedial math, reading, and writing. Math and writing are available for drop-in tutoring; tutoring in all other subjects is available upon request. **Library/Resources:** The 2 libraries contain 59,750 volumes, 15,471 microform items, and 4,950 audio/video tapes/CDs/DVDs, and subscribe to 67,113 periodicals including electronic. Computerized library services include interlibrary loans, database searching, Internet access, and Wi-Fi capability. Special learning facilities include an art gallery, radio station, an astronomy observatory, Alice James books poetry journal, assistive learning center, and on-site nursery school and day care as a teaching environment. **Physically Challenged Students:** 95% of the campus is accessible. Facilities include wheelchair ramps, elevators, special parking, specially equipped restrooms, special class scheduling, lowered drinking fountains, and special housing. **Special:** Many opportunities for travel courses to countries such as Costa Rica, Italy, St. Johns, Ireland, Peru, Spain and more. Semester-long study abroad programs in China or France are available, as well as numerous other countries through co-operative arrangements with other universities. There are opportunities to participate in the National Student Exchange program. Student teaching is required of all education majors. Internships are required in rehabilitation and health and are also available in other disciplines under the sponsorship of the Partnership for Civic Advancement. There are multiple opportunities for student employment, including positions funded by the President's Work Initiative, which are available to all students. There are eight interdisciplinary majors offered, and individualized, student-designed majors are available and encouraged. UMF also offers 3+2 programs in Engineering and in Counseling. There are 4 national honor societies, a freshman honors program, and 9 departmental honors programs. **Visiting:** There are regularly scheduled orientations for prospective students, which include sessions on financial aid, majors, student life, the admissions process, and special opportunities such as study abroad, and tours of the campus. There are guides for informal visits and visitors may sit in on classes. To schedule a visit, contact the UMF Admissions Office at (207) 778-7086. **Campus Safety and Security:** Measures include 24-hour foot and vehicle patrol, emergency notification system, self-defense education, and security escort services. There are shuttle buses, emergency telephones, lighted pathways/sidewalks, controlled access to dorms/residences, and safety whistles.

REQUIREMENTS: Applicants are required to have 4 credits in English, 3 each in math, sciences (2 that are labs), and social sciences. An essay and a counselor recommendation are required, and an interview is recommended for some. The GED is accepted for highly motivated students. AP and CLEP credits are accepted. Important factors in the admissions decision are advanced placement or honors courses, recommendations by school officials, and extracurricular activities record. All students must maintain a minimum GPA of 2.0 while earning 128 semester hours, including 40 or more credits in their majors, and at least 40 credits in General Education. Core requirements include first-year seminar, English composition, mathematics, two courses in natural sciences, two courses in social sciences, humanities, fine arts, and a physical activity requirement. **Procedure:** Freshmen are admitted fall and spring. There are early admissions, deferred admissions, and rolling admissions plans. Application deadlines are open. Notification is sent on a rolling basis. Applications are accepted on-line. Application fees are waived if application is completed on-line. **Transfer Students:** 129 transfer students enrolled in 2015-2016. Applicants must have a minimum GPA of 2.0 (2.5 or 2.75 for some majors). Submission of passing Praxis Core scores are required of all students seeking transfer into teacher education programs leading to certification. 32 of 128 credits required for the bachelor's degree must be completed at UMF. **International Students:** There are 4 international students enrolled. The school actively recruits these students. They must take the TOEFL with a minimum score of 550 on the paper-based TOEFL (PBT) or 79 on the Internet-based version (iBT), or take the IELTS. The SAT is optional for admittance, but recommended for placement of matriculating first-year students.

ADMISSIONS: 80% of the 2016-2017 applicants were accepted. The SAT scores for the 2016-2017 freshman class were: Critical Reading-- 42% below 500, 39% between 500 and 599, 17% between 600 and 699, and 2% between 700 and 800. Math-- 51% below 500, 36% between 500 and 599, 11% between 600 and 699, and 2% between 700 and 800. Writing-- 50% below 500, 39% between 500 and 599, 10% between 600 and 699, and 1% between 700 and 800. 35% of the current freshmen were in the top fifth of their class; 67% were in the top two fifths. 3 freshmen graduated first in their class. **Admissions Contact:** UMF Admissions Email: *umfadmit@maine.edu* Web: *www.umf.maine.edu*

FINANCIAL AID: In 2016-2017, 82% of all full-time freshmen and 78%

of continuing full-time students received some form of financial aid. 79% of all full-time freshmen and 73% of continuing full-time students received need-based aid. The average freshman award was $14,568. Need-based scholarships or need-based grants averaged $8,916; need-based self-help aid (loans and jobs) averaged $6,237; and other non-need-based awards and non-need-based scholarships averaged $3,026. 47% of undergraduate students work part-time. Average annual earnings from campus work are $1337. The average financial indebtedness of the 2016 graduate was $30,517. The FAFSA code is 002040. The priority date for freshman financial aid applications for fall entry is March 1. The deadline for filing freshman financial aid applications for fall entry is May 1.

UNIVERSITY OF MAINE AT FORT KENT *(The complete profile is made available exclusively on our website, www.barronspac.com)*

UNIVERSITY OF MAINE AT MACHIAS E-4

www.machias.edu

Machias, ME 04654 (207) 255-1318
(888) 468-6866

Fax: (207) 255-1363 **Email: ummadmissions@maine.edu**

Full-time: 200 men, 300 women
Part-time: 145 men, 542 women
Graduate: n/av
Year: semesters, summer session
Room & Board: $8000

Faculty: 31; IIB, --$
Ph.D.s: 71%
Student/Faculty: 15 to 1
Tuition: $14,960 ($38,600)
Freshman Class: 374 applied, 312 accepted, 120 enrolled

SAT: recommended **ACT:** 22
Application Deadline: August 15

CEEB CODE: 3956
COMPETITIVE

University of Maine at Machias, founded in 1909, is a publicly funded liberal arts institution in the University of Maine System. Figures in the above capsule and in this profile are approximate. There are 4 undergraduate schools. In addition to regional accreditation, UMM has baccalaureate program accreditation with NRPA. The 243-acre campus is in a rural area 85 miles east of Bangor. Including any residence halls, there are 8 buildings.

STUDENT LIFE: 82% of undergraduates are from Maine. Others are from 26 states, 16 foreign countries, and Canada. 98% are from public schools. 90% are White; 4% American Indian/Alaska Native; 4% Foreign; 1% African American; 1% Hispanic. **Female To Male Ratio:** 2.4:1. The average age of freshmen is 20; all undergraduates, 29. 28% do not continue beyond their first year; 45% remain to graduate. **Housing:** 353 students can be accommodated in college housing, which includes single-sex and coed dorms. On-campus housing is guaranteed for all 4 years. 76% of students commute. All students may keep cars.

FACULTY/CLASSROOMS: 54% of faculty are male; 46% are female. All teach undergraduates. No introductory courses are taught by graduate students. The average class size in an introductory lecture is 21; in a laboratory is 16; and in a regular course is 17.

PROGRAMS OF STUDY: UMM confers B.A., B.S., and B.C.S. degrees. Associate degrees are also awarded. Bachelor's degrees are awarded in AGRICULTURE (agricultural business management, agricultural sciences, environmental studies, fish and game management, fishing and fisheries, and natural resources), BIOLOGICAL SCIENCE (biology ecology and field biology, biology/biological science, biological sciences, marine biology, marine science, wildlife conservation biology, and wildlife biology), BUSINESS (accounting, business administration and management, business administration marketing, entrepreneurial studies, environment & natnl resource economics, marketing/retailing/merchandising, recreation and leisure services, recreation/leisure (adventure leadership), recreation/leisure (community recreation), recreational facilities management, small business management, sports management, sustainable management, and tourism), COMMUNICATIONS AND THE ARTS (creative writing, English, fine arts, fine/studio arts, general, printmaking, recreation administration, sport & lifestyle studies, and writing), EDUCATION (business education, elementary education, English education, general studies, physical education, physical science secondary school education, recreation education, social studies education, social studies secondary school education, special education, and sports and wellness studies), ENGINEERING AND ENVIRONMENTAL DESIGN (environmental science and survey and mapping technology), HEALTH PROFESSIONS (allied health, biology, exercise science, mental health/human services, preallied health, predentistry, premedicine, pre-physician assistant, and preveterinary science), SOCIAL SCIENCE (behavioral science, criminal justice, human services, interdisciplinary studies, liberal arts/general studies, liberal arts, sciences, general studies, humanities, parks and recreation management, and psychology). Elementary education, marine biology, and environmental studies are the strongest academically. Elementary education, business administration, and behavioral science have the largest enrollments.

ACTIVITIES: 7% of men belong to 2 local and 2 national fraternities; 3% of women belong to 1 local and 3 national sororities. There are 34 groups on campus, including art, band, pop band, chorale, chorus, communications, computers, dance, drama, ethnic, honors, international, LGBT, literary magazine, musical theater, outing club, photography, professional, radio and TV, religious, social service, and student government. Popular campus events include Winter Carnival, Spring Weekend, Homecoming Weekend, and Greek Week. **Sports:** There are 2 intercollegiate sports for men and 3 for women, and 10 intramural sports for men and 10 for women. Facilities include 2 gyms, weight/exercise rooms, handball/raquetball courts, a pool, and a 64-acre recreational center with a lodge and cabins on the lake. **Graduates:** From July 1, 2015 to June 30, 2016, 100 bachelor's degrees were awarded. The most popular majors were behavioral science (15%), business administration (13%), and recreation management (13%). 10 companies recruited on campus in 2015-2016. In an average class, 19% graduate in 4 years or less, 42% graduate in 5 years or less, and 46% graduate in 6 years or less.

SERVICES: Counseling and information services are available, as is tutoring in every subject. There is remedial math, reading, and writing. The Student Services Coordinator provides one-on-one services, including learning strategies, study skills, and assistance with papers and learning styles. **Library/Resources:** The library contains 82,000 volumes, 5,000 microform items, and 3,000 audio/video tapes/CDs/DVDs, and subscribes to 320 periodicals including electronic. Computerized library services include interlibrary loans, database searching, Internet access, and Wi-Fi capability. Special learning facilities include an art gallery, radio station, and aquariums for marine and aquaculture studies. **Physically Challenged Students:** 85% of the campus is accessible. Facilities include wheelchair ramps, elevators, special parking, specially equipped restrooms, lowered drinking fountains, and automatic doors. **Special:** Co-op programs in all majors except education, cross-registration, internships, work-study programs, a B.A.-B.S. degree, study abroad in England and Wales, and a student-designed concentration in environmental science are available. UMM also offers a Bachelor of College Studies program, credit for prior learning, nondegree study, and a pass/fail option in certain courses. There are a freshman honors program. **Visiting:** There are regularly scheduled orientations for prospective students, consisting of traditional orientations prior to the fall and spring semesters, which include programming to guide students in all aspects of starting college—academic, student services and activities, and administrative. UMM also offers two summer student orientations, which include aspects of the fall orientations plus a parent orientation. There are guides for informal visits and visitors may sit in on classes. To schedule a visit, contact the Admissions Office at ummadmissions@maine.edu. **Campus Safety and Security:** Measures include emergency notification system, self-defense education, and security escort services. There are lighted pathways/sidewalks, controlled access to dorms/residences, a keyless entry system for residence halls, and security patrol from 5 p.m. to 5 a.m. daily.

REQUIREMENTS: The SAT or ACT is recommended. All candidates must be graduates of an accredited secondary school, although the GED/HiSET is accepted. UMM recommends that students place in the top half of their graduating class and that composite SAT scores be satisfactory. UMM also recommends completion of 4 units of English, 3 units of math, 2 each of lab science, social science/history, and fine arts or foreign language, and 3 units of electives. An essay is required, and an interview is strongly recommended. UMM requires applicants to be in the upper 50% of their class. AP and CLEP credits are accepted. Important factors in the admissions decision are extracurricular activities record, leadership record, and recommendations by school officials. To graduate, students must complete a minimum of 120 credit hours with a GPA of 2.0. The environmental core curriculum consists of 40-43 hours in the areas of communication skills, science and math, humans in social context, fine arts, historical and cultural perspectives, and lifetime fitness. **Proce-**

dure: Freshmen are admitted fall, spring, and summer. There are early admissions, deferred admissions, and rolling admissions plans. Applications should be filed by August 15 for fall entry, along with a $40 fee. Notification is sent on a rolling basis. Applications are accepted on-line. **Transfer Students:** 36 transfer students enrolled in 2015-2016. A minimum college GPA of 2.0 and evidence of good standing are required of transfer applicants. 30 of 120 credits required for the bachelor's degree must be completed at UMM. **International Students:** There are 10 international students enrolled. The school actively recruits these students. They must take the TOEFL with a minimum score of 5 on the paper-based TOEFL (PBT) or 5 on the Internet-based version (iBT).

ADMISSIONS: 83% of the 2016-2017 applicants were accepted. The ACT scores were 43% below 12, 14% between 12 and 17, 29% between 18 and 23, 7% between 24 and 29, and 7% above 30. 23% of the current freshmen were in the top fifth of their class; 53% were in the top two fifths. **Admissions Contact:** PJ Singh, Admissions Counselor. Email: *ummadmissions@maine.edu* Web: *www.machias.edu*

FINANCIAL AID: In 2016-2017, 88% of all full-time freshmen and 80% of continuing full-time students received some form of financial aid. 78% of all full-time freshmen and 82% of continuing full-time students received need-based aid. The average freshman award was $8,488. Need-based scholarships or need-based grants averaged $5,884; need-based self-help aid (loans and jobs) averaged $3,439; and other non-need-based awards and non-need-based scholarships averaged $6,420. The FAFSA code is 002055. The deadline for filing freshman financial aid applications for fall entry is March 1.

UNIVERSITY OF MAINE AT PRESQUE ISLE D-2

www.umpi.edu

Presque Isle, ME 04769 (207) 768-9453

Fax: (207) 768-9777	Email: umpi-admissions@maine.edu
Full-time: 267 men, 394 women	Faculty: 42; IIB, --$
Part-time: 46 men, 126 women	Ph.D.s: 56%
Graduate: n/av	Student/Faculty: 15 to 1
Year: semesters, summer session	Tuition: $7435 ($11,065)
Room & Board: $7844	Freshman Class: 1442 applied, 1112 accepted, 196 enrolled
ACT: 21	CEEB CODE: 3008
Application Deadline: n/av	COMPETITIVE

University of Maine at Presque Isle, founded in 1903, is a public institution within the University of Maine System offering liberal arts, teacher education, and professional programs leading to post-secondary certificates, and associate and bachelor's degrees. Figures in the above capsule and in this profile are approximate. There are 3 undergraduate schools. In addition to regional accreditation, UMPI has baccalaureate program accreditation with CSWE, CAATE, and NAACLS. The 150-acre campus is in a rural area 150 miles north of Bangor. Including any residence halls, there are 15 buildings.

STUDENT LIFE: 73% of undergraduates are from Maine. Others are from 14 states, 5 foreign countries, and Canada. 8% are Foreign; 67% White; 4% American Indian/Alaska Native; 1% Asian American; 1% Hispanic. **Female To Male Ratio:** 1.7:1. The average age of freshmen is 19; all undergraduates, 24. 45% do not continue beyond their first year; 28% remain to graduate. **Housing:** 359 students can be accommodated in college housing, which includes coed dorms, off-campus apartments, and married student housing. On-campus housing is guaranteed for all 4 years. 71% of students commute. All students may keep cars.

FACULTY/CLASSROOMS: 56% of faculty are male; 44% are female. All teach undergraduates. No introductory courses are taught by graduate students. The average class size in an introductory lecture is 20; in a laboratory is 12; and in a regular course is 15.

PROGRAMS OF STUDY: UMPI confers B.A., B.S., B.A.A.E., B.F.A., B.L.S., and B.S.W. degrees. Associate degrees are also awarded. Bachelor's degrees are awarded in BIOLOGICAL SCIENCE (biology/biological science), BUSINESS (accounting, business administration and management, and recreation and leisure services), COMMUNICATIONS AND THE ARTS (applied art, art, and English), EDUCATION (art education, athletic training, elementary education, health education, physical education, and secondary education), ENGINEERING AND ENVIRONMENTAL DESIGN (environmental science), SOCIAL SCIENCE (criminal justice, international studies, liberal arts/general studies, and social work). Education, social work, and criminal justice have the largest enrollments.

ACTIVITIES: 2% of men belong to 1 national fraternity; 1% of women belong to 1 national sorority. There are 25 groups on campus, including activities board, diversity club, non-traditional students club, a Cappella group, art, band, chess, communications, drama, environmental, ethnic, honors, international, LGBT, literary magazine, newspaper, professional, radio and TV, religious, social, social service, and student government. Popular campus events include Spring Ball, Winter Blast, and Spring Fest. **Sports:** There are 6 intercollegiate sports for men and 6 for women, and 15 intramural sports for men and 15 for women. Facilities include a facility that houses a swimming pool, gymnasium, track, fitness room and climbing wall. Another multifunctional structure houses a gym, a weight room, phys ed labs, a sports medicine facility, Athletic Hall of Fame, and an auditorium. A large playing field contains baseball, soccer, and tennis courts. There are also hiking trails, a bike path, and a ropes course. The campus also hosts a ice hockey team. **Graduates:** From July 1, 2015 to June 30, 2016, 149 bachelor's degrees were awarded. The most popular majors were education (17%), business/marketing (17%), and liberal arts/general studies (15%). 35 companies recruited on campus in 2015-2016. In an average class, 7% graduate in 4 years or less, 21% graduate in 5 years or less, and 28% graduate in 6 years or less. Of the 2015 graduating class, 7% were enrolled in graduate school within 6 months of graduation.

SERVICES: Counseling and information services are available, as is tutoring in most subjects. There is remedial math, reading, and writing. **Library/Resources:** The library contains 75,000 volumes, 750,000 microform items, and 1,400 audio/video tapes/CDs/DVDs, and subscribes to 2,000 periodicals including electronic. Computerized library services include interlibrary loans, database searching, and Internet access. Special learning facilities include an art gallery, natural history museum, radio station, and a theater. **Physically Challenged Students:** All of the campus is accessible. Facilities include wheelchair ramps, elevators, special parking, specially equipped restrooms, special class scheduling, lowered drinking fountains, lowered telephones, and special housing. **Special:** The university participates in transfer programs in agriculture, nutrition science, and animal and veterinary science. There is a nursing program with the University of Maine at Fort Kent. There are study-abroad programs in France, Ireland, and Canada (other countries are available), and internships in many majors. UM-Presque Isle offers work-study programs, dual and student-designed majors, a B.A.-B.S. degree, and nondegree study. Students can apply for credit by exam and credit for life, military, and work experience. A credit/no credit option is available. There is 1 national honor society, a freshman honors program, and 5 departmental honors programs. **Visiting:** There are regularly scheduled orientations for prospective students, including advisement, a campus tour, and meetings with faculty and coaches. There are guides for informal visits, visitors may sit in on classes, and stay overnight. **Campus Safety and Security:** Measures include security escort services. There are lighted pathways/sidewalks.

REQUIREMENTS: Applicants should have completed 16 academic credits recommended at an accredited secondary school, including 4 in English, 3 each in math and social studies, 2 each in science with a lab, foreign language, and electives. A GED certificate may be substituted. The university recommends an essay and an interview for all candidates. Art majors must submit a portfolio. AP and CLEP credits are accepted. Important factors in the admissions decision are advanced placement or honors courses, recommendations by school officials, and extracurricular activities record. Core requirements for B.A. degrees include 18 credits in humanities, 12 in social science, 11 in math/science, and 4 in phys ed/health. The student must complete a minimum number of credits, which varies according to major, with a cumulative GPA of 2.0 in 120 to 128 credit hours. Requirements for the B.S. and other degrees vary considerably with each major. **Procedure:** Freshmen are admitted fall, spring, and summer. Entrance exams should be taken by January 1. There are early decision, deferred admissions, and rolling admissions plans. Application deadlines are open. The fall 2016 application fee was $40. Applications are accepted on-line. **Transfer Students:** 203 transfer students enrolled in 2015-2016. Applicants must have a 2.0 GPA from a regionally accredited two-or four-year college. Applicants must submit official transcripts from all colleges attended, along with an official ranscript from the high school from which they graduated. 30 of 120 credits required for the bachelor's degree must be completed at UMPI. **International Students:** There are 368 international students enrolled. The school actively recruits these students. They must take the TOEFL.

ADMISSIONS: 77% of the 2016-2017 applicants were accepted. 16% of the current freshmen were in the top fifth of their class; 38% were in the top two fifths. **Admissions Contact:** Erin Benson, Director of Admissions. Email: *umpi-admissions@maine.edu* Web: *www.umpi.edu*

FINANCIAL AID: In 2016-2017, 74% of all full-time freshmen and 79% of continuing full-time students received some form of financial aid. 89% of all full-time freshmen and 89% of continuing full-time students received need-based aid. The average freshman award was $12,268. Need-based scholarships or need-based grants averaged $8,150; need-based self-help aid (loans and jobs) averaged $4,223; other non-need-based awards and non-need-based scholarships averaged $2,063; and $2,403 from other forms of aid. The average financial indebtedness of the 2016 graduate was $5,193. The FAFSA code is 002033. The priority date for freshman financial aid applications for fall entry is April 1.

UNIVERSITY OF NEW ENGLAND — B-6

www.une.edu

Biddeford, ME 04005	**1-800-477-4863** **(800) 477-4863**
Fax: 207-602-4900	**Email: admissions@une.edu**
Full-time: 640 men, 1701 women	**Faculty:** 153; IIA, av$
Part-time: 11 men, 22 women	**Ph.D.s:** 73%
Graduate: 1170 men, 2818 women	**Student/Faculty:** 15 to 1
Year: semesters, summer session	**Tuition:** $35,630
Room & Board: $13,250	**Freshman Class:** 4883 applied, 4056 accepted, 722 enrolled
SAT CR/M/W: 523/529/510 **ACT:** 23	**CEEB CODE:** 3751
Application Deadline: February 15	**COMPETITIVE**

University of New England is leading the transformation of global health sciences education. Beyond mere "training," we provide a full and integrated education preparing our graduates for evolving health care professions. In addition to our 27 health sciences disciplines, the full range of liberal arts classes and majors makes UNE a unique participatory educational environment. No matter what degree or profession you are pursuing, the interdisciplinary learning turns out scholars and professionals who can adapt and prosper. In Dental Medicine, Pharmacy, Medicine, Nursing and 11 allied health programs, UNE prepares future health care professionals to practice comprehensive and collaborative team-based care the new gold standard. We have three beautiful campuses: in Portland and Biddeford, Maine, and in Tangier, Morocco. This newest campus in Tangier allows UNE students to experience the world while staying on track for their majors. It gives our future professionals a unique understanding of the world they will lead. There are 2 undergraduate schools and 6 graduate schools. In addition to regional accreditation, UNE has baccalaureate program accreditation with ACBSP, ADA, APTA, CSWE, NLN, CAAHEP, AOA, CAATE, and NLNAC. The 623-acre campus is in a small town on the banks of the Saco River and the shore of the Atlantic Ocean in Biddeford, ME. The Portland campus is located about 5 miles from Portland's Old Port in Maine's largest city. Including any residence halls, there are 61 buildings.

STUDENT LIFE: 70% of undergraduates are from out of state, mostly the Northeast. Students are from 40 states, 6 foreign countries, and Canada. 9% are race unknown; 74% White; 7% African American; 6% Asian American; 1% Hispanic; 1% Foreign; 1% two or more races. **Female To Male Ratio:** 2.5:1. The average age of freshmen is 18; all undergraduates, 20. 20% do not continue beyond their first year; 80% remain to graduate. **Housing:** 1525 students can be accommodated in college housing, which includes single-sex and coed dorms. In addition, there are special-interest houses. On-campus housing is guaranteed for the freshman year only. 65% of students live on campus. All students may keep cars.

FACULTY/CLASSROOMS: 42% of faculty are male; 58% are female. 45% teach undergraduates. No introductory courses are taught by graduate students. The average class size in a laboratory is 18 and in a regular course is 21.

PROGRAMS OF STUDY: UNE confers B.A., B.S., B.S.W., and B.S.N. degrees. Master's and doctoral degrees are also awarded. Bachelor's degrees are awarded in AGRICULTURE (animal science, aquaculture & fishery technology, and environmental studies), BIOLOGICAL SCIENCE (biochemistry, biology/biological science, marine affairs, marine science, neurosciences, and nutrition), BUSINESS (business administration and management and sports management), COMMUNICATIONS AND THE ARTS (art and design, communications, English, and recreation administration), COMPUTER AND PHYSICAL SCIENCE (applied mathematics, chemistry, and oceanography), EDUCATION (art education, athletic training, education, elementary education, and secondary education), ENGINEERING AND ENVIRONMENTAL DESIGN (environmental science), HEALTH PROFESSIONS (biomedical science, dental hygiene, exercise science, medical laboratory science, nursing, occupational therapy, predentistry, prepharmacy, pre-physician assistant, and public health), SOCIAL SCIENCE (applied social science, history, liberal arts/general studies, political science/government, psychology, social work, and sociology). Medical biology/medical sciences, nursing, and applied exercise science have the largest enrollments.

ACTIVITIES: There are no fraternities or sororities. There are 70 groups on campus, including and skiing, surfing, additional clubs for sailing, art, cheerleading, communications, dance, debate, drama, environmental, ethnic, honors, international, LGBT, literary magazine, musical theater, newspaper, pep band, political, professional, religious, social, social service, student government, and yearbook. Popular campus events include Welcome Week, Family and Friends Weekend, and Full Leadership Retreat. **Sports:** There are 7 intercollegiate sports for men and 10 for women, and 15 intramural sports for men and 15 for women. Facilities include The Harold Alfond Forum facility that includes an ice hockey arena, a performance court, fitness center, and athletic training rooms. The Campus Center houses a gym, indoor track, fitness center, six-lane pool, and a racquetball court. **Graduates:** From July 1, 2015 to June 30, 2016, 531 bachelor's degrees were awarded. The most popular majors were nursing (14%), medical biology/medical science (11%), and health wellness occupational studies (9%). 50 companies recruited on campus in 2015-2016. In an average class, 59% graduate in 4 years or less, 60% graduate in 5 years or less, and 60% graduate in 6 years or less.

SERVICES: Counseling and information services are available, as is tutoring in most subjects. There is a reader service for the blind, and remedial math, reading, and writing. **Library/Resources:** The 2 libraries contain 135,000 volumes, 536 microform items, 12,500 audio/video tapes/CDs/DVDs, and subscribe to 130,000 periodicals including electronic. Computerized library services include interlibrary loans, database searching, Internet access, and Wi-Fi capability. Special learning facilities include an Art Gallery, and a Marine Science Education Center. **Physically Challenged Students:** 85% of the campus is accessible. Facilities include wheelchair ramps, elevators, special parking, specially equipped restrooms, special class scheduling, lowered drinking fountains, lowered telephones, and special housing. **Special:** UNE offers cross-registration with the Greater Portland Alliance of Colleges and Universities, internships in all majors, work-study programs, and study abroad and dual majors in all departments. There are transfer articulation agreements with Central Maine Community College and Great Bay Community College. Additionally, the University offers several pre-medical tracks for students interested in pursuing a medical field as a graduate student, including several accelerated programs: social work, health/wellness/occupational studies, pre-pharmacy, physician assistant, medicine and dental medicine all offer undergrad/grad level tracks. There are 2 national honor societies. **Visiting:** There are regularly scheduled orientations for prospective students, which includes a tour and information session. There are guides for informal visits and visitors may sit in on classes. To schedule a visit, contact the Office of Undergraduate Admissions. **Campus Safety and Security:** Measures include 24-hour foot and vehicle patrol, emergency notification system, self-defense education, and security escort services. There are shuttle buses, emergency telephones, lighted pathways/sidewalks, controlled access to dorms/residences, and a safe-ride program for students.

REQUIREMENTS: Applicants should be high school graduates with 4 years of English, 3 years each of math and science, and 2 years each of history and social studies. The GED is accepted. SAT or ACT scores are required (students do not need to submit scores from both exams.) AP and CLEP credits are accepted. Important factors in the admissions decision are recommendations by school officials, geographical diversity, and advanced placement or honors courses. A total of at least 120 credits with a minimum GPA of 2.0 is required for graduation. Some programs require more than 120 credits. Students must take 43 credits in a liberal arts core curriculum of humanities, sciences, and social sciences. Most majors require 1-semester internships. Courses in English composition, human traditions, environmental studies, lab science, creative arts, and math are required. **Procedure:** Freshmen are admitted fall and spring. Entrance exams should be taken in the spring of the junior year or the fall of the senior year. There are early admissions and deferred admissions plans. Early decision applications should be filed by December 1; regular applications, by February 15 for fall entry; and December 1 for spring entry, along with a $40 fee. Notification is sent on a rolling basis. Applications are accepted on-line. Application fees are waived if application is completed on-line. **Transfer Students:** 158 transfer students enrolled in 2015-2016. Transfer applicants should present a GPA of at least 2.5 in prior college work. 30 of 120 credits required for the bachelor's degree must be completed at UNE. **International Students:** There are 12 international students enrolled. They must take the TOEFL with a minimum score of 550 on the paper-based TOEFL (PBT) or 79 on the Internet-based version (iBT). They must also take the SAT or ACT.

ADMISSIONS: 83% of the 2016-2017 applicants were accepted. The SAT scores for the 2016-2017 freshman class were: Critical Reading-- 39% below 500, 45% between 500 and 599, 14% between 600 and 699, and 2% between 700 and 800. Math-- 35% below 500, 43% between 500 and 599, 20% between 600 and 699, and 2% between 700 and 800. Writing-- 42% below 500, 45% between 500 and 599, and 13% between 600 and 699. The ACT scores were 4% between 12 and 17, 46% between 18 and 23, 45% between 24 and 29, and 4% above 30. **Admissions Contact:** Scott Steinberg, Dean of University Admission. Email: *admissions@une.edu* Web: *www.une.edu*

FINANCIAL AID: In 2016-2017, 100% of all full-time freshmen and 99% of continuing full-time students received some form of financial aid. The average freshman award was $34,702. 34% of undergraduate students work part-time. The FAFSA code is 002050. The deadline for filing freshman financial aid applications for fall entry is May 1.

UNIVERSITY OF SOUTHERN MAINE A-5

www.usm.maine.edu

Gorham, ME 04038 — (207) 780-5670, (800) 800-4876

Fax: (207) 780-5640	**Email:** admitusm@maine.edu
Full-time: 2166 men, 2665 women	**Faculty:** IIA, av$
Part-time: 1128 men, 1659 women	**Ph.D.s:** 74%
Graduate: 686 men, 1351 women	**Student/Faculty:** n/av
Year: semesters, summer session	**Tuition:** $8920 ($21,280)
Room & Board: $9400	**Freshman Class:** 3676 applied, 924 enrolled
SAT CR/M/W: 500/500/490 **ACT:** 21	**CEEB CODE:** 3691
Application Deadline: February 15	**COMPETITIVE**

University of Southern Maine, founded in 1878, is a publicly funded, multi-campus, comprehensive, residential, liberal arts institution serving the University of Maine system. Figures in the above capsule and in this profile are approximate. There are 5 undergraduate schools and 8 graduate schools. In addition to regional accreditation, USM has baccalaureate program accreditation with AACSB, ABET, CSAB, CSWE, NASM, NCATE, NLN, and NRPA. The 144-acre campus is in an urban area 110 miles north of Boston, MA. Including any residence halls, there are 66 buildings.

STUDENT LIFE: 90% of undergraduates are from Maine. Others are from 35 states, 27 foreign countries, and Canada. 97% are White; 1% African American; 1% Asian American; 1% American Indian/Alaska Native; 1% Hispanic. **Female To Male Ratio:** 1.4:1. The average age of freshmen is 19; all undergraduates, 25. **Housing:** 1835 students can be accommodated in college housing, which includes coed dorms, on-campus apartments, and married student housing. In addition, there are honors houses, special-interest houses, and a fine arts house. On-campus housing is guaranteed for all 4 years. 81% of students commute. All students may keep cars.

FACULTY/CLASSROOMS: 53% of faculty are male; 47% are female. 80% teach undergraduates and do research. No introductory courses are taught by graduate students. The average class size in an introductory lecture is 50; in a laboratory is 20; and in a regular course is 22.

PROGRAMS OF STUDY: USM confers B.A., B.S., B.F.A., and B.M. degrees. Associate, master's, and doctoral degrees are also awarded. Bachelor's degrees are awarded in BIOLOGICAL SCIENCE (biology/biological science), BUSINESS (accounting and business administration and management), COMMUNICATIONS AND THE ARTS (communications, dramatic arts, English, fine arts, French, music, and music performance), COMPUTER AND PHYSICAL SCIENCE (chemistry, computer science, geology, geoscience, mathematics, and physics), EDUCATION (music education and technical education), ENGINEERING AND ENVIRONMENTAL DESIGN (electrical/electronics engineering, environmental science, and industrial engineering technology), HEALTH PROFESSIONS (environmental health science, health science, nursing, recreation therapy, and sports medicine), SOCIAL SCIENCE (anthropology, economics, geography, history, philosophy, political science/government, psychology, social work, sociology, and women's studies). Electrical engineering, computer science, and nursing are the strongest academically. Business administration, nursing, and psychology have the largest enrollments.

ACTIVITIES: 2% of men belong to 1 local and 3 national fraternities; 2% of women belong to 2 local and 2 national sororities. There are 100 groups on campus, including ski, commuter, environmental, art, band, cheerleading, chess, choir, chorale, chorus, computers, dance, drama, ethnic, honors, international, jazz band, LGBT, literary magazine, musical theater, opera, orchestra, outing, photography, political, professional, religious, social, social service, and student government. Popular campus events include Winter Weekend, Spring Fling, and Comedy Nights. **Sports:** There are 12 intercollegiate sports for men and 13 for women, and 14 intramural sports for men and 14 for women. Facilities include gyms, tennis courts, athletic fields, racquetball and squash courts, cross-country ski trails, two weight-training and fitness facilities, an ice arena, a field house, and an indoor track. **Graduates:** From July 1, 2015 to June 30, 2016, 1101 bachelor's degrees were awarded. The most popular majors were health professions (20%), social sciences (19%), and business (13%).

SERVICES: Counseling and information services are available, as is tutoring in most subjects. There is a reader service for the blind, and remedial math, reading, and writing. **Library/Resources:** The 3 libraries contain 455,129 volumes, 731,755 microform items, and 5,288 audio/video tapes/CDs/DVDs, and subscribe to 3,249 periodicals including electronic. Computerized library services include interlibrary loans and database searching. Special learning facilities include an art gallery, planetarium, TV station, and cartography collections. **Physically Challenged Students:** All of the campus is accessible. Facilities include wheelchair ramps, elevators, special parking, specially equipped restrooms, special class scheduling, lowered drinking fountains, and lowered telephones. **Special:** Cross-registration within the University of Maine system and 4 Greater Portland colleges, a Washington semester, and study abroad in more than 12 countries are offered. Internships, co-op and work-study programs, a B.A.-B.S. degree, dual and student-designed majors, a 2-2 engineering program with the University of Maine, credit for life experience, nondegree study, and pass/fail options are also available. There is a January intersession. There are 2 national honor societies, a freshman honors program, and 1 departmental honors program. **Visiting:** There are regularly scheduled orientations for prospective students, including regularly scheduled campus tours and group information sessions, as well as special events such as fall open houses. Interviews are also available on request. There are guides for informal visits and visitors may sit in on classes. To schedule a visit, contact the Admissions Office. **Campus Safety and Security:** Measures include 24-hour foot and vehicle patrol, self-defense education, and security escort services. There are shuttle buses, emergency telephones, lighted pathways/sidewalks, and preventive programs within residence halls.

REQUIREMENTS: The SAT or ACT is required. Applicants must be graduates of an accredited secondary school. The GED is accepted. Either 41 academic credits or 20 1/2 Carnegie units are required. Secondary school courses should include 4 years of English, 3 of math, 2 each of a foreign language and lab science, and 1 each of history and social studies. An essay is required, as are auditions for music applicants and interviews for applicants to the School of Applied Science. Guidance counselor recommendations are required for those students applying during their senior year. AP and CLEP credits are accepted. Important factors in the admissions decision are advanced placement or honors courses, recommendations by school officials, and extracurricular activities record. A total of 120 hours, of which 36 to 94 are in the major, and a minimum GPA of 2.0 are required for graduation. All students must fulfill the distribution requirements of the 3-part core curriculum: basic competence, methods of inquiry/ways of knowing, and interdisciplinary studies. **Procedure:** Freshmen are admitted fall and spring. Entrance exams should be taken by May of the junior year or January of the senior year. There are deferred admissions and rolling admissions plans. Applications should be filed by February 15 for fall entry; December 1 for spring entry. The fall 2016 application fee was $40. Applications are accepted on-line. **Transfer Students:** 848 transfer students enrolled in 2015-2016. Applicants must have a minimum GPA of 2.0 or 2.75 for those from non-regionally accredited institutions. Students who have been out of high school for less than 3 years must submit SAT scores. 30 of 120 credits required for the bachelor's degree must be completed at USM. **International Students:** They must take the TOEFL.

ADMISSIONS: The SAT scores for the 2016-2017 freshman class were: Critical Reading-- 47% below 500, 39% between 500 and 599, 12% between 600 and 699, and 2% between 700 and 800. Math-- 50% below 500, 40% between 500 and 599, 9% between 600 and 699, and 1% between 700 and 800. Writing-- 51% below 500, 37% between 500 and 599, 11% between 600 and 699, and 1% between 700 and 800. The ACT scores were 45% below 12, 32% between 12 and 17, 15% between 18 and 23, 3% between 24 and 29, and 5% above 30. 22% of the current freshmen were in the top fifth of their class; 51% were in the top two fifths. **Admissions Contact:** Scott Steinberg, Dean of Undergraduate Admission. Email: *admitusm@maine.edu* Web: *www.usm.maine.edu*

FINANCIAL AID: The FAFSA code is 009762. The priority date for freshman financial aid applications for fall entry is February 15. The deadline for filing freshman financial aid applications for fall entry is March 1.

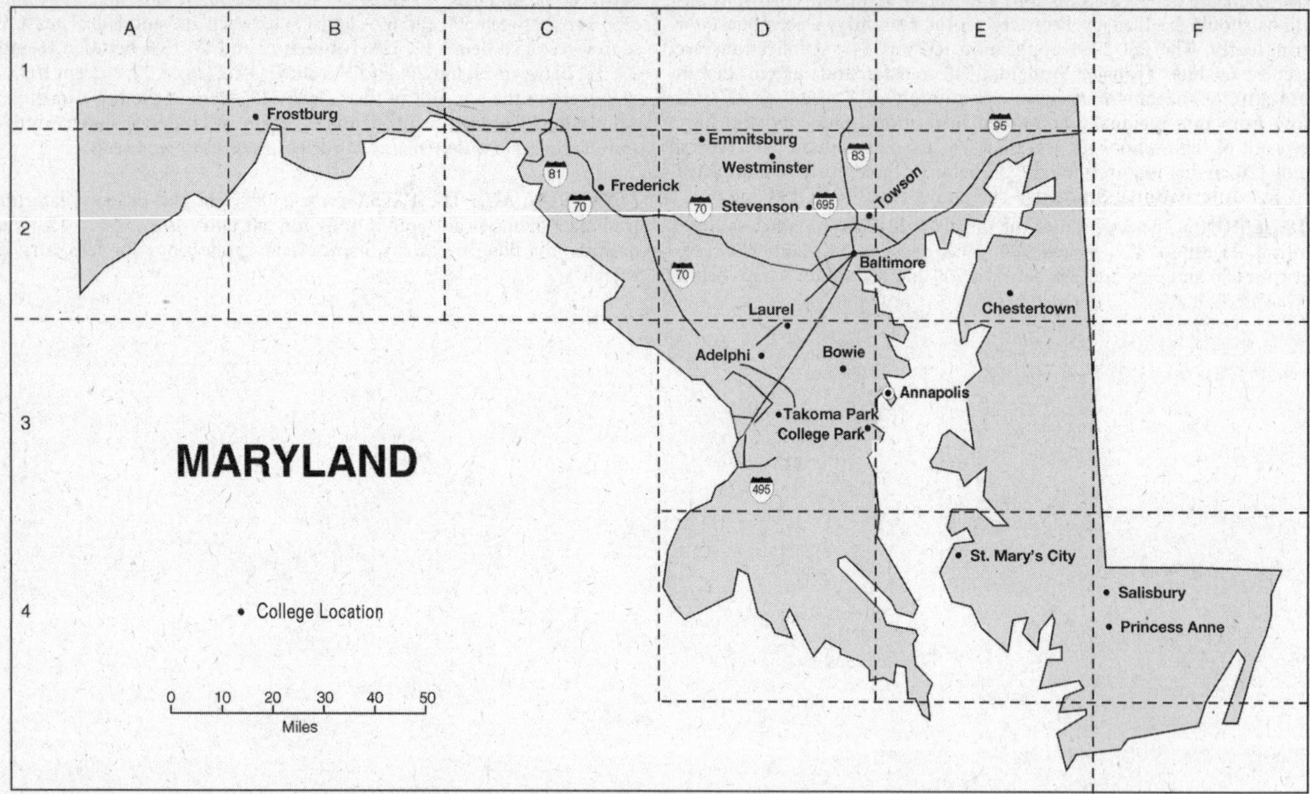

BOWIE STATE UNIVERSITY *(The complete profile is made available exclusively on our website, www.barronspac.com)*

CAPITOL TECHNOLOGY UNIVERSITY D-3

Capitol College
www.captechu.edu

Laurel, MD 20708 | **(301) 369-2800** **(800) 950-1992**

Fax: (301) 953-1442 | **Email: admissions@captechu.edu**

Full-time: 100 men, 40 women	**Faculty:** n/av
Part-time: 130 men, 30 women	**Ph.D.s:** n/av
Graduate: 340 men, 130 women	**Student/Faculty:** n/av
Year: semesters, summer session	**Tuition:** $25,430
Room & Board: $5980	**Freshman Class:** n/av
SAT: required	**CEEB CODE:** 5101
Application Deadline: open	**COMPETITIVE**

Capitol Technology University, was founded in 1927 as the Capitol Radio Engineering Institute, a correspondence school. Today it is a private college offering undergraduate programs in engineering and computer technology, as well as graduate programs in management and electronic commerce. Cost varies by program. The figures in the above capsule and in this profile are approximate. There are 4 undergraduate schools and 1 graduate school. In addition to regional accreditation, Capitol has baccalaureate program accreditation with ABET. The 52-acre campus is in a rural area in the south of Laurel Maryland, 19 miles north of Washington, D.C. Including any residence halls, there are 9 buildings.

STUDENT LIFE: 72% of undergraduates are from Maryland. Others are from 16 states, and 21 foreign countries. 7% are Foreign; 5% Asian American; 5% Hispanic; 43% White; 39% African American; 1% American Indian/Alaska Native. **Male To Female Ratio:** 2.9:1. The average age of freshmen is 23; all undergraduates, 28. 41% do not continue beyond their first year. **Housing:** 100 students can be accommodated in college housing, which includes coed on-campus apartments. On-campus housing is available on a first-come and first-served basis. Priority is given to out-of-town students. 87% of students commute. All students may keep cars.

FACULTY/CLASSROOMS: All teach undergraduates. No introductory courses are taught by graduate students. The average class size in an introductory lecture is 20 and in a regular course is 22.

PROGRAMS OF STUDY: Capitol confers B.S. degrees. Associate and master's degrees are also awarded. Bachelor's degrees are awarded in COMMUNICATIONS AND THE ARTS (telecommunications), COMPUTER AND PHYSICAL SCIENCE (optics), ENGINEERING AND ENVIRONMENTAL DESIGN (computer engineering, electrical/electronics engineering, and engineering technology). Electrical/electronics engineering is the strongest academically and has the largest enrollment.

ACTIVITIES: There are no fraternities or sororities. There are 17 groups on campus, including chess, computers, literary magazine, newspaper, professional, and student government. Popular campus events include Octoberfest and Spring Bash. **Sports:** Facilities include an off-campus gym, a basketball court, a student center, and athletic field.

SERVICES: Counseling and information services are available, as is tutoring in most subjects, such as math, electronics, English, and developmental English. **Library/Resources:** The library contains 10,000 volumes, and subscribes to 100 periodicals including electronic. Computerized library services include interlibrary loans and database searching. **Physically Challenged Students:** All of the campus is accessible. Facilities include wheelchair ramps, elevators, special parking, specially equipped restrooms, and lowered drinking fountains. **Special:** Internships and work-study programs are offered through the school's cooperative education program. There are 2 national honor societies. **Visiting:** There are regularly scheduled orientations for prospective students. There are guides for informal visits, visitors may sit in on classes, and stay overnight. To schedule a visit, contact the Admissions Office. **Campus Safety and Security:** There are lighted pathways/sidewalks.

REQUIREMENTS: The SAT is required with a minimum composite score of 860. Applicants should be graduates of an accredited secondary school. The GED is accepted. 20 academic credits or 20 Carnegie units are required. Secondary school courses must include 4 units of English, 3 of math, and 2 each of science and social studies. An essay and an interview are recommended. A GPA of 2.8 is required. AP and CLEP credits are accepted. Important factors in the admissions decision are advanced placement or honors courses, recommendations by school officials, and extracurricular activities record. A minimum GPA of 2.0 and 130 to 137 credit hours are required for graduation. Additional curriculum requirements vary with the major. **Procedure:** Freshmen are admitted to all sessions. Entrance exams should be taken by March 1. There is a rolling admissions plan. Application deadlines are open. Application fee is $25. Applications are accepted online. **Transfer Students:** Transfer students must have earned 15 college credits and a minimum GPA of 2.0. 40 of 130 credits required for the bachelor's degree must be completed at Capitol. **International Students:** The school actively recruits these students. They must take the TOEFL.

Admissions Contact: Darnell Edwards, Director of Admissions. Email: *admissions@captechu.edu* Web: *www.captechu.edu*

FINANCIAL AID: Capitol is a member of CSS. The CSS/Profile is required. Check with the school for current application deadlines.

COPPIN STATE UNIVERSITY D-2

www.coppin.edu

Baltimore, MD 21216	**(410) 951-3600** **(800) 635-3674**
Fax: (410) 523-7351	**Email: admissions@coppin.edu**
Full-time: 554 men, 1935 women	**Faculty:** 143; IIA, av$
Part-time: 137 men, 616 women	**Ph.D.s:** 55%
Graduate: 174 men, 516 women	**Student/Faculty:** 17 to 1
Year: semesters, summer session	**Tuition:** $7438 ($13,168)
Room & Board: $9603	**Freshman Class:** 5593 applied, 1988 accepted, 632 enrolled
SAT or ACT: required	**CEEB CODE:** 5122
Application Deadline: June 15	**VERY COMPETITIVE**

Coppin State University, founded in 1900 and part of the University System of Maryland, offers undergraduate programs in liberal arts, teacher education, and nursing. There are 5 undergraduate schools and 1 graduate school. In addition to regional accreditation, Coppin has baccalaureate program accreditation with NCATE, NLN, and NCSWE. The 65-acre campus is in an urban area in Baltimore, Maryland. Including any residence halls, there are 13 buildings.

STUDENT LIFE: 90% of undergraduates are from Maryland. Others are from 10 states, 5 foreign countries, and Canada. 90% are from public schools. 86% are African American; 4% Foreign; 3% Asian American; 2% Hispanic; 1% White; 1% American Indian/Alaska Native. **Female To Male Ratio:** 3.5:1. The average age of freshmen is 19; all undergraduates, 23. **Housing:** 600 students can be accommodated in college housing, which includes coed dorms. On-campus housing is available on a first-come and first-served basis. 79% of students commute. Upperclassmen may keep cars. Alcohol is not permitted.

FACULTY/CLASSROOMS: 55% of faculty are male; 45% are female. No introductory courses are taught by graduate students. The average class size in a regular course is 25.

PROGRAMS OF STUDY: Coppin confers B.A., B.S. and B.S.N. degrees. Master's degrees are also awarded. Bachelor's degrees are awarded in BIOLOGICAL SCIENCE (biology/biological science), BUSINESS (accounting, business administration and management, management science, and sports management), COMMUNICATIONS AND THE ARTS (English and visual and performing arts), COMPUTER AND PHYSICAL SCIENCE (chemistry, computer science, and mathematics), EDUCATION (elementary education, health information management, and special education), HEALTH PROFESSIONS (health, nursing, and rehabilitation therapy), SOCIAL SCIENCE (applied psychology, criminal justice, history, interdisciplinary studies, international studies, liberal arts/general studies, political science/government, psychology, social science, social work, and urban studies). Business, psychology, and criminal justice, and nursing are the strongest academically and have the largest enrollments.

ACTIVITIES: 27% of women belong to 4 national sororities. There are 35 groups on campus, including art, cheerleading, choir, chorus, computers, dance, drama, ethnic, film, honors, international, marching band, musical theater, newspaper, political, professional, religious, social, social service, and student government. Popular campus events include The Lyceum Series, Honors Program, and Black History Month. **Sports:** There are 7 intercollegiate sports for men and 7 for women, and 5 intramural sports for men and 5 for women. Facilities include a gym, indoor swimming pool, handball and racquetball courts, a soccer field, dance studio, weight room, an outdoor track, softball field, and tennis courts. **Graduates:** From July 1, 2015 to June 30, 2016, 484 bachelor's degrees were awarded. The most popular majors were nursing (16%), criminal justice (12%), and applied psychology (10%).

SERVICES: Counseling and information services are available, as is tutoring in every subject, and remedial math, reading, and writing. **Library/Resources:** The library contains 200,000 volumes, 233,000 microform items, and subscribes to 715 periodicals including electronic. Computerized library services include interlibrary loans, database searching, and Internet access. Special learning facilities include an art gallery. **Physically Challenged Students:** 95% of the campus is accessible. Facilities include wheelchair ramps, elevators, special parking, specially equipped restrooms, lowered drinking fountains, and lowered telephones. Individual attention for students requiring specialized materials, equipment, or instructional style accommodation. **Special:** Internships are available in business, as are B.A.-B.S. degrees in all majors. Student-designed majors are possible with approval. There are 3 national honor societies, Phi Beta Kappa, and a freshman honors program. **Visiting:** There are regularly scheduled orientations for prospective students, consisting of open houses. There are guides for informal visits and visitors may sit in on classes. To schedule a visit, contact the Office of Admissions. **Campus Safety and Security:** Measures include 24-hour foot and vehicle patrol, emergency notification system, and security escort services. There are also shuttle buses, emergency telephones, lighted pathways/sidewalks, and controlled access to dorms/residences.

REQUIREMENTS: The SAT or ACT is required. Applicants must be graduates of an accredited secondary school with a minimum GPA of 2.0 or have a GED certificate. Students must have completed 4 in English, 2 each in history, math, science, and social studies, and 1 in foreign language. Up to 15% of a freshman class may be admitted conditionally without these requirements, and those students who graduated high school more than 5 years ago will be reviewed individually. AP and CLEP credits are accepted. Important factors in the admissions decision are advanced placement or honors courses, extracurricular activities record, and evidence of special talent. To graduate, all students must have a minimum 2.0 GPA and complete a minimum of 120 credit hours (varies by program of study), with 36 to 40 hours in the major. Students must complete about 50 hours of liberal arts courses in English, math, speech, history, health, physical education, natural and social sciences, and philosophy. All seniors must take a standardized exit exam relevant to their major. **Procedure:** Freshmen are admitted to all sessions. There is a rolling admissions plan. Applications should be filed by June 15 for fall entry; December 15 for spring entry. The fall 2016 application fee was $50. Applications are accepted online. **Transfer Students:** Transfer students must have a minimum 2.0 GPA and be in good academic standing at their former institutions. Applicants with fewer than 25 credits must meet freshman requirements. 30 of 120 credits required for the bachelor's degree must be completed at Coppin. **International Students:** They must take the TOEFL with a minimum score of 500 on the paper-based TOEFL (PBT), in addition to the SAT or ACT.

ADMISSIONS: 36% of the 2016-2017 applicants were accepted. **Admissions Contact:** Michelle Gross, Director of Admissions. Email: *admissions@coppin.edu* Web: *www.coppin.edu*

FINANCIAL AID: Coppin is a member of CSS. The college's own financial statement is required. The FAFSA code is 002068. The priority date for freshman financial aid applications for fall entry is March 1.

FROSTBURG STATE UNIVERSITY *(The complete profile is made available exclusively on our website, www.barronspac.com)*

GOUCHER COLLEGE D-2

www.goucher.edu

Baltimore, MD 21204	**(410) 337-6100** **(800) 468-2437**
Fax: (410) 337-6354	**Email: admissions@goucher.edu**
Full-time: 460 men, 984 women	**Faculty:** 129; IIB, av$
Part-time: 14 men, 15 women	**Ph.D.s:** 91%
Graduate: 132 men, 567 women	**Student/Faculty:** 10 to 1
Year: semesters	**Tuition:** $43,416
Room & Board: $12,300	**Freshman Class:** 3443 applied, 2728 accepted, 440 enrolled
SAT CR/M/W: 590/570/560 **ACT:** 26	**CEEB CODE:** 5257
Application Deadline: February 1	**VERY COMPETITIVE**

Goucher College is an innovative liberal arts college and graduate school preparing students for 21st-century careers, including undergraduate studies abroad. Since 1885, Goucher has been a small college with a big view of the world. The college offers more than 30 majors and several interdisciplinary areas for undergraduates and 12 graduate programs. Every undergraduate studies abroad, helps students learn how to live, study, and work in different cultures through three-week, semester, or yearlong study abroad experiences. Goucher students receive a broad-based education with skills to last a lifetime such as critical thinking, abstract reasoning, and problem-solving to prepare them for the jobs of the future. They put their education into action through collaborative research in the natural sciences, service-learning programs that support local communities, and leadership opportunities. Goucher helps students become nimble, creative, confident, and capable of carving their own successes. Goucher graduates offer employers distinct advantages in a quickly changing, increasingly global economy. There is 1 undergraduate school and 1 graduate school. The 287-acre campus is in a suburban area 8 miles north of downtown Baltimore. Including any residence halls, there are 21 buildings.

STUDENT LIFE: 72% of undergraduates are from out of state, mostly the Middle Atlantic. Students are from 47 states, 30 foreign countries, and Canada. 62% are from public schools. 8% are Hispanic; 67% White; 4% two or more races; 4% race unknown; 3% Asian American; 3% Foreign; 10% African American. **Female To Male Ratio:** 2.6:1. The average age of freshmen is 18; all undergraduates, 20. 21% do not continue beyond their first year; 77% remain to graduate. **Housing:** 1285 students can be accommodated in college housing, which includes single-sex and coed dorms and on-campus apartments. In addition, there are language houses, special-interest houses, healthy living house, language house, peace house, and gaming house. On-campus housing is available on a lottery system for upperclassmen. 84% of students live on campus; of those, 80% remain on campus on weekends. All students may keep cars.

FACULTY/CLASSROOMS: 40% of faculty are male; 60% are female. All teach undergraduates. No introductory courses are taught by graduate students. The average class size in an introductory lecture is 18 and in a laboratory is 18.

PROGRAMS OF STUDY: Goucher confers B.A. degrees. Master's degrees are also awarded. Bachelor's degrees are awarded in AGRICULTURE (environmental studies), BIOLOGICAL SCIENCE (biochemistry and biology/biological science), BUSINESS (business administration and management), COMMUNICATIONS AND THE ARTS (art history, art, communications, dance, English, French, music, Russian, Spanish, and theatre arts), COMPUTER AND PHYSICAL SCIENCE (chemistry, computer science, mathematics, and physics), EDUCATION (education and special education), SOCIAL SCIENCE (American studies, anthropology, economics, history, interdisciplinary studies, international relations, peace studies, philosophy, political science/government, psychology, religion, sociology, and women's studies). Biology, chemistry, and history are the strongest academically. Psychology, business management, and English have the largest enrollments.

ACTIVITIES: There are no fraternities or sororities. There are 60 groups on campus, including art, campus agricultural co-op, chorale, chorus, communications, computers, dance, debate, drama, environmental, ethnic, film, honors, international, jazz band, LGBT, literary magazine, musical theater, newspaper, opera, orchestra, political, professional, radio and TV, religious, social, social service, student government, symphony, and yearbook. Popular campus events include Get into Goucher Day, Spring Gala, Opening Celebration, African-American Heritage, Hispanic Heritage, Fisher Music Residency, Rosenberg Lecture-Performance, and Meyerhoff Visiting Professorship. **Sports:** There are 9 intercollegiate sports for men and 11 for women, and 3 intramural sports for men and 3 for women. Facilities include gyms, indoor pool, strength and conditioning, training room, cardio fitness, racquetball, squash, tennis courts, indoor/outdoor equestrian, outdoor track, outdoor volleyball court, disc golf, and nature trails. **Graduates:** From July 1, 2015 to June 30, 2016, 327 bachelor's degrees were awarded. The most popular majors were psychology (12%), communications (10%), and business management (9%). 67 companies recruited on campus in 2015-2016. In an average class, 51% graduate in 4 years or less, 61% graduate in 5 years or less, and 63% graduate in 6 years or less.

SERVICES: There are many academic support options available through the college's Academic Center for Excellence (ACE). **Library/Resources:** The library contains 550,000 volumes, 22,268 microform items, 5,700 audio/video tapes/CDs/DVDs, and subscribes to 96,000 periodicals including electronic. Computerized library services include interlibrary loans, database searching, Internet access, and Wi-Fi capability. Special learning facilities include an art gallery, radio station, The Sanford J. Ungar Athenaeum, that features a technologically superior library, a forum for public events, classrooms, art gallery, and a center for community service programming. The academic center for excellence offers study-skills workshops, peer-led supplemental instruction, yoga, meditation, and Reiki sessions, a TV studio, three multi-purpose performance spaces, a robotics lab, a rooftop observatory, advanced teaching labs for physics, neuroscience, and computer science, research labs for math, physics, and psychology, a technology/learning center, international technology and media center, and centers for writing, math, and politics. **Physically Challenged Students:** All of the campus is accessible. Facilities include wheelchair ramps, elevators, special parking, specially equipped restrooms, special class scheduling, lowered drinking fountains, and special housing. **Special:** Goucher offers internships in Baltimore and Washington D.C., study abroad in 32 countries, and other off-campus experiences. The college also collaborates with many of the 14 other colleges in the Baltimore Collegetown Network. Students may cross-register with Johns Hopkins, Towson University, Peabody Institute, Stevenson University, Coppin State College, University of Maryland Baltimore, University of Maryland Baltimore County, Loyola College, the Community College of Baltimore County, and Maryland Institute College of Art. 3-2 engineering degrees with Johns Hopkins University and Columbia University are offered. Dual majors and student-designed, interdisciplinary majors are an option. There is 1 national honor society and a chapter of Phi Beta Kappa. **Visiting:** There are regularly scheduled orientations for prospective students. A full day experience introducing students to Goucher, academic life, and the campus community. There are guides for informal visits, visitors may sit in on classes, and stay overnight. To schedule a visit, contact Office of Admissions at admissions@goucher.edu. **Campus Safety and Security:** Measures include 24-hour foot and vehicle patrol, emergency notification system, self-defense education, and security escort services. There are also shuttle buses, emergency telephones, lighted pathways/sidewalks, controlled access to dorms/residences, an officer-manned gatehouse 24/7 during academic sessions, and a green dot program.

REQUIREMENTS: Applicants should be graduates of an accredited high school or have earned the GED. A personal essay is required, and an interview is recommended. Prospective performing or visual arts majors are urged to seek an audition or submit a portfolio through our Fine and Performing Arts Scholarship program. As an alternative to the traditional Common Application, Goucher has created the Goucher Video Application. AP credits are accepted. Important factors in the admissions decision are extracurricular activities record, recommendations by school officials, and advanced placement or honors courses. To graduate, all students must complete 120 credit hours, with a minimum GPA of 2.0. The number of required hours for each major varies by major. Requirements include; 1 lab-related course in the natural sciences; 1 course each in social sciences, mathematical reasoning, artistic/creative expression, textual analysis/critical perspectives, understanding diverse perspectives, environmental sustainability, and a physical education activity course. Students are also required to demonstrate proficiency in college writing, and a foreign language. Other requirements include a study abroad experience, for which students receive a voucher to help offset the cost. First year students attending college full-time for the first time must also complete a transitions course and a Frontiers course. **Procedure:** Freshmen are admitted in the fall and spring. Entrance exams should be taken in spring of the junior year or fall of the senior year. There are early decision, early admissions, and deferred admissions plans. Early decision applications should be filed by November 15; regular applications, by February 1 for fall entry; and December 1 for spring entry, along with a $55 fee. Notification of early decision is sent December 15; regular decision, April 1. 22 early decision candidates were accepted for the 2016-2017 class. 46 applicants were on the 2016 waiting list; 20 were admitted. Applications are accepted online. **Transfer Students:** 32 transfer students enrolled in 2015-2016. Common Application with personal essay, recommendation from college professor or academic teacher, and high school transcript (if a student has attempted less than 30 credits) 60 of 120 credits required for the bachelor's degree must be completed at Goucher. **International Students:** There are 38 international students enrolled. The school actively recruits these students. They must take the TOEFL with a minimum score of 550 on the paper-based TOEFL (PBT) or 80 on the Internet-based version (iBT).

ADMISSIONS: 79% of the 2016-2017 applicants were accepted. The SAT scores for the 2016-2017 freshman class were: Critical Reading--24% below 500, 34% between 500 and 599, 32% between 600 and 699, and 10% between 700 and 800. Math-- 22% below 500, 45% between 500 and 599, 23% between 600 and 699, and 10% between 700 and 800. Writing-- 27% below 500, 37% between 500 and 599, 30% between 600 and 699, and 6% between 700 and 800. The ACT scores were 5% between 12 and 17, 35% between 18 and 23, 46% between 24 and 29, and 14% above 30. 42% of the current freshmen were in the top fifth of their class; 76% were in the top two fifths. 3 freshmen graduated first in their class. **Admissions Contact:** Carlton E. Surbeck, Director of Admissions. Email: *admissions@goucher.edu* Web: *www.goucher.edu*

FINANCIAL AID: In 2016-2017, 71% of all full-time freshmen and 93% of continuing full-time students received some form of financial aid. 71% of all full-time freshmen and 92% of continuing full-time students received need-based aid. The average freshman award was $26,444. Need-based scholarships or need-based grants averaged $28,191; need-based self-help aid (loans and jobs) averaged $4,667; and other non-need-based awards and non-need-based scholarships averaged $16,099. 63% of undergraduate students work part-time. Average annual earnings from campus work are $2100. The average financial indebtedness of the 2016 graduate was $25,580. Goucher is a member of CSS. The CSS/Profile, and the college's own financial statement are required. The FAFSA code is 002073. The priority date for freshman financial aid applications for fall entry is February 1. The filing deadline for filing for fall entry is April 1.

HOOD COLLEGE — C-2

www.hood.edu

Frederick, MD 21701	**(301) 696-3400** **(800) 922-1599**
Fax: (301) 696-3819	**Email: admission@hood.edu**
Full-time: 446 men, 733 women	**Faculty:** 92; IIA, --$
Part-time: 32 men, 66 women	**Ph.D.s:** 95%
Graduate: 347 men, 664 women	**Student/Faculty:** 11 to 1
Year: semesters, summer session	**Tuition:** $34,120
Room & Board: $11,610	**Freshman Class:** 1636 applied, 1286 accepted, 258 enrolled
SAT CR/M/W: 520/515/500 **ACT:** 22	**CEEB CODE:** 5296
Application Deadline: August 15	**COMPETITIVE**

Hood College, founded in 1893, is an independent, comprehensive college that offers an integration of the liberal arts, and professional preparation, as well as undergraduate majors in the natural sciences. There are 4 undergraduate schools and 1 graduate school. In addition to regional accreditation, Hood has baccalaureate program accreditation with AACSB, CSWE, and NCATE. The 50-acre campus is in a suburban area 45 miles northwest of Washington, D.C. and 45 miles west of Baltimore. Including any residence halls, there are 38 buildings.

STUDENT LIFE: 77% of undergraduates are from Maryland. Others are from 27 states, 21 foreign countries, and Canada. 79% are from public schools. 8% are Hispanic; 65% White; 4% Asian American; 4% two or more races; 4% race unknown; 2% Foreign; 13% African American. 57% are Protestant; 18% Catholic; 12% claim no religious affiliation. **Female To Male Ratio:** 1.8:1. The average age of freshmen is 18; all undergraduates, 22. 22% do not continue beyond their first year; 66% remain to graduate. **Housing:** 823 students can be accommodated in college housing, which includes coed dorms, off-campus apartments, honors houses, and language houses. Special-interest floors in the residence halls include living/learning communities and a community service floor. On-campus housing is guaranteed for all 4 years, and is available on a first-come, first-served basis, and is available on a lottery system for upperclassmen. 55% of students live on campus; of those, 65% remain on campus on weekends. All students may keep cars.

FACULTY/CLASSROOMS: 42% of faculty are male; 58% are female. All teach undergraduates, and do research. No introductory courses are taught by graduate students. The average class size in an introductory lecture is 16; in a laboratory is 10; and in a regular course is 15.

PROGRAMS OF STUDY: Hood confers B.A., B.S. and B.S.N degrees. Master's and doctoral degrees are also awarded. Bachelor's degrees are awarded in BIOLOGICAL SCIENCE (biochemistry and biology/biological science), BUSINESS (accounting, business administration and management, business administration marketing, and marketing), COMMUNICATIONS AND THE ARTS (art, communications, English, French, German, music, and Spanish), COMPUTER AND PHYSICAL SCIENCE (chemistry, computer science, and mathematics), EDUCATION (early childhood education, elementary education, English education, foreign languages education, mathematics education, science education, secondary education, and special education), ENGINEERING AND ENVIRONMENTAL DESIGN (computational sciences and environmental science), HEALTH PROFESSIONS (nursing), SOCIAL SCIENCE (archeology, economics, history, international studies, Latin American studies, law, Middle Eastern studies, philosophy, political science/government, psychology, religion, social work, and sociology). Chemistry, social work, and psychology are the strongest academically. Business administration, psychology, and biology have the largest enrollments.

ACTIVITIES: There are no fraternities or sororities. There are 79 groups on campus, including art, band, cheerleading, choir, chorale, chorus, communications, computers, dance, drama, environmental, ethnic, film, honors, international, jazz band, LGBT, literary magazine, musical theater, newspaper, orchestra, political, professional, radio and TV, religious, social, social service, and student government. Popular campus events include Ring Formal, Liberation of the Black Mind Weekend, and Crab Fest. **Sports:** There are 9 intercollegiate sports for men and 10 for women, and 4 intramural sports for men and 5 for women. Facilities include men's and women's basketball and volleyball, with two-level fitness center and cardio room, a full-service athletic training room, pool, and fields for field hockey, soccer, and lacrosse. **Graduates:** From July 1, 2015 to June 30, 2016, 352 bachelor's degrees were awarded. The most popular majors were education (11%), psychology (9%), and biology (8%). 110 companies recruited on campus in 2015-2016. In an average class, 2% graduate in 3 years or less, 55% graduate in 4 years or less, 64% graduate in 5 years or less, and 66% graduate in 6 years or less. Of the 2015 graduating class, 33% were enrolled in graduate school within 6 months of graduation, and 63% were employed.

SERVICES: Counseling and information services are available, as is tutoring in some subjects. Readers for the blind and interpreters for the hearing impaired are available. There are also services for students with learning disabilities, a language lab, and courses in time management and study skills. **Library/Resources:** Computerized library services include interlibrary loans, database searching, Internet access, and Wi-Fi capability. Special learning facilities include an art gallery, radio station, aquatic center, a child development lab, an observatory, information technology center, mock trial court room, and financial trading room. **Physically Challenged Students:** 50% of the campus is accessible. Facilities include wheelchair ramps, elevators, special parking, specially equipped restrooms, special class scheduling, and special housing. **Special:** The college offers a Washington semester with American University, dual majors, student-designed majors, credit for life experience, nondegree study, pass/fail options, and cross-registration with area colleges and the Duke University Marine Sciences Education Consortium. Internships of up to 15 credits are available in all majors throughout the United States and abroad. Students may study abroad in the Dominican Republic, Japan, Spain, France, and other countries. There is a 4-year honors program featuring one interdisciplinary course per semester and special co-curricular activities. There are 16 national honor societies, a freshman honors program, and 8 departmental honors programs. **Visiting:** There are regularly scheduled orientations for prospective students, including tours and meetings with faculty, students and administrators, and admissions interviews. There are guides for informal visits, visitors may sit in on classes, and stay overnight. To schedule a visit, contact Lisa Troth at admission@hood.edu. **Campus Safety and Security:** Measures include 24-hour foot and vehicle patrol, emergency notification system, self-defense education, security escort services, emergency telephones, lighted pathways/sidewalks, and controlled access to dorms/residences.

REQUIREMENTS: The SAT or ACT is recommended. Applicants should be graduates of an accredited secondary school. The GED is accepted. Hood recommends the completion of at least 16 academic credits in high school, including courses in English, social sciences, natural sciences, foreign languages, and math. Hood College is SAT Optional for students with a high school GPA of 3.25 or higher on a 4.0 scale. AP and CLEP credits are accepted. Important factors in the admissions decision are advanced placement or honors courses, leadership record, and extracurricular activities record. To graduate, students must complete a total of 124 credit hours, with a minimum GPA of 2.0, and a 2.0 GPA in the major. 24 to 52 credits are required in a student's major. All students must complete 41 to 45 credits in the core curriculum, which includes first-year seminar, English, math, language courses, courses in methods of inquiry, and phys ed courses. Enrollment in the final 30 credits must be on the Hood Campus as a degree candidate. **Procedure:** Freshmen are admitted in the fall and spring. Entrance exams should be taken in spring of the junior year or fall of the senior year. There is a rolling admissions plan. Applications should be filed by August 15 for fall entry; December 31 for spring entry. Notifications are sent October 1. Application fees are waived if application is completed online. **Transfer Students:** 127 transfer students enrolled in 2015-2016. Applicants must have at least 12 college credits and a minimum GPA of 2.5. A total of 70 credits may be transferred. 30 of 124 credits required for the bachelor's degree must be completed at Hood. **International Students:** There are 33 international students enrolled. The school actively recruits these students. They must take the TOEFL with a minimum score of 550 on the paper-based TOEFL (PBT) or 79 on the Internet-based version (iBT), or take the IELTS. They must also take the SAT or ACT. SAT scores may be substituted for the TOEFL.

ADMISSIONS: 79% of the 2016-2017 applicants were accepted. The SAT scores for the 2016-2017 freshman class were: Critical Reading-- 42% below 500, 35% between 500 and 599, 20% between 600 and 699, and 3% between 700 and 800. Math-- 42% below 500, 37% between 500 and 599, 19% between 600 and 699, and 2% between 700 and 800. Writing-- 43% below 500, 44% between 500 and 599, 11% between 600 and 699, and 2% between 700 and 800. The ACT scores were 12% between 12 and 17, 44% between 18 and 23, 36% between 24 and 29, and 8% above 30. 25% of the current freshmen were in the top fifth of their class; 58% were in the top two fifths. 3 freshmen graduated first in their class. **Admissions Contact:** Jennifer Decker, Director of Admissions. Email: *admission@hood.edu* Web: *www.hood.edu*

FINANCIAL AID: In 2016-2017, 77% of all full-time freshmen and 79% of continuing full-time students received some form of financial aid. 85% of all full-time freshmen and 98% of continuing full-time students received need-based aid. The average freshman award was $28,376. Need-based scholarships or need-based grants averaged $25,594; need-based self-help aid (loans and jobs) averaged $3,728; and other non-need-based awards and non-need-based scholarships averaged $18,077. 24% of undergraduate students work part-time. Average annual earnings from campus work are $2000. The average financial indebtedness of the 2016 graduate was $23,750. Hood is a member of CSS. The FAFSA code is 002076. The priority date for freshman financial aid applications for fall entry is February 15.

JOHNS HOPKINS UNIVERSITY — D-2

www.jhu.edu

Baltimore, MD 21218	(410) 516-8171
Fax: (410) 516-6025	Email: gotojhu@jhu.edu
Full-time: 2741 men, 2594 women	Faculty: 623; I, +$
Part-time: 17 men, 13 women	Ph.D.s: 92%
Graduate: 1264 men, 677 women	Student/Faculty: 12 to 1
Year: 4-1-4, summer session	Tuition: $48,710
Room & Board: $14,540	Freshman Class: 14848 applied, 3603 accepted, 1206 enrolled
SAT CR/M/W: 680/710/680 ACT: 31	CEEB CODE: 5532
Application Deadline: January 1	MOST COMPETITIVE

Johns Hopkins University, founded in 1876, is a private multicampus institution offering undergraduate degrees at the Homewood campus through the Krieger School of Arts and Sciences, the Whiting School of Engineering, and the Peabody Institute of Music. There are 5 undergraduate schools and 9 graduate schools. In addition to regional accreditation, Johns Hopkins has baccalaureate program accreditation with ABET. The 140-acre campus is in a suburban area in a residential setting in northern Baltimore. Including any residence halls, there are 40 buildings.

STUDENT LIFE: 88% of undergraduates are from out of state, mostly the Middle Atlantic. Students are from 50 states, 49 foreign countries, and Canada. 60% are from public schools. 44% are White; 22% Asian American; 13% Hispanic. **Male To Female Ratio:** 1.2:1. The average age of freshmen is 18; all undergraduates, 20. 3% do not continue beyond their first year; 93% remain to graduate. **Housing:** 2700 students can be accommodated in college housing, which includes single-sex and coed dorms, on-campus apartments, off-campus apartments, special-interest houses, non-university-sponsored fraternity, and sorority houses. On-campus housing is available on a lottery system for upperclassmen. 61% of students live on campus. Upperclassmen may keep cars.

FACULTY/CLASSROOMS: 68% of faculty are male; 32% are female. No introductory courses are taught by graduate students.

PROGRAMS OF STUDY: Johns Hopkins confers B.A. and B.S. degrees. Master's and doctoral degrees are also awarded. Bachelor's degrees are awarded in BIOLOGICAL SCIENCE (biology/biological science, biophysics, cell biology, molecular biology, and neurosciences), BUSINESS (business administration and management), COMMUNICATIONS AND THE ARTS (art history and appreciation, classics, creative writing, English, French, German, Germanic languages and literature, Italian, Latin, media arts, music composition, romance languages and literature, and Spanish), COMPUTER AND PHYSICAL SCIENCE (applied mathematics, chemistry, computer science, earth science, mathematics, natural sciences, and physics), EDUCATION (music education), ENGINEERING AND ENVIRONMENTAL DESIGN (biomedical engineering, chemical engineering, civil engineering, computer engineering, electrical/electronics engineering, engineering, engineering mechanics, environmental engineering, environmental science, materials engineering, materials science, mechanical engineering, and systems engineering), HEALTH PROFESSIONS (public health), SOCIAL SCIENCE (African studies, anthropology, archeology, behavioral science, cognitive science, East Asian studies, economics, history, history of science, humanities, interdisciplinary studies, international studies, Latin American studies, Near Eastern studies, philosophy, political science/government, psychology, social science, and sociology). Engineering, public health, international studies, and writing seminars are the strongest academically. International studies, public health, and biomedical engineering have the largest enrollments.

ACTIVITIES: 24% of men belong to 13 national fraternities; 23% of women belong to 9 national sororities. There are 250 groups on campus, including art, band, cheerleading, chess, choir, chorale, chorus, clubs for volunteer organizations, computers, dance, debate, drama, ethnic, film, forensics, honors, international, jazz band, LGBT, literary magazine, marching band, musical theater, newspaper, opera, orchestra, pep band, photography, political, professional, radio and TV, religious, social, social service, student government, and symphony. Popular campus events include Fall Fest, Spring Fair, Homecoming, and Hoptoberfest. **Sports:** There are 12 intercollegiate sports for men and 10 for women, and 20 intramural sports for men and 20 for women. Facilities include a recreation center with pool and a diving pool, wrestling, fencing, weight room, fitness center, a climbing wall, an indoor jogging track, multipurpose rooms, and courts for basketball, badminton, squash, volleyball and handball. There is also a stadium, outdoor playing fields, and tennis courts. **Graduates:** From July 1, 2015 to June 30, 2016, 1004 bachelor's degrees were awarded. The most popular majors were biomedical engineering (11%), international studies (10%), and public health studies (9%). 224 companies recruited on campus in 2015-2016. In an average class, 3% graduate in 3 years or less, 83% graduate in 4 years or less, 91% graduate in 5 years or less, and 92% graduate in 6 years or less. Of the 2015 graduating class, 38% were enrolled in graduate school within 6 months of graduation, and 47% were employed.

SERVICES: Counseling and information services are available, as is tutoring in most subjects, and a reader service for the blind. **Library/Resources:** The 4 libraries contain 2.6 million volumes, 4.1 million microform items, 9,707 audio/video tapes/CDs/DVDs, and subscribe to 30,120 periodicals including electronic. Computerized library services include interlibrary loans, database searching, Internet access, and Wi-Fi capability. Special learning facilities include an art gallery, radio station, and a space telescope science institute. **Physically Challenged Students:** Facilities include wheelchair ramps, elevators, special parking, specially equipped restrooms, special class scheduling, lowered drinking fountains, and lowered telephones. JHU works with all individuals to ensure access to all programs. **Special:** Internships, dual majors in music and arts and sciences/engineering, cross-registration with Baltimore-area colleges and Johns Hopkins divisions, a cooperative double degree with Peabody Conservatory of Music, a cooperative film center with the Maryland Institute College of Arts (MICA), a student-designed semester at the Johns Hopkins School of International Studies in Washington, D.C., and various multidisciplinary programs are offered. Students may enroll at Johns Hopkins in Bologna, Italy, or Nanjing, China, Europe, South America, the Far East, and Australia. Combined BA/BS-MA/MS programs are available in many departments. There are 4 national honor societies, Phi Beta Kappa, and 25 departmental honors programs. **Visiting:** There are regularly scheduled orientations for prospective students, including scheduled open house programs, campus tours led by current students, and group information sessions offered weekday mornings and afternoons. There are guides for informal visits, visitors may sit in on classes, and stay overnight. To schedule a visit, contact Office of Undergraduate Admissions. **Campus Safety and Security:** Measures include 24-hour foot and vehicle patrol, emergency notification system, self-defense education, and security escort services. There are also shuttle buses, emergency telephones, and lighted pathways/sidewalks.

REQUIREMENTS: The SAT Reasoning Test or the ACT is required for all first-year applicants. The Writing section of the ACT is optional. The essay section of the redesigned SAT will be optional once it's administered. Applicants may also choose to submit SAT Subject Tests in one or more areas of interest as a way to demonstrate an academic strength. Johns Hopkins will consider the two highest Subject Test scores when reviewing applications, but your application will not be negatively affected if you choose not to submit Subject Test scores. The university encourages applicants interested in an engineering major to submit scores from the mathematics Level 2 SAT Subject Test and at least one science SAT Subject Test as a way to demonstrate their strengths in relevant subject areas. In addition, applicants should be graduates of an accredited secondary school or have the GED. The university recommends that secondary preparation include 4 years each of English and math, 2 (prefer 3) of social science or history and lab science, and 3-4 of a foreign language (2 for engineering majors). 2 personal essays are required, and interviews are available but not required. AP credits are accepted. Important factors in the admissions decision are advanced placement or honors courses, extracurricular activities record, and personality/intangible qualities. The B.A. requires a total of 120 hours; the B.S. in engineering requires 120 to 128 hours, depending on the major. A GPA of at least 2.0 is required for graduation. All students must take at least 4 courses (2 for engineers) with a writing-intensive component to graduate. **Procedure:** Freshmen are admitted in the fall. There are early decision and deferred admissions plans. Early decision applications should be filed by November 1; regular applications, by January 1 for fall entry, along with a $70 fee. Notification of early decision is sent December 15; regular decision, April 1. 447 early decision candidates were accepted for the 2016-2017 class. 1319 applicants were on the 2016 waiting list; 446 were admitted. Applications are accepted on-line. **Transfer Students:** 40 transfer students enrolled in 2015-2016. Transfer students from two- and four-year colleges and universities may apply for admission into the Johns Hopkins sophomore and junior classes in the fall semester only. Applicants must have completed more than 12 semester based credits (either matriculated or not) with a minimum cumulative grade point average of 3.0. Applications must include a written essay and at least 1 letter of recommendation. High school records are also required. 60 of 120 credits required for the bachelor's degree must be completed at Johns Hopkins. **International Students:** There are 494 international students enrolled. The school actively recruits these students. They must take the TOEFL with a minimum score of 600 on the paper-based TOEFL (PBT), as well as the SAT or ACT.

ADMISSIONS: 24% of the 2016-2017 applicants were accepted. The SAT scores for the 2016-2017 freshman class were: Critical Reading-- 1% below 500, 3% between 500 and 599, 35% between 600 and 699, and 62% between 700 and 800. Math-- 1% between 500 and 599, 23% between 600 and 699, and 75% between 700 and 800. Writing-- 3% between 500 and 599, 29% between 600 and 699, and 67% between 700 and 800. The ACT scores were 2% between 12 and 17, 13% between 18 and 23, 11% between 24 and 29, and 74% above 30. 92% of the current freshmen were in the top fifth of their class; 98% were in the top two fifths. 81 freshmen graduated first in their class. **Admissions Contact:** Alexandra Leikin, Office of Undergraduate Admissions. Email: *gotojhu@jhu.edu* Web: *www.jhu.edu*

FINANCIAL AID: The average freshman award was $38,105. Johns Hopkins is a member of CSS. The CSS/Profile and FAFSA are required. The deadline for filing freshman financial aid applications for fall entry is March 1.

LOYOLA UNIVERSITY MARYLAND D-2

www.loyola.edu

Baltimore, MD 21210 (410) 617-5012 (800) 221-9107
Email: admission@loyola.edu

Full-time: 1691 men, 2344 women	**Faculty:** I, ++$
Part-time: 21 men, 28 women	**Ph.D.s:** n/av
Graduate: 589 men, 1294 women	**Student/Faculty:** 12 to 1
Year: semesters, summer session	**Tuition:** $46,430
Room & Board: $13,870	**Freshman Class:** 13,863 applied, 8266 accepted, 1137 enrolled
SAT CR/M: 591/599 **ACT:** 27	**CEEB CODE:** 5379
Application Deadline: January 15	**VERY COMPETITIVE**

Loyola University Maryland, is a Catholic, Jesuit comprehensive university, which commits to the ideals of liberal education, and the development of the whole person. This mission is embraced through an undergraduate curriculum, rooted in the Jesuit tradition of the liberal arts, which prepares students for success in wide-ranging professional pursuits, and graduate studies. Loyola's undergraduate experience is complemented by its graduate programs, the region's leaders in professional education. This ideal is underscored by a thriving program of community service that takes Loyola students into the greater Baltimore community and beyond to serve individuals who are materially disadvantaged, creating a synergy of mind, body and spirit that transforms lives. There are 3 undergraduate schools and 3 graduate schools. In addition to regional accreditation, has baccalaureate program accreditation with AACSB, ABET, CSAB, NASDTEC, NCATE, and MSHEC. The 89-acre campus is in an urban area 3 miles from downtown Baltimore. Including any residence halls, there are 51 buildings.

STUDENT LIFE: 83% of undergraduates are from out of state, mostly the Middle Atlantic. 9% are Hispanic; 78% White; 5% African American; 3% Asian American; 2% two or more races. **Female To Male Ratio:** 1.6:1. **Housing:** 3291 students can be accommodated in college housing, which includes single-sex and coed dorms, on-campus apartments, honors houses, and special-interest houses. On-campus housing is guaranteed for the freshman year only, and on a first-come, first-served basis, and is available on a lottery system for upperclassmen. Upperclassmen may keep cars.

FACULTY/CLASSROOMS: 51% of faculty are male; 49% are female. All teach undergraduates. No introductory courses are taught by graduate students.

PROGRAMS OF STUDY: Loyola confers B.A., B.S., B.B.A., and B.S.E. degrees. Master's and doctoral degrees are also awarded. Bachelor's degrees are awarded in BIOLOGICAL SCIENCE (biology/biological science), BUSINESS (accounting and business administration and management), COMMUNICATIONS AND THE ARTS (communications, creative writing, English, fine arts, French, German, Latin, and Spanish), COMPUTER AND PHYSICAL SCIENCE (chemistry, computer science, mathematics, and physics), EDUCATION (elementary education), ENGINEERING AND ENVIRONMENTAL DESIGN (engineering), HEALTH PROFESSIONS (speech pathology/audiology), SOCIAL SCIENCE (classical/ancient civilization, economics, history, philosophy, political science/government, psychology, sociology, and theological studies). General business, communication, and social sciences have the largest enrollments.

ACTIVITIES: There are no fraternities or sororities. There are 194 groups on campus, including art, band, cheerleading, chess, choir, chorale, chorus, computers, dance, drama, ethnic, film, honors, international, jazz band, LGBT, literary magazine, musical theater, newspaper, orchestra, pep band, photography, political, professional, radio and TV, religious, social, social service, student government, symphony, and yearbook. Popular campus events include Modern Masters Series, Humanities Symposium, Loyolapalooza, International Festival, Evergreen Players, ChordBusters, Luna Fest, Poisened Cup Players, and Bull and Oyster Roast. **Sports:** There are 8 intercollegiate sports for men and 9 for women, and 8 intramural sports for men and 8 for women. Facilities include lacrosse, soccer, practice field, training facilities, a natatorium, aquatic center, indoor climbing wall, a fitness center, indoor track, racquetball, squash courts, areobic/martial arts studios, gymnasium, indoor soccer, and floor hockey. **Graduates:** From July 1, 2015 to June 30, 2016, 903 bachelor's degrees were awarded. The most popular majors were business/marketing (32%), communications/journalism (12%), and psychology (9%). 94 companies recruited on campus in 2015-2016. In an average class, 79% graduate in 4 years or less, 5% graduate in 5 years or less, and 84% graduate in 6 years or less. Of the 2015 graduating class, 25% were enrolled in graduate school within 6 months of graduation, and 26% were employed.

SERVICES: Counseling and information services are available, as is tutoring in most subjects, a reader service for the blind, and remedial math. **Library/Resources:** The library contains 1.1 million volumes, 691 microform items, 19,086 audio/video tapes/CDs/DVDs, and subscribes to 56,888 periodicals including electronic. Computerized library services include interlibrary loans, database searching, and Internet access. Special learning facilities include an art gallery, radio station, and TV station. **Physically Challenged Students:** 99% of the campus is accessible. Facilities include wheelchair ramps, elevators, special parking, specially equipped restrooms, special class scheduling, lowered drinking fountains, and lowered telephones. **Special:** Loyola offers cross-registration with Johns Hopkins, Towson, and Morgan State Universities, Goucher College, the College of Notre Dame, Maryland Art Institute, and Peabody Conservatory. Credit-bearing internships are available in most majors and study abroad is possible in 27 countries. Work-study programs and dual majors are also offered. There is a chapter of Phi Beta Kappa and a freshman honors program. **Visiting:** There are regularly scheduled orientations for prospective students, we offer daily visits on most weekdays, Monday through Friday, and reservations are required. The visit lasts approximately 2.5 to 3 hours and includes a group information session, a campus tour, and an interview (optional). There are guides for informal visits and visitors may sit in on classes. To schedule a visit, contact the Admission Office. **Campus Safety and Security:** Measures include 24-hour foot and vehicle patrol, emergency notification system, self-defense education, and security escort services. There are also shuttle buses, emergency telephones, lighted pathways/sidewalks, and controlled access to dorms/residences.

REQUIREMENTS: Loyola University is Test Optional. SAT and ACT are considered if submitted. All applicants should have graduated from an accredited secondary school or have earned the GED. Secondary preparation should include 4 years of English, 4 each of math, foreign language, natural science, and classical or modern foreign language, and 2 to 3 of history. AP and CLEP credits are accepted. Important factors in the admissions decision are advanced placement or honors courses, recommendations by school officials, and extracurricular activities record. All students must complete 120 hours, including 36 in the major, with at least a 2.0 GPA. The required core curriculum includes 2 courses each in history, language (at the second-year level), literature, philosophy, social sciences, and theology, 1 course each in composition, ethics, fine arts, math, humanities, and natural sciences, and 1 additional course in math, natural science, or computer science. **Procedure:** Freshmen are admitted in the fall, spring, and summer. Entrance exams should be taken by December of the senior year. There are early admissions, deferred admissions, and rolling admissions plans. Early decision applications should be filed by November 1; regular applications, by January 15 for fall entry, along with a $50 fee. Notification of early decision is sent January 15; regular decision, March 15. Applications are accepted online. **Transfer Students:** 60 of 120 credits required for the bachelor's degree must be completed at Loyola. **International Students:** There are 22 international students enrolled. The school actively recruits these students. They must take the TOEFL with a minimum score of 550 on the paper-based TOEFL (PBT) or 79 on the Internet-based version (iBT).

ADMISSIONS: 60% of the 2016-2017 applicants were accepted. The SAT scores for the 2016-2017 freshman class were: Critical Reading-- 4% below 500, 51% between 500 and 599, 39% between 600 and 699, and 6% between 700 and 800. Math-- 6% below 500, 40% between 500 and 599, 48% between 600 and 699, and 6% between 700 and 800. The ACT scores were 19% above 30. **Admissions Contact:** Office of Admission Email: *admission@loyola.edu* Web: *www.loyola.edu*

FINANCIAL AID: Loyola is a member of CSS. The CSS/Profile and a noncustodial parent's profile are required. The FAFSA code is 002078. The deadline for filing freshman financial aid applications for fall entry is February 15.

MARYLAND INSTITUTE COLLEGE OF ART *(The complete profile is made available exclusively on our website, www.barronspac.com)*

MCDANIEL COLLEGE — D-2

www.mcdaniel.edu

Westminster, MD 21157 — (410) 857-2230, (800) 638-5005

Fax: (410) 857-2757	**Email:** admissions@mcdaniel.edu
Full-time: 746 men, 779 women	**Faculty:** IIB, av$
Part-time: 18 men, 16 women	**Ph.D.s:** 87%
Graduate: 267 men, 1077 women	**Student/Faculty:** 11 to 1
Year: 4-1-4, summer session	**Tuition:** $40,580
Room & Board: $10,800	**Freshman Class:** 2403 applied, 1876 accepted, 388 enrolled
SAT CR/M: 545/546 **ACT:** 24	**CEEB CODE:** 5898
Application Deadline: February 1	**VERY COMPETITIVE**

McDaniel College, founded in 1867, is a four-year independent college of the liberal arts and sciences offering more than 70 undergraduate programs of study, including dual and student-designed majors, plus highly regarded graduate and professional studies programs. McDaniel College is the only American college with a European campus in Budapest, Hungary. There is 1 undergraduate school and 1 graduate school. In addition to regional accreditation, McDaniel has baccalaureate program accreditation with CSWE, NCATE, and ACS. The 160-acre campus is in a suburban area 30 miles from Baltimore's Inner Harbor, and 60 miles from Washington, D.C. Including any residence halls, there are 73 buildings.

STUDENT LIFE: 65% of undergraduates are from Maryland. Others are from 33 states, 15 foreign countries, and Canada. 79% are from public schools. 7% are Hispanic; 66% White; 6% race unknown; 4% Asian American; 3% two or more races; 14% African American. **Female To Male Ratio:** 1.8:1. The average age of freshmen is 18; all undergraduates, 20. 21% do not continue beyond their first year; 71% remain to graduate. **Housing:** 1384 students can be accommodated in college housing, which includes single-sex and coed dorms and on-campus apartments. In addition, there are honors houses, language houses, special-interest houses, fraternity and sorority floors, academic clusters, living-learning communities, substance-free floors, coed dorms, special housing for disabled students and theme housing. On-campus housing is guaranteed for all 4 years. 78% of students live on campus; of those, 60% remain on campus on weekends. Some may keep cars.

FACULTY/CLASSROOMS: 44% of faculty are male; 56% are female. All teach undergraduates, and 50% do research. No introductory courses are taught by graduate students. The average class size in an introductory lecture is 18; in a laboratory is 17; and in a regular course is 16.

PROGRAMS OF STUDY: McDaniel confers B.A. degrees. Master's degrees are also awarded. Bachelor's degrees are awarded in BIOLOGICAL SCIENCE (biology/biological science), BUSINESS (business administration and management), COMMUNICATIONS AND THE ARTS (art history and appreciation, communications, dramatic arts, English, fine arts, French, German, music, and Spanish), COMPUTER AND PHYSICAL SCIENCE (chemistry, computer science, mathematics, and physics), EDUCATION (Asian studies and physical education), ENGINEERING AND ENVIRONMENTAL DESIGN (environmental science), SOCIAL SCIENCE (economics, history, Middle Eastern studies, philosophy, political science/government, psychology, religion, social work, and sociology). Psychology, health & physical education/fitness, and biology have the largest enrollments.

ACTIVITIES: 15% of men belong to 1 local and 3 national fraternities; 18% of women belong to 1 local and 5 national sororities. There are 100 groups on campus, including art, band, Canine Companions for Independence, cheerleading, choir, chorale, chorus, computers, dance, drama, environmental, ethnic, film, forensics, honors, international, jazz band, LGBT, literary magazine, musical theater, newspaper, opera, orchestra, pep band, photography, political, professional, radio and TV, religious, social, social service, student government, symphony, and yearbook. Popular campus events include Homecoming, Late Night Carnival, Fall Fest, Midnight Madness, Cultural dinners, Spring Fling, Relay for Life, and Improv Performances. **Sports:** There are 12 intercollegiate sports for men and 12 for women, and 12 intramural sports for men and 12 for women. Facilities include football, field hockey, lacrosse, a fitness center with an aerobic conditioning area, a power/free weight room, basketball and volleyball, multi-purpose synthetic courts, a wrestling room, a sports medicine center, baseball, softball, a soccer complex, and two practice/intramural venues, a pool, squash/racquetball, golf, and tennis.

Graduates: From July 1, 2015 to June 30, 2016, 376 bachelor's degrees were awarded. The most popular majors were exercise science (13%), psychology (10%), and biology (9%). 50 companies recruited on campus in 2015-2016. In an average class, 63% graduate in 4 years or less and 70% graduate in 6 years or less.

SERVICES: Counseling and information services are available, as is tutoring in most subjects. There is a reader service for the blind, and remedial math, reading, and writing. **Library/Resources:** The library contains 409,875 volumes, 1.4 million microform items, 14,035 audio/video tapes/CDs/DVDs, and subscribes to 65,155 periodicals including electronic. Computerized library services include interlibrary loans, database searching, Internet access, and Wi-Fi capability. Special learning facilities include an art gallery, radio station, TV station, an observatory, human performance lab, video production lab, photography studio, graphics lab, and student research science labs. **Physically Challenged Students:** 85% of the campus is accessible. Facilities include wheelchair ramps, elevators, special parking, specially equipped restrooms, special class scheduling, lowered drinking fountains, lowered telephones, and special housing. **Special:** The Center for Experience and Opportunity (CEO) provides students with experiential learning opportunities including community outreach, service learning, internships, work/study, undergraduate research, post-graduate fellowships, preprofessional studies, and learning communities. Global Initiatives offers programming and activities for members of the Global Fellows program in addition to innovative approaches to travel learning, such as study abroad either around the world or at McDaniel's campus in Budapest, Hungary, and global experiential and civic engagement opportunities. There is a Washington semester in conjunction with American University. The college offers dual and student-designed majors, credit by exam (in foreign languages), and pass/fail options. McDaniel College has 5-year B.A./M.S. programs and offers certification in elementary and secondary education. The college also offers advanced standing for international baccalaureate recipients. There are 20 national honor societies, Phi Beta Kappa, a freshman honors program, and 24 departmental honors programs. **Visiting:** There are regularly scheduled orientations for prospective students, including an information session conducted by a counselor and/or the Director or Dean of Admissions and a student-led tour of campus. Individual visits and fall visit days include a class visit and lunch on campus. There are guides for informal visits and visitors may sit in on classes. **Campus Safety and Security:** Measures include 24-hour foot and vehicle patrol, emergency notification system, and security escort services. There are shuttle buses, emergency telephones, and lighted pathways/sidewalks.

REQUIREMENTS: The SAT or ACT is required. Applicants must be graduates of an accredited secondary school or have a GED. A minimum of 16 academic credits are required, including 4 years of English, 3 each of foreign language, math, and social studies, and lab science. SAT Subject Tests and an interview are recommended. An essay and academic recommendations are required. AP and CLEP credits are accepted. Important factors in the admissions decision are advanced placement or honors courses, recommendations by alumni, leadership record, parents or siblings attended your school, recommendations by school officials, evidence of special talent, personality/intangible qualities, and extracurricular activities record. All students are required to complete the McDaniel Plan, which provides a liberal arts education combining a comprehensive program of general education and a rigorous program in the major, complemented by electives and a range of special opportunities. For the B.A. degree, students must complete at least 128 credit hours distributed among the requirements of the McDaniel Plan, including a first year seminar, introduction to college writing, sophomore interdisciplinary studies course, global citizenship, second language study, departmental writing, critical inquiries in the liberal arts, at least one January term course, four physical activity, and wellness courses, up to 50 credit hours of required coursework in the major, and electives. The minimum GPA for graduation is 2.0. **Procedure:** Freshmen are admitted in the fall and spring. Entrance exams should be taken at the end of the junior year. There are early admissions and deferred admissions plans. February 15 for fall entry, along with a $50 fee. Notifications are sent in rolling. Applications are accepted online. **Transfer Students:** 69 transfer students enrolled in 2015-2016. A minimum college GPA of 2.5 is required. 32 of 128 credits required for the bachelor's degree must be completed at McDaniel. **International Students:** The school actively recruits these students. They must take the TOEFL. They must also take the SAT.

ADMISSIONS: 78% of the 2016-2017 applicants were accepted. The SAT scores for the 2016-2017 freshman class were: Critical Reading-- 31% below 500, 43% between 500 and 599, 19% between 600 and 699, and 7% between 700 and 800. Math-- 27% below 500, 45% between 500 and 599, 23% between 600 and 699, and 5% between 700 and 800. The ACT scores were 2% between 12 and 17, 43% between 18 and 23, 42% between 24 and 29, and 13% above 30. **Admissions Contact:** Florence W. Hines, VP, Dean of Admissions. Email: *admissions@mcdaniel.edu* Web: *www.mcdaniel.edu*

FINANCIAL AID: The college's own financial statement is required. The FAFSA code is 002109. The priority date for freshman financial aid applications for fall entry is March 1.

MORGAN STATE UNIVERSITY *(The complete profile is made available exclusively on our website, www.barronspac.com)*

MOUNT ST. MARY'S UNIVERSITY D-2

www.msmary.edu

Emmitsburg, MD 21727	**(301) 447-5214** **(800) 448-4347**
Fax: (301) 447-5860	**Email: admissions@msmary.edu**
Full-time: 746 men, 883 women	**Faculty:** 114
Part-time: 48 men, 52 women	**Ph.D.s:** 90%
Graduate: 264 men, 193 women	**Student/Faculty:** 12 to 1
Year: semesters, summer session	**Tuition:** $39,000
Room & Board: $12,610	**Freshman Class:** 6086 applied, 3746 accepted, 417 enrolled
SAT CR/M/W: 530/520/500 **ACT:** 21	**CEEB CODE:** 5421
Application Deadline: March 1	**COMPETITIVE**

Mount St. Mary's University, founded in 1808, is a private liberal arts institution affiliated with the Roman Catholic Church. The figures given in the above capsule and in this profile are approximate. There are 4 undergraduate schools and 6 graduate schools. In addition to regional accreditation, The Mount has baccalaureate program accreditation with NASDTEC, NCATE, and IACBE. The 1400-acre campus is in a rural area 60 miles northwest of Washington, D.C., and 50 miles west of Baltimore. Including any residence halls, there are 32 buildings.

STUDENT LIFE: 57% of undergraduates are from Maryland. Others are from 37 states, 9 foreign countries, and Canada. 63% are from public schools. 67% are White; 4% two or more races; 3% Asian American; 13% African American; 10% Hispanic; 1% Foreign; 1% race unknown. 70% are Catholic; 20% Protestant. **Female To Male Ratio:** 1.1:1. The average age of freshmen is 18; all undergraduates, 21. 25% do not continue beyond their first year; 68% remain to graduate. **Housing:** 1459 students can be accommodated in college housing, which includes coed dorms, special-interest houses, wellness floors, and quiet floors. On-campus housing is guaranteed for all 4 years. 80% of students live on campus; of those, 80% remain on campus on weekends. All students may keep cars.

FACULTY/CLASSROOMS: 57% of faculty are male; 43% are female. 87% teach undergraduates, 50% do research, and 50% do both. No introductory courses are taught by graduate students. The average class size in an introductory lecture is 20; in a laboratory is 10; and in a regular course is 19.

PROGRAMS OF STUDY: The Mount confers B.A. and B.S. degrees. Master's degrees are also awarded. Bachelor's degrees are awarded in BIOLOGICAL SCIENCE (biochemistry and biology/biological science), BUSINESS (accounting, business administration and management, and sports management), COMMUNICATIONS AND THE ARTS (communications, English, fine arts, French, German, and Spanish), COMPUTER AND PHYSICAL SCIENCE (chemistry, computer science, information sciences and systems, and mathematics), EDUCATION (elementary education), ENGINEERING AND ENVIRONMENTAL DESIGN (environmental science), HEALTH PROFESSIONS (health science), SOCIAL SCIENCE (criminal justice, economics, history, human services, interdisciplinary studies, international studies, philosophy, political science/government, psychology, social studies, sociology, and theological studies). Business, criminal justice, and elementary education have the largest enrollments.

ACTIVITIES: There are no fraternities or sororities. There are 70 groups on campus, including art, band, cheerleading, chess, choir, chorale, computers, dance, debate, drama, environmental, ethnic, honors, international, literary magazine, musical theater, newspaper, pep band, political, professional, radio and TV, religious, social, social service, student government, and yearbook. Popular campus events include Acoustic Battle, Christmas Dance, Crab Feast, Homecoming and Special Olympics. **Sports:** There are 8 intercollegiate sports for men and 9 for women, and 25 intramural sports for men and 25 for women. Facilities include multipurpose indoor courts, a track, pool, aerobics, sauna, a weight room, basketball, tennis courts, and playing fields. **Graduates:** From July 1, 2015 to June 30, 2016, 383 bachelor's degrees were awarded. The most popular majors were business (24%), criminal justice (13%), and accounting (7%). 86 companies recruited on campus in 2015-2016. In an average class, 2% graduate in 3 years or less, 65% graduate in 4 years or less, 70% graduate in 5 years or less, and 71% graduate in 6 years or less. Of the 2015 graduating class, 16% were enrolled in graduate school within 6 months of graduation, and 89% were employed.

SERVICES: Counseling and information services are available, as is tutoring in every subject, a reader service for the blind, and remedial math. There is a study skills and language lab, a writing center, and closed-caption TV and software for sight-impaired students are also available. **Library/Resources:** The library contains 149,287 volumes, 2,459 audio/video tapes/CDs/DVDs, and subscribes to 26,777 periodicals including electronic. Computerized library services include interlibrary loans, database searching, Internet access, and Wi-Fi capability. Special learning facilities include an art gallery, radio station, and TV station. **Physically Challenged Students:** 85% of the campus is accessible. Facilities include wheelchair ramps, elevators, special parking, specially equipped restrooms, special class scheduling, lowered drinking fountains, and lowered telephones. **Special:** Mount Saint Mary's offers cross-registration with an area community college, study abroad in the U.K., Europe, and South America, and secondary teacher certification in English, foreign languages, math, and social studies. Dual majors, interdisciplinary majors in biopsychology, American culture, and classical studies, a general studies degree, 3 dual degree programs, and non-degree and accelerated study are possible. A number of independently designed internships, work-study programs, and pass/fail options are available. The Core curriculum is a common 4 year curriculum integrated with every academic major. There are 20 national honor societies and a freshman honors program. **Visiting:** There are regularly scheduled orientations for prospective students, including campus tours and information sessions on academic programs, community life, admissions, and financial aid. There are guides for informal visits, visitors may sit in on classes, and stay overnight. To schedule a visit, contact the Admissions Office. **Campus Safety and Security:** Measures include 24-hour foot and vehicle patrol, emergency notification system, security escort services, emergency telephones, lighted pathways/sidewalks, and controlled access to dorms/residences.

REQUIREMENTS: The SAT is required. Applicants should be graduates of an accredited secondary school or hold the GED. Secondary preparation should include 4 years of English, 3 each of math, history, natural science, and social sciences, and 2 of a foreign language. An interview is recommended. AP and CLEP credits are accepted. Important factors in the admissions decision are recommendations by school officials, advanced placement or honors courses, and extracurricular activities record. Students are required to take a 4-year, 49 credit core curriculum in liberal arts (a number of which will overlap with/contribute to a student's major). The common educational experience includes a liberal arts symposium, a Western civilization sequence including art and literature, and courses in philosophy, theology, foreign language, math, American culture, and ethics. Graduation requirements include 120 credits, with most majors requiring 36 credits (30 to 36 in the major) and a minimum GPA of 2.0. **Procedure:** Freshmen are admitted in the fall and spring. Entrance exams should be taken by January of the senior year. There are early admissions, deferred admissions, and rolling admissions plans. Application deadlines are open. Application fee is $45. Applications are accepted online. **Transfer Students:** 47 transfer students enrolled in 2015-2016. Transfer applicants should have at least a 2.0 GPA in previous college work, be in good academic and disciplinary standing, and account for all time elapsed since graduation from high school. 30 of 120 credits required for the bachelor's degree must be completed at The Mount. **International Students:** There are 15 international students enrolled. They must take the TOEFL with a minimum score of 550 on the paper-based TOEFL (PBT) or 83 on the Internet-based version (iBT). They must also take the SAT or ACT.

ADMISSIONS: 62% of the 2016-2017 applicants were accepted. The SAT scores for the 2016-2017 freshman class were: Critical Reading-- 36% below 500, 43% between 500 and 599, 18% between 600 and 699, and 3% between 700 and 800. Math-- 38% below 500, 42% between 500 and 599, 19% between 600 and 699, and 1% between 700 and 800. Writing-- 50% below 500, 38% between 500 and 599, 11% between 600 and 699, and 1% between 700 and 800. The ACT scores were 1% below 12, 8% between 12 and 17, 61% between 18 and 23, 26% between 24 and 29, and 4% above 30. 27% of the current freshmen were in the top fifth of their class; 58% were in the top two fifths. 3 freshmen graduated first in their class. **Admissions Contact:** Michael Post, VP for Enrollment & Student Affairs. Email: *admissions@msmary.edu* Web: *www.msmary.edu*

FINANCIAL AID: In 2016-2017, 99% of all full-time freshmen and 98% of continuing full-time students received some form of financial aid. 78% of all full-time freshmen and 71% of continuing full-time students received need-based aid. The average freshman award was $27,021. Need-based scholarships or need-based grants averaged $3,000 ($18,850 maximum); need-based self-help aid (loans and jobs) averaged $5,570 ($7,030 maximum); non-need-based athletic scholarships averaged $1,340 ($51,610 maximum); and other non-need-based awards and non-need-based scholarships averaged $16,050 ($37,700 maximum). 42% of undergraduate students work part-time. Average annual earnings from campus work are $1424. The average financial indebtedness of the 2016 graduate was $33,894. The FAFSA code is 002086. The priority date for freshman financial aid applications for fall entry is December 1. The filing deadline for fall entry is March 1.

NOTRE DAME OF MARYLAND UNIVERSITY — D-2

www.ndm.edu

Baltimore, MD 21210	(410) 532-5330 (800) 435-0200
Fax: (410) 532-6287	Email: admiss@ndm.edu
Full-time: 650 women	**Faculty:** 74
Part-time: 90 men, 880 women	**Ph.D.s:** 65%
Graduate: 270 men, 1190 women	**Student/Faculty:** 8 to 1
Year: 4-1-4, summer session	**Tuition:** $35,019
Room & Board: $11,446	**Freshman Class:** n/av
SAT or ACT: required	**CEEB CODE:** 5114
Application Deadline: open	**VERY COMPETITIVE**

The College of Notre Dame of Maryland, founded in 1873, is a private liberal arts institution is primarily for women, and affiliated with the Catholic Church. The figures in the above capsule and in this profile are approximate. There are 4 undergraduate schools and 1 graduate school. In addition to regional accreditation, Notre Dame has baccalaureate program accreditation with NLN. The 58-acre campus is in a suburban area 10 miles north of Baltimore. Including any residence halls, there are 11 buildings.

STUDENT LIFE: 70% of undergraduates are from Maryland. Others are from 21 states. **Female To Male Ratio:** 7.6:1. **Housing:** 450 students can be accommodated in college housing, which includes single-sex dorms. On-campus housing is guaranteed for all 4 years. 65% of students live on campus; of those, 60% remain on campus on weekends. All students may keep cars. Alcohol is not permitted.

FACULTY/CLASSROOMS: 30% of faculty are male; 70% are female. All teach undergraduates. No introductory courses are taught by graduate students. The average class size in an introductory lecture is 30; in a laboratory is 20; and in a regular course is 20.

PROGRAMS OF STUDY: Notre Dame confers B.A., and B.S. degrees. Master's degrees are also awarded. Bachelor's degrees are awarded in BIOLOGICAL SCIENCE (biology/biological science), BUSINESS (accounting, banking and finance, business administration and management, international business management, and marketing/retailing/merchandising), COMMUNICATIONS AND THE ARTS (art history and appreciation, classics, communications, English, graphic design, modern language, music, photography, and studio art), COMPUTER AND PHYSICAL SCIENCE (chemistry, computer science, information sciences and systems, mathematics, and physics), EDUCATION (art education, early childhood education, elementary education, foreign languages education, music education, science education, secondary education, and special education), ENGINEERING AND ENVIRONMENTAL DESIGN (preengineering), HEALTH PROFESSIONS (nursing, predentistry, premedicine, and prepharmacy), SOCIAL SCIENCE (economics, history, interdisciplinary studies, international relations, liberal arts/general studies, political science/government, prelaw, psychology, and religion). Business, education, and communication arts are the strongest academically.

ACTIVITIES: There are no fraternities or sororities. There are 24 groups on campus, including art, choir, dance, drama, ethnic, honors, international, literary magazine, newspaper, political, professional, radio and TV, religious, social, social service, student government, and yearbook. Popular campus events include Honors Convocation, Antostal Day, and Multicultural Awareness Week. **Sports:** Facilities include a sports/activities complex, racquetball courts, a dance studio, fitness center, an indoor walking track, game room, activities resource center, and a basketball court.

SERVICES: Counseling and information services are available, as is tutoring in most subjects. **Library/Resources:** The library contains 290,000 volumes, 378,138 microform items, 24,000 audio/video tapes/CDs/DVDs, and subscribes to 2,000 periodicals including electronic. Computerized library services include database searching. Special learning facilities include an art gallery, planetarium, radio station, TV station, a graphic arts studio, roof-top greenhouse, and cultural center. **Physically Challenged Students:** 98% of the campus is accessible. Facilities include wheelchair ramps, elevators, special parking, specially equipped restrooms, and lowered drinking fountains. **Special:** The college offers cross-registration with Johns Hopkins, Towson State, and Morgan State Universities; Coppin State, Goucher, and Loyola Colleges; and the Maryland Institute College of Art. Study abroad, internships, dual bachelor's degrees in nursing and engineering, 3-2 engineering degrees with Johns Hopkins University and the University of Maryland, and pass/fail options are available. Notre Dame's Weekend College offers bachelor's degree programs for employed adults. There are 8 national honor societies, a freshman honors program, and 4 departmental honors programs. **Visiting:** There are regularly scheduled orientations for prospective students, consisting of programs in June and January, each of which includes a stay in the dormitory, registration, and advisement. There are guides for informal visits and visitors may sit in on classes. To schedule a visit, contact the Office of Admissions. **Campus Safety and Security:** Measures include 24-hour foot and vehicle patrol, self-defense education, security escort services, and lighted pathways/sidewalks.

REQUIREMENTS: The SAT or ACT is required. For scholarship purposes, applicants should be graduates of an accredited secondary school. 18 academic credits are required; 4 units of English, 3 each of math, and a foreign language, and 2 each of history, and science, plus 4 electives. An essay is required and an interview is recommended. AP credits are accepted. Important factors in the admissions decision are recommendations by school officials, advanced placement or honors courses, and leadership record. To graduate, students must complete a total of 128 credit hours with a minimum GPA of 2.0 (2.5 in many majors). All students must fulfill the distribution requirements in the general education core, the major, and electives, and must demonstrate proficiency in writing, public speaking, computer literacy, and library research. In most majors, a minimum of 42 hours is required. All students must take a speech course, and 2 courses in phys ed, and some majors require senior practicums. **Procedure:** Freshmen are admitted in the fall and spring. Entrance exams should be taken no later than January of the senior year. There are early decision, early admissions, deferred admissions, and rolling admissions plans. Application deadlines are open. Notification is sent on a rolling basis. Applications are accepted online. **Transfer Students:** Notre Dame requires a minimum GPA of 2.5 for transfer students but recommends a GPA of 3.0. A combined score of 800 is required for the SAT I and 18 for the ACT. Students must also submit a letter of recommendation and an essay. 60 of 128 credits required for the bachelor's degree must be completed at Notre Dame. **International Students:** The school actively recruits these students. They must take the TOEFL.

Admissions Contact: Sharon Bogdan, Director of Admissions. Email: *admiss@ndm.edu* Web: *www.ndm.edu*

FINANCIAL AID: In 2016-2017, 85% of all full-time freshmen and 89% of continuing full-time students received some form of financial aid. 80% of all full-time freshmen and 75% of continuing full-time students received need-based aid. The average freshman award was $20,796. Need-based scholarships or need-based grants averaged $15,600 ($22,750 maximum); need-based self-help aid (loans and jobs) averaged $4,011 ($6,125 maximum); and other non-need-based awards and non-need-based scholarships averaged $9,202 ($18,700 maximum). Notre Dame is a member of CSS. The CSS/Profile is required. The FAFSA code is 002065. Check with the school for current application deadlines.

SALISBURY UNIVERSITY — F-4

www.salisbury.edu

Salisbury, MD 21801 — (410) 543-6161, (800) 543-0148

Fax: (410) 546-6016 — **Email:** admissions@salisbury.edu

Full-time: 3096 men, 4154 women	**Faculty:** 410; IIA, av$
Part-time: 308 men, 303 women	**Ph.D.s:** 85%
Graduate: 215 men, 672 women	**Student/Faculty:** 16 to 1
Year: 4-1-4, summer session	**Tuition:** $9364 ($17,776)
Room & Board: $11,350	**Freshman Class:** 8307 applied, 5477 accepted, 1329 enrolled
SAT CR/M/W: 570/580/560 **ACT:** 23	**CEEB CODE:** 5403
Application Deadline: January 15	**VERY COMPETITIVE**

Salisbury University, founded in 1925, is a member of the University System of Maryland, offering 58 distinct graduate and undergraduate programs. There are 4 undergraduate schools and 1 graduate school. In addition to regional accreditation, SU has baccalaureate program accreditation with AACSB, CSWE, NASM, ACS-CPT, CoARC, CAAHEP, CAATE, CCNE, NAACLS, and CAEP. The 184-acre campus is in a rural area on the historic Eastern Shore of Maryland, 30 miles from Ocean City and 2.5 hours from Baltimore and Washington, D.C. Including any residence halls, there are 79 buildings.

STUDENT LIFE: 85% of undergraduates are from Maryland. Others are from 31 states, 63 foreign countries, and Canada. 80% are from public schools. 70% are White; 14% African American; 4% Hispanic; 3% Asian American; 3% two or more races; 3% race unknown; 2% Foreign; 1% American Indian/Alaska Native. **Female To Male Ratio:** 1.4:1. The average age of freshmen is 18; all undergraduates, 21. 16% do not continue beyond their first year; 67% remain to graduate. **Housing:** 3158 students can be accommodated in college housing, which includes coed dorms, on-campus apartments, off-campus apartments. In addition, there are special-interest houses, international, and living/learning. On-campus housing is guaranteed for all 4 years, and is available on a first-come, and first-served basis. 59% of students commute. All students may keep cars.

FACULTY/CLASSROOMS: 44% of faculty are male; 56% are female. 93% teach undergraduates, 9% do research, and 9% do both. Graduate students teach 2% of introductory courses. The average class size in an introductory lecture is 30; in a laboratory is 21; and in a regular course is 25.

PROGRAMS OF STUDY: SU confers B.A., B.S., B.A.S.W., and B.F.A. degrees. Master's and doctoral degrees are also awarded. Bachelor's degrees are awarded in AGRICULTURE (environmental studies), BIOLOGICAL SCIENCE (biology/biological science), BUSINESS (accounting, business administration and management, business economics, finance, international business management, management science, and marketing), COMMUNICATIONS AND THE ARTS (art, communications, English, English as a second/foreign language, fine arts, French, music, Spanish, and theatre arts), COMPUTER AND PHYSICAL SCIENCE (chemistry, computer science, earth science, information sciences and systems, mathematics, and physics), EDUCATION (athletic training, early childhood education, elementary education, physical education, and physical education/exercise science), HEALTH PROFESSIONS (community health work, medical laboratory technology, nursing, and respiratory therapy), SOCIAL SCIENCE (economics, geography, history, international studies, liberal arts/general studies, peace studies, philosophy, political science/government, psychology, social work, and sociology). Communication arts, psychology, and social work are the strongest academically. Biology, exercise science, and nursing have the largest enrollments.

ACTIVITIES: 12% of men belong to 9 national fraternities; 7% of women belong to 7 national sororities. There are 100 groups on campus, including art, band, cheerleading, choir, chorale, chorus, communications, computers, dance, debate, drama, environmental, ethnic, film, honors, international, jazz band, LGBT, literary magazine, musical theater, newspaper, opera, orchestra, pep band, photography, political, professional, radio and TV, religious, social, social service, student government, and symphony. Popular campus events include Gullfest, Homecoming Week, The Big Event, and I Love Salisbury (community service projects). **Sports:** There are 9 intercollegiate sports for men and 11 for women, and 19 intramural sports for men and 20 for women. Facilities include a stadium, gym, pool, indoor climbing walls, dance studio, indoor and outdoor tennis courts, baseball, varsity and practice fields, all-weather track, fitness center, 2 strength rooms, lighted intramural fields, and outdoor sand volleyball courts. **Graduates:** From July 1, 2015 to June 30, 2016, 1967 bachelor's degrees were awarded. The most popular majors were communication arts (9%), psychology (7%), and social work (7%). 400 companies recruited on campus in 2015-2016. In an average class, 45% graduate in 4 years or less, 65% graduate in 5 years or less, and 67% graduate in 6 years or less.

SERVICES: Counseling and information services are available, as is tutoring in most subjects, such as math, reading, and writing. There is a reader service for the blind. **Library/Resources:** The 3 libraries contain 205,155 volumes, 646,036 microform items, 2,105 audio/video tapes/CDs/DVDs, and subscribe to 843 periodicals including electronic. Computerized library services include interlibrary loans, database searching, Internet access, and Wi-Fi capability. Special learning facilities include an art gallery, radio station, TV station, Nabb Research Center for Delmarva History & Culture, Scarborough Student Leadership Center, Center for Conflict Resolution, Richard A Henson Medical Simulation Center, Ward Museum of Wildfowl Art, Center for Integrated Media, Center for Conflict Resolution, Guerrieri University Center, BEACON, Small Business Development Center, Franklin P Perdue Museum of Business and Entrepreneurship, and Guerrieri Academic Commons. **Physically Challenged Students:** 95% of the campus is accessible. Facilities include wheelchair ramps, elevators, special parking, specially equipped restrooms, special class scheduling, lowered drinking fountains, lowered telephones, and special housing. **Special:** Cross-registration with schools in the University System of Maryland and study abroad in numerous countries are offered. SU also offers an Annapolis semester, a Washington semester, internships, work-study programs, accelerated degree programs in dentistry, optometry, podiatric medicine, and pharmacy, dual majors in biology/environmental marine science, social work/sociology, and physical engineering, interdisciplinary and student-designed majors including physics/microelectronics, a 3-2 engineering degree with the University of Maryland at College Park, Old Dominion University, and Widener University, a Co-op program in electrical engineering, and pass/fail options. There are 23 national honor societies and a freshman honors program. **Visiting:** Regularly scheduled orientations are available for prospective students, consisting of presentations, tours, students meet with faculty and staff, and Saturday open house programs. There are guides for informal visits and visitors may sit in on classes. To schedule a visit, contact Admissions Office. **Campus Safety and Security:** Measures include 24-hour foot and vehicle patrol, emergency notification system, self-defense education, and security escort services. There are also shuttle buses, emergency telephones, lighted pathways/sidewalks, controlled access to dorms/residences, 24-hour university police protection, video surveillance system, information meetings/discussions, student patrols, pamphlets/posters/fliers, student patrols, and 911 Shield app.

REQUIREMENTS: Applicants must be graduates of accredited secondary schools or have earned a GED. The university requires 15 academic credits, including 4 in English, 3 each in math and social studies, 3 in science (2 with labs), and 2 in foreign language. Auditions are required for admission into the music and B.F.A. programs once admission to the university is granted. Essays are recommended but not required. A campus visit is recommended for all students. The SAT is not required for student with a 3.5 or greater GPA. AP and CLEP credits are accepted. Important factors in the admissions decision are leadership record, extracurricular activities record, and advanced placement or honors courses. Students must successfully complete at least 120 credit hours of coursework with a cumulative GPA of 2.0 or higher. Students must take 30 of the last 37 credit hours at SU (special cooperative programs are exempt). Students completing their course requirements through an approved study abroad program are exempt from this policy. Complete at least 30 credit hours at SU by direct classroom instruction and/or lab experience and not through credit by examination. Complete at least 30 credit hours at the 300/400 level with grades of C or better. Transfer students must complete at least 15 hours of their 30 upper-level credits at SU (note: other than field-based courses in the Seidel School of Education & Professional Studies, courses taken on a PS/F basis do not satisfy this requirement). Satisfy the General Education requirements. Satisfy the requirements in at least one major program of study including the major's required GPA. Earn grades of C or better in English 101, 102 or 103. **Procedure:** Freshmen are admitted in the fall and spring. Entrance exams should be taken in the fall of your junior year. There are early decision, early admissions, and deferred admissions plans. Early decision applications should be filed by November 15; regular applications, by January 15 for fall entry. The fall 2016 application fee was $50. Notification of early decision is sent December 15; regular decision, March 15. 208 early decision candidates were accepted for the 2016-2017 class. Applications are accepted online. Application fees are waived if application is completed online. **Transfer Students:** 1224 transfer students enrolled in 2015-2016. Applicants must present a minimum GPA of 2.0 with at least 24 transferable credit hours earned from a regionally accredited community college or 4-year college or university. Contractural admission is extended to individuals who have complete 12 credit hours of transferable coursework and present a minimum GPA of 2.5 Students with fewer than 24 credit hours must be eligible for freshman admission in addition to maintaining at least a 2.0 GPA in college courses. 30 of 120 credits required for the bachelor's degree must be completed at SU. **International Students:** There are 126 international students enrolled. The school actively recruits these students. They must take the TOEFL with a minimum score of 550 on the paper-based TOEFL (PBT) or 79 on the Internet-based version (iBT). Students must take the SAT or ACT, IELTS, Cambridge English, Elken, ELI (SU) Completer, or any other approved proof of English competency. They must also take the SAT or ACT. Test optional admission for eligible applicants with GPA if 3.5 or higher (on 4.0 scale).

ADMISSIONS: 66% of the 2016-2017 applicants were accepted. The SAT scores for the 2016-2017 freshman class were: Critical Reading-- 6% below 500, 60% between 500 and 599, 31% between 600 and 699, and 3% between 700 and 800. Math-- 6% below 500, 55% between 500 and 599, 37% between 600 and 699, and 2% between 700 and 800. Writing-- 9% below 500, 62% between 500 and 599, 27% between 600 and 699, and 2% between 700 and 800. The ACT scores were 4% between 12 and 17, 57% between 18 and 23, 35% between 24 and 29, and 4% above 30. 45% of the current freshmen were in the top fifth of their class; 78% were in the top two fifths. 1 freshman graduated first in the class. **Admissions Contact:** Elizabeth Skoglund, Director of Admissions. Email: *admissions@salisbury.edu* Web: *www.salisbury.edu*

FINANCIAL AID: In 2016-2017, 85% of all full-time freshmen and 76% of continuing full-time students received some form of financial aid. 51% of all full-time freshmen and 52% of continuing full-time students received need-based aid. Average annual earnings from campus work are $3750. The average financial indebtedness of the 2016 graduate was $26,940. SU is a member of CSS. The FAFSA code is 002091. The priority date for freshman financial aid applications for fall entry is February 15. The filing deadline for fall entry is March 1.

ST. JOHN'S COLLEGE-ANNAPOLIS — E-3

www.sjc.edu

Annapolis, MD 21401	(410) 626-2522 (800) 727-9238
Fax: (410) 269-7916	**Email:** annapolis.admissions@sjc.edu
Full-time: 231 men, 181 women	**Faculty:** 73
Part-time: n/av	**Ph.D.s:** 78%
Graduate: 29 men, 16 women	**Student/Faculty:** 8 to 1
Year: semesters	**Tuition:** $48,544
Room & Board: $11,598	**Freshman Class:** 345 applied, 299 accepted, 124 enrolled
SAT CR/M: 680/640 **ACT:** 29	**CEEB CODE:** 5598
Application Deadline: open	**MOST COMPETITIVE**

St. John's is a liberal arts college with a distinct purpose: reading and discussing the great books of Western civilization. Alongside names such as Plato, Shakespeare, Euclid, Nietzsche, Einstein, and Austen, Johnnies wrestle with ideas in interdisciplinary seminars with two faculty and fewer than 20 students. Johnnies are original and unconventional, love big questions and discussion, and debate the ideas of thinkers, authors, scientists, philosophers, musicians, mathematicians, politicians, and more who changed our world. St. John's, founded in 1696 and chartered in 1784, but Johnnies explore the great books on two different campuses one in Annapolis, Maryland, and the other in Santa Fe, New Mexico. There is 1 undergraduate school and 1 graduate school. The 36-acre campus is in a small town in the heart of Annapolis, Maryland, near the Chesapeake Bay, 35 miles east of Washington, D.C., and 32 miles south of Baltimore. Including any residence halls, there are 18 buildings.

STUDENT LIFE: 83% of undergraduates are from out of state, mostly

the Middle Atlantic. Students are from 49 states, 27 foreign countries, and Canada. 90% are White; 3% Asian American; 2% African American; 2% Hispanic; 1% Foreign. 58% claim no religious affiliation **Male To Female Ratio:** 1.3:1. The average age of freshmen is 19; all undergraduates, 21. 18% do not continue beyond their first year; 82% remain to graduate. **Housing:** 375 students can be accommodated in college housing, which includes single-sex and coed dorms. On-campus housing is guaranteed for the freshman year only and is available on a lottery system for upperclassmen. 82% of students live on campus. Upperclassmen may keep cars.

FACULTY/CLASSROOMS: 73% of faculty are male; 27% are female. All teach undergraduates. No introductory courses are taught by graduate students. The average class size in a laboratory is 15 and in a regular course is 15.

PROGRAMS OF STUDY: St. John's confers B.A. in Liberal Arts degrees. Master's degrees are also awarded. Bachelor's degrees are awarded in BIOLOGICAL SCIENCE (biology/biological science), COMMUNICATIONS AND THE ARTS (languages, literature, and music), COMPUTER AND PHYSICAL SCIENCE (chemistry, mathematics, and physics), SOCIAL SCIENCE (economics, history, liberal arts/general studies, liberal arts, sciences, general studies, humanities, philosophy, political science/government, theological studies, Western European studies, and Western civilization/culture). Liberal arts is the strongest academically, and have the largest enrollments.

ACTIVITIES: There are no fraternities or sororities. There are 40 groups on campus, including Jewish fellowship, vegetarian, waltz and swing, woodshop, chorus, dance, drama, film, international, LGBT, literary magazine, newspaper, orchestra, photography, poetry, religious, and student government. Popular campus events include Reality Weekend, Senior Prank, and College Navy Croquet Match. **Sports:** There are 4 intercollegiate sports for men and 4 for women, and 19 intramural sports for men and 19 for women. Facilities include a gym/weight room, cardio room, and indoor running track, tennis, sailing, and playing fields. Including martial arts and yoga, fencing, rafting, skiing, and rock climbing. **Graduates:** From July 1, 2015 to June 30, 2016, 104 bachelor's degrees were awarded. The most popular majors were liberal arts (100%). 7 companies recruited on campus in 2015-2016. In an average class, 63% graduate in 4 years or less, 71% graduate in 5 years or less, and 68% graduate in 6 years or less. Of the 2015 graduating class, 27% were enrolled in graduate school within 6 months of graduation, and 84% were employed.

SERVICES: Counseling and information services are available, as is tutoring in some subjects. There is remedial math and writing. **Library/Resources:** The 2 libraries contain 133,000 volumes, 2,000 microform items, 5,000 audio/video tapes/CDs/DVDs, and subscribe to 240 periodicals including electronic. Computerized library services include interlibrary loans, database searching, Internet access, and Wi-Fi capability. Special learning facilities include an art gallery, planetarium, including soundproof music practice rooms, dark room, an art gallery and a music library. **Physically Challenged Students:** 70% of the campus is accessible. Facilities include wheelchair ramps, elevators, special parking, specially equipped restrooms, special class scheduling, lowered drinking fountains, lowered telephones, and special housing. **Special:** St. John's offers summer internships and an informal study-abroad program. **Visiting:** There are regularly scheduled orientations for prospective students, consisting of an overnight stay on campus, class visits, and a tour. There are guides for informal visits, visitors may sit in on classes, and stay overnight. To schedule a visit, contact the Admission Office. **Campus Safety and Security:** Measures include 24-hour foot and vehicle patrol, emergency notification system, self-defense education, and security escort services. There are emergency telephones, lighted pathways/sidewalks, and controlled access to dorms/residences.

REQUIREMENTS: Applicants need not be high school graduates, some students are admitted before they complete high school. Test scores may be submitted but are not required. Secondary preparation should include 4 years of English, 3 years of math, and 2 years each of foreign language, science, history, and music. equivalent to 132 credits, covers a range of classic to modern works. Students attend small seminars; 9-week preceptorials on specific works or topics, language, music, and math tutorials, and a 3-year natural sciences lab. Active learning occurs through discussion, translations, writing, experiment, mathematical demonstration, and musical analysis. Students take oral exams each semester and submit annual essays. Sophomores also take a math exam and seniors an oral exam that admits them to degree Applicants must submit written essays, which are critical to the admissions decision, and are strongly urged to visit. Important factors in the admissions decision are recommendations by school officials, advanced placement or honors courses, and personality/intangible qualities. The common curriculum, candidacy. Seniors also present a final essay to the faculty and take a 1-hour public oral exam. **Procedure:** Freshmen are admitted fall. There are early admissions, deferred admissions, and rolling admissions plans. Application deadlines are open. Notification is sent on a rolling basis. Applications are accepted online. **Transfer Students:** 20 transfer students enrolled in 2015-2016. Transfer students may enter only as freshmen and must complete the entire program at St. John's. The admissions criteria are the same as for regular students. Students in good academic standing may transfer to the Santa Fe campus at the beginning of any academic year. 132 of 132 credits required for the bachelor's degree must be completed at St. John's. **International Students:** There are 66 international students enrolled. The school actively recruits these students. They must take the TOEFL and the IELTS. They must also take the SAT.

ADMISSIONS: 87% of the 2016-2017 applicants were accepted. The SAT scores for the 2016-2017 freshman class were: Critical Reading-- 6% below 500, 17% between 500 and 599, 38% between 600 and 699, and 39% between 700 and 800. Math-- 4% below 500, 19% between 500 and 599, 45% between 600 and 699, and 29% between 700 and 800. Writing-- 4% below 500, 17% between 500 and 599, 47% between 600 and 699, and 33% between 700 and 800. The ACT scores were 16% between 18 and 23, 42% between 24 and 29, and 42% above 30. **Admissions Contact:** Benjamin Baum, Director of Admissions. Email: *annapolis.admissions@sjc.edu* Web: *www.sjc.edu*

FINANCIAL AID: In 2016-2017, 100% of all full-time freshmen received some form of financial aid. 94% of all full-time freshmen and 86% of continuing full-time students received need-based aid. The average freshman award was $38,219. Need-based scholarships or need-based grants averaged $23,445; and need-based self-help aid (loans and jobs) averaged $7,100. 78% of undergraduate students work part-time. Average annual earnings from campus work are $2700. The average financial indebtedness of the 2016 graduate was $27,613. St. John's is a member of CSS. The FAFSA code is 002092. The priority date for freshman financial aid applications for fall entry is February 15.

ST. MARY'S COLLEGE OF MARYLAND E-4

www.smcm.edu

St. Marys City, MD 20686	**(240) 895-5000** **(800) 492-7181**
Fax: (240) 895-5001	**Email: admissions@smcm.edu**
Full-time: 720 men, 958 women	**Faculty:** 141; IIB, +$
Part-time: 34 men, 35 women	**Ph.D.s:** 97%
Graduate: 8 men, 19 women	**Student/Faculty:** 12 to 1
Year: semesters, summer session	**Tuition:** $13,895 ($28,745)
Room & Board: $12,080	**Freshman Class:** 1675 applied, 1320 accepted, 394 enrolled
SAT CR/M/W: 580/570/585 **ACT:** 25	**CEEB CODE:** 5601
Application Deadline: February 15	**VERY COMPETITIVE**

St. Mary's College of Maryland, founded in 1840, is a small public liberal arts college designated by law as a Maryland honors college in 1992. There is 1 undergraduate school and 1 graduate school. In addition to regional accreditation, SMCM has baccalaureate program accreditation with ACS. The 319-acre campus is in a rural area 70 miles southeast of Washington, D.C. Including any residence halls, there are 42 buildings.

STUDENT LIFE: 92% of undergraduates are from Maryland. Others are from 21 states, 10 foreign countries, and Canada. 80% are from public schools. 8% are African American; 8% Hispanic; 73% White; 5% two or more races; 3% Asian American; 2% race unknown; 1% Foreign. **Female To Male Ratio:** 1.3:1. The average age of freshmen is 18; all undergraduates, 20. 14% do not continue beyond their first year; 78% remain to graduate. **Housing:** 1571 students can be accommodated in college housing, which includes single-sex and coed dorms, on-campus apartments, language houses, and special-interest houses. On-campus housing is guaranteed for all 4 years, and is available on a first-come, and first-served basis. 84% of students live on campus; of those, 80% remain on campus on weekends. All students may keep cars.

FACULTY/CLASSROOMS: 51% of faculty are male; 49% are female. All teach undergraduates, and all do research. No introductory courses are taught by graduate students. The average class size in an introductory lecture is 16 and in a laboratory is 17.

PROGRAMS OF STUDY: SMCM confers B.A. degrees. Master's degrees are also awarded. Bachelor's degrees are awarded in AGRICULTURE (environmental studies), BIOLOGICAL SCIENCE (biochemistry and biology/biological science), COMMUNICATIONS AND THE ARTS (art, art history and appreciation, dramatic arts, English, film arts, languages, music, and visual and performing arts), COMPUTER AND PHYSICAL SCIENCE (chemistry, computer science, mathematics, natural sciences, and physics), SOCIAL SCIENCE (anthropology, Asian/Oriental studies, economics, history, philosophy, political science/government, psychology, public affairs, religion, and sociology). Biology, psychology, and economics have the largest enrollments.

ACTIVITIES: There are no fraternities or sororities. There are 92 groups on campus, including art, cheerleading, choir, chorale, chorus, dance, drama, drum and bugle corps, environmental, ethnic, honors, international, jazz band, LGBT, literary magazine, musical theater, newspaper, orchestra, outdoors, political, professional, radio and TV, religious, social, sports club, student government, symphony, and yearbook. Popular campus events include World Carnival, River Concert Series, the Great Cardboard-Boat Race, Dance Club Shows, Burlesque Club Shows, Acapella Group Shows. **Sports:** There are 8 intercollegiate sports for men and 9 for women, and 10 intramural sports for men and 10 for women. Facilities include swimming pools, basketball and volleyball arena, health and fitness center, weight room, training room, exercise room, and gymnasiums. Physical education, athletics, and recreation facilities also include 5varsity practice fields, a track, tennis courts, an outdoor stadium, rowing center, and baseball facilities. **Graduates:** From July 1, 2015 to June 30, 2016, 501 bachelor's degrees were awarded. The most popular majors were psychology (13%), biology (12%), and economics (11%). 32 companies recruited on campus in 2015-2016. In an average class, 67% graduate in 4 years or less, 76% graduate in 5 years or less, and 78% graduate in 6 years or less.

SERVICES: Counseling and information services are available, as is tutoring in some subjects, such as anthropology, biology, chemistry, computer science, economics, English, foreign languages, history, mathematics, physics, psychology, sociology, and writing. There is also a reader service for the blind. **Library/Resources:** The library contains 172,545 volumes, 18,832 microform items, and 7,284 audio/video tapes/CDs/DVDs, and subscribes to 514 periodicals including electronic. Computerized library services include interlibrary loans, database searching, Internet access, and Wi-Fi capability. Special learning facilities include an art gallery, radio station, TV station, Historic archaeological site, and estuarine research facilities. **Physically Challenged Students:** 95% of the campus is accessible. Facilities include wheelchair ramps, elevators, special parking, specially equipped restrooms, special class scheduling, lowered drinking fountains, lowered telephones, and special housing. Living suites that meet ADA standards are also available. **Special:** St. Mary's offers internships, study abroad, national and international exchange programs, work-study, and both dual and student-designed majors. Credit bearing internships offered by St. Mary's include a Computer Science co-op program and the Washington Program in Political science. St. Mary's has an MOU with the George Washington University's Semester in Washington program. Non-degree study and pass/fail options are possible. There are 8 national honor societies and a chapter of Phi Beta Kappa. **Visiting:** There are regularly scheduled orientations for prospective students, student visits include personal interviews, group presentations, open house programs, meetings with faculty and students, and campus tours. There are guides for informal visits and visitors may sit in on classes. To schedule a visit, contact Kyle Wise at (800) 492-7181. **Campus Safety and Security:** Measures include 24-hour foot and vehicle patrol, emergency notification system, self-defense education, security escort services, emergency telephones, lighted pathways/sidewalks, controlled access to dorms/residences, Student security-assistant foot patrols, and nighthawk program from 8 pm- midnight.

REQUIREMENTS: The St. Mary's College of Maryland admissions committee takes pride in reviewing applications holistically, and we consider many facets of a student's application when making admissions decisions. A student's high school record is most important to us, with careful attention paid to co-curricular activities (including work and family responsibilities), essays, letters of recommendation, and standardized test scores (either SAT Reasoning or ACT required). A competitive candidate pursues a rigorous high school curriculum which includes four years of English, three years of social science, three years of mathematics, three years of science, and a range of academic electives. Study of a foreign language is strongly recommended. Advanced placement, international baccalaureate, and honors courses are highly valued. First-year applicants must possess an earned high school diploma or a satisfactory score on the General Education Development (GED) examination. AP and CLEP credits are accepted. Important factors in the admissions decision are advanced placement or honors courses, leadership record, and recommendations by school officials. Students must complete complete core curriculum requirements, which include a liberal arts seminar, a foreign language course, six breadth categories, and an academic experience that takes students outside the classroom (e.g., study abroad, internships, service-learning). There is also a St. Mary's Project or a senior capstone experience. Students must meet additional requirements in their major fields and complete at least 128 semester hours, with at least 44 upper division credits and at least a 2.0 GPA. **Procedure:** Freshmen are admitted in the fall and spring. Entrance exams should be taken by January of the senior year. There are early admissions and deferred admissions plans. Applications should be filed by February 15 for fall entry; November 1 for spring entry, along with a $50 fee. Notifications are sent February 15. Applications are accepted online. **Transfer Students:** 108 transfer students enrolled in 2015-2016. The St. Mary's College of Maryland admissions committee takes pride in reviewing applications holistically, and we consider many facets of a student's application when making admissions decisions. A student's success at their prior institution is most important to us, with careful attention paid to co-curricular activities (including work and family responsibilities), writing, and recommendations. A competitive candidate has completed at least 12 hours of credit with a minimum grade point average of 2.75 in all college courses and has earned a high school diploma or satisfactory score on the General Education Development (GED) examination. 38 of 128 credits required for the bachelor's degree must be completed at SMCM. **International Students:** There are 22 international students enrolled. The school actively recruits these students. They must take the TOEFL with a minimum score of 550 on the paper-based TOEFL (PBT) or 90 on the Internet-based version (iBT). They must also take the SAT or ACT.

ADMISSIONS: 79% of the 2016-2017 applicants were accepted. The SAT scores for the 2016-2017 freshman class were: Critical Reading-- 15% below 500, 41% between 500 and 599, 33% between 600 and 699, and 11% between 700 and 800. Math-- 22% below 500, 41% between 500 and 599, 32% between 600 and 699, and 5% between 700 and 800. Writing-- 20% below 500, 45% between 500 and 599, 31% between 600 and 699, and 5% between 700 and 800. The ACT scores were 12, 4% between 12 and 17, 37% between 18 and 23, 41% between 24 and 29, and 18% above 30. 3 freshmen graduated first in their class. **Admissions Contact:** Gary Sherman, Vice President of Enrollment Management. Email: *admissions@smcm.edu* Web: *www.smcm.edu*

FINANCIAL AID: In 2016-2017, 53% of all full-time freshmen and 45% of continuing full-time students received some form of financial aid. 47% of all full-time freshmen and 31% of continuing full-time students received need-based aid. The average freshman award was $14,166. Need-based scholarships or need-based grants averaged $10,377; need-based self-help aid (loans and jobs) averaged $3,303; and other non-need-based awards and non-need-based scholarships averaged $3,859. 55% of undergraduate students work part-time. Average annual earnings from campus work are $1593. The average financial indebtedness of the 2016 graduate was $19,420. The FAFSA code is 002095. The priority date for freshman financial aid applications for fall entry is February 15. The deadline for filing freshman financial aid applications for fall entry is February 28.

STEVENSON UNIVERSITY — D-2
www.stevenson.edu

Stevenson, MD 21153	**(410) 486-7001** **(877) 468-6852**
Fax: (443) 352-4440	**Email: admissions@stevenson.edu**
Full-time: 1094 men, 1971 women	**Faculty:** 126; IIB, +$
Part-time: 121 men, 412 women	**Ph.D.s:** 105%
Graduate: 87 men, 415 women	**Student/Faculty:** 22 to 1
Year: semesters, summer session	**Tuition:** $64,052
Room & Board: $8718	**Freshman Class:** n/av
SAT CR/M/W: 510/510/500 **ACT:** 22	**CEEB CODE:** 5856
Application Deadline: March 1	**COMPETITIVE**

Stevenson University, founded as Villa Julie College in 1947, is the third-largest independent university in Maryland and offers more than 25 undergraduate degree programs. Stevenson is committed providing career-focused programs based in theory, practice, and mentoring whereby students develop a deep knowledge coupled with practical application and mastery in their major areas. The figures given in the above capsule under room and board is for room only. There are 5 undergraduate schools and 1 graduate school. In addition to regional accreditation, Stevenson has baccalaureate program accreditation with NCATE, NLN, ABA, CCNE, and CSHSE. The 60-acre campus is in a suburban area 12 miles from downtown Baltimore. Including any residence halls, there are 31 buildings.

STUDENT LIFE: 80% of undergraduates are from Maryland. Others are from 35 states, and 1 foreign country. 81% are from public schools. 56% are White; 5% Hispanic; 5% two or more races; 3% Asian American; 3% race unknown; 27% African American. **Female To Male Ratio:** 2.1:1. The average age of freshmen is 18; all undergraduates, 23. 21% do not continue beyond their first year; 56% remain to graduate. **Housing:** 2000 students can be accommodated in college housing, which includes coed dorms and on-campus apartments, special-interest houses, and theme houses. On-campus housing is available on a first-come, first-served basis, and on a lottery system for upperclassmen. 57% of students commute. All students may keep cars.

FACULTY/CLASSROOMS: 49% of faculty are male; 51% are female. 99% teach undergraduates. No introductory courses are taught by graduate students. The average class size in an introductory lecture is 18; in a laboratory is 15; and in a regular course is 15.

PROGRAMS OF STUDY: Stevenson confers B.A. and B.S. degrees. Master's degrees are also awarded. Bachelor's degrees are awarded in BIOLOGICAL SCIENCE (biology/biological science and biotechnology), BUSINESS (accounting, business administration and management, business communications, business systems analysis, fashion merchandising, and marketing management), COMMUNICATIONS AND THE ARTS (art, dramatic arts, English literature, film arts, video, and visual design), COMPUTER AND PHYSICAL SCIENCE (applied mathematics, chemistry, computer security and information assurance, information sciences and systems, and mathematics), EDUCATION (early childhood education, elementary education, and middle school education), HEALTH PROFESSIONS (medical laboratory technology and nursing), SOCIAL SCIENCE (fashion design and technology, history, human services, interdisciplinary studies, paralegal studies, psychology, and public affairs). Sciences, and education are the strongest academically. Nursing, and business have the largest enrollments.

ACTIVITIES: There are no fraternities; 2% of women belong to 1 local and 1 national sororities. There are 55 groups on campus, including band, cheerleading, chess, choir, computers, dance, debate, drama, environmental, ethnic, forensics, honors, international, jazz band, LGBT, literary magazine, marching band, musical theater, mustang activities and programming board, newspaper, orchestra, pep band, photography, political, professional, radio and TV, religious, social, social service, and student government. Popular campus events include Rockland Blow Out, Relay for Life, Taste of Cultures, Wet-n-Wild, Homecoming, Humans vs Zombies, Welcome Week, Spring Fling, Founder's Day, The Q Group Gala, and Night of the Arts. **Sports:** There are 12 intercollegiate sports for men and 14 for women, and 25 intramural sports for men and 27 for women. Facilities include football, lacrosse, soccer and field hockey, basketball, volleyball, tennis courts, ice hockey, softball, baseball, and golf. **Graduates:** From July 1, 2015 to June 30, 2016, 912 bachelor's degrees were awarded. The most popular majors were health professions and related programs (25%), business/marketing (18%), and computer and informatin sciences (9%). 226 companies recruited on campus in 2015-2016. In an average class, 42% graduate in 4 years or less, 53% graduate in 5 years or less, and 56% graduate in 6 years or less. Of the 2015 graduating class, 6% were enrolled in graduate school within 6 months of graduation, and 84% were employed.

SERVICES: Counseling and information services are available, as is tutoring in most subjects. Stevenson also provide textbooks in alternate formats for students who are blind or low vision. There is a reader service for the blind, and remedial math, reading, and writing. Free individual tutoring as well as study groups led by a tutor, peer tutoring, paraprofessional tutoring, and faculty tutoring is available. Academic Link is provided at both campuses. **Library/Resources:** The 2 libraries contain 77,377 volumes, 199,324 microform items, 3,154 audio/video tapes/CDs/DVDs, and subscribe to 68,582 periodicals including electronic. Computerized library services include interlibrary loans, database searching, Internet access, and Wi-Fi capability. Special learning facilities include an art gallery, radio station, a theater, and a video studio. **Physically Challenged Students:** All of the campus is accessible. Facilities include wheelchair ramps, elevators, special parking, specially equipped restrooms, special class scheduling, lowered drinking fountains, lowered telephones, and special housing. **Special:** Co-op programs and internships are available. In addition, study abroad, service learning, field placements, independent study and research, and other experiential learning opportunities are offered as part of classes. Cross-registration, work study, accelerated degree programs, and student-designed majors are possible. There are 19 national honor societies and a freshman honors program. **Visiting:** There are regularly scheduled orientations for prospective students, including a general overview, information on how to apply and how to finance a college education, special academic presentations, tours, meetings with faculty and students, and lunch. There are guides for informal visits, visitors may sit in on classes, and stay overnight. To schedule a visit, contact the Admissions Office at admissions@stevenson.edu. **Campus Safety and Security:** Measures include 24-hour foot and vehicle patrol, emergency notification system, self-defense education, and security escort services. There are also shuttle buses, emergency telephones, lighted pathways/sidewalks, and controlled access to dorms/residences.

REQUIREMENTS: The SAT or ACT is required. Applicants must be graduates of an accredited secondary school. Although a secondary transcript is required, particular secondary preparation is not stipulated for all programs. Some degree programs do require specific high school courses. Stevenson requires 17 units of 4 in English, 3 each in math, science with 2 units of lab, 2 units each in social studies, and 1 unit in history, and 4 unites in other academic program. An essay is required and an interview is recommended. A GPA of 2.0 is required. AP and CLEP credits are accepted. Important factors in the admissions decision are evidence of special talent, personality/intangible qualities, extracurricular activities record, recommendations by alumni, and recommendations by school officials. In order to obtain a bachelor's degree from Stevenson University, a student must earn a minimum of 120 credits, which must include a minimum of 30 credits at the 300- or 400-level. Complete the core curriculum for a bachelor's degree. Successfully complete the courses required by the major. "I" grades (incompletes) must be cleared from the student's record. Achieve a cumulative grade point average of at least 2.00; the GPA is calculated on the basis of work done at Stevenson University only. Earn a minimum cumulative grade point average in the major of 2.00. Majors may have additional grade or GPA requirements. Earn at least 30 credits at Stevenson University. Earn the final 30 credits at Stevenson University unless permission is granted in writing by the Assistant Vice President for Academic Support Services.Comply with the general regulations of the University. File the official application for Graduation in accordance with published deadlines. **Procedure:** Freshmen are admitted in the fall, spring, and summer. Entrance exams should be taken between September and November of the senior year. There are deferred admissions and rolling admissions plans. Application deadlines are open. Application fee is $40. Applications are accepted online. **Transfer Students:** 217 transfer students enrolled in 2015-2016. Transfer applicants must provide both college and high school transcripts and have a minimum 2.5 GPA. Transfer students with a 2.0 cumulative GPA and other accomplishments or experience may be granted conditional admission to the college. Students may enroll in the fall, August 1. 30 of 120 credits required for the bachelor's degree must be completed at Stevenson. **International Students:** There are 2 international students enrolled. They must take the TOEFL with a minimum score of 550 on the paper-based TOEFL (PBT) or 80 on the Internet-based version (iBT).

ADMISSIONS: The SAT scores for the 2016-2017 freshman class were: Critical Reading-- 44% below 500, 42% between 500 and 599, 13% between 600 and 699, and 1% between 700 and 800. Math-- 43% below 500, 40% between 500 and 599, 16% between 600 and 699, and 1% between 700 and 800. Writing-- 49% below 500, 40% between 500 and 599, and 11% between 600 and 699. The ACT scores were 12% between 12 and 17, 53% between 18 and 23, 32% between 24 and 29, and 3% above 30. 42% of the current freshmen were in the top fifth of their class; 69% were in the top two fifths. **Admissions Contact:** Mark J. Hergan, Vice President for Enrollment Management. Email: *admissions@stevenson.edu* Web: *www.stevenson.edu*

FINANCIAL AID: In 2016-2017, 99% of all full-time freshmen and 96% of continuing full-time students received some form of financial aid. 75% of all full-time freshmen and 69% of continuing full-time students

received need-based aid. The average freshman award was $43,526. Need-based scholarships or need-based grants averaged $4,424 ($12,320 maximum); need-based self-help aid (loans and jobs) averaged $3,163 ($3,500 maximum); other non-need-based awards and non-need-based scholarships averaged $4,757 ($28,864 maximum); and $3,159 from other forms of aid. 21% of undergraduate students work part-time. Average annual earnings from campus work are $2004. The average financial indebtedness of the 2016 graduate was $33,726. Stevenson is a member of CSS. The FAFSA code is 002107. The priority date for freshman financial aid applications for fall entry is February 1.

TOWSON UNIVERSITY D-2

www.towson.edu

Towson, MD 21252 (410) 704-2113
(888) 4-TOWSON
Fax: (410) 704-3030 Email: admissions@towson.edu

Full-time: 5540 men, 8645 women	**Faculty:** IIA, av$
Part-time: 940 men, 1105 women	**Ph.D.s:** 52%
Graduate: 890 men, 2655 women	**Student/Faculty:** n/av
Year: semesters, summer session	**Tuition:** $9408 ($18,228)
Room & Board: $8000	**Freshman Class:** n/av
SAT or ACT: required	**CEEB CODE:** 5404
Application Deadline: n/av	**VERY COMPETITIVE**

Towson University, founded in 1866, is part of the University System of Maryland and offers undergraduate and graduate programs in liberal arts and sciences, allied health sciences, education, fine arts, communication, and business and economics. Figures in the above capsule and in this profile are approximate. There are 7 undergraduate schools and 1 graduate school. In addition to regional accreditation, Towson has baccalaureate program accreditation with AACSB, CAHEA, NASDTEC, NASM, NCATE, NLN, ACOTE, AOTA, CAAHEP, and NCATE. The 328-acre campus is in a suburban area 8 miles north of Baltimore City's Inner Harbor. Including any residence halls, there are 44 buildings.

STUDENT LIFE: 80% of undergraduates are from Maryland. Others are from 28 states, 12 foreign countries, and Canada. 69% are White; 4% Asian American; 3% Foreign; 2% Hispanic; 12% African American. **Female To Male Ratio:** 1.7:1. The average age of freshmen is 19; all undergraduates, 22. **Housing:** 3518 students can be accommodated in college housing, which includes coed dorms, on-campus apartments, honors houses, and as well as special-interest houses. There are also separate floors that are alcohol-free, smoke-free, and substance-free, leadership and quiet floors, and an international house. On-campus housing is available on a first-come, first-served basis, and on a lottery system for upperclassmen. Priority is given to out-of-town students. 78% of students commute. Upperclassmen may keep cars.

FACULTY/CLASSROOMS: 50% of faculty are male; 50% are female. No introductory courses are taught by graduate students. The average class size in an introductory lecture is 25; in a laboratory is 24; and in a regular course is 25.

PROGRAMS OF STUDY: Towson confers B.A., B.S., B.F.A., and B.M. degrees. Master's and doctoral degrees are also awarded. Bachelor's degrees are awarded in BIOLOGICAL SCIENCE (biology/biological science and molecular biology), BUSINESS (accounting, business administration and management, and sports management), COMMUNICATIONS AND THE ARTS (art, communications, dance, English, French, German, media arts, music, Spanish, and theater design), COMPUTER AND PHYSICAL SCIENCE (chemistry, computer science, earth science, geology, geoscience, information sciences and systems, mathematics, and physics), EDUCATION (art education, athletic training, dance education, early childhood education, education, education of the deaf and hearing impaired, elementary education, music education, physical education, and special education), ENGINEERING AND ENVIRONMENTAL DESIGN (environmental science), HEALTH PROFESSIONS (exercise science, health care administration, health science, medical laboratory technology, nursing, occupational therapy, speech pathology/audiology, and sports medicine), SOCIAL SCIENCE (anthropology, crosscultural studies, economics, family/consumer studies, geography, gerontology, history, interdisciplinary studies, international studies, law, philosophy, political science/government, psychology, religion, social science, sociology, and women's studies). Fine arts, business, and education are the strongest academically. Business disciplines, mass communications, and psychology have the largest enrollments.

ACTIVITIES: 8% of men belong to 13 national fraternities; 6% of women belong to 11 national sororities. Groups on campus include art, band, cheerleading, choir, chorale, chorus, computers, dance, drama, drill team, environmental, ethnic, forensics, honors, international, jazz band, LGBT, literary magazine, marching band, musical theater, orchestra, pep band, photography, political, professional, religious, social, social service, student government, and symphony. Popular campus events include Fraternity and Sorority Dances, Ethics Forum, and Tiger Fest. **Sports:** There are 7 intercollegiate sports for men and 12 for women. Facilities include an athletic center, a stadium, baseball and softball fields, tennis courts, a pool, a soccer field, and practice fields. Recreation facilities include gyms, a weight room, a pool, playing fields, and an indoor climbing wall. **Graduates:** From July 1, 2015 to June 30, 2016, 3120 bachelor's degrees were awarded. The most popular majors were business administration (16%), psychology (8%), and mass communication (7%). 115 companies recruited on campus in 2015-2016.

SERVICES: Counseling and information services are available, as is tutoring in most subjects. There is also a reader service for the blind and remedial math, reading, and writing. Note takers, English language and tutorial services centers, a writing lab, and signers for the hearing impaired are also available. **Library/Resources:** The library contains 364,468 volumes, 830,286 microform items, and 14,174 audio/video tapes/CDs/DVDs, and subscribes to 2,164 periodicals including electronic. Computerized library services include interlibrary loans, database searching, and Internet access. Special learning facilities include an art gallery, planetarium, TV station, an curriculum center, a herbarium, animal museum, observatory, and greenhouse. **Physically Challenged Students:** 85% of the campus is accessible. Facilities include wheelchair ramps, elevators, special parking, specially equipped restrooms, special class scheduling, lowered drinking fountains, lowered telephones, and special housing. Automatic doors, assistive listening devices in theaters and concert halls, and interior and exterior signage. **Special:** Towson University offers cooperative programs with other institutions in the University System of Maryland and at Loyola College, the College of Notre Dame, and Johns Hopkins University, cross-registration at more than 80 colleges through the National Student Exchange, and study abroad. Students may pursue a dual major in physics and engineering, an interdisciplinary studies degree, which allows them to design their own majors, a 3-2 engineering program with the University of Maryland at College Park and Penn State, or nondegree study. There are pass/fail options, extensive evening offerings, and opportunities to earn credits between semesters. Internships are available in most majors, and work-study programs are offered both on and off campus. There are 20 national honor societies, a freshman honors program, and 12 departmental honors programs. **Visiting:** There are regularly scheduled orientations for prospective students, including campus tours, a session for parents, a session on the admissions process for transfers and freshmen, and a roundtable discussion. There are guides for informal visits. To schedule a visit, contact the Admissions Office. **Campus Safety and Security:** Measures include 24-hour foot and vehicle patrol, emergency notification system, self-defense education, and security escort services. There are also shuttle buses, emergency telephones, lighted pathways/sidewalks, controlled access to dorms/residences, operation ID, and a police dog on campus.

REQUIREMENTS: The SAT or ACT and the ACT Optional Writing test are required. Applicants should have graduated from an accredited secondary school or earned the GED. Secondary preparation should include 4 years of English, 3 each of math, lab science, and social studies, and 2 of foreign language. Prospective music and dance majors must audition. AP and CLEP credits are accepted. Important factors in the admissions decision are advanced placement or honors courses, recommendations by school officials, and leadership record. Students must complete course work in the arts, English, humanities, math, biological or physical science, social science, information technology, and global awareness. **Procedure:** Freshmen are admitted in the fall and spring. Entrance exams should be taken in the junior or senior year. There are deferred admissions and rolling admissions plans. Check with the school for current application deadlines. The fall 2016 application fee was $45. Notification is sent on a rolling basis. Applications are accepted online. **Transfer Students:** 2500 transfer students enrolled in 2015-2016. Transfer applicants should have earned at least 30 academic credits. For those with fewer than 30 attempted, freshmen requirements must be met. Minimum GPA requirements range from 2.0 to 2.5, depending on the number of credits completed. Transcripts are required. 30 of 120 credits required for the bachelor's degree must be completed at Towson. **International Students:** The school actively recruits these students. They must take the TOEFL and the college's own test. The TOEFL is required at preadmission; a college test is required at postadmission. They must also take the SAT or ACT, scoring 550. Towson accepts the TOEFL as a substitute for the verbal SAT.

ADMISSIONS: 9 freshmen graduated first in their class. **Admissions Contact:** Louise Shulack, Director of Admissions. Email: *admissions@towson.edu* Web: *www.towson.edu*

FINANCIAL AID: In 2016-2017, 70% of all full-time freshmen and 62% of continuing full-time students received some form of financial aid. 43% of all full-time freshmen and 39% of continuing full-time students received need-based aid. The average freshman award was $12,131. Need-based scholarships or need-based grants averaged $7,019; need-based self-help aid (loans and jobs) averaged $3,503; non-need-based athletic scholarships averaged $9,663; and other non-need-based awards and non-need-based scholarships averaged $3,502. 72% of undergraduate students work part-time. Average annual earnings from campus work are $1185. The average financial indebtedness of the 2016 graduate was $14,085. The FAFSA code is 002099. Check with the school for current application deadlines.

UNITED STATES NAVAL ACADEMY E-3

www.usna.edu

Annapolis, MD 21402	(410) 293-4361 (888) 249-7707
Fax: (410) 293-4348	Email: webmail@usna.edu
Full-time: 3334 men, 1153 women	Faculty: 592; IIB, ++$
Part-time: n/av	Ph.D.s: 66%
Graduate: n/av	Student/Faculty: 8 to 1
Year: semesters, summer session	Tuition: see profile
Room & Board: see profile	Freshman Class: 17043 applied, 1355 accepted, 1177 enrolled
SAT CR/M: 674/667 ACT: required	CEEB CODE: 5809
Application Deadline: January 31	MOST COMPETITIVE

United States Naval Academy, founded in 1845, is a national military service college offering undergraduate degree programs and professional training in aviation, surface ships, submarines, and various military, maritime, and technical fields. The U.S. Navy pays tuition, room and board, medical and dental care, and a monthly stipend to all Naval Academy students. Graduates earn a Bachelor of Science degree and a commission in the United States Navy or the United States Marine Corps, and have a five year obligation of active military service. There is 1 undergraduate school. In addition to regional accreditation, Navy; Annapolis has baccalaureate program accreditation with ABET and ACS. The 338-acre campus is in a small town on the Chesapeake Bay 30 miles southeast of Baltimore, Maryland and 32 miles east of Washington, D.C. Including any residence halls, there are 343 buildings.

STUDENT LIFE: 94% of undergraduates are from out of state, mostly the Middle Atlantic. Students are from 50 states, and 29 foreign countries. 64% are White; 11% Hispanic; 8% two or more races; 7% African American; 7% Asian American; 1% American Indian/Alaska Native; 1% Foreign; 1% race unknown. **Male To Female Ratio:** 2.9:1. The average age of freshmen is 18; all undergraduates, 20. 3% do not continue beyond their first year; 89% remain to graduate. **Housing:** 4650 students can be accommodated in college housing, which includes coed dorms. On-campus housing is guaranteed for all 4 years. Some may keep cars.

FACULTY/CLASSROOMS: 71% of faculty are male; 29% are female. All teach undergraduates, 67% do research, and 67% do both. No introductory courses are taught by graduate students. The average class size in an introductory lecture is 20; in a laboratory is 18; and in a regular course is 18.

PROGRAMS OF STUDY: Navy; Annapolis confers B.S. degrees. Bachelor's degrees are awarded in BUSINESS (operations research), COMMUNICATIONS AND THE ARTS (Arabic, Chinese, and English), COMPUTER AND PHYSICAL SCIENCE (chemistry, computer science, cyber operations, information sciences and systems, mathematics, oceanography, physics, and science), ENGINEERING AND ENVIRONMENTAL DESIGN (aerospace engineering, computer engineering, electrical/electronics engineering, engineering, marine engineering, mechanical engineering, naval architecture and marine engineering, nuclear engineering, ocean engineering, and systems engineering), SOCIAL SCIENCE (economics, history, and political science/government).

ACTIVITIES: There are no fraternities or sororities. There are 100 groups on campus, including bagpipe, band, cheerleading, chess, choir, chorale, chorus, communications, computers, dance, debate, drama, drill team, drum and bugle corps, ethnic, honors, international, jazz band, LGBT, literary magazine, marching band, Military Professional, musical theater, orchestra, pep band, photography, professional, radio and TV, religious, social, social service, student government, and yearbook. Popular campus events include Induction Day, Commissioning Week, which includes the Plebe Recognition Ceremony, Ring Dance, Graduation, and Army/Navy sporting events. **Sports:** There are 33 intercollegiate sports for men and 23 for women and 15 intramural sports for men and 15 for women. Facilities include a stadium, basketball arena, Olympic pool with a diving well for 10-meter diving boards, wrestling arena, hydraulically banked indoor track, outdoor track, indoor ice rink, nautilus and weight rooms, facilities for gymnastics, boxing, volleyball, swimming, water polo, racquetball, basketball and personal conditioning, squash courts, climbing wall, baseball stadium, a crew house, 18 hole golf course, soccer facility, a sailing center, indoor and outdoor tennis courts, and athletic field houses. **Graduates:** From July 1, 2015 to June 30, 2016, 1084 bachelor's degrees were awarded. The most popular majors were political science (11%), systems engineering (10%), and economics (10%). 2 companies recruited on campus in 2015-2016. In an average class, 91% graduate in 4 years or less. Of the 2015 graduating class, 6% were enrolled in graduate school within 6 months of graduation, and 100% were employed.

SERVICES: Counseling and information services are available, as is tutoring in some subjects, such as mathematics, chemistry, physics, and cybersecurity. **Library/Resources:** The library contains 682,396 volumes, 614 microform items, 8,518 audio/video tapes/CDs/DVDs, and subscribes to 68,224 periodicals including electronic. Computerized library services include interlibrary loans, database searching, Internet access, and Wi-Fi capability. Special learning facilities include a planetarium, radio station, propulsion lab; wind tunnels -both subsonic and supersonic; flight simulator; space environment simulators; clean room to assemble space parts; vibration lab; oceanographic research vessel; field laboratory which includes a NOAA tide guide guage and equipment for biogeochemical analysis; rotating wave tank laboratory; weather and oceanographic monitoring equipment; autonomous surface and underwater vehicles; high capacity server which provides access to near-real-time and archived geoscience data and forecast model output available to the university community; a Two Million Volt Pellatron Accelerator; state of the art liquid crystal laboratory; state of the art dielectrics lab; acoustics lab with two anechoic chambers; robotic 20 inch Cassegrain telescope; 2 warship bridge simulators; fleet of Yard Patrol Craft; fleet of 44 foot keelboats; fleet of 26 foot keelboats; fleet of 20 foot dinghies, fleet of lasers; fleet of 420's; 380 foot towing tank; 120 foot towing tank; recirculating water channel; ballasting tank; circular water basin; 2-D wave tank; ship structures lab; autonomous surface vessels lab; naval history museum; 50 yard rifle range; 15 yard pistol range; trap and skeet range; 200 yard rifle range; 50 foot indoor shooting range. **Physically Challenged Students:** All of the campus is accessible. Facilities include wheelchair ramps, elevators, special parking, and specially equipped restrooms. **Special:** A voluntary graduate program is available for those midshipmen who complete academic graduation requirements by the end of their seventh semester and are selected to begin master's work at nearby universities. Midshipmen selected as Trident Scholars spend their senior year in independent research at the Naval Academy. Study abroad for one semester is available in countries around the world. Honors programs are available in selected majors. There are 8 national honor societies and 10 departmental honors programs. **Visiting:** There are regularly scheduled orientations for prospective students, visitation weekends for highly competitive candidates for admission, and summer seminar weeks for rising high school seniors. There are guides for informal visits, visitors may sit in on classes, and stay overnight. To schedule a visit, contact USNA Admissions at (888) 49-7707. **Campus Safety and Security:** Measures include 24-hour foot and vehicle patrol, emergency notification system, self-defense education, emergency telephones, lighted pathways/sidewalks, controlled access to dorms/residences, gate guards, and dorm room lockers.

REQUIREMENTS: The SAT or ACT is required. Candidates must be unmarried with no dependents, U.S. citizens of good moral character, and between 17 and 22 years of age. Candidates should have a solid secondary school background, including 4 years each of English and math, 2 years of a foreign language, and 1 year each of U.S. history, world or European history, chemistry, physics, and computer literacy. Candidates must obtain an official nomination from congressional or military sources. An interview is conducted, and medical and physical aptitude exams must be passed to qualify for admission. AP credits are accepted. Students must complete approximately 140 semester hours, including core requirements in mathematics, engineering, natural sciences, humanities, cybersecurity, and social sciences. Professional Development courses and Physical Education are required during all 4 years. Physical readiness test must be passed semi-annually. During required summer training sessions, students train aboard U.S. Navy ships, submarines, and aircraft and with units of the U.S. Marine Corps. Graduates are obligated to serve at least 5 years on active duty as commissioned officers of the United States Navy or United States Marine Corps. **Procedure:** Freshmen are admitted in the summer. Entrance exams should be taken December of the junior year in high school. There are early admissions and rolling admissions plans. Applications should be filed by January 31 for fall entry. Notifications are sent April 15. Applications are accepted online. **Transfer Students:** All students enter as freshmen/plebes and must complete the entire 47 month program. 140 of 140 credits required for the bachelor's degree must be completed at Navy; Annapolis. **International Students:** There are 56 international students enrolled. The school actively recruits these students. They must take the TOEFL, as well as the SAT or ACT.

ADMISSIONS: 8% of the 2016-2017 applicants were accepted. The SAT scores for the 2016-2017 freshman class were: Critical Reading-- 2% below 500, 19% between 500 and 599, 37% between 600 and 699, and 41% between 700 and 800. Math-- 15% between 500 and 599, 41% between 600 and 699, and 40% between 700 and 800. 78% of the current freshmen were in the top fifth of their class; 91% were in the top two fifths. 177 freshmen graduated first in their class. **Admissions Contact:** USNA Admissions Office Email: *webmail@usna.edu* Web: *www.usna.edu*

FINANCIAL AID: Check with the school for current application deadlines.

UNIVERSITY OF MARYLAND/BALTIMORE COUNTY D-2

www.umaryland.edu

Baltimore, MD 21250 **(410) 455-2291**

Fax: (410) 455-1094	**Email:** admissions@umbc.edu
Full-time: 5298 men, 4343 women	**Faculty:** I, av$
Part-time: 894 men, 739 women	**Ph.D.s:** 85%
Graduate: 1323 men, 1277 women	**Student/Faculty:** 20 to 1
Year: 4-1-4, summer session	**Tuition:** $10,384 ($22,682)
Room & Board: $10,912	**Freshman Class:** 10629 applied, 6316 accepted, 1555 enrolled
SAT CR/M/W: 540/570/530 **ACT:** required	**CEEB CODE:** 5835
Application Deadline: February 1	**VERY COMPETITIVE**

University of Maryland/Baltimore County, is a dynamic public research university integrating teaching, research and service to benefit the citizens of Maryland. As an Honors University, the campus offers academically talented students a strong undergraduate liberal arts foundation that prepares them for graduate and professional study, entry into the workforce, and community service and leadership. UMBC emphasizes science, engineering, information technology, human services and public policy at the graduate level. There are 6 undergraduate schools and 4 graduate schools. In addition to regional accreditation, UMBC has baccalaureate program accreditation with ABET, CSWE, and NCATE. The 500-acre campus is in a suburban area 5 miles southwest of Baltimore and 35 miles north of Washington, D.C. Including any residence halls, there are 50 buildings.

STUDENT LIFE: 89% of undergraduates are from Maryland. Others are from 45 states, 104 foreign countries, and Canada. 6% are Hispanic; 6% Foreign; 43% White; 20% Asian American; 17% African American. **Male To Female Ratio:** 1.2:1. The average age of freshmen is 18; all undergraduates, 22. 13% do not continue beyond their first year; 86% remain to graduate. **Housing:** 5000 students can be accommodated in college housing, which includes coed dorms, on-campus apartments, honors houses, language houses, special-interest houses, wellness and quiet-study floors, living learning communities, and gender neutral housing. On-campus housing is guaranteed for the freshman year only, is available on a first-come, and first-served basis. 66% of students commute. All students may keep cars. Alcohol is not permitted.

FACULTY/CLASSROOMS: 61% of faculty are male; 39% are female. No introductory courses are taught by graduate students. The average class size in an introductory lecture is 41; in a laboratory is 28; and in a regular course is 30.

PROGRAMS OF STUDY: UMBC confers B.A., B.S., B.F.A., and B.S.E. degrees. Master's and doctoral degrees are also awarded. Bachelor's degrees are awarded in AGRICULTURE (environmental studies), BIOLOGICAL SCIENCE (biology ecology and field biology, biochemistry, bioinformatics, biology/biological science, biological sciences, and cell & molecular biology), BUSINESS (entrepreneurial studies), COMMUNICATIONS AND THE ARTS (acting, Africana studies, applied art, art history, art, art/art studies, art and design, art history and appreciation, art/visual culture, arts administration/management, communications, dance, design, dramatic arts, English, fine arts, French, German, linguistics, modern language, music, Russian, Spanish, theater design, and visual and performing arts), COMPUTER AND PHYSICAL SCIENCE (applied physics, chemistry, computer science, cybernetics, cyber operations, cyber intelligence/security studies, information sciences and systems, mathematics, physics, and statistics), EDUCATION (art education and childhood education), ENGINEERING AND ENVIRONMENTAL DESIGN (chemical engineering, computer engineering, environmental science, and mechanical engineering), HEALTH PROFESSIONS (allied health, biology, emergency medical technologies, and health science), SOCIAL SCIENCE (African American studies, American studies, anthropology, classical/ancient civilization, cultural studies/critical theory & analysis, cultural anthropology, economics, gender studies, geography, history, interdisciplinary studies, philosophy, political science/government, psychology, social work, sociology, women & gender studies, and women's studies). Biological & biomedical sciences, computer & information sciences, and support services are the strongest academically. Information systems, computer science, and biological sciences have the largest enrollments.

ACTIVITIES: 4% of men belong to 11 national fraternities; 5% of women belong to 8 national sororities. There are 268 groups on campus, including and Intellectual Sports Council, Council of Majors, art, band, cheerleading, chess, choir, chorale, chorus, computers, dance, debate, drama, environmental, ethnic, film, forensics, honors, international, jazz band, LGBT, literary magazine, Model United Nations, musical theater, newspaper, opera, orchestra, pep band, photography, political, professional, radio and TV, religious, social, social service, student government, and symphony. Popular campus events include Quadmania, Welcome Week, and Homecoming. **Sports:** There are 8 intercollegiate sports for men and 9 for women, and 16 intramural sports for men and 16 for women. Facilities include a multipurpose arena, aquatic center, fitness center, tennis courts, a stadium, playing and practice fields, an indoor track, an outdoor cross-country course, golf, a track and field complex, and a soccer stadium. **Graduates:** From July 1, 2015 to June 30, 2016, 1914 bachelor's degrees were awarded. The most popular majors were psychology (12%), information systems (11%), and biological sciences (11%). 572 companies recruited on campus in 2015-2016. In an average class, 1% graduate in 3 years or less, 34% graduate in 4 years or less, 21% graduate in 5 years or less, and 61% graduate in 6 years or less. Of the 2015 graduating class, 7% were enrolled in graduate school within 6 months of graduation, and 83% were employed.

SERVICES: Counseling and information services are available, as is tutoring in every subject, a reader service for the blind, and remedial math, reading, and writing. Other services include notetakers, readers, mobility training, American Sign Language interpreters, and scribes for students who have a need based on a manual or learning disability. **Library/Resources:** The library contains 1.0 million volumes, 1.1 million microform items, 1.9 million audio/video tapes/CDs/DVDs, and subscribes to 33,000 periodicals including electronic. Computerized library services include interlibrary loans, database searching, and Internet access. Special learning facilities include an art gallery, radio station, the imaging research center, the Howard Hughes Medical Institute, and a telescope, a center for art design and visual culture and the Albin O Kuhn Library, and 2 professional dance companies. **Physically Challenged**

Students: 95% of the campus is accessible. Facilities include wheelchair ramps, elevators, special parking, specially equipped restrooms, special class scheduling, lowered drinking fountains, and lowered telephones. Braille writer, tape recorders, talking book machines, TTY, talking calculators, Optacon and information on the talking computer. **Special:** Dual and student-designed majors, cooperative education programs in all majors, a Washington semester, the Sondheim Public Affairs Scholars Program, cross-registration with University of Maryland schools and Johns Hopkins University, internships, both paid and nonpaid, in public, private, and nonprofit organizations, study abroad in 19 countries, work-study programs, B.A.-B.S. degrees, pass/fail options, and nondegree study are available. UMBC also offers various opportunities in interdisciplinary studies and in such fields as artificial intelligence and optical communications. There are 15 national honor societies, Phi Beta Kappa, a freshman honors program, and 17 departmental honors programs. **Visiting:** There are regularly scheduled orientations for prospective students, including a group information session with an admissions counselor followed by a student-guided walking tour of campus. Saturday information sessions and 4 campus open houses are also scheduled each fall. Summer preview days are in July and August. There are two transfer open houses. There are guides for informal visits, visitors may sit in on classes, and stay overnight. To schedule a visit, contact the Office of Undergraduate Admissions. **Campus Safety and Security:** Measures include 24-hour foot and vehicle patrol, emergency notification system, self-defense education, and security escort services. There are shuttle buses, emergency telephones, lighted pathways/sidewalks, controlled access to dorms/residences, a 24-hour police department, and a campus risk management department.

REQUIREMENTS: The SAT or ACT is required. Minimum high school preparation should include 4 years of English, 3 years each of social science/history and math, including algebra I and II and geometry, 3 years of lab sciences, and 2 years of a foreign language. An essay is required of all freshman applicants. UMBC requires applicants to be in the upper 50% of their class. AP and CLEP credits are accepted. Important factors in the admissions decision are advanced placement or honors courses, recommendations by school officials, and leadership record. To graduate, students are required to complete at least 120 credits, including 45 at the upper-division level, with a minimum GPA of 2.0. The core curriculum includes courses in arts and humanities, social sciences, math and natural sciences, phys ed, and modern or classical language and culture. Students must pass an English composition course with a C or better. **Procedure:** Freshmen are admitted to all sessions. Entrance exams should be taken by fall of the senior year. There is an early admissions plan. Early decision applications should be filed by November 1; regular applications, by February 1 for fall entry. The fall 2016 application fee was $50. Notification of early decision is sent December 15; regular decision, 433 applicants were on the 2016 waiting list; 281 were admitted. Applications are accepted online. **Transfer Students:** 1070 transfer students enrolled in 2015-2016. A 2.5 cumulative GPA for all previous college work is recommended. Applicants with fewer than 30 semester hours should submit SAT scores and the high school transcript, they must also meet freshman admission requirements. 30 of 120 credits required for the bachelor's degree must be completed at UMBC. **International Students:** There are 1042 international students enrolled. The school actively recruits these students. They must take the TOEFL with a minimum score of 550 on the paper-based TOEFL (PBT) or 80 on the Internet-based version (iBT).

ADMISSIONS: 59% of the 2016-2017 applicants were accepted. The SAT scores for the 2016-2017 freshman class were: Critical Reading-- 46% between 500 and 599, 36% between 600 and 699, and 10% between 700 and 800. Math-- 3% below 500, 35% between 500 and 599, 46% between 600 and 699, and 16% between 700 and 800. Writing-- 10% below 500, 44% between 500 and 599, 38% between 600 and 699, and 8% between 700 and 800. The ACT scores were 1% between 12 and 17, 19% between 18 and 23, 53% between 24 and 29, and 26% above 30. 25% of the current freshmen were in the top fifth of their class; 54% were in the top two fifths. There were 4 National Merit finalists. **Admissions Contact:** Dale Bittinger, Director of Admissions. Email: *admissions@umbc.edu* Web: *www.umaryland.edu*

FINANCIAL AID: In 2016-2017, 46% of all full-time freshmen and 45% of continuing full-time students received some form of financial aid. 39% of all full-time freshmen and 43% of continuing full-time students received need-based aid. The average freshman award was $10,282. Need-based scholarships or need-based grants averaged $12,276; need-based self-help aid (loans and jobs) averaged $3,376; non-need-based athletic scholarships averaged $10,038; and other non-need-based awards and non-need-based scholarships averaged $8,009. 100% of undergraduate students work part-time. Average annual earnings from campus work are $1335. The average financial indebtedness of the 2016 graduate was $20,298. The priority date for freshman financial aid applications for fall entry is February 14. The filing deadline for fall entry is June 30.

UNIVERSITY OF MARYLAND/COLLEGE PARK D-3

www.umd.edu

College Park, MD 20742	(301) 314-8385 (800) 422-5867
Fax: (301) 314-9693	**Email:** ApplyMaryland@umd.edu
Full-time: 13,906 men, 12,444 women	**Faculty:** 1803; IB, +$
	Ph.D.s: 91%
Part-time: 1240 men, 882 women	**Student/Faculty:** 15 to 1
Graduate: 5521 men, 5090 women	**Tuition:** $10,180 ($32,044)
Year: semesters, summer session	**Freshman Class:** 30272 applied, 14538 accepted, 4553 enrolled
Room & Board: $11,758	
SAT or ACT: required	**CEEB CODE:** 5814
Application Deadline: January 20	**HIGHLY COMPETITIVE**

University of Maryland/College Park, founded in 1856, is a land-grant institution, the flagship campus of the state's university system, offering undergraduate and graduate degrees. There are 12 undergraduate schools and 13 graduate schools. In addition to regional accreditation, Maryland has baccalaureate program accreditation with AACSB, ABET, ACEJMC, ASLA, NASM, NCATE, and CADE. The 1339-acre campus is in a suburban area 3 miles northeast of Washington, D.C., and 35 miles south of Baltimore. Including any residence halls, there are 253 buildings.

STUDENT LIFE: 79% of undergraduates are from Maryland. Others are from 48 states, 57 foreign countries, and Canada. 50% are White; 5% Foreign; 4% two or more races; 2% race unknown; 16% Asian American; 13% African American; 10% Hispanic. **Male To Female Ratio:** 1.1:1. The average age of freshmen is 18; all undergraduates, 21. 5% do not continue beyond their first year; 87% remain to graduate. **Housing:** 12525 students can be accommodated in college housing, which includes single-sex and coed dorms, on-campus apartments, honors houses, language houses, special-interest houses, fraternity houses, and sorority houses. On-campus housing is guaranteed for the freshman year only and is available on a lottery system for upperclassmen. 60% of students commute. All students may keep cars.

FACULTY/CLASSROOMS: 62% of faculty are male; 38% are female. 57% teach undergraduates, and 43% do research. Graduate students teach 12% of introductory courses. The average class size in an introductory lecture is 37; in a laboratory is 21; and in a regular course is 35.

PROGRAMS OF STUDY: Maryland confers B.A., B.S., B.L.A., B.M., and B.M.E. degrees. Master's and doctoral degrees are also awarded. Bachelor's degrees are awarded in AGRICULTURE (agricultural business management, agricultural economics, agriculture, animal science, natural resource management, and plant science), BIOLOGICAL SCIENCE (biochemistry, biology/biological science, microbiology, and nutrition), BUSINESS (accounting, business administration and management, finance, international business management, logistics, management information systems, marketing, operations management, and supply chain management), COMMUNICATIONS AND THE ARTS (Arabic, art history and appreciation, Chinese, classics, communications, dance, dramatic arts, English, English literature, film arts, foreign language, French, Germanic languages and literature, Japanese, journalism, linguistics, music, music performance, music theory and composition, romance languages and literature, Russian, Spanish, studio art, and theatre arts), COMPUTER AND PHYSICAL SCIENCE (astronomy, atmospheric sciences and meteorology, chemistry, computer science, geology, information sciences and systems, mathematics, physical sciences, and physics), EDUCATION (art education, drama education, early childhood education, education, elementary education, middle school education, music education, physical education, secondary education, and special education), ENGINEERING AND ENVIRONMENTAL DESIGN (aerospace engineering, architecture, bioengineering, chemical engineering, civil engineering, computer engineering, electrical/electronics engineering, engineering, environmental science, fire protection engineering, landscape architecture/design, materials engineering, and mechanical engineering), HEALTH PROFESSIONS (community health work, predentistry, preveterinary science, public health, speech pathology/audiology, and veterinary science), SOCIAL SCIENCE (African American studies, American studies, anthropology, criminal justice, criminology, early childhood studies, economics, family/consumer studies, geography, history, interdisciplinary studies, Italian studies, Judaic studies, philosophy, political science/government, prelaw, psychology, Russian and Slavic studies, sociology, and women's studies). Engineering, computer science, and business are the strongest academically. Biological sciences, economics, and psychology have the largest enrollments.

ACTIVITIES: 13% of men belong to 21 national fraternities; 14% of women belong to 24 national sororities. There are 675 groups on campus, including art, band, cheerleading, chess, choir, chorale, chorus, computers, dance, debate, drama, drill team, environmental, ethnic, film, forensics, honors, international, jazz band, LGBT, literary magazine, marching band, musical theater, newspaper, opera, orchestra, pep band, photography, political, professional, radio and TV, religious, social, social service, student government, symphony, and yearbook. Popular campus events include Art Attack, Union All-Niter and Maryland Day. **Sports:** There are 8 intercollegiate sports for men and 11 for women, and 16 intramural sports for men and 16 for women. Facilities include indoor and outdoor pools, tennis, squash, racquetball, volleyball, basketball courts, a fitness center/weight rooms, aerobic rooms, martial arts, saunas, indoor track, bowling, and golf. Athletic facilities include a stadium, gym, and indoor and outdoor artificial turf practice fields. **Graduates:** From July 1, 2015 to June 30, 2016, 7253 bachelor's degrees were awarded. The most popular majors were engineering (14%), biological sciences (7%), and economics (5%). In an average class, 70% graduate in 4 years or less, 83% graduate in 5 years or less, and 87% graduate in 6 years or less.

SERVICES: Counseling and information services are available, as is tutoring in most subjects, including all 100- and 200-level courses. There is also a reader service for the blind, and remedial math. **Library/Resources:** The 7 libraries contain 4.8 million volumes, 519,086 microform items, 445,966 audio/video tapes/CDs/DVDs, and subscribe to 155,601 periodicals including electronic. Computerized library services include interlibrary loans, database searching, Internet access, and Wi-Fi capability. Special learning facilities include an art gallery, radio station, TV station, an observatory. **Physically Challenged Students:** 95% of the campus is accessible. Facilities include wheelchair ramps, elevators, special parking, specially equipped restrooms, special class scheduling, lowered drinking fountains, lowered telephones. Special shuttle service, and electronic doors. **Special:** Each of the 12 undergraduate schools offers special programs, and there is a campus-wide co-op education program offering engineering and other majors. In addition, the university offers cross-registration with other colleges in the Consortium of Universities of the Washington Metropolitan area, several living-learning programs for undergraduates, the B.A./B.S. degree in most majors, dual and student-designed majors, non-degree study, an accelerated veterinary medicine program, varied study abroad opportunities, work-study programs with government and nonprofit organizations, and internship opportunities with federal and state legislators, the local media, and various federal agencies. There are 49 national honor societies, a chapter of Phi Beta Kappa, a freshman honors program, and 39 departmental honors programs. **Visiting:** There are regularly scheduled orientations for prospective students, consisting of 3 fall and 4 spring open house programs for admitted students, as well as regularly scheduled information sessions followed by a campus tour. There are guides for informal visits, visitors may sit in on classes, and stay overnight. To schedule a visit, contact the Office of Undergraduate Admissions. **Campus Safety and Security:** Measures include 24-hour foot and vehicle patrol, emergency notification system, self-defense education, and security escort services. There are also shuttle buses, emergency telephones, lighted pathways/sidewalks, controlled access to dorms/residences, and video surveillance.

REQUIREMENTS: The SAT or ACT and the ACT Optional Writing test are required. The university evaluates exam scores along with GPA, curriculum, and other criteria. Applicants should be graduates of accredited secondary schools or have the GED. Secondary preparation should include 4 years of English, 3 of history or social sciences, 2 of algebra and 1 of plane geometry, and 2 of lab sciences. An essay and counselor recommendation are required. Music majors must also audition. Applicants who submit the ACT rather than the SAT must submit the ACT Writing Test. AP and CLEP credits are accepted. Important factors in the admissions decision are advanced placement or honors courses, recommendations by school officials, parents or siblings attended your school, evidence of special talent, extracurricular activities record, and geographical diversity. Most programs require a minimum of 120 credits for graduation; the number of hours required in the major varies. All students are required to complete a set of General Education courses. **Procedure:** Freshmen are admitted in the fall, spring, and summer. Entrance exams should be taken at the end of the junior year or the beginning of the senior year. There are deferred admissions and rolling admissions plans. Early decision applications should be filed by November 1; regular applications, by January 20 for fall entry; and December 1 for spring entry, along with a $75 fee. Notification of early decision is sent February 15; regular decision, April 1. Applications are accepted online. **Transfer Students:** 2197 transfer students enrolled in 2015-2016. Transfer applicants from regionally accredited institutions should have attempted at least 12 credits and have earned at least a 2.0 GPA, although this requirement varies depending on space available. Applicants from Maryland community colleges may be given special consideration. 30 of 120 credits required for the bachelor's degree must be completed at Maryland. **International Students:** There are 1238 international students enrolled. They must take the TOEFL with a minimum score of 100 on the Internet-based version (iBT), or take the IELTS. They must also take the SAT or ACT.

ADMISSIONS: 48% of the 2016-2017 applicants were accepted. The SAT scores for the 2016-2017 freshman class were: Critical Reading-- 5% below 500, 22% between 500 and 599, 49% between 600 and 699, and 24% between 700 and 800. Math-- 4% below 500, 15% between 500 and 599, 43% between 600 and 699, and 38% between 700 and 800. The ACT scores were 7% between 18 and 23, 35% between 24 and 29, and 58% above 30. **Admissions Contact:** Admissions Officer. Email: *ApplyMaryland@umd.edu* Web: *www.umd.edu*

FINANCIAL AID: In 2016-2017, 86% of all full-time freshmen received some form of financial aid. 37% of all full-time freshmen received need-based aid. The average freshman award was $14,586. Need-based scholarships or need-based grants averaged $11,040; need-based self-help aid (loans and jobs) averaged $5,194; non-need-based athletic scholarships averaged $20,282; and other non-need-based awards and non-need-based scholarships averaged $6,577. 19% of undergraduate students work part-time. Average annual earnings from campus work are $5000. The average financial indebtedness of the 2016 graduate was $26,818. The FAFSA code is 002103. The priority date for freshman financial aid applications for fall entry is February 15.

UNIVERSITY OF MARYLAND/EASTERN SHORE F-4
www.umes.edu

Princess Anne, MD 21853 **(410) 651-6410**

Fax: (410) 651-7922	**Email:** umesadmissions@umes.edu
Full-time: 1480 men, 1810 women	**Faculty:** 230; IIA, +$
Part-time: 147 men, 136 women	**Ph.D.s:** 80%
Graduate: 279 men, 445 women	**Student/Faculty:** 15 to 1
Year: semesters, summer session	**Tuition:** $7625 ($17,188)
Room & Board: $9388	**Freshman Class:** 7249 applied, 3556 accepted, 1020 enrolled
SAT or ACT: required	**CEEB CODE:** 5400
Application Deadline: June 30	**COMPETITIVE**

University of Maryland/Eastern Shore, founded in 1886, is a public university, and part of the University of Maryland System offering undergraduate and graduate programs in the arts and sciences, professional studies, and agricultural sciences. The figures in the above capsule and in this profile are approximate. There are 3 undergraduate schools and 1 graduate school. The 620-acre campus is in a small town of Princess Anne, on the Eastern Shore of Maryland, 3 hrs to Washington D.C., Baltimore, Philadelphia, and Virginia Beach. Including any residence halls, there are 40 buildings.

STUDENT LIFE: 84% of undergraduates are from Maryland. Others are from 32 states, 48 foreign countries, and Canada. 85% are from public schools. 76% are African American; 5% Foreign; 18% White; 1% Asian

American; 1% Hispanic. 90% are Protestant. **Female To Male Ratio:** 1.3:1. The average age of freshmen is 18; all undergraduates, 21. 25% do not continue beyond their first year; 36% remain to graduate. **Housing:** 1530 students can be accommodated in college housing, which includes single-sex dorms, on-campus apartments, off-campus apartments, honors houses, fraternity houses, a residential complex, and wellness housing. On-campus housing on a first-come, first-served basis, and is available on a lottery system for upperclassmen. 63% of students live on campus; of those, 30% remain on campus on weekends. All students may keep cars.

FACULTY/CLASSROOMS: 45% of faculty are male; 55% are female. 85% teach undergraduates, and 15% do research. Graduate students teach 1% of introductory courses. The average class size in an introductory lecture is 75; in a laboratory is 18; and in a regular course is 30.

PROGRAMS OF STUDY: UMES confers B.A., B.S., B.G.S., and B.M. degrees. Master's and doctoral degrees are also awarded. Bachelor's degrees are awarded in AGRICULTURE (agriculture and poultry science), BIOLOGICAL SCIENCE (biology/biological science), BUSINESS (accounting, business administration and management, and hotel/motel and restaurant management), COMMUNICATIONS AND THE ARTS (English), COMPUTER AND PHYSICAL SCIENCE (chemistry, computer science, and mathematics), EDUCATION (agricultural education, art education, business education, elementary education, health education, home economics education, industrial arts education, mathematics education, music education, physical education, science education, secondary education, and social science education), ENGINEERING AND ENVIRONMENTAL DESIGN (aeronautical science, construction technology, engineering technology, and environmental science), HEALTH PROFESSIONS (physical therapy and rehabilitation therapy), SOCIAL SCIENCE (criminal justice, history, home economics, liberal arts/general studies, and sociology). Physical therapy, engineering, and environmental science are the strongest academically. Business, hotel restaurant management, and biology have the largest enrollments.

ACTIVITIES: 20% of men belong to 4 national fraternities; 20% of women belong to 4 national sororities. There are 25 groups on campus, including art, band, cheerleading, choir, chorale, chorus, computers, dance, drama, drill team, ethnic, honors, international, jazz band, literary magazine, newspaper, pep band, photography, political, professional, radio and TV, religious, social, social service, student government, and yearbook. Popular campus events include Parents Day, Spring Festival, and Ethnic Festival. **Sports:** There are 5 intercollegiate sports for men and 5 for women, and 4 intramural sports for men and 4 for women. Facilities include an indoor pool and stadium. **Graduates:** From July 1, 2015 to June 30, 2016, 577 bachelor's degrees were awarded. The most popular majors were homeland security (19%), business/marketing (13%), history, and and biological/life sciences (11%). In an average class, 37% graduate in 6 years or less.

SERVICES: Counseling and information services are available, as is tutoring in every subject, and remedial math, reading, and writing. **Library/Resources:** The library contains 150,000 volumes. Computerized library services include interlibrary loans and database searching. Special learning facilities include an art gallery and radio station. **Physically Challenged Students:** 20% of the campus is accessible. Facilities include wheelchair ramps, elevators, special parking, specially equipped restrooms, special class scheduling, lowered drinking fountains, and lowered telephones. **Special:** Students may cross-register at Salisbury State University. A cooperative education program, internships, a winter term, work-study programs, a general studies degree, and dual and student-designed majors are offered. Also available are an accelerated degree program and a 3-2 engineering degree with the University of Maryland/College Park. There are pass/fail options. There is 1 national honor society, a freshman honors program, and 10 departmental honors programs. **Visiting:** There are regularly scheduled orientations for prospective students, including 2 formal orientation sessions and 9 visitation/open house days. There are guides for informal visits and visitors may sit in on classes. To schedule a visit, contact the Office of Recruitment at (410) 651-6178. **Campus Safety and Security:** Measures include 24-hour foot and vehicle patrol and security escort services. There are also shuttle buses, emergency telephones, lighted pathways/sidewalks, and student security team.

REQUIREMENTS: Applicants should be graduates of accredited secondary schools or have the GED. High school preparation should include 4 years each of English and math, 3 years of social science, and 2 years each of science and foreign language, and 6 years of academic electives. An essay and interview are recommended. UMES recommends that prospective art education majors submit a portfolio. AP and CLEP credits are accepted. Important factors in the admissions decision are advanced placement or honors courses, personality/intangible qualities, leadership record, evidence of special talent, extracurricular activities record, and recommendations by school officials. Students must complete 122 hours, including 36 hours in the major, 15 in communicative and quantitative skills, 9 in humanities, 7 in natural sciences, 6 in social sciences, and 4 in health and phys ed. A minimum 2.0 overall GPA is required. **Procedure:** Freshmen are admitted to all sessions. Entrance exams should be taken in April before the senior year. There are early decision, early admissions, deferred admissions, and rolling admissions plans. Applications should be filed by June 30 for fall entry, along with a $25 fee. **Transfer Students:** 198 transfer students enrolled in 2015-2016. Transfer applicants must have attempted at least 9 credits at another institution and have at least a cumulative GPA of 2.0 or have earned an associate degree or completed 56 hours of community college work. Students may enroll in the fall, winter, spring and summer. 75 of 122 credits required for the bachelor's degree must be completed at UMES. **International Students:** They must take the TOEFL as well as the SAT, scoring 800.

ADMISSIONS: 49% of the 2016-2017 applicants were accepted. **Admissions Contact:** Cheryll Collier-Mills, Director of Admissions and Recruitment. Email: *umesadmissions@umes.edu* Web: *www.umes.edu*

FINANCIAL AID: UMES is a member of CSS. The college's own financial statement and the International Student's Certification of Finances are required. The FAFSA code is 002106. The priority date for freshman financial aid applications for fall entry is March 1. The filing deadline for fall entry is April 1.

UNIVERSITY OF MARYLAND/UNIVERSITY COLLEGE *(The complete profile is made available exclusively on our website, www.barronspac.com)*

WASHINGTON ADVENTIST UNIVERSITY *(The complete profile is made available exclusively on our website, www.barronspac.com)*

WASHINGTON COLLEGE — E-2

www.washcoll.edu

Chestertown, MD 21620	(410) 778-7700 (800) 422-1782 Email: wc_admissions@washcoll.edu
Full-time: 639 men, 819 women	**Faculty:** 117; IIB, av$
Part-time: 9 men, 12 women	**Ph.D.s:** 98%
Graduate: n/av	**Student/Faculty:** 12 to 1
Year: semesters	**Tuition:** $43,850
Room & Board: $10,612	**Freshman Class:** 6847 applied, 3702 accepted, 391 enrolled
SAT CR/M: 590/590	**CEEB CODE:** 5888
Application Deadline: February 15	**VERY COMPETITIVE**

Washington College, founded in 1782, is an independent college offering programs in the liberal arts and sciences, business management, and teacher preparation. There are 4 undergraduate schools. The 112-acre campus is in a small town 75 miles from Baltimore, Washington DC, and Philadelphia. Including any residence halls, there are 75 buildings.

STUDENT LIFE: 59% of undergraduates are from out of state, mostly the Middle Atlantic. Students are from 37 states, 31 foreign countries, and Canada. 67% are from public schools. 72% are White; 11% Foreign; 5% African American; 5% race unknown; 3% Hispanic; 2% Asian American; 2% two or more races; 1% American Indian/Alaska Native. **Female To Male Ratio:** 1.3:1. The average age of freshmen is 18; all undergraduates, 20. 17% do not continue beyond their first year; 75% remain to graduate. **Housing:** 1226 students can be accommodated in college housing, which includes single-sex and coed dorms, on-campus apartments, special-interest houses, fraternity houses, International house, a science house. There is also substance-free housing, theme housing, and wellness housing. On-campus housing is guaranteed for the freshman year only and is available on a lottery system for upperclassmen. 85% of students live on campus; of those, 65% remain on campus on weekends. All students may keep cars.

FACULTY/CLASSROOMS: 56% of faculty are male; 44% are female. All

teach undergraduates. No introductory courses are taught by graduate students. The average class size in an introductory lecture is 15; in a laboratory is 16; and in a regular course is 15.

PROGRAMS OF STUDY: WC confers B.A. and B.S. degrees. Master's degrees are also awarded. Bachelor's degrees are awarded in AGRICULTURE (environmental studies), BIOLOGICAL SCIENCE (biology/biological science), BUSINESS (business administration and management), COMMUNICATIONS AND THE ARTS (art, dramatic arts, English, fine arts, French, German, music, and Spanish), COMPUTER AND PHYSICAL SCIENCE (chemistry, computer science, mathematics, and physics), ENGINEERING AND ENVIRONMENTAL DESIGN (environmental science), SOCIAL SCIENCE (American studies, anthropology, economics, history, humanities, interdisciplinary studies, international studies, liberal arts, sciences, general studies, humanities, philosophy, political science/government, psychology, and sociology). Biology, business management, and psychology have the largest enrollments.

ACTIVITIES: 8% of men belong to 3 national fraternities; 14% of women belong to 3 national sororities. There are 100 groups on campus, including band, chorale, chorus, computers, dance, debate, drama, environmental, ethnic, honors, international, jazz band, LGBT, literary magazine, minority and human rights, newspaper, orchestra, photography, political, professional, radio and TV, religious, social, social service, student government, and yearbook. Popular campus events include Fall and Spring Convocations, George Washington Birthday Ball, War on the Shore, and May Day. **Sports:** There are 8 intercollegiate sports for men and 10 for women, and 12 intramural sports for men and 11 for women. Facilities include a stadium, swim center, gym, field house, squash and racquetball courts, fitness center, playing and practice fields, and a boathouse. **Graduates:** From July 1, 2015 to June 30, 2016, 340 bachelor's degrees were awarded. The most popular majors were social sciences (20%), business and marketing (15%), and biological and life sciences (11%). 75 companies recruited on campus in 2015-2016. In an average class, 2% graduate in 3 years or less, 72% graduate in 4 years or less, 74% graduate in 5 years or less, and 76% graduate in 6 years or less. Of the 2015 graduating class, 15% were enrolled in graduate school within 6 months of graduation, and 75% were employed.

SERVICES: Counseling and information services are available, as is tutoring in every subject, and remedial math and writing. **Library/Resources:** The library contains 325,000 volumes, 100,635 microform items, 8,750 audio/video tapes/CDs/DVDs, and subscribes to 28,300 periodicals including electronic. Computerized library services include interlibrary loans, database searching, Internet access, and Wi-Fi capability. Special learning facilities include an art gallery, and radio station. The Center for the American Experience, the Center for Environment and Society, the Kohl Gallery, the Rose O'Neill Literary House, the Geographic Information Systems (GIS) laboratory, and the Chester River Watershed Observatory. **Physically Challenged Students:** 95% of the campus is accessible. Facilities include wheelchair ramps, elevators, special parking, specially equipped restrooms, special class scheduling, lowered drinking fountains, lowered telephones, motorized carts, and curb cuts. **Special:** A program that provides internships, externships, and job shadowing during all four years is available in all majors. There is study abroad in 26 countries and a Washington, DC semester. The college offers a 3-2 nursing program with Johns Hopkins University and a 3-2 pharmacology program, along with an option for a student-designed interdisciplinary major. There are 19 national honor societies and a chapter of Phi Beta Kappa. **Visiting:** Regularly scheduled orientations are available for prospective students consisting of weekday visits. There are also guides for informal visits and visitors may sit in on classes. To schedule a visit, contact the Admissions Office. **Campus Safety and Security:** Measures include 24-hour foot and vehicle patrol, emergency notification system, security escort services, emergency telephones, lighted pathways/sidewalks, controlled access to dorms/residences, and peer education through student groups.

REQUIREMENTS: Applicants must be graduates of an accredited secondary school or have a GED. 16 Carnegie units are required; 20 are recommended. Applicants should take high school courses in English, foreign language, history, math, science, and social studies. An essay is required, and an interview is recommended. Either the SAT or the ACT is required. AP and CLEP credits are accepted. Important factors in the admissions decision are advanced placement or honors courses, recommendations by school officials, and leadership record. All students are required to take a freshman Global Perspective seminar and courses distributed among the social sciences, natural sciences, humanities, quantitative studies, foreign languages, and a writing requirement. The Senior Capstone Experience consists of a comprehensive exam, thesis, or independent project. Students must complete 128 credit hours, including at least 32 in the major, to graduate. A minimum GPA of 2.0 is required. **Procedure:** Freshmen are admitted in the fall and spring. Entrance exams should be taken in the spring of the junior year or fall of the senior year. There are early decision, deferred admissions, and rolling admissions plans. Early decision applications should be filed by November 1; regular applications, by February 15 for fall entry; and December 1 for spring entry, along with a $50 fee. Notification is sent on a rolling basis. 64 early decision candidates were accepted for the 2016-2017 class. 384 applicants were on the 2016 waiting list; 2 were admitted. Applications are accepted online. **Transfer Students:** 36 transfer students enrolled in 2015-2016. Requirements for students are a minimum GPA of 2.3, a high school transcript, college transcript(s) and essay or personal statement. An interview and standardized test scores are recommended. 56 of 128 credits required for the bachelor's degree must be completed at WC. **International Students:** There are 136 international students enrolled. The school actively recruits these students. They must take the TOEFL with a minimum score of 550 on the paper-based TOEFL (PBT) or 79 on the Internet-based version (iBT). They must also take the SAT or ACT.

ADMISSIONS: 54% of the 2016-2017 applicants were accepted. The SAT scores for the 2016-2017 freshman class were: Critical Reading-- 7% below 500, 42% between 500 and 599, 43% between 600 and 699, and 8% between 700 and 800. Math-- 11% below 500, 41% between 500 and 599, 42% between 600 and 699, and 6% between 700 and 800. 55% of the current freshmen were in the top fifth of their class; 82% were in the top two fifths. **Admissions Contact:** Satyajit Dattagupta, Vice President of Enrollment Management. Email: *wc_admissions@washcoll.edu* Web: *www.washcoll.edu*

FINANCIAL AID: In 2016-2017, 92% of all full-time freshmen and 90% of continuing full-time students received some form of financial aid. 100% of all full-time freshmen and 98% of continuing full-time students received need-based aid. The average freshman award was $31,250. Need-based scholarships or need-based grants averaged $27,166; need-based self-help aid (loans and jobs) averaged $4,723; other non-need-based awards and non-need-based scholarships averaged $16,766; and $4,472 from other forms of aid. 40% of undergraduate students work part-time. Average annual earnings from campus work are $1000. The average financial indebtedness of the 2016 graduate was $36,911. WC is a member of CSS. The college's own financial statement, signed copies of the student's and parents' federal tax returns, and W2s are required. The FAFSA code is 002108. The deadline for filing freshman financial aid applications for fall entry is February 15.

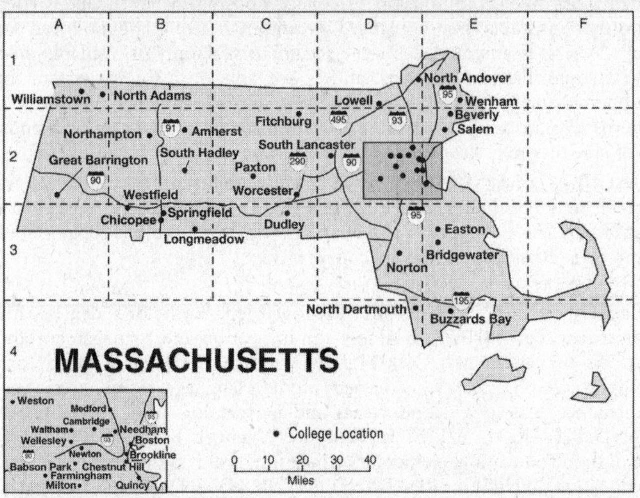

AMERICAN INTERNATIONAL COLLEGE *(The complete profile is made available exclusively on our website, www.barronspac.com)*

AMHERST COLLEGE B-2

www.amherst.edu

Amherst, MA 01002 **(413) 542-2328**

Email: admission@amherst.edu

Full-time: 929 men, 863 women	**Faculty:** 220; IIB, ++$
Part-time: n/av	**Ph.D.s:** 97%
Graduate: n/av	**Student/Faculty:** 8 to 1
Year: semesters	**Tuition:** $ ($52,476)
Room & Board: n/app	**Freshman Class:** n/av
SAT or ACT: required	**CEEB CODE:** 3003
Application Deadline: January 1	**HIGHLY COMPETITIVE+**

Amherst College, founded in 1821, is a private liberal arts institution. The figures in the above capsule for tuition is for out of state students. In addition to regional accreditation, Amherst has baccalaureate program accreditation with NEASC-CIHE. The 1015-acre campus is in a small town 90 miles west of Boston. Including any residence halls, there are 75 buildings.

STUDENT LIFE: 88% of undergraduates are from out of state, mostly the Middle Atlantic. Students are from 49 states, 55 foreign countries, and Canada. 58% are from public schools. 5% are two or more races; 5% race unknown; 42% White; 13% Asian American; 13% Hispanic; 12% African American; 10% Foreign. **Male To Female Ratio:** 1.1:1. The average age of freshmen is 22; all undergraduates, 20. 2% do not continue beyond their first year; 94% remain to graduate. **Housing:** 618 students can be accommodated in college housing, which includes coed dorms. In addition, there are language houses, special-interest houses, and a cooperative house. On-campus housing is guaranteed for all 4 years. 98% of students live on campus; of those, 95% remain on campus on weekends. Upperclassmen may keep cars.

FACULTY/CLASSROOMS: 52% of faculty are male; 48% are female. All teach undergraduates, and all do research. No introductory courses are taught by graduate students. The average class size in a regular course is 16.

PROGRAMS OF STUDY: Amherst confers B.A. degrees. Bachelor's degrees are awarded in AGRICULTURE (environmental studies), BIOLOGICAL SCIENCE (biochemistry, biology/biological science, biophysics, and neurosciences), COMMUNICATIONS AND THE ARTS (art history, art/art studies, classics, dance, English, film, television and digital media, fine arts, French, German, music, Russian, Spanish, and theatre studies), COMPUTER AND PHYSICAL SCIENCE (astronomy, chemistry, computer science, geology, mathematics, physics, and statistics), EDUCATION (Asian studies), SOCIAL SCIENCE (African American studies, American studies, anthropology, architectural studies, economics, European studies, history, interdisciplinary studies, law, philosophy, political science/government, psychology, religion, sociology, and women & gender studies). Economics, English, and political science have the largest enrollments.

ACTIVITIES: There are no fraternities or sororities. There are 150 groups on campus, including art, band, cheerleading, chess, choir, chorale, chorus, communications, computers, dance, debate, drama, environmental, ethnic, film, honors, international, jazz band, LGBT, literary magazine, musical theater, newspaper, opera, orchestra, photography, political, professional, radio and TV, religious, social, social service, student government, symphony, and yearbook. Popular campus events include Fall Festival, Harlem Renaissance, and Spring Weekend Concert. **Sports:** There are 13 intercollegiate sports for men and 14 for women, and 6 intramural sports for men and 6 for women. Facilities include 2 gyms, a pool, a field house, a hockey rink, an outdoor track, a fitness center, 10 international squash courts, an indoor jogging track, 3 indoor and 30 outdoor tennis courts, baseball and softball diamonds, a 9-hole golf course, and playing fields. Our athletics program is the oldest in the country. Number of NCAA titles won: 76 Division III individual titles and 11 team championships. **Graduates:** From July 1, 2015 to June 30, 2016, 464 bachelor's degrees were awarded. The most popular majors were economics (17%), English (11%), and psychology (10%). 46 companies recruited on campus in 2015-2016. In an average class, 87% graduate in 4 years or less, 93% graduate in 5 years or less, and 94% graduate in 6 years or less. Of the 2015 graduating class, 16% were enrolled in graduate school within 6 months of graduation, and 69% were employed.

SERVICES: Counseling and information services are available, as is tutoring in every subject. There is a reader service for the blind. A quantitative skills center and a writing center are also available. **Library/Resources:** The 5 libraries contain 1.5 million volumes, 448,680 microform items, and 60,547 audio/video tapes/CDs/DVDs, and subscribe to 16,069 periodicals including electronic. Computerized library services include interlibrary loans, database searching, Internet access, and Wi-Fi capability. Special learning facilities include an art gallery, natural history museum, planetarium, radio station, an observatory, the Emily Dickinson Museum, the Amherst Center for Russian Culture, and the Center for Humanistic Inquiry. **Physically Challenged Students:** Facilities include wheelchair ramps, elevators, special parking, specially equipped restrooms, special class scheduling, lowered drinking fountains, lowered telephones, and special housing. **Special:** Students may cross-register through the Five College Consortium, the other members of which are all within 10 miles of Amherst, or through the Twelve College Exchange Program. A number of interterm and summer internships are available, as is study-abroad in 40 countries. Dual majors, triple majors, student-designed interdisciplinary majors based on independent study as of junior or senior year, and work-study programs are possible. There are limited pass/fail options. There are 2 national honor societies, Phi Beta Kappa, and 38 departmental honors programs. **Visiting:** There are regularly scheduled orientations for prospective students, dean-led information sessions and student-led tours. There are guides for informal visits, visitors may sit in on classes, and stay overnight. To schedule a visit, contact the Admission Office. **Campus Safety and Security:** Measures include 24-hour foot and vehicle patrol, emergency notification system, self-defense education, and security escort services. There are emergency telephones, lighted pathways/sidewalks, controlled access to dorms/residences, ACEMS (Amherst College Emergency Medical Service), and access code pad security to dorms.

REQUIREMENTS: The SAT or ACT is required, plus 2 SAT: Subject tests are required for admission. Amherst strongly recommends that applicants take 4 years of English, math through calculus, 3 or 4 years of a foreign language, 2 years of history and social science, and at least 2 years of natural science, including a lab science. 2 essays are required. Important factors in the admissions decision are advanced placement or honors courses, recommendations by school officials, and evidence of special talent. To earn the B.A., all students must complete 32 courses, equivalent to 128 credits, 8 to 14 of which are in the major, with at least a C average. Other than a 1-semester freshman seminar in liberal studies, there are no specific course requirements. A thesis or comparable work is required for honors candidates. **Procedure:** Freshmen are admitted fall. Entrance exams should be taken no later than December of the senior year. There are early decision and deferred admissions plans. Early decision applications should be filed by November 15; regular applications, by January 1 for fall entry, along with a $60 fee. Notification of early decision is sent December 15; regular decision, April 1. 169 early decision candidates were accepted for the 2016-2017 class. 600 applicants were on the 2016 waiting list; 61 were admitted. Applications are accepted on-line. **Transfer Students:** 15 transfer students enrolled in 2015-2016. Applicants must have full sophomore standing prior to applying and a minimum 3.0 GPA in previous college work. Transfers are accepted for the sophomore and junior classes only, and Amherst recommends that they submit SAT or ACT scores, plus high school and college transcripts, and seek a personal interview. 64 of 128 credits required for the bachelor's degree must be completed at Amherst. **International Students:** There are 175 international students enrolled. The school actively recruits these students. They must take the TOEFL with a minimum score of 600 on the paper-based TOEFL (PBT) or 100 on the Internet-based version (iBT) or take the MELAB or the SAT: ELAP if English is not the applicant's first language. They must also take the SAT or ACT.

ADMISSIONS: The SAT scores for the 2016-2017 freshman class were: Critical Reading-- 3% between 500 and 599, 30% between 600 and 699, and 67% between 700 and 800. Math-- 4% between 500 and 599, 27% between 600 and 699, and 69% between 700 and 800. Writing-- 6% between 500 and 599, 30% between 600 and 699, and 64% between 700 and 800. The ACT scores were 82% above 30. 99% were in the top two fifths. **Admissions Contact:** Katharine L. Fretwell, Dean of Admission and Financial Aid. Email: *admission@amherst.edu* Web: *www.amherst.edu*

FINANCIAL AID: In 2016-2017, 54% of all full-time freshmen and 58% of continuing full-time students received some form of financial aid. 54% of all full-time freshmen and 58% of continuing full-time students received need-based aid. The average freshman award was $49,469. Need-based scholarships or need-based grants averaged $48,105; and need-based self-help aid (loans and jobs) averaged $1,655. 60% of undergraduate students work part-time. Average annual earnings from campus work are $1250. The CSS/Profile is required. The FAFSA code is 002115. The deadline for filing freshman financial aid applications for fall entry is February 15.

ANNA MARIA COLLEGE C-2

www.annamaria.edu

Paxton, MA 01612	(508) 849-3586 (800) 344-4586
Fax: (508) 849-3362	Email: admission@annamaria.edu
Full-time: 305 men, 506 women	**Faculty:** 38
Part-time: 140 men, 177 women	**Ph.D.s:** 55%
Graduate: 179 men, 161 women	**Student/Faculty:** n/av
Year: semesters, summer session	**Tuition:** $35,074
Room & Board: $13,112	**Freshman Class:** n/av **CEEB CODE:** 3005
Application Deadline: n/av	**COMPETITIVE**

Anna Maria College is a private, Catholic, co-educational institution founded in 1946 by the Sisters of Saint Anne. Anna Maria offers a variety of undergraduate majors, as well as many graduate and certificate programs, both on-ground and online. The small student-faculty ratio allows for a highly personalized learning experience, while the modest class and campus size allow for optimal student involvement. Anna Maria offers more than 30 undergraduate degree programs with popular majors including Criminal Justice, Education, Fire Science, Health Science, Music and Art Therapy, Nursing, Social Work, and Sport Management. In addition, combined bachelor-master programs provide a fast track to receiving both one's undergraduate and graduate degrees in just five years. Programs available include Public Administration, Health Emergency Management, Criminal Justice, Counseling Psychology, Education, and Business. There are 5 undergraduate schools and 1 graduate school. In addition to regional accreditation, AMC has baccalaureate program accreditation with CSWE, NASM, NLN, TEAC, ACEN, and AMTA. The 192-acre campus is in a rural area 8 miles northwest of Worcester. Including any residence halls, there are 13 buildings.

STUDENT LIFE: 72% of undergraduates are from Massachusetts. Others are from 32 states, 1 foreign country, and Canada. 8% are Hispanic; 8% race unknown; 68% White; 2% Asian American; 2% two or more races; 10% African American. **Female To Male Ratio:** 1.4:1. The average age of freshmen is 19; all undergraduates, 20. 36% do not continue beyond their first year; 49% remain to graduate. **Housing:** 710 students can be accommodated in college housing, which includes coed dorms. Substance-free housing. On-campus housing is guaranteed for all 4 years, is guaranteed for the freshman year only, is available on a first-come, first-served basis, and is available on a lottery system for upperclassmen. Priority is given to out-of-town students. 59% of students live on campus; of those, 20% remain on campus on weekends. All students may keep cars.

FACULTY/CLASSROOMS: 50% of faculty are male; 50% are female. All teach undergraduates. No introductory courses are taught by graduate students. The average class size in an introductory lecture is 20; in a laboratory is 20; and in a regular course is 13.

PROGRAMS OF STUDY: AMC confers B.A., B.S., B.M. and B.S.N. degrees. Master's degrees are also awarded. Bachelor's degrees are awarded in BUSINESS (business administration and management and sports management), COMMUNICATIONS AND THE ARTS (art, English, graphic design, media arts, modern language, music, music performance, studio art, and visual and performing arts), COMPUTER AND PHYSICAL SCIENCE (computer science), EDUCATION (early childhood education, elementary education, health education, and music education), ENGINEERING AND ENVIRONMENTAL DESIGN (environmental science), HEALTH PROFESSIONS (art therapy, emergency medical services, music therapy, and nursing), SOCIAL SCIENCE (counseling/psychology, criminal justice, fire science, history, human development, humanities, liberal arts/general studies, paralegal studies, political science/government, psychology, public administration, religion, social science, social work, and sociology). Nursing is the strongest academically. Nursing, criminal justice, and fire science have the largest enrollments.

ACTIVITIES: There are no fraternities or sororities. There are 25 groups on campus, including art, cheerleading, choir, chorus, computers, dance, drama, ethnic, honors, international, jazz band, LGBT, musical theater, newspaper, political, professional, religious, social, social service, student government, and yearbook. Popular campus events include Highlighter Party, Sporting Events and the Annual Pig Roast/Spring Weekend. **Sports:** There are 6 intercollegiate sports for men and 7 for women, and 3 intramural sports for men and 3 for women. Facilities include a gym, basketball court, volleyball court, and locker rooms. Additionally we have a multipurpose center and weigh/fitness room. We also have an outdoor field turf stadium that serves our football, soccer, field hockey and lacrosse fields. **Graduates:** From July 1, 2015 to June 30, 2016, 251 bachelor's degrees were awarded. The most popular majors were nursing (32%), fire science (22%), and criminal justice (10%). In an average class, 36% graduate in 4 years or less and 40% graduate in 6 years or less.

SERVICES: Counseling and information services are available, as is tutoring in every subject. There is a reader service for the blind, and remedial math, reading, and writing. **Library/Resources:** The library contains 62,536 volumes, 12 microform items, and 819 audio/video tapes/CDs/DVDs, and subscribes to 1,841 periodicals including electronic. Computerized library services include interlibrary loans, database searching, and Internet access. Special learning facilities include an art gallery, an audiovisual center, and a nature trail. **Physically Challenged Students:** 80% of the campus is accessible. Facilities include wheelchair ramps, elevators, special parking, specially equipped restrooms, special class scheduling, lowered drinking fountains, and special housing. **Special:** Cross-registration with the Higher Education Consortium of Central Massachusetts, and internships in all majors are available. The college offers study abroad, a Washington semester, student-designed majors, accelerated degree programs, a general studies degree, credit by exam, work-study programs, and 5-year advanced degree programs in business, counseling psychology, criminal justice, education, and public administration. There are 6 national honor societies. **Visiting:** There are regularly scheduled orientations for prospective students, including on-campus interviews, campus tours, day visitation program by appointment, and a fall open house. There are guides for informal visits, visitors may sit in on classes, and stay overnight. To schedule a visit, contact Nancy Dowd at ndowd@annamaria.edu. **Campus Safety and Security:** Measures include 24-hour foot and vehicle patrol, emergency notification system, and security escort services. There are shuttle buses, emergency telephones, and lighted pathways/sidewalks.

REQUIREMENTS: A GED is accepted. 16 academic units are recommended, including 4 years of English, 2 years each of foreign language, history or social studies, math, and sciences. An interview is recommended. When applicable, an audition and portfolio are required. An essay and one letter of recommendation are required. A GPA of 2.0 is required. AP and CLEP credits are accepted. The 54-credit core curriculum consists of classes in English, literature, math, natural science, foreign language, fine arts, history, philosophy, social/behavioral sciences, and religious studies. A total of 120 credits is required for graduation, with a minimum of 30 in the major and a 2.0 GPA. **Procedure:** Freshmen are admitted fall and spring. There are deferred admissions and rolling admissions plans. Application deadlines are open. Application fee is $25. Notification is sent on a rolling basis. Applications are accepted on-line. **Transfer Students:** 65 transfer students enrolled in 2015-2016. Transfers with a minimum GPA of 2.0 are accepted for upper-division work. High school and college transcripts are required. An essay or personal statement and a statement of good standing from prior institutions are also required. 45 of 120 credits required for the bachelor's degree must be completed at AMC. **International Students:** There was 1 international student enrolled. The school actively recruits these students. They must take the TOEFL with a minimum score of 550 on the paper-based TOEFL (PBT) or 79 on the Internet-based version (iBT).

Admissions Contact: Peter Miller, Dean of Admissions & Financial Aid. Email: *admission@annamaria.edu* Web: *www.annamaria.edu*

FINANCIAL AID: In 2016-2017, 97% of all full-time freshmen and 99% of continuing full-time students received some form of financial aid. 86% of all full-time freshmen and 88% of continuing full-time students received need-based aid. The average freshman award was $28,969. Need-based scholarships or need-based grants averaged $7,635; and need-based self-help aid (loans and jobs) averaged $5,097. 22% of undergraduate students work part-time. The state aid form is required. The FAFSA code is 002117. Check with the school for current application deadlines.

ASSUMPTION COLLEGE C-2
www.assumption.edu

Worcester, MA 01609	(508) 767-7285 (866) 477-7776
Fax: (508) 799-4412	Email: admiss@assumption.edu
Full-time: 820 men, 1140 women	Faculty: 141; IIB, +$
Part-time: 6 men, 6 women	Ph.D.s: 91%
Graduate: 127 men, 291 women	Student/Faculty: 11 to 1
Year: semesters, summer session	Tuition: $36,260
Room & Board: $11,660	Freshman Class: 4559 applied, 3544 accepted, 579 enrolled
SAT CR/M: 550/560 ACT: 25	CEEB CODE: 3009
Application Deadline: February 15	COMPETITIVE+

Assumption College, founded in 1904 by Augustinians of the Assumption, offers a Catholic liberal arts and sciences education to undergraduates, along with programs for graduate and continuing education students. There is 1 undergraduate school and 1 graduate school. In addition to regional accreditation, Assumption has baccalaureate program accreditation with CRE and ACS. The 180-acre campus is in a suburban area 45 miles west of Boston in New England's second-largest city, Worcester, MA. Including any residence halls, there are 49 buildings.

STUDENT LIFE: 65% of undergraduates are from Massachusetts. Others are from 28 states, 22 foreign countries, and Canada. 62% are from public schools. 75% are White; 7% Hispanic; 6% African American; 6% race unknown; 3% Foreign; 2% Asian American; 2% two or more races; 1% American Indian/Alaska Native. **Female To Male Ratio:** 1.5:1. The average age of freshmen is 18; all undergraduates, 20. 18% do not continue beyond their first year; 74% remain to graduate. **Housing:** 1918 students can be accommodated in college housing, which includes single-sex dorms and on-campus apartments. In addition, there are special-interest houses, freshman dorms, substance-free dorms, first-year experience dorm, and a living/learning center. On-campus housing is guaranteed for all 4 years. 87% of students live on campus; of those, 80% remain on campus on weekends. Upperclassmen may keep cars.

FACULTY/CLASSROOMS: 54% of faculty are male; 46% are female. All teach undergraduates. No introductory courses are taught by graduate students. The average class size in a laboratory is 15 and in a regular course is 20.

PROGRAMS OF STUDY: Assumption confers B.A. degrees. Master's degrees are also awarded. Bachelor's degrees are awarded in BIOLOGICAL SCIENCE (biology/biological science and molecular biology), BUSINESS (accounting, business administration and management, international business management, marketing management, and organizational behavior), COMMUNICATIONS AND THE ARTS (art history, classics, English, French, graphic design, languages, music, Spanish, and studio art), COMPUTER AND PHYSICAL SCIENCE (actuarial science, chemistry, computer science, and mathematics), EDUCATION (education), ENGINEERING AND ENVIRONMENTAL DESIGN (environmental science), SOCIAL SCIENCE (criminology, economics, history, human services, international studies, Italian studies, Latin American studies, philosophy, political science/government, psychology, sociology, and theological studies). Business studies, natural sciences, and English have the largest enrollments.

ACTIVITIES: There are no fraternities or sororities. There are 60 groups on campus, including art, band, cheerleading, choir, chorale, chorus, computers, dance, drama, environmental, ethnic, film, honors, international, jazz band, literary magazine, musical theater, newspaper, orchestra, pep band, photography, political, professional, radio and TV, religious, social, social service, student government, and yearbook. Popular campus events include Midnight Madness Baketball Kickoff, Campus Concert, and Duck Day. **Sports:** There are 10 intercollegiate sports for men and 11 for women. Facilities include a 1,200-seat multi-sports stadium, a 3,000-seat gym, baseball and softball diamonds, a field hockey area, a soccer field, and tennis courts. A recreation center houses a 6-lane swimming pool, a jogging/walking track, 2 racquetball courts, an aerobics/dance studio, a multi-purpose room with TRX equipment, fully equipped Bodymaster and free-weight rooms, a fitness center, a varsity weight room, and a field house with 3 multipurpose courts for basketball, volleyball, and floor hockey. **Graduates:** From July 1, 2015 to June 30, 2016, 459 bachelor's degrees were awarded. The most popular majors were human services and rehabilitation studies (15%), biology (10%), and English (9%). 95 companies recruited on campus in 2015-2016. In an average class, 72% graduate in 4 years or less, and 74% graduate in 5 years or less. Of the 2015 graduating class, 23% were enrolled in graduate school within 6 months of graduation, and 62% were employed.

SERVICES: Counseling and information services are available, as is tutoring in most subjects. There is a reader service for the blind, signing for the deaf, and technology services for the disabled. **Library/Resources:** The library contains 289,146 volumes, 1,392 microform items, and 29,869 audio/video tapes/CDs/DVDs, and subscribes to 41,086 periodicals including electronic. Computerized library services include interlibrary loans, database searching, Internet access, and Wi-Fi capability. Special learning facilities include a radio station and TV station. **Physically Challenged Students:** 71% of the campus is accessible. Facilities include wheelchair ramps, elevators, special parking, specially equipped restrooms, special class scheduling, lowered drinking fountains, lowered telephones, and special housing. **Special:** Co-op program in marine studies available. Cross-registration with the Higher Education Consortium of Central Massachusetts is offered. The college has its own study abroad campus in Rome, and study abroad is available through other providers as well. The college offers internships, a Washington semester, student-designed and dual majors, credit by exam, and credit for military experience. The college offers 6-in-5 programs in accounting (BA/MBA), special education(BA/MA), school counseling (BA/MA), and rehabilitation counseling (BA/MA); a 3-in-2 program in engineering with the University of Notre Dame, and multiple combined degree programs with other institutions. There are 11 national honor societies and a freshman honors program. **Visiting:** There are regularly scheduled orientations for prospective students, consisting of new student orientation, meetings with future classmates, choosing roommates, registration, testing, conferences with academic advisers, and discussions of aspects of college life. There are guides for informal visits and visitors may sit in on classes. To schedule a visit, contact Maureen Langhammer at (866) 477-7776. **Campus Safety and Security:** Measures include 24-hour foot and vehicle patrol, emergency notification system, self-defense education, and security escort services. There are shuttle buses, emergency telephones, lighted pathways/sidewalks, controlled access to dorms/residences, and a gated entrance.

REQUIREMENTS: Applicants must graduate from an accredited secondary school or have a GED. 18 academic units are required, including 4 years of English, 3 of math, and 2 each of history, science, and foreign language. An essay and an interview are recommended. AP and CLEP credits are accepted. Important factors in the admissions decision are advanced placement or honors courses, leadership record, and recommendations by school officials. Assumption College's core curriculum centers around three reading and writing intensive seminar sequences in English, Philosophy, and Theology taken in the first and second years. From these seminars four areas of skill or expertise branch: Scientific and Quantitative Reasoning, comprising courses in mathematics and laboratory science; Person and Society, comprising courses in history and a wide range of the social sciences; Culture and Expression, comprising courses in the fine arts and foreign language, and The Great Conversation, comprising further coursework in literature, political science, philosophy, or theology. A global awareness requirement ensures all students experience non-Western traditions. The baccalaureate degree is completed with 120 credit hours, and a grade point average of 2.0. **Procedure:** Freshmen are admitted fall and spring. Entrance exams should be taken in May of the junior year or November of the senior year. There are early decision, early admissions, and deferred admissions plans. Early decision applications should be filed by November 1; regular applications, by February 15 for fall entry; and December 15 for spring entry, along with a $50 fee. Notification of early decision is sent December 1; regular decision, March 15. 47 applicants were on the 2016 waiting list; 10 were admitted. Applications are accepted on-line. **Transfer Students:** 56 transfer students enrolled in 2015-2016. Transfer students must have maintained a minimum 2.5 GPA at their previous college. SAT scores and high school and college transcripts are required. 60 of 120 credits required for the bachelor's degree must be completed at Assumption. **International Students:** There are 48 international students enrolled. The school actively recruits these students. They must take the TOEFL with a minimum score of 550 on the paper-based TOEFL (PBT) or 80 on the Internet-based version (iBT).

ADMISSIONS: 78% of the 2016-2017 applicants were accepted. The SAT scores for the 2016-2017 freshman class were: Critical Reading-- 24% below 500, 48% between 500 and 599, 26% between 600 and 699, and 2% between 700 and 800. Math-- 17% below 500, 55% between 500 and 599, 26% between 600 and 699, and 2% between 700 and 800. The ACT scores were 3% between 12 and 17, 31% between 18 and 23, 53% between 24 and 29, and 13% above 30. 29% of the current freshmen were in the top fifth of their class; 63% were in the top two fifths. **Admissions Contact:** Evan E. Lipp, Vice President for Enrollment Management. Email: *admiss@assumption.edu* Web: *www.assumption.edu*

FINANCIAL AID: In 2016-2017, 99% of all full-time freshmen and 97% of continuing full-time students received some form of financial aid. 79% of all full-time freshmen and 72% of continuing full-time students received need-based aid. The average freshman award was $24,076. Need-based scholarships or need-based grants averaged $21,837 ($51,388 maximum); need-based self-help aid (loans and jobs) averaged $3,681 ($9,000 maximum); non-need-based athletic scholarships averaged $12,909 ($49,109 maximum); and other non-need-based awards and non-need-based scholarships averaged $15,171 ($44,712 maximum). The FAFSA code is 002118. The deadline for filing freshman financial aid applications for fall entry is February 15.

ATLANTIC UNION COLLEGE — D-2

www.atlanticuc.edu

South Lancaster, MA 01561	**(978) 368-2239** **(800) 282-2030**
Fax: (978) 368-2517	**Email: enroll@atlanticuc.edu**
Full-time: 150 men, 250 women	**Faculty:** n/av
Part-time: 20 men, 30 women	**Ph.D.s:** 42%
Graduate: 5 men, 10 women	**Student/Faculty:** n/av
Year: semesters, summer session	**Tuition:** $17,998
Room & Board: $9230	**Freshman Class:** n/av
SAT or ACT: required	**CEEB CODE:** 3010
Application Deadline: August 1	**COMPETITIVE**

Atlantic Union College, established in 1882, is a private liberal arts institution associated with the Seventh-Day Adventist church and offers limited professional and pre-professional programs. The figures in the above capsule and in this profile are approximate. There is 1 undergraduate school. In addition to regional accreditation, AUC has baccalaureate program accreditation with NASM. The 135-acre campus is in a small town 50 miles west of Boston. Including any residence halls, there are 54 buildings.

STUDENT LIFE: 55% of undergraduates are from out of state, mostly the Northeast. Students are from 14 states, 21 foreign countries, and Canada. 53% are African American; 22% Hispanic; 20% White; 15% Foreign; 1% Asian American; 1% American Indian/Alaska Native. **Female To Male Ratio:** 1.7:1. The average age of freshmen is 21; all undergraduates, 23. 27% do not continue beyond their first year. **Housing:** 469 students can be accommodated in college housing, which includes single-sex dorms, on-campus apartments, and married student housing. On-campus housing is guaranteed for all 4 years. 56% of students live on campus; of those, 85% remain on campus on weekends. Alcohol is not permitted. All students may keep cars.

FACULTY/CLASSROOMS: 45% of faculty are male; 55% are female. All teach undergraduates, 10% do research, and 10% do both. No introductory courses are taught by graduate students. The average class size in an introductory lecture is 18; in a laboratory is 30; and in a regular course is 16.

PROGRAMS OF STUDY: AUC confers B.A., B.S., and B.M. degrees. Associate and master's degrees are also awarded. Bachelor's degrees are awarded in BIOLOGICAL SCIENCE (biology/biological science and life science), BUSINESS (accounting and business administration and management), COMMUNICATIONS AND THE ARTS (art, English, and music), COMPUTER AND PHYSICAL SCIENCE (computer science, information sciences and systems, and mathematics), EDUCATION (early childhood education, elementary education, and music education), HEALTH PROFESSIONS (nursing), SOCIAL SCIENCE (culinary arts, history, liberal arts/general studies, ministries, psychology, religion, social work, and theological studies). Nursing, business, and psychology are the strongest academically. Nursing, business, and education have the largest enrollments.

ACTIVITIES: There are no fraternities or sororities. There are 13 groups on campus, including art, band, choir, chorale, drama, ethnic, honors, newspaper, orchestra, religious, social, student government, and yearbook. Popular campus events include Fall Picnic, Cultural Heritage Weeks, and Fine Arts Week. **Sports:** There are 7 intramural sports for men and 7 for women. Facilities include a gym and field house with a weight room and tennis/volleyball/badminton, racquetball/handball, and basketball courts, a swimming pool, and athletic fields for flag football, soccer, softball, and baseball.

SERVICES: Counseling and information services are available, as is tutoring in most subjects. There is remedial math, reading, and writing. Additional services are provided upon request. **Library/Resources:** The library contains 139,000 volumes, 17,336 microform items, and 4,754 audio/video tapes/CDs/DVDs, and subscribes to 469 periodicals including electronic. Computerized library services include interlibrary loans, database searching, Internet access, and Wi-Fi capability. **Physically Challenged Students:** 73% of the campus is accessible. Facilities include wheelchair ramps, elevators, special parking, specially equipped restrooms, special class scheduling, and lowered drinking fountains. **Special:** There is cross-registration with Mount Wachusett Community College and the Colleges of Worcester Consortium. Students may study abroad in 6 countries. AUC also offers newspaper and biology research internships, cooperative programs in several majors, pass/fail options, and nondegree study. The Summer Advantage in New England program offers precollege credit to high school honor students. There is also an adult degree program, in which most study is done at home, and student-designed majors are permited. Dual majors, an accelerated degree in management and professional studies, a 1-3 engineering degree with Walla Walla College, and preprofessional curricula in dentistry, dental hygiene, medicine, respiratory therapy, radiologic technology, and veterinary medicine in conjunction with Loma Linda University are offered. There are 3 national honor societies, a freshman honors program, and 4 departmental honors programs. **Visiting:** There are regularly scheduled orientations for prospective students, including campus tours, class visits, and financial aid and admissions information sessions. There are guides for informal visits, visitors may sit in on classes, and stay overnight. **Campus Safety and Security:** Measures include self-defense education and security escort services. There are lighted pathways/sidewalks.

REQUIREMENTS: The SAT or ACT is required. Applicants should be graduates of an accredited secondary school. The GED is accepted with a minimum score of 250. Required academic credits include 4 years of high school English and 2 years each of a foreign language, math, history, and science. A GPA of 2.2 is required. AP and CLEP credits are accepted. Important factors in the admissions decision are recommendations by school officials, recommendations by alumni, and personality/intangible qualities. Students must complete 9 hours each in humanities, science, and social science and 12 hours in religion/ethics. Foreign language proficiency, a phys ed requirement, 40 hours of community service, and a course in college writing must also be completed. AUC requires 128 to 143 credit hours for the bachelor's degree, with 30 to 60 in the major, and a 2.0 GPA. **Procedure:** Freshmen are admitted fall and spring. Entrance exams should be taken during the senior year of high school. There is a rolling admissions plan. Applications should be filed by August 1 for fall entry; January 2 for spring entry. The fall 2016 application fee was $25. Notification is sent on a rolling basis. Applications are accepted on-line. **Transfer Students:** Applicants who have completed at least 24 semester hours are not required to submit SAT or ACT scores. Applicants from junior colleges may receive credit for up to 72 semester hours. Only a grade of C or better transfers for credit. 30 of 128 credits required for the bachelor's degree must be completed at AUC. **International Students:** The school actively recruits these students. They must take the TOEFL. They must also take the ACT.

Admissions Contact: Rosita Lashley, Director of Admissions. Email: *enroll@atlanticuc.edu* Web: *www.atlanticuc.edu*

FINANCIAL AID: AUC is a member of CSS. Check with the school for current application deadlines.

BABSON COLLEGE D-2

www.babson.edu

Babson Park, MA 02457 (781) 239-5522
(800) 488-3696

Fax: (781) 239-4135 **Email:** ugradadmission@babson.edu

Full-time: 1070 men, 730 women	**Faculty:** IIB
Part-time: n/av	**Ph.D.s:** 72%
Graduate: 1200 men, 440 women	**Student/Faculty:** n/av
Year: semesters, summer session	**Tuition:** $48,288
Room & Board: $15,376	**Freshman Class:** n/av
SAT or ACT: required	**CEEB CODE:** 3075
Application Deadline: January 4	**HIGHLY COMPETITIVE**

Babson College, founded in 1919, is a private business school. All students start their own businesses during their freshman year with money loaned by the college. The figures in the above capsule and in this profile are approximate. There are 4 undergraduate schools and 1 graduate school. In addition to regional accreditation, Babson has baccalaureate program accreditation with AACSB. The 370-acre campus is in a suburban area in Wellesley MA, 14 miles west of Boston. Including any residence halls, there are 53 buildings.

STUDENT LIFE: 70% of undergraduates are from out of state, mostly the Northeast. Students are from 47 states, 60 foreign countries, and Canada. 50% are from public schools. 8% are Hispanic; 44% White; 4% African American; 18% Foreign; 11% Asian American. **Male To Female Ratio:** 1.9:1. The average age of freshmen is 18; all undergraduates, 20. 5% do not continue beyond their first year; 85% remain to graduate. **Housing:** 1441 students can be accommodated in college housing, which includes single-sex and coed dorms, on-campus apartments, and married student housing. In addition, there are special-interest houses, substance-free living, fraternity and sorority towers, and a cultural house. On-campus housing is guaranteed for all 4 years. 85% of students live on campus; of those, 80% remain on campus on weekends. All students may keep cars.

FACULTY/CLASSROOMS: 69% of faculty are male; 31% are female. No introductory courses are taught by graduate students. The average class size in an introductory lecture is 34; in a laboratory is 20; and in a regular course is 27.

PROGRAMS OF STUDY: Babson confers B.S.M. degrees. Master's degrees are also awarded. Bachelor's degrees are awarded in BUSINESS (business administration and management).

ACTIVITIES: 10% of men belong to 7 national fraternities; 12% of women belong to 3 national sororities. There are 60 groups on campus, including art, band, cappella , cheerleading, choir, chorus, dance, drama, ethnic, honors, international, jazz band, LGBT, literary magazine, musical theater, newspaper, photography, political, professional, radio and TV, religious, social, social service, student government, and yearbook. Popular campus events include Multicultural Week. **Sports:** There are 11 intercollegiate sports for men and 11 for women, and 11 intramural sports for men and 11 for women. Facilities include a sports complex with an indoor swimming pool/diving, a 200-meter, 6-lane indoor track, a 1500-square-foot field house, a 600-seat gym with 3 basketball courts, 5 squash and 2 racquetball courts, a fitness center, a dance aerobics studio, locker rooms with saunas, and a sports medicine facility, badminton, baseball, softball, cricket, golf, lacrosse, rugby, table tennis, ultimate disk, ice hockey, alpine skiing, cross county, yoga, and volleyball. **Graduates:** From July 1, 2015 to June 30, 2016, 424 bachelor's degrees were awarded. 301 companies recruited on campus in 2015-2016. In an average class, 80% graduate in 4 years or less, 85% graduate in 5 years or less, and 85% graduate in 6 years or less. Of the 2015 graduating class, 3% were enrolled in graduate school within 6 months of graduation, and 92% were employed.

SERVICES: Counseling and information services are available, as is tutoring in most subjects. There are writing/speech skills and math/science skills centers. **Library/Resources:** The library contains 132,024 volumes, 346,941 microform items, and 4,645 audio/video tapes/CDs/DVDs, and subscribes to 511 periodicals including electronic. Computerized library services include interlibrary loans, database searching, and Internet access. Special learning facilities include an art gallery, radio station, performing arts theater, and centers for entrepreneurial studies, management, language and culture, writing, math, visual arts, executive education, and women's leadership. **Physically Challenged Students:** 75% of the campus is accessible. Facilities include wheelchair ramps, elevators, special parking, specially equipped restrooms, special class scheduling, lowered drinking fountains, and special housing. **Special:** There is cross-registration with Brandeis University, Wellesley College, and F.W. Olin College of Engineering. Internships and study abroad in 27 countries are available. There is a freshman honors program and 10 departmental honors programs. **Visiting:** There are regularly scheduled orientations for prospective students, including an open house each year, personal interviews, campus tours, group information sessions and fall preview days. There are guides for informal visits. To schedule a visit, contact the Admission Office. **Campus Safety and Security:** Measures include 24-hour foot and vehicle patrol, self-defense education, and security escort services. There are shuttle buses, emergency telephones, lighted pathways/sidewalks, a motorist assist program, a transportation service for the cross-registration program, vans available to students for school activities, and crime prevention programs.

REQUIREMENTS: The SAT or ACT is required. Applicants must be graduates of an accredited secondary school or have a GED. 16 academic courses are required, including 4 credits of English, 3 of math, 2 of social studies, and 1 of science. A fourth year of math is strongly recommended. Essays are required. SAT Subject tests in math are recommended. AP credits are accepted. Important factors in the admissions decision are advanced placement or honors courses, evidence of special talent, and leadership record. Students must complete a curriculum of general management and liberal arts, with 50% in management and 50% in liberal arts. A total of 128 semester hours is required for graduation. A minimum GPA of 2.0 is required. **Procedure:** Freshmen are admitted fall. Entrance exams should be taken prior to application (SAT or ACT). There are early decision, early admissions, and deferred admissions plans. Early decision applications should be filed by November 1; regular applications, by January 4 for fall entry. The fall 2016 application fee was $60. Notification of early decision is sent December 15; regular decision, March 20. Applications are accepted on-line. **Transfer Students:** Transfer applicants are expected to demonstrate solid academic performance at their prior institution and must submit 1 essay and 1 recommendation from a college teacher or administrator, in addition to a high school transcript and SAT scores. They must also submit course descriptions and syllabi for any courses they have taken. 64 of 128 credits required for the bachelor's degree must be completed at Babson. **International Students:** There are 318 international students enrolled. The school actively recruits these students. They must take the TOEFL with a minimum score of 600 on the paper-based TOEFL (PBT) or 100 on the Internet-based version (iBT), English Language Proficiency Test. They must also take the SAT or ACT.

Admissions Contact: Grant Gosselin, Dean of Undergraduate Admission. Email: *ugradadmission@babson.edu* Web: *www.babson.edu*

FINANCIAL AID: In 2016-2017, 45% of all full-time freshmen and 41% of continuing full-time students received some form of financial aid. 45% of all full-time freshmen and 41% of continuing full-time students received need-based aid. The average freshman award was $26,171. Need-based scholarships or need-based grants averaged $29,787; and need-based self-help aid (loans and jobs) averaged $5,013. 32% of undergraduate students work part-time. Average annual earnings from campus work are $1580. The average financial indebtedness of the 2016 graduate was $24,900. The CSS/Profile, and tax returns are required. The

FAFSA code is 002121. The deadline for filing freshman financial aid applications for fall entry is April 15.

BARD COLLEGE AT SIMON'S ROCK A-2

www.simons-rock.edu

Great Barrington, MA 01230 (413) 528-7228 (800) 235-7186

Fax: (413) 541-0081 Email: admit@simons-rock.edu

Full-time: 140 men, 219 women	**Faculty:** 51
Part-time: 2 men, 1 women	**Ph.D.s:** 90%
Graduate: n/av	**Student/Faculty:** 6 to 1
Year: semesters	**Tuition:** $51,735
Room & Board: $14,060	**Freshman Class:** 304 applied, 272 accepted, 143 enrolled
SAT CR/M/W: 692/656/661 **ACT:** 28	**CEEB CODE:** 3795
Application Deadline: n/av	**MOST COMPETITIVE**

Bard College at Simon's Rock is the only four-year college in the United States specifically designed to allow bright, highly motivated adolescents to fully realize their intellectual and creative potential by beginning college immediately after the tenth or eleventh grade. Offering students both significant autonomy and appropriate support, Simon's Rock fosters a diverse community of intellectual and chronological peers. Under the guidance of talented and dedicated faculty, students learn to formulate and defend their own ideas; to engage with the ideas of others; and to become innovative thinkers who contribute with purpose to the world around them. There is 1 undergraduate school. The 210-acre campus is in a small town in the Berkshire Hills of Western MA, approximately 2 hours from New York City and Boston. Including any residence halls, there are 47 buildings.

STUDENT LIFE: 77% of undergraduates are from out of state, mostly the Middle Atlantic. Students are from 37 states, and 16 foreign countries. 65% are from public schools. 57% are White; 16% Foreign; 9% race unknown; 6% Asian American; 5% African American; 4% Hispanic; 3% two or more races; 1% American Indian/Alaska Native. **Female To Male Ratio:** 1.5:1. The average age of freshmen is 16; all undergraduates, 18. 17% do not continue beyond their first year; 75% remain to graduate. **Housing:** 347 students can be accommodated in college housing, which includes single-sex and coed dorms and on-campus apartments, as well as senior only housing. On-campus housing is guaranteed for all 4 years. 93% of students live on campus; of those, 93% remain on campus on weekends. Alcohol is not permitted. Upperclassmen may keep cars.

FACULTY/CLASSROOMS: 51% of faculty are male; 49% are female. All teach undergraduates, and all do research. No introductory courses are taught by graduate students. The average class size in an introductory lecture is 14; in a laboratory is 10; and in a regular course is 12.

PROGRAMS OF STUDY: Simon's Rock confers B.A. degrees. Associate degrees are also awarded. Bachelor's degrees are awarded in AGRICULTURE (environmental studies), BIOLOGICAL SCIENCE (biology/biological science), COMMUNICATIONS AND THE ARTS (art history and appreciation, creative writing, dance, dramatic arts, drawing, intermedia/multimedia, linguistics, literature, music, studio art ceramics, and studio art painting), COMPUTER AND PHYSICAL SCIENCE (chemistry, computer science, mathematics, physics, and quantitative methods), EDUCATION (global studies), ENGINEERING AND ENVIRONMENTAL DESIGN (preengineering), HEALTH PROFESSIONS (premedicine), SOCIAL SCIENCE (African American studies, Asian/Oriental studies, crosscultural studies, cultural studies/critical theory & analysis, French studies, gender studies, geography, German area studies, history, philosophy, political science/government, psychology, and Spanish studies). Pre-engineering is the strongest academically. Literary studies, music, and politics have the largest enrollments.

ACTIVITIES: There are no fraternities or sororities. There are 29 groups on campus, including art, choir, chorus, computers, dance, debate, drama, environmental, ethnic, film, international, jazz band, LGBT, literary magazine, musical theater, newspaper, orchestra, photography, political, religious, social, social service, and student government. Popular campus events include Mayfest, Spring Formal, Dance Concert, Rock the Community Day of Service, Chinese New Year, Bollywood, Dolly Drag, Black Student Union Ball. **Sports:** There are 3 intercollegiate sports for men and 3 for women, and 6 intramural sports for men and 6 for women. Facilities include an 8-lane swimming pool, multicourt gym, 3 racquetball courts, an elevated running track, fitness, weight-training center, rock-climbing wall, soccer field, 4 tennis courts, and hiking trails. **Graduates:** From July 1, 2015 to June 30, 2016, 51 bachelor's degrees were awarded. The most popular majors were mathematics (10%), creative writing (8%), and pre-engineering (8%). In an average class, 1% graduate in 3 years or less, 69% graduate in 4 years or less.

SERVICES: Counseling and information services are available, as is tutoring in most subjects. There is a reader service for the blind, and remedial writing. Study skills instruction is available. Writing is with adult tutors and other subjects are with trained peer tutors. **Library/Resources:** The library contains 69,517 volumes, 3,896 microform items, and 6,425 audio/video tapes/CDs/DVDs, and subscribes to 43,313 periodicals including electronic. Computerized library services include interlibrary loans, database searching, Internet access, and Wi-Fi capability. Special learning facilities include an art gallery. **Physically Challenged Students:** 75% of the campus is accessible. Facilities include wheelchair ramps, elevators, special parking, specially equipped restrooms, special class scheduling, lowered drinking fountains, lowered telephones, and special housing. **Special:** 3-2 BA/BS engineering degree programs with Columbia University and Dartmouth University. 3-2 BA/MS program in environmental science with Bard College's Center for Environmental Policy. Articulated junior-year study abroad agreements with two colleges at Oxford University (Lincoln College and St. Catherine's College), the University of Manchester's Center for New Writing, Qingdao University in China, the University of Glasgow in Scotland, the London Dramatic Academy in London, Eastern Carolina University's Italy Intensives abroad, and the Umbra Institute, Perugia, Italy. There are also domestic study away opportunities with the Bard Globalization and International Affairs (BGIA) program in NYC, the Eugene O'Neil Theater in CT, the Washington Center in Washington DC, and the International Center of Photography in NYC. Internships may be completed for course credit through the Extended Campus Project program, and students are encouraged to work with the Director of Career Development to develop internships for credit or personal development that connect with their academic and career interests. Most Simon's Rock BA graduates complete more than one of the College's BA concentrations, and students have the option of creating a self-designed second concentration. Work-study opportunities are available on campus, as well as with several non-profit organizations and schools in the community. **Visiting:** There are regularly scheduled orientations for prospective students, that includes a sample class, a campus tour, and an interview. There are guides for informal visits and visitors may sit in on classes. To schedule a visit, contact the Office of Admission. **Campus Safety and Security:** Measures include 24-hour foot and vehicle patrol, emergency notification system, and security escort services. There are shuttle buses, lighted pathways/sidewalks, and controlled access to dorms/residences.

REQUIREMENTS: Applicants are required to submit application form, parent statement, 3 letters of recommendation, personal interview, high school transcript and school report, and application essays. Test scores are optional, but will be considered if submitted. Important factors in the admissions decision are personality/intangible qualities, recommendations by school officials, advanced placement or honors courses, evidence of special talent, recommendations by alumni, ability to finance college education, leadership record, parents or siblings attended your school, extracurricular activities record, and geographical diversity. AA degree requirements: Writing and Thinking Workshop; General Education Seminars; courses in Intercultural Perspectives, Arts course; Mathematics, Natural Sciences and World Languages. Students in the BA program must complete at least one BA concentration, a tutorial, internship, independent study and/or study abroad; and a senior thesis. **Procedure:** Freshmen are admitted fall and spring. There is a rolling admissions plan. Application deadlines are open. Notification is sent on a rolling basis. Applications are accepted on-line. **Transfer Students:** 2 transfer students enrolled in 2015-2016. Transfer students must be evaluated by Admission, although review of transfer credit is done by the Dean of Academic Affairs and the Registrar. 60 of 120 credits required for the bachelor's degree must be completed at Simon's Rock. **International Students:** There are 51 international students enrolled. The school actively recruits these students. They must take the TOEFL with a minimum score of 600 on the paper-based TOEFL (PBT) or 100 on the Internet-based version (iBT), and take the IELTS.

ADMISSIONS: 89% of the 2016-2017 applicants were accepted. The SAT scores for the 2016-2017 freshman class were: Critical Reading-- 4% between 500 and 599, 41% between 600 and 699, and 52% between 700 and 800. Math-- 22% between 500 and 599, 48% between 600 and 699, and 30% between 700 and 800. Writing-- 11% between 500 and 599, 26% between 600 and 699, and 19% between 700 and 800. The ACT scores were 14% between 18 and 23, 57% between 24 and 29, and 14% above 30. 75% of the current freshmen were in the top fifth of their class; 83% were in the top two fifths. **Admissions Contact:** Office of Admission Email: *admit@simons-rock.edu* Web: *www.simons-rock.edu*

FINANCIAL AID: In 2016-2017, 99% of all full-time freshmen and 97% of continuing full-time students received some form of financial aid. 68% of all full-time freshmen and 66% of continuing full-time students received need-based aid. The average freshman award was $30,220. Need-based scholarships or need-based grants averaged $32,929; need-based self-help aid (loans and jobs) averaged $6,252; and other non-need-based awards and non-need-based scholarships averaged $13,897. The average financial indebtedness of the 2016 graduate was $27,544. Simon's Rock is a member of CSS. The CSS/Profile is required. The FAFSA code is 009645. The priority date for freshman financial aid applications for fall entry is February 1. The deadline for filing freshman financial aid applications for fall entry is May 1.

BAY PATH UNIVERSITY B-3

www.baypath.edu

Longmeadow, MA 01106	**(413) 565-6806** **(800) 782-7284**
Fax: (413) 565-1336	**Email: kamartin@baypath.edu**
Full-time: 1415 women	**Faculty:** 31
Part-time: 478 women	**Ph.D.s:** 36%
Graduate: 184 men, 1148 women	**Student/Faculty:** 11 to 1
Year: semesters	**Tuition:** $32,739
Room & Board: $12,610	**Freshman Class:** 1542 applied, 942 accepted, 153 enrolled
	CEEB CODE: 3078
Application Deadline: n/av	**COMPETITIVE**

Bay Path University, founded in 1897, is a comprehensive, private college offering innovative undergraduate programs for women only and graduate programs for men and women. The figures in the above capsule and in this profile are approximate. There are 3 undergraduate schools and 1 graduate school. In addition to regional accreditation, Bay Path has baccalaureate program accreditation with ABA, Mass. Dept. of Education & Secondary Education, and ACOTE. The 48-acre campus is in a suburban area in Longmeadow MA, 90 minutes to Boston and 2 hours to New York City. Including any residence halls, there are 17 buildings.

STUDENT LIFE: 58% of undergraduates are from Massachusetts. Others are from 24 states, and 5 foreign countries. 94% are from public schools. 7% are race unknown; 62% White; 3% two or more races; 2% Asian American; 14% Hispanic; 11% African American; 1% Foreign. **Female To Male Ratio:** 16.5:1. The average age of freshmen is 18; all undergraduates, 21. 28% do not continue beyond their first year; 72% remain to graduate. **Housing:** 411 students can be accommodated in college housing, which includes single-sex dorms, and themed floors in residence halls. On-campus housing is guaranteed for all 4 years, is available on a first-come, first-served basis, and is available on a lottery system for upperclassmen. 55% of students commute. Alcohol is not permitted. All students may keep cars.

FACULTY/CLASSROOMS: 29% of faculty are male; 71% are female. 63% teach undergraduates. No introductory courses are taught by graduate students. The average class size in a laboratory is 18 and in a regular course is 13.

PROGRAMS OF STUDY: Bay Path confers B.A., and B.S. degrees. Associate and master's degrees are also awarded. Bachelor's degrees are awarded in BIOLOGICAL SCIENCE (biochemistry, biology/biological science, biology/gen sci/envir sci second ed, biotechnology, forensic psychology, forensic science, and neurosciences), BUSINESS (accounting, business administration and management, business administration marketing, human resources/organizational mgmt, marketing/retailing/merchandising, and small business management), COMMUNICATIONS AND THE ARTS (communications and writing), COMPUTER AND PHYSICAL SCIENCE (cyber intelligence/security studies), EDUCATION (early childhood education, educational studies, and elementary education), ENGINEERING AND ENVIRONMENTAL DESIGN (interior design), HEALTH PROFESSIONS (biomedical science, medical science, and pre-occupational therapy), SOCIAL SCIENCE (child psychology/development, criminal justice, forensic studies, legal studies, liberal arts/general studies, paralegal studies, and psychology). Medical science, cybersecurity, and business are the strongest academically. Pre-OT, psychology, and forensic science have the largest enrollments.

ACTIVITIES: There are no fraternities or sororities. There are 32 groups on campus, including Diverse Step Sisters, Habitat for Humanity, Wellness Wildcats, Women of Cultures, cheerleading, chorale, computers, dance, drama, ethnic, forensics, honors, international, LGBT, musical theater, political, professional, religious, social, social service, student government, and Tactical Team. Popular campus events include Campus Awakening, Generations Banquets, Karaoke Unplugged, and Dinner with the President. **Sports:** There are 8 intercollegiate sports for women. Facilities include a fitness center that houses a weight-training room, a dance studio, and an aerobics room and a nearby 12-acre playing field with soccer and softball fields, a walking/jogging track, and a field house. **Graduates:** From July 1, 2015 to June 30, 2016, 429 bachelor's degrees were awarded. The most popular majors were business (20%), psychology (15%), and liberal studies (11%). In an average class, 53% graduate in 4 years or less, 60% graduate in 5 years or less, and 61% graduate in 6 years or less.

SERVICES: Counseling and information services are available, as is tutoring in every subject. **Library/Resources:** The library contains 367,343 volumes, and 35,000 audio/video tapes/CDs/DVDs, and subscribes to 49,120 periodicals including electronic. Computerized library services include interlibrary loans, database searching, and Internet access. **Physically Challenged Students:** 90% of the campus is accessible. Facilities include wheelchair ramps, elevators, special parking, and specially equipped restrooms. **Special:** Cross-registration is possible with other member schools of the Cooperating Colleges of Greater Springfield Consortium. Bay Path's Capital of the World program allows students to visit a different world center during each spring break. Most academic programs require an internship or other experiential learning opportunity. There are 4 national honor societies, a freshman honors program, and 2 departmental honors programs. **Visiting:** There are regularly scheduled orientations for prospective students. There are guides for informal visits, visitors may sit in on classes, and stay overnight. To schedule a visit, contact Dawn Bryden at dbryden@baypath.edu. **Campus Safety and Security:** Measures include 24-hour foot and vehicle patrol, emergency notification system, self-defense education, and security escort services. There are shuttle buses, emergency telephones, lighted pathways/sidewalks, controlled access to dorms/residences, fire, vehicle, and driving safety education programs.

REQUIREMENTS: Applicants should have completed at least 4 academic courses each year, including 4 years of English, 3 of math, at least 2 each of social studies and lab sciences, and 2 of a foreign language. An essay is required, as are letters of recommendation from a guidance counselor and a teacher. An interview is strongly recommended. AP and CLEP credits are accepted. To graduate, students must complete at least 120 credits with a minimum GPA of 2.0. The 46-hour core curriculum includes course work in communication, science, social science, math, and fine and performing arts. **Procedure:** Freshmen are admitted fall and spring. Entrance exams should be taken in the spring of the junior year or by December of the senior year. There are deferred admissions and rolling admissions plans. Application deadlines are open. Applications are accepted on-line. Application fees are waived if application is completed on-line. **Transfer Students:** 84 transfer students enrolled in 2015-2016. Applicants must be in good standing at their previous school and are encouraged to arrange for an interview at Bay Path. Students who have earned fewer than 12 credits must submit SAT or ACT scores. 30 of 120 credits required for the bachelor's degree must be completed at Bay Path. **International Students:** There are 9 international students enrolled. The school actively recruits these students. They must take the TOEFL with a minimum score of 76 on the Internet-based version (iBT), and the IELTS.

ADMISSIONS: 61% of the 2016-2017 applicants were accepted. The SAT scores for the 2016-2017 freshman class were: Critical Reading-- 55% below 500, 33% between 500 and 599, 11% between 600 and 699, and 1% between 700 and 800. Math-- 63% below 500, 32% between 500 and 599, and 5% between 600 and 699. Writing-- 60% below 500, 34% between 500 and 599, 5% between 600 and 699, and 1% between 700 and 800. The ACT scores were 19% between 12 and 17, 48% between 18 and 23, 26% between 24 and 29, and 7% above 30. 15% of the current freshmen were in the top fifth of their class; 59% were in the top two fifths. **Admissions Contact:** Kathleen Martin, Vice Provost. Email: *kamartin@baypath.edu* Web: *www.baypath.edu*

FINANCIAL AID: In 2016-2017, 97% of all full-time freshmen and 90% of continuing full-time students received some form of financial aid. 92% of all full-time freshmen and 86% of continuing full-time students received need-based aid. The average freshman award was $30,322. Need-based scholarships or need-based grants averaged $14,176 ($18,843 maximum); need-based self-help aid (loans and jobs) averaged $5,707 ($5,746 maximum); and other non-need-based awards and non-need-based scholarships averaged $14,515 ($18,500 maximum). 40% of undergraduate students work part-time. Average annual earnings from campus work are $2205. The average financial indebtedness of the 2016 graduate was $28,204. Bay Path is a member of CSS. The college's own financial statement, and and parent and student income tax forms is required. The FAFSA code is 002122. Check with the school for current application deadlines.

BECKER COLLEGE — C-2

www.becker.edu

Worcester, MA 01609 (508) 373-9400 (877) 523-2537

Fax: (508) 890-1500	**Email:** admissions@becker.edu
Full-time: 670 men, 733 women	**Faculty:** 193
Part-time: 98 men, 325 women	**Ph.D.s:** 61%
Graduate: n/av	**Student/Faculty:** n/av
Year: semesters, summer session	**Tuition:** $40,082
Room & Board: $17,546	**Freshman Class:** 3350 applied, 2088 accepted, 381 enrolled
SAT or ACT: required	**CEEB CODE:** 3079
Application Deadline: open	**COMPETITIVE**

Becker College, founded in 1784, offers baccalaureate degree programs on the College's two distinctive campuses, located in Worcester and Leicester, Massachusetts. Both undergraduate and adult learning programs make Becker a place where students gain the experience they need to contribute to a global society and rise to the top of their chosen professions. Figures in the above capsule and in this profile are approximate. There are 4 undergraduate schools. In addition to regional accreditation, Becker has baccalaureate program accreditation with NLN and AVMA-Vet Tech. The campus is in an urban area about 40 miles west of Boston in Worcester. Including any residence halls, there are 49 buildings.

STUDENT LIFE: 69% of undergraduates are from Massachusetts. Others are from 33 states, and 13 foreign countries. 67% are from public schools. 9% are African American; 76% White; 2% Asian American; 2% two or more races; 10% Hispanic; 1% Foreign. **Female To Male Ratio:** 1.4:1. The average age of freshmen is 18; all undergraduates, 24. 35% do not continue beyond their first year; 30% remain to graduate. **Housing:** 700 students can be accommodated in college housing, which includes single-sex and coed dorms. In addition, there are special-interest houses, and living learning communities. On-campus housing is available on a first-come and first-served basis. 61% of students commute. All students may keep cars.

FACULTY/CLASSROOMS: 40% of faculty are male; 60% are female. 77% teach undergraduates, 23% do research, and 23% do both. No introductory courses are taught by graduate students. The average class size in an introductory lecture is 17; in a laboratory is 12; and in a regular course is 17.

PROGRAMS OF STUDY: Becker confers B.A., and B.S. degrees. Associate degrees are also awarded. Bachelor's degrees are awarded in AGRICULTURE (animal science), BIOLOGICAL SCIENCE (biology/biological science), BUSINESS (business administration and management, marketing and distribution, and sports management), COMMUNICATIONS AND THE ARTS (communications, design, and graphic design), COMPUTER AND PHYSICAL SCIENCE (computer game design/development), EDUCATION (early childhood education and elementary education), HEALTH PROFESSIONS (exercise science, nursing, preveterinary science, and veterinary science), SOCIAL SCIENCE (criminal justice, early childhood studies, forensic studies, liberal arts/general studies, and psychology). Interactive media (game design), and veterinary science are the strongest academically. Interactive media (game design) has the largest enrollment.

ACTIVITIES: There are no fraternities or sororities. There are 22 groups on campus, including art, cheerleading, chorale, chorus, communications, dance, drama, ethnic, honors, international, LGBT, musical theater, newspaper, professional, religious, social, social service, student government, and yearbook. **Sports:** There are 8 intercollegiate sports for men and 8 for women, and 5 intramural sports for men and 5 for women. **Graduates:** From July 1, 2015 to June 30, 2016, 347 bachelor's degrees were awarded. The most popular majors were business (28%), animal studies (including pre-veterinary science) (26%), and nursing (17%). In an average class, 31% graduate in 6 years or less. Of the 2015 graduating class, 15% were enrolled in graduate school within 6 months of graduation, and 79% were employed.

SERVICES: Counseling and information services are available, as is tutoring in most subjects. There is remedial math and writing. There is also an academic support center for students. **Library/Resources:** Computerized library services include interlibrary loans, database searching, Internet access, and Wi-Fi capability. **Physically Challenged Students:** Facilities include wheelchair ramps, elevators, special parking, specially equipped restrooms, lowered drinking fountains, lowered telephones, and special housing. All classes are accessible. **Special:** Cross-registration is offered through the Worcester Consortium of Higher Education. There are co-op programs, internships, study abroad, work-study programs. There are 3 national honor societies and a freshman honors program. **Visiting:** There are regularly scheduled orientations for prospective students. There are guides for informal visits, visitors may sit in on classes, and stay overnight. To schedule a visit, contact the Admissions Office. **Campus Safety and Security:** Measures include 24-hour foot and vehicle patrol, self-defense education, and security escort services. There are shuttle buses, emergency telephones, and lighted pathways/sidewalks.

REQUIREMENTS: The SAT is required. The ACT is recommended. In addition, a high school transcript is required. A GPA of 2.0 is required. AP and CLEP credits are accepted. To graduate, baccalaureate students must complete at least 122 semester hours and maintain a 2.0 minimum GPA. Distribution requirements vary with the program of study. **Procedure:** Freshmen are admitted fall and spring. Entrance exams should be taken before submitting the application. There are early admissions, deferred admissions, and rolling admissions plans. Application deadlines are open. Notifications are sent November 15. Applications are accepted on-line. **Transfer Students:** 207 transfer students enrolled in 2015-2016. Requirements for transfer students depend on the program. Must have at least a 2.0 GPA from prior institution. 30 of 15 credits required for the bachelor's degree must be completed at Becker. **International Students:** There are 11 international students enrolled. The school actively recruits these students. They must take the TOEFL with a minimum score of 550 on the paper-based TOEFL (PBT) or 80 on the Internet-based version (iBT). They must also take the SAT or ACT.

ADMISSIONS: 62% of the 2016-2017 applicants were accepted. 17% of the current freshmen were in the top fifth of their class; 48% were in the top two fifths. **Admissions Contact:** Debbie Gallo, Associate Director of Admissions. Email: *admissions@becker.edu* Web: *www.becker.edu*

FINANCIAL AID: In 2016-2017, 100% of all full-time freshmen and 93% of continuing full-time students received some form of financial aid. 57% of all full-time freshmen and 61% of continuing full-time students received need-based aid. Average annual earnings from campus work are $993. The average financial indebtedness of the 2016 graduate was $41,666. The state aid form and the college's own financial statement are required. The priority date for freshman financial aid applications for fall entry is March 15.

BENJAMIN FRANKLIN INSTITUTE OF TECHNOLOGY — E-2

Franklin Institute of Boston

www.bfit.edu

Boston, MA 02116 (617) 423-4630

Fax: (617) 482-3706	**Email:** nkraft@bfit.edu
Full-time: n/av	**Faculty:** n/av
Part-time: n/av	**Ph.D.s:** 3%
Graduate: n/av	**Student/Faculty:** 11 to 1
Year: semesters, summer session	**Tuition:** $18,190
Room & Board: $10,000	**Freshman Class:** n/av
	CEEB CODE: 3394
Application Deadline: n/av	**COMPETITIVE**

Benjamin Franklin Institute of Technology, founded in 1908, is a private technical college offering degree programs in industrial and engineering technologies. A bachelor's degree is offered in several majors, including automotive technology. There are 7 undergraduate schools. In addition to regional accreditation, BFIT has baccalaureate program accreditation with ABET. The 3-acre campus is in an urban area. Including any residence halls, there are 3 buildings.

STUDENT LIFE: 95% of undergraduates are from Massachusetts. Others are from 5 states, and 7 foreign countries. 35% are White; 35% African American; 2% Foreign; 14% Hispanic; 12% Asian American. The average age of freshmen is 22; all undergraduates, 22. **Housing:** 20 students can be accommodated in college housing, which includes coed dorms. On-campus housing is available on a first-come and first-served basis. Priority is given to out-of-town students. 90% of students commute. Alcohol is not permitted. No one may keep cars.

FACULTY/CLASSROOMS: 74% of faculty are male; 26% are female. All teach undergraduates. No introductory courses are taught by graduate students. The average class size in an introductory lecture is 30; in a laboratory is 12; and in a regular course is 25.

PROGRAMS OF STUDY: BFIT confers B.S. degrees. Associate degrees are also awarded. Bachelor's degrees are awarded in ENGINEERING AND ENVIRONMENTAL DESIGN (automotive technology). Mechanical and electronic engineering technology are the strongest academically. Automotive and computers have the largest enrollments.

ACTIVITIES: There are no fraternities or sororities. There are 2 groups on campus, including honors and student government. Popular campus events include Technology Olympics and International Culture Day. **Sports:** There are 2 intercollegiate sports for men, and 2 intramural sports for men.

SERVICES: Counseling and information services are available, as is tutoring in every subject. There is remedial math, reading, and writing. **Library/Resources:** The library contains 10,000 volumes and subscribes to 70 periodicals including electronic. Computerized library services include interlibrary loans, database searching, and Internet access. **Physically Challenged Students:** 50% of the campus is accessible. Facilities include elevators and specially equipped restrooms. **Special:** There is a chapter of Phi Beta Kappa. **Visiting:** Visitors may sit in on classes. To schedule a visit, contact the Office of Admission.

REQUIREMENTS: The ACT Optional Writing test is required. Applicants should be high school graduates or have the GED. To graduate, students must earn a minimum cumulative GPA of 2.0. 2 college English courses are required. **Procedure:** Freshmen are admitted fall and spring. There is a rolling admissions plan. Check with the school for current application deadlines. The fall 2016 application fee was $25. **Transfer Students:** **International Students:** They must take the TOEFL and the college's own test, or satisfactorily complete Franklin's or another recognized ESL program.

Admissions Contact: Norman Kraft, Dean of Enrollment Services. Email: *nkraft@bfit.edu* Web: *www.bfit.edu*

FINANCIAL AID: BFIT is a member of CSS. The FAFSA code is 002151. Check with the school for current application deadlines.

BENTLEY UNIVERSITY — D-2
www.bentley.edu

Waltham, MA 02452	**(781) 891-2244** **(800) 523-2354**
Fax: (781) 891-3414	**Email: ugadmission@bentley.edu**
Full-time: 2458 men, 1679 women	**Faculty:** 232; IIA, ++$
Part-time: 41 men, 25 women	**Ph.D.s:** 78%
Graduate: 641 men, 708 women	**Student/Faculty:** 12 to 1
Year: semesters, summer session	**Tuition:** $44,085
Room & Board: $14,520	**Freshman Class:** 8346 applied, 3532 accepted, 915 enrolled
SAT CR/M/W: 590/640/600 **ACT:** 28	**CEEB CODE:** 3096
Application Deadline: January 7	**HIGHLY COMPETITIVE**

Bentley University is one of the nation's leading business schools, dedicated to preparing a new kind of business leader and one with the deep technical skills, the broad global perspective, and the high ethical standards required to make a difference in an ever-changing world. To achieve our goal, we infuse our advanced business curriculum with the richness of a liberal arts education. The results are graduates who are making an impact in their chosen fields and turning their passions into success stories. There is 1 undergraduate school and 1 graduate school. In addition to regional accreditation, Bentley has baccalaureate program accreditation with AACSB and EQUIS. The 163-acre campus is in a suburban area in Waltham, Massachusetts. Including any residence halls, there are 45 buildings.

STUDENT LIFE: 57% of undergraduates are from out of state, mostly the Middle Atlantic. Students are from 44 states, 76 foreign countries, and Canada. 67% are from public schools. 8% are Asian American; 8% Hispanic; 61% White; 4% race unknown; 3% African American; 2% two or more races; 15% Foreign. **Male To Female Ratio:** 1.2:1. The average age of freshmen is 18; all undergraduates, 20. 6% do not continue beyond their first year; 89% remain to graduate. **Housing:** College-sponsored housing includes coed dorms and on-campus apartments. Honors and special interest floors are available for first-year students. Special interest buildings exist for upperclass students. On-campus housing is guaranteed for all 4 years. 80% of students live on campus; of those, 85% remain on campus on weekends. Upperclassmen may keep cars.

FACULTY/CLASSROOMS: 60% of faculty are male; 40% are female. 83% teach undergraduates, and 64% do research. No introductory courses are taught by graduate students. The average class size in an introductory lecture is 27; in a laboratory is 18; and in a regular course is 27.

PROGRAMS OF STUDY: Bentley confers B.A. and B.S. degrees. Master's and doctoral degrees are also awarded. Bachelor's degrees are awarded in AGRICULTURE (environmental studies), BUSINESS (accounting, accounting (finance), accounting (information systems), applied economics/management, business administration and management, business (dual major program), business communications, business economics, business information systems, business and technology, finance, information & communication technology, business management, marketing, and sustainable management), COMMUNICATIONS AND THE ARTS (English, foreign language, and media arts), COMPUTER AND PHYSICAL SCIENCE (actuarial science, computer information systems, and mathematics), EDUCATION (global studies), HEALTH PROFESSIONS (health), SOCIAL SCIENCE (economics, history, interdisciplinary studies, liberal arts/general studies, philosophy, public administration, and Spanish studies). Marketing, accounting, finance, and management are the strongest academically. Finance, economics-finance, and marketing have the largest enrollments.

ACTIVITIES: 12% of men belong to 2 local and 6 national fraternities; 15% of women belong to 3 national sororities. There are 110 groups on campus, including art, band, cheerleading, chess, choir, chorus, computers, dance, debate, drama, environmental, ethnic, film, honors, international, jazz band, LGBT, literary magazine, musical theater, newspaper, orchestra, photography, political, professional, radio and TV, religious, social, social service, student government, and yearbook. Popular campus events include Spring Day, Welcome Back Concert, Halloween Dance Party, Homecoming, Diwali, Culture Fest, Football games, Take Back the Night. **Sports:** There are 12 intercollegiate sports for men and 11 for women, and 7 intramural sports for men and 7 for women. Facilities include The Dana Center, a 118,000 square foot multipurpose facility, that features a field house, two story fitness center, fitness center for varsity athletics, general locker rooms, a competition-sized swimming pool, athletic training rooms and rehabilitation area, athletic team and general locker rooms, and 24 athletic offices. **Graduates:** From July 1, 2015 to June 30, 2016, 1059 bachelor's degrees were awarded. The most popular majors were finance (18%), economics-finance (17%), and marketing (15%). 317 companies recruited on campus in 2015-2016. In an average class, 83% graduate in 4 years or less, 88% graduate in 5 years or less, and 89% graduate in 6 years or less. Of the 2015 graduating class, 10% were enrolled in graduate school within 6 months of graduation, and 87% were employed.

SERVICES: Counseling and information services are available, as is tutoring in most subjects. There is a reader service for the blind, and remedial math, reading, and writing. There is a Natural Reader, and additional assistive programs available upon request. **Library/Resources:** The library contains 183,873 volumes, 9,079 microform items, and 43,053 audio/video tapes/CDs/DVDs, and subscribes to 85,454 periodicals including electronic. Computerized library services include interlibrary loans, database searching, Internet access, and Wi-Fi capability. Special learning facilities include an art gallery, radio station, TV station,

Academic Technology Center, Winer Accounting Center for Electronic Learning and Business Measurement, the Bentley Library, Center for Languages and International Collaboration, Center for Marketing Technology, Computer Information Systems, Sandbox, Design and Usability Center, Media and Culture Labs and Studio, Trading Room, Hughey Center for Financial Services, Center for Arts and Sciences, Valente Center, Center for Business Ethics, Service-Learning Center, Center for Women in Business, Center for Quantitative Analysis, and Center for International Students and Scholars, The Multicultural Center, The Writing Center, Spiritual Life Center, The Cronin Office of International Education, Bentley Global Cyberlaw Center, Center for Integration of Science and Industry. **Physically Challenged Students:** 80% of the campus is accessible. Facilities include wheelchair ramps, elevators, special parking, specially equipped restrooms, special class scheduling, and special housing. All other items available upon request. **Special:** 93% of Bentley seniors report that they complete at least one professional internships and 71% have two or more internships. Internships can be paid, for-credit and not-for-credit. Bentley offers more than 50 study abroad programs in 26 countries as well as Semester at Sea. In addition, Bentley offers faculty-lead international courses which are 3-credit intensive study abroad experiences offered during semester breaks. During these courses, a Bentley professor leads students on an immersive learning experience in a multitude of world regions offering students the opportunity to combine cultural activities with business, or other relevant site visits. Corporate Partnerships pair students with leaders from top companies to work on real-world issues. Every student participates in this hands-on learning experience usually in their junior year. More than 1,000 students participate in Service Learning in over 80 locations throughout Greater Boston and the world. A fourth credit option is available. Work-study is offered through various departments throughout campus. Students can access available openings through an on-campus employment website. There are 14 Bachelor of Science majors and 10 Bachelor of Arts majors in addition to 35 minors and multiple concentrations. Bentley offers a Liberal Studies second (dual) major in American Studies, Diversity and Society, Earth, Environment and Global Sustainability, Ethics and Social Responsibility, Global Perspectives, Health and Industry, Media Arts and Society, and Quantitative Perspectives. Through our Master's Candidate Program, academically talented and highly motivated students from any undergraduate major can take graduate-level courses during their senior year, obtaining their undergraduate and graduate degrees in 5 years. Possible graduate majors include the emerging leaders MBA or one of six MS programs: accounting, business analytics, finance, financial planning, information technology, marketing analytics, and taxation. There are 5 national honor societies, a freshman honors program, and 17 departmental honors programs. **Visiting:** There are regularly scheduled orientations for prospective students, fall, spring, and summer open house programs, interviews are arranged by appointment, campus tours and group information sessions take place regularly throughout the year, visits are available during the week and some selected Saturdays. There are guides for informal visits and visitors may sit in on classes. To schedule a visit, contact the Office of Undergraduate Admission. **Campus Safety and Security:** Measures include 24-hour foot and vehicle patrol, emergency notification system, self-defense education, and security escort services. There are shuttle buses, emergency telephones, lighted pathways/sidewalks, controlled access to dorms/residences, new student and parent orientation safety presentation anonymous crime reporting through website Emergency Response Guidebook (flipbooks) in all classrooms, faculty/staff offices and an app available to all students, and faculty and staff to use on electronic devices, and emergency information web page.

REQUIREMENTS: The SAT or ACT is required. The ACT Optional Writing test is also required. In addition, All students need to submit the Common Application, official secondary school transcript, standardized test scores (either the SAT or ACT), 2 letters of recommendation. International and transfer applicants also have additional required documents which can be viewed at www.bentley.edu/undergraduate/applying. AP and CLEP credits are accepted. Important factors in the admissions decision are advanced placement or honors courses, extracurricular activities record, and recommendations by school officials. All undergraduate students complete general education courses in areas such as IT, writing and literature, mathematics, economics, history and social science. Students in B.S. programs take a common core of nine courses covering areas such as business ethics, accounting, finance, business statistics and strategic management. All students take elective courses that fulfill diversity, international and communication intensive requirements. A total of 122 credit hours for students beginning as freshmen, 121 for transfer students with a minimum GPA of 2.0 overall and 2.0 in the major are required for graduation. All first year students must take a first year seminar. Majors are anywhere from 24-30 credit hours. **Procedure:** Freshmen are admitted fall and spring. Entrance exams should be received by January 15. There are early decision and deferred admissions plans. Early decision applications should be filed by November 15; regular applications, by January 7 for fall entry, along with a $50 fee. Notification of early decision is sent December 22; regular decision, March 31. 220 early decision candidates were accepted for the 2016-2017 class. 1877 applicants were on the 2016 waiting list. Applications are accepted on-line. Application fees are waived if application is completed on-line. **Transfer Students:** 84 transfer students enrolled in 2015-2016. Transfer application, personal statement, official transcripts, mid-year progress report and two letters of recommendation, transfer college report, standardized test scores 60 of 122 credits required for the bachelor's degree must be completed at Bentley. **International Students:** There are 617 international students enrolled. The school actively recruits these students. They must take the TOEFL with a minimum score of 577 on the paper-based TOEFL (PBT) or 90 on the Internet-based version (iBT) and the Comprehensive English Language Test, or take the IELTS. They must also take the SAT or ACT.

ADMISSIONS: 42% of the 2016-2017 applicants were accepted. The SAT scores for the 2016-2017 freshman class were: Critical Reading-- 9% below 500, 42% between 500 and 599, 44% between 600 and 699, and 5% between 700 and 800. Math-- 2% below 500, 19% between 500 and 599, 56% between 600 and 699, and 24% between 700 and 800. Writing-- 7% below 500, 39% between 500 and 599, 45% between 600 and 699, and 9% between 700 and 800. The ACT scores were 1% below 12, 7% between 12 and 17, 24% between 18 and 23, 27% between 24 and 29, and 41% above 30. 66% of the current freshmen were in the top fifth of their class; 91% were in the top two fifths. 9 freshmen graduated first in their class. **Admissions Contact:** Erik Vardaro, Director of Undergraduate Admission. Email: *ugadmission@bentley.edu* Web: *www.bentley.edu*

FINANCIAL AID: In 2016-2017, 73% of all full-time freshmen and 73% of continuing full-time students received some form of financial aid. 50% of all full-time freshmen and 43% of continuing full-time students received need-based aid. The average freshman award was $35,965. Need-based scholarships or need-based grants averaged $30,356 ($50,000 maximum); need-based self-help aid (loans and jobs) averaged $4,400 ($7,500 maximum); non-need-based athletic scholarships averaged $24,617 ($60,890 maximum); and other non-need-based awards and non-need-based scholarships averaged $17,311 ($44,210 maximum). 30% of undergraduate students work part-time. Average annual earnings from campus work are $1450. The average financial indebtedness of the 2016 graduate was $31,046. Bentley is a member of CSS. The CSS/Profile, and federal tax returns, including all schedules for parents and student are required. The FAFSA code is 002124. The deadline for filing freshman financial aid applications for fall entry is January 7.

BERKLEE COLLEGE OF MUSIC *(The complete profile is made available exclusively on our website, www.barronspac.com)*

BOSTON ARCHITECTURAL COLLEGE *(The complete profile is made available exclusively on our website, www.barronspac.com)*

BOSTON COLLEGE — E-2

www.bc.edu

Chestnut Hill, MA 02467 — **(617) 552-3100**, **(800) 360-2522**

Fax: (617) 552-0798

Full-time: 4308 men, 5001 women	**Faculty:** I, ++$
Part-time: n/av	**Ph.D.s:** 96%
Graduate: 1970 men, 2572 women	**Student/Faculty:** 12 to 1
Year: semesters, summer session	**Tuition:** $51,480
Room & Board: $14,441	**Freshman Class:** 28956 applied, 9017 accepted, 2359 enrolled
SAT CR/M/W: 670/690/685 **ACT:** 32	**CEEB CODE:** 3083
Application Deadline: January 1	**MOST COMPETITIVE**

Boston College, founded in 1863, is an independent institution affiliated with the Roman Catholic Church and the Jesuit Order. It offers undergraduate programs in the arts and sciences, business, nursing, and education, and graduate and professional programs. There are 4 undergraduate schools and 7 graduate schools. In addition to regional accreditation, BC has baccalaureate program accreditation with AACSB, CSWE, NCATE, and NLN. The 338-acre campus is in a suburban area 6 miles west of Boston. Including any residence halls, there are 148 buildings.

STUDENT LIFE: 75% of undergraduates are from out of state, mostly the Northeast. Students are from 49 states, 59 foreign countries, and Canada. 45% are from public schools. 7% are Foreign; 63% White; 4% African American; 4% race unknown; 3% two or more races; 10% Asian American; 10% Hispanic. **Female To Male Ratio:** 1.2:1. The average age of freshmen is 18; all undergraduates, 21. 5% do not continue beyond their first year; 91% remain to graduate. **Housing:** 7450 students can be accommodated in college housing, which includes single-sex and coed dorms and on-campus apartments. In addition, there are honors houses, special-interest houses, community and multicultural housing, quiet residences, single-sex freshman halls, perspectives academic program housing, and a substance-free residence. On-campus housing is guaranteed for the freshman year only and is available on a lottery system for upperclassmen. 85% of students live on campus; of those, 90% remain on campus on weekends. Upperclassmen may keep cars.

FACULTY/CLASSROOMS: 56% of faculty are male; 44% are female. All teach undergraduates, and all do research. Graduate students teach 14% of introductory courses. The average class size in a laboratory is 15 and in a regular course is 30.

PROGRAMS OF STUDY: BC confers B.A., and B.S. degrees. Master's and doctoral degrees are also awarded. Bachelor's degrees are awarded in BIOLOGICAL SCIENCE (biochemistry and biology/biological science), BUSINESS (accounting, banking and finance, business administration and management, business economics, human resources, management science, marketing/retailing/merchandising, and operations research), COMMUNICATIONS AND THE ARTS (art history and appreciation, classics, communications, dramatic arts, English, film arts, French, Italian, linguistics, music, romance languages and literature, and studio art), COMPUTER AND PHYSICAL SCIENCE (chemistry, computer science, geology, geophysics and seismology, information sciences and systems, mathematics, and physics), EDUCATION (early childhood education, elementary education, secondary education, and special education), ENGINEERING AND ENVIRONMENTAL DESIGN (environmental science), HEALTH PROFESSIONS (nursing), SOCIAL SCIENCE (applied psychology, classical/ancient civilization, developmental psychology, economics, German area studies, Hispanic American studies, history, human development, philosophy, political science/government, psychology, Russian and Slavic studies, sociology, and theological studies). Finance, economics, and chemistry are the strongest academically. Communications, finance and economics have the largest enrollments.

ACTIVITIES: There are no fraternities or sororities. There are 230 groups on campus, including art, band, cheerleading, chess, choir, chorale, chorus, communications, computers, dance, debate, drama, environmental, ethnic, film, honors, international, jazz band, LGBT, literary magazine, marching band, musical theater, newspaper, orchestra, pep band, photography, political, professional, radio and TV, religious, social, social service, student government, symphony, and yearbook. Popular campus events include Middlemarch Ball, Senior Week, and Sporting Events. **Sports:** There are 12 intercollegiate sports for men and 15 for women, and 38 intramural sports for men and 30 for women. Facilities include a 44,500-seat stadium, a forum that seats 8500 for basketball and 7600 for ice hockey, soccer fields, baseball fields, and a track. BC also has a student recreation complex with: equipment for cardio, weight, strength training, dozens of group exercise class options including spinning, yoga, pilates, an indoor pool diving, swimming, and dedicated indoor courts for basketball, racquetball, squash, tennis and volleyball. **Graduates:** From July 1, 2015 to June 30, 2016, 2315 bachelor's degrees were awarded. The most popular majors were economics (11%), finance (9%), and communication (8%). 300 companies recruited on campus in 2015-2016. In an average class, 89% graduate in 4 years or less and 92% graduate in 6 years or less. Of the 2015 graduating class, 19% were enrolled in graduate school within 6 months of graduation, and 69% were employed.

SERVICES: Counseling and information services are available, as is tutoring in most subjects. There is a reader service for the blind. There is a academic development center that serves all students. **Library/Resources:** The 8 libraries contain 3.0 million volumes, 4.3 million microform items, and subscribe to 48,347 periodicals including electronic. Computerized library services include interlibrary loans, database searching, and Internet access. Special learning facilities include an art gallery, radio station, and TV station. **Physically Challenged Students:** 95% of the campus is accessible. Facilities include wheelchair ramps, elevators, special parking, specially equipped restrooms, special class scheduling, lowered drinking fountains, lowered telephones, and special housing. **Special:** There are internship programs in management and in arts and sciences. Students may cross-register with Boston University, Brandeis University, Hebrew College, Hellenic College, Pine Manor College, Regis College, or Tufts University. BC also offers a Washington semester in cooperation with American University, work-study programs with nonprofit agencies, study abroad, and dual and student-designed majors. Students may pursue a 3-2 engineering program with Boston University and accelerated 5-year programs in social work and education. There are 12 national honor societies, Phi Beta Kappa, a freshman honors program, and 4 departmental honors programs. **Visiting:** There are regularly scheduled orientations for prospective students, group information sessions and campus tours Monday through Friday. There are guides for informal visits and visitors may sit in on classes. To schedule a visit, contact Office of Undergraduate Admission. **Campus Safety and Security:** Measures include 24-hour foot and vehicle patrol, emergency notification system, self-defense education, and security escort services. There are shuttle buses, emergency telephones, lighted pathways/sidewalks, controlled access to dorms/residences, and safety seminars and safety walking tours are offered for incoming students during orientation. A fire safety awareness week is held every year with a mock dorm room burning demonstration, distribution of fire safety education materials, and drills. Students and faculty/staff members can also opt into an emergency alert system that can send emergency messages from the university to cell phones.

REQUIREMENTS: For fall 2017 entry, students may submit either the newly designed SAT Test or ACT test or the old SAT test with Writing or the ACT test with Writing. Applicants must be graduates of an accredited high school completing 4 units each of English, foreign language, science, and math. Those students applying to the school of nursing must complete at least 2 years of a lab science including 1 unit of chemistry. Applicants to the school of management are strongly encouraged to take 4 years of college preparatory math. An essay is required. AP credits are accepted. Core requirements include 2 courses each in natural science, social science, history, philosophy, and theology; 1 course each in literature, writing, math, and cultural diversity, and proficiency in a foreign language for College of Arts and Science students. To graduate, students must complete 120 credits (or 117 for nursing majors) including at least 30 in the major with a minimum 1.667 GPA (1.5 in management). Computer science is required for management majors, and a freshman writing seminar for all students except honors and AP students. Students in the honors program may elect to take courses in lieu of a thesis. Scholars of the college must complete a scholar's project before graduation. **Procedure:** Freshmen are admitted fall and spring. Entrance exams should be taken no later than January of the senior year. There are early admissions and deferred admissions plans. Early decision applications should be filed by November 1; regular applications, by January 1 for fall entry; and November 1 for spring entry, along with a $75 fee. Notification of early decision is sent December 25; regular decision, April 15. 5689 applicants were on the 2016 waiting list; 112 were admitted. Applications are accepted on-line. **Transfer Students:** 153 transfer students enrolled in 2015-2016. Applicants must have a current GPA of at least 3.0 and must have earned a minimum of 9 semester hours. High school transcripts, letters of recommendation, and SAT or ACT scores are required. 60 of 120 credits required for the bachelor's degree must be completed at BC. **International Students:** There are 578 international students enrolled. The school actively recruits these students. They must take the TOEFL with a minimum score of 600 on the paper-based TOEFL (PBT) or 100 on the Internet-based version (iBT), TOEFL requirement will be waived if student scores 600+ on SAT Critical Reading or 27+ on ACT English. SAT Subject Tests will be considered if submitted, but are not required.

ADMISSIONS: 31% of the 2016-2017 applicants were accepted. The SAT scores for the 2016-2017 freshman class were: Critical Reading-- 2% below 500, 13% between 500 and 599, 50% between 600 and 699, and 34% between 700 and 800. Math-- 1% below 500, 10% between 500 and 599, 44% between 600 and 699, and 44% between 700 and 800. Writing-- 2% below 500, 12% between 500 and 599, 41% between 600 and 699, and 44% between 700 and 800. The ACT scores were 2% between

18 and 23, 15% between 24 and 29, and 83% above 30. 95% of the current freshmen were in the top fifth of their class; 99% were in the top two fifths. **Admissions Contact:** John L. Mahoney Jr., Director Undergraduate Admission. Web: *www.bc.edu*

FINANCIAL AID: 40% of all full-time freshmen and 40% of continuing full-time students received need-based aid. The average freshman award was $37,639. Need-based scholarships or need-based grants averaged $35,519; need-based self-help aid (loans and jobs) averaged $5,203; non-need-based athletic scholarships averaged $49,353; and other non-need-based awards and non-need-based scholarships averaged $21,093. 26% of undergraduate students work part-time. Average annual earnings from campus work are $2500. The average financial indebtedness of the 2016 graduate was $20,849. BC is a member of CSS. The CSS/Profile, the federal IRS income tax form, W-2s, and Divorced/Separated Statement (when applicable) are required. The FAFSA code is 002128. The deadline for filing freshman financial aid applications for fall entry is February 1.

BOSTON UNIVERSITY E-2

www.bu.edu

Boston, MA 02215	(617) 353-2300
Fax: (617) 353-9695	**Email:** admissions@bu.edu
Full-time: 6430 men, 10198 women	**Faculty:** 1285; I, +$
Part-time: 631 men, 685 women	**Ph.D.s:** 90%
Graduate: 6409 men, 8342 women	**Student/Faculty:** 12 to 1
Year: semesters, summer session	**Tuition:** $50,240
Room & Board: $14,870	**Freshman Class:** 57441 applied, 16907 accepted, 3552 enrolled
SAT CR/M/W: 650/660/660 **ACT:** 30	**CEEB CODE:** 3087
Application Deadline: January 3	**MOST COMPETITIVE**

Boston University is a private teaching and research university committed to excellence in undergraduate education. BU offers students more than 250 programs of study, internships in the US and abroad, one of the nations's most extensive study abroad programs, and cutting-edge research with faculty mentors. BU students engage with their campus community through nearly 500 student organizations, club and intramural sports, and 22 NCAA Division-I varsity sports teams. Students experience the city of Boston as an extension of the campus for study, internships, employment, and cultural and recreational activities. There are 10 undergraduate schools and 14 graduate schools. In addition to regional accreditation, BU has baccalaureate program accreditation with AACSB, ABET, and NASM. The 134-acre campus is in an urban area on the Charles River in Boston's Back Bay. Including any residence halls, there are 321 buildings.

STUDENT LIFE: 81% of undergraduates are from out of state, mostly the Northeast. Students are from 49 states, 106 foreign countries, and Canada. 64% are from public schools. 41% are White; 4% African American; 4% two or more races; 4% race unknown; 22% Foreign; 14% Asian American; 11% Hispanic. **Female To Male Ratio:** 1.4:1. The average age of freshmen is 19; all undergraduates, 20. 7% do not continue beyond their first year; 87% remain to graduate. **Housing:** 11096 students can be accommodated in college housing, which includes single-sex and coed dorms, on-campus apartments, off-campus apartments, and married student housing. In addition, there are honors houses, language houses, special-interest houses, international floors, and gender neutral floors. On-campus housing is guaranteed for all 4 years. 75% of students live on campus; of those, 80% remain on campus on weekends. All students may keep cars.

FACULTY/CLASSROOMS: 58% of faculty are male; 42% are female. 61% teach undergraduates. No introductory courses are taught by graduate students. The average class size in an introductory lecture is 80; in a laboratory is 17; and in a regular course is 16.

PROGRAMS OF STUDY: BU confers B.A., B.S., B.F.A., B.L.S., Mus.B. and B.S.B.A. degrees. Master's and doctoral degrees are also awarded. Bachelor's degrees are awarded in AGRICULTURE (environmental studies), BIOLOGICAL SCIENCE (biochemistry, biology/biological science, ecology, environmental biology, marine science, neurosciences, nutrition, and physiology), BUSINESS (business administration and management, hospitality management services, and hotel/motel and restaurant management), COMMUNICATIONS AND THE ARTS (acting, art history and appreciation, Chinese, classical languages, classics, communications, dramatic arts, English, film arts, French, Germanic languages and literature, graphic design, Greek (classical), guitar, journalism, Latin, linguistics, film and media studies, music, music composition, music history and appreciation, music performance, music theory and composition, organ performance, painting, percussion, performing arts, piano performance, printmaking, Russian languages and literature, scenic and lighting design, sculpture, Spanish, stage management, theatre arts, theater design, theatre production, theater management, and voice), COMPUTER AND PHYSICAL SCIENCE (astronomy, astronomy and physics, astrophysics, chemistry, chemistry education, computer science, earth science, geophysics and seismology, mathematics, mathematics – philosophy, physics, and planetary and space science), EDUCATION (art education, Asian studies, athletic training, bilingual/bicultural education, early childhood education, education, education of the deaf and hearing impaired, elementary education, English education, foreign languages education, mathematics education, music education, physical education, science education, social studies education, and special education), ENGINEERING AND ENVIRONMENTAL DESIGN (architectural history, biomedical engineering, computer engineering, electrical/electronics engineering, engineering, manufacturing engineering, and mechanical engineering), HEALTH PROFESSIONS (biomedical science, health science, medical science, occupational therapy, physical therapy, predentistry, and speech pathology/audiology), SOCIAL SCIENCE (American studies, anthropology, archeology, architectural studies, classical/ancient civilization, criminal justice, economics, European studies, French studies, geography, Hispanic American studies, history, hotel, rest/tourism management, interdisciplinary studies, international relations, Italian studies, Japanese studies, Latin American studies, Middle Eastern studies, philosophy, philosophy and religion, political science/government, psychology, religion, sociology, and urban studies). Kilachand Honors College, 7-yr accelerated medical & dental programs, and engineering are the strongest academically. Communications, business, and engineering have the largest enrollments.

ACTIVITIES: 3% of men belong to 1 local and 8 national fraternities; 5% of women belong to 10 national sororities. There are 500 groups on campus, including sports club, art, band, cheerleading, chess, choir, chorale, chorus, communications, computers, dance, debate, drama, environmental, ethnic, film, honors, international, jazz band, LGBT, literary magazine, marching band, multicultural club, musical theater, newspaper, opera, orchestra, pep band, photography, political, professional, radio and TV, religious, social, social service, student government, and yearbook. Popular campus events include Fall Welcome (Splash), World Fair and Culture Fest, Fringe Festival, Lobster Night, Pumpkin Drop, and Head of the Charles River Regatta. **Sports:** There are 9 intercollegiate sports for men and 13 for women, and 16 intramural sports for men and 16 for women. Facilities include 2 multipurpose fields, softball field, indoor track and tennis center, 3 outdoor tennis courts, two ice rinks, competition pool, 2 recreational pools, rock wall, 3-court multipurpose gymnasium, 4-court wood gymnasium, 6 squash/racquetball courts, dance studio, fitness center, boathouse, and sailing pavilion. **Graduates:** From July 1, 2015 to June 30, 2016, 4495 bachelor's degrees were awarded. The most popular majors were management (18%), communications (12%), and engineering (8%). 650 companies recruited on campus in 2015-2016. In an average class, 4% graduate in 3 years or less, 81% graduate in 4 years or less, 85% graduate in 5 years or less, and 87% graduate in 6 years or less. Of the 2015 graduating class, 12% were enrolled in graduate school within 6 months of graduation, and 69% were employed.

SERVICES: Counseling and information services are available, as is tutoring in most subjects, such as liberal arts, science, engineering, management, and writing. There is a reader service for the blind. Comprehensive learning strategy for learning disabled is available. **Library/Resources:** The 23 libraries contain 5.7 million volumes. Computerized library services include interlibrary loans, database searching, Internet access, and Wi-Fi capability. Special learning facilities include an art gallery, planetarium, radio station, and TV station. BU has over 2,000 research laboratories on campus, 3 supercomputers that are available for student use, and four specialized high-performance computer labs. BU also has an astronomy observatory, 20th-century archives, a theater company in residence, the Geddes language lab, a speech, language, and hearing clinic, a performance center, a multi-media center, the Life Sciences and Engineering building, the Engineering Product Innovation Center, and the Photonics Center which houses state-of-the-art laboratories for developing new light-based technologies. **Physically Chal-**

lenged Students: 90% of the campus is accessible. Facilities include wheelchair ramps, elevators, special parking, specially equipped restrooms, special class scheduling, lowered drinking fountains, lowered telephones, special housing, and on-campus transportation, relocation of classes/events for access, tactile and access maps, visual fire alarms for the deaf, adaptive computers, and readers, notetakers and ASL interpreters. **Special:** Boston University offers many opportunities for students to excel, including: Kilachand Honors College, a university-wide honors program, BU's Seven-Year Accelerated Medical and Dental Programs, which allow highly motivated students to complete their bachelor's degree and medical or dental doctorate in seven years, and the MMEDIC/ENGMEDIC integrated curriculums where students begin their medical studies as undergraduates. BU's Dual Degree program enables students to earn two degrees simultaneously. Combined bachelors and masters programs are also available in many disciplines. Students conduct research with faculty or independently though our Undergraduate Research Opportunities Program and Work for Distinction. Students have many opportunities to intern in the US and abroad, and participate in more than 100 BU study abroad programs around the world. There are 16 national honor societies, Phi Beta Kappa, and a freshman honors program. **Visiting:** There are regularly scheduled orientations for prospective students. Admissions at the Alan & Sherry Leventhal center is open Mon.-Fri. and some Saturdays during the academic year. Appointments can be made for class visits or lunch with current students. Campus tours and information sessions are also offered. There are guides for informal visits, visitors may sit in on classes, and stay overnight. **Campus Safety and Security:** Measures include 24-hour foot and vehicle patrol, emergency notification system, self-defense education, and security escort services. There are shuttle buses, emergency telephones, lighted pathways/sidewalks, controlled access to dorms/residences, mountain bicycle patrol system. There is a uniformed safety/security assistant on duty 24 hours a day in large residence halls, and there are 60 academy-trained officers in the university police department.

REQUIREMENTS: The SAT or ACT is required. The ACT Optional Writing test is also required. Applicants are evaluated on an individual basis. For most BU programs, the recommended curriculum includes 4 years of English, 3 to 4 years of math (pre-calculus/calculus recommended), 3 to 4 years of lab sciences, 3 to 4 years of history/social science, and 2 to 4 years of a foreign language. Students may submit the ACT or SAT. Students applying to the Accelerated Medical or Dental Programs are required to submit Subject Tests in chemistry, math (level 2), and a foreign language (recommended). Candidates for the College of Fine Arts are not required to submit standardized test scores, but must present a portfolio or participate in an audition. Boston University does not require the optional essay on the new SAT test. For students applying for fall 2018, BU will accept only the new SAT or the ACT. You can find more information about the new SAT on the College Board website. AP and CLEP credits are accepted. Important factors in the admissions decision are advanced placement or honors courses, recommendations by school officials, and extracurricular activities record. All students are required to complete at least 128 credit hours to qualify for graduation from Boston University. The individual schools and colleges within BU have specific academic requirements and standards for determining satisfactory completion of a program of study such as grades, majors, concentrations, divisional studies, or internships. **Procedure:** Freshmen are admitted fall and spring. Entrance exams should be taken in the junior year or early in the senior year. There are early decision, early admissions, and deferred admissions plans. Early decision applications should be filed by November 1; regular applications, by January 3 for fall entry, along with a $80 fee. Notification of early decision is sent December 15; regular decision, April 1. 1098 early decision candidates were accepted for the 2016-2017 class. 4107 applicants were on the 2016 waiting list. Applications are accepted on-line. Application fees are waived if application is completed on-line. **Transfer Students:** 575 transfer students enrolled in 2015-2016. College transcript and secondary school transcripts, including proof of high school graduation (or GED), must be submitted. Recommendations, Transfer College Report, and an essay are also required. **International Students:** There are 3595 international students enrolled. The school actively recruits these students. They must take the TOEFL with a minimum score of 90 on the Internet-based version (iBT), or take the IELTS. They must also take the SAT or ACT.

ADMISSIONS: 29% of the 2016-2017 applicants were accepted. The SAT scores for the 2016-2017 freshman class were: Critical Reading-- 1% below 500, 16% between 500 and 599, 60% between 600 and 699, and 23% between 700 and 800. Math-- 14% between 500 and 599, 56% between 600 and 699, and 29% between 700 and 800. Writing-- 1% below 500, 13% between 500 and 599, 59% between 600 and 699, and 27% between 700 and 800. The ACT scores were 1% between 12 and 17, 8% between 18 and 23, 18% between 24 and 29, and 73% above 30. 85% of the current freshmen were in the top fifth of their class; 98% were in the top two fifths. There were 27 National Merit finalists. 49 freshmen graduated first in their class. **Admissions Contact:** Kelly Walter, Assoc VP & Exec Dir of Undergraduate Adm. Email: *admissions@bu.edu* Web: *www.bu.edu*

FINANCIAL AID: In 2016-2017, 54% of all full-time freshmen and 53% of continuing full-time students received some form of financial aid. 39% of all full-time freshmen and 37% of continuing full-time students received need-based aid. The average freshman award was $36,848. Need-based scholarships or need-based grants averaged $35,594 ($71,366 maximum); need-based self-help aid (loans and jobs) averaged $5,730 ($9,500 maximum); non-need-based athletic scholarships averaged $45,742 ($70,259 maximum); and other non-need-based awards and non-need-based scholarships averaged $22,204 ($57,000 maximum). 35% of undergraduate students work part-time. Average annual earnings from campus work are $2000. The average financial indebtedness of the 2016 graduate was $41,098. BU is a member of CSS. The CSS/Profile is required. The FAFSA code is 002130. The deadline for filing freshman financial aid applications for fall entry is February 1.

BRANDEIS UNIVERSITY D-2

www.brandeis.edu

Waltham, MA 02454 **(781) 736-3500**
(800) 622-0622

Fax: (781) 736-3536 **Email: admissions@brandeis.edu**

Full-time: 1521 men, 2070 women	**Faculty:** 317; I, +$
Part-time: 7 men, 10 women	**Ph.D.s:** 95%
Graduate: 971 men, 1150 women	**Student/Faculty:** 10 to 1
Year: semesters, summer session	**Tuition:** $51,545
Room & Board: $14,380	**Freshman Class:** 11351 applied, 3796 accepted, 841 enrolled
SAT CR/M/W: 680/690/690 **ACT:** 31	**CEEB CODE:** 3092
Application Deadline: January 1	**MOST COMPETITIVE**

Brandeis University is a highly competitive private liberal arts and research university. Founded in 1948 by the American Jewish community and named for Supreme Court Justice Louis D. Brandeis, Brandeis embraces the values of academic excellence, critical thinking, openness to all, and making the world a better place. Brandeis is a member of the Association of American Universities (AAU), which represents the 62 leading research universities in the United States and Canada. There is 1 undergraduate school and 4 graduate schools. The 235-acre campus is in a suburban area 10 miles west of Boston. Including any residence halls, there are 96 buildings.

STUDENT LIFE: 72% of undergraduates are from out of state, mostly the Middle Atlantic. Students are from 47 states, 58 foreign countries, and Canada. 8% are Hispanic; 5% African American; 46% White; 4% race unknown; 3% two or more races; 21% Foreign; 13% Asian American. **Female To Male Ratio:** 1.3:1. The average age of freshmen is 18; all undergraduates, 20. 7% do not continue beyond their first year; 91% remain to graduate. **Housing:** 2900 students can be accommodated in college housing, which includes coed dorms. Leader Scholar Communities for first-year students and Common Cause Communities for upperclassmen. On-campus housing is guaranteed for the freshman year only, and is available on a first-come, first-served basis, and is available on a lottery system for upperclassmen. 79% of students live on campus; of those, 80% remain on campus on weekends. Upperclassmen may keep cars.

FACULTY/CLASSROOMS: 58% of faculty are male; 42% are female. All teach undergraduates, and all do research. No introductory courses are taught by graduate students.

PROGRAMS OF STUDY: Brandeis confers B.A., and B.S. degrees. Master's and doctoral degrees are also awarded. Bachelor's degrees are awarded in AGRICULTURE (environmental studies), BIOLOGICAL SCIENCE (biochemistry, biology/biological science, biophysics, and neurosciences), BUSINESS (business administration and management), COMMUNICATIONS AND THE ARTS (art history, classics, comparative literature, creative writing, English, film arts, French, German, linguistics, music, Russian languages and literature, Spanish, studio art, and theatre arts), COMPUTER AND PHYSICAL SCIENCE (chemistry, computer science, mathematics, and physics), EDUCATION (education), HEALTH PROFESSIONS (health science), SOCIAL SCIENCE (African American studies, American studies, anthropology, East Asian studies, economics, European studies, history, interdisciplinary studies, international studies, Islamic studies, Judaic studies, Latin American studies, Middle Eastern studies, Near Eastern studies, philosophy, political science/government, psychology, sociology, and women's studies). Economics, biology, and psychology have the largest enrollments.

ACTIVITIES: There are no fraternities or sororities. There are 246 groups on campus, including art, band, cheerleading, chess, choir, chorale, chorus, computers, dance, debate, drama, environmental, ethnic, film, honors, international, jazz band, LGBT, literary magazine, musical theater, newspaper, orchestra, pep band, photography, political, professional, radio and TV, religious, social, social service, student government, Waltham Group, Student Events (programming board), Triskelion (GLBTQIA organization), BEMCO (EMTs), and yearbook. Popular campus events include Library Party, MELA, Concerts, Night for Africa, Culture X, SpringFest, Speakers, Festival of the Arts, Deis Impact, Liquid Latex Show, and Purim. **Sports:** There are 9 intercollegiate sports for men and 10 for women, and 30 intramural sports for men and 30 for women. Facilities include a 70,000 square foot field house including a 1800 seat basketball arena, 3 indoor tennis courts, 3 indoor basketball courts, 7 squash courts, 6 lane indoor track, several multipurpose rooms for aerobics, dance, group fitness, sauna in men's and women's lockerrooms, fencing room, weight room, turf soccer field, grass club field, baseball and softball diamonds, 12 outdoor tennis courts, 6 lane indoor pool, and 8 lane outdoor track. **Graduates:** From July 1, 2015 to June 30, 2016, 915 bachelor's degrees were awarded. The most popular majors were business (10%), economics (10%), and biology (9%). 520 companies recruited on campus in 2015-2016. In an average class, 1% graduate in 3 years or less, 83% graduate in 4 years or less, 87% graduate in 5 years or less, and 90% graduate in 6 years or less. Of the 2015 graduating class, 24% were enrolled in graduate school within 6 months of graduation, and 60% were employed.

SERVICES: Counseling and information services are available, as is tutoring in most subjects. We produce Alt-Format Text for our blind students. Students with disabilities access the peer tutoring program available to all students. **Library/Resources:** The library contains 2.2 million volumes, 960,812 microform items, and 64,879 audio/video tapes/CDs/DVDs, and subscribes to 31,922 periodicals including electronic. Computerized library services include interlibrary loans, database searching, Internet access, and Wi-Fi capability. Special learning facilities include an art gallery, radio station, TV station, a spatial orientation laboratory, an astronomical observatory, an emotion laboratory, a cultural center, a treasure hall, an art museum, and an audiovisual center. **Physically Challenged Students:** 85% of the campus is accessible. Facilities include wheelchair ramps, elevators, special parking, specially equipped restrooms, special class scheduling, lowered drinking fountains, lowered telephones, and special housing. Libraries, student centers, several other buildings, sports facilities, and the majority of residence halls are accessible. **Special:** Students may pursue interdepartmental programs in 18 different fields. Students may cross-register with Boston, Wellesley, Babson, Bentley and Olin Colleges and Boston and Tufts Universities. Study abroad is possible in 69 countries. Internships are available in virtually every field, and work-study is also available. Dual and student-designed majors can be arranged. Brandeis University and the Fu Foundation School of Engineering and Applied Science of Columbia University have established a dual degree program whereby students complete three years of course work at Brandeis, then spend two years at Columbia University to complete the requirements for an engineering degree. The university also offers credit by exam, nondegree study, and pass/fail options. Opportunities for early acceptance to area medical schools are offered to Brandeis students. There is 1 national honor society and a chapter of Phi Beta Kappa. **Visiting:** There are regularly scheduled orientations for prospective students. Most weekdays we offer morning and afternoon information sessions led by admissions counselors and followed by student-led tours. Information sessions are typically held Mon-Fri at 10:15 a.m., 2:15 p.m.; tours at 9am, 11am, 1pm and 3pm. There are guides for informal visits and visitors may sit in on classes. To schedule a visit, contact the Office of Admissions. **Campus Safety and Security:** Measures include 24-hour foot and vehicle patrol, emergency notification system, self-defense education, and security escort services. There are shuttle buses, emergency telephones, lighted pathways/sidewalks, controlled access to dorms/residences, extensive closed circuit television system on campus, a student EMT division that responds to medical calls during the academic year, and a personal safety committee with student involvement.

REQUIREMENTS: Brandeis has a test-flexible policy and no longer requires that citizens and permanent residents of the US or Canada submit SAT or ACT scores for the purposes of admission. Eligible applicants can choose one of the following three submission options: Option 1: Submit SAT or ACT; Option 2: Submit a combination of three SAT Subject Tests and/or AP tests (or IB exams); Option 3: Submit an academic portfolio through the Common Application including: One graded analytical paper from 11th or 12th grade and a second academic Teacher Evaluation. *Home-schooled applicants and candidates applying from secondary schools that provide written evaluations rather than grades are required to submit the SAT or the ACT test with the writing section. *All international applicants who are not US/Canadian citizens or permanent residents must submit either the SAT or the ACT test section. AP credits are accepted. Important factors in the admissions decision are advanced placement or honors courses, recommendations by school officials, and geographical diversity. All candidates for a bachelor's degree must satisfactorily complete 128 credits, a major, a writing requirement, a foreign language requirement, a group of courses designed to provide a strong foundation in general education, and the phys ed requirement. Oral communication, quantitative reasoning, and non-Western and comparative studies requirements also must be met. One course may be used to fulfill a general university requirement, excepting University Writing Seminars, writing-intensive and oral communication courses, with the pass/fail grading. No more than one course (and never the final one) in the foreign language sequence may be taken pass/fail if the language is being offered in satisfaction of the foreign language requirement. **Procedure:** Freshmen are admitted fall, spring, and summer. Entrance exams should be taken by January of the senior year. There are early decision and deferred admissions plans. Early decision applications should be filed by November 1; regular applications, by January 1 for fall entry; and November 1 for spring entry, along with an $80 fee. Notification of early decision is sent December 1; regular decision, April 1. 273 early decision candidates were accepted for the 2016-2017 class. 1478 applicants were on the 2016 waiting list; 89 were admitted. Applications are accepted on-line. Application fees are waived if application is completed on-line. **Transfer Students:** 52 transfer students enrolled in 2015-2016. Major consideration is given to the quality of college-level work completed, the secondary school record, professors' and deans' evaluations as well as the students fit for our institution. Because there is a 2-year residence requirement, students should apply before entering their junior year. 64 of 128 credits required for the bachelor's degree must be completed at Brandeis. **International Students:** There are 742 international students enrolled. The school actively recruits these students. They must take the TOEFL with a minimum score of 600 on the paper-based TOEFL (PBT) or 100 on the Internet-based version (iBT), or take the IELTS. They must also take the SAT or ACT.

ADMISSIONS: 33% of the 2016-2017 applicants were accepted. The SAT scores for the 2016-2017 freshman class were: Critical Reading-- 2% below 500, 8% between 500 and 599, 49% between 600 and 699, and 41% between 700 and 800. Math-- 2% below 500, 6% between 500 and 599, 47% between 600 and 699, and 46% between 700 and 800. Writing-- 2% below 500, 7% between 500 and 599, 45% between 600 and 699, and 47% between 700 and 800. The ACT scores were 1% between 18 and 23, 23% between 24 and 29, and 76% above 30. 89% of the current freshmen were in the top fifth of their class; 99% were in the top two fifths. 28 freshmen graduated first in their class. **Admissions Contact:** Jennifer Walker, Dean of Admissions. Email: *admissions@brandeis.edu* Web: *www.brandeis.edu*

FINANCIAL AID: In 2016-2017, 65% of all full-time freshmen and 59% of continuing full-time students received some form of financial aid. 51% of all full-time freshmen and 47% of continuing full-time students received need-based aid. The average freshman award was $44,670. Need-based scholarships or need-based grants averaged $41,280 ($68,226 maximum); need-based self-help aid (loans and jobs) averaged $3,390 ($8,500 maximum); and other non-need-based awards and non-need-based scholarships averaged $14,105 ($17,500 maximum). 60% of undergraduate students work part-time. Average annual earnings from campus work are $2367. The average financial indebtedness of the 2016 graduate was $32,922. Brandeis is a member of CSS. The CSS/Profile, and copies of student and parent tax returns are required. The FAFSA code is 002133. The deadline for filing freshman financial aid applications for fall entry is January 1.

BRIDGEWATER STATE UNIVERSITY E-3

wwwbridgew.edu

Bridgewater, MA 02325 **(508) 531-1237**

Fax: (508) 531-1746	**Email:** admissions@bridgew.edu
Full-time: 3198 men, 4628 women	**Faculty:** n/av
Part-time: 763 men, 973 women	**Ph.D.s:** 92%
Graduate: 394 men, 1042 women	**Student/Faculty:** 19 to 1
Year: semesters, summer session	**Tuition:** $9610 ($15,750)
Room & Board: $12,200	**Freshman Class:** 6007 applied, 4863 accepted, 1420 enrolled
SAT CR/M: 490/500 **ACT:** 21	**CEEB CODE:** 3517
Application Deadline: February 15	**COMPETITIVE**

Bridgewater State University provides a broad range of baccalaureate degree programs through its College of Humanities and Social Sciences, Bartlett College of Science and Mathematics, College of Education and Allied Studies and Ricciardi College of Business. Bridgewater State University offers 32 undergraduate academic programs with 90 different areas of concentration as well as internships, research programs, study abroad and honors programs. There are 5 undergraduate schools and 1 graduate school. In addition to regional accreditation, BSU has baccalaureate program accreditation with CSWE, NASAD, NASDTEC, NASM, NCATE, ACS, FAA, CAATE, NASPAA, and CACREP. The 278-acre campus is in a suburban area 28 miles from Boston. Including any residence halls, there are 44 buildings.

STUDENT LIFE: 96% of undergraduates are from Massachusetts. Others are from 27 states, 27 foreign countries, and Canada. 75% are White; 7% Hispanic; 4% two or more races; 2% Asian American; 2% race unknown; 10% African American. **Female To Male Ratio:** 1.5:1. The average age of freshmen is 19; all undergraduates, 23. 21% do not continue beyond their first year; 58% remain to graduate. **Housing:** 3295 students can be accommodated in college housing, which includes coed dorms and on-campus apartments. Break housing for athletes, student teachers, visiting lecturers, international students and special housing for disabled students. On-campus housing is available on a first-come and first-served basis. Alcohol is not permitted. Upperclassmen may keep cars.

FACULTY/CLASSROOMS: 48% of faculty are male; 52% are female. No introductory courses are taught by graduate students.

PROGRAMS OF STUDY: BSU confers B.A., B.S. and B.S.Ed. degrees. Master's degrees are also awarded. Bachelor's degrees are awarded in BIOLOGICAL SCIENCE (biology/biological science), BUSINESS (accounting, finance, and management science), COMMUNICATIONS AND THE ARTS (art, art history and appreciation, English, fine arts, music, Spanish, and speech/debate/rhetoric), COMPUTER AND PHYSICAL SCIENCE (chemistry, computer science, earth science, geochemistry, mathematics, and physics), EDUCATION (art education, athletic training, dance education, drama education, early childhood education, elementary education, health education, music education, physical education, and special education), ENGINEERING AND ENVIRONMENTAL DESIGN (aeronautical science), SOCIAL SCIENCE (anthropology, criminal justice, economics, geography, philosophy, political science/government, psychology, social work, and sociology). Counselor education, special education, and business are the strongest academically. Early childhood and elementary education, management, and criminal justice have the largest enrollments.

ACTIVITIES: There are 90 groups on campus, including art, band, chorale, communications, computers, dance, drama, environmental, ethnic, forensics, honors, international, jazz band, LGBT, musical theater, newspaper, political, professional, religious, social, social service, student government, and yearbook. Popular campus events include Homecoming, Springfest and Campus Movie Fest. **Sports:** There are 10 intercollegiate sports for men and 12 for women. Facilities include the Adrian Tinsley Center which has a Competition Court with NCAA regulation basketball and volleyball venue that seats 1000 spectators, synthetic multipurpose courts which are lined for basketball, volleyball, badminton, and tennis, a walking/jogging track which is a 1/8 mile three lane track that encircles the 32,000 square foot gymnasium area, a 9,000 square foot Thornburg Fitness Center which is equipped with a cardiovascular machines, selectorized weight machines, a plate-loaded equipment, free-weights, and Olympic lifting platforms, the John J. Kelly Gymnasium which houses a large and small gym, the Dr. Mary Jo Moriarty pool, weight room, classrooms and offices, the Edward C. Swenson Athletic Complex where the BSU Bears compete in football, field hockey and soccer, Alumni Park where our baseball and softball players compete, and Dr. Henry Rosen Memorial tennis courts. **Graduates:** From July 1, 2015 to June 30, 2016, 1942 bachelor's degrees were awarded. The most popular majors were education (19%), business/marketing (16%), homeland security, law enforcement, and firefighting (12%). 196 companies recruited on campus in 2015-2016. In an average class, 29% graduate in 4 years or less, 53% graduate in 5 years or less, and 58% graduate in 6 years or less. Of the 2015 graduating class, 17% were enrolled in graduate school within 6 months of graduation, and 84% were employed.

SERVICES: Counseling and information services are available, as is tutoring in most subjects. There is a reader service for the blind, and remedial math, reading, and writing. There are recorded texts, classroom interpreters, scribes and note takers, testing accommodations, and a speech/hearing/language center. **Library/Resources:** Computerized library services include interlibrary loans, database searching, Internet access, and Wi-Fi capability. Special learning facilities include an art gallery, planetarium, an observatory, and a greenhouse. **Physically Challenged Students:** 95% of the campus is accessible. Facilities include wheelchair ramps, elevators, special parking, specially equipped restrooms, special class scheduling, lowered drinking fountains, lowered telephones, and special housing. **Special:** Opportunities are provided for cross-registration with other Massachusetts Colleges and Universities, internships are available in most majors, double majors, joint/dual degree in B.S. & M.S. in Criminal Justice and B.S.Ed. in Elementary Education & M.Ed. in Special Education, core curriculum requirements, non-degree study, and study abroad programs. Bridgewater State University participates in The Washington Center Internship Program, National Student Exchange, Southeastern Association for Cooperation in Higher Education, and the College Academic Program sharing, and accelerated degree program available for MSW and some post-bacs. There is a chapter of Phi Beta Kappa, a freshman honors program, and 27 departmental honors programs. **Visiting:** There are regularly scheduled orientations for prospective students, Campus tours for prospective students Monday through Thursday at 11 a.m. and 3 p.m. when college is in session and 10 a.m. and 2 p.m. during summer months. BSU also allows prospective students and their families to participate in an interactive open classroom session. There are guides for informal visits and visitors may sit in on classes. To schedule a visit, contact the Admissions Office. **Campus Safety and Security:** Measures include 24-hour foot and vehicle patrol, emergency notification system, self-defense education, and security escort services. There are shuttle buses, emergency telephones, lighted pathways/sidewalks, controlled access to dorms/residences, BSU police department, university-operated transit system that runs from 7:15 a.m. to 8:00 p.m., Monday through Friday, and a safety-escort van that runs from 7 p.m. to 3 a.m, 7 days a week.

REQUIREMENTS: Graduation from an accredited secondary school is required; SAT or ACT scores required, a GED will be accepted. Applicants must have successfully completed 17 Carnegie units, including 4 units of English, 4 units of mathematics, 3 units of science with 2 lab units, 2 units of a foreign language, 2 units of social studies, and 2 in other college preparatory electives. An essay is recommended. AP and CLEP credits are accepted. Students are required to complete a minimum of 120 semester hours. Students must maintain a minimum GPA of 2.0. **Procedure:** Freshmen are admitted fall and spring. There is no deadline for the entrance exams. There are early admissions and deferred admissions plans. Applications should be filed by February 15 for fall entry; November 1 for spring entry, along with a $50 fee. Notifications are sent April 15. Applications are accepted on-line. Application fees are waived if application is completed on-line. **Transfer Students:** 113 transfer students enrolled in 2015-2016. Transfer students must have maintained a minimum GPA of 2.5 from 1 to 23 credits or 2.0 from more than 24 credits at a previous institution. College transcripts and an essay are required of all transfer students; some students must submit high school transcripts and standardized test scores. 30 of 120 credits required for the bachelor's degree must be completed at BSU. **International Students:** There are 57 international students enrolled. They must take the TOEFL with a minimum score of 500 on the paper-based TOEFL (PBT) or 61 on the Internet-based version (iBT), or take the IELTS-International English Lanuage Testing System. They must also take the SAT or ACT.

ADMISSIONS: 81% of the 2016-2017 applicants were accepted. The SAT scores for the 2016-2017 freshman class were: Critical Reading--

53% below 500, 38% between 500 and 599, and 9% between 600 and 699. Math-- 49% below 500, 41% between 500 and 599, and 10% between 600 and 699. The ACT scores were 14% between 12 and 17, 58% between 18 and 23, 26% between 24 and 29, and 2% above 30. **Admissions Contact:** Gregg A. Meyer, Dean of University Admissions. Email: *admissions@bridgew.edu* Web: *wwwbridgew.edu*

FINANCIAL AID: In 2016-2017, 69% of all full-time freshmen and 70% of continuing full-time students received some form of financial aid. 54% of all full-time freshmen and 52% of continuing full-time students received need-based aid. The average freshman award was $5,510. Need-based scholarships or need-based grants averaged $3,289; need-based self-help aid (loans and jobs) averaged $1,962; other non-need-based awards and non-need-based scholarships averaged $2,195; and $1,860 from other forms of aid. The FAFSA code is 002183. The deadline for filing freshman financial aid applications for fall entry is March 1.

CAMBRIDGE COLLEGE *(The complete profile is made available exclusively on our website, www.barronspac.com)*

CLARK UNIVERSITY C-2
www.clarku.edu

Worcester, MA 01610 | **(508) 793-7431** **(800) 462-5275**
Fax: (508) 793-8821 | **Email: admissions@clarku.edu**

Full-time: 865 men, 1358 women	**Faculty:** 206; IIA, +$
Part-time: 28 men, 38 women	**Ph.D.s:** 97%
Graduate: 434 men, 575 women	**Student/Faculty:** 9 to 1
Year: semesters, summer session	**Tuition:** $43,150
Room & Board: $8450	**Freshman Class:** 7914 applied, 4328 accepted, 548 enrolled
SAT CR/M/W: 620/610/610 **ACT:** 29	**CEEB CODE:** 3279
Application Deadline: January 15	**HIGHLY COMPETITIVE+**

Clark University, founded in 1887, is a liberal arts based research university. There are 2 undergraduate schools and 3 graduate schools. In addition to regional accreditation, Clark has baccalaureate program accreditation with AACSB and NASDTEC. The 50-acre campus is in an urban area 50 miles west of Boston. Including any residence halls, there are 79 buildings.

STUDENT LIFE: 68% of undergraduates are from out of state, mostly the Northeast. Students are from 41 states, 68 foreign countries, and Canada. 78% are from public schools. 8% are Asian American; 8% Hispanic; 7% race unknown; 57% White; 4% African American; 2% two or more races; 14% Foreign. 49% claim no religious affiliation; 15% Protestant; 13% Catholic. **Female To Male Ratio:** 1.5:1. The average age of freshmen is 19; all undergraduates, 20. 12% do not continue beyond their first year; 78% remain to graduate. **Housing:** 1739 students can be accommodated in college housing, which includes single-sex and coed dorms, on-campus apartments, and off-campus apartments. In addition, there are special-interest houses, wellness, and quiet houses. On-campus housing is guaranteed for the freshman year only and is available on a lottery system for upperclassmen. 69% of students live on campus. All students may keep cars.

FACULTY/CLASSROOMS: 56% of faculty are male; 44% are female. All teach undergraduates, and all do research. No introductory courses are taught by graduate students. The average class size in an introductory lecture is 25; in a laboratory is 17; and in a regular course is 21.

PROGRAMS OF STUDY: Clark confers B.A., and B.S. degrees. Master's and doctoral degrees are also awarded. Bachelor's degrees are awarded in BIOLOGICAL SCIENCE (biochemistry and biology/biological science), BUSINESS (business administration and management), COMMUNICATIONS AND THE ARTS (art history and appreciation, communications, comparative literature, dramatic arts, English, film arts, fine arts, French, languages, music, romance languages and literature, Spanish, studio art, and visual and performing arts), COMPUTER AND PHYSICAL SCIENCE (chemistry, computer science, mathematics, and physics), ENGINEERING AND ENVIRONMENTAL DESIGN (environmental science), HEALTH PROFESSIONS (predentistry and premedicine), SOCIAL SCIENCE (Asian/Oriental studies, classical/ancient civilization, economics, geography, history, international relations, international studies, philosophy, political science/government, prelaw, psychology, sociology, and women's studies). Psychology, and geography are the strongest academically. Psychology, biology/biochemistry, and political science have the largest enrollments.

ACTIVITIES: There are no fraternities or sororities. There are 130 groups on campus, including art, band, chess, choir, chorale, chorus, computers, dance, debate, drama, environmental, ethnic, film, honors, international, jazz band, LGBT, literary magazine, musical theater, newspaper, orchestra, pep band, photography, political, professional, radio and TV, religious, social, social service, student government, symphony, and yearbook. Popular campus events include Gryphon and Pleiades Honor Society Variety Show, International Gala, and Spree Day. **Sports:** There are 8 intercollegiate sports for men and 9 for women, and 12 intramural sports for men and 12 for women. Facilities include athletic center with a 2000-seat gym, pool, fitness center, tennis courts, and outdoor fields utilized for soccer, lacrosse, football, baseball and softball. **Graduates:** From July 1, 2015 to June 30, 2016, 510 bachelor's degrees were awarded. The most popular majors were psychology (23%), biology and biochemistry (11%), and management (10%). 89 companies recruited on campus in 2015-2016. In an average class, 1% graduate in 3 years or less, 72% graduate in 4 years or less, 77% graduate in 5 years or less, and 78% graduate in 6 years or less. Of the 2015 graduating class, 32% were enrolled in graduate school within 6 months of graduation, and 41% were employed.

SERVICES: Counseling and information services are available, as is tutoring in some subjects, such as biology, chemistry, economics, management, math and writing. For learning-disabled students, the university provides early orientation, alternative test-taking accommodations, and a learning specialist. **Library/Resources:** The 9 libraries contain 667,967 volumes, 61,404 microform items, and 2,489 audio/video tapes/CDs/DVDs, and subscribe to 2,133 periodicals including electronic. Computerized library services include interlibrary loans, database searching, Internet access, and Wi-Fi capability. Special learning facilities include an art gallery and radio station. **Physically Challenged Students:** 95% of the campus is accessible. Facilities include wheelchair ramps, elevators, special parking, specially equipped restrooms, special class scheduling, lowered drinking fountains, lowered telephones, and special housing. **Special:** For-credit internships are available in all disciplines with private corporations and small businesses, medical centers, and government agencies. There is cross-registration with members of the Higher Education Consortium of Central Massachusetts, including 9 other colleges and universities. Clark also offers study abroad in 24 countries, a Washington semester with American University, work-study programs, accelerated degree programs, dual and student-designed majors, pass/no record options, and a 3-2 engineering degree with Columbia University. There are 10 national honor societies, Phi Beta Kappa, and 21 departmental honors programs. **Visiting:** There are regularly scheduled orientations for prospective students, consisting of open houses during fall and spring semesters, which include tours, information sessions, and talks with faculty, administration, and coaches. There are guides for informal visits and visitors may sit in on classes. To schedule a visit, contact the Admissions Office. **Campus Safety and Security:** Measures include 24-hour foot and vehicle patrol, emergency notification system, self-defense education, and security escort services. There are shuttle buses, emergency telephones, lighted pathways/sidewalks, and controlled access to dorms/residences.

REQUIREMENTS: SAT or ACT are optional. Applicants must graduate from an accredited secondary school or have a GED. 16 Carnegie units are required, including 4 years of English, 3 each of math and science, and 2 each of foreign languages and social studies, including history. AP credits are accepted. Each student is required to complete 2 critical thinking courses in 2 categories of verbal expression and formal analysis, and 6 perspectives courses, representing the categories of aesthetics, comparative, historical, language and culture, science, and values. A student must receive passing grades in a minimum of 32 full courses, with a C- or better in at least 24 of these courses, and maintain a minimum 2.0 GPA to graduate. **Procedure:** Freshmen are admitted fall and spring. Entrance exams should be taken by November of the senior year. There are early decision, early admissions, and deferred admissions plans. Applications should be filed by January 15 for fall entry; November 15 for spring entry, along with a $60 fee. Notifications are sent April 1. 35 early decision candidates were accepted for the 2016-2017 class. 357 applicants were on the 2016 waiting list; 6 were admitted. Applications are accepted on-line. **Transfer Students:** 24 transfer students enrolled in 2015-2016. Applicants should have a minimum GPA of about 2.8. At least one full semester of college course work is required. High school and college transcripts, recent SAT or ACT test scores, a statement of good standing from previous institutions attended, and a transfer statement are required. Grades of C or better in comparable course work transfer for credit. 16 of 32 credits required for the bachelor's degree must be completed at Clark. **International Students:** There are 320 international students enrolled. The school actively recruits these students. They must take the TOEFL with a minimum score of 550 on the paper-based TOEFL (PBT) or 80 on the Internet-based version (iBT), or take the IELTS, scoring 6.5.

ADMISSIONS: 55% of the 2016-2017 applicants were accepted. The SAT scores for the 2016-2017 freshman class were: Critical Reading-- 6% below 500, 34% between 500 and 599, 44% between 600 and 699, and 16% between 700 and 800. Math-- 6% below 500, 36% between 500 and 599, 47% between 600 and 699, and 11% between 700 and 800. Writing-- 8% below 500, 33% between 500 and 599, 47% between 600 and 699, and 12% between 700 and 800. The ACT scores were 6% between 18 and 23, 50% between 24 and 29, and 44% above 30. 62% of the current freshmen were in the top fifth of their class; 91% were in the top two fifths. 3 freshmen graduated first in their class. **Admissions Contact:** Donald Honeman, Dean of Admissions. Email: *admissions@clarku.edu* Web: *www.clarku.edu*

FINANCIAL AID: In 2016-2017, 92% of all full-time freshmen and 91% of continuing full-time students received some form of financial aid. 64% of all full-time freshmen and 56% of continuing full-time students received need-based aid. The average freshman award was $31,290. Need-based scholarships or need-based grants averaged $29,463; and need-based self-help aid (loans and jobs) averaged $5,998. 75% of undergraduate students work part-time. Average annual earnings from campus work are $2000. The average financial indebtedness of the 2016 graduate was $24,990. Clark is a member of CSS. The CSS/Profile is required. The FAFSA code is 002139. The deadline for filing freshman financial aid applications for fall entry is February 1.

COLLEGE OF ART AND DESIGN AT LESLEY UNIVERSITY *(The complete profile is made available exclusively on our website, www.barronspac.com)*

COLLEGE OF THE HOLY CROSS — C-2

www.holycross.edu

Worcester, MA 01610	**(508) 793-2443** **(800) 442-2421**
Fax: (508) 793-3888	**Email: admissions@holycross.edu**
Full-time: 1427 men, 1483 women	**Faculty:** 279; IIB, +$
Part-time: 11 men, 20 women	**Ph.D.s:** 93%
Graduate: n/av	**Student/Faculty:** 10 to 1
Year: semesters	**Tuition:** $48,940
Room & Board: $13,225	**Freshman Class:** 6693 applied, 2574 accepted, 765 enrolled
SAT CR/M/W: 640/654/648 **ACT:** 29	**CEEB CODE:** 3282
Application Deadline: January 15	**MOST COMPETITIVE**

College of the Holy Cross is the only liberal arts college that embraces a Catholic, Jesuit identity. And of the 28 Jesuit colleges and universities in the United States, Holy Cross stands alone in its exclusive commitment to undergraduate education. There is 1 undergraduate school. In addition to regional accreditation, Holy Cross has baccalaureate program accreditation with NAST. The 174-acre campus is in a suburban area 45 miles west of Boston. Including any residence halls, there are 35 buildings.

STUDENT LIFE: 60% of undergraduates are from out of state, mostly the Northeast. Students are from 46 states, 18 foreign countries, and Canada. 50% are from public schools. 70% are White; 5% Asian American; 5% race unknown; 4% African American; 3% Foreign; 3% two or more races; 10% Hispanic. 64% are Catholic; 18% Unknown denominations. **Female To Male Ratio:** 1.0:1. The average age of freshmen is 18; all undergraduates, 20. 4% do not continue beyond their first year; 92% remain to graduate. **Housing:** 2503 students can be accommodated in college housing, which includes coed dorms and on-campus apartments. In addition, there are special-interest houses, substance-free housing, and first-year living and learning housing. On-campus housing is guaranteed for all 4 years. 89% of students live on campus; of those, 90% remain on campus on weekends. Upperclassmen may keep cars.

FACULTY/CLASSROOMS: 55% of faculty are male; 45% are female. All teach undergraduates, and all do research. No introductory courses are taught by graduate students. The average class size in a regular course is 18.

PROGRAMS OF STUDY: Holy Cross confers A.B. degrees. Bachelor's degrees are awarded in AGRICULTURE (environmental studies), BIOLOGICAL SCIENCE (biology/biological science), BUSINESS (accounting), COMMUNICATIONS AND THE ARTS (art history and appreciation, Chinese, classics, English, French, German, Italian, literature, music, Russian, Spanish, studio art, and theatre arts), COMPUTER AND PHYSICAL SCIENCE (chemistry, computer science, mathematics, and physics), SOCIAL SCIENCE (anthropology, architectural studies, Asian/Oriental studies, economics, history, international studies, Latin American studies, philosophy, political science/government, psychology, religion, and sociology). Economics, psychology, and political science have the largest enrollments.

ACTIVITIES: There are no fraternities or sororities. There are 97 groups on campus, including art, band, cheerleading, choir, chorale, chorus, computers, dance, debate, drama, environmental, ethnic, film, honors, international, jazz band, LGBT, literary magazine, marching band, musical theater, newspaper, orchestra, pep band, photography, political, professional, religious, social, social service, student government, symphony, and yearbook. Popular campus events include Family Weekend, Purple Pride Day, Winter Homecoming, and Spring Weekend. **Sports:** There are 13 intercollegiate sports for men and 14 for women, and 11 intramural sports for men and 10 for women. Facilities include baseball, football, soccer fields and stadiums, indoor and outdoor running tracks, a swimming pool, ice rink, indoor crew tanks, basketball arena, weight and exercise rooms, wellness centers, tennis, squash, and racquetball courts. **Graduates:** From July 1, 2015 to June 30, 2016, 699 bachelor's degrees were awarded. The most popular majors were economics (17%), psychology (13%), and political science (10%). 119 companies recruited on campus in 2015-2016. In an average class, 88% graduate in 4 years or less, 92% graduate in 5 years or less, and 92% graduate in 6 years or less. Of the 2015 graduating class, 13% were enrolled in graduate school within 6 months of graduation, and 70% were employed.

SERVICES: Counseling and information services are available, as is tutoring in some subjects, such as calculus, biology, chemistry, physics, economics, accounting, and statistics. **Library/Resources:** The 6 libraries contain 646,531 volumes, 16,595 microform items, and 37,841 audio/video tapes/CDs/DVDs, and subscribe to 10,409 periodicals including electronic. Computerized library services include interlibrary loans, database searching, Internet access, and Wi-Fi capability. Special learning facilities include an art gallery, greenhouses, research-level laboratories and equipment, and multimedia resource center. **Physically Challenged Students:** 85% of the campus is accessible. Facilities include wheelchair ramps, elevators, special parking, specially equipped restrooms, special class scheduling, lowered drinking fountains, lowered telephones, and special housing. **Special:** Academic internships are available through the Center for Interdisciplinary Studies. Internship program includes a student-managed large-cap investment portfolio. Student-designed majors, dual majors, Washington semester, New York City semester, and study abroad in approximately 15 countries are possible. The College also offers several 4- to 6-week programs in locations such as Jerusalem, Kenya, London, Luxembourg, Moscow, Paris, Rome and South Africa. There is a 3-2 engineering program in conjunction with Columbia University, internships, and an accelerated degree program. Students may also cross-register with 10 other colleges and universities in a local higher education consortium. There are 2 national honor societies, Phi Beta Kappa, and 8 departmental honors programs. **Visiting:** There are regularly scheduled orientations for prospective students, open houses in October and November consist of informational panels on academics, admissions, financial aid, and student life, as well as tours of the facilities. There are guides for informal visits, visitors may sit in on classes, and stay overnight. To schedule a visit, contact the Admissions Office. **Campus Safety and Security:** Measures include 24-hour foot and vehicle patrol, emergency notification system, self-defense education, and security escort services. There are shuttle buses, emergency telephones, lighted pathways/sidewalks, controlled access to dorms/residences, and card access control system.

REQUIREMENTS: Applicants should be graduates of an accredited secondary school or hold the GED. Recommended preparatory courses include English, foreign language, history, math, and science. An essay is required. Students have the option to submit standardized test scores if they believe the results represent a fuller picture of their achievements and potential; students who opt not to submit scores will not be at any disadvantage in admissions decisions. An interview is recommended. AP credits are accepted. Important factors in the admissions decision are extracurricular activities record, recommendations by school officials, and advanced placement or honors courses. Distribution requirements include social science, natural and mathematical science, cross-cultural studies, religious and philosophical studies, historical studies and the arts, and literature. In addition, students must demonstrate competence in a classical or modern language or American sign language. A total of 32 courses worth at least 1 unit each is required for graduation, with 10 to 14 courses in the major. The minimum GPA for graduation is 2.0. **Procedure:** Freshmen are admitted fall. Entrance exams should be taken no later than January 15th of the senior year. There are early decision and deferred admissions plans. Early decision applications should be filed by December 15; regular applications, by January 15 for fall entry, along with a $60 fee. Notification of early decision is sent January 15; regular decision, April 1. 347 early decision candidates were accepted for the 2016-2017 class. 459 applicants were on the 2016 waiting list; 14 were admitted. Applications are accepted on-line. Application fees are waived if application is completed on-line. **Transfer Students:** 14 transfer students enrolled in 2015-2016. Standardized test scores are not required but applicants must provide transcripts and 2 professor recommendations. Personal interviews are highly recommended. 64 of 128 credits required for the bachelor's degree must be completed at Holy Cross. **International Students:** There are 75 international students enrolled. The school actively recruits these students. They must take the TOEFL with a minimum score of 600 on the paper-based TOEFL (PBT) or 100 on the Internet-based version (iBT).

ADMISSIONS: 38% of the 2016-2017 applicants were accepted. The SAT scores for the 2016-2017 freshman class were: Critical Reading-- 2% below 500, 21% between 500 and 599, 58% between 600 and 699, and 19% between 700 and 800. Math-- 1% below 500, 14% between 500 and 599, 61% between 600 and 699, and 24% between 700 and 800. Writing-- 1% below 500, 21% between 500 and 599, 52% between 600 and 699, and 26% between 700 and 800. The ACT scores were 3% between 18 and 23, 47% between 24 and 29, and 50% above 30. 19 freshmen graduated first in their class. **Admissions Contact:** Ann McDermott, Director. Email: *admissions@holycross.edu* Web: *www.holycross.edu*

FINANCIAL AID: In 2016-2017, 64% of all full-time freshmen and 55% of continuing full-time students received some form of financial aid. 55% of all full-time freshmen and 48% of continuing full-time students received need-based aid. The average freshman award was $39,937. Need-based scholarships or need-based grants averaged $38,039; need-based self-help aid (loans and jobs) averaged $5,605; non-need-based athletic scholarships averaged $28,502; and other non-need-based awards and non-need-based scholarships averaged $30,908. 51% of undergraduate students work part-time. Average annual earnings from campus work are $1786. The average financial indebtedness of the 2016 graduate was $25,446. Holy Cross is a member of CSS. The CSS/Profile, student and parent federal tax returns, business/farm supplement, if applicable are required. The FAFSA code is 002141. The deadline for filing freshman financial aid applications for fall entry is January 15.

CURRY COLLEGE — E-2

www.curry.edu

Milton, MA 02186	**(617) 333-2210** **(800) 669-0686**
Fax: (617) 333-2114	**Email: adm@curry.edu**
Full-time: 981 men, 1130 women	**Faculty:** 119; IIB, +$
Part-time: 116 men, 461 women	**Ph.D.s:** 82%
Graduate: 101 men, 136 women	**Student/Faculty:** 18 to 1
Year: semesters, summer session	**Tuition:** $37,505
Room & Board: $14,310	**Freshman Class:** 6346 applied, 5635 accepted, 736 enrolled
SAT: required **ACT:** 21	**CEEB CODE:** 3285
Application Deadline: April 1	**COMPETITIVE**

Curry College, founded in 1879, is a private, four-year, liberal arts based institution. Curry extends its educational programs offering 22 undergraduate majors, as well as graduate degrees in business, education, criminal justice and nursing. The Curry College mission is to educate and graduate students prepared to engage in successful careers and active citizenship with a global perspective. We are an inclusive community of diverse learners and educators, committed to continuing our legacy of developing effective communicators with reflective and critical thinking skills. We mentor and empower our students, building meaningful relationships that inspire them to achieve their ambitions. Curry College provides rigorous and relevant academic programs to undergraduate and graduate students, and our rich blend of liberal arts and career-directed programs is enhanced by practical field experiences and co-curricular activities. There is 1 undergraduate school and 1 graduate school. In addition to regional accreditation, Curry has baccalaureate program accreditation with CCNE and PCIPP. The 131-acre campus is in a suburban area 7 miles south of downtown Boston. Including any residence halls, there are 44 buildings.

STUDENT LIFE: 75% of undergraduates are from Massachusetts. Others are from 31 states, 23 foreign countries, and Canada. 78% are from public schools. 9% are race unknown; 67% White; 6% Hispanic; 2% Asian American; 2% Foreign; 2% two or more races; 11% African American. **Female To Male Ratio:** 1.4:1. The average age of freshmen is 18; all undergraduates, 20. 29% do not continue beyond their first year; 48% remain to graduate. **Housing:** 1599 students can be accommodated in college housing, which includes single-sex and coed dorms. In addition, there are special-interest houses. On-campus housing is available on a first-come, first-served basis, and is available on a lottery system for upperclassmen. 73% of students live on campus. Upperclassmen may keep cars.

FACULTY/CLASSROOMS: 35% of faculty are male; 65% are female. All teach undergraduates. No introductory courses are taught by graduate students. The average class size in an introductory lecture is 19; in a laboratory is 14; and in a regular course is 19.

PROGRAMS OF STUDY: Curry confers B.A. and B.S. degrees. Master's degrees are also awarded. Bachelor's degrees are awarded in BIOLOGICAL SCIENCE (biochemistry and biology/biological science), BUSINESS (accounting and business administration and management), COMMUNICATIONS AND THE ARTS (communications, English, graphic design, and visual and performing arts), COMPUTER AND PHYSICAL SCIENCE (computer programming and information sciences and systems), EDUCATION (early childhood education, education, elementary education, health education, and special education), HEALTH PROFESSIONS (nursing), SOCIAL SCIENCE (criminal justice, history, liberal arts/general studies, philosophy, political science/government, psychology, and sociology). Nursing, and communication are the strongest academically. Nursing, business, and criminal justice have the largest enrollments.

ACTIVITIES: There are no fraternities or sororities. There are 34 groups on campus, including art, cheerleading, chorale, dance, drama, ethnic, film, honors, international, LGBT, literary magazine, musical theater, newspaper, photography, political, professional, radio and TV, religious, social, social service, student government, and yearbook. Popular campus events include Dances, Late Night Programs, and Theater Productions. **Sports:** There are 7 intercollegiate sports for men and 7 for women, and 10 intramural sports for men and 10 for women. Facilities include athletic and recreational, a 1,000 seat gymnasium, a 300 seat gymnasium, a fitness center, a dance studio, an athletic weight room, 9 outdoor tennis courts, an outdoor pool, 4 grass athletic fields, a 2,000-seat turf stadium, a 500-seat auditorium, and a 5,000-meter cross-country trail. **Graduates:** From July 1, 2015 to June 30, 2016, 687 bachelor's degrees were awarded. The most popular majors were nursing (40%), business (13%), and criminal justice (12%). 72 companies recruited on campus in 2015-2016. In an average class, 45% graduate in 4 years or less, 51% graduate in 5 years or less, and 48% graduate in 6 years or less.

SERVICES: Counseling and information services are available, as is tutoring in most subjects. There is a reader service for the blind, and remedial math, reading, and writing. General development courses in writing, reading, and math are designed to develop the student's basic skills. **Library/Resources:** The library contains 231,347 volumes, and 2,927 audio/video tapes/CDs/DVDs, and subscribes to 43,558 periodicals including electronic. Computerized library services include interlibrary loans, database searching, Internet access, and Wi-Fi capability. Special learning facilities include a radio station and TV station. **Physically Challenged Students:** 80% of the campus is accessible. Facilities include wheelchair ramps, elevators, special parking, specially equipped restrooms, special class scheduling, and special housing. **Special:** Curry College provides rigorous and relevant academic programs to undergraduate and graduate students, and our rich blend of liberal arts and career-directed programs is enhanced by practical field experiences and co-curricular activities. The First-Year Learning Communities program at Curry College allows students to collaborate with faculty and other first-year students both in and out of the classroom as they investigate a theme and complete required courses. Some first-year learning communities are living/learning communities which allow students to reside with classmates who share similar academic goals and interests. Six distinct communities include first-year honors students, communication scholars students, students majoring in the sciences, students focused on community service and action, exploratory health students, and students focused on wellness, resources, and communication as they transition to college. Curry has received great recognition for our communication program. TV and film students can garner real-word experience through the Semester in Los Angeles, New York City, and Washington D.C. programs which allows students to complete internships with leading industry employers. The Program for Advancement of Learning (PAL) provides academically focused assistance to bright, college-able students with specific language-based learning disabilities, executive function disorders, and/or AD/HD. Since its inception, PAL has focused on providing comprehensive, strength-based support to college students with learning differences in a proactive environment. Curry College offers English for Speakers of Other Languages (ESOL) coursework for both domestic and international students, and has exchange partnerships which allow Curry College students to study abroad at Richmond University in London and Saint Francis University in Ambialet, France. There are 6 national honor societies and a freshman honors program. **Visiting:** There are regularly scheduled orientations for prospective students, student visits consist of interviews with an admissions counselor and tours with a student. There are guides for informal visits and visitors may sit in on classes. To schedule a visit, contact The Admissions Office. **Campus Safety and Security:** Measures include 24-hour foot and vehicle patrol, emergency notification system, self-defense education, and security escort services. There are shuttle buses, emergency telephones, lighted pathways/sidewalks, controlled access to dorms/residences, and a campus safety office.

REQUIREMENTS: The College's Program for the Advancement of Learning does not require nor does it consider SAT or ACT scores during the admission process. AP and CLEP credits are accepted. Important factors in the admissions decision are recommendations by school officials, leadership record, and extracurricular activities record. Successful completion of the liberal arts core curriculum and a total of 120 semester hours, completion of a major, and a minimum 2.0 GPA, are required for graduation. Transfer students have modified liberal arts requirements. **Procedure:** Freshmen are admitted fall and spring. Entrance exams should be taken during the junior year or in November of the senior year. There are early admissions, deferred admissions, and rolling admissions plans. Applications should be filed by April 1 for fall entry; December 1 for spring entry, along with a $50 fee. Notification is sent on a rolling basis. 83 applicants were on the 2016 waiting list; 28 were admitted. Applications are accepted on-line. **Transfer Students:** 58 transfer students enrolled in 2015-2016. Transfer applicants must be in good academic and judicial standing at their previous colleges, with a minimum GPA of 2.0. 30 of 120 credits required for the bachelor's degree must be completed at Curry. **International Students:** There are 48 international students enrolled. They must take the TOEFL with a minimum score of 525 on the paper-based TOEFL (PBT) or 71 on the Internet-based version (iBT).

ADMISSIONS: 89% of the 2016-2017 applicants were accepted. The SAT scores for the 2016-2017 freshman class were: Critical Reading-- 60% below 500, 30% between 500 and 599, and 3% between 600 and 699. Math-- 58% below 500, 30% between 500 and 599, and 5% between 600 and 699. Writing-- 63% below 500, 27% between 500 and 599, and 3% between 600 and 699. The ACT scores were 21% between 12 and 17, 58% between 18 and 23, 19% between 24 and 29, and 2% above 30. 20% of the current freshmen were in the top fifth of their class; 40% were in the top two fifths. **Admissions Contact:** Jane Fidler, VP of Admission & Dean of Undergrad. Adm. Email: *curryadm@curry.edu* Web: *www.curry.edu*

FINANCIAL AID: In 2016-2017, 99% of all full-time freshmen and 95% of continuing full-time students received some form of financial aid. 70% of all full-time freshmen and 66% of continuing full-time students received need-based aid. The average freshman award was $29,026. Need-based scholarships or need-based grants averaged $9,334 ($26,715 maximum); need-based self-help aid (loans and jobs) averaged $4,874 ($9,500 maximum); and other non-need-based awards and non-need-based scholarships averaged $17,433 ($26,000 maximum). 36% of undergraduate students work part-time. Average annual earnings from campus work are $1127. The average financial indebtedness of the 2016 graduate was $42,191. The FAFSA code is 002143. The priority date for freshman financial aid applications for fall entry is March 1.

EASTERN NAZARENE COLLEGE E-2

www.enc.edu

Quincy, MA 02170 (617) 745-3711 (800) 883-6288

Fax: (617) 745-3980 **Email: admissio@enc.edu**

Full-time: 245 men, 355 women	**Faculty:** n/av
Part-time: 15 men, 25 women	**Ph.D.s:** 57%
Graduate: 30 men, 140 women	**Student/Faculty:** n/av
Year: 4-1-4, summer session	**Tuition:** $30,815
Room & Board: $9140	**Freshman Class:** n/av
SAT or ACT: required	**CEEB CODE:** 3365
Application Deadline: September 1	**COMPETITIVE**

Eastern Nazarene College, founded in 1918, is a private college affiliated with the Church of the Nazarene. It offers a program in the liberal arts. The figures in the above capsule and in this profile are approximate. There are 5 undergraduate schools and 1 graduate school. In addition to regional accreditation, ENC has baccalaureate program accreditation with CSWE. The 15-acre campus is in a suburban area 6 miles south of Boston. Including any residence halls, there are 16 buildings.

STUDENT LIFE: 55% of undergraduates are from out of state, mostly the Northeast. Students are from 27 states, 24 foreign countries, and Canada. 88% are White; 5% African American; 4% Asian American; 3% Foreign; 1% Hispanic. 88% are Protestant. **Female To Male Ratio:** 1.8:1. The average age of freshmen is 18; all undergraduates, 20. 25% do not continue beyond their first year; 60% remain to graduate. **Housing:** 638 students can be accommodated in college housing, which includes single-sex dorms and married student housing. On-campus housing is guaranteed for all 4 years. 75% of students live on campus; of those, 75% remain on campus on weekends. Alcohol is not permitted. All students may keep cars.

FACULTY/CLASSROOMS: 72% of faculty are male; 28% are female. 83% teach undergraduates. No introductory courses are taught by graduate students. The average class size in an introductory lecture is 75; in a laboratory is 20; and in a regular course is 22.

PROGRAMS OF STUDY: ENC confers B.A., and B.S. degrees. Associate and master's degrees are also awarded. Bachelor's degrees are awarded in BIOLOGICAL SCIENCE (biology/biological science and marine biology), BUSINESS (accounting and business administration and management), COMMUNICATIONS AND THE ARTS (advertising, broadcasting, communications, dramatic arts, English, French, journalism, literature, music, music performance, Spanish, and speech/debate/rhetoric), COMPUTER AND PHYSICAL SCIENCE (chemistry, computer science, mathematics, physics, and science), EDUCATION (athletic training, education, elementary education, music education, science education, and social science education), ENGINEERING AND ENVIRONMENTAL DESIGN (computer engineering, engineering physics, and environmental science), HEALTH PROFESSIONS (sports medicine), SOCIAL SCIENCE (child psychology/development, Christian studies, clinical psychology, history, ministries, physical fitness/movement, psychology, religion, religious music, social studies, social work, and sociology). Chemistry, physics, and history are the strongest academically. Education, business, and psychology have the largest enrollments.

ACTIVITIES: There are no fraternities or sororities. There are 34 groups on campus, including band, cheerleading, choir, chorale, chorus, drama, jazz band, literary magazine, musical theater, newspaper, pep band, photography, professional, radio and TV, religious, social service, student government, and yearbook. Popular campus events include Freshmen Breakout, All-School Outing, and Junior/Senior Banquet. **Sports:** There are 5 intercollegiate sports for men and 5 for women, and 4 intramural sports for men and 5 for women. Facilities include a phys ed center equipped with a basketball area, a batting cage, and playing courts.

SERVICES: Counseling and information services are available, as is tutoring in most subjects. There is remedial math, reading, and writing. **Library/Resources:** The library contains 115,000 volumes, and subscribes to 600 periodicals including electronic. Computerized library services include interlibrary loans and database searching. Special learning facilities include a radio station. **Physically Challenged Students:** 65% of the campus is accessible. Facilities include wheelchair ramps, elevators, special parking, and specially equipped restrooms. **Special:** Internships are available in the metropolitan Boston area. Study abroad in Costa Rica, a Washington semester, a 3-2 engineering degree with Boston University, and a cooperative program with the Massachusetts College of Pharmacy are offered. Work-study programs, dual majors, credit for life, military, work experience, and pass/fail options are available. An off-campus degree-completion program for adults in business administration is offered. There is 1 national honor society. **Visiting:** There are regularly scheduled orientations for prospective students. There are guides for informal visits, visitors may sit in on classes, and stay overnight. To schedule a visit, contact the Office of Admissions. **Campus Safety and Security:** Measures include 24-hour foot and vehicle patrol, self-defense education, and security escort services. There are emergency telephones and lighted pathways/sidewalks.

REQUIREMENTS: The SAT or ACT is required. Applicants must be graduates of an accredited secondary school or have a GED. They must have a minimum of 16 academic credits, including 4 of English, 2 to 4 each of math and foreign language, 1 to 4 of science, and 1 to 2 each of history and social studies. Music students must audition. An essay and interview are recommended. AP and CLEP credits are accepted. Important factors in the admissions decision are advanced placement or honors courses, recommendations by school officials, and leadership record. All students must complete the core curriculum of writing and rhetoric, biblical history, social science, science or math, symbolic systems and intercultural awareness, philosophy and religion, and phys ed. A total of 130 credits is required for the B.A. or B.S., with 32 to 40 in the major. Minimum GPA for graduation is 2.0. **Procedure:** Freshmen are admitted to all sessions. Entrance exams should be taken in the spring of the junior year. There are deferred admissions and rolling admissions plans. Applications should be filed by September 1 for fall entry. The fall 2016 application fee was $25. **Transfer Students:** A minimum 2.0 GPA is required. An interview is recommended. 60 of 130 credits required for the bachelor's degree must be completed at ENC. **International Students:** They must take the TOEFL.

Admissions Contact: Rodney Rogers, Director of Admissions. Email: *admissio@enc.edu* Web: *www.enc.edu*

FINANCIAL AID: ENC is a member of CSS. The college's own financial statement is required. The FAFSA code is 002145. Check with the school for current application deadlines.

ELMS COLLEGE — B-3

www.elms.edu

Chicopee, MA 01013	(413) 592-3189 (800) 255-ELMS
Fax: (413) 594-2781	Email: admissions@elms.edu
Full-time: 65 men, 360 women	Faculty: IIA, --$
Part-time: 25 men, 190 women	Ph.D.s: 76%
Graduate: 20 men, 80 women	Student/Faculty: n/av
Year: semesters	Tuition: $33,410
Room & Board: $12,236	Freshman Class: n/av
SAT or ACT: required	CEEB CODE: 3283
Application Deadline: open	VERY COMPETITIVE

Elms College, founded in 1928 as College of Our Lady of the Elms, is a Roman Catholic institution offering undergraduate degrees in liberal arts and sciences and graduate degrees in liberal arts, education, and theology. The figures in the above capsule and in this profile are approximate. There are 4 undergraduate schools. In addition to regional accreditation, College of Our Lady of the Elms has baccalaureate program accreditation with CSWE and NLN. The 32-acre campus is in a suburban area 2 miles north of Springfield and 90 miles west of Boston. Including any residence halls, there are 11 buildings.

STUDENT LIFE: 85% of undergraduates are from Massachusetts. Others are from 9 states, and 10 foreign countries. 74% are from public schools. 80% are White; 4% African American; 4% Hispanic; 1% Asian American; 1% Foreign. 60% are Catholic. **Female To Male Ratio:** 5.7:1. The average age of freshmen is 20; all undergraduates, 22. 11% do not continue beyond their first year. **Housing:** 315 students can be accommodated in college housing, which includes single-sex and coed dorms. On-campus housing is guaranteed for all 4 years. 60% of students commute. All students may keep cars.

FACULTY/CLASSROOMS: 35% of faculty are male; 65% are female. 90% teach undergraduates, and 90% do research. No introductory courses are taught by graduate students. The average class size in an introductory lecture is 13; in a laboratory is 8; and in a regular course is 11.

PROGRAMS OF STUDY: College of Our Lady of the Elms confers B.A., and B.S. degrees. Associate and master's degrees are also awarded. Bachelor's degrees are awarded in BIOLOGICAL SCIENCE (biology/biological science), BUSINESS (accounting, business administration and management, international business management, and marketing/retailing/merchandising), COMMUNICATIONS AND THE ARTS (English, fine arts, and Spanish), COMPUTER AND PHYSICAL SCIENCE (chemistry, computer science, mathematics, and natural sciences), EDUCATION (bilingual/bicultural education, early childhood education, elementary education, foreign languages education, middle school education, science education, secondary education, special education, and teaching English as a second/foreign language (TESOL/TEFOL)), HEALTH PROFESSIONS (health science, medical laboratory technology, nursing, predentistry, premedicine, and speech pathology/audiology), SOCIAL SCIENCE (American studies, international studies, paralegal studies, prelaw, psychology, religion, social work, and sociology). Nursing, education, and biology are the strongest academically. Education, business, and nursing have the largest enrollments.

ACTIVITIES: There are no fraternities or sororities. There are 41 groups on campus, including art, choir, chorale, chorus, computers, dance, drama, ethnic, honors, international, literary magazine, musical theater, newspaper, photography, professional, radio and TV, religious, social, social service, student government, and yearbook. Popular campus events include Soph Show, Cap and Gown, and Ring Ceremony. **Sports:** There are 6 intercollegiate sports for men and 9 for women, and 6 intramural sports for men and 6 for women. Facilities include fitness and athletic center housing a suspended indoor track, a 25-meter, 6-lane pool, a weight and aerobics room, a multipurpose arena, a basketball court, and a volleyball court.

SERVICES: Counseling and information services are available, as is tutoring in every subject. There is a reader service for the blind, and remedial math, reading, and writing. There also is an academic advising and resource center, a counseling service office, career services, wellness services, student activities, a campus ministry office, and resident advisers. **Library/Resources:** The library contains 103,136 volumes, 77,784 microform items, and 2,208 audio/video tapes/CDs/DVDs, and subscribes to 695 periodicals including electronic. Computerized library services include interlibrary loans and database searching. Special learning facilities include an art gallery, radio station, TV station, and a rare books collection. **Physically Challenged Students:** 40% of the campus is accessible. Facilities include wheelchair ramps, elevators, special parking, specially equipped restrooms, special class scheduling, lowered drinking fountains, and lowered telephones. **Special:** Students may cross-register at any of the Cooperating Colleges of Greater Springfield or Consortium of Sisters of St. Joseph Colleges. Internships are available with local hospitals, businesses, and schools. Study abroad, student-designed interdepartmental majors, accelerated degree programs, work-study, dual majors, nondegree study, and pass/fail options are offered. There are 5 national honor societies, Phi Beta Kappa, and a freshman honors program. **Visiting:** There are regularly scheduled orientations for prospective students, including tours and interviews scheduled weekdays between 9 a.m. and 4 p.m. as well as 2 open houses in the fall and 1 in the spring. There are guides for informal visits, visitors may sit in on classes, and stay overnight. To schedule a visit, contact the Admission Office. **Campus Safety and Security:** Measures include 24-hour foot and vehicle patrol, self-defense education, and security escort services. There are emergency telephones, lighted pathways/sidewalks, a safety and security manual is published each year, and there is a safety and security committee of administrators, students, faculty, and staff.

REQUIREMENTS: The SAT or ACT is required. Applicants should be graduates of accredited high schools or have earned the GED. Secondary preparation should include 4 units of English, 3 each of math and science, and 2 each of foreign language, history, and social studies. A personal essay is required; an interview is recommended. AP and CLEP credits are accepted. Important factors in the admissions decision are advanced placement or honors courses, recommendations by school officials, and extracurricular activities record. To graduate, all students must complete 120 hours with a 2.0 GPA. 54 hours are required in courses in rhetoric, computer science, history, religion, phys ed, philosophy, sociology, fine arts, humanities, foreign language, math, senior seminar, and service learning experience. **Procedure:** Freshmen are admitted fall and spring. Entrance exams should be taken no later than November of the senior year. There are early admissions, deferred admissions, and rolling admissions plans. Application deadlines are open. The fall 2016 application fee was $30. Applications are accepted on-line. **Transfer Students:** Applicants must have a minimum 2.0 GPA. 45 of 120 credits required for the bachelor's degree must be completed at College of Our Lady of the Elms. **International Students:** The school actively recruits these students.

Admissions Contact: Joseph P. Wagner, Director of Admission. Email: *admissions@elms.edu* Web: *www.elms.edu*

FINANCIAL AID: College of Our Lady of the Elms is a member of CSS. The college's own financial statement is required. The FAFSA code is 002140. Check with the school for current application deadlines.

EMERSON COLLEGE E-2

www.emerson.edu

Boston, MA 02116	(617) 824-8600
Fax: (617) 824-8609	**Email:** admission@emerson.edu
Full-time: 1496 men, 2237 women	**Faculty:** 202; IIA, +$
Part-time: 24 men, 27 women	**Ph.D.s:** 73%
Graduate: 153 men, 518 women	**Student/Faculty:** 13 to 1
Year: semesters, summer session	**Tuition:** $39,036
Room & Board: $15,700	**Freshman Class:** 8618 applied, 4225 accepted, 915 enrolled
SAT CR/M/W: 620/590/610 **ACT:** 27	**CEEB CODE:** 3367
Application Deadline: January 15	**HIGHLY COMPETITIVE**

Emerson College, founded in 1880, is the premier college in the United States for the study of communication and the arts. There are 2 undergraduate schools and 2 graduate schools. The 8-acre campus is in an urban area on Boston Common in the Theater District. Including any residence halls, there are 13 buildings.

STUDENT LIFE: 78% of undergraduates are from out of state, mostly the Middle Atlantic. Students are from 47 states, 30 foreign countries, and Canada. 75% are from public schools. 9% are Foreign; 65% White; 5% Asian American; 4% two or more races; 3% African American; 2% race unknown; 12% Hispanic. **Female To Male Ratio:** 1.7:1. The average age of freshmen is 18; all undergraduates, 20. 13% do not continue beyond their first year; 80% remain to graduate. **Housing:** 2101 students can be accommodated in college housing, which includes coed dorms, and living and learning communities such as a writers' block and digital culture floors. On-campus housing is guaranteed for the freshman year only, and is available on a first-come, first-served basis, and is available on a lottery system for upperclassmen. 58% of students live on campus; of those, 75% remain on campus on weekends. No one may keep cars.

FACULTY/CLASSROOMS: 55% of faculty are male; 45% are female. All teach undergraduates. Graduate students teach 4% of introductory courses. The average class size in an introductory lecture is 35; in a laboratory is 18; and in a regular course is 24.

PROGRAMS OF STUDY: Emerson confers B.A., B.S. and B.F.A. degrees. Master's and doctoral degrees are also awarded. Bachelor's degrees are awarded in BUSINESS (marketing management), COMMUNICATIONS AND THE ARTS (advertising, broadcasting, communications, creative writing, dramatic arts, film arts, journalism, media arts, musical theater, performing arts, public relations, publishing, radio/television technology, speech/debate/rhetoric, theater design, and theater management), HEALTH PROFESSIONS (speech pathology/audiology), SOCIAL SCIENCE (interdisciplinary studies). Visual & media arts, writing, and literature & publishing are the strongest academically. Visual & media arts, performing arts, and communication have the largest enrollments.

ACTIVITIES: 3% of women belong to 2 local and 1 national sororities. There are 80 groups on campus, including digital media, marketing/PR clubs, radio stations, chorale, computers, dance, debate, drama, environmental, ethnic, film, forensics, honors, international, LGBT, literary magazine, musical theater, newspaper, photography, political, professional, radio and TV, religious, social, social service, student government, theatre troupes, and yearbook. Popular campus events include Evvy's Award Show, and Emerson Recognition and Achievement Awards. **Sports:** There are 7 intercollegiate sports for men and 8 for women. Facilities include a gymnasium, 10,000-square-foot fitness center, and lighted athletic field. **Graduates:** From July 1, 2015 to June 30, 2016, 969 bachelor's degrees were awarded. The most popular majors were communication/journalism (36%), visual and performing arts (30%), and business/marketing (15%). In an average class, 77% graduate in 4 years or less, 79% graduate in 5 years or less, and 80% graduate in 6 years or less. Of the 2015 graduating class, 8% were enrolled in graduate school within 6 months of graduation, and 81% were employed.

SERVICES: Counseling and information services are available, as is tutoring in most subjects. There is remedial math, reading, and writing. **Library/Resources:** The library contains 163,314 volumes, 9,414 microform items, and 16,574 audio/video tapes/CDs/DVDs, and subscribes to 57,169 periodicals including electronic. Computerized library services include interlibrary loans, database searching, Internet access, and Wi-Fi capability. Special learning facilities include an art gallery, radio station, TV station, sound-treated television studios, film production facilities and digital production labs, speech-language-hearing clinics, several theaters, 2 radio stations, marketing research suite, and digital newsroom. **Physically Challenged Students:** 85% of the campus is accessible. Facilities include wheelchair ramps, elevators, specially equipped restrooms, special class scheduling, and special housing. **Special:** Student-designed, interdisciplinary, and dual majors are available. Cross-registration is offered with the 6-member Boston ProArts consortium. Nearly 800 internships are possible, 600 in Boston and 200 in Los Angeles. Internships bear credit and are graded. Emerson has nondegree study as well as study abroad in the Netherlands, China, and a summer film program in Prague. There is 1 national honor society and a freshman honors program. **Visiting:** There are regularly scheduled orientations for prospective students, including an information session with an admission representative and a tour lead by a current student. There are guides for informal visits and visitors may sit in on classes. To schedule a visit, contact the Admissions Office. **Campus Safety and Security:** Measures include 24-hour foot and vehicle patrol, emergency notification system, self-defense education, and security escort services. There are shuttle buses, emergency telephones, lighted pathways/sidewalks, and controlled access to dorms/residences.

REQUIREMENTS: The SAT or ACT is required. The ACT Optional Writing test is also required. Emerson is a member of the Common Application and requires an Application Supplement. Candidates must have graduated from high school (or have a GED) and present 4 years of English and 3 years each in science, social studies, foreign language, and math. Candidates for performing arts programs are required to submit a theatre-related resume and either audition or interview, or submit a portfolio or an essay. Candidates for film are required to submit either a 5-8 minute video sample and statement, or a 5-10 page script. AP and CLEP credits are accepted. Important factors in the admissions decision are advanced placement or honors courses, evidence of special talent, and recommendations by school officials. All students must complete 128 credit hours, with 40 to 64 in their major and a minimum GPA of 2.0. The general education curriculum consists of 4 foundations courses (oral and written communication and quantitative reasoning), 7 perspectives courses (liberal arts humanities), and 2 global/U.S. diversity courses. **Procedure:** Freshmen are admitted fall and spring. Entrance exams should be taken before December of the senior year. There are early decision and deferred admissions plans. Early decision applications should be filed by November 1; regular applications, by January 15 for fall entry; and November 1 for spring entry, along with a $65 fee. Notification of early decision is sent December 15; regular decision, April 1. 1569 applicants were on the 2016 waiting list; 44 were admitted. Applications are accepted on-line. **Transfer Students:** 172 transfer students enrolled in 2015-2016. Requirements for transfer students are the same as for all students. 48 of 128 credits required for the bachelor's degree must be completed at Emerson. **International Students:** There are 282 international students enrolled. The school actively recruits these students. They must take the TOEFL with a minimum score of 550 on the paper-based TOEFL (PBT) or 80 on the Internet-based version (iBT), or take the IELTS. They must also take the SAT or ACT.

ADMISSIONS: 49% of the 2016-2017 applicants were accepted. The SAT scores for the 2016-2017 freshman class were: Critical Reading-- 5% below 500, 33% between 500 and 599, 48% between 600 and 699, and 14% between 700 and 800. Math-- 9% below 500, 42% between 500 and

599, 40% between 600 and 699, and 9% between 700 and 800. Writing--6% below 500, 34% between 500 and 599, 47% between 600 and 699, and 13% between 700 and 800. The ACT scores were 1% between 12 and 17, 9% between 18 and 23, 66% between 24 and 29, and 24% above 30. 60% of the current freshmen were in the top fifth of their class; 89% were in the top two fifths. 8 freshmen graduated first in their class. **Admissions Contact:** Michael Lynch, Director of Undergraduate Admission. Email: *admission@emerson.edu* Web: *www.emerson.edu*

FINANCIAL AID: In 2016-2017, 64% of all full-time freshmen and 58% of continuing full-time students received some form of financial aid. 52% of all full-time freshmen and 50% of continuing full-time students received need-based aid. The average freshman award was $28,595. Need-based scholarships or need-based grants averaged $20,145 ($58,752 maximum); need-based self-help aid (loans and jobs) averaged $4,193 ($9,000 maximum); and other non-need-based awards and non-need-based scholarships averaged $15,280 ($49,609 maximum). 61% of undergraduate students work part-time. Average annual earnings from campus work are $2008. The CSS/Profile is required. The FAFSA code is 002146. The priority date for freshman financial aid applications for fall entry is March 1.

EMMANUEL COLLEGE — E-2

www.emmanuel.edu

Boston, MA 02115 — **(617) 735-9715**

Fax: (617) 735-9801	**Email: enroll@emmanuel.edu**
Full-time: 478 men, 1295 women	**Faculty:** 94; IIB, +$
Part-time: 12 men, 80 women	**Ph.D.s:** 82%
Graduate: 41 men, 149 women	**Student/Faculty:** 13 to 1
Year: semesters, summer session	**Tuition:** $37,840
Room & Board: $14,270	**Freshman Class:** 5692 applied, 4006 accepted, 555 enrolled
SAT CR/M/W: 565/555/555 **ACT:** 25	**CEEB CODE:** 3368
Application Deadline: February 15	**COMPETITIVE+**

Emmanuel College, founded by the Sisters of Notre Dame de Namur in 1919, is a coed, residential, Catholic liberal arts and sciences college. Figures in the above capsule and in this profile are approximate. There are 4 undergraduate schools and 1 graduate school. In addition to regional accreditation, EC has baccalaureate program accreditation with CCNE. The 17-acre campus is in an urban area in the city of Boston. Including any residence halls, there are 10 buildings.

STUDENT LIFE: 55% of undergraduates are from Massachusetts. Others are from 29 states, 44 foreign countries, and Canada. 71% are White; 6% Hispanic; 4% African American; 3% Asian American; 3% two or more races; 11% race unknown; 1% Foreign. **Female To Male Ratio:** 2.9:1. The average age of freshmen is 18; all undergraduates, 20. 19% do not continue beyond their first year; 58% remain to graduate. **Housing:** 1290 students can be accommodated in college housing, which includes coed dorms. In addition, there are special-interest houses, and theme housing. On-campus housing is guaranteed for all 4 years. 73% of students live on campus; of those, 75% remain on campus on weekends. Alcohol is not permitted. Upperclassmen may keep cars.

FACULTY/CLASSROOMS: 40% of faculty are male; 60% are female. All teach undergraduates. No introductory courses are taught by graduate students. The average class size in an introductory lecture is 22; in a laboratory is 18; and in a regular course is 20.

PROGRAMS OF STUDY: EC confers B.A., B.F.A. and B.S. degrees. Master's degrees are also awarded. Bachelor's degrees are awarded in AGRICULTURE (environmental studies), BIOLOGICAL SCIENCE (biochemistry, biology/biological science, biomathematics, and neurosciences), BUSINESS (accounting, business administration and management, and sports management), COMMUNICATIONS AND THE ARTS (communications, English, English literature, Spanish, and studio art), COMPUTER AND PHYSICAL SCIENCE (chemistry and mathematics), EDUCATION (elementary education and secondary education), ENGINEERING AND ENVIRONMENTAL DESIGN (graphic arts technology), HEALTH PROFESSIONS (art therapy and nursing), SOCIAL SCIENCE (American studies, counseling/psychology, developmental psychology, forensic studies, history, interdisciplinary studies, international studies, liberal arts/general studies, philosophy, political science/government, psychology, religion, and sociology). English & communication, management, and psychology have the largest enrollments.

ACTIVITIES: There are no fraternities or sororities. There are 48 groups on campus, including art, band, cheerleading, chess, choir, chorus, dance, debate, drama, ethnic, honors, international, jazz band, LGBT, literary magazine, musical theater, newspaper, orchestra, pep band, photography, political, professional, radio and TV, religious, social, social service, student government, and yearbook. Popular campus events include Moonlight Breakfast, Student Leadership Reception, Latin Explosion, Midnight Madness, and Family Weekend. **Sports:** There are 8 intercollegiate sports for men and 8 for women, and 19 intramural sports for men and 19 for women. Facilities include the Jean Yawkey Center gymnasium which includes one NCAA regulation court or two full-size practice courts for volleyball, and basketball with bleacher seating for 1200-1400, a fitness center, locker rooms, and training room. The Roberto Clemente field for softball, soccer and women's lacrosse teams, as well as the practice facility for track and field. **Graduates:** From July 1, 2015 to June 30, 2016, 487 bachelor's degrees were awarded. The most popular majors were business/marketing (16%), biological/life sciences (14%), and health professions & related programs (10%). 124 companies recruited on campus in 2015-2016. In an average class, 57% graduate in 5 years or less and 64% graduate in 6 years or less.

SERVICES: Counseling and information services are available, as is tutoring in every subject. There is a reader service for the blind, and remedial math and writing. **Library/Resources:** The library contains 185,400 volumes, and 1,883 audio/video tapes/CDs/DVDs, and subscribes to 2,100 periodicals including electronic. Computerized library services include interlibrary loans, database searching, Internet access, and Wi-Fi capability. Special learning facilities include an art gallery and radio station. **Physically Challenged Students:** 90% of the campus is accessible. Facilities include wheelchair ramps, elevators, special parking, specially equipped restrooms, special class scheduling, lowered drinking fountains, lowered telephones, and special housing. **Special:** There is cross-registration with Wheelock College, Simmons College, Massachusetts College of Art, Massachusetts College of Pharmacy, and Wentworth Institute of Technology. The college offers internships, study abroad, a Washington semester, work-study programs on campus and in Boston-area organizations, an accelerated degree program in business administration for nontraditional students, dual and student-designed majors, and prelaw/prehealth preparation. There are 14 national honor societies, a freshman honors program, and 100 departmental honors programs. **Visiting:** There are regularly scheduled orientations for prospective students, consisting of 2 open houses and weekday and weekend information sessions. There are guides for informal visits, visitors may sit in on classes, and stay overnight. To schedule a visit, contact the Office of Admissions. **Campus Safety and Security:** Measures include 24-hour foot and vehicle patrol, emergency notification system, self-defense education, and security escort services. There are shuttle buses, emergency telephones, lighted pathways/sidewalks, controlled access to dorms/residences, 24-hour staffed residence hall desks and security office, closed-circuit surveillance in public areas, off-campus escorts, bike patrol, first responders program, a Rape Agression Defense program, and a mass notification system.

REQUIREMENTS: The SAT or ACT is required. Applicants must be graduates of an accredited secondary school or have a GED. 16 academic credits are required, including 4 years of English, 3 years each of math, science with 2 units of lab, foreign language, and social studies. An essay and an interview are encouraged but not required. AP credits are accepted. Important factors in the admissions decision are advanced placement or honors courses, recommendations by school officials, leadership record, evidence of special talent, personality/intangible qualities, extracurricular activities record, recommendations by alumni, parents or siblings attended your school, and geographical diversity. Students must complete a total of 128 credit hours with 40 to 48 in the major and a 2.0 GPA to graduate. Distribution requirements include 15 general ed courses, 10 to 17 courses for the major, and 5 to 7 elective or minor courses. A capstone experience and first-year seminar is required. **Procedure:** Freshmen are admitted fall and spring. Entrance exams should be taken by November of the senior year. There are early admissions and deferred admissions plans. Applications should be filed by February 15 for fall entry, along with a $60 fee. Notifications are sent December 15. Applications are accepted on-line. Application fees are waived if application is completed on-line. **Transfer Students:** 34 transfer students enrolled in 2015-2016. Students must submit essays, college and high school transcripts, and 2 letters of recommendation. They must be financially and academically eligible to return to the previously attended institution. 64 of 128 credits required for the bachelor's degree must be completed at Emmanuel College. **International Students:** There are 26 international students enrolled. The school actively recruits these students. They must take the TOEFL with a minimum score of 550 on the paper-based TOEFL (PBT) or 79 on the Internet-based version (iBT), or take ELS level 109 or the equivalent. They must also take the SAT or ACT.

ADMISSIONS: 70% of the 2016-2017 applicants were accepted. The SAT scores for the 2016-2017 freshman class were: Critical Reading-- 10% below 500, 56% between 500 and 599, 33% between 600 and 699, and 1% between 700 and 800. Math-- 17% below 500, 56% between 500 and 599, and 26% between 600 and 699. Writing-- 18% below 500, 54% between 500 and 599, 26% between 600 and 699, and 2% between 700 and 800. The ACT scores were 33% between 18 and 23, 57% between 24 and 29, and 10% above 30. 43% of the current freshmen were in the top fifth of their class; 75% were in the top two fifths. **Admissions Contact:** Sandra Robbins, Dean of Enrollment. Email: *enroll@emmanuel.edu* Web: *www.emmanuel.edu*

FINANCIAL AID: In 2016-2017, 99% of all full-time freshmen and 95% of continuing full-time students received some form of financial aid. 84% of all full-time freshmen and 80% of continuing full-time students received need-based aid. The average freshman award was $27,356. Need-based scholarships or need-based grants averaged $23,170; need-based self-help aid (loans and jobs) averaged $3,660; other non-need-based awards and non-need-based scholarships averaged $4,836; and $14,720 from other forms of aid. 38% of undergraduate students work part-time. Average annual earnings from campus work are $1800. The college's own financial statement is required. The FAFSA code is 002147. The priority date for freshman financial aid applications for fall entry is February 15.

ENDICOTT COLLEGE E-2

www.endicott.edu

Beverly, MA 01915 (978) 921-1000 (800) 325-1114

Fax: (978) 232-2520 Email: admissio@endicott.edu

Full-time: 1023 men, 1590 women	**Faculty:** 91; IIB, +$
Part-time: 104 men, 238 women	**Ph.D.s:** 70%
Graduate: 368 men, 917 women	**Student/Faculty:** 27 to 1
Year: 4-1-4, summer session	**Tuition:** $29,494
Room & Board: $13,734	**Freshman Class:** 3842 applied, 2809 accepted, 765 enrolled
SAT CR/M/W: 532/543/530 **ACT:** 27	**CEEB CODE:** 3369
Application Deadline: February 15	**VERY COMPETITIVE+**

Endicott College, founded in 1939, offers programs in the professional and liberal arts. Endicott provides an education built upon a combination of theory and practice, which is tested through internships and work experience. There are 8 undergraduate schools and 1 graduate school. In addition to regional accreditation, Endicott has baccalaureate program accreditation with NASAD, NCATE, NLN, NASAD, CIDA, and AHPCA. The 235-acre campus is in a suburban area 20 miles north of Boston. Including any residence halls, there are 53 buildings.

STUDENT LIFE: 52% of undergraduates are from out of state, mostly the Northeast. Students are from 30 states, and 29 foreign countries. 79% are from public schools. 86% are White. **Female To Male Ratio:** 1.8:1. The average age of freshmen is 18; all undergraduates, 19. 17% do not continue beyond their first year; 73% remain to graduate. **Housing:** 2130 students can be accommodated in college housing, which includes single-sex and coed dorms, on-campus apartments, and off-campus apartments. In addition, there are honors houses, special-interest houses, single-parent, international, academic themed, healthy living and ocean-front housing available. On-campus housing is guaranteed for the freshman year only, and is available on a first-come, first-served basis, and is available on a lottery system for upperclassmen. 86% of students live on campus; of those, 85% remain on campus on weekends. Upperclassmen may keep cars.

FACULTY/CLASSROOMS: 44% of faculty are male; 56% are female. No introductory courses are taught by graduate students. The average class size in an introductory lecture is 18 and in a laboratory is 10.

PROGRAMS OF STUDY: Endicott confers B.A., B.S. and B.F.A. degrees. Associate, master's, and doctoral degrees are also awarded. Bachelor's degrees are awarded in BIOLOGICAL SCIENCE (biotechnology), BUSINESS (accounting, business administration and management, entrepreneurial studies, finance, hospitality management services, hotel/motel and restaurant management, international business management, marketing management, and sports management), COMMUNICATIONS AND THE ARTS (communications, digital communications, English, fine arts, graphic design, photography, and studio art), COMPUTER AND PHYSICAL SCIENCE (applied mathematics, computer science, and mathematics), EDUCATION (athletic training, education, and physical education), ENGINEERING AND ENVIRONMENTAL DESIGN (bioengineering, environmental science, and interior design), HEALTH PROFESSIONS (art therapy, exercise science, and nursing), SOCIAL SCIENCE (criminal justice, history, international studies, liberal arts/general studies, political science/government, and psychology). Business management, nursing, and sport management have the largest enrollments.

ACTIVITIES: There are no fraternities or sororities. There are 60 groups on campus, including crew, outdoor adventure and fitness, art, band, cheerleading, chorale, chorus, computers, dance, debate, drama, environmental, ethnic, film, honors, international, jazz band, LGBT, literary magazine, musical theater, newspaper, pep band, photography, political, professional, radio and TV, religious, Sailing, social, social service, student government, and yearbook. Popular campus events include Family/Homecoming Weekend, Annual Regatta, Festival of Lights, Performing Arts Events, and Ice Skating on campus ponds. **Sports:** There are 10 intercollegiate sports for men and 9 for women, and 9 intramural sports for men and 9 for women. Outdoor facilities include a 2,200-seat multi-purpose turf stadium with an athletic support building, a new turf baseball/soccer field, 6 outdoor tennis courts, a separate softball stadium, and sailing/kayaking based out of Winter Island, Salem, MA, and cross country courses (5k and 8k). Indoor facilities include a 1400-seat gym with a racquetball, indoor tennis, and basketball courts, weight, fitness, and group fitness rooms, indoor track, rock climbing wall, and a field house. **Graduates:** From July 1, 2014 to June 30, 2015, 633 bachelor's degrees were awarded. The most popular majors were business administration (17%), sport management (12%), and nursing (9%). 98 companies recruited on campus in 2014-2015. In an average class, 71% graduate in 4 years or less, 73% graduate in 5 years or less, and 73% graduate in 6 years or less. Of the 2014 graduating class, 21% were enrolled in graduate school within 6 months of graduation, and 75% were employed.

SERVICES: Counseling and information services are available, as is tutoring in every subject. There is a reader service for the blind. **Library/Resources:** The library contains 120,600 volumes, 6,987 microform items, and 1,975 audio/video tapes/CDs/DVDs, and subscribes to 80,316 periodicals including electronic. Computerized library services include interlibrary loans, database searching, Internet access, and Wi-Fi capability. Special learning facilities include an art gallery, radio station, TV station, state-of-the-art nursing and science labs, several fine art studios (interior design, graphic design, photography, painting, and ceramics) recital hall, black box theater, nature trails, private beaches and marshland, a student-run restaurant, and an archives museum. **Physically Challenged Students:** 95% of the campus is accessible. Facilities include wheelchair ramps, elevators, special parking, specially equipped restrooms, special class scheduling, and lowered drinking fountains. **Special:** Three internships are required of most undergraduates. Students may study abroad. There are accelerated degree programs in Business Administration, Hospitality Management, Liberal Studies, Liberal Studies/Education, Nursing and Psychology. Cross-registration available through NECCUM. Five-year bachelor/master's programs available. There are 14 national honor societies, a freshman honors program, and 1 departmental honors program. **Visiting:** There are regularly scheduled orientations for prospective students, includes testing, preregistration, and an introduction to general student life. There are guides for informal visits, visitors may sit in on classes, and stay overnight. To schedule a visit, contact the Office of Admission. **Campus Safety and Security:** Measures include 24-hour foot and vehicle patrol, emergency notification system, self-defense education, and security escort services. There are shuttle buses, emergency telephones, lighted pathways/sidewalks, controlled access to dorms/residences, license plate reecognition system, security cameras, property identification, crime prevention workshops, and alcohol safety programs.

REQUIREMENTS: The SAT or ACT is recommended. Essays and two science and math recommendations are required for nursing (including chemistry) and athletic training majors. AP and CLEP credits are accepted. All undergraduates complete a senior thesis and multiple internships. Core requirements for undergraduate students include the areas of writing and academic inquiry. General education requirements include completing at least 3 credits in each of the College's eight thematic categories. **Procedure:** Freshmen are admitted fall and spring. Entrance exams should be taken In fall of the senior year. Applications should be filed by February 15 for fall entry; December 15 for spring entry, along with a $50 fee. 42 applicants were on the 2015 waiting list. Applications are accepted on-line. **Transfer Students:** 99 transfer students enrolled in 2014-2015. Official high school and college transcripts and a letter of recommendation are required. 24 of 124 credits required for the bachelor's degree must be completed at Endicott. **International Students:** There are 43 international students enrolled. The school actively recruits these students. They must take the TOEFL with a minimum score of 550 on the paper-based TOEFL (PBT) or 79 on the Internet-based version (iBT). They must also take the SAT or ACT.

ADMISSIONS: 73% of the 2015-2016 applicants were accepted. The SAT scores for the 2015-2016 freshman class were: Critical Reading-- 29% below 500, 53% between 500 and 599, 17% between 600 and 699, and 1% between 700 and 800. Math-- 23% below 500, 53% between 500 and 599, 22% between 600 and 699, and 2% between 700 and 800. Writing-- 31% below 500, 51% between 500 and 599, 17% between 600 and 699, and 1% between 700 and 800. **Admissions Contact:** Thomas J. Redman, Vice President Admissions. E-Mail: *admissio@endicott.edu* Web: *www.endicott.edu*

FINANCIAL AID: In 2015-2016, 91% of all full-time freshmen and 88% of continuing full-time students received some form of financial aid. 64% of all full-time freshmen and 63% of continuing full-time students received need-based aid. The average freshman award was $21,354.. 36% of undergraduate students work part-time. Average annual earnings from campus work are $1500. The average financial indebtedness of the 2015 graduate was $39,178. Endicott is a member of CSS. The FAFSA and the college's own financial statement are required. The priority date for freshman financial aid applications for fall entry is March 15.

FITCHBURG STATE UNIVERSITY C-2

www.fitchburgstate.edu

Fitchburg, MA 01420 (978) 665-3140
(800) 705-9692
Fax: (978) 665-3140 Email: admissions@fitchburgstate.edu

Full-time: 1624 men, 1803 women	**Faculty:** 198
Part-time: 335 men, 403 women	**Ph.D.s:** 91%
Graduate: 633 men, 2420 women	**Student/Faculty:** 15 to 1
Year: semesters	**Tuition:** $10,135 ($16,215)
Room & Board: $11,684	**Freshman Class:** n/av
SAT: required **ACT:** 21	**CEEB CODE:** 3519
Application Deadline: March 1	**COMPETITIVE**

Fitchburg State University, founded in 1894, is a comprehensive public university offering undergraduate, graduate and continuing education programs. There are 4 undergraduate schools and 1 graduate school. In addition to regional accreditation, Fitchburg State has baccalaureate program accreditation with ABET, NCATE, CCNE, IACBE, and CSHSE. The 78-acre campus is in a suburban area 45 miles west of Boston. Including any residence halls, there are 35 buildings.

STUDENT LIFE: 91% of undergraduates are from Massachusetts. Others are from 15 states, 4 foreign countries, and Canada. 80% are from public schools. 8% are Hispanic; 78% White; 7% African American; 3% Asian American; 2% race unknown; 1% Foreign; 1% two or more races. **Female To Male Ratio:** 1.8:1. The average age of freshmen is 18; all undergraduates, 22. 25% do not continue beyond their first year; 51% remain to graduate. **Housing:** 1623 students can be accommodated in college housing, which includes coed dorms and on-campus apartments. In addition, there are special-interest houses. 56% of students commute. All students may keep cars.

FACULTY/CLASSROOMS: 55% of faculty are male; 45% are female. All teach undergraduates. No introductory courses are taught by graduate students. The average class size in an introductory lecture is 27; in a laboratory is 15; and in a regular course is 24.

PROGRAMS OF STUDY: Fitchburg State confers B.A., B.S., and B.S.Ed. degrees. Master's degrees are also awarded. Bachelor's degrees are awarded in BIOLOGICAL SCIENCE (biology/biological science, biotechnology, environmental biology, and neurosciences), BUSINESS (accounting, business administration and management, international business management, international economics, management science, and marketing management), COMMUNICATIONS AND THE ARTS (communications, dramatic arts, English, graphic design, literature, photography, theater management, and video), COMPUTER AND PHYSICAL SCIENCE (applied mathematics, chemistry, computer science, earth science, and mathematics), EDUCATION (early childhood education, education, elementary education, industrial arts education, middle school education, secondary education, special education, technical education, and vocational education), ENGINEERING AND ENVIRONMENTAL DESIGN (architectural technology, construction technology, electrical/electronics engineering technology, energy management technology, industrial engineering technology, and manufacturing technology), HEALTH PROFESSIONS (exercise science, health science, and nursing), SOCIAL SCIENCE (cognitive science, criminal justice, developmental psychology, economics, geography, history, human services, industrial and organizational psychology, interdisciplinary studies, political science/government, prelaw, psychology, and sociology). Nursing, and communications/media are the strongest academically. Communications/media, business administration, and education have the largest enrollments.

ACTIVITIES: 1% of men belong to 2 national fraternities; 3% of women belong to 3 national sororities. There are 70 groups on campus, including band, cheerleading, choir, chorus, computers, dance, drama, environmental, ethnic, film, honors, international, jazz band, LGBT, literary magazine, newspaper, photography, political, professional, radio and TV, religious, social, social service, and student government. Popular campus events include Falcon Fest, Rock the Block, and Center Stage Performing Arts Series. **Sports:** There are 8 intercollegiate sports for men and 8 for women, and 10 intramural sports for men and 10 for women. Facilities include a 1,000-seat gym, an indoor/outdoor track, a weight room, varsity and intramural fields, a student union, volleyball, basketball, and racquetball courts, a swimming pool, and a dance studio. **Graduates:** From July 1, 2015 to June 30, 2016, 807 bachelor's degrees were awarded. The most popular majors were communications media (15%), business administration (13%), and nursing (8%). In an average class, 24% graduate in 4 years or less, 43% graduate in 5 years or less, and 51% graduate in 6 years or less. Of the 2015 graduating class, 10% were enrolled in graduate school within 6 months of graduation.

SERVICES: Counseling and information services are available, as is tutoring in most subjects. There is a reader service for the blind, and remedial math, reading, and writing. **Library/Resources:** The library contains 208,450 volumes, 125,344 microform items, and 2,774 audio/video tapes/CDs/DVDs, and subscribes to 757 periodicals including electronic. Computerized library services include interlibrary loans, database searching, Internet access, and Wi-Fi capability. Special learning facilities include an art gallery, and radio station. **Physically Challenged Students:** 85% of the campus is accessible. Facilities include wheelchair ramps, elevators, special parking, specially equipped restrooms, special class scheduling, lowered drinking fountains, lowered telephones, and special housing. **Special:** Students may cross-register at any other Massachusetts state universities. Internships in a variety of fields, study abroad in 9 countries, B.A. B.S. degrees, dual majors, and a student-designed interdisciplinary studies major are offered. There are 13 national honor societies, a freshman honors program, and 9 departmental honors programs. **Visiting:** There are regularly scheduled orientations for prospective students, tours of the campus, and residence halls, admissions/financial aid information, and academic program advising. There are guides for informal visits and visitors may sit in on classes. To schedule a visit, contact the Admissions Office. **Campus Safety and Security:** Measures include 24-hour foot and vehicle patrol, emergency notification system, self-defense education, and security escort services. There are shuttle buses, emergency telephones, lighted pathways/sidewalks, and controlled access to dorms/residences.

REQUIREMENTS: The SAT or ACT is required. Applicants should be graduates of accredited high schools or have the GED. Secondary preparation should include 4 years of English, 3 years each of math and liberal arts or phys ed, and 2 years each of a foreign language, social studies, including U.S. history, and science. AP and CLEP credits are accepted. Important factors in the admissions decision are advanced placement or honors courses, leadership record, and extracurricular activities record. All students must complete a minimum of 120 credit hours with a GPA of at least 2.0 overall and in the major (some majors require a higher GPA). Core coursework is required in the arts, science/math and technology, citizenship and the world, and global diversity. Also required are 2 introductory semesters of writing. **Procedure:** Freshmen are admitted fall and spring. Entrance exams should be taken in the junior or senior year. There are deferred admissions and rolling admissions plans. Applications should be filed by March 1 for fall entry; December 1 for spring entry, along with a $50 fee. Notification is sent on a rolling basis. Applications are accepted on-line. **Transfer Students:** 355 transfer students enrolled in 2015-2016. Applicants should have a minimum GPA of 2.0 in at least 12 credits of transferable college work. 45 of 120 credits required for the bachelor's degree must be completed at Fitchburg State. **International Students:** There are 133 international students enrolled. The school actively recruits these students. They must take the TOEFL with a minimum score of 550 on the paper-based TOEFL (PBT) or 79 on the Internet-based version (iBT). They must also take the SAT or ACT.

ADMISSIONS: 36% of the 2016-2017 applicants were accepted. The SAT scores for the 2016-2017 freshman class were: Critical Reading-- 48% below 500, 40% between 500 and 599, 11% between 600 and 699, and 1% between 700 and 800. Math-- 40% below 500, 46% between 500 and 599, 14% between 600 and 699, and 1% between 700 and 800. Writing-- 51% below 500, 39% between 500 and 599, 9% between 600 and 699, and 1% between 700 and 800. The ACT scores were 41% below 12, 37% between 12 and 17, 11% between 18 and 23, 7% between 24 and 29, and 4% above 30. **Admissions Contact:** Sean Ganas, irector of Admissions. Email: *admissions@fitchburgstate.edu* Web: *www.fitchburgstate.edu*

FINANCIAL AID: In 2016-2017, 83% of all full-time freshmen and 83% of continuing full-time students received some form of financial aid. The FAFSA code is 002184. The deadline for filing freshman financial aid applications for fall entry is March 1.

FRAMINGHAM STATE UNIVERSITY D-2

www.framingham.edu

Framingham, MA 01701 **(508) 626-4500**

Fax: (508) 626-4017 **Email: admissions@framingham.edu**

Full-time: 1456 men, 2245 women	**Faculty:** 194; IIA, av$
Part-time: 246 men, 390 women	**Ph.D.s:** 89%
Graduate: 393 men, 1247 women	**Student/Faculty:** 15 to 1
Year: semesters, summer session	**Tuition:** $9340 ($15,420)
Room & Board: $11,244	**Freshman Class:** 6204 applied, 4021 accepted, 749 enrolled
SAT CR/M/W: 480/500/480 **ACT:** 22	**CEEB CODE:** 3518
Application Deadline: February 15	**COMPETITIVE**

Framingham State University, founded in 1839, is a comprehensive public institution offering degree programs based on a liberal arts foundation that includes unique career programs. There are 4 undergraduate schools and 1 graduate school. In addition to regional accreditation, FSU has baccalaureate program accreditation with ADA and NLN. The 54-acre campus is in a suburban area 20 miles west of Boston. Including any residence halls, there are 23 buildings.

STUDENT LIFE: 95% of undergraduates are from Massachusetts. Others are from 21 states, 14 foreign countries, and Canada. 68% are White; 4% two or more races; 3% Asian American; 3% race unknown; 12% Hispanic; 10% African American. **Female To Male Ratio:** 1.9:1. The average age of freshmen is 18; all undergraduates, 22. 25% do not continue beyond their first year; 55% remain to graduate. **Housing:** 1996 students can be accommodated in college housing, which includes single-sex and coed dorms. On-campus housing is available on a first-come and first-served basis. 52% of students live on campus; of those, 72% remain on campus on weekends. Alcohol is not permitted. Upperclassmen may keep cars.

FACULTY/CLASSROOMS: 42% of faculty are male; 58% are female. All teach undergraduates. No introductory courses are taught by graduate students.

PROGRAMS OF STUDY: FSU confers B.A., B.S. and B.S.Ed. degrees. Master's degrees are also awarded. Bachelor's degrees are awarded in BIOLOGICAL SCIENCE (biochemistry, biology/biological science, and nutrition), BUSINESS (accounting, business administration and management, business and technology, fashion merchandising, finance, management, and marketing), COMMUNICATIONS AND THE ARTS (American Sign Language, art history and appreciation, communications, English, modern language, Spanish, and studio art), COMPUTER AND PHYSICAL SCIENCE (chemistry, computer science, and mathematics), EDUCATION (early childhood education, elementary education, and global studies), ENGINEERING AND ENVIRONMENTAL DESIGN (environmental science), HEALTH PROFESSIONS (nursing), SOCIAL SCIENCE (criminology, economics, fashion design and technology, food science, geography, history, interdisciplinary studies, political science/government, psychology, sociology, and textiles and clothing). Psychology, education, and management have the largest enrollments.

ACTIVITIES: There are no fraternities or sororities. There are 50 groups on campus, including art, cheerleading, chorus, computers, dance, drama, environmental, ethnic, honors, international, LGBT, literary magazine, musical theater, newspaper, political, professional, radio and TV, religious, social, social service, and student government. Popular campus events include Sandbox Festival, Homecoming and Family Weekend, Super Weekends and Semi-Formal Dance. **Sports:** There are 6 intercollegiate sports for men and 7 for women, and 9 intramural sports for men and 9 for women. Facilities include an athletic and recreation center, a gym, and student center. In addition, there are two all-weather turf fields for soccer, football, field hockey, softball, women's lacrosse, and intramural sports available on lower campus fields. **Graduates:** From July 1, 2015 to June 30, 2016, 969 bachelor's degrees were awarded. The most popular majors were psychology (10%), communication arts (8%), and business administration (8%). 250 companies recruited on campus in 2015-2016. In an average class, 36% graduate in 4 years or less, 53% graduate in 5 years or less, and 55% graduate in 6 years or less. Of the 2015 graduating class, 19% were enrolled in graduate school within 6 months of graduation, and 92% were employed.

SERVICES: Counseling and information services are available, as is tutoring in most subjects. There is a reader service for the blind, and remedial math, reading, and writing. The Center for Academic Success and Achievement is also available for tutoring. **Library/Resources:** The library contains 216,902 volumes, and 4,288 audio/video tapes/CDs/DVDs, and subscribes to 163 periodicals including electronic. Computerized library services include interlibrary loans, database searching, Internet access, and Wi-Fi capability. Special learning facilities include an art gallery, planetarium, radio station, Center for Global Education, Center for Social Research, Metrowest Economic Research Center, McAuliffe Center for Education and Teaching Excellence, Challenger Learning Center, NASA Educator Resource Center, Metrowest STEM Education Network, Child Development Laboratory, Education Curriculum Library, Entrepreneur Innovation Center, John C. Stalker Institute for Food and Nutrition, Framingham State/Boston Children's Hospital Food Study, Greenhouse, and a Planetarium. **Physically Challenged Students:** 95% of the campus is accessible. Facilities include wheelchair ramps, elevators, special parking, specially equipped restrooms, special class scheduling, lowered drinking fountains, and lowered telephones. **Special:** The university offers a 2-3 preengineering program in cooperation with the University of Massachusetts at Amherst, Lowell, and Dartmouth. Study abroad in 8 countries, a Washington semester, and various internships are available. Pass/fail options are limited to 2 courses. There are 11 national honor societies, a freshman honors program, and 8 departmental honors programs. **Visiting:** There are regularly scheduled orientations for prospective students, include campus tours, advising, and information sessions (majors, computing, campus life and resources). There are guides for informal visits and visitors may sit in on classes. To schedule a visit, contact the Office of Undergraduate Admissions. **Campus Safety and Security:** Measures include 24-hour foot and vehicle patrol, emergency notification system, self-defense education, and security escort services. There are shuttle buses, emergency telephones, lighted pathways/sidewalks, security cameras, and residence hall security and card access.

REQUIREMENTS: The SAT is required. Applicants must have a high school diploma or the GED. Secondary preparation must total 17 college-preparatory credits, including 4 years of English, 4 years of math, and 3 years of science (3 with lab), and 2 each of foreign language and social science. The required 2 years of electives may include additional academic subjects or art, music, or computer courses. Prospective studio art majors must submit a portfolio. AP and CLEP credits are accepted. Important factors in the admissions decision are advanced placement or honors courses, leadership record, and recommendations by school officials. The university's goal-based general education model includes writing, math, language, literature or philosophy, visual or performing arts, physical science, life science, historical studies, social and behavioral sciences, forces in the United States, study of Constitutions, gender, class, and race; and non-Western studies. Every student must take 12 general education courses and fulfill all required goals. A total of 128 credits (32 courses), including 40 to 68 credits in the major, and a 2.0 GPA are required to graduate. **Procedure:** Freshmen are admitted fall and spring. Entrance exams should be taken in the spring of the junior year or fall of the senior year. There are early admissions, deferred admissions, and rolling admissions plans. Applications should be filed by February 15 for fall entry; December 1 for spring entry, along with a $50 fee. Notification is sent on a rolling basis. Applications are accepted on-line. **Transfer Students:** 379 transfer students enrolled in 2015-2016. Applicants with more than 24 transferable college credits must present a college GPA between 2.00-2.50 for admission consideration; those with fewer than 24 transferable credits must also meet freshman admission requirements. Official transcripts must be submitted from all colleges previously attended at the time of application. 32 of 128 credits required for the bachelor's degree must be completed at FSU. **International Students:** They must take the TOEFL with a minimum score of 550 on the paper-based TOEFL (PBT) or 79 on the Internet-based version (iBT). They must also take the SAT or ACT.

ADMISSIONS: 65% of the 2016-2017 applicants were accepted. The SAT scores for the 2016-2017 freshman class were: Critical Reading-- 55% below 500, 34% between 500 and 599, 9% between 600 and 699, and 1% between 700 and 800. Math-- 48% below 500, 42% between 500 and 599, and 10% between 600 and 699. Writing-- 58% below 500, 35% between 500 and 599, 6% between 600 and 699, and 1% between 700 and 800. The ACT scores were 1% below 12, 11% between 12 and 17, 48% between 18 and 23, 38% between 24 and 29, and 2% above 30. **Admissions Contact:** Shayna Eddy, Director of Undergraduate Admissions. Email: *admissions@framingham.edu* Web: *www.framingham.edu*

FINANCIAL AID: In 2016-2017, 88% of all full-time freshmen and 78% of continuing full-time students received some form of financial aid. 71% of all full-time freshmen and 63% of continuing full-time students received need-based aid. The average freshman award was $9,911. Need-based scholarships or need-based grants averaged $3,229; need-based self-help aid (loans and jobs) averaged $5,254; and other non-need-based awards and non-need-based scholarships averaged $1,428. 60% of undergraduate students work part-time. Average annual earnings from campus work are $1050. The average financial indebtedness of the 2016 graduate was $19,300. FSU is a member of CSS. The FAFSA code is 002185. The priority date for freshman financial aid applications for fall entry is March 1.

FRANKLIN W. OLIN COLLEGE OF ENGINEERING D-2

www.olin.edu

Needham, MA 02492	781-292-2222
Fax: 781-292-2210	Email: info@olin.edu
Full-time: 178 men, 164 women	**Faculty:** 38
Part-time: 8 men, 20 women	**Ph.D.s:** 100%
Graduate: n/av	**Student/Faculty:** 8 to 1
Year: semesters	**Tuition:** $45,525
Room & Board: $15,600	**Freshman Class:** 983 applied, 118 accepted, 79 enrolled
SAT CR/M/W: 730/770/715 **ACT:** 33	**CEEB CODE:** 2824
Application Deadline: January 1	**MOST COMPETITIVE**

Olin College is an undergraduate engineering institution that has been exploring innovative approaches to engineering education since its founding in 1997. Olin's dual mission is to offer an innovative engineering program to talented undergraduate students and to play a leading role in the transformation of engineering education in the U.S. and abroad. Olin is increasingly recognized as a leader in engineering education reform for its interdisciplinary, hands-on curriculum and distinctive learning culture. There is 1 undergraduate school. In addition to regional accreditation, Olin College of Engineering has baccalaureate program accreditation with ABET. The 75-acre campus is in a suburban area 12 miles west of Boston. Including any residence halls, there are 10 buildings.

STUDENT LIFE: 86% of undergraduates are from out of state, mostly the West. Students are from 38 states, 12 foreign countries, and Canada. 8% are Foreign; 7% two or more races; 53% White; 5% Hispanic; 16% Asian American; 10% race unknown; 1% African American. **Male To Female Ratio:** 1.0:1. The average age of freshmen is 18; all undergraduates, 20. 4% do not continue beyond their first year; 95% remain to graduate. **Housing:** 354 students can be accommodated in college housing, which includes coed dorms. On-campus housing is guaranteed for all 4 years. All students may keep cars.

FACULTY/CLASSROOMS: 55% of faculty are male; 45% are female. All teach undergraduates. No introductory courses are taught by graduate students. The average class size in an introductory lecture is 20; in a laboratory is 15; and in a regular course is 20.

PROGRAMS OF STUDY: Olin College of Engineering confers B.S. degrees. Bachelor's degrees are awarded in ENGINEERING AND ENVIRONMENTAL DESIGN (electrical and computer engineering, engineering, and mechanical engineering).

ACTIVITIES: There are no fraternities or sororities. There are 55 groups on campus, including art, band, chess, chorus, computers, dance, drama, environmental, ethnic, film, international, LGBT, musical theater, newspaper, orchestra, political, professional, religious, social, social service, student government, and yearbook. Popular campus events include Candidates' Weekend, Family Weekend, SAC Carnival, and EXPO. **Sports:** **Graduates:** From July 1, 2015 to June 30, 2016, 84 bachelor's degrees were awarded. The most popular majors were engineering (47%), mechanical engineering (32%), and electrical and computer engineering (21%). 50 companies recruited on campus in 2015-2016. In an average class, 83% graduate in 4 years or less, 95% graduate in 5 years or less, and 95% graduate in 6 years or less. Of the 2015 graduating class, 10% were enrolled in graduate school within 6 months of graduation, and 85% were employed.

SERVICES: Counseling and information services are available, as is tutoring in every subject. **Library/Resources:** Computerized library services include interlibrary loans, database searching, Internet access, and Wi-Fi capability. **Physically Challenged Students:** All of the campus is accessible. Facilities include wheelchair ramps, elevators, special parking, specially equipped restrooms, special class scheduling, lowered drinking fountains, lowered telephones, and special housing. **Special:** Students may cross-register for courses at Babson College, Brandeis University, and Wellesley College. Many students choose to study away from Olin in an array of programs inside and outside of the US. **Visiting:** There are regularly scheduled orientations for prospective students, Information sessions are one hour long and are immediately followed by a one hour student-led tour (when student tour guides are available). Schedules vary. There are guides for informal visits, visitors may sit in on classes, and stay overnight. **Campus Safety and Security:** Measures include 24-hour foot and vehicle patrol and emergency notification system. There are shuttle buses, emergency telephones, lighted pathways/ sidewalks, and controlled access to dorms/residences.

REQUIREMENTS: The SAT or ACT is required. The ACT Optional Writing test is also required. A high school profile with a counselor's letter of recommendation and letters of recommendation from a core math or science teacher and one other teacher, as well as two essays (of 300 and 500 words in length) are required. All finalists for admission must have an on-campus interview. All students must complete a minimum of 120 credits, and must maintain a minimum cumulative GPA of 2.0 in order to graduate from Olin. Students must complete their program specific graduation requirements, as well as general requirements including 46 credits in Engineering, 30 credits in Math and Science, and 28 credits in Arts, Humanities, Social Sciences, and Entrepreneurship. All students complete an ambitious year-long culminating capstone that engages interdisciplinary student teams in significant design problems with realistic constraints for an external partner and prepares students for work in their chosen fields. **Procedure:** Freshmen are admitted fall. Entrance exams should be taken by December of the senior year. There is a deferred admissions plan. Applications should be filed by January 1 for fall entry, along with a $80 fee. Notifications are sent March 21. 57 applicants were on the 2016 waiting list; 5 were admitted. Applications are accepted on-line. **Transfer Students:** 8 transfer students enrolled in 2015-2016. Transfer students are subject to the same requirements, application process and deadlines as first-time students. **International Students:** There are 23 international students enrolled. They must also take the SAT or ACT.

ADMISSIONS: 12% of the 2016-2017 applicants were accepted. The SAT scores for the 2016-2017 freshman class were: Critical Reading-- 1% between 500 and 599, 25% between 600 and 699, and 74% between 700 and 800. Math-- 15% between 600 and 699 and 85% between 700 and 800. Writing-- 2% between 500 and 599, 35% between 600 and 699, and 63% between 700 and 800. The ACT scores were 3% between 24 and 29, and 97% above 30. There were 14 National Merit finalists. 10 freshmen graduated first in their class. **Admissions Contact:** Emily Roper-Doten, Dean of Admission and Financial Aid. Email: *info@olin.edu* Web: *www.olin.edu*

FINANCIAL AID: In 2016-2017, 100% of all full-time freshmen and 100% of continuing full-time students received some form of financial aid. 52% of all full-time freshmen and 48% of continuing full-time students received need-based aid. The average freshman award was $43,005. Need-based scholarships or need-based grants averaged $38,050 ($64,901 maximum); need-based self-help aid (loans and jobs) averaged $3,133 ($3,500 maximum); and other non-need-based awards and non-need-based scholarships averaged $20,177 ($22,750 maximum). 47% of undergraduate students work part-time. Average annual earnings from campus work are $4000. The average financial indebtedness of the 2016 graduate was $19,992. The FAFSA code is 039463. The deadline for filing freshman financial aid applications for fall entry is February 15.

GORDON COLLEGE — E-1
www.gordon.edu

Wenham, MA 01984	**(978) 867-4218** **(866) 464-6736**
Fax: (978) 867-4682	**Email: admissions@gordon.edu**
Full-time: 580 men, 994 women	**Faculty:** 90; IIB, +$
Part-time: 31 men, 52 women	**Ph.D.s:** 86%
Graduate: 83 men, 264 women	**Student/Faculty:** 12 to 1
Year: semesters, summer session	**Tuition:** $36,060
Room & Board: $10,412	**Freshman Class:** n/av
SAT CR/M/W: 557/551/549 **ACT:** 26	**CEEB CODE:** 3417
Application Deadline: February 1	**COMPETITIVE+**

The mission of Gordon College is to graduate men and women distinguished by intellectual maturity and Christian character, dedicated to lives of service and prepared for leadership worldwide. Gordon combines an exceptional liberal arts education with an informed Christian faith. Three pillars undergird this mission: stretch the mind, deepen the faith, and elevate the contribution. Gordon offers more than 90 areas of undergraduate study, as well as several graduate programs. There is 1 undergraduate school and 2 graduate schools. In addition to regional accreditation, Gordon has baccalaureate program accreditation with CSWE, NASDTEC, NASM, DECM, MBHE, and NEASC. The 485-acre campus is in a suburban area 25 miles north of Boston. Including any residence halls, there are 40 buildings.

STUDENT LIFE: 63% of undergraduates are from out of state, mostly the Northeast. Students are from 44 states, 55 foreign countries, and Canada. 63% are from public schools. 9% are Foreign; 7% Hispanic; 69% White; 5% African American; 5% Asian American; 4% two or more races; 1% race unknown. 94% are Protestant. **Female To Male Ratio:** 1.9:1. The average age of freshmen is 18; all undergraduates, 20. 14% do not continue beyond their first year; 71% remain to graduate. **Housing:** 1448 students can be accommodated in college housing, which includes single-sex and coed dorms, on-campus apartments, and married student housing. In addition, there are special-interest houses, and respond and reveal (reconciliation emphasis). On-campus housing is guaranteed for all 4 years. 96% of students live on campus; of those, 70% remain on campus on weekends. Alcohol is not permitted. All students may keep cars.

FACULTY/CLASSROOMS: 45% of faculty are male; 55% are female. 3% teach undergraduates, and 97% do both. No introductory courses are taught by graduate students. The average class size in an introductory lecture is 36; in a laboratory is 15; and in a regular course is 15.

PROGRAMS OF STUDY: Gordon confers B.A., B.S. and B.Mu. degrees. Master's degrees are also awarded. Bachelor's degrees are awarded in BIOLOGICAL SCIENCE (biology/biological science), BUSINESS (accounting, banking and finance, business administration and management, finance, and recreation and leisure services), COMMUNICATIONS AND THE ARTS (art, communications, dramatic arts, English, French, German, languages, linguistics, music, music performance, and Spanish), COMPUTER AND PHYSICAL SCIENCE (chemistry, computer science, mathematics, and physics), EDUCATION (early childhood education, elementary education, middle school education, music education, secondary education, and special education), HEALTH PROFESSIONS (physical therapy), SOCIAL SCIENCE (biblical studies, economics, history, international studies, philosophy, political science/government, psychology, social work, sociology, and youth ministry). Biology, biblical studies, psychology, education, music, and art are the strongest academically. Business administration, psychology, and biology have the largest enrollments.

ACTIVITIES: There are no fraternities or sororities. There are 120 groups on campus, including band, choir, chorale, chorus, computers, dance, debate, drama, environmental, extensive options for student outreaches, and off-campus ministries, film, honors, international, jazz band, literary magazine, musical theater, newspaper, orchestra, photography, political, professional, radio and TV, religious, social, social service, student government, and symphony. Popular campus events include Golden Goose, Gordon Globes, Senior Formal, Winter Ball, Gordon's Got Talent, Gordon's Amazing Race, Founders Ball, Christmas Gala, and Highland Games. **Sports:** There are 8 intercollegiate sports for men and 10 for women, and 14 intramural sports for men and 14 for women. Facilities include a gym, weight rooms, tennis courts, athletic fields, training room, indoor swimming pool, climbing wall, racquetball courts, aerobics room, ski/running trails, outdoor ropes course, sauna, indoor walking track, outdoor track, and field facilities. **Graduates:** From July 1, 2015 to June 30, 2016, 396 bachelor's degrees were awarded. The most popular majors were business admin & management (9%), English language & literature (7%), and social work (7%). 137 companies recruited on campus in 2015-2016. In an average class, 61% graduate in 4 years or less and 69% graduate in 6 years or less. Of the 2015 graduating class, 15% were enrolled in graduate school within 6 months of graduation, and 71% were employed.

SERVICES: There is a reader service for the blind, writing and academic support centers, and student tutors in many subjects. **Library/Resources:** The library contains 132,914 volumes, 154 microform items, and 5,987 audio/video tapes/CDs/DVDs, and subscribes to 1,540 periodicals including electronic. Computerized library services include interlibrary loans, database searching, Internet access, and Wi-Fi capability. Special learning facilities include an art gallery, radio station, electronic microscope, and human anatomy (cadaver) lab. **Physically Challenged Students:** 84% of the campus is accessible. Facilities include wheelchair ramps, elevators, special parking, specially equipped restrooms, special class scheduling, lowered drinking fountains, lowered telephones, and special housing. **Special:** Gordon offers a variety of internship experiences, including a package of global internship opportunities for students. The College permits cross-registration with other institutions in the Northeast Consortium of Colleges and Universities in Massachusetts. There is a 3-2 engineering program with the University of Southern California. B.A.- B.S. degrees, dual majors, student-designed majors, nondegree study, and pass/fail options are available. Off-campus study opportunities include a Washington semester, the Christian College Consortium Visitor Program, the LaVida Wilderness Expedition, and study abroad in Europe and Asia. Center for Entrepreneurial Leadership offers practical, creative, cross-disiplinary programs, and seeks to promote entrepreneurial thinking. There are 8 national honor societies, a freshman honors program, and 13 departmental honors programs. **Visiting:** There are regularly scheduled orientations for prospective students, consisting of numerous open house programs throughout the fall, winter and spring. There are guides for informal visits, visitors may sit in on classes, and stay overnight. To schedule a visit, contact Leah LaPalombara at (866) 464-6736. **Campus Safety and Security:** Measures include 24-hour foot and vehicle patrol, emergency notification system, self-defense education, and security escort services. There are shuttle buses, emergency telephones, lighted pathways/sidewalks, controlled access to dorms/residences, gated entrance, active threat training, and video surveillance.

REQUIREMENTS: The SAT or ACT is required. The ACT Optional Writing test is also required. Applicants must graduate from an accredited secondary school or have a GED. Home-schooled students are not required to provide a GED. A minimum of 17 Carnegie units is required, including 4 English courses and 2 courses each in math, science and social studies. Foreign language is a recommended elective. A personal statement, a personal reference, and an interview are required. Music majors must audition. Art majors must submit a portfolio for acceptance to the program. AP and CLEP credits are accepted. Important factors in the admissions decision are advanced placement or honors courses, evidence of special talent, personality/intangible qualities, extracurricular activities record, leadership record, recommendations by alumni, and geographical diversity. All students must demonstrate competency in writing, and foreign language. The common core curriculum consists of 36 credits 8 credits in biblical studies, 4 credits each in theology, social science, natural sciences, and humanities, 8 in language studies, and 4 in freshman seminar. 3 Physical and outdoor education courses. The general core consists of 12-16 credits (depending on foreign language fulfillment). 4 credits in natural science and 2-4 credits in each division (social science, fine arts, and literature). A total of 124 credits is required for graduation, with 20 or more Gordon credits in a major and a minimum cumulative GPA of 2.0. **Procedure:** Freshmen are admitted fall and spring. Entrance exams should be taken spring of the junior year and the fall of the senior year. There are deferred admissions and rolling admissions plans. Early decision applications should be filed by October 15; regular applications, by February 1 for fall entry; and December 15 for spring entry, along with a $50 fee. Notification of early decision is sent November 1; regular decision, February 15. 16 applicants were on the 2016 waiting list; 2 were admitted. Applications are accepted on-line. **Transfer Students:** 42 transfer students enrolled in 2015-2016. Applicants must have a minimum GPA of 2.00. College transcripts, high school transcripts, and SAT or ACT scores, if the applicant has completed less than 1 year of full time study, an interview, and personal and academic references are required. If you have less than 24 credit we also need office high and ACT/SAT scores in addtion to college transcript. 32 of 124 credits required for the bachelor's degree must be completed at Gordon. **International Students:** There are 152 international students enrolled. The school actively recruits these students. They must take the TOEFL with a minimum score of 85 on the Internet-based version (iBT), or take the SAT or ACT.

ADMISSIONS: The SAT scores for the 2016-2017 freshman class were: Critical Reading-- 29% below 500, 38% between 500 and 599, 25% between 600 and 699, and 8% between 700 and 800. Math-- 30% below 500, 38% between 500 and 599, 26% between 600 and 699, and 6% between 700 and 800. Writing-- 31% below 500, 38% between 500 and 599, 28% between 600 and 699, and 3% between 700 and 800. The ACT scores were 3% between 12 and 17, 30% between 18 and 23, 45% between 24 and 29, and 22% above 30. 49% of the current freshmen were in the top fifth of their class; 77% were in the top two fifths. There were 9 National Merit finalists. 24 freshmen graduated first in their class. **Admissions Contact:** June Bodoni, Associate Vice President for Enrollment. Email: *admissions@gordon.edu* Web: *www.gordon.edu*

FINANCIAL AID: In 2016-2017, 100% of all full-time freshmen and 98% of continuing full-time students received some form of financial aid. 62% of all full-time freshmen and 69% of continuing full-time students received need-based aid. The average freshman award was $24,811. Need-based scholarships or need-based grants averaged $20,550; need-based self-help aid (loans and jobs) averaged $4,832; and other non-need-based awards and non-need-based scholarships averaged $15,187. 70% of undergraduate students work part-time. Average annual earnings from campus work are $1470. The average financial indebtedness of the 2016 graduate was $36,557. Gordon is a member of CSS. The FAFSA code is 002153. The priority date for freshman financial aid applications for fall entry is March 1.

HAMPSHIRE COLLEGE — B-2

www.hampshire.edu

Amherst, MA 01002 — (413) 559-5752

Email: mtwombly@hampshire.edu

Full-time: 548 men, 848 women
Part-time: n/av
Graduate: n/av
Year: 4-1-4
Room & Board: $13,274
Application Deadline: January 15

Faculty: 119; IIB, +$
Ph.D.s: 93%
Student/Faculty: 12 to 1
Tuition: $50,550
Freshman Class: 2071 applied, 1450 accepted, 374 enrolled
CEEB CODE: 3447
MOST COMPETITIVE

Hampshire College, founded in 1965, is a private institution offering a liberal arts education with an emphasis on independent research, creative work, and multidisciplinary study. There are 5 undergraduate schools. The 800-acre campus is in a rural area in Amherst, Massachusetts. Including any residence halls, there are 30 buildings.

STUDENT LIFE: 81% of undergraduates are from out of state, mostly the Northeast. Students are from 46 states, and Canada. 65% are from public schools. 66% are White; 11% Hispanic; 7% two or more races; 5% Foreign; 4% African American; 4% race unknown; 2% Asian American; 1% American Indian/Alaska Native. **Female To Male Ratio:** 1.5:1. The average age of freshmen is 18; all undergraduates, 20. 18% do not continue beyond their first year; 74% remain to graduate. **Housing:** 1400 students can be accommodated in college housing, which includes single-sex and coed dorms and on-campus apartments. In addition, there are special-interest houses. We have 3 living and learning communities plus various themed housing options. On-campus housing is guaranteed for all 4 years. 82% of students live on campus. All students may keep cars.

FACULTY/CLASSROOMS: 44% of faculty are male; 56% are female. All teach undergraduates. No introductory courses are taught by graduate students. The average class size in a regular course is 14.

PROGRAMS OF STUDY: Hampshire confers B.A. degrees. Bachelor's degrees are awarded in AGRICULTURE (agriculture and animal science), BIOLOGICAL SCIENCE (biology/biological science, botany, ecology, marine biology, nutrition, and physiology), COMMUNICATIONS AND THE ARTS (art history and appreciation, communications, comparative literature, creative writing, dance, dramatic arts, film arts, fine arts, journalism, linguistics, literature, media arts, music, performing arts, photography, and video), COMPUTER AND PHYSICAL SCIENCE (chemistry, computer science, geology, mathematics, physics, and science), EDUCATION (education), ENGINEERING AND ENVIRONMENTAL DESIGN (architecture, environmental design, and environmental science), HEALTH PROFESSIONS (health science and premedicine), SOCIAL SCIENCE (African studies, African American studies, American studies, anthropology, Asian/Oriental studies, cognitive science, crosscultural studies, economics, family/consumer studies, geography, history, humanities, international relations, international studies, Judaic studies, Latin American studies, law, Middle Eastern studies, peace studies, philosophy, political science/government, psychology, religion, sociology, urban studies, and women's studies). Film, photography, and video are the strongest academically. Social sciences has the largest enrollment.

ACTIVITIES: There are no fraternities or sororities. There are 100 groups on campus, including art, chorus, computers, dance, drama, environmental, ethnic, film, international, LGBT, literary magazine, musical theater, newspaper, orchestra, photography, political, radio and TV, religious, social, social service, and student government. Popular campus events include Div Days, Hampshire Halloween, and Spring Jam. **Sports:** There are 3 intercollegiate sports for men and 3 for women, and 18 intramural sports for men and 18 for women. Facilities include 2 multipurpose sports centers housing a glass-enclosed swimming pool, a 12,000-square-foot playing floor, a 30-foot climbing wall, a weight-lifting area, 4 indoor tennis courts, and a jogging track. Other facilities include soccer fields, 10 outdoor tennis courts, 2 softball diamonds, and a 2-mile nature trail. **Graduates:** From July 1, 2015 to June 30, 2016, 291 bachelor's degrees were awarded. In an average class, 68% graduate in 6 years or less.

SERVICES: Counseling and information services are available, as is tutoring in most subjects. There is a reader service for the blind. There are also an advising center, a writing and reading program, and a lab quantitative skills program. **Library/Resources:** The library contains 129,804 volumes, 4,534 microform items, and 9,134 audio/video tapes/CDs/DVDs, and subscribes to 53,366 periodicals including electronic. Computerized library services include interlibrary loans, database searching, Internet access, and Wi-Fi capability. Special learning facilities include an art gallery, radio station, multimedia center, farm center, music and dance studios, optics lab, electronics shop, integrated greenhouse and aquaculture facility, fabrication shop, performing arts center, and the R.W. Kern Center Living Building Challenge is multi-functional as a living laboratory. **Physically Challenged Students:** 90% of the campus is accessible. Facilities include wheelchair ramps, elevators, special parking, specially equipped restrooms, special class scheduling, lowered drinking fountains, and lowered telephones. The college provides a variety of support services to meet individual special needs. **Special:** Cross-registration is possible with other members of the Five College Consortium (Amherst College, the University of Massachusetts, Smith

College, and Mount Holyoke). Internships, multidisciplinary dual majors, and study abroad (in the ISEP program, Tibetan Center, or a Costa Rica semester) are offered. All majors are student-designed. Students may complete their programs in fewer than 4 years. **Visiting:** There are regularly scheduled orientations for prospective students, including interviews, information sessions, campus tours, Discover Hampshire Days, Campus Visitation Days, and an overnight program. There are guides for informal visits, visitors may sit in on classes, and stay overnight. To schedule a visit, contact the Admissions Office. **Campus Safety and Security:** Measures include 24-hour foot and vehicle patrol and security escort services. There are lighted pathways/sidewalks, EMT on-call program, and dorm doors accessible by students only.

REQUIREMENTS: Applicants must submit all transcripts from 9th grade on or GED/state equivalency exam results. Students are required to submit a personal statement and an analytic essay or academic paper. An interview is recommended. AP credits are accepted. Important factors in the admissions decision are evidence of special talent, personality/intangible qualities, extracurricular activities record, and recommendations by school officials. All students must complete 3 divisions of study. In Division I: Basic Studies, students complete courses in cognitive science, humanities, arts and cultural studies, natural science, interdisciplinary arts, and social science and must complete 2 courses or the Division I exam project. In Division II: Concentration, students explore their field or fields of emphasis through individually designed internships or field studies. In Division III: Advanced Studies, students complete a major independent study project centered on a specific topic, question, or idea. Students must also partcipate in service to the college or the surrounding community and consider some aspect of their work from a non-Western perspective. **Procedure:** Freshmen are admitted fall and spring. There are early decision, early admissions, and deferred admissions plans. Early decision applications should be filed by November 15; regular applications, by January 15 for fall entry; and November 1 for spring entry. Notification of early decision is sent December 15; regular decision, April 1. 47 applicants were on the 2016 waiting list; 5 were admitted. Applications are accepted on-line. **Transfer Students:** 68 transfer students enrolled in 2015-2016. A proposed program of study, high school and college transcripts, and 1 recommendation must be submitted. Students can transfer in the fall, and spring. **International Students:** The school actively recruits these students. They must take the TOEFL.

ADMISSIONS: 70% of the 2016-2017 applicants were accepted. **Admissions Contact:** Meredith Twombly, Dean of Enrollment and Retention. Email: *mtwombly@hampshire.edu* Web: *www.hampshire.edu*

FINANCIAL AID: In 2016-2017, 61% of all full-time freshmen received some form of financial aid. 61% of all full-time freshmen received need-based aid. The average freshman award was $42,087. Need-based scholarships or need-based grants averaged $37,941; need-based self-help aid (loans and jobs) averaged $4,576; other non-need-based awards and non-need-based scholarships averaged $8,854; and $3,026 from other forms of aid. Hampshire is a member of CSS. The CSS/Profile, the college's own financial statement, and noncustodial parent statement are required. The FAFSA code is 004661. The priority date for freshman financial aid applications for fall entry is January 15.

HARVARD COLLEGE/HARVARD UNIVERSITY — D-2

www.college.harvard.edu

Cambridge, MA 02138 — **(617) 495-1551**

Fax: (617) 495-8821	**Email:** college@harvard.edu
Full-time: 3510 men, 3140 women	**Faculty:** I, ++$
Part-time: 10 men, 10 women	**Ph.D.s:** n/av
Graduate: 5565 men, 5350 women	**Student/Faculty:** n/av
Year: semesters, summer session	**Tuition:** $45,278
Room & Board: $15,381	**Freshman Class:** n/av
SAT or ACT: required	**CEEB CODE:** 3434
Application Deadline: January 1	**MOST COMPETITIVE**

Harvard College, founded in 1636, is the undergraduate college of Harvard University. The figures in the above capsule and in this profile are approximate. There are 4 undergraduate schools and 10 graduate schools. In addition to regional accreditation, Harvard has baccalaureate program accreditation with ABET. The 380-acre campus is in an urban area across the Charles River from Boston. Including any residence halls, there are 400 buildings.

STUDENT LIFE: 81% of undergraduates are from out of state, mostly the Middle Atlantic. Students are from 50 states, 118 foreign countries, and Canada. 67% are from public schools. 8% are African American; 8% Hispanic; 7% Foreign; 43% White; 17% Asian American; 1% American Indian/Alaska Native. **Male To Female Ratio:** 1.1:1. The average age of freshmen is 18; all undergraduates, 20. 96% remain to graduate. **Housing:** 6325 students can be accommodated in college housing, which includes coed dorms and on-campus apartments. On-campus housing is guaranteed for all 4 years. 97% of students live on campus. All students may keep cars.

FACULTY/CLASSROOMS: 98% teach undergraduates, 97% do research, and 95% do both. No introductory courses are taught by graduate students. The average class size in a regular course is 25.

PROGRAMS OF STUDY: Harvard confers A.B. and S.B. degrees. Master's and doctoral degrees are also awarded. Bachelor's degrees are awarded in BIOLOGICAL SCIENCE (biochemistry, biology/biological science, and biophysics), COMMUNICATIONS AND THE ARTS (art history and appreciation, Chinese, classics, creative writing, English, fine arts, folklore and mythology, French, German, Greek, Hebrew, Italian, Japanese, Latin, linguistics, literature, music, Portuguese, Russian, and Spanish), COMPUTER AND PHYSICAL SCIENCE (applied mathematics, astronomy, chemistry, computer science, geology, geophysics and seismology, mathematics, physical sciences, physics, and statistics), ENGINEERING AND ENVIRONMENTAL DESIGN (engineering, environmental design, environmental science, and preengineering), SOCIAL SCIENCE (African American studies, American studies, anthropology, Asian/Oriental studies, economics, European studies, history, humanities, Middle Eastern studies, philosophy, political science/government, psychology, religion, Russian and Slavic studies, Sanskrit and Indian studies, social science, social studies, sociology, and women's studies). Economics, government, and biology have the largest enrollments.

ACTIVITIES: There are no fraternities or sororities. There are 250 groups on campus, including art, band, cheerleading, chess, choir, chorale, chorus, computers, dance, debate, drama, ethnic, film, honors, international, jazz band, LGBT, literary magazine, marching band, musical theater, newspaper, opera, orchestra, pep band, photography, political, professional, radio and TV, religious, social, social service, student government, symphony, and yearbook. Popular campus events include Harvard/Yale Football, Head of the Charles Crew Regatta, and Cultural Rhythms Festival. **Sports:** There are 21 intercollegiate sports for men and 20 for women, and 16 intramural sports for men and 16 for women. Facilities include several gyms and athletic centers, pools, a track, boat houses, a sailing center, a hockey rink, and various courts and playing fields.

SERVICES: There is a reader service for the blind. Tutoring is available in all subjects. **Library/Resources:** The 97 libraries contain 15.0 million volumes, and subscribe to 100,000 periodicals including electronic. Computerized library services include interlibrary loans and database searching. Special learning facilities include an art gallery, natural history museum, planetarium, and radio station. **Physically Challenged Students:** Facilities include wheelchair ramps, elevators, special parking, specially equipped restrooms, special class scheduling, lowered drinking fountains, and lowered telephones. **Special:** Students may cross-register with MIT and with other schools within the university and may design their own concentrations or enroll for nondegree study. Internships and study abroad may be arranged. Accelerated degree programs, dual majors, a 3-2 engineering degree, and a combined A.B.-S.B. in engineering are offered. There are pass/fail options. There is a chapter of Phi Beta Kappa. **Visiting:** There are regularly scheduled orientations for prospective students, consisting of group information sessions and tours. There are guides for informal visits, visitors may sit in on classes, and stay overnight. To schedule a visit, contact the Undergraduate Admissions Office. **Campus Safety and Security:** Measures include 24-hour foot and vehicle patrol, self-defense education, and security escort services. There are shuttle buses, emergency telephones, and lighted pathways/sidewalks.

REQUIREMENTS: The ACT is required, as well as 3 SAT Subject tests. Applicants need not be high school graduates but are expected to be well prepared academically. An essay and an interview are required, in addition to a transcript, a counselor report, and 2 teacher recommendations from academic disciplines. AP credits are accepted. Important factors in the admissions decision are evidence of special talent, personality/intangible qualities, and recommendations by school officials. In 8 semesters, students must pass a minimum of 32 1-semester courses. The average course load is 4 courses per semester, but the course rate may be varied for special reasons. A typical balanced program devotes about one-fourth of its courses to core curriculum requirements, one-half to the concentration (or major field), and the remaining one-fourth to electives. **Procedure:** Freshmen are admitted fall. Entrance exams should be taken by January of the senior year. There is a deferred admissions plan. Early decision applications should be filed by November 1; regular applications, by January 1 for fall entry. The fall 2016 application fee was $65. Notification of early decision is sent December 1; regular decision, March 15. Applications are accepted on-line. **Transfer Students:** Transfer applicants must have completed at least 1 full year of daytime study in a degree-granting program at 1 institution. Students are required to submit the SAT or ACT, 2 letters of recommendation, high school and college transcripts with a dean's report, and several essays. 16 of 32 credits required for the bachelor's degree must be completed at Harvard. **International Students:** The school actively recruits these students. They must also take the SAT or ACT.

Admissions Contact: Marlyn McGrath, Director of Admissions. Email: *college@harvard.edu* Web: *www.college.harvard.edu*

FINANCIAL AID: Harvard is a member of CSS. The CSS/Profile, the college's own financial statement, and federal tax forms are required. The FAFSA code is E00468. Check with the school for current application deadlines.

HELLENIC COLLEGE/HOLY CROSS GREEK ORTHODOX SCHOOL OF THEOLOGY D-2

www.hchc.edu

Brookline, MA 02445	(617) 850-1285 (866) 424-2338
Fax: (617) 850-1460	Email: gfloor@hchc.edu
Full-time: 61 men, 38 women	**Faculty:** 13
Part-time: n/av	**Ph.D.s:** 90%
Graduate: 125 men, 16 women	**Student/Faculty:** 9 to 1
Year: semesters	**Tuition:** $23,714
Room & Board: $16,192	**Freshman Class:** 64 applied, 52 accepted, 38 enrolled
SAT CR/M/W: 550/450/460 **ACT:** 22	**CEEB CODE:** 3449
Application Deadline: August 1	**COMPETITIVE**

Hellenic College, founded in 1968, is a private college affiliated with the Greek Orthodox Church. It offers programs in the classics, elementary education, religious studies, human development, management and leadership, and literature and history. Figures in the above capsule and in this profile are approximate. There is 1 undergraduate school and 1 graduate school. In addition to regional accreditation, HCHC has baccalaureate program accreditation with NASDTEC. The 59-acre campus is in an urban area 4 miles southwest of Boston. Including any residence halls, there are 7 buildings.

STUDENT LIFE: 90% of undergraduates are from out of state, mostly the Midwest. Students are from 25 states, 9 foreign countries, and Canada. 90% are from public schools. 95% are White; 5% Hispanic; 13% Foreign. 95% are Eastern Orthodox. **Male To Female Ratio:** 3.4:1. The average age of freshmen is 20; all undergraduates, 22. 5% do not continue beyond their first year; 95% remain to graduate. **Housing:** 220 students can be accommodated in college housing, which includes coed dorms, on-campus apartments, and married student housing. On-campus housing is available on a first-come and first-served basis. 90% of students live on campus; of those, 90% remain on campus on weekends. Alcohol is not permitted. All students may keep cars.

FACULTY/CLASSROOMS: 70% of faculty are male; 30% are female. No introductory courses are taught by graduate students. The average class size in an introductory lecture is 20; in a laboratory is 20; and in a regular course is 15.

PROGRAMS OF STUDY: HCHC confers B.A. degrees. Master's degrees are also awarded. Bachelor's degrees are awarded in BUSINESS (business administration and management), COMMUNICATIONS AND THE ARTS (classics and literature), EDUCATION (elementary education), SOCIAL SCIENCE (history, human development, and religion). Religious studies, and elementary education are the strongest academically. Religious studies, and human development have the largest enrollments.

ACTIVITIES: There are no fraternities or sororities. Groups on campus include choir, ethnic, religious, social, social service, and student government. Popular campus events include Feast of the Holy Cross, Matriculation Day, and Campus Christmas Party. **Sports:** There are 4 intramural sports for men and 3 for women. Facilities include a gym, tennis, basketball, and racquetball courts, and a soccer field. **Graduates:** From July 1, 2015 to June 30, 2016, 12 bachelor's degrees were awarded. The most popular majors were religious studies (50%), management and leadership (25%), and human development (25%). In an average class, 97% graduate in 4 years or less. Of the 2015 graduating class, 60% were enrolled in graduate school within 6 months of graduation, and 30% were employed.

SERVICES: Counseling and information services are available, as is tutoring in some subjects. There is remedial math, reading, and writing. **Library/Resources:** The library contains 63,374 volumes, 883 microform items, and 3,015 audio/video tapes/CDs/DVDs, and subscribes to 720 periodicals including electronic. Computerized library services include interlibrary loans, database searching, and Internet access. **Physically Challenged Students:** 10% of the campus is accessible. Facilities include wheelchair ramps, elevators, special parking, specially equipped restrooms, and lowered drinking fountains. **Special:** The college offers cross-registration with Boston Theological Institute, Newbury College, and Boston College, credit by examination, and study abroad in Greece. There is a freshman honors program. **Visiting:** There are regularly scheduled orientations for prospective students, including observation of classroom and student life. There are guides for informal visits, visitors may sit in on classes, and stay overnight. To schedule a visit, contact the Office of Admissions. **Campus Safety and Security:** There are shuttle buses, lighted pathways/sidewalks, a 16-hour security patrol.

REQUIREMENTS: The SAT or ACT is required. Applicants should graduate from an accredited secondary school or have a GED. 15 academic credits are required, including 4 units of English, 2 each of math, foreign language, and social studies, and 1 of science. An essay is required. A GPA of 2.5 is required. AP and CLEP credits are accepted. Important factors in the admissions decision are recommendations by school officials, advanced placement or honors courses, and recommendations by alumni. To graduate, students must complete 129 credits, with 39 in the major, and maintain a minimum overall GPA of 2.0. General education requirements include 72 credits, with courses in English language and literature, music, history, science, philosophy, and social science. **Procedure:** Freshmen are admitted fall and spring. There are deferred admissions and rolling admissions plans. Early decision applications should be filed by December 1; regular applications, by August 1 for fall entry; and December 1 for spring entry. The fall 2016 application fee was $50. Notification of early decision is sent February 1; regular decision, June 15. **Transfer Students:** 11 transfer students enrolled in 2015-2016. An essay, college transcripts, recommendation letters, an interview, and a health certificate are required. SAT or ACT scores and high school transcripts are waived if the student has 24 or more college credit hours. 60 of 129 credits required for the bachelor's degree must be completed at HCHC. **International Students:** There are 5 international students enrolled. They must take the TOEFL with a minimum score of 500 on the paper-based TOEFL (PBT) or 61 on the Internet-based version (iBT).

ADMISSIONS: 81% of the 2016-2017 applicants were accepted. The SAT scores for the 2016-2017 freshman class were: Critical Reading-- 30% below 500, 35% between 500 and 599, 30% between 600 and 699, and 5% between 700 and 800. Math-- 55% below 500, 35% between 500 and 599, 5% between 600 and 699, and 5% between 700 and 800. Writing-- 45% below 500, 35% between 500 and 599, and 20% between 600 and 699. The ACT scores were 20% below 12, 60% between 12 and 17, 20% between 18 and 23. **Admissions Contact:** Gregory Floor , Director for Admissions. Email: *gfloor@hchc.edu* Web: *www.hchc.edu*

FINANCIAL AID: In 2016-2017, 95% of all full-time freshmen and 95% of continuing full-time students received some form of financial aid. 95% of all full-time freshmen and 95% of continuing full-time students received need-based aid. 36% of undergraduate students work part-time. Average annual earnings from campus work are $1600. The average financial indebtedness of the 2016 graduate was $31,000. The college's own financial statement is required. The FAFSA code is 002154. Check with the school for current application deadlines.

LASELL COLLEGE D-2
www.lasell.edu

Newton, MA 02466 (617) 243-2225
(888) LASELL-4
Fax: (617) 243-2380 Email: info@lasell.edu

Full-time: 605 men, 1142 women
Part-time: 17 men, 14 women
Graduate: 95 men, 221 women
Year: semesters, summer session
Room & Board: $13,900
SAT: required **ACT:** 21
Application Deadline: September 1

Faculty: 93; IIB, av$
Ph.D.s: 78%
Student/Faculty: 19 to 1
Tuition: $33,600
Freshman Class: 3240 applied, 2456 accepted, 439 enrolled
CEEB CODE: 3481
COMPETITIVE

An innovator in education for over 160 years, Lasell College today is a comprehensive coeducational college offering professionally oriented bachelor's and masters degree programs. Lasell encourages students to explore new ideas and shared interests through high impact learning experiences including internships, service learning, international study and a collaborative, problem based learning approach that engages students in the work of their field. The College offers over 40 undergraduate majors and minors. There is 1 undergraduate school and 1 graduate school. In addition to regional accreditation, Lasell has baccalaureate program accreditation with ACBSP, NCATE, CAATE, CAHE, and COSMA. The 53-acre campus is in a suburban area in Newton, Massachusetts, at the interchange of Route 95 and the Massachusetts Turnpike, 8 miles west of Boston. Including any residence halls, there are 51 buildings.

STUDENT LIFE: 54% of undergraduates are from Massachusetts. Others are from 26 states, and 26 foreign countries. 80% are from public schools. 9% are Hispanic; 70% White; 6% Foreign; 5% African American; 5% race unknown; 2% Asian American; 2% two or more races. **Female To Male Ratio:** 1.9:1. The average age of freshmen is 18; all undergraduates, 20. 20% do not continue beyond their first year; 51% remain to graduate. **Housing:** 1325 students can be accommodated in college housing, which includes single-sex and coed dorms and on-campus apartments. In addition, there are special-interest houses, and community service house. On-campus housing is guaranteed for all 4 years, and is available on a first-come, first-served basis, and is available on a lottery system for upperclassmen. 75% of students live on campus; of those, 55% remain on campus on weekends. Upperclassmen may keep cars.

FACULTY/CLASSROOMS: 44% of faculty are male; 56% are female. All teach undergraduates. No introductory courses are taught by graduate students. The average class size in a regular course is 17.

PROGRAMS OF STUDY: Lasell confers B.A., and B.S. degrees. Master's degrees are also awarded. Bachelor's degrees are awarded in AGRICULTURE (environmental studies), BUSINESS (accounting, banking and finance, business administration and management, entrepreneurial studies, fashion merchandising, hospitality management services, international business management, marketing/retailing/merchandising, sports management, and tourism), COMMUNICATIONS AND THE ARTS (advertising, communications, English, graphic design, journalism, media arts, multimedia, public relations, sports media, and video), COMPUTER AND PHYSICAL SCIENCE (applied mathematics and web technology), EDUCATION (athletic training, early childhood education, elementary education, secondary education, and sports studies), SOCIAL SCIENCE (child care/child and family studies, criminal justice, fashion design and technology, history, human services, humanities, interdisciplinary studies, law, liberal arts/general studies, physical fitness/movement, psychology, and sociology). Athletic training, fashion design, and management are the strongest academically. Communication, fashion & retail management, and sport management have the largest enrollments.

ACTIVITIES: There are no fraternities or sororities. There are 74 groups on campus, including art, cheerleading, chorale, chorus, dance, drama, environmental, ethnic, honors, international, jazz band, LGBT, literary magazine, newspaper, political, professional, radio and TV, religious, social, social service, student government, and yearbook. Popular campus events include River Day, Torchlight Parade, Awards Night, and Rugby. **Sports:** There are 8 intercollegiate sports for men and 9 for women, and 5 intramural sports for men and 5 for women. Facilities include an athletic center with basketball courts, volleyball court, an indoor track, dance studio, locker rooms, tennis courts, 2 fitness centers, 2 athletic fields, and a Stoller Boat House on the Charles River. **Graduates:** From July 1, 2015 to June 30, 2016, 421 bachelor's degrees were awarded. The most popular majors were communication (11%), fashion and retail merchandising (10%), and fashion design and production (9%). 43 companies recruited on campus in 2015-2016. In an average class, 46% graduate in 4 years or less, 50% graduate in 5 years or less, and 51% graduate in 6 years or less. Of the 2015 graduating class, 10% were enrolled in graduate school within 6 months of graduation, and 83% were employed.

SERVICES: Counseling and information services are available, as is tutoring in most subjects. There is remedial math and writing. The Academic Achievement Center offers individual assistance in math, accounting, and many other subjects, as well as in techniques for writing, coaching on presentation skills, and improving reading comprehension, as well as providing special resources for students with documented learning disabilities. **Library/Resources:** The library contains 35,832 volumes, and 4,392 audio/video tapes/CDs/DVDs, and subscribes to 131 periodicals including electronic. Computerized library services include interlibrary loans, database searching, Internet access, and Wi-Fi capability. Special learning facilities include an art gallery, and radio station. Special learning facilities includes our academic achievement center, Lasell Village (continuing care retirement community), the Center for Community-Based Learning, the Center for Teaching and Learning, two child study centers, a cultural center, and a fashion collection. **Physically Challenged Students:** Facilities include wheelchair ramps, elevators, special parking, specially equipped restrooms, special class scheduling, and lowered drinking fountains. **Special:** All academic programs require at least one internship, and student employment options are available on campus. Student-designed majors are possible, as is a 5th year master's degree option. Over 25% of Lasell graduates have a college sponsored international learning experience, including study abroad (over 90 options), international service and departmental trips. Over 90% of graduates participated in service learning programs. Multiple programs can be completed in three years under guidance from professional advisor. All programs feature connected learning, which is an ongoing practical application of classroom theory. Additionally, the College has cross registration with Regis College and participates in the Washington semester program at American University. There is a freshman honors program. **Visiting:** There are regularly scheduled orientations for prospective students, consisting of the president's welcome, faculty presentations, tours, and student panels. There are guides for informal visits, visitors may sit in on classes, and stay overnight. To schedule a visit, contact The Office of Undergraduate Admission. **Campus Safety and Security:** Measures include 24-hour foot and vehicle patrol, emergency notification system, self-defense education, and security escort services. There are shuttle buses, emergency telephones, lighted pathways/sidewalks, and controlled access to dorms/residences.

REQUIREMENTS: The SAT is required. Applicants should have completed 16 Carnegie units of high school study. The GED is accepted. Two letters of recommendation and a personal essay are required, and an interview is recommended. AP and CLEP credits are accepted. Important factors in the admissions decision are advanced placement or honors courses, personality/intangible qualities, and leadership record. A graduate of Lasell receives the degree of Bachelor of Arts or Bachelor of Science. Specific requirements of the various curricula are described under each major. In order to graduate, each student must earn a minimum of 120 credits of academic work; out of these 120 credits, students must complete a minimum of 42 credits in the arts and sciences. Most degree programs at the College require between 120 and 127 credits to graduate. Lasell College allows a maximum of 90 transferable credits, the final semester of which must be at Lasell College, attain a cumulative GPA of 2.0 or higher, complete a major degree program, and meet Lasell's Core Curriculum competencies. All degree programs have additional requirements described in the catalog. **Procedure:** Freshmen are admitted fall and spring. There are early admissions, deferred admissions, and rolling admissions plans. Applications should be filed by September 1 for fall entry, along with a $40 fee. Notifications are sent December 1. Applications are accepted on-line. Application fees are waived if application is completed on-line. **Transfer Students:** 67 transfer students enrolled in 2015-2016. Applicants must submit an application, final secondary school transcript if 24 college credits), official college/university transcripts, official SAT/ACT scores (if 24 college credits), personal statement or essay, 2 recommendations (1 must be academic), and if English is not the native language, applicants must submit

TOEFL or other English proficiency exam score. 30 of 120 credits required for the bachelor's degree must be completed at Lasell. **International Students:** There are 113 international students enrolled. The school actively recruits these students. They must take the TOEFL with a minimum score of 525 on the paper-based TOEFL (PBT) or 71 on the Internet-based version (iBT), and take the IELTS. They must also take the SAT or ACT.

ADMISSIONS: 76% of the 2016-2017 applicants were accepted. The SAT scores for the 2016-2017 freshman class were: Critical Reading-- 55% below 500, 36% between 500 and 599, 8% between 600 and 699, and 1% between 700 and 800. Math-- 59% below 500, 33% between 500 and 599, 7% between 600 and 699, and 1% between 700 and 800. Writing-- 59% below 500, 33% between 500 and 599, 7% between 600 and 699, and 1% between 700 and 800. The ACT scores were 17% between 12 and 17, 55% between 18 and 23, 26% between 24 and 29, and 2% above 30. **Admissions Contact:** James M. Tweed, AVP Enroll Mgmt, Dean UG Admis & Fin Aid. Email: *info@lasell.edu* Web: *www.lasell.edu*

FINANCIAL AID: In 2016-2017, 94% of all full-time freshmen and 94% of continuing full-time students received some form of financial aid. 87% of all full-time freshmen and 79% of continuing full-time students received need-based aid. The average freshman award was $26,718. Need-based scholarships or need-based grants averaged $22,814 ($46,760 maximum); need-based self-help aid (loans and jobs) averaged $4,158 ($5,500 maximum); and other non-need-based awards and non-need-based scholarships averaged $10,249 ($42,348 maximum). 70% of undergraduate students work part-time. Average annual earnings from campus work are $1500. The average financial indebtedness of the 2016 graduate was $39,852. Lasell is a member of CSS. The priority date for freshman financial aid applications for fall entry is March 1.

LESLEY UNIVERSITY D-2

www.lesley.edu

Cambridge, MA 02138	(617) 349-8800 (800) 999-1959
Fax: (617) 349-8810	Email: admissions@lesley.edu
Full-time: 331 men, 1019 women	Faculty: 80; IIA, av$
Part-time: 19 men, 49 women	Ph.D.s: 85%
Graduate: 444 men, 2641 women	Student/Faculty: 20 to 1
Year: semesters, summer session	Tuition: $26,250
Room & Board: $15,300	Freshman Class: 3115 applied, 2135 accepted, 379 enrolled
SAT CR/M/W: 545/520/540 ACT: 23	CEEB CODE: 3483
Application Deadline: February 15	COMPETITIVE

Lesley University, founded in 1909, is a private undergraduate institution, offering degree programs in education, human services, and the arts. Expanded resources, course work, and opportunities are available to students through the larger coeducational Lesley University system, including cross-registration with the Lesley University College of Art and Design. Figures in the above capsule and in this profile are approximate. Tuition and fees, varies by undergraduate and graduate programs. There are 2 undergraduate schools and 2 graduate schools. In addition to regional accreditation, Lesley has baccalaureate program accreditation with NASAD, TEAC, AACTE, and CACREP. The 5-acre campus is in an urban area outside of Harvard Square in Cambridge, MA. Including any residence halls, there are 53 buildings.

STUDENT LIFE: 57% of undergraduates are from out of state, mostly the Northeast. Students are from 33 states, 24 foreign countries, and Canada. 84% are from public schools. 71% are White; 7% Hispanic; 4% Asian American; 4% Foreign; 4% two or more races; 2% African American; 12% race unknown. **Female To Male Ratio:** 4.7:1. The average age of freshmen is 18; all undergraduates, 20. 27% do not continue beyond their first year; 73% remain to graduate. **Housing:** 803 students can be accommodated in college housing, which includes single-sex and coed dorms. In addition, there are special-interest houses, theme housing, and wellness housing. There are also Victorian houses, and suite-style residence. On-campus housing is available on a first-come and first-served basis. 60% of students live on campus. All students may keep cars.

FACULTY/CLASSROOMS: 44% of faculty are male; 56% are female. All teach undergraduates, and all do research. No introductory courses are taught by graduate students. The average class size in an introductory lecture is 20; in a laboratory is 14; and in a regular course is 14.

PROGRAMS OF STUDY: Lesley confers B.S. and B.F.A. degrees. Associate, master's, and doctoral degrees are also awarded. Bachelor's degrees are awarded in BUSINESS (management science), COMMUNICATIONS AND THE ARTS (creative writing and visual and performing arts), COMPUTER AND PHYSICAL SCIENCE (natural sciences), EDUCATION (early childhood education, elementary education, middle school education, and special education), SOCIAL SCIENCE (human services, humanities, psychology, and social science). Education, counseling, and photography & art therapy have the largest enrollments.

ACTIVITIES: There are no fraternities or sororities. There are 25 groups on campus, including Third Wave (a women's group), Student Athlete Advisory Committee, choir, chorus, dance, drama, ethnic, international, LGBT, literary magazine, musical theater, newspaper, photography, political, professional, religious, Second Start, social, social service, and student government. Popular campus events include Family and Friends Weekend, Quad Fest, and World Fest. **Sports:** There are 7 intercollegiate sports for men and 7 for women, and 3 intramural sports for men and 5 for women. Facilities include outdoor tennis courts, and a fitness center with Nautilus circuit, free weights, and cardiovascular equipment. Students may also use an Olympic-size swimming pool at a nearby school as well as the indoor and outdoor facilities, including two full-size basketball courts, two racquetball courts, a rowing tank, a softball court, an indoor track and a lighted outdoor soccer field. **Graduates:** From July 1, 2015 to June 30, 2016, 453 bachelor's degrees were awarded. The most popular majors were visual and performing arts (25%), psychology (19%), and education (13%). 100 companies recruited on campus in 2015-2016. In an average class, 33% graduate in 4 years or less, 10% graduate in 5 years or less, and 3% graduate in 6 years or less.

SERVICES: Counseling and information services are available, as is tutoring in most subjects. There is a reader service for the blind, and remedial math. **Library/Resources:** The 2 libraries contain 124,022 volumes, 878,938 microform items, and 42,680 audio/video tapes/CDs/DVDs, and subscribe to 861 periodicals including electronic. Computerized library services include interlibrary loans, database searching, Internet access, and Wi-Fi capability. Special learning facilities include an art gallery, center for teaching resources, media production facility, and instructional computing and math achievement center. **Physically Challenged Students:** 85% of the campus is accessible. Facilities include wheelchair ramps, elevators, special parking, specially equipped restrooms, special class scheduling, lowered drinking fountains. The Disability Services Office provides document review and arranges for reasonable accommodations for special needs students. **Special:** Study abroad in Cuba, England, and Sweden, and 6 others by arrangement, a Washington Justice semester, and on-campus work-study programs are offered. All students participate in at least 3 field placement experiences, beginning in their freshman year. There are combined accelerated degree programs in management, counseling, and education majors. Dual majors and student-designed majors are also available. Accelerated and weekend course programs as well as cross-registration with AIB are offered for Adult Baccalaureate College and School of Education. There is a freshman honors program and 2 departmental honors programs. **Visiting:** There are regularly scheduled orientations for prospective students, which includes personal interviews with professional staff, student campus tours, information sessions, class visits, and meetings with financial aid. There are guides for informal visits, visitors may sit in on classes, and stay overnight. To schedule a visit, contact the Admissions Office. **Campus Safety and Security:** Measures include 24-hour foot and vehicle patrol, self-defense education, and security escort services. There are shuttle buses, emergency telephones, lighted pathways/sidewalks, and watch tours.

REQUIREMENTS: It is recommended that students complete 20 academic units in high school, including 4 in English, 3 each in science, with 2 units in lab, and math, and 1 each in history, and social studies, and 4 in academic electives. SAT or ACT scores, a writing sample, and 2 recommendations are also required as part of the application, and a personal interview is recommended. Applicants must have a high school diploma from an accredited secondary school or a GED. AP and CLEP credits are accepted. Important factors in the admissions decision are evidence of special talent, personality/intangible qualities, recommendations by school officials, and advanced placement or honors courses. Students must complete 45 hours of general education requirements, including 15 of humanities, 12 of natural science, 9 of social science, 6 of multicultural perspectives, and 3 of first-year seminar, emphasis is given to cross-curriculum components in writing, critical and quantitative reasoning, global perspectives, and leadership and ethics. Art Institute of Boston Students must also complete a foundation year. To graduate, students need 128 total credit hours, including 30 to 33 in the liberal arts majors or 41 to 43 in professional majors. **Procedure:** Freshmen are admitted fall and spring. Entrance exams should be taken by February 15. There are deferred admissions and rolling admissions plans. Early decision applications should be filed by December 1; regular applications, by February 15 for fall entry; and November 1 for spring entry, along with a $50 fee. Notification of early decision is sent January 1; regular decision, on a rolling basis. 2 applicants were on the 2016 waiting list. Applications are accepted on-line. **Transfer Students:** 124 transfer students enrolled in 2015-2016. Applicants must have a minimum 2.5 GPA. They must provide high school and college transcripts, complete an essay or personal statement, and have a statement of good standing from prior institution. An interview is recommended for all Lesley College students and required of all Art Institute of Boston Students. 45 of 124 credits required for the bachelor's degree must be completed at Lesley. **International Students:** There are 32 international students enrolled. The school actively recruits these students. They must take the TOEFL with a minimum score of 500 on the paper-based TOEFL (PBT).

ADMISSIONS: The SAT scores for the 2016-2017 freshman class were: Critical Reading-- 26% below 500, 48% between 500 and 599, 22% between 600 and 699, and 3% between 700 and 800. Math-- 37% below 500, 46% between 500 and 599, and 16% between 600 and 699. Writing-- 29% below 500, 47% between 500 and 599, 22% between 600 and 699, and 2% between 700 and 800. The ACT scores were 5% between 12 and 17, 36% between 18 and 23, 54% between 24 and 29, and 5% above 30. 40% of the current freshmen were in the top fifth of their class; 75% were in the top two fifths. **Admissions Contact:** Deb Kocar, Director of Admissions. Email: *admissions@lesley.edu* Web: *www.lesley.edu*

FINANCIAL AID: In 2016-2017, 75% of all full-time freshmen and 70% of continuing full-time students received some form of financial aid. 75% of all full-time freshmen and 71% of continuing full-time students received need-based aid. The average freshman award was $14,886. Need-based scholarships or need-based grants averaged $8,614; need-based self-help aid (loans and jobs) averaged $4,996; other non-need-based awards and non-need-based scholarships averaged $10,553; and $3,805 from other forms of aid. 25% of undergraduate students work part-time. Average annual earnings from campus work are $1400. The average financial indebtedness of the 2016 graduate was $18,000. The college's own financial statement, and parent and student federal tax returns are required. The FAFSA code is 002160. The priority date for freshman financial aid applications for fall entry is February 15.

MASSACHUSETTS COLLEGE OF ART AND DESIGN *(The complete profile is made available exclusively on our website, www.barronspac.com)*

MASSACHUSETTS COLLEGE OF LIBERAL ARTS A-1

www.mcla.edu

North Adams, MA 01247 **(413) 662-5410**

Fax: (413) 662-5179	**Email: admissions@mcla.edu**
Full-time: 489 men, 766 women	**Faculty:** 91
Part-time: 51 men, 137 women	**Ph.D.s:** 86%
Graduate: 73 men, 127 women	**Student/Faculty:** 12 to 1
Year: semesters, summer session	**Tuition:** $11,080 ($18,995)
Room & Board: $10,078	**Freshman Class:** 2013 applied, 1551 accepted, 327 enrolled
SAT CR/M: 520/500 **ACT:** 23	**CEEB CODE:** 3521
Application Deadline: open	**COMPETITIVE**

Massachusetts College of Liberal Arts delivers a high-quality, affordable education that provides students with the critical thinking and communication skills of greatest value to their development, their community, and their future employers. As the public liberal arts college of the Commonwealth, MCLA is committed to preparing students for success at work and in life. MCLA provides unmatched, hands-on growth opportunities early, and often, in an inspiring, creative community. In addition to regional accreditation, MCLA has baccalaureate program accreditation with CAATE. The 80-acre campus is in a rural area 45 miles east of Albany, NY. Including any residence halls, there are 20 buildings.

STUDENT LIFE: 74% of undergraduates are from Massachusetts. Others are from 19 states, and 2 foreign countries. 9% are African American; 73% White; 7% Hispanic; 5% race unknown; 2% Asian American; 2% two or more races. **Male To Female Ratio:** 5.6:1. The average age of freshmen is 18; all undergraduates, 22. 22% do not continue beyond their first year; 52% remain to graduate. **Housing:** 1020 students can be accommodated in college housing, which includes single-sex and coed dorms and on-campus apartments. In addition, there are special-interest houses. On-campus housing is guaranteed for all 4 years. 60% of students live on campus. All students may keep cars.

FACULTY/CLASSROOMS: 48% of faculty are male; 52% are female. No introductory courses are taught by graduate students.

PROGRAMS OF STUDY: MCLA confers B.A. and B.S. degrees. Master's degrees are also awarded. Bachelor's degrees are awarded in AGRICULTURE (environmental studies), BIOLOGICAL SCIENCE (biology/biological science), BUSINESS (accounting and business administration and management), COMMUNICATIONS AND THE ARTS (art, arts administration/management, communications, English, English literature, English Writing, fine arts, performing arts, and visual and performing arts), COMPUTER AND PHYSICAL SCIENCE (chemistry, computer science, mathematics, and physics), EDUCATION (athletic training, childhood education, education, mathematics education, middle school education, and secondary education), HEALTH PROFESSIONS (allied health, cytotechnology, and pre-health studies), SOCIAL SCIENCE (history, interdisciplinary studies, liberal arts/general studies, philosophy, philosophy and religion, political science/government, psychology, public administration, and sociology).

ACTIVITIES: There are 50 groups on campus, including band, cheerleading, choir, chorale, chorus, computers, dance, drama, environmental, ethnic, honors, international, jazz band, LGBT, literary magazine, musical theater, newspaper, photography, political, professional, radio and TV, religious, social, social service, student government, and yearbook. **Sports:** There are 6 intercollegiate sports for men and 7 for women. Facilities include a campus center with a swimming pool, weight rooms, a fitness center, handball, squash, and racquetball courts. The campus also features an outdoor complex with tennis courts and soccer, baseball, and softball fields, a 1,750-seat gym, and a 5-mile cross-country running trail. **Graduates:** From July 1, 2015 to June 30, 2016, 354 bachelor's degrees were awarded. The most popular majors were business (18%), English (13%), and biology (11%). In an average class, 38% graduate in 4 years or less, 50% graduate in 5 years or less, and 53% graduate in 6 years or less.

SERVICES: Counseling and information services are available, as is tutoring in some subjects. There is remedial math, reading, and writing. **Library/Resources:** The library contains 170,000 volumes, 290,000 microform items, and 6,300 audio/video tapes/CDs/DVDs, and subscribes to 70 periodicals including electronic. Computerized library services include interlibrary loans, database searching, and Internet access. Special learning facilities include an art gallery, radio station, and TV station. **Physically Challenged Students:** 98% of the campus is accessible. Facilities include wheelchair ramps, elevators, special parking, specially equipped restrooms, and special class scheduling. **Special:** There are 8 national honor societies, a freshman honors program, and 7 departmental honors programs. **Visiting:** There are regularly scheduled orientations for prospective students. There are guides for informal visits and visitors may sit in on classes. To schedule a visit, contact Admissions Office. **Campus Safety and Security:** Measures include 24-hour foot and vehicle patrol, emergency notification system, self-defense education, and security escort services. There are emergency telephones and lighted pathways/sidewalks.

REQUIREMENTS: The SAT or ACT is required. MCLA's admission criteria can be described as moderately selective with a strong emphasis placed on a student's academic performance in high school. Successful candidates for admission should meet MCLA's sliding scale which correlates high school grade point average with SAT or ACT scores. Secondly, applicants should demonstrate completion of 17 Carnegie units, including 4 courses in English, 4 each in science and math, and 2 each in foreign language, history/social science, and electives. The GED is also accepted. A GPA of 2.0 is required. AP and CLEP credits are accepted. All students must complete at least 120 credits, including 40 in the core curriculum, and maintain a GPA of at least 2.0. **Procedure:** Freshmen are admitted fall and spring. Entrance exams should be taken by January of the senior year. There are early decision, early admissions, deferred admissions, and rolling admissions plans. Application deadlines are open. The fall 2016 application fee was $40. Notification is sent on a rolling basis. Applications are accepted on-line. **Transfer Students:** 144

transfer students enrolled in 2015-2016. MCLA's transfer policy is highly dependent on a student's performance at their previous college (s). A minimum grade point average of 2.5 is expected for admission. Students applying without an earned Associate's degree must submit official high school transcript and standardized test scores as well. 45 of 120 credits required for the bachelor's degree must be completed at MCLA. **International Students:** There are 7 international students enrolled. The school actively recruits these students. They must take the TOEFL with a minimum score of 550 on the paper-based TOEFL (PBT). They must also take the SAT.

Admissions Contact: Gina Puc, Director of Admissions. Email: *admissions@mcla.edu* Web: *www.mcla.edu*

FINANCIAL AID: In 2016-2017, 80% of all full-time freshmen and 81% of continuing full-time students received some form of financial aid. 70% of all full-time freshmen and 69% of continuing full-time students received need-based aid. The average freshman award was $15,549. Need-based scholarships or need-based grants averaged $6,942; and need-based self-help aid (loans and jobs) averaged $3,540. The average financial indebtedness of the 2016 graduate was $29,933. MCLA is a member of CSS. The priority date for freshman financial aid applications for fall entry is March 1.

MASSACHUSETTS INSTITUTE OF TECHNOLOGY D-2
web.mit.edu

Cambridge, MA 02139 **(617) 253-3400**

Fax: (617) 258-8304	**Email:** admissions@mit.edu
Full-time: 2426 men, 2066 women	**Faculty:** 1022; I, ++$
Part-time: 19 men, 16 women	**Ph.D.s:** 97%
Graduate: 4539 men, 2265 women	**Student/Faculty:** 4 to 1
Year: 4-1-4, summer session	**Tuition:** $46,704
Room & Board: $13,730	**Freshman Class:** 18,306 applied, 1519 accepted, 1107 enrolled
SAT CR/M/W: 730/780/740 **ACT:** 34	**CEEB CODE:** 3514
Application Deadline: January 1	**MOST COMPETITIVE**

MIT, founded in 1861, is a private, independent, institution offering programs in architecture and planning, engineering, humanities, arts, social sciences, management, science, health sciences, and technology. There are 5 undergraduate schools and 5 graduate schools. In addition to regional accreditation, MIT has baccalaureate program accreditation with AACSB, ABET, CSAB, and ACS. The 168-acre campus is in an urban area 1 mile north of Boston. Including any residence halls, there are 158 buildings.

STUDENT LIFE: 90% of undergraduates are from out of state, mostly the Middle Atlantic. Students are from 50 states, 96 foreign countries, and Canada. 6% are African American; 6% two or more races; 36% White; 25% Asian American; 2% race unknown; 15% Hispanic; 11% Foreign. **Male To Female Ratio:** 1.6:1. The average age of freshmen is 19; all undergraduates, 20. 2% do not continue beyond their first year; 98% remain to graduate. **Housing:** 3420 students can be accommodated in college housing, which includes single-sex and coed dorms, on-campus apartments, and married student housing. In addition, there are language houses, special-interest houses, fraternity houses, sorority houses, off-campus independent living groups, and non-Greek cooperative houses. On-campus housing is guaranteed for all 4 years. 74% of students live on campus. Some may keep cars.

FACULTY/CLASSROOMS: 78% of faculty are male; 22% are female. All teach undergraduates, and all do research. No introductory courses are taught by graduate students.

PROGRAMS OF STUDY: MIT confers B.S. degrees. Master's and doctoral degrees are also awarded. Bachelor's degrees are awarded in BIOLOGICAL SCIENCE (biology/biological science and neurosciences), BUSINESS (management science), COMMUNICATIONS AND THE ARTS (creative writing, digital communications, linguistics, literature, media arts, and music), COMPUTER AND PHYSICAL SCIENCE (chemistry, computer science, earth science, mathematics, physics, and science technology), ENGINEERING AND ENVIRONMENTAL DESIGN (aeronautical engineering, aerospace studies, architecture, bioengineering, biomedical engineering, chemical engineering, civil engineering, electrical/electronics engineering, engineering, environmental engineering, materials engineering, materials science, mechanical engineering, nuclear engineering, and ocean engineering), SOCIAL SCIENCE (anthropology, archeology, cognitive science, economics, history, humanities, interdisciplinary studies, philosophy, political science/government, and urban studies). Engineering, science, and management & social science programs are the strongest academically. Engineering has the largest enrollment.

ACTIVITIES: 32% of women belong to 6 national sororities. Groups on campus include art, band, cheerleading, chess, choir, chorale, chorus, computers, dance, debate, drama, environmental, ethnic, film, honors, international, jazz band, LGBT, literary magazine, marching band, musical theater, newspaper, orchestra, over 400 recognized organizations on campus, photography, political, professional, radio and TV, religious, social, social service, student government, symphony, and yearbook. Popular campus events include Independent Activities Period, and Spring Weekend. **Sports:** There are 16 intercollegiate sports for men and 15 for women, and 20 intramural sports for men and 20 for women. Facilities include an athletic complex with 10 buildings and 26 acres of playing fields. **Graduates:** From July 1, 2015 to June 30, 2016, 1011 bachelor's degrees were awarded. The most popular majors were computer science and engineering (9%), mechanical engineering 2-A (7%), and electrical engineering/computer science (7%). 307 companies recruited on campus in 2015-2016. In an average class, 84% graduate in 4 years or less, 91% graduate in 5 years or less, and 93% graduate in 6 years or less. Of the 2015 graduating class, 33% were enrolled in graduate school within 6 months of graduation, and 58% were employed.

SERVICES: Counseling and information services are available, as is tutoring in most subjects. There is a reader service for the blind. Accommodations for students with documented disabilities are determined on an individual basis. **Library/Resources:** The 5 libraries contain 2.9 million volumes, 2.4 million microform items, and 49,480 audio/video tapes/CDs/DVDs. Computerized library services include interlibrary loans, database searching, Internet access, and Wi-Fi capability. Special learning facilities include an art gallery, radio station, and TV station. **Physically Challenged Students:** Facilities include wheelchair ramps, elevators, special parking, specially equipped restrooms, special class scheduling, lowered drinking fountains, lowered telephones, wheelchair lifts, and automatic doors. An assistive technology lab and assistance with library services are available, upon determination of need. **Special:** MIT offers cross-registration with Harvard, Wellesley, the Massachusetts College of Art and Design, and the School of the Museum of Fine Arts. Internships are offered in a number of programs. Short and long-term study abroad options are offered. The Undergraduate Research Opportunities Program (UROP) cultivates and supports research partnerships between MIT undergraduates and faculty. There are 10 national honor societies and a chapter of Phi Beta Kappa. **Visiting:** There are regularly scheduled orientations for prospective students, including daily tours (Monday through Friday) preceded by an information session with admissions staff. Visitors may sit in on classes and stay overnight. To schedule a visit, contact the Office of Admissions. **Campus Safety and Security:** Measures include 24-hour foot and vehicle patrol, emergency notification system, self-defense education, and security escort services. There are shuttle buses, emergency telephones, lighted pathways/sidewalks, and automated external defibrillators (AEDs) are stationed across campus.

REQUIREMENTS: The SAT or ACT is required. The ACT Optional Writing test is also required. In addition, 2 SAT Subject Tests, including 1 each of math and science, are required. 16 academic units are recommended, including 4 each of English, math, and science, 2 of social studies, and 2 foreign language. The GED is accepted. Essays, 2 teacher evaluations, an official transcript, and a guidance counselor report are required. An interview is strongly recommended. AP credits are accepted. To graduate, students must fulfill the General Institute Requirements, as well as communication and physical education requirements, and fulfill departmental program requirements. The General Institute Requirements consist of 6 courses in science, 1 in lab science, 2 in restricted science and technology electives, and 8 in humanities, arts, and social sciences for a total of 17 courses. **Procedure:** Freshmen are admitted fall. Entrance exams should be taken by the January test date. There are early admissions and deferred admissions plans. Applications should be filed by January 1 for fall entry, along with a $75 fee. Notifications are sent March 20. 652 applicants were on the 2016 waiting list; 52 were admitted. Applications are accepted on-line. **Transfer Students:** 16 transfer students enrolled in 2015-2016. In order to apply, applicant must have minimum of 2 semesters of college, but not more than 5 semesters, at the time they would enroll. Transfer credit is assessed by each academic department on a course by course basis. Enrolling transfer students are required to complete at least 3 semesters at MIT to earn a bachelors degree. For entry in the spring semester, only U.S. citizens and permanent residents may apply. Applicants who are not U.S. citizens or permanent residents must apply for entry in the fall semester. **International Students:** There are 484 international students enrolled. The school actively recruits these students. They must also take the SAT or ACT. Non-English speakers may substitute the TOEFL for the SAT or ACT.

ADMISSIONS: 8% of the 2016-2017 applicants were accepted. The SAT scores for the 2016-2017 freshman class were: Critical Reading-- 4% between 500 and 599, 27% between 600 and 699, and 69% between 700 and 800. Math-- 5% between 600 and 699 and 95% between 700 and 800. Writing-- 2% between 500 and 599, 27% between 600 and 699, and 71% between 700 and 800. The ACT scores were 3% between 24 and 29, and 97% above 30. 100% of the current freshmen were in the top fifth of their class. 208 freshmen graduated first in their class. **Admissions Contact:** Stuart Schmill, Dean of Admissions. Email: *admissions@mit.edu* Web: *web.mit.edu*

FINANCIAL AID: MIT is a member of CSS. The CSS/Profile, parent W-2s, 1040s, and the business tax form are required. The FAFSA code is 002178. The deadline for filing freshman financial aid applications for fall entry is February 15.

MASSACHUSETTS MARITIME ACADEMY E-4
www.maritime.edu

Buzzards Bay, MA 02532	**(508) 830-5000** **(800) 544-3411** **Email: admissions@maritime.edu**
Full-time: 1403 men, 202 women	**Faculty:** n/av
Part-time: 59 men, 13 women	**Ph.D.s:** 63%
Graduate: 58 men, 16 women	**Student/Faculty:** n/av
Year: 4-1-4, summer session	**Tuition:** $8004 ($24,600)
Room & Board: $11,978	**Freshman Class:** 825 applied, 664 accepted, 402 enrolled
SAT CR/M/W: 500/540/490 **ACT:** 22	**CEEB CODE:** 3515
Application Deadline: rolling	**COMPETITIVE**

Massachusetts Maritime Academy, founded in 1891, is the oldest continuously operating maritime academy in the country. Cooperative educational learning and leadership training opportunities prepare graduates for professional positions within private industry or, if opted, military commissions. There is 1 undergraduate school and 1 graduate school. In addition to regional accreditation, MMA has baccalaureate program accreditation with IACBE. The 54-acre campus is in a small town 60 miles south of Boston. Including any residence halls, there are 12 buildings.

STUDENT LIFE: 79% of undergraduates are from Massachusetts. Others are from 33 states, and 3 foreign countries. 85% are White; 4% Hispanic; 4% race unknown; 3% two or more races; 2% Asian American; 1% African American; 1% Foreign. **Male To Female Ratio:** 6.6:1. The average age of freshmen is 18; all undergraduates, 20. **Housing:** 1500 students can be accommodated in college housing, which includes coed dorms. On-campus housing is guaranteed for all 4 years. 95% of students live on campus; of those, 15% remain on campus on weekends. Alcohol is not permitted. All students may keep cars.

FACULTY/CLASSROOMS: 70% of faculty are male; 30% are female. No introductory courses are taught by graduate students.

PROGRAMS OF STUDY: MMA confers B.S. degrees. Master's degrees are also awarded. Bachelor's degrees are awarded in BUSINESS (international business management), ENGINEERING AND ENVIRONMENTAL DESIGN (engineering, engineering/mechanical emp/energy sys focus, environmental science, marine engineering, and marine transportation), SOCIAL SCIENCE (homeland security/emergency preparedness). Marine engineering, and Marine transportation are the strongest academically and have the largest enrollment.

ACTIVITIES: There are no fraternities or sororities. There are 20 groups on campus, including regimental leadership, band, communications, drama, international, intramurals, jazz band, LGBT, literary magazine, marching band, pep band, professional, social service, student government, and yearbook. Popular campus events include Ring Dance, Emory Rice Day, and Change of Command. **Sports:** There are 8 intercollegiate sports for men and 8 for women. Facilities include multi-purpose stadium for football, soccer & lacrosse, baseball & softball fields, sailing center to accommodate co-ed sailing and rowing programs, an Olympic-size swimming pool, 3 weight rooms, cardiovascular center, and indoor gymnasium that seats 500 and an auxiliary gymnasium used for recreation and club sports. **Graduates:** From July 1, 2015 to June 30, 2016, 278 bachelor's degrees were awarded. The most popular majors were marine engineering (34%), marine transportation (21%), and facilities engineering (14%).

SERVICES: Counseling and information services are available, as is tutoring in most subjects. **Library/Resources:** The library contains 177,582 volumes, and 812 audio/video tapes/CDs/DVDs, and subscribes to 52,704 periodicals including electronic. Computerized library services include interlibrary loans, database searching, Internet access, and Wi-Fi capability. **Physically Challenged Students:** 90% of the campus is accessible. Facilities include wheelchair ramps, elevators, special parking, specially equipped restrooms, special class scheduling, and lowered drinking fountains. **Special:** Spring semester study abroad opportunities are available via exchange programs with Dalian Maritime University and Shanghai Maritime University. Students with a minimum cumulative grade point average of 3.0 may enroll in a dual-degree program with the permission of the department chairperson of each program. Interested students may pursue dual-degree combinations by presenting their proposals for approval by the chairperson of each department. In order to officially declare a dual major before the end of the third semester, a student must have completed either Calculus I or Applied Calculus. **Visiting:** There are regularly scheduled orientations for prospective students, Campus tours, admissions interviews, and overnight visits can be arranged. There are also Open House programs. There are guides for informal visits, visitors may sit in on classes, and stay overnight. To schedule a visit, contact the Admissions Office. **Campus Safety and Security:** Measures include 24-hour foot and vehicle patrol and emergency notification system. There are emergency telephones, lighted pathways/sidewalks, controlled access to dorms/residences, and late night transport/escort service when available.

REQUIREMENTS: The SAT or ACT is required. Applicants must have graduated from an accredited secondary school or hold a GED certificate. They should have completed 17 Carnegie units, including 4 each in English, and math, 3-4 in science (3 of which must be lab), 2 in a foreign language, 1 each in social studies, and history, and 2 in academic electives. An essay, official school transcripts, copy of passport/birth certificate, and two letters of recommendation are also required. An interview is strongly recommended. A GPA of 2.0 is required. AP and CLEP credits are accepted. Important factors in the admissions decision are advanced placement or honors courses, leadership record, and extracurricular activities record. A major program at Massachusetts Maritime Academy includes approximately 128 credits of academic semester courses plus sea terms, experiential learning, and/or cooperative programs. Within each program the academic courses are designated in the categories of Major courses, General Education courses, and Support courses. Each major program includes at least two free electives. Students may choose to add more free elective courses or a minor or concentration sequence of elective courses. During August orientation, all first-year students are required to participate in a freshman mini-cruise. Students in license majors (Marine Engineering and Marine Transportation) are required to participate in four seagoing experiences, three aboard the USTS Kennedy (freshman, sophomore and senior years) and one aboard a commercial vessel (junior year). Students enrolled in shore-side majors must complete cooperative education placements as required by the program. Depending upon the major, students completing a non-license degree program may be required to complete experiential learning opportunities. **Procedure:** Freshmen are admitted fall. There are early admissions and rolling admissions plans. Application deadlines are open. The fall 2016 application fee was $50. Notifications are sent December 31. Applications are accepted online. **Transfer Students:** Minimum number of credits completed for transfer admissions must be 12 to 23 transferable credits with a 2.5 minimum college GPA OR 24 or more transferable credits with a 2.0 minimum college GPA. Transfer students must have successfully completed college-level algebra, college-level English composition, and Chemistry I with a lab. 30 credits required for the bachelor's degree must be completed at MMA. **International Students:** There are 10 international students enrolled. They must take the TOEFL with a minimum score of 530 on the paper-based TOEFL (PBT) or 75 on the Internet-based version (iBT). MMA accepts proof of attendance in an English instructed school for at least one year, IELTS, and TOEFL. They must also take the SAT or ACT.

ADMISSIONS: 80% of the 2016-2017 applicants were accepted. The SAT scores for the 2016-2017 freshman class were: Critical Reading-- 47% below 500, 41% between 500 and 599, and 12% between 600 and 699. Math-- 25% below 500, 52% between 500 and 599, 22% between 600 and 699, and 1% between 700 and 800. Writing-- 53% below 500, 41% between 500 and 599, and 6% between 600 and 699. The ACT scores were 9% between 12 and 17, 55% between 18 and 23, and 36% between 24 and 29. **Admissions Contact:** Captain Elizabeth Stevenson, Vice President of Enrollment Management. Email: *admissions@maritime.edu* Web: *www.maritime.edu*

FINANCIAL AID: The college's own financial statement is required. The FAFSA code is 002181. The priority date for freshman financial aid applications for fall entry is May 1.

MCPHS UNIVERSITY *(The complete profile is made available exclusively on our website, www.barronspac.com)*

MERRIMACK COLLEGE — D-1

www.merrimack.edu

North Andover, MA 01845 — **(978) 837-5100**

Fax: (978) 837-5133	**Email:** admissions@merrimack.edu
Full-time: 1135 men, 1035 women	**Faculty:** IIB, +$
Part-time: 76 men, 73 women	**Ph.D.s:** 84%
Graduate: 18 men, 116 women	**Student/Faculty:** n/av
Year: semesters, summer session	**Tuition:** $38,425
Room & Board: $14,345	**Freshman Class:** 3869 applied, 3400 accepted, 610 enrolled
	CEEB CODE: 3525
Application Deadline: February 15	**COMPETITIVE**

Founded in 1947, by the Order of St. Augustine. Merrimack offers over 40 undergraduate majors, as well as graduate programs in education and part-time degree completion and certificate programs. Figures in the above capsule and in this profile are approximate. There are 4 undergraduate schools and 1 graduate school. In addition to regional accreditation, Merrimack has baccalaureate program accreditation with ABET, CAATE, and ACS. The 220-acre campus is in a suburban area 25 miles north of Boston. Including any residence halls, there are 34 buildings.

STUDENT LIFE: 74% of undergraduates are from Massachusetts. Others are from 20 states, 22 foreign countries, and Canada. 73% are White; 7% Hispanic; 3% African American; 2% Asian American; 2% Foreign. **Male To Female Ratio:** 1.0:1. The average age of freshmen is 18; all undergraduates, 20. 13% do not continue beyond their first year; 69% remain to graduate. **Housing:** 1634 students can be accommodated in college housing, which includes single-sex and coed dorms and on-campus apartments. In addition, there are special-interest houses, international, wellness, and theme housing, including Austin Scholars housing. On-campus housing is guaranteed for all 4 years. 81% of students live on campus; of those, 81% remain on campus on weekends. Upperclassmen may keep cars.

FACULTY/CLASSROOMS: 53% of faculty are male; 47% are female. No introductory courses are taught by graduate students. The average class size in an introductory lecture is 25; in a laboratory is 15; and in a regular course is 15.

PROGRAMS OF STUDY: Merrimack confers B.A. and B.S. degrees. Associate and master's degrees are also awarded. Bachelor's degrees are awarded in BIOLOGICAL SCIENCE (biochemistry and biology/biological science), BUSINESS (accounting, business administration and management, business economics, international business management, and marketing/retailing/merchandising), COMMUNICATIONS AND THE ARTS (communications, English, and modern language), COMPUTER AND PHYSICAL SCIENCE (chemistry, computer science, mathematics, and physics), EDUCATION (elementary education and secondary education), ENGINEERING AND ENVIRONMENTAL DESIGN (civil engineering, electrical/electronics engineering, and environmental science), HEALTH PROFESSIONS (allied health, predentistry, premedicine, and sports medicine), SOCIAL SCIENCE (economics, history, philosophy, political science/government, prelaw, psychology, religion, and sociology). Science, engineering, and business are the strongest academically. Biology, business administration, and sports medicine have the largest enrollments.

ACTIVITIES: 3% of men belong to 2 national fraternities; 9% of women belong to 3 national sororities. There are 57 groups on campus, including art, cheerleading, choir, chorale, chorus, communications, computers, dance, drama, environmental, ethnic, film, honors, international, jazz band, LGBT, literary magazine, musical theater, newspaper, pep band, photography, political, professional, radio and TV, religious, social, social service, student government, and yearbook. Popular campus events include Spring Weekend, Mr. Merrimack, Cram Jam, Merrimack Survivor, and Relay for Life. **Sports:** There are 10 intercollegiate sports for men and 12 for women, and 6 intramural sports for men and 5 for women. Facilities include an athletic complex, including an ice rink, a basketball court, an aerobics studio, and a well-equipped exercise room, and outdoor facilities including 2 sets of tennis courts, baseball, football, softball, soccer, lacrosse, and field hockey fields, and a turf field. **Graduates:** From July 1, 2015 to June 30, 2016, 402 bachelor's degrees were awarded. The most popular majors were business administration (11%), finance (8%), and marketing (8%). 100 companies recruited on campus in 2015-2016. In an average class, 51% graduate in 4 years or less, 62% graduate in 5 years or less, and 69% graduate in 6 years or less.

SERVICES: Counseling and information services are available, as is tutoring in every subject. There is a reader service for the blind. Math and writing resource centers are available to all students. **Library/Resources:** The library contains 176,908 volumes, and 2,672 audio/video tapes/CDs/DVDs, and subscribes to 4,800 periodicals including electronic. Computerized library services include interlibrary loans, database searching, Internet access, and Wi-Fi capability. Special learning facilities include an art gallery, planetarium, radio station, TV station, astronomy dome and telescope, Rogers Center for the Arts, Diversity Education Center, Center for Augustinian Study & Legacy, Center for Biotechnology and Biomedical Sciences, Center for the Study of Jewish-Christian-Muslim Relations, and RFID (Radio Frequency Identification) technology lab. **Physically Challenged Students:** 95% of the campus is accessible. Facilities include wheelchair ramps, elevators, special parking, specially equipped restrooms, special class scheduling, lowered drinking fountains, lowered telephones, and special housing. **Special:** Merrimack offers cooperative programs in business, engineering, liberal arts, and computer science, cross-registration through the Northeast Consortium, internships in all arts and science programs, study abroad in 9 countries, and a Washington semester at American University. Work-study programs, a 5-year combined B.A.-B.S. degree in many major fields, and dual and self-designed majors are available. General studies, nondegree study, and pass/fail options are possible. There are 7 national honor societies and 3 departmental honors programs. **Visiting:** There are regularly scheduled orientations for prospective students, including campus open houses (total of 4) and several Saturday information sessions for prospective freshman candidates during the fall months. Transfer students have 2 fall semester open house/information session and 2 during the winter/spring mont. Visitors may sit in on classes. To schedule a visit, contact the Office of Admissions. **Campus Safety and Security:** Measures include 24-hour foot and vehicle patrol, emergency notification system, self-defense education, and security escort services. There are shuttle buses, emergency telephones, lighted pathways/sidewalks, controlled access to dorms/residences. There is a Rape Aggressive Defense program available through police services.

REQUIREMENTS: For business administration, humanities, and social science majors, Merrimack recommends that applicants complete 4 units of English, 3 math and 2 science, 3 of social studies, and 2 foreign language. For other majors, an additional math course and 1 additional course in science are needed. An essay is required, and an interview is recommended. Applicants should have completed 19 Carnegie units. AP and CLEP credits are accepted. **Procedure:** Freshmen are admitted fall and spring. Entrance exams should be taken during the spring of the junior year and the fall of the senior year. There are early decision, early admissions, and deferred admissions plans. Early decision applications should be filed by November 15; regular applications, by February 15 for fall entry. Notification of early decision is sent January 1; regular decision, March 15. Applications are accepted on-line. **Transfer Students:** 72 transfer students enrolled in 2015-2016. Applicants must have maintained a minimum 2.5 GPA; some programs require a higher GPA. Transfer students must complete the transfer application and essay and must submit official college/university transcript (from each college/university attended), course descriptions of all courses completed from each college/university (needed for evaluation and determination of transfer credit), and a letter of recommendation. Student must not be under disciplinary censure and must be eligible to return to previous institution. A high school transcript is required if the student has less than 30 semester hours of college-level credit completed at the time of application. 48 of 124 credits required for the bachelor's degree must be completed at Merrimack. **International Students:** There are 55 international students enrolled. The school actively recruits these students. They must take the TOEFL with a minimum score of 550 on the paper-based TOEFL (PBT) or 75 on the Internet-based version (iBT).

ADMISSIONS: 88% of the 2016-2017 applicants were accepted. 16% of the current freshmen were in the top fifth of their class; 44% were in the top two fifths. 1 freshman graduated first in the class. **Admissions Contact:** Mark Barrett, Dean, Undergraduate Admissions. Email: *admissions@merrimack.edu* Web: *www.merrimack.edu*

FINANCIAL AID: Merrimack is a member of CSS. The FAFSA code is 002120. The deadline for filing freshman financial aid applications for fall entry is February 1.

MONTSERRAT COLLEGE OF ART *(The complete profile is made available exclusively on our website, www.barronspac.com)*

MOUNT HOLYOKE COLLEGE — B-2
www.mtholyoke.edu

South Hadley, MA 01075 — **(413) 538-2023**

Fax: (413) 538-2409	**Email:** admission@mtholyoke.edu
Full-time: 2095 women	**Faculty:** 186; IIB, +$
Part-time: 1 men, 30 women	**Ph.D.s:** 98%
Graduate: 12 men, 77 women	**Student/Faculty:** 10 to 1
Year: semesters, summer session	**Tuition:** $43,886
Room & Board: $12,860	**Freshman Class:** n/av
SAT or ACT: required	**CEEB CODE:** 3529
Application Deadline: January 15	**MOST COMPETITIVE**

Mount Holyoke College, founded in 1837, is an independent liberal arts college and the oldest institution of higher learning for women in the United States. The 800-acre campus is in a small town 90 miles west of Boston and 160 miles north of New York City. Including any residence halls, there are 68 buildings.

STUDENT LIFE: 75% of undergraduates are from out of state, mostly the Middle Atlantic. Students are from 44 states, 69 foreign countries, and Canada. 65% are from public schools. 8% are Hispanic; 6% African American; 45% White; 4% two or more races; 27% Foreign; 10% Asian American; 1% race unknown. **Female To Male Ratio:** 169.4:1. The average age of freshmen is 18; all undergraduates, 20. 10% do not continue beyond their first year; 85% remain to graduate. **Housing:** 2111 students can be accommodated in college housing, which includes single-sex dorms and on-campus apartments, and special accommodations are available by need. On-campus housing is guaranteed for all 4 years. 95% of students live on campus; of those, 70% remain on campus on weekends. All students may keep cars.

FACULTY/CLASSROOMS: 42% of faculty are male; 58% are female. All teach undergraduates, and all do research. No introductory courses are taught by graduate students. The average class size in an introductory lecture is 20; in a laboratory is 12; and in a regular course is 15.

PROGRAMS OF STUDY: Mount Holyoke confers A.B. degrees. Master's degrees are also awarded. Bachelor's degrees are awarded in AGRICULTURE (environmental studies), BIOLOGICAL SCIENCE (biochemistry, biology/biological science, and neurosciences), COMMUNICATIONS AND THE ARTS (Africana studies, art history and appreciation, classics, dance, dramatic arts, English, film arts, French, Greek, Italian, Latin, music, romance languages and literature, Spanish, and studio art), COMPUTER AND PHYSICAL SCIENCE (astronomy, chemistry, computer science, geology, mathematics, physics, and statistics), EDUCATION (psychology education), ENGINEERING AND ENVIRONMENTAL DESIGN (architecture), SOCIAL SCIENCE (anthropology, Asian/Oriental studies, classical/ancient civilization, East Asian studies, economics, gender studies, geography, German area studies, history, international relations, Latin American studies, medieval studies, Middle Eastern studies, philosophy, political science/government, psychology, religion, Russian and Slavic studies, sociology, and South Asian studies). Sciences, social sciences, and international relations are the strongest academically. Psychology, biology, and economics have the largest enrollments.

ACTIVITIES: There are no fraternities or sororities. There are 130 groups on campus, including art, band, cheerleading, choir, chorale, chorus, computers, dance, debate, drama, environmental, ethnic, film, honors, international, jazz band, LGBT, literary magazine, newspaper, orchestra, photography, political, professional, radio and TV, religious, social, social service, student government, symphony, and yearbook. Popular campus events include Nightfest, Mountain Day, Fall Fest, No Study Zone, Pangy Day, Cultural Nights, and Spring Weekend. **Sports:** There are 14 intercollegiate sports for women. Facilities include indoor athletic and recreational facilities are housed in the Kendall Sports & Dance Complex, fitness center, gymnasium, natatorium, field house, turf & track complex, soccer field, activity field and tennis courts. Also in close proximity are the college's Canoe House and a scenic one-mile loop around Upper Lake for running, walking, or riding a horse, and the Mount Holyoke College Equestrian Center. **Graduates:** From July 1, 2015 to June 30, 2016, 628 bachelor's degrees were awarded. The most popular majors were psychology (10%), economics (9%), and English (8%). 87 companies recruited on campus in 2015-2016. In an average class, 78% graduate in 4 years or less, 84% graduate in 5 years or less, and 85% graduate in 6 years or less. Of the 2015 graduating class, 22% were enrolled in graduate school within 6 months of graduation, and 85% were employed.

SERVICES: Counseling and information services are available, as is tutoring in every subject. There is a writing center available to all students at all levels. There is a reader service for the blind. Special testing accommodations, diagnostic testing services, note-taking services, as well as readers and tutors, are available. There is also an adaptive technology lab. **Library/Resources:** The 2 libraries contain 1.4 million volumes, 24,481 microform items, and 12,030 audio/video tapes/CDs/DVDs, and subscribe to 7,525 periodicals including electronic. Computerized library services include interlibrary loans, database searching, Internet access, and Wi-Fi capability. Special learning facilities include an art gallery, radio station, an observatory, a child study center, a botanical garden and greenhouse, an equestrian center, a conference center, and centers for global initiatives, leadership, and the environment. **Physically Challenged Students:** Facilities include wheelchair ramps, elevators, special parking, specially equipped restrooms, special class scheduling, lowered drinking fountains, and special housing. **Special:** Mount Holyoke offers students cross-registration through the Five-College Consortium. Other opportunities include the 12-College Exchange Program, science and international studies internships, study abroad in over 50 countries (semester or full-year), a Washington semester, work-study, student-designed majors, dual majors, accelerated degrees, nondegree study, and pass/fail options. A teacher licensure program is available. Mount Holyoke's "The Lynk" Program enables students to meaningfully link their liberal arts education with their career goals through internships, research projects, and summer employment. There are 5 national honor societies and a chapter of Phi Beta Kappa. **Visiting:** There are regularly scheduled orientations for prospective students, including tours, on-campus interviews, overnight stays, and meetings with professors and coaches. There are guides for informal visits, visitors may sit in on classes, and stay overnight. To schedule a visit, contact the Admission Office. **Campus Safety and Security:** Measures include 24-hour foot and vehicle patrol, emergency notification system, self-defense education, and security escort services. There are shuttle buses, emergency telephones, lighted pathways/sidewalks, and controlled access to dorms/residences.

REQUIREMENTS: The school recommends that applicants have 4 years each of English and foreign language, 3 each of math and science, and 2 of social studies. An essay is required and an interview is strongly recommended. AP credits are accepted. Important factors in the admissions decision are advanced placement or honors courses, leadership record, and recommendations by school officials. Students must complete 128 total credits with a final GPA of 2.0. Students must complete a first-year seminar and a major (generally 32-56 credits). At least 68 credits must be earned from course work outside the major department. Students must complete one course each in the humanities, science/math, and social sciences. Students must also complete a foreign language course, a multicultural perspectives course, and 4 units (2 semesters) of physical education courses. While not required, students may also elect to complete any number (or none) of the following: a second major, a minor (but not both a second major and a minor), a Five College certificate, or a Nexus program. At least 64 of the student's 128 credits must be earned at Mount Holyoke over a minimum of 4 semesters during the student's sophomore, junior and senior years. **Procedure:** Freshmen are admitted fall and spring. Entrance exams should be taken before the application deadline. There are early decision and deferred admissions plans. Early decision applications should be filed by November 15; regular applications, by January 15 for fall entry, along with a $60 fee. Notification of early decision is sent January 1; regular decision, April 1. 161 early decision candidates were accepted for the 2016-2017 class. 459 applicants were on the 2016 waiting list; 7 were admitted. Applications are accepted on-line. Application fees are waived if application is completed on-line. **Transfer Students:** 77 transfer students enrolled in 2015-2016. A statement of good standing, transcripts of secondary school or college-level work, and an essay are required of transfer applicants. An interview is recommended. SAT scores will be considered if submitted but are not required. 64 of 128 credits required for the bachelor's degree must be completed at Mount Holyoke. **International Students:** There are 564 international students enrolled. The school actively recruits these students. They must take the TOEFL with a minimum score of 100 on the Internet-based version (iBT).

ADMISSIONS: 50% of the 2016-2017 applicants were accepted. 81% of the current freshmen were in the top fifth of their class; 96% were in the top two fifths. 14 freshmen graduated first in their class. **Admissions Contact:** Gail Berson, VP of Enrollment and Dean of Admissions. Email: *admission@mtholyoke.edu* Web: *www.mtholyoke.edu*

FINANCIAL AID: In 2016-2017, 79% of all full-time freshmen and 78% of continuing full-time students received some form of financial aid. 66% of all full-time freshmen and 65% of continuing full-time students received need-based aid. The average freshman award was $36,894. Need-based scholarships or need-based grants averaged $32,332; need-based self-help aid (loans and jobs) averaged $5,360; and other non-need-based awards and non-need-based scholarships averaged $19,312. 64% of undergraduate students work part-time. Average annual earnings from campus work are $1152. Mount Holyoke is a member of CSS. The CSS/Profile, parent and student tax returns, and noncustodial parent form are required. The FAFSA code is 002192. The priority date for freshman financial aid applications for fall entry is February 15. The deadline for filing freshman financial aid applications for fall entry is March 1.

MOUNT IDA COLLEGE — D-2

www.mountida.edu

Newton, MA 02459	(617) 928-4553
Fax: (617) 928-4507	Email: admissions@mountida.edu
Full-time: 400 men, 700 women	Faculty: 56; IIB, -$
Part-time: 10 men, 20 women	Ph.D.s: 61%
Graduate: n/av	Student/Faculty: 19 to 1
Year: semesters, summer session	Tuition: $33,820
Room & Board: $13,000	Freshman Class: n/av
SAT or ACT: required	CEEB CODE: 3530
Application Deadline: August 15	COMPETITIVE

Mount Ida College, founded in 1899, is an independent baccalaureate college that prepares students for a profession through a curriculum that emphasizes career studies integrated with liberal learning. The figures in the above capsule and in this profile are approximate. There are 5 undergraduate schools. In addition to regional accreditation, Mount Ida has baccalaureate program accreditation with ABFSE, ADA, FIDER, and NASAD. The 72-acre campus is in a suburban area 8 miles west of downtown Boston. Including any residence halls, there are 18 buildings.

STUDENT LIFE: 54% of undergraduates are from Massachusetts. Others are from 23 states, 33 foreign countries, and Canada. 80% are from public schools. 7% are Hispanic; 63% White; 3% Asian American; 16% African American; 10% Foreign; 1% American Indian/Alaska Native. **Female To Male Ratio:** 1.8:1. The average age of freshmen is 19; all undergraduates, 21. **Housing:** 803 students can be accommodated in college housing, which includes single-sex and coed dorms. In addition, there are honors houses, and housing for students over age 21. On-campus housing is guaranteed for all 4 years. 60% of students live on campus. Upperclassmen may keep cars.

FACULTY/CLASSROOMS: 46% of faculty are male; 54% are female. All teach undergraduates. No introductory courses are taught by graduate students. The average class size in an introductory lecture is 25; in a laboratory is 16; and in a regular course is 20.

PROGRAMS OF STUDY: Mount Ida confers B.A., B.S. and B.L.S. degrees. Associate degrees are also awarded. Bachelor's degrees are awarded in AGRICULTURE (equine science), BUSINESS (business administration and management, fashion merchandising, funeral home services, hospitality management services, marketing/retailing/merchandising, retailing, and small business management), COMMUNICATIONS AND THE ARTS (American literature, art and design, communications, English, graphic design, journalism, media arts, and radio/television technology), EDUCATION (early childhood education and history education), ENGINEERING AND ENVIRONMENTAL DESIGN (interior design), HEALTH PROFESSIONS (veterinary science), SOCIAL SCIENCE (American studies, child psychology/development, criminal justice, fashion design and technology, law, liberal arts/general studies, and sociology). Veterinary technology, dental hygiene, and funeral service are the strongest academically. Business and veterinary technology has the largest enrollment.

ACTIVITIES: There are no fraternities or sororities. There are 25 groups on campus, including art, cheerleading, chess, choir, dance, drama, ethnic, fashion, honors, international, LGBT, literary magazine, newspaper, photography, professional, radio and TV, religious, social, social service, student government, and yearbook. Popular campus events include Welcome Week, Spring Fling, and Senior Week. **Sports:** There are 7 intercollegiate sports for men and 6 for women, and 8 intramural sports for men and 10 for women. Facilities include a gym, playing fields, a fitness center, tennis courts, an outdoor swimming pool, athletic fields, and an athletic center. **Graduates:** From July 1, 2015 to June 30, 2016, 128 bachelor's degrees were awarded. The most popular majors were criminal justice (16%), graphic design (13%), and management (11%).

SERVICES: Counseling and information services are available, as is tutoring in most subjects. There is remedial math, reading, and writing. There is a program for learning-disabled students, for which a fee is charged. Studies skills courses are also available. The Learning Circle is another innovative campuswide initiative that provides a professional learning specialist to assist students and monitor their academic progress. **Library/Resources:** The library contains 62,500 volumes, 68 microform items, and 2,000 audio/video tapes/CDs/DVDs, and subscribes to 530 periodicals including electronic. Computerized library services include interlibrary loans, database searching, and Internet access. Special learning facilities include an art gallery, radio station, TV station, communication lab, darkroom, sewing rooms, blueprint-making facility, and dental labs. **Physically Challenged Students:** 75% of the campus is accessible. Facilities include wheelchair ramps, elevators, special parking, specially equipped restrooms, special class scheduling, lowered drinking fountains, lowered telephones, and special housing. **Special:** Internships in the form of work experience are available in each department. Work-study provided by the college, student-designed majors, study abroad in 14 countries, exchange program with Strasbourg, France, a general studies degree, an interdisciplinary major in legal studies, nondegree study, and an accelerated degree program in funeral service are also available. There are 4 national honor societies, a freshman honors program, and 4 departmental honors programs. **Visiting:** There are regularly scheduled orientations for prospective students, consisting of fall and spring open houses, Saturday sessions, and weekday appointments. There are guides for informal visits, visitors may sit in on classes, and stay overnight. To schedule a visit, contact the Admissions Office. **Campus Safety and Security:** Measures include 24-hour foot and vehicle patrol, self-defense education, and security escort services. There are shuttle buses, emergency telephones, and lighted pathways/sidewalks.

REQUIREMENTS: The SAT or ACT is required. Applicants are required to have 4 units of English, 2 of social studies, and 3 each of math and science. A portfolio is recommended for certain programs, while an interview is recommended for all applicants. The GED is accepted. AP and CLEP credits are accepted. Important factors in the admissions decision are advanced placement or honors courses, evidence of special talent, and recommendations by school officials. Candidates for a bachelor's degree require 128 credits with a 2.0 GPA. The distribution requirement varies for each major. 1 phys ed course is required. The all-college curriculum includes these common experiences for all students: a college success course, a junior year interdisciplinary seminar, and a senior capstone project. **Procedure:** Freshmen are admitted fall and spring. Entrance exams should be taken as early as possible by the junior year.

There are early admissions, deferred admissions, and rolling admissions plans. Applications should be filed by August 15 for fall entry, along with a $35 fee. Applications are accepted on-line. **Transfer Students:** 144 transfer students enrolled in 2015-2016. Applicants need a minimum GPA of C and must submit college and high school transcripts. 32 of 120 credits required for the bachelor's degree must be completed at Mount Ida. **International Students:** There are 93 international students enrolled. The school actively recruits these students. They must take the TOEFL. They must also take the SAT or ACT.

Admissions Contact: Matthew Morrison, Director of Admissions. Email: *admissions@mountida.edu* Web: *www.mountida.edu*

FINANCIAL AID: 70% of undergraduate students work part-time. Average annual earnings from campus work are $1500. The average financial indebtedness of the 2016 graduate was $19,268. Mount Ida is a member of CSS. The FAFSA code is 002193. The priority date for freshman financial aid applications for fall entry is May 1.

NEW ENGLAND CONSERVATORY OF MUSIC *(The complete profile is made available exclusively on our website, www.barronspac.com)*

NEWBURY COLLEGE D-2

www.newbury.edu

Brookline, MA 02445 **(617) 730-7007**

Fax: (617) 731-9618	**Email:** admissions@newbury.edu
Full-time: 293 men, 390 women	**Faculty:** 28
Part-time: 25 men, 43 women	**Ph.D.s:** n/av
Graduate: n/av	**Student/Faculty:** 26 to 1
Year: semesters, summer session	**Tuition:** $32,750
Room & Board: $14,200	**Freshman Class:** n/av
SAT or ACT: recommended	**CEEB CODE:** 3639
Application Deadline: n/av	**COMPETITIVE**

Newbury College, founded in 1962, is a private institution offering career-relevant degree programs in business, graphic design, legal studies, computer science, interior design, communication, culinary arts, hotel and restaurant management, and psychology. The figures in the above capsule and in this profile are approximate. There are 4 undergraduate schools. In addition to regional accreditation, Newbury has baccalaureate program accreditation with NEASC. The 10-acre campus is in a suburban area 3 miles west of Boston. Including any residence halls, there are 10 buildings.

STUDENT LIFE: 75% of undergraduates are from Massachusetts. Others are from 24 states, 12 foreign countries, and Canada. 7% are Asian American; 37% White; 36% African American; 3% Foreign; 16% Hispanic; 1% race unknown. **Female To Male Ratio:** 1.4:1. The average age of freshmen is 19; all undergraduates, 21. 42% do not continue beyond their first year; 40% remain to graduate. **Housing:** College-sponsored housing includes coed dorms. In addition, there are special-interest houses. On-campus housing is guaranteed for all 4 years, and is available on a first-come, first-served basis, and is available on a lottery system for upperclassmen. Priority is given to out-of-town students. 63% of students commute. Alcohol is not permitted. Some may keep cars.

FACULTY/CLASSROOMS: All teach undergraduates. No introductory courses are taught by graduate students. The average class size in a regular course is 20.

PROGRAMS OF STUDY: Newbury confers B.S. and B.A. degrees. Associate degrees are also awarded. Bachelor's degrees are awarded in BUSINESS (accounting, business administration and management, fashion merchandising, hotel/motel and restaurant management, international business management, marketing management, and sports management), COMMUNICATIONS AND THE ARTS (communications and graphic design), COMPUTER AND PHYSICAL SCIENCE (computer science), ENGINEERING AND ENVIRONMENTAL DESIGN (interior design), HEALTH PROFESSIONS (health care administration), SOCIAL SCIENCE (criminal justice, food production/management/services, legal studies, and psychology). Psychology, and legal studies are the strongest academically. Psychology, criminal justice, and business management have the largest enrollments.

ACTIVITIES: There are no fraternities or sororities. There are 20 groups on campus, including choir, chorus, communications, dance, ethnic, honors, international, LGBT, professional, radio and TV, religious, social, social service, and student government. Popular campus events include Multicultural Week, Spring Fling and Fall Fest. **Sports:** There are 6 intercollegiate sports for men and 6 for women, and 9 intramural sports for men and 9 for women. Facilities include an off-site gym and a cardiovascular/weight room. **Graduates:** From July 1, 2015 to June 30, 2016, 152 bachelor's degrees were awarded. The most popular majors were psychology (17%), culinary management (10%), and criminal justice (7%). 60 companies recruited on campus in 2015-2016. In an average class, 37% graduate in 4 years or less, 41% graduate in 5 years or less, and 42% graduate in 6 years or less.

SERVICES: Counseling and information services are available, as is tutoring in every subject. There is a reader service for the blind, and remedial math, reading, and writing. **Library/Resources:** The library contains 61,529 volumes, and 311 audio/video tapes/CDs/DVDs, and subscribes to 18,200 periodicals including electronic. Computerized library services include interlibrary loans, database searching, Internet access, and Wi-Fi capability. Special learning facilities include an art gallery, radio station, and TV station. **Physically Challenged Students:** 80% of the campus is accessible. Facilities include wheelchair ramps, elevators, special parking, specially equipped restrooms, special class scheduling, and lowered drinking fountains. **Special:** Internships are part of the bachelor's degree program. Dual majors are available. Credits earned for associate degrees in professional areas can be applied toward the college's bachelor's degree programs. There are 4 national honor societies, a freshman honors program, and 4 departmental honors programs. **Visiting:** There are regularly scheduled orientations for prospective students, including fall and spring open houses, daily interviews, and campus tours. There are guides for informal visits and visitors may sit in on classes. To schedule a visit, contact the Office of Admissions. **Campus Safety and Security:** Measures include 24-hour foot and vehicle patrol, emergency notification system, and security escort services. There are shuttle buses and lighted pathways/sidewalks.

REQUIREMENTS: The SAT or ACT is recommended. Applicants must submit an application, 2 letters of recommendation, high school transcripts, and an essay. AP and CLEP credits are accepted. Important factors in the admissions decision are leadership record, recommendations by alumni, and extracurricular activities record. Candidates for a bachelor's degree must earn 120 credits or 60 credits beyond the associate degree, with a 2.0 GPA. Distribution requirements include courses in math, lab science, literature, and social science, as well as 3 additional credits in arts and sciences. A minimum of 45 credits as well as a minimum of 50% of the courses in the major must be taken at Newbury College. **Procedure:** Freshmen are admitted fall and spring. Entrance exams should be taken following acceptance. There are deferred admissions and rolling admissions plans. Application deadlines are open. Application fee is $25. Notification is sent on a rolling basis. Applications are accepted on-line. Application fees are waived if application is completed on-line. **Transfer Students:** 43 transfer students enrolled in 2015-2016. Transfer students must submit an application, 1 recommendation, high school and college transcripts, and an essay. 60 of 120 credits required for the bachelor's degree must be completed at Newbury. **International Students:** There are 16 international students enrolled. The school actively recruits these students. They must take the TOEFL with a minimum score of 71 on the Internet-based version (iBT).

Admissions Contact: Yavuz Kiremit, Director of Admissions. Email: *admissions@newbury.edu* Web: *www.newbury.edu*

FINANCIAL AID: In 2016-2017, 84% of all full-time freshmen and 85% of continuing full-time students received some form of financial aid. 98% of all full-time freshmen and 98% of continuing full-time students received need-based aid. The average freshman award was $28,610. Need-based scholarships or need-based grants averaged $14,813 ($13,759 maximum); need-based self-help aid (loans and jobs) averaged $3,460 ($5,500 maximum); and other non-need-based awards and non-need-based scholarships averaged $6,064 ($18,000 maximum). 22% of undergraduate students work part-time. Average annual earnings from campus work are $1472. The average financial indebtedness of the 2016 graduate was $30,875. Newbury is a member of CSS. The FAFSA code is 007484. The priority date for freshman financial aid applications for fall entry is March 1. The deadline for filing freshman financial aid applications for fall entry is May 1.

NICHOLS COLLEGE *(The complete profile is made available exclusively on our website, www.barronspac.com)*

NORTHEASTERN UNIVERSITY E-2

www.northeastern.edu

Boston, MA 02115	(617) 373-2200
Fax: (617) 373-8780	Email: admissions@neu.edu
Full-time: 8466 men, 8461 women	Faculty: I, +$
Part-time: n/av	Ph.D.s: 95%
Graduate: 4128 men, 3510 women	Student/Faculty: 13 to 1
Year: semesters, summer session	Tuition: $47,653
Room & Board: $15,050	Freshman Class: n/av
SAT or ACT: required	CEEB CODE: 3667
Application Deadline: January 1	MOST COMPETITIVE

Northeastern University, founded in 1898, is a private research university. Northeastern is the leader in worldwide experiential learning, urban engagement, and interdisciplinary research that meets global and societal needs. Our broad mix of experience-based education programs our signature cooperative education program, as well as student research, service learning, and global learning build the connections that enable students to transform their lives. The University offers a comprehensive range of undergraduate and graduate programs leading to degrees through the doctorate in nine colleges and schools. There are 7 undergraduate schools and 8 graduate schools. In addition to regional accreditation, Northeastern has baccalaureate program accreditation with AACSB, ABET, ACPE, NAAB, CAATE, CCNE, and ACS. The 73-acre campus is in an urban area in the heart of Boston, on Huntington Avenue, also known as the Avenue of the Arts. Including any residence halls, there are 88 buildings.

STUDENT LIFE: 67% of undergraduates are from out of state, mostly the Northeast. Students are from 48 states, 119 foreign countries, and Canada. **Male To Female Ratio:** 1.1:1. The average age of freshmen is 18; all undergraduates, 20. **Housing:** 8354 students can be accommodated in college housing, which includes single-sex and coed dorms, on-campus apartments, and off-campus apartments. In addition, there are honors houses, special-interest houses, academic/college-based, innovation, global perspective, leadership, creative expression, green living, and community service housing. On-campus housing is guaranteed for the freshman year only, and is available on a first-come, first-served basis, and is available on a lottery system for upperclassmen. Upperclassmen may keep cars.

FACULTY/CLASSROOMS: 57% of faculty are male; 43% are female. No introductory courses are taught by graduate students.

PROGRAMS OF STUDY: Northeastern confers B.A., B.S., B.F.A. and B.L.A. degrees. Master's and doctoral degrees are also awarded. Bachelor's degrees are awarded in AGRICULTURE (environmental studies), BIOLOGICAL SCIENCE (biochemistry, biology/biological science, marine biology, and neurosciences), BUSINESS (accounting, business administration and management, international business management, and management information systems), COMMUNICATIONS AND THE ARTS (American Sign Language, art, communications, dramatic arts, English, film arts, graphic design, journalism, languages, linguistics, multimedia, music, music technology, studio art, and theatre arts), COMPUTER AND PHYSICAL SCIENCE (applied physics, chemistry, computer programming, computer science, digital arts/technology, earth science, information sciences and systems, mathematics, and physics), ENGINEERING AND ENVIRONMENTAL DESIGN (architecture, chemical engineering, civil engineering, computer engineering, electrical/electronics engineering, environmental science, industrial engineering, landscape architecture/design, and mechanical engineering), HEALTH PROFESSIONS (health science, nursing, pharmaceutical science, pharmacy, physical therapy, and speech pathology/audiology), SOCIAL SCIENCE (African American studies, anthropology, Asian/Oriental studies, criminal justice, economics, history, interdisciplinary studies, Judaic studies, philosophy, philosophy and religion, political science/government, psychology, religion, and sociology). Business administration, engineering, and sciences have the largest enrollments.

ACTIVITIES: 8% of men belong to 18 national fraternities; 12% of women belong to 11 national sororities. There are 331 groups on campus, including art, band, cheerleading, chess, chorale, chorus, computers, dance, debate, drama, environmental, ethnic, film, honors, international, jazz band, LGBT, literary magazine, musical theater, newspaper, orchestra, pep band, political, professional, radio and TV, religious, resident student association, social, social service, student government, symphony, and yearbook. Popular campus events include Springfest, Senior Week, Welcome Week and Carnevale. **Sports:** There are 7 intercollegiate sports for men and 9 for women, and 31 intramural sports for men and 31 for women. Facilities include an outdoor and indoor tracks, a indoor hockey arena, swimming pool, indoor and outdoor tennis courts, racquetball, squash, volleyball, basketball courts, and three fitness centers. **Graduates:** From July 1, 2015 to June 30, 2016, 3368 bachelor's degrees were awarded. The most popular majors were business (20%), health professions (13%), and engineering (12%). 500 companies recruited on campus in 2015-2016. In an average class, 82% graduate in 6 years or less.

SERVICES: Counseling and information services are available, as is tutoring in most subjects. There is remedial math, reading, and writing. **Library/Resources:** The 3 libraries contain 896,213 volumes, 1.3 million microform items, and 18,210 audio/video tapes/CDs/DVDs, and subscribe to 128,027 periodicals including electronic. Computerized library services include interlibrary loans, database searching, Internet access, and Wi-Fi capability. Special learning facilities include an art gallery, radio station, architecture studio, TV production suite, and various research labs. **Physically Challenged Students:** 95% of the campus is accessible. Facilities include wheelchair ramps, elevators, special parking, specially equipped restrooms, special class scheduling, lowered drinking fountains, lowered telephones, special housing, specially equipped labs, and a tunnel system connecting the major administrative and academic buildings. **Special:** Northeastern offers a variety of experiential learning opportunities such as co-op, research, global experience, and service-learning in Boston, throughout the U.S., and around the world to integrate classroom instruction with professional experience. Northeastern takes a flexible student-centered approach to academics that allows you to create the education that best suits your goals and aspirations. We offer four- and five-year programs, combined degree programs, interdisciplinary study options, study abroad in dozens of countries, undergraduate research opportunities, an honors program, work-study through the university and in neighboring public and private agencies, and student-designed majors. There are 14 national honor societies and a freshman honors program. **Visiting:** There are regularly scheduled orientations for prospective students. There are guides for informal visits. To schedule a visit, contact the Office of Undergraduate Admissions. **Campus Safety and Security:** Measures include 24-hour foot and vehicle patrol, emergency notification system, self-defense education, and security escort services. There are shuttle buses, emergency telephones, lighted pathways/sidewalks, controlled access to dorms/residences, and in-room safes.

REQUIREMENTS: The ACT Optional Writing test is required. Northeastern requires that applicants have 17 academic units, including 4 in English, 3 each in math, science, and social studies, and 2 each in foreign language and history. Recommended are 4 units in math and science, and a foreign language. An essay is required. The SAT or ACT is required. AP credits are accepted. Important factors in the admissions decision are advanced placement or honors courses, leadership record, evidence of special talent, extracurricular activities record, geographical diversity, and recommendations by school officials. Although each college has its own requirements, students must generally complete at least 128 semester hours with a minimum GPA of 2.0. Students must also fulfill the university-wide general education requirement. **Procedure:** Freshmen are admitted fall. Entrance exams should be taken from May of the junior year through December of the senior year. There are early admissions and deferred admissions plans. Early decision applications should be filed by November 1; regular applications, by January 1 for fall entry, along with a $75 fee. Notification of early decision is sent December 31; regular decision, April 1. Applications are accepted on-line. **Transfer Students:** 683 transfer students enrolled in 2015-2016. The most successful transfer students have earned a cumulative GPA of 3.3. Students have also completed the introductory-level courses for their intended majors. Transfer students with less than 24 semester hours of college-level credit must also submit their high school transcripts and SAT or ACT scores. **International Students:** There are 2881 international students enrolled. The school actively recruits these students. They must take the TOEFL with a minimum score of 92 on the Internet-based version (iBT).

ADMISSIONS: 86% of the current freshmen were in the top fifth of their class; 97% were in the top two fifths. **Admissions Contact:** Kurt Heissenbuttel, Director of Admissions. Email: *admissions@neu.edu* Web: *www.northeastern.edu*

FINANCIAL AID: The CSS/Profile is required. The FAFSA code is

002199. The priority date for freshman financial aid applications for fall entry is February 15.

PINE MANOR COLLEGE *(The complete profile is made available exclusively on our website, www.barronspac.com)*

REGIS COLLEGE D-2

www.regiscollege.edu

Weston, MA 02493	**(781) 768-7100** **(866) 438-7344**
Fax: (781) 768-7071	**Email: admission@regiscollege.edu**
Full-time: 231 men, 727 women	**Faculty:** 70
Part-time: 33 men, 244 women	**Ph.D.s:** 70%
Graduate: 94 men, 625 women	**Student/Faculty:** 13 to 1
Year: semesters, summer session	**Tuition:** $37,540
Room & Board: $14,380	**Freshman Class:** 2025 applied, 1705 accepted, 268 enrolled
SAT or ACT: required	**CEEB CODE:** 3723
Application Deadline: June 1	**COMPETITIVE**

Regis College, through education in the arts, sciences, and professions, empowers women and men to challenge themselves academically, to serve and to lead. A Catholic college, Regis is a diverse and welcoming community guided by the values of the Sisters of St. Joseph of Boston. Figures in the above capsule and in this profile are approximate. There are 2 undergraduate schools and 1 graduate school. In addition to regional accreditation, Regis has baccalaureate program accreditation with CSWE, NASDTEC, NLN, and NEASC. The 131-acre campus is in a suburban area 12 miles west of Boston. Including any residence halls, there are 15 buildings.

STUDENT LIFE: 81% of undergraduates are from Massachusetts. Others are from 22 states, 25 foreign countries, and Canada. 75% are from public schools. 5% are Asian American; 49% White; 2% Foreign; 19% African American; 13% race unknown; 11% Hispanic; 1% two or more races. **Female To Male Ratio:** 4.5:1. The average age of freshmen is 18; all undergraduates, 23. 18% do not continue beyond their first year; 55% remain to graduate. **Housing:** 786 students can be accommodated in college housing, which includes single-sex and coed dorms, and quiet housing floors. On-campus housing is guaranteed for all 4 years. 60% of students live on campus; of those, 60% remain on campus on weekends. Upperclassmen may keep cars.

FACULTY/CLASSROOMS: 25% of faculty are male; 75% are female. 77% teach undergraduates. No introductory courses are taught by graduate students. The average class size in an introductory lecture is 18; in a laboratory is 10; and in a regular course is 11.

PROGRAMS OF STUDY: Regis confers B.A., B.S.N. and B.S.W. degrees. Associate, master's, and doctoral degrees are also awarded. Bachelor's degrees are awarded in BIOLOGICAL SCIENCE (biochemistry and biology/biological science), BUSINESS (business administration - international), COMMUNICATIONS AND THE ARTS (communications, English, and Spanish), COMPUTER AND PHYSICAL SCIENCE (chemistry), EDUCATION (mathematics education), HEALTH PROFESSIONS (health, nursing, public health, and radiological science), SOCIAL SCIENCE (criminal justice, history, international relations, law, liberal arts/general studies, political science/government, psychology, social work, and sociology). Nursing, medical imaging, and business management have the largest enrollments.

ACTIVITIES: There are no fraternities or sororities. There are 27 groups on campus, including choir, chorale, chorus, computers, dance, drama, ethnic, honors, international, literary magazine, musical theater, newspaper, photography, political, professional, radio and TV, religious, social, social service, student government, and yearbook. **Sports:** There are 7 intercollegiate sports for men and 9 for women, and 4 intramural sports for men and 4 for women. Facilities include an athletic facility, a softball diamond, soccer field, 4 tennis courts, an aerobics and dance studio, squash courts, a pool, sauna and Jacuzzi. The on campus fitness center provides a full range of cardiovascular machines as well as free weights and Nautilus equipment. **Graduates:** From July 1, 2015 to June 30, 2016, 319 bachelor's degrees were awarded. The most popular majors were health professions and related programs (70%), business/marketing (5%), and biological/life sciences (4%). In an average class, 41% graduate in 4 years or less, 53% graduate in 5 years or less, and 53% graduate in 6 years or less.

SERVICES: Counseling and information services are available, as is tutoring in most subjects. There is a reader service for the blind, and remedial math, reading, and writing. There are academic support services for learning-disabled students. **Library/Resources:** The library contains 134,706 volumes, 10,826 microform items, and 7,856 audio/video tapes/CDs/DVDs, and subscribes to 24,774 periodicals including electronic. Computerized library services include interlibrary loans, database searching, Internet access, and Wi-Fi capability. Special learning facilities include an art gallery, radio station, museum of stamps and postal history, and fine arts center. **Physically Challenged Students:** 87% of the campus is accessible. Facilities include wheelchair ramps, elevators, special parking, specially equipped restrooms, special class scheduling, lowered drinking fountains, and special housing. **Special:** Regis offers cross-registration with Boston, Babson, and Bentley Colleges and through the Sisters of St. Joseph Consortium. Students may study abroad at Regis affiliates in London, Ireland, and Kyoto, Japan, or through programs of other American colleges. Regis also offers internships, an accelerated degree program, a Washington semester at American University, dual and self-designed majors, work-study, nondegree study, and pass/fail options. Students have the option of pursuing a minor in addition to their major field of study. There are 10 national honor societies and a freshman honors program. **Visiting:** There are regularly scheduled orientations for prospective students, visiting students can participate in a welcome tour, lunch, speaker panels, and overnight programs offering class participation. There are guides for informal visits, visitors may sit in on classes, and stay overnight. To schedule a visit, contact the Admissions Office. **Campus Safety and Security:** Measures include 24-hour foot and vehicle patrol, self-defense education, and security escort services. There are shuttle buses, emergency telephones, lighted pathways/sidewalks, and controlled access to dorms/residences.

REQUIREMENTS: Applicants should have 4 years of English, 3 or 4 electives, 3 years of math, and 2 years each of foreign language, social studies, and natural science, including a lab science. An essay and 2 letters of recommendation are required. An interview is strongly encouraged. The GED is accepted. On-line applications must be accompanied by the transcript, letters of recommendation, and official SAT or ACT scores for some programs. Regis requires applicants to be in the upper 50% of their class. A GPA of 2.5 is required. AP and CLEP credits are accepted. Important factors in the admissions decision are recommendations by school officials, extracurricular activities record, and ability to finance college education. The Baccalaureate degree is conferred upon candidates who have satisfactorily completed a minimum of 120 semester credit hours, with a cumulative gradepoint average of at least 2.00 and who have completed the requirements for a major field, as well as the General Education Program requirements. Certain programs, such as nursing, nuclear medicine technology, social work, and elementary and secondary teaching licensure programs, require the student to earn a higher GPA. **Procedure:** Freshmen are admitted fall and spring. Entrance exams should be taken during the fall before enrollment. There are early admissions, deferred admissions, and rolling admissions plans. Applications should be filed by June 1 for fall entry, along with a $50 fee. Notifications are sent December 20. Applications are accepted online. **Transfer Students:** 27 transfer students enrolled in 2015-2016. Transfer students must complete an admission application and fee. In addition, an official high school transcript is required if the applicant has completed fewer than 9 college courses, an official college transcript, 1 letter of recommendation from a professor at the previous college attended, the academic catalog of the previous college, an essay, SAT or ACT scores if fewer than 16 courses have been completed, and health records. 54 of 120 credits required for the bachelor's degree must be completed at Regis. **International Students:** There are 21 international students enrolled. The school actively recruits these students. They must take the TOEFL with a minimum score of 550 on the paper-based TOEFL (PBT) or 79 on the Internet-based version (iBT).

ADMISSIONS: 84% of the 2016-2017 applicants were accepted. **Admissions Contact:** Zakaree Harris, Director of Admission. Email: *admission@regiscollege.edu* Web: *www.regiscollege.edu*

FINANCIAL AID: In 2016-2017, 91% of all full-time freshmen and 72% of continuing full-time students received some form of financial aid. 77% of all full-time freshmen and 82% of continuing full-time students received need-based aid. The average freshman award was $36,730. Need-based scholarships or need-based grants averaged $6,204; need-based self-help aid (loans and jobs) averaged $7,500; and other non-need-based awards and non-need-based scholarships averaged $18,085 ($37,540 maximum). 28% of undergraduate students work part-time. Average annual earnings from campus work are $934. Regis is a member of CSS. The FAFSA code is 002206. The priority date for freshman financial aid applications for fall entry is February 15.

SALEM STATE UNIVERSITY *(The complete profile is made available exclusively on our website, www.barronspac.com)*

SIMMONS COLLEGE — E-2

www.simmons.edu

Boston, MA 02115	(617) 521-2515 (800) 345-8468
Fax: (617) 521-3190	**Email:** ugadm@simmons.edu
Full-time: 3 men, 1591 women	**Faculty:** 126
Part-time: 10 men, 198 women	**Ph.D.s:** n/av
Graduate: 529 men, 3882 women	**Student/Faculty:** 13 to 1
Year: semesters, summer session	**Tuition:** $38,590
Room & Board: $14,500	**Freshman Class:** 2923 applied, 2139 accepted, 458 enrolled
SAT CR/M/W: 600/580/570 **ACT:** 26	**CEEB CODE:** 3761
Application Deadline: February 1	**VERY COMPETITIVE**

Simmons College, founded in 1899, is a private institution with an undergraduate college for women that offers a comprehensive education combining the arts, sciences, and humanities with preprofessional training. All graduate programs are co-ed, with the exception of the women-only MBA program. There are 5 undergraduate schools and 5 graduate schools. In addition to regional accreditation, Simmons has baccalaureate program accreditation with AACSB, APTA, CSWE, ACS, CCNE, and ACEND. The 12-acre campus is in an urban area in Boston. Including any residence halls, there are 17 buildings.

STUDENT LIFE: 60% of undergraduates are from Massachusetts. Others are from 42 states, 53 foreign countries, and Canada. 9% are Asian American; 7% African American; 7% Hispanic; 65% White; 4% Foreign; 4% two or more races; 4% race unknown. **Female To Male Ratio:** 10.5:1. The average age of freshmen is 19; all undergraduates, 22. 17% do not continue beyond their first year; 74% remain to graduate. **Housing:** 1100 students can be accommodated in college housing, which includes single-sex dorms and off-campus apartments. In addition, there are special-interest houses, theme housing, wellness housing, cooperative housing, women's dorms, and non-trad students with dependents. On-campus housing is guaranteed for the freshman year only, is available on a first-come, first-served basis, and is available on a lottery system for upperclassmen. 61% of students live on campus; of those, 70% remain on campus on weekends. No one may keep cars.

FACULTY/CLASSROOMS: 17% of faculty are male; 83% are female. 70% teach undergraduates. No introductory courses are taught by graduate students. The average class size in an introductory lecture is 15; in a laboratory is 11; and in a regular course is 14.

PROGRAMS OF STUDY: Simmons confers B.A., B.S. and B.S.W. degrees. Master's and doctoral degrees are also awarded. Bachelor's degrees are awarded in AGRICULTURE (environmental studies), BIOLOGICAL SCIENCE (biochemistry, biology/biological science, and biometrics and biostatistics), BUSINESS (business administration and management, finance, management information systems, marketing and distribution, and retailing), COMMUNICATIONS AND THE ARTS (arts administration/management, communications, English, French, information technology, music, and Spanish), COMPUTER AND PHYSICAL SCIENCE (chemistry, computer science, mathematics, and physics), EDUCATION (education, elementary education, health information management, secondary education, special education, and teaching English as a second/foreign language (TESOL/TEFOL)), HEALTH PROFESSIONS (exercise science, nursing, physical therapy, and public health), SOCIAL SCIENCE (African American studies, biopsychology, dietetics, East Asian studies, economics, food production/management/services, food science, history, interdisciplinary studies, international relations, philosophy, political science/government, psychobiology, psychology, social work, sociology, and women's studies). Nursing has the largest enrollment.

ACTIVITIES: There are no fraternities or sororities. There are 66 groups on campus, including art, campus ministries, choir, chorale, chorus, communications, dance, drama, ethnic, film, honors, international, jazz band, LGBT, literary magazine, newspaper, orchestra, political, professional, radio and TV, religious, social service, student government, symphony, and yearbook. Popular campus events include Connections Carnival - the Simmons Student Organization and Involvement Fair, Winter Wonderland, and Almost Midnight Breakfast. **Sports:** There are 10 intercollegiate sports for women. Facilities include an 8-lane pool, a spa and sauna, 1 racquetball and 2 squash courts, 2 rowing tanks, 3 fitness rooms, a dance studio, an indoor running area, 2 volleyball courts, and a basketball court. **Graduates:** From July 1, 2015 to June 30, 2016, 531 bachelor's degrees were awarded. The most popular majors were nursing (32%), biology (15%), and business administration (6%). 178 companies recruited on campus in 2015-2016. In an average class, 1% graduate in 3 years or less, 66% graduate in 4 years or less, 72% graduate in 5 years or less, and 73% graduate in 6 years or less. Of the 2015 graduating class, 23% were enrolled in graduate school within 6 months of graduation, and 67% were employed.

SERVICES: Counseling and information services are available, as is tutoring in every subject. There is a reader service for the blind, and remedial writing. **Library/Resources:** The library contains 280,302 volumes, 13,580 microform items, and 3,460 audio/video tapes/CDs/DVDs, and subscribes to 3,825 periodicals including electronic. Computerized library services include interlibrary loans, database searching, Internet access, and Wi-Fi capability. Special learning facilities include an art gallery, radio station, a writing center, tutoring, and disability services. **Physically Challenged Students:** 95% of the campus is accessible. Facilities include wheelchair ramps, elevators, special parking, specially equipped restrooms, special class scheduling, and lowered drinking fountains. **Special:** Cross-registration is available with the New England Conservatory of Music, Hebrew, Emmanuel, and Wheelock Colleges, Massachusetts College of Art, Massachusetts College of Pharmacy and Health Sciences, and Wentworth Institute of Technology. Simmons offers study abroad in Europe through the Institute of European studies. A Washington semester at American University, accelerated degree programs, profit and nonprofit internship programs, a B.A.-B.S. degree, dual majors, interdisciplinary majors, student-designed majors, work-study programs, and pass/fail options are also offered. There is a dual-degree program in chemistry, pharmacy, and physician's assistant with Massachusetts College of Pharmacy. There are 9 national honor societies, a freshman honors program, and 12 departmental honors programs. **Visiting:** There are regularly scheduled orientations for prospective students. There are guides for informal visits, visitors may sit in on classes, and stay overnight. To schedule a visit, contact Sara Purisky at (800) 345-8468. **Campus Safety and Security:** Measures include 24-hour foot and vehicle patrol, emergency notification system, self-defense education, and security escort services. There are emergency telephones, lighted pathways/sidewalks, and controlled access to dorms/residences.

REQUIREMENTS: The SAT or ACT is required. Simmons recommends that applicants have 4 years of English, math, foreign language, and social studies, as well as 3 years of science and history. An essay is required, and an interview is strongly recommended. A GPA of 3.0 is required. AP and CLEP credits are accepted. Important factors in the admissions decision are leadership record, advanced placement or honors courses, parents or siblings attended your school, evidence of special talent, personality/intangible qualities, extracurricular activities record, recommendations by alumni, geographical diversity, and recommendations by school officials. To graduate, students must complete 128 semester hours, including 24 to 48 in the major, and maintain a minimum GPA of 2.0. Eight semester hours in a supervised independent learning experience or an internship are also required. Students must also fulfill foreign language, math competency, and technology competency requirements. In addition to completing the multidisciplinary core courses, students must complete 1 course from each of the following 6 modes of inquiry categories: creative and performing arts, language, literature, and culture, quantitative analysis and reasoning, scientific inquiry, social and historical perspectives, and psychological and ethical development. A thesis is optional. **Procedure:** Freshmen are admitted fall and spring. There are early admissions and deferred admissions plans. Applications should be filed by February 1 for fall entry; December 1 for spring entry, along with a $55 fee. Notification of early decision is sent December 15; regular decision, March 15. Applications are accepted on-line. Application fees are waived if application is completed on-line. **Transfer Students:** 48 transfer students enrolled in 2015-2016. Applicants should have a GPA of 2.8, at least 17 college-level credit hours, official transcripts from all colleges attended, and a faculty recommendation and dean's report from the previous college attended. 48 of 128 credits required for the bachelor's degree must be completed at Simmons. **International Students:** There are 69 international students enrolled. The school actively recruits these students. They must take the TOEFL with a minimum score of 83 on the Internet-based version (iBT), or take the IELTS or SAT/ACT. They must also take the SAT or ACT.

ADMISSIONS: 73% of the 2016-2017 applicants were accepted. The SAT scores for the 2016-2017 freshman class were: Critical Reading-- 8% below 500, 42% between 500 and 599, 35% between 600 and 699, and 10% between 700 and 800. Math-- 12% below 500, 55% between 500 and 599, 31% between 600 and 699, and 2% between 700 and 800. Writing-- 13% below 500, 45% between 500 and 599, 35% between 600 and 699, and 7% between 700 and 800. The ACT scores were 19% between 18 and 23, 53% between 24 and 29, and 28% above 30. 53% of the current freshmen were in the top fifth of their class; 82% were in the top two fifths. 2 freshmen graduated first in their class. **Admissions Contact:** Ellen Johnson, Director. Email: *ugadm@simmons.edu* Web: *www.simmons.edu*

FINANCIAL AID: In 2016-2017, 100% of all full-time freshmen and 96% of continuing full-time students received some form of financial aid. 80% of all full-time freshmen and 77% of continuing full-time students received need-based aid. The average freshman award was $31,398. Need-based scholarships or need-based grants averaged $22,881 ($57,115 maximum); need-based self-help aid (loans and jobs) averaged $3,341 ($6,000 maximum); and other non-need-based awards and non-need-based scholarships averaged $5,090 ($59,740 maximum). 34% of undergraduate students work part-time. Average annual earnings from campus work are $1250. Simmons is a member of CSS. The college's own financial statement, federal tax returns, and an institutional form is required. The FAFSA code is 002208. The priority date for freshman financial aid applications for fall entry is February 15.

SMITH COLLEGE — B-2

www.smith.edu

Northampton, MA 01063 — **(413) 585-2500**

Fax: (413) 585-2527	**Email:** admission@smith.edu
Full-time: 2490 women	**Faculty:** 270; IIB, ++$
Part-time: 11 women	**Ph.D.s:** 99%
Graduate: 59 men, 323 women	**Student/Faculty:** 9 to 1
Year: semesters	**Tuition:** $47,904
Room & Board: $16,010	**Freshman Class:** 5254 applied, 1956 accepted, 654 enrolled
SAT CR/M/W: 685/670/685 **ACT:** 31	**CEEB CODE:** 3762
Application Deadline: January 15	**MOST COMPETITIVE**

Smith College, founded in 1871, is an independent women's college, and offers a liberal arts education. Figures in the above capsule and in this profile are approximate. There is 1 undergraduate school and 1 graduate school. In addition to regional accreditation, Smith has baccalaureate program accreditation with ABET. The 156-acre campus is in a small town 90 miles west of Boston. Including any residence halls, there are 118 buildings.

STUDENT LIFE: 82% of undergraduates are from out of state, mostly the Northeast. Students are from 48 states, 72 foreign countries, and Canada. 64% are from public schools. 8% are race unknown; 6% African American; 5% two or more races; 45% White; 14% Foreign; 12% Asian American; 10% Hispanic. 40% are Hindu, Buddhist, Muslim, Unitarian, and Christian Scientists; 20% Protestant; 18% claim no religious affiliation; 14% Catholic. **Female To Male Ratio:** 47.9:1. The average age of freshmen is 18; all undergraduates, 20. 9% do not continue beyond their first year; 86% remain to graduate. **Housing:** 2440 students can be accommodated in college housing, which includes single-sex. In addition, there are language houses, special-interest houses, non-smoking houses, 2 cooperative houses, housing for non-traditional-age students, an apartment complex for a limited number of juniors and seniors, a non-trad students with dependents, and women's dorms. On-campus housing is guaranteed for all 4 years. 96% of students live on campus. Upperclassmen may keep cars.

FACULTY/CLASSROOMS: 45% of faculty are male; 55% are female. All teach undergraduates, and do research. No introductory courses are taught by graduate students. The average class size in an introductory lecture is 25; in a laboratory is 13; and in a regular course is 20.

PROGRAMS OF STUDY: Smith confers A.B., and B.S.Eng. degrees. Master's and doctoral degrees are also awarded. Bachelor's degrees are awarded in BIOLOGICAL SCIENCE (biochemistry, biology/biological science, and neurosciences), COMMUNICATIONS AND THE ARTS (art history and appreciation, classics, comparative literature, creative writing, dance, dramatic arts, East Asian languages and literature, English, film arts, French, Germanic languages and literature, Greek, Italian, Latin, music, Russian, Spanish, and studio art), COMPUTER AND PHYSICAL SCIENCE (astronomy, chemistry, computer science, geology, mathematics, and physics), EDUCATION (early childhood education, education, and elementary education), ENGINEERING AND ENVIRONMENTAL DESIGN (architecture, engineering, and environmental science), HEALTH PROFESSIONS (exercise science), SOCIAL SCIENCE (African studies, African American studies, American studies, anthropology, classical/ancient civilization, cognitive science, economics, ethics, politics, and social policy, European studies, French studies, history, international relations, Japanese studies, Judaic studies, Latin American studies, Luso-Brazilian studies, medieval studies, Middle Eastern studies, philosophy, political science/government, psychology, religion, Russian and Slavic studies, sociology, urban studies, and women's studies). Art, economics, and government have the largest enrollments.

ACTIVITIES: There are no fraternities or sororities. There are 127 groups on campus, including art, cheerleading, chess, chorus, computers, dance, debate, drama, environmental, ethnic, honors, international, jazz band, LGBT, literary magazine, musical theater, newspaper, photography, political, professional, radio and TV, religious, social, social service, student government, symphony, and yearbook. Popular campus events include International Student Day, Spring and Winter Weekends and Rally Day. **Sports:** There are 14 intercollegiate sports for women, and 4 intramural sports for women. Facilities include indoor and outdoor tracks, tennis courts, riding rings, gyms, a climbing wall, indoor pool with 1- and 3-meter diving boards, weight-training rooms, dance studio, athletic training rooms, a human performance lab, squash courts, field hockey, soccer, lacrosse, and softball fields. There is a performing arts center, and a concert hall. **Graduates:** From July 1, 2015 to June 30, 2016, 682 bachelor's degrees were awarded. The most popular majors were social sciences (22%), area, ethnic, and genger studies (11%), and psychology (10%). 71 companies recruited on campus in 2015-2016. In an average class, 82% graduate in 4 years or less, 85% graduate in 5 years or less, and 89% graduate in 6 years or less.

SERVICES: Counseling and information services are available, as is tutoring in every subject. There is a reader service for the blind. Numerous services are provided for learning-disabled students, including note taking, oral tests, readers, tutors, books on tape, reading software, voice recognition, tape recorders, extended-timed tests, and writing counselors. **Library/Resources:** The 4 libraries contain 1.5 million volumes, 149,402 microform items, and 76,662 audio/video tapes/CDs/DVDs, and subscribe to 60,916 periodicals including electronic. Computerized library services include interlibrary loans, database searching, Internet access, and Wi-Fi capability. Special learning facilities include an art gallery, radio station, TV station, astronomy observatories, center for foreign languages and culture, digital design studio, plant and horticultural labs, art studios with casting, printmaking, darkroom facilities, specialized libraries for science, music, art, the Quantitative Learning Center, and the Jacobson Center for writing, teaching and learning. **Physically Challenged Students:** 85% of the campus is accessible. Facilities include wheelchair ramps, elevators, special parking, specially equipped restrooms, special class scheduling, lowered drinking fountains, and lowered telephones. **Special:** Smith offers study abroad in more than 50 countries including Italy, France, Germany, and Switzerland. There are also affiliated programs in India, Japan, Russia, China, South Africa, Peru, Brazil, and Spain. Other opportunities include cross-registration with 5 area colleges, a Washington semester, Smithsonian internships, exchanges with historically Black colleges, and other liberal arts colleges, and at BioSphere2. A 3-2 engineering degree is offered with Dartmouth College. Support for nontraditional-age students and for international students is provided, and funding for a summer internship is available for every undergraduate. Accelerated degree programs, student-designed majors, dual majors, and non-degree study are offered. There are 3 national honor societies and a chapter of Phi Beta Kappa. **Visiting:** There are regularly scheduled orientations for prospective students, including student-guided tours available 4 times a day, Monday through Friday, when school is in full session and on Saturday mornings from September to

January. Interviews may also be scheduled during these times. Information sessions are offered twice daily most of the year. There are guides for informal visits, visitors may sit in on classes, and stay overnight. To schedule a visit, contact the Office of Admissions. **Campus Safety and Security:** Measures include 24-hour foot and vehicle patrol, emergency notification system, self-defense education, and security escort services. There are shuttle buses, emergency telephones, lighted pathways/sidewalks, First-year students are required to attend panel discussions on campus safety. Specialized personal safety presentations, including self defense and sexual assault information, are provided to various houses and organizations. There are crime prevention programs including bicycle registration.

REQUIREMENTS: Smith highly recommends that applicants have 4 years of English, 3 years each of math, science (3 units with lab) and foreign language, and 2 years of history, and 1 year of academic electives. SAT and ACT are considered but not required. Interviews are recommended. The GED is accepted. AP credits are accepted. Important factors in the admissions decision are personality/intangible qualities, recommendations by school officials, evidence of special talent, and extracurricular activities record. All students plan individual programs in consultation with faculty advisers and take 64 credits outside their major and 36 to 64 credits in the major. Students must maintain a minimum 2.0 GPA in all academic work and during the senior year. A total of 128 credits is needed to graduate. A writing-intensive course is required for first-year students. A thesis is required for departmental honors programs. Distribution requirements are necessary for Latin honors eligibility. **Procedure:** Freshmen are admitted fall. Entrance exams should be taken before January of the senior year. There are early decision, early admissions, and deferred admissions plans. Early decision applications should be filed by November 15; regular applications, by January 15 for fall entry, along with a $60 fee. Notification of early decision is sent December 15; regular decision, April 1. 158 early decision candidates were accepted for the 2016-2017 class. 432 applicants were on the 2016 waiting list; 1 was admitted. Applications are accepted online. **Transfer Students:** 34 transfer students enrolled in 2015-2016. Criteria for transfer students are similar to those for entering freshmen, with more emphasis on the college record. 64 credits required for the bachelor's degree must be completed at Smith. **International Students:** The school actively recruits these students. They must take the TOEFL with a minimum score of 600 on the paper-based TOEFL (PBT) or 95 on the Internet-based version (iBT). They must also take the SAT or ACT if the language of instruction is English.

ADMISSIONS: 37% of the 2016-2017 applicants were accepted. The SAT scores for the 2016-2017 freshman class were: Critical Reading-- 1% below 500, 9% between 500 and 599, 42% between 600 and 699, and 47% between 700 and 800. Math-- 1% below 500, 21% between 500 and 599, 42% between 600 and 699, and 36% between 700 and 800. Writing-- 1% below 500, 12% between 500 and 599, 44% between 600 and 699, and 43% between 700 and 800. The ACT scores were 1% between 12 and 17, 5% between 18 and 23, 29% between 24 and 29, and 65% above 30. **Admissions Contact:** Debra Shaver, Director of Admissions. Email: *admission@smith.edu* Web: *www.smith.edu*

FINANCIAL AID: In 2016-2017, 67% of all full-time freshmen and 69% of continuing full-time students received some form of financial aid. 58% of all full-time freshmen and 63% of continuing full-time students received need-based aid. The average freshman award was $48,887. Need-based scholarships or need-based grants averaged $43,839; need-based self-help aid (loans and jobs) averaged $3,981; other non-need-based awards and non-need-based scholarships averaged $15,484; and $3,011 from other forms of aid. The average financial indebtedness of the 2016 graduate was $41,969. Smith is a member of CSS. The CSS/Profile, the college's own financial statement, noncustodial profile, and parent and student federal tax returns are required. The FAFSA code is 002209. The deadline for filing freshman financial aid applications for fall entry is February 15.

SPRINGFIELD COLLEGE — B-3
www.springfieldcollege.edu

Springfield, MA 01109 — (413) 748-3136, (800) 343-1257

Fax: (413) 748-3694 — Email: admissions@spfldcol.edu

Full-time: 100 men, 2000 women	**Faculty:** 210; IIA, av$
Part-time: 50 men, 50 women	**Ph.D.s:** 62%
Graduate: 400 men, 500 women	**Student/Faculty:** 10 to 1
Year: semesters, summer session	**Tuition:** $34,455
Room & Board: $11,540	**Freshman Class:** n/av
SAT or ACT: required	**CEEB CODE:** 3763
Application Deadline: December 1	**COMPETITIVE**

Springfield College, established in 1885, is a private liberal arts and sciences institution. Figures in the above capsule and in this profile are approximate. There are 3 undergraduate schools and 1 graduate school. In addition to regional accreditation, S.C. has baccalaureate program accreditation with APTA, CAHEA, and NRPA. The 160-acre campus is in a suburban area 26 miles north of Hartford, Connecticut. Including any residence halls, there are 38 buildings.

STUDENT LIFE: Students are from 30 states, 12 foreign countries, and Canada. 83% are from public schools. 93% are White; 4% African American; 2% Hispanic; 1% Asian American. **Female To Male Ratio:** 4.6:1. The average age of freshmen is 18; all undergraduates, 21. 12% do not continue beyond their first year. **Housing:** 1980 students can be accommodated in college housing, which includes single-sex and coed dorms, on-campus apartments, off-campus apartments, and married student housing. In addition, there are special-interest houses, and a wellness dorm. On-campus housing is guaranteed for all 4 years. 85% of students live on campus; of those, 70% remain on campus on weekends. Alcohol is not permitted. Upperclassmen may keep cars.

FACULTY/CLASSROOMS: 52% of faculty are male; 48% are female. No introductory courses are taught by graduate students. The average class size in an introductory lecture is 125; in a laboratory is 20; and in a regular course is 30.

PROGRAMS OF STUDY: S.C. confers B.A. and B.S. degrees. Master's and doctoral degrees are also awarded. Bachelor's degrees are awarded in BIOLOGICAL SCIENCE (biochemistry, biology/biological science, and biotechnology), BUSINESS (business administration and management and sports management), COMMUNICATIONS AND THE ARTS (English and fine arts), COMPUTER AND PHYSICAL SCIENCE (chemistry, information sciences and systems, and mathematics), EDUCATION (early childhood education, elementary education, health education, middle school education, physical education, science education, and secondary education), ENGINEERING AND ENVIRONMENTAL DESIGN (computer graphics), HEALTH PROFESSIONS (art therapy, emergency medical technologies, environmental health science, health care administration, predentistry, premedicine, recreation therapy, and rehabilitation therapy), SOCIAL SCIENCE (gerontology, history, human services, parks and recreation management, physical fitness/movement, political science/government, prelaw, psychology, and sociology). Physical therapy, and athletic training are the strongest academically. Physical education has the largest enrollment.

ACTIVITIES: There are no fraternities or sororities. There are 58 groups on campus, including art, band, cheerleading, choir, chorus, club sports, communications, computers, dance, drama, ethnic, film, honors, international, jazz band, LGBT, literary magazine, musical theater, newspaper, pep band, professional, radio and TV, religious, social, social service, student government, and yearbook. Popular campus events include Parents Weekend and Stepping Up Day. **Sports:** There are 13 intercollegiate sports for men and 11 for women, and 10 intramural sports for men and 10 for women. Facilities include a 2000-seat stadium, a 2000-seat gym, a superturf football/soccer/lacrosse/field hockey field, 8 tennis courts, baseball and softball fields, and free weight and Nautilus rooms. **Graduates:** Of the 2015 graduating class, 19% were enrolled in graduate school within 6 months of graduation, and 78% were employed.

SERVICES: Counseling and information services are available, as is tutoring in every subject. There is remedial math and writing. **Library/Resources:** The library contains 168,332 volumes, 736,056 microform items, and 3,200 audio/video tapes/CDs/DVDs, and subscribes to 831 periodicals including electronic. Computerized library services include interlibrary loans and database searching. Special learning facilities include an art gallery, radio station, and outdoor center. **Physically Challenged Students:** 75% of the campus is accessible. Facilities include wheelchair ramps, elevators, special parking, specially equipped restrooms, special class scheduling, and lowered drinking fountains. **Special:** There is a co-op program and cross-registration with cooperating colleges in the greater Springfield area. Internships are required in most majors, and there is limited study abroad. There are 2 national honor societies. **Visiting:** There are guides for informal visits, visitors may sit in on classes, and stay overnight. To schedule a visit, contact the Admissions Office. **Campus Safety and Security:** Measures include 24-hour foot and vehicle patrol, self-defense education, and security escort services. There are shuttle buses, emergency telephones, and lighted pathways/sidewalks.

REQUIREMENTS: The SAT or ACT is required. Applicants must be graduates of an accredited secondary school and have completed 4 years of English and 3 years each of history, math, and science. The school accepts the GED. An essay is required and an interview is recommended. Applications are accepted on-line. AP and CLEP credits are accepted. Important factors in the admissions decision are advanced placement or honors courses, leadership record, and extracurricular activities record. To graduate, students must complete a total of 130 credits with a 2.0 GPA. Core requirements include 50 semester hours in English, social and natural sciences, health, religion, philosophy, and art, and 4 credits in phys ed. **Procedure:** Freshmen are admitted fall and spring. Entrance exams should be taken by November of the senior year. There are early decision, early admissions, deferred admissions, and rolling admissions plans. Early decision applications should be filed by December 1; regular applications, by December 1 for fall entry, along with a $40 fee. Notification of early decision is sent February 1; regular decision, March 15. Applications are accepted on-line. **Transfer Students:** Grades of 2.0 transfer for credit. Transfer students are admitted in the fall and spring. **International Students:** There are 20 international students enrolled. The school actively recruits these students. They must take the TOEFL. They must also take the SAT or ACT.

Admissions Contact: Mary N. DeAngelo, Director of Admissions. Email: *admissions@spfldcol.edu* Web: *www.springfieldcollege.edu*

FINANCIAL AID: The CSS/Profile, and tax returns from parents and student are required. The FAFSA code is 002211. The deadline for filing freshman financial aid applications for fall entry is March 15.

STONEHILL COLLEGE — E-3

www.stonehill.edu

Easton, MA 02357 — **(508) 565-1373**

Fax: (508) 565-1545	**Email: admissions@stonehill.edu**
Full-time: 985 men, 1485 women	**Faculty:** 156; IIB, +$
Part-time: 5 men, 6 women	**Ph.D.s:** 85%
Graduate: n/av	**Student/Faculty:** 12 to 1
Year: semesters, summer session	**Tuition:** $39,900
Room & Board: $15,130	**Freshman Class:** n/av
SAT or ACT: required	**CEEB CODE:** 3770
Application Deadline: January 15	**COMPETITIVE+**

Stonehill is a selective Catholic college with a welcoming community and beautiful campus. Dedicated, supportive faculty mentor students in 80+ academic programs in the liberal arts, sciences, and business. Nearly 90% of students participate in internships, study abroad, research, practicum, and field work. Stonehill is a vibrant community where students learn to live lives that make a difference. Figures in the above capsule and in this profile are approximate. There are 4 undergraduate schools. In addition to regional accreditation, Stonehill has baccalaureate program accreditation with ACS and AUPHA. The 384-acre campus is in a suburban area 22 miles south of Boston. Including any residence halls, there are 65 buildings.

STUDENT LIFE: 58% of undergraduates are from Massachusetts. Others are from 29 states, and 10 foreign countries. 90% are White; 3% Hispanic; 2% African American. 71% are Catholic; 13% claim no religious affiliation. **Female To Male Ratio:** 1.5:1. The average age of freshmen is 18; all undergraduates, 20. 8% do not continue beyond their first year; 85% remain to graduate. **Housing:** 2199 students can be accommodated in college housing, which includes single-sex dorms. In addition, there are special-interest houses, substance-free/wellness housing, theme housing, and community service housing. On-campus housing is guaranteed for all 4 years. 91% of students live on campus; of those, 85% remain on campus on weekends. Upperclassmen may keep cars.

FACULTY/CLASSROOMS: 58% of faculty are male; 42% are female. All teach undergraduates, and all do research. No introductory courses are taught by graduate students. The average class size in an introductory lecture is 21.

PROGRAMS OF STUDY: Stonehill confers B.A., B.S. and B.S.B.A. degrees. Bachelor's degrees are awarded in AGRICULTURE (environmental studies), BIOLOGICAL SCIENCE (biochemistry, biology/biological science, and neurosciences), BUSINESS (accounting, banking and finance, business administration and management, international business management, and marketing/retailing/merchandising), COMMUNICATIONS AND THE ARTS (art history and appreciation, communications, English, fine arts, French, music, and Spanish), COMPUTER AND PHYSICAL SCIENCE (chemistry, computer science, mathematics, and physics), EDUCATION (education), HEALTH PROFESSIONS (health care administration), SOCIAL SCIENCE (American studies, Christian studies, criminology, economics, gender studies, history, interdisciplinary studies, international studies, philosophy, political science/government, psychology, public administration, religion, and sociology). Business, biology, and psychology have the largest enrollments.

ACTIVITIES: There are no fraternities or sororities. There are 77 groups on campus, including art, band, cheerleading, choir, chorale, chorus, computers, dance, drama, environmental, ethnic, film, honors, international, LGBT, literary magazine, musical theater, newspaper, pep band, photography, political, professional, radio and TV, religious, social, social service, student government, and yearbook. Popular campus events include Skyhawk Weekend, Spring Weekend, and Halloween Mixer. **Sports:** There are 9 intercollegiate sports for men and 11 for women, and 20 intramural sports for men and 20 for women. Facilities include a 2400-seat stadium for football, field hockey, soccer, and lacrosse, a 500-seat field for men's and women's soccer, a 2000-seat gym with basketball and volleyball courts, 5000 square feet of weight and cardiovascular fitness areas, a recreational and intramural sports complex, tennis courts, baseball, softball, and field hockey fields, a regulation beach volleyball court, and 3 recreational fields for intramural and club sports. **Graduates:** From July 1, 2015 to June 30, 2016, 515 bachelor's degrees were awarded. The most popular majors were business/marketing (20%), social sciences (14%), and mathematics and statistics/homeland security (10%). 356 companies recruited on campus in 2015-2016. In an average class, 80% graduate in 4 years or less, 84% graduate in 5 years or less, and 87% graduate in 6 years or less. Of the 2015 graduating class, 41% were enrolled in graduate school within 6 months of graduation, and 71% were employed.

SERVICES: Counseling and information services are available, as is tutoring in most subjects. A learning disabilities specialist and free diagnostic testing are also available as are auxiliary aids for hearing impaired students. There are note takers, and other resources based on need. There is a reader service for the blind, and remedial writing. **Library/Resources:** The library contains 243,500 volumes, 150,431 microform items, and 9,593 audio/video tapes/CDs/DVDs, and subscribes to 13,111 periodicals including electronic. Computerized library services include interlibrary loans, database searching, Internet access, and Wi-Fi capability. Special learning facilities include an art gallery, radio station, an observatory, an institute for the study of law and society, and several archives and special collections. **Physically Challenged Students:** All of the campus is accessible. Facilities include wheelchair ramps, elevators, special parking, specially equipped restrooms, special class scheduling, lowered drinking fountains, lowered telephones, and special housing. **Special:** Stonehill College offers cross registration, double major, duel enrollment, exchange student program (domestic), honors program and independent study, internships liberal arts/career combination, student-designed major, study abroad, and teachers certification program. There are fall-semester international internships sites in Belgrade, Dublin, London, Madrid, Paris, and Yerevan. Stonehill also offers BA/BS programs with the University of Notre Dame, Indiana, Los Angeles semester, New York semester, Washington DC semester, and SEA semester, and the Stonehill undergraduate research experience (SURE) program. There are 20 national honor societies and a freshman honors program. **Visiting:** There are regularly scheduled orientations for prospective students, consisting of group information sessions and guided campus tours available by appointment throughout the year. Visitors may sit in on classes. To schedule a visit, contact the Admissions Office. **Campus Safety and Security:** Measures include 24-hour foot and vehicle patrol, emergency notification system, self-defense education, and security escort services. There are emergency telephones, lighted pathways/sidewalks, controlled access to dorms/residences, bicycle patrols, and a weekend guest sign-in policy.

REQUIREMENTS: Applicants should be graduates of an accredited high school or have earned the GED. Secondary preparation should include 4 units of English, 3 units each of foreign language, science, 3-4 units of math, 3-4 units of science with 3 units of lab, and 3-4 history. An essay, school report, 2 teacher evaluations, and a completed common application sent with a Stonehill Supplemental Information Form are required. AP credits are accepted. Important factors in the admissions decision are advanced placement or honors courses, evidence of special talent, leadership record, extracurricular activities record, recommendations by school officials, parents or siblings attended your school, personality/intangible qualities, recommendations by alumni, and geographical diversity. All students must complete a cornerstone program, which consists of 4 common courses within history/literature and philosophy/religious studies; a learning community consisting of 2 linked courses and a 3rd integrated course; a moral inquiry course; and a senior capstone experience within the major. Distribution requirements include 2 semesters of a foreign language and 1 course each in in natural scientific inquiry, social scientific inquiry, and statistical reasoning. Students must complete 120 hours 40 3- to 4-credit courses while maintaining a minimum GPA of 2.0. **Procedure:** Freshmen are admitted fall and spring. There are early decision, early admissions, and deferred admissions plans. Early decision applications should be filed by December 1; regular applications, by January 15 for fall entry; and November 1 for spring entry, along with a $60 fee. Notification of early decision is sent December 31; regular decision, March 15. 44 early decision candidates were accepted for the 2016-2017 class. 98 applicants were on the 2016 waiting list; 24 were admitted. Applications are accepted on-line. Application fees are waived if application is completed on-line. **Transfer Students:** 27 transfer students enrolled in 2015-2016. Applicants must have a minimum GPA of 2.0. Official high school transcripts and college transcripts along with catalogs with course descriptions from all colleges attended are required. An essay and 2 recommendations are required, and an interview is recommended. Application for transfer admission is in the fall and spring. 60 of 120 credits required for the bachelor's degree must be completed at Stonehill. **International Students:** There are 12 international students enrolled. The school actively recruits these students. They must take the TOEFL.

ADMISSIONS: 65% of the current freshmen were in the top fifth of their class; 92% were in the top two fifths. 7 freshmen graduated first in their class. **Admissions Contact:** Emma Brown, Assistant Dean of Admissions. Email: *admissions@stonehill.edu* Web: *www.stonehill.edu*

FINANCIAL AID: In 2016-2017, 78% of all full-time freshmen received some form of financial aid. The average freshman award was $31,017. Need-based scholarships or need-based grants averaged $25,498; need-based self-help aid (loans and jobs) averaged $5,007; non-need-based athletic scholarships averaged $13,471; and other non-need-based awards and non-need-based scholarships averaged $17,439. 47% of undergraduate students work part-time. Average annual earnings from campus work are $2120. The average financial indebtedness of the 2016 graduate was $31,622. Stonehill is a member of CSS. The CSS/Profile, noncustodial profile and business/farm supplement are required. The FAFSA code is 002217. The deadline for filing freshman financial aid applications for fall entry is February 1.

SUFFOLK UNIVERSITY — E-2
www.suffolk.edu

Boston, MA 02108 — (617) 573-8460, (800) 6SUFFOL

Fax: (617) 742-4291 — **Email:** admission@suffolk.edu

Full-time: 2248 men, 2756 women
Part-time: 133 men, 153 women
Graduate: 950 men, 1320 women
Year: semesters, summer session
Room & Board: $14,730
SAT CR/M/W: 508/512/502 **ACT:** 23
Application Deadline: March 1

Faculty: 258
Ph.D.s: 82%
Student/Faculty: 19 to 1
Tuition: $35,440
Freshman Class: 8642 applied, 7289 accepted, 1205 enrolled
CEEB CODE: 3771
COMPETITIVE

Founded in 1906, Suffolk University offers students experiential learning, a campus set amid Boston's world-renowned landmarks, and enviable access to top employers. Thanks to small classes, students work closely with their professors experts in their fields who mentor and connect them with career-shaping internships. Suffolk students enjoy a vibrant campus life that features over 80 clubs and organizations and meaningful community service opportunities. They also gain global insights at Suffolk's campus in Madrid, Spain, and partner institutions around the world. Suffolk's strong emphasis on hands-on learning equips students to define and successfully pursue their professional careers upon graduation. There are 2 undergraduate schools and 3 graduate schools. In addition to regional accreditation, Suffolk has baccalaureate program accreditation with AACSB, ABET, FIDER, and NASAD. The 2-acre campus is in an urban area in the heart of downtown Boston. Including any residence halls, there are 14 buildings.

STUDENT LIFE: 68% of undergraduates are from Massachusetts. Others are from 45 states, 100 foreign countries, and Canada. 65% are from public schools. 8% are Asian American; 6% African American; 6% race unknown; 44% White; 22% Foreign; 2% two or more races; 11% Hispanic. **Female To Male Ratio:** 1.3:1. The average age of freshmen is 18; all undergraduates, 21. 25% do not continue beyond their first year; 76% remain to graduate. **Housing:** 1299 students can be accommodated in college housing, which includes coed dorms. On-campus housing is available on a first-come, first-served basis, and is available on a lottery system for upperclassmen. Alcohol is not permitted. No one may keep cars.

FACULTY/CLASSROOMS: 54% of faculty are male; 46% are female. All teach undergraduates. No introductory courses are taught by graduate students. The average class size in an introductory lecture is 22 and in a laboratory is 15.

PROGRAMS OF STUDY: Suffolk confers B.A., B.S., B.F.A., B.S.B.A., B.S.G.S. and B.S.J. degrees. Associate, master's, and doctoral degrees are also awarded. Bachelor's degrees are awarded in AGRICULTURE (environmental studies), BIOLOGICAL SCIENCE (biochemistry, biology/biological science, biotechnology, life science, and marine science), BUSINESS (accounting, banking and finance, entrepreneurial studies, international business management, international economics, management science, and marketing/retailing/merchandising), COMMUNICATIONS AND THE ARTS (advertising, art history and appreciation, broadcasting, communications, creative writing, dramatic arts, English, film arts, fine arts, French, graphic design, journalism, media arts, music history and appreciation, performing arts, public relations, Spanish, and speech/debate/rhetoric), COMPUTER AND PHYSICAL SCIENCE (chemistry, computer programming, computer science, information sciences and systems, mathematics, and physics), EDUCATION (business education, English education, mathematics education, and science education), ENGINEERING AND ENVIRONMENTAL DESIGN (computer engineering, electrical/electronics engineering, environmental engineering, environmental science, and interior design), HEALTH PROFESSIONS (medical laboratory technology and radiological science), SOCIAL SCIENCE (African American studies, American studies, criminal justice, economics, European studies, German area studies, history, human development, human services, humanities, international relations, paralegal studies, philosophy, political science/government, psychology, social science, sociology, and women's studies). Business, sociology, and communications are the strongest academically. Finance, communication & journalism, and marketing have the largest enrollments.

ACTIVITIES: There are more than 75 groups on campus, including art, choir, chorale, chorus, computers, dance, debate, drama, ethnic, film, forensics, honors, international, jazz band, LGBT, literary magazine, musical theater, newspaper, orientation, photography, political, professional, radio and TV, religious, social, social service, and student government. Popular campus events include Fallfest Talent Show, Temple Street Fair, and Diversity Services-Coffee Hour. **Sports:** There are 7 intercollegiate sports for men and 6 for women, and 2 intramural sports for men and 2 for women. Facilities include a basketball, volleyball, and aerobics facility, indoor baseball/softball practice and a fully equipped fitness center. **Graduates:** From July 1, 2015 to June 30, 2016, 1269 bachelor's degrees were awarded. The most popular majors were communications (13%), finance (11%), and marketing (10%). 250 companies recruited on campus in 2015-2016. In an average class, 1% graduate in 3 years or less, 53% graduate in 4 years or less, 58% graduate in 5 years or less, and 59% graduate in 6 years or less. Of the 2015 graduating class, 76% were enrolled in graduate school within 6 months of graduation, and 52% were employed.

SERVICES: Counseling and information services are available, as is tutoring in every subject. There is a reader service for the blind, and remedial math, reading, and writing. **Library/Resources:** The 3 libraries contain 159,014 volumes, 199,622 microform items, and 1,904 audio/video tapes/CDs/DVDs, and subscribe to 478 periodicals including electronic. Computerized library services include interlibrary loans, database searching, Internet access, and Wi-Fi capability. Special learning facilities include an art gallery, radio station, and TV station. **Physically Challenged Students:** Facilities include wheelchair ramps, elevators, specially equipped restrooms, special class scheduling, lowered drinking fountains, and lowered telephones. **Special:** There are 15 national honor societies, a freshman honors program, and 11 departmental honors programs. **Visiting:** There are regularly scheduled orientations for prospective students. Students visits include a general presentation and an overview panel presentation of student life, career and co-op opportunities, learning center services, and athletics and academic department meetings, and campus tours. There are guides for informal visits and visitors may sit in on classes. To schedule a visit, contact the Admissions Office. **Campus Safety and Security:** Measures include 24-hour foot and vehicle patrol, emergency notification system, self-defense education, and security escort services. There are emergency telephones and lighted pathways/sidewalks.

REQUIREMENTS: The SAT or ACT is required. The ACT Optional Writing test is also required. Applicants should have a high school diploma or the GED. Recommended secondary preparation includes 4 years of English, 3 of math, 2 each of a foreign language and science, and 1 of American history. Exact requirements differ by degree program. A personal essay is required, and an interview is recommended. AP and CLEP credits are accepted. Important factors in the admissions decision are advanced placement or honors courses, recommendations by school officials, and leadership record. All students must complete their semester hours with at least a 2.0 GPA. Distribution requirements vary by degree program. **Procedure:** Freshmen are admitted fall, spring, and summer. Entrance exams should be taken by December of the senior year. There are early admissions and deferred admissions plans. Early decision applications should be filed by November 15; regular applications, by March 1 for fall entry; and December 15 for spring entry, along with a $50 fee. Notification of early decision is sent December 20; regular decision, January 15. Applications are accepted on-line. **Transfer Students:** 391 transfer students enrolled in 2015-2016. Applicants should have a minimum 2.5 GPA from an accredited college. Those with fewer than 15 college credits must submit a high school transcript. 30 of 124 credits required for the bachelor's degree must be completed at Suffolk. **International Students:** There are 1147 international students enrolled. The school actively recruits these students. They must take the TOEFL with a minimum score of 550 on the paper-based TOEFL (PBT) or 80 on the Internet-based version (iBT). They must also take the SAT or ACT and the college's own entrance exam.

ADMISSIONS: 84% of the 2016-2017 applicants were accepted. The SAT scores for the 2016-2017 freshman class were: Critical Reading-- 45% below 500, 40% between 500 and 599, 13% between 600 and 699, and 2% between 700 and 800. Math-- 41% below 500, 44% between 500 and 599, 14% between 600 and 699, and 1% between 700 and 800. Writing-- 45% below 500, 43% between 500 and 599, 11% between 600 and 699, and 1% between 700 and 800. The ACT scores were 10% between 12 and 17, 46% between 18 and 23, 39% between 24 and 29, and 5% above 30. 29% of the current freshmen were in the top fifth of their class; 59% were in the top two fifths. One freshman graduated first in the class. **Admissions Contact:** Donna Grand Pre, Director, Undergraduate Admissions. Email: *admission@suffolk.edu* Web: *www.suffolk.edu*

FINANCIAL AID: In 2016-2017, 94% of all full-time freshmen and 83% of continuing full-time students received some form of financial aid. 66% of all full-time freshmen and 52% of continuing full-time students received need-based aid. The average freshman award was $31,238. Need-based scholarships or need-based grants averaged $8,501 ($35,440 maximum); need-based self-help aid (loans and jobs) averaged $4,683 ($9,000 maximum); and other non-need-based awards and non-need-based scholarships averaged $22,252 ($55,686 maximum). 11% of undergraduate students work part-time. Average annual earnings from campus work are $1818. The average financial indebtedness of the 2016 graduate was $26,856. The college's own financial statement, and verification of income are required. The FAFSA code is 002218. The deadline for filing freshman financial aid applications for fall entry is February 15.

THE BOSTON CONSERVATORY AT BERKLEE — E-2

Boston Conservatory
www.bostonconservatory.edu

Boston, MA 02215 — **(617) 912-9153**

Full-time: 217 men, 286 women	**Faculty:** n/av
Part-time: 2 men, 7 women	**Ph.D.s:** n/av
Graduate: 100 men, 107 women	**Student/Faculty:** 5 to 1
Year: semesters	**Tuition:** $43,800
Room & Board: $17,242	**Freshman Class:** n/av
SAT CR/M: 549/577 **ACT:** 25	**CEEB CODE:** 3084
Application Deadline: December 1	**COMPETITIVE+**

Boston Conservatory at Berklee, which merged with Berklee College of music (2016), and was founded in 1867, is a private college providing degree programs in music, musical theater, and dance. Figures in the above capsule and in this profile are approximate. Cost varies by programs. There are 4 undergraduate schools and 3 graduate schools. In addition to regional accreditation, BoCo has baccalaureate program accreditation with NASM. The campus is in an urban area in Boston's Back Bay. Including any residence halls, there are 9 buildings.

STUDENT LIFE: 80% of undergraduates are from out of state, mostly the Northeast. Students are from 40 states, 24 foreign countries, and Canada. **Female To Male Ratio:** 1.3:1. The average age of freshmen is 18. 19% do not continue beyond their first year. **Housing:** 182 students can be accommodated in college housing, which includes coed dorms. On-campus housing is guaranteed for the freshman year only and is available on a lottery system for upperclassmen. 72% of students commute. Alcohol is not permitted. No one may keep cars.

FACULTY/CLASSROOMS: All teach undergraduates. No introductory courses are taught by graduate students. The average class size in an introductory lecture is 15; in a laboratory is 5; and in a regular course is 15.

PROGRAMS OF STUDY: BoCo confers B.F.A., and B.M. degrees. Master's degrees are also awarded. Bachelor's degrees are awarded in COMMUNICATIONS AND THE ARTS (dance, guitar, music, music performance, music theory and composition, musical theater, opera, and piano/organ), EDUCATION (music education). Music has the largest enrollment.

ACTIVITIES: There are 19 groups on campus, including band, choir, chorale, chorus, dance, drama, international, LGBT, musical theater, newspaper, opera, orchestra, political, professional, religious, social service, student government, and yearbook. Popular campus events include Parents Weekend, Off the Block Program, Drag Show, and Thanksgiving Dinner. **Sports:** There is no sports program at BoCo. **Graduates:** From July 1, 2015 to June 30, 2016, 117 bachelor's degrees were awarded. The most popular majors were musical theater (46%), music (40%), and dance (14%).

SERVICES: Counseling and information services are available, as is tutoring in some subjects, such as writing, music theory, and music history. **Library/Resources:** The library contains 40,000 volumes, and subscribes to 120 periodicals including electronic. Computerized library services include interlibrary loans and database searching. **Physically Challenged Students:** 20% of the campus is accessible. Facilities include elevators. **Special:** There are 3 national honor societies and 1 departmental honors program. **Visiting:** Visitors may sit in on classes. To schedule a visit, contact the Admissions Office. **Campus Safety and Security:** Measures include 24-hour foot and vehicle patrol. There are emergency telephones and controlled access to dorms/residences.

REQUIREMENTS: Either the SAT or the ACT is required for undergraduate admission. An audition is the most important factor for acceptance and merit scholarship. GPA and standardized test scores are considered in concert with each other to determine ability to undertake the academic, liberal arts component of the undergraduate degree. A GPA of 2.7 is required. AP and CLEP credits are accepted. Important factors in the admissions decision are evidence of special talent, extracurricular activities record, and personality/intangible qualities. **Procedure:** Freshmen are admitted fall. Entrance exams should be taken as early as possible. There is a deferred admissions plan. Applications should be filed by December 1 for fall entry, along with a $110 fee. Notifications are sent April 1. 30 applicants were on the 2016 waiting list. Applications are accepted on-line. **Transfer Students:** 15 transfer students enrolled in 2015-2016. A successful audition and a 3.0 GPA are required. Transfer credits are determined through transcript review conducted by the dean and Registrar. The high school transcript is required if fewer than 2 semesters worth of college-level work have been undertaken/earned. **International Students:** There are 62 international students enrolled. The school actively recruits these students. They must take the TOEFL or MELAB. They must also take the SAT or ACT. An audition also is required.

Admissions Contact: Meghan Cadwallader, Director of Admissions. Web: *www.bostonconservatory.edu*

FINANCIAL AID: BoCo is a member of CSS. The FAFSA code is 002129. Check with the school for current application deadlines.

TUFTS UNIVERSITY D-2

www.tufts.edu

Medford, MA 02155 (617) 627-3170

Fax: (617) 627-3860 Email: undergraduate.admissions@tufts.edu

Full-time: 2701 men, 2734 women	**Faculty:** 543; I, +$
Part-time: 33 men, 40 women	**Ph.D.s:** 93%
Graduate: 2392 men, 3589 women	**Student/Faculty:** 8 to 1
Year: semesters, summer session	**Tuition:** $50,604
Room & Board: $13,094	**Freshman Class:** 20223 applied, 2889 accepted, 1338 enrolled
SAT CR/M/W: 680/710/690 **ACT:** 32	**CEEB CODE:** 3901
Application Deadline: January 1	**MOST COMPETITIVE**

Tufts University, founded in 1852, is a private institution offering undergraduate programs in liberal arts and sciences, engineering, and fine arts. Figures in the above capsule and in this profile are from a recent year, and apply to the Medford/Somerville campus resources unless otherwise noted. There are 3 undergraduate schools and 9 graduate schools. In addition to regional accreditation, Tufts has baccalaureate program accreditation with ABET, ADA, CAHEA, NASAD, and MA Dept of Elementary and Secondary Education. The 150-acre campus is in a suburban area 5 miles northwest of Boston. Including any residence halls, there are 135 buildings.

STUDENT LIFE: 74% of undergraduates are from out of state, mostly the Northeast. Students are from 50 states, 76 foreign countries, and Canada. 59% are from public schools. 7% are Hispanic; 6% race unknown; 56% White; 5% two or more races; 4% African American; 12% Asian American; 10% Foreign. **Female To Male Ratio:** 1.2:1. The average age of freshmen is 18; all undergraduates, 20. 4% do not continue beyond their first year; 92% remain to graduate. **Housing:** 3372 students can be accommodated in college housing, which includes single-sex and coed dorms and on-campus apartments. In addition, there are language houses, special-interest houses, fraternity houses, sorority houses, and theme and wellness houses. On-campus housing is available on a lottery system for upperclassmen. 62% of students live on campus. Upperclassmen may keep cars.

FACULTY/CLASSROOMS: 53% of faculty are male; 47% are female. All teach undergraduates, and all do research. No introductory courses are taught by graduate students. The average class size in a regular course is 20.

PROGRAMS OF STUDY: Tufts confers B.A., B.S.(inc. Engineering options), and B.F.A. degrees. Master's and doctoral degrees are also awarded. Bachelor's degrees are awarded in BIOLOGICAL SCIENCE (biochemistry, biology/biological science, biophysics, and biotechnology), COMMUNICATIONS AND THE ARTS (Africana studies, Arabic, art history, Chinese, classics, dramatic arts, English, French, German, Greek, interdisciplinary art, Italian, Japanese, Latin, film and media studies, music, Russian, and Spanish), COMPUTER AND PHYSICAL SCIENCE (applied mathematics, applied physics, astrophysics, chemistry, computer science, geology, mathematics, and physics), EDUCATION (education), ENGINEERING AND ENVIRONMENTAL DESIGN (architecture, biomedical engineering, chemical engineering, civil engineering, computer engineering, electrical/electronics engineering, engineering, engineering and applied science, engineering physics, environmental engineering, environmental science, and mechanical engineering), HEALTH PROFESSIONS (biology, biomedical science, and community health work), SOCIAL SCIENCE (American studies, anthropology, archeology, Asian/Oriental studies, biopsychology, child psychology/development, cognitive science, economics, feminist, gender, sexuality studies, German area studies, history, interdisciplinary studies, international relations, Judaic studies, Latin American studies, Middle Eastern studies, peace studies, philosophy, political science/government, psychology, religion, Russian and Slavic studies, sociology, and urban studies). International relations, engineering, and philosophy are the strongest academically. International relations, computer science, and biology have the largest enrollments.

ACTIVITIES: 16% of men belong to 3 local and 6 national fraternities; 17% of women belong to 4 national sororities. There are 325 groups on campus, including Tufts Dance Collective, Leonard Carmichael Society, art, band, cheerleading, chess, choir, chorale, chorus, communications, computers, dance, debate, drama, environmental, ethnic, film, forensics, honors, international, jazz band, LGBT, literary magazine, musical theater, newspaper, opera, orchestra, pep band, photography, political, professional, radio and TV, religious, social, social service, student government, symphony, Tufts Mountain Club, and yearbook. Popular campus events include Tuftonia's Day, Fan the Fire Athletics Event, student and faculty directed arts performances, school-wide concerts, Fall Gala, Winter Bash, Spring Fling, and the EPIIC International Symposium. **Sports:** There are 15 intercollegiate sports for men and 16 for women, and 7 intramural sports for men and 7 for women. Facilities include sports and fitness center, football stadium, 2 gyms, an 8-lane all-weather track, 9 tennis courts, a field house, an indoor cage, an indoor track, 7 squash courts, a swimming pool, multiple dance rooms, a weight room, spin studio, yoga studio, a sauna, a sailing center, an exercise center, film room, and baseball, softball, soccer, lacrosse, field hockey, and playing fields. **Graduates:** From July 1, 2015 to June 30, 2016, 1374 bachelor's degrees were awarded. The most popular majors were social sciences (27%), engineering (10%), and biological/life sciences (8%). 150 companies recruited on campus in 2015-2016. In an average class, 87% graduate in 4 years or less and 92% graduate in 6 years or less. Of the 2015 graduating class, 14% were enrolled in graduate school within 6 months of graduation, and 80% were employed.

SERVICES: Counseling and information services are available, as is tutoring in every subject, as needed, through the Academic Resources Center with weekly standing tutoring sessions for larger (typically introductory) classes. There is a reader service for the blind. Services are also available through other campus offices, groups, and classes. **Library/Resources:** The 3 libraries contain 1.2 million volumes, 1.3 million microform items, and 61,809 audio/video tapes/CDs/DVDs. Computerized library services include interlibrary loans, database searching, Internet access, and Wi-Fi capability. Special learning facilities include an art gallery, radio station, TV station, a recital hall, theater in the round, and a center for scientific visualization. **Physically Challenged Students:** 90% of the campus is accessible. Facilities include wheelchair ramps, elevators, special parking, specially equipped restrooms, special class scheduling, lowered drinking fountains, lowered telephones, and special housing. **Special:** The university offers cross-registration at Boston University, Boston College, and Brandeis University, a Washington semester, domestic exchanges with Swarthmore College, and study abroad in England, Spain, France, Chile, Japan, Ghana, China, Hong Kong, and Germany. Many internships are available. Double majors in the liberal arts are common; student-designed majors are possible. There is a 5-year B.A./M.A. or B.S./M.S. program in liberal arts or engineering, a 5-year B.A.-B.F.A. program with the School of the Museum of Fine Arts, and a B.A.-B.M. program with the New England Conservatory of Music. There are 5 national honor societies and a chapter of Phi Beta Kappa. **Visiting:** There are regularly scheduled orientations for prospective students. There are guides for informal visits and visitors may sit in on classes. To schedule a visit, contact the Admissions Office. **Campus Safety and Security:** Measures include 24-hour foot and vehicle patrol, emergency notification system, self-defense education, and security escort services. There are shuttle buses, emergency telephones, lighted pathways/sidewalks, and controlled access to dorms/residences.

REQUIREMENTS: The university accepts either the SAT Reasoning Test and the results of two SAT: Subject tests or the ACT. Liberal arts applicants should take two SAT: Subject test of their choice, engineering applicants should take a math level I or II, and either physics or chemistry. Students applying for the Bachelors of Fine Arts do not need to submit subject tests but are required to provide a portfolio. In addition, all applicants should be high school graduates or hold the GED. Academic preparation is expected to include 4 years each of English, foreign language, social studies, math, and natural sciences. For the Class of 2022, we will be accepting the old or new SAT and will not be requiring the Writing section for the ACT. AP credits are accepted. Important factors in the admissions decision are leadership record, advanced placement or honors courses, evidence of special talent, extracurricular activities record, recommendations by school officials, parents or siblings attended your school, personality/intangible qualities, recommendations by alumni, and geographical diversity. Liberal arts students must complete 34 courses. 10 of them in the area of concentration. Requirements include foundation courses in writing, quantitative reasoning, and foreign language or culture and courses in humanities, arts, social sciences, math, and natural sciences. Requirements for engineering students include a total of 38 courses, 10 are engineering introduction courses, 8 are engineering foundation courses, 12 of them in the area of concentration, and distribution requirements in English, humanities, arts, and social sciences. Students in the Bachelors of Fine Arts program at the School of the Museum of Fine Arts must complete 14 academic courses in addition to 76 credits of studio art to complete their degree in Interdisciplinary Art. **Procedure:** Freshmen are admitted fall. Entrance exams should be taken by January of the senior year unless applying Early Decision. There are early decision and deferred admissions plans. Early decision applications should be filed by November 1; regular applications, by January 1 for fall entry, along with a $75 fee. Notification of early decision is sent December 15; regular decision, April 1. Applications are accepted on-line. **Transfer Students:** 67 transfer students enrolled in 2015-2016. Primary consideration is given to college and secondary school achievement and record of personal involvement. Transfer students must submit the Common Application for Transfer Students, the Tufts Supplement, transcripts from both high school and college, a college official's report, letters of recommendation, as well as either the SAT or the ACT with Writing. **International Students:** There are 570 international students enrolled. The school actively recruits these students. They must take the TOEFL with a minimum score of 650 on the paper-based TOEFL (PBT) or 100 on the Internet-based version (iBT), the IELTS exam is also accepted. ACT or SAT with two Subject Tests (portfolio is required in lieu of subject tests for BFA applicants).

ADMISSIONS: 14% of the 2016-2017 applicants were accepted. The SAT scores for the 2016-2017 freshman class were: Critical Reading-- 4% between 500 and 599, 32% between 600 and 699, and 64% between 700 and 800. Math-- 2% between 500 and 599, 25% between 600 and 699, and 73% between 700 and 800. Writing-- 1% below 500, 2% between 500 and 599, 31% between 600 and 699, and 66% between 700 and 800. The ACT scores were 1% between 18 and 23, 10% between 24 and 29, and 89% above 30. There were 54 National Merit finalists. **Admissions Contact:** Karen Richardson, Dean of Admissions. Email: *undergraduate.admissions@tufts.edu* Web: *www.tufts.edu*

FINANCIAL AID: In 2016-2017, 38% of all full-time freshmen and 36% of continuing full-time students received some form of financial aid. 36% of all full-time freshmen and 34% of continuing full-time students received need-based aid. The average freshman award was $43,518. Need-based scholarships or need-based grants averaged $42,971; need-based self-help aid (loans and jobs) averaged $3,772; and other non-need-based awards and non-need-based scholarships averaged $500. The average financial indebtedness of the 2016 graduate was $24,267. Tufts is a member of CSS. The CSS/Profile, and parent and student federal income tax forms are required. The deadline for filing freshman financial aid applications for fall entry is February 15.

UNIVERSITY OF MASSACHUSETTS AMHERST — B-2

www.umass.edu

Amherst, MA 01003	(413) 545-0222
Fax: (413) 545-4312	**Email:** mail@admissions.umass.edu
Full-time: n/av	**Faculty:** 1295; I, av$
Part-time: n/av	**Ph.D.s:** 94%
Graduate: n/av	**Student/Faculty:** 17 to 1
Year: semesters, summer session	**Tuition:** $14,171 ($30,504)
Room & Board: $12,028	**Freshman Class:** 40,010 applied, 23,308 accepted, 4661 enrolled
SAT CR/M: 600/630 **ACT:** 27	**CEEB CODE:** 0917
Application Deadline: January 15	**VERY COMPETITIVE+**

UMass Amherst, established in 1863, is a public research, land-grant institution offering over 100 bachelor's degree programs. There are 8 undergraduate schools and 8 graduate schools. In addition to regional accreditation, UMass Amherst has baccalaureate program accreditation with AACSB, ABET, ASLA, FIDER, NASM, NCATE, NLN, SAF, ACBSP, ACPHA, ACS, APA, ASLHA, CCNE, and CEPH. The 1463-acre campus is in a small town 90 miles west of Boston and 60 miles north of Hartford, Connecticut. Including any residence halls, there are 320 buildings.

STUDENT LIFE: 77% of undergraduates are from Massachusetts. Others are from 48 states, 69 foreign countries, and Canada. 9% are Asian American; 8% race unknown; 67% White; 5% Hispanic; 4% African American; 4% Foreign; 3% two or more races. The average age of freshmen is 18; all undergraduates, 21. 9% do not continue beyond their first year; 78% remain to graduate. **Housing:** 13590 students can be accommodated in college housing, which includes single-sex and coed dorms, on-campus apartments, and married student housing. In addition, there are honors houses, language houses, special-interest houses, fraternity houses, sorority houses, and first-year housing. On-campus housing is guaranteed for the freshman year only and is available on a lottery system for upperclassmen. 58% of students live on campus. All students may keep cars.

FACULTY/CLASSROOMS: 55% of faculty are male; 45% are female. All teach undergraduates, and all do research. No introductory courses are taught by graduate students.

PROGRAMS OF STUDY: UMass Amherst confers B.A., B.S., B.B.A., B.F.A., B.G.S. and B.Mus. degrees. Associate, master's, and doctoral degrees are also awarded. Bachelor's degrees are awarded in AGRICULTURE (agricultural economics, animal science, natural resource management, plant science, soil science, and wood science), BIOLOGICAL SCIENCE (biochemistry, biology/biological science, microbiology, and nutrition), BUSINESS (accounting, banking and finance, business administration and management, hospitality management services, marketing management, operations management, and sports management), COMMUNICATIONS AND THE ARTS (art history and appreciation, Chinese, classics, communications, comparative literature, dance, dramatic arts, English, Germanic languages and literature, Japanese, journalism, linguistics, music, music performance, Portuguese, Spanish, and studio art), COMPUTER AND PHYSICAL SCIENCE (astronomy, chemistry, computer science, earth science, geology, mathematics, physics, and science), EDUCATION (education), ENGINEERING AND ENVIRONMENTAL DESIGN (architecture, chemical engineering, civil engineering, computer engineering, construction technology, electrical/electronics engineering, environmental design, environmental science, industrial engineering, landscape architecture/design, and mechanical engineering), HEALTH PROFESSIONS (exercise science, nursing, predentistry, premedicine, preveterinary science, public health, and speech pathology/audiology), SOCIAL SCIENCE (African American studies, anthropology, economics, food science, French studies, gender studies, geography, history, interdisciplinary studies, Italian studies, Judaic studies, law, liberal arts/general studies, Middle Eastern studies, philosophy, political science/government, psychology, Russian and Slavic studies, sociology, and women's studies). Psychology, biology, and management have the largest enrollments.

ACTIVITIES: 8% of men belong to 1 local and 18 national fraternities; 6% of women belong to 1 local and 11 national sororities. There are 402 groups on campus, including art, band, cheerleading, chess, choir, chorale, chorus, communications, computers, dance, debate, drama, environmental, ethnic, film, honors, international, jazz band, LGBT, literary magazine, marching band, musical theater, newspaper, opera, orchestra, pep band, photography, political, professional, radio and TV, religious, social, social service, student government, student-owned businesses, and symphony. Popular campus events include First Week, Festival of the Arts, Multicultural Film Festival, Cultural Night, Jazz in July, and Center Series Events. **Sports:** There are 9 intercollegiate sports for men and 10 for women, and 21 intramural sports for men and 23 for women. Facilities include an 120 acres of multipurpose fields, softball and soccer fields, a 20,000-seat football stadium, a track, and 22 tennis courts. Indoor facilities include a 120,000-sq-ft recreation center with weight and fitness equipment, a 3-court gym, a wellness center, and an elevated jogging track. Other facilities include 3 pools, 3 handball/squash, racquetball courts, 2 gyms, 2 dance studios, weight-training rooms, fitness centers, basketball/volleyball/badminton courts, and an indoor track. The indoor sports arena has 10,500 seats and 2 Olympic-sized ice sheets. Body shops are also available in residential areas. **Graduates:** From July 1, 2015 to June 30, 2016, 5683 bachelor's degrees were awarded. The most popular majors were psychology (8%), communication (4%), and biology (4%). 557 companies recruited on campus in 2015-2016. In an average class, 2% graduate in 3 years or less, 66% graduate in 4 years or less, 77% graduate in 5 years or less, and 78% graduate in 6 years or less.

SERVICES: Counseling and information services are available, as is tutoring in most subjects. There is a reader service for the blind. **Library/Resources:** The 2 libraries contain 4.5 million volumes, 2.6 million microform items, and 47,873 audio/video tapes/CDs/DVDs, and subscribe to 122,636 periodicals including electronic. Computerized library services include interlibrary loans, database searching, Internet access, and Wi-Fi capability. Special learning facilities include an art gallery, radio station, TV station, botanical gardens, an astronomical observatory, and learning commons. **Physically Challenged Students:** All of the campus is accessible. Facilities include wheelchair ramps, elevators, special parking, specially equipped restrooms, special class scheduling, lowered drinking fountains, lowered telephones, and special housing. All programs are made accessible through accommodations. **Special:** Cross-registration is possible with Smith, Mount Holyoke, Hampshire, and Amherst Colleges. Co-op programs, internships in every major, study abroad in more than 70 countries, domestic exchange, a Washington semester, work-study programs, dual majors, and B.A.-B.S. degrees are available. Accelerated degrees are currently offered in economics, communication, and environmental design and are being planned for other programs, including management. The Bachelor's Degree with Individual Concentration (BDIC) is also available. The Commonwealth Honors College welcomes honor students who meet entrance requirements. There are also teacher certification, distance learning, independent study, and ESL programs. There are 46 national honor societies, Phi Beta Kappa, a freshman honors program, and 76 departmental honors programs. **Visiting:** There are regularly scheduled orientations for prospective students, including 3 guided tours daily weekdays, 2 tours daily on weekends and twice-daily information sessions. There are guides for informal visits and visitors may sit in on classes.. **Campus Safety and Security:** Measures include 24-hour foot and vehicle patrol, emergency notification system, self-defense education, and security escort services. There are shuttle buses, emergency telephones, lighted pathways/sidewalks, and controlled access to dorms/residences.

REQUIREMENTS: The SAT is required. Applicants must be graduates of an accredited secondary school or have the GED. The university recommends that students complete 16 Carnegie units including 4 years of English, 4 years each of math (including math during their senior year and a minimum of Algebra II) and science (including 2 years lab), and 2 years each of electives, foreign language, and social studies. Students must present a portfolio for admission to the art program and must audition for admission to music and dance. A GPA of 2.0 is required. AP and CLEP credits are accepted. Important factors in the admissions decision are advanced placement or honors courses, extracurricular activities record, and recommendations by school officials. Students must complete 120 credit hours and maintain a minimum GPA of 2.0 overall and in the major. For the general education requirement, students must take 4 courses in Social World, 2 courses in Social and Cultural Diversity, 2 courses in Biological and Physical World, 2 courses in Writing, and 1 each in Basic Math Skills, Integrative Experience, and Analytic Reasoning. There is an Interdisciplinary option. **Procedure:** Freshmen are admitted fall and spring. Entrance exams should be taken as soon as possible after admissions deadline. There are early admissions, deferred admissions, and rolling admissions plans. Applications should be filed by January 15 for fall entry; October 1 for spring entry, along with a $75 fee. Notifications are sent in March. 1278 applicants were on the 2016 waiting list; 26 were admitted. Applications are accepted online. **Transfer Students:** Transfer applicants must submit transcripts from all colleges or universities attended and an essay. Those with fewer than 27 credits must submit high school transcripts and SAT scores. Priority is given to students with an associate degree. Grades of C- or better in comparable coursework transfer for credit. Students completing an approved MassTransfer associate degree program with a 2.5 or higher cumulative GPA, who are in good academic, financial, and disciplinary status at all previously attended colleges, are guaranteed admission. Some UMass Amherst majors may require a higher GPA and/or prerequisite coursework. 45 of 120 credits required for the bachelor's degree must be completed at UMass Amherst. **International Students:** There are 980 international students enrolled. The school actively recruits these students. They must take the TOEFL with a minimum score of 80 on the Internet-based version (iBT). They must also take the SAT or ACT.

ADMISSIONS: 58% of the 2016-2017 applicants were accepted. The SAT scores for the 2016-2017 freshman class were: Critical Reading-- 8% below 500, 42% between 500 and 599, 42% between 600 and 699, and 9% between 700 and 800. Math-- 3% below 500, 29% between 500 and 599, 42% between 600 and 699, and 16% between 700 and 800. The ACT scores were 9% between 18 and 23, 63% between 24 and 29, and 28% above 30. 62% of the current freshmen were in the top fifth of their class; 92% were in the top two fifths. **Admissions Contact:** Jon Westover, Assoc. Director of Freshmen Admissions. Email: *mail@admissions.umass.edu* Web: *www.umass.edu*

FINANCIAL AID: The average freshman award was $15,551. Need-based scholarships or need-based grants averaged $10,480; need-based self-help aid (loans and jobs) averaged $3,773; non-need-based athletic scholarships averaged $22,625; other non-need-based awards and non-need-based scholarships averaged $5,904; and $3,685 from other forms of aid. UMass Amherst is a member of CSS. The FAFSA code is 002221. The priority date for freshman financial aid applications for fall entry is March 1.

UNIVERSITY OF MASSACHUSETTS BOSTON (E-2)

www.umb.edu

Boston, MA 02125 (617) 287-6100

Fax: (617) 287-5999 **Email:** undergrad.admissions@umb.edu

Full-time: 4367 men, 4916 women	**Faculty:** 714; I, -$
Part-time: 1615 men, 1949 women	**Ph.D.s:** 98%
Graduate: 1295 men, 2705 women	**Student/Faculty:** 16 to 1
Year: semesters, summer session	**Tuition:** $13,435 ($32,023)
Room & Board: $11,100	**Freshman Class:** 9886 applied, 6774 accepted, 1651 enrolled
SAT CR/M: 520/540 **ACT:** required	**CEEB CODE:** 3924
Application Deadline: March 1	**COMPETITIVE**

UMass Boston, established in 1964, is a public research institution offering undergraduate studies in arts and sciences and in preprofessional training. There are 10 undergraduate schools and 11 graduate schools. In addition to regional accreditation, UMass Boston has baccalaureate program accreditation with AACSB, ABET, AACTE, ACS, APA, CCNE, and AACSB. The 187-acre campus is in an urban area 5 miles south of downtown Boston. Including any residence halls, there are 9 buildings.

STUDENT LIFE: 95% of undergraduates are from Massachusetts. Others are from 35 states, 143 foreign countries, and Canada. 8% are race unknown; 39% White; 3% two or more races; 14% African American; 13% Foreign; 12% Hispanic; 11% Asian American. **Female To Male Ratio:** 1.3:1. The average age of freshmen is 19; all undergraduates, 25. 21% do not continue beyond their first year; 44% remain to graduate. **Housing:** Alcohol is not permitted. All students commute. All students may keep cars.

FACULTY/CLASSROOMS: 49% of faculty are male; 51% are female. All teach undergraduates. No introductory courses are taught by graduate students. The average class size in an introductory lecture is 26; in a laboratory is 16; and in a regular course is 26.

PROGRAMS OF STUDY: UMass Boston confers B.A., and B.S. degrees. Master's and doctoral degrees are also awarded. Bachelor's degrees are awarded in BIOLOGICAL SCIENCE (biochemistry and biology/biological science), BUSINESS (labor studies and management science), COMMUNICATIONS AND THE ARTS (art, classical languages, classics, communications, dramatic arts, English, French, information technology, Italian, music, and Spanish), COMPUTER AND PHYSICAL SCIENCE (chemistry, computer science, earth science, information sciences and systems, mathematics, and physics), EDUCATION (Asian studies and early childhood education), ENGINEERING AND ENVIRONMENTAL DESIGN (electrical and computer engineering, engineering, engineering physics, and environmental science), HEALTH PROFESSIONS (exercise science, medical technology, and nursing), SOCIAL SCIENCE (African American studies, American studies, anthropology, community services, criminal justice, economics, ethics, politics, and social policy, geography, gerontology, Hispanic American studies, history, human services, paralegal studies, philosophy, physical fitness/movement, political science/government, psychology, sociology, and women & gender studies). Management, nursing, and psychology have the largest enrollments.

ACTIVITIES: There are no fraternities or sororities. There are 100 groups on campus, including art, band, campus ministries, cheerleading, chess, choir, chorale, chorus, computers, dance, drama, ethnic, film, honors, international, jazz band, LGBT, literary magazine, musical theater, newspaper, orchestra, photography, political, professional, religious, social, social service, and student government. Popular campus events include Convocation Day, Seasonal Festivals, and Lecture Series. **Sports:** There are 8 intercollegiate sports for men and 8 for women, and 12 intramural sports for men and 12 for women. Facilities include an athletic center with a 3500-seat gym with 4 basketball and 2 volleyball courts, an ice rink that seats 1000, a Olympic-size swimming pool with high-dive area, a multipurpose weight room, a sports medicine area, an 8-lane, 400-meter track, 8 tennis courts, a softball diamond, 3 multipurpose fields primarily used for soccer and lacrosse, other recreational fields, a boat house, dock, and fleet of sailboats and rowing dories, and a fitness center with strength-training equipment. **Graduates:** From July 1, 2015 to June 30, 2016, 2564 bachelor's degrees were awarded. The most popular majors were business/marketing (18%), health professions and related programs (17%), and psychology (13%). 100 companies recruited on campus in 2015-2016. In an average class, 18% graduate in 4 years or less, 38% graduate in 5 years or less, and 44% graduate in 6 years or less.

SERVICES: Counseling and information services are available, as is tutoring in every subject. There is a reader service for the blind, and remedial math, reading, and writing. There are also reading study skills workshops and a math resource center available. **Library/Resources:** The library contains 1.0 million volumes. Computerized library services include interlibrary loans, database searching, Internet access, and Wi-Fi capability. Special learning facilities include an art gallery, planetarium, tropical greenhouse, observatory, adaptive computer lab, languages lab, applied language and math center. **Physically Challenged Students:** All of the campus is accessible. Facilities include wheelchair ramps, elevators, special parking, specially equipped restrooms, special class scheduling, lowered drinking fountains, and lowered telephones. Amplified phones, powered doors, indoor-connected building access, an accessible shuttle bus, an adaptive computer lab, and a center for students with disabilities. **Special:** Students may cross-register with Boston Public Colleges, Massachusetts College of Art, Bunker Hill Community College, Roxbury Community College, and Hebrew College. UMass Boston also offers cooperative programs, internships, study abroad, work-study programs, student-designed majors, B.A.-B.S. degrees, nondegree study, pass/fail options, and dual and interdisciplinary majors, including anthropology/history, biology/medical technology, philosophy/public policy, and psychology/sociology. Also available are 3-1 and 2-2 engineering programs with various area institutions. The College of Public and Community Service provides social-oriented education. There are 3 national honor societies and a freshman honors program. **Visiting:** There are regularly scheduled orientations for prospective students, including general information sessions about the university and the admissions process and a tour of the campus. There are guides for informal visits and visitors may sit in on classes. To schedule a visit, contact Enrollment Information Services at (617) 287-6000. **Campus Safety and Security:** Measures include 24-hour foot and vehicle patrol, emergency notification system, self-defense education, and security escort services. There are shuttle buses, emergency telephones, lighted pathways/sidewalks, Operation ID, motorist assistance, and crime prevention programs.

REQUIREMENTS: The SAT or ACT is required. Applicants should be graduates of an accredited secondary school. The GED is accepted. The university requires the completion of 16 Carnegie units, including 4 years of English, 3 of college preparatory math and science, 2 each of a foreign language and social studies, and 2 electives in the above academic areas or in humanities, arts, or computer science. A GPA of 3.0 is required. AP and CLEP credits are accepted. For graduation, students must complete 120 credit hours (123 hours in the College of Nursing) and maintain a minimum GPA of 2.0. Distribution requirements vary by college. All students must demonstrate writing proficiency. **Procedure:** Freshmen are admitted fall and spring. Entrance exams should be taken by the fall of the senior year. There are deferred admissions and rolling admissions plans. Applications should be filed by March 1 for fall entry, along with a $60 fee. Notification is sent on a rolling basis. Applications are accepted on-line. **Transfer Students:** 1535 transfer students enrolled in 2015-2016. Applicants with fewer than 24 credits must meet freshman requirements. To transfer, students must have a minimum college GPA of 2.5. Grades of C- or better transfer for credit. 30 of 120 credits required for the bachelor's degree must be completed at UMass Boston. **International Students:** There are 1356 international students enrolled. The school actively recruits these students. They must take the TOEFL with a minimum score of 550 on the paper-based TOEFL (PBT) or 79 on the Internet-based version (iBT). They must also take the SAT or ACT if the language of instruction is English.

ADMISSIONS: 69% of the 2016-2017 applicants were accepted. The SAT scores for the 2016-2017 freshman class were: Critical Reading-- 37% below 500, 44% between 500 and 599, 17% between 600 and 699, and 3% between 700 and 800. Math-- 27% below 500, 47% between 500 and 599, 24% between 600 and 699, and 2% between 700 and 800. The ACT scores were 3% between 12 and 17, 48% between 18 and 23, 43% between 24 and 29, and 6% above 30. **Admissions Contact:** Corey Ford, Director of Undergraduate Admissions. Email: *undergrad.admissions@umb.edu* Web: *www.umb.edu*

FINANCIAL AID: The FAFSA code is 002222. The priority date for freshman financial aid applications for fall entry is March 1.

UNIVERSITY OF MASSACHUSETTS DARTMOUTH D-4

www.umassd.edu

North Dartmouth, MA 02747 **(508) 999-8605**

Fax: (508) 999-8755	**Email:** admissions@umassd.edu
Full-time: 3124 men, 2887 women	**Faculty:** 357; IIA, ++$
Part-time: 431 men, 557 women	**Ph.D.s:** 89%
Graduate: 782 men, 866 women	**Student/Faculty:** 17 to 1
Year: semesters, summer session	**Tuition:** $13,188 ($27,473)
Room & Board: $12,470	**Freshman Class:** 8211 applied, 5789 accepted, 1367 enrolled
SAT CR/M/W: 500/520/487 **ACT:** 23	**CEEB CODE:** 3786
Application Deadline: open	**COMPETITIVE**

UMass Dartmouth, founded in 1895, is a public institution that provides undergraduate and graduate programs in the liberal and creative arts and sciences and in professional training. There are 5 undergraduate schools and 3 graduate schools. In addition to regional accreditation, UMass Dartmouth has baccalaureate program accreditation with AACSB, ABET, NASAD, NASDTEC, ACS, NAACLS, and CCNE. The 710-acre campus is in a suburban area approximately 60 miles south of Boston and 28 miles east of Providence, Rhode Island. Including any residence halls, there are 35 buildings.

STUDENT LIFE: 91% of undergraduates are from Massachusetts. Others are from 43 states, 46 foreign countries, and Canada. 89% are from public schools. 8% are Hispanic; 7% Foreign; 6% race unknown; 59% White; 4% Asian American; 3% two or more races; 13% African American. **Male To Female Ratio:** 1.0:1. The average age of freshmen is 18; all undergraduates, 22. 27% do not continue beyond their first year; 49% remain to graduate. **Housing:** 4494 students can be accommodated in college housing, which includes coed dorms and on-campus apartments. In addition, there are honors houses, special-interest houses, quiet housing, substance awareness housing, and apartments and townhouses for upperclassmen. On-campus housing is guaranteed for the freshman year only, and is available on a first-come, first-served basis, and is available on a lottery system for upperclassmen. Priority is given to out-of-town students. 54% of students live on campus; of those, 35% remain on campus on weekends. All students may keep cars.

FACULTY/CLASSROOMS: 49% of faculty are male; 51% are female. All teach undergraduates, 60% do research, and 60% do both. Graduate students teach 1% of introductory courses. The average class size in an introductory lecture is 33; in a laboratory is 23; and in a regular course is 29.

PROGRAMS OF STUDY: UMass Dartmouth confers B.A., B.S. and B.F.A. degrees. Master's and doctoral degrees are also awarded. Bachelor's degrees are awarded in BIOLOGICAL SCIENCE (biochemistry, biology/biological science, and marine biology), BUSINESS (accounting, business administration and management, finance, management information systems, management, marketing/retailing/merchandising, and operations management), COMMUNICATIONS AND THE ARTS (art history and appreciation, ceramic art and design, drawing with printmaking focus, English literature, English writing, fiber/textiles/weaving, French, graphic design, illustration, metal/jewelry, music, painting, photography, Portuguese, sculpture, Spanish, and visual design), COMPUTER AND PHYSICAL SCIENCE (astronomy and physics, chemistry, computer science, mathematics, physics, and software engineering), EDUCATION (art education), ENGINEERING AND ENVIRONMENTAL DESIGN (bioengineering, civil engineering, computer engineering, electrical/electronics engineering, and mechanical engineering), HEALTH PROFESSIONS (clinical science, cytotechnology, medical laboratory science, and nursing), SOCIAL SCIENCE (anthropology, criminal justice, economics, history, interdisciplinary studies, liberal arts/general studies, philosophy, political science/government, psychology, sociology, and women & gender studies). Engineering, physical/life sciences, and nursing are the strongest academically. Nursing, psychology, and mechanical engineering have the largest enrollments.

ACTIVITIES: 1% of men belong to 3 local and 2 national fraternities; 1% of women belong to 4 local and 4 national sororities. There are 148 groups on campus, including art, band, cheerleading, choir, chorale, chorus, computers, dance, drama, ethnic, film, honors, international, jazz band, LGBT, literary magazine, musical theater, newspaper, orchestra, photography, political, professional, radio and TV, religious, social, social service, student government, symphony, and yearbook. Popular campus events include Welcome Back Week, Homecoming Weekend, and Family Fall Weekend. **Sports:** There are 11 intercollegiate sports for men and 12 for women, and 7 intramural sports for men and 7 for women. Facilities include a 1650-seat gym, a 1250-seat football stadium, an aquatic sports center, 10 tennis courts, a 10,000-sq-ft fitness center, a running track, and soccer, softball, and intramural fields. **Graduates:** From July 1, 2015 to June 30, 2016, 1385 bachelor's degrees were awarded. The most popular majors were psychology (8%), accounting (8%), and marketing (7%).

SERVICES: Counseling and information services are available, as is tutoring in most subjects, through the writing/reading, science/engineering, math/business, and academic resource centers. There is a reader service for the blind, and remedial math. **Library/Resources:** The 2 libraries contain 431,678 volumes, and 7,921 audio/video tapes/CDs/DVDs. Computerized library services include interlibrary loans, database searching, Internet access, and Wi-Fi capability. Special learning facilities include an art gallery, radio station, an observatory, marine research vessels, and a number of cultural and research centers. **Physically Challenged Students:** 97% of the campus is accessible. Facilities include wheelchair ramps, elevators, special parking, specially equipped restrooms, special class scheduling, lowered drinking fountains, lowered telephones, and special housing. **Special:** The university permits cross-registration through the SACHEM Consortium of 9 schools in Massachusetts. Study abroad in 9 countries, an engineering or business co-op program, a Washington semester, internships, numerous work-study programs, dual majors, service learning opportunities and student-designed majors are available. Non-degree study, pass/fail options, B.S. to M.S. degrees in chemistry, nursing, computer science, electrical engineering, civil engineering, computer engineering, and mechanical engineering, a B.A.-M.A. in psychology, a English B.A. to Professional Writing Master's, a BA-MAT in several fields, along with MPP-JD and MBA-JD programs are available. There is a freshman honors program. **Visiting:** There are regularly scheduled orientations for prospective students, including scheduled campus tours Monday through Friday and most Saturdays. There are guides for informal visits and visitors may sit in on classes. To schedule a visit, contact Tabitha Marsden at tmarsden@umassd.edu. **Campus Safety and Security:** Measures include 24-hour foot and vehicle patrol, emergency notification system, self-defense education, and security escort services. There are shuttle buses, emergency telephones, lighted pathways/sidewalks, controlled access to dorms/residences, and a bicycle patrol.

REQUIREMENTS: The SAT is required. Applicants should have 4 years each of English and mathematics, 3 of science, 2 of the same foreign language, 2 social science (which includes 1 in US History), and 2 of college-preparatory electives. The GED is accepted. An audition is necessary for music majors, and a portfolio is recommended for studio arts and design applicants. All applicants must submit an essay. AP and CLEP credits are accepted. Important factors in the admissions decision are recommendations by school officials, advanced placement or honors courses, and evidence of special talent. Each student must complete the requirements of the 5 clusters that comprise the University Studies curriculum: Cluster 1 Foundations for Engagement, Cluster 2 the Natural World, Cluster 3 the Cultural World, Cluster 4 the Social World, and Cluster 5 the Educated and Engaged Citizen. A freshman English composition course is required. Colleges set some additional distribution course requirements. The B.A. requires foreign language study. To graduate, students must complete 120 to 132 credit hours and maintain a 2.0 GPA. **Procedure:** Freshmen are admitted fall and spring. Entrance exams should be taken spring of the junior year or early fall of the senior year. There are early decision, deferred admissions, and rolling admissions plans. Application deadlines are open. Application fee is $60. Notification of early decision is sent December 15; regular decision, on a rolling basis. 1762 early decision candidates were accepted for the 2016-2017 class. Applications are accepted on-line. **Transfer Students:** 564 transfer students enrolled in 2015-2016. Applicants must submit all official college transcripts and must take the SAT unless they graduated from high school more than 3 years prior to applying. Those with fewer than 24 transferable credits may need to submit high school records. 45 of 120 credits required for the bachelor's degree must be completed at UMass Dartmouth. **International Students:** There are 145 international students enrolled. The school actively recruits these students. They must take the TOEFL with a minimum score of 550 on the paper-based TOEFL (PBT) or 79 on the Internet-based version (iBT). They must also take the SAT or ACT.

ADMISSIONS: 71% of the 2016-2017 applicants were accepted. The SAT scores for the 2016-2017 freshman class were: Critical Reading--46% below 500, 40% between 500 and 599, 12% between 600 and 699, and 2% between 700 and 800. Math-- 37% below 500, 45% between 500 and 599, 16% between 600 and 699, and 2% between 700 and 800. Writing-- 55% below 500, 36% between 500 and 599, 8% between 600 and 699, and 1% between 700 and 800. The ACT scores were 9% between 12 and 17, 49% between 18 and 23, 37% between 24 and 29, and 5% above 30. 30% of the current freshmen were in the top fifth of their class; 60% were in the top two fifths. 2 freshmen graduated first in their class. **Admissions Contact:** Hanan Khamis, Director of Admissions. Email: *admissions@umassd.edu* Web: *www.umassd.edu*

FINANCIAL AID: The FAFSA code is 002210. The priority date for freshman financial aid applications for fall entry is March 1.

UNIVERSITY OF MASSACHUSETTS LOWELL — D-1

www.uml.edu

Lowell, MA 01854	**(978) 934-3931** **(800) 410-4607**
Fax: (978) 934-3086	**Email: admissions@uml.edu**
Full-time: n/av	**Faculty:** I, av$
Part-time: n/av	**Ph.D.s:** n/av
Graduate: n/av	**Student/Faculty:** n/av
Year: semesters, summer session	**Tuition:** $14,307 ($30,875)
Room & Board: $12,073	**Freshman Class:** n/av **CEEB CODE:** 3911
Application Deadline: n/av	**COMPETITIVE**

UMass Lowell, founded in 1895, is a public institution offering undergraduate programs through the colleges of fine arts and social sciences, sciences, engineering, health, and management, as well as a graduate school in education. There are 5 undergraduate schools and 1 graduate school. In addition to regional accreditation, UMass Lowell has baccalaureate program accreditation with AACSB, ABET, APTA, CAHEA, CSAB, NASAD, NASM, NCATE, NLN, CCNE, EHAC, and NAACL. The 125-acre campus is in an urban area 30 miles northwest of Boston. Including any residence halls, there are 47 buildings.

STUDENT LIFE: **Housing:** 4238 students can be accommodated in college housing, which includes single-sex and coed dorms, on-campus apartments, and off-campus apartments. In addition, there are honors houses, special-interest houses, theme housing, wellness housing, and living learning communities. On-campus housing is guaranteed for the freshman year only, and is available on a first-come, first-served basis, and is available on a lottery system for upperclassmen. All students may keep cars.

FACULTY/CLASSROOMS: No introductory courses are taught by graduate students.

PROGRAMS OF STUDY: UMass Lowell confers B.A., B.F.A., B.L.A., B.M., B.S., B.S.B.A., B.S.E., B.S.E.T. and B.S.I.T degrees. Associate, master's, and doctoral degrees are also awarded. Bachelor's degrees are awarded in BIOLOGICAL SCIENCE (biology/biological science and nutritional sciences), BUSINESS (business administration and management), COMMUNICATIONS AND THE ARTS (English, English literature, English Writing, fine arts, modern language, music, and music performance), COMPUTER AND PHYSICAL SCIENCE (applied mathematics, chemistry, computer science, inform, science, systms & tech, information sciences and systems, mathematics, and physics), ENGINEERING AND ENVIRONMENTAL DESIGN (biomedical engineering, chemical engineering, civil engineering, civil engineering technology, computer engineering, electrical/electronics engineering, engineering technology, environmental science, industrial administration/management, industrial engineering technology, mechanical engineering, mechanical engineering technology, and plastics engineering), HEALTH PROFESSIONS (clinical science, community health work, environmental health science, exercise science, nursing, and public health), SOCIAL SCIENCE (American studies, criminal justice, economics, history, liberal arts/general studies, peace studies, philosophy, political science/government, psychology, and sociology). Business administration, mechanical engineering, and criminal justice have the largest enrollments.

ACTIVITIES: There are 220 groups on campus, including art, band, cheerleading, chess, choir, chorale, computers, dance, drama, environmental, ethnic, film, honors, international, LGBT, literary magazine, marching band, newspaper, orchestra, pep band, photography, political, professional, radio and TV, religious, social, social service, student government, and yearbook. Popular campus events include Homecoming Weekend, Spring Carnival, Battle of the Bands, Concrete Canoe Competition, Fox Hall Common Events, Athletic Events, and Club Sports. **Sports:** There are 7 intercollegiate sports for men and 8 for women, and 28 intramural sports for men and 28 for women. Facilities include a 65,000-square-foot Campus Recreation Center, a 9,000-square-foot fitness center. The Cushing Field Complex features two separate fields. They host home events for field hockey, women's and men's lacrosse, and men's and women's soccer. The Tsongas Center hosts men's ice hockey as well as men's and women's basketball. LeLacheur Park hosts men's baseball and serves as the home site for the Lowell Spinners, a Class-A affiliate of the Boston Red Sox. **Graduates:** From July 1, 2015 to June 30, 2016, 2388 bachelor's degrees were awarded. The most popular majors were business/marketing (18%), engineering (15%), health professions and related programs, homeland security, and computer and information sciences (11%). In an average class, 56% graduate in 6 years or less.

SERVICES: Counseling and information services are available, as is tutoring in most subjects. There is a reader service for the blind, and remedial writing. **Library/Resources:** The 3 libraries contain 382,599 volumes, 91,022 microform items, and 14,353 audio/video tapes/CDs/DVDs, and subscribe to 32,744 periodicals including electronic. Computerized library services include interlibrary loans, database searching, Internet access, and Wi-Fi capability. Special learning facilities include an art gallery, natural history museum, and radio station. The Health & Social Sciences building provides state-of-the-art simulation laboratories, observation rooms, a demonstration hospital wing and true-to-life exam room in the nursing facilities. **Physically Challenged Students:** 90% of the campus is accessible. Facilities include wheelchair ramps, elevators, special parking, specially equipped restrooms, special class scheduling, lowered drinking fountains, and lowered telephones. **Special:** Cross-registration, co-op, and work-study programs are available, as are opportunities for internships, undergraduate research, and study abroad. The university offers a combined B.S.-M.S. degree in multiple majors, dual majors, nondegree study, and pass/fail options. There are 8 national honor societies, Phi Beta Kappa, and a freshman honors program. **Visiting:** There are regularly scheduled orientations for prospective students. **Campus Safety and Security:** Measures include 24-hour foot and vehicle patrol, self-defense education, and security escort services. There are shuttle buses, emergency telephones, and lighted pathways/sidewalks.

REQUIREMENTS: The university recommends that secondary preparation include 4 courses each in English, and math, 3 in social science with lab, 1 of 2 required in history and social studies, 2 in foreign language, and 2 academic electives. Prospective music majors must audition, and an interview is recommended for all students. AP and CLEP credits are accepted. All students must complete a minimum of 120 credits with a 2.0 GPA. Core requirements are 36 credits: 2 College Writing Courses, 3 Arts and Humanities Perspectives Courses, 3 Social Sciences Perspective Courses, 2 Sciences with Lab Perspective Courses, 1 Mathematics Perspective Course, and 1 Science, Technology, Engineering and Mathematics Perspective Course. **Procedure:** Freshmen are admitted fall and spring. There are early admissions, deferred admissions, and rolling admissions plans. Check with the school for current application deadlines. The application fee is $60. Applications are accepted on-line. **Transfer Students:** Transfer applicants must present at least a 2.0 GPA in previous college work. Those with fewer than 30 credits must meet freshman admission requirements. Students may enroll in the fall, and spring. 30 of 120 credits required for the bachelor's degree must be completed at UMass Lowell. **International Students:** They must take the TOEFL with a minimum score of 550 on the paper-based TOEFL (PBT) or 79 on the Internet-based version (iBT). They must also take the SAT or ACT.

Admissions Contact: Christine Bryan, Senior Associate Director of Admissions. Email: *admissions@uml.edu* Web: *www.uml.edu*

FINANCIAL AID: In 2016-2017, 90% of all full-time freshmen received some form of financial aid. 90% of all full-time freshmen received need-based aid. The average freshman award was $15,247. Need-based scholarships or need-based grants averaged $9,343; need-based self-help aid (loans and jobs) averaged $4,457; non-need-based athletic scholarships averaged $11,266; other non-need-based awards and non-need-based scholarships averaged $3,438; and $4,501 from other forms of aid. 16% of undergraduate students work part-time. Average annual earnings from campus work are $3090. The average financial indebtedness of the 2016 graduate was $30,915. The FAFSA code is 002161. The priority date for freshman financial aid applications for fall entry is March 1.

WELLESLEY COLLEGE — D-2

www.wellesley.edu

Wellesley, MA 02481 — **(781) 283-2270**

Fax: (781) 283-3678	**Email: admission@wellesley.edu**
Full-time: 2187 women	**Faculty:** 356; IIB, ++$
Part-time: 10 women	**Ph.D.s:** 98%
Graduate: n/av	**Student/Faculty:** 7 to 1
Year: semesters, summer session	**Tuition:** $48,802
Room & Board: $15,114	**Freshman Class:** 4555 applied, 1380 accepted, 595 enrolled
SAT CR/M/W: 694/703/696 **ACT:** 31	**CEEB CODE:** 3957
Application Deadline: January 15	**MOST COMPETITIVE**

Wellesley College, ranked among the United States' top liberal arts and sciences colleges, has a deep tradition of educating women who will make a difference in the world. Living and learning on a campus, just outside of Boston, full of self-directed and intellectually curious women helps students develop the skills needed to succeed in all professional fields, including those traditionally dominated by men. Every resource at the College is devoted to undergraduate women. Students have extraordinary opportunities to cultivate their leadership abilities and gain lifelong access to a legendary network of accomplished Wellesley alumnae. There is 1 undergraduate school. The 500-acre campus is in a suburban area 12 miles west of Boston. Including any residence halls, there are 64 buildings.

STUDENT LIFE: 87% of undergraduates are from out of state, mostly the West. Students are from 50 states, 84 foreign countries, and Canada. 65% are from public schools. 6% are two or more races; 5% African American; 4% race unknown; 39% White; 21% Asian American; 12% Foreign; 10% Hispanic. The student base is all female. The average age of freshmen is 18; all undergraduates, 20. 5% do not continue beyond their first year; 93% remain to graduate. **Housing:** 2211 students can be accommodated in college housing, which includes single-sex dorms. In addition, there are special-interest houses, language corridors, and co-ops. On-campus housing is guaranteed for all 4 years. 98% of students live on campus; of those, 97% remain on campus on weekends. Upperclassmen may keep cars.

FACULTY/CLASSROOMS: 43% of faculty are male; 57% are female. All teach undergraduates, and all do research. No introductory courses are taught by graduate students. The average class size in an introductory lecture is 25 and in a regular course is 18.

PROGRAMS OF STUDY: Wellesley confers B.A. degrees. Bachelor's degrees are awarded in AGRICULTURE (environmental studies), BIOLOGICAL SCIENCE (biochemistry, biology/biological science, biological sciences, and neurosciences), COMMUNICATIONS AND THE ARTS (American literature, Arabic, art history, art, art/art studies, art history and appreciation, China Asia-Pacific studies, Chinese, classical languages, classics, comparative literature, creative writing, dramatic arts, East Asian languages and literature, English, English literature, English Writing, film arts, fine/studio arts, general, French, French and Francophone studies, German, German studies, Greek, Greek (classical), Hebrew, Italian, Japanese, Korean, Latin, linguistics, literature, media arts, film and media studies, music, Portuguese, Russian, Russian languages and literature, Spanish, studio art, studio art graphic design, studio art painting, and theatre arts), COMPUTER AND PHYSICAL SCIENCE (astronomy, astrophysics, chemistry, computer science, geology, mathematics, and physics), EDUCATION (childhood education, classical studies, early childhood education, elementary education, and secondary education), ENGINEERING AND ENVIRONMENTAL DESIGN (architecture and preengineering), HEALTH PROFESSIONS (biology, predentistry, premedicine, preoptometry, pre-physician assistant, prepodiatry, and preveterinary science), SOCIAL SCIENCE (African American studies, American studies, anthropology, archeology, Asian/American studies, Asian/Oriental studies, biopsychology, child psychology/development, Chinese Studies, classical/ancient civilization, cognitive science, economics, government, feminist, gender, sexuality studies, French studies, gender studies, German area studies, Hispanic American studies, history, international relations, Italian studies, Japanese studies, Judaic studies, Latin American studies, law, liberal arts/general studies, liberal arts, sciences, general studies, humanities, liberal arts/engineering studies, medieval studies, Middle Eastern studies, peace studies, philosophy, political science/government, prelaw, psychobiology, psychology, religion, sociology, women & gender studies, and women's studies). Economics, psychology, and political science have the largest enrollments.

ACTIVITIES: There are no fraternities or sororities. There are 160 groups on campus, including art, cheerleading, chess, choir, chorale, chorus, communications, computers, dance, debate, drama, environmental, ethnic, film, honors, international, jazz band, LGBT, literary magazine, musical theater, newspaper, orchestra, photography, political, professional, radio and TV, religious, social, social service, student government, symphony, and yearbook. Popular campus events include Lake Day, Marathon Monday/Scream Tunnel, and Spring Concert. **Sports:** There are 14 intercollegiate sports for women, and 21 intramural sports for women. Facilities include an indoor pool, dance studios, a weight room, an indoor track, golf course, courts for racquetball, squash, tennis, and volleyball. **Graduates:** From July 1, 2015 to June 30, 2016, 545 bachelor's degrees were awarded. The most popular majors were economics (15%), political science (11%), and psychology (10%). 80 companies recruited on campus in 2015-2016. In an average class, 86% graduate in 4 years or less, 92% graduate in 5 years or less, and 93% graduate in 6 years or less.

SERVICES: Counseling and information services are available, as is tutoring in every subject. There is a reader service for the blind. **Library/Resources:** The 5 libraries contain 1.1 million volumes, 313 microform items, and 33,536 audio/video tapes/CDs/DVDs, and subscribe to 414,382 periodicals including electronic. Computerized library services include interlibrary loans, database searching, Internet access, and Wi-Fi capability. Special learning facilities include an art gallery, radio station, a science center, a botanic greenhouse, an observatory, a center for child developmental studies, centers for research on women, and a media and technology center. **Physically Challenged Students:** 85% of the campus is accessible. Facilities include wheelchair ramps, elevators, special parking, specially equipped restrooms, special class scheduling, lowered drinking fountains, lowered telephones, special housing. Signage in braille. **Special:** Students may cross-register at MIT, Brandeis University, or Babson College. Exchange programs are available with Spelman College in Georgia and Mills College in California, with members of the Twelve College Exchange Program, with Williams College's maritime studies program, and with Connecticut College's National Theater Institute. Study abroad is possible through Wellesley-administered programs in France and Germany, exchange programs in Argentina, Japan, Korea, and the United Kingdom, and other programs in Italy, Japan, Spain, South Africa, and China. There are more than 150 approved study abroad programs available. There are summer internship programs in Boston and Washington, D.C. Dual majors, student-designed majors, non-degree study, and pass/fail options are possible. A 3-2 program with MIT, Dartmouth, and Columbia awards a B.A.-B.S. degree. There are 2 national honor societies, Phi Beta Kappa, and 51 departmental honors programs. **Visiting:** There are regularly scheduled orientations for prospective students, that include an information session followed by campus tour. There are guides for informal visits, visitors may sit in on classes, and stay overnight. To schedule a visit, contact the Admission Office at admission@wellesley.edu. **Campus Safety and Security:** Measures include 24-hour foot and vehicle patrol, emergency notification system, self-defense education, and security escort services. There are shuttle buses, emergency telephones, lighted pathways/sidewalks, and controlled access to dorms/residences.

REQUIREMENTS: The SAT Reasoning Test and 2 SAT subject tests, or the ACT with Writing are required. Wellesley College does not require a fixed plan of secondary school course preparation. Entering students normally have completed 4 years of college preparatory studies in secondary school that include training in clear and coherent writing and interpreting literature, history, principles of math (typically 4 years), competence in at least 1 foreign language, ancient or modern (usually 4 years of study), and experience in at least 2 lab sciences. An essay is required, and an interview is recommended. AP credits are accepted. Important factors in the admissions decision are advanced placement or honors courses, extracurricular activities record, and leadership record. All students must complete 32 units, at least 8 of which are in the major field, with a minimum 2.0 GPA. Requirements include 3 courses each in humanities, social science, and natural science and math, 1 multicultural course, 1 semester of expository writing in any department, and 2 credits in phys ed. Students must also possess proficiency in a modern or ancient foreign language. A thesis is required for departmental honors. A quantitative reasoning requirement must be satisfied by all students. **Procedure:** Freshmen are admitted fall. Entrance exams should be taken spring of the junior year or fall of the senior year. There are early decision and deferred admissions plans. Early decision applications should be filed by November 1; regular applications, by January 15 for fall entry. Notification of early decision is sent December 15; regular decision, April 1. 166 early decision candidates were accepted for the 2016-2017 class. 843 applicants were on the 2016 waiting list; 30 were admitted. Applications are accepted on-line. Application fees are waived if application is completed on-line. **Transfer Students:** 11 transfer students enrolled in 2015-2016. Applicants must provide high school and college transcripts, SAT or ACT scores if they submitted them to their current institution, a personal statement, and a statement of good standing from institutions previously attended. 16 of 32 credits required for the bachelor's degree must be completed at Wellesley. **International Students:** There are 276 international students enrolled. The school actively recruits these students. They must also take the SAT or ACT.

ADMISSIONS: 30% of the 2016-2017 applicants were accepted. The SAT scores for the 2016-2017 freshman class were: Critical Reading-- 6% between 500 and 599, 44% between 600 and 699, and 49% between 700 and 800. Math-- 9% between 500 and 599, 44% between 600 and 699, and 46% between 700 and 800. Writing-- 7% between 500 and 599, 35% between 600 and 699, and 57% between 700 and 800. The ACT scores were 1% between 18 and 23, 26% between 24 and 29, and 73% above 30. 95% of the current freshmen were in the top fifth of their class; 100% were in the top two fifths. **Admissions Contact:** Board of Admission Email: *admission@wellesley.edu* Web: *www.wellesley.edu*

FINANCIAL AID: In 2016-2017, 59% of all full-time freshmen and 63% of continuing full-time students received some form of financial aid. 59% of all full-time freshmen and 63% of continuing full-time students received need-based aid. The average freshman award was $43,423. Need-based scholarships or need-based grants averaged $46,277; and need-based self-help aid (loans and jobs) averaged $3,562. 63% of undergraduate students work part-time. Average annual earnings from campus work are $2000. The average financial indebtedness of the 2016 graduate was $12,455. Wellesley is a member of CSS. The CSS/Profile, and the most recent income tax returns of parents and student are required. The FAFSA code is 002224. The priority date for freshman financial aid applications for fall entry is March 1.

WENTWORTH INSTITUTE OF TECHNOLOGY — E-2

www.wit.edu

Boston, MA 02115	**(617) 989-4000** **(800) 556-0610**
Fax: (617) 989-4910	
Full-time: 3129 men, 773 women	**Faculty:** 151
Part-time: 349 men, 73 women	**Ph.D.s:** 70%
Graduate: 180 men, 72 women	**Student/Faculty:** 15 to 1
Year: semesters, summer session	**Tuition:** $33,724
Room & Board: $13,388	**Freshman Class:** 6975 applied, 4650 accepted, 964 enrolled
SAT CR/M: 520/580 **ACT:** 23	**CEEB CODE:** 3958
Application Deadline: February 15	**COMPETITIVE**

Wentworth Institute of Technology, founded in 1904, is a private college specializing in architecture, design, engineering, and management. The figures in the above capsule and in this profile are approximate. There are 4 undergraduate schools and 2 graduate schools. In addition to regional accreditation, Wentworth has baccalaureate program accreditation with ABET, ACCE, FIDER, NAAB, IACBE, IFMA, and CIDA. The 35-acre campus is in an urban area in Boston. Including any residence halls, there are 27 buildings.

STUDENT LIFE: 63% of undergraduates are from Massachusetts. Others are from 38 states, 60 foreign countries, and Canada. 60% are White; 12% race unknown; 7% Asian American; 7% Foreign; 6% two or more races; 4% African American; 3% Hispanic; 1% American Indian/Alaska Native. **Male To Female Ratio:** 4.0:1. The average age of freshmen is 18; all undergraduates, 20. 16% do not continue beyond their first year; 66% remain to graduate. **Housing:** 2143 students can be accommodated in college housing, which includes coed dorms and on-campus apartments. On-campus housing is guaranteed for the freshman year only. 51% of students live on campus; of those, 85% remain on campus on weekends. Alcohol is not permitted. Upperclassmen may keep cars.

FACULTY/CLASSROOMS: 63% of faculty are male; 37% are female. All teach undergraduates. No introductory courses are taught by graduate students. The average class size in a regular course is 21.

PROGRAMS OF STUDY: Wentworth confers B.S. degrees. Associate and master's degrees are also awarded. Bachelor's degrees are awarded in BUSINESS (business management), COMMUNICATIONS AND THE ARTS (industrial design), COMPUTER AND PHYSICAL SCIENCE (applied mathematics, computer networks & systems, computer information systems, computer science, and information sciences and systems), ENGINEERING AND ENVIRONMENTAL DESIGN (architecture, biomedical engineering, civil engineering, computer engineering, construction management, electrical/electronics engineering, electromechanical technology, engineering, industrial administration/management, interior design, and technological management). Computer science and all engineering majors are the strongest academically. Architecture, construction management, computer science, and mechanical engineering have the largest enrollments.

ACTIVITIES: There are no fraternities or sororities. There are 58 groups on campus, including choir, communications, computers, dance, drama, ethnic, honors, international, LGBT, literary magazine, musical theater, orchestra, professional, radio and TV, religious, social, social service, and student government. Popular campus events include Beaux Arts Ball, and Homecoming. **Sports:** There are 11 intercollegiate sports for men and 6 for women, and 13 intramural sports for men and 13 for women. Facilities include gyms, tennis courts, two fitness centers, and softball, soccer,lacrosse and rugby playing fields. **Graduates:** From July 1, 2015 to June 30, 2016, 784 bachelor's degrees were awarded. The most popular majors were architecture (22%), mechanical engineering technology (7%), and construction management (7%). 189 companies recruited on campus in 2015-2016. In an average class, 1% graduate in 3 years or less, 49% graduate in 4 years or less, 64% graduate in 5 years or less, and 66% graduate in 6 years or less. Of the 2015 graduating class, 9% were enrolled in graduate school within 6 months of graduation, and 84% were employed.

SERVICES: Counseling and information services are available, as is tutoring in every subject. There is remedial math and writing. Free tutoring is available to all students through the Center of Academic Excellennce. **Library/Resources:** The library contains 61,000 volumes, 90 microform items, and 20,000 audio/video tapes/CDs/DVDs, and subscribes to 350 periodicals including electronic. Computerized library services include interlibrary loans, database searching, and Internet access. Special learning facilities include a radio station, design studios, Flanagan campus center, computer networking lab, and a center for sciences and biomedical engineering. **Physically Challenged Students:** 30% of the campus is accessible. Facilities include wheelchair ramps, elevators, special parking, specially equipped restrooms, special class scheduling, lowered drinking fountains, and lowered telephones. **Special:** Wentworth offers extensive cooperative programs; cross-registration with other members of the Colleges of the Fenway Consortium; study abroad, including study in France for third-year architecture students. Most students at the bachelor's level attend school in the summer, as most cooperative work occurs during the academic year. There are 5 national honor societies and a chapter of Phi Beta Kappa. **Visiting:** There are regularly scheduled orientations for prospective students, including daily tours and information programs, Monday to Friday. There are guides for informal visits and visitors may sit in on classes. To schedule a visit, contact The Admissions Office. **Campus Safety and Security:** Measures include 24-hour foot and vehicle patrol, emergency notification system, self-defense education, and security escort services. There are emergency telephones, lighted pathways/sidewalks, and controlled access to dorms/residences. All campus police officers have emergency medical training.

REQUIREMENTS: The SAT or ACT is required. Applicants must be graduates of an accredited secondary school or have the GED. High school course requirements vary by major. AP and CLEP credits are accepted. Important factors in the admissions decision are advanced placement or honors courses, leadership record, and extracurricular activities record. For a bachelor's degree, students must complete a total of 136 to 176 hours, depending on the major, with a minimum GPA of 2.0 overall and 2.5 in the major. An introductory computer course is required of all students. All full-time bachelor's degree candidates must complete 2 semesters of co-op, beginning after the first 2 years of study. **Procedure:** Freshmen are admitted fall and spring. Entrance exams should be taken in the spring of the junior year or the fall of the senior year. There are deferred admissions and rolling admissions plans. Applications should be filed by February 15 for fall entry. The fall 2016 application fee was $50. Notification is sent on a rolling basis. Applications are accepted on-line. **Transfer Students:** 136 transfer students enrolled in 2015-2016. Requirements for transfer students vary by program. All applicants must submit official college and high school transcripts. Portfolios and faculty reviews are recommended of applicants to industrial design, interior design, and architecture programs. Grades of C or better transfer for credit. Transfer students must take 50% of the course work in their degree program at Wentworth to graduate. 68 of 136 credits required for the bachelor's degree must be completed at Wentworth. **International Students:** There are 316 international students enrolled. The school actively recruits these students. They must take the TOEFL with a minimum score of 550 on the paper-based TOEFL (PBT) or 79 on the Internet-based version (iBT), and take the IELTS, Pearson Test of English, 3 or more years at an English-based high school. They must also take the SAT or ACT.

ADMISSIONS: 67% of the 2016-2017 applicants were accepted. The SAT scores for the 2016-2017 freshman class were: Critical Reading-- 33% below 500, 48% between 500 and 599, 18% between 600 and 699, and 2% between 700 and 800. Math-- 12% below 500, 48% between 500 and 599, 35% between 600 and 699, and 6% between 700 and 800. Writing-- 43% below 500, 42% between 500 and 599, 13% between 600 and 699, and 1% between 700 and 800. The ACT scores were 1% below 12, 2% between 12 and 17, 43% between 18 and 23, 48% between 24 and 29, and 7% above 30. **Admissions Contact:** Amy Dufour, Associate Director of Admissions. Web: *www.wit.edu*

FINANCIAL AID: In 2016-2017, 88% of all full-time freshmen and 52% of continuing full-time students received some form of financial aid. 78% of all full-time freshmen and 43% of continuing full-time students received need-based aid. The average freshman award was $18,344. Need-based scholarships or need-based grants averaged $5,423; need-based self-help aid (loans and jobs) averaged $4,578; and other non-need-based awards and non-need-based scholarships averaged $9,800. 40% of undergraduate students work part-time. Average annual earnings from campus work are $1373. The average financial indebtedness of the 2016 graduate was $36,691. The FAFSA code is 002225. The priority date for freshman financial aid applications for fall entry is March 1.

WESTERN NEW ENGLAND UNIVERSITY B-3

www.wne.edu

Springfield, MA 01119	(413) 782-1321 (800) 325-1122
Fax: (413) 782-1777	**Email:** learn@wne.edu
Full-time: 1593 men, 987 women	**Faculty:** 188
Part-time: 85 men, 59 women	**Ph.D.s:** 88%
Graduate: 470 men, 639 women	**Student/Faculty:** 12 to 1
Year: semesters, summer session	**Tuition:** $34,874
Room & Board: $13,214	**Freshman Class:** 6399 applied, 5094 accepted, 723 enrolled
SAT CR/M: 530/560 **ACT:** 24	**CEEB CODE:** 3962
Application Deadline: open	**COMPETITIVE**

Western New England University, founded in 1919, is a private nonsectarian institution offering undergraduate programs in business, engineering and arts and sciences. There are 3 undergraduate schools and 5 graduate schools. In addition to regional accreditation, WNE has baccalaureate program accreditation with AACSB, ABET, ACPE, CSWE, and ABA. The 215-acre campus is in a suburban area 90 miles west of Boston, MA, 30 miles from Hartford, CT, and 150 miles from New York City. Including any residence halls, there are 26 buildings.

STUDENT LIFE: 52% of undergraduates are from Massachusetts.

Others are from 30 states, 18 foreign countries, and Canada. 73% are White; 8% Hispanic; 6% African American; 4% race unknown; 3% Asian American; 3% Foreign; 2% two or more races; 1% American Indian/Alaska Native. 98% claim no religious affiliation. **Male To Female Ratio:** 1.3:1. The average age of freshmen is 18; all undergraduates, 20. 23% do not continue beyond their first year; 60% remain to graduate. **Housing:** 2000 students can be accommodated in college housing, which includes coed dorms, on-campus apartments, and married student housing, and freshmen are grouped by academic interest areas or theme housing. On-campus housing is guaranteed for all 4 years. 62% of students live on campus; of those, 70% remain on campus on weekends. All students may keep cars.

FACULTY/CLASSROOMS: 59% of faculty are male; 41% are female. Graduate students teach 1% of introductory courses. The average class size in an introductory lecture is 20; in a laboratory is 17; and in a regular course is 19.

PROGRAMS OF STUDY: WNE confers B.A., B.S., B.B.A., B.A.L.S., B.S.B.A., B.S.B.E., B.S.C.J., B.S.E.E., B.S.H.S., B.S.I.E., B.S.M.E., B.S.W., B.S.B.M.E. and B.S.C.E. degrees. Associate, master's, and doctoral degrees are also awarded. Bachelor's degrees are awarded in BIOLOGICAL SCIENCE (biology/biological science and neurosciences), BUSINESS (accounting, business administration and management, entrepreneurial studies, finance, international business, management science, marketing, and sports management), COMMUNICATIONS AND THE ARTS (advertising, communications, creative writing, English, and public relations), COMPUTER AND PHYSICAL SCIENCE (actuarial science, chemistry, chemistry/forensic chemistry, computer information systems, computer science, information sciences and systems, and mathematics), EDUCATION (elementary education and secondary education), ENGINEERING AND ENVIRONMENTAL DESIGN (biomedical engineering, civil engineering, computer engineering, electrical/electronics engineering, industrial engineering, mechanical engineering, and preengineering), HEALTH PROFESSIONS (health science, premedicine, preoptometry, prepharmacy, and pre-physician assistant), SOCIAL SCIENCE (American studies, criminal justice, economics, forensic studies, history, international studies, law, liberal arts/general studies, liberal arts, sciences, general studies, humanities, philosophy, political science/government, psychology, social work, and sociology). Engineering is the strongest academically. Psychology, sports management, and mechanical engineering have the largest enrollments.

ACTIVITIES: There are no fraternities or sororities. There are 70 groups on campus, including art, band, cheerleading, chorus, computers, dance, drama, environmental, ethnic, film, forensics, honors, international, jazz band, LGBT, literary magazine, musical theater, newspaper, pep band, photography, political, professional, radio and TV, religious, social, social service, student government, and yearbook. Popular campus events include Spring Week, Family and Friends Weekend, Midnight Madness, and Mr. University. **Sports:** There are 10 intercollegiate sports for men and 9 for women, and 13 intramural sports for men and 13 for women. Facilities include a healthful living center equipped for basketball, wrestling, racquetball, squash, aerobics, fitness, and volleyball, as well as a weight room, an 8-lane pool, and a track. The 1,200-seat Golden Bear Stadium serves multiple varsity sports including football, field hockey, and lacrosse. There are tennis courts, baseball and softball fields. Suprenant Field which is home to the Golden Bear men's and women's soccer teams. **Graduates:** From July 1, 2015 to June 30, 2016, 606 bachelor's degrees were awarded. The most popular majors were psychology (8%), accounting (8%), and mechanical engineering (7%). 70 companies recruited on campus in 2015-2016. In an average class, 1% graduate in 3 years or less, 50% graduate in 4 years or less, 59% graduate in 5 years or less, and 60% graduate in 6 years or less.

SERVICES: Counseling and information services are available, as is tutoring in most subjects. There is a reader service for the blind. **Library/Resources:** The 2 libraries contain 107,000 volumes, 119,369 microform items, and 9,029 audio/video tapes/CDs/DVDs, and subscribe to 304 periodicals including electronic. Computerized library services include interlibrary loans, database searching, Internet access, and Wi-Fi capability. Special learning facilities include an art gallery, radio station, TV station, math, and writing and science centers. **Physically Challenged Students:** Facilities include wheelchair ramps, elevators, special parking, specially equipped restrooms, special class scheduling, lowered drinking fountains, lowered telephones, and special housing. **Special:** Students may cross-register with cooperating colleges of Greater Springfield. The college offers internships, study abroad, a Washington semester, work-study programs, B.A.-B.S. degrees, an accelerated degree program, and dual and student-designed majors. The 3+3 law program offers qualified students the opportunity to earn a J.D. in 6 years. There is also a 6-year biomedical engineering/law program, a 5-year Bachelor/M.B.A., a 5-year Bachelor/Masters in Organizational Leadership,a 5-year accounting/M.S.A., a 5-year B.S./M.S. in Engineering Management and Electrical Engineering and Mechanical Engineering and Industrial Engineering and Civil Engineering. There are 14 national honor societies and a freshman honors program. **Visiting:** There are regularly scheduled orientations for prospective students, including multiple open houses. There are guides for informal visits, visitors may sit in on classes, and stay overnight. To schedule a visit, contact the Undergraduate Admissions Office. **Campus Safety and Security:** Measures include 24-hour foot and vehicle patrol, emergency notification system, self-defense education, and security escort services. There are emergency telephones, lighted pathways/sidewalks, controlled access to dorms/residences, security cameras, medical response, fire response, and a comprehensive public safety awareness program.

REQUIREMENTS: Applicants must be graduates of an approved secondary school and must have completed 4 years of high school English, 2 or more years of math, 1 or more years of science, and 1 year of history and social science. An interview is recommended. ACT is accepted in lieu of SAT. AP and CLEP credits are accepted. Important factors in the admissions decision are advanced placement or honors courses, extracurricular activities record, and recommendations by school officials. To graduate, students must complete 122 credit hours, with a minimum GPA of 2.0. Requirements include 2 courses each in English, math, lab science, and phys ed, and 1 course each in history, culture, and computers. A first-year seminar is also required for freshmen. Each student needs to complete two Learning Beyond the Classroom experiences to be eligible for graduation. These are to help them make connections between coursework and applied learning experiences. Other requirements vary according to the major. **Procedure:** Freshmen are admitted fall and spring. Entrance exams should be taken in the spring of the junior year or fall of the senior year. There are early admissions, deferred admissions, and rolling admissions plans. Application deadlines are open. Application fee is $40. Notification is sent on a rolling basis. Applications are accepted on-line. Application fees are waived if application is completed on-line. **Transfer Students:** 109 transfer students enrolled in 2015-2016. Applicants must have a minimum GPA of 2.3. Grades of C- or better transfer for credit. The university admits transfer students in the fall and spring. 30 of 122 credits required for the bachelor's degree must be completed at WNE. **International Students:** There are 93 international students enrolled. The school actively recruits these students. They must take the TOEFL with a minimum score of 550 on the paper-based TOEFL (PBT) or 79 on the Internet-based version (iBT). They must also take the SAT or ACT.

ADMISSIONS: 80% of the 2016-2017 applicants were accepted. The SAT scores for the 2016-2017 freshman class were: Critical Reading-- 30% below 500, 50% between 500 and 599, 18% between 600 and 699, and 2% between 700 and 800. Math-- 19% below 500, 49% between 500 and 599, 29% between 600 and 699, and 3% between 700 and 800. The ACT scores were 2% between 12 and 17, 37% between 18 and 23, 51% between 24 and 29, and 10% above 30. 32% of the current freshmen were in the top fifth of their class; 61% were in the top two fifths. One freshman graduated first in the class. **Admissions Contact:** Bryan Gross, Vice President for Enrollment Management. Email: *learn@wne.edu* Web: *www.wne.edu*

FINANCIAL AID: In 2016-2017, 99% of all full-time freshmen and 94% of continuing full-time students received some form of financial aid. 84% of all full-time freshmen and 77% of continuing full-time students received need-based aid. The average freshman award was $30,900. Need-based scholarships or need-based grants averaged $18,650. 40% of undergraduate students work part-time. Average annual earnings from campus work are $1800. The FAFSA code is 002226. The priority date for freshman financial aid applications for fall entry is rolling. The deadline for filing freshman financial aid applications for fall entry is rolling.

WESTFIELD STATE UNIVERSITY B-3

www.westfield.ma.edu

Westfield, MA 01086 **(413) 572-5218**

Fax: (413) 572-0520 **Email:** admissions@westfield.ma.edu

Full-time: 2304 men, 2678 women	**Faculty:** 234
Part-time: 300 men, 328 women	**Ph.D.s:** 90%
Graduate: 240 men, 533 women	**Student/Faculty:** 21 to 1
Year: semesters, summer session	**Tuition:** $9275 ($15,355)
Room & Board: $10,396	**Freshman Class:** 4740 applied, 3695 accepted, 1068 enrolled
SAT CR/M/W: 490/500/480 **ACT:** 21	**CEEB CODE:** 3523
Application Deadline: March 1	**COMPETITIVE**

Westfield State University, founded in 1839, is a public university with liberal arts and sciences, teacher preparation programs and professional training in business, nursing and allied health fields. There is 1 undergraduate school and 1 graduate school. In addition to regional accreditation, Westfield State has baccalaureate program accreditation with ABET, CSWE, NASM, NCATE, CAAHEP, and CCNE. The 256-acre campus is in a suburban area in western Massachusetts, 15 miles west of Springfield, 100 miles west of Boston. Including any residence halls, there are 26 buildings.

STUDENT LIFE: 93% of undergraduates are from Massachusetts. Others are from 22 states, 15 foreign countries, and Canada. 9% are Hispanic; 76% White; 5% African American; 5% two or more races; 3% race unknown; 2% Asian American. **Female To Male Ratio:** 1.2:1. The average age of freshmen is 18; all undergraduates, 21. 22% do not continue beyond their first year; 66% remain to graduate. **Housing:** 3059 students can be accommodated in college housing, which includes coed dorms, on-campus apartments, and off-campus apartments. In addition, there are honors houses, special-interest houses, special housing for disabilities students, and special housing for international students. On-campus housing is available on a first-come and first-served basis. 54% of students live on campus. Upperclassmen may keep cars.

FACULTY/CLASSROOMS: 48% of faculty are male; 52% are female. 99% teach undergraduates. No introductory courses are taught by graduate students. The average class size in an introductory lecture is 22; in a laboratory is 15; and in a regular course is 19.

PROGRAMS OF STUDY: Westfield State confers B.A., B.S., B.S.E., B.S.N. and B.S.W. degrees. Master's degrees are also awarded. Bachelor's degrees are awarded in BIOLOGICAL SCIENCE (biology/biological science), BUSINESS (business administration and management), COMMUNICATIONS AND THE ARTS (art, communications, English, music, Spanish, and theatre arts), COMPUTER AND PHYSICAL SCIENCE (chemistry, computer science, information sciences and systems, mathematics, and science), EDUCATION (athletic training, early childhood education, elementary education, special education, and vocational education), ENGINEERING AND ENVIRONMENTAL DESIGN (city/community/regional planning and environmental science), HEALTH PROFESSIONS (nursing), SOCIAL SCIENCE (criminal justice, economics, ethnic studies, history, liberal arts/general studies, physical fitness/movement, political science/government, psychology, social work, and sociology). Business managment, education, and criminal justice have the largest enrollments.

ACTIVITIES: There are no fraternities or sororities. There are 91 groups on campus, including art, band, choir, chorale, chorus, communications, computers, dance, drama, environmental, ethnic, honors, international, jazz band, LGBT, literary magazine, musical theater, newspaper, orchestra, pep band, political, professional, radio and TV, religious, social, social service, student government, and symphony. Popular campus events include Homecoming, Spring Weekend and Comedy Night. **Sports:** There are 8 intercollegiate sports for men and 10 for women, and 8 intramural sports for men and 5 for women. Facilities include a track, baseball and softball fields, a 400-seat gym, and a 5,000-seat stadium. **Graduates:** From July 1, 2015 to June 30, 2016, 1215 bachelor's degrees were awarded. The most popular majors were liberal studies (15%), business management (13%), and criminal justice (13%). In an average class, 53% graduate in 4 years or less, 64% graduate in 5 years or less, and 66% graduate in 6 years or less.

SERVICES: Counseling and information services are available, as is tutoring in every subject. There is a reader service for the blind. **Library/Resources:** The library contains 139,363 volumes, 481,154 microform items, and 4,916 audio/video tapes/CDs/DVDs, and subscribes to 1,418 periodicals including electronic. Computerized library services include interlibrary loans, database searching, Internet access, and Wi-Fi capability. Special learning facilities include an art gallery, natural history museum, radio station, TV station, a geology museum, a greenhouse, and a science center. **Physically Challenged Students:** 75% of the campus is accessible. Facilities include wheelchair ramps, elevators, special parking, specially equipped restrooms, special class scheduling, and special housing. **Special:** Students may cross-register through College Academic Program Sharing, National Student Exchange, and Cooperating Colleges of Greater Springfield. Internships are for credit only in conjunction with all major programs. The University offers international exchange programs in China, Ireland and Poland and hundreds of study abroad programs in over 35 countries, a Washington semester for political science, criminal justice, and psychology majors, an internship program with Walt Disney World, dual majors, student-designed majors, some credit for military experience and a multi-department Honors Program. There are 16 national honor societies and a freshman honors program. **Visiting:** There are regularly scheduled orientations for prospective students, including a campus tour, classroom observation, academic department presentations, lunch with faculty, staff, and students, and a question-and-answer session moderated by a panel of administrators. There are guides for informal visits. To schedule a visit, contact the Admissions Office. **Campus Safety and Security:** Measures include 24-hour foot and vehicle patrol, emergency notification system, self-defense education, and security escort services. There are shuttle buses, emergency telephones, lighted pathways/sidewalks, and controlled access to dorms/residences.

REQUIREMENTS: The SAT or ACT is required. Applicants must achieve a minimum 3.0 cumulative average in academic subjects. Students who have between a 2.0 and a 3.0 GPA may be accepted via a sliding scale, contingent upon the SAT or ACT scores. They must be graduates of an accredited secondary school and must have completed 4 years of college preparatory level English, 4 years of math (algebra I and II and geometry), 2 years of social sciences (including 1 year of U.S history), 3 years of sciences, including 2 with lab, 2 foreign language, and 2 years of electives. The GED is accepted. A portfolio is required for admission to the art program, and an audition is necessary for admission to the music program. All applicants must submit either SAT or ACT scores unless they have a documented learning disability. A GPA of 2.0 is required. AP and CLEP credits are accepted. Students must complete a total of 120 credit hours, with 43 or more credits in 9 specified areas and 30 to 40 hours in the major. The college requires a 2.0 GPA overall and 2.0 in major courses. U.S. history or government and diversity awareness courses are required. **Procedure:** Freshmen are admitted fall and spring. Entrance exams should be taken in the spring of the junior year and fall of the senior year. There are deferred admissions and rolling admissions plans. Applications should be filed by March 1 for fall entry; December 1 for spring entry, along with a $50 fee. Notifications are sent March 15. Applications are accepted on-line. Application fees are waived if application is completed on-line. **Transfer Students:** 431 transfer students enrolled in 2015-2016. Transfer students must have 24 transferable credits with a minimum cumulative GPA of 2.0 (higher for some majors). A grade of C- or better with a 2.0 GPA will transfer for credit. Transfer students are admitted in the fall and spring. For students transferring from a Massachusetts Community College, a D may be transferred for credit. 30 of 120 credits required for the bachelor's degree must be completed at Westfield State. **International Students:** There are 38 international students enrolled. The school actively recruits these students. They must take the TOEFL with a minimum score of 550 on the paper-based TOEFL (PBT) or 79 on the Internet-based version (iBT), or take the IELTS. They must also take the SAT or ACT.

ADMISSIONS: 78% of the 2016-2017 applicants were accepted. The SAT scores for the 2016-2017 freshman class were: Critical Reading-- 44% below 500, 45% between 500 and 599, 10% between 600 and 699, and 1% between 700 and 800. Math-- 40% below 500, 48% between 500 and 599, and 11% between 600 and 699. Writing-- 50% below 500, 43% between 500 and 599, and 6% between 600 and 699. The ACT scores were 2% below 12, 15% between 12 and 17, 60% between 18 and 23, and 23% between 24 and 29. **Admissions Contact:** Kelly Hart, Director of Admissions. Email: *admissions@westfield.ma.edu* Web: *www.westfield.ma.edu*

FINANCIAL AID: Westfield State is a member of CSS. The FAFSA code is 002189. The deadline for filing freshman financial aid applications for fall entry is March 1.

WHEATON COLLEGE D-3
wheatoncollege.edu

Norton, MA 02766	(508) 286-8251 (800) 394-6003
Fax: (508) 286-8271	Email: admission@wheatoncollege.edu
Full-time: 622 men, 1015 women	**Faculty:** 137; IIB, +$
Part-time: 5 men, 8 women	**Ph.D.s:** 65%
Graduate: n/av	**Student/Faculty:** 10 to 1
Year: semesters	**Tuition:** $49,012
Room & Board: $12,500	**Freshman Class:** 4478 applied, 2779 accepted, 528 enrolled
SAT CR/M/W: 580/580/580 **ACT:** 27	**CEEB CODE:** 3963
Application Deadline: January 1	**VERY COMPETITIVE**

Wheaton College, established in 1834, is an independent liberal arts institution. There is 1 undergraduate school. The 478-acre campus is in a suburban area 35 miles south of Boston and 20 miles north of Providence. Including any residence halls, there are 81 buildings.

STUDENT LIFE: 67% of undergraduates are from out of state, mostly the Northeast. Students are from 34 states, 76 foreign countries, and Canada. 76% are from public schools. 7% are Hispanic; 65% White; 6% African American; 5% Asian American; 3% two or more races; 2% race unknown; 12% Foreign. **Female To Male Ratio:** 1.6:1. The average age of freshmen is 18; all undergraduates, 20. 14% do not continue beyond their first year; 79% remain to graduate. **Housing:** 1612 students can be accommodated in college housing, which includes single-sex and coed dorms. In addition, there are language houses, special-interest houses, House of REPS, ECCO House, Emerson House, Farm House, House of the Living Arts, Hungry Lyons House, Jewish Life House, KNUTH-Computer Science House, MAD-Media Amelioration Discernibly, Outdoors House, Peace House, Renaissance House, Safe Haus, TWAP House, UWC Davis House, and SOHL House. On-campus housing is guaranteed for all 4 years and is available on a lottery system for upperclassmen. 97% of students live on campus. All students may keep cars.

FACULTY/CLASSROOMS: 48% of faculty are male; 52% are female. All teach undergraduates, 88% do research, and 88% do both. No introductory courses are taught by graduate students. The average class size in an introductory lecture is 24; in a laboratory is 17; and in a regular course is 18.

PROGRAMS OF STUDY: Wheaton confers B.A. degrees. Bachelor's degrees are awarded in BIOLOGICAL SCIENCE (biochemistry, bioinformatics, biology/biological science, and neurosciences), BUSINESS (business administration and management), COMMUNICATIONS AND THE ARTS (Africana studies, art history, classics, creative writing, dramatic arts, English, film arts, fine arts, fine/studio arts, general, German, German studies, Germanic languages and literature, Greek, Greek (classical), Latin, literature, film and media studies, music, Russian, Russian languages and literature, studio art, and theatre/dance), COMPUTER AND PHYSICAL SCIENCE (astronomy, astronomy and physics, chemistry, computer mathematics, computer science, mathematics, mathematics – economics, and physics), EDUCATION (Asian studies, classical studies, early childhood education, and secondary education), ENGINEERING AND ENVIRONMENTAL DESIGN (environmental science), HEALTH PROFESSIONS (biology and multidisciplinary studies), SOCIAL SCIENCE (African studies, African American studies, American studies, anthropology, area studies, classical/ancient civilization, economics, French studies, Hispanic American studies, history, international relations, Italian studies, philosophy, philosophy and religion, political science/government, psychology, religion, religious studies, sociology, women & gender studies, and women's studies). Arts and sciences is the strongest academically. Psychology, business & management, and biology have the largest enrollments.

ACTIVITIES: There are no fraternities or sororities. There are 120 groups on campus, including art, band, cheerleading, choir, chorale, chorus, communications, computers, dance, debate, drama, ethnic, film, honors, international, jazz band, LGBT, literary magazine, newspaper, orchestra, photography, political, professional, radio and TV, religious, social, social service, student government, symphony, and yearbook. Popular campus events include Head of the Peacock (boat races), Candle Lighting, Spring Weekend, HOLI, and Vespers & Luminaria. **Sports:** There are 10 intercollegiate sports for men and 13 for women, and 3 intramural sports for men and 3 for women. Facilities include an 8-lane stretch pool, a field house with 5 tennis courts, 1 outdoor and 5 indoor basketball courts, 200-meter track, golf/archery range and batting cage, an 850-seat gym, 7 lighted outdoor tennis courts, running course, baseball stadium, 2 athletic fields, softball field, artificial turf field, aerobics/dance studio, and a fitness center. **Graduates:** From July 1, 2015 to June 30, 2016, 386 bachelor's degrees were awarded. The most popular majors were social sciences (18%), biological/life sciences (14%), and visual and performing arts (13%). 47 companies recruited on campus in 2015-2016. In an average class, 76% graduate in 4 years or less, 79% graduate in 5 years or less, and 79% graduate in 6 years or less.

SERVICES: Counseling and information services are available, as is tutoring in most subjects. There is a reader service for the blind. Peer tutoring and note takers for hearing-impaired students are also available. **Library/Resources:** The library contains 343,772 volumes, 108,137 microform items, and 11,015 audio/video tapes/CDs/DVDs, and subscribes to 29,037 periodicals including electronic. Computerized library services include interlibrary loans, database searching, Internet access, and Wi-Fi capability. Special learning facilities include an art gallery, planetarium, radio station, a greenhouse, and an observatory. **Physically Challenged Students:** Facilities include wheelchair ramps, elevators, special parking, specially equipped restrooms, and special class scheduling. **Special:** Students may cross-register with Brown University as well as with colleges in the Southeastern Association for Cooperation in Higher Education in Massachusetts and with schools participating in the 12 College Exchange Program. Wheaton offers study abroad in 90 countries, internship programs, nondegree study, dual majors, student-designed majors, a Washington semester at American University, and interdisciplinary majors, including math and economics, math and computer science, physics and astronomy, and theater and English dramatic literature. Dual-degree programs exist with the following institutions: Thayer School of Engineering, Dartmouth College (B.S. Engineering); Graduate School of Management, University of Rochester (M.B.A.); and New England School of Optometry (Doctor of Optometry). There is a chapter of Phi Beta Kappa and a freshman honors program. **Visiting:** There are regularly scheduled orientations for prospective students. Campus visits may include campus tours, class visits, interviews, faculty & coach visits, and overnight dorm stays. There are guides for informal visits, visitors may sit in on classes, and stay overnight. To schedule a visit, contact the Admissions Office. **Campus Safety and Security:** Measures include 24-hour foot and vehicle patrol, emergency notification system, self-defense education, and security escort services. There are emergency telephones, lighted pathways/sidewalks, and controlled access to dorms/residences.

REQUIREMENTS: Applicants must be graduates of an accredited secondary school. Recommended courses include English with emphasis on composition skills, 4 years each of foreign language, math, and social studies, 3 years of history, 2-3 years of science, 2 of which must include lab. Wheaton requires an essay and strongly recommends an interview. AP credits are accepted. Among the requirements for graduation are 32 course units (4 semester hours each), with a minimum of 10 courses in the major. The requirements for each major are determined by the department. The core classes consist of First-year Seminar, English, quantitative skills, foreign language, and non-Western course. Students must maintain a minimum GPA of 2.0 (C-) in all courses to remain in good academic standing. **Procedure:** Freshmen are admitted fall and spring. Entrance exams should be taken in October or November. There are early decision and deferred admissions plans. Early decision applications should be filed by November 1; regular applications, by January 1 for fall entry; and November 1 for spring entry, along with a $60 fee. Notification of early decision is sent December 15; regular decision, April 1. 104 early decision candidates were accepted for the 2016-2017 class. 112 applicants were on the 2016 waiting list; 1 was admitted. Applications are accepted on-line. Application fees are waived if application is completed on-line. **Transfer Students:** 14 transfer students enrolled in 2015-2016. Transfer students are encouraged to present a strong B average in their college work to date. Preference will be given to college over high school work. The college transcript is evaluated. High school and college transcripts, an essay or personal statement, a statement of good standing, instructor recommendation, and a midterm evaluation are required. 16 of 32 credits required for the bachelor's degree must be completed at Wheaton. **International Students:** There are 196 international students enrolled. The school actively recruits these students. They must take the TOEFL with a minimum score of 580 on the paper-based TOEFL (PBT) or 90 on the Internet-based version (iBT).

ADMISSIONS: 62% of the 2016-2017 applicants were accepted. The

SAT scores for the 2016-2017 freshman class were: Critical Reading-- 14% below 500, 48% between 500 and 599, 29% between 600 and 699, and 9% between 700 and 800. Math-- 11% below 500, 48% between 500 and 599, 35% between 600 and 699, and 7% between 700 and 800. Writing-- 16% below 500, 44% between 500 and 599, 34% between 600 and 699, and 6% between 700 and 800. The ACT scores were 1% between 12 and 17, 16% between 18 and 23, 57% between 24 and 29, and 26% above 30. 45% of the current freshmen were in the top fifth of their class; 76% were in the top two fifths. 3 freshmen graduated first in their class. **Admissions Contact:** Grant Gosselin, VP for Enrollment and Dean of Admissions & Student Aid. Email: *admission@wheatoncollege.edu* Web: *wheatoncollege.edu*

FINANCIAL AID: In 2016-2017, 99% of all full-time freshmen and 96% of continuing full-time students received some form of financial aid. 65% of all full-time freshmen and 64% of continuing full-time students received need-based aid. The average freshman award was $30,354. Need-based scholarships or need-based grants averaged $23,276 ($63,740 maximum); need-based self-help aid (loans and jobs) averaged $5,777 ($42,312 maximum); and other non-need-based awards and non-need-based scholarships averaged $8,335 ($34,938 maximum). 56% of undergraduate students work part-time. Average annual earnings from campus work are $1066. The average financial indebtedness of the 2016 graduate was $33,040. Wheaton is a member of CSS. The CSS/Profile, noncustodial profile and business/farm supplement are required. The FAFSA code is 002227. The deadline for filing freshman financial aid applications for fall entry is February 1.

WHEELOCK COLLEGE E-2
www.wheelock.edu

Boston, MA 02215	**(617) 879-2038** **(800) 734-5212**
Fax: (617) 879-2449	**Email: undergrad@wheelock.edu**
Full-time: 126 men, 587 women	**Faculty:** IIA, -$
Part-time: 3 men, 10 women	**Ph.D.s:** 61%
Graduate: 28 men, 299 women	**Student/Faculty:** 11 to 1
Year: semesters, summer session	**Tuition:** $34,825
Room & Board: $14,400	**Freshman Class:** 1305 applied, 1095 accepted, 158 enrolled **CEEB CODE:** 3964
Application Deadline: March 1	**COMPETITIVE**

Wheelock College, established in 1888, is a private institution with programs in education, child life and family studies, social work, juvenile justice and youth advocacy, and human services. There are 2 undergraduate schools and 2 graduate schools. In addition to regional accreditation, Wheelock has baccalaureate program accreditation with CSWE, NCATE, and NEASC. The 7-acre campus is in an urban area Fenway of Boston. Including any residence halls, there are 12 buildings.

STUDENT LIFE: 63% of undergraduates are from Massachusetts. Others are from 27 states, and 10 foreign countries. 83% are from public schools. 58% are White; 5% race unknown; 4% Asian American; 4% two or more races; 2% Foreign; 15% African American; 12% Hispanic. **Female To Male Ratio:** 5.7:1. The average age of freshmen is 18; all undergraduates, 20. 32% do not continue beyond their first year; 61% remain to graduate. **Housing:** 675 students can be accommodated in college housing, which includes single-sex and coed dorms. an all-female dorm. On-campus housing is guaranteed for all 4 years. 60% of students live on campus. Some may keep cars.

FACULTY/CLASSROOMS: 26% of faculty are male; 74% are female. No introductory courses are taught by graduate students.

PROGRAMS OF STUDY: Wheelock confers B.A., B.S. and B.S.W. degrees. Master's degrees are also awarded. Bachelor's degrees are awarded in AGRICULTURE (environmental studies), COMMUNICATIONS AND THE ARTS (communications and performing arts), COMPUTER AND PHYSICAL SCIENCE (mathematics), EDUCATION (early childhood education, educational studies, elementary education, science education, and special education), SOCIAL SCIENCE (American studies, child care/child and family studies, humanities, political science/government, psychology, and social work). Education, social work, and child life are the strongest academically. Counseling psychology, developmental psychology, and early childhood education have the largest enrollments.

ACTIVITIES: There are no fraternities or sororities. There are 25 groups on campus, including Ukulele Union, Nerd and Gaming Alliance, Commuter Council, dance, drama, environmental, ethnic, honors, international, LGBT, musical theater, newspaper, professional, social, and student government. **Sports:** There are 7 intercollegiate sports for men and 7 for women, and 9 intramural sports for men and 9 for women. Facilities include a sports complex at a neighboring college with a pool and diving board, racquetball courts, a weight room, an indoor track, a basketball court, crew tanks, and cardiovascular equipment. **Graduates:** From July 1, 2015 to June 30, 2016, 169 bachelor's degrees were awarded. The most popular majors were psychology (37%), education (26%), and public administration and social services (13%). In an average class, 57% graduate in 4 years or less, 60% graduate in 5 years or less, and 61% graduate in 6 years or less.

SERVICES: Counseling and information services are available, as is tutoring in some subjects. There is a reader service for the blind, and remedial writing. **Library/Resources:** The library contains 83,573 volumes, 483,257 microform items, and 3,633 audio/video tapes/CDs/DVDs, and subscribes to 12,629 periodicals including electronic. Computerized library services include interlibrary loans, database searching, Internet access, and Wi-Fi capability. Special learning facilities include an art gallery, center for learning and innovation, and the Wheelock Family Theater. **Physically Challenged Students:** 67% of the campus is accessible. Facilities include wheelchair ramps, elevators, special parking, specially equipped restrooms, special class scheduling, lowered drinking fountains, and lowered telephones. Assistive technology available in the learning center. **Special:** Wheelock offers cross-registration with the Colleges of the Fenway Consortium and internships that include student teaching and social work practice. Dual majors, study-abroad programs and pass/fail options are available. There are service-learning opportunities in Barbados, Belize, Northern Ireland, Ghana, Spain, South Africa, Germany, Nicaragua, and Guatemala. Students may receive credit for life and work experience. Students begin practical fieldwork their freshman year. There is 1 national honor society, a freshman honors program, and 3 departmental honors programs. **Visiting:** There are regularly scheduled orientations for prospective students, Information sessions are held on select Saturdays in the fall and spring. Students hear a presentation from a counselor, have a tour, and may speak to a counselor individually. There are guides for informal visits, visitors may sit in on classes, and stay overnight. To schedule a visit, contact the Undergraduate Admissions Office. **Campus Safety and Security:** Measures include 24-hour foot and vehicle patrol and security escort services. There are emergency telephones and lighted pathways/sidewalks.

REQUIREMENTS: Applicants must be graduates of an accredited secondary school and must have completed 4 years of English, 3 years of math, and 2 years each of science with 1 lab, and history, and 1 of social studies, plus 3 academic electives. The GED is accepted. The college requires an essay and two letters of recommendation. AP and CLEP credits are accepted. To graduate, students must complete a minimum of 134 credit hours with a minimum GPA of 2.0. Students must complete courses in first-year seminar, reading, writing, and speaking, quantitative reasoning and mathematical thinking, human growth and development, self and society, languages and literature, creativity and the arts, historical perspectives, investigations in science and technology, ethics and social justice, interdisciplinary capstone seminar, perspectives on diversity, and upper-level writing. **Procedure:** Freshmen are admitted fall and spring. There are early decision, deferred admissions, and rolling admissions plans. Early decision applications should be filed by December 1; regular applications, by March 1 for fall entry; and December 1 for spring entry. Notification of early decision is sent December 20; regular decision, on a rolling basis. Applications are accepted on-line. Application fees are waived if application is completed on-line. **Transfer Students:** 24 transfer students enrolled in 2015-2016. 67 of 134 credits required for the bachelor's degree must be completed at Wheelock. **International Students:** There are 11 international students enrolled. They must take the TOEFL with a minimum score of 550 on the paper-based TOEFL (PBT) or 79 on the Internet-based version (iBT). They must also take the SAT or ACT. Applicants should submit SAT or ACT scores or TOEFL scores if English is not their official language.

ADMISSIONS: 84% of the 2016-2017 applicants were accepted. The SAT scores for the 2016-2017 freshman class were: Critical Reading-- 70% below 500, 23% between 500 and 599, and 7% between 600 and 699. Math-- 69% below 500, 29% between 500 and 599, and 2% between 600 and 699. Writing-- 67% below 500, 27% between 500 and 599, and 6% between 600 and 699. The ACT scores were 43% between 12 and 17,

47% between 18 and 23, and 10% between 24 and 29. **Admissions Contact:** Allison Sherlock, Senior Associate Director of Undergraduate. Email: *undergrad@wheelock.edu* Web: *www.wheelock.edu*

FINANCIAL AID: In 2016-2017, 97% of all full-time freshmen received some form of financial aid. 97% of all full-time freshmen received need-based aid. The average freshman award was $26,960. Need-based scholarships or need-based grants averaged $23,325; need-based self-help aid (loans and jobs) averaged $4,151; other non-need-based awards and non-need-based scholarships averaged $13,428; and $3,373 from other forms of aid. 33% of undergraduate students work part-time. Average annual earnings from campus work are $1800. The average financial indebtedness of the 2016 graduate was $29,038. The FAFSA code is 002228. The priority date for freshman financial aid applications for fall entry is February 15.

WILLIAMS COLLEGE — A-1
www.williams.edu

Williamstown, MA 01267 — (413) 597-2211

Email: cwade@williams.edu

Full-time: 1013 men, 1052 women
Part-time: 15 men, 19 women
Graduate: 25 men, 27 women
Year: 4-1-4
Room & Board: $13,220
SAT CR/M/W: 730/720/730 **ACT:** 33
Application Deadline: January 1

Faculty: 264; IIB, ++$
Ph.D.s: 97%
Student/Faculty: 7 to 1
Tuition: $50,070
Freshman Class: 6883 applied, 1212 accepted, 551 enrolled
CEEB CODE: 3965
MOST COMPETITIVE

Williams College, founded in 1793, is a private institution offering undergraduate degrees in liberal arts and graduate degrees in art history and development economics. There are 5 undergraduate schools and 2 graduate schools. The 450-acre campus is in a small town 150 miles north of New York City and west of Boston. Including any residence halls, there are 97 buildings.

STUDENT LIFE: 87% of undergraduates are from out of state, mostly the Northeast. Students are from 46 states, 53 foreign countries, and Canada. 8% are African American; 8% Foreign; 6% two or more races; 49% White; 13% Hispanic; 12% Asian American. **Female To Male Ratio:** 1.0:1. The average age of freshmen is 19; all undergraduates, 20. 2% do not continue beyond their first year; 95% remain to graduate. **Housing:** College-sponsored housing includes coed dorms, on-campus apartments, and cooperative housing, in which students prepare their own meals. On-campus housing is guaranteed for all 4 years and is available on a lottery system for upperclassmen. Upperclassmen may keep cars.

FACULTY/CLASSROOMS: 56% of faculty are male; 44% are female. No introductory courses are taught by graduate students.

PROGRAMS OF STUDY: Williams confers B.A. degrees. Master's degrees are also awarded. Bachelor's degrees are awarded in BIOLOGICAL SCIENCE (biology/biological science), COMMUNICATIONS AND THE ARTS (Arabic, art, art history and appreciation, classics, dramatic arts, English, fine arts, French, German, literature, music, Russian, and Spanish), COMPUTER AND PHYSICAL SCIENCE (astronomy, astrophysics, chemistry, computer science, geology, mathematics, physics, and statistics), SOCIAL SCIENCE (American studies, anthropology, Asian/Oriental studies, economics, history, philosophy, political science/government, psychology, religion, sociology, and women's studies).

ACTIVITIES: There are no fraternities or sororities. Groups on campus include a capella singing groups, handbell choir, art, band, chess, choir, chorale, chorus, comedy group, communications, computers, dance, debate, drama, environmental, ethnic, film, honors, international, jazz band, LGBT, literary magazine, marching band, musical theater, newspaper, opera, orchestra, pep band, photography, political, professional, radio and TV, religious, social, social service, student government, symphony, and yearbook. Popular campus events include Winter Carnival, Mountain Day, and Claiming Williams. **Sports:** There are 16 intercollegiate sports for men and 15 for women, and 17 intramural sports for men and 17 for women. Facilities include 2 gyms, a 50-meter pool, a dance studio, a weight room, rowing tanks, a boathouse, a golf course, playing fields, artificial turf field, indoor and outdoor tracks, and courts for tennis, squash, and paddle tennis. **Graduates:** From July 1, 2015 to June 30, 2016, 522 bachelor's degrees were awarded. The most popular majors were economics (17%), English (13%), and history (12%). In an average class, 88% graduate in 4 years or less, 95% graduate in 5 years or less, and 96% graduate in 6 years or less.

SERVICES: Counseling and information services are available, as is tutoring in every subject. There is a reader service for the blind, and remedial math, reading, and writing. Services include a peer health program, rape and sexual assault hotline, and 10-1 counseling service. **Library/Resources:** Computerized library services include interlibrary loans, database searching, Internet access, and Wi-Fi capability. Special learning facilities include an art gallery, planetarium, radio station, a 2500-acre experimental forest, an environmental studies center, a center for foreign languages, literatures, and cultures, a rare book library, a studio art center, and a three-stage center for the performing arts. **Physically Challenged Students:** Facilities include wheelchair ramps, elevators, special parking, specially equipped restrooms, special class scheduling, lowered drinking fountains, lowered telephones, and special housing. **Special:** Students may cross-register at Bennington or Massachusetts College of Liberal Arts and study abroad in Madrid, Oxford, Cairo, Beijing, and Kyoto, or any approved program with another college or university. Teaching and medical field experiences, dual and student-designed majors, internships, and a 3-2 engineering program with Columbia University is offered. There are pass/fail options during the winter term. Each department offers Oxford-style tutorials where students meet with the professor weekly in groups of 2-3. There are 2 national honor societies and a chapter of Phi Beta Kappa. **Visiting:** There are regularly scheduled orientations for prospective students, including panels, forums, class visits, and campus tours. There are guides for informal visits, visitors may sit in on classes, and stay overnight. To schedule a visit, contact the Admission Office. **Campus Safety and Security:** Measures include 24-hour foot and vehicle patrol, emergency notification system, self-defense education, and security escort services. There are emergency telephones, lighted pathways/sidewalks, and controlled access to dorms/residences.

REQUIREMENTS: Williams requires the following standardized tests: SAT or ACT with Writing, and Two SAT Subject Tests. Applicants to Williams should pursue the strongest program of study offered by their secondary schools. While there are no absolute requirements for admission, competitive candidates typically study English, math, natural science, foreign language and social studies in four-year sequences and present a distinguished record throughout their secondary school career. AP credits are accepted. All students must complete 4 winter study courses and 32 regular semester courses, 9 of which are in the major field, with a C- or higher. Requirements include 3 semester-long courses in each of 3 academic divisions: languages and arts, social sciences, and science and math. **Procedure:** Freshmen are admitted fall. There are early decision and deferred admissions plans. Early decision applications should be filed by November 15; regular applications, by January 1 for fall entry. The fall 2016 application fee was $65. Notification of early decision is sent 12 15; regular decision, 244 early decision candidates were accepted for the 2016-2017 class. 573 applicants were on the 2016 waiting list; 53 were admitted. Applications are accepted on-line. **Transfer Students:** Transfer applicants should present a 3.5 GPA in previous college work and must submit either SAT or ACT scores. 16 of 32 credits required for the bachelor's degree must be completed at Williams. **International Students:** There are 161 international students enrolled. The school actively recruits these students. They must take the TOEFL, if English is not the applicant's first language. They must also take the SAT or ACT.

ADMISSIONS: 18% of the 2016-2017 applicants were accepted. The SAT scores for the 2016-2017 freshman class were: Critical Reading-- 6% between 500 and 599, 28% between 600 and 699, and 66% between 700 and 800. Math-- 7% between 500 and 599, 31% between 600 and 699, and 62% between 700 and 800. Writing-- 1% below 500, 5% between 500 and 599, 29% between 600 and 699, and 65% between 700 and 800. The ACT scores were 1% between 18 and 23, 14% between 24 and 29, and 85% above 30. **Admissions Contact:** Courtney Wade, Director of Institutional Research. Email: *cwade@williams.edu* Web: *www.williams.edu*

FINANCIAL AID: 50% of all full-time freshmen and 49% of continuing full-time students received need-based aid. The average freshman award was $53,433. Need-based scholarships or need-based grants averaged $48,376; and need-based self-help aid (loans and jobs) averaged $5,057. The average financial indebtedness of the 2016 graduate was $16,593. The CSS/Profile is required. The FAFSA code is 002229. The deadline for filing freshman financial aid applications for fall entry is February 1.

WORCESTER POLYTECHNIC INSTITUTE C-2

www.wpi.edu

Worcester, MA 01609	(508) 831-5286
Fax: (508) 831-5875	**Email:** admissions@wpi.edu
Full-time: 2814 men, 1461 women	**Faculty:** 368
Part-time: 117 men, 40 women	**Ph.D.s:** 92%
Graduate: 1546 men, 664 women	**Student/Faculty:** 12 to 1
Year: quarters, summer session	**Tuition:** $46,994
Room & Board: $13,736	**Freshman Class:** 10468 applied, 5071 accepted, 1120 enrolled
SAT CR/M/W: 630/680/620 **ACT:** 30	**CEEB CODE:** 3969
Application Deadline: February 1	**MOST COMPETITIVE**

Founded in 1865 as one of the nation's earliest technological universities, Worcester Polytechnic Institute is known for its project-based curriculum and Global Perspective Program, through which students complete projects at more than 25 sites on five continents. WPI's 14 academic departments offer more than 50 undergraduate and graduate programs in the arts and sciences, business, and engineering, while its interdisciplinary research programs advance fields as diverse as the life sciences, energy, information security, and robotics. There is 1 undergraduate school and 2 graduate schools. In addition to regional accreditation, WPI has baccalaureate program accreditation with AACSB, ABET, CSAB, and ACS. The 90-acre campus is in a suburban area 40 miles west of Boston. Including any residence halls, there are 54 buildings.

STUDENT LIFE: 62% of undergraduates are from out of state, mostly the Northeast. Students are from 43 states, 69 foreign countries, and Canada. 9% are Hispanic; 7% race unknown; 63% White; 4% Asian American; 3% African American; 3% two or more races; 11% Foreign. **Male To Female Ratio:** 2.1:1. The average age of freshmen is 18; all undergraduates, 20. 5% do not continue beyond their first year; 86% remain to graduate. **Housing:** 2072 students can be accommodated in college housing, which includes coed dorms, on-campus apartments, and off-campus apartments. In addition, there are special-interest houses, fraternity houses, and sorority houses. On-campus housing is guaranteed for the freshman year only and is available on a lottery system for upperclassmen. Upperclassmen may keep cars.

FACULTY/CLASSROOMS: 73% of faculty are male; 27% are female. All teach undergraduates. No introductory courses are taught by graduate students. The average class size in an introductory lecture is 100; in a laboratory is 20; and in a regular course is 20.

PROGRAMS OF STUDY: WPI confers B.A. and B.S. degrees. Master's and doctoral degrees are also awarded. Bachelor's degrees are awarded in AGRICULTURE (environmental studies), BIOLOGICAL SCIENCE (biochemistry, bioinformatics, and biology/biological science), BUSINESS (business administration and management, management engineering, and management information systems), COMMUNICATIONS AND THE ARTS (game design and development and technical and business writing), COMPUTER AND PHYSICAL SCIENCE (actuarial science, applied physics, chemistry, computer science, mathematics, and physics), ENGINEERING AND ENVIRONMENTAL DESIGN (aerospace engineering, architectural engineering, biomedical engineering, chemical engineering, civil engineering, electrical/electronics engineering, environmental engineering, industrial engineering, mechanical engineering, mechatronics engineering, and technology and public affairs), SOCIAL SCIENCE (economics, humanities, interdisciplinary studies, international studies, liberal arts/engineering studies, and social science). Engineering, computer science, and biology have the largest enrollments.

ACTIVITIES: 28% of men belong to 13 national fraternities; 45% of women belong to 6 national sororities. There are 200 groups on campus, including art, band, cheerleading, chess, choir, chorale, chorus, communications, computers, dance, debate, drama, environmental, ethnic, forensics, honors, international, jazz band, LGBT, literary magazine, musical theater, newspaper, orchestra, pep band, photography, political, professional, radio and TV, religious, robotics and design teams, social, social service, student government, symphony, and yearbook. Popular campus events include Campus Tradition Days, New Voices Festival, Quad Fest, Winter Carnival, Greek Week, International Dinner, Family Weekend, Community Service Day, Relay For Life, and Homecoming. **Sports:** There are 10 intercollegiate sports for men and 10 for women, and 7 intramural sports for men and 7 for women. Facilities include an aerobics area, softball fields, an 8-lane synthetic surface track, a fitness center, a crew center, a playing field with artificial turf, a pool, basketball, tennis, racquetball and squash courts, and a 2800-seat gym. The sports and recreation center holds a 4-court gym, an indoor track, 14,000-sq-ft of fitness space, a rowing tank, and a 25-meter competition pool. **Graduates:** From July 1, 2015 to June 30, 2016, 904 bachelor's degrees were awarded. The most popular majors were mechanical engineering (22%), electrical & computer engineering (10%), and chemical engineering (9%). 400 companies recruited on campus in 2015-2016. In an average class, 80% graduate in 4 years or less, 85% graduate in 5 years or less, and 86% graduate in 6 years or less. Of the 2015 graduating class, 19% were enrolled in graduate school within 6 months of graduation, and 68% were employed.

SERVICES: Counseling and information services are available, as is tutoring in most subjects, such as math, physics, chemistry, computer science, and other select subjects. **Library/Resources:** The library contains 242,660 volumes, 189,960 microform items, and 5,772 audio/video tapes/CDs/DVDs, and subscribes to 75,696 periodicals including electronic. Computerized library services include interlibrary loans, database searching, Internet access, and Wi-Fi capability. Special learning facilities include an art gallery, radio station, state-of-the-art specialized laboratories in all science and engineering research departments, including: two atomic-force microscopes, medical imaging lab, fire science lab, laser holography lab, computer music lab, satellite navigation lab, and Life Sciences and Bioengineering Center at Gateway Park. **Physically Challenged Students:** 96% of the campus is accessible. Facilities include wheelchair ramps, elevators, special parking, specially equipped restrooms, special class scheduling, and lowered drinking fountains. **Special:** Students may cross-register with 10 other colleges in the Higher Education Consortium of Central Massachusetts. Co-op programs in all majors, internships, work-study programs, dual majors in every subject, student-designed majors, non-degree study, pass/fail options and an accelerated 5 year BS/MS degree program are all available. There is also a distinctive Global Projects Program with over 40 project centers in 25 countries where students complete immersive 7-week experiences that benefit communities and organizations around the world. There are 14 national honor societies. **Visiting:** There are regularly scheduled orientations for prospective students, daily information sessions & student-led tours, and large-scale open house events in fall & spring. There are guides for informal visits, visitors may sit in on classes, and stay overnight. To schedule a visit, contact Barbara Hassett at admissions@wpi.edu. **Campus Safety and Security:** Measures include 24-hour foot and vehicle patrol, emergency notification system, self-defense education, and security escort services. There are shuttle buses, emergency telephones, lighted pathways/sidewalks, controlled access to dorms/residences, and student-run emergency medical service supervised by the campus police department.

REQUIREMENTS: Applicants must have completed 4 years each of math, with pre-calculus, and English, and 2 years of lab sciences. An essay is required and a letter of recommendation from either a math or science teacher and the guidance counselor. Those opting for Flex Path will submit academic work in place of the SAT or ACT. AP credits are accepted. Important factors in the admissions decision are advanced placement or honors courses, recommendations by school officials, and extracurricular activities record. For a B.S. degree, WPI requires that students in science and engineering complete an individual project in the humanities. Students must also complete 2 major team projects. Distribution requirements vary according to the major, and all students must take courses in social sciences and phys ed. **Procedure:** Freshmen are admitted fall. Entrance exams should be taken between April and January. There are early admissions and deferred admissions plans. Applications should be filed by February 1 for fall entry, along with a $65 fee. Notifications are sent April 1. 1519 applicants were on the 2016 waiting list. Applications are accepted on-line. Application fees are waived if application is completed on-line. **Transfer Students:** 39 transfer students enrolled in 2015-2016. Grades of B or better transfer for credit. A high school transcript or GED is required. Students who have been out of school for a year or more must present a resume or personal biography, and 2 academic recommendations. Also they must have completed a calculus course and 2 lab sciences courses. 72 of 135 credits required for the bachelor's degree must be completed at WPI. **International Students:** There are 507 international students enrolled. The school actively recruits these students. They must take the TOEFL with a minimum score of 550 on the paper-based TOEFL (PBT) or 80 on the Internet-based version (iBT) or take the MELAB, or can take IELTS, GCSE, or Pearson's Test of English. They must also take the SAT or ACT or a Flex Path Supplement.

ADMISSIONS: 48% of the 2016-2017 applicants were accepted. The SAT scores for the 2016-2017 freshman class were: Critical Reading-- 3% below 500, 29% between 500 and 599, 50% between 600 and 699, and 18% between 700 and 800. Math-- 9% between 500 and 599, 54% between 600 and 699, and 37% between 700 and 800. Writing-- 5% below 500, 32% between 500 and 599, 50% between 600 and 699, and 12% between 700 and 800. The ACT scores were 4% between 18 and 23, 40% between 24 and 29, and 56% above 30. 87% of the current freshmen were in the top fifth of their class; 98% were in the top two fifths. 44 freshmen graduated first in their class. **Admissions Contact:** Jennifer Cluett, Director of Admissions. Email: *admissions@wpi.edu* Web: *www.wpi.edu*

FINANCIAL AID: In 2016-2017, 68% of all full-time freshmen and 63% of continuing full-time students received some form of financial aid. 68% of all full-time freshmen and 62% of continuing full-time students received need-based aid. The average freshman award was $36,113. Need-based scholarships or need-based grants averaged $23,865; and need-based self-help aid (loans and jobs) averaged $3,132. WPI is a member of CSS. The CSS/Profile, and CSS Noncustodial Profile are required. The FAFSA code is 002233. The deadline for filing freshman financial aid applications for fall entry is February 1.

WORCESTER STATE UNIVERSITY C-2

www.worcester.edu

Worcester, MA 01602	**(508) 929-8040** **(866) 972-2255**
Fax: (508) 929-8183	**Email: admissions@worcester.edu**
Full-time: 1670 men, 2363 women	**Faculty:** 208; IIA, +$
Part-time: 507 men, 841 women	**Ph.D.s:** 80%
Graduate: 223 men, 867 women	**Student/Faculty:** 20 to 1
Year: semesters, summer session	**Tuition:** $9202 ($15,282)
Room & Board: $11,775	**Freshman Class:** 789 enrolled
SAT CR/M: 501/509 **ACT:** 23	**CEEB CODE:** 3524
Application Deadline: May 1	**COMPETITIVE**

Worcester State University, established in 1874, is part of the Massachusetts public higher education system, and offer undergraduate and graduate programs. A liberal arts core is emphasized, as are selected areas of science, the health professions, education, business, and management. There are 2 undergraduate schools and 1 graduate school. In addition to regional accreditation, WSU has baccalaureate program accreditation with ASHA, ACOTE, JRCEP, NASP, CAEP, CCNE, MACN, and CEC. The 58-acre campus is in an urban area on the west side of Worcester, Massachusetts, 45 miles west of Boston. Including any residence halls, there are 12 buildings.

STUDENT LIFE: 96% of undergraduates are from Massachusetts. Others are from 24 states, 27 foreign countries, and Canada. 8% are African American; 7% race unknown; 67% White; 4% Asian American; 3% two or more races; 10% Hispanic; 1% Foreign. **Female To Male Ratio:** 1.7:1. The average age of freshmen is 19; all undergraduates, 25. **Housing:** 1577 students can be accommodated in college housing, which includes single-sex and coed dorms and on-campus apartments. In addition, there are honors houses, special-interest houses, and Eco-House (students interested in sustainability and green living). On-campus housing is available on a first-come and first-served basis. Priority is given to out-of-town students. 73% of students commute. Alcohol is not permitted. All students may keep cars.

FACULTY/CLASSROOMS: 41% of faculty are male; 59% are female. No introductory courses are taught by graduate students.

PROGRAMS OF STUDY: WSU confers B.A. and B.S. degrees. Master's degrees are also awarded. Bachelor's degrees are awarded in BIOLOGICAL SCIENCE (biology/biological science and biotechnology), BUSINESS (business administration and management), COMMUNICATIONS AND THE ARTS (communications, English, Spanish, and visual and performing arts), COMPUTER AND PHYSICAL SCIENCE (chemistry, computer science, mathematics, and natural sciences), EDUCATION (early childhood education, elementary education, and health education), ENGINEERING AND ENVIRONMENTAL DESIGN (environmental science), HEALTH PROFESSIONS (nursing, occupational therapy, public health, and speech pathology/audiology), SOCIAL SCIENCE (criminal justice, economics, geography, history, liberal arts/general studies, psychology, sociology, and urban studies). Occupational therapy, and nursing are the strongest academically. Business administration, psychology, and criminal justice have the largest enrollments.

ACTIVITIES: There are no fraternities or sororities. There are 40 groups on campus, including cheerleading, chess, chorale, computers, dance, drama, environmental, ethnic, honors, LGBT, newspaper, political, professional, radio and TV, religious, social, social service, student government, and yearbook. Popular campus events include Multicultural Festival, Homecoming, SGA Auction to Benefit Homeless and Lecture Series. **Sports:** There are 9 intercollegiate sports for men and 10 for women, and 10 intramural sports for men and 10 for women. Facilities include the John Coughlin stadium, a weight room, softball and baseball fields, and ice rink. **Graduates:** From July 1, 2015 to June 30, 2016, 1115 bachelor's degrees were awarded. The most popular majors were business administration (17%), psychology (12%), and criminal justice (9%).

SERVICES: Counseling and information services are available, as is tutoring in most subjects. There is a reader service for the blind, and remedial math, reading, and writing. **Library/Resources:** The library contains 144,910 volumes, and 4,213 audio/video tapes/CDs/DVDs, and subscribes to 198,507 periodicals including electronic. Computerized library services include interlibrary loans, database searching, Internet access, and Wi-Fi capability. Special learning facilities include a radio station, photographic labs, a audiovisual center, multimedia classrooms with satellite connectivity, discipline-specific computer labs, and a speech, language, and hearing clinic. **Physically Challenged Students:** All of the campus is accessible. Facilities include wheelchair ramps, elevators, special parking, specially equipped restrooms, lowered drinking fountains, lowered telephones, and special housing. **Special:** Cross-registration with the Worcester Consortium for Higher Education is available, as are internships, study abroad (more than 60 countries), a Washington semester, work-study, non-degree study, and a pass/fail option. There are 20 national honor societies, a freshman honors program, and 16 departmental honors programs. **Visiting:** There are regularly scheduled orientations for prospective students, including a campus tour and review of campus life and organizations, success in college, special opportunities, and available services. To schedule a visit, contact Admissions Office. **Campus Safety and Security:** Measures include 24-hour foot and vehicle patrol, emergency notification system, self-defense education, and security escort services. There are shuttle buses, emergency telephones, lighted pathways/sidewalks, controlled access to dorms/residences, and crime prevention programs offered throughout the year to both students and faculty/staff.

REQUIREMENTS: For students with a GPA of 2.9 or above, a minimum SAT or ACT score may be required. For students whose GPA is below 2.9, a minimum SAT or ACT score is applied according to a scale established by WSC. Applicants must graduate from an accredited secondary school. They should have completed 4 years of English, 3 of math, 2 each of a foreign language, a lab science, and social studies, including 1 year of U.S. history and government, and 2 electives. The College Board Student Descriptive questionnaire must be submitted. AP and CLEP credits are accepted. Candidates for a baccalaureate degree must complete 120 semester-hour credits with a 2.0 cumulative grade point average (GPA) and a minimum of 2.0 GPA or higher in the departmental and ancillary courses of the major field of concentration. To receive a baccalaureate degree from Worcester State University, a student must complete 30 of the last 40 credits at Worcester State University, earn a majority of credits in the major at Worcester State University and earn a majority of credits in the minor (if elected) at the University. **Procedure:** Freshmen are admitted fall, spring, and summer. Entrance exams should be taken in spring of the junior year or fall of the senior year. There is a rolling admissions plan. Applications should be filed by May 1 for fall entry, along with a $50 fee. Notifications are sent in rolling. Applications are accepted on-line. **Transfer Students:** 522 transfer students enrolled in 2015-2016. Transfer applicants must have earned a minimum of 12 college credits with a minimum 2.5 GPA or 13 to 23 credits with a minimum 2.0 GPA. Students with fewer than 24 transfer credits may be admitted under the same criteria as first-time freshmen. 30 of 120 credits required for the bachelor's degree must be completed at WSU. **International Students:** There are 36 international students enrolled. They must take the TOEFL with a minimum score of 79 on the Internet-based version (iBT). They must also take the SAT.

ADMISSIONS: The SAT scores for the 2016-2017 freshman class were: Critical Reading-- 50% below 500, 39% between 500 and 599, 11%

between 600 and 699, and 1% between 700 and 800. Math-- 44% below 500, 44% between 500 and 599, 11% between 600 and 699, and 1% between 700 and 800. The ACT scores were 5% between 12 and 17, 48% between 18 and 23, 43% between 24 and 29, and 3% above 30. **Admissions Contact:** Joseph DiCarlo, Director of Admissions. Email: *admissions@worcester.edu* Web: *www.worcester.edu*

FINANCIAL AID: WSU is a member of CSS. The college's own financial statement is required. The FAFSA code is 002190. The priority date for freshman financial aid applications for fall entry is March 1. The deadline for filing freshman financial aid applications for fall entry is May 1.

ADRIAN COLLEGE E-5

www.adrian.edu

Adrian, MI 49221	**(517) 265-5161** **(800) 877-2246**
Fax: (517) 264-3878	**Email: admissions@adrian.edu**
Full-time: 810 men, 735 women	**Faculty:** 89; IIB, av$
Part-time: 26 men, 35 women	**Ph.D.s:** 92%
Graduate: 9 men, 10 women	**Student/Faculty:** 13 to 1
Year: semesters, summer session	**Tuition:** $32,660
Room & Board: $9740	**Freshman Class:** 5153 applied, 3189 accepted, 487 enrolled
SAT CR/M: 480/500 **ACT:** 22	**CEEB CODE:** 1001
Application Deadline: March 30	**COMPETITIVE**

Adrian College, founded in 1859, is a private liberal arts institution affiliated with the United Methodist Church. The figures in the above capsule and in this profile are approximate. There is 1 undergraduate school and 4 graduate schools. In addition to regional accreditation, Adrian has baccalaureate program accreditation with CSWE, NCATE, TEAC, and CAATE. The 132-acre campus is in a small town 35 miles southwest of Ann Arbor. Including any residence halls, there are 41 buildings.

STUDENT LIFE: 75% of undergraduates are from Michigan. Others are from Canada. 9% are African American; 80% White; 5% race unknown; 4% two or more races; 3% Foreign; 2% Hispanic; 1% Asian American. 48% claim no religious affiliation; 23% Protestant; 18% Catholic. **Male To Female Ratio:** 1.1:1. 46% remain to graduate. **Housing:** 1600 students can be accommodated in college housing, which includes single-sex and coed dorms, on-campus apartments, off-campus apartments, honors houses, special-interest houses, fraternity houses, substance-free, smoke-free, extended quiet hours, upperclassmen only residence halls, and theme housing. On-campus housing is guaranteed for all 4 years. All students may keep cars.

FACULTY/CLASSROOMS: 52% of faculty are male; 48% are female. All teach undergraduates. No introductory courses are taught by graduate students. The average class size in an introductory lecture is 19; in a laboratory is 15; and in a regular course is 12.

PROGRAMS OF STUDY: Adrian confers B.A., B.S., B.B.A., B.F.A., B.M., B.M.E. and B.S.W. degrees. Associate and master's degrees are also awarded. Bachelor's degrees are awarded in AGRICULTURE (environmental studies), BIOLOGICAL SCIENCE (biology/biological science), BUSINESS (accounting, business administration and management, international business management, marketing management, and sports management), COMMUNICATIONS AND THE ARTS (arts administration/management, communications, dramatic arts, English, French, German, journalism, literature, music, music performance, musical theater, Spanish, and studio art), COMPUTER AND PHYSICAL SCIENCE (chemistry, earth science, mathematics, and physics), EDUCATION (elementary education, physical education, and secondary education), ENGINEERING AND ENVIRONMENTAL DESIGN (environmental science and interior design), HEALTH PROFESSIONS (exercise science), SOCIAL SCIENCE (criminal justice, economics, history, international studies, Japanese studies, philosophy, political science/government, psychology, religion, social work, and sociology). Accounting & business administration, and exercise science have the largest enrollments.

ACTIVITIES: 18% of men belong to 4 national fraternities; 19% of women belong to 3 national sororities. There are 79 groups on campus, including and exercise groups, equestrian team, gamers council, sports, various outdoors, art, band, cheerleading, choir, chorale, chorus, computers, dance, drama, environmental, ethnic, feminist empowerment movement, honors, international, jazz band, LGBT, literary magazine, marching band, musical theater, newspaper, orchestra, pep band, photography, political, professional, radio and TV, religious, social, social service, student government, symphony, and yearbook. Popular campus events include Family Weekend, International Week, Dance Marathon, One-Act Plays, Sadie Hawkins Dance, Sibs 'n' Kids Weekend. **Sports:** There are 13 intercollegiate sports for men and 18 for women, and 6 intramural sports for men and 6 for women. Facilities include a sport and fitness center featuring a multipurpose forum with courts for basketball, volleyball, and tennis, and an indoor track, racquetball courts, a weight room, and a performance gym, a football stadium, baseball and softball fields, soccer fields, tennis courts, track, and numerous intramural fields. **Graduates:** From July 1, 2015 to June 30, 2016, 314 bachelor's degrees were awarded. The most popular majors were business and accounting (22%), exercise science and athletic training (11%), and biology (10%). 22 companies recruited on campus in 2015-2016. In an average class, 54% graduate in 6 years or less. Of the 2015 graduating class, 20% were enrolled in graduate school within 6 months of graduation, and 22% were employed.

SERVICES: Counseling and information services are available, as is tutoring in most subjects, a reader service for the blind, and remedial math, reading, and writing. **Library/Resources:** The library contains 163,727 volumes, 51,188 microform items, 4,032 audio/video tapes/CDs/DVDs, and subscribes to 10,373 periodicals including electronic. Computerized library services include interlibrary loans, database searching, Internet access, and Wi-Fi capability. Special learning facilities include an art gallery, planetarium, radio station, a solar greenhouse, palatinate lab, and an observatory. **Physically Challenged Students:** Facilities include wheelchair ramps, elevators, special parking, specially equipped restrooms, lowered drinking fountains, lowered telephones, special housing. Diagnostic testing, learning services, note-taking services, oral testing, extended time, priority seating, readers, tape recording, texts on tape, tutors, and student and psychological support groups. **Special:** Adrian offers preprofessional programs in architectture, engineering, health sciences, law, ministry, medical technology, and art therapy. Study abroad in 16 countries and a Washington Semester. Student-designed majors and internships in more than 450 locations, and a 3-2 engineering degree with Washington University in St. Louis and the University of Detroit Mercy. There are 15 national honor societies and a freshman honors program. **Visiting:** There are regularly scheduled orientations for prospective students, including a student-guided campus tour and visits with an admissions counselor, professors from the student's area of interest, and an athletics coach. There are guides for informal visits, visitors may sit in on classes, and stay overnight. To schedule a visit, contact the Office of Admissions. **Campus Safety and Security:** Measures include 24-hour foot and vehicle patrol, self-defense education, security escort services, emergency telephones and lighted pathways/sidewalks.

REQUIREMENTS: The SAT or ACT is required. In addition, Applicants must be graduates of an accredited secondary school. The GED is accepted. Each student is reviewed individually based on GPA and test scores. Adrian requires applicants to be in the upper 50% of their class. A GPA of 3.0 is required. AP and CLEP credits are accepted. Important factors in the admissions decision are advanced placement or honors courses, leadership record, and extracurricular activities record. To graduate, students must maintain a 2.0 average over 124 credit hours, 30 of which must be in upper-division courses. 22 hours of distribution requirements and 21 of basic educational proficiency are required, including 2 semesters of foreign language and 1 each of communication, English, fine arts, fitness, humanities, math, natural or physical science, religion or philosophy, and social science. **Procedure:** Freshmen are admitted in the fall and spring. Entrance exams should be taken during the spring of the junior year or fall of the senior year. There are deferred admissions and rolling admissions plans. Application deadlines are open. Applications are accepted online. **Transfer Students:** 65 transfer students enrolled in 2015-2016. Applicants must have an above-average GPA and provide final high school transcripts. If the student has completed fewer than 24 semester hours, ACT or SAT test scores are also required. Grades of 2.0 and above transfer for credit. The college admits transfer students every semester. 34 of 124 credits required for the bachelor's degree must be completed at Adrian. **International Students:** There are 69 international students enrolled. The school actively recruits these students. They must take the TOEFL with a minimum score of 500 on the paper-based TOEFL (PBT) or 73 on the Internet-based version (iBT). They must also take the SAT or ACT.

ADMISSIONS: 62% of the 2016-2017 applicants were accepted. The SAT scores for the 2016-2017 freshman class were: Critical Reading-- 55% below 500 and 45% between 500 and 599. Math-- 41% below 500, 52% between 500 and 599, and 7% between 600 and 699. The ACT scores were 38% below 12, 34% between 12 and 17, 16% between 18 and 23, 6% between 24 and 29, and 6% above 30. 11 freshmen graduated first in their class. **Admissions Contact:** Erin DeSmet, Director of Admissions. Email: *admissions@adrian.edu* Web: *www.adrian.edu*

FINANCIAL AID: In 2016-2017, 99% of all full-time freshmen and continuing full-time students received some form of financial aid. 83% of all full-time freshmen and 86% of continuing full-time students received need-based aid. The average freshman award was $33,831. Need-based scholarships or need-based grants averaged $22,666 ($38,806 maximum); need-based self-help aid (loans and jobs) averaged $12,008 ($45,500 maximum); and other non-need-based awards and non-need-based scholarships averaged $15,472 ($31,870 maximum). 39% of undergraduate students work part-time. Average annual earnings from campus work are $1500. The average financial indebtedness of the 2016 graduate was $41,000. Adrian is a member of CSS. The FAFSA code is 002234. The priority date for freshman financial aid applications for fall entry is March 1.

ALBION COLLEGE — D-5

www.albion.edu

Albion, MI 49224 — **(517) 629-0321** **(800) 858-6770**

Fax: (517) 629-0569	**Email: admission@albion.edu**
Full-time: 667 men, 726 women	**Faculty:** 104; IIB, av$
Part-time: 12 men, 13 women	**Ph.D.s:** 94%
Graduate: n/av	**Student/Faculty:** 12 to 1
Year: semesters, summer session	**Tuition:** $41,040
Room & Board: $11,610	**Freshman Class:** 3338 applied, 2412 accepted, 402 enrolled
SAT: required **ACT:** 23	**CEEB CODE:** 1007
Application Deadline: open	**COMPETITIVE**

Albion College, established in 1835, is a nationally-ranked private institution affiliated with the United Methodist Church offering undergraduate degrees in liberal arts curricula. There is 1 undergraduate school. In addition to regional accreditation, Albion has baccalaureate program accreditation with NASM, TEAC, ACS, and CAATE. The 574-acre campus is in a small town in south central Michigan, 65 miles from Detroit. Including any residence halls, there are 94 buildings.

STUDENT LIFE: 83% of undergraduates are from Michigan. Others are from 28 states, 21 foreign countries, and Canada. 9% are African American; 7% Hispanic; 69% White; 6% race unknown; 3% Asian American; 3% Foreign; 2% two or more races. 73% claim no religious affiliation; 11% Catholic. **Female To Male Ratio:** 1.1:1. The average age of freshmen is 18; all undergraduates, 19. 19% do not continue beyond their first year; 70% remain to graduate. **Housing:** 1625 students can be accommodated in college housing, which includes single-sex and coed dorms, on-campus apartments, married student housing, and fraternity houses. On-campus housing is guaranteed for all 4 years. 93% of students live on campus. All students may keep cars.

FACULTY/CLASSROOMS: 56% of faculty are male; 44% are female. All teach undergraduates, 97% do research, and 97% do both. No introductory courses are taught by graduate students. The average class size in an introductory lecture is 24; in a laboratory is 14; and in a regular course is 20.

PROGRAMS OF STUDY: Albion confers B.A. and B.F.A. degrees. Bachelor's degrees are awarded in AGRICULTURE (environmental studies and forestry and related sciences), BIOLOGICAL SCIENCE (biochemistry and biology/biological science), BUSINESS (accounting, business administration and management, and finance), COMMUNICATIONS AND THE ARTS (art, art history and appreciation, communication studies, creative writing, English, French, German, music, music performance, Spanish, theatre arts, and visual and performing arts), COMPUTER AND PHYSICAL SCIENCE (actuarial mathematics, astronomy and physics, chemistry, earth science, geology, mathematics, and physics), EDUCATION (athletic training, English education, and music education), ENGINEERING AND ENVIRONMENTAL DESIGN (engineering, engineering physics, and environmental science), HEALTH PROFESSIONS (exercise science), SOCIAL SCIENCE (anthropology, economics, ethnic studies, gender studies, history, international studies, philosophy, political science/government, psychology, public affairs, religion, sociology, and women's studies). Economics & management, biology, and psychology have the largest enrollments.

ACTIVITIES: 37% of men belong to 6 national fraternities; 30% of women belong to 6 national sororities. There are 110 groups on campus, including art, band, cheerleading, chess, choir, chorale, chorus, computers, dance, drama, environmental, ethnic, film, honors, international, jazz band, LGBT, literary magazine, marching band, musical theater, newspaper, opera, orchestra, pep band, photography, political, professional, radio and TV, religious, social, social service, student government, symphony, and yearbook. Popular campus events include Briton Bash, Day of Woden and The Big Show: National Concert/Comedy Artist Performance. **Sports:** There are 12 intercollegiate sports for men and 12 for women, and 4 intramural sports for men and 4 for women. Facilities include fields for soccer, and lacrosse, fields baseball and softball, aquatic center, a cardiovascular fitness room, physical conditioning, health and wellness programs, space for intramural sports, track, racquetball courts, weight room, and an equestrian center. **Graduates:** From July 1, 2015 to June 30, 2016, 264 bachelor's degrees were awarded. The most popular majors were biology (16%), economics and management (12%), and psychological science (11%). 55 companies recruited on campus in 2015-2016. In an average class, 61% graduate in 4 years or less, 69% graduate in 5 years or less, and 70% graduate in 6 years or less. Of the 2015 graduating class, 43% were enrolled in graduate school within 6 months of graduation, and 54% were employed.

SERVICES: Counseling and information services are available, as is tutoring in most subjects, and a reader service for the blind. Also available is the Quantitative Studies center, and the writing center. **Library/Resources:** The library contains 346,622 volumes, 51,080 microform items, 9,257 audio/video tapes/CDs/DVDs, and subscribes to 76,603 periodicals including electronic. Computerized library services include interlibrary loans, database searching, Internet access, and Wi-Fi capability. Special learning facilities include an art gallery, planetarium, radio station, a nature center, an equestrian center, and a Dow analytical science laboratory. **Physically Challenged Students:** 90% of the campus is accessible. Facilities include wheelchair ramps, elevators, special parking, specially equipped restrooms, special class scheduling, lowered drinking fountains, lowered telephones, and special housing. **Special:** Albion offers study abroad in 40 countries, and study/internship programs in New York City, Philadelphia, Washington, D.C., Oak Ridge, and Chicago. Students may earn a dual engineering degree in conjunction with Columbia University, Michigan Technological University, or the University of Michigan. Student-designed majors and interdisciplinary majors in fields including environmental science, ethnic studies, international studies, and women's and gender studies are available. There are 6 national honor societies, Phi Beta Kappa, a freshman honors program, and 13 departmental honors programs. **Visiting:** There are regularly scheduled orientations for prospective students, SOAR (Student Orientation, Advising & Registration): consists of 4 programs held in early June and 1 in August for students and parents. There are guides for informal visits, visitors may sit in on classes, and stay overnight. To schedule a visit, contact Martha Bunde at (517) 629-0769. **Campus Safety and Security:** Measures include 24-hour foot and vehicle patrol, emergency notification system, self-defense education, and security escort services. There are also shuttle buses, emergency telephones, lighted pathways/sidewalks, and controlled access to dorms/residences.

REQUIREMENTS: Applicants must graduate from an accredited secondary school or earn a GED. Completion of 15 Carnegie credits is required. A strong background in English, math, and the lab and social sciences is recommended as the best preparation for academic success. The Admission Committee will consider courses taken, grades earned, the academic rigor of the program and SAT/ACT scores as corroborative evidence. Applications are accepted online at the Albion web site and through the Common App. A GPA of 3.0 is required. AP and CLEP credits are accepted. Important factors in the admissions decision are advanced placement or honors courses, extracurricular activities record, and personality/intangible qualities. Requirements for graduation are: 32 units (128 semester hours) a minimum of the last 12 units must be taken at Albion College. A minimum of one major, completion of the core, and pass the Writing Competence Exam. Have a minimum of 2.0 cum GPA. Submission of an Application for Degree. The CORE Requirement; at Albion, the general education requirement is referred to as "the core." Students begin to fulfill the core in their first semester with Liberal Arts 101; some will be able to complete much of the core requirement by the end of their first year. Liberal Arts 101 (First-Year Seminar, 1 unit), Modes of Inquiry (1 unit in each), Textual Analysis, Artistic Creation and Analysis, Scientific Analysis, Modeling and Analysis, Historical and Cultural Analysis. Category Requirements (1 unit in each), Environmental Studies, Ethnicity Studies, Gender Studies, and Global Studies. Distribution Requirement: one unit in fine arts (art and art history, music, theatre, honors), 2 units in humanities (English, foreign languages, philosophy, religious studies, honors), 2 units in mathematics or natural sciences (biology, chemistry, computer science, geological sciences, mathematics, physics, honors), 2 units each in social science (anthropology and sociology, economics and management, history, political science, psychology, speech communication, honors). **Procedure:** Freshmen are admitted in the fall and spring. Entrance exams should be taken in April or June of the junior year. There are early admissions, deferred admissions, and rolling admissions plans. Application deadlines are open. Notification is sent on a rolling basis. Applications are accepted on-line. Application fees are waived if application is completed on-line. **Transfer Students:** 35 transfer students enrolled in 2015-2016. Transfer applicants must submit official college transcripts. Grades of 2.0 or better are considered for transfer credit. Albion evaluates the applicant's course work before conferring transfer credit. 48 of 128 credits required for the bachelor's degree must be completed at Albion. **International Students:** There are 39 international students enrolled. The school actively recruits these students. They must take the TOEFL with a minimum score of 550 on the paper-based TOEFL (PBT) or 79 on the Internet-based version (iBT). They must also take the SAT or ACT.

ADMISSIONS: 72% of the 2016-2017 applicants were accepted. The ACT scores were 6% between 12 and 17, 46% between 18 and 23, 40% between 24 and 29, and 7% above 30. **Admissions Contact:** Mandy Dubiel, Director of Admissions. Email: *admission@albion.edu* Web: *www.albion.edu*

FINANCIAL AID: In 2016-2017, 100% of all full-time freshmen and continuing full-time students received some form of financial aid. 83% of all full-time freshmen and 75% of continuing full-time students received need-based aid. The average freshman award was $40,574. Need-based scholarships or need-based grants averaged $35,581 ($52,925 maximum); and need-based self-help aid (loans and jobs) averaged $5,870 ($7,500 maximum). 53% of undergraduate students work part-time. Average annual earnings from campus work are $1252. The average financial indebtedness of the 2016 graduate was $38,356. The FAFSA code is 002235. The priority date for freshman financial aid applications for fall entry is December 1.

ALMA COLLEGE D-4

www.alma.edu

Alma, MI 48801-1599 (989) 463-7139
(800) 321-ALMA

Fax: (989) 463-7057 Email: admissions@alma.edu

Full-time: 596 men, 783 women	**Faculty:** 103; IIB, -$
Part-time: 17 men, 55 women	**Ph.D.s:** 82%
Graduate: n/av	**Student/Faculty:** 11 to 1
Year: other	**Tuition:** $37,310
Room & Board: $10,238	**Freshman Class:** 4696 applied, 3186 accepted, 447 enrolled
SAT CR/M/W: 503/526/496 **ACT:** 24	**CEEB CODE:** 1010
Application Deadline: open	**COMPETITIVE**

Alma College, a selective, residential college, offers a personalized education with multiple paths and experiences leading to success. Strong academic programs and a deep regard for students as individuals are fundamental to an Alma education, with small classes and many opportunities for one-on-one collaboration with dedicated faculty. In addition to regional accreditation, Alma has baccalaureate program accreditation with NASM, TEAC, and ACS. The 128-acre campus is in a small town Alma, Michigan, which is about 50 miles north of Lansing. Including any residence halls, there are 29 buildings.

STUDENT LIFE: 90% of undergraduates are from Michigan. Others are from 30 states, 8 foreign countries, and Canada. 8% are race unknown; 77% White; 5% Hispanic; 4% African American; 2% Asian American; 2% Foreign; 2% two or more races. 39% are Protestant; 39% claim no religious affiliation; 18% Catholic. **Female To Male Ratio:** 1.4:1. The average age of freshmen is 18; all undergraduates, 20. 20% do not continue beyond their first year; 67% remain to graduate. **Housing:** 1323 students can be accommodated in college housing, which includes coed dorms, on-campus apartments, special-interest houses, fraternity houses, sorority houses, and an international house for students who live or have traveled overseas. On-campus housing is guaranteed for all 4 years. 91% of students live on campus; of those, 75% remain on campus on weekends. All students may keep cars.

FACULTY/CLASSROOMS: 54% of faculty are male; 46% are female. All teach undergraduates, and all do research. No introductory courses are taught by graduate students. The average class size in an introductory lecture is 18; in a laboratory is 12; and in a regular course is 17.

PROGRAMS OF STUDY: Alma confers B.A., B.S., B.M., B.S.N., and B.F.A. degrees. Bachelor's degrees are awarded in AGRICULTURE (environmental studies), BIOLOGICAL SCIENCE (biochemistry, biology/biological science, biotechnology, and neurosciences), BUSINESS (accounting, business administration and management, finance, international business management, and marketing), COMMUNICATIONS AND THE ARTS (art, communications, dance, English, French, German, music, Spanish, and theatre arts), COMPUTER AND PHYSICAL SCIENCE (chemistry, computer science, mathematics, and physics), EDUCATION (athletic training, early childhood education, educational studies, elementary education, secondary education, and special education), HEALTH PROFESSIONS (exercise science, health care administration, health science, and nursing), SOCIAL SCIENCE (anthropology, economics, history, philosophy, political science/government, psychology, religion, and sociology). New media studies, environmental studies, integrative physiology and health science are the strongest academically. Education, business administration, and nursing have the largest enrollments.

ACTIVITIES: 30% of men belong to 2 local and 4 national fraternities; 33% of women belong to 1 local and 4 national sororities. There are 81 groups on campus, including art, bagpipe, band, cheerleading, chess, choir, chorale, chorus, communications, computers, dance, drama, environmental, ethnic, honors, international, jazz band, LGBT, literary magazine, marching band, newspaper, orchestra, photography, political, professional, religious, social, social service, student government, symphony, and yearbook. Popular campus events include Homecoming, Songfest, and Honors Day. **Sports:** There are 12 intercollegiate sports for men and 12 for women, and 16 intramural sports for men and 16 for women. Facilities include a recreation center with a climbing wall, fitness center, courts, and suspended track, an indoor gym and pool, an outdoor sports complex with an artificial turf playing field, an track, baseball, soccer, and softball fields, a weight training room, and racquetball and tennis courts. **Graduates:** From July 1, 2015 to June 30, 2016, 308 bachelor's degrees were awarded. The most popular majors were business administration (16%), education (12%), and psychology (10%). In an average class, 1% graduate in 3 years or less, 51% graduate in 4 years or less, 66% graduate in 5 years or less, and 67% graduate in 6 years or less. Of the 2015 graduating class, 20% were enrolled in graduate school within 6 months of graduation, and 70% were employed.

SERVICES: Counseling and information services are available, as is tutoring in every subject. Individual and group tutoring are also available. There is a reader service for the blind. **Library/Resources:** The library contains 245,000 volumes, 247,000 microform items, 10,700 audio/video tapes/CDs/DVDs, and subscribes to 1,000 periodicals including electronic. Computerized library services include interlibrary loans, database searching, Internet access, and Wi-Fi capability. Special learning facilities include an art gallery, planetarium, writing lab, digital media commons, Dow Digital Science Center, and a human performance laboratory. **Physically Challenged Students:** 75% of the campus is accessible. Facilities include wheelchair ramps, elevators, special parking, specially equipped restrooms, special class scheduling, and lowered drinking fountains. There are 2 residence halls with private baths, and several small housing units. **Special:** Alma offers internships in many fields, study abroad in 18 countries, and an experiential learning program at the Philadelphia Center. There are work-study programs, dual majors, and student-designed majors in a wide variety of subjects. The college confers 3-2 engineering degrees in conjunction with the University of Michigan and Kettering University. Non-degree study may be pursued, and students have a pass/fail grading option. A 4-week spring term provides intensive study in 1 course, often combined with travel. There are 3 national honor societies, Phi Beta Kappa, a freshman honors program, and 19 departmental honors programs. **Visiting:** There are regularly scheduled orientations for prospective students, Faculty talks, campus tours, a meal on campus, financial aid information, admissions sessions. There are guides for informal visits, visitors may sit in on classes, and stay overnight. To schedule a visit, contact the Admissions Office. **Campus Safety and Security:** Measures include 24-hour foot and vehicle patrol, emergency notification system, security escort services, emergency telephones, lighted pathways/sidewalks, controlled access to dorms/residences, and ID card access to residence halls.

REQUIREMENTS: Either the SAT or the ACT is required. Applicants must have graduated from an accredited secondary school and have earned 16 Carnegie units, including 4 years of English and 3 each of math, science, and social studies, with 2 of a foreign language recommended. Alma prefers applicants in the upper 25% of their class. Portfolio and audition are required for performing arts scholarships. A GPA of 3.0 is required. AP credits are accepted. Important factors in the admissions decision are advanced placement or honors courses, leadership record, and recommendations by school officials. Degree requirements include completion of a minimum of 136 credit hours; 148 hours are required for the B.F.A. degree, 136 to 156 for the B.M. degree. Students must attain a minimum GPA of 2.0, or 3.0 for fine arts majors. All students must demonstrate proficiency in English, second language/international awareness, communication, and computation, and they must complete distribution requirements, which include 12 fine arts and humanities credits and 12 each of social science and natural science credits. The total number of program credits is 36 for a departmental major, 56 for an interdepartmental major, and 56 to 68 for self-directed majors. **Procedure:** Freshmen are admitted in the fall and winter. Entrance exams should be taken in the spring of the junior year or as late as the winter of the senior year. There are deferred admissions and rolling admissions plans. Application deadlines are open. Application fee is $25. Notification is sent on a rolling basis. Applications are accepted on-line. Application fees are waived if application is completed on-line. **Transfer Students:** 42 transfer students enrolled in 2015-2016. Students wishing to transfer to Alma must have a minimum GPA of 2.0 from other colleges attended. 34 of 136 credits required for the bachelor's degree must be completed at Alma. **International Students:** There are 22 international students enrolled. The school actively recruits these students. They must take the TOEFL with a minimum score of 550 on the paper-based TOEFL (PBT) or 79 on the Internet-based version (iBT). The SAT or ACT is required if the TOEFL is not submitted.

ADMISSIONS: 68% of the 2016-2017 applicants were accepted. The SAT scores for the 2016-2017 freshman class were: Critical Reading-- 54% below 500, 23% between 500 and 599, 15% between 600 and 699, and 8% between 700 and 800. Math-- 35% below 500, 38% between 500 and 599, 23% between 600 and 699, and 4% between 700 and 800. Writing-- 61% below 500, 11% between 500 and 599, 22% between 600 and 699, and 6% between 700 and 800. The ACT scores were 2% between 12 and 17, 46% between 18 and 23, 46% between 24 and 29, and 6% above 30. 39% of the current freshmen were in the top fifth of their class; 71% were in the top two fifths. 8 freshmen graduated first in their class. **Admissions Contact:** Craig Aimar, Director of Admissions. Email: *admissions@alma.edu* Web: *www.alma.edu*

FINANCIAL AID: In 2016-2017, 99% of all full-time freshmen and 100% of continuing full-time students received some form of financial aid. 97% of all full-time freshmen and 91% of continuing full-time students received need-based aid. The average freshman award was $24,698. Need-based scholarships or need-based grants averaged $25,234. 22% of undergraduate students work part-time. Average annual earnings from campus work are $1500. The FAFSA code is 002236. The priority date for freshman financial aid applications for fall entry is March 1.

ANDREWS UNIVERSITY — C-5

www.andrews.edu

Berrien Springs, MI 49104 — (616) 471-6343, (800) 253-2874

Fax: (616) 471-3228 — **Email:** undergraduate@andrews.edu

Full-time: 783 men, 931 women	**Faculty:** 148
Part-time: 107 men, 143 women	**Ph.D.s:** 72%
Graduate: 1097 men, 528 women	**Student/Faculty:** 12 to 1
Year: semesters, summer session	**Tuition:** $21,170
Room & Board: $6860	**Freshman Class:** 1809 applied, 879 accepted, 377 enrolled
SAT: required **ACT:** 23	**CEEB CODE:** 1030
Application Deadline: open	**COMPETITIVE+**

Andrews University, established in 1874, is a private institution affiliated with the Seventh-day Adventist Church that offers undergraduate degrees in business, education, arts and sciences, architecture, and technology. There are 5 undergraduate schools and 6 graduate schools. In addition to regional accreditation, Andrews has baccalaureate program accreditation with AACSB, ABET, ADA, AHEA, APTA, CAHEA, CSWE, NAAB, NASM, NCATE, NLN, and IACBE. The 1600-acre campus is in a rural area 10 miles south of Benton Harbor. Including any residence halls, there are 51 buildings.

STUDENT LIFE: 56% of undergraduates are from out of state, mostly the Middle Atlantic. Students are from 46 states, 51 foreign countries, and Canada. 23% are from public schools. 42% are White; 25% African American; 12% Foreign; 10% Asian American; 10% Hispanic; 1% American Indian/Alaska Native. 89% are Protestant; 12% unknown denominations. **Male To Female Ratio:** 1.2:1. The average age of freshmen is 18; all undergraduates, 22. 21% do not continue beyond their first year; 58% remain to graduate. **Housing:** 1500 students can be accommodated in college housing, which includes single-sex dorms, on-campus apartments, and married student housing. On-campus housing is available on a first-come and first-served basis. 54% of students live on campus. All students may keep cars. Alcohol is not permitted.

FACULTY/CLASSROOMS: 64% of faculty are male; 36% are female. No introductory courses are taught by graduate students. The average class size in a laboratory is 16 and in a regular course is 18.

PROGRAMS OF STUDY: Andrews confers B.A., B.S., B.B.A., B.F.A., B.Mus., B.S.D., B.S.Educ., B.S.El.Ed., B.S.Eng., B.S.W., and B.T. degrees. Associate, master's, and doctoral degrees are also awarded. Bachelor's degrees are awarded in AGRICULTURE (agriculture, animal science, and horticulture), BIOLOGICAL SCIENCE (anatomy, biochemistry, biology/biological science, biophysics, botany, molecular biology, nutrition, and zoology), BUSINESS (accounting, banking and finance, business administration and management, business economics, management information systems, and marketing/retailing/merchandising), COMMUNICATIONS AND THE ARTS (art, ceramic art and design, communications, creative writing, design, English, French, graphic design, journalism, literature, music, music performance, painting, photography, public relations, Spanish, and visual and performing arts), COMPUTER AND PHYSICAL SCIENCE (applied mathematics, chemistry, computer science, information sciences and systems, mathematics, and physics), EDUCATION (art education, elementary education, English education, mathematics education, music education, science education, secondary education, social studies education, and teaching English as a second/foreign language (TESOL/TEFOL)), ENGINEERING AND ENVIRONMENTAL DESIGN (aeronautical technology, aircraft mechanics, architecture, aviation administration/management, aviation computer technology, biomedical equipment technology, computer graphics, computer technology, electrical/electronics engineering, engineering, environmental science, graphic arts technology, and landscape architecture/design), HEALTH PROFESSIONS (allied health, art therapy, biomedical science, medical laboratory technology, nursing, preveterinary science, public health, and speech pathology/audiology), SOCIAL SCIENCE (anthropology, behavioral science, crosscultural studies, dietetics, economics, family/consumer studies, history, human development, interdisciplinary studies, pastoral studies, political science/government, psychology, religion, religious education, social studies, social work, sociology, theological studies, and youth ministry). Health sciences, business, and architecture have the largest enrollments.

ACTIVITIES: There are 30 groups on campus, including band, choir, chorale, chorus, computers, drama, ethnic, honors, international, newspaper, professional, religious, social, social service, and student government. Popular campus events include Alumni Weekend and International Food Fair. **Sports:** There are 6 intramural sports for men and 4 for women. Facilities include a gym, pool, racquetball courts, and health clubs in 2 of 3 dorms. **Graduates:** From July 1, 2015 to June 30, 2016, 341 bachelor's degrees were awarded. The most popular majors were health professions (20%), business (10%), and biology/life science (8%). In an average class, 34% graduate in 4 years or less, 51% graduate in 5 years or less, and 58% graduate in 6 years or less.

SERVICES: Counseling and information services are available, as is tutoring in most subjects, such as math, writing, and reading. Learning and assessment centers. are also available. **Library/Resources:** The library contains 747,764 volumes, 83,520 microform items, and 48,447 audio/video tapes/CDs/DVDs, and subscribes to 2,874 periodicals including electronic. Computerized library services include interlibrary loans, database searching, and Internet access. Special learning facilities include an art gallery, natural history museum, and an archeological museum. **Physically Challenged Students:** 50% of the campus is accessible. Facilities include wheelchair ramps, elevators, special parking, specially equipped restrooms, special class scheduling, lowered drinking fountains, lowered telephones, special housing. A special committee handles needs as they arise. **Special:** Students may pursue a second major in business administration. Study abroad, student-designed majors, nondegree study, and pass/fail options are available. There is a freshman honors program. **Visiting:** There are regularly scheduled orientations for prospective students, consisting of tours, meetings with faculty, and social activities. There are guides for informal visits, visitors may sit in on classes, and stay overnight. To schedule a visit, contact the Admissions Office. **Campus Safety and Security:** Measures include 24-hour foot and vehicle patrol, security escort services, lighted pathways/sidewalks, and CPR training.

REQUIREMENTS: The SAT or ACT is required. Candidates for admission must graduate from an accredited secondary school or earn a GED. 10 Carnegie units are required, and students must have completed 4 courses in English and 2 courses each in history, math, and science. Interviews are recommended for all applicants. A GPA of 2.3 is required. CLEP credits are accepted. Important factors in the admissions decision are advanced placement or honors courses, recommendations by school officials, and evidence of special talent. Students must complete a minimum of 124 semester credits. Specific course requirements include religion, English, behavioral sciences, fine arts, and phys ed. **Procedure:** Freshmen are admitted in the fall, spring, and summer. Entrance exams should be taken as early as possible. There are deferred admissions and rolling admissions plans. Application deadlines are open. Application fee is $30. **Transfer Students:** 131 transfer students enrolled in 2015-2016. Transfer applicants must submit a high school transcript and transcripts from all colleges attended. A maximum of 70 semester credits from a 2-year school or 90 semester credits from a 4-year school may be transferred toward a bachelor's degree. Credits should be relevant to the student's major at Andrews University. The minimum GPA is 2.25, and the ACT is preferred. Students must meet freshman entrance requirements if they are transferring with less than sophomore standing from an accredited college. 30 of 124 credits required for the bachelor's degree must be completed at Andrews. **International Students:** There are 230 international students enrolled. The school actively recruits these students. They must take the TOEFL with a minimum score of 550 on the paper-based TOEFL (PBT). They must also take the SAT or ACT.

ADMISSIONS: 49% of the 2016-2017 applicants were accepted. The ACT scores were 34% below 12, 26% between 12 and 17, 21% between 18 and 23, 11% between 24 and 29, and 8% above 30. 32% of the current freshmen were in the top fifth of their class; 55% were in the top two fifths. There were 2 National Merit finalists. **Admissions Contact:** Shanna Leak, Undergraduate Admissions Supervisor. Email: *undergraduate@andrews.edu* Web: *www.andrews.edu*

FINANCIAL AID: The FAFSA code is 002238. The priority date for freshman financial aid applications for fall entry is open.

AQUINAS COLLEGE - MICHIGAN — D-4

www.aquinas.edu

Grand Rapids, MI 49506 — (616) 632-2860, (800) 678-9593

Fax: (616) 732-4469	**Email:** admissions@aquinas.edu
Full-time: 527 men, 889 women	**Faculty:** 86; IIB, --$
Part-time: 114 men, 124 women	**Ph.D.s:** 80%
Graduate: 21 men, 89 women	**Student/Faculty:** 13 to 1
Year: semesters, summer session	**Tuition:** $30,062
Room & Board: $8814	**Freshman Class:** n/av
ACT: 24	**CEEB CODE:** 5750
Application Deadline: open	**HIGHLY COMPETITIVE**

Aquinas College, established in 1866, is a private liberal arts institution affiliated with the Roman Catholic Church and offers undergraduate and graduate degrees through day and evening programs. Figures in the above capsule and in this profile are approximate. There is 1 undergraduate school and 2 graduate schools. In addition to regional accreditation, Aquinas has baccalaureate program accreditation with TEAC and CAATE. The 117-acre campus is in a suburban area east of downtown Grand Rapids. Including any residence halls, there are 35 buildings.

STUDENT LIFE: 93% of undergraduates are from Michigan. Others are from 22 states, 18 foreign countries, and Canada. 8% are race unknown; 77% White; 6% Hispanic; 3% African American; 2% Foreign; 2% two or more races; 1% Asian American. 47% are Catholic; 28% Nondenominational and Unknown; 21% Protestant. **Female To Male Ratio:** 1.7:1. The average age of freshmen is 18; all undergraduates, 21. 23% do not continue beyond their first year; 52% remain to graduate. **Housing:** 909 students can be accommodated in college housing, which includes single-sex and coed dorms, on-campus apartments, special-interest houses, including service learning houses. On-campus housing is available on a first-come, first-served basis, and on a lottery system for upperclassmen. 29% of students commute. All students may keep cars.

FACULTY/CLASSROOMS: 54% of faculty are male; 46% are female. All teach undergraduates. No introductory courses are taught by graduate students. The average class size in an introductory lecture is 20; in a laboratory is 20; and in a regular course is 17.

PROGRAMS OF STUDY: Aquinas confers B.A., B.S. B.APMC, B.A.AT, B.A.AT-HY, B.A.CL, B.A.CN, B.A.CN-TH, B.A.DL-BSAT, B.A.EH, B.A.ES, B.A.FH, B.A.GN, B.A.GY, B.A.HY, B.A.ICN, B.A.ILSTDUES, B.A.LANGARTS, B.A.LNGDIS, B.A.MC, B.A.PG, B.A.PH, B.A.POHI, B.A.PS, B.A.SH., B.A.SS-CONT, B.A.SST.EDUC.SEC, B.A.SST-ED, B.A.SY, B.A.TH, B.A.TY, BAGE, BFA.AT-CER, BFA.AT-DRW, BFA.AT-PHOTO, BFA.AT-PRNT, BFA.AT-PTG, BFA.AT-SCUL, BM.LITMC, BMED.CHSPVN, BMED.INSPVN, BPA.PA, B.S.AP, B.S.BSCY, B.S.BY, B.S.CS, B.S.CY, B.S.CYPC, B.S.DL-BDAD/SPTS, B.S.ELSTUD, B.S.EX.SCI, B.S.GY, BS.HPE-ATG, B.S.IS, B.S.MIS, B.S.MS, B.S.PE, B.S.PG, BSBA.BA, BSBA.DL.AGBS, BSBA.DL.BSMC, BSBA.DL-BSCN, BSBA.DL-BSTH, BSIB.ISB, and BSSB degrees. Associate and master's degrees are also awarded. Bachelor's degrees are awarded in AGRICULTURE (environmental studies), BIOLOGICAL SCIENCE (biology/biological science and environmental biology), BUSINESS (accounting, business administration and management, business administration - international, business administration marketing, business communications, business economics, human resources, information & communication technology, international business management, management information systems, marketing and distribution, marketing management, nonprofit/public organization management, recreation and leisure services, recreational facilities management, and sports management), COMMUNICATIONS AND THE ARTS (art history, art, art history and appreciation, arts administration/management, ceramic art and design, communications, drawing, English, English literature, English writing, fine arts, French, German, jazz, journalism, keyboard - piano concentration, language arts, literature, modern language, music, music business management, music history and appreciation, music performance, music theory and composition, musical theater, painting, performing arts, photography, piano performance, printmaking, sculpture, Spanish, theatre arts, theatre production, theatre studies, theater management, visual and performing arts, vocal performance, voice, vocal music education, and writing), COMPUTER AND PHYSICAL SCIENCE (chemistry, information sciences and systems, mathematics, mathematics/computational, mathematics/theoretical, and physical chemistry), EDUCATION (art education, athletic training, early childhood education, education, education of the multiply handicapped, education of the physically handicapped, elementary education, English education, general studies, global studies, health education, health and education science, health and physical education, mathematics education, music education, physical education, physical science secondary school education, science education, secondary education, social science education, social studies education, social studies secondary school education, Spanish education K-12, special education, specific learning disabilities, sports and wellness studies, and teaching English as a second/foreign language (TESOL/TEFOL)), ENGINEERING AND ENVIRONMENTAL DESIGN (environmental science and preengineering), HEALTH PROFESSIONS (health, health and physical activity, kinesiology, pre-health studies, predentistry, premedicine, and sports medicine), SOCIAL SCIENCE (Christian studies, community services, economics, French studies, geography, history, human services, interdisciplinary studies, international relations, international studies, Japanese studies, liberal arts/general studies, liberal arts, sciences, general studies, humanities, philosophy, political science/government, prelaw, psychology, public administration, religion, religious studies, religious music, social science, social studies, sociology, theology, theological studies, women & gender studies, and women's studies). Sustainable business, pre-health sciences, accounting and communication are the strongest academically. Business administration, biology, and psychology have the largest enrollments.

ACTIVITIES: There are no fraternities or sororities. There are 55 groups on campus, including art, band, cheerleading, choir, chorale, chorus, computers, dance, drama, environmental, ethnic, honors, international, jazz band, LGBT, literary magazine, musical theater, newspaper, pep band, photography, political, professional, radio and TV, religious, social, social service, and student government. Popular campus events include Spring Fling, Moose Cafe, Refresh Yourself, and AQ Idol. **Sports:** There are 11 intercollegiate sports for men and 13 for women, and 4 intramural sports for men and 4 for women. Facilities include a health and fitness center with volleyball and basketball competition courts, athletic training lab, work out equipment, soccer and lacrosse field, and indoor track. **Graduates:** From July 1, 2015 to June 30, 2016, 381 bachelor's degrees were awarded. The most popular majors were business administration (10%), biology (8%), and education (6%). 50 companies recruited on campus in 2015-2016. In an average class, 34% graduate in 4 years or less, 51% graduate in 5 years or less, and 52% graduate in 6 years or less. Of the 2015 graduating class, 13% were enrolled in graduate school within 6 months of graduation, and 72% were employed.

SERVICES: Counseling and information services are available, as is tutoring in most subjects, a reader service for the blind, and remedial math, reading, and writing. **Library/Resources:** The library contains 283,187 volumes, 36,972 microform items, and 4,773 audio/video tapes/CDs/DVDs, and subscribes to 234 periodicals including electronic. Computerized library services include interlibrary loans, database searching, Internet access, and Wi-Fi capability. Special learning facilities include an art gallery, radio station, a theatre, greenhouse, observatory, and nature trails. **Physically Challenged Students:** 95% of the campus is accessible. Facilities include wheelchair ramps, elevators, special parking, specially equipped restrooms, special class scheduling, lowered drinking fountains, lowered telephones, and special housing. **Special:** Students may cross-register with the Dominican Consortium and may study abroad in Ireland, Germany, France, Spain, Costa Rica, Italy, or Japan. Co-op programs and internships are available in all majors, and work-study programs are also available. Students may pursue dual majors in business administration and accounting, sports management, communication arts, or art and B.A.-B.S. degrees in business, geography, or psychology. Student-designed majors can be arranged. Aquinas offers a general studies degree and may confer credit for life, military experience. A pass/fail grading option is available. Preengineering, prehealth, and teacher certification programs are all available in conjunction with majors offered at Aquinas. There are 5 national honor societies, a freshman honors program, and 5 departmental honors programs. **Visiting:** There are regularly scheduled orientations for prospective students, consisting of a tour of the campus and presentations by financial aid personnel, program directors, coaches, and faculty. There are guides for informal visits, visitors may sit in on classes, and stay overnight. To schedule a visit, contact the Admissions Office. **Campus Safety and Security:** Measures include 24-hour foot and vehicle patrol, emergency notification system, self-defense education, security escort services, emergency telephones, lighted pathways/sidewalks, and controlled access to dorms/residences.

REQUIREMENTS: The ACT is required. Candidates for admission must graduate from an accredited secondary school. Students must have completed 15 Carnegie units and 4 years of English and social studies and 3 to 4 years each of math and science. AP and CLEP credits are accepted. Important factors in the admissions decision are advanced placement or honors courses, leadership record, and extracurricular activities record. To graduate, students must complete 124 semester hours, with 30 to 48 in the major, and maintain a minimum GPA of 2.0. The general education program consists of a core of 18 to 30 hours, which includes, from the first to the fourth year, foreign language and a yearlong integrated skills course, and courses in the humanities, religion, and global perspectives; and distribution requirements of 30 to 33 hours, which include courses in cultural diversity, mythology and spirituality, natural sciences, the fine arts, and quantitative reasoning and technology. **Procedure:** Freshmen are admitted in the fall and winter. Entrance exams should be taken during the spring of the junior year. There is a rolling admissions plan. Application deadlines are open. Applications are accepted online. **Transfer Students:** 59 transfer students enrolled in 2015-2016. Transfer applicants must have earned at least 12 credits in academic course work from an accredited junior or 4-year college with a minimum GPA of 2.0. Interviews are recommended. 30 of 124 credits required for the bachelor's degree must be completed at Aquinas. **International Students:** There are 29 international students enrolled. The school actively recruits these students. They must take the TOEFL with a minimum score of 550 on the paper-based TOEFL (PBT). They must also take the ACT.

ADMISSIONS: The ACT scores were 2% between 12 and 17, 45% between 18 and 23, 47% between 24 and 29, and 7% above 30. **Admissions Contact:** Angela Schlosser Bacon, Director of Admissions. Email: *admissions@aquinas.edu* Web: *www.aquinas.edu*

FINANCIAL AID: In 2016-2017, 100% of all full-time freshmen and 86% of continuing full-time students received some form of financial aid. 83% of all full-time freshmen and 80% of continuing full-time students received need-based aid. The average freshman award was $23,572. Need-based scholarships or need-based grants averaged $21,588; need-based self-help aid (loans and jobs) averaged $1,984; non-need-based athletic scholarships averaged $2,906; and other non-need-based awards and non-need-based scholarships averaged $16,026. 35% of undergraduate students work part-time. Average annual earnings from campus work are $1900. The average financial indebtedness of the 2016 graduate was $32,047. The FAFSA code is 002239. The priority date for freshman financial aid applications for fall entry is March 1.

BAKER COLLEGE OF FLINT *(The complete profile is made available exclusively on our website, www.barronspac.com)*

CALVIN COLLEGE — D-4

www.calvin.edu

Grand Rapids, MI 49546 — (616) 526-6106, (800) 688-0122

Fax: (616) 526-6777 — **Email:** admissions@calvin.edu

Full-time: 1637 men, 1965 women	**Faculty:** 252; IIB, +$
Part-time: 105 men, 100 women	**Ph.D.s:** 89%
Graduate: 27 men, 84 women	**Student/Faculty:** 13 to 1
Year: 4-1-4, summer session	**Tuition:** $31,730
Room & Board: $9840	**Freshman Class:** 3981 applied, 2970 accepted, 909 enrolled
SAT CR/M: 620/600 **ACT:** 27	**CEEB CODE:** 1095
Application Deadline: August 15	**VERY COMPETITIVE+**

Calvin College, established in 1876, is a private institution affiliated with the Christian Reformed Church, offering undergraduate and graduate degrees in liberal arts and in some professional programs. Calvin is perhaps best known for the integration of learning and Christian faith. In every aspect of college life teaching and learning, athletics and the arts, campus life and community activities Calvin offers an outstanding education of the mind and heart. There is 1 undergraduate school and 2 graduate schools. In addition to regional accreditation, Calvin has baccalaureate program accreditation with ABET, CSWE, NASM, NCATE, ACS, and CCNE. The 390-acre campus is in a suburban area 7 miles southeast of downtown Grand Rapids. Including any residence halls, there are 40 buildings.

STUDENT LIFE: 50% of undergraduates are from out of state, mostly the Midwest. Students are from 47 states, 58 foreign countries, and Canada. 47% are from public schools. 73% are White; 10% Foreign; 4% Asian American; 4% Hispanic; 3% African American; 3% two or more races; 2% race unknown; 1% American Indian/Alaska Native. 57% are Protestant. **Female To Male Ratio:** 1.2:1. The average age of freshmen is 18; all undergraduates, 20. 15% do not continue beyond their first year; 76% remain to graduate. **Housing:** 2400 students can be accommodated in college housing, which includes single-sex dorms, on-campus apartments, off-campus apartments, honors houses, language houses, and special-interest houses. The college offers residence halls with living-learning floors that are focused on outdoor recreation, environmental care, race and ethnicity, and honors living. The college also offers an intentional living-learning community for athletes and students who are seeking to live an active lifestyle. There are also five off-campus urban houses with a community/urban focus. On-campus housing is available on a lottery system for upperclassmen. 60% of students live on campus; of those, 90% remain on campus on weekends. All students may keep cars. Alcohol is not permitted.

FACULTY/CLASSROOMS: 64% of faculty are male; 36% are female. All teach undergraduates, and all do research. No introductory courses are taught by graduate students. The average class size in an introductory lecture is 27; in a laboratory is 19; and in a regular course is 24.

PROGRAMS OF STUDY: Calvin confers B.A., B.S., B.A.S.P.A., B.C.S., B.F.A., B.M.E., B.S.A., B.S.E., B.S.N., B.S.P.A., B.S.R. and B.S.W. degrees. Master's degrees are also awarded. Bachelor's degrees are awarded in AGRICULTURE (environmental studies), BIOLOGICAL SCIENCE (biochemistry and biology/biological science), BUSINESS (accounting, business administration and management, business (dual major program), business communications, finance, human resources, management information systems, marketing management, small business management, and sports management), COMMUNICATIONS AND THE ARTS (American literature, art, art/art studies, art and design, art/visual culture, Chinese, communications, creative writing, digital communications, Dutch, English, English literature, English Writing, film arts, film, television and digital media, fine arts, French, German, graphic design, information technology, Japanese, language arts, linguistics, literature, media arts, film and media studies, music, music history and appreciation, music performance, music theory and composition, piano/organ, Spanish, strategic communication, video, voice, vocal music education, and writing), COMPUTER AND PHYSICAL SCIENCE (actuarial science, chemistry, computer programming, computer science, data processing, digital arts/technology, earth science, environmental geology, geology, information sciences and systems, mathematics, mathematics – economics, natural sciences, and physics), EDUCATION (art education, Asian studies, early childhood education, education, elementary education, English secondary education, English education, mathematics education, music education, physical education, science education, secondary education, and special education), ENGINEERING AND ENVIRONMENTAL DESIGN (chemical engineering, civil engineering, computer engineering, electrical/electronics engineering, engineering, environmental science, and mechanical engineering), HEALTH PROFESSIONS (biology, exercise science, kinesiology, nursing, occupational therapy, predentistry, premedicine, preoptometry, pre-occupational therapy, prepharmacy, prephysical therapy, preveterinary science, public health, recreation therapy, and speech pathology/audiology), SOCIAL SCIENCE (area studies, Asian/Oriental studies, classical and near eastern civilization, development economics, economics, geography, history, interdisciplinary studies, international relations, international studies, philosophy, political science/government, prelaw, psychology, public administration, religion, religious music, social work, sociology, theology, and theological studies). Nursing, biology, accounting, and philosophy are the strongest academically. Education, business, and engineering have the largest enrollments.

ACTIVITIES: There are no fraternities or sororities. There are 40 groups on campus, including art, band, chess, choir, chorale, chorus, computers, dance, drama, environmental, ethnic, film, honors, international, jazz band, LGBT, literary magazine, musical theater, newspaper, orchestra, pep band, political, professional, radio and TV, religious, social, social service, student government, symphony, and yearbook. Popular campus events include Festival of Faith and Writing, Festival of Faith and Music, Sem Pond Jump, Rangeela, The January Series, Dance Guild, and Cardboard Canoe Contest. **Sports:** There are 9 intercollegiate sports for men and 10 for women, and 18 intramural sports for men and 14 for women. Facilities include an arena, a fitness center, climbing wall, pool, basketball courts, a dance studio, an indoor track and tennis center with a 200-meter track and four full-size indoor tennis courts, a soccer facility, baseball and softball diamonds, cross-country course, track, a weight-training/exercise room, outdoor tennis courts, sand beach volleyball courts, an ice skating rink, and a recreational trail around campus. **Graduates:** From July 1, 2015 to June 30, 2016, 848 bachelor's degrees were awarded. The most popular majors were engineering (8%), business administration and management general (6%), and nursing (6%). 390 companies recruited on campus in 2015-2016. In an average class, 1% graduate in 3 years or less, 58% graduate in 4 years or less, 73% graduate in 5 years or less, and 76% graduate in 6 years or less. Of the 2015 graduating class, 25% were enrolled in graduate school within 6 months of graduation, and 73% were employed.

SERVICES: Counseling and information services are available, as is tutoring in most subjects. There is a reader service for the blind, and remedial math, reading, and writing. There is also a braille print service for the blind, books on tape, note taking, interpreting, diagnostic testing, special advising, and early registration. **Library/Resources:** The library contains 714,950 volumes, 598,135 microform items, and 17,192 audio/video tapes/CDs/DVDs, and subscribes to 5,500 periodicals including electronic. Computerized library services include interlibrary loans, database searching, Internet access, and Wi-Fi capability. Special learning facilities include an art gallery, radio station, the college has a TV studio, an ecosystem preserve, an interpretive center, an integrated scientific research experimental laboratory, an observatory with a 16-inch telescope, a greenhouse, a human performance lab, two community gardens and an audiology and speech pathology clinic. **Physically Challenged Students:** 95% of the campus is accessible. Facilities include wheelchair ramps, elevators, special parking, specially equipped restrooms, special class scheduling, lowered drinking fountains, lowered telephones, and special housing. **Special:** Dual and student-designed majors are available. Students may study off-campus in semester-long programs in China, Hungary, Britain, France, Ghana, Honduras, Peru, Spain, Washington, D.C. and New Mexico. In addition, Calvin's January Interim takes students to more than 30 countries. The college also offers cooperative programs in a variety of majors and locations around the world. Calvin also offers a master's degree in speech pathology and audiology (SPAUD) and education. Experiential learning opportunities are a staple at Calvin as well. In the college's most recent Career Outcomes Report, 86-percent of 2015 grads reported completing at least one internship/practicum while at Calvin. There are 6 national honor societies, a freshman honors program, and 25 departmental honors programs. **Visiting:** There are regularly scheduled orientations for prospective students, prospective students and their families are invited to explore Calvin firsthand by scheduling an individual visit through the admissions office or through participating in a regularly scheduled Fridays at Calvin visit. There are guides for informal visits, visitors may sit in on classes, and stay overnight. To schedule a visit, contact the Admissions Office. **Campus Safety and Security:** Measures include 24-hour foot and vehicle patrol, emergency notification system, self-defense education, and security escort services. There are emergency telephones, lighted pathways/sidewalks, controlled access to dorms/residences, a crime alert bulletin, and reports in the school newspaper.

REQUIREMENTS: Either the ACT or the SAT are acceptable. In selecting students for admission, Calvin College looks for evidence of a student's Christian commitment and his or her capacity and desire to learn. Students who are interested in the Christian perspective and curriculum of Calvin, and who show interest in its aims, are eligible for consideration. Although the prospect of academic success is of primary consideration, the aspirations of the applicant, the recommendation of a high school teacher, and the ability of Calvin to be of service, will also be considered. AP and CLEP credits are accepted. Important factors in the admissions decision are recommendations by school officials, leadership record, and extracurricular activities record. Degree requirements include completion of 124 credit hours, with 28 credits in the major. All students must complete specific course work in English, religion, history, science, math, communication, fine arts, psychology or sociology, economics or political science, philosophy, kinesiology, research and information technology, foreign language and cross-cultural engagement. A minimum GPA of 2.0 is required. **Procedure:** Freshmen are admitted in the fall and spring. Entrance exams should be taken during the spring of the junior year or fall of the senior year. There are deferred admissions and rolling admissions plans. Applications should be filed by August 15 for fall entry; January 15 for spring entry, along with a $35 fee. Applications are accepted online. **Transfer Students:** 75 transfer students enrolled in 2015-2016. Applicants from 4-year colleges are required to have a minimum GPA of 2.0; from 2-year colleges, 2.5. The SAT minimum requirements are 510 on the critical reading section and 510 on the math section. A minimum score of 20 is required on the ACT. 32 of 124 credits required for the bachelor's degree must be completed at Calvin. **International Students:** There are 414 international students enrolled. The school actively recruits these students. They must take the TOEFL with a minimum score of 550 on the paper-based TOEFL (PBT) or 80 on the Internet-based version (iBT), must take the MELAB if they scored low on the TOEFL. They must also take the SAT or ACT, scoring 20. Exceptions are made for strong students without easy access to standardized exams.

ADMISSIONS: 75% of the 2016-2017 applicants were accepted. The SAT scores for the 2016-2017 freshman class were: Critical Reading-- 7% below 500, 34% between 500 and 599, 42% between 600 and 699, and 17% between 700 and 800. Math-- 9% below 500, 38% between 500 and 599, 39% between 600 and 699, and 14% between 700 and 800. The ACT scores were 19% between 18 and 23, 54% between 24 and 29, and 27% above 30. 55% of the current freshmen were in the top fifth of their class; 78% were in the top two fifths. There were 13 National Merit finalists. **Admissions Contact:** Ben Arendt, Director of Admissions. Email: *admissions@calvin.edu* Web: *www.calvin.edu*

FINANCIAL AID: In 2016-2017, 99% of all full-time freshmen and 94% of continuing full-time students received some form of financial aid. 68% of all full-time freshmen and 69% of continuing full-time students received need-based aid. The average freshman award was $23,000. Need-based scholarships or need-based grants averaged $7,500 ($26,000 maximum); need-based self-help aid (loans and jobs) averaged $5,500 ($5,500 maximum); and other non-need-based awards and non-need-based scholarships averaged $14,000 ($32,000 maximum). 85% of undergraduate students work part-time. Average annual earnings from campus work are $2500. The average financial indebtedness of the 2016 graduate was $30,998. Calvin is a member of CSS. The college's own financial statement is required. The FAFSA code is 002241. The priority date for freshman financial aid applications for fall entry is January 15. The deadline for filing freshman financial aid applications for fall entry is August 1.

CENTRAL MICHIGAN UNIVERSITY D-4

www.cmich.edu

Mount Pleasant, MI 48859	**(989) 774-3076** **(888) 292-5366**
Fax: (989) 774-7267	**Email: cmuadmit@cmich.edu**
Full-time: 8465 men, 10946 women	**Faculty:** 629; I, --$
Part-time: 1159 men, 1669 women	**Ph.D.s:** 81%
Graduate: 2568 men, 3767 women	**Student/Faculty:** 21 to 1
Year: semesters, summer session	**Tuition:** $11,550 ($23,670)
Room & Board: $8780	**Freshman Class:** 18025 applied, 12565 accepted, 3733 enrolled
ACT: 23	**CEEB CODE:** 1106
Application Deadline: open	**COMPETITIVE**

Central Michigan University, founded in 1892, is a public university offering programs in liberal arts, business, and health, education, and human services. There are 8 undergraduate schools and 1 graduate school. In addition to regional accreditation, CMU has baccalaureate program accreditation with AACSB, ABET, ACEJMC, CSWE, NASAD, NASM, NCATE, NRPA, and CADE. The 480-acre campus is in a small town 70 miles north of Lansing. Including any residence halls, there are 56 buildings.

STUDENT LIFE: 93% of undergraduates are from Michigan. Others are from 50 states, 71 foreign countries, and Canada. 70% are from public schools. 73% are White; 5% Foreign; 4% race unknown; 3% Hispanic; 2% Asian American; 12% African American; 1% American Indian/Alaska Native. **Female To Male Ratio:** 1.3:1. The average age of freshmen is 19; all undergraduates, 23. 23% do not continue beyond their first year; 60% remain to graduate. **Housing:** 7529 students can be accommodated in college housing, which includes single-sex and coed dorms, on-campus apartments, married student housing, honors houses. There are also residential colleges for business, education, and human services, health professions, science and technology, and music. On-campus housing is guaranteed for all 4 years. 67% of students commute. All students may keep cars. Alcohol is not permitted.

FACULTY/CLASSROOMS: 56% of faculty are male; 44% are female. All teach undergraduates. Graduate students teach 2% of introductory courses. The average class size in an introductory lecture is 39 and in a laboratory is 22.

PROGRAMS OF STUDY: CMU confers B.A., B.S., B.A.A., B.F.A., B.Indiv.S., B.Mus., B.S.B.A., B.S.E., and B.S.E.T. degrees. Master's and doctoral degrees are also awarded. Bachelor's degrees are awarded in AGRICULTURE (environmental studies and natural resource management), BIOLOGICAL SCIENCE (biochemistry, biology/biological science, and neurosciences), BUSINESS (accounting, business administration and management, entrepreneurial studies, hospitality management services, human resources, international business management, logistics, management information systems, management science, marketing and distribution, marketing management, marketing/retailing/merchandising, purchasing/inventory management, real estate, recreational facilities management, and retailing), COMMUNICATIONS AND THE ARTS (advertising, apparel design, art, broadcasting, communications, design, dramatic arts, English, French, German, graphic design, journalism, language arts, music, music history and appreciation, music performance, music theory and composition, musical theater, photography, piano/organ, public relations, Spanish, speech/debate/rhetoric, theater design, visual and performing arts, and voice), COMPUTER AND PHYSICAL SCIENCE (actuarial science, chemistry, computer science, earth science, geology, information sciences and systems, mathematics, oceanography, physical sciences, physics, science, and statistics), EDUCATION (athletic training, education, elementary education, foreign languages education, music education, and physical education), ENGINEERING AND ENVIRONMENTAL DESIGN (computer technology, electrical/electronics engineering, engineering technology, environmental science, industrial administration/management, interior design, manufacturing technology, mechanical engineering, and mechanical engineering technology), HEALTH PROFESSIONS (biomedical science, community health work, health, health care administration, public health, recreation therapy, rehabilitation therapy, speech pathology/audiology, and sports medicine), SOCIAL SCIENCE (anthropology, child psychology/development, cognitive science, community services, criminal justice, dietetics, early childhood studies, economics, ethics, politics, and social policy, European studies, family/consumer studies, food production/management/services, geography, history, interdisciplinary studies, law, parks and recreation management, philosophy, psychology, religion, social science, social studies, social work, sociology, and women's studies). Psychology, marketing, and accounting have the largest enrollments.

ACTIVITIES: 5% of men belong to 14 national fraternities; 10% of women belong to 14 national sororities. There are 400 groups on campus, including art, band, cheerleading, choir, chorus, communications, computers, dance, drama, environmental, ethnic, forensics, honors, international, jazz band, LGBT, literary magazine, marching band, musical theater, orchestra, pep band, photography, political, professional, religious, social, social service, student government, and symphony. Popular campus events include Homecoming, Michigan Story Festival, and Native American Pow Wow. **Sports:** There are 6 intercollegiate sports for men and 10 for women, and 21 intramural sports for men and 21 for women. Facilities include a football stadium, softball fields, field hockey complex, an indoor athletic complex, indoor and outdoor track, soccer field, baseball stadium, arena, and student activity center. **Graduates:** From July 1, 2015 to June 30, 2016, 4063 bachelor's degrees were awarded. The most popular majors were business (23%), teacher education (11%), and fitness and exercise science (9%). 400 companies recruited on campus in 2015-2016. In an average class, 1% graduate in 3 years or less, 18% graduate in 4 years or less, 45% graduate in 5 years or less, and 57% graduate in 6 years or less. Of the 2015 graduating class, 15% were enrolled in graduate school within 6 months of graduation, and 80% were employed.

SERVICES: Counseling and information services are available, as is tutoring in most subjects, a reader service for the blind, and remedial math, reading, and writing. **Library/Resources:** The library contains 1.5 million volumes, 1.4 million microform items, 23,061 audio/video tapes/CDs/DVDs, and subscribes to 2,731 periodicals including electronic. Computerized library services include interlibrary loans, database searching, Internet access, and Wi-Fi capability. Special learning facilities include an art gallery, natural history museum, TV station, Museum of Cultural and Natural History, Clarke Historical Library, Gerald L. Poor School Museum, Brooks Astronomical Observatory, leadership institute, and a multicultural education center. **Physically Challenged Students:** 95% of the campus is accessible. Facilities include wheelchair ramps, elevators, special parking, specially equipped restrooms, special class scheduling, lowered drinking fountains, lowered telephones, special housing, and a Student Disability Services office. **Special:** CMU offers internships in business administration, study abroad in 43 countries, and dual majors in chemistry/physics and computer science/math. Student-designed majors are available for a bachelor of individualized studies, and there is credit for life, military, and work experience. Students may take up to 25 hours for pass/fail grades. CMU off-campus programs offers external degree programs in which students can get degrees without attending classes on campus. There are 13 national honor societies, a freshman honors program, and 21 departmental honors programs. **Visiting:** There are guides for informal visits, visitors may sit in on classes, and stay overnight. To schedule a visit, contact the Admissions Office. **Campus Safety and Security:** Measures include emergency notification system and security escort services. There are also shuttle buses, emergency telephones, lighted pathways/sidewalks, and blue light phone system.

REQUIREMENTS: The ACT is required. Applicants must be high school graduates or hold a GED. The university strongly recommends 4 years each of English and math, 3 each of science and social studies, and 2 of foreign language, as well as 1 course each in computer science and fine arts. AP and CLEP credits are accepted. Students must complete 124 credit hours, including 30 in the major, with a GPA of 2.0. They must fulfill the requirements in the University Program (27-30 semester hours of coursework in humanities, natural science, and social science, an integrative and area studies), and fulfill University competency requirements in written English (Freshmen and Advanced Composition), oral English, and math. **Procedure:** Freshmen are admitted to all sessions. Entrance exams should be taken Junior or senior year of high school. There are deferred admissions and rolling admissions plans. Application deadlines are open. Application fee is $35. Applications are accepted on-line. **Transfer Students:** 1091 transfer students enrolled in 2015-2016. Transfer students must have a GPA of 2.0. 30 of 124 credits required for the bachelor's degree must be completed at CMU. **International Students:** There are 527 international students enrolled. The school actively recruits these students. They must take the TOEFL with a minimum score of 550 on the paper-based TOEFL (PBT) or 79 on the Internet-based version (iBT).

ADMISSIONS: 70% of the 2016-2017 applicants were accepted. The ACT scores were 29% below 12, 34% between 12 and 17, 22% between 18 and 23, 9% between 24 and 29, and 6% above 30. 33% of the current freshmen were in the top fifth of their class; 62% were in the top two fifths. 59 freshmen graduated first in their class. **Admissions Contact:** Krista Casey, Assistant Director of Admissions. Email: *cmuadmit@cmich.edu* Web: *www.cmich.edu*

FINANCIAL AID: In 2016-2017, 66% of all full-time freshmen and 62% of continuing full-time students received some form of financial aid. 56% of all full-time freshmen and 57% of continuing full-time students received need-based aid. The average freshman award was $13,814. Need-based scholarships or need-based grants averaged $8,069; need-based self-help aid (loans and jobs) averaged $6,249; non-need-based athletic scholarships averaged $15,110; and other non-need-based awards and non-need-based scholarships averaged $4,161. 25% of undergraduate students work part-time. Average annual earnings from campus work are $3500. The average financial indebtedness of the 2016 graduate was $33,545. The FAFSA code is 002243. The priority date for freshman financial aid applications for fall entry is March 1.

COLLEGE FOR CREATIVE STUDIES *(The complete profile is made available exclusively on our website, www.barronspac.com)*

CONCORDIA UNIVERSITY, ANN ARBOR E-5

www.cuaa.edu

Ann Arbor, MI 48105	(734) 995-7311 (800) 253-0680
Fax: (734) 995-4610	**Email:** admissions@cuaa.edu
Full-time: 186 men, 242 women	**Faculty:** 39
Part-time: 53 men, 40 women	**Ph.D.s:** 60%
Graduate: 154 men, 400 women	**Student/Faculty:** 11 to 1
Year: semesters, summer session	**Tuition:** $26,965
Room & Board: $8980	**Freshman Class:** 429 applied, 281 accepted, 94 enrolled
SAT CR/M/W: 575/550/560 **ACT:** 22	**CEEB CODE:** 1094
Application Deadline: August 15	**VERY COMPETITIVE**

Concordia University, established in 1963, is a private institution affiliated with the Missouri Synod of the Lutheran Church, offering undergraduate and graduate degrees in the arts and sciences, business, education, and human services. The figures in the above capsule and in this profile are approximate. There are 4 undergraduate schools and 2 graduate schools. In addition to regional accreditation, Concordia has baccalaureate program accreditation with NCATE. The 187-acre campus is in a suburban area 40 miles west of Detroit. Including any residence halls, there are 30 buildings.

STUDENT LIFE: 83% of undergraduates are from Michigan. Others are from 20 states, 6 foreign countries, and Canada. 85% are White; 8% African American; 2% Asian American; 2% American Indian/Alaska Native; 2% Hispanic; 1% Foreign. 30% are Protestant. **Female To Male Ratio:** 1.7:1. The average age of freshmen is 18; all undergraduates, 23. 31% do not continue beyond their first year; 47% remain to graduate. **Housing:** 436 students can be accommodated in college housing, which includes single-sex dorms and married student housing. On-campus housing is guaranteed for all 4 years. 57% of students live on campus; of those, 60% remain on campus on weekends. All students may keep cars. Alcohol is not permitted.

FACULTY/CLASSROOMS: 47% of faculty are male; 53% are female. All teach undergraduates. No introductory courses are taught by graduate students. The average class size in an introductory lecture is 24; in a laboratory is 12; and in a regular course is 11.

PROGRAMS OF STUDY: Concordia confers B.A. degrees. Associate and master's degrees are also awarded. Bachelor's degrees are awarded in BIOLOGICAL SCIENCE (biology/biological science), BUSINESS (accounting, business administration and management, finance, hospitality management services, and human resources), COMMUNICATIONS AND THE ARTS (art, communications, dramatic arts, English, Greek, journalism, language arts, music, and Spanish), COMPUTER AND PHYSICAL SCIENCE (chemistry, computer science, mathematics, physical sciences, physics, and science), EDUCATION (early childhood education, elementary education, health education, physical education, and secondary education), ENGINEERING AND ENVIRONMENTAL DESIGN (preengineering), HEALTH PROFESSIONS (predentistry and premedicine), SOCIAL SCIENCE (biblical languages, criminal justice, family/consumer studies, history, humanities, justice and society, philosophy, psychology, religion, religious studies, religious music, safety management, social science, social studies, and sociology). Education, business, and family life are the strongest academically. Business administration, teacher education, and English have the largest enrollments.

ACTIVITIES: There are no fraternities or sororities. There are 21 groups on campus, including band, choir, chorale, communications, computers, dance, debate, drama, ethnic, jazz band, musical theater, newspaper, pep band, religious, social, social service, student government, and yearbook. Popular campus events include Boar's Head Festival, Servant Events, and a Fall Carnival. **Sports:** There are 5 intercollegiate sports for men and 5 for women, and 10 intramural sports for men and 10 for women. Facilities include a soccer field, baseball and softball diamonds, sand volleyball courts, a gym, and an open field for intramurals. **Graduates:** From July 1, 2015 to June 30, 2016, 112 bachelor's degrees were awarded. The most popular majors were teacher education (21%), business (21%), and criminal justice (10%). In an average class, 1% graduate in 3 years or less, 19% graduate in 4 years or less, 35% graduate in 5 years or less, and 37% graduate in 6 years or less.

SERVICES: Counseling and information services are available, as is tutoring in every subject, and remedial math. There is also a writing lab with consultants. **Library/Resources:** The library contains 117,000 volumes, 300,000 microform items, 1,400 audio/video tapes/CDs/DVDs, and subscribes to 660 periodicals including electronic. Computerized library services include interlibrary loans, database searching, Internet access, and Wi-Fi capability. Special learning facilities include an art gallery. **Physically Challenged Students:** 90% of the campus is accessible. Facilities include wheelchair ramps, elevators, special parking, specially equipped restrooms, and lowered drinking fountains. **Special:** Internships are available in most academic majors. Cross-registration is available with Eastern Michigan and Kettering Universities, Schoolcraft College, Henry Ford Community College, Michigan State Police Training Division, and Michigan Academy of Emergency Services. Students may study abroad in 6 countries. Accelerated degree programs are available in business administration, criminal justice administration, communication, hospitality management, and public safety. The college confers credit for life, military, and work experience through the School of Adult and Continuing Education. Nondegree study, dual majors in many combinations, student-designed majors, a 3-2 engineering degree with Kettering University, and a pass/fail grading option are available. **Visiting:** There are regularly scheduled orientations for prospective students, including several preview days, Senior Day, Junior Day, Art Day, Music Day, and Theatre Day. Individual tours are arranged by appointment. There are guides for informal visits, visitors may sit in on classes, and stay overnight. To schedule a visit, contact the Admissions Office. **Campus Safety and Security:** Measures include 24-hour foot and vehicle patrol, security escort services, lighted pathways/sidewalks, and controlled access to dorms/residences.

REQUIREMENTS: The SAT is required. The ACT is preferred. Applicants must graduate from an accredited secondary school or have the GED. 20 Carnegie units are recommended, including 4 units in English, 3 in math, and 2 each in science, social studies, and foreign language. AP and CLEP credits are accepted. Important factors in the admissions decision are leadership record, advanced placement or honors courses, and evidence of special talent. Degree requirements include completion of 128 credit hours, with at least 30 in the major, and up to 49 credit hours of general studies, and a minimum GPA of 2.0. The student must also demonstrate proficiency in foreign language, writing, speech, and math. Required courses include upper-level general studies, writing-intensive courses, a freshman seminar, physical activities, computer applications, religion, humanities, social science, language/communication, and science. A senior project is required. Education students must take the Michigan Test for Teacher Certification. **Procedure:** Freshmen are admitted in the fall and spring. There are deferred admissions and rolling admissions plans. Applications should be filed by August 15 for fall entry. The fall 2016 application fee was $25. Notification is sent on a rolling basis. Applications are accepted on-line. **Transfer Students:** 91 transfer students enrolled in 2015-2016. A GPA of 2.0 is required for transfer students; a GPA of 2.5 is required for admittance to the teacher education program. Transfer students who have earned 12 or more credits are not required to take the ACT. Interviews are recommended. 30 of 128 credits required for the bachelor's degree must be completed at Concordia. **International Students:** There are 7 international students enrolled. They must take the TOEFL with a minimum score of 520 on the paper-based TOEFL (PBT) or 68 on the Internet-based version (iBT) or take the MELAB. They must also take the SAT or ACT.

ADMISSIONS: 66% of the 2016-2017 applicants were accepted. The SAT scores for the 2016-2017 freshman class were: Critical Reading-- 36% below 500, 21% between 500 and 599, 21% between 600 and 699, and 22% between 700 and 800. Math-- 28% below 500, 43% between 500 and 599, and 29% between 600 and 699. Writing-- 43% below 500, 7% between 500 and 599, 29% between 600 and 699, and 21% between 700 and 800. The ACT scores were 36% below 12, 20% between 12 and 17, 27% between 18 and 23, 11% between 24 and 29, and 6% above 30. **Admissions Contact:** Amy Becher, Executive Director of Enrollment Services. Email: *admissions@cuaa.edu* Web: *www.cuaa.edu*

FINANCIAL AID: In 2016-2017, 100% of all full-time freshmen and continuing full-time students received some form of financial aid. 65% of all full-time freshmen and 69% of continuing full-time students received need-based aid. The average freshman award was $18,392. Need-based scholarships or need-based grants averaged $5,047 ($13,505 maximum); need-based self-help aid (loans and jobs) averaged $7,766 ($9,000 maximum); non-need-based athletic scholarships averaged $8,274 ($17,500 maximum); and other non-need-based awards and non-need-based scholarships averaged $6,500 ($19,700 maximum). 42% of undergraduate students work part-time. Average annual earnings from campus work are $1781. The average financial indebtedness of the 2016 graduate was $25,000. The the college's own financial statement is required. The filing deadline for fall entry is March 1.

DAVENPORT UNIVERSITY *(The complete profile is made available exclusively on our website, www.barronspac.com)*

EASTERN MICHIGAN UNIVERSITY D-5
www.emich.edu

Ypsilanti, MI 48197 (734) 487-3060
(800) GO TO EMU
Fax: (734) 487-6559 Email: undergraduate.admissions@emich.edu

Full-time: 5276 men, 7795 women | **Faculty:** 773; IIA, +$
Part-time: 2026 men, 2683 women | **Ph.D.s:** 75%
Graduate: 1395 men, 2459 women | **Student/Faculty:** 17 to 1
Year: semesters, summer session | **Tuition:** $10,417 ($27,712)
Room & Board: $9344 | **Freshman Class:** 14228 applied, 10639 accepted, 2888 enrolled
SAT CR/M/W: 483/509/486 **ACT:** 22 | **CEEB CODE:** 1201
Application Deadline: August 30 | **COMPETITIVE**

Eastern Michigan University, founded in 1849, is a public institution offering programs in arts and sciences, business, education, health and human services, and technology. There are 6 undergraduate schools and 1 graduate school. In addition to regional accreditation, EMU has baccalaureate program accreditation with AACSB, ACCE, CSWE, NASM, NCATE, ACPHA, ACOTE, ABA, ACS, APA, ASHA, CCNE, CADE, CAAHEP, CAAT, CIDA, HLC, MDOE, NAACLS, NASPAA, CNSS, and PAB. The 460-acre campus is in a suburban area 8 miles east of Ann Arbor. Including any residence halls, there are 120 buildings.

STUDENT LIFE: 88% of undergraduates are from Michigan. Others are from 49 states, 30 foreign countries, and Canada. 90% are from public schools. 65% are White; 5% Hispanic; 4% two or more races; 3% Asian American; 2% Foreign; 2% race unknown; 19% African American. **Female To Male Ratio:** 1.5:1. The average age of freshmen is 18; all undergraduates, 23. 25% do not continue beyond their first year; 40% remain to graduate. **Housing:** 3688 students can be accommodated in college housing, which includes coed dorms, on-campus apartments, married student housing, honors houses, special-interest houses, sorority houses, special housing known as community of scholars, upper-class halls, and a first-year center. On-campus housing is available on a first-come and first-served basis. 78% of students commute. All students may keep cars.

FACULTY/CLASSROOMS: 46% of faculty are male; 54% are female. 95% teach undergraduates. Graduate students teach 2% of introductory courses.

PROGRAMS OF STUDY: EMU confers B.A., B.S., B.A.E., B.A. in Language and World Business, B.B.A., B.B.E., B.F.A., B.M.E., B.M.T., B.M.U., B.S.N. and B.S.W. degrees. Master's and doctoral degrees are also awarded. Bachelor's degrees are awarded in BIOLOGICAL SCIENCE (biochemistry, biology/biological science, and nutrition), BUSINESS (accounting, apparel and accessories marketing, banking and finance, business administration and management, business data processing, business economics, business systems analysis, entrepreneurial studies, fashion merchandising, hospitality management services, hotel/motel and restaurant management, international business management, labor studies, management information systems, management science, marketing management, marketing/retailing/merchandising, office supervision and management, personnel management, supply chain management, tourism, and trade and industrial supervision and management), COMMUNICATIONS AND THE ARTS (advertising, American literature, animation, applied music, art, art history and appreciation, arts administration/management, classical languages, communications, communications technology, creative writing, dance, design, dramatic arts, English, English literature, film arts, fine arts, French, German, graphic design, historic preservation, Japanese, journalism, language arts, linguistics, literature, media arts, music, music performance, percussion, performing arts, piano/organ, public relations, Spanish, speech/debate/rhetoric, strings, technical and business writing, telecommunications, visual and performing arts, voice, and winds),

COMPUTER AND PHYSICAL SCIENCE (actuarial science, applied mathematics, astronomy, chemistry, computer programming, computer science, computer security and information assurance, earth science, geology, hydrogeology, information sciences and systems, mathematics, physics, polymer science, science, and statistics), EDUCATION (art education, athletic training, bilingual/bicultural education, business education, computer education, drama education, early childhood education, education, education of the deaf and hearing impaired, education of the emotionally handicapped, education of the mentally handicapped, education of the multiply handicapped, education of the physically handicapped, education of the visually handicapped, educational media, elementary education, English education, foreign languages education, health education, industrial arts education, mathematics education, middle school education, music education, physical education, psychology education, reading education, school psychology, science education, secondary education, social foundations, social studies education, special education, technical education, and trade and industrial education), ENGINEERING AND ENVIRONMENTAL DESIGN (airline piloting and navigation, applied aviation, aviation administration/management, city/community/regional planning, computer engineering, computer graphics, computer technology, construction management, electrical/electronics engineering technology, engineering physics, engineering technology, interior design, land use management and reclamation, manufacturing engineering, manufacturing technology, mechanical engineering technology, military science, plastics technology, and urban planning technology), HEALTH PROFESSIONS (allied health, exercise science, health care administration, medical laboratory science, medical laboratory technology, music therapy, nursing, occupational therapy, recreation therapy, speech pathology/audiology, and sports medicine), SOCIAL SCIENCE (African studies, African American studies, anthropology, area studies, Asian/Oriental studies, child care/child and family studies, clothing and textiles management/production/services, counseling/psychology, criminal justice, dietetics, economics, gender studies, geography, gerontology, history, interdisciplinary studies, international relations, Latin American studies, Middle Eastern studies, paralegal studies, philosophy, political science/government, psychology, public administration, Russian and Slavic studies, social studies, social work, sociology, textiles and clothing, urban studies, and women's studies). Education, business, and health/nursing are the strongest academically. Elementary education, arts/sciences, and business have the largest enrollments.

ACTIVITIES: 4% of men belong to 1 local and 10 national fraternities; 4% of women belong to 1 local and 11 national sororities. There are 300 groups on campus, including art, band, cheerleading, chess, choir, chorale, chorus, computers, dance, debate, drama, drill team, environmental, ethnic, film, forensics, honors, international, jazz band, LGBT, literary magazine, marching band, musical theater, newspaper, opera, orchestra, pep band, photography, political, professional, radio and TV, religious, social, social service, student government, and symphony. Popular campus events include Martin Luther King Birthday Celebration and Family Weekend. **Sports:** There are 12 intercollegiate sports for men and 15 for women, and 20 intramural sports for men and 20 for women. Facilities include a stadium, outdoor playing fields, a field house, a student recreation and intramural center, basketball courts, volleyball courts, swimming pools, softball and soccer fields, weight rooms, an aerobic studio, and a pro shop. **Graduates:** From July 1, 2015 to June 30, 2016, 3321 bachelor's degrees were awarded. The most popular majors were business/marketing (20%), health professions and related programs (15%), and education (11%). 600 companies recruited on campus in 2015-2016. In an average class, 1% graduate in 3 years or less, 13% graduate in 4 years or less, 27% graduate in 5 years or less, and 37% graduate in 6 years or less.

SERVICES: Counseling and information services are available, as is tutoring in every subject, a reader service for the blind, and remedial math, reading, and writing. Notetakers and interpreters are also provided for students with disabilities. **Library/Resources:** The library contains 1.1 million volumes, 994,057 microform items, and 37,078 audio/video tapes/CDs/DVDs, and subscribes to 28,034 periodicals including electronic. Computerized library services include interlibrary loans, database searching, Internet access, and Wi-Fi capability. Special learning facilities include an art gallery, radio station, and TV station. **Physically Challenged Students:** 93% of the campus is accessible. Facilities include wheelchair ramps, elevators, special parking, specially equipped restrooms, special class scheduling, lowered drinking fountains, lowered telephones, and special housing. **Special:** EMU offers internships, work-study programs, a Washington semester in public administration, and co-op programs and cross-registration with the University of Michigan at Ann Arbor, Concordia College, and Washtenaw Community College. Students may study abroad in more than 23 countries. EMU allows dual majors, nondegree study, B.A.-B.S. degrees in all majors, student-designed majors, and accelerated degree programs, and confers a general studies degree, as well as a B.A.-B.B.A. degree in language and world business. Students may receive credit for life, military, and work experience, and pass/fail options are open. There are 9 national honor societies, a freshman honors program, and 36 departmental honors programs. **Visiting:** There are regularly scheduled orientations for prospective students, including tours scheduled every morning and afternoon, as well as Saturday morning, with trained student tour guides. There are guides for informal visits, visitors may sit in on classes, and stay overnight. To schedule a visit, contact the Admissions On-Campus Programs. **Campus Safety and Security:** Measures include 24-hour foot and vehicle patrol, emergency notification system, self-defense education, and security escort services. There are also shuttle buses, emergency telephones, lighted pathways/sidewalks, controlled access to dorms/residences, bicycle patrols, a crime prevention officer, area police officers in dorms, an anonymous tip line, operation identification, vehicle glass etching, a bike lock lease program, and surveillance cameras.

REQUIREMENTS: A minimum composite of 17 on the ACT, or a satisfactory score on the SAT is required. Applicants should be high school graduates or hold a GED. The university recommends that students complete 21 academic credits in high school, consisting of 4 credits each in English, math, and science, 2 credits each in foreign language and social studies, 1 credit in history, and 4 credits in other traditional college-preparatory courses. A portfolio is required for applicants to the art program, and an audition is required for music students. AP and CLEP credits are accepted. To graduate, students must have a GPA of 2.0, and complete a minimum of 124 semester hours, including usually 30 in the major, 20 in the minor (or 50 in a comprehensive major), and 40 in General Education. In addition to distribution requirements, students must have a course in global awareness, a course in U.S. diversity, and satisfy requirements for learning beyond the classroom. **Procedure:** Freshmen are admitted to all sessions. Entrance exams should be taken by November of the senior year of high school. There are early admissions and rolling admissions plans. Applications should be filed by August 30 for fall entry; January 2 for winter entry; April 25 for spring entry; and June 21 for summer entry. The fall 2016 application fee was $35. Notification is sent on a rolling basis. Applications are accepted online. **Transfer Students:** 1697 transfer students enrolled in 2015-2016. Transfer students must have at least 12 semester hours of college credit, with a GPA of 2.0. 30 of 124 credits required for the bachelor's degree must be completed at EMU. **International Students:** There are 360 international students enrolled. The school actively recruits these students. They must take the TOEFL with a minimum score of 500 on the paper-based TOEFL (PBT) or 61 on the Internet-based version (iBT) or take the MELAB, or take the IELTS.

ADMISSIONS: 75% of the 2016-2017 applicants were accepted. The SAT scores for the 2016-2017 freshman class were: Critical Reading-- 47% below 500, 26% between 500 and 599, 14% between 600 and 699, and 3% between 700 and 800. Math-- 41% below 500, 40% between 500 and 599, 17% between 600 and 699, and 2% between 700 and 800. Writing-- 57% below 500, 33% between 500 and 599, 9% between 600 and 699, and 1% between 700 and 800. The ACT scores were 11% between 12 and 17, 54% between 18 and 23, 32% between 24 and 29, and 3% above 30. 22 freshmen graduated first in their class. **Admissions Contact:** Brian Selfridge, Freshmen Admissions. Email: *undergraduate.admissions@emich.edu* Web: *www.emich.edu*

FINANCIAL AID: In 2016-2017, 97% of all full-time freshmen and 75% of continuing full-time students received some form of financial aid. 61% of all full-time freshmen and 62% of continuing full-time students received need-based aid. The average freshman award was $13,104. Need-based scholarships or need-based grants averaged $6,283 ($9,061 maximum); need-based self-help aid (loans and jobs) averaged $3,533 ($5,500 maximum); non-need-based athletic scholarships averaged $17,719 ($34,795 maximum); and other non-need-based awards and non-need-based scholarships averaged $7,919 ($28,128 maximum). 16% of undergraduate students work part-time. Average annual earnings from campus work are $3400. The average financial indebtedness of the 2016 graduate was $24,402. The FAFSA code is 002259. The priority date for freshman financial aid applications for fall entry is February 1. The filing deadline for fall entry is December 19.

FERRIS STATE UNIVERSITY D-4
www.ferris.edu

Big Rapids, MI 49307 (231) 591-2100

Fax: (231) 591-3944	**Email:** admissions@ferris.edu
Full-time: 4445 men, 4340 women	**Faculty:** IIA, --$
Part-time: 1660 men, 2421 women	**Ph.D.s:** 35%
Graduate: 522 men, 799 women	**Student/Faculty:** 16 to 1
Year: semesters, summer session	**Tuition:** $11,144 ($17,910)
Room & Board: $10,301	**Freshman Class:** 10883 applied, 8455 accepted, 1830 enrolled
SAT: required **ACT:** 22	**CEEB CODE:** 1222
Application Deadline: August 1	**COMPETITIVE**

Ferris State University, established in 1884, is a public institution offering day and evening courses through its Schools of Arts and Sciences, Education and Human Services, Health Professions, Engineering Technology, Business, and Pharmacy, MI College of Optometry, and Kendall College of Art and Design. There are 6 undergraduate schools and 5 graduate schools. In addition to regional accreditation, Ferris State has baccalaureate program accreditation with ABET, ACBSP, ACCE, and ACPE. The 935-acre campus is in a small town 55 miles north of Grand Rapids. Including any residence halls, there are 110 buildings.

STUDENT LIFE: 91% of undergraduates are from Michigan. Others are from 44 states, 38 foreign countries, and Canada. 78% are White; 7% African American; 5% Hispanic; 3% Foreign; 3% two or more races; 3% race unknown; 2% Asian American; 1% American Indian/Alaska Native. **Female To Male Ratio:** 1.1:1. The average age of freshmen is 19; all undergraduates, 24. 25% do not continue beyond their first year. **Housing:** 3607 students can be accommodated in college housing, which includes single-sex and coed dorms, on-campus apartments, and married student housing. In addition, there are honors houses, language houses, special-interest houses, substance free, 1st year experience, quiet house, graphic design, and sophomore leadership. On-campus housing is guaranteed for all 4 years. 77% of students live on campus. All students may keep cars.

FACULTY/CLASSROOMS: 54% of faculty are male; 46% are female. All teach undergraduates. No introductory courses are taught by graduate students. The average class size in an introductory lecture is 22; in a laboratory is 11; and in a regular course is 17.

PROGRAMS OF STUDY: Ferris State confers B.A., B.S., B.F.A., B.S.N., B.S.W., and B.A.S. degrees. Associate, master's, and doctoral degrees are also awarded. Bachelor's degrees are awarded in BIOLOGICAL SCIENCE (biochemistry, biology/biological science, biology/ gen science secondary education, and biotechnology), BUSINESS (accounting, accounting (finance), accounting (information systems), business administration w/legal studies, business administration and management, business administration/aviation, business data processing, collaborative design, facilities management, finance, hospitality management services, hotel and restaurant administration, hotel/motel and restaurant management, human resources, insurance and risk management, integrative studies, marketing, marketing/retailing/merchandising, operations management, recreation and leisure services, resort management, professional golf management, and professional tennis management), COMMUNICATIONS AND THE ARTS (advertising, applied speech communication, art history, art history and appreciation, communications, digital media, digital media software engineering, drawing, drawing with printmaking focus, English, fashion studies, fine arts, graphic communications management, graphic design, illustration, industrial design, journalism & technical communications, metal/jewelry, music industry, painting, photography, printmaking, printing management, public relations, sculpture, sports communication, technical communication, and television & digital media production), COMPUTER AND PHYSICAL SCIENCE (actuarial science, applied mathematics, chemistry, chemistry education, computer networks & systems, computer information technology, computer information systems, digital animation & game design, and industrial technology), EDUCATION (art education, business education, early childhood education, elementary education, English education, health information management, history education, mathematics education, pro-mo-ted-technical education, social studies education, and technical education), ENGINEERING AND ENVIRONMENTAL DESIGN (architecture & sustainability, automotive technology, construction management, construction mgmt/commercial/industrial, construction mgmt/highway/bridge, electrical/electronics engineering technology, engineering technology, furniture design, HVACR eng tech & energy management, HVACR engineering technology, heavy equip service engineering, manufacturing engineering, mechanical engineering technology, plastics engineering, preengineering, product design engineering technology, surveying engineering, and welding engineering), HEALTH PROFESSIONS (allied health, biology, dental hygiene, health care administration, healthcare marketing, medical laboratory science, medical records administration/services, molecular diagnostics, nuclear medical technology, nursing, pre-health studies, prephysical therapy, and public health), SOCIAL SCIENCE (criminal justice, history, political science/government, psychology, social studies, social work, and sociology). Pharmacy, and optometry are the strongest academically. Pharmacy/pre pharmacy, nursing, and criminal justice have the largest enrollments.

ACTIVITIES: 2% of men belong to 8 national fraternities; 2% of women belong to 10 national sororities. There are 239 groups on campus, including art, band, cheerleading, choir, chorus, communications, dance, debate, drama, drill team, ethnic, forensics, honors, international, jazz band, LGBT, musical theater, newspaper, orchestra, pep band, political, professional, radio and TV, religious, social, social service, student government, and symphony. Popular campus events include Ferris Fest and Autumn a LIVE Concert, Bulldawg Beginnings, Homecoming, Big Event, Spring Concert, and Bulldawg Weekends. **Sports:** There are 7 intercollegiate sports for men and 8 for women, and 32 intramural sports for men and 31 for women. Facilities include a golf course, racquetball and fitness club, an ice arena, stadium, and a student recreation center with a pool, and tennis courts. **Graduates:** From July 1, 2015 to June 30, 2016, 2600 bachelor's degrees were awarded. The most popular majors were nursing (6%), criminal justice (4%), and business administration (4%). 280 companies recruited on campus in 2015-2016. In an average class, 12% graduate in 3 years or less, 29% graduate in 4 years or less, 42% graduate in 5 years or less, and 49% graduate in 6 years or less.

SERVICES: Counseling and information services are available, as is tutoring in most subjects, a reader service for the blind, and remedial math, reading, and writing. **Library/Resources:** The library contains 267,362 volumes, 3.1 million microform items, 5,071 audio/video tapes/CDs/DVDs, and subscribes to 77,847 periodicals including electronic. Computerized library services include interlibrary loans, database searching, Internet access, and Wi-Fi capability. Special learning facilities include an art gallery, natural history museum, radio station, TV station, and Jim Crow Museum. **Physically Challenged Students:** 98% of the campus is accessible. Facilities include wheelchair ramps, elevators, special parking, specially equipped restrooms, special class scheduling, lowered drinking fountains, lowered telephones, and special housing. **Special:** Ferris State offers co-op programs in automotive service technology. Ferris also offers internships, study abroad, work-study programs, accelerated degrees, dual and student-designed majors, credit for life, military, and work experience. There are 18 national honor societies and a freshman honors program. **Visiting:** There are regularly scheduled orientations for prospective students, consisting of an admission's presentation, lunch, and a campus tour. There are guides for informal visits. To schedule a visit, contact the Admissions Office. **Campus Safety and Security:** Measures include 24-hour foot and vehicle patrol, emergency notification system, self-defense education, and security escort services. There are also shuttle buses, emergency telephones, lighted pathways/sidewalks, and controlled access to dorms/residences.

REQUIREMENTS: The SAT or ACT is required. Applicants must graduate from an accredited secondary school or earn a GED. 4 years each of English and math. 3 years of science (2 lab) and 3 social studies. 2 years of foreign language, 1 visual/performing arts and 1 physical education/health. AP and CLEP credits are accepted. Important factors in the admissions decision are personality/intangible qualities, leadership record, and advanced placement or honors courses. Degree requirements include a minimum 2.0 GPA. The total number of credit hours required varies. General education courses required include English, speech, math, humanities, social science, cultural enrichment, and natural science subjects. **Procedure:** Freshmen are admitted in the fall, spring, and summer. Entrance exams should be taken before course registration. There is a rolling admissions plan. Applications should be filed by August 1 for fall entry. Application fees are waived if application is completed online. **Transfer Students:** 1259 transfer students enrolled in 2015-2016. A GPA of at least 2.0 is required, as are college transcripts, and a statement of good standing from previously attended institutions. Some students may need to submit high school transcripts and test scores. 30 of 120 credits required for the bachelor's degree must be completed at Ferris State. **International Students:** There are 326 international students enrolled. The school actively recruits these students. They must take the TOEFL with a minimum score of 500 on the paper-based TOEFL (PBT) or 61 on the Internet-based version (iBT). They must also take the SAT or ACT, scoring 17, and a supplemental math exam.

ADMISSIONS: 78% of the 2016-2017 applicants were accepted. The SAT scores for the 2016-2017 freshman class were: The ACT scores were 15% between 12 and 17, 53% between 18 and 23, 27% between 24 and 29, and 5% above 30. **Admissions Contact:** Kristen Salomonson, Dean of Enrollment Service & Director of Admissions. Email: *admissions@ferris.edu* Web: *www.ferris.edu*

FINANCIAL AID: In 2016-2017, 95% of all full-time freshmen and 88% of continuing full-time students received some form of financial aid. 68% of all full-time freshmen and 63% of continuing full-time students received need-based aid. The average freshman award was $15,546. Need-based scholarships or need-based grants averaged $3,140; need-based self-help aid (loans and jobs) averaged $2,160; non-need-based athletic scholarships averaged $283; and other non-need-based awards and non-need-based scholarships averaged $9,970. 17% of undergraduate students work part-time. Average annual earnings from campus work are $2720. The average financial indebtedness of the 2016 graduate was $35,710. Ferris State is a member of CSS. The FAFSA code is 002260. The priority date for freshman financial aid applications for fall entry is December 1. The filing deadline for fall entry is rolling.

GRACE BIBLE COLLEGE D-4

www.gbcol.edu

Grand Rapids, MI 49509	**(616) 538-2330** **(800) 968-1887**
Fax: (616) 538-2330	**Email: graceadmissions@gbcol.edu**
Full-time: 145 men, 144 women	**Faculty:** 7
Part-time: 6 men, 8 women	**Ph.D.s:** 43%
Graduate: n/av	**Student/Faculty:** 26 to 1
Year: semesters	**Tuition:** $17,850
Room & Board: $7400	**Freshman Class:** 234 applied, 217 accepted, 110 enrolled
SAT CR/M/W: 560/540/500 **ACT:** 21	**CEEB CODE:** 0809
Application Deadline: n/av	**COMPETITIVE**

Grace Bible College, founded in 1939, is a private institution affiliated with the Grace Gospel Fellowship. It's mission is to provide a curriculum that integrates general education and biblical studies and prepares students for service in their career, church, and society. Figures in the above capsule and in this profile are approximate. There is 1 undergraduate school and 1 graduate school. In addition to regional accreditation, GBC has baccalaureate program accreditation with ABHES and AABC. The 21-acre campus is in a suburban area on the southwest side of Grand Rapids. Including any residence halls, there are 21 buildings.

STUDENT LIFE: 80% of undergraduates are from Michigan. Others are from 15 states, and 2 foreign countries. 93% are White; 3% African American; 1% Asian American; 1% Hispanic. 97% are Protestant. **Female To Male Ratio:** 1.0:1. The average age of freshmen is 19; all undergraduates, 21. 21% do not continue beyond their first year; 60% remain to graduate. **Housing:** 240 students can be accommodated in college housing, which includes single-sex dorms, on-campus apartments, and off-campus apartments. On-campus housing is guaranteed for all 4 years. 60% of students live on campus; of those, 75% remain on campus on weekends. Alcohol is not permitted. All students may keep cars.

FACULTY/CLASSROOMS: 72% of faculty are male; 28% are female. All teach undergraduates. No introductory courses are taught by graduate students. The average class size in an introductory lecture is 60 and in a regular course is 16.

PROGRAMS OF STUDY: GBC confers B.S., B.Mus., B.R.E. and B.Th. degrees. Associate and master's degrees are also awarded. Bachelor's degrees are awarded in BUSINESS (business administration and management), COMMUNICATIONS AND THE ARTS (music), EDUCATION (elementary education and secondary education), SOCIAL SCIENCE (biblical studies, criminal justice, early childhood studies, human services, interdisciplinary studies, missions, pastoral studies, religious education, and youth ministry). Youth Ministry, worship arts, and human services have the largest enrollments.

ACTIVITIES: There are no fraternities or sororities. Groups on campus include cheerleading, choir, drama, jazz band, musical theater, religious, and student government. Popular campus events include Winter Formal, Missions Conference, and Campus Service Days. **Sports:** There are 3 intercollegiate sports for men and 4 for women. Facilities include a 300-seat soccer field and an athletic center with a 500-seat gym for basketball and volleyball, a racquetball court, and an exercise and weight room. **Graduates:** From July 1, 2015 to June 30, 2016, 31 bachelor's degrees were awarded. The most popular majors were education (33%), youth and pastoral ministries (17%), and visual performing arts and digital media (17%). In an average class, 20% graduate in 3 years or less, 46% graduate in 4 years or less, 62% graduate in 5 years or less, and 75% graduate in 6 years or less.

SERVICES: Counseling and information services are available, as is tutoring in most subjects. There is remedial writing. **Library/Resources:** The library contains 42,867 volumes, 53 microform items, and 2,582 audio/video tapes/CDs/DVDs, and subscribes to 54,292 periodicals including electronic. Computerized library services include interlibrary loans, database searching, Internet access, and Wi-Fi capability. **Physically Challenged Students:** 85% of the campus is accessible. Facilities include wheelchair ramps, elevators, special parking, specially equipped restrooms, and lowered drinking fountains. **Special:** Cross-registration is available with Cornerstone and Davenport Universities. GBC offers 6-month internships for theology majors. Most 4-year degree programs require a semester practicum. **Visiting:** There are regularly scheduled orientations for prospective students, consisting of 7 Friday programs a year that include workshops, class visits, and campus tours. There are guides for informal visits, visitors may sit in on classes, and stay overnight. To schedule a visit, contact Lizz Niles at lniles@gbcol.edu. **Campus Safety and Security:** Measures include emergency notification system and security escort services. There are lighted pathways/sidewalks, controlled access to dorms/residences, an evening and overnight foot patrol.

REQUIREMENTS: The ACT is preferred. Applicants must be graduates of accredited secondary schools or have earned a GED. The application must show involvement in Christian activities and personal salvation through Jesus Christ. GBC requires applicants to be in the upper 50% of their class. AP and CLEP credits are accepted. To graduate, students must complete 126 to 158 credits, depending on the major, with a minimum GPA of 2.0 and must be considered worthy in character and conduct by the faculty. Course work is required in arts and sciences, ministry studies, Bible/theology, math/computer science, lab science, and phys ed. Attendance is expected at worship services twice a week. **Procedure:** Freshmen are admitted fall and spring. There is a rolling admissions plan. Application deadlines are open. Applications are accepted on-line. Application fees are waived if application is completed on-line. **Transfer Students:** 20 transfer students enrolled in 2015-2016. Applicants must present a GPA of 2.0 and be in good standing at their previous school. Those with fewer than 24 college credit hours must submit high school records. 63 of 126 credits required for the bachelor's degree must be completed at GBC. **International Students:** They must take the TOEFL.

ADMISSIONS: 93% of the 2016-2017 applicants were accepted. The SAT scores for the 2016-2017 freshman class were: Critical Reading-- 35% below 500 and 66% between 500 and 599. Math-- 34% below 500 and 66% between 500 and 599. Writing-- 34% below 500, 33% between 500 and 599, and 33% between 600 and 699. The ACT scores were 20% between 12 and 17, 70% between 18 and 23, 7% between 24 and 29, and 3% above 30. 32% of the current freshmen were in the top fifth of their class; 41% were in the top two fifths. **Admissions Contact:** Kevin Gilliam, Associate Vice President of Enrollment. Email: *graceadmissions@gbcol.edu* Web: *www.gbcol.edu*

FINANCIAL AID: In 2016-2017, 98% of all full-time freshmen and 97% of continuing full-time students received some form of financial aid. 74% of all full-time freshmen and 81% of continuing full-time students received need-based aid. The average freshman award was $7,780. Need-based scholarships or need-based grants averaged $3,383 ($5,350 maximum); need-based self-help aid (loans and jobs) averaged $2,063 ($3,500 maximum); and other non-need-based awards and non-need-based scholarships averaged $3,946 ($4,500 maximum). 43% of undergraduate students work part-time. Average annual earnings from campus work are $2300. The average financial indebtedness of the 2016 graduate was $16,689. The FAFSA code is 002265. The priority date for freshman financial aid applications for fall entry is February 1.

GRAND RAPIDS THEOLOGICAL SEMINARY/CORNERSTONE UNIVERSITY D-4

www.cornerstone.edu

Grand Rapids, MI 49525 (616) 222-1426
(800) 787-9778
Fax: (616) 222-1418 Email: admissions@cornerstone.edu

Full-time: 600 men, 881 women	**Faculty:** 55
Part-time: 251 men, 420 women	**Ph.D.s:** 40%
Graduate: 327 men, 291 women	**Student/Faculty:** 21 to 1
Year: semesters, summer session	**Tuition:** $25,112
Room & Board: $8226	**Freshman Class:** 1962 applied, 1648 accepted, 303 enrolled
SAT CR/M/W: 544/529/504 **ACT:** 23	**CEEB CODE:** 1253
Application Deadline: August 15	**COMPETITIVE**

Grand Rapids Theological Seminary/Cornerstone University, founded in 1941, is a private liberal arts college and graduate seminary educating students from a Christian perspective. Major undergraduate programs include business, media studies, teacher education, and religion. There are 3 undergraduate schools and 2 graduate schools. In addition to regional accreditation, Cornerstone University has baccalaureate program accreditation with CSWE, NASM, ATS, NASM, and CSWE. The 132-acre campus is in a suburban area on the northeast side of Grand Rapids. Including any residence halls, there are 37 buildings.

STUDENT LIFE: 85% of undergraduates are from Michigan. Others are from 37 states, 30 foreign countries, and Canada. 62% are from public schools. 9% are African American; 84% White; 3% Hispanic; 2% Asian American; 1% American Indian/Alaska Native; 1% Foreign. 66% are Protestant. **Female To Male Ratio:** 1.4:1. The average age of freshmen is 18; all undergraduates, 24. 22% do not continue beyond their first year; 48% remain to graduate. **Housing:** 880 students can be accommodated in college housing, which includes single-sex dorms, on-campus apartments, married student housing, and honors houses. On-campus housing is guaranteed for the freshman year only, and is available on a first-come, and first-served basis. Priority is given to out-of-town students. 65% of students live on campus; of those, 50% remain on campus on weekends. Alcohol is not permitted. All students may keep cars.

FACULTY/CLASSROOMS: 67% of faculty are male; 33% are female. All teach undergraduates, 50% do research, and 50% do both. No introductory courses are taught by graduate students. The average class size in an introductory lecture is 60; in a laboratory is 24; and in a regular course is 21.

PROGRAMS OF STUDY: Cornerstone University confers B.A., B.Mus., and B.S. degrees. Associate and master's degrees are also awarded. Bachelor's degrees are awarded in BIOLOGICAL SCIENCE (biology/biological science), BUSINESS (accounting, business administration and management, international business management, international economics, marketing/retailing/merchandising, and sports management), COMMUNICATIONS AND THE ARTS (advertising, applied music, audio technology, communications, English, English Writing, fine arts, graphic design, literature, media arts, music, music performance, musical theater, speech/debate/rhetoric, and video), COMPUTER AND PHYSICAL SCIENCE (chemistry), EDUCATION (education, elementary education, English education, middle school education, music education, physical education, science education, and secondary education), HEALTH PROFESSIONS (exercise science, pre-health studies, predentistry, premedicine, and preveterinary science), SOCIAL SCIENCE (biblical studies, Christian studies, family/consumer studies, history, humanities, interdisciplinary studies, liberal arts/general studies, philosophy, psychology, religion, religious education, social work, and youth ministry). English, music, and education are the strongest academically. Education, business, psychology, and media/film have the largest enrollments.

ACTIVITIES: There are no fraternities or sororities. There are 22 groups on campus, including band, cheerleading, choir, chorale, chorus, dance, drama, environmental, ethnic, film, honors, international, jazz band, musical theater, newspaper, orchestra, pep band, photography, political, professional, radio and TV, religious, social, social service, student government, and symphony. Popular campus events include Sibling Weekends, Friends Weekend and Variety Show. **Sports:** There are 5 intercollegiate sports for men and 5 for women, and 4 intramural sports for men and 4 for women. Facilities include a basketball/volleyball arena, tennis, volleyball, basketball, soccer, and softball, a baseball diamond, soccer fields/intramural fields, a softball field, a sand volleyball court, a fitness center, a training room, and racquetball courts. **Graduates:** From July 1, 2015 to June 30, 2016, 461 bachelor's degrees were awarded. The most popular majors were business (45%), psychology (12%), and education (8%). 30 companies recruited on campus in 2015-2016. In an average class, 30% graduate in 4 years or less, 43% graduate in 5 years or less, and 48% graduate in 6 years or less. Of the 2015 graduating class, 8% were enrolled in graduate school within 6 months of graduation, and 91% were employed.

SERVICES: Counseling and information services are available, as is tutoring in every subject. There is also a Learning Center with a computer lab and special adaptive software that specialize in writing and math, tutoring by appointment in the residence halls, test-taking assistance, and readers and typists as needed. There is a reader service for the blind, and remedial math and writing. **Library/Resources:** The library contains 375,000 volumes, 276,107 microform items, 5,226 audio/video tapes/CDs/DVDs, and subscribes to 39,500 periodicals including electronic. Computerized library services include interlibrary loans, database searching, Internet access, and Wi-Fi capability. Special learning facilities include a radio station, the Center for Excellence in Teaching and Learning, and the Cornerstone University Learning Center. **Physically Challenged Students:** All of the campus is accessible. Facilities include wheelchair ramps, elevators, special parking, specially equipped restrooms, special class scheduling, special housing. large computer monitors for the visually impaired, and soundproof rooms for using tape recorders that read books-on-tape. **Special:** All students choose a student-ministries assignment each semester. Cornerstone requires internships in many areas of study. Study abroad programs, accelerated degrees in organizational leadership, management, business administration, ministry leadership, and education, and a Washington semester are available. There are 3 national honor societies, Phi Beta Kappa, a freshman honors program, and 3 departmental honors programs. **Visiting:** There are regularly scheduled orientations for prospective students, Admissions and financial aid presentations, class visits, meeting with a faculty member, and course preregistration. There are guides for informal visits, visitors may sit in on classes, and stay overnight. To schedule a visit, contact Kayleigh Boston, Admissions Office. **Campus Safety and Security:** Measures include 24-hour foot and vehicle patrol, emergency notification system, self-defense education, security escort services, emergency telephones, lighted pathways/sidewalks, and controlled access to dorms/residences.

REQUIREMENTS: The college requires an official high school transcript or GED certificate with a minimum 2.5 high school GPA. Either an ACT or SAT score must be submitted, with a minimum score of 19 for the ACT and a minimum score of 1350 (total) for the SAT. A reference from a pastor or other Christian leader is required. Auditions are required for music scholarships. In addition, the following program is recommended for college preparation: 14 Carnegie units (including 4 years of English, 3 each of math and social sciences, 2 each of science and foreign language), as well as 8 semesters of academic electives. AP and CLEP credits are accepted. Important factors in the admissions decision are personality/intangible qualities, advanced placement or honors courses, and extracurricular activities record. To graduate, students must complete 120 to 129 credit hours depending on the degree, including 46 in the liberal arts core. The number of hours in the major varies. The student must have an overall GPA of 2.0, 2.5 in the major, 2.0 in the minor, and pass a comprehensive exam in his or her field. **Procedure:** Freshmen are admitted to all sessions. Entrance exams should be taken during the junior or senior year of high school. There are deferred admissions and rolling admissions plans. Applications should be filed by August 15 for fall entry; January 15 for spring entry, along with a $25 fee. Application fees are waived if application is completed online. **Transfer Students:** 37 transfer students enrolled in 2015-2016. The college requires official college transcript(s) from students (minimum college GPA of 2.0), as well as a reference from a pastor or other Christian leader. In addition, if the applicant has fewer than 24 hours of college credit, an official high school transcript is required (minimum high school GPA of 2.5) and official ACT or SAT scores (minimum ACT score of 19, SAT score of 1350). 32 of 120 credits required for the bachelor's degree must be completed at Cornerstone University. **International Students:** There are 49 international students enrolled. The school actively recruits these students. They must take the TOEFL with a minimum score of 500 on the paper-based TOEFL (PBT) or 61 on the Internet-based version (iBT). They must also take the SAT or ACT, scoring 900.

ADMISSIONS: 84% of the 2016-2017 applicants were accepted. The

SAT scores for the 2016-2017 freshman class were: Critical Reading-- 31% below 500, 34% between 500 and 599, 31% between 600 and 699, and 3% between 700 and 800. Math-- 34% below 500, 46% between 500 and 599, 17% between 600 and 699, and 3% between 700 and 800. Writing-- 20% below 500, 23% between 500 and 599, and 6% between 600 and 699. The ACT scores were 27% below 12, 30% between 12 and 17, 26% between 18 and 23, 9% between 24 and 29, and 8% above 30. 31% of the current freshmen were in the top fifth of their class; 64% were in the top two fifths. 5 freshmen graduated first in their class. **Admissions Contact:** Lisa Link, Director of Admissions. Email: *admissions@cornerstone.edu* Web: *www.cornerstone.edu*

FINANCIAL AID: In 2016-2017, 100% of all full-time freshmen and 98% of continuing full-time students received some form of financial aid. 85% of all full-time freshmen and 81% of continuing full-time students received need-based aid. The average freshman award was $23,811. Need-based scholarships or need-based grants averaged $15,028 ($36,098 maximum); need-based self-help aid (loans and jobs) averaged $2,366 ($5,500 maximum); non-need-based athletic scholarships averaged $1,069 ($15,000 maximum); and other non-need-based awards and non-need-based scholarships averaged $5,348 ($20,306 maximum). 34% of undergraduate students work part-time. Average annual earnings from campus work are $1011. The average financial indebtedness of the 2016 graduate was $27,919. The priority date for freshman financial aid applications for fall entry is March 1.

GRAND VALLEY STATE UNIVERSITY D-4

www.gvsu.edu

Allendale, MI 49401	**(616) 331-5000** **(800) 748-0246**
Fax: (616) 331-2000	**Email: admissions@gvsu.edu**
Full-time: 7699 men, 10964 women	**Faculty:** 1069; IIA, av$
Part-time: 1136 men, 1432 women	**Ph.D.s:** 78%
Graduate: 1102 men, 2235 women	**Student/Faculty:** 17 to 1
Year: semesters, summer session	**Tuition:** $14,220
Room & Board: $8030	**Freshman Class:** 17880 applied, 14596 accepted, 3966 enrolled
SAT: required **ACT:** 24	**CEEB CODE:** 1258
Application Deadline: July 23	**COMPETITIVE+**

Grand Valley State University, founded in 1960, is a comprehensive public institution offering graduate and undergraduate liberal arts and professional education. Figures in the above capsule and in this profile are approximate. There are 8 undergraduate schools and 7 graduate schools. In addition to regional accreditation, GVSU has baccalaureate program accreditation with AACSB, ABET, APTA, CSWE, NASAD, NASM, NCATE, and NLN. The 1342-acre campus is in a small town 12 miles west of Grand Rapids. Including any residence halls, there are 72 buildings.

STUDENT LIFE: 95% of undergraduates are from Michigan. Others are from 40 states, 73 foreign countries, and Canada. 75% are from public schools. 91% are White; 7% African American; 4% Hispanic; 4% two or more races; 3% Asian American; 2% American Indian/Alaska Native; 1% Foreign; 1% race unknown. **Female To Male Ratio:** 1.5:1. The average age of freshmen is 18; all undergraduates, 21. 18% do not continue beyond their first year; 56% remain to graduate. **Housing:** 5820 students can be accommodated in college housing, which includes single-sex and coed dorms, on-campus apartments, off-campus apartments, married student housing, honors houses, language houses, special-interest houses, fraternity houses, and sorority houses. On-campus housing is guaranteed for the freshman year only, and is available on a first-come, first-served basis, and is available on a lottery system for upperclassmen. Priority is given to out-of-town students. 73% of students commute. All students may keep cars. Alcohol is not permitted.

FACULTY/CLASSROOMS: 51% of faculty are male; 49% are female. 97% teach undergraduates. No introductory courses are taught by graduate students. The average class size in an introductory lecture is 37; in a laboratory is 21; and in a regular course is 27.

PROGRAMS OF STUDY: GVSU confers B.A., B.S., B.B.A., B.F.A., B.M., B.M.E., B.S.E., B.S.N. and B.S.W. degrees. Master's and doctoral degrees are also awarded. Bachelor's degrees are awarded in AGRICULTURE (natural resource management), BIOLOGICAL SCIENCE (biology/biological science and cell biology), BUSINESS (accounting, banking and finance, business administration and management, business economics, hotel/motel and restaurant management, international business management, management science, marketing/retailing/merchandising, and personnel management), COMMUNICATIONS AND THE ARTS (advertising, art, art history and appreciation, broadcasting, Chinese, classics, communications, creative writing, dance, design, dramatic arts, English, film arts, fine arts, French, German, journalism, languages, music, photography, and Spanish), COMPUTER AND PHYSICAL SCIENCE (chemistry, computer science, earth science, geochemistry, geology, information sciences and systems, mathematics, physics, science, and statistics), EDUCATION (art education, athletic training, elementary education, foreign languages education, middle school education, music education, science education, secondary education, and special education), ENGINEERING AND ENVIRONMENTAL DESIGN (engineering, industrial engineering technology, and occupational safety and health), HEALTH PROFESSIONS (biomedical science, clinical science, exercise science, health science, medical laboratory technology, nursing, physical therapy, physician's assistant, predentistry, premedicine, and recreation therapy), SOCIAL SCIENCE (anthropology, behavioral science, biopsychology, criminal justice, economics, geography, history, international relations, law, liberal arts/general studies, philosophy, political science/government, prelaw, psychology, public administration, Russian and Slavic studies, social science, social work, and sociology). Health sciences, English, and psychology have the largest enrollments.

ACTIVITIES: 5% of women belong to 10 national sororities. There are 250 groups on campus, including art, band, cheerleading, chess, choir, chorale, chorus, computers, dance, drama, environmental, ethnic, film, honors, international, jazz band, LGBT, literary magazine, marching band, musical theater, newspaper, opera, orchestra, pep band, photography, political, professional, radio and TV, religious, social, social service, student government, and symphony. Popular campus events include Family Day, Hispanic Awareness Week and Black History Month. **Sports:** There are 9 intercollegiate sports for men and 10 for women, and 26 intramural sports for men and 26 for women. Facilities include a football stadium, a baseball field, a basketball arena, swimming and diving pools, an indoor track, a weight room, a fitness building/intramural center, an outdoor cross-country track, and an outdoor soccer field. **Graduates:** From July 1, 2015 to June 30, 2016, 4301 bachelor's degrees were awarded. The most popular majors were business/marketing (16%), biological/life sciences (9%), and health sciences (8%). 192 companies recruited on campus in 2015-2016. In an average class, 30% graduate in 4 years or less, 56% graduate in 5 years or less, and 63% graduate in 6 years or less. Of the 2015 graduating class, 25% were enrolled in graduate school within 6 months of graduation, and 79% were employed.

SERVICES: Counseling and information services are available, as is tutoring in most subjects, a reader service for the blind, and remedial math, reading, and writing. **Library/Resources:** The 2 libraries contain 708,000 volumes, 868,850 microform items, 19,804 audio/video tapes/CDs/DVDs, and subscribe to 73,759 periodicals including electronic. Computerized library services include interlibrary loans, database searching, Internet access, and Wi-Fi capability. Special learning facilities include an art gallery, radio station, TV station, a cadaver lab, 2 Great Lakes research vessels, a performance auditorium, and dance studios. **Physically Challenged Students:** 98% of the campus is accessible. Facilities include wheelchair ramps, elevators, special parking, specially equipped restrooms, special class scheduling, lowered drinking fountains, and lowered telephones. **Special:** Many programs offer dual majors and internships, and most majors qualify for B.A.-B.S. degrees. There is an engineering cooperative program, a student-designed major in liberal studies, and many work-study programs. Outside opportunities include study abroad in 10 countries and a Washington semester. There are 14 national honor societies, a freshman honors program, and 12 departmental honors programs. **Visiting:** There are regularly scheduled orientations for prospective students, including registration activities. There are guides for informal visits, visitors may sit in on classes, and stay overnight. To schedule a visit, contact the Admissions Office. **Campus Safety and Security:** Measures include 24-hour foot and vehicle patrol, emergency notification system, self-defense education, and security escort services. There are also shuttle buses, emergency telephones, and lighted pathways/sidewalks.

REQUIREMENTS: Michigan residents must submit ACT test scores, nonresidents either ACT or SAT scores. In addition, high school transcripts should indicate 4 years of English with 1 composition course, 3 each of math (including 2 years of algebra), science (including 1 lab), and social studies, and 2 of a foreign language. Applicants who graduated from high school more than 3 years ago need not show test results. The GED is accepted. A GPA of 3.0 is required. AP and CLEP credits are accepted. Important factors in the admissions decision are extracurricular activities record, recommendations by school officials, and advanced placement or honors courses. To graduate, students must have earned 30 credits in general education, composed of 10 courses selected from specific groups, and have completed the university's required courses in English and math, as well as the upper-division writing course. A total of 120 credits, with 36 to 60 in the major, and a GPA of 2.0, are required to graduate. **Procedure:** Freshmen are admitted to all sessions. Entrance exams should be taken during the junior year. There is a rolling admissions plan. Applications should be filed by July 23 for fall entry, along with a $30 fee. Notification is sent on a rolling basis. Applications are accepted online. **Transfer Students:** 1800 transfer students enrolled in 2015-2016. Transfer students must have a minimum of 30 college credits with a 2.0 GPA. They must submit previous college transcripts and a statement of good standing from prior institutions. 30 of 120 credits required for the bachelor's degree must be completed at GVSU. **International Students:** There are 272 international students enrolled. The school actively recruits these students. They must take the TOEFL with a minimum score of 550 on the paper-based TOEFL (PBT) or 80 on the Internet-based version (iBT) or take the MELAB and the Comprehensive English Language Test. They must also take the SAT or ACT.

ADMISSIONS: 82% of the 2016-2017 applicants were accepted. The ACT scores were 19% below 12, 31% between 12 and 17, 28% between 18 and 23, 12% between 24 and 29, and 10% above 30. 45% of the current freshmen were in the top fifth of their class; 80% were in the top two fifths. 18 freshmen graduated first in their class. **Admissions Contact:** Jodi Chycinski, Director of Admissions. Email: *admissions@gvsu.edu* Web: *www.gvsu.edu*

FINANCIAL AID: In 2016-2017, 67% of all full-time freshmen and 65% of continuing full-time students received some form of financial aid. 60% of all full-time freshmen and 59% of continuing full-time students received need-based aid. The average freshman award was $10,949. Need-based scholarships or need-based grants averaged $7,469; and need-based self-help aid (loans and jobs) averaged $4,937. 12% of undergraduate students work part-time. Average annual earnings from campus work are $3330. The average financial indebtedness of the 2016 graduate was $24,876. GVSU is a member of CSS. The FAFSA code is 002268. The deadline for filing freshman financial aid applications for fall entry is February 15.

HILLSDALE COLLEGE D-5

www.hillsdale.edu

Hillsdale, MI 49242 (517) 607-2327

Fax: (517) 607-2223 Email: admissions@hillsdale.edu

Full-time: 725 men, 715 women	**Faculty:** 127
Part-time: 2 men, 23 women	**Ph.D.s:** 95%
Graduate: 29 men, 11 women	**Student/Faculty:** 11 to 1
Year: semesters, summer session	**Tuition:** $25,522
Room & Board: $10,200	**Freshman Class:** 1934 applied, 874 accepted, 377 enrolled
SAT CR/M/W: 680/640/660 **ACT:** 31	**CEEB CODE:** 1295
Application Deadline: April 1	**MOST COMPETITIVE**

Hillsdale College distinguishes itself from most other academic institutions by its rigorous, traditional, liberal arts core curriculum and its principled determination never to accept federal taxpayer funding. Hillsdale's core curriculum contains the essence of the classical liberal arts education. Through it, our students are introduced to the history, the philosophical and theological ideas, the works of literature, and the scientific discoveries that set Western Civilization apart. As explained in Hillsdale mission statement, "The College considers itself a trustee of modern man's intellectual and spiritual inheritance from the Judeo-Christian faith and Greco-Roman culture, a heritage finding its clearest expression in the American experiment of self-government under law". There is 1 undergraduate school and 1 graduate school. The 400-acre campus is in a small town 120 miles southwest of Detroit. Including any residence halls, there are 75 buildings.

STUDENT LIFE: 65% of undergraduates are from out of state, mostly the Midwest. Students are from 48 states, 13 foreign countries, and Canada. 56% are from public schools. 100% are race unknown **Male To Female Ratio:** 1.0:1. The average age of freshmen is 18; all undergraduates, 20. 5% do not continue beyond their first year; 83% remain to graduate. **Housing:** 1081 students can be accommodated in college housing, which includes single-sex dorms, on-campus apartments, honors houses, fraternity houses, and sorority houses. On-campus housing is guaranteed for all 4 years. 69% of students live on campus; of those, 95% remain on campus on weekends. All students may keep cars. Alcohol is not permitted.

FACULTY/CLASSROOMS: 74% of faculty are male; 26% are female. All teach undergraduates. No introductory courses are taught by graduate students. The average class size in an introductory lecture is 32; in a laboratory is 13; and in a regular course is 17.

PROGRAMS OF STUDY: Hillsdale confers B.A. and B.S. degrees. Master's and doctoral degrees are also awarded. Bachelor's degrees are awarded in BIOLOGICAL SCIENCE (biochemistry and biology/biological science), BUSINESS (accounting, finance, international business management, marketing/retailing/merchandising, and sports management), COMMUNICATIONS AND THE ARTS (art, classics, comparative literature, English, French, German, Greek, Latin, music, Spanish, speech/debate/rhetoric, and theatre arts), COMPUTER AND PHYSICAL SCIENCE (applied mathematics, chemistry, mathematics, and physics), EDUCATION (physical education), HEALTH PROFESSIONS (exercise science and sports psychology), SOCIAL SCIENCE (American studies, Christian studies, economics, European studies, history, philosophy, philosophy and religion, political science/government, psychology, religion, and sociology). Biology, business, economics, English, and history are the strongest academically. Economics, English, and history have the largest enrollments.

ACTIVITIES: There are 143 groups on campus, including art, band, cheerleading, chess, choir, chorale, chorus, communications, computers, dance, debate, drama, ethnic, film, forensics, honors, international, jazz band, literary magazine, musical theater, newspaper, opera, orchestra, pep band, photography, political, professional, radio and TV, religious, social, social service, student government, symphony, and yearbook. Popular campus events include Centralhallapalooza, President's Ball, Mock Rock, Garden Party, Welcome Party, and Kickoff Cookout. **Sports:** There are 13 intercollegiate sports for men and 11 for women, and 10 intramural sports for men and 10 for women. Facilities include an athletic complex with a football field, swimming pool, indoor track and tennis facility, a basketball arena, weight room, outdoor track, an exercise/physiology room, and volleyball, handball, racquetball, and wallyball courts. **Graduates:** From July 1, 2015 to June 30, 2016, 345 bachelor's degrees were awarded. The most popular majors were English (12%), history (11%), and economics (10%). 74 companies recruited on campus in 2015-2016. In an average class, 3% graduate in 3 years or less, 73% graduate in 4 years or less, 83% graduate in 5 years or less, and 83% graduate in 6 years or less.

SERVICES: Counseling and information services are available, as is tutoring in every subject. **Library/Resources:** The library contains 268,001 volumes, 56,805 microform items, and 21,801 audio/video tapes/CDs/DVDs, subscribes to 86,687 periodicals including electronic. Computerized library services include interlibrary loans, database searching, Internet access, and Wi-Fi capability. Special learning facilities include an art gallery, natural history museum, radio station, auditorium, recreational area, greenhouse, music hall, media center, K-8 private academy, arboretum, rare books library, shooting range, science building, science center, and preschool. **Physically Challenged Students:** 85% of the campus is accessible. Facilities include wheelchair ramps, elevators, special parking, specially equipped restrooms, lowered drinking fountains, special housing. Special accommodations according to individual needs. **Special:** Special academic programs include the Washington Journalism Internship at the National Journalism Center and the Washington-Hillsdale Intern Program (WHIP), which places students in congressional or government offices. Students may study abroad in France, Germany, or Spain, and qualified students are chosen to attend Oxford University for a year. A business internship is offered in London at Regents College. The Thomas Professional Sales Intern program is also available. The college offers an accelerated degree; interdisciplinary majors, including political economy combining economics, history, and political science; 3-2 and 2-2 engineering degrees; and work-study programs at the city radio station WCSR and the city newspaper, the Hillsdale Daily News. There are 33 national honor societies and 26 departmental honors programs. **Visiting:** There are regularly scheduled orientations for prospective students, agenda is customized based on visitor request; almost all visits include a campus tour and meeting with an Admissions Representative. Visitors may sit in on classes and stay overnight. To schedule a visit, contact Margaret Braman in Admissions. **Campus Safety and Security:** Measures include 24-hour foot and vehicle patrol, emergency notification system, self-defense education, and security escort services. There are also shuttle buses, emergency telephones, lighted pathways/sidewalks, and controlled access to dorms/residences.

REQUIREMENTS: The student must be a high school graduate or have earned a GED, and also completed 4 years of English, 3 each of math and science, and 2 each of history, social studies, and foreign language. The ACT or SAT is required. The college requires 2 letters of recommendation and an essay. An interview is also recommended. For music majors, an audition is required for a scholarship. For art majors, a portfolio must be submitted for review. The school recommends taking SAT: Subject tests, but they are not required. Some AP/CLEP credits do count as college credit. AP and CLEP credits are accepted. Important factors in the admissions decision are advanced placement or honors courses, leadership record, and extracurricular activities record. To graduate, the student must complete 124 semester hours with a GPA of 2.0. Required courses include 1 year of English, 1 year of science, 1 semester of Western Heritage and 1 semester of American Heritage, 1 semester of political science, 15 hours of the humanities, 12 of the natural sciences and math, 12 of the social sciences, and 2 of phys ed. Students must also enroll in 2 seminars at the school's Center for Constructive Alternatives. 12 credit hours in a foreign language for a B.A. degree and 34 credit hours in math and science for a B.S. degree are also required. **Procedure:** Freshmen are admitted in the fall and spring. Entrance exams should be taken spring junior year, fall senior year. There is a early decision plan. Early decision applications should be filed by November 1; regular applications, by April 1 for fall entry; and December 1 for spring entry, along with a $35 fee. Notification of early decision is sent December 1; regular decision, on a rolling basis. 119 early decision candidates were accepted for the 2016-2017 class. 16 applicants were on the 2016 waiting list; 4 were admitted. Applications are accepted on-line. Application fees are waived if application is completed online. **Transfer Students:** 12 transfer students enrolled in 2015-2016. high school transcript, college transcripts, essay or personal statement, standardized test scores, statement of good standing from prior institution. **International Students:** There are 23 international students enrolled. The school actively recruits these students. They must also take the SAT or ACT.

ADMISSIONS: 45% of the 2016-2017 applicants were accepted. The SAT scores for the 2016-2017 freshman class were: Critical Reading-- 2% below 500, 11% between 500 and 599, 42% between 600 and 699, and 45% between 700 and 800. Math-- 5% below 500, 25% between 500 and 599, 46% between 600 and 699, and 24% between 700 and 800. Writing-- 20% between 500 and 599, 46% between 600 and 699, and 34% between 700 and 800. The ACT scores were 1% between 18 and 23, 40% between 24 and 29, and 59% above 30. There were 7 National Merit finalists. **Admissions Contact:** Doug Banbury, Associate VP of Admissions. Email: *admissions@hillsdale.edu* Web: *www.hillsdale.edu*

FINANCIAL AID: In 2016-2017, 97% of all full-time freshmen and 98% of continuing full-time students received some form of financial aid. 39% of all full-time freshmen and 40% of continuing full-time students received need-based aid. The average freshman award was $20,071. Need-based scholarships or need-based grants averaged $6,960 ($12,335 maximum); need-based self-help aid (loans and jobs) averaged $5,437 ($11,000 maximum); non-need-based athletic scholarships averaged $10,723 ($36,922 maximum); and other non-need-based awards and non-need-based scholarships averaged $15,745 ($24,670 maximum). 67% of undergraduate students work part-time. Average annual earnings from campus work are $1344. The average financial indebtedness of the 2016 graduate was $23,981. Hillsdale is a member of CSS. The CSS/Profile and the college's own financial statement are required. The priority date for freshman financial aid applications for fall entry is rolling. The filing deadline for fall entry is April 1.

HOPE COLLEGE C-4

www.hope.edu

Holland, MI 49422 (616) 395-7850
(800) 968-7850
Fax: (616) 395-7130
Email: admissions@hope.edu

Full-time: 1282 men, 1959 women	**Faculty:** 243; IIB, av$
Part-time: 74 men, 89 women	**Ph.D.s:** 76%
Graduate: n/av	**Student/Faculty:** 12 to 1
Year: semesters, summer session	**Tuition:** $30,550
Room & Board: $9390	**Freshman Class:** 4720 applied, 3184 accepted, 794 enrolled
	CEEB CODE: 1301
Application Deadline: open	**VERY COMPETITIVE**

Hope College, founded by Dutch pioneers in 1866, is a private liberal arts institution affiliated with the Reformed Church in America. There are 4 undergraduate schools. In addition to regional accreditation, Hope has baccalaureate program accreditation with ABET, CSWE, NASAD, NASM, TEAC, ACS, CCNE, NASD, NAST, and CAATE. The 120-acre campus is in an urban area 26 miles southwest of Grand Rapids and 5 miles east of Lake Michigan. Including any residence halls, there are 133 buildings.

STUDENT LIFE: 67% of undergraduates are from Michigan. Others are from 41 states, 37 foreign countries, and Canada. 77% are from public schools. 83% are White; 8% Hispanic; 3% African American; 2% Asian American; 2% Foreign; 2% two or more races. 30% are Protestant; 26% unknown denominations; 18% Catholic; 16% claim no religious affiliation. **Female To Male Ratio:** 1.5:1. The average age of freshmen is 18; all undergraduates, 20. 10% do not continue beyond their first year; 78% remain to graduate. **Housing:** 2636 students can be accommodated in college housing, which includes single-sex and coed dorms, on-campus apartments, and married student housing, language houses, special-interest houses, fraternity houses, sorority houses. Additional accommodations include student cottages. On-campus housing is guaranteed for all 4 years. 78% of students live on campus; of those, 75% remain on campus on weekends. All students may keep cars. Alcohol is not permitted.

FACULTY/CLASSROOMS: 56% of faculty are male; 44% are female. All teach undergraduates. No introductory courses are taught by graduate students. The average class size in an introductory lecture is 21; in a laboratory is 17; and in a regular course is 19.

PROGRAMS OF STUDY: Hope confers B.A., B.S., B.Mus. and B.S.N. degrees. Bachelor's degrees are awarded in BIOLOGICAL SCIENCE (biochemistry, biology/adolescence education, biology/biological science, and cell biology), BUSINESS (accounting and business administration and management), COMMUNICATIONS AND THE ARTS (art, art history and appreciation, classical languages, communications, creative writing, dance, dramatic arts, English, fine arts, French, German, language arts, Latin, music, music performance, piano/organ, piano performance, Spanish, theatre arts, and vocal music education), COMPUTER AND PHYSICAL SCIENCE (chemistry, chemistry education, computer science, geology, mathematics, and physics), EDUCATION (art education, athletic training, dance education, elementary education, English education, foreign languages education, history education, music education, science education, secondary education, and special education), ENGINEERING AND ENVIRONMENTAL DESIGN (engineering), HEALTH PROFESSIONS (exercise science and nursing), SOCIAL SCIENCE (economics, history, international studies, Japanese studies, philosophy, physical fitness/movement, political science/government, psychology, religion, social work, sociology, and women's studies). Chemistry, biological sciences, and psychology are the strongest academically. Management, psychology and biology have the largest enrollments.

ACTIVITIES: 12% of men belong to 7 local and 1 national fraternities; 14% of women belong to 7 local and 1 national sororities. There are 78 groups on campus, including art, band, cheerleading, chess, choir, chorale, chorus, computers, dance, drama, environmental, ethnic, honors, international, jazz band, literary magazine, musical theater, newspaper, orchestra, pep band, political, professional, radio and TV, religious, social, social service, student government, symphony, and yearbook. Popular campus events include The Pull, Spring Festival, and Nykerk Cup Competition. **Sports:** There are 11 intercollegiate sports for men and 11 for women, and 14 intramural sports for men and 15 for women. Facilities include soccer fields, basketball/volleyball courts, a running track, a swimming and diving pool, exercise rooms, dance studios, racquetball courts, weight training, and cardiovascular equipment. **Graduates:** From July 1, 2015 to June 30, 2016, 722 bachelor's degrees were awarded. The most popular majors were managemet (9%), biology (9%), and psychology (8%). 36 companies recruited on campus in 2015-2016. In an average class, 1% graduate in 3 years or less, 69% graduate in 4 years or less, 75% graduate in 5 years or less, and 80% graduate in 6 years or less. Of the 2015 graduating class, 25% were enrolled in graduate school within 6 months of graduation, and 72% were employed.

SERVICES: Counseling and information services are available, as is tutoring in most subjects, and a reader service for the blind. **Library/Resources:** The 2 libraries contain 368,869 volumes, 382,734 microform items, 17,879 audio/video tapes/CDs/DVDs, and subscribe to 7,329 periodicals including electronic. Computerized library services include interlibrary loans, database searching, Internet access, and Wi-Fi capability. Special learning facilities include an art gallery, planetarium, radio station, TV station, an academic support center, and a modern and classical language lab. **Physically Challenged Students:** 95% of the campus is accessible. Facilities include wheelchair ramps, elevators, special parking, specially equipped restrooms, special class scheduling, lowered drinking fountains, and special housing. **Special:** The college offers internships in all academic areas as well as on-campus work-study programs, student-designed majors, study abroad in more than 57 countries, and Washington, Chicago, New York, and Philadelphia semesters. Students may have dual majors. There are 20 national honor societies, Phi Beta Kappa, and 1 departmental honors program. **Visiting:** There are regularly scheduled orientations for prospective students, including tours, classes, lunch with a current student, and appointments with professors. There are guides for informal visits, visitors may sit in on classes, and stay overnight. To schedule a visit, contact the Admissions Office. **Campus Safety and Security:** Measures include 24-hour foot and vehicle patrol and security escort services. There are also shuttle buses, emergency telephones, and lighted pathways/sidewalks.

REQUIREMENTS: All applicants must submit either an ACT or SAT score. The college requires a high school transcript, which must include 4 years of English, 2 each of math, a foreign language, and social science, and 1 year of a lab science, as well as 5 other academic courses. The college requires submission of an essay and recommends an interview. A portfolio or audition is required for certain majors. The GED is considered. AP and CLEP credits are accepted. Important factors in the admissions decision are advanced placement or honors courses, evidence of special talent, and leadership record. To graduate with a B.A. or B.S. degree, students must complete 126 semester hours with a 2.0 GPA. All students must take 56 hours of the general education program, including a first-year seminar, 10 hours of math and natural science, 8 of cultural heritage, 6 each of social science, performing and fine arts, and religion, 4 each of a language and writing, 4 in a senior seminar, 4 credits of cultural diversity courses, and 2 hours of health dynamics. **Procedure:** Freshmen are admitted in the fall and spring. Entrance exams should be taken during spring of the junior year or fall of the senior year. There are deferred admissions and rolling admissions plans. Application deadlines are open. The fall 2016 application fee was $35. Notifications are sent December 3. 820 applicants were on the 2016 waiting list; 174 were admitted. Applications are accepted online. **Transfer Students:** 64 transfer students enrolled in 2015-2016. Transfer students must have a GPA of 2.0 in at least 1 year of liberal arts courses. 30 of 126 credits required for the bachelor's degree must be completed at Hope. **International Students:** There are 95 international students enrolled. The school actively recruits these students. They must take the TOEFL with a minimum score of 79 on the Internet-based version (iBT). They must also take the SAT or ACT.

ADMISSIONS: 67% of the 2016-2017 applicants were accepted. The SAT scores for the 2016-2017 freshman class were: Critical Reading-- 13% below 500, 36% between 500 and 599, 42% between 600 and 699, and 9% between 700 and 800. Math-- 7% below 500, 323% between 500 and 599, 44% between 600 and 699, and 15% between 700 and 800. The ACT scores were 1% between 12 and 17, 24% between 18 and 23, 54% between 24 and 29, and 21% above 30. 60% of the current freshmen were in the top fifth of their class; 89% were in the top two fifths. **Admissions Contact:** William C. Vanderbilt, Vice President for Admissions. Email: *admissions@hope.edu* Web: *www.hope.edu*

FINANCIAL AID: In 2016-2017, 94% of all full-time freshmen and 92% of continuing full-time students received some form of financial aid. 61% of all full-time freshmen and 59% of continuing full-time students received need-based aid. The average freshman award was $18,226. Need-based scholarships or need-based grants averaged $11,066; need-based self-help aid (loans and jobs) averaged $2,520; and other non-need-based awards and non-need-based scholarships averaged $4,249. The average financial indebtedness of the 2016 graduate was $20,600. Hope is a member of CSS. The college's own financial statement is required. The FAFSA code is 002273. The priority date for freshman financial aid applications for fall entry is March 1.

KALAMAZOO COLLEGE — D-5

www.kzoo.edu

Kalamazoo, MI 49006	(269) 337-7166 (800) 253-3602
Fax: (269) 337-7390	**Email:** admissions@kzoo.edu
Full-time: 640 men, 978 women	**Faculty:** 103
Part-time: 2 men, 3 women	**Ph.D.s:** 91%
Graduate: none	**Student/Faculty:** 13 to 1
Year: quarters	**Tuition:** $44,418
Room & Board: $9174	**Freshman Class:** 3469 applied, 2377 accepted, 348 enrolled
SAT CR/M/W: 610/640/610 **ACT:** 28	**CEEB CODE:** 1365
Application Deadline: January 15	**HIGHLY COMPETITIVE+**

As a highly selective, nationally renowned, and internationally oriented four-year college of arts and sciences, Kalamazoo College has developed a tradition of excellence in the fulfillment of this mission. Founded in 1833, "K" College is among the 100 oldest colleges and universities in the nation. There are 5 undergraduate schools. The 60-acre campus is in a suburban area 140 miles from the Detroit and Chicago area. Including any residence halls, there are 30 buildings.

STUDENT LIFE: 61% of undergraduates are from Michigan. Others are from 43 states, and 30 foreign countries. 81% are from public schools. **Female To Male Ratio:** 1.5:1. The average age of freshmen is 18; all undergraduates, 20. 8% do not continue beyond their first year. **Housing:** 875 students can be accommodated in college housing, which includes single-sex and coed dorms, special-interest houses, and a wellness house. On-campus housing is available on a lottery system for upperclassmen. 66% of students live on campus; of those, 75% remain on campus on weekends. Upperclassmen may keep cars.

FACULTY/CLASSROOMS: 48% of faculty are male; 52% are female. All teach undergraduates. No introductory courses are taught by graduate students. The average class size in an introductory lecture is 26; in a laboratory is 14; and in a regular course is 22.

PROGRAMS OF STUDY: Kalamazoo confers B.A. degrees. Bachelor's degrees are awarded in BIOLOGICAL SCIENCE (biochemistry, biology/biological science, and neurosciences), BUSINESS (business economics), COMMUNICATIONS AND THE ARTS (art, art history and appreciation, dramatic arts, English, film, television and digital media, French, German, music, and Spanish), COMPUTER AND PHYSICAL SCIENCE (chemistry, computer science, mathematics, and physics), EDUCATION (physical education), ENGINEERING AND ENVIRONMENTAL DESIGN (engineering and environmental science), HEALTH PROFESSIONS (health science and pre-health studies), SOCIAL SCIENCE (African studies, anthropology, classical/ancient civilization, East Asian studies, economics, ethnic studies, history, human development, interdisciplinary studies, international studies, philosophy, political science/government, psychology, public administration, religion, and sociology). Foreign languages, international studies, and commerce are the strongest academically. Public administration, physical sciences, and biological sciences have the largest enrollments.

ACTIVITIES: There are no fraternities or sororities. There are 70 groups on campus, including art, cheerleading, chess, choir, chorus, computers, dance, drama, environmental, ethnic, film, honors, international, jazz band, LGBT, literary magazine, musical theater, newspaper, orchestra, photography, political, professional, radio and TV, religious, social, social service, student government, and symphony. Popular campus events include Homecoming-dance, pep rally, Monte Carlo-Casino night games and dancing, K-Fest-Student Involvement, and Outdoor Movies. **Sports:** There are 9 intercollegiate sports for men and 9 for women, and 8 intramural sports for men and 7 for women. Facilities include a field house with a gym, basketball and volleyball courts, weight-training rooms, dance studio, tennis courts and racquetball courts, a natatorium, an athletic field complex and field house, turf football and soccer/lacrosse fields, baseball and softball fields. **Graduates:** From July 1, 2015 to June 30, 2016, 348 bachelor's degrees were awarded. The most popular majors were social sciences (18%), biological/life sciences (12%), and psychology (12%). In an average class, 76% graduate in 4 years or less, 81% graduate in 5 years or less, and 83% graduate in 6 years or less.

SERVICES: Counseling and information services are available, as is tutoring in most subjects. There is also a writing center, language labs, and supplemental instructions. **Library/Resources:** The library contains 397,384 volumes, 15,025 microform items, 7,523 audio/video tapes/CDs/DVDs, and subscribes to 1,364 periodicals including electronic. Computerized library services include interlibrary loans, database searching, Internet access, and Wi-Fi capability. Special learning facilities include an art gallery, radio station, and TV station. **Physically Challenged Students:** 25% of the campus is accessible. Facilities include wheelchair ramps, elevators, special parking, specially equipped restrooms, special class scheduling, and special housing. **Special:** Kalamazoo College through the Center for International Programs currently sends students to 59 programs in 25 countries on 6 continents. Over the past four years, the K-College graduate participation rate in our study abroad programs is 80% to 85% and the school allows dual and interdisciplinary majors, and has Inter-Institutional enrollment with Western Michigan University. A 3-2 engineering degree is offered with Washington University and the University of Michigan. There are 3 national honor societies and a chapter of Phi Beta Kappa. **Visiting:** There are regularly scheduled orientations for prospective students, including interviews, tours, overnight and class visits as requested. Special preview events include formal presentation of the unique curriculum and financial aid seminars. There are guides for informal visits, visitors may sit in on classes, and stay overnight. To schedule a visit, contact Sharayl Moore at (877)557-9755. **Campus Safety and Security:** Measures include 24-hour foot and vehicle patrol, emergency notification system, self-defense education, and security escort services, emergency telephones, lighted pathways/sidewalks, and controlled access to dorms/residences.

REQUIREMENTS: The college requires a high school transcript, an essay, supplement and teacher and counselor recommendations; an interview is recommended. Applications are online only. The College is a Common Application exclusive member. AP credits are accepted. Important factors in the admissions decision are recommendations by school officials, leadership record, and advanced placement or honors courses. To graduate, students must complete 36 academic units, including a minimum of 8 units in the major, with a minimum 2.0 GPA. The college requires sophomore and senior seminars and completion of a senior individualized project. The student must also take 5 noncredit courses in phys ed and show proficiency in writing as well as in a foreign language. **Procedure:** Freshmen are admitted fall. Entrance exams should be taken by December of the senior year. There are early decision, early admissions, and deferred admissions plans. Early decision applications should be filed by November 1; regular applications, by January 15 for fall entry. Notification of early decision is sent December 1; regular decision, April 1. 27 early decision candidates were accepted for the 2016-2017 class. 317 applicants were on the 2016 waiting list; 65 were admitted. Application fees are waived if application is completed online. **Transfer Students:** 14 transfer students enrolled in 2015-2016. In addition to the Transfer Application, we require the College Official's Report, Instructor Evaluation, official high school and college transcripts. While an interview is not required, it is strongly recommended. And most cases, successful transfer applicants present grades of a B average or better in their current courses. 18 of 36 credits required for the bachelor's degree must be completed at Kalamazoo. **International Students:** There are 132 international students enrolled. The school actively recruits these students. They must take the TOEFL with a minimum score of 550 on the paper-based TOEFL (PBT) or 84 on the Internet-based version (iBT), or the SAT, IELTS, or IB programs.

ADMISSIONS: 69% of the 2016-2017 applicants were accepted. The SAT scores for the 2016-2017 freshman class were: Critical Reading-- 16% below 500, 29% between 500 and 599, 33% between 600 and 699, and 22% between 700 and 800. Math-- 9% below 500, 22% between 500 and 599, 37% between 600 and 699, and 31% between 700 and 800. Writing-- 13% below 500, 28% between 500 and 599, 39% between 600 and 699, and 19% between 700 and 800. The ACT scores were 2% between 12 and 17, 13% between 18 and 23, 48% between 24 and 29, and 37% above 30. 9 freshmen graduated first in their class. **Admissions Contact:** Eric P. Staab, Dean of Admission. Email: *admissions@kzoo.edu* Web: *www.kzoo.edu*

FINANCIAL AID: In 2016-2017, 98% of all full-time freshmen and continuing full-time students received some form of financial aid. 74% of all full-time freshmen and 67% of continuing full-time students received need-based aid. The average freshman award was $36,012. Need-based scholarships or need-based grants averaged $29,445; need-based self-help aid (loans and jobs) averaged $6,481; and other non-need-based awards and non-need-based scholarships averaged $20,273. The average financial indebtedness of the 2016 graduate was $28,764. The college's own financial statement is required. The FAFSA code is 002275. The priority date for freshman financial aid applications for fall entry is February 15.

KETTERING UNIVERSITY E-4

www.kettering.edu

Flint, MI 48504	**(810) 762-9500** **(800) 955-4464**
Fax: (810) 762-9837	**Email: admissions@kettering.edu**
Full-time: 1438 men, 329 women	**Faculty:** 116; IIB, av$
Part-time: 85 men, 14 women	**Ph.D.s:** 93%
Graduate: 319 men, 103 women	**Student/Faculty:** 14 to 1
Year: semesters, summer session	**Tuition:** $39,790
Room & Board: $7780	**Freshman Class:** 2251 applied, 1617 accepted, 418 enrolled
SAT CR/M: 590/640 **ACT:** 27	**CEEB CODE:** 1246
Application Deadline: n/av	**HIGHLY COMPETITIVE**

Kettering University, is a private college, founded in 1919. Student in the undergraduate program alternate 11-week terms of full-time classes with 12-week terms of full-time paid professional cooperative education (co-op) work experience in industry. Students typically begin co-op during their freshman year and co-op in 43 states and several countries. There are 3 undergraduate schools and 1 graduate school. In addition to regional accreditation, Kettering has baccalaureate program accreditation with ABET and ACBSP. The 85-acre campus is in a suburban area 60 miles north of Detroit. Including any residence halls, there are 10 buildings.

STUDENT LIFE: 66% of undergraduates are from Michigan. Others are from 49 states, 18 foreign countries, and Canada. 85% are from public schools. 75% are White; 6% race unknown; 5% Hispanic; 4% Asian American; 4% Foreign; 3% African American; 3% two or more races. **Male To Female Ratio:** 4.1:1. The average age of freshmen is 18; all undergraduates, 21. 86% do not continue beyond their first year; 64% remain to graduate. **Housing:** 623 students can be accommodated in college housing, which includes coed dorms, on-campus apartments, fraternity houses and sorority houses. On-campus housing is guaranteed for the freshman year only and is available on a lottery system for upperclassmen. Priority is given to out-of-town students. 60% of students commute. All students may keep cars. Alcohol is not permitted.

FACULTY/CLASSROOMS: 80% of faculty are male; 20% are female. All teach undergraduates, 16% do research, and 16% do both. No introductory courses are taught by graduate students. The average class size in an introductory lecture is 40; in a laboratory is 14; and in a regular course is 20.

PROGRAMS OF STUDY: Kettering confers B.S. degrees. Master's degrees are also awarded. Bachelor's degrees are awarded in BIOLOGICAL SCIENCE (biochemistry), COMPUTER AND PHYSICAL SCIENCE (applied mathematics, applied physics, chemistry, and computer science), ENGINEERING AND ENVIRONMENTAL DESIGN (computer engineering, electrical/electronics engineering, engineering physics, industrial engineering, and mechanical engineering). Mechanical, electrical, and computer engineering have the largest enrollments.

ACTIVITIES: 39% of men belong to 13 national fraternities; 32% of women belong to 6 national sororities. There are 43 groups on campus, including art, band, computers, dance, drama, environmental, ethnic, honors, international, LGBT, literary magazine, newspaper, photography, political, professional, radio and TV, religious, social, social service, student government, and yearbook. Popular campus events include Greek Week, Diversity Week, and Student and Alumni Industry Speaker

Series. **Sports:** There is no sports program at Kettering. Facilities include a recreation center with basketball, tennis/basketball/courts, racquetball and squash courts, a track, pool, free weights, Nautilus, fitness room with comprehensive assortment of fitness machines and group exercise room. A sports and recreation complex includes softball, multipurpose fields, a golf green, outdoor track, and sand volleyball courts. **Graduates:** From July 1, 2015 to June 30, 2016, 320 bachelor's degrees were awarded. The most popular majors were engineering (83%), computer and information sciences (8%), and business/marketing (4%). 303 companies recruited on campus in 2015-2016. In an average class, 53% graduate in 6 years or less. Of the 2015 graduating class, 40% were enrolled in graduate school within 6 months of graduation, and 96% were employed.

SERVICES: Counseling and information services are available, as is tutoring in most subjects. Tutoring is routinely available for most subjects in the Academic Support Center. Supplemental tutoring is coordinated through the Academic Services Department. Math and writing labs are available. A Strategies for Academic Success program is also available. **Library/Resources:** The library contains 133,210 volumes, 35,000 microform items, and 800 audio/video tapes/CDs/DVDs, and subscribes to 400 periodicals including electronic. Computerized library services include interlibrary loans, database searching, and Internet access. Special learning facilities include an art gallery, radio station, and an industrial history archives. **Physically Challenged Students:** All of the campus is accessible. Facilities include wheelchair ramps, elevators, special parking, specially equipped restrooms, special class scheduling, lowered drinking fountains, and lowered telephones. **Special:** All undergraduate students participate in paid professional cooperative education work experience. Students may pursue a dual major in any degree combination. Accelerated degree programs in engineering are available in most majors, as is study abroad in 3 countries. There are 8 national honor societies. **Visiting:** There are regularly scheduled orientations for prospective students, including 2 open house programs for prospective students. There are guides for informal visits, visitors may sit in on classes, and stay overnight. To schedule a visit, contact the Admissions Office. **Campus Safety and Security:** Measures include 24-hour foot and vehicle patrol, self-defense education, security escort services, emergency telephones, lighted pathways/sidewalks, controlled access to dorms/residences, and after-hours access is secure via the tunnel from the residence hall and campus center.

REQUIREMENTS: The SAT or ACT is required. Applicants must graduate from an accredited secondary school with a minimum of 10.5 academic credits (21 recommended). Applicants must have completed 3-4 years of English, and math, and 2-3 years of science with lab, 2 years of social studies and history, and 1 year of academic electives AP credits are accepted. Important factors in the admissions decision are extracurricular activities record and advanced placement or honors courses. Degree requirements include completion of 160 credit hours, with 60 in the major. All students must take specific courses in math, chemistry, physics, written and oral communication, humanities, and economics, and complete at least 5 terms of co-op experience in industry plus 2 work terms designated for a senior thesis project. A minimum grade average of 80 on a scale of 100 is required for graduation. The GPA is determined by a formula combining the numerical grades achieved and the number of credits attempted. Students must complete a thesis. **Procedure:** Freshmen are admitted in the fall, winter, and summer. Entrance exams should be taken during the spring of the junior year and fall of the senior year. There are deferred admissions and rolling admissions plans. Application deadlines are open. Notifications are sent December 15. Applications are accepted online. **Transfer Students:** 38 transfer students enrolled in 2015-2016. Transfer applicants must present the same minimum preparation as freshmen in math and science and must submit both high school and college transcripts and SAT or ACT scores. Required courses can be taken in high school or college. A minimum GPA of 3.0 in English, math, and science is expected. Transfers who present less than 30 credits of full-time study will be judged on both their college and high school record and test scores. 88 of 160 credits required for the bachelor's degree must be completed at Kettering. **International Students:** There are 33 international students enrolled. The school actively recruits these students. They must take the TOEFL or MELAB.

ADMISSIONS: 72% of the 2016-2017 applicants were accepted. The SAT scores for the 2016-2017 freshman class were: Critical Reading-- 4% below 500, 50% between 500 and 599, 33% between 600 and 699, and 13% between 700 and 800. Math-- 4% below 500, 30% between 500 and 599, 39% between 600 and 699, and 26% between 700 and 800. The ACT scores were 10% between 18 and 23, 66% between 24 and 29, and 35% above 30. 64% of the current freshmen were in the top fifth of their class; 94% were in the top two fifths. 18 freshmen graduated first in their class. **Admissions Contact:** Barbara Sosin, Director of Admissions. Email: *admissions@kettering.edu* Web: *www.kettering.edu*

FINANCIAL AID: In 2016-2017, 89% of all full-time freshmen and 84% of continuing full-time students received some form of financial aid. 79% of all full-time freshmen and 67% of continuing full-time students received need-based aid. The average freshman award was $20,532. Need-based scholarships or need-based grants averaged $19,330; need-based self-help aid (loans and jobs) averaged $3,585; other non-need-based awards and non-need-based scholarships averaged $15,499; and $3,484 from other forms of aid. 18% of undergraduate students work part-time. The college's own financial statement is required. The FAFSA code is 002262. The priority date for freshman financial aid applications for fall entry is March 1.

LAKE SUPERIOR STATE UNIVERSITY — D-2

www.lssu.edu

Sault Sainte Marie, MI 49783	(906) 635-2231 (888) 800-5778
Fax: (906) 635-6696	Email: admissions@lssu.edu
Full-time: 897 men, 910 women	**Faculty:** 99
Part-time: 176 men, 239 women	**Ph.D.s:** n/av
Graduate: 1 men, 1 women	**Student/Faculty:** 23 to 1
Year: semesters, summer session	**Tuition:** $11,019
Room & Board: $9442	**Freshman Class:** n/av
SAT CR/M/W: 470/500/480 **ACT:** 21	**CEEB CODE:** 1421
Application Deadline: August 15	**COMPETITIVE**

Lake Superior State University, founded in 1946, is a public university that provides a blend of liberal and technical studies, offering undergraduate degrees in 45 areas of study. There are 12 undergraduate schools. In addition to regional accreditation, Lake State has baccalaureate program accreditation with ABET, ACBSP, NLN, CAAHEP, CAATE, HEHPAC, ABA, and AAMC. The 115-acre campus is in a small town Michigan's Upper Peninsula, 45 minutes north of the Mackinac Bridge. Including any residence halls, there are 37 buildings.

STUDENT LIFE: 99% of undergraduates are from Michigan. Others are from 29 states, 11 foreign countries, and Canada. 79% are White; 9% American Indian/Alaska Native; 7% Foreign; 2% African American; 2% Hispanic; 1% Asian American; 1% two or more races; 1% race unknown. **Female To Male Ratio:** 1.1:1. The average age of freshmen is 18; all undergraduates, 22. 30% do not continue beyond their first year; 48% remain to graduate. **Housing:** 900 students can be accommodated in college housing, which includes single-sex and coed dorms, on-campus apartments, honors houses, fraternity houses, sorority houses, and theme housing. On-campus housing is guaranteed for the freshman year only, on a first-come, first-served basis, and is available on a lottery system for upperclassmen. 66% of students commute. All students may keep cars.

FACULTY/CLASSROOMS: 51% of faculty are male; 49% are female. All teach undergraduates. No introductory courses are taught by graduate students. The average class size in an introductory lecture is 23; in a laboratory is 15; and in a regular course is 27.

PROGRAMS OF STUDY: Lake State confers B.A. and B.S. degrees. Associate degrees are also awarded. Bachelor's degrees are awarded in AGRICULTURE (aquaculture & fishery technology, fish and game management, and wildlife management), BIOLOGICAL SCIENCE (biochemistry, biology/biological science, and wildlife conservation biology), BUSINESS (accounting, banking and finance, business administration and management, business administration - international, business administration marketing, international business, international business management, and marketing/retailing/merchandising), COMMUNICATIONS AND THE ARTS (communications, creative writing, fine arts, and literature), COMPUTER AND PHYSICAL SCIENCE (actuarial mathematics, chemistry, clinical laboratory science, chemistry/forensic chemistry, chemistry secondary education, computer management, computer networks & systems, computer science, environmental chemistry, environmental geology, geology, and mathematics), EDUCATION (athletic training, early childhood education, elementary education, general studies, and secondary education), ENGINEERING AND ENVIRONMENTAL DESIGN (computer engineering, electrical/electronics engineering, engineering, engineering management, engineering technology, environmental engineering technology, environmental science, fire protection science, manufacturing technology, and mechanical engineering), HEALTH PROFESSIONS (clinical science, emergency medical services, environmental health science, exercise science, medical laboratory technology, nursing, predentistry, premedicine, prepharmacy, and recreation therapy), SOCIAL SCIENCE (criminal justice, economics, fire science, forensic studies, French studies, history, homeland security, human services, law enforcement and corrections, parks and recreation management, political science/government, prelaw, psychology, social science, and sociology). Engineering, biological science, nursing, and physical science are the strongest academically. Criminal justice, and business have the largest enrollments.

ACTIVITIES: There are 60 groups on campus, including art, band, choir, chorale, chorus, computers, dance, drama, environmental, ethnic, honors, jazz band, LGBT, newspaper, pep band, political, professional, radio and TV, religious, social, social service, and student government. Popular campus events include Winter Carnival, Spring Fling, and Great Lake State Weekend. **Sports:** There are 5 intercollegiate sports for men and 6 for women. Facilities include an ice arena, gym, swimming and diving pools, handball/squash courts, a weight-training and isometric room, and a dance studio. **Graduates:** From July 1, 2015 to June 30, 2016, 402 bachelor's degrees were awarded. The most popular majors were nursing (11%), accounting (6%), and criminal justice generalist (6%). In an average class, 3% graduate in 3 years or less, 27% graduate in 4 years or less, 53% graduate in 5 years or less, and 59% graduate in 6 years or less. Of the 2015 graduating class, 13% were enrolled in graduate school within 6 months of graduation, and 83% were employed.

SERVICES: Counseling and information services are available, as is tutoring in every subject, on request and free of charge. There is a reader service for the blind, and remedial math, reading, and writing. In addition, math, reading, and writing labs are also available. **Library/Resources:** The library contains 106,618 volumes, 810 audio/video tapes/CDs/DVDs, and subscribes to 950 periodicals including electronic. Computerized library services include interlibrary loans, database searching, Internet access, and Wi-Fi capability. Special learning facilities include an art gallery, natural history museum, planetarium, radio station, fish hatchery and aquatics lab, SIM Lab, and firing range. **Physically Challenged Students:** Facilities include wheelchair ramps, elevators, special parking, specially equipped restrooms, special class scheduling, lowered drinking fountains, and lowered telephones. **Special:** Lake State offers internships in criminal justice, medical science lab, human services, natural resources technology, work-study programs, co-op programs in engineering technology, and cross-registration with the Canadian Colleges of Sault and Algoma and Bridge International Consortium. Study abroad and student-designed majors are available, as are B.A.-B.S. degrees and dual majors. Distance learning is also offered. There are a freshman honors program. **Visiting:** There are regularly scheduled orientations for prospective students. There are guides for informal visits and visitors may sit in on classes. To schedule a visit, contact the Admissions Office. **Campus Safety and Security:** Measures include 24-hour foot and vehicle patrol, emergency notification system, self-defense education, and security escort services, and lighted pathways/sidewalks.

REQUIREMENTS: The ACT is required. Applicants should be high school graduates with 4 years of English, 3 each of math and science, 2 each of a foreign language and social studies, and 1 of history and should have a GPA of 2.4. The GED is accepted. Students below a 2.4 GPA and 19 act (or equivalent SAT) will go through a pending process and be evaluated on a case by case basis. AP and CLEP credits are accepted. Important factors in the admissions decision are advanced placement or honors courses, recommendations by school officials, and recommendations by alumni. To graduate, students must complete 124 semester hours with a GPA of 2.0. The core curriculum includes course-work in computer literacy, English, oral communications, aesthetics, critical thinking, humanities, math, science, social science, ethics, and cultural diversity. At least 30 of the final credits, and 50% of all upper-level courses, must be taken in residence at Lake State. Math and English competency must be met. **Procedure:** Freshmen are admitted to all sessions. There are deferred admissions and rolling admissions plans. Applications should be filed by August 15 for fall entry, along with a $25 fee. Applications are accepted on-line. **Transfer Students:** 137 transfer students enrolled in 2015-2016. Applicants must be eligible to return to the last institution attended and must have an overall college GPA of 2.0. High school transcripts, ACT scores, and/or GED scores are required if transferring with fewer than 19 semester hours of credit. 30 of 124 credits required for the bachelor's degree must be completed at Lake State. **International Students:** There are 20 international students enrolled. The school actively recruits these students. They must take the TOEFL with a minimum score of 500 on the paper-based TOEFL (PBT) or 61 on the Internet-based version (iBT).

ADMISSIONS: The SAT scores for the 2016-2017 freshman class were: Critical Reading-- 67% below 500, 22% between 500 and 599, and 11% between 600 and 699. Math-- 45% below 500 and 55% between 500 and 599. Writing-- 55% below 500, 33% between 500 and 599, and 11% between 600 and 699. The ACT scores were 1% below 12, 12% between 12 and 17, 59% between 18 and 23, 20% between 24 and 29, and 1% above 30. **Admissions Contact:** Michelle Markstrom, Assistant Director of Admissions. Email: *admissions@lssu.edu* Web: *www.lssu.edu*

FINANCIAL AID: In 2016-2017, 73% of all full-time freshmen and 69% of continuing full-time students received some form of financial aid. 61% of all full-time freshmen and 62% of continuing full-time students received need-based aid. The average freshman award was $8,519. Need-based scholarships or need-based grants averaged $4,984 ($5,477 maximum); need-based self-help aid (loans and jobs) averaged $7,394 ($13,882 maximum); non-need-based athletic scholarships averaged $3,489 ($12,762 maximum); and other non-need-based awards and non-need-based scholarships averaged $7,418 ($1,400 maximum). 18% of undergraduate students work part-time. Average annual earnings from campus work are $1864. The FAFSA code is 002293. The priority date for freshman financial aid applications for fall entry is March 1.

LAWRENCE TECHNOLOGICAL UNIVERSITY — E-5

www.ltu.edu

Southfield, MI 48075	**(248) 204-3160** **(800) CALL-LTU**
Fax: (248) 204-3188	**Email: admissions@ltu.edu**
Full-time: 1237 men, 474 women	**Faculty:** 116
Part-time: 311 men, 142 women	**Ph.D.s:** 67%
Graduate: 844 men, 301 women	**Student/Faculty:** 15 to 1
Year: semesters, summer session	**Tuition:** $30,300 ($31,140)
Room & Board: $10,107	**Freshman Class:** 2318 applied, 1607 accepted, 375 enrolled
SAT CR/M/W: 540/610/530 **ACT:** 25	**CEEB CODE:** 1399
Application Deadline: n/av	**VERY COMPETITIVE**

Lawrence Technological University, founded in 1932 as Lawrence Institute of Technology, is a private institution housing colleges of engineering, management, arts and sciences, and architecture and design. There are 4 undergraduate schools and 4 graduate schools. In addition to regional accreditation, Lawrence Tech has baccalaureate program accreditation with AACSB, ABET, ACBSP, FIDER, NAAB, NASAD, CIDA, ASC, and IACBE. The 107-acre campus is in a suburban area 30 minutes north of downtown Detroit. Including any residence halls, there are 20 buildings.

STUDENT LIFE: 94% of undergraduates are from Michigan. Others are from 31 states, 44 foreign countries, and Canada. 8% are race unknown; 7% African American; 61% White; 4% Hispanic; 3% Asian American; 2% two or more races; 15% Foreign. **Male To Female Ratio:** 2.6:1. The average age of freshmen is 18; all undergraduates, 22. 20% do not continue beyond their first year; 55% remain to graduate. **Housing:** 724 students can be accommodated in college housing, which includes coed on-campus apartments and off-campus apartments. There is also Arbor Lofts, a private apartment complex for student use. On-campus housing is available on a first-come and first-served basis. 67% of students commute. All students may keep cars.

FACULTY/CLASSROOMS: 69% of faculty are male; 31% are female. 95% teach undergraduates. No introductory courses are taught by graduate students. The average class size in an introductory lecture is 16; in a laboratory is 17; and in a regular course is 14.

PROGRAMS OF STUDY: Lawrence Tech confers B.A., B.S., B.F.A. and B.F.M. degrees. Associate, master's, and doctoral degrees are also awarded. Bachelor's degrees are awarded in BIOLOGICAL SCIENCE (biochemistry, biotechnology, and molecular biology), BUSINESS (business administration and management and international business management), COMMUNICATIONS AND THE ARTS (animation, audio technology, communications, English, game design and development, illustration, industrial design, information technology, media arts, and technical and business writing), COMPUTER AND PHYSICAL SCIENCE (chemistry, computer science, environmental chemistry, information sciences and systems, mathematics, mathematics/computational, and physics), ENGINEERING AND ENVIRONMENTAL DESIGN (architectural engineering, architecture, biomedical engineering, civil engineering, computer engineering, computer graphics, construction management, electrical/electronics engineering, engineering, engineering technology, industrial administration/management, industrial engineering, interior architecture, interior design, mechanical engineering, technological management, and transportation engineering), SOCIAL SCIENCE (architectural studies, humanities, and psychology). Mathematics, computer science, and engineering are the strongest academically. Engineering and architecture has the largest enrollment.

ACTIVITIES: 10% of men belong to 5 local and 4 national fraternities; 18% of women belong to 4 local and 2 national sororities. There are 46 groups on campus, including chess, chorus, communications, computers, dance, international, LGBT, literary magazine, newspaper, pep band, photography, religious, robotics, social, social service, and student government. Popular campus events include Discovery Days, New Student Convocation, and Welcome Back Picnic, Homecoming, Winterfest, Chinese New Year, International Fest, and Greek Week. **Sports:** There are 11 intercollegiate sports for men and 9 for women, and 12 intramural sports for men and 12 for women. Facilities include an indoor recreation/athletic facility with cardio equipment (treadmills, elipticles, bikes, etc), free weights and weight machines, a track around the gym, full court basketball floor, racquetball courts, table tennis table, heavy bag and recreational sports (including IM flag football, soccer, and club ultimate Frisbee). **Graduates:** From July 1, 2015 to June 30, 2016, 332 bachelor's degrees were awarded. The most popular majors were engineering (42%), architecture (22%), and computer science (11%). 202 companies recruited on campus in 2015-2016. In an average class, 46% graduate in 4 years or less, 52% graduate in 5 years or less, and 55% graduate in 6 years or less. Of the 2015 graduating class, 12% were enrolled in graduate school within 6 months of graduation, and 88% were employed.

SERVICES: Counseling and information services are available, as is tutoring in most subjects. There is a reader service for the blind, and remedial math, reading, and writing. There is also an Academic Achievement Center **Library/Resources:** The library contains 38,508 volumes, 49,630 microform items, 2,261 audio/video tapes/CDs/DVDs, and subscribes to 45,297 periodicals including electronic. Computerized library services include interlibrary loans, database searching, Internet access, and Wi-Fi capability. **Physically Challenged Students:** 97% of the campus is accessible. Facilities include wheelchair ramps, elevators, special parking, specially equipped restrooms, special class scheduling, lowered drinking fountains, lowered telephones, and special housing. **Special:** There are co-op programs in a number of majors, internships, study abroad in 8 countries and dual majors available. There is 1 national honor society and 2 departmental honors programs. **Visiting:** There are regularly scheduled orientations for prospective students. There are guides for informal visits, visitors may sit in on classes, and stay overnight. To schedule a visit, contact the Admissions Office. **Campus Safety and Security:** Measures include 24-hour foot and vehicle patrol, emergency notification system, and security escort services. There are also shuttle buses, emergency telephones, lighted pathways/sidewalks, and closed-circuit camera monitoring.

REQUIREMENTS: The ACT is required. The SAT is recommended. Students must have a high school diploma and a GPA of no lower than 2.5, at least 2.0 in each subject area pertaining to their major. Applicants should have taken 4 years each of math, science, and English, and 3 years of social science. The GED is accepted. An interview is recommended. AP and CLEP credits are accepted. Important factors in the admissions decision are advanced placement or honors courses, personality/intangible qualities, and leadership record. To graduate, students must have completed, depending on the major, 120 to 131 semester credit hours, with a GPA no lower than 2.0. Senior projects are required in most degree programs. **Procedure:** Freshmen are admitted to all sessions. Entrance exams should be taken in the semester preceding entry. There are deferred admissions and rolling admissions plans. Application deadlines are open. Application fee is $30. Notification is sent on a rolling basis. Applications are accepted online. **Transfer Students:** 146 transfer students enrolled in 2015-2016. Admission is based on the college GPA, which must be 2.0 or higher, with 30 or more semester hours. If less than 30 hours have been completed, admission is based on high school transcripts. 30 of 120 credits required for the bachelor's degree must be completed at Lawrence Tech. **International Students:** There are 349 international students enrolled. The school actively recruits these students. They must take the TOEFL with a minimum score of 550 on the paper-based TOEFL (PBT) or 79 on the Internet-based version (iBT) or take the MELAB and the Comprehensive English Language Test, and placement exams for incoming freshman only.

ADMISSIONS: 69% of the 2016-2017 applicants were accepted. The SAT scores for the 2016-2017 freshman class were: Critical Reading-- 30% below 500, 40% between 500 and 599, 27% between 600 and 699, and 3% between 700 and 800. Math-- 15% below 500, 24% between 500 and 599, 58% between 600 and 699, and 3% between 700 and 800. Writing-- 28% below 500, 53% between 500 and 599, and 19% between 600 and 699. The ACT scores were 5% between 12 and 17, 27% between 18 and 23, 49% between 24 and 29, and 19% above 30. 46% of the current freshmen were in the top fifth of their class; 73% were in the top two fifths. 3 freshmen graduated first in their class. **Admissions Contact:** Jane Rohrback, Admissions Director. Email: *admissions@ltu.edu* Web: *www.ltu.edu*

FINANCIAL AID: In 2016-2017, 95% of all full-time freshmen and 81% of continuing full-time students received some form of financial aid. 72% of all full-time freshmen and 58% of continuing full-time students received need-based aid. The average freshman award was $27,992. Need-based scholarships or need-based grants averaged $4,587 ($11,593 maximum); need-based self-help aid (loans and jobs) averaged $4,058 ($7,500 maximum); non-need-based athletic scholarships averaged $8,401 ($20,000 maximum); and other non-need-based awards and non-need-based scholarships averaged $13,203 ($30,000 maximum). 85% of undergraduate students work part-time. Average annual earnings from campus work are $2838. The average financial indebtedness of the 2016 graduate was $36,894. Lawrence Tech is a member of CSS. The deadline for filing freshman financial aid applications for fall entry is April 1.

MADONNA UNIVERSITY E-5

www.madonna.edu

Livonia, MI 48150

(734) 432-5341
(800) 852-4951
Email: admissions@madonna.edu

Full-time: 443 men, 910 women
Part-time: 405 men, 871 women
Graduate: 107 men, 562 women
Year: semesters, summer session
Room & Board: $9550
ACT: 21
Application Deadline: April 1

Faculty: 86
Ph.D.s: 58%
Student/Faculty: 10 to 1
Tuition: $19,500
Freshman Class: 843 applied, 635 accepted, 219 enrolled
CEEB CODE: 1437
COMPETITIVE

Madonna University, with its rich Catholic heritage, was established in 1937 by the Felician Sisters, with the values of St. Francis of Assisi. Strong academic programs, career preparation, and service learning projects change the lives of students, who, in turn, change the lives of others. Students enjoy personal instruction from skilled professors dedicated to student success. Madonna boasts more than 100 undergraduate and 35 graduate programs including signature programs in nursing, business, teacher education, criminal justice, sign language, broadcast and cinema arts, forensic science, hospice, and social work. Courses are offered online and on site in Livonia, and at centers in Gaylord, Detroit, and Macomb, Mich, and through Study Abroad. The first-year experience eases the transition from high school to college. Madonna Champions of Character Crusaders field 19 men's and women's sports teams. Students of all ages and varied religious, socio-economic and cultural backgrounds. Alumni have earned the reputation as effective leaders and socially-responsible citizens who create positive change. There are 6 undergraduate schools and 1 graduate school. In addition to regional accreditation, MU has baccalaureate program accreditation with AACSB, CSWE, NCATE, ACEND, CCNE, and FEPAC. The 85-acre campus is in a suburban area 6 miles west of Detroit, 20 miles from Ann Arbor. Including any residence halls, there are 5 buildings.

STUDENT LIFE: 88% of undergraduates are from Michigan. Others are from 8 states, 4 foreign countries, and Canada. 85% are from public schools. 59% are White; 15% Foreign; 12% African American; 6% race unknown; 4% Hispanic; 2% two or more races; 1% Asian American; 1% American Indian/Alaska Native. 53% are Hindu, Islam/Muslim, and Undeclared; 30% Catholic. **Female To Male Ratio:** 2.5:1. The average age of freshmen is 18; all undergraduates, 24. 18% do not continue beyond their first year; 58% remain to graduate. **Housing:** 308 students can be accommodated in college housing, which includes single-sex dorms. On-campus housing is available on a first-come and first-served basis. 89% of students commute. All students may keep cars. Alcohol is not permitted.

FACULTY/CLASSROOMS: 41% of faculty are male; 59% are female. 84% teach undergraduates. No introductory courses are taught by graduate students. The average class size in an introductory lecture is 16; in a laboratory is 14; and in a regular course is 16.

PROGRAMS OF STUDY: MU confers B.A., B.S., B.A.S., B.Mus, B.S.N., B.S.W., B.A.P.M. and B.A.P.T. degrees. Associate, master's, and doctoral degrees are also awarded. Bachelor's degrees are awarded in BIOLOGICAL SCIENCE (biochemistry, biology/biological science, forensic science, nutrition, and nutritional sciences), BUSINESS (accounting, applied management, business administration and management, hospitality management services, international business management, management information systems, management science, marketing, and sports management), COMMUNICATIONS AND THE ARTS (broadcasting, church music, communication studies, English, fine arts, graphic design, instrumental performance, journalism, language arts, music, music business management, piano performance, Spanish, technical and business writing, video, vocal performance, and writing), COMPUTER AND PHYSICAL SCIENCE (applied science, chemistry, computer science, mathematics, natural sciences, physics, and science), EDUCATION (art education, early childhood education, music education, physical education, secondary education, and Spanish education K-12), ENGINEERING AND ENVIRONMENTAL DESIGN (environmental science, occupational safety and health, and preengineering), HEALTH PROFESSIONS (biomedical science, health science, hospice care, nursing, predentistry, premedicine, preoptometry, preosteopathy, prepharmacy, prephysician assistant, prepodiatry, and preveterinary science), SOCIAL SCIENCE (child psychology/development, criminal justice, dietetics, family/consumer studies, fire science, food science, gerontology, history, interdisciplinary studies, interpreter for the deaf, liberal arts/general studies, paralegal studies, pastoral studies, prelaw, psychology, religious studies, religious music, social studies, social work, and sociology). Nursing is the strongest academically. Nursing, criminal justice, and business administration have the largest enrollments.

ACTIVITIES: There are no fraternities or sororities. There are 41 groups on campus, including Red Cross club, art, choir, chorale, computers, dance, environmental, ethnic, film, forensics, honors, international, LGBT, literary magazine, musical theater, newspaper, nursing student association, pep band, photography, professional, radio and TV, religious, social, social service, and student government. Popular campus events include Week of Welcome, Alternative Spring Breaks, Retreats, Recitals, Art Gallery Exhibits, Musical Theater events, Blood Drives, Welcome Events, 5K, Madonna Mile and International Festival. **Sports:** There are 8 intercollegiate sports for men and 9 for women. Facilities include basketball and volleyball, baseball, soccer and lacrosse field, softball, golf courses, weight training room, and gym. **Graduates:** From July 1, 2015 to June 30, 2016, 750 bachelor's degrees were awarded. The most popular majors were nursing (18%), international business (15%), and criminal justice (13%). 48 companies recruited on campus in 2015-2016. In an average class, 1% graduate in 3 years or less, 30% graduate in 4 years or less, 50% graduate in 5 years or less, and 58% graduate in 6 years or less.

SERVICES: Counseling and information services are available, as is tutoring in most subjects, 1000 and 2000 level courses. **Library/Resources:** The library contains 242,797 volumes, 583 microform items, 944 audio/video tapes/CDs/DVDs, and subscribes to 70,158 periodicals including electronic. Computerized library services include interlibrary loans, database searching, Internet access, and Wi-Fi capability. Special learning facilities include an art gallery, radio station, TV station, writing center, personalized instruction, and sign language studies lab. Franciscan Center for science & media, nursing simulation labs, and center for students in transition. **Physically Challenged Students:** All of the campus is accessible. Facilities include wheelchair ramps, elevators, special parking, specially equipped restrooms, special class scheduling, lowered drinking fountains, and lowered telephones. Interpreters and notetakers for hearing-impaired and visually-impaired students, telecommunication devices, specially equipped rooms and visible fire alarms for hearing-impaired students, talking books, tape recorders, diagnostic testing service, early syllabus, recorded exams, a Learning Center, oral exams, proofreading service, reading machine, take-home exams, software for vision impaired students, special testing arrangements, private rooms, extended time testing and adjustable computer monitors. **Special:** Madonna University undergraduate students have opportunities for a variety of special programs. Under the guidance of faculty and program chairs/directors, all majors have the opportunity for co-op and internship experiences. Madonna University also participates in multiple consortium arrangements including the Detroit Area Catholic Higher Education Consortium (DACHEC) with Marygrove College, Sacred Heart Major Seminary and University of Detroit Mercy, and the Online Consortium of Independent Colleges and Universities (OCICU) with a number of institutions, including St. Leo's University and Regis University. Study Abroad opportunities are available yearly to over 17 destinations. Work-study opportunities are available in a number of offices at Madonna University. Discipline-specific degrees are available, including a Bachelor of Science in Nursing (B.S.N. degree), Bachelor of Social Work (B.S.W. degree), Bachelor of Music (B.MUS. degree), Bachelor of Applied Science (B.A.S. degree), a Bachelor of Applied Management (B.Ap.M. degree) and a Bachelor of Applied Technology (B.Ap.T. degree). Additionally, students have the opportunity to customize a major with our B.A. degree with a major of Interdisciplinary Studies. There are 12 national honor societies. **Visiting:** There are regularly scheduled orientations for prospective students, Including an interview and a tour of the campus. This provides an opportunity to learn about academic and support services, opportunities, and programs for a successful college experience. There are guides for informal visits, visitors may sit in on classes, and stay overnight. To schedule a visit, contact Sarah Gombar at sgombar@madonna.edu. **Campus Safety and Security:** Measures include 24-hour foot and vehicle patrol, emergency notification system, and security escort services, emergency telephones, lighted pathways/sidewalks, controlled access to dorms/residences, and emergency car care servive.

REQUIREMENTS: The ACT is required. Candidates should have completed 4 years of English, 3 years of math, 2 years of science and 1 year of History. An essay is required. For some majors, students are asked to submit a portfolio or to appear for an interview or audition. AP and CLEP credits are accepted. Important factors in the admissions decision are advanced placement or honors courses, recommendations by school officials, and evidence of special talent. To graduate, undergraduate students seeking a Baccalaureate degree must complete at least 120 credit hours with a grade of C (2.0) or better in every major sequence course, and a final semester and cumulative GPA of 2.0 or better. Students are required to complete a major (required credit hours in the major vary from 30 to 65 including a capstone senior seminar), and a minimum of 52 credit hours of general education and university core courses. Students must complete a writing assessment, unless waived by a minimum ACT or SAT writing score, and to complete up to 3 credit hours of remediation coursework as determined by their score on the writing assessment. Baccalaureate degree students also have a 30 credit hour residency requirement that must be completed at Madonna University. Undergraduate students seeking an Associate's degree must complete at least 60 credit hours with a grade of C (2.0) or better in every major sequence course, and a final semester and cumulative GPA of 2.0 or better. Students are required to complete a major (required credit hours in the major vary from 24 to 32), and a minimum of 21 credit hours of general education and university core courses. Students are also required to complete a writing assessment, unless waived by a minimum ACT or SAT writing score and to complete up to 3 credit hours of remediation coursework as determined by their score on the writing assessment. Associate degree students also have a 15 credit hour residency requirement that must be completed at Madonna University. **Procedure:** Freshmen are admitted to all sessions. Entrance exams should be taken During either the junior or senior year. There are early decision, early admissions, and rolling admissions plans. Early decision applications should be filed by December 1; regular applications, by April 1 for fall entry; November 1 for winter entry; and March 1 for summer entry, along with a $25 fee. Notification of early decision is sent January 15; regular decision, on a rolling basis. 8 early decision candidates were accepted for the 2016-2017 class. Application fees are waived if application is completed online. **Transfer Students:** 539 transfer students enrolled in 2015-2016. Applicants must be in good academic and personal standing at their previous colleges and must submit official transcripts of college and high school work. Courses completed at an accredited institution with a grade of C or better will be considered for transfer credit. 30 of 120 credits required for the bachelor's degree must be completed at MU. **International Students:** There are 85 international students enrolled. The school actively recruits these students. They must also take the SAT or ACT.

ADMISSIONS: 75% of the 2016-2017 applicants were accepted. The SAT scores for the 2016-2017 freshman class were: The ACT scores were 23% between 12 and 17, 53% between 18 and 23, 23% between 24 and 29, and 1% above 30. **Admissions Contact:** Mark A Schroeder, Director of Undergraduate Admissions. Email: *admissions@madonna.edu* Web: *www.madonna.edu*

FINANCIAL AID: 17% of undergraduate students work part-time. Average annual earnings from campus work are $1453. The average financial indebtedness of the 2016 graduate was $29,244. The FAFSA code is 002282. The priority date for freshman financial aid applications for fall entry is March 1.

MARYGROVE COLLEGE *(The complete profile is made available exclusively on our website, www.barronspac.com)*

MICHIGAN STATE UNIVERSITY D-4

www.msu.edu

East Lansing, MI 48824 **(517) 355-8332**

Fax: (517) 353-1647	**Email: admissions.msu.edu**
Full-time: 17,315 men, 18,132 women	**Faculty:** I, av$
	Ph.D.s: 90%
Part-time: 1997 men, 1646 women	**Student/Faculty:** 17 to 1
Graduate: 4993 men, 6261 women	**Tuition:** $14,114 ($37,942)
Year: semesters, summer session	**Freshman Class:** 37480 applied, 24641 accepted, 7911 enrolled
Room & Board: $9784	
SAT: required **ACT:** 26	
Application Deadline: July 25	**VERY COMPETITIVE+**

Michigan State University Spartans work to advance the common good in uncommon ways. The nation's pioneer land-grant university, MSU began as a bold experiment that democratized higher education and helped bring science and innovation into everyday life. Today, MSU is one of the top research universities in the world on one of the biggest, greenest campuses in the nation and is home to a diverse community of dedicated students and scholars, athletes and artists, scientists and leaders. There are 17 undergraduate schools and 17 graduate schools. In addition to regional accreditation, MSU has baccalaureate program accreditation with AACSB, ABET, ACCE, ACEJMC, ASLA, CAHEA, CSWE, FIDER, NASM, NLN, and SAF. The 5200-acre campus is in a suburban area in East Lansing, three miles east of Michigan's capitol in Lansing. Including any residence halls, there are 545 buildings.

STUDENT LIFE: 75% of undergraduates are from Michigan. Others are from 50 states, 130 foreign countries, and Canada. 7% are African American; 65% White; 5% Asian American; 4% Hispanic; 3% two or more races; 14% Foreign; 1% American Indian/Alaska Native. **Female To Male Ratio:** 1.1:1. The average age of freshmen is 18; all undergraduates, 20. 8% do not continue beyond their first year; 78% remain to graduate. **Housing:** 18000 students can be accommodated in college housing, which includes single-sex and coed dorms, on-campus apartments, married student housing, honors houses, special-interest houses, residential colleges, living-learning communities, quiet floors, and substance-free environments. On-campus housing is guaranteed for all 4 years. 60% of students commute. Upperclassmen may keep cars.

FACULTY/CLASSROOMS: 57% of faculty are male; 43% are female. No introductory courses are taught by graduate students. The average class size in an introductory lecture is 100; in a laboratory is 30; and in a regular course is 30.

PROGRAMS OF STUDY: MSU confers B.A., B.S., B.F.A., B.Land.Arch., B.Mus., and B.S. in Nursing degrees. Master's and doctoral degrees are also awarded. Bachelor's degrees are awarded in AGRICULTURE (agricultural business management, agriculture, animal science, environmental studies, fishing and fisheries, forestry and related sciences, horticulture, natural resource management, soil science, and wildlife management), BIOLOGICAL SCIENCE (biochemistry, bioinformatics, biology/biological science, biological sciences, biotechnology, botany, entomology, environmental biology, microbiology, neurosciences, nutrition, physiology, plant pathology, and zoology), BUSINESS (accounting, apparel and textiles, banking and finance, business administration and management, finance, hospitality management services, human resources, human resources/organizational management, marketing, marketing management, marketing/retailing/merchandising, packaging, personnel management, supply chain management, and tourism), COMMUNICATIONS AND THE ARTS (advertising, Arabic, art history and appreciation, Chinese, communications, composition, dramatic arts, East Asian languages and literature, English, film arts, French, German, graphic design, jazz, journalism, Latin, linguistics, music, music performance, music theory and composition, Russian, Spanish, studio art, telecommunications, and theatre studies), COMPUTER AND PHYSICAL SCIENCE (actuarial science, astrophysics, chemical physics, chemistry, computer science, earth science, geology, geophysics and seismology, geoscience, information sciences and systems, mathematics, natural sciences, physical sciences, physics, and statistics), EDUCATION (agricultural education, art education, education, music education, physical education, and special education), ENGINEERING AND ENVIRONMENTAL DESIGN (chemical engineering, city/community/regional planning, civil engineering, computational sciences, computer engineering, construction management, electrical/electronics engineering, engineering, engineering mechanics, environmental engineering technology, interior design, landscape architecture, landscape architecture/design, manufacturing engineering, materials engineering, materials science and engineering, mechanical engineering, textile technology, and urban planning technology), HEALTH PROFESSIONS (clinical science, human biology, medical laboratory technology, music therapy, nursing, predentistry, preveterinary science, speech pathology/audiology, and veterinary science), SOCIAL SCIENCE (American studies, anthropology, child psychology/development, classical/ancient civilization, criminal justice, dietetics, economics, family and community services, family/consumer resource management, family/consumer studies, food production/management/services, food science, geography, history, human development & family studies, humanities, interdisciplinary studies, international relations, parks and recreation management, philosophy, political science/government, prelaw, psychology, public administration, religion, social science, social work, sociology, and women's studies). Education, business, and physics are the strongest academically. Business, social science, and natural science have the largest enrollments.

ACTIVITIES: There are 700 groups on campus, including art, band, cheerleading, chess, choir, chorale, chorus, communications, computers, dance, debate, drama, drill team, environmental, ethnic, film, forensics, honors, international, jazz band, LGBT, literary magazine, marching band, musical theater, newspaper, opera, orchestra, pep band, photography, political, professional, radio and TV, religious, social, social service, student government, symphony, and yearbook. Popular campus events include Athletic Events (football, basketball, hockey in particular), Welcome Week, and Homecoming. **Sports:** There are 12 intercollegiate sports for men and 13 for women, and 10 intramural sports for men and 10 for women. Facilities include a stadium, a gym and field house, ice arena, and a multipurpose student events center, indoor football practice facility, intramural facilities, indoor and outdoor tennis courts, ball fields, a running track, golf courses, and swimming pools. **Graduates:** From July 1, 2015 to June 30, 2016, 8724 bachelor's degrees were awarded. The most popular majors were business (18%), communications (13%), and social science (11%). In an average class, 78% graduate in 6 years or less.

SERVICES: Counseling and information services are available, as is tutoring in most subjects, a reader service for the blind, and remedial math, reading, and writing. **Library/Resources:** The 3 libraries contain 4.5 million volumes, 1.2 million microform items, 40,000 audio/video tapes/CDs/DVDs, and subscribe to 33,000 periodicals including electronic. Computerized library services include interlibrary loans, database searching, Internet access, and Wi-Fi capability. Special learning facilities include an art gallery, natural history museum, planetarium, radio station, TV station, a botanical garden, superconducting cyclotron lab, environmental toxicology center, pesticide research center, center for the performing arts, center for computer-aided and engineering and manufacturing. **Physically Challenged Students:** Facilities include wheelchair ramps, elevators, special parking, specially equipped restrooms, special class scheduling, lowered drinking fountains, lowered telephones, special housing. Tape recorders, videotaped classes, reading machines, readers and note takers. **Special:** Special academic programs include an engineering co-op program with business and industry; internships in business, education, political science, agriculture, and communication arts, study abroad in more than 70 countries, on-campus work-study programs, and a sea semester. An accelerated degree program in all majors and student-designed majors are offered at the Honors College. Nondegree study, pass/fail options in some courses, and dual majors are possible. Educationally disadvantaged students may avail themselves of the College Achievement Admissions Program (CAAP). Cross-registration with the Committee on Institutional Cooperation schools is available. There are 48 national honor societies, Phi Beta Kappa, and a freshman honors program. **Visiting:** Regularly scheduled orientations are available for prospective students, including a presentation and a tour of the campus. There are guides for informal visits, visitors may sit in on classes, and stay overnight. To schedule a visit, contact the Office of Admissions. **Campus Safety and Security:** Measures include 24-hour foot and vehicle patrol, emergency notification system, self-defense education, and security escort services. There are also shuttle buses, emergency telephones, lighted pathways/sidewalks, controlled access to dorms/residences, and regional/campus bus service.

REQUIREMENTS: The SAT or ACT is required. Applicants must be graduates of an accredited secondary school and have completed 4 years of English, 3 years each of math and social studies, 2 years of science, and 2 years of a single foreign language. A personal statement is strongly recommended. The GED is accepted. Music majors must audition. AP and CLEP credits are accepted. Important factors in the admissions decision are recommendations by school officials, advanced placement or honors courses, and evidence of special talent. To graduate, students must complete a freshman writing course and a writing course specified by the major and degree program. Students must complete the 26-credit University Integrative Studies requirement consisting of 8 credits of arts and humanitites, 8 of social, behavioral, and economic sciences, 8 of general science, and 3 of a transcollegiate course. Students must also complete a math requirement determined by each undergraduate college (minimum of college algebra plus trigonometry/finite math/statistics.) A minimum 2.0 GPA and 120 semester hours are required. **Procedure:** Freshmen are admitted in the fall, spring, and summer. Entrance exams should be taken during the junior year of high school. There are deferred admissions and rolling admissions plans. Applications should be filed by July 25 for fall entry; December 1 for spring entry; and April 15 for summer entry, along with a $65 fee. Applications are accepted online. **Transfer Students:** 1640 transfer students enrolled in 2015-2016. To transfer, a minimum GPA of 2.0 is required, (prefer 3.0 overall GPA). MSU Integrative Studies requirement should be fulfilled (28 general graduation credits), and college algebra completed. 30 of 120 credits required for the bachelor's degree must be completed at MSU. **International Students:** There are 4846 international students enrolled. The school actively recruits these students. They must take the TOEFL with a minimum score of 550 on the paper-based TOEFL (PBT) or 79 on the Internet-based version (iBT) or take the MELAB and the college's own test, or take the MSUELT.

ADMISSIONS: 66% of the 2016-2017 applicants were accepted. The SAT scores for the 2016-2017 freshman class were: Critical Reading-- 41% below 500, 35% between 500 and 599, 18% between 600 and 699, and 6% between 700 and 800. Math-- 37% below 500, 41% between 500 and 599, 18% between 600 and 699, and 3% between 700 and 800. Writing-- 38% below 500, 43% between 500 and 599, 15% between 600 and 699, and 4% between 700 and 800. The ACT scores were 2% between 12 and 17, 22% between 18 and 23, 57% between 24 and 29, and 19% above 30. 66% of the current freshmen were in the top fifth of their class; 94% were in the top two fifths. **Admissions Contact:** James Cotter, Director of Admissions. Email: *admissions.msu.edu* Web: *www.msu.edu*

FINANCIAL AID: In 2016-2017, 45% of all full-time freshmen and 46% of continuing full-time students received some form of financial aid. 35% of all full-time freshmen and 37% of continuing full-time students received need-based aid. The average freshman award was $13,208. Need-based scholarships or need-based grants averaged $10,138; need-based self-help aid (loans and jobs) averaged $3,802; non-need-based athletic scholarships averaged $28,376; and other non-need-based awards and non-need-based scholarships averaged $9,915. The average financial indebtedness of the 2016 graduate was $25,724. The FAFSA code is 002290. The priority date for freshman financial aid applications for fall entry is October 1. The filing deadline for fall entry is March 1.

MICHIGAN TECHNOLOGICAL UNIVERSITY — B-2

www.mtu.edu

Houghton, MI 49931	**(906) 487-2335** **(888) 688-1885**
Fax: (906) 487-2125	**Email: mtu4u@mtu.edu**
Full-time: 3997 men, 1463 women	**Faculty:** 408; I, -$
Part-time: 258 men, 111 women	**Ph.D.s:** 88%
Graduate: 1057 men, 384 women	**Student/Faculty:** 12 to 1
Year: semesters, summer session	**Tuition:** $14,634 ($30,968)
Room & Board: $10,105	**Freshman Class:** 5589 applied, 4272 accepted, 1381 enrolled
SAT CR/M/W: 590/620/560 **ACT:** 27	**CEEB CODE:** 1464
Application Deadline: n/av	**VERY COMPETITIVE+**

Michigan Technological University is a leading public research university whose mission is preparing students to create the future. The University's world-class faculty conducts research and develops new technologies to help build a prosperous and sustainable world. Michigan Tech's five colleges and schools offer more than 120 undergraduate and graduate degree programs in engineering, forest resources, computing, technology, business and economics, natural, physical and environmental sciences, arts, humanities, and social sciences. There are 5 undergraduate schools and 1 graduate school. In addition to regional accreditation, Michigan Tech has baccalaureate program accreditation with AACSB, ABET, ACCE, SAF, and TEAC. The 925-acre campus is in a small town 325 miles north of Milwaukee, Wisconsin. Including any residence halls, there are 34 buildings.

STUDENT LIFE: 75% of undergraduates are from Michigan. Others are from 42 states, 34 foreign countries, and Canada. 87% are White; 3% Foreign; 3% two or more races; 2% Hispanic; 2% race unknown; 1% African American; 1% Asian American. **Male To Female Ratio:** 2.7:1. The average age of freshmen is 18; all undergraduates, 21. 17% do not continue beyond their first year; 67% remain to graduate. **Housing:** 3175 students can be accommodated in college housing, which includes coed dorms, on-campus apartments, married student housing, honors houses and special-interest houses. On-campus housing is guaranteed for the freshman year only, and is available on a first-come, and first-served basis. 53% of students commute. All students may keep cars.

FACULTY/CLASSROOMS: 68% of faculty are male; 32% are female. All teach undergraduates, 74% do research, and 74% do both. Graduate students teach 5% of introductory courses. The average class size in an introductory lecture is 73; in a laboratory is 26; and in a regular course is 31.

PROGRAMS OF STUDY: Michigan Tech confers B.A. and B.S. degrees. Associate, master's, and doctoral degrees are also awarded. Bachelor's degrees are awarded in AGRICULTURE (forestry and related sciences, natural resource management, and wildlife management), BIOLOGICAL SCIENCE (biochemistry, bioinformatics, biology/biological science, and ecology), BUSINESS (accounting, finance, management engineering, management information systems, management science, marketing, and sports management), COMMUNICATIONS AND THE ARTS (audio technology, communications, English, technical and business writing, theater design, and theatre studies), COMPUTER AND PHYSICAL SCIENCE (applied physics, chemistry, computer information systems, computer science, geology, geophysics and seismology, mathematics, physics, software engineering, and statistics), EDUCATION (secondary education), ENGINEERING AND ENVIRONMENTAL DESIGN (biomedical engineering, chemical engineering, civil engineering, computer engineering, construction management, electrical/electronics engineering, electrical/electronics engineering technology, engineering, environmental engineering, environmental science, geological engineering, materials engineering, mechanical engineering, mechanical engineering technology, and surveying engineering), HEALTH PROFESSIONS (exercise science, medical laboratory science, pharmaceutical chemistry, predentistry, premedicine, prepharmacy, and prephysical therapy), SOCIAL SCIENCE (anthropology, economics, history, liberal arts/general studies, psychology, and social science). Engineering and sciences is the strongest academically. Mechanical engineering, chemical engineering, and electrical engineering have the largest enrollments.

ACTIVITIES: 8% of men belong to 3 local and 9 national fraternities;

14% of women belong to 4 local and 4 national sororities. There are 225 groups on campus, including art, band, cheerleading, chess, choir, chorale, chorus, communications, computers, dance, drama, environmental, ethnic, film, honors, international, jazz band, LGBT, literary magazine, musical theater, newspaper, orchestra, pep band, photography, political, professional, radio and TV, religious, social, social service, student government, and symphony. Popular campus events include Winter Carnival, K-Day, Homecoming, Spring Fling, Make a Difference Day, International Night, Parade of Nations, Safe House Halloween, Division I Hockey, Design Expo, LeaderShape Institute, and Afternoon on the Town. **Sports:** There are 7 intercollegiate sports for men and 7 for women, and 24 intramural sports for men and 24 for women. Facilities include Student Development Complex (SDC) is comprised of facilities including ice arena, a fitness center, swimming pool, a climbing wall, varsity gym, outdoor softball fields and sand volleyball courts, football and soccer fields, practice fields, golf course, tennis, golf course, and skiing. **Graduates:** From July 1, 2015 to June 30, 2016, 1065 bachelor's degrees were awarded. The most popular majors were mechanical engineering (24%), chemical engineering (10%), and civil engineering (8%). 450 companies recruited on campus in 2015-2016. In an average class, 28% graduate in 4 years or less, 61% graduate in 5 years or less, and 67% graduate in 6 years or less.

SERVICES: Counseling and information services are available, as is tutoring in most subjects, and a reader service for the blind. There are also Academic Success Coaches; Biological Sciences Learning Center; Business and Economics Tidwell Learning Center; Career Services Learning Center; Chemical Engineering Learning Center; Chemistry Learning Center; Civil and Environmental Engineering Learning Center; Computer Science Learning Center; Electrical and Computer Engineering Learning Center; Engineering Learning Center; First-Year Engineering Learning Center; Forestry Learning Center; Materials Science and Engineering Learning Center; Mathematics Learning Center; Multiliteracies Center; Physics Learning Center. **Library/Resources:** The library contains 478,976 volumes, 454,059 microform items, 910 audio/video tapes/CDs/DVDs, and subscribes to 53,784 periodicals including electronic. Computerized library services include interlibrary loans, database searching, Internet access, and Wi-Fi capability. Special learning facilities include an art gallery, radio station, The A.E. Seaman Mineral Museum, which is the official mineral museum of Michigan, the Rozsa Center for the Performing Arts, state-of-the-art theater, Ford Center with 4,000-acre Ford Forest, Cosmic Ray Observatory, X-ray Fluorescence Spectrometer, Unit Operations Lab and Process Simulation and Control Center, Earth, Planetary and Space Sciences Institute, Computer-aided Engineering Lab, Microfabrication Facility, and the Great Lakes Research Center. **Physically Challenged Students:** 80% of the campus is accessible. Facilities include wheelchair ramps, elevators, special parking, specially equipped restrooms, special class scheduling, lowered drinking fountains, and special housing. **Special:** Michigan Technological University is a leading public research university developing new technologies and preparing students to create the future for a prosperous and sustainable world. Michigan Tech offers more than 120 undergraduate and graduate degree programs in engineering, forest resources, computing, technology, business and economics, natural, physical and environmental sciences, arts, humanities, and social sciences. Accelerated Master's Degrees are available in nearly 20 areas. Over 420 companies visit campus annually to recruit students for co-ops, internships, and full-time jobs. The Pavlis Honors College provides opportunities for students to participate in the Enterprise Program (teams of students working on large-scale government- and industry-sponsored projects), the Pavlis Institute for Global Technological Leadership, Research Scholars Program, and more. Students may also participate in industry-sponsored senior design or international senior design. Study abroad opportunities exist in over 40 countries. Undergraduate research is also available. Last year, students spent over 126,000 hours working on paid undergraduate research. Michigan Tech offers dual degrees, double majors, minors, and certificate programs. Students looking to enroll in professional health programs will find an early assurance program with Michigan State University for medical school and Central Michigan University for physical therapy (DPT). Agreements for 3+2 programs with many institutions in the Midwest are in place. There are 11 national honor societies and 23 departmental honors programs. **Visiting:** Regularly scheduled orientations are available for prospective students. There are guides for informal visits, visitors may sit in on classes, and stay overnight. To schedule a visit, contact Admissions Office at mtu4u@mtu.edu. **Campus Safety and Security:** Measures include 24-hour foot and vehicle patrol, emergency notification system, self-defense education, and security escort services. There are also shuttle buses, emergency telephones, lighted pathways/sidewalks, controlled access to dorms/residences, and emergency medical services.

REQUIREMENTS: First-year applicants are required to submit an official high school transcript with grades through at least the junior year and official ACT or SAT scores. Scores may be sent directly from the testing agency, or reported on the official high school transcript or on Michigan Tech's Counselor Information Page. Transfer student applicants are required to submit official college transcripts from all institutions previously attended. An official high school transcript is required for transfer applicants who have not earned an Associate's degree or higher at time of application to Michigan Tech. Applicants to programs in the Visual and Performing Arts Department must provide essay responses; select majors must submit examples of creative work. We encourage GED and home school applicants to apply. A GPA of 2.8 is required. AP and CLEP credits are accepted. To graduate, students must complete 120 to 145 credit hours and maintain a minimum GPA (both cumulative and in the major department) of 2.0. The general education curriculum, required for all baccalaureate students and included in the 120-145 credits, consists of 4 core courses, a 12 credit hour distribution requirement, physical education, and a 15 credit hour science/math requirement. Students must take 30 credit hours of upper-level courses at MTU that apply to the degree requirements, and 30 of the last 36 credit hours, regardless of level, must be completed at MTU. **Procedure:** Freshmen are admitted to all sessions. Entrance exams should be taken Scores will be accepted until time of enrollment. There are deferred admissions and rolling admissions plans. Application deadlines are open. Notifications are sent June 15. Application fees are waived if application is completed online. **Transfer Students:** 184 transfer students enrolled in 2015-2016. Transfer students must have a minimum GPA of 2.75 on a 4.0 scale; grades of B or better are expected in math and science courses. Some selected programs require a 2.5 cumulative transfer GPA. 30 of 120 credits required for the bachelor's degree must be completed at Michigan Tech. **International Students:** There are 176 international students enrolled. The school actively recruits these students. They must take the TOEFL with a minimum score of 550 on the paper-based TOEFL (PBT) or 79 on the Internet-based version (iBT) or take the MELAB, IELTS, TOEIC, Pearson Test of English, and Eiken STEP.

ADMISSIONS: 76% of the 2016-2017 applicants were accepted. The SAT scores for the 2016-2017 freshman class were: Critical Reading-- 16% below 500, 35% between 500 and 599, 28% between 600 and 699, and 20% between 700 and 800. Math-- 4% below 500, 29% between 500 and 599, 49% between 600 and 699, and 18% between 700 and 800. Writing-- 32% below 500, 37% between 500 and 599, 30% between 600 and 699, and 1% between 700 and 800. The ACT scores were 15% between 18 and 23, 58% between 24 and 29, and 27% above 30. 52% of the current freshmen were in the top fifth of their class; 83% were in the top two fifths. There were 9 National Merit finalists. 55 freshmen graduated first in their class. **Admissions Contact:** Allison Carter, Director of Admissions. Email: *mtu4u@mtu.edu* Web: *www.mtu.edu*

FINANCIAL AID: 23% of undergraduate students work part-time. Average annual earnings from campus work are $5736. The FAFSA code is 002292. The priority date for freshman financial aid applications for fall entry is March 1.

NORTHERN MICHIGAN UNIVERSITY C-2

www.nmu.edu

Marquette, MI 49855	**(906) 227-2650** **(800) 682-9797**
Fax: (906) 227-1747	**Email: admissions@nmu.edu**
Full-time: 2883 men, 3413 women	**Faculty:** 291; IIA, av$
Part-time: 336 men, 450 women	**Ph.D.s:** 75%
Graduate: 233 men, 435 women	**Student/Faculty:** 22 to 1
Year: semesters, summer session	**Tuition:** $9766 ($15,262)
Room & Board: $9838	**Freshman Class:** 5346 applied, 4056 accepted, 1544 enrolled
ACT: 23	**CEEB CODE:** 1560
Application Deadline: open	**COMPETITIVE**

Northern Michigan University, founded in 1899, is the university of choice in the Midwest for students seeking quality academic programs in a high-tech learning environment. There are 4 undergraduate schools and 1 graduate school. In addition to regional accreditation, NMU has baccalaureate program accreditation with AACSB, ADA, CSWE, NASM, NCATE, NLN, TEAC, CAAHEP, and CCNE. The 360-acre campus is in an urban area on the southern shores of Lake Superior. Including any residence halls, there are 55 buildings.

STUDENT LIFE: 80% of undergraduates are from Michigan. Others are from 48 states, 39 foreign countries, and Canada. 84% are White; 3% Hispanic; 3% two or more races; 3% race unknown; 2% African American; 2% American Indian/Alaska Native; 2% Foreign; 1% Asian American. **Female To Male Ratio:** 1.2:1. The average age of freshmen is 18.2; all undergraduates, 22.1. 28% do not continue beyond their first year; 49% remain to graduate. **Housing:** 3250 students can be accommodated in college housing, which includes coed dorms, on-campus apartments, married student housing, honors houses, special-interest houses, and smoke-free and chemical-free houses. On-campus housing is guaranteed for all 4 years, is available on a first-come, and first-served basis. 58% of students commute. All students may keep cars.

FACULTY/CLASSROOMS: 51% of faculty are male; 49% are female. All teach undergraduates, 41% do research, and 41% do both. Graduate students teach 1% of introductory courses. The average class size in an introductory lecture is 30; in a laboratory is 17; and in a regular course is 23.

PROGRAMS OF STUDY: NMU confers B.A., B.S., B.F.A., B.M.Ed., B.S.N., B.S.W. and D.N.P. degrees. Associate, master's, and doctoral degrees are also awarded. Bachelor's degrees are awarded in AGRICULTURE (environmental studies, fishing and fisheries, and wildlife management), BIOLOGICAL SCIENCE (biochemistry, biology/biological science, biology/gen sci/envir sci second ed, botany, ecology, forensic science, genetics, microbiology, physiology, and zoology), BUSINESS (accounting, accounting (finance), accounting (information systems), banking and finance, business administration and management, entrepreneurial studies, finance, and marketing/retailing/merchandising), COMMUNICATIONS AND THE ARTS (art and design, broadcasting, communications, design, English, fine arts, French, language arts, music, public relations, Spanish, speech/debate/rhetoric, and theatre arts), COMPUTER AND PHYSICAL SCIENCE (chemistry, computer programming, computer science, cyber intelligence/security studies, earth science, information sciences and systems, mathematics, and physics), EDUCATION (art education, business education, computer education, elementary education, health education, industrial arts education, music education, physical education, science education, and secondary education), ENGINEERING AND ENVIRONMENTAL DESIGN (construction management, electrical/electronics engineering technology, furniture design, industrial engineering technology, and manufacturing technology), HEALTH PROFESSIONS (clinical science, exercise science, medical laboratory technology, nursing, physician's assistant, predentistry, premedicine, preveterinary science, speech pathology/audiology, and speech therapy), SOCIAL SCIENCE (criminal justice, economics, gender studies, geography, history, international studies, parks and recreation management, philosophy, physical fitness/movement, political science/government, prelaw, psychology, public administration, social work, sociology, Spanish studies, and water resources). Nursing, construction management, MPA, education, and criminal justice are the strongest academically. Nursing, art & design and biology have the largest enrollments.

ACTIVITIES: 1% of men belong to 2 national fraternities; 1% of women belong to 1 local and 2 national sororities. There are 318 groups on campus, including and health, philosophy, art, band, cheerleading, chess, choir, chorale, chorus, communications, computers, dance, drama, drill team, environmental, ethnic, film, honors, international, international dance club, jazz band, LGBT, literary magazine, marching band, musical theater, newspaper, orchestra, pep band, photography, political, professional, radio and TV, religious, social, social service, student government, and symphony. Popular campus events include Winterfest, Homecoming, and U.P. 200 Dog Sled Race. **Sports:** There are 7 intercollegiate sports for men and 9 for women, and 12 intramural sports for men and 12 for women. Facilities include indoor and outdoor playing fields, an aerobic and fitness training area, ice rink, swimming pool, diving tank, field house, stadium, basketball and hockey arena, rock-climbing wall, golf stimulator and racquetball courts. **Graduates:** From July 1, 2015 to June 30, 2016, 1802 bachelor's degrees were awarded. The most popular majors were business (10%), tech/occupational studies (10%), and biology (9%). In an average class, 5% graduate in 3 years or less, 22% graduate in 4 years or less, 41% graduate in 5 years or less, and 47% graduate in 6 years or less. Of the 2015 graduating class, 25% were enrolled in graduate school within 6 months of graduation, and 60% were employed.

SERVICES: Counseling and information services are available, as is tutoring in most subjects, a reader service for the blind, and remedial math, reading, and writing. **Library/Resources:** The library contains 750,000 volumes, 131,919 microform items, 5,641 audio/video tapes/CDs/DVDs, and subscribes to 35,686 periodicals including electronic. Computerized library services include interlibrary loans, database searching, Internet access, and Wi-Fi capability. Special learning facilities include an art gallery, radio station, TV station, Special learning facilities on campus include a learning resource center, computing help desk, regional heritage center, and an observatory. **Physically Challenged Students:** All of the campus is accessible. Facilities include wheelchair ramps, elevators, special parking, specially equipped restrooms, lowered drinking fountains, lowered telephones, and special housing. **Special:** NMU offers internships, a co-op program in business, study abroad in a number of countries, a Washington semester, dual majors in computer information and accounting and student-designed majors in individual studies and liberal arts. There are 7 national honor societies, a freshman honors program, and 1 departmental honors program. **Visiting:** There are regularly scheduled orientations for prospective students, including an admissions interview, a tour and a faculty visit. Visitors may sit in on classes and stay overnight. To schedule a visit, contact Campus Visit at https:/www.nmu.edu/admissions/visit-register. **Campus Safety and Security:** Measures include 24-hour foot and vehicle patrol, emergency notification system, self-defense education, and security escort services. There are also shuttle buses, emergency telephones, lighted pathways/sidewalks, controlled access to dorms/residences, and a crime prevention program with a full-time staff.

REQUIREMENTS: NMU requires a GPA of 2.25 and a minimum composite score of 980 for the SAT and 19 for the ACT. Applicants must be graduates of accredited secondary schools or have earned a GED. NMU requires 12 to 16 Carnegie units; recommended secondary school preparation includes 4 years of English, 3 each of math, history, social studies, foreign language, and science, 2 of fine arts or performing arts, and 1 of computer instruction. Students seeking art scholarships must submit a portfolio; those seeking music and theater scholarships must audition. AP and CLEP credits are accepted. Students must earn 40 semester credits in liberal studies, including courses in humanities, composition, natural sciences/math, social sciences, communications and visual and performing arts. Graduation requirements vary by degree program, but at the minimum, students must earn 124 semester credits, including 32 in a major field, with a GPA of 2.0. Courses in phys ed/health and world culture are also required. **Procedure:** Freshmen are admitted to all sessions. Entrance exams should be taken The year prior to enrollment. There are deferred admissions and rolling admissions plans. Application deadlines are open. The fall 2016 application fee was $35. Notification is sent on a rolling basis. Application fees are waived if application is completed online. **Transfer Students:** 396 transfer students enrolled in 2015-2016. Applicants must present a minimum GPA of 2.0 in at least 12 semester credits of college-level work. 32 of 124 credits required for the bachelor's degree must be completed at NMU. **International Students:** There are 214 international students enrolled. The school actively recruits these students. They must take the TOEFL with a minimum score of 500 on the paper-based TOEFL (PBT) or 61 on the Internet-based version (iBT). Students must also take the SAT or ACT, scoring 19. Canadian students must take the SAT or ACT.

ADMISSIONS: 76% of the 2016-2017 applicants were accepted. **Admissions Contact:** Gerri Daniels, Director of Admissions. Email: *admissions@nmu.edu* Web: *www.nmu.edu*

FINANCIAL AID: In 2016-2017, 94% of all full-time freshmen and 88% of continuing full-time students received some form of financial aid. 59% of all full-time freshmen and 58% of continuing full-time students received need-based aid. The average freshman award was $12,830. Need-based scholarships or need-based grants averaged $5,282 ($10,000 maximum); need-based self-help aid (loans and jobs) averaged $4,195 ($9,500 maximum); non-need-based athletic scholarships averaged $9,240 ($26,363 maximum); and other non-need-based awards and non-need-based scholarships averaged $7,597 ($26,463 maximum). 31% of undergraduate students work part-time. Average annual earnings from campus work are $2179. The average financial indebtedness of the 2016 graduate was $25,500. The FAFSA code is 002301. The priority date for freshman financial aid applications for fall entry is March 1.

NORTHWOOD UNIVERSITY - MICHIGAN *(The complete profile is made available exclusively on our website, www.barronspac.com)*

OAKLAND UNIVERSITY E-4
www.oakland.edu

Rochester, MI 48309 (248) 370-3360
(800) OAK-UNIV
Email: visit@oakland.edu

Full-time: 5344 men, 7543 women
Part-time: 1962 men, 2312 women
Graduate: 1519 men, 2031 women
Year: semesters, summer session
Room & Board: $9250
ACT: 22
Application Deadline: March 24

Faculty: I, --$
Ph.D.s: n/av
Student/Faculty: n/av
Tuition: $11,513 ($23,873)
Freshman Class: 12152 applied, 7551 accepted, 2464 enrolled
CEEB CODE: 1497
COMPETITIVE

Oakland University, established in 1957, is a comprehensive state-supported institution serving a primarily commuter student body. Figures in the above capsule and in this profile are approximate. There are 7 undergraduate schools and 7 graduate schools. In addition to regional accreditation, Oakland has baccalaureate program accreditation with AACSB, ABET, CSWE, NASM, TEAC, NASPAA, NAST, NASD, ACS, CCNE, CACREP, and CAPTE. The 1444-acre campus is in a suburban area 25 miles north of Detroit. Including any residence halls, there are 46 buildings.

STUDENT LIFE: 97% of undergraduates are from Michigan. Others are from 39 states, 45 foreign countries, and Canada. 8% are African American; 75% White; 4% Asian American; 4% race unknown; 3% Hispanic; 3% two or more races; 2% Foreign. **Female To Male Ratio:** 1.3:1. The average age of freshmen is 19; all undergraduates, 23. 24% do not continue beyond their first year. **Housing:** College-sponsored housing includes single-sex and coed dorms, on-campus apartments, and married student housing. In addition, there are honors houses, special-interest houses, fraternity houses, sorority houses, living learning communities, international village, and eco Interest, pre-business, pre-nursing, and scholars tower. On-campus housing is guaranteed for all 4 years. All students may keep cars.

FACULTY/CLASSROOMS: 54% of faculty are male; 46% are female. No introductory courses are taught by graduate students.

PROGRAMS OF STUDY: Oakland confers B.A., B.S., B.F.A., B.I.S., B.Mus., B.S.E., B.S.N. and B.S.W. degrees. Master's and doctoral degrees are also awarded. Bachelor's degrees are awarded in BIOLOGICAL SCIENCE (biochemistry and biology/biological science), BUSINESS (accounting, banking and finance, business administration and management, business economics, human resources, management information systems, marketing/retailing/merchandising, operations management, and personnel management), COMMUNICATIONS AND THE ARTS (art history and appreciation, Chinese, communications, dance, dramatic arts, English, film arts, French, German, Japanese, journalism, linguistics, music, performing arts, Spanish, and studio art), COMPUTER AND PHYSICAL SCIENCE (chemistry, computer science, information sciences and systems, mathematics, medical physics, physics, and statistics), EDUCATION (elementary education and music education), ENGINEERING AND ENVIRONMENTAL DESIGN (computer engineering, electrical/electronics engineering, engineering chemistry, engineering physics, environmental science, industrial engineering, mechanical engineering, and occupational safety and health), HEALTH PROFESSIONS (allied health, health science, medical laboratory science, nursing, and preventive/wellness health care), SOCIAL SCIENCE (African American studies, anthropology, East Asian studies, economics, history, international relations, Latin American studies, liberal arts/general studies, philosophy, political science/government, psychology, public administration, Russian and Slavic studies, social work, sociology, South Asian studies, and women's studies). Business, health sciences, and engineering have the largest enrollments.

ACTIVITIES: 2% of men belong to 6 national fraternities; 2% of women belong to 6 national sororities. There are 258 groups on campus, including art, band, cheerleading, choir, chorale, chorus, computers, dance, drama, environmental, ethnic, film, forensics, honors, international, jazz band, LGBT, musical theater, newspaper, orchestra, pep band, political, professional, radio and TV, religious, social, social service, student government, and symphony. Popular campus events include Welcome Week, Hispanic Celebration, and Week of Champions at OU. **Sports:** There are 7 intercollegiate sports for men and 9 for women, and 18 intramural sports for men and 18 for women. Facilities include a student recreation and athletic center that includes softball and baseball diamonds, an indoor track, soccer and touch football fields, and facilities for swimming, basketball, weight training, dance, fencing, handball, squash, racquetball, and golf. **Graduates:** From July 1, 2015 to June 30, 2016, 2345 bachelor's degrees were awarded. The most popular majors were nursing (14%), business (13%), and education (8%). 190 companies recruited on campus in 2015-2016.

SERVICES: Counseling and information services are available, as is tutoring in most subjects, such as 100 and 200 level classes. There is a reader service for the blind, and remedial math, reading, and writing. There is also a mentorship program. **Library/Resources:** The 2 libraries contain 851,190 volumes, 1.2 million microform items, 29,868 audio/video tapes/CDs/DVDs, and subscribe to 43,501 periodicals including electronic. Computerized library services include interlibrary loans, database searching, Internet access, and Wi-Fi capability. Special learning facilities include an art gallery, radio station, TV station, the Product Development and Manufacturing Center, the Historical House Museum, and the Lean-Learning Institute. **Physically Challenged Students:** 99% of the campus is accessible. Facilities include wheelchair ramps, elevators, special parking, specially equipped restrooms, special class scheduling, lowered drinking fountains, lowered telephones, and special housing, with automatic door openers. **Special:** Special academic programs include internships, cooperative programs for most disciplines, and many work-study opportunities. There are organized programs for study abroad in 8 countries; independent programs can be arranged. Oakland also offers a B.A. or B.S. degree in biology and economics, a general studies program, dual majors, a student-designed major, cross-registration with Macomb Community College, and preprofessional studies in medicine, dentistry, optometry, and veterinary medicine. There are 12 national honor societies and a freshman honors program. **Visiting:** There are regularly scheduled orientations for prospective students, including a review of services, academic advising, and course registration. There are guides for informal visits, visitors may sit in on classes, and stay overnight. To schedule a visit, contact the Admissions Office. **Campus Safety and Security:** Measures include 24-hour foot and vehicle patrol, emergency notification system, self-defense education, and security escort services. There are also shuttle buses, emergency telephones, lighted pathways/sidewalks, controlled access to dorms/residences, and a text alert.

REQUIREMENTS: The ACT is required. Admissions requirements include graduation from an accredited secondary school and high school level college preparatory work, including 4 years of English and 3 years each of math, science, and social studies. 2 years of foreign language is recommended as well. Music and dance majors must audition. A GPA of 2.5 is required. AP and CLEP credits are accepted. To graduate, students must complete 124 credit hours (153 to 161 for the B.Mus. or 128 for the B.S.Env.Health). All students must complete 40 credits of general education requirements, including at least 1 course (3 or more credits) from the list of approved courses in each of the 10 knowledge areas: writing, formal reasoning, arts, foreign language and culture, global perspective, literature, natural science and technology, social science, Western civilization, and knowledge application. A GPA of 2.0 is required. **Procedure:** Freshmen are admitted to all sessions. Entrance exams should be taken during the spring of the junior year or early fall of the senior year. There are deferred admissions and rolling admissions plans. Applications should be filed by March 24 for fall entry. Notification is sent on a rolling basis. Applications are accepted online. **Transfer Students:** 1891 transfer students enrolled in 2015-2016. Applicants must have at least a 2.5 GPA; a higher GPA is required in some majors. 32 of 124 credits required for the bachelor's degree must be completed at Oakland. **International Students:** They must take the TOEFL with a minimum score of 550 on the paper-based TOEFL (PBT) or 79 on the Internet-based version (iBT) or take the MELAB. They must also take the ACT.

ADMISSIONS: 62% of the 2016-2017 applicants were accepted. **Admissions Contact:** Eleanor Reynolds, Assistant Vice President Student Affairs Admissions. Email: *visit@oakland.edu* Web: *www.oakland.edu*

FINANCIAL AID: The average freshman award was $12,885. Need-based scholarships or need-based grants averaged $5,645; need-based self-help aid (loans and jobs) averaged $3,173; and non-need-based athletic scholarships averaged $11,515. The FAFSA code is 002307. The priority date for freshman financial aid applications for fall entry is January 1.

OLIVET COLLEGE *(The complete profile is made available exclusively on our website, www.barronspac.com)*

ROCHESTER COLLEGE *(The complete profile is made available exclusively on our website, www.barronspac.com)*

SAGINAW VALLEY STATE UNIVERSITY D-4

www.svsu.edu

University Center, MI 48710	(989) 964-4200 (800) 968-9500
Fax: (989) 790-0180	**Email:** admissions@svsu.edu
Full-time: 2884 men, 4104 women	**Faculty:** n/av
Part-time: 652 men, 757 women	**Ph.D.s:** 83%
Graduate: 207 men, 561 women	**Student/Faculty:** n/av
Year: semesters, summer session	**Tuition:** $9345 ($21,947)
Room & Board: $9185	**Freshman Class:** 6700 applied, 5083 accepted, 1353 enrolled
ACT: 22	**CEEB CODE:** 1766
Application Deadline: December 1	**COMPETITIVE**

Saginaw Valley State University, founded in 1963, is a state-supported institution offering undergraduate and graduate degrees in arts and behavioral sciences, business and management, education, nursing and health sciences, and science, engineering, and technology. Figures in the above capsule and in this profile are approximate. There are 5 undergraduate schools and 5 graduate schools. In addition to regional accreditation, SVSU has baccalaureate program accreditation with AACSB, ABET, CSWE, NASM, NCATE, ACS, NAACLS, ACOTE, CCNE, and CAATE. The 782-acre campus is in a suburban area 5 miles north of Saginaw. Including any residence halls, there are 90 buildings.

STUDENT LIFE: 91% of undergraduates are from Michigan. Others are from 26 states, 43 foreign countries, and Canada. 95% are from public schools. 8% are African American; 8% Foreign; 71% White; 6% race unknown; 4% Hispanic; 2% two or more races; 1% Asian American. **Female To Male Ratio:** 1.4:1. The average age of freshmen is 18; all undergraduates, 22. 32% do not continue beyond their first year; 68% remain to graduate. **Housing:** 2736 students can be accommodated in college housing, which includes coed dorms, on-campus apartments, healthy life-style floors and buildings, and first-year suites. On-campus housing is available on a first-come and first-served basis. 71% of students commute. All students may keep cars.

FACULTY/CLASSROOMS: No introductory courses are taught by graduate students. The average class size in an introductory lecture is 25 and in a laboratory is 17.

PROGRAMS OF STUDY: SVSU confers B.A., B.S., B.A.S., B.B.A., B.F.A., B.P.A., B.S.E.E., B.S.M.E., B.S.N., and B.S.W. degrees. Master's and doctoral degrees are also awarded. Bachelor's degrees are awarded in BIOLOGICAL SCIENCE (biochemistry and biology/biological science), BUSINESS (accounting, banking and finance, business administration and management, business economics, finance, international business management, and marketing management), COMMUNICATIONS AND THE ARTS (art, communications, creative writing, design, dramatic arts, English, fine arts, French, music, Spanish, and technical and business writing), COMPUTER AND PHYSICAL SCIENCE (applied mathematics, applied science, chemical physics, chemistry, computer science, information sciences and systems, mathematics, optics, and physics), EDUCATION (art education, athletic training, drama education, elementary education, English education, foreign languages education, mathematics education, music education, physical education, science education, social studies education, and special education), ENGINEERING AND ENVIRONMENTAL DESIGN (electrical/electronics engineering, engineering technology, industrial administration/management, mechanical engineering, and preengineering), HEALTH PROFESSIONS (exercise science, health science, medical laboratory science, medical technology, nursing, predentistry, premedicine, and prephysical therapy), SOCIAL SCIENCE (criminal justice, economics, geography, history, interdisciplinary studies, international studies, political science/government, prelaw, psychology, public administration, social work, and sociology). Nursing, social work, and criminal justice have the largest enrollments.

ACTIVITIES: 3% of men belong to 7 national fraternities; 3% of women belong to 1 local and 3 national sororities. There are 165 groups on campus, including art, band, cheerleading, chess, choir, chorus, computers, dance, drama, environmental, ethnic, film, honors, international, jazz band, LGBT, literary magazine, marching band, musical theater, newspaper, orchestra, pep band, photography, political, professional, radio and TV, religious, social, social service, and student government. Popular campus events include Battle of the Valleys, Cards Party and International Food Festival. **Sports:** There are 8 intercollegiate sports for men and 8 for women, and 16 intramural sports for men and 16 for women. Facilities include a health and phys ed complex with a pool, indoor track, basketball courts, badminton courts, volleyball courts, racquetball courts, fitness center, tennis courts, intramural, baseball, softball, soccer fields, archery range, fitness trail, football stadium, golf driving range, putting green, and horse shoe pits. **Graduates:** From July 1, 2015 to June 30, 2016, 1324 bachelor's degrees were awarded. The most popular majors were nursing (8%), social work (7%), and criminal justice (7%). 370 companies recruited on campus in 2015-2016. In an average class, 11% graduate in 4 years or less, 30% graduate in 5 years or less, and 38% graduate in 6 years or less. Of the 2015 graduating class, 24% were enrolled in graduate school within 6 months of graduation, and 87% were employed.

SERVICES: Counseling and information services are available, as is tutoring in most subjects, a reader service for the blind, and remedial math, reading, and writing. **Library/Resources:** The library contains 368,865 volumes, 354,265 microform items, 27,210 audio/video tapes/CDs/DVDs, and subscribes to 50,291 periodicals including electronic. Computerized library services include interlibrary loans, database searching, Internet access, and Wi-Fi capability. Special learning facilities include an art gallery, radio station, an observatory. **Physically Challenged Students:** 99% of the campus is accessible. Facilities include wheelchair ramps, elevators, special parking, specially equipped restrooms, special class scheduling, lowered drinking fountains, lowered telephones, and special housing. Electronically opened doors, and special access to the library. All buildings are interconnected on the second floor. **Special:** Study abroad in 53 countries, internships, and Michigan Work Study and Federal College Work Study job opportunities within several on-campus departments. There are 4 national honor societies. **Visiting:** There are regularly scheduled orientations for prospective students, including tours, help with schedules, basic information and counseling. There are guides for informal visits. To schedule a visit, contact the Office of Admissions at tours@svsu.edu. **Campus Safety and Security:** Measures include 24-hour foot and vehicle patrol, emergency notification system, self-defense education, and security escort services, emergency telephones, and lighted pathways/sidewalks. In addition the SVSU public safety department has commissioned law enforcement to provide police services.

REQUIREMENTS: Applicants must submit a completed undergraduate application for admission, an official high school transcript or GED, and ACT results. SVSU recommends high school students take a rigorous college preparatory curriculum prior to enrolling at SVSU: four years of English, three years of math, three years of natural sciences, three years of social sciences, and two years of the same foreign language. A GPA of 2.5 is required. AP and CLEP credits are accepted. Students must complete a minimum of 124 credits, satisfy basic skills and general education requirements, and maintain a minimum GPA of 2.0. The General Education Program consists of 35 credit hours in 10 categories. **Procedure:** Freshmen are admitted to all sessions. There are deferred admissions and rolling admissions plans. Application deadlines are open. Application fee is $30. Applications are accepted online. **Transfer Students:** 599 transfer students enrolled in 2015-2016. Transfer students with fewer than 24 credits from a previous college must submit high school and college transcripts. ACT or SAT scores must be submitted. A minimum GPA of 2.0 is needed. An interview may be required. 31 of 124 credits required for the bachelor's degree must be completed at SVSU. **International Students:** There are 465 international students enrolled. The school actively recruits these students. They must take the TOEFL with a minimum score of 500 on the paper-based TOEFL (PBT) or 61 on the Internet-based version (iBT).

ADMISSIONS: 76% of the 2016-2017 applicants were accepted. The ACT scores were 7% between 12 and 17, 55% between 18 and 23, 32% between 24 and 29, and 5% above 30. 32% of the current freshmen were in the top fifth of their class; 62% were in the top two fifths. 33 freshmen graduated first in their class. **Admissions Contact:** Jennifer Pahl, Director of Admissions. Email: *admissions@svsu.edu* Web: *www.svsu.edu*

FINANCIAL AID: In 2016-2017, 94% of all full-time freshmen and 91% of continuing full-time students received some form of financial aid. 65% of all full-time freshmen and 64% of continuing full-time students received need-based aid. Average annual earnings from campus work are

$1500. The FAFSA code is 002314. Check with the school for current application deadlines.

SIENA HEIGHTS UNIVERSITY E-5

www.sienaheights.edu

Adrian, MI 49221 (517) 264-7185
(800) 521-0009
Email: admissions@sienaheights.edu

Full-time: 606 men, 639 women	**Faculty:** 76; IIA
Part-time: 442 men, 715 women	**Ph.D.s:** 66%
Graduate: 80 men, 160 women	**Student/Faculty:** 12 to 1
Year: semesters, summer session	**Tuition:** $22,740
Room & Board: $9300	**Freshman Class:** 1422 applied, 962 accepted, 300 enrolled
ACT: 21	**CEEB CODE:** 1719
Application Deadline: August 1	**COMPETITIVE**

Siena Heights University, founded in 1919 is a Catholic university sponsored by the Adrian Dominican Sisters. Enrolling a diverse community of traditional-age and working adult students, Siena Heights is a coeducational North Central accredited institution founded in the liberal arts tradition, offering associate's, bachelor's, master's and specialist's degrees. The University is headquartered in Adrian, Michigan, where it offers a traditional undergraduate experience, and degree completion centers are Dearborn, Southfield, Benton Harbor, Monroe, Battle Creek, Lansing, Jackson, as well as online. There are 2 undergraduate schools and 1 graduate school. In addition to regional accreditation, Siena has baccalaureate program accreditation with CSWE, NASAD, TEAC, and CCNE. The 140-acre campus is in a small town. Including any residence halls, there are 14 buildings.

STUDENT LIFE: 89% of undergraduates are from Michigan. Others are from 37 states, 12 foreign countries, and Canada. 67% are White; 12% African American; 12% race unknown; 5% Hispanic; 2% two or more races; 1% Asian American; 1% American Indian/Alaska Native; 1% Foreign. 35% are Protestant; 26% claim no religious affiliation; 21% Catholic. **Female To Male Ratio:** 1.3:1. The average age of freshmen is 18; all undergraduates, 29. 43% do not continue beyond their first year; 53% remain to graduate. **Housing:** 605 students can be accommodated in college housing, which includes single-sex and coed dorms, on-campus apartments, married student housing, special housing for international students, and dorm floors exclusively for men and women. On-campus housing is available on a first-come, first-served basis, and is available on a lottery system for upperclassmen. 71% of students commute. All students may keep cars.

FACULTY/CLASSROOMS: 46% of faculty are male; 54% are female. All teach undergraduates. No introductory courses are taught by graduate students.

PROGRAMS OF STUDY: Siena confers B.A., B.S., B.A.S., and B.F.A. degrees. Associate and master's degrees are also awarded. Bachelor's degrees are awarded in BIOLOGICAL SCIENCE (biology/biological science), BUSINESS (accounting and business administration and management), COMMUNICATIONS AND THE ARTS (art history and appreciation, communications, English, fine arts, graphic design, music, Spanish, studio art, theatre arts, and visual and performing arts), COMPUTER AND PHYSICAL SCIENCE (chemistry, computer information systems, information sciences and systems, mathematics, and natural sciences), EDUCATION (art education, elementary education, music education, science education, special education, and trade and industrial education), HEALTH PROFESSIONS (pre-health studies and premedicine), SOCIAL SCIENCE (child psychology/development, criminal justice, history, human services, humanities, liberal arts/general studies, philosophy, psychology, public administration, religion, social science, and social work). Business administration, nursing, and biology have the largest enrollments.

ACTIVITIES: 2% of men belong to 1 national fraternity; 2% of women belong to 1 national sorority. There are 30 groups on campus, including art, band, cheerleading, choir, chorus, computers, dance, drama, environmental, ethnic, international, jazz band, LGBT, literary magazine, marching band, musical theater, newspaper, pep band, photography, professional, religious, social, social service, student government, and symphony. Popular campus events include Alumni/Family Weekend, International Dinner, Athletic Banquets, Homecoming, and Common Dialog Day. **Sports:** There are 10 intercollegiate sports for men and 11 for women. Facilities include a stadium football, soccer, track, and lacrosse, basketball and volleyball courts, practice courts, baseball diamond, and track and field areas. **Graduates:** From July 1, 2015 to June 30, 2016, 849 bachelor's degrees were awarded. The most popular majors were health professions and related programs (24%), business (22%), and law enforcement and related programs (11%). In an average class, 43% graduate in 6 years or less.

SERVICES: Counseling and information services are available, as is tutoring in most subjects, and remedial math, reading, and writing. **Library/Resources:** The library contains 206,966 volumes, 3,134 microform items, 1,543 audio/video tapes/CDs/DVDs, and subscribes to 47,565 periodicals including electronic. Computerized library services include interlibrary loans, database searching, Internet access, and Wi-Fi capability. Special learning facilities include an art gallery. **Physically Challenged Students:** 90% of the campus is accessible. Facilities include wheelchair ramps, elevators, special parking, specially equipped restrooms, special class scheduling, and lowered drinking fountains. We have an Office of Disability Resources and have long been a Student Support Services grant recipient. **Special:** The most unique program is the Bachelors in Applied Science for adult learners looking to complete their degree. SHU also offers Completely Online Programs and many additional distance learning opportunities. There is a Liberal Arts core curriculum that includes traditional general studies groupings of courses as well as liberal arts studies courses that reflect Dominican and University values. SHU also offers dual enrollment credit for high school students and a variety of study abroad opportunities. There is 1 national honor society. **Visiting:** There are regularly scheduled orientations for prospective students. There are guides for informal visits, visitors may sit in on classes, and stay overnight. To schedule a visit, contact Trudy Mohre at tmohre@sienaheights.edu. **Campus Safety and Security:** Measures include 24-hour foot and vehicle patrol, emergency notification system, self-defense education, and security escort services. There are lighted pathways/sidewalks, and StormReady Community-National Weather Service.

REQUIREMENTS: The ACT is required, with a minimum score of 17. Admissions requirements include graduation from an accredited secondary school. The GED is accepted. Applications are accepted on-line. AP and CLEP credits are accepted. Degree requirements may vary according to which College you attend and which major you select. Generally, the following requirement applies at least 120 semester hours with a minimum of a 2.0 GPA. At least 30 semester hours at SHU. At least 12 of the last 30 semester hours at SHU. At least 30 semester hours at the 300/400 level and at least 15 of those at SHU. demonstration of writing and math proficiency, and the liberal arts core curriculum. **Procedure:** Freshmen are admitted in the fall and spring. There are deferred admissions and rolling admissions plans. Applications should be filed by August 1 for fall entry. Notifications are sent July 1. Applications are accepted online. Application fees are waived if application is completed on-line. **Transfer Students:** 474 transfer students enrolled in 2015-2016. 2.5 High School GPA, 2.0 College GPA for College of Arts and Sciences, which offers the traditional undergraduate experience. Please refer to our online catalog or contact a representative from the College for Professional Studies if you are an adult learner looking to complete a degree. 30 of 120 credits required for the bachelor's degree must be completed at Siena. **International Students:** There are 25 international students enrolled. The school actively recruits these students. They must take the TOEFL, and also take the ACT, scoring 18.

ADMISSIONS: 68% of the 2016-2017 applicants were accepted. **Admissions Contact:** Trudy Mohre, Director of Admissions. Email: *admissions@sienaheights.edu* Web: *www.sienaheights.edu*

FINANCIAL AID: In 2016-2017, 96% of all full-time freshmen and 80% of continuing full-time students received some form of financial aid. 73% of all full-time freshmen and 69% of continuing full-time students received need-based aid. Siena is a member of CSS. The FAFSA code is 002316. The deadline for filing freshman financial aid applications for fall entry is August 1.

SPRING ARBOR UNIVERSITY D-5

www.arbor.edu

Spring Arbor, MI 49283	**(517) 750-6468**
	(800) 968-0011
Fax: (517) 750-6620	**Email: admissions@arbor.edu**
Full-time: 555 men, 815 women	**Faculty:** IIA
Part-time: 65 men, 120 women	**Ph.D.s:** 61%
Graduate: 290 men, 950 women	**Student/Faculty:** n/av
Year: semesters, summer session	**Tuition:** $26,730
Room & Board: $9270	**Freshman Class:** n/av
ACT: recommended	**CEEB CODE:** 1732
Application Deadline: August 1	**COMPETITIVE**

Spring Arbor University, founded in 1873 by leaders of the Free Methodist Church, offers a Christ-centered, liberal arts education with more than 50 undergraduate programs, 7 degree-completion programs, and 7 graduate programs. The figures in the above capsule are approximate. There are 3 undergraduate schools and 7 graduate schools. In addition to regional accreditation, SAU has baccalaureate program accreditation with CSWE, NCATE, and CCNE. The 123-acre campus is in a small town 8 miles south west of Jackson. Including any residence halls, there are 36 buildings.

STUDENT LIFE: 85% of undergraduates are from Michigan. Others are from 30 states, 6 foreign countries, and Canada. 90% are White; 5% African American; 2% Asian American; 2% Hispanic; 1% Foreign. 67% are Protestant; 20% unknown nondenominations; 11% claim no religious affiliation. **Female To Male Ratio:** 2.1:1. 28% do not continue beyond their first year; 59% remain to graduate. **Housing:** 1060 students can be accommodated in college housing, which includes single-sex dorms, on-campus apartments, and married student housing. On-campus housing is guaranteed for all 4 years. 68% of students live on campus; of those, 60% remain on campus on weekends. Upperclassmen may keep cars. Alcohol is not permitted.

FACULTY/CLASSROOMS: 60% of faculty are male; 40% are female. 94% teach undergraduates. No introductory courses are taught by graduate students. The average class size in a regular course is 18.

PROGRAMS OF STUDY: SAU confers B.A., and B.S.W. degrees. Associate and master's degrees are also awarded. Bachelor's degrees are awarded in BIOLOGICAL SCIENCE (biochemistry and biology/biological science), BUSINESS (accounting, business administration and management, and management information systems), COMMUNICATIONS AND THE ARTS (advertising, art, broadcasting, communications, English, film arts, language arts, music, Spanish, video, and visual and performing arts), COMPUTER AND PHYSICAL SCIENCE (chemistry, computer science, mathematics, and physics), EDUCATION (Christian education, music education, and special education), HEALTH PROFESSIONS (exercise science and nursing), SOCIAL SCIENCE (biblical studies, history, missions, philosophy, philosophy and religion, physical fitness/movement, psychology, social science, social studies, social work, sociology, theological studies, and youth ministry). Business, teacher education, and English are the strongest academically. Teacher education, business, and philosophy/religion have the largest enrollments.

ACTIVITIES: There are no fraternities or sororities. There are 41 groups on campus, including art, band, choir, chorale, drama, ethnic, film, honors, international, jazz band, literary magazine, musical theater, newspaper, pep band, radio and TV, religious, social, social service, student government, symphony, and yearbook. Popular campus events include Porchfest, Arbor Games, and Midnight Breakfast. **Sports:** There are 7 intercollegiate sports for men and 7 for women, and 7 intramural sports for men and 6 for women. Facilities include a weight room, basketball courts and volleyball courts, a indoor track, swimming pool, a training room, batting cages, baseball, softball, a soccer field, outdoor track, and tennis courts (2 lighted). **Graduates:** From July 1, 2015 to June 30, 2016, 684 bachelor's degrees were awarded. The most popular majors were business (36%), family life (17%), and teacher education (16%). In an average class, 1% graduate in 3 years or less, 38% graduate in 4 years or less, 54% graduate in 5 years or less, and 59% graduate in 6 years or less. Of the 2015 graduating class, 25% were enrolled in graduate school within 6 months of graduation, and 63% were employed.

SERVICES: Counseling and information services are available, as is tutoring in most subjects, a reader service for the blind, and remedial math, reading, and writing. Religious counseling and health services are also available. **Library/Resources:** The library contains 112,811 volumes, 576,594 microform items, 3,943 audio/video tapes/CDs/DVDs, and subscribes to 587 periodicals including electronic. Computerized library services include interlibrary loans, database searching, and Internet access. Special learning facilities include an art gallery, radio station, TV production facilities and equipment. **Physically Challenged Students:** 80% of the campus is accessible. Facilities include wheelchair ramps, elevators, special parking, specially equipped restrooms, lowered drinking fountains, lowered telephones, and special housing. **Special:** Study abroad is available in more than 12 countries. A Washington semester is available through the American Studies Program. The university also offers cross-registration with Jackson Community College, work-study, a dual major in physics/math, student-designed majors, pass/fail options, and nondegree study. Alternative programs for adult learners provide field-based study and assign credit for life experience. An accelerated B.A. program for such students is offered. A 3-2 engineering degree is offered with the University of Michigan, Western Michigan University, and Tri-State University. There are 3 national honor societies and a freshman honors program. **Visiting:** There are regularly scheduled orientations for prospective students, including a tour, class and chapel attendance, lunch, and a student panel discussion. There are guides for informal visits, visitors may sit in on classes, and stay overnight. To schedule a visit, contact the Admissions Office. **Campus Safety and Security:** Measures include 24-hour foot and vehicle patrol, emergency notification system, self-defense education, and security escort services, lighted pathways/sidewalks, controlled access to dorms/residences, and key card entry to some dorms.

REQUIREMENTS: The ACT is recommended. Applicants must be graduates of accredited secondary schools or have a GED. ACT or SAT test scores are required. An interview is advised for those who do not meet the requirements. Home-schooled applicants must take the ACT or the SAT, provide transcripts of course work, and submit a 2- to 3-page paper. A GPA of 2.6 is required. AP and CLEP credits are accepted. Important factors in the admissions decision are personality/intangible qualities, parents or siblings attended your school, and leadership record. Students must complete 4 Christian perspective courses plus cross-cultural studies, writing skills, speech, and physical fitness. Liberal arts requirements are in fine arts, humanities, natural science/math, philosophy/religion, and social science. To graduate, at least 124 semester hours, with 40 hours in upper-division courses and including 30 to 60 in the major, are needed. A minimum GPA of 2.0 overall and 2.2 in the major is also required. Students must also complete the University CORE, which includes communication skills, physical fitness, and liberal arts requirements. **Procedure:** Freshmen are admitted to all sessions. Entrance exams should be taken in the spring of the junior year or fall of the senior year. There are deferred admissions and rolling admissions plans. Applications should be filed by August 1 for fall entry. The fall 2016 application fee was $30. Notification is sent on a rolling basis. Applications are accepted online. **Transfer Students:** 102 transfer students enrolled in 2015-2016. Applicants should have a minimum GPA of 2.0 and are encouraged to arrange an interview. A release of information form is required from the previous college attended. 30 of 124 credits required for the bachelor's degree must be completed at SAU. **International Students:** There are 20 international students enrolled. They must take the TOEFL with a minimum score of 525 on the paper-based TOEFL (PBT). The SAT or ACT may be required for some students.

ADMISSIONS: 8 freshmen graduated first in their class. **Admissions Contact:** Randy Comfort, Director of Admissions. Email: *admissions@arbor.edu* Web: *www.arbor.edu*

FINANCIAL AID: In 2016-2017, 100% of all full-time freshmen and 87% of continuing full-time students received some form of financial aid. 84% of all full-time freshmen and 83% of continuing full-time students received need-based aid. The average freshman award was $19,168. Need-based scholarships or need-based grants averaged $9,643; need-based self-help aid (loans and jobs) averaged $3,699; and non-need-based athletic scholarships averaged $3,677. 32% of undergraduate students work part-time. Average annual earnings from campus work are $1250. The average financial indebtedness of the 2016 graduate was $13,834. The FAFSA code is 002318. Check with the school for current application deadlines.

UNIVERSITY OF DETROIT MERCY E-5

www.udmercy.edu

Detroit, MI 48221 (313) 993-1245
(800) 635-5020
Fax: (313) 993-3317 Email: admissions@udmercy.edu

Full-time: 810 men, 1355 women
Part-time: 154 men, 327 women
Graduate: 1014 men, 1215 women
Year: semesters, summer session
Room & Board: $8934
SAT CR/M/W: 526/543/517 **ACT:** 25
Application Deadline: n/av
Faculty: 334
Ph.D.s: 92%
Student/Faculty: 10 to 1
Tuition: $39,882
Freshman Class: n/av
CEEB CODE: 1835
COMPETITIVE+

University of Detroit Mercy, founded in 1877, is a private, independent institution affiliated with the Jesuits and Sisters of Mercy. It offers undergraduate programs in liberal arts, education and human services, business administration, engineering and science, architecture, and nursing and health sciences. There are 6 undergraduate schools and 7 graduate schools. In addition to regional accreditation, UDM, Detroit Mercy has baccalaureate program accreditation with AACSB, ABET, ADA, CSWE, NAAB, NLN, TEAC, CCNE, CAHIIM, and CAHME. The 70-acre campus is in an urban area 7 miles north of downtown Detroit. Including any residence halls, there are 21 buildings.

STUDENT LIFE: 87% of undergraduates are from Michigan. Others are from 34 states, 41 foreign countries, and Canada. 7% are race unknown; 60% White; 6% Foreign; 5% Asian American; 5% Hispanic; 3% two or more races; 13% African American. 42% are Muslim, Hindu, Christian and other denominations and religions.; 37% Catholic; 19% claim no religious affiliation. **Female To Male Ratio:** 1.5:1. The average age of freshmen is 18; all undergraduates, 23. 17% do not continue beyond their first year; 68% remain to graduate. **Housing:** 955 students can be accommodated in college housing, which includes coed dorms, a freshman residence program, honors floors, and peace & justice floor. On-campus housing is guaranteed for all 4 years. 69% of students commute. All students may keep cars.

FACULTY/CLASSROOMS: 47% of faculty are male; 53% are female. No introductory courses are taught by graduate students.

PROGRAMS OF STUDY: UDM, Detroit Mercy confers B.A., B.A.E., B.C.E., B.C.I., B.D.H., B.E.E., B.M.E., B.R.M., B.S., B.S.A., B.S.N., B.S.ARCH, B.S.W, B.ENG., and B.F.A. degrees. Master's and doctoral degrees are also awarded. Bachelor's degrees are awarded in BIOLOGICAL SCIENCE (biochemistry, biology/biological science, and industrial/organizational psychology), BUSINESS (accounting, business administration and management, and finance), COMMUNICATIONS AND THE ARTS (communications, digital media, dramatic arts, English, and theatre acting), COMPUTER AND PHYSICAL SCIENCE (chemistry, computer science, information sciences and systems, mathematics, software engineering, and software production & management), EDUCATION (elementary education, middle school education, secondary education, and special education), ENGINEERING AND ENVIRONMENTAL DESIGN (architectural engineering, architecture, civil engineering, electrical/electronics engineering, engineering, mechanical engineering, and robotic & mechatronic systems engineering), HEALTH PROFESSIONS (dental hygiene, health care administration, health services administration, nursing, predentistry, and premedicine), SOCIAL SCIENCE (addiction studies, criminal justice, developmental psychology, economics, history, legal studies, liberal arts/general studies, paralegal studies, philosophy, political science/government, prelaw, psychology, religion, social work, and sociology). Nursing, biology, and engineering are the strongest academically. Nursing, and biology (pre-med/pre-dent), and business have the largest enrollments.

ACTIVITIES: 12% of men belong to 6 national fraternities; 6% of women belong to 5 national sororities. There are 50 groups on campus, including cheerleading, chorale, drama, ethnic, film, honors, international, LGBT, literary magazine, musical theater, newspaper, pep band, political, professional, radio and TV, religious, social, social service, and student government. Popular campus events include Engineering and Architecture Week, Ethics Bowl, and Alternative Spring Break. **Sports:** There are 8 intercollegiate sports for men and 10 for women, and 4 intramural sports for men and 4 for women. Facilities include a fitness center with a gym, basketball courts and an indoor track, racquetball/handball courts, soccer field, softball field, outdoor track, and tennis courts. **Graduates:** From July 1, 2015 to June 30, 2016, 729 bachelor's degrees were awarded. The most popular majors were health professions and related programs (52%), biological/life sciences (22%), and business/marketing (9%). In an average class, 53% graduate in 4 years or less, 59% graduate in 5 years or less, and 68% graduate in 6 years or less.

SERVICES: Counseling and information services are available, as is tutoring in most subjects, and remedial math, reading, and writing. **Library/Resources:** The 3 libraries contain 741,046 volumes, 1.0 million microform items, 81,219 audio/video tapes/CDs/DVDs, and subscribe to 4,049 periodicals including electronic. Computerized library services include interlibrary loans, database searching, Internet access, and Wi-Fi capability. Special learning facilities include a radio station. **Physically Challenged Students:** 80% of the campus is accessible. Facilities include wheelchair ramps, elevators, special parking, and special class scheduling. **Special:** Cooperative education is mandatory for engineering and architecture majors and is optional for others. Internships are available for many programs. Cross-registration is available with a consortium of Catholic colleges in the Detroit area. Many accelerated programs that combine a bachelor and master degree are available. Some programs include BS to DDS, BA to MBA, BEE to MEE etc. Study abroad experiences are available to students in many different countries, for example Cuba, Poland and Italy. Academic exploration courses are provided to help students who are undecided about a future vocation. There are 3 national honor societies and a freshman honors program. **Visiting:** There are regularly scheduled orientations for prospective students, including a look at student life, testing and advising, and registration. There are guides for informal visits, visitors may sit in on classes, and stay overnight. To schedule a visit, contact Admissions Office. **Campus Safety and Security:** Measures include 24-hour foot and vehicle patrol, emergency notification system, self-defense education, security escort services, emergency telephones, lighted pathways/sidewalks, and controlled access to dorms/residences.

REQUIREMENTS: The SAT or ACT is required. Graduation from an accredited secondary school is required; a GED will be accepted. Students must submit 15 academic units, 4 units of English, 3 of math, and 2 of history, and natural science, including a lab course. Remaining credits are recommended 1 each in foreign language, social studies, an academic electives, and visual/performing arts. An interview is recommended. A GPA of 2.5 is required. AP and CLEP credits are accepted. Students must successfully complete at least 126 credit hours, including a core curriculum, and maintain a minimum GPA of 2.0. Required courses include English composition, religion, philosophy, speech fundamentals, math, and a computer course. **Procedure:** Freshmen are admitted to all sessions. Entrance exams should be taken during the junior or senior year. There are early admissions, deferred admissions, and rolling admissions plans. Check with the school for current application deadlines. Applications are accepted online. Application fees are waived if application is completed on-line. **Transfer Students:** 170 transfer students enrolled in 2015-2016. Transfer applicants with fewer than 24 semester hours of credit at an accredited institution must submit SAT or ACT scores and must have maintained a minimum GPA of 2.0. If the student is older than 23 years of age, SAT /ACT scores need not be submitted. Application for transfer admission may enroll in the fall, winter, and summer. Open admission policy does not apply to transfer students. 32 of 126 credits required for the bachelor's degree must be completed at UDM, Detroit Mercy. **International Students:** There are 107 international students enrolled. The school actively recruits these students. They must take the college's own test.

ADMISSIONS: The SAT scores for the 2016-2017 freshman class were: Critical Reading-- 39% below 500, 32% between 500 and 599, and 29% between 600 and 699. Math-- 32% below 500, 32% between 500 and 599, 29% between 600 and 699, and 7% between 700 and 800. Writing-- 50% below 500, 21% between 500 and 599, 21% between 600 and 699, and 7% between 700 and 800. The ACT scores were 2% between 12 and 17, 45% between 18 and 23, 45% between 24 and 29, and 9% above 30. 20 freshmen graduated first in their class. **Admissions Contact:** Tyra Rounds, Director of Admissions. Email: *admissions@udmercy.edu* Web: *www.udmercy.edu*

FINANCIAL AID: In 2016-2017, 100% of all full-time freshmen and 99% of continuing full-time students received some form of financial aid. 100% of all full-time freshmen and 99% of continuing full-time students received need-based aid. The average freshman award was $33,282. Need-based scholarships or need-based grants averaged $27,115; need-based self-help aid (loans and jobs) averaged $4,315; non-need-based athletic scholarships averaged $18,902; other non-need-based awards and non-need-based scholarships averaged $21,817; and $3,764 from other forms of aid. The average financial indebtedness of the 2016 graduate was $21,309. UDM, Detroit Mercy is a member of CSS. The FAFSA code is 002323. The priority date for freshman financial aid applications for fall entry is April 1.

UNIVERSITY OF MICHIGAN/ANN ARBOR E-5

www.umich.edu

Ann Arbor, MI 48109 (734) 764-7433

Fax: (734) 936-0740
Email: ua-admissions@umich.edu
Full-time: 13642 men, 13519 women
Faculty: 2735; I, +$
Ph.D.s: 91%
Part-time: 541 men, 418 women
Student/Faculty: 15 to 1
Graduate: 8321 men, 7018 women
Tuition: $13,856 ($43,476)
Year: trimesters, summer session
Freshman Class: 51761 applied, 13584 accepted, 12142 enrolled
Room & Board: $10,554
SAT or ACT: required
CEEB CODE: 1839
Application Deadline: February 1
MOST COMPETITIVE

University of Michigan/Ann Arbor, founded in 1817, is the main campus of the University of Michigan. The public institution offers undergraduate programs in the arts and sciences, architecture, business administration, education, engineering, fine arts, kinesiology, natural resources, nursing, and professional studies, as well as a wide range of graduate and professional programs. Figures in the above capsule and in this profile are approximate. There are 12 undergraduate schools and 18 graduate schools. In addition to regional accreditation, UM has baccalaureate program accreditation with AACSB, ABET, ACEJMC, ACPE, ADA, ASLA, CSWE, NAAB, NASAD, NASM, NCATE, NLN, and SAF. The 3177-acre campus is in a suburban area 38 miles west of Detroit. Including any residence halls, there are 538 buildings.

STUDENT LIFE: 62% of undergraduates are from Michigan. Others are from 50 states, 86 foreign countries, and Canada. 66% are White; 6% Foreign; 4% African American; 4% Hispanic; 11% Asian American. **Male To Female Ratio:** 1.1:1. The average age of freshmen is 18; all undergraduates, 20. 90% remain to graduate. **Housing:** 11664 students can be accommodated in college housing, which includes single-sex and coed dorms, on-campus apartments, and married student housing. In addition, there are honors houses, language houses, special-interest houses, fraternity houses, sorority houses, substance-free dorm rooms, women-in-science housing, theme and wellness housing, gender neutral, and cooperative housing. On-campus housing is guaranteed for the freshman year only, and on a first-come, first-served basis, and is available on a lottery system for upperclassmen. 66% of students commute. All students may keep cars.

FACULTY/CLASSROOMS: 60% of faculty are male; 40% are female. All teach undergraduates, and all do research. No introductory courses are taught by graduate students. The average class size in an introductory lecture is 70; in a laboratory is 18; and in a regular course is 31.

PROGRAMS OF STUDY: UM confers B.A., B.S., A.B.Ed., B.B.A., B.D.A., B.F.A., B.G.S., B.Mus., B.Mus.A., B.S.Chem., B.S.E., B.S.Ed. and B.S.N. degrees. Master's and doctoral degrees are also awarded. Bachelor's degrees are awarded in AGRICULTURE (environmental studies), BIOLOGICAL SCIENCE (biochemistry, biology/biological science, biophysics, botany, cell biology, ecology, evolutionary biology, microbiology, molecular biology, and neurosciences), BUSINESS (business administration and management, organizational behavior, and sports management), COMMUNICATIONS AND THE ARTS (Arabic, art, art history and appreciation, audio technology, ceramic art and design, classical languages, classics, communications, comparative literature, creative writing, dance, design, dramatic arts, drawing, English, English literature, fiber/textiles/weaving, film arts, French, German, Germanic languages and literature, graphic design, Greek, Greek (modern), Hebrew, historic preservation, illustration, industrial design, Italian, jazz, Latin, linguistics, literature, metal/jewelry, music, music history and appreciation, music performance, music technology, music theory and composition, musical theater, painting, performing arts, photography, printmaking, Russian, Russian languages and literature, sculpture, Spanish, speech/debate/rhetoric, theater design, video, and winds), COMPUTER AND PHYSICAL SCIENCE (astronomy, astrophysics, atmospheric sciences and meteorology, chemistry, computer science, earth science, environmental geology, geology, geoscience, mathematics, oceanography, physics, and statistics), EDUCATION (athletic training, elementary education, music education, and physical education), ENGINEERING AND ENVIRONMENTAL DESIGN (aeronautical engineering, aerospace studies, architecture, biomedical engineering, chemical engineering, civil engineering, computer engineering, electrical/electronics engineering, engineering, engineering physics, environmental engineering, geological engineering, geophysical engineering, industrial engineering, materials engineering, materials science, mechanical engineering, naval architecture and marine engineering, and nuclear engineering), HEALTH PROFESSIONS (dental hygiene, exercise science, nursing, pharmaceutical chemistry, pharmaceutical science, pharmacy, and radiological science), SOCIAL SCIENCE (African studies, African American studies, American studies, anthropology, archeology, Asian/Oriental studies, behavioral science, biblical studies, Caribbean studies, classical/ancient civilization, cognitive science, Eastern European studies, economics, European studies, Hispanic American studies, history, humanities, interdisciplinary studies, international studies, Islamic studies, Judaic studies, Latin American studies, liberal arts/general studies, medieval studies, Mexican-American/Chicano studies, Middle Eastern studies, Near Eastern studies, philosophy, physical fitness/movement, political science/government, psychology, public affairs, Puerto Rican studies, religion, Russian and Slavic studies, social science, sociology, Western European studies, and women's studies). Psychology, engineering, and business administration have the largest enrollments.

ACTIVITIES: 17% of men belong to 40 national fraternities; 24% of women belong to 1 local and 27 national sororities. There are 1303 groups on campus, including art, band, cheerleading, chess, choir, chorale, chorus, computers, dance, debate, drama, environmental, ethnic, film, forensics, honors, international, jazz band, LGBT, literary magazine, marching band, musical theater, newspaper, opera, orchestra, pep band, photography, political, professional, radio and TV, religious, social, social service, student government, symphony, and yearbook. Popular campus events include Martin Luther King Day, Native American Powwow, and FestiFall. **Sports:** There are 14 intercollegiate sports for men and 14 for women, and 23 intramural sports for men and 23 for women. Facilities include a stadium, athletic areas, gym, indoor track and tennis complex, indoor practice center, recreational buildings, golf courses, a natatorium, swimming pools, ice arena, soccer and field hockey fields. **Graduates:** From July 1, 2015 to June 30, 2016, 7091 bachelor's degrees were awarded. The most popular majors were engineering (15%), social sciences (14%), and psychology (10%). In an average class, 70% graduate in 4 years or less, 86% graduate in 5 years or less, and 88% graduate in 6 years or less.

SERVICES: Counseling and information services are available, as is tutoring in some subjects, a reader service for the blind. **Library/Resources:** The 27 libraries contain 10.6 million volumes, 10.6 million microform items, 126,011 audio/video tapes/CDs/DVDs, and subscribe to 83,062 periodicals including electronic. Computerized library services include interlibrary loans, database searching, Internet access, and Wi-Fi capability. Special learning facilities include an art gallery, natural history museum, planetarium, radio station, TV station, archeology museum, botanical gardens, two historical museums, electronics music studio, and digital media commons. **Physically Challenged Students:** 99% of the campus is accessible. Facilities include wheelchair ramps, elevators, special parking, specially equipped restrooms, special class scheduling, lowered drinking fountains, lowered telephones, special housing. paratransit service, specially equipped vans, talking calculators, telecommunication devices for the deaf, and an adaptive technology computing site that includes a high-speed scanner, voice input and voice output, braille display and large-print screens, and a braille printer. **Special:** There are 22 national honor societies, a chapter of Phi Beta Kappa, and a freshman honors program. **Visiting:** There are regularly scheduled orientations for prospective students. Student visits also include placement testing, academic advising, course registration, social activities, and informational programs on student life, computing resources, campus safety, and career planning. There are guides for informal visits and visitors may sit in on classes. To schedule a visit, contact the Office of Undergraduate Admissions. **Campus Safety and Security:** Measures include 24-hour foot and vehicle patrol, emergency notification system, self-defense education, and security escort services. There are also shuttle buses, emergency telephones, lighted pathways/sidewalks, controlled access to dorms/residences, a nite-owl bus service, officer bicycle patrols, and a taxi service.

REQUIREMENTS: Applicants must submit either SAT or ACT scores (or both), and be graduates of accredited secondary schools or have earned a GED. The university requires 16 Carnegie units, including 4 in English, 3 in math (4 for engineering majors), 3 each in history, science with 1 unit lab, and 1 unit in social studies, 2 (for LSA) in foreign language. The following are recommended electives: 1 unit of hands-on computer study and 2 units of fine or performing arts. An essay is required for all applicants. Students applying to the School of Art must submit a portfolio; those applying to the School of Music must present an audition. AP and CLEP credits are accepted. Important factors in the admissions decision are advanced placement or honors courses, evidence of special talent, and geographical diversity. Academic requirements vary by program. For the College of Literature, Science, and the Arts, most students must fulfill requirements in English, race and ethnicity, and foreign language. Students must also complete 9 semester hours each of humanities, social science, and natural science/math. Students must meet the quantitative reasoning requirement, designed to ensure proficiency in using and analyzing quantitative information. To graduate, students must complete 120 to 128 semester hours, including 24 to 30 in a major field, with a minimum GPA of 2.0. **Procedure:** Freshmen are admitted to all sessions. Entrance exams should be taken by the end of the junior year or the beginning of the senior. There are deferred admissions and rolling admissions plans. Applications should be filed by February 1 for fall entry. The fall 2016 application fee was $65. Notifications are sent April 1. 4512 applicants were on the 2016 waiting list; 90 were admitted. Applications are accepted online. **Transfer Students:** 888 transfer students enrolled in 2015-2016. A minimum college GPA of 3.0 is required for junior-level transfers. Student may enroll in the fall February 1. As for winter-October 1, spring-February 1, summer-February 1 are for some colleges, check with University of Michigan/Ann Arbor on these schools, admissions.umich.edu/apply/transfer-students. 60 of 120 credits required for the bachelor's degree must be completed at UM. **International Students:** There are 1644 international students enrolled. They must take the TOEFL with a minimum score of 570 on the paper-based TOEFL (PBT) or 88 on the Internet-based version (iBT) or take the MELAB. They must also take the SAT or ACT.

ADMISSIONS: 26% of the 2016-2017 applicants were accepted. 95% of the current freshmen were in the top fifth of their class; 99% were in the top two fifths. There were 83 National Merit finalists. **Admissions Contact:** Bernadette Lis, Associate Vice Provost. Email: *ua-admissions@umich.edu* Web: *www.umich.edu*

FINANCIAL AID: In 2016-2017, 47% of all full-time freshmen and 48% of continuing full-time students received some form of financial aid. 48% of all full-time freshmen and continuing full-time students received need-based aid. The average freshman award was $21,649. Need-based scholarships or need-based grants averaged $15,006; need-based self-help aid (loans and jobs) averaged $4,962; non-need-based athletic scholarships averaged $30,285; other non-need-based awards and non-need-based scholarships averaged $5,720; and $1,221 from other forms of aid. The average financial indebtedness of the 2016 graduate was $34,191. UM is a member of CSS. The FAFSA code is 002325. The priority date for freshman financial aid applications for fall entry is April 30.

UNIVERSITY OF MICHIGAN/DEARBORN E-5

www.umdearborn.edu

Dearborn, MI 48128 **(313) 593-5100**

Fax: (313) 436-9167 **Email: umd-admissions@umich.edu**

Full-time: 2678 men, 2307 women	**Faculty:** IIA, +$
Part-time: 1059 men, 1097 women	**Ph.D.s:** 80%
Graduate: 1346 men, 644 women	**Student/Faculty:** n
Year: semesters, summer session	**Tuition:** $11,757 ($24,487)
Room & Board: n/app	**Freshman Class:** 5312 applied, 3318 accepted, 951 enrolled
SAT: required **ACT:** 24	**CEEB CODE:** 1861
Application Deadline: open	**VERY COMPETITIVE**

University of Michigan/Dearborn, founded in 1959, is a public, comprehensive commuter institution that is part of the University of Michigan system. The emphasis of its degree programs is on the liberal arts, management, engineering, and education. There are 4 undergraduate schools and 4 graduate schools. In addition to regional accreditation, UM-Dearborn has baccalaureate program accreditation with AACSB, ABET, NCATE, TEAC, and ACS. The 196-acre campus is in a suburban area 10 miles from Detroit. Including any residence halls, there are 20 buildings.

STUDENT LIFE: 90% of undergraduates are from Michigan. Others are from 17 states, 59 foreign countries, and Canada. 8% are Asian American; 68% White; 6% Hispanic; 3% Foreign; 3% two or more races; 3% race unknown; 10% African American. **Male To Female Ratio:** 1.3:1. The average age of freshmen is 18; all undergraduates, 23. Alcohol is not permitted. All students commute. All students may keep cars.

FACULTY/CLASSROOMS: No introductory courses are taught by graduate students. The average class size in a regular course is 29.

PROGRAMS OF STUDY: UM-Dearborn confers B.A., B.S., B.B.A., B.G.S., B.S.A., and B.S.E. degrees. Master's degrees are also awarded. Bachelor's degrees are awarded in AGRICULTURE (environmental studies), BIOLOGICAL SCIENCE (biochemistry, biology/biological science, and microbiology), BUSINESS (accounting, business administration and management, management information systems, management science, marketing management, and supply chain management), COMMUNICATIONS AND THE ARTS (art history and appreciation, communications, English, French, language arts, and music history and appreciation), COMPUTER AND PHYSICAL SCIENCE (applied mathematics, chemistry, computer science, geology, mathematics, physics, science, and software engineering), EDUCATION (early childhood education, education, elementary education, mathematics education, science education, secondary education, social studies education, and special education), ENGINEERING AND ENVIRONMENTAL DESIGN (bioengineering, biomedical engineering, computer engineering, electrical/electronics engineering technology, engineering, environmental science, industrial engineering technology, manufacturing engineering, and mechanical engineering), HEALTH PROFESSIONS (biology and health), SOCIAL SCIENCE (African studies, African American studies, American studies, anthropology, area studies, criminal justice, economics, Hispanic American studies, history, humanities, international studies, liberal arts/general studies, philosophy, political science/government, psychology, social studies, sociology, urban studies, women & gender studies, and women's studies). Electrical engineering, and business administration are the strongest academically. Mechanical engineering, prebusiness, and business administration have the largest enrollments.

ACTIVITIES: 4% of women belong to 4 national sororities. There are 117 groups on campus, including art, cheerleading, chess, computers, dance, debate, drama, environmental, ethnic, film, honors, international, LGBT, literary magazine, musical theater, newspaper, pep band, political, professional, radio and TV, radio station, religious, social, social service, and student government. Popular campus events include Martin Luther King Diversity Celebration, Native American Pow Wow, and Fall Fest. **Sports:** There are 1 intercollegiate sports for men and 2 for women, and 21 intramural sports for men and 20 for women. Facilities include a gym, ice rink, indoor/outdoor track, playing field, sand volleyball courts, weight and exercise rooms, outdoor tennis courts, and River Rouge Trail. **Graduates:** From July 1, 2015 to June 30, 2016, 1292 bachelor's degrees were awarded. The most popular majors were business/marketing (18%), engineering (12%), and psychology (11%). In an average class, 14% graduate in 4 years or less, 41% graduate in 5 years or less, and 53% graduate in 6 years or less.

SERVICES: Counseling and information services are available, as is tutoring in most subjects, such as science, computer classes, composition, and math. There is a reader service for the blind and remedial math, reading, and writing. **Library/Resources:** The library contains 382,065 volumes, 544,977 microform items, 6,070 audio/video tapes/CDs/DVDs, and subscribes to 16,828 periodicals including electronic. Computerized library services include interlibrary loans, database searching, and Internet access. Special learning facilities include an art gallery, natural history museum, radio station, TV station, a nature preserve, an Armenian research center, early childhood education center, an engineering education and practice center, a national historic landmark, and an astronomy dome. **Physically Challenged Students:** All of the campus is accessible. Facilities include wheelchair ramps, elevators, special parking, specially equipped restrooms, lowered drinking fountains, and lowered telephones. **Special:** UM-Dearborn offers internships, study abroad, work-study and accelerated degree programs, a general studies degree, a dual major in engineering math, student-designed majors, and co-op programs in engineering, business administration, and arts and sciences. Non-degree study and pass/fail options are possible. There is 1 national honor society, a freshman honors program, and 2 departmental honors programs. **Visiting:** There are regularly scheduled orientations for prospective students, consisting of a tour, a student panel, academic unit introduction, and campus life sessions. There are guides for informal visits and visitors may sit in on classes. To schedule a visit, contact the Admissions Office. **Campus Safety and Security:** Measures include 24-hour foot and vehicle patrol, self-defense education, and security escort services, emergency telephones, lighted pathways/sidewalks, vehicle etching, crime prevention day, CPR training, and a rape awareness seminar.

REQUIREMENTS: The SAT or ACT is required. Other admissions requirements normally include graduation from an accredited secondary school; recommended high school units include 4 years each in math, English, social studies, and history, 2 each in science, with 1 unit of lab, and foreign language. The GED is accepted with a minimum score of 55. An essay and interview are recommended. AP credits are accepted. Important factors in the admissions decision are advanced placement or honors courses, recommendations by school officials, and leadership record. Each college within the university has its own requirements. To graduate, students must complete 120 to 128 credit hours. **Procedure:** Freshmen are admitted to all sessions. Entrance exams should be taken in the spring of the junior year or the fall of the senior year. There are deferred admissions and rolling admissions plans. Check with the school for current application deadlines. The application fee is $30. Notification is sent on a rolling basis. Application fees are waived if application is completed online. **Transfer Students:** 843 transfer students enrolled in 2015-2016. Applicants are required to have 25 to 30 transferable semester/credit hours; if they have fewer than 25, the SAT or ACT is mandatory. The required minimum GPA ranges from 2.5 to 3.0, depending on major. Application for admission is rolling, in the fall, winter, and summer. 60 of 128 credits required for the bachelor's degree must be completed at UM-Dearborn. **International Students:** There are 75 international students enrolled. They must take the TOEFL with a minimum score of 550 on the paper-based TOEFL (PBT) or 80 on the Internet-based version (iBT) or take the MELAB, or the APIEL exam. They must also take the SAT or ACT, scoring 22.

ADMISSIONS: 62% of the 2016-2017 applicants were accepted. The ACT scores were 44% between 18 and 23, 43% between 24 and 29, and 13% above 30. 14 freshmen graduated first in their class. **Admissions Contact:** Christine Kelly-Williams, Associate Director. Email: *admissions@umich.edu* Web: *www.umdearborn.edu*

FINANCIAL AID: The average freshman award was $9,549. Need-based scholarships or need-based grants averaged $6,909; need-based self-help aid (loans and jobs) averaged $3,605; non-need-based athletic scholarships averaged $4,338; and $2,868 from other forms of aid. The average financial indebtedness of the 2016 graduate was $10,875. The FAFSA code is 002326. The priority date for freshman financial aid applications for fall entry is March 1.

UNIVERSITY OF MICHIGAN-FLINT — E-4

www.umflint.edu

Flint, MI 48502	(810) 762-3300
Fax: (810) 762-3272	Email: admissions@umflint.edu
Full-time: 1960 men, 2530 women	Faculty: 287; IIA, av$
Part-time: 889 men, 1764 women	Ph.D.s: 69%
Graduate: 556 men, 856 women	Student/Faculty: 15 to 1
Year: semesters, summer session	Tuition: $9904 ($18,796)
Room & Board: $7703	Freshman Class: 3003 applied, 2345 accepted, 724 enrolled
SAT CR/M/W: 610/595/580 ACT: 21	CEEB CODE: 1853
Application Deadline: August 20	COMPETITIVE+

University of Michigan-Flint, established in 1956, is a public institution offering programs in the liberal arts and sciences, education, health professions, and business. Figures in the above capsule and in this profile are approximate. Fee cost are upper or lower division and varies by programs. There are 4 undergraduate schools and 6 graduate schools. In addition to regional accreditation, UM-Flint has baccalaureate program accreditation with AACSB, APTA, CSWE, NASM, NCATE, NLN, AACN, ACS, CCNE, and JRCERT. The 73-acre campus is in an urban area 60 miles northwest of Detroit, 50 miles east of Lansing, and 55 miles north of Ann Arbor. Including any residence halls, there are 9 buildings.

STUDENT LIFE: 92% of undergraduates are from Michigan. Others are from 37 states, 34 foreign countries, and Canada. 97% are from public schools. 68% are White; 11% African American; 6% Foreign; 5% race unknown; 4% Hispanic; 3% two or more races; 2% Asian American; 1% American Indian/Alaska Native. **Female To Male Ratio:** 1.5:1. The average age of freshmen is 19; all undergraduates, 26. 20% do not continue beyond their first year; 40% remain to graduate. **Housing:** 310 students can be accommodated in college housing, which includes coed dorms and off-campus apartments. On-campus housing is available on a first-come and first-served basis. 96% of students commute. Alcohol is not permitted. All students may keep cars.

FACULTY/CLASSROOMS: 42% of faculty are male; 58% are female. All teach undergraduates, and all do research. No introductory courses are taught by graduate students. The average class size in an introductory lecture is 24; in a laboratory is 17; and in a regular course is 20.

PROGRAMS OF STUDY: UM-Flint confers B.A., B.S., B.A.S., B.B.A., B.F.A., B.S.E., B.S.N., B.S.W., B.M., B.M.E. and B.I.S. degrees. Master's and doctoral degrees are also awarded. Bachelor's degrees are awarded in BIOLOGICAL SCIENCE (biology/biological science and ecology), BUSINESS (accounting, banking and finance, business administration and management, human resources, and marketing/retailing/merchandising), COMMUNICATIONS AND THE ARTS (art, communications, dramatic arts, English, French, music, and Spanish), COMPUTER AND PHYSICAL SCIENCE (applied science, chemistry, computer science, mathematics, physical sciences, physics, and science), EDUCATION (early childhood education, education, elementary education, foreign languages education, music education, and secondary education), ENGINEERING AND ENVIRONMENTAL DESIGN (engineering), HEALTH PROFESSIONS (environmental health science, health care administration, health science, medical laboratory technology, nursing, physical therapy, and radiation therapy), SOCIAL SCIENCE (anthropology, applied psychology, community psychology, criminal justice, economics, geography, history, philosophy, political science/government, psychology, public administration, social science, social work, sociology, and urban studies). Business, and nursing are the strongest academically. Business, education, and health sciences have the largest enrollments.

ACTIVITIES: 5% of men belong to 6 national fraternities; 4% of women belong to 7 national sororities. There are 103 groups on campus, including art, band, cheerleading, choir, chorale, chorus, computers, dance, debate, drama, ethnic, honors, jazz band, LGBT, literary magazine, musical theater, newspaper, political, professional, radio and TV, religious, social, social service, and student government. Popular campus events include Welcome Back Week, Winter Block Party and Presidents Ball. **Sports:** There are 13 intramural sports for men and 12 for women. Facilities include a recreation building housing a multipurpose gym, racquetball courts, a weight training area, and a swimming pool. **Graduates:** From July 1, 2015 to June 30, 2016, 1102 bachelor's degrees were awarded. The most popular majors were registered nursing (18%), health care administration/management (7%), and business administration/management (5%). 179 companies recruited on campus in 2015-2016. In an average class, 11% graduate in 4 years or less, 31% graduate in 5 years or less, and 39% graduate in 6 years or less.

SERVICES: Counseling and information services are available, as is tutoring in every subject. There is a reader service for the blind, and remedial math, reading, and writing. Sign language interpreters, note takers, and testing accomodations. **Library/Resources:** The library contains 353,617 volumes, 600,610 microform items, and 10,581 audio/video tapes/CDs/DVDs, and subscribes to 559 periodicals including electronic. Computerized library services include interlibrary loans, database searching, and Internet access. Special learning facilities include an art gallery and radio station. **Physically Challenged Students:** 97% of the campus is accessible. Facilities include wheelchair ramps, elevators, special parking, specially equipped restrooms, special class scheduling, lowered drinking fountains, lowered telephones. Telephone for the hearing impaired. Reasonable accommodations may be made for students with documented disabilities. **Special:** Special arrangements include co-op programs and dual majors, student-designed majors, cross-registration with Mott Community College, internships, study abroad, work-study, a 3-2 engineering program, an accelerated business degree, a general studies degree, nondegree study, and pass/fail options. There are 5 national honor societies, a chapter of Phi Beta Kappa, a freshman honors program, and 47 departmental honors programs. **Visiting:** There are regularly scheduled orientations for prospective students. There are guides for informal visits and visitors may sit in on classes. To schedule a visit, contact the Admissions Office at (810) 762-3300. **Campus Safety**

and Security: Measures include 24-hour foot and vehicle patrol, emergency notification system, self-defense education, and security escort services. There are shuttle buses, emergency telephones, and lighted pathways/sidewalks.

REQUIREMENTS: The SAT or ACT is required. In addition, , with the ACT preferred. Graduation from secondary school is required, with 4 years of English, 3 each of math and social studies, and 2 of science. The GED is accepted. SAT: Subject tests and an interview are recommended. Applied music students must audition. A GPA of 2.7 is required. AP and CLEP credits are accepted. Important factors in the admissions decision are advanced placement or honors courses, evidence of special talent, and leadership record. To graduate, all students must complete at least 120 credits, including 30 to 70 in the major along with satisfying all major requirements, and maintain a GPA of 2.0. Distribution requirements total 50 credits in English composition, humanities, fine arts, social science, and natural science. **Procedure:** Freshmen are admitted to all sessions. Entrance exams should be taken in the spring of the junior year or fall of the senior year. There are deferred admissions and rolling admissions plans. Applications should be filed by August 20 for fall entry; December 1 for winter entry. The fall 2016 application fee was $30. Notification is sent on a rolling basis. Applications are accepted on-line. **Transfer Students:** 857 transfer students enrolled in 2015-2016. Applicants must have at least 12 college credits and a minimum GPA of 2.0 in transferable courses. An associate degree and an interview are recommended. 45 of 120 credits required for the bachelor's degree must be completed at UM-Flint. **International Students:** There are 425 international students enrolled. The school actively recruits these students. They must take the TOEFL with a minimum score of 500 on the paper-based TOEFL (PBT) or 61 on the Internet-based version (iBT) or take the MELAB, or take the IELTS. They must also take the SAT or ACT.

ADMISSIONS: 78% of the 2016-2017 applicants were accepted. The SAT scores for the 2016-2017 freshman class were: Critical Reading-- 30% below 500, 10% between 500 and 599, 40% between 600 and 699, and 20% between 700 and 800. Math-- 20% below 500, 30% between 500 and 599, 30% between 600 and 699, and 20% between 700 and 800. Writing-- 20% below 500, 50% between 500 and 599, and 30% between 700 and 800. The ACT scores were 45% below 12, 25% between 12 and 17, 16% between 18 and 23, 7% between 24 and 29, and 7% above 30. 34% of the current freshmen were in the top fifth of their class; 63% were in the top two fifths. 7 freshmen graduated first in their class. **Admissions Contact:** Jon Davidson, Director of Admissions. Email: *admissions@umflint.edu* Web: *www.umflint.edu*

FINANCIAL AID: In 2016-2017, 61% of all full-time freshmen and 73% of continuing full-time students received some form of financial aid. 41% of all full-time freshmen and 54% of continuing full-time students received need-based aid. The average freshman award was $10,259. Need-based scholarships or need-based grants averaged $5,897; need-based self-help aid (loans and jobs) averaged $3,699; and other non-need-based awards and non-need-based scholarships averaged $4,246. Average annual earnings from campus work are $2398. The average financial indebtedness of the 2016 graduate was $27,336. The deadline for filing freshman financial aid applications for fall entry is March 1.

WAYNE STATE UNIVERSITY — E-5

www.wayne.edu

Detroit, MI 48202 — **(313) 577-2100**

Email: admissions@wayne.edu

Full-time: 5311 men, 6730 women	**Faculty:** I, -$
Part-time: 2373 men, 2866 women	**Ph.D.s:** n/av
Graduate: 4634 men, 5384 women	**Student/Faculty:** 15 to 1
Year: semesters, summer session	**Tuition:** $12,269 ($26,219)
Room & Board: $9747	**Freshman Class:** 11093 applied, 9036 accepted, 2588 enrolled
ACT: 24	**CEEB CODE:** 1898
Application Deadline: August 1	**COMPETITIVE**

Wayne State University, founded in 1868, is a premier public, urban research institution offering more than 380 academic programs through 13 schools and colleges. Wayne State's five satellite campuses offer higher education to students throughout Southeast Michigan. Wayne State is dedicated to preparing students to excel by combining the academic excellence of a major research university with the practical experience of an institution that by its history, location and diversity represents a microcosm of the world we live in. There are 9 undergraduate schools and 11 graduate schools. In addition to regional accreditation, WSU has baccalaureate program accreditation with AACSB, ABET, ABFSE, ACPE, CSWE, NASM, ACS, CAA, CCNE, IAA, MDE, ABFSE, JRCERT, ACEND, NAACLS, NASD, NAST, and NASM. The 194-acre campus is in an urban area 2 miles north of downtown Detroit in the New Center area. Including any residence halls, there are 104 buildings.

STUDENT LIFE: 96% of undergraduates are from Michigan. Others are from 34 states, 38 foreign countries, and Canada. 9% are Asian American; 58% White; 5% Hispanic; 4% two or more races; 4% race unknown; 3% Foreign; 17% African American. **Female To Male Ratio:** 1.2:1. The average age of freshmen is 18; all undergraduates, 24. 82% remain to graduate. **Housing:** 2437 students can be accommodated in college housing, which includes single-sex and coed dorms, on-campus apartments, special Interest living communities are also available in the dormitories. On-campus housing is available on a first-come and first-served basis. 87% of students commute. All students may keep cars.

FACULTY/CLASSROOMS: 54% of faculty are male; 46% are female. Graduate students teach 17% of introductory courses. The average class size in a laboratory is 21 and in a lecture course is 32.

PROGRAMS OF STUDY: Wayne State; WSU confers B.S., B.A., B.F.A., B.A.ED, B.S.ED, B.MUS, B.S.RT, B.S.PA, B.S.RDLT, B.S.CLS, B.S.DT, B.H.S., B.S.N., B.S.W., B.S.P., B.S.CHM, B.S.CRJ, B.P.A., B.S.BS, B.S.CT, B.S.CM, B.S.ETME, B.S.MAET, B.S.ETEM, B.S.ETT, B.S.ETEE, B.S.IE, B.S.ME, B.S.E.E., B.S.CIVL, B.S.C.E., B.S.BME, B.S.M.S., and B.S.C.S. degrees. Master's and doctoral degrees are also awarded. Bachelor's degrees are awarded in BIOLOGICAL SCIENCE (biochemistry, biology/biological science, biophysics, and nutrition), BUSINESS (accounting, banking and finance, business administration and management, funeral home services, labor studies, management information systems, marketing/retailing/merchandising, organizational leadership and management, and supply chain management), COMMUNICATIONS AND THE ARTS (art, art history and appreciation, classics, communications, communication science, dance, design, dramatic arts, English, film arts, film, television and digital media, fine arts, German, journalism, linguistics, media arts, music, public relations, romance languages and literature, Slavic languages, and theatre arts), COMPUTER AND PHYSICAL SCIENCE (astronomy, chemistry, computer science, geology, information sciences and systems, mathematics, mathematics – economics, physics, and radiological technology), EDUCATION (art education, elementary education, English education, global studies, health education, mathematics education, physical education, science education, secondary education, social studies education, and special education), ENGINEERING AND ENVIRONMENTAL DESIGN (biomedical engineering, chemical engineering, civil engineering, computer technology, construction management, electrical and computer engineering, electrical/electronics engineering, electrical/electronics engineering technology, electromechanical technology, environmental science, industrial engineering, manufacturing technology, mechanical engineering, and mechanical engineering technology), HEALTH PROFESSIONS (biology, clinical science, exercise science, health science, kinesiology, nursing, public health, radiation therapy, and speech pathology/audiology), SOCIAL SCIENCE (African studies, anthropology, Asian/Oriental studies, communication sciences & disorders, criminal justice, dietetics, economics, food science, history, Near Eastern studies, philosophy, political science/government, psychology, public affairs, social work, sociology, urban studies, and women's studies). Medical school, engineering, and social work are the strongest academically. Biology, psychology, and engineering have the largest enrollments.

ACTIVITIES: There are 511 groups on campus, including art, band, cheerleading, chess, choir, chorale, chorus, communications, computers, dance, debate, environmental, ethnic, film, forensics, honors, international, jazz band, LGBT, literary magazine, marching band, musical theater, newspaper, orchestra, pep band, photography, political, professional, radio and TV, religious, social, social service, student government, and symphony. Popular campus events include Student Organization Day, International Fair, and Detroit Festival of the Arts, and Alternative Spring Break Detroit. **Sports:** There are 8 intercollegiate sports for men and 9 for women. Facilities include two full gymnasiums, a weight room, racquetball and squash courts, a competition swimming pool, outdoor track, tennis courts, baseball fields, softball, and football fields and a football stadium, weight rooms, exercise equipment, indoor basketball courts, an indoor track, climbing wall, ropes course, women's only workout area, and indoor putting greens. **Graduates:** From July 1, 2015 to June 30, 2016, 3072 bachelor's degrees were awarded. The most popular majors were psychology (12%), biology, general (6%), health professions, and and related sciences (4%). In an average class, 18% graduate in 4 years or less, 37% graduate in 5 years or less, and 39% graduate in 6 years or less. Of the 2015 graduating class, 90% were employed within 6 months of graduation.

SERVICES: Counseling and information services are available, as is tutoring in every subject, a reader service for the blind, and remedial math, reading, and writing. Tutorial services are available through centralized counseling or academic departments. **Library/Resources:** The 5 libraries contain 3.0 million volumes. Computerized library services include interlibrary loans, database searching, Internet access, and Wi-Fi capability. Special learning facilities include an art gallery, natural history museum, planetarium, and a radio station. **Physically Challenged Students:** All of the campus is accessible. Facilities include wheelchair ramps, elevators, special parking, specially equipped restrooms, lowered drinking fountains, lowered telephones, and special housing. **Special:** Special academic programs include internships, study abroad, on-campus work-study programs, accelerated degree programs in liberal arts and science, engineering, and nursing, co-op programs, non-degree study, double majors, one 3-2 engineering and computer science programs. There is a chapter of Phi Beta Kappa, a freshman honors program, and 49 departmental honors programs. **Visiting:** There are regularly scheduled orientations for prospective students, The agenda includes meeting with advisors, registering for classes, meeting upperclassmen, and touring the campus. There are guides for informal visits, visitors may sit in on classes, and stay overnight. To schedule a visit, contact the Office of Undergraduate Admissions. **Campus Safety and Security:** Measures include 24-hour foot and vehicle patrol, emergency notification system, self-defense education, and security escort services. There are also shuttle buses, emergency telephones, lighted pathways/sidewalks, and controlled access to dorms/residences.

REQUIREMENTS: At Wayne State, we know that students come from different backgrounds and experiences, which are things that make our students so great! That's why we look at each individual applicant as that, an individual. The Office of Undergraduate Admissions will review your grade-point average, ACT or SAT score and any other supporting documentation you provide us or we request from you. AP and CLEP credits are accepted. To graduate, students must complete at least 120 credit hours and have a minimum GPA of 2.0 for all WSU course work. Students must complete general education requirements, all school/college, departmental and program requirements, and complete at least thirty credits at Wayne State. **Procedure:** Freshmen are admitted to all sessions. The ACT or SAT should be taken in the junior year. There are deferred admissions and rolling admissions plans. Applications should be filed by August 1 for fall entry; December 1 for winter entry; April 1 for spring entry; and April 1 for summer entry, along with a $25 fee. Applications are accepted online. **Transfer Students:** 2410 transfer students enrolled in 2015-2016. You can be admitted to Wayne State as a transfer student if you have at least 24 transferable credits of previous college work and a minimum 2.5 cumulative grade-point average from all higher education institutions you've attended. Students who have completed an Associate Degree may be admitted with a grade point average of a 2.0 or better. 30 of 120 credits required for the bachelor's degree must be completed at WSU. **International Students:** There are 404 international students enrolled. The school actively recruits these students. They must take the TOEFL with a minimum score of 550 on the paper-based TOEFL (PBT) or 79 on the Internet-based version (iBT) or take the MELAB. They must also take the SAT or ACT.

ADMISSIONS: 81% of the 2016-2017 applicants were accepted. The ACT scores were 4% between 12 and 17, 44% between 18 and 23, 40% between 24 and 29, and 12% above 30. 43% of the current freshmen were in the top fifth of their class; 72% were in the top two fifths. **Admissions Contact:** Ericka M. Jackson, Director of Undergraduate Admissions. Email: *admissions@wayne.edu* Web: *www.wayne.edu*

FINANCIAL AID: In 2016-2017, 93% of all full-time freshmen and 85% of continuing full-time students received some form of financial aid. 63% of all full-time freshmen and 67% of continuing full-time students received need-based aid. WSU is a member of CSS. The FAFSA code is 002329. The priority date for freshman financial aid applications for fall entry is March 31.

WESTERN MICHIGAN UNIVERSITY D-5

www.wmich.edu

Kalamazoo, MI 49008 — **(269) 387-2000** **(800) 400-4968**

Fax: (269) 387-2096 — **Email: ask-wmu@wmich.edu**

Full-time: 7662 men, 7337 women	**Faculty:** 714; I, --$
Part-time: 1444 men, 1541 women	**Ph.D.s:** 77%
Graduate: 2066 men, 2873 women	**Student/Faculty:** 22 to 1
Year: semesters, summer session	**Tuition:** $11,493 ($26,851)
Room & Board: $9561	**Freshman Class:** 13613 applied, 11205 accepted, 2930 enrolled
SAT: required **ACT:** 22	**CEEB CODE:** 1902
Application Deadline: open	**COMPETITIVE**

Western Michigan University, founded in 1903, is a dynamic, globally engaged institution that combines the resources of a national research university with the support and personal attention often found at a small college. Additional locations in Battle Creek, Benton Harbor, Grand Rapids, Lansing, Metro Detroit, Muskegon, and Traverse City. There are 7 undergraduate schools and 1 graduate school. In addition to regional accreditation, WMU has baccalaureate program accreditation with AACSB, ABET, ADA, CSWE, FIDER, NASAD, NASM, NCATE, AABI, ACOTE, ACCGC, CAATE, CCNE, NASD, and NAST. The 1289-acre campus is in an urban area 140 miles west of Detroit and 140 miles east of Chicago in Kalamazoo. Including any residence halls, there are 170 buildings.

STUDENT LIFE: 88% of undergraduates are from Michigan. Others are from 40 states, 63 foreign countries, and Canada. 71% are White; 6% Hispanic; 4% Foreign; 4% two or more races; 2% Asian American; 13% African American; 1% race unknown. **Female To Male Ratio:** 1.1:1. The average age of freshmen is 18; all undergraduates, 22. 21% do not continue beyond their first year; 53% remain to graduate. **Housing:** 6713 students can be accommodated in college housing, which includes single-sex and coed dorms, on-campus apartments, married student housing, honors houses, special-interest houses, fraternity houses, sorority houses, second year experience, and transfer student communities. On-campus housing is guaranteed for the freshman year only, is available on a first-come, and first-served basis. 74% of students commute. All students may keep cars.

FACULTY/CLASSROOMS: 50% of faculty are male; 50% are female. Graduate students teach 23% of introductory courses. The average class size in an introductory lecture is 104; in a laboratory is 22; and in a regular course is 31.

PROGRAMS OF STUDY: WMU confers B.A., B.S., B.B.A., B.F.A., B.M., B.M.A., B.S.E., B.S.N., and B.S.W. degrees. Master's and doctoral degrees are also awarded. Bachelor's degrees are awarded in AGRICULTURE (environmental studies), BIOLOGICAL SCIENCE (biochemistry, biology/biological science, and biology/ gen science secondary education), BUSINESS (accounting, apparel and accessories marketing, business economics, business intelligence and analytics, business law, entrepreneurial studies, fashion merchandising, finance, human resources/organizational management, management information systems, management & strategic leadership, marketing/retailing/merchandising, personal financial planning, recreation and leisure services, sports management, supply chain management, and tourism), COMMUNICATIONS AND THE ARTS (advertising, Africana studies, apparel design, art history, art, communication studies, communications, creative writing, dance, English, film, television and digital media, French, German, graphic design, instrumental performance, instrumental music education, Japanese, jazz, journalism, keyboard - piano concentration, Latin, music, music composition, music performance, music theory and composition, musical theater, performing arts, public relations, Spanish, telecommunications, theatre acting, theater design, theatre studies, theater management, vocal performance, and writing & rhetoric), COMPUTER AND PHYSICAL SCIENCE (applied mathematics, chemistry, chemistry secondary education, computer information systems, computer science, earth science, geochemistry, geology, geophysics and seismology, hydrogeology, mathematics, physics secondary education, physics, and statistics), EDUCATION (art education, athletic training, business education, early childhood education, education, education of the emotionally handicapped, education of the mentally handicapped, elementary education, English secondary education, English comm secondary education, foreign languages education, general studies, health education, health information management, learner designed area of study, middle school education, music education, physical education, secondary education, social studies secondary school education, Spanish education K-12, special education, specific learning disabilities, university studies, and vocational education), ENGINEERING AND ENVIRONMENTAL DESIGN (aerospace engineering, airline piloting and navigation, aviation administration/management, aviation maintenance technology, chemical engineering, city/community/regional planning, civil engineering, computer engineering, construction engineering, drafting and design technology, electrical and computer engineering, engineering graphics & design, engineering management, graphic and printing production, industrial engineering, interior design, manufacturing engineering, manufacturing technology, mechanical engineering, paper engineering, textile, and fashion merchandising & design), HEALTH PROFESSIONS (biomedical science, community health work, exercise science, music therapy, nursing, occupational therapy, and speech pathology/audiology), SOCIAL SCIENCE (anthropology, behavioral science, child care/child and family studies, child psychology/development, clothing and textiles management/production/services, criminal justice, dietetics, economics, family/consumer studies, fashion design and technology, food production/management/services, gender studies, geography, history, interdisciplinary studies, international studies, philosophy, political science/government, psychology, public history/archives, religion, social work, sociology, textiles and clothing, and women's studies). Nursing, business, and biomedical sciences have the largest enrollments.

ACTIVITIES: 5% of men belong to 19 national fraternities; 7% of women belong to 14 national sororities. There are 396 groups on campus, including art, band, cheerleading, chess, choir, chorale, chorus, communications, computers, dance, drama, environmental, ethnic, film, honors, international, jazz band, LGBT, literary magazine, marching band, musical theater, newspaper, orchestra, pep band, photography, political, professional, radio and TV, religious, social, social service, student government, and symphony. Popular campus events include Bronco Bash, Homecoming, Campus Classic, CommUniversity, Relay for Life, and Family Weekend. **Sports:** There are 6 intercollegiate sports for men and 10 for women, and 16 intramural sports for men and 15 for women. Facilities include a recreation center, which includes a swimming pool, weight and fitness room, basketball, floor hockey, indoor soccer, a climbing wall, an elevated track for jogging, aerobics, indoor cycling, badminton, tennis, and volleyball. The field house includes an arena for basketball and volleyball competition and facilities for gymnastics. There is also an outdoor track, tennis courts, football stadium, swimming pool, ice arena, baseball stadium, and softball stadium. **Graduates:** From July 1, 2015 to June 30, 2016, 3644 bachelor's degrees were awarded. The most popular majors were business/marketing (20%), health professions and related programs (11%), and interdisciplinary studies (8%). 622 companies recruited on campus in 2015-2016. In an average class, 22% graduate in 4 years or less, 45% graduate in 5 years or less, and 53% graduate in 6 years or less.

SERVICES: Counseling and information services are available, as is tutoring in most subjects, a reader service for the blind, and remedial math, reading, and writing. Also available are Day care, health insurance, health service, non-remedial tutoring, placement service, content tutoring, and supplemental instruction. **Library/Resources:** The 4 libraries contain 2.1 million volumes, 109,111 microform items, 170,578 audio/video tapes/CDs/DVDs, and subscribe to 186,031 periodicals including electronic. Computerized library services include interlibrary loans, database searching, Internet access, and Wi-Fi capability. Special learning facilities include an art gallery, radio station, Archives & Regional History Library, Aviation flight simulators, Behavioral research and development center, Business incubator for student entrepreneurs and inventors, Business technology and research park, Center for electron microscopy, Historic farm sustainability living/learning community with permaculture landscape, Nuclear accelerator, Particle accelerator, Pilot plant for manufacturing and printing of paper and fiber recovery, Stock trading room with electronic ticker and terminals. **Physically Challenged Students:** 85% of the campus is accessible. Facilities include wheelchair ramps, elevators, special parking, specially equipped restrooms, special class scheduling, lowered drinking fountains, lowered telephones, and special housing. **Special:** Cross-registration is available through the Kalamazoo Consortium. Opportunities are provided for internships in occupational and music therapy, teaching, business, history, and engineering and accelerated degree programs in audiology, engineering, communication, music, social work, Spanish, statistics, orientation & mobility and vision rehabilitation therapy. Also available are work-study programs, student-designed majors, pass/fail options, and credit by exam. WMU offers students study abroad programs in 41 countries, and access to foreign study opportunities in almost every country in the world through linkages with other universities and organizations. There are 37 national honor societies, a chapter of Phi Beta Kappa, a freshman honors program, and 32 departmental honors programs. **Visiting:** There are regularly scheduled orientations for prospective students, visiting students can participate in an admission presentation, departmental advising, lunch, and a campus tour. There are guides for informal visits and visitors may sit in on classes. To schedule a visit, contact The Campus Visit Center. **Campus Safety and Security:** Measures include 24-hour foot and vehicle patrol, emergency notification system, and security escort services. There are also shuttle buses, emergency telephones, lighted pathways/sidewalks, controlled access to dorms/residences, Residence hall security system, engravers for identification of items, free bicycle registration, a select group of residence halls have been assigned WMU community police officers to assist residence life staff with a variety of functions and to develop crime prevention programs; all interior residence hall doors to the living areas are locked 24 hours a day, and all front doors are locked during the night and early morning hours; Several resident assistants live on each floor; Each residence hall room has a deadbolt door lock, and an effective lock changing procedure is in place.

REQUIREMENTS: Applicants must submit an official high school transcript (or GED test scores). ACT or SAT test scores are required unless the applicant has been out of high school for two or more years. An audition is required for music majors. An interview may be recommended. The College of Fine Arts requires an audition, portfolio, or interview of all applicants. A GPA of 2.5 is required. AP and CLEP credits are accepted. Important factors in the admissions decision are advanced placement or honors courses, extracurricular activities record, and recommendations by school officials. Students must complete a minimum of 122 credit hours, including a minimum of 30 hours at WMU. They must complete a major with a minimum of 24 hours and, if required by the curriculum, a minor with a minimum of 15 hours. A minimum GPA of 2.0 is required. Students must complete or qualify for 37 credit hours of general education courses in college-level writing, college-level mathematics, fine arts, humanities, US culture, non-Western world, social science, natural science with lab, science and technology, and health and well-being. Comprehensive exams are required in some departments. All students must demonstrate computer literacy. **Procedure:** Freshmen are admitted to all sessions. Entrance exams should be taken During the junior year or early in the senior year. There is a rolling admissions plan. Application deadlines are open. Application fee is $40. Notification is sent on a rolling basis. Applications are accepted online. **Transfer Students:** 2565 transfer students enrolled in 2015-2016. Transfer students must have a minimum 2.0 GPA in transferable courses (as calculated by the Office of Admissions) to be considered for admission. Courses completed and trend of grades will also be taken into account. 30 of 122 credits required for the bachelor's degree must be completed at WMU. **International Students:** There are 666 international students enrolled. The school actively recruits these students. They must take the TOEFL with a minimum score of 550 on the paper-based TOEFL (PBT) or 80 on the Internet-based version (iBT) or take the MELAB, or take the IELTS.

ADMISSIONS: 82% of the 2016-2017 applicants were accepted. The ACT scores were 14% between 12 and 17, 50% between 18 and 23, 31% between 24 and 29, and 5% above 30. 25% of the current freshmen were in the top fifth of their class; 56% were in the top two fifths. 24 freshmen graduated first in their class. **Admissions Contact:** Dachea Hill, Director of Admissions. Email: *ask-wmu@wmich.edu* Web: *www.wmich.edu*

FINANCIAL AID: In 2016-2017, 78% of all full-time freshmen and 51% of continuing full-time students received some form of financial aid. 54% of all full-time freshmen and 35% of continuing full-time students received need-based aid. The average freshman award was $17,144. Need-based scholarships or need-based grants averaged $6,154 ($15,000 maximum); need-based self-help aid (loans and jobs) averaged $5,565 ($7,500 maximum); non-need-based athletic scholarships averaged $26,707 ($40,000 maximum); and other non-need-based awards and non-need-based scholarships averaged $6,162 ($18,500 maximum). 19% of undergraduate students work part-time. Average annual earnings from campus work are $5152. The average financial indebtedness of the 2016 graduate was $26,587. The FAFSA code is 002330. The priority date for freshman financial aid applications for fall entry is March 1.

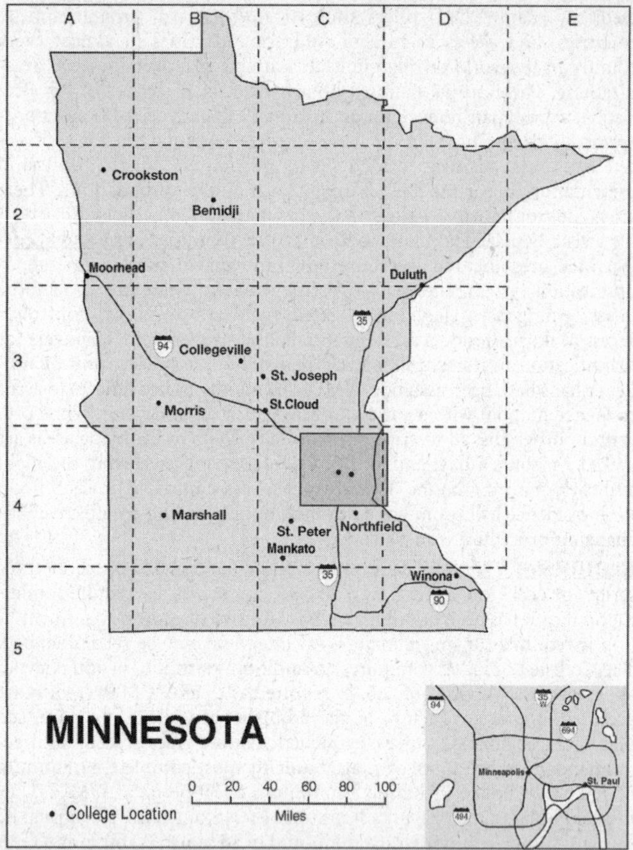

AUGSBURG COLLEGE C-4

www.augsburg.edu

Minneapolis, MN 55454 (612) 330-1001
(800) 788-5678
Fax: (612) 330-1581 **Email:** admissions@augsburg.edu

Full-time: 1231 men, 1343 women
Part-time: 197 men, 353 women
Graduate: 286 men, 606 women
Year: varies, summer session
Room & Board: $7514
SAT CR/M: 505/565 **ACT:** 22
Application Deadline: August 15

Faculty: 195; IIB, av$
Ph.D.s: 85%
Student/Faculty: 15 to 1
Tuition: $36,415
Freshman Class: 2346 applied, 1217 accepted, 449 enrolled
CEEB CODE: 6014
COMPETITIVE

Augsburg College, established in 1869, is a private liberal arts institution affiliated with the Evangelical Lutheran Church. Figures in the above capsule and in this profile are approximate. There is 1 undergraduate school and 1 graduate school. In addition to regional accreditation, Augsburg has baccalaureate program accreditation with ACCE, AHEA, CSWE, NASM, NCATE, NLN, ARC-PA, CIC, and AAHE. The 18-acre campus is in an urban area in Minneapolis. Including any residence halls, there are 26 buildings.

STUDENT LIFE: 89% of undergraduates are from Minnesota. Others are from 34 states, 51 foreign countries, and Canada. 8% are African American; 71% White; 6% Asian American; 3% Hispanic; 2% American Indian/Alaska Native; 1% Foreign. 51% are Protestant; 30% claim no religious affiliation; 22% Buddhist, Orthodox, Hindu, 21 %Lutheran, and Muslim; 13% Catholic. **Female To Male Ratio:** 1.3:1. The average age of freshmen is 19; all undergraduates, 26. 19% do not continue beyond their first year; 60% remain to graduate. **Housing:** 1150 students can be accommodated in college housing, which includes coed dorms, on-campus apartments, married student housing, and special-interest houses. On-campus housing is guaranteed for the freshman year only, and on a first-come, first-served basis, and on a lottery system for upperclassmen. Priority is given to out-of-town students. 54% of students live on campus; of those, 50% remain on campus on weekends. All students may keep cars.

FACULTY/CLASSROOMS: 49% of faculty are male; 51% are female. 99% teach undergraduates. No introductory courses are taught by graduate students. The average class size in an introductory lecture is 20; in a laboratory is 16; and in a regular course is 16.

PROGRAMS OF STUDY: Augsburg confers B.A., B.S., B.M., B.S.N., M.A., M.B.A., M.S., M.S.W., and D.N.P. degrees. Master's degrees are also awarded. Bachelor's degrees are awarded in AGRICULTURE (environmental studies), BIOLOGICAL SCIENCE (biology/biological science), BUSINESS (accounting, business administration and management, economics – statistics, international business management, management information systems, and marketing/retailing/merchandising), COMMUNICATIONS AND THE ARTS (art, art history and appreciation, communications, dramatic arts, English, French, German, languages, music, Scandinavian languages, Spanish, speech/debate/rhetoric, and studio art), COMPUTER AND PHYSICAL SCIENCE (chemistry, computer science, mathematics, and physics), EDUCATION (education, elementary education, health education, music education, physical education, and secondary education), HEALTH PROFESSIONS (music therapy and pre-health studies), SOCIAL SCIENCE (East Asian studies, economics, history, international relations, philosophy, political science/government, psychology, religion, Russian and Slavic studies, Scandinavian studies, social work, sociology, urban studies, women's studies, and youth ministry). Physics, chemistry, and English are the strongest academically. Business, communication, and education have the largest enrollments.

ACTIVITIES: There are no fraternities or sororities. There are 40 groups on campus, including art, band, cheerleading, choir, chorus, dance, drama, ethnic, honors, international, jazz band, LGBT, literary magazine, newspaper, orchestra, pep band, political, professional, radio and TV, religious, social, social service, and student government. Popular campus events include Days in May, Spring Affair, Advent Vespers, Peace, Justice & Hunger Concerns, and Concerts. **Sports:** There are 9 intercollegiate sports for men and 7 for women, and 4 intramural sports for men and 4 for women. Facilities include a sports field, a gym, tennis courts, ice arena, and a domed field facility for winter sports. **Graduates:** From July 1, 2015 to June 30, 2016, 539 bachelor's degrees were awarded. The most popular majors were business management (10%), accounting/public accounting (6%), and elementary education (6%). 66 companies recruited on campus in 2015-2016. In an average class, 7% graduate in 3 years or less, 38% graduate in 4 years or less, 53% graduate in 5 years or less, and 55% graduate in 6 years or less. Of the 2015 graduating class, 24% were enrolled in graduate school within 6 months of graduation, and 85% were employed.

SERVICES: Counseling and information services are available, as is tutoring in every subject, and a reader service for the blind, and remedial math and writing. Taped textbooks and adaptive computer technology, including a text scanner, speaking software, a touch tablet, and text magnification software are also available. **Library/Resources:** The library contains 190,000 volumes, 21,355 microform items, 3,477 audio/video tapes/CDs/DVDs, and subscribes to 686 periodicals including electronic. Computerized library services include interlibrary loans, database searching, Internet access, and Wi-Fi capability. Special learning facilities include an art gallery, planetarium, radio station, The James G. Lindell Family Library, the Gage Family Art Gallery, and the Christensen Center Art Gallery. **Physically Challenged Students:** 95% of the campus is accessible. Facilities include wheelchair ramps, elevators, special parking, specially equipped restrooms, special class scheduling, lowered drinking fountains, lowered telephones, and special housing. **Special:** Special academic programs include internships and co-op programs in business, government, and nonprofit and community-based organizations, a Washington semester, and study abroad in Europe, Latin America, and Africa. There are student-designed majors, cross-registration through the Associated Colleges of the Twin Cities (ACTC), dual and 3-2 engineering degrees with Washington University, Michigan Technological University, and the University of Minnesota, and preprofessional programs in dentistry, law, medicine, physical therapy, pharmacy, theology, and veterinary medicine. Credit for previous learning experience may be granted, and pass/fail options are possible. There is 1 national honor society, a freshman honors program, and 1 departmental honors program. **Visiting:** There are regularly scheduled orientations for prospective students, including admissions interviews and campus tours.

Students may also arrange to meet with professors and coaches and to attend lectures. There are guides for informal visits, visitors may sit in on classes, and stay overnight. To schedule a visit, contact the Admissions Counselor. **Campus Safety and Security:** Measures include 24-hour foot and vehicle patrol, self-defense education, security escort services, emergency telephones, lighted pathways/sidewalks, and controlled access to dorms/residences.

REQUIREMENTS: The SAT is recommended. The ACT is required, with a minimum score of 22 on the ACT. Admissions requirements include graduation from an accredited secondary school with 4 years of English. The GED is also accepted. An essay is required, and an interview is recommended. AP and CLEP credits are accepted. Important factors in the admissions decision are advanced placement or honors courses, leadership record, and recommendations by school officials. To graduate, all students must have a minimum GPA of 2.0 and a total of 32 courses, with 10 to 15 in the major. They must complete 15 courses from 8 perspective areas and a first-year fall orientation and seminar. Students must also satisfy entry-level and graduation skills requirements in writing, critical thinking, math, quantitative reasoning, and speaking and demonstrate proficiency in 2 sports. **Procedure:** Freshmen are admitted in the fall and spring. Entrance exams should be taken during the fall of the senior year in high school. There are deferred admissions and rolling admissions plans. Applications should be filed by August 15 for fall entry; December 1 for spring entry, along with a $25 fee. Notification is sent on a rolling basis. Applications are accepted online. **Transfer Students:** 282 transfer students enrolled in 2015-2016. Applicants must have a minimum GPA of 2.2 in college course work. 9 of 32 credits required for the bachelor's degree must be completed at Augsburg. **International Students:** There are 44 international students enrolled. The school actively recruits these students. They must take the TOEFL with a minimum score of 550 on the paper-based TOEFL (PBT) or 80 on the Internet-based version (iBT). They must also take the SAT or ACT.

ADMISSIONS: 52% of the 2016-2017 applicants were accepted. The SAT scores for the 2016-2017 freshman class were: Critical Reading--50% below 500, 25% between 500 and 599, 21% between 600 and 699, and 4% between 700 and 800. Math-- 21% below 500, 33% between 500 and 599, 38% between 600 and 699, and 8% between 700 and 800. The ACT scores were 38% below 12, 27% between 12 and 17, 23% between 18 and 23, 8% between 24 and 29, and 4% above 30. 28% of the current freshmen were in the top fifth of their class; 55% were in the top two fifths. 5 freshmen graduated first in their class. **Admissions Contact:** Carola Thorson, Director of Admissions. Email: *admissions@augsburg.edu* Web: *www.augsburg.edu*

FINANCIAL AID: In 2016-2017, 98% of all full-time freshmen received some form of financial aid. 98% of all full-time freshmen received need-based aid. The average freshman award was $12,883. Need-based scholarships or need-based grants averaged $11,308 ($27,892 maximum); and $1,631 from other forms of aid. 44% of undergraduate students work part-time. Average annual earnings from campus work are $1710. The average financial indebtedness of the 2016 graduate was $27,000. The college's own financial statement is required. The FAFSA code is 002334. The priority date for freshman financial aid applications for fall entry is April 15. The filing deadline for fall entry is August 1.

BEMIDJI STATE UNIVERSITY — B-2
www.bemidjistate.edu

Bemidji, MN 56601	(218) 755-2040 (877) 236-4354
Fax: (218) 755-2074	**Email:** admissions@bemidjistate.edu
Full-time: 1701 men, 1823 women	**Faculty:** n/av
Part-time: 419 men, 801 women	**Ph.D.s:** 79%
Graduate: 79 men, 194 women	**Student/Faculty:** n/av
Year: semesters, summer session	**Tuition:** $8366
Room & Board: $7690	**Freshman Class:** 3343 applied, 1317 accepted, 743 enrolled
ACT: required	**CEEB CODE:** 6676
Application Deadline: open	**VERY COMPETITIVE**

Bemidji State University, founded in 1919, is a public liberal arts university. Figures in the above capsule and in this profile are approximate. There are 3 undergraduate schools and 1 graduate school. In addition to regional accreditation, Bemidji has baccalaureate program accreditation with CSWE, NASM, and NLN. The 89-acre campus is in a small town 220 miles northwest of Minneapolis. Including any residence halls, there are 21 buildings.

STUDENT LIFE: 87% of undergraduates are from Minnesota. Others are from 46 states, 34 foreign countries, and Canada. 95% are from public schools. 89% are White; 5% Foreign; 3% American Indian/Alaska Native; 1% African American; 1% Asian American; 1% Hispanic. **Female To Male Ratio:** 1.3:1. The average age of freshmen is 18; all undergraduates, 24. 28% do not continue beyond their first year; 44% remain to graduate. **Housing:** 1700 students can be accommodated in college housing, which includes single-sex and coed dorms, on-campus apartments, special-interest houses, fraternity houses, and single-parent apartments. On-campus housing on a first-come and first-served basis. 68% of students commute. All students may keep cars. Alcohol is not permitted.

FACULTY/CLASSROOMS: 59% of faculty are male; 41% are female. 99% teach undergraduates, and 15% do research. Graduate students teach 1% of introductory courses. The average class size in an introductory lecture is 35; in a laboratory is 20; and in a regular course is 23.

PROGRAMS OF STUDY: Bemidji confers B.A., B.S., and B.F.A. degrees. Associate and master's degrees are also awarded. Bachelor's degrees are awarded in AGRICULTURE (environmental studies), BIOLOGICAL SCIENCE (biology/biological science), BUSINESS (accounting and business administration and management), COMMUNICATIONS AND THE ARTS (broadcasting, communications, English, fine arts, German, journalism, languages, music, and Spanish), COMPUTER AND PHYSICAL SCIENCE (chemistry, computer science, earth science, geology, mathematics, and physics), EDUCATION (art education, early childhood education, elementary education, foreign languages education, health education, industrial arts education, middle school education, science education, and secondary education), ENGINEERING AND ENVIRONMENTAL DESIGN (industrial engineering technology), HEALTH PROFESSIONS (medical laboratory technology, nursing, predentistry, and premedicine), SOCIAL SCIENCE (community services, criminal justice, economics, geography, history, parks and recreation management, philosophy, political science/government, prelaw, psychology, social science, social work, and sociology). Nursing, accounting, and engineering are the strongest academically. Business administration, and elementary & secondary education have the largest enrollments.

ACTIVITIES: 1% of men belong to 2 national fraternities; 1% of women belong to 1 national sorority. There are 80 groups on campus, including art, band, cheerleading, choir, chorus, computers, dance, drama, environmental, ethnic, honors, international, jazz band, LGBT, literary magazine, musical theater, newspaper, opera, orchestra, pep band, political, professional, radio and TV, religious, social, social service, and student government. Popular campus events include Funtastic Dance Follies, Madrigal Music, Plays, and Concerts. **Sports:** There are 7 intercollegiate sports for men and 7 for women, and 7 intramural sports for men and 4 for women. Facilities include a basketball gym, a pool, a hockey arena, a football stadium, indoor and outdoor tracks, baseball and softball fields, tennis, racquetball, and handball courts, weight rooms, and a dance studio. **Graduates:** From July 1, 2015 to June 30, 2016, 888 bachelor's degrees were awarded. The most popular majors were business/marketing (18%), education (16%), and health professions and related programs (11%). 45 companies recruited on campus in 2015-2016. In an average class, 42% graduate in 6 years or less. Of the 2015 graduating class, 14% were enrolled in graduate school within 6 months of graduation, and 90% were employed.

SERVICES: Counseling and information services are available, as is tutoring in every subject, and a reader service for the blind, and remedial math, reading, and writing. **Library/Resources:** The library contains 190,000 volumes, 721,255 microform items, 2,500 audio/video tapes/CDs/DVDs, and subscribes to 907 periodicals including electronic. Computerized library services include interlibrary loans and database searching. Special learning facilities include an art gallery, radio station, and TV station. **Physically Challenged Students:** 95% of the campus is accessible. Facilities include wheelchair ramps, elevators, special parking, specially equipped restrooms, lowered drinking fountains, and lowered telephones. **Special:** Students may attend other schools within the Minnesota State University system and study abroad in 10 countries. Paid internships and work-study programs are available in many fields. Students may receive credit for life, military, and work experience. Student-designed dual majors, nondegree study, and pass/fail options are offered. There are 2 national honor societies and a freshman honors program.

Visiting: There are regularly scheduled orientations for prospective students, including an interview with an admissions counselor, a tour of the campus, and visits with faculty. There are guides for informal visits, visitors may sit in on classes, and stay overnight. To schedule a visit, contact the Admissions Office. **Campus Safety and Security:** Measures include 24-hour foot and vehicle patrol, emergency notification system, self-defense education, and security escort services. There are also shuttle buses, emergency telephones, lighted pathways/sidewalks, controlled access to dorms/residences, in-room safes, all buildings are locked overnight, controlled sportsman's weapons storage, and 24/7 campus security team.

REQUIREMENTS: Applicants must have a minimum high school rank of 50% or a composite score of 21 on the ACT. They should have had 4 years of English and 3 years each of math, science, and social studies. Bemidji requires applicants to be in the upper 50% of their class. AP and CLEP credits are accepted. Important factors in the admissions decision are recommendations by school officials, advanced placement or honors courses, and extracurricular activities record. All students must complete at least 128 semester hours, of which 42 are general education, including courses in freshman English, the humanities, social science, physical science, liberal education activities, and phys ed. Students must maintain a minimum GPA of 2.0, a 2.3 GPA is required in the major (2.5 for education majors). **Procedure:** Freshmen are admitted to all sessions. Entrance exams should be taken during the junior year. There are deferred admissions and rolling admissions plans. Application deadlines are open. The fall 2016 application fee was $20. Applications are accepted online. **Transfer Students:** 349 transfer students enrolled in 2015-2016. Applicants must have a minimum GPA of 2.0. 32 of 128 credits required for the bachelor's degree must be completed at Bemidji. **International Students:** There are 150 international students enrolled. The school actively recruits these students. They must take the TOEFL.

ADMISSIONS: 39% of the 2016-2017 applicants were accepted. **Admissions Contact:** Paul Muller, Director for Admissions. Email: *pmuller@bemidjistate.edu* Web: *www.bemidjistate.edu*

FINANCIAL AID: In 2016-2017, 83% of all full-time freshmen and 78% of continuing full-time students received some form of financial aid. 78% of all full-time freshmen and continuing full-time students received need-based aid. The average freshman award was $9,457. Need-based scholarships or need-based grants averaged $6,030; need-based self-help aid (loans and jobs) averaged $4,436; non-need-based athletic scholarships averaged $4,080; other non-need-based awards and non-need-based scholarships averaged $3,598; and $9,967 from other forms of aid. 25% of undergraduate students work part-time. Average annual earnings from campus work are $1490. The average financial indebtedness of the 2016 graduate was $20,470. The college's own financial statement is required. Check with the school for current application deadlines.

BETHEL UNIVERSITY C-4

www.bethel.edu

St. Paul, MN 55112 (651) 638-6242 (800) 255-8706

Fax: (651) 635-1490 Email: undergrad-admissions@bethel.edu

Full-time: 1131 men, 1642 women	**Faculty:** 188; IIA, -$
Part-time: 191 men, 457 women	**Ph.D.s:** 78%
Graduate: 994 men, 1023 women	**Student/Faculty:** 15 to 1
Year: 4-1-4, summer session	**Tuition:** $35,160
Room & Board: $10,110	**Freshman Class:** 2179 applied, 1734 accepted, 727 enrolled
SAT CR/M: 590/580 **ACT:** 25	**CEEB CODE:** 6038
Application Deadline: n/av	**VERY COMPETITIVE**

Bethel University, established in 1871, is a private liberal arts university affiliated with the Converge Worldwide (Baptist General Conference). The figures in the above capsule and in this profile are approximate. There are 2 undergraduate schools and 2 graduate schools. In addition to regional accreditation, Bethel has baccalaureate program accreditation with CSWE, TEAC, CAATE, and CCNE. The 247-acre campus is in a suburban area 10 miles north of Minneapolis/St. Paul. Including any residence halls, there are 39 buildings.

STUDENT LIFE: 78% of undergraduates are from Minnesota. Others are from 43 states, 22 foreign countries, and Canada. 80% are from public schools. 90% are White; 2% African American; 2% Asian American; 2% Hispanic. 97% are Protestant. **Female To Male Ratio:** 1.3:1. The average age of freshmen is 18; all undergraduates, 20. 15% do not continue beyond their first year; 75% remain to graduate. **Housing:** 2076 students can be accommodated in college housing, which includes coed dorms, on-campus apartments, and off-campus apartments. On-campus housing is available on a first-come, first-served basis, and on a lottery system for upperclassmen. 70% of students live on campus; of those, 60% remain on campus on weekends. Upperclassmen may keep cars. Alcohol is not permitted.

FACULTY/CLASSROOMS: 51% of faculty are male; 49% are female. All teach undergraduates. No introductory courses are taught by graduate students. The average class size in a laboratory is 20 and in a regular course is 22.

PROGRAMS OF STUDY: Bethel confers B.A., B.S., B.Mus., and B.Mus.Ed degrees. Associate, master's, and doctoral degrees are also awarded. Bachelor's degrees are awarded in AGRICULTURE (environmental studies), BIOLOGICAL SCIENCE (biochemistry, biology/biological science, and molecular biology), BUSINESS (accounting, banking and finance, and business administration and management), COMMUNICATIONS AND THE ARTS (art, communications, dramatic arts, English, English literature, French, journalism, multimedia, music, music performance, Spanish, and visual and performing arts), COMPUTER AND PHYSICAL SCIENCE (applied physics, chemistry, computer science, mathematics, and physics), EDUCATION (athletic training, business education, early childhood education, education, elementary education, English education, foreign languages education, health education, mathematics education, middle school education, music education, physical education, science education, secondary education, social studies education, and teaching English as a second/foreign language (TESOL/TEFOL)), ENGINEERING AND ENVIRONMENTAL DESIGN (engineering and applied science and environmental science), HEALTH PROFESSIONS (community health work, exercise science, and nursing), SOCIAL SCIENCE (biblical studies, economics, history, international relations, philosophy, political science/government, psychology, religious music, social studies, social work, theological studies, Third World studies, and youth ministry). Physics, chemisty, and nursing are the strongest academically. Business, education, and nursing have the largest enrollments.

ACTIVITIES: There are no fraternities or sororities. There are 74 groups on campus, including art, band, choir, chorale, chorus, dance, debate, drama, drill team, environmental, ethnic, film, forensics, honors, international, jazz band, literary magazine, musical theater, newspaper, orchestra, pep band, political, professional, radio and TV, religious, social, social service, student government, and symphony. Popular campus events include Nikdg and Gadkin and Festival of Christmas. **Sports:** There are 9 intercollegiate sports for men and 9 for women, and 6 intramural sports for men and 6 for women. Facilities include a gym, an indoor recreation center, with track and multipurpose courts, weight room, racquetball courts, soccer fields, tennis courts, and a football, baseball, and softball stadium. **Graduates:** From July 1, 2015 to June 30, 2016, 756 bachelor's degrees were awarded. The most popular majors were education (16%), business/marketing (14%), and health professions and related (11%). 125 companies recruited on campus in 2015-2016. In an average class, 63% graduate in 4 years or less, 73% graduate in 5 years or less, and 75% graduate in 6 years or less. Of the 2015 graduating class, 22% were enrolled in graduate school within 6 months of graduation, and 74% were employed.

SERVICES: Counseling and information services are available, as is tutoring in every subject, and a reader service for the blind. The Academic Enrichment and Support Center offers individual peer tutoring, student-led help sessions, a writing lab, and consultation on a variety of topics. **Library/Resources:** The library contains 194,196 volumes, 195,650 microform items, 15,503 audio/video tapes/CDs/DVDs, and subscribes to 38,080 periodicals including electronic. Computerized library services include interlibrary loans, database searching, Internet access, and Wi-Fi capability. Special learning facilities include an art gallery and radio station. **Physically Challenged Students:** 99% of the campus is accessible. Facilities include wheelchair ramps, elevators, special parking, specially equipped restrooms, special class scheduling, lowered drinking fountains, lowered telephones, and special housing. **Special:** Cross-registration is available through the Council for Christian Colleges and Universities. Students may arrange internships and study abroad in various countries. Students may design their own major and earn a 3-2 engineering degree. An adult degree completion program is offered. There are 6 national honor societies, a freshman honors program, and 6 departmental honors programs. **Visiting:** There are regularly scheduled orientations for prospective students, consisting of a campus tour, visits with advisors, faculty, coaches, Chapel and class visits, and meals in the dining center. There are guides for informal visits, visitors may sit in on classes, and stay overnight. To schedule a visit, contact the Admissions Office. **Campus Safety and Security:** Measures include 24-hour foot and vehicle patrol, emergency notification system, self-defense education, and security escort services. There are also shuttle buses, emergency telephones, lighted pathways/sidewalks, controlled access to dorms/residences, and surveillance cameras in parking lots and buildings.

REQUIREMENTS: The SAT or ACT is required. The PSAT is accepted. An interview is recommended. Requirements include a personal statement, contact information for an academic or spiritual reference, and an official transcript and class ranking from an accredited secondary school (GED is accepted). Bethel requires applicants to be in the upper 50% of their class. A GPA of 2.5 is required. AP and CLEP credits are accepted. Important factors in the admissions decision are advanced placement or honors courses, extracurricular activities record, and personality/intangible qualities. Students must complete a minimum of 122 semester credit hours, with 30 to 60 in the major and 51 to 52 in general education. Specific general education courses include Introduction to the Bible, Christianity and Western Culture, College Writing, Creativity in Fine Arts, and Physical Wellness. An overall GPA of 2.0 and a GPA of 2.25 in the major are needed. **Procedure:** Freshmen are admitted in the fall and spring. Entrance exams should be taken spring of junior year. There is a rolling admissions plan. Application deadlines are open. Notifications are sent October 1. 43 applicants were on the 2016 waiting list; 10 were admitted. Applications are accepted online. **Transfer Students:** 164 transfer students enrolled in 2015-2016. Applicants must have a minimum GPA of 2.5 and must submit all college transcripts. 28 of 122 credits required for the bachelor's degree must be completed at Bethel. **International Students:** There are 8 international students enrolled. They must take the TOEFL with a minimum score of 525 on the paper-based TOEFL (PBT) or 70 on the Internet-based version (iBT).

ADMISSIONS: 80% of the 2016-2017 applicants were accepted. The SAT scores for the 2016-2017 freshman class were: Critical Reading-- 20% below 500, 31% between 500 and 599, 30% between 600 and 699, and 19% between 700 and 800. Math-- 20% below 500, 39% between 500 and 599, 28% between 600 and 699, and 14% between 700 and 800. The ACT scores were 17% below 12, 23% between 12 and 17, 26% between 18 and 23, 14% between 24 and 29, and 21% above 30. 45% of the current freshmen were in the top fifth of their class; 74% were in the top two fifths. 31 freshmen graduated first in their class. **Admissions Contact:** Jay Fedje, Director of Admissions. Email: *undergrad-admissions@bethel.edu* Web: *www.bethel.edu*

FINANCIAL AID: In 2016-2017, 99% of all full-time freshmen and 94% of continuing full-time students received some form of financial aid. 71% of all full-time freshmen and 68% of continuing full-time students received need-based aid. The average freshman award was $19,129. Need-based scholarships or need-based grants averaged $7,041 ($27,794 maximum); need-based self-help aid (loans and jobs) averaged $3,753 ($8,700 maximum); and other non-need-based awards and non-need-based scholarships averaged $8,335 ($31,020 maximum). 56% of undergraduate students work part-time. Average annual earnings from campus work are $1500. The average financial indebtedness of the 2016 graduate was $30,496. Bethel is a member of CSS. The college's own financial statement is required. The FAFSA code is 002338. The priority date for freshman financial aid applications for fall entry is April 15.

CARLETON COLLEGE C-4

www.carleton.edu

Northfield, MN 55057	**(507) 222-4190** **(800) 995-CARL**
Fax: (507) 222-4526	**Email: admissions@carleton.edu**
Full-time: 1013 men, 1032 women	**Faculty:** 209; IIB, ++$
Part-time: 3 men, 15 women	**Ph.D.s:** 91%
Graduate: n/av	**Student/Faculty:** 9 to 1
Year: trimesters	**Tuition:** $50,874
Room & Board: $13,197	**Freshman Class:** 6485 applied, 1455 accepted, 568 enrolled
SAT or ACT: required	**CEEB CODE:** 6081
Application Deadline: January 15	**MOST COMPETITIVE**

Carleton College, founded in 1866, is a private liberal arts college. There are 3 undergraduate schools. The 1040-acre campus is in a small town 35 miles south of Minneapolis-St. Paul. Including any residence halls, there are 49 buildings.

STUDENT LIFE: 85% of undergraduates are from out of state, mostly the Midwest. Students are from 50 states, 35 foreign countries, and Canada. 60% are from public schools. 59% are White; 9% Hispanic; 9% Foreign; 7% Asian American; 7% two or more races; 6% African American; 2% race unknown; 1% American Indian/Alaska Native. 49% claim no religious affiliation; 14% Buddhist, Hindu, Muslim, Taoist, and Unitarian Universalist; 13% Protestant. **Female To Male Ratio:** 1.0:1. The average age of freshmen is 18; all undergraduates, 20. 4% do not continue beyond their first year; 96% remain to graduate. **Housing:** 1819 students can be accommodated in college housing, which includes single-sex and coed dorms, on-campus apartments, off-campus apartments, language houses and special-interest houses. On-campus housing is guaranteed for all 4 years. 96% of students live on campus; of those, 97% remain on campus on weekends. No one may keep cars.

FACULTY/CLASSROOMS: 52% of faculty are male; 48% are female. All teach undergraduates, and all do research. No introductory courses are taught by graduate students. The average class size in an introductory lecture is 20; in a laboratory is 16; and in a regular course is 17.

PROGRAMS OF STUDY: Carleton confers B.A. degrees. Bachelor's degrees are awarded in AGRICULTURE (environmental studies), BIOLOGICAL SCIENCE (biology/biological science), COMMUNICATIONS AND THE ARTS (art history and appreciation, classics, English, French, German, Greek, Latin, linguistics, media arts, music, romance languages and literature, Russian, Spanish, and studio art), COMPUTER AND PHYSICAL SCIENCE (chemistry, computer science, geology, mathematics, and physics), SOCIAL SCIENCE (African studies, African American studies, American studies, anthropology, Asian/Oriental studies, classical/ancient civilization, economics, history, international relations, Latin American studies, philosophy, political science/government, psychology, religion, sociology, and women's studies). Sciences, biological, and physical sciences are the strongest academically. Social sciences, history, and physical sciences have the largest enrollments.

ACTIVITIES: There are no fraternities or sororities. There are 300 groups on campus, including hobby club, art, band, chess, choir, chorale, chorus, computers, dance, debate, drama, educational, environmental, ethnic, film, honors, international, jazz band, LGBT, literary magazine, musical theater, newspaper, orchestra, photography, political, professional, radio and TV, religious, social, social service, student government, and symphony. Popular campus events include Mai Fete, Spring Concert, Mid-Winter Ball, Ebony, and Golden Shillers Film Festival. **Sports:** There are 23 intercollegiate sports for men and 23 for women, and 14 intramural sports for men and 14 for women. Facilities include a gym with an arena, swimming pool, and wrestling room. There is also a recreation center with a gym, dance studio, indoor tennis court, swimming pool, stadium complex with handball and racquetball courts, indoor track, baseball batting cage, weight room, and an additional recreation center with an indoor track, sport courts, weight room, dance studio, and climbing wall. Additional facilities include a field for baseball, softball, soccer, ultimate frisbee, lacrosse, rugby, field hockey, outdoor tennis courts, running, biking, hiking, and cross-country skiing trails. **Graduates:** From July 1, 2015 to June 30, 2016, 487 bachelor's degrees were awarded. The most popular majors were biology (11%), computer science (11%), and economics (10%). In an average class, 89% graduate in 4 years or less, 91% graduate in 5 years or less, and 95% graduate in 6 years or less.

SERVICES: Counseling and information services are available, as is tutoring in every subject. There are also writing and math skills assistance centers, as well as a reader service for the blind. **Library/Resources:** The library contains 1.6 million volumes, 356,954 microform items, and 63,998 audio/video tapes/CDs/DVDs, and subscribes to 82,879 periodicals including electronic. Computerized library services include interlibrary loans, database searching, Internet access, and Wi-Fi capability. Special learning facilities include an art gallery, radio station, an observatory, an 880-acre arboretum, and Weitz center for creativity. **Physically Challenged Students:** 39% of the campus is accessible. Facilities include wheelchair ramps, elevators, special parking, specially equipped restrooms, special class scheduling, lowered drinking fountains, lowered telephones, and special housing. **Special:** Students may cross-register with St. Olaf College and pursue a variety of internships. The college offers study abroad in over 50 countries. Dual majors in all areas and student designed majors are available. Students may earn a 3-2 engineering degree with Washington or Columbia Universities. There are 3 national honor societies and a chapter of Phi Beta Kappa. **Visiting:** There are regularly scheduled orientations for prospective students, Prospective students can attend an information session, take a tour, have an interview, sit in on classes have a meal in the dining halls or attend panels on particular topics pertinent to study abroad, financial aid or other topics. There are guides for informal visits, visitors may sit in on classes, and stay overnight. To schedule a visit, contact the Admissions Office. **Campus Safety and Security:** Measures include 24-hour foot and vehicle patrol, emergency notification system, self-defense education, security escort services, emergency telephones, lighted pathways/sidewalks, controlled access to dorms/residences, and nighttime transport service.

REQUIREMENTS: The SAT or ACT is required, as well as the ACT Optional Writing test. There are no secondary school requirements, but it is recommended that applicants have completed 4 years of English, 3 years each of math and a foreign language, 2 years each of history and science, and 1 year of social studies. An essay and 2 teacher recommendations are required. AP credits are accepted. Important factors in the admissions decision are advanced placement or honors courses, personality/intangible qualities, and evidence of special talent. To graduate, you must complete 210 credits and maintain a 2.0 cumulative GPA. A normal course load is 18 credits per term (there are 3 terms). Students also explore an integrated exercise in their major in the form of a comprehensive exam, an extensive research project, paper or public presentation. The goal is to demonstrate proficiency within your major. A first-year seminar and course work in Quantitative Reasoning and Global Citizenship are also required. **Procedure:** Freshmen are admitted in the fall. Entrance exams should be taken before February 15. There are early decision and deferred admissions plans. Early decision applications should be filed by November 15; regular applications, by January 15 for fall entry, along with a $30 fee. Notification of early decision is sent December 15; regular decision, April 15. 219 early decision candidates were accepted for the 2016-2017 class. 533 applicants were on the 2016 waiting list; 2 were admitted. Application fees are waived if application is completed online. **Transfer Students:** Transfers are usually accepted for sophomore and junior classes. A 3.0 GPA is recommended. 108 of 210 credits required for the bachelor's degree must be completed at Carleton. **International Students:** There are 208 international students enrolled. The school actively recruits these students. They must take the TOEFL with a minimum score of 600 on the paper-based TOEFL (PBT) or 100 on the Internet-based version (iBT). They must also take the SAT or ACT.

ADMISSIONS: 22% of the 2016-2017 applicants were accepted. 91% of the current freshmen were in the top fifth of their class; 100% were in the top two fifths. **Admissions Contact:** Paul Thiboutot, VP & Dean of Admissions & Financial Aid. Email: *admissions@carleton.edu* Web: *www.carleton.edu*

FINANCIAL AID: In 2016-2017, 77% of all full-time freshmen and 86% of continuing full-time students received some form of financial aid. 55% of all full-time freshmen and 56% of continuing full-time students received need-based aid. The average freshman award was $47,719. Need-based scholarships or need-based grants averaged $42,019; need-based self-help aid (loans and jobs) averaged $5,441; and other non-need-based awards and non-need-based scholarships averaged $2,000. 91% of undergraduate students work part-time. Average annual earnings from campus work are $1720. The average financial indebtedness of the 2016 graduate was $22,641. Carleton is a member of CSS. The CSS/Profile is required. The FAFSA code is 002340. The deadline for filing freshman financial aid applications for fall entry is January 15.

COLLEGE OF SAINT BENEDICT — C-3

www.csbsju.edu

St. Joseph, MN 56374	(320) 363-5060 (800) 544-1489
Fax: (320) 363-3206	Email: admissions@csbsju.edu
Full-time: 1939 women	**Faculty:** 144; IIB, +$
Part-time: 19 women	**Ph.D.s:** 92%
Graduate: n/av	**Student/Faculty:** 12 to 1
Year: semesters	**Tuition:** $42,271
Room & Board: $10,535	**Freshman Class:** 1859 applied, 1631 accepted, 503 enrolled
SAT or ACT: required	**CEEB CODE:** 6104
Application Deadline: January 15	**COMPETITIVE**

College of Saint Benedict, and Saint John's University are nationally-leading liberal arts colleges whose unique partnership offers students the educational choices of a large university and the individual attention of a premier small college. There is 1 undergraduate school. In addition to regional accreditation, Saint Ben's has baccalaureate program accreditation with ADA, NASM, NCATE, ACS, and CCNE. The 600-acre campus is in a small town 70 miles northwest of Minneapolis and 10 miles west of St. Cloud. Including any residence halls, there are 52 buildings.

STUDENT LIFE: 80% of undergraduates are from Minnesota. Others are from 34 states, and 16 foreign countries. 79% are from public schools. 78% are White; 7% Hispanic; 6% Asian American; 4% Foreign; 3% African American; 1% American Indian/Alaska Native; 1% two or more races. 53% are Catholic; 29% Protestant; 16% claim no religious affiliation. The student base is all female. The average age of freshmen is 18; all undergraduates, 20. 13% do not continue beyond their first year; 84% remain to graduate. **Housing:** 1665 students can be accommodated in college housing, which includes single-sex dorms and on-campus apartments, there are special-interest houses, Health and Wellness community, 2 Eco houses and Benedictine Living Community. On-campus housing is guaranteed for the freshman year only, and on a first-come, first-served basis, and is available on a lottery system for upperclassmen. 89% of students live on campus; of those, 75% remain on campus on weekends. All students may keep cars.

FACULTY/CLASSROOMS: 47% of faculty are male; 53% are female. All teach undergraduates and do research. No introductory courses are taught by graduate students. The average class size in an introductory lecture is 18; in a laboratory is 13; and in a regular course is 19.

PROGRAMS OF STUDY: Saint Ben's confers B.A., and B.S.N. degrees. Bachelor's degrees are awarded in AGRICULTURE (environmental studies), BIOLOGICAL SCIENCE (biochemistry, biology/biological science, and nutrition), BUSINESS (accounting and management science), COMMUNICATIONS AND THE ARTS (art, classics, communications, English, French, German, music, Spanish, and theatre arts), COMPUTER AND PHYSICAL SCIENCE (chemistry, computer science, mathematics, natural sciences, and physics), EDUCATION (elementary education), ENGINEERING AND ENVIRONMENTAL DESIGN (pre-engineering), HEALTH PROFESSIONS (nursing, occupational therapy, predentistry, premedicine, preoptometry, prepharmacy, prephysical therapy, and preveterinary science), SOCIAL SCIENCE (Asian/Oriental studies, economics, gender studies, Hispanic American studies, history, humanities, liberal arts/general studies, peace studies, philosophy, political science/government, prelaw, psychology, social science, sociology, and theological studies). Biology, nursing , and psychology have the largest enrollments.

ACTIVITIES: There are no fraternities or sororities. There are 110 groups on campus, including art, band, choir, chorale, chorus, computers, dance, debate, drama, environmental, ethnic, film, honors, international, jazz band, LGBT, literary magazine, musical theater, newspaper, opera, orchestra, outdoor leadership center and academic clubs., pep band, political, professional, radio and TV, religious, social, social service, student government, and symphony. Popular campus events include the Club Involvement Fair, Festival of Cultures, Family Weekend, Homecoming, weekly Praise in the Pub, Meditation Sessions, Asian New Year and Martin Luther King Jr. Week. **Sports:** There are 11 intercollegiate sports for women, and 12 intramural sports for women. Facilities include a volleyball and basketball arena, racquetball courts, indoor and outdoor tennis courts, an indoor pool, a field house with an indoor running track, aerobics studio, fitness center and exercise and weight-training equipment, a softball field, a soccer field. Students have access to Saint John's University facilities as well, where they can also access lakes for canoeing, fishing, swimming, rowing and kayaking and 20 miles of on-campus wooded hiking and jogging trails. **Graduates:** From July 1, 2015 to June 30, 2016, 422 bachelor's degrees were awarded. The most popular majors were biology (11%), nursing (11%), and communication (11%). 188 companies recruited on campus in 2015-2016. In an average class, 1% graduate in 3 years or less, 77% graduate in 4 years or less, 84% graduate in 5 years or less, and 85% graduate in 6 years or less. Of the 2015 graduating class, 20% were enrolled in graduate school within 6 months of graduation, and 77% were employed.

SERVICES: Counseling and information services are available, as is tutoring in most subjects, such as math, writing, global languages and natural sciences. The College of Saint Benedict and Saint John's University established a Disability Services Office. Accomodations are provided on a case by case basis for enrolled students who provide adequate documentation of a disability. Individual tutoring is available as needed. Academic and psychological counseling are available on an unlimited basis. **Library/Resources:** The 2 libraries contain 764,960 volumes, 121,426 microform items, 28,047 audio/video tapes/CDs/DVDs, and subscribe to 46,204 periodicals including electronic. Computerized library services include interlibrary loans, database searching, Internet access, and Wi-Fi capability. Special learning facilities include an art gallery, radio station, TV station, a pottery studio and kiln, a labyrinth, dance studio, green house and Saint Benedict's Monastery Heritage Museum. At Saint John's University there is Saint John's Outdoor University, an observatory, greenhouse, herbarium, natural history museum, Sommers digital video studio and the Hill Museum and Manuscript library. **Physically Challenged Students:** 80% of the campus is accessible. Facilities include wheelchair ramps, elevators, special parking, specially equipped restrooms, special class scheduling, lowered drinking fountains, and special housing. Exterior power assist doors, and accessible busing options. **Special:** Students may cross-register with St. Cloud State University. There are study-abroad programs in Australia, Austria, Chile, China, France,Germany, Guatemala, Greece, Ireland (Cork and Galway), Italy, India, Japan, London-England, Northern Ireland, South Africa, and Spain. Many short term study abroad opportunities are also offered. Internships, dual and student-designed majors, preprofessional programs, and liberal studies degrees may be pursued. A 3-2 engineering program is offered through the University of Minnesota, as is a 3-1 program in dentistry. Nondegree study and a pass/fail grading option are also available. There are 5 national honor societies, Phi Beta Kappa, and a freshman honors program. **Visiting:** There are regularly scheduled orientations for prospective students, programs include Admissions and Financial Aid presentations, campus tours and student panels. There are guides for informal visits, visitors may sit in on classes, and stay overnight. **Campus Safety and Security:** Measures include 24-hour foot and vehicle patrol, emergency notification system, self-defense education, and security escort services. There are also shuttle buses, emergency telephones, lighted pathways/sidewalks, and controlled access to dorms/residences.

REQUIREMENTS: The SAT or ACT is required. Students should be graduates of an accredited secondary school. Academic preparation should include 17 units, including 4 of English, 3 of math, 2 each of a lab science and social studies, and 4 electives. A foreign language is recommended. The GED is accepted. Home-schooled applicants are not required to have a high school diploma but are required to provide appropriate documentation of college preparatory curriculum. Saint Ben's requires applicants to be in the upper 50% of their class. A GPA of 3.0 is required. AP and CLEP credits are accepted. Important factors in the admissions decision are advanced placement or honors courses, extracurricular activities record, and parents or siblings attended your school. To graduate students must complete a first-year seminar and a junior-senior ethics seminar intended as a capstone for the liberal arts experience, and fulfill gender, intercultural, experiential learning, and fine arts requirements. Distribution requirements include 4 credits in fine arts, 2 courses each in humanities and theology, and 1 course each in math, natural science, and social science. All students must prove math and foreign language proficiency. A total of 124 credits must be earned, with a minimum GPA of 2.0. Attendance at 8 fine arts experiences is also required. **Procedure:** Freshmen are admitted in the fall and spring. Entrance exams should be taken during the spring of the junior year or fall of the senior year. There are early admissions and deferred admissions plans. Application deadlines are open. Notifications are sent April 1. Applications are accepted online. **Transfer Students:** 18 transfer students enrolled in 2015-2016. Transfer applicants must have a minimum college GPA of 2.75. An essay or personal statement, high school and college transcripts, and a transfer student evaluation form are required. Standardized test scores may be required of some. 76 of 124 credits required for the bachelor's degree must be completed at Saint Ben's. **International Students:** There are 87 international students enrolled. The school actively recruits these students. They must take the TOEFL with a minimum score of 550 on the paper-based TOEFL (PBT) or 80 on the Internet-based version (iBT), IELTS also accepted with minimum score of 6.5. In certain cases, the SAT or ACT may replace TOEFL.

ADMISSIONS: 88% of the 2016-2017 applicants were accepted. The SAT scores for the 2016-2017 freshman class were: Critical Reading-- 38% below 500, 41% between 500 and 599, 18% between 600 and 699, and 3% between 700 and 800. Math-- 51% below 500, 39% between 500 and 599, and 10% between 600 and 699. Writing-- 41% below 500, 51% between 500 and 599, 3% between 600 and 699, and 5% between 700 and 800. The ACT scores were 1% between 12 and 17, 35% between 18 and 23, 46% between 24 and 29, and 18% above 30. 61% of the current freshmen were in the top fifth of their class; 85% were in the top two fifths. There was 1 National Merit finalist. **Admissions Contact:** Dr. Calvin Mosley, Vice President for Admission & Financial. Email: *admissions@csbsju.edu* Web: *www.csbsju.edu*

FINANCIAL AID: In 2016-2017, 96% of all full-time freshmen and 94% of continuing full-time students received some form of financial aid. 75% of all full-time freshmen and 69% of continuing full-time students received need-based aid. The average freshman award was $35,516. Need-based scholarships or need-based grants averaged $29,368; need-based self-help aid (loans and jobs) averaged $6,635; and other non-need-based awards and non-need-based scholarships averaged $17,950. 60% of undergraduate students work part-time. Average annual earnings from campus work are $2445. The average financial indebtedness of the 2016 graduate was $39,110. Saint Ben's is a member of CSS. The college's own financial statement is required. The FAFSA code is 002341. The priority date for freshman financial aid applications for fall entry is March 15.

COLLEGE OF ST. SCHOLASTICA D-2

www.css.edu

Duluth, MN 55811	(218) 723-6046 (800) 447-5444
Fax: (218) 723-5991	**Email:** admissions@css.edu
Full-time: 679 men, 1576 women	**Faculty:** 190; IIB, -$
Part-time: 124 men, 462 women	**Ph.D.s:** 61%
Graduate: 431 men, 1134 women	**Student/Faculty:** 15 to 1
Year: semesters, summer session	**Tuition:** $35,326
Room & Board: $9314	**Freshman Class:** 3589 applied, 2206 accepted, 439 enrolled
SAT CR/M/W: 520/490/490 **ACT:** 24	**CEEB CODE:** 6107
Application Deadline: n/av	**COMPETITIVE**

The College of St. Scholastica, founded in 1912, is an independent private college that provides intellectual and moral preparation for responsible living and meaningful work, St. Scholastica has extended campuses in St. Paul, Brainerd, Rochester, and St. Cloud, MN. The college is guided by the Benedictine values of community, hospitality, respect, stewardship, and love of learning. Figures in the above capsule and in this profile are approximate. There are 6 undergraduate schools and 1 graduate school. In addition to regional accreditation, Saints has baccalaureate program accreditation with APTA, CSWE, TEAC, ACOTE, CAHIIM, and CAATE. The 186-acre campus is in a suburban area 150 miles north of Minneapolis and St. Paul. Including any residence halls, there are 18 buildings.

STUDENT LIFE: 85% of undergraduates are from Minnesota. Others are from 50 states, 32 foreign countries, and Canada. 83% are White; 4% Hispanic; 3% African American; 3% Foreign; 3% two or more races; 2% Asian American; 1% American Indian/Alaska Native; 1% race unknown. 18% are Catholic; 11% Protestant. **Female To Male Ratio:** 2.6:1. The average age of freshmen is 18; all undergraduates, 25. 20% do not continue beyond their first year; 70% remain to graduate. **Housing:** 961 students can be accommodated in college housing, which includes single-sex and coed dorms and on-campus apartments. On-campus housing is available on a first-come, first-served basis, and on a lottery system for upperclassmen. 51% of students live on campus; of those, 75% remain on campus on weekends. All students may keep cars.

FACULTY/CLASSROOMS: 34% of faculty are male; 66% are female. All teach undergraduates. No introductory courses are taught by graduate students. The average class size in an introductory lecture is 21; in a laboratory is 16; and in a regular course is 21.

PROGRAMS OF STUDY: Saints confers B.A. and B.S. degrees. Master's and doctoral degrees are also awarded. Bachelor's degrees are awarded in BIOLOGICAL SCIENCE (biochemistry and biology/biological science), BUSINESS (accounting, business administration and management, finance, business management, marketing management, and organizational behavior), COMMUNICATIONS AND THE ARTS (advertising, art, communications, English, journalism, languages, and music), COMPUTER AND PHYSICAL SCIENCE (chemistry, computer science, mathematics, and natural sciences), EDUCATION (education, global studies, and social science education), HEALTH PROFESSIONS (exercise science, health care administration, health science, nursing, and physical therapy), SOCIAL SCIENCE (behavioral science, economics, history, humanities, Native American studies, peace studies, philosophy, psychology, religion, and social work). Nursing, management, and biological sciences have the largest enrollments.

ACTIVITIES: There are no fraternities or sororities. There are 68 groups on campus, including band, cheerleading, choir, chorale, chorus, computers, dance, drama, ethnic, honors, international, jazz band, LGBT, literary magazine, newspaper, pep band, photography, political, professional, radio and TV, religious, social, social service, and student government. Popular campus events include Mayfest Week, Fall Fest, and International Week. **Sports:** There are 10 intercollegiate sports for men and 10 for women, and 14 intramural sports for men and 14 for women. Facilities include a wellness center, which includes a track, aerobic studio, free weight room, complete machine fitness space, athletic trainer's room, and climbing wall. **Graduates:** From July 1, 2015 to June 30, 2016, 816 bachelor's degrees were awarded. The most popular majors were nursing (49%), management (15%), and biological sciences (10%). In an average class, 57% graduate in 4 years or less, 65% graduate in 5 years or less, and 66% graduate in 6 years or less. Of the 2015 graduating class, 29% were enrolled in graduate school within 6 months of graduation, and 63% were employed.

SERVICES: Counseling and information services are available, as is tutoring in most subjects, and a reader service for the blind, and remedial writing. Sign language interpreters, a note-taking service, tape recorders, voice input computers, and remedial study skills are also available. **Library/Resources:** The library contains 111,943 volumes, 1,915 microform items, 14,932 audio/video tapes/CDs/DVDs, and subscribes to 55,088 periodicals including electronic. Computerized library services include interlibrary loans, database searching, Internet access, and Wi-Fi capability. Special learning facilities include a radio station, TV station, a music library. **Physically Challenged Students:** 95% of the campus is accessible. Facilities include wheelchair ramps, elevators, special parking, specially equipped restrooms, special class scheduling, lowered drinking fountains, lowered telephones, and special housing. **Special:** Students may cross-register with the University of Minnesota of Duluth and the University of Wisconsin of Superior. Self-designed majors, a Washington semester with American University, internships, study abroad in several countries, accelerated degrees, non-degree study, pass/fail options, and credit for life, military, or work experience are available. There is a 3-2 engineering degree with the Institute of Technology of the University of Minnesota. There are 2 national honor societies. **Visiting:** There are regularly scheduled orientations for prospective students, visting students can participate in a class placement survey, peer and academic advisement, and registration. There are guides for informal visits, visitors may sit in on classes, and stay overnight. To schedule a visit, contact the Admissions Office. **Campus Safety and Security:** Measures include 24-hour foot and vehicle patrol, emergency notification system, self-defense education, security escort services, emergency telephones, lighted pathways/sidewalks, and controlled access to dorms/residences.

REQUIREMENTS: The SAT or ACT is required. Students are also required to send official high school transcripts. AP and CLEP credits are accepted. To graduate, students must complete 128 semester credits, with a 2.0 GPA. Approximately 52 credits of general education courses are required. The hours required in the major vary. Some majors require an internship for graduation. A senior project may be required. **Procedure:** Freshmen are admitted to all sessions. Entrance exams should be taken by January of the senior year of high school. There are deferred admissions and rolling admissions plans. Application deadlines are open. Notification is sent on a rolling basis. Applications are accepted online. **Transfer Students:** 489 transfer students enrolled in 2015-2016. Applicants must have a GPA of 2.0. 32 of 128 credits required for the bachelor's degree must be completed at Saints. **International Students:** There are 79 international students enrolled. The school actively recruits these students. They must take the TOEFL with a minimum score of 550 on the paper-based TOEFL (PBT) or 79 on the Internet-based version (iBT).

ADMISSIONS: 61% of the 2016-2017 applicants were accepted. The SAT scores for the 2016-2017 freshman class were: Critical Reading-- 47% below 500, 42% between 500 and 599, and 11% between 600 and 699. Math-- 58% below 500, 32% between 500 and 599, and 11% between 600 and 699. Writing-- 58% below 500 and 42% between 500 and 599. The ACT scores were 6% between 12 and 17, 46% between 18 and 23, 41% between 24 and 29, and 6% above 30. 38% of the current freshmen were in the top fifth of their class; 76% were in the top two fifths. 19 freshmen graduated first in their class. **Admissions Contact:** Eric Berg, Vice President for Enrollment Management. Email: *admissions@css.edu* Web: *www.css.edu*

FINANCIAL AID: In 2016-2017, 81% of all full-time freshmen and 78% of continuing full-time students received some form of financial aid. 76% of all full-time freshmen and 74% of continuing full-time students received need-based aid. The average freshman award was $29,883. Need-based scholarships or need-based grants averaged $7,000; need-based self-help aid (loans and jobs) averaged $4,059; and other non-need-based awards and non-need-based scholarships averaged $20,080. 29% of undergraduate students work part-time. Average annual earnings from campus work are $1970. The average financial indebtedness of the 2016 graduate was $40,774. The FAFSA code is 002343. The priority date for freshman financial aid applications for fall entry is March 1.

CONCORDIA COLLEGE - MOORHEAD — A-2

www.concordiacollege.edu

Moorhead, MN 56562	(218) 299-3004 (800) 699-9897
Fax: (218) 299-4720	**Email:** admissions@cord.edu
Full-time: 952 men, 1536 women	**Faculty:** 181; IIB, -$
Part-time: 16 men, 27 women	**Ph.D.s:** 85%
Graduate: 4 men, 23 women	**Student/Faculty:** 14 to 1
Year: semesters, summer session	**Tuition:** $43,278
Room & Board: $7810	**Freshman Class:** 2493 applied, 1944 accepted, 684 enrolled
SAT CR/M: 570/550 **ACT:** 25	**CEEB CODE:** 6113
Application Deadline: open	**COMPETITIVE+**

Concordia College, founded in 1891, is a private, liberal arts institution affiliated with the Evangelical Lutheran Church in America. Figures in the above capsule and in this profile are approximate. There are 2 undergraduate schools and 1 graduate school. In addition to regional accreditation, Concordia has baccalaureate program accreditation with CSWE, NASM, CCNE, ACEND, and MN Board of Examiners for Nursing Home Administration. The 113-acre campus is in a suburban area 230 miles northwest of Minneapolis and St. Paul. Including any residence halls, there are 42 buildings.

STUDENT LIFE: 67% of undergraduates are from Minnesota. Others are from 33 states, 31 foreign countries, and Canada. 94% are from public schools. 83% are White; 6% race unknown; 4% Foreign; 2% African American; 2% Asian American; 2% Hispanic; 1% American Indian/Alaska Native; 1% two or more races. 43% are Protestant; 36% unknown religion; 17% Catholic. **Female To Male Ratio:** 1.6:1. The average age of freshmen is 18; all undergraduates, 20. 16% do not continue beyond their first year; 71% remain to graduate. **Housing:** 1792 students can be accommodated in college housing, which includes single-sex and coed dorms, on-campus apartments, language houses, special-interest houses, and townhouses available. On-campus housing is guaranteed for the freshman year only, and on a first-come, first-served basis, and is available on a lottery system for upperclassmen. 64% of students live on campus. All students may keep cars. Alcohol is not permitted.

FACULTY/CLASSROOMS: 51% of faculty are male; 49% are female. All teach undergraduates and do research. No introductory courses are taught by graduate students. The average class size in an introductory lecture is 23; in a laboratory is 17; and in a regular course is 19.

PROGRAMS OF STUDY: Concordia confers B.A. and B.M. degrees. Master's degrees are also awarded. Bachelor's degrees are awarded in BIOLOGICAL SCIENCE (biology/biological science and nutrition), BUSINESS (accounting, business administration and management, and international business management), COMMUNICATIONS AND THE ARTS (art, Chinese, classical languages, classics, communications, dramatic arts, English, French, German, journalism, Latin, music, music performance, music theory and composition, and Spanish), COMPUTER AND PHYSICAL SCIENCE (applied science, chemistry, mathematics, and physics), EDUCATION (art education, business education, elementary education, foreign languages education, health education, mathematics education, music education, physical education, secondary education, and social studies education), ENGINEERING AND ENVIRONMENTAL DESIGN (environmental science), HEALTH PROFESSIONS (clinical science, exercise science, health, and nursing), SOCIAL

SCIENCE (history, humanities, international studies, philosophy, political science/government, psychology, religion, Scandinavian studies, social work, and sociology). Natural sciences is the strongest academically. Education, business, and biology have the largest enrollments.

ACTIVITIES: There are no fraternities or sororities. There are 106 groups on campus, including art, band, cheerleading, choir, chorale, chorus, communications, dance, debate, drama, environmental, ethnic, forensics, honors, international, jazz band, LGBT, literary magazine, musical theater, newspaper, orchestra, pep band, photography, political, professional, radio and TV, religious, social, social service, student government, and symphony. Popular campus events include Christmas Concert, Martin Luther King Jr. Day, and National Book Award Celebration. **Sports:** There are 11 intercollegiate sports for men and 11 for women, and 6 intramural sports for men and 5 for women. Facilities include an indoor track with multipurpose volleyball/basketball/tennis courts, an indoor swimming pool, an all-weather track, a field house, basketball courts, an auxiliary gym, a weight room, outdoor tennis courts, softball and soccer competition fields, a baseball complex, and soccer practice fields. **Graduates:** From July 1, 2015 to June 30, 2016, 540 bachelor's degrees were awarded. The most popular majors were business (17%), education (15%), and biology (12%). In an average class, 65% graduate in 4 years or less, 71% graduate in 5 years or less, and 71% graduate in 6 years or less. Of the 2015 graduating class, 32% were enrolled in graduate school within 6 months of graduation, and 82% were employed.

SERVICES: Counseling and information services are available, as is tutoring in most subjects, and a reader service for the blind, and an interpreter service for the deaf. **Library/Resources:** The library contains 346,744 volumes, 44,055 microform items, 26,572 audio/video tapes/CDs/DVDs, and subscribes to 4,342 periodicals including electronic. Computerized library services include interlibrary loans, database searching, Internet access, and Wi-Fi capability. Special learning facilities include an art gallery, radio station, TV station, an observatory, a field biology research facility, a laser facility, a nursing simulation lab, and a 2MeV hypervelocity dust particle accelerator. **Physically Challenged Students:** 95% of the campus is accessible. Facilities include wheelchair ramps, elevators, special parking, specially equipped restrooms, special class scheduling, lowered drinking fountains, and special housing. **Special:** Co-op programs and internships are available in most majors, and dual majors are available in all majors. There is a Washington semester and an urban studies semester in Chicago. Study abroad in 26 countries, on- and off-campus work-study, a B.A.-B.M. degree in music, and a 3-2 engineering degree with the University of Minnesota are available. Nondegree study for special students and pass/fail options also are possible. Cross-registration is offered through the Tri-College University Consortium. There are 18 national honor societies, a freshman honors program, and 16 departmental honors programs. **Visiting:** There are regularly scheduled orientations for prospective students, including an extensive campus tour and meetings with admissions counselors and faculty members. There are guides for informal visits, visitors may sit in on classes, and stay overnight. To schedule a visit, contact the Office of Admissions. **Campus Safety and Security:** Measures include 24-hour foot and vehicle patrol, emergency notification system, security escort services, emergency telephones, lighted pathways/sidewalks, and controlled access to dorms/residences.

REQUIREMENTS: The SAT or ACT is required. Two character references are required, and an interview is recommended. The GED is accepted. Academic performance and preparation, as evidenced in a high school transcript, are the most important factors in the admissions decision. AP and CLEP credits are accepted. Important factors in the admissions decision are advanced placement or honors courses, recommendations by school officials, and leadership record. All students must maintain a minimum GPA of 2.0 while taking 126 semester hours, including at least 32 in the major. Required courses include written communication, oral communication, an introduction to liberal arts, and 2 courses each in physical education and religion. Exploration requirements include 7 courses taken from 6 areas: science and math, social science, world language, humanities and arts plus 2 Perspectives courses to include 1 U.S. Cultural Diversity course and 1 International and Global Perspectives course. The final course in the Core Curriculum is a writing-intensive capstone course. **Procedure:** Freshmen are admitted to all sessions. Entrance exams should be taken by the first semester of the senior year. There are early admissions, deferred admissions, and rolling admissions plans. Application deadlines are open. Application fee is $20. Notification is sent on a rolling basis. Applications are accepted online. **Transfer Students:** 42 transfer students enrolled in 2015-2016. Transfer applicants must have a minimum 2.0 GPA and provide official transcripts from previously attended schools. 28 of 126 credits required for the bachelor's degree must be completed at Concordia. **International Students:** There are 102 international students enrolled. The school actively recruits these students. They must take the TOEFL with a minimum score of 73 on the Internet-based version (iBT).

ADMISSIONS: 78% of the 2016-2017 applicants were accepted. The SAT scores for the 2016-2017 freshman class were: Critical Reading-- 23% below 500, 33% between 500 and 599, 35% between 600 and 699, and 10% between 700 and 800. Math-- 33% below 500, 29% between 500 and 599, 23% between 600 and 699, and 15% between 700 and 800. Writing-- 31% below 500, 37% between 500 and 599, 23% between 600 and 699, and 10% between 700 and 800. The ACT scores were 13% below 12, 22% between 12 and 17, 29% between 18 and 23, 16% between 24 and 29, and 20% above 30. 53% of the current freshmen were in the top fifth of their class; 81% were in the top two fifths. There were 4 National Merit finalists. **Admissions Contact:** Peter A Lien, Admissions Director. Email: *admissions@cord.edu* Web: *www.concordiacollege.edu*

FINANCIAL AID: In 2016-2017, 99% of all full-time freshmen and 97% of continuing full-time students received some form of financial aid. 77% of all full-time freshmen and 73% of continuing full-time students received need-based aid. The average freshman award was $27,769. Need-based scholarships or need-based grants averaged $21,188; and need-based self-help aid (loans and jobs) averaged $7,676. 52% of undergraduate students work part-time. Average annual earnings from campus work are $1405. Concordia is a member of CSS. The FAFSA code is 002346. The deadline for filing freshman financial aid applications for fall entry is rolling.

CONCORDIA UNIVERSITY SAINT PAUL C-4

www.csp.edu

St. Paul, MN 55104 (651) 641-8230
(800) 333-4705

Fax: (651) 603-6320 Email: admissions@csp.edu

Full-time: 636 men, 746 women
Part-time: 434 men, 751 women
Graduate: 559 men, 1254 women
Year: semesters, summer session
Room & Board: $8300
ACT: 21
Application Deadline: August 1
Faculty: 81
Ph.D.s: 76%
Student/Faculty: 16 to 1
Tuition: $20,750
Freshman Class: 1483 applied, 822 accepted, 229 enrolled
CEEB CODE: 6114
COMPETITIVE

Concordia University, founded in 1893 and a member of the Concordia University System, is a private institution affiliated with the Lutheran Church Missouri Synod and offering programs in teacher education, business, church vocations, and the liberal arts. Master's programs and bachelor's degree completion programs for adult learners are also offered. There are 3 undergraduate schools and 1 graduate school. In addition to regional accreditation, CSP has baccalaureate program accreditation with ACBSP and NCATE. The 37-acre campus is in an urban area in the Midway area of the Twin Cities, between Minneapolis and St. Paul. Including any residence halls, there are 24 buildings.

STUDENT LIFE: 73% of undergraduates are from Minnesota. Others are from 30 states, 17 foreign countries, and Canada. 8% are Asian American; 63% White; 5% Foreign; 4% Hispanic; 4% two or more races; 4% race unknown; 12% African American. 52% are Protestant. **Female To Male Ratio:** 1.7:1. The average age of freshmen is 18; all undergraduates, 26. 30% do not continue beyond their first year; 50% remain to graduate. **Housing:** 514 students can be accommodated in college housing, which includes single-sex and coed dorms, on-campus apartments, and married student housing. On-campus housing is guaranteed for the freshman year only, and is available on a first-come, and first-served basis. Priority is given to out-of-town students. 79% of students commute. All students may keep cars.

FACULTY/CLASSROOMS: 48% of faculty are male; 52% are female. 79% teach undergraduates. No introductory courses are taught by graduate students. The average class size in an introductory lecture is 15; in a laboratory is 19; and in a regular course is 15.

PROGRAMS OF STUDY: CUSP confers B.A., B.S., B.B.A., and B.F.A.

degrees. Associate, master's, and doctoral degrees are also awarded. Bachelor's degrees are awarded in BIOLOGICAL SCIENCE (biology/biological science), BUSINESS (accounting, banking and finance, business administration and management, marketing management, organizational leadership and management, and sports management), COMMUNICATIONS AND THE ARTS (art, choral music, church music, communications, creative writing, design, dramatic arts, English, English Writing, graphic design, instrumental music education, music, music business management, strategic communication, studio art, theatre arts, and vocal music education), COMPUTER AND PHYSICAL SCIENCE (computer science, information sciences and systems, and mathematics), EDUCATION (art education, Christian education, early childhood education, education of the emotionally handicapped, elementary education, English education, mathematics education, middle school education, music education, physical education, science education, secondary education, social studies education, social studies secondary school education, and special education), HEALTH PROFESSIONS (community health work, nursing, and radiological science), SOCIAL SCIENCE (child care/child and family studies, criminal justice, history, physical fitness/movement, psychology, religion, religious education, religious music, sociology, and theological studies). Business, teacher education, and criminal justice have the largest enrollments.

ACTIVITIES: There are no fraternities or sororities. There are 40 groups on campus, including art, band, cheerleading, choir, chorus, dance, drama, ethnic, honors, international, jazz band, musical theater, newspaper, pep band, political, professional, religious, social, social service, and student government. Popular campus events include Fine Arts Christmas Concert, and Spring Honors Convocation. **Sports:** There are 6 intercollegiate sports for men and 7 for women, and 8 intramural sports for men and 8 for women. Facilities include a gym, health and wellness center, a stadium for football, soccer, track and field, and baseball and softball playing fields. **Graduates:** From July 1, 2015 to June 30, 2016, 557 bachelor's degrees were awarded. The most popular majors were organizational leadership/business (18%), marketing (8%), and teacher education (7%). 60 companies recruited on campus in 2015-2016. In an average class, 1% graduate in 3 years or less, 27% graduate in 4 years or less, 43% graduate in 5 years or less, and 46% graduate in 6 years or less. Of the 2015 graduating class, 15% were enrolled in graduate school within 6 months of graduation, and 79% were employed.

SERVICES: Counseling and information services are available, as is tutoring in every subject, and a reader service for the blind, and remedial math, reading, and writing. **Library/Resources:** The library contains 161,959 volumes, 11,516 microform items, 3,128 audio/video tapes/CDs/DVDs, and subscribes to 297 periodicals including electronic. Computerized library services include interlibrary loans, database searching, Internet access, and Wi-Fi capability. Special learning facilities include an art gallery. **Physically Challenged Students:** 90% of the campus is accessible. Facilities include wheelchair ramps, elevators, special parking, specially equipped restrooms, special class scheduling, lowered drinking fountains, and lowered telephones. **Special:** Concordia, St. Paul offers cross-registration with other members of the Concordia University System, internships in many programs, and study-abroad opportunities. Accelerated degree programs and interdisciplinary majors are also available. Credit for life experience, nondegree study, and pass/fail options are possible. Degree completion programs designed for working adults are offered in cohort-delivered format via face-to-face or on-line learning. There is 1 national honor society, a freshman honors program, and 1 departmental honors program. **Visiting:** There are regularly scheduled orientations for prospective students, including a campus tour, class visits, and a meeting with professors. There are guides for informal visits, visitors may sit in on classes, and stay overnight. To schedule a visit, contact the Office of Undergraduate Admission. **Campus Safety and Security:** Measures include 24-hour foot and vehicle patrol, emergency notification system, self-defense education, security escort services, emergency telephones, lighted pathways/sidewalks, and controlled access to dorms/residences.

REQUIREMENTS: The ACT is required. Applicants are normally expected to have 4 years of English, 2 each of math, science, fine arts, and history/social studies, and 1 of health or phys ed. An interview is recommended. 2 letters of recommendation are required. The GED is accepted. AP and CLEP credits are accepted. To graduate, students must complete 128 credit hours in the form of 1 major or 2 minors, GPA varies from 2.0 to 2.75, and required hours in the major vary from 32 to 44, depending on the program. The core curriculum consists of 48 hours of liberal arts courses. **Procedure:** Freshmen are admitted in the fall and spring. Entrance exams should be taken during the senior year. There are deferred admissions and rolling admissions plans. Applications should be filed by August 1 for fall entry; December 1 for spring entry, along with a $30 fee. Applications are accepted online. **Transfer Students:** 940 transfer students enrolled in 2015-2016. Applicants must have a 2.0 GPA and submit 2 letters of recommendation. Students with fewer than 1 year of college credits must also submit ACT scores and an official high school transcript. 32 of 128 credits required for the bachelor's degree must be completed at CSP. **International Students:** There are 114 international students enrolled. The school actively recruits these students. They must take the TOEFL with a minimum score of 513 on the paper-based TOEFL (PBT) or 65 on the Internet-based version (iBT) or take the MELAB.

ADMISSIONS: 55% of the 2016-2017 applicants were accepted. The ACT scores were 16% between 12 and 17, 54% between 18 and 23, 25% between 24 and 29, and 5% above 30. 22% of the current freshmen were in the top fifth of their class; 45% were in the top two fifths. 3 freshmen graduated first in their class. **Admissions Contact:** Kristin Vogel, Assoc VP for Traditional Enrollment. Email: *admissions@csp.edu* Web: *www.csp.edu*

FINANCIAL AID: In 2016-2017, 75% of all full-time freshmen and 72% of continuing full-time students received some form of financial aid. 75% of all full-time freshmen and 72% of continuing full-time students received need-based aid. The average freshman award was $16,832. Need-based scholarships or need-based grants averaged $12,382; need-based self-help aid (loans and jobs) averaged $4,037; and other non-need-based awards and non-need-based scholarships averaged $4,244. 14% of undergraduate students work part-time. Average annual earnings from campus work are $1896. The average financial indebtedness of the 2016 graduate was $25,000. The college's own financial statement, and federal tax return are required. The FAFSA code is 002347. The priority date for freshman financial aid applications for fall entry is March 1.

GUSTAVUS ADOLPHUS COLLEGE C-4

www.gustavus.edu

St. Peter, MN 56082	(507) 933-7676 (800) GUSTAVU
Fax: (507) 933-6270	**Email:** admission@gustavus.edu
Full-time: 1117 men, 1306 women	**Faculty:** 201; IIB, -$
Part-time: 21 men, 11 women	**Ph.D.s:** 85%
Graduate: n/av	**Student/Faculty:** 12 to 1
Year: 4-1-4	**Tuition:** $43,033
Room & Board: $9400	**Freshman Class:** 4804 applied, 3037 accepted, 610 enrolled
ACT: 27	**CEEB CODE:** 6253
Application Deadline: November 1	**HIGHLY COMPETITIVE**

Gustavus Adolphus College, founded in 1862, is a private liberal arts college affiliated with the Evangelical Luteran Church in America. Figures in the above capsule and in this profile are approximate. There are 3 undergraduate schools. In addition to regional accreditation, Gustavus has baccalaureate program accreditation with NASM, NCATE, NLN, CCNE, and NASPE. The 340-acre campus is in a small town 65 miles southwest of Minneapolis. Including any residence halls, there are 56 buildings.

STUDENT LIFE: 81% of undergraduates are from Minnesota. Others are from 43 states, 15 foreign countries, and Canada. 94% are from public schools. 85% are White; 4% Asian American; 3% Hispanic; 2% African American; 2% Foreign; 2% two or more races; 1% American Indian/Alaska Native; 1% race unknown. 72% are Protestant; 21% Catholic. **Female To Male Ratio:** 1.2:1. The average age of freshmen is 18; all undergraduates, 20. 9% do not continue beyond their first year; 80% remain to graduate. **Housing:** 2103 students can be accommodated in college housing, which includes coed dorms, on-campus apartments, language houses, and special-interest houses. On-campus housing is guaranteed for all 4 years and available on a lottery system for upperclassmen. 85% of students live on campus; of those, 75% remain on campus on weekends. All students may keep cars.

FACULTY/CLASSROOMS: 52% of faculty are male; 48% are female. All teach undergraduates and do research. No introductory courses are taught by graduate students. The average class size in an introductory lecture is 25; in a laboratory is 15; and in a regular course is 15.

PROGRAMS OF STUDY: Gustavus confers B.A. degrees. Bachelor's degrees are awarded in AGRICULTURE (environmental studies), BIOLOGICAL SCIENCE (biochemistry and biology/biological science), BUSINESS (accounting, business administration and management, business economics, and international business management), COMMUNICATIONS AND THE ARTS (classics, communications, dance, dramatic arts, English, fine arts, French, music, Russian, Scandinavian languages, Spanish, and speech/debate/rhetoric), COMPUTER AND PHYSICAL SCIENCE (chemistry, computer science, geology, mathematics, and physics), EDUCATION (art education, business education, elementary education, foreign languages education, health education, middle school education, music education, science education, and secondary education), HEALTH PROFESSIONS (nursing, physical therapy, predentistry, and premedicine), SOCIAL SCIENCE (anthropology, economics, geography, history, philosophy, political science/government, prelaw, psychology, religion, social science, sociology, and women's studies). Physical science, and social science are the strongest academically. Business, biology, and communication studies have the largest enrollments.

ACTIVITIES: 14% of men belong to 6 local and 1 national fraternities; 14% of women belong to 5 local and 1 national sororities. There are 125 groups on campus, including art, band, cheerleading, choir, chorus, computers, dance, debate, drama, environmental, ethnic, film, forensics, honors, international, jazz band, LGBT, literary magazine, musical theater, newspaper, orchestra, pep band, political, professional, radio and TV, religious, social, social service, student government, symphony, and yearbook. Popular campus events include Christmas in Christ Chapel, Earth Jam All-Day Music Festival, and Building Bridges Diversity Conference. **Sports:** There are 12 intercollegiate sports for men and 13 for women, and 17 intramural sports for men and 10 for women. Facilities include an ice arena, a pool, gymnastics area, an indoor tennis center, an arena, playing fields, football field, racquetball and tennis courts, a weight room, an indoor and an outdoor running track, varsity and intramural fields for soccer, softball, baseball, lacrosse, rugby, and ultimate frisbee. **Graduates:** From July 1, 2015 to June 30, 2016, 603 bachelor's degrees were awarded. The most popular majors were biology (9%), economics/management (6%), and psychology (5%). 40 companies recruited on campus in 2015-2016. In an average class, 2% graduate in 3 years or less, 80% graduate in 4 years or less, 82% graduate in 5 years or less, and 82% graduate in 6 years or less. Of the 2015 graduating class, 34% were enrolled in graduate school within 6 months of graduation, and 66% were employed.

SERVICES: Counseling and information services are available, as is tutoring in most subjects. A writing lab, ESL services and disability assistance are also available. **Library/Resources:** The library contains 311,480 volumes, 43,075 microform items, and 105,799 audio/video tapes/CDs/DVDs, and subscribes to 32,340 periodicals including electronic. Computerized library services include interlibrary loans, database searching, Internet access, and Wi-Fi capability. Special learning facilities include an art gallery, radio station, an arboretum, observatory, greenhouses,bronze-casting facility, geology museum, and many specialized laboratories. **Physically Challenged Students:** All of the campus is accessible. Facilities include wheelchair ramps, elevators, special parking, specially equipped restrooms, special class scheduling, lowered drinking fountains, lowered telephones, and special housing. **Special:** Co-op programs in nursing with St. Olaf College and cross-registration with Minnesota State University are available. The college offers internships, a Washington semester, study abroad in 22 countries, student-designed majors, nondegree study, work-study, and pass/fail options for some courses. A 3-2 engineering degree program with the University of Minnesota and Minnesota State University, Mankato is offered. The Curriculum II core offers a 12-course interdisciplinary program. There are 16 national honor societies, Phi Beta Kappa, and 12 departmental honors programs. **Visiting:** There are regularly scheduled orientations for prospective students, consisting of an interview, a tour, and meetings with faculty and students. There are guides for informal visits, visitors may sit in on classes, and stay overnight. To schedule a visit, contact the Admissions Office. **Campus Safety and Security:** Measures include 24-hour foot and vehicle patrol, emergency notification system, and security escort services. There are also shuttle buses, emergency telephones, lighted pathways/sidewalks, and controlled access to dorms/residences.

REQUIREMENTS: Applicants must have completed 4 years of English, 3 each of math and science, and 2 each of a foreign language, history, and social studies. AP credits are accepted. Important factors in the admissions decision are advanced placement or honors courses and evidence of special talent. All students are required to complete 32 courses plus 2 January interim courses and two-half courses in personal fitness and lifetime activity. Nine courses must be in the following areas (1 each): the arts, biblical, and theological studies, literary and rhetorical studies, historical and philosophical studies, mathematical and logical reasoning, natural science perspective, human behavior and social institutions, and non-western cultures. A minimum GPA of 2.0 is necessary for graduation. A total of 7 to 11 courses is required in the major. **Procedure:** Freshmen are admitted in the fall, winter, and spring. Entrance exams should be taken in the fall of the senior year. There are deferred admissions and rolling admissions plans. Applications should be filed by November 1 for fall entry; December 1 for winter entry; and January 1 for spring entry. Notifications are sent in November. Applications are accepted online. **Transfer Students:** 32 transfer students enrolled in 2015-2016. Transfer applicants must have earned a 2.4 GPA at their previous college. 72 of 140 credits required for the bachelor's degree must be completed at Gustavus. **International Students:** There are 58 international students enrolled. The school actively recruits these students. They must take the TOEFL.

ADMISSIONS: 63% of the 2016-2017 applicants were accepted. The SAT scores for the 2016-2017 freshman class were: The ACT scores were 2% below 12, 13% between 12 and 17, 31% between 18 and 23, 20% between 24 and 29, and 34% above 30. 56% of the current freshmen were in the top fifth of their class; 88% were in the top two fifths. There were 4 National Merit finalists. 23 freshmen graduated first in their class. **Admissions Contact:** Bob Neuman, Senior Associate Dean. Email: *admission@gustavus.edu* Web: *www.gustavus.edu*

FINANCIAL AID: In 2016-2017, 93% of all full-time freshmen and 92% of continuing full-time students received some form of financial aid. 69% of all full-time freshmen and 65% of continuing full-time students received need-based aid. The average freshman award was $31,279. Need-based scholarships or need-based grants averaged $26,732; and need-based self-help aid (loans and jobs) averaged $9,317. 71% of undergraduate students work part-time. Average annual earnings from campus work are $1600. The average financial indebtedness of the 2016 graduate was $33,523. Gustavus is a member of CSS. The CSS/Profile and the college's own financial statement are required. The FAFSA code is 002353. The priority date for freshman financial aid applications for fall entry is January 1. The filing deadline for fall entry is April 15.

HAMLINE UNIVERSITY C-4

www.hamline.edu

St. Paul, MN 55104	(651) 523-2207 (800) 753-9753
Fax: (651) 523-2458	Email: admission@hamline.edu
Full-time: 903 men, 1259 women	**Faculty:** n/av
Part-time: 30 men, 50 women	**Ph.D.s:** 88%
Graduate: 766 men, 1461 women	**Student/Faculty:** 13 to 1
Year: 4-1-4, summer session	**Tuition:** $36,286
Room & Board: $9392	**Freshman Class:** 3417 applied, 2378 accepted, 521 enrolled
SAT CR/M/W: 550/540/540 **ACT:** 24	**CEEB CODE:** 6265
Application Deadline: n/av	**VERY COMPETITIVE**

Hamline University, founded in 1854, is a private liberal arts and sciences university affiliated with the United Methodist Church. There are 3 undergraduate schools and 4 graduate schools. In addition to regional accreditation, Hamline has baccalaureate program accreditation with NASM, NCATE, ABA, and ACS. The 60-acre campus is in an urban area between the downtowns of Minneapolis and St. Paul.

STUDENT LIFE: 78% of undergraduates are from Minnesota. Others are from 44 states, 34 foreign countries, and Canada. 72% are White; 6% African American; 6% Asian American; 6% Hispanic; 6% two or more races; 2% race unknown; 1% American Indian/Alaska Native; 1% Foreign. 28% are Lutheran, Buddhist and unknown; 19% Catholic; 17% claim no religious affiliation. **Female To Male Ratio:** 1.6:1. The average age of freshmen is 18; all undergraduates, 20. 17% do not continue beyond their first year; 65% remain to graduate. **Housing:** 955 students can be accommodated in college housing, which includes coed dorms, on-campus apartments, married student housing, language houses, special-interest houses, fraternity houses, PRIDE black student alliance house, Hmong student asociation house, and Amity scholar house. On-campus housing is guaranteed for all 4 years. 58% of students commute. All students may keep cars.

FACULTY/CLASSROOMS: 43% of faculty are male; 57% are female. No introductory courses are taught by graduate students.

PROGRAMS OF STUDY: Hamline confers B.A., B.S., B.B.A., and B.F.A degrees. Master's and doctoral degrees are also awarded. Bachelor's degrees are awarded in AGRICULTURE (environmental studies), BIOLOGICAL SCIENCE (biochemistry and biology/biological science), BUSINESS (accounting, business administration and management, global/general management, and international business management), COMMUNICATIONS AND THE ARTS (art history, art, communications, creative writing, dramatic arts, English, fine arts, French, German, music, music performance, Spanish, and theatre arts), COMPUTER AND PHYSICAL SCIENCE (chemistry, digital arts/technology, mathematics, and physics), EDUCATION (athletic training, education, elementary education, foreign languages education, music education, science education, and secondary education), HEALTH PROFESSIONS (exercise science and premedicine), SOCIAL SCIENCE (anthropology, criminal justice, East Asian studies, economics, forensic studies, history, Latin American studies, paralegal studies, peace studies, philosophy, political science/government, prelaw, psychology, religion, social science, social studies, sociology, urban studies, and women's studies). Social sciences, business, and psychology have the largest enrollments.

ACTIVITIES: There are 60 groups on campus, including art, band, cheerleading, chess, choir, chorale, chorus, computers, dance, drama, environmental, ethnic, film, forensics, honors, international, jazz band, LGBT, literary magazine, musical theater, newspaper, orchestra, pep band, photography, political, professional, radio and TV, religious, social, social service, student government, and symphony. Popular campus events include World Fest, Fall Organization Fair, and Women's Leadership Retreat. **Sports:** There are 9 intercollegiate sports for men and 10 for women, and 11 intramural sports for men and 11 for women. Facilities include a stadium, field house, swimming pool, playing field, and an athletic center. **Graduates:** From July 1, 2015 to June 30, 2016, 428 bachelor's degrees were awarded. The most popular majors were social sciences (15%), psychology (13%), and business (5%). 85 companies recruited on campus in 2015-2016. In an average class, 56% graduate in 4 years or less, 6% graduate in 5 years or less, and 2% graduate in 6 years or less.

SERVICES: Counseling and information services are available, as is tutoring in every subject, and a reader service for the blind, and remedial math, reading, and writing. **Library/Resources:** Computerized library services include interlibrary loans, database searching, Internet access, and Wi-Fi capability. Special learning facilities include an art gallery, radio station, centers for global and environmental education, and for excellence in urban teaching. There are also centers for writing and quantitative reasoning. **Physically Challenged Students:** Facilities include wheelchair ramps, elevators, special parking, specially equipped restrooms, special class scheduling, lowered drinking fountains, lowered telephones, and special housing. **Special:** Cross-registration with Augsburg, Macalester, Saint Catherine Colleges and the University of Saint Thomas is possible. Students may select cooperative programs, study abroad, a Washington semester with American University, dual majors, student-designed majors, and pass/fail options. Students may earn a 3-2 or 4-2 engineering degree at the University of Minnesota or Washington University. On-campus work-study is available, as are extensive internship opportunities on and off campus. There is a chapter of Phi Beta Kappa and a freshman honors program. **Visiting:** There are guides for informal visits, visitors may sit in on classes, and stay overnight. To schedule a visit, contact the Admissions Office at (651) 523-2014. **Campus Safety and Security:** Measures include 24-hour foot and vehicle patrol, emergency notification system, self-defense education, security escort services, emergency telephones, lighted pathways/sidewalks, and controlled access to dorms/residences.

REQUIREMENTS: The SAT or ACT is required. It is recommended that candidates for admission complete 4 years each of English (with 1 year of college preparatory writing), social studies, academic electives, math, and social science, 3 years of lab science, and 2 years of a foreign language. The GED is accepted. AP and CLEP credits are accepted. To graduate, students must complete a minimum of 32 course credits within their field of concentration with a minimum overall GPA of 2.0. 63 course credits must be outside the major. In their first year, all students are required to take a freshman seminar and freshman English and demonstrate computer literacy. All students must also take a variety of general education courses to apply toward the "Hamline Plan." An independent study project and an internship are also required. **Procedure:** Freshmen are admitted to all sessions. There are early decision, early admissions, deferred admissions, and rolling admissions plans. Application deadlines are open. Notification of early decision is sent December 20; regular decision. Applications are accepted on-line. **Transfer Students:** 140 transfer students enrolled in 2015-2016. Transfer applicants must submit the application form, transcript copies, teacher/advisor recommendation, and a secondary school transcript, if fewer than 32 semester hours have been competed. Applicants must submit an essay or personal statement. A minimum college GPA of 2.0 is required. 56 of 128 credits required for the bachelor's degree must be completed at Hamline. **International Students:** There are 30 international students enrolled. The school actively recruits these students. They must take the TOEFL with a minimum score of 550 on the paper-based TOEFL (PBT) or 80 on the Internet-based version (iBT). They must also take the SAT or ACT.

ADMISSIONS: 70% of the 2016-2017 applicants were accepted. The SAT scores for the 2016-2017 freshman class were: Critical Reading-- 36% below 500, 32% between 500 and 599, 22% between 600 and 699, and 10% between 700 and 800. Math-- 27% below 500, 51% between 500 and 599, 19% between 600 and 699, and 3% between 700 and 800. Writing-- 31% below 500, 36% between 500 and 599, 31% between 600 and 699, and 3% between 700 and 800. The ACT scores were 20% below 12, 24% between 12 and 17, 21% between 18 and 23, 11% between 24 and 29, and 19% above 30. **Admissions Contact:** Undergraduate Admission Email: *admission@hamline.edu* Web: *www.hamline.edu*

FINANCIAL AID: In 2016-2017, 99% of all full-time freshmen and 98% of continuing full-time students received some form of financial aid. 89% of all full-time freshmen and 84% of continuing full-time students received need-based aid. The average freshman award was $31,477. The average financial indebtedness of the 2016 graduate was $36,006. The FAFSA code is 002354. The priority date for freshman financial aid applications for fall entry is March 15.

MACALESTER COLLEGE C-4

www.macalester.edu

St. Paul, MN 55105	**(651) 696-6357** **(800) 231-7974**
Fax: (651) 696-6724	**Email: admissions@macalester.edu**
Full-time: 846 men, 1262 women	**Faculty:** 182; IIB, +$
Part-time: 20 men, 18 women	**Ph.D.s:** 82%
Graduate: n/av	**Student/Faculty:** 10 to 1
Year: semesters	**Tuition:** $50,639
Room & Board: $11,266	**Freshman Class:** 5946 applied, 2206 accepted, 506 enrolled
SAT CR/M/W: 700/680/690 **ACT:** 31	**CEEB CODE:** 6390
Application Deadline: January 15	**MOST COMPETITIVE**

Macalester College, founded in 1874, has been preparing students for world citizenship and providing an integrated international education for over seven decades. The academic program ranks among the top 20 in the nation at a liberal arts and sciences college. Most students study abroad for 15 weeks or more, providing time for substantial experience and study in another country. Graduates reap the benefits of a multicultural student body and global education in the job market and at the nations top graduate programs. There is 1 undergraduate school. In addition to regional accreditation, Macalester has baccalaureate program accreditation with NASM. The 53-acre campus is in an urban area midway between downtown St. Paul and Minneapolis. Including any residence halls, there are 43 buildings.

STUDENT LIFE: 70% of undergraduates are from out of state, mostly the Midwest. Students are from 49 states, 87 foreign countries, and Canada. 61% are from public schools. 64% are White; 15% Foreign; 7% Asian American; 6% Hispanic; 5% two or more races; 3% African American; 1% American Indian/Alaska Native; 1% race unknown. **Female To Male Ratio:** 1.5:1. The average age of freshmen is 18; all undergraduates, 20. 7% do not continue beyond their first year; 88% remain to graduate. **Housing:** 1300 students can be accommodated in college housing, which includes single-sex and coed dorms, on-campus apartments, language houses, special-interest houses, vegetarian co-op, a cultural house, interfaith house, and a section for gender neutral. On-campus housing is available on a lottery system for upperclassmen. 66% of students live on campus; of those, 90% remain on campus on weekends. Upperclassmen may keep cars.

FACULTY/CLASSROOMS: 46% of faculty are male; 54% are female. All teach undergraduates, and 80% do research. No introductory courses are taught by graduate students. The average class size in an introductory lecture is 20; in a laboratory is 13; and in a regular course is 17.

PROGRAMS OF STUDY: Macalester confers B.A. degrees. Bachelor's degrees are awarded in AGRICULTURE (environmental studies), BIOLOGICAL SCIENCE (biology/biological science and neurosciences), COMMUNICATIONS AND THE ARTS (art, Chinese, classics, dramatic arts, English, French, Japanese, linguistics, media arts, music, Russian, and Spanish), COMPUTER AND PHYSICAL SCIENCE (chemistry, computer science, geology, mathematics, and physics), EDUCATION (education), SOCIAL SCIENCE (American studies, anthropology, Asian/Oriental studies, economics, geography, German area studies, history, humanities, international studies, Latin American studies, philosophy, political science/government, psychology, religion, sociology, and women's studies). International studies, biology and political science are the strongest academically. Mathematics, biology and political science have the largest enrollments.

ACTIVITIES: There are no fraternities or sororities. There are 115 groups on campus, including social justice organizations, art, bagpipe, band, chess, choir, chorale, chorus, computers, dance, debate, drama, environmental, ethnic, forensics, honors, international, jazz band, LGBT, literary magazine, multi faith council, newspaper, orchestra, photography, political, professional, radio and TV, religious, social, social service, student government, and symphony. Popular campus events include Midnight Breakfast, Mac Idol, Spring Fest and Founders Day. **Sports:** There are 10 intercollegiate sports for men and 11 for women, and 12 intramural sports for men and 12 for women. Facilities include a field house, a gym, swimming pool, a stadium for football, soccer, and outdoor track, racquetball courts, tennis courts, an indoor track and field facility, weight room/fitness center, dance studios, health & wellness center, athletic training room, squash courts, and baseball and softball diamonds. **Graduates:** From July 1, 2015 to June 30, 2016, 488 bachelor's degrees were awarded. The most popular majors were biology (10%), political science (10%), and economics (9%). 88 companies recruited on campus in 2015-2016. In an average class, 84% graduate in 4 years or less, 87% graduate in 5 years or less, and 88% graduate in 6 years or less. Of the 2015 graduating class, 14% were enrolled in graduate school within 6 months of graduation, and 80% were employed.

SERVICES: Counseling and information services are available, as is tutoring in some subjects, such as math, chemistry, physics, and writing. There is also a reader service for the blind. **Library/Resources:** The library contains 348,727 volumes, 87,004 microform items, and 16,769 audio/video tapes/CDs/DVDs, and subscribes to 12,151 periodicals including electronic. Computerized library services include interlibrary loans, database searching, Internet access, and Wi-Fi capability. Special learning facilities include an art gallery, radio station, an academic support center, a 280-acre natural history study area 25 miles from campus. **Physically Challenged Students:** 90% of the campus is accessible. Facilities include wheelchair ramps, elevators, special parking, specially equipped restrooms, special class scheduling, lowered drinking fountains, lowered telephones, and special housing. **Special:** Cross-registration is offered at Augsburg College, Hamline University, St. Catherine University, the University of St. Thomas and Minneapolis College of Art and Design. There also are cooperative programs in liberal arts and architecture with Washington University in St. Louis, engineering with the same school and the University of Minnesota. Internships are available in government, financial services, law, medicine, research, the arts, and other fields. Students study abroad in more than 68 countries. Student-designed majors and pass/fail options for no more than 1 course per semester also are available. There are 16 national honor societies, Phi Beta Kappa, and 30 departmental honors programs. **Visiting:** There are regularly scheduled orientations for prospective students, including interviews, information sessions, a class visit, and a tour of campus. There are guides for informal visits, visitors may sit in on classes, and stay overnight. To schedule a visit, contact the Admissions Office. **Campus Safety and Security:** Measures include 24-hour foot and vehicle patrol, emergency notification system, self-defense education, security escort services, emergency telephones, lighted pathways/sidewalks, controlled access to dorms/residences, and security site on the school's web site.

REQUIREMENTS: The SAT or ACT is required. Applicants should have earned at least 16 academic credits, including 4 years of English and 3 each in math, laboratory science, foreign language, and social studies/history. The college also expects applicants to have taken honors, AP, or IB courses where available. An essay is required, and an interview is recommended. AP credits are accepted. Important factors in the admissions decision are advanced placement or honors courses, extracurricular activities record, and recommendations by school officials. All students are required to complete 128 semester credits, with 32 to 44 in the major, and an overall minimum GPA of 2.0. Required courses include 12 credits in humanities and fine arts, 8 credits in natural science and/or math, 8 credits in social science, 4 credits each in US identities & differences, internationalism 12 credits on writing, 4 to 12 credits in quantitative reasoning, and a first-year course. Second language proficiency equivalent to 2 years of college-level language must be shown, and every major requires a capstone experience. **Procedure:** Freshmen are admitted in the fall. Entrance exams should be taken in the fall of the senior year or before. There are early decision and deferred admissions plans. Early decision applications should be filed by November 15; regular applications, by January 15 for fall entry, along with a $40 fee. Notification of early decision is sent December 15; regular decision, March 30. 150 early decision candidates were accepted for the 2016-2017 class. 430 applicants were on the 2016 waiting list. Application fees are waived if application is completed online. **Transfer Students:** 16 transfer students enrolled in 2015-2016. Transfer students should follow the application instructions found on the Admissions website for U.S. Transfer Students and for International Transfer Students. Transfer applicants should usually present a cumulative grade point average of "B+" (or 3.33 average) or better. The application fee for transfer students is $40. Students considering transferring to Macalester may have their transcripts evaluated for the transfer of course credits prior to applying by sending an official transcript and specifically requesting this service from the Registrar's Office. This evaluation is only preliminary, but is complete enough to be helpful in planning for transfer. 64 of 128 credits required for the bachelor's degree must be completed at Macalester. **International Students:** There are 318 international students enrolled. The school actively recruits these students. They must take the TOEFL with a minimum score of 600 on the paper-based TOEFL (PBT) or 100 on the Internet-based version (iBT), and take the IELTS 7.0 minimum. They must also take the SAT or ACT.

ADMISSIONS: 37% of the 2016-2017 applicants were accepted. The SAT scores for the 2016-2017 freshman class were: Critical Reading-- 2% below 500, 12% between 500 and 599, 31% between 600 and 699, and 55% between 700 and 800. Math-- 1% below 500, 14% between 500 and 599, 49% between 600 and 699, and 36% between 700 and 800. Writing-- 1% below 500, 10% between 500 and 599, 44% between 600 and 699, and 45% between 700 and 800. The ACT scores were 3% between 18 and 23, 29% between 24 and 29, and 68% above 30. 84% of the current freshmen were in the top fifth of their class; 99% were in the top two fifths. There were 24 National Merit finalists. 29 freshmen graduated first in their class. **Admissions Contact:** Lorne T. Robinson, Dean of Admissions and Financial Aid. Email: *admissions@macalester.edu* Web: *www.macalester.edu*

FINANCIAL AID: In 2016-2017, 88% of all full-time freshmen and 85% of continuing full-time students received some form of financial aid. 69% of all full-time freshmen and 68% of continuing full-time students received need-based aid. The average freshman award was $43,701. Need-based scholarships or need-based grants averaged $37,960; and need-based self-help aid (loans and jobs) averaged $5,741. 70% of undergraduate students work part-time. Average annual earnings from campus work are $2200. The average financial indebtedness of the 2016 graduate was $23,875. Macalester is a member of CSS. The CSS/Profile, the parent's W-2 and income tax forms are required. The FAFSA code is 002358. The priority date for freshman financial aid applications for fall entry is February 1.

METROPOLITAN STATE UNIVERSITY C-4

www.metrostate.edu

St. Paul, MN 55106 **(651) 793-1306**

Fax: (651) 793-1310 **Email: jill.peterson@metrostate.edu**

Full-time: 1232 men, 1787 women	**Faculty:** 115
Part-time: 1383 men, 2572 women	**Ph.D.s:** 81%
Graduate: 340 men, 473 women	**Student/Faculty:** 15 to 1
Year: semesters, summer session	**Tuition:** $7566 ($14,394)
Room & Board: n/app	**Freshman Class:** n/av
SAT or ACT: recommended	**CEEB CODE:** 1245
Application Deadline: June 15	**COMPETITIVE**

Metropolitan State University, founded in 1971, is a public institution primarily serving working adults through a variety of majors and individually designed degree programs. Figures in the above capsule and in this profile are approximate. There are 6 undergraduate schools and 2 graduate schools. In addition to regional accreditation, Metro State has baccalaureate program accreditation with NLN. The campus is in an urban area throughout the Twin Cities Metro area. Including any residence halls, there are 7 buildings.

STUDENT LIFE: 98% of undergraduates are from Minnesota. Others are from 21 states, 53 foreign countries, and Canada. 95% are from public schools. 69% are White; 2% Hispanic; 2% Foreign; 16% African American; 10% Asian American; 1% American Indian/Alaska Native. **Female To Male Ratio:** 1.6:1. The average age of freshmen is 26; all undergraduates, 31. All students commute. Alcohol is not permitted.

FACULTY/CLASSROOMS: 55% of faculty are male; 45% are female. All teach undergraduates. No introductory courses are taught by graduate students. The average class size in an introductory lecture is 24; in a laboratory is 24; and in a regular course is 19.

PROGRAMS OF STUDY: Metro State confers B.A., B.S., B.A.S. and B.S.N. degrees. Master's and doctoral degrees are also awarded. Bachelor's degrees are awarded in BIOLOGICAL SCIENCE (biology/biological science), BUSINESS (accounting, banking and finance, business administration and management, hospitality management services, human resources, international business management, management information systems, marketing and distribution, marketing management, operations management, and trade and industrial supervision and management), COMMUNICATIONS AND THE ARTS (advertising, communications, dramatic arts, English, playwriting/screenwriting, and technical and business writing), COMPUTER AND PHYSICAL SCIENCE (applied mathematics, computer science, computer security and information assurance, and information sciences and systems), EDUCATION (early childhood education), HEALTH PROFESSIONS (dental hygiene and nursing), SOCIAL SCIENCE (addiction studies, child psychology/development, criminal justice, developmental psychology, early childhood studies, economics, ethnic studies, food production/management/services, history, human services, law enforcement and corrections, liberal arts/general studies, philosophy, psychology, public administration, social science, social work, and women's studies). Nursing is the strongest academically. Accounting, and business administration have the largest enrollments.

ACTIVITIES: There are no fraternities or sororities. There are 26 groups on campus, including drama, ethnic, honors, international, LGBT, literary magazine, newspaper, professional, religious, social, and student government. **Sports:** There is no sports program at Metro State. **Graduates:** From July 1, 2015 to June 30, 2016, 1505 bachelor's degrees were awarded. The most popular majors were business (37%), individualized studies (15%), and law enforcement and criminal justice (9%).

SERVICES: Counseling and information services are available, as is tutoring in some subjects, such as accounting, finance, economics, writing, math, and ESL. **Library/Resources:** The library contains 77,378 volumes, 7,218 audio/video tapes/CDs/DVDs, and subscribes to 242 periodicals including electronic. Computerized library services include interlibrary loans, database searching, Internet access, and Wi-Fi capability. Special learning facilities include an art gallery. **Physically Challenged Students:** All of the campus is accessible. Facilities include elevators, special parking, specially equipped restrooms, lowered drinking fountains, and lowered telephones. **Special:** Internships, co-op programs in many areas, study abroad, dual majors, and student-designed programs are offered. There is 1 departmental honors program. **Visiting:** There are regularly scheduled orientations for prospective students, including a campus tour, meetings with a financial aid adviser, faculty, and students, and a general information session. To schedule a visit, contact the Admissions Office. **Campus Safety and Security:** Measures include security escort services.

REQUIREMENTS: Metro State requires applicants to be in the upper 50% of their class or have ACT, PSAT, or SAT scores at or above the national median. Applicants not meeting these requirements will be considered in the alternative admissions process. The GED is accepted. AP and CLEP credits are accepted. To graduate, all students must complete 120 to 124 semester credits, with a varying number of hours required in the major, 48 credits in a core curriculum, and a 2.0 GPA. Other requirements include natural/physical science, math/logic, global awareness, humanities, and fine arts. **Procedure:** Freshmen are admitted to all sessions. There is a deferred admissions plan. Applications should be filed by June 15 for fall entry; August 15 for spring entry; and March 15 for summer entry, along with a $20 fee. Notification is sent on a rolling basis. Applications are accepted online. **Transfer Students:** Applicants must have at least a C average. 30 of 120 credits required for the bachelor's degree must be completed at Metro State. **International Students:** There are 93 international students enrolled. They must take the TOEFL with a minimum score of 500 on the paper-based TOEFL (PBT).

Admissions Contact: Jill Peterson, Admissions Director. Email: *jill.peterson@metrostate.edu* Web: *www.metrostate.edu*

FINANCIAL AID: Metro State is a member of CSS. The FAFSA code is 010374. Check with the school for current application deadlines.

MINNEAPOLIS COLLEGE OF ART AND DESIGN *(The complete profile is made available exclusively on our website, www.barronspac.com)*

MINNESOTA STATE UNIVERSITY, MANKATO — C-4

www.mnsu.edu

Mankato, MN 56001	**(507) 389-1822** **(800) 722-0544**
Fax: (507) 389-1511	**Email: admissions@mnsu.edu**
Full-time: 5554 men, 5588 women	**Faculty:** n/av
Part-time: 871 men, 1321 women	**Ph.D.s:** 80%
Graduate: 746 men, 1235 women	**Student/Faculty:** 20 to 1
Year: semesters, summer session	**Tuition:** $7574 ($15,052)
Room & Board: $8042	**Freshman Class:** 5605 applied, 5292 accepted, 2215 enrolled
ACT: 23	**CEEB CODE:** 6677
Application Deadline: August 24	**COMPETITIVE**

Minnesota State University, Mankato, founded in 1868 and a unit of Minnesota State Colleges and Universities, offers programs in the liberal arts and sciences, as well as business, education, engineering and technology, and nursing. The figures in the above capsule and in this profile are approximate. There are 6 undergraduate schools and 1 graduate school. In addition to regional accreditation, Minnesota State or MSU has baccalaureate program accreditation with AACSB, ABET, ADA, CSWE, NASAD, NASM, NCATE, NLN, and NRPA. The 354-acre campus is in a rural area 85 miles southwest of Minneapolis-St. Paul. Including any residence halls, there are 25 buildings.

STUDENT LIFE: 83% of undergraduates are from Minnesota. Others are from 48 states, 68 foreign countries, and Canada. 94% are from public schools. 76% are White; 7% Foreign; 4% African American; 4% race unknown; 3% Asian American; 3% Hispanic; 2% two or more races. **Female To Male Ratio:** 1.1:1. The average age of freshmen is 19; all undergraduates, 22. 26% do not continue beyond their first year; 49% remain to graduate. **Housing:** 3100 students can be accommodated in college housing, which includes single-sex and coed dorms, on-campus apartments, special-interest floors including freshman quiet-study, upperclass, engineering, and computer science floors. On-campus housing is guaranteed for the freshman year only, and is available on a first-come, first-served basis. 82% of students commute. All students may keep cars. Alcohol is not permitted.

FACULTY/CLASSROOMS: 51% of faculty are male; 49% are female. 96% teach undergraduates, and 51% do research. Graduate students teach 4% of introductory courses. The average class size in an introductory lecture is 43; in a laboratory is 11; and in a regular course is 21.

PROGRAMS OF STUDY: Minnesota State or MSU confers B.A., B.S., B.F.A., B.Mus., B.S.EE., and B.S.ME. degrees. Associate, master's, and doctoral degrees are also awarded. Bachelor's degrees are awarded in BIOLOGICAL SCIENCE (biochemistry, biology/biological science, biotechnology, life science, and life science secondary school education), BUSINESS (accounting, banking and finance, business administration and management, finance, international business, international business management, management science, marketing, recreation and leisure services, and sports management), COMMUNICATIONS AND THE ARTS (art, communication studies, communications, dance, dramatic arts, English, English as a second/foreign language, French, German, journalism, media management, music, music business management, music industry, Spanish, speech/debate/rhetoric, technical communication, and theatre studies), COMPUTER AND PHYSICAL SCIENCE (chemistry, chemistry/adolescence education, computer engineering technology, computer information technology, computer security and information assurance, earth science, information sciences and systems, mathematics, and physics), EDUCATION (art education, dance education, early childhood education, education, elementary education, foreign languages education, general studies, health education, mathematics education, middle school education, music education, physical education, science education, secondary education, social studies education, and special education), ENGINEERING AND ENVIRONMENTAL DESIGN (automotive technology, aviation administration/management, civil engineering, computer engineering, construction management, electrical/electronics engineering, electrical/electronics engineering technology, engineering technology, environmental science, food services technology, manufacturing engineering, manufacturing technology, mechanical engineering, military science, and preengineering), HEALTH PROFESSIONS (allied health, clinical science, community health work, dental hygiene, exercise science, health science, medical laboratory science, nursing, predentistry, premedicine, prepharmacy, preveterinary science, public health, and speech pathology/audiology), SOCIAL SCIENCE (American Indian studies, anthropology, communication sciences & disorders, cognitive science, corrections, criminal justice, dietetics, economics, ethnic studies, family/consumer studies, geography, history, human development, humanities, international relations, law enforcement and corrections, parks and recreation management, philosophy, political science/government, prelaw, psychology, Scandinavian studies, social studies, social work, sociology, urban studies, and women's studies). Engineering, nursing, and sciences are the strongest academically. Business, nursing, and education have the largest enrollments.

ACTIVITIES: 4% of men belong to 7 national fraternities; 3% of women belong to 4 national sororities. There are 250 groups on campus, including art, band, cheerleading, choir, chorale, chorus, computers, dance, drama, ethnic, film, forensics, honors, international, jazz band, LGBT, literary magazine, musical theater, newspaper, opera, orchestra, pep band, photography, political, professional, radio and TV, religious, social, social service, and student government. Popular campus events include Multicultural Activities, Celebrations, Greek Week, and the Big Event. **Sports:** There are 11 intercollegiate sports for men and 11 for women, and 55 intramural sports for men and 55 for women. Facilities include a stadium, a field house, an indoor swimming pool, racquetball courts, a walking/jogging track, multipurpose rooms, weights, workout machines, gyms; an indoor track, tennis courts, and a ice hockey arena. **Graduates:** From July 1, 2015 to June 30, 2016, 2414 bachelor's degrees were awarded. The most popular majors were nursing (9%), management (5%), and psychology (5%). 238 companies recruited on campus in 2015-2016. In an average class, 2% graduate in 3 years or less, 18% graduate in 4 years or less, 42% graduate in 5 years or less, and 49% graduate in 6 years or less.

SERVICES: Counseling and information services are available, as is tutoring in most subjects, and a reader service for the blind, and remedial math, reading, and writing. Also available are alternative testing accommodations, note taking, sign language interpreting, and taped texts. **Library/Resources:** The library contains 1.2 million volumes, 253,560 microform items, 30,686 audio/video tapes/CDs/DVDs, and subscribes to 3,126 periodicals including electronic. Computerized library services include interlibrary loans, database searching, Internet access, and Wi-Fi capability. Special learning facilities include an art gallery, radio station, 2 observatories, and high ropes course. **Physically Challenged Students:** All of the campus is accessible. Facilities include wheelchair ramps, elevators, special parking, specially equipped restrooms, special class scheduling, lowered drinking fountains, lowered telephones, special housing. **Special:** The university offers cross-registration within the Minnesota State University System and with Bethany Lutheran College and Gustavus Adolphus College. Students may serve internships, study abroad, or participate in an accelerated degree program. B.A.-B.S. degrees, dual and student-designed majors, nondegree study, and pass/fail options also are available. There are 25 national honor societies and a freshman honors program. **Visiting:** There are regularly scheduled orientations for prospective students, consisting of overview presentations, campus tours, and academic information fairs. There are guides for informal visits and visitors may sit in on classes. To schedule a visit, contact the Office of Admission. **Campus Safety and Security:** Measures include 24-hour foot and vehicle patrol, emergency notification system, self-defense education, and security escort services. There are also shuttle buses, emergency telephones, lighted pathways/sidewalks, controlled access to dorms/residences, closed-circuit parking lot surveillance cameras, and motion-sensitive lights in low traffic areas.

REQUIREMENTS: Applicants must be graduates of an accredited secondary school and rank in the top 50% of their high school class or have an ACT composite score of 21 or higher along with a satisfactory class rank. AP and CLEP credits are accepted. To graduate, students must complete 128 semester hours of credit, with a minimum GPA of 2.0 and at least 45 hours in the major. Most programs require 44 hours of general education, including courses in English, speech, science, math, social/behavioral science, arts and humanities, cultural diversity, global perspective, ethnic/civic responsibility, and people and the environment. **Procedure:** Freshmen are admitted to all sessions. Entrance exams should be taken in the spring of the junior year or the fall of the senior year. There are deferred admissions and rolling admissions plans. Applications should be filed by August 24 for fall entry, along with a $20 fee. Notification is sent on a rolling basis. Applications are accepted online. **Transfer Students:** 1014 transfer students enrolled in 2015-2016. Transfer applicants must have a minimum GPA of 2.0 and have completed at least 67% of all college-level courses attempted. 30 of 128 credits required for the bachelor's degree must be completed at Minnesota State or MSU. **International Students:** There are 1040 international students enrolled. The school actively recruits these students. They must take the TOEFL with a minimum score of 500 on the paper-based TOEFL (PBT) or 61 on the Internet-based version (iBT), an English placement test at matriculation.

ADMISSIONS: 94% of the 2016-2017 applicants were accepted. The SAT scores for the 2016-2017 freshman class were: The ACT scores were 9% below 12, 62% between 12 and 17, 16% between 18 and 23, 12% between 24 and 29, and 1% above 30. 20% of the current freshmen were in the top fifth of their class; 55% were in the top two fifths. 20 freshmen graduated first in their class. **Admissions Contact:** Admissions Office, the Officer of Admissions. Email: *admissions@mnsu.edu* Web: *www.mnsu.edu*

FINANCIAL AID: In 2016-2017, 80% of all full-time freshmen and continuing full-time students received some form of financial aid. 80% of all full-time freshmen and continuing full-time students received need-based aid. The average freshman award was $6,134. Need-based scholarships or need-based grants averaged $5,290; need-based self-help aid (loans and jobs) averaged $4,409; non-need-based athletic scholarships averaged $5,827; and other non-need-based awards and non-need-based scholarships averaged $2,271. 21% of undergraduate students work part-time. Average annual earnings from campus work are $1960. The FAFSA code is 002360. The priority date for freshman financial aid applications for fall entry is March 15.

MINNESOTA STATE UNIVERSITY, MOORHEAD — A-2

www.mnstate.edu

Moorhead, MN 56563 — **(218)477-2161**

Fax: (218) 477-4374	**Email:** admissions@mnstate.edu
Full-time: 2526 men, 3304 women	**Faculty:** n/av
Part-time: 484 men, 698 women	**Ph.D.s:** n/av
Graduate: 106 men, 379 women	**Student/Faculty:** n/av
Year: semesters, summer session	**Tuition:** $7617 ($14,749)
Room & Board: $8324	**Freshman Class:** 3393 applied, 2489 accepted, 2238 enrolled
ACT: required	**CEEB CODE:** 6678
Application Deadline: August 1	**COMPETITIVE**

Minnesota State University Moorhead, founded in 1887, is a public comprehensive institution. There are 4 undergraduate schools and 1 graduate school. In addition to regional accreditation, MSU Moorhead has baccalaureate program accreditation with AACSB, ACCE, CSWE, NASAD, NASM, NCATE, ABA, BSN, MS (in nursing), ACS, and ASLH. The 119-acre campus is in a suburban area in Moorehead, Minnesota, just 240 miles northwest of Minneapolis-St. Paul and across the river from Fargo, North Dakota. Including any residence halls, there are 28 buildings.

STUDENT LIFE: 83% are White; 6% Foreign; 3% African American; 1% Asian American; 1% Hispanic. **Female To Male Ratio:** 1.4:1. The average age of freshmen is 19; all undergraduates, 23. **Housing:** 1844 students can be accommodated in college housing, which includes single-sex and coed dorms, on-campus apartments, sorority houses, and living learning communities. On-campus housing is available on a first-come and first-served basis. 81% of students commute. All students may keep cars. Alcohol is not permitted.

FACULTY/CLASSROOMS: 61% of faculty are male; 39% are female. No introductory courses are taught by graduate students.

PROGRAMS OF STUDY: MSU Moorhead confers B.A., B.S., B.F.A., B.M., B.S.N., and B.S.W. degrees. Associate, master's, and doctoral degrees are also awarded. Bachelor's degrees are awarded in BIOLOGICAL SCIENCE (biology/biological science), BUSINESS (accounting, banking and finance, business administration and management, international business management, management science, marketing/retailing/merchandising, and operations management), COMMUNICATIONS AND THE ARTS (broadcasting, communications, dramatic arts, English, film arts, fine arts, journalism, music, music technology, public relations, Spanish, and speech/debate/rhetoric), COMPUTER AND PHYSICAL SCIENCE (chemistry, computer science, computer security and information assurance, earth science, geoscience, mathematics, and physics), EDUCATION (art education, athletic training, early childhood education, elementary education, English education, foreign languages education, health education, mathematics education, music education, physical education, science education, social studies education, and special education), ENGINEERING AND ENVIRONMENTAL DESIGN (construction management, graphic arts technology, and industrial engineering technology), HEALTH PROFESSIONS (community health work, exercise science, health care administration, medical laboratory technology, nursing, predentistry, premedicine, prepharmacy, preveterinary science, and speech pathology/audiology), SOCIAL SCIENCE (anthropology, criminal justice, East Asian studies, economics, gerontology, history, international studies, law, paralegal studies, philosophy, political science/government, prelaw, psychology, social work, sociology, Spanish studies, and women's studies).

ACTIVITIES: 2% of men belong to 1% of women belong to 2 local and 2 national sororities. There are 150 groups on campus, including art, band, cheerleading, choir, chorus, computers, dance, drama, drill team, ethnic, film, honors, international, jazz band, LGBT, literary magazine, musical theater, newspaper, orchestra, pep band, photography, political, professional, radio and TV, religious, social, social service, and student government. Popular campus events include Celebrations of Nations, Straw Hat Summer Theatre, Dragon Frost, Grass Volleyball Tournament, and Muggle Quidditch. **Sports:** There are 5 intercollegiate sports for men and 9 for women, and 14 intramural sports for men and 14 for women. Facilities include a wellness center, basketball/volleyball courts, exercise room with cardio and strength training equipment, a rock climbing wall, and an elevated indoor running track. Sports include baseball, fencing, lacrosse, rugby, Tae Kwon Do, soccer, wrestling, and martial arts. **Graduates:** From July 1, 2015 to June 30, 2016, 1229 bachelor's degrees were awarded. The most popular majors were mass communication (8%), elementary education (5%), and social work (5%).

SERVICES: Counseling and information services are available, as is tutoring in every subject, and a reader service for the blind, and remedial math, reading, and writing. **Library/Resources:** The library contains 656,104 volumes, 872,378 microform items, 25,290 audio/video tapes/CDs/DVDs, and subscribes to 2,245 periodicals including electronic. Computerized library services include interlibrary loans and database searching. Special learning facilities include an art gallery, planetarium, radio station, TV station, and a regional science center. **Physically Challenged Students:** Facilities include wheelchair ramps, elevators, special parking, specially equipped restrooms, lowered drinking fountains, and lowered telephones. **Special:** Internships are available in most disciplines. The university offers cross-registration with North Dakota State University and Concordia College and is a member of the National Student Exchange. Study abroad program allows students to study at any of 125 member universities. Variety of internships are available at local, state & federal government agencies, service organizations and in the private sector. There are 7 national honor societies, a freshman honors program, and 1 departmental honors program. **Visiting:** There are regularly scheduled orientations for prospective students, including a campus tour, lunch, and meetings with faculty and an admissions officer. There are guides for informal visits. To schedule a visit, contact the Admissions Office. **Campus Safety and Security:** Measures include 24-hour foot and vehicle patrol, emergency notification system, self-defense education, security escort services, emergency telephones, lighted pathways/sidewalks, and in-room safes.

REQUIREMENTS: A high school diploma is required, and the GED is accepted. A SAT satisfactory score or ACT score of 21 is required for applicants whose high school rank is below the top half. MSU Moorhead requires applicants to be in the upper 50% of their class. AP and CLEP credits are accepted. To graduate students must have a 2.0 GPA and complete 120 semester hours, including a liberal arts core of 45 credits and 43 semester hours in upper-division courses. Required courses include 2 in English, 6 credits each of natural science, social science, humanities, and communication systems, and 5 credits in cultural diversity. All students must complete an upper-level writing requirement. **Procedure:** Freshmen are admitted in the fall, spring, and summer. Entrance exams should be taken in the junior or senior year of high school. There is a rolling admissions plan. Applications should be filed by August 1 for fall entry; November 15 for spring entry. The fall 2016 application fee was $20. Applications are accepted online. **Transfer Students:** 659 transfer students enrolled in 2015-2016. Applicants must submit a high school transcript or GED score and all other transcripts for post-secondary schools attended. A minimum GPA of 2.0 (higher for entry in some departments) is necessary for transfer credit. 30 of 120 credits required for the bachelor's degree must be completed at MSU Moorhead. **International Students:** There are 320 international students enrolled. The school actively recruits these students. They must take the TOEFL with a minimum score of 500 on the paper-based TOEFL (PBT) or 61 on the Internet-based version (iBT).

ADMISSIONS: 73% of the 2016-2017 applicants were accepted. **Admissions Contact:** Richard DePaolis-Metz, Director of Undergraduate Admissions. Email: *admissions@mnstate.edu* Web: *www.mnstate.edu*

FINANCIAL AID: The FAFSA code is 002367. Check with the school for current application deadlines.

NORTH CENTRAL UNIVERSITY — C-4
www.northcentral.edu

Minneapolis, MN 55404	(612) 343-4469 800-289-6222
Fax: (612) 343-4146	Email: admissions@northcentral.edu
Full-time: 587 men, 718 women	Faculty: 60
Part-time: n/av	Ph.D.s: 50%
Graduate: n/av	Student/Faculty: 18 to 1
Year: semesters, summer session	Tuition: $23,050
Room & Board: $3350	Freshman Class: n/av
SAT: required ACT: 21	CEEB CODE: 0051
Application Deadline: June 1	COMPETITIVE

North Central University, founded in 1930 and affiliated with the Assemblies of God, is a Christian University that emphasizes rigorous academic training and spiritual passion. There are 5 undergraduate schools. The 12-acre campus is in an urban area in downtown Minneapolis. Including any residence halls, there are 24 buildings.

STUDENT LIFE: 54% of undergraduates are from Minnesota. Others are from 40 states, 11 foreign countries, and Canada. 88% are from public schools. 82% are White; 6% Hispanic; 4% African American; 4% two or more races; 2% Asian American. 99% are Protestant. **Female To Male Ratio:** 1.2:1. The average age of freshmen is 18; all undergraduates, 20. 25% do not continue beyond their first year; 40% remain to graduate. **Housing:** 950 students can be accommodated in college housing, which includes single-sex dorms, on-campus apartments, and married student housing. On-campus housing is available on a first-come and first-served basis. 80% of students live on campus; of those, 80% remain on campus on weekends. All students may keep cars. Alcohol is not permitted.

FACULTY/CLASSROOMS: 63% of faculty are male; 37% are female. All teach undergraduates. No introductory courses are taught by graduate students. The average class size in an introductory lecture is 80; in a laboratory is 15; and in a regular course is 25.

PROGRAMS OF STUDY: NCU confers B.A. and B.S. degrees. Associate degrees are also awarded. Bachelor's degrees are awarded in COMMUNICATIONS AND THE ARTS (communications), EDUCATION (elementary education), SOCIAL SCIENCE (behavioral science, biblical languages, ministries, pastoral studies, religion, religious education, and religious music). Pastoral studies, youth ministry, and psychology are the strongest academically. Pastoral Studies, youth ministry, and business administration have the largest enrollments.

ACTIVITIES: There are no fraternities or sororities. There are 28 groups on campus, including art, band, choir, chorale, chorus, drama, jazz band, literary magazine, musical theater, newspaper, orchestra, photography, political, professional, radio and TV, religious, social, and student government. Popular campus events include All-College Picnic, Community Outreach Day, and Spring Banquet. **Sports:** There are 6 intercollegiate sports for men and 6 for women, and 4 intramural sports for men and 4 for women. Facilities include Elliot Park, the Clark-Danielson College Life Center Gym, and the National Sports Complex.

SERVICES: Counseling and information services are available, as is tutoring in every subject. **Library/Resources:** The library contains 70,041 volumes, 29 microform items, 200 audio/video tapes/CDs/DVDs, and subscribes to 325 periodicals including electronic. Computerized library services include interlibrary loans, database searching, and Internet access. Special learning facilities include a radio station. **Physically Challenged Students:** All of the campus is accessible. Facilities include wheelchair ramps, elevators, special parking, specially equipped restrooms, special class scheduling, lowered drinking fountains, and lowered telephones. **Special:** Students may pursue co-op programs in nursing or secondary education, study abroad in 6 countries, and nondegree study. Credit for life, military, or work experience is possible. Work-study, dual majors, and student-designed majors are available. There is 1 national honor society and 1 departmental honors program. **Visiting:** There are regularly scheduled orientations for prospective students. There are guides for informal visits, visitors may sit in on classes, and stay overnight. To schedule a visit, contact the Admissions Office. **Campus Safety and Security:** Measures include 24-hour foot and vehicle patrol, emergency notification system, self-defense education, and security escort services. There are also shuttle buses, lighted pathways/sidewalks, and controlled access to dorms/residences.

REQUIREMENTS: The SAT or ACT is required. The college requires a minimum ACT score of 18, high school transcripts, and academic and pastoral references. AP and CLEP credits are accepted. Students must complete 129 to 144 credits for their particular bachelor's degree. Each program has specific requirements, including general education and Biblical studies core classes. Internships are required for all programs. Students must take 60 or more total hours in their major, with a minimum overall GPA of 2.0 (2.2 for teacher education). **Procedure:** Freshmen are admitted in the fall and spring. Entrance exams should be taken during junior or senior year of high school. There is a rolling admissions plan. Applications should be filed by June 1 for fall entry; December 31 for spring entry, along with a $25 fee. Notification is sent on a rolling basis. **Transfer Students:** Transfer applicants must submit a completed application, a pastor's reference, a high school transcript or the GED, and college transcripts. Applicants with less than a year of college credit must also submit ACT or SAT scores and academic references. 27 of 129 credits required for the bachelor's degree must be completed at NCU. **International Students:** They must take the TOEFL, in additional to the SAT and ACT, scoring 18.

Admissions Contact: Joshua Martin, Admissions Director. Email: *admissions@northcentral.edu* Web: *www.northcentral.edu*

FINANCIAL AID: 100% of undergraduate students work part-time. The FFS and the college's own financial statement are required. The FAFSA code is 002369. Check with the school for current application deadlines.

SAINT JOHN'S UNIVERSITY — B-3

www.csbsju.edu

Collegeville, MN 56321	(320) 363-5060 (800) 544-1489
Fax: (320) 363-3206	**Email:** admissions@csbsju.edu
Full-time: 1731 men	**Faculty:** 139; IIB, +$
Part-time: 17 men	**Ph.D.s:** 88%
Graduate: 52 men, 43 women	**Student/Faculty:** 12 to 1
Year: semesters	**Tuition:** $41,732
Room & Board: $9892	**Freshman Class:** 1457 applied, 1279 accepted, 461 enrolled
SAT or ACT: required	**CEEB CODE:** 6624
Application Deadline: January 15	**COMPETITIVE**

Saint John's University, and The College of Saint Benedict are nationally-leading liberal arts colleges whose unique partnership offers students the educational choices of a large university and the individual attention of a premier small college. There is 1 undergraduate school and 1 graduate school. In addition to regional accreditation, St. John's has baccalaureate program accreditation with ADA, NASM, NCATE, ACS, ATS, and CCNE. The 2700-acre campus is in a rural area 15 miles west of St. Cloud and 75 miles northwest of Minneapolis and St. Paul. Including any residence halls, there are 61 buildings.

STUDENT LIFE: 76% of undergraduates are from Minnesota. Others are from 39 states, 15 foreign countries, and Canada. 71% are from public schools. 8% are Hispanic; 78% White; 5% African American; 4% Foreign; 3% Asian American; 1% American Indian/Alaska Native; 1% two or more races. 52% are Catholic; 30% Protestant; 17% claim no religious affiliation. **Male To Female Ratio:** 41.9:1. The average age of freshmen is 19; all undergraduates, 20. 13% do not continue beyond their first year; 79% remain to graduate. **Housing:** 1529 students can be accommodated in college housing, which includes single-sex dorms, on-campus apartments, special-interest houses, Eco-houses, and Benedictine living community. On-campus housing is guaranteed for the freshman year only, and is available on a first-come, first-served basis, and is available on a lottery system for upperclassmen. 90% of students live on campus. All students may keep cars.

FACULTY/CLASSROOMS: 48% of faculty are male; 52% are female. All teach undergraduates and do research. No introductory courses are taught by graduate students. The average class size in an introductory lecture is 18; in a laboratory is 13; and in a regular course is 19.

PROGRAMS OF STUDY: St. John's confers B.A. and B.S.N. degrees. Master's degrees are also awarded. Bachelor's degrees are awarded in AGRICULTURE (environmental studies), BIOLOGICAL SCIENCE (biochemistry, biology/biological science, and nutrition), BUSINESS (accounting and management science), COMMUNICATIONS AND THE ARTS (art, classics, communications, English, French, German, music, Spanish, and theatre arts), COMPUTER AND PHYSICAL SCIENCE (chemistry, computer science, mathematics, natural sciences, and physics), EDUCATION (elementary education), ENGINEERING AND ENVIRONMENTAL DESIGN (preengineering), HEALTH PROFESSIONS (nursing, occupational therapy, predentistry, premedicine, preoptometry, prepharmacy, prephysical therapy, and preveterinary science), SOCIAL SCIENCE (Asian/Oriental studies, economics, gender studies, Hispanic American studies, history, humanities, liberal arts/general studies, peace studies, philosophy, political science/government, prelaw, psychology, social science, sociology, and theological studies). Global business leadership, accounting and biology have the largest enrollments.

ACTIVITIES: There are no fraternities or sororities. There are 110 groups on campus, including a outdoor leadership center, academic clubs, art, band, choir, chorale, chorus, computers, dance, debate, drama, environmental, ethnic, film, honors, international, jazz band, LGBT, literary magazine, musical theater, newspaper, opera, orchestra, pep band, political, professional, radio and TV, religious, social, social service, student government, and symphony. Popular campus events include Club Involvement Fair, Festival of Cultures, Family Weekend, Homecoming, weekly Praise in the Pub, Meditation Sessions, Asian New Year and Martin Luther King Jr. Week. **Sports:** There are 12 intercollegiate sports for men, and 13 intramural sports for men. Facilities include a football field, stadium, basketball arena, baseball field, soccer field, seasonal dome with connected indoor golf center, lacrosse and rugby fields, indoor and outdoor tennis courts, indoor and outdoor tracks, a complete fitness center, hardwood racquetball courts, swimming pool, climbing wall, wrestling room, training room, outdoor intramural hockey rink, seven lakes for canoeing, fishing, swimming, rowing and kayaking, on-campus wooded hiking and jogging trails, and access to all athletic facilities at the College of Saint Benedict. **Graduates:** From July 1, 2015 to June 30, 2016, 373 bachelor's degrees were awarded. The most popular majors were business management (21%), accounting (14%), and biology (7%). 188 companies recruited on campus in 2015-2016. In an average class, 1% graduate in 3 years or less, 68% graduate in 4 years or less, 76% graduate in 5 years or less, and 77% graduate in 6 years or less. Of the 2015 graduating class, 12% were enrolled in graduate school within 6 months of graduation, and 87% were employed.

SERVICES: Counseling and information services are available, as is tutoring in most subjects, such as math, writing, global languages and natural sciences. The College of Saint Benedict and Saint John's University established a Disability Services Office. Accomodations are provided on a case by case basis for enrolled students who provide adequate documentation of a disability. Individual tutoring is available as needed. Academic and psychological counseling are available on an unlimited basis. **Library/Resources:** The 2 libraries contain 764,960 volumes, 121,426 microform items, 28,047 audio/video tapes/CDs/DVDs, and subscribe to 46,204 periodicals including electronic. Computerized library services include interlibrary loans, database searching, Internet access, and Wi-Fi capability. Special learning facilities include an art gallery, natural history museum, radio station, TV station, a pottery studio and kiln, Saint John's Outdoor University, an observatory, greenhouse, herbarium, Sommers digital video studio and the Hill Museum and Manuscript Library, a labyrinth, pottery studio, kiln, greenhouse, dance studio and Saint Benedict's Monastery Heritage Museum at the College of Saint Benedict. **Physically Challenged Students:** 90% of the campus is accessible. Facilities include wheelchair ramps, elevators, special parking, specially equipped restrooms, special class scheduling, lowered drinking fountains, and special housing. **Special:** Students may cross-register with St. Cloud State University. There are study-abroad programs in Australia, Austria, Chile, China, Coventry-England, France, Germany, Guatemala, Greece, Ireland(Cork and Galway), Italy, India, Japan,London-England, Northern Ireland, South Africa, and Spain. Many short term study abroad opportunities are also offered. Internships, dual and student-designed majors, preprofessional programs, and liberal studies degrees may be pursued. A 3-2 engineering program is offered through the University of Minnesota, as is a 3-1 program in dentistry. Nondegree study and a pass/fail grading option are also available. There are 4 national honor societies, Phi Beta Kappa, and a freshman honors program. **Visiting:** There are regularly scheduled orientations for prospective students, programs include Admissions and Financial Aid presentations, campus tours and student panels. There are guides for informal visits, visitors may sit in on classes, and stay overnight. **Campus Safety and Security:** Measures include 24-hour foot and vehicle patrol, emergency notification system, self-defense education, and security escort services. There are also shuttle buses, emergency telephones, lighted pathways/sidewalks, and controlled access to dorms/residences.

REQUIREMENTS: The SAT or ACT is required. Students should be graduates of an accredited secondary school. Academic preparation should include 17 units, including 4 of English, 3 of math, 2 each of a lab science and social studies, and 4 electives. A foreign language is recommended. The GED is accepted. Home-schooled applicants are not required to have a high school diploma but are required to provide appropriate documentation of college preparatory curriculum and standardized test scores. St. John's requires applicants to be in the upper 50% of their class. A GPA of 3.0 is required. AP and CLEP credits are accepted. Important factors in the admissions decision are advanced placement or honors courses, extracurricular activities record, and parents or siblings attended your school. To graduate students must complete a first-year seminar and a junior-senior ethics seminar intended as a capstone for the liberal arts experience, and fulfill gender, intercultural, experiential learning, and fine arts requirements. Distribution requirements include 4 credits in fine arts, 2 courses each in humanities and theology, and 1 course each in math, natural science, and social science. All students must prove math and foreign language proficiency. A total of 124 credits must be earned, with a minimum GPA of 2.0. Attendance at 8 fine arts experiences is also required. **Procedure:** Freshmen are admitted in the fall and spring. Entrance exams should be taken during the spring of the junior year or fall of the senior year. There are early admissions and deferred admissions plans. Application deadlines are open. Notifications are sent April 1. Applications are accepted online. **Transfer Students:** 23 transfer students enrolled in 2015-2016. Transfer applicants must have a minimum college GPA of 2.75. An essay or personal statement, high school and college transcripts, and a transfer student evaluation form are required. Standardized test scores and an interview may be required of some. 76 of 124 credits required for the bachelor's degree must be completed at St. John's. **International Students:** There are 76 international students enrolled. The school actively recruits these students. They must take the TOEFL with a minimum score of 550 on the paper-based TOEFL (PBT) or 80 on the Internet-based version (iBT). IELTS also accepted with minimum score of 6.5. in certain cases, the SAT or ACT may replace TOEFL.

ADMISSIONS: 88% of the 2016-2017 applicants were accepted. The SAT scores for the 2016-2017 freshman class were: Critical Reading-- 33% below 500, 53% between 500 and 599, 12% between 600 and 699, and 2% between 700 and 800. Math-- 35% below 500, 41% between 500 and 599, and 24% between 600 and 699. Writing-- 59% below 500, 31% between 500 and 599, 8% between 600 and 699, and 2% between 700 and 800. The ACT scores were 2% between 12 and 17, 34% between 18 and 23, 47% between 24 and 29, and 17% above 30. 34% of the current freshmen were in the top fifth of their class; 65% were in the top two fifths. **Admissions Contact:** Dr. Calvin Mosley, Vice President Admission and Financial Aid. Email: *admissions@csbsju.edu* Web: *www.csbsju.edu*

FINANCIAL AID: In 2016-2017, 96% of all full-time freshmen and 93% of continuing full-time students received some form of financial aid. 74% of all full-time freshmen and 67% of continuing full-time students received need-based aid. The average freshman award was $34,795. Need-based scholarships or need-based grants averaged $28,696; need-based self-help aid (loans and jobs) averaged $5,885; and other non-need-based awards and non-need-based scholarships averaged $16,890. 60% of undergraduate students work part-time. Average annual earnings from campus work are $2445. The average financial indebtedness of the 2016 graduate was $40,067. St. John's is a member of CSS. The college's own financial statement is required. The priority date for freshman financial aid applications for fall entry is March 15.

SAINT MARY'S UNIVERSITY OF MINNESOTA — D-5

www.smumn.edu

Winona, MN 55987 — **(507) 457-1700** **(800) 635-5987**

Fax: (507) 457-1722 — **Email: admission@smumn.edu**

Full-time: 563 men, 605 women	**Faculty:** IIA, --$
Part-time: 173 men, 249 women	**Ph.D.s:** 91%
Graduate: 1256 men, 2794 women	**Student/Faculty:** 20 to 1
Year: semesters	**Tuition:** $32,575
Room & Board: $8635	**Freshman Class:** 1686 applied, 1336 accepted, 283 enrolled
SAT CR/M/W: 501/497/485 **ACT:** 23	**CEEB CODE:** 6632
Application Deadline: May 1	**COMPETITIVE**

Saint Mary's University of Minnesota, founded in 1912, is a private, Lasallian Catholic, comprehensive institution, guided by the De La Salle Christian Brothers since 1933. At the coeducational, residential Winona campus, the undergraduate College combines traditional liberal arts and sciences with career preparation in a student-centered environment. The Schools of Graduate and Professional Programs (SGPP) is one of the largest graduate schools in Minnesota. A pioneer in outreach education since 1984, SGPP offers certificate, bachelor completion, master's, specialist, and doctoral programs at the university's Twin Cities and Winona campuses, and centers in Rochester, Apple Valley, and Oakdale. Courses are also offered in greater Minnesota and Wisconsin, Kenya and Jamaica. There are 4 undergraduate schools and 3 graduate schools. In addition to regional accreditation, SMUMN has baccalaureate program accreditation with NASM, IACBE, and JRCNMT. The 350-acre campus is in a small town 110 miles southeast of Twin Cities and 275 miles northwest of Chicago. Including any residence halls, there are 47 buildings.

STUDENT LIFE: 71% of undergraduates are from Minnesota. Others are from 30 states, 18 foreign countries, and Canada. 70% are from public schools. 57% are White; 24% race unknown; 6% African American; 5% Hispanic; 4% Foreign; 2% Asian American; 1% American Indian/Alaska Native; 1% two or more races. 45% are Catholic; 14% Protestant. **Female To Male Ratio:** 1.8:1. The average age of freshmen is 19; all undergraduates, 20. 20% do not continue beyond their first year; 61% remain to graduate. **Housing:** 1046 students can be accommodated in college housing, which includes single-sex and coed dorms, on-campus apartments, special-interest houses, living learning communities, first-year residence halls, and substance-free residence halls. On-campus housing is guaranteed for all 4 years. 93% of students live on campus; of those, 75% remain on campus on weekends. All students may keep cars.

FACULTY/CLASSROOMS: 61% of faculty are male; 39% are female. No introductory courses are taught by graduate students. The average class size in an introductory lecture is 16; in a laboratory is 14; and in a regular course is 15.

PROGRAMS OF STUDY: SMUMN confers B.A. and B.S. degrees. Master's and doctoral degrees are also awarded. Bachelor's degrees are awarded in BIOLOGICAL SCIENCE (biochemistry, biology/biological science, biophysics, environmental biology, and life science secondary school education), BUSINESS (accounting, business administration and management, business intelligence and analytics, entrepreneurial studies, finance, international business, marketing, and sports management), COMMUNICATIONS AND THE ARTS (art, graphic design, journalism, literature, music, music industry, music performance, public relations, Spanish, studio art, and theatre arts), COMPUTER AND PHYSICAL SCIENCE (actuarial science, chemistry, chemistry/adolescence education, computer science, mathematics, and physics), EDUCATION (elementary education, English education, global studies, mathematics education, music education, secondary education, social studies education, and Spanish adolescense education), ENGINEERING AND ENVIRONMENTAL DESIGN (engineering physics and nuclear medicine technology), HEALTH PROFESSIONS (cardiac sonography, cytotechnology, medical laboratory science, and prephysical therapy), SOCIAL SCIENCE (criminal justice, history, human services, pastoral studies, philosophy, political science/government, psychology, social science, sociology, theology, and youth ministry). biology, biochemistry, and theology are the strongest academically. marketing, biology, and accounting have the largest enrollments.

ACTIVITIES: 4% of men belong to 2 national fraternities; 3% of women belong to 1 national sorority. There are 85 groups on campus, including art, band, cheerleading, choir, chorale, chorus, dance, drama, environmental, ethnic, honors, international, jazz band, LGBT, literary magazine, musical theater, newspaper, political, professional, radio and TV, religious, social, social service, student government, and yearbook. Popular campus events include Cardinal Days, Taylor Richmond Benefit Dance, and Finals Breakfast. **Sports:** There are 10 intercollegiate sports for men and 11 for women. Facilities include basketball, indoor tennis, and racquetball courts, an indoor ice arena, exercise and weight rooms, baseball, softball, and soccer fields, Nordic ski and running trails, an indoor track, an indoor swimming pool, a dance studio, a Frisbee disc course, an outdoor track, and a high ropes course. **Graduates:** From July 1, 2015 to June 30, 2016, 234 bachelor's degrees were awarded. The most popular majors were health professions and related programs (12%), law enforcement, criminal justice (7%), and education (5%). 8 companies recruited on campus in 2015-2016. In an average class, 2% graduate in 3 years or less, 51% graduate in 4 years or less, 60% graduate in 5 years or less, and 61% graduate in 6 years or less.

SERVICES: Counseling and information services are available, as is tutoring in most subjects, and a reader service for the blind, and remedial math, reading, and writing. **Library/Resources:** The library contains 209,807 volumes, 200,692 microform items, 9,789 audio/video tapes/CDs/DVDs, and subscribes to 40,015 periodicals including electronic. Computerized library services include interlibrary loans, database searching, Internet access, and Wi-Fi capability. Special learning facilities include an art gallery, radio station, an observatory. **Physically Challenged Students:** 93% of the campus is accessible. Facilities include wheelchair ramps, elevators, special parking, specially equipped restrooms, lowered drinking fountains, lowered telephones, special housing. **Special:** Students may cross-register with Winona State University. Internships, co-op programs, student teaching and study abroad, work-study programs, and a Washington semester are available. The university also offers dual and student-designed majors, non-degree study, pass/fail options, credit for life, military, and work experience, and an honors program that also serves as an alternative general education program. There are 14 national honor societies and 13 departmental honors programs. **Visiting:** There are regularly scheduled orientations for prospective students, including an interview, a tour, class visits, and lunch. There are guides for informal visits, visitors may sit in on classes, and stay overnight. To schedule a visit, contact the Office of Admissions. **Campus Safety and Security:** Measures include 24-hour foot and vehicle patrol, emergency notification system, security escort services, emergency telephones, lighted pathways/sidewalks, and controlled access to dorms/residences.

REQUIREMENTS: The SAT or ACT is required. In addition, Candidates for admission should have completed 4 units of English, 3 each of math and natural science, 2 of social studies, and 6 academic electives. Completion of 2 units of foreign language is recommended. A GPA of 2.5 is required. AP and CLEP credits are accepted. Important factors in the admissions decision are advanced placement or honors courses, leadership record, and extracurricular activities record. Students must have a 2.0 cumulative major GPA and complete a minimum of 122 semester credits, including at least 45 at the upper-division level. Students must complete a major program and the general education program. **Procedure:** Freshmen are admitted in the fall and spring. Entrance exams should be taken by the fall of the senior year. There are early admissions, deferred admissions, and rolling admissions plans. Applications should be filed by May 1 for fall entry; December 1 for spring entry, along with a $25 fee. Notification is sent on a rolling basis. Applications are accepted online. **Transfer Students:** 171 transfer students enrolled in 2015-2016. Applicants must have a 2.0 GPA with at least 12 credits. 60 of 122 credits required for the bachelor's degree must be completed at SMUMN. **International Students:** There are 54 international students enrolled. The school actively recruits these students. They must take the TOEFL with a minimum score of 550 on the paper-based TOEFL (PBT) or 79 on the Internet-based version (iBT).

ADMISSIONS: 79% of the 2016-2017 applicants were accepted. The SAT scores for the 2016-2017 freshman class were: Critical Reading-- 48% below 500, 43% between 500 and 599, 5% between 600 and 699, and 5% between 700 and 800. Math-- 48% below 500, 33% between 500 and 599, 14% between 600 and 699, and 5% between 700 and 800. Writing-- 59% below 500, 29% between 500 and 599, 6% between 600 and 699, and 6% between 700 and 800. The ACT scores were % below 12, 8% between 12 and 17, 51% between 18 and 23, 36% between 24 and 29, and 5% above 30. **Admissions Contact:** Mark Kormann, Assistant Vice President Admission. Email: *admission@smumn.edu* Web: *www.smumn.edu*

FINANCIAL AID: In 2016-2017, 99% of all full-time freshmen and 94% of continuing full-time students received some form of financial aid. 73% of all full-time freshmen and 71% of continuing full-time students received need-based aid. The average financial indebtedness of the 2016 graduate was $39,196. The college's own financial statement is required. The FAFSA code is 002380. The priority date for freshman financial aid applications for fall entry is March 15. The filing deadline for fall entry is open.

SOUTHWEST MINNESOTA STATE UNIVERSITY B-4

www.smsu.edu

Marshall, MN 56258	**(507) 537-6286** **(800) 642-0684**
Fax: (507) 537-7154	**Email: admissions@smsu.edu**
Full-time: 1075 men, 1250 women	**Faculty:** n/av
Part-time: 150 men, 235 women	**Ph.D.s:** 76%
Graduate: 155 men, 370 women	**Student/Faculty:** n/av
Year: semesters, summer session	**Tuition:** $8773 ($18,557)
Room & Board: $9010	**Freshman Class:** n/av
SAT: recommended **ACT:** required	**CEEB CODE:** 6703
Application Deadline: August 1	**COMPETITIVE**

Southwest Minnesota State University, founded in 1963, is a public institution offering programs in liberal arts, technology, and preprofessional training. The figures in the above capsule and in this profile are approximate. There are 4 undergraduate schools. In addition to regional accreditation, SMSU has baccalaureate program accreditation with CSWE and ACS. The 216-acre campus is in a rural area 150 miles southwest of Minneapolis. Including any residence halls, there are 24 buildings.

STUDENT LIFE: 75% of undergraduates are from Minnesota. Others are from 29 states, 33 foreign countries, and Canada. 95% are from public schools. 85% are White; 7% Foreign; 4% African American; 2% Asian American; 1% American Indian/Alaska Native; 1% Hispanic. **Female To Male Ratio:** 1.3:1. The average age of freshmen is 19; all undergraduates, 22. 25% do not continue beyond their first year; 35% remain to graduate. **Housing:** 1182 students can be accommodated in college housing, which includes single-sex and coed dorms, on-campus apartments, special-interest houses, a quiet house, and a weekend programming house. On-campus housing is guaranteed for the freshman year only. All students may keep cars. Alcohol is not permitted.

FACULTY/CLASSROOMS: 56% of faculty are male; 44% are female. All teach undergraduates. No introductory courses are taught by graduate students. The average class size in an introductory lecture is 26; in a laboratory is 19; and in a regular course is 21.

PROGRAMS OF STUDY: SMSU confers B.A., B.S., and B.A.S. degrees. Associate and master's degrees are also awarded. Bachelor's degrees are awarded in AGRICULTURE (agricultural business management), BIOLOGICAL SCIENCE (biology/biological science), BUSINESS (accounting, business administration and management, hotel/motel and restaurant management, and marketing/retailing/merchandising), COMMUNICATIONS AND THE ARTS (art, communications, creative writing, dramatic arts, literature, music, and Spanish), COMPUTER AND PHYSICAL SCIENCE (applied science, chemistry, computer science, and mathematics), EDUCATION (art education, early childhood education, elementary education, foreign languages education, health education, mathematics education, music education, physical education, and science education), ENGINEERING AND ENVIRONMENTAL DESIGN (environmental science), HEALTH PROFESSIONS (dental laboratory technology and medical technology), SOCIAL SCIENCE (history, interdisciplinary studies, law enforcement and corrections, political science/government, psychology, public administration, social work, and sociology). Education, business administration, and psychology have the largest enrollments.

ACTIVITIES: There are no fraternities or sororities. There are 100 groups on campus, including art, band, cheerleading, chess, choir, chorus, computers, dance, debate, drama, ethnic, forensics, honors, international, jazz band, literary magazine, marching band, musical theater, newspaper, orchestra, pep band, political, professional, radio and TV, religious, social, social service, student government, and symphony. Popular campus events include Martin Luther King Celebration, Cinco de Mayo, and Dakota Indigenous Nations Studies Conference. **Sports:** There are 5 intercollegiate sports for men and 6 for women, and 14 intramural sports for men and 13 for women. Facilities include a gym, baseball complex, softball facilities, racquetball courts, football stadium, wrestling rooms, weight room, pool, a mulitipurpose facility, a soccer field, and a fitness center.

SERVICES: Counseling and information services are available, as is tutoring in most subjects, and a reader service for the blind, and remedial math, reading, and writing. **Library/Resources:** The library contains 168,000 volumes, 228,000 microform items, 12,000 audio/video tapes/CDs/DVDs, and subscribes to 950 periodicals including electronic. Computerized library services include interlibrary loans, database searching, Internet access, and Wi-Fi capability. Special learning facilities include an art gallery, natural history museum, planetarium, radio station, and TV station. **Physically Challenged Students:** 98% of the campus is accessible. Facilities include wheelchair ramps, elevators, special parking, specially equipped restrooms, special class scheduling, lowered drinking fountains, lowered telephones, and special housing. **Special:** SMSU has cooperative programs with various local colleges, cross-registration with several state universities, and an accelerated degree. SMSU also offers internships in every discipline, work-study programs, student-designed and interdisciplinary majors including speech communication and theater arts, nondegree study, pass/fail options, and credit for life, military, and work experience. There are 2 national honor societies and a freshman honors program. **Visiting:** Regularly scheduled orientations for prospective students. There are guides for informal visits, visitors may sit in on classes, and stay overnight. To schedule a visit, contact the Admissions Office. **Campus Safety and Security:** Measures include 24-hour foot and vehicle patrol, self-defense education, security escort services, emergency telephones, and lighted pathways/sidewalks.

REQUIREMENTS: The SAT is recommended. The ACT is preferred. Admission is based on class rank or ACT/SAT composite. Students should be graduates of an accredited secondary school or have a GED certificate. An interview is recommended. SMSU requires applicants to be in the upper 50% of their class. AP and CLEP credits are accepted. Important factors in the admissions decision are recommendations by school officials, leadership record, and personality/intangible qualities. To graduate, students must complete at least 128 semester credit hours, a minimum of 27 of which must be at the 300 or 400 level, and a liberal arts core curriculum, with a minimum GPA of 2.0. **Procedure:** Freshmen are admitted to all sessions. Entrance exams should be taken during the junior or senior year. There are deferred admissions and rolling admissions plans. Applications should be filed by August 1 for fall entry; January 1 for spring entry. The fall 2016 application fee was $20. Notification is sent on a rolling basis. Applications are accepted online. **Transfer Students:** Applicants need a minimum GPA of 2.0 in previous college-level work at an accredited institution. High school transcripts are required if students are transferring with fewer than 24 semester credits. 48 of 128 credits required for the bachelor's degree must be completed at SMSU. **International Students:** The school actively recruits these students. They must take the TOEFL.

Admissions Contact: Richard Shearer, Director of Enrollment. Email: *admissions@smsu.edu* Web: *www.smsu.edu*

FINANCIAL AID: The college's own financial statement is required. The FAFSA code is 002375. Check with the school for current application deadlines.

ST. CATHERINE UNIVERSITY — C-4

www.stkate.edu

St. Paul, MN 55105 — **(651) 690-8850** — **(800) 656-KATE**

Fax: (651) 690-8824 — **Email: admissions@stkate.edu**

Full-time: 20 men, 2168 women	**Faculty:** 292; IIA, --$
Part-time: 103 men, 1268 women	**Ph.D.s:** 55%
Graduate: 150 men, 1308 women	**Student/Faculty:** 12 to 1
Year: 4-1-4, summer session	**Tuition:** $37,628
Room & Board: $8002	**Freshman Class:** 2375 applied, 1473 accepted, 682 enrolled
SAT CR/M: 560/525 **ACT:** 24	**CEEB CODE:** 6105
Application Deadline: open	**VERY COMPETITIVE**

A dynamic university educating students to lead and influence, St. Catherine prepares students to make a difference in their professions, their communities and the world. At the University's heart is the largest, most innovative college for women in the nation. St. Catherine also offers a range of graduate and associate programs for women and men. The figures in the above capsule and in this profile are approximate. There are 4 undergraduate schools and 1 graduate school. In addition to regional accreditation, SCU has baccalaureate program accreditation with ADA, APTA, CSWE, NASM, NLN, and NAACLS. The 110-acre campus is in an urban area 6 miles southwest of downtown St. Paul. Including any residence halls, there are 22 buildings.

STUDENT LIFE: 89% of undergraduates are from Minnesota. Others are from 30 states, 34 foreign countries, and Canada. 86% are from public schools. 68% are White; 3% Hispanic; 11% African American; 10% Asian American; 1% American Indian/Alaska Native; 1% Foreign. 50% are Catholic; 20% Protestant. **Female To Male Ratio:** 17.4:1. The average age of freshmen is 18; all undergraduates, 22. 16% do not continue beyond their first year; 67% remain to graduate. **Housing:** 900 students can be accommodated in college housing, which includes single-sex dorms, on-campus apartments, apartments for student-parents, and theme housing. On-campus housing is available on a first-come, first-served basis, and on a lottery system for upperclassmen. 56% of students commute. All students may keep cars.

FACULTY/CLASSROOMS: 21% of faculty are male; 79% are female. All teach undergraduates. No introductory courses are taught by graduate students. The average class size in an introductory lecture is 19; in a laboratory is 14; and in a regular course is 13.

PROGRAMS OF STUDY: SCU confers B.A. and B.S. degrees. Associate, master's, and doctoral degrees are also awarded. Bachelor's degrees are awarded in BIOLOGICAL SCIENCE (biochemistry, biology/biological science, and nutrition), BUSINESS (accounting, business administration and management, fashion merchandising, international business management, international economics, management information systems, and marketing/retailing/merchandising), COMMUNICATIONS AND THE ARTS (American Sign Language, art, classics, communications, dramatic arts, English, fine arts, French, Latin, media arts, music, musical theater, Spanish, and speech/debate/rhetoric), COMPUTER AND PHYSICAL SCIENCE (chemistry, information sciences and systems, and mathematics), EDUCATION (art education, early childhood education, elementary education, home economics education, music education, physical education, and secondary education), ENGINEERING AND ENVIRONMENTAL DESIGN (food services technology), HEALTH PROFESSIONS (exercise science, health care administration, medical records administration/services, nursing, occupational therapy, rehabilitation therapy, and respiratory therapy), SOCIAL SCIENCE (dietetics, economics, ethnic studies, family/consumer studies, fashion design and technology, history, international relations, interpreter for the deaf, philosophy, political science/government, psychology, social studies, social work, sociology, theological studies, and women's studies). Biology, chemistry, and psychology are the strongest academically. Nursing, social work, and accounting have the largest enrollments.

ACTIVITIES: There are no fraternities or sororities. There are 42 groups on campus, including art, band, cheerleading, choir, chorale, chorus, dance, drama, ethnic, honors, international, LGBT, literary magazine, musical theater, newspaper, photography, political, professional, radio and TV, religious, social, social service, and student government. Popular campus events include Winter Charity Ball, Dew Drop Bop, and Kat-Walk Fashion Show. **Sports:** There are 11 intercollegiate sports for women, and 8 intramural sports for women. Facilities include a gym, weight room, swimming pool, outdoor fitness course, tennis courts, soccer field, and a softball field. **Graduates:** From July 1, 2015 to June 30, 2016, 534 bachelor's degrees were awarded. The most popular majors were health professions and related programs (32%), business/marketing (14%), and public administration and social service/education (7%). 13 companies recruited on campus in 2015-2016. In an average class, 45% graduate in 4 years or less, 63% graduate in 5 years or less, and 67% graduate in 6 years or less. Of the 2015 graduating class, 22% were enrolled in graduate school within 6 months of graduation, and 84% were employed.

SERVICES: Counseling and information services are available, as is tutoring in most subjects, and a reader service for the blind, and remedial math, reading, and writing. **Library/Resources:** The 2 libraries contain 250,865 volumes, 180,946 microform items, 7,844 audio/video tapes/CDs/DVDs, and subscribe to 2,763 periodicals including electronic. Computerized library services include interlibrary loans, database searching, Internet access, and Wi-Fi capability. Special learning facilities include an art gallery, radio station, an observatory, and anatomy lab. **Physically Challenged Students:** 90% of the campus is accessible. Facilities include wheelchair ramps, elevators, special parking, specially equipped restrooms, special class scheduling, lowered drinking fountains, and lowered telephones. **Special:** SCU offers co-op programs with Carondolet College, the University of Minnesota, and George Washington University, and cross-registration with the Associated Colleges of the Twin Cities and other colleges sponsored by the Sisters of St. Joseph. Students may arrange internships, a Washington semester, and study abroad. Dual majors are available in the sciences and engineering. Students may receive credit for life, military, or work experience. Student-designed majors, non-degree study, and pass/fail options are available. The Weekend College offers a B.A. degree. There are 24 national honor societies, a chapter of Phi Beta Kappa, and a freshman honors program. **Visiting:** There are regularly scheduled orientations for prospective students, including a tour, an admissions interview, and an appointment with a faculty member. There are guides for informal visits, visitors may sit in on classes, and stay overnight. To schedule a visit, contact the Admissions Office. **Campus Safety and Security:** Measures include 24-hour foot and vehicle patrol, emergency notification system, self-defense education, security escort services, emergency telephones, lighted pathways/sidewalks, and controlled access to dorms/residences.

REQUIREMENTS: The SAT or ACT is required. Applicants must have completed a college preparatory program including 4 courses in English, 3 in math, and 2 each in a foreign language, science, and social studies. SCU requires applicants to be in the upper 50% of their class. AP and CLEP credits are accepted. Important factors in the admissions decision are advanced placement or honors courses, recommendations by school officials, and extracurricular activities record. To graduate, students must complete 130 semester credits, including a liberal arts core with courses in history, foreign language, philosophy, math, fine arts, literature, and theology, and 80 credits outside the major. Required courses are the Reflective Woman and the Global Search for Justice. At least 36 hours are required in the major. Students must have a minimum 2.0 GPA and demonstrate proficiency in composition, math, and computer literacy. **Procedure:** Freshmen are admitted in the fall and winter. Entrance exams should be taken during the senior year. There are deferred admissions and rolling admissions plans. Application deadlines are open. Notification is sent on a open basis. Applications are accepted online. **Transfer Students:** 354 transfer students enrolled in 2015-2016. Transfer applicants must submit high school and college transcripts. 48 of 130 credits required for the bachelor's degree must be completed at SCU. **International Students:** There are 48 international students enrolled. The school actively recruits these students. They must take the TOEFL with a minimum score of 500 on the paper-based TOEFL (PBT) or 61 on the Internet-based version (iBT) or take the MELAB and the college's own test. The SAT is required only if the student attended a U.S. high school, whether in this country or overseas.

ADMISSIONS: 62% of the 2016-2017 applicants were accepted. The SAT scores for the 2016-2017 freshman class were: Critical Reading-- 27% below 500, 39% between 500 and 599, 17% between 600 and 699, and 17% between 700 and 800. Math-- 27% below 500, 56% between 500 and 599, and 17% between 600 and 699. The ACT scores were 1% below 12, 48% between 18 and 23, 44% between 24 and 29, and 7% above 30. 53% of the current freshmen were in the top fifth of their class; 85% were in the top two fifths. 11 freshmen graduated first in their class. **Admissions Contact:** Marlene Mohs, Associate Dean of Admissions. Email: *admissions@stkate.edu* Web: *www.stkate.edu*

FINANCIAL AID: In 2016-2017, 99% of all full-time freshmen and 91% of continuing full-time students received some form of financial aid. 63% of all full-time freshmen and 60% of continuing full-time students received need-based aid. The average freshman award was $30,592. Need-based scholarships or need-based grants averaged $10,581; need-based self-help aid (loans and jobs) averaged $5,504; other non-need-based awards and non-need-based scholarships averaged $11,278; and $5,215 from other forms of aid. 100% of undergraduate students work part-time. Average annual earnings from campus work are $3200. The average financial indebtedness of the 2016 graduate was $39,607. SCU is a member of CSS. The college's own financial statement is required. The FAFSA code is 002342. The priority date for freshman financial aid applications for fall entry is April 15.

ST. CLOUD STATE UNIVERSITY C-3

www.stcloudstate.edu

St. Cloud, MN 56301 **(320) 308-2244**
(800) 369-4260
Fax: (320) 308-2243 **Email: scsu4u@stcloudstate.edu**

Full-time: 5400 men, 6250 women	**Faculty:** n/av
Part-time: 1190 men, 1685 women	**Ph.D.s:** n/av
Graduate: 555 men, 925 women	**Student/Faculty:** n/av
Year: semesters, summer session	**Tuition:** $6100 ($12,700)
Room & Board: $4500	**Freshman Class:** n/av
ACT: required	**CEEB CODE:** 6679
Application Deadline: n/av	**COMPETITIVE**

St. Cloud State University, founded in 1869, is a comprehensive university offering programs that include the liberal arts and career preparation with emphasis on diversity, hands-on learning, and service to the community. There are 6 undergraduate schools and 1 graduate school. In addition to regional accreditation, SCSU has baccalaureate program accreditation with AACSB, ABET, ACEJMC, ASLA, CSWE, NASAD, NASM, and NCATE. The 100-acre campus is in a suburban area 60 miles northwest of Minneapolis. Including any residence halls, there are 50 buildings.

STUDENT LIFE: 92% of undergraduates are from Minnesota. Others are from 50 states, 85 foreign countries, and Canada. 77% are White; 5% Foreign; 2% African American; 2% Asian American; 1% American Indian/Alaska Native; 1% Hispanic. **Female To Male Ratio:** 1.2:1. The average age of freshmen is 19; all undergraduates, 22. 29% do not continue beyond their first year. **Housing:** 3000 students can be accommodated in college housing, which includes single-sex and coed dorms, as well as special housing for international students. 82% of students commute. All students may keep cars. Alcohol is not permitted.

FACULTY/CLASSROOMS: 56% of faculty are male; 44% are female. All teach undergraduates. No introductory courses are taught by graduate students.

PROGRAMS OF STUDY: SCSU confers B.A., B.S., B.E.S., B.F.A., and B.Mus. degrees. Associate, master's, and doctoral degrees are also awarded. Bachelor's degrees are awarded in BIOLOGICAL SCIENCE (biology/biological science), BUSINESS (accounting, banking and finance, business administration and management, business economics, international business management, marketing/retailing/merchandising, and personnel management), COMMUNICATIONS AND THE ARTS (advertising, broadcasting, communications, dramatic arts, English, fine arts, journalism, languages, music, and speech/debate/rhetoric), COMPUTER AND PHYSICAL SCIENCE (atmospheric sciences and meteorology, chemistry, computer science, earth science, geology, mathematics, physics, and statistics), EDUCATION (art education, early childhood education, elementary education, foreign languages education, guidance education, health education, industrial arts education, music education, science education, and secondary education), ENGINEERING AND ENVIRONMENTAL DESIGN (aviation administration/management, electrical/electronics engineering, engineering technology, and manufacturing engineering), HEALTH PROFESSIONS (predentistry, premedicine, public health, and speech pathology/audiology), SOCIAL SCIENCE (anthropology, criminal justice, economics, geography, history, international relations, philosophy, political science/government, prelaw, psychology, public administration, social science, social work, sociology, and urban studies). Mass communication, elementary education, and special education have the largest enrollments.

ACTIVITIES: There are 240 groups on campus, including entrepreneurial, travel, art, band, cheerleading, chess, choir, chorale, chorus, computers, dance, drama, ethnic, film, honors, international, jazz band, LGBT, literary magazine, marching band, musical theater, opera, orchestra, pep band, photography, political, professional, radio and TV, religious, social, social service, sports, student government, symphony, and yearbook. Popular campus events include Music Festival, Ethnic Awareness Week, and Major Speakers and Workshops.

SERVICES: Counseling and information services are available, as is tutoring in every subject, and a reader service for the blind, and remedial math, reading, and writing. **Library/Resources:** The library contains 887,462 volumes, 1.8 million microform items, 24,244 audio/video tapes/CDs/DVDs, and subscribes to 1,762 periodicals including electronic. Computerized library services include interlibrary loans, database searching, Internet access, and Wi-Fi capability. Special learning facilities include an art gallery, natural history museum, planetarium, radio station, TV station, Herb Brooks National Hockey and Events Center. **Physically Challenged Students:** 86% of the campus is accessible. Facilities include wheelchair ramps, elevators, special parking, specially equipped restrooms, special class scheduling, lowered drinking fountains, and lowered telephones. **Special:** The university offers cross-registration, internships in almost all majors, work-study programs, and study abroad in 25 countries. Students may take dual majors, design their own majors for a Bachelor of Elective Studies degree, and earn a general degree or a B.A.-B.S. degree in all majors, including meteorology and photographic technology. The university gives credit for military experience and allows nondegree study and pass/fail options. There are 4 national honor societies and a freshman honors program. **Visiting:** There are regularly scheduled orientations for prospective students. There are guides for informal visits and visitors may sit in on classes. To schedule a visit, contact the Admissions Office. **Campus Safety and Security:** Measures include 24-hour foot and vehicle patrol, security escort services, shuttle buses, emergency telephones, lighted pathways/sidewalks, and a required short safety course.

REQUIREMENTS: The ACT is required. SCSU requires applicants to be in the upper 50% of their class. AP and CLEP credits are accepted. Students must complete a minimum of 120 semester credit hours, including 40 hours of general education requirements and 60 to 180 hours in the major, and maintain at least a 2.0 GPA (higher for many majors). Students must complete English 191, English 192, Speech 192, 2 credits in phys ed, and 24 credits in philosophy, humanities, fine arts, natural science and math, social and behavioral science, and diversity courses. **Procedure:** Freshmen are admitted in the fall, spring, and summer. Entrance exams should be taken in the junior or senior year. Application deadlines are open. The fall 2016 application fee was $20. Notification is sent on a rolling basis. **Transfer Students:** Applicants must have a minimum 2.0 GPA from their previous college if they transfer with 12 or more credits. If they have fewer than 12 credits, they are treated as entering freshmen. 30 of 120 credits required for the bachelor's degree must be completed at SCSU. **International Students:** The school actively recruits these students. They must take the TOEFL.

Admissions Contact: Pat Krueger, Associate Director of Admissions. Email: *scsu4u@stcloudstate.edu* Web: *www.stcloudstate.edu*

FINANCIAL AID: The college's own financial statement is required. The FAFSA code is 002377. Check with the school for current application deadlines.

ST. OLAF COLLEGE — C-4

www.stolaf.edu

Northfield, MN 55057 — **(507) 786-3025, (800) 800-3025**

Fax: (507) 786-3832 — **Email: admissions@stolaf.edu**

Full-time: 1289 men, 1716 women	**Faculty:** 213; IIB, +$
Part-time: 10 men, 31 women	**Ph.D.s:** 93%
Graduate: n/av	**Student/Faculty:** 14 to 1
Year: 4-1-4, summer session	**Tuition:** $42,940
Room & Board: $9790	**Freshman Class:** 7571 applied, 2723 accepted, 763 enrolled
SAT CR/M/W: 635/640/650 **ACT:** 29	**CEEB CODE:** 6638
Application Deadline: January 15	**HIGHLY COMPETITIVE+**

One of the nation's leading liberal arts colleges, St. Olaf College offers a distinctive education grounded in academic rigor, residential learning, global engagement, and a vibrant Lutheran faith tradition. St. Olaf provides an uncommon educational experience that fully prepares students to make a meaningful difference in our changing world. There is 1 undergraduate school. In addition to regional accreditation, St. Olaf has baccalaureate program accreditation with CSWE, NASM, NCATE, CCNE, NASD, and NAST. The 300-acre campus is in a small town 35 miles south of Minneapolis/St. Paul. Including any residence halls, there are 55 buildings.

STUDENT LIFE: 58% of undergraduates are from out of state, mostly the Midwest. Students are from 49 states, 79 foreign countries, and Canada. 74% are White. 44% are Protestant; 23% other Christian, and unkown; 17% claim no religious affiliation; 16% Catholic. **Female To Male Ratio:** 1.3:1. The average age of freshmen is 18; all undergraduates, 20. 7% do not continue beyond their first year; 87% remain to graduate. **Housing:** 2970 students can be accommodated in college housing, which includes coed dorms, honors houses, language houses, and special-interest houses. On-campus housing is guaranteed for all 4 years. 93% of students live on campus. Alcohol is not permitted. Some may keep cars.

FACULTY/CLASSROOMS: 52% of faculty are male; 48% are female. All teach undergraduates and do research. No introductory courses are taught by graduate students. The average class size in an introductory lecture is 24; in a laboratory is 18; and in a regular course is 22.

PROGRAMS OF STUDY: St. Olaf confers B.A., and B.Mus. degrees. Bachelor's degrees are awarded in AGRICULTURE (environmental studies), BIOLOGICAL SCIENCE (biology/biological science), COMMUNICATIONS AND THE ARTS (art history and appreciation, classics, dance, English, French, German, Greek, Latin, music, music performance, music theory and composition, Norwegian, Russian, Spanish, studio art, and theatre arts), COMPUTER AND PHYSICAL SCIENCE (chemistry, computer science, mathematics, and physics), EDUCATION (music education and social studies education), HEALTH PROFESSIONS (exercise science and nursing), SOCIAL SCIENCE (American studies, Asian/American studies, classical/ancient civilization, economics, ethnic studies, Hispanic American studies, history, interdisciplinary studies, medieval studies, philosophy, political science/government, psychology, religion, religious music, Russian and Slavic studies, social work, sociology, and women's studies). Biology, psychology, and economics have the largest enrollments.

ACTIVITIES: There are no fraternities or sororities. There are 221 groups on campus, including art, band, chess, choir, chorus, communications, computers, dance, drama, drill team, environmental, ethnic, film, honors, international, jazz band, LGBT, literary magazine, musical theater, newspaper, opera, orchestra, pep band, photography, political, professional, radio and TV, religious, social, social service, student government, and symphony. Popular campus events include Christmas Festival and President's Ball. **Sports:** There are 22 intercollegiate sports for men and 19 for women, and 35 intramural sports for men and 32 for women. Facilities include a fitness center, with weight-training and exercise machines, a ventilated waxing room for Nordic and alpine skiing, a climbing wall, batting cages, elevated running track, and volleyball, basketball, and tennis courts. The gymnasium features basketball and volleyball facilities, a pool, and a field house with indoor tennis courts, racquetball courts, a wrestling room, and an indoor running track. Outdoor facilities include an all weather track, tennis courts, and fields for football, baseball, softball, and soccer. There is also a sand volleyball court, broomball rink, and golf courses. **Graduates:** From July 1, 2014 to June 30, 2015, 677 bachelor's degrees were awarded. The most popular majors were biology (12%), psychology (8%), and economics (8%). 144 companies recruited on campus in 2014-2015. In an average class, 84% graduate in 4 years or less, 87% graduate in 5 years or less, and 87% graduate in 6 years or less.

SERVICES: Counseling and information services are available, as is tutoring in every subject, and a reader service for the blind. Study sessions are available upon request. **Library/Resources:** The 4 libraries contain 798,216 volumes, 13,103 microform items, 773,160 audio/video tapes/CDs/DVDs, and subscribe to 85,059 periodicals including electronic. Computerized library services include interlibrary loans, database searching, Internet access, and Wi-Fi capability. Special learning facilities include an art gallery, radio station, 700 acres of land dedicated to natural habitat, sustainable agriculture, and conventional agriculture. **Physically Challenged Students:** 76% of the campus is accessible. Facilities include wheelchair ramps, elevators, special parking, specially equipped restrooms, special class scheduling, lowered drinking fountains, lowered telephones, and special housing. Electric door openers, curb cuts, and a sling for swimming pool entry. **Special:** St. Olaf offers cross-registration with Carleton College, study abroad in more than 50 countries, 20 domestic off-campus programs, pre-professional programs, internships, and a 3-2 B.A.-B.S.E. degree in engineering with Washington University in St. Louis or the University of Minnesota. There are dual majors, non-degree study, on-campus work study, and pass/fail options. The Center for Integrative Studies allows students to design individual majors with an emphasis on tutorials and seminars. St. Olaf's Conversation programs, focusing on the great books, American studies, Asian studies, environmental studies, scientific inquiry, and public affairs, foster intimate learning communities that engage students in interdisciplinary study, critical thinking, and thoughtful discussion of major issues that transcend disciplinary borders and historical, cultural, and social contexts. There are 22 national honor societies, and a chapter of Phi Beta Kappa. **Visiting:** There are regularly scheduled orientations for prospective students, offerings include: tours, class visits, information sessions, and interviews. There are guides for informal visits, visitors may sit in on classes, and stay overnight. **Campus Safety and Security:** Measures include 24-hour foot and vehicle patrol, emergency notification system, self-defense education, security escort services, emergency telephones, lighted pathways/sidewalks, and controlled access to dorms/residences.

REQUIREMENTS: The SAT or ACT is required. It is recommended that applicants complete 4 years of English, 4 of math and social studies/history, 4 of science (2 labs), and 4 of a foreign language. AP credits are accepted. In addition to the distribution requirements, students are required to demonstrate skills at an intermediate level in a foreign language and proficiency in English composition, and to complete the phys ed requirement and to have taken a 1/4-credit oral communication course and a 1-credit mathematical reasoning course. A first-year writing course is also required. Distribution requirements include courses in history, literature, art, science, human behavior, Bible and theology, multicultural studies, and ethical issues. A minimum of 24 full-course credits out of 35 must be graded, and 18 must be upper-division. A minimum of 8 full-credit courses in a disciplinary or interdisciplinary major are required. All majors include writing requirements. Students must complete 35 credits and maintain a minimum GPA of 2.0. **Procedure:** Freshmen are admitted in the fall, winter, and spring. Entrance exams should be taken in the spring of the junior year or the fall of the senior year. There are early decision and deferred admissions plans. Early decision applications should be filed by November 15; regular applications, by January 15 for fall entry. Notification of early decision is sent December 15; regular decision, March 15. 180 early decision candidates were accepted for the 2015-2016 class. 729 applicants were on the 2015 waiting list; 113 were admitted. Applications are accepted on-line. **Transfer Students:** 36 transfer students enrolled in 2014-2015. 17 of 35 credits required for the bachelor's degree must be completed at St. Olaf. **International Students:** There are 233 international students enrolled. The school actively recruits these students. They must take the TOEFL with a minimum score of 90 on the Internet-based version (iBT), or take the IELTS. They must also take the SAT or ACT.

ADMISSIONS: 36% of the 2015-2016 applicants were accepted. The SAT scores for the 2015-2016 freshman class were: Critical Reading-- 10% below 500, 24% between 500 and 599, 37% between 600 and 699, and 29% between 700 and 800. Math-- 4% below 500, 27% between 500 and 599, 43% between 600 and 699, and 26% between 700 and 800. The ACT scores were 12% between 18 and 23, 41% between 24 and 29, and 47% above 30. 70% of the current freshmen were in the top fifth of their class; 93% were in the top two fifths. There were 19 National Merit finalists. 43 freshmen graduated first in their class. **Admissions Contact:** David Wagner, Director of Admissions. Email: *admissions@stolaf.edu* Web: *www.stolaf.edu*

FINANCIAL AID: In 2015-2016, 95% of all full-time freshmen and 93% of continuing full-time students received some form of financial aid. 68% of all full-time freshmen and continuing full-time students received need-based aid. The average freshman award was $33,935. Need-based scholarships or need-based grants averaged $32,224 ($52,730 maximum); need-based self-help aid (loans and jobs) averaged $4,809 ($5,800 maximum); and other non-need-based awards and non-need-based scholarships averaged $16,256 ($26,365 maximum). 70% of undergraduate students work part-time. Average annual earnings from campus work are $1130. The average financial indebtedness of the 2015 graduate was $29,950. St. Olaf is a member of CSS. The CSS/Profile and FAFSA are required. The deadline for filing freshman financial aid applications for fall entry is February 1.

UNIVERSITY OF MINNESOTA CROOKSTON — A-2

www.umcrookston.edu

Crookston, MN 56716 — **(218) 281-8569** / **(800) 232-6466**

Fax: (218) 281-8575 — **Email: umcinfo@umn.edu**

Full-time: 724 men, 669 women	**Faculty:** 73; IIB, -$
Part-time: 590 men, 781 women	**Ph.D.s:** 40%
Graduate: n/av	**Student/Faculty:** 20 to 1
Year: semesters, summer session	**Tuition:** $11,646
Room & Board: $8093	**Freshman Class:** 670 applied, 472 accepted, 121 enrolled
SAT CR/M/W: 480/520/490 **ACT:** 22	**CEEB CODE:** 6893
Application Deadline: August 15	**COMPETITIVE**

University of Minnesota/Crookston, founded in 1965, is a public institution offering applied bachelor degree programs, including on-line opportunities, in agriculture, arts, humanities, and social sciences, business, math, science, technology and natural resources. There are 4 undergraduate schools. The 108-acre campus is in a small town 290 miles northwest of Minneapolis, and 25 miles southeast of Grand Forks, North Dakota. Including any residence halls, there are 35 buildings.

STUDENT LIFE: 67% of undergraduates are from Minnesota. Others are from 42 states, 16 foreign countries, and Canada. 76% are White; 7% African American; 7% Foreign; 2% Asian American; 2% Hispanic; 2% two or more races; 2% race unknown; 1% American Indian/Alaska Native. **Female To Male Ratio:** 1.1:1. The average age of freshmen is 19; all undergraduates, 26. 24% do not continue beyond their first year; 51% remain to graduate. **Housing:** 563 students can be accommodated in college housing, which includes coed dorms and on-campus apartments. On-campus housing is available on a first-come and first-served basis. Priority is given to out-of-town students. 20% of students commute. All students may keep cars. Alcohol is not permitted.

FACULTY/CLASSROOMS: 58% of faculty are male; 48% are female. All teach undergraduates, 40% do research, and 40% do both. No introductory courses are taught by graduate students. The average class size in an introductory lecture is 25; in a laboratory is 18; and in a regular course is 25.

PROGRAMS OF STUDY: UMC confers B.S., B.A.H., and B.M.M. degrees. Bachelor's degrees are awarded in AGRICULTURE (agricultural business management, agronomy, animal science, equine science, horticulture, and natural resource management), BIOLOGICAL SCIENCE (biology/biological science), BUSINESS (accounting, business administration and management, marketing management, organizational behavior, and sports management), COMMUNICATIONS AND THE ARTS (communications), COMPUTER AND PHYSICAL SCIENCE (information sciences and systems and software engineering), EDUCATION (early childhood education and elementary education), ENGINEERING AND ENVIRONMENTAL DESIGN (agricultural engineering technology, airline piloting and navigation, applied aviation, computer technology, environmental science, and industrial administration/management), HEALTH PROFESSIONS (health, health care administration, and health science), SOCIAL SCIENCE (criminal justice). Business management, natural resources, and equine science have the largest enrollments.

ACTIVITIES: 1% of women belong to 1 national sorority. There are 39 groups on campus, including cheerleading, chess, choir, chorale, chorus, computers, drama, environmental, ethnic, honors, international, LGBT, pep band, political, professional, religious, social, social service, and student government. Popular campus events include What's on Wednesday (WOW), Ag-Arama and Winter Wonderland. **Sports:** There are 4 intercollegiate sports for men and 7 for women, and 10 intramural sports for men and 10 for women. Facilities include a gym, an indoor complex with basketball/volleyball and racquetball courts, a training room, a fitness center, a football field surrounded by an all-weather track, tennis courts, soccer, baseball, and softball fields. **Graduates:** From July 1, 2015 to June 30, 2016, 314 bachelor's degrees were awarded. The most popular majors were business management (18%), natural resources (15%), and applied studies (7%). 30 companies recruited on campus in 2015-2016. In an average class, 11% graduate in 3 years or less, 36% graduate in 4 years or less, 42% graduate in 5 years or less, and 53% graduate in 6 years or less. Of the 2015 graduating class, 8% were enrolled in graduate school within 6 months of graduation, and 92% were employed.

SERVICES: Counseling and information services are available, as is tutoring in most subjects, and a reader service for the blind, and remedial math and writing. The Academic Assistance Center also provides help with study strategies and English as a second language, and federally funded student support services are available to those who are eligible. **Library/Resources:** The library contains 244,686 volumes, 26,204 microform items, and 2,222 audio/video tapes/CDs/DVDs. Computerized library services include interlibrary loans, database searching, Internet access, and Wi-Fi capability. **Physically Challenged Students:** 95% of the campus is accessible. Facilities include wheelchair ramps, elevators, special parking, specially equipped restrooms, special class scheduling, lowered drinking fountains, lowered telephones, and special housing. **Special:** UMC offers cross-registration with the University of North Dakota Air Force ROTC. The internship or field experience requirement may be completed through on-the-job experience in the private sector, with a government agency, or through other appropriate work experience; a minimum of 450 hours of employment or volunteer assignments is usually required for satisfactory evaluation of the student's progress. Study abroad in more than 200 locations and student-designed majors are available. There is 1 national honor society, a freshman honors program, and 1 departmental honors program. **Visiting:** There are regularly scheduled orientations for prospective students. There are guides for informal visits, visitors may sit in on classes, and stay overnight. To schedule a visit, contact the Admissions Office. **Campus Safety and Security:** Measures include emergency notification system, self-defense education, and security escort services. There are also shuttle buses, emergency telephones, and lighted pathways/sidewalks.

REQUIREMENTS: A minimum score of 21 on the ACT or 980 on the SAT. Applicants must have successfully completed a high school or college preparatory program; the GED is accepted. The strength of the high school curriculum is considered. Students failing to meet minimum requirements of GPA and ACT or SAT scores will be referred to the Admissions Committee for an admission decision. AP and CLEP credits are accepted. To graduate, students must complete 120 credit hours, including 40 credits of liberal education and 40 upper-division credits, with a minimum GPA of 2.0. 3 credits of technology are required. **Procedure:** Freshmen are admitted in the fall and spring. Entrance exams should be taken by May 1. There are deferred admissions and rolling admissions plans. Applications should be filed by August 15 for fall entry, along with a $30 fee. Notification is sent on a rolling basis. Applications are accepted online. **Transfer Students:** 240 transfer students enrolled in 2015-2016. Transfer students with fewer than 24 earned college credits need to submit an official high school transcript, ACT or SAT scores, and official transcripts from previous colleges. Transfer students with 24 or more semester credits need to submit only official transcripts from previous colleges. A minimum 2.0 college GPA is required. 30 of 120 credits required for the bachelor's degree must be completed at UMC. **International Students:** There are 145 international students enrolled. The school actively recruits these students. They must take the TOEFL with a minimum score of 520 on the paper-based TOEFL (PBT) or 68 on the Internet-based version (iBT) or take the MELAB, or take the IELTS. Native English speaking students are not required to submit TOEFL scores but are required to submit ACT, SAT, or other standardized college entrance exams.

ADMISSIONS: 70% of the 2016-2017 applicants were accepted. The SAT scores for the 2016-2017 freshman class were: Critical Reading--53% below 500, 27% between 500 and 599, and 13% between 600 and 699. Math-- 20% below 500, 53% between 500 and 599, 7% between 600 and 699, and 7% between 700 and 800. Writing-- 57% below 500 and 43% between 500 and 599. The ACT scores were 41% below 12, 29% between 12 and 17, 19% between 18 and 23, 9% between 24 and 29, and 2% above 30. 37% of the current freshmen were in the top fifth of their class; 60% were in the top two fifths. 3 freshmen graduated first in their class. **Admissions Contact:** Peter Phaiah, Admissions Director. Email: *umcinfo@umn.edu* Web: *www.umcrookston.edu*

FINANCIAL AID: In 2016-2017, 74% of all full-time freshmen and 70% of continuing full-time students received some form of financial aid. 71% of all full-time freshmen and 64% of continuing full-time students received need-based aid. The average freshman award was $13,370. Need-based scholarships or need-based grants averaged $9,574; need-based self-help aid (loans and jobs) averaged $4,780; and other non-need-based awards and non-need-based scholarships averaged $3,640. Average annual earnings from campus work are $1200. The average financial indebtedness of the 2016 graduate was $27,608. The FAFSA code is 004069. The priority date for freshman financial aid applications for fall entry is March 1.

UNIVERSITY OF MINNESOTA/DULUTH D-2
www.d.umn.edu

Duluth, MN 55812	**(218) 726-7171** **(800) 232-1339**
Fax: (218) 726-6394	**Email: umdadmis@d.umn.edu**
Full-time: 4875 men, 4041 women	**Faculty:** 454; IIA, -$
Part-time: n/av	**Ph.D.s:** 63%
Graduate: 430 men, 576 women	**Student/Faculty:** 20 to 1
Year: semesters, summer session	**Tuition:** $13,082 ($17,032)
Room & Board: $7210	**Freshman Class:** 7456 applied, 5694 accepted, 2105 enrolled
SAT CR/M/W: 510/540/530 **ACT:** 24	**CEEB CODE:** 6873
Application Deadline: August 1	**COMPETITIVE+**

University of Minnesota Duluth, founded in 1895, is a liberal arts institution offering undergraduate and graduate programs as a campus of the University of Minnesota. There are 5 undergraduate schools and 1 graduate school. In addition to regional accreditation, UMD has baccalaureate program accreditation with AACSB, ABET, ACPE, ASLA, CSAB, CSWE, NASM, NCATE, ASLHA, CAA, NASM, and NRPA. The 244-acre campus is in an urban area 150 miles north of Minneapolis and St. Paul. Including any residence halls, there are 58 buildings.

STUDENT LIFE: 82% of undergraduates are from Minnesota. Others are from 44 states, 47 foreign countries, and Canada. 95% are from public schools. 81% are White; 5% race unknown; 4% Asian American; 3% African American; 3% Foreign; 2% American Indian/Alaska Native; 2% Hispanic. **Male To Female Ratio:** 1.1:1. The average age of freshmen is 18; all undergraduates, 20. 19% do not continue beyond their first year; 53% remain to graduate. **Housing:** 3171 students can be accommodated in college housing, which includes single-sex and coed dorms, on-campus apartments, honors houses, global home living learning community, greenhouse sustainability community, and a wellness dwelling community. On-campus housing is available on a first-come and first-served basis. 72% of students commute. All students may keep cars. Alcohol is not permitted.

FACULTY/CLASSROOMS: 55% of faculty are male; 45% are female. All teach undergraduates, 75% do research, and 75% do both. No introductory courses are taught by graduate students. The average class size in an introductory lecture is 60; in a laboratory is 20; and in a regular course is 30.

PROGRAMS OF STUDY: UMD confers B.A., B.S., B.A.A., B.Acc., B.A.Sc., B.B.A., B.F.A., B.Mus., B.S.Ch.E., B.S.C.E., B.S.E.C.E. and B.S.M.E. degrees. Master's and doctoral degrees are also awarded. Bachelor's degrees are awarded in AGRICULTURE (environmental studies), BIOLOGICAL SCIENCE (biochemistry, biology/biological science, cell biology, and molecular biology), BUSINESS (accounting, business administration and management, management information systems, and organizational leadership and management), COMMUNICATIONS AND THE ARTS (art, art history and appreciation, communications, dramatic arts, English, graphic design, jazz, music, music performance, Spanish, and studio art), COMPUTER AND PHYSICAL SCIENCE (actuarial science, applied physics, chemistry, computer science, geology, information sciences and systems, mathematics, physics, and statistics), EDUCATION (art education, athletic training, elementary education, foreign languages education, health education, mathematics education, middle school education, music education, physical education, recreation education, science education, secondary education, and social studies education), ENGINEERING AND ENVIRONMENTAL DESIGN (chemical engineering, civil engineering, computer engineering, electrical/electronics engineering, environmental science, industrial engineering, and mechanical engineering), HEALTH PROFESSIONS (hospital administration), SOCIAL SCIENCE (anthropology, criminology, early childhood studies, economics, geography, German area studies, history, interdisciplinary studies, international studies, Native American studies, philosophy, political science/government, prelaw, psychology, sociology, urban studies, and women's studies). Business, sciences, and engineering are the strongest academically. Business administration, biology, and psychology have the largest enrollments.

ACTIVITIES: 1% of men belong to 2 local and 3 national fraternities; 1% of women belong to 1 local and 3 national sororities. There are 270 groups on campus, including and wind ensemble, jazz choir, art, band, chamber orchestra, cheerleading, chess, choir, chorale, chorus, computers, dance, drama, environmental, ethnic, film, honors, international, jazz band, LGBT, literary magazine, marching band, musical theater, newspaper, opera, orchestra, pep band, photography, political, professional, radio and TV, religious, social, social service, and student government. Popular campus events include Out Cold Winter Festival, Black History Month, Hispanic Heritage Month, and Drag Show. **Sports:** There are 6 intercollegiate sports for men and 8 for women, and 26 intramural sports for men and 26 for women. Facilities include a rock-climbing walls, a multipurpose ice center, a football and track-and-field stadium, a baseball park, softball and soccer fields, a field house for track and tennis, a gym for basketball and volleyball, a nearby country club for cross-country and golf, and a cardio and weight facility. **Graduates:** From July 1, 2015 to June 30, 2016, 2168 bachelor's degrees were awarded. The most popular majors were psychology (7%), communication (5%), and finance (5%). 126 companies recruited on campus in 2015-2016. In an average class, 1% graduate in 3 years or less, 28% graduate in 4 years or less, 49% graduate in 5 years or less, and 54% graduate in 6 years or less. Of the 2015 graduating class, 12% were enrolled in graduate school within 6 months of graduation, and 75% were employed.

SERVICES: Counseling and information services are available, as is tutoring in some subjects, math, business, economics, sciences, accounting, computer science, engineering, physics, statistics, biology, American Sign Language, and writing. There is a reader service for the blind, and remedial math and writing. Workshops and seminars are also offered on study skills, note taking, time management, test-taking strategies, and goal setting. **Library/Resources:** The library contains 777,708 volumes, 756,339 microform items, 13,724 audio/video tapes/CDs/DVDs, and subscribes to 65,686 periodicals including electronic. Computerized library services include interlibrary loans, database searching, Internet access, and Wi-Fi capability. Special learning facilities include an art gallery, planetarium, radio station, Glensheen historic mansion, child care center, speech and hearing clinic, performing arts centers (theatre and music), a visual imaging lab, and a motion and media across disciplines lab. **Physically Challenged Students:** All of the campus is accessible. Facilities include wheelchair ramps, elevators, special parking, specially equipped restrooms, lowered drinking fountains, lowered telephones, and special housing. **Special:** Students may study abroad in England, Sweden, and Finland, and Australia. UMD also offers cross-registration with the College of St. Scholastica and the University of Wisconsin/Superior, internships, work-study programs, a B.A.-B.S. degree in several fields, student-designed majors, and nondegree study. There is 1 national honor society, Phi Beta Kappa, a freshman honors program, and 28 departmental honors programs. **Visiting:** There are regularly scheduled orientations for prospective students, including an information session, a campus tour, and a chance to meet with admissions counselors, faculty, or coaches and representatives from the five collegiate units. There are guides for informal visits and visitors may sit in on classes. To schedule a visit, contact UMD Office of Admissions. **Campus Safety and Security:** Measures include 24-hour foot and vehicle patrol, emergency notification system, self-defense education, security escort services, emergency telephones and lighted pathways/sidewalks.

REQUIREMENTS: The ACT is required. Applicants must have completed 4 years in English, 4 years in math, 3 years in sciences, 3 years in social sciences, and 2 years each in a single second language. Course work in the visual and performing arts and computer skills is recommended. Students with a GED certificate will be admitted selectively as space permits. AP and CLEP credits are accepted. To graduate, students must complete 120 to 136 semester credits, including 2 courses in college writing, and a liberal education distribution of at least 35 credits in 10 academic areas. At least 4 credits of course work must emphasize cultural diversity, and 4 should emphasize an international perspective. **Procedure:** Freshmen are admitted in the fall and spring. Entrance exams should be taken at the end of junior year or the beginning of senior year. There is a rolling admissions plan. Applications should be filed by August 1 for fall entry; December 1 for spring entry, along with a $40 fee. Notification is sent on a rolling basis. Applications are accepted online. **Transfer Students:** 544 transfer students enrolled in 2015-2016. Applicants who have completed 26 or more semester credits must have a minimum 2.0 GPA and a 75% completion ratio; applicants who have attempted fewer than 26 semester credits must have a high school rank at or above the 50th percentile, a 1.8 GPA in their previous college work, and a 75% completion ratio. **International Students:** There are 153 international students enrolled. The school actively recruits these students. They must take the TOEFL with a minimum score of 550 on the paper-based TOEFL (PBT) or 80 on the Internet-based version (iBT).

ADMISSIONS: 76% of the 2016-2017 applicants were accepted. The SAT scores for the 2016-2017 freshman class were: Critical Reading-- 40% below 500, 34% between 500 and 599, 23% between 600 and 699, and 3% between 700 and 800. Math-- 28% below 500, 46% between 500 and 599, 21% between 600 and 699, and 5% between 700 and 800. Writing-- 36% below 500, 41% between 500 and 599, 21% between 600 and 699, and 2% between 700 and 800. The ACT scores were 15% below 12, 33% between 12 and 17, 33% between 18 and 23, 11% between 24 and 29, and 8% above 30. 33% of the current freshmen were in the top fifth of their class; 71% were in the top two fifths. **Admissions Contact:** Scott Schulz, Director of Admissions. Email: *umdadmis@d.umn.edu* Web: *www.d.umn.edu*

FINANCIAL AID: In 2016-2017, 63% of all full-time freshmen and 61% of continuing full-time students received some form of financial aid. 63% of all full-time freshmen and 60% of continuing full-time students received need-based aid. The average freshman award was $10,478. Need-based scholarships or need-based grants averaged $7,658; need-based self-help aid (loans and jobs) averaged $3,740; and other non-need-based awards and non-need-based scholarships averaged $3,391. 14% of undergraduate students work part-time. The average financial indebtedness of the 2016 graduate was $18,214. The FAFSA code is 002388. The priority date for freshman financial aid applications for fall entry is February 15.

UNIVERSITY OF MINNESOTA/MORRIS B-3

www.morris.umn.edu

Morris, MN 56267 (320) 589-6035 (888) 866-3382

Fax: (320) 589-6051	**Email:** admissions@morris.umn.edu
Full-time: 722 men, 924 women	**Faculty:** 118; IIB, -$
Part-time: 57 men, 68 women	**Ph.D.s:** 92%
Graduate: n/av	**Student/Faculty:** 12 to 1
Year: semesters, summer session	**Tuition:** $12,846 ($14,846)
Room & Board: $7914	**Freshman Class:** 3414 applied, 1982 accepted, 375 enrolled
SAT CR/M/W: 560/590/540 **ACT:** 25	**CEEB CODE:** 6890
Application Deadline: March 15	**VERY COMPETITIVE**

University of Minnesota, Morris, founded in 1959, is a public liberal arts institution within the University of Minnesota system. The figures in the above capsule and in this profile are approximate. There is 1 undergraduate school. In addition to regional accreditation, UMM has baccalaureate program accreditation with NCATE. The 130-acre campus is in a small town 150 miles northwest of Minneapolis. Including any residence halls, there are 33 buildings.

STUDENT LIFE: 76% of undergraduates are from Minnesota. Others are from 32 states, and 24 foreign countries. 95% are from public schools. 60% are White; 6% American Indian/Alaska Native; 4% Hispanic; 3% Asian American; 2% African American; 12% two or more races; 1% race unknown. **Female To Male Ratio:** 1.3:1. The average age of freshmen is 18; all undergraduates, 20. 17% do not continue beyond their first year; 83% remain to graduate. **Housing:** 1032 students can be accommodated in college housing, which includes coed dorms, on-campus apartments, and housing for disabled students. On-campus housing is guaranteed for all 4 years, and is available on a first-come, first-served basis, and on a lottery system for upperclassmen. 60% of students live on campus; of those, 80% remain on campus on weekends. All students may keep cars. Alcohol is not permitted.

FACULTY/CLASSROOMS: 58% of faculty are male; 42% are female. All teach undergraduates, 63% do research, and 63% do both. No introductory courses are taught by graduate students. The average class size in an introductory lecture is 23; in a laboratory is 16; and in a regular course is 18.

PROGRAMS OF STUDY: UMM confers B.A. degrees. Bachelor's degrees are awarded in AGRICULTURE (environmental studies), BIOLOGICAL SCIENCE (biology/biological science), BUSINESS (management science), COMMUNICATIONS AND THE ARTS (art history and appreciation, communications, dramatic arts, English, French, German, music, Spanish, speech/debate/rhetoric, and studio art), COMPUTER AND PHYSICAL SCIENCE (chemistry, computer science, geology, mathematics, physics, and statistics), EDUCATION (education, elementary education, secondary education, and sports studies), ENGINEER-

ING AND ENVIRONMENTAL DESIGN (environmental science), HEALTH PROFESSIONS (premedicine), SOCIAL SCIENCE (American Indian studies, anthropology, economics, European studies, history, interdisciplinary studies, Latin American studies, liberal arts/general studies, philosophy, political science/government, prelaw, psychology, social science, sociology, and women's studies). Sciences, education, and performing arts are the strongest academically. Education, psychology, and biology have the largest enrollments.

ACTIVITIES: There are no fraternities or sororities. There are 100 groups on campus, including art, band, cheerleading, chess, choir, chorale, chorus, computers, dance, debate, drama, ethnic, forensics, honors, horseback riding, international, jazz band, LGBT, literary magazine, musical theater, newspaper, orchestra, photography, political, professional, radio and TV, religious, social, social service, student government, and yearbook. Popular campus events include Cultural Heritage Week, Diversity Jam, and Jazz Fest. **Sports:** There are 8 intercollegiate sports for men and 9 for women, and 19 intramural sports for men and 19 for women. Facilities include a stadium, phys ed center, gyms, wrestling, exercise and weight rooms, a pool, handball and racquetball courts, a track, fields for softball, baseball, soccer, and football, a diving well, a warm-water pool and slide, an indoor track, and a cardiovascular fitness room. **Graduates:** From July 1, 2015 to June 30, 2016, 374 bachelor's degrees were awarded. The most popular majors were biology (12%), economics (11%), and psychology (10%). 66 companies recruited on campus in 2015-2016. In an average class, 53% graduate in 4 years or less, 68% graduate in 5 years or less, and 70% graduate in 6 years or less. Of the 2015 graduating class, 23% were enrolled in graduate school within 6 months of graduation, and 71% were employed.

SERVICES: Counseling and information services are available, as is tutoring in every subject, and a reader service for the blind, and remedial math, reading, and writing. **Library/Resources:** The library contains 223,472 volumes, 2,215 microform items, 7,892 audio/video tapes/CDs/DVDs, and subscribes to 81,943 periodicals including electronic. Computerized library services include interlibrary loans, database searching, Internet access, and Wi-Fi capability. Special learning facilities include an art gallery, radio station, and TV station. UMM also houses a language lab, an observatory, and an agricultural experiment station. **Physically Challenged Students:** 70% of the campus is accessible. Facilities include wheelchair ramps, elevators, special parking, specially equipped restrooms, special class scheduling, lowered drinking fountains, special housing. A disability services coordinator is also available. Special learning equipment and services are available through the academic assistance center. **Special:** UMM offers work-study programs, internships, study abroad, dual majors, student-designed majors, nondegree study, pass/fail options, and credit for life, military, and work experience. There is a 3-2 engineering degree with the University of Minnesota at Twin Cities. A competitive, merit-based program that pairs students and professors to undertake creative projects is available. There is a freshman honors program and 34 departmental honors programs. **Visiting:** There are regularly scheduled orientations for prospective students, Visits include a campus tour, lunch with faculty, a session with admissions staff, and a student panel. There are guides for informal visits, visitors may sit in on classes, and stay overnight. To schedule a visit, contact the Admissions Office at admissions@morris.umn.edu. **Campus Safety and Security:** Measures include 24-hour foot and vehicle patrol, emergency notification system, self-defense education, and security escort services. There are also shuttle buses, emergency telephones, lighted pathways/sidewalks, and controlled access to dorms/residences.

REQUIREMENTS: The SAT or ACT is required, as well as the ACT Optional Writing test are required. Applicants should be graduates of an accredited secondary school or have a GED certificate. They must have completed 4 years of English, 3 each of math and science, 2 of a single foreign language, and 1 each of social studies and American history. A GPA of 3.0 is required. AP and CLEP credits are accepted. Important factors in the admissions decision are leadership record, extracurricular activities record, and advanced placement or honors courses. In addition to 40 semester hours in the major, students are required to complete 60 credits of a general education curriculum, including courses in writing, computing, foreign language or equivalent, and advanced study, as well as courses focusing on the arts, the physical and abstract worlds, and the self and others. All first-year students participate in a freshman seminar, and the cumulative of their major work is presented in the senior seminar, which is a requirement for all seniors. **Procedure:** Freshmen are admitted in the fall and spring. Entrance exams should be taken before December 1 of the senior year. There are deferred admissions and rolling admissions plans. Applications should be filed by March 15 for fall entry; September 15 for spring entry, along with a $35 fee. Notification is sent on a rolling basis. Applications are accepted online. **Transfer Students:** 101 transfer students enrolled in 2015-2016. Applicants must complete the application for admission, submit all college transcripts, and have maintained a minimum GPA of 2.5. 30 of 120 credits required for the bachelor's degree must be completed at UMM. **International Students:** There are 191 international students enrolled. They must take the TOEFL with a minimum score of 79 on the Internet-based version (iBT), or any one of theses tests SAT, ACT, or IETLS.

ADMISSIONS: 58% of the 2016-2017 applicants were accepted. The SAT scores for the 2016-2017 freshman class were: Critical Reading-- 32% below 500, 44% between 500 and 599, 12% between 600 and 699, and 12% between 700 and 800. Math-- 16% below 500, 40% between 500 and 599, 24% between 600 and 699, and 20% between 700 and 800. Writing-- 28% below 500, 44% between 500 and 599, 24% between 600 and 699, and 4% between 700 and 800. The ACT scores were 2% between 12 and 17, 33% between 18 and 23, 49% between 24 and 29, and 15% above 30. There was 1 National Merit finalist. 11 freshmen graduated first in their class. **Admissions Contact:** Jennifer Zych-Herrmann, Director of Admissions. Email: *admissions@morris.umn.edu* Web: *www.morris.umn.edu*

FINANCIAL AID: In 2016-2017, 72% of all full-time freshmen and 59% of continuing full-time students received some form of financial aid. 71% of all full-time freshmen and 56% of continuing full-time students received need-based aid. The average freshman award was $12,768. Need-based scholarships or need-based grants averaged $10,266; need-based self-help aid (loans and jobs) averaged $4,175; and other non-need-based awards and non-need-based scholarships averaged $3,483. 40% of undergraduate students work part-time. Average annual earnings from campus work are $1500. The average financial indebtedness of the 2016 graduate was $25,732. The FAFSA code is 002389. The priority date for freshman financial aid applications for fall entry is April 1.

UNIVERSITY OF MINNESOTA/TWIN CITIES C-4

www.twin-cities.umn.edu

Minneapolis, MN 55455	**(612) 625-2008** **(800) 752-1000**
Fax: (612) 625-1693	**Email: admissions@tc.umn.edu.**
Full-time: 14211 men, 15356 women	**Faculty:** 1, av$
	Ph.D.s: 78%
Part-time: 2561 men, 2743 women	**Student/Faculty:** 17 to 1
Graduate: 7830 men, 8879 women	**Tuition:** $14,142 ($23,806)
Year: semesters, summer session	**Freshman Class:** n/av
Room & Board: $9377	
SAT or ACT: required	**CEEB CODE:** 6874
Application Deadline: n/av	**HIGHLY COMPETITIVE+**

University of Minnesota/Twin Cities, founded in 1851, is a land-grant institution offering programs in liberal and fine arts, physical and biological sciences, health sciences, education, natural resources, human ecology, business, agriculture, and engineering and professional training in law, medicine, dentistry, pharmacy, and veterinary medicine. There are 12 undergraduate schools and 17 graduate schools. In addition to regional accreditation, The U has baccalaureate program accreditation with AACSB, ABET, ABFSE, ACEJMC, ADA, APTA, ASLA, CSWE, FIDER, NAAB, NASM, NCATE, NLN, and SAF. The 2000-acre campus is in an urban area within both Minneapolis and St. Paul. Including any residence halls, there are 205 buildings.

STUDENT LIFE: 73% of undergraduates are from Minnesota. Others are from 50 states, 139 foreign countries, and Canada. 85% are from public schools. 8% are Asian American; 64% White; 4% African American; 4% race unknown; 3% Hispanic; 3% two or more races; 13% Foreign. **Female To Male Ratio:** 1.1:1. The average age of freshmen is 18; all undergraduates, 21. 7% do not continue beyond their first year; 78% remain to graduate. **Housing:** 6956 students can be accommodated in college housing, which includes single-sex and coed dorms, on-campus apartments, off-campus apartments, married student housing, honors houses, special-interest houses, fraternity houses, sorority houses, and cooperative housing. On-campus housing is guaranteed for the freshman year only, is available on a first-come, first-served basis, and is available on a lottery system for upperclassmen. 78% of students commute. All students may keep cars. Alcohol is not permitted.

FACULTY/CLASSROOMS: 57% of faculty are male; 43% are female. All teach undergraduates, and all do research. No introductory courses are taught by graduate students.

PROGRAMS OF STUDY: The U confers B.A., B.S., B.A.E.M., B.C.E., B.S.Ch., B.Ch.E., B.Comp.Sci., B.E.E., B.F.A., B.G.E., B.I.S., B.Materials Sci.E., B.S. Mathematics, B.M.E., B.S.Bus., B.S.G., B.S. in Astrophysics, B.S. in Geophysics, B.S.N., B.S. Statistics, B.A.S., B.A.Sc., B.B.A.E., B.B.P.E., B.Bm.E., B.Comp.E., B.D.A., B.E.D., B.Mus., and B.S.Phys. degrees. Master's and doctoral degrees are also awarded. Bachelor's degrees are awarded in AGRICULTURE (agricultural business management, agricultural communications, animal science, fishing and fisheries, forestry production and processing, forestry and related sciences, and natural resource management), BIOLOGICAL SCIENCE (biochemistry, biology/biological science, biology and society, botany, cell biology, ecology, evolutionary biology, genetics, microbiology, nutrition, physiology, and wildlife biology), BUSINESS (accounting, applied economics / management, business administration and management, management science, marketing/retailing/merchandising, recreation and leisure services, recreational facilities management, and retailing), COMMUNICATIONS AND THE ARTS (acting, apparel design, art, art history and appreciation, Chinese, classical languages, dance, English, film arts, French, German, Greek, Hebrew, Italian, Japanese, languages, Latin, linguistics, music, Russian, Scandinavian languages, Spanish, speech/debate/rhetoric, and studio art), COMPUTER AND PHYSICAL SCIENCE (astrophysics, chemistry, computer science, geology, geophysics and seismology, mathematics, physics, and statistics), EDUCATION (agricultural education, Asian studies, bilingual/bicultural education, business education, classical studies, early childhood education, elementary education, English education, home economics education, industrial arts education, mathematics education, music education, physical education, science education, social studies education, and teaching English as a second/foreign language (TESOL/TEFOL)), ENGINEERING AND ENVIRONMENTAL DESIGN (aerospace engineering, architecture, bioengineering, biomedical engineering, chemical engineering, civil engineering, electrical/electronics engineering, environmental design, geological engineering, industrial engineering, interior design, landscape architecture/design, materials engineering, materials science, mechanical engineering, and metallurgical engineering), HEALTH PROFESSIONS (biology, dental hygiene, medical laboratory technology, music therapy, nursing, occupational therapy, pharmacy, physical therapy, predentistry, premedicine, prepharmacy, preveterinary science, and speech pathology/audiology), SOCIAL SCIENCE (African American studies, American Indian studies, American studies, anthropology, biblical studies, child psychology/development, East Asian studies, economics, food science, geography, history, humanities, international relations, Mexican-American/Chicano studies, Middle Eastern studies, philosophy, political science/government, prelaw, psychology, Russian and Slavic studies, sociology, South Asian studies, textiles and clothing, urban studies, and women's studies). Engineering, psychology, and economics are the strongest academically and have the largest enrollments are the strongest academically.

ACTIVITIES: There are 600 groups on campus, including art, band, cheerleading, chess, choir, chorale, chorus, computers, dance, debate, drama, drill team, environmental, ethnic, film, honors, international, jazz band, LGBT, literary magazine, marching band, musical theater, newspaper, orchestra, pep band, photography, political, professional, radio and TV, religious, social, social service, student government, and symphony. Popular campus events include Homecoming. **Sports:** There are 12 intercollegiate sports for men and 11 for women, and 16 intramural sports for men and 16 for women. Facilities include an outdoor stadium, gyms, field houses, a hockey rink, an aquatic center, and a student recreation center. **Graduates:** From July 1, 2015 to June 30, 2016, 7687 bachelor's degrees were awarded. The most popular majors were psychology (4%), journalism (4%), and communication studies (3%). In an average class, 3% graduate in 3 years or less, 61% graduate in 4 years or less, 76% graduate in 5 years or less, and 78% graduate in 6 years or less.

SERVICES: Counseling and information services are available, as is tutoring in every subject, and a reader service for the blind, and remedial math, reading, and writing. There are also test proctoring, and sign language interpreters. **Library/Resources:** The 14 libraries contain 6.2 million volumes, 5.4 million microform items, 500,000 audio/video tapes/CDs/DVDs, and subscribe to 48,105 periodicals including electronic. Computerized library services include interlibrary loans, database searching, and Internet access. Special learning facilities include an art gallery, natural history museum, planetarium, radio station, and TV station. **Physically Challenged Students:** Facilities include wheelchair ramps, elevators, special parking, specially equipped restrooms, special class scheduling, lowered drinking fountains, lowered telephones, special housing. listening devices, TTY and volume-control phones, print enlargers, and adaptive computers. In addition, support groups and counselors provide assistance with all areas of university life and career planning. **Special:** The university offers cooperative programs, cross-registration with the Minnesota Community College system, internships, study abroad in 65 countries, work-study programs both on and off campus, a B.A.-B.S. degree in all majors, a general studies degree, and dual and student-designed majors. Pass/fail options and credit for life, military, or work experience are available. There are 21 national honor societies, Phi Beta Kappa, a freshman honors program, and 8 departmental honors programs. **Visiting:** There are regularly scheduled orientations are available for prospective students. There are guides for informal visits, visitors may sit in on classes, and stay overnight. To schedule a visit, contact the Visit Line at (612) 625-0000. **Campus Safety and Security:** Measures include 24-hour foot and vehicle patrol, emergency notification system, self-defense education, and security escort services. There are also shuttle buses, emergency telephones, lighted pathways/sidewalks, a 20-member university police force, and blue-light phone centers.

REQUIREMENTS: The university uses a formula index in evaluating high school rank and ACT test scores. A portfolio is required for studio arts and architecture, an audition for music, and an interview for architecture and education. A high school diploma is required; the GED is accepted. AP and CLEP credits are accepted. Important factors in the admissions decision are advanced placement or honors courses, evidence of special talent, and leadership record. To graduate, students must complete 120 to 130 semester credits, including 45 in the major, with a minimum GPA of 2.0. Distribution requirements include course work in the 4 areas of communication, language, and symbolic systems, physical and biological sciences, the individual and society, and artistic expression. Other requirements vary by program. **Procedure:** Freshmen are admitted to all sessions. Entrance exams should be taken by the end of the junior year or October/November/December of the senior year. There are early admissions, deferred admissions, and rolling admissions plans. Application deadlines are open. Application fee is $55. Notification is sent on a rolling basis. Applications are accepted online. **Transfer Students:** 2114 transfer students enrolled in 2015-2016. Admission requirements vary by major/program, with a minimum 2.2 GPA needed for consideration. College transcripts are required. 30 of 120 credits required for the bachelor's degree must be completed at The U. **International Students:** There are 2643 international students enrolled. They must take the MELAB, and Minnesota Battery and the Institutional TOEFL. ACT for residents of Minnesota and neighboring states, SAT for residents of other states.

ADMISSIONS: 75% of the current freshmen were in the top fifth of their class; 98% were in the top two fifths. **Admissions Contact:** Rachelle Hernandez, Director of Admissions. Email: *admissions@tc.umn.edu.* Web: *http:/twin-cities.umn.edu*

FINANCIAL AID: In 2016-2017, 50% of all full-time freshmen received some form of financial aid. The average freshman award was $13,165. Need-based scholarships or need-based grants averaged $10,456; and need-based self-help aid (loans and jobs) averaged $5,046. The college's own financial statement is required. The FAFSA code is 003969. Check with the school for current application deadlines.

UNIVERSITY OF NORTHWESTERN - ST. PAUL C-4

Northwestern College
www.unwsp.edu

St. Paul, MN 55113 **(651) 631-5141**

Email: admissions@unwsp.edu

Full-time: 770 men, 1040 women	**Faculty:** IIB, -$
Part-time: 25 men, 30 women	**Ph.D.s:** 81%
Graduate: 52 men, 42 women	**Student/Faculty:** 13 to 1
Year: semesters, summer session	**Tuition:** $29,470
Room & Board: $5460	**Freshman Class:** n/av
ACT: required	**CEEB CODE:** 6489
Application Deadline: August 1	**COMPETITIVE**

Since 1902, students have come to Northwestern to learn and develop as leaders through Christ-centered, academically excellent education. University of Northwestern (UNW) is a Christ-centered liberal arts university. All members of the UNW community students, faculty, staff profess faith in Jesus Christ as Lord and Savior. Our shared faith brings us together in a powerful way as we learn and grow together in Christ. There are 4 undergraduate schools. In addition to regional accreditation, Northwestern has baccalaureate program accreditation with NASM. The 107-acre campus is in a suburban area in Roseville, MN which just 3 miles from St. Paul and 5 miles from Minneapolis. Including any residence halls, there are 17 buildings.

STUDENT LIFE: 68% of undergraduates are from Minnesota. Others are from 31 states, and 89 foreign countries. 68% are from public schools. 90% are White; 4% Asian American; 3% African American; 2% Hispanic; 1% Foreign. 99% are Protestant. **Female To Male Ratio:** 1.3:1. The average age of freshmen is 18; all undergraduates, 20. 21% do not continue beyond their first year; 61% remain to graduate. **Housing:** 1335 students can be accommodated in college housing, which includes single-sex dorms, on-campus apartments, married student housing, special-interest houses. On-campus housing is guaranteed for the freshman year only, and is available on a first-come, and first-served basis. Priority is given to out-of-town students. 89% of students live on campus. Upperclassmen may keep cars. Alcohol is not permitted.

FACULTY/CLASSROOMS: 56% of faculty are male; 44% are female. All teach undergraduates. No introductory courses are taught by graduate students. The average class size in an introductory lecture is 39; in a laboratory is 17; and in a regular course is 22.

PROGRAMS OF STUDY: Northwestern confers B.A., B.S., B.M.E., and B.Mus. degrees. Associate and master's degrees are also awarded. Bachelor's degrees are awarded in BIOLOGICAL SCIENCE (biochemistry and biology/biological science), BUSINESS (accounting, banking and finance, business administration and management, international business management, management information systems, and marketing management), COMMUNICATIONS AND THE ARTS (animation, broadcasting, communications, dramatic arts, English, English as a second/foreign language, graphic design, journalism, music, music performance, music theory and composition, piano/organ, public relations, Spanish, strings, studio art, and voice), COMPUTER AND PHYSICAL SCIENCE (mathematics), EDUCATION (art education, early childhood education, elementary education, English education, mathematics education, music education, physical education, and social studies education), HEALTH PROFESSIONS (exercise science), SOCIAL SCIENCE (biblical studies, criminal justice, crosscultural studies, history, interdisciplinary studies, ministries, pastoral studies, psychology, religious education, urban studies, and youth ministry). Education, music, and communication are the strongest academically. Education, business, and Christian ministries have the largest enrollments.

ACTIVITIES: There are no fraternities or sororities. There are 30 groups on campus, including band, cheerleading, chess, choir, chorale, chorus, computers, dance, debate, drama, ethnic, film, forensics, honors, international, jazz band, literary magazine, musical theater, newspaper, opera, orchestra, pep band, photography, political, professional, radio and TV, religious, social, social service, student government, and yearbook. Popular campus events include Spring Variety Shows, Christmas at Northwestern, Five16 Film Festival, Multicultural Festival, and Day of Prayer and Service. **Sports:** There are 9 intercollegiate sports for men and 9 for women, and 8 intramural sports for men and 8 for women. Facilities include softball, baseball, soccer, lacrosse, and football fields, as well as outdoor tennis courts. There are aquatic sports in summer and broomball in winter. A health and physical education center, has a basketball court, racquetball courts, an elevated jogging surface, a fitness center, and an athletic training room. Other sports include cross country, soccer, golf, track and field, volleyball, wrestling, badminton, dodgeball, flag football, pickleball, table tennis, foosball, 8-ball and 9-ball, and wallyball. One residence (Akenson) has a swimming pool. **Graduates:** From July 1, 2015 to June 30, 2016, 433 bachelor's degrees were awarded. The most popular majors were education (19%), Christian ministries/biblical studies (19%), and business (15%). 150 companies recruited on campus in 2015-2016. In an average class, 8% graduate in 3 years or less, 45% graduate in 4 years or less, 59% graduate in 5 years or less, and 61% graduate in 6 years or less. Of the 2015 graduating class, 6% were enrolled in graduate school within 6 months of graduation, and 89% were employed.

SERVICES: Counseling and information services are available, as is tutoring in some subjects, such as writing, math, Spanish, Greek, science, accounting, and statistics for psychology. There is also remedial math, reading, and writing. **Library/Resources:** The library contains 124,574 volumes, 70,350 microform items, 5,092 audio/video tapes/CDs/DVDs, and subscribes to 1,263 periodicals including electronic. Computerized library services include interlibrary loans, database searching, Internet access, and Wi-Fi capability. Special learning facilities include an art gallery, radio station, TV station, Northwestern's DeWitt Library is part of the DeWitt Learning Commons. **Physically Challenged Students:** 70% of the campus is accessible. Facilities include wheelchair ramps, elevators, special parking, specially equipped restrooms, special class scheduling, lowered drinking fountains, and special housing. **Special:** The university offers 8 study-abroad programs and 4 U.S. off-campus programs through the Council for Christian Colleges and Universities. Additionally, students can choose from 35 countries to study abroad in. International business majors are placed in overseas internships. A 3-2 engineering degree with the University of Minnesota-Twin Cities is offered. There are 6 national honor societies, a freshman honors program, and 11 departmental honors programs. **Visiting:** There are regularly scheduled orientations for prospective students. There are guides for informal visits, visitors may sit in on classes, and stay overnight. To schedule a visit, contact the Admissions Office. **Campus Safety and Security:** Measures include 24-hour foot and vehicle patrol, emergency notification system, self-defense education, and security escort services. There are also shuttle buses, emergency telephones, lighted pathways/sidewalks, and controlled access to dorms/residences. The campus also has limited accessibility due to being surrounded on 3 sides by Lake Johanna, and the main entrance to the campus is gated.

REQUIREMENTS: The ACT is preferred but the SAT is accepted. A high school diploma is required; the GED is accepted. The minimum high school GPA is 2.0, but a 3.0 or higher is recommended. Applicants are expected to have completed the following Carnegie units: 4 in English, 3 each in math, science, and social studies, and 2 others. 2 in foreign language are recommended. A statement of Christian faith and an assent to a lifestyle agreement are required. 2 letters of reference must be submitted, including 1 from the applicant's pastor. A personal interview is required for some students. Northwestern requires applicants to be in the upper 50% of their class. A GPA of 2.0 is required. AP and CLEP credits are accepted. Important factors in the admissions decision are personality/intangible qualities, recommendations by school officials, and leadership record. To graduate, students must complete 125 to 166 semester credits (depends on specific major) with a 2.0 GPA. The number of credits required in the major varies from 36 to 100 (average of 58). A core curriculum of 64 to 68 credits is built around a biblical worldview theme, thoroughly integrating general education and biblical worldview studies. **Procedure:** Freshmen are admitted to all sessions. Entrance exams should be taken during the fall of the senior year of high school. There are deferred admissions and rolling admissions plans. Applications should be filed by August 1 for fall entry; December 15 for spring entry; and May 1 for summer entry, along with a $30 fee. Notification is sent on a rolling basis. Applications are accepted online. **Transfer Students:** 108 transfer students enrolled in 2015-2016. Applicants must have an average of C or better from an accredited institution. 30 of 125 credits required for the bachelor's degree must be completed at Northwestern. **International Students:** There are 9 international students enrolled. They must take the TOEFL or MELAB, or take the ACT or SAT.

Admissions Contact: Erick Klein, Director of Admissions. Email: *admissions@unwsp.edu* Web: *www.unwsp.edu*

FINANCIAL AID: In 2016-2017, 99% of all full-time freshmen received some form of financial aid. 99% of all full-time freshmen received need-based aid. The average freshman award was $24,700. Average annual earnings from campus work are $2516. The average financial indebtedness of the 2016 graduate was $25,162. The college's own financial statement is required. The FAFSA code is 002371. The priority date for freshman financial aid applications for fall entry is January 1.

UNIVERSITY OF ST. THOMAS — C-4

www.stthomas.edu

St. Paul, MN 55105 — **(651) 962-6150**, **(800) 328-6819**

Fax: (651) 962-6160 — **Email: admissions@stthomas.edu**

Full-time: 3158 men, 2691 women	**Faculty:** 377
Part-time: 150 men, 112 women	**Ph.D.s:** n/av
Graduate: 1768 men, 2104 women	**Student/Faculty:** 14 to 1
Year: 4-1-4, summer session	**Tuition:** $39,594
Room & Board: $9760	**Freshman Class:** 5540 applied, 4774 accepted, 1368 enrolled
SAT CR/M: 580/590 **ACT:** 26	**CEEB CODE:** 6110
Application Deadline: January 15	**VERY COMPETITIVE+**

University of St. Thomas, founded in 1885, is a private liberal arts institution affiliated with the Roman Catholic Church. There is 1 undergraduate school and 7 graduate schools. In addition to regional accreditation, St. Thomas has baccalaureate program accreditation with AACSB, ABET, CSWE, NASM, NCATE, and ACS. The 78-acre campus is in an urban area 5 miles west of St. Paul and 5 miles east of Minneapolis. Including any residence halls, there are 60 buildings.

STUDENT LIFE: 79% of undergraduates are from Minnesota. Others are from 43 states, 83 foreign countries, and Canada. 72% are from public schools. 77% are White; 6% Foreign; 5% Asian American; 4% African American; 4% Hispanic; 3% two or more races; 2% race unknown. 38% are Catholic; 29% Protestant; 27% Buddhist, Muslim, and Hindu. **Male To Female Ratio:** 1.0:1. The average age of freshmen is 18; all undergraduates, 20. 12% do not continue beyond their first year; 88% remain to graduate. **Housing:** College-sponsored housing includes single-sex dorms, on-campus apartments, off-campus apartments, special-interest houses, LLC's, chemical-free lifestyle, first-year experience, women in science housing, special housing for disabled students, theme housing, wellness housing, and housing options for Catholic women and Catholic men. On-campus housing on a first-come, first-served basis, and is available on a lottery system for upperclassmen. 60% of students commute. All students may keep cars.

FACULTY/CLASSROOMS: 58% of faculty are male; 42% are female. 86% teach undergraduates. No introductory courses are taught by graduate students. The average class size in a laboratory is 15 and in a regular course is 20.

PROGRAMS OF STUDY: St. Thomas confers B.A., B.S., B.S.M.E., B.S.E.E. and B.M. degrees. Master's and doctoral degrees are also awarded. Bachelor's degrees are awarded in Engineering, and business are the strongest academically. Business has the largest enrollment.

ACTIVITIES: There are no fraternities or sororities. There are 140 groups on campus, including band, choir, chorus, computers, dance, drama, ethnic, honors, international, jazz band, LGBT, literary magazine, newspaper, pep band, political, professional, radio and TV, religious, social, social service, student government, and yearbook. **Sports:** There are 10 intercollegiate sports for men and 10 for women. Facilities include a basketball and volleyball arena, swimming pool, diving area, field house with a fitness center, a weight room, aerobics rooms. **Graduates:** From July 1, 2015 to June 30, 2016, 1557 bachelor's degrees were awarded. The most popular majors were marketing (9%), financial management (9%), and accounting (7%). In an average class, 62% graduate in 4 years or less, 75% graduate in 5 years or less, and 76% graduate in 6 years or less.

SERVICES: Counseling and information services are available, as is tutoring in every subject. There is a reader service for the blind. **Library/Resources:** The 4 libraries contain 695,137 volumes, 1.1 million microform items, 76,383 audio/video tapes/CDs/DVDs, and subscribe to 193,510 periodicals including electronic. Computerized library services include interlibrary loans, database searching, and Wi-Fi capability. Special learning facilities include an art gallery, radio station, and TV station. **Physically Challenged Students:** 5% of the campus is accessible. Facilities include wheelchair ramps, elevators, special parking, specially equipped restrooms, lowered drinking fountains, and special housing. **Special:** There is a freshman honors program. **Visiting:** There are regularly scheduled orientations for prospective students. There are guides for informal visits, visitors may sit in on classes, and stay overnight. To schedule a visit, contact the Visit Coordinator at admvisit@stthomas.edu. **Campus Safety and Security:** Measures include 24-hour foot and vehicle patrol, emergency notification system, and security escort services. There are also shuttle buses, emergency telephones, lighted pathways/sidewalks, and controlled access to dorms/residences.

REQUIREMENTS: The ACT is required, the SAT is recommended, and application writing sample, standardized test score (ACT or SAT), recommendations 3 years of high school Math. The GED is accepted in place of high school transcript(s). AP and CLEP credits are accepted. Important factors in the admissions decision are recommendations by school officials, advanced placement or honors courses, and evidence of special talent. **Procedure:** Freshmen are admitted in the fall and spring. Entrance exams should be taken by the fall of the senior year. There are deferred admissions and rolling admissions plans. Application deadlines are open. Notification of early decision is sent December 15; regular decision, February 15. Applications are accepted online. **Transfer Students:** 271 transfer students enrolled in 2015-2016. Transfer applicants must have a minimum GPA of 2.3 in transferable college credits. 32 of 132 credits required for the bachelor's degree must be completed at St. Thomas. **International Students:** There are 186 international students enrolled. They must take the TOEFL or MELAB, as well as the SAT or ACT.

ADMISSIONS: 86% of the 2016-2017 applicants were accepted. The SAT scores for the 2016-2017 freshman class were: Critical Reading-- 20% below 500, 34% between 500 and 599, 32% between 600 and 699, and 14% between 700 and 800. Math-- 6% below 500, 40% between 500 and 599, 42% between 600 and 699, and 12% between 700 and 800. The ACT scores were 19% between 18 and 23, 62% between 24 and 29, and 19% above 30. 53% of the current freshmen were in the top fifth of their class; 87% were in the top two fifths. There were 4 National Merit finalists. 15 freshmen graduated first in their class. **Admissions Contact:** Kristen Hatfield, Director of Admissions. Email: *admissions@stthomas.edu* Web: *www.stthomas.edu*

FINANCIAL AID: In 2016-2017, 61% of all full-time freshmen and 56% of continuing full-time students received some form of financial aid. 47% of all full-time freshmen and 46% of continuing full-time students received need-based aid. The average freshman award was $28,360. The FAFSA code is 002345. The priority date for freshman financial aid applications for fall entry is April 1.

WINONA STATE UNIVERSITY — D-5

www.winona.edu

Winona, MN 55987	**(507) 457-5100** **(800) DIAL-WSU**
Fax: (507) 457-5620	**Email: admissions@winona.edu**
Full-time: 2517 men, 4180 women	**Faculty:** n/av
Part-time: 342 men, 617 women	**Ph.D.s:** 77%
Graduate: 127 men, 343 women	**Student/Faculty:** 20 to 1
Year: semesters, summer session	**Tuition:** $9075 ($14,772)
Room & Board: $8460	**Freshman Class:** 7476 applied, 4467 accepted, 1586 enrolled
ACT: 23	**CEEB CODE:** 6680
Application Deadline: July 14	**COMPETITIVE**

Winona State University, founded in 1858, is a mid-sized comprehensive regional university and a member of the Minnesota State. There are 5 undergraduate schools and 1 graduate school. In addition to regional accreditation, WSU has baccalaureate program accreditation with AACSB, ABET, CSWE, NASM, NCATE, CCNE, CAATE, and NAST. The 125-acre campus is in an urban area 120 miles southeast of Minneapolis and St. Paul. Including any residence halls, there are 35 buildings.

STUDENT LIFE: 67% of undergraduates are from Minnesota. Others are from 40 states, 51 foreign countries, and Canada. 85% are White; 3% African American; 3% Hispanic; 3% Foreign; 2% Asian American; 2% two or more races; 1% race unknown. **Female To Male Ratio:** 1.7:1. The average age of freshmen is 18; all undergraduates, 22. 23% do not continue beyond their first year; 59% remain to graduate. **Housing:** 2722 students can be accommodated in college housing, which includes single-sex and coed dorms, on-campus apartments, special-interest houses. On-campus housing is guaranteed for the freshman year only, and is available on a first-come, and first-served basis. 71% of students commute. All students may keep cars. Alcohol is not permitted.

FACULTY/CLASSROOMS: 44% of faculty are male; 56% are female. No introductory courses are taught by graduate students. The average class size in a laboratory is 19 and in a regular course is 28.

PROGRAMS OF STUDY: WSU confers B.A.S., B.A., B.S., B.S.Ed., B.S.W., and B.M. degrees. Associate, master's, and doctoral degrees are also awarded. Bachelor's degrees are awarded in BIOLOGICAL SCIENCE (biology/biological science), BUSINESS (accounting, banking and finance, business administration and management, business economics, human resources/organizational management, management information systems, marketing, and recreation and leisure services), COMMUNICATIONS AND THE ARTS (broadcasting, communication studies, dramatic arts, English, fine arts, graphic design, journalism, music, music performance, Spanish, and speech/debate/rhetoric), COMPUTER AND PHYSICAL SCIENCE (applied science, chemistry, computer science, earth science, earth science/adolescence education, geology, mathematics, physics, and statistics), EDUCATION (art education, athletic training, business education, early childhood education, elementary education, foreign languages education, global studies, health education, mathematics education, music education, physical education, science education, secondary education, social studies education, special education, specific learning disabilities, and teaching English as a second/foreign language (TESOL/TEFOL)), ENGINEERING AND ENVIRONMENTAL DESIGN (materials engineering and preengineering), HEALTH PROFESSIONS (community health work, cytotechnology, exercise science, health care administration, movement science, nursing, predentistry, premedicine, preoptometry, prepharmacy, prephysical therapy, prepodiatry, preveterinary science, and public health), SOCIAL SCIENCE (criminal justice, economics, history, paralegal studies, physical fitness/movement, political science/government, prelaw, psychology, public administration, social work, sociology, and women & gender studies). Nursing, education, and engineering are the strongest academically. Nursing, elementary education, and business administration have the largest enrollments.

ACTIVITIES: There are 155 groups on campus, including art, band, cheerleading, chess, choir, chorale, chorus, computers, dance, debate, drama, environmental, ethnic, film, forensics, honors, international, jazz band, LGBT, literary magazine, musical theater, newspaper, orchestra, pep band, photography, political, professional, radio and TV, religious, social, social service, student government, and symphony. Popular campus events include Homecoming. **Sports:** There are 5 intercollegiate sports for men and 10 for women, and 16 intramural sports for men and 16 for women. Facilities include a stadium, baseball field, softball field, gyms in multiples buildings, weight room, gymnastic practice area, a swimming pool, handball/racquetball courts, cardio-fitness center, and a walking/jogging inside track. **Graduates:** From July 1, 2015 to June 30, 2016, 1790 bachelor's degrees were awarded. The most popular majors were business/marketing (22%), health professions and related programs (19%), and education (10%). In an average class, 57% graduate in 5 years or less and 59% graduate in 6 years or less.

SERVICES: Counseling and information services are available, as is tutoring in most subjects. **Library/Resources:** The library contains 404,647 volumes, 27,501 microform items, 13,967 audio/video tapes/CDs/DVDs, and subscribes to 34,393 periodicals including electronic. Computerized library services include interlibrary loans, database searching, Internet access, and Wi-Fi capability. Special learning facilities include an art gallery and radio station. **Physically Challenged Students:** 5% of the campus is accessible. Facilities include wheelchair ramps, elevators, special parking, specially equipped restrooms, special class scheduling, lowered drinking fountains, lowered telephones, and special housing. **Special:** WSU offers cross-registration with St. Mary's University, study abroad in 12 countries, internships, work-study programs, student-designed majors, dual majors, pass/fail options, and credit for life, military, and work experience. Students may earn accelerated degrees in all majors and a general studies degree. There are 9 national honor societies and 6 departmental honors programs. **Visiting:** Regularly scheduled orientations are available for prospective students, including daily tours and admissions visits from October through January on select Saturday mornings. There are guides for informal visits and visitors may sit in on classes. To schedule a visit, contact the Office of Admissions. **Campus Safety and Security:** Measures include 24-hour foot and vehicle patrol, emergency notification system, self-defense education, and security escort services. There are also shuttle buses, emergency telephones, lighted pathways/sidewalks, and controlled access to dorms/residences.

REQUIREMENTS: The ACT is required. Candidates should have completed 4 units of English, 1 of which may be speech; 3 each of math and science; 2 each of a foreign language and social studies; 1 of history; and 1 elective, preferably in world culture, the arts, or computer science. AP and CLEP credits are accepted. To graduate, students must complete 120 credit hours with a minimum GPA of 2.0. General education requirements include 3 credits in public speaking, 3 credits in English, 7 credits in natural sciences, 3 in math and logical reasoning, 9 in history and social sciences, 9 in humanities and fine arts, and 2 in phys ed. Majors average 46 credits, and some require a capstone experience. **Procedure:** Freshmen are admitted in the fall, spring, and summer. Entrance exams should be taken in the junior year. There is a rolling admissions plan. Applications should be filed by July 14 for fall entry; November 24 for spring entry. The fall 2016 application fee was $20. Applications are accepted on-line. Application fees are waived if application is completed online. **Transfer Students:** 564 transfer students enrolled in 2015-2016. Applicants must have completed 24 semester hours of credit with a minimum GPA of 2.4. 30 of 120 credits required for the bachelor's degree must be completed at WSU. **International Students:** There are 264 international students enrolled. The school actively recruits these students. They must take the TOEFL with a minimum score of 520 on the paper-based TOEFL (PBT) or 68 on the Internet-based version (iBT).

ADMISSIONS: 60% of the 2016-2017 applicants were accepted. **Admissions Contact:** Carl Stange, Director of Admissions. Email: *admissions@winona.edu* Web: *www.winona.edu*

FINANCIAL AID: In 2016-2017, 60% of all full-time freshmen and 57% of continuing full-time students received some form of financial aid. 50% of all full-time freshmen and 51% of continuing full-time students received need-based aid. The average freshman award was $7,135. Need-based scholarships or need-based grants averaged $5,112; need-based self-help aid (loans and jobs) averaged $3,387; non-need-based athletic scholarships averaged $2,417; and other non-need-based awards and non-need-based scholarships averaged $2,485. The average financial indebtedness of the 2016 graduate was $35,221. The FAFSA code is 002394. The priority date for freshman financial aid applications for fall entry is May 15.

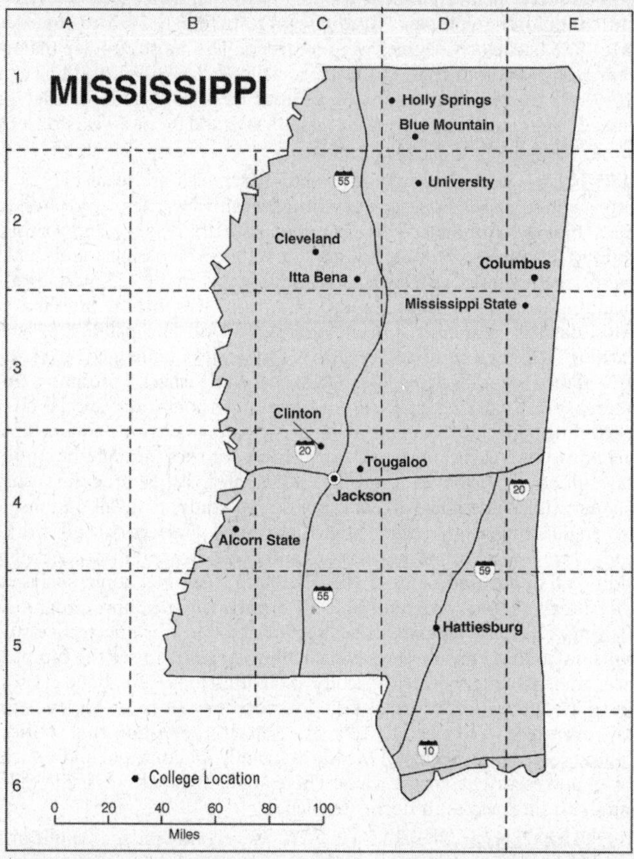

ALCORN STATE UNIVERSITY B-4

www.alcorn.edu

Lorman, MS 39096 **(601) 877-6147**

Fax: (601) 877-6347 **Email: ebarnes@alcorn.edu**

Full-time: 980 men, 1725 women	**Faculty:** IIB, -$
Part-time: 60 men, 245 women	**Ph.D.s:** 64%
Graduate: 165 men, 505 women	**Student/Faculty:** 17 to 1
Year: semesters, summer session	**Tuition:** $6858
Room & Board: $8996	**Freshman Class:** n/av
SAT: recommended **ACT:** required	**CEEB CODE:** 1008
Application Deadline: open	**COMPETITIVE**

Alcorn State University, founded in 1871, is a public institution offering programs in agriculture, the arts and sciences, business, engineering, and nursing. The figures in the above capsule and in this profile are approximate. There are 6 undergraduate schools and 1 graduate school. In addition to regional accreditation, Alcorn has baccalaureate program accreditation with AACSB, ADA, AHEA, NASM, NCATE, NLN, AAFCS, and NAIT. The 1756-acre campus is in a rural area in Clairborne county, 45 miles south of Vicksburg and 7 miles west of Lorman. Including any residence halls, there are 128 buildings.

STUDENT LIFE: 81% of undergraduates are from Mississippi. Others are from 32 states, 13 foreign countries, and Canada. 95% are from public schools. 91% are African American; 7% White; 2% Foreign. **Female To Male Ratio:** 2.1:1. The average age of freshmen is 24; all undergraduates, 25. 28% do not continue beyond their first year; 45% remain to graduate. **Housing:** 2495 students can be accommodated in college housing, which includes single-sex dorms. In addition, there are honors houses. On-campus housing is guaranteed for all 4 years. 56% of students commute. Alcohol is not permitted. All students may keep cars.

FACULTY/CLASSROOMS: 55% of faculty are male; 45% are female. 92% teach undergraduates. No introductory courses are taught by graduate students.

PROGRAMS OF STUDY: Alcorn confers B.A., B.S., B.M., B.M.E., and B.S.N. degrees. Associate and master's degrees are also awarded. Bachelor's degrees are awarded in AGRICULTURE (agricultural business management and agricultural economics), BIOLOGICAL SCIENCE (biology/biological science and nutrition), BUSINESS (accounting, business administration and management, and recreation and leisure services), COMMUNICATIONS AND THE ARTS (communications, English, and music), COMPUTER AND PHYSICAL SCIENCE (applied science, chemistry, computer science, and mathematics), EDUCATION (elementary education and special education), ENGINEERING AND ENVIRONMENTAL DESIGN (computer technology), HEALTH PROFESSIONS (health science, nursing, and sports medicine), SOCIAL SCIENCE (child psychology/development, criminal justice, economics, history, political science/government, psychology, social work, and sociology). Business administration, biology, and elementary education have the largest enrollments.

ACTIVITIES: 7% of men belong to 4 local and 4 national fraternities; 10% of women belong to 4 local and 4 national sororities. There are 79 groups on campus, including band, cheerleading, choir, chorus, dance, drama, honors, jazz band, marching band, newspaper, photography, radio and TV, religious, student government, and yearbook. Popular campus events include High School Day and Career Development Day. **Sports:** There are 8 intercollegiate sports for men and 10 for women, and 9 intramural sports for men and 9 for women. Facilities include a 10,000-seat stadium and a 5000-seat gym. **Graduates:** From July 1, 2015 to June 30, 2016, 399 bachelor's degrees were awarded. The most popular majors were general studies (20%), biology (12%), and nursing (9%). 214 companies recruited on campus in 2015-2016. In an average class, 45% graduate in 6 years or less. Of the 2015 graduating class, 38% were enrolled in graduate school within 6 months of graduation, and 99% were employed.

SERVICES: Counseling and information services are available, as is tutoring in most subjects. There is remedial math, reading, and writing. **Library/Resources:** The library contains 225,423 volumes, 581,883 microform items, and 17,200 audio/video tapes/CDs/DVDs, and subscribes to 40,741 periodicals including electronic. Computerized library services include interlibrary loans, database searching, Internet access, and Wi-Fi capability. Special learning facilities include a radio station. **Physically Challenged Students:** 15% of the campus is accessible. Facilities include wheelchair ramps, elevators, special parking, specially equipped restrooms, and lowered drinking fountains. **Special:** The university offers internships and work-study programs. There is 1 national honor society, a chapter of Phi Beta Kappa, a freshman honors program, and 5 departmental honors programs. **Visiting:** There are regularly scheduled orientations for prospective students. There are guides for informal visits, visitors may sit in on classes, and stay overnight. To schedule a visit, contact the Admissions Office. **Campus Safety and Security:** Measures include 24-hour foot and vehicle patrol. There are lighted pathways/sidewalks.

REQUIREMENTS: The ACT is required. The SAT is recommended. Students must have graduated from an accredited high school with at least a C average and have completed 15 1/2 units of a college prep curriculum. AP and CLEP credits are accepted. To graduate, students must complete at least 128 semester hours with a minimum GPA of 2.0. Core requirements include 12 hours of social science, 9 each of natural science and creative arts, 6 of English, 4 of phys ed or military science, and 3 each of math and oral communications, as well as 1 of student adjustment. **Procedure:** Freshmen are admitted to all sessions. Entrance exams should be taken so that scores may be submitted at the time application is made. There are early decision, deferred admissions, and rolling admissions plans. Application deadlines are open. Notification is sent on a rolling basis. **Transfer Students:** 286 transfer students enrolled in 2015-2016. Applicants must have at least 6 hours each of composition and lab sciences, 3 hours of college algebra or above, and 9 other transferable elective hours and must have maintained an overall minimum GPA of 2.0. 104 of 128 credits required for the bachelor's degree must be completed at Alcorn. **International Students:** There are 30 international students enrolled. The school actively recruits these students. They must take the TOEFL with a minimum score of 525 on the paper-based TOEFL (PBT). They must also take the SAT or ACT, scoring 21.

Admissions Contact: Emanuel F. Barnes, Director of Admissions. Email: *ebarnes@alcorn.edu* Web: *www.alcorn.edu*

FINANCIAL AID: In 2016-2017, 42% of all full-time freshmen received some form of financial aid. 31% of all full-time freshmen received need-based aid. The average freshman award was $6,199. Need-based scholarships or need-based grants averaged $3,974 ($4,310 maximum); need-based self-help aid (loans and jobs) averaged $3,308 ($3,500 maximum); non-need-based athletic scholarships averaged $9,192 ($14,696 maximum); and other non-need-based awards and non-need-based scholarships averaged $5,162 ($9,550 maximum). 27% of undergraduate students work part-time. Average annual earnings from campus work are $1700. The average financial indebtedness of the 2016 graduate was $22,842. Alcorn is a member of CSS. The college's own financial statement is required. Check with the school for current application deadlines.

BELHAVEN UNIVERSITY C-4

www.belhaven.edu

Jackson, MS 39202	(601) 968-5940 (800) 960-5940
Fax: (601) 968-8946	Email: admission@belhaven.edu
Full-time: 550 men, 782 women	Faculty: 108
Part-time: 358 men, 951 women	Ph.D.s: 63%
Graduate: 512 men, 1574 women	Student/Faculty: 8 to 1
Year: semesters, summer session	Tuition: $23,016
Room & Board: $8000	Freshman Class: 2465 applied, 1048 accepted, 236 enrolled
SAT CR/M: 540/515 ACT: 21	CEEB CODE: 1055
Application Deadline: August 12	COMPETITIVE

Belhaven University, founded in 1883, is a private liberal arts institution with a Presbyterian heritage. Figures in the above capsule and in this profile are approximate. There is 1 undergraduate school and 1 graduate school. In addition to regional accreditation, Belhaven has baccalaureate program accreditation with NASAD and NASM. The 42-acre campus is in an urban area in Jackson, MS. Including any residence halls, there are 19 buildings.

STUDENT LIFE: 69% of undergraduates are from Mississippi. Others are from 45 states, and 28 foreign countries. 59% are African American; 28% White; 6% race unknown; 3% Hispanic; 1% Asian American; 1% American Indian/Alaska Native; 1% Foreign; 1% two or more races. 65% are Protestant. **Female To Male Ratio:** 2.3:1. The average age of freshmen is 20; all undergraduates, 30. 34% do not continue beyond their first year; 51% remain to graduate. **Housing:** 718 students can be accommodated in college housing, which includes single-sex dorms and on-campus apartments. On-campus housing is guaranteed for all 4 years, and is available on a first-come, first-served basis. 78% of students commute. Alcohol is not permitted. All students may keep cars.

FACULTY/CLASSROOMS: 52% of faculty are male; 48% are female. All teach undergraduates. No introductory courses are taught by graduate students. The average class size in a regular course is 18.

PROGRAMS OF STUDY: Belhaven confers B.A., B.S., B.A.A., B.B.A., B.F.A., B.H.A., B.S.M., and B.S.N. degrees. Associate and master's degrees are also awarded. Bachelor's degrees are awarded in BIOLOGICAL SCIENCE (biology/biological science), BUSINESS (accounting and business administration and management), COMMUNICATIONS AND THE ARTS (art, arts administration/management, ballet, broadcasting, communications, creative writing, dance, dramatic arts, English, and music), COMPUTER AND PHYSICAL SCIENCE (chemistry, computer science, information sciences and systems, and mathematics), EDUCATION (athletic training and elementary education), HEALTH PROFESSIONS (exercise science, nursing, and sports medicine), SOCIAL SCIENCE (applied psychology, biblical studies, history, humanities, interdisciplinary studies, international studies, philosophy, political science/government, psychology, religious music, and social work). Biology, and chemistry are the strongest academically. Business administration, education, and social services have the largest enrollments.

ACTIVITIES: There are no fraternities or sororities. There are 24 groups on campus, including art, band, cheerleading, choir, chorus, dance, drama, ethnic, honors, jazz band, literary magazine, marching band, musical theater, newspaper, orchestra, political, professional, religious, social service, student government, and yearbook. Popular campus events include Singing Christmas Tree, Concert and Lecture Series, and Lake Day. **Sports:** There are 9 intercollegiate sports for men and 8 for women, and 6 intramural sports for men and 6 for women. Facilities include a gym, a lake, an intramural and soccer field, baseball field, football/soccer field, an athletic training facility, and an exercise, weight, and conditioning complex. **Graduates:** From July 1, 2015 to June 30, 2016, 572 bachelor's degrees were awarded. The most popular majors were business administration (33%), social sciences (12%), and fine arts (10%). 51 companies recruited on campus in 2015-2016. In an average class, 35% graduate in 4 years or less, 48% graduate in 5 years or less, and 49% graduate in 6 years or less.

SERVICES: Counseling and information services are available, as is tutoring in some subjects, such as writing, worldview, chemistry, physics, math, biology, and Bible. There is remedial math, reading, and writing. **Library/Resources:** The library contains 100,957 volumes, and 1,926 audio/video tapes/CDs/DVDs, and subscribes to 38,922 periodicals including electronic. Computerized library services include interlibrary loans, database searching, Internet access, and Wi-Fi capability. Special learning facilities include an art gallery. **Physically Challenged Students:** 90% of the campus is accessible. Facilities include wheelchair ramps, elevators, special parking, specially equipped restrooms, and special class scheduling. **Special:** Students may participate in various internships, including one in Washington, D.C., or in 6 countries through the study-travel program. Belhaven also offers accelerated degree programs, dual majors, student-designed majors, nondegree study, pass/fail options, a 3-2 engineering degree with Mississippi State University, and work-study. Two 1-month summer sessions and two 2-week minisessions offer additional opportunities for credit. There are 7 national honor societies, a freshman honors program, and 17 departmental honors programs. **Visiting:** There are regularly scheduled orientations for prospective students, including Preview Days, which allow students to see the campus, meet students, interview with faculty and admissions, and attend classes. There are guides for informal visits, visitors may sit in on classes, and stay overnight. To schedule a visit, contact the Admissions Office. **Campus Safety and Security:** Measures include 24-hour foot and vehicle patrol and security escort services. There are lighted pathways/sidewalks and controlled access to dorms/residences.

REQUIREMENTS: The SAT or ACT is recommended. Applicants should be graduates of an accredited secondary school, with 16 academic units, including 4 of English, 2 of math, 1 each of history and natural science, a recommended 2 of a foreign language, and 6 of electives. A personal recommendation and essay are also required. AP and CLEP credits are accepted. Requirements for graduation vary by degree, but students must complete at least 124 semester hours, including 25 hours of World View Curriculum courses, with a minimum 2.0 GPA. **Procedure:** Freshmen are admitted to all sessions. Entrance exams should be taken in the junior year. There is a rolling admissions plan. Applications should be filed by August 12 for fall entry, along with a $25 fee. Applications are accepted on-line. **Transfer Students:** 491 transfer students enrolled in 2015-2016. Transfer applicants must have a minimum 2.0 GPA and submit all college transcripts. 31 of 124 credits required for the bachelor's degree must be completed at Belhaven. **International Students:** There are 74 international students enrolled. They must take the TOEFL. They must also take the SAT or ACT.

ADMISSIONS: 43% of the 2016-2017 applicants were accepted. The SAT scores for the 2016-2017 freshman class were: Critical Reading-- 32% below 500, 35% between 500 and 599, and 33% between 600 and 699. Math-- 40% below 500, 46% between 500 and 599, and 14% between 600 and 699. The ACT scores were 3% between 12 and 17, 65% between 18 and 23, 28% between 24 and 29, and 4% above 30. 32% of the current freshmen were in the top fifth of their class; 60% were in the top two fifths. **Admissions Contact:** Suzanne Sullivan, Assistant VP for University Advancement. Email: *admission@belhaven.edu* Web: *www.belhaven.edu*

FINANCIAL AID: In 2016-2017, 94% of all full-time freshmen and 96% of continuing full-time students received some form of financial aid. 90% of all full-time freshmen and 92% of continuing full-time students received need-based aid. The average freshman award was $17,514. Need-based scholarships or need-based grants averaged $4,595 ($10,250 maximum); need-based self-help aid (loans and jobs) averaged $2,761 ($3,500 maximum); other non-need-based awards and non-need-based scholarships averaged $4,426 ($11,236 maximum); and $5,632 from other forms of aid. 21% of undergraduate students work part-time. Average annual earnings from campus work are $2400. The average financial indebtedness of the 2016 graduate was $23,419. The FAFSA code is 002397. The priority date for freshman financial aid applications for fall entry is March 1.

BLUE MOUNTAIN COLLEGE D-1
www.bmc.edu

Blue Mountain, MS 38610	(662) 685-4771 (800) 235-0136
Fax: (662) 685-4776	Email: lgibson@bmc.edu
Full-time: 231 men, 264 women	**Faculty:** 34
Part-time: 13 men, 36 women	**Ph.D.s:** 82%
Graduate: 3 men, 24 women	**Student/Faculty:** 15 to 1
Year: semesters, summer session	**Tuition:** $10,185
Room & Board: $5764	**Freshman Class:** 386 applied, 185 accepted, 111 enrolled
SAT CR/M/W: 555/480/495 **ACT:** 21	**CEEB CODE:** 1066
Application Deadline: n/av	**VERY COMPETITIVE**

Blue Mountain College is a Christian liberal arts institution supported by the Mississippi Baptist Convention. Deeply committed to the education of its students since its founding in 1873, the College has continued to attract capable, confident students who desire to pursue knowledge through a Christian worldview in a caring, person-centered environment. There is 1 undergraduate school and 1 graduate school. In addition to regional accreditation, BMC has baccalaureate program accreditation with MCC, Board of Trustees/State Institutions Higher Learning, and MS Commission on Teacher/Admin.Licensure/Certificate. The 190-acre campus is in a rural area 35 miles from Tupelo, MS, and 65 miles from Memphis, TN. Including any residence halls, there are 23 buildings.

STUDENT LIFE: 78% of undergraduates are from Mississippi. Others are from 15 states, 10 foreign countries, and Canada. 88% are from public schools. 83% are White; 2% Hispanic; 2% Foreign; 2% two or more races; 10% African American; 1% American Indian/Alaska Native. 95% are Protestant. **Female To Male Ratio:** 1.3:1. The average age of freshmen is 19; all undergraduates, 23. 31% do not continue beyond their first year; 55% remain to graduate. **Housing:** 346 students can be accommodated in college housing, which includes single-sex dorms. On-campus housing is available on a first-come, first-served basis. 59% of students live on campus; of those, 30% remain on campus on weekends. Alcohol is not permitted. All students may keep cars.

FACULTY/CLASSROOMS: 46% of faculty are male; 54% are female. 98% teach undergraduates. No introductory courses are taught by graduate students. The average class size in an introductory lecture is 20; in a laboratory is 18; and in a regular course is 15.

PROGRAMS OF STUDY: BMC confers B.A., B.S., and B.S.Ed. degrees. Master's degrees are also awarded. Bachelor's degrees are awarded in BIOLOGICAL SCIENCE (biology/biological science), BUSINESS (business administration and management), COMMUNICATIONS AND THE ARTS (church music, English, fine arts, and music), COMPUTER AND PHYSICAL SCIENCE (mathematics), EDUCATION (elementary education, English education, mathematics education, music education, physical education, science education, social science education, and Spanish adolescense education), HEALTH PROFESSIONS (exercise science and medical technology), SOCIAL SCIENCE (biblical studies, Christian studies, criminal justice, history, liberal arts/general studies, psychology, and Spanish studies). Elementary education, biology, and business administration are the strongest academically. Elementary education, business administration, and psychology have the largest enrollments.

ACTIVITIES: There are no fraternities or sororities. There are 31 groups on campus, including art, band, cheerleading, choir, chorale, chorus, drama, honors, literary magazine, musical theater, pep band, professional, religious, social, student government, and yearbook. Popular campus events include Society Rush, Founder's Day, Homecoming on the Hill, Ministerial Alumni Day, Homecoming, and Topper Fest. **Sports:** There are 6 intercollegiate sports for men and 6 for women, and 8 intramural sports for men and 9 for women. The athletic and recreation facilities are a gymnasium, swimming pool, a fitness center, and sportsplex. **Graduates:** From July 1, 2015 to June 30, 2016, 115 bachelor's degrees were awarded. The most popular majors were psychology (18%), business administration (18%), and elementary education (14%). 21 companies recruited on campus in 2015-2016. In an average class, 1% graduate in 3 years or less, 37% graduate in 4 years or less, 49% graduate in 5 years or less, and 50% graduate in 6 years or less. Of the 2015 graduating class, 19% were enrolled in graduate school within 6 months of graduation, and 80% were employed.

SERVICES: Counseling and information services are available, as is tutoring in every subject. There is remedial math, reading, and writing. **Library/Resources:** The 2 libraries contain 80,354 volumes, 1 microform items, and 1,474 audio/video tapes/CDs/DVDs, and subscribe to 146 periodicals including electronic. Computerized library services include interlibrary loans, database searching, Internet access, and Wi-Fi capability. **Physically Challenged Students:** All of the campus is accessible. Facilities include wheelchair ramps, elevators, special parking, specially equipped restrooms, special class scheduling, lowered drinking fountains, and special housing. **Special:** The College offers dual majors and internships (maximum 6 credits); consortial relationship with Union University resulting in dual degrees in Biology/Nursing, Psychology/Nursing; a consortial relationship with Baptist Memorial College of Health Sciences resulting in dual degrees in Biology/Nursing, Biology/Diagnostic Medical Sonography, Biology/Medical Laboratory Technology, Biology/Medical Radiography, Biology/Nuclear Medicine Technology, Biology/Radiation Therapy, Biology/Respiratory Care and a joint program in Business Administration with concentration in Health Care Management; two online degree programs: Business Administration and Psychology. The College offers a Junior-Senior Honors Program. There are 8 national honor societies and 8 departmental honors programs. **Visiting:** There are regularly scheduled orientations for prospective students, first-year experience, and a designated orientation time set aside for transfers prior to first class day. There are guides for informal visits, visitors may sit in on classes, and stay overnight. To schedule a visit, contact Nancy McDonald at (662) 685-4771. **Campus Safety and Security:** Measures include 24-hour foot and vehicle patrol and emergency notification system. There are lighted pathways/sidewalks and controlled access to dorms/residences.

REQUIREMENTS: The SAT or ACT is required. BMC recommends that applicants for admission have completed 4 units of English, 3 each of math, science, and social studies, and 2 of a foreign language. AP and CLEP credits are accepted. Important factors in the admissions decision are ability to finance college education, recommendations by alumni, and recommendations by school officials. All students must take a minimum of 120 semester hours, with a minimum of 40 hours on the junior-senior level; 25% of total degree hours required must be earned at Blue Mountain. No more than 42 hours of course work carrying the same prefix may be credited toward the degree (with few exceptions). Core curriculum requirements include 12 semester hours of English, 6 each of history and biblical studies, 4 of biological science, 3 each of psychology, fine arts, math, physical science, computer applications, and electives, and 2 of phys ed. A 2.0 GPA overall is required (2.5 for teacher education). Most degrees require a minor. **Procedure:** Freshmen are admitted to all sessions. Entrance exams should be taken during junior or senior year. There are deferred admissions and rolling admissions plans. Application deadlines are open. Applications are accepted on-line. **Transfer Students:** 137 transfer students enrolled in 2015-2016. Transfer students who have been enrolled in other colleges must submit official transcripts from each college attended and must be eligible to re-enter the last college attended. A maximum of 70 semester hours of credit may be transferred from a community or junior college. 30 of 120 credits required for the bachelor's degree must be completed at BMC. **International Students:** There are 9 international students enrolled. The school actively recruits these students. They must take the TOEFL with a minimum score of 500 on the paper-based TOEFL (PBT) or 61 on the Internet-based version (iBT). They must also take the SAT or ACT.

ADMISSIONS: 48% of the 2016-2017 applicants were accepted. 31% of the current freshmen were in the top fifth of their class; 62% were in the top two fifths. 3 freshmen graduated first in their class. **Admissions Contact:** Lynn Gibson, Vice President for Enrollment Services. Email: *lgibson@bmc.edu* Web: *www.bmc.edu*

FINANCIAL AID: In 2016-2017, 100% of all full-time freshmen and 97% of continuing full-time students received some form of financial aid. 64% of all full-time freshmen and 61% of continuing full-time students received need-based aid. The average freshman award was $13,047. Need-based scholarships or need-based grants averaged $5,011 ($6,215 maximum); need-based self-help aid (loans and jobs) averaged $3,125 ($5,124 maximum); non-need-based athletic scholarships averaged $5,003 ($15,282 maximum); and other non-need-based awards and non-need-based scholarships averaged $6,534 ($19,000 maximum). 17% of undergraduate students work part-time. Average annual earnings from campus work are $1157. The average financial indebtedness of the 2016 graduate was $15,256. The FAFSA code is 002398. The priority date for freshman financial aid applications for fall entry is April 1. The deadline for filing freshman financial aid applications for fall entry is December 1.

DELTA STATE UNIVERSITY C-2
www.deltastate.edu

Cleveland, MS 38733 (662) 846-4020
(800) 468-6378
Fax: (662) 846-4683 Email: admissions@deltastate.edu

Full-time: 936 men, 1326 women	**Faculty:** 182; IIA
Part-time: 128 men, 269 women	**Ph.D.s:** 76%
Graduate: 242 men, 559 women	**Student/Faculty:** 12 to 1
Year: semesters, summer session	**Tuition:** $6112
Room & Board: $7064	**Freshman Class:** 845 applied, 735 accepted
SAT CR/M: 510/475 **ACT:** required	**CEEB CODE:** 1163
Application Deadline: August 1	**COMPETITIVE**

Delta State University, founded in 1924, is a public liberal arts institution offering degrees in arts and sciences, business, education, and nursing. Figures in the above capsule and in this profile are approximate. There are 4 undergraduate schools and 4 graduate schools. In addition to regional accreditation, DSU has baccalaureate program accreditation with ACBSP, CSWE, NASAD, NASM, NCATE, AABI, AAFCS, ACEND, ACS, CAATE, CACREP, CCNE, MDE, and NASPE. The 274-acre campus is in a small town 110 miles south of Memphis, TN, and 130 miles north of Jackson. Including any residence halls, there are 80 buildings.

STUDENT LIFE: 85% of undergraduates are from Mississippi. Others are from 40 states, 37 foreign countries, and Canada. 62% are White; 34% African American; 2% Hispanic; 1% Asian American; 1% two or more races; 1% race unknown. **Female To Male Ratio:** 1.6:1. The average age of freshmen is 19; all undergraduates, 23. 41% do not continue beyond their first year; 41% remain to graduate. **Housing:** 1094 students can be accommodated in college housing, which includes single-sex and coed dorms, on-campus apartments, and married student housing. On-campus housing is available on a first-come, first-served basis. 64% of students commute. Alcohol is not permitted. All students may keep cars.

FACULTY/CLASSROOMS: 44% of faculty are male; 56% are female. 90% teach undergraduates. No introductory courses are taught by graduate students. The average class size in an introductory lecture is 42; in a laboratory is 22; and in a regular course is 22.

PROGRAMS OF STUDY: DSU confers B.A., B.S., B.B.A., B.C.A., B.F.A., B.M., B.M.Ed., B.S.J.C., B.S.Ed., B.S.I.S., B.S.N. and B.S.W. degrees. Master's and doctoral degrees are also awarded. Bachelor's degrees are awarded in BIOLOGICAL SCIENCE (biology/biological science), BUSINESS (accounting, accounting (finance), business administration and management, management science, and marketing/retailing/merchandising), COMMUNICATIONS AND THE ARTS (art, English, music, and music business management), COMPUTER AND PHYSICAL SCIENCE (chemistry, computer information systems, digital arts/technology, and mathematics), EDUCATION (elementary education, English education, health and physical education, mathematics education, music education, and social science education), ENGINEERING AND ENVIRONMENTAL DESIGN (aviation administration/management, aviation flight technology, and environmental science), HEALTH PROFESSIONS (health care administration, nursing, and speech pathology/audiology), SOCIAL SCIENCE (criminal justice, family/consumer studies, history, interdisciplinary studies, political science/government, psychology, social science, and social work). Entertainment industry studies, commercial aviation, and nursing are the strongest academically. Elementary education, biology, and health have the largest enrollments.

ACTIVITIES: 16% of men belong to 9 national fraternities; 17% of women belong to 6 national sororities. There are 91 groups on campus, including art, band, cheerleading, choir, chorale, chorus, computers, dance, debate, drama, environmental, ethnic, film, honors, international, jazz band, LGBT, literary magazine, marching band, musical theater, newspaper, opera, orchestra, Pageant Board and Programming Council, pep band, photography, political, professional, radio and TV, religious, social, social service, student government, and yearbook. Popular campus events include Welcome Week, Pig Pickin', Homecoming, Springfest, and Go Green Weekend. **Sports:** There are 8 intercollegiate sports for men and 7 for women, and 28 intramural sports for men and 28 for women. Facilities include a coliseum, indoor pool, gym, baseball field, baseball practice center, softball field, soccer field, football stadium, student performance center, 9-hole golf course, outdoor tennis courts, 4 racquetball courts, 2 intramural fields, outdoor walking facility, and fitness center. **Graduates:** From July 1, 2015 to June 30, 2016, 503 bachelor's degrees were awarded. The most popular majors were elementary education (11%), family and consumer science (8%), and nursing (8%). In an average class, 2% graduate in 3 years or less, 17% graduate in 4 years or less, 31% graduate in 5 years or less, and 34% graduate in 6 years or less.

SERVICES: Counseling and information services are available, as is tutoring in every subject. There is remedial math, reading, and writing. **Library/Resources:** The library contains 374,284 volumes, 832,822 microform items, and 20,028 audio/video tapes/CDs/DVDs, and subscribes to 24,018 periodicals including electronic. Computerized library services include interlibrary loans, database searching, and Internet access. Special learning facilities include an art gallery, natural history museum, planetarium, radio station, and a performing arts center. **Physically Challenged Students:** 95% of the campus is accessible. Facilities include wheelchair ramps, elevators, special parking, specially equipped restrooms, special class scheduling, lowered drinking fountains, lowered telephones, and special housing. **Special:** Internships are degree requirements for several majors such as athletic training, family and consumer sciences and others. DSU also offers an interdisciplinary studies degree as well as a few special non-degree certification programs. There are 33 national honor societies and a freshman honors program. **Visiting:** There are regularly scheduled orientations for prospective students, including campus tours and introduction to faculty and staff. There are guides for informal visits, visitors may sit in on classes, and stay overnight. To schedule a visit, contact the Undergraduate Admissions Office. **Campus Safety and Security:** Measures include 24-hour foot and vehicle patrol, emergency notification system, self-defense education, and security escort services. There are emergency telephones, lighted pathways/sidewalks, and controlled access to dorms/residences.

REQUIREMENTS: The ACT is required. Students may gain admission by completing the college prep curriculum with a minimum 3.2 GPA; by completing the college prep curriculum with a minimum of 2.5 GPA and scoring at least 16 on the ACT (650 on the SAT) by ranking in the upper 50% of the class and scoring at least 16 on the ACT (650 on the SAT); or by completing the college prep curriculum with a minimum 2.0 GPA and scoring 18 or higher on the ACT (740 on the SAT). The Nelson Denny Reading Test and Math Placement Test must also be taken. Applicants must be graduates of an accredited secondary school or have the GED. They should have completed 4 courses in English, 3 each in math, science, and social studies, 2 each in a foreign language, world geography, or additional science/math, and .5 in computer applications. AP and CLEP credits are accepted. To graduate, students must complete 124 to 130 semester hours, including 30 to 74 in the major, depending on the program, with a minimum GPA of 2.0. General education requirements include 6 hours of English composition, 3 hours each of communication studies and mathematics, 12 hours of humanities and fine arts, minimum of 6 hours lab science, 6 hours of perspectives on society and 2 hours minimum of personal development. In addition, all students must satisfy a writing proficiency requirement. **Procedure:** Freshmen are admitted to all sessions. Entrance exams should be taken as early as possible. There is a rolling admissions plan. Applications should be filed by August 1 for fall entry; January 1 for spring entry. The fall 2016 application fee was $25. Applications are accepted on-line. **Transfer Students:** 485 transfer students enrolled in 2015-2016. A minimum GPA of 2.0 is required, as is an associate degree and ACT or SAT scores; students must be in good standing with last college or university attended. 30 of 124 credits required for the bachelor's degree must be completed at DSU. **International Students:** There are 106 international students enrolled. They must take the TOEFL with a minimum score of 525 on the paper-based TOEFL (PBT) or 70 on the Internet-based version (iBT), and take the IELTS. They must also take the SAT or ACT, scoring SAT=770(Math+Reading) ACT=16 (Composite).

ADMISSIONS: The SAT scores for the 2016-2017 freshman class were: Critical Reading-- 38% below 500, 38% between 500 and 599, 13% between 600 and 699, and 13% between 700 and 800. Math-- 63% below 500, 25% between 600 and 699, and 13% between 700 and 800. The ACT scores were 23% between 12 and 17, 59% between 18 and 23, 15% between 24 and 29, and 2% above 30. **Admissions Contact:** Debbie Heslep, Dean of Enrollment Management. Email: *admissions@deltastate.edu* Web: *www.deltastate.edu*

FINANCIAL AID: In 2016-2017, 82% of all full-time freshmen and 93% of continuing full-time students received some form of financial aid. 52% of all full-time freshmen and 63% of continuing full-time students received need-based aid. The average freshman award was $6,735. Need-based scholarships or need-based grants averaged $3,406 ($5,753 maximum); need-based self-help aid (loans and jobs) averaged $2,070 ($3,500 maximum); non-need-based athletic scholarships averaged $1,990 ($6,571 maximum); and other non-need-based awards and non-need-based scholarships averaged $3,451 ($19,145 maximum). 8% of undergraduate students work part-time. Average annual earnings from campus work are $1017. The average financial indebtedness of the 2016 graduate was $27,089. The FAFSA code is 002403. The deadline for filing freshman financial aid applications for fall entry is March 1.

JACKSON STATE UNIVERSITY *(The complete profile is made available exclusively on our website, www.barronspac.com)*

MILLSAPS COLLEGE C-4

www.millsaps.edu

Jackson, MS 39210 (601) 974-1050
(800) 352-1050

Fax: (601) 974-1059 **Email: admissions@millsaps.edu**

Full-time: 384 men, 346 women	**Faculty:** 86; IIB, av$
Part-time: 5 men, 9 women	**Ph.D.s:** 95%
Graduate: 41 men, 19 women	**Student/Faculty:** 8 to 1
Year: semesters, summer session	**Tuition:** $37,110
Room & Board: $12,970	**Freshman Class:** 1901 applied, 902 accepted, 171 enrolled
SAT CR/M: 540/560 **ACT:** 26	**CEEB CODE:** 1471
Application Deadline: rolling	**COMPETITIVE+**

Millsaps College, founded in 1890, is an independent liberal arts institution affiliated with the United Methodist Church. Millsaps College is known for its academic strength, national-caliber faculty, small class size, and spirit of community service. Figures in the above capsule and in this profile are approximate. There are 4 undergraduate schools and 1 graduate school. In addition to regional accreditation, Millsaps has baccalaureate program accreditation with AACSB, NCATE, and ACS. The 100-acre campus is in an urban area in the capital city of Jackson. Including any residence halls, there are 33 buildings.

STUDENT LIFE: 58% of undergraduates are from out of state, mostly the South. Students are from 25 states, 14 foreign countries, and Canada. 61% are from public schools. 76% are White; 5% Asian American; 3% Foreign; 3% race unknown; 2% Hispanic; 10% African American; 1% American Indian/Alaska Native. 51% claim no religious affiliation; 33% Protestant; 14% Catholic. **Male To Female Ratio:** 1.1:1. The average age of freshmen is 18; all undergraduates, 20. 21% do not continue beyond their first year; 67% remain to graduate. **Housing:** 950 students can be accommodated in college housing, which includes single-sex and coed dorms. In addition, there are special-interest houses, fraternity houses, designated housing for freshmen, special housing for disabled students, and a service learning residence hall dedicated to community service and leadership. On-campus housing is available on a first-come, first-served basis, and is available on a lottery system for upperclassmen. 88% of students live on campus; of those, 75% remain on campus on weekends. All students may keep cars.

FACULTY/CLASSROOMS: 50% of faculty are male; 50% are female. All teach undergraduates, 90% do research, and 90% do both. No introductory courses are taught by graduate students. The average class size in an introductory lecture is 20; in a laboratory is 20; and in a regular course is 13.

PROGRAMS OF STUDY: Millsaps confers B.A., B.S., and B.B.A. degrees. Master's degrees are also awarded. Bachelor's degrees are awarded in BIOLOGICAL SCIENCE (biochemistry, biology/biological science, and neurosciences), BUSINESS (accounting and business administration and management), COMMUNICATIONS AND THE ARTS (art history and appreciation, classics, communications, creative writing, English, music, Spanish, and studio art), COMPUTER AND PHYSICAL SCIENCE (applied mathematics, chemistry, geology, mathematics, and physics), EDUCATION (education), SOCIAL SCIENCE (anthropology, economics, European studies, history, Latin American studies, philosophy, political science/government, psychology, public administration, religion, and sociology). Biology, chemistry, and premed are the strongest academically. Business administration, biology and psychology have the largest enrollments.

ACTIVITIES: 60% of men belong to 6 national fraternities; 64% of women belong to 4 national sororities. There are 80 groups on campus, including art, cheerleading, choir, chorale, chorus, computers, dance, debate, drama, environmental, ethnic, honors, international, LGBT, literary magazine, musical theater, newspaper, pep band, photography, political, professional, religious, social, social service, student government, and yearbook. Popular campus events include Major Madness, Project Midtown, and Homecoming. **Sports:** There are 9 intercollegiate sports for men and 9 for women, and 9 intramural sports for men and 9 for women. Facilities include a 63,300-square-foot activities center containing a fitness center with basketball and volleyball courts, a cardio theater, an aerobics room, fitness and weight-training equipment, a free-weight room, an outdoor pool, racquetball and handball courts, and a squash court. Outdoor areas include 6 tennis courts, a sand volleyball court, and softball, baseball, football, soccer, and multipurpose fields. **Graduates:** From July 1, 2015 to June 30, 2016, 202 bachelor's degrees were awarded. The most popular majors were biology (13%), accounting (13%), and business administration (12%). 276 companies recruited on campus in 2015-2016. In an average class, 1% graduate in 3 years or less, 62% graduate in 4 years or less, 66% graduate in 5 years or less, and 67% graduate in 6 years or less. Of the 2015 graduating class, 40% were enrolled in graduate school within 6 months of graduation, and 33% were employed.

SERVICES: Counseling and information services are available, as is tutoring in most subjects, by request, as needed. There is a writing center, a language lab, and math lab. **Library/Resources:** The library contains 200,396 volumes, 35,525 microform items, and 8,984 audio/video tapes/CDs/DVDs, and subscribes to 38,588 periodicals including electronic. Computerized library services include interlibrary loans, database searching, Internet access, and Wi-Fi capability. Special learning facilities include an art gallery, an observatory, a multi-disciplinary laboratory, and a molecular biology/functional genomics research lab. **Physically Challenged Students:** 90% of the campus is accessible. Facilities include wheelchair ramps, elevators, special parking, specially equipped restrooms, special class scheduling, lowered drinking fountains, lowered telephones, and special housing. Other needs can be addressed through the ADA coordinator on an individual basis. **Special:** Millsaps sponsors international studies programs in Africa, Asia, Europe, and Latin America. Direct exchange options are offered in Japan and Ireland. Students may also participate in a wide variety of field research, honors, internship, fellowships, and service learning programs. There are 28 national honor societies, Phi Beta Kappa, and 19 departmental honors programs. **Visiting:** There are regularly scheduled orientations for prospective students, including meetings with faculty and student services personneland tours of the campus. There are guides for informal visits, visitors may sit in on classes, and stay overnight. To schedule a visit, contact the Admissions Office. **Campus Safety and Security:** Measures include 24-hour foot and vehicle patrol, emergency notification system, self-defense education, and security escort services. There are emergency telephones, lighted pathways/sidewalks, controlled access to dorms/residences, and controlled access to all buildings during specified hours; entrances to campus are gated and staffed at night.

REQUIREMENTS: The SAT or ACT is required. Applicants should be graduates of an accredited secondary school or have a GED certificate, and have completed at least 14 academic units, including 4 in English, 3 in math, 2 in social studies, and 2 in histroy. An essay is required. AP and CLEP credits are accepted. Important factors in the admissions decision are advanced placement or honors courses, extracurricular activities record, and recommendations by school officials. To graduate, students must complete 128 credit hours with 32 to 48 hours in the major and a minimum GPA of 2.0. The core curriculum includes 4 interdisciplinary courses in humanities and 4 in the sciences and math. Students must also take Introduction to Liberal Studies during the freshman year and Reflections on Liberal Studies during the senior year. Other requirements include satisfactory completion of a 7-paper writing proficiency portfolio and a comprehensive exam in the specific field of study. **Procedure:** Freshmen are admitted fall and spring. Entrance exams should be taken in the spring of the junior year or fall of the senior year. There are early admissions, deferred admissions, and rolling admissions plans. Early decision applications should be filed by January 12. Notification is sent on a rolling basis. Applications are accepted on-line. **Transfer Stu-**

dents: 36 transfer students enrolled in 2015-2016. Applicants must have a minimum GPA of 2.75 and be in good standing at their previous school. Requirements include high school and college transcripts, an essay or personal statement, and ACT or SAT scores. 32 of 128 credits required for the bachelor's degree must be completed at Millsaps. **International Students:** There are 23 international students enrolled. The school actively recruits these students. They must take the TOEFL with a minimum score of 550 on the paper-based TOEFL (PBT) or 80 on the Internet-based version (iBT), or take the IELTS. The SAT or ACT are accepted in lieu of the TOEFL.

ADMISSIONS: 47% of the 2016-2017 applicants were accepted. The SAT scores for the 2016-2017 freshman class were: Critical Reading-- 25% below 500, 39% between 500 and 599, 28% between 600 and 699, and 8% between 700 and 800. Math-- 17% below 500, 47% between 500 and 599, 33% between 600 and 699, and 3% between 700 and 800. The ACT scores were 9% below 12, 23% between 12 and 17, 27% between 18 and 23, 18% between 24 and 29, and 23% above 30. 48% of the current freshmen were in the top fifth of their class; 79% were in the top two fifths. 6 freshmen graduated first in their class. **Admissions Contact:** Catherine Box, Director of Admissions. Email: *admissions@millsaps.edu* Web: *www.millsaps.edu*

FINANCIAL AID: In 2016-2017, 99% of all full-time freshmen and 98% of continuing full-time students received some form of financial aid. 67% of all full-time freshmen and 57% of continuing full-time students received need-based aid. The average freshman award was $30,461. Need-based scholarships or need-based grants averaged $24,248 ($44,890 maximum); need-based self-help aid (loans and jobs) averaged $8,358 ($28,790 maximum); and other non-need-based awards and non-need-based scholarships averaged $20,865 ($44,890 maximum). 76% of undergraduate students work part-time. The average financial indebtedness of the 2016 graduate was $27,926. The FAFSA code is 002414. The priority date for freshman financial aid applications for fall entry is March 1.

MISSISSIPPI COLLEGE — C-4

www.mc.edu

Clinton, MS 39058	(601) 925-3800
Fax: (601) 925-3950	**Email:** kylebrantley@mc.edu
Full-time: n/av	**Faculty:** IIA, -$
Part-time: n/av	**Ph.D.s:** n/av
Graduate: n/av	**Student/Faculty:** n/av
Year: semesters, summer session	**Tuition:** $16,660
Room & Board: $9190	**Freshman Class:** 3050 applied, 1827 accepted, 585 enrolled
SAT CR/M: 550/520 **ACT:** 24	**CEEB CODE:** 1477
Application Deadline: open	**COMPETITIVE**

Mississippi College, founded in 1826 and affiliated with the Southern Baptist Church, is a private institution offering degrees in liberal arts, business, education, and health sciences. The figures in the above capsule and in this profile are approximate. There are 6 undergraduate schools and 8 graduate schools. In addition to regional accreditation, MC has baccalaureate program accreditation with ACBSP, CSWE, NASM, and NCATE. The 320-acre campus is in a suburban area 15 minutes outside of Jackson, MS. Including any residence halls, there are 30 buildings.

STUDENT LIFE: 60% of undergraduates are from Mississippi. Others are from 42 states, and 34 foreign countries. 94% are Protestant. The average age of freshmen is 18; all undergraduates, 24. **Housing:** 1800 students can be accommodated in college housing, which includes single-sex dorms, on-campus apartments, and off-campus apartments. On-campus housing is available on a first-come, first-served basis. 55% of students live on campus. Alcohol is not permitted. All students may keep cars.

FACULTY/CLASSROOMS: No introductory courses are taught by graduate students. The average class size in an introductory lecture is 30; in a laboratory is 25; and in a regular course is 25.

PROGRAMS OF STUDY: MC confers B.A., B.S., B.M., B.M.Ed., B.S.B.A., B.S.Ed., B.S.N., and B.S.W. degrees. Master's and doctoral degrees are also awarded. Bachelor's degrees are awarded in BIOLOGICAL SCIENCE (biochemistry and biology/biological science), BUSINESS (accounting, business administration and management, and marketing/retailing/merchandising), COMMUNICATIONS AND THE ARTS (applied music, art, communications, English, French, graphic design, languages, modern language, music, music theory and composition, piano/organ, Spanish, voice, and winds), COMPUTER AND PHYSICAL SCIENCE (chemistry, computer science, mathematics, and physics), EDUCATION (art education, business education, elementary education, music education, and special education), ENGINEERING AND ENVIRONMENTAL DESIGN (engineering physics and interior design), HEALTH PROFESSIONS (nursing), SOCIAL SCIENCE (American studies, Christian studies, criminal justice, family/consumer studies, history, paralegal studies, political science/government, psychology, religious music, social studies, social work, and sociology). Biology, chemistry, education, business, and nursing are the strongest academically. Business, kinesiology, and education have the largest enrollments.

ACTIVITIES: There are 70 groups on campus, including art, band, cheerleading, chess, choir, chorale, chorus, communications, computers, dance, debate, drama, environmental, ethnic, forensics, honors, international, jazz band, literary magazine, marching band, musical theater, newspaper, opera, pep band, political, professional, radio and TV, religious, social, social service, student government, symphony, and yearbook. Popular campus events include I Love America Day, Derby Day, and Spring Fever Week. **Sports:** There are 9 intercollegiate sports for men and 8 for women, and 8 intramural sports for men and 8 for women. Facilities include a coliseum, an 8300-seat stadium, tennis courts, soccer and softball fields, a swimming pool, 4000-seat gym, fitness facility, and a campus weight-training facility.

SERVICES: Counseling and information services are available, as is tutoring in most subjects, such as study skills classes. There is remedial math, reading, and writing. **Library/Resources:** The 2 libraries contain 370,404 volumes, 540,471 microform items, and 18,348 audio/video tapes/CDs/DVDs, and subscribe to 4,742 periodicals including electronic. Computerized library services include interlibrary loans, database searching, Internet access, and Wi-Fi capability. Special learning facilities include an art gallery, radio station, and TV station. **Physically Challenged Students:** Facilities include wheelchair ramps, elevators, special parking, specially equipped restrooms, special class scheduling, lowered drinking fountains, lowered telephones, and special housing. Wide doors and special dorm rooms equipped for the physically disabled. **Special:** MC also offers study abroad in up to 10 countries, a 3-3 program with the School of Law, work-study programs, internships, B.A.-B.S. degrees, and credit for military experience and by exam. There are 25 national honor societies and a freshman honors program. **Visiting:** There are regularly scheduled orientations for prospective students, Including attending classes, touring the campus, and meeting with administrators and departmental advisers. There are guides for informal visits, visitors may sit in on classes, and stay overnight. **Campus Safety and Security:** Measures include 24-hour foot and vehicle patrol, emergency notification system, self-defense education, and security escort services. There are shuttle buses, emergency telephones, lighted pathways/sidewalks, and controlled access to dorms/residences.

REQUIREMENTS: An official high school transcript and an official ACT and/or SAT score meeting our standard admission requirement must be submitted in order to be considered for admission. AP and CLEP credits are accepted. To graduate, students must complete 130 credit hours, with an average of C or better in the major. The core curriculum includes English, history, economics, computer science, religion, math, art, social science, phys ed, and chapel. 30 hours are usually required in the major; some majors require 36 to 45. Students must pass a writing proficiency exam. B.A. candidates and English majors must take 12 hours of a foreign language. **Procedure:** Freshmen are admitted fall, spring, and summer. Entrance exams should be taken by June prior to the fall semester. There is a rolling admissions plan. Application deadlines are open. Application fee is $25. Notification is sent on a rolling basis. Applications are accepted on-line. Application fees are waived if application is completed on-line. **Transfer Students:** 315 transfer students enrolled in 2015-2016. Applicants must be junior college graduates or students in good academic standing with the college they last attended. They must have a minimum GPA of 2.0. Applicants must submit transcripts from all schools previously attended. 33 of 130 credits required for the bachelor's degree must be completed at MC. **International Students:** There are 350 international students enrolled. The school actively recruits these students. They must take the TOEFL.

ADMISSIONS: 60% of the 2016-2017 applicants were accepted. There were 2 National Merit finalists. **Admissions Contact:** Kyle Brantley, Director of Admissions. Email: *kylebrantley@mc.edu* Web: *www.mc.edu*

FINANCIAL AID: In 2016-2017, 96% of all full-time freshmen and 95% of continuing full-time students received some form of financial aid. The FAFSA code is 002415. The priority date for freshman financial aid applications for fall entry is October 1.

MISSISSIPPI STATE UNIVERSITY E-3

www.msstate.edu

Mississippi State, MS 39762	(662) 325-2224
Fax: (662) 325-7360	Email: admit@msstate.edu
Full-time: 8344 men, 8351 women	Faculty: 385; I, --$
Part-time: 782 men, 612 women	Ph.D.s: 73%
Graduate: 1790 men, 1742 women	Student/Faculty: 43 to 1
Year: semesters, summer session	Tuition: $7780 ($20,900)
Room & Board: $3674	Freshman Class: 10162 applied, 9866 accepted, 3624 enrolled
SAT: required ACT: 24	CEEB CODE: 1480
Application Deadline: August 1	COMPETITIVE+

Mississippi State University is "The People's University". We have students from every state and many countries. MSU helps students prepare for success with nationally ranked academic programs, transformative leadership experiences, and abundant social opportunities. MSU is big enough to find your place, but small enough to feel like home. MSU has over 80 majors, and is ranked Top 100 in research schools. There are 9 undergraduate schools and 1 graduate school. In addition to regional accreditation, MSU has baccalaureate program accreditation with AACSB, ABET, ASLA, CSAB, FIDER, NAAB, NASAD, NASM, NCATE, SAF, ACCI, ACEND, AAHA, AAVLD, AAFCS, ACS, APA, AVMA, AAALAC, CACREP, CHEA, ASPA, NALP, NASPAA, NASP, and and SWST. The 4200-acre campus is in a small town 125 miles northeast of Jackson, MS.

STUDENT LIFE: 66% of undergraduates are from Mississippi. Others are from 50 states, 78 foreign countries, and Canada. 71% are White; 4% Foreign; 3% Hispanic; 2% two or more races; 19% African American; 1% Asian American. 44% are Jewish; 40% Catholic; 16% other religious affliation unknown. **Male To Female Ratio:** 1.0:1. The average age of freshmen is 19; all undergraduates, 22. 18% do not continue beyond their first year; 60% remain to graduate. **Housing:** 5250 students can be accommodated in college housing, which includes single-sex and coed dorms. In addition, there are special-interest houses. On-campus housing is guaranteed for the freshman year only, and is available on a first-come, first-served basis. 72% of students commute. Alcohol is not permitted. All students may keep cars.

FACULTY/CLASSROOMS: 59% of faculty are male; 41% are female. 36% teach undergraduates, 29% do research, and 20% do both. Graduate students teach 1% of introductory courses. The average class size in an introductory lecture is 25 and in a laboratory is 33.

PROGRAMS OF STUDY: MSU confers B.A., B.B.A, B.F.A., B.S., B.L.A., B.M.E., B.ARC., BACC, and B.S.W. degrees. Master's and doctoral degrees are also awarded. Bachelor's degrees are awarded in AGRICULTURE (agricultural business management, agricultural economics, agriculture, agronomy, animal science, fishing and fisheries, forestry production and processing, horticulture, plant protection (pest management), poultry science, and wildlife management), BIOLOGICAL SCIENCE (biochemistry, biology/biological science, and microbiology), BUSINESS (accounting, banking and finance, business administration and management, insurance, marketing/retailing/merchandising, real estate, and trade and industrial supervision and management), COMMUNICATIONS AND THE ARTS (art, communications, English, and languages), COMPUTER AND PHYSICAL SCIENCE (chemistry, computer science, geoscience, information sciences and systems, mathematics, physics, and science), EDUCATION (agricultural education, business education, education, elementary education, music education, physical education, secondary education, special education, and technical education), ENGINEERING AND ENVIRONMENTAL DESIGN (aerospace studies, agricultural engineering technology, architecture, bioengineering, chemical engineering, civil engineering, computer engineering, electrical/electronics engineering, industrial engineering, industrial engineering technology, landscape architecture/design, and mechanical engineering), HEALTH PROFESSIONS (medical technology), SOCIAL SCIENCE (anthropology, economics, food science, history, interdisciplinary studies, liberal arts/general studies, philosophy, political science/government, psychology, social work, and sociology). Accounting, biochemistry, and physics are the strongest academically. Engineering, business/marketing, and parks and recreation have the largest enrollments.

ACTIVITIES: 18% of men belong to 20 national fraternities; 25% of women belong to 13 national sororities. There are 386 groups on campus, including departmental/academic ambassador programs, art, band, chess, choir, communications, computers, dance, debate, drama, environmental, ethnic, fashion, film, forensics, honors, international, LGBT, literary magazine, marching band, musical theater, newspaper, pep band, photography, political, professional, radio and TV, religious, social, and student government. Popular campus events include Outdoor films, concerts, Salsa in the Streets, Magicians, comedy shows, and speakers. **Sports:** There are 7 intercollegiate sports for men and 9 for women, and 40 intramural sports for men and 40 for women. Facilities include a gym, an 1/8 mile jogging track, racquetball courts, a swimming pool, table tennis, strength and aerobic conditioning room, a climbing wall, aerobics/dancing studios, and training rooms, and soccer and multi-purpose fields.**Graduates:** From July 1, 2015 to June 30, 2016, 3692 bachelor's degrees were awarded. The most popular majors were kinesiology (9%), interdisciplinary studies (7%), and communication (5%). In an average class, 31% graduate in 4 years or less, 54% graduate in 5 years or less, and 60% graduate in 6 years or less.

SERVICES: Counseling and information services are available, as is tutoring in every subject, such as math, English, chemistry, physics, and study skills. There is a reader service for the blind, and remedial math, reading, and writing. There is also a writing effectiveness class, study assistance, preparation for professional exams and credit courses in reading and study skills. **Library/Resources:** The 3 libraries contain 2.6 million volumes, 3.5 million microform items, and 107,443 audio/video tapes/CDs/DVDs, and subscribe to 114,771 periodicals including electronic. Computerized library services include interlibrary loans, database searching, Internet access, and Wi-Fi capability. Special learning facilities include an art gallery, natural history museum, planetarium, radio station, TV station, Cullis & Gladys Wade Clock Museum, Dunn-Seiler Museum, Giles Hall Gallery, Lois Dowdle Cobb Museum, Mississippi Entomological Museum, and many others. **Physically Challenged Students:** 90% of the campus is accessible. Facilities include wheelchair ramps, elevators, special parking, specially equipped restrooms, special class scheduling, lowered drinking fountains, lowered telephones, special housing, and phones equipped with TTY in the union and library. **Special:** Cooperative education, cross-registration with the Academic Common Market, internships, and study abroad in 15 countries are offered. Work-study programs, a Washington semester, accelerated degree programs, a general studies degree, nondegree study, student-designed majors, B.A.-B.S. degrees, and pass/fail options for some courses are available. There are 27 national honor societies, a freshman honors program, and 2 departmental honors programs. **Visiting:** There are regularly scheduled orientations for prospective students, including 2-day sessions for freshmen, and 1-day session for transfers. There are guides for informal visits, visitors may sit in on classes, and stay overnight. To schedule a visit, contact Lindsey Norman at lcn32@msstate .edu. **Campus Safety and Security:** Measures include 24-hour foot and vehicle patrol, emergency notification system, self-defense education, and security escort services. There are shuttle buses, emergency telephones, lighted pathways/sidewalks, and controlled access to dorms/ residences.

REQUIREMENTS: The SAT or ACT is required. Applicants should have completed 16 1/2 high school academic credits, including 4 in English, 3 in math, 2 each in science with lab, and history, 1 each in academic electives, foreign language, social studies, visual/performing arts and 1/ 2 credit in the computer as a productivity tool (not keyboarding). Student must also have a minimum 3.2 GPA on required high school courses; 2.5 GPA on required high school classes or class standing in top 50% with an ACT score of 16 or higher/SAT I combined score of 750 or higher; 2.0 GPA on required high school classes with ACT score of 18 or higher/SAT I combined 840 or higher; or satisfy National Collegiate Athletic Association standards for student-athletes who are full qualifiers under Division I guidelines. Students with a GED are accepted with the required ACT/SAT I score. A GPA of 2.0 is required. AP and CLEP credits are accepted. To complete a baccalaureate degree, a student must (1) satisfactorily complete the degree curriculum requirements, (2) make an overall C average (2.00 GPA) on all hours scheduled and rescheduled at all institutions attended, including Mississippi State University, (3) make a C average (2.00 GPA) on all hours scheduled and rescheduled at Mississippi State University, (4) complete from Mississippi State University no less than 25 percent of his/her degree program in junior and senior subjects (courses numbered 3000 through 5000) approved by the dean of the college or school in which he or she is enrolled, and (5) complete at least the last 25 percent of semester credit hours of coursework taken to fulfill degree requirements from Mississippi State University. (Any exception to the 25 percent requirement must be approved in writing by the student's dean prior to taking course work at another institution.) Any course in the student's degree program that carries academic credit from Mississippi State University will fulfill these requirements. Hours earned at an approved exchange institution will count toward the 25 percent requirement. (6) Not more than 25 percent of any curriculum may be earned by Advanced Placement (AP) course, advanced standing examinations, College-Level Examination Program (CLEP), International Baccalaureate (IB), Cambridge International, evaluated military service credits, tutorial, and extension courses. Evaluated military training courses granted academic credit are classified as MSU (institutional) academic pass/fail credit with a grade of S and annotated as "ACE Guide Military Credit." Military training courses include all branches of the United States Armed Services, except the United States Air Force. The Air Force provides a Community College of the Air Force transcript and credit is entered as transfer courses. (7) Not more than 20 percent of any curriculum may be earned through correspondence courses. Correspondence courses must be approved by the dean before being taken by students in residence. USAFI credits are classified as correspondence work. (8) No more than 12 hours of Directed Individual Study (DIS) may be used to complete degree requirements. The creation of DIS courses must be approved in advance by the department head. (9) Prior job/work experience alone can not count as academic credit at MSU. **Procedure:** Freshmen are admitted fall, spring, and summer. Entrance exams should be taken in the spring of junior year or fall semester of senior year. There are deferred admissions and rolling admissions plans. Applications should be filed by August 1 for fall entry; November 15 for spring entry; and May 15 for summer entry, along with a $40 fee. Notification is sent on a rolling basis. Applications are accepted on-line. **Transfer Students:** 1832 transfer students enrolled in 2015-2016. Applicants must submit an official college transcript from each college attended, indicating a minimum GPA of 2.0 (some departments require 2.5) and must be in good standing at their previous school. Transfers may enroll in fall, spring, and summer. 30 of 124 credits required for the bachelor's degree must be completed at MSU. **International Students:** There are 232 international students enrolled. The school actively recruits these students. They must take the TOEFL with a minimum score of 525 on the paper-based TOEFL (PBT) or 71 on the Internet-based version (iBT). They must also take the SAT.

ADMISSIONS: 97% of the 2016-2017 applicants were accepted. The ACT scores were 5% between 12 and 17, 41% between 18 and 23, 39% between 24 and 29, and 15% above 30. 48% of the current freshmen were in the top fifth of their class; 27% were in the top two fifths. There were 36 National Merit finalists. 95 freshmen graduated first in their class. **Admissions Contact:** Crystal Sloan, Assistant Director of Admissions. Email: *admit@msstate.edu* Web: *www.msstate.edu*

FINANCIAL AID: In 2016-2017, 91% of all full-time freshmen and 86% of continuing full-time students received some form of financial aid. 50% of all full-time freshmen and 48% of continuing full-time students received need-based aid. The average freshman award was $14,012. Need-based scholarships or need-based grants averaged $6,108 ($15,277 maximum); need-based self-help aid (loans and jobs) averaged $3,879 ($13,494 maximum); non-need-based athletic scholarships averaged $21,188 ($49,822 maximum); and other non-need-based awards and non-need-based scholarships averaged $7,821 ($41,710 maximum). 24% of undergraduate students work part-time. Average annual earnings from campus work are $2727. The average financial indebtedness of the 2016 graduate was $36,561. The FAFSA code is 002423. The priority date for freshman financial aid applications for fall entry is April 1. The deadline for filing freshman financial aid applications for fall entry is May 1.

MISSISSIPPI UNIVERSITY FOR WOMEN E-2

www.muw.edu

Columbus, MS 39701	(662) 329-7106 (877) 462-8439
Fax: (662) 241-7481	**Email:** admissions@muw.edu
Full-time: 300 men, 1600 women	**Faculty:** IIA
Part-time: 300 men, 1000 women	**Ph.D.s:** 68%
Graduate: 20 men, 100 women	**Student/Faculty:** n/av
Year: semesters, summer session	**Tuition:** $7882 ($21,956)
Room & Board: $9183	**Freshman Class:** n/av
SAT or ACT: recommended	**CEEB CODE:** 1481
Application Deadline: open	**COMPETITIVE**

Mississippi University for Women (The W), founded in 1884, is a public institution offering degrees in liberal arts, education, business and communications, nursing, human sciences, science and math, health and kinesiology, and culinary arts. Figures in the above capsule and in this profile are approximate. There are 4 undergraduate schools and 4 graduate schools. In addition to regional accreditation, The W has baccalaureate program accreditation with ACBSP, NASAD, NASM, NCATE, and NLN. The 110-acre campus is in a small town 120 miles west of Birmingham, Alabama. Including any residence halls, there are 53 buildings.

STUDENT LIFE: 89% of undergraduates are from Mississippi. Others are from 20 states, 25 foreign countries, and Canada. 84% are from public schools. 70% are White; 27% African American; 2% Foreign; 1% Asian American. **Female To Male Ratio:** 4.4:1. The average age of freshmen is 19; all undergraduates, 29. 30% do not continue beyond their first year; 43% remain to graduate. **Housing:** 1100 students can be accommodated in college housing, which includes single-sex dorms, on-campus apartments, and married student housing. On-campus housing is available on a first-come, first-served basis. 77% of students commute. Alcohol is not permitted. All students may keep cars.

FACULTY/CLASSROOMS: 39% of faculty are male; 61% are female. 94% teach undergraduates. No introductory courses are taught by graduate students. The average class size in an introductory lecture is 35; in a laboratory is 23; and in a regular course is 25.

PROGRAMS OF STUDY: The W confers B.A., B.S., B.F.A., B.M., and B.S.N. degrees. Associate, master's, and doctoral degrees are also awarded. Bachelor's degrees are awarded in BIOLOGICAL SCIENCE (biology/biological science and microbiology), BUSINESS (accounting, business administration and management, and sports management), COMMUNICATIONS AND THE ARTS (communications, English, fine arts, music, and Spanish), COMPUTER AND PHYSICAL SCIENCE (chemistry, mathematics, and physical sciences), EDUCATION (art education, elementary education, and music education), HEALTH PROFESSIONS (nursing, public health, and speech pathology/audiology), SOCIAL SCIENCE (culinary arts, food production/management/services, history, paralegal studies, physical fitness/movement, political science/government, psychology, and social science). Biology, chemistry, and English are the strongest academically. Business, nursing, and elementary education have the largest enrollments.

ACTIVITIES: 10% of men belong to 2 local and 1 national fraternities; 20% of women belong to 12 local and 3 national sororities. There are 84 groups on campus, including art, band, choir, chorale, chorus, computers, dance, drama, ethnic, film, honors, international, jazz band, literary magazine, musical theater, newspaper, orchestra, photography, political, professional, radio and TV, religious, social, social service, student government, and yearbook. Popular campus events include Mardi Gras and Oktoberfest. **Sports:** There are 5 intramural sports for men and 5 for women. Facilities include a gym, tennis and racquetball courts, indoor swimming pool, a gymnastics room, weight room, dance studio, 3-hole pitch-and-putt golf course, soccer, and flag football field. **Graduates:** From July 1, 2015 to June 30, 2016, 617 bachelor's degrees were awarded. The most popular majors were nursing (40%), elementary education (7%), and general studies (7%).

SERVICES: Counseling and information services are available, as is tutoring in most subjects. There is remedial math, reading, and writing. **Library/Resources:** The library contains 232,638 volumes, 569,448 microform items, and 98 audio/video tapes/CDs/DVDs, and subscribes to 1,620 periodicals including electronic. Computerized library services include interlibrary loans and database searching. Special learning facilities include an art gallery, radio station, and a distance learning studio. **Physically Challenged Students:** 95% of the campus is accessible. Facilities include wheelchair ramps, elevators, special parking, specially equipped restrooms, special class scheduling, lowered drinking fountains, and lowered telephones. **Special:** Cross-registration and a 3-2 engineering degree are available with Mississippi State University. MUW also offers internships in all colleges, co-op and work-study programs, several combinations of dual majors, study abroad in 5 countries, credit for experience, nondegree study, and a pass/fail option. There are 15 national honor societies, a freshman honors program, and 3 departmental honors programs. **Visiting:** There are regularly scheduled orientations for prospective students, including talks with various student services officers and preregistration. There are guides for informal visits, visitors may sit in on classes, and stay overnight. To schedule a visit, contact the Director of Admissions. **Campus Safety and Security:** Measures include 24-hour foot and vehicle patrol and security escort services. There are lighted pathways/sidewalks, controlled access to dorms/residences, guard gates, and freshman orientation class.

REQUIREMENTS: The SAT or ACT is recommended. Prospective students should have completed 4 units of English; 3 each of math, science, and social studies courses in U.S. history, world history, government, and economics or geography; 2 of advanced electives, including foreign language or geography; and a course in computer applications. AP and CLEP credits are accepted. Important factors in the admissions decision are recommendations by school officials, leadership record, and advanced placement or honors courses. To graduate, students must complete 124 credit hours, including 30 to 39 in a major, with a minimum GPA of 2.0. The core curriculum requires 12 hours of English, 8 of lab-based science, 6 each of history and social sciences, 3 each of speech or philosophy, fine arts, and math, 1 each of phys ed, and a freshman seminar. **Procedure:** Freshmen are admitted to all sessions. Entrance exams should be taken as early as possible. There are early decision, early admissions, and rolling admissions plans. Application deadlines are open. The fall 2016 application fee was $25. **Transfer Students:** Applicants must have a GPA of 2.0 in 6 semester hours of both English composition and a lab science, 3 of college algebra or above, and 9 of transferable electives. High school and college transcripts are required. 32 of 128 credits required for the bachelor's degree must be completed at The W. **International Students:** The school actively recruits these students. They must take the TOEFL. They must also take the SAT or ACT, scoring 16.

Admissions Contact: Shelley Moss, Director of Admissions. Email: *admissions@muw.edu* Web: *www.muw.edu*

FINANCIAL AID: The W is a member of CSS. The FAFSA code is 002422. Check with the school for current application deadlines.

MISSISSIPPI VALLEY STATE UNIVERSITY *(The complete profile is made available exclusively on our website, www.barronspac.com)*

RUST COLLEGE — D-1

www.rustcollege.edu

Holly Springs, MS 38635	(662) 252-8000 (888) 886-8492
Fax: (662) 252-8895	Email: jmcsonald@rustcollege.edu
Full-time: 300 men, 550 women	**Faculty:** n/av
Part-time: 60 men, 105 women	**Ph.D.s:** 47%
Graduate: n/av	**Student/Faculty:** n/av
Year: semesters, summer session	**Tuition:** $7400
Room & Board: $3200	**Freshman Class:** n/av
SAT or ACT: required	**CEEB CODE:** 1669
Application Deadline: rolling	**COMPETITIVE**

Rust College, founded in 1866, is a private liberal arts college affiliated with the United Methodist Church. The academic year consists of semesters, each divided into two 8-week modules, plus a summer term. Figures in the above capsule and in this profile are approximate. There are 5 undergraduate schools. The 126-acre campus is in a small town 35 miles southeast of Memphis, Tennessee. Including any residence halls, there are 23 buildings.

STUDENT LIFE: 55% of undergraduates are from Mississippi. Others are from 24 states, and 6 foreign countries. 90% are from public schools. 93% are African American; 6% Foreign; 1% White. 60% are Protestant; 29% claim no religious affiliation. **Female To Male Ratio:** 1.8:1. The average age of freshmen is 19; all undergraduates, 22. 57% do not continue beyond their first year. **Housing:** 856 students can be accommodated in college housing, which includes single-sex dorms. In addition, there are honors houses. On-campus housing is guaranteed for all 4 years. 65% of students live on campus; of those, 50% remain on campus on weekends. Alcohol is not permitted. All students may keep cars.

FACULTY/CLASSROOMS: 67% of faculty are male; 33% are female. All teach undergraduates. No introductory courses are taught by graduate students. The average class size in an introductory lecture is 10; in a laboratory is 10; and in a regular course is 25.

PROGRAMS OF STUDY: Rust confers B.A., B.S., and B.S.W. degrees. Associate degrees are also awarded. Bachelor's degrees are awarded in BIOLOGICAL SCIENCE (biology/biological science), BUSINESS (business administration and management), COMMUNICATIONS AND THE ARTS (communications, English, journalism, and music), COMPUTER AND PHYSICAL SCIENCE (chemistry, computer science, and mathematics), EDUCATION (business education, elementary education, English education, mathematics education, science education, secondary education, and social science education), HEALTH PROFESSIONS (health), SOCIAL SCIENCE (political science/government, social work, and sociology). Business administration and management are the strongest academically. Biology, computer science, and social work have the largest enrollments.

ACTIVITIES: 2% of men belong to 3 local and 3 national fraternities; 6% of women belong to 4 local and 4 national sororities. There are 32 groups on campus, including band, cheerleading, choir, chorale, computers, drama, ethnic, honors, international, marching band, newspaper, political, radio and TV, religious, social, social service, and student government. Popular campus events include Career Day, Religious Emphasis Week, and African American Student Leadership Conference. **Sports:** There are 7 intercollegiate sports for men and 7 for women. Facilities include a gym, swimming pool, tennis courts, track, stadium, bowling alley, pool tables, and the Magic Johnson Sports Arena.

SERVICES: Counseling and information services are available, as is tutoring in most subjects. There is remedial math, reading, and writing. **Library/Resources:** The library contains 123,055 volumes, and 106 audio/video tapes/CDs/DVDs, and subscribes to 340 periodicals including electronic. Computerized library services include interlibrary loans, database searching, and Internet access. Special learning facilities include a radio station, TV station, and the Dr. Ron Trojak collection of African Tribal Art. **Physically Challenged Students:** All of the campus is accessible. Facilities include wheelchair ramps, elevators, special parking, specially equipped restrooms, and lowered drinking fountains. **Special:** Internships are available in all areas and may be required for some majors. On-campus work-study, study abroad, credit by examination, independent study, B.A.-B.S. degrees, and dual majors in a variety of programs are available. There are 3-2 degrees in preprofessional programs and medical technology and a 3-2 engineering degree with the student's school of choice. There are 3 national honor societies, a freshman honors program, and 5 departmental honors programs. **Visiting:** There are regularly scheduled orientations for prospective students, including a campus tour, departmental visits, introduction to the application process, financial aid orientation, and question-and-answer session. There are guides for informal visits, visitors may sit in on classes, and stay overnight. To schedule a visit, contact Enrollment Services. **Campus Safety and Security:** Measures include 24-hour foot and vehicle patrol and security escort services. There are lighted pathways/sidewalks.

REQUIREMENTS: The SAT or ACT is required. Students must submit 19 academic credits, including 4 in English, 3 each in math, science, and social studies, and 6 electives. An audition, interview, and 2 letters of recommendation are required. The GED is accepted. An essay and portfolio are recommended. AP and CLEP credits are accepted. Important factors in the admissions decision are evidence of special talent, extracurricular activities record, and recommendations by school officials. All students must earn a minimum of 124 semester hours while maintaining a cumulative GPA of 2.0. Distribution requirements include 59 1/2 general education credits in the fields of education, humanities, science, and math and a required freshman program. A minimum of 50 credits constitutes a major, and comprehensive exams are given in all programs. Required courses in addition to the freshman program include math, biology, physical science, computer science, English, foreign language, literature, speech, social science, and history. **Procedure:** Freshmen are admitted fall, spring, and summer. Entrance exams should be taken prior to the first semester of the freshman year. There is a rolling admissions plan. Check with the school for current application deadlines. The fall 2016 application fee was $10. Applications are accepted on-line. **Transfer Stu-**

dents: Transfer applicants with at least 15 semester hours of credit need not take the ACT or SAT. No credits for courses with a grade below C and no credits for any course that is not in keeping with the college's catalog will be accepted. 30 of 124 credits required for the bachelor's degree must be completed at Rust. **International Students:** They must take the TOEFL. They must also take the SAT or ACT.

Admissions Contact: Johnny McDonald, Director Enrollment Services. Email: *jmcsonald@rustcollege.edu* Web: *www.rustcollege.edu*

FINANCIAL AID: The FFS and the college's own financial statement are required. The FAFSA code is 002433. Check with the school for current application deadlines.

TOUGALOO COLLEGE *(The complete profile is made available exclusively on our website, www.barronspac.com)*

UNIVERSITY OF MISSISSIPPI D-2

www.olemiss.edu

University, MS 38677 | **(662) 915-7226** | **(800) OLE-MISS**

Fax: (662) 915-1831 | **Email: admissions@olemiss.edu**

Full-time: n/av	**Faculty:** I
Part-time: n/av	**Ph.D.s:** n/av
Graduate: n/av	**Student/Faculty:** n/av
Year: semesters, summer session	**Tuition:** $7744 ($22,012)
Room & Board: $10,002	**Freshman Class:** 17918 applied, 14029 accepted, 3895 enrolled
SAT CR/M: 562/564 **ACT:** 25	**CEEB CODE:** 1840
Application Deadline: July 1	**COMPETITIVE+**

University of Mississippi, the flagship university for the state of Mississippi, opened in 1848. It offers nationally recognized programs across a broad range of undergraduate and graduate studies, from medicine and law to creative writing and accountancy. Ole Miss is the state's largest university, and was named the nation's 13th-fastest growing university. There are 10 undergraduate schools and 7 graduate schools. In addition to regional accreditation, Ole Miss has baccalaureate program accreditation with AACSB, ABET, ACEJMC, CSWE, NASAD, NASM, NCATE, NRPA, ACS, ACEND, FEPAC, CAPRA, and NAST. The 3684-acre campus is in a small town 70 miles southeast of Memphis, TN. Including any residence halls, there are 284 buildings.

STUDENT LIFE: Housing: 5597 students can be accommodated in college housing, which includes single-sex dorms, on-campus apartments, off-campus apartments, and married student housing. In addition, there are honors houses, special-interest houses, fraternity houses, sorority houses, living-learning communities and freshman interest groups. On-campus housing is guaranteed for the freshman year only, and is available on a first-come, first-served basis, and is available on a lottery system for upperclassmen. Alcohol is not permitted. All students may keep cars.

FACULTY/CLASSROOMS: No introductory courses are taught by graduate students.

PROGRAMS OF STUDY: Ole Miss confers B.A., B.A.Ed, B.A.J., B.A.P.R.M., B.Accy, B.B.A., B.F.A., B.G.S., B.M., B.P.S., B.S., B.S.C.E., B.S.C.J., B.S.Ch.E, B.S.C.S., B.S.E.E., B.S.E.S., B.S.F.C.S., B.S.G.E., B.S.J., B.S.M.E., B.S.N., B.E., and B.S.W. degrees. Master's and doctoral degrees are also awarded. Bachelor's degrees are awarded in BIOLOGICAL SCIENCE (biology/biological science), BUSINESS (accounting (finance), banking and finance, business administration and management, business economics, finance, hospitality management services, insurance, management information systems, management science, marketing/retailing/merchandising, and real estate), COMMUNICATIONS AND THE ARTS (Arabic, art, art history and appreciation, Chinese, communication science, English, French, German, journalism, linguistics, music, Spanish, and theatre arts), COMPUTER AND PHYSICAL SCIENCE (chemistry, computer science, geology, mathematics, and physics), EDUCATION (elementary education, English education, health information management, mathematics education, science education, social science education, and special education), ENGINEERING AND ENVIRONMENTAL DESIGN (chemical engineering, civil engineering, electrical/electronics engineering, engineering, geological engineering, and mechanical engineering), HEALTH PROFESSIONS (cytotechnology, dental hygiene, exercise science, health science, medical laboratory science, medical technology, nursing, pharmaceutical science, and radiological science), SOCIAL SCIENCE (African American studies, anthropology, area studies, classical/ancient civilization, criminal justice, dietetics, economics, forensic studies, history, international studies, liberal arts/general studies, paralegal studies, parks and recreation management, philosophy, political science/government, psychology, public administration, religion, social work, and sociology). Accountancy, pharmacy, and creative writing are the strongest academically. Business, accountancy, and integrated marketing communications have the largest enrollments.

ACTIVITIES: Groups on campus include art, band, cheerleading, chess, choir, chorale, chorus, computers, dance, drama, drill team, ethnic, honors, international, jazz band, LGBT, literary magazine, marching band, musical theater, newspaper, orchestra, pep band, political, professional, radio and TV, religious, social, social service, student government, symphony, and yearbook. Popular campus events include Welcome Week, Red and Blue Week, The Big Event, Faulkner and Yoknapatawpha Conference, and Oxford Conference for the Book. **Sports:** There are 6 intercollegiate sports for men and 8 for women. Facilities include a football stadium, basketball coliseum, baseball stadium, intramural fields, women's soccer complex, softball complex, volleyball courts, an indoor tennis facility, golf course, track and field complex, athletics training center, fitness center with indoor pool, racquetball courts and basketball courts, equipment rental and guides for high-adventure outdoor activities, including camping, skiing, scuba, canoeing, kayaking, and backpacking. **Graduates:** From July 1, 2015 to June 30, 2016, 3394 bachelor's degrees were awarded. The most popular majors were general studies (7%), marketing (6%), and accountancy/finance (6%).

SERVICES: Counseling and information services are available, as is tutoring in most subjects. There is a reader service for the blind, and remedial math and reading. **Library/Resources:** The 2 libraries contain 3.1 million volumes, 296,313 microform items, 22,176 audio/video tapes/CDs/DVDs, and subscribe to 146,257 periodicals including electronic. Computerized library services include interlibrary loans, database searching, Internet access, and Wi-Fi capability. Special learning facilities include an art gallery, radio station, and TV station. There are also the Mary Buie Museum, the Center for the Study of Southern Culture, the National Center for Physical Acoustics, Rowan Oak, the home of William Faulkner, the National Center for Natural Products Research, the National Food Service Management Institute, the Croft Institute for International Studies, the Sally McDonnell Barksdale Honors College, the Center for Manufacturing Excellence, and the Center for Intelligence and Security Studies. **Physically Challenged Students:** Facilities include wheelchair ramps, elevators, special parking, specially equipped restrooms, special class scheduling, lowered drinking fountains, lowered telephones, and special housing. **Special:** Online programs, dual majors, a general studies degree, credit by exam, special testing in music and languages, credit for military experience, and limited pass/fail options also are available. Co-op programs in the School of Engineering offered. Study abroad and internships are available in numerous countries. There are 17 national honor societies, a chapter of Phi Beta Kappa, and a freshman honors program. **Visiting:** There are regularly scheduled orientations for prospective students. There are guides for informal visits, visitors may sit in on classes, and stay overnight. To schedule a visit, contact Martin Barret Fisher at (662) 915-7226. **Campus Safety and Security:** Measures include 24-hour foot and vehicle patrol, emergency notification system, self-defense education, and security escort services. There are shuttle buses, emergency telephones, lighted pathways/sidewalks, and controlled access to dorms/residences.

REQUIREMENTS: Applicants need 15 academic credits, including 4 units in English, 3 each in math (4 recommended), 3 sciences with lab (4 recommended), 3 in social studies, 1 in foreign language, and 1/2 in computer applications. Electives should include a second year of foreign language or world geography. A portfolio for art majors and an audition for theater and music majors are required. A GPA of 2.0 is required. AP and CLEP credits are accepted. The core curriculum is a set of 30 hours of course-work taken by students. The core includes the following courses required for all entering freshmen students: 6 hours of English composition (Honors students may satisfy English composition requirements by taking Hon 101 and 102), 3 hours of college algebra or quantitative reasoning or statistics (taken from a department of mathematics) or a more advanced mathematics course; 6 hours of natural science; 9 hours of humanities and fine arts, and 6 hours of social or behavioral science courses. For the award of a bachelor's degree from any school or college of the University of Mississippi, a student must earn a GPA of at least 2.00 on all course-work submitted in fulfillment of the course requirements for the degree. In addition, the student must earn a minimum GPA of 2.0 on all course work attempted at the University of Mississippi. Finally, the student must have a minimum 2.0 GPA on all college work attempted at any institution of higher learning. There may be additional grade requirements for the College of Liberal Arts or the professional schools. It is the student's responsibility to check on the requirements applicable to the specific degree for which he or she is a candidate. **Procedure:** Freshmen are admitted to all sessions. There are early admissions, deferred admissions, and rolling admissions plans. Applications should be filed by July 1 for fall entry, along with a $40 fee. **Transfer Students:** Transfer students must have earned a minimum 2.0 GPA on previous college work. The SAT or ACT may be required depending on credits earned. 30 of 126 credits required for the bachelor's degree must be completed at Ole Miss. **International Students:** There are 836 international students enrolled. The school actively recruits these students. They must take the TOEFL with a minimum score of 550 on the paper-based TOEFL (PBT) or 79 on the Internet-based version (iBT) and the college's own test, the IELTS & Pearson are also accepted. They must also take the SAT or ACT. If GPA is between 2.75-2.99; SAT of 1150 or above required.

ADMISSIONS: 78% of the 2016-2017 applicants were accepted. The SAT scores for the 2016-2017 freshman class were: Critical Reading-- 22% below 500, 46% between 500 and 599, 24% between 600 and 699, and 8% between 700 and 800. Math-- 18% below 500, 48% between 500 and 599, 26% between 600 and 699, and 8% between 700 and 800. The ACT scores were 2% between 12 and 17, 33% between 18 and 23, 46% between 24 and 29, and 19% above 30. 43% of the current freshmen were in the top fifth of their class; 71% were in the top two fifths. There were 43 National Merit finalists. **Admissions Contact:** Whitman Smith, Director of Enrollment Services. Email: *admissions@olemiss.edu* Web: *www.olemiss.edu*

FINANCIAL AID: In 2016-2017, 87% of all full-time freshmen and 80% of continuing full-time students received some form of financial aid. 73% of all full-time freshmen and 56% of continuing full-time students received need-based aid. The average freshman award was $15,273. Need-based scholarships or need-based grants averaged $9,452 ($47,739 maximum); need-based self-help aid (loans and jobs) averaged $9,749 ($34,467 maximum); non-need-based athletic scholarships averaged $17,578 ($48,294 maximum); and other non-need-based awards and non-need-based scholarships averaged $8,086 ($46,418 maximum). The average financial indebtedness of the 2016 graduate was $38,597. Ole Miss is a member of CSS. The FAFSA code is 002440. The priority date for freshman financial aid applications for fall entry is March 1. The deadline for filing freshman financial aid applications for fall entry is February 15.

UNIVERSITY OF SOUTHERN MISSISSIPPI D-5

www.usm.edu

Hattiesburg, MS 39406 **(601) 266-5000**

Fax: (601) 266-5148	**Email: admissions@usm.edu**
Full-time: 4250 men, 7143 women	**Faculty:** 687
Part-time: 967 men, 1298 women	**Ph.D.s:** 76%
Graduate: 1039 men, 1771 women	**Student/Faculty:** 18 to 1
Year: semesters, summer session	**Tuition:** $6336 ($14,448)
Room & Board: $6834	**Freshman Class:** 4436 applied, 2473 accepted, 1787 enrolled
ACT: 22	**CEEB CODE:** 1479
Application Deadline: June 30	**COMPETITIVE**

University of Southern Mississippi, founded in 1910, is a public institution offering comprehensive undergraduate and graduate programs. Figures in the above capsule and in this profile are approximate. There are 6 undergraduate schools and 1 graduate school. In addition to regional accreditation, Southern Miss has baccalaureate program accreditation with AACSB, ABET, ACEJMC, ADA, AHEA, ASLA, CAHEA, CSAB, CSWE, FIDER, NASAD, NASM, NCATE, NLN, and NRPA. The 1090-acre campus is in a suburban area 90 miles southeast of Jackson, and 105 miles north of New Orleans, LA. Including any residence halls, there are 176 buildings.

STUDENT LIFE: 88% of undergraduates are from Mississippi. Others are from 50 states, 57 foreign countries, and Canada. 65% are White; 29% African American; 1% Asian American; 1% American Indian/Alaska Native; 1% Hispanic; 1% Foreign; 1% two or more races; 1% race unknown. **Female To Male Ratio:** 1.6:1. The average age of freshmen is 18; all undergraduates, 23. 25% do not continue beyond their first year; 50% remain to graduate. **Housing:** 3400 students can be accommodated in college housing, which includes single-sex dorms and married student housing. In addition, there are special-interest houses, fraternity houses, and sorority houses. There is a section in one dorm that is reserved for honor students. Freshmen are housed together. On-campus housing is available on a first-come, first-served basis. 72% of students commute. Alcohol is not permitted. All students may keep cars.

FACULTY/CLASSROOMS: 49% of faculty are male; 51% are female. 64% teach undergraduates, and 64% do research. No introductory courses are taught by graduate students.

PROGRAMS OF STUDY: Southern Miss confers B.A., B.S., B.F.A., B.M., B.M.E. and B.S.B.A degrees. Master's and doctoral degrees are also awarded. Bachelor's degrees are awarded in BIOLOGICAL SCIENCE (biology/biological science), BUSINESS (accounting, banking and finance, business administration and management, business economics, hotel/motel and restaurant management, international business management, marketing/retailing/merchandising, and personnel management), COMMUNICATIONS AND THE ARTS (advertising, communications, dance, design, dramatic arts, English, fine arts, journalism, languages, music, radio/television technology, and speech/debate/rhetoric), COMPUTER AND PHYSICAL SCIENCE (chemistry, computer science, geology, information sciences and systems, mathematics, physics, polymer science, and statistics), EDUCATION (art education, business education, early childhood education, elementary education, foreign languages education, guidance education, health education, home economics education, industrial arts education, middle school education, music education, science education, and secondary education), ENGINEERING AND ENVIRONMENTAL DESIGN (architectural technology, computer technology, construction technology, electrical/electronics engineering technology, engineering technology, and mechanical engineering technology), HEALTH PROFESSIONS (medical laboratory technology, nursing, predentistry, premedicine, and speech pathology/audiology), SOCIAL SCIENCE (anthropology, criminal justice, economics, geography, history, international studies, parks and recreation management, philosophy, political science/government, prelaw, psychology, social science, social work, and sociology). Curriculum instruction special education, human performance, and management international business have the largest enrollments.

ACTIVITIES: 15% of men belong to 14 national fraternities; 17% of women belong to 11 national sororities. There are 239 groups on campus, including art, band, cheerleading, choir, chorale, chorus, computers, dance, drama, drum and bugle corps, ethnic, film, honors, international, jazz band, LGBT, literary magazine, marching band, musical theater, newspaper, opera, orchestra, pep band, photography, political, professional, radio and TV, religious, social, social service, student government, and symphony. **Sports:** There are 6 intercollegiate sports for men and 6 for women, and 36 intramural sports for men and 36 for women. Facilities include a recreational lake, a football stadium, a basketball coliseum, baseball park, softball stadium, track and field stadium, fitness institute, a natatorium, volleyball courts, and playing fields for softball, flag football, and soccer. **Graduates:** From July 1, 2015 to June 30, 2016, 2520 bachelor's degrees were awarded. The most popular majors were nursing (9%), elementary education (6%), and psychology (6%). 918 companies recruited on campus in 2015-2016. In an average class, 8% graduate in 4 years or less, 43% graduate in 5 years or less, and 49% graduate in 6 years or less.

SERVICES: Counseling and information services are available, as is tutoring in most subjects. There is a reader service for the blind, and remedial math, reading, and writing. **Library/Resources:** The 2 libraries contain 122,428 volumes, 4.9 million microform items, and 33,189 audio/video tapes/CDs/DVDs, and subscribe to 24,369 periodicals including electronic. Computerized library services include interlibrary loans, database searching, and Internet access. Special learning facilities include an art gallery, natural history museum, radio station, TV production studios, the museum of natural science, and a music resource center. **Physically Challenged Students:** 80% of the campus is accessible. Facilities include wheelchair ramps, elevators, special parking, specially equipped restrooms, special class scheduling, lowered drinking fountains, lowered telephones, and special housing. **Special:** USM offers many cooperative programs, internships, dual majors, nondegree study, limited pass/fail options, credit for life experience, and study abroad in 12 countries. The university also participates in the Title IV College Work-Study Program. Accelerated degrees, distance learning, ESL, independent study, and a teacher certification program are also available. There are 27 national honor societies and a freshman honors program. **Visiting:** There are regularly scheduled orientations for prospective students, including campus tours and general session orientations. There are guides for informal visits and visitors may sit in on classes. To schedule a visit, contact Office of Admissions. **Campus Safety and Security:** Measures include 24-hour foot and vehicle patrol, emergency notification system, self-defense education, and security escort services. There are shuttle buses, emergency telephones, lighted pathways/sidewalks, and controlled access to dorms/residences.

REQUIREMENTS: Full admission will be granted to the following: All students completing the College Preparatory Curriculum (CPC) with a minimum of a 3.2 high school GPA on the CPC and a submitted ACT (composite) or SAT score. All students completing the College Preparatory Curriculum (CPC) with a minimum of a 2.5 high school GPA on the CPC or a class rank in the top 50 percent, as well as a score of 16 or higher on the ACT (composite) or a combined SAT score of 760. All students completing the College Preparatory Curriculum (CPC) with a minimum of 2.0 high school GPA on the CPC and a score of 18 or higher on the ACT (composite) or a combined SAT score of 860. Students who satisfy the National Collegiate Athletic Association (NCAA) standards for student-athletes who are full qualifiers under Division I guidelines. AP and CLEP credits are accepted. To graduate, students must complete at least 128 semester hours, including 64 at the senior college level, with a minimum GPA of 2.0. Core requirements include courses in reasoning and communication skills, English, including composition, history, humanities and fine arts, social and behavioral sciences, human wellness, and natural and applied sciences. **Procedure:** Freshmen are admitted fall, spring, and summer. Entrance exams should be taken in the fall of the senior year. Applications should be filed by June 30 for fall entry; January 1 for spring entry; and May 1 for summer entry, along with a $35 fee. Notification is sent on a rolling basis. Applications are accepted on-line. **Transfer Students:** 1787 transfer students enrolled in 2015-2016. Students must have either an associate degree intended for transfer from a regionally accredited institution or have completed the 30 semester hours of designated coursework outlined below with a minimum 2.0 cumulative grade point average for admission. 6 semester hours of English Composition (English Composition I and II), 3 semester hours of mathematics (college algebra, quantitative reasoning, or higher mathematics), 6 semester hours of natural science (courses must be laboratory-based, with the lecture courses accompanied by the respective lab course), 9 semester hours of humanities and fine arts (common examples of acceptable coursework are history, philosophy, religion, world literature, art, music), 6 semester hours of social or behavioral sciences (common examples of acceptable coursework are anthropology, geography, sociology, psychology, and social work). 32 of 128 credits required for the bachelor's degree must be completed at Southern Miss. **International Students:** The school actively recruits these students. They must take the TOEFL with a minimum score of 525 on the paper-based TOEFL (PBT). They must also take the SAT or ACT, scoring 18.

ADMISSIONS: 56% of the 2016-2017 applicants were accepted. The SAT scores for the 2016-2017 freshman class were: Critical Reading-- 35% below 500, 43% between 500 and 599, 18% between 600 and 699, and 4% between 700 and 800. Math-- 42% below 500, 40% between 500 and 599, and 18% between 600 and 699. The ACT scores were 41% below 12, 24% between 12 and 17, 19% between 18 and 23, 7% between 24 and 29, and 9% above 30. There were 6 National Merit finalists. **Admissions Contact:** Amanda King, Admissions Office. Email: *admissions@usm.edu* Web: *www.usm.edu*

FINANCIAL AID: In 2016-2017, 66% of all full-time freshmen and 64% of continuing full-time students received some form of financial aid. 75% of all full-time freshmen and 70% of continuing full-time students received need-based aid. The average freshman award was $10,446. Need-based scholarships or need-based grants averaged $4,505; need-based self-help aid (loans and jobs) averaged $3,552; non-need-based athletic scholarships averaged $7,396; and other non-need-based awards and non-need-based scholarships averaged $5,568. The average financial indebtedness of the 2016 graduate was $29,502. The college's own financial statement is required. The FAFSA code is 002441. Check with the school for current application deadlines.

WILLIAM CAREY UNIVERSITY *(The complete profile is made available exclusively on our website, www.barronspac.com)*

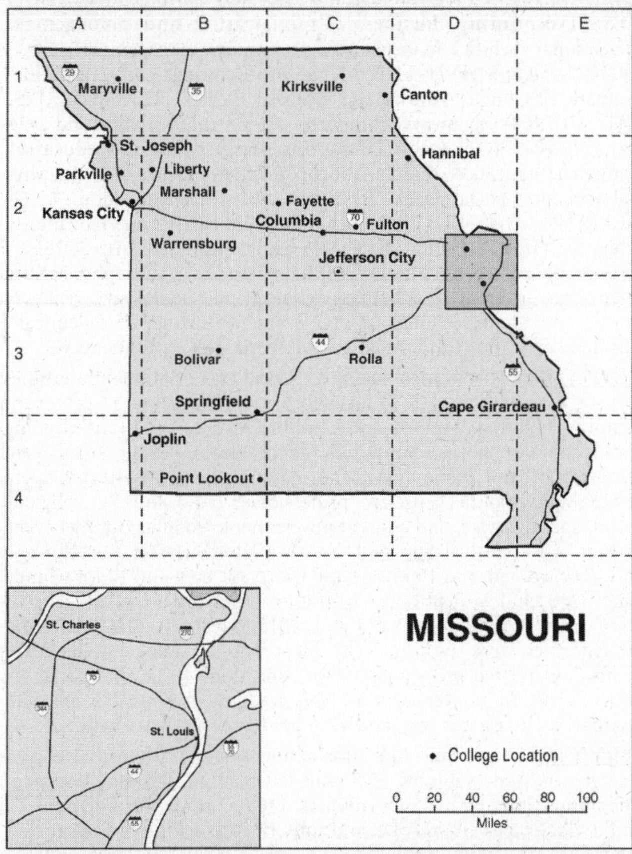

AVILA UNIVERSITY A-2

www.avila.edu

Kansas City, MO 64145	**(816) 501-2400** **(800) GO-AVILA**
Fax: (816) 501-2453	**Email: admissions@avila.edu**
Full-time: 320 men, 605 women	**Faculty:** IIB, -$
Part-time: 60 men, 150 women	**Ph.D.s:** 69%
Graduate: 225 men, 480 women	**Student/Faculty:** n/av
Year: semesters, summer session	**Tuition:** $27,980
Room & Board: $7500	**Freshman Class:** n/av
ACT: required	**CEEB CODE:** 6109
Application Deadline: August 25	**COMPETITIVE**

Avila University, founded in 1916, is a comprehensive liberal arts institution sponsored by the Sisters of St. Joseph of Carondelet. Avila has over 60 undergraduate majors and concentrations and six graduate degree programs. The figures in the above capsule and in this profile are approximate. There are 7 undergraduate schools and 3 graduate schools. In addition to regional accreditation, Avila has baccalaureate program accreditation with CAHEA, CSWE, and CCNE. The 50-acre campus is in a suburban area in Kansas City, MO. Including any residence halls, there are 11 buildings.

STUDENT LIFE: 55% of undergraduates are from Missouri. Others are from 21 states, 34 foreign countries, and Canada. 87% are from public schools. 9% are Foreign; 7% Hispanic; 61% White; 2% two or more races; 19% African American; 1% Asian American; 1% American Indian/Alaska Native. 26% are Catholic. **Female To Male Ratio:** 2.0:1. The average age of freshmen is 18; all undergraduates, 23. 33% do not continue beyond their first year; 51% remain to graduate. **Housing:** 310 students can be accommodated in college housing, which includes single-sex and coed dorms and on-campus apartments. On-campus housing is guaranteed for the freshman year only, is available on a first-come, first-served basis, and on a lottery system for upperclassmen. Priority is given to out-of-town students. 71% of students commute. All students may keep cars.

FACULTY/CLASSROOMS: 33% of faculty are male; 67% are female. All teach undergraduates, and all do research. No introductory courses are taught by graduate students. The average class size in an introductory lecture is 22; in a laboratory is 25; and in a regular course is 14.

PROGRAMS OF STUDY: Avila confers B.A., B.S., B.F.A., B.S.B.A., B.S.N., and B.S.W. degrees. Master's degrees are also awarded. Bachelor's degrees are awarded in BIOLOGICAL SCIENCE (biochemistry and biology/biological science), BUSINESS (accounting, banking and finance, business administration and management, international business management, management science, and marketing/retailing/merchandising), COMMUNICATIONS AND THE ARTS (art, communications, dramatic arts, English, and music), COMPUTER AND PHYSICAL SCIENCE (chemistry, computer science, information sciences and systems, mathematics, and radiological technology), EDUCATION (business education, educational studies, elementary education, middle school education, and special education), HEALTH PROFESSIONS (medical laboratory technology, nursing, premedicine, and sports medicine), SOCIAL SCIENCE (history, paralegal studies, political science/government, psychology, religious studies, social work, sociology, and theological studies). Nursing, education, and communications are the strongest academically. Nursing, education, and radiologic technology have the largest enrollments.

ACTIVITIES: There are no fraternities or sororities. There are 37 groups on campus, including art, cheerleading, choir, chorale, chorus, computers, dance, drama, ethnic, film, honors, international, LGBT, literary magazine, musical theater, newspaper, photography, political, professional, radio and TV, religious, social, social service, and student government. Popular campus events include Student Appreciation Day, Organization Fair, and International Festival. **Sports:** There are 4 intercollegiate sports for men and 7 for women. Facilities include a field house with basketball and volleyball courts, a training room, and weight and fitness equipment. There is also an athletic complex with baseball, softball, and soccer fields, tennis courts, and practice fields. **Graduates:** From July 1, 2015 to June 30, 2016, 222 bachelor's degrees were awarded. The most popular majors were business (18%), nursing (15%), and radiologic science (12%). In an average class, 32% graduate in 4 years or less, 35% graduate in 5 years or less, and 46% graduate in 6 years or less. Of the 2015 graduating class, 29% were enrolled in graduate school within 6 months of graduation, and 90% were employed.

SERVICES: Counseling and information services are available, as is tutoring in most subjects. There is a reader service for the blind, and remedial math, reading, and writing. **Library/Resources:** The library contains 81,755 volumes, 493,760 microform items, 2,910 audio/video tapes/CDs/DVDs, and subscribes to 550 periodicals including electronic. Computerized library services include interlibrary loans, database searching, Internet access, and Wi-Fi capability. Special learning facilities include an art gallery, radio station, TV station, a theater, an interactive video library, video production facilities, a Nursing Education and Resource Center, and a dance studio. **Physically Challenged Students:** 95% of the campus is accessible. Facilities include wheelchair ramps, elevators, special parking, specially equipped restrooms, special class scheduling, lowered drinking fountains, and lowered telephones. **Special:** Students may cross-register with the Kansas City Area Student Exchange, the Sisters of Saint Joseph College Consortium, and the Council of Independent Colleges Student Exchange. Avila also offers internships in business, communication, graphic design, paralegal, and other majors, work-study, a Washington center program, dual majors in science, math, and health professions, and accelerated degree programs in business administration and psychology. There are 6 national honor societies and 4 departmental honors programs. **Visiting:** There are regularly scheduled orientations for prospective students, including a visit with admissions and a faculty member a campus tour, and an appointment with the athletics or performance grant manager. There are guides for informal visits, visitors may sit in on classes, and stay overnight. To schedule a visit, contact the Campus Visit Coordinator. **Campus Safety and Security:** Measures include 24-hour foot and vehicle patrol, security escort services, emergency telephones, lighted pathways/sidewalks, controlled access to dorms/residences, 24-hour closed-circuit television in residence hall entryways, computer labs, and the student lounge. Another closed circuit system monitors gym areas. In addition, all University parking lot entrances are monitored by a closed circuit system.

REQUIREMENTS: The ACT is required. Applicants must be graduates of an accredited secondary school or have a GED certificate. They should have completed 16 academic units, including 4 in English, 3 in math, 2 to 4 in foreign language, 2 to 3 in natural and social sciences, and 1 to 2 in fine arts. A GPA of 2.5 is required. AP and CLEP credits are accepted. Important factors in the admissions decision are recommendations by school officials, extracurricular activities record, and leadership record. To graduate, students must complete at least 128 semester hours with a minimum 2.0 GPA. The 41- to 46-hour core curriculum consists of courses in composition, communication, math, history, literature, theology, philosophy, the arts, the sciences, and social institutions. The average hours in a major range from 36 to 60. **Procedure:** Freshmen are admitted to all sessions. Entrance exams should be taken in the spring or summer of the junior year. There is a rolling admissions plan. Applications should be filed by August 25 for fall entry, along with a $25 fee. Notification is sent on a rolling basis. Applications are accepted online. **Transfer Students:** 194 transfer students enrolled in 2015-2016. Applicants must have a minimum GPA of 2.0. 30 of 128 credits required for the bachelor's degree must be completed at Avila. **International Students:** There are 94 international students enrolled. The school actively recruits these students. They must take the TOEFL with a minimum score of 500 on the paper-based TOEFL (PBT) or 61 on the Internet-based version (iBT).

ADMISSIONS: 1 freshman graduated first in the class. **Admissions Contact:** Patti Harper, Director of Admissions. Email: *admissions@avila.edu* Web: *www.avila.edu*

FINANCIAL AID: In 2016-2017, 97% of all full-time freshmen and 87% of continuing full-time students received some form of financial aid. 76% of all full-time freshmen and 74% of continuing full-time students received need-based aid. 92% of undergraduate students work part-time. Average annual earnings from campus work are $1200. The FAFSA code is 002449. Check with the school for current application deadlines.

CENTRAL METHODIST UNIVERSITY — C-2

www.centralmethodist.edu

Fayette, MO 65248 — **(660) 248-6251**, **(877) CMU-1854**

Fax: (660) 248-1872 — **Email: admissions@centralmethodist.edu**

Full-time: 575 men, 583 women	**Faculty:** 63
Part-time: 5 men, 10 women	**Ph.D.s:** 83%
Graduate: n/av	**Student/Faculty:** 16 to 1
Year: semesters, summer session	**Tuition:** $29,700
Room & Board: $7130	**Freshman Class:** 1344 applied, 897 accepted, 302 enrolled
ACT: required	**CEEB CODE:** 6089
Application Deadline: n/av	**VERY COMPETITIVE**

Central Methodist University, founded in 1854, is a private liberal arts institution affiliated with the Methodist Church. There are 4 undergraduate schools. In addition to regional accreditation, CMU has baccalaureate program accreditation with NASM and CCNE. The 83-acre campus is in a small town 30 miles northwest of Columbia. Including any residence halls, there are 16 buildings.

STUDENT LIFE: 90% of undergraduates are from Missouri. Others are from 23 states, 8 foreign countries, and Canada. 96% are from public schools. 85% are White; 8% African American; 2% Hispanic; 1% Asian American; 1% American Indian/Alaska Native; 1% Foreign. 86% are Protestant; 14% Catholic. **Female To Male Ratio:** 1.0:1. The average age of freshmen is 18; all undergraduates, 21. 35% do not continue beyond their first year; 43% remain to graduate. **Housing:** 700 students can be accommodated in college housing, which includes single-sex and coed dorms, off-campus apartments, and married student housing. On-campus housing is guaranteed for all 4 years. 59% of students live on campus. All students may keep cars. Alcohol is not permitted.

FACULTY/CLASSROOMS: 60% of faculty are male; 63% are female. All teach undergraduates. No introductory courses are taught by graduate students. The average class size in an introductory lecture is 30; in a laboratory is 24; and in a regular course is 12.

PROGRAMS OF STUDY: CMU confers B.A., B.S., B.M., B.M.E., B.S.E. and B.S.N., B.G.S., B.A.S.M. and B.ACC. degrees. Associate and master's degrees are also awarded. Bachelor's degrees are awarded in BIOLOGICAL SCIENCE (biology/biological science and marine biology), BUSINESS (accounting, business administration and management, recreational facilities management, and sports management), COMMUNICATIONS AND THE ARTS (broadcasting, communications, dramatic arts, English, music, and Spanish), COMPUTER AND PHYSICAL SCIENCE (chemistry, computer science, mathematics, and physics), EDUCATION (athletic training, early childhood education, elementary education, middle school education, music education, physical education, social science education, and special education), ENGINEERING AND ENVIRONMENTAL DESIGN (environmental science), HEALTH PROFESSIONS (nursing), SOCIAL SCIENCE (criminal justice, history, interdisciplinary studies, philosophy, political science/government, psychology, religion, and sociology). Sciences, music, and preprofessional programs are the strongest academically. Business, education, and nursing have the largest enrollments.

ACTIVITIES: 21% of men belong to 3 local and 2 national fraternities; 24% of women belong to 4 local sororities. There are 37 groups on campus, including premed and criminal justice, band, cheerleading, choir, chorale, chorus, computers, dance, debate, drama, drill team, honors, jazz band, literary magazine, marching band, newspaper, opera, photography, political, prelaw, professional, radio and TV, religious, social, social service, and student government. Popular campus events include Music Festival. **Sports:** There are 5 intercollegiate sports for men and 4 for women, and 10 intramural sports for men and 10 for women. Facilities include a field house with a gym, playing fields, and a recreation center. **Graduates:** From July 1, 2015 to June 30, 2016, 149 bachelor's degrees were awarded. The most popular majors were health professions/related programs (19%), education (19%), and social sciences (15%). In an average class, 30% graduate in 4 years or less, 38% graduate in 5 years or less, and 42% graduate in 6 years or less.

SERVICES: Counseling and information services are available, as is tutoring in some subjects, and remedial reading. **Library/Resources:** The library contains 102,695 volumes, 140,812 microform items, 3,736 audio/video tapes/CDs/DVDs, and subscribes to 447 periodicals including electronic. Computerized library services include interlibrary loans, database searching, Internet access, and Wi-Fi capability. Special learning facilities include an art gallery, natural history museum, radio station, TV station, and observatory. **Physically Challenged Students:** 65% of the campus is accessible. Facilities include wheelchair ramps, elevators, special parking, specially equipped restrooms, special class scheduling, and lowered drinking fountains. **Special:** CMU offers cooperative programs in medical technology and physical therapy and 3-2 engineering degrees with the University of Missouri at Rolla, the University of Evansville, Stanford University, and Washington University in St. Louis. Work-study programs, internships, study abroad, dual majors, a general studies degree, and nondegree study are also available. There are 14 national honor societies and a freshman honors program. **Visiting:** There are regularly scheduled orientations for prospective students, including meeting with admissions and financial assistance staff, a campus tour, and visits with faculty members. There are guides for informal visits, visitors may sit in on classes, and stay overnight. To schedule a visit, contact the Admissions Office at (660) 248-6241. **Campus Safety and Security:** Measures include 24-hour foot and vehicle patrol, emergency notification system, and security escort services, emergency telephones, lighted pathways/sidewalks, controlled access to dorms/residences, and key-card access to student housing.

REQUIREMENTS: A minimum score of 21 on the ACT is required. Those students with a GPA lower than 2.5 may request conditional admission. Applicants should be graduates of an accredited secondary school or have a GED certificate. Recommended preparatory courses include 4 units of English, 3 of math, and 2 each of science, social studies, and humanities. AP and CLEP credits are accepted. Important factors in the admissions decision are advanced placement or honors courses, evidence of special talent, and extracurricular activities record. To graduate, students must complete 124 to 131 credit hours, including at least 24 in the major, depending on the degree. A minimum GPA of 2.0 is required for all but the athletic training and education programs, which require a 2.5. Students must complete 53 hours of a distribution curriculum, including computer literacy, computer science, phys ed, religion, philosophy, freshman orientation to college life, and a senior capstone. **Procedure:** Freshmen are admitted to all sessions. There is a rolling admissions plan. Application deadlines are open. The fall 2016 application fee was $20. Applications are accepted online. **Transfer Students:** 105 transfer students enrolled in 2015-2016. Transfer applicants must be in good academic standing at their previous college and have a 2.0 cumulative GPA. 30 of 124 credits required for the bachelor's degree must be completed at CMU. **International Students:** There are 11 international students enrolled. They must take the TOEFL with a minimum score of 550 on the paper-based TOEFL (PBT).

ADMISSIONS: 67% of the 2016-2017 applicants were accepted. 4 freshmen graduated first in their class. **Admissions Contact:** Adam Jenkins, Director of Admission. Email: *admissions@centralmethodist.edu* Web: *www.centralmethodist.edu*

FINANCIAL AID: In 2016-2017, 100% of all full-time freshmen and 96% of continuing full-time students received some form of financial aid. 89% of all full-time freshmen and 81% of continuing full-time students received need-based aid. The average freshman award was $17,813. Need-based scholarships or need-based grants averaged $5,030; need-based self-help aid (loans and jobs) averaged $3,187; non-need-based athletic scholarships averaged $4,725; other non-need-based awards and non-need-based scholarships averaged $8,871; and $3,467 from other forms of aid. 27% of undergraduate students work part-time. Average annual earnings from campus work are $1045. The average financial indebtedness of the 2016 graduate was $21,828. The FAFSA code is 002453. Check with the school for current application deadlines.

COLLEGE OF THE OZARKS B-4

www.cofo.edu

Point Lookout, MO 65726	**(417) 334-6411** **(800) 222-0525**
Fax: (417) 335-2618	**Email: admiss4@cofo.edu**
Full-time: 678 men, 821 women	**Faculty:** 89; IIB, -$
Part-time: 6 men, 7 women	**Ph.D.s:** 58%
Graduate: n/av	**Student/Faculty:** 14 to 1
Year: semesters	**Tuition:** see profile
Room & Board: $6800	**Freshman Class:** 1130 applied, 419 accepted, 384 enrolled
SAT CR/M/W: 595/530/570 **ACT:** 23	**CEEB CODE:** 6713
Application Deadline: December 31	**COMPETITIVE**

The cost to College of the Ozarks for providing an educational opportunity is approximately $18,500 per year for each student. While most colleges and universities pass along a portion of this cost as tuition, this is not the case at College of the Ozarks. The College guarantees to meet all of this cost for each full-time student by using a combination of earnings from its endowment, operating its own mandatory student Work Education Program, and accepting student aid grants, as well as gifts, and other sources. As a result, each full-time student's Cost of Education is met 100% by participating in the Work Education Program and a combination of private, institutional, and federal/state student aid – but without loans of any kind. There is 1 undergraduate school. In addition to regional accreditation, C of O has baccalaureate program accreditation with ADA, NCACS, CNE, and Missouri State Board of Nursing. The 1000-acre campus is in a small town 40 miles south of Springfield, adjacent to the resort town of Branson. Including any residence halls, there are 99 buildings.

STUDENT LIFE: 78% of undergraduates are from Missouri. Others are from 27 states, and 18 foreign countries. 78% are from public schools. 92% are White; 2% Hispanic; 1% African American; 1% Asian American; 1% American Indian/Alaska Native; 1% Foreign; 1% two or more races; 1% race unknown. 91% are Protestant. **Female To Male Ratio:** 1.2:1. The average age of freshmen is 18; all undergraduates, 20. 15% do not continue beyond their first year; 69% remain to graduate. **Housing:** 1344 students can be accommodated in college housing, which includes single-sex dorms. Student members of the volunteer fire department have living facilities at the fire department. On-campus housing is guaranteed for all 4 years. 87% of students live on campus; of those, 60% remain on campus on weekends. All students may keep cars. Alcohol is not permitted.

FACULTY/CLASSROOMS: 53% of faculty are male; 47% are female. All teach undergraduates. No introductory courses are taught by graduate students. The average class size in an introductory lecture is 40; in a laboratory is 18; and in a regular course is 30.

PROGRAMS OF STUDY: C of O confers B.A. and B.S. degrees. Bachelor's degrees are awarded in AGRICULTURE (agricultural business management, agricultural sciences, agriculture, agronomy, animal science, conservation and regulation, and horticulture), BIOLOGICAL SCIENCE (biology ecology and field biology, biology/adolescence education, and biology/biological science), BUSINESS (accounting, business administration and management, business administration - international, business administration, management operations, business administration marketing, business economics, hotel/motel and restaurant management, international business management, marketing management, and meeting/special event management), COMMUNICATIONS AND THE ARTS (art, communications, communications technology, dramatic arts, English, journalism, media arts, music, music business management, music ministry, music theatre accompanying, music theory and composition, musical theater, performing arts, public relations, Spanish, communication arts - speech, speech and theatre education, studio art, studio art ceramics, studio art computer art, studio art fibers, studio art graphic design, studio art painting, theater design, theatre studies, and theatre ministry), COMPUTER AND PHYSICAL SCIENCE (chemistry, chemistry/adolescence education, computer science, information sciences and systems, and mathematics), EDUCATION (agricultural education, art education, business education, early childhood education, elementary education, English education, mathematics education, music education, physical education, physical education/exercise science, recreation education, secondary education, social studies education, Spanish education K-12, and vocational education), ENGINEERING AND ENVIRONMENTAL DESIGN (graphic arts technology and preengineering), HEALTH PROFESSIONS (allied health, health, medical technology, nursing, premedicine, prepharmacy, and preveterinary science), SOCIAL SCIENCE (biblical studies, child care/child and family studies, Christian studies, clothing and textiles management/production/services, corrections, criminal justice, criminology, culinary arts, dietetics, family/consumer studies, food science, history, home economics, interdisciplinary studies, law enforcement and corrections, ministries, philosophy, prelaw, psychology, religion, religious music, social science, family studies/soc serv/marriage family, social work, and sociology). Business, agriculture, education, and health services are the strongest academically. Education, business, and health services have the largest enrollments.

ACTIVITIES: There are no fraternities or sororities. There are 50 groups on campus, including art, band, cheerleading, choir, chorale, computers, dance, drama, honors, international, jazz band, musical theater, newspaper, orchestra, pep band, photography, political, professional, religious, social service, student government, and yearbook. Popular campus events include Honor America, 9/11 Remembrance Ceremony, Convocation Speakers, Spring Fest, Mud Fest, Lip Sync, Homecoming, NAIA Division II Men's Championship Tournament. **Sports:** There are 5 intercollegiate sports for men and 5 for women, and 10 intramural sports for men and 10 for women. Facilities include an athletic complex with a main gym, training room, swimming pool, dance studio, racquetball courts, weight room, basketball court, indoor running track, gymnasium, intramural fields, tennis courts, baseball field, outdoor tennis and basketball courts, outdoor track and jump pits. **Graduates:** From July 1, 2015 to June 30, 2016, 293 bachelor's degrees were awarded. The most popular majors were education (15%), health services (11%), and business (10%). 200 companies recruited on campus in 2015-2016. In an average class, 54% graduate in 4 years or less, 68% graduate in 5 years or less, and 69% graduate in 6 years or less. Of the 2015 graduating class, 7% were enrolled in graduate school within 6 months of graduation.

SERVICES: Counseling and information services are available, as is tutoring in some subjects. Services provided on an individual basis. There is remedial math and writing. **Library/Resources:** The library contains 445,045 volumes, 30,720 microform items, 3,805 audio/video tapes/CDs/DVDs, and subscribes to 53,095 periodicals including electronic. Computerized library services include interlibrary loans, database searching, Internet access, and Wi-Fi capability. Special learning facilities include an art gallery, the Ralph Foster Museum, Edwards Mill (replica of a 1800s working grist mill) and weaving studio, fire department, print shop, greenhouses, fruitcake and jelly kitchen, day care center, farm operations, farmers market, Gaetz Tractor Museum and the Ozarkiana room, containing historical periodicals and pictures of the Ozarks, The Missouri Vietnam Veterans Memorial, and a 911 Memorial. **Physically Challenged Students:** 80% of the campus is accessible. Facilities include wheelchair ramps, elevators, special parking, specially equipped restrooms, and special housing. **Special:** Interdisciplinary programs, Medical Technology through reverse transfer from Cox Health Systems, and pre-professional programs: Pre-Law, Pre-Dentistry, Pre-Medicine, Pre-Pharmacy, Pre-Physician's Assistant, and Pre-Veterinary Medicine, and Patriotic Education Travel Program. There are 8 national honor societies, a freshman honors program, and 8 departmental honors programs. **Visiting:** There are regularly scheduled orientations for prospective students, Monday through Friday, as well as guides for informal visits, and visitors may sit in on classes. To schedule a visit, contact the Admissions Office. **Campus Safety and Security:** Measures include 24-hour foot and vehicle patrol, emergency notification system, and security escort services, emergency telephones, lighted pathways/sidewalks, controlled access to dorms/residences, fire department on campus, and security cameras.

REQUIREMENTS: The ACT and the ACT Optional Writing test are required. Students should be in the top half of their graduating class and score at least a 20 on the ACT (950 SAT). Students should have a 3.00 grade point average. Students who have taken the college preparatory curriculum in high school are more competitive in the admission process than those who have not. Current college preparatory courses include 4 units of English, 3 units each of mathematics, social studies, and science. The College is most concerned with the core courses of English, history/social science, mathematics, and science. Because the College's mission focuses on serving students with financial need, students must demonstrate a significant level of financial need. C of O requires applicants to be in the upper 50% of their class. A GPA of 3.2 is required. AP and CLEP credits are accepted. Important factors in the admissions decision are recommendations by school officials, leadership record, advanced placement or honors courses, evidence of special talent, personality/intangible qualities, extracurricular activities record, geographical diversity, ability to finance college education, parents or siblings attended your school, and recommendations by alumni. Graduation Requirements; Completion of a minimum of 125 semester hours of credit with a 2.0 or higher cumulative grade point average (GPA). Remedial classes, including all College of the Ozarks classes beginning with a zero (0) do not count toward graduation. Completion of at least one major with a minimum of a 2.0 GPA for the major. Some majors have higher GPA requirements. A major must include at least 30 required hours (major/collateral) with at least 15 hours upper division (300-400 level) courses. Completion of all general education courses with a minimum of a 2.0 GPA. Completion of at least 36 credit hours of upper division courses. No more than six of those hours may be in internship. Students with transfer hours must complete a minimum of 45 credit hours at the College of the Ozarks. At least 12 credit hours must be in the major field including nine upper division hours. Exceptions may be made with the approval of the Dean of the College. Participation in the College Work Education Program as a full-time student for at least one semester is required for completion of degree. The last 30 hours of credit must be completed at the College of the Ozarks unless a waiver is granted in writing from the Dean of the College. The faculty and the Board of Trustees vote on all graduates. To be approved for graduation, all students must have satisfied all current degree and instructional requirements, as well as be in compliance with all College regulations at time of graduation. Students will graduate with either a Bachelor of Arts degree, Bachelor of Science degree, or a Bachelor of Science in Nursing degree. **Procedure:** Freshmen are admitted in the fall and spring. Entrance exams should be taken during junior year, and October of Senior year. There is a rolling admissions plan. Applications should be filed by December 31 for fall entry; December 31 for spring entry. Notifications are sent January 15. 520 applicants were on the 2016 waiting list; 35 were admitted. Applications are accepted online. **Transfer Students:** 35 transfer students enrolled in 2015-2016. Transfer Student Admissions: Students with fewer than 24 transferable college semester hours completed elsewhere should submit the materials listed above plus the transfer student documents that are noted. This includes a college transcript (from all institutions attended) and a transfer student form. The transfer student form attests to the positive character of the student and must be completed by the dean of students at the institution from which the student is transferring. Transfer students with 24 or more transferable college semester hours need not submit ACT scores and high school transcripts, but they are required to submit college transcripts and the transfer student form. Reference forms for transfer students should be submitted by college academic personnel. Transfer applicants with over 60 hours may be ineligible for admission. 45 of 125 credits required for the bachelor's degree must be completed at C of O. **International Students:** There are 27 international students enrolled. They must take the TOEFL with a minimum score of 550 on the paper-based TOEFL (PBT) or 79 on the Internet-based version (iBT). Student must also take the ACT or SAT, the SAT is preferred.

ADMISSIONS: 37% of the 2016-2017 applicants were accepted. The SAT scores for the 2016-2017 freshman class were: Critical Reading-- 14% below 500, 36% between 500 and 599, 43% between 600 and 699, and 7% between 700 and 800. Math-- 21% below 500, 50% between 500 and 599, 21% between 600 and 699, and 7% between 700 and 800. Writing-- 29% below 500, 43% between 500 and 599, 21% between 600 and 699, and 7% between 700 and 800. The ACT scores were 1% between 12 and 17, 55% between 18 and 23, 40% between 24 and 29, and 4% above 30. 50% of the current freshmen were in the top fifth of their class; 86% were in the top two fifths. 14 freshmen graduated first in their class. **Admissions Contact:** Dr. Marci Linson, Dean of Admissions. Email: *admiss4@cofo.edu* Web: *www.cofo.edu*

FINANCIAL AID: In 2016-2017, 100% of all full-time freshmen and continuing full-time students received some form of financial aid. 90% of all full-time freshmen and 65% of continuing full-time students received need-based aid. The average freshman award was $19,871. Need-based scholarships or need-based grants averaged $13,433 ($14,016 maximum); need-based self-help aid (loans and jobs) averaged $4,284 ($4,284 maximum); and non-need-based athletic scholarships averaged $4,109 ($6,800 maximum). 100% of undergraduate students work part-time. Average annual earnings from campus work are $4284. The average financial indebtedness of the 2016 graduate was $5,088. The FAFSA code is 002500. The priority date for freshman financial aid applications for fall entry is November 15. The filing deadline for fall entry is February 15.

COLUMBIA COLLEGE - MISSOURI C-2

www.ccis.edu

Columbia, MO 65216	(573) 875-7352 (800) 231-7352
Fax: (573) 875-7506	**Email:** admissions@ccis.edu
Full-time: 336 men, 468 women	**Faculty:** 68; IIB, av$
Part-time: 51 men, 81 women	**Ph.D.s:** 80%
Graduate: 53 men, 104 women	**Student/Faculty:** 12 to 1
Year: semesters, summer session	**Tuition:** $20,963
Room & Board: $6940	**Freshman Class:** 1580 applied, 801 accepted, 203 enrolled
SAT CR/M: 500/550 **ACT:** 23	**CEEB CODE:** 6095
Application Deadline: August 12	**COMPETITIVE**

Columbia College-Missouri, founded in 1851, has been helping students advance their lives through higher education for more than 160 years. As a private, nonprofit, liberal arts and sciences institution, the college takes pride in its small classes, experienced faculty and quality educational programs. Students may enroll in day, evening or online classes. The college is accredited by the Higher Learning Commission. There are 3 undergraduate schools and 1 graduate school. The 36-acre campus is in an urban area 120 miles east of Kansas City and 120 miles west of St. Louis. Including any residence halls, there are 29 buildings.

STUDENT LIFE: 87% of undergraduates are from Missouri. Others are from 24 states, 33 foreign countries, and Canada. 76% are White; 9% Foreign; 5% two or more races; 4% race unknown; 3% African American; 2% Hispanic; 1% Asian American; 1% American Indian/Alaska Native. 85% claim no religious affiliation. **Female To Male Ratio:** 1.5:1. The average age of freshmen is 18; all undergraduates, 22. **Housing:** 395 students can be accommodated in college housing, which includes single-sex and coed dorms, on-campus apartments, and living learning communities. On-campus housing is guaranteed for all 4 years, and is available on a first-come, and first-served basis. 60% of students commute. All students may keep cars. Alcohol is not permitted.

FACULTY/CLASSROOMS: 53% of faculty are male; 47% are female. All teach undergraduates. No introductory courses are taught by graduate students. The average class size in an introductory lecture is 15 and in a laboratory is 15.

PROGRAMS OF STUDY: Columbia-Missouri confers B.A., B.S., B.G.S., and B.F.A. degrees. Associate and master's degrees are also awarded. Bachelor's degrees are awarded in AGRICULTURE (environmental studies), BIOLOGICAL SCIENCE (biology/biological science), BUSINESS (accounting, banking and finance, business administration and management, entrepreneurial studies, finance, human resources, international business management, marketing/retailing/merchandising, and sports management), COMMUNICATIONS AND THE ARTS (art, ceramic art and design, communications, English, fine arts, graphic design, painting, photography, printmaking, and public relations), COMPUTER AND PHYSICAL SCIENCE (chemistry, computer science, information sciences and systems, and mathematics), EDUCATION (education, education administration, elementary education, middle school education, and secondary education), ENGINEERING AND ENVIRONMENTAL DESIGN (military science), HEALTH PROFESSIONS (health administration and policy, health care administration, and nursing), SOCIAL SCIENCE (American studies, criminal justice, fire services administration, forensic studies, history, human services, interdisciplinary studies, liberal arts/general studies, philosophy, political science/government, psychology, social work, and sociology). Psychology, chemisty, and computer science are the strongest academically. Visual arts & music, humanities, and biology have the largest enrollments.

ACTIVITIES: There are no fraternities or sororities. Groups on campus include art, choir, chorale, drama, drum and bugle corps, environmental, ethnic, forensics, honors, international, international student, LGBT, orchestra, photography, political, professional, religious, social, social service, and student government. Popular campus events include Ivy Chain, Holiday Lighting Ceremony, and Schiffman Ethics. **Sports:** There are 7 intercollegiate sports for men and 8 for women, and 16 intramural sports for men and 16 for women. Facilities include softball and soccer fields, a dance studio, indoor tennis courts, an exercise/weight room, and a gym and sports complex. **Graduates:** From July 1, 2015 to June 30, 2016, 189 bachelor's degrees were awarded. The most popular majors were general studies (17%), criminal justice (6%), and management (6%). In an average class, 67% graduate in 6 years or less.

SERVICES: Counseling and information services are available, as is tutoring in some subjects, such as American or world history, speech, intro to computer information systems and ethics. **Library/Resources:** The library contains 344,382 volumes, 152,224 audio/video tapes/CDs/DVDs, and subscribes to 349,070 periodicals including electronic. Computerized library services include interlibrary loans, database searching, Internet access, and Wi-Fi capability. Special learning facilities include an art gallery. **Physically Challenged Students:** All of the campus is accessible. Facilities include wheelchair ramps, elevators, special parking, specially equipped restrooms, special class scheduling, lowered drinking fountains, lowered telephones, and special housing. **Special:** Columbia offers cross-registration with the University of Missouri/Columbia and Stephens College, internships, study abroad in more than 20 countries, B.A.-B.S. degrees in most disciplines, an interdisciplinary studies degree, student-designed and dual majors, nondegree study, and pass/fail options. Select students who complete a special 2-semester project earn a bachelor's degree with distinction (B.A.D.). There are 16 national honor societies, a freshman honors program, and 1 departmental honors program. **Visiting:** There are regularly scheduled orientations for prospective students, including a campus tour, a workshop in financial aid, an academic/organization fair, and a luncheon. There are guides for informal visits, visitors may sit in on classes, and stay overnight. To schedule a visit, contact the Admissions Office. **Campus Safety and Security:** Measures include 24-hour foot and vehicle patrol, emergency notification system, self-defense education, security escort services, emergency telephones, lighted pathways/sidewalks, and controlled access to dorms/residences.

REQUIREMENTS: The SAT or ACT and ACT Writing Test are recommended. Applicants must be graduates of an accredited secondary school or have a GED certificate. Students should have completed 4 units of English, 3 units of math including 2 units of algebra and 1 unit of geometry, and 3 units each of natural science and social studies, and 2 units of foreign language A GPA of 2.5 is required. AP and CLEP credits are accepted. To graduate, students must complete 60 credit hours for an Associate's degree or 120 credit hours for a Bachelors degree with a minimum GPA of 2.0. Distribution requirements include 12 hours in basic skills (English Composition, Speech, Computer Information Systems and Math); 6 hours in humanities, history, social and behavioral science; 5-6 hours in math/science and three hours in ethics. Bachelor of Art degrees require six hours of a foreign language or culture and society courses, ethics course, and 39 hours of upper-level course work. Most majors require students to complete a capstone course with the exception of Bachelors in General Studies and Associates degrees. **Procedure:** Freshmen are admitted to all sessions. Entrance exams should be taken in spring of the junior year or fall of the senior year. There are deferred admissions and rolling admissions plans. Applications should be filed by August 12 for fall entry; January 1 for spring entry, along with a $35 fee. Applications are accepted online. **Transfer Students:** 146 transfer students enrolled in 2015-2016. Applicants must have a minimum GPA of 2.0 overall and in the last semester attended and must submit a high school transcript and SAT or ACT scores, and a good standing from prior institution. 24 of 120 credits required for the bachelor's degree must be completed at Columbia. **International Students:** There are 85 international students enrolled. The school actively recruits these students. They must take the TOEFL with a minimum score of 500 on the paper-based TOEFL (PBT) or 61 on the Internet-based version (iBT). They must also take the ACT.

ADMISSIONS: 51% of the 2016-2017 applicants were accepted. The SAT scores for the 2016-2017 freshman class were: Critical Reading-- 46% below 500, 31% between 500 and 599, 8% between 600 and 699, and 15% between 700 and 800. Math-- 22% below 500, 62% between 500 and 599, 8% between 600 and 699, and 8% between 700 and 800. The ACT scores were 3% between 12 and 17, 52% between 18 and 23, 39% between 24 and 29, and 6% above 30. **Admissions Contact:** Stephanie Johnson, Director of Admissions. Email: *admissions@ccis.edu* Web: *www.ccis.edu*

FINANCIAL AID: In 2016-2017, 69% of all full-time freshmen and 64% of continuing full-time students received some form of financial aid. 53% of all full-time freshmen and 48% of continuing full-time students received need-based aid. The average freshman award was $7,559. Need-based scholarships or need-based grants averaged $3,271 ($12,055 maximum); need-based self-help aid (loans and jobs) averaged $1,515 ($5,500 maximum); non-need-based athletic scholarships averaged $2,837 ($23,207 maximum); and other non-need-based awards and non-need-based scholarships averaged $12,018 ($28,911 maximum). Average annual earnings from campus work are $2110. Columbia is a member of CSS. The college's own financial statement is required. The FAFSA code is 002456. The priority date for freshman financial aid applications for fall entry is March 1. The filing deadline for fall entry is April 30.

COX COLLEGE *(The complete profile is made available exclusively on our website, www.barronspac.com)*

CULVER-STOCKTON COLLEGE — C-1

www.culver.edu

Canton, MO 63435	**(573) 288-6331** **(800) 537-1883**
Fax: (573) 288-6618	**Email: admissions@culver.edu**
Full-time: 467 men, 477 women	**Faculty:** 50
Part-time: 48 men, 66 women	**Ph.D.s:** 64%
Graduate: 14 men, 23 women	**Student/Faculty:** 15 to 1
Year: semesters, summer session	**Tuition:** $25,415
Room & Board: $8110	**Freshman Class:** 2913 applied, 1628 accepted, 269 enrolled
SAT: recommended **ACT:** 21	**CEEB CODE:** 6123
Application Deadline: n/av	**COMPETITIVE**

Culver-Stockton College, established in 1853, is a private liberal arts institution affiliated with the Christian Church (Disciples of Christ). There is 1 undergraduate school. In addition to regional accreditation, C-SC has baccalaureate program accreditation with NASM, NLN, IACBE, and CAATE. The 143-acre campus is in a small town 125 miles north of St. Louis. Including any residence halls, there are 21 buildings.

STUDENT LIFE: 53% of undergraduates are from Missouri. Others are from 34 states, 13 foreign countries, and Canada. 95% are from public schools. 74% are White; 6% Foreign; 5% Hispanic; 2% two or more races; 11% African American; 1% Asian American; 1% American Indian/Alaska Native. 72% are Protestant; 17% Catholic. **Female To Male Ratio:** 1.1:1. The average age of freshmen is 18; all undergraduates, 20. 35% do not continue beyond their first year; 52% remain to graduate. **Housing:** 806 students can be accommodated in college housing, which includes single-sex and coed dorms, fraternity houses, and sorority houses. On-campus housing is guaranteed for all 4 years. 72% of students live on campus; of those, 50% remain on campus on weekends. All students may keep cars.

FACULTY/CLASSROOMS: 52% of faculty are male; 48% are female. All teach undergraduates. No introductory courses are taught by graduate students. The average class size in an introductory lecture is 19; in a laboratory is 17; and in a regular course is 16.

PROGRAMS OF STUDY: C-SC confers B.A., B.S., B.F.A., B.M.E., and B.S.N. degrees. Master's degrees are also awarded. Bachelor's degrees are awarded in BIOLOGICAL SCIENCE (biochemistry and biology/biological science), BUSINESS (accounting, business administration and management, finance, marketing management, and sports management), COMMUNICATIONS AND THE ARTS (art, arts administration/management, communications, dramatic arts, English, fine arts, graphic design, music, music technology, and musical theater), COMPUTER AND PHYSICAL SCIENCE (mathematics), EDUCATION (art education, athletic training, drama education, education, elementary education, music education, and physical education), HEALTH PROFESSIONS (health science and nursing), SOCIAL SCIENCE (criminal justice, history, international studies, legal studies, political science/government, psychology, and religion). Accounting, atlhletic training, biological chemistry, education and nursing are the strongest academically. Business, criminal justice, and nursing have the largest enrollments.

ACTIVITIES: 37% of men belong to 5 national fraternities; 38% of women belong to 3 national sororities. There are 45 groups on campus, including art, band, cheerleading, choir, chorus, communications, dance, drama, environmental, ethnic, honors, international, jazz band, LGBT, literary magazine, musical theater, newspaper, photography, political, professional, radio and TV, religious, social, social service, and student government. Popular campus events include National Collegiate Alcohol Awareness Week, Honors Day, Hillstock, Up 'til Dawn, Wildcat Welcome, and Greek Week. **Sports:** There are 10 intercollegiate sports for men and 9 for women, and 8 intramural sports for men and 8 for women. Facilities include a football stadium, soccer field, baseball field, softball field, intramural fields, a dance studio, a weight room, exercise equipment, a field house with basketball, volleyball, tennis, and racquetball courts. **Graduates:** From July 1, 2015 to June 30, 2016, 165 bachelor's degrees were awarded. The most popular majors were business (20%), psychology (15%), and sport management (13%). 30 companies recruited on campus in 2015-2016. In an average class, 44% graduate in 4 years or less, 52% graduate in 5 years or less, and 52% graduate in 6 years or less. Of the 2015 graduating class, 23% were enrolled in graduate school within 6 months of graduation, and 74% were employed.

SERVICES: Counseling and information services are available, as is tutoring in most subjects, and remedial math and writing. **Library/Resources:** The library contains 262,796 volumes, 112 microform items, 2,435 audio/video tapes/CDs/DVDs, and subscribes to 25,561 periodicals including electronic. Computerized library services include interlibrary loans, database searching, Internet access, and Wi-Fi capability. Special learning facilities include an art gallery, planetarium, radio station, TV station, a phage genomics research facility with DNA sequencer, astronomy observation deck, biological research station, collegiate teaching greenhouse, rare books collection, a performing arts center with a multi-media editing suite and recording studio, a publications lab, a photography studio, a simulated classroom, mock trial courtroom with legal research library, 17 computer labs and a tutoring center. **Physically Challenged Students:** 40% of the campus is accessible. Facilities include wheelchair ramps, elevators, special parking, specially equipped restrooms, and lowered drinking fountains. **Special:** Culver-Stockton offers a joint-degree program in nursing in conjunction with Blessing-Rieman College of Nursing and a 3-2 occupational therapy degree with Washington University in St. Louis. Study abroad, internships, and individualized majors are also available. There are 11 national honor societies, a freshman honors program, and 9 departmental honors programs. **Visiting:** There are regularly scheduled orientations for prospective students, includes meetings with professors, students, coaches,financial aid and extracurricular advisers, financial aid information, a student life panel, and campus tours. There are guides for informal visits, visitors may sit in on classes, and stay overnight. To schedule a visit, contact Gaye Redd at (800) 537-1883. **Campus Safety and Security:** Measures include 24-hour foot and vehicle patrol, emergency notification system, self-defense education, security escort services, lighted pathways/sidewalks and controlled access to dorms/residences.

REQUIREMENTS: Requirements include secondary school records with GPA and SAT or ACT (preferred) scores. Recommended is a college preparatory program including 4 years of English, 2 to 4 of science, 3 years of social studies, and 2 of math. The GED is accepted. AP and CLEP credits are accepted. To graduate, students must complete 120 credit hours, including 36 to 60 in the major, with a minimum GPA of 2.0. Distribution requirements include 1 course each in humanities, fine arts, intercultural learning, social science, natural science, and quantitative literacy. English composition I&II, speech, religion, phys ed; 2 courses in experiential learning and Academic and Cultural Events are also required. **Procedure:** Freshmen are admitted in the fall and spring. Entrance exams should be taken by April of the entering school year. There are deferred admissions and rolling admissions plans. Application deadlines are open. Applications are accepted online. **Transfer Students:** 71 transfer students enrolled in 2015-2016. Transfer applicants must submit college transcripts and must have a minimum college GPA of 2.0. 30 of 120 credits required for the bachelor's degree must be completed at C-SC. **International Students:** There are 66 international students enrolled. The school actively recruits these students. They must take the TOEFL with a minimum score of 550 on the paper-based TOEFL (PBT) or 79 on the Internet-based version (iBT), International students are not required to take the TOEFL if they have resided in this country for 1 semester or submit SAT or ACT scores.

ADMISSIONS: 56% of the 2016-2017 applicants were accepted. The SAT scores for the 2016-2017 freshman class were: Critical Reading--53% below 500, 40% between 500 and 599, and 7% between 600 and 699. Math-- 33% below 500 and 67% between 500 and 599. The ACT scores were 13% between 12 and 17, 69% between 18 and 23, 17% between 24 and 29, and 1% above 30. 16% of the current freshmen were in the top fifth of their class; 38% were in the top two fifths. 1 freshman graduated first in the class. **Admissions Contact:** Misty McBee, Exec Director of Marketing and Admission. Email: *admissions@culver.edu* Web: *www.culver.edu*

FINANCIAL AID: In 2016-2017, 98% of all full-time freshmen and 97% of continuing full-time students received some form of financial aid. 87% of all full-time freshmen and 77% of continuing full-time students received need-based aid. The average freshman award was $20,056. Need-based scholarships or need-based grants averaged $17,146 ($33,525 maximum); need-based self-help aid (loans and jobs) averaged $3,511 ($37,940 maximum); non-need-based athletic scholarships averaged $6,097 ($9,000 maximum); and other non-need-based awards and non-need-based scholarships averaged $10,013 ($33,525 maximum). 44% of undergraduate students work part-time. Average annual earnings from campus work are $1214. The average financial indebtedness of the 2016 graduate was $25,769. C-SC is a member of CSS. The FAFSA code is 002460. The priority date for freshman financial aid applications for fall entry is January 1. The filing deadline for fall entry is June 1.

DRURY UNIVERSITY B-3

www.drury.edu

Springfield, MO 65802	**(417) 873-7205** **(800) 922-2274**
Fax: (417) 866-3873	**Email: druryad@drury.edu**
Full-time: 622 men, 720 women	**Faculty:** 144; IIB, --$
Part-time: 9 men, 19 women	**Ph.D.s:** 94%
Graduate: 73 men, 168 women	**Student/Faculty:** 12 to 1
Year: semesters, summer session	**Tuition:** $25,755
Room & Board: $8036	**Freshman Class:** 1563 applied, 1088 accepted, 390 enrolled
ACT: 25	**CEEB CODE:** 6169
Application Deadline: August 22	**VERY COMPETITIVE**

Drury is a small, liberal arts university that has held to its core values since its establishment in 1873. Drury values find their origins in Drury's unique church affiliation, and they are responsible for an academic and spiritual environment that provides students with unique opportunities and advantages. There are 3 undergraduate schools and 5 graduate schools. In addition to regional accreditation, Drury has baccalaureate program accreditation with AACSB, ACBSP, NAAB, NASM, NCATE, AMTS, and ACS. The 80-acre campus is in an urban area 200 miles southwest of St. Louis and 150 miles southeast of Kansas City. Including any residence halls, there are 44 buildings.

STUDENT LIFE: 85% of undergraduates are from Missouri. Others are from 27 states, 53 foreign countries, and Canada. 85% are from public schools. 78% are White; 3% African American; 3% Hispanic; 3% two or more races; 10% Foreign; 1% Asian American; 1% American Indian/Alaska Native. 70% are Protestant; 16% Catholic. **Female To Male Ratio:** 1.3:1. The average age of freshmen is 18; all undergraduates, 21. 16% do not continue beyond their first year; 64% remain to graduate. **Housing:** 1022 students can be accommodated in college housing, which includes coed dorms, on-campus apartments, off-campus apartments, married student housing, honors houses, fraternity houses, and leadership, and living-learning communities. On-campus housing is guaranteed for all 4 years. 65% of students live on campus; of those, 80% remain on campus on weekends. All students may keep cars.

FACULTY/CLASSROOMS: 58% of faculty are male; 42% are female. All teach undergraduates, 40% do research, and 40% do both. No introductory courses are taught by graduate students. The average class size in an introductory lecture is 21; in a laboratory is 21; and in a regular course is 18.

PROGRAMS OF STUDY: Drury confers B.A., B.S., M.Arch., B.M.T., B.B.A., A.S., and B.Ed. degrees. Associate and master's degrees are also awarded. Bachelor's degrees are awarded in AGRICULTURE (environmental studies and natural resource management), BIOLOGICAL SCIENCE (biology/biological science), BUSINESS (accounting, banking and finance, business administration and management, management information systems, marketing management, organizational leadership and management, and sports management), COMMUNICATIONS AND THE ARTS (advertising, art history and appreciation, arts administration/management, communications, design, dramatic arts, English, fine arts, French, German, media arts, music, public relations, radio/television technology, Spanish, and visual design), COMPUTER AND PHYSICAL SCIENCE (chemistry, computer science, mathematics, and physics), EDUCATION (elementary education, music education, physical education, and secondary education), ENGINEERING AND ENVIRONMENTAL DESIGN (architecture and environmental science), HEALTH PROFESSIONS (environmental health science, exercise science, health science, music therapy, predentistry, premedicine, preoptometry, preosteopathy, prepharmacy, prephysical therapy, preveterinary science, and respiratory therapy), SOCIAL SCIENCE (American studies, criminal justice, criminology, economics, history, human services, international studies, philosophy, political science/government, prelaw, psychology, religion, sociology, and Spanish studies). Premedicine, business and architecture are the strongest academically. Business/marketing, visual and performing arts, and biology have the largest enrollments.

ACTIVITIES: 21% of men belong to 4 national fraternities; 25% of women belong to 4 national sororities. There are 100 groups on campus, including academic interests, environment, leadership, student life, art, band, cheerleading, chess, choir, chorale, chorus, computers, dance, debate, drama, environmental, ethnic, film, forensics, honors, international, jazz band, LGBT, literary magazine, minority students, musical theater, newspaper, opera, orchestra, pep band, photography, political, professional, radio and TV, religious, social, social service, student government, and symphony. Popular campus events include Homecoming, Fireworks on Sunderland Field, Fall Festival, Earth Day and Christmas Vespers. **Sports:** There are 9 intercollegiate sports for men and 10 for women, and 5 intramural sports for men and 5 for women. Facilities include a gym, tennis court, racquetball courts, a soccer stadium, a practice field for soccer, a baseball training center, baseball field (off-campus), a tennis stadium (off-campus), a pool, a fitness center, a running track, and a Wellness Program. **Graduates:** From July 1, 2015 to June 30, 2016, 317 bachelor's degrees were awarded. The most popular majors were business/marketing (23%), biological/life sciences (12%), and visual and performing arts (11%). 50 companies recruited on campus in 2015-2016. In an average class, 1% graduate in 3 years or less, 47% graduate in 4 years or less, 63% graduate in 5 years or less, and 66% graduate in 6 years or less. Of the 2015 graduating class, 39% were enrolled in graduate school within 6 months of graduation.

SERVICES: Counseling and information services are available, as is tutoring in every subject, a reader service for the blind, and remedial writing. There is also a math and reading learning center, a writing center, and a communications center. **Library/Resources:** The library contains 185,811 volumes, 13,565 microform items, 5,344 audio/video tapes/CDs/DVDs, and subscribes to 469 periodicals including electronic. Computerized library services include interlibrary loans, database searching, Internet access, and Wi-Fi capability. Special learning facilities include an art gallery, radio station, TV station, an astronomical observatory, a greenhouse, teleconference facility, art and architecture slide collection, speech communication center, and writing center. **Physically Challenged Students:** 95% of the campus is accessible. Facilities include wheelchair ramps, elevators, special parking, specially equipped restrooms, special class scheduling, lowered drinking fountains, and lowered telephones. **Special:** Drury offers study abroad in Aigina, Greece and 19 other countries as well as cross-registration with colleges in 8 countries; nearly 50% of students study abroad. Premedical early admission arrangements with St. Louis University, the University of Missouri, and Kirksville College of Osteopathic Medicine and a 3-2 engineering dual-degree program in conjunction with the University of Missouri and Washington University are available. Co-op programs include computer information systems and arts administration. 75% of students complete a professional internship; options include public and private sectors and a Washington semester. Work study, credit by exam, non-degree study, dual majors in most majors, and satisfactory/unsatisfactory options are also possible. There are 11 national honor societies, Phi Beta Kappa, a freshman honors program, and 8 departmental honors programs. **Visiting:** There are regularly scheduled orientations for prospective students, including visit days for all students as well as visit days specialized for premed, architecture, preengineering, math, physics, computer sciences, arts and sciences, and social sciences students. There are guides for informal visits, visitors may sit in on classes, and stay overnight. To schedule a visit, contact Kim Atkison in Admissions. **Campus Safety and Security:** Measures include 24-hour foot and vehicle patrol, emergency notification system, self-defense education, and security escort services. There are shuttle buses, emergency telephones, lighted pathways/sidewalks, controlled access to dorms/residences, lighted parking lots with security cameras.

REQUIREMENTS: The ACT is required. Applicants must be graduates of an accredited secondary school or have a GED certificate. Recommended high school credits include 4 units of English and at least 3 each of math through algebra II, natural science, and social studies. An essay and a reference from the high school counselor or principal are required. A GPA of 3.0 is required. AP and CLEP credits are accepted. Important factors in the admissions decision are ability to finance college education, recommendations by school officials, and personality/intangible qualities. To graduate, students must complete 124 credit hours (150 for accounting and 170 for B.Arch.). They must also maintain a minimum GPA of 2.0 and complete 26 to 32 credit hours in the major (99 for architecture). Students pursue a broad curriculum called CORE that includes requirements in science, math, humanities, fine arts, fitness, foreign language, and social science, **Procedure:** Freshmen are admitted to all sessions. Entrance exams should be taken in the spring of the junior year or fall of the senior year. There are deferred admissions and rolling admissions plans. Applications should be filed by August 22 for fall entry; January 10 for spring entry, along with a $50 fee. Notifications are sent October 1. Applications are accepted online. **Transfer Students:** 106 transfer students enrolled in 2015-2016. Applicants must have a minimum GPA of 2.0 in all college work completed and supply an essay or writing sample. 30 of 124 credits required for the bachelor's degree must be completed at Drury. **International Students:** There are 141 international students enrolled. The school actively recruits these students. They must take the TOEFL with a minimum score of 530 on the paper-based TOEFL (PBT) or 71 on the Internet-based version (iBT), or take the IELTS, ACT, or SAT.

ADMISSIONS: 70% of the 2016-2017 applicants were accepted. The SAT scores for the 2016-2017 freshman class were: Critical Reading--17% below 500, 39% between 500 and 599, 22% between 600 and 699, and 22% between 700 and 800. Math-- 13% below 500, 52% between 500 and 599, 30% between 600 and 699, and 5% between 700 and 800. Writing-- 43% below 500, 26% between 500 and 599, 22% between 600 and 699, and 9% between 700 and 800. The ACT scores were 1% between 12 and 17, 39% between 18 and 23, 46% between 24 and 29, and 14% above 30. 61% of the current freshmen were in the top fifth of their class; 84% were in the top two fifths. **Admissions Contact:** Kevin Kropf, Executive VP of Enrollment Management. Email: *druryad@drury.edu* Web: *www.drury.edu*

FINANCIAL AID: In 2016-2017, 68% of all full-time freshmen and

63% of continuing full-time students received some form of financial aid. 68% of all full-time freshmen and 63% of continuing full-time students received need-based aid. The average freshman award was $19,022. Need-based scholarships or need-based grants averaged $15,353; need-based self-help aid (loans and jobs) averaged $4,504; non-need-based athletic scholarships averaged $15,936; and other non-need-based awards and non-need-based scholarships averaged $7,325. 74% of undergraduate students work part-time. Average annual earnings from campus work are $2000. The average financial indebtedness of the 2016 graduate was $31,011. Drury is a member of CSS. The college's own financial statement is required. The FAFSA code is 002461. The priority date for freshman financial aid applications for fall entry is December 1.

EVANGEL UNIVERSITY — B-3

www.evangel.edu

Springfield, MO 65802 — (417) 865-2811, (800) EVANGEL

Fax: (417) 865-9599 — **Email:** admissions@evangel.edu

Full-time: 726 men, 978 women	**Faculty:** n/av
Part-time: 90 men, 85 women	**Ph.D.s:** 63%
Graduate: 66 men, 134 women	**Student/Faculty:** n/av
Year: semesters, summer session	**Tuition:** $21,316
Room & Board: $7582	**Freshman Class:** 1163 applied, 857 accepted, 432 enrolled
SAT or ACT: recommended	**CEEB CODE:** 6198
Application Deadline: n/av	**COMPETITIVE**

Evangel University, established in 1955, is a comprehensive Christian college affiliated with the Assemblies of God, offering more than 100 academic programs, including adult and graduate studies degree programs, and a embedded seminary. Figures in the above capsule and in this profile are approximate. There are 2 undergraduate schools and 1 graduate school. In addition to regional accreditation, Evangel has baccalaureate program accreditation with CSWE, NASM, and NCATE. The 80-acre campus is in an urban area in Springfield, just 225 miles west of St. Louis. Including any residence halls, there are 21 buildings.

STUDENT LIFE: 55% of undergraduates are from Missouri. Others are from 50 states, 62 foreign countries, and Canada. 79% are from public schools. 74% claim no religious affiliation; 12% Protestant. **Female To Male Ratio:** 1.4:1. The average age of freshmen is 18; all undergraduates, 21. 31% do not continue beyond their first year. **Housing:** 1460 students can be accommodated in college housing, which includes single-sex and coed dorms, married student housing, honors houses, and six residents halls. On-campus housing is guaranteed for all 4 years. 75% of students live on campus; of those, 100% remain on campus on weekends. All students may keep cars. Alcohol is not permitted.

FACULTY/CLASSROOMS: All teach undergraduates. No introductory courses are taught by graduate students. The average class size in an introductory lecture is 40 and in a regular course is 20.

PROGRAMS OF STUDY: Evangel confers B.A., B.S., B.B.A., B.F.A., B.M., and B.S.W. degrees. Associate and master's degrees are also awarded. Bachelor's degrees are awarded in BIOLOGICAL SCIENCE (biology/biological science), BUSINESS (accounting, management science, and marketing/retailing/merchandising), COMMUNICATIONS AND THE ARTS (art, broadcasting, communications, design, dramatic arts, English, journalism, music, music performance, Spanish, and speech/debate/rhetoric), COMPUTER AND PHYSICAL SCIENCE (chemistry, computer science, and mathematics), EDUCATION (business education, early childhood education, elementary education, foreign languages education, music education, physical education, science education, secondary education, and special education), HEALTH PROFESSIONS (medical laboratory technology), SOCIAL SCIENCE (biblical studies, criminal justice, history, international studies, missions, parks and recreation management, political science/government, psychology, public administration, religion, religious music, social science, social work, and sociology). Science and technology and behavioral science is the strongest academically. Business has the largest enrollment.

ACTIVITIES: There are no fraternities or sororities. There are 19 groups on campus, including band, cheerleading, choir, chorale, chorus, drama, forensics, honors, jazz band, marching band, musical theater, newspaper, orchestra, pep band, photography, political, professional, radio and TV, religious, student government, symphony, and yearbook. Popular campus events include College Weekend, Harvest Fest, Homecoming, and Spring Fling. **Sports:** There are 5 intercollegiate sports for men and 6 for women, and 4 intramural sports for men and 4 for women. Facilities include a student activities center and a gym. **Graduates:** From July 1, 2014 to June 30, 2015, 322 bachelor's degrees were awarded. The most popular majors were business/marketing (23%), education (13%), and communications/journalism (10%). 88 companies recruited on campus in 2014-2015. In an average class, 25% graduate in 4 years or less, 36% graduate in 5 years or less, and 37% graduate in 6 years or less.

SERVICES: Counseling and information services are available, as is tutoring in every subject. There is a reader service for the blind, remedial math, reading, and writing. **Library/Resources:** The library contains 96,487 volumes, 11,386 microform items, 6,801 audio/video tapes/CDs/DVDs, and subscribes to 748 periodicals including electronic. Computerized library services include interlibrary loans, database searching, Internet access, and Wi-Fi capability. Special learning facilities include an art gallery, radio station, and TV station. **Physically Challenged Students:** All of the campus is accessible. Facilities include wheelchair ramps, elevators, special parking, specially equipped restrooms, lowered drinking fountains, and lowered telephones. **Special:** There are 3-2 engineering degrees available in conjunction with the University of Missouri at Columbia. Other options include work-study, credit by exam, and a Washington semester. There are 9 national honor societies and 8 departmental honors programs. **Visiting:** There are regularly scheduled orientations for prospective students, consisting of scheduled visits every Friday and by appointment. There are guides for informal visits, visitors may sit in on classes, and stay overnight. To schedule a visit, contact the Office of Admissions. **Campus Safety and Security:** Measures include 24-hour foot and vehicle patrol, emergency notification system, and security escort services, emergency telephones, lighted pathways/sidewalks, and controlled access to dorms/residences.

REQUIREMENTS: The SAT or ACT is recommended. The preparatory curriculum includes 3 credits in English, 2 each in math and social studies, and 1 in lab science. The GED is accepted. AP and CLEP credits are accepted. All students must complete 50 to 53 general education hours, including courses in phys ed, computer literacy, English composition, English literature, and Bible study. A minimum GPA of 2.0 is required for graduation. Students must complete 124 credit hours, 36 of which are upper division level, with approximately 30 credit hours in the major. **Procedure:** Freshmen are admitted to all sessions. Entrance exams should be taken before high school graduation. There is a rolling admissions plan. Application deadlines are open. Application fee is $25. Applications are accepted on-line. **Transfer Students:** 134 transfer students enrolled in 2014-2015. Transfer applicants must be in good standing with their previous institutions and have a cumulative GPA of 2.0. 30 of 124 credits required for the bachelor's degree must be completed at Evangel. **International Students:** There are 9 international students enrolled. They must take the TOEFL, as well as take the SAT or ACT.

ADMISSIONS: 74% of the 2015-2016 applicants were accepted. **Admissions Contact:** Cheir Meyer, Director of Admissions. Email: *admissions@evangel.edu* Web: *www.evangel.edu*

FINANCIAL AID: In 2015-2016, 84% of all full-time freshmen and 99% of continuing full-time students received some form of financial aid. 47% of all full-time freshmen and 58% of continuing full-time students received need-based aid. The average freshman award was $11,729. 21% of undergraduate students work part-time. Average annual earnings from campus work are $1100. The average financial indebtedness of the 2015 graduate was $34,434. The FAFSA is required. Check with the school for current application deadlines.

FONTBONNE UNIVERSITY — D-3

www.fontbonne.edu

St. Louis, MO 63105 — (314) 889-1413, (800) 205-5862

Fax: (314) 889-1451 — **Email:** fbyou@fontbonne.edu

Full-time: 460 men, 1075 women	**Faculty:** n/av
Part-time: 160 men, 390 women	**Ph.D.s:** 69%
Graduate: 250 men, 645 women	**Student/Faculty:** n/av
Year: semesters, summer session	**Tuition:** $24,610
Room & Board: $9107	**Freshman Class:** n/av
SAT or ACT: required	**CEEB CODE:** 6216
Application Deadline: n/av	**COMPETITIVE**

Fontbonne University, a Catholic coeducational institution of higher learning sponsored by the Sisters of St. Joseph of Carondelet, is rooted in the Judeo-Christian tradition. The university is dedicated to the discovery, understanding, preservation and dissemination of truth. Undergraduate and graduate programs are offered in an atmosphere characterized by a commitment to open communication, personal concern and diversity. Fontbonne University seeks to educate students to think critically, to act ethically and to assume responsibility as citizens and leaders. Figures in the above capsule and in this profile are approximate. There are 2 undergraduate schools and 19 graduate schools. In addition to regional accreditation, Fontbonne has baccalaureate program accreditation with ACBSP, ADA, CSWE, NCATE, CAA of ASHA, CED, and ACEND. The 16-acre campus is in a suburban area in Clayton, 1 mile west of St. Louis city limits. Including any residence halls, there are 10 buildings.

STUDENT LIFE: 88% of undergraduates are from Missouri. Others are from 21 states, and 19 foreign countries. 55% are from public schools. 63% are White; 33% African American; 1% Asian American; 1% American Indian/Alaska Native; 1% Hispanic; 1% Foreign. 55% are Catholic; 23% Protestant. **Female To Male Ratio:** 2.4:1. The average age of freshmen is 19; all undergraduates, 29. 42% do not continue beyond their first year; 51% remain to graduate. **Housing:** 270 students can be accommodated in college housing, which includes coed dorms, on-campus apartments, and off-campus apartments. On-campus housing is available on a first-come and first-served basis. Priority is given to out-of-town students. 90% of students commute. All students may keep cars.

FACULTY/CLASSROOMS: No introductory courses are taught by graduate students. The average class size in an introductory lecture is 12; in a laboratory is 13; and in a regular course is 12.

PROGRAMS OF STUDY: Fontbonne confers B.A., B.S., B.B.A. and B.F.A. degrees. Master's degrees are also awarded. Bachelor's degrees are awarded in BIOLOGICAL SCIENCE (biology/biological science and nutritional sciences), BUSINESS (accounting, apparel and accessories marketing, business administration and management, fashion merchandising, marketing management, marketing/retailing/merchandising, sports management, and supply chain management), COMMUNICATIONS AND THE ARTS (advertising, art, communications, dramatic arts, English, English literature, English writing, fine arts, performing arts, theatre acting, theatre arts, theatre production, theater management, and writing), COMPUTER AND PHYSICAL SCIENCE (computer science, computer security and information assurance, information sciences and systems, and mathematics), EDUCATION (drama education, early childhood education, education, education of the deaf and hearing impaired, elementary education, English education, general studies, mathematics education, middle school education, secondary education, and special education), HEALTH PROFESSIONS (predentistry, premedicine, prephysical therapy, and speech pathology/audiology), SOCIAL SCIENCE (behavioral science, child care/child and family studies, communication sciences & disorders, dietetics, family/consumer studies, history, human services, liberal arts/general studies, prelaw, psychology, religion, religious studies, social work, and sociology). Education, computer science, and math are the strongest academically. Business administration, organizational studies, and education have the largest enrollments.

ACTIVITIES: There are no fraternities or sororities. There are 32 groups on campus, including Griffin Gang (althletic support club), computers, dance, drama, environmental, ethnic, Fontbonne Activities Board (planning of on campus activites, honors, international, LGBT, literary magazine, musical theater, newspaper, photography, political, professional, religious, social, social service, and student government. Popular campus events include Spring Fest, Art Shows, International Bazaar, Lip Sync Contest, Comedy Nights, and Musical Performances. **Sports:** There are 9 intercollegiate sports for men and 9 for women. Facilities include a student activity center that houses a 1000-seat gym, weight room, track, and aerobics room. **Graduates:** From July 1, 2015 to June 30, 2016, 466 bachelor's degrees were awarded. The most popular majors were business administration (37%), special education (10%), and organizational behavior studies (10%). 25 companies recruited on campus in 2015-2016. In an average class, 33% graduate in 4 years or less, 51% graduate in 5 years or less, and 54% graduate in 6 years or less.

SERVICES: Counseling and information services are available, as is tutoring in every subject. There is remedial math, reading, and writing. **Library/Resources:** The library contains 91,172 volumes, and 3,564 audio/video tapes/CDs/DVDs, and subscribes to 23,463 periodicals including electronic. Computerized library services include interlibrary loans, database searching, Internet access, and Wi-Fi capability. Special learning facilities include an art gallery, a biological green house, test and demo kitchens for dietetics, and speech-language and audiology clinics. **Physically Challenged Students:** All of the campus is accessible. Facilities include wheelchair ramps, elevators, special parking, specially equipped restrooms, special class scheduling, lowered drinking fountains, and special housing. **Special:** Fontbonne offers cross-registration with several area colleges and a student exchange program with the Sisters of St. Joseph Consortium. There are also cooperative programs in all majors except education, internships with major companies, study abroad in 2 countries, work-study programs, student-designed and dual majors, credit by exam, nondegree study, pass/fail options, and B.A.-B.S. degrees. In addition, an accelerated degree program in business is available, as are 3-2 degrees in engineering and social work with Washington University. There is 1 national honor society and a freshman honors program. **Visiting:** There are regularly scheduled orientations for prospective students, including a campus tour, a financial aid presentation, and visits with faculty and current students. There are guides for informal visits, visitors may sit in on classes, and stay overnight. To schedule a visit, contact the Admissions Office. **Campus Safety and Security:** Measures include 24-hour foot and vehicle patrol, emergency notification system, and security escort services. There are also shuttle buses and controlled access to dorms/residences.

REQUIREMENTS: The SAT or ACT is required. Applicants must be graduates of an accredited secondary school or have a GED certificate. They must have completed 16 academic credits, including 4 in English, 3 in math, 2 each in science and social studies, and 1 in history. An audition or portfolio may be required. Fontbonne requires applicants to be in the upper 50% of their class. A GPA of 2.5 is required. AP and CLEP credits are accepted. Important factors in the admissions decision are advanced placement or honors courses, extracurricular activities record, and leadership record. To graduate, students must complete 128 credit hours, including 44 in general education requirements, with a minimum GPA of 2.0. The number of hours required for the major varies. **Procedure:** Freshmen are admitted to all sessions. Entrance exams should be taken prior to registration. There are deferred admissions and rolling admissions plans. Check with the school for current application deadlines. The application fee is $25. Applications are accepted online. **Transfer Students:** 233 transfer students enrolled in 2015-2016. Applicants must have a minimum GPA of 2.0 and either submit ACT or the SAT scores or take a placement test. Students with fewer than 30 credits must submit a high school transcript. An interview is recommended. 32 of 128 credits required for the bachelor's degree must be completed at Fontbonne. **International Students:** There are 26 international students enrolled. The school actively recruits these students. They must take the TOEFL.

ADMISSIONS: 1 freshman graduated first in the class. **Admissions Contact:** Keith Quigley, Director of Freshman Recruitment. Email: *fbyou@fontbonne.edu* Web: *www.fontbonne.edu*

FINANCIAL AID: The CSS/Profile, FFS, and the college's own financial statement are required. The FAFSA code is 002464. Check with the school for current application deadlines.

HANNIBAL-LAGRANGE UNIVERSITY D-2

www.hlg.edu

Hannibal, MO 63401	**(800) HLG-1119**
Fax: (573) 221-6594	**Email: admissions@hlg.edu**
Full-time: 483 men, 808 women	**Faculty:** n/av
Part-time: n/av	**Ph.D.s:** n/av
Graduate: 30 men, 44 women	**Student/Faculty:** n/av
Year: semesters, summer session	**Tuition:** $21,710
Room & Board: $8105	**Freshman Class:** 696 applied, 448 accepted, 184 enrolled
ACT: required	**CEEB CODE:** 6266
Application Deadline: August	**COMPETITIVE**

Hannibal-LaGrange University, founded in 1858, is a private facility affiliated with the Southern Baptist Church. There are 4 undergraduate schools and 1 graduate school. In addition to regional accreditation, HLGU has baccalaureate program accreditation with NLN. The 165-acre campus is in a small town 100 miles north of St. Louis. Including any residence halls, there are 22 buildings.

STUDENT LIFE: 80% of undergraduates are from Missouri. Others are from 29 states, and 27 foreign countries. 83% are White; 5% African American; 5% Hispanic; 5% Foreign; 1% Asian American; 1% American Indian/Alaska Native. 80% are Protestant. **Female To Male Ratio:** 1.7:1. 37% do not continue beyond their first year; 54% remain to graduate. **Housing:** 550 students can be accommodated in college housing, which includes single-sex dorms and on-campus apartments. On-campus housing is available on a first-come, first-served basis. 53% of students commute. All students may keep cars. Alcohol is not permitted.

FACULTY/CLASSROOMS: 45% of faculty are male; 55% are female. All teach undergraduates. No introductory courses are taught by graduate students. The average class size in an introductory lecture is 25 and in a laboratory is 15.

PROGRAMS OF STUDY: HLGU confers B.A., B.S., B.A.S., B.S.E., and B.S.N. degrees. Associate and master's degrees are also awarded. Bachelor's degrees are awarded in BIOLOGICAL SCIENCE (biology/biological science), BUSINESS (accounting, business administration and management, organizational behavior, and recreation and leisure services), COMMUNICATIONS AND THE ARTS (art, communications, dramatic arts, English, music, music performance, and speech/debate/rhetoric), COMPUTER AND PHYSICAL SCIENCE (computer programming, information sciences and systems, and mathematics), EDUCATION (Christian education, early childhood education, elementary education, and secondary education), HEALTH PROFESSIONS (exercise science and nursing), SOCIAL SCIENCE (biblical studies, criminal justice, history, liberal arts/general studies, missions, psychology, religious music, social work, and sociology). Nursing, and education are the strongest academically. Education, criminal justice, and nusing have the largest enrollments.

ACTIVITIES: There are no fraternities or sororities. There are 24 groups on campus, including Alpha Tau Beta, and Lambda Alpha Epsilon, Fellowship of Christian Athletes, Gatekeepers, Naturea Investigato Circulus, Phi Beta Lambda (Future Business Leaders), Pi Gamam Mu, Alpha Chi, art, cheerleading, choir, chorus, drama, ethnic, honors, international, musical theater, newspaper, professional, radio and TV, religious, social, social service, student government, and yearbook. Popular campus events include Campus Visitation Days, Experience HLGU Day, Trojan Turkey Trek, Homecoming, and Booster Banquet. **Sports:** There are 8 intercollegiate sports for men and 9 for women, and 7 intramural sports for men and 7 for women. Facilities include baseball, softball, and soccer fields a sports complex that has a gym, weight and aerobics rooms, volleyball, tennis, and racquetball courts. **Graduates:** From July 1, 2015 to June 30, 2016, 167 bachelor's degrees were awarded. The most popular majors were education (50%), nursing (25%), and criminal justice (25%).

SERVICES: Counseling and information services are available, as is tutoring in some subjects. Based on available tutors, math, English, writing, literature, science, behavioral science, accounting and business, history, and Bible. There is also remedial math and writing. **Library/Resources:** The library contains 121,840 volumes, 22,152 microform items, 6,702 audio/video tapes/CDs/DVDs, and subscribes to 266 periodicals including electronic. Computerized library services include interlibrary loans, database searching, and Internet access. Special learning facilities include an art gallery, radio station, a theatre, mission center, sports complex, nature trail and testing lab. **Physically Challenged Students:** 70% of the campus is accessible. Facilities include wheelchair ramps, elevators, special parking, specially equipped restrooms, special class scheduling, and special housing. **Special:** Credit by examination, prior learning assessment, online courses, adult programs, and self-designed liberal arts degree. There are 2 national honor societies, a freshman honors program, and 2 departmental honors programs. **Visiting:** There are regularly scheduled orientations for prospective students, consisting of Encounter Days, which are organized tours of the campus covering financial aid, student affairs, and academic areas, and which include lunch in the cafeteria. There are guides for informal visits, visitors may sit in on classes, and stay overnight. To schedule a visit, contact Ray Carty at rcarty@hlg.edu. **Campus Safety and Security:** Measures include 24-hour foot and vehicle patrol, emergency notification system, self-defense education, security escort services, emergency telephones, lighted pathways/sidewalks, and controlled access to dorms/residences.

REQUIREMENTS: The ACT is required. Applicants must be graduates of an accredited secondary school or have the GED. AP and CLEP credits are accepted. All students must complete a minimum of 124 credit hours with a 2.0 GPA to graduate. The major usually requires 36 or more credit hours of study. General education requirements include 8 hours of natural science, 6 hours each of Bible, composition, literature, foreign language, history, fine arts, and social science, 3 hours each of speech and algebra, 2 hours in phys ed, and 1 hour in success in education. Different core requirements pertain to education and nursing students. **Procedure:** Freshmen are admitted to all sessions. Entrance exams should be taken before registration. There is a rolling admissions plan. Check with the school for current application deadlines. The fall 2016 application fee was $25. Applications are accepted on-line. **Transfer Students:** 187 transfer students enrolled in 2015-2016. Applicants must submit transcripts from all colleges attended. Students applying with fewer than 30 credit hours must also submit a high school transcript along with ACT or SAT scores. 32 of 124 credits required for the bachelor's degree must be completed at HLGU. **International Students:** There are 74 international students enrolled. The school actively recruits these students. They must take the TOEFL with a minimum score of 520 on the paper-based TOEFL (PBT) or 68 on the Internet-based version (iBT). They must also take the SAT or ACT, scoring 20.

ADMISSIONS: 64% of the 2016-2017 applicants were accepted. The ACT scores were 20% below 12, 43% between 12 and 17, 27% between 18 and 23, 4% between 24 and 29, and 6% above 30. 21% of the current freshmen were in the top fifth of their class; 52% were in the top two fifths. **Admissions Contact:** Dr. Ray Carty, Vice President of Enrollment Management. Email: *admissions@hlg.edu* Web: *www.hlg.edu*

FINANCIAL AID: Average annual earnings from campus work are $1500. The FAFSA code is 009089. Check with the school for current application deadlines.

HARRIS-STOWE STATE UNIVERSITY *(The complete profile is made available exclusively on our website, www.barronspac.com)*

KANSAS CITY ART INSTITUTE — A-2

www.kcai.edu

Kansas City, MO 64111	**(816) 474-5224** **(800) 522-5224**
Fax: (816) 802-3309	**Email: admiss@kcai.edu**
Full-time: 225 men, 419 women	**Faculty:** 56
Part-time: 7 men, 9 women	**Ph.D.s:** 14%
Graduate: n/av	**Student/Faculty:** 9 to 1
Year: semesters, summer session	**Tuition:** $34,418
Room & Board: $9890	**Freshman Class:** 428 applied, 400 accepted, 150 enrolled
SAT CR/M/W: 580/440/560 **ACT:** 24	**CEEB CODE:** 6330
Application Deadline: August 1	**COMPETITIVE+**

The Kansas City Art Institute, founded in 1885, is an independent college of art and design. The figures in the above capsule and in this profile are approximate. There are 5 undergraduate schools. In addition to regional accreditation, KCAI has baccalaureate program accreditation with NASAD. The 15-acre campus is in an urban area in midtown Kansas City. Including any residence halls, there are 15 buildings.

STUDENT LIFE: 61% of undergraduates are from out of state, mostly the Midwest. Students are from 35 states, and 9 foreign countries. 90% are from public schools. 7% are Hispanic; 61% White; 5% African American; 2% Asian American; 12% race unknown; 10% two or more races. **Female To Male Ratio:** 1.8:1. The average age of freshmen is 18; all undergraduates, 20.5. 15% do not continue beyond their first year; 60% remain to graduate. **Housing:** 180 students can be accommodated in college housing, which includes single-sex and coed dorms and off-campus apartments. The Student Affairs Office offers assistance finding off-campus housing. On-campus housing is guaranteed for the freshman year only, and is available on a first-come, and first-served basis. 77% of students commute. All students may keep cars. Alcohol is not permitted.

FACULTY/CLASSROOMS: 57% of faculty are male; 43% are female.

All teach undergraduates. No introductory courses are taught by graduate students. The average class size in an introductory lecture is 22; in a laboratory is 15; and in a regular course is 22.

PROGRAMS OF STUDY: KCAI confers B.F.A. degrees. Bachelor's degrees are awarded in COMMUNICATIONS AND THE ARTS (animation, art history and appreciation, ceramic art and design, creative writing, design, digital communications, fiber/textiles/weaving, film arts, film, television and digital media, fine arts, game programming, illustration, painting, photography, printmaking, and sculpture), COMPUTER AND PHYSICAL SCIENCE (digital arts/technology). Foundation, art history, and ceramics are the strongest academically. Illustration, painting, and animation have the largest enrollments.

ACTIVITIES: There are no fraternities or sororities. There are 19 groups on campus, including art, ethnic, LGBT, literary magazine, professional, radio and TV, religious, social, social service, and student government. Popular campus events include Dances, Film Series, Drag Show and Social Events. **Sports:** There is no sports program at KCAI. **Graduates:** From July 1, 2015 to June 30, 2016, 154 bachelor's degrees were awarded. The most popular majors were painting (23%), illustration (19%), and fiber and animation (9%). 15 companies recruited on campus in 2015-2016. In an average class, 49% graduate in 4 years or less, 56% graduate in 5 years or less, and 62% graduate in 6 years or less. Of the 2015 graduating class, 5% were enrolled in graduate school within 6 months of graduation, and 46% were employed.

SERVICES: Counseling and information services are available, as is tutoring in every subject, and remedial reading and writing. **Library/Resources:** The library contains 30,403 volumes, and 493 audio/video tapes/CDs/DVDs, and subscribes to 84 periodicals including electronic. Computerized library services include interlibrary loans, database searching, Internet access, and Wi-Fi capability. Special learning facilities include an art gallery, radio station, a generous studio space, digital labs, media center, and central woodshop. **Physically Challenged Students:** 75% of the campus is accessible. Facilities include wheelchair ramps, elevators, special parking, specially equipped restrooms, special class scheduling. Students with hearing disabilities (vibrating alarms, lights to notify resident of a visitor at their door. **Special:** KCAI offers internships with major corporations such as Hallmark, independent study, work-study programs, study abroad in 7 countries, cross-registration, an exchange program, and nondegree study. There are two certificate programs in Social Practice and Asian Studies. We also offer a Post-Baccalaureate Art Education certification program. **Visiting:** There are regularly scheduled orientations for prospective students, information sessions are offered once a month. There are guides for informal visits and visitors may sit in on classes. To schedule a visit, contact the Admissions Office. **Campus Safety and Security:** Measures include 24-hour foot and vehicle patrol, emergency notification system, security escort services, and emergency telephones.

REQUIREMENTS: The SAT or ACT is required. Applicants must submit a portfolio consisting of 15 to 25 pieces of artwork, 1 letter of recommendation, and high school transcripts. The GED is accepted. A statement of purpose is required. AP and CLEP credits are accepted. Important factors in the admissions decision are evidence of special talent, advanced placement or honors courses, and recommendations by school officials. Students must maintain a minimum GPA of 2.0 overall and within their studio major. A total of 126 credit hours is needed, including 78 in studio classes; 42 distributed among courses in history of Western thought, art history, literature, humanities, and other liberal arts, and 6 in electives. **Procedure:** Freshmen are admitted in the fall and spring. Entrance exams should be taken in spring of the junior year or fall of the senior year. There are deferred admissions and rolling admissions plans. Applications should be filed by August 1 for fall entry; November 1 for spring entry, along with a $45 fee. Notification is sent on a rolling basis. Applications are accepted online. **Transfer Students:** 67 transfer students enrolled in 2015-2016. Transfer applicants must submit official transcripts and a portfolio. A minimum GPA of 2.5 is required. 63 of 126 credits required for the bachelor's degree must be completed at KCAI. **International Students:** There are 3 international students enrolled. The school actively recruits these students. They must take the TOEFL with a minimum score of 550 on the paper-based TOEFL (PBT) or 79 on the Internet-based version (iBT).

ADMISSIONS: 93% of the 2016-2017 applicants were accepted. The SAT scores for the 2016-2017 freshman class were: Critical Reading-- 13% below 500, 50% between 500 and 599, 34% between 600 and 699, and 3% between 700 and 800. Math-- 34% below 500 and 66% between 500 and 599. Writing-- 38% below 500, 53% between 500 and 599, and 9% between 600 and 699. The ACT scores were 28% below 12, 22% between 12 and 17, 21% between 18 and 23, 14% between 24 and 29, and 15% above 30. 32% of the current freshmen were in the top fifth of their class; 60% were in the top two fifths. **Admissions Contact:** Julia Welles, Dean of Admissions and Recruitment. Email: *admiss@kcai.edu* Web: *www.kcai.edu*

FINANCIAL AID: In 2016-2017, 100% of all full-time freshmen and 99% of continuing full-time students received some form of financial aid. 70% of all full-time freshmen and 69% of continuing full-time students received need-based aid. The average freshman award was $20,405. Need-based scholarships or need-based grants averaged $6,857 ($9,250 maximum); need-based self-help aid (loans and jobs) averaged $6,000 ($8,500 maximum); and other non-need-based awards and non-need-based scholarships averaged $17,929 ($25,680 maximum). 61% of undergraduate students work part-time. Average annual earnings from campus work are $1035. The average financial indebtedness of the 2016 graduate was $26,000. The FAFSA code is 002473. The priority date for freshman financial aid applications for fall entry is March 15.

LINCOLN UNIVERSITY *(The complete profile is made available exclusively on our website, www.barronspac.com)*

LINDENWOOD UNIVERSITY — D-2

www.lindenwood.edu

St. Charles, MO 63301 — (636) 949-4949

Fax: (636) 949-4989	**Email:** admissions@lindenwood.edu
Full-time: 2460 men, 3185 women	**Faculty:** IIA, -$
Part-time: 100 men, 160 women	**Ph.D.s:** 87%
Graduate: 1065 men, 2680 women	**Student/Faculty:** 29 to 1
Year: 4-1-4, summer session	**Tuition:** $16,632
Room & Board: $8500	**Freshman Class:** n/av
SAT or ACT: required	**CEEB CODE:** 6367
Application Deadline: December 8	**COMPETITIVE**

Lindenwood University, founded in 1827, is a private institution offering undergraduate and graduate degree programs in the arts and sciences, business, education, and preprofessional fields. The figures in the above capsule and in this profile are approximate. There are 8 undergraduate schools and 5 graduate schools. In addition to regional accreditation, Lindenwood has baccalaureate program accreditation with TEAC and CAAHEP. The 500-acre campus is in a suburban area in St. Charles, just 25 miles west of St. Louis. Including any residence halls, there are 37 buildings.

STUDENT LIFE: 73% of undergraduates are from Missouri. Others are from 43 states, 63 foreign countries, and Canada. 9% are Foreign; 76% White; 12% African American; 1% Hispanic. **Female To Male Ratio:** 1.7:1. The average age of freshmen is 19; all undergraduates, 25. 38% do not continue beyond their first year; 40% remain to graduate. **Housing:** 3500 students can be accommodated in college housing, which includes single-sex dorms, on-campus apartments, married student housing, and sorority houses. On-campus housing is guaranteed for all 4 years. 68% of students live on campus; of those, 67% remain on campus on weekends. All students may keep cars. Alcohol is not permitted.

FACULTY/CLASSROOMS: 49% of faculty are male; 51% are female. 99% teach undergraduates. No introductory courses are taught by graduate students. The average class size in an introductory lecture is 30; in a laboratory is 25; and in a regular course is 25.

PROGRAMS OF STUDY: Lindenwood confers B.A., B.S., and B.F.A. degrees. Master's and doctoral degrees are also awarded. Bachelor's degrees are awarded in BIOLOGICAL SCIENCE (biology/biological science), BUSINESS (accounting, banking and finance, business administration and management, human resources, management information systems, marketing/retailing/merchandising, and sports management), COMMUNICATIONS AND THE ARTS (art history and appreciation, communications, creative writing, dance, dramatic arts, English, French, music, performing arts, Spanish, and studio art), COMPUTER AND PHYSICAL SCIENCE (chemistry, computer science, and mathematics), EDUCATION (athletic training, business education, early childhood education, elementary education, music education, physical education, science education, and secondary education), ENGINEERING AND ENVIRONMENTAL DESIGN (engineering), HEALTH PROFESSIONS (medical technology), SOCIAL SCIENCE (criminal justice, fashion design and technology, history, human services, international studies, liberal arts/general studies, ministries, political science/government, prelaw, psychology, public administration, religion, social work, and sociology). Biology, education, and mass communications, are the strongest academically and have the largest enrollments are the strongest academically.

ACTIVITIES: 1% of men belong to 1 local and 2 national fraternities; 1% of women belong to 1 national sorority. There are 75 groups on campus, including art, band, cheerleading, chess, choir, chorale, chorus, computers, dance, debate, drama, drill team, ethnic, film, forensics, honors, international, jazz band, literary magazine, marching band, musical theater, newspaper, pep band, photography, political, professional, radio and TV, religious, social, social service, and student government. Popular campus events include Spring Fling, Alumni Weekend, and Christmas Walk. **Sports:** There are 20 intercollegiate sports for men and 19 for women, and 9 intramural sports for men and 9 for women. Facilities include an indoor pool, a gym, weight rooms, a stadium, a performance arena, a sand volleyball court, tennis courts, softball, baseball, and soccer fields, an all-weather track, and ice rink. Students may use the local golf course and bowling alley for a discounted fee. **Graduates:** From July 1, 2015 to June 30, 2016, 1010 bachelor's degrees were awarded. The most popular majors were business administration (24%), elementary education (7%), and criminology (6%). 84 companies recruited on campus in 2015-2016. In an average class, 26% graduate in 4 years or less, 38% graduate in 5 years or less, and 40% graduate in 6 years or less. Of the 2015 graduating class, 14% were enrolled in graduate school within 6 months of graduation, and 94% were employed.

SERVICES: Counseling and information services are available, as is tutoring in every subject, and a reader service for the blind, and remedial math, reading, and writing. **Library/Resources:** The library contains 171,562 volumes, 26,128 microform items, and 2,138 audio/video tapes/CDs/DVDs, and subscribes to 115,000 periodicals including electronic. Computerized library services include interlibrary loans, database searching, Internet access, and Wi-Fi capability. Special learning facilities include an art gallery, radio station, TV station, a greenhouse, wetlands program facility, a success center, and the Boone Home historic site. **Physically Challenged Students:** 50% of the campus is accessible. Facilities include wheelchair ramps, elevators, special parking, specially equipped restrooms, special class scheduling, lowered drinking fountains, and lowered telephones. **Special:** The university offers internships in most majors, a co-op program in computer science, study abroad and a Washington semester for juniors, and cross-registration through a consortium of Greater St. Louis College and Universities. Dual and student-designed majors, accelerated degree programs, 3-2 degrees in engineering with Washington University in St. Louis and the University of Missouri-Columbia, work-study programs, and nondegree study are also available. There are evening and weekend classes for working adults and 5-year bachelor's programs. There are 9 national honor societies, a freshman honors program, and 6 departmental honors programs. **Visiting:** There are regularly scheduled orientations for prospective students, including an admissions interview, a campus tour and advising. There are guides for informal visits, visitors may sit in on classes, and stay overnight. To schedule a visit, contact the Office of Undergraduate Admissions. **Campus Safety and Security:** Measures include 24-hour foot and vehicle patrol, emergency notification system, self-defense education, security escort services, emergency telephones, and lighted pathways/sidewalks.

REQUIREMENTS: The SAT or ACT is required. Applicants must be graduates of an accredited secondary school or have a GED. High school preparation should include at least 16 academic units, including 4 years of English, 2 to 3 each of math, science, and social studies, 2 of a foreign language, and some study of fine or performing arts. An essay and an interview are recommended. Lindenwood requires applicants to be in the upper 50% of their class. A GPA of 2.5 is required. AP and CLEP credits are accepted. Important factors in the admissions decision are leadership record, evidence of special talent, and advanced placement or honors courses. In order to graduate, students must complete a minimum of 128 credit hours, including at least 36 in the major and 42 in upper-division courses, with a minimum GPA of 2.0. Core curriculum courses include 10 hours of math and science, 9 each of social sciences, humanities, and civilization, 6 of English, and 3 each of fine arts and communications. They must score at proficiency level on a writing assessment. **Procedure:** Freshmen are admitted to all sessions. There are deferred admissions and rolling admissions plans. Application deadlines are open. Application fee is $30. **Transfer Students:** 803 transfer students enrolled in 2015-2016. Applicants must have a minimum GPA of 2.0 and should submit official college transcripts in order to transfer credits. 38 of 128 credits required for the bachelor's degree must be completed at Lindenwood. **International Students:** There are 557 international students enrolled. The school actively recruits these students. They must take the TOEFL with a minimum score of 500 on the paper-based TOEFL (PBT) or 61 on the Internet-based version (iBT). They must also take the SAT or ACT.

ADMISSIONS: 3 freshmen graduated first in their class. **Admissions Contact:** Joe Parisi, Associate Dean of Admissions. Email: *admissions@lindenwood.edu* Web: *www.lindenwood.edu*

FINANCIAL AID: In 2016-2017, 98% of all full-time freshmen and continuing full-time students received some form of financial aid. 66% of all full-time freshmen and continuing full-time students received need-based aid. 72% of undergraduate students work part-time. Average annual earnings from campus work are $2400. The average financial indebtedness of the 2016 graduate was $15,500. The FAFSA code is 002480. Check with the school for current application deadlines.

MARYVILLE UNIVERSITY OF SAINT LOUIS D-3

www.maryville.edu

St. Louis, MO 63141	(314) 529-9350/9359 (800) 627-9855
Fax: (314) 529-9927	**Email:** admissions@maryville.edu
Full-time: 804 men, 1343 women	**Faculty:** IIA, -$
Part-time: 174 men, 646 women	**Ph.D.s:** 69%
Graduate: 629 men, 3232 women	**Student/Faculty:** n/av
Year: semesters, summer session	**Tuition:** $27,958
Room & Board: $10,088	**Freshman Class:** 1846 applied, 1713 accepted, 554 enrolled
ACT: 26	**CEEB CODE:** 6399
Application Deadline: August 19	**VERY COMPETITIVE+**

Maryville University, founded in 1872, is a selective, comprehensive and nationally ranked private institution. Maryville offers more than 90 degrees at the undergraduate, masters and doctoral levels. Maryville's athletics teams compete at the NCAA Division II level in the Great Lakes Valley Conference. There are 5 undergraduate schools and 5 graduate schools. In addition to regional accreditation, Maryville has baccalaureate program accreditation with ACBSP, FIDER, NASAD, NASM, NCATE, AOTA, CAPTE, and CCNE. The 130-acre campus is in a suburban area 20 miles west of downtown St. Louis. Including any residence halls, there are 31 buildings.

STUDENT LIFE: 76% of undergraduates are from Missouri. Others are from 50 states, 54 foreign countries, and Canada. 91% are from public schools. 8% are African American; 73% White; 5% Foreign; 5% race unknown; 4% Hispanic; 3% Asian American; 2% two or more races. 64% claim no religious affiliation; 15% Catholic. **Female To Male Ratio:** 3.2:1. The average age of freshmen is 18; all undergraduates, 24. 14% do not continue beyond their first year; 75% remain to graduate. **Housing:** 866 students can be accommodated in college housing, which includes single-sex and coed dorms and on-campus apartments. On-campus housing is available on a first-come, first-served basis, and on a lottery system for upperclassmen. 75% of students commute. All students may keep cars.

FACULTY/CLASSROOMS: 36% of faculty are male; 64% are female. No introductory courses are taught by graduate students. The average class size in an introductory lecture is 16 and in a laboratory is 14.

PROGRAMS OF STUDY: Maryville confers B.A., B.S., B.F.A., B.S.C.L.S., B.S.M.T., and B.S.N. degrees. Master's and doctoral degrees are also awarded. Bachelor's degrees are awarded in BIOLOGICAL SCIENCE (biochemistry and biology/biological science), BUSINESS (accounting, business administration and management, international business management, marketing management, organizational leadership and management, and sports management), COMMUNICATIONS AND THE ARTS (communications, English, game design and development, graphic design, and studio art), COMPUTER AND PHYSICAL SCIENCE (actuarial science, chemistry, cyber intelligence/security studies, information sciences and systems, mathematics, and science), EDUCATION (art education, early childhood education, elementary education, middle school education, and secondary education), ENGINEERING AND ENVIRONMENTAL DESIGN (engineering, environmental science, and interior design), HEALTH PROFESSIONS (clinical science, health science, music therapy, nursing, occupational therapy, physical therapy, rehabilitation therapy, and speech pathology/audiology), SOCIAL SCIENCE (criminology, forensic studies, history, international studies, liberal arts/general studies, paralegal studies, psychology, and sociology). Actuarial science, nursing, and physical therapy are the strongest academically. Nursing, business administration, and psychology have the largest enrollments.

ACTIVITIES: There are no fraternities or sororities. There are 100 groups on campus, including art, cheerleading, chorale, dance, environmental, ethnic, forensics, honors, international, LGBT, literary magazine, marching band, newspaper, orchestra, pep band, political, professional, religious, social, social service, and student government. Popular campus events include Saturday Night Live Comedy Series, Fall Festival, and Bingo and Brew. **Sports:** There are 9 intercollegiate sports for men and 10 for women, and 10 intramural sports for men and 10 for women. Facilities include lacrosse and soccer field, baseball fields, softball, wrestling facility, a gym, outdoor and indoor basketball arena, and a fitness center. **Graduates:** From July 1, 2015 to June 30, 2016, 608 bachelor's degrees were awarded. The most popular majors were nursing/health professions (71%), business administration (12%), and education (6%). 150 companies recruited on campus in 2015-2016. In an average class, 75% graduate in 6 years or less. Of the 2015 graduating class, 9% were enrolled in graduate school within 6 months of graduation, and 86% were employed.

SERVICES: Counseling and information services are available, as is tutoring in every subject, and a reader service for the blind. There is also a writing center, learning styles inventory, and help with time management and test-taking skills, study skills materials, workshops, and individual consultations. **Library/Resources:** The library contains 60,082 volumes, 29,773 microform items, 182,199 audio/video tapes/CDs/DVDs, and subscribes to 94,642 periodicals including electronic. Computerized library services include interlibrary loans, database searching, Internet access, and Wi-Fi capability. Special learning facilities include an art gallery, an observatory, a teaching lab, art and design labs, clinical labs for nursing, occupational therapy, and physical therapy, communications lab, cyber security virtual lab, and multimedia classrooms. **Physically Challenged Students:** All of the campus is accessible. Facilities include wheelchair ramps, elevators, special parking, specially equipped restrooms, special class scheduling, lowered drinking fountains, and lowered telephones. **Special:** There is cross-registration with Missouri Baptist College and Fontbonne, Webster, and Lindenwood Universities. Students may choose internships in various fields, and cooperative programs are available with various employers Other options include dual and student-designed majors, study abroad in China, England, France, Italy, Japan, Spain, and other countries, a 3-2 engineering degree with Washington University, and a Washington semester. Accelerated degree programs are offered in actuarial science and nursing. A 3+4 B.S/O.D. optometry degree with the University of Missouri-St. Louis and a B.A. criminal justice/criminology degree in association with St. Louis County and Municipal Police Academy are possible. There are 12 national honor societies, a freshman honors program, and 8 departmental honors programs. **Visiting:** There are regularly scheduled orientations for prospective students, including visiting the campus and arranging a personal interview with an admissions counselor. There are guides for informal visits, visitors may sit in on classes, and stay overnight. To schedule a visit, contact the Admissions Office. **Campus Safety and Security:** Measures include 24-hour foot and vehicle patrol, emergency notification system, self-defense education, and security escort services. There are emergency telephones, lighted pathways/sidewalks, video security systems in residence halls, and security key operated dorm entrances.

REQUIREMENTS: The ACT is recommended. Students must have graduated from an accredited secondary school with 22 academic credits or have the GED. Expected preparatory courses include 4 units of English, 3 of math, and 2 each of science and social studies, plus 3 additional units in any of the preceding areas or in a foreign language. Some majors have additional admission requirements. AP and CLEP credits are accepted. Important factors in the admissions decision are recommendations by school officials, advanced placement or honors courses, and leadership record. To graduate, all students must complete a minimum of 128 credit hours, with a minimum GPA of 2.0. The core curriculum consists of 12 credit hours each of humanities, math and science, and social and behavioral science, and 8 credit hours each of communication skills and fine arts. 48 upper-division credits must be completed. **Procedure:** Freshmen are admitted to all sessions. Entrance exams should be taken during the junior year. There are deferred admissions and rolling admissions plans. Applications should be filed by August 19 for fall entry. Notification is sent on a rolling basis. Applications are accepted on-line. **Transfer Students:** 361 transfer students enrolled in 2015-2016. A minimum GPA of 2.0, or higher for some majors, is required. Some majors may require ACT or SAT. 30 of 128 credits required for the bachelor's degree must be completed at Maryville. **International Students:** There are 171 international students enrolled. The school actively recruits these students. They must take the TOEFL with a minimum score of 500 on the paper-based TOEFL (PBT) or 61 on the Internet-based version (iBT).

ADMISSIONS: 93% of the 2016-2017 applicants were accepted. The ACT scores were 6% between 12 and 17, 31% between 18 and 23, 53% between 24 and 29, and 10% above 30. 51% of the current freshmen were in the top fifth of their class; 77% were in the top two fifths. 16 freshmen graduated first in their class. **Admissions Contact:** Shani Lenore-Jenkins, Associate Vice President of Enrollment. Email: *admissions@maryville.edu* Web: *www.maryville.edu*

FINANCIAL AID: 12% of undergraduate students work part-time. Average annual earnings from campus work are $2200. The FAFSA code is 002482. The priority date for freshman financial aid applications for fall entry is March 1. The deadline for filing freshman financial aid applications for fall entry is April 1.

MISSOURI BAPTIST UNIVERSITY D-3

www.mobap.edu

St. Louis, MO 63141	(314) 392-2296 (877) 434-1115
Fax: (314) 434-7596	Email: admissions@mobap.edu
Full-time: 684 men, 755 women	**Faculty:** IIB, --$
Part-time: 1106 men, 2086 women	**Ph.D.s:** 60%
Graduate: 280 men, 821 women	**Student/Faculty:** 20 to 1
Year: semesters, summer session	**Tuition:** $24,924
Room & Board: $10,670	**Freshman Class:** 303 applied, 300 accepted, 286 enrolled
ACT: 21	**CEEB CODE:** 2258
Application Deadline: open	**COMPETITIVE**

Missouri Baptist University, established in 1964, is a private liberal arts institution. There is 1 undergraduate school and 1 graduate school. In addition to regional accreditation, MBU has baccalaureate program accreditation with NASM, NCATE, NACEP, CAAHEP, and CoAES. The 65-acre campus is in a suburban area 15 miles west of St. Louis. Including any residence halls, there are 16 buildings.

STUDENT LIFE: 88% of undergraduates are from Missouri. Others are from 33 states, 21 foreign countries, and Canada. 55% are White; 32% race unknown; 6% African American; 2% two or more races; 1% Asian American; 1% American Indian/Alaska Native; 1% Hispanic; 1% Foreign. 34% are Protestant; 11% Catholic. **Female To Male Ratio:** 1.8:1. The average age of freshmen is 19; all undergraduates, 20. **Housing:** 346 students can be accommodated in college housing, which includes single-sex dorms, on-campus apartments, and off-campus apartments. On-campus housing is available on a first-come and first-served basis. 80% of students commute. All students may keep cars. Alcohol is not permitted.

FACULTY/CLASSROOMS: 51% of faculty are male; 49% are female. No introductory courses are taught by graduate students. The average class size in an introductory lecture is 30; in a laboratory is 20; and in a regular course is 25.

PROGRAMS OF STUDY: MBU confers B.A., B.S., B.M., B.M.E., B.P.S., and B.S.E. degrees. Associate, master's, and doctoral degrees are also awarded. Bachelor's degrees are awarded in BIOLOGICAL SCIENCE (biochemistry, biology/biological science, and biotechnology), BUSI-

NESS (accounting, applied management, business administration and management, management science, marketing management, organizational leadership and management, and sports management), COMMUNICATIONS AND THE ARTS (broadcasting, communications, English, journalism, music, music performance, music technology, musical theater, public relations, speech and theatre education, and theatre arts), COMPUTER AND PHYSICAL SCIENCE (chemistry, chemistry/forensic chemistry, information sciences and systems, and mathematics), EDUCATION (business education, early childhood education, elementary education, health education, middle school education, music education, physical education, secondary education, and special education), HEALTH PROFESSIONS (exercise science, health care administration, and health science), SOCIAL SCIENCE (behavioral science, child psychology/development, Christian studies, criminal justice, gender studies, history, human services, liberal arts/general studies, ministries, psychology, religious music, and social science). Business administration, elementary education, and criminal justice have the largest enrollments.

ACTIVITIES: There are no fraternities or sororities. There are 25 groups on campus, including band, business, cheerleading, choir, chorale, chorus, communications, computers, dance, drama, ethnic, film, honors, international, jazz band, literary magazine, musical theater, opera, orchestra, photography, political, professional, radio and TV, religious, social, social service, and student government. Popular campus events include Spring Musical, Christmas Concert, and Hanging of the Green. **Sports:** There are 13 intercollegiate sports for men and 14 for women, and 4 intramural sports for men and 4 for women. Facilities include a sports and recreation complex with a gymnasium, indoor track, training and fitness centers, and baseball, softball, and soccer fields. **Graduates:** From July 1, 2015 to June 30, 2016, 330 bachelor's degrees were awarded. The most popular majors were business administration (10%), accounting (9%), and elementary education (7%).

SERVICES: Counseling and information services are available, as is tutoring in some subjects, by appointment: accounting, economics, grammar, Greek, Music Appreciation, Old and New Testament History, psychology, and Spanish. There is a reader service for the blind, and remedial math and writing. Walk-in tutoring in math, biology and chemistry **Library/Resources:** The library contains 82,337 volumes, 3,708 microform items, and 4,615 audio/video tapes/CDs/DVDs, and subscribes to 25,459 periodicals including electronic. Computerized library services include interlibrary loans, database searching, Internet access, and Wi-Fi capability. Special learning facilities include a radio station, and audiovisual production lab. **Physically Challenged Students:** 80% of the campus is accessible. Facilities include wheelchair ramps, elevators, special parking, specially equipped restrooms, special class scheduling, lowered drinking fountains, and special housing. **Special:** There is cross-registration with Fontbonne, and Maryville, Lindenwood, and Webster Universities. Students may opt for credit by examination, non-degree study, and student-designed majors. A 3-2 engineering degree with the University of Missouri/Columbia or a 2-2 engineering degree with the Missouri University of Science and Technology is available. Study abroad is possible at Harlaxton College in England, Hong Kong Baptist University, or through Webster University, Best Semester, Consortium for Global Education, or the Center for Cross Cultural Study. MBU also offers internships in various disciplines and dual majors in some fields. There are 5 national honor societies and a freshman honors program. **Visiting:** There are regularly scheduled orientations for prospective students, Student visits include a welcome weekend, open houses, and campus tours. There are guides for informal visits, visitors may sit in on classes, and stay overnight. To schedule a visit, contact the Admissions Office. **Campus Safety and Security:** Measures include 24-hour foot and vehicle patrol, emergency notification system, self-defense education, and security escort services. There are also shuttle buses, emergency telephones, lighted pathways/sidewalks, and controlled access to dorms/residences.

REQUIREMENTS: Applicants must have a minimum score of 20 on the ACT or a satisfactory score on the SAT. Applicants must be graduates of an accredited secondary school. GED and home-schooled students are accepted. MBU requires applicants to be in the upper 50% of their class. AP and CLEP credits are accepted. Important factors in the admissions decision are advanced placement or honors courses, leadership record, and evidence of special talent. All students must take courses in the humanities/fine arts, social and behavioral sciences, natural sciences, phys ed, computer literacy, and Old and New Testament History. A minimum GPA of 2.0 is required (some majors require a GPA of 2.5 or better). To graduate, students must complete at least 128 credit hours, with a minimum of 30 hours in the major and 45 hours of upper-division courses; pass a general education exam and an exit exam or other assessment in the major; and complete a capstone project. **Procedure:** Freshmen are admitted to all sessions. Entrance exams should be taken during the junior year. There is a rolling admissions plan. Application deadlines are open. Application fee is $35. Application fees are waived if application is completed online. **Transfer Students:** 366 transfer students enrolled in 2015-2016. Applicants must have a 2.0 GPA, with some programs requiring 2.5 or better. Students must submit official transcripts from all previous colleges attended, along with a character reference. 24 of 128 credits required for the bachelor's degree must be completed at MBU. **International Students:** There are 42 international students enrolled. The school actively recruits these students. They must take the TOEFL with a minimum score of 550 on the paper-based TOEFL (PBT) or 80 on the Internet-based version (iBT).

ADMISSIONS: 99% of the 2016-2017 applicants were accepted. There was 1 National Merit finalist. 9 freshmen graduated first in their class. **Admissions Contact:** Cynthia Sutton, Director of Admissions. Email: *admissions@mobap.edu* Web: *www.mobap.edu*

FINANCIAL AID: In 2016-2017, 100% of all full-time freshmen received some form of financial aid. The college's own financial statement is required. The FAFSA code is 007540. The priority date for freshman financial aid applications for fall entry is February 1.

MISSOURI SOUTHERN STATE UNIVERSITY — A-4

www.mssu.edu

Joplin, MO 64801	**(417) 625-9379** **(866) 818-6778**
Fax: (417) 659-4429	**Email: admissions@mssu.edu**
Full-time: 1799 men, 2411 women	**Faculty:** 202; IIB, -$
Part-time: 750 men, 772 women	**Ph.D.s:** 57%
Graduate: 19 men, 32 women	**Student/Faculty:** 18 to 1
Year: semesters, summer session	**Tuition:** $5877 ($11,188)
Room & Board: $6622	**Freshman Class:** 2333 applied, 2196 accepted, 925 enrolled
ACT: 22	**CEEB CODE:** 6322
Application Deadline: September 1	**COMPETITIVE**

Missouri Southern State University, founded in 1937, is a public, primarily commuter institution offering undergraduate degree programs in the arts and sciences, business, education, psychology, and technology. There are 4 undergraduate schools and 3 graduate schools. In addition to regional accreditation, Missouri Southern has baccalaureate program accreditation with ABET, ACBSP, ADA, NCATE, NLN, and NAACLS. The 365-acre campus is in a small town in the southwest corner of the state, 138 miles south of Kansas City. Including any residence halls, there are 50 buildings.

STUDENT LIFE: 79% of undergraduates are from Missouri. Others are from 40 states, 31 foreign countries, and Canada. 76% are White; 6% African American; 5% Hispanic; 4% Foreign; 3% American Indian/Alaska Native; 3% race unknown; 2% Asian American; 1% two or more races. **Female To Male Ratio:** 1.3:1. The average age of freshmen is 19; all undergraduates, 24. 37% do not continue beyond their first year; 36% remain to graduate. **Housing:** 900 students can be accommodated in college housing, which includes single-sex and coed dorms and on-campus apartments. On-campus housing is available on a first-come and first-served basis. 86% of students commute. All students may keep cars. Alcohol is not permitted.

FACULTY/CLASSROOMS: 50% of faculty are male; 50% are female. 99% teach undergraduates. No introductory courses are taught by graduate students. The average class size in a regular course is 21.

PROGRAMS OF STUDY: Missouri Southern confers B.A., B.S., B.G.S., B.S.B.A. and B.S.E. degrees. Associate and master's degrees are also awarded. Bachelor's degrees are awarded in AGRICULTURE (conservation and regulation), BIOLOGICAL SCIENCE (biochemistry, bioinformatics, biology/adolescence education, ecology, forensic science, life science, marine biology, microbiology, and physiology), BUSINESS (accounting, business administration and management, finance, financial services, human resources/organizational management, international business, international business information systems, logistics, management information systems, marketing, and marketing management), COMMUNICATIONS AND THE ARTS (art, art and design, art/visual culture, choral music, communications, English, English literature, English writing, fine arts, fine/studio arts, general, French, graphic design, instrumental music education, language arts, literature, music, music industry, piano performance, public relations, speech and theatre education, studio art, studio art painting, theatre arts, theatre studies, and vocal performance), COMPUTER AND PHYSICAL SCIENCE (applied science, chemistry, computer engineering technology, computer information systems, computer science, industrial technology, mathematics, mathematics/computational, physics and mathematics, physics, radiological technology, science, and science technology), EDUCATION (business education, childhood education, computer education, early childhood education, elementary education, English education, mathematics education, middle school education, physical education, reading education, science education, social science education, social studies education, social studies secondary school education, Spanish education K-12, special education, and teaching English as a second/foreign language (TESOL/TEFOL)), ENGINEERING AND ENVIRONMENTAL DESIGN (manufacturing technology and transportation technology), HEALTH PROFESSIONS (dental hygiene, environmental health science, health, health promotion, health science, medical technology, predentistry, premedicine, preoptometry, preoccupational therapy, prepharmacy, pre-physician assistant, prephysical therapy, preveterinary science, and respiratory therapy), SOCIAL SCIENCE (criminal justice, early childhood studies, economics, forensic studies, history, justice and society, law enforcement and corrections, political science/government, psychology, social studies, and sociology). Criminal justice, health professions & related programs, and business/marketing are the strongest academically. Teacher education, criminal justice, and biology-environmental health have the largest enrollments.

ACTIVITIES: 1% of men belong to 3 national fraternities; 2% of women belong to 2 national sororities. There are 84 groups on campus, including art, band, cheerleading, chess, choir, chorale, chorus, communications, computers, dance, debate, drama, ethnic, film, forensics, honors, international, jazz band, literary magazine, marching band, musical theater, newspaper, orchestra, pep band, photography, political, professional, radio and TV, religious, social, social service, student government, and symphony. Popular campus events include Spring Fling, Natural High, and International Semesters. **Sports:** There are 6 intercollegiate sports for men and 6 for women, and 10 intramural sports for men and 10 for women. Facilities include a football stadium, gym, basketball court, indoor track, training and weight room, cross-country course, and soccer, softball, and baseball fields. **Graduates:** From July 1, 2015 to June 30, 2016, 833 bachelor's degrees were awarded. The most popular majors were business/marketing (24%), criminal justice (18%), and health professions and related programs (14%). 1467 companies recruited on campus in 2015-2016. In an average class, 16% graduate in 4 years or less, 31% graduate in 5 years or less, and 36% graduate in 6 years or less.

SERVICES: Counseling and information services are available, as is tutoring in most subjects. There is a reader service for the blind, and remedial math, reading, and writing. Assistance is also provided for improving time management, and test-taking skills. **Library/Resources:** The library contains 1.4 million volumes, 784,368 microform items, 5,031 audio/video tapes/CDs/DVDs, and subscribes to 236 periodicals including electronic. Computerized library services include interlibrary loans, database searching, Internet access, and Wi-Fi capability. Special learning facilities include an art gallery, radio station, TV station, a biology pond, child development center, a crime lab, small business development center, performing arts center, a greenhouse, and an international trade and quality center. **Physically Challenged Students:** 99% of the campus is accessible. Facilities include wheelchair ramps, elevators, special parking, specially equipped restrooms, special class scheduling, lowered drinking fountains, lowered telephones, and special housing. **Special:** There are co-op programs in radiological and medical technology, respiratory therapy, paramedical studies, aviation, and engineering. Students may study abroad at Oxford or Cambridge and in 100 countries through ISEP. Missouri Southern also offers internships in many majors, accelerated degree programs in all majors, a 3-2 engineering degree with the University of Missouri-Rolla, a general studies degree, and credit for life experience. Nondegree study is possible. There are 12 national honor societies, a freshman honors program, and 1 departmental honors program. **Visiting:** There are regularly scheduled orientations for prospective students, tour of campus, advising with a faculty member in the student's chosen field of study. There are guides for informal visits, visitors may sit in on classes, and stay overnight. To schedule a visit, contact Derek Skaggs at skaggs-d@mssu.edu. **Campus Safety and Security:** Measures include 24-hour foot and vehicle patrol, emergency notification system, and self-defense education. There are emergency telephones, lighted pathways/sidewalks, controlled access to dorms/residences, officers on duty 24/7, even on holidays. We have a redundancy of notification systems, including Rave messaging. The RAD self-defense for girls is taught as a regular class in Fall/Spring. We also teach the ALICE concepts (active shooter response) to students in the University Experience classes.

REQUIREMENTS: The ACT is required. Applicants must be graduates of accredited secondary schools or have earned a GED. The college requires completion of 16 Carnegie units in core courses for high school graduates. Missouri Southern requires applicants to be in the upper 50% of their class. AP and CLEP credits are accepted. General education requirements include a total of 51 credit hours, with 15 in basic studies, 12 each in science and cultural studies, 9 in humanities, and 3 in international studies. Students must also demonstrate proficiency in computer skills and writing. To graduate, students must complete at least 124 credit hours, including a minimum of 40 in the major, and present a minimum GPA of 2.0 (2.75 for the B.S.E.). **Procedure:** Freshmen are admitted to all sessions. Entrance exams should be taken during the junior or senior year of high school. There are deferred admissions and rolling admissions plans. Applications should be filed by September 1 for fall entry, along with a $25 fee. Notification is sent on a rolling basis. Applications are accepted on-line. **Transfer Students:** 652 transfer students enrolled in 2015-2016. Applicants must have a GPA of 2.0 and must be able to return to their previous college. 30 of 124 credits required for the bachelor's degree must be completed at Missouri Southern. **International Students:** There are 209 international students enrolled. The school actively recruits these students. They must take the TOEFL with a minimum score of 68 on the Internet-based version (iBT). They must also take the SAT or ACT, scoring 18.

ADMISSIONS: 94% of the 2016-2017 applicants were accepted. The ACT scores were 15% between 12 and 17, 53% between 18 and 23, 28% between 24 and 29, and 4% above 30. 32% of the current freshmen were in the top fifth of their class; 57% were in the top two fifths. **Admissions Contact:** Derek S. Skaggs, Director of Admissions. Email: *admissions@mssu.edu* Web: *www.mssu.edu*

FINANCIAL AID: In 2016-2017, 96% of all full-time freshmen and 85% of continuing full-time students received some form of financial aid. 59% of all full-time freshmen and 60% of continuing full-time students received need-based aid. The average freshman award was $8,332. Need-based scholarships or need-based grants averaged $5,183 ($5,775 maximum); need-based self-help aid (loans and jobs) averaged $3,161 ($5,000 maximum); non-need-based athletic scholarships averaged $3,906 ($19,468 maximum); and other non-need-based awards and non-need-based scholarships averaged $3,963 ($9,752 maximum). 8% of undergraduate students work part-time. The average financial indebtedness of the 2016 graduate was $20,638. The FAFSA code is 002488. The priority date for freshman financial aid applications for fall entry is April 1. The filing deadline for fall entry is October 1.

MISSOURI STATE UNIVERSITY B-3

www.missouristate.edu

Springfield, MO 65897 — **(417) 836-5000**, **(800) 492-7900**

Fax: (417) 836-5137 — **Email: info@MissouriState.edu**

Full-time: 6281 men, 8750 women	**Faculty:** n/av
Part-time: 1011 men, 1258 women	**Ph.D.s:** 71%
Graduate: 1185 men, 2037 women	**Student/Faculty:** 22 to 1
Year: semesters, summer session	**Tuition:** $7060 ($13,930)
Room & Board: $8130	**Freshman Class:** 9038 applied, 7626 accepted, 3194 enrolled
SAT CR/M: 540/552 **ACT:** 24	**CEEB CODE:** 6665
Application Deadline: July 20	**COMPETITIVE+**

Missouri State University, founded in 1905, is a public institution offering undergraduate programs in arts & letters, business administration, humanities and social sciences, education and psychology, health & applied sciences, science and math. There are 7 undergraduate schools and 1 graduate school. In addition to regional accreditation, MSU has baccalaureate program accreditation with AACSB, ABET, ACCE, ACPE, APTA, CSWE, NASM, NCATE, ACEND, ACPHA, and ARC-PA. The 304-acre campus is in a suburban area 220 miles southwest of St. Louis. Including any residence halls, there are 61 buildings.

STUDENT LIFE: 90% of undergraduates are from Missouri. Others are from 50 states, 83 foreign countries, and Canada. 81% are White; 5% African American; 4% Foreign; 4% two or more races; 3% Hispanic; 1% Asian American; 1% race unknown. **Female To Male Ratio:** 1.4:1. The average age of freshmen is 18; all undergraduates, 22. 25% do not continue beyond their first year; 55% remain to graduate. **Housing:** 4000 students can be accommodated in college housing, which includes coed dorms, on-campus apartments, married student housing, honors houses, fraternity houses, sorority houses, apartments for single students, international students, and theme housing. On-campus housing is guaranteed for all 4 years. 77% of students commute. All students may keep cars. Alcohol is not permitted.

FACULTY/CLASSROOMS: 52% of faculty are male; 48% are female. No introductory courses are taught by graduate students. The average class size in a regular course is 23.

PROGRAMS OF STUDY: MSU confers B.S.A.T., B.A., B.A.S., B.F.A., B.M.U.S., B.M.E., B.S., B.S.Ed., B.S.N., and B.S.W. degrees. Master's and doctoral degrees are also awarded. Bachelor's degrees are awarded in AGRICULTURE (agriculture, animal science, environmental studies, plant science, and wildlife management), BIOLOGICAL SCIENCE (biology/biological science and cell biology), BUSINESS (accounting, apparel and textiles, business administration and management, entrepreneurial studies, fashion merchandising, finance, logistics, management science, marketing/retailing/merchandising, and recreation and leisure services), COMMUNICATIONS AND THE ARTS (art history, art, communications, communication science, design, English, French, German, information technology, journalism, Latin, music, musical theater, performing arts, Spanish, speech/debate/rhetoric, and theatre arts), COMPUTER AND PHYSICAL SCIENCE (chemistry, computer science, geology, mathematics, and natural sciences), EDUCATION (agricultural education, athletic training, business education, computer education, early childhood education, education administration, elementary education, global studies, middle school education, physical education, science education, and special education), ENGINEERING AND ENVIRONMENTAL DESIGN (construction management, interior design, and materials science), HEALTH PROFESSIONS (clinical science, exercise science, health care administration, health promotion, hospital administration, nursing, physical therapy, physician's assistant, radiological science, respiratory therapy, and speech pathology/audiology), SOCIAL SCIENCE (anthropology, child psychology/development, counseling/psychology, criminology, dietetics, economics, family/consumer studies, fashion design and technology, geography, gerontology, history, philosophy, political science/government, religion, social work, and sociology). Business, and education have the largest enrollments.

ACTIVITIES: 40% of men belong to 36% of women belong to Groups on campus include art, band, campus ministries, cheerleading, chess, choir, chorale, chorus, communications, computers, dance, drama, drill team, environmental, ethnic, film, honors, international, jazz band, LGBT, literary magazine, marching band, musical theater, newspaper, opera, orchestra, pep band, political, professional, radio and TV, religious, social, social service, student government, and symphony. Popular campus events include Tent Theater, Spring Fling, Community Service Fair and Leadership Conference. **Sports:** There are 6 intercollegiate sports for men and 10 for women, and 23 intramural sports for men and 22 for women. Facilities include a stadium, arena, swimming pool, softball and practice fields, tennis courts, bowling, and a recreation center. **Graduates:** From July 1, 2015 to June 30, 2016, 3114 bachelor's degrees were awarded. The most popular majors were business/marketing (29%), education (13%), and social sciences (8%). 610 companies recruited on campus in 2015-2016. In an average class, 32% graduate in 4 years or less, 50% graduate in 5 years or less, and 52% graduate in 6 years or less. Of the 2015 graduating class, 70% were employed within 6 months of graduation.

SERVICES: Counseling and information services are available, as is tutoring in some subjects. There is a reader service for the blind, and remedial math, reading, and writing. Proctors are available for tests given to those with disabilities. **Library/Resources:** The library contains 782,257 volumes, 1.1 million microform items, and 19,708 audio/video tapes/CDs/DVDs, and subscribes to 37,000 periodicals including electronic. Computerized library services include interlibrary loans, database searching, Internet access, and Wi-Fi capability. Special learning facilities include an art gallery, radio station, and TV station. **Physically Challenged Students:** All of the campus is accessible. Facilities include wheelchair ramps, elevators, special parking, specially equipped restrooms, special class scheduling, lowered drinking fountains, lowered telephones, special housing. **Special:** MSU offers co-op programs, internships, study abroad in 40 countries, and work-study programs. Also available are B.A.-B.S. degrees in 12 majors, preprofessional programs in law and medicine, accelerated degree programs and student-designed and interdisciplinary majors, including antiquities, agriculture business and agriculture education, chemistry/biochemistry, communication management, and finance/real estate. A 3-2 engineering degree is available through the University of Missouri-Rolla. Credit for military experience and pass/not-pass options are offered. There are 27 national honor societies and a freshman honors program. **Visiting:** There are regularly scheduled orientations for prospective students, guests can request an appointment with an admissions advisor, an academic department, or other areas of interest. There are guides for informal visits. To schedule a visit, contact the Admissions Office. **Campus Safety and Security:** Measures include 24-hour foot and vehicle patrol, emergency notification system, self-defense education, and security escort services. There are shuttle buses, emergency telephones, lighted pathways/sidewalks, and controlled access to dorms/residences.

REQUIREMENTS: Either SAT or ACT is required for admittance; with the ACT preferred. Admission is based on a sliding scale of rank or GPA and test score. Freshmen must also have a 17-unit high school core curriculum, including 4 in English, 3 each in math, science (with 1 lab), and in academic electives, 2 in social studies, and 1 each in visual and performing arts, and history. AP and CLEP credits are accepted. Important factors in the admissions decision are leadership record, advanced placement or honors courses, and extracurricular activities record. A total of 125 to 130 semester hours, including 30 to 60 in the major, and a minimum GPA of 2.0 are required. 45 general education semester hours are required, to include 8 in natural sciences, 6 to 9 each in social sciences and humanities, 6 in American studies, 4 in phys ed, 3 to 6 in English composition, 3 each in math and speech, and 1 in freshman orientation. Arts/fine arts and computer literacy classes are also required. **Procedure:** Freshmen are admitted fall, spring, and summer. Entrance exams should be taken as early as possible. There is a rolling admissions plan. Applications should be filed by July 20 for fall entry, along with a $35 fee. Notification is sent on a rolling basis. Application fees are waived if application is completed online. **Transfer Students:** 1644 transfer students enrolled in 2015-2016. Applicants must present a minimum GPA of 2.0 on transferable courses. College transcripts are required. If they have completed less than 24 semester hours, they are also required to meet freshman admission requirements. Application for Admission is in the fall, spring, and summer. 30 of 125 credits required for the bachelor's degree must be completed at MSU. **International Students:** There are 780 international students enrolled. The school actively recruits these students. They must take the TOEFL with a minimum score of 500 on the paper-based TOEFL (PBT) or 61 on the Internet-based version (iBT). They must also take the ACT.

ADMISSIONS: 84% of the 2016-2017 applicants were accepted. The SAT scores for the 2016-2017 freshman class were: Critical Reading--33% below 500, 31% between 500 and 599, 33% between 600 and 699, and 3% between 700 and 800. Math-- 27% below 500, 41% between 500 and 599, 25% between 600 and 699, and 7% between 700 and 800. The ACT scores were 2% between 12 and 17, 47% between 18 and 23, 43% between 24 and 29, and 8% above 30. 37% of the current freshmen were in the top fifth of their class; 62% were in the top two fifths. **Admissions Contact:** Michelle Olsen, Ph.D., Director of Institutional Research. Email: *info@MissouriState.edu* Web: *www.missouristate.edu*

FINANCIAL AID: In 2016-2017, 64% of all full-time freshmen and 59% of continuing full-time students received some form of financial aid. 64% of all full-time freshmen and 59% of continuing full-time students received need-based aid. The average freshman award was $9,620. Need-based scholarships or need-based grants averaged $6,452; need-based self-help aid (loans and jobs) averaged $5,568; non-need-based athletic scholarships averaged $14,241; other non-need-based awards and non-need-based scholarships averaged $3,440; and $3,039 from other forms of aid. The average financial indebtedness of the 2016 graduate was $24,734. MSU is a member of CSS. The FAFSA code is 002503. The priority date for freshman financial aid applications for fall entry is March 31. The deadline for filing freshman financial aid applications for fall entry is rolling.

MISSOURI UNIVERSITY OF SCIENCE AND TECHNOLOGY C-3

www.mst.edu

Rolla, MO 65409	(573) 341-4164 (800) 522-0938
Fax: (573) 341-4082	Email: admissions@mst.edu
Full-time: 4227 men, 1245 women	Faculty: 361; I, av$
Part-time: 487 men, 187 women	Ph.D.s: 89%
Graduate: 1577 men, 407 women	Student/Faculty: 15 to 1
Year: semesters, summer session	Tuition: $9510 ($24,675)
Room & Board: $9145	Freshman Class: n/av
SAT CR/M: 590/640 ACT: 28	CEEB CODE: 6876
Application Deadline: July 1	HIGHLY COMPETITIVE

Missouri University of Science and Technology, founded in 1870, is part of the University of Missouri system. A public research institution, it offers comprehensive undergraduate and graduate programs and confers degrees in arts and sciences, engineering, mines and metallurgy, and management and information systems. There are 4 undergraduate schools. In addition to regional accreditation, Missouri S&T has baccalaureate program accreditation with AACSB, ABET, CSAB, EAC, and CAC. The 284-acre campus is in a small town 100 miles southwest of St. Louis, and 100 miles northeast of Springfield. Including any residence halls, there are 72 buildings.

STUDENT LIFE: 77% of undergraduates are from Missouri. Others are from 49 states, 60 foreign countries, and Canada. 78% are White; 6% Foreign; 4% African American; 4% race unknown; 2% Asian American; 2% Hispanic; 2% two or more races. **Male To Female Ratio:** 3.4:1. The average age of freshmen is 18; all undergraduates, 21. 17% do not continue beyond their first year; 63% remain to graduate. **Housing:** 2152 students can be accommodated in college housing, which includes coed dorms, on-campus apartments, and married student housing. In addition, there are honors houses, fraternity houses, sorority houses, residential college, learning community, and holistic community. On-campus housing is guaranteed for the freshman year only, and is available on a first-come, and first-served basis. All students may keep cars. Alcohol is not permitted.

FACULTY/CLASSROOMS: 75% of faculty are male; 25% are female. No introductory courses are taught by graduate students.

PROGRAMS OF STUDY: Missouri S&T confers B.A. and B.S. degrees. Master's and doctoral degrees are also awarded. Bachelor's degrees are awarded in BIOLOGICAL SCIENCE (biology/biological science, environmental biology, and life science), BUSINESS (business administration and management and management information systems), COMMUNICATIONS AND THE ARTS (English and technical and business writing), COMPUTER AND PHYSICAL SCIENCE (applied mathematics, chemistry, computer science, geology, geophysics and seismology, information sciences and systems, mathematics, physics, and statistics), EDUCATION (secondary education), ENGINEERING AND ENVIRONMENTAL DESIGN (aeronautical engineering, architectural engineering, ceramic engineering, chemical engineering, civil engineering, computer engineering, electrical/electronics engineering, engineering management, engineering mechanics, environmental engineering, geological engineering, manufacturing engineering, materials engineering, mechanical engineering, metallurgical engineering, mining and mineral engineering, nuclear engineering, petroleum/natural gas engineering, and systems engineering), HEALTH PROFESSIONS (premedicine), SOCIAL SCIENCE (economics, history, philosophy, prelaw, and psychology). Engineering, and science & technology are the strongest academically. Engineering, arts, and science have the largest enrollments.

ACTIVITIES: 19% of women belong to 5 national sororities. There are 221 groups on campus, including art, band, cheerleading, chess, choir, chorale, chorus, computers, dance, drama, drill team, ethnic, honors, international, jazz band, LGBT, literary magazine, marching band, musical theater, newspaper, orchestra, pep band, political, professional, radio and TV, religious, social, social service, student government, symphony, and yearbook. Popular campus events include St. Patrick's Day, Homecoming, Campus Block Party, and Celebration of Nations. **Sports:** There are 8 intercollegiate sports for men and 7 for women, and 20 intramural sports for men and 19 for women. Facilities include a gym, weight room, pool, a golf course, track, racquetball and tennis courts, baseball and soccer fields, and a stadium. **Graduates:** From July 1, 2015 to June 30, 2016, 1118 bachelor's degrees were awarded. The most popular majors were mechanical engineering (15%), civil engineering (12%), and electrical engineering (8%). 872 companies recruited on campus in 2015-2016. In an average class, 63% graduate in 6 years or less. Of the 2015 graduating class, 16% were enrolled in graduate school within 6 months of graduation, and 57% were employed.

SERVICES: Counseling and information services are available, as is tutoring in most subjects, and a reader service for the blind. **Library/Resources:** The library contains 479,874 volumes, 423,403 microform items, 4,634 audio/video tapes/CDs/DVDs, and subscribes to 3,901 periodicals including electronic. Computerized library services include interlibrary loans, database searching, Internet access, and Wi-Fi capability. Special learning facilities include a radio station, a writing center, a student design center, nuclear reactor, observatory, explosives testing labs, an underground mine, and a hot glass shop. **Physically Challenged Students:** 95% of the campus is accessible. Facilities include wheelchair ramps, elevators, special parking, specially equipped restrooms, special class scheduling, lowered drinking fountains, lowered telephones, and special housing. **Special:** MS&T offers internships in business and government, co-op programs in which students work and attend school on alternating schedules, and study abroad in more than 40 countries. Accelerated degrees in science and engineering, dual majors, B.A.-B.S. degrees, a 3-2 engineering degree, work-study programs, credit for life/military/work experience, and pass/fail options in certain courses are also available. There are 28 national honor societies, a freshman honors program, and 16 departmental honors programs. **Visiting:** There are regularly scheduled orientations for prospective students, including a tour with a student, admissions and financial aid counseling, special interest contact, and a departmental visit with a faculty member. There are guides for informal visits, visitors may sit in on classes, and stay overnight. To schedule a visit, contact Admissions Office at admissions@mst.edu. **Campus Safety and Security:** Measures include 24-hour foot and vehicle patrol, emergency notification system, self-defense education, and security escort services. There are also shuttle buses, emergency telephones, lighted pathways/sidewalks, crime prevention and rape/sexual assault programs.

REQUIREMENTS: The sum of the student's class rank percentile and aptitude exam percentile must be 120 or higher. Candidates must be graduates of an accredited secondary school or have the GED. The applicant must have completed 16 academic credit units, including 4 each in English and math, 3 each in science and social studies, and 2 in a foreign language. Students may take the SAT or the ACT, however the ACT is recommended. A GPA of 2.0 is required. AP and CLEP credits are accepted. Important factors in the admissions decision are leadership record, extracurricular activities record, and advanced placement or honors courses. Candidates for graduation must maintain at least a 2.0 GPA. A total of 120 credits is required. A Senior assessment exam is required. **Procedure:** Freshmen are admitted in the fall, winter, and summer. Entrance exams should be taken late in the junior year or early in the senior year. There are deferred admissions and rolling admissions plans. Early decision applications should be filed by December 1; regular applications, by July 1 for fall entry; December 1 for spring entry; and May 1 for summer entry, along with a $50 fee. Applications are accepted online. **Transfer Students:** 427 transfer students enrolled in 2015-2016. Applicants with fewer than 24 semester hours of college-level work must apply as freshmen; those with 24 or more must have attained at least a 2.0 GPA in all college-level courses. 60 of 120 credits required for the bachelor's degree must be completed at Missouri S&T. **International Students:** There are 384 international students enrolled. The school actively recruits these students. They must take the TOEFL with a minimum score of 550 on the paper-based TOEFL (PBT) or 79 on the Internet-based version (iBT). They must also take the SAT or ACT.

ADMISSIONS: The SAT scores for the 2016-2017 freshman class were: Critical Reading-- 14% below 500, 35% between 500 and 599, 36% between 600 and 699, and 15% between 700 and 800. Math-- 5% below 500, 21% between 500 and 599, 54% between 600 and 699, and 21%

between 700 and 800. The ACT scores were 1% below 12, 8% between 12 and 17, 26% between 18 and 23, 19% between 24 and 29, and 46% above 30. 60% of the current freshmen were in the top fifth of their class; 88% were in the top two fifths. **Admissions Contact:** Lynn Stichnote, Director. Email: *admissions@mst.edu* Web: *www.mst.edu*

FINANCIAL AID: In 2016-2017, 88% of all full-time freshmen and 90% of continuing full-time students received some form of financial aid. 43% of all full-time freshmen and 52% of continuing full-time students received need-based aid. The average freshman award was $11,773. Need-based scholarships or need-based grants averaged $9,131; need-based self-help aid (loans and jobs) averaged $3,755; non-need-based athletic scholarships averaged $5,569; and other non-need-based awards and non-need-based scholarships averaged $6,300. The average financial indebtedness of the 2016 graduate was $6,166. Missouri S&T is a member of CSS. The FAFSA code is 002517. The priority date for freshman financial aid applications for fall entry is March 1.

MISSOURI VALLEY COLLEGE B-2

www.moval.edu

Marshall, MO 65340 (660) 831-4157

Fax: (660) 831-4233	**Email:** admissions@moval.edu
Full-time: 840 men, 550 women	**Faculty:** n/av
Part-time: 20 men, 20 women	**Ph.D.s:** 44%
Graduate: n/av	**Student/Faculty:** n/av
Year: semesters, summer session	**Tuition:** $19,750
Room & Board: $8400	**Freshman Class:** n/av
SAT or ACT: required	**CEEB CODE:** 6413
Application Deadline: September 1	**COMPETITIVE**

Missouri Valley College, founded in 1889, is a private liberal arts college, affiliated with the Presbyterian Church, offering 35 majors. The figures in the above capsule and in this profile are approximate. There is 1 undergraduate school and 1 graduate school. In addition to regional accreditation, MVC has baccalaureate program accreditation with CAATE and Missouri State Board of Nursing. The 150-acre campus is in a small town 50 miles northwest of Columbia, and 80 miles northeast of Kansas City. Including any residence halls, there are 17 buildings.

STUDENT LIFE: 66% of undergraduates are from Missouri. Others are from 43 states, 26 foreign countries, and Canada. 75% are from public schools. 83% are White; 6% Hispanic; 4% Asian American; 17% African American; 10% Foreign; 1% American Indian/Alaska Native. 45% are Protestant; 32% Islamic, Mormon, Orthodox, Agnostic and unknown; 14% Catholic. **Male To Female Ratio:** 1.5:1. The average age of freshmen is 19; all undergraduates, 21. 48% do not continue beyond their first year; 20% remain to graduate. **Housing:** 1100 students can be accommodated in college housing, which includes single-sex and coed dorms, on-campus apartments, and off-campus apartments. In addition, there are honors houses, special-interest houses, fraternity houses, and sorority houses. On-campus housing is guaranteed for all 4 years. 72% of students live on campus; of those, 50% remain on campus on weekends. All students may keep cars. Alcohol is not permitted.

FACULTY/CLASSROOMS: 73% of faculty are male; 27% are female. All teach undergraduates. No introductory courses are taught by graduate students. The average class size in an introductory lecture is 30; in a laboratory is 25; and in a regular course is 18.

PROGRAMS OF STUDY: MVC confers B.A., B.S., B.F.A., and B.S.N degrees. Associate and master's degrees are also awarded. Bachelor's degrees are awarded in BIOLOGICAL SCIENCE (biology/biological science), BUSINESS (accounting, business administration and management, and recreational facilities management), COMMUNICATIONS AND THE ARTS (art, communications, dramatic arts, English, and speech/debate/rhetoric), COMPUTER AND PHYSICAL SCIENCE (information sciences and systems and mathematics), EDUCATION (elementary education, physical education, and social studies education), HEALTH PROFESSIONS (exercise science), SOCIAL SCIENCE (addiction studies, anthropology, criminal justice, economics, history, human services, liberal arts/general studies, philosophy, political science/government, psychology, public administration, religion, and sociology). Education is the strongest academically. Business administration (multiple areas), exercise science, psychology have the largest enrollments.

ACTIVITIES: 15% of men belong to 4 national fraternities; 8% of women belong to 2 national sororities. There are 40 groups on campus, including art, cheerleading, choir, chorale, chorus, computers, dance, drama, ethnic, film, honors, international, jazz band, literary magazine, musical theater, newspaper, photography, radio and TV, religious, social, social service, student government, and yearbook. Popular campus events include Springfest, Maastricht Institute of Entrepreneurship, and Guerilla Film Festival. **Sports:** There are 13 intercollegiate sports for men and 12 for women, and 7 intramural sports for men and 7 for women. Facilities include a gym, tennis and basketball courts, football and soccer fields, a stadium, and horse stables. **Graduates:** From July 1, 2015 to June 30, 2016, 251 bachelor's degrees were awarded. The most popular majors were exercise science (12%), criminal justice (11%), and management (7%). In an average class, 3% graduate in 3 years or less, 20% graduate in 4 years or less, 27% graduate in 5 years or less, and 22% graduate in 6 years or less.

SERVICES: Counseling and information services are available, as is tutoring in most subjects, and remedial math, reading, and writing. **Library/Resources:** The 2 libraries contain 83,000 volumes, 31,000 microform items, 3,400 audio/video tapes/CDs/DVDs, and subscribe to 250 periodicals including electronic. Computerized library services include interlibrary loans, database searching, Internet access, and Wi-Fi capability. Special learning facilities include an art gallery, radio station, and TV station. **Physically Challenged Students:** 65% of the campus is accessible. Facilities include wheelchair ramps, elevators, special parking, specially equipped restrooms, and special class scheduling. **Special:** interdisciplinary studies (personalized plan of study), internships, study abroad, work-study, co-op programs, nondegree study, and pass/fail options are available. There are 3 national honor societies and 3 departmental honors programs. **Visiting:** There are regularly scheduled orientations for prospective students, and there are 4 Open Houses a year. In addition there are guides for informal visits, visitors may sit in on classes, and stay overnight. To schedule a visit, contact Jessica Green at admissions@moval.edu. **Campus Safety and Security:** Measures include 24-hour foot and vehicle patrol, emergency notification system, and security escort services. There are shuttle buses, emergency telephones, lighted pathways/sidewalks, and controlled access to dorms/residences.

REQUIREMENTS: The SAT or ACT is required. Students must have graduated from an accredited secondary school or have the GED. Auditions required for performance-based scholarships MVC requires applicants to be in the upper 50% of their class. AP and CLEP credits are accepted. Important factors in the admissions decision are advanced placement or honors courses, evidence of special talent, and extracurricular activities record. Students must complete 120 credit hours, including the core curriculum (about 47 credits), a major (typically 40-60 credits) and upper division credits (at least 40). A 2.0 GPA is also required for graduation. **Procedure:** Freshmen are admitted to all sessions. Entrance exams should be taken as early as possible. There are early admissions and rolling admissions plans. Application deadlines are open. Application fee is $20. Notification is sent on a rolling basis. Applications are accepted online. **Transfer Students:** A minimum GPA of 2.0 is recommended; D grades do not transfer. Official transcripts are required for all previous colleges attended. Students with fewer than 27 credits transferring must submit high school transcripts as well. 30 of 120 credits required for the bachelor's degree must be completed at MVC. **International Students:** There are 247 international students enrolled. The school actively recruits these students. They must take the TOEFL, as well as the SAT or ACT.

Admissions Contact: Tennille Langdon, Director of Admissions. Email: *admissions@moval.edu* Web: *www.moval.edu*

FINANCIAL AID: In 2016-2017, 99% of all full-time freshmen and continuing full-time students received some form of financial aid. MVC is a member of CSS. The FAFSA code is 002489. The priority date for freshman financial aid applications for fall entry is March 15.

MISSOURI WESTERN STATE UNIVERSITY *(The complete profile is made available exclusively on our website, www.barronspac.com)*

NORTHWEST MISSOURI STATE UNIVERSITY A-1
www.nwmissouri.edu

Maryville, MO 64468 (660) 562-1146
(800) 633-1175
Fax: (660) 562-1121 Email: admissions@nwmissouri.edu

Full-time: 2091 men, 2827 women
Part-time: 323 men, 387 women
Graduate: 497 men, 405 women
Year: trimesters, summer session
Room & Board: $8558
ACT: 22
Application Deadline: open
Faculty: 252; IIA, --$
Ph.D.s: 64%
Student/Faculty: 21 to 1
Tuition: $9179 ($15,499)
Freshman Class: 5009 applied, 3754 accepted, 1499 enrolled
CEEB CODE: 6488
COMPETITIVE

Northwest Missouri State University, founded in 1905, is a public institution offering undergraduate courses in agriculture, science, arts and humanities, business, government, computer science, health and wellness, and education. There are 7 undergraduate schools and one graduate school. In addition to regional accreditation, Northwest has baccalaureate program accreditation with AACSB, ACBSP, ADA, AHEA, NASM, NCATE, AACTE, AAFCS, and ACS. The 370-acre campus is in a small town 90 miles north of Kansas City. Including any residence halls, there are 35 buildings.

STUDENT LIFE: 70% of undergraduates are from Missouri. Others are from 38 states, 34 foreign countries, and Canada. 98% are from public schools. 75% are White; 5% African American; 3% Hispanic; 3% two or more races; 2% race unknown; 10% Foreign; 1% Asian American. **Female To Male Ratio:** 1.2:1. The average age of freshmen is 18; all undergraduates, 20. 33% do not continue beyond their first year; 47% remain to graduate. **Housing:** 2992 students can be accommodated in college housing, which includes single-sex and coed dorms, on-campus apartments, and married student housing. In addition, there are fraternity houses and sorority houses. On-campus housing is guaranteed for all 4 years and is guaranteed for the freshman year only. 63% of students commute. Alcohol is not permitted. All students may keep cars.

FACULTY/CLASSROOMS: 49% of faculty are male; 51% are female. All teach undergraduates. No introductory courses are taught by graduate students. The average class size in an introductory lecture is 33; in a laboratory is 21; and in a regular course is 25.

PROGRAMS OF STUDY: Northwest confers B.A., B.S., B.F.A., B.S.ED., B.S.Med.Tech., B.S.N. and B.Tech degrees. Associate and master's degrees are also awarded. Bachelor's degrees are awarded in AGRICULTURE (agricultural business management, agricultural economics, agricultural mechanics, agricultural sciences, agriculture, agronomy, animal science, conservation and regulation, forestry and related sciences, horticulture, and wildlife management), BIOLOGICAL SCIENCE (biology/biological science, botany, ecology, marine biology, and zoology), BUSINESS (accounting, apparel and textiles, banking and finance, business administration and management, business economics, finance, international business, international business management, marketing/retailing/merchandising, and recreation and leisure services), COMMUNICATIONS AND THE ARTS (advertising, art, broadcasting, communications, dramatic arts, English, fine arts, journalism, music, public relations, Spanish, and speech/debate/rhetoric), COMPUTER AND PHYSICAL SCIENCE (chemistry, computer management, computer science, data processing, earth science, geology, information sciences and systems, mathematics, physics, science, and statistics), EDUCATION (agricultural education, art education, business education, early childhood education, education of the mentally handicapped, elementary education, English education, mathematics education, middle school education, music education, physical education, recreation education, science education, secondary education, special education, and specific learning disabilities), ENGINEERING AND ENVIRONMENTAL DESIGN (emergency/disaster science and preengineering), HEALTH PROFESSIONS (biology, predentistry, premedicine, prepharmacy, and preveterinary science), SOCIAL SCIENCE (child care/child and family studies, criminology, dietetics, economics, food science, geography, history, humanities, industrial and organizational psychology, philosophy, political science/government, prelaw, psychology, public administration, social psychology, social science, sociology, and textiles and clothing). Teacher education, business management, psychology, and agriculture are the strongest and have the largest enrollments are the strongest academically.

ACTIVITIES: 12% of men belong to 9 national fraternities; 18% of women belong to 7 national sororities. There are 157 groups on campus, including band, cheerleading, choir, chorale, chorus, computers, dance, debate, drama, drill team, drum and bugle corps, ethnic, film, forensics, international, jazz band, LGBT, literary magazine, marching band, newspaper, orchestra, pep band, photography, political, professional, radio and TV, religious, social, student government, symphony, and yearbook. Popular campus events include SAC Fall and Spring Concerts, Homecoming events, Football Games, Up 'Til Dawn Colden Pond Plunge, SAC Grocery Bingo, SAC Late Night events, Greek Life Bid Day, Advantage Week Fireworks, Distinguished Lecture Series, and Bearcat Basketball Games. **Sports:** There are 7 intercollegiate sports for men and 9 for women, and 12 intramural sports for men and 13 for women. Facilities include A 7000-seat stadium, a 3000-seat basketball arena, 3 gyms, 4 racquetball courts, a weight-lifting area, baseball and softball fields, volleyball and tennis courts, dance areas, Disc golf course, Cricket pitch and state of the art Foster Fitness center and human performance laboratory. **Graduates:** From July 1, 2015 to June 30, 2016, 992 bachelor's degrees were awarded. The most popular majors were business/marketing (20%), education (19%), and psychology (11%). 182 companies recruited on campus in 2015-2016. In an average class, 27% graduate in 4 years or less, 48% graduate in 5 years or less, and 50% graduate in 6 years or less. Of the 2015 graduating class, 17% were enrolled in graduate school within 6 months of graduation, and 80% were employed.

SERVICES: Counseling and information services are available, as is tutoring in most subjects. There is a reader service for the blind, and remedial math, reading, and writing. **Library/Resources:** The library contains 240,370 volumes, 8,421 microform items, and 5,234 audio/video tapes/CDs/DVDs, and subscribes to 33,868 periodicals including electronic. Computerized library services include interlibrary loans, database searching, Internet access, and Wi-Fi capability. Special learning facilities include an art gallery, radio station, TV station, Missouri Arboretum, Mozingo Outdoor Education Recreation Area (observatory, ropes challenge course, trap and archery, canoes and kayaks), Horace Mann Laboratory School, R.T. Wright Farm (dairy operation, swine herd, horticulture complex, experimental farmland), Center for Innovation and Entrepreneurship (business incubator), Studio Theater and Black Box experimental theater, online Northwest History Museum, Science Museum, Agriculture Museum, Jean Jennings Bartik Computing Museum, Warren Stucki Museum of Broadcasting, Student Media Converged Newsroom, Joyce and Harvey White International Plaza. Anita Aldrich Human Performance Lab and Foster Fitness Center. A state of the art Michael L. Faust student media laboratory. **Physically Challenged Students:** All of the campus is accessible. Facilities include wheelchair ramps, elevators, special parking, specially equipped restrooms, special class scheduling, lowered drinking fountains, and lowered telephones. **Special:** Campus-wide internships, study abroad program (England, Mexico, Spain, Netherlands, Japan and many others. Work-study programs, student designed majors, a 3-2 engineering degree with the Missouri University of Science and Technology, credit for military experience, service learning, non degree study, and pass/fail options are possible. There are 3 national honor societies and a freshman honors program. **Visiting:** There are regularly scheduled orientations for prospective students. There are guides for informal visits, visitors may sit in on classes, and stay overnight. To schedule a visit, contact Mabel Cook Recruitment and Visitors Center at admissions@nwmissouri.edu. **Campus Safety and Security:** Measures include 24-hour foot and vehicle patrol, emergency notification system, self-defense education, and security escort services. There are shuttle buses, lighted pathways/sidewalks, and controlled access to dorms/residences.

REQUIREMENTS: Students are required to have a minimum composite score of 980 or 1060* on the SAT or 21 on the ACT; if scores are below those levels, a combined percentile index obtained from the SAT or ACT score and high school rank will be used, (*per 2016 SAT redesign). AP and CLEP credits are accepted. Important factors in the admissions decision are evidence of special talent and personality/intangible qualities. All students must maintain a minimum GPA of 2.0 while taking at least 124 credit hours. Distribution requirements include 9 hours each in social science and humanities, 8 hours in natural science, 6 hours in composition, 4 hours each in math and phys ed, 3 hours each in oral communications and behavioral sciences, and 1 hour in the freshman seminar. **Procedure:** Freshmen are admitted fall, spring, and summer. Entrance exams should be taken in the fall of the senior year. There is a rolling admissions plan. Application deadlines are open. Application fee is $25. Notifications are sent September 1. Applications are accepted on-line. Application fees are waived if application is completed on-line. **Transfer Students:** 253 transfer students enrolled in 2015-2016. Applicants must present a minimum GPA of 2.0. 30 of 124 credits required for the bachelor's degree must be completed at Northwest. **International Students:** There are 175 international students enrolled. The school actively recruits these students. They must take the TOEFL with a minimum score of 500 on the paper-based TOEFL (PBT) or 61 on the Internet-based version (iBT).

ADMISSIONS: 75% of the 2016-2017 applicants were accepted. 31% of the current freshmen were in the top fifth of their class; 63% were in the top two fifths. 34 freshmen graduated first in their class. **Admissions Contact:** Tamera Grow, Associate Director of Admissions. Email: *admissions@nwmissouri.edu* Web: *www.nwmissouri.edu*

FINANCIAL AID: In 2016-2017, 71% of all full-time freshmen and 67% of continuing full-time students received some form of financial aid. 63% of all full-time freshmen and 57% of continuing full-time students received need-based aid. The average freshman award was $11,074. Need-based scholarships or need-based grants averaged $7,375; need-based self-help aid (loans and jobs) averaged $3,290; and non-need-based athletic scholarships averaged $6,366. 53% of undergraduate students work part-time. Average annual earnings from campus work are $2526. The FAFSA code is 002496. The priority date for freshman financial aid applications for fall entry is April 1.

PARK UNIVERSITY — A-2
www.park.edu

Parkville, MO 64152 — **(816) 584-6215** / **(800) 745-7275**

Fax: (816) 741-4462	**Email: admissions@park.edu**
Full-time: 547 men, 657 women	**Faculty:** 94
Part-time: 182 men, 288 women	**Ph.D.s:** 54%
Graduate: 336 men, 448 women	**Student/Faculty:** 11 to 1
Year: semesters, summer session	**Tuition:** $13,284
Room & Board: $7045	**Freshman Class:** 778 applied, 539 accepted, 212 enrolled
ACT: 21	**CEEB CODE:** 6574
Application Deadline: n/av	**COMPETITIVE**

Park University, founded in 1875, is a private institution offering degree programs in the humanities, performing arts, natural and life sciences, and social and administrative sciences. Figures in the above capsule and in this profile are approximate. There are 3 undergraduate schools and 1 graduate school. In addition to regional accreditation, Park has baccalaureate program accreditation with NLN and CAATE. The 700-acre campus is in a suburban area 12 miles north of Kansas City. Including any residence halls, there are 17 buildings.

STUDENT LIFE: 80% of undergraduates are from Missouri. Others are from 50 states, 103 foreign countries, and Canada. 80% are from public schools. 52% are White; 5% Hispanic; 19% Foreign; 10% African American; 1% Asian American; 1% American Indian/Alaska Native. 88% claim no religious affiliation. **Female To Male Ratio:** 1.3:1. The average age of freshmen is 18; all undergraduates, 24. 39% do not continue beyond their first year; 41% remain to graduate. **Housing:** 410 students can be accommodated in college housing, which includes coed dorms, on-campus apartments, and honors houses. On-campus housing is guaranteed for all 4 years. 80% of students commute. All students may keep cars. Alcohol is not permitted.

FACULTY/CLASSROOMS: 62% of faculty are male; 38% are female. All teach undergraduates, and 80% do research. No introductory courses are taught by graduate students. The average class size in an introductory lecture is 20; in a laboratory is 10; and in a regular course is 15.

PROGRAMS OF STUDY: Park confers B.A., B.S., B.P.A., B.S.W., B.S.N., and B.F.A. degrees. Associate and master's degrees are also awarded. Bachelor's degrees are awarded in BIOLOGICAL SCIENCE (biology/biological science), BUSINESS (accounting, business administration and management, business economics, human resources, management information systems, and marketing management), COMMUNICATIONS AND THE ARTS (communications, dramatic arts, English, fine arts, graphic design, music, public relations, and Spanish), COMPUTER AND PHYSICAL SCIENCE (chemistry, computer science, information sciences and systems, mathematics, and natural sciences), EDUCATION (athletic training, early childhood education, and elementary education), ENGINEERING AND ENVIRONMENTAL DESIGN (aviation administration/management, computational sciences, engineering management, and interior design), HEALTH PROFESSIONS (health care administration), SOCIAL SCIENCE (child care/child and family studies, criminal justice, economics, fire protection, fire services administration, geography, history, human services, law, liberal arts/general studies, political science/government, psychology, public administration, social psychology, social work, and sociology). Management, management/computer information systems, and management/human resources have the largest enrollments.

ACTIVITIES: There are no fraternities or sororities. There are 30 groups on campus, including cheerleading, computers, drama, ethnic, honors, international, literary magazine, newspaper, photography, political, professional, radio and TV, religious, social, social service, and student government. Popular campus events include Fall Harvest Festival, Spring Fling, and International Week. **Sports:** There are 6 intercollegiate sports for men and 7 for women, and 3 intramural sports for men and 3 for women. Facilities include indoor gyms with basketball and volleyball courts, outdoor track, soccer and softball fields, tennis courts, and outdoor sand volleyball and basketball courts. **Graduates:** From July 1, 2015 to June 30, 2016, 398 bachelor's degrees were awarded. The most popular majors were business/management (24%), education (14%), and computer and information systems (13%). 15 companies recruited on campus in 2015-2016. In an average class, 6% graduate in 3 years or less, 53% graduate in 4 years or less, 36% graduate in 5 years or less, and 5% graduate in 6 years or less.

SERVICES: Counseling and information services are available, as is tutoring in most subjects, and a reader service for the blind, and remedial math, reading, and writing. **Library/Resources:** The library contains 158,422 volumes, 195,530 microform items, and 670 audio/video tapes/CDs/DVDs, and subscribes to 775 periodicals including electronic. Computerized library services include interlibrary loans and database searching. Special learning facilities include an art gallery, radio station, and TV station. **Physically Challenged Students:** 95% of the campus is accessible. Facilities include wheelchair ramps, elevators, special parking, specially equipped restrooms, special class scheduling, and lowered drinking fountains. **Special:** Cross-registration is available through a Kansas City consortium, and study abroad is possible through other schools. The university also offers internships in most majors, work-study programs with local companies, a Washington semester, credit for life and military experience, pass/fail options, and nondegree study. An accelerated degree program is offered in some majors. There are 2 national honor societies and a freshman honors program. **Visiting:** There are regularly scheduled orientations for prospective students, including a campus tour, lunch, an information session with a student panel, sessions on admissions, scholarships, and financial aid, and a chance to attend a class and meet with a faculty member. There are guides for informal visits, visitors may sit in on classes, and stay overnight. To schedule a visit, contact the Admissions and Student Financial Services. **Campus Safety and Security:** Measures include 24-hour foot and vehicle patrol, security escort services, emergency telephones, and lighted pathways/sidewalks.

REQUIREMENTS: The ACT is required. The GED is accepted with a minimum total score of 225 and no area less than 35. Park requires applicants to be in the upper 50% of their class. A GPA of 2.0 is required. AP and CLEP credits are accepted. Important factors in the admissions decision are advanced placement or honors courses, leadership record, and extracurricular activities record. All students must complete core requirements, including 3 semesters of English composition and 1 of algebra, as well as 1 science course. They must also complete 24 to 27 hours of general education courses and 9 hours of liberal learning courses. Of the 120 credit hours needed for the bachelor's degree, 45 must be completed in upper-division work and 30 to 60 in the major, with a minimum GPA of 2.0. **Procedure:** Freshmen are admitted in the fall, spring, and summer. Entrance exams should be taken during the junior year or early in the senior year. There is a rolling admissions plan. Check with the school for current application deadlines. The application fee is $25. Notification is sent on a rolling basis. Applications are accepted online. **Transfer Students:** The college requires a GPA of at least 2.0. A minimum ACT composite score of 20 is recommended but is waived for students age 25 or older. 30 of 120 credits required for the bachelor's degree must be completed at Park. **International Students:** There are 324 international students enrolled. The school actively recruits these students. They must take the TOEFL, as well as the ACT.

ADMISSIONS: 69% of the 2016-2017 applicants were accepted. The ACT scores were 50% below 12, 29% between 12 and 17, 9% between 18 and 23, 5% between 24 and 29, and 7% above 30. 29% of the current freshmen were in the top fifth of their class; 54% were in the top two fifths. **Admissions Contact:** Eric Blair, Director of Undergraduate Admissions. Email: *admissions@park.edu* Web: *www.park.edu*

FINANCIAL AID: In 2016-2017, 62% of all full-time freshmen and 57% of continuing full-time students received some form of financial aid. 49% of all full-time freshmen and 42% of continuing full-time students received need-based aid. The average freshman award was $10,524. The average financial indebtedness of the 2016 graduate was $22,218. The the college's own financial statement is required. The FAFSA code is 002498. The priority date for freshman financial aid applications for fall entry is March 15. The filing deadline for fall entry is August 1.

RESEARCH COLLEGE OF NURSING *(The complete profile is made available exclusively on our website, www.barronspac.com)*

ROCKHURST UNIVERSITY — A-2
www.rockhurst.edu

Kansas City, MO 64110 — **(816) 501-4100** **(800) 842-6776**
Fax: (816) 501-4241 — **Email: admission@rockhurst.edu**

Full-time: 615 men, 850 women	**Faculty:** n/av
Part-time: 320 men, 540 women	**Ph.D.s:** 84%
Graduate: 335 men, 475 women	**Student/Faculty:** n/av
Year: semesters, summer session	**Tuition:** $17,440
Room & Board: $11,780	**Freshman Class:** n/av
SAT : recommended **ACT:** required	**CEEB CODE:** 6611
Application Deadline: n/av	**COMPETITIVE**

Rockhurst University, founded in 1910, is a private Catholic Jesuit institution that offers undergraduate programs in the arts and sciences, education, nursing, and business. The figures in the above capsule and in this profile are approximate. There are 4 undergraduate schools and 2 graduate schools. In addition to regional accreditation, Rockhurst has baccalaureate program accreditation with APTA, CAHEA, NLN, TEAC, and AACTE. The 55-acre campus is in an urban area in Kansas City. Including any residence halls, there are 19 buildings.

STUDENT LIFE: 58% of undergraduates are from Missouri. Others are from 17 states. 49% are from public schools. 82% are White; 5% African American; 3% Asian American; 3% Hispanic; 1% American Indian/Alaska Native; 1% Foreign. 46% are Catholic; 34% Buddhist, Hindu, Muslim, and Islamic; 20% Protestant. **Female To Male Ratio:** 1.5:1. The average age of freshmen is 18; all undergraduates, 21. 11% do not continue beyond their first year; 66% remain to graduate. **Housing:** 815 students can be accommodated in college housing, which includes single-sex and coed dorms, on-campus apartments, honors houses, and special-interest houses. On-campus housing is available on a first-come and first-served basis. Priority is given to out-of-town students. 61% of students live on campus; of those, 45% remain on campus on weekends. All students may keep cars.

FACULTY/CLASSROOMS: 52% of faculty are male; 48% are female. 87% teach undergraduates. No introductory courses are taught by graduate students. The average class size in an introductory lecture is 20; in a laboratory is 14; and in a regular course is 21.

PROGRAMS OF STUDY: Rockhurst confers B.A., B.S., B.S.B.A., and B.S.N. degrees. Master's and doctoral degrees are also awarded. Bachelor's degrees are awarded in BIOLOGICAL SCIENCE (biochemistry, bioinformatics, and biology/biological science), BUSINESS (business administration and management, business communications, business economics, and nonprofit/public organization management), COMMUNICATIONS AND THE ARTS (communications, English, French, and Spanish), COMPUTER AND PHYSICAL SCIENCE (chemistry, computer science, mathematics, and physics), EDUCATION (elementary education, foreign languages education, and secondary education), ENGINEERING AND ENVIRONMENTAL DESIGN (computer technology), HEALTH PROFESSIONS (clinical science, nursing, and speech pathology/audiology), SOCIAL SCIENCE (economics, history, international relations, philosophy, political science/government, psychology, and theological studies). Nursing, and business administration are the strongest academically.

ACTIVITIES: 7% of men belong to 4 national fraternities; 7% of women belong to 2 national sororities. There are 55 groups on campus, including art, cheerleading, choir, chorale, chorus, computers, drama, ethnic, honors, international, literary magazine, musical theater, newspaper, photography, political, professional, radio and TV, religious, social, social service, and student government. Popular campus events include Fraternity Socials, Coffee House Events, and Rockstock (live bands). **Sports:** There are 5 intercollegiate sports for men and 5 for women, and 12 intramural sports for men and 12 for women. Facilities include athletic and soccer fields, tennis, handball, racquetball, badminton, basketball, and volleyball courts, a weight and exercise room, gymnastics, and a baseball field. **Graduates:** From July 1, 2015 to June 30, 2016, 366 bachelor's degrees were awarded. The most popular majors were business (35%), nursing/health professions (21%), and psychology/social science/history (13%). In an average class, 51% graduate in 4 years or less, 63% graduate in 5 years or less, and 66% graduate in 6 years or less.

SERVICES: Counseling and information services are available. The Learning Center offers tutoring in many subject assistance with any college task, writing task, and study strategies, SI courses, support for various professional tests, plus a computer bank. **Library/Resources:** The library contains 314,890 volumes, 596,850 microform items, 8,078 audio/video tapes/CDs/DVDs, and subscribes to 38,934 periodicals including electronic. Computerized library services include interlibrary loans, database searching, Internet access, and Wi-Fi capability. Special learning facilities include an art gallery, radio station, and a multimedia classrooms. **Physically Challenged Students:** 90% of the campus is accessible. Facilities include wheelchair ramps, elevators, special parking, specially equipped restrooms, lowered drinking fountains, and lowered telephones. **Special:** Students may obtain career-related work experience through the Cooperative Education Program. Internships for credit and salary are available. Students are encouraged to study abroad in 1 of 5 countries for a semester, to take a semester in New York at Fordham University, or to participate in a congressional intern/study program in Washington, D.C., through Marquette University. B.A.-B.S. degrees are available in business administration. Work-study and an accelerated degree in nursing are also available. Students may pursue dual majors, a 3-2 engineering degree, and interdisciplinary majors. There are 7 national honor societies, Phi Beta Kappa, a freshman honors program, and 12 departmental honors programs. **Visiting:** There are regularly scheduled orientations for prospective students, including a campus tour, an interview with an admissions counselor, and a classroom visit or meeting with a faculty member. There are guides for informal visits, visitors may sit in on classes, and stay overnight. To schedule a visit, contact the Admissions Office. **Campus Safety and Security:** Measures include 24-hour foot and vehicle patrol, self-defense education, and security escort services. There are also shuttle buses, emergency telephones, lighted pathways/sidewalks, and formal presentations. There is also a full in-house security program geared toward integration of security into the overall campus operation.

REQUIREMENTS: The ACT is required. The SAT is recommended. In addition, applicants must be a graduate of an accredited secondary school or have earned a GED. The university requires completion of 15 academic credits, including 4 years of English, 3 to 4 of history/social science, 3 of math, 2 to 4 of a foreign language, and 1 of visual or performing arts. An interview is recommended, and a recommendation is required. Rockhurst requires applicants to be in the upper 50% of their class. A GPA of 2.0 is required. AP and CLEP credits are accepted. Important factors in the admissions decision are advanced placement or honors courses, recommendations by school officials, and leadership record. Students must complete 128 credit hours with a minimum of 18 in the major, with at least a 2.0 GPA. 52 prescribed semester hours in philosophy, theology, history, literature, science, social studies, and the arts are required. Students must also demonstrate proficiency in oral and written communication and math. **Procedure:** Freshmen are admitted to all sessions. Entrance exams should be taken in April or June of the junior year or October, December, or February of the senior year.

There are deferred admissions and rolling admissions plans. Check with the school for current application deadlines. The application fee is $25. Applications are accepted online. **Transfer Students:** 95 transfer students enrolled in 2015-2016. Transfer applicants must have a GPA of at least 2.25. An interview is recommended. All college transcripts must be submitted; a high school transcript and test scores are required if the applicant has completed fewer than 24 college semester hours. 30 of 128 credits required for the bachelor's degree must be completed at Rockhurst. **International Students:** There are 2 international students enrolled. The school actively recruits these students. They must take the TOEFL with a minimum score of 550 on the paper-based TOEFL (PBT) or 79 on the Internet-based version (iBT). They must also take the SAT or ACT, scoring 20.

ADMISSIONS: 5 freshmen graduated first in their class. **Admissions Contact:** Phil Gebauer, Associate Vice President for Enrollment. Email: *admission@rockhurst.edu* Web: *www.rockhurst.edu*

FINANCIAL AID: In 2016-2017, 91% of all full-time freshmen and 81% of continuing full-time students received some form of financial aid. 69% of all full-time freshmen and 67% of continuing full-time students received need-based aid. The average freshman award was $21,879. 22% of undergraduate students work part-time. Average annual earnings from campus work are $1500. The average financial indebtedness of the 2016 graduate was $16,579. The FAFSA code is 002499. Check with the school for current application deadlines.

SAINT LOUIS UNIVERSITY — D-2

www.slu.edu

St. Louis, MO 63103	(314) 977-2500 (800) SLUFORU
Fax: (314) 977-7136	Email: admission@slu.edu
Full-time: 3156 men, 4332 women	Faculty: 776; I, -$
Part-time: 255 men, 505 women	Ph.D.s: 86%
Graduate: 1898 men, 2768 women	Student/Faculty: 11 to 1
Year: semesters, summer session	Tuition: $39,226
Room & Board: $10,640	Freshman Class: 13216 applied, 8273 accepted, 1618 enrolled
SAT: required ACT: 28	CEEB CODE: 6629
Application Deadline: December 1	HIGHLY COMPETITIVE

Saint Louis University, founded in 1818, is a Catholic, Jesuit institution that values academic excellence, life-changing research, compassionate health care, and a strong commitment to faith and service. SLU is the second oldest Jesuit university in the United States, offering a complete range of undergraduate, graduate and professional programs including law, and medicine. the University fosters the intellectual and character development of nearly 13,000 students on campuses in St. Louis and Madrid, Spain. Building on a legacy of nearly 200 years, Saint Louis University continues to move forward with an unwavering commitment to a higher purpose, and a greater good. There are 10 undergraduate schools and 12 graduate schools. In addition to regional accreditation, SLU has baccalaureate program accreditation with AACSB, ABET, CSWE, NASAD, NCATE, ACS, AABI, CEPH, CAHIIM, ACEND, CAAHEP, CCNE, JRCERT, JRCNMT, NAACLS, and DESE. The 270-acre campus is in an urban area midtown section of St. Louis, approximately 4 miles west of the Gateway Arch. Including any residence halls, there are 134 buildings.

STUDENT LIFE: 63% of undergraduates are from out of state, mostly the Midwest. Students are from 48 states, 52 foreign countries, and Canada. 9% are Asian American; 66% White; 6% African American; 6% Hispanic; 6% Foreign; 4% two or more races; 2% race unknown. 42% claim no religious affiliation; 38% Catholic; 13% Protestant. **Female To Male Ratio:** 1.4:1. The average age of freshmen is 18; all undergraduates, 20. 10% do not continue beyond their first year; 73% remain to graduate. **Housing:** 3865 students can be accommodated in college housing, which includes single-sex and coed dorms, on-campus apartments, fraternity houses, sorority houses, women's dorms, men's dorms, coed dorms, special housing for disabled students, and learning community houses. On-campus housing is available on a first-come, first-served basis, and on a lottery system for upperclassmen. 51% of students live on campus; of those, 80% remain on campus on weekends. All students may keep cars.

FACULTY/CLASSROOMS: 59% of faculty are male; 41% are female. 39% teach undergraduates, 46% do research, and 21% do both. Graduate students teach 7% of introductory courses. The average class size in an introductory lecture is 19; in a laboratory is 17; and in a regular course is 19.

PROGRAMS OF STUDY: SLU confers B.A. and B.S. degrees. Master's and doctoral degrees are also awarded. Bachelor's degrees are awarded in AGRICULTURE (environmental studies), BIOLOGICAL SCIENCE (biochemistry, biology/biological science, forensic science, neurosciences, and nutritional sciences), BUSINESS (accounting, business administration and management, business economics, entrepreneurial studies, finance, international business, international economics, management information systems, marketing, marketing management, organizational behavior, organizational leadership and management, and sustainable management), COMMUNICATIONS AND THE ARTS (art history, classical languages, classics, communications, dramatic arts, English, English literature, English writing, fine/studio arts, general, French, Germanic languages and literature, information technology, Italian, music, Russian languages and literature, Spanish, studio art, theatre arts, and theater management), COMPUTER AND PHYSICAL SCIENCE (applied mathematics, atmospheric sciences and meteorology, chemistry, clinical laboratory science, computer programming, computer information technology, computer information systems, computer science, earth science, geology, mathematics, and physics), EDUCATION (drama education, education, elementary education, English education, general studies, health information management, mathematics education, middle school education, nutrition education, physical science secondary school education, science education, secondary education, and social science education), ENGINEERING AND ENVIRONMENTAL DESIGN (aeronautical engineering, aeronautical technology, aerospace engineering, aerospace studies, airline piloting and navigation, bioengineering, biomedical engineering, civil engineering, civil engineering technology, computer engineering, computer technology, electrical/electronics engineering, electrical technology, electrical/electronics engineering technology, emergency/disaster science, engineering, engineering management, engineering physics, environmental science, and mechanical engineering), HEALTH PROFESSIONS (allied health, biology, biomedical science, clinical science, cytotechnology, exercise science, health, health administration and policy, health care administration, kinesiology, medical laboratory science, medical laboratory technology, medical records administration/services, nuclear medical technology, nursing, nutrition and dietetics, occupational therapy, public health, radiation therapy, radiograph medical technology, radiologic imaging modalities, and speech pathology/audiology), SOCIAL SCIENCE (African American studies, American studies, anthropology, behavioral science, communication sciences & disorders, criminal justice, forensic studies, French studies, history, homeland security/emergency preparedness, international relations, Latin American studies, legal studies, philosophy, political science/government, psychology, safety and security technology, safety management, social work, sociology, theology, theological studies, urban studies, and women's studies). Engineering, public health, business, Theology, physical therapy, and athletic training are the strongest academically. Nursing, physical therapy, and accounting have the largest enrollments.

ACTIVITIES: 18% of men belong to 8 national fraternities; 27% of women belong to 6 national sororities. There are 155 groups on campus, including games/hobbies, improvisational comedy, minority student groups, model UN, singing groups, speakers forum, sports/fitness club, theatre program, wilderness/outdoor programs, art, band, campus ministry, cheerleading, chess, choir, chorale, chorus, computers, dance, debate, drama, drill team, environmental, ethnic, honors, international, jazz band, LGBT, literary magazine, musical theater, newspaper, pep band, photography, political, professional, radio and TV, religious, social, social service, and student government. Popular campus events include comedians, major concerts in fall and spring, Make a Difference Day, Fall Welcome, Winter Welcome, SLU Involvement Fair, Homecoming, Billikens After Dark events, Sunday Night Mass, Relay for Life, Dance Marathon, Atlas Week, and International Banquet, LA. **Sports:** There are 8 intercollegiate sports for men and 10 for women, and 23 intramural sports for men and 23 for women. Facilities include a basketball court, soccer playing field, practice soccer, courts for baseball field and softball diamond, swimming and diving pool, and a hockey field. **Graduates:** From July 1, 2015 to June 30, 2016, 1988 bachelor's degrees were awarded. The most popular majors were business administration (17%), nursing (8%), and biology (6%). 321 companies recruited on campus in 2015-2016. In an average class, 64% graduate in 4 years or less, 73% graduate in 5 years or less, and 74% graduate in 6 years or less. Of the 2015 graduating class, 31% were enrolled in graduate school within 6 months of graduation, and 59% were employed.

SERVICES: Counseling and information services are available, as is tutoring in most subjects. **Library/Resources:** The 3 libraries contain 1.9 million volumes, 2.8 million microform items, 127,907 audio/video tapes/CDs/DVDs, and subscribe to 11,147 periodicals including electronic. Computerized library services include interlibrary loans, database searching, Internet access, and Wi-Fi capability. Special learning facilities include an art gallery, radio station, TV station, the Vatican Manuscripts microfilm library, student unions, LEED Certified Research Facility, Doisy Research Center, biological station, entrepreneurial studies center, earthquake research center, performing arts center, supersonic wind tunnel, water tunnel, shock tube, fabrication labs, flight simulators, airport, sculpture/ceramics studio, physiology/gait research labs, Madrid, Spain Campus, Law School in the heart of the downtown legal community, demonstration clinics (practice with actual clients): counseling and family therapy, child development, speech and hearing, psychology, dental, occupational and physical therapy, organic garden. **Physically Challenged Students:** 95% of the campus is accessible. Facilities include wheelchair ramps, elevators, special parking, specially equipped restrooms, special class scheduling, lowered drinking fountains, lowered telephones, and special housing. **Special:** There are internships available in many departments. We have accelerated degree programs in Nursing (B.S.), Leadership and Organizational Development (M.A.), and Organizational Informatics (M.S.). We have Dual Majors and Student-designed majors. We have 3-2 Engineering and program degrees with Washington University in St. Louis. We have cross registration with Washington University in St. Louis, University of Missouri at St. Louis, Aquinas Institute of Theology, and Harris-Stowe State College. Students may also participate in university-sponsored mission trips. Students may also study abroad in 30 countries: Argentina, Australia, Austria, Belgium, Chile, China, Denmark, Ecuador, El Salvador, England, France, Germany, Hong Kong, Hungary, India, Ireland, Italy, Mexico, The Netherlands, Nicaragua, Philippines, Russia, South Africa, South Korea, Spain, Sweden, Switzerland, Taiwan, Thailand, and Vietnam. There are 3 national honor societies, Phi Beta Kappa, and a freshman honors program. **Visiting:** There are regularly scheduled orientations for prospective students, Events & visits are available year round. Options include campus tours, residence hall tours, academic meetings, class visits, & presentations on admission, student development, studying abroad, stud. life/campus culture, & staying in residence halls. There are guides for informal visits, visitors may sit in on classes, and stay overnight. To schedule a visit, contact Andrea Hitsman at admission@slu.edu. **Campus Safety and Security:** Measures include 24-hour foot and vehicle patrol, emergency notification system, self-defense education, and security escort services. There are also shuttle buses, emergency telephones, lighted pathways/sidewalks, controlled access to dorms/residences, video cameras, identification of valuables, smoke detectors in halls, informal safety and security discussions, bike patrols, prevention/awareness programs, mobile security patrols, motorist assistance, security officers, and 24 hour emergency telephone/alarm devices.

REQUIREMENTS: The SAT or ACT is required. A complete application is required for admission consideration, which also consists of an essay, a high school transcript, and test scores. Auditions and portfolios are required for the music and art programs. AP and CLEP credits are accepted. Important factors in the admissions decision are advanced placement or honors courses, leadership record, and extracurricular activities record. Students must maintain a 2.0 GPA while completing a minimum of 120 credit hours. The core curriculum includes courses in English, Philosophy, Theology, Mathematics, a Foreign Language and Cultural Diversity. **Procedure:** Freshmen are admitted in the fall, spring, and summer. Entrance exams should be taken Junior or Senior year. Junior is recommended. There are deferred admissions and rolling admissions plans. Applications should be filed by December 1 for fall entry; January 1 for spring entry; and June 1 for summer entry. Notification is sent on a rolling basis. 164 applicants were on the 2016 waiting list; 107 were admitted. Application fees are waived if application is completed online. **Transfer Students:** 274 transfer students enrolled in 2015-2016. The university requires original transcripts from each institution even if the student is not planning on transferring credit to SLU. 30 of 120 credits required for the bachelor's degree must be completed at SLU. **International Students:** There are 530 international students enrolled. The school actively recruits these students. They must take the TOEFL with a minimum score of 550 on the paper-based TOEFL (PBT) or 80 on the Internet-based version (iBT) and the college's own test, and the IELTS.

ADMISSIONS: 63% of the 2016-2017 applicants were accepted. The SAT scores for the 2016-2017 freshman class were: Critical Reading-- 13% below 500, 31% between 500 and 599, 44% between 600 and 699, and 12% between 700 and 800. Math-- 7% below 500, 32% between 500 and 599, 45% between 600 and 699, and 16% between 700 and 800. The ACT scores were 13% between 18 and 23, 51% between 24 and 29, and 36% above 30. 65% of the current freshmen were in the top fifth of their class; 87% were in the top two fifths. There were 8 National Merit finalists. **Admissions Contact:** Jean M. Gilman, Asst. Vice President, Office of Admissions. Email: *admission@slu.edu* Web: *www.slu.edu*

FINANCIAL AID: In 2016-2017, 95% of all full-time freshmen and 90% of continuing full-time students received some form of financial aid. 52% of all full-time freshmen and 54% of continuing full-time students received need-based aid. 25% of undergraduate students work part-time. Average annual earnings from campus work are $2300. The average financial indebtedness of the 2016 graduate was $34,361. SLU is a member of CSS. The FAFSA code is 002506. The priority date for freshman financial aid applications for fall entry is March 1. The filing deadline for fall entry is May 1.

SOUTHEAST MISSOURI STATE UNIVERSITY — E-3

www.semo.edu

Cape Girardeau, MO 63701 — (573) 651-2539

Fax: 573-651-5936	**Email:** admissions@semo.edu
Full-time: 3424 men, 4472 women	**Faculty:** 403; IIA, --$
Part-time: 1167 men, 1630 women	**Ph.D.s:** 74%
Graduate: 481 men, 804 women	**Student/Faculty:** 21 to 1
Year: semesters, summer session	**Tuition:** $6990 ($12,375)
Room & Board: $8508	**Freshman Class:** 5184 applied, 4293 accepted, 1858 enrolled
SAT: required **ACT:** 23	**CEEB CODE:** 6655
Application Deadline: July 1	**COMPETITIVE**

Southeast Missouri State University, founded in 1873, is a public institution offering undergraduate and graduate programs in arts and sciences, agriculture, business, education, health and human services, and technology. It includes a school of visual and performing arts. There are 7 undergraduate schools and 1 graduate school. In addition to regional accreditation, Southeast has baccalaureate program accreditation with AACSB, ABET, ACEJMC, CSWE, NASM, NCATE, NRPA, ACEND, ACS, ASHA, ATMAE, AND, CAC, EAC, ETC, CAA, CAATE, CACREP, CCNE, CEPR/PRSA, CHRIE, COSMA, NAST, NAEYC, NCATE, NCFR/CFLE, NIBS, and NKBA. The 400-acre campus is in a small town 120 miles south of St. Louis. Including any residence halls, there are 105 buildings.

STUDENT LIFE: 78% of undergraduates are from Missouri. Others are from 39 states, 54 foreign countries, and Canada. 9% are African American; 8% Foreign; 76% White; 3% race unknown; 2% Hispanic; 1% Asian American; 1% two or more races. **Female To Male Ratio:** 1.4:1. The average age of freshmen is 18; all undergraduates, 21. 27% do not continue beyond their first year; 51% remain to graduate. **Housing:** 3104 students can be accommodated in college housing, which includes single-sex and coed dorms, honors houses, special-interest houses, fraternity houses, and sorority houses. Honors program students may choose to live in a designated honors community. A variety of other learning and theme communities are available for students. Examples include education, science, transfer students, and health care. On-campus housing is guaranteed for the freshman year only, is available on a first-come, and first-served basis. 75% of students commute. All students may keep cars. Alcohol is not permitted.

FACULTY/CLASSROOMS: 45% of faculty are male; 55% are female. All teach undergraduates and do research. Graduate students teach 5% of introductory courses. The average class size in an introductory lecture is 22; in a laboratory is 19; and in a regular course is 24.

PROGRAMS OF STUDY: Southeast confers B.A., B.F.A., B.G.S., B.S.,

B.S.A.T., B.S.B.A., B.S.Ed., B.F.C.S.E., B.M.E., B.M., and B.S.N. degrees. Associate and master's degrees are also awarded. Bachelor's degrees are awarded in AGRICULTURE (agricultural business management, animal science, and horticulture), BIOLOGICAL SCIENCE (environmental biology, forensic science, and marine biology), BUSINESS (accounting, business administration and management, business communications, business economics, entrepreneurial studies, fashion merchandising, finance, hospitality management services, human resources/organizational mgmt, international business management, management, marketing, and sports management), COMMUNICATIONS AND THE ARTS (advertising, art, communication studies, dance, English, German, historic preservation, information technology, instrumental performance, journalism, music, public relations, recreation administration, and theatre acting), COMPUTER AND PHYSICAL SCIENCE (actuarial science, chemistry, computer information systems, computer science, cyber intelligence/security studies, environmental chemistry, mathematics, and physics), EDUCATION (art education, athletic training, early childhood education, education of the exceptional child, elementary education, English education, foreign languages education, general studies, global studies, industrial arts education, mathematics education, middle school education, music education, physical education/exercise science, science education, and social studies education), ENGINEERING AND ENVIRONMENTAL DESIGN (emergency/disaster science, engineering physics, engineering technology, environmental science, interior design, mechanical design technology, and technological management), HEALTH PROFESSIONS (biology, biomedical science, health, health communication, health care administration, health science, medical laboratory science, and nursing), SOCIAL SCIENCE (criminal justice, economics, history, interdisciplinary studies, philosophy, political science/government, psychology, social science, and social work). Nursing and general studies has the largest enrollment.

ACTIVITIES: 15% of men belong to 11 national fraternities; 21% of women belong to 8 national sororities. There are 174 groups on campus, including and residence hall association, student activities council, art, band, cheerleading, choir, chorus, dance, debate, drama, drill team, environmental, ethnic, forensics, Fraternities and sororities, honors, international, jazz band, LGBT, literary magazine, marching band, musical theater, newspaper, opera, orchestra, pep band, photography, political, professional, radio and TV, religious, social, social service, student government, and symphony. Popular campus events include Family Weekend, Homecoming, Late Night Breakfast, Spring Fling, Ice Cream PigOut and International Week. **Sports:** There are 5 intercollegiate sports for men and 8 for women, and 18 intramural sports for men and 18 for women. Facilities include an indoor track, a rock climbing wall, racquetball courts, basketball/volleyball/badminton/multi-purpose courts, free-weight room, a weight machine circuit area, a plyometrics/calisthenics room, a private dumbbell/abs room, two cardio areas complete with treadmills/bikes/cross-trainers/steppers/rowers, two group fitness studios with aerial silks, group exercise bikes, suspension training, a pool, volleyball court, basketball goal, bouldering wall, zip line, rope swing, softball/soccer/multi-purpose fields, a large flag-football/cricket/multipurpose field, and tennis courts, a challenge course with 300' zip-line, outdoor sand volleyball courts, and indoor soccer/hockey. **Graduates:** From July 1, 2015 to June 30, 2016, 1697 bachelor's degrees were awarded. The most popular majors were general studies (9%), nursing (7%), and elementary education (4%). In an average class, 1% graduate in 3 years or less, 29% graduate in 4 years or less, 44% graduate in 5 years or less, and 51% graduate in 6 years or less.

SERVICES: Counseling and information services are available, as is tutoring in most subjects, such as mathematics, chemistry, physics, biology, anatomy and physiology, political science, psychology and Spanish. There is also remedial math. **Library/Resources:** The library contains 424,364 volumes, 1.2 million microform items, 14,511 audio/video tapes/CDs/DVDs, and subscribes to 78,593 periodicals including electronic. Computerized library services include interlibrary loans, database searching, Internet access, and Wi-Fi capability. Special learning facilities include an art gallery, natural history museum, radio station, Center for regional history, school of visual and performing arts, center for innovation and entrepreneurship, agriculture research center, horticulture greenhouse, center for speech and hearing, Southeast Missouri State University Autism Center for Diagnosis and Treatment, Southeast Missouri Music Academy, University School for Young Children, River Campus Art Gallery, center for writing excellence, Academic Support Centers, Rosemary Berkel and Harry L. Crisp II Museum, Center for Scholarship in Teaching and Learning, CATAPULT Creative House (student incubator) and The Faulkner Center. **Physically Challenged Students:** All of the campus is accessible. Facilities include wheelchair ramps, elevators, special parking, specially equipped restrooms, special class scheduling, lowered drinking fountains, lowered telephones, and special housing. **Special:** Southeast offers a Cooperative Doctorate of Education in Educational Leadership with the University of Missouri and Cooperative Master of Science in Criminal Justice with Missouri Southern State University. Opportunities are provided for individually arranged internships and work-study, study abroad in 40 countries, a general studies degree, dual and student-designed majors (interdisciplinary studies), credit by exam, non-degree study, and pass/fail options. A 3-2 engineering degree is possible in conjunction with the University of Missouri at Rolla or at Columbia. There is cross registration with Three Rivers College to facilitate completion of an AA degree and transfer to a Southeast four-year degree program. There are pre-professional programs in architecture, chiropractic, dentistry, engineering, law, medicine, optometry, pharmacy, physical therapy, occupational therapy, and veterinary medicine. There are 28 national honor societies and a freshman honors program. **Visiting:** There are regularly scheduled orientations for prospective students, includes academic advising and other university information. There are guides for informal visits. To schedule a visit, contact the Office of Admissions. **Campus Safety and Security:** Measures include 24-hour foot and vehicle patrol, emergency notification system, self-defense education, and security escort services. There are shuttle buses, emergency telephones, lighted pathways/sidewalks, and controlled access to dorms/residences.

REQUIREMENTS: The SAT or ACT is required. Graduation from an accredited secondary school is required; the GED is accepted. Applicants should submit an academic record with 4 units in English, 2 units in social studies, 1 unit in history, 3 units in mathematics, 3 units in science (1 unit must be lab course), 1 unit in visual and performing arts, and 3 units of academic electives. A GPA of 2.0 is required. AP and CLEP credits are accepted. Students must complete a minimum of 120 credit hours (24 to 97 hours in the major). The core includes 51 credit hours in the University Studies program, as well as in interdisciplinary studies, English, and math. Minimum GPA of 2.0. Other graduation requirements varies by program. Students must also pass a writing exam and complete 4 career proficiency checks and, at the freshman and senior level, Measure of Academic Proficiency and Progress (MAPP). **Procedure:** Freshmen are admitted in the fall, spring, and summer. Entrance exams should be taken in the spring of the junior year or fall of the senior year. There is a rolling admissions plan. Applications should be filed by July 1 for fall entry; November 1 for spring entry; and May 1 for summer entry, along with a $30 fee. Applications are accepted online. **Transfer Students:** 588 transfer students enrolled in 2015-2016. Transcripts from the student's previous college must be submitted, listing at least 24 credits earned and a minimum GPA of 2.0. The ACT is required for those students who have fewer than 24 credit hours. 30 of 120 credits required for the bachelor's degree must be completed at Southeast. **International Students:** There are 645 international students enrolled. The school actively recruits these students. They must take the TOEFL with a minimum score of 500 on the paper-based TOEFL (PBT) or 61 on the Internet-based version (iBT). They must also take the SAT or ACT, scoring 18.

ADMISSIONS: 83% of the 2016-2017 applicants were accepted. The ACT scores were 5% between 12 and 17, 58% between 18 and 23, 32% between 24 and 29, and 5% above 30. 36% of the current freshmen were in the top fifth of their class; 65% were in the top two fifths. 41 freshmen graduated first in their class. **Admissions Contact:** Lenell Hahn, Director of Admissions. Email: *admissions@semo.edu* Web: *www.semo.edu*

FINANCIAL AID: In 2016-2017, 92% of all full-time freshmen and 89% of continuing full-time students received some form of financial aid. 59% of all full-time freshmen and 55% of continuing full-time students received need-based aid. The average freshman award was $10,979. Need-based scholarships or need-based grants averaged $4,819 ($15,750 maximum); need-based self-help aid (loans and jobs) averaged $3,582 ($12,500 maximum); non-need-based athletic scholarships averaged $10,608 ($24,923 maximum); other non-need-based awards and non-need-based scholarships averaged $5,008 ($25,256 maximum); and $3,641 from other forms of aid. 20% of undergraduate students work part-time. Average annual earnings from campus work are $2172. The average financial indebtedness of the 2016 graduate was $26,260. The FAFSA code is 002501. The priority date for freshman financial aid applications for fall entry is March 1.

SOUTHWEST BAPTIST UNIVERSITY *(The complete profile is made available exclusively on our website, www.barronspac.com)*

STEPHENS COLLEGE C-2
www.stephens.edu

Columbia, MO 65215 (573) 876-2391

Fax: (573) 876-7237	**Email:** inquiry@stephens.edu
Full-time: 1 men, 556 women	**Faculty:** n/av
Part-time: 6 men, 116 women	**Ph.D.s:** 83%
Graduate: 24 men, 172 women	**Student/Faculty:** n/av
Year: semesters, summer session	**Tuition:** $28,510
Room & Board: $9532	**Freshman Class:** 748 applied, 725 accepted, 259 enrolled
SAT or ACT: required	**CEEB CODE:** 6683
Application Deadline: August 1	**COMPETITIVE**

Stephens College, founded in 1833, is a private college primarily for women, offering undergraduate programs in the arts and sciences, business, education, and fine arts. There are 5 undergraduate schools and 3 graduate schools. The 59-acre campus is in an urban area 120 miles west of St. Louis. Including any residence halls, there are 35 buildings.

STUDENT LIFE: 64% of undergraduates are from Missouri. Others are from 41 states, and 2 foreign countries. 93% are from public schools. 73% are White; 13% African American; 5% two or more races; 4% Hispanic; 3% race unknown; 2% Asian American; 1% American Indian/Alaska Native; 1% Foreign. **Female To Male Ratio:** 27.2:1. The average age of freshmen is 18; all undergraduates, 24. 33% do not continue beyond their first year; 45% remain to graduate. **Housing:** 724 students can be accommodated in college housing, which includes single-sex dorms and on-campus apartments, and honors houses. There is also special interest houses for intercultural scholars and fine arts majors, and houses with designated academic floors, nonsmoking floors and pet floors. On-campus housing is guaranteed for all 4 years. 72% of students live on campus; of those, 90% remain on campus on weekends. All students may keep cars.

FACULTY/CLASSROOMS: 40% of faculty are male; 60% are female. 92% teach undergraduates, 92% do research, and 92% do both. No introductory courses are taught by graduate students. The average class size in an introductory lecture is 30; in a laboratory is 12; and in a regular course is 20.

PROGRAMS OF STUDY: Stephens confers B.A., B.S. and B.F.A. degrees. Master's degrees are also awarded. Bachelor's degrees are awarded in AGRICULTURE (equine science), BIOLOGICAL SCIENCE (biology/biological science), BUSINESS (accounting, business administration and management, and fashion merchandising), COMMUNICATIONS AND THE ARTS (creative writing, dance, dramatic arts, English, film arts, graphic design, public relations, and theater design), EDUCATION (early childhood education and elementary education), ENGINEERING AND ENVIRONMENTAL DESIGN (interior design), SOCIAL SCIENCE (fashion design and technology and liberal arts/general studies). Education, and biology are the strongest academically. Performing arts, fashion, and biology have the largest enrollments.

ACTIVITIES: There are no fraternities; 8% of women belong to 2 national sororities. There are 38 groups on campus, including art, choir, chorale, chorus, dance, drama, ethnic, honors, international, LGBT, literary magazine, musical theater, newspaper, photography, political, professional, radio and TV, religious, social, social service, student government, and yearbook. Popular campus events include Opening Convocation, Honors Convocation, and Performing Arts Events. **Sports:** There are 4 intercollegiate sports for women. Facilities include a 300-seat gym and tennis courts. **Graduates:** From July 1, 2015 to June 30, 2016, 164 bachelor's degrees were awarded. The most popular majors were health information administration (11%), fashion - marketing and manegment (10%), and counseling (7%). In an average class, 71% graduate in 3 years or less, 96% graduate in 4 years or less, 99% graduate in 5 years or less, and 100% graduate in 6 years or less. Of the 2015 graduating class, 2% were enrolled in graduate school within 6 months of graduation.

SERVICES: Counseling and information services are available, as is tutoring in most subjects, and remedial writing. **Library/Resources:** The library contains 143,229 volumes, 10,792 microform items, 3,356 audio/video tapes/CDs/DVDs, and subscribes to 45,699 periodicals including electronic. Computerized library services include interlibrary loans, database searching, and Internet access. Special learning facilities include an art gallery, radio station, and TV station. **Physically Challenged Students:** 80% of the campus is accessible. Facilities include wheelchair ramps, elevators, special parking, specially equipped restrooms, special class scheduling, lowered drinking fountains, and special housing. **Special:** Students may study abroad in England, Italy, Mexico, France, Ecuador, South Korea, and Spain. Stephens also offers cross-registration with the Mid-Missouri Association of Colleges and Universities, many internships, a Washington semester, dual and student-designed majors, a 3-2 occupational therapy degree program with Washington University, accelerated degree programs in dance and theater arts, and pass/fail options for electives. There are 8 national honor societies and a freshman honors program. **Visiting:** There are regularly scheduled orientations for prospective students, consisting of attendance at classes, a campus tour, an appointment with instructors, and an interview. There are guides for informal visits, visitors may sit in on classes, and stay overnight. To schedule a visit, contact the Campus Visit Coordinator at apply@stephens.edu. **Campus Safety and Security:** Measures include 24-hour foot and vehicle patrol, emergency notification system, self-defense education, security escort services, emergency telephones, lighted pathways/sidewalks, and controlled access to dorms/residences.

REQUIREMENTS: The SAT or ACT is required. Applicants must be graduates of accredited secondary schools or have earned a GED. An essay is also required, and an interview is recommended. A GPA of 2.5 is required. AP and CLEP credits are accepted. Important factors in the admissions decision are advanced placement or honors courses, leadership record, and recommendations by school officials. All students must complete 6 hours of English and a distribution of 9 courses in lower-division work, including 6 hours of social sciences and 3 hours each of math, science, literary studies, history, cultural studies, and ethics. The bachelor's degree requires completion of at least 120 semester hours, including 30 to 72 in a major field, with a minimum GPA of 2.0. **Procedure:** Freshmen are admitted in the fall and spring. There are deferred admissions and rolling admissions plans. Applications should be filed by August 1 for fall entry, along with a $50 fee. Applications are accepted online. **Transfer Students:** 68 transfer students enrolled in 2015-2016. Applicants must submit official transcripts from all college work attempted or completed as well as a recommendation from an academic college instructor. Transfers must submit an official high school transcript. 36 of 120 credits required for the bachelor's degree must be completed at Stephens. **International Students:** There are 2 international students enrolled. The school actively recruits these students. They must take the TOEFL with a minimum score of 79 on the Internet-based version (iBT).

ADMISSIONS: 97% of the 2016-2017 applicants were accepted. The ACT scores were 29% below 12, % between 12 and 17, 14% between 18 and 23, 43% between 24 and 29, and 0% above 30. 27% of the current freshmen were in the top fifth of their class; 60% were in the top two fifths. **Admissions Contact:** Tiffany Goalder Email: *inquiry@stephens.edu* Web: *www.stephens.edu*

FINANCIAL AID: In 2016-2017, 99% of all full-time freshmen and 54% of continuing full-time students received some form of financial aid. 82% of all full-time freshmen and 49% of continuing full-time students received need-based aid. The average freshman award was $7,025. Need-based scholarships or need-based grants averaged $9,878; need-based self-help aid (loans and jobs) averaged $3,574; non-need-based athletic scholarships averaged $7,656; and other non-need-based awards and non-need-based scholarships averaged $15,398. 10% of undergraduate students work part-time. Average annual earnings from campus work are $1630. The average financial indebtedness of the 2016 graduate was $37,467. The FAFSA code is 002512. The priority date for freshman financial aid applications for fall entry is March 1.

TRUMAN STATE UNIVERSITY C-1
www.truman.edu

Kirksville, MO 63501 (660) 785-4114

Fax: (660) 785-7456	**Email:** admissions@truman.edu
Full-time: 2153 men, 3034 women	**Faculty:** 332; IIA, --$
Part-time: 325 men, 500 women	**Ph.D.s:** 84%
Graduate: 89 men, 251 women	**Student/Faculty:** 16 to 1
Year: semesters, summer session	**Tuition:** $7456 ($13,940)
Room & Board: $8558	**Freshman Class:** 5178 applied, 3505 accepted, 1263 enrolled
SAT CR/M: 600/590 **ACT:** 27	**CEEB CODE:** 6483
Application Deadline: March 1	**HIGHLY COMPETITIVE**

Truman State University, founded in 1867, is a highly selective public liberal arts and sciences institution offering 37 undergraduate areas of study and 7 graduate degrees within the liberal arts and sciences and select pre-professional programs. There are 5 undergraduate schools and 5 graduate schools. In addition to regional accreditation, Truman has baccalaureate program accreditation with AACSB, NASM, NCATE, ACS, CCNE, and CAATE ASHA. The 140-acre campus is in a small town in the northeast corner of Missouri. 170 miles from Kansas City, 200 miles from St. Louis, and 90 miles north of Columbia. Including any residence halls, there are 32 buildings.

STUDENT LIFE: 83% of undergraduates are from Missouri. Others are from 43 states, 50 foreign countries, and Canada. 83% are from public schools. 80% are White; 6% Foreign; 4% African American; 3% Hispanic; 3% two or more races; 2% Asian American; 2% race unknown. 41% claim no religious affiliation; 34% Protestant; 20% Catholic. **Female To Male Ratio:** 1.5:1. The average age of freshmen is 18; all undergraduates, 20. 13% do not continue beyond their first year; 72% remain to graduate. **Housing:** 2725 students can be accommodated in college housing, which includes single-sex and coed dorms, on-campus apartments, and married student housing. In addition, there are language houses and special-interest houses. On-campus housing is guaranteed for the freshman year only, is available on a first-come, first-served basis, and is available on a lottery system for upperclassmen. 54% of students commute. Alcohol is not permitted. All students may keep cars.

FACULTY/CLASSROOMS: 55% of faculty are male; 45% are female. All teach undergraduates. Graduate students teach 2% of introductory courses. The average class size in an introductory lecture is 25; in a laboratory is 20; and in a regular course is 21.

PROGRAMS OF STUDY: Truman confers B.A., B.S., B.F.A., B.M. and B.S.N. degrees. Master's degrees are also awarded. Bachelor's degrees are awarded in AGRICULTURE (agricultural business management, agriculture, agronomy, animal science, equine science, and horticulture), BIOLOGICAL SCIENCE (biology/biological science), BUSINESS (accounting, business administration and management, and international business management), COMMUNICATIONS AND THE ARTS (art, art history and appreciation, classics, communications, creative writing, dramatic arts, English, fine arts, French, German, journalism, linguistics, music, music performance, romance languages and literature, Russian, Spanish, studio art, and visual design), COMPUTER AND PHYSICAL SCIENCE (chemistry, computer science, mathematics, and physics), EDUCATION (athletic training and physical education), ENGINEERING AND ENVIRONMENTAL DESIGN (preengineering), HEALTH PROFESSIONS (clinical science, exercise science, health science, nursing, physical therapy, predentistry, premedicine, prepharmacy, preveterinary science, public health, and speech pathology/audiology), SOCIAL SCIENCE (anthropology, criminal justice, economics, history, interdisciplinary studies, philosophy, physical fitness/movement, political science/government, prelaw, psychology, religion, and sociology). Chemistry, biology, and accounting are the strongest academically. Business administration, biology, and English have the largest enrollments.

ACTIVITIES: 26% of men belong to 14 national fraternities; 25% of women belong to 7 national sororities. There are 250 groups on campus, including art, band, cheerleading, chess, choir, chorale, chorus, computers, dance, debate, drama, drill team, environmental, ethnic, film, forensics, honors, international, jazz band, LGBT, literary magazine, marching band, musical theater, newspaper, opera, orchestra, pep band, political, professional, radio and TV, religious, social, social service, student government, and symphony. Popular campus events include Final Blowout, Kohlenberg Lyceum Series, and the Big Event. **Sports:** There are 10 intercollegiate sports for men and 10 for women, and 33 intramural sports for men and 33 for women. Facilities include a football stadium, a soccer field, tennis courts, softball diamond, baseball diamond, arena with basketball courts, pool, weight training rooms, indoor and outdoor track facilities, and a 60,000-square-foot student recreation center. **Graduates:** From July 1, 2015 to June 30, 2016, 1140 bachelor's degrees were awarded. The most popular majors were business administration (10%), exercise science (10%), and biology (9%). 327 companies recruited on campus in 2015-2016. In an average class, 3% graduate in 3 years or less, 56% graduate in 4 years or less, 70% graduate in 5 years or less, and 72% graduate in 6 years or less. Of the 2015 graduating class, 40% were enrolled in graduate school within 6 months of graduation, and 56% were employed.

SERVICES: Counseling and information services are available, as is tutoring in most subjects, services for the hearing impaired, and a braille scanner and printer. There is a reader service for the blind. Disability services provides reasonable accommodations to qualified students which include, but are not limited to: classroom accommodations such as test or note taking services, housing including placement & bathroom configurations, assistance for hearing & visually impaired students. Client accommodations are based on individualized, qualified guidelines per ADA standards and are determined through a collaborative approach between the student and the Disability Services Coordinator. **Library/Resources:** The library contains 495,359 volumes, 1.5 million microform items, 44,441 audio/video tapes/CDs/DVDs, and subscribes to 3,912 periodicals including electronic. Computerized library services include interlibrary loans, database searching, Internet access, and Wi-Fi capability. Special learning facilities include an art gallery, planetarium, radio station, nursing simulation lab, an observatory, greenhouse chamber, speech and hearing clinic, a broadcasting studio, language learning center, farm, herpetology lab, writing center, convergent media center, midi music studio and various labs for science programs. **Physically Challenged Students:** 99% of the campus is accessible. Facilities include wheelchair ramps, elevators, special parking, specially equipped restrooms, special class scheduling, lowered drinking fountains, and special housing. The swimming pool is equipped with a lift to assist physically disabled swimmers. **Special:** Study abroad in over 50 countries is offered through Truman's own programs and those of the College Consortium for International Studies, the Council on International Educational Exchange, and the International Student Exchange Program. The university requires internships in education and health and exercise science. Voluntary legislative internships are offered to all students at the state capitol, and internships through the Washington Center. There is a dual-degree program with Physics and Engineering where Truman provides the Physics and the student then transfers to another institution for Engineering and upon completion of that work Truman will award a Physics degree along with earned Engineering degree from the other school. Work-study programs, B.A.-B.S. degrees, dual majors, student-designed interdisciplinary majors, credit for military experience, pass/fail options for internships, and non-degree study are available. There are 16 national honor societies, Phi Beta Kappa, a freshman honors program, and 19 departmental honors programs. **Visiting:** There are regularly scheduled orientations for prospective students, campus visits include a personalized meeting with an admission counselor, a student-led campus tour, and appointments with a faculty member in the student's major or in any areas of special interest upon request. There are guides for informal visits, visitors may sit in on classes, and stay overnight. To schedule a visit, contact Sophie Krautmann at (660) 785-4114. **Campus Safety and Security:** Measures include 24-hour foot and vehicle patrol, emergency notification system, self-defense education, security escort services, emergency telephones, lighted pathways/sidewalks, and controlled access to dorms/residences.

REQUIREMENTS: Truman must have a standardized test score on file for admission consideration, either the ACT or the SAT. Applicants should have completed 4 units of English, 3 each of science and social studies, 2 of foreign language, and 1 of art or music. 4 units of math are strongly recommended. An essay is required and list of activities is strongly recommended. AP and CLEP credits are accepted. Important factors in the admissions decision are advanced placement or honors courses, leadership record, and extracurricular activities record. All students must complete 63 hours of course work in the liberal arts, 16 of which must be in written and oral communication, math and statistics, computer literacy, and personal well-being, and 23 of which must be in history, science, social science, philosophy/religion, math, and aesthetics. Elementary proficiency in a foreign language is required of all majors. The B.A., B.F.A., and B.M. degree require intermediate proficiency in one foreign language, and the B.S. and B.S.N. require additional course work in science, math, statistics, computer science, social sciences, or logic. Skills such as writing, quantitative analysis, problem solving, and critical thinking are reinforced throughout the curriculum, and all seniors end their studies with a capstone, or culminating experience, in their majors. Students must also complete a nationally normed exam in their subject areas as part of Truman's assessment program. **Procedure:** Freshmen are in the admitted fall, spring, and summer. Entrance exams should be taken spring of junior year, summer, or fall of senior year. There are deferred admissions and rolling admissions plans. Applications should be filed by March 1 for fall entry; November 15 for spring entry; and March 1 for summer entry. Notification is sent on a rolling basis. Applications are accepted on-line. **Transfer Students:**

240 transfer students enrolled in 2015-2016. Transfer applicants are considered for admission through a competitive individualized review process that emphasizes preparedness for study based upon a variety of criteria. Cumulative grade point average in transferable college credit, strength of college curriculum, and the admission essay are considered for all transfer admission candidates. Cumulative high school record and ACT/SAT scores will also be reviewed for applicants who have completed fewer than 24 hours of transferable post high school college credit at the time of application. 45 of 120 credits required for the bachelor's degree must be completed at Truman. **International Students:** There are 440 international students enrolled. The school actively recruits these students. They must take the TOEFL with a minimum score of 550 on the paper-based TOEFL (PBT) or 79 on the Internet-based version (iBT) and the Comprehensive English Language Test. They must also take the SAT or ACT.

ADMISSIONS: 68% of the 2016-2017 applicants were accepted. The SAT scores for the 2016-2017 freshman class were: Critical Reading-- 10% below 500, 39% between 500 and 599, 33% between 600 and 699, and 18% between 700 and 800. Math-- 16% below 500, 35% between 500 and 599, 33% between 600 and 699, and 16% between 700 and 800. The ACT scores were 18% between 18 and 23, 54% between 24 and 29, and 28% above 30. 76% of the current freshmen were in the top fifth of their class; 95% were in the top two fifths. There were 7 National Merit finalists. 197 freshmen graduated first in their class. **Admissions Contact:** Melody Chambers, Director of Admission. Email: *admissions@truman.edu* Web: *www.truman.edu*

FINANCIAL AID: In 2016-2017, 99% of all full-time freshmen and 80% of continuing full-time students received some form of financial aid. 45% of all full-time freshmen and 37% of continuing full-time students received need-based aid. The average freshman award was $12,830. Need-based scholarships or need-based grants averaged $4,931 ($14,399 maximum); need-based self-help aid (loans and jobs) averaged $4,404 ($9,650 maximum); non-need-based athletic scholarships averaged $3,555 ($22,171 maximum); and other non-need-based awards and non-need-based scholarships averaged $9,300 ($27,856 maximum). 34% of undergraduate students work part-time. Average annual earnings from campus work are $1152. The average financial indebtedness of the 2016 graduate was $24,811. The FAFSA code is 002495. The priority date for freshman financial aid applications for fall entry is February 15. The filing deadline for fall entry is April 1.

UNIVERSITY OF CENTRAL MISSOURI — B-2

www.ucmo.edu

Warrensburg, MO 64093 — **(660) 543-4290**

Fax: (660) 543-8517	**Email:** admit@ucmo.edu
Full-time: 3764 men, 4428 women	**Faculty:** 452; IIA, --$
Part-time: 680 men, 867 women	**Ph.D.s:** 67%
Graduate: 810 men, 1399 women	**Student/Faculty:** 17 to 1
Year: semesters, summer session	**Tuition:** $8610 ($13,435)
Room & Board: $10,372	**Freshman Class:** n/av
ACT: required	**CEEB CODE:** 6090
Application Deadline: August 19	**COMPETITIVE**

University of Central Missouri, founded in 1871, is a public liberal arts institution offering a comprehensive range of degree programs. There are 4 undergraduate schools and 1 graduate school. In addition to regional accreditation, Central has baccalaureate program accreditation with AACSB, ABET, ACCE, ADA, ASLA, CSWE, NASAD, NASM, NCATE, NLN, ACS, ADDA, ASLHA, CAA, CADE, CCNE, NAIT, NASPE, and SOA. The 1561-acre campus is in a small town 50 miles southeast of Kansas City. Including any residence halls, there are 107 buildings.

STUDENT LIFE: 89% of undergraduates are from Missouri. Others are from 42 states, 59 foreign countries, and Canada. 92% are from public schools. 9% are African American; 85% White; 6% Foreign; 3% Hispanic; 1% Asian American. 54% are Protestant; 20% Catholic; 12% claim no religious affiliation. **Female To Male Ratio:** 1.3:1. The average age of freshmen is 19; all undergraduates, 22. 32% do not continue beyond their first year; 51% remain to graduate. **Housing:** 3540 students can be accommodated in college housing, which includes single-sex and coed dorms, on-campus apartments, off-campus apartments, married student housing, honors houses, special-interest houses, fraternity houses, sorority houses, and quiet dorms. On-campus housing is guaranteed for the freshman year only, is available on a first-come, and first-served basis. 72% of students commute. All students may keep cars.

FACULTY/CLASSROOMS: 54% of faculty are male; 46% are female. No introductory courses are taught by graduate students. The average class size in an introductory lecture is 30 and in a regular course is 23.

PROGRAMS OF STUDY: Central confers B.A., B.S., B.F.A., B.M., B.M.E., B.S.B.A., B.S.Ed. and B.S.W. degrees. Associate and master's degrees are also awarded. Bachelor's degrees are awarded in AGRICULTURE (agricultural business management and conservation and regulation), BIOLOGICAL SCIENCE (biology/biological science), BUSINESS (accounting, business administration and management, hotel/motel and restaurant management, human resources, management science, marketing/retailing/merchandising, organizational behavior, recreation and leisure services, and tourism), COMMUNICATIONS AND THE ARTS (broadcasting, communications, English, French, German, journalism, music, photography, public relations, Spanish, speech/debate/rhetoric, studio art, and theater design), COMPUTER AND PHYSICAL SCIENCE (actuarial science, chemistry, computer science, earth science, geology, information sciences and systems, mathematics, and physics), EDUCATION (agricultural education, art education, business education, early childhood education, elementary education, English education, foreign languages education, industrial arts education, mathematics education, middle school education, music education, physical education, science education, secondary education, social studies education, and special education), ENGINEERING AND ENVIRONMENTAL DESIGN (agricultural engineering technology, automotive technology, aviation computer technology, commercial art, construction management, drafting and design technology, electrical/electronics engineering, electrical/electronics engineering technology, engineering, engineering technology, graphic arts technology, industrial engineering technology, interior design, manufacturing technology, and occupational safety and health), HEALTH PROFESSIONS (medical laboratory technology, nursing, predentistry, premedicine, preveterinary science, and speech pathology/audiology), SOCIAL SCIENCE (criminal justice, dietetics, economics, geography, history, political science/government, prelaw, psychology, safety management, social work, sociology, and textiles and clothing). School of technology, elementary education and early childhood, criminal justice and nursing have the largest enrollments.

ACTIVITIES: 6% of men belong to 12 national fraternities; 6% of women belong to 11 national sororities. There are 250 groups on campus, including art, band, cheerleading, chess, choir, chorale, chorus, computers, dance, debate, drama, drill team, ethnic, film, forensics, honors, international, jazz band, LGBT, literary magazine, marching band, musical theater, newspaper, opera, orchestra, pep band, photography, political, professional, radio and TV, religious, social, social service, student government, and symphony. Popular campus events include Performing Arts Series, Technology Fair, and Repertory Theater. **Sports:** There are 7 intercollegiate sports for men and 7 for women, and 32 intramural sports for men and 32 for women. Facilities include a stadium with gyms, baseball, softball, women's soccer, and practice fields, a bowling alley, tennis courts, and a multipurpose building that contains a swimming pool, weight rooms, and courts for basketball, racquetball, and volleyball. A nearby outdoor recreation area has an 18-hole golf course and facilities for swimming and other activities. The Student Recreation and Wellness Center includes fitness rooms for aerobics, spinning, kickboxing, sport courts, a free weight room, additional fitness areas with fitness equipment, a passive recreation room, inside walking track, and climbing wall. **Graduates:** From July 1, 2015 to June 30, 2016, 1805 bachelor's degrees were awarded. The most popular majors were technology (8%), criminal justice (7%), and elementary education and early childhood (6%). 330 companies recruited on campus in 2015-2016. In an average class, 28% graduate in 4 years or less, 45% graduate in 5 years or less, and 49% graduate in 6 years or less. Of the 2015 graduating class, 18% were enrolled in graduate school within 6 months of graduation, and 91% were employed.

SERVICES: Counseling and information services are available, as is tutoring in some subjects, for a fee including math, chemistry, physics, biology, accounting, economics, and business. There is a reader service for the blind, and remedial math. Writing and learning labs are available for all students. Tutoring is available through TRIO Student Support

Services. **Library/Resources:** The library contains 2.2 million volumes, 815,787 microform items, 20,544 audio/video tapes/CDs/DVDs, and subscribes to 783 periodicals including electronic. Computerized library services include interlibrary loans, database searching, Internet access, and Wi-Fi capability. Special learning facilities include an art gallery, natural history museum, planetarium, radio station, TV station, an instructional airport, a 200-acre farm, a driving/safety range, a speech and hearing clinic, a child development lab, and an English Language Center. **Physically Challenged Students:** 95% of the campus is accessible. Facilities include wheelchair ramps, elevators, special parking, specially equipped restrooms, special class scheduling, lowered drinking fountains, lowered telephones, and special housing. **Special:** Central offers cross-registration with the Midwest Student Exchange program, credit and non-credit internships, study abroad in more than 15 countries, a B.A. - B.S. degree, dual and student-designed majors, credit for military service, pass/fail options, nondegree study, and a 3-2 engineering degree with the University of Missouri at Columbia and at Rolla and with the University of Indiana. There are 25 national honor societies, a freshman honors program, and 7 departmental honors programs. **Visiting:** There are regularly scheduled orientations for prospective students, including orientation sessions on housing, general education requirements, and enrollment for fall classes. There are guides for informal visits, visitors may sit in on classes, and stay overnight. To schedule a visit, contact the Office of Admissions. **Campus Safety and Security:** Measures include 24-hour foot and vehicle patrol, emergency notification system, self-defense education, security escort services, emergency telephones, lighted pathways/sidewalks, a bike patrol, and a canine patrol.

REQUIREMENTS: The ACT is required. Applicants must have completed 16 academic credits, including 4 credits in English with a writing emphasis, 3 credits each in math (algebra and beyond) and social science, 2 credits in natural sciences, and 1 credit in fine or performing arts, as well as 3 credits in academic electives. A foreign language is recommended. The GED is accepted. AP and CLEP credits are accepted. To graduate, students must complete a minimum of 120 hours, including 35 to 64 in the major, and have a minimum GPA of 2.0; several majors require a higher cumulative GPA. General education requirements include a total of 39 to 45 hours in humanities, social sciences, multicultural studies, technology, English and oral communications, math, science, and individual development. A comprehensive exam may be part of the exit assessment in selected majors. **Procedure:** Freshmen are admitted to all sessions. Entrance exams should be taken in the junior year of high school. There is a rolling admissions plan. Applications should be filed by August 19 for fall entry, along with a $30 fee. Notification is sent on a rolling basis. Applications are accepted online. **Transfer Students:** 1006 transfer students enrolled in 2015-2016. Applicants must have a minimum GPA of 2.0, as indicated by an official college transcript. 30 of 120 credits required for the bachelor's degree must be completed at Central. **International Students:** There are 540 international students enrolled. The school actively recruits these students. They must take the TOEFL with a minimum score of 500 on the paper-based TOEFL (PBT), and participate in institutional assessment. They must also take the ACT.

ADMISSIONS: 24% of the current freshmen were in the top fifth of their class; 55% were in the top two fifths. 20 freshmen graduated first in their class. **Admissions Contact:** Dr. Richard Sluder, Assistant Provost of Enrollment Management. Email: *admit@ucmo.edu* Web: *www.ucmo.edu*

FINANCIAL AID: In 2016-2017, 94% of all full-time freshmen and 71% of continuing full-time students received some form of financial aid. 66% of all full-time freshmen and 62% of continuing full-time students received need-based aid. The average freshman award was $9,825. 11% of undergraduate students work part-time. Average annual earnings from campus work are $3300. The average financial indebtedness of the 2016 graduate was $23,766. Central is a member of CSS. The FAFSA code is 002454. The priority date for freshman financial aid applications for fall entry is April 1.

UNIVERSITY OF MISSOURI/COLUMBIA C-2

www.missouri.edu

Columbia, MO 65211 (573) 882-7786

Fax: (573) 882-7887	**Email:** MU4U@missouri.edu
Full-time: 12,097 men, 13,081 women	**Faculty:** 1241; I, -$
Part-time: 924 men, 894 women	**Ph.D.s:** 93%
Graduate: 3290 men, 4462 women	**Student/Faculty:** 20 to 1
Year: semesters, summer session	**Tuition:** $9257 ($23,366)
Room & Board: $8944	**Freshman Class:** n/av
ACT: required	**CEEB CODE:** 6875
Application Deadline: May 1	**MOST COMPETITIVE**

University of Missouri/Columbia, established in 1839, offers a comprehensive array of undergraduate and graduate programs as well as professional training in law, medicine, and veterinary medicine. There are 16 undergraduate schools and 19 graduate schools. In addition to regional accreditation, Mizzou has baccalaureate program accreditation with AACSB, ABET, ACEJMC, ADA, APTA, CAHEA, CSWE, FIDER, NASM, NCATE, NRPA, SAF, ACOTE, CAAHEP, and CADE. The 1262-acre campus is in a suburban area 120 miles west of St. Louis and 120 miles east of Kansas City. Including any residence halls, there are 350 buildings.

STUDENT LIFE: 71% of undergraduates are from Missouri. Others are from 50 states, 115 foreign countries, and Canada. 81% are White; 8% African American; 3% Hispanic; 3% Foreign; 2% Asian American. **Female To Male Ratio:** 1.1:1. The average age of freshmen is 18; all undergraduates, 20. 16% do not continue beyond their first year; 71% remain to graduate. **Housing:** 7177 students can be accommodated in college housing, which includes single-sex and coed dorms, off-campus apartments, married student housing, honors houses, language houses, special-interest houses, fraternity houses, sorority houses, international houses, quiet houses, graduate/professional houses, and learning/living communities by major. 74% of students commute. All students may keep cars. Alcohol is not permitted.

FACULTY/CLASSROOMS: 63% of faculty are male; 37% are female. No introductory courses are taught by graduate students.

PROGRAMS OF STUDY: Mizzou confers B.A., B.S., B.E.S., B.F.A., B.G.S., B.H.S., B.J., B.M., B.S.Acc., B.S.B.A., B.S.B.E., B.S.ChE., B.S.CiE., B.O.S., B.S.E.E., B.S.Ed., B.S.F., B.S.F.W., B.S.H.E.S., B.S.I.E., B.S.M.E., B.S.N. and B.S.W. degrees. Master's and doctoral degrees are also awarded. Bachelor's degrees are awarded in AGRICULTURE (agricultural business management, agricultural economics, agriculture, animal science, fishing and fisheries, forestry and related sciences, plant science, and soil science), BIOLOGICAL SCIENCE (biochemistry, biology/biological science, microbiology, and nutrition), BUSINESS (accounting, banking and finance, business administration and management, business economics, hotel/motel and restaurant management, marketing/retailing/merchandising, real estate, and tourism), COMMUNICATIONS AND THE ARTS (advertising, art, art history and appreciation, broadcasting, classics, communications, creative writing, design, dramatic arts, English, English literature, French, German, journalism, linguistics, music, Russian, and Spanish), COMPUTER AND PHYSICAL SCIENCE (atmospheric sciences and meteorology, chemistry, computer science, geology, mathematics, physics, and statistics), EDUCATION (art education, early childhood education, education, education administration, elementary education, English education, mathematics education, middle school education, music education, science education, secondary education, and social studies education), ENGINEERING AND ENVIRONMENTAL DESIGN (biomedical engineering, chemical engineering, civil engineering, computer engineering, electrical/electronics engineering, engineering, industrial engineering, and mechanical engineering), HEALTH PROFESSIONS (nursing, occupational therapy, physical therapy, public health, radiological science, respiratory therapy, and veterinary science), SOCIAL SCIENCE (anthropology, archeology, child care/child and family studies, counseling/psychology, early childhood studies, economics, family/consumer resource management, food science, geography, history, human development, international studies, liberal arts/general studies, parks and recreation management, philosophy, political science/government, psychology, public administration, public affairs, religion, rural sociology, social science, social work, sociology, and textiles and clothing). Biological sciences, accounting, and journalism are the strongest academically. Business administration, journalism, and biological sciences have the largest enrollments.

ACTIVITIES: 22% of men belong to 32 national fraternities; 28% of women belong to 18 national sororities. There are 700 groups on campus, including art, band, cheerleading, chess, choir, chorale, chorus, computers, dance, debate, drama, drill team, drum and bugle corps, environmental, ethnic, film, honors, international, jazz band, LGBT, literary magazine, marching band, musical theater, newspaper, orchestra, pep band, photography, political, professional, radio and TV, religious, social, social service, student government, symphony, and yearbook. Popular campus events include Big Twelve athletics, Academic Weeks, and Meet Mizzou Day. **Sports:** There are 8 intercollegiate sports for men and 10 for women, and 35 intramural sports for men and 37 for women. Facilities include recreation complex with a 50-meter competition pool and diving well, a club pool, a high-tech fitness club, a heavy-lifting gym, a climbing and bouldering wall, multicourts, racquetball courts, and an indoor track. There is a 62,000-seat stadium, a 1,300-seat indoor gym, and an 18,000-seat auditorium. **Graduates:** From July 1, 2015 to June 30, 2016, 5528 bachelor's degrees were awarded. The most popular majors were business (17%), journalism (12%), and health professions and related sciences (10%). 1786 companies recruited on campus in 2015-2016. In an average class, 46% graduate in 4 years or less, 67% graduate in 5 years or less, and 71% graduate in 6 years or less.

SERVICES: Counseling and information services are available, as is tutoring in some subjects, and a reader service for the blind. **Library/Resources:** The 11 libraries contain 2.7 million volumes, 8.1 million microform items, and 35,711 audio/video tapes/CDs/DVDs. Computerized library services include interlibrary loans, database searching, Internet access, and Wi-Fi capability. Special learning facilities include an art gallery, natural history museum, radio station, TV station, astronomy observatory, freedom of information center, herbarium, State Historical Society of Missouri, Western Historical Manuscripts, and anthropology, fishery, wildlife collections, and the Life Sciences Center. **Physically Challenged Students:** All of the campus is accessible. Facilities include wheelchair ramps, elevators, special parking, specially equipped restrooms, special class scheduling, lowered drinking fountains, lowered telephones, and special housing. **Special:** Available academic programs include co-op programs and cross-registration with other schools, internships, study abroad, a Washington semester, and work-study programs. Special degrees or studies include an accelerated degree, dual majors, a general studies degree, and student-designed majors. For highly motivated students, there is an honors college and the possibility of early admission to the schools of law and medicine. There are 25 national honor societies, Phi Beta Kappa, a freshman honors program, and 34 departmental honors programs. **Visiting:** There are regularly scheduled orientations for prospective students, consisting of a campus tour, a visit with an admissions representative, and a visit with an academic representative on request. There are guides for informal visits and visitors may sit in on classes. To schedule a visit, contact the Admissions Office. **Campus Safety and Security:** Measures include 24-hour foot and vehicle patrol, emergency notification system, self-defense education, and security escort services. There are also shuttle buses, emergency telephones, lighted pathways/sidewalks, a 24-hour bicycle patrol.

REQUIREMENTS: The ACT is required. Students may gain probationary admission with sufficient GED scores. The usual requirements are completion of 17 Carnegie units, including 4 each in English and math, 3 each in social studies and science, 2 in a foreign language, and 1 in fine arts. Admission is determined by these units and a combination of class rank and ACT score. AP and CLEP credits are accepted. Important factors in the admissions decision are advanced placement or honors courses and evidence of special talent. To graduate, students must maintain a minimum 2.0 GPA and complete at least 120 credits, of which at least 30 must be in their major, although credit requirements can vary by degree program. All students must take English, plus 2 additional writing-intensive courses, demonstrate competency in college algebra, take 1 additional course in development math and reasoning skills, and complete a course in American history or government. Students must complete 9 hours in social and behavioral sciences, 9 in physical and biological sciences (including 1 lab course), and 9 in humanities and fine arts. A capstone experience is also required. **Procedure:** Freshmen are admitted to all sessions. Entrance exams should be taken late in the junior year or in the senior year. There are deferred admissions and rolling admissions plans. Applications should be filed by May 1 for fall entry, along with a $50 fee. Notification is sent on a rolling basis. Applications are accepted online. **Transfer Students:** 1407 transfer students enrolled in 2015-2016. Transfer students must present 24 hours of completed college-level course work with a minimum 2.5 GPA. Students must also complete college algebra or equivalent as well as freshman English or equivalent with a C- or better. 30 of 120 credits required for the bachelor's degree must be completed at Mizzou. **International Students:** There are 798 international students enrolled. The school actively recruits these students. They must take the TOEFL.

ADMISSIONS: The ACT scores were 6% below 12, 23% between 12 and 17, 31% between 18 and 23, 18% between 24 and 29, and 23% above 30. There were 29 National Merit finalists. 235 freshmen graduated first in their class. **Admissions Contact:** Barbara Rupp, Director of Undergraduate Admissions. Email: *MU4U@missouri.edu* Web: *www.missouri.edu*

FINANCIAL AID: In 2016-2017, 52% of all full-time freshmen and 48% of continuing full-time students received some form of financial aid. 46% of all full-time freshmen and 39% of continuing full-time students received need-based aid. The average financial indebtedness of the 2016 graduate was $23,588. The FAFSA code is 002516. The priority date for freshman financial aid applications for fall entry is March 1.

UNIVERSITY OF MISSOURI-KANSAS CITY A-2
www.umkc.edu

Kansas City, MO 64110	**(816) 235-1111** **(800) 775-8652**
Fax: (816) 235-5544	**Email: admit@umkc.edu**
Full-time: 2851 men, 3818 women	**Faculty:** 1, --$
Part-time: 2119 men, 2920 women	**Ph.D.s:** 68%
Graduate: 2496 men, 2740 women	**Student/Faculty:** 14 to 1
Year: semesters, summer session	**Tuition:** $9553 ($22,714)
Room & Board: $10,010	**Freshman Class:** 5138 applied, 3179 accepted, 1212 enrolled
SAT M/W: 609/578	**CEEB CODE:** 6872
Application Deadline: July 1	**VERY COMPETITIVE**

University of Missouri/Kansas City, which opened in 1933, is a public institution offering undergraduate and graduate programs in the arts and sciences, engineering, business, education, health fields, preprofessional, and professional studies. There are 10 undergraduate schools and 12 graduate schools. In addition to regional accreditation, UMKC has baccalaureate program accreditation with AACSB, ABET, ACPE, ADA, NASM, NCATE, NLN, NASM, NAST, and CCNE. The 149-acre campus is in an urban area in Kansas City. Including any residence halls, there are 68 buildings.

STUDENT LIFE: 81% of undergraduates are from Missouri. Others are from 51 states, 45 foreign countries, and Canada. 60% are White; 11% African American; 8% Foreign; 7% Hispanic; 6% Asian American; 4% race unknown; 3% two or more races; 1% American Indian/Alaska Native. **Female To Male Ratio:** 1.3:1. The average age of freshmen is 18; all undergraduates, 21. 25% do not continue beyond their first year; 75% remain to graduate. **Housing:** 1399 students can be accommodated in college housing, which includes coed dorms, on-campus apartments, married student housing, fraternity houses and sorority houses. On-campus housing is available on a first-come and first-served basis. 77% of students commute. Alcohol is not permitted. All students may keep cars.

FACULTY/CLASSROOMS: 53% of faculty are male; 47% are female. No introductory courses are taught by graduate students. The average class size in an introductory lecture is 30; in a laboratory is 16; and in a regular course is 24.

PROGRAMS OF STUDY: UMKC confers B.A., B.S., B.B.A., B.F.A., B.I.T., B.L.A., B.M., B.M.E., B.S.C.I.E., B.S.D.H., B.S.E.E., B.S.M.E., B.H.S. and B.S.N. degrees. Master's and doctoral degrees are also awarded. Bachelor's degrees are awarded in BIOLOGICAL SCIENCE (bioinformatics, biology/biological science, and biotechnology), BUSINESS (accounting and business administration and management), COMMUNICATIONS AND THE ARTS (art history and appreciation, communications, dance, dramatic arts, English, French, German, information technology, music, music performance, music theory and composition, performing arts, Spanish, and studio art), COMPUTER AND

PHYSICAL SCIENCE (chemistry, computer science, geology, mathematics, and physics), EDUCATION (early childhood education, elementary education, middle school education, music education, and secondary education), ENGINEERING AND ENVIRONMENTAL DESIGN (civil engineering, electrical/electronics engineering, environmental science, and mechanical engineering), HEALTH PROFESSIONS (dental hygiene, health, health science, music therapy, and nursing), SOCIAL SCIENCE (criminal justice, economics, geography, history, Judaic studies, liberal arts/general studies, philosophy, political science/government, psychology, sociology, and urban studies). Health sciences and performing arts is the strongest academically. Liberal arts, business, and computing/engineering have the largest enrollments.

ACTIVITIES: 4% of men belong to 6 national fraternities; 6% of women belong to 2 local and 7 national sororities. There are 255 groups on campus, including art, band, cheerleading, chess, choir, chorale, chorus, computers, dance, debate, drama, ethnic, honors, international, jazz band, LGBT, literary magazine, newspaper, opera, orchestra, photography, political, professional, radio and TV, religious, social, social service, student government, and yearbook. Popular campus events include International Food and Culture Night, Welcome Back Week, Spring Fling, Homecoming, and Court Warming. **Sports:** There are 6 intercollegiate sports for men and 8 for women, and 13 intramural sports for men and 13 for women. Facilities include a recreation center with gyms, indoor/outdoor pool, indoor and outdoor tracks, a fitness center, and handball, racquetball, and squash courts. There are also recreation facilities at the University Center. **Graduates:** From July 1, 2015 to June 30, 2016, 1812 bachelor's degrees were awarded. The most popular majors were liberal arts (14%), business administration (11%), and nursing (10%). In an average class, 2% graduate in 3 years or less, 23% graduate in 4 years or less, 40% graduate in 5 years or less, and 53% graduate in 6 years or less.

SERVICES: Counseling and information services are available, as is tutoring in some subjects, such as accounting, biology, chemistry, foreign languages, writing, and math and statistics. There is also a reader service for the blind. **Library/Resources:** The 4 libraries contain 1.1 million volumes, 1.2 million microform items, 353,243 audio/video tapes/CDs/DVDs, and subscribe to 7,222 periodicals including electronic. Computerized library services include interlibrary loans, database searching, and Internet access. Special learning facilities include a natural history museum, planetarium, and radio station. **Physically Challenged Students:** 95% of the campus is accessible. Facilities include wheelchair ramps, elevators, special parking, specially equipped restrooms, special class scheduling, lowered drinking fountains, lowered telephones, and special housing. **Special:** Special academic programs include co-op programs and internships in several majors, study abroad in 8 countries, an accelerated degree program, and dual majors. Special degrees include a B.A.-B.S. degree in the computer science program and a liberal arts degree offered by the adult program. The pass/fail option is available in some courses. Freshmen may enter 6-year medical and dental programs. There are 4 national honor societies, a freshman honors program, and 1 departmental honors program. **Visiting:** There are regularly scheduled orientations for prospective students, consisting of a 1-day program for new freshmen or a half-day optional program for transfer students. There are guides for informal visits. To schedule a visit, contact the Welcome Center at (816) 235-8652. **Campus Safety and Security:** Measures include 24-hour foot and vehicle patrol, emergency notification system, self-defense education, and security escort services. There are also shuttle buses, emergency telephones, lighted pathways/sidewalks, and controlled access to dorms/residences.

REQUIREMENTS: A combination of the student's test score and class rank determines admissibility; if the rank is 47 or below, the ACT score must be 23 or higher. Graduation from an accredited secondary school is a requirement for admission; the GED is also accepted. Required high school subjects include 4 units each of English and math, 3 each of social studies and science, 1 of arts, and 2 of a foreign language. A portfolio is required for art majors, an audition for music majors, and an interview for only those students applying for the pharmacy degree or the 6-year medical and dental programs. AP and CLEP credits are accepted. Most candidates for the B.A. and B.S. degrees must complete a core curriculum that consists of courses in English, a foreign language, math, philosophy, fine arts, history, literature, natural sciences, and social sciences. They must complete 120 credit hours, including 30 in their major, with a 2.0 GPA. **Procedure:** Freshmen are admitted to all sessions. Entrance exams should be taken by March of the senior year. There is a rolling admissions plan. Applications should be filed by July 1 for fall entry; November 1 for spring entry, along with a $45 fee. Applications are accepted online. **Transfer Students:** 1226 transfer students enrolled in 2015-2016. Transfer Students need to have an overall 2.0 GPA on a 4.0 scale in all coursework, which includes repeated coursework, attempted at previous institutions. Transfer students must send in all official college transcripts from all colleges and universities where coursework was attempted. Transfer students with fewer than 24 hours of transferable college credit must also send in official high school transcripts. Some academic units and departments have specific admission requirements in addition to general university requirements. 30 of 120 credits required for the bachelor's degree must be completed at UMKC. **International Students:** There are 447 international students enrolled. The school actively recruits these students. They must take the TOEFL with a minimum score of 550 on the paper-based TOEFL (PBT) or 80 on the Internet-based version (iBT).

ADMISSIONS: 62% of the 2016-2017 applicants were accepted. The SAT scores for the 2016-2017 freshman class were: Math-- 27% below 500, 37% between 500 and 599, 19% between 600 and 699, and 16% between 700 and 800. Writing-- 23% below 500, 33% between 500 and 599, 30% between 600 and 699, and 14% between 700 and 800. The ACT scores were 5% between 12 and 17, 39% between 18 and 23, 40% between 24 and 29, and 16% above 30. 56% of the current freshmen were in the top fifth of their class; 84% were in the top two fifths. 30 freshmen graduated first in their class. **Admissions Contact:** Tamara Byland, Director of Admissions. Email: *admit@umkc.edu* Web: *www.umkc.edu*

FINANCIAL AID: In 2016-2017, 69% of all full-time freshmen received some form of financial aid. 66% of all full-time freshmen received need-based aid. The average freshman award was $10,463. Need-based scholarships or need-based grants averaged $7,401; and need-based self-help aid (loans and jobs) averaged $6,935. The FAFSA code is 002518. The priority date for freshman financial aid applications for fall entry is March 1.

UNIVERSITY OF MISSOURI-ST. LOUIS D-2

www.umsl.edu

St. Louis, MO 63121	(314) 516-5451
Fax: (314) 516-5310	**Email:** admissions@umsl.edu
Full-time: 2366 men, 3068 women	**Faculty:** 686; I, --$
Part-time: 3563 men, 4926 women	**Ph.D.s:** 75%
Graduate: 1042 men, 2049 women	**Student/Faculty:** 15 to 1
Year: semesters, summer session	**Tuition:** n/av
Room & Board: n/app	**Freshman Class:** 1949 applied, 1377 accepted, 441 enrolled
SAT CR/M/W: 520/560/560 **ACT:** 24	**CEEB CODE:** 6889
Application Deadline: August 25	**COMPETITIVE**

University of Missouri/St. Louis, founded in 1963, is a public institution offering undergraduate and graduate programs and conferring degrees in arts and sciences, business, nursing, education, engineering, and optometry. UMSL is recognized for its contributions to the social and economic advancement of the St. Louis region. Nationally recognized programs include criminology and criminal justice, biology and the Harris World Ecology Center, business, and counseling. UMSL students consistently score high on licensing exams in nursing, optometry, clinical psychology, and education. There are 7 undergraduate schools and 5 graduate schools. In addition to regional accreditation, UMSL has baccalaureate program accreditation with AACSB, ABET, CSWE, NASM, NCATE, and CCNE. The 350-acre campus is in an urban area 10 miles north of downtown St. Louis. Including any residence halls, there are 47 buildings.

STUDENT LIFE: 94% of undergraduates are from Missouri. Others are from 42 states, 44 foreign countries, and Canada. 81% are from public schools. 69% are White; 5% Asian American; 4% race unknown; 3% Hispanic; 2% Foreign; 2% two or more races; 15% African American. **Female To Male Ratio:** 1.4:1. The average age of freshmen is 18; all undergraduates, 26. 22% do not continue beyond their first year; 53% remain to graduate. **Housing:** 1202 students can be accommodated in college housing, which includes coed dorms, on-campus apartments, married student housing, honors houses, language houses, special-interest houses, fraternity houses, sorority houses, theme house, wellness house, students over 21 apartments, and graduate/professional school housing. On-campus housing is available on a first-come and first-served basis. 91% of students commute. All students may keep cars.

FACULTY/CLASSROOMS: 43% of faculty are male; 57% are female. 44% teach undergraduates, 11% do research, and 22% do both. Graduate students teach 18% of introductory courses. The average class size in an introductory lecture is 25; in a laboratory is 16; and in a regular course is 17.

PROGRAMS OF STUDY: UMSL confers B.A., B.S., B.F.A., B.L.S., B.M., B.M.E., B.M, B.S.Acc., B.S.B.A., B.S.C.I.E., B.S.Ed., B.S.E.E., B.S.M.E., B.E.S., B.S.N., B.S.P.P.A., B.S.W., B.I.S., and B.S.I.S. degrees. Master's and doctoral degrees are also awarded. Bachelor's degrees are awarded in BIOLOGICAL SCIENCE (biochemistry, biology/biological science, and biotechnology), BUSINESS (accounting, business administration and management, finance, international business management, logistics, management information systems, marketing management, and operations management), COMMUNICATIONS AND THE ARTS (art history and appreciation, communications, dance, dramatic arts, English, French, German, Germanic languages and literature, Japanese, media arts, music, Spanish, and studio art), COMPUTER AND PHYSICAL SCIENCE (chemistry, computer science, information sciences and systems, mathematics, and physics), EDUCATION (early childhood education, education, elementary education, music education, physical education, secondary education, and special education), ENGINEERING AND ENVIRONMENTAL DESIGN (civil engineering, electrical/electronics engineering, and mechanical engineering), HEALTH PROFESSIONS (nursing), SOCIAL SCIENCE (anthropology, criminal justice, economics, history, interdisciplinary studies, liberal arts/general studies, philosophy, political science/government, psychology, public administration, social work, and sociology). Biology, chemistry, and biochem/biotech are the strongest academically. Business, education, and nursing have the largest enrollments.

ACTIVITIES: 3% of men belong to 3 national fraternities; 2% of women belong to 3 national sororities. There are 110 groups on campus, including art, band, cheerleading, choir, chorale, chorus, computers, dance, debate, drama, environmental, ethnic, forensics, honors, international, jazz band, LGBT, literary magazine, newspaper, opera, pep band, photography, political, professional, radio and TV, religious, social, social service, and student government. Popular campus events include Expo, Weeks of Welcome, Family Weekend, MLK Day of Service, and Mirthday Week. **Sports:** There are 6 intercollegiate sports for men and 7 for women, and 16 intramural sports for men and 16 for women. Facilities include open fitness space, treadmills, ellipticals, strength & functional training equipment, gym courts for basketball, volleyball, badminton and open recreation, multi-activity court with dasher board system for indoor soccer and floor hockey, indoor track, climbing walls, aquatic facility for classes and therapy, and rooms for fitness classes. **Graduates:** From July 1, 2015 to June 30, 2016, 2246 bachelor's degrees were awarded. The most popular majors were business administration (25%), health professions (12%), and education (11%). 325 companies recruited on campus in 2015-2016. In an average class, 22% graduate in 3 years or less, 14% graduate in 4 years or less, 5% graduate in 5 years or less, and 41% graduate in 6 years or less. Of the 2015 graduating class, 9% were enrolled in graduate school within 6 months of graduation, and 78% were employed.

SERVICES: Counseling and information services are available, as is tutoring in most subjects, such as math and writing labs, and remedial math. **Library/Resources:** The 2 libraries contain 1.3 million volumes, 1.3 million microform items, 4,083 audio/video tapes/CDs/DVDs, and subscribe to 2,539 periodicals including electronic. Computerized library services include interlibrary loans, database searching, Internet access, and Wi-Fi capability. Special learning facilities include an art gallery, planetarium, radio station, TV station. Libraries include the Thomas Jefferson library, and the St. Louis Mercantile library that host a collection of American Art. There are also art galleries, observatory, on-campus pre-school, honors college, nonprofit management/leadership program, women in public life institute, centers for nanoscience, neurodynamics, emerging technologies, entrepreneurship and economic education, international studies, transportation studies, gerontology, teaching and learning, performing arts, world ecology, technology and learning, math, science education, eye care, ELS language, trauma recovery, student success, and French, German, and Greek cultural centers. **Physically Challenged Students:** All of the campus is accessible. Facilities include wheelchair ramps, elevators, special parking, specially equipped restrooms, special class scheduling, lowered drinking fountains, lowered telephones, and special housing. **Special:** Cross-registration with Washington University, St. Louis University, and St. Louis Community College and cooperative programs in all majors are offered. Study abroad in 32 countries, including England, France, and Germany is available. Most degree programs are available through the Evening Courses. Some work-study is available. There is an accelerated nursing degree program and student-designed majors for the B.L.S. There are 24 national honor societies and a freshman honors program. **Visiting:** There are regularly scheduled orientations for prospective students, 20-minute info session, special appointments if needed and a campus walking tour. There are guides for informal visits, visitors may sit in on classes, and stay overnight. To schedule a visit, contact Yolanda Weathersby at (314) 516-6877. **Campus Safety and Security:** Measures include 24-hour foot and vehicle patrol, emergency notification system, self-defense education, and security escort services. There are shuttle buses, emergency telephones, lighted pathways/sidewalks, controlled access to dorms/residences, and criminal investigations.

REQUIREMENTS: The SAT or ACT is required. Applicants are required to have a total of 17 units, such as 4 each in English and math, 3 each in social studies and science, 2 in the same foreign language, and 1 in fine arts. Class rank and test scores are used to determine eligibility for admission. A GPA of 2.3 is graduation. The number of hours required for the major varies. **Procedure:** Freshmen are admitted in the fall, spring, and summer. Entrance exams should be taken Late in the junior year or early in the senior year. There is a rolling admissions plan. Applications should be filed by August 25 for fall entry; January 3 for winter entry; January 21 for spring entry; and May 1 for summer entry, along with a $35 fee. Notification is sent on a rolling basis. Applications are accepted online. AP and CLEP credits are accepted. To graduate, students must complete a minimum 120 credit hours, 42 of which must be in the area of general education. They must maintain a 2.3 GPA. **Transfer Students:** 1435 transfer students enrolled in 2015-2016. Transfer students must have earned a minimum of 24 credit hours and maintained a minimum 2.3 GPA. 30 of 120 credits required for the bachelor's degree must be completed at UMSL. **International Students:** There are 299 international students enrolled. The school actively recruits these students. They must take the TOEFL with a minimum score of 500 on the paper-based TOEFL (PBT) or 61 on the Internet-based version (iBT) and the college's own test.

ADMISSIONS: 71% of the 2016-2017 applicants were accepted. The SAT scores for the 2016-2017 freshman class were: Critical Reading-- 67% below 500 and 33% between 500 and 599. Math-- 36% below 500, 45% between 500 and 599, and 18% between 600 and 699. Writing-- 38% below 500, 38% between 500 and 599, 15% between 600 and 699, and 38% between 700 and 800. 42% of the current freshmen were in the top fifth of their class; 75% were in the top two fifths. 14 freshmen graduated first in their class. **Admissions Contact:** Drew Griffin, Director of Admissions. Email: *admissions@umsl.edu* Web: *www.umsl.edu*

FINANCIAL AID: The average freshman award was $17,075. Need-based scholarships or need-based grants averaged $7,541 ($20,967 maximum); need-based self-help aid (loans and jobs) averaged $3,332 ($7,820 maximum); non-need-based athletic scholarships averaged $12,024 ($26,132 maximum); and other non-need-based awards and non-need-based scholarships averaged $10,888 ($34,173 maximum). Average annual earnings from campus work are $2923. The average financial indebtedness of the 2016 graduate was $24,266. The FAFSA code is 002519. The priority date for freshman financial aid applications for fall entry is January 1.

WASHINGTON UNIVERSITY IN ST. LOUIS D-3

www.wustl.edu

St. Louis, MO 63130	**(314) 935-6000** **(800) 638-0700**
Fax: (314) 935-4290	**Email: admissions@wustl.edu**
Full-time: 3298 men, 3617 women	**Faculty:** I, ++$
Part-time: 220 men, 405 women	**Ph.D.s:** 94%
Graduate: 3775 men, 3717 women	**Student/Faculty:** 8 to 1
Year: semesters, summer session	**Tuition:** $49,770
Room & Board: $15,596	**Freshman Class:** 29197 applied, 4827 accepted, 1776 enrolled
SAT or ACT: required	**CEEB CODE:** 6929
Application Deadline: January 15	**VERY COMPETITIVE**

Washington University in St. Louis, founded in 1853, is a private institution offering undergraduate and graduate programs in arts and sciences, business, architecture, engineering, art, and professional programs in law, medicine (including physical therapy and occupational therapy), and social work. There are 5 undergraduate schools and 8 graduate schools. In addition to regional accreditation, Washington U. has baccalaureate program accreditation with AACSB, ABET, and NASAD. The 169-acre campus is in a suburban area 7 miles west of St. Louis. Including any residence halls, there are 116 buildings.

STUDENT LIFE: 92% of undergraduates are from out of state, mostly the Midwest. Students are from 50 states, 48 foreign countries, and Canada. 57% are from public schools. 8% are African American; 8% Foreign; 7% Hispanic; 53% White; 4% two or more races; 2% race unknown; 18% Asian American. **Female To Male Ratio:** 1.1:1. The average age of freshmen is 18; all undergraduates, 20. 4% do not continue beyond their first year; 94% remain to graduate. **Housing:** 5378 students can be accommodated in college housing, which includes single-sex and coed dorms, on-campus apartments, off-campus apartments, married student housing, special-interest houses, fraternity houses, special-interest suites, and upper-class housing. There is also small group housing for students who share common interests and goals. On-campus housing is guaranteed for the freshman year only and is available on a lottery system for upperclassmen. 62% of students live on campus; of those, 97% remain on campus on weekends. Upperclassmen may keep cars.

FACULTY/CLASSROOMS: 61% of faculty are male; 39% are female. No introductory courses are taught by graduate students. The average class size in an introductory lecture is 30.

PROGRAMS OF STUDY: Washington U. confers B.A., B.S., B.F.A., B.M., B.S.B.A., B.S.B.M.E., B.S.C.E., B.S.Ch.E., B.S.C.S., B.S.Co.E., B.S.E.E., B.S.I.M., B.S.M.E. and B.S.S.S.E. degrees. Associate, master's, and doctoral degrees are also awarded. Bachelor's degrees are awarded in AGRICULTURE (environmental studies, natural resource management, and plant science), BIOLOGICAL SCIENCE (biochemistry, bioinformatics, biology/biological science, biomathematics, biophysics, ecology, environmental biology, and neurosciences), BUSINESS (accounting, banking and finance, business administration and management, business economics, entrepreneurial studies, finance, human resources, international business management, international economics, marketing management, marketing/retailing/merchandising, and trade and industrial supervision and management), COMMUNICATIONS AND THE ARTS (advertising, American literature, Arabic, art history and appreciation, ceramic art and design, Chinese, classical languages, classics, communications, comparative literature, creative writing, dance, design, dramatic arts, drawing, East Asian languages and literature, English, English literature, film arts, fine arts, French, German, Germanic languages and literature, graphic design, Greek (classical), Hebrew, illustration, Italian, Japanese, journalism, languages, Latin, linguistics, literature, music, music theory and composition, painting, performing arts, photography, printmaking, romance languages and literature, sculpture, Spanish, studio art, and visual and performing arts), COMPUTER AND PHYSICAL SCIENCE (applied mathematics, chemistry, computer programming, computer science, earth science, geochemistry, geology, geophysics and seismology, information sciences and systems, mathematics, physical sciences, physics, and statistics), EDUCATION (art education, education, elementary education, foreign languages education, mathematics education, middle school education, science education, secondary education, social science education, and social studies education), ENGINEERING AND ENVIRONMENTAL DESIGN (architectural technology, architecture, bioengineering, biomedical engineering, chemical engineering, civil engineering, commercial art, computer engineering, electrical/electronics engineering, engineering, engineering mechanics, environmental science, mechanical engineering, systems engineering, and technology and public affairs), HEALTH PROFESSIONS (allied health, health care administration, health science, pharmacy, predentistry, premedicine, prepharmacy, and preveterinary science), SOCIAL SCIENCE (African studies, African American studies, American studies, anthropology, archeology, area studies, Asian/Oriental studies, biopsychology, East Asian studies, Eastern European studies, economics, ethnic studies, European studies, fashion design and technology, history, humanities, industrial and organizational psychology, interdisciplinary studies, international relations, international studies, Islamic studies, Judaic studies, Latin American studies, Middle Eastern studies, Near Eastern studies, philosophy, political science/government, psychology, religion, social science, South Asian studies, systems science, urban studies, Western European studies, and women's studies). Social sciences, engineering, and business are the strongest academically and have the largest enrollments.

ACTIVITIES: 33% of men belong to 10 national fraternities; 33% of women belong to 8 national sororities. There are 350 groups on campus, including art, band, cheerleading, chess, choir, chorale, chorus, computers, dance, debate, drama, environmental, ethnic, film, forensics, honors, international, jazz band, LGBT, literary magazine, musical theater, newspaper, opera, orchestra, pep band, photography, political, professional, radio and TV, religious, social, social service, student government, symphony, and yearbook. Popular campus events include Multicultural Celebrations, W.I.L.D. (concert festival), and student-run carnival. **Sports:** There are 9 intercollegiate sports for men and 10 for women, and 33 intramural sports for men and 33 for women. Facilities include cardio and strength training equipment, cycling studio, group exercise studios, indoor running track, gymnasium, athletics complex, varsity basketball and volleyball courts, pool and diving well, racquetball and squash courts, and weight room and practice gym, football field, and outdoor track. **Graduates:** From July 1, 2015 to June 30, 2016, 1762 bachelor's degrees were awarded. The most popular majors were biology and psychology (20%), engineering (19%), and business (12%). 442 companies recruited on campus in 2015-2016. In an average class, 88% graduate in 4 years or less, 93% graduate in 5 years or less, and 94% graduate in 6 years or less. Of the 2015 graduating class, 23% were enrolled in graduate school within 6 months of graduation, and 68% were employed.

SERVICES: Counseling and information services are available, as is tutoring in every subject, and a reader service for the blind. **Library/Resources:** The 12 libraries contain 5.4 million volumes, 3.4 million microform items, and 102,156 audio/video tapes/CDs/DVDs, and subscribe to 140,541 periodicals including electronic. Computerized library services include interlibrary loans, database searching, Internet access, and Wi-Fi capability. Special learning facilities include an art gallery, planetarium, radio station, TV station, a dance studio, a professional theater, observatory, and studio theater. **Physically Challenged Students:** 95% of the campus is accessible. Facilities include wheelchair ramps, elevators, special parking, specially equipped restrooms, special class scheduling, lowered drinking fountains, and lowered telephones. **Special:** Opportunities are provided for cooperative programs with other schools, internships, work-study programs, study abroad, a Washington (D.C.) semester, accelerated degree programs, a B.A.-B.S. engineering degree, credit by examination, nondegree study, pass/fail options, and dual and student-designed majors. There are 19 national honor societies and a chapter of Phi Beta Kappa. **Visiting:** There are regularly scheduled orientations for prospective students, student visits consist of group presentations followed by a campus tour, as well as class visits and meetings with current students and faculty. There are guides for informal visits, visitors may sit in on classes, and stay overnight. To schedule a visit, contact the Office of Undergraduate Admissions. **Campus Safety and Security:** Measures include 24-hour foot and vehicle patrol, emergency notification system, self-defense education, and security escort services. There are also shuttle buses, emergency telephones, lighted pathways/sidewalks, and controlled access to dorms/residences.

REQUIREMENTS: The SAT or ACT is required. An essay is required from all applicants. Portfolios are required for students applying to the College of Art. Portfolios are encouraged for students applying to the College of Architecture. 4 years of english, math, science, and social studies are recommended. Up to 4 years of a foreign language and history are recommended. Also required are recommendations from a teacher and a counselor. AP credits are accepted. Academic requirements for graduation are set by the undergraduate divisions and vary by major. There are no requirements that every student in every degree program must satisfy. **Procedure:** Freshmen are admitted in the fall. Entrance exams should be taken By December of the senior year. There are early decision and deferred admissions plans. Early decision applications should be filed by November 15; regular applications, by January 15 for fall entry, along with a $75 fee. Notification of early decision is sent December 15; regular decision, April 1. 624 early decision candidates were accepted for the 2016-2017 class. Applications are accepted on-line. Application fees are waived if application is completed on-line. **Transfer Students:** 73 transfer students enrolled in 2015-2016. Academic requirements for graduation are set by the undergraduate divisions and vary by major. There are no requirements that every student in every degree program must satisfy. **International Students:** There are 584 international students enrolled. The school actively recruits these students. They must take the TOEFL with a minimum score of 550 on the paper-based TOEFL (PBT) or 100 on the Internet-based version (iBT). They must also take the SAT or ACT.

ADMISSIONS: 17% of the 2016-2017 applicants were accepted. The SAT scores for the 2016-2017 freshman class were: Critical Reading-- 1% between 500 and 599, 27% between 600 and 699, and 72% between 700 and 800. Math-- 2% between 500 and 599, 18% between 600 and 699, and 80% between 700 and 800. Writing-- 2% between 500 and 599, 26% between 600 and 699, and 72% between 700 and 800. The ACT scores were 7% between 24 and 29, and 93% above 30. 96% of the current freshmen were in the top fifth of their class; 100% were in the top two fifths. **Admissions Contact:** Office of Undergraduate Admissions Email: *admissions@wustl.edu* Web: *www.wustl.edu*

FINANCIAL AID: In 2016-2017, 50% of all full-time freshmen and 54% of continuing full-time students received some form of financial aid. 38% of all full-time freshmen and 43% of continuing full-time students received need-based aid. The average freshman award was $42,389. Average annual earnings from campus work are $2257. The average financial indebtedness of the 2016 graduate was $23,577. Washington U. is a member of CSS. The CSS/Profile, and Finalized FAFSA using IRS Data Retrieval Tool is required. The FAFSA code is 002519. The deadline for filing freshman financial aid applications for fall entry is February 1.

WEBSTER UNIVERSITY — D-2

www.webster.edu

St. Louis, MO 63119	**(314) 246-7080** **(800) 753-6765**
Fax: (314) 246-7116	**Email: admissions@webster.edu**
Full-time: 987 men, 1244 women	**Faculty:** 199
Part-time: 210 men, 181 women	**Ph.D.s:** 87%
Graduate: 536 men, 1065 women	**Student/Faculty:** 11 to 1
Year: semesters, summer session	**Tuition:** $26,300
Room & Board: $11,190	**Freshman Class:** 2630 applied, 1235 accepted, 433 enrolled
ACT: 24	**CEEB CODE:** 6933
Application Deadline: August 1	**COMPETITIVE**

Webster University is committed to delivering high-quality learning experiences that transform students for global citizenship and individual excellence. With its home campus in St. Louis, Webster University is the only Tier 1, private, non-profit U.S.-based university providing a network of international residential campuses. Founded in 1915, Webster University's campus network includes traditional, metropolitan, military and corporate locations around the world. Webster University is an independent institution with programs in fine and performing arts, liberal arts and sciences, media communications, education, nursing, and business. There are 5 undergraduate schools and 5 graduate schools. In addition to regional accreditation, Webster has baccalaureate program accreditation with ACBSP, NASM, NCATE, NLN, ABA, and COA. The 47-acre campus is in a suburban area 6 miles southwest of St. Louis. Including any residence halls, there are 41 buildings.

STUDENT LIFE: 71% of undergraduates are from Missouri. Others are from 44 states, 80 foreign countries, and Canada. 9% are race unknown; 62% White; 5% Hispanic; 4% Asian American; 3% two or more races; 17% African American. **Female To Male Ratio:** 1.4:1. The average age of freshmen is 18; all undergraduates, 23. 25% do not continue beyond their first year; 59% remain to graduate. **Housing:** 855 students can be accommodated in college housing, which includes single-sex and coed dorms, on-campus apartments, and special-interest houses. On-campus housing is available on a first-come, first-served basis, and on a lottery system for upperclassmen. Priority is given to out-of-town students. 67% of students commute. All students may keep cars.

FACULTY/CLASSROOMS: 54% of faculty are male; 46% are female. All teach undergraduates. No introductory courses are taught by graduate students. The average class size in an introductory lecture is 13; in a laboratory is 10; and in a regular course is 12.

PROGRAMS OF STUDY: Webster confers B.A., B.S., B.F.A., B.M., B.M.Ed. and B.S.N. degrees. Master's and doctoral degrees are also awarded. Bachelor's degrees are awarded in AGRICULTURE (environmental studies), BIOLOGICAL SCIENCE (biology/biological science), BUSINESS (accounting, business administration and management, finance, management science, and marketing management), COMMUNICATIONS AND THE ARTS (acting, advertising, animation, art history, art, art history and appreciation, audio technology, ballet, ceramic art and design, choral music, communications, costume design, creative writing, dance, digital communications, dramatic arts, English, film arts, French, German, graphic design, information technology, instrumental performance, instrumental music education, jazz, journalism, media arts, music, music performance, music theory and composition, musical theater, painting, photography, piano performance, playwriting/screenwriting, printmaking, public relations, scenic and lighting design, sculpture, Spanish, studio art, theater design, video, vocal performance, voice, and vocal music education), COMPUTER AND PHYSICAL SCIENCE (computer management, computer science, information sciences and systems, and mathematics), EDUCATION (art education, early childhood education, education, elementary education, foreign languages education, journalism education, mathematics education, middle school education, music education, secondary education, social studies education, social studies secondary school education, and special education), HEALTH PROFESSIONS (exercise science and nursing), SOCIAL SCIENCE (American studies, area studies, criminology, cultural anthropology, economics, European studies, history, interdisciplinary studies, international relations, legal studies, philosophy, political science/government, psychology, religion, religious studies, sociology, and women's studies). Fine arts, and communications are the strongest academically. Business, computer science, and education have the largest enrollments.

ACTIVITIES: There are no fraternities; 3% of women belong to 1 local sorority. There are 68 groups on campus, including art, band, cheerleading, chess, choir, chorale, chorus, communications, computers, dance, debate, departmental clubs, drama, environmental, ethnic, film, forensics, international, jazz band, LGBT, literary magazine, musical theater, newspaper, opera, orchestra, photography, political, professional, radio and TV, religious, social, social service, student government, and symphony. Popular campus events include Homecoming, Webster Works Worldwide and Spring Fest. **Sports:** There are 8 intercollegiate sports for men and 8 for women, and 4 intramural sports for men and 4 for women. Facilities include a gym, an athletic training center, a fitness center, and indoor swimming pool. **Graduates:** From July 1, 2015 to June 30, 2016, 739 bachelor's degrees were awarded. The most popular majors were management (13%), psychology (5%), and computer science (5%). 120 companies recruited on campus in 2015-2016. In an average class, 1% graduate in 3 years or less, 43% graduate in 4 years or less, 56% graduate in 5 years or less, and 59% graduate in 6 years or less.

SERVICES: Counseling and information services are available, as is tutoring in most subjects. There is also a reader service for the blind, and peer tutoring and study skills training. **Library/Resources:** The library contains 281,548 volumes, 138,000 microform items, and 30,909 audio/video tapes/CDs/DVDs, and subscribes to 1,175 periodicals including electronic. Computerized library services include interlibrary loans, database searching, Internet access, and Wi-Fi capability. Special learning facilities include an art gallery, radio station, TV station, a media center, a theater, and a community music school. **Physically Challenged Students:** 75% of the campus is accessible. Facilities include wheelchair ramps, elevators, special parking, specially equipped restrooms, special class scheduling, lowered drinking fountains, lowered telephones, special housing. Telephones for the hearing impaired, automatic door openers, a reading machine, computer for paraplegic students, reading and writing software, deaf interpreters, note takers, and alternate format textbooks. All TV monitors in classrooms have closed caption capabilities. **Special:** Webster University offers co-op programs, work-study programs, internships, dual majors, student-designed majors, and a 3-2 engineering degree with the University of Missouri/Columbia and Washington University. Study abroad in over 14 countries is available. **Visiting:** There are regularly scheduled orientations for prospective students, Students visiting campus may participate in a personal tour, meeting with an admissions representative and faculty member, sit in on a class, and attend a campus activity. There are guides for informal visits, visitors may sit in on classes, and stay overnight. To schedule a visit, contact The Office of Admission. **Campus Safety and Security:** Measures include 24-hour foot and vehicle patrol, emergency notification system, self-defense education, and security escort services. There are emergency telephones, lighted pathways/sidewalks, and controlled access to dorms/residences.

REQUIREMENTS: The ACT is required. Applicants must be graduates of an accredited secondary school. The GED is accepted. Webster recommends that students complete 19 high school academic units, including 4 units of English, 3 each of social studies/history, science, math, and electives, 2 units of foreign language, and 1 unit of visual/performing arts. An essay is required of all students, and a portfolio or audition is required for art, dance, music, musical theater, and film. Webster requires applicants to be in the upper 50% of their class. AP and CLEP credits are accepted. To graduate, students must complete at least 128 semester hours, with a minimum GPA of 2.0. They must successfully complete an approved major, which may or may not require more than 128 credit hours, and successfully complete the global citizenship program or general education program requirements. All new degree-seeking freshmen with fewer than 16 college credit hours are required to take a freshman seminar. At least 30 semester credits of a student's final 36 credits must be earned at Webster. **Procedure:** Freshmen are admitted fall, spring, and summer. Entrance exams should be taken in the spring of the junior year. There are deferred admissions and rolling admissions plans. Applications should be filed by August 1 for fall entry; December 1 for spring entry, along with a $35 fee. Notification is sent on a rolling basis. Applications are accepted on-line. **Transfer Students:** 441 transfer students enrolled in 2015-2016. Applicants for transfer must have a minimum GPA of 2.0 for college credit completed. If they have fewer than 30 transferable hours, they must submit high school transcripts. 30 of 128 credits required for the bachelor's degree must be completed at Webster. **International Students:** There are 100 international students enrolled. The school actively recruits these students. They must take the TOEFL with a minimum score of 80 on the Internet-based version (iBT) and the Comprehensive English Language Test, Equivalent current Cambridge, Oxford, NAEB, TEEP, Academic IELTS, London Certificate, and Pearson tests in lieu of TOEFL. SAT or ACT if they are graduates of U.S. high schools or international secondary schools that use English as the language of instruction.

ADMISSIONS: 47% of the 2016-2017 applicants were accepted. The ACT scores were 7% between 12 and 17, 39% between 18 and 23, 44% between 24 and 29, and 10% above 30. 30% of the current freshmen were in the top fifth of their class; 64% were in the top two fifths. 3 freshmen graduated first in their class. **Admissions Contact:** James Myers, Associate VP Undergraduate Admissions. Email: *admissions@webster.edu* Web: *www.webster.edu*

FINANCIAL AID: In 2016-2017, 97% of all full-time freshmen and 91% of continuing full-time students received some form of financial aid. 76% of all full-time freshmen and 69% of continuing full-time students received need-based aid. The average freshman award was $28,334. Need-based scholarships or need-based grants averaged $10,695; need-based self-help aid (loans and jobs) averaged $5,900; other non-need-based awards and non-need-based scholarships averaged $13,461; and $3,738 from other forms of aid. 26% of undergraduate students work part-time. Average annual earnings from campus work are $3000. The average financial indebtedness of the 2016 graduate was $26,792. The college's own financial statement is required. The FAFSA code is 002521. The priority date for freshman financial aid applications for fall entry is March 1. The filing deadline for fall entry is August 1.

WESTMINSTER COLLEGE C-2

www.westminister-mo.edu

Fulton, MO 65251 (573) 592-5251 (800) 475-3361

Fax: (573) 592-5255 Email: admissions@westminstercollege.edu

Full-time: 520 men, 397 women	**Faculty:** 61; IIB, --$
Part-time: 13 men, 3 women	**Ph.D.s:** 89%
Graduate: n/av	**Student/Faculty:** 14 to 1
Year: semesters, summer session	**Tuition:** $23,480
Room & Board: $9340	**Freshman Class:** 1356 applied, 910 accepted, 219 enrolled
SAT: recommended **ACT:** 24	**CEEB CODE:** 6937
Application Deadline: open	**COMPETITIVE**

Westminster College, founded in 1851, is a private liberal arts and sciences college affiliated with the Presbyterian Church. There is 1 undergraduate school. In addition to regional accreditation, Westminster has baccalaureate program accreditation with ACBSP. The 87-acre campus is in a small town 20 miles east of Columbia and 25 miles north of Jefferson City. Including any residence halls, there are 26 buildings.

STUDENT LIFE: 65% of undergraduates are from Missouri. Others are from 28 states, and 70 foreign countries. 75% are from public schools. 65% are White; 16% Foreign; 9% African American; 3% Hispanic; 2% American Indian/Alaska Native; 2% race unknown; 1% Asian American; 1% two or more races. 56% are Protestant; 20% Catholic; 15% claim no religious affiliation. **Male To Female Ratio:** 1.3:1. The average age of freshmen is 18; all undergraduates, 20. 17% do not continue beyond their first year; 70% remain to graduate. **Housing:** 900 students can be accommodated in college housing, which includes single-sex and coed dorms, off-campus apartments, special-interest houses and fraternity houses. On-campus housing is guaranteed for all 4 years. 84% of students live on campus; of those, 90% remain on campus on weekends. All students may keep cars.

FACULTY/CLASSROOMS: 59% of faculty are male; 41% are female. All teach undergraduates, 75% do research, and 75% do both. No introductory courses are taught by graduate students. The average class size in an introductory lecture is 19; in a laboratory is 20; and in a regular course is 14.

PROGRAMS OF STUDY: Westminster confers B.A. degrees. Bachelor's degrees are awarded in BIOLOGICAL SCIENCE (biochemistry and biology/biological science), BUSINESS (accounting, business administration and management, business communications, international business management, management information systems, and sports management), COMMUNICATIONS AND THE ARTS (English, French, and Spanish), COMPUTER AND PHYSICAL SCIENCE (chemistry, computer science, mathematics, and physics), EDUCATION (elementary education, middle school education, physical education, secondary education, and sports and wellness studies), ENGINEERING AND ENVIRONMENTAL DESIGN (environmental science), HEALTH PROFESSIONS (nursing), SOCIAL SCIENCE (anthropology, economics, history, international studies, philosophy, political science/government, psychology, religion, and sociology). English, biology, and psychology are the strongest academically. Business administration, biology, and psychology have the largest enrollments.

ACTIVITIES: 45% of men belong to 5 national fraternities; 34% of women belong to 3 national sororities. There are 65 groups on campus, including and Multicultural Club, International Club, art, Blue Blazers investment club, cheerleading, choir, chorale, chorus, computers, dance, drama, environmental, ethnic, honors, international, jazz band, LGBT, literary magazine, musical theater, newspaper, pep band, photography, political, professional, religious, social, social service, and student government. Popular campus events include Alumni Weekend, Westminster Symposium, Undergraduate Scholars Forum, What if..? Conference and International Week. **Sports:** There are 8 intercollegiate sports for men and 8 for women, and 16 intramural sports for men and 10 for women. Facilities include a gym, aerobic training center, weight room, training room, football, baseball, softball, soccer fields, field sports area, tennis, racquetball, sand volleyball courts, a swimming pool, indoor rifle range, and a auditorium/arena. **Graduates:** From July 1, 2015 to June 30, 2016, 205 bachelor's degrees were awarded. The most popular majors were business administration/management (29%), biology and psychology (19%), and education (10%). 71 companies recruited on campus in 2015-2016. In an average class, 53% graduate in 4 years or less, 62% graduate in 5 years or less, and 68% graduate in 6 years or less. Of the 2015 graduating class, 24% were enrolled in graduate school within 6 months of graduation, and 90% were employed.

SERVICES: Counseling and information services are available, as is tutoring in most subjects, and remedial math, reading, and writing. **Library/Resources:** The 2 libraries contain 100,265 volumes, 6,912 microform items, 9,691 audio/video tapes/CDs/DVDs, and subscribe to 30,201 periodicals including electronic. Computerized library services include interlibrary loans, database searching, Internet access, and Wi-Fi capability. **Physically Challenged Students:** 80% of the campus is accessible. Facilities include wheelchair ramps, elevators, special parking, specially equipped restrooms, special class scheduling, lowered drinking fountains, and lowered telephones. **Special:** Westminster offers co-op programs with colleges of the Mid-Missouri Associated Colleges and Universities, cross-registration with William Woods University, internships in all areas, study abroad in 15 countries, a Washington semester, a United Nations semester, and an urban studies program in Chicago. Student-designed majors are available as well as a dual degree nursing program with Golfarb School of Nursing at Barnes-Jewish College, dual degree program with Logan University of Chiropractic, and a 3-2 engineering degree with Washington University in St. Louis. The pass/fail option and dual majors are available. There are 16 national honor societies, a freshman honors program, and 8 departmental honors programs. **Visiting:** There are regularly scheduled orientations for prospective students, including 1-day summer programs with a general orientation and class registration. There are guides for informal visits, visitors may sit in on classes, and stay overnight. To schedule a visit, contact Robert Andrews, VP & Dean Enrollment Services. **Campus Safety and Security:** Measures include 24-hour foot and vehicle patrol, emergency notification system, self-defense education, security escort services, emergency telephones and lighted pathways/sidewalks.

REQUIREMENTS: The ACT is required.The SAT is recommended. Applicants must be graduates of an accredited secondary school. The GED is also accepted. Students must have completed 4 years each of social studies and English, 3 years each of math and science, and 2 years each of a foreign language and history. An essay is required and an interview is recommended. Westminster requires applicants to be in the upper 50% of their class. AP and CLEP credits are accepted. Important factors in the admissions decision are advanced placement or honors courses, leadership record, and extracurricular activities record. To graduate, students must complete 122 credit hours, including a maximum of 40 hours in their major, with a minimum GPA of 2.0. All students are required to take Westminster seminar, academic writing, statistics or calculus, 4 hours of foreign language, and 1 hour of phys ed. Students must also take 6 to 10 hours (37 to 42 total) in scientific inquiry, historical awareness, fundamental questions, artistic expression, human behaviors and institutions, cultural diversity, and global interdependence. In addition, an integrative upper-level course, 2 writing intensive courses, and an upper-level course from a non-major academic division are required. **Procedure:** Freshmen are admitted to all sessions. Entrance exams should be taken in the junior year of high school. There are early decision, deferred admissions, and rolling admissions plans. Application deadlines are open. Applications are accepted on-line. **Transfer Students:** 49 transfer students enrolled in 2015-2016. Applicants must have taken either the ACT or the SAT and must complete at least 4 semesters at Westminster as full-time students. 60 of 122 credits required for the bachelor's degree must be completed at Westminster. **International Students:** There are 159 international students enrolled. The school actively recruits these students. They must take the TOEFL.

ADMISSIONS: 67% of the 2016-2017 applicants were accepted. The ACT scores were 17% below 12, 28% between 12 and 17, 22% between 18 and 23, 17% between 24 and 29, and 18% above 30. 44% of the current freshmen were in the top fifth of their class; 69% were in the top two fifths. 5 freshmen graduated first in their class. **Admissions Contact:** Robert Andrews, VP & Dean of Enrollment Services. Email: *admissions@westminstercollege.edu* Web: *www.westminister-mo.edu*

FINANCIAL AID: In 2016-2017, 99% of all full-time freshmen and continuing full-time students received some form of financial aid. 53% of all full-time freshmen and 57% of continuing full-time students received need-based aid. The average freshman award was $20,155. Need-based scholarships or need-based grants averaged $15,940; and need-based self-help aid (loans and jobs) averaged $4,660. 66% of undergraduate students work part-time. Average annual earnings from campus work are $2000. The average financial indebtedness of the 2016 graduate was $26,723. The FAFSA code is 002523. The priority date for freshman financial aid applications for fall entry is February 15.

WILLIAM JEWELL COLLEGE — B-2

www.jewell.edu

Liberty, MO 64068	**(816) 781-7700, ext. 5137** **(800) 753-7009**
Fax: (816) 415-5027	**Email: admission@william.jewell.edu**
Full-time: 414 men, 616 women	**Faculty:** 70
Part-time: n/av	**Ph.D.s:** 86%
Graduate: n/av	**Student/Faculty:** 15 to 1
Year: semesters, summer session	**Tuition:** $32,330
Room & Board: $8880	**Freshman Class:** 2497 applied, 1374 accepted, 282 enrolled
SAT: required **ACT:** 26	**CEEB CODE:** 6941
Application Deadline: August 15	**COMPETITIVE+**

William Jewell College, founded in 1849, is an academically selective liberal arts college and offers undergraduate programs in the arts and sciences, business, education, and nursing fields. The figures in the above capsule and in this profile are approximate. There are 4 undergraduate schools. In addition to regional accreditation, Jewell has baccalaureate program accreditation with NASM and CCNE. The 200-acre campus is in a suburban area 15 miles northeast of Kansas City. Including any residence halls, there are 28 buildings.

STUDENT LIFE: 69% of undergraduates are from Missouri. Others are from 30 states, and 11 foreign countries. 91% are from public schools. 82% are White; 4% African American; 3% Hispanic; 2% Asian American; 2% Foreign; 1% American Indian/Alaska Native. 51% are Protestant; 35% claim no religious affiliation; 11% Catholic. **Female To Male Ratio:** 1.5:1. The average age of freshmen is 19; all undergraduates, 20. 22% do not continue beyond their first year; 63% remain to graduate. **Housing:** 1013 students can be accommodated in college housing, which includes single-sex and coed dorms, honors houses, language houses, fraternity houses, and sorority houses. On-campus housing is guaranteed for all 4 years. 75% of students live on campus; of those, 60% remain on campus on weekends. All students may keep cars. Alcohol is not permitted.

FACULTY/CLASSROOMS: 51% of faculty are male; 49% are female. 80% teach undergraduates, 20% do research, and 20% do both. No introductory courses are taught by graduate students. The average class size in an introductory lecture is 20; in a laboratory is 18; and in a regular course is 15.

PROGRAMS OF STUDY: Jewell confers B.A. and B.S. degrees. Bachelor's degrees are awarded in BIOLOGICAL SCIENCE (biochemistry and biology/biological science), BUSINESS (accounting, business administration and management, business economics, and international business management), COMMUNICATIONS AND THE ARTS (art, communications, dramatic arts, English, French, music, and Spanish), COMPUTER AND PHYSICAL SCIENCE (chemistry, mathematics, and physics), EDUCATION (elementary education, music education, and secondary education), HEALTH PROFESSIONS (medical laboratory technology and nursing), SOCIAL SCIENCE (history, international relations, Japanese studies, philosophy, political science/government, psychology, and religion). Business has the largest enrollment.

ACTIVITIES: 31% of men belong to 3 national fraternities; 34% of women belong to 4 national sororities. There are 60 groups on campus, including cheerleading, choir, chorale, chorus, computers, dance, debate, drama, drill team, ethnic, honors, international, jazz band, LGBT, musical theater, newspaper, orchestra, pep band, photography, political, professional, radio and TV, religious, social, social service, student government, and symphony. Popular campus events include Hanging of the Green/Lighting of the Quad and Family Weekend. **Sports:** There are 9 intercollegiate sports for men and 9 for women, and 12 intramural sports for men and 12 for women. Facilities include a football and soccer stadium, a complex for baseball and softball, and a phys ed center with an indoor track, a dance room, and facilities for basketball, racquetball, swimming, indoor tennis, volleyball, and weight lifting, and gym. **Graduates:** From July 1, 2015 to June 30, 2016, 267 bachelor's degrees were awarded. The most popular majors were business/marketing (22%), health professions and related sciences (17%), and psychology (11%). 36 companies recruited on campus in 2015-2016. In an average class, 54% graduate in 4 years or less, 62% graduate in 5 years or less, and 63% graduate in 6 years or less. Of the 2015 graduating class, 25% were enrolled in graduate school within 6 months of graduation, and 75% were employed.

SERVICES: Counseling and information services are available, as is tutoring in most subjects. **Library/Resources:** The library contains 231,031 volumes, 1,050 microform items, 11,232 audio/video tapes/CDs/DVDs, and subscribes to 500 periodicals including electronic. Computerized library services include interlibrary loans, database searching, and Internet access. Special learning facilities include an art gallery, planetarium, and a radio station. **Physically Challenged Students:** 85% of the campus is accessible. Facilities include wheelchair ramps, elevators, special parking, specially equipped restrooms, special class scheduling, lowered drinking fountains, lowered telephones, and special housing. **Special:** Internships for juniors or seniors, study abroad in Europe, Japan, Mexico, Australia, and Hong Kong, and a Washington semester are offered. B.A.-B.S. degrees, dual majors of any combination, internships, an accelerated degree in nursing, student-designed majors, and 3-2 engineering degrees with Washington University and the Universities of Missouri and Kansas are available. The Oxbridge Honors Program for major study is patterned after the teaching methods of Oxford and Cambridge and includes a year at either Oxford or Cambridge. Leadership and service learning programs are offered. There are 13 national honor societies, a freshman honors program, and 13 departmental honors programs. **Visiting:** There are regularly scheduled orientations for prospective students, and personalized visits can be arranged upon request. There are guides for informal visits and visitors may sit in on classes. To schedule a visit, contact the Admission Office. **Campus Safety and Security:** Measures include 24-hour foot and vehicle patrol, emergency notification system, self-defense education, emergency telephones, lighted pathways/sidewalks, and controlled access to dorms/residences.

REQUIREMENTS: The SAT or ACT is required. Students must be graduates of an accredited secondary school; the GED is also accepted. The college requires that applicants have taken 4 English courses and 4 academic electives, 3 courses each in math, social studies, and science; of these, 1 must be a lab, 2 in foreign language. An interview is recommended. An audition is advised for music applicants. AP and CLEP credits are accepted. Important factors in the admissions decision are advanced placement or honors courses, extracurricular activities record, and leadership record. To graduate, students must complete a minimum of 124 credits with a minimum 2.0 GPA, fulfilling the proper core requirements for their major and degree. All students must take the Responsible Self in their first year, and must also take courses in oral and written communication, phys ed, math, and foreign language, interdisciplinary courses in 4 categories, and a core curriculum capstone course. Comprehensive exams in most majors are required. **Procedure:** Freshmen are admitted in the fall, spring, and summer. Entrance exams should be taken in the junior year. There are deferred admissions and rolling admissions plans. Applications should be filed by August 15 for fall entry, along with a $25 fee. Notification is sent on a rolling basis. Applications are accepted online. **Transfer Students:** 44 transfer students enrolled in 2015-2016. Transfer students must have maintained a 2.5 GPA and be in good academic standing with their former schools and submit all college transcripts. Education majors must take the ACT, achieving a minimum score of 20. An interview is recommended for all students. 30 of 124 credits required for the bachelor's degree must be completed at Jewell. **International Students:** There are 22 international students enrolled. The school actively recruits these students. They must take the TOEFL with a minimum score of 550 on the paper-based TOEFL (PBT) or 80 on the Internet-based version (iBT) or take the MELAB.

ADMISSIONS: 55% of the 2016-2017 applicants were accepted. The SAT scores for the 2016-2017 freshman class were: Critical Reading-- 24% below 500, 30% between 500 and 599, 39% between 600 and 699, and 7% between 700 and 800. Math-- 21% below 500, 34% between 500 and 599, 39% between 600 and 699, and 11% between 700 and 800. The ACT scores were 9% below 12, 22% between 12 and 17, 25% between 18 and 23, 18% between 24 and 29, and 26% above 30. 68% of the current freshmen were in the top fifth of their class; 92% were in the top two fifths. 28 freshmen graduated first in their class. **Admissions Contact:** Bridget Gramling, Dean of Admissions. Email: *admission@william.jewell.edu* Web: *www.jewell.edu*

FINANCIAL AID: In 2016-2017, 99% of all full-time freshmen and 96% of continuing full-time students received some form of financial aid. 72% of all full-time freshmen and 69% of continuing full-time students received need-based aid. The average freshman award was $25,316.. The average financial indebtedness of the 2016 graduate was $24,102. Jewell is a member of CSS. The FAFSA code is 002524. The priority date for freshman financial aid applications for fall entry is March 1.

WILLIAM WOODS UNIVERSITY C-2

www.williamwoods.edu

Fulton, MO 65251	(573) 592-1106 (800) 995-3159
Fax: (573) 592-1180	**Email:** admissions@williamwoods.edu
Full-time: 220 men, 616 women	**Faculty:** 56; IIB
Part-time: 39 men, 98 women	**Ph.D.s:** 60%
Graduate: 420 men, 683 women	**Student/Faculty:** 11 to 1
Year: semesters, summer session	**Tuition:** $22,740
Room & Board: $9300	**Freshman Class:** 863 applied, 631 accepted, 184 enrolled
SAT CR/M: 490/500 **ACT:** 22	**CEEB CODE:** 6944
Application Deadline: August 15	**COMPETITIVE**

William Woods University, founded in 1870, is an independent professions-oriented, liberal arts institution affiliated with the Christian Church (Disciples of Christ). Unique programs of study include an equestrian studies program and a four-year American Sign Language Interpreting program. There is 1 undergraduate school and 1 graduate school. In addition to regional accreditation, William Woods has baccalaureate program accreditation with CSWE, CAATE, and CAAHEP. The 170-acre campus is in a small town 100 miles west of St. Louis. Including any residence halls, there are 35 buildings.

STUDENT LIFE: 60% of undergraduates are from Missouri. Others are from 42 states, 19 foreign countries, and Canada. 80% are White; 5% Hispanic; 4% African American; 4% Foreign; 3% race unknown; 2% two or more races; 1% Asian American; 1% American Indian/Alaska Native. 42% are Baptist, Christian, Methodist, Lutheran, Presbyterian, and Pentecost; 30% claim no religious affiliation; 21% Catholic. **Female To Male Ratio:** 2.1:1. The average age of freshmen is 19; all undergraduates, 21. 26% do not continue beyond their first year; 52% remain to graduate. **Housing:** 760 students can be accommodated in college housing, which includes single-sex, and coed dorms, on-campus apartments, special-interest houses, fraternity houses, sorority houses, nonsmoking, and independent housing. On-campus housing is guaranteed for all 4 years. 76% of students live on campus; of those, 70% remain on campus on weekends. All students may keep cars.

FACULTY/CLASSROOMS: 46% of faculty are male; 54% are female. All teach undergraduates. No introductory courses are taught by graduate students. The average class size in an introductory lecture is 20; in a laboratory is 15; and in a regular course is 15.

PROGRAMS OF STUDY: William Woods confers B.A., B.S., B.F.A. and B.S.W. degrees. Associate, master's, and doctoral degrees are also awarded. Bachelor's degrees are awarded in AGRICULTURE (equine science), BIOLOGICAL SCIENCE (biology/biological science), BUSINESS (accounting, accounting (finance), and business administration and management), COMMUNICATIONS AND THE ARTS (American Sign Language, art, communications, dramatic arts, English, graphic design, journalism, and studio art), COMPUTER AND PHYSICAL SCIENCE (computer science, information sciences and systems, mathematics, and science), EDUCATION (athletic training, early childhood education, elementary education, middle school education, physical education, physical ed teacher education, and special education), SOCIAL SCIENCE (family/juvenile justice, history, interdisciplinary studies, international studies, interpreter for the deaf, paralegal studies, political science/government, psychology, and social work). Business and equestrian studies are the largest enrollments.

ACTIVITIES: 43% of men belong to 2 national fraternities; 45% of women belong to 4 national sororities. There are 40 groups on campus, including art, cheerleading, choir, drama, honors, international, musical theater, newspaper, professional, radio and TV, religious, social, social service, and student government. Popular campus events include Salute to the Arts, Campus Involvement and Activities Fair, and Autumn at the Woods. **Sports:** There are 5 intercollegiate sports for men and 6 for women, and 7 intramural sports for men and 7 for women. Facilities include a gym, a fitness center, sand volleyball court, tennis courts, soccer, baseball, and softball fields, a weight room, a lake with a sand beach, table tennis and pool tables, and a cross-country trail equipped with FitTrail stations. **Graduates:** From July 1, 2015 to June 30, 2016, 212 bachelor's degrees were awarded. The most popular majors were business (19%), equestrian studies/equestrian (16%), and education (12%). 50 companies recruited on campus in 2015-2016. In an average class, 49% graduate in 4 years or less, 52% graduate in 5 years or less, and 52% graduate in 6 years or less.

SERVICES: Counseling and information services are available, as is tutoring in most subjects, and a reader service for the blind, and remedial math and writing. Interpreting is provided for the deaf upon request and receipt of supporting documentation. **Library/Resources:** The library contains 134,338 volumes, 11,072 microform items, 28,711 audio/video tapes/CDs/DVDs, and subscribes to 15,796 periodicals including electronic. Computerized library services include interlibrary loans, database searching, Internet access, and Wi-Fi capability. Special learning facilities include an art gallery, radio station, 12 "smart classrooms" equipped with smartboards and networked computers, labs for photography, foreign languages, art, and American Sign Language interpreting, equestrian studies stables, a model courtroom, and an observatory. **Physically Challenged Students:** 85% of the campus is accessible. Facilities include wheelchair ramps, elevators, special parking, specially equipped restrooms, special class scheduling, and lowered telephones. Campus access to TTY phones. **Special:** William Woods University offers cross-registration with schools in the Mid-Missouri Association of Colleges and Universities, internships in various fields, including equestrian studies and computer information systems, study abroad, and work-study. We also offer an accelerated degree program in several majors, and student-designed and dual majors are also possible. Credit for life, and credit for military experience, are available. The LEAD (Leading, Educating, Achieving, and Developing) program provides awards ($5000 to residential students) to any incoming student who makes a commitment to attend a minimum number of campus activities and participate within the surrounding community. There are 12 national honor societies and a freshman honors program. **Visiting:** There are regularly scheduled orientations for prospective students, including the opportunity to talk with an academic adviser, and an extensive student development-directed orientation to campus life. There are guides for informal visits, visitors may sit in on classes, and stay overnight. To schedule a visit, contact Ashley Sundin. **Campus Safety and Security:** Measures include 24-hour foot and vehicle patrol, self-defense education, security escort services, emergency telephones, lighted pathways/sidewalks, and controlled access to dorms/residences.

REQUIREMENTS: A high-school GPA of 2.5 on a 4.0 scale, and a score of 19 on the ACT or 900 on the SAT is generally required for admission. AP and CLEP credits are accepted. Students must complete a minimum of 120 credits to graduate, including at least 30 in the major and 43 in Common Studies. They must have maintained a minimum GPA of 2.0. An internship or other culminating project is required for many majors. **Procedure:** Freshmen are admitted to all sessions. Entrance exams should be taken in the spring of the junior year or the fall of the senior year. There are deferred admissions and rolling admissions plans. Applications should be filed by August 15 for fall entry. Application fees are waived if application is completed online. **Transfer Students:** 79 transfer students enrolled in 2015-2016. Transfer students are required to have at least 12 college credit hours from an accredited college or university and have at least a 2.0 GPA. 30 of 120 credits required for the bachelor's degree must be completed at William Woods. **International Students:** There are 46 international students enrolled. The school actively recruits these students. They must take the TOEFL with a minimum score of 500 on the paper-based TOEFL (PBT) or 61 on the Internet-based version (iBT). They must also take the SAT or ACT, scoring 19.

ADMISSIONS: 73% of the 2016-2017 applicants were accepted. The SAT scores for the 2016-2017 freshman class were: Critical Reading-- 53% below 500, 31% between 500 and 599, and 16% between 600 and 699. Math-- 47% below 500, 27% between 500 and 599, and 16% between 600 and 699. The ACT scores were 14% between 12 and 17, 49% between 18 and 23, 28% between 24 and 29, and 9% above 30. 45% of the current freshmen were in the top fifth of their class; 65% were in the top two fifths. **Admissions Contact:** Kathy Groves, Vice President. Email: *admissions@williamwoods.edu* Web: *www.williamwoods.edu*

FINANCIAL AID: In 2016-2017, 100% of all full-time freshmen and 95% of continuing full-time students received some form of financial aid. 70% of all full-time freshmen and continuing full-time students received need-based aid. The average freshman award was $12,633. The college's own financial statement is required. The FAFSA code is 002525. The deadline for filing freshman financial aid applications for fall entry is March 1.

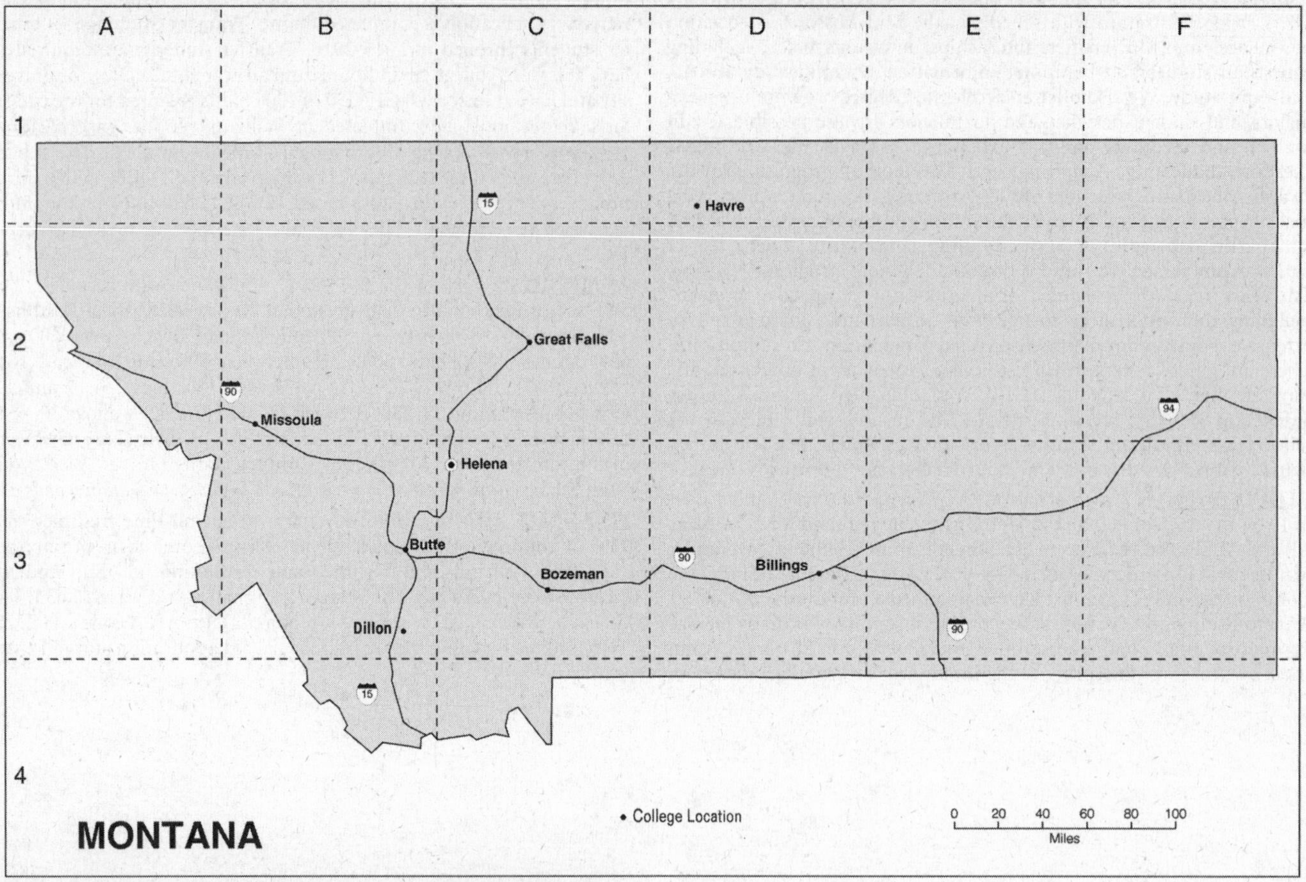

A B C D E F

1 2 3 4

Havre
Great Falls
Missoula
Helena
Butte
Bozeman
Billings
Dillon
15 90 94

MONTANA

• College Location

0 20 40 60 80 100
Miles

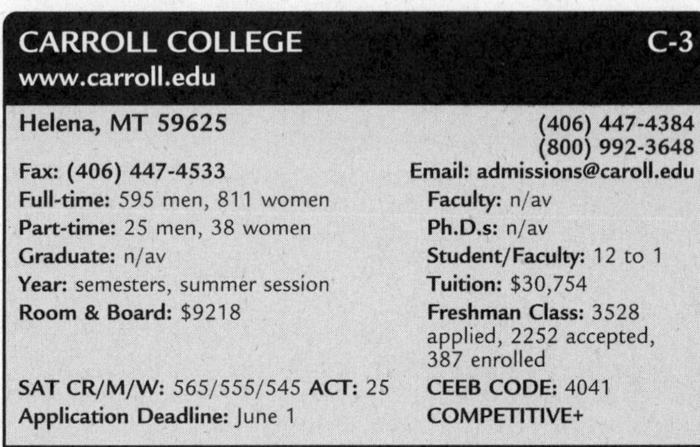

CARROLL COLLEGE C-3

www.carroll.edu

Helena, MT 59625 (406) 447-4384
(800) 992-3648

Fax: (406) 447-4533 **Email: admissions@caroll.edu**

Full-time: 595 men, 811 women	**Faculty:** n/av
Part-time: 25 men, 38 women	**Ph.D.s:** n/av
Graduate: n/av	**Student/Faculty:** 12 to 1
Year: semesters, summer session	**Tuition:** $30,754
Room & Board: $9218	**Freshman Class:** 3528 applied, 2252 accepted, 387 enrolled
SAT CR/M/W: 565/555/545 **ACT:** 25	**CEEB CODE:** 4041
Application Deadline: June 1	**COMPETITIVE+**

Carroll College, founded in 1909, is a small liberal arts college affiliated with the Roman Catholic Church. It offers undergraduate programs in arts and sciences, business, engineering, nursing, education, religion, and selected preprofessional training. There are 2 undergraduate schools. In addition to regional accreditation, Carroll has baccalaureate program accreditation with ABET, CAHEA, CSWE, NASDTEC, NLN, and NRPA. The 64-acre campus is in a small town 110 miles east of Missoula and 100 miles west of Bozeman. Including any residence halls, there are 20 buildings.

STUDENT LIFE: 51% of undergraduates are from out of state, mostly the Northwest. Students are from 35 states, 13 foreign countries, and Canada. 81% are from public schools. 80% are White; 8% race unknown; 5% Hispanic; 2% Asian American; 2% Foreign; 2% two or more races; 1% African American; 1% American Indian/Alaska Native. 44% are Catholic; 33% Lutheran, Methodist and Baptist; 22% claim no religious affiliation. **Female To Male Ratio:** 1.4:1. The average age of freshmen is 18; all undergraduates, 20. 21% do not continue beyond their first year; 60% remain to graduate. **Housing:** 950 students can be accommodated in college housing, which includes coed dorms, on-campus apartments, married student housing, and a dorm for freshman students. On-campus housing is guaranteed for all 4 years. 69% of students live on campus. All students may keep cars.

FACULTY/CLASSROOMS: 56% of faculty are male; 44% are female. All teach undergraduates. No introductory courses are taught by graduate students. The average class size in an introductory lecture is 22; in a laboratory is 13; and in a regular course is 17.

PROGRAMS OF STUDY: Carroll confers B.A. and B.S. degrees. Associate degrees are also awarded. Bachelor's degrees are awarded in BIOLOGICAL SCIENCE (biochemistry and biology/biological science), BUSINESS (accounting, business administration and management, and finance), COMMUNICATIONS AND THE ARTS (classical languages, communications, creative writing, dramatic arts, English, English literature, English Writing, French, performing arts, public relations, and Spanish), COMPUTER AND PHYSICAL SCIENCE (chemistry, computer science, and mathematics), EDUCATION (elementary education, foreign languages education, physical education, secondary education, and teaching English as a second/foreign language (TESOL/TEFOL)), ENGINEERING AND ENVIRONMENTAL DESIGN (civil engineering and environmental science), HEALTH PROFESSIONS (clinical science, health care administration, health science, nursing, predentistry, premedicine, preoptometry, prepharmacy, and preveterinary science), SOCIAL SCIENCE (history, international relations, philosophy, political science/government, prelaw, psychology, public administration, religion, social science, and sociology). Business, nursing, and biology have the largest enrollments.

ACTIVITIES: There are no fraternities or sororities. Groups on campus include backpacking, climbing, fishing, floating, hiking, skiing, snowshoeing, wilderness training, art, CAMP (explore the great outdoors via mountain biking), cheerleading, choir, dance, drama, drill team, ethnic, film, forensics, honors, international, jazz band, LGBT, literary magazine, musical theater, newspaper, pep band, political, professional, radio and TV, religious, social, social service, student government, and yearbook. Popular campus events include Theme Dances, Casino Night, Spring Softball Tournament, Piano Night, Set-Up Your Roommate Dance, SEARCH, Literary and film festival, retreats, coffee nights, community service. **Sports:** There are 6 intercollegiate sports for men and

7 for women, and 13 intramural sports for men and 13 for women. Facilities include basketball, tennis, racquetball courts, weight-lifting, aerobics, dance rooms, football stadium, soccer field, track and field, cross country, golf, swimming, yoga, martial arts, kickboxing, bowling, dodge ball, ultimate frisbee, volleyball, softball, a fitness center, and a gym. **Graduates:** From July 1, 2015 to June 30, 2016, 264 bachelor's degrees were awarded. The most popular majors were health professions and related programs (26%), biological/life sciences (16%), and business/marketing (12%). In an average class, 63% graduate in 6 years or less.

SERVICES: Counseling and information services are available, as is tutoring in most subjects, such as writing, math, statistics, economics, chemistry, accounting, anatomy, and physiology. There is also remedial math, reading, and writing. **Library/Resources:** The library contains 89,003 volumes, 64,500 microform items, 3,890 audio/video tapes/CDs/DVDs, and subscribes to 504 periodicals including electronic. Computerized library services include interlibrary loans, database searching, Internet access, and Wi-Fi capability. Special learning facilities include a radio station, TV station, civil engineering lab, nursing lab (SimMan), performing arts theater and astronomical observatory. **Physically Challenged Students:** 90% of the campus is accessible. Facilities include wheelchair ramps, elevators, special parking, specially equipped restrooms, special class scheduling, lowered drinking fountains, and special housing. **Special:** Carroll College offers a 3-2 engineering program leading to acceptance to any of 6 cooperating universities. In addition, internships, study abroad in Paris, Japan, Spain, Germany, Korea, and many other countries through a consortium for international studies, and work-study programs in certain fields are available. Students may take a dual major in any two fields of study, select an interdisciplinary major such as health information management, earn credit for life, military, and work experience, or pursue nondegree study. The pass/fail option is available. There are 6 national honor societies, Phi Beta Kappa, a freshman honors program, and 5 departmental honors programs. **Visiting:** There are regularly scheduled orientations for prospective students. There are guides for informal visits, visitors may sit in on classes, and stay overnight. To schedule a visit, contact the Admissions Office. **Campus Safety and Security:** Measures include emergency notification system, security escort services, emergency telephones, lighted pathways/sidewalks, and controlled access to dorms/residences.

REQUIREMENTS: Satisfactory scores on the SAT or on the ACT are recommended. Students must be graduates of an accredited secondary school or have a GED. An essay is required. High school recommended units are: 4 in English, 3 in math, 2 each for Science (1 must be a lab), social studies, history, academic electives, and 1 in visual performing arts. A GPA of 2.5 is required. AP and CLEP credits are accepted. Important factors in the admissions decision are advanced placement or honors courses, evidence of special talent, personality/intangible qualities, recommendations by school officials, leadership record, and parents or siblings attended your school. To graduate, students must complete 122 semester hours and maintain the specific GPA and credit concentration required by their major. The college's general liberal arts requirements include courses in writing, communications, history, math, natural and social sciences, philosophy, theology, and fine arts. **Procedure:** Freshmen are admitted in the fall and spring. Entrance exams should be taken in the fall of the senior year. There are deferred admissions and rolling admissions plans. Applications should be filed by June 1 for fall entry, along with a $35 fee. Notification is sent on a rolling basis. Application fees are waived if application is completed online. **Transfer Students:** 34 transfer students enrolled in 2015-2016. Transfer students need a 2.5 GPA and must submit ACT or SAT scores if fewer than 30 college credits have been completed. Letters of recommendation are required. 30 of 122 credits required for the bachelor's degree must be completed at Carroll. **International Students:** The school actively recruits these students. They must take the TOEFL. English-speaking students must submit SAT or ACT scores.

ADMISSIONS: 64% of the 2016-2017 applicants were accepted. **Admissions Contact:** Cynthia Thornquist, Director of Admissions & Enrollment. Email: *admissions@caroll.edu* Web: *www.carroll.edu*

FINANCIAL AID: In 2016-2017, 77% of all full-time freshmen and 66% of continuing full-time students received some form of financial aid. 71% of all full-time freshmen and 65% of continuing full-time students received need-based aid. The average freshman award was $24,493. Need-based scholarships or need-based grants averaged $16,384; need-based self-help aid (loans and jobs) averaged $3,698; non-need-based athletic scholarships averaged $9,115; other non-need-based awards and non-need-based scholarships averaged $3,237; and $12,981 from other forms of aid. The average financial indebtedness of the 2016 graduate was $26,996. The FAFSA code is 002526. The priority date for freshman financial aid applications for fall entry is March 1.

MONTANA STATE UNIVERSITY — C-3

www.montana.edu

Bozeman, MT 59717	**(406) 994-2452** **(888) MSU-CATS**
Fax: (406) 994-1923	**Email: admissions@montana.edu**
Full-time: 6466 men, 5205 women	**Faculty:** I, --$
Part-time: 1070 men, 966 women	**Ph.D.s:** 79%
Graduate: 895 men, 1086 women	**Student/Faculty:** 19 to 1
Year: semesters, summer session	**Tuition:** $6850 ($22,081)
Room & Board: $8650	**Freshman Class:** 13799 applied, 11570 accepted, 2943 enrolled
SAT CR/M/W: 570/565/545 **ACT:** 25	**CEEB CODE:** 4488
Application Deadline: n/av	**COMPETITIVE+**

Montana State University, the state's land-grant institution, educates students creates knowledge and art and serves communities by integrating learning, discovery and engagement. There are 9 undergraduate schools and 1 graduate school. In addition to regional accreditation, MSU has baccalaureate program accreditation with AACSB, ABET, ADA, CSAB, NAAB, NASAD, NASM, NCATE, NLN, AAFCS, CACREP, and CCNE. The 1850-acre campus is in a small town 140 miles west of Billings and 90 miles north of Yellowstone National Park. Including any residence halls, there are 90 buildings.

STUDENT LIFE: 69% of undergraduates are from Montana. Others are from 50 states, 65 foreign countries, and Canada. 88% are White; 3% Foreign; 2% Hispanic; 1% Asian American; 1% American Indian/Alaska Native; 1% two or more races; 1% race unknown. **Male To Female Ratio:** 1.2:1. The average age of freshmen is 18; all undergraduates, 22. 29% do not continue beyond their first year; 47% remain to graduate. **Housing:** 5400 students can be accommodated in college housing, which includes single-sex and coed dorms and married student housing. In addition, there are honors houses, fraternity houses, sorority houses, floors for older students, nonsmoking floors, theme, and wellness floors. On-campus housing is guaranteed for the freshman year only, is available on a first-come, and first-served basis. 75% of students commute. All students may keep cars.

FACULTY/CLASSROOMS: 62% of faculty are male; 38% are female. All teach undergraduates and do research. Graduate students teach 21% of introductory courses. The average class size in an introductory lecture is 66; in a laboratory is 18; and in a regular course is 22.

PROGRAMS OF STUDY: MSU confers B.A., B.S., B.F.A. and B.Mus.Ed. degrees. Associate, master's, and doctoral degrees are also awarded. Bachelor's degrees are awarded in AGRICULTURE (agricultural business management, animal science, horticulture, natural resource management, and plant science), BIOLOGICAL SCIENCE (biology/biological science, biotechnology, cell biology, microbiology, and neurosciences), BUSINESS (business administration and management), COMMUNICATIONS AND THE ARTS (art, English, fine arts, media arts, modern language, and music), COMPUTER AND PHYSICAL SCIENCE (chemistry, computer science, earth science, mathematics, and physics), EDUCATION (agricultural education, elementary education, music education, secondary education, and technical education), ENGINEERING AND ENVIRONMENTAL DESIGN (agricultural engineering technology, chemical engineering, civil engineering, computer engineering, construction engineering, electrical/electronics engineering, environmental design, environmental science, industrial engineering, land use management and reclamation, mechanical engineering, and mechanical engineering technology), HEALTH PROFESSIONS (health and nursing), SOCIAL SCIENCE (anthropology, economics, history, human development, liberal arts/general studies, philosophy, political science/government, psychology, and sociology). Engineering, physical science, and architecture are the strongest academically. Business, education, and nursing have the largest enrollments.

ACTIVITIES: 4% of men belong to 7 national fraternities; 3% of women belong to 4 national sororities. There are 150 groups on campus, including art, band, cheerleading, chess, choir, chorale, chorus, computers, dance, drama, drill team, environmental, ethnic, film, honors, international, jazz band, LGBT, literary magazine, marching band, musical theater, newspaper, opera, orchestra, pep band, photography, political, professional, radio and TV, religious, social, social service, student government, and symphony. Popular campus events include International Food Bazaar and Native American Pow-Wow. **Sports:** There are 6 intercollegiate sports for men and 7 for women, and 38 intramural sports for men and 40 for women. **Graduates:** From July 1, 2015 to June 30, 2016, 2223 bachelor's degrees were awarded. The most popular majors were engineering (12%), business (12%), and health professions and related sciences (10%). 126 companies recruited on campus in 2015-2016. In an average class, 49% graduate in 6 years or less. Of the 2015 graduating class, 15% were enrolled in graduate school within 6 months of graduation, and 95% were employed.

SERVICES: Counseling and information services are available, as is tutoring in most subjects, a reader service for the blind, and remedial math, reading, and writing. **Library/Resources:** The 2 libraries contain 744,989 volumes, 2.2 million microform items, 13,446 audio/video tapes/CDs/DVDs, and subscribe to 10,131 periodicals including electronic. Computerized library services include interlibrary loans, database searching, and Internet access. Special learning facilities include an art gallery, natural history museum, planetarium, radio station, TV station, Blackstone Business Launchpad, Museum of the Rockies, Jake Jabs College of Business and Entrepreneurship Center, Nursing Simulation Lab, Subzero Science/Engineering Research, Optical Technology Center. Burns Telecommunication Center. **Physically Challenged Students:** 90% of the campus is accessible. Facilities include wheelchair ramps, elevators, special parking, specially equipped restrooms, special class scheduling, lowered drinking fountains, and lowered telephones. There are also services through the resource center, and a taping service for the blind. **Special:** Montana State University offers internships in selected majors, study in 40 countries, cross-registration in selected programs, B.A.-B.S. degrees, dual and interdisciplinary majors, nondegree study, and pass/fail options. There are 23 national honor societies and a freshman honors program. **Visiting:** There are regularly scheduled orientations for prospective students. There are guides for informal visits, visitors may sit in on classes, and stay overnight. To schedule a visit, contact the Office of New Student Services at orientation@montana.edu. **Campus Safety and Security:** Measures include 24-hour foot and vehicle patrol, emergency notification system, self-defense education, and security escort services. There are emergency telephones, lighted pathways/sidewalks, and controlled access to dorms/residences.

REQUIREMENTS: The SAT or ACT is required. MSU requires applicants to have a minimum GPA of 2.5, rank in the upper 50% of their graduating class or have minimum composite scores of 22 on the ACT or a satisfactory score on the SAT. They must be graduates of an accredited secondary school. The GED is accepted. Students should have completed 4 years of English, 3 years each of social studies and math, 2 years of lab science, of these units, 2 must be lab and 2 years of language, computer science, visual and performing arts, or vocational education. MSU requires applicants to be in the upper 50% of their class. A GPA of 2.5 is required. AP and CLEP credits are accepted. To graduate, students must complete a core curriculum of 8 credits of natural sciences, 6 credits each of multicultural studies, humanities, social science, and communications, and 3 credits each of fine arts and math. The total number of credits required varies by program, with 120 being the minimum; at least one third must be in upper-division courses. A minimum 2.0 GPA is needed. Students must be officially registered in their chosen curriculum for at least 2 semesters before graduation. **Procedure:** Freshmen are admitted in the fall, spring, and summer. Entrance exams should be taken in the fall of the senior year. There are deferred admissions and rolling admissions plans. Application deadlines are open. Application fee is $30. Notification is sent on a rolling basis. Applications are accepted online. **Transfer Students:** 848 transfer students enrolled in 2015-2016. Applicants must have a minimum GPA of 2.0, grades of D or better transfer for credit. 30 credits required for the bachelor's degree must be completed at MSU. **International Students:** The school actively recruits these students. They must take the TOEFL with a minimum score of 525 on the paper-based TOEFL (PBT). Students must also submit proof of American Cultural Exchange Language Institute Level 6 (available at MSU).

ADMISSIONS: 84% of the 2016-2017 applicants were accepted. The SAT scores for the 2016-2017 freshman class were: Critical Reading-- 22% below 500, 39% between 500 and 599, 32% between 600 and 699, and 7% between 700 and 800. Math-- 22% below 500, 38% between 500 and 599, 33% between 600 and 699, and 7% between 700 and 800. Writing-- 32% below 500, 39% between 500 and 599, 25% between 600 and 699, and 4% between 700 and 800. There were 6 National Merit finalists. 114 freshmen graduated first in their class. **Admissions Contact:** Ronda Russell, Director, Admissions. Email: *admissions@montana.edu* Web: *www.montana.edu*

FINANCIAL AID: In 2016-2017, 64% of all full-time freshmen received some form of financial aid. 64% of all full-time freshmen received need-based aid. The average freshman award was $12,022. Need-based scholarships or need-based grants averaged $5,226; need-based self-help aid (loans and jobs) averaged $4,286; non-need-based athletic scholarships averaged $5,925; other non-need-based awards and non-need-based scholarships averaged $1,641; and $4,200 from other forms of aid. 50% of undergraduate students work part-time. The average financial indebtedness of the 2016 graduate was $24,421. Check with the school for current application deadlines.

MONTANA STATE UNIVERSITY-BILLINGS D-3

www.msubillings.edu

Billings, MT 59101 | **(406) 657-2158** | **(800) 565-MSUB**

Fax: (406) 657-2302 | **Email: admissions@msubillings.edu**

Full-time: 1097 men, 1575 women	**Faculty:** 174; IIA, --$
Part-time: 317 men, 755 women	**Ph.D.s:** 86%
Graduate: 91 men, 304 women	**Student/Faculty:** 17 to 1
Year: semesters, summer session	**Tuition:** $7660 ($17,843)
Room & Board: $15,300	**Freshman Class:** 1470 applied, 1463 accepted, 689 enrolled
SAT CR/M: 480/500 **ACT:** 21	**CEEB CODE:** 4298
Application Deadline: open	**COMPETITIVE**

Montana State University-Billings, founded in 1927, is a comprehensive, regional, public university offering instructional and learning opportunities in the arts and sciences as well as professional programs in business, technology, human services, rehabilitation, health professions, and education. The figures in the above capsule and in this profile are approximate. There are 5 undergraduate schools and 1 graduate school. In addition to regional accreditation, MSU-Billings has baccalaureate program accreditation with AACSB, NASAD, NASM, and NCATE. The 92-acre campus is in an urban area in Billings. Including any residence halls, there are 22 buildings.

STUDENT LIFE: 90% of undergraduates are from Montana. Others are from 39 states, 21 foreign countries, and Canada. 97% are from public schools. 83% are White; 6% American Indian/Alaska Native; 4% Hispanic; 3% Foreign; 1% African American; 1% Asian American; 1% two or more races; 1% race unknown. **Female To Male Ratio:** 1.8:1. The average age of freshmen is 21; all undergraduates, 25. 42% do not continue beyond their first year; 33% remain to graduate. **Housing:** 558 students can be accommodated in college housing, which includes single-sex and coed dorms and married student housing. On-campus housing is available on a first-come and first-served basis. 81% of students commute. All students may keep cars.

FACULTY/CLASSROOMS: 58% of faculty are male; 42% are female. All teach undergraduates. No introductory courses are taught by graduate students. The average class size in an introductory lecture is 30 and in a laboratory is 19.

PROGRAMS OF STUDY: MSU-Billings confers B.A., B.S., B.A.S., B.S.Ed., B.S.H.S., and B.S.L.S. degrees. Associate and master's degrees are also awarded. Bachelor's degrees are awarded in BIOLOGICAL SCIENCE (biology/biological science), BUSINESS (business administration and management), COMMUNICATIONS AND THE ARTS (art, communications, dramatic arts, English, music, music performance, and public relations), COMPUTER AND PHYSICAL SCIENCE (applied science, chemistry, information sciences and systems, and mathematics), EDUCATION (art education, athletic training, early childhood education, education, elementary education, health education, mathematics education, middle school education, music education, outdoor leadership/education, physical education, science education, secondary education, social science education, social studies education, and special education), ENGINEERING AND ENVIRONMENTAL DESIGN (environmental science), HEALTH PROFESSIONS (exercise science, health care administration, and rehabilitation therapy), SOCIAL SCIENCE (criminal justice, history, human services, liberal arts/general studies, liberal arts, sciences, general studies, humanities, political science/government, psychology, sociology, and Spanish studies). The sciences, business, and education are the strongest academically. Education, and business have the largest enrollments.

ACTIVITIES: There are no fraternities or sororities. There are 53 groups on campus, including art, band, cheerleading, choir, chorale, chorus, computers, drama, ethnic, honors, international, jazz band, literary magazine, newspaper, orchestra, pep band, political, professional, radio and TV, religious, social, social service, and student government. Popular campus events include Powwow and Native American Day. **Sports:** There are 6 intercollegiate sports for men and 7 for women, and 6 intramural sports for men and 5 for women. Facilities include a phys ed building with a pool, gyms, running track, weight-training equipment, racquetball courts, and a soccer/softball field. **Graduates:** From July 1, 2015 to June 30, 2016, 582 bachelor's degrees were awarded. The most popular majors were business/marketing (28%), education (24%), and liberal arts/general studies (8%). 100 companies recruited on campus in 2015-2016. In an average class, 24% graduate in 6 years or less. Of the 2015 graduating class, 9% were enrolled in graduate school within 6 months of graduation, and 90% were employed.

SERVICES: Counseling and information services are available, as is tutoring in most subjects, a reader service for the blind, and remedial math, reading, and writing. There is also an Academic support center for students. **Library/Resources:** The 2 libraries contain 245,859 volumes, 51,660 microform items, 2,275 audio/video tapes/CDs/DVDs, and subscribe to 790 periodicals including electronic. Computerized library services include interlibrary loans, database searching, Internet access, and Wi-Fi capability. Special learning facilities include an art gallery, radio station, a scientific field station, a small business institute, an urban institute, a special education learning center, a disabilities center, a center for business enterprise, and a center for applied economic research. **Physically Challenged Students:** All of the campus is accessible. Facilities include wheelchair ramps, elevators, special parking, specially equipped restrooms, special class scheduling, lowered drinking fountains, lowered telephones, special housing. **Special:** MSU-Billings offers co-op programs in business, human services, and liberal arts, internships, work-study programs, B.A.-B.S. degrees, dual majors, nondegree study, and pass/fail options. There are 10 national honor societies, a freshman honors program, and 1 departmental honors program. **Visiting:** There are regularly scheduled orientations for prospective students. There are guides for informal visits, visitors may sit in on classes, and stay overnight. To schedule a visit, contact Tammi Watson at (406) 657-2044. **Campus Safety and Security:** Measures include 24-hour foot and vehicle patrol, emergency notification system, self-defense education, and security escort services, shuttle buses, emergency telephones, lighted pathways/sidewalks, and controlled access to dorms/residences.

REQUIREMENTS: The SAT or ACT is required. Applicants must be graduates of an accredited secondary school; the GED is also accepted. The applicant must have taken 4 years of English, 3 each of math, and social studies, and 2 each of science with lab, and computer science, visual/performing arts, foreign language or vocational education. Students need to meet 1 of 3 criteria: be in the upper 50% of their class; have a GPA of 2.0 or better; or have minimum composite scores of 22 on the ACT or satisfactory scores on the SAT. A GPA of 2.0 is required. AP and CLEP credits are accepted. Important factors in the admissions decision are advanced placement or honors courses, geographical diversity, and evidence of special talent. To graduate, students must have earned a minimum of 120 semester credits, including 30 in their major. They must maintain a minimum 2.0 GPA; education and human services majors must maintain a minimum 2.7 GPA. General education requirements must also be fulfilled. **Procedure:** Freshmen are admitted to all sessions. Entrance exams should be taken in the senior year of high school. There are deferred admissions and rolling admissions plans. Application deadlines are open. Application fee is $30. Notification is sent on a rolling basis. Applications are accepted online. **Transfer Students:** 455 transfer students enrolled in 2015-2016. Out-of-state transfer students must have earned a 2.0 GPA; in-state transfer students must be in good academic standing. Students may enroll in the fall, spring, and summer. 20 of 120 credits required for the bachelor's degree must be completed at MSU-Billings. **International Students:** There are 156 international students enrolled. The school actively recruits these students. They must take the TOEFL with a minimum score of 515 on the paper-based TOEFL (PBT) or 68 on the Internet-based version (iBT). They must also take the SAT or ACT.

ADMISSIONS: 31% of the current freshmen were in the top fifth of their class; 62% were in the top two fifths. **Admissions Contact:** Dr. Cheri Johanenes, Director of Admissions and Records and Registrar. Email: *cjohannes@msubillings.edu* Web: *www.msubillings.edu*

FINANCIAL AID: In 2016-2017, 80% of all full-time freshmen and 79% of continuing full-time students received some form of financial aid. 68% of all full-time freshmen and 67% of continuing full-time students received need-based aid. The average freshman award was $8,715. Need-based scholarships or need-based grants averaged $4,599; need-based self-help aid (loans and jobs) averaged $5,165; non-need-based athletic scholarships averaged $2,774; and other non-need-based awards and non-need-based scholarships averaged $1,765. 75% of undergraduate students work part-time. Average annual earnings from campus work are $1340. The average financial indebtedness of the 2016 graduate was $15,562. The college's own financial statement is required. The FAFSA code is 002530. The priority date for freshman financial aid applications for fall entry is March 1. The filing deadline for fall entry is September 30.

MONTANA STATE UNIVERSITY-NORTHERN *(The complete profile is made available exclusively on our website, www.barronspac.com)*

MONTANA TECH OF THE UNIVERSITY OF MONTANA — B-3

www.mtech.edu

Butte, MT 59701	**(406) 496-4568** **(800) 445-TECH**
Fax: (406) 496-4710	**Email: enrollment@mtech.edu**
Full-time: 1485 men, 750 women	**Faculty:** n/av
Part-time: 231 men, 304 women	**Ph.D.s:** 60%
Graduate: 134 men, 76 women	**Student/Faculty:** n/av
Year: semesters, summer session	**Tuition:** $6797 ($20,512)
Room & Board: $8650	**Freshman Class:** 969 applied, 857 accepted, 425 enrolled
SAT CR/M/W: 560/600/510 **ACT:** 25	**CEEB CODE:** 4487
Application Deadline: open	**COMPETITIVE+**

Montana Tech of the University of Montana possesses an internationally esteemed, century-old tradition of excellence in higher education. The university offers degrees and certificates focused in areas such as nursing, health and safety, responsible development of natural resources, engineering, ecology and restoration, business, information technology, energy, and workforce development. Montana Tech has a long-standing reputation for producing outstanding graduates. Figures in the above capsule and in this profile are approximate. There are 3 undergraduate schools and 1 graduate school. In addition to regional accreditation, Montana Tech has baccalaureate program accreditation with ABET, CSAB, ACS, and IACBE. The 56-acre campus is in a small town in Butte, Montana. Including any residence halls, there are 19 buildings.

STUDENT LIFE: 79% of undergraduates are from Montana. Others are from 36 states, 14 foreign countries, and Canada. 9% are Foreign; 79% White; 6% race unknown; 2% American Indian/Alaska Native; 2% Hispanic; 1% African American; 1% Asian American. **Male To Female Ratio:** 1.6:1. 24% do not continue beyond their first year; 45% remain to graduate. **Housing:** College-sponsored housing includes coed dorms, off-campus apartments, and married student housing. On-campus housing is guaranteed for the freshman year only, and is available on a first-come, and first-served basis. Priority is given to out-of-town students. 89% of students commute. All students may keep cars.

FACULTY/CLASSROOMS: 66% of faculty are male; 34% are female. No introductory courses are taught by graduate students.

PROGRAMS OF STUDY: Montana Tech confers B.S. and B.A.S degrees. Associate and master's degrees are also awarded. Bachelor's degrees are awarded in BIOLOGICAL SCIENCE (biology/biological science), BUSINESS (business information systems and business systems analysis), COMMUNICATIONS AND THE ARTS (communications and communications technology), COMPUTER AND PHYSICAL SCIENCE (chemistry, computer programming, computer science, mathematics, science, and statistics), EDUCATION (health information management), ENGINEERING AND ENVIRONMENTAL DESIGN (computer engineering, engineering, environmental engineering, geological engineering, geophysical engineering, metallurgical engineering, mining and mineral engineering, occupational safety and health, and petroleum/natural gas engineering), HEALTH PROFESSIONS (nursing), SOCIAL SCIENCE (liberal arts/general studies). Engineering is the strongest academically and has the largest enrollment is the strongest academically.

ACTIVITIES: There are no fraternities or sororities. There are 50 groups on campus, including rodeo club, shooting and archery club, band, cheerleading, chess, choir, chorale, computers, dance, environmental, ethnic, honors, international, LGBT, newspaper, pep band, political, professional, radio and TV, religious, ski and snowboard club, social, social service, and student government. Popular campus events include M-Day, and Homecoming. **Sports:** There are 3 intercollegiate sports for men and 3 for women. Facilities include HPER; contains Kelvin Sampson Court, cardio room, weight room, racquetball courts, locker rooms, classrooms, and offices. The Alumni Coliseum provides an outstanding football experience for Digger home games. **Graduates:** From July 1, 2015 to June 30, 2016, 294 bachelor's degrees were awarded. The most popular majors were petroleum engineering (22%), general engineering (15%), and businees (13%). In an average class, 17% graduate in 4 years or less, 38% graduate in 5 years or less, and 43% graduate in 6 years or less.

SERVICES: Counseling and information services are available, as is tutoring in most subjects, such as accounting, algebra, basic math, biology, business, calculus, chemistry, differential equations, dynamics, E-circuits, engineering economics, fluids, nursing, physics, psychology, statics, strengths, survey of metallurgical & materials and engineering. There is a reader service for the blind, remedial math and writing. There are also available career exploration, student/parent mentoring program, financial management workshops, and study skills workshops. **Library/Resources:** The library contains 144,204 volumes, 60,704 microform items, and 5,995 audio/video tapes/CDs/DVDs, and subscribes to 73,241 periodicals including electronic. Computerized library services include interlibrary loans, database searching, Internet access, and Wi-Fi capability. Special learning facilities include a radio station, a mineral museum, and METNET 2-way interactive communication studio. **Physically Challenged Students:** 75% of the campus is accessible. Facilities include wheelchair ramps, elevators, special parking, specially equipped restrooms, special class scheduling, lowered drinking fountains, lowered telephones, and special housing. **Special:** 3-2 liberal arts-engineering program with Carroll College, dual enrollment agreement with Flathead Valley Community College, collaborative programs with UM Helena (BAS Business, BS BIT, BAS General Studies), UM Western (Elementary Education Certification and Secondary Education Certification in Biological Sciences, General Sciences, and Mathematical Sciences), and UM-COT (AAS Surgical Technology)Additionally, Tech offers double majors, honors program, independent study, internships, and work study. There are 3 national honor societies, Phi Beta Kappa, and a freshman honors program. **Visiting:** There are regularly scheduled orientations for prospective students, there is an official fall orientation, though visits are welcome any time. There are guides for informal visits, visitors may sit in on classes, and stay overnight. To schedule a visit, contact the Enrollment Services at (406) 496-4256. **Campus Safety and Security:** Measures include 24-hour foot and vehicle patrol, emergency notification system, self-defense education, and security escort services. There are emergency telephones and lighted pathways/sidewalks.

REQUIREMENTS: The SAT or ACT is required. The ACT Optional Writing test is also required. Applicants must be graduates of an accredited secondary school. The GED is accepted. 14 academic credits are required, including English, 4 years; math and social studies, 3 years each; science, 2 years; plus 2 years chosen from foreign language, computer science, visual and performing arts, or vocational education. Applicants must have minimum composite scores of 22 on the ACT or satisfactory scores on the SAT or a 2.5 GPA, or be in the top half of their graduating class. Other factors regarding admissions are considered only if the preceding standards are not met. Montana Tech requires applicants to be in the upper 50% of their class. A GPA of 2.5 is required. AP and CLEP credits are accepted. For graduation, students must complete at least 120 semester credits (more for engineering degrees) and maintain a minimum 2.0 GPA. Requirements include 6 hours each of communications, humanities/fine arts, mathematical sciences, and social sciences, and 6 to 7 hours of physical and life sciences with a lab required for 1 course. Engineering students must satisfy specific requirements within the individual curriculum. **Procedure:** Freshmen are admitted to all sessions. Entrance exams should be taken in the senior year. There are deferred admissions and rolling admissions plans. Application deadlines are open. Application fee is $30. Notification is sent on a rolling basis. Applications are accepted online. **Transfer Students:** 226 transfer students enrolled in 2015-2016. Transfer applicants must have a minimum GPA of 2.0. Grades of C and above transfer for credit. **International Students:** There are 260 international students enrolled. The school actively recruits these students. They must take the TOEFL with a minimum score of 525 on the paper-based TOEFL (PBT) or 71 on the Internet-based version (iBT). They must also take the SAT or ACT, scoring 22.

ADMISSIONS: 88% of the 2016-2017 applicants were accepted. The SAT scores for the 2016-2017 freshman class were: Critical Reading-- 21% below 500, 52% between 500 and 599, 25% between 600 and 699, and 2% between 700 and 800. Math-- 10% below 500, 35% between 500 and 599, 52% between 600 and 699, and 3% between 700 and 800. Writing-- 40% below 500, 54% between 500 and 599, and 6% between 600 and 699. The ACT scores were 33% between 18 and 23, 59% between 24 and 29, and 8% above 30. 28 freshmen graduated first in their class. **Admissions Contact:** Stephanie Crowe, Director of Recruiting. Email: *enrollment@mtech.edu* Web: *www.mtech.edu*

FINANCIAL AID: In 2016-2017, 59% of all full-time freshmen and 57% of continuing full-time students received some form of financial aid. 53% of all full-time freshmen and 49% of continuing full-time students received need-based aid. The average freshman award was $9,477. Need-based scholarships or need-based grants averaged $5,575; need-based self-help aid (loans and jobs) averaged $3,224; non-need-based athletic scholarships averaged $4,026; and other non-need-based awards and non-need-based scholarships averaged $2,054. The average financial indebtedness of the 2016 graduate was $26,198. The college's own financial statement is required. The FAFSA code is 002531. Check with the school for current application deadlines.

ROCKY MOUNTAIN COLLEGE D-3

www.rocky.edu

Billings, MT 59102 **(406) 657-1000 (406) 657-1026 (800) 877-6259**

Fax: (406) 657-1189 **Email: admissions@rocky.edu**

Full-time: 434 men, 423 women
Part-time: 23 men, 28 women
Graduate: 34 men, 58 women
Year: semesters, summer session
Room & Board: $8134

Faculty: 62; IIB, --$
Ph.D.s: 83%
Student/Faculty: 14 to 1
Tuition: $26,136
Freshman Class: 1545 applied, 959 accepted, 217 enrolled

SAT CR/M/W: 500/495/445 **ACT:** 22
Application Deadline: n/av

CEEB CODE: 4660
COMPETITIVE

Rocky Mountain College is a private college founded on the unique practice of joining the liberal arts tradition along with practical training for professional development. Established in 1878, RMC functions on a mission of educating students through liberal arts and professional programs that cultivate critical thinking, creative expression, ethical decision-making, informed citizenship, and professional excellence. The College supports its mission through core themes of academic excellence, transformational learning, and shared responsibility and stewardship. There is 1 undergraduate school and 1 graduate school. In addition to regional accreditation, Rocky has baccalaureate program accreditation with ARC-PA and AABI. The 60-acre campus is in a suburban area in a residential section of Billings, Montana. Including any residence halls, there are 16 buildings.

STUDENT LIFE: 54% of undergraduates are from Montana. Others are from 41 states, 14 foreign countries, and Canada. 77% are White; 6% Hispanic; 4% Foreign; 4% two or more races; 3% race unknown; 2% African American; 2% American Indian/Alaska Native; 1% Asian American. **Female To Male Ratio:** 1.0:1. The average age of freshmen is 18; all undergraduates, 21. 31% do not continue beyond their first year; 44% remain to graduate. **Housing:** 570 students can be accommodated in college housing, which includes coed dorms, on-campus apartments, and married student housing. On-campus housing is guaranteed for the freshman year only, and is available on a first-come, and first-served basis. 55% of students commute. All students may keep cars. Alcohol is not permitted.

FACULTY/CLASSROOMS: 54% of faculty are male; 46% are female. All teach undergraduates, 5% do research, and 5% do both. No introductory courses are taught by graduate students. The average class size in an introductory lecture is 15; in a laboratory is 11; and in a regular course is 15.

PROGRAMS OF STUDY: Rocky confers B.A. and B.S. degrees. Associate and master's degrees are also awarded. Bachelor's degrees are awarded in AGRICULTURE (environmental studies, equestrian studies, and equine science), BUSINESS (accounting, business administration and management, and sports management), COMMUNICATIONS AND THE ARTS (art, communications, creative writing, literature, music performance, and theatre arts), COMPUTER AND PHYSICAL SCIENCE (chemistry, computer science, geology, mathematics, and petroleum systems/geology), EDUCATION (art education, education, elementary education, English education, health and physical education, mathematics education, music education, psychology education, science education, social science education, and social studies education), ENGINEERING AND ENVIRONMENTAL DESIGN (aeronautical science, aviation administration/management, and environmental science), HEALTH PROFESSIONS (biology and exercise science), SOCIAL SCIENCE (history, philosophy and religion, political science/government, psychology, and sociology). Business, biology, and health and human performance. have the largest enrollments.

ACTIVITIES: There are no fraternities or sororities. There are 28 groups on campus, including art, aviation and equestrian, band, cheerleading, choir, chorale, chorus, computers, debate, drama, environmental, forensics, honors, international, jazz band, LGBT, literary magazine, musical theater, newspaper, pep band, professional, radio and TV, religious, social, social service, student government, and yearbook. Popular campus events include Convocations, Intercollegiate Athletics, Homecoming, Candlelight Dinner, Yule Log Dinner, and International Week. **Sports:** There are 8 intercollegiate sports for men and 8 for women, and 10 intramural sports for men and 10 for women. Facilities include a football stadium, soccer field, gymnasium, auxiliary exercise areas, weight room, swimming pool, and a climbing wall. **Graduates:** From July 1, 2015 to June 30, 2016, 156 bachelor's degrees were awarded. The most popular majors were business (23%), education (14%), and health and human performance (14%). 18 companies recruited on campus in 2015-2016. In an average class, 29% graduate in 4 years or less, 42% graduate in 5 years or less, and 44% graduate in 6 years or less. Of the 2015 graduating class, 17% were enrolled in graduate school within 6 months of graduation, and 80% were employed.

SERVICES: Counseling and information services are available, as is tutoring in most subjects, such as accounting, biology, chemistry, economics, mathematics, physics, and writing. There is a reader service for the blind, and remedial math, reading, and writing. Note-taking is available for qualified students. **Library/Resources:** The library contains 106,639 volumes, 2 microform items, 1,702 audio/video tapes/CDs/DVDs, and subscribes to 202 periodicals including electronic. Computerized library services include interlibrary loans, database searching, Internet access, and Wi-Fi capability. Special learning facilities include an art gallery, radio station, a flight school and equestrian facilities. **Physically Challenged Students:** 75% of the campus is accessible. Facilities include wheelchair ramps, elevators, special parking, specially equipped restrooms, special class scheduling, lowered drinking fountains, and special housing. **Special:** Rocky Mountain College offers internships with local, regional, and national employers. Various study abroad opportunities with formal exchange contracts in the United Kingdom, Finland, Japan, Sweden, and China. There are dual majors, individualized programs of study, credit for life, military, and work experience. Juniors and seniors may elect to take 1 course on a pass/fail basis each semester. Specialized programs offered by Rocky Mountain College include aviation and equestrian studies. There is 1 national honor society and 1 departmental honors program. **Visiting:** There are regularly scheduled orientations for prospective students, students may visit year-round and will meet with admission representatives, tour campus, with opportunities to sit in on a class and meet with a faculty member. There are guides for informal visits, visitors may sit in on classes, and stay overnight. To schedule a visit, contact Megan Cabe at (406) 657-1026. **Campus Safety and Security:** Measures include emergency notification system, self-defense education, and security escort services. There are emergency telephones, lighted pathways/sidewalks, controlled access to dorms/residences, and security cameras and electronic access systems.

REQUIREMENTS: The SAT or ACT is required. Applicants must be graduates of an accredited secondary school. The GED is also accepted. Students must have completed 4 units of English, 4 units of math, 3 units in the natural sciences, 3 units in the socal sciences, and 2 units of history. The school recommends a portfolio for admission to the art program, an audition for admission to the music or theatre program, and an interview for academically challenged students. A GPA of 2.5 is required. AP and CLEP credits are accepted. Important factors in the admissions decision are personality/intangible qualities, extracurricular activities record, and advanced placement or honors courses. To graduate, students must complete a minimum of 124 credit hours, complete all major requirements with a minimum overall GPA of 2.0 and 2.25 in the major. If a minor area is chosen, a minimum of 18 hours is required. There are core curriculum requirements in fine arts, humanities, communication, and the natural and social sciences, as well as writing, communication, and math. **Procedure:** Freshmen are admitted fall, spring, and summer. Entrance exams should be taken during the first half of the senior year. There are deferred admissions and rolling admissions plans. Application deadlines are open. Application fee is $35. Application fees are waived if application is completed on-line. **Transfer Students:** 65 transfer students enrolled in 2015-2016. Transfer students must have a minimum GPA of 2.0 and grades of 2.0 and higher transfer for credit. Transfers are admitted every term. 30 of 124 credits required for the bachelor's degree must be completed at Rocky. **International Students:** There are 33 international students enrolled. The school actively recruits these students. They must take the TOEFL with a minimum score of 570 on the paper-based TOEFL (PBT) or 88 on the Internet-based version (iBT), or take the IELTS. They must also take the SAT or ACT, scoring 860/SAT (critical reading and math) or 18/ACT.

ADMISSIONS: 62% of the 2016-2017 applicants were accepted. The SAT scores for the 2016-2017 freshman class were: Critical Reading-- 48% below 500, 41% between 500 and 599, and 11% between 600 and 699. Math-- 50% below 500, 38% between 500 and 599, 11% between 600 and 699, and 1% between 700 and 800. Writing-- 67% below 500, 29% between 500 and 599, 2% between 600 and 699, and 2% between 700 and 800. The ACT scores were 11% between 12 and 17, 60% between 18 and 23, 24% between 24 and 29, and 5% above 30. 29% of the current freshmen were in the top fifth of their class; 61% were in the top two fifths. 7 freshmen graduated first in their class. **Admissions Contact:** Austin Mapston, Dean of Enrollment Services. Email: *admissions@rocky.edu* Web: *www.rocky.edu*

FINANCIAL AID: In 2016-2017, 99% of all full-time freshmen and continuing full-time students received some form of financial aid. 92% of all full-time freshmen and 89% of continuing full-time students received need-based aid. The average freshman award was $27,180. Need-based scholarships or need-based grants averaged $18,459 ($43,287 maximum); need-based self-help aid (loans and jobs) averaged $7,629 ($34,164 maximum); non-need-based athletic scholarships averaged $4,688 ($26,136 maximum); and other non-need-based awards and non-need-based scholarships averaged $9,946 ($26,136 maximum). 26% of undergraduate students work part-time. Average annual earnings from campus work are $1184. The average financial indebtedness of the 2016 graduate was $37,082. The college's own financial statement is required. The FAFSA code is 002534. The priority date for freshman financial aid applications for fall entry is March 1.

UNIVERSITY OF GREAT FALLS — C-2

www.ugf.edu

Great Falls, MT 59405	(406) 791-5210 (800) 856-9544
Fax: (406) 791-5209	**Email:** enroll@ugf.edu
Full-time: 268 men, 309 women	**Faculty:** n/av
Part-time: n/av	**Ph.D.s:** n/av
Graduate: n/av	**Student/Faculty:** n/av
Year: semesters, summer session	**Tuition:** $30,604
Room & Board: $7920	**Freshman Class:** n/av
SAT or ACT: recommended	**CEEB CODE:** 4058
Application Deadline: September 1	**COMPETITIVE**

University of Great Falls, established in 1932, is a private, liberal arts university affiliated with the Roman Catholic Church. Great Falls offers 40 undergraduate, 2 graduate (3 concentrations), and 4 distance learning degrees. The figures in the above capsule and in this profile are approximate. There are 3 undergraduate schools and 2 graduate schools. The 44-acre campus is in an urban area in Great Falls Montana. Including any residence halls, there are 14 buildings.

STUDENT LIFE: 56% of undergraduates are from out of state, mostly

the West. Students are from 30 states, 10 foreign countries, and Canada. 70% are White; 7% race unknown; 4% Foreign. 40% are other Christian; 30% claim no religious affiliation; 29% Catholic. **Female To Male Ratio:** 1.2:1. **Housing:** 189 students can be accommodated in college housing, which includes single-sex and coed dorms, on-campus apartments, and off-campus apartments. On-campus housing is available on a first-come and first-served basis. All students may keep cars. Alcohol is not permitted.

FACULTY/CLASSROOMS: 59% of faculty are male; 42% are female. All teach undergraduates. No introductory courses are taught by graduate students. The average class size in an introductory lecture is 15; in a laboratory is 10; and in a regular course is 14.

PROGRAMS OF STUDY: UGF confers B.A. and B.S. degrees. Associate and master's degrees are also awarded. Bachelor's degrees are awarded in BIOLOGICAL SCIENCE (biology/biological science, microbiology, molecular biology, and physiology), BUSINESS (accounting, business administration and management, and management science), COMMUNICATIONS AND THE ARTS (art, English, and fine arts), COMPUTER AND PHYSICAL SCIENCE (chemistry (pre-MBA), computer science, mathematics, physical sciences, and science), EDUCATION (education of the exceptional child, elementary education, health and physical education, mathematics education, middle school education, physical education, reading education, science education, secondary education, social studies education, and special education), HEALTH PROFESSIONS (predentistry and premedicine), SOCIAL SCIENCE (addiction studies, counseling/psychology, criminal justice, history, law enforcement and corrections, paralegal studies, political science/government, prelaw, psychology, religion, religious studies, social science, social studies, sociology, and theological studies). Biology, paralegal studies, and computer science are the strongest academically. Biology, education, and business administration have the largest enrollments.

ACTIVITIES: There are no fraternities or sororities. There are 18 groups on campus, including art, cheerleading, chess, choir, chorus, computers, debate, drama, ethnic, forensics, honors, literary magazine, musical theater, orchestra, photography, professional, religious, social, social service, student government, and symphony. Popular campus events include Orientation Barbecue, Spook-a-Roo (Halloween community activity), Alumni Weekend, and Friends and Family Weekend. **Sports:** There are 2 intercollegiate sports for men and 3 for women, and 7 intramural sports for men and 7 for women. Facilities include UGF has a gymnasium with training facilities, a game room, and workout room.

SERVICES: Counseling and information services are available, as is tutoring in some subjects, such as 090-level courses, 100-level courses, 200-level courses, and selected 300-level courses. There is also a reader service for the blind, and remedial math, reading, and writing, and tutoring in basic skills. **Library/Resources:** The library contains 106,135 volumes, 124,608 microform items, and 3,894 audio/video tapes/CDs/DVDs, and subscribes to 587 periodicals including electronic. Computerized library services include interlibrary loans, database searching, Internet access, and Wi-Fi capability. Special learning facilities include an art gallery. **Physically Challenged Students:** All of the campus is accessible. Facilities include wheelchair ramps, special parking, specially equipped restrooms, special class scheduling, and lowered drinking fountains. **Special:** There are 1 national honor societies and a freshman honors program. **Visiting:** There are regularly scheduled orientations for prospective students, including meeting with prospective advisers and staff, financial aid presentation, campus tour, and lunch. There are guides for informal visits, visitors may sit in on classes, and stay overnight. To schedule a visit, contact the Admissions Office at enroll@ugf.edu. **Campus Safety and Security:** Measures include 24-hour foot and vehicle patrol, emergency notification system, self-defense education, and security escort services, shuttle buses, emergency telephones, and lighted pathways/sidewalks.

REQUIREMENTS: The SAT or ACT is recommended. In addition, Graduation from an accredited secondary school is required; the GED is accepted. Applicants should have 4 years of English, 3 years of math, and 2 years each of social studies, science, and electives, including foreign language, art, music, and vocational education. A GPA of 2.0 is required. AP and CLEP credits are accepted. Students must complete 128 credit hours, including 30 to 65 in the major, plus 15 to 21 minor credits, maintaining a minimum GPA of 2.0. The 52-credit-hour core curriculum includes math, computer science, art, behavioral science, history, literature, philosophy, science, writing, theology, and religion. Specific disciplines required include human nature, intellectual inquiry, and religious dimension. **Procedure:** Freshmen are admitted in the fall, spring, and summer. Entrance exams should be taken prior to registration. There are deferred admissions and rolling admissions plans. Applications should be filed by September 1 for fall entry. The fall 2016 application fee was $25. **Transfer Students:** Transfer applicants must be in good academic standing from another accredited college or university, and must submit official transcripts from all colleges or universities attended. Transfer students must also submit an official high school transcript. 30 of 128 credits required for the bachelor's degree must be completed at UGF. **International Students:** There are 27 international students enrolled. The school actively recruits these students. They must take the TOEFL with a minimum score of 500 on the paper-based TOEFL (PBT) or 80 on the Internet-based version (iBT).

Admissions Contact: Melanie Houge, Assistant Director of Admission. Email: *enroll@ugf.edu* Web: *www.ugf.edu*

FINANCIAL AID: In 2016-2017, 95% of all full-time freshmen received some form of financial aid. 52% of all full-time freshmen received need-based aid. The average freshman award was $15,002. Non-need-based athletic scholarships averaged $15,527; and other non-need-based awards and non-need-based scholarships averaged $13,971. UGF is a member of CSS. The FAFSA code is 002527. Check with the school for current application deadlines.

UNIVERSITY OF MONTANA — B-2

www.umt.edu

Missoula, MT 59812	(406) 243-5672 (800) 462-8636
Fax: (406) 243-5711	**Email:** admiss@umontana.edu
Full-time: 4303 men, 4978 women	**Faculty:** n/av
Part-time: 1143 men, 1268 women	**Ph.D.s:** 77%
Graduate: 923 men, 1337 women	**Student/Faculty:** 16 to 1
Year: semesters, summer session	**Tuition:** $6099 ($22,372)
Room & Board: $8006	**Freshman Class:** 5345 applied, 4956 accepted, 2013 enrolled
SAT CR/M/W: 550/542/530 **ACT:** 23	**CEEB CODE:** 4489
Application Deadline: March 1	**COMPETITIVE**

University of Montana, founded in 1893, is a public institution with programs in arts and sciences, business administration, visual and performing arts, education and human sciences, forestry, journalism, and pharmacy and allied health sciences. It is part of the Montana University System. The figures in the above capsule and in this profile are approximate. There are 8 undergraduate schools and 2 graduate schools. In addition to regional accreditation, UM has baccalaureate program accreditation with AACSB, ACCE, ACPE, APTA, CAHEA, CSAB, CSWE, NASAD, NASDTEC, NASM, NCATE, and SAF. The 220-acre campus is in an urban area 200 miles east of Spokane. Including any residence halls, there are 57 buildings.

STUDENT LIFE: 73% of undergraduates are from Montana. Others are from 50 states, 68 foreign countries, and Canada. 80% are from public schools. 76% are White; 7% race unknown; 4% Hispanic; 4% Foreign; 4% two or more races; 3% American Indian/Alaska Native; 1% African American; 1% Asian American. **Female To Male Ratio:** 1.2:1. The average age of freshmen is 19; all undergraduates, 23. 28% do not continue beyond their first year; 50% remain to graduate. **Housing:** 3430 students can be accommodated in college housing, which includes single-sex and coed dorms, off-campus apartments, married student housing, honors houses, special-interest houses, an international house, and nontraditional houses. On-campus housing is guaranteed for the freshman year only. 70% of students commute. All students may keep cars.

FACULTY/CLASSROOMS: 56% of faculty are male; 44% are female. All teach undergraduates and do research. Graduate students teach 2% of introductory courses. The average class size in an introductory lecture is 35; in a laboratory is 25; and in a regular course is 35.

PROGRAMS OF STUDY: UM confers B.A., B.S., B.A.S., B.A.E., B.A.R.TV., B.F.A., B.M., B.M.E., B.S.B.A.D, B.S.F., B.S.M.T., and B.S.W. degrees. Associate, master's, and doctoral degrees are also awarded. Bachelor's degrees are awarded in AGRICULTURE (conservation and regulation, environmental studies, and forestry and related sciences), BIOLOGICAL SCIENCE (biochemistry, biology/biological science, botany, ecology, microbiology, wildlife biology, and zoology), BUSINESS (accounting, banking and finance, business administration and management, international business management, management information systems, marketing/retailing/merchandising, recreational facilities management, and small business management), COMMUNICATIONS AND THE ARTS (classics, communications, dramatic arts, English, fine arts, French, German, Japanese, journalism, linguistics, media arts, music, music performance, radio/television technology, Russian, and Spanish), COMPUTER AND PHYSICAL SCIENCE (applied science, chemistry, combined science, computer science, geology, geoscience, mathematics, and physics), EDUCATION (athletic training, elementary education, music education, physical education / exercise science, science education, and secondary education), HEALTH PROFESSIONS (health promotion, medical technology, and pharmacology), SOCIAL SCIENCE (anthropology, communication sciences & disorders, economics, geography, history, liberal arts/general studies, Native American studies, philosophy, political science/government, psychology, social work, and sociology). Business, forestry, and education have the largest enrollments.

ACTIVITIES: 6% of men belong to 7 national fraternities; 6% of women belong to 4 national sororities. There are 150 groups on campus, including academic, and forestry clubs, art, band, cheerleading, chess, choir, chorale, chorus, computers, creative writing dance, drill team, ethnic, honors, international, jazz band, LGBT, literary magazine, marching band, newspaper, opera, orchestra, pep band, political, professional, radio and TV, religious, social, social service, student government, and symphony. Popular campus events include Foresters Day, Founders Day, International Week, Griz-Cat Football Game, and Kyi-Yo Pow-wow. **Sports:** There are 6 intercollegiate sports for men and 9 for women, and 16 intramural sports for men and 12 for women. Facilities include a field house with an arena and gyms, stadium, student and faculty fitness center, golf course, soccer and rugby fields, swimming pool, game room, climbing wall, athlete weight training rooms, and mountain trails. **Graduates:** The most popular majors were business administration and related (accounting, MIS) (16%), physical sciences (13%), communications, journalism, and and natural resources and conservation (8%). In an average class, 25% graduate in 4 years or less, 43% graduate in 5 years or less, and 50% graduate in 6 years or less.

SERVICES: Counseling and information services are available, as is tutoring in every subject. There is a reader service for the blind, and remedial math, reading, and writing. Mentors and note takers are also available, as are books on tape for LD students. **Library/Resources:** The 4 libraries contain 1.4 million volumes, 347,441 microform items, 73,946 audio/video tapes/CDs/DVDs, and subscribe to 5,000 periodicals including electronic. Computerized library services include interlibrary loans, database searching, Internet access, and Wi-Fi capability. Special learning facilities include an art gallery, radio station, TV station, experimental forest, biological station, ranch, center for people and forests, geology field camp, international language lab, wilderness institute, observatory, and freshwater research center. **Physically Challenged Students:** 75% of the campus is accessible. Facilities include wheelchair ramps, elevators, special parking, specially equipped restrooms, special class scheduling, lowered drinking fountains, lowered telephones, special housing. **Special:** Students may cross-register with Montana Tech of UM (Butte) and UM-Western (Dillon). Co-op programs exist in business, communications, economics, management, and liberal studies; internships in most majors, work-study programs with nonprofit organizations and on campus, and study abroad in 12 countries are available. The school offers a B.A.-B.S. degree in chemistry, pass/fail options in classes other than major requirements, and dual majors in physics and computer science as well as history and political science. There are 7 national honor societies, Phi Beta Kappa, a freshman honors program, and 5 departmental honors programs. **Visiting:** There are regularly scheduled orientations for prospective students, including placement testing, advising, workshops, and social events. There are guides for informal visits and visitors may sit in on classes. To schedule a visit, contact Enrollment Services (406) 243-2332. **Campus Safety and Security:** Measures include 24-hour foot and vehicle patrol, emergency notification system, self-defense education, and security escort services. There are shuttle buses, emergency telephones, lighted pathways/sidewalks, controlled access to dorms/residences, and shuttle buses between campus and downtown after hours on weekends.

REQUIREMENTS: The SAT or ACT is required, with a minimum composite ACT score of 22 or a satisfactory SAT verbal-math-writing composite score. Applicants must be graduates of an accredited secondary school. The GED is accepted. Students should have completed 4 years of English, 3 of math, 3 of social studies, 2 of lab science, and 2 from foreign language, computer science, visual arts, or vocational education. UM requires applicants to be in the upper 50% of their class. A GPA of 2.5 is required. AP and CLEP credits are accepted. Important factors in the admissions decision are advanced placement or honors courses, evidence of special talent, and geographical diversity. A total of 120 credits is required for graduation in most majors. The number of hours in the major varies; some majors require a thesis. There are competency requirements in writing, math, and foreign language or symbolic systems. Distribution requirements include courses in expressive arts, literary and artistic studies, historical and cultural studies, social sciences, ethical and human values, and natural sciences. A minimum GPA of 2.0 must be maintained. **Procedure:** Freshmen are admitted to all sessions. There are deferred admissions and rolling admissions plans. Applications should be filed by March 1 for fall entry; November 15 for spring entry, along with a $36 fee. Notification is sent on a rolling basis. Applications are accepted online. **Transfer Students:** 1215 transfer students enrolled in 2015-2016. Applicants must have a minimum GPA of 2.0. Grades of 2.0 or better transfer for credit. 30 of 120 credits required for the bachelor's degree must be completed at UM. **International Students:** There are 379 international students enrolled. The school actively recruits these students. They must take the TOEFL with a minimum score of 500 on the paper-based TOEFL (PBT). They must also take the ACT English - minimum score 18.

ADMISSIONS: 93% of the 2016-2017 applicants were accepted. The SAT scores for the 2016-2017 freshman class were: Critical Reading-- 26% below 500, 44% between 500 and 599, 25% between 600 and 699, and 5% between 700 and 800. Math-- 26% below 500, 50% between 500 and 599, 20% between 600 and 699, and 3% between 700 and 800. Writing-- 35% below 500, 45% between 500 and 599, 18% between 600 and 699, and 2% between 700 and 800. **Admissions Contact:** Sharon O'Hare, Associate VP for Enrollment. Email: *admiss@umontana.edu* Web: *www.umt.edu*

FINANCIAL AID: In 2016-2017, 62% of all full-time freshmen and 60% of continuing full-time students received some form of financial aid. The average freshman award was $10,836.. The average financial indebtedness of the 2016 graduate was $29,918. UM is a member of CSS. The FAFSA code is 002536. The priority date for freshman financial aid applications for fall entry is February 15.

UNIVERSITY OF MONTANA-WESTERN *(The complete profile is made available exclusively on our website, www.barronspac.com)*

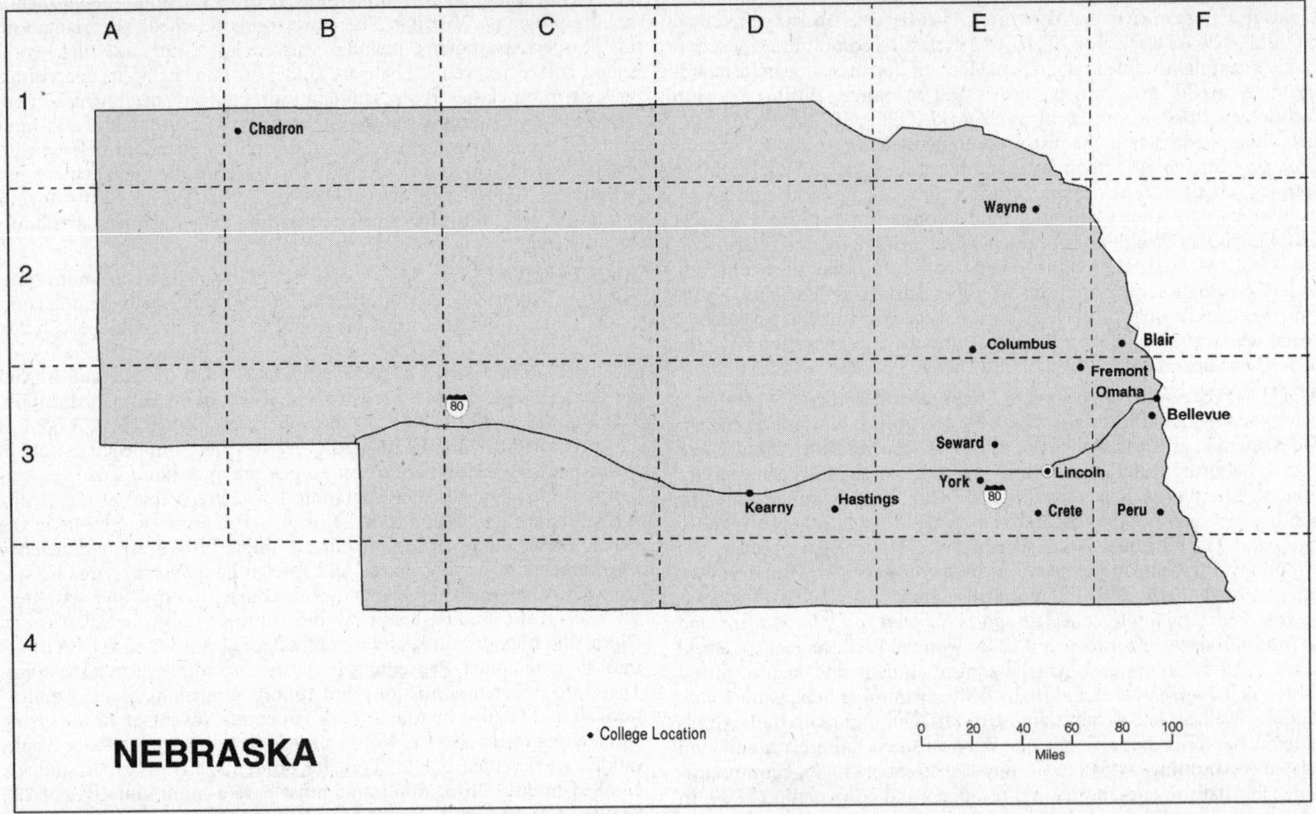

BELLEVUE UNIVERSITY *(The complete profile is made available exclusively on our website, www.barronspac.com)*

CHADRON STATE COLLEGE *(The complete profile is made available exclusively on our website, www.barronspac.com)*

CLARKSON COLLEGE F-3
www.clarksoncollege.edu

Omaha, NE 68131 **(402) 552-3041**
(800) 647-5500
Fax: (402) 552-6057 **Email: admissions@clarksoncollege.edu**

Full-time: 200 men, 350 women	**Faculty:** n/av
Part-time: 100 men, 120 women	**Ph.D.s:** n/av
Graduate: 67 men, 73 women	**Student/Faculty:** n/av
Year: semesters, summer session	**Tuition:** $17,964
Room & Board: $13,904	**Freshman Class:** n/av
SAT or ACT: required	**CEEB CODE:** 2250
Application Deadline: August 16	**COMPETITIVE**

Clarkson College, established in 1888 and affiliated with the Episcopal Church, offers undergraduate and graduate degrees in the health care professions and business. The figures in the above capsule and in this profile are approximate. Cost for room and board is based on 13 credit hours, per semester. There are 3 undergraduate schools and 2 graduate schools. In addition to regional accreditation, Clarkson has baccalaureate program accreditation with NLN. The 3-acre campus is in an urban area in Omaha. Including any residence halls, there are 4 buildings.

STUDENT LIFE: 61% of undergraduates are from Nebraska. Others are from 13 states, and 2 foreign countries. 90% are from public schools. 90% are White; 3% African American; 2% Asian American; 2% Hispanic; 1% American Indian/Alaska Native. 50% are Catholic; 45% Protestant. **Female To Male Ratio:** 1.5:1. The average age of all undergraduates is 22. 87% remain to graduate. **Housing:** 140 students can be accommodated in college housing, which includes coed on-campus apartments. On-campus housing is available on a first-come and first-served basis. Priority is given to out-of-town students. 90% of students commute. All students may keep cars. Alcohol is not permitted.

FACULTY/CLASSROOMS: 16% of faculty are male; 84% are female. All teach undergraduates. No introductory courses are taught by graduate students. The average class size in an introductory lecture is 30; in a laboratory is 20; and in a regular course is 20.

PROGRAMS OF STUDY: Clarkson confers B.S. and B.S.N. degrees. Associate and master's degrees are also awarded. Bachelor's degrees are awarded in BUSINESS (business administration and management), COMPUTER AND PHYSICAL SCIENCE (radiological technology), HEALTH PROFESSIONS (nursing and radiograph medical technology). Radiological technology, and nursing are the strongest academically. Nursing has the largest enrollment.

ACTIVITIES: There are no fraternities or sororities. There are 12 groups on campus, including newspaper, professional, religious, social, social service, and student government. Popular campus events include Talent Show, Game Nights, and Intramural Volleyball. **Sports:** There is no sports program at Clarkson. Facilities include an exercise room available 24 hours, and a small gym area with basketball, and volleyball courts.

SERVICES: Counseling and information services are available, as is tutoring in every subject. **Library/Resources:** The library contains 7,613 volumes, 698 audio/video tapes/CDs/DVDs, and subscribes to 217 periodicals including electronic. Computerized library services include interlibrary loans, database searching, and Internet access. **Physically Challenged Students:** 95% of the campus is accessible. Facilities include wheelchair ramps, elevators, special parking, specially equipped restrooms, special class scheduling, lowered drinking fountains, lowered telephones, and special housing. **Special:** A co-op program in nursing, work-study programs, and dual majors are available. Credit is given for military experience, and nondegree study is possible. The distance education option allows advanced placement students living a distance from the campus to complete their studies at home. There is 1 national honor society. **Visiting:** There are regularly scheduled orientations for prospective students. There are guides for informal visits and visitors may sit in on classes. To schedule a visit, contact the Admissions Office. **Campus Safety and Security:** Measures include 24-hour foot and vehicle patrol, emergency notification system, self-defense education, and security escort services, emergency telephones, and lighted pathways/sidewalks.

REQUIREMENTS: The SAT or ACT is required, with a minimum composite score of 20 on the ACT or a satisfactory score on the SAT. Tests are not required for applicants more than 2 years out of high school.

Applicants must be graduates of an accredited secondary school, with 3 years of English and 2 each of social science, algebra, and science (including lab science). The GED is accepted. Clarkson requires applicants to be in the upper 50% of their class. AP and CLEP credits are accepted. Important factors in the admissions decision are advanced placement or honors courses, extracurricular activities record, and evidence of special talent. To graduate, students must complete 128 credit hours, including 68 in the major, and maintain a minimum GPA of 2.0. General education requirements include courses in the humanities, English, behavioral and social sciences, science and math, and phys ed. A 9-hour core curriculum is also required. **Procedure:** Freshmen are admitted to all sessions. Entrance exams should be taken during the junior year or first semester of the senior year. There is a deferred admissions plan. Applications should be filed by August 16 for fall entry, along with a $35 fee. Notification of early decision is sent April 1; regular decision, June 1. **Transfer Students:** Transfer students must have a minimum GPA of 2.5. Grades of C or better transfer for credit. Transfers are admitted for fall and spring. An interview is sometimes required. 64 of 128 credits required for the bachelor's degree must be completed at Clarkson. **International Students:** They must take the TOEFL, 85 on the MELAB, and 5 on the TWE. They must also take the SAT or ACT.

Admissions Contact: Denise Work, Director of Admissions. Email: *admissions@clarksoncollege.edu* Web: *www.clarksoncollege.edu*

FINANCIAL AID: In 2016-2017, 90% of all full-time freshmen and continuing full-time students received some form of financial aid. Clarkson is a member of CSS. The college's own financial statement is required. The FAFSA code is 009862. Check with the school for current application deadlines.

COLLEGE OF SAINT MARY — F-3

www.csm.edu

Omaha, NE 68106	**(402) 399-2407** **(800) 926-5534**
Fax: (402) 399-2412	**Email: enroll@csm.edu**
Full-time: 679 women	**Faculty:** 40
Part-time: 9 men, 82 women	**Ph.D.s:** 70%
Graduate: 14 men, 234 women	**Student/Faculty:** 15 to 1
Year: semesters, summer session	**Tuition:** $27,984
Room & Board: $7200	**Freshman Class:** 193 applied, 183 accepted, 71 enrolled
ACT: 23	**CEEB CODE:** 6106
Application Deadline: open	**COMPETITIVE**

College of Saint Mary, founded in 1923, is a women's college committed to the works, values and aspirations of the Sisters of Mercy and dedicated to the education of women in an environment that calls forth potential and fosters leadership. There is 1 undergraduate school and 1 graduate school. In addition to regional accreditation, CSM has baccalaureate program accreditation with NLN, ACOTE, IACBE, and ABA. The 40-acre campus is in an urban area within metro Omaha. Including any residence halls, there are 9 buildings.

STUDENT LIFE: 80% of undergraduates are from Nebraska. Others are from 21 states, and 9 foreign countries. 90% are from public schools. 78% are White; 6% African American; 2% Asian American; 2% two or more races; 10% Hispanic; 1% American Indian/Alaska Native; 1% Foreign. 58% are Unknown religion; 42% Catholic. **Female To Male Ratio:** 43.3:1. The average age of freshmen is 20; all undergraduates, 25. 21% do not continue beyond their first year; 49% remain to graduate. **Housing:** 289 students can be accommodated in college housing, which includes single-sex dorms. Residence hall for single student mothers with children. On-campus housing is guaranteed for all 4 years. 68% of students commute. All students may keep cars.

FACULTY/CLASSROOMS: 16% of faculty are male; 84% are female. 95% teach undergraduates, and 10% do research. No introductory courses are taught by graduate students. The average class size in an introductory lecture is 16; in a laboratory is 14; and in a regular course is 14.

PROGRAMS OF STUDY: CSM confers B.A., B.S., B.B.L.M., B.G.S., and B.R.S. degrees. Associate, master's, and doctoral degrees are also awarded. Bachelor's degrees are awarded in BIOLOGICAL SCIENCE (biology/biological science), BUSINESS (business intelligence and analytics), COMMUNICATIONS AND THE ARTS (art, English, language arts, and Spanish), COMPUTER AND PHYSICAL SCIENCE (chemistry, mathematics, and natural sciences), EDUCATION (early childhood education, education, elementary education, and special education), HEALTH PROFESSIONS (medical laboratory technology and nursing), SOCIAL SCIENCE (applied psychology, humanities, liberal arts/general studies, paralegal studies, psychology, social science, and theological studies). Biology, chemistry, occupational therapy, and nursing are the strongest academically. Occupational therapy, nursing, and education have the largest enrollments.

ACTIVITIES: There are no fraternities or sororities. There are 20 groups on campus, including campus activities board, business, green team, art, choir, chorus, dance, drama, environmental, ethnic, forensics, honors, international, multicultural, professional, religious, social, social service, and student government. Popular campus events include Heritage Week, Queen of Hearts Celebration, Casino and Comedian Night. **Sports:** There are 8 intercollegiate sports for women, and 5 intramural sports for women. Facilities include a gym, swimming pool, weight room, running track, exercise room, training room, soccer fields, and softball fields. **Graduates:** From July 1, 2015 to June 30, 2016, 132 bachelor's degrees were awarded. The most popular majors were rehabilitation studies/occupational therapy (33%), nursing (17%), and business (9%). 30 companies recruited on campus in 2015-2016. In an average class, 41% graduate in 4 years or less, 43% graduate in 5 years or less, and 49% graduate in 6 years or less. Of the 2015 graduating class, 37% were enrolled in graduate school within 6 months of graduation, and 39% were employed.

SERVICES: Counseling and information services are available, as is tutoring in most subjects, and a reader service for the blind, and remedial math, reading, and writing. There are also study groups and learning circles. **Library/Resources:** The library contains 89,613 volumes, and 2,770 audio/video tapes/CDs/DVDs, and subscribes to 375 periodicals including electronic. Computerized library services include interlibrary loans, database searching, Internet access, and Wi-Fi capability. Special learning facilities include an art gallery, cadaver lab, digital piano lab, native fish aquarium, nursing/occupational therapy/physician assistant laboratories,lecture capture system, and online learning platform. **Physically Challenged Students:** All of the campus is accessible. Facilities include wheelchair ramps, elevators, special parking, specially equipped restrooms, special class scheduling, lowered drinking fountains, and special housing. **Special:** Students may pursue internships in any major, including research courses in the sciences. CSM also offers dual majors, study abroad, nondegree study, pass/fail options, an accelerated degree program in business leadership and management, and credit for military and work experience. There are 2 national honor societies, a freshman honors program, and 30 departmental honors programs. **Visiting:** There are regularly scheduled orientations for prospective students, consisting of a tour of the campus, a meeting with a financial aid representative, student-life presentations, and lunch. There are guides for informal visits, visitors may sit in on classes, and stay overnight. To schedule a visit, contact Amy Miller at (402) 399-2355. **Campus Safety and Security:** Measures include 24-hour foot and vehicle patrol, emergency notification system, self-defense education, security escort services, lighted pathways/sidewalks, controlled access to dorms/residences, and camera-monitored entrances to residence halls.

REQUIREMENTS: Students are accepted with a minimum composite score of 18 on the ACT or comparable SAT score. Students must also have a GPA of at least 2.0. Applicants must be graduates of an accredited secondary school. The GED is accepted. Students should have completed 16 academic units, including 4 years of English and 2 each of math, social studies, and science, with biology and chemistry required for the various health profession majors. An interview is recommended. A GPA of 2.0 is required. AP and CLEP credits are accepted. To graduate, students must complete 128 semester hours, with a minimum of 30 hours in the major and a 2.0 GPA in the major and overall. Required general education courses total 47 hours, with 10 in quantitative reasoning and science, 6 each in English and theology, 3 each in communications, moral reasoning, fine arts, global cultural diversity, history, philosophy, and social science, and 1 in a first year seminar. Each student prior to graduation completes and presents a research project in her major either individually or with a team. **Procedure:** Freshmen are admitted in the fall, spring, and summer. Entrance exams should be taken in the junior or senior year. There are deferred admissions and rolling admissions plans. Application deadlines are open. Application fee is $30. Applications are accepted online. **Transfer Students:** 149 transfer students enrolled in

2015-2016. Applicants should have a minimum GPA of 2.0 and submit official transcripts from previous colleges attended. Students with fewer than 12 credit hours must also submit ACT or SAT scores. Grades of C or better transfer for credit. Students are admitted every term. 30 of 128 credits required for the bachelor's degree must be completed at CSM. **International Students:** There are 7 international students enrolled. They must take the TOEFL with a minimum score of 550 on the paper-based TOEFL (PBT) or 79 on the Internet-based version (iBT). They must also take the SAT or ACT, scoring 18.

ADMISSIONS: 95% of the 2016-2017 applicants were accepted. The ACT scores were 26% below 12, 35% between 12 and 17, 23% between 18 and 23, 10% between 24 and 29, and 6% above 30. 41% of the current freshmen were in the top fifth of their class; 81% were in the top two fifths. **Admissions Contact:** Greg Fritz, VP Enrollment Services. Email: *enroll@csm.edu* Web: *www.csm.edu*

FINANCIAL AID: In 2016-2017, 100% of all full-time freshmen and 99% of continuing full-time students received some form of financial aid. 77% of all full-time freshmen and 84% of continuing full-time students received need-based aid. The average freshman award was $29,270. Need-based scholarships or need-based grants averaged $9,933; need-based self-help aid (loans and jobs) averaged $5,598; non-need-based athletic scholarships averaged $6,257; and other non-need-based awards and non-need-based scholarships averaged $14,356. 80% of undergraduate students work part-time. Average annual earnings from campus work are $1556. The average financial indebtedness of the 2016 graduate was $29,538. The FAFSA code is 002540. The priority date for freshman financial aid applications for fall entry is March 15.

CONCORDIA UNIVERSITY NEBRASKA E-3

www.cune.edu

Seward, NE 68434	(402) 643-7233 (800) 535-5494
Fax: (402) 643-4073	Email: admiss@cune.edu
Full-time: 500 men, 550 women	**Faculty:** IIB, --$
Part-time: 15 men, 20 women	**Ph.D.s:** n/av
Graduate: 100 men, 105 women	**Student/Faculty:** n/av
Year: semesters, summer session	**Tuition:** $28,480
Room & Board: $7800	**Freshman Class:** n/av
SAT or ACT: required	**CEEB CODE:** 6116
Application Deadline: n/av	**VERY COMPETITIVE**

Concordia University Nebraska, founded in 1894, is a private university owned and operated by the Lutheran Church-Missouri Synod, with degree programs in professional education and liberal arts. Among Concordia's major programs are those for professional work in the Lutheran Church: teacher education, director of Christian education, preseminary pastoral training, and church music. The figures in the above capsule and in this profile are approximate. There is 1 undergraduate school and 1 graduate school. In addition to regional accreditation, Concordia has baccalaureate program accreditation with NCATE. The 120-acre campus is in a small town 25 miles west of Lincoln. Including any residence halls, there are 26 buildings.

STUDENT LIFE: 59% of undergraduates are from out of state, mostly the Midwest. Students are from 37 states, and 9 foreign countries. 95% are White; 2% African American; 2% Asian American; 1% Hispanic. 95% are Protestant. **Female To Male Ratio:** 1.1:1. The average age of freshmen is 18; all undergraduates, 21. 22% do not continue beyond their first year; 48% remain to graduate. **Housing:** 815 students can be accommodated in college housing, which includes single-sex dorms, off-campus apartments, and married student housing. On-campus housing is guaranteed for all 4 years. 85% of students live on campus; of those, 90% remain on campus on weekends. All students may keep cars. Alcohol is not permitted.

FACULTY/CLASSROOMS: 71% of faculty are male; 29% are female. All teach undergraduates. Graduate students teach 1% of introductory courses. The average class size in an introductory lecture is 20; in a laboratory is 15; and in a regular course is 15.

PROGRAMS OF STUDY: Concordia confers B.A., B.S., B.F.A., B.S.Med.Tech., B.Mus., and B.Sacred Music degrees. Master's degrees are also awarded. Bachelor's degrees are awarded in BIOLOGICAL SCIENCE (biology/biological science), BUSINESS (accounting, business administration and management, and sports management), COMMUNICATIONS AND THE ARTS (communications, dramatic arts, English, fine arts, music, speech/debate/rhetoric, and studio art), COMPUTER AND PHYSICAL SCIENCE (chemistry, computer science, mathematics, natural sciences, and physical sciences), EDUCATION (business education, Christian education, early childhood education, elementary education, home economics education, industrial arts education, middle school education, music education, physical education, science education, secondary education, and special education), HEALTH PROFESSIONS (exercise science, health, medical laboratory technology, predentistry, and premedicine), SOCIAL SCIENCE (behavioral science, geography, history, physical fitness/movement, prelaw, psychology, and theological studies). Education, business, and art are the strongest academically. Education has the largest enrollment.

ACTIVITIES: There are no fraternities or sororities. There are 35 groups on campus, including band, cheerleading, choir, chorale, chorus, computers, dance, debate, drama, drill team, ethnic, forensics, honors, international, jazz band, literary magazine, musical theater, newspaper, orchestra, pep band, photography, professional, religious, social, social service, student government, and yearbook. Popular campus events include Spring Weekend and Multicultural Awareness Week. **Sports:** There are 8 intercollegiate sports for men and 8 for women, and 7 intramural sports for men and 7 for women. Facilities include a gym, weight-training room, indoor pool, football, baseball, soccer fields, a track, and field stadium.

SERVICES: Counseling and information services are available, as is tutoring in every subject, and a reader service for the blind. Talking books and tape recorders are also available. **Library/Resources:** The 3 libraries contain 177,683 volumes, 10,719 microform items, and 13,214 audio/video tapes/CDs/DVDs, and subscribe to 545 periodicals including electronic. Computerized library services include database searching. Special learning facilities include an art gallery, natural history museum, and observatory. **Physically Challenged Students:** 35% of the campus is accessible. Facilities include wheelchair ramps, elevators, special parking, specially equipped restrooms, lowered drinking fountains, and lowered telephones. **Special:** Concordia offers cross-registration with the University of Nebraska in Lincoln. Internships are available in education, business, and Christian education. B.A.-B.S. degrees, student-designed majors, dual majors, study abroad in England and China, nondegree studies, and pass/fail options are available. There is an accelerated degree program in organizational management. There is a freshman honors program. **Visiting:** There are regularly scheduled orientations for prospective students, including a campus tour, visits with professors/coaches, and an admission interview. There are guides for informal visits, visitors may sit in on classes, and stay overnight. To schedule a visit, contact the Office of Admission. **Campus Safety and Security:** Measures include 24-hour foot and vehicle patrol, self-defense education, and security escort services, emergency telephones, lighted pathways/sidewalks, vehicle and bicycle registration, and a possession ID engraving program.

REQUIREMENTS: A minimum composite score of 18 is recommended for the ACT. Applicants need not be graduates of an accredited secondary school. The GED is accepted. The school strongly encourages high school courses in art, English, foreign language, history, math, music, phys ed, science, and social studies. An interview is recommended. A GPA of 2.8 is required. AP and CLEP credits are accepted. Important factors in the admissions decision are ability to finance college education, leadership record, and recommendations by alumni. To graduate, students must complete a minimum of 128 credits with a GPA of at least 2.0. Required general education courses include 12 hours of theology, 9 hours each of English/speech, social science, and science, 6 of fine arts, 3 each of math and health and phys ed, 2 to 3 of electives, and 1 hour minimum of computer literacy. **Procedure:** Freshmen are admitted to all sessions. Entrance exams should be taken in the junior or senior year. There is a rolling admissions plan. Application deadlines are open. Applications are accepted on-line. **Transfer Students:** 58 transfer students enrolled in 2015-2016. Applicants should have a minimum GPA of 2.5 and a minimum ACT score of 18. An interview is recommended. Passing grades transfer for credit. Transfers are admitted every term. 30 of 128 credits required for the bachelor's degree must be completed at Concordia. **International Students:** There are 9 international students enrolled. They must take the TOEFL.

Admissions Contact: Aaron Roberts, Director of Undergraduate Admissions. Email: *admiss@cune.edu* Web: *www.cune.edu*

FINANCIAL AID: In 2016-2017, 98% of all full-time freshmen received some form of financial aid. The college's own financial statement is required. The FAFSA code is 002541. Check with the school for current application deadlines.

CREIGHTON UNIVERSITY F-3

www.creighton.edu

Omaha, NE 68178 (402) 280-2703
(800) 282-5835
Fax: (402) 280-2685 **Email:** admissions@creighton.edu

Full-time: 1719 men, 2262 women	**Faculty:** 354; IIA, +$
Part-time: 90 men, 132 women	**Ph.D.s:** 91%
Graduate: 1667 men, 2523 women	**Student/Faculty:** 11 to 1
Year: semesters, summer session	**Tuition:** $37,606
Room & Board: $10,600	**Freshman Class:** 10352 applied, 7315 accepted, 1033 enrolled
SAT CR/M/W: 580/590/560 **ACT:** 27	**CEEB CODE:** 6121
Application Deadline: February 15	**VERY COMPETITIVE+**

Creighton University, founded in 1878, is a private Jesuit Catholic institution offering undergraduate programs in arts and sciences, business administration, and nursing. The graduate institution offers programs in dental, medical, law, pharmacy, physical therapy, and occupational therapy programs. There are 3 undergraduate schools and 1 graduate school. In addition to regional accreditation, Creighton has baccalaureate program accreditation with AACSB, ACPE, ADA, CSWE, NCATE, ABA, LCME, ACGME, ACCME, ACOTE, CAPTE, CCNE, ANCC, AACN, and CAAHEP. The 139-acre campus is in an urban area near downtown Omaha Nebraska. Including any residence halls, there are 61 buildings.

STUDENT LIFE: 76% of undergraduates are from out of state, mostly the Midwest. Students are from 46 states, 34 foreign countries, and Canada. 52% are from public schools. 70% are White; 9% Asian American; 8% Hispanic; 4% two or more races; 3% Foreign; 2% African American; 2% race unknown; 1% American Indian/Alaska Native. 43% are Jewish, Hinduism, Buddhism, Islam and Unknown; 37% Catholic; 16% Protestant. **Female To Male Ratio:** 1.4:1. The average age of freshmen is 18; all undergraduates, 21. 11% do not continue beyond their first year; 79% remain to graduate. **Housing:** 2522 students can be accommodated in college housing, which includes coed dorms, on-campus apartments, married student housing, honors houses, special-interest houses. There are also the Cortina Community and Freshman Leadership Program housing. On-campus housing is available on a first-come, first-served basis, and on a lottery system for upperclassmen. 58% of students live on campus; of those, 90% remain on campus on weekends. All students may keep cars.

FACULTY/CLASSROOMS: 48% of faculty are male; 52% are female. 61% teach undergraduates, and 61% do both. No introductory courses are taught by graduate students. The average class size in an introductory lecture is 24 and in a laboratory is 15.

PROGRAMS OF STUDY: Creighton confers B.A., B.F.A., B.S., B.S.B.A., B.S.N., B.S.Physics, and B.S.W. degrees. Associate, master's, and doctoral degrees are also awarded. Bachelor's degrees are awarded in BIOLOGICAL SCIENCE (neurosciences), BUSINESS (accounting, business intelligence and analytics, finance, international business, leadership, management, and marketing), COMMUNICATIONS AND THE ARTS (art history, classical languages, communication studies, English, French and Francophone studies, German studies, graphic design & media, journalism, music, musical theater, Spanish and Hispanic studies, studio art, and theatre arts), COMPUTER AND PHYSICAL SCIENCE (applied physics analysis, chemistry, computer science & informatics, mathematics, physics, sustainable energy, and sustainable energy science), EDUCATION (elementary education), ENGINEERING AND ENVIRONMENTAL DESIGN (environmental science), HEALTH PROFESSIONS (biology, dental hygiene, emergency medical services, exercise science, health administration and policy, healthy lifestyle management, and nursing), SOCIAL SCIENCE (American studies, classical and near eastern civilization, cultural anthropology, economics, history, international relations, justice and society, medical anthropology, philosophy, political science/government, psychology, social work, sociology, and theology). Business, science, health science, nursing, biological sciences, and psychology are the strongest academically, and have the largest enrollments.

ACTIVITIES: 37% of men belong to 6 national fraternities; 56% of women belong to 7 national sororities. There are 217 groups on campus, including art, cheerleading, chess, choir, chorale, chorus, computers, dance, debate, drama, drill team, environmental, ethnic, forensics, honors, international, LGBT, musical theater, newspaper, orchestra, pep band, photography, political, professional, radio and TV, religious, social, social service, student government, and symphony. Popular campus events include Fallapalooza Concert, Skutt Shutdown, Lip Sync, Spring Fling Week, Luau, Greek Week, FLP Thanksgiving Dinner, Greek Philanthropies, Christmas at Creighton, Homecoming Week, Paint Party, Hazing Prevention Week, and One Creighton Harvest Fest. **Sports:** There are 18 intercollegiate sports for men and 16 for women, and 23 intramural sports for men and 23 for women. Facilities include The Creighton Championship Center which is the athletic practice, training, and academic support facility that is part of the east campus athletic/fitness/recreation corridor. This corridor also consists of an intercollegiate soccer facility, an arena for women's basketball and volleyball. The Creighton campus has two physical fitness centers with space for basketball, volleyball, badminton, soccer, and other recreational and intramural play, weight rooms, and jogging tracks. Additionally, the Creighton Sports Complex includes playing fields for softball, intramural teams, and indoor batting cages for softball and baseball. **Graduates:** From July 1, 2015 to June 30, 2016, 947 bachelor's degrees were awarded. The most popular majors were business/marketing (22%), health professions and related programs (22%), and biological/life sciences (10%). 397 companies recruited on campus in 2015-2016. In an average class, 6% graduate in 3 years or less, 72% graduate in 4 years or less, 78% graduate in 5 years or less, and 79% graduate in 6 years or less.

SERVICES: Counseling and information services are available, as is tutoring in most subjects. **Library/Resources:** The 3 libraries contain 772,560 volumes, 800,483 microform items, 9,950 audio/video tapes/CDs/DVDs, and subscribe to 89,787 periodicals including electronic. Computerized library services include interlibrary loans, database searching, Internet access, and Wi-Fi capability. Special learning facilities include a radio station, St John's Church is at the center of the Creighton University campus and serves the Omaha community as well. The Lied Art Gallery is open seven days a week and is free to the public. The University is home to a wind energy collection system and the state's largest solar array that acts as an outdoor classroom for students in the energy technology program. iJAY, an Apple Authorized Campus Store, uniquely blends commercial and educational interests by doubling as a learning center, giving students the opportunity to gain hands-on experience running a retail store as part of a practicum course. The Heider Securities Investment and Analysis Center in the business college is a trading room complete with a real-time stock ticker, interactive market boards, and 11 Bloomberg terminals. **Physically Challenged Students:** 87% of the campus is accessible. Facilities include wheelchair ramps, elevators, special parking, specially equipped restrooms, special class scheduling, lowered drinking fountains, and special housing. **Special:** The University offers study abroad, numerous internship, volunteer and service opportunities in countries all over the world. Students may take an accelerated degree program in creative writing, organizational communication, and administration and policy. B.A.-B.S. degrees and dual majors are possible as well as the Art-Engineering degree program with the University of Detroit Mercy, and with Marquette University. Army ROTC is offered on campus, and is available through an arrangement with the University of Nebraska Omaha. There are 15 national honor societies, Phi Beta Kappa, and a freshman honors program. **Visiting:** There are regularly scheduled orientations for prospective students, consisting of open house programs with various presentations and campus tours. A daily visit can be scheduled by either calling the Admissions office or completing online request at https:/choose.creighton.edu/portal/campus-visit. There are guides for informal visits, visitors may sit in on classes, and stay overnight. To schedule a visit, contact the Admissions Office. **Campus Safety and Security:** Measures include 24-hour foot and vehicle patrol, emergency notification system, self-defense education, and security escort services. There are shuttle buses, emergency telephones, lighted pathways/sidewalks, controlled access to dorms/residences, an pedestrian escort service, full-time crime prevention officer, violence intervention and prevention center, electronic card access systems, blue light emergency phones, security alarm systems, panic buttons, and a surveillance camera.

REQUIREMENTS: The SAT or ACT is required. Applicants must be graduates of an accredited secondary school. The GED is accepted. Students should have completed 16 credits including 4 credits in English, 3 each in math and electives, and 2 each in foreign language, natural science (with labs), and social sciences. Home-schooled students are welcome. Creighton requires applicants to be in the upper 50% of their class. A GPA of 2.5 is required. AP and CLEP credits are accepted. Important factors in the admissions decision are advanced placement or honors courses, extracurricular activities record, and recommendations by school officials. To graduate with a bachelor's degree, students must complete a minimum of 128 credit hours, with at least 48 credit hours in courses numbered 300 or above and maintain a CGPA of 2.0. Total number of credit hours required in major and specific disciplines varies by college and major. In addition, a completion of Magis Common Core and College Core Curriculum are required for a bachelor's degree. **Procedure:** Freshmen are admitted in the fall, spring, and summer. Entrance exams should be taken fall of the senior year. There are early admissions, deferred admissions, and rolling admissions plans. Applications should be filed by February 15 for fall entry; December 15 for spring entry, along with a $40 fee. Notification is sent on a rolling basis. Applications are accepted on-line. Application fees are waived if application is completed on-line. **Transfer Students:** 49 transfer students enrolled in 2015-2016. Applicants must be in good academic standing at another accredited university, college, or junior college. Both college-level work and high school academic record are considered for admission, and an overall college GPA of 2.75 (4.0 scale) or higher is recommended for acceptance. Credit hours earned with grades of "C-" or better at an accredited institution of higher education prior to admission to Creighton University may be transferred at the discretion of the respective College. Transfers are admitted every semester. 48 of 128 credits required for the bachelor's degree must be completed at Creighton. **International Students:** There are 128 international students enrolled. The school actively recruits these students. They must take the TOEFL with a minimum score of 570 on the paper-based TOEFL (PBT) or 88 on the Internet-based version (iBT), or take the IELTS. They must also take the SAT or ACT.

ADMISSIONS: 71% of the 2016-2017 applicants were accepted. The SAT scores for the 2016-2017 freshman class were: Critical Reading-- 16% below 500, 42% between 500 and 599, 34% between 600 and 699, and 8% between 700 and 800. Math-- 8% below 500, 45% between 500 and 599, 37% between 600 and 699, and 10% between 700 and 800. Writing-- 18% below 500, 49% between 500 and 599, 27% between 600 and 699, and 6% between 700 and 800. The ACT scores were 17% between 18 and 23, 56% between 24 and 29, and 27% above 30. 61% of the current freshmen were in the top fifth of their class; 85% were in the top two fifths. There were 3 National Merit finalists. 27 freshmen graduated first in their class. **Admissions Contact:** Sarah Richardson, Director of Admissions and Scholarships. Email: *SarahRichardson@creighton.edu* Web: *www.creighton.edu*

FINANCIAL AID: In 2016-2017, 100% of all full-time freshmen and 96% of continuing full-time students received some form of financial aid. 58% of all full-time freshmen and 53% of continuing full-time students received need-based aid. The average freshman award was $30,597.. The average financial indebtedness of the 2016 graduate was $36,195. The college's own financial statement is required. The FAFSA code is 002542. The priority date for freshman financial aid applications for fall entry is January 15. The deadline for filing freshman financial aid applications for fall entry is April 1.

DOANE UNIVERSITY — E-3

www.doane.edu

Crete, NE 68333	(402) 826-8222 (800) 333-6263
Fax: (402) 826-8600	**Email:** admissions@doane.edu
Full-time: 530 men, 508 women	**Faculty:** 82; IIB, --$
Part-time: 6 men, 3 women.	**Ph.D.s:** 83%
Graduate: n/av	**Student/Faculty:** 11 to 1
Year: 4-1-4	**Tuition:** $30,434
Room & Board: $8750	**Freshman Class:** 1892 applied, 1449 accepted, 331 enrolled
SAT: recommended **ACT:** 23	**CEEB CODE:** 6165
Application Deadline: n/av	**VERY COMPETITIVE**

Doane University is known for its leadership in higher education, grounded in the university's commitment to academic excellence, innovation, community and a special sense of place for each individual. These are the values that have made Doane successful for more than 140 years and will help build an even stronger university for the future. There are 3 undergraduate schools and 3 graduate schools. In addition to regional accreditation, Doane has baccalaureate program accreditation with NCATE. The 300-acre campus is in a small town 25 miles southwest of Lincoln. Including any residence halls, there are 28 buildings.

STUDENT LIFE: 77% of undergraduates are from Nebraska. Others are from 27 states, 9 foreign countries, and Canada. 77% are from public schools. 82% are White; 7% Hispanic; 3% African American; 3% two or more races; 2% Foreign; 2% race unknown; 1% Asian American. 19% are Catholic. **Male To Female Ratio:** 1.1:1. The average age of freshmen is 18; all undergraduates, 20. 23% do not continue beyond their first year; 77% remain to graduate. **Housing:** 832 students can be accommodated in college housing, which includes single-sex and coed dorms, on-campus apartments, honors houses and special-interest houses. On-campus housing is guaranteed for all 4 years. 78% of students live on campus; of those, 79% remain on campus on weekends. All students may keep cars.

FACULTY/CLASSROOMS: 46% of faculty are male; 54% are female. All teach undergraduates. No introductory courses are taught by graduate students. The average class size in an introductory lecture is 24; in a laboratory is 16; and in a regular course is 18.

PROGRAMS OF STUDY: Doane confers B.A. and B.S. degrees. Bachelor's degrees are awarded in AGRICULTURE (environmental studies), BIOLOGICAL SCIENCE (biochemistry and biology/biological science), BUSINESS (accounting and business administration and management), COMMUNICATIONS AND THE ARTS (art, art and design, dramatic arts, English, English as a second/foreign language, French, German, journalism, music, and Spanish), COMPUTER AND PHYSICAL SCIENCE (chemistry, computer science, information sciences and systems, mathematics, natural sciences, and physics), EDUCATION (elementary education, physical education, and special education), ENGINEERING AND ENVIRONMENTAL DESIGN (engineering physics and environmental science), SOCIAL SCIENCE (economics, history, international studies, philosophy, political science/government, psychology, public administration, religion, and sociology). Biology, and economics (emphasis business, management) are the strongest academically. Education, and business administration have the largest enrollments.

ACTIVITIES: 22% of women belong to 4 local sororities. There are 50 groups on campus, including alternative spring break, wildlife/conservation, Hanson Leadership program, investment, art, band, cheerleading, choir, chorale, chorus, computers, dance, drama, ethnic, forensics, honors, international, jazz band, LGBT, literary magazine, marching band, musical theater, newspaper, pep band, photography, political, professional, radio and TV, religious, social, social service, speech team, and student government. Popular campus events include Parents Day, Stop Day, Christmas Festival, and Concerts. **Sports:** There are 6 intercollegiate sports for men and 6 for women, and 4 intramural sports for men and 4 for women. Facilities include a phys ed building, field house, sports field, fitness center, a gym, pool, nature and cross-country trails, challenge course, indoor and outdoor tracks. **Graduates:** From July 1, 2015 to June 30, 2016, 235 bachelor's degrees were awarded. The most popular majors were elementary education (21%), business (15%), and biology (12%). 45 companies recruited on campus in 2015-2016. In an average class, 1% graduate in 3 years or less, 60% graduate in 4 years or less, 63% graduate in 5 years or less, and 66% graduate in 6 years or less. Of the 2015 graduating class, 20% were enrolled in graduate school within 6 months of graduation, and 79% were employed.

SERVICES: Counseling and information services are available, as is tutoring in every subject, and remedial math, reading, and writing. **Library/Resources:** The library contains 331,014 volumes, 7,420 microform items, 12,433 audio/video tapes/CDs/DVDs, and subscribes to 237,588 periodicals including electronic. Computerized library services include interlibrary loans, database searching, Internet access, and Wi-Fi capability. Special learning facilities include an art gallery, radio station, TV station, and observatory. **Physically Challenged Students:** 60% of the campus is accessible. Facilities include wheelchair ramps, elevators, special parking, specially equipped restrooms, and special class scheduling. **Special:** Internships for sophomores through seniors, a Washington semester, and study abroad in numerous countries are possible. A 3-2 engineering program in conjunction with Washington at St. Louis and Columbia Universities, work-study, student-designed and interdisciplinary majors, dual majors and accelerated degrees in all areas, credit by exam, nondegree study, and pass/fail options are available. Doane also offers the HELPS program, designed for Doane College graduates who wish to return as full-time students to seek further education in preparation for career advancement. Students may pursue a 3-2 environmental studies/forestry degree in conjunction with Duke University. Doane's Lincoln campus, designed for adults, offers intensive 8-week classes in the evening and on weekends in both undergraduate and graduate programs. Doane offers an honors program, leadership development program, and the opportunity to conduct summer research projects with faculty. There are 7 national honor societies, a freshman honors program, and 3 departmental honors programs. **Visiting:** There are regularly scheduled orientations for prospective students, including 4 scheduled half-day visits that incorporate a parents program. There are guides for informal visits, visitors may sit in on classes, and stay overnight. To schedule a visit, contact the Admissions Office. **Campus Safety and Security:** Measures include security escort services, emergency telephones, lighted pathways/sidewalks, and evening patrols by trained security personnel.

REQUIREMENTS: The ACT is required. The SAT is recommended. Applicants must be graduates of an accredited secondary school. The GED is accepted. It is recommended that 4 units of English and 3 units each of math, science, and the social sciences be completed. An interview is recommended. Art students must submit a portfolio, and music and drama students must audition. A GPA of 2.0 is required. AP and CLEP credits are accepted. Important factors in the admissions decision are advanced placement or honors courses, leadership record, parents or siblings attended your school, evidence of special talent, personality/intangible qualities, extracurricular activities record, recommendations by alumni, geographical diversity, recommendations by school officials, and ability to finance college education. The Doane Plan requires students to complete 60 to 70 credits in heritage studies, contemporary issues, international/multicultural perspective, natural science, quantitative reasoning, communication, aesthetic perspective, health and well-being, and community and leadership. Students are also required to complete 2 hours of phys ed, demonstrate computer skills in word processing, and in most disciplines, complete a senior seminar. Students must complete 132 credit hours and have a minimum GPA of 2.0 in the major to graduate. **Procedure:** Freshmen are admitted in the fall, winter, and spring. Entrance exams should be taken by spring of the junior year or early senior year. There are deferred admissions and rolling admissions plans. Application deadlines are open. Notification is sent on a rolling basis. Applications are accepted online. **Transfer Students:** 44 transfer students enrolled in 2015-2016. Transfer students must submit a transcript from previously attended colleges and have been in good standing. The SAT or ACT is usually required. Grades of 2.0 or higher generally transfer for credit. 30 of 132 credits required for the bachelor's degree must be completed at Doane. **International Students:** There are 19 international students enrolled. The school actively recruits these students. They must take the TOEFL with a minimum score of 525 on the paper-based TOEFL (PBT) or 70 on the Internet-based version (iBT), and take the IELTS with a minimum score of 5.5. They must also take the SAT or ACT, scoring 21. 21 on the ACT English subsection, or a satisfactory score on the SAT.

ADMISSIONS: 77% of the 2016-2017 applicants were accepted. The ACT scores were 3% between 12 and 17, 52% between 18 and 23, 41% between 24 and 29, and 4% above 30. 36% of the current freshmen were in the top fifth of their class; 80% were in the top two fifths. There were 2 National Merit finalists. 9 freshmen graduated first in their class. **Admissions Contact:** Dr. Raja Tayeh, Vice President for Enrollment. Email: *admissions@doane.edu* Web: *www.doane.edu*

FINANCIAL AID: In 2016-2017, 100% of all full-time freshmen and 98% of continuing full-time students received some form of financial aid. 87% of all full-time freshmen and 89% of continuing full-time students received need-based aid. The average freshman award was $23,848. Need-based scholarships or need-based grants averaged $20,993 ($28,170 maximum); need-based self-help aid (loans and jobs) averaged $4,467 ($10,650 maximum); non-need-based athletic scholarships averaged $5,204 ($16,500 maximum); and other non-need-based awards and non-need-based scholarships averaged $13,464 ($9,748 maximum). 41% of undergraduate students work part-time. Average annual earnings from campus work are $1016. The average financial indebtedness of the 2016 graduate was $26,609. The FAFSA code is 002544. The deadline for filing freshman financial aid applications for fall entry is March 1.

HASTINGS COLLEGE D-3

www.hastings.edu

Hastings, NE 68901	**(402) 461-7403** **(800) 532-7642**
Fax: (402) 461-7490	**Email: hcadmissions@hastings.edu**
Full-time: 564 men, 519 women	**Faculty:** 86; IIB, --$
Part-time: 10 men, 11 women	**Ph.D.s:** 72%
Graduate: 22 men, 28 women	**Student/Faculty:** 13 to 1
Year: 4-1-4, summer session	**Tuition:** $27,300
Room & Board: $8080	**Freshman Class:** 11186 applied, 1126 accepted, 289 enrolled
SAT: required **ACT:** 24	**CEEB CODE:** 6270
Application Deadline: August 1	**COMPETITIVE+**

Hastings College, founded in 1882, and affiliated with the Presbyterian Church, offers programs in the liberal arts and sciences, education, business, and pre-health professions. Figures in the above capsule and in this profile are approximate. There is 1 undergraduate school and 1 graduate school. In addition to regional accreditation, Hastings College has baccalaureate program accreditation with NASM and NCATE. The 120-acre campus is in a rural area in south-central, Nebraska, and 2 1/2 hours west of Omaha. Including any residence halls, there are 40 buildings.

STUDENT LIFE: 69% of undergraduates are from Nebraska. Others are from 23 states, 8 foreign countries, and Canada. 86% are from public schools. 89% are White; 4% Hispanic; 3% African American; 1% Asian American; 1% American Indian/Alaska Native; 1% Foreign. 38% are Protestant; 34% claim no religious affiliation; 21% Catholic. **Male To Female Ratio:** 1.1:1. The average age of freshmen is 19; all undergraduates, 21. 27% do not continue beyond their first year; 63% remain to graduate. **Housing:** 842 students can be accommodated in college housing, which includes single-sex and coed dorms, on-campus apartments, and honors houses. On-campus housing is guaranteed for the freshman year only, and is available on a first-come, first-served basis. Priority is given to out-of-town students. 73% of students live on campus; of those, 60% remain on campus on weekends. All students may keep cars.

FACULTY/CLASSROOMS: 56% of faculty are male; 44% are female. All teach undergraduates, 25% do research, and 25% do both. No introductory courses are taught by graduate students. The average class size in an introductory lecture is 25; in a laboratory is 24; and in a regular course is 23.

PROGRAMS OF STUDY: Hastings College confers B.A. and B.M. degrees. Master's degrees are also awarded. Bachelor's degrees are awarded in BIOLOGICAL SCIENCE (biology/biological science), BUSINESS (accounting and business administration and management), COMMUNICATIONS AND THE ARTS (broadcasting, communications, dramatic arts, English, fine arts, German, music, Spanish, and speech/debate/rhetoric), COMPUTER AND PHYSICAL SCIENCE (chemistry, computer science, mathematics, and physics), EDUCATION (art education, business education, elementary education, foreign languages education, music education, science education, secondary education, and special education), HEALTH PROFESSIONS (health care administration), SOCIAL SCIENCE (economics, history, human services, philosophy, political science/government, psychology, religion, social science, and sociology). Physics, mathematics, and religion are the strongest academically. Business administration, teacher education, and biology have the largest enrollments.

ACTIVITIES: 30% of men belong to 4 local fraternities; 30% of women belong to 4 local sororities. There are 80 groups on campus, including public relations, health advisory council, nontraditional students, peer educators, art, band, cheerleading, choir, chorus, computers, dance, debate, drama, environmental, ethnic, flag team, forensics, honors, international, jazz band, LGBT, literary magazine, marching band, musical theater, newspaper, orchestra, pep band, photography, political, professional, radio and TV, religious, social, social service, student government, and symphony. Popular campus events include May Fete, Festival of Lessons and Carols, and Artist Lecture Series. **Sports:** There are 9 intercollegiate sports for men and 10 for women, and 12 intramural sports for men and 12 for women. Facilities include a physical fitness center, a pool, weight room, indoor and outdoor tennis courts, stadium, basketball, cross country, track and field, golf, soccer, volleyball, softball, rodeo, archery, bowling, gym, wellness center, and an all-weather track. **Graduates:** From July 1, 2015 to June 30, 2016, 238 bachelor's degrees were awarded. The most popular majors were business administration (9%), psychology (9%), and biology (8%). 80 companies recruited on campus in 2015-2016. In an average class, 52% graduate in 4 years or less, 62% graduate in 5 years or less, and 63% graduate in 6 years or less. Of the 2015 graduating class, 27% were enrolled in graduate school within 6 months of graduation, and 71% were employed.

SERVICES: Counseling and information services are available, as is tutoring in most subjects, such as all core subjects and most lower-division courses. **Library/Resources:** The library contains 135,450 volumes, 87,723 microform items, 3,802 audio/video tapes/CDs/DVDs, and subscribes to 1,050 periodicals including electronic. Computerized library services include interlibrary loans, database searching, Internet access, and Wi-Fi capability. Special learning facilities include an art gallery, radio station, TV station, an observatory, a glass blowing studio, a greenhouse, and infant study lab. **Physically Challenged Students:** 90% of the campus is accessible. Facilities include wheelchair ramps, elevators, special parking, specially equipped restrooms, special class scheduling, lowered drinking fountains, and lowered telephones. **Special:** There is a co-op nursing program, a 3-2 engineering program with Columbia and Washington Universities and Georgia Institute of Technology, and a 3-2 degree in occupational therapy with Boston and Washington Universities. Internships, study abroad in England, Spain, Russia, Ireland, Holland, and Germany, dual majors in all areas, and student-designed majors are possible. There are 12 national honor societies. **Visiting:** There are regularly scheduled orientations for prospective students, including academic department presentations, a financial aid session, a student panel discussion, a student guided tour, and an activities fair. There are guides for informal visits, visitors may sit in on classes, and stay overnight. To schedule a visit, contact the Admissions Office. **Campus Safety and Security:** Measures include emergency notification system, security escort service, emergency telephones, lighted pathways/sidewalks, and night security patrol.

REQUIREMENTS: The SAT or ACT is required. Applicants should graduate from an accredited secondary school with a minimum of 4 academic credits in English and 2 each in math, science, social studies, and a foreign language. Generally, placement in the upper half of the graduating class, a minimum GPA of 2.0, or a composite score of 20 on the enhanced ACT, is a minimal requirement for consideration for admission. Hastings College requires applicants to be in the upper 50% of their class. A GPA of 2.0 is required. AP and CLEP credits are accepted. Important factors in the admissions decision are advanced placement or honors courses, leadership record, and personality/intangible qualities. Students are required to take courses in written and oral communication, physical and life science, foreign language, history, social and political science, literature, philosophy, religion, health/wellness, computer science, the fine arts, and phys ed. A minimum 2.0 GPA and 127 credit hours, with 30 to 36 in the major, are required to graduate. **Procedure:** Freshmen are admitted to all sessions. Entrance exams should be taken before November. There is a rolling admissions plan. Applications should be filed by August 1 for fall entry; December 1 for winter entry; January 1 for spring entry; and May 15 for summer entry. The fall 2016 application fee was $20. Applications are accepted online. **Transfer Students:** 48 transfer students enrolled in 2015-2016. Transfer students must have completed course work equivalent by description to that of Hastings and have earned grades of C or better. 30 of 127 credits required for the bachelor's degree must be completed at Hastings College. **International Students:** There are 16 international students enrolled. The school actively recruits these students. They must take the TOEFL. International athletes should take a standardized test for athletic eligibility.

ADMISSIONS: 10% of the 2016-2017 applicants were accepted. The ACT scores were 37% below 12, 23% between 12 and 17, 20% between 18 and 23, 10% between 24 and 29, and 10% above 30. 36% of the current freshmen were in the top fifth of their class; 64% were in the top two fifths. 18 freshmen graduated first in their class. **Admissions Contact:** Chris Schukei, Director of Admissions. Email: *cschukei@hastings.edu* Web: *www.hastings.edu*

FINANCIAL AID: In 2016-2017, 100% of all full-time freshmen received some form of financial aid, and need-based aid. 40% of undergraduate students work part-time. Average annual earnings from campus work are $1200. The average financial indebtedness of the 2016 graduate was $22,882. Hastings College is a member of CSS. The FAFSA code is 002548. The deadline for filing freshman financial aid applications for fall entry is May 1.

MIDLAND UNIVERSITY *(The complete profile is made available exclusively on our website, www.barronspac.com)*

NEBRASKA METHODIST COLLEGE *(The complete profile is made available exclusively on our website, www.barronspac.com)*

NEBRASKA WESLEYAN UNIVERSITY E-3

www.nebrwesleyan.edu

Lincoln, NE 68504 **(402) 465-2544**

Fax: (402) 465-2179 **Email:** admissions@nebrwesleyan.edu

Full-time: 690 men, 980 women	**Faculty:** 105; IIB, --$
Part-time: 78 men, 155 women	**Ph.D.s:** 89%
Graduate: 66 men, 179 women	**Student/Faculty:** 13 to 1
Year: semesters, summer session	**Tuition:** $29,800
Room & Board: $8340	**Freshman Class:** n/av
SAT: required **ACT:** 26	**CEEB CODE:** 6470
Application Deadline: August 15	**COMPETITIVE+**

Nebraska Wesleyan University, founded in 1887, is a private liberal arts institution affiliated with the United Methodist Church. NWU offers 106 majors, minors, and pre-professional programs. Figures in the above capsule and in this profile are approximate. There are 18 undergraduate schools and 3 graduate schools. In addition to regional accreditation, NWU has baccalaureate program accreditation with ACBSP, CSWE, NASM, NCATE, and NLN. The 50-acre campus is in a suburban area in the city of Lincoln, 50 miles west of Omaha. Including any residence halls, there are 31 buildings.

STUDENT LIFE: 88% of undergraduates are from Nebraska. Others are from 25 states, 14 foreign countries, and Canada. 93% are White; 2% African American; 2% Asian American; 2% Hispanic; 1% American Indian/Alaska Native. 36% are Protestant; 24% Catholic; 14% claim no religious affiliation. **Female To Male Ratio:** 1.6:1. The average age of freshmen is 18; all undergraduates, 20. 18% do not continue beyond their first year; 70% remain to graduate. **Housing:** 1055 students can be accommodated in college housing, which includes single-sex and coed dorms, on-campus apartments, off-campus apartments, fraternity houses, and sorority houses. On-campus housing is guaranteed for all 4 years. 65% of students live on campus; of those, 70% remain on campus on weekends. All students may keep cars.

FACULTY/CLASSROOMS: 45% of faculty are male; 55% are female. All teach undergraduates. No introductory courses are taught by graduate students. The average class size in an introductory lecture is 22; in a laboratory is 17; and in a regular course is 19.

PROGRAMS OF STUDY: NWU confers B.A., B.S., B.F.A., B.M. and B.S.N. degrees. Master's degrees are also awarded. Bachelor's degrees are awarded in BIOLOGICAL SCIENCE (biochemistry, biology/biological science, and molecular biology), BUSINESS (accounting, business administration and management, international business management, and sports management), COMMUNICATIONS AND THE ARTS (applied music, art, communications, dramatic arts, English, French, German, language arts, music, Spanish, and studio art), COMPUTER AND PHYSICAL SCIENCE (chemistry, computer science, information sciences and systems, mathematics, and physics), EDUCATION (athletic training, elementary education, English education, middle school education, music education, physical education, science education, social science education, and special education), HEALTH PROFESSIONS (exercise science, health, and nursing), SOCIAL SCIENCE (biopsychology, economics, history, international studies, paralegal studies, philosophy, political science/government, psychology, religion, social work, sociology, and women's studies). Business administration, biology, and psychology have the largest enrollments.

ACTIVITIES: 12% of men belong to 1 local and 3 national fraternities; 19% of women belong to 2 local and 2 national sororities. There are 80 groups on campus, including art, band, cheerleading, choir, chorus, computers, debate, drama, drill team, ethnic, forensics, honors, international, jazz band, LGBT, literary magazine, musical theater, newspaper, opera, orchestra, pep band, political, professional, religious, social, social service, student government, and yearbook. Popular campus events include International Dinners, Mosaic Week (week emphasizing multicultural activities), and Visions. **Sports:** There are 8 intercollegiate sports for men and 8 for women, and 8 intramural sports for men and 8 for women. Facilities include a recreation and fitness center, field house and gym, a football/soccer stadium, swimming pool, outdoor track, baseball fields, tennis courts, racquetball courts, and volleyball courts.

Graduates: From July 1, 2015 to June 30, 2016, 403 bachelor's degrees were awarded. The most popular majors were business administration (23%), nursing (13%), and education (9%). 82 companies recruited on campus in 2015-2016. In an average class, 1% graduate in 3 years or less, 52% graduate in 4 years or less, 66% graduate in 5 years or less, and 70% graduate in 6 years or less.

SERVICES: Counseling and information services are available, as is tutoring in some subjects, such as sciences, social sciences, humanities, and math. **Library/Resources:** The library contains 221,084 volumes, 4,897 microform items, 8,826 audio/video tapes/CDs/DVDs, and subscribes to 832 periodicals including electronic. Computerized library services include interlibrary loans, database searching, Internet access, and Wi-Fi capability. Special learning facilities include an art gallery, planetarium, laboratory theater, sleep lab, greenhouse, herbarium, and nuclear magnetic resonance lab. **Physically Challenged Students:** 92% of the campus is accessible. Facilities include wheelchair ramps, elevators, special parking, specially equipped restrooms, special class scheduling, lowered drinking fountains, lowered telephones, and special housing. All academic programs can be moved or adapted as needed to accommodate students. **Special:** NWU offers the Capitol Hill Internship Program, study abroad in 38 countries through the International Student Exchange Program and sister schools in Mexico, Japan, and Estonia. A global studies major, and many other interdisciplinary studies majors and minors. Internships are available in most departments and required in many. Natural sciences majors can complete summer research fellowships at labs, universities, and agencies nationwide and internationally. Other options include pass/fail options, dual majors, credit by exam, and a 3-2 engineering degree in conjunction with Washington and Columbia Universities. There are 25 national honor societies. **Visiting:** There are regularly scheduled orientations for prospective students, consisting of a tour, classroom visits, and meetings with faculty, financial aid and admissions personnel, and current students. There are guides for informal visits, visitors may sit in on classes, and stay overnight. To schedule a visit, contact the Admissions Office. **Campus Safety and Security:** Measures include emergency notification system, security escort services, emergency telephones, lighted pathways/sidewalks, controlled access to dorms/residences, security service, night time foot patrol, and a uniformed police officer during the day.

REQUIREMENTS: The SAT or ACT is required. Freshmen must be graduates of an accredited secondary school or submit the GED. A campus visit is recommended. NWU requires applicants to be in the upper 50% of their class. AP and CLEP credits are accepted. To graduate, students must complete approximately 42 to 48 hours of general education requirements, including 9 hours in First-year Experience, 8 in Developing Foundations courses, 7 in Scientific Inquiry, 6 in U.S. Culture and Society, 3 to 11 in Global Perspectives, 3 in Western Intellectual and Religious Traditions, and 3 in Fine Arts. At least 126 credit hours, including 30 in the major, must be completed with a minimum GPA of 2.0. A senior comprehensive is also needed, consisting of a comprehensive exam in the major discipline, a thesis or independent study, or an internship, presentation, or performance. **Procedure:** Freshmen are admitted in the fall and spring. Entrance exams should be taken no later than December of the senior year. There are early decision and deferred admissions plans. Early decision applications should be filed by November 15; regular applications, by August 15 for fall entry; December 15 for spring entry; and April 15 for summer entry, along with a $20 fee. Notification of early decision is sent December 15; regular decision, January 15. 338 early decision candidates were accepted for the 2016-2017 class. Applications are accepted online. **Transfer Students:** 61 transfer students enrolled in 2015-2016. Applicants must be in good standing at their previous school and have a 2.0 GPA or higher. Grades of C- or better transfer for credit. 30 of 126 credits required for the bachelor's degree must be completed at NWU. **International Students:** There are 33 international students enrolled. The school actively recruits these students. They must take the TOEFL with a minimum score of 525 on the paper-based TOEFL (PBT) or 71 on the Internet-based version (iBT). The SAT or ACT is recommended.

ADMISSIONS: 48% of the current freshmen were in the top fifth of their class; 79% were in the top two fifths. 22 freshmen graduated first in their class. **Admissions Contact:** Gordie Coffin, Director of Admissions. Email: *admissions@nebrwesleyan.edu* Web: *www.nebrwesleyan.edu*

FINANCIAL AID: In 2016-2017, 99% of all full-time freshmen and 96% of continuing full-time students received some form of financial aid. 77% of all full-time freshmen and 71% of continuing full-time students received need-based aid. The average freshman award was $16,769. Need-based scholarships or need-based grants averaged $10,040; need-based self-help aid (loans and jobs) averaged $3,648; and other non-need-based awards and non-need-based scholarships averaged $2,690. 102% of undergraduate students work part-time. Average annual earnings from campus work are $1318. The average financial indebtedness of the 2016 graduate was $24,708. The FAFSA code is 002555. The priority date for freshman financial aid applications for fall entry is rolling.

PERU STATE COLLEGE *(The complete profile is made available exclusively on our website, www.barronspac.com)*

UNION COLLEGE — E-3
www.ucollege.edu

Lincoln, NE 68506	**(402) 486-2504** **(800) 228-4600**
Fax: (402) 486-2566	**Email: enrol@ucollege.edu**
Full-time: 284 men, 380 women	**Faculty:** 53
Part-time: 53 men, 69 women	**Ph.D.s:** 52%
Graduate: 21 men, 49 women	**Student/Faculty:** 15 to 1
Year: semesters, summer session	**Tuition:** $17,430
Room & Board: $5840	**Freshman Class:** n/av
ACT: 22	**CEEB CODE:** 6865
Application Deadline: open	**COMPETITIVE**

Union College, established in 1891, is a private liberal arts institution affiliated with the Seventh-Day Adventist Church. There is 1 undergraduate school. In addition to regional accreditation, Union has baccalaureate program accreditation with CSWE and NCATE. The 26-acre campus is in a suburban area in southeast Lincoln Nebraska. Including any residence halls, there are 13 buildings.

STUDENT LIFE: 86% of undergraduates are from out of state, mostly the Midwest. Students are from 45 states, 21 foreign countries, and Canada. 30% are from public schools. 8% are Hispanic; 72% White; 6% Foreign; 3% African American; 3% Asian American; 1% American Indian/Alaska Native. **Female To Male Ratio:** 1.4:1. The average age of freshmen is 18; all undergraduates, 22. 35% do not continue beyond their first year; 54% remain to graduate. **Housing:** 642 students can be accommodated in college housing, which includes single-sex dorms, on-campus apartments, and married student housing. On-campus housing is guaranteed for the freshman year only, and is available on a first-come, and first-served basis. 52% of students commute. All students may keep cars. Alcohol is not permitted.

FACULTY/CLASSROOMS: 55% of faculty are male; 45% are female. No introductory courses are taught by graduate students. The average class size in an introductory lecture is 21 and in a regular course is 16.

PROGRAMS OF STUDY: Union confers B.A., B.S., B.A.T., B.Ed., B.M., B.S.W. and B.T. degrees. Associate and master's degrees are also awarded. Bachelor's degrees are awarded in BIOLOGICAL SCIENCE (biology/biological science), BUSINESS (accounting, banking and finance, business administration and management, management science, marketing and distribution, and small business management), COMMUNICATIONS AND THE ARTS (communications, English, French, German, graphic design, journalism, literature, music, music performance, public relations, Spanish, and studio art), COMPUTER AND PHYSICAL SCIENCE (chemistry, computer science, mathematics, physics, and science), EDUCATION (art education, business education, computer education, elementary education, English education, mathematics education, music education, physical education, secondary education, and social science education), HEALTH PROFESSIONS (medical laboratory technology, nursing, and physician's assistant), SOCIAL SCIENCE (history, international public service, international studies, pastoral studies, physical fitness/movement, psychology, religion, religious education, social science, social work, and theological studies). Physician's assistant, and physical science are the strongest academically. Nursing and international rescue and relief has the largest enrollment.

ACTIVITIES: There are no fraternities or sororities. There are 18 groups on campus, including art, band, choir, chorale, chorus, computers, drama, ethnic, honors, international, literary magazine, newspaper, orchestra, photography, religious, social, student government, and yearbook. **Sports:** There are 2 intercollegiate sports for men and 3 for women, and 8 intramural sports for men and 8 for women. Facilities include an indoor swimming pool, weight room, tennis courts, and a sandlot volleyball court. **Graduates:** From July 1, 2015 to June 30, 2016, 170 bachelor's degrees were awarded. The most popular majors were nursing (16%), business administration (15%), and elementary education (8%). 32 companies recruited on campus in 2015-2016. In an average class, 29% graduate in 4 years or less and 57% graduate in 6 years or less. Of the 2015 graduating class, 15% were enrolled in graduate school within 6 months of graduation, and 80% were employed.

SERVICES: Counseling and information services are available, as is tutoring in most subjects, and a reader service for the blind, and remedial math, reading, and writing. **Library/Resources:** The library contains 161,728 volumes, 1,938 microform items, 2,066 audio/video tapes/CDs/DVDs, and subscribes to 604 periodicals including electronic. Computerized library services include interlibrary loans, database searching, Internet access, and Wi-Fi capability. Special learning facilities include an art gallery, and a state-run natural arboretum. **Physically Challenged Students:** 75% of the campus is accessible. Facilities include wheelchair ramps, elevators, special parking, specially equipped restrooms, and lowered telephones. **Special:** Special academic programs include study abroad in 7 countries, co-op programs with 9 Adventist institutions abroad, and cross-registration with the University of Nebraska, Nebraska Wesleyan University, and Southeast Community College. Student-designed majors are available through the Personalized Bachelor's Degree Program. There are pass/fail options in electives for upperclassmen with a minimum cumulative GPA of 2.0. Some internships are available. There is a freshman honors program. **Visiting:** There are regularly scheduled orientations for prospective students. There are guides for informal visits, visitors may sit in on classes, and stay overnight. To schedule a visit, contact the Admissions Office Campus Hostess. **Campus Safety and Security:** Measures include 24-hour foot and vehicle patrol, security escort services, emergency telephones and lighted pathways/sidewalks.

REQUIREMENTS: Freshmen with a high school GPA below 2.5 and/or an ACT composite score below the 20th percentile will be enrolled in the freshman development program. Applicants must have graduated from an accredited secondary school with 18 academic credits, including 3 units of English and 1 unit each of math, science, and history. For math and science programs, 2 units of algebra and 1 unit each of geometry and trigonometry are recommended. For majors in nursing, biology, chemistry, physics, or engineering, applicants should complete physics and chemistry courses. The GED is also accepted. An essay and interview are advised, and music students should audition. A GPA of 2.5 is required. AP and CLEP credits are accepted. Students must complete 128 semester hours, with fulfillment of a major, and maintain a minimum GPA of 2.0. There are 56 hours of core classes, including those in art/fine arts, computer science, English, history, math, science, and philosophy/religion. Courses in phy ed are also required. **Procedure:** Freshmen are admitted in the fall and spring. Entrance exams should be taken by fall of the senior year. There is a rolling admissions plan. Application deadlines are open. **Transfer Students:** Transfer students must have a minimum GPA of 2.0. The ACT is required, and high school and college transcripts must be submitted. 30 of 128 credits required for the bachelor's degree must be completed at Union. **International Students:** There are 109 international students enrolled. The school actively recruits these students. They must take the TOEFL with a minimum score of 550 on the paper-based TOEFL (PBT) or 80 on the Internet-based version (iBT). They must also take the ACT, scoring 18.

ADMISSIONS: 32% of the current freshmen were in the top fifth of their class; 69% were in the top two fifths. **Admissions Contact:** Kevin Ericks, Director of Admissions. Email: *ucenrol@ucollege.edu* Web: *www.ucollege.edu*

FINANCIAL AID: In 2016-2017, 99% of all full-time freshmen and 91% of continuing full-time students received some form of financial aid. 97% of all full-time freshmen and 79% of continuing full-time students received need-based aid. 54% of undergraduate students work part-time. Average annual earnings from campus work are $2400. Check with the school for current application deadlines.

UNIVERSITY OF NEBRASKA - KEARNEY *(The complete profile is made available exclusively on our website, www.barronspac.com)*

UNIVERSITY OF NEBRASKA - LINCOLN E-3
www.admissions.unl.edu

Lincoln, NE 68588 (402) 472-2023 (800) 742-8800

Fax: (402) 472-0670 **Email:** admissions@unl.edu

Full-time: 9905 men, 8912 women	**Faculty:** 959; I, -$
Part-time: 796 men, 569 women	**Ph.D.s:** 93%
Graduate: 2410 men, 2668 women	**Student/Faculty:** 18 to 1
Year: semesters, summer session	**Tuition:** $8279 ($22,446)
Room & Board: $10,310	**Freshman Class:** 9724 applied, 7425 accepted, 4628 enrolled
SAT CR/M: 560/580 **ACT:** 25	**CEEB CODE:** 6877
Application Deadline: May 1	**VERY COMPETITIVE**

University of Nebraska–Lincoln, founded in 1869, is a public institution. UNL is an educational institution of international stature, listed by the Carnegie Foundation within the "Research Universities (very high research activity)" category. UNL is a land-grant university and a member of the Association of Public and Land-grant Universities (APLU). Programs are offered through the Colleges of Agricultural Sciences and Natural Resources, Architecture, Arts and Sciences, Business Administration, Education and Human Sciences, Engineering, Fine and Performing Arts, Journalism and Mass Communications, and Law; and the Exploratory and Pre-Professonal Advising Center. There are 8 undergraduate schools and 1 graduate school. In addition to regional accreditation, UN-L has baccalaureate program accreditation with AACSB, ABET, ACCE, ACEJMC, ADA, ASLA, NAAB, NASAD, NASM, TEAC, NASD, NAST, and CAEP. The 622-acre campus is in an urban area 55 miles southwest of Omaha. Including any residence halls, there are 270 buildings.

STUDENT LIFE: 72% of undergraduates are from Nebraska. Others are from 50 states, 106 foreign countries, and Canada. 8% are Foreign; 77% White; 5% Hispanic; 3% African American; 3% two or more races; 2% Asian American; 2% race unknown. **Male To Female Ratio:** 1.1:1. The average age of freshmen is 18; all undergraduates, 20. 18% do not continue beyond their first year; 67% remain to graduate. **Housing:** 9931 students can be accommodated in college housing, which includes single-sex and coed dorms, on-campus apartments, off-campus apartments, and married student housing. In addition, there are honors houses, special-interest houses, fraternity houses, sorority houses, and special floors/sections for first-year students in 26 interest groups; 9 scholar communities. On-campus housing is guaranteed for the freshman year only, and is available on a first-come, and first-served basis. 59% of students commute. All students may keep cars. Alcohol is not permitted.

FACULTY/CLASSROOMS: 69% of faculty are male; 31% are female. 89% teach undergraduates, 89% do research, and 86% do both. No introductory courses are taught by graduate students. The average class size in an introductory lecture is 44; in a laboratory is 23; and in a regular course is 27.

PROGRAMS OF STUDY: UN-L confers B.A., B.S., B.F.A., B.J., B.M., B.M.Ed., and B.L.A. degrees. Master's and doctoral degrees are also awarded. Bachelor's degrees are awarded in AGRICULTURE (agricultural business management, agricultural communications, agricultural economics, agricultural mechanics, agriculture, agronomy, animal science, environmental studies, fish and game management, food technology for companion animals, horticulture, natural resource/environmental economics, natural resource management, plant science, ranch management, range/farm management, turfgrass and landscape management, and wildlife management), BIOLOGICAL SCIENCE (biochemistry, biology/biological science, entomology, forensic science, life science secondary school education, microbiology, and nutrition), BUSINESS (accounting, apparel and accessories marketing, apparel and textiles, banking and finance, business administration and management, business economics, entrepreneurial studies, fashion merchandising, finance, hospitality management services, human resources, insurance and risk management, international business management, investments and securities, management science, marketing management, marketing/retailing/merchandising, organizational leadership and management, and supply chain management), COMMUNICATIONS AND THE ARTS (advertising, apparel design, art history, art, art history and appreciation, broadcasting, classical languages, classics, communications, communication rhetoric/communication, dance, dramatic arts, English, film arts, film, television and digital media, fine arts, Great Plains studies, French, German, information technology, journalism, language arts, Latin, music, public relations, Russian, Spanish, speech/debate/rhetoric, studio art, theatre arts, and theater design), COMPUTER AND PHYSICAL SCIENCE (actuarial science, applied science, astronomy, atmospheric sciences and meteorology, chemistry, chemistry/adolescence education, computer science, earth science/adolescence education, geology, mathematics, physics, physics with astrophysics option, and science), EDUCATION (agricultural education, athletic training, business education, childhood education, computer education, drama education, early childhood education, education, elementary education, English education, environmental education, foreign languages education, golf enterprise management, home economics education, journalism education, marketing and distribution education, mathematics education, music education, physical science secondary school education, science education, secondary education, social science education, and special education), ENGINEERING AND ENVIRONMENTAL DESIGN (agricultural engineering, architectural engineering, architecture, bioengineering, chemical engineering, civil engineering, computer engineering, construction engineering, construction management, electrical/electronics engineering, environmental science, interior design, landscape architecture, landscape architecture/design, and mechanical engineering), HEALTH PROFESSIONS (exercise science, health science, predentistry, premedicine, prepharmacy, speech pathology/audiology, and veterinary science), SOCIAL SCIENCE (anthropology, architectural studies, child care/child and family studies, classical/ancient civilization, culinary arts, dietetics, early childhood studies, economics, ethnic studies, family/consumer studies, food production/management/services, food science, geography, history, interdisciplinary studies, Latin American studies, liberal arts/general studies, medieval studies, parks and recreation management, philosophy, political science/government, prelaw, psychology, religious studies, sociology, textiles and clothing, water resources, and women & gender studies). Agriculture, biochemistry, and biological sciences are the strongest academically. Business administration, psychology, and pre-health have the largest enrollments.

ACTIVITIES: 19% of men belong to 28 national fraternities; 22% of women belong to 19 national sororities. There are 551 groups on campus, including art, band, cheerleading, choir, chorale, chorus, communications, computers, dance, debate, drama, drill team, environmental, ethnic, film, forensics, honors, international, jazz band, LGBT, literary magazine, marching band, musical theater, newspaper, opera, orchestra, pep band, photography, political, professional, radio and TV, religious, social, social service, student government, and symphony. Popular campus events include Homecoming, Big Red Welcome, The Big Event, Dance Marathon, and Football Games. **Sports:** There are 9 intercollegiate sports for men and 13 for women, and 76 intramural sports for men and 76 for women. Facilities include campus recreation center, multi-sport competition center, soccer and tennis complex, bowling alley, rifle range, athletic conditioning and training center, football stadium, indoor and outdoor practice facilities, soccer fields, track, tennis courts, swimming pools, also arena and baseball/softball stadiums shared with city of Lincoln. **Graduates:** From July 1, 2015 to June 30, 2016, 3855 bachelor's degrees were awarded. The most popular majors were business marketing (23%), engineering (10%), and agriculture (9%). 174 companies recruited on campus in 2015-2016. In an average class, 33% graduate in 4 years or less, 62% graduate in 5 years or less, and 67% graduate in 6 years or less. Of the 2015 graduating class, 22% were enrolled in graduate school within 6 months of graduation, and 60% were employed.

SERVICES: There is a reader service for the blind. **Library/Resources:** The 8 libraries contain 3.8 million volumes, 255,917 microform items, and 429,764 audio/video tapes/CDs/DVDs, subscribe to 96,522 periodicals including electronic. Computerized library services include interlibrary loans, database searching, Internet access, and Wi-Fi capability. Special learning facilities include an art gallery, natural history museum, planetarium, radio station, TV station, Nebraska State Museum, International Quilt Study Center and Museum, Sheldon Museum of Art, Diocles Laser/Extreme Light Lab, Krueger Collection of Miniatures, Jackie Gaughan Multicultural Center, Larsen Tractor Test and Power Museum, Great Plains Art Museum, Behlen Observatory, Midwest Roadside Safety Facility. **Physically Challenged Students:** All of the campus is accessible. Facilities include wheelchair ramps, elevators, special parking, specially equipped restrooms, special class scheduling, lowered drinking fountains, lowered telephones, and special housing. Assistance from Services for Students with Disabilities. **Special:** There is cross-registration with many schools and co-op programs are available in the Colleges of Engineering and Agriculture. Through membership in the International Student Exchange Program, the university can place students in more than 90 universities around the world. Internship opportunities abound, as do work-study programs and undergraduate research opportunities. Accelerated degree programs, a Washington semester, B.A.-B.S. degrees, dual majors, combined pre-professional programs, student-designed majors, credit by exam, nondegree study, and pass/fail options are also available. There are 35 national honor societies, Phi Beta Kappa, a freshman honors program, and 39 departmental honors programs. **Visiting:** There are regularly scheduled orientations for prospective students, a campus tour, an information session about academics, scholarships and financial aid, living and dining options, how to get involved, Greek Life and career connections for your future. There are guides for informal visits and visitors may sit in on classes. To schedule a visit, contact the Admissions Office. **Campus Safety and Security:** Measures include 24-hour foot and vehicle patrol, emergency notification system, and self-defense education. There are also shuttle buses, emergency telephones, lighted pathways/sidewalks, and controlled access to dorms/residences.

REQUIREMENTS: The SAT or ACT is recommended. Applicants must be graduates of an accredited secondary school. The GED is accepted. Students must have completed 4 years each of English and math, 3 years of science and social studies, and 2 years of a foreign language. Applicants must have a minimum composite ACT score of 20, or a combined SAT score of 950, or rank in the top 50% of their high school class. UNL requires applicants to be in the upper 50% of their class. AP and CLEP credits are accepted. Important factors in the admissions decision are advanced placement or honors courses, recommendations by school officials, and evidence of special talent. All students matriculating beginning Fall 2009 must complete the general education requirements for the Achievement-Centered Education (ACE) program. The program is based on a set of four institutional objectives and 10 student learning outcomes. Students complete the equivalent of 3 credit hours for each of the ten student learning outcomes. A minimum GPA of 2.0 is required. Each college and major has its own requirements; few graduation requirements apply to all students. **Procedure:** Freshmen are admitted to all sessions. Entrance exams should be taken in April of the junior year. There is a rolling admissions plan. Applications should be filed by May 1 for fall entry; December 1 for spring entry; and May 1 for summer entry, along with a $45 fee. Applications are accepted on-line. **Transfer Students:** 923 transfer students enrolled in 2015-2016. Transfer students must have a 2.0 GPA for both the cumulative average of all post-secondary facilities attended and for the most recent term of attendance. In certain majors, a higher GPA and/or extra course work may be required. **International Students:** There are 1474 international students enrolled. The school actively recruits these students. ACT or SAT may be required for admission into some colleges.

ADMISSIONS: 76% of the 2016-2017 applicants were accepted. The SAT scores for the 2016-2017 freshman class were: Critical Reading-- 25% below 500, 37% between 500 and 599, 25% between 600 and 699, and 13% between 700 and 800. Math-- 23% below 500, 33% between 500 and 599, 30% between 600 and 699, and 14% between 700 and 800. The ACT scores were 3% between 12 and 17, 35% between 18 and 23, 43% between 24 and 29, and 19% above 30. 44% of the current freshmen were in the top fifth of their class; 73% were in the top two fifths. There were 46 National Merit finalists. 346 freshmen graduated first in their class. **Admissions Contact:** Amber Williams, Associate Dean of Enrollment Management. Email: *admissions@unl.edu* Web: *www.admissions.unl.edu*

FINANCIAL AID: In 2016-2017, 85% of all full-time freshmen and 70% of continuing full-time students received some form of financial aid. 54% of all full-time freshmen and 40% of continuing full-time students received need-based aid. 71% of undergraduate students work part-time. Average annual earnings from campus work are $5168. The average financial indebtedness of the 2016 graduate was $20,930. The FAFSA code is 002565. The priority date for freshman financial aid applications for fall entry is April 1.

UNIVERSITY OF NEBRASKA - OMAHA F-3

www.unomaha.edu

Omaha, NE 68182 **(402) 554-2393**

Fax: (402) 554-3472 **Email:** unoadmissions@unomaha.edu

Full-time: 4000 men, 4725 women	**Faculty:** IIA, av$
Part-time: 1300 men, 1500 women	**Ph.D.s:** n/av
Graduate: 1090 men, 1720 women	**Student/Faculty:** n/av
Year: semesters, summer session	**Tuition:** $7204 ($16,918)
Room & Board: $8916	**Freshman Class:** n/av
SAT or ACT: required	**CEEB CODE:** 6420
Application Deadline: August 1	**COMPETITIVE**

University of Nebraska at Omaha, established in 1908, is a public institution and part of the University of Nebraska system. The figures in the above capsule and in this profile are approximate. There are 9 undergraduate schools and 1 graduate school. In addition to regional accreditation, UNOmaha has baccalaureate program accreditation with AACSB, ABET, CSWE, NASAD, NASM, NCATE, CACREP, NASPAA, CAAHEP, CAA, and ACS. The 158-acre campus is in a suburban area within the Omaha city limits. Including any residence halls, there are 46 buildings.

STUDENT LIFE: 93% of undergraduates are from Nebraska. Others are from 34 states, 78 foreign countries, and Canada. 86% are from public schools. 82% are White; 6% African American; 3% Asian American; 3% Hispanic; 2% Foreign; 1% American Indian/Alaska Native. **Female To Male Ratio:** 1.2:1. The average age of freshmen is 18; all undergraduates, 23. 29% do not continue beyond their first year; 39% remain to graduate. **Housing:** 1212 students can be accommodated in college housing, which includes single-sex and coed dorms and on-campus apartments, and honors houses. On-campus housing is available on a first-come and first-served basis. 91% of students commute. All students may keep cars. Alcohol is not permitted.

FACULTY/CLASSROOMS: 59% of faculty are male; 41% are female. 97% teach undergraduates. Graduate students teach 4% of introductory courses. The average class size in an introductory lecture is 38; in a laboratory is 12; and in a regular course is 21.

PROGRAMS OF STUDY: UN-Omaha confers B.A., B.S., B.A.A.H., B.A.S.A., B.A.T.H., B.F.A., B.I.S., B.G.S., B.M., B.S.B.A., B.S.C.N., B.S.C.S., B.S.E.D., B.S.P.A. and B.S.S.W. degrees. Master's and doctoral degrees are also awarded. Bachelor's degrees are awarded in AGRICULTURE (environmental studies), BIOLOGICAL SCIENCE (bioinformatics, biology/biological science, and biotechnology), BUSINESS (accounting, banking and finance, business communications, management information systems, management science, marketing/retailing/merchandising, real estate, and recreation and leisure services), COMMUNICATIONS AND THE ARTS (art, art history and appreciation, broadcasting, communications, creative writing, dramatic arts, English, fine arts, French, German, journalism, music, Spanish, and speech/debate/rhetoric), COMPUTER AND PHYSICAL SCIENCE (chemistry, computer science, geology, information sciences and systems, mathematics, and physics), EDUCATION (elementary education, library science, physical education, and secondary education), ENGINEERING AND ENVIRONMENTAL DESIGN (aviation administration/management and engineering physics), HEALTH PROFESSIONS (community health work and health care administration), SOCIAL SCIENCE (African American studies, criminal justice, economics, geography, history, interdisciplinary studies, international studies, Latin American studies, liberal arts/general studies, philosophy, political science/government, psychology, public administration, social work, sociology, and women's studies). Elementary education, criminal justice, and marketing management have the largest enrollments.

ACTIVITIES: 2% of men belong to 7 national fraternities; 2% of women belong to 9 national sororities. There are 112 groups on campus, including band, cheerleading, chess, choir, chorale, chorus, dance, drama, drill team, ethnic, film, honors, international, jazz band, LGBT, literary magazine, marching band, musical theater, newspaper, opera, orchestra, pep band, political, professional, radio and TV, religious, social, social service, student government, and symphony. Popular campus events include Celebrate UNO, International Week, and Black History Month. **Sports:** There are 5 intercollegiate sports for men and 8 for women, and 16 intramural sports for men and 16 for women. Facilities include a football field, afield house, and a recreation building housing basketball and volleyball courts, weight rooms, and a swimming pool.

SERVICES: Counseling and information services are available, as is tutoring in some subjects, such as math and psychology There is a reader service for the blind. **Library/Resources:** The library contains 700,000 volumes, 2.0 million microform items, 7,000 audio/video tapes/CDs/DVDs, and subscribes to 3,000 periodicals including electronic. Computerized library services include interlibrary loans, database searching, and Internet access. Special learning facilities include an art gallery, radio station, and TV station. **Physically Challenged Students:** 99% of the campus is accessible. Facilities include wheelchair ramps, elevators, special parking, specially equipped restrooms, special class scheduling, lowered drinking fountains, and lowered telephones. **Special:** UNOmaha offers internships for business students, cooperative programs, and credit by examination. Students may study abroad in various European countries. There are 15 national honor societies, a freshman honors program, and 10 departmental honors programs. **Visiting:** There are regularly scheduled orientations for prospective students. There are guides for informal visits and visitors may sit in on classes. To schedule a visit, contact the Office of Orientation at (402) 554-2677. **Campus Safety and Security:** Measures include 24-hour foot and vehicle patrol, self-defense education, and security escort services. There are also shuttle buses, emergency telephones, and lighted pathways/sidewalks.

REQUIREMENTS: The SAT or ACT is required. Students must be graduates of an accredited secondary school. The GED is accepted. Students must have completed 4 units of English and 2 each of math, social sciences, and sciences. UN-Omaha requires applicants to be in the upper 50% of their class. AP and CLEP credits are accepted. Important factors in the admissions decision are recommendations by school officials, evidence of special talent, and personality/intangible qualities. To graduate, students must complete 30 hours of distribution requirements in natural and physical sciences, humanities and fine arts, and social and behavioral sciences; 15 hours in fundamental academic skills in English writing, math, and public speaking; and 6 hours in cultural diversity. **Procedure:** Freshmen are admitted in the fall, spring, and summer. Entrance exams should be taken by the senior year. There is a rolling admissions plan. Applications should be filed by August 1 for fall entry; December 1 for spring entry; and June 1 for summer entry, along with a $45 fee. Applications are accepted online. **Transfer Students:** Applicants must present evidence of good standing at the last institution they attended. Grades of C or better transfer for credit. A minimum GPA of 2.0 is required. 30 of 125 credits required for the bachelor's degree must be completed at UNOmaha. **International Students:** The school actively recruits these students. They must take the TOEFL.

ADMISSIONS: 27 freshmen graduated first in their class. **Admissions Contact:** Maureen Pope, Undergrad Associate Director of Operations. Email: *unoadmissions@unomaha.edu* Web: *www.unomaha.edu*

FINANCIAL AID: The FAFSA code is 002554. Check with the school for current application deadlines.

WAYNE STATE COLLEGE E-2

www.wsc.edu

Wayne, NE 68787 **(402) 375-7000** **(866) 972-2287**

Fax: (402) 375-7204 **Email:** admissions@wsc.edu

Full-time: 1173 men, 1562 women	**Faculty:** IIA, --$
Part-time: 104 men, 152 women	**Ph.D.s:** 81%
Graduate: 231 men, 284 women	**Student/Faculty:** 20 to 1
Year: semesters, summer session	**Tuition:** $6042 ($10,634)
Room & Board: $6760	**Freshman Class:** 2070 applied, 2070 accepted, 691 enrolled
ACT: 21	**CEEB CODE:** 6469
Application Deadline: open	**COMPETITIVE**

Wayne State College, founded in 1910, is a public liberal arts institution. Figures in the above capsule and in this profile are approximate. Tuition cost is based on residency location. There are 4 undergraduate schools and 2 graduate schools. In addition to regional accreditation, Wayne State has baccalaureate program accreditation with NASAD, NASM, NCATE, and IACBE. The 128-acre campus is in a rural area 45 miles southwest of Sioux City. Including any residence halls, there are 25 buildings.

STUDENT LIFE: 87% of undergraduates are from Nebraska. Others are from 27 states, 18 foreign countries, and Canada. 79% are White; 7%

Hispanic; 6% race unknown; 3% African American; 2% two or more races; 1% Asian American; 1% American Indian/Alaska Native; 1% Foreign. **Female To Male Ratio:** 1.3:1. The average age of freshmen is 18; all undergraduates, 21. 38% do not continue beyond their first year; 53% remain to graduate. **Housing:** 1571 students can be accommodated in college housing, which includes coed dorms. On-campus housing is guaranteed for the freshman year only, and is available on a first-come, first-served basis. 54% of students commute. Alcohol is not permitted. All students may keep cars. Alcohol is not permitted.

FACULTY/CLASSROOMS: 55% of faculty are male; 45% are female. No introductory courses are taught by graduate students.

PROGRAMS OF STUDY: Wayne State confers B.A. and B.S. degrees. Master's degrees are also awarded. Bachelor's degrees are awarded in BIOLOGICAL SCIENCE (biology/biological science and life science), BUSINESS (business administration and management and sports management), COMMUNICATIONS AND THE ARTS (art, communications, dramatic arts, English, graphic design, modern language, music, Spanish, and speech/debate/rhetoric), COMPUTER AND PHYSICAL SCIENCE (chemistry, computer science, and mathematics), EDUCATION (elementary education, health education, home economics education, industrial arts education, middle school education, music education, science education, and special education), ENGINEERING AND ENVIRONMENTAL DESIGN (technological management), HEALTH PROFESSIONS (exercise science), SOCIAL SCIENCE (counseling/psychology, criminal justice, early childhood studies, family/consumer studies, geography, history, interdisciplinary studies, political science/government, psychology, social science, and sociology). Business, elementary education, and criminal justice have the largest enrollments.

ACTIVITIES: There are 100 groups on campus, including art, band, cheerleading, chess, choir, chorale, chorus, computers, dance, drama, drill team, ethnic, forensics, honors, international, jazz band, LGBT, marching band, musical theater, newspaper, orchestra, pep band, political, professional, radio and TV, religious, social, student government, and symphony. Popular campus events include International Dinner, Elizabethan Dinners and Greek Olympics. **Sports:** There are 6 intercollegiate sports for men and 7 for women, and 37 intramural sports for men and 37 for women. Facilities include tennis courts, softball, flag football, soccer fields, gym, a recreation center, which has an indoor track, weight room, pool, handball, volleyball, basketball, and tennis courts, a football stadium, an outdoor track, and a baseball/softball complex. **Graduates:** From July 1, 2015 to June 30, 2016, 522 bachelor's degrees were awarded. The most popular majors were education (28%), business (15%), and psychology (9%). In an average class, 27% graduate in 4 years or less, 48% graduate in 5 years or less, and 53% graduate in 6 years or less.

SERVICES: Counseling and information services are available, as is tutoring in most subjects. There is a reader service for the blind. **Library/Resources:** The library contains 348,951 volumes, 620,128 microform items, and 19,820 audio/video tapes/CDs/DVDs, and subscribes to 45,026 periodicals including electronic. Computerized library services include interlibrary loans, database searching, Internet access, and Wi-Fi capability. Special learning facilities include an art gallery, natural history museum, planetarium, radio station, TV station, and arboretum. **Physically Challenged Students:** Facilities include wheelchair ramps, elevators, special parking, specially equipped restrooms, special class scheduling, lowered drinking fountains, lowered telephones, special housing, a pool equipped with special steps. **Special:** Pass/fail options, internships, study abroad, credit by exam, any combination of dual majors, a B.A.-B.S. degree in certain instances, and some student-designed majors. There is also a Regional Health Opportunities Program. There is a freshman honors program and 14 departmental honors programs. **Visiting:** There are regularly scheduled orientations for prospective students. There are guides for informal visits, visitors may sit in on classes, and stay overnight. To schedule a visit, contact the Admissions Office. **Campus Safety and Security:** Measures include 24-hour foot and vehicle patrol, emergency notification system, security escort services, emergency telephones and lighted pathways/sidewalks.

REQUIREMENTS: Applicants must be graduates of an accredited secondary school. The GED is accepted. Entering freshmen should have completed 18 credits, with a recommended 4 units of English, 3 each of math and social studies, and 2 each of science, foreign language, computer science, and visual/performing arts. AP and CLEP credits are accepted. Students must complete a specified 44-credit general education curriculum. A minimum of 120 credit hours is required for graduation, of which at least 40 must be in upper-level courses. Students must maintain at least a 2.0 overall GPA for nonteaching majors and a 2.5 overall GPA for teaching majors. **Procedure:** Freshmen are admitted to all sessions. Entrance exams should be taken in the spring of the junior year or fall of the senior year. There are deferred admissions and rolling admissions plans. Application deadlines are open. Applications are accepted online. **Transfer Students:** 184 transfer students enrolled in 2015-2016. Transfer students must have a minimum GPA of 2.0. Grades of C and above transfer for credit. 30 of 120 credits required for the bachelor's degree must be completed at Wayne State. **International Students:** They must take the TOEFL with a minimum score of 550 on the paper-based TOEFL (PBT).

ADMISSIONS: 100% of the 2016-2017 applicants were accepted. The ACT scores were 45% below 12, 26% between 12 and 17, 15% between 18 and 23, 8% between 24 and 29, and 6% above 30. **Admissions Contact:** Kevin Halle, Director of Admissions. Email: *admissions@wsc.edu* Web: *www.wsc.edu*

FINANCIAL AID: The FAFSA code is 002566. The priority date for freshman financial aid applications for fall entry is April 1.

YORK COLLEGE — E-3

www.york.edu

York, NE 68467	**(402) 363-5627** **(800) 950-9675**
Fax: (402) 363-5623	**Email: enroll@york.edu**
Full-time: 180 men, 190 women	**Faculty:** n/av
Part-time: 25 men, 20 women	**Ph.D.s:** n/av
Graduate: none	**Student/Faculty:** n/av
Year: semesters, summer session	**Tuition:** $17,700
Room & Board: $6600	**Freshman Class:** n/av
ACT: recommended	**CEEB CODE:** 6984
Application Deadline: August 31	**COMPETITIVE**

York College, founded in 1890, is an independent undergraduate college affiliated with the Churches of Christ. The figures in the above capsule and in this profile are approximate. There is 1 undergraduate school. In addition to regional accreditation, York has baccalaureate program accreditation with NCATE. The 40-acre campus is in a small town 45 miles west of Lincoln. Including any residence halls, there are 18 buildings.

STUDENT LIFE: 67% of undergraduates are from out of state, mostly the Midwest. Students are from 30 states, 5 foreign countries, and Canada. 90% are from public schools. 87% are White; 5% African American; 4% Foreign; 3% Hispanic; 1% Asian American. 22% are Protestant. **Female To Male Ratio:** 1.0:1. The average age of freshmen is 18; all undergraduates, 21. 15% do not continue beyond their first year; 50% remain to graduate. **Housing:** 472 students can be accommodated in college housing, which includes single-sex dorms and on-campus apartments. On-campus housing is guaranteed for all 4 years. 72% of students live on campus; of those, 85% remain on campus on weekends. All students may keep cars. Alcohol is not permitted.

FACULTY/CLASSROOMS: 67% of faculty are male; 33% are female. All teach undergraduates. No introductory courses are taught by graduate students. The average class size in an introductory lecture is 30; in a laboratory is 20; and in a regular course is 25.

PROGRAMS OF STUDY: York confers B.A., B.S., B.B.A. and B.Mus. degrees. Associate and master's degrees are also awarded. Bachelor's degrees are awarded in BIOLOGICAL SCIENCE (biology/biological science), BUSINESS (accounting, business administration and management, and human resources), COMMUNICATIONS AND THE ARTS (communications, English, music performance, and voice), COMPUTER AND PHYSICAL SCIENCE (natural sciences), EDUCATION (drama education, education, elementary education, English education, middle school education, music education, psychology education, science education, secondary education, social science education, and special education), SOCIAL SCIENCE (biblical studies, biopsychology, history, human services, liberal arts/general studies, psychology, and youth ministry). Education, natural science, and psychology are the strongest academically. Education, and business have the largest enrollments.

ACTIVITIES: 57% of men belong to 4 local fraternities; 62% of women belong to 4 local sororities. There are 25 groups on campus, including art, choir, chorus, computers, drama, honors, international, literary magazine, musical theater, newspaper, photography, political, professional, religious, social, social service, student government, and yearbook. Popular campus events include High School Days, Fall Musical and an All School Banquet. **Sports:** There are 4 intercollegiate sports for men and 3 for women, and 6 intramural sports for men and 6 for women. Facilities include a gym, basketball and volleyball courts, soccer, baseball, and intramural fields, a weight room and an indoor track. **Graduates:** From July 1, 2015 to June 30, 2016, 57 bachelor's degrees were awarded. The most popular majors were education (29%), business (26%), and psychology (9%). 7 companies recruited on campus in 2015-2016. In an average class, 8% graduate in 3 years or less, 35% graduate in 4 years or less, 49% graduate in 5 years or less, and 50% graduate in 6 years or less. Of the 2015 graduating class, 6% were enrolled in graduate school within 6 months of graduation, and 90% were employed.

SERVICES: Counseling and information services are available, as is tutoring in most subjects, and remedial math, reading, and writing. A peer tutoring program is available for students. **Library/Resources:** The library contains 126,086 volumes, 21,578 microform items, and 7,017 audio/video tapes/CDs/DVDs, and subscribes to 301 periodicals including electronic. Computerized library services include interlibrary loans and database searching. **Physically Challenged Students:** 50% of the campus is accessible. Facilities include wheelchair ramps, elevators, special parking, specially equipped restrooms, lowered drinking fountains, lowered telephones, and special housing. **Special:** Summer internships are required in biblical studies,and psychology, and work-study is available on campus. Honors and independent study are available as adjuncts to a normal course load. There are 2 national honor societies, a freshman honors program, and 2 departmental honors programs. **Visiting:** There are regularly scheduled orientations for prospective students, including a campus tour visit with financial aid and admissions representatives, and a visit with the registrar and possibly with a faculty member within the student's major area of concentration. There are guides for informal visits, visitors may sit in on classes, and stay overnight. **Campus Safety and Security:** Measures include self-defense education, emergency telephones, lighted pathways/sidewalks, and an evening foot patrol.

REQUIREMENTS: For regular acceptance, students must meet 2 of the following 3 requirements: a 2.0 cumulative GPA; graduate in the top half of their graduating class; satisfactory scores on the ACT or SAT. York requires applicants to be in the upper 50% of their class. AP and CLEP credits are accepted. Important factors in the admissions decision are ability to finance college education, personality/intangible qualities, and evidence of special talent. To graduate, students must complete a minimum of 128 credits with a 2.0 GPA. Course work includes a general education requirement of 18 hours of humanities, 16 of Bible, 12 of social science, 6 of science, and 3 of math or computer science. The major requirements vary according to concentration, typically, 40 hours or more are required. Some majors and minors require a 2.5 GPA. **Procedure:** Freshmen are admitted to all sessions. Entrance exams should be taken during March, but before April. There is a rolling admissions plan. Applications should be filed by August 31 for fall entry, along with a $20 fee. **Transfer Students:** 48 transfer students enrolled in 2015-2016. Transfer students with less than 24 semester hours must have a high school transcript, ACT scores, college transcripts, and 1 reference. Transfers with 24 to 60 hours must have proof of high school graduation (diploma or final), a college transcript, and 1 reference. Transfers with more than 60 hours must have a college transcript and 1 reference letter. 30 of 128 credits required for the bachelor's degree must be completed at York. **International Students:** There are 6 international students enrolled. They must take the TOEFL, as well as the SAT or ACT.

ADMISSIONS: 7 freshmen graduated first in their class. **Admissions Contact:** Morgan DeBoer, Admissions Recruiter. Email: *mdeboer@york.edu* Web: *www.york.edu*

FINANCIAL AID: In 2016-2017, 99% of all full-time freshmen and continuing full-time students received some form of financial aid. 98% of all full-time freshmen and 99% of continuing full-time students received need-based aid. The average freshman award was $14,765. Need-based scholarships or need-based grants averaged $7,182; need-based self-help aid (loans and jobs) averaged $2,762; non-need-based athletic scholarships averaged $1,835; and other non-need-based awards and non-need-based scholarships averaged $2,986. 72% of undergraduate students work part-time. Average annual earnings from campus work are $825. The average financial indebtedness of the 2016 graduate was $19,634. Check with the school for current application deadlines.

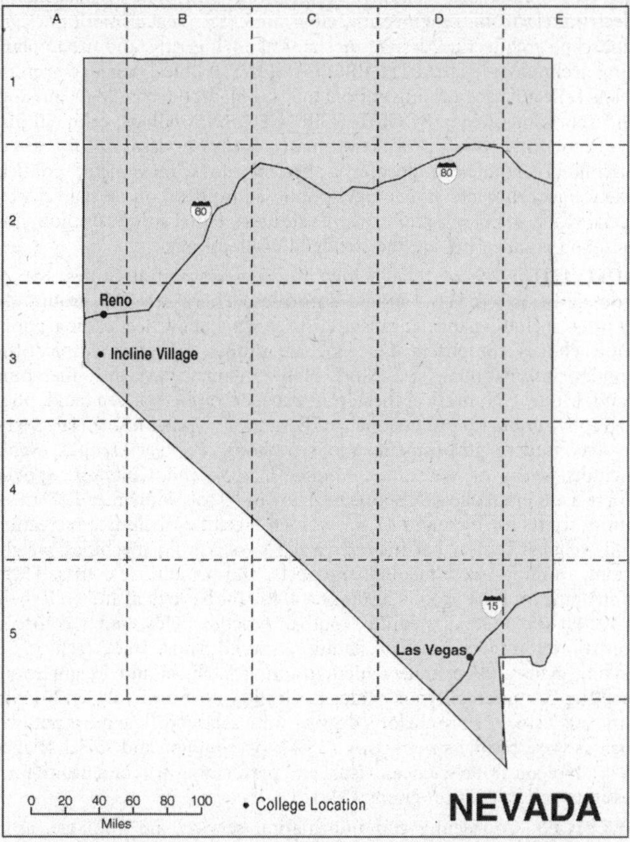

SIERRA NEVADA COLLEGE A-3

www.sierranevada.edu

Incline Village, NV 89451	**(775) 831-1314** **(866) 412-4636**
Fax: (775) 831-6223	**Email: admissions@sierranevada.edu**
Full-time: 301 men, 185 women	**Faculty:** 43
Part-time: 4 men, 8 women	**Ph.D.s:** n/av
Graduate: 156 men, 381 women	**Student/Faculty:** 9 to 1
Year: semesters, summer session	**Tuition:** $31,150
Room & Board: $12,332	**Freshman Class:** 554 applied, 364 accepted, 90 enrolled
ACT: 23	**CEEB CODE:** 4757
Application Deadline: August 22	**COMPETITIVE**

Sierra Nevada College, founded in 1969, is a private institution offering programs in liberal arts, fine arts, business, hotel resort management, ski business management, environmental science, and teacher education. The figures in the above capsule and in this profile are approximate. There are 7 undergraduate schools. In addition to regional accreditation, SNC has baccalaureate program accreditation with NWCCU. The 17-acre campus is in a rural area 25 miles west of Reno. Including any residence halls, there are 7 buildings.

STUDENT LIFE: 80% of undergraduates are from out of state, mostly the West. Students are from 35 states, 30 foreign countries, and Canada. 60% are from public schools. 93% are White; 3% African American; 2% Foreign. **Female To Male Ratio:** 1.2:1. The average age of freshmen is 19; all undergraduates, 22. 14% do not continue beyond their first year; 62% remain to graduate. **Housing:** 120 students can be accommodated in college housing, which includes coed dorms and on-campus apartments. On-campus housing is guaranteed for all 4 years. 60% of students commute. All students may keep cars. Alcohol is not permitted.

FACULTY/CLASSROOMS: 60% of faculty are male; 40% are female. All teach undergraduates, 15% do research, and 25% do both. No introductory courses are taught by graduate students. The average class size in an introductory lecture is 12; in a laboratory is 8; and in a regular course is 12.

PROGRAMS OF STUDY: SNC confers B.A., B.S. and B.F.A. degrees. Bachelor's degrees are awarded in BUSINESS (business administration and management and recreational facilities management), COMMUNICATIONS AND THE ARTS (fine arts and music), COMPUTER AND PHYSICAL SCIENCE (science), ENGINEERING AND ENVIRONMENTAL DESIGN (environmental science), SOCIAL SCIENCE (humanities). Environmental and science/ecology is the strongest academically. Business administration has the largest enrollment.

ACTIVITIES: There are no fraternities or sororities. Groups on campus include art, choir, chorale, chorus, computers, dance, environmental, ethnic, honors, international, newspaper, political, professional, social, social service, and student government. Popular campus events include Bohemia Night, Nevada Day, and Game Show Take-off. **Sports:** There are 2 intercollegiate sports for men and 2 for women, and 2 intramural sports for men and 2 for women. Facilities include hiking and mountain biking trails, volleyball and softball areas, community tennis courts and golf courses. **Graduates:** From July 1, 2015 to June 30, 2016, 127 bachelor's degrees were awarded. The most popular majors were business/marketing, visual/performing arts, and biological/life sciences. In an average class, 40% graduate in 6 years or less.

SERVICES: Counseling and information services are available, as is tutoring in every subject, and remedial math, reading, and writing. **Library/Resources:** The library contains 20,000 volumes, 10,000 microform items, and subscribes to 100 periodicals including electronic. Computerized library services include interlibrary loans, database searching, Internet access, and Wi-Fi capability. Special learning facilities include an art gallery, an observatory, and a recording studio. **Physically Challenged Students:** All of the campus is accessible. Facilities include wheelchair ramps, elevators, special parking, specially equipped restrooms, special class scheduling, and special housing. **Special:** Business administration concentrations are offered in ski business and resort management and in hotel, restaurant, and resort management. Student-designed majors, work-study programs, internships, credit for life experiences and volunteer community work, and nondegree study are available. **Visiting:** There are regularly scheduled orientations for prospective students, including a student-led campus tour that is available by appointment and 1-night overnight stays. There are guides for informal visits, visitors may sit in on classes, and stay overnight. To schedule a visit, contact the Office of Admissions. **Campus Safety and Security:** Measures include 24-hour foot and vehicle patrol, emergency notification system, security escort services, lighted pathways/sidewalks, and controlled access to dorms/residences.

REQUIREMENTS: The ACT is required, as is the ACT Optional Writing test is also required. All applicants are reviewed individually. Official transcripts, an essay, and 2 letters of recommendation are required, and an interview is recommended. Recommended by Carnegie units 13 academic units such as 4 in English, 3 units in math, 2 units each in science with lab, and foreign language. AP and CLEP credits are accepted. Important factors in the admissions decision are advanced placement or honors courses, recommendations by school officials, and personality/intangible qualities. All students must complete at least 120 semester hours, including 40 in upper-division courses with a minimum GPA of 2.0. Students also must pass the writing proficiency exam and meet distribution requirements in 4 interdisciplinary themes: symbols, relationships with nature and humans, memberships in groups and institutions, and ethics, values, and beliefs. **Procedure:** Freshmen are admitted to all sessions. Entrance exams should be taken in the spring of junior year or fall of senior year. There are early decision, early admissions, deferred admissions, and rolling admissions plans. Applications should be filed by August 22 for fall entry. Notifications are sent February 15. Applications are accepted online. **Transfer Students:** 67 transfer students enrolled in 2015-2016. The college accepts applications from students who have completed course work at an accredited post-secondary institution. If fewer than 15 credits have been earned, the high school transcript and standardized test scores are also required. Transfer applicants are expected to be in good academic standing at their college or university. Students may enroll in the fall, spring and summer. 68 of 120 credits required for the bachelor's degree must be completed at SNC. **International Students:** The school actively recruits these students. They must take the TOEFL, or take any other English proficiency test.

ADMISSIONS: 66% of the 2016-2017 applicants were accepted. The ACT scores were 21% between 12 and 17, 42% between 18 and 23, 34% between 24 and 29, and 3% above 30. **Admissions Contact:** Jon Cherry,

Interim Director/Undergradute Admission. Email: *admissions@sierranevada.edu* Web: *www.sierranevada.edu*

FINANCIAL AID: In 2016-2017, 80% of all full-time freshmen and continuing full-time students received some form of financial aid. 80% of all full-time freshmen and continuing full-time students received need-based aid. The average freshman award was $31,140. Need-based scholarships or need-based grants averaged $26,237; need-based self-help aid (loans and jobs) averaged $4,928; non-need-based athletic scholarships averaged $13,950; other non-need-based awards and non-need-based scholarships averaged $15,639; and $3,299 from other forms of aid. 37% of undergraduate students work part-time. The college's own financial statement is required. The FAFSA code is 009192. The priority date for freshman financial aid applications for fall entry is August.

UNIVERSITY OF NEVADA, LAS VEGAS D-5

www.unlv.edu

Las Vegas, NV 89154	(702) 774-UNLV
Fax: (702) 774-8008	**Email:** admissions@unlv.edu
Full-time: 7616 men, 9724 women	**Faculty:** 676; I, -$
Part-time: 2785 men, 3211 women	**Ph.D.s:** 95%
Graduate: 1851 men, 2331 women	**Student/Faculty:** 24 to 1
Year: semesters, summer session	**Tuition:** $6823 ($20,732)
Room & Board: $10,730	**Freshman Class:** 7408 applied, 6437 accepted, 3865 enrolled
SAT CR/M/W: 495/500/475 **ACT:** 22	**CEEB CODE:** 4861
Application Deadline: February 1	**COMPETITIVE**

University of Nevada, Las Vegas, established in 1957, is a state-supported institution offering undergraduate and graduate programs in business, education, health science, engineering, science and math, hotel administration, fine arts, liberal arts, urban affairs, and honors. Figures in the above capsule and in this profile are approximate. There are 10 undergraduate schools and 1 graduate school. In addition to regional accreditation, UNLV has baccalaureate program accreditation with AACSB, ABET, ACCE, ADA, APTA, ASLA, CSAB, CSWE, FIDER, NAAB, NASAD, NASM, NCATE, and NLN. The 353-acre campus is in an urban area on the southern tip of Nevada, just east of the Las Vegas strip. Including any residence halls, there are 90 buildings.

STUDENT LIFE: 87% of undergraduates are from Nevada. Others are from 50 states, 57 foreign countries, and Canada. 9% are African American; 46% White; 4% Foreign; 18% Asian American; 14% Hispanic; 1% American Indian/Alaska Native. **Female To Male Ratio:** 1.2:1. The average age of freshmen is 18; all undergraduates, 21. 26% do not continue beyond their first year; 39% remain to graduate. **Housing:** 2500 students can be accommodated in college housing, which includes coed dorms, are honors houses, special-interest houses, substance-free, study-intensive recess housing, major-specific houses, a global house, and a leadership focus house. On-campus housing is guaranteed for the freshman year only, is available on a first-come, and first-served basis. Priority is given to out-of-town students. 93% of students commute. All students may keep cars.

FACULTY/CLASSROOMS: 65% of faculty are male; 35% are female. 95% teach undergraduates, and 5% do research. No introductory courses are taught by graduate students. The average class size in an introductory lecture is 21 and in a laboratory is 20.

PROGRAMS OF STUDY: UNLV confers B.A., B.S. and B.F.A. degrees. Master's and doctoral degrees are also awarded. Bachelor's degrees are awarded in BIOLOGICAL SCIENCE (biology/biological science), BUSINESS (accounting, banking and finance, hotel/motel and restaurant management, human resources, international business management, management information systems, management science, marketing/retailing/merchandising, real estate, and recreational facilities management), COMMUNICATIONS AND THE ARTS (art history and appreciation, communications, dance, dramatic arts, English, film arts, fine arts, French, German, music, romance languages and literature, and Spanish), COMPUTER AND PHYSICAL SCIENCE (applied physics, chemistry, computer science, earth science, geology, mathematics, physics, and radiological technology), EDUCATION (elementary education, health education, physical education, recreation education, secondary education, special education, and trade and industrial education), ENGINEERING AND ENVIRONMENTAL DESIGN (architectural engineering, civil engineering, computer engineering, construction management, electrical/electronics engineering, environmental science, interior design, landscape architecture/design, mechanical engineering, and urban planning technology), HEALTH PROFESSIONS (clinical science, exercise science, health care administration, nuclear medical technology, nursing, and sports medicine), SOCIAL SCIENCE (anthropology, criminal justice, economics, food production/management/services, history, interdisciplinary studies, philosophy, physical fitness/movement, political science/government, psychology, public administration, social science, social work, sociology, and women's studies). Hotel administration, fine arts, and engineering are the strongest academically.

ACTIVITIES: 8% of men belong to 18 national fraternities; 8% of women belong to 11 national sororities. There are 160 groups on campus, including and campus ministries, art, band, cheerleading, chess, choir, chorus, computers, dance, debate, drama, drill team, ethnic, film, honors, international, jazz band, LGBT, literary magazine, marching band, Model UN, musical theater, newspaper, orchestra, pep band, photography, political, professional, radio and TV, religious, social, social service, student government, and symphony. Popular campus events include Weeks of Welcome, Premier UNLV, and Unityfest. **Sports:** There are 8 intercollegiate sports for men and 9 for women, and 47 intramural sports for men and 47 for women. Facilities include a recreation and wellness center that includes a lap pool, cardio machines, weight room, running track, racquetball courts, and 5 multiuse courts. There is an arena for basketball, a 3,000-seat arena for basketball and volleyball, a 40,000-seat football stadium, football practice fields, tennis courts, a softball stadium, a baseball stadium, soccer fields, track facilities, a boxing gym, and separate athletic/training facilities and weight room facilities for intercollegiate athletes. **Graduates:** From July 1, 2015 to June 30, 2016, 3726 bachelor's degrees were awarded. The most popular majors were business/marketing (35%), psychology, and social science (7%), biological/life sciences, visual and performing arts, and health professions and related programs (5%).

SERVICES: Counseling and information services are available, as is tutoring in every subject. There is a reader service for the blind, and remedial math, reading, and writing. **Library/Resources:** The 6 libraries contain 950,600 volumes, 1.8 million microform items, 13,500 audio/video tapes/CDs/DVDs, and subscribe to 1,759 periodicals including electronic. Computerized library services include interlibrary loans, database searching, Internet access, and Wi-Fi capability. Special learning facilities include an art gallery, natural history museum, and radio station. **Physically Challenged Students:** All of the campus is accessible. Facilities include wheelchair ramps, elevators, special parking, specially equipped restrooms, special class scheduling, lowered drinking fountains, lowered telephones, and special housing. **Special:** Opportunities are provided for internships, an accelerated degree program, B.A.-B.S. degrees, dual majors, credit by examination, credit for military service, nondegree study, pass/fail options, and study abroad in 25 countries. There are 16 national honor societies, including Phi Beta Kappa, a freshman honors program, and 11 departmental honors programs. **Visiting:** There are regularly scheduled orientations for prospective students, consisting of a complete introduction to the campus, student services, and parent orientation. There are guides for informal visits and visitors may sit in on classes. To schedule a visit, contact the Office of Admissions. **Campus Safety and Security:** Measures include 24-hour foot and vehicle patrol, emergency notification system, self-defense education, and security escort services. There are shuttle buses, emergency telephones, and lighted pathways/sidewalks.

REQUIREMENTS: Graduation from an accredited secondary school is required. Applicants must also meet the academic core requirements, which include 4 credits in English and 3 each in history, social studies, math (must include algebra 1 and algebra 2), and science, of these units 2 must be lab. A GPA of 3.0 is required. AP and CLEP credits are accepted. Important factors in the admissions decision are recommendations by school officials, advanced placement or honors courses, and geographical diversity. Students must complete 124 credits, with 45 in the major, and maintain a minimum GPA of 2.0. All students must meet core requirements that include courses in English, logic and math, the Constitution, social science, fine arts, science, humanities, and international and multicultural diversity. **Procedure:** Freshmen are admitted to all sessions. Entrance exams should be taken by February 1. There is a rolling admissions plan. Applications should be filed by February 1 for fall entry; October 1 for spring entry; and February 1 for summer entry, along with a $60 fee. Applications are accepted on-line. **Transfer Stu-**

dents: 2378 transfer students enrolled in 2015-2016. Applicants should present a minimum GPA of 2.5 and a minimum of 24 credits for transfer. The SAT or the ACT is recommended. Applicants must be in good academic standing and eligible to return to the educational institution last attended. 30 of 124 credits required for the bachelor's degree must be completed at UNLV. **International Students:** They must take the TOEFL with a minimum score of 500 on the paper-based TOEFL (PBT) or 61 on the Internet-based version (iBT) or take the MELAB, or take the IELTS, or prove English proficiency by other means.

ADMISSIONS: 87% of the 2016-2017 applicants were accepted. The SAT scores for the 2016-2017 freshman class were: Critical Reading-- 49% below 500, 39% between 500 and 599, 11% between 600 and 699, and 1% between 700 and 800. Math-- 48% below 500, 37% between 500 and 599, 13% between 600 and 699, and 2% between 700 and 800. Writing-- 62% below 500, 30% between 500 and 599, 7% between 600 and 699, and 1% between 700 and 800. 51% of the current freshmen were in the top fifth of their class; 83% were in the top two fifths. There were 3 National Merit finalists. **Admissions Contact:** Wendell Staszkow, Assistant Director of Admissions. Email: *admissions@unlv.edu* Web: *www.unlv.edu*

FINANCIAL AID: In 2016-2017, 66% of all full-time freshmen and 70% of continuing full-time students received some form of financial aid. The average freshman award was $11,374. Need-based scholarships or need-based grants averaged $5,959; need-based self-help aid (loans and jobs) averaged $3,328; non-need-based athletic scholarships averaged $18,533; other non-need-based awards and non-need-based scholarships averaged $3,254; and $3,647 from other forms of aid. 75% of undergraduate students work part-time. UNLV is a member of CSS. The CCS/Profile, FAFSA, FFS, or SFS and the college's own financial statement, and a singlefile form are required. The FAFSA code is 002569. The priority date for freshman financial aid applications for fall entry is February 1.

UNIVERSITY OF NEVADA/RENO — A-3

www.unr.edu

Reno, NV 89557 — **(775) 784-1110**

Fax: (775) 784-4283	**Email:** asknevada@unr.edu
Full-time: 7215 men, 8193 women	**Faculty:** I, -$
Part-time: 1355 men, 1428 women	**Ph.D.s:** 84%
Graduate: 1445 men, 1727 women	**Student/Faculty:** 21 to 1
Year: semesters, summer session	**Tuition:** $7142 ($21,052)
Room & Board: $10,868	**Freshman Class:** 9646 applied, 7988 accepted, 3353 enrolled
SAT CR/M/W: 540/550/520 **ACT:** 24	**CEEB CODE:** 4844
Application Deadline: February 1	**COMPETITIVE**

University of Nevada/Reno, established in 1874, is a land-grant institution and part of the Nevada System of Higher Education. It offers programs in agriculture, arts and science, business administration, education, engineering, human and community sciences, journalism, medicine, and mining, as well as interdisciplinary studies. There are 10 undergraduate schools and 1 graduate school. In addition to regional accreditation, Nevada has baccalaureate program accreditation with AACSB, ABET, ACEJMC, AHEA, CSWE, NASM, NCATE, and NLN. The 268-acre campus is in an urban area 200 miles east of San Francisco, 35 miles from Lake Tahoe. Including any residence halls, there are 128 buildings.

STUDENT LIFE: 70% of undergraduates are from Nevada. Others are from 46 states, 65 foreign countries, and Canada. 59% are White; 19% Hispanic; 7% Asian American; 6% two or more races; 3% African American; 3% Foreign; 2% race unknown; 1% American Indian/Alaska Native. **Female To Male Ratio:** 1.1:1. The average age of freshmen is 18; all undergraduates, 22. 20% do not continue beyond their first year; 54% remain to graduate. **Housing:** 2611 students can be accommodated in college housing, which includes single-sex and coed dorms, on-campus apartments, off-campus apartments, married student housing, honors houses, special-interest houses, fraternity houses, sorority houses, and living learning center. On-campus housing is available on a first-come and first-served basis. 78% of students commute. Alcohol is not permitted. All students may keep cars.

FACULTY/CLASSROOMS: 53% of faculty are male; 47% are female. All teach undergraduates and do research. Graduate students teach 10% of introductory courses. The average class size in an introductory lecture is 45; in a laboratory is 23; and in a regular course is 34.

PROGRAMS OF STUDY: Nevada confers B.A., B.S., B.A.C.J., B.A.Ed., B.F.A., B.G.S., B.M., B.S.Bus.Ad., B.S.C.E., B.S.Chem.E., B.S.Chem., B.S.C.S., B.S.Ed., B.S.E.E., B.S.E.P., B.S.Geog., B.S.Geol., B.S.Geol.E., B.S.Geophys., B.S.M.E., B.S.Met.E., B.S.Min.E., B.S.Nurs. and B.S.Vet.Sc. degrees. Master's and doctoral degrees are also awarded. Bachelor's degrees are awarded in AGRICULTURE (agricultural sciences, natural resource management, and wildlife management), BIOLOGICAL SCIENCE (biochemistry, biology/biological science, biotechnology, neurosciences, nutrition, and nutritional sciences), BUSINESS (accounting, business administration - international, finance, management science, marketing, and marketing/retailing/merchandising), COMMUNICATIONS AND THE ARTS (applied music, art history, art, communications, dramatic arts, English, French, journalism, music, and Spanish), COMPUTER AND PHYSICAL SCIENCE (chemistry, computer science, geology, geophysics and seismology, hydrology, information sciences and systems, mathematics, and physics), EDUCATION (early childhood education, elementary education, general studies, music education, secondary education, and special education), ENGINEERING AND ENVIRONMENTAL DESIGN (chemical engineering, civil engineering, civil and environmental engineering, electrical/electronics engineering, engineering physics, environmental science, geological engineering, mechanical engineering, metallurgical engineering, and mining and mineral engineering), HEALTH PROFESSIONS (kinesiology, nursing, nutrition and dietetics, and speech pathology/audiology), SOCIAL SCIENCE (anthropology, child care/child and family studies, criminal justice, economics, geography, history, international relations, philosophy, political science/government, psychology, social work, sociology, and women's studies). Biology, psychology, and criminal justice have the largest enrollments.

ACTIVITIES: 7% of men belong to 2 local and 7 national fraternities; 7% of women belong to 9 national sororities. There are 240 groups on campus, including art, band, cheerleading, chess, choir, chorale, chorus, computers, dance, debate, drama, drill team, environmental, ethnic, film, forensics, honors, international, jazz band, LGBT, literary magazine, marching band, musical theater, newspaper, orchestra, pep band, photography, political, professional, radio and TV, religious, social, social service, student government, and symphony. Popular campus events include Mackay Week. **Sports:** There are 6 intercollegiate sports for men and 10 for women, and 6 intramural sports for men and 6 for women. Facilities include a recreation center, stadium, gym, baseball field, a movie theater, and an indoor events center. **Graduates:** From July 1, 2015 to June 30, 2016, 3372 bachelor's degrees were awarded. The most popular majors were business (17%), health sciences (13%), and engineering (11%). In an average class, 23% graduate in 4 years or less, 47% graduate in 5 years or less, and 54% graduate in 6 years or less.

SERVICES: Counseling and information services are available, as is tutoring in most subjects. There is also reader service for the blind, and remedial math, reading, and writing. Students are mainstreamed with special services for the disabled. **Library/Resources:** The 6 libraries contain 1.2 million volumes, 3.3 million microform items, 49,433 audio/video tapes/CDs/DVDs, and subscribe to 19,058 periodicals including electronic. Computerized library services include interlibrary loans, database searching, and Internet access. Special learning facilities include an art gallery, planetarium, radio station, TV station, the Nevada Historical Society Museum, and the Keck Mineral Museum. **Physically Challenged Students:** 99% of the campus is accessible. Facilities include wheelchair ramps, elevators, special parking, specially equipped restrooms, special class scheduling, lowered drinking fountains, lowered telephones, special housing, and automatic door openers. **Special:** Students may study abroad in 24 countries, pursue internships, and complete dual majors in many subject areas. There is 1 national honor society and a freshman honors program. **Visiting:** There are regularly scheduled orientations for prospective students, meetings with academic representatives. Campus tours include visiting residence halls. There are guides for informal visits and visitors may sit in on classes. To schedule a visit, contact the Office for Prospective Students. **Campus Safety and Security:** Measures include 24-hour foot and vehicle patrol, emergency notification system, self-defense education, and security escort services. There are shuttle buses, emergency telephones, lighted pathways/sidewalks, and controlled access to dorms/residences.

REQUIREMENTS: The SAT or ACT is required. Test scores are used for placement purposes only. Applicants should have completed 13 1/2 academic credits, including 4 in English, 3 each in math, science, and social studies/history, and a half credit in computer literacy. The GED is not accepted. A GPA of 3.0 is required. AP and CLEP credits are accepted. To graduate, all students must complete 124 to 138 semester credits and earn a GPA of 2.0. The core curriculum includes 9 credits of Western Traditions, 6 each of capstone courses and natural science, 3 to 6 of writing, 3 each of math, social science, and fine arts, and fulfillment of the diversity requirement. **Procedure:** Freshmen are admitted in the fall and spring. Entrance exams should be taken in October of the senior year. There are deferred admissions and rolling admissions plans. Applications should be filed by February 1 for fall entry; November 1 for spring entry. The fall 2016 application fee was $60. Notification is sent on a rolling basis. **Transfer Students:** 1324 transfer students enrolled in 2015-2016. Applicants should have a GPA of 2.5 and 24 transferable credits. College transcripts are required. 32 of 120 credits required for the bachelor's degree must be completed at Nevada. **International Students:** There are 283 international students enrolled. The school actively recruits these students. They must take the TOEFL. The SAT or ACT may also be submitted.

ADMISSIONS: 83% of the 2016-2017 applicants were accepted. The SAT scores for the 2016-2017 freshman class were: Critical Reading-- 29% below 500, 46% between 500 and 599, 22% between 600 and 699, and 3% between 700 and 800. Math-- 27% below 500, 44% between 500 and 599, 26% between 600 and 699, and 3% between 700 and 800. Writing-- 39% below 500, 43% between 500 and 599, 16% between 600 and 699, and 1% between 700 and 800. The ACT scores were 7% between 12 and 17, 47% between 18 and 23, 39% between 24 and 29, and 7% above 30. 45% of the current freshmen were in the top fifth of their class; 76% were in the top two fifths. **Admissions Contact:** Dr. Melisa N. Choroszy, Assistant Vice President, Records/Enrollment Services. Email: *asknevada@unr.edu* Web: *www.unr.edu*

FINANCIAL AID: In 2016-2017, 56% of all full-time freshmen and 53% of continuing full-time students received some form of financial aid. 40% of all full-time freshmen and 41% of continuing full-time students received need-based aid. The average freshman award was $8,293. The average financial indebtedness of the 2016 graduate was $23,110. The FAFSA code is 002568. The priority date for freshman financial aid applications for fall entry is February 1.

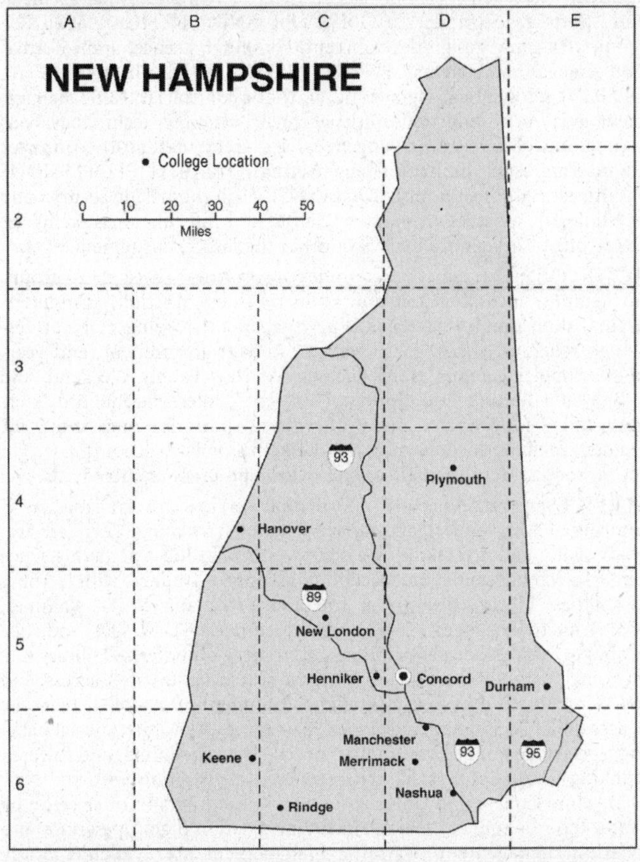

COLBY-SAWYER COLLEGE C-5

www.colby-sawyer.edu

New London, NH 03257 (603) 526-3700
(800) 272-1015
Fax: (603) 526-3452 Email: admissions@colby-sawyer.edu

Full-time: 677 men, 679 women	**Faculty:** n/av
Part-time: 6 men, 12 women	**Ph.D.s:** n/av
Graduate: n/av	**Student/Faculty:** 14 to 1
Year: semesters	**Tuition:** $38,040
Room & Board: $12,750	**Freshman Class:** n/av
SAT or ACT: required	**CEEB CODE:** 3281
Application Deadline: open	**COMPETITIVE**

Colby-Sawyer College, established in 1837, is a private, independent institution offering programs of study that innovatively integrate liberal arts and sciences with professional preparation. Undergraduate majors include environmental studies, graphic design, child development, education, exercise and sport sciences, studio arts, nursing, business, biology, English, psychology, communications, and history, society, and culture, as well as education certification. The figures in the above capsule and in this profile are approximate. There are 2 undergraduate schools. In addition to regional accreditation, Colby-Sawyer has baccalaureate program accreditation with CCNE and CAATE. The 200-acre campus is in a small town 90 minutes north of Boston. Including any residence halls, there are 30 buildings.

STUDENT LIFE: 68% of undergraduates are from out of state, mostly the Northeast. Students are from 28 states, 38 foreign countries, and Canada. 83% are from public schools. 89% are White; 2% Hispanic; 10% Foreign; 1% African American; 1% Asian American. **Female To Male Ratio:** 1.0:1. The average age of freshmen is 18; all undergraduates, 19. 19% do not continue beyond their first year; 64% remain to graduate. **Housing:** 870 students can be accommodated in college housing, which includes single-sex and coed dorms, on-campus apartments, and off-campus apartments, and a substance-free residence hall. On-campus housing is guaranteed for all 4 years. 90% of students live on campus; of those, 70% remain on campus on weekends. All students may keep cars.

FACULTY/CLASSROOMS: 48% of faculty are male; 52% are female. All teach undergraduates. No introductory courses are taught by graduate students. The average class size in a regular course is 17.

PROGRAMS OF STUDY: Colby-Sawyer confers B.A., B.S. and B.F.A. degrees. Associate degrees are also awarded. Bachelor's degrees are awarded in AGRICULTURE (environmental studies), BIOLOGICAL SCIENCE (biology/biological science), BUSINESS (accounting, business administration and management, and sports management), COMMUNICATIONS AND THE ARTS (art, communications, creative writing, English, graphic design, performing arts, and studio art), COMPUTER AND PHYSICAL SCIENCE (natural sciences), EDUCATION (art education, athletic training, early childhood education, English education, social science education, and social studies education), ENGINEERING AND ENVIRONMENTAL DESIGN (environmental science), HEALTH PROFESSIONS (exercise science, nursing, and public health), SOCIAL SCIENCE (child psychology/development, history, humanities, philosophy, psychology, and sociology). Exercise & sport sciences, business administration, and nursing have the largest enrollments.

ACTIVITIES: There are no fraternities or sororities. There are 40 groups on campus, including student academic counselors, key association (campus tour guides), art, chorus, dance, drama, environmental, film, honors, international, LGBT, literary magazine, musical theater, newspaper, outing, photography, political, professional, radio and TV, religious, social, social service, and student government. Popular campus events include Fall and Spring Weekends, and Mountain Day. **Sports:** There are 8 intercollegiate sports for men and 9 for women, and 15 intramural sports for men and 15 for women. Facilities include outdoor and indoor tennis courts, a fitness center, an NCAA-approved swimming pool, a suspended indoor track, squash and racquetball courts, outdoor competitive fields, and nearby golf courses, ski and biking trails, and an indoor riding arena. **Graduates:** From July 1, 2015 to June 30, 2016, 216 bachelor's degrees were awarded. The most popular majors were business administration (22%), health and phusical education (13%), and teacher education (11%). In an average class, 51% graduate in 4 years or less, 59% graduate in 5 years or less, and 60% graduate in 6 years or less. Of the 2015 graduating class, 11% were enrolled in graduate school within 6 months of graduation, and 90% were employed.

SERVICES: Counseling and information services are available, as is tutoring in every subject. There is a reader service for the blind, and remedial math, reading, and writing. **Library/Resources:** The library contains 93,861 volumes, 204,109 microform items, 2,400 audio/video tapes/CDs/DVDs, and subscribes to 32,019 periodicals including electronic. Computerized library services include interlibrary loans, database searching, and Internet access. Special learning facilities include an art gallery, radio station, academic development center, Windy Hill Laboratory School (K-3), weather station, and the Curtis L.Ivey Science Center. **Physically Challenged Students:** 50% of the campus is accessible. Facilities include wheelchair ramps, elevators, special parking, specially equipped restrooms, special class scheduling, and special housing. **Special:** There is cross-registration through the New Hampshire College and University Council. Students may choose internships (required in some majors) and may study abroad in Australia, Canada, and several European countries. A Washington semester with American University is available. Other options include education certification, credit by exam, and interdisciplinary majors such as history, society, and culture. There are 4 national honor societies and a freshman honors program. **Visiting:** There are regularly scheduled orientations for prospective students, including tours and interviews. Open house programs offer tours as well as academic, athletic, campus life, career development, and academic development presentations; several visiting-day programs offer tours, interviews, and class visits. There are guides for informal visits, visitors may sit in on classes, and stay overnight. To schedule a visit, contact the Admissions Office. **Campus Safety and Security:** Measures include 24-hour foot and vehicle patrol, emergency notification system, self-defense education, security escort services. There are also shuttle buses, emergency telephones, lighted pathways/sidewalks, controlled access to dorms/residences, and monthly meetings between students and campus safety personnel.

REQUIREMENTS: The SAT or ACT is required, as is the ACT Optional Writing test. The GED is accepted. A minimum of 15 college preparatory credits is recommended for admission, including 4 years of English, 3 or more of social studies, 3 of math, 2 of the same foreign language, and 3 or more of lab science. An essay is required, as are 2 letters of recommendation. Interviews are strongly recommended. A GPA of 2.0 is required. AP and CLEP credits are accepted. Required courses include writing, math, and computer literacy. Each pathway is a set of five courses that all relate to a theme. Each student is required to take a total of eight Exploration courses: 1 course each in fne and performing arts, history, humanities, literature, social sciences, and laboratory science course, and 1 course from 2 of the following areas: environmental literacy, media literacy, global perspectives, and wellness. Most majors must also complete an internship or a senior research project. A total of 120 credit hours, with a minimum GPA of 2.0, is required for graduation. **Procedure:** Freshmen are admitted in the fall and spring. Entrance exams should be taken in the fall of the senior year. There are early decision, deferred admissions, and rolling admissions plans. Early decision applications should be filed by December 1, along with a $45 fee. Notification of early decision is sent December 15; regular decision, on a rolling basis. Applications are accepted online. **Transfer Students:** 17 transfer students enrolled in 2015-2016. College-level work will be emphasized. College transcripts, course descriptions, and a dean's form are required in addition to the standard requirements. 60 of 120 credits required for the bachelor's degree must be completed at Colby-Sawyer. **International Students:** There are 13 international students enrolled. The school actively recruits these students. They must take the TOEFL.

Admissions Contact: Admissions Office Email: *admissions@colby-sawyer.edu* Web: *www.colby-sawyer.edu*

FINANCIAL AID: In 2016-2017, 97% of all full-time freshmen and 78% of continuing full-time students received some form of financial aid. 81% of all full-time freshmen and 78% of continuing full-time students received need-based aid. The average freshman award was $24,043. The average financial indebtedness of the 2016 graduate was $13,578. Colby-Sawyer is a member of CSS. The FAFSA code is 002572. Check with the school for current application deadlines.

DANIEL WEBSTER COLLEGE — D-6

www.dwc.edu

Nashua, NH 03063	(603) 577-6600 (800) 325-6876
Fax: (603) 577-6001	Email: admissions@dwc.edu
Full-time: 555 men, 135 women	Faculty: n/av
Part-time: 25 men, 10 women	Ph.D.s: n/av
Graduate: 75 men, 70 women	Student/Faculty: 16 to 1
Year: semesters, summer session	Tuition: $15,630
Room & Board: $11,354	Freshman Class: n/av
SAT: required	CEEB CODE: 3648
Application Deadline: open	COMPETITIVE

Daniel Webster College, founded in 1965, is a non-denominational private college offering study in the fields of aviation, business, computer sciences, engineering, sports management, homeland security and psychology. The figures in the above capsule and in this profile are approximate. There are 4 undergraduate schools and 1 graduate school. In addition to regional accreditation, DWC has baccalaureate program accreditation with ABET, AABI, AT-CTl CAA, FAA, NASSM, and SMPRC. The 54-acre campus is in a suburban area in Southern New Hampshire in Nashua, 36 miles to Boston and 20 miles to Manchester, NH. Including any residence halls, there are 14 buildings.

STUDENT LIFE: 66% of undergraduates are from out of state, mostly the Northeast. Students are from 22 states, 15 foreign countries, and Canada. 91% are White; 5% African American; 2% Hispanic; 2% Foreign. **Male To Female Ratio:** 3.0:1. The average age of freshmen is 18; all undergraduates, 21. 24% do not continue beyond their first year. **Housing:** 500 students can be accommodated in college housing, which includes single-sex and coed dorms, on-campus apartments, suites, quiet floors in residence halls, smoke-free, and substance-free areas, and a 10-month housing option. On-campus housing is guaranteed for all 4 years. 68% of students live on campus; of those, 80% remain on campus on weekends. All students may keep cars.

FACULTY/CLASSROOMS: 80% of faculty are male; 20% are female. All teach undergraduates and do research. No introductory courses are taught by graduate students. The average class size in an introductory lecture is 17; in a laboratory is 12; and in a regular course is 20.

PROGRAMS OF STUDY: DWC confers B.S. and M.B.A. degrees. Associate and master's degrees are also awarded. Bachelor's degrees are awarded in BUSINESS (accounting, business administration and management, management information systems, marketing management, and sports management), COMPUTER AND PHYSICAL SCIENCE (computer game design/development, computer science, and information sciences and systems), ENGINEERING AND ENVIRONMENTAL DESIGN (aeronautical engineering, air traffic control, air traffic management, aviation administration/management, computer technology, construction, construction engineering, electrical and computer engineering, and mechanical engineering), HEALTH PROFESSIONS (health care administration), SOCIAL SCIENCE (homeland security and psychology). Aviation, computer science, and information systems are the strongest academically. Aviation has the largest enrollment.

ACTIVITIES: There are no fraternities or sororities. There are 26 groups on campus, including golf and culinary clubs, ski club, computers, drama, film, honors, jazz band, newspaper, off reading club, professional, religious, social, social service, student government, and yearbook. Popular campus events include Ski Day, Family Weekend, and Whitewater Rafting Trip. **Sports:** There are 7 intercollegiate sports for men and 7 for women, and 6 intramural sports for men and 5 for women. Facilities include an indoor basketball/volleyball court, a weight room, soccer, lacrosse, and softball fields, and cross-country trails.

SERVICES: Counseling and information services are available, as is tutoring in every subject, and remedial math and writing. There are also study skills and test skills workshops, study groups, a math/science center, a writing center, and accommodations for students with learning disabilities. **Library/Resources:** The library contains 32,000 volumes, 55,294 microform items, 1,457 audio/video tapes/CDs/DVDs, and subscribes to 390 periodicals including electronic. Computerized library services include interlibrary loans, database searching, Internet access, and Wi-Fi capability. **Physically Challenged Students:** 75% of the campus is accessible. Facilities include wheelchair ramps, elevators, special parking, specially equipped restrooms, special class scheduling, and lowered drinking fountains. **Special:** There is cross-registration with the New Hampshire College and University Council. All programs offer credit by exam. Interdisciplinary majors, including aviation flight operations and aviation management/air traffic management are available. Study abroad, internships in aviation, business management, computer sciences, and sport management, a general studies degree, and a 2-2 engineering program with the universities of New Hampshire and Massachusetts at Lowell, Kettering University, and Clarkson University are additional options. There is 1 national honor society and 1 departmental honors program. **Visiting:** Regularly scheduled orientations are available for prospective students, including a tour and an admissions interview; also available are meetings with faculty and coaches and an aerial tour of the campus as well as sitting in on class. There are guides for informal visits, visitors may sit in on classes, and stay overnight. To schedule a visit, contact the Office of Admissions. **Campus Safety and Security:** Measures include 24-hour foot and vehicle patrol, emergency notification system, self-defense education, security escort services, emergency telephones, lighted pathways/sidewalks, and controlled access to dorms/residences.

REQUIREMENTS: The SAT is required. Applicants must be graduates of an accredited secondary school or submit the GED. Students should have taken 4 years of English, 3 of math, 2 each of social studies and science, and 1 of history. An essay and an interview are recommended. AP and CLEP credits are accepted. Important factors in the admissions decision are advanced placement or honors courses, recommendations by school officials, and leadership record. Students must complete general education courses in communication, computer literacy, math, natural science, the humanities, and the social sciences. At least 120 credits, with 45 to 58 in the major, are required for graduation. Students must maintain a minimum overall GPA of 2.0. and grades of C or better in their major. **Procedure:** Freshmen are admitted to all sessions. There are early decision, deferred admissions, and rolling admissions plans. Application deadlines are open. Application fee is $35. Applications are accepted online. **Transfer Students:** Transfer students must have a minimum college GPA of 2.0. The SAT is required. Grades of C or better transfer for credit. 30 of 120 credits required for the bachelor's degree must be completed at DWC. **International Students:** They must take the TOEFL, as well as the SAT or ACT.

Admissions Contact: Daniel P. Monahan, Dean of Admissions. Email: *admissions@dwc.edu* Web: *www.dwc.edu*

FINANCIAL AID: The college's own financial statement is required. The FAFSA code is 004731. Check with the school for current application deadlines.

DARTMOUTH COLLEGE B-4

www.dartmouth.edu

Hanover, NH 03755 (603) 646-2875

Fax: (603) 646-1216 Email: admissions.office@dartmouth.edu

Full-time: 2137 men, 2133 women	**Faculty:** 582; I, ++$
Part-time: n/av	**Ph.D.s:** n/av
Graduate: 1098 men, 973 women	**Student/Faculty:** 7 to 1
Year: quarters, summer session	**Tuition:** $51,438
Room & Board: $14,736	**Freshman Class:** 20,507 applied, 2250 accepted, 1116 enrolled
SAT or ACT: required	**CEEB CODE:** 3351
Application Deadline: January 1	**MOST COMPETITIVE**

Founded in 1769, Dartmouth is a member of the Ivy League and consistently ranks among the world's greatest academic institutions. Dartmouth has forged a singular identity for combining its deep commitment to outstanding undergraduate liberal arts and graduate education with distinguished research and scholarship in the Arts & Sciences and its three leading professional schools the Geisel School of Medicine, Thayer School of Engineering, and the Tuck School of Business. There are 4 undergraduate schools and 4 graduate schools. The 269-acre campus is in a rural area 140 miles northwest of Boston. Including any residence halls, there are 172 buildings.

STUDENT LIFE: 99% of undergraduates are from out of state, mostly the Middle Atlantic. Students are from 50 states, 82 foreign countries, and Canada. 55% are from public schools. 50% are White; 15% Asian American; 9% Hispanic; 9% Foreign; 7% African American; 5% two or more races; 3% race unknown; 2% American Indian/Alaska Native. **Male To Female Ratio:** 1.0:1. The average age of freshmen is 18; all undergraduates, 20. 2% do not continue beyond their first year; 97% remain to graduate. **Housing:** 3500 students can be accommodated in college housing, which includes coed dorms, on-campus apartments, off-campus apartments, and married student housing. In addition, there are language houses, special-interest houses, fraternity houses, sorority houses, substance- and smoke-free residence halls, faculty-in-residence and academic affinity programs, cooperative housing, theme housing, wellness housing, and gender-neutral housing available. On-campus housing is guaranteed for the freshman year only and is available on a lottery system for upperclassmen. 88% of students live on campus. Upperclassmen may keep cars.

FACULTY/CLASSROOMS: 62% of faculty are male; 38% are female. All teach undergraduates and do research. No introductory courses are taught by graduate students. The average class size in an introductory lecture is 34; in a laboratory is 16; and in a regular course is 23.

PROGRAMS OF STUDY: Dartmouth confers B.A. and B.Eng. degrees. Master's and doctoral degrees are also awarded. Bachelor's degrees are awarded in AGRICULTURE (environmental studies), BIOLOGICAL SCIENCE (biochemistry, biology/biological science, genetics, and neurosciences), COMMUNICATIONS AND THE ARTS (Arabic, art history and appreciation, Chinese, classical languages, classics, comparative literature, dramatic arts, English, film arts, French, German, Italian, linguistics, music, Portuguese, romance languages and literature, Russian, Spanish, and studio art), COMPUTER AND PHYSICAL SCIENCE (astronomy, astronomy and physics, astrophysics, chemistry, computer science, earth science, mathematics, and physics), ENGINEERING AND ENVIRONMENTAL DESIGN (engineering and applied science, engineering physics, and environmental science), SOCIAL SCIENCE (African American studies, anthropology, Asian/Oriental studies, classical/ancient civilization, cognitive science, economics, French studies, geography, German area studies, history, Latin American studies, Middle Eastern studies, Native American studies, philosophy, psychology, religion, Russian and Slavic studies, sociology, Spanish studies, and women's studies). Economics, government, psychological and brain sciences have the largest enrollments.

ACTIVITIES: 44% of men belong to 9 local and 5 national fraternities; 47% of women belong to 3 local and 6 national sororities. There are 160 groups on campus, including art, band, cheerleading, chess, choir, chorale, chorus, computers, dance, debate, drama, environmental, ethnic, film, forensics, honors, international, jazz band, LGBT, literary magazine, marching band, musical theater, newspaper, opera, orchestra, pep band, photography, political, professional, radio and TV, religious, social, social service, student government, symphony, and yearbook. Popular campus events include Dartmouth Night/Homecoming Weekend, Winter Carnival, and Green Key Service Weekend. **Sports:** There are 17 intercollegiate sports for men and 18 for women, and 25 intramural sports for men and 25 for women. Facilities include an arena, fitness center, squash and racquetball courts, dance studio, ice-hockey arena, a gym, football stadium, boat house, a tennis center with indoor and outdoor courts, golf course, ski slope with 3 chairlifts, and a riding farm. **Graduates:** From July 1, 2015 to June 30, 2016, 1094 bachelor's degrees were awarded. The most popular majors were social sciences (39%), biological/life sciences (12%), and history (7%). In an average class, 95% graduate in 6 years or less.

SERVICES: Counseling and information services are available, as is tutoring in every subject, and a reader service for the blind. There is an academic skills center for all students, as well as readers, note takers, tape recorders and support for learning-disabled students are available. **Library/Resources:** The 10 libraries contain 2.6 million volumes, 2.6 million microform items, 789,236 audio/video tapes/CDs/DVDs, and subscribe to 72,726 periodicals including electronic. Computerized library services include interlibrary loans, database searching, Internet access, and Wi-Fi capability. Special learning facilities include an art gallery, radio station, a creative and performing arts center, life sciences lab, a physical and social sciences centers, and observatory. **Physically Challenged Students:** All of the campus is accessible. Facilities include wheelchair ramps, elevators, special parking, specially equipped restrooms, special class scheduling, lowered drinking fountains, lowered telephones, and special housing. **Special:** Students may design programs using the college's unique Dartmouth Plan, which divides the academic calendar into 4 10-week terms, based on the seasons. The plan permits greater flexibility for vacations and for the 45 study-abroad programs in 23 countries in Latin America, Europe, Asia, and Africa. Cross-registration is offered through the Twelve College Exchange Network. Exchange programs also exist with the University of California at San Diego, Stanford, Oxford, and McGill Universities, selected German universities, Keio University in Tokyo, and Beijing Normal University in China. Students may design their own interdisciplinary majors involving multiple departments, take dual majors in all fields, or create a modified major involving 2 departments, with emphasis in 1. Hands-on computer science education, internships, and work-study programs also are available. A 3-2 engineering degree is offered with Dartmouth's Thayer School of Engineering. There are 3 national honor societies and a chapter of Phi Beta Kappa. **Visiting:** Regularly scheduled orientations are available for prospective students, including a campus tour, a group information session, and a student forum. There are guides for informal visits, visitors may sit in on classes, and stay overnight. To schedule a visit, contact the Office of Admissions. **Campus Safety and Security:** Measures include 24-hour foot and vehicle patrol, emergency notification system, self-defense education, and security escort services. There are also shuttle buses, emergency telephones, and lighted pathways/sidewalks.

REQUIREMENTS: The SAT or ACT, as well as the ACT Optional Writing test are required. Evidence of intellectual capacity, motivation, and personal integrity are important factors in the highly competitive admissions process, which also considers talent, accomplishment, and involvement in nonacademic areas. Course requirements are flexible, but students are recommended to take 4 units in English, foreign language, math, science, and social studies. The GED is accepted. AP credits are accepted. Important factors in the admissions decision are leadership record, advanced placement or honors courses, personality/intangible qualities, extracurricular activities record, evidence of special talent, parents or siblings attended your school, recommendations by alumni, and geographical diversity. All students must pass 35 courses, 10 of which must be distributed in the following fields: arts, social analysis, literature, quantitative or deductive science, philosophical, religious, or historical analysis, natural science, technology or applied science, and international or comparative study. 3 world culture courses are required from the U.S., Europe, and at least 1 non-Western society. A multidisciplinary or interdisciplinary course, a freshman seminar, a senior project, and foreign language proficiency are also required. **Procedure:** Freshmen are admitted in the fall. Entrance exams should be taken no later than November or January of the senior year. There are early decision and deferred admissions plans. Early decision applications should be filed by November 1; regular applications, by January 1 for fall entry, along with a $80 fee. Notification of early decision is sent December 15; regular decision, April 10. 482 early decision candidates were accepted for the 2016-2017 class. 963 applicants were on the 2016 waiting list; 129 were admitted. Applications are accepted on-line. **Transfer Students:** 17 transfer students enrolled in 2015-2016. Applicants must demonstrate high achievement and intellectual motivation through college transcripts as well as standardized test scores and high school transcripts. Fall closing date is March 1. Notification will be May 15, and must reply by June 1. 18 of 35 credits required for the bachelor's degree must be completed at Dartmouth. **International Students:** There are 286 international students enrolled. The school actively recruits these students. They must take the TOEFL, as well as the SAT or ACT.

ADMISSIONS: 11% of the 2016-2017 applicants were accepted. 95% of the current freshmen were in the top fifth of their class; 100% were in the top two fifths. 323 freshmen graduated first in their class. **Admissions Contact:** Maria Laskaris, Dean of Admissions. Email: *admissions.office@dartmouth.edu* Web: *www.dartmouth.edu*

FINANCIAL AID: In 2016-2017, 46% of all full-time freshmen received some form of financial aid, or need-based aid. The average freshman award was $49,373. Need-based scholarships or need-based grants averaged $46,917; need-based self-help aid (loans and jobs) averaged $4,520; and other non-need-based awards and non-need-based scholarships averaged $4,312. The average financial indebtedness of the 2016 graduate was $17,171. Dartmouth is a member of CSS. The CSS/Profile, parents' and student's federal income tax returns, and noncustodial and business/farm supplement are required. The FAFSA code is 002573. The deadline for filing freshman financial aid applications for fall entry is February 1.

FRANKLIN PIERCE UNIVERSITY C-6

www.franklinpierce.edu

Rindge, NH 03461 (603) 899-4050
(800) 437-0048

Fax: (603) 899-4394 Email: admissions@franklinpierce.edu

Full-time: 591 men, 716 women	**Faculty:** 71; IIB, -$
Part-time: 95 men, 285 women	**Ph.D.s:** 70%
Graduate: 205 men, 324 women	**Student/Faculty:** 14 to 1
Year: semesters, summer session	**Tuition:** $34,050
Room & Board: $12,700	**Freshman Class:** 4419 applied, 3681 accepted, 450 enrolled
SAT CR/M/W: required **ACT:** 21	**CEEB CODE:** 3395
Application Deadline: n/av	**COMPETITIVE**

Franklin Pierce University, founded in 1962, is a private liberal arts institution with an extensive continuing education program. Many degrees are offered with emphasis in health care, business, education, mass communications, psychology, humanities, visual and performing arts, and leadership studies. Figures in the above capsule and in this profile are approximate. There are 2 undergraduate schools and 1 graduate school. In addition to regional accreditation, FPU has baccalaureate program accreditation with NEASC. The 1200-acre campus is in a rural area in Rindge, New Hampshire, 65 miles northwest of Boston. Including any residence halls, there are 30 buildings.

STUDENT LIFE: 78% of undergraduates are from out of state, mostly the Northeast. Students are from 40 states, 14 foreign countries, and Canada. 83% are from public schools. 74% are White; 5% Hispanic; 4% African American; 3% Foreign; 2% two or more races; 13% race unknown; 1% Asian American. **Female To Male Ratio:** 1.5:1. The average age of freshmen is 18; all undergraduates, 20. 31% do not continue beyond their first year; 52% remain to graduate. **Housing:** 1492 students can be accommodated in college housing, which includes coed dorms, on-campus apartments, off-campus apartments, special-interest houses, wellness living, and apartments for single student. On-campus housing is guaranteed for all 4 years. 85% of students live on campus. All students may keep cars.

FACULTY/CLASSROOMS: 48% of faculty are male; 52% are female. All teach undergraduates, 50% do research, and 50% do both. No introductory courses are taught by graduate students. The average class size in an introductory lecture is 60; in a laboratory is 16; and in a regular course is 16.

PROGRAMS OF STUDY: FPU confers B.A. and B.S. degrees. Associate, master's, and doctoral degrees are also awarded. Bachelor's degrees are awarded in BIOLOGICAL SCIENCE (biology/biological science), BUSINESS (accounting, banking and finance, business administration and management, management science, marketing/retailing/merchandising, and sports management), COMMUNICATIONS AND THE ARTS (arts administration/management, communications, dance, dramatic arts, English, fine arts, graphic design, music, and theatre arts), COMPUTER AND PHYSICAL SCIENCE (mathematics), EDUCATION (education, elementary education, and secondary education), ENGINEERING AND ENVIRONMENTAL DESIGN (environmental science), HEALTH PROFESSIONS (health care administration, health science, and nursing), SOCIAL SCIENCE (American studies, anthropology, criminal justice, history, interdisciplinary studies, political science/government, psychology, and social work). Anthropology, health sciences, and biology are the strongest academically. Biology, health sciences, and criminal justice have the largest enrollments.

ACTIVITIES: There are no fraternities or sororities. There are 35 groups on campus, including art, cheerleading, choir, chorale, chorus, computers, dance, drama, environmental, ethnic, film, forensics, honors, international, jazz band, LGBT, literary magazine, musical theater, newspaper, photography, political, professional, radio and TV, religious, social, social service, student government, and yearbook. Popular campus events include Winter Carnival, Spring and Fall Weekend, and Up All Night Mardi Gras. **Sports:** There are 9 intercollegiate sports for men and 11 for women, and 32 intramural sports for men and 32 for women. Facilities include air-frame activity center, with tennis courts, indoor turf soccer field, basketball courts, track, fitness center, volleyball courts, a field house, a fitness center, a gym, an athletic training facility, playing fields including an artificial turf baseball field, and artificial turf soccer/lacrosse and field hockey field, a softball field, and another all-purpose field, a lake with a beach, a fleet of sailboats and kayaks, cross-country and hiking trails, and courts for tennis, basketball, and volleyball. **Graduates:** From July 1, 2015 to June 30, 2016, 378 bachelor's degrees were awarded. The most popular majors were business/marketing (18%), health professions and related sciences (14%), and biological/life sciences (7%). In an average class, 2% graduate in 3 years or less, 37% graduate in 4 years or less, 48% graduate in 5 years or less, and 50% graduate in 6 years or less. Of the 2015 graduating class, 37% were enrolled in graduate school within 6 months of graduation, and 79% were employed.

SERVICES: Counseling and information services are available, as is tutoring in every subject, and a reader service for the blind, and remedial math, reading, and writing. Note takers, a professional reading specialist, alternative testing, reduced course loads, study skills workshops, and content-area study skills courses are also available. **Library/Resources:** The library contains 132,015 volumes, 26,182 microform items, 10,312 audio/video tapes/CDs/DVDs, and subscribes to 13,365 periodicals including electronic. Computerized library services include interlibrary loans, database searching, Internet access, and Wi-Fi capability. Special learning facilities include an art gallery, radio station, TV station, computer labs, theaters, recording studios, athletic training facility, and glass-blowing hut. **Physically Challenged Students:** 70% of the campus is accessible. Facilities include wheelchair ramps, elevators, special parking, specially equipped restrooms, special class scheduling, and special housing. **Special:** Cross-registration is offered in nearly every subject through the New Hampshire College and University Council, a 13-member consortium of area institutions. Study abroad in 9 countries, Pierce on the Camino, internships in most majors on or off campus, a Washington semester, and work-study through the college are possible. In addition, accelerated degree programs in all majors, dual majors in most fields, student-designed majors, credit for life experience, and nondegree study are available. Pathway programs from undergraduate to M.D. and D.V.M. programs at St. George's University in Grenada afford students special graduate study opportunities, along with pathways and consideration to Franklin Pierce's Doctor of Physical Therapy and Master of Physician Assistant Studies programs. Pathway and accelerated Franklin Pierce M.B.A., M.Ed., and M.S. in Information Technology Management degree programs provide additional options. There are 7 national honor societies and a freshman honors program. **Visiting:** Regularly scheduled orientations are available for prospective students, including open houses held each spring and fall and interviews and tours available weekdays and most Saturdays. There are guides for informal visits, visitors may sit in on classes, and stay overnight. To schedule a visit, contact the Admissions Office. **Campus Safety and Security:** Measures include 24-hour foot and vehicle patrol, emergency notification system, self-defense education, and security escort services. There are also shuttle buses, emergency telephones, lighted pathways/sidewalks, On campus student-run fire department and EMS squad.

REQUIREMENTS: The SAT is required. The ACT and ACT Writing Test are recommended. In addition, Applicants must have earned 10 academic units or 16 Carnegie units in high school, including 4 years of English, 3 each in math and social studies, and 3 in science. An interview is recommended. The GED is accepted. FPU requires applicants to be in the upper 60% of their class. A GPA of 2.9 is required. AP and CLEP credits are accepted. Important factors in the admissions decision are recommendations by school officials, advanced placement or honors courses, and extracurricular activities record. Students must complete 120 semester hours with a cumulative GPA of at least 2.0 and pass exams for writing and math competency. General and liberal education core curricular requirements include mastery of an established set of learning outcomes in the following areas: Knowledge & Understanding, Intellectual & Practical Skills, Personal & Social Responsibility, Engaged Learning & Thinking. These learning outcomes focus on preparing our students for life and careers in an increasingly complex and challenging 21st-century world. **Procedure:** Freshmen are admitted to all sessions. Entrance exams should be taken in the spring of junior year or the fall of the senior year. There are deferred admissions and rolling admissions plans. Application deadlines are open. Application fee is $40. Notification is sent on a rolling basis. Applications are accepted online. **Transfer Students:** 21 transfer students enrolled in 2015-2016. A minimum 2.0 GPA in college work is required. Students with fewer than 30 credits must submit SAT results (no minimum score) and official high school transcripts. A personal recommendation is necessary, and an interview is recommended. 30 of 120 credits required for the bachelor's degree must be completed at FPU. **International Students:** There are 25 international students enrolled. The school actively recruits these students. They must take the TOEFL with a minimum score of 61 on the Internet-based version (iBT), and also take ELS Level 109. The SAT or ACT may be substituted for the TOEFL.

ADMISSIONS: 83% of the 2016-2017 applicants were accepted. The SAT scores for the 2016-2017 freshman class were: Critical Reading-- 58% below 500, 36% between 500 and 599, and 6% between 600 and 699. Math-- 54% below 500, 37% between 500 and 599, and 7% between 600 and 699. Writing-- 63% below 500, 32% between 500 and 599, and 5% between 600 and 699. The ACT scores were 9% below 12, 72% between 12 and 17, and 19% above 30. 44% of the current freshmen were in the top fifth of their class; 56% were in the top two fifths. **Admissions Contact:** Linda Quimby, Director. Email: *admissions@franklinpierce.edu* Web: *www.franklinpierce.edu*

FINANCIAL AID: In 2016-2017, 86% of all full-time freshmen and 85% of continuing full-time students received some form of financial aid. 86% of all full-time freshmen and 85% of continuing full-time students received need-based aid. The average freshman award was $23,887. Need-based scholarships or need-based grants averaged $19,445; need-based self-help aid (loans and jobs) averaged $5,484; non-need-based athletic scholarships averaged $12,919; and other non-need-based awards and non-need-based scholarships averaged $13,304. 50% of undergraduate students work part-time. Average annual earnings from campus work are $618. The average financial indebtedness of the 2016 graduate was $36,087. FPU is a member of CSS. The FAFSA code is 002575. The priority date for freshman financial aid applications for fall entry is March 1.

GRANITE STATE COLLEGE *(The complete profile is made available exclusively on our website, www.barronspac.com)*

KEENE STATE COLLEGE *(The complete profile is made available exclusively on our website, www.barronspac.com)*

NEW ENGLAND COLLEGE C-5

www.nec.edu

Henniker, NH 03242 (603) 428-2223 (800) 521-7642

Fax: (608) 428-3155
Email: admission@nec.nec.edu
Full-time: 709 men, 1021 women
Part-time: 12 men, 14 women
Graduate: 475 men, 394 women
Year: varies, summer session
Room & Board: $13,536
Application Deadline: open
Faculty: 43
Ph.D.s: 80%
Student/Faculty: 15 to 1
Tuition: $34,887
Freshman Class: 4209 applied, 4163 accepted, 286 enrolled
CEEB CODE: 3657
COMPETITIVE

New England College, founded in 1946, is an independent liberal arts institution emphasizing small classes and a cocurricular leadership program. Figures in the above capsule and in this profile are approximate. There is 1 undergraduate school and 1 graduate school. In addition to regional accreditation, NEC has baccalaureate program accreditation with NEASC. The 225-acre campus is in a small town 17 miles west of Concord and 80 miles north of Boston, Massachusetts. Including any residence halls, there are 31 buildings.

STUDENT LIFE: 82% of undergraduates are from out of state, mostly the South. Students are from 50 states, 19 foreign countries, and Canada. 83% are from public schools. 52% are White; 24% African American; 8% Hispanic; 8% race unknown; 4% Foreign; 2% two or more races; 1% Asian American; 1% American Indian/Alaska Native. 100% claim no religious affiliation **Female To Male Ratio:** 1.2:1. The average age of freshmen is 20; all undergraduates, 28. 27% do not continue beyond their first year; 40% remain to graduate. **Housing:** 685 students can be accommodated in college housing, which includes coed dorms, on-campus apartments, special-interest houses, cooperative substance-free housing, and living learning housing. On-campus housing is guaranteed for all 4 years and is available on a lottery system for upperclassmen. 64% of students commute. All students may keep cars.

FACULTY/CLASSROOMS: 49% of faculty are male; 51% are female. 67% teach undergraduates, and 20% do both. No introductory courses are taught by graduate students. The average class size in an introductory lecture is 16; in a laboratory is 14; and in a regular course is 13.

PROGRAMS OF STUDY: NEC confers B.A. and B.S. degrees. Associate, master's, and doctoral degrees are also awarded. Bachelor's degrees are awarded in BIOLOGICAL SCIENCE (biology/biological science), BUSINESS (business administration and management, recreation and leisure services, and sports management), COMMUNICATIONS AND THE ARTS (art history and appreciation, communications, creative writing, dramatic arts, fine arts, and game programming), COMPUTER AND PHYSICAL SCIENCE (computer science), EDUCATION (education, elementary education, physical education, secondary education, and special education), ENGINEERING AND ENVIRONMENTAL DESIGN (environmental science), HEALTH PROFESSIONS (health care administration and health science), SOCIAL SCIENCE (criminal justice, philosophy, physical fitness/movement, political science/government, psychology, and sociology). Business, education, and biology/health science are the strongest academically and have the largest enrollments are the strongest academically. Business, health science, and psycology have the largest enrollments.

ACTIVITIES: 3% of men belong to 1 local and 1 national fraternities; 3% of women belong to 1 local and 1 national sororities. There are 37 groups on campus, including chorus, dance, drama, environmental, ethnic, film, honors, including sport clubs, international, LGBT, literary magazine, newspaper, photography, political, professional, radio and TV, religious, social, social service, student government, and yearbook. Popular campus events include International Week, Snow Day, and Spring Weekend. **Sports:** There are 8 intercollegiate sports for men and 8 for women, and 7 intramural sports for men and 7 for women. Facilities include a gym, field house, playing fields, indoor and outdoor basketball and tennis courts, cross-country ski trails, Alpine skiing (free) at a local ski area, turf field, and a fitness center. **Graduates:** From July 1, 2015 to June 30, 2016, 159 bachelor's degrees were awarded. The most popular majors were business (21%), health science (15%), and psychology (12%). 21 companies recruited on campus in 2015-2016. In an average class, 6% graduate in 3 years or less, 41% graduate in 4 years or less, 43% graduate in 5 years or less, and 43% graduate in 6 years or less. Of the 2015 graduating class, 18% were enrolled in graduate school within 6 months of graduation, and 94% were employed.

SERVICES: Counseling and information services are available, as is tutoring in most subjects, and remedial math and writing. The mentor program provides both academic and life coaching. **Library/Resources:** The library contains 110,000 volumes, 36,000 microform items, and 2,000 audio/video tapes/CDs/DVDs, and subscribes to 756 periodicals including electronic. Computerized library services include interlibrary loans, database searching, Internet access, and Wi-Fi capability. Special learning facilities include an art gallery, radio station, the center for educational innovation, a high-tech classroom, and the John Lyons center for business. **Physically Challenged Students:** 80% of the campus is accessible. Facilities include wheelchair ramps, elevators, special parking, specially equipped restrooms, and special class scheduling. **Special:** Cross-registration is available with the New Hampshire College and University Council. Also available are internships for juniors and seniors with a GPA of 2.5, study abroad in most countries, work-study programs, dual majors, student-designed majors, interdisciplinary majors, nondegree study, pass/fail options, and 3+3 Law program at New York Law School are also offered. Washington semeste; Double majors; Individually designed majors; Work Study on and off campus; fully on-line programs both at undergraduate and graduate levels. There is 1 national honor society, a freshman honors program, and 32 departmental honors programs. **Visiting:** There are regularly scheduled orientations for prospective students, including class registration and meeting faculty and other students. There are guides for informal visits, visitors may sit in on classes, and stay overnight. To schedule a visit, contact the Admissions Office. **Campus Safety and Security:** Measures include 24-hour foot and vehicle patrol, emergency notification system, and security escort services. There are also shuttle buses, emergency telephones, lighted pathways/sidewalks, and controlled access to dorms/residences.

REQUIREMENTS: New England College, requirements are 4 years of English, 3 years each of math and social studies, and 2 years each of science and electives are recommended. An essay is required and an interview is recommended. AP and CLEP credits are accepted. Important factors in the admissions decision are personality/intangible qualities, extracurricular activities record, and leadership record. All students must earn a minimum GPA of 2.0 and take 120 credit hours, including an average of 50 in their major. 4 credits of college writing, 1 math course, LAS 1 on being human, LAS 2 communities in America, LAS 3 creative arts, LAS 4 Social Science, LAS 5 laboratory science, LAS 6 humanities, and LAS 7 global perspectives, and 1 LAS elective. **Procedure:** Freshmen are admitted to all sessions. There are deferred admissions and rolling admissions plans. Application deadlines are open. Application fee is $30. Notification is sent on a rolling basis. Applications are accepted on-line. **Transfer Students:** 59 transfer students enrolled in 2015-2016. Transfer students should have a 2.0 minimum GPA from the previous college. A recommendation from the dean of students is required. An interview is recommended. 30 of 120 credits required for the bachelor's degree must be completed at NEC. **International Students:** There are 72 international students enrolled. The school actively recruits these students. They must take the TOEFL with a minimum score of 550 on the paper-based TOEFL (PBT) or 80 on the Internet-based version (iBT) or take the MELAB, the Comprehensive English Language Test, and the college's own test.

ADMISSIONS: 99% of the 2016-2017 applicants were accepted. 12% of the current freshmen were in the top fifth of their class; 41% were in the top two fifths. **Admissions Contact:** Brad Poznaski, Director of UG Admissions. Email: *admission@nec.nec.edu* Web: *www.nec.edu*

FINANCIAL AID: In 2016-2017, 89% of all full-time freshmen and 84% of continuing full-time students received some form of financial aid. 92% of all full-time freshmen and 83% of continuing full-time students received need-based aid. The average freshman award was $31,111. Need-based scholarships or need-based grants averaged $25,229 ($40,620 maximum); need-based self-help aid (loans and jobs) averaged $7,187 ($32,936 maximum); and other non-need-based awards and non-need-based scholarships averaged $21,601 ($34,984 maximum). 85% of undergraduate students work part-time. Average annual earnings from campus work are $1121. The average financial indebtedness of the 2016 graduate was $35,230. The college's own financial statement is required. The FAFSA code is 002579. The priority date for freshman financial aid applications for fall entry is March 1. The filing deadline for fall entry is September 5.

PLYMOUTH STATE UNIVERSITY *(The complete profile is made available exclusively on our website, www.barronspac.com)*

RIVIER UNIVERSITY — D-6

www.rivier.edu

Nashua, NH 03060 — (603) 897-8507, (800) 44-RIVIER

Fax: (603) 891-1799	**Email:** rivadmit@rivier.edu
Full-time: 310 men, 610 women	**Faculty:** n/av
Part-time: 205 men, 505 women	**Ph.D.s:** n/av
Graduate: 255 men, 625 women	**Student/Faculty:** n/av
Year: semesters, summer session	**Tuition:** $28,800
Room & Board: $11,610	**Freshman Class:** n/av
SAT: required	**CEEB CODE:** 3728
Application Deadline: open	**VERY COMPETITIVE**

Rivier College, founded in 1933 by the Sisters of the Presentation of Mary, is a private Roman Catholic college offering a liberal arts and professional curriculum. The figures in the above capsule and in this profile are approximate. There is 1 undergraduate school and 1 graduate school. In addition to regional accreditation, Rivier has baccalaureate program accreditation with NLN. The 68-acre campus is in a suburban area 45 miles north of Boston. Including any residence halls, there are 44 buildings.

STUDENT LIFE: 68% of undergraduates are from New Hampshire. Others are from 13 states, 13 foreign countries, and Canada. 80% are from public schools. 93% are White; 2% Hispanic; 1% African American; 1% Asian American; 1% Foreign. 80% are Catholic. **Female To Male Ratio:** 2.3:1. The average age of freshmen is 18; all undergraduates, 28. 29% do not continue beyond their first year. **Housing:** 425 students can be accommodated in college housing, which includes coed dorms, and a substance-free/wellness residence hall. On-campus housing is guaranteed for all 4 years, and is available on a first-come, and first-served basis. 56% of students commute. All students may keep cars.

FACULTY/CLASSROOMS: 38% of faculty are male; 62% are female. 88% teach undergraduates. No introductory courses are taught by graduate students. The average class size in an introductory lecture is 25; in a laboratory is 20; and in a regular course is 17.

PROGRAMS OF STUDY: Rivier confers B.A., B.S., and B.F.A. degrees. Associate and master's degrees are also awarded. Bachelor's degrees are awarded in BIOLOGICAL SCIENCE (biology/biological science), BUSINESS (business administration and management, management information systems, and management science), COMMUNICATIONS AND THE ARTS (communications, English, graphic design, illustration, and studio art), COMPUTER AND PHYSICAL SCIENCE (computer science and mathematics), EDUCATION (art education, early childhood education, elementary education, English education, mathematics education, secondary education, and social studies education), HEALTH PROFESSIONS (nursing, predentistry, premedicine, and preveterinary science), SOCIAL SCIENCE (history, human development, liberal arts/general studies, political science/government, prelaw, psychology, and sociology). Art, education, and nursing are the strongest academically. Education, psychology, and business have the largest enrollments.

ACTIVITIES: There are no fraternities or sororities. There are 32 groups on campus, including nursing, behavioral sciences, history, paralegal, art, chorus, computers, debate, drama, ethnic, honors, international, literary magazine, newspaper, political, professional, religious, social, social sciences, social service, student government, and yearbook. Popular campus events include Spirit Week, Black History Month, and Women's History Month. **Sports:** There are 5 intercollegiate sports for men and 5 for women, and 7 intramural sports for men and 7 for women. Facilities include a gym, a weight room, and soccer and softball fields.

SERVICES: Counseling and information services are available, as is tutoring in some subjects, such as math, English, business, and languages. Tutoring is also available in other subjects, as well as remedial math and writing. There is a full-service writing center. **Library/Resources:** The library contains 107,200 volumes, 89,572 microform items, 29,094 audio/video tapes/CDs/DVDs, and subscribes to 480 periodicals including electronic. Computerized library services include interlibrary loans and database searching. Special learning facilities include an art gallery, TV station, education curriculum resources center, legal reference center, early childhood center/laboratory school, and language lab. **Physically Challenged Students:** 75% of the campus is accessible. Facilities include wheelchair ramps, elevators, special parking, specially equipped restrooms, and lowered drinking fountains. **Special:** Rivier offers cross-registration through the New Hampshire College and University Council, internships in most majors, an accelerated master's program in English, dual majors, a liberal studies degree, credit by challenge examination, nondegree study, and pass/fail options. There is 1 national honor society and a freshman honors program. **Visiting:** There are regularly scheduled orientations for prospective students, including an opportunity to interview, a tour, class visits, and opportunities to meet with faculty, coaches, and current students. There are guides for informal visits, visitors may sit in on classes, and stay overnight. To schedule a visit, contact the Office of Undergraduate Admissions. **Campus Safety and Security:** Measures include 24-hour foot and vehicle patrol, security escort services, emergency telephones, lighted pathways/sidewalks, 24-hour access by telephone or walkie-talkie, and electronically operated dorm entrances using security cards.

REQUIREMENTS: The SAT is required. Applicants must be high school graduates or hold the GED. The recommended college preparatory curriculum includes 4 years of English, 3 of math, 2 or more each of foreign language and social studies, 1 of lab science, and 4 academic electives. An essay and 1 or 2 letters of recommendation are required, and an interview is highly recommended. Prospective art majors must submit a portfolio. A GPA of 2.5 is required. AP and CLEP credits are accepted. Important factors in the admissions decision are advanced placement or honors courses, recommendations by school officials, and extracurricular activities record. A writing sample is required at entry, and a demonstration of writing proficiency must be shown prior to graduation. Students must complete at least 120 credit hours, ordinarily consisting of 40 3-credit courses with 35 to 60 credits in the student's major, and they must maintain a minimum GPA of 2.0. Distribution requirements include 17 core courses in basic skills of writing and math, the humanities, and the sciences. These courses include religious studies, philosophy, physical and life sciences, fine arts, modern languages, literature, behavioral and social sciences, and Western civilization. **Procedure:** Freshmen are admitted in the fall and spring. Entrance exams should be taken in the junior or senior year. There are deferred admissions and rolling admissions plans. Application deadlines are open. The fall 2016 application fee was $25. Notification of early decision is sent December 1; regular decision, on a rolling basis. Applications are accepted online. **Transfer Students:** Transfer applicants should have a minimum GPA of 2.5 and submit SAT I or ACT scores if they have earned fewer than 12 credits at the previous institution. Official college transcripts are required and an interview is recommended. 60 of 120 credits required for the bachelor's degree must be completed at Rivier. **International Students:** The school actively recruits these students. They must take the TOEFL and the college's own test.

Admissions Contact: David A. Boisvert, Director of Undergraduate Admissions. Email: *rivadmit@rivier.edu* Web: *www.rivier.edu*

FINANCIAL AID: Rivier is a member of CSS. The FAFSA code is 002586. Check with the school for current application deadlines.

SAINT ANSELM COLLEGE — D-6

www.anselm.edu

Manchester, NH 03102	(603) 641-7500 (888)-4-ANSELM
Fax: (603) 641-7550	Email: admission@anselm.edu
Full-time: 762 men, 1116 women	Faculty: 146; IIB, av$
Part-time: 17 men, 28 women	Ph.D.s: 98%
Graduate: n/av	Student/Faculty: 11 to 1
Year: semesters, summer session	Tuition: $36,336
Room & Board: $13,040	Freshman Class: 3568 applied, 2716 accepted, 532 enrolled
SAT CR/M/W: 560/570/570 ACT: 25	CEEB CODE: 3748
Application Deadline: February 1	COMPETITIVE+

Saint Anselm College, founded in 1889, is a private Roman Catholic institution offering a liberal arts education. There is 1 undergraduate school. In addition to regional accreditation, Saint Anselm has baccalaureate program accreditation with NLN. The 380-acre campus is in a suburban area in Southern New Hampshire, minutes from downtown Manchester. 50 miles north of Boston and under an hour from the white mountains and seacoast. Including any residence halls, there are 64 buildings.

STUDENT LIFE: 79% of undergraduates are from out of state, mostly the Northeast. Students are from 28 states, 21 foreign countries, and Canada. 67% are from public schools. 78% are White; 3% Hispanic; 2% African American; 2% two or more races; 13% race unknown; 1% Asian American; 1% Foreign. 55% are Catholic. **Female To Male Ratio:** 1.5:1. The average age of freshmen is 18; all undergraduates, 20. 12% do not continue beyond their first year; 75% remain to graduate. **Housing:** 1794 students can be accommodated in college housing, which includes single-sex and coed dorms, on-campus apartments, special-interest houses, and substance-free housing. On-campus housing is guaranteed for all 4 years. 90% of students live on campus; of those, 88% remain on campus on weekends. All students may keep cars.

FACULTY/CLASSROOMS: 60% of faculty are male; 40% are female. All teach undergraduates. No introductory courses are taught by graduate students. The average class size in a laboratory is 18 and in a regular course is 18.

PROGRAMS OF STUDY: Saint Anselm confers B.A. and B.S.N. degrees. Bachelor's degrees are awarded in BIOLOGICAL SCIENCE (biochemistry and biology/biological science), BUSINESS (accounting, banking and finance, and business administration and management), COMMUNICATIONS AND THE ARTS (classics, English, fine arts, French, and Spanish), COMPUTER AND PHYSICAL SCIENCE (chemistry, computer science, mathematics, and natural sciences), EDUCATION (education and secondary education), ENGINEERING AND ENVIRONMENTAL DESIGN (engineering and environmental science), HEALTH PROFESSIONS (nursing, predentistry, and premedicine), SOCIAL SCIENCE (criminal justice, economics, forensic studies, German area studies, history, liberal arts/general studies, philosophy, political science/government, prelaw, psychology, sociology, and theological studies). Nursing is the strongest academically. Nursing, business, and biology have the largest enrollments.

ACTIVITIES: There are no fraternities or sororities. There are 60 groups on campus, including art, band, chess, choir, chorale, chorus, communications, computers, dance, debate, drama, environmental, ethnic, film, forensics, honors, international, jazz band, LGBT, literary magazine, musical theater, newspaper, orchestra, pep band, photography, political, professional, radio and TV, religious, social, social service, student government, and yearbook. Popular campus events include Family Weekend, Road for Hope, Spring Weekend, Running of the Bells, Gingerbread House Competition, and Shakespeare's Birthday. **Sports:** There are 10 intercollegiate sports for men and 10 for women, and 8 intramural sports for men and 8 for women. Facilities include a gym, ice hockey arena, activity center that houses basketball, volleyball, tennis, racquetball courts, weight and training rooms, a football stadium, a baseball stadium, athletic fields and state-of-the-art fitness center. **Graduates:** From July 1, 2015 to June 30, 2016, 417 bachelor's degrees were awarded. The most popular majors were social sciences (20%), business/marketing (19%), and health professions and related programs (19%). In an average class, 71% graduate in 4 years or less, 74% graduate in 5 years or less, and 75% graduate in 6 years or less.

SERVICES: Counseling and information services are available, as is tutoring in most subjects, and a reader service for the blind. **Library/Resources:** The library contains 219,000 volumes, 65,000 microform items, 8,000 audio/video tapes/CDs/DVDs, and subscribes to 3,900 periodicals including electronic. Computerized library services include interlibrary loans, database searching, Internet access, and Wi-Fi capability. Special learning facilities include an art gallery, planetarium, radio station, TV station, New Hampshire Institute of Politics and Political Library. **Physically Challenged Students:** 80% of the campus is accessible. Facilities include wheelchair ramps, elevators, special parking, specially equipped restrooms, special class scheduling, lowered drinking fountains, lowered telephones, and special housing. **Special:** Saint Anselm offers a 5-year liberal arts and a 3-2 engineering program in cooperation with Manhattan College, University of Notre Dame, University of Massachusetts Lowell, and Catholic University of America. Cross-registration is possible. In addition, internships, work-study, a Washington semester, a New York City semester, study abroad, and nondegree study are available. There are 11 national honor societies and a freshman honors program. **Visiting:** There are regularly scheduled orientations for prospective students, consisting of daily individual interviews and/or group information sessions followed by a campus tour. There are guides for informal visits and visitors may sit in on classes. To schedule a visit, contact the Office of Admission. **Campus Safety and Security:** Measures include 24-hour foot and vehicle patrol, emergency notification system, and self-defense education. There are emergency telephones, lighted pathways/sidewalks, and controlled access to dorms/residences.

REQUIREMENTS: Applicants must have 16 academic credits and 16 Carnegie units, including 4 years of English, 3 each of math and science, 2 of foreign language, and 1 each of history and social studies. An essay is required, and an interview is recommended. The GED is accepted. AP and CLEP credits are accepted. Important factors in the admissions decision are advanced placement or honors courses, leadership record, extracurricular activities record, recommendations by school officials, parents or siblings attended your school, evidence of special talent, personality/intangible qualities, recommendations by alumni, and geographical diversity. In the spirit of what is best in a liberal arts education, the academic core at Saint Anselm College has been designed to offer students a breadth of experience that will prepare them for life, an education that not only provides professional and career preparation, but also encourages a lifelong pursuit of truth that will sustain and enrich their lives. The core is characterized by its balance between common courses that foster a sense of academic community and elective courses that allow for individual student choice. Core Learning Outcomes: Aesthetic & Creative Engagement, Citizenship & Global Engagement, Historical Awareness, Linguistic Awareness, Philosophical Reasoning, Theological Reasoning, Quantitative Reasoning, Scientific Reasoning, Social Scientific Awareness. The new core includes three major elements: Humanities, College Writing, Core Learning Outcomes, Humanities Program - Conversatio. Each student is welcomed into the academic community at Saint Anselm College through a year-long interdisciplinary course in the humanities program - Conversatio. The course title is taken from the Benedictine vow that encourages faithfulness to a way of life within community, and in this first year course students are provided with an orientation to studies in the Liberal Arts and an introduction to the distinctive value of those studies within the Catholic Benedictine intellectual tradition. College Writing Program: Writing is fundamental to the pursuit of knowledge in the tradition of the liberal arts. The College Writing Program offers students the opportunity to develop written communication skills across and within disciplines. The ability to write well also prepares students for success in professions and graduate study. In order to fulfill the requirements of the College Writing Program, all students must take Freshman English and three additional course offerings designated as Writing Intensive. Core Learning Outcomes: The majority of course requirements in the core curriculum will be taken as elective courses that fulfill core learning outcomes. Saint Anselm College has identified nine core learning outcomes that are considered essential for the education of each student. Because the core curriculum is based on student learning outcomes, rather than on specific required courses, students are given greater choice in completing their core requirements as they are able to select from among a variety of courses that fulfill each of the different student learning outcomes. Core learning outcomes are specific to the core curriculum and are a subset of a broader list of student learning outcomes that are integrated throughout the entire curriculum. **Procedure:** Freshmen are admitted fall and spring. Entrance exams should be taken during the spring of the junior year or fall of the senior year. There are early admissions and deferred admissions plans. Early decision applications should be filed by November 15; regular applications, by February 1 for fall entry; and November 15 for spring entry, along with a $50 fee. Notifications are sent March 10. 196 applicants were on the 2016 waiting list; 38 were admitted. Applications are accepted online. **Transfer Students:** 21 transfer students enrolled in 2015-2016. 20 of 40 credits required for the bachelor's degree must be completed at Saint Anselm. **International Students:** There are 12 international students enrolled. They must take the TOEFL with a minimum score of 80 on the Internet-based version (iBT), International students must submit either scores from the SAT or TOEFL if they have not taken the SAT.

ADMISSIONS: 76% of the 2016-2017 applicants were accepted. The SAT scores for the 2016-2017 freshman class were: Critical Reading-- 10% below 500, 57% between 500 and 599, 29% between 600 and 699, and 4% between 700 and 800. Math-- 11% below 500, 51% between 500 and 599, 36% between 600 and 699, and 2% between 700 and 800. Writing-- 11% below 500, 51% between 500 and 599, 34% between 600 and 699, and 4% between 700 and 800. The ACT scores were 6% below 12, 23% between 12 and 17, 37% between 18 and 23, 22% between 24 and 29, and 12% above 30. 56% of the current freshmen were in the top fifth of their class; 87% were in the top two fifths. **Admissions Contact:** Eric Nichols, Deam of Admission. Email: *admission@anselm.edu* Web: *www.anselm.edu*

FINANCIAL AID: In 2016-2017, 96% of all full-time freshmen and 97% of continuing full-time students received some form of financial aid. The average freshman award was $25,200. Need-based scholarships or need-based grants averaged $20,050. Saint Anselm is a member of CSS. The CSS/Profile is required. The FAFSA code is 002580. The deadline for filing freshman financial aid applications for fall entry is March 15.

SOUTHERN NEW HAMPSHIRE UNIVERSITY D-6

www.snhu.edu

Manchester, NH 03106	(603) 645-9611 (800) 642-4968
Fax: (603) 645-9693	**Email:** admission@snhu.edu
Full-time: 1415 men, 1560 women	**Faculty:** 122
Part-time: 28 men, 24 women	**Ph.D.s:** n/av
Graduate: 42 men, 76 women	**Student/Faculty:** 15 to 1
Year: semesters, summer session	**Tuition:** $31,136
Room & Board: $12,062	**Freshman Class:** n/av
ACT: 23	**CEEB CODE:** 3649
Application Deadline: November 15	**COMPETITIVE**

Southern New Hampshire University, founded in 1932, is a private university offering academic programs in business, education, liberal arts, culinary arts, and community economic development. SNHU also has continuing education and online education programs. There are 5 undergraduate schools and 4 graduate schools. In addition to regional accreditation, SNHU has baccalaureate program accreditation with ACBSP, CIHE, and NEASC. The 338-acre campus is in a suburban area 55 miles north of Boston. Including any residence halls, there are 28 buildings.

STUDENT LIFE: 51% of undergraduates are from out of state, mostly the Northeast. Students are from 29 states, 35 foreign countries, and Canada. 9% are Foreign; 68% White; 3% Hispanic; 2% African American; 2% two or more races; 15% race unknown; 1% Asian American. 29% claim no religious affiliation **Female To Male Ratio:** 1.1:1. The average age of freshmen is 18; all undergraduates, 21. 25% do not continue beyond their first year; 50% remain to graduate. **Housing:** 2025 students can be accommodated in college housing, which includes single-sex and coed dorms and on-campus apartments. On-campus housing is guaranteed for all 4 years, and is available on a first-come, and first-served basis. 69% of students live on campus; of those, 65% remain on campus on weekends. All students may keep cars.

FACULTY/CLASSROOMS: 52% of faculty are male; 48% are female. No introductory courses are taught by graduate students. The average class size in an introductory lecture is 20; in a laboratory is 15; and in a regular course is 21.

PROGRAMS OF STUDY: SNHU confers B.A., B.S. and B.B.A. degrees. Associate, master's, and doctoral degrees are also awarded. Bachelor's degrees are awarded in AGRICULTURE (environmental studies), BUSINESS (accounting, business administration and management, fashion merchandising, hospitality management services, international business management, marketing management, marketing/retailing/merchandising, retailing, sports management, and tourism), COMMUNICATIONS AND THE ARTS (advertising, communications, creative writing, English, English as a second/foreign language, English literature, and graphic design), COMPUTER AND PHYSICAL SCIENCE (computer science, digital arts/technology, and information sciences and systems), EDUCATION (business education, early childhood education, education, elementary education, English education, secondary education, social studies education, and special education), ENGINEERING AND ENVIRONMENTAL DESIGN (technological management), SOCIAL SCIENCE (child psychology/development, culinary arts, history, liberal arts/general studies, political science/government, psychology, public affairs, and social science). Business administration is the strongest academically. Business, psychology, and education have the largest enrollments.

ACTIVITIES: 2% of men belong to 2 national fraternities; 3% of women belong to 3 local and 1 national sororities. There are 62 groups on campus, including and field hockey, crew club, band, cheerleading, chess, choir, chorus, dance, debate, drama, ethnic, honors, international, jazz band, LGBT, literary magazine, musical theater, newspaper, orchestra, political, professional, radio and TV, religious, social, social service, sports club, student government, and yearbook. Popular campus events include Fall, Winter, and Spring Weekends, International Night, and Trips Abroad to Italy, Greece, and England. **Sports:** There are 8 intercollegiate sports for men and 7 for women, and 15 intramural sports for men and 15 for women. Facilities include gyms, a swimming pool, tennis courts, a game field, fitness room, natural grass baseball, softball, and practice fields, a racquetball court, and an aerobic/exercise room. **Graduates:** From July 1, 2015 to June 30, 2016, 595 bachelor's degrees were awarded. The most popular majors were business/marketing (40%), psychology (11%), and education (10%). 75 companies recruited on campus in 2015-2016. Of the 2015 graduating class, 11% were enrolled in graduate school within 6 months of graduation, and 85% were employed.

SERVICES: Counseling and information services are available, as is tutoring in every subject, and a reader service for the blind, and remedial math and writing. Peer mentoring and structured learning assistance services are also available. There is also a Jump Start program available for the summer of pre-college. **Library/Resources:** The library contains 94,042 volumes, 378,319 microform items, 3,170 audio/video tapes/CDs/DVDs, and subscribes to 755 periodicals including electronic. Computerized library services include interlibrary loans, database searching, Internet access, and Wi-Fi capability. Special learning facilities include an art gallery, radio station, a center for financial studies, an advertising agency, an audiovisual studio, a psychology observation lab, a career development center, and an iMAC graphics lab. **Physically Challenged Students:** Facilities include wheelchair ramps, elevators, special parking, specially equipped restrooms, special class scheduling, lowered drinking fountains, lowered telephones, and special housing. **Special:** There are co-ops available, a choice of over 35 study abroad opportunities through the University Studies Abroad Consortium, work-study positions throughout the campus, dual majors, and a 3-year bachelor's degree that is an accelerated degree program in business administration. SNHU also offers cross-registration, distance learning, English as a second language, independent study, internships, and student-design major. There are 6 national honor societies, a freshman honors program, and 1 departmental honors program. **Visiting:** There are regularly scheduled orientations for prospective students, including a greeting from college administrators, campus tours with students, and informal presentation/discussions with faculty and staff. There are guides for informal visits and visitors may sit in on classes. To schedule a visit, contact Office of Admission. **Campus Safety and Security:** Measures include 24-hour foot and vehicle patrol, emergency notification system, and security escort services. There are also emergency telephones, lighted pathways/sidewalks, controlled access to dorms/residences, winter driving seminars for international students, and public safety officers.

REQUIREMENTS: A general college-preparatory program is required for degree seeking students. Students must have completed 4 years of English, and 3 years each of math, science with 1 unit of lab, and social studies. An essay, a high school transcript, and a letter of recommendation from a guidance counselor or teacher is required. An interview is strongly recommended. SAT or ACT scores are optional. The GED is accepted. AP and CLEP credits are accepted. Important factors in the admissions decision are leadership record, extracurricular activities record, and recommendations by school officials. To graduate, students must complete a minimum of 120 credit hours, including 39 in their majors, with a GPA of 2.0. Distribution requirements total 45 credits from the college core, including 2 to 3 courses in writing, and 2 math, information technology, public speaking, statistics, behavioral, social and natural sciences, courses and electives in fine arts and literature. **Procedure:** Freshmen are admitted in the fall and spring. There are early admissions and rolling admissions plans. Application deadlines are open. Application fee is $40. Notification is sent on a rolling basis. Applications are accepted online. **Transfer Students:** 283 transfer students enrolled in 2015-2016. Transfer applicants must submit a completed application, an attestation form that confirms high school graduation, and official college transcripts from each institution previously attended. Most successful applicants for transfer admission have a cumulative GPA of 2.5 or higher. Students may enroll in the fall and spring semesters on-campus. Military applicants must submit a completed application, an attestation form or final, official high school transcript, Military transcripts and official college transcripts from each institution previously attended (if applicable). Military experience is considered in the admission process and most successful applicants hold a cumulative GPA of 2.5 or higher. Students may enroll in the fall and spring semesters on-campus. 30 of 120 credits required for the bachelor's degree must be completed at SNHU. **International Students:** There are 89 international students enrolled. The school actively recruits these students. They must take the TOEFL.

ADMISSIONS: The ACT scores were 12% between 12 and 17, 51% between 18 and 23, 37% between 24 and 29, and % above 30. **Admissions Contact:** Tim Whittum, Director of Admission. Email: *admission@snhu.edu* Web: *www.snhu.edu*

FINANCIAL AID: The average freshman award was $22,924. Need-based scholarships or need-based grants averaged $4,220; need-based self-help aid (loans and jobs) averaged $3,001; and non-need-based athletic scholarships averaged $9,971. The average financial indebtedness of the 2016 graduate was $38,574. SNHU is a member of CSS. The FAFSA code is 002580. The priority date for freshman financial aid applications for fall entry is March 15. The deadline for filing freshman financial aid applications for fall entry is June 30.

THOMAS MORE COLLEGE OF LIBERAL ARTS D-6

www.thomasmorecollege.edu

Merrimack, NH 03054 (603) 880-8308 (800) 880-8308

Fax: (603) 880-9280 **Email: admissions@thomasmorecollege.edu**

Full-time: 52 men, 44 women	**Faculty:** 5
Part-time: n/av	**Ph.D.s:** 100%
Graduate: n/av	**Student/Faculty:** 14 to 1
Year: semesters	**Tuition:** $20,400
Room & Board: $9700	**Freshman Class:** n/av
SAT or ACT: required	**CEEB CODE:** 3892
Application Deadline: open	**COMPETITIVE**

Thomas More College of Liberal Arts, founded in 1978, by Roman Catholic educators, is an undergraduate institution that combines intensive reading of the Great Books with lectures and seminar discussions placing those works in their historical, cultural, and theological context. Thomas More welcomes students of all faiths. Figures in the above capsule and in this profile are approximate. There is 1 undergraduate school. In addition to regional accreditation, Thomas More College has baccalaureate program accreditation with AALE. The 14-acre campus is in a small town 40 miles north of Boston. Including any residence halls, there are 5 buildings.

STUDENT LIFE: 81% of undergraduates are from out of state, mostly the Northeast. Students are from 20 states, 2 foreign countries, and Canada. 84% are White; 4% American Indian/Alaska Native; 4% Hispanic; 3% Foreign. **Male To Female Ratio:** 1.2:1. The average age of freshmen is 18; all undergraduates, 20. 9% do not continue beyond their first year. **Housing:** College-sponsored housing includes single-sex dorms. On-campus housing is guaranteed for all 4 years. All students may keep cars. Alcohol is not permitted. All students commute.

FACULTY/CLASSROOMS: 80% of faculty are male; 20% are female. All teach undergraduates, 80% do research, and 80% do both. No introductory courses are taught by graduate students.

PROGRAMS OF STUDY: Thomas More College confers B.A. degrees. Bachelor's degrees are awarded in SOCIAL SCIENCE (liberal arts/general studies).

ACTIVITIES: There are no fraternities or sororities. Groups on campus include art, choir, chorale, chorus, dance, debate, drama, literary magazine, musical theater, newspaper, photography, radio and TV, and yearbook. Popular campus events include St. Patrick's Day. **Sports:** **Graduates:** From July 1, 2015 to June 30, 2016, 12 bachelor's degrees were awarded. The most popular majors were liberal arts (100%). In an average class, 100% graduate in 4 years or less. Of the 2015 graduating class, 27% were enrolled in graduate school within 6 months of graduation, and 73% were employed.

SERVICES: Counseling and information services are available, as is tutoring in most subjects. Informal tutoring is available by request. **Library/Resources:** The library contains 50,000 volumes, and subscribes to 20 periodicals including electronic. Computerized library services include Internet access. Special learning facilities include a radio station. **Physically Challenged Students:** 70% of the campus is accessible. Facilities include wheelchair ramps, special parking, and specially equipped restrooms. **Special:** A semester in Rome for sophomores is required. Internships are available at Vatican Radio, Zenit News, and the United Nations. **Visiting:** There are regularly scheduled orientations for prospective students. There are guides for informal visits, visitors may sit in on classes, and stay overnight. To schedule a visit, contact the Director of Admissions. **Campus Safety and Security:** Measures include security escort services, and lighted pathways/sidewalks.

REQUIREMENTS: The SAT or ACT is required. Applicants should be high school graduates with 4 college preparatory units of English, 3 of math, and 2 each of foreign language, social science, and lab science. The GED is accepted. An essay and 2 letters of recommendation are required. An interview is strongly recommended. Important factors in the admissions decision are personality/intangible qualities, evidence of special talent, and leadership record. To graduate, students in the classes of 2013 and beyond must complete 121 credit hours, including 32 in humanities, 12 each in classical languages, tutorials, philosophy, and Sacred Scripture, 9 in writing/rhetoric/poetics, 7 in fine arts, and 6 each in math, natural science, and theology. In addition, students must complete a junior project of independent study and a senior thesis and seminar. **Procedure:** Freshmen are admitted in the fall and spring. There is a rolling admissions plan. Application deadlines are open. Applications are accepted online. **Transfer Students:** 4 transfer students enrolled in 2015-2016. Applicants must submit a transcript from all higher institutions attended. **International Students:** There are 2 international students enrolled. The school actively recruits these students.

ADMISSIONS: There were 2 National Merit finalists. **Admissions Contact:** Mark Schwerdt, Director of Admissions. Email: *admissions@thomasmorecollege.edu* Web: *www.thomasmorecollege.edu*

FINANCIAL AID: In 2016-2017, 80% of all full-time freshmen and 90% of continuing full-time students received some form of financial aid. 65% of all full-time freshmen and 77% of continuing full-time students received need-based aid. The average freshman award was $8,768. 59% of undergraduate students work part-time. Average annual earnings from campus work are $1960. The average financial indebtedness of the 2016 graduate was $13,056. Thomas More College is a member of CSS. The FAFSA code is 030431. Check with the school for current application deadlines.

UNIVERSITY OF NEW HAMPSHIRE E-5

www.unh.edu

Durham, NH 03824	**(603) 862-1360**
Fax: (603) 862-0077	**Email: admissions@unh.edu**
Full-time: 5647 men, 6820 women	**Faculty:** 644
Part-time: 245 men, 159 women	**Ph.D.s:** 88%
Graduate: 1017 men, 1348 women	**Student/Faculty:** 19 to 1
Year: semesters, summer session	**Tuition:** $17,624 ($31,424)
Room & Board: $10,938	**Freshman Class:** 20203 applied, 15326 accepted, 2880 enrolled
SAT CR/M: 590/570 **ACT:** 25	**CEEB CODE:** 3918
Application Deadline: February 1	**VERY COMPETITIVE**

The University of New Hampshire is the state's flagship public research university, providing comprehensive, high-quality undergraduate programs in liberal arts, engineering, physical sciences, business, life sciences, agriculture, and health and human services, as well as graduate programs (certificate, master's, doctoral). UNH has the feel of a small New England liberal arts college and provides the educational opportunities of a world-class research university, including a distinctive commitment to undergraduate research and one of the nation's largest undergraduate research conferences. There are 7 undergraduate schools and 2 graduate schools. In addition to regional accreditation, UNH has baccalaureate program accreditation with AACSB, ABET, ADA, CSWE, NASM, NRPA, SAF, TEAC, AACN, ACOTE, AEE, ASHA, AUPHA, CCIE, CEPH, COAMFTE, JRC-AT, NAACLS, and NAEYC. The 2600-acre campus is in a small town 60 miles north of Boston. Including any residence halls, there are 150 buildings.

STUDENT LIFE: 54% of undergraduates are from out of state, mostly the Northeast. Students are from 42 states, 38 foreign countries, and Canada. 81% are from public schools. 81% are White; 7% race unknown; 3% Hispanic; 3% Foreign; 2% Asian American; 2% two or more races; 1% African American. **Female To Male Ratio:** 1.2:1. The average age of freshmen is 18; all undergraduates, 20. 14% do not continue beyond their first year; 77% remain to graduate. **Housing:** 7000 students can be accommodated in college housing, which includes coed dorms, on-campus apartments, married student housing, honors houses, special-interest houses, international and substance-free residence halls. On-campus housing is guaranteed for the freshman year only, is available on a first-come, and first-served basis. 55% of students live on campus; of those, 65% remain on campus on weekends. Upperclassmen may keep cars.

FACULTY/CLASSROOMS: 49% of faculty are male; 51% are female. 98% teach undergraduates, 2% do research, and 98% do both. Graduate students teach 2% of introductory courses. The average class size in an introductory lecture is 52; in a laboratory is 21; and in a regular course is 35.

PROGRAMS OF STUDY: UNH confers B.A., B.F.A., B.M., and B.S. degrees. Associate, master's, and doctoral degrees are also awarded. Bachelor's degrees are awarded in AGRICULTURE (animal science, dairy science, EcoGastronomy, environmental studies, environmental horticulture, equine studies, and forestry and related sciences), BIOLOGICAL SCIENCE (biochemistry, biology/biological science, genetics, marine biology, microbiology, molecular biology, neurosciences, nutrition, sustainability, wildlife biology, and zoology), BUSINESS (business administration and management, environment & natnl resource economics, and hospitality management services), COMMUNICATIONS AND THE ARTS (art history, classics, communications, English, fine arts, French, German, information technology, linguistics, music, recreation administration, Russian, Spanish, studio art, and theatre arts), COMPUTER AND PHYSICAL SCIENCE (applied mathematics, chemistry, computer science, earth science, earth science/adolescence education, geology, mathematics, physics, and statistics), EDUCATION (athletic training, mathematics education, and physical education), ENGINEERING AND ENVIRONMENTAL DESIGN (bioengineering, chemical engineering, city/community/regional planning, civil engineering, computer engineering, electrical/electronics engineering, engineering physics, environmental engineering, environmental science, mechanical engineering, and ocean engineering), HEALTH PROFESSIONS (biomedical science, health administration and policy, kinesiology, nursing, occupational therapy, and speech pathology/audiology), SOCIAL SCIENCE (anthropology, economics, European studies, family/consumer studies, French studies, geography, history, human development & family studies, humanities, international studies, Italian studies, justice and society, philosophy, physical fitness/movement, political science/government, psychology, social work, sociology, and women's studies). business, biology and life sciences, and engineering are the strongest academically. Business administration, psychology, and biomedical science have the largest enrollments.

ACTIVITIES: 11% of men belong to 11 national fraternities; 14% of women belong to 8 national sororities. There are 281 groups on campus, including art, band, cheerleading, chess, choir, chorale, chorus, computers, dance, debate, drama, environmental, ethnic, film, honors, international, jazz band, LGBT, literary magazine, marching band, musical theater, newspaper, opera, orchestra, pep band, photography, political, professional, radio and TV, religious, social, social service, student government, symphony, and yearbook. Popular campus events include Jukebox, Student Activities Fair, Concerts and Comedians, Winter Carnival, Athletic Events, Homecoming, MUB Lecture Series, May Day, and Kwanzaa Celebration. **Sports:** There are 36 intercollegiate sports for men and 43 for women, and 34 intramural sports for men and 34 for women. Facilities include indoor and outdoor swimming pools, tracks, tennis courts, gyms, wrestling and gymnastics rooms, dance studio, playing fields, indoor ice rink, cross-country ski trails, and a pond for sailing. There is also a recreation and sports complex, for hockey special events, a fitness center, jogging track, weight room, racquetball courts, international squash court, aerobics and martial arts studios, multipurpose courts, basketball courts, recreation equipment and programming for people with disabilities. **Graduates:** From July 1, 2015 to June 30, 2016, 2870 bachelor's degrees were awarded. The most popular majors were business administration (18%), psychology (8%), and communication (6%). 200 companies recruited on campus in 2015-2016. In an average class, 66% graduate in 4 years or less, 76% graduate in 5 years or less, and 77% graduate in 6 years or less. Of the 2015 graduating class, 30% were enrolled in graduate school within 6 months of graduation, and 50% were employed.

SERVICES: Counseling and information services are available, as is tutoring in most subjects. Instruction in learning strategies, study skills, time management, and organizational skills is also available. The university writing center offers free assistance by trained consultants. **Library/Resources:** The 4 libraries contain 1.4 million volumes, 129,763 microform items, 69,250 audio/video tapes/CDs/DVDs, and subscribe to 76,791 periodicals including electronic. Computerized library services include interlibrary loans, database searching, Internet access, and Wi-Fi capability. Special learning facilities include an art gallery, radio station, art gallery, radio station, optical observatory, marine research labs (coastal, estuarine, island), interoperability lab, experiential learning center with challenge course, electron microscope, child development center, journalism lab, experimental wind tunnel, agricultural and equine facilities including an organic research dairy farm and sustainable agriculture facilities, advanced manufacturing center (coming in 2017), nursing simulation lab, instructional and recreational climbing wall, exercise physiology lab, sawmill, language labs, performing arts center, and survey center. **Physically Challenged Students:** 88% of the campus is accessible. Facilities include wheelchair ramps, elevators, special parking, specially equipped restrooms, special class scheduling, lowered drinking fountains, lowered telephones, and special housing. Accommodations made on a case-by-case basis include sign language interpreters, reduced course loads, extended exam time, accessible transportation, academic modifications, note takers, text on tape, and note takers. **Special:** UNH is committed to providing students with an absorbing and comprehensive educational experience that fosters the development of the whole person. A central mission is to offer students a wide variety of enriching co-curricular programs. There is nationwide study through the National Student Exchange and worldwide study through the Center for International Education. Exciting opportunities for undergraduate research are supported by faculty and the prospect of special funding. Many majors include an internship or service-learning experience. A Washington semester, Semester in the City, work-study, BA/BS degrees, dual majors, student-designed majors and bachelor's/graduate degree plans are also available. Joint programs with Cornell University in marine science are offered. Extensive cross-registration is possible through the New Hampshire College and University Council Consortium. UNH has a vast range of interdisciplinary minors designed to complement a major's focus with intellectual interests and pre-professional experience. There are 20 national honor societies, Phi Beta Kappa, a freshman honors program, and 67 departmental honors programs. **Visiting:** There are regularly scheduled orientations for prospective students, campus tours, group information sessions, and open house programs. There are guides for informal visits and visitors may sit in on classes. To schedule a visit, contact the Admissions Office. **Campus Safety and Security:** Measures include 24-hour foot and vehicle patrol, emergency notification system, self-defense education, and security escort services. There are also shuttle buses, emergency telephones, lighted pathways/sidewalks, controlled access to dorms/residences, and prevention awareness programs.

REQUIREMENTS: The SAT or ACT is required, as is the ACT Optional Writing test also required: 15 academic units: 4 English, 3 mathematics, 3 science (at least 2 must include lab), 2 foreign language, and 3 social studies. Recommended: 19 academic units: 4 units each in English, mathematics, and science (3 that include lab), 3 units each in foreign language, social studies, 1 in visual/performing arts. Essay required for all students. Audition is required for music and theatre students. A portfolio is required for students wishing to major in Studio Arts. AP and CLEP credits are accepted. Important factors in the admissions decision are advanced placement or honors courses, recommendations by school officials, and evidence of special talent. To graduate, all students must maintain a GPA of 2.0 and complete at least 128 credits, with a minimum of 36 credits and 10 classes in the major. General education requirements include 4 writing-intensive courses, including freshman composition, 3 courses in biological/physical science, 1 course each in quantitative reasoning, historical perspectives, social science, fine arts, foreign culture, and philosophy/literature. All seniors must complete a senior thesis or project. **Procedure:** Freshmen are admitted in the fall and spring. Entrance exams should be taken before February 1 of the senior year. There are early decision, deferred admissions, and rolling admissions plans. Early decision applications should be filed by November 15; regular applications, by February 1 for fall entry; and October 15 for spring entry, along with a $50 fee. Notification of early decision is sent January 15; regular decision, April 15. 6275 early decision candidates were accepted for the 2016-2017 class. Application fees are waived if application is completed online. **Transfer Students:** 587 transfer students enrolled in 2015-2016. Applicants must submit an overall minimum GPA of 2.8 in a general education curriculum. The SAT or the ACT is required unless waived. An essay is required. A letter of recommendation is optional. 32 of 128 credits required for the bachelor's degree must be completed at UNH. **International Students:** There are 399 international students enrolled. The school actively recruits these students. They must take the TOEFL with a minimum score of 550 on the paper-based TOEFL (PBT) or 80 on the Internet-based version (iBT). They must also take the SAT or ACT.

ADMISSIONS: 76% of the 2016-2017 applicants were accepted. The SAT scores for the 2016-2017 freshman class were: Critical Reading-- 8% below 500, 42% between 500 and 599, 43% between 600 and 699, and 7% between 700 and 800. Math-- 10% below 500, 52% between 500 and 599, 31% between 600 and 699, and 7% between 700 and 800. The ACT scores were 3% between 12 and 17, 34% between 18 and 23, 53% between 24 and 29, and 10% above 30. 40% of the current freshmen were in the top fifth of their class; 76% were in the top two fifths. 14 freshmen graduated first in their class. **Admissions Contact:** Robert McGann, Director of Admissions. Email: *robert.mcgann@unh.edu* Web: *http:/admissions.unh.edu/*

FINANCIAL AID: In 2016-2017, 87% of all full-time freshmen and 81% of continuing full-time students received some form of financial aid. 71% of all full-time freshmen and 64% of continuing full-time students received need-based aid. The average freshman award was $23,442. Need-based scholarships or need-based grants averaged $11,051 ($31,821 maximum); need-based self-help aid (loans and jobs) averaged $5,807 ($8,000 maximum); non-need-based athletic scholarships averaged $26,223 ($40,876 maximum); and other non-need-based awards and non-need-based scholarships averaged $11,006 ($44,500 maximum). 14% of undergraduate students work part-time. Average annual earnings from campus work are $2490. The average financial indebtedness of the 2016 graduate was $38,979. The FAFSA code is 002589. The deadline for filing freshman financial aid applications for fall entry is March 1.

UNIVERSITY OF NEW HAMPSHIRE - MANCHESTER D6

www.manchester.unh.edu

Manchester, NH 03101 **(603) 641-4150**

Fax: (603) 641-4342 **Email: manchester.admissions@unh.edu**

Full-time: 264 men, 295 women	**Faculty:** n/av
Part-time: 164 men, 119 women	**Ph.D.s:** n/av
Graduate: 98 men, 182 women	**Student/Faculty:** 13 to 1
Year: semesters, summer session	**Tuition:** $14,490 ($28,290)
Room & Board: n/app	**Freshman Class:** 205 applied, 149 accepted, 57 enrolled
SAT CR/M/W: 520/517/494 **ACT:** 21	**CEEB CODE:** 002094
Application Deadline: n/av	**COMPETITIVE**

University of New Hampshire at Manchester, founded in 1985, is the sixth college under the University of New Hampshire. Manchester provides associate's, bachelor's and master's degrees, with a special emphasis on programs that address urban issues and integrate undergraduate and graduate studies with professional and business communities. In addition to regional accreditation, Manchester has baccalaureate program accreditation with ABET and CCIE. The campus is 53 miles from Boston. Including any residence halls, there is 1 building.

STUDENT LIFE: 97% of undergraduates are from New Hampshire. 73% are White; 4% Hispanic; 3% Asian American; 2% two or more races; 16% race unknown; 1% African American. **Female To Male Ratio:** 1.1:1. The average age of freshmen is 18; all undergraduates, 24. 19% do not continue beyond their first year; 67% remain to graduate. **Housing:** College-sponsored housing includes single-sex and coed off-campus apartments. All students commute. All students may keep cars.

FACULTY/CLASSROOMS: No introductory courses are taught by graduate students. The average class size in a regular course is 6.

PROGRAMS OF STUDY: Manchester confers B.A. and B.S. degrees. Associate and master's degrees are also awarded. Bachelor's degrees are awarded in BIOLOGICAL SCIENCE (biological sciences and biotechnology), BUSINESS (business (dual major program)), COMMUNICATIONS AND THE ARTS (communications and English), COMPUTER AND PHYSICAL SCIENCE (computer information technology and computer science), EDUCATION (English education), ENGINEERING AND ENVIRONMENTAL DESIGN (electrical and computer engineering and mechanical engineering technology), SOCIAL SCIENCE (history, homeland security, humanities, and psychology). ASL/English interpreting, engineering technology, homeland security, and neuropsychology are the strongest academically. Biological sciences, business, and communication arts have the largest enrollments.

ACTIVITIES: There are no fraternities or sororities. There are 32 groups on campus, including art, band, chorus, communications, computers, dance, drama, environmental, ethnic, film, international, LGBT, literary magazine, musical theater, newspaper, political, professional, and social service. **Sports:** There is no sports program at Manchester. **Graduates:** From July 1, 2015 to June 30, 2016, 177 bachelor's degrees were awarded. The most popular majors were business, biological science, and communication arts. In an average class, 38% graduate in 4 years or less and 67% graduate in 6 years or less.

SERVICES: Counseling and information services are available, as is tutoring in every subject, and a reader service for the blind. **Library/Resources:** Computerized library services include interlibrary loans, database searching, Internet access, and Wi-Fi capability. **Physically Challenged Students:** Facilities include wheelchair ramps, elevators, special parking, specially equipped restrooms, special class scheduling, lowered drinking fountains, and lowered telephones. **Visiting:** There are regularly scheduled orientations for prospective students, campus tours, open house porgrams, and information sesssions. There are guides for informal visits. To schedule a visit, contact Office of Admissions. **Campus Safety and Security:** Measures include emergency notification system, self-defense education, and security escort services. There are lighted pathways/sidewalks.

REQUIREMENTS: AP and CLEP credits are accepted. Important factors in the admissions decision are advanced placement or honors courses, leadership record, and personality/intangible qualities. **Procedure:** Freshmen are admitted in the fall and spring. There are early admissions and deferred admissions plans. Application deadlines are open. Application fee is $50. Applications are accepted online. **Transfer Students:** 157 transfer students enrolled in 2015-2016. 32 of 128 credits required for the bachelor's degree must be completed at Manchester. **International Students:** They must take the TOEFL with a minimum score of 550 on the paper-based TOEFL (PBT) or 79 on the Internet-based version (iBT). They must also take the SAT or ACT.

ADMISSIONS: 73% of the 2016-2017 applicants were accepted. The SAT scores for the 2016-2017 freshman class were: Critical Reading-- 41% below 500, 46% between 500 and 599, 11% between 600 and 699, and 2% between 700 and 800. Math-- 41% below 500, 44% between 500 and 599, and 15% between 600 and 699. Writing-- 50% below 500, 41% between 500 and 599, and 9% between 600 and 699. The ACT scores were 40% below 12, 40% between 12 and 17, 40% between 18 and 23, and 20% above 30. **Admissions Contact:** Erika Couture, Senior Associate Director of Admissions. Email: *manchester.admissions@unh.edu* Web: *www.manchester.unh.edu*

FINANCIAL AID: In 2016-2017, 86% of all full-time freshmen received some form of financial aid. 73% of all full-time freshmen received need-based aid. The priority date for freshman financial aid applications for fall entry is March 1.

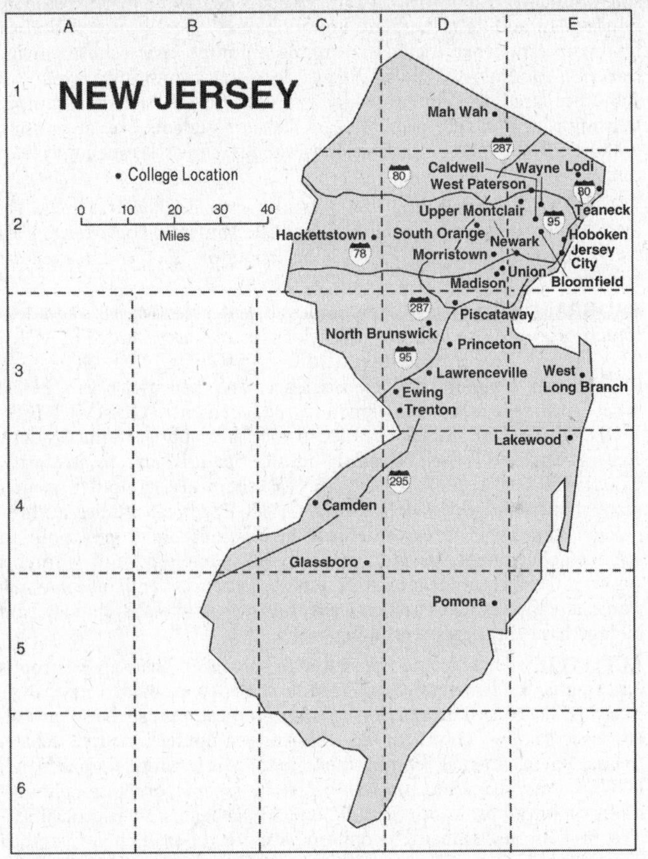

BERKELEY COLLEGE/NEW JERSEY *(The complete profile is made available exclusively on our website, www.barronspac.com)*

BLOOMFIELD COLLEGE *(The complete profile is made available exclusively on our website, www.barronspac.com)*

CALDWELL UNIVERSITY *(The complete profile is made available exclusively on our website, www.barronspac.com)*

CENTENARY COLLEGE C-2

www.centenarycollege.edu

Hackettstown, NJ 07840	**(908) 852-1400** **(800) 236-8679**
Fax: (908) 852-3454	**Email: admissions@centenarycollege.edu**
Full-time: 680 men, 1160 women	**Faculty:** 72; IIB, -$
Part-time: 58 men, 95 women	**Ph.D.s:** 54%
Graduate: 229 men, 472 women	**Student/Faculty:** 26 to 1
Year: semesters, summer session	**Tuition:** $32,656
Room & Board: $10,946	**Freshman Class:** 753 applied, 672 accepted, 272 enrolled
SAT CR/M: required **ACT:** 21	**CEEB CODE:** 2080
Application Deadline: open	**COMPETITIVE**

Centenary College, founded in 1867, is a private institution affiliated with the United Methodist Church. The college offers undergraduate and graduate programs in liberal arts, business, international studies, education, equine studies, fashion, and fine arts. Figures in the above capsule and in this profile are approximate. There is 1 undergraduate school and 1 graduate school. In addition to regional accreditation, Centenary has baccalaureate program accreditation with CSWE, NASDTEC, and TEAC. The 42-acre campus is in a suburban area 55 miles west of New York City. Including any residence halls, there are 22 buildings.

STUDENT LIFE: 88% of undergraduates are from New Jersey. Others are from 21 states, 8 foreign countries, and Canada. 85% are from public schools. 9% are African American; 7% Hispanic; 66% White; 3% Asian American; 1% American Indian/Alaska Native; 1% Foreign. **Female To Male Ratio:** 1.8:1. The average age of freshmen is 18; all undergraduates, 24. 24% do not continue beyond their first year; 51% remain to graduate. **Housing:** 756 students can be accommodated in college housing, which includes single-sex and coed dorms and on-campus apartments. On-campus housing is available on a first-come, first-served basis, and on a lottery system for upperclassmen. 54% of students live on campus; of those, 70% remain on campus on weekends. All students may keep cars.

FACULTY/CLASSROOMS: 44% of faculty are male; 56% are female. All teach undergraduates, and all do research. No introductory courses are taught by graduate students. The average class size in an introductory lecture is 25; in a laboratory is 20; and in a regular course is 15.

PROGRAMS OF STUDY: Centenary confers B.A., B.F.A. and B.S. degrees. Associate and master's degrees are also awarded. Bachelor's degrees are awarded in AGRICULTURE (equine science), BIOLOGICAL SCIENCE (biology/biological science), BUSINESS (accounting and business administration and management), COMMUNICATIONS AND THE ARTS (applied art, communications, dramatic arts, and English), COMPUTER AND PHYSICAL SCIENCE (mathematics), EDUCATION (elementary education and secondary education), SOCIAL SCIENCE (criminal justice, fashion design and technology, history, interdisciplinary studies, international studies, political science/government, psychology, and sociology). Equine studies, business, and education are the strongest academically.

ACTIVITIES: 3% of men belong to 1 local fraternity; 5% of women belong to 3 local sororities. There are 30 groups on campus, including art, chorus, dance, debate, drama, environmental, ethnic, honors, international, LGBT, literary magazine, newspaper, photography, political, professional, radio and TV, religious, social, social service, student government, and yearbook. Popular campus events include President's Ball, Community Plunge, and Tis the Season. **Sports:** There are 7 intercollegiate sports for men and 7 for women. Facilities include a gym, a fitness center and indoor pool, tennis courts, playing fields, and an equine center and stables. **Graduates:** From July 1, 2015 to June 30, 2016, 524 bachelor's degrees were awarded. The most popular majors were business administration (51%), social sciences (9%), and psychology (8%). 35 companies recruited on campus in 2015-2016. In an average class, 51% graduate in 4 years or less, 51% graduate in 5 years or less, and 52% graduate in 6 years or less. Of the 2015 graduating class, 10% were enrolled in graduate school within 6 months of graduation, and 75% were employed.

SERVICES: Counseling and information services are available, as is tutoring in every subject. There is remedial math, reading, and writing. Learning associates provide personalized support in many subjects. **Library/Resources:** The library contains 68,000 volumes, 20,000 microform items, 5,000 audio/video tapes/CDs/DVDs, and subscribes to 375 periodicals including electronic. Computerized library services include interlibrary loans, database searching, Internet access, and Wi-Fi capability. Special learning facilities include a radio station, TV station, an equestrian center, and CAD lab. **Physically Challenged Students:** 60% of the campus is accessible. Facilities include wheelchair ramps, special parking, specially equipped restrooms, special class scheduling, and lowered telephones. **Special:** Centenary offers internships in every major. The college offers study abroad in England and other countries, dual majors, as long as they are covered under the same degree, an accelerated degree program in liberal arts and business administration, student-designed majors, work-study on-campus, and a pass/fail option. Students ages 25 or older may earn life experience credits. There is 1 national honor society and a freshman honors program. **Visiting:** There are regularly scheduled orientations for prospective students, including basic skills testing, advising, registration, and social events. Visitors may sit in on classes and stay overnight. To schedule a visit, contact the Admissions Office. **Campus Safety and Security:** Measures include 24-hour foot and vehicle patrol, emergency notification system, security escort services, emergency telephones, lighted pathways/sidewalks, and controlled access to dorms/residences.

REQUIREMENTS: Minimum scores include a satisfactory SAT score or an ACT composite of 18. Applicants must be graduates of accredited secondary schools or have earned a GED. Centenary requires 16 academic credits or Carnegie units, based on 4 years of English, math, and science, and 2 years each of foreign language and history. An essay is required for freshmen, and an interview is recommended. Applicants to specific fine arts programs must also submit a portfolio. A GPA of 2.0 is required. AP and CLEP credits are accepted. Important factors in the admissions decision are advanced placement or honors courses, leadership record, and ability to finance college education. Students must complete a distribution of 40 to 46 semester hours in core courses, including college seminars, and 9 credits in liberal arts studies, as well as the required number of credits, usually 48, for their majors. At least 128 semester hours and a minimum GPA of 2.0 are needed to earn the bachelor's degree. **Procedure:** Freshmen are admitted in the fall and spring. Entrance exams should be taken as early as possible in the senior year. There are deferred admissions and rolling admissions plans. Application deadlines are open. Application fee is $30. Notification is sent on a rolling basis. Applications are accepted online. **Transfer Students:** 178 transfer students enrolled in 2015-2016. Applicants must have a minimum college GPA of 2.0 and submit proof of high school graduation or the equivalent. 32 of 128 credits required for the bachelor's degree must be completed at Centenary. **International Students:** There are 54 international students enrolled. The school actively recruits these students. They must take the TOEFL with a minimum score of 520 on the paper-based TOEFL (PBT) or 80 on the Internet-based version (iBT), or IELTS with a score of 5.0. They must also take the SAT or ACT.

ADMISSIONS: 89% of the 2016-2017 applicants were accepted. The SAT scores for the 2016-2017 freshman class were: Critical Reading-- 67% below 500, 25% between 500 and 599, 7% between 600 and 699, and 1% between 700 and 800. Math-- 65% below 500, 30% between 500 and 599, and 5% between 600 and 699. The ACT scores were 29% below 12, 43% between 12 and 17, 7% between 18 and 23, 7% between 24 and 29, and 14% above 30. **Admissions Contact:** Glenna Warren, Dean of Admissions and Financial Aid. Email: *admissions@centenarycollege.edu* Web: *www.centenarycollege.edu*

FINANCIAL AID: In 2016-2017, 85% of all full-time freshmen and 88% of continuing full-time students received some form of financial aid. 84% of all full-time freshmen and 85% of continuing full-time students received need-based aid. The average freshman award was $19,100. Need-based scholarships or need-based grants averaged $14,806; and need-based self-help aid (loans and jobs) averaged $5,279. 75% of undergraduate students work part-time. Average annual earnings from campus work are $1200. The average financial indebtedness of the 2016 graduate was $28,104. The FAFSA code is 002599. The priority date for freshman financial aid applications for fall entry is March 15. The filing deadline for fall entry is September 1.

COLLEGE OF SAINT ELIZABETH *(The complete profile is made available exclusively on our website, www.barronspac.com)*

DREW UNIVERSITY/COLLEGE OF LIBERAL ARTS D-2

www.drew.edu

Madison, NJ 07940 **(973) 408-DREW**

Email: cadm@drew.edu

Full-time: 599 men, 877 women	**Faculty:** 128; IIA, +$
Part-time: 19 men, 26 women	**Ph.D.s:** 98%
Graduate: 282 men, 326 women	**Student/Faculty:** 12 to 1
Year: semesters, summer session	**Tuition:** $47,752
Room & Board: $13,296	**Freshman Class:** n/av
SAT CR/M/W: 590/560/570 **ACT:** 26	**CEEB CODE:** 2193
Application Deadline: February 1	**VERY COMPETITIVE**

The College of Liberal Arts was added to Drew University in 1928 and is part of an educational complex that includes a theological school and a graduate school. Drew is a private, independent institution. There is 1 undergraduate school and 2 graduate schools. The 186-acre campus is in a suburban area 30 miles west of New York City. Including any residence halls, there are 57 buildings.

STUDENT LIFE: 62% of undergraduates are from New Jersey. Others are from 43 states, 45 foreign countries, and Canada. 9% are African American; 8% Foreign; 7% race unknown; 6% Asian American; 55% White; 5% two or more races; 11% Hispanic. **Female To Male Ratio:** 1.4:1. The average age of freshmen is 18; all undergraduates, 20. 13% do not continue beyond their first year; 67% remain to graduate. **Housing:** 1451 students can be accommodated in college housing, which includes single-sex and coed dorms, on-campus apartments, and married student housing. In addition, there are honors houses, special-interest houses, first year experience living learning community, civic scholars living learning community, global village learning community, wellness/substance-free floors, single gender floors, and quiet floors. On-campus housing is guaranteed for all 4 years. 78% of students live on campus; of those, 70% remain on campus on weekends. Upperclassmen may keep cars.

FACULTY/CLASSROOMS: 50% of faculty are male; 50% are female. No introductory courses are taught by graduate students. The average class size in an introductory lecture is 20; in a laboratory is 14; and in a regular course is 17.

PROGRAMS OF STUDY: Drew confers B.A. degrees. Master's and doctoral degrees are also awarded. Bachelor's degrees are awarded in AGRICULTURE (environmental studies), BIOLOGICAL SCIENCE (biochemistry, biology/biological science, and neurosciences), BUSINESS (business administration and management), COMMUNICATIONS AND THE ARTS (art, art history and appreciation, Chinese, classics, English, French, German, music, Spanish, and theatre arts), COMPUTER AND PHYSICAL SCIENCE (chemistry, computer science, mathematics, and physics), SOCIAL SCIENCE (African studies, anthropology, economics, history, international relations, philosophy, political science/government, psychology, religion, sociology, and women's studies). Theatre arts, natural & physical sciences, and international studies are the strongest academically. Business studies, psychology, and biology have the largest enrollments.

ACTIVITIES: There are no fraternities or sororities. There are 80 groups on campus. Students are encouraged to start new clubs that meet their interests. There are currently over 70 clubs on campus, such as political, art, cheerleading, choir, chorale, chorus, computers, dance, debate, drama, environmental, ethnic, film, honors, international, jazz band, LGBT, literary magazine, musical theater, newspaper, orchestra, photography, political, professional, radio and TV, religious, social, social service, student government, symphony, and yearbook. Popular campus events include Drew Forum Lecture Series, First Annual Picnic, Holiday Ball, JamFest a Capella Concert, Chamber Music Society of Lincoln Center Concert Series, Drew Theatre productions, MedFest - That Medieval Thing, Bear-B-Que, Boardwalk Night, Hoyt Halloween. **Sports:** There are 9 intercollegiate sports for men and 11 for women, and 12 intramural sports for men and 12 for women. Facilities include an artificial turf athletic field, a gym, a field house with an indoor track and practice space, pool with diving board, tennis complex, weight training room, fitness center, a game room, and baseball and softball fields. **Graduates:** From July 1, 2015 to June 30, 2016, 266 bachelor's degrees were awarded. The most popular majors were business studies (14%), psychology (9%), and biology (9%). In an average class, 63% graduate in 4 years or less, 66% graduate in 5 years or less, and 67% graduate in 6 years or less.

SERVICES: Counseling and information services are available, as is tutoring in most subjects, and a reader service for the blind. Drew's Center for Academic Excellence includes academic coaching, and math and science resource center. **Library/Resources:** The 2 libraries contain 743,441 volumes, 526,964 microform items, and 6,170 audio/video tapes/CDs/DVDs, and subscribe to 1,405 periodicals including electronic. Computerized library services include interlibrary loans, database searching, Internet access, and Wi-Fi capability. Special learning facilities include an art gallery, planetarium, and radio station. An observatory and an arboretum. It is also home to the Charles A. Dana Center for Research Scientists Emeriti and the Shakespeare Theatre of New Jersey. **Physically Challenged Students:** Facilities include wheelchair ramps, elevators, special parking, specially equipped restrooms, special class scheduling, lowered drinking fountains, lowered telephones, special housing. The main dining facility, the student center and commons, and the ground floor of every dorm and classroom building are accessible to students with physical disabilities. **Special:** Civic Scholars program, five-year dual degree program (BA/MA in teaching) program with Drew's Caspersen School of Graduate Studies, seven-year dual degree program (BA/MD) with Rutgers-New Jersey Medical School, five-year dual degree program (BA/BS in engineering) with Columbia University, six-year dual degree (BA/JD) program with Seton Hall Law School, six-year dual degree program (BA/JD) with New York Law School, five-year dual degree program (BA/MEM or MF) in Environmental Management or Forestry with Duke University, five-year dual degree program (BA/MA in Business Management) with Wake Forest University, five-year dual degree program (BA/MS in Software Engineering) with Stevens Institute of Technology, study abroad opportunities. There are 15 national honor societies, Phi Beta Kappa, a freshman honors program, and 30 departmental honors programs. **Visiting:** There are regularly scheduled orientations for prospective students. Hour-long student-led campus tours, and information sessions that give prospective students and parents the opportunity to meet with admission counselors, explore our programs, learn about admission and enrollment procedures, and ask questions. There are guides for informal visits and visitors may sit in on classes. To schedule a visit, contact the Office of College Admissions. **Campus Safety and Security:** Measures include 24-hour foot and vehicle patrol, emergency notification system, self-defense education, security escort services, emergency telephones, lighted pathways/sidewalks, and controlled access to dorms/residences.

REQUIREMENTS: Standardized test scores are not required for admission to Drew, but will be considered along with other academic credentials when submitted. Students electing to apply to Drew without submitting the results from the SAT or ACT must typically have strong high school transcripts in a college-prep or honors program with no grade below a B. Note: some academic scholarships will require standardized test scores. The university strongly recommends 18 academic credits or Carnegie units, including 4 in English, 3 each in math, the same foreign language, science including 2 lab courses, and history, with the remaining 2 in other academic courses. An essay is also required, and an interview is strongly recommended, especially for students interested in competing for an academic scholarship. AP and CLEP credits are accepted. To graduate, students must earn at least 128 credits, of which at least 64 must be beyond the lower level and at least 32 must be at the upper level. All students must fulfill the requirements of a major and those of the general education program. For graduation, the cumulative GPA, both overall and in the major, must be at least 2.0. General education requirements include a first-year seminar, demonstration of writing competency by completion of at least three writing courses, intermediate proficiency in a foreign language, two quantitative courses, two diversity courses, five breadth courses (one each from the following areas: natural science, social science, humanities, arts, and interdisciplinary) and an off-campus experience. Students may complete a minor, but one is not required. **Procedure:** Freshmen are admitted in the fall and spring. Entrance exams should be taken by fall of the senior year of high school. There are early decision, early admissions, and deferred admissions plans. Early decision applications should be filed by Janurary 15; regular applications, by February 1 for fall entry, along with a $40 fee. Notification of early decision is sent February 15; regular decision, March 18. 98 early decision candidates were accepted for the 2016-2017 class. 84 applicants were on the 2016 waiting list; 58 were admitted. Application fees are waived if application is completed online. **Transfer Students:** 78 transfer students enrolled in 2015-2016. Applicants must submit official high school and college transcripts, a personal essay, and a statement of good standing from previous schools attended. An interview also may be required. Drew takes a holistic approach to reviewing the application for admission. Admission decisions are based on the strength of the academic record as well as extra-curricular involvement. We consider college grade-point average, essay and recommendations. If the applicant has earned less than 24 college credits, we may also consider high school grades and course of study. Transfer students are not required to submit the results from standardized tests such as the SAT or ACT, but may choose to do so. 48 of 128 credits required for the bachelor's degree must be completed at Drew. **International Students:** There are 198 international students enrolled. The school actively recruits these students. They must take the TOEFL with a minimum score of 550 on the paper-based TOEFL (PBT) or 80 on the Internet-based version (iBT).

ADMISSIONS: 57% of the 2016-2017 applicants were accepted. The SAT scores for the 2016-2017 freshman class were: Critical Reading-- 15% below 500, 37% between 500 and 599, 36% between 600 and 699, and 12% between 700 and 800. Math-- 15% below 500, 54% between 500 and 599, 27% between 600 and 699, and 4% between 700 and 800. Writing-- 17% below 500, 45% between 500 and 599, 31% between 600 and 699, and 7% between 700 and 800. The ACT scores were 1% between 12 and 17, 23% between 18 and 23, 60% between 24 and 29, and 16% above 30. **Admissions Contact:** James Skiff, Executive Director of College Admissions. Email: *cadm@drew.edu* Web: *www.drew.edu*

FINANCIAL AID: The average financial indebtedness of the 2016 graduate was $24,964. The FAFSA code is 002603. The deadline for filing freshman financial aid applications for fall entry is February 15.

FAIRLEIGH DICKINSON UNIVERSITY/ COLLEGE AT FLORHAM — D-2

www.fdu.edu

Madison, NJ 07940 — (973) 443-8900, (800) 338-8803

Fax: (973) 443-8088 — **Email:** globaleducation@fdu.edu

Full-time: 1076 men, 1205 women — **Faculty:** n/av
Part-time: 98 men, 101 women — **Ph.D.s:** n/av
Graduate: 512 men, 517 women — **Student/Faculty:** n/av
Year: semesters, summer session — **Tuition:** $39,222
Room & Board: $12,840 — **Freshman Class:** 3907 applied, 2601 accepted, 646 enrolled
SAT CR/M/W: 520/530/520 **ACT:** required — **CEEB CODE:** 2262
Application Deadline: open — **COMPETITIVE**

Fairleigh Dickinson University/College at Florham, founded in 1942, is an independent university offering undergraduate, graduate, and professional level programs. Studies are rooted in the liberal arts but also offer hands-on opportunities in business and professional internships, cooperative education, and global studies abroad. Figures in the above capsule and in this profile are approximate. There are 3 undergraduate schools and 2 graduate schools. In addition to regional accreditation, College at Florham has baccalaureate program accreditation with AACSB, NASDTEC, and ACS. The 166-acre campus is in a suburban area 27 miles west of New York City. Including any residence halls, there are 36 buildings.

STUDENT LIFE: 85% of undergraduates are from New Jersey. Others are from 27 states, 12 foreign countries, and Canada. 8% are African American; 8% Hispanic; 69% White; 3% Asian American; 1% American Indian/Alaska Native; 1% Foreign. **Female To Male Ratio:** 1.1:1. The average age of freshmen is 18; all undergraduates, 20. 25% do not continue beyond their first year; 52% remain to graduate. **Housing:** 1500 students can be accommodated in college housing, which includes coed dorms, honors houses, and special-interest houses. On-campus housing is available on a first-come and first-served basis. Priority is given to out-of-town students. 60% of students live on campus; of those, 75% remain on campus on weekends. Upperclassmen may keep cars.

FACULTY/CLASSROOMS: No introductory courses are taught by graduate students.

PROGRAMS OF STUDY: College at Florham confers B.A., B.S., B.S.A.H.T., B.S.C.L.S. and B.S.N. degrees. Master's degrees are also awarded. Bachelor's degrees are awarded in BIOLOGICAL SCIENCE (biochemistry and biology/biological science), BUSINESS (accounting, banking and finance, business administration and management, entrepreneurial studies, hotel/motel and restaurant management, and marketing/retailing/merchandising), COMMUNICATIONS AND THE ARTS (animation, communications, creative writing, dramatic arts, film arts, fine arts, literature, and video), COMPUTER AND PHYSICAL SCIENCE (chemistry, computer science, mathematics, and radiological technology), HEALTH PROFESSIONS (allied health, clinical science, medical laboratory technology, and nursing), SOCIAL SCIENCE (economics, French studies, history, humanities, liberal arts/general studies, philosophy, political science/government, psychology, sociology, and Spanish studies). Psychology, business management, and communications have the largest enrollments.

ACTIVITIES: There are 44 groups on campus, including cheerleading, chorale, computers, dance, environmental, ethnic, honors, international, LGBT, literary magazine, newspaper, political, professional, radio and TV, religious, social, social service, and student government. Popular campus events include Florham Fest and Haunted Mansion. **Sports:** There are 9 intercollegiate sports for men and 9 for women, and 7 intramural sports for men and 5 for women. Facilities include a turf field for football, field hockey, soccer, and lacrosse. **Graduates:** From July 1, 2015 to June 30, 2016, 522 bachelor's degrees were awarded. The most popular majors were psychology (14%), business/marketing (12%), and communications (8%). 200 companies recruited on campus in 2015-2016. In an average class, 35% graduate in 4 years or less, 48% graduate in 5 years or less, and 52% graduate in 6 years or less.

SERVICES: Counseling and information services are available, as is tutoring in most subjects, a reader service for the blind, and remedial math, reading, and writing. There is oral interpretation for the hearing impaired. Workshops also offer assistance with learning disabilities that offers comprehensive support to students admitted to the program. **Library/Resources:** The library contains 149,850 volumes, 19,236 microform items,689 audio/video tapes/CDs/DVDs, and subscribes to 1,182 periodicals including electronic. Computerized library services include interlibrary loans, database searching, Internet access, and Wi-Fi capability. Special learning facilities include an art gallery, radio station, an weblab, ITV multimedia classrooms, and theaters. **Physically Challenged Students:** 34% of the campus is accessible. Facilities include wheelchair ramps, elevators, special parking, specially equipped restrooms, special class scheduling, lowered drinking fountains, lowered telephones, and special housing. **Special:** The college offers co-op programs in most majors, internships, and study abroad. A Washington semester, work-study, accelerated degrees, and student-designed majors in the humanities and general studies are possible. Prepharmacy and joint baccalaureate dental programs are available. There are 10 national honor societies, a freshman honors program, and 11 departmental honors programs. **Visiting:** There are regularly scheduled orientations for prospective students, including standardized placement testing, faculty advisement, class registration, and educational and social activities to prepare students for entrance. There are guides for informal visits, visitors may sit in on classes, and stay overnight. To schedule a visit, contact the Admissions Office. **Campus Safety and Security:** Measures include 24-hour foot and vehicle patrol, emergency notification system, self-defense education, and security escort services. There are also shuttle buses, emergency telephones, and lighted pathways/sidewalks.

REQUIREMENTS: The SAT or ACT is required. Applicants should be graduates of an accredited high school or have a GED certificate. They should have completed a minimum of 16 academic units, including 4 in English, 3 in math, 2 each in history, foreign language, and lab science (3 are recommended), and 3 in electives. Those students applying to science and health sciences programs must meet additional requirements. An interview may be requested. AP and CLEP credits are accepted. Important factors in the admissions decision are leadership record, recommendations by school officials, and extracurricular activities record. To graduate, students must complete a 120 to 128 credits, including 30 to 44 in the major, with an overall minimum 2.0 GPA (2.5 in the major). Distribution requirements include courses in English, communications, math, phys ed, foreign language, humanities, social and behavioral sciences, lab and computer science, an integrated, interdisciplinary university core sequence, and freshman seminar. **Procedure:** Freshmen are admitted to all sessions. Entrance exams should be taken May of their junior year. There are early admissions, deferred admissions, and rolling admissions plans. Check with the school for current application deadlines. The application fee is $40. Notification is sent on a rolling basis. Applications are accepted online. **Transfer Students:** 131 transfer students enrolled in 2015-2016. All transfer applicants must submit official transcripts for all college work taken. Those students with fewer than 24 credits must also submit a high school transcript or a copy of their state department of education's equivalency score and SAT scores. 32 of 120 credits required for the bachelor's degree must be completed at College at Florham. **International Students:** There are 14 international students enrolled. The school actively recruits these students. They must take the TOEFL with a minimum score of 550 on the paper-based TOEFL (PBT) or 79 on the Internet-based version (iBT), or take the IELTS. SAT or ACT is highly recommended.

ADMISSIONS: 67% of the 2016-2017 applicants were accepted. The SAT scores for the 2016-2017 freshman class were: Critical Reading-- 36% below 500, 51% between 500 and 599, 13% between 600 and 699, and 1% between 700 and 800. Math-- 31% below 500, 49% between 500 and 599, 18% between 600 and 699, and 1% between 700 and 800. Writing-- 36% below 500, 50% between 500 and 599, 13% between 600 and 699, and 1% between 700 and 800. 32% of the current freshmen were in the top fifth of their class; 62% were in the top two fifths. 5 freshmen graduated first in their class. **Admissions Contact:** Jonathan Wexler, Associate Vice President of Enrollment Management. Email: *globaleducation@fdu.edu* Web: *www.fdu.edu*

FINANCIAL AID: The FAFSA code is 004738. The priority date for freshman financial aid applications for fall entry is February 15.

FAIRLEIGH DICKINSON UNIVERSITY/ METROPOLITAN CAMPUS E-2

www.fdu.edu

Teaneck, NJ 07666 — **(201) 692-2553**, **(800) 338-8803**

Fax: (201) 692-7319 — **Email: globaleducation@fdu.edu**

Full-time: 983 men, 1488 women — **Faculty:** IIA, +$

Part-time: 1567 men, 2006 women — **Ph.D.s:** n/av

Graduate: 1126 men, 1634 women — **Student/Faculty:** n/av

Year: semesters, summer session — **Tuition:** $28,886

Room & Board: $11,368 — **Freshman Class:** 5108 applied, 2916 accepted, 711 enrolled

SAT CR/M/W: 510/530/500 **ACT:** required — **CEEB CODE:** 2263

Application Deadline: March 15 — **COMPETITIVE**

Farleigh Dickinson University/Metropolitan Campus, founded in 1942, is an independent university offering undergraduate and graduate degrees in business, arts and sciences, professional studies, public administration, and hotel, restaurant, and tourism management. There are 3 undergraduate schools and 3 graduate schools. In addition to regional accreditation, FDU-Metropolitan has baccalaureate program accreditation with AACSB, ABET, TEAC, JR, and ABA. The 92-acre campus is in a suburban area 13 miles from midtown Manhattan, New York City. Including any residence halls, there are 55 buildings.

STUDENT LIFE: 87% of undergraduates are from New Jersey. Others are from 25 states, 64 foreign countries, and Canada. 9% are Asian American; 9% Foreign; 33% White; 20% Hispanic; 18% African American. **Female To Male Ratio:** 1.4:1. The average age of freshmen is 18; all undergraduates, 22. 27% do not continue beyond their first year; 40% remain to graduate. **Housing:** 982 students can be accommodated in college housing, which includes single-sex, coed dorms, honors houses, special-interest houses, L.I.F.E. house and Global Scholar houses. On-campus housing is available on a first-come, first-served basis, and is available on a lottery system for upperclassmen. 79% of students commute. All students may keep cars. Alcohol is not permitted.

FACULTY/CLASSROOMS: No introductory courses are taught by graduate students.

PROGRAMS OF STUDY: FDU-Metropolitan confers B.A., B.S., B.S.Civ.E.T., B.S.C.L.S., B.S.Con.E.T., B.S.E.E., B.S.E.E.T., B.S.M.E.T. and B.S.N. degrees. Associate, master's, and doctoral degrees are also awarded. Bachelor's degrees are awarded in BIOLOGICAL SCIENCE (biochemistry, biology/biological science, and marine biology), BUSINESS (accounting, business administration and management, business economics, entrepreneurial studies, hotel/motel and restaurant management, and marketing/retailing/merchandising), COMMUNICATIONS AND THE ARTS (communications, English literature, and fine arts), COMPUTER AND PHYSICAL SCIENCE (chemistry, computer science, information sciences and systems, mathematics, radiological technology, and science), ENGINEERING AND ENVIRONMENTAL DESIGN (civil engineering technology, construction engineering, electrical/electronics engineering, electrical/electronics engineering technology, and mechanical engineering technology), HEALTH PROFESSIONS (allied health, clinical science, medical laboratory technology, nursing, and physical therapy), SOCIAL SCIENCE (criminal justice, economics, history, humanities, interdisciplinary studies, international studies, liberal arts/general studies, philosophy, political science/government, psychology, and Spanish studies). Nursing, psychology, and business management have the largest enrollments.

ACTIVITIES: 1% of men belong to 5 national fraternities; 1% of women belong to 7 national sororities. There are 72 groups on campus, including cheerleading, chorus, computers, dance, drama, environmental, ethnic, film, honors, international, LGBT, literary magazine, newspaper, pep band, photography, political, professional, radio and TV, religious, social, social service, and student government. Popular campus events include Welcome Back Week, Spring Fest, and Dances. **Sports:** There are 7 intercollegiate sports for men and 10 for women, and 7 intramural sports for men and 7 for women. Facilities include a track, basketball courts, volleyball courts, racquetball courts, weight room, outdoor tennis courts, a baseball field, soccer field, training rooms, a softball field, a fitness center with aerobics room, selectorized weight room, and cardio room. **Graduates:** From July 1, 2015 to June 30, 2016, 784 bachelor's degrees were awarded. The most popular majors were psychology (7%), nursing (6%), and criminal justice (6%). 201 companies recruited on campus in 2015-2016. In an average class, 21% graduate in 4 years or less, 37% graduate in 5 years or less, and 40% graduate in 6 years or less.

SERVICES: Counseling and information services are available, as is tutoring in every subject, a reader service for the blind, and remedial math, reading, and writing. Workshops offer assistance with academic study skills, time management, and advanced reading and writing. Support services for basic skills students and freshmen are available. There is also a Regional Center for College Students with Learning Disabilities that offers comprehensive support to students admitted to the program. **Library/Resources:** The 3 libraries contain 196,703 volumes, 103,808 microform items, 1,311 audio/video tapes/CDs/DVDs, and subscribe to 1,601 periodicals including electronic. Computerized library services include interlibrary loans, database searching, and Internet access. Special learning facilities include an art gallery, radio station, computer labs, ITV multimedia classrooms, photonics lab, theater, art galleries, web-lab, cyber crime lab, and the Regional Center for College Students with Learning Disabilities. **Physically Challenged Students:** 41% of the campus is accessible. Facilities include wheelchair ramps, elevators, special parking, specially equipped restrooms, special class scheduling, lowered drinking fountains, lowered telephones, and special housing. Oral interpretation for the hearing impaired. **Special:** FDU-Metropolitan offers co-op programs in most majors, cross-registration, internships, and study abroad in England and Vancouver. A Washington semester, work-study, accelerated degrees, and student-designed majors in the humanities and general studies are possible. A 7-year medical program is available with Karol Marcinkowski School of Medicine in Poland, as is an accelerated chiropractic program with New York Chiropractic College and Logan Chiropractic College (B.S.,B.A./M.A.T.). There are 12 national honor societies, a freshman honors program, and 16 departmental honors programs. **Visiting:** There are regularly scheduled orientations for prospective students, including standardized placement testing, faculty advisement, class registration, and educational and social activities to prepare students for entrance. There are guides for informal visits, visitors may sit in on classes, and stay overnight. To schedule a visit, contact the Admissions Office. **Campus Safety and Security:** Measures include 24-hour foot and vehicle patrol, emergency notification system, self-defense education, security escort services, emergency telephones and lighted pathways/sidewalks.

REQUIREMENTS: The SAT or ACT is required. Applicants should be graduates of an accredited high school or have a GED certificate. They should have completed a minimum of 16 academic units, including 4 in English, 3 in math, 2 each in history, foreign language, and lab science (3 are recommended), and 3 in electives. Those students applying to science, engineering, and health sciences programs must meet additional requirements. An interview may be required. AP and CLEP credits are accepted. Important factors in the admissions decision are leadership record, recommendations by school officials, and extracurricular activities record. To graduate, students must complete 120 to 128 credits, including 30 to 44 in the major, with an overall minimum 2.0. GPA. Students must complete a 4-semester interdisciplinary sequence and 1 course in freshman seminar. The core curriculum includes 6 credits in English, 12 in university core, and 3 each in math and computer science. **Procedure:** Freshmen are admitted to all sessions. Entrance exams should be taken by May of the junior year. There are deferred admissions and rolling admissions plans. Applications should be filed by March 15 for fall entry, along with a $40 fee. Notification is sent on a rolling basis. Applications are accepted online. **Transfer Students:** 499 transfer students enrolled in 2015-2016. All applicants must submit official transcripts for all college work taken. Those students with fewer than 24 credits must also submit a high school transcript or a copy of their state department of education's equivalency score and SAT scores. 32 of 128 credits required for the bachelor's degree must be completed at FDU. **International Students:** There are 243 international students enrolled. The school actively recruits these students. They must take the TOEFL with a minimum score of 550 on the paper-based TOEFL (PBT) or 79 on the Internet-based version (iBT), or take the IELTS. The ACT or SAT is highly recommended.

ADMISSIONS: 57% of the 2016-2017 applicants were accepted. The SAT scores for the 2016-2017 freshman class were: Critical Reading-- 42% below 500, 46% between 500 and 599, and 11% between 600 and 699. Math-- 30% below 500, 52% between 500 and 599, 16% between 600 and 699, and 2% between 700 and 800. Writing-- 43% below 500, 49% between 500 and 599, and 8% between 600 and 699. 30% of the current freshmen were in the top fifth of their class; 62% were in the top two fifths. 1 freshman graduated first in the class. **Admissions Contact:** Jonathan Wexler, Associate Vice President of Enrollment Management. Email: *globaleducation@fdu.edu* Web: *www.fdu.edu*

FINANCIAL AID: Check with the school for current application deadlines.

FELICIAN UNIVERSITY *(The complete profile is made available exclusively on our website, www.barronspac.com)*

GEORGIAN COURT UNIVERSITY *(The complete profile is made available exclusively on our website, www.barronspac.com)*

KEAN UNIVERSITY D-2
www.kean.edu

Union, NJ 07083 **(908) 737-7100**

Fax: (908) 737-7105	**Email:** admitme@kean.edu
Full-time: 3707 men, 5532 women	**Faculty:** IIA, ++$
Part-time: 926 men, 1647 women	**Ph.D.s:** 82%
Graduate: 494 men, 1764 women	**Student/Faculty:** 16 to 1
Year: semesters, summer session	**Tuition:** $11,870 ($18,637)
Room & Board: $12,780	**Freshman Class:** 8785 applied, 6536 accepted, 1526 enrolled
SAT CR/M: 480/500 **ACT:** 21	**CEEB CODE:** 2517
Application Deadline: April 30	**COMPETITIVE**

Kean University is a public university serving undergraduate and graduate students in the liberal arts, the sciences, and other professions. There are also campuses in Toms River, New Jersey, and Wenzhou China. There are 6 undergraduate schools and 1 graduate school. In addition to regional accreditation, Kean has baccalaureate program accreditation with ABET, NASAD, NASM, NCATE, NLN, NAST, CIDA, CAATE, and CAHIIM. The 185-acre campus is in a suburban area Union, New Jersey with additional locations in Toms River, NJ and Wenzhou, China. Including any residence halls, there are 47 buildings.

STUDENT LIFE: 98% of undergraduates are from New Jersey. Others are from 18 states, and 45 foreign countries. 8% are race unknown; 5% Asian American; 35% White; 27% Hispanic; 2% Foreign; 2% two or more races; 19% African American. **Female To Male Ratio:** 1.7:1. The average age of freshmen is 18; all undergraduates, 24. 27% do not continue beyond their first year; 50% remain to graduate. **Housing:** 2045 students can be accommodated in college housing, which includes single-sex and coed dorms and on-campus apartments. In addition, there are special-interest houses, freshman housing, and women-only floor, living learning communities for SIMS (success in math & science), GREEN (gearing residents toward environment, exercise & nutrition) and WELL (women empowered toward leadership and learning). On-campus housing is available on a first-come and first-served basis. 85% of students commute. Upperclassmen may keep cars. Alcohol is not permitted.

FACULTY/CLASSROOMS: 46% of faculty are male; 54% are female. No introductory courses are taught by graduate students. The average class size in a regular course is 21.

PROGRAMS OF STUDY: Kean confers B.A., B.S., B.F.A., B.I.D., and B.S.N. degrees. Master's and doctoral degrees are also awarded. Bachelor's degrees are awarded in BIOLOGICAL SCIENCE (biology/biological science), BUSINESS (accounting, finance, international business management, management science, marketing management, recreational facilities management, and sustainable management), COMMUNICATIONS AND THE ARTS (art history and appreciation, communications, English, fine arts, fine/studio arts, general, industrial design, information technology, music, music performance, performing arts, Spanish, studio art, theatre arts, theater design, and visual and performing arts), COMPUTER AND PHYSICAL SCIENCE (chemistry, computer science, earth science, mathematics, and science and technology studies), EDUCATION (athletic training, early childhood education, elementary education, health information management, middle school education, music education, physical education, secondary education, and special education), ENGINEERING AND ENVIRONMENTAL DESIGN (architecture and interior design), HEALTH PROFESSIONS (medical technology, nursing, and speech pathology/audiology), SOCIAL SCIENCE (Asian/Oriental studies, criminal justice, economics, history, political science/government, psychology, public administration, and sociology). Science/technology and education is the strongest academically. Business, education, and psychology have the largest enrollments.

ACTIVITIES: There are 157 groups on campus, including art, band, choir, chorale, chorus, communications, computers, dance, drama, environmental, ethnic, film, forensics, honors, international, jazz band, LGBT, musical theater, newspaper, orchestra, pep band, photography, political, professional, radio and TV, religious, social, social service, student government, symphony, and yearbook. Popular campus events include Homecoming, Kean Day, Comedy Show, Unity Week, Concerts, Meet the Greeks, Food Bank Luncheon, Student Group Expo, Martin Luther King Jr. Week of Service, Black History Month, Latin Festival Month, Chinese New Year Celebration, and Creolefest. **Sports:** There are 6 intercollegiate sports for men and 7 for women, and 6 intramural sports for men and 6 for women. Facilities include a stadium, track, soccer, baseball, softball, practice fields, an arena, indoor basketball courts, outdoor basketball courts, outdoor tennis courts, a pool, fitness rooms, and pool tables. **Graduates:** From July 1, 2015 to June 30, 2016, 2549 bachelor's degrees were awarded. The most popular majors were psychology (18%), management science (7%), and biology (7%). 157 companies recruited on campus in 2015-2016. In an average class, 21% graduate in 4 years or less, 43% graduate in 5 years or less, and 50% graduate in 6 years or less.

SERVICES: Counseling and information services are available, as is tutoring in most subjects, and remedial math, reading, and writing. **Library/Resources:** The library contains 217,852 volumes, and subscribes to 62,000 periodicals including electronic. Computerized library services include interlibrary loans, database searching, Internet access, and Wi-Fi capability. Special learning facilities include an art gallery, planetarium, radio station, TV station, New Jersey Center for science, technology, and mathematics, Holocaust Resource Center, Wynona Moore Lipman Ethnic Studies Center, Liberty Hall Museum, and Human Rights Institute, and New Jersey Highlands. **Physically Challenged Students:** All of the campus is accessible. Facilities include wheelchair ramps, elevators, special parking, specially equipped restrooms, special class scheduling, lowered drinking fountains, and special housing. **Special:** There are 28 national honor societies, a freshman honors program, and 9 departmental honors programs. **Visiting:** There are regularly scheduled orientations for prospective students. We host a variety of events for prospective students, ranging from student for a day and open house to information sessions and campus tours. Our Center for Academic Success Office manages all orientation activities for accepted students. There are guides for informal visits and visitors may sit in on classes. To schedule a visit, contact Office of Admissions. **Campus Safety and Security:** Measures include 24-hour foot and vehicle patrol, emergency notification system, self-defense education, and security escort services. There are also shuttle buses, emergency telephones, lighted pathways/sidewalks, controlled access to dorms/residences, all residence halls have surveillance cameras in floors, lounges, elevators and exit doors, and all residence halls have fire sprinkler systems.

REQUIREMENTS: Applicants must be graduates of accredited secondary schools or have earned a GED. College preparatory study includes 4 courses in English, 3 in math, 2 each in lab science and history, and 5 in academic electives. An official transcript and SAT/ACT scores are required. An essay and 2 letters of recommendation are recommended, but not required. AP and CLEP credits are accepted. Important factors in the admissions decision are advanced placement or honors courses, recommendations by school officials, and extracurricular activities record. **Procedure:** Freshmen are admitted in the fall and spring. Entrance exams should be taken April-June of the junior year & Oct-Jan of the senior year. There are early admissions, deferred admissions, and rolling admissions plans. Applications should be filed by April 30 for fall entry; December 15 for spring entry; and April 1 for summer entry, along with a $75 fee. Notifications are sent November 1. Applications are accepted online. **Transfer Students:** 1525 transfer students enrolled in 2015-2016. NACES evaluation of transcripts for any foreign institution attended. The minimum number of credits to transfer with a 2.0 is 30. Between 15-30 credit (semester) hours students must have a 3.0 GPA. 32 of 124 credits required for the bachelor's degree must be completed at Kean. **International Students:** There are 248 international students enrolled. The school actively recruits these students. They must take the TOEFL with a minimum score of 550 on the paper-based TOEFL (PBT) or 79 on the Internet-based version (iBT), IELTS. They must also take the SAT or ACT.

ADMISSIONS: 74% of the 2016-2017 applicants were accepted. **Admissions Contact:** Jennifer Kanellis, Director of Admissions. Email: *admitme@kean.edu* Web: *www.kean.edu*

FINANCIAL AID: In 2016-2017, 86% of all full-time freshmen received some form of financial aid. 71% of all full-time freshmen received need-based aid. The average freshman award was $10,100. Need-based scholarships or need-based grants averaged $8,910; need-based self-help aid (loans and jobs) averaged $3,579; and other non-need-based awards and non-need-based scholarships averaged $3,798. 8% of undergraduate students work part-time. Average annual earnings from campus work are $5363. The average financial indebtedness of the 2016 graduate was $33,693. The FAFSA code is 002622. The priority date for freshman financial aid applications for fall entry is April 17.

MONMOUTH UNIVERSITY — E-3

www.monmouth.edu

West Long Branch, NJ 07764 — (732) 571-3456, (800) 543-9671

Fax: (732) 263-5166 — **Email:** admission@monmouth.edu

Full-time: 1862 men, 2588 women	**Faculty:** 253; IIA, +$
Part-time: 101 men, 142 women	**Ph.D.s:** 80%
Graduate: 402 men, 1299 women	**Student/Faculty:** 18 to 1
Year: semesters, summer session	**Tuition:** $33,728
Room & Board: $12,506	**Freshman Class:** 8486 applied, 6651 accepted, 1128 enrolled
SAT CR/M/W: 511/525/518 **ACT:** 23	**CEEB CODE:** 2416
Application Deadline: March 1	**COMPETITIVE**

Monmouth University, founded in 1933, is a leading private institution that offers a comprehensive array of undergraduate and graduate degree programs. The University provides students with a highly personalized education that builds the knowledge and confidence of tomorrow's leaders. There are 7 undergraduate schools and 1 graduate school. In addition to regional accreditation, Monmouth has baccalaureate program accreditation with AACSB, ABET, CSWE, NCATE, NLN, ACS, CCNE, and CACREP. The 159-acre campus is in a suburban area 55 miles from New York City, and 75 miles from Philadelphia. Including any residence halls, there are 55 buildings.

STUDENT LIFE: 85% of undergraduates are from New Jersey. Others are from 29 states, 24 foreign countries, and Canada. 85% are from public schools. 74% are White; 5% African American; 4% race unknown; 3% Asian American; 2% two or more races; 11% Hispanic; 1% Foreign. **Female To Male Ratio:** 1.7:1. The average age of freshmen is 18; all undergraduates, 20. 17% do not continue beyond their first year; 67% remain to graduate. **Housing:** 2092 students can be accommodated in college housing, which includes coed dorms, on-campus apartments, off-campus apartments, and honors houses. On-campus housing is available on a first-come, first-served basis, and on a lottery system for upperclassmen. Priority is given to out-of-town students. 59% of students commute. All students may keep cars.

FACULTY/CLASSROOMS: 49% of faculty are male; 51% are female. 91% teach undergraduates, 61% do research, and 56% do both. No introductory courses are taught by graduate students. The average class size in an introductory lecture is 22; in a laboratory is 14; and in a regular course is 22.

PROGRAMS OF STUDY: Monmouth confers B.A., B.S., B.F.A., B.S.N. and B.S.W. degrees. Associate, master's, and doctoral degrees are also awarded. Bachelor's degrees are awarded in BIOLOGICAL SCIENCE (biology/biological science and marine biology), BUSINESS (accounting, banking and finance, business administration and management, business administration international, business administration marketing, business economics, international business management, marketing management, and real estate), COMMUNICATIONS AND THE ARTS (art, art history and appreciation, communications, English, graphic design, modern language, music, music business management, music industry, and Spanish), COMPUTER AND PHYSICAL SCIENCE (chemistry, clinical laboratory science, chemistry education, computer science, mathematics, and software engineering), EDUCATION (art education, early childhood education, education, elementary education, English education, foreign languages education, health education, mathematics education, music education, physical education, science education, secondary education, social studies education, social studies secondary school education, Spanish education K-12, and special education), ENGINEERING AND ENVIRONMENTAL DESIGN (computer graphics), HEALTH PROFESSIONS (medical laboratory science, medical laboratory technology, nursing, and premedicine), SOCIAL SCIENCE (anthropology, criminal justice, history, homeland security, legal studies, political science/government, prelaw, psychology, social work, and sociology). Business, education, and communication have the largest enrollments.

ACTIVITIES: 15% of women belong to 8 national sororities. There are 109 groups on campus, including art, band, cheerleading, choir, chorus, computers, dance, debate, drama, environmental, ethnic, honors, international, jazz band, LGBT, literary magazine, musical theater, newspaper, pep band, photography, political, professional, radio and TV, religious, social, social service, student activities board, student government, and yearbook. Popular campus events include The Big Event, Springfest, Welcome Week, Greek Week, Winter Ball, and Haunted Tours. **Sports:** There are 16 intercollegiate sports for men and 17 for women, and 15 intramural sports for men and 12 for women. Facilities include an arena, indoor track, indoor practice facility with basketball courts, football field, soccer field, outdoor tennis courts, all-weather track, pool, exercise and weight facility, a varsity athletics weight room, and baseball, softball, and field hockey fields. **Graduates:** From July 1, 2015 to June 30, 2016, 1107 bachelor's degrees were awarded. The most popular majors were business (23%), communication (12%), and education (11%). 237 companies recruited on campus in 2015-2016. In an average class, 57% graduate in 4 years or less, 69% graduate in 5 years or less, and 67% graduate in 6 years or less. Of the 2015 graduating class, 42% were enrolled in graduate school within 6 months of graduation, and 65% were employed.

SERVICES: Counseling and information services are available, as is tutoring in every subject, a reader service for the blind, and remedial math, reading, and writing. **Library/Resources:** The library contains 285,358 volumes, and 1,862 audio/video tapes/CDs/DVDs, and subscribes to 65,000 periodicals including electronic. Computerized library services include interlibrary loans, database searching, Internet access, and Wi-Fi capability. Special learning facilities include an art gallery, radio station, TV station, theater, financial markets lab, a greenhouse, and a community garden. **Physically Challenged Students:** 95% of the campus is accessible. Facilities include wheelchair ramps, elevators, special parking, specially equipped restrooms, special class scheduling, lowered drinking fountains, and special housing. Academic assistance provided within the classroom. **Special:** Students may study abroad in England, Australia, Italy, and Spain. Experiential learning is a graduation requirement. There are cooperative and internship programs and a Washington semester. Five Year Baccalaureate/Mater's Programs in many academice areas. Monmouth also offers student-designed majors, dual major in history/political science, flexible studies programs, and credit for life experience. There are 22 national honor societies and a freshman honors program. **Visiting:** There are regularly scheduled orientations for prospective students, students visits include campus tours. There are guides for informal visits and visitors may sit in on classes. To schedule a visit, contact the Admission Office at visitmu@monmouth.edu. **Campus Safety and Security:** Measures include 24-hour foot and vehicle patrol, emergency notification system, self-defense education, security escort services, emergency telephones, lighted pathways/sidewalks, controlled access to dorms/residences, and the university police.

REQUIREMENTS: The SAT or ACT is required. The ACT Optional Writing test is also required. Applicants must be graduates of accredited secondary schools or have earned a GED. The university requires 16 Carnegie units, based on 4 years of English, 3 of math, and 2 each of social studies/history and science, with the remaining 5 units in academic electives. An essay and a letter of recommendation are required. AP and CLEP credits are accepted. Important factors in the admissions decision are advanced placement or honors courses, extracurricular activities record, and leadership record. To graduate, students must earn at least 128 credits, including 30 to 81 in a major, with a minimum GPA of 2.0 overall and 2.1 in the major. Education majors are required to have a cumulative GPA of 3.0. **Procedure:** Freshmen are admitted in the fall and spring. Entrance exams should be taken by December of the senior year. There is a deferred admissions plan. Applications should be filed by March 1 for fall entry; January 1 for spring entry, along with a $50 fee. Notifications are sent April 1. Applications are accepted online. **Transfer Students:** 421 transfer students enrolled in 2015-2016. Transfer applicants with fewer than 24 transferable college credits must provide a high school transcript and SAT or ACT scores. All transfer applicants must submit official college transcripts for all institutions attended. A 2.25 minimum college GPA is required for general admission consideration,does not guarantee acceptance. For education majors, a minimum cumulative GPA of 3.0 is required. 32 of 128 credits required for the bachelor's degree must be completed at Monmouth. **International Students:** There are 37 international students enrolled. The school actively recruits these students. They must take the TOEFL with a minimum score of 550 on the paper-based TOEFL (PBT) or 79 on the Internet-based version (iBT) or take the MELAB, the IELTS, or the Cambridge ESOL (CAE). They must also take the SAT or ACT, scoring varies by student profile. Students from English speaking countries must take the SAT or ACT.

ADMISSIONS: 78% of the 2016-2017 applicants were accepted. The SAT scores for the 2016-2017 freshman class were: Critical Reading-- 42% below 500, 48% between 500 and 599, 9% between 600 and 699, and 1% between 700 and 800. Math-- 34% below 500, 51% between 500 and 599, 14% between 600 and 699, and 2% between 700 and 800. Writing-- 38% below 500, 48% between 500 and 599, 13% between 600 and 699, and 1% between 700 and 800. The ACT scores were 3% between 12 and 17, 61% between 18 and 23, 34% between 24 and 29, and 3% above 30. 29% of the current freshmen were in the top fifth of their class; 65% were in the top two fifths. **Admissions Contact:** Victoria Bobik, Director of Undergraduate Admission. Email: *admission@monmouth.edu* Web: *www.monmouth.edu*

FINANCIAL AID: In 2016-2017, 99% of all full-time freshmen and 94% of continuing full-time students received some form of financial aid. 68% of all full-time freshmen and 59% of continuing full-time students received need-based aid. The average freshman award was $30,803. Need-based scholarships or need-based grants averaged $13,843 ($46,190 maximum); need-based self-help aid (loans and jobs) averaged $4,941 ($9,500 maximum); non-need-based athletic scholarships averaged $24,027 ($52,077 maximum); other non-need-based awards and non-need-based scholarships averaged $10,448 ($33,729 maximum); and $12,234 from other forms of aid. 26% of undergraduate students work part-time. Average annual earnings from campus work are $1000. The average financial indebtedness of the 2016 graduate was $27,281. The state aid form is required. The FAFSA code is 002616. Check with the school for current application deadlines.

MONTCLAIR STATE UNIVERSITY *(The complete profile is made available exclusively on our website, www.barronspac.com)*

NEW JERSEY CITY UNIVERSITY *(The complete profile is made available exclusively on our website, www.barronspac.com)*

NEW JERSEY INSTITUTE OF TECHNOLOGY E-2

www.njit.edu

Newark, NJ 07102 (973) 596-3300

Fax: (973) 596-3461	**Email:** admissions@njit.edu
Full-time: 4801 men, 1298 women	**Faculty:** 410; I, +$
Part-time: 787 men, 163 women	**Ph.D.s:** 100%
Graduate: 2268 men, 844 women	**Student/Faculty:** 17 to 1
Year: semesters, summer session	**Tuition:** $16,269 ($27,929)
Room & Board: $13,300	**Freshman Class:** 6045 applied, 3673 accepted, 1108 enrolled
SAT CR/M/W: 575/635/570	**CEEB CODE:** 2513
Application Deadline: March 1	**VERY COMPETITIVE**

New Jersey Institute of Technology is a public research university providing instruction, research, and public service in engineering, computer science, management, architecture, digital design, industrial design, interior design, engineering technology, applied sciences, and related fields. The figures in the above capsule and in this profile are approximate. There are 6 undergraduate schools and 1 graduate school. In addition to regional accreditation, NJIT has baccalaureate program accreditation with AACSB, ABET, NAAB, and CIDA. The 45-acre campus is in an urban area 10 miles west of New York City. Including any residence halls, there are 27 buildings.

STUDENT LIFE: 92% of undergraduates are from New Jersey. Others are from 24 states, 86 foreign countries, and Canada. 80% are from public schools. 9% are African American; 8% two or more races; 8% race unknown; 4% Foreign; 35% White; 21% Asian American; 14% Hispanic. **Male To Female Ratio:** 3.4:1. The average age of freshmen is 18; all undergraduates, 22. 18% do not continue beyond their first year; 54% remain to graduate. **Housing:** 1663 students can be accommodated in college housing, which includes coed dorms. On-campus housing is available on a first-come, first-served basis, and on a lottery system for upperclassmen. Priority is given to out-of-town students. 77% of students commute. All students may keep cars.

FACULTY/CLASSROOMS: 82% of faculty are male; 18% are female. All teach undergraduates and do research. Graduate students teach 10% of introductory courses. The average class size in an introductory lecture is 30; in a laboratory is 27; and in a regular course is 25.

PROGRAMS OF STUDY: NJIT confers B.A., B.S. and B.Arch. degrees. Master's and doctoral degrees are also awarded. Bachelor's degrees are awarded in BIOLOGICAL SCIENCE (biology/biological science), BUSINESS (management science), COMMUNICATIONS AND THE ARTS (communications and technical and business writing), COMPUTER AND PHYSICAL SCIENCE (applied mathematics, applied physics, chemistry, computer management, computer science, information sciences and systems, and mathematics), ENGINEERING AND ENVIRONMENTAL DESIGN (architecture, biomedical engineering, chemical engineering, civil engineering, computer engineering, computer technology, electrical/electronics engineering, engineering and applied science, engineering technology, environmental engineering, environmental science, geophysical engineering, industrial engineering, manufacturing engineering, mechanical engineering, technological management, and technology and public affairs), SOCIAL SCIENCE (history). Engineering, computer science, and architecture are the strongest academically.

ACTIVITIES: 8% of men belong to 19 local and 10 national fraternities; 5% of women belong to 4 local and 5 national sororities. There are 92 groups on campus, including art, band, chess, computers, dance, drama, drum and bugle corps, ethnic, honors, international, LGBT, marching band, musical theater, newspaper, photography, professional, religious, social, social service, student government, and yearbook. Popular campus events include Miniversity, International Students Food Festival, and Leadership Training Weekend. **Sports:** There are 9 intercollegiate sports for men and 6 for women, and 13 intramural sports for men and 7 for women. Facilities include a stadium, a fitness center with an indoor track, a swimming pool, tennis courts, racquet sport courts, playing fields, bowling lanes, a table tennis and billiards area, and gyms. **Graduates:** From July 1, 2015 to June 30, 2016, 1352 bachelor's degrees were awarded. The most popular majors were engineering (41%), engineering technology/ computer and information sciences (15%), and architecture (10%). 170 companies recruited on campus in 2015-2016. In an average class, 1% graduate in 3 years or less, 23% graduate in 4 years or less, 46% graduate in 5 years or less, and 59% graduate in 6 years or less.

SERVICES: Counseling and information services are available, as is tutoring in most subjects, a reader service for the blind, and remedial math, reading, and writing. **Library/Resources:** The 2 libraries contain 171,180 volumes, 7,650 microform items, and 100,502 audio/video tapes/CDs/DVDs. Computerized library services include interlibrary loans and database searching. Special learning facilities include an art gallery, and 3 TV studios. NJIT is home to many government, and industry sponsored labs, and research centers, including EPA Northeast Hazardous Substance Research Center, National Center for Transportation and Industrial Productivity, Center for Manufacturing Systems, Emission Reduction Research Center, Microelectronics Research Center, Center for Microwave and Lightwave Engineering, and the Multi-Lifecycle Engineering Center. **Physically Challenged Students:** 95% of the campus is accessible. Facilities include wheelchair ramps, elevators, special parking, specially equipped restrooms, special class scheduling, lowered drinking fountains, and lowered telephones. **Special:** Cross-registration is offered in conjunction with Essex County College, Rutgers University's Newark campus, and the University of Medicine and Dentistry of New Jersey. Cooperative programs, available in all majors, include two 6-month internships. There are 3-2 engineering degree programs with Stockton State College and Lincoln and Seton Hall Universities. NJIT also offers work-study programs, study abroad in 18 countries, dual and interdisciplinary majors, accelerated degree programs, distance learning, and nondegree study. There is 1 national honor society, a freshman honors program, and 17 departmental honors programs. **Visiting:** There are regularly scheduled orientations for prospective students, including tours and meetings with admissions personnel, students, and faculty. There are guides for informal visits, visitors may sit in on classes, and stay overnight. To schedule a visit, contact the Director of Admissions. **Campus Safety and Security:** Measures include 24-hour foot and vehicle patrol, self-defense education, and security escort services. There are also shuttle buses, emergency telephones, and lighted pathways/sidewalks.

REQUIREMENTS: The SAT and the SAT: Subject test in math I or II are required. Applicants should have completed 16 secondary school units, including 4 each in English and math, 2 units in science, of these, 2 units must be laboratory science. Recommended units include, 2 in foreign language, 2 in academic electives, and 1 unit in social studies, and 1 unit in history. NJIT requires applicants to be in the upper 30% of their class. AP and CLEP credits are accepted. Important factors in the admissions decision are leadership record, advanced placement or honors courses, recommendations by school officials, evidence of special talent, personality/intangible qualities, extracurricular activities record, recommendations by alumni, and geographical diversity. General university requirements include 9 credits of humanities and social science electives, 7 of natural sciences, 6 each of math, cultural history, basic social sciences, and engineering technology, 3 each of English and management, and 2 of computer science. Students must also complete 2 courses in phys ed. To graduate, students must earn between 124 and 164 credits, depending on the program, including 50 in the major, with a minimum GPA of 2.0 in upper-level major courses. **Procedure:** Freshmen are admitted in the fall and spring. Entrance exams should be taken in May of the junior year or November of the senior year. There is a rolling admissions plan. Applications should be filed by March 1 for fall entry, along with a $70 fee. Notifications are sent November 15. Applications are accepted online. **Transfer Students:** 717 transfer students enrolled in 2015-2016. A minimum college GPA of 2.0 is required, but 2.5 or higher is recommended. Students must submit transcripts of all attempted postsecondary academic work. Applicants with fewer than 30 credits may be asked to provide scores on the SAT and the SAT: Subject test in math, as well as high school transcripts. Engineering technology students must present an associate degree. Admission to the School of Architecture is very competitive for transfer students. 33 credits required for the bachelor's degree must be completed at NJIT. **International Students:** There are 271 international students enrolled. The school actively recruits these students. They must take the TOEFL with a minimum score of 550 on the paper-based TOEFL (PBT) or 79 on the Internet-based version (iBT). They must also take the SAT.

ADMISSIONS: 61% of the 2016-2017 applicants were accepted. The SAT scores for the 2016-2017 freshman class were: Critical Reading-- 21% below 500, 45% between 500 and 599, 28% between 600 and 699, and 6% between 700 and 800. Math-- 36% between 500 and 599, 47% between 600 and 699, and 17% between 700 and 800. Writing-- 24% below 500, 44% between 500 and 599, 25% between 600 and 699, and 7% between 700 and 800. 40% of the current freshmen were in the top fifth of their class; 73% were in the top two fifths. **Admissions Contact:** Kathy Kelly, Director of Admissions. Email: *admissions@njit.edu* Web: *www.njit.edu*

FINANCIAL AID: In 2016-2017, 94% of all full-time freshmen and 71% of continuing full-time students received some form of financial aid. 88% of all full-time freshmen and 66% of continuing full-time students received need-based aid. The average freshman award was $14,728. Need-based scholarships or need-based grants averaged $13,675; need-based self-help aid (loans and jobs) averaged $4,238; non-need-based athletic scholarships averaged $22,612; other non-need-based awards and non-need-based scholarships averaged $13,735; and $3,692 from other forms of aid. The average financial indebtedness of the 2016 graduate was $21,653. The FAFSA code is 002621. The priority date for freshman financial aid applications for fall entry is March 15.

PRINCETON UNIVERSITY — D-3

www.princeton.edu

Princeton, NJ 08544	(609) 258-3060
Fax: (609) 258-6743	**Email:** uaoffice@princeton.edu
Full-time: 2673 men, 2571 women	**Faculty:** 904
Part-time: n/av	**Ph.D.s:** 94%
Graduate: 1675 men, 1016 women	**Student/Faculty:** 6 to 1
Year: semesters	**Tuition:** $43,450
Room & Board: $14,160	**Freshman Class:** 26498 applied, 1963 accepted, 1285 enrolled
SAT CR/M/W: 740/760/750 **ACT:** 33	**CEEB CODE:** 2672
Application Deadline: January 1	**MOST COMPETITIVE**

Princeton University, established in 1746, is a private institution offering degrees in the liberal arts and sciences, engineering, applied science, architecture, public and international affairs, interdisciplinary and regional studies, and the creative arts. There are 4 undergraduate schools and 4 graduate schools. In addition to regional accreditation, Princeton has baccalaureate program accreditation with ABET and NAAB. The 500-acre campus is in a small town 50 miles south of New York City. Including any residence halls, there are 160 buildings.

STUDENT LIFE: 84% of undergraduates are from out of state, mostly the Middle Atlantic. Students are from 50 states, 88 foreign countries, and Canada. 8% are African American; 8% Hispanic; 47% White; 4% two or more races; 20% Asian American; 2% race unknown; 11% Foreign. **Male To Female Ratio:** 1.2:1. The average age of freshmen is 18; all undergraduates, 20. 2% do not continue beyond their first year; 96% remain to graduate. **Housing:** 6729 students can be accommodated in college housing, which includes single-sex and coed dorms, on-campus apartments, off-campus apartments, and married student housing. Freshmen and sophomores are assigned to 1 of 6 residential colleges; most juniors and seniors live in upper-class dorms and select from among such dining options as co-ops and private clubs. On-campus housing is guaranteed for all 4 years. 98% of students live on campus. Upperclassmen may keep cars.

FACULTY/CLASSROOMS: 68% of faculty are male; 32% are female. All teach undergraduates, and all do research. No introductory courses are taught by graduate students.

PROGRAMS OF STUDY: Princeton confers A.B. and B.S.E. degrees. Master's and doctoral degrees are also awarded. Bachelor's degrees are awarded in BIOLOGICAL SCIENCE (ecology, evolutionary biology, and molecular biology), BUSINESS (operations research), COMMUNICATIONS AND THE ARTS (classics, comparative literature, English, French, German, Italian, music, Portuguese, Slavic languages, and Spanish), COMPUTER AND PHYSICAL SCIENCE (astrophysics, chemistry, computer science, geoscience, mathematics, and physics), ENGINEERING AND ENVIRONMENTAL DESIGN (aeronautical engineering, architectural engineering, architecture, chemical engineering, civil engineering, electrical/electronics engineering, and mechanical engineering), SOCIAL SCIENCE (anthropology, archeology, East Asian studies, economics, history, international relations, Near Eastern studies, philosophy, political science/government, psychology, religion, and sociology). Economics, politics, and public policy have the largest enrollments.

ACTIVITIES: There are no fraternities or sororities. There are 250 groups on campus, including art, band, cheerleading, chess, choir, chorale, chorus, communications, computers, dance, debate, drama, environmental, ethnic, forensics, honors, international, jazz band, LGBT, literary magazine, marching band, musical theater, newspaper, opera, orchestra, pep band, photography, political, professional, religious, social, social service, student government, symphony, and yearbook. Popular campus events include Communiversity Day. **Sports:** There are 20 intercollegiate sports for men and 18 for women, and 20 intramural sports for men and 20 for women. Facilities include a gymnasium, a fitness center, pool with diving facilities, football, track and field, lacrosse, field hockey, a hockey rink, tennis courts, golf course, baseball, rugby, soccer, and softball. **Graduates:** From July 1, 2015 to June 30, 2016, 1271 bachelor's degrees were awarded. The most popular majors were social science (26%), engineering (20%), and life sciences (10%). In an average class, 88% graduate in 4 years or less, 95% graduate in 5 years or less, and 97% graduate in 6 years or less.

SERVICES: Counseling and information services are available, as is tutoring in every subject, a reader service for the blind. There is also a center for teaching and learning workshops, and individual consultations in which students can learn to manage large reading loads, problem-solve, take effective notes, create study tools, prepare for long-term projects, oral presentations, prepare for exams, manage time, and overcome test anxiety. Princeton's Writing Program works to ensure freshmen and others to master college-level writing. **Library/Resources:** The 11 libraries contain 8.2 million volumes, 395,285 microform items, 120,600 audio/video tapes/CDs/DVDs, and subscribe to 84,283 periodicals including electronic. Computerized library services include interlibrary loans, database searching, Internet access, and Wi-Fi capability. Special learning facilities include an art gallery, natural history museum, a music center, a visual and performing arts center, several theaters, an observatory, a plasma physics lab, and a center for environmental and energy studies. **Physically Challenged Students:** Facilities include wheelchair ramps, elevators, special parking, specially equipped restrooms, lowered drinking fountains, lowered telephones, and special housing. Each student's needs are assessed individually. Accommodations may include additional testing time, sign language translators, and dietary accommodations for food allergies. **Special:** Princeton offers independent study, accelerated degree programs, student-proposed courses and majors, field study, community-based learning courses that enrich course work with related service projects, study abroad, freshman seminars, and independent work in the junior and senior year. They also offer a Program in Teacher Preparation. There are 2 national honor societies and a chapter of Phi Beta Kappa. **Visiting:** There are regularly scheduled orientations for prospective students, including information sessions on Monday to Friday within the Admission Office, and some saturdays in the fall. Also, Princeton has an open campus, with many free and public events, and students are welcome to attend such events. They may visit www.princeton.edu/admission for more information. Visitors may sit in on classes. To schedule a visit, contact the Undergraduate Admission Office. **Campus Safety and Security:** Measures include 24-hour foot and vehicle patrol, emergency notification system, self-defense education, and security escort services. There are also shuttle buses, emergency telephones, lighted pathways/sidewalks, and controlled access to dorms/residences.

REQUIREMENTS: The ACT is accepted in lieu of SAT Reasoning test. Three SAT Subject tests are also required for all applicants. Recommended college preparatory courses include 4 years each of English, math, science, and a foreign language, 2 years each of lab science, history, and some study of art and music. Essays are required as part of the application and an interview is recommended. Students with special talent in visual or performing arts may supplement tapes, CDs or DVDs. AP credits are accepted. Important factors in the admissions decision are personality/intangible qualities, recommendations by school officials, and advanced placement or honors courses. To graduate, students must complete 8 semesters, or academic units. Candidates for the A.B. degree must demonstrate proficiency in English composition and a foreign language and they must complete distribution requirements in 7 academic areas. Candidates for the B.S.E., must satisfy the English composition requirement and complete a minimum of 7 courses in the humanities and social sciences spread over 4 distribution areas. A junior project and senior thesis are required of virtually all students. **Procedure:** Freshmen are admitted in the fall. Entrance exams should be taken by January of the senior year at the latest. There are early admissions and deferred admissions plans. Applications should be filed by January 1 for fall entry, along with a $65 fee. Notifications are sent April 1. 1395 applicants were on the 2016 waiting list; 33 were admitted. Applications are accepted online. **Transfer Students:** Princeton does not have a transfer admissions option. **International Students:** There are 569 international students enrolled. The school actively recruits these students. They must take the TOEFL. The SAT: Writing Test may be substituted for the TOEFL. Students must take the ACT, plus three SAT Subject Tests.

ADMISSIONS: 7% of the 2016-2017 applicants were accepted. The SAT scores for the 2016-2017 freshman class were: Critical Reading-- 3% between 500 and 599, 21% between 600 and 699, and 76% between 700 and 800. Math-- 1% between 500 and 599, 19% between 600 and 699, and 80% between 700 and 800. Writing-- 3% between 500 and 599, 18% between 600 and 699, and 79% between 700 and 800. The ACT scores were 1% between 18 and 23, 6% between 24 and 29, and 93% above 30. 98% of the current freshmen were in the top fifth of their class; 99% were in the top two fifths. 137 freshmen graduated first in their class. **Admissions Contact:** Janet Lavin Rapelye, Dean of Admissions. Email: *uaoffice@princeton.edu* Web: *www.princeton.edu*

FINANCIAL AID: Princeton is a member of CSS. The FAFSA code is 002627. Check with the school for current application deadlines.

RAMAPO COLLEGE OF NEW JERSEY D-1

www.ramapo.edu

Mahwah, NJ 07430 **(201) 684-7300**

Fax: (201) 684-7964	**Email: admissions@ramapo.edu**
Full-time: 2269 men, 2654 women	**Faculty:** 218; IIB, +$
Part-time: 215 men, 287 women	**Ph.D.s:** 94%
Graduate: 104 men, 258 women	**Student/Faculty:** 17 to 1
Year: semesters, summer session	**Tuition:** $13,698 ($22,563)
Room & Board: $11,640	**Freshman Class:** 7106 applied, 3783 accepted, 918 enrolled
SAT CR/M/W: 540/552/535	**CEEB CODE:** 2884
Application Deadline: March 1	**COMPETITIVE**

Ramapo College, founded in 1969, is a public institution offering undergraduate programs in the arts and sciences, American and international studies, business administration, and human services. Personal interaction is incorporated throughout the curriculum as is an international and multicultural component including telecommunications and computer technology. Figures in the above capsule and in this profile are approximate. There are 5 undergraduate schools and 4 graduate schools. In addition to regional accreditation, Ramapo has baccalaureate program accreditation with AACSB, CSWE, TEAC, MSCHE, NLNAC, and ACS. The 314-acre campus is in a suburban area 25 miles northwest of New York City. Including any residence halls, there are 62 buildings.

STUDENT LIFE: 95% of undergraduates are from New Jersey. Others are from 17 states, and 27 foreign countries. 7% are race unknown; 66% White; 6% Asian American; 5% African American; 13% Hispanic; 1% Foreign; 1% two or more races. **Female To Male Ratio:** 1.2:1. The average age of freshmen is 18; all undergraduates, 22. 12% do not continue beyond their first year; 72% remain to graduate. **Housing:** 3062 students can be accommodated in college housing, which includes coed dorms on-campus apartments, honors houses, special-interest houses. There are also blocks of rooms that are reserved for scholars and honors students, and theme and wellness housing. On-campus housing is guaranteed for all 4 years, and is available on a first-come, first-served basis. 53% of students live on campus. All students may keep cars.

FACULTY/CLASSROOMS: 51% of faculty are male; 49% are female. All teach undergraduates. No introductory courses are taught by graduate students. The average class size in an introductory lecture is 26; in a laboratory is 19; and in a regular course is 23.

PROGRAMS OF STUDY: Ramapo confers B.A., B.S., B.S.N. and B.S.W. degrees. Master's degrees are also awarded. Bachelor's degrees are awarded in AGRICULTURE (environmental studies), BIOLOGICAL SCIENCE (biochemistry, bioinformatics, and biology/biological science), BUSINESS (accounting, business administration and management, and international business management), COMMUNICATIONS AND THE ARTS (art, communications, dramatic arts, literature, music, and visual and performing arts), COMPUTER AND PHYSICAL SCIENCE (chemistry, computer science, information sciences and systems, and mathematics), ENGINEERING AND ENVIRONMENTAL DESIGN (engineering physics and environmental science), HEALTH PROFESSIONS (allied health, clinical science, and nursing), SOCIAL SCIENCE (African studies, American studies, economics, history, international studies, law, liberal arts/general studies, political science/government, psychology, science and society, social science, social work, sociology, and Spanish studies). Physics, bioinformatics, and biology are the strongest academically. Business administration, psychology, and communication arts have the largest enrollments.

ACTIVITIES: 17% of men belong to 15 national fraternities; 17% of women belong to 13 national sororities. There are 100 groups on campus, including theme housing, environmental clubs, cheerleading, choir, chorale, chorus, computers, dance, debate, drama, environmental, ethnic, honors, international, LGBT, literary magazine, musical theater, newspaper, pep band, photography, political, professional, radio and TV, religious, social, social service, student government, volunteer/community service, and yearbook. Popular campus events include LollaNoBooza, Octoberfest, and Stress Busters. **Sports:** There are 8 intercollegiate sports for men and 10 for women, and 16 intramural sports for men and 16 for women. Facilities include 10% Varsity and 80% Intramural participation. Facilities include a stadium, a track, tennis courts, and baseball, softball, field hockey, and soccer fields, an arena for basketball and volleyball courts, a gym, a fitness center includes cardio machines, machine weight stations, and free weights. Also available is an athletic training room, and swimming pool. **Graduates:** From July 1, 2015 to June 30, 2016, 1250 bachelor's degrees were awarded. The most popular majors were business/marketing (23%), psychology (15%), and communication arts (11%). 130 companies recruited on campus in 2015-2016. In an average class, 2% graduate in 3 years or less, 60% graduate in 4 years or less, 70% graduate in 5 years or less, and 72% graduate in 6 years or less.

SERVICES: Counseling and information services are available, as is tutoring in every subject. There is a reader service for the blind, and remedial math, reading, and writing. Students also have access to resources at the Center for Academic Success. **Library/Resources:** The library contains 191,031 volumes, 2,500 microform items, 9,373 audio/video tapes/CDs/DVDs, and subscribes to 488 periodicals including electronic. Computerized library services include interlibrary loans, database searching, Internet access, and Wi-Fi capability. Special learning facilities include a radio station, TV station, astronomical observatory, international telecommunications satellite center, the Marge Roukema Center for International Education and Entrepreneurship, a solar greenhouse center, a spirituality center, and a sustainability education center. **Physically Challenged Students:** All of the campus is accessible. Facilities include wheelchair ramps, elevators, special parking, specially equipped restrooms, special class scheduling, lowered drinking fountains, lowered telephones, and special housing. **Special:** Ramapo's curriculum emphasizes the interdependence of global society and includes an international dimension in all academic programs. Students may study abroad in many countries. Cooperative programs are available with various corporations and in foreign countries. Cross-registration is possible with local state colleges. Ramapo offers accelerated degree programs, dual and student-designed majors, credit for life experience, pass/fail options, internships, work-study programs, and certificate programs in gerontology and substance abuse. A teachers education program is offered. There are 23 national honor societies, a freshman honors program, and 5 departmental honors programs. **Visiting:** There are regularly scheduled orientations for prospective students, Student visits include orientation, advisement, registration, and immediate decision days (that follow the early action plan). There are guides for informal visits and visitors may sit in on classes. To schedule a visit, contact the Admissions Office at admissions@ramapo.edu. **Campus Safety and Security:** Measures include 24-hour foot and vehicle patrol, emergency notification system, and security escort services. There are also shuttle buses, emergency telephones, lighted pathways/sidewalks, and surveillance cameras.

REQUIREMENTS: The SAT is required. Applicants must be graduates of an accredited secondary schools or have earned a GED. The college requires 18 academic credits, including 4 in English, 3 each in math, science (2 with lab), social studies, and academic electives, and 2 in foreign language. Students must also submit an essay. An interview is recommended. AP and CLEP credits are accepted. Important factors in the admissions decision are advanced placement or honors courses, recommendations by school officials, and evidence of special talent. Students must complete general education requirements of approximately 50 credits in science, social science, humanities, and English composition, as well as core requirements in their school of study and their particular major. A senior seminar is also required. To graduate, students must earn at least 128 credits with a minimum GPA of 2.0. **Procedure:** Freshmen are admitted in the fall and spring. Entrance exams should be taken during the senior year. There are early admissions, deferred admissions, and rolling admissions plans. Early decision applications should be filed by November 1; regular applications, by March 1 for fall entry; and December 1 for spring entry. The fall 2016 application fee was $60. Notification of early decision is sent December 5; regular decision, on a rolling basis. Applications are accepted on-line. **Transfer Students:** 555 transfer students enrolled in 2015-2016. Applicants must supply a completed admission application, official transcripts from all previously attended colleges, and an official high school transcript (if fewer than 60 credits from another college attempted). 48 of 128 credits required for the bachelor's degree must be completed at Ramapo. **International Students:** There are 77 international students enrolled. The school actively recruits these students. They must take the TOEFL with a minimum score of 550 on the paper-based TOEFL (PBT) or 90 on the Internet-based version (iBT) and the Comprehensive English Language Test. They must also take the SAT.

ADMISSIONS: 53% of the 2016-2017 applicants were accepted. The SAT scores for the 2016-2017 freshman class were: Critical Reading-- 27% below 500, 51% between 500 and 599, 19% between 600 and 699, and 3% between 700 and 800. Math-- 21% below 500, 50% between 500 and 599, 25% between 600 and 699, and 4% between 700 and 800. Writing-- 30% below 500, 47% between 500 and 599, 20% between 600 and 699, and 3% between 700 and 800. 57% of the current freshmen were in the top fifth of their class; 89% were in the top two fifths. 2 freshmen graduated first in their class. **Admissions Contact:** Peter Rice, Director of Admissions. Email: *admissions@ramapo.edu* Web: *www.ramapo.edu*

FINANCIAL AID: In 2016-2017, 80% of all full-time freshmen and 82% of continuing full-time students received some form of financial aid. 60% of all full-time freshmen and 50% of continuing full-time students received need-based aid. 4% of undergraduate students work part-time. Average annual earnings from campus work are $2000. The average financial indebtedness of the 2016 graduate was $27,909. The FAFSA code is 009344. The priority date for freshman financial aid applications for fall entry is March 1. The filing deadline for fall entry is March 15.

RIDER UNIVERSITY D-3
www.rider.edu

Lawrenceville, NJ 08648	**(609) 896-5042** **(800) 257-9026**
Fax: (609) 895-6645	**Email: admissions@rider.edu**
Full-time: 1520 men, 2119 women	**Faculty:** 235; IIA, ++$
Part-time: 159 men, 262 women	**Ph.D.s:** 98%
Graduate: 364 men, 682 women	**Student/Faculty:** 16 to 1
Year: semesters, summer session	**Tuition:** $39,820 ($38,360)
Room & Board: $14,230	**Freshman Class:** 9172 applied, 6366 accepted, 871 enrolled
SAT CR/M/W: 490/500/480 **ACT:** 21	**CEEB CODE:** 2758
Application Deadline: n/av	**COMPETITIVE**

Rider University, founded in 1865, is a private institution offering undergraduate programs in the areas of business administration, liberal arts, education, sciences, and continuing studies. Westminster Choir College, located in nearby Princeton, is Rider's fourth college. Figures in the above capsule and in this profile are approximate. There are 4 undergraduate schools and 2 graduate schools. In addition to regional accreditation, Rider has baccalaureate program accreditation with AACSB, NASM, NCATE, CACREP, and NASP. The 280-acre campus is in a suburban area 3 miles north of Trenton and 7 miles south of Princeton. Including any residence halls, there are 41 buildings.

STUDENT LIFE: 75% of undergraduates are from New Jersey. Others are from 37 states, 76 foreign countries, and Canada. 60% are White; 5% Asian American; 3% Foreign; 3% two or more races; 3% race unknown; 14% Hispanic; 12% African American. **Female To Male Ratio:** 1.5:1. The average age of freshmen is 18; all undergraduates, 21. 20% do not continue beyond their first year; 64% remain to graduate. **Housing:** 2515 students can be accommodated in college housing, which includes single-sex and coed dorms, on-campus apartments, honors houses, language houses, special-interest houses, fraternity houses, sorority houses, learning community, wellness, quiet, science area, and first-year experience housing. On-campus housing is available on a lottery system for upperclassmen. 55% of students live on campus; of those, 50% remain on campus on weekends. All students may keep cars.

FACULTY/CLASSROOMS: 51% of faculty are male; 49% are female. 98% teach undergraduates, and all do research. No introductory courses are taught by graduate students. The average class size in an introductory lecture is 26; in a laboratory is 14; and in a regular course is 20.

PROGRAMS OF STUDY: Rider confers B.A., B.M., B.S., and B.S.B.A. degrees. Associate and master's degrees are also awarded. Bachelor's degrees are awarded in BIOLOGICAL SCIENCE (biochemistry, biology/biological science, and marine science), BUSINESS (accounting, banking and finance, business administration and management, business economics, human resources, international business management, management science, marketing/retailing/merchandising, and office supervision and management), COMMUNICATIONS AND THE ARTS (advertising, communications, dance, dramatic arts, English, English literature, fine arts, French, German, journalism, multimedia, music, piano/organ, public relations, Russian, Spanish, and voice), COMPUTER AND PHYSICAL SCIENCE (actuarial science, chemistry, geoscience, information sciences and systems, mathematics, and physics), EDUCATION (business education, early childhood education, elementary education, English education, foreign languages education, marketing and distribution education, mathematics education, music education, science education, secondary education, and social studies education), ENGINEERING AND ENVIRONMENTAL DESIGN (environmental science), HEALTH PROFESSIONS (premedicine), SOCIAL SCIENCE (American studies, biopsychology, economics, history, liberal arts/general studies, philosophy, political science/government, prelaw, psychology, and sociology). Elementary education, accounting, and business administration have the largest enrollments.

ACTIVITIES: 5% of men belong to 4 national fraternities; 10% of women belong to 7 national sororities. There are 130 groups on campus, including art, band, cheerleading, choir, chorale, chorus, computers, dance, drama, environmental, ethnic, film, honors, international, jazz band, LGBT, literary magazine, musical theater, newspaper, opera, orchestra, pep band, photography, political, professional, radio and TV, religious, social, social service, student government, symphony, and yearbook. Popular campus events include Cranberry Fest, Fall Concert, Family Weekend, and R Factor. **Sports:** There are 10 intercollegiate sports for men and 10 for women, and 10 intramural sports for men and 6 for women. Facilities include a recreation center with basketball, volleyball, and tennis courts, and an elevated jogging/walking track, a fitness center with cardio equipment, weight room machines, and free weights. **Graduates:** From July 1, 2015 to June 30, 2016, 983 bachelor's degrees were awarded. The most popular majors were accounting (11%), psychology (10%), and early childhood education (9%). 150 companies recruited on campus in 2015-2016. In an average class, 58% graduate in 4 years or less, 64% graduate in 5 years or less, and 66% graduate in 6 years or less.

SERVICES: Counseling and information services are available, as is tutoring in most subjects, and remedial math, reading, and writing. **Library/Resources:** The library contains 451,460 volumes, 661,743 microform items, 5,889 audio/video tapes/CDs/DVDs, and subscribes to 45,016 periodicals including electronic. Computerized library services include interlibrary loans, database searching, Internet access, and Wi-Fi capability. Special learning facilities include an art gallery, radio station, TV station, a journalism and sociology lab, and a holocaust/genocide center. **Physically Challenged Students:** 75% of the campus is accessible. Facilities include wheelchair ramps, elevators, special parking, specially equipped restrooms, special class scheduling, lowered drinking fountains, and lowered telephones. **Special:** Internships in many programs, a co-op program in retail marketing, work-study, study abroad in 14 countries, a B.A.-B.S. degree in all liberal arts and sciences, dual majors in education, a liberal studies degree, and nondegree study are possible. There is a freshman honors program. **Visiting:** There are regularly scheduled orientations for prospective students, including 3 open houses, Saturday information sessions and other programs that consist of a welcome, a campus tour, and a variety of formal and informal activities to meet faculty, staff, current students, and alumni. There are guides for informal visits and visitors may sit in on classes. To schedule a visit, contact The Office of Admissions. **Campus Safety and Security:** Measures include 24-hour foot and vehicle patrol, emergency notification system, self-defense education, and security escort services. There are also shuttle buses, emergency telephones, lighted pathways/sidewalks, a shuttle car, a staffed kiosk at the entrance, a security system in residence halls, video camera surveillance, bike patrol, and a property ID program.

REQUIREMENTS: The SAT or ACT is required. Applicants need 16 Carnegie units, including 4 years of English and 2 of math. 3 units of math are required for prospective math, science, and business majors. An essay is recommended. An audition is required for theater scholarships. The GED is accepted. AP and CLEP credits are accepted. Important factors in the admissions decision are advanced placement or honors courses, extracurricular activities record, and leadership record. To graduate, all students must maintain a minimum GPA of 2.0 while taking 120 semester hours. Students also must fulfill core curriculum requirements, including 9 hours in humanities, 7 to 8 in science, 6 each in English writing and foreign language (may be waived if proficiency is demonstrated), social sciences/communications, and history, and 3 in math. 30 to 76 credits are required in the major. A thesis is required in the honors program and some science majors. **Procedure:** Freshmen are admitted in the fall and spring. Entrance exams should be taken by January of the senior year. There are deferred admissions and rolling admissions plans. Application deadlines are open. Application fee is $50. Notification is sent on a rolling basis. 62 applicants were on the 2016 waiting list; 28 were admitted. Applications are accepted online. **Transfer Students:** 242 transfer students enrolled in 2015-2016. A GPA of 2.5 or better is required for applicants. If students have fewer than 30 credits, they also must submit high school transcripts and SAT scores. An essay or personal statement is required, and an interview is recommended. 30 of 120 credits required for the bachelor's degree must be completed at Rider. **International Students:** There are 201 international students enrolled. The school actively recruits these students. They must take the TOEFL with a minimum score of 550 on the paper-based TOEFL (PBT) or 80 on the Internet-based version (iBT). They must also take the SAT or ACT.

ADMISSIONS: 69% of the 2016-2017 applicants were accepted. The SAT scores for the 2016-2017 freshman class were: Critical Reading-- 52% below 500, 36% between 500 and 599, 11% between 600 and 699, and 2% between 700 and 800. Math-- 44% below 500, 40% between 500 and 599, 14% between 600 and 699, and 1% between 700 and 800. Writing-- 53% below 500, 34% between 500 and 599, 12% between 600 and 699, and 1% between 700 and 800. The ACT scores were 12% between 12 and 17, 53% between 18 and 23, 30% between 24 and 29, and 5%

above 30. **Admissions Contact:** Susan C. Christian, Director of Admissions. Email: *admissions@rider.edu* Web: *www.rider.edu*

FINANCIAL AID: In 2016-2017, 81% of all full-time freshmen and 74% of continuing full-time students received some form of financial aid. 80% of all full-time freshmen and 73% of continuing full-time students received need-based aid. The average freshman award was $31,784. Need-based scholarships or need-based grants averaged $27,328; need-based self-help aid (loans and jobs) averaged $5,490; and $3,147 from other forms of aid. The SFS is required. The FAFSA code is 002628. The priority date for freshman financial aid applications for fall entry is March 1.

ROWAN UNIVERSITY C-4

www.rowan.edu

Glassboro, NJ 08028 **(855) 256-4200**

Fax: (856) 256-4430	**Email:** admissions@rowan.edu
Full-time: 6405 men, 5300 women	**Faculty:** 362
Part-time: 680 men, 779 women	**Ph.D.s:** 83%
Graduate: 1128 men, 1858 women	**Student/Faculty:** 18 to 1
Year: semesters, summer session	**Tuition:** $12,864 ($20,978)
Room & Board: $11,627	**Freshman Class:** 12158 applied, 6860 accepted, 1770 enrolled
SAT CR/M/W: 582/622/565	**CEEB CODE:** 2515
Application Deadline: March 1	**VERY COMPETITIVE+**

Rowan University, a leading state-designated comprehensive public research institution, combines liberal education with professional preparation from the baccalaureate through the doctorate. Rowan provides a collaborative, learning-centered environment in which highly qualified and diverse faculty, staff, and students integrate teaching, research, scholarship, creative activity, and community service. There are 9 undergraduate schools and 1 graduate school. In addition to regional accreditation, Rowan has baccalaureate program accreditation with AACSB, ABET, CSAB, NASAD, NASDTEC, NASM, NCATE, LCME, LOCA, COPTI, MUS, CAATE, THEA, NASD, and NAST. The 921-acre campus is in a suburban area 20 miles southeast of Philadelphia. Including any residence halls, there are 85 buildings.

STUDENT LIFE: 95% of undergraduates are from New Jersey. Others are from 33 states, and 19 foreign countries. 90% are from public schools. 66% are White; 4% Asian American; 4% race unknown; 3% two or more races; 12% Hispanic; 10% African American; 1% Foreign. **Male To Female Ratio:** 1.0:1. The average age of freshmen is 18; all undergraduates, 21. 12% do not continue beyond their first year; 66% remain to graduate. **Housing:** 4500 students can be accommodated in college housing, which includes coed dorms, on-campus apartments, honors houses and special-interest houses. On-campus housing is guaranteed for the freshman year only and is available on a lottery system for upperclassmen. Priority is given to out-of-town students. 63% of students commute. Upperclassmen may keep cars.

FACULTY/CLASSROOMS: 53% of faculty are male; 47% are female. 92% teach undergraduates, 8% do research, and 8% do both. No introductory courses are taught by graduate students. The average class size in an introductory lecture is 22; in a laboratory is 16; and in a regular course is 22.

PROGRAMS OF STUDY: Rowan confers B.A., B.S., B.S.N., B.F.A., B.G.S. and B.M. degrees. Master's and doctoral degrees are also awarded. Bachelor's degrees are awarded in AGRICULTURE (environmental studies), BIOLOGICAL SCIENCE (biochemistry, bioinformatics, and biology/biological science), BUSINESS (accounting, business administration and management, entrepreneurial studies, human resources, marketing/retailing/merchandising, personnel management, and small business management), COMMUNICATIONS AND THE ARTS (advertising, art, broadcasting, communications, dramatic arts, English, fine arts, jazz, journalism, music, public relations, radio/television technology, Spanish, speech/debate/rhetoric, and theatre arts), COMPUTER AND PHYSICAL SCIENCE (chemistry, computer science, mathematics, physical sciences, and physics), EDUCATION (art education, athletic training, collaborative education, early childhood education, education, elementary education, foreign languages education, general studies, music education, and science education), ENGINEERING AND ENVIRONMENTAL DESIGN (biomedical engineering, chemical engineering, civil engineering, engineering, and mechanical engineering), HEALTH PROFESSIONS (health and nursing), SOCIAL SCIENCE (African studies, American studies, criminal justice, economics, geography, history, liberal arts/general studies, philosophy and religion, political science/government, psychology, and sociology). Engineering, biology, and education are the strongest academically. Biological science, psychology, and elementary education have the largest enrollments.

ACTIVITIES: 5% of men belong to 16 national fraternities; 4% of women belong to 10 national sororities. There are 150 groups on campus, including art, band, cheerleading, chess, choir, chorale, chorus, communications, computers, dance, drama, environmental, ethnic, film, honors, international, jazz band, LGBT, literary magazine, music ensembles, musical theater, newspaper, opera, orchestra, pep band, photography, political, professional, radio and TV, religious, social, social service, student government, symphony, and yearbook. Popular campus events include Prof Stock, Back to the Boro, Senior Send Off, Home Coming, and Leadership Conference. **Sports:** There are 8 intercollegiate sports for men and 10 for women, and 15 intramural sports for men and 15 for women. Facilities include a stadium, gym, football and soccer, field hockey, and women's lacrosse. The NCAA sports for men are football, soccer, cross country, basketball, swimming, indoor track, outdoor track and baseball. For women there are volleyball, cross country, field hockey, soccer, basketball, indoor track, swimming, lacrosse, outdoor track and softball. Regarding men's and women's intramural sports breakdown: many of our sports are either open to either gender or we have co-rec or co-ed divisions available. The majority of open divisions are men's teams such as wiffleball, bowling, billiards, racquetball, ping pong, tennis, badminton, dodgeball, battleship, horse, golf, sand volleyball, punt, pass and kick, free throw and 3 point competition (15 offerings). Men's specific – basketball, outdoor soccer, softball, volleyball, flag football, indoor soccer, 1 on 1 basketball, kickball, regional dodgeball (9 offerings). Women's specific basketball, outdoor soccer, softball, volleyball, flag football, indoor soccer, 1 on 1 basketball, regional dodgeball (8 offerings). A student recreation center includes: competition pools, multi-purpose wood courts, indoor jogging track, group fitness studio, cycling studio, racquetball courts, free weight room, cardiovascular, and selectorized equipment areas. **Graduates:** From July 1, 2015 to June 30, 2016, 2856 bachelor's degrees were awarded. The most popular majors were psychology (9%), biological science (6%), and law/justice (6%). 106 companies recruited on campus in 2015-2016. In an average class, 43% graduate in 4 years or less, 61% graduate in 5 years or less, and 66% graduate in 6 years or less.

SERVICES: Counseling and information services are available, as is tutoring in every subject, a reader service for the blind, and remedial math, reading, and writing. **Library/Resources:** The 4 libraries contain 641,430 volumes, 519,817 microform items, 18,984 audio/video tapes/CDs/DVDs, and subscribe to 77,727 periodicals including electronic. Computerized library services include interlibrary loans, database searching, Internet access, and Wi-Fi capability. Special learning facilities include an art gallery, planetarium, radio station, TV station, a virtual reality cave, exercise science research laboratory, assessment and learning center. **Physically Challenged Students:** 95% of the campus is accessible. Facilities include wheelchair ramps, elevators, special parking, specially equipped restrooms, special class scheduling, lowered drinking fountains, lowered telephones, and special housing. **Special:** Honors program is a special interdisciplinary program that is not housed in any department per se; rather departments provide courses to the stand alone honors program. Students may study abroad in 40 countries. Internships are available in all majors both with and without pay. Rowan also offers accelerated degree programs and 3-2 degrees in optometry, podiatry, and pharmacy as well as a 4-1 degree in business. There are dual majors, pass/fail options, and credit for military experience. BS/MS accelerated degrees. Joint BS/MS accelerated degrees with Stockton College. There are 12 national honor societies and a freshman honors program. **Visiting:** There are regularly scheduled orientations for prospective students, visiting students may participate in a 2-day summer program providing schedule confirmation/adjustment, student activities updates, and workshops for students and parents. There are guides for informal visits and visitors may sit in on classes. To schedule a visit, contact Albert Betts at betts@rowan.edu. **Campus Safety and Security:** Measures include 24-hour foot and vehicle patrol, emergency notification system, self-defense education, and security escort services. There are shuttle buses, emergency telephones, lighted pathways/sidewalks, controlled access to dorms/residences, and Rowan Department of Public Safety and EMS service.

REQUIREMENTS: The SAT is required, students are required to score an 1080, or no less than 500 on either part. Students submitting ACT scores should have a minimum composite score of 23. Applicants must be graduates of accredited secondary schools or have earned a GED. Rowan requires 16 academic credits or Carnegie units, including 4 in English, 3 each in math and college preparatory electives, and 2 each in foreign language, history, and lab science. A portfolio or audition is required for specific majors. A GPA of 2.0 is required. AP and CLEP credits are accepted. Important factors in the admissions decision are advanced placement or honors courses, evidence of special talent, and leadership record. General education requirements include 6-12 credits of social and behavior sciences; 6-12 credits of history, humanities and language; 7-15 credits of math and science (one science course must be 4 credits with a lab component), 9 credits of communication, and 6 credits in non-program courses. Students also take requirements in the Rowan Experience, which includes the Rowan Seminar and courses with the following designations: multicultural/global, artistic/creative experience, literature, and writing intensive. The Bachelor's degree requires 120-132 semester hours, including 30-42 in a major field, with a minimum GPA of 2.0. **Procedure:** Freshmen are admitted in the fall and spring. Entrance exams should be taken by May or June of the junior year, or by December of the senior year. There is a deferred admissions plan. Applications should be filed by March 1 for fall entry; November 1 for spring entry, along with a $65 fee. Notifications are sent April 15. 150 applicants were on the 2016 waiting list; 56 were admitted. Applications are accepted online. **Transfer Students:** 1634 transfer students enrolled in 2015-2016. Applicants must have a minimum GPA of 2.0, but should present a GPA of 2.5 to be competitive. An associate degree is recommended. Students who have earned fewer than 24 semester hours must also submit a high school transcript and SAT I results. 30 of 120 credits required for the bachelor's degree must be completed at Rowan. **International Students:** There are 110 international students enrolled. The school actively recruits these students. They must take the TOEFL with a minimum score of 550 on the paper-based TOEFL (PBT) or 79 on the Internet-based version (iBT), or take the IELTS. They must also take ACT, and SAT for students whose first language is English, and in all engineering majors.

ADMISSIONS: 56% of the 2016-2017 applicants were accepted. The SAT scores for the 2016-2017 freshman class were: Critical Reading-- 28% below 500, 46% between 500 and 599, 23% between 600 and 699, and 3% between 700 and 800. Math-- 20% below 500, 43% between 500 and 599, 31% between 600 and 699, and 6% between 700 and 800. Writing-- 35% below 500, 44% between 500 and 599, 19% between 600 and 699, and 2% between 700 and 800. **Admissions Contact:** Albert Betts, Director of Admissions. Email: *admissions@rowan.edu* Web: *www.rowan.edu*

FINANCIAL AID: The average freshman award was $10,662. Need-based scholarships or need-based grants averaged $9,121; need-based self-help aid (loans and jobs) averaged $3,314; and other non-need-based awards and non-need-based scholarships averaged $6,699. 10% of undergraduate students work part-time. Average annual earnings from campus work are $1200. The average financial indebtedness of the 2016 graduate was $25,348. The FAFSA code is 002609. The priority date for freshman financial aid applications for fall entry is January 1. The filing deadline for fall entry is March 15.

RUTGERS UNIVERSITY - CAMDEN C-4

www.camden.rutgers.edu

Camden, NJ 08102 **(856) 225-6510**

Email: camdem@admissions.rutgers.edu

Full-time: 1676 men, 2380 women	**Faculty:** IIA, ++$
Part-time: 373 men, 592 women	**Ph.D.s:** 99%
Graduate: 721 men, 733 women	**Student/Faculty:** 10 to 1
Year: semesters, summer session	**Tuition:** $14,238 ($29,381)
Room & Board: $11,908	**Freshman Class:** 8725 applied, 5016 accepted, 675 enrolled
SAT CR/M/W: 510/530/500	**CEEB CODE:** 2742
Application Deadline: open	**COMPETITIVE**

Rutgers University - Camden Campus was founded in 1926. On July 1, 2013, the New Jersey Medical and Health Sciences Education Restructuring Act went into effect, integrating Rutgers, The State University of New Jersey, with all units of the University of Medicine and Dentistry of New Jersey (UMDNJ), except University Hospital in Newark and the School of Osteopathic Medicine in Stratford. The integration of the legacy elements of UMDNJ into Rutgers has created a fourth unit, Rutgers Biomedical and Health Sciences (RBHS), which consists of a number of schools and units located on various sites but closely aligned with the campuses in Newark and New Brunswick. The campus is comprised of 4 undergraduate, degree-granting schools: College of the Arts and Sciences, University College-Camden, the School of Nursing-Camden and the School of Business-Camden. Each school has individual requirements, policies, and fees. There are 4 undergraduate schools and 4 graduate schools. In addition to regional accreditation, RU-Camden has baccalaureate program accreditation with AACSB, APTA, CSWE, TEAC, and CCNE. The 32-acre campus is in an urban area 1 mile east of Philadelphia. Including any residence halls, there are 47 buildings.

STUDENT LIFE: 97% of undergraduates are from New Jersey. Others are from 18 states, 18 foreign countries, and Canada. 9% are Asian American; 53% White; 4% two or more races; 2% race unknown; 17% African American; 14% Hispanic; 1% Foreign. **Female To Male Ratio:** 1.3:1. The average age of freshmen is 18; all undergraduates, 22. 17% do not continue beyond their first year; 83% remain to graduate. **Housing:** 680 students can be accommodated in college housing, which includes coed dorms, on-campus apartments, fraternity houses, and sorority houses. 88% of students commute. Alcohol is not permitted.

FACULTY/CLASSROOMS: 52% of faculty are male; 48% are female. No introductory courses are taught by graduate students. The average class size in an introductory lecture is 30; in a laboratory is 20; and in a regular course is 30.

PROGRAMS OF STUDY: RU-Camden confers B.A., B.S., and B.H.M. degrees. Master's and doctoral degrees are also awarded. Bachelor's degrees are awarded in BIOLOGICAL SCIENCE (biochemistry and biology/biological science), BUSINESS (accounting, banking and finance, hospitality management services, management science, and marketing/retailing/merchandising), COMMUNICATIONS AND THE ARTS (art, art history and appreciation, dramatic arts, English, French, German, music, and Spanish), COMPUTER AND PHYSICAL SCIENCE (chemistry, computer science, mathematics, physics, and science), HEALTH PROFESSIONS (medical laboratory technology and nursing), SOCIAL SCIENCE (African American studies, child care/child and family studies, criminal justice, economics, history, interdisciplinary studies, liberal arts/general studies, philosophy, political science/government, psychology, religion, social work, sociology, and urban studies). Nursing, psychology, business, and criminal justice are the strongest academically. Nursing, business management, and psychology have the largest enrollments.

ACTIVITIES: There are no fraternities or sororities. There are 75 groups on campus, including computers, drama, ethnic, honors, international, LGBT, newspaper, political, professional, radio and TV, religious, social, social service, student government, and yearbook. Popular campus events include Raptor Day, Springfest and Basketball Team Sports. **Sports:** There are 9 intercollegiate sports for men and 10 for women. **Graduates:** From July 1, 2015 to June 30, 2016, 1391 bachelor's degrees were awarded. The most popular majors were nursing (19%), psychology (12%), and business administration and management (10%). In an average class, 26% graduate in 4 years or less, 50% graduate in 5 years or less, and 57% graduate in 6 years or less.

SERVICES: Counseling and information services are available, as is tutoring in some subjects, a reader service for the blind, and remedial math, reading, and writing. **Library/Resources:** The 2 libraries contain 729,987 volumes, 974,491 microform items, 591 audio/video tapes/CDs/DVDs, and subscribe to 15,013 periodicals including electronic. Computerized library services include interlibrary loans, database searching, and Internet access. Special learning facilities include an art gallery and radio station. **Physically Challenged Students:** 95% of the campus is accessible. Facilities include wheelchair ramps, elevators, special parking, specially equipped restrooms, special class scheduling, lowered drinking fountains, lowered telephones, and special housing. Facilities vary from building to building. All classes are scheduled in accessible locations for disabled students. **Special:** The University offers a cooperative baccalaureate program in engineering with School of Engineering (New Brunswick Campus). Interdisciplinary programs in African-American studies, general science. Cooperative baccalaureate in medical technology with approved hospital. B.A./M.A. in Childhood Studies, English, history, liberal studies or psychology; B.A./M.S. in biology, chemistry or mathematics (with the Graduate School-Camden). B.A. in economics or political science/Master of Public Administration (with the Graduate School-Camden); BS/Master of Business and Science (MBS). In addition, there is an 8-year B.A./M.D. program and many combined bachelor's and master's programs. There is distance learning, English as a Second Language, honors, and independent study programs available. There is a freshman honors program. **Visiting:** There are regularly scheduled orientations for prospective students, including an information session with an admissions officer and a campus tour. Visitors may sit in on classes. To schedule a visit, contact the Admissions Office (Camden). **Campus Safety and Security:** Measures include 24-hour foot and vehicle patrol, emergency notification system, self-defense education, and security escort services. There are also shuttle buses, emergency telephones, lighted pathways/sidewalks. The police department is supplemented by security guards.

REQUIREMENTS: The SAT or ACT is required, but not for students who have been out of high school for 2 years or more. SAT: Subject tests are required of students without a high school diploma from an accredited high school and from some GED holders. A high school diploma is required; the GED is accepted. Students must have completed a general college-preparatory program, including 16 academic credits or Carnegie units, with 4 years of English, 3 years of math (4 recommended), and 2 years each of a foreign language and science, plus 5 in electives. AP and CLEP credits are accepted. Important factors in the admissions decision are advanced placement or honors courses, evidence of special talent, and leadership record. To graduate, students must complete 120 credits, with 30 to 48 in the major, and maintain a minimum GPA of 2.0. A core curriculum of 60 credits is required, including 3 credits each in literary masterpieces, art, music or theater arts, and a foreign language, with an additional 3 credits in English or a foreign language, and 3 credits in math, with an additional 3 credits in math, computer science, or statistics. 1 interdisciplinary course is required, as are 9 credits from social science disciplines, 6 credits in English composition, 6 credits in history, 6 credits in the natural science disciplines, and an additional 9 credits in courses offered outside the major department. **Procedure:** Freshmen are admitted in the fall. Entrance exams should be taken by December of senior year is recommended, but not required. There are early admissions and rolling admissions plans. Application deadlines are open. Application fee is $70. Notifications are sent March 1. Applications are accepted online. **Transfer Students:** 733 transfer students enrolled in 2015-2016. Applicants must have a minimum of 12 credit hours. Grades of C or better in courses that correspond in content and credit to those offered by the college transfer for credit. Transfer students are admitted in the fall and spring semesters. All high school and previous college transcripts are required. 30 of 120 credits required for the bachelor's degree must be completed at RU-Camden. **International Students:** There are 59 international students enrolled. They must take the TOEFL with a minimum score of 550 on the paper-based TOEFL (PBT) or 79 on the Internet-based version (iBT). They must also take the SAT or ACT. or the IELTS, scoring 7.

ADMISSIONS: 57% of the 2016-2017 applicants were accepted. The SAT scores for the 2016-2017 freshman class were: Critical Reading-- 47% below 500, 41% between 500 and 599, 11% between 600 and 699, and 1% between 700 and 800. Math-- 41% below 500, 41% between 500 and 599, 16% between 600 and 699, and 2% between 700 and 800. Writing-- 51% below 500, 40% between 500 and 599, 8% between 600 and 699, and 1% between 700 and 800. 35% of the current freshmen were in the top fifth of their class; 68% were in the top two fifths. **Admissions Contact:** Craig Westman, Associate Chancellor, Enrollment Management. Email: *admissions@ugadm.rutgers.edu* Web: *www.camden.rutgers.edu*

FINANCIAL AID: In 2016-2017, 95% of all full-time freshmen and 97% of continuing full-time students received some form of financial aid. 80% of all full-time freshmen and 96% of continuing full-time students received need-based aid. The average freshman award was $18,236. Need-based scholarships or need-based grants averaged $12,115; need-based self-help aid (loans and jobs) averaged $4,194; and other non-need-based awards and non-need-based scholarships averaged $7,735. Average annual earnings from campus work are $1525. The average financial indebtedness of the 2016 graduate was $28,813. The FAFSA code is 002629. The priority date for freshman financial aid applications for fall entry is March 15. The filing deadline for fall entry is open.

RUTGERS UNIVERSITY - NEW BRUNSWICK D-3

Rutgers, The State University of New Jersey New Brunswick
www.newbrunswick.rutgers.edu

Piscataway, NJ 08854 **(732) 932-4636**

Fax: (732) 445-0237
Email: admissions@rutgers.edu
Full-time: 17,016 men, 17,004 women
Faculty: I, +$
Ph.D.s: 99%
Part-time: 910 men, 1238 women
Student/Faculty: 13 to 1
Graduate: 5489 men, 8489 women
Tuition: $14,372 ($30,023)
Year: semesters, summer session
Freshman Class: 36677 applied, 20884 accepted, 6460 enrolled
Room & Board: $12,260
SAT or ACT: required
CEEB CODE: 2753
Application Deadline: n/av
HIGHLY COMPETITIVE

Rutgers University - New Brunswick was founded in 1766. The New Jersey Medical and Health Sciences Education Restructuring Act went into effect, integrating Rutgers, with all units of the University of Medicine and Dentistry of New Jersey (UMDNJ), except University Hospital in Newark and the School of Osteopathic Medicine in Stratford. The integration of the legacy elements of UMDNJ into Rutgers has created a fourth unit, Rutgers Biomedical and Health Sciences (RBHS), which consists of a number of schools and units located on various sites but closely aligned with the campus in New Brunswick. Undergraduate students in New Brunswick enroll in the School of Arts and Sciences, the liberal arts college, and/or in one of the professional schools: School of Environmental and Biological Sciences (formerly Cook College); Mason Gross School of the Arts; Rutgers Business School: Undergraduate-New Brunswick; School of Communication, and Information; School of Engineering; Edward J. Bloustein School of Planning and Public Policy; the School of Management and Labor Relations; Ernest Mario School of Pharmacy; College of Nursing; School of Nursing; School of Health Related Professions; or the School of Public Health. Some schools located in New Brunswick and/or Newark are also part of the Rutgers Biomedical and Health Sciences unit and are listed for each campus. Each school has individual requirements, policies, and fees. There are 12 undergraduate schools and 17 graduate schools. In addition to regional accreditation, RU-New Brunswick has baccalaureate program accreditation with AACSB, ABET, ACPE, ADA, APTA, ASLA, CSWE, NASM, TEAC, ABOG, ACEND, ACGME, ACME, ACOTE, ANFP, APA, ARC-PA, ARRT, CAAHEP, CACREP, CAHIIM, CCNE, CEPH, COA, COARC, CORE LCME, NAACLS, and NASD. The 2688-acre campus is in an urban area 33 miles south of New York City. Including any residence halls, there are 670 buildings.

STUDENT LIFE: 86% of undergraduates are from New Jersey. Others are from 48 states, 54 foreign countries, and Canada. 8% are African American; 8% Foreign; 40% White; 3% two or more races; 26% Asian American; 2% race unknown; 13% Hispanic. **Female To Male Ratio:** 1.1:1. The average age of freshmen is 18; all undergraduates, 25. 8% do not continue beyond their first year; 92% remain to graduate. **Housing:** 15925 students can be accommodated in college housing, which includes single-sex and coed dorms and married student housing. In addition, there are language houses, special-interest houses, fraternity houses, sorority houses, substance-free house, math/science/engineering house for women, first-year residence, transfer center, and residence for single mothers with children. 58% of students commute. Upperclassmen may keep cars. Alcohol is not permitted.

FACULTY/CLASSROOMS: 51% of faculty are male; 49% are female. No introductory courses are taught by graduate students. The average class size in an introductory lecture is 30; in a laboratory is 20; and in a regular course is 30.

PROGRAMS OF STUDY: RU-New Brunswick confers B.A., B.S., B.F.A., B.Mus. and B.S.N. degrees. Associate, master's, and doctoral degrees are also awarded. Bachelor's degrees are awarded in AGRICULTURE (agriculture, animal science, natural resource/environmental economics, natural resource management, and plant science), BIOLOGICAL SCIENCE (biochemistry, biology/biological science, biomathematics, biotechnology, botany, cell biology, ecology, evolutionary biology, genetics, marine science, microbiology, molecular biology, nutrition, and physiology), BUSINESS (accounting, banking and finance, business administration and management, finance, human resources, labor studies, management information systems, management science, marketing, and marketing/retailing/merchandising), COMMUNICATIONS AND THE ARTS (art, art history and appreciation, Chinese, classics, communications, comparative literature, dance, dramatic arts, East Asian languages and literature, English, French, German, Italian, journalism, Latin, linguistics, music, Portuguese, Russian, Spanish, and visual and performing arts), COMPUTER AND PHYSICAL SCIENCE (astrophysics, atmospheric sciences and meteorology, chemistry, computer science, geology, information sciences and systems, mathematics, physics, and statistics), EDUCATION (health information management), ENGINEERING AND ENVIRONMENTAL DESIGN (biomedical engineering, bioresource engineering, ceramic engineering, chemical engineering, civil engineering, electrical/electronics engineering, engineering and applied science, environmental design, environmental science, industrial engineering, materials science and engineering, and mechanical engineering), HEALTH PROFESSIONS (allied health, biomedical science, exercise science, medical laboratory technology, medical technology, nursing, pharmacy, public health, and rehabilitation therapy), SOCIAL SCIENCE (African American studies, American studies, anthropology, Asian/Oriental studies, criminal justice, economics, food science, geography, Hispanic American studies, history, humanities, Judaic studies, Latin American studies, medieval studies, Middle Eastern studies, philosophy, political science/government, psychology, religion, Russian and Slavic studies, social work, sociology, urban studies, and women's studies). Business administration & management, nursing, and pharmacy have the largest enrollments.

ACTIVITIES: There are 400 groups on campus, including art, band, cheerleading, chess, choir, chorale, chorus, computers, dance, drama, drill team, ethnic, film, honors, international, jazz band, LGBT, literary magazine, marching band, musical theater, newspaper, opera, orchestra, pep band, photography, political, professional, radio and TV, religious, social, social service, student government, symphony, and yearbook. Popular campus events include Theater Trips, Rutgers Day, Football and Basketball. **Sports:** There are 9 intercollegiate sports for men and 13 for women, and 50 intramural sports for men and 50 for women. **Graduates:** From July 1, 2015 to June 30, 2016, 8815 bachelor's degrees were awarded. The most popular majors were business/marketing (14%), engineering (10%), and health professions and related programs (10%). 1000 companies recruited on campus in 2015-2016. In an average class, 58% graduate in 4 years or less, 77% graduate in 5 years or less, and 80% graduate in 6 years or less.

SERVICES: Counseling and information services are available, as is tutoring in most subjects, with specific assistance in difficult first- and second-level courses, as well as reading assistance. There is also remedial math, reading, and writing, computer software with aids, library technology, and assistance. **Library/Resources:** The 15 libraries contain 5.5 million volumes, 3.6 million microform items, 57,166 audio/video tapes/CDs/DVDs, and subscribe to 195,296 periodicals including electronic. Computerized library services include interlibrary loans, database searching, Internet access, and Wi-Fi capability. Special learning facilities include an art gallery, radio station, TV station, a geology museum, and various research centers. **Physically Challenged Students:** Facilities include wheelchair ramps, elevators, special parking, specially equipped restrooms, special class scheduling, lowered drinking fountains, lowered telephones, and special housing. All classes are scheduled in accessible locations for disabled students. **Special:** 5-year B.A. or B.S./MBA program in Rutgers Business School, BS in Business Discipline/MBA; BA or BS in Science Discipline/MBA; 8-year Bachelor/Medical Dual Degree program with Robert Wood Johnson Medical School, 5-year BS/BS in Bioenvironmental engineering with the School of Engineering, 5-year accelerated baccalaureate-M.B.A with Rutgers Business School, Bureau of Engineering Research, supported by the university, industry, state and federal government, provides research opportunities for students and faculty; Continuing professional education, Exchange program between School of Engineering and the City University of London for qualified students majoring in civil, electrical, or mechanical engineering, 5-year (BA/BS degree) program in liberal arts and engineering, 5-year BA or BS/M.Ed. with the Graduate School of Education, Interdepartmental programs, and certificate programs are also available. There is Study Abroad in England, France, Italy, Ireland, Germany, Greece, Mexico, Israel, Australia, India, Japan, Netherlands, Scotland, South Africa, South Korea, Spain and several others. Alumnae externship program, Language and Cultural House Program, B.A. in Religion/M.A. in Religious Studies, B.A./Master of Communication and Information Studies (with SC&I), B.A./MLER (with School of Management and Labor Relations), Baccalaureate/M.C.R.P. or M.P.P with EJB School of Planning and Public Policy, Baccalaureate in Business major/Master of Human Resource Management (with School of Management and Labor Relations-SMLR), BS/Master of Business and Science (MBS). Pharm.D./MBA program with Rutgers Business School, Pharm.D./M.P.H., Pharm.D./Ph.D.in Pharmaceutical Science, Pharm.D./Ph.D. in Toxicology, and Pharm.D./M.D. There are 2 national honor societies, including Phi Beta Kappa, and a freshman honors program. **Visiting:** There are regularly scheduled orientations for prospective students, including a preadmission orientation. To schedule a visit, contact the University Undergraduate Admissions. **Campus Safety and Security:** Measures include 24-hour foot and vehicle patrol, self-defense education, and security escort services. There are also shuttle buses, emergency telephones, lighted pathways/sidewalks, and student safety officers.

REQUIREMENTS: The SAT or ACT is required. A high school diploma is required. The GED is accepted. Students must have completed a general college-preparatory program, including 16 academic credits or Carnegie units, with 4 years of English, 3 years of math 4 recommended, including (algebra I and II, and geometry), 2 years each of a foreign language and science, and 5 in electives. Engineering students need 4 years of math and must take chemistry and physics for sciences; nursing and pharmacy students must take biology and chemistry. AP and CLEP credits are accepted. Important factors in the admissions decision are evidence of special talent, extracurricular activities record, and ability to finance college education. To graduate, students must complete 120 credits, with a minimum GPA of 2.0. A liberal arts core requirement includes 6 credits in writing, 6 credits in quantitative reasoning, 6 credits in natural sciences, social sciences and 12 credits in humanities, 3 credits in diversity, and 3 credits in global awareness. Check with the individual college for specific program requirements. **Procedure:** Freshmen are admitted in the fall. It is recommended but not required, that entrance exams be taken December of your senior year. There are early admissions and rolling admissions plans. Application deadlines are open. Application fee is $70. Applications are accepted online. **Transfer Students:** 2667 transfer students enrolled in 2015-2016. Applicant must have a minimum of 12 credit hours earned. High school and college transcripts are required. Transfers are admitted in the fall or spring. 30 of 120 credits required for the bachelor's degree must be completed at RU-New Brunswick. **International Students:** There are 2905 international students enrolled. They must take the TOEFL with a minimum score of 550 on the paper-based TOEFL (PBT) or 79 on the Internet-based version (iBT). Student's are required to take the IELTS, scoring 7.

ADMISSIONS: 57% of the 2016-2017 applicants were accepted. The SAT scores for the 2016-2017 freshman class were: Critical Reading-- 8% below 500, 40% between 500 and 599, 38% between 600 and 699, and 14% between 700 and 800. Math-- 4% below 500, 26% between 500 and 599, 44% between 600 and 699, and 27% between 700 and 800. Writing-- 6% below 500, 37% between 500 and 599, 38% between 600 and 699, and 18% between 700 and 800. 67% of the current freshmen were in the top fifth of their class; 93% were in the top two fifths. **Admissions Contact:** Office of University Undergraduate Admissions Email: *admissions@ugadm.rutgers.edu* Web: *www.newbrunswick.rutgers.edu*

FINANCIAL AID: In 2016-2017, 71% of all full-time freshmen and 76% of continuing full-time students received some form of financial aid. 49% of all full-time freshmen and 59% of continuing full-time students received need-based aid. The average freshman award was $18,455. Need-based scholarships or need-based grants averaged $12,659; need-based self-help aid (loans and jobs) averaged $4,717; non-need-based athletic scholarships averaged $21,322; and other non-need-based awards and non-need-based scholarships averaged $10,063. Average annual earnings from campus work are $1528. The average financial indebtedness of the 2016 graduate was $24,861. The FAFSA code is 002629. The priority date for freshman financial aid applications for fall entry is March 15.

RUTGERS UNIVERSITY - NEWARK E-2

Rutgers, The State University of New Jersey-Newark Campus
www.newark.rutgers.edu

Newark, NJ 07102 **(973) 353-1374**

Fax: (973) 353-3789 **Email: newarkadmissions@ugadm.rutgers.edu**

Full-time: 3102 men, 3578 women
Part-time: 696 men, 794 women
Graduate: 2244 men, 1907 women
Year: semesters, summer session
Room & Board: $13,459
Faculty: I, ++$
Ph.D.s: 99%
Student/Faculty: 11 to 1
Tuition: $13,829 ($29,480)
Freshman Class: 13085 applied, 8546 accepted, 1337 enrolled
SAT CR/M/W: 500/530/510 **ACT:** required
CEEB CODE: 2753
Application Deadline: open
COMPETITIVE

Rutgers University - Newark, was founded in 1908. On July 1, 2013, the New Jersey Medical and Health Sciences Education Restructuring Act went into effect, integrating Rutgers, The State University of New Jersey, with all units of the University of Medicine and Dentistry of New Jersey (UMDNJ), except University Hospital in Newark and the School of Osteopathic Medicine in Stratford. The integration of the legacy elements of UMDNJ into Rutgers has created a fourth unit, Rutgers Biomedical and Health Sciences (RBHS), which consists of a number of schools and units located on various sites but closely aligned with the campus in New Brunswick. The campus is comprised of 5 undergraduate, degree-granting schools: Newark College of Arts and Sciences, University College-Newark, Rutgers Business School, Undergraduate-Newark, College of Nursing, School of Nursing, School of Criminal Justice and the School of Public Affairs and Administration. Some schools located in Newark and/or New Brunswick are also part of the Rutgers Biomedical and Health Sciences unit and are listed for each campus. Each school has individual requirements, policies, and fees. There are 5 undergraduate schools and 5 graduate schools. In addition to regional accreditation, RU-Newark has baccalaureate program accreditation with AACSB, CSWE, TEAC, and CCNE. The 106-acre campus is in an urban area 7 miles west of New York City. Including any residence halls, there are 51 buildings.

STUDENT LIFE: 94% of undergraduates are from New Jersey. Others are from 25 states, 41 foreign countries, and Canada. 4% are Foreign; 4% race unknown; 3% two or more races; 27% Hispanic; 24% White; 20% Asian American; 18% African American. **Female To Male Ratio:** 1.0:1. The average age of freshmen is 18; all undergraduates, 23. 14% do not continue beyond their first year; 86% remain to graduate. **Housing:** 2046 students can be accommodated in college housing, which includes coed dorms, on-campus apartments, and fraternity houses. 90% of students commute. All students may keep cars. Alcohol is not permitted.

FACULTY/CLASSROOMS: 64% of faculty are male; 36% are female. No introductory courses are taught by graduate students. The average class size in an introductory lecture is 30; in a laboratory is 20; and in a regular course is 30.

PROGRAMS OF STUDY: RU-Newark confers B.A., B.S., and B.F.A. degrees. Associate, master's, and doctoral degrees are also awarded. Bachelor's degrees are awarded in BIOLOGICAL SCIENCE (biology/biological science, botany, and zoology), BUSINESS (accounting, banking and finance, business administration and management, finance, management science, marketing, marketing/retailing/merchandising, and supply chain management), COMMUNICATIONS AND THE ARTS (art, creative writing, dramatic arts, English, French, German, Italian, journalism, music, Portuguese, Spanish, and visual and performing arts), COMPUTER AND PHYSICAL SCIENCE (applied mathematics, applied physics, chemistry, computer science, geology, geoscience, information sciences and systems, mathematics, and physics), ENGINEERING AND ENVIRONMENTAL DESIGN (environmental science and geological engineering), HEALTH PROFESSIONS (allied health, clinical science, medical laboratory technology, and nursing), SOCIAL SCIENCE (African American studies, American studies, anthropology, area studies, classical/ancient civilization, criminal justice, Eastern European studies, economics, history, interdisciplinary studies, medieval studies, philosophy, political science/government, psychology, public administration, Puerto Rican studies, science and society, social work, sociology, and women's studies). Business, and criminal justice are the strongest academically. Accounting, criminal justice, and finance have the largest enrollments.

ACTIVITIES: There are no fraternities or sororities. There are 85 groups on campus, including chess, chorale, chorus, drama, newspaper, outreach, radio and TV, and student government. Popular campus events include Alpha Sigma Lambda, Black History Month and Honors Convocation. **Sports:** There are 7 intercollegiate sports for men and 7 for women. Athletics facilities, utilized by varsity sports and recreation, are available to all members of the Rutgers community. The facilities complement the diversified program offerings. Rutgers-Newark pledges to provide its constituencies modern facilities and equipment in sufficient numbers that conform to optimum standards for health and safety. **Graduates:** From July 1, 2015 to June 30, 2016, 1588 bachelor's degrees were awarded. The most popular majors were accounting (15%), psychology (13%), and criminal justice (12%). In an average class, 33% graduate in 4 years or less, 62% graduate in 5 years or less, and 68% graduate in 6 years or less.

SERVICES: Counseling and information services are available, as is tutoring in most subjects. There is a reader service for the blind, and remedial math, reading, and writing. **Library/Resources:** The 4 libraries contain 729,987 volumes, 974,491 microform items, 591 audio/video tapes/CDs/DVDs, and subscribe to 15,013 periodicals including electronic. Computerized library services include interlibrary loans, database searching, and Internet access. Special learning facilities include an art gallery, radio station, a molecular and behavioral neuroscience center, and institutes of jazz and animal behavior. **Physically Challenged Students:** 80% of the campus is accessible. Facilities include wheelchair ramps, elevators, special parking, specially equipped restrooms, special class scheduling, lowered drinking fountains, lowered telephones, and special housing. Facilities vary from building to building. However, all classes are scheduled in accessible locations for disabled students. **Special:** Students may cross-register with the New Jersey Institute of Technology. Internships are available. The school offers study abroad in over 30 countries, accelerated degree programs in business administration and criminal justice, co-op programs, independent study, distance learning, English as a Second Language, dual majors, student-designed majors, nondegree study, and pass/fail options. Contact the school for information on the Honors College. 5-year baccalaureate-MBA with Rutgers Business School; BS in Business Discipline/MBA; BA or BS in Science Discipline/MBA; Baccalaureate/M.A. in Criminal Justice with the School of Criminal Justice; Baccalaureate/MPA with the School of Public Affairs and Administration; Cooperative baccalaureate program with School of Engineering (New Brunswick campus); Cooperative baccalaureate in medical technology with affiliated hospitals; Interdisciplinary programs in archaeology, international affairs, legal studies, women's studies; continuing professional education; Baccalaureate in Business Major/Master of Human Resource Management (with School of Management and Labor Relations in New Brunswick); Baccalaureate-master's dual degree programs with the School of Criminal Justice and Rutgers Business School; BA or BS in Biology/MS in Biology; BA in Chemistry/MS in Chemistry; BA in Economics/MA in Economics; BS in Environmental Sciences/MS In Environmental Geology; BS in Environmental Sciences/MS in Environmental Sciences; BA in Political Science, Sociology or Anthropology/MS in Global Affairs; BA in History/MA in History; BA in History, Sociology or Anthropology/MA in Jazz History and Research; BA in Political Science/MA in Political Science; BA/MA in Peace and Conflict Studies; BS in Computer Science or Information Science/Master of Information Technology; BS in Accounting/Master of Accountancy (Governmental Accounting or Financial Accounting); BS in Accounting/MBA in Professional Accounting; BS in Finance/Master of Quantitative Finance; BS/Master of Business and Science (MBS); BS in Nursing/MS in Nursing; BA in Psychology/MA in Psychology; Master of Public Administration/Master of Accountancy in Governmental Accounting; MS in Global Affairs/Master of Public Policy (with Bloustein School in New Brunswick); Pharm.D./M.B.A. program with Rutgers Business School. There are 12 national honor societies, including Phi Beta Kappa, and a freshman honors program. **Visiting:** There are regularly scheduled orientations for prospective students, including an information session with an admissions counselor and a tour of the campus. There are guides for informal visits and visitors may sit in on classes. To schedule a visit, contact the Admissions Office (Newark). **Campus Safety and Security:** Measures include 24-hour foot and vehicle patrol, self-defense education, and security escort services. There are also shuttle buses, emergency telephones, lighted pathways/sidewalks, security guards assist Rutgers police in providing public safety services, and a student marshal program.

REQUIREMENTS: The SAT or ACT is required. A high school diploma is required; the GED is accepted. SAT: Subject tests are required of students without a high school diploma from an accredited high school and from some GED holders. Students should have completed 16 high school academic credits or Carnegie units, with 4 years of English, 3 years of math, (4 recommended) 2 years each of science, a general college-preparatory program, including and a foreign language, and 5 electives. Biology and chemistry are required for nursing students. AP and CLEP credits are accepted. Important factors in the admissions decision are advanced placement or honors courses, evidence of special talent, and leadership record. To graduate, students must complete 124 credits with a minimum GPA of 2.0. Distribution requirements include 8 credits in natural science/math or 3 courses in nonlab science, math, or computer science; 6 credits each in history, literature, social sciences, humanities, and fine arts; 1 course in critical thinking; and 15 credits of electives. All students must take English composition and demonstrate math proficiency either by exam or by successfully completing a college algebra course or any other advanced course in math, a college calculus course, (with a grade of C or better) or a precalculus course (with a grade of B or better). **Procedure:** Freshmen are admitted in the fall. Entrance exams should be taken by December of senior year is recommended, but not required. There are early admissions and rolling admissions plans. Application deadlines are open. Application fee is $70. Notifications are sent March 1. Applications are accepted online. **Transfer Students:** 1088 transfer students enrolled in 2015-2016. Students who have completed at least 12 credit hours at another college with a cumulative GPA of 2.0 are considered for admission as transfer students. Transfers are admitted in the fall and spring. High school and college transcripts are required. 30 of 124 credits required for the bachelor's degree must be completed at RU-Newark. **International Students:** There are 356 international students enrolled. They must take the TOEFL with a minimum score of 550 on the paper-based TOEFL (PBT) or 79 on the Internet-based version (iBT) and the college's own test. Students are required to take the IELTS, scoring 6.

ADMISSIONS: 65% of the 2016-2017 applicants were accepted. The SAT scores for the 2016-2017 freshman class were: Critical Reading-- 55% below 500, 36% between 500 and 599, 8% between 600 and 699, and 1% between 700 and 800. Math-- 36% below 500, 46% between 500 and 599, 16% between 600 and 699, and 2% between 700 and 800. Writing-- 50% below 500, 39% between 500 and 599, 9% between 600 and 699, and 1% between 700 and 800. 38% of the current freshmen were in the top fifth of their class; 76% were in the top two fifths. **Admissions Contact:** Latoya Battle-Brown, Assistant Provost and Dean of Admissions. Email: *newarkadmissions@ugadm.rutgers.edu* Web: *www.newark.rutgers.edu*

FINANCIAL AID: In 2016-2017, 82% of all full-time freshmen and 92% of continuing full-time students received some form of financial aid. 72% of all full-time freshmen and 84% of continuing full-time students received need-based aid. The average freshman award was $17,228. Need-based scholarships or need-based grants averaged $12,493; need-based self-help aid (loans and jobs) averaged $4,227; and other non-need-based awards and non-need-based scholarships averaged $7,071. Average annual earnings from campus work are $1528. The average financial indebtedness of the 2016 graduate was $26,823. The FAFSA code is 002629. The priority date for fall entry is March 15. The filing

SAINT PETER'S UNIVERSITY E-2

www.spc.edu

Jersey City, NJ 07306	(201) 915-9213 (888) SPC-9933
Fax: (201) 432-5860	**Email:** admissions@spc.edu
Full-time: 825 men, 1077 women	**Faculty:** IIA, av$
Part-time: 101 men, 314 women	**Ph.D.s:** 80%
Graduate: 282 men, 446 women	**Student/Faculty:** 13 to 1
Year: semesters, summer session	**Tuition:** $34,198
Room & Board: $14,994	**Freshman Class:** 3256 applied, 1973 accepted, 393 enrolled
SAT or ACT: required	**CEEB CODE:** 2806
Application Deadline: open	**COMPETITIVE**

Saint Peter's University, founded in 1872, is a private liberal arts and business college affiliated with the Roman Catholic Church and known as New Jersey's Jesuit College. The figures in the above capsule and in this profile are approximate. There is 1 undergraduate school and 3 graduate schools. In addition to regional accreditation, SPU has baccalaureate program accreditation with TEAC, CCNE, and IACBE. The 30-acre campus is in an urban area in New Jersey City, 2 miles west of New York City. Including any residence halls, there are 29 buildings.

STUDENT LIFE: 87% of undergraduates are from New Jersey. Others are from 29 states, and 36 foreign countries. 56% are from public schools. 44% are White; 30% Hispanic; 29% African American; 10% Asian American; 1% American Indian/Alaska Native. 68% are Catholic. **Female To Male Ratio:** 1.5:1. The average age of freshmen is 18; all undergraduates, 24. 23% do not continue beyond their first year; 51% remain to graduate. **Housing:** 863 students can be accommodated in college housing, which includes single-sex and coed dorms and on-campus apartments. In addition, there are special-interest houses, and community service houses. On-campus housing is guaranteed for all 4 years. 50% of students commute. Upperclassmen may keep cars.

FACULTY/CLASSROOMS: 50% of faculty are male; 50% are female. All teach undergraduates. No introductory courses are taught by graduate students. The average class size in an introductory lecture is 23; in a laboratory is 14; and in a regular course is 16.

PROGRAMS OF STUDY: SPU confers B.A., B.S. and B.S.N. degrees. Associate, master's, and doctoral degrees are also awarded. Bachelor's degrees are awarded in BIOLOGICAL SCIENCE (biochemistry and biology/biological science), BUSINESS (accounting, business administration and management, international business management, and marketing/retailing/merchandising), COMMUNICATIONS AND THE ARTS (art history and appreciation, classical languages, communications, English, fine arts, graphic design, modern language, Spanish, and visual and performing arts), COMPUTER AND PHYSICAL SCIENCE (chemistry, computer science, mathematics, natural sciences, and physics), EDUCATION (elementary education and secondary education), HEALTH PROFESSIONS (biomedical science, health care administration, medical laboratory technology, nursing, predentistry, and premedicine), SOCIAL SCIENCE (African American studies, American studies, classical/ancient civilization, criminal justice, economics, history, humanities, interdisciplinary studies, international studies, Latin American studies, philosophy, political science/government, prelaw, psychology, social science, sociology, theological studies, and urban studies). Natural sciences, and accounting are the strongest academically. Business management, accounting, and computer sciences have the largest enrollments.

ACTIVITIES: There are no fraternities or sororities. There are 50 groups on campus, including cheerleading, chess, choir, chorus, computers, debate, drama, ethnic, forensics, honors, international, literary magazine, newspaper, pep band, political, professional, radio and TV, religious, social, social service, and student government. Popular campus events include International Day, Career Fairs and SpringFest. **Sports:** There are 10 intercollegiate sports for men and 8 for women, and 20 intramural sports for men and 18 for women. Facilities include a recreational center, a gym, and an athletic field, baseball, basketball, cross country, golf, indoor-outdoor track, swimming/diving, tennis, and volleyball. **Graduates:** From July 1, 2015 to June 30, 2016, 489 bachelor's degrees were awarded. The most popular majors were business/marketing (29%), biological/life sciences (10%), and health professions and related programs (9%). In an average class, 53% graduate in 6 years or less.

SERVICES: Counseling and information services are available, as is tutoring in every subject. There is a reader service for the blind, and remedial math, reading, and writing. **Library/Resources:** The 2 libraries contain 285,000 volumes, 70,000 microform items, and 3,800 audio/video tapes/CDs/DVDs, and subscribe to 1,800 periodicals including electronic. Computerized library services include interlibrary loans and database searching. Special learning facilities include an art gallery, radio station, and TV station. **Physically Challenged Students:** 80% of the campus is accessible. Facilities include wheelchair ramps, elevators, special parking, specially equipped restrooms, special class scheduling, lowered drinking fountains, lowered telephones, and special housing. **Special:** There are co-op programs with local companies, as well as departmental programs, and many internships available in Jersey City and nearby New York City. A Washington semester and study abroad in any of 60 countries are offered. There are preprofessional programs in dentistry, pharmacy, physician assistant, and physical therapy. The college also offers dual majors and student-designed majors, credit for life, military, and work experience, nondegree study, and pass/fail options. There are 9 national honor societies, a freshman honors program, and 1 departmental honors program. **Visiting:** There are regularly scheduled orientations for prospective students, including open houses, weekend and weekday visit days with a tour and class and information sessions, as well as tours and interviews by appointment. There are guides for informal visits, visitors may sit in on classes, and stay overnight. To schedule a visit, contact the Admissions Office. **Campus Safety and Security:** Measures include 24-hour foot and vehicle patrol, self-defense education, and security escort services. There are shuttle buses, emergency telephones, and security desk monitoring of access to residence halls.

REQUIREMENTS: The SAT or ACT is required. Applicants must be high school graduates or submit the GED certificate. Students should have completed 16 Carnegie units of high school study, including 4 years of English, 3 of math, 2 each of science, history, and a foreign language, and another 3 of additional work in any of these subjects. An essay and 2 letters of recommendation are required, and an interview is recommended. SPC requires applicants to be in the upper 97% of their class. A GPA of 3.1 is required. AP and CLEP credits are accepted. Important factors in the admissions decision are advanced placement or honors courses, extracurricular activities record, and recommendations by school officials. To graduate, students must complete 129 credit hours, including 57 in the core curriculum, 12 in core electives, between 30 and 45 in the major, and the rest in subjects related to the major. The core curriculum requires 9 credits of natural sciences, 6 to 8 of math, and 3 each of social science, philosophy, history, literature, a modern language, fine arts, and composition. Students must earn a GPA of 2.0. **Procedure:** Freshmen are admitted fall and spring. Entrance exams should be taken by the fall of the senior year. There are early admissions, deferred admissions, and rolling admissions plans. Application deadlines are open. Notification is sent on a rolling basis. 299 applicants were on the 2016 waiting list; 290 were admitted. Applications are accepted on-line. **Transfer Students:** 164 transfer students enrolled in 2015-2016. The school requires a 2.0 college GPA of transfer students, as well as a high school transcript and a satisfactory composite SAT score for students less than 2 years out of high school. An interview is recommended. 30 of 129 credits required for the bachelor's degree must be completed at SPU. **International Students:** The school actively recruits these students. They must take the TOEFL.

ADMISSIONS: 61% of the 2016-2017 applicants were accepted. **Admissions Contact:** Joseph Giglio, Director of Admissions. Email: *admissions@spc.edu* Web: *www.spc.edu*

FINANCIAL AID: SPU is a member of CSS. The FAFSA code is 002638. Check with the school for current application deadlines.

SETON HALL UNIVERSITY — D-2

www.shu.edu

South Orange, NJ 07079 — **(973) 313-6146**

Fax: (973) 275-2040	**Email:** thehall@shu.edu
Full-time: 1939 men, 2698 women	**Faculty:** 339
Part-time: 189 men, 322 women	**Ph.D.s:** 88%
Graduate: 1992 men, 2516 women	**Student/Faculty:** 14 to 1
Year: semesters, summer session	**Tuition:** $38,458
Room & Board: $17,056	**Freshman Class:** 6436 applied, 5474 accepted, 993 enrolled
SAT CR/M/W: 530/540/550 **ACT:** 23	**CEEB CODE:** 2811
Application Deadline: March 1	**COMPETITIVE**

Seton Hall University, founded in 1856, is a oldest U.S. diocesan Catholic university, under the Archdiocese of Newark. The University is home to eight schools that offer degrees at the baccalaureate, master, and doctoral and professional levels. Figures in the above capsule and in this profile are approximate. There are 8 undergraduate schools and 8 graduate schools. In addition to regional accreditation, Seton Hall has baccalaureate program accreditation with AACSB, CSWE, NCATE, and CCNE. The 58-acre campus is in a suburban area in south Orange, New Jersey, 14 miles west of New York City. Including any residence halls, there are 35 buildings.

STUDENT LIFE: 76% of undergraduates are from New Jersey. Others are from 43 states, 70 foreign countries, and Canada. 69% are from public schools. 8% are Asian American; 51% White; 3% Foreign; 14% Hispanic; 13% African American. 69% are Catholic; 14% Protestant. **Female To Male Ratio:** 1.3:1. The average age of freshmen is 18; all undergraduates, 21. 19% do not continue beyond their first year; 65% remain to graduate. **Housing:** 2236 students can be accommodated in college housing, which includes coed dorms, off-campus apartments, honors houses and special-interest houses. On-campus housing is available on a lottery system for upperclassmen. Priority is given to out-of-town students. 80% of students live on campus. Upperclassmen may keep cars.

FACULTY/CLASSROOMS: 53% of faculty are male; 47% are female. No introductory courses are taught by graduate students. The average class size in an introductory lecture is 26; in a laboratory is 17; and in a regular course is 21.

PROGRAMS OF STUDY: Seton Hall confers B.A., B.S., B.A.B.A., B.S.B., B.S.E., B.S.I.R. and B.S.N. degrees. Master's and doctoral degrees are also awarded. Bachelor's degrees are awarded in AGRICULTURE (environmental studies), BIOLOGICAL SCIENCE (biochemistry and biology/biological science), BUSINESS (accounting, business administration and management, business economics, finance, management information systems, marketing management, and sports management), COMMUNICATIONS AND THE ARTS (applied music, art history, broadcasting, classics, communications, creative writing, English, fine arts, French, graphic design, Italian, journalism, modern language, music, Spanish, and theatre arts), COMPUTER AND PHYSICAL SCIENCE (chemistry, computer science, mathematics, and physics), EDUCATION (elementary education, secondary education, and special education), HEALTH PROFESSIONS (nursing), SOCIAL SCIENCE (African American studies, anthropology, Asian/Oriental studies, criminal justice, economics, history, international relations, Latin American studies, liberal arts/general studies, philosophy, political science/government, psychology, religion, social science, social work, sociology, and theological studies). Business, biology, and diplomacy are the strongest academically. Nursing has the largest enrollment.

ACTIVITIES: 7% of men belong to 11 national fraternities; 11% of women belong to 14 national sororities. There are 124 groups on campus, including art, cheerleading, chess, choir, chorus, commuter council, computers, dance, drama, drill team, environmental, ethnic, film, forensics, honors, international, literary magazine, musical theater, newspaper, pep band, photography, political, professional, radio and TV, religious, social, social service, and student government. Popular campus events include University Day, Theatre-in-the-Round, and Career Day. **Sports:** There are 6 intercollegiate sports for men and 8 for women, and 13 intramural sports for men and 13 for women. Facilities include an arena, recreational field house, indoor track, indoor pool, fitness and aerobics rooms, a soccer and baseball field, a softball field, tennis and racquetball courts, and men's basketball. **Graduates:** From July 1, 2015 to June 30, 2016, 993 bachelor's degrees were awarded. The most popular majors were nursing (10%), finance (7%), and biology (7%). 400 companies recruited on campus in 2015-2016. In an average class, 51% graduate in 4 years or less, 62% graduate in 5 years or less, and 65% graduate in 6 years or less. Of the 2015 graduating class, 29% were enrolled in graduate school within 6 months of graduation, and 77% were employed.

SERVICES: Counseling and information services are available, as is tutoring in most subjects, a reader service for the blind, and remedial math, reading, and writing. The Academic Resource Center also offers support for students interested in national scholarship opportunities and aids students who are pursuing interdisciplinary and pre-professional majors. **Library/Resources:** The 2 libraries contain 629,978 volumes, 500,000 microform items, 5,340 audio/video tapes/CDs/DVDs, and subscribe to 29,000 periodicals including electronic. Computerized library services include interlibrary loans, database searching, Internet access, and Wi-Fi capability. Special learning facilities include an art gallery, radio station, TV station, various institutes, and centers for learning and research. **Physically Challenged Students:** 95% of the campus is accessible. Facilities include wheelchair ramps, elevators, special parking, specially equipped restrooms, special class scheduling, lowered drinking fountains, and special housing. **Special:** Co-op and work-study are possible through the College of Arts & Sciences and the School of Business; internships are available through the College of Arts & Sciences and School of Diplomacy. Education majors go into the field during their sophomore year. Engineering 3+2 degrees are available with the New Jersey Institute of Technology. Study abroad is available in 15 countries.

An accelerated B.S.N. degree is offered. There are a total of 17 bachelor/graduate dual degree programs. Non-degree study is permitted. There are 27 national honor societies, a freshman honors program, and 5 departmental honors programs. **Visiting:** There are regularly scheduled orientations for prospective students, including campus tours weekdays and Saturdays during the academic year and on weekdays during the summer. Open houses for prospective applicants are available each fall. Visitors may sit in on classes. To schedule a visit, contact the Enrollment Services Office. **Campus Safety and Security:** Measures include 24-hour foot and vehicle patrol, emergency notification system, self-defense education, and security escort services. There are also shuttle buses, emergency telephones, lighted pathways/sidewalks, controlled access to dorms/residences, and security attendants posted at residence hall entrances.

REQUIREMENTS: Seton Hall recommends a satisfactory score on the SAT or a minimum composite score on the ACT. Applicants must supply high school transcripts or a GED certificate. Students should have completed 16 Carnegie units of high school study, including 4 years of English, 3 of Math, 2 each of a foreign language and either History or Social Studies, 1 of Science, and 4 academic electives. An essay is required and an interview is recommended. AP and CLEP credits are accepted. Important factors in the admissions decision are advanced placement or honors courses, leadership record, and parents or siblings attended your school. To graduate, students must complete the University Core Curriculum and complete at least 120 credit hours earning a minimum GPA of 2.0. **Procedure:** Freshmen are admitted in the fall and spring. Entrance exams should be taken by January of the senior year. There are early admissions, deferred admissions, and rolling admissions plans. Application deadlines are open. Application fee is $55. Notification is sent on a rolling basis. Applications are accepted online. **Transfer Students:** 315 transfer students enrolled in 2015-2016. Applicants should have earned 30 hours of college credit, with a minimum GPA of 2.5, or 2.8 for the business and science schools. The SAT is required for students with fewer than 30 credits of college-level work at the time of application, and an interview is recommended. 30 of 120 credits required for the bachelor's degree must be completed at Seton Hall. **International Students:** There are 90 international students enrolled. The school actively recruits these students. They must take the TOEFL with a minimum score of 550 on the paper-based TOEFL (PBT) or 79 on the Internet-based version (iBT). They must also take the SAT.

ADMISSIONS: 85% of the 2016-2017 applicants were accepted. The SAT scores for the 2016-2017 freshman class were:, Critical Reading-- 29% below 500, 49% between 500 and 599, 21% between 600 and 699, and 1% between 700 and 800. Math-- 26% below 500, 49% between 500 and 599, 24% between 600 and 699, and 2% between 700 and 800. Writing-- 24% below 500, 48% between 500 and 599, 26% between 600 and 699, and 2% between 700 and 800. The ACT scores were 20% below 12, 33% between 12 and 17, 27% between 18 and 23, 8% between 24 and 29, and 13% above 30. 48% of the current freshmen were in the top fifth of their class; 72% were in the top two fifths. 1 freshman graduated first in the class. **Admissions Contact:** Wendy Lin-Cook, Assistant Vice President for Admissions. Email: *thehall@shu.edu* Web: *www.shu.edu*

FINANCIAL AID: The FAFSA code is 002632. The priority date for freshman financial aid applications for fall entry is March 1. The filing deadline for fall entry is open.

STEVENS INSTITUTE OF TECHNOLOGY E-2

www.stevens.edu

Hoboken, NJ 07030	**(201) 216-5699** **(800) 458-5323** **Email: student_life@stevens.edu**
Full-time: 2087 men, 868 women	**Faculty:** 255; I, +$
Part-time: 14 men, 7 women	**Ph.D.s:** 90%
Graduate: 2411 men, 972 women	**Student/Faculty:** 10 to 1
Year: semesters, summer session	**Tuition:** $48,838
Room & Board: $13,500	**Freshman Class:** 6540 applied, 2849 accepted, 686 enrolled
SAT CR/M: 635/698 **ACT:** 31	**CEEB CODE:** 2819
Application Deadline: December 15	**MOST COMPETITIVE**

Stevens Institute of Technology, founded in 1870, is a private institution offering programs of study in science, computer science, engineering, business, and humanities. Figures in the above capsule and in this profile are approximate. There are 4 undergraduate schools and 3 graduate schools. In addition to regional accreditation, Stevens has baccalaureate program accreditation with ABET, CSAB, MSCHE, ACS, and AACSB. The 55-acre campus is in an urban area on the banks of the Hudson River, overlooking the Manhattan skyline. Including any residence halls, there are 25 buildings.

STUDENT LIFE: 59% of undergraduates are from New Jersey. Others are from 42 states, 30 foreign countries, and Canada. 80% are from public schools. 9% are Hispanic; 8% race unknown; 66% White; 4% Foreign; 2% African American; 11% Asian American. **Male To Female Ratio:** 2.4:1. The average age of freshmen is 18; all undergraduates, 20. 10% do not continue beyond their first year; 76% remain to graduate. **Housing:** 1358 students can be accommodated in college housing, which includes coed dorms, on-campus apartments, off-campus apartments, married student housing, special-interest houses, fraternity houses, sorority houses, and wellness housing. On-campus housing is guaranteed for all 4 years. 71% of students live on campus; of those, 70% remain on campus on weekends. Upperclassmen may keep cars. Alcohol is not permitted.

FACULTY/CLASSROOMS: 80% of faculty are male; 20% are female. 75% teach undergraduates, and 75% do research. No introductory courses are taught by graduate students. The average class size in an introductory lecture is 75; in a laboratory is 20; and in a regular course is 25.

PROGRAMS OF STUDY: Stevens confers B.A., B.S., B.E., M.S., M.B.A., and M.A. Engineer degrees. Master's and doctoral degrees are also awarded. Bachelor's degrees are awarded in BIOLOGICAL SCIENCE (biochemistry and bioinformatics), BUSINESS (business administration and management), COMMUNICATIONS AND THE ARTS (literature and music technology), COMPUTER AND PHYSICAL SCIENCE (chemistry, computer science, computer security and information assurance, digital arts/technology, information sciences and systems, mathematics, physics, and science technology), ENGINEERING AND ENVIRONMENTAL DESIGN (biomedical engineering, chemical engineering, civil engineering, computational sciences, computer engineering, electrical/electronics engineering, engineering management, engineering physics, environmental engineering, mechanical engineering, naval architecture and marine engineering, and systems engineering), SOCIAL SCIENCE (history and philosophy). Engineering is the strongest academically. Mechanical engineering, civil engineering, and business have the largest enrollments.

ACTIVITIES: 25% of men belong to 11 national fraternities; 25% of women belong to 1 local and 3 national sororities. There are 105 groups on campus, including anime, paintball, SAE, art, band, chess, choir, chorus, computers, dance, debate, drama, engineers without borders, environmental, ethnic, film, honors, international, jazz band, literary magazine, musical theater, newspaper, pep band, photography, political, professional, radio and TV, religious, social, social service, and student government. Popular campus events include Fall Tech Fest, Spring Boken Festival, and Midnight Breakfast. **Sports:** There are 13 intercollegiate sports for men and 13 for women, and 12 intramural sports for men and 12 for women. Facilities include a swimming pool, basketball arena, fitness rooms, racquetball/squash courts, a playing field, and several outdoor courts. **Graduates:** From July 1, 2015 to June 30, 2016, 541 bachelor's degrees were awarded. The most popular majors were engineering (62%), business/marketing (13%), and computer and informatin sciences (9%). 380 companies recruited on campus in 2015-2016. In an average class, 25% graduate in 4 years or less, 72% graduate in 5 years or less, and 76% graduate in 6 years or less. Of the 2015 graduating class, 20% were enrolled in graduate school within 6 months of graduation, and 75% were employed.

SERVICES: Counseling and information services are available, as is tutoring in every subject. **Library/Resources:** The library contains 123,063 volumes, and subscribes to 39,500 periodicals including electronic. Computerized library services include interlibrary loans, database searching, Internet access, and Wi-Fi capability. Special learning facilities include a radio station, TV station, a lab for ocean and coastal engineering, an environmental lab, a design and manufacturing institute, a technology center, a telecommunications institute, a computer vision lab, an ultrafast laser spectroscopy and high-speed communications lab, and a wireless network security center. **Physically Challenged Students:** All of the campus is accessible. Facilities include wheelchair ramps, elevators, special parking, specially equipped restrooms, lowered drinking fountains, and special housing. **Special:** Stevens offers cross-registration and a 3-2 engineering degree with New York University, a work-study program within the school, co-op programs, corporate and research internships through the undergraduate projects in technology and medicine, study abroad in 7 countries, and pass/fail options for extra courses. Students may undertake dual majors as well as accelerated degree programs in medicine, dentistry, and law and can receive a B.A.-B.E. degree or a B.A.-B.S. degree in all majors. Undergraduates may take graduate courses. There are 9 national honor societies and a freshman honors program. **Visiting:** There are regularly scheduled orientations for prospective students, including interviews and campus tours. There are guides for informal visits, visitors may sit in on classes, and stay overnight. To schedule a visit, contact the Admissions Office. **Campus Safety and Security:** Measures include 24-hour foot and vehicle patrol, emergency notification system, self-defense education, security escort services, emergency telephones, lighted pathways/sidewalks, and controlled access to dorms/residences.

REQUIREMENTS: The SAT or ACT is required. Applicants must provide official high school transcripts. Students should have taken 4 years of English, math, and 3-4 units of science, with lab, and 2 units each are recommended foreign language, social studies, and history. An interview, essay, and 2 letters of recommendation are required. AP credits are accepted. Important factors in the admissions decision are advanced placement or honors courses, evidence of special talent, personality/intangible qualities, extracurricular activities record, leadership record, parents or siblings attended your school, recommendations by alumni, and geographical diversity. To graduate, the student must have earned 122 to 150 credit hours (dependent on program) with a minimum 2.0 GPA; the total hours in the major vary by program. The core curriculum includes courses in engineering, science, computer science, math, liberal arts, and phys ed. **Procedure:** Freshmen are admitted fall. Entrance exams should be taken by February of the senior year. There are early decision and deferred admissions plans. Early decision applications should be filed by November 15; regular applications, by December 15 for fall entry, along with a $55 fee. Notification of early decision is sent December 15; regular decision, February 15. 338 early decision candidates were accepted for the 2016-2017 class. 358 applicants were on the 2016 waiting list; 187 were admitted. Applications are accepted online. **Transfer Students:** 36 transfer students enrolled in 2015-2016. Applicants should have a minimum GPA of 3.0. They must submit all college transcripts, including course descriptions; SAT or ACT scores are required of those students with fewer than 30 hours of college credit. Students may enroll in the fall, July 1 - rolling, and spring, November 1 - rolling. 50 of 122 credits required for the bachelor's degree must be completed at Stevens. **International Students:** There are 92 international students enrolled. The school actively recruits these students. They must take the TOEFL. They must also take the SAT or ACT.

ADMISSIONS: 44% of the 2016-2017 applicants were accepted. The SAT scores for the 2016-2017 freshman class were: Critical Reading-- 27% between 500 and 599, 57% between 600 and 699, and 16% between 700 and 800. Math-- 4% between 500 and 599, 47% between 600 and 699, and 49% between 700 and 800. The ACT scores were 1% between 18 and 23, 33% between 24 and 29, and 66% above 30. 78% of the current freshmen were in the top fifth of their class; 95% were in the top two fifths. 9 freshmen graduated first in their class. **Admissions Contact:** Ken Nilsen, Dean of Students. Email: *student_life@stevens.edu* Web: *www.stevens.edu*

FINANCIAL AID: In 2016-2017, 93% of all full-time freshmen and 90% of continuing full-time students received some form of financial aid. 84% of all full-time freshmen and 80% of continuing full-time students received need-based aid. The average freshman award was $33,123. Need-based scholarships or need-based grants averaged $13,691; need-based self-help aid (loans and jobs) averaged $4,751; other non-need-based awards and non-need-based scholarships averaged $4,536; and $19,855 from other forms of aid. 24% of undergraduate students work part-time. Average annual earnings from campus work are $1202. Stevens is a member of CSS. The CSS/Profile is required. The FAFSA code is 002639. The priority date for freshman financial aid applications for fall entry is February 15.

STOCKTON UNIVERSITY *(The complete profile is made available exclusively on our website, www.barronspac.com)*

THE COLLEGE OF NEW JERSEY — D-3
www.tcnj.edu

Ewing, NJ 08628	**(609) 771-2131** **(800) 624-0967**
Fax: (609) 637-5174	**Email: tcnjinfo@tcnj.edu**
Full-time: 2706 men, 3658 women	**Faculty:** IIA, ++$
Part-time: 77 men, 95 women	**Ph.D.s:** 88%
Graduate: 94 men, 454 women	**Student/Faculty:** 13 to 1
Year: semesters, summer session	**Tuition:** $19,908 ($30,840)
Room & Board: $12,001	**Freshman Class:** 10937 applied, 5356 accepted, 1417 enrolled
SAT CR/M/W: 595/620/605 **ACT:** 27	**CEEB CODE:** 2519
Application Deadline: January 15	**HIGHLY COMPETITIVE**

The College of New Jersey, founded in 1855, is a public institution offering programs in the liberal arts, sciences, business, engineering, nursing, and education. There are 7 undergraduate schools and 1 graduate school. In addition to regional accreditation, TCNJ has baccalaureate program accreditation with AACSB, ABET, NASM, NCATE, and NLN. The 289-acre campus is in a suburban area between Princeton and Trenton, NJ. Including any residence halls, there are 61 buildings.

STUDENT LIFE: 94% of undergraduates are from New Jersey. Others are from 23 states, 30 foreign countries, and Canada. 70% are from public schools. 9% are Asian American; 7% race unknown; 66% White; 5% African American; 11% Hispanic; 1% two or more races. 48% are Catholic; 17% Protestant; 15% claim no religious affiliation; 15% Eastern Orthodox, Buddhist, Muslim, Islamic and Quaker. **Female To Male Ratio:** 1.5:1. The average age of freshmen is 18; all undergraduates, 21. 6% do not continue beyond their first year; 86% remain to graduate. **Housing:** 4000 students can be accommodated in college housing, which includes single-sex and coed dorms, on-campus apartments, off-campus apartments, special-interest houses. All freshman participate in the First Seminar Program, and are housed in learning communities that connect the academic and social aspects of the college environment. This includes wellness housing and housing for international students. On-campus housing is guaranteed for the freshman year only and is available on a lottery system for upperclassmen. 60% of students live on campus. Upperclassmen may keep cars.

FACULTY/CLASSROOMS: 49% of faculty are male; 51% are female. All teach undergraduates, 85% do research, and 85% do both. No introductory courses are taught by graduate students. The average class size in an introductory lecture is 25; in a laboratory is 17; and in a regular course is 21.

PROGRAMS OF STUDY: TCNJ confers B.A., B.S., B.A.B.M.E., B.F.A., B.M., B.S.C.E., B.S.Co.E., B.S.E.E., B.S.M.E. and B.S.N. degrees. Master's degrees are also awarded. Bachelor's degrees are awarded in BIOLOGICAL SCIENCE (biology/biological science), BUSINESS (accounting and business administration and management), COMMUNICATIONS AND THE ARTS (art, art history and appreciation, communications, English, fine arts, graphic design, multimedia, music, and Spanish), COMPUTER AND PHYSICAL SCIENCE (chemistry, computer science, digital arts/technology, mathematics, and physics), EDUCATION (art education, early childhood education, education of the deaf and hearing impaired, elementary education, English education, health education, mathematics education, music education, physical education, science education, social science education, social studies education, special education, and technical education), ENGINEERING AND ENVIRONMENTAL DESIGN (biomedical engineering, civil engineering, computer engineering, electrical/electronics engineering, engineering and applied science, and mechanical engineering), HEALTH PROFESSIONS (exercise science and nursing), SOCIAL SCIENCE (criminal justice, economics, history, international studies, philosophy, political science/government, psychology, sociology, and women's studies). Biology, education, and engineering are the strongest academically. Psychology, biology, and elementary education have the largest enrollments.

ACTIVITIES: 14% of men belong to 14 national fraternities; 11% of women belong to 13 national sororities. There are 226 groups on campus, including art, band, cheerleading, chess, choir, chorale, chorus, computers, dance, drama, environmental, ethnic, film, forensics, honors, international, jazz band, LGBT, literary magazine, musical theater, newspaper, opera, orchestra, pep band, photography, political, professional, radio and TV, religious, social, social service, student government, symphony, and yearbook. Popular campus events include Lallanobozza, Mystique of the EAST, and TCNJ Later Nighter. **Sports:** There are 9 intercollegiate sports for men and 9 for women, and 14 intramural sports for men and 14 for women. Facilities include a stadium, an aquatic center, baseball and softball, a soccer/multipurpose field, an all-weather track, a sand volleyball court, playing fields, a gym, a physical enhancement center, recreation center, tennis, racquetball, basketball/volleyball courts, and a free weight room. **Graduates:** From July 1, 2015 to June 30, 2016, 1582 bachelor's degrees were awarded. The most popular majors were business/finance (18%), psychology (7%), and education (3%). 400 companies recruited on campus in 2015-2016. In an average class, 1% graduate in 3 years or less, 76% graduate in 4 years or less, 87% graduate in 5 years or less, and 87% graduate in 6 years or less. Of the 2015 graduating class, 33% were enrolled in graduate school within 6 months of graduation, and 95% were employed.

SERVICES: Counseling and information services are available, as is tutoring in most subjects, a reader service for the blind, and remedial math, reading, and writing. **Library/Resources:** The library contains 694,144 volumes, 426,253 microform items, and 40,127 audio/video tapes/CDs/DVDs, and subscribes to 73,733 periodicals including electronic. Computerized library services include interlibrary loans, database searching, Internet access, and Wi-Fi capability. Special learning facilities include an art gallery, planetarium, radio station, TV station, electron microscopy lab, nuclear magnetic resonance lab, optical spectroscopy lab, observatory, planetarium, and greenhouse. **Physically Challenged Students:** 90% of the campus is accessible. Facilities include wheelchair ramps, elevators, special parking, specially equipped restrooms, special class scheduling, lowered drinking fountains, lowered telephones, and special housing. **Special:** TCNJ offers cross-registration with the New Jersey Marine Science Consortium, a limited number of overseas internship possibilities, numerous internships in the public and private sectors, a Washington semester, and study abroad in more than a dozen countries. Pass/fail options and some dual majors are possible. Specially designed research courses allow students to participate in collaborative scholarly projects with members of the faculty, and the Bonner Center offers opportunities for community-engaged initiatives. Combined advanced and accelerated degree programs are offered in education of the deaf and hard of hearing, special education, medicine, and optometry. There are 16 national honor societies, Phi Beta Kappa, a freshman honors program, and 40 departmental honors programs. **Visiting:** There are regularly scheduled orientations for prospective students, consisting of an admissions presentation and a tour of campus. Reservations are required. There are guides for informal visits, visitors may sit in on classes, and stay overnight. To schedule a visit, contact the Admissions Office. **Campus Safety and Security:** Measures include 24-hour foot and vehicle patrol, emergency notification system, self-defense education, security escort services, emergency telephones, lighted pathways/sidewalks, and controlled access to dorms/residences.

REQUIREMENTS: The SAT is required. Applicants must have earned 18 academic credits in high school, consisting of 4 each in English, math and science, of those 2 must be lab, 2 each in foreign language and social studies. An essay is required. Art majors must submit a portfolio, and music majors must audition. The GED is accepted. AP and CLEP credits are accepted. Important factors in the admissions decision are advanced placement or honors courses, leadership record, parents or siblings attended your school, personality/intangible qualities, geographical diversity, recommendations by school officials, and evidence of special talent. To graduate, students must complete a liberal learning curriculum of 128 to 136 credit hours that includes at least 1 major, as well as a suite of courses that address 3 interdependent structural elements: intellectual and scholarly growth, civic responsibilities, and the broad sectors of human inquiry within the arts and humanities, social sciences, natural sciences, and quantitative reasoning. **Procedure:** Freshmen are admitted in the fall and spring. Entrance exams should be taken by the end of the junior year or early in the senior year. There are early decision and rolling admissions plans. Early decision applications should be filed by November 15; regular applications, by January 15 for fall entry; and November 15 for spring entry, along with a $75 fee. Notification of early decision is sent December 15; regular decision, January 15. 344 early decision candidates were accepted for the 2016-2017 class. 520 applicants were on the 2016 waiting list; 238 were admitted. Applications are accepted on-line. **Transfer Students:** 262 transfer students enrolled in 2015-2016. Transfer students must have a minimum GPA of 2.5, and those with fewer than 33 credits must submit SAT scores. An associate degree is recommended. All transfer students must submit high school transcripts. 12 of 34 credits required for the bachelor's degree must be completed at TCNJ. **International Students:** There are 23 international students enrolled. They must take the TOEFL with a minimum score of 550 on the paper-based TOEFL (PBT) or 90 on the Internet-based version (iBT). They must also take the SAT or ACT. The SAT is required for merit scholarship consideration.

ADMISSIONS: 49% of the 2016-2017 applicants were accepted. The SAT scores for the 2016-2017 freshman class were: Critical Reading-- 8% below 500, 44% between 500 and 599, 40% between 600 and 699, and 8% between 700 and 800. Math-- 4% below 500, 32% between 500 and 599, 49% between 600 and 699, and 15% between 700 and 800. Writing-- 9% below 500, 36% between 500 and 599, 43% between 600 and 699, and 12% between 700 and 800. 87% of the current freshmen were in the top fifth of their class; 98% were in the top two fifths. 13 freshmen graduated first in their class. **Admissions Contact:** Grecia Montero, Director of Admissions. Email: *tcnjinfo@tcnj.edu* Web: *www.tcnj.edu*

FINANCIAL AID: In 2016-2017, 41% of all full-time freshmen and 60% of continuing full-time students received some form of financial aid. 46% of all full-time freshmen and 60% of continuing full-time students received need-based aid. The average freshman award was $11,065. Need-based scholarships or need-based grants averaged $14,316; need-based self-help aid (loans and jobs) averaged $3,709; other non-need-based awards and non-need-based scholarships averaged $4,550; and $3,632 from other forms of aid. 21% of undergraduate students work part-time. Average annual earnings from campus work are $2400. The average financial indebtedness of the 2016 graduate was $33,635. TCNJ is a member of CSS. The FAFSA code is 002642. The priority date for freshman financial aid applications for fall entry is March 1. The filing deadline for fall entry is October 1.

THOMAS EDISON STATE UNIVERSITY *(The complete profile is made available exclusively on our website, www.barronspac.com)*

WESTMINSTER CHOIR COLLEGE *(The complete profile is made available exclusively on our website, www.barronspac.com)*

WILLIAM PATERSON UNIVERSITY OF NEW JERSEY E-2

www.wpunj.edu

Wayne, NJ 07470 (973) 720-2125

Fax: (973) 720-2910	**Email:** admissions@wpunj.edu
Full-time: 3814 men, 4522 women	**Faculty:** 400; IIA, ++$
Part-time: 755 men, 935 women	**Ph.D.s:** 92%
Graduate: 322 men, 1004 women	**Student/Faculty:** 21 to 1
Year: semesters, summer session	**Tuition:** $12,573 ($19,094)
Room & Board: $10,560	**Freshman Class:** 6968 applied, 4234 accepted, 1240 enrolled
SAT CR/M: 517/526 **ACT:** required	**CEEB CODE:** 2518
Application Deadline: June 1	**COMPETITIVE**

William Paterson University of New Jersey, founded in 1855, is a public institution comprised of the colleges of Arts and Communication, Education, Humanities, and Social Sciences, Science and Health, and Business. Figures in the above capsule and in this profile are approximate. There are 5 undergraduate schools and 5 graduate schools. In addition to regional accreditation, WPUNJ has baccalaureate program accreditation with ASLA, NASM, NCATE, and NLN. The 370-acre campus is in a suburban area 25 miles west of New York City. Including any residence halls, there are 35 buildings.

STUDENT LIFE: 98% of undergraduates are from New Jersey. Others are from 22 states, 58 foreign countries, and Canada. 75% are from public schools. 63% are White; 4% Asian American; 15% Hispanic; 12% African American; 1% Foreign. **Female To Male Ratio:** 1.3:1. The average age of freshmen is 18; all undergraduates, 24. **Housing:** College-sponsored housing includes coed dorms, on-campus apartments, and honors houses. On-campus housing is guaranteed for all 4 years. 77% of students commute. Upperclassmen may keep cars.

FACULTY/CLASSROOMS: 51% of faculty are male; 49% are female. All teach undergraduates, and all do research. No introductory courses are taught by graduate students. The average class size in an introductory lecture is 32; in a laboratory is 24; and in a regular course is 19.

PROGRAMS OF STUDY: WPUNJ confers B.A., B.S., B.F.A. and B.M.

degrees. Master's and doctoral degrees are also awarded. Bachelor's degrees are awarded in BIOLOGICAL SCIENCE (biology/biological science and biotechnology), BUSINESS (accounting, banking and finance, and business administration and management), COMMUNICATIONS AND THE ARTS (art history and appreciation, communications, dramatic arts, English, fine arts, music, Spanish, and studio art), COMPUTER AND PHYSICAL SCIENCE (chemistry, computer science, and mathematics), EDUCATION (health education, music education, physical education, and special education), ENGINEERING AND ENVIRONMENTAL DESIGN (environmental science), HEALTH PROFESSIONS (community health work, health science, and nursing), SOCIAL SCIENCE (African American studies, anthropology, economics, geography, history, philosophy, political science/government, psychology, and sociology). Biology/biotechnology, computer science, and English are the strongest academically. Management, communications, and education have the largest enrollments.

ACTIVITIES: 2% of men belong to 13 national fraternities; 3% of women belong to 12 national sororities. There are 100 groups on campus, including art, cheerleading, chorus, computers, dance, drama, ethnic, film, honors, international, jazz band, LGBT, literary magazine, musical theater, newspaper, opera, orchestra, photography, political, professional, radio and TV, religious, social, social service, student government, and yearbook. Popular campus events include Pioneer Pride Week, Latin Heritage Celebration, Welcome Week, African Heritage Celebration, WinterFest, Springfest, and Meet the Greeks. **Sports:** There are 7 intercollegiate sports for men and 7 for women, and 24 intramural sports for men and 24 for women. Facilities include a recreation center with courts for basketball, tennis, racquetball, volleyball, and badminton, weight and exercise rooms, pool, and an athletic complex with fields for baseball, field hockey, football, soccer, softball, and track. **Graduates:** From July 1, 2015 to June 30, 2016, 1984 bachelor's degrees were awarded. The most popular majors were business/marketing (19%), education (13%), and psychology (11%). In an average class, 14% graduate in 4 years or less, 40% graduate in 5 years or less, and 47% graduate in 6 years or less.

SERVICES: Counseling and information services are available, as is tutoring in most subjects, and remedial math, reading, and writing. There is a science enrichment center, a writing center, and a business tutorial lab. **Library/Resources:** The library contains 300,000 volumes, 1,000,000 microform items, 20,000 audio/video tapes/CDs/DVDs, and subscribes to 5,000 periodicals including electronic. Computerized library services include interlibrary loans and database searching. Special learning facilities include an art gallery, radio station, TV station, a speech and hearing clinic, an academic support center, a computerized writing center, and a teleconference center. **Physically Challenged Students:** Facilities include wheelchair ramps, elevators, special parking, specially equipped restrooms, special class scheduling, lowered drinking fountains, lowered telephones, and special housing. **Special:** Study abroad in 33 countries, cross-registration, internships, work-study programs on campus, accelerated degree programs, dual majors, individual curriculum design, and credit for military experience are available. Nondegree study and some pass/fail options are also possible. In the Learning Clusters Project, students experience how 3 general education courses, taken together, reinforce and better integrate each other. There is a professional program in teacher education leading to certification in early childhood, elementary, middle, and secondary education. There are 19 national honor societies, a freshman honors program, and 11 departmental honors programs. **Visiting:** There are regularly scheduled orientations for prospective students, including a campus tour, guest speakers, and dissemination of printed information. There are guides for informal visits and visitors may sit in on classes. To schedule a visit, contact the Admissions Office. **Campus Safety and Security:** Measures include 24-hour foot and vehicle patrol, emergency notification system, and security escort services. There are also shuttle buses, emergency telephones, lighted pathways/sidewalks, and controlled access to dorms/residences.

REQUIREMENTS: The SAT or ACT is required. Applicants must have 16 academic credits or Carnegie units, including 4 in English, 3 in math, 2 each in science lab and social studies, and 5 electives such as foreign language and history. An essay and interview are recommended for some applicants, as are a portfolio and audition. The GED is accepted. AP and CLEP credits are accepted. Important factors in the admissions decision are advanced placement or honors courses, recommendations by school officials, and evidence of special talent. All students must maintain a cumulative GPA of at least 2.0 and take 120 credit hours, typically including 30 to 40 in their major. The University Core Curriculum (the Core) will be the general education program of William Paterson it is a 40 credit program, which constitutes a third of the entire undergraduate curriculum. Students create their Core experience by choosing a sequence of 13 courses from each of the following six areas of study. Each area and sub-area will have a variety of courses to choose from. Also required are 1 course in health or movement science, 1 course dealing with racism or sexism. Courses in areas Four, Five and Six (Diversity and Justice, Community and Civic Engagement, and Global Awareness) may be within student majors. Such courses can thus be used to satisfy both, Core and major requirements. Students at WPU are required to complete four Writing Intensive courses and two Technology Intensive courses. These courses are not additional "stand-alone" courses but any course within the Core, or any major or any minor or any free elective that has been designated as a WI or TI course. **Procedure:** Freshmen are admitted in the fall and spring. Entrance exams should be taken by January 31. There are early admissions, deferred admissions, and rolling admissions plans. Applications should be filed by June 1 for fall entry; December 1 for spring entry, along with a $50 fee. Notification is sent on a rolling basis. Applications are accepted online. **Transfer Students:** Transfer students must present at least 12 college level credits with a minimum 2.0 GPA. Nursing Majors are encouraged to have a minimum of a 3.0 GPA or higher. Communication Disorders must have a minimum GPA of 3.5. Allied Health, Public Health, and Business Majors have specific requirements for admission please check our website, www.wpunj.edu for those requirements. 30 of 120 credits required for the bachelor's degree must be completed at WPUNJ. **International Students:** There are 99 international students enrolled. They must take the TOEFL with a minimum score of 550 on the paper-based TOEFL (PBT) or 80 on the Internet-based version (iBT), or take the IELTS - overall band score of 6.0 or higher. TOEFL could be waived based on submission of sufficient SAT/ACT scores.

ADMISSIONS: 61% of the 2016-2017 applicants were accepted. The SAT scores for the 2016-2017 freshman class were: Critical Reading-- 49% below 500, 39% between 500 and 599, 9% between 600 and 699, and 2% between 700 and 800. Math-- 42% below 500, 46% between 500 and 599, and 12% between 600 and 699. **Admissions Contact:** Rohan Howell, Director of Undergraduate Admissions. Email: *admissions@wpunj.edu* Web: *www.wpunj.edu*

FINANCIAL AID: In 2016-2017, 86% of all full-time freshmen and 84% of continuing full-time students received some form of financial aid. 64% of all full-time freshmen and 66% of continuing full-time students received need-based aid. The average freshman award was $13,247. Need-based scholarships or need-based grants averaged $8,359 ($13,800 maximum); need-based self-help aid (loans and jobs) averaged $3,285 ($5,000 maximum); and other non-need-based awards and non-need-based scholarships averaged $5,622 ($18,000 maximum). 72% of undergraduate students work part-time. Average annual earnings from campus work are $1500. The average financial indebtedness of the 2016 graduate was $29,906. WPUNJ is a member of CSS. The FAFSA code is 002625. The priority date for freshman financial aid applications for fall entry is April 1.

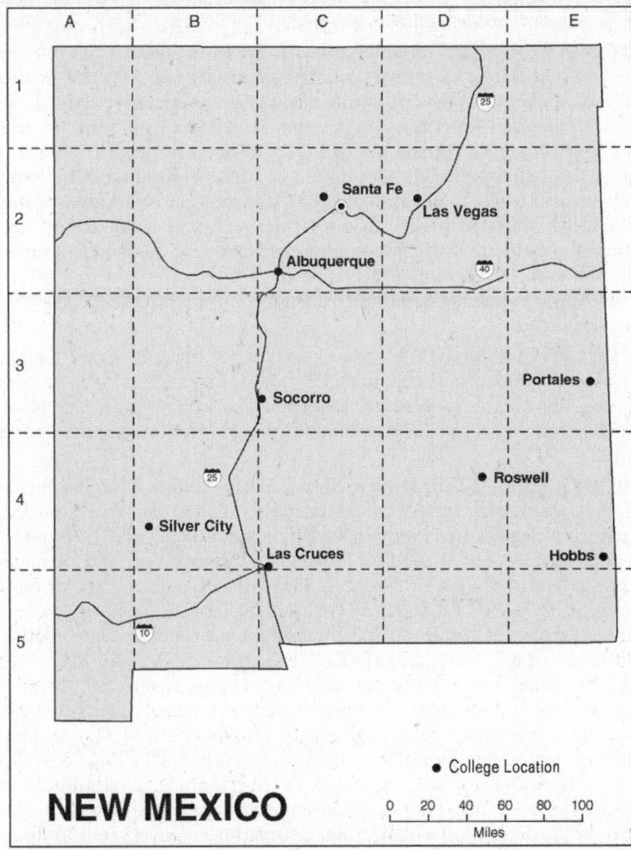

EASTERN NEW MEXICO UNIVERSITY E-3

www.enmu.edu

Portales, NM 88130	(575) 562-2178 (800) 367-3668
Fax: (575) 562-2118	**Email:** enrollment.services@enmu.edu
Full-time: 1204 men, 1555 women	**Faculty:** 151
Part-time: 796 men, 1017 women	**Ph.D.s:** 80%
Graduate: 324 men, 959 women	**Student/Faculty:** 17 to 1
Year: semesters, summer session	**Tuition:** $7656 ($13,430)
Room & Board: $9808	**Freshman Class:** 2291 applied, 1515 accepted, 709 enrolled
SAT CR/M: required **ACT:** 21	**CEEB CODE:** 4116
Application Deadline: August 20	**COMPETITIVE**

Eastern New Mexico University, founded in 1934, is a public institution offering programs in the liberal arts and sciences, as well as education, business, fine arts, and vocational and technical fields. Figures in the above capsule and in this profile are approximate. There are 4 undergraduate schools and 1 graduate school. In addition to regional accreditation, Eastern has baccalaureate program accreditation with ACBSP, ASLA, CSWE, NASM, NCATE, NLN, and TEAC. The 400-acre campus is in a small town in Portales, NM. Including any residence halls, there are 40 buildings.

STUDENT LIFE: 80% of undergraduates are from New Mexico. Others are from 47 states, 16 foreign countries, and Canada. 47% are White; 33% Hispanic; 6% race unknown; 4% African American; 4% American Indian/Alaska Native; 3% Foreign; 2% two or more races; 1% Asian American. **Female To Male Ratio:** 1.5:1. The average age of freshmen is 19; all undergraduates, 25. 39% do not continue beyond their first year. **Housing:** 1098 students can be accommodated in college housing, which includes single-sex and coed dorms, on-campus apartments, married student housing, sorority houses, and female freshmen-only living areas. On-campus housing is guaranteed for all 4 years, and is available on a first-come, and first-served basis. Priority is given to out-of-town students. 67% of students commute. Alcohol is not permitted. All students may keep cars.

FACULTY/CLASSROOMS: 49% of faculty are male; 51% are female. 93% teach undergraduates and do research. Graduate students teach 10% of introductory courses. The average class size in an introductory lecture is 30; in a laboratory is 15; and in a regular course is 19.

PROGRAMS OF STUDY: Eastern confers B.A., B.S., B.A.E., B.B.A., B.F.A., B.M., B.M.E., B.S.E., B.U.S., B.A.A.S., B.S.N., B.S.W., and B.O.E. degrees. Associate and master's degrees are also awarded. Bachelor's degrees are awarded in AGRICULTURE (agricultural business management, agriculture, animal science, and wildlife management), BIOLOGICAL SCIENCE (avian sciences, biochemistry, and biology/biological science), BUSINESS (accounting, business administration and management, and marketing/retailing/merchandising), COMMUNICATIONS AND THE ARTS (art, communications, dramatic arts, English, music, Spanish, and visual design), COMPUTER AND PHYSICAL SCIENCE (chemistry, computer science, geology, information sciences and systems, and mathematics), EDUCATION (agricultural education, business education, early childhood education, elementary education, home economics education, music education, physical education, special education, and technical education), ENGINEERING AND ENVIRONMENTAL DESIGN (electrical/electronics engineering technology and environmental science), HEALTH PROFESSIONS (medical laboratory technology, nursing, and speech pathology/audiology), SOCIAL SCIENCE (anthropology, counseling/psychology, criminal justice, forensic studies, history, human services, political science/government, psychology, religion, social studies, social work, and sociology). Elementary education, business administration, and nursing (BSN only) are the strongest academically. Business, education, and criminal justice have the largest enrollments.

ACTIVITIES: There are 55 groups on campus, including art, band, cheerleading, choir, chorus, communications, computers, dance, debate, drama, drill team, environmental, ethnic, film, forensics, honors, international, jazz band, LGBT, marching band, musical theater, newspaper, pep band, photography, political, professional, radio and TV, religious, social, social service, student government, symphony, and yearbook. Popular campus events include Green and Silver Preview, and Dawg Days (freshman orientation). **Sports:** There are 7 intercollegiate sports for men and 7 for women, and 15 intramural sports for men and 15 for women. Facilities include an indoor arena, outdoor stadium, indoor/outdoor tennis courts, handball and racquetball courts, and an indoor pool. **Graduates:** From July 1, 2015 to June 30, 2016, 615 bachelor's degrees were awarded. The most popular majors were university studies (9%), elementary education (9%), and applied arts and science (9%). 91 companies recruited on campus in 2015-2016. In an average class, 11% graduate in 4 years or less, 24% graduate in 5 years or less, and 29% graduate in 6 years or less.

SERVICES: Counseling and information services are available, as is tutoring in every subject, and a reader service for the blind, and remedial math, reading, and writing. **Library/Resources:** The 3 libraries contain 329,003 volumes, 467,017 microform items, 28,321 audio/video tapes/CDs/DVDs, and subscribe to 62,670 periodicals including electronic. Computerized library services include interlibrary loans, database searching, and Internet access. Special learning facilities include an art gallery, natural history museum, radio station, TV station, Eastern New Mexico University is home to a broadcasting center, a science fiction library, a teacher education library, a mineral museum, an anthropology museum, an archeological dig site, and a corresponding museum to the dig site at Blackwater Draw. **Physically Challenged Students:** All of the campus is accessible. Facilities include wheelchair ramps, elevators, special parking, specially equipped restrooms, special class scheduling, lowered drinking fountains, and special housing. ADA compliant campus, reserved parking, automatic doors, curb cuts, and elevators. **Special:** The school offers co-op programs in wildlife and fisheries and communication, internships, work-study programs, student-designed majors, a general studies degree, credit for military experience, and non-degree study. There are 2 national honor societies. **Visiting:** There are regularly scheduled orientations for prospective students, including meetings with admissions, financial aid, meeting advisor/faculty in field of interest, a tour of campus, and a meal in the dining hall. There are guides for informal visits, visitors may sit in on classes, and stay overnight. To schedule a visit, contact the Admissions Office at (575) 562-2178. **Campus Safety and Security:** Measures include 24-hour foot and vehicle patrol, emergency notification system, self-defense education, and security escort services. There are emergency telephones, lighted pathways/sidewalks, controlled access to dorms/residences, and security cameras to deter crime/theft.

REQUIREMENTS: A minimum composite score of 17 on the ACT or 810 on the SAT, or a GPA of 2.5, is required. Applicants must be high school graduate or possess a GED certificate and be in good standing with all previously attended institutions. A GPA of 2.5 is required. AP and CLEP credits are accepted. To graduate, students must earn 128 credit hours, 36 in the major, 40 total upper division, with a minimum GPA of 2.0. Minimum 32 hours must be from ENMU-Main campus; 15 of final 33 hours must be upper division. **Procedure:** Freshmen are admitted in the fall, spring, and summer. Entrance exams should be taken in the junior or senior year of high school. There is a rolling admissions plan. Applications should be filed by August 20 for fall entry. Applications are accepted online. **Transfer Students:** 615 transfer students enrolled in 2015-2016. Transfer students must have a minimum cumulative college GPA of 2.0 and be in good standing with all previously attended institutions. 32 of 128 credits required for the bachelor's degree must be completed at Eastern. **International Students:** There are 151 international students enrolled. They must take the TOEFL with a minimum score of 550 on the paper-based TOEFL (PBT) or 61 on the Internet-based version (iBT).

ADMISSIONS: 66% of the 2016-2017 applicants were accepted. The SAT scores for the 2016-2017 freshman class were: Critical Reading-- 60% below 500, 23% between 500 and 599, and 9% between 600 and 699. Math-- 54% below 500, 33% between 500 and 599, 9% between 600 and 699, and 1% between 700 and 800. The ACT scores were 56% below 12, 25% between 12 and 17, 15% between 18 and 23, 2% between 24 and 29, and 2% above 30. 36% of the current freshmen were in the top fifth of their class; 68% were in the top two fifths. 14 freshmen graduated first in their class. **Admissions Contact:** Cody Spitz, Director of Enrollment Services. Email: *enrollment.services@enmu.edu* Web: *www.enmu.edu*

FINANCIAL AID: In 2016-2017, 98% of all full-time freshmen and 89% of continuing full-time students received some form of financial aid. 42% of all full-time freshmen and 44% of continuing full-time students received need-based aid. The average freshman award was $10,356. Need-based scholarships or need-based grants averaged $4,736; need-based self-help aid (loans and jobs) averaged $3,892; non-need-based athletic scholarships averaged $3,382; other non-need-based awards and non-need-based scholarships averaged $4,213; and $2,905 from other forms of aid. The average financial indebtedness of the 2016 graduate was $14,821. The college's own financial statement, and institutional scholarship application is required. The FAFSA code is 002651. The priority date for freshman financial aid applications for fall entry is March 1. The filing deadline for fall entry is August 15.

NEW MEXICO HIGHLANDS UNIVERSITY *(The complete profile is made available exclusively on our website, www.barronspac.com)*

NEW MEXICO INSTITUTE OF MINING AND TECHNOLOGY C-3

www.nmt.edu

Socorro, NM 87801	**(575) 835-5424** **(800) 428-TECH**
Fax: (575) 835-5989	**Email: admission@nmt.edu**
Full-time: 1013 men, 375 women	**Faculty:** 128
Part-time: 85 men, 96 women	**Ph.D.s:** 95%
Graduate: 334 men, 232 women	**Student/Faculty:** 12 to 1
Year: semesters, summer session	**Tuition:** $6891 ($20,041)
Room & Board: $7942	**Freshman Class:** 1663 applied, 390 accepted, 302 enrolled
SAT CR/M: 630/620 **ACT:** 27	**CEEB CODE:** 4533
Application Deadline: August 1	**HIGHLY COMPETITIVE**

New Mexico Institute of Mining and Technology, founded in 1889 as the New Mexico School of Mines, is a science and engineering university. It has 4 research-associated divisions: the New Mexico Bureau of Geology and Mineral Resources, the Energetic Materials Research and Testing Center, the Petroleum Recovery Research Center, and the Langmuir Laboratory for Atmospheric Research. There is 1 undergraduate school and 1 graduate school. In addition to regional accreditation, New Mexico Tech has baccalaureate program accreditation with ABET. The 320-acre campus is in a small town 75 miles south of Albuquerque. Including any residence halls, there are 28 buildings.

STUDENT LIFE: 84% of undergraduates are from New Mexico. Others are from 30 states, 13 foreign countries, and Canada. 51% are White; 31% Hispanic; 5% two or more races; 4% American Indian/Alaska Native; 3% Asian American; 3% Foreign; 2% African American; 1% race unknown. **Male To Female Ratio:** 2.0:1. The average age of freshmen is 18; all undergraduates, 21. 25% do not continue beyond their first year; 49% remain to graduate. **Housing:** 807 students can be accommodated in college housing, which includes single-sex and coed dorms, on-campus apartments, off-campus apartments, and married student housing. On-campus housing is available on a first-come and first-served basis. 55% of students commute. Alcohol is not permitted. All students may keep cars.

FACULTY/CLASSROOMS: 78% of faculty are male; 22% are female. 95% teach undergraduates and 95% do research. No introductory courses are taught by graduate students. The average class size in an introductory lecture is 21; in a laboratory is 15; and in a regular course is 19.

PROGRAMS OF STUDY: New Mexico Tech confers B.S., and B.G.S. degrees. Associate, master's, and doctoral degrees are also awarded. Bachelor's degrees are awarded in BIOLOGICAL SCIENCE (biology/biological science), BUSINESS (business administration and management), COMMUNICATIONS AND THE ARTS (technical and business writing), COMPUTER AND PHYSICAL SCIENCE (chemistry, computer science, earth science, information sciences and systems, mathematics, and physics), ENGINEERING AND ENVIRONMENTAL DESIGN (chemical engineering, civil engineering, electrical/electronics engineering, environmental engineering, environmental science, materials engineering, mechanical engineering, mining and mineral engineering, and petroleum/natural gas engineering), HEALTH PROFESSIONS (biomedical science), SOCIAL SCIENCE (liberal arts/general studies and psychology). Physics, and electrical engineering are the strongest academically. Mechanical engineering, petroleum engineering, and computer science have the largest enrollments.

ACTIVITIES: There are no fraternities or sororities. There are 55 groups on campus, including art, band, chess, chorus, computers, drama, ethnic, honors, international, jazz band, LGBT, musical theater, orchestra, political, professional, radio and TV, religious, social, social service, student government, and yearbook. Popular campus events include 49ers, Spring Fling, and International Student Exhibit. **Sports:** There are 9 intramural sports for men and 9 for women. Facilities include a swimming pool, two gyms, an 18-hole golf course, an athletic field, climbing wall, weight/fitness room, racquetball/squash, tennis courts, sand volleyball court, ping-pong area, and a martial arts/combatives room. **Graduates:** From July 1, 2015 to June 30, 2016, 223 bachelor's degrees were awarded. The most popular majors were mechanical engineering (27%), petroleum engineering (13%), and biology (10%). In an average class, 20% graduate in 4 years or less, 44% graduate in 5 years or less, and 49% graduate in 6 years or less.

SERVICES: Counseling and information services are available, as is tutoring in most subjects, and a reader service for the blind. **Library/Resources:** The library contains 385,987 volumes, 79,926 microform items, and 2,899 audio/video tapes/CDs/DVDs, and subscribes to 50,000 periodicals including electronic. Computerized library services include interlibrary loans, database searching, Internet access, and Wi-Fi capability. Special learning facilities include a radio station, a mineral museum, a seismic research mine, and an astronomical observatory. **Physically Challenged Students:** Facilities include wheelchair ramps, elevators, special parking, specially equipped restrooms, lowered drinking fountains, lowered telephones. The majority of the campus is wheelchair accessible. **Special:** New Mexico Tech offers co-op programs in computer science and all engineering majors, internships in technical communications, and cross-registration with New Mexico State, University of New Mexico, and Los Alamos National Laboratories in the WERC consortium. Dual majors are offered in engineering, computer science, physics, and math. Work-study, student-designed majors in environmental science, general studies, and basic science, nondegree study, and pass/fail options are also available. There are 4 national honor societies. **Visiting:** There are regularly scheduled orientations for prospective students, including 2 days of get-acquainted social activities, information sessions for parents and students, and transition sessions for parents. There are guides for informal visits, visitors may sit in on classes, and stay overnight. To schedule a visit, contact the Admission Office. **Campus Safety**

and Security: Measures include 24-hour foot and vehicle patrol, self-defense education, security escort services, and emergency telephones and lighted pathways/sidewalks.

REQUIREMENTS: The SAT is required. The ACT is recommended, with a minimum score of 21. Applicants must be high school graduates or present a GED certificate. Students should have earned 15 academic credits, consisting of 4 units of English, 3 each of social science and math (2 beyond general math), 2 of lab science, and electives. A GPA of 2.5 is required. AP credits are accepted. Important factors in the admissions decision are advanced placement or honors courses, evidence of special talent, and extracurricular activities record. Students must earn at least 130 credit hours to graduate, including 42 hours of basic science, consisting in part of 10 hours of physics and 8 each of chemistry, calculus, biology, geology, and engineering. Further distribution requirements include 9 hours each of written and spoken English, 18 hours of literature, philosophy, the arts, and social science, and a senior seminar or senior design project. The credit hours required in the major vary by program. The student must also maintain a cumulative GPA of 2.0. **Procedure:** Freshmen are admitted to all sessions. Entrance exams should be taken by December of the senior year. There are deferred admissions and rolling admissions plans. Applications should be filed by August 1 for fall entry; December 1 for spring entry, along with a $15 fee. Notifications are sent March 1. **Transfer Students:** 79 transfer students enrolled in 2015-2016. Transfer students must have a GPA of 2.0 and have completed 30 semester hours of transferable credit. Those who have fewer than 30 credit hours, or who have not completed freshman English, must present a minimum ACT score of 21, as well as high school transcripts. 30 of 130 credits required for the bachelor's degree must be completed at New Mexico Tech. **International Students:** There are 38 international students enrolled. They must take the TOEFL with a minimum score of 540 on the paper-based TOEFL (PBT) or 76 on the Internet-based version (iBT).

ADMISSIONS: 23% of the 2016-2017 applicants were accepted. The SAT scores for the 2016-2017 freshman class were: Critical Reading-- 12% below 500, 24% between 500 and 599, 46% between 600 and 699, and 18% between 700 and 800. Math-- 9% below 500, 30% between 500 and 599, 47% between 600 and 699, and 14% between 700 and 800. The ACT scores were 26% between 18 and 23, 50% between 24 and 29, and 24% above 30. 56% of the current freshmen were in the top fifth of their class; 81% were in the top two fifths. 1 freshman graduated first in the class. **Admissions Contact:** Tony Ortiz, Director of Admission. Email: *admission@nmt.edu* Web: *www.nmt.edu*

FINANCIAL AID: In 2016-2017, 95% of all full-time freshmen and 85% of continuing full-time students received some form of financial aid. 40% of all full-time freshmen and 37% of continuing full-time students received need-based aid. The average freshman award was $2,785. Need-based scholarships or need-based grants averaged $4,126 ($5,775 maximum); need-based self-help aid (loans and jobs) averaged $3,225 ($6,000 maximum); and other non-need-based awards and non-need-based scholarships averaged $2,278 ($5,683 maximum). The average financial indebtedness of the 2016 graduate was $22,355. The FAFSA code is 002654. The priority date for freshman financial aid applications for fall entry is March 1. The filing deadline for fall entry is May 1.

NEW MEXICO STATE UNIVERSITY C-4

www.nmsu.edu

Las Cruces, NM 88003	**(505) 646-3121** **(800) 662-6678**
Fax: (505) 646-6330	**Email: admissions@nmsu.edu**
Full-time: 5036 men, 5632 women	**Faculty:** 555; I, --$
Part-time: 966 men, 1150 women	**Ph.D.s:** 79%
Graduate: 1329 men, 1716 women	**Student/Faculty:** 19 to 1
Year: semesters, summer session	**Tuition:** $5950 ($19,112)
Room & Board: $8100	**Freshman Class:** 7116 applied, 4952 accepted, 1862 enrolled
SAT: required **ACT:** 21	**CEEB CODE:** 4531
Application Deadline: open	**COMPETITIVE**

New Mexico State University, founded in 1888, is a public institution offering undergraduate and graduate programs that include study in liberal arts, agriculture, business, engineering, health science, education, and visual and performing arts. There are 6 undergraduate schools and 1 graduate school. In addition to regional accreditation, NMSU has baccalaureate program accreditation with AACSB, ABET, ADA, CSWE, NASM, NCATE, AAHE, ACS, NASPAA, ASHA, ASEE, AAAHC, AER, APA, CADE, CACREP, CAATE, CAA, CEPH, IACS, NASP, CCNE, NMPED, and SRM. The 900-acre campus is in a small town 40 miles north of El Paso. Including any residence halls, there are 294 buildings.

STUDENT LIFE: 71% of undergraduates are from New Mexico. Others are from 48 states, 44 foreign countries, and Canada. 49% are Hispanic; 32% White; 8% Foreign; 3% African American; 3% race unknown; 2% American Indian/Alaska Native; 2% two or more races; 1% Asian American. **Female To Male Ratio:** 1.2:1. The average age of freshmen is 19; all undergraduates, 23. 26% do not continue beyond their first year; 74% remain to graduate. **Housing:** 3385 students can be accommodated in college housing, which includes single-sex and coed dorms, on-campus apartments, married student housing, honors houses, fraternity houses, and sorority houses. On-campus housing is available on a first-come and first-served basis. 81% of students commute. All students may keep cars.

FACULTY/CLASSROOMS: 51% of faculty are male; 49% are female. Graduate students teach 23% of introductory courses. The average class size in an introductory lecture is 40 and in a laboratory is 20.

PROGRAMS OF STUDY: NMSU confers B.A., and B.S. degrees. Associate, master's, and doctoral degrees are also awarded. Bachelor's degrees are awarded in AGRICULTURE (agricultural business management, agricultural economics, agriculture, agronomy, animal science, horticulture, natural resource management, range/farm management, soil science, turfgrass and landscape management, and wildlife science), BIOLOGICAL SCIENCE (biochemistry, biology/biological science, ecology, genetics, microbiology, molecular biology, nutrition, and plant pathology), BUSINESS (accounting, business administration and management, business economics, fashion merchandising, finance, hotel/motel and restaurant management, international business management, management information systems, marketing, marketing/retailing/merchandising, and tourism), COMMUNICATIONS AND THE ARTS (animation, art, communications, dance, dramatic arts, English, film arts, fine arts, foreign language, journalism, music, music performance, theatre arts, video, and visual and performing arts), COMPUTER AND PHYSICAL SCIENCE (astronomy, chemistry, computer science, geology, information sciences and systems, mathematics, and physics), EDUCATION (agricultural education, athletic training, bilingual/bicultural education, early childhood education, elementary education, home economics education, music education, physical education, secondary education, and special education), ENGINEERING AND ENVIRONMENTAL DESIGN (aerospace engineering, aerospace studies, chemical engineering, city/community/regional planning, civil engineering, computer technology, electrical/electronics engineering, engineering physics, engineering technology, environmental engineering, environmental science, industrial engineering, mechanical engineering, and surveying engineering), HEALTH PROFESSIONS (clinical science, community health work, environmental health science, kinesiology, nursing, and speech pathology/audiology), SOCIAL SCIENCE (anthropology, community services, criminal justice, economics, family/consumer studies, geography, history, philosophy, physical fitness/movement, political science/government, psychology, social work, sociology, textiles and clothing, and women's studies). Criminal justice, nursing, and biology have the largest enrollments.

ACTIVITIES: 2% of men belong to 10 national fraternities; 2% of women belong to 6 national sororities. There are 226 groups on campus, including art, band, cheerleading, choir, chorale, chorus, computers, dance, drama, drill team, drum and bugle corps, environmental, ethnic, film, honors, international, jazz band, LGBT, literary magazine, marching band, musical theater, newspaper, opera, orchestra, pep band, photography, political, professional, radio and TV, religious, social, social service, student government, and symphony. Popular campus events include Fiestas Latinas, American Indian Week, Noche De Luminarias, Greek Week, Halloween Howl, and NMSU Homecoming. **Sports:** There are 6 intercollegiate sports for men and 9 for women, and 21 intramural sports for men and 21 for women. Facilities include campus stadiums, a game room, natatorium, tennis courts, playing fields, a gym, and rodeo grounds. **Graduates:** From July 1, 2015 to June 30, 2016, 2714 bachelor's degrees were awarded. The most popular majors were criminal justice (7%), individualized studies (5%), and psychology (4%). 341 companies recruited on campus in 2015-2016. In an average class, 16% graduate in 4 years or less, 37% graduate in 5 years or less, and 46% graduate in 6 years or less.

SERVICES: Counseling and information services are available, as is

tutoring in most subjects, and a reader service for the blind. There is also an interpreter for the hearing impaired. **Library/Resources:** The 2 libraries contain 1.8 million volumes, 1.5 million microform items, 17,232 audio/video tapes/CDs/DVDs, and subscribe to 79,830 periodicals including electronic. Computerized library services include interlibrary loans, database searching, Internet access, and Wi-Fi capability. Special learning facilities include an art gallery, natural history museum, radio station, TV station, a experimental farm and orchard, a cattle and experimental ranch, and a recreational area in the Organ Mountains. **Physically Challenged Students:** 95% of the campus is accessible. Facilities include wheelchair ramps, elevators, special parking, specially equipped restrooms, lowered drinking fountains, lowered telephones. **Special:** Internships, cooperative programs in engineering, math, science, teacher education, business, agriculture, social services, health, government, and other majors, dual majors, study abroad in 56 countries, work-study, and B.A.-B.S. degrees are available. WICHE and National Student Exchange are also available. There are 25 national honor societies, a freshman honors program, and 18 departmental honors programs. **Visiting:** There are regularly scheduled orientations for prospective students, including a tour of the campus and meetings with admissions counselors, faculty members, and financial aid advisers. There are guides for informal visits, visitors may sit in on classes, and stay overnight. To schedule a visit, contact the Office of Admissions. **Campus Safety and Security:** Measures include 24-hour foot and vehicle patrol, emergency notification system, self-defense education, and security escort services. There are also shuttle buses, lighted pathways/sidewalks, controlled access to dorms/residences, and recycled phones with 911 programmed in for emergencies.

REQUIREMENTS: Applicants must score 20 on the ACT or may take the SAT (accepted, but not recommended), and submit a composite score of 780. The GED is accepted. Minimum high school preparation includes 4 units of English, 3 of math, 2 beyond general science, and 1 foreign language/fine arts. A GPA of 2.0 is required. AP and CLEP credits are accepted. All students must complete a minimum of 128 credits, including at least 50 upper-division credits. Distribution requirements include communications, humanities, math, natural sciences, and social sciences. **Procedure:** Freshmen are admitted to all sessions. Entrance exams should be taken during the high school junior or senior year. There is a rolling admissions plan. Application deadlines are open. Application fee is $20. Notification is sent on a rolling basis. Applications are accepted online. **Transfer Students:** 1019 transfer students enrolled in 2015-2016. Applicants must have a minimum GPA of 2.0. 30 credits are required to avoid freshman admission requirements. If the applicant has earned 30 academic credit hours or more, the ACT score will be waived. If the applicant has earned 48 academic credit hours or more, the high school transcript will be waived. 30 of 128 credits required for the bachelor's degree must be completed at NMSU. **International Students:** There are 570 international students enrolled. The school actively recruits these students. They must take the TOEFL with a minimum score of 550 on the paper-based TOEFL (PBT) or 79 on the Internet-based version (iBT) or take the MELAB.

ADMISSIONS: 70% of the 2016-2017 applicants were accepted. The SAT scores for the 2016-2017 freshman class were: Critical Reading-- 60% below 500, 30% between 500 and 599, 9% between 600 and 699, and 1% between 700 and 800. Math-- 55% below 500, 34% between 500 and 599, and 11% between 600 and 699. Writing-- 65% below 500, 28% between 500 and 599, and 7% between 600 and 699. The ACT scores were 49% below 12, 24% between 12 and 17, 17% between 18 and 23, 6% between 24 and 29, and 4% above 30. 33% of the current freshmen were in the top fifth of their class; 57% were in the top two fifths. 28 freshmen graduated first in their class. **Admissions Contact:** Delia De Leon, Interim Director of Admissions. Email: *admissions@nmsu.edu* Web: *www.nmsu.edu*

FINANCIAL AID: In 2016-2017, 97% of all full-time freshmen and 88% of continuing full-time students received some form of financial aid. 70% of all full-time freshmen and 66% of continuing full-time students received need-based aid. The average freshman award was $11,033. Need-based scholarships or need-based grants averaged $6,651 ($24,840 maximum); need-based self-help aid (loans and jobs) averaged $4,140 ($13,392 maximum); non-need-based athletic scholarships averaged $10,006 ($20,358 maximum); other non-need-based awards and non-need-based scholarships averaged $4,200 ($16,971 maximum); and $11,577 from other forms of aid. 7% of undergraduate students work part-time. Average annual earnings from campus work are $7566. The average financial indebtedness of the 2016 graduate was $21,589. The FAFSA code is 002657. The deadline for filing freshman financial aid applications for fall entry is March 1.

SANTA FE UNIVERSITY OF ART AND DESIGN *(The complete profile is made available exclusively on our website, www.barronspac.com)*

ST. JOHN'S COLLEGE, SANTA FE — C-2

www.sjc.edu

Santa Fe, NM 87505	(505) 984-6060 (800) 331-5232
Fax: (505) 984-6162	Email: SantaFe.Admissions@sjcsf.edu
Full-time: 186 men, 139 women	**Faculty:** 45
Part-time: 3 men, 2 women	**Ph.D.s:** 80%
Graduate: 41 men, 26 women	**Student/Faculty:** 8 to 1
Year: semesters, summer session	**Tuition:** $49,219
Room & Board: $10,890	**Freshman Class:** 188 applied, 167 accepted, 94 enrolled
SAT CR/M/W: 695/592/642 **ACT:** 28	**CEEB CODE:** 4737
Application Deadline: February 15	**HIGHLY COMPETITIVE+**

St. John's College, Santa Fe, founded in 1696, offers a curriculum based on the great books of western civilization in which students and faculty learn together in small discussion-based classes. There is 1 undergraduate school and 1 graduate school. The 298-acre campus is in a suburban area in Santa Fe, New Mexico. Including any residence halls, there are 42 buildings.

STUDENT LIFE: 94% of undergraduates are from out of state, mostly the Southwest. Students are from 41 states, and 18 foreign countries. 68% are from public schools. 60% are White; 20% Foreign; 12% Hispanic; 4% two or more races; 3% Asian American; 1% African American; 1% American Indian/Alaska Native; 1% race unknown. **Male To Female Ratio:** 1.4:1. The average age of freshmen is 20; all undergraduates, 21. 22% do not continue beyond their first year; 60% remain to graduate. **Housing:** 327 students can be accommodated in college housing, which includes single-sex and coed dorms, on-campus apartments, married student housing, special-interest houses, substance free residences, and green/sustainable housing. On-campus housing is guaranteed for the freshman year only and is available on a lottery system for upperclassmen. 75% of students live on campus; of those, 75% remain on campus on weekends. All students may keep cars.

FACULTY/CLASSROOMS: 75% of faculty are male; 25% are female. All teach undergraduates. No introductory courses are taught by graduate students. The average class size in a laboratory is 15 and in a regular course is 15.

PROGRAMS OF STUDY: St. John's confers B.A. degrees. Master's degrees are also awarded. Bachelor's degrees are awarded in COMPUTER AND PHYSICAL SCIENCE (mathematics and science), SOCIAL SCIENCE (liberal arts/general studies and philosophy). Liberal arts is the strongest academically.

ACTIVITIES: There are no fraternities or sororities. There are 27 groups on campus, including art, chess, chorus, dance, drama, environmental, ethnic, film, international, LGBT, literary magazine, newspaper, orchestra, outdoor leadership program, political, social service, and student government. Popular campus events include Oktoberfest, Halloween and Christmas parties. **Sports:** There are 7 intramural sports for men and 7 for women. Facilities include mountain biking, soccer field, track, outdoor tennis courts, gym with weight room and cardio equipment, racquetball, squash, and basketball courts, a ski mountain 30 minutes from campus, and hiking trails which depart from campus. **Graduates:** From July 1, 2015 to June 30, 2016, 84 bachelor's degrees were awarded. The most popular majors were liberal arts and sciences and liberal studies (100%). 50 companies recruited on campus in 2015-2016. In an average class, 60% graduate in 4 years or less, 8% graduate in 5 years or less, and 2% graduate in 6 years or less. Of the 2015 graduating class, 13% were enrolled in graduate school within 6 months of graduation, and 51% were employed.

SERVICES: Counseling and information services are available, as is tutoring in every subject. **Library/Resources:** The library contains 68,711 volumes, and 4,707 audio/video tapes/CDs/DVDs, and subscribes to 80 periodicals including electronic. Computerized library services include interlibrary loans, database searching, Internet access, and Wi-Fi capability. Special learning facilities include an art gallery, art studio, wood working studio, ceramics studio, music practice rooms, Ptolemy stone, and laboratories. **Physically Challenged Students:** 75% of the campus is accessible. Facilities include wheelchair ramps, elevators, special parking, specially equipped restrooms, special class scheduling, lowered drinking fountains, and special housing. **Special:** Internships with alumni in a wide range of fields are available and students may transfer between the Santa Fe and Annapolis campuses. Ariel Internship Program provides stipends to undergraduates for a limited number of summer intership opportunities. Work study programs are available with the state government, museums, galleries, the Santa Fe Institute, businesses, and schools. Pre-medical studies at universities around the country. **Visiting:** There are regularly scheduled orientations for prospective students, student-led walking tour of the campus, audit a seminar and math and language tutorials, spend the night in student housing, interview with admission's counselor and faculty member. There are guides for informal visits, visitors may sit in on classes, and stay overnight. To schedule a visit, contact Anne Young at ahyoung@sjc.edu. **Campus Safety and Security:** Measures include 24-hour foot and vehicle patrol, emergency notification system, and security escort services. There are also shuttle buses, emergency telephones, lighted pathways/sidewalks, controlled access to dorms/residences, informal discussions and pamphlets/posters/films.

REQUIREMENTS: Applicants must write personal essays and submit 2 references, a secondary school report including a reference from a school official, and transcripts of all academic work in high school and college. A campus visit and interview are recommended. 3 years of math and 2 years of foreign language are required; 4 years each of math, foreign language, and English, and 3 years of science are recommended. The GED is accepted. Important factors in the admissions decision are parents or siblings attended your school, recommendations by alumni, and evidence of special talent. The college has 1 curriculum, based on the great books of western civilization for a total of 136 credits. Students attend seminars, preceptorials on specific works or topics, language, music, and math tutorials, and a 3-year science lab. Students take oral exams each semester and write annual essays. Sophomores take a math exam and seniors write a final essay and take an oral exam. **Procedure:** Freshmen are admitted in the fall and spring. There are deferred admissions and rolling admissions plans. Early decision applications should be filed by November 15; regular applications, by February 15 for fall entry. Notification of early decision is sent December 15; regular decision. Application fees are waived if application is completed online. **Transfer Students:** 14 transfer students enrolled in 2015-2016. St. John's accepts transfer students only for its freshman class; no previous college credit is recognized. Admission requirements are the same as is for freshmen students. 136 of 136 credits required for the bachelor's degree must be completed at St. John's. **International Students:** There are 65 international students enrolled. The school actively recruits these students. They must take the TOEFL with a minimum score of 550 on the paper-based TOEFL (PBT).

ADMISSIONS: 89% of the 2016-2017 applicants were accepted. The SAT scores for the 2016-2017 freshman class were: Critical Reading-- 11% between 500 and 599, 37% between 600 and 699, and 52% between 700 and 800. Math-- 15% below 500, 41% between 500 and 599, 37% between 600 and 699, and 7% between 700 and 800. Writing-- 4% below 500, 22% between 500 and 599, 52% between 600 and 699, and 19% between 700 and 800. The ACT scores were 14% between 12 and 17, 19% between 18 and 23, 14% between 24 and 29, and 52% above 30. 47% of the current freshmen were in the top fifth of their class; 78% were in the top two fifths. There was 1 National Merit finalist. 4 freshmen graduated first in their class. **Admissions Contact:** Yvette Sobky-Shaffer, Director of Admissions. Email: *SantaFe.Admissions@sjcsf.edu* Web: *www.sjc.edu*

FINANCIAL AID: In 2016-2017, 98% of all full-time freshmen and 97% of continuing full-time students received some form of financial aid. 90% of all full-time freshmen and 84% of continuing full-time students received need-based aid. The average freshman award was $45,292. Need-based scholarships or need-based grants averaged $27,729; need-based self-help aid (loans and jobs) averaged $6,763; other non-need-based awards and non-need-based scholarships averaged $15,511; and $35,365 from other forms of aid. 94% of undergraduate students work part-time. Average annual earnings from campus work are $2960. The average financial indebtedness of the 2016 graduate was $27,093. St. John's is a member of CSS. The FAFSA code is 002093. The priority date for freshman financial aid applications for fall entry is February 15.

UNIVERSITY OF NEW MEXICO — C-2

www.unm.edu

Albuquerque, NM 87131	(505) 277-8900 (800) CALL UNM ext. 1
Fax: (505) 277-6809	**Email:** apply@unm.edu
Full-time: 7401 men, 8939 women	**Faculty:** I, --$
Part-time: 1875 men, 2637 women	**Ph.D.s:** 85%
Graduate: 2744 men, 3425 women	**Student/Faculty:** 20 to 1
Year: semesters, summer session	**Tuition:** $6950 ($20,688)
Room & Board: $8454	**Freshman Class:** 11652 applied, 7350 accepted, 3518 enrolled
SAT or ACT: required	**CEEB CODE:** 4845
Application Deadline: June 15	**COMPETITIVE**

University of New Mexico, founded in 1889, is a public university offering instruction in liberal and fine arts, business, engineering, health science, teacher preparation, law, and technology. In addition, to the main Campus there are four branch campuses. The figures provided in this profile are approximate. There are 10 undergraduate schools and 5 graduate schools. In addition to regional accreditation, UNM has baccalaureate program accreditation with AACSB, ABET, ACCE, ACEJMC, ACPE, ADA, CAHEA, NAAB, NASM, NCATE, CDA, CAATE, and NAST/NASD. The 783-acre campus is in an urban area within the city of Albuquerque. Including any residence halls, there are 339 buildings.

STUDENT LIFE: 90% of undergraduates are from New Mexico. Others are from 50 states, 56 foreign countries, and Canada. 45% are Hispanic; 37% White; 6% American Indian/Alaska Native; 3% African American; 3% Asian American; 3% two or more races; 2% race unknown; 1% Foreign. **Female To Male Ratio:** 1.2:1. The average age of freshmen is 19; all undergraduates, 23. 22% do not continue beyond their first year; 48% remain to graduate. **Housing:** 3700 students can be accommodated in college housing, which includes single-sex and coed dorms, on-campus apartments, and married student housing. In addition, honors houses, special-interest houses, fraternity houses, sorority houses, freshman living learning communities, scholar's wing, graduates and senior undergraduate unit, global learning community, and combined BA/MD degree program quarters. 89% of students commute. All students may keep cars. Alcohol is not permitted.

FACULTY/CLASSROOMS: 52% of faculty are male; 48% are female. No introductory courses are taught by graduate students.

PROGRAMS OF STUDY: UNM confers B.A., B.S., B.A.A., B.A.E.P.D., B.A.Ed., B.A.F.A., B.B.A., B.F.A., B.I.S., B.L.A., B.M., B.M.E., B.S.C.E., B.S.Ch.E., B.S.Cp.E., B.S.Cn.E., B.S.C.S., B.S.D.H., B.S.E.E., B.S.Ed., B.S.M.E., B.S.M.L., B.S.N., B.S.D.H., and B.S.N.E degrees. Associate, master's, and doctoral degrees are also awarded. Bachelor's degrees are awarded in BIOLOGICAL SCIENCE (biochemistry, biology/biological science, and nutrition), BUSINESS (business administration and management), COMMUNICATIONS AND THE ARTS (Africana studies, American Sign Language, art history, art, classics, communications, comparative literature, dance, English, film, television and digital media, French, German, journalism, languages, linguistics, media arts, music, Portuguese, Russian, Spanish, studio art, theater design, and theatre studies), COMPUTER AND PHYSICAL SCIENCE (astrophysics, chemistry, computer science, earth science, mathematics, physics, and statistics), EDUCATION (art education, athletic training, drama education, early childhood education, elementary education, health education, music education, physical education, secondary education, special education, and technical education), ENGINEERING AND ENVIRONMENTAL DESIGN (architecture, chemical engineering, civil engineering, computer engineering, construction engineering, construction management, electrical/electronics engineering, environmental design, environmental science, mechanical engineering, and nuclear engineering), HEALTH PROFESSIONS (dental hygiene, emergency medical technologies, exercise science, health, medical laboratory technology, nursing, radiological science, and speech pathology/audiology), SOCIAL SCIENCE (American studies, anthropology, Asian/Oriental studies, child care/child and family studies, criminology, economics, European studies, family/consumer studies, geography, history, human development, human services, interdisciplinary studies, international studies, Latin American studies, liberal arts/general studies, Mexican-American/Chicano studies, Native American studies, philosophy, political science/government, psychology, religion, sociology, and women's studies). Business administration, psychology, and biology have the largest enrollments.

ACTIVITIES: 2% of men belong to 15 national fraternities; 3% of women belong to 10 national sororities. There are 400 groups on campus, including art, band, cheerleading, chess, choir, chorale, chorus, communications, dance, drama, drill team, environmental, ethnic, honors, international, jazz band, LGBT, literary magazine, marching band, musical theater, opera, orchestra, pep band, political, professional, religious, social, social service, student government, and symphony. Popular campus events include Spring Fiesta, Welcome Back Days, and Hanging of the Greens. **Sports:** There are 8 intercollegiate sports for men and 11 for women, and 5 intramural sports for men and 5 for women. Facilities include a football field, gyms, pools, weights, racquetball, basketball, and tennis courts. **Graduates:** From July 1, 2015 to June 30, 2016, 3493 bachelor's degrees were awarded. The most popular majors were business administration (20%), psychology (8%), and elementary education (6%). 414 companies recruited on campus in 2015-2016. In an average class, 48% graduate in 6 years or less.

SERVICES: Counseling and information services are available, as is tutoring in most subjects, and remedial math, reading, and writing. **Library/Resources:** The 8 libraries contain 3.6 million volumes, 713,958 microform items, and 54,238 audio/video tapes/CDs/DVDs, and subscribe to 71,932 periodicals including electronic. Computerized library services include interlibrary loans, database searching, Internet access, and Wi-Fi capability. Special learning facilities include an art gallery, planetarium, TV station, a robotics lab, lithography and meteoritic institutes, observatory, arts lab, and museums of geology, anthropology, and biology. **Physically Challenged Students:** All of the campus is accessible. Facilities include wheelchair ramps, elevators, special parking, specially equipped restrooms, lowered drinking fountains, and special housing. **Special:** There is a 3-2 engineering program with the Anderson School of Management. Study abroad is available in 28 countries. The university offers cooperative programs in arts and sciences management, engineering, and fine arts, a Washington semester, work-study, dual and student-designed majors, a general studies degree, credit for military experience, nondegree study, and pass/fail options. There are 20 national honor societies, Phi Beta Kappa, a freshman honors program, and 46 departmental honors programs. **Visiting:** There are regularly scheduled orientations for prospective students, includes academic advisement and registration. There are guides for informal visits, visitors may sit in on classes, and stay overnight. To schedule a visit, contact Admissions & Recrutiment Services. **Campus Safety and Security:** Measures include 24-hour foot and vehicle patrol, emergency notification system, self-defense education, and security escort services. There are also shuttle buses, emergency telephones, lighted pathways/sidewalks, crime stoppers, jump starts, operation ID, bicycle registration, and a 911 emergency system.

REQUIREMENTS: The SAT or ACT is required. A total of 13 academic credits is required, including 4 years of English, 3 years of math, and 2 years each of foreign language, natural science (with 1 lab), and social science (with 1 in U.S. history). A GED is accepted. Freshman applicants must be graduates of a high school accredited by a regional accrediting association or by the state department of education or state university of the state in which the high school is located. The minimum GPA requirement for admission to bachelor degree programs is 2.25 (on a 4.00 scale) in all previous academic work from an accredited high school. Grades in all courses allowed toward high school graduation are computed in the average. A GPA of 2.5 is required. AP and CLEP credits are accepted. All students must take 2 English courses or pass an English composition competence examination and complete the University Core Curriculum. A minimum of 128 credit hours is required, along with a GPA of 2.0. **Procedure:** Freshmen are admitted in the fall, spring, and summer. Entrance exams should be taken during the summer following the junior year. There are early admissions, deferred admissions, and rolling admissions plans. June 15 for fall entry; November 15 for spring entry; and May 1 for summer entry. The fall 2016 application fee was $20. Notification is sent on a rolling basis. Applications are accepted online. **Transfer Students:** 927 transfer students enrolled in 2015-2016. Applicants must have at least a 2.0 GPA in all transferable courses. Please note that admission requirements are subject to change. 30 of 128 credits required for the bachelor's degree must be completed at UNM. **International Students:** There are 208 international students enrolled. The school actively recruits these students. They must take the TOEFL, University of Cambridge English Examination (CPE or CAE) and IELTS. They must also take the SAT or ACT.

ADMISSIONS: 63% of the 2016-2017 applicants were accepted. The ACT scores were 7% above 30. **Admissions Contact:** Matthew Hulett, Director of Admissions & Recruitment. Email: *apply@unm.edu* Web: *www.unm.edu*

FINANCIAL AID: In 2016-2017, 85% of continuing full-time students received some form of financial aid. The FAFSA code is 002663. Check with the school for current application deadlines.

UNIVERSITY OF THE SOUTHWEST — E-4

www.usw.edu

Hobbs, NM 88240	**(575) 392-6563** **(800) 530-4400**
Fax: (575) 392-6006	**Email: admission@usw.edu**
Full-time: 150 men, 200 women	**Faculty:** IIB
Part-time: 20 men, 55 women	**Ph.D.s:** n/av
Graduate: 40 men, 125 women	**Student/Faculty:** 15 to 1
Year: semesters, summer session	**Tuition:** $15,456
Room & Board: $7310	**Freshman Class:** n/av
SAT or ACT: required	**CEEB CODE:** 4116
Application Deadline: open	**COMPETITIVE**

University of the Southwest, founded in 1962, is an independent college offering 53 majors (including specialties) undergraduate programs in arts and sciences, business, education, psychology, and criminal justice. Graduate programs are offered in education. The figures in the above capsule and in this profile are approximate. There is 1 undergraduate school and 1 graduate school. The 162-acre campus is in a small town in Hobbs, New Mexico, 110 miles southwest of Lubbock, TX. Including any residence halls, there are 11 buildings.

STUDENT LIFE: 70% of undergraduates are from New Mexico. Others are from 11 states, 5 foreign countries, and Canada. 7% are Foreign; 43% White; 38% Hispanic; 3% African American; 1% Asian American; 1% American Indian/Alaska Native. **Female To Male Ratio:** 1.8:1. The average age of freshmen is 20; all undergraduates, 26. 35% do not continue beyond their first year; 35% remain to graduate. **Housing:** 172 students can be accommodated in college housing, which includes single-sex and coed dorms and on-campus apartments. On-campus housing is available on a first-come and first-served basis. Priority is given to out-of-town students. 59% of students live on campus. All students may keep cars. Alcohol is not permitted.

FACULTY/CLASSROOMS: 51% of faculty are male; 49% are female. 99% teach undergraduates. No introductory courses are taught by graduate students. The average class size in an introductory lecture is 11; in a laboratory is 7; and in a regular course is 12.

PROGRAMS OF STUDY: USW confers B.S., B.A.S., and B.B.A. degrees. Master's degrees are also awarded. Bachelor's degrees are awarded in BIOLOGICAL SCIENCE (biology/biological science), BUSINESS (accounting and business administration and management), COMMUNICATIONS AND THE ARTS (English and fine arts), COMPUTER AND PHYSICAL SCIENCE (mathematics), EDUCATION (elementary education, secondary education, and special education), SOCIAL SCIENCE (criminal justice, history, humanities, psychology, and sociology). Education, and business are the strongest academically. Education, business, and criminal justice have the largest enrollments.

ACTIVITIES: There are no fraternities or sororities. There are 7 groups on campus, including debate, drama, honors, international, newspaper, professional, religious, and student government. Popular campus events include Annual Students in Free Enterprise Dinner and Award Presentation, Family Week, and Speakers' Presentations. **Sports:** There are 4 intercollegiate sports for men and 6 for women, and 5 intramural sports for men and 5 for women. Facilities include soccer, and baseball fields, a game room, a physical fitness center with a multipurpose gym, racquetball courts, softball, and volleyball. **Graduates:** From July 1, 2015 to June 30, 2016, 98 bachelor's degrees were awarded. The most popular majors were education (29%), psychology (11%), and accounting (10%). 10 companies recruited on campus in 2015-2016. In an average class, 19% graduate in 5 years or less. Of the 2015 graduating class, 5% were enrolled in graduate school within 6 months of graduation.

SERVICES: Counseling and information services are available, as is tutoring in most subjects, and remedial math and writing. **Library/Resources:** The library contains 76,450 volumes, 25,750 microform items, 1,553 audio/video tapes/CDs/DVDs, and subscribes to 333 periodicals including electronic. Computerized library services include interlibrary loans, database searching, and Internet access. **Physically Challenged Students:** All of the campus is accessible. Facilities include wheelchair ramps, special parking, and specially equipped restrooms. **Special:** The school offers co-op programs in early childhood education. Internships are available for students majoring in business, psychology, and education. CSW also offers nondegree study and credit for military experience. There are 2 national honor societies and 1 departmental honors program. **Visiting:** There are guides for informal visits, visitors may sit in on classes, and stay overnight. To schedule a visit, contact Coordinator of Admissions. **Campus Safety and Security:** Measures include 24-hour foot and vehicle patrol.

REQUIREMENTS: The ACT Optional Writing test is required. Students must have a minimum composite score of 18 on the ACT or a satisfactory score on the SAT. Applicants must be graduates of an accredited secondary school or have a GED certificate. Southwest requires applicants to be in the upper 50% of their class. AP and CLEP credits are accepted. Important factors in the admissions decision are advanced placement or honors courses, extracurricular activities record, and ability to finance college education. To graduate, students must complete 128 semester hours with a minimum GPA of 2.0 (2.5 for education majors). General education requirements include 12 semester hours each of social science and math/science, 9 each of humanities/fine arts and communications, 6 of religion, and 3 of economics, as well as a course in free enterprise and a senior seminar in leadership and ethics. **Procedure:** Freshmen are admitted to all sessions. There is a rolling admissions plan. Application deadlines are open. Application fee is $25. Notification is sent on a rolling basis. Applications are accepted online. **Transfer Students:** 135 transfer students enrolled in 2015-2016. Applicants must present a minimum GPA of 2.0 and official transcripts from all colleges attended. 30 of 128 credits required for the bachelor's degree must be completed at University of the Southwest. **International Students:** There are 27 international students enrolled. They must take the TOEFL, as well as the SAT or ACT.

Admissions Contact: Shelbie Faught, Undergraduate Prigrams Admissions Coordinator, Director New Fresh. Email: *staught@csw.edu* Web: *www.usw.edu*

FINANCIAL AID: In 2016-2017, 97% of all full-time freshmen and 88% of continuing full-time students received some form of financial aid. 64% of all full-time freshmen and 70% of continuing full-time students received need-based aid. 17% of undergraduate students work part-time. The the college's own financial statement is required. The FAFSA code is 013935. Check with the school for current application deadlines.

WESTERN NEW MEXICO UNIVERSITY *(The complete profile is made available exclusively on our website, www.barronspac.com)*

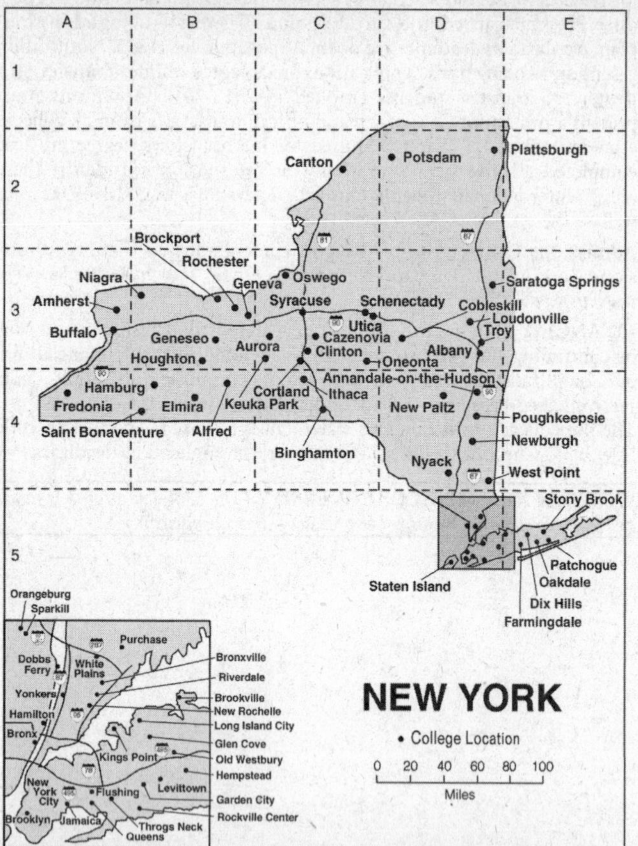

ADELPHI UNIVERSITY D-5

www.adelphi.edu

Garden City, NY 11530 (516) 877-3050
(800) ADELPHI

Fax: (516) 877-3039
Email: admissions@adelphi.edu

Full-time: 1403 men, 2997 women
Part-time: 111 men, 302 women
Graduate: 547 men, 1857 women
Year: semesters, summer session
Room & Board: $14,210
SAT CR/M/W: 550/565/560 **ACT:** 22
Application Deadline: open

Faculty: 317; I, av$
Ph.D.s: 87%
Student/Faculty: 11 to 1
Tuition: $34,034
Freshman Class: 9367 applied, 6762 accepted, 868 enrolled
CEEB CODE: 2003
COMPETITIVE

Adelphi University, founded in 1896, is a private institution. The figure for tuition and fees in the above capsule is for first-year students. Tuition varies by programs. There are 8 undergraduate schools and 7 graduate schools. In addition to regional accreditation, Adelphi has baccalaureate program accreditation with AACSB, CSWE, NCATE, NLN, APA, ASHA, and CCNE. The 75-acre campus is in a suburban area 20 miles east of New York City. Including any residence halls, there are 26 buildings.

STUDENT LIFE: 93% of undergraduates are from New York. Others are from 38 states, 40 foreign countries, and Canada. 74% are from public schools. 8% are African American; 55% White; 5% race unknown; 4% Foreign; 2% two or more races; 15% Hispanic; 11% Asian American. 47% are Catholic; 17% Hindu, Buddhist, Muslim, Christian and unknown; 16% claim no religious affiliation; 12% Jewish. **Female To Male Ratio:** 2.5:1. The average age of freshmen is 18; all undergraduates, 22. 19% do not continue beyond their first year; 67% remain to graduate. **Housing:** 1282 students can be accommodated in college housing, which includes coed dorms. In addition, there are honors houses, special-interest houses, and theme housing. On-campus housing is available on a first-come, and first-served basis, and is available on a lottery system for upperclassmen. Priority is given to out-of-town students. 76% of students commute. Alcohol is not permitted. All students may keep cars.

FACULTY/CLASSROOMS: 46% of faculty are male; 54% are female. All teach undergraduates. No introductory courses are taught by graduate students. The average class size in a regular course is 20.

PROGRAMS OF STUDY: Adelphi confers B.A., B.S., B.B.A., B.F.A., B.S.Ed. and B.S.S.W. degrees. Associate, master's, and doctoral degrees are also awarded. Bachelor's degrees are awarded in AGRICULTURE (environmental studies), BIOLOGICAL SCIENCE (biochemistry and biology/biological science), BUSINESS (accounting, banking and finance, business administration and management, human resources, and management information systems), COMMUNICATIONS AND THE ARTS (art history and appreciation, communications, dance, design, dramatic arts, English, fine arts, French, languages, music, performing arts, Spanish, and theater design), COMPUTER AND PHYSICAL SCIENCE (chemistry, computer science, mathematics, and physics), EDUCATION (art education and physical education), HEALTH PROFESSIONS (nursing and speech pathology/audiology), SOCIAL SCIENCE (anthropology, criminal justice, economics, history, Latin American studies, philosophy, political science/government, psychology, social science, social work, and sociology). Nursing, business, and social work are the strongest academically. Nursing, biology, and psychology have the largest enrollments.

ACTIVITIES: 10% of men belong to 7 national fraternities; 8% of women belong to 10 national sororities. There are 80 groups on campus, including model UN, radio station, art, band, campus ministries, cheerleading, chorale, chorus, computers, dance, debate, drama, environmental, ethnic, film, honors, international, jazz band, LGBT, literary magazine, musical theater, newspaper, opera, orchestra, political, professional, religious, social, social service, student government, and yearbook. Popular campus events include Family Week, Student Holiday Party, Spring-In Festival, Spring Concert, and Commuter Appreciation Week. **Sports:** There are 9 intercollegiate sports for men and 11 for women, and 14 intramural sports for men and 14 for women. Facilities include a stadium, gym, swimming pool, finess center, racquetball, squash, tennis courts, dance studio, an indoor track, baseball field, and softball field. **Graduates:** From July 1, 2015 to June 30, 2016, 1219 bachelor's degrees were awarded. The most popular majors were health professions (33%), business/marketing (13%), and social science (8%). 200 companies recruited on campus in 2015-2016. In an average class, 5% graduate in 3 years or less, 54% graduate in 4 years or less, 61% graduate in 5 years or less, and 64% graduate in 6 years or less. Of the 2015 graduating class, 41% were enrolled in graduate school within 6 months of graduation, and 88% were employed.

SERVICES: Counseling and information services are available, as is tutoring in most subjects, such as a learning center that offers tutoring in writing, quantitative skills and help with class assignments. There is also a reader service for the blind. **Library/Resources:** The library contains 632,180 volumes, 789,749 microform items, and 26,746 audio/video tapes/CDs/DVDs, and subscribes to 929 periodicals including electronic. Computerized library services include interlibrary loans, database searching, Internet access, and Wi-Fi capability. Special learning facilities include an art gallery, observatory, theater, sculpture and ceramics studios, a bronze casting foundry, and language labs. **Physically Challenged Students:** 95% of the campus is accessible. Facilities include wheelchair ramps, elevators, special parking, specially equipped restrooms, special class scheduling, lowered drinking fountains, lowered telephones, and special housing. **Special:** Cross-registration is possible with New York University College of Dentistry, Tufts University School of Dental Medicine, Columbia University, New York Law School, SUNY State College of Optometry, and New York Medical College. Internships are available in accounting, banking and money management, and communications, among others. Study abroad is available in 65 countries, including Spain, France, Denmark, and England. A 5-year bachelor's/master's degree in a number of fields, including biology, social work, and education is offered. In addition, work-study programs, double majors, the B.A.-B.S. degree, an accelerated degree program, student-designed majors, and a Washington semester are available. A 3-2 engineering degree is offered with Rensselaer Polytechnic, Columbia, Polytechnic, and Stevens Institute of Technology, and joint degree programs are offered in computer science, dentistry, engineering, environmental studies, law, optometry, and physical therapy with other universities and technical institutions. Credit for life experience for adult students, nondegree study in special cases, and pass/fail options are possible. There are 27 national honor societies and a freshman honors program. **Visiting:** There are regularly scheduled orientations for prospective students, including a campus tour, interview, and information sessions. There are guides for informal visits and visitors may sit in on classes. To schedule a visit, contact the Undergraduate Admissions. **Campus Safety and Security:** Measures include 24-hour foot and vehicle patrol, emergency notification system, self-defense education, and security escort services. There are shuttle buses, emergency telephones, lighted pathways/sidewalks. Dorm main entrances are videotaped and are locked 24 hours a day.

REQUIREMENTS: Applicants should have 16 academic credits, including a recommended 4 units of English, history, and social studies, 3 each of math and science, and 2 or 3 of foreign language. An essay is required and An interview recommended for all applicants. A portfolio for art and technical theater candidates, an audition for music, dance, and theater candidates, and an interview for nursing, social work, and honors candidates are required. The SAT is recommended for the general studies and learning disabilities programs. A GPA of 2.5 is required. AP credits are accepted. Important factors in the admissions decision are advanced placement or honors courses, leadership record, and personality/intangible qualities. To graduate, students need at least a 2.0 cumulative GPA (higher in some programs) and 120 credit hours with a minimum of 27 in the major. 6 credits each are required in the arts, humanities, and languages, natural sciences and math, and social sciences. Other course requirements include English composition, freshman seminar (3 credits each), and a 1-credit freshman orientation experience, and a capstone experience for seniors. **Procedure:** Freshmen are admitted fall and spring. Entrance exams should be taken in October of the senior year or May of the junior year. There are early admissions, deferred admissions, and rolling admissions plans. Application deadlines are open. The fall 2016 application fee was $40. Applications are accepted online. **Transfer Students:** 376 transfer students enrolled in 2015-2016. A GPA of 2.5 is recommended in addition to an essay, an high school transcript, and records of all work completed or in progress from previous colleges and universities. An interview is required for students in social work and nursing, while an audition is needed for music, dance, and theater students and a portfolio for art and technical theater students. 30 of 120 credits required for the bachelor's degree must be completed at Adelphi. **International Students:** There are 203 international students enrolled. The school actively recruits these students. They must take the TOEFL with a minimum score of 550 on the paper-based TOEFL (PBT) or 80 on the Internet-based version (iBT). They must also take the SAT or ACT.

ADMISSIONS: 72% of the 2016-2017 applicants were accepted. The SAT scores for the 2016-2017 freshman class were: Critical Reading-- 21% below 500, 53% between 500 and 599, 22% between 600 and 699, and 3% between 700 and 800. Math-- 20% below 500, 45% between 500 and 599, 27% between 600 and 699, and 8% between 700 and 800. Writing-- 20% below 500, 47% between 500 and 599, 27% between 600 and 699, and 6% between 700 and 800. The ACT scores were 9% between 12 and 17, 55% between 18 and 23, 34% between 24 and 29, and 2% above 30. 46% of the current freshmen were in the top fifth of their class; 81% were in the top two fifths. **Admissions Contact:** Christine Murphy, Director of Admissions. Email: *admissions@adelphi.edu* Web: *www.adelphi.edu*

FINANCIAL AID: In 2016-2017, 75% of all full-time freshmen received some form of financial aid. 73% of all full-time freshmen received need-based aid. The average freshman award was $22,000. Need-based scholarships or need-based grants averaged $7,417; need-based self-help aid (loans and jobs) averaged $5,171; non-need-based athletic scholarships averaged $19,999; other non-need-based awards and non-need-based scholarships averaged $18,224; and $3,902 from other forms of aid. The average financial indebtedness of the 2016 graduate was $33,485. Adelphi is a member of CSS. The state aid form is required. The FAFSA code is 002666. The priority date for freshman financial aid applications for fall entry is March 1.

ALBANY COLLEGE OF PHARMACY AND HEALTH SCIENCES *(The complete profile is made available exclusively on our website, www.barronspac.com)*

ALFRED STATE COLLEGE — B-4

www.alfredstate.edu

Alfred, NY 14802 — (607) 587-4215, (800) 4-ALFRED

Fax: (607) 587-4299 — **Email:** admissions@alfredstate.edu

Full-time: 1780 men, 1820 women	**Faculty:** n/av
Part-time: n/av	**Ph.D.s:** n/av
Graduate: n/av	**Student/Faculty:** n/av
Year: semesters, summer session	**Tuition:** $8075
Room & Board: $11,820	**Freshman Class:** n/av
SAT CR/M/W: 520/540/490 **ACT:** 23	**CEEB CODE:** 2522
Application Deadline: rolling	**COMPETITIVE**

Alfred State College, founded in 1908, is a public institution conferring associate and bachelor's degrees. Figures in the above capsule and in this profile are approximate. There are 5 undergraduate schools. In addition to regional accreditation, Alfred State College has baccalaureate program accreditation with ABET. The 150-acre campus is in a rural area 15 miles north of Pennsylvania, 75 miles south of Rochester, and 90 miles southeast of Buffalo. Including any residence halls, there are 50 buildings.

STUDENT LIFE: 97% of undergraduates are from New York. Others are from 7 states, 12 foreign countries, and Canada. 73% are White; 7% race unknown; 6% Hispanic; 3% American Indian/Alaska Native; 2% two or more races; 11% African American; 1% Asian American. **Female To Male Ratio:** 1.0:1. The average age of freshmen is 18; all undergraduates, 19. 67% remain to graduate. **Housing:** College-sponsored housing includes coed dorms and on-campus apartments. In addition, there are honors houses, language houses, special-interest houses, wellness, computerized, and adult housing. On-campus housing is guaranteed for all 4 years. 70% of students live on campus; of those, 50% remain on campus on weekends. Alcohol is not permitted. All students may keep cars.

FACULTY/CLASSROOMS: 66% of faculty are male; 34% are female. All teach undergraduates. No introductory courses are taught by graduate students. The average class size in an introductory lecture is 40; in a laboratory is 20; and in a regular course is 20.

PROGRAMS OF STUDY: Alfred State College confers B.S., B.B.A., and B.T. degrees. Associate degrees are also awarded. Bachelor's degrees are awarded in BUSINESS (banking and finance), COMPUTER AND PHYSICAL SCIENCE (information sciences and systems), ENGINEERING AND ENVIRONMENTAL DESIGN (architectural technology, computer technology, construction management, electrical/electronics engineering technology, manufacturing technology, mechanical engineering technology, survey and mapping technology, and technological management). Engineering technology programs are the strongest academically and have the largest enrollments.

ACTIVITIES: There are 90 groups on campus, including rescue and response team, band, cheerleading, chess, choir, chorale, chorus, computers, dance, drama, environmental, ethnic, forensics, honors, international, jazz band, LGBT, literary magazine, musical theater, newspaper, orchestra, peer education network, pep band, professional, radio and TV, social, social service, student government, and yearbook. Popular campus events include Family Weekend, and Hot Dog Day. **Sports:** There are 9 intercollegiate sports for men and 7 for women, and 26 intramural sports for men and 23 for women. Facilities include a fitness center/weight room, indoor swimming pool, wrestling room, gym, tennis courts, outdoor track, baseball and softball fields, and practice fields. **Graduates:** Of the 2015 graduating class, 99% were enrolled in graduate school within 6 months of graduation, and 99% were employed.

SERVICES: Counseling and information services are available, as is tutoring in most subjects. There is a reader service for the blind, and remedial math, reading, and writing. **Library/Resources:** The 2 libraries contain 61,500 volumes, and 8,148 audio/video tapes/CDs/DVDs, and subscribe to 5,500 periodicals including electronic. Computerized library services include interlibrary loans, database searching, Internet access, and Wi-Fi capability. Special learning facilities include an art gallery and radio station. **Physically Challenged Students:** All of the campus is accessible. Facilities include wheelchair ramps, elevators, special parking, specially equipped restrooms, special class scheduling, lowered drinking fountains, lowered telephones, and special housing. **Special:** Cross-registration is offered with Alfred University, Houghton College, Rochester area colleges, and the Western New York Consortium. On-campus work-study programs are available, as are summer internships. There are 2 national honor societies, a freshman honors program, and 52 departmental honors programs. **Visiting:** There are regularly scheduled orientations for prospective students, including open houses during the fall and spring semesters. All aspects of the campus are open for visitation, and accepted students are invited to participate in an overnight visit. There are guides for informal visits, visitors may sit in on classes, and stay overnight. To schedule a visit, contact the Admissions Office. **Campus Safety and Security:** Measures include 24-hour foot and vehicle patrol, emergency notification system, self-defense education, and security escort services. There are shuttle buses, emergency telephones, lighted pathways/sidewalks, and controlled access to dorms/residences.

REQUIREMENTS: The SAT or ACT is required. Applicants must have graduated from an accredited secondary school or earned a GED. Specific course requirements vary by curriculum. A portfolio is required for applicants interested in computer art and design and digital media and animation. AP and CLEP credits are accepted. Important factors in the admissions decision are advanced placement or honors courses, extracurricular activities record, and recommendations by school officials. To graduate, candidates for a bachelor's degree must complete a total of 120 credits. A core sequence, including courses in math, physical sciences, and liberal studies, and a year-long senior technical project, are required. A phys ed course is also required. **Procedure:** Freshmen are admitted to all sessions. Entrance exams should be taken November 1. There is a rolling admissions plan. Application deadlines are open. Application fee is $50. Notifications are sent November 1. Applications are accepted online. **Transfer Students:** 263 transfer students enrolled in 2015-2016. Transfer applicants must have a minimum 2.4 GPA. 30 of 120 credits required for the bachelor's degree must be completed at Alfred State College. **International Students:** There are 50 international students enrolled. The school actively recruits these students. They must take the TOEFL.

Admissions Contact: Deborah Goodrich, Associate Vice President for Enrollment Management. Email: *admissions@alfredstate.edu* Web: *www.alfredstate.edu*

FINANCIAL AID: In 2016-2017, 80% of all full-time freshmen received some form of financial aid, and continuing full-time students received need-based aid. Average annual earnings from campus work are $1000. The priority date for freshman financial aid applications for fall entry is December. The deadline for filing freshman financial aid applications for fall entry is January.

ALFRED UNIVERSITY — B-4

www.alfred.edu

Alfred, NY 14802	(607) 871-2115 (800) 541-9229
Fax: (607) 871-2198	**Email:** admissions@alfred.edu
Full-time: 939 men, 970 women	**Faculty:** 150
Part-time: 24 men, 27 women	**Ph.D.s:** 93%
Graduate: 157 men, 314 women	**Student/Faculty:** 12 to 1
Year: semesters, summer session	**Tuition:** $30,100
Room & Board: $12,196	**Freshman Class:** 3417 applied, 2385 accepted, 535 enrolled
SAT CR/M/W: 530/550/510 **ACT:** 24	**CEEB CODE:** 2005
Application Deadline: August 1	**COMPETITIVE+**

Alfred University, founded in 1836, is composed of the privately endowed college of Liberal Arts and Sciences, and College of Ceramics (Inamori School of Engineering, and School of Art and Design). AU offers more than 40 undergraduate majors/programs. The figures in the above capsule and in this profile are approximate. There are 5 undergraduate schools and 1 graduate school. In addition to regional accreditation, AU has baccalaureate program accreditation with AACSB, ABET, NASAD, TEAC, CAATE, and ACS. The 232-acre campus is in a rural area in Alfred, NY, about 1 hour west of Corning, 1.5 hours south of Rochester and 2 hours from Buffalo. Including any residence halls, there are 52 buildings.

STUDENT LIFE: 76% of undergraduates are from New York. Others are from 42 states, 19 foreign countries, and Canada. 8% are African American; 7% Hispanic; 66% White; 3% Foreign; 2% Asian American; 2% two or more races; 12% race unknown. **Female To Male Ratio:** 1.2:1. The average age of freshmen is 18; all undergraduates, 20. 26% do not continue beyond their first year; 62% remain to graduate. **Housing:** 1469 students can be accommodated in college housing, which includes single-sex and coed dorms and on-campus apartments. In addition, there are honors houses, language houses, special-interest houses, and theme housing. On-campus housing is guaranteed for the freshman year only, is available on a first-come, first-served basis, and is available on a lottery system for upperclassmen. 76% of students live on campus; of those, 90% remain on campus on weekends. All students may keep cars.

FACULTY/CLASSROOMS: 54% of faculty are male; 46% are female. 90% teach undergraduates, and 90% do research. No introductory courses are taught by graduate students. The average class size in an introductory lecture is 30; in a laboratory is 20; and in a regular course is 18.

PROGRAMS OF STUDY: AU confers B.A., B.F.A. and B.S. degrees. Master's and doctoral degrees are also awarded. Bachelor's degrees are awarded in AGRICULTURE (environmental studies), BIOLOGICAL SCIENCE (biology/biological science), BUSINESS (accounting, business administration and management, and marketing/retailing/merchandising), COMMUNICATIONS AND THE ARTS (art history and appreciation, ceramic art and design, communications, dramatic arts, English, fine arts, glass, Spanish, and theatre arts), COMPUTER AND PHYSICAL SCIENCE (chemistry, geology, mathematics, physics, and science), EDUCATION (art education, athletic training, business education, early childhood education, mathematics education, science education, secondary education, and social studies education), ENGINEERING AND ENVIRONMENTAL DESIGN (ceramic engineering, materials engineering, and mechanical engineering), SOCIAL SCIENCE (criminal justice, crosscultural studies, gerontology, history, interdisciplinary studies, philosophy, political science/government, psychology, and sociology). Engineering is the strongest academically. Art & design, business administration, and mechanical engineering have the largest enrollments.

ACTIVITIES: There are no fraternities or sororities. There are 90 groups on campus, including business, communications, cultural, diversity and multicultural, engineering, entertainment, math and science, service and leadership, spiritual life, art, athletics, band, cheerleading, chorale, chorus, computers, dance, drama, environmental, ethnic, film, honors, international, jazz band, LGBT, literary magazine, musical theater, newspaper, orchestra, pep band, photography, political, professional, radio and TV, religious, social, social service, student government, and yearbook. Popular campus events include Homecoming Weekend, Family Weekend, and Hot Dog Day. **Sports:** There are 10 intercollegiate sports for men and 11 for women, and 14 intramural sports for men and 13 for women. Facilities include a field for football, soccer, and lacrosse, pool, softball field, tennis courts, racquetball, squash courts, weight room, dance and exercise studios, indoor gym, fitness center, equestrian center, hiking trails, indoor track, and easy access to cross-country skiing, and basketball courts. **Graduates:** From July 1, 2015 to June 30, 2016, 356 bachelor's degrees were awarded. The most popular majors were fine arts (31%), engineering (17%), and biology (8%). 80 companies recruited on campus in 2015-2016. In an average class, 44% graduate in 4 years or less, 61% graduate in 5 years or less, and 62% graduate in 6 years or less.

SERVICES: Counseling and information services are available, as is tutoring in most subjects. Time management, study skills workshops, and a writing center are available. There are also services for students with learning and physical disabilities. **Library/Resources:** The 2 libraries contain 286,995 volumes, 79,704 microform items, and 179,255 audio/video tapes/CDs/DVDs, and subscribe to 93,502 periodicals including electronic. Computerized library services include interlibrary loans, database searching, Internet access, and Wi-Fi capability. Special learning facilities include an art gallery, radio station, John L. Stull Observatory, and a Museum of Ceramic Art. **Physically Challenged Students:** 45% of the campus is accessible. Facilities include wheelchair ramps, elevators, special parking, specially equipped restrooms, special class scheduling, and lowered drinking fountains. **Special:** There are cooperative programs in engineering with Duke and Columbia Universities. AU participates in a cross-registration program with more than 15 area colleges and universities through the Rochester Area Colleges consortium. AU also offers study abroad, Washington and Albany semesters, student-designed majors, and a 4+1 MBA program for students majoring in Liberal Arts & Sciences or Engineering. There are 16 national honor societies and a chapter of Phi Beta Kappa. **Visiting:** There are regularly scheduled orientations for prospective students, with an agenda customized per student's needs. There are guides for informal visits, visitors may sit in on classes, and stay overnight. To schedule a visit, contact the Admissions Office. **Campus Safety and Security:** Measures include 24-hour foot and vehicle patrol, emergency notification system, and security escort services. There are emergency telephones, lighted pathways/sidewalks, and controlled access to dorms/residences.

REQUIREMENTS: The SAT or ACT is required. A GED is accepted. A minimum of 16 Carnegie units is required, including 4 years of English, 2 to 3 years each of math, history/social studies, and science. Depending on the school/college applied to, the remaining units may be either in a foreign language, the categories listed above, or business, art, or computer science. Official high school transcripts, one letter of recommendation, an essay, and a $50 fee (may be waived by visiting campus or with a NACAC or College Board waiver) is required of all applicants. Applicants to the School of Art and Design must submit a portfolio. Interviews are encouraged. AP credits are accepted. Important factors in the admissions decision are recommendations by school officials, extracurricular activities record, and leadership record. To satisfy the requirements for a Bachelors Degree a student must: complete all course requirements, including those required for the major, general education, and the minimum number of credits for the degree sought depending on the school or college of enrollment; earn a cumulative GPA of at least 2.0; satisfy the Global Perspective Requirement; satisfy the Physical Education requirement; request legal conferral of degree and satisfy financial obligations to the University; earn at least 45 semester credit hours at AU; and be in residence at AU at least during the final 30 credit hours earned toward the degree. **Procedure:** Freshmen are admitted fall and spring. Entrance exams should be taken spring of junior year. There are early decision, deferred admissions, and rolling admissions plans. Early decision applications should be filed by December 1; regular applications, by August 1 for fall entry; and December 1 for spring entry, along with a $50 fee. Notification of early decision is sent December 15; regular decision, on a rolling basis. 45 early decision candidates were accepted for the 2016-2017 class. 91 applicants were on the 2016 waiting list; 11 were admitted. Applications are accepted on-line. **Transfer Students:** 49 transfer students enrolled in 2015-2016. Transfer applicants must have a GPA of at least 2.5 on a 4.0 scale. They must submit at least 1 letter of recommendation and official high school and college transcripts. Applicants to the School of Art and Design must also submit a portfolio. 45 of 120 credits required for the bachelor's degree must be completed at AU. **International Students:** There are 51 international students enrolled. The school actively recruits these students. They must take the TOEFL with a minimum score of 550 on the paper-based TOEFL (PBT) or 80 on the Internet-based version (iBT). The IELTS must be taken if they do not submit the SAT or ACT.

ADMISSIONS: 70% of the 2016-2017 applicants were accepted. The SAT scores for the 2016-2017 freshman class were: Critical Reading-- 27% below 500, 51% between 500 and 599, 19% between 600 and 699, and 3% between 700 and 800. Math-- 20% below 500, 49% between 500 and 599, 27% between 600 and 699, and 4% between 700 and 800. Writing-- 43% below 500, 40% between 500 and 599, 15% between 600 and 699, and 2% between 700 and 800. The ACT scores were 16% below 12, 28% between 12 and 17, 30% between 18 and 23, 15% between 24 and 29, and 11% above 30. 36% of the current freshmen were in the top fifth of their class; 70% were in the top two fifths. 3 freshmen graduated first in their class. **Admissions Contact:** Earl E. Pierce, VP for Enrollment Management. Email: *admissions@alfred.edu* Web: *www.alfred.edu*

FINANCIAL AID: In 2016-2017, 95% of all full-time freshmen received some form of financial aid, or need-based aid. The average freshman award was $26,623. Need-based scholarships or need-based grants averaged $20,371; need-based self-help aid (loans and jobs) averaged $6,640; and $4,986 from other forms of aid. 40% of undergraduate students work part-time. Average annual earnings from campus work are $1800. The average financial indebtedness of the 2016 graduate was $33,467. AU is a member of CSS. The state aid form, college's own financial statement, business/farm supplement, and the noncustodial parent statement are required. The FAFSA code is 002671. The priority date for freshman financial aid applications for fall entry is March 15. The deadline for filing for fall entry is May 1.

BARD COLLEGE — D-4

www.bard.edu

Annandale-on-Hudson, NY 12504 — **(845) 758-7472**

Fax: (845) 758-5208	**Email: admission@bard.edu**
Full-time: 871 men, 1075 women	**Faculty:** 152; IIB, ++$
Part-time: 32 men, 45 women	**Ph.D.s:** 96%
Graduate: 105 men, 162 women	**Student/Faculty:** 13 to 1
Year: 4-1-4	**Tuition:** $49,906
Room & Board: $14,118	**Freshman Class:** 7044 applied, 2266 accepted, 447 enrolled
SAT CR/M: 650/620	**CEEB CODE:** 2037
Application Deadline: January 1	**HIGHLY COMPETITIVE**

Bard College, founded in 1860, is an independent liberal arts and sciences institution affiliated historically with the Association of Episcopal Colleges. Discussion-oriented seminars and independent study are encouraged, tutorials are on a one-to-one basis, and most classes are kept small. Figures in the above capsule and in this profile are approximate. There is 1 undergraduate school and 12 graduate schools. The 600-acre campus is in a rural area 100 miles north of New York City. Including any residence halls, there are 70 buildings.

STUDENT LIFE: 66% of undergraduates are from out of state, mostly the Middle Atlantic. Students are from 47 states, 57 foreign countries, and Canada. 8% are African American; 61% White; 5% Asian American; 2% Hispanic; 11% Foreign; 11% race unknown; 1% American Indian/Alaska Native. **Female To Male Ratio:** 1.3:1. The average age of freshmen is 18; all undergraduates, 20. 14% do not continue beyond their first year; 78% remain to graduate. **Housing:** 1450 students can be accommodated in college housing, which includes single-sex and coed dorms. In addition, there are special-interest houses, suites, and quiet dorms available. On-campus housing is guaranteed for the freshman year only and is available on a lottery system for upperclassmen. All students may keep cars.

FACULTY/CLASSROOMS: 57% of faculty are male; 43% are female. All teach undergraduates, and all do research. No introductory courses are taught by graduate students.

PROGRAMS OF STUDY: Bard confers B.A., B.S., B.Music, and B.P.S. (returning to college). Five-year dual-degree programs: B.M./B.A in music and in another liberal arts field; B.S. in Economics and Finance/B.A. degree in another liberal arts field. degrees. Associate, master's, and doctoral degrees are also awarded. Bachelor's degrees are awarded in AGRICULTURE (environmental studies), BIOLOGICAL SCIENCE (biology/biological science), COMMUNICATIONS AND THE ARTS (Arabic, art history and appreciation, Chinese, classical languages, creative writing, dance, dramatic arts, English literature, film arts, French, Germanic languages and literature, Hebrew, Italian, Japanese, literature, music, photography, Russian, Spanish, studio art, and theatre arts), COMPUTER AND PHYSICAL SCIENCE (chemistry, computer science, mathematics, and physics), SOCIAL SCIENCE (African studies, American studies, anthropology, area studies, Asian/Oriental studies, Celtic studies, classical/ancient civilization, economics, French studies, gender studies, German area studies, history, interdisciplinary studies, international studies, Italian studies, Judaic studies, Latin American studies, medieval studies, Middle Eastern studies, philosophy, political science/government, psychology, religion, Russian and Slavic studies, Sanskrit and Indian studies, science and society, sociology, Spanish studies, theological studies, and Victorian studies). Social studies, visual & performing arts, and languages & literatures have the largest enrollments.

ACTIVITIES: There are no fraternities or sororities. There are 150 groups on campus, including and Model UN, art, band, chamber groups, chess, choir, chorus, computers, dance, debate, drama, environmental, ethnic, film, forensics, international, jazz band, LGBT, literary magazine, musical theater, newspaper, opera, orchestra, photography, political, radio and TV, religious, social, social service, student government, and symphony. Popular campus events include Winter Carnival, Spring Festival, and International Students Cultural Show. **Sports:** There are 10 intercollegiate sports for men and 8 for women, and 9 intramural sports for men and 9 for women. Facilities include a gym with pool, baseball field, fitness & weight facilities, rugby, soccer and lacrosse fields, squash and tennis courts, cross-country trails, bike paths, and multi-purpose fields for activities such as ultimate frisbee and open recreation. **Gradu-**

ates: From July 1, 2015 to June 30, 2016, 436 bachelor's degrees were awarded. The most popular majors were social studies (32%), visual and performing arts (28%), and language and literature (21%). In an average class, 69% graduate in 4 years or less, 77% graduate in 5 years or less, and 78% graduate in 6 years or less.

SERVICES: Counseling and information services are available, as is tutoring in every subject. There is a reader service for the blind. **Library/ Resources:** The library contains 434,580 volumes, 8,120 microform items, and 5,083 audio/video tapes/CDs/DVDs, and subscribes to 36,900 periodicals including electronic. Computerized library services include interlibrary loans, database searching, Internet access, and Wi-Fi capability. Special learning facilities include an art gallery, radio station, ecology field station, the Levy Economics Institute, the Institute for Writing and Thinking, the Institute for Advanced Theology, the Center for Curatorial Studies and Art in Contemporary Culture, and an archeological station. **Physically Challenged Students:** 70% of the campus is accessible. Facilities include wheelchair ramps, elevators, special parking, specially equipped restrooms, lowered drinking fountains, and lowered telephones. **Special:** Bard offers opportunities for study abroad, internships, Washington and New York semesters, dual majors, student-designed majors, accelerated degree programs, and pass/fail options. A 3-2 engineering degree is available with the Columbia University, Washington University (St. Louis), and Dartmouth College Schools of Engineering. Other 3-2 degrees are available in forestry and environmental studies, social work, architecture, city and regional planning, public health, and business administration. There are also opportunities for independent study, multicultural and ethnic studies, area studies, human rights, and globalization and international affairs. **Visiting:** There are regularly scheduled orientations for prospective students, consisting of regularly scheduled daily tours and information sessions. Visitors may sit in on classes. To schedule a visit, contact the Admissions Office. **Campus Safety and Security:** Measures include 24-hour foot and vehicle patrol, emergency notification system, self-defense education, and security escort services. There are shuttle buses, emergency telephones, and lighted pathways/sidewalks. Volunteer emergency medical technicians on call 24 hours a day. There is also the Bard response to Rape and Associated Violence Education (BRAVE).

REQUIREMENTS: Bard places strong emphasis on the academic background and intellectual curiosity of applicants, as well as indications of the student's commitment to social and environmental concerns, independent research, volunteer work, and other important extracurricular activities. Students applying for admission are expected to have graduated from an accredited secondary school (the GED is accepted) and must submit written essays with the application. The high school record should include a full complement of college-preparatory courses. Honors and advanced placement courses are also considered. A GPA of 3.0 is required. AP credits are accepted. Important factors in the admissions decision are ability to finance college education, advanced placement or honors courses, recommendations by school officials, and extracurricular activities record. All students must complete a 3-week workshop in Language and Thinking (August of first year), a two and a half week Citizen Science program (January of first year); a first-year seminar; and a senior project. A conference in the junior year is required, and through a moderation process in the sophomore year, the student chooses a concentration in an academic department. A distribution of at least 1 course in each of the 9 academic areas is required, with 40 credits outside the division of the student's major and a total of 128 credit hours needed to graduate. "Rethinking Differences" a course fulfilling the diversity requirement, is also required. **Procedure:** Freshmen are admitted fall. There are early admissions and deferred admissions plans. Applications should be filed by January 1 for fall entry; November 1 for spring entry, along with a $50 fee. Notifications are sent April 1. 200 applicants were on the 2016 waiting list. Applications are accepted online. **Transfer Students:** 62 transfer students enrolled in 2015-2016. Admission requirements are the same as for regular applicants. A minimum GPA of 3.0 and an interview are recommended. High School transcript (when less than 2 years of college-level study completed), transfer questionnaire, and dean's report are required. 64 of 128 credits required for the bachelor's degree must be completed at Bard. **International Students:** There are 229 international students enrolled. The school actively recruits these students. They must take the TOEFL with a minimum score of 600 on the paper-based TOEFL (PBT) or 100 on the Internet-based version (iBT).

ADMISSIONS: 32% of the 2016-2017 applicants were accepted. **Admissions Contact:** Mary Backlund, Director of Admissions. Email: *admission@bard.edu* Web: *www.bard.edu*

FINANCIAL AID: In 2016-2017, 69% of all full-time freshmen and 70% of continuing full-time students received some form of financial aid. 64% of all full-time freshmen and 67% of continuing full-time students received need-based aid. The average freshman award was $41,950. Need-based scholarships or need-based grants averaged $38,766 ($49,226 maximum); need-based self-help aid (loans and jobs) averaged $6,361 ($6,500 maximum); and other non-need-based awards and non-need-based scholarships averaged $16,000 ($20,000 maximum). 30% of undergraduate students work part-time. Average annual earnings from campus work are $2000. The average financial indebtedness of the 2016 graduate was $28,261. Bard is a member of CSS. The CSS/Profile, state aid form, non-custodial profile, and/or business/farm supplement if applicable are required. The priority date for freshman financial aid applications for fall entry is February 1.

BARNARD COLLEGE/COLUMBIA UNIVERSITY — D-5

www.barnard.edu

New York, NY 10027 — **(212) 854-2014**

Fax: (212) 854-6220	**Email: admissions@barnard.edu**
Full-time: 2510 women	**Faculty:** IIB, ++$
Part-time: 38 women	**Ph.D.s:** n/av
Graduate: n/av	**Student/Faculty:** n/av
Year: semesters	**Tuition:** $47,631
Room & Board: $15,110	**Freshman Class:** 1306 accepted, 635 enrolled
SAT or ACT: required	**CEEB CODE:** 2038
Application Deadline: January 1	**MOST COMPETITIVE**

Barnard College, founded in 1889, is an undergraduate womens' liberal arts college and independent affiliate of Columbia University. The figures in the above capsule and in this profile are approximate. There is 1 undergraduate school. The 4-acre campus is in an urban area Manhattan's Upper West Side. Including any residence halls, there are 18 buildings.

STUDENT LIFE: 74% of undergraduates are from out of state, mostly the Middle Atlantic. Students are from 48 states, 35 foreign countries, and Canada. 53% are from public schools. 8% are Foreign; 7% African American; 6% two or more races; 53% White; 14% Asian American; 12% Hispanic; 1% race unknown. The student base is all female. The average age of freshmen is 18; all undergraduates, 20. 5% do not continue beyond their first year; 89% remain to graduate. **Housing:** 2057 students can be accommodated in college housing, which includes single-sex and coed dorms, on-campus apartments, and off-campus apartments. In addition, there are special-interest houses. On-campus housing is guaranteed for all 4 years. 90% of students live on campus; of those, 75% remain on campus on weekends. Alcohol is not permitted. All students may keep cars.

FACULTY/CLASSROOMS: 35% of faculty are male; 65% are female. All teach undergraduates, and do research. No introductory courses are taught by graduate students. The average class size in an introductory lecture is 30; in a laboratory is 11; and in a regular course is 13.

PROGRAMS OF STUDY: Barnard College confers B.A. degrees. Bachelor's degrees are awarded in BIOLOGICAL SCIENCE (biochemistry and biology/biological science), COMMUNICATIONS AND THE ARTS (art history and appreciation, classics, comparative literature, dance, dramatic arts, English, film arts, French, German, Greek, Italian, Latin, linguistics, music, Russian, and Spanish), COMPUTER AND PHYSICAL SCIENCE (astronomy, chemistry, computer science, mathematics, physics, and statistics), ENGINEERING AND ENVIRONMENTAL DESIGN (architecture and environmental science), SOCIAL SCIENCE (American studies, anthropology, biopsychology, classical/ancient civilization, East Asian studies, economics, European studies, history, international studies, medieval studies, Middle Eastern studies, philosophy, political science/government, psychology, religion, sociology, urban studies, and women's studies). English, psychology, and economics are the strongest academically, and have the largest enrollments.

ACTIVITIES: There are no fraternities or sororities. There are 100 groups on campus, including art, band, cheerleading, choir, chorale, chorus, dance, debate, drama, environmental, ethnic, film, international, jazz band, LGBT, literary magazine, marching band, Model UN, musical theater, newspaper, opera, orchestra, pep band, photography, political, professional, radio and TV, religious, social, social service, student government, symphony, and yearbook. Popular campus events include Spring and Winter Festivals, Founders Day and Take Back the Night. **Sports:** There are 16 intercollegiate sports for women, and 16 intramural sports for women. Facilities include pools, weight rooms, gyms, tennis courts, an indoor track, and a boat slip. **Graduates:** From July 1, 2015 to June 30, 2016, 692 bachelor's degrees were awarded. The most popular majors were social sciences (30%), psychology (13%), and visual and performing arts (10%). In an average class, 2% graduate in 3 years or less, 82% graduate in 4 years or less, 88% graduate in 5 years or less, and 89% graduate in 6 years or less.

SERVICES: Counseling and information services are available, as is tutoring in every subject. There is a reader service for the blind. A student-staffed writing room is available for students of all levels of writing ability, and a math help room is also available to students in all math courses. **Library/Resources:** The library contains 204,906 volumes, 17,705 microform items, and 17,448 audio/video tapes/CDs/DVDs, and subscribes to 543 periodicals including electronic. Computerized library services include interlibrary loans, database searching, Internet access, and Wi-Fi capability. Special learning facilities include an art gallery, radio station, greenhouses, science laboratories, child development research and study center, dance studios, modern theaters, womens' research archives within a womens' center, and multimedia labs and classrooms. **Physically Challenged Students:** 90% of the campus is accessible. Facilities include wheelchair ramps, elevators, special parking, specially equipped restrooms, special class scheduling, lowered drinking fountains, lowered telephones, and special housing. The Office of Disability Services provides a variety of support services to students with permanent and temporary disabilities. **Special:** Barnard offers cross-registration with Columbia University. There are more than 2500 internships with New York City companies and research centers, and study abroad worldwide. A 3-2 engineering program with the Columbia School of Engineering and double-degree programs with the Columbia University Schools of International and Public Affairs, Law, and Dentistry, and the Jewish Theological Seminary are possible. Cross registration programs also with the Juilliard School and the Manhattan School of Music. The college offers selective dual and student-designed majors and multidisciplinary majors. There is 1 national honor society and a chapter of Phi Beta Kappa. **Visiting:** There are regularly scheduled orientations for prospective students, as well as open house programs for prospective students regularly scheduled throughout the year. There are guides for informal visits, visitors may sit in on classes, and stay overnight. To schedule a visit, contact The Office of Admissions at admissions@barnard.edu. **Campus Safety and Security:** Measures include 24-hour foot and vehicle patrol and security escort services. There are shuttle buses, emergency telephones, lighted pathways/sidewalks, safety and security education programs.

REQUIREMENTS: The SAT or ACT is required. If taking the SAT, an applicant must also take 2 SAT Subject tests. A GED is accepted. Applicants should prepare with 4 years of English, and at least 3 years each of math, science, a foreign language and history. An interview is recommended. AP credits are accepted. Important factors in the admissions decision are advanced placement or honors courses, personality/intangible qualities, recommendations by school officials, leadership record, parents or siblings attended your school, evidence of special talent, geographical diversity, and extracurricular activities record. A total of 120 credits is required, with a minimum GPA of 2.0. All students must complete a major and may elect a double major or minor as well. Students must take 2 semesters each of a foreign language, and complete a series of other foundation courses that encompass the humanities, social sciences and sciences with global, technological, quantitative and cultural diversity coursework. Students must also complete 1 semester each in first-year seminar, and first-year English. **Procedure:** Freshmen are admitted in the fall. Entrance exams should be taken by January of the senior year. There are early decision, early admissions, and deferred admissions plans. Early decision applications should be filed by November 1; regular applications, by January 1 for fall entry, along with a $70 fee. Notification of early decision is sent December 15; regular decision, April 1. 280 early decision candidates were accepted for the 2016-2017 class. Applications are accepted online. **Transfer Students:** 80 transfer students enrolled in 2015-2016. The SAT or ACT is required. Deadline for transfer applicants is April 1 (fall term) and November 1 (spring term). They must submit the common application, a writing supplement, and high school and college transcripts. Applicants and be in good standing from prior institutions attended and will only be considered at sophomore or junior year entry. 60 of 120 credits required for the bachelor's degree must be completed at Barnard College. **International Students:** There are 211 international students enrolled. The school actively recruits these students. They must take the TOEFL with a minimum score of 600 on the paper-based TOEFL (PBT) or 100 on the Internet-based version (iBT), IELTS is also accepted. They must also take the SAT or ACT. Applicants who take the SAT must also take 2 SAT Subject tests.

ADMISSIONS: The SAT scores for the 2016-2017 freshman class were: Critical Reading-- 2% below 500, 12% between 500 and 599, 41% between 600 and 699, and 46% between 700 and 800. Math-- 2% below 500, 16% between 500 and 599, 47% between 600 and 699, and 35% between 700 and 800. Writing-- 3% below 500, 8% between 500 and 599, 38% between 600 and 699, and 51% between 700 and 800. The ACT scores were 2% between 18 and 23, 34% between 24 and 29, and 64% above 30. **Admissions Contact:** Jennifer Fondiller, Dean of Enrollment Management. Email: *admissions@barnard.edu* Web: *www.barnard.edu*

FINANCIAL AID: In 2016-2017, 45% of all full-time freshmen and 30% of continuing full-time students received some form of financial aid. 45% of all full-time freshmen and 30% of continuing full-time students received need-based aid. The average freshman award was $48,352. Need-based scholarships or need-based grants averaged $44,840; and need-based self-help aid (loans and jobs) averaged $7,707. 46% of undergraduate students work part-time. The average financial indebtedness of the 2016 graduate was $16,733. Barnard College is a member of CSS. The CSS/Profile, state aid form, college's own financial statement, parents' and student's federal tax returns, and the business and/or farm supplement are required. The priority date for freshman financial aid applications for fall entry is February 15.

BERKELEY COLLEGE/NEW YORK CITY CAMPUS *(The complete profile is made available exclusively on our website, www.barronspac.com)*

BERKELEY COLLEGE/WHITE PLAINS CAMPUS *(The complete profile is made available exclusively on our website, www.barronspac.com)*

BORICUA COLLEGE — D-5
www.boricuacollege.edu

New York, NY 10032	**(212) 694-1000** **(718) 782-2200**
Fax: (212) 694-1015 or (718) 782-2050	**Email: acruz@ boricuacolleg**
Full-time: 260 men, 910 women	**Faculty:** n/av
Part-time: n/av	**Ph.D.s:** n/av
Graduate: n/av	**Student/Faculty:** n/av
Year: 4-1-4, summer session	**Tuition:** $10,100
Room & Board: n/app	**Freshman Class:** n/av **CEEB CODE:** 2901
Application Deadline: n/av	**COMPETITIVE**

Boricua College, founded in 1974, is a private college for bilingual students, designed to meet the needs of the Spanish-speaking community. Figures in the above capsule and in this profile are approximate. There are 4 undergraduate schools and 2 graduate schools. In addition to regional accreditation, Boricua has baccalaureate program accreditation with MSCHE. The campus is in an urban area in Upper Manhattan, New York, in the historic Audubon Terrace complex. Including any residence halls, there are 4 buildings.

STUDENT LIFE: 100% of undergraduates are from New York. 70% are from public schools. 85% are Hispanic; 10% African American; 1% White. 85% are Catholic. **Female To Male Ratio:** 3.5:1. The average age of freshmen is 29; all undergraduates, 32. 12% do not continue beyond their first year; 80% remain to graduate. **Housing:** Alcohol is not permitted. No one may keep cars.

FACULTY/CLASSROOMS: No introductory courses are taught by graduate students.

PROGRAMS OF STUDY: Boricua confers B.A. degrees. Associate degrees are also awarded. Bachelor's degrees are awarded in BUSINESS (business administration and management), EDUCATION (elementary education), SOCIAL SCIENCE (human services and liberal arts/general studies). Applied science paralegal studies is the strongest academically. Human services has the largest enrollment.

ACTIVITIES: There are no fraternities or sororities. There are 5 groups

on campus, including art, chorus, drama, newspaper, and student government. Popular campus events include Cultural Programs, Puerto Rican Discovery Day, Christmas and Spring concerts with a chorus and orchestra. **Sports:** Facilities include a gymnasium that hosts yoga, dance, martial arts, volleyball, basketball, and lectures on personal health and physical activities. **Graduates:** From July 1, 2015 to June 30, 2016, 90 bachelor's degrees were awarded. The most popular majors were human services, early childhood education, and business administration. In an average class, 65% graduate in 4 years or less and 35% graduate in 5 years or less.

SERVICES: Counseling and information services are available, as is tutoring in most subjects. **Library/Resources:** The 4 libraries contain 15,778 volumes, 5,000 audio/video tapes/CDs/DVDs, and subscribe to 5,000 periodicals including electronic. Computerized library services include interlibrary loans, database searching, Internet access, and Wi-Fi capability. Special learning facilities include an art gallery, Puerto Rican Disapora collection, a map collection, museum, theatre, cultural center, and natural science laboratories. **Physically Challenged Students:** Facilities include elevators and specially equipped restrooms. **Visiting:** There are regularly scheduled orientations for prospective students. To schedule a visit, contact Abraham Cruzat or Miriam Prefferat. **Campus Safety and Security:** There are shuttle buses, emergency telephones, and lighted pathways/sidewalks.

REQUIREMENTS: Boricua administers its own tests to prospective students, although either the SAT or ACT is accepted. Applicants must be graduates of an accredited secondary school or have a GED. 2 letters of recommendation and an admissions interview are required. Applicants must demonstrate a working knowledge of English and Spanish to a faculty panel. CLEP credits are accepted. Important factors in the admissions decision are leadership record, personality/intangible qualities, and recommendations by school officials. **Procedure:** Freshmen are admitted in the fall, spring, and summer. There are early decision and rolling admissions plans. Application deadlines are open. Application fee is $30. **Transfer Students:** Applicants with associate degrees may transfer up to 60 credits. All college credits passed with grade C and above are accepted. 80 of 124 credits required for the bachelor's degree must be completed at Boricua.

Admissions Contact: Abraham Cruz, Director of Student Services. Email: *acruz@boricuacolleg* Web: *www.boricuacollege.edu*

FINANCIAL AID: In 2016-2017, 100% of all full-time freshmen and continuing full-time students received some form of financial aid. 100% of all full-time freshmen and continuing full-time students received need-based aid. The average freshman award was $100. Boricua is a member of CSS. The FAFSA code is 013029. Check with the school for current application deadlines.

CANISIUS COLLEGE — A-3

www.canisius.edu

Buffalo, NY 14208 — **(716) 888-2200**

Fax: (716) 888-3230	**Email:** admissions@canisius.edu
Full-time: 1180 men, 1294 women	**Faculty:** 172; IIA, av$
Part-time: 75 men, 46 women	**Ph.D.s:** 98%
Graduate: 439 men, 700 women	**Student/Faculty:** 11 to 1
Year: semesters, summer session	**Tuition:** $34,515
Room & Board: $13,022	**Freshman Class:** 4620 applied, 3537 accepted, 600 enrolled
SAT CR/M: 535/545 **ACT:** 25	**CEEB CODE:** 2073
Application Deadline: March 1	**COMPETITIVE**

Canisius College, founded in 1870, is a private Roman Catholic college in the Jesuit tradition. It offers undergraduate programs in the liberal arts and sciences, business, education, and human services. The figures in the above capsule and in this profile are approximate. There are 3 undergraduate schools and 3 graduate schools. In addition to regional accreditation, Canisius has baccalaureate program accreditation with AACSB, CAHEA, NCATE, CACREP, CAATE, CED, and CAEP. The 72-acre campus is in an urban area in Buffalo NY. Including any residence halls, there are 56 buildings.

STUDENT LIFE: 91% of undergraduates are from New York. Others are from 38 states, 19 foreign countries, and Canada. 70% are from public schools. 8% are African American; 8% race unknown; 70% White; 5% Hispanic; 5% Foreign; 2% Asian American; 2% two or more races. **Female To Male Ratio:** 1.2:1. The average age of freshmen is 18; all undergraduates, 20. 17% do not continue beyond their first year; 71% remain to graduate. **Housing:** 1200 students can be accommodated in college housing, which includes single-sex and coed dorms, on-campus apartments, and off-campus apartments. In addition, there are special-interest houses, an intercultural hall, townhouses, honor's dorm, and Bosch or Frisch halls (suite-style rooms) for first-year students. On-campus housing is guaranteed for all 4 years, and is available on a first-come, first-served basis, and is available on a lottery system for upperclassmen. 54% of students commute. All students may keep cars.

FACULTY/CLASSROOMS: 58% of faculty are male; 42% are female. All teach undergraduates, and do research. No introductory courses are taught by graduate students. The average class size in an introductory lecture is 23; in a laboratory is 18; and in a regular course is 20.

PROGRAMS OF STUDY: Canisius confers B.A., B.S., B.A.Ed. and B.S.Ed. degrees. Master's degrees are also awarded. Bachelor's degrees are awarded in AGRICULTURE (environmental studies), BIOLOGICAL SCIENCE (biochemistry, bioinformatics, biology/biological science, cell biology, neurosciences, and zoology), BUSINESS (accounting, banking and finance, business administration and management, business communications, business economics, entrepreneurial studies, fashion merchandising, finance, international business management, management information systems, management science, marketing management, marketing/retailing/merchandising, operations research, and sports management), COMMUNICATIONS AND THE ARTS (art history, classical languages, communications, creative writing, digital communications, English, fine arts, French, German, journalism, media arts, modern language, music, music performance, Spanish, speech/debate/rhetoric, and theatre arts), COMPUTER AND PHYSICAL SCIENCE (chemistry, computer science, information sciences and systems, mathematics, and physics), EDUCATION (athletic training, business education, childhood education, early childhood education, education, education administration, education of the deaf and hearing impaired, education of the exceptional child, elementary education, English education, foreign languages education, mathematics education, middle school education, physical education, science education, social studies education, special education, and teaching English as a second/foreign language (TESOL/TEFOL)), ENGINEERING AND ENVIRONMENTAL DESIGN (computational sciences, environmental science, and preengineering), HEALTH PROFESSIONS (clinical science, exercise science, medical laboratory technology, predentistry, premedicine, prepharmacy, preveterinary science, and sports medicine), SOCIAL SCIENCE (anthropology, biblical studies, cognitive science, criminal justice, European studies, gerontology, history, humanities and social science, international relations, Latin American studies, liberal arts/general studies, philosophy, prelaw, psychology, social science, sociology, urban studies, and women's studies). Accounting, biology, and finance are the strongest academically. Psychology, business administration/management, and communication studies have the largest enrollments.

ACTIVITIES: 1% of women belong to 1 national sorority. There are 140 groups on campus, including art, band, cheerleading, chess, choir, chorale, computers, dance, drama, drill team, environmental, ethnic, honors, international, jazz band, LGBT, literary magazine, musical theater, newspaper, orchestra, pep band, political, professional, radio and TV, religious, social, social service, student government, and yearbook. Popular campus events include Fall Semiformal, International Fest, and Canisius Concert Series. **Sports:** There are 8 intercollegiate sports for men and 9 for women, and 12 intramural sports for men and 12 for women. Facilities include an athletic center with a 25-yard pool, training rooms, a sports complex with Astroturf playing fields, rifle range, and a mirrored dance studio. **Graduates:** From July 1, 2015 to June 30, 2016, 648 bachelor's degrees were awarded. The most popular majors were business/marketing (32%), biological/life science (14%), and communication (10%). 30 companies recruited on campus in 2015-2016. In an average class, 61% graduate in 4 years or less, 70% graduate in 5 years or less, and 71% graduate in 6 years or less.

SERVICES: Counseling and information services are available, as is tutoring in every subject. There is a reader service for the blind, and remedial math, reading, and writing. **Library/Resources:** The library contains 313,916 volumes, 599,947 microform items, 14,674 audio/video tapes/CDs/DVDs, and subscribes to 52,472 periodicals including electronic. Computerized library services include interlibrary loans, database searching, Internet access, and Wi-Fi capability. Special learning facilities include an art gallery, radio station, TV station, television studio, foreign language lab, media-assisted classrooms, digital media lab, and a musical instrument digital interface classroom. **Physically Challenged Students:** 90% of the campus is accessible. Facilities include wheelchair ramps, elevators, special parking, specially equipped restrooms, special class scheduling, lowered drinking fountains, lowered telephones, automatic doors, TDD, a shuttle service, distraction-free testing spaces, and adjustable classroom desks. **Special:** Canisius offers internships, credit by exam, pass/fail options, dual majors, a Washington semester, work-study programs, and study abroad in over a dozen countries. Cooperative programs are available with the Fashion Institute of Technology in New York City. Cross-registration is permitted with the schools in the Western New York Consortium of Higher Education. Canisius also offers early assurance and joint degree programs, with SUNY health professions schools in Buffalo and Syracuse, and a 3-2 MBA. There are 16 national honor societies, a freshman honors program, and 5 departmental honors programs. **Visiting:** There are regularly scheduled orientations for prospective students, including an admissions interview or group session, campus tour, and financial aid appointment by request. Also available are summer visitations for families, selected Saturday visits, multiple Fall Open Houses and an Open House in the Spring, a Financial Aid Workshop in January, and overnight stays for admitted students. There are guides for informal visits and visitors may sit in on classes. To schedule a visit, contact the Admissions Office. **Campus Safety and Security:** Measures include 24-hour foot and vehicle patrol, emergency notification system, self-defense education, and security escort services. There are shuttle buses, emergency telephones, lighted pathways/sidewalks, controlled access to dorms/residences, crime prevention officer, bicycle patrols, crime prevention programs, and blue light emergency stations around campus.

REQUIREMENTS: All students must submit high school transcript (or GED) and SAT or ACT results. College preparatory course work should include 4 units each of English and social science, 3 units each of math, science, and foreign language. Students with a B+ average and a satisfactory SAT score are most competitive. An essay and an interview are recommended. AP and CLEP credits are accepted. Important factors in the admissions decision are leadership record, recommendations by school officials, and advanced placement or honors courses. Students take 12 required courses and complete 6 knowledge and skills requirement areas to satisfy their requirements. In addition, students must take 10 3-credit courses in the major. A minimum of 120 credit hours and a GPA of 2.0 are required for graduation. **Procedure:** Freshmen are admitted fall, spring, and summer. Entrance exams should be taken during the junior or senior year. There are deferred admissions and rolling admissions plans. Applications should be filed by March 1 for fall entry, along with a $40 fee. Notification is sent on a rolling basis. Applications are accepted on-line. **Transfer Students:** 117 transfer students enrolled in 2015-2016. Applicants must present a minimum GPA of 2.0 and a Transfer Recommendation Form. Students may enroll during the fall, spring, and summer. 30 of 120 credits required for the bachelor's degree must be completed at Canisius. **International Students:** There are 127 international students enrolled. The school actively recruits these students. They must take the TOEFL with a minimum score of 550 on the paper-based TOEFL (PBT) or 79 on the Internet-based version (iBT). The IELTS or STEPs are also acceptable. They must also take the SAT or ACT.

ADMISSIONS: 77% of the 2016-2017 applicants were accepted. The SAT scores for the 2016-2017 freshman class were: Critical Reading-- 33% below 500, 45% between 500 and 599, 20% between 600 and 699, and 2% between 700 and 800. Math-- 27% below 500, 45% between 500 and 599, 24% between 600 and 699, and 4% between 700 and 800. The ACT scores were 2% between 12 and 17, 37% between 18 and 23, 50% between 24 and 29, and 11% above 30. 48% of the current freshmen were in the top fifth of their class; 75% were in the top two fifths. 6 freshmen graduated first in their class. **Admissions Contact:** Justin Rogers, Director of Admissions. Email: *admissions@canisius.edu* Web: *www.canisius.edu*

FINANCIAL AID: In 2016-2017, 98% of all full-time freshmen and 97% of continuing full-time students received some form of financial aid. 86% of all full-time freshmen and 80% of continuing full-time students received need-based aid. The average freshman award was $33,160. Need-based scholarships or need-based grants averaged $10,090 ($45,186 maximum); need-based self-help aid (loans and jobs) averaged $4,735 ($7,900 maximum); non-need-based athletic scholarships averaged $18,922 ($48,426 maximum); other non-need-based awards and non-need-based scholarships averaged $17,337 ($46,003 maximum); and $23,879 from other forms of aid. 22% of undergraduate students work part-time. Average annual earnings from campus work are $1440. The average financial indebtedness of the 2016 graduate was $33,973. Canisius is a member of CSS. The FAFSA code is 002681. The priority date for freshman financial aid applications for fall entry is February 15.

CAZENOVIA COLLEGE — C-3

www.cazenovia.edu

Cazenovia, NY 13035	(315) 655-7208 (800) 654-3210
Fax: (315) 655-2190	**Email:** admission@cazcollege.edu
Full-time: 250 men, 700 women	**Faculty:** IIB, -$
Part-time: 35 men, 120 women	**Ph.D.s:** n/av
Graduate: n/av	**Student/Faculty:** 15 to 1
Year: semesters, summer session	**Tuition:** $32,674
Room & Board: $13,796	**Freshman Class:** n/av
SAT or ACT: recommended	**CEEB CODE:** 2078
Application Deadline: open	**COMPETITIVE**

Cazenovia College, founded in 1824, is a private institution offering degree programs in liberal arts and pre-professional studies. The figures in the above capsule and in this profile are approximate. There is 1 undergraduate school. In addition to regional accreditation, Cazenovia has baccalaureate program accreditation with IACBE and TEAC. The 40-acre campus is in a small town in Madison County, and 18 miles southeast of Syracuse, NY. Including any residence halls, there are 26 buildings.

STUDENT LIFE: 80% of undergraduates are from New York. Others are from 26 states, 4 foreign countries, and Canada. 90% are from public schools. 86% are White; 4% African American; 4% Hispanic; 2% Asian American; 2% American Indian/Alaska Native; 1% Foreign. **Female To Male Ratio:** 2.9:1. The average age of freshmen is 18. **Housing:** 817 students can be accommodated in college housing, which includes single-sex and coed dorms, on-campus apartments, off-campus apartments, and all-female residence hall, and upperclass-only housing. 90% of students live on campus. Upperclassmen may keep cars.

FACULTY/CLASSROOMS: 40% of faculty are male; 60% are female. All teach undergraduates. No introductory courses are taught by graduate students. The average class size in an introductory lecture is 20; in a laboratory is 15; and in a regular course is 16.

PROGRAMS OF STUDY: Cazenovia confers B.A., B.S., B.F.A., and B.P.S. degrees. Associate degrees are also awarded. Bachelor's degrees are awarded in AGRICULTURE (environmental studies), BUSINESS (business administration and management and management science), COMMUNICATIONS AND THE ARTS (communications, English, studio art, and visual design), EDUCATION (early childhood education and elementary education), ENGINEERING AND ENVIRONMENTAL DESIGN (commercial art and interior design), SOCIAL SCIENCE (criminology, fashion design and technology, human services, liberal arts/general studies, psychology, and social science). Interior design, and equine management are the strongest academically. Management has the largest enrollment.

ACTIVITIES: There are no fraternities or sororities. There are 52 groups on campus, including art, band, cheerleading, choir, chorale, computers, debate, drama, environmental, ethnic, honors, LGBT, literary magazine, musical theater, newspaper, political, professional, religious, social, social service, student government, and yearbook. **Sports:** There are 10 intercollegiate sports for men and 10 for women, and 9 intramural sports for men and 9 for women. Facilities include an athletic center with a pool, 2 gyms, a fitness center, baseball, basketball, cross country, equestrian riding, lacrosse, soccer, softball, women's volleyball, dodge ball, flag football, floor hockey, ultimate frisbee, cheeringleading, crew, coed golf, and tennis. **Graduates:** From July 1, 2015 to June 30, 2016, 163 bachelor's degrees were awarded. The most popular majors were management (39%), human services (25%), and visual communications (19%).

SERVICES: Counseling and information services are available, as is tutoring in most subjects. There is a reader service for the blind, and remedial math, reading, and writing. **Library/Resources:** The library contains 83,340 volumes, 14,727 microform items, and 4,160 audio/video tapes/CDs/DVDs, and subscribes to 61,000 periodicals including electronic. Computerized library services include interlibrary loans, database searching, Internet access, and Wi-Fi capability. Special learning facilities include an art gallery. **Physically Challenged Students:** 86% of the campus is accessible. Facilities include wheelchair ramps, elevators, special parking, specially equipped restrooms, special class scheduling, lowered telephones, and special housing. **Special:** Cazenovia offers internships, a Washington semester, work-study, B.A.-B.S. degrees in liberal studies and liberal and professional studies. There is a study-abroad program at Canterbury Christ Church University in the United Kingdom. There are 3 national honor societies, a freshman honors program, and 2 departmental honors programs. **Visiting:** There are regularly scheduled orientations for prospective students, consist of a welcome by the president and deans, financial aid sessions, placement testing, academic advising, and registration. There are guides for informal visits, visitors may sit in on classes, and stay overnight. To schedule a visit, contact the Admissions Office. **Campus Safety and Security:** Measures include 24-hour foot and vehicle patrol, emergency notification system, and security escort services. There are emergency telephones, lighted pathways/sidewalks, and controlled access to dorms/residences.

REQUIREMENTS: The SAT or ACT is recommended. Applicants should be graduates of an accredited secondary school or the equivalent. A recommendation from a guidance counselor or teacher is required. AP and CLEP credits are accepted. Important factors in the admissions decision are advanced placement or honors courses and leadership record. A total of 120 semester credits and a GPA of 2.0 are required for the bachelor's degree. Students must take courses in speech, academic writing, diversity and social consciousness, science or math, visual literacy, communications, ethics, cultural literacy, and research methods. They must also demonstrate math proficiency and complete a senior capstone course. **Procedure:** Freshmen are admitted in the fall and spring. Entrance exams should be taken by the fall of the senior year. There are deferred admissions and rolling admissions plans. Application deadlines are open. Application fee is $30. Applications are accepted online. **Transfer Students:** 66 transfer students enrolled in 2015-2016. Applicants must present at least 12 college credits, with a minimum GPA of 2.0, and official transcripts from previous colleges attended. Students with fewer than 24 credits must also submit a high school transcript. 30 of 120 credits required for the bachelor's degree must be completed at Cazenovia. **International Students:** There are 4 international students enrolled. The school actively recruits these students. They must take the TOEFL.

Admissions Contact: Robert A. Croot, Dean for Admissions and Financial Aid. Email: *admission@cazcollege.edu* Web: *www.cazenovia.edu*

FINANCIAL AID: Cazenovia is a member of CSS. The FAFSA code is 002685. The priority date for freshman financial aid applications for fall entry is March 1.

CITY UNIVERSITY OF NEW YORK/ BARUCH COLLEGE — D-5

www.cuny.edu

New York, NY 10010 — **(646) 312-2010**

Fax: (646) 312-1361	**Email:** admissions@baruch.cuny.edu
Full-time: 5712 men, 5153 women	**Faculty:** IIA, ++$
Part-time: 1884 men, 2108 women	**Ph.D.s:** 59%
Graduate: 1550 men, 1683 women	**Student/Faculty:** 16 to 1
Year: semesters, summer session	**Tuition:** $6561 ($16,581)
Room & Board: $15,048	**Freshman Class:** 19768 applied, 5516 accepted, 1282 enrolled
SAT or ACT: required	**CEEB CODE:** 2034
Application Deadline: February 1	**HIGHLY COMPETITIVE**

Baruch College, was founded in 1919, and became a separate unit of the City University of New York in 1968. It offers undergraduate programs in business and public administration and liberal arts and sciences. There are 3 undergraduate schools and 3 graduate schools. In addition to regional accreditation, Baruch has baccalaureate program accreditation with AACSB. The 4-acre campus is in an urban area in New York City. Including any residence halls, there are 6 buildings.

STUDENT LIFE: 85% of undergraduates are from New York. Others are from 2 states, and 168 foreign countries. 62% are from public schools. 9% are African American; 30% Asian American; 29% White; 18% Hispanic; 12% Foreign; 1% two or more races. **Male To Female Ratio:** 1.0:1. The average age of freshmen is 18; all undergraduates, 24. 12% do not continue beyond their first year; 66% remain to graduate. **Housing:** 236 students can be accommodated in college housing, which includes coed dorms. On-campus housing is available on a lottery system for upperclassmen. 98% of students commute. Alcohol is not permitted. No one may keep cars.

FACULTY/CLASSROOMS: 60% of faculty are male; 40% are female. 93% teach undergraduates, and 89% do research. Graduate students teach 8% of introductory courses. The average class size in an introductory lecture is 275; in a laboratory is 20; and in a regular course is 35.

PROGRAMS OF STUDY: Baruch confers B.A., B.S. and B.B.A. degrees. Master's degrees are also awarded. Bachelor's degrees are awarded in BUSINESS (accounting, investments and securities, management science, marketing management, marketing/retailing/merchandising, operations research, personnel management, and real estate), COMMUNICATIONS AND THE ARTS (advertising, communications, English, journalism, music, and Spanish), COMPUTER AND PHYSICAL SCIENCE (actuarial science, information sciences and systems, mathematics, and statistics), SOCIAL SCIENCE (economics, history, industrial and organizational psychology, philosophy, political science/government, psychology, public affairs, and sociology). Economics, English, and math are the strongest academically. Accounting, finance, and marketing have the largest enrollments.

ACTIVITIES: There are no fraternities or sororities. There are 130 groups on campus, including cheerleading, chess, chorus, computers, dance, debate, drama, ethnic, honors, international, LGBT, literary magazine, newspaper, photography, political, professional, radio and TV, religious, social, social service, student government, and yearbook. Popular campus events include Club Fairs, Relay for Life and Caribbean Week. **Sports:** There are 7 intercollegiate sports for men and 7 for women, and 5 intramural sports for men and 5 for women. Facilities include a swimming pool, two gyms, a weight room, an exercise room, and racquetball courts. **Graduates:** From July 1, 2015 to June 30, 2016, 3082 bachelor's degrees were awarded. The most popular majors were finance and investments (23%), accounting (20%), and marketing (10%). 172 companies recruited on campus in 2015-2016. In an average class, 5% graduate in 4 years or less, 63% graduate in 5 years or less, and 67% graduate in 6 years or less.

SERVICES: Counseling and information services are available, as is tutoring in most subjects. There is a reader service for the blind. Note takers and large-print computer screens are available, as well as interpreters for the deaf. **Library/Resources:** The library contains 655,671 volumes, 2.1 million microform items, and 52,880 audio/video tapes/CDs/DVDs, and subscribes to 89,951 periodicals including electronic. Computerized library services include interlibrary loans, database searching, Internet access, and Wi-Fi capability. Special learning facilities include an art gallery, radio station, journalism lab, and a newspaper lab. **Physically Challenged Students:** All of the campus is accessible. Facilities include wheelchair ramps, elevators, specially equipped restrooms, special class scheduling, lowered drinking fountains, and lowered telephones. **Special:** Students may take courses at all CUNY schools. The college offers internships and study abroad in Great Britain, France, Germany, Mexico, and Israel. Students may design their own liberal arts major. A federal work-study program is available, and pass/fail options are permitted for liberal arts majors. Students may combine any undergraduate major with a master's in accountancy. There are 4 national honor societies, a freshman honors program, and 17 departmental honors programs. **Visiting:** There are regularly scheduled orientations for prospective students, including a meeting with an admissions counselor. There are guides for informal visits. To schedule a visit, contact the Admissions Office. **Campus Safety and Security:** Measures include 24-hour foot and vehicle patrol, self-defense education, and security escort services. There are lighted pathways/sidewalks, controlled access to dorms/residences. There are fire safety directors and an ID system that uses card swipe in turnstiles for entry.

REQUIREMENTS: The SAT or ACT is required. Applicants must provide a high school transcript a GED will be accepted indicating a minimum average grade of 81% in academic subjects, with a minimum of 14 credits. AP and CLEP credits are accepted. Important factors in the admissions decision are personality/intangible qualities, advanced placement or honors courses, and leadership record. Students must complete a minimum of 120 credits for the B.A. or B.S. and 124 for the B.B.A., with at least 24 hours in the major, and maintain a GPA of 2.0. Students' core curriculum should include courses in English, literature, communications, history, philosophy, psychology, microeconomics, and fine and performing arts. **Procedure:** Freshmen are admitted fall and spring. Entrance exams should be taken March 1. There are early decision and rolling admissions plans. Early decision applications should be filed by December 1; regular applications, by February 1 for fall entry; and October 1 for spring entry, along with a $65 fee. Notifications are sent February 1. Applications are accepted on-line. **Transfer Students:** 2085 transfer students enrolled in 2015-2016. Applicants must have a minimum GPA of 2.5 for 12 to 34.9 credits submitted, a minimum GPA of 2.25 for 35 to 59.9 credits, and a minimum GPA of 2.0 for 60 or more credits. Business applicants must have a 2.75 GPA. Students applying for transfer with fewer than 12 credits earned must have a minimum GPA of 2.5 and a minimum high school average of 80%. 32 of 128 credits required for the bachelor's degree must be completed at Baruch. **International Students:** There are 1281 international students enrolled. They must take the TOEFL with a minimum score of 550 on the paper-based TOEFL (PBT) or 80 on the Internet-based version (iBT). They must also take the SAT or ACT.

ADMISSIONS: 28% of the 2016-2017 applicants were accepted. The SAT scores for the 2016-2017 freshman class were: Critical Reading-- 14% below 500, 43% between 500 and 599, 35% between 600 and 699, and 8% between 700 and 800. Math-- 3% below 500, 25% between 500 and 599, 51% between 600 and 699, and 22% between 700 and 800. **Admissions Contact:** Marisa Delacruz, Director of Undergraduate Admissions. Email: *marisa.delacruz@baruch.cuny.edu* Web: *www.cuny.edu*

FINANCIAL AID: The FAFSA code is 007273. The deadline for filing freshman financial aid applications for fall entry is August 12.

CITY UNIVERSITY OF NEW YORK/ BROOKLYN COLLEGE — D-5

www.brooklyn.cuny.edu

Brooklyn, NY 11210 — **(718) 951-5001**

Fax: (718) 951-4506	**Email: admissions@brooklyn.cuny.edu**
Full-time: 3852 men, 5386 women	**Faculty:** 543; IIA, ++$
Part-time: 1472 men, 2389 women	**Ph.D.s:** 96%
Graduate: 1169 men, 2256 women	**Student/Faculty:** 15 to 1
Year: semesters, summer session	**Tuition:** $5884 ($15,004)
Room & Board: n/app	**Freshman Class:** 19843 applied, 6346 accepted, 1148 enrolled
SAT or ACT: required	**CEEB CODE:** 2046
Application Deadline: October 1	**COMPETITIVE+**

Brooklyn College, established in 1930, is a publicly supported college of liberal arts, sciences, pre-professional, and professional studies. It is part of the City University of New York and serves the commuter student. Figures in the above capsule and in this profile are approximate. There are 5 undergraduate schools and 5 graduate schools. In addition to regional accreditation, Brooklyn has baccalaureate program accreditation with ADA, NCATE, and ASLHA. The 36-acre campus is in an urban area in Brooklyn, NY. Including any residence halls, there are 15 buildings.

STUDENT LIFE: 99% of undergraduates are from New York. Others are from 10 states, 140 foreign countries, and Canada. 78% are from public schools. 40% are White; 4% Foreign; 25% African American; 16% Asian American; 14% Hispanic; 1% two or more races. **Female To Male Ratio:** 1.5:1. The average age of freshmen is 18; all undergraduates, 23. 16% do not continue beyond their first year; 84% remain to graduate. **Housing:** Alcohol is not permitted. All students commute. No one may keep cars.

FACULTY/CLASSROOMS: 51% of faculty are male; 49% are female. No introductory courses are taught by graduate students. The average class size in a laboratory is 16 and in a regular course is 32.

PROGRAMS OF STUDY: Brooklyn confers B.A., B.S., B.F.A., B.B.A. and B.Mus. degrees. Master's degrees are also awarded. Bachelor's degrees are awarded in AGRICULTURE (environmental studies), BIOLOGICAL SCIENCE (biology/biological science), BUSINESS (accounting, banking and finance, business administration and management, business (dual major program), business information systems, and business systems analysis), COMMUNICATIONS AND THE ARTS (art, art history and appreciation, broadcasting, classics, communications, comparative literature, creative writing, English, film arts, French, Italian, journalism, linguistics, multimedia, music, music performance, music theory and composition, radio/television technology, Russian, Spanish, speech/debate/rhetoric, theater management, and visual and performing arts), COMPUTER AND PHYSICAL SCIENCE (chemistry, computer science, earth science, geology, information sciences and systems, mathematics, and physics), EDUCATION (art education, bilingual/bicultural education, childhood education, early childhood education, elementary education, English education, foreign languages education, mathematics education, music education, physical education, science education, secondary education, and social studies education), HEALTH PROFESSIONS (health science and speech pathology/audiology), SOCIAL SCIENCE (African studies, American studies, anthropology, Caribbean studies, child care/child and family studies, economics, Hispanic American studies, history, interdisciplinary studies, Judaic studies, Latin American studies, philosophy, political science/government, psychology, Puerto Rican studies, religion, sociology, and women's studies). Business, accounting, and education have the largest enrollments.

ACTIVITIES: 3% of men belong to 2 local and 6 national fraternities; 3% of women belong to 4 local and 4 national sororities. There are 161 groups on campus, including academic club, art, chess, computers, dance, drama, ethnic, film, forensics, honors, international, LGBT, literary magazine, musical theater, newspaper, political, professional, radio and TV, religious, social, social service, student government, symphony, and yearbook. Popular campus events include Welcome Back Bash, Fall Festival and Make a Difference Day. **Sports:** There are 6 intercollegiate sports for men and 7 for women, and 3 intramural sports for men and 3 for women. Facilities include a swimming pool, soccer field, softball field, volleyball, tennis, basketball courts, fitness center, and a jogging track. **Graduates:** From July 1, 2015 to June 30, 2016, 2474 bachelor's degrees were awarded. The most popular majors were business (21%), psychology (13%), and accounting (11%). 330 companies recruited on campus in 2015-2016. In an average class, 46% graduate in 5 years or less and 54% graduate in 6 years or less.

SERVICES: Counseling and information services are available, as is tutoring in every subject. There is a reader service for the blind. **Library/ Resources:** The library contains 1.7 million volumes, 1.3 million microform items, 130,093 audio/video tapes/CDs/DVDs, and subscribes to 185,516 periodicals including electronic. Computerized library services include interlibrary loans, database searching, and Internet access. Special learning facilities include an art gallery, radio station, TV station, three color studios, and a speech and hearing clinic. **Physically Challenged Students:** All of the campus is accessible. Facilities include wheelchair ramps, elevators, special parking, specially equipped restrooms, special class scheduling, and lowered drinking fountains. **Special:** There are numerous cross-registration programs with colleges and universities in the area. Many internships and work-study programs are available. Study abroad is possible in more than 29 countries. A B.A.-M.D., B.S.-M.P.S., and accelerated B.A.-M.A. programs are available. A number of B.A.-B.S. degrees, dual majors, a 3-2 engineering degree, and student-designed majors are possible. Credit by exam, credit for life experience, non-degree study, and pass/fail options are offered. There is a Latin and Greek Institute offered during the summer through the Graduate Center. There are 9 national honor societies, Phi Beta Kappa, a freshman honors program, and 6 departmental honors programs. **Visiting:** There are regularly scheduled orientations for prospective students, including campus tours, presentations, and meetings with faculty. There are guides for informal visits. To schedule a visit, contact Christopher Milton, Asst. Director for Recruitment at (718) 951-5001. **Campus Safety and Security:** Measures include 24-hour foot and vehicle patrol, emergency notification system, and security escort services. There are shuttle buses, emergency telephones, lighted pathways/sidewalks, CCTV cameras, and informational assistants.

REQUIREMENTS: The SAT or ACT is required. Applicants applying directly from high school must have completed 81% GPA requirements with 5 units of math and English, with no less than 2 years of either combined (critical reading and math) SAT score, or ACT equivalent of 1000 for regular freshmen admissions. Students will be admitted with GED score of 3000 and have the equivalent of 2 years of high school math. AP and CLEP credits are accepted. There are 11 required, interrelated courses that cover the following core curriculum areas: classics, art, music, political science, sociology, history, literature, math, computer science, chemistry, physics, biology, geology, philosophy, and comparative cultures. There are basic skills requirements in reading, composition, speech, and math, as well as a foreign language requirement. A 2.0 GPA and a minimum of 120 credit hours, with 31 to 36 in the major (67 to

70 for chemistry), are required to graduate. **Procedure:** Freshmen are admitted fall and spring. There are early admissions and rolling admissions plans. Applications should be filed by October 1 for fall entry; February 1 for spring entry, along with a $65 fee. Notification of early decision is sent December 15; regular decision, on a rolling basis. Applications are accepted online. **Transfer Students:** 2879 transfer students enrolled in 2015-2016. Transfer students must have 24 credits; 2.5 GPA and freshman requirements: 25 and over credits, a 2.3 GPA. 30 of 120 credits required for the bachelor's degree must be completed at Brooklyn. **International Students:** There are 352 international students enrolled. The school actively recruits these students. They must take the TOEFL with a minimum score of 500 on the paper-based TOEFL (PBT) or 61 on the Internet-based version (iBT), and the college's own test.

Admissions Contact: Penelope Terry, Director of Undergraduate Admissions. Email: *pterry@brooklyn.cuny.edu* Web: *www.brooklyn.cuny.edu*

FINANCIAL AID: In 2016-2017, 69% of all full-time freshmen and 76% of continuing full-time students received some form of financial aid. 61% of all full-time freshmen and 74% of continuing full-time students received need-based aid. The average freshman award was $7,500. Need-based scholarships or need-based grants averaged $3,300 ($10,500 maximum); need-based self-help aid (loans and jobs) averaged $3,200 ($3,500 maximum); and other non-need-based awards and non-need-based scholarships averaged $1,500 ($10,500 maximum). 71% of undergraduate students work part-time. Average annual earnings from campus work are $1200. The average financial indebtedness of the 2016 graduate was $12,300. The FAFSA code is 002687. The priority date for freshman financial aid applications for fall entry is April 1.

CITY UNIVERSITY OF NEW YORK/CITY COLLEGE D-5

www.ccny.cuny.edu

New York, NY 10031 (212) 650-6977

Fax: (212) 650-6417	**Email:** admissions@ccny.cuny.edu
Full-time: 4508 men, 4792 women	**Faculty:** 510; IIA, ++$
Part-time: 1437 men, 1434 women	**Ph.D.s:** 87%
Graduate: 1095 men, 1396 women	**Student/Faculty:** 14 to 1
Year: semesters, summer session	**Tuition:** $6471 ($13,281)
Room & Board: $13,848	**Freshman Class:** 24497 applied, 1530 accepted, 1441 enrolled
SAT CR/M/W: 520/580/515	**CEEB CODE:** 2083
Application Deadline: December 1	**VERY COMPETITIVE**

City College, founded in 1847, is a public liberal arts college that is part of the City University of New York. The college offers programs through 4 undergraduate and 4 graduate schools and 2 professional centers. There are 6 undergraduate schools and 6 graduate schools. In addition to regional accreditation, CCNY has baccalaureate program accreditation with ABET, ABFSE, NAAB, and NCATE. The 35-acre campus is in an urban area in New York City. Including any residence halls, there are 14 buildings.

STUDENT LIFE: 96% of undergraduates are from New York. Others are from 40 states, 158 foreign countries, and Canada. 84% are from public schools. 25% are Hispanic; 23% African American; 21% Asian American; 20% White; 10% Foreign; 1% American Indian/Alaska Native. **Female To Male Ratio:** 1.1:1. The average age of freshmen is 19; all undergraduates, 24. 22% do not continue beyond their first year; 42% remain to graduate. **Housing:** 580 students can be accommodated in college housing, which includes single-sex and coed on-campus apartments and married student housing, as well as apartments for single students. On-campus housing is available on a first-come and first-served basis. Priority is given to out-of-town students. 97% of students commute. Alcohol is not permitted. All students may keep cars.

FACULTY/CLASSROOMS: 56% of faculty are male; 44% are female. 77% teach undergraduates, 65% do research, and 53% do both. No introductory courses are taught by graduate students. The average class size in an introductory lecture is 29; in a laboratory is 15; and in a regular course is 19.

PROGRAMS OF STUDY: CCNY-City confers B.A., B.S., B.Arch., B.E., B.F.A., B.M.E., and B.S.Ed. degrees. Master's and doctoral degrees are also awarded. Bachelor's degrees are awarded in BIOLOGICAL SCIENCE (biology/biological science), BUSINESS (business administration and management), COMMUNICATIONS AND THE ARTS (art, communications, comparative literature, dramatic arts, English, film arts, fine arts, French, multimedia, music, performing arts, romance languages and literature, Spanish, and video), COMPUTER AND PHYSICAL SCIENCE (atmospheric sciences and meteorology, chemistry, computer science, earth science, geology, mathematics, physics, and quantitative methods), EDUCATION (art education, bilingual/bicultural education, early childhood education, education of the emotionally handicapped, education of the mentally handicapped, elementary education, English education, foreign languages education, mathematics education, secondary education, social studies education, and special education), ENGINEERING AND ENVIRONMENTAL DESIGN (architecture, biomedical engineering, chemical engineering, civil engineering, computer engineering, electrical/electronics engineering, environmental engineering, environmental science, landscape architecture/design, and mechanical engineering), HEALTH PROFESSIONS (biomedical science, physician's assistant, predentistry, and premedicine), SOCIAL SCIENCE (American studies, anthropology, area studies, Asian/Oriental studies, economics, ethnic studies, history, international studies, Latin American studies, philosophy, political science/government, prelaw, psychology, sociology, and urban studies). Engineering, architecture, and sciences are the strongest academically. Engineering, architecture, and psychology have the largest enrollments.

ACTIVITIES: There are 170 groups on campus, including choral groups, art, band, cheerleading, chess, chorus, computers, dance, debate, drama, ethnic, film, honors, international, jazz band, LGBT, literary magazine, Model UN, newspaper, orchestra, photography, political, professional, radio and TV, religious, social, social service, student government, and yearbook. Popular campus events include Langston Hughes Poetry Contest, Dance Theater of Harlem Performances at Davis Center, and Architecture Lecture Series. **Sports:** There are 9 intercollegiate sports for men and 9 for women, and 9 intramural sports for men and 9 for women. Facilities include a weight room, swimming pools, and two gyms. **Graduates:** From July 1, 2015 to June 30, 2016, 2126 bachelor's degrees were awarded. The most popular majors were psychology (15%), engineering (13%), and social sciences (11%). 850 companies recruited on campus in 2015-2016. In an average class, 8% graduate in 4 years or less, 30% graduate in 5 years or less, and 42% graduate in 6 years or less. Of the 2015 graduating class, 18% were enrolled in graduate school within 6 months of graduation.

SERVICES: Counseling and information services are available, as is tutoring in most subjects. There is a reader service for the blind. **Library/Resources:** The 47 libraries contain 1.8 million volumes, 901,300 microform items, 225,480 audio/video tapes/CDs/DVDs, and subscribe to 56,476 periodicals including electronic. Computerized library services include interlibrary loans, database searching, Internet access, and Wi-Fi capability. Special learning facilities include an art gallery, planetarium, radio station, TV station, weather station, laser labs, microwave labs, and structural biology lab. **Physically Challenged Students:** 94% of the campus is accessible. Facilities include wheelchair ramps, elevators, special parking, specially equipped restrooms, special class scheduling, lowered drinking fountains, and lowered telephones. **Special:** Cross-registration is permitted with other City University colleges. A 7-year biomedical education degree is available. Opportunities are provided for a co-op program in engineering, internships, a Washington semester, work-study programs, a wide variety of accelerated degree programs, dual majors, credit by exam, credit for life experience, study abroad in 12 countries, and a B.A.-B.S. degree in biomedical engineering, math, physics, and psychology. There are 2 national honor societies, Phi Beta Kappa, a freshman honors program, and 100 departmental honors programs. **Visiting:** There are regularly scheduled orientations for prospective students. There are guides for informal visits and visitors may sit in on classes. To schedule a visit, contact the Admissions Office. **Campus Safety and Security:** Measures include 24-hour foot and vehicle patrol, emergency notification system, and security escort services. There are shuttle buses, emergency telephones, lighted pathways/sidewalks, controlled access to dorms/residences, bicycle patrols, IDs, criminal investigations, and security systems.

REQUIREMENTS: Students who apply should have a recommended satisfactory minimum SAT score or an ACT score of 22. Graduation from an accredited secondary school is generally required, but a GED will be accepted. 14 academic credits should be presented with a minimum grade average of 80%. AP credits are accepted. Students must successfully complete 120 credits, with 32 to 48 in the major, and maintain a minimum GPA of 2.0. A core curriculum must be met, including courses in anthropology, art, English, psychology, and sociology. Students must complete a college proficiency exam. **Procedure:** Freshmen are admitted to all sessions. Entrance exams should be taken prior to registration. There is a rolling admissions plan. Applications should be filed by December 1 for fall entry; October 15 for spring entry, along with a $65 fee. Notifications are sent January 15. Applications are accepted online. **Transfer Students:** 1498 transfer students enrolled in 2015-2016. Transfer applicants must have earned a minimum of 24 credit hours and maintained a GPA of 2.0. Selected programs have more competitive requirements. 32 of 120 credits required for the bachelor's degree must be completed at CCNY. **International Students:** There are 1758 international students enrolled. They must take the TOEFL with a minimum score of 500 on the paper-based TOEFL (PBT) or 61 on the Internet-based version (iBT). They must also take the ACT, and the CUNY Placement Exam.

ADMISSIONS: 6% of the 2016-2017 applicants were accepted. The SAT scores for the 2016-2017 freshman class were: Critical Reading-- 43% below 500, 34% between 500 and 599, 16% between 600 and 699, and 6% between 700 and 800. Math-- 14% below 500, 45% between 500 and 599, 29% between 600 and 699, and 12% between 700 and 800. 60% of the current freshmen were in the top fifth of their class; 87% were in the top two fifths. **Admissions Contact:** Joe Fantozzi, Director of Admissions. Email: *admissions@ccny.cuny.edu* Web: *www.ccny.cuny.edu*

FINANCIAL AID: In 2016-2017, 84% of all full-time freshmen and 82% of continuing full-time students received some form of financial aid. 84% of all full-time freshmen and 82% of continuing full-time students received need-based aid. The average freshman award was $8,757. Need-based scholarships or need-based grants averaged $7,989; need-based self-help aid (loans and jobs) averaged $7,210; other non-need-based awards and non-need-based scholarships averaged $3,106; and $5,530 from other forms of aid. The average financial indebtedness of the 2016 graduate was $16,944. The state aid form is required. The FAFSA code is 002688. The priority date for freshman financial aid applications for fall entry is April 1. The deadline for fall entry is rolling.

CITY UNIVERSITY OF NEW YORK/COLLEGE OF STATEN ISLAND

(The complete profile is made available exclusively on our website, www.barronspac.com)

CITY UNIVERSITY OF NEW YORK/COLLEGE OF TECHNOLOGY

(The complete profile is made available exclusively on our website, www.barronspac.com)

CITY UNIVERSITY OF NEW YORK/ HUNTER COLLEGE — D-5

www.hunter.cuny.edu

New York, NY 10065

(212) 772-4490
(800) 772-4000
Email: admissions@hunter.cuny.edu

Full-time: 4185 men, 7611 women	**Faculty:** 750; IIA, ++$
Part-time: 1664 men, 3178 women	**Ph.D.s:** 86%
Graduate: 1434 men, 4752 women	**Student/Faculty:** 15 to 1
Year: semesters, summer session	**Tuition:** $17,250
Room & Board: $13,848	**Freshman Class:** n/av
SAT CR/M: 574/598	**CEEB CODE:** 2301
Application Deadline: open	**VERY COMPETITIVE**

Hunter College, the City University of New York, (CUNY) a comprehensive, institution established in 1870, is part of the City University of New York, and is both city and state-supported. Primarily a commuter college, it emphasizes liberal arts in its undergraduate and graduate programs. Figures in the above capsule and in this profile are approximate. There are 3 undergraduate schools and 4 graduate schools. In addition to regional accreditation, Hunter has baccalaureate program accreditation with ADA, APTA, ASLA, CSWE, NCATE, and NLN. The 3-acre campus is in an urban area in New York City. Including any residence halls, there are 6 buildings.

STUDENT LIFE: 98% of undergraduates are from New York. Others are from 42 states, 151 foreign countries, and Canada. 71% are from public schools. 6% are Foreign; 44% White; 21% Asian American; 17% Hispanic; 12% African American. **Female To Male Ratio:** 2.1:1. The average age of freshmen is 18; all undergraduates, 24. 17% do not continue beyond their first year. **Housing:** 662 students can be accommodated in college housing, which includes coed dorms. On-campus housing is available on a first-come, and first-served basis, and is available on a lottery system for upperclassmen. 99% of students commute. No one may keep cars.

FACULTY/CLASSROOMS: No introductory courses are taught by graduate students. The average class size in a laboratory is 20 and in a regular course is 30.

PROGRAMS OF STUDY: Hunter confers B.A., B.S., B.F.A., B.Mus. and B.S.Ed degrees. Master's degrees are also awarded. Bachelor's degrees are awarded in BIOLOGICAL SCIENCE (biology/biological science and nutrition), BUSINESS (accounting), COMMUNICATIONS AND THE ARTS (Chinese, classics, comparative literature, creative writing, dance, dramatic arts, English, English literature, film arts, fine arts, French, German, Greek, Hebrew, Italian, languages, Latin, media arts, music, Russian, and Spanish), COMPUTER AND PHYSICAL SCIENCE (chemistry, computer science, mathematics, physics, and statistics), EDUCATION (art education, early childhood education, elementary education, foreign languages education, health education, middle school education, music education, science education, and secondary education), ENGINEERING AND ENVIRONMENTAL DESIGN (energy management technology, environmental science, and preengineering), HEALTH PROFESSIONS (medical laboratory technology, nursing, physical therapy, predentistry, premedicine, and public health), SOCIAL SCIENCE (African American studies, anthropology, archeology, economics, geography, Hispanic American studies, history, international relations, Judaic studies, Latin American studies, philosophy, political science/government, prelaw, psychology, religion, social science, sociology, urban studies, and women's studies). Nursing is the strongest academically. Psychology has the largest enrollment.

ACTIVITIES: There are 150 groups on campus, including art, band, cheerleading, choir, chorale, chorus, drama, ethnic, film, honors, international, jazz band, LGBT, literary magazine, musical theater, newspaper, orchestra, political, professional, radio and TV, religious, social, social service, student government, and symphony. Popular campus events include Major Day Fair. **Sports:** There are 9 intercollegiate sports for men and 11 for women. Facilities include fencing, dance, weight rooms, racquetball courts, a pool, outdoor tennis courts, and a gym. **Graduates:** From July 1, 2015 to June 30, 2016, 2707 bachelor's degrees were awarded. The most popular majors were psychology (21%), social sciences (18%), and English (14%). In an average class, 46% graduate in 6 years or less.

SERVICES: Counseling and information services are available, as is tutoring in every subject. There is a reader service for the blind, and remedial math, reading, and writing. Review of graduate-level papers through the writing center and a math tutoring center are available. **Library/Resources:** The library contains 865,240 volumes, 651,000 microform items, 75,000 audio/video tapes/CDs/DVDs, and subscribes to 36,000 periodicals including electronic. Computerized library services include database searching. Special learning facilities include an art gallery, radio station, a geography/geology lab, on-campus elementary and secondary schools, and a theater. **Physically Challenged Students:** All of the campus is accessible. Facilities include wheelchair ramps, elevators, special parking, specially equipped restrooms, special class scheduling, lowered drinking fountains, and lowered telephones. **Special:** Special academic programs include internships, student-designed majors, work-study, study abroad in 24 countries, and dual majors. There is cross-registration with the Brooklyn School of Law, Marymount Manhattan College, and the YIVO Institute. Through the National Student Exchange Program, Hunter students can study for 1 or 2 semesters at any of 150 U.S. campuses. Accelerated degree programs are offered in anthropology, biopharmacology, economics, English, history, math, physics, sociology, and social research. Exchange programs in Paris or Puerto Rico are possible. There are 2 national honor societies, Phi Beta Kappa, a freshman honors program, and 19 departmental honors programs. **Visiting:** There are regularly scheduled orientations for prospective students, consisting of presentations and tours. There are guides for informal visits and visitors may sit in on classes. To schedule a visit, contact the Admissions Office. **Campus Safety and Security:** Measures include self-defense education. There are shuttle buses, emergency telephones, and 24-hour foot patrol.

REQUIREMENTS: Student admission is based on a combination of high school grade average, high school academic credits, including

English and math, and SAT scores. AP and CLEP credits are accepted. To graduate, students must complete 120 credits. The total number of hours in a major varies from 24 credits for a liberal arts major to 63 credits for a professional concentration; a minimum GPA of 2.0 is needed overall and in the major. Distribution requirements include 12 credits of social sciences, up to 12 credits of a foreign language, 10 or more of math and science, 9 of humanities and the arts, 6 of literature, and 3 of English composition. **Procedure:** Freshmen are admitted fall and spring. Entrance exams should be taken by October of the junior year. There are early admissions, deferred admissions, and rolling admissions plans. Application deadlines are open. Application fee is $65. Notification of early decision are sent December 15; regular decision, January 1. 4 early decision candidates were accepted for the 2016-2017 class. Applications are accepted on-line. **Transfer Students:** 1877 transfer students enrolled in 2015-2016. Applicants must have at least a 2.0 GPA. All students must complete 30 of the 120 to 131 credits required for a bachelor's degree at the college, including half of those needed for both the major and the minor. **International Students:** There are 1352 international students enrolled. They must take the TOEFL with a minimum score of 500 on the paper-based TOEFL (PBT) and the college's own test.

ADMISSIONS: The SAT scores for the 2016-2017 freshman class were: Critical Reading-- 12% below 500, 54% between 500 and 599, 26% between 600 and 699, and 8% between 700 and 800. Math-- 3% below 500, 50% between 500 and 599, 37% between 600 and 699, and 10% between 700 and 800. **Admissions Contact:** Joseph Fantozzie Jr., Associate Director for Undergraduate Adm. Email: *admissions@hunter.cuny.edu* Web: *www.hunter.cuny.edu*

FINANCIAL AID: The college's own financial statement is required. The FAFSA code is 002689. The deadline for filing freshman financial aid applications for fall entry is May 1.

CITY UNIVERSITY OF NEW YORK/JOHN JAY COLLEGE OF CRIMINAL JUSTICE *(The complete profile is made available exclusively on our website, www.barronspac.com)*

CITY UNIVERSITY OF NEW YORK/LEHMAN COLLEGE *(The complete profile is made available exclusively on our website, www.barronspac.com)*

CITY UNIVERSITY OF NEW YORK/MEGER EVERS COLLEGE *(The complete profile is made available exclusively on our website, www.barronspac.com)*

CITY UNIVERSITY OF NEW YORK/ QUEENS COLLEGE — D-5

www.qc.cuny.edu

Queens, NY 11367 — **(718) 997-5600**

Fax: (718) 997-5617	**Email:** admissions@qc.cuny.edu
Full-time: 5259 men, 6434 women	**Faculty:** 430; IIA, ++$
Part-time: 2010 men, 2623 women	**Ph.D.s:** 87%
Graduate: 1026 men, 2280 women	**Student/Faculty:** 19 to 1
Year: semesters, summer session	**Tuition:** $6938 ($14,048)
Room & Board: $14,020	**Freshman Class:** 19032 applied, 11236 accepted, 1475 enrolled
SAT CR/M/W: 520/560/510	**CEEB CODE:** 2750
Application Deadline: February 1	**COMPETITIVE**

Queens College, established in 1937, and part of the City University of New York, offers a rigorous education in the liberal arts and sciences under the guidance of a faculty dedicated to both teaching and research. Students graduate with the ability to think critically, address complex problems, explore various cultures, and use modern technologies and information resources. Queens College was cited in a report published by the Education Trust as being one of only five colleges in the U.S. that do a good job serving low-income students. This was based on the college's graduation rate, low tuition, and the amount of need-based financial aid it awards to students. Queens College participates in CUNY's Macaulay Honors College, a challenging program open to the most academically gifted students, and offers qualified students its own honors programs in the arts and humanities, sciences, and social sciences. There is 1 undergraduate school and 1 graduate school. In addition to regional accreditation, Queens has baccalaureate program accreditation with ADA, NASM, NCATE, TEAC, APA, ACEND, CAA, CAEP, New York State Board of Regents, ALA, and AAFCS. The 80-acre campus is in an urban area 11 miles from Manhattan. Including any residence halls, there are 30 buildings.

STUDENT LIFE: 94% of undergraduates are from New York. Others are from 29 states, 77 foreign countries, and Canada. 70% are from public schools. 9% are African American; 5% Foreign; 29% White; 28% Asian American; 28% Hispanic; 1% two or more races. **Female To Male Ratio:** 1.4:1. The average age of freshmen is 19; all undergraduates, 24. 15% do not continue beyond their first year; 58% remain to graduate. **Housing:** 506 students can be accommodated in college housing, which includes coed on-campus apartments. On-campus housing is available on a first-come and first-served basis. 98% of students commute. Alcohol is not permitted. All students may keep cars.

FACULTY/CLASSROOMS: 50% of faculty are male; 50% are female. 75% teach undergraduates. No introductory courses are taught by graduate students. The average class size in an introductory lecture is 31; in a laboratory is 22; and in a regular course is 30.

PROGRAMS OF STUDY: Queens confers B.A., B.S., B.B.A., B.F.A., BA/MA combined degree, and B.Mus. degrees. Master's degrees are also awarded. Bachelor's degrees are awarded in AGRICULTURE (environmental studies), BIOLOGICAL SCIENCE (neurosciences and nutritional sciences), BUSINESS (accounting, business administration - international, finance, and labor studies), COMMUNICATIONS AND THE ARTS (art history, Chinese, classics, comparative literature, design, English, film, television and digital media, French, German, graphic design, Greek, Hebrew, Italian, Latin, linguistics, film and media studies, music, music performance, Russian, Spanish, communication arts - speech, and studio art), COMPUTER AND PHYSICAL SCIENCE (actuarial science, chemistry, computer science, geology, mathematics, and physics), EDUCATION (art education, early childhood education, elementary education, music education, physical education, physical education/exercise science, secondary education, Spanish education K-12, and teaching English as a second/foreign language (TESOL/TEFOL)), HEALTH PROFESSIONS (biology, nutrition and dietetics, and speech pathology/audiology), SOCIAL SCIENCE (African studies, American studies, anthropology, applied social science, East Asian studies, economics, family/consumer studies, history, home economics, Latin American studies, Middle Eastern studies, modern jewish studies, philosophy, political science/government, psychology, religion, sociology, urban studies, and women's studies). psychology, computer science and accounting have the largest enrollments.

ACTIVITIES: 1% of women belong to 1 local and 4 national sororities. There are 105 groups on campus, Chabad of QC, La Tertulia, Muslim Students Association, PRISM, art, band, choir, chorus, communications, computers, dance, debate, drama, environmental, ethnic, film, honors, international, jazz band, LGBT, literary magazine, musical theater, newspaper, political, professional, radio and TV, religious, science fiction and animation, social, social service, student government, symphony, and yearbook. Popular campus events include Welcome Day, Orientation Sessions for Freshmen and Transfers, and Career Fair. **Sports:** There are 7 intercollegiate sports for men and 10 for women, and 8 intramural sports for men and 8 for women. Facilities include a gym complex, swimming pool, dance studios, weight rooms, outdoor track, soccer, lacrosse, baseball fields, and tennis courts. **Graduates:** From July 1, 2015 to June 30, 2016, 2926 bachelor's degrees were awarded. The most popular majors were psychology (18%), accounting (14%), and economics (6%). In an average class, 28% graduate in 4 years or less, 51% graduate in 5 years or less, and 58% graduate in 6 years or less.

SERVICES: Counseling and information services are available, as is tutoring in most subjects. There is a reader service for the blind. **Library/Resources:** The library contains 1.1 million volumes, 988,133 microform items, 49,690 audio/video tapes/CDs/DVDs, and subscribes to 134,400 periodicals including electronic. Computerized library services include interlibrary loans, database searching, Internet access, and Wi-Fi capability. Special learning facilities include an art gallery, radio station, small museum, and a theater. **Physically Challenged Students:** All of the campus is accessible. Facilities include wheelchair ramps, elevators, special parking, specially equipped restrooms, special class scheduling, lowered drinking fountains, lowered telephones, and special housing. **Special:** Queens offers co-op programs, cross-registration with other CUNY campuses, internships in business, liberal arts, journalism, and social sciences and other fields, study abroad, work-study, accelerated degrees, dual majors, pass/fail options, and nondegree study. There are preprofessional programs in engineering, law, and medical/dental/health sciences. The SEEK program provides financial and educational resources for underprepared freshmen. The Macaulay Honors Program is for high achieving freshmen, which eligible students receive a full tuition scholarship, a generous Opportunities Fund study grant, and a laptop computer. There are 3 national honor societies, Phi Beta Kappa, and a freshman honors program. **Visiting:** There are regularly scheduled orientations for prospective students, including information sessions and a campus tour. Visitors may sit in on classes. To schedule a visit, contact the Admissions Office. **Campus Safety and Security:** Measures include 24-hour foot and vehicle patrol and emergency notification system. There are shuttle buses, emergency telephones, lighted pathways/ sidewalks, and controlled access to dorms/residences.

REQUIREMENTS: The SAT is required. High school preparation should include 4 years each of English, and social studies, 3 each of math and foreign language, and 2 of lab science. AP and CLEP credits are accepted. To graduate, students must complete 120 credits with a minimum GPA of 2.0. They must fulfill requirements in the major and liberal arts core curriculum. Entering freshmen and transfer students will follow a revised liberal arts curriculum to meet the requirements of the CUNY Pathways Initiative. The Pathways General Education framework is common to all CUNY colleges. This guarantees that the core curriculum requirements fulfilled at one CUNY college will carry over seamlessly if a student transfers to another CUNY college. **Procedure:** Freshmen are admitted fall and spring. Entrance exams should be taken in the spring of the junior year or the fall of the senior year. There are deferred admissions and rolling admissions plans. Application deadlines are open. Application fee is $65. Notifications are sent February 1. Applications are accepted online. **Transfer Students:** 4099 transfer students enrolled in 2015-2016. Admissions requirements vary depending on the number of credits to be transferred; students should consult with the Admissions Office. 45 of 120 credits required for the bachelor's degree must be completed at Queens. **International Students:** There are 623 international students enrolled. The school actively recruits these students. They must take the TOEFL with a minimum score of 500 on the paper-based TOEFL (PBT) or 62 on the Internet-based version (iBT). They must also take the SAT or ACT, or the CUNY Skills Assessment Test.

ADMISSIONS: 59% of the 2016-2017 applicants were accepted. The SAT scores for the 2016-2017 freshman class were: Critical Reading-- 37% below 500, 46% between 500 and 599, 14% between 600 and 699, and 3% between 700 and 800. Math-- 13% below 500, 54% between 500 and 599, 26% between 600 and 699, and 7% between 700 and 800. Writing-- 42% below 500, 40% between 500 and 599, 9% between 600 and 699, and 2% between 700 and 800. **Admissions Contact:** Mr. Vincent J. Angrisani, Executive Director of Enrollment. Email: *vincent.angrisani@qc.cuny.edu* Web: *www.qc.cuny.edu*

FINANCIAL AID: In 2016-2017, 71% of all full-time freshmen and 66% of continuing full-time students received some form of financial aid. 51% of all full-time freshmen and 62% of continuing full-time students received need-based aid. The average freshman award was $8,792. Need-based scholarships or need-based grants averaged $9,236; need-based self-help aid (loans and jobs) averaged $2,590; and non-need-based athletic scholarships averaged $6,028. The average financial indebtedness of the 2016 graduate was $2,610. The state aid form is required. The priority date for freshman financial aid applications for fall entry is February 15.

CITY UNIVERSITY OF NEW YORK/YORK COLLEGE *(The complete profile is made available exclusively on our website, www.barronspac.com)*

CLARKSON UNIVERSITY — D-2
www.clarkson.edu

Potsdam, NY 13699 — **(315) 268-6480**

Fax: (315) 268-7647	**Email:** admission@clarkson.edu
Full-time: 2249 men, 954 women	**Faculty:** 188
Part-time: 39 men, 26 women	**Ph.D.s:** 89%
Graduate: 686 men, 430 women	**Student/Faculty:** 15 to 1
Year: semesters, summer session	**Tuition:** $46,132
Room & Board: $14,260	**Freshman Class:** 7066 applied, 4820 accepted, 797 enrolled
SAT CR/M/W: 570/610/540 **ACT:** 26	**CEEB CODE:** 2084
Application Deadline: January 15	**HIGHLY COMPETITIVE**

Clarkson University is a nationally recognized research university pursuing degrees in 60 plus academic programs of study in engineering, business, arts, education, sciences and the health professions. We are the institution of choice for enterprising, high-ability scholars from diverse backgrounds who embrace challenge and thrive in a rigorous, highly collaborative learning environment. In partnership with leading business and industry, we are reshaping education to meet the needs of a modern world by connecting knowledge, discipline, nations and cultures. We encourage our students to push the limits of what is known, and to apply their ingenuity to develop fresh solutions to real-world challenges. For 120 years, our graduates have achieved extraordinary professional success and advanced the global economy ethically and responsibly. There are 4 undergraduate schools and 4 graduate schools. In addition to regional accreditation, Clarkson has baccalaureate program accreditation with AACSB, ABET, APTA, ARC-PA, CAPTE, CAHME, and CAEP. The 640-acre campus is in a small town in Potsdam, N.Y., 135 miles northeast of Syracuse, N.Y., 85 miles south of Ottawa, Ontario and in Schenectady, N.Y., 15 miles northwest of Albany, N.Y. Including any residence halls, there are 84 buildings.

STUDENT LIFE: 73% of undergraduates are from New York. Others are from 39 states, 22 foreign countries, and Canada. 87% are from public schools. 83% are White; 5% Hispanic; 3% Asian American; 3% two or more races; 2% African American; 2% Foreign; 2% race unknown. **Male To Female Ratio:** 2.1:1. The average age of freshmen is 18; all undergraduates, 20. 11% do not continue beyond their first year; 72% remain to graduate. **Housing:** 2509 students can be accommodated in college housing, which includes single-sex and coed dorms, on-campus apartments, and off-campus apartments. In addition, there are honors houses, special-interest houses, fraternity houses, and sorority houses. On-campus housing is guaranteed for all 4 years and is available on a lottery system for upperclassmen. 82% of students live on campus; of those, 90% remain on campus on weekends. All students may keep cars.

FACULTY/CLASSROOMS: 70% of faculty are male; 30% are female. 82% teach undergraduates, and do research. No introductory courses are taught by graduate students. The average class size in an introductory lecture is 42; in a laboratory is 20; and in a regular course is 29.

PROGRAMS OF STUDY: Clarkson confers B.S. and B.P.S. degrees. Master's and doctoral degrees are also awarded. Bachelor's degrees are awarded in BIOLOGICAL SCIENCE (biology/biological science and molecular biology), BUSINESS (business intelligence and analytics, entrepreneurial studies, finance, and supply chain management), COMMUNICATIONS AND THE ARTS (communications), COMPUTER AND PHYSICAL SCIENCE (applied mathematics, chemistry, computer science, digital arts/technology, information sciences and systems, mathematics, physics, and software engineering), ENGINEERING AND ENVIRONMENTAL DESIGN (aeronautical engineering, chemical engineering, civil engineering, computer engineering, electrical/electronics engineering, engineering management, environmental engineering, environmental science, and mechanical engineering), HEALTH PROFESSIONS (environmental health science), SOCIAL SCIENCE (history, humanities, interdisciplinary studies, political science/government, and psychology). Engineering, business, and physical/life sciences, are the strongest academically and have the largest enrollments.

ACTIVITIES: 13% of men belong to 2 local and 7 national fraternities; 14% of women belong to 4 national sororities. There are 235 groups on campus, including outing club, cheerleading, chess, chorus, computers, dance, debate, drama, drill team, environmental, ethnic, honors, international, jazz band, LGBT, musical theater, newspaper, orchestra, pep band, photography, political, professional, radio and TV, religious, social, social service, student government, and yearbook. Popular campus events include SpringFest, NCAA Division I Men's and Women's Hockey Games, First Saturday, and Cold Out Gold Out. **Sports:** There are 10 intercollegiate sports for men and 10 for women, and 10 intramural sports for men and 10 for women. Facilities include a multipurpose ice arena, fitness center, gym, swimming pool, weight room, field house, tennis courts, all-purpose indoor and outdoor turf fields, baseball and softball fields, and multi-purpose grass fields. **Graduates:** From July 1, 2015 to June 30, 2016, 729 bachelor's degrees were awarded. The most popular majors were mechanical engineering (18%), civil engineering (10%), and engineering & management (9%). 445 companies recruited on campus in 2015-2016. In an average class, 2% graduate in 3 years or less, 60% graduate in 4 years or less, 73% graduate in 5 years or less, and 72% graduate in 6 years or less. Of the 2015 graduating class, 14% were enrolled in graduate school within 6 months of graduation, and 64% were employed.

SERVICES: Counseling and information services are available, as is

tutoring in most subjects. There is a reader service for the blind, and remedial math and writing. **Library/Resources:** The 2 libraries contain 429,473 volumes, 258,640 microform items, 435 audio/video tapes/CDs/ DVDs, and subscribe to 31,596 periodicals including electronic. Computerized library services include interlibrary loans, database searching, Internet access, and Wi-Fi capability. Special learning facilities include a radio station, TV station, design, prototyping and testing facilities for SPEED team competitions, Institute for a Sustainable Environment, Center for Air Resources Engineering and Science, Center for Advanced Materials Processing, Adirondack, Semester study program in Saranac Lake, Trudeau Semester study program in immunology and infectious disease, Beacon Institute for Rivers and Estuaries, Center for Rehabilitation Engineering, Science, and Technology, Shipley Center for Innovation, wind turbine test site, wind turbine blade test facility, wind tunnel facility, water tunnel facility, greenhouse, observatory, nature preserve with hiking/cross country ski trail, food digester, 20 kW wood pellet boiler coupled to a 2 kW solar thermal system, and 2MW solar power production facility, and a working laboratory. **Physically Challenged Students:** 85% of the campus is accessible. Facilities include wheelchair ramps, elevators, special parking, specially equipped restrooms, special class scheduling, lowered drinking fountains, lowered telephones, and special housing. **Special:** Students can take advantage of many unique educational experiences at Clarkson. For example students can sign up for the Washington Semester or Semester at Sea. Also available is an Adirondack semester in Saranac Lake, and the Trudeau Semester in immunology, and the infectious disease. Students can cross-register at St. Lawrence University, SUNY Potsdam or SUNY Canton, or transfer to Clarkson through one of our many 3-2 engineering degree agreements. Our 3-2 agreements allow students to take their first 3 years of college at a 4-year liberal arts institution and then transfer with junior standing into one of Clarkson's 4-year engineering programs. Students can choose one of Clarkson's may pre-designed interdisciplinary majors, or design their own with a dual major or BPS degree. All Clarkson students are required to complete a professional experience, which usually takes place through a co-op or internship, with one of Clarkson's many industry partners including General Dynamics, General Electric, IBM, Global-Founrdries, and Proctor & Gamble. Many programs of study also require a study abroad experience, with instructor-led summer trips or a semester/year abroad in Australia, Austria, China, Croatia, Denmark, England, France, Germany, Hong Kong, Hungary, Ireland, Italy, South Korea, Mexico, Netherlands, New Zealand, Scotland, Singapore, Spain, South Africa, Sweden, Urugyay. Work-study programs are also available. There are 23 national honor societies, a freshman honors program, and 9 departmental honors programs. **Visiting:** There are regularly scheduled orientations for prospective students. Visits are individually customized to your interests, and include a personalized tour with a Clarkson student and one-on-one meetings with admissions officers, faculty members, and coaches. There are guides for informal visits, visitors may sit in on classes, and stay overnight. To schedule a visit, contact the Undergraduate Admission at (800) 527-6577. **Campus Safety and Security:** Measures include 24-hour foot and vehicle patrol, emergency notification system, self-defense education, and security escort services. There are emergency telephones, lighted pathways/sidewalks, controlled access to dorms/residences, and numerous surveillance cameras in the majority of the academic buildings, laundry rooms, and some parking lots.

REQUIREMENTS: SAT or ACT scores are required. SAT subject tests are recommended. Applicants must have graduated from an accredited secondary school or have a GED. A campus visit and interview are also recommended. AP and CLEP credits are accepted. Important factors in the admissions decision are advanced placement or honors courses, recommendations by school officials, and extracurricular activities record. Students must complete a least 120 credit hours, 30 in a major field of study, with a minimum 2.0 cumulative GPA. Students must also meet the requirements of the Clarkson Common Experience, which includes a professional co-op or internship, and any additional requirements determined by their major department. A student entering as a first-year freshman must have been in residence for at least four semesters including the final undergraduate semester or, if entering with advanced standing, have completed at least half the remaining upper-level undergraduate work in residence at Clarkson. **Procedure:** Freshmen are admitted in the fall and spring. There are early decision, early admissions, and deferred admissions plans. Early decision applications should be filed by December 1; regular applications, by January 15 for fall entry; and October 15 for spring entry. The fall 2016 application fee was $50. Notification of early decision is sent January 1; regular decision, February 1. 131 early decision candidates were accepted for the 2016-2017 class. 65 applicants were on the 2016 waiting list; 11 were admitted. Application fees are waived if application is completed online. **Transfer Students:** 123 transfer students enrolled in 2015-2016. They must submit two letters of recommendation, including one from an academic professor or instructor. Applicants must also submit official secondary school transcripts if not earning an associate's degree, and SAT or ACT scores if less than 24 credits at time of application. The student must also submit Clarkson's Dean of Students recommendation. Transfer applicants into engineering or other majors requiring calculus should have completed at least one college-level calculus course. International students whose first language is not English must submit TOEFL or IELTS scores. 120 of 30 credits required for the bachelor's degree must be completed at Clarkson. **International Students:** There are 114 international students enrolled. The school actively recruits these students. They must take the TOEFL with a minimum score of 550 on the paper-based TOEFL (PBT) or 80 on the Internet-based version (iBT). They must also take the SAT or ACT.

ADMISSIONS: 68% of the 2016-2017 applicants were accepted. The SAT scores for the 2016-2017 freshman class were: Critical Reading-- 17% below 500, 45% between 500 and 599, 33% between 600 and 699, and 5% between 700 and 800. Math-- 6% below 500, 34% between 500 and 599, 47% between 600 and 699, and 13% between 700 and 800. Writing-- 30% below 500, 47% between 500 and 599, 20% between 600 and 699, and 3% between 700 and 800. The ACT scores were 18% between 18 and 23, 58% between 24 and 29, and 24% above 30. 64% of the current freshmen were in the top fifth of their class; 91% were in the top two fifths. 19 freshmen graduated first in their class. **Admissions Contact:** Brian T. Grant, VP for Enrollment & Student Advancement. Email: *admission@clarkson.edu* Web: *www.clarkson.edu*

FINANCIAL AID: In 2016-2017, 99% of all full-time freshmen and continuing full-time students received some form of financial aid. 81% of all full-time freshmen and 80% of continuing full-time students received need-based aid. The average freshman award was $42,486. Need-based scholarships or need-based grants averaged $30,000 ($63,514 maximum); need-based self-help aid (loans and jobs) averaged $7,700 ($30,000 maximum); non-need-based athletic scholarships averaged $43,993 ($49,161 maximum); and other non-need-based awards and non-need-based scholarships averaged $14,397 ($63,448 maximum). 33% of undergraduate students work part-time. Average annual earnings from campus work are $924. The average financial indebtedness of the 2016 graduate was $23,500. The FAFSA code is 002699. The priority date for freshman financial aid applications for fall entry is February 15. The deadline for fall entry is March 1.

COLGATE UNIVERSITY — D-5

www.colgate.edu

Hamilton, NY 13346 — **(315) 228-7401**

Fax: (315) 228-7544	**Email: admission@colgate.edu**
Full-time: 1289 men, 1626 women	**Faculty:** 295; IIB, ++$
Part-time: n/av	**Ph.D.s:** 99%
Graduate: 2 men, 6 women	**Student/Faculty:** 9 to 1
Year: semesters	**Tuition:** $51,955
Room & Board: $13,075	**Freshman Class:** n/av
SAT CR/M: 670/690 **ACT:** 31	**CEEB CODE:** 2086
Application Deadline: January 15	**MOST COMPETITIVE**

Colgate University is a highly selective residential liberal arts institution that offers 54 majors and supports 25 Division I athletic teams. Colgate is distinguished by its commitment to global engagement, student-faculty research, off-campus study, sustainable practices, and utilizing technology to enhance learning. The figures in the above capsule and in this profile are approximate. There is 1 undergraduate school and 1 graduate school. The 575-acre campus is in a rural area in the geographic center of New York State, about four hours northwest of New York City. Including any residence halls, there are 88 buildings.

STUDENT LIFE: 76% of undergraduates are from out of state, mostly the Northeast. Students are from 47 states, 75 foreign countries, and Canada. 57% are from public schools. 66% are White; 9% Hispanic; 9% Foreign; 4% African American; 4% Asian American; 4% race unknown; 3% two or more races; 1% American Indian/Alaska Native. **Female To**

Male Ratio: 1.3:1. The average age of freshmen is 18; all undergraduates, 19. 5% do not continue beyond their first year; 90% remain to graduate. **Housing:** 2680 students can be accommodated in college housing, which includes coed dorms and on-campus apartments. In addition, there are language houses, special-interest houses, fraternity houses, sorority houses, and residential commons (living-learning community). On-campus housing is guaranteed for all 4 years. All students may keep cars.

FACULTY/CLASSROOMS: 59% of faculty are male; 41% are female. All teach undergraduates and do research. No introductory courses are taught by graduate students. The average class size in a regular course is 18.

PROGRAMS OF STUDY: Colgate confers B.A. degrees. Master's degrees are also awarded. Bachelor's degrees are awarded in BIOLOGICAL SCIENCE (biochemistry, biology/biological science, environmental biology, molecular biology, and neurosciences), COMMUNICATIONS AND THE ARTS (art/art studies, art history and appreciation, Chinese, classics, dramatic arts, English, French, German, Greek, Japanese, Latin, music, Russian, Spanish, studio art, and theatre studies), COMPUTER AND PHYSICAL SCIENCE (astronomy, astrophysics, chemistry, computer science, environmental geology, geology, geophysics and seismology, mathematics, natural sciences, physical sciences, and physics), EDUCATION (Asian studies, classical studies, and education), ENGINEERING AND ENVIRONMENTAL DESIGN (environmental science), HEALTH PROFESSIONS (biology), SOCIAL SCIENCE (African studies, anthropology, economics, geography, history, humanities, international relations, Latin American studies, Middle Eastern studies, Native American studies, peace studies, philosophy, philosophy and religion, political science/government, psychology, religion, Russian and Slavic studies, social science, sociology, and women's studies). Economics, political science, and English have the largest enrollments.

ACTIVITIES: 34% of men belong to 5 national fraternities; 63% of women belong to 3 national sororities. There are 200 groups on campus, including art, band, cheerleading, chess, choir, chorale, chorus, communications, computers, dance, debate, drama, environmental, ethnic, film, forensics, honors, international, jazz band, LGBT, literary magazine, musical theater, newspaper, orchestra, pep band, photography, political, professional, radio and TV, religious, social, social service, student government, symphony, and yearbook. Popular campus events include Colgate/Cornell hockey game, Global Leaders Lecture Series, DanceFest, and Spring Party Weekend. **Sports:** There are 11 intercollegiate sports for men and 11 for women, and 29 intramural sports for men and 30 for women. Facilities include Crown Field at Andy Kerr Stadium, Cotterell Court, Starr Rink, Lineberry Natatorium, Tyler's Field, Beyer-Small '76 Field, Eaton Street Softball Complex, Trudy Fitness Center, Glendening Boathouse, Seven Oaks Golf Course, Mark P. Buttitta '74 Varsity Weight Room, R.L. Browning '37 Outdoor Track, Huntington Gymnasium, Sanford Field House, J.W. Abrahamson Memorial Courts, Harry H. Lang Cross Country Course, Reid Athletic Center, Class of 1965 Arena, Angert Family Climbing Wall, and The Beattie Reserve. **Graduates:** From July 1, 2015 to June 30, 2016, 676 bachelor's degrees were awarded. 130 companies recruited on campus in 2015-2016. In an average class, 84% graduate in 4 years or less and 88% graduate in 6 years or less. Of the 2015 graduating class, 15% were enrolled in graduate school within 6 months of graduation, and 81% were employed.

SERVICES: Counseling and information services are available, as is tutoring in every subject. There is a reader service for the blind, and remedial writing. **Library/Resources:** The 2 libraries contain 899,850 volumes, 443,423 microform items, 26,768 audio/video tapes/CDs/DVDs, and subscribe to 92,091 periodicals including electronic. Computerized library services include interlibrary loans, database searching, Internet access, and Wi-Fi capability. Special learning facilities include an art gallery, planetarium, radio station, TV station, anthropology museum, observatory, visualization lab with planetarium, and geology museum. **Physically Challenged Students:** Facilities include wheelchair ramps, elevators, special parking, specially equipped restrooms, special class scheduling, lowered drinking fountains, and special housing. **Special:** Colgate offers various internships, semester and summer research opportunities with faculty, work-study programs, off-campus study programs in over 20 countries, accelerated degree programs, dual majors, and student-designed majors. A 3-2 engineering degree with Columbia University, Washington University in St. Louis, and Rensselaer Polytechnic Institute, an early assurance medical program with George Washington University and University of Rochester, credit by exam, and pass/fail options are available. There are 11 national honor societies and a chapter of Phi Beta Kappa. **Visiting:** There are regularly scheduled orientations for prospective students, nonevaluative interviews, information sessions, and student-led tours. There are guides for informal visits, visitors may sit in on classes, and stay overnight. To schedule a visit, contact Office of Admission. **Campus Safety and Security:** Measures include 24-hour foot and vehicle patrol, emergency notification system, self-defense education, and security escort services. There are shuttle buses, emergency telephones, lighted pathways/sidewalks, and controlled access to dorms/residences.

REQUIREMENTS: Students must submit an application, supplement, standardized test scores (SAT or ACT), and the application fee. Students must also submit the school report, counselor recommendation, two teacher recommendations, transcript, and senior grades. AP credits are accepted. Important factors in the admissions decision are recommendations by school officials, advanced placement or honors courses, and extracurricular activities record. To graduate, students must complete a first-year seminar course and the core curriculum, including 4 general education courses and 2 courses each in the natural sciences, social sciences, and humanities. A total of 32 courses is required, with 8 to 12 courses in the major. Study in a foreign language and a physical education credit are also required. **Procedure:** Freshmen are admitted in the fall. Entrance exams should be taken prior to application submission. There are early decision and deferred admissions plans. Early decision applications should be filed by November 15; regular applications, by January 15 for fall entry, along with a $60 fee. Notifications are sent in March. 369 early decision candidates were accepted for the 2016-2017 class. Application fees are waived if application is completed online. **Transfer Students:** 27 transfer students enrolled in 2015-2016. The application fee, official high school transcripts, college official's report, mid-term report, faculty recommendation, essay on application, and test scores from SAT/ACT. International students must submit the TOEFL. 16 of 32 credits required for the bachelor's degree must be completed at Colgate. **International Students:** There are 273 international students enrolled. The school actively recruits these students. They must take the TOEFL. The IELTS is accepted. They must also take the SAT or ACT.

ADMISSIONS: 29% of the 2016-2017 applicants were accepted. 88% of the current freshmen were in the top fifth of their class; 98% were in the top two fifths. 19 freshmen graduated first in their class. **Admissions Contact:** Gary L. Ross, VP & Dean of Admission & Financial Aid. Email: *admission@colgate.edu* Web: *www.colgate.edu*

FINANCIAL AID: In 2016-2017, 42% of all full-time freshmen received some form of financial aid, and received need-based aid. The average freshman award was $49,442. Need-based scholarships or need-based grants averaged $44,142; and need-based self-help aid (loans and jobs) averaged $5,300. 45% of undergraduate students work part-time. Average annual earnings from campus work are $2800. The average financial indebtedness of the 2016 graduate was $16,000. Colgate is a member of CSS. The CSS/Profile is required. The FAFSA code is 002701. The deadline for filing freshman financial aid applications for fall entry is January 15.

COLLEGE OF MOUNT SAINT VINCENT D-5

www.cmsv.edu

Riverdale, NY 10471 (718) 405-3200 (800) 665-CMSV

Fax: (718) 549-7945 **Email:** admissions@mountsaintvincent.edu

Full-time: 305 men, 1105 women	**Faculty:** IIB, +$
Part-time: 30 men, 155 women	**Ph.D.s:** n/av
Graduate: 105 men, 310 women	**Student/Faculty:** n/av
Year: semesters, summer session	**Tuition:** $35,620
Room & Board: $9500	**Freshman Class:** 2991 applied, 2446 accepted, 450 enrolled
SAT CR/M: 500/500 **ACT:** required	**CEEB CODE:** 2088
Application Deadline: March 1	**COMPETITIVE**

College of Mount Saint Vincent, founded as an academy in 1847 and chartered as a college in 1911, is a private liberal arts institution in the Catholic tradition. The figures in the above capsule and in this profile are approximate. There is 1 undergraduate school and 1 graduate school. In addition to regional accreditation, The Mount has baccalaureate program accreditation with ACBSP and NLN. The 70-acre campus is in an urban area 12 miles north of New York City. Including any residence halls, there are 11 buildings.

STUDENT LIFE: 89% of undergraduates are from New York. Others are from 28 states, and 9 foreign countries. 45% are from public schools. 8% are two or more races; 5% Foreign; 38% Hispanic; 32% White; 14% African American; 10% Asian American. 81% are Catholic. **Female To Male Ratio:** 3.6:1. The average age of freshmen is 18; all undergraduates, 22. 25% do not continue beyond their first year; 62% remain to graduate. **Housing:** 778 students can be accommodated in college housing, which includes coed dorms. On-campus housing is guaranteed for all 4 years, and is available on a first-come, first-served basis, and is available on a lottery system for upperclassmen. 70% of students live on campus; of those, 65% remain on campus on weekends. All students may keep cars.

FACULTY/CLASSROOMS: 39% of faculty are male; 61% are female. All teach undergraduates, and 80% do research. No introductory courses are taught by graduate students. The average class size in an introductory lecture is 25; in a laboratory is 15; and in a regular course is 15.

PROGRAMS OF STUDY: The Mount confers B.A. and B.S. degrees. Master's and doctoral degrees are also awarded. Bachelor's degrees are awarded in BIOLOGICAL SCIENCE (biochemistry and biology/biological science), BUSINESS (business administration and management), COMMUNICATIONS AND THE ARTS (communications, English, French, modern language, and Spanish), COMPUTER AND PHYSICAL SCIENCE (chemistry, computer science, mathematics, and physics), EDUCATION (health education, physical education, and special education), HEALTH PROFESSIONS (allied health and nursing), SOCIAL SCIENCE (economics, history, liberal arts/general studies, philosophy, psychology, religion, sociology, and urban studies). Nursing, and biology are the strongest academically. Nursing, psychology, and business have the largest enrollments.

ACTIVITIES: There are no fraternities or sororities. There are 30 groups on campus, including art, cheerleading, chess, choir, chorus, computers, dance, debate, drama, ethnic, film, honors, international, LGBT, literary magazine, musical theater, newspaper, photography, professional, radio and TV, religious, social, social service, student government, and yearbook. Popular campus events include Phin Fest, Mount Madness, Brown Bag Bingo, Spring Concert and Theater Thursdays. **Sports:** There are 7 intercollegiate sports for men and 7 for women, and 5 intramural sports for men and 5 for women. Facilities include gyms, athletic and recreation center, a weight room, dance studio, fitness center with aerobic and Nautilus facilities, basketball court, and squash.

SERVICES: Counseling and information services are available, as is tutoring in most subjects, such as computer science, math, chemistry, biology, languages, psychology, sociology, writing, and economics. There is a reader service for the blind, and remedial math, reading, and writing. **Library/Resources:** The library contains 129,000 volumes, 7,000 microform items, 6,500 audio/video tapes/CDs/DVDs, and subscribes to 234 periodicals including electronic. Computerized library services include interlibrary loans, database searching, Internet access, and Wi-Fi capability. Special learning facilities include a radio station and TV station. **Physically Challenged Students:** 90% of the campus is accessible. Facilities include wheelchair ramps, elevators, special parking, specially equipped restrooms, lowered drinking fountains, and lowered telephones. **Special:** Cross-registration with Manhattan College offers cooperative B.A. programs in international studies, philosophy, phys ed, physics, religious studies, and urban affairs. Internships, work-study, study abroad in 6 countries, a 3-2 engineering degree with Manhattan College, dual majors, and student-designed majors in liberal arts are available. B.A.-B.S. degrees in computer science, health education, math, and psychology, and teacher dual certification programs with special education and elementary, middle school, and secondary education are possible. There are 15 national honor societies, a freshman honors program, and 5 departmental honors programs. **Visiting:** There are regularly scheduled orientations for prospective students, Upon request, students may have an interview with an admissions counselor, sit in on classes, and tour the campus. All students are invited to an open house. Accepted students may have a one-on-one meeting with a student on campus. There are guides for informal visits, visitors may sit in on classes, and stay overnight. To schedule a visit, contact the Admissions Office. **Campus Safety and Security:** Measures include 24-hour foot and vehicle patrol, emergency notification system, and security escort services. There are shuttle buses, emergency telephones, lighted pathways/sidewalks, controlled access to dorms/residences, a college committee on safety and security on campus.

REQUIREMENTS: The SAT or ACT is required. Applicants should have completed 4 high school academic units of English, 3 of science, and 2 each of math, foreign language, and social sciences, as well as electives. An essay is required, and an interview is recommended. One letter of recommendation is required, and additional letters are encouraged. AP and CLEP credits are accepted. Important factors in the admissions decision are advanced placement or honors courses, recommendations by school officials, and extracurricular activities record. All students must complete a 49-credit core curriculum with courses in humanities, social sciences, math and computers, and natural sciences. A total of 120 credits for a B.A. or 126 credits for a B.S., with a minimum of 30 credits in the major, and a minimum GPA of 2.0 are required. **Procedure:** Freshmen are admitted fall and spring. Entrance exams should be taken during the junior year and/or fall of the senior year. There are early admissions and rolling admissions plans. Early decision applications should be filed by November 15; regular applications, by March 1 for fall entry. Notification of early decision is sent December 15; regular decision, on a rolling basis. 50 applicants were on the 2016 waiting list; 35 were admitted. Applications are accepted on-line. **Transfer Students:** 41 transfer students enrolled in 2015-2016. Transfer applicants should have a minimum GPA of 2.0. Those majoring in nursing, the sciences, math, or computer science need at least a 2.5 GPA. An interview is recommended. 45 of 120 credits required for the bachelor's degree must be completed at The Mount. **International Students:** There are 30 international students enrolled. The school actively recruits these students. They must take the TOEFL with a minimum score of 80 on the paper-based TOEFL (PBT) or 80 on the Internet-based version (iBT), or complete ELS Level 109, available on campus. They must also take the SAT or ACT, scoring 900.

ADMISSIONS: 82% of the 2016-2017 applicants were accepted. **Admissions Contact:** Curt Dircks, Director for Admission. Email: *admissions@mountsaintvincent.edu* Web: *www.cmsv.edu*

FINANCIAL AID: In 2016-2017, 98% of all full-time freshmen received some form of financial aid. The average freshman award was $17,000. The Mount is a member of CSS. The FAFSA code is 002703. The priority date for freshman financial aid applications for fall entry is February 15. The filing deadline for fall entry is June 30.

COLUMBIA UNIVERSITY/ SCHOOL OF GENERAL STUDIES D-5

www.gs.columbia.edu

New York, NY 10027	**(212) 854-2772** **(800) 895-1169**
Fax: (212) 854-6316	**Email: gs-admit@columbia.edu**
Full-time: 949 men, 586 women	**Faculty:** n/av
Part-time: 224 men, 246 women	**Ph.D.s:** 100%
Graduate: n/av	**Student/Faculty:** 6 to 1
Year: semesters, summer session	**Tuition:** $51,114
Room & Board: $10,356	**Freshman Class:** n/av
SAT or ACT: recommended	**CEEB CODE:** 2095
Application Deadline: June 1	**MOST COMPETITIVE**

School of General Studies, is a liberal arts college created specifically for returning and nontraditional students seeking a rigorous, traditional, Ivy League undergraduate degree full or part time. GS is also home to the oldest and largest Postbaccalaureate Premedical Program in the United States, the Joint Program with Jewish Theological Seminary, the Dual BA Program Between Columbia University and Sciences Po, and the Joint Bachelor's Degree Program between City University of Hong Kong and Columbia University. There are 3 undergraduate schools and 14 graduate schools. The 36-acre campus is in an urban area in the Morningside Heights neighborhood on the Upper West Side of Manhattan in New York City.

STUDENT LIFE: 56% of undergraduates are from out of state. 9% are race unknown; 8% Asian American; 5% African American; 49% White; 10% Hispanic; 1% two or more races. **Male To Female Ratio:** 1.4:1. The average age of freshmen is 20; all undergraduates, 27. **Housing:** College-sponsored housing includes single-sex and coed off-campus apartments and married student housing. In addition, there are special-interest houses, fraternity houses, and international house. On-campus housing is available on a first-come and first-served basis. Priority is given to out-of-town students. 72% of students commute. Alcohol is not permitted. No one may keep cars.

FACULTY/CLASSROOMS: 66% of faculty are male; 34% are female. No introductory courses are taught by graduate students.

PROGRAMS OF STUDY: GS confers B.A. degrees. Bachelor's degrees are awarded in BIOLOGICAL SCIENCE (biology/biological science), COMMUNICATIONS AND THE ARTS (art history and appreciation, classics, comparative literature, dance, dramatic arts, English literature, film arts, French, German, Italian, literature, music, Slavic languages, Spanish, and visual and performing arts), COMPUTER AND PHYSICAL SCIENCE (applied mathematics, astronomy, chemistry, computer science, geoscience, mathematics, physics, and statistics), ENGINEERING AND ENVIRONMENTAL DESIGN (architecture and environmental science), SOCIAL SCIENCE (African American studies, anthropology, archeology, classical/ancient civilization, East Asian studies, economics, French studies, German area studies, Hispanic American studies, history, Italian studies, Latin American studies, Middle Eastern studies, philosophy, political science/government, psychology, religion, sociology, urban studies, and women's studies). Political science, economics, and English have the largest enrollments.

ACTIVITIES: There are 541 groups on campus, including art, band, cheerleading, chess, choir, chorale, chorus, computers, dance, debate, drama, environmental, ethnic, film, forensics, honors, international, jazz band, LGBT, literary magazine, marching band, musical theater, newspaper, opera, orchestra, photography, political, professional, radio and TV, religious, social, social service, student government, symphony, and yearbook. **Sports:** There are 14 intercollegiate sports for men and 16 for women, and 11 intramural sports for men and 11 for women. Facilities include 2 gyms, swimming pool, tennis, squash, and racquetball courts, a training center, dance/martial arts studios, a fencing room, a wrestling room, and an indoor track. **Graduates:** The most popular majors were economics, political science, and history. 300 companies recruited on campus in 2015-2016.

SERVICES: Counseling and information services are available, as is tutoring in most subjects, such as English, math, foreign languages, and sciences. **Library/Resources:** The 21 libraries contain 12.0 million volumes, 6.4 million microform items, and 179,457 audio/video tapes/CDs/DVDs, and subscribe to 167,884 periodicals including electronic. Computerized library services include interlibrary loans, database searching, Internet access, and Wi-Fi capability. Special learning facilities include an art gallery, radio station, and an observatory. **Physically Challenged Students:** All of the campus is accessible. Facilities include wheelchair ramps, elevators, specially equipped restrooms, lowered drinking fountains, and lowered telephones. **Special:** Pre-professional studies in allied health and medical fields and interdisciplinary majors, minors, and concentrations are offered. Internships in New York City, work-study programs on campus, study abroad, a 3-2 engineering degree at Columbia University School of Engineering and Applied Science, and combined and dual majors are available. There is a chapter of Phi Beta Kappa. **Visiting:** There are regularly scheduled orientations for prospective students, information session and campus tour. There are guides for informal visits and visitors may sit in on classes. To schedule a visit, contact Office of Admissions and Financial Aid. **Campus Safety and Security:** Measures include 24-hour foot and vehicle patrol, emergency notification system, self-defense education, and security escort services. There are shuttle buses, emergency telephones, lighted pathways/sidewalks, and controlled access to dorms/residences.

REQUIREMENTS: SAT, ACT, or Columbia's General Studies Admissions Exam (GSAE) scores are required, and must be submitted along with high school and all college transcripts. Students who have not taken the SAT or ACT within the last 8 years may take the GSAE. An autobiographical essay statement is required. Some students are required to complete an interview. GEDs are accepted. AP credits are accepted. Important factors in the admissions decision are extracurricular activities record, personality/intangible qualities, and evidence of special talent. All students must complete 124 credit hours, including 56 distribution requirement credits in literature, humanities, foreign language or literature, social science, science, and global studies, as well as the requirements for a major. At least 64 of the 124 credit hours required to graduate must be completed at Columbia University. Proficiency in English composition and math is required. A GPA of 2.0 is necessary to graduate. **Procedure:** Freshmen are admitted fall, spring, and summer. Entrance exams should be taken as early as possible. There are deferred admissions and rolling admissions plans. Early decision applications should be filed by March 1; regular applications, by June 1 for fall entry; November 1 for spring entry; and March 1 for summer entry, along with a $80 fee. Notification of early decision is sent May 1. Applications are accepted online. **Transfer Students:** 324 transfer students enrolled in 2015-2016. 64 of 124 credits required for the bachelor's degree must be completed at GS. **International Students:** The school actively recruits these students. They must take the TOEFL with a minimum score of 600 on the paper-based TOEFL (PBT) or 100 on the Internet-based version (iBT) and the college's own test. International students must take either the TOEFL or an English placement test administered by Columbia's American Language Program. They must also take the SAT or ACT, and the college's own entrance exam. Submission of recent SAT scores is encouraged. Students with no scores must take the General Studies Admissions Exam.

Admissions Contact: Matthew Rotstein, Dean of Admissions. Email: *mr2185@columbia.edu* Web: *www.gs.columbia.edu*

FINANCIAL AID: GS is a member of CSS. The college's own financial statement is required. The priority date for freshman financial aid applications for fall entry is March 1. The filing deadline for fall entry is June 1.

COLUMBIA UNIVERSITY/CITY OF NEW YORK — D-5

www.columbia.edu

New York, NY 10027 — **(212) 854-2522**

Fax: (212) 854-1209	**Email:** ugrad-ask@columbia.edu
Full-time: 3174 men, 2910 women	**Faculty:** I, ++$
Part-time: n/av	**Ph.D.s:** n/av
Graduate: n/av	**Student/Faculty:** 6 to 1
Year: semesters, summer session	**Tuition:** $50,526
Room & Board: $12,432	**Freshman Class:** 33531 applied, 2131 accepted, 1416 enrolled
SAT CR/M/W: 740/750/750 **ACT:** 33	**CEEB CODE:** 2116
Application Deadline: January 1	**MOST COMPETITIVE**

Columbia University in the City of New York, was founded in 1754. We offer undergraduate programs in liberal arts, and science programs in Columbia College and 1,500 major in The Fu Foundation School of Engineering & Applied Science. Students also have access to our more than a dozen graduate and professional schools, a traditional college campus in the neighborhood of Morningside Heights. The figures in the above capsule and in this profile are approximate. There are 4 undergraduate schools and 1 graduate school. The 36-acre campus is in an urban area in New York City. Including any residence halls, there are 50 buildings.

STUDENT LIFE: 77% of undergraduates are from out of state, mostly the Middle Atlantic. Students are from 50 states, 90 foreign countries, and Canada. 36% are White; 3% race unknown; 22% Asian American; 2% American Indian/Alaska Native; 13% Hispanic; 13% Foreign; 11% African American. **Male To Female Ratio:** 1.1:1. The average age of freshmen is 18; all undergraduates, 20. 1% do not continue beyond their first year; 99% remain to graduate. **Housing:** 5606 students can be accommodated in college housing, which includes single-sex and coed dorms and on-campus apartments. In addition, there are language houses, special-interest houses, and fraternity houses. On-campus housing is guaranteed for all 4 years and is available on a lottery system for upperclassmen. 94% of students live on campus. All students may keep cars.

FACULTY/CLASSROOMS: All teach undergraduates and do research. No introductory courses are taught by graduate students.

PROGRAMS OF STUDY: Columbia confers B.A. and B.S. degrees. Master's and doctoral degrees are also awarded. Bachelor's degrees are awarded in BIOLOGICAL SCIENCE (biochemistry, biology/biological science, biophysics, environmental biology, and neurosciences), BUSINESS (operations research), COMMUNICATIONS AND THE ARTS (art history and appreciation, classics, comparative literature, dance, dramatic arts, English, film arts, French, German, Germanic languages and literature, Greek, Latin, linguistics, music, Russian, Spanish, and visual and performing arts), COMPUTER AND PHYSICAL SCIENCE (applied mathematics, applied physics, astronomy, astrophysics, chemistry, computer science, earth science, geochemistry, geology, geophysics and seismology, mathematics, physics, and statistics), EDUCATION (education), ENGINEERING AND ENVIRONMENTAL DESIGN (architecture, biomedical engineering, chemical engineering, civil engineering, computer engineering, electrical/electronics engineering, engineering management, engineering mechanics, environmental science, industrial engineering technology, materials science, mechanical engineering, metallurgical engineering, and mining and mineral engineering), SOCIAL SCIENCE (African American studies, American studies, anthropology, archeology, area studies, Asian/American studies, classical/ancient civilization, East Asian studies, economics, Hispanic American studies, history, Italian studies, Latin American studies, medieval studies, Middle Eastern studies, philosophy, political science/ government, psychology, religion, Russian and Slavic studies, sociology, urban studies, and women's studies). Political science, economics, and engineering have the largest enrollments.

ACTIVITIES: 19% of men belong to 22 national fraternities; 9% of women belong to 11 national sororities. There are 500 groups on campus, including art, band, cheerleading, chess, choir, chorale, chorus, communications, computers, dance, debate, drama, environmental, ethnic, film, forensics, honors, international, jazz band, LGBT, literary magazine, marching band, musical theater, newspaper, opera, orchestra, pep band, photography, political, professional, radio and TV, religious, social, social service, student government, symphony, and yearbook. Popular campus events include New Student Orientation Program, Orgo Night, Bacchanal Spring Concert, and Tree Lighting Ceremony/Yule Log. **Sports:** There are 14 intercollegiate sports for men and 15 for women, and 20 intramural sports for men and 20 for women. Facilities include a football stadium, indoor and outdoor track, and field facilities, a baseball field, a soccer stadium, a recreational gym with a swimming pool, basketball/volleyball courts, aerobic, fencing, wrestling, martial arts, weight rooms, boat house, and tennis, squash, handball, and racquetball courts. **Graduates:** From July 1, 2015 to June 30, 2016, 1580 bachelor's degrees were awarded. The most popular majors were social sciences (22%), engineering (21%), and biological/life sciences (10%). 370 companies recruited on campus in 2015-2016. In an average class, 89% graduate in 4 years or less, 94% graduate in 5 years or less, and 96% graduate in 6 years or less.

SERVICES: Counseling and information services are available, as is tutoring in every subject. There is a reader service for the blind. **Library/ Resources:** The 22 libraries contain 12.0 million volumes. Computerized library services include interlibrary loans, database searching, Internet access, and Wi-Fi capability. Special learning facilities include an art gallery, planetarium, radio station, and an observatory. **Physically Challenged Students:** All of the campus is accessible. Facilities include wheelchair ramps, elevators, special parking, specially equipped restrooms, special class scheduling, lowered drinking fountains, lowered telephones, and special housing. **Special:** There are study abroad programs at more than 200 locations, including France, Oxford, Cambridge, Universities in England, and the Kyoto Center for Japanese Studies in Japan, and Biosphere 2 (Arizona). Cross-registration is possible with the Juilliard School and Barnard College. Combined B.A.-B.S. degrees are offered via 3-2 or 4-1 engineering programs. A 3-2 engineering degree is offered with Columbia's Fu Foundation School of Engineering and Applied Science. There is also a 5-year B.A./M.I.A. with Columbia's School of International and Public Affairs. The college offers work-study, internships, credit by exam, pass/fail options, and dual, student-designed, and interdisciplinary majors, including regional studies and ancient studies. There is a chapter of Phi Beta Kappa. **Visiting:** There are regularly scheduled orientations for prospective students, consisting of group information sessions and student-led tours as well as special science tours and engineering tours. There are guides for informal visits, visitors may sit in on classes, and stay overnight. To schedule a visit, contact the Visitors Center at (212) 854-4900. **Campus Safety and Security:** Measures include 24-hour foot and vehicle patrol, emergency notification system, self-defense education, and security escort services. There are shuttle buses, emergency telephones, lighted pathways/sidewalks, and controlled access to dorms/residences.

REQUIREMENTS: The SAT or ACT is required, as is the ACT Optional Writing test. The admissions application consists of the Common Application and Columbia Supplement; HS transcript; SAT and 2 SAT Subject Tests or ACT with Writing; 3 letters of reference; and an essay. AP credits are accepted. All students must complete a core curriculum consisting of classes in Western and non-Western cultures, literature and philosophy, history, social science, art, sculpture and architecture, and music of the Western tradition and science; 2 courses in non-Western areas are also required. Distribution requirements include 2 years of foreign language (unless competency can be demonstrated), 2 semesters of science, 1 year of phys ed, and 1 semester of writing. A thesis may be required for departmental honors in certain departments. A total of 124 credit hours is required; usually 30 to 40 of these are in the major. The engineering students are required to take Calculus, Physics, Chemistry and Economics and specific introductory engineering design courses in addition to half of the Columbia College core. The minimum required GPA is 2.0. **Procedure:** Freshmen are admitted fall. Entrance exams should be taken by Jan. of the senior year (RD) or Nov. (if ED). There are early decision and deferred admissions plans. Early decision applications should be filed by November 1; regular applications, by January 1 for fall entry, along with a $85 fee. Notification of early decision is sent December 15; regular decision, April 1. Applications are accepted on-line. **Transfer Students:** 123 transfer students enrolled in 2015-2016. Applicants must have completed 1 full year of college (24 credits). They must submit high school and college transcripts. 60 of 128 credits required for the bachelor's degree must be completed at Columbia. **International Students:** The school actively recruits these students. They must take the TOEFL with a minimum score of 100 on the Internet-based version (iBT), or take the IELTS. They must also take the SAT or ACT.

ADMISSIONS: 6% of the 2016-2017 applicants were accepted. The SAT scores for the 2016-2017 freshman class were: Critical Reading-- 3% between 500 and 599, 21% between 600 and 699, and 76% between 700 and 800. Math-- 2% between 500 and 599, 20% between 600 and 699, and 78% between 700 and 800. Writing-- 2% between 500 and 599, 24% between 600 and 699, and 74% between 700 and 800. The ACT scores were 10% between 24 and 29, and 90% above 30. **Admissions Contact:** Admissions Officer, Office of Undergraduate Admissions. Email: *ugrad-ask@columbia.edu* Web: *www.columbia.edu*

FINANCIAL AID: In 2016-2017, 51% of all full-time freshmen and 52% of continuing full-time students received some form of financial aid. 49% of all full-time freshmen and 50% of continuing full-time students received need-based aid. The average freshman award was $43,087. Need-based scholarships or need-based grants averaged $42,785; and need-based self-help aid (loans and jobs) averaged $2,263. Columbia is a member of CSS. The CSS/Profile, college's own financial statement, federal tax returns, business/farm supplement, and/or the divorced/ separated parents statement, if applicable, are required. The deadline for filing freshman financial aid applications for fall entry is March 1.

CONCORDIA COLLEGE - NEW YORK *(The complete profile is made available exclusively on our website, www.barronspac.com)*

COOPER UNION FOR THE ADVANCEMENT OF SCIENCE AND ART — D-5

www.cooper.edu

New York, NY 10003 — **(212) 353-4120**

Fax: (212) 353-4342	**Email:** admissions@cooper.edu
Full-time: 556 men, 307 women	**Faculty:** 50
Part-time: 1 men, 4 women	**Ph.D.s:** 90%
Graduate: 36 men, 16 women	**Student/Faculty:** 17 to 1
Year: semesters, summer session	**Tuition:** $42,650
Room & Board: $15,560	**Freshman Class:** 3193 applied, 247 accepted, 186 enrolled
SAT CR/M: 650/730 **ACT:** 31	**CEEB CODE:** 2097
Application Deadline: January 1	**MOST COMPETITIVE**

Cooper Union, offers degrees in architecture, art, and engineering. As of the Fall of 2014, new students receive a half-tuition scholarship, plus additional financial aid to help offset the costs of attendance. The figures in the above capsule and in this profile are approximate. There are 3 undergraduate schools and 1 graduate school. In addition to regional accreditation, Cooper Union has baccalaureate program accreditation with ABET, NAAB, and NASAD. The campus is in an urban area in New York City. Including any residence halls, there are 4 buildings.

STUDENT LIFE: 55% of undergraduates are from New York. Others are from 39 states, 14 foreign countries, and Canada. 70% are from public schools. 33% are White; 21% Asian American; 15% African American; 14% race unknown; 10% Foreign; 9% Hispanic; 4% two or more races; 1% American Indian/Alaska Native. **Male To Female Ratio:** 1.8:1. The average age of freshmen is 18; all undergraduates, 20. 5% do not continue beyond their first year; 81% remain to graduate. **Housing:** 178 students can be accommodated in college housing, which includes coed dorms. On-campus housing is available on a first-come, and first-served basis, and is available on a lottery system for upperclassmen. 80% of students commute. Some may keep cars.

FACULTY/CLASSROOMS: 73% of faculty are male; 27% are female. All teach undergraduates and do research. No introductory courses are taught by graduate students. The average class size in an introductory lecture is 25; in a laboratory is 16; and in a regular course is 20.

PROGRAMS OF STUDY: The Cooper Union confers B.S., B.Arch., B.E., and B.F.A. degrees. Master's degrees are also awarded. Bachelor's degrees are awarded in COMMUNICATIONS AND THE ARTS (fine arts and graphic design), ENGINEERING AND ENVIRONMENTAL DESIGN (architecture, chemical engineering, civil engineering, electrical/electronics engineering, engineering, and mechanical engineering). Architecture, fine art, and engineering are the strongest academically. Engineering has the largest enrollment.

ACTIVITIES: There are 90 groups on campus, including art, band, chess, chorale, computers, dance, drama, environmental, ethnic, film, honors, international, jazz band, LGBT, literary magazine, musical theater, newspaper, orchestra, photography, political, professional, religious, social, social service, student government, and yearbook. Popular campus events include Annual Culture Show, Annual Talent Show, End-of-the-Year Student Art, Architecture and Engineering Exhibit and ongoing events in the Great Hall. **Sports:** There are 5 intercollegiate sports for men and 3 for women, and 12 intramural sports for men and 12 for women. Facilities include access to local gyms on weekends, a nearby swimming pool, and basketball courts. **Graduates:** From July 1, 2015 to June 30, 2016, 184 bachelor's degrees were awarded. The most popular majors were fine arts (30%), electrical engineering (16%), and mechanical engineering (15%). 110 companies recruited on campus in 2015-2016. In an average class, 1% graduate in 3 years or less, 70% graduate in 4 years or less, 81% graduate in 5 years or less, and 82% graduate in 6 years or less. Of the 2015 graduating class, 42% were enrolled in graduate school within 6 months of graduation, and 42% were employed.

SERVICES: Counseling and information services are available, as is tutoring in some subjects, such as math, physics, speech, writing, and other forms of communication. **Library/Resources:** The library contains 147,552 volumes, 24,217 microform items, 2,228 audio/video tapes/CDs/DVDs, and subscribes to 9,730 periodicals including electronic. Computerized library services include interlibrary loans, database searching, and Internet access. Special learning facilities include an art gallery, center for speaking and writing, electronic resources center, and a visual resources center. **Physically Challenged Students:** 80% of the campus is accessible. Facilities include wheelchair ramps, elevators, specially equipped restrooms, special class scheduling, and special housing. **Special:** Cross-registration with New School University, internships, formal study abroad for art and engineering students. Non-degree study is possible. An accelerated degree in engineering is also available (combined bachelors and masters degree program). Cooper Union also participates in a joint MEng/MD degree program with SUNY Downstate Medical Center. Students are permitted, with approval, to take an elective leave to further pursue their interests and long term goals. There are 4 national honor societies and 1 departmental honors program. **Visiting:** There are regularly scheduled orientations for prospective students, consisting of open house and portfolio review days for art and open house for engineering; architecture tours are by appointment. There are guides for informal visits and visitors may sit in on classes. To schedule a visit, contact the Office of Admissions and Records. **Campus Safety and Security:** Measures include emergency notification system, emergency telephones, lighted pathways/sidewalks, and controlled access to dorms/residences. There are security guards in all building lobbies and hand-scan technology in the residence hall.

REQUIREMENTS: The SAT or ACT is required. Engineering applicants must take SAT Subject Tests in mathematics I or II and physics or chemistry. Graduation from an approved secondary school is required. Applicants should have completed 16 to 18 high school academic credits, depending on their major. An essay is part of the application process. Art students must submit a portfolio. Art and architecture applicants must complete a project called the home test. AP credits are accepted. Important factors in the admissions decision are personality/intangible qualities, evidence of special talent, and advanced placement or honors courses. The 5-year architecture program requires 160 credits, including 30 in liberal arts and electives, for graduation. Art students must complete 128 credits, including 38 in liberal arts and electives. Engineering students are required to complete a minimum of 135 credits, including a computer programming course and approximately 12-28 credits in humanities and social sciences, with a minimum GPA of 2.0. All students must complete a four semester sequence of humanities and social science courses. **Procedure:** Freshmen are admitted fall. Entrance exams should be taken before February 1. There are early decision, early admissions, and deferred admissions plans. Early decision applications should be filed by December 1; regular applications, by January 1 for fall entry, along with a $70 fee. Notification of early decision is sent February 1; regular decision, April 1. 75 early decision candidates were accepted for the 2016-2017 class. 75 applicants were on the 2016 waiting list; 15 were admitted. Applications are accepted on-line. **Transfer Students:** 20 transfer students enrolled in 2015-2016. Art and architecture transfer applicants must present a portfolio and a minimum of 24 credits in studio classes. Engineering transfer applicants must submit a transcript with grades of B or better in at least 24 credits of appropriate courses. 68 of 128 credits required for the bachelor's degree must be completed at The Cooper Union. **International Students:** There are 86 international students enrolled. They must take the TOEFL with a minimum score of 600 on the paper-based TOEFL (PBT) or 100 on the Internet-based version (iBT). They must also take the SAT or ACT, and the college's own entrance exam. All freshman applicants must take the SAT. Art and architecture students must also take the home test.

ADMISSIONS: 8% of the 2016-2017 applicants were accepted. The SAT scores for the 2016-2017 freshman class were: Critical Reading-- 3% below 500, 19% between 500 and 599, 47% between 600 and 699, and 31% between 700 and 800. Math-- 9% below 500, 17% between 500 and 599, 18% between 600 and 699, and 57% between 700 and 800. The ACT scores were 25% between 24 and 29, and 75% above 30. 90% of the current freshmen were in the top fifth of their class; 95% were in the top two fifths. 10 freshmen graduated first in their class. **Admissions Contact:** Mitchell Lipton, Dean of Admissions and Records. Email: *admissions@cooper.edu* Web: *www.cooper.edu*

FINANCIAL AID: In 2016-2017, 100% of all full-time freshmen and continuing full-time students received some form of financial aid. 36% of all full-time freshmen and 35% of continuing full-time students received need-based aid. The average freshman award was $37,500. Need-based scholarships or need-based grants averaged $5,254 ($5,500 maximum); need-based self-help aid (loans and jobs) averaged $3,217 ($3,768 maximum); and other non-need-based awards and non-need-based scholarships averaged $37,500 ($37,500 maximum). 47% of undergraduate students work part-time. Average annual earnings from campus work are $1001. The average financial indebtedness of the 2016 graduate was $14,902. The Cooper Union is a member of CSS. The CSS/Profile is required. The FAFSA code is 002710. The priority date for freshman financial aid applications for fall entry is April 15. The filing deadline for fall entry is May 1.

CORNELL UNIVERSITY — C-4

www.cornell.edu

Ithaca, NY 14850 — **(607) 255-5241**

Fax: (607) 255-0659	**Email:** admissions@cornell.edu
Full-time: 6989 men, 7577 women	**Faculty:** n/av
Part-time: n/av	**Ph.D.s:** n/av
Graduate: 4322 men, 3431 women	**Student/Faculty:** n/av
Year: semesters, summer session	**Tuition:** $50,953
Room & Board: $13,900	**Freshman Class:** 44965 applied, 6337 accepted, 3315 enrolled
SAT or ACT: required	**CEEB CODE:** 2098
Application Deadline: January 2	**MOST COMPETITIVE**

Cornell University, was founded in 1865, as the federal land-grant institution of New York State. It is a private endowed university, a member of the Ivy League/Ancient Eight, and a partner of the State University of New York. It has seven undergraduate units and four graduate and professional units in Ithaca, two medical graduate and professional units in New York City, and one in Doha, Qatar. The Cornell NYC Tech Campus in New York City is the latest addition. In addition to regional accreditation, Cornell has baccalaureate program accreditation with AACSB, ABET, ASLA, NAAB, CIDA, ABA, and PAB. The 745-acre campus is in a rural area 60 miles south of Syracuse, NY. Including any residence halls, there are 657 buildings.

STUDENT LIFE: 66% of undergraduates are from out of state, mostly

the Middle Atlantic. Students are from 50 states, 93 foreign countries, and Canada. 8% are race unknown; 6% African American; 5% two or more races; 39% White; 18% Asian American; 12% Hispanic; 11% Foreign. **Male To Female Ratio:** 1.0:1. The average age of freshmen is 18; all undergraduates, 20. 3% do not continue beyond their first year; 97% remain to graduate. **Housing:** 8806 students can be accommodated in college housing, which includes single-sex and coed dorms, on-campus apartments, and married student housing. In addition, there are language houses, special-interest houses, fraternity houses, and sorority houses. On-campus housing is available on a lottery system for upperclassmen. 54% of students live on campus; of those, 90% remain on campus on weekends. All students may keep cars.

FACULTY/CLASSROOMS: No introductory courses are taught by graduate students.

PROGRAMS OF STUDY: Cornell confers B.A., B.S., B.Arch. and B.F.A. degrees. Master's and doctoral degrees are also awarded. Bachelor's degrees are awarded in AGRICULTURE (agricultural sciences, animal science, international agriculture/rural development, plant science, and viticulture and enology), BIOLOGICAL SCIENCE (biology/biological science, biology and society, biometrics and biostatistics, entomology, human biology, health, and society, and nutritional sciences), BUSINESS (applied economics/management, hotel and restaurant administration, industrial and labor relations, and policy analysis and management), COMMUNICATIONS AND THE ARTS (Africana studies, art history, China Asia-Pacific studies, classics, communications, comparative literature, design and environmental analysis, English, fiber science and apparel design, fine arts, French, German, Italian, linguistics, music, performing and media arts, and Spanish), COMPUTER AND PHYSICAL SCIENCE (astronomy, atmospheric science, chemistry/ chemical biology, computer science, inform, science, systems & technology, information science, mathematics, physics, science of earth systems, science of natural and environmental systems, science and technology studies, and statistics), EDUCATION (Asian studies), ENGINEERING AND ENVIRONMENTAL DESIGN (architecture, bioengineering, chemical engineering, civil engineering, electrical and computer engineering, engineering physics, environmental engineering, landscape architecture, materials science and engineering, mechanical engineering, and operations research and engineering), HEALTH PROFESSIONS (global & public health sciences), SOCIAL SCIENCE (American studies, anthropology, archeology, developmental sociology, economics, government, feminist, gender, sexuality studies, food science, German area studies, history, human development, Near Eastern studies, philosophy, psychology, religious studies, sociology, and urban and regional studies). Engineering, business, and liberal arts & sciences have the largest enrollments.

ACTIVITIES: 25% of men belong to 2 local and 42 national fraternities; 25% of women belong to 21 national sororities. There are 1017 groups on campus, including art, band, cheerleading, chess, choir, chorale, chorus, communications, computers, dance, debate, drama, drill team, environmental, ethnic, film, forensics, honors, international, jazz band, LGBT, literary magazine, marching band, musical theater, newspaper, orchestra, pep band, photography, political, professional, radio and TV, religious, social, social service, student government, symphony, and yearbook. Popular campus events include Dragon Day, Third World Festival of the Arts, Slope Day, ClubFest, Festival of Black Gospel, A Capella Concerts, Fashion Shows, Bhangra Dance Shows, Filthy Gorgeous (LGBTQ Celebration), Mid Autumn Festival, Yamatai, HOLI, Israel Day. **Sports:** There are 18 intercollegiate sports for men and 19 for women, and 24 intramural sports for men and 24 for women. Facilities include indoor and outdoor track, arena, swimming pools, football/ lacrosse stadium, strength & conditioning center, bowling alley, rowing center, golf course, fencing Salle, community recreation center, rink, indoor and outdoor tennis courts, international squash courts, equestrian center, wrestling center, sailing center, and climbing wall. **Graduates:** From July 1, 2015 to June 30, 2016, 3674 bachelor's degrees were awarded. The most popular majors were agriculture, biological/life sciences, and business marketing (39%), engineering (16%), and social sciences (10%). 369 companies recruited on campus in 2015-2016. In an average class, 8% graduate in 3 years or less, 87% graduate in 4 years or less, 93% graduate in 5 years or less, and 94% graduate in 6 years or less. Of the 2015 graduating class, 24% were enrolled in graduate school within 6 months of graduation, and 62% were employed.

SERVICES: Counseling and information services are available, as is tutoring in some subjects. There is a reader service for the blind. Peer-facilitated, active-learning study groups are available for many introductory science classes. Biology and math student support centers, and writing workshops are also available. **Library/Resources:** The 17 libraries contain 9.2 million volumes, 175,144 audio/video tapes/CDs/DVDs, and subscribe to 125,023 periodicals including electronic. Computerized library services include interlibrary loans, database searching, Internet access, and Wi-Fi capability. Special learning facilities include an art gallery, radio station, biotechnology institute, woods sanctuary, national resource centers, optical observatories, Africana studies, research center, arboretum, particle accelerator, supercomputers, national research centers, performing arts center, lab of ornithology, vertebrates museum, living and learning communities, campus orchard, dairy pilot plant, mineralogical museum, animal teaching hospital, 2 agricultural experiment stations, student farm, and a marine laboratory. **Physically Challenged Students:** Facilities include wheelchair ramps, elevators, special parking, specially equipped restrooms, lowered drinking fountains, lowered telephones, and special housing. They also offer testing accommodations, course materials in alternate formats, transportation assistance around campus, assistive listening devices, assistive technology, dining options to address dietary restrictions, classes located in accessible locations. **Special:** Cornell's colleges and schools offer nearly unlimited opportunities for international study internships and exchanges. There are opportunities for dual-majors and minors throughout the university. Refer to information provided by the individual schools, colleges, and programs for details. There are 7 national honor societies and a chapter of Phi Beta Kappa. **Visiting:** There are regularly scheduled orientations for prospective students, Student visits consist of campus tours and information sessions. There are guides for informal visits, visitors may sit in on classes, and stay overnight. To schedule a visit, contact The Red Carpet Society at (607) 255-3447. **Campus Safety and Security:** Measures include 24-hour foot and vehicle patrol, emergency notification system, self-defense education, and security escort services. There are shuttle buses, emergency telephones, lighted pathways/sidewalks, controlled access to dorms/residences. Cornell also has specially assigned crime prevention officers who create and maintain educational outreach programs and conduct security reviews of on campus locations. A building Security Committee comprised of Crime Prevention, the Chief's office, University Architect, Planning and Construction and Project Management personnel, ensure new facilities and major renovations take full advantage of reasonable security devices and measures. The Public Safety Advisory Committee comprised of students, staff and faculty representatives who meet regularly to review on campus crime prevention and education efforts. There are also larger councils on hazing, alcohol, sexual and domestic violence and mental health and wellness, which are comprise of students, faculty and staff, and chaired by executive level administrators. These committees include more members and meet often.

REQUIREMENTS: The SAT or ACT is required. An essay is required as part of the application process. Other requirements vary by division or program, including specific SAT Subject tests and selection of courses within the minimum 16 secondary-school academic units needed. An interview and/or portfolio is required for specific majors. AP credits are accepted. A student's college determines degree requirements such as residency, number of credits, distribution of credits, and grade averages. See the individual requirements listed by each college or school or contact the college registrar's office. **Procedure:** Freshmen are admitted fall and spring. There are early decision and deferred admissions plans. Early decision applications should be filed by November 1; regular applications, by January 2 for fall entry. The fall 2016 application fee was $80. Notifications are sent in April. 1196 early decision candidates were accepted for the 2016-2017 class. 2874 applicants were on the 2016 waiting list; 61 were admitted. Application fees are waived if application is completed online. **Transfer Students:** 585 transfer students enrolled in 2015-2016. All applicants must submit high school and college transcripts, as well as scores from the SAT or ACT. Other admission requirements vary by program, including the number of credits that must be completed at Cornell. 60 of 120 credits required for the bachelor's degree must be completed at Cornell. **International Students:** There are 1554 international students enrolled. The school actively recruits these students. They must take the TOEFL with a minimum score of 600 on the paper-based TOEFL (PBT) or 100 on the Internet-based version (iBT), the IELTS (International English Language Testing System) is also accepted. They must also take the SAT or ACT.

ADMISSIONS: 14% of the 2016-2017 applicants were accepted. The SAT scores for the 2016-2017 freshman class were: Critical Reading-- 8% between 500 and 599, 37% between 600 and 699, and 55% between 700 and 800. Math-- 5% between 500 and 599, 25% between 600 and 699, and 70% between 700 and 800. The ACT scores were 1% between 18 and 23, 14% between 24 and 29, and 85% above 30. **Admissions Contact:** Shawn Felton, Director of Undergraduate Admissions. Email: *admissions@cornell.edu* Web: *www.cornell.edu*

FINANCIAL AID: In 2016-2017, 60% of all full-time freshmen and 54% of continuing full-time students received some form of financial aid. 46% of all full-time freshmen and 45% of continuing full-time students received need-based aid. The average freshman award was $46,569. Need-based scholarships or need-based grants averaged $40,333; and need-based self-help aid (loans and jobs) averaged $5,327. 40% of undergraduate students work part-time. Average annual earnings from campus work are $2300. The average financial indebtedness of the 2016 graduate was $23,389. The CSS/Profile, college's own financial statement, and the IRS form is required after enrollment. The FAFSA code is 002711. The deadline for filing freshman financial aid applications for fall entry is February 15.

DAEMEN COLLEGE — A-3

www.daemen.edu

Amherst, NY 14226	(716) 566-7861 (800) 462-7652
Fax: (716) 839-8229	**Email:** admissions@daemen.edu
Full-time: 470 men, 1207 women	**Faculty:** IIA, -$
Part-time: 98 men, 270 women	**Ph.D.s:** n/av
Graduate: 177 men, 578 women	**Student/Faculty:** n/av
Year: semesters, summer session	**Tuition:** $25,995
Room & Board: $12,050	**Freshman Class:** n/av **CEEB CODE:** 2762
Application Deadline: open	**COMPETITIVE**

Daemen College, founded in 1947, is a private institution offering undergraduate and graduate programs in the liberal and fine arts, business, education, allied health professions, and natural sciences. The figures in the above capsule and in this profile are approximate. There is 1 undergraduate school and 1 graduate school. In addition to regional accreditation, Daemen has baccalaureate program accreditation with APTA, CSWE, NLN, TEAC, ARC-PA, IACBE, and ACEN. The 35-acre campus is in a suburban area 9 miles northeast of downtown Buffalo. Including any residence halls, there are 16 buildings.

STUDENT LIFE: 96% of undergraduates are from New York. Others are from 30 states, 4 foreign countries, and Canada. 9% are African American; 85% White; 2% Hispanic; 1% Asian American; 1% American Indian/Alaska Native; 1% Foreign. 42% are Catholic; 15% Protestant. **Female To Male Ratio:** 2.8:1. The average age of freshmen is 18; all undergraduates, 23. 26% do not continue beyond their first year; 54% remain to graduate. **Housing:** 800 students can be accommodated in college housing, which includes coed dorms, quiet dorms, on-campus apartments, and off-campus apartments. On-campus housing is guaranteed for all 4 years. 65% of students commute. All students may keep cars.

FACULTY/CLASSROOMS: 40% of faculty are male; 60% are female. 64% teach undergraduates, 1% do research, and 1% do both. No introductory courses are taught by graduate students. The average class size in an introductory lecture is 17; in a laboratory is 10; and in a regular course is 14.

PROGRAMS OF STUDY: Daemen confers B.A., B.S., B.S./M.S. and B.F.A. degrees. Master's and doctoral degrees are also awarded. Bachelor's degrees are awarded in AGRICULTURE (environmental studies), BIOLOGICAL SCIENCE (biochemistry and biology/biological science), BUSINESS (accounting and business administration and management), COMMUNICATIONS AND THE ARTS (animation, applied art, art, arts administration/management, English, fine arts, French, graphic design, and Spanish), COMPUTER AND PHYSICAL SCIENCE (mathematics and natural sciences), EDUCATION (art education, early childhood education, elementary education, English education, foreign languages education, mathematics education, science education, and social studies education), HEALTH PROFESSIONS (health science, nursing, physician's assistant, and preventive/wellness health care), SOCIAL SCIENCE (history, paralegal studies, political science/government, psychology, religion, and social work). Physical therapy, physician assistant, and natural science are the strongest academically. Nursing, physical therapy, and natural science have the largest enrollments.

ACTIVITIES: 6% of men belong to 1 local fraternity; 4% of women belong to 4 local sororities. There are 47 groups on campus, including amnesty international, academic clubs, athletic clubs, pre-law association, student without borders, art, cheerleading, choir, dance, drama, environmental, ethnic, honors, LGBT, literary magazine, musical theater, newspaper, political, professional, social, social service, student government, wellness club, and yearbook. Popular campus events include Homecoming, Battle of the Bands, and Spring Fest. **Sports:** There are 7 intercollegiate sports for men and 9 for women, and 4 intramural sports for men and 2 for women. Facilities include basketball, cross country, golf, soccer, tennis, track and field, a gym, weight and exercise rooms, and volleyball sand court. **Graduates:** From July 1, 2015 to June 30, 2016, 279 bachelor's degrees were awarded. The most popular majors were nursing (18%), natural science (16%), and early childhood/childhood education (15%). 80 companies recruited on campus in 2015-2016. In an average class, 35% graduate in 4 years or less, 50% graduate in 5 years or less, and 54% graduate in 6 years or less. Of the 2015 graduating class, 25% were enrolled in graduate school within 6 months of graduation, and 90% were employed.

SERVICES: Counseling and information services are available, as is tutoring in every subject. There is remedial math, reading, and writing. **Library/Resources:** The library contains 140,576 volumes, 28,055 microform items, 2,354 audio/video tapes/CDs/DVDs, and subscribes to 31,925 periodicals including electronic. Computerized library services include interlibrary loans, database searching, Internet access, and Wi-Fi capability. Special learning facilities include an art gallery, and a video conference center. **Physically Challenged Students:** 83% of the campus is accessible. Facilities include wheelchair ramps, elevators, special parking, specially equipped restrooms, lowered drinking fountains, and lowered telephones. **Special:** Daemen offers cooperative programs in all majors, internships, cross-registration within the Western New York Consortium of Colleges and Universities, student-designed majors, work-study programs, an accelerated degree program in nursing, dual majors, a Washington semester, and study abroad in 6 countries. There is also an International Studies, Program that leads to a minor in international studies. There are 8 national honor societies, a freshman honors program, and 20 departmental honors programs. **Visiting:** There are regularly scheduled orientations for prospective students, two 5-day orientations that includes a campus tour, an interview, and placement testing in math and English during July and August. Fall Open House is in October, College Night in September, and Day @ Daemen in September and November are also offered. There are guides for informal visits, visitors may sit in on classes, and stay overnight. To schedule a visit, contact the Admissions Office. **Campus Safety and Security:** Measures include 24-hour foot and vehicle patrol, emergency notification system, and security escort services. There are emergency telephones, lighted pathways/sidewalks, including video monitors.

REQUIREMENTS: Applicants must be graduates of an accredited secondary school or have the GED equivalent. Some departments have further admissions requirements, including a portfolio review for art majors, 3-year sequences of math and science for all natural science programs, and 2 essays, 3 letters of recommendation, and a supplemental application for the physician assistant program. A GPA of 86.0 is required. AP and CLEP credits are accepted. Important factors in the admissions decision are advanced placement or honors courses, leadership record, and evidence of special talent. To graduate, students must complete 120 to 199 hours (depending on the degree program) with a minimum GPA of 2.0. Students are required to complete a minimum of 30 credit hours of course work in residence. The final semester's course work must be taken in residence. **Procedure:** Freshmen are admitted fall, spring, and summer. Entrance exams should be taken by the summer following the senior year. There are early admissions, deferred admissions, and rolling admissions plans. Application deadlines are open. Application fee is $25. Notification is sent on a rolling basis. Applications are accepted online. **Transfer Students:** 266 transfer students enrolled in 2015-2016. Applicants must present college transcripts and an indication of good standing from the last institution attended and a minimum GPA of 2.0. to 2.8. Physician assistant applicants should submit essays, 3 letters of recommendation, and supplemental applications. 30 of 120 credits required for the bachelor's degree must be completed at Daemen. **International Students:** There are 15 international students enrolled. The school actively recruits these students. They must take the TOEFL.

Admissions Contact: Frank Williams, Associate Vice President for Enrollment Management and Dean of Admissions. Email: *admissions@daemen.edu* Web: *daemen.edu*

FINANCIAL AID: In 2016-2017, 94% of all full-time freshmen and 94% of continuing full-time students received some form of financial aid. 83% of all full-time freshmen and 82% of continuing full-time students received need-based aid. The average freshman award was $12,769. Need-based scholarships or need-based grants averaged $8,931; need-based self-help aid (loans and jobs) averaged $4,356; non-need-based athletic scholarships averaged $6,833; and other non-need-based awards and non-need-based scholarships averaged $3,149. 20% of undergraduate students work part-time. Average annual earnings from campus work are $1077. The average financial indebtedness of the 2016 graduate was $20,465. The state aid form, and foreign student certification of finances is required. The FAFSA code is 002808. The deadline for filing freshman financial aid applications for fall entry is March 15.

DOMINICAN COLLEGE *(The complete profile is made available exclusively on our website, www.barronspac.com)*

D'YOUVILLE COLLEGE — A-3
www.dyc.edu

Buffalo, NY 14201	**(716) 829-7600** **(800) 777-3921**
Fax: (716) 829-7900	**Email: admiss@dyc.edu**
Full-time: 378 men, 1041 women	**Faculty:** 189
Part-time: 98 men, 298 women	**Ph.D.s:** 51%
Graduate: 373 men, 721 women	**Student/Faculty:** 10 to 1
Year: semesters, summer session	**Tuition:** $24,420
Room & Board: $11,180	**Freshman Class:** 1216 applied, 854 accepted, 233 enrolled
SAT CR/M/W: 521/531/499 **ACT:** 23	**CEEB CODE:** 2197
Application Deadline: open	**COMPETITIVE**

D'Youville College, founded in 1908, is a private, nonsectarian liberal arts institution granting degrees at the bachelors, masters, first professional and doctoral levels. Figures in the above capsule and in this profile are approximate. There is 1 undergraduate school and 1 graduate school. In addition to regional accreditation, D'Youville has baccalaureate program accreditation with ADA, APTA, CCNE, MACHE, and IACBE. The 10-acre campus is in an urban area 1 mile north of downtown Buffalo. Including any residence halls, there are 12 buildings.

STUDENT LIFE: 93% of undergraduates are from New York. Others are from 22 states, 46 foreign countries, and Canada. 80% are from public schools. 72% are White; 9% African American; 5% Foreign; 4% Asian American; 4% Hispanic; 4% race unknown; 2% two or more races; 1% American Indian/Alaska Native. 51% are Anglican, Buddhist, Christian, Hindu, Muslim, and unknown; 23% Catholic; 23% claim no religious affiliation. **Female To Male Ratio:** 2.4:1. The average age of freshmen is 18; all undergraduates, 22. 22% do not continue beyond their first year; 44% remain to graduate. **Housing:** 478 students can be accommodated in college housing, which includes single-sex and coed dorms,on-campus apartments, quiet levels, and 21 and older floors. On-campus housing is guaranteed for all 4 years. 83% of students commute. All students may keep cars.

FACULTY/CLASSROOMS: 33% of faculty are male; 67% are female. All teach undergraduates, and do research. No introductory courses are taught by graduate students.

PROGRAMS OF STUDY: D'Youville confers B.A., B.S., B.S./M.S., and B.S.N. degrees. Master's and doctoral degrees are also awarded. Bachelor's degrees are awarded in BIOLOGICAL SCIENCE (biology/biological science), BUSINESS (accounting and business administration and management), COMMUNICATIONS AND THE ARTS (English), COMPUTER AND PHYSICAL SCIENCE (information sciences and systems and mathematics), HEALTH PROFESSIONS (exercise science, health care administration, nursing, and physician's assistant), SOCIAL SCIENCE (dietetics, history, interdisciplinary studies, international studies, philosophy, psychology, and sociology). Education, and health professions are the strongest academically. Health professions, business, and nursing have the largest enrollments.

ACTIVITIES: There are no fraternities or sororities. There are 35 groups on campus, including cheerleading, chorus, computers, dance, drama, drill team, ethnic, honors, international, LGBT, literary magazine, newspaper, professional, religious, social, social service, and student government. Popular campus events include Moving Up Days, International Fiesta, and Honors Convocation. **Sports:** There are 7 intercollegiate sports for men and 7 for women. Facilities include a gym with basketball and volleyball courts, indoor batting cage, athletic fields, fitness facility with aerobic and free weights, swimming pool, and dance studio. **Graduates:** From July 1, 2015 to June 30, 2016, 389 bachelor's degrees were awarded. The most popular majors were health professions and related sciences (71%), business/marketing (8%), and interdisciplinary studies (6%). In an average class, 23% graduate in 4 years or less, 36% graduate in 5 years or less, and 44% graduate in 6 years or less.

SERVICES: Counseling and information services are available, as is tutoring in some subjects. There is a reader service for the blind, and remedial math, reading, and writing. **Library/Resources:** The library contains 96,876 volumes, 205,411 microform items, and 4,246 audio/video tapes/CDs/DVDs, and subscribes to 683 periodicals including electronic. Computerized library services include interlibrary loans, database searching, Internet access, and Wi-Fi capability. **Physically Challenged Students:** 95% of the campus is accessible. Facilities include wheelchair ramps, elevators, special parking, specially equipped restrooms, lowered drinking fountains, and special housing. **Special:** D'Youville has cross-registration with member colleges of the Western New York Consortium. Internships, work-study programs, dual majors, study abroad in 5 countries, and pass/fail options are available. Accelerated 5-year B.S.-M.S. programs in occupational therapy, international business, elementary education, physician's assistant and nursing, and dietetics are offered. For freshmen with undecided majors, the Career Discovery Program offers special courses, internships, and faculty advisers. There are 3 national honor societies and 2 departmental honors programs. **Visiting:** There are regularly scheduled orientations for prospective students as well as guides for informal visits, visitors may sit in on classes, and stay overnight. To schedule a visit, contact the Admissions Office. **Campus Safety and Security:** Measures include 24-hour foot and vehicle patrol, emergency notification system, self-defense education, and security escort services. There are emergency telephones, lighted pathways/sidewalks, a special focus program, and a security committee.

REQUIREMENTS: The SAT or ACT is required. Applicants should have completed 16 Carnegie units, including 4 years of high school English, 3 years of social studies, and 1 year each of math and science. Some majors require additional years of math and science. The GED is accepted as is AP and CLEP credits. All students must complete general program and core curriculum requirements, including 5 courses in humanities, 2 each in English and natural sciences, and 1 each in ethics, philosophy or religion, history, sociology, psychology, economics or political science, math, and computer science. A minimum of 120 to 144 credit hours, varying by major, with a minimum GPA of 2.0, (higher for some programs), is required to graduate. **Procedure:** Freshmen are admitted fall and spring. Entrance exams should be taken by the end of the junior year. There are deferred admissions and rolling admissions plans. Application deadlines are open. Applications are accepted online. **Transfer Students:** 252 transfer students enrolled in 2015-2016. Applicants need a minimum GPA of 2.0, or 2.5 for some programs. 30 of 120 credits required for the bachelor's degree must be completed at D'Youville. **International Students:** There are 86 international students enrolled. The school actively recruits these students. They must take the TOEFL with a minimum score of 500 on the paper-based TOEFL (PBT) or 61 on the Internet-based version (iBT). They must also take the SAT or ACT, scoring 900.

ADMISSIONS: 70% of the 2016-2017 applicants were accepted. The SAT scores for the 2016-2017 freshman class were: Critical Reading-- 32% below 500, 46% between 500 and 599, 21% between 600 and 699, and 1% between 700 and 800. Math-- 36% below 500, 49% between 500 and 599, and 45% between 600 and 699. Writing-- 53% below 500, 36% between 500 and 599, 10% between 600 and 699, and 1% between 700 and 800. The ACT scores were 5% between 12 and 17, 41% between 18 and 23, and 54% between 24 and 29. **Admissions Contact:** Steven Smith, Director of Undergraduate Admissions. Email: *admiss@dyc.edu* Web: *www.dyc.edu*

FINANCIAL AID: In 2016-2017, 89% of all full-time freshmen and 87% of continuing full-time students received some form of financial aid. 88% of all full-time freshmen and 84% of continuing full-time students received need-based aid. The average freshman award was $18,923. The state aid form is required. The FAFSA code is 002712. The priority date for freshman financial aid applications for fall entry is March 1. The filing deadline for fall entry is April 15.

EASTMAN SCHOOL OF MUSIC/UNIVERSITY OF ROCHESTER

(The complete profile is made available exclusively on our website, www.barronspac.com)

ELMIRA COLLEGE — B-4
www.elmira.edu

Elmira, NY 14901	(607) 735-1724 (800) 935-6472
Fax: (607) 735-1718	Email: admissions@elmira.edu
Full-time: 305 men, 669 women	**Faculty:** 71
Part-time: 26 men, 101 women	**Ph.D.s:** 87%
Graduate: 29 men, 57 women	**Student/Faculty:** 11 to 1
Year: other, summer session	**Tuition:** $41,900
Room & Board: $12,000	**Freshman Class:** 2103 applied, 1728 accepted, 208 enrolled
SAT CR/M/W: 510/530/500 **ACT:** 24	**CEEB CODE:** 2226
Application Deadline: rolling	**COMPETITIVE**

Elmira College, founded in 1855, is a private coeducational liberal arts college emphasizing both general and professional education. There is 1 undergraduate school and 1 graduate school. In addition to regional accreditation, Elmira has baccalaureate program accreditation with NLN, TEAC, and ACEN. The 55-acre campus is in a suburban area 90 miles southwest of Syracuse and 50 miles west of Binghamton. Including any residence halls, there are 26 buildings.

STUDENT LIFE: 62% of undergraduates are from New York. Others are from 31 states, 12 foreign countries, and Canada. 78% are White; 5% African American; 5% race unknown; 4% Hispanic; 4% Foreign; 2% Asian American; 2% two or more races. **Female To Male Ratio:** 2.3:1. The average age of freshmen is 18; all undergraduates, 22. 24% do not continue beyond their first year; 60% remain to graduate. **Housing:** 1218 students can be accommodated in college housing, which includes single-sex and coed dorms as well as on-campus apartments, quiet floors, alcohol and tobacco free floors, and honors floor. On-campus housing is guaranteed for all 4 years. 88% of students live on campus; of those, 90% remain on campus on weekends. All students may keep cars.

FACULTY/CLASSROOMS: 44% of faculty are male; 56% are female. 94% teach undergraduates. No introductory courses are taught by graduate students. The average class size in an introductory lecture is 15; in a laboratory is 9; and in a regular course is 14.

PROGRAMS OF STUDY: Elmira confers B.A. and B.S. degrees. Associate and master's degrees are also awarded. Bachelor's degrees are awarded in BIOLOGICAL SCIENCE (biochemistry and biology/biological science), BUSINESS (accounting, business administration and management, and business economics), COMMUNICATIONS AND THE ARTS (classics, dramatic arts, English literature, fine arts, languages, music, and theatre arts), COMPUTER AND PHYSICAL SCIENCE (chemistry and mathematics), EDUCATION (art education, early childhood education, education of the deaf and hearing impaired, foreign languages education, science education, secondary education, and special education), HEALTH PROFESSIONS (community health work, nursing, predentistry, premedicine, and speech pathology/audiology), SOCIAL SCIENCE (American studies, criminal justice, history, human services, international studies, liberal arts, sciences, general studies, humanities, philosophy and religion, political science/government, prelaw, psychology, and sociology). Education and nursing is the strongest academically. Nursing, business administration, and psychology have the largest enrollments.

ACTIVITIES: There are no fraternities or sororities. There are 80 groups on campus, including Active Minds, Model UN, Orchesis, Relay for Life, Student Alumni Council, art, cheerleading, chorale, chorus, communications, dance, drama, environmental, ethnic, honors, international, LGBT, literary magazine, musical theater, newspaper, photography, political, professional, religious, social, social service, Student Activities Board, student government, and yearbook. Popular campus events include Candlelight, Mountain Day, Octagon Fair, Holiday Banquet, and May Days. **Sports:** There are 9 intercollegiate sports for men and 11 for women, and 6 intramural sports for men and 6 for women. Facilities are available for baseball, basketball, cheerleading, cross country, field hockey, golf, ice hockey, lacrosse, soccer, softball, tennis, and volleyball. There is also a soccer field, gymnasium, dance studio, racquetball courts, and a swimming pool. Our Murray Athletic Center, (located about 9 miles from campus) features a hockey arena, gymnasium, field house with indoor tennis courts, squash courts and playing fields. **Graduates:** From July 1, 2015 to June 30, 2016, 319 bachelor's degrees were awarded. The most popular majors were business/marketing/finance (23%), nursing (18%), and education (13%). 50 companies recruited on campus in 2015-2016. In an average class, 56% graduate in 4 years or less, 59% graduate in 5 years or less, and 60% graduate in 6 years or less.

SERVICES: Counseling and information services are available, as is tutoring in most subjects, a reader service for the blind. A writing center, tutoring center, math lab, learning and disabilities specialist, and IT Help Desk are all available for students with needs. **Library/Resources:** The library contains 122,904 volumes, 35,678 microform items, and 2,811 audio/video tapes/CDs/DVDs, and subscribes to 6 periodicals including electronic. Computerized library services include interlibrary loans, database searching, Internet access, and Wi-Fi capability. Special learning facilities include an art gallery, finance trading room, speech and hearing clinic, state-of-the-art simulation labs for our nursing program, and Mark Twain's study and exhibit. **Physically Challenged Students:** 25% of the campus is accessible. Facilities include wheelchair ramps, elevators, special parking, specially equipped restrooms, special class scheduling, and special housing. **Special:** Term III Travel trips; Honors Program; Student-designed majors; 3-2 chemical engineering degree is offered with Clarkson University; 4+1 MBA with Alfred University, Clarkson University, Rochester Institute of Technology, and Union College. 4+1 MBA with specialization in Accounting or MS in Accounting with Rochester Institute of Technology or University of Buffalo. There are 19 national honor societies, Phi Beta Kappa, a freshman honors program, and 15 departmental honors programs. **Visiting:** There are regularly scheduled orientations for prospective students, consisting of an open house format and overview, a tour, lunch, a student panel, a faculty panel, general admissions and scholarship information, and an optional interview. Individual visits for interviews and tours are available year-round, including Saturday mornings. There are guides for informal visits, visitors may sit in on classes, and stay overnight. To schedule a visit, contact the Office of Admissions. **Campus Safety and Security:** Measures include 24-hour foot and vehicle patrol, emergency notification system, and security escort services. There are emergency telephones, lighted pathways/sidewalks, controlled access to dorms/residences. On a limited basis we provide shuttles to off-campus activities.

REQUIREMENTS: The SAT or ACT is recommended. Applicants should have completed 4 years of high school English, 3 of math, and 2 of science. An essay is part of the application process. An interview is strongly recommended. Test scores are optional. A GPA of 2.0 is required. AP and CLEP credits are accepted. Important factors in the admissions decision are advanced placement or honors courses, extracurricular activities record, and recommendations by school officials. A total of 120 credit hours with a minimum GPA of 2.0 overall is required to graduate. All students must complete the following graduation requirements in addition to the requirements of their selected major: Academic Writing Program (3-6 credits; depends on whether entering as a first-time student or transfer); "W" Course (3 credits) a course in the student's major with an emphasis on written communication; Mathematical Competency and Quantitative Reasoning (3-8 credits); Core Program (3 credits) First-Year Seminar foundation course in the liberal arts and sciences for all entering freshmen; The Pillars and World Engagement (Pillars=27 credits, World Engagement=9 credits) - The Pillars include coursework in the following subject areas: Fine Arts, Humanities and Languages, Social Sciences, Mathematics and Natural Sciences; World Engagement consists of 3 courses designed to help students view the world from multiple perspectives; Physical Education requirement (2 credits) may be waived with participation in sports, ROTC, or other approved campus physical activities; Community Service (60 hours total); and an Internship Requirement (minimum 80 hours in a career-related internship) or project submission if completing the Pre-Grad School internship. **Procedure:** Freshmen are admitted fall and winter. Entrance exams should be taken by April of the entry year. There are deferred admissions and rolling admissions plans. Application deadlines are open. Notification is sent on a rolling basis. 28 early decision candidates were accepted for the 2016-2017 class. Applications are accepted online. **Transfer Students:** 44 transfer students enrolled in 2015-2016. Applicants must have a minimum GPA of 2.0. Transcripts from all schools previously attended are required, along with a letter of recommendation from a Dean, faculty member, college placement, counselor, etc. from your most recently attended institution. If you have earned less than 12 credits, a secondary school transcript is also required.

A student conduct form must be completed by the Dean of Students from your most recently attended institution. 30 of 120 credits required for the bachelor's degree must be completed at Elmira. **International Students:** There are 48 international students enrolled. The school actively recruits these students. They must take the TOEFL with a minimum score of 79 on the Internet-based version (iBT). Student's must also take the IELTS, or PTE.

ADMISSIONS: 82% of the 2016-2017 applicants were accepted. 36% of the current freshmen were in the top fifth of their class; 68% were in the top two fifths. 3 freshmen graduated first in their class. **Admissions Contact:** Christopher R. Coons, Vice President of Enrollment Management. Email: *admissions@elmira.edu* Web: *www.elmira.edu*

FINANCIAL AID: In 2016-2017, 100% of all full-time freshmen and 97% of continuing full-time students received some form of financial aid. 82% of all full-time freshmen and 81% of continuing full-time students received need-based aid. The average freshman award was $30,560. Need-based scholarships or need-based grants averaged $27,537; need-based self-help aid (loans and jobs) averaged $3,751; and other non-need-based awards and non-need-based scholarships averaged $21,312. 50% of undergraduate students work part-time. Average annual earnings from campus work are $1500. The average financial indebtedness of the 2016 graduate was $27,757. The state aid form is required. The FAFSA code is 002718. The priority date for freshman financial aid applications for fall entry is February 1. The filing deadline for fall entry is March 15.

EUGENE LANG COLLEGE/THE NEW SCHOOL FOR LIBERAL ARTS D-5

www.newschool.edu/lang

New York, NY 10011	(212) 229-5150 (800) 292-3040
Fax: (212) 229-5355	**Email:** lang@newschool.edu
Full-time: 425 men, 930 women	**Faculty:** 65
Part-time: 42 men, 60 women	**Ph.D.s:** 80%
Graduate: n/av	**Student/Faculty:** 22 to 1
Year: semesters	**Tuition:** $39,976
Room & Board: $15,674	**Freshman Class:** n/av
SAT or ACT: required	**CEEB CODE:** 2521
Application Deadline: January 6	**COMPETITIVE**

Eugene Lang College, established in 1978, is the liberal arts undergraduate division of the New School. Figures in the above capsule and in this profile are approximate. There is 1 undergraduate school. In addition to regional accreditation, Eugene Lang College has baccalaureate program accreditation with MSCHE. The 37-acre campus is in an urban area in Greenwich Village, Manhattan, New York City. Including any residence halls, there are 23 buildings.

STUDENT LIFE: 72% of undergraduates are from out of state, mostly the Middle Atlantic. Students are from 43 states, 46 foreign countries, and Canada. 61% are from public schools. 6% are African American; 57% White; 5% Asian American; 5% Foreign; 4% two or more races; 13% Hispanic; 10% race unknown. **Female To Male Ratio:** 2.1:1. The average age of freshmen is 19; all undergraduates, 20. 20% do not continue beyond their first year; 52% remain to graduate. **Housing:** 1945 students can be accommodated in college housing, which includes coed dorms. In addition, there are special-interest houses. Honors community housing is focused more on academics than an actual GPA. On-campus housing is available on a first-come, first-served basis, and is available on a lottery system for upperclassmen. 70% of students commute. All students may keep cars. Alcohol is not permitted.

FACULTY/CLASSROOMS: 43% of faculty are male; 57% are female. All teach undergraduates. No introductory courses are taught by graduate students.

PROGRAMS OF STUDY: Lang College confers B.A. degrees. Bachelor's degrees are awarded in AGRICULTURE (environmental studies), COMMUNICATIONS AND THE ARTS (dance, dramatic arts, literature, music, theatre acting, theater design, and theatre studies), EDUCATION (education and foreign languages education), SOCIAL SCIENCE (anthropology, Chinese Studies, economics, gender studies, history, interdisciplinary studies, philosophy, political science/government, psychology, religion, sociology, and urban studies). Creative writing, history, and Urban studies are the strongest academically. Writing, and cultural studies have the largest enrollments.

ACTIVITIES: There are no fraternities or sororities. There are 46 groups on campus, including art, band, choir, chorus, communications, computers, dance, debate, drama, environmental, ethnic, film, honors, international, jazz band, LGBT, literary magazine, museum club, musical theater, newspaper, opera, orchestra, photography, political, professional, radio and TV, religious, social, social service, student government, and symphony. Popular campus events include Welcome Back Block Party, Seek Relief Week, Midnight Breakfast, 100 Nights Dinner, Leadership Retreat, Service Trips, Leadership Awards Banquet. **Sports:** There are 4 intramural sports for men and 4 for women. Facilities include a fitness room where they host group fitness classes and personal training. **Graduates:** From July 1, 2015 to June 30, 2016, 420 bachelor's degrees were awarded. The most popular majors were liberal arts (32%), literary studies (16%), and arts (15%). In an average class, 39% graduate in 4 years or less, 48% graduate in 5 years or less, and 52% graduate in 6 years or less. Of the 2015 graduating class, 10% were enrolled in graduate school within 6 months of graduation, and 6% were employed.

SERVICES: **Library/Resources:** The 3 libraries contain 15.7 million volumes, 1,184 microform items, and 17,426 audio/video tapes/CDs/DVDs, and subscribe to 76,012 periodicals including electronic. Computerized library services include interlibrary loans, database searching, Internet access, and Wi-Fi capability. Special learning facilities include an art gallery, radio station, a writing center. **Physically Challenged Students:** 95% of the campus is accessible. Facilities include wheelchair ramps, elevators, specially equipped restrooms, special class scheduling, lowered drinking fountains, and special housing. **Special:** Eugene Lang offers a concentration rather than a traditional major; there is no core curriculum and students are instructed in small seminars. Students may cross-register with other New School divisions. A large variety of internships for credit, study abroad, B.A./M.A. and B.A./M.S.T. options, a B.A./B.F.A. degree with Parsons The New School for Design and The New School for Jazz and Contemporary Music Program, student-designed majors, and nondegree study are available. **Visiting:** There are regularly scheduled orientations for prospective students, consisting of information sessions every weekday at 2 o'clock; tours every weekday at 3 o'clock. Walk in meetings with counselors available every weekday between 9 AM and 5 PM. There are guides for informal visits and visitors may sit in on classes. To schedule a visit, contact Denise Rodriguez at rodrigud@newschool.edu. **Campus Safety and Security:** Measures include self-defense education.

REQUIREMENTS: Freshmen Requirements: Common App (online); 2 essays; secondary school transcript; counselor recommendation; teacher evaluation; SAT or ACT scores (or a graded academic paper); TOEFL score (for ESL students). Transfers: college transcripts. AP and CLEP credits are accepted. Important factors in the admissions decision are recommendations by school officials, advanced placement or honors courses, and extracurricular activities record. To graduate, students must complete 120 credit hours, with a GPA of 2.0 and a minimum of 36 hours in 1 of 11 paths of study: writing, literature, the arts (includes dance and theater, urban studies, social and historical inquiry, cultural studies, media, philosophy, religious studies, psychology, education studies, science, technology, and society). Also required are 88 credit hours in Lang College courses and 4 credits of senior work. Required courses include a first-year writing seminar and a freshman workshop program. **Procedure:** Freshmen are admitted fall and spring. Entrance exams should be taken in May of the junior year or October of the senior year. There are early decision and deferred admissions plans. Early decision applications should be filed by November 1; regular applications, by January 6 for fall entry; and November 1 for spring entry, along with a $50 fee. Notification of early decision is sent December 15; regular decision, April 1. Application fees are waived if application is completed online. **Transfer Students:** Applicants must have a minimum college GPA of 2.5 and must submit high school transcripts, ACT or SAT scores (if taken in the last 5 years), and 2 recommendations. An interview is recommended. Grades of C or better transfer for credit. 60 of 120 credits required for the bachelor's degree must be completed at Eugene Lang College. **International Students:** There are 96 international students enrolled. The school actively recruits these students. They must take the TOEFL with a minimum score of 100 on the paper-based TOEFL (PBT) or 100 on the Internet-based version (iBT), or take the IELTS, or the PTE.

Admissions Contact: Candice MacLusky, Director of Undergraduate Admissions. Email: *macluskc@newschool.edu* Web: *www.newschool.edu/lang*

FINANCIAL AID: In 2016-2017, 47% of all full-time freshmen received some form of financial aid. 41% of all full-time freshmen received need-based aid. The average financial indebtedness of the 2016 graduate was $23,170. Eugene Lang College is a member of CSS. The state aid form is required. The priority date for freshman financial aid applications for fall entry is March 1. The filing deadline for fall entry is June 30.

EXCELSIOR COLLEGE *(The complete profile is made available exclusively on our website, www.barronspac.com)*

FARMINGDALE STATE COLLEGE E-5

www.farmingdale.edu

Farmingdale, NY 11735 **(631) 420-2200**

Fax: (631) 420-2633 **Email:** admissions@farmingdale.edu

Full-time: 4091 men, 2851 women	**Faculty:** 228; IIB, +$
Part-time: 1085 men, 1208 women	**Ph.D.s:** 73%
Graduate: n/av	**Student/Faculty:** 30 to 1
Year: semesters, summer session	**Tuition:** $7860 ($17,710)
Room & Board: $12,764	**Freshman Class:** 1329 enrolled
SAT CR/M: 480/500 **ACT:** 21	**CEEB CODE:** 2526
Application Deadline: June 1	**COMPETITIVE**

Farmingdale State College, also known as SUNY Farmingdale State College founded in 1912, is a public institution offering associate, bachelor's, and master's degrees in the applied sciences and technology. There are 4 undergraduate schools. In addition to regional accreditation, SUNY Farmingdale has baccalaureate program accreditation with ABET, ADA, ATMAE, NAACLS, and CCNE. The 380-acre campus is in a suburban area on Long Island, about 35 miles east of New York City. Including any residence halls, there are 40 buildings.

STUDENT LIFE: 98% of undergraduates are from New York. Others are from 13 states, 68 foreign countries, and Canada. 92% are from public schools. 8% are Asian American; 59% White; 2% Foreign; 2% two or more races; 18% Hispanic; 10% African American; 1% race unknown. **Male To Female Ratio:** 1.3:1. The average age of freshmen is 18; all undergraduates, 23. 20% do not continue beyond their first year; 52% remain to graduate. **Housing:** 600 students can be accommodated in college housing, which includes coed dorms. On-campus housing is available on a first-come and first-served basis. 94% of students commute. All students may keep cars. Alcohol is not permitted.

FACULTY/CLASSROOMS: 54% of faculty are male; 46% are female. All teach undergraduates. No introductory courses are taught by graduate students. The average class size in an introductory lecture is 30; in a laboratory is 18; and in a regular course is 26.

PROGRAMS OF STUDY: SUNY Farmingdale confers B.S., and B.Tech. degrees. Associate and master's degrees are also awarded. Bachelor's degrees are awarded in AGRICULTURE (horticulture), BIOLOGICAL SCIENCE (biology/biological science), BUSINESS (applied economics / management, business administration and management, facilities management, global management, and sports management), COMMUNICATIONS AND THE ARTS (English and Professional Communication, telecommunications engineering technology, and visual design), COMPUTER AND PHYSICAL SCIENCE (applied mathematics, computer engineering technology, computer programming, and information sciences and systems), ENGINEERING AND ENVIRONMENTAL DESIGN (aeronautical science, architectural technology, automotive technology, aviation administration/management, construction technology, electrical/electronics engineering technology, industrial engineering technology, manufacturing technology, and mechanical engineering technology), HEALTH PROFESSIONS (dental hygiene, medical technology, and nursing), SOCIAL SCIENCE (applied psychology, criminal justice, and safety and security technology). Nursing, dental hygiene, and bioscience are the strongest academically. Business management, science technology & society, and criminal justice/ law enforcement technology have the largest enrollments.

ACTIVITIES: 3% of men belong to 4 national fraternities; 4% of women belong to 2 national sororities. There are 60 groups on campus, including art, computers, dance, drama, environmental, ethnic, honors, LGBT, musical theater, newspaper, photography, professional, radio and TV, religious, social, social service, student government, and yearbook. Popular campus events include RAMFEST, Club Challenge, Bingo for Books, Casino Night, Spring Concert, and Farewell to Farmingdale. **Sports:** There are 9 intercollegiate sports for men and 9 for women, and 11 intramural sports for men and 11 for women. Facilities include basketball, badminton, volleyball, racquetball, handball, squash, tennis courts, a wrestling room, weight training rooms, indoor and outdoor tracks, a golf driving range and 3-hole golf layout, baseball, softball, soccer/lacrosse, and multipurpose fields. **Graduates:** From July 1, 2015 to June 30, 2016, 1605 bachelor's degrees were awarded. The most popular majors were business management (21%), science, technology and society (12%), criminal justice, and law enforcement tech. (8%). 90 companies recruited on campus in 2015-2016. In an average class, 52% graduate in 6 years or less. Of the 2015 graduating class, 83% were employed within 6 months of graduation.

SERVICES: Counseling and information services are available, as is tutoring in most subjects. There is a reader service for the blind, and remedial math, reading, and writing. There is also a learning disabilities specialist counselor available. **Library/Resources:** The library contains 180,000 volumes, 27,000 microform items, 1,446 audio/video tapes/CDs/DVDs, and subscribes to 706 periodicals including electronic. Computerized library services include interlibrary loans, database searching, Internet access, and Wi-Fi capability. Special learning facilities include an art gallery, radio station, a dental hygiene clinic, CAD/CAM and CIM labs, fleet of multi & single engine airplanes, and a greenhouse complex. **Physically Challenged Students:** 90% of the campus is accessible. Facilities include wheelchair ramps, elevators, special parking, specially equipped restrooms, special class scheduling, lowered drinking fountains, and lowered telephones. **Special:** Internships are available, as well as study abroad opportunities. In addition there are 12 national honor societies. **Visiting:** Regularly scheduled orientations are available for prospective students, including a tour of the campus and general information about the college, admissions, financial aid, and residence life, and guides for informal visits. To schedule a visit, contact the Admissions Office. **Campus Safety and Security:** Measures include 24-hour foot and vehicle patrol, emergency notification system, and security escort services. There are shuttle buses, emergency telephones, lighted pathways/sidewalks, and controlled access to dorms/residences.

REQUIREMENTS: The SAT is required. Applicants must be graduates of an accredited secondary school or have earned a GED. Specific entrance requirements vary by program, but recommended preparation includes 4 units of English and 3 each of math, science, and social science. AP and CLEP credits are accepted. Important factors in the admissions decision are advanced placement or honors courses, recommendations by school officials, and your extracurricular activities record. To graduate, students must complete 120 to 130 credits with a minimum GPA of 2.0. The core curriculum includes at least 60 credits of liberal arts and sciences courses in the Bachelor of Science programs and 45 credits in the Bachelor of Technology programs, as well as credits in major coursework. One writing-intensive course and all general education requirements must be satisfactorily completed. **Procedure:** Freshmen are admitted fall and spring. There are deferred admissions and rolling admissions plans. Applications should be filed by June 1 for fall entry; November 1 for spring entry, along with a $50 fee. Notification is sent on a rolling basis. Application fees are waived if application is completed online. **Transfer Students:** 3436 transfer students enrolled in 2015-2016. Applicants must have a minimum GPA of 2.5. 30 of 120 credits required for the bachelor's degree must be completed at SUNY Farmingdale. **International Students:** There are 140 international students enrolled. The school actively recruits these students. They must take the TOEFL with a minimum score of 550 on the paper-based TOEFL (PBT) or 79 on the Internet-based version (iBT), IELTS (6.0), SAT Critical Reading (400). They must also take the SAT or ACT, scoring 1000. The SAT exam is not required for international students who attended high school outside of the United States.

ADMISSIONS: The SAT scores for the 2016-2017 freshman class were: Critical Reading-- 63% below 500, 32% between 500 and 599, and 5% between 600 and 699. Math-- 49% below 500, 42% between 500 and 599, and 8% between 600 and 699. The ACT scores were 12% between 12 and 17, 67% between 18 and 23, 20% between 24 and 29, and 1% above 30. 18% of the current freshmen were in the top fifth of their class; 47% were in the top two fifths. **Admissions Contact:** Jim Hall, Director of Admissions. Email: *admissions@farmingdale.edu* Web: *www.farmingdale.edu*

FINANCIAL AID: In 2016-2017, 65% of all full-time freshmen and 64% of continuing full-time students received some form of financial aid. 50% of all full-time freshmen and 52% of continuing full-time students received need-based aid. The average freshman award was $8,429. Need-based scholarships or need-based grants averaged $6,283 ($18,125 maximum); need-based self-help aid (loans and jobs) averaged $3,791 ($11,290 maximum); and other non-need-based awards and non-need-based scholarships averaged $2,413 ($12,933 maximum). The state aid form and the college's own financial statement are required. The priority date for freshman financial aid applications for fall entry is April 1. The filing deadline for fall entry is July 15.

FASHION INSTITUTE OF TECHNOLOGY/STATE UNIVERSITY OF NEW YORK *(The complete profile is made available exclusively on our website, www.barronspac.com)*

FIVE TOWNS COLLEGE — E-5

www.ftc.edu

Dix Hills, NY 11746 — (631) 656-2110

Fax: (631) 656-2172	**Email:** admissions@ftc.edu
Full-time: 479 men, 213 women	**Faculty:** 24
Part-time: 41 men, 16 women	**Ph.D.s:** 33%
Graduate: 29 men, 10 women	**Student/Faculty:** 14 to 1
Year: semesters, summer session	**Tuition:** $21,480
Room & Board: $13,870	**Freshman Class:** 598 applied, 331 accepted, 239 enrolled
SAT CR/M/W: required **ACT:** 21	**CEEB CODE:** 3142
Application Deadline: rolling	**COMPETITIVE**

Five Towns College, founded in 1972, is a private institution offering undergraduate programs in the music business, liberal arts, theater, elementary education, mass communication in broadcasting, as well as journalism, audio recording technology, and film/video. Graduate programs in music, music education, and childhood education are also offered. Figures in the above capsule and in this profile are approximate. There is 1 undergraduate school and 1 graduate school. In addition to regional accreditation, FTC has baccalaureate program accreditation with NCATE. The 40-acre campus is in a suburban area in Dix Hills, Long Island, 48 miles east of New York City. Including any residence halls, there are 5 buildings.

STUDENT LIFE: 94% of undergraduates are from New York. Others are from 9 states, and 1 foreign county. 91% are from public schools. 6% are race unknown; 51% White; 5% two or more races; 4% Asian American; 20% African American; 13% Hispanic; 1% Foreign. **Male To Female Ratio:** 2.3:1. The average age of freshmen is 19; all undergraduates, 21. 23% do not continue beyond their first year; 55% remain to graduate. **Housing:** 200 students can be accommodated in college housing, which includes coed dorms. Priority is given to out-of-town students. 80% of students commute. Upperclassmen may keep cars. Alcohol is not permitted.

FACULTY/CLASSROOMS: 56% of faculty are male; 42% are female. 98% teach undergraduates, 20% do research, and 20% do both. No introductory courses are taught by graduate students. The average class size in an introductory lecture is 30 and in a regular course is 15.

PROGRAMS OF STUDY: FTC confers B.S., B.F.A., B.P.S. and Mus.B. degrees. Associate, master's, and doctoral degrees are also awarded. Bachelor's degrees are awarded in BUSINESS (business administration, management, and operations), COMMUNICATIONS AND THE ARTS (audio technology, communications, dramatic arts, film, television and digital media, jazz, music business management, music performance, music theory and composition, theatre arts, and video), EDUCATION (elementary education and music education). Music, business, and childhood education are the strongest academically. Business management with a concentration in audio recording technology, and film & video have the largest enrollments.

ACTIVITIES: There are no fraternities or sororities. There are 16 groups on campus, including hip-hop, barbershop quartets, music business, theatrical concert, art, band, choir, chorale, chorus, dance, drama, film, international, jazz band, musical theater, newspaper, orchestra, professional, radio and TV, readers theater, social, student government, symphony, and yearbook. Popular campus events include Lunch and Lecture Series, Annual Picnic, and Spring and Fall Festivals. **Sports:** There is no sports program at FTC. Facilities include a gym with basketball and volleyball courts, an outdoor baseball/soccer field, and a fitness center.

Graduates: From July 1, 2015 to June 30, 2016, 178 bachelor's degrees were awarded. The most popular majors were business management (48%), film and video (16%), and music (11%). 64 companies recruited on campus in 2015-2016. In an average class, 54% graduate in 4 years or less, 64% graduate in 5 years or less, and 75% graduate in 6 years or less. Of the 2015 graduating class, 15% were enrolled in graduate school within 6 months of graduation, and 81% were employed.

SERVICES: Counseling and information services are available, as is tutoring in most subjects. There is also a reader service for the blind. **Library/Resources:** The 2 libraries contain 44,771 volumes, 50 microform items, 16,416 audio/video tapes/CDs/DVDs, and subscribe to 500 periodicals including electronic. Computerized library services include interlibrary loans, database searching, Internet access, and Wi-Fi capability. Special learning facilities include a radio station, a 72-, 48-, and 24-track recording studios, a MIDI studio, and a film video/TV studio. **Physically Challenged Students:** All of the campus is accessible. Facilities include wheelchair ramps, special parking, specially equipped restrooms, and special housing. **Special:** Internships are required in business management (concentrations in audio recording technology and music business), mass communication (concentrations in broadcasting and journalism), and are available for all other degree programs. There is 1 national honor society. **Visiting:** There are regularly scheduled orientations for prospective students, including a campus tour, academic counseling, financial aid counseling, and educational workshops. Students also learn about student support services and how to become involved in student activities. There are guides for informal visits and visitors may sit in on classes. To schedule a visit, contact the Admissions Office. **Campus Safety and Security:** Measures include 24-hour foot and vehicle patrol, emergency notification system, and security escort services. There are shuttle buses, lighted pathways/sidewalks, and controlled access to dorms/residences.

REQUIREMENTS: The SAT or ACT is required. A minimum high school average of 80 is required. A GED with a minimum score of 2500 is accepted. An audition is required for students in music, music education and theater arts program. We recommend a 1350 on all three parts of the SAT. We offer an entrance exam for students that do not meet our academic standards. AP and CLEP credits are accepted. Important factors in the admissions decision are evidence of special talent, recommendations by school officials, and extracurricular activities record. To graduate, all students must complete a total of 134 credits for a Mus.B. or B.F.A. degree, 127 for a B.S. degree, or 121 for a B.P.S. degree. Students must maintain at least a C average in their major concentration and have a minimum GPA of 2.0 to graduate. Distribution requirements include 45 credits in core courses in liberal arts. The core curriculum consists of English Composition 101 and 102, Speech 101, 3 credits each of either psychology or sociology, and various upper-division liberal arts and social science courses. All music students must pass a jury exam. Music majors and elementary education majors must take a comprehensive exam. **Procedure:** Freshmen are admitted fall, spring, and summer. Entrance exams should be taken prior to admission. There are early decision, deferred admissions, and rolling admissions plans. Early decision applications should be filed by December 1, along with a $35 fee. Notification is sent on a rolling basis. 5 early decision candidates were accepted for the 2016-2017 class. Applications are accepted online. **Transfer Students:** 70 transfer students enrolled in 2015-2016. Students must be in good academic standing at their former school and have a minimum GPA of 2.5. 60 of 121 credits required for the bachelor's degree must be completed at FTC. **International Students:** There are 7 international students enrolled. The school actively recruits these students. They must take the TOEFL with a minimum score of 520 on the paper-based TOEFL (PBT) or 79 on the Internet-based version (iBT).

ADMISSIONS: 55% of the 2016-2017 applicants were accepted. The SAT scores for the 2016-2017 freshman class were: Critical Reading-- 67% below 500, 26% between 500 and 599, 5% between 600 and 699, and 2% between 700 and 800. Math-- 68% below 500, 24% between 500 and 599, 7% between 600 and 699, and 1% between 700 and 800. Writing-- 75% below 500, 21% between 500 and 599, 3% between 600 and 699, and 1% between 700 and 800. The ACT scores were 40% below 12, 45% between 12 and 17, 15% between 18 and 23. 15% of the current freshmen were in the top fifth of their class; 40% were in the top two fifths. **Admissions Contact:** Jerry Cohen, Dean of Enrollment Services. Email: *admissions@ftc.edu* Web: *www.ftc.edu*

FINANCIAL AID: In 2016-2017, 82% of all full-time freshmen received some form of financial aid, or need-based aid. The average freshman award was $14,000. Need-based scholarships or need-based grants averaged $3,900; need-based self-help aid (loans and jobs) averaged $4,000; and other non-need-based awards and non-need-based scholarships averaged $7,000. 90% of undergraduate students work part-time. Average annual earnings from campus work are $3000. The average financial indebtedness of the 2016 graduate was $22,000. The college's own financial statement is required. The FAFSA code is 012561. The priority date for freshman financial aid applications for fall entry is March 31. The filing deadline for fall entry is August 25.

FORDHAM UNIVERSITY D-5

www.fordham.edu

Bronx, NY 10458 (718) 817-4000 (800) FORDHAM

Fax: (718) 367-9404 **Email:** enroll@fordham.edu

Full-time: 3765 men, 4998 women **Faculty:** I, +$

Part-time: 199 men, 296 women **Ph.D.s:** 95%

Graduate: 2237 men, 4087 women **Student/Faculty:** 14 to 1

Year: semesters, summer session **Tuition:** $49,073

Room & Board: $16,845 **Freshman Class:** 44816 applied, 20268 accepted, 2199 enrolled

SAT CR/M/W: 640/640/650 **ACT:** 29 **CEEB CODE:** 2259

Application Deadline: January 1 **MOST COMPETITIVE**

Fordham University, an independent institution offering an education based in the Jesuit tradition, has two major campuses in New York City. Fordham has four full-time undergraduate colleges, and six graduate/professional schools, offering a broad range of studies in liberal arts and sciences, business administration, social service, education and law. Pre-professional studies in law and medicine are popular programs, as well as the opportunity to study abroad. Fordham also works with more than 2,000 organizations in the New York metropolitan area to arrange internships for students in fields such as business, communications, medicine, law and education. There are 4 undergraduate schools and 6 graduate schools. In addition to regional accreditation, Fordham has baccalaureate program accreditation with AACSB and NCATE. The 93-acre campus is in an urban area Rose Hill campus is located in the Bronx adjacent to the Bronx Zoo and New York Botanical Gardens. The Lincoln Center campus is located in Manhattan at 60th Street and Columbus Avenue, next to Lincoln Center for the Performing Arts. Including any residence halls, there are 42 buildings.

STUDENT LIFE: 57% of undergraduates are from out of state, mostly the Northeast. Students are from 45 states, 73 foreign countries, and Canada. 59% are White; 14% Hispanic; 10% Asian American; 8% Foreign; 4% African American; 3% two or more races; 2% race unknown; 1% American Indian/Alaska Native. 50% are Catholic. **Female To Male Ratio:** 1.5:1. The average age of freshmen is 18; all undergraduates, 20. 91% remain to graduate. **Housing:** 4490 students can be accommodated in college housing, which includes coed dorms, on-campus apartments, and off-campus apartments, and integrated learning communities. On-campus housing is guaranteed for all 4 years, is available on a first-come, first-served basis, and on a lottery system for upperclassmen. 51% of students live on campus. All students may keep cars.

FACULTY/CLASSROOMS: 53% of faculty are male; 47% are female. No introductory courses are taught by graduate students. The average class size in an introductory lecture is 23.

PROGRAMS OF STUDY: Fordham confers B.A., B.S., and B.F.A. degrees. Master's and doctoral degrees are also awarded. Bachelor's degrees are awarded in BIOLOGICAL SCIENCE (biology/biological science and neurosciences), BUSINESS (accounting, business administration and management, business economics, finance, international business management, and marketing management), COMMUNICATIONS AND THE ARTS (art history, classical languages, classics, communication studies, comparative literature, dance, digital media, digital media technologies, dramatic arts, English, English literature, English Writing, film, television and digital media, fine arts, French, German, graphic design, Italian, journalism, Latin, music, music theory and composition, performing arts, Spanish, studio art, theatre acting, theater design, theatre production, and visual and performing arts), COMPUTER AND PHYSICAL SCIENCE (chemistry, computer science, information sciences and systems, mathematics, mathematics – economics, natural sciences, physics, science, and statistics), ENGINEERING AND ENVIRONMENTAL DESIGN (architecture, engineering physics, and environmental science), HEALTH PROFESSIONS (pre-health studies), SOCIAL SCIENCE (African studies, African American studies, American studies, anthropology, classical/ancient civilization, economics, French studies, German area studies, history, international studies, Italian studies, Latin American studies, medieval studies, Middle Eastern studies, philosophy, political science/government, prelaw, psychology, religion, social science, social work, sociology, Spanish studies, theological studies, urban studies, and women's studies). Biology, political science, and English are the strongest academically. Business, communications, and social sciences have the largest enrollments.

ACTIVITIES: There are no fraternities or sororities. There are 185 groups on campus, including campus activities board, art, band, cheerleading, chess, choir, chorale, chorus, communications, computers, dance, debate, drama, environmental, ethnic, film, honors, international, jazz band, LGBT, literary magazine, marching band, musical theater, newspaper, orchestra, pep band, photography, political, professional, radio and TV, religious, social, social service, student admission ambassadors, student government, symphony, and yearbook. Popular campus events include Spring Weekend, Spring Semiformal, and Senior Week. **Sports:** There are 12 intercollegiate sports for men and 11 for women, and 7 intramural sports for men and 7 for women. Facilities include a football stadium, pool with diving area, indoor track, gym, tennis, squash, and racquetball courts, and student workout room. **Graduates:** From July 1, 2015 to June 30, 2016, 1969 bachelor's degrees were awarded. The most popular majors were business administration (27%), social sciences (18%), and communication and media studies (13%). In an average class, 75% graduate in 4 years or less, 80% graduate in 5 years or less, and 81% graduate in 6 years or less.

SERVICES: Counseling and information services are available, as is tutoring in most subjects. **Library/Resources:** The 3 libraries contain 2.3 million volumes, 3.2 million microform items, 64,833 audio/video tapes/CDs/DVDs, and subscribe to 68,957 periodicals including electronic. Computerized library services include interlibrary loans, database searching, Internet access, and Wi-Fi capability. Special learning facilities include an art gallery, radio station, a seismic station, an archeological site, two trade rooms, and a biological field station. **Physically Challenged Students:** 80% of the campus is accessible. Facilities include wheelchair ramps, elevators, special parking, specially equipped restrooms, special class scheduling, and lowered drinking fountains. **Special:** Fordham University offers career-oriented internships during the junior or senior year with New York City companies and institutions. A combined 3-2 engineering program is available with Columbia and Case Western Reserve Universities. Accelerated degrees, dual and student-designed majors, and pass/fail options are available. Study abroad programs are available around the globe and include Fordham specific programs in London, England; Grenada, Spain; and Pretoria, South Africa. Fordham additionally offers a B.F.A program in conjunction with the Alvin Ailey School of Dance and a B.A. program in Theatre. There are 6 national honor societies, Phi Beta Kappa, and a freshman honors program. **Visiting:** There are regularly scheduled orientations for prospective students, an information session with a tour, guided tour, or self-guided tour. There are also partial day visits consisting of presentations, Q&A session with current students and tour over the summer. There are guides for informal visits and visitors may sit in on classes. To schedule a visit, contact Office of Undergraduate Admission. **Campus Safety and Security:** Measures include 24-hour foot and vehicle patrol, emergency notification system, and security escort services. There are shuttle buses, emergency telephones, lighted pathways/sidewalks, and controlled access to dorms/residences.

REQUIREMENTS: The SAT or ACT is required. Applicants should complete 4 years of high school English, 3 years of math, science, social studies, and history, and 2 years of a foreign language. Applicants should submit the Common Application which includes an essay and questions on the Fordham member screen. A secondary school report and counselor or teacher letter of recommendation is required. Fordham requires either the SAT or ACT. SAT II subject tests are not required. Auditions are required for theatre and dance majors. Additionally, Fordham has a no interview policy. AP credits are accepted. Important factors in the admissions decision are advanced placement or honors courses, leadership record, extracurricular activities record, parents or siblings attended your school, evidence of special talent, personality/intangible qualities, geographical diversity, and recommendations by school officials. All students must complete a core curriculum, including courses each in literature, history, philosophy, theology, natural sciences, social sciences, math, English composition, fine arts and foreign language competency. A total of 124 credits and a 2.0 minimum GPA are required for graduation. **Procedure:** Freshmen are admitted in the fall and spring. Entrance exams should be taken by January of the senior year. There are early decision, early admissions, and deferred admissions plans. Early decision applications should be filed by November 1; regular applications, by January 1 for fall entry; and November 1 for spring entry, along with a $70 fee. Notification of early decision is sent December 20; regular decision, April 1. 154 early decision candidates were accepted for the 2016-2017 class. 8573 applicants were on the 2016 waiting list; 402 were admitted. Applications are accepted online. **Transfer Students:** 260 transfer students enrolled in 2015-2016. A 3.0 minimum GPA is recommended. All applicants are required to submit the Common Application and essay, official high school and college transcripts, and a letter of good standing from the Dean or University Registrar from the institution the student currently attends. Applicants with less than one full year of full-time course work at a post-secondary institution must submit SAT or ACT scores. 64 of 124 credits required for the bachelor's degree must be completed at Fordham. **International Students:** There are 716 international students enrolled. The school actively recruits these students. They must take the TOEFL with a minimum score of 90 on the Internet-based version (iBT) and the college's own test. They must also take the SAT or ACT.

ADMISSIONS: 45% of the 2016-2017 applicants were accepted. The SAT scores for the 2016-2017 freshman class were: Critical Reading-- 2% below 500, 24% between 500 and 599, 53% between 600 and 699, and 21% between 700 and 800. Math-- 1% below 500, 22% between 500 and 599, 57% between 600 and 699, and 19% between 700 and 800. Writing-- 2% below 500, 23% between 500 and 599, 54% between 600 and 699, and 21% between 700 and 800. The ACT scores were 3% between 18 and 23, 51% between 24 and 29, and 46% above 30. 74% of the current freshmen were in the top fifth of their class; 100% were in the top two fifths. 25 freshmen graduated first in their class. **Admissions Contact:** Patricia Peek, Ph.D., Director of Admission. Email: *enroll@fordham.edu* Web: *www.fordham.edu*

FINANCIAL AID: In 2016-2017, 91% of all full-time freshmen received some form of financial aid. Fordham is a member of CSS. The CSS/Profile, noncustodial profile, business, and farm supplement are required. The FAFSA code is 002722. The priority date for freshman financial aid applications for fall entry is December 4. The filing deadline for fall entry is February 10.

HAMILTON COLLEGE — C-3

www.hamilton.edu

Clinton, NY 13323	**(315) 859-4421** **(800) 843-2655**
Fax: (315) 859-4457	**Email: admission@hamilton.edu**
Full-time: 918 men, 972 women	**Faculty:** IIB, ++$
Part-time: n/av	**Ph.D.s:** 94%
Graduate: n/av	**Student/Faculty:** 9 to 1
Year: semesters	**Tuition:** $49,500
Room & Board: $12,570	**Freshman Class:** 5071 applied, 1336 accepted, 469 enrolled
SAT CR/M/W: 690/700/695 **ACT:** 32	**CEEB CODE:** 2286
Application Deadline: January 1	**MOST COMPETITIVE**

Hamilton College, chartered in 1812, is a private, nonsectarian, liberal arts school offering undergraduate programs in the arts and sciences. Figures in the above capsule and in this profile are approximate. There is 1 undergraduate school. The 1300-acre campus is in a rural area 9 miles southwest of Utica. Including any residence halls, there are 106 buildings.

STUDENT LIFE: 70% of undergraduates are from out of state, mostly the Middle Atlantic. Students are from 46 states, 39 foreign countries, and Canada. 61% are from public schools. 63% are White; 11% race unknown. 40% claim no religious affiliation; 24% Protestant; 21% Catholic. **Female To Male Ratio:** 1.1:1. The average age of freshmen is 18; all undergraduates, 20. 4% do not continue beyond their first year; 91% remain to graduate. **Housing:** 1835 students can be accommodated in college housing, which includes coed dorms, on-campus apartments, and married student housing. In addition, there are special-interest houses, quiet floors, and substance-free areas, cooperative housing and first year housing. On-campus housing is guaranteed for all 4 years. 97% of students live on campus. Upperclassmen may keep cars.

FACULTY/CLASSROOMS: 57% of faculty are male; 43% are female. All teach undergraduates. No introductory courses are taught by graduate students. The average class size in a regular course is 16.

PROGRAMS OF STUDY: Hamilton confers A.B. degrees. Bachelor's degrees are awarded in AGRICULTURE (environmental studies), BIOLOGICAL SCIENCE (biochemistry, biology/biological science, and neurosciences), COMMUNICATIONS AND THE ARTS (art, art history and appreciation, Chinese, classics, communications, comparative literature, creative writing, dance, dramatic arts, English, English literature, French, languages, music, and studio art), COMPUTER AND PHYSICAL SCIENCE (chemical physics, chemistry, computer science, geoscience, mathematics, and physics), SOCIAL SCIENCE (African studies, American studies, anthropology, archeology, Asian/Oriental studies, economics, German area studies, Hispanic American studies, history, interdisciplinary studies, international relations, philosophy, political science/government, psychobiology, psychology, public affairs, religion, Russian and Slavic studies, sociology, and women's studies). Economics, mathematics, and psychology have the largest enrollments.

ACTIVITIES: 28% of men belong to 11 national fraternities; 21% of women belong to 6 local and 1 national sororities. There are 189 groups on campus, including art, band, chess, choir, chorale, chorus, communications, computers, dance, debate, drama, environmental, ethnic, film, honors, international, jazz band, LGBT, literary magazine, musical theater, newspaper, orchestra, photography, political, professional, radio and TV, religious, social, social service, student government, and yearbook. Popular campus events include Class and Charter Day, and Feb Fest (Winter Carnival). **Sports:** There are 14 intercollegiate sports for men and 15 for women, and 16 intramural sports for men and 16 for women. Facilities include a gym, field house, fitness and dance center, squash and racquetball courts, indoor and outdoor tennis courts, an artificial grass football stadium, 9-hole golf course, swimming pool, indoor and outdoor tracks, baseball and softball fields, an artificial turf field, paddle tennis courts, and an ice rink. **Graduates:** From July 1, 2014 to June 30, 2015, 500 bachelor's degrees were awarded. The most popular majors were social sciences (27%), biological/life sciences, foreign languages, literatures and linguistics (12%), and English (7%). In an average class, 85% graduate in 4 years or less, 90% graduate in 5 years or less, and 91% graduate in 6 years or less.

SERVICES: Counseling and information services are available, as is tutoring in some subjects. There is tutoring through the New York State Higher Education Opportunity Program (HEOP). **Library/Resources:** The 2 libraries contain 625,376 volumes, 293,834 microform items, and 35,217 audio/video tapes/CDs/DVDs, and subscribe to 4,546 periodicals including electronic. Computerized library services include interlibrary loans, database searching, Internet access, and Wi-Fi capability. Special learning facilities include an art gallery, radio station, TV station, an observatory, electron microscope, and the Wellin Museum of Art. **Physically Challenged Students:** Facilities include wheelchair ramps, elevators, special parking, specially equipped restrooms, special class scheduling, and special housing. **Special:** Cross-registration is permitted with Colgate University and Utica College. Opportunities are provided for a Washington semester and a New York City semester. Student-designed majors and study abroad in many countries are available, and 3-2 engineering degrees are offered with Washington University in St. Louis, Rensselaer Polytechnic Institute, and Columbia University. There are 8 national honor societies and a chapter of Phi Beta Kappa. **Visiting:** There are regularly scheduled orientations for prospective students, consisting of an interview, tour, class visit, and open house program. There are guides for informal visits, visitors may sit in on classes, and stay overnight. To schedule a visit, contact the Office of Admission. **Campus Safety and Security:** Measures include 24-hour foot and vehicle patrol, emergency notification system, self-defense education, and security escort services. There are shuttle buses, emergency telephones, lighted pathways/sidewalks, and controlled access to dorms/residences.

REQUIREMENTS: The SAT or ACT is required. Although graduation from an accredited secondary school or a GED is desirable, and a full complement of college-preparatory courses is recommended, Hamilton will consider all highly recommended candidates who demonstrate an ability and desire to perform at intellectually demanding levels. Students can fulfill test requirements with the SAT, ACT, 3 SAT Subject tests, 3 AP exams, or any combination of these. An essay is required, and an interview is recommended. AP credits are accepted. Important factors in the admissions decision are advanced placement or honors courses, personality/intangible qualities, extracurricular activities record, recommendations by school officials, parents or siblings attended your school, and evidence of special talent. Students must successfully complete 128 credits, with 32 to 40 of these in the student's major, and must maintain at least a 72 average in half the courses taken. **Procedure:** Freshmen are admitted fall. Entrance exams should be taken prior to February of the senior year. There are early decision and deferred admissions plans. Early decision applications should be filed by November 15; regular applications, by January 1 for fall entry, along with a $70 fee. Notification of early decision is sent December 15; regular decision, February 15. 251 early decision candidates were accepted for the 2015-2016 class. 438 applicants were on the 2015 waiting list; 21 were admitted. Applications are accepted on-line. **Transfer Students:** 9 transfer students enrolled in 2014-2015. Transfer applicants must submit high school and college transcripts, an essay or personal statement, and standardized test scores and must present a minimum GPA of 3.0 in all college-level work. 64 of 128 credits required for the bachelor's degree must be completed at Hamilton. **International Students:** There are 90 international students enrolled. The school actively recruits these students. They must take the TOEFL. They must also take the SAT or ACT.

ADMISSIONS: 26% of the 2015-2016 applicants were accepted. The SAT scores for the 2015-2016 freshman class were: Critical Reading-- 9% between 500 and 599, 42% between 600 and 699, and 49% between 700 and 800. Math-- 6% between 500 and 599, 42% between 600 and 699, and 53% between 700 and 800. Writing-- 11% between 500 and 599, 35% between 600 and 699, and 54% between 700 and 800. 95% of the current freshmen were in the top fifth of their class; 100% were in the top two fifths. **Admissions Contact:** Monica Inzer, Vice President and Dean of Admission and Financial Aid. E-Mail: *admission@hamilton.edu* Web: *www.hamilton.edu*

FINANCIAL AID: In 2015-2016, 44% of all full-time freshmen received some form of financial aid. 44% of all full-time freshmen received need-based aid. The average freshman award was $43,909. Need-based scholarships or need-based grants averaged $40,165; need-based self-help aid (loans and jobs) averaged $4,452; and $3,286 from other forms of aid. The average financial indebtedness of the 2015 graduate was $18,941. Hamilton is a member of CSS. The CSS/Profile, FAFSA, and the college's own financial statement are required. The deadline for filing freshman financial aid applications for fall entry is February 15.

HARTWICK COLLEGE — D-3

www.hartwick.edu

Oneonta, NY 13820	(607) 431-4150 (888) HARTWICK
Fax: (607) 431-4102	Email: admissions@hartwick.edu
Full-time: 540 men, 812 women	Faculty: 105; IIB, +$
Part-time: 12 men, 19 women	Ph.D.s: 91%
Graduate: n/av	Student/Faculty: 13 to 1
Year: 4-1-4, summer session	Tuition: $41,840
Room & Board: $11,120	Freshman Class: n/av
SAT: required ACT: 24	CEEB CODE: 2288
Application Deadline: rolling	COMPETITIVE

Hartwick College, founded in 1797, is a private undergraduate liberal arts and sciences college. There is 1 undergraduate school. In addition to regional accreditation, Hartwick has baccalaureate program accreditation with NASAD, NASM, TEAC, CCNE, and ACS. The 425-acre campus is in a small town 75 miles southwest of Albany, NY. Including any residence halls, there are 20 buildings.

STUDENT LIFE: 75% of undergraduates are from New York. Others are from 29 states, 20 foreign countries, and Canada. 85% are from public schools. 9% are African American; 7% Hispanic; 67% White; 3% Foreign; 2% Asian American; 12% race unknown. 30% are Protestant; 26% claim no religious affiliation; 24% Catholic. **Female To Male Ratio:** 1.5:1. The average age of freshmen is 18; all undergraduates, 20. 26% do not continue beyond their first year; 51% remain to graduate. **Housing:** 1201 students can be accommodated in college housing, which includes coed dorms and on-campus apartments. In addition, there are honors houses, fraternity houses, sorority houses, substance-free housing, a community engagement floor, and an environmental campus. On-campus housing is available on a lottery system for upperclassmen. 77% of students live on campus; of those, 80% remain on campus on weekends. All students may keep cars.

FACULTY/CLASSROOMS: 57% of faculty are male; 43% are female. All teach undergraduates. No introductory courses are taught by graduate students. The average class size in an introductory lecture is 20; in a laboratory is 20; and in a regular course is 17.

PROGRAMS OF STUDY: Hartwick confers B.A., and B.S. degrees. Bachelor's degrees are awarded in BIOLOGICAL SCIENCE (biochemistry and biology/biological science), BUSINESS (accounting and business administration and management), COMMUNICATIONS AND THE ARTS (art, art history and appreciation, dramatic arts, English, French, German, languages, music, and Spanish), COMPUTER AND PHYSICAL SCIENCE (chemistry, computer science, geology, information sciences and systems, mathematics, and physics), EDUCATION (music education), ENGINEERING AND ENVIRONMENTAL DESIGN (environmental science), HEALTH PROFESSIONS (medical technology and nursing), SOCIAL SCIENCE (anthropology, economics, history, philosophy, political science/government, psychology, religion, and sociology). Psychology, business administration/accounting, and nursing have the largest enrollments.

ACTIVITIES: 10% of men belong to 2 national fraternities; 8% of women belong to 2 local and 1 national sororities. There are 70 groups on campus, including art, band, cheerleading, choir, chorale, chorus, dance, drama, environmental, ethnic, honors, international, jazz band, LGBT, literary magazine, musical theater, newspaper, pep band, political, professional, radio and TV, religious, social, social service, student government, and yearbook. Popular campus events include Hawk Night Fever (pep rally), Oneonta State and Hartwick Fest (street fair and concert), and Scholar Showcase. **Sports:** There are 7 intercollegiate sports for men and 10 for women, and 5 intramural sports for men and 5 for women. Facilities include 2 gyms, an indoor pool, dance room, athletic and training facilities, track, fitness centers, lighted all-weather playing field, lighted soccer field, an equestrian complex (off-campus), and courts for handball, racquetball, squash, and tennis. **Graduates:** From July 1, 2015 to June 30, 2016, 333 bachelor's degrees were awarded. The most popular majors were nursing (16%), business administration (15%), and biology (10%). In an average class, 50% graduate in 4 years or less, 54% graduate in 5 years or less, and 56% graduate in 6 years or less. Of the 2015 graduating class, 21% were enrolled in graduate school within 6 months of graduation, and 29% were employed.

SERVICES: Counseling and information services are available, as is tutoring in most subjects. There is a reader service for the blind, a writing center and an academic support center. **Library/Resources:** The library contains 300,606 volumes, 29,700 microform items, 3,644 audio/video tapes/CDs/DVDs, and subscribes to 13,112 periodicals including electronic. Computerized library services include interlibrary loans, database searching, Internet access, and Wi-Fi capability. Special learning facilities include an art gallery, radio station, an environmental campus, art and culture museum, and an observatory. **Physically Challenged Students:** 50% of the campus is accessible. Facilities include wheelchair ramps, elevators, special parking, and specially equipped restrooms. **Special:** Hartwick's innovative approach emphasizes personalized instruction and practical experiences both inside and outside the classroom: study abroad, internships, collaborative research, and more. Hartwick offers more than 30 courses of study leading to a bachelor of arts (B.A.) or bachelor of science (B.S.) degree, four pre-professional programs, five cooperative programs, and a series of interesting minors and other options, including certification in education. Plus, you can design you own major. Within Hartwick's Three-Year Bachelor's Degree Program, there are 24 major areas of study leading to a bachelor of arts (B.A.) or bachelor of science (B.S.) degree. There is a 3-2 engineering program with Clarkson University or Columbia University, and a 3-3 program with Albany Law School. There are 9 national honor societies and a freshman honors program. **Visiting:** There are regularly scheduled orientations for prospective students, consisting of an interview and tour, lunch, departmental open houses, presentations on student life, off-campus programs, and a career planning process. There are guides for informal visits, visitors may sit in on classes, and stay overnight. To schedule a visit, contact the Admissions Office at admissions@hartwick.edu. **Campus Safety and Security:** Measures include 24-hour foot and vehicle patrol, emergency notification system, self-defense education, and security escort services. There are emergency telephones, lighted pathways/sidewalks, and controlled access to dorms/residences.

REQUIREMENTS: Reporting of SAT and ACT scores is optional. The recommended secondary course of study includes 4 years of English and

3 years each of math, a foreign language, history, and lab science. Hartwick strongly recommends that applicants plan a campus visit and interview. Prospective art majors should submit a portfolio, and music majors must audition. AP and CLEP credits are accepted. Important factors in the admissions decision are advanced placement or honors courses, recommendations by school officials, and ability to finance your college education. Students must complete 120 credit hours with at least a 2.0 GPA. The core curriculum as established by Hartwick's Liberal Arts in Practice. Distribution requirements include a first-year seminar, 9 credits in humanities, physical and life sciences, and social and behavioral sciences. There should also be 3 credits in quantitative and formal reasoning, foreign language (intermediate-level proficiency), and attainment of writing level 4, and a senior capstone. **Procedure:** Freshmen are admitted in the fall and spring. Entrance exams should be taken in the spring of the junior year and/or the fall of the senior year. There are early decision, deferred admissions, and rolling admissions plans. Application deadlines are open. Notification is sent on a rolling basis. 17 early decision candidates were accepted for the 2016-2017 class. 51 applicants were on the 2016 waiting list; 45 were admitted. Applications are accepted online. **Transfer Students:** 34 transfer students enrolled in 2015-2016. Applicants should present a minimum GPA of 2.0. 60 of 120 credits required for the bachelor's degree must be completed at Hartwick. **International Students:** There are 42 international students enrolled. They must take the TOEFL with a minimum score of 550 on the paper-based TOEFL (PBT) or 79 on the Internet-based version (iBT). They must also take the SAT, scoring 420.

Admissions Contact: Lisa Starkey-Wood, Director of Admissions. Email: *admissions@hartwick.edu* Web: *www.hartwick.edu*

FINANCIAL AID: In 2016-2017, 87% of all full-time freshmen and 83% of continuing full-time students received some form of financial aid. 86% of all full-time freshmen and 80% of continuing full-time students received need-based aid. The average freshman award was $27,415. Need-based scholarships or need-based grants averaged $25,788; need-based self-help aid (loans and jobs) averaged $6,942; non-need-based athletic scholarships averaged $19,984; and other non-need-based awards and non-need-based scholarships averaged $23,742. 66% of undergraduate students work part-time. Average annual earnings from campus work are $1640. The average financial indebtedness of the 2016 graduate was $27,653. Hartwick is a member of CSS. The college's own financial statement is required. The FAFSA code is 002729. The deadline for filing freshman financial aid applications for fall entry is February 15.

HILBERT COLLEGE — A-4
www.hilbert.edu

Hamburg, NY 14075 — **(716) 926-8785**, **(800) 649-8003**

Fax: (716) 649-0702 — **Email: admissions@hilbert.edu**

Full-time: 326 men, 414 women	**Faculty:** 47; IIB, -$
Part-time: 30 men, 40 women	**Ph.D.s:** 53%
Graduate: 15 men, 42 women	**Student/Faculty:** 18 to 1
Year: semesters, summer session	**Tuition:** $21,250
Room & Board: $9600	**Freshman Class:** n/av
SAT or ACT: required	**CEEB CODE:** 2334
Application Deadline: rolling	**COMPETITIVE**

Hilbert College, founded in 1957, is a private four-year college, in the Catholic Franciscan tradition. Hilbert is a dynamic Western New York college that offering career-focused majors, including one of the top criminal justice programs in the region, and more than 50 minors and concentrations. The college's engaging, student-centered campus community offers numerous leadership, internship, and service learning opportunities from which students launch successful careers while making positive changes in their communities. The Hilbert Blueprint promotes a well-rounded student experience over four years – starting with the Foundations Seminar in the freshman year, followed by Sophomore Service, Junior Symposium, and culminating with the Senior Capstone. Hilbert has expanded its academic offerings with the college's first graduate programs and new Accelerated Degree Programs geared to adult learners. There is 1 undergraduate school and 1 graduate school. The 44-acre campus is in a suburban area about 10 miles south of Buffalo. Including any residence halls, there are 11 buildings.

STUDENT LIFE: 94% of undergraduates are from New York. Others are from 21 states, 2 foreign countries, and Canada. 80% are from public schools. 75% are White; 7% African American; 7% two or more races; 6% race unknown; 4% Hispanic; 1% Asian American; 1% American Indian/Alaska Native; 1% Foreign. **Female To Male Ratio:** 1.3:1. The average age of freshmen is 18; all undergraduates, 22. 25% do not continue beyond their first year; 51% remain to graduate. **Housing:** 304 students can be accommodated in college housing, which includes coed dorms and on-campus apartments. On-campus housing is guaranteed for the freshman year only, and is available on a first-come, first-served basis, and is available on a lottery system for upperclassmen. 68% of students commute. All students may keep cars.

FACULTY/CLASSROOMS: 51% of faculty are male; 49% are female. All teach undergraduates, 10% do research, and 10% do both. No introductory courses are taught by graduate students. The average class size in an introductory lecture is 20 and in a regular course is 15.

PROGRAMS OF STUDY: Hilbert confers B.A. and B.S. degrees. Associate and master's degrees are also awarded. Bachelor's degrees are awarded in BIOLOGICAL SCIENCE (forensic science), BUSINESS (accounting, business administration and management, international business management, organizational leadership and management, and sports management), COMMUNICATIONS AND THE ARTS (digital communications and English), COMPUTER AND PHYSICAL SCIENCE (computer security and information assurance and cyber intelligence/security studies), HEALTH PROFESSIONS (rehabilitation therapy), SOCIAL SCIENCE (criminal justice, criminology, forensic studies, human services, liberal arts/general studies, paralegal studies, political science/government, and psychology). Paralegal studies, forensic science, psychology, and accounting are the strongest academically. Criminal justice, forensic science, and business administration have the largest enrollments.

ACTIVITIES: There are no fraternities or sororities. There are 20 groups on campus, including Rugby Speedball, hockey club, cheerleading, computers, ethnic, film, forensics, honors, literary magazine, newspaper, photography, professional, religious, social, social service, student government, and student veterans association. Popular campus events include Quad Party, Fall Fest, and Fall Family Weekend. **Sports:** There are 5 intercollegiate sports for men and 6 for women, and 4 intramural sports for men and 4 for women. Facilities include a soccer/lacrosse field, baseball and softball diamonds, a practice field, a fitness center, and a indoor athletic facility. **Graduates:** From July 1, 2015 to June 30, 2016, 227 bachelor's degrees were awarded. The most popular majors were criminal justice (28%), forensic science/crime scene invetigation (15%), and business administration (9%). 50 companies recruited on campus in 2015-2016. In an average class, 40% graduate in 4 years or less, 48% graduate in 5 years or less, and 50% graduate in 6 years or less. Of the 2015 graduating class, 14% were enrolled in graduate school within 6 months of graduation, and 80% were employed.

SERVICES: Counseling and information services are available, as is tutoring in most subjects. Remedial math and writing are also available. **Library/Resources:** The library contains 36,076 volumes, 3,616 microform items, 1,500 audio/video tapes/CDs/DVDs, and subscribes to 23,190 periodicals including electronic. Computerized library services include interlibrary loans, database searching, Internet access, and Wi-Fi capability. **Physically Challenged Students:** 95% of the campus is accessible. Facilities include wheelchair ramps, elevators, special parking, specially equipped restrooms, special class scheduling, lowered drinking fountains, and lowered telephones. **Special:** Hilbert offers study abroad, cross-registration with the 17-member Western New York College Consortium, internships in most majors, and work-study programs. The college maintains articulation agreements with 22 New York State community colleges. There are 5 national honor societies, a freshman honors program, and 3 departmental honors programs. **Visiting:** There are regularly scheduled orientations for prospective students. There are guides for informal visits and visitors may sit in on classes. To schedule a visit, contact Office of Admissions at admissions@hilbert.edu. **Campus Safety and Security:** Measures include 24-hour foot and vehicle patrol, emergency notification system, self-defense education, and security escort services. There are emergency telephones, lighted pathways/sidewalks, and controlled access to dorms/residences.

REQUIREMENTS: The SAT or ACT is recommended. Admission is based upon past academic performance, demonstrated ability, and personal characteristics. Applicants must submit an official high school transcript or GED certificate. AP and CLEP credits are also accepted. Important factors in the admissions decision are leadership record, advanced placement or honors courses, and recommendations by school officials. To graduate, students must complete 120 credit hours, including at least 36 in the major and 60 in liberal arts, with a minimum 2.0 GPA. Students must fulfill General Education requirements in interdisciplinary studies, intercultural awareness, arts & literature, math, religious studies, moral reasoning, political science/geography/history, sociology/psychology/economics, and physical sciences. **Procedure:** Freshmen are admitted to all sessions. There are deferred admissions and rolling admissions plans. Application deadlines are open. Application fee is $25. Application fees are waived if application is completed online. **Transfer Students:** 301 transfer students enrolled in 2015-2016. Applicants must submit official transcripts from all colleges attended and, in somes cases, the high school transcript. 30 of 120 credits required for the bachelor's degree must be completed at Hilbert. **International Students:** There are 4 international students enrolled. They must take the TOEFL.

Admissions Contact: Jacob Yale, Director of Admissions. Email: *admissions@hilbert.edu* Web: *www.hilbert.edu*

FINANCIAL AID: In 2016-2017, 88% of all full-time freshmen and 83% of continuing full-time students received some form of financial aid. 100% of all full-time freshmen and 98% of continuing full-time students received need-based aid. The average freshman award was $15,206. Need-based scholarships or need-based grants averaged $11,620; need-based self-help aid (loans and jobs) averaged $3,971; and other non-need-based awards and non-need-based scholarships averaged $5,087. 7% of undergraduate students work part-time. Average annual earnings from campus work are $1735. Hilbert is a member of CSS. The FAFSA code is 002735. The priority date for freshman financial aid applications for fall entry is March 1. The filing deadline for fall entry is December 1.

HOBART AND WILLIAM SMITH COLLEGES — B-3

www.hws.edu

Geneva, NY 14456	**(315) 781-3622** **(800) 852-2256**
Fax: (315) 781-3914	**Email: admissions@hws.edu**
Full-time: 1109 men, 1137 women	**Faculty:** 221; IIB, +$
Part-time: 11 men, 5 women	**Ph.D.s:** 100%
Graduate: 2 men, 7 women	**Student/Faculty:** 10 to 1
Year: semesters, summer session	**Tuition:** $51,559
Room & Board: $13,050	**Freshman Class:** 4614 applied, 2788 accepted, 590 enrolled
SAT or ACT: required	**CEEB CODE:** 2294
Application Deadline: February 1	**HIGHLY COMPETITIVE**

Hobart and William Smith are selective, residential, liberal arts colleges defined by a longstanding focus on educating across academic disciplines and the close work of research and creativity that connects faculty and students. With a strong commitment to diversity, the Colleges have a distinguished history of interdisciplinary teaching and scholarship, curricular innovation and exceptional outcomes. Sixty percent of HWS students study abroad and all participate in community service activities. Originally founded as two separate colleges (Hobart for men in 1822 and William Smith for women in 1908), Hobart and William Smith students share the same campus, faculty, administration and curriculum. Each College maintains its own traditions, deans, student government and athletic department, providing students with an innovative, 21st century construct to interrogate gender and difference. There are 2 undergraduate schools and 1 graduate school. The 320-acre campus is in a small town in Geneva, New York, in the Finger Lakes region on the north shore of Seneca Lake. Including any residence halls, there are 97 buildings.

STUDENT LIFE: 60% of undergraduates are from out of state, mostly the Northeast. Students are from 40 states, 35 foreign countries, and Canada. 57% are from public schools. 72% are White; 7% Foreign; 6% African American; 6% race unknown; 5% Hispanic; 4% Asian American. **Female To Male Ratio:** 1.0:1. The average age of freshmen is 18; all undergraduates, 20. 16% do not continue beyond their first year; 77% remain to graduate. **Housing:** 1980 students can be accommodated in college housing, which includes single-sex and coed dorms, on-campus apartments, and off-campus apartments. In addition, there are honors houses, language houses, special-interest houses, fraternity houses, cooperative, and themed houses, and townhouses for upper class years. On-campus housing is guaranteed for all 4 years. 85% of students live on campus; of those, 93% remain on campus on weekends. All students may keep cars.

FACULTY/CLASSROOMS: 51% of faculty are male; 49% are female. All teach undergraduates and do research. No introductory courses are taught by graduate students. The average class size in an introductory lecture is 21; in a laboratory is 13; and in a regular course is 20.

PROGRAMS OF STUDY: HWS confers B.A. and B.S. degrees. Master's degrees are also awarded. Bachelor's degrees are awarded in BIOLOGICAL SCIENCE (biochemistry and biology/biological science), COMMUNICATIONS AND THE ARTS (Africana studies, art history, classics, communication rhetoric/communication, comparative literature, dance, English, film, television and digital media, fine arts, French, Greek, Latin, modern language, music, Russian languages and literature, Spanish and Hispanic studies, and studio art), COMPUTER AND PHYSICAL SCIENCE (chemistry, computer science, geoscience, mathematics, and physics), ENGINEERING AND ENVIRONMENTAL DESIGN (architecture and environmental science), SOCIAL SCIENCE (African studies, American studies, anthropology, architectural studies, Asian/Oriental studies, economics, European studies, history, international relations, Latin American studies, philosophy, political science/government, psychology, religion, Russian and Slavic studies, sociology, Spanish studies, urban studies, and women's studies). Natural sciences, environmental studies, and economics are the strongest academically. Economics, media & society, and environmental studies have the largest enrollments.

ACTIVITIES: There are 108 groups on campus, including women's collective, club sports, first generation, art, chess, choir, chorale, chorus, computers, dance, debate, drama, environmental, ethnic, film, honors, HWS Debate Team, international, jazz band, LGBT, literary magazine, musical theater, newspaper, orchestra, photography, political, professional, radio and TV, religious, social, social service, student government, symphony, and yearbook. Popular campus events include Stu Lieblein '90 Pitch Contest (entrepreneurship), Koshare Dance performances, Charter Day and Moving Up Day, as well as Convocation and Homecoming. **Sports:** There are 11 intercollegiate sports for men and 12 for women, and 18 intramural sports for men and 18 for women. Facilities include a sport and recreation center, gyms, athletic fields, swimming pool, indoor tennis courts, outdoor tennis courts, weight rooms, basketball courts, racquetball court, indoor track, international squash courts, boathouse, and a rowing facility. **Graduates:** From July 1, 2015 to June 30, 2016, 475 bachelor's degrees were awarded. The most popular majors were economics (13%), environmental studies (8%), and media and society (7%). In an average class, 73% graduate in 4 years or less, 76% graduate in 5 years or less, and 77% graduate in 6 years or less. Of the 2015 graduating class, 15% were enrolled in graduate school within 6 months of graduation, and 83% were employed.

SERVICES: Counseling and information services are available, as is tutoring in most subjects. HWS offer peer facilitated learning in anthropology, music, art history, biology, chemistry, computer science, economics, French, philosophy, sociology and Spanish. There is a reader service for the blind. Students can get writing and quantitative reasoning support regardless of discipline/course. Study mentors are also available to help with time management, test taking and note taking skills. **Library/Resources:** The library contains 387,217 volumes, 16,670 microform items, and 13,255 audio/video tapes/CDs/DVDs, and subscribes to 55,938 periodicals including electronic. Computerized library services include interlibrary loans, database searching, Internet access, and Wi-Fi capability. Special learning facilities include an art gallery, radio station, performing arts center, observatory, natural preserve, 35 acres of farmland, the HWS Finger Lakes Institute, a research vessel, and solar farms. **Physically Challenged Students:** 69% of the campus is accessible. Facilities include wheelchair ramps, elevators, special parking, specially equipped restrooms, special class scheduling, and lowered drinking fountains. **Special:** Each HWS student completes both a major and a minor (or a second major). Students have the option to design, with a faculty adviser, their own major. The colleges offer special degree programs in business administration (4 + 1 joint degree in conjunction University of Rochester, Syracuse University, Clarkson University and Rochester Institute of Technology), engineering (3 + 2 joint degree in conjunction with Dartmouth College and Columbia University), education (NYS certification for various education levels and disciplines), and Master of Arts in Teaching (HWS graduates only). Through the Salisbury Center for Career, Professional and Experiential Education, students have numerous opportunities to find credit-bearing internships nationally and internationally. The colleges guarantee that students of good academic standing, who successfully complete the HWS career development Pathways program, are able to participate in at least one internship or research opportunity. Sixty percent of students study abroad in programs available in more than 50 locations. Additionally, the colleges offer a semester in Washington, D.C. Academic scholarships are available, including The Elizabeth Blackwell Class of 1849 Pioneer in Science Scholarship, which is awarded to applicants who have completed advanced science coursework, relevant research or participated in science related experiences; and Arts Scholarships which are awarded for excellence in the fine and performing arts. There are 10 national honor societies, Phi Beta Kappa, and 100 departmental honors programs. **Visiting:** There are regularly scheduled orientations for prospective students, and daily information sessions and tours offered year round, with admissions interviews strongly recommended. Special Open House events are held throughout the winter, spring, summer and fall designed for high school juniors and seniors. There are guides for informal visits, visitors may sit in on classes, and stay overnight. To schedule a visit, contact Office of Admissions. **Campus Safety and Security:** Measures include 24-hour foot and vehicle patrol, emergency notification system, and security escort services. There are shuttle buses, emergency telephones, lighted pathways/sidewalks, controlled access to dorms/residences, and student EMS corps.

REQUIREMENTS: SAT Subject tests are not required but will be considered if taken. A GED is accepted. A total of 19 academic credits is required, including 4 years of English, 3 of math, and at least 3 each of lab science, foreign language, and history. An essay is also required. An interview is highly recommended. AP credits are accepted. Important factors in the admissions decision are advanced placement or honors courses, evidence of special talent, and leadership record. At HWS, we've built our education around exploring the world from multiple perspectives. A course of study must include: a first-year seminar that introduces students to the intellectual community and provides academic mentorship; passing 32 courses (including achieving a minimum grade and GPA standards); completing the requirements for an academic major, including a capstone course or experience, and a minor (or a second major); completing potential faculty-mandated writing requirements through a writing enriched curriculum; and addressing each of the eight goals of our general curriculum. Two goals are integrated across the four-year curriculum and six are aspirational goals satisfied through the completion of specific coursework that address each goal. The aim or the student should include the two integrated goals of critical thinking and communication, and six aspirational goals covering: the ability to reason quantitatively, experiential understanding of scientific inquiry, critical and experiential understanding of artistic process, critical understanding of social inequalities, critical understanding of cultural difference, and intellectual foundation for ethical judgment as a basis for socially responsible action. **Procedure:** Freshmen are admitted fall and spring. Entrance exams should be taken no later than December of the senior year. There are early decision, early admissions, and deferred admissions plans. Early decision applications should be filed by November 15; regular applications, by February 1 for fall entry, along with a $45 fee. Notification of early decision is sent December 15; regular decision, March 23. 291 early decision candidates were accepted for the 2016-2017 class. 566 applicants were on the 2016 waiting list; 88 were admitted. Application fees are waived if application is completed online. **Transfer Students:** 11 transfer students enrolled in 2015-2016. Applicants must have a 2.7 GPA and have completed 1 year of college study. They are required to take the SAT or ACT. An interview is highly recommended. 16 of 32 credits required for the bachelor's degree must be completed at HWS. **International Students:** There are 143 international students enrolled. The school actively recruits these students. They must take the TOEFL with a minimum score of 80 on the Internet-based version (iBT), or take the iELTS. They must also take the SAT or ACT.

ADMISSIONS: 60% of the 2016-2017 applicants were accepted. 45% of the current freshmen were in the top fifth of their class; 88% were in the top two fifths. 32 freshmen graduated first in their class. **Admissions Contact:** John W. Young, Director of Admissions. Email: *jyoung@hws.edu* Web: *www.hws.edu*

FINANCIAL AID: In 2016-2017, 92% of all full-time freshmen and 94% of continuing full-time students received some form of financial aid. 60% of all full-time freshmen and 57% of continuing full-time students received need-based aid. The average freshman award was $36,683. Need-based scholarships or need-based grants averaged $29,312 ($51,543 maximum); need-based self-help aid (loans and jobs) averaged $7,145 ($9,800 maximum); and other non-need-based awards and non-need-based scholarships averaged $17,534 ($52,000 maximum). 38% of undergraduate students work part-time. Average annual earnings from campus work are $934. The average financial indebtedness of the 2016 graduate was $34,432. HWS is a member of CSS. The CSS/Profile is required. The FAFSA code is 002731. The priority date for freshman financial aid applications for fall entry is February 1.

HOFSTRA UNIVERSITY — D-5

www.hofstra.edu

Hempstead, NY 11549	**(516) 463-6700** **(800) HOFSTRA**
Fax: (516) 463-7660	**Email: admission@hofstra.edu**
Full-time: 2989 men, 3485 women	**Faculty:** 371; I, +$
Part-time: 219 men, 211 women	**Ph.D.s:** 92%
Graduate: 1606 men, 2443 women	**Student/Faculty:** 17 to 1
Year: semesters, summer session	**Tuition:** $38,900
Room & Board: $12,910	**Freshman Class:** 26388 applied, 16258 accepted, 1714 enrolled
SAT CR/M: 560/570 **ACT:** 25	**CEEB CODE:** 2295
Application Deadline: open	**COMPETITIVE+**

Hofstra University, founded in 1935, is an independent institution offering programs in liberal arts and sciences, business, communications, education, engineering and applied sciences, health and human services, honors studies, law, and medicine. There are 7 undergraduate schools and 8 graduate schools. In addition to regional accreditation, Hofstra has baccalaureate program accreditation with AACSB, ABET, ACEJMC, TEAC, ABA, ACS, APA, MSCHE, ARC-PA, CAATE, CAA, AATA, CORE, LCME, NASP, and TEAC. The 240-acre campus is in a suburban area 25 miles east of New York City. Including any residence halls, there are 115 buildings.

STUDENT LIFE: 63% of undergraduates are from New York. Others are from 46 states, 51 foreign countries, and Canada. 9% are African American; 9% Asian American; 56% White; 4% Foreign; 4% race unknown; 2% two or more races; 14% Hispanic. **Female To Male Ratio:** 1.3:1. The average age of freshmen is 18; all undergraduates, 20. 20% do not continue beyond their first year; 60% remain to graduate. **Housing:** 3600 students can be accommodated in college housing, which includes single-sex and coed dorms and on-campus apartments. In addition, there are honors houses, and special-interest houses. There is a living-learning center, quiet floors, women's floors, themed living communities and freshman housing. On-campus housing is guaranteed for all 4 years, and is available on a first-come, first-served basis, and on a lottery system for upperclassmen. Priority is given to out-of-town students. 50% of students commute. All students may keep cars.

FACULTY/CLASSROOMS: 55% of faculty are male; 45% are female. 81% teach undergraduates, 81% do research, and 81% do both. No introductory courses are taught by graduate students. The average class size in an introductory lecture is 28; in a laboratory is 16; and in a regular course is 21.

PROGRAMS OF STUDY: Hofstra confers B.A., B.S., B.B.A., B.E., B.F.A., and B.S.Ed. degrees. Master's and doctoral degrees are also awarded. Bachelor's degrees are awarded in AGRICULTURE (environmental studies), BIOLOGICAL SCIENCE (biochemistry and biology/biological science), BUSINESS (accounting, banking and finance, business administration and management, business economics, business law, entrepreneurial studies, international business management, labor studies, management information systems, marketing management, and supply chain management), COMMUNICATIONS AND THE ARTS (American literature, art history and appreciation, audio technology, ceramic art and design, China Asia-Pacific studies, Chinese, classics, comparative literature, creative writing, dance, design, dramatic arts, film arts, fine arts, French, German, Hebrew, Italian, Japanese, jazz, journalism, Latin, linguistics, media arts, metal/jewelry, music, music business management, music history and appreciation, music performance, music theory and composition, painting, photography, public relations, publishing, radio/television technology, Russian, Spanish, speech/debate/rhetoric, theater design, theater management, video, and visual and performing arts), COMPUTER AND PHYSICAL SCIENCE (applied mathematics, applied physics, chemistry, computer science, geology, information sciences and systems, mathematics, and physics), EDUCATION (art education, athletic training, business education, childhood education, dance education, elementary education, English education, foreign languages education, global studies, health education, mathematics education, music education, physical education, science education, secondary education, and social studies education), ENGINEERING AND ENVIRONMENTAL DESIGN (biomedical engineering, civil engineering, computer engineering, electrical/electronics engineering, engineering and applied science, industrial engineering, manufacturing engineering, and mechanical engineering), HEALTH PROFESSIONS (allied health, community health work, exercise science, health science, pre-health studies, predentistry, premedicine, preoptometry, preosteopathy, prepodiatry, preveterinary science, and speech pathology/audiology), SOCIAL SCIENCE (African studies, American studies, anthropology, Caribbean studies, Chinese Studies, criminology, economics, forensic studies, geography, Hispanic American studies, history, Japanese studies, Judaic studies, Latin American studies, liberal arts/general studies, philosophy, political science/government, psychology, religion, sociology, urban ecology, and women's studies). Engineering, communication/radio, business/marketing, education, humanities, physician assistant are the strongest academically. Biology, psychology, and accounting have the largest enrollments.

ACTIVITIES: 7% of women belong to 1 local and 11 national sororities. There are 249 groups on campus, including art, band, cheerleading, chess, choir, chorale, chorus, communications, computers, dance, debate, drama, environmental, ethnic, film, forensics, honors, international, jazz band, LGBT, literary magazine, musical theater, newspaper, opera, orchestra, pep band, photography, political, professional, radio and TV, religious, social, social service, student government, symphony, and yearbook. Popular campus events include New Student Convocation, Welcome Week, Hofstra Celebrates the Holidays, Student Leadership Awards, Hofstra Music Fest, Hofstra Fall Festival, Jail & Bail, Alt Spring Break, Greek Week, Relay for Life, Leadership Programs, Senior Week, Heritage Month. **Sports:** There are 8 intercollegiate sports for men and 9 for women, and 6 intramural sports for men and 6 for women. Facilities include a stadium, an arena, soccer stadium, physical education building, swim center, softball stadium, intramural fields, fitness center with a multipurpose gym, indoor track, and a weight room. **Graduates:** From July 1, 2015 to June 30, 2016, 1403 bachelor's degrees were awarded. The most popular majors were psychology (8%), marketing (6%), and management (6%). 239 companies recruited on campus in 2015-2016. In an average class, 50% graduate in 4 years or less, 59% graduate in 5 years or less, and 60% graduate in 6 years or less. Of the 2015 graduating class, 27% were enrolled in graduate school within 6 months of graduation, and 76% were employed.

SERVICES: Counseling and information services are available, as is tutoring in most subjects. There is a reader service for the blind. **Library/Resources:** The 3 libraries contain 1.2 million volumes, 3.4 million microform items, 17,433 audio/video tapes/CDs/DVDs, and subscribe to 14,628 periodicals including electronic. Computerized library services include interlibrary loans, database searching, Internet access, and Wi-Fi capability. Special learning facilities include an art gallery, radio station, science labs and state-of-the-art bio-engineering labs, robotics and big data labs, rooftop observatory, 6 theaters including a black box teaching theater, financial trading room, multi-media converged news room, comprehensive media production facility including a 24-hr radio station, multiple 3-D printers, digital language lab, state-of-the-art medical school, 100% wireless campus, child care institute, cultural center, museum, arboretum, and a bird sanctuary. **Physically Challenged Students:** All of the campus is accessible. Facilities include wheelchair ramps, elevators, special parking, specially equipped restrooms, special class scheduling, lowered drinking fountains, lowered telephones, and special housing. **Special:** Internships in numerous career fields, Engineering Co-Op Program, SUNY Brockport/Washington Semester, utilization of the Washington Center for internship conferences and programming, an Albany internship with the NY State Assembly, NY State Senate Internship, Study Abroad, and dual and individually designed majors are offered. Credits for prior learning and credit by exam are given with proper credentials. Hofstra offers over 100 dual degree programs. There are 36 national honor societies, Phi Beta Kappa, a freshman honors program, and 35 departmental honors programs. **Visiting:** There are regularly scheduled orientations for prospective students, a group information session, a campus tour and an optional interview with a admission counselor. There are guides for informal visits, visitors may sit in on classes, and stay overnight. To schedule a visit, contact Andrea Nadler at (516) 463-6798. **Campus Safety and Security:** Measures include 24-hour foot and vehicle patrol, emergency notification system, self-defense education, and security escort services. There are shuttle buses, emergency telephones, lighted pathways/sidewalks, and controlled access to dorms/residences. Residence halls have security cameras, require card access to enter, and are monitored by resident student safety representative 24/7, with the help of a CCTV, bike patrol, and a motorist assistance program.

REQUIREMENTS: Applicants should graduate from an accredited secondary school or have a GED. Preparatory work should include 4 years of English, 3 each of history and social studies, math, and science, and 2 of foreign language. Engineering students are required to have 4 years of math and 1 each of chemistry and physics. An essay is required. Interviews are recommended. One counselor or teacher recommendation is helpful. Hofstra is test optional, standardized test scores are not required for most programs with the exception of home schooled and international applicants. AP and CLEP credits are accepted. Important factors in the admissions decision are advanced placement or honors courses, recommendations by school officials, and leadership record. A total of 124 to 134 credit hours is required for graduation, (152 for 5 year Accounting) with approximately 30 to 60 in the major depending on degree program and a minimum GPA of 2.0. Some majors have a higher GPA requirement. Students must pass writing studies and composition 1 and 2, and pass a writing proficiency exam. For the B.A. degree, 33 credits in distribution/general education are required: 9 each in humanities, social science, natural science/math/computer science, 3 each in cross culture, and interdisciplinary. Foreign language study is required for the B.A., the B.B.A. in international business, and some B.S. programs. **Procedure:** Freshmen are admitted fall and spring. Entrance exams should be taken in the junior or senior year. There are early admissions, deferred admissions, and rolling admissions plans. Early decision applications should be filed by December 15, along with a $70 fee. Notification of early decision is sent January 15; regular decision, February 1. 47 applicants were on the 2016 waiting list; 10 were admitted. Applications are accepted online. **Transfer Students:** 599 transfer students enrolled in 2015-2016. Admission is based primarily on prior college work. A maximum of 64 credits from a 2-year school or 94 credits from a 4-year school is accepted. There is a 30-credit maximum on AP/CLEP credits. 30 of 124 credits required for the bachelor's degree must be completed at Hofstra. **International Students:** There are 294 international students enrolled. The school actively recruits these students. They must take the TOEFL with a minimum score of 550 on the paper-based TOEFL (PBT) or 80 on the Internet-based version (iBT).

ADMISSIONS: 62% of the 2016-2017 applicants were accepted. The SAT scores for the 2016-2017 freshman class were: Critical Reading-- 12% below 500, 56% between 500 and 599, 27% between 600 and 699, and 5% between 700 and 800. Math-- 9% below 500, 52% between 500 and 599, 33% between 600 and 699, and 6% between 700 and 800. The ACT scores were 3% below 12, 28% between 12 and 17, 32% between 18 and 23, 17% between 24 and 29, and 21% above 30. 50% of the current freshmen were in the top fifth of their class; 78% were in the top two fifths. 8 freshmen graduated first in their class. **Admissions Contact:** Jessica Eads, Vice President of Enrollment Management. Email: *admission@hofstra.edu* Web: *www.hofstra.edu*

FINANCIAL AID: In 2016-2017, 93% of all full-time freshmen and 88% of continuing full-time students received some form of financial aid. 71% of all full-time freshmen and 64% of continuing full-time students received need-based aid. The average freshman award was $27,000. Need-based scholarships or need-based grants averaged $22,000 ($53,000 maximum); need-based self-help aid (loans and jobs) averaged $7,000 ($14,000 maximum); non-need-based athletic scholarships averaged $22,000 ($48,000 maximum); and other non-need-based awards and non-need-based scholarships averaged $18,000 ($40,000 maximum). 41% of undergraduate students work part-time. Average annual earnings from campus work are $3000. The state aid form is required. The FAFSA code is 002732. The priority date for freshman financial aid applications for fall entry is February 15.

HOUGHTON COLLEGE B-3

www.houghton.edu

Houghton, NY 14744 (585) 567-9348 (800) 777-2556
Fax: (585) 567-9522 Email: admission@houghton.edu

Full-time: 354 men, 636 women
Part-time: 9 men, 10 women
Graduate: 10 men, 10 women
Year: semesters, summer session
Room & Board: $8754
Faculty: 73
Ph.D.s: 88%
Student/Faculty: 11 to 1
Tuition: $30,336
Freshman Class: 737 applied, 696 accepted, 244 enrolled
SAT CR/M/W: 565/555/540 **ACT:** required
CEEB CODE: 2299
Application Deadline: March 1
COMPETITIVE

Houghton College, founded in 1883, provides a residential educational experience integrating academic instruction with Christian faith. Figures in the above capsule and in this profile are approximate. In addition to regional accreditation, Houghton has baccalaureate program accreditation with NASM and TEAC. The 1300-acre campus is in a rural area 65 miles southeast of Buffalo and 70 miles southwest of Rochester. Including any residence halls, there are 20 buildings.

STUDENT LIFE: 68% of undergraduates are from out of state, mostly the Middle Atlantic. Students are from 36 states, 31 foreign countries, and Canada. 66% are from public schools. 84% are White; 7% Foreign; 3% African American; 2% Hispanic; 2% two or more races; 1% Asian American; 1% race unknown. 95% are Protestant. **Female To Male Ratio:** 1.8:1. The average age of freshmen is 18; all undergraduates, 20. 12% do not continue beyond their first year; 74% remain to graduate. **Housing:** 1066 students can be accommodated in college housing, which includes single-sex dorms, on-campus apartments, and married student housing. In addition, there are special-interest houses, Equestrian students can live in housing on site, and cooperative housing. On-campus housing is guaranteed for all 4 years. Priority is given to out-of-town students. 81% of students live on campus; of those, 67% remain on campus on weekends. All students may keep cars. Alcohol is not permitted.

FACULTY/CLASSROOMS: 64% of faculty are male; 36% are female. All teach undergraduates, and 20% do research. No introductory courses are taught by graduate students. The average class size in an introductory lecture is 26; in a laboratory is 13; and in a regular course is 17.

PROGRAMS OF STUDY: Houghton confers B.A., B.S., B.F.A., and B.Mus. degrees. Associate and master's degrees are also awarded. Bachelor's degrees are awarded in AGRICULTURE (equine science), BIOLOGICAL SCIENCE (biochemistry, biology/adolescence education, biology/biological science, and environmental biology), BUSINESS (accounting, business administration and management, recreation and leisure services, and recreational facilities management), COMMUNICATIONS AND THE ARTS (art, communications, English, ESL, English literature, English Writing, instrumental performance, media arts, music, music performance, music theory and composition, organ performance, printmaking, Spanish, studio art, vocal performance, voice, vocal music education, and writing), COMPUTER AND PHYSICAL SCIENCE (applied physics, chemistry, chemistry/adolescence education, computer science, mathematics, physics, and science), EDUCATION (art education, childhood education, Christian education, early childhood education, education of the exceptional child, elementary education, English education, foreign languages education, general studies, health education, mathematics education, music education, physical education, science education, secondary education, special education, and teaching English as a second/foreign language (TESOL/TEFOL)), ENGINEERING AND ENVIRONMENTAL DESIGN (environmental science and preengineering), HEALTH PROFESSIONS (medical technology, predentistry, premedicine, preoptometry, prepharmacy, prephysical therapy, preveterinary science, and recreation therapy), SOCIAL SCIENCE (biblical studies, Christian studies, counseling/psychology, crosscultural studies, history, humanities, interdisciplinary studies, international studies, liberal arts/general studies, ministries, parks and recreation management, pastoral studies, philosophy, political science/government, prelaw, psychobiology, psychology, religion, religious education, religious studies, religious music, and sociology). Biology, religion, and art are the strongest academically. Management/business administration, biology, and inclusive childhood education have the largest enrollments.

ACTIVITIES: There are no fraternities or sororities. There are 50 groups on campus, including art, bagpipe, band, choir, chorale, chorus, communications, drama, environmental, ethnic, honors, international, jazz band, literary magazine, musical theater, newspaper, opera, orchestra, pep band, photography, political, professional, religious, social, social service, student government, symphony, volunteer service, and yearbook. Popular campus events include Christian Life Emphasis Week, Film Festival, SPOT Variety Show, Purple and Gold Week, Faith and Justice Symposium and Martin Luther King Jr. Service Day. **Sports:** There are 7 intercollegiate sports for men and 9 for women, and 7 intramural sports for men and 7 for women. Facilities include basketball, racquetball courts, swimming pool, indoor track, ski slope, cross-country ski trails, tennis courts, climbing wall, all-weather track, ropes course, equestrian center with an indoor riding ring, gym, and baseball and softball fields. **Graduates:** From July 1, 2015 to June 30, 2016, 260 bachelor's degrees were awarded. The most popular majors were business/marketing (22%), education (18%), and biology/life sciences (12%). 54 companies recruited on campus in 2015-2016. In an average class, 2% graduate in 3 years or less, 64% graduate in 4 years or less, 72% graduate in 5 years or less, and 71% graduate in 6 years or less. Of the 2015 graduating class, 18% were enrolled in graduate school within 6 months of graduation, and 86% were employed.

SERVICES: Counseling and information services are available, as is tutoring in some subjects, and a reader service for the blind. There is also support for students with learning-related disabilities. **Library/Resources:** The 2 libraries contain 314,183 volumes, 47,163 microform items, and 21,092 audio/video tapes/CDs/DVDs, and subscribe to 57,591 periodicals including electronic. Computerized library services include interlibrary loans, database searching, Internet access, and Wi-Fi capability. Special learning facilities include an art gallery, digital media lab, greenhouse, and an outdoor classroom. **Physically Challenged Students:** 85% of the campus is accessible. Facilities include wheelchair ramps, elevators, special parking, specially equipped restrooms, special class scheduling, lowered drinking fountains, lowered telephones, and special housing. **Special:** Students may cross-register with members of the Western New York Consortium, the Christian College Consortium, and the Five College Committee. Internships are available in psychology, social work, business, educational ministries, physical fitness, political science, graphic design, communication, athletic training, recreation, English, and Christian education. Study abroad is available in 25 countries, as well as a Washington semester, and dual majors. A 3-2 engineering degree with Clarkson and Washington Universities is offered as well as a 4-1 BS/MBA degree with Alfred U, Clarkson U, Niagara U and Rochester Institute of Technology. A PharmD 3-4 degree program with University of Buffalo is also available. Students may design their own major as an Interdisciplinary Studies major. Credit for military experience and nondegree study are possible. There are 3 national honor societies, Phi Beta Kappa, a freshman honors program, and 3 departmental honors programs. **Visiting:** There are regularly scheduled orientations for prospective students, including a campus tour, an admissions interview, a financial aid session, a class visit, and an academic information session. There are guides for informal visits, visitors may sit in on classes, and stay overnight. To schedule a visit, contact the Admissions Office. **Campus Safety and Security:** Measures include 24-hour foot and vehicle patrol, emergency notification system, and security escort services. There are also emergency telephones, lighted pathways/sidewalks, and controlled access to dorms/residences. A campus emergency preparedness plan includes agreements with local police departments, the American Red Cross, and local schools/businesses for cooperative assistance as needed.

REQUIREMENTS: The SAT or ACT is required. Applicants must graduate from an accredited secondary school, be home-schooled, or have a GED. A total of 16 academic credits is recommended, including 4 of English, 3 each of social studies, science with 2 units of lab, and history, and 2 of foreign language. An essay is required. Music students must audition. An interview is recommended. AP and CLEP credits are accepted. Important factors in the admissions decision are advanced placement or honors courses, personality/intangible qualities, parents or siblings attended your school, evidence of special talent, extracurricular activities record, and recommendations by school officials. Integrative studies courses are required in the following disciplines: writing, literature, Bible, foreign language, history, math, science, physical education, theology, philosophy, fine arts, social science, and humanities. A minimum GPA of 2.0 is required to graduate. **Procedure:** Freshmen are admitted fall and spring. Entrance exams should be taken in the spring of the junior year or fall of the senior year. There are deferred admissions and rolling admissions plans. Application deadlines are open. Application fee is $40. Notification of early decision is sent November 1; regular decision, on a rolling basis. Applications are accepted online. **Transfer Students:** 40 transfer students enrolled in 2015-2016. Applicants should have a 2.75 or better GPA. A character recommendation and high school transcripts must be submitted. The essay, an SAT or ACT and an interview are optional but encouraged. 30 of 125 credits required for the bachelor's degree must be completed at Houghton. **International Students:** There are 64 international students enrolled. The school actively recruits these students. They must take the TOEFL with a minimum score of 550 on the paper-based TOEFL (PBT) or 80 on the Internet-based version (iBT). They must also take the SAT or ACT.

ADMISSIONS: 94% of the 2016-2017 applicants were accepted. The SAT scores for the 2016-2017 freshman class were: Critical Reading-- 25% below 500, 37% between 500 and 599, 29% between 600 and 699, and 9% between 700 and 800. Math-- 26% below 500, 40% between 500 and 599, 31% between 600 and 699, and 2% between 700 and 800. Writing-- 30% below 500, 42% between 500 and 599, 21% between 600 and 699, and 6% between 700 and 800. The ACT scores were 9% between 12 and 17, 32% between 18 and 23, 43% between 24 and 29, and 16% above 30. 51% of the current freshmen were in the top fifth of their class; 80% were in the top two fifths. There was 1 National Merit finalist. 8 freshmen graduated first in their class. **Admissions Contact:** Ryan Spear, Director of Admission. Email: *john.wise@houghton.edu* Web: *www.houghton.edu*

FINANCIAL AID: In 2016-2017, 100% of all full-time freshmen and 97% of continuing full-time students received some form of financial aid. 85% of all full-time freshmen and 86% of continuing full-time students received need-based aid. The average freshman award was $24,707. Need-based scholarships or need-based grants averaged $12,334; need-based self-help aid (loans and jobs) averaged $5,668; non-need-based athletic scholarships averaged $17,178; and other non-need-based awards and non-need-based scholarships averaged $4,067. 43% of undergraduate students work part-time. Average annual earnings from campus work are $1561. The average financial indebtedness of the 2016 graduate was $30,494. Houghton is a member of CSS. The college's own financial statement is required. The FAFSA code is 002734. The priority date for freshman financial aid applications for fall entry is March 1.

IONA COLLEGE — D-5

www.iona.edu

New Rochelle, NY 10801	(914) 637-2702 (800) 231-IONA
Fax: (914) 633-2182	**Email:** admissions@iona.edu
Full-time: 1267 men, 1660 women	**Faculty:** 169; IIA, +$
Part-time: 248 men, 287 women	**Ph.D.s:** 90%
Graduate: 320 men, 459 women	**Student/Faculty:** 16 to 1
Year: semesters, summer session	**Tuition:** $36,584
Room & Board: $14,400	**Freshman Class:** 8741 applied, 7556 accepted, 722 enrolled
SAT CR/M: 500/500 **ACT:** 22	**CEEB CODE:** 2324
Application Deadline: February 15	**COMPETITIVE**

Iona College, founded in 1940, is a private college in the tradition of the Christian Brothers and American Catholic higher education, offering programs through schools of general studies, arts and science, and business. Figures in the above capsule and in this profile are approximate. There are 2 undergraduate schools and 2 graduate schools. In addition to regional accreditation, Iona has baccalaureate program accreditation with AACSB, ABET, ACEJMC, CSWE, NCATE, CLRA, NASP, and ACS. The 43-acre campus is in a suburban area in New Rochelle (Westchester county) New York, two miles from Long Island Sound and 20 miles north of Midtown Manhattan and 20 miles south of Stamford, CT. Including any residence halls, there are 49 buildings.

STUDENT LIFE: 76% of undergraduates are from New York. Others are from 34 states, 40 foreign countries, and Canada. 6% are African American; 57% White; 2% Asian American; 17% race unknown; 16% Hispanic; 1% Foreign; 1% two or more races. **Female To Male Ratio:** 1.3:1. The average age of freshmen is 18; all undergraduates, 19. 19% do not continue beyond their first year; 65% remain to graduate. **Housing:** 1358 students can be accommodated in college housing, which includes single-sex dorms, on-campus apartments, and off-campus apartments. On-campus housing is available on a first-come, first-served basis, and on a lottery system for upperclassmen. 63% of students live on campus. Upperclassmen may keep cars.

FACULTY/CLASSROOMS: 58% of faculty are male; 42% are female. 88% teach undergraduates. No introductory courses are taught by graduate students. The average class size in an introductory lecture is 25; in a laboratory is 17; and in a regular course is 14.

PROGRAMS OF STUDY: Iona confers B.A., B.S., B.B.A. and B.P.S. degrees. Master's degrees are also awarded. Bachelor's degrees are awarded in BIOLOGICAL SCIENCE (biochemistry and biology/biological science), BUSINESS (accounting, business administration and management, finance, international business management, management science, and marketing management), COMMUNICATIONS AND THE ARTS (communications, English, French, Italian, Spanish, and speech/debate/rhetoric), COMPUTER AND PHYSICAL SCIENCE (applied mathematics, chemistry, computer science, information sciences and systems, mathematics, and physics), EDUCATION (childhood education and early childhood education), ENGINEERING AND ENVIRONMENTAL DESIGN (environmental science), HEALTH PROFESSIONS (speech pathology/audiology), SOCIAL SCIENCE (criminal justice, economics, history, international studies, liberal arts/general studies, philosophy, political science/government, psychology, religion, social work, and sociology). Computer science, speech pathology, and biology/biochemistry are the strongest academically. Mass communication, business, and criminal justice have the largest enrollments.

ACTIVITIES: 6% of men belong to 1 local and 2 national fraternities; 9% of women belong to 4 local and 1 national sororities. There are 80 groups on campus, including black student union, democracy matters, Gaelic society), Hispanic organization of Latin awareness, Italian society, karate club, national student speech and hearing/language association, inter-residence hall council, students against destructive, students association, community service, veterans students for peace, bagpipe, cheerleading, dance public relations, chorale, communications, computers, dance, debate, drama, environmental, film, honors, international, LGBT, literary magazine, multi cultural groups, Caribbean ancestry, musical theater, newspaper, political, professional, radio and TV, religious, social, social service, student government, and yearbook. Popular campus events include Spring Weekend/Concert Event, Travel Series, Heritage Week, Fashion Show, Campus Coffee House, Homecoming Carnivel, Week of the Peacemaker and Make a Difference Week, Black History Month, Hispanic Heritage Month and Alcohol Awareness Week. **Sports:** There are 10 intercollegiate sports for men and 11 for women. Facilities include gymnasiums, weight rooms, cardio room, core studio, aerobics studio, rowing tank, swimming pool/diving/water polo, soccer/lacrosse field, and a softball field. **Graduates:** From July 1, 2015 to June 30, 2016, 727 bachelor's degrees were awarded. The most popular majors were business (38%), mass communication (17%), and education (10%). 65 companies recruited on campus in 2015-2016. In an average class, 1% graduate in 3 years or less, 56% graduate in 4 years or less, 63% graduate in 5 years or less, and 66% graduate in 6 years or less. Of the 2015 graduating class, 40% were enrolled in graduate school within 6 months of graduation, and 68% were employed.

SERVICES: Counseling and information services are available, as is tutoring in most subjects, and a reader service for the blind. Assistance is also available for students with acquiring electronic versions of texts. **Library/Resources:** The 3 libraries contain 268,476 volumes, 510,213 microform items, and 4,176 audio/video tapes/CDs/DVDs, and subscribe to 742 periodicals including electronic. Computerized library services include interlibrary loans, database searching, Internet access, and Wi-Fi capability. Special learning facilities include an art gallery, radio station, TV station, an electron microscope, and a speech and hearing clinic. **Physically Challenged Students:** 70% of the campus is accessible. Facilities include wheelchair ramps, elevators, special parking, specially equipped restrooms, special class scheduling, lowered drinking fountains, and special housing. **Special:** There are internships available for students. Study abroad is available in 9 countries. Work-study positions are available in several locations throughout the college. Students may earn either a BA or BS degree in Adolescent Education, Computer Science, Economics, or Mathematics. There is an articulation agreement with New York Medical College for Physical Therapy. Five-year programs are offered in the following areas: Chemistry and Adolescent Education; Chemistry and Computer Science; Computer Science; Criminal Justice; English; History, Mathematics and Computer Science; and Psychology. There are 2 national honor societies, a freshman honors program, and 24 departmental honors programs. **Visiting:** There are regularly scheduled orientations for prospective students, including a meeting with an admissions counselor, a campus tour, and a variety of on-campus programs during the summer and fall. There are guides for informal visits and visitors may sit in on classes. To schedule a visit, contact Raymond Garo at (914) 633-2622. **Campus Safety and Security:** Measures include 24-hour foot and vehicle patrol, emergency notification system, and security escort services. There are shuttle buses, emergency telephones, lighted pathways/sidewalks, and controlled access to dorms/residences.

REQUIREMENTS: The SAT or ACT is required. Applicants must complete 16 academic credits, including 4 units of English, 3 of math, 3 science, 2 each of foreign language and social studies, and 1 each of history, and academic electives. A GED is accepted. An essay is required, and an interview is recommended. AP and CLEP credits are accepted. Important factors in the admissions decision are recommendations by school officials, extracurricular activities record, and leadership record. All students are required to take courses in humanities, social sciences, science and technology, natural and/or symbolic languages, and communication skills, as a part of the college core. Students enrolled in BBA programs, BS programs, and the Honors Program take specific core courses that are unique to each program. Students who earn BA degrees must take a total of 90 liberal arts credits; students who earn BS degrees must take a total of 60 liberal arts credits; and students who earn BBA degrees must take a total of 63 liberal arts credits in order to complete the bachelor's degree. Computer literacy is required. The total number of credits required to graduate is at least 120, depending on the major, with at least 30 in the major. The minimum GPA requirement is 2.0. **Procedure:** Freshmen are admitted fall and spring. Entrance exams should be taken in the spring of the junior year. There are early admissions and deferred admissions plans. Applications should be filed by February 15 for fall entry; January 1 for spring entry, along with a $50 fee. 1184 applicants were on the 2016 waiting list; 1120 were admitted. Application fees are waived if application is completed online. **Transfer Students:** 161 transfer students enrolled in 2015-2016. Transfer applicants must have a GPA of at least 2.0 and must submit high school transcripts if they have earned fewer than 30 college credits. An interview is recommended. 30 of 120 credits required for the bachelor's degree must be completed at Iona. **International Students:** There are 48 international students enrolled. The school actively recruits these students. They must take the TOEFL with a minimum score of 550 on the paper-based TOEFL (PBT) or 80 on the Internet-based version (iBT). They must also take the SAT or ACT.

ADMISSIONS: 86% of the 2016-2017 applicants were accepted. The SAT scores for the 2016-2017 freshman class were: Critical Reading-- 49% below 500, 41% between 500 and 599, 9% between 600 and 699, and 1% between 700 and 800. Math-- 44% below 500, 42% between 500 and 599, 13% between 600 and 699, and 2% between 700 and 800. The ACT scores were 28% below 12, 37% between 12 and 17, 20% between 18 and 23, 6% between 24 and 29, and 10% above 30. 34% of the current freshmen were in the top fifth of their class; 66% were in the top two fifths. **Admissions Contact:** Joanna Cavallo, Associate Director of Admissions. Email: *admissions@iona.edu* Web: *www.iona.edu*

FINANCIAL AID: In 2016-2017, 98% of all full-time freshmen and 96% of continuing full-time students received some form of financial aid. 72% of all full-time freshmen and 65% of continuing full-time students received need-based aid. The average freshman award was $27,908. Need-based scholarships or need-based grants averaged $6,704 ($20,400 maximum); need-based self-help aid (loans and jobs) averaged $3,871 ($9,800 maximum); non-need-based athletic scholarships averaged $17,643 ($49,102 maximum); and other non-need-based awards and non-need-based scholarships averaged $20,153 ($48,611 maximum). 15% of undergraduate students work part-time. Average annual earnings from campus work are $1261. The average financial indebtedness of the 2016 graduate was $31,960. Iona is a member of CSS. The state aid form is required. The FAFSA code is 002737. The deadline for filing freshman financial aid applications for fall entry is April 15.

ITHACA COLLEGE — C-4

www.ithaca.edu

Ithaca, NY 14850 — (607) 274-3124, (800) 429-4274

Fax: (607) 274-1900 — **Email:** admission@ithaca.edu

Full-time: 2537 men, 3566 women	**Faculty:** 515
Part-time: 62 men, 56 women	**Ph.D.s:** 88%
Graduate: 145 men, 312 women	**Student/Faculty:** 11 to 1
Year: semesters, summer session	**Tuition:** $41,776
Room & Board: $14,990	**Freshman Class:** 14380 applied, 10054 accepted, 1634 enrolled
SAT CR/M/W: 600/590/580 **ACT:** 27	**CEEB CODE:** 2325
Application Deadline: February 1	**VERY COMPETITIVE**

Ithaca College is home to both undergraduates and graduate students and offers more than 100 degree programs in its schools of business, communications, health sciences and human performance, humanities and sciences, and music. IC's integrative core curriculum builds bridges across disciplines and uniquely blends liberal arts with professional study. There are 5 undergraduate schools and 1 graduate school. In addition to regional accreditation, Ithaca has baccalaureate program accreditation with AACSB, APTA, NASM, NCATE, NRPA, AOTA, CAAHEP, CAPTE, CAA ASHA, ACS, NYS Board of Public Accounting, and National Association of Schools of Theatre. The 669-acre campus is in a small town 250 miles northwest of New York City. Including any residence halls, there are 86 buildings.

STUDENT LIFE: 56% of undergraduates are from out of state, mostly the Middle Atlantic. Students are from 48 states, 53 foreign countries, and Canada. 83% are from public schools. 8% are Hispanic; 71% White; 6% African American; 6% race unknown; 4% Asian American; 3% two or more races; 2% Foreign. **Female To Male Ratio:** 1.4:1. The average age of freshmen is 18; all undergraduates, 20. 15% do not continue beyond their first year; 75% remain to graduate. **Housing:** 4526 students can be accommodated in college housing, which includes single-sex and coed dorms and on-campus apartments. In addition, there are honors houses, language houses, special-interest houses, first-year students only housing, quiet study residence hall, service and music honor fraternities, smoke-free buildings and floors, coed by buildings, honors floors, substance-free building, multicultural housing, and several freshman seminar groups housed together. On-campus housing is guaranteed for all 4 years. 71% of students live on campus; of those, 95% remain on campus on weekends. All students may keep cars.

FACULTY/CLASSROOMS: 50% of faculty are male; 50% are female. All teach undergraduates. Graduate students teach 5% of introductory courses. The average class size in an introductory lecture is 22.

PROGRAMS OF STUDY: Ithaca confers B.A., B.S., B.F.A., and Mus.B. degrees. Master's and doctoral degrees are also awarded. Bachelor's degrees are awarded in AGRICULTURE (environmental studies), BIOLOGICAL SCIENCE (biochemistry and biology/biological science), BUSINESS (accounting, applied economics/management, business administration with legal studies, business administration and management, business communications, organizational behavior, recreation and leisure services, and sports management), COMMUNICATIONS AND THE ARTS (art, art history and appreciation, audio technology, broadcasting, communications, creative writing, dramatic arts, English, English literature, English writing, film arts, fine arts, French, German, Germanic languages and literature, jazz, journalism, languages, media arts, modern language, music, music performance, music theory and composition, musical theater, performing arts, photography, piano pedagogy, public relations, Spanish, sports media, studio art, telecommunications, theater design, theater management, video, and visual and performing arts), COMPUTER AND PHYSICAL SCIENCE (chemistry, computer mathematics, computer programming, computer science, mathematics, mathematics – economics, physics secondary education, physics and mathematics, and physics), EDUCATION (art education, athletic training, education, education of the deaf and hearing impaired, English secondary education, English comm secondary education, English education, foreign languages education, health education, mathematics education, middle school education, music education, physical education, secondary education, social science education, social studies education, speech correction, sports and wellness studies, and sports studies), ENGINEERING AND ENVIRONMENTAL DESIGN (engineering chemistry, engineering physics, and environmental science), HEALTH PROFESSIONS (allied health, clinical science, community health work, exercise science, health, health science, occupational therapy, physical therapy, preallied health, pre-health studies, predentistry, premedicine, preoptometry, public health, recreation therapy, rehabilitation therapy, speech pathology/audiology, speech therapy, and sports medicine), SOCIAL SCIENCE (anthropology, applied psychology, architectural studies, area studies, economics, German area studies, gerontology, history, industrial and organizational psychology, interdisciplinary studies, Italian studies, legal studies, liberal arts/general studies, philosophy, philosophy and religion, physical fitness/movement, political science/government, prelaw, psychology, social studies, and sociology). Physical therapy, theater, and music are the strongest academically. Business administration, music, and television/radio have the largest enrollments.

ACTIVITIES: There are 200 groups on campus, including academic clubs, cultural, art, band, cheerleading, chess, choir, chorale, chorus, computers, dance, debate, drama, environmental, ethnic, film, forensics, honors, international, jazz band, LGBT, literary magazine, musical theater, newspaper, opera, orchestra, pep band, photography, political, professional, radio and TV, religious, social, social service, sports, student government, and symphony. Popular campus events include Pep Rallies, Student Involvement Fair, and various multicultural awareness events. **Sports:** There are 11 intercollegiate sports for men and 14 for women, and 16 intramural sports for men and 16 for women. Facilities include gyms, dance studios, student union, indoor and outdoor pools, fitness center and wellness clinic, outdoor track, and baseball, football, lacrosse, field hockey, and soccer fields. The Athletics and Events Center has an indoor track, tennis courts, aquatics pavilion, and stadium. **Graduates:** From July 1, 2015 to June 30, 2016, 1481 bachelor's degrees were awarded. The most popular majors were business administration (8%), music (8%), and integrated marketing communications (6%). 200 companies recruited on campus in 2015-2016. In an average class, 2% graduate in 3 years or less, 66% graduate in 4 years or less, 74% graduate in 5 years or less, and 75% graduate in 6 years or less. Of the 2015 graduating class, 26% were enrolled in graduate school within 6 months of graduation, and 33% were employed.

SERVICES: We provide content-based tutoring in over 50 courses. **Library/Resources:** The library contains 311,396 volumes, 19,603 microform items, 33,540 audio/video tapes/CDs/DVDs, and subscribes to 72,576 periodicals including electronic. Computerized library services include interlibrary loans, database searching, Internet access, and Wi-Fi capability. Special learning facilities include an art gallery, radio station, TV station, digital audio/video labs, photography labs, cinematography postproduction studio, film animation lab, lighting studio, physical therapy and occupational therapy clinics, speech and hearing clinic, athletic training clinic, wellness clinic, human anatomy lab, movement analysis lab, financial trading room, recording and electroacoustic music studio, music and theatre performance halls, art gallery, psychology labs, biology, chemistry, and physics labs (including single crystal x-ray diffractometer and 3D printer), observatory, natural lands, greenhouse, organic garden, and apiary. **Physically Challenged Students:** Facilities include wheelchair ramps, elevators, special parking, specially equipped restrooms, special class scheduling, lowered drinking fountains, lowered telephones, and special housing. **Special:** Cross-registration is available with Cornell University and Wells College. Opportunities are also provided for internships, study abroad (in more than 50 countries), a semester of study/internship in NYC, Los Angeles, and/or London, work-study programs, accelerated degree programs, dual majors, non-degree study, pass/fail options, and student-designed majors. A 3-2 engineering degree with Cornell University, Clarkson University, Rensselaer Polytechnic Institute, and Binghamton University is available. A 4-1 B.S./M.B.A. program, a pre-med and pre-law program, and a one-semester program in marine biology with Duke University and the Sea Education Association are also available. There are 34 national honor societies, a freshman honors program, and 33 departmental honors programs. **Visiting:** There are regularly scheduled orientations for prospective students, which includes a campus tour, and an interview with an admissions counselor. Fall open house programs offering personal meetings with faculty are available by appointment. There are guides for informal visits and visitors may sit in on classes. To schedule a visit, contact the Admission Office. **Campus Safety and Security:** Measures include 24-hour foot and vehicle patrol, emergency notification system, self-defense education, and security escort services. There are emergency telephones, lighted pathways/sidewalks, controlled access to dorms/residences, and crime prevention programs.

REQUIREMENTS: Applicants should be graduates of an accredited secondary school with a minimum of 16 Carnegie units, including 4 years of English, 3 years each of math, science, and social studies, 2 years of foreign language, and other college-preparatory electives. The GED is accepted. An essay is required, as is an audition for music and theater students. In some majors, a portfolio and an interview are recommended. AP and CLEP credits are accepted. Students must successfully complete a minimum of 120 credits including the course requirements of their specific major. All students participate in Ithaca College's Integrative Core Curriculum (ICC). The centerpiece of the ICC is a "Themes and Perspectives" sequence where students take a minimum of one course each in the natural sciences, creative arts, humanities, and social sciences, all focusing on one of six general themes, such as "Inquiry, Imagination, and Innovation" or "Quest for a Sustainable Future." The Themes and Perspectives sequence kicks off with a first-semester Ithaca Seminar introducing students to the theme and helping them transition to college life and learning. Additional elements of the ICC include coursework in writing, diversity, and quantitative literacy, as well as a capstone experience and learning portfolio. **Procedure:** Freshmen are admitted in the fall and spring. Entrance exams should be taken in spring of the junior year or fall of the senior year. There are early decision, early admissions, deferred admissions, and rolling admissions plans. Early decision applications should be filed by November 1; regular applications, by February 1 for fall entry; and December 1 for spring entry, along with a $60 fee. Notification of early decision is sent December 15; regular decision, April 15. 169 early decision candidates were accepted for the 2016-2017 class. 1219 applicants were on the 2016 waiting list; 23 were admitted. Application fees are waived if application is completed online. **Transfer Students:** 100 transfer students enrolled in 2015-2016. Transfer applicants must submit a high school transcript, transcripts from previously attended colleges, and a personal recommendation from their adviser or Dean of Students. A minimum college GPA of 2.75 is recommended. 30 of 120 credits required for the bachelor's degree must be completed at Ithaca. **International Students:** There are 115 international students enrolled. The school actively recruits these students. They must take the TOEFL with a minimum score of 550 on the paper-based TOEFL (PBT) or 80 on the Internet-based version (iBT), or take the IELTS.

ADMISSIONS: 70% of the 2016-2017 applicants were accepted. The SAT scores for the 2016-2017 freshman class were: Critical Reading-- 8% below 500, 41% between 500 and 599, 43% between 600 and 699, and 8% between 700 and 800. Math-- 10% below 500, 43% between 500 and 599, 42% between 600 and 699, and 5% between 700 and 800. Writing-- 8% below 500, 47% between 500 and 599, 37% between 600 and 699, and 7% between 700 and 800. The ACT scores were 12% between 18 and 23, 65% between 24 and 29, and 23% above 30. 50% of the current freshmen were in the top fifth of their class; 80% were in the top two fifths. 9 freshmen graduated first in their class. **Admissions Contact:** Nicole Eversley Bradwell, Director of Admission. Email: *admission@ithaca.edu* Web: *www.ithaca.edu*

FINANCIAL AID: In 2016-2017, 97% of all full-time freshmen and 93% of continuing full-time students received some form of financial aid. 70% of all full-time freshmen and 67% of continuing full-time students received need-based aid. The average freshman award was $38,128. Need-based scholarships or need-based grants averaged $26,477 ($61,720 maximum); need-based self-help aid (loans and jobs) averaged $7,388 ($16,100 maximum); and other non-need-based awards and non-need-based scholarships averaged $11,841 ($59,918 maximum). 39% of undergraduate students work part-time. Average annual earnings from campus work are $2342. Ithaca is a member of CSS. The CSS/Profile is required. The FAFSA code is 002739. The deadline for filing freshman financial aid applications for fall entry is February 1.

JUILLIARD SCHOOL *(The complete profile is made available exclusively on our website, www.barronspac.com)*

KEUKA COLLEGE — B-3

www.keuka.edu

Keuka Park, NY 14478	(315) 279-5254 (800) 33-KEUKA
Fax: (315) 279-5386	**Email:** admissions@keuka.edu
Full-time: 377 men, 959 women	**Faculty:** 80; IIA, -$
Part-time: 68 men, 320 women	**Ph.D.s:** 78%
Graduate: 42 men, 167 women	**Student/Faculty:** 14 to 1
Year: 4-1-4, summer session	**Tuition:** $28,692
Room & Board: $11,070	**Freshman Class:** n/av
SAT or ACT: required	**CEEB CODE:** 2350
Application Deadline: open	**COMPETITIVE**

Keuka College, founded in 1890, is a private college offering undergraduate and graduate, bachelor's and master's degrees through its Accelerated Studies for Adults Program and international programs in China and Vietnam. There is 1 undergraduate school and 6 graduate schools. In addition to regional accreditation, Keuka has baccalaureate program accreditation with CSWE, TEAC, IACBE, CCNE, and ACOTE. The 203-acre campus is in a rural area 60 miles south of Rochester. Including any residence halls, there are 19 buildings.

STUDENT LIFE: 94% of undergraduates are from New York. Others are from 26 states, 9 foreign countries, and Canada. 80% are from public schools. 74% are White; 9% African American; 7% race unknown; 4% Hispanic; 3% Foreign; 1% Asian American; 1% American Indian/Alaska Native; 1% two or more races. **Female To Male Ratio:** 3.0:1. The average age of freshmen is 18; all undergraduates, 23. 30% do not continue beyond their first year; 51% remain to graduate. **Housing:** 873 students can be accommodated in college housing, which includes single-sex and coed dorms. In addition, there are honors houses, special-interest houses, cooperative living, leadership, and wellness housing. On-campus housing is guaranteed for all 4 years. 80% of students live on campus. Alcohol is not permitted. All students may keep cars.

FACULTY/CLASSROOMS: 45% of faculty are male; 55% are female. All teach undergraduates. No introductory courses are taught by graduate students. The average class size in an introductory lecture is 20; in a laboratory is 15; and in a regular course is 20.

PROGRAMS OF STUDY: Keuka confers B.A. and B.S. degrees. Master's degrees are also awarded. Bachelor's degrees are awarded in BIOLOGICAL SCIENCE (biochemistry and biology/biological science), BUSINESS (accounting, business administration and management, and marketing/retailing/merchandising), COMMUNICATIONS AND THE ARTS (American Sign Language, communications, and English), COMPUTER AND PHYSICAL SCIENCE (mathematics), EDUCATION (elementary education and secondary education), ENGINEERING AND ENVIRONMENTAL DESIGN (environmental science), HEALTH PROFESSIONS (medical laboratory technology, nursing, occupational therapy, predentistry, premedicine, and preveterinary science), SOCIAL SCIENCE (criminal justice, political science/government, prelaw, psychology, social work, and sociology). Occupational therapy, criminal justice, and management are the strongest academically. Occupational therapy, education, and management have the largest enrollments.

ACTIVITIES: There are no fraternities or sororities. There are 45 groups on campus, including art, cheerleading, choir, chorale, communications, community service, dance, drama, ethnic, honors, international, LGBT, literary magazine, newspaper, political, professional, religious, social, social service, student government, and yearbook. Popular campus events include Spring Weekend, May Day and Family Weekend. **Sports:** There are 8 intercollegiate sports for men and 9 for women, and 5 intramural sports for men and 5 for women. Facilities include a gym, fitness center, weight room, and an outdoor athletic facility. **Graduates:** From July 1, 2015 to June 30, 2016, 547 bachelor's degrees were awarded. The most popular majors were nursing (26%), social work (22%), and business (20%). In an average class, 51% graduate in 4 years or less, 5% graduate in 5 years or less, and 1% graduate in 6 years or less. Of the 2015 graduating class, 39% were enrolled in graduate school within 6 months of graduation, and 90% were employed.

SERVICES: Counseling and information services are available, as is tutoring in every subject. There is also a reader service for the blind, and remedial math, reading, and writing. Individual and group tutoring is available free through the college's academic support services. **Library/Resources:** The library contains 112,297 volumes, 4,190 microform items, 4,190 audio/video tapes/CDs/DVDs, and subscribes to 18,151 periodicals including electronic. Computerized library services include interlibrary loans, database searching, Internet access, and Wi-Fi capability. Special learning facilities include an art gallery. **Physically Challenged Students:** 72% of the campus is accessible. Facilities include wheelchair ramps, elevators, special parking, specially equipped restrooms, special class scheduling, lowered drinking fountains, and special housing. **Special:** There are co-op programs with other members of the Rochester Area Colleges Consortium. The college offers internships, study abroad, a Washington semester, dual majors, and student-designed majors. Credit is also given by exam and for work experience. There are 16 national honor societies. **Visiting:** There are regularly scheduled orientations for prospective students, presentation by a division leader, and breakout sessions based on discipline, tours and lunch. There are guides for informal visits, visitors may sit in on classes, and stay overnight. **Campus Safety and Security:** Measures include 24-hour foot and vehicle patrol, emergency notification system, self-defense education, and security escort services. There are also shuttle buses, emergency telephones, and lighted pathways/sidewalks.

REQUIREMENTS: The SAT or ACT is recommended. The GED is accepted AP and CLEP credits are accepted. Important factors in the admissions decision are advanced placement or honors courses, extracurricular activities record, and leadership record. Students must complete 1 field period combining academic study and professional experience for each year of enrollment. The core curriculum consists of 43 to 46 credits, including but not limited to required courses in phys ed, computer science, and integrative studies. A total of 120 credit hours is required for graduation with a minimum of 30 credits in the major and a major and cumulative GPA of 2.0. **Procedure:** Freshmen are admitted in the fall and spring. There are deferred admissions and rolling admissions plans. Application deadlines are open. Notification is sent on a rolling basis. Applications are accepted online. **Transfer Students:** 47 transfer students enrolled in 2015-2016. Applicants must take the SAT or ACT and submit transcripts. An interview is recommended. A minimum GPA of 2.5 is required in college work. 30 of 120 credits required for the bachelor's degree must be completed at Keuka. **International Students:** There are 54 international students enrolled. The school actively recruits these students. They must take the TOEFL with a minimum score of 59 on the Internet-based version (iBT).

Admissions Contact: Meg Ryan, Director of Admissions. Email: *admissions@keuka.edu* Web: *www.keuka.edu*

FINANCIAL AID: In 2016-2017, 95% of all full-time freshmen and 93% of continuing full-time students received some form of financial aid. 93% of all full-time freshmen and 90% of continuing full-time students received need-based aid. The average freshman award was $26,408. Need-based scholarships or need-based grants averaged $9,280; need-based self-help aid (loans and jobs) averaged $5,092; and other non-need-based awards and non-need-based scholarships averaged $13,303. 65% of undergraduate students work part-time. Average annual earnings from campus work are $1250. The average financial indebtedness of the 2016 graduate was $20,156. The college's own financial statement is required. The FAFSA code is 002744. The priority date for freshman financial aid applications for fall entry is March 15. The filing deadline for fall entry is rolling.

LE MOYNE COLLEGE — C-3
www.lemoyne.edu

Syracuse, NY 13214	**(315) 445-4300** **(800) 333-4733**
Fax: (315) 445-4711	**Email: admission@lemoyne.edu**
Full-time: 1060 men, 1474 women	**Faculty:** 155; IIA, +$
Part-time: 83 men, 280 women	**Ph.D.s:** 91%
Graduate: 197 men, 455 women	**Student/Faculty:** 15 to 1
Year: semesters, summer session	**Tuition:** $33,030
Room & Board: $12,970	**Freshman Class:** 6832 applied, 4462 accepted, 631 enrolled
SAT CR/M: 540/560 **ACT:** required	**CEEB CODE:** 2366
Application Deadline: February 1	**COMPETITIVE**

Le Moyne College, founded in 1946, is a private liberal arts and sciences institution affiliated with the Roman Catholic Society of Jesus (Jesuit) and offers undergraduate and graduate degrees in a variety of disciplines. There is 1 undergraduate school and 3 graduate schools. In addition to regional accreditation, Le Moyne has baccalaureate program accreditation with AACSB, TEAC, CCNE, and ACS. The 161-acre campus is in a suburban area on the eastern edge of Syracuse. Including any residence halls, there are 46 buildings.

STUDENT LIFE: 94% of undergraduates are from New York. Others are from 24 states, 45 foreign countries, and Canada. 87% are from public schools. 77% are White; 6% African American; 6% race unknown; 5% Hispanic; 3% Asian American; 2% two or more races; 1% Foreign. 41% are Catholic; 39% claim no religious affiliation. **Female To Male Ratio:** 1.6:1. The average age of freshmen is 18; all undergraduates, 21. 14% do not continue beyond their first year; 67% remain to graduate. **Housing:** 1615 students can be accommodated in college housing, which includes coed dorms, on-campus apartments, and off-campus apartments. In addition, there are special-interest houses, as well as living learning communities. On-campus housing is guaranteed for all 4 years, and is available on a first-come, first-served basis, and is available on a lottery system for upperclassmen. Priority is given to out-of-town students. 57% of students live on campus; of those, 85% remain on campus on weekends. All students may keep cars.

FACULTY/CLASSROOMS: 57% of faculty are male; 43% are female. 91% teach undergraduates, and 90% do research. No introductory courses are taught by graduate students. The average class size in an introductory lecture is 21; in a laboratory is 15; and in a regular course is 21.

PROGRAMS OF STUDY: Le Moyne confers B.A. and B.S. degrees. Master's degrees are also awarded. Bachelor's degrees are awarded in BIOLOGICAL SCIENCE (biochemistry, biology/biological science, and ecology), BUSINESS (accounting, banking and finance, human resources, management information systems, marketing management, operations management, and organizational leadership and management), COMMUNICATIONS AND THE ARTS (communications, creative writing, dramatic arts, English, French, literature, and Spanish), COMPUTER AND PHYSICAL SCIENCE (actuarial science, applied mathematics, chemistry, computer programming, computer science, information sciences and systems, mathematics, physical sciences, physics, science, and statistics), EDUCATION (elementary education, English education, foreign languages education, mathematics education, science education, secondary education, social studies education, special education, and teaching English as a second/foreign language (TESOL/TEFOL)), ENGINEERING AND ENVIRONMENTAL DESIGN (environmental science and preengineering), HEALTH PROFESSIONS (nursing, predentistry, premedicine, preoptometry, prepharmacy, prepodiatry, and preveterinary science), SOCIAL SCIENCE (anthropology, criminology, economics, history, human services, international relations, international studies, peace studies, philosophy, political science/government, prelaw, psychology, religion, and sociology). Biology, psychology, and accounting, are the strongest academically, and have the largest enrollments.

ACTIVITIES: There are no fraternities or sororities. There are 86 groups on campus, including art, band, cheerleading, choir, chorale, chorus, communications, computers, dance, drama, environmental, ethnic, film, honors, international, jazz band, LGBT, literary magazine, musical theater, newspaper, orchestra, photography, political, professional, radio and TV, religious, social, social service, student government, and yearbook. Popular campus events include Spring Olympics, Halloween Dance, Spring Semi-Formal, Senior Week Activities, Fall Fest, Earth Jam, Welcome Week and Le Moyne's Got Talent. **Sports:** There are 10 intercollegiate sports for men and 11 for women, and 12 intramural sports for men and 12 for women. Facilities include a gym, athletic weightroom, team rooms, pool with diving board, fitness center, athletic training room, jogging track, racquetball courts, fitness studio, recreational gym, fields for intercollegiate baseball, softball, soccer, lacrosse, and a cross-country trail. **Graduates:** From July 1, 2015 to June 30, 2016, 631 bachelor's degrees were awarded. The most popular majors were biology (18%), psychology (13%), and nursing (9%). 300 companies recruited on campus in 2015-2016. In an average class, 56% graduate in 4 years or less, 66% graduate in 5 years or less, and 67% graduate in 6 years or less. Of the 2015 graduating class, 27% were enrolled in graduate school within 6 months of graduation, and 30% were employed.

SERVICES: Counseling and information services are available, as is tutoring in some subjects. Le Moyne offers tutoring in math, biology, chemistry, physics, economics, philosophy, Spanish, French, German, Latin, Arabic, history, Japanese, Italian, Chinese, psychology, finance and statistics. There is a reader service for the blind, and remedial math and writing. Study groups are available for selected courses. A writing tutor is available for all subjects. **Library/Resources:** The library contains 227,857 volumes, 282,309 microform items, 9,896 audio/video tapes/CDs/DVDs, and subscribes to 182,325 periodicals including electronic. Computerized library services include interlibrary loans, database searching, Internet access, and Wi-Fi capability. Special learning facilities include an art gallery, radio station, TV station, a performing arts center, a media center, and a tutor/writing center. **Physically Challenged Students:** 98% of the campus is accessible. Facilities include wheelchair ramps, elevators, special parking, specially equipped restrooms, lowered drinking fountains, lowered telephones, special housing, automatic door openers, strobe fire alarm system, and wheelchair tables in classrooms, and braille signage. **Special:** Internships are available to students in all majors. A campus work-study program, study abroad in 15 countries, dual majors, and a Washington semester are also offered. Accelerated Bachelor's/Master's Degree Collaborations in engineering, computer science, communication, public administration, information management, library and information sciences, forensic science with Syracuse University is available. A 3+3 Bachelor's and Law arrangement with Syracuse University; as well as Accelerated Bachelor's/Master's Degree and early assurance collaborative arrangements in medical, dental, podiatry and optometry fields of graduate study with other partner institutions, e.g., a DPT with Update Medical University, dental with University of Buffalo and accelerated entry into Physician Assistant Studies are also offered. There are 16 national honor societies, a freshman honors program, and 15 departmental honors programs. **Visiting:** There are regularly scheduled orientations for prospective students, including a campus tour, and an interview with admissions counselors. Accepted students are invited to attend class, meet with faculty, and stay overnight in a residence hall. There are guides for informal visits, visitors may sit in on classes, and stay overnight. To schedule a visit, contact the Admission Office. **Campus Safety and Security:** Measures include 24-hour foot and vehicle patrol, emergency notification system, self-defense education, and security escort services. There are shuttle buses, emergency telephones, lighted pathways/sidewalks, controlled access to dorms/residences, 8 blue light security phones, 190 stationary closed-circuit security cameras, campus-wide card access, and 13 pan tilt zoom closed-circuit security cameras.

REQUIREMENTS: Students should graduate from an accredited high school, completed 17 academic units that include 4 each in English and social studies, 3 to 4 each in math and science, and 3 in foreign language. A personal statement and letters of recommendation from a teacher, and a counselor are required. AP and CLEP credits are accepted. Important factors in the admissions decision are recommendations by school officials, advanced placement or honors courses, and extracurricular activities record. A core curriculum of courses in the humanities, natural sciences, and social sciences is also required. Students must earn a GPA of 2.0 overall and in their major, complete one half of their major in residence and a minimum of 120 total credit hours to graduate. **Procedure:** Freshmen are admitted fall and spring. Entrance exams should be taken in the spring of the junior year or fall of the senior year. There are early admissions, deferred admissions, and rolling admissions plans. Applications should be filed by February 1 for fall entry; December 1 for spring entry, along with a $35 fee. Notification is sent on a rolling basis. 199 applicants were on the 2016 waiting list; 1 was admitted. Application fees are waived if application is completed online. **Transfer Students:** 251 transfer students enrolled in 2015-2016. A 2.6 GPA is required for admission to most programs. A completed application for transfer admission, official college transcripts, and a personal statement must be submitted. Official high school transcripts should be submitted if fewer than 24 college credits are completed. SAT or ACT scores are now optional for students with fewer than 24 college credits. 30 of 120 credits required for the bachelor's degree must be completed at Le Moyne. **International Students:** There are 27 international students enrolled. The school actively recruits these students. They must take the TOEFL with a minimum score of 550 on the paper-based TOEFL (PBT) or 79 on the Internet-based version (iBT). They must also take the SAT or ACT.

ADMISSIONS: 65% of the 2016-2017 applicants were accepted. The SAT scores for the 2016-2017 freshman class were: Critical Reading--24% below 500, 48% between 500 and 599, 23% between 600 and 699, and 5% between 700 and 800. Math-- 16% below 500, 53% between 500 and 599, 27% between 600 and 699, and 4% between 700 and 800. The ACT scores were 1% between 12 and 17, 39% between 18 and 23, 49% between 24 and 29, and 11% above 30. 44% of the current freshmen were in the top fifth of their class; 75% were in the top two fifths. 8 freshmen graduated first in their class. **Admissions Contact:** Mary M. Chandler, Sr. Director of Admission. Email: *admission@lemoyne.edu* Web: *www.lemoyne.edu*

FINANCIAL AID: In 2016-2017, 97% of all full-time freshmen and 82% of continuing full-time students received some form of financial aid. 84% of all full-time freshmen and 82% of continuing full-time students received need-based aid. The average freshman award was $26,507. Need-based scholarships or need-based grants averaged $22,529 ($45,200 maximum); need-based self-help aid (loans and jobs) averaged $4,234 ($9,500 maximum); non-need-based athletic scholarships averaged $15,013 ($47,300 maximum); and other non-need-based awards and non-need-based scholarships averaged $16,196 ($24,250 maximum). 40% of undergraduate students work part-time. Average annual earnings from campus work are $1298. The average financial indebtedness of the 2016 graduate was $29,951. Le Moyne is a member of CSS. The state aid form is required. The FAFSA code is 002748. The deadline for filing freshman financial aid applications for fall entry is February 15.

LIM COLLEGE *(The complete profile is made available exclusively on our website, www.barronspac.com)*

LIST COLLEGE D-5
www.jtsa.edu

New York, NY 10027	(212) 678-8832
Fax: (212) 678-8947	**Email:** lcadmissions@jtsa.edu
Full-time: 90 men, 90 women	**Faculty:** n/av
Part-time: 15 men, 15 women	**Ph.D.s:** n/av
Graduate: n/av	**Student/Faculty:** n/av
Year: semesters, summer session	**Tuition:** $23,470
Room & Board: $14,400	**Freshman Class:** n/av
SAT or ACT: required	**CEEB CODE:** 0339
Application Deadline: open	**COMPETITIVE**

Albert A. List College of Jewish Studies, the undergraduate division of the Jewish Theological Seminary, and founded in 1886, is a private institution affiliated with the Conservative branch of the Jewish faith. List College offers programs in all aspects of Judaism, including Bible, Rabbinics, literature, history, philosophy, education, and communal service. There is also a combined liberal arts program with Columbia University and Barnard College. The 1-acre campus is in an urban area in New York, NY. Including any residence halls, there are 6 buildings.

STUDENT LIFE: 75% of undergraduates are from out of state, mostly the Middle Atlantic. Students are from 12 states, 3 foreign countries, and Canada. 70% are from public schools. 100% are White. 100% are Jewish. **Male To Female Ratio:** Is 1:1. The average age of freshmen is 18; all undergraduates, 20. 96% remain to graduate. **Housing:** 212 students can be accommodated in college housing, which includes coed dorms, on-campus apartments, off-campus apartments, married student housing, and kosher housing. On-campus housing is guaranteed for all 4 years. 93% of students live on campus; of those, 95% remain on campus on weekends. Alcohol is not permitted. All students may keep cars.

FACULTY/CLASSROOMS: 68% of faculty are male; 32% are female. All teach undergraduates and do research. No introductory courses are taught by graduate students. The average class size in an introductory lecture is 30 and in a regular course is 10.

PROGRAMS OF STUDY: List College confers B.A. degrees. Bachelor's degrees are awarded in SOCIAL SCIENCE (biblical studies and Judaic studies).

ACTIVITIES: There are no fraternities or sororities. List College students have access to all clubs and organizations at Columbia and Barnard. These groups include art, band, choir, chorus, computers, dance, drama, ethnic, film, honors, international, LGBT, literary magazine, musical theater, newspaper, orchestra, photography, political, professional, radio and TV, religious, social, social service, student government, and yearbook. Popular campus events include Purim, Simchat Torah and Orientation. **Sports:** There are 3 intramural sports for men and 3 for women. Students may also use the facilities at Columbia University.

SERVICES: Counseling and information services are available, as is tutoring in most subjects. **Library/Resources:** The library contains 320,000 volumes, 3,500 microform items, and subscribes to 750 periodicals including electronic. Computerized library services include interlibrary loans and database searching. Special learning facilities include an art gallery, radio station, music center, Jewish education, research center, and the Jewish Museum Archives Center. **Physically Challenged Students:** All of the campus is accessible. Facilities include wheelchair ramps, elevators, special parking, specially equipped restrooms, lowered drinking fountains, lowered telephones, and elevators with braille panels. **Special:** There is a joint program with Columbia University and a double-degree program with Barnard College, which enable students to earn 2 B.A. degrees in 4 to 4 1/2 years. Study abroad is available in Israel, England, France, and Spain. Student-designed majors, credit by exam, and nondegree study are also offered. There is a chapter of Phi Beta Kappa and a freshman honors program. **Visiting:** There are regularly scheduled orientations for prospective students, including a tour of the campus and Columbia University, an interview with the dean, and an overnight dormitory stay. There are guides for informal visits, visitors may sit in on classes, and stay overnight. To schedule a visit, contact the Admissions Office. **Campus Safety and Security:** Measures include 24-hour foot and vehicle patrol and security escort services. There are emergency telephones and lighted pathways/sidewalks.

REQUIREMENTS: The SAT or ACT is required. Applicants must be graduates of an accredited secondary school or have the GED. An essay and 2 recommendations are required; an interview is strongly recommended. AP credits are accepted. Important factors in the admissions decision are advanced placement or honors courses, extracurricular activities record, and personality/intangible qualities. Students must take a Hebrew language requirement, 24 credits in Jewish history, 9 in literature, and 6 each in Bible, Jewish philosophy, and Talmud. In addition, there are 60 required credits in liberal arts, including 6 credits each in English, history/philosophy/social science, and math or lab science to be completed at another college or university. A total of 156 credits (96 taken at List College) is required for graduation, with 21 in a major field. **Procedure:** Freshmen are admitted fall and spring. Entrance exams should be taken in the spring of the junior year. There are early decision, early admissions, and deferred admissions plans. Early decision applications should be filed by November 1. The fall 2016 application fee was $60. Notification of early decision is sent December 15; regular decision, **Transfer Students:** Applicants must submit SAT or ACT scores, an essay, high school and college transcripts, and 2 academic recommendations. A minimum college GPA of 2.5 is required. An interview is recommended. 48 of 156 credits required for the bachelor's degree must be completed at List College. **International Students:** They must take the TOEFL and the college's own test, the American Language English Placement Test. They must also take the SAT or ACT.

Admissions Contact: Shuly Rubin Schwartz, Director of Admissions. Email: *lcadmissions@jtsa.edu* Web: *www.jtsa.edu*

FINANCIAL AID: List College is a member of CSS. The CSS/Profile and the college's own financial statement, and 1040 tax forms are required. Check with the school for current application deadlines.

LIU BROOKLYN D-5
www.liu.edu/brooklyn

Brooklyn, NY 11201	(718) 488-1011 (800) LIU-PLAN
Fax: (718) 780-6110	**Email:** bkln-admissions@liu.edu
Full-time: 1181 men, 2593 women	**Faculty:** 205
Part-time: 138 men, 393 women	**Ph.D.s:** 90%
Graduate: 973 men, 2361 women	**Student/Faculty:** 20 to 1
Year: semesters, summer session	**Tuition:** $36,256
Room & Board: $13,426	**Freshman Class:** 7273 applied, 6364 accepted, 732 enrolled
SAT CR/M/W: required **ACT:** 21	**CEEB CODE:** 2369
Application Deadline: rolling	**COMPETITIVE**

LIU Brooklyn, a comprehensive, private university, offers nearly 200 academic programs through its School of Health Professions, Harriet Rothkopf Heilbrunn School of Nursing, College of Liberal Arts and Science, School of Education, School of Communication and Visual Arts, School of Business, Public Administration, and Information Science, Honors College, LIU Pharmacy (Arnold and Marie Schwartz College of Pharmacy and Health Sciences), and School of Professional and Continuing Studies. In addition to 18 championship award-winning NCAA Division I athletics teams and a vibrant campus life, the university is home to the internationally acclaimed George Polk Awards, one of the most coveted honors in investigative journalism. There are 8 undergraduate schools and 7 graduate schools. In addition to regional accreditation, LIU has baccalaureate program accreditation with ACPE, CSWE, TEAC, AACN, AOTA, and CAAHEP. The 11-acre campus is in an urban area in Brooklyn, NY. Including any residence halls, there are 11 buildings.

STUDENT LIFE: 88% of undergraduates are from New York. Others are from 37 states, 59 foreign countries, and Canada. 3% are Foreign; 25% African American; 21% White; 2% two or more races; 19% Asian American; 19% race unknown; 14% Hispanic. **Female To Male Ratio:** 2.3:1. The average age of freshmen is 19; all undergraduates, 23. 35% do not continue beyond their first year; 65% remain to graduate. **Housing:** 910 students can be accommodated in college housing, which includes coed dorms and on-campus apartments. On-campus housing is guaranteed for all 4 years, and is available on a first-come, and first-served basis. 86% of students commute. No one may keep cars.

FACULTY/CLASSROOMS: 44% of faculty are male; 56% are female. No introductory courses are taught by graduate students.

PROGRAMS OF STUDY: LIU Brooklyn confers B.A. B.S. and B.F.A. degrees. Associate, master's, and doctoral degrees are also awarded. Bachelor's degrees are awarded in BIOLOGICAL SCIENCE (biochemistry and biology/biological science), BUSINESS (accounting, business administration and management, entrepreneurial studies, finance, human resources/organizational mgmt, marketing, operations research, and sports management), COMMUNICATIONS AND THE ARTS (communication science, dance, English, fine arts, French, jazz, journalism, media arts, music, music performance, Spanish, communication arts - speech, studio art, and visual and performing arts), COMPUTER AND PHYSICAL SCIENCE (chemistry, computer science, information sciences and systems, and mathematics), EDUCATION (art education, athletic training, early childhood education, elementary education, English education, middle school education, music education, physical education, science education, secondary education, and social studies education), ENGINEERING AND ENVIRONMENTAL DESIGN (commercial art), HEALTH PROFESSIONS (clinical science, health science, kinesiology, nursing, occupational therapy, pharmacy, physician's assistant, public health, and respiratory therapy), SOCIAL SCIENCE (economics, history, humanities, interdisciplinary studies, liberal arts/general studies, philosophy, political science/government, psychology, social science, social work, and sociology). Pharmacy, nursing, and health science have the largest enrollments.

ACTIVITIES: There are 65 groups on campus, including art, band, choir, chorale, chorus, communications, computers, dance, debate, drama, environmental, ethnic, film, honors, international, jazz band, LGBT, literary magazine, newspaper, pep band, political, professional, radio and TV, religious, social, social service, student government, and yearbook. Popular campus events include Homecoming Week, LIU Blackbird Madness, Relay for Life, Holiday Party for Kids, LIU Spring Concert, LIU Spring Week, LIU Gives Back Month, Last Class Bash, Midnight Breakfast, Welcome Week, and Culture Fest. **Sports:** There are 5 intercollegiate sports for men and 12 for women, and 4 intramural sports for men and 4 for women. Facilities include Steinberg Wellness Center, an NCAA-regulation swimming pool, therapy pool, 2,500-seat arena, campus fitness center, workout and track facilities, and health and fitness programs. **Graduates:** From July 1, 2015 to June 30, 2016, 887 bachelor's degrees were awarded. The most popular majors were health professions (57%), business/marketing (8%), and biological/life sciences (8%). 175 companies recruited on campus in 2015-2016. In an average class, 1% graduate in 3 years or less, 11% graduate in 4 years or less, 22% graduate in 5 years or less, and 28% graduate in 6 years or less.

SERVICES: Counseling and information services are available, as is tutoring in every subject. There is a reader service for the blind, and remedial math, reading, and writing. **Library/Resources:** The library contains 548,873 volumes, 260,844 microform items, 10,072 audio/video tapes/CDs/DVDs, and subscribes to 398,358 periodicals including electronic. Computerized library services include interlibrary loans, database searching, Internet access, and Wi-Fi capability. Special learning facilities include an art gallery, radio station, and TV station. Honors College: school for highly motivated students seeking challenging academics. Kumble Theater for the Performing Arts: state-of-the art performance venue that welcomes artistic exploration for students and features world-renowned performance artists from the areas of dance, music, and theater. Student-Run Businesses: These fully functional business operations afford students unique experiential learning opportunities as they make executive-level decisions. They include: Browse: a high-tech, Apple-licensed technology store, with "Genius Bar" customer service that employs students, Student Innovation Incubator: is a physical and virtual workspace for students to launch startup businesses and collaborate with successful entrepreneurs, Wall Street Trading Floor: featuring Bloomberg terminals and other business technology, this simulated trading floor empowers students to utilize the latest financial tools and learn in a real-time trading environment. LIU Pharmacy students have access to three labs: The Lachman Institute for Pharmaceutical Analysis provides opportunities for industry-supported research, The Joan B. and Samuel J. Williamson Institute for Pharmacometrics trains students to use computer-based predictive models of drug safety and efficacy, The Natoli Engineering Institute for Industrial Pharmacy Development and Research welcomes industry scientists to partner with academia to research solid dosage forms and instrumentation. **Physically Challenged Students:** 95% of the campus is accessible. Facilities include wheelchair ramps, elevators, special parking, specially equipped restrooms, special class scheduling, lowered drinking fountains, lowered telephones, and special housing. **Special:** Paid internships help students build a resume while still in classes. Study abroad options include Europe, Asia, China, Australia and many other locations. LIU Global offers study options in several locations around the world. Dual majors, accelerated degrees, and a nationally recognized Honors College help motivated students shape a challenging academic schedule. The Arthur O. Eve Higher Education Opportunity Program is specially designed for New York State residents who are economically and educationally disadvantaged. LIU Promise is the University's commitment to assist students with their personal Success Coach who advises them from admission to graduation. A wide range of support services include tutoring, academic advisement, financial aid, career, and personal counseling. There is a freshman honors program. **Visiting:** There are regularly scheduled orientations for prospective students, including a guided campus tour, admissions overview, a meet-and-greet with faculty and deans, interacting with student leaders, attending mini classes, becoming a student for a day, and touring our student-run businesses and high tech incubator. There are guides for informal visits and visitors may sit in on classes. **Campus Safety and Security:** Measures include 24-hour foot and vehicle patrol, emergency notification system, and security escort services. There are emergency telephones, lighted pathways/sidewalks, and controlled access to dorms/residences.

REQUIREMENTS: The SAT or ACT are optional but recommended for most programs and required for some programs. Average GPA: Solid "B" / 82–85 / 3.0. High school students seeking admission to LIU Brooklyn are expected to have completed a college preparatory program includes 4 years of English, 3 years each of math, social studies, science, and 2 years of foreign language. Students must also submit the following: completed application for admission, official high school transcript or evidence of completion of high school graduation requirements (GED), non-refundable application fee, tests results from the SAT (optional) or ACT (school codes: ACT 2687; SAT 2070), personal statement/essay, and letters of recommendation from high school teacher or guidance counselor. Students applying for admission to programs in the visual and performing arts must also schedule an audition or portfolio review through the department. AP and CLEP credits are accepted. General Requirements for Graduation: 2.0 cumulative average (higher in some areas), 2.25 minor subject average (higher in some areas) if attempted, Core and major requirements fulfilled, and minor requirements if attempted, 128 credits (more in some departments), 129 credits including freshman seminar, writing across the curriculum courses (3-5 depending on admissions status), and minimum liberal arts requirements (varies depending on degree being earned). CORE: Competency Requirements (library use, computer literacy, oral communication competency), English Comp (6 credits), laboratory sciences (8 credits), history and philosophy (9 credits), literature or foreign language (6 credits), arts (6 credits), economics or political science (6 credits), anthropology, geography, psychology or sociology (6 credits), and mathematics (3 credits). **Procedure:** Freshmen are admitted fall and spring. Entrance exams should be taken by Spring 2017. There are early admissions, deferred admissions, and rolling admissions plans. Application deadlines are open. Application fee is $50. Notification is sent on a rolling basis. Applications are accepted online. **Transfer Students:** 664 transfer students enrolled in 2015-2016. A high school GPA or college GPA of 2.0 is required. Some programs require a 2.75-3.0 minimum GPA. 32 of 128 credits required for the bachelor's degree must be completed at LIU-Brooklyn. **International Students:** There are 121 international students enrolled. The school actively recruits these students. They must take the TOEFL with a minimum score of 527 on the paper-based TOEFL (PBT) or 75 on the Internet-based version (iBT). The SAT or ACT are optional but recommended.

ADMISSIONS: 88% of the 2016-2017 applicants were accepted. The SAT scores for the 2016-2017 freshman class were: Critical Reading-- 68% below 500, 25% between 500 and 599, 6% between 600 and 699, and 1% between 700 and 800. Math-- 56% below 500, 29% between 500 and 599, 13% between 600 and 699, and 2% between 700 and 800. Writing-- 67% below 500, 25% between 500 and 599, 7% between 600 and 699, and 1% between 700 and 800. The ACT scores were 24% between 12 and 17, 38% between 18 and 23, 33% between 24 and 29, and 5% above 30. **Admissions Contact:** Richard Sunday, Dean of Admissions. Email: *bkln-admissions@liu.edu* Web: *www.liu.edu/brooklyn*

FINANCIAL AID: In 2016-2017, 90% of all full-time freshmen and 87% of continuing full-time students received some form of financial aid. 80% of all full-time freshmen and 82% of continuing full-time students

received need-based aid. The average freshman award was $11,762. Need-based scholarships or need-based grants averaged $8,178; need-based self-help aid (loans and jobs) averaged $3,734; non-need-based athletic scholarships averaged $15,458; and other non-need-based awards and non-need-based scholarships averaged $4,918. The average financial indebtedness of the 2016 graduate was $32,000. LIU Brooklyn is a member of CSS. The priority date for freshman financial aid applications for fall entry is February 15. The filing deadline for fall entry is rolling.

LIU POST D-5

www.liu.edu/post

Brookville, NY 11548	(516) 299-2900 (800) LIU-PLAN
Fax: (516) 299-2137	Email: post-enroll@liu.edu
Full-time: 1230 men, 1860 women	**Faculty:** 194; IIA, ++$
Part-time: 1364 men, 1770 women	**Ph.D.s:** 90%
Graduate: 614 men, 1785 women	**Student/Faculty:** 16 to 1
Year: semesters, summer session	**Tuition:** $36,256
Room & Board: $13,426	**Freshman Class:** 6725 applied, 5479 accepted, 536 enrolled
SAT CR/M/W: 510/510/490 **ACT:** 22	**CEEB CODE:** 2070
Application Deadline: rolling	**COMPETITIVE**

LIU Post, a comprehensive, private university, offers more than 200 academic programs through its School of Computer Science, Innovation and Management Engineering, School of Business, School of Professional Accountancy, School of Visual Arts, Communications and Digital Technologies, School of Performing Arts, College of Education, Information and Technology, College of Liberal Arts and Sciences, School of Health Professions and Nursing, and Honors College. Our students receive all of the resources of a major university, with world-class faculty that includes Fulbright fellows, a vibrant campus life, and 22 championship award-winning NCAA Division II athletic teams. There are 8 undergraduate schools and 8 graduate schools. In addition to regional accreditation, LIU Post has baccalaureate program accreditation with AACSB, CSWE, TEAC, AACN, JRCERT, and NAACLS. The 308-acre campus is in a suburban area in Nassau County on Long Island, 25 miles east of New York City. Including any residence halls, there are 46 buildings.

STUDENT LIFE: 92% of undergraduates are from New York. Others are from 34 states, 45 foreign countries, and Canada. 7% are African American; 6% Asian American; 51% White; 4% Foreign; 2% two or more races; 18% race unknown; 12% Hispanic. **Female To Male Ratio:** 1.7:1. The average age of freshmen is 18; all undergraduates, 23. 26% do not continue beyond their first year; 74% remain to graduate. **Housing:** 1381 students can be accommodated in college housing, which includes coed dorms. international students, and theme housing. On-campus housing is guaranteed for all 4 years, and is available on a first-come, and first-served basis. 68% of students commute. All students may keep cars.

FACULTY/CLASSROOMS: 46% of faculty are male; 54% are female. No introductory courses are taught by graduate students.

PROGRAMS OF STUDY: confers B.A., B.F.A., B.S. and B.M. degrees. Associate, master's, and doctoral degrees are also awarded. Bachelor's degrees are awarded in BIOLOGICAL SCIENCE (biology/adolescence education, biology/biological science, cell biology, and nutrition), BUSINESS (accounting, business administration and management, and marketing/retailing/merchandising), COMMUNICATIONS AND THE ARTS (art, art history and appreciation, arts administration/management, broadcasting, dance, dramatic arts, English, film arts, fine arts, French, instrumental performance, Italian, journalism, music, music performance, photography, public relations, radio/tv, Spanish, theatre arts, and vocal performance), COMPUTER AND PHYSICAL SCIENCE (applied mathematics, chemistry, chemistry/adolescence education, computer science, digital arts/technology, earth science / adolescence education, geology, information sciences and systems, mathematics, physics, and radiological technology), EDUCATION (art education, early childhood education, elementary education, English education, foreign languages education, health education, mathematics education, music education, physical education, social studies education, and Spanish adolescense education), ENGINEERING AND ENVIRONMENTAL DESIGN (commercial art), HEALTH PROFESSIONS (art therapy, biomedical science, clinical science, health care administration, health science, medical laboratory technology, nursing, and speech pathology/audiology), SOCIAL SCIENCE (American studies, criminal justice, economics, forensic studies, geography, history, humanities, interdisciplinary studies, international studies, liberal arts, sciences, general studies, humanities, philosophy, political science/government, psychology, public administration, social science, social work, and sociology). Business administration, criminal justice, and health sciences have the largest enrollments.

ACTIVITIES: 8% of men belong to 6 national fraternities; 11% of women belong to 6 national sororities. There are 73 groups on campus, including art, band, cheerleading, choir, chorale, chorus, computers, dance, drama, environmental, ethnic, film, forensics, honors, international, LGBT, literary magazine, marching band, musical theater, newspaper, pep band, photography, political, professional, radio and TV, religious, social, social service, student government, and yearbook. Popular campus events include Homecoming & Spirit Week, Midnight Madness, Founder's Day, Move-a-thon, Holidays at Hillwood, Pratt After Dark, Relay for Life, Midnight Breakfast, LIU Gives Back Month, Spring Concert, and Senior Week. **Sports:** There are 9 intercollegiate sports for men and 15 for women, and 5 intramural sports for men and 5 for women. Facilities include The LIU Post, Pratt Recreation Center which is an eight-lane swimming pool, basketball courts, racquetball courts, and an elevated jogging track. Home to the LIU Post Pioneers' 24 Division II NCAA men's and women's sports teams, the campus has 70-acres of playing fields, including the Bethpage Federal Credit Union Stadium. **Graduates:** From July 1, 2015 to June 30, 2016, 1067 bachelor's degrees were awarded. The most popular majors were health professions (23%), business/marketing (19%), and education (10%). 125 companies recruited on campus in 2015-2016. In an average class, 2% graduate in 3 years or less, 27% graduate in 4 years or less, 42% graduate in 5 years or less, and 46% graduate in 6 years or less.

SERVICES: Counseling and information services are available, as is tutoring in every subject. There is a reader service for the blind, as well as remedial math, reading, and writing. **Library/Resources:** The library contains 890,216 volumes, 406,803 microform items, 4,494 audio/video tapes/CDs/DVDs, and subscribes to 399,045 periodicals including electronic. Computerized library services include interlibrary loans, database searching, Internet access, and Wi-Fi capability. Other special learning facilities include an art gallery, radio station, TV station, Tilles Center for the Performing Arts, a 2,242-seat concert hall that features a wide range of dance, music, and theater events, and where students in the School of Visual and Performing Arts are able to perform alongside world-renowned performers and engage in live stage productions. The school also offers student-run businesses. These fully functional business operations afford students unique experiential learning opportunities as they make executive-level decisions. **Physically Challenged Students:** 80% of the campus is accessible. Facilities include wheelchair ramps, elevators, special parking, specially equipped restrooms, special class scheduling, lowered drinking fountains, lowered telephones, and special housing. **Special:** Paid internships help students build a resume while still taking classes. Study abroad options include Europe, Asia, China, Australia, Costa Rica and many other locations. LIU Global offers study options in several locations around the world. Dual majors, accelerated degrees, and a nationally recognized Honors Program help motivated students shape a challenging academic schedule. The Higher Education Opportunity Program is specially designed for New York State residents who are economically disadvantaged and educationally underprepared. LIU Post also offers a wide range of support services including tutoring, academic advisement, financial aid, and career and personal counseling. There is a freshman honors program. **Visiting:** There are regularly scheduled orientations for prospective students, events include a guided campus tour, admissions overview, a meet-and-greet with faculty & deans, interacting with student leaders, attending mini classes, becoming a student for a day, and touring our student-run businesses and high tech incubato. There are guides for informal visits and visitors may sit in on classes. **Campus Safety and Security:** Measures include 24-hour foot and vehicle patrol, emergency notification system, and security escort services. There are shuttle buses, emergency telephones, lighted pathways/sidewalks, and controlled access to dorms/residences.

REQUIREMENTS: Average GPA: Solid "B" (82–85) 3.0, Average SAT: Math and Critical Reading combined: 1000 or ACT Composite: 20. High school students seeking admission to LIU Post are expected to have completed a college preparatory program (including 4 years of English, 3 years each of math, social studies, and science, and 2 years of foreign language). Students applying for admission to programs in the visual and performing arts must schedule an audition or portfolio review through the department. Students must also submit the following: completed application for admission, official high school transcript or evidence of completion of high school graduation requirements (GED), Non-refundable application fee, tests results from the SAT or ACT (school codes: ACT-2687; SAT-2070), personal statement/essay, and one letter of recommendation from high school teacher or guidance counselor AP and CLEP credits are accepted. General Requirements for Graduation: 2.00 cumulative average (higher in some areas), 2.25 minor subject average (higher in some areas) if attempted, core and major requirements fulfilled, and minor requirements if attempted, 128 credits (more in some departments), 129 credits including freshman seminar, writing across the curriculum courses 3-5 depending on admissions status, and minimum liberal arts requirements (varies depending on degree being earned). Core: Competency Requirements (library use, computer literacy, oral communication competency), English Comp (6 credits), laboratory sciences (8 credits), history and philosophy (9 credits), literature or foreign language (6 credits), arts (6 credits), economics or political science (6 credits), anthropology, geography, psychology or sociology (6 credits), and mathematics (3 credits). **Procedure:** Freshmen are admitted fall and spring. Entrance exams should be taken by Spring 2017. There are early decision, early admissions, deferred admissions, and rolling admissions plans. Early decision applications should be filed by December 1, along with a $50 fee. Notification of early decision is sent December 31; regular decision, on a rolling basis. Applications are accepted on-line. Application fees are waived if application is completed on-line. **Transfer Students:** 371 transfer students enrolled in 2015-2016. A high school GPA of 2.5 or college GPA of 2.0 is required. 32 of 128 credits required for the bachelor's degree must be completed at LIU Post. **International Students:** There are 238 international students enrolled. The school actively recruits these students. They must take the TOEFL with a minimum score of 550 on the paper-based TOEFL (PBT) or 75 on the Internet-based version (iBT). They must also take the SAT or ACT.

ADMISSIONS: 81% of the 2016-2017 applicants were accepted. The SAT scores for the 2016-2017 freshman class were: Critical Reading-- 32% below 500, 50% between 500 and 599, 16% between 600 and 699, and 2% between 700 and 800. Math-- 28% below 500, 49% between 500 and 599, 21% between 600 and 699, and 2% between 700 and 800. Writing-- 42% below 500, 43% between 500 and 599, 14% between 600 and 699, and 1% between 700 and 800. The ACT scores were 3% between 12 and 17, 41% between 18 and 23, 53% between 24 and 29, and 3% above 30. **Admissions Contact:** Rita Langdon, Director of Undergraduate Admissions. Email: *post-enroll@liu.edu* Web: *www.liu.edu/post*

FINANCIAL AID: In 2016-2017, 88% of all full-time freshmen and 80% of continuing full-time students received some form of financial aid. 52% of all full-time freshmen and 57% of continuing full-time students received need-based aid. The average freshman award was $12,012. Need-based scholarships or need-based grants averaged $5,302; need-based self-help aid (loans and jobs) averaged $4,035; non-need-based athletic scholarships averaged $6,924; and other non-need-based awards and non-need-based scholarships averaged $8,033. The average financial indebtedness of the 2016 graduate was $18,700. LIU Post is a member of CSS. The state aid form is recommended. The FAFSA code is 2751. The priority date for freshman financial aid applications for fall entry is February 15. The filing deadline for fall entry is rolling.

MANHATTAN COLLEGE — D-5

www.manhattan.edu

Riverdale, NY 10471	**(718) 862-7200** **(800) 622-9235**
Fax: (718) 862-8019	**Email: admit@manhattan.edu**
Full-time: 1713 men, 1428 women	**Faculty:** IIA, ++$
Part-time: 151 men, 59 women	**Ph.D.s:** 93%
Graduate: 196 men, 253 women	**Student/Faculty:** 12 to 1
Year: semesters, summer session	**Tuition:** $37,320
Room & Board: $14,430	**Freshman Class:** 6546 applied, 4555 accepted, 842 enrolled
SAT CR/M/W: 526/535/528 **ACT:** 24	**CEEB CODE:** 2395
Application Deadline: March 1	**COMPETITIVE+**

Manhattan College, founded in 1853, offers an exceptional college education enriched by Lasallian Catholic values and access to New York City. Our celebrated faculty and students are committed to the lifelong pursuit of academic excellence, career achievement, and reflection on values, ethics and principles. Figures in the above capsule and in this profile are approximate. There are 5 undergraduate schools and 4 graduate schools. In addition to regional accreditation, Manhattan has baccalaureate program accreditation with AACSB, ABET, AHEA, CAHEA, and TEAC. The 23-acre campus is in an urban area in Riverdale NY, 10 miles north of midtown Manhattan. Including any residence halls, there are 21 buildings.

STUDENT LIFE: 75% of undergraduates are from New York. Others are from 32 states, 37 foreign countries, and Canada. 60% are from public schools. 60% are White; 4% African American; 3% Asian American; 19% Hispanic; 1% Foreign. 55% are Catholic. **Male To Female Ratio:** 1.2:1. The average age of freshmen is 18; all undergraduates, 23. 12% do not continue beyond their first year; 75% remain to graduate. **Housing:** 2095 students can be accommodated in college housing, which includes coed dorms, on-campus apartments, off-campus apartments, and married student housing. Arches - a living/learning environment. On-campus housing is guaranteed for all 4 years. 75% of students live on campus. All students may keep cars.

FACULTY/CLASSROOMS: 60% of faculty are male; 40% are female. All teach undergraduates, 80% do research, and 80% do both. No introductory courses are taught by graduate students. The average class size in an introductory lecture is 15 and in a regular course is 22.

PROGRAMS OF STUDY: Manhattan confers B.A., B.S., and B.S.E. degrees. Master's degrees are also awarded. Bachelor's degrees are awarded in BIOLOGICAL SCIENCE (biochemistry and biology/biological science), BUSINESS (accounting, banking and finance, business economics, international business management, labor studies, and marketing/retailing/merchandising), COMMUNICATIONS AND THE ARTS (broadcasting, communications, English, French, journalism, and Spanish), COMPUTER AND PHYSICAL SCIENCE (chemistry, computer science, information sciences and systems, mathematics, and physics), EDUCATION (early childhood education, education, education of the emotionally handicapped, elementary education, foreign languages education, health education, middle school education, physical education, science education, secondary education, and special education), ENGINEERING AND ENVIRONMENTAL DESIGN (chemical engineering, civil engineering, electrical/electronics engineering, environmental engineering, and mechanical engineering), HEALTH PROFESSIONS (predentistry, premedicine, and radiological science), SOCIAL SCIENCE (economics, history, peace studies, philosophy, political science/government, prelaw, psychology, religion, sociology, and urban studies). Engineering, and business are the strongest academically. Engineering, business, and liberal arts have the largest enrollments.

ACTIVITIES: 3% of men belong to 2 local and 1 national fraternities; 1% of women belong to 2 local sororities. There are 70 groups on campus, including bagpipe, cheerleading, choir, chorus, computers, dance, debate, drama, ethnic, honors, international, jazz band, literary magazine, musical theater, newspaper, orchestra, pep band, political, professional, radio and TV, religious, social, social service, student government, and yearbook. Popular campus events include Annual Springfest, Special Olympics, and Jasper Jingle. **Sports:** There are 8 intercollegiate sports for men and 8 for women, and 7 intramural sports for men and 7 for women. Facilities include a gym with basketball courts, volleyball, dodge ball, indoor soccer, dorm wars, indoor track, and a weight room with free weights and weightlifting machines, a fitness center, dance studio use for dancing and fitness classes, a large turf field used for football, soccer, lacrosse, softball and frisbee. **Graduates:** From July 1, 2015 to June 30, 2016, 784 bachelor's degrees were awarded. The most popular majors were civil engineering, communication, management, and childhood education and biology. In an average class, 63% graduate in 4 years or less and 70% graduate in 6 years or less. Of the 2015 graduating class, 18% were enrolled in graduate school within 6 months of graduation, and 65% were employed.

SERVICES: Counseling and information services are available, as is tutoring in every subject. The center for Academic Success is comprised of 3 offices with open door policy and extended hours, for students with needs. **Library/Resources:** The library contains 292,438 volumes, 675,489 microform items, 2,676 audio/video tapes/CDs/DVDs, and subscribes to 343 periodicals including electronic. Computerized library services include interlibrary loans, database searching, Internet access, and Wi-Fi capability. Special learning facilities include a radio station, research and learning center, Internet, Holocaust, Genocide and Interfaith Education Center, and Center for Academic Success. **Physically Challenged Students:** All of the campus is accessible. Facilities include wheelchair ramps, elevators, special parking, specially equipped restrooms, and special housing. **Special:** Manhattan offers credit and non-credit based internships and experiential learning opportunities in for-profit, not-for-profit, social, cultural, educational, religious, government and non-government organizations. Students may enroll in numerous study abroad programs that are offered throughout the world. Five year Bachelors/Masters degrees in Business, Education and Engineering are offered and a dual major in international business, credit by exam, and non-degree study are also available. There are 22 national honor societies, Phi Beta Kappa, a freshman honors program, and 28 departmental honors programs. **Visiting:** There are regularly scheduled orientations for prospective students, during 2 days in the summer, which include scheduling, parent workshops, loan seminars, and English and math testing. There are guides for informal visits, visitors may sit in on classes, and stay overnight. To schedule a visit, contact the Admission Center. **Campus Safety and Security:** Measures include 24-hour foot and vehicle patrol and emergency notification system. There are also emergency telephones, lighted pathways/sidewalks, and controlled access to dorms/residences.

REQUIREMENTS: The SAT or ACT is required. Applicants must graduate from an accredited secondary school or have earned a GED. 16 academic units are required, 4 of English, 3 each of math and social studies, 2 of foreign language, 2 of lab sciences, and electives. An essay is required and an interview is recommended. AP and CLEP credits are also accepted. Important factors in the admissions decision are advanced placement or honors courses, leadership record, and recommendations by school officials. All students must take courses in English composition and literature, religious studies, philosophy, humanities, social science, science, math, and a modern foreign language. About 130 credit hours are required for graduation, with about 36 in the major. The minimum GPA is 2.0. **Procedure:** Freshmen are admitted fall and spring. Entrance exams should be taken in the spring of the junior year or the fall of the senior year. There are early decision, deferred admissions, and rolling admissions plans. Early decision applications should be filed by November 15; regular applications, by March 1 for fall entry; and December 1 for spring entry, along with a $75 fee. Notification of early decision is sent December 15; regular decision, December 15. 38 early decision candidates were accepted for the 2016-2017 class. 272 applicants were on the 2016 waiting list; 52 were admitted. Applications are accepted online. **Transfer Students:** 143 transfer students enrolled in 2015-2016. Applicants must have a GPA of 2.5 and meet subject course requirements according to their course of study. They must submit transcripts from colleges and high schools attended. An interview is recommended. 66 of 130 credits required for the bachelor's degree must be completed at Manhattan. **International Students:** There are 85 international students enrolled. The school actively recruits these students. They must take the TOEFL with a minimum score of 550 on the paper-based TOEFL (PBT) or 80 on the Internet-based version (iBT), or take the IELTS. They must also take the SAT or ACT.

ADMISSIONS: 70% of the 2016-2017 applicants were accepted. The SAT scores for the 2016-2017 freshman class were: Critical Reading-- 38% below 500, 44% between 500 and 599, 16% between 600 and 699, and 2% between 700 and 800. Math-- 29% below 500, 40% between 500 and 599, 27% between 600 and 699, and 4% between 700 and 800. Writing-- 35% below 500, 45% between 500 and 599, 19% between 600 and 699, and 2% between 700 and 800. The ACT scores were 16% below 12, 27% between 12 and 17, 30% between 18 and 23, 12% between 24 and 29, and 15% above 30. **Admissions Contact:** William J. Bisset, Ph.D., Vice President for Enrollment Management. Email: *admit@manhattan.edu* Web: *www.manhattan.edu*

FINANCIAL AID: In 2016-2017, 94% of all full-time freshmen and 48% of continuing full-time students received some form of financial aid. 94% of all full-time freshmen and 48% of continuing full-time students received need-based aid. The average freshman award was $22,566. Need-based scholarships or need-based grants averaged $14,551; need-based self-help aid (loans and jobs) averaged $4,900; and non-need-based athletic scholarships averaged $31,336. 26% of undergraduate students work part-time. Average annual earnings from campus work are $1500. The average financial indebtedness of the 2016 graduate was $34,375. The college's own financial statement is required. The priority date for freshman financial aid applications for fall entry is February 15.

MANHATTAN SCHOOL OF MUSIC *(The complete profile is made available exclusively on our website, www.barronspac.com)*

MANHATTANVILLE COLLEGE — D-5

www.manhattanville.edu

Purchase, NY 10577	(914) 323-5129 (800) 32 VILLE
Fax: (914) 694-1732	**Email:** admissions@mville.edu
Full-time: 608 men, 1100 women	**Faculty:** 110; IIA, +$
Part-time: 39 men, 51 women	**Ph.D.s:** 74%
Graduate: 339 men, 728 women	**Student/Faculty:** 15 to 1
Year: semesters, summer session	**Tuition:** $36,220
Room & Board: $14,520	**Freshman Class:** 3929 applied, 2902 accepted, 459 enrolled
SAT or ACT: recommended	**CEEB CODE:** 2397
Application Deadline: August 1	**COMPETITIVE+**

Manhattanville College, founded in 1841, is an independent, coeducational liberal arts institution dedicated to academic excellence. Manhattanville prepares students to be ethical and socially responsible leaders in a global community. The college has a rich history of preparing highly motivated students who value ethical integrity and social responsibility with the highest-quality education amongst a globally diverse campus community. The undergraduate programs combine the intellectual strength and passion of a liberal arts education with the hands-on, real-world experiences to turn a student's passion into an exciting career. The college offers more than 50 undergraduate areas of study including majors in sport studies, digital media production, accounting and marketing. Students can combine in-class learning with on-the-job experiences through access to over 700 internships ranging from Fortune 500 companies to non-profits, arts and entertainment venues to research opportunities and more. At Manhattanville, students get an insider's view of how the world works through powerful internships, international study and services learning, and four years of life on a campus. The Manhattanville School of Business offers six master's degrees, including, Business Leadership, Finance, Human Resource Management and Organizational Effectiveness, International Management, Marketing Communication Management and Sport Business Management. Manhattanville welcomes writers and aspiring writers to join its dynamic literary community. There is 1 undergraduate school and 2 graduate schools. In addition to regional accreditation, M'ville has baccalaureate program accreditation with NCATE and IACBE. The 100-acre campus is in a suburban area 30 miles north of New York City. Including any residence halls, there are 20 buildings.

STUDENT LIFE: 64% of undergraduates are from New York. Others are from 43 states, 47 foreign countries, and Canada. 40% are race unknown; 28% White; 13% Hispanic. **Female To Male Ratio:** 1.9:1. The average age of freshmen is 18; all undergraduates, 20. 21% do not continue beyond their first year; 54% remain to graduate. **Housing:** 1260 students can be accommodated in college housing, which includes coed dorms, and honors houses. There is a wellness community housing available which promotes a substance-free, holistic environment. On-campus housing is guaranteed for all 4 years, and is available on a first-come, and first-served basis. 64% of students live on campus; of those, 70% remain on campus on weekends. All students may keep cars.

FACULTY/CLASSROOMS: 50% of faculty are male; 50% are female. All teach undergraduates. No introductory courses are taught by graduate students. The average class size in a regular course is 19.

PROGRAMS OF STUDY: M'ville confers B.A., B.S., B.F.A., and B.Mus. degrees. Master's and doctoral degrees are also awarded. Bachelor's degrees are awarded in AGRICULTURE (environmental studies), BIOLOGICAL SCIENCE (biochemistry and biology/biological science), BUSINESS (accounting, banking and finance, business administration and management, and marketing), COMMUNICATIONS AND THE ARTS (art history and appreciation, communications, dance, digital media, dramatic arts, English, French, music, Spanish, and studio art), COMPUTER AND PHYSICAL SCIENCE (chemistry, computer science, and mathematics), EDUCATION (education and sports studies), SOCIAL SCIENCE (American studies, Asian/Oriental studies, economics, history, international studies, legal studies, philosophy, political science/government, psychology, religion, and sociology). Psychology, business management, and communication studies have the largest enrollments.

ACTIVITIES: There are no fraternities or sororities. There are 40 groups on campus, including art, band, cheerleading, chess, chorale, chorus, computers, dance, debate, drama, environmental, ethnic, film, honors, international, jazz band, LGBT, literary magazine, musical theater, newspaper, opera, orchestra, photography, political, professional, radio and TV, religious, social, social service, student government, and yearbook. Popular campus events include Fall Fest'ville, Quad Jam, end of semester brunches and nights parties which are provided as a countdown to graduation. **Sports:** There are 8 intercollegiate sports for men and 11 for women. Facilities include an athletic and recreation, gym, which has batting cages, indoor pool, tennis courts, strength and conditioning center, field for lacrosse, field hockey, and a soccer, baseball field and softball field. **Graduates:** From July 1, 2014 to June 30, 2015, 292 bachelor's degrees were awarded. The most popular majors were management (13%), psychology (12%), and communications (8%). 80 companies recruited on campus in 2014-2015. In an average class, 54% graduate in 4 years or less, 58% graduate in 5 years or less, and 58% graduate in 6 years or less. Of the 2014 graduating class, 21% were enrolled in graduate school within 6 months of graduation, and 52% were employed.

SERVICES: Counseling and information services are available, as is tutoring in every subject. **Library/Resources:** The library contains 429,051 volumes, 259,230 microform items, and 12,786 audio/video tapes/CDs/DVDs, and subscribes to 56,314 periodicals including electronic. Computerized library services include interlibrary loans, database searching, Internet access, and Wi-Fi capability. Special learning facilities include an art gallery, radio station, multimedia production labs, environmental sciences lab, performance theatre and dance studio. **Physically Challenged Students:** 70% of the campus is accessible. Facilities include wheelchair ramps, elevators, special parking, specially equipped restrooms, special class scheduling, and special housing. **Special:** Manhattanville college offers two Study Abroad programs (cooperative and non-cooperative) to successful candidates to further their education through international institutions. Manhattanville is pleased to announce a new partnership with EF International Language Centers (EF). Manhattanville offers cross-registration with SUNY Purchase. Dual, student-designed and interdisciplinary majors are also available at the college. There are 3 national honor societies, a freshman honors program, and 18 departmental honors programs. **Visiting:** There are regularly scheduled orientations for prospective students, consisting of weekday information sessions and tours. There are guides for informal visits, visitors may sit in on classes, and stay overnight. To schedule a visit, contact Joseph Garzione in the Office of Admissions at joseph.garzione@mville.edu. **Campus Safety and Security:** Measures include 24-hour foot and vehicle patrol, emergency notification system, and security escort services. There are also shuttle buses, emergency telephones, lighted pathways/sidewalks, and controlled access to dorms/residences.

REQUIREMENTS: The SAT or ACT is recommended. Applicants should graduate in the upper 50% of their class with 4 years of English, 3 each of history, math, and science, including 2 of lab science, and 1 half-year each of art and music. The GED is accepted. Interviews are strongly encouraged. Art applicants must submit a portfolio, and music applicants must audition. A GPA of 2.5 is required. AP and CLEP credits are accepted. Important factors in the admissions decision are advanced placement or honors courses, evidence of special talent, and extracurricular activities record. To qualify for a Bachelor's degree and be eligible for participation in the college's commencement ceremony, undergraduate students must complete all of the following degree requirements: general education requirements for all students regardless of major or program. A minimum of 120 total credits (though some major programs may exceed 120). A minimum cumulative G.P.A. of 2.0. Completion of a Major (normally with final grades of C or better, though some majors accept C- or higher). Minimum number of liberal arts credits for B.A. degree: 90 liberal arts credits, B.S. degree: 60 liberal arts credits, B.F.A. degree: 30 liberal arts credits, B.Mus degree: 30 liberal arts credits. All undergraduate students must complete all of the the following general education credit requirements (competency and distribution) to fulfill the college's general education requirements for degree completion. A minimum letter grade of "C-" must be earned to fulfill a requirement. I: Competency Requirements: Quantitative Reasoning (6 credits), Critical Analysis and Reasoning (6 credits), Scientific Reasoning (6 credits), Oral Communication (3 credits), Written Communication (6 credits), Second Language (minimum of 6 introductory-level credits in one language or demonstration of equivalent competency), and Technological Competency (3 credits). II: Distribution Area Requirements: All Manhattanville undergraduates must complete the indicated credit requirement in all four of the following curricular distribution areas in addition to Competency requirements: Humanities (6 credits), Social Science (6 credits), Mathematical (3 credits) and Scientific (3 credits), Fine Arts (6 credits). A minimum C- letter grade must be earned in any general education competency or distribution course to fulfill a requirement. **Procedure:** Freshmen are admitted fall and spring. We adhere to early action policy, December 1 deadline application. There are early admissions, deferred admissions, and rolling admissions plans. Application deadlines are open. Application fee is $50. Notification of early decision is sent December 31; regular decision. Applications are accepted online. **Transfer Students:** 77 transfer students enrolled in 2014-2015. 30 or more credits - application, recommendations, college transcripts, applicants can adhere to college-wide test-optional policy, interview recommended for some. If less than 30 credits - application, recommendations, college/high school transcripts, applicants can adhere to college-wide test-optional policy, interview recommended for some. 30 of 120 credits required for the bachelor's degree must be completed at M'ville. **International Students:** There are 236 international students enrolled. The school actively recruits these students. They must take the TOEFL with a minimum score of 550 on the paper-based TOEFL (PBT) or 80 on the Internet-based version (iBT). They must take the IELTS. They must take the Cambridge English, CEFR B2 or higher, IB. They must also take the SAT or ACT.

ADMISSIONS: 74% of the 2015-2016 applicants were accepted. The SAT scores for the 2015-2016 freshman class were: Critical Reading--26% below 500, 57% between 500 and 599, 15% between 600 and 699, and 2% between 700 and 800. Math-- 32% below 500, 48% between 500 and 599, 17% between 600 and 699, and 3% between 700 and 800. Writing-- 29% below 500, 48% between 500 and 599, 21% between 600 and 699, and 2% between 700 and 800. **Admissions Contact:** Nik Kumar, Vice President, Enrollment Management. Email: *admissions@mville.edu* Web: *www.manhattanville.edu*

FINANCIAL AID: In 2015-2016, 97% of all full-time freshmen and 95% of continuing full-time students received some form of financial aid. 61% of all full-time freshmen and 66% of continuing full-time students received need-based aid. The average freshman award was $26,805. Need-based scholarships or need-based grants averaged $4,883 ($45,410 maximum); need-based self-help aid (loans and jobs) averaged $2,227 ($8,500 maximum); and other non-need-based awards and non-need-based scholarships averaged $17,718 ($34,870 maximum). The average financial indebtedness of the 2015 graduate was $25,171. The FAFSA and the state aid form are required. International students can apply for need based aid using the International Student Financial Aid Application (ISFAA). The deadline for filing freshman financial aid applications for fall entry is March 1.

MANNES SCHOOL FOR MUSIC *(The complete profile is made available exclusively on our website, www.barronspac.com)*

MARIST COLLEGE D-4

www.marist.edu

Poughkeepsie, NY 12601	**(845) 575-3226** **(800) 436-5483**
Fax: (845) 575-3215	**Email: admissions@marist.edu**
Full-time: 2046 men, 2920 women	**Faculty:** 232; IIA, +$
Part-time: 284 men, 366 women	**Ph.D.s:** 75%
Graduate: 450 men, 503 women	**Student/Faculty:** 22 to 1
Year: semesters, summer session	**Tuition:** $35,210
Room & Board: $14,650	**Freshman Class:** 11087 applied, 4545 accepted, 1225 enrolled
SAT CR/M/W: 580/600/590 **ACT:** 27	**CEEB CODE:** 2400
Application Deadline: February 1	**VERY COMPETITIVE**

Marist College, founded in 1929, is private liberal arts college. Marist is dedicated to helping students develop the intellect and character required for enlightened, ethical, and productive lives in the global community of the 21st century. There are 7 undergraduate schools and 5 graduate schools. In addition to regional accreditation, Marist has baccalaureate program accreditation with AACSB, CSWE, NCATE, NAACLS, and CAATE. The 210-acre campus is in a suburban area 75 miles north of New York City on the Hudson River. Including any residence halls, there are 75 buildings.

STUDENT LIFE: 52% of undergraduates are from New York. Others are

from 48 states, 52 foreign countries, and Canada. 66% are from public schools. 9% are Hispanic; 73% White; 6% race unknown; 4% African American; 3% Asian American; 2% Foreign; 2% two or more races. **Female To Male Ratio:** 1.4:1. The average age of freshmen is 18; all undergraduates, 21. 10% do not continue beyond their first year; 83% remain to graduate. **Housing:** 3176 students can be accommodated in college housing, which includes coed dorms, on-campus apartments, and off-campus apartments. In addition, there are special-interest houses, freshman dorms with mentors, and housing for upperclassmen. 61% of students live on campus; of those, 90% remain on campus on weekends. Alcohol is not permitted. Upperclassmen may keep cars.

FACULTY/CLASSROOMS: 53% of faculty are male; 47% are female. All teach undergraduates. No introductory courses are taught by graduate students.

PROGRAMS OF STUDY: Marist confers B.A., B.S. and B.P.S. degrees. Master's degrees are also awarded. Bachelor's degrees are awarded in AGRICULTURE (conservation and regulation), BIOLOGICAL SCIENCE (biochemistry, biology/adolescence education, and biology/biological science), BUSINESS (accounting, business administration and management, and fashion merchandising), COMMUNICATIONS AND THE ARTS (communications, digital media, English, fashion studies, fine arts, French, game design and development, Italian, film and media studies, Spanish, and studio art), COMPUTER AND PHYSICAL SCIENCE (applied mathematics, chemistry, chemistry/adolescence education, computer game design/development, computer science, information sciences and systems, and mathematics), EDUCATION (athletic training, English education, history education, mathematics education, and special education), ENGINEERING AND ENVIRONMENTAL DESIGN (environmental science and interior design), HEALTH PROFESSIONS (medical technology), SOCIAL SCIENCE (American studies, criminal justice, economics, fashion design and technology, history, liberal arts/general studies, philosophy, political science/government, psychology, religion, and social work). Fashion, computer science/software development, business administration, chemistry/biochemistry, and education are the strongest academically. Business administration, communications, and fashion merchandising have the largest enrollments.

ACTIVITIES: 3% of women belong to 1 local and 3 national sororities. There are 81 groups on campus, including art, band, cheerleading, chess, choir, chorale, chorus, communications, computers, dance, debate, drama, environmental, ethnic, film, honors, international, jazz band, LGBT, literary magazine, marching band, musical theater, newspaper, orchestra, pep band, photography, political, professional, radio and TV, religious, social, social service, student government, and symphony. Popular campus events include Activities Fair, Foxfest, and Giving Tree Program. **Sports:** There are 11 intercollegiate sports for men and 12 for women, and 11 intramural sports for men and 11 for women. Facilities include a boathouse, basketball arena, stadium, playing fields, a field house, swimming pool, diving well, racquetball courts, tennis pavilion, dance, and aerobics studio, weight room, intramural basketball courts, and a fitness center. **Graduates:** From July 1, 2015 to June 30, 2016, 1300 bachelor's degrees were awarded. The most popular majors were business (30%), communications (20%), and psychology (13%). 200 companies recruited on campus in 2015-2016. In an average class, 1% graduate in 3 years or less, 68% graduate in 4 years or less, 76% graduate in 5 years or less, and 78% graduate in 6 years or less. Of the 2015 graduating class, 10% were enrolled in graduate school within 6 months of graduation, and 74% were employed.

SERVICES: Counseling and information services are available, as is tutoring in every subject. There is a reader service for the blind, as well as remedial math, reading, and writing. **Library/Resources:** The library contains 196,914 volumes, 10,828 audio/video tapes/CDs/DVDs, and subscribes to 145,583 periodicals including electronic. Computerized library services include interlibrary loans, database searching, Internet access, and Wi-Fi capability. Special learning facilities include an art gallery, radio station, TV station, a gallery of Lowell Thomas memorabilia, estuarine and environmental studies lab, public opinion institute, and economic research center. **Physically Challenged Students:** All of the campus is accessible. Facilities include wheelchair ramps, elevators, special parking, specially equipped restrooms, special class scheduling, lowered drinking fountains, lowered telephones, and special housing. **Special:** Marist offers cross-registration with schools in the Mid-Hudson Career Consortium and study abroad in 38 countries. The school also offers a 3-year degree in social work, co-op programs in computer science and computer information systems, information technology, accounting, and business, work-study programs, and dual and student-designed majors. There are internships available with more than 1100 organizations in the United States and abroad, including New York State Legislature and White House programs. There are 15 national honor societies and a freshman honors program. **Visiting:** There are regularly scheduled orientations for prospective students, including 1-day June visits for freshmen and a 1-week welcome program. There are guides for informal visits, visitors may sit in on classes, and stay overnight. To schedule a visit, contact the Admission Office at admission@marist.edu. **Campus Safety and Security:** Measures include 24-hour foot and vehicle patrol, emergency notification system, and security escort services. There are also emergency telephones, lighted pathways/sidewalks, and controlled access to dorms/residences.

REQUIREMENTS: Applicants should have 17 high school units, including at least 4 years in English, 3 each in math and science, 2 each in social studies, foreign language, and an elective, and 1 in American history. An essay and 2 letters of recommendation are also required. AP and CLEP credits are accepted. Important factors in the admissions decision are advanced placement or honors courses, leadership record, and recommendations by school officials. To graduate, students must maintain a GPA of 2.0 in the major while taking 120 credits. A 30-credit core curriculum and 30 to 36 credits in a major are required. Distribution requirements include 6 credits each in natural sciences, social sciences, history, literature, and math and 3 credits each in fine arts and philosophy/religious studies. Specific course requirements include English writing skills and foundation courses in those areas defined by major programs. **Procedure:** Freshmen are admitted in the fall and spring. Entrance exams should be taken during the fall of the senior year. There are early decision and deferred admissions plans. Early decision applications should be filed by November 15; regular applications, by February 1 for fall entry; and November 15 for spring entry, along with a $50 fee. Notification of early decision is sent December 15; regular decision, April 1. 270 early decision candidates were accepted for the 2016-2017 class. Applications are accepted online. **Transfer Students:** 274 transfer students enrolled in 2015-2016. Applicants must have at least a 2.8 GPA (depending on the college and major program) in at least 30 college credits. Students with fewer than 25 credits will be treated as freshmen. Grades of C or better transfer. 30 of 120 credits required for the bachelor's degree must be completed at Marist. **International Students:** There are 124 international students enrolled. The school actively recruits these students. They must take the TOEFL with a minimum score of 550 on the paper-based TOEFL (PBT) or 80 on the Internet-based version (iBT) and the college's own test. The IELTS is accepted.

ADMISSIONS: 41% of the 2016-2017 applicants were accepted. The SAT scores for the 2016-2017 freshman class were: Critical Reading-- 9% below 500, 47% between 500 and 599, 37% between 600 and 699, and 7% between 700 and 800. Math-- 7% below 500, 41% between 500 and 599, 46% between 600 and 699, and 6% between 700 and 800. Writing-- 9% below 500, 44% between 500 and 599, 38% between 600 and 699, and 9% between 700 and 800. The ACT scores were 12% between 18 and 23, 66% between 24 and 29, and 22% above 30. 49% of the current freshmen were in the top fifth of their class; 80% were in the top two fifths. 3 freshmen graduated first in their class. **Admissions Contact:** Kent Rinehart, Dean of Admission. Email: *admissions@marist.edu* Web: *www.marist.edu*

FINANCIAL AID: In 2016-2017, 90% of all full-time freshmen and continuing full-time students received some form of financial aid. 52% of all full-time freshmen and 54% of continuing full-time students received need-based aid. The average freshman award was $18,946. Need-based scholarships or need-based grants averaged $14,026 ($50,350 maximum); need-based self-help aid (loans and jobs) averaged $6,185 ($9,500 maximum); non-need-based athletic scholarships averaged $15,189 ($56,106 maximum); and other non-need-based awards and non-need-based scholarships averaged $9,435 ($49,860 maximum). 28% of undergraduate students work part-time. Average annual earnings from campus work are $694. The average financial indebtedness of the 2016 graduate was $39,584. Marist is a member of CSS. The FAFSA code is 002765. The priority date for freshman financial aid applications for fall entry is February 15.

MARYMOUNT MANHATTAN COLLEGE D-5

www.mmm.edu

New York, NY 10021	(212) 517-0430 (800) 627-9668
Fax: (212) 517-0448	**Email:** admissions@mmm.edu
Full-time: 396 men, 1296 women	**Faculty:** 96; IIB, +$
Part-time: 42 men, 211 women	**Ph.D.s:** 91%
Graduate: n/av	**Student/Faculty:** 17 to 1
Year: semesters, summer session	**Tuition:** $30,290
Room & Board: $15,990	**Freshman Class:** 4174 applied, 2995 accepted, 504 enrolled
SAT or ACT: required	**CEEB CODE:** 2405
Application Deadline: open	**VERY COMPETITIVE**

Marymount Manhattan College is an urban, independent liberal arts college, offering programs in the arts and sciences for all ages, as well as substantial preprofessional preparation. Figures in the above capsule and in this profile are approximate. There is 1 undergraduate school. The campus is in an urban area in Manhattan. Including any residence halls, there are 3 buildings.

STUDENT LIFE: 55% of undergraduates are from out of state, mostly the Middle Atlantic. Students are from 44 states, 26 foreign countries, and Canada. 57% are from public schools. 68% are White; 3% Asian American; 3% Foreign; 14% Hispanic; 12% African American. **Female To Male Ratio:** 3.4:1. The average age of freshmen is 19; all undergraduates, 21. 38% do not continue beyond their first year; 49% remain to graduate. **Housing:** 780 students can be accommodated in college housing, which includes single-sex and coed dorms and off-campus apartments. On-campus housing is available on a first-come, first-served basis, and on a lottery system for upperclassmen. Priority is given to out-of-town students. 64% of students commute. Alcohol is not permitted. All students may keep cars.

FACULTY/CLASSROOMS: 49% of faculty are male; 51% are female. 65% teach undergraduates, 35% do research, and 35% do both. No introductory courses are taught by graduate students. The average class size in an introductory lecture is 25; in a laboratory is 15; and in a regular course is 20.

PROGRAMS OF STUDY: MMC confers B.A., B.S. and B.F.A. degrees. Associate degrees are also awarded. Bachelor's degrees are awarded in BIOLOGICAL SCIENCE (biology/biological science), BUSINESS (accounting and business administration and management), COMMUNICATIONS AND THE ARTS (communications, dance, dramatic arts, English, and fine arts), COMPUTER AND PHYSICAL SCIENCE (information sciences and systems), EDUCATION (elementary education), HEALTH PROFESSIONS (premedicine and speech pathology/audiology), SOCIAL SCIENCE (history, international studies, liberal arts/general studies, philosophy and religion, political science/government, psychology, and sociology). Theater, communications, and business are the strongest academically.

ACTIVITIES: There are no fraternities; 1% of women belong to 2 national sororities. There are 29 groups on campus, including art, choir, computers, dance, drama, ethnic, honors, international, LGBT, literary magazine, musical theater, newspaper, photography, political, professional, radio and TV, religious, social, social service, student government, and yearbook. Popular campus events include Strawberry Festival, Honors Day and Holiday Soiree. **Sports:** There are 3 intramural sports for men and 3 for women. Facilities include a 300-seat auditorium. **Graduates:** From July 1, 2015 to June 30, 2016, 389 bachelor's degrees were awarded. The most popular majors were visual/performing arts (38%), journalism (27%), and business/marketing (9%). 37 companies recruited on campus in 2015-2016. In an average class, 39% graduate in 4 years or less, 48% graduate in 5 years or less, and 49% graduate in 6 years or less. Of the 2015 graduating class, 23% were enrolled in graduate school within 6 months of graduation, and 63% were employed.

SERVICES: Counseling and information services are available, as is tutoring in every subject. There is remedial math, reading, and writing. **Library/Resources:** The library contains 75,000 volumes, 70 microform items, 4,000 audio/video tapes/CDs/DVDs, and subscribes to 2,740 periodicals including electronic. Computerized library services include interlibrary loans, database searching, Internet access, and Wi-Fi capability. Special learning facilities include an art gallery, radio station, TV station, and communications arts multimedia suite featuring digital editing technology. **Physically Challenged Students:** All of the campus is accessible. Facilities include wheelchair ramps, elevators, specially equipped restrooms, special class scheduling, and lowered drinking fountains. **Special:** MMC offers study abroad, interdisciplinary courses, pass/fail options, nondegree study, credit for life experience, and some 250 internships in all majors. Cooperative programs in business and finance, dance, music, languages, nursing, and urban education are offered in conjunction with local colleges and institutes. There is a January mini-session, cross-registration with Hunter College, and the China Institute, and a 5-year masters in publishing with Pace University. There are 7 national honor societies and 5 departmental honors programs. **Visiting:** There are regularly scheduled orientations for prospective students, including an interview with an admissions counselor, a tour of the school and dorms, and a meeting with a financial aid adviser. There are guides for informal visits and visitors may sit in on classes. To schedule a visit, contact the Admissions Office. **Campus Safety and Security:** Measures include 24-hour foot and vehicle patrol and self-defense education. There are also shuttle buses, lighted pathways/sidewalks, security cameras, and photo ID check-in.

REQUIREMENTS: The SAT or ACT is required. Applicants should be graduates of an accredited secondary school or have a GED certificate. MMC recommends completion of 16 academic units, including 4 each in English and electives, and 3 each in language, math, social science, and science. A recommendations is needed, and an interview is strongly advised. Applicants to the dance and acting programs must audition. AP and CLEP credits are accepted. Important factors in the admissions decision are personality/intangible qualities, evidence of special talent, and leadership record. To graduate, students must complete 120 credit hours, including 31 to 71 in the major, with a minimum GPA of 2.0. The core plus shared curriculum totals 48 credits in the areas of critical thinking, psychology and philosophy, quantitative reasoning and science, the modern world, communications/language, and the arts. **Procedure:** Freshmen are admitted to all sessions. Entrance exams should be taken as early as possible. There are deferred admissions and rolling admissions plans. Application deadlines are open. Application fee is $60. Notification of early decision is sent December 15; regular decision, on a rolling basis. Applications are accepted online. **Transfer Students:** 141 transfer students enrolled in 2015-2016. Applicants who have graduated from high school less then 5 years ago must meet standard freshman requirements and must submit official transcripts from all colleges attended. 30 of 120 credits required for the bachelor's degree must be completed at MMC. **International Students:** There are 58 international students enrolled. The school actively recruits these students. They must take the TOEFL, as well as the SAT or ACT, scoring 900.

ADMISSIONS: 72% of the 2016-2017 applicants were accepted. **Admissions Contact:** James Rogers, Dean of Admissions. Email: *admissions@mmm.edu* Web: *www.mmm.edu*

FINANCIAL AID: In 2016-2017, 77% of all full-time freshmen and 75% of continuing full-time students received some form of financial aid. 77% of all full-time freshmen and 59% of continuing full-time students received need-based aid. The average freshman award was $13,068. Need-based scholarships or need-based grants averaged $10,521; need-based self-help aid (loans and jobs) averaged $3,477; and $3,477 from other forms of aid. 75% of undergraduate students work part-time. Average annual earnings from campus work are $2500. The average financial indebtedness of the 2016 graduate was $15,206. The FAFSA code is 002769. The deadline for filing freshman financial aid applications for fall entry is March 15.

MEDAILLE COLLEGE A-1

www.medaille.edu

Buffalo, NY 14214	(716) 880-2200
Fax: (716) 880-2007	**Email:** admissionsug@medaille.edu
Full-time: 580 men, 1069 women	**Faculty:** IIA, --$
Part-time: 42 men, 152 women	**Ph.D.s:** 62%
Graduate: 179 men, 611 women	**Student/Faculty:** 16 to 1
Year: semesters, summer session	**Tuition:** $23,812
Room & Board: $11,300	**Freshman Class:** 1497 applied, 895 accepted, 400 enrolled
SAT CR/M: required **ACT:** 21	**CEEB CODE:** 2422
Application Deadline: rolling	**COMPETITIVE**

Medaille College, founded in 1875, is a private, nonsectarian institution offering undergraduate programs in liberal arts, education, business, and sciences, and graduate programs in business and education, to a primarily commuter student body. There is 1 undergraduate school and 1 graduate school. In addition to regional accreditation, Medaille has baccalaureate program accreditation with AVMA. The 13-acre campus is in an urban area 3 miles from downtown Buffalo. Including any residence halls, there are 17 buildings.

STUDENT LIFE: 92% of undergraduates are from New York. Others are from 17 states, 4 foreign countries, and Canada. 61% are White; 5% Hispanic; 3% Asian American; 16% African American; 1% American Indian/Alaska Native; 1% Foreign. **Female To Male Ratio:** 2.3:1. The average age of freshmen is 18; all undergraduates, 24. 32% do not continue beyond their first year; 68% remain to graduate. **Housing:** 420 students can be accommodated in college housing, which includes single-sex and coed dorms and on-campus apartments. On-campus housing is available on a first-come and first-served basis. 80% of students commute. All students may keep cars.

FACULTY/CLASSROOMS: 50% of faculty are male; 50% are female. No introductory courses are taught by graduate students. The average class size in an introductory lecture is 20; in a laboratory is 10; and in a regular course is 14.

PROGRAMS OF STUDY: Medaille confers B.A., B.S., B.B.A. and B.S.Ed. degrees. Associate and master's degrees are also awarded. Bachelor's degrees are awarded in BIOLOGICAL SCIENCE (biology/biological science), BUSINESS (business administration and management and sports management), COMMUNICATIONS AND THE ARTS (communications and English), EDUCATION (early childhood education, elementary education, and middle school education), HEALTH PROFESSIONS (veterinary science), SOCIAL SCIENCE (criminal justice, liberal arts/general studies, psychology, and social science). Education, business, and communication are the strongest academically. Education, business administration, and veterinary technology have the largest enrollments.

ACTIVITIES: There are no fraternities or sororities. There are 26 groups on campus, including academic clubs, art, cheerleading, dance, drama, environmental, ethnic, honors, LGBT, literary magazine, musical theater, newspaper, photography, professional, radio and TV, social, and student government. Popular campus events include Founders Day, Silent Auction, Campus Carnival, and Honors Convocation. **Sports:** There are 7 intercollegiate sports for men and 8 for women, and 3 intramural sports for men and 3 for women. Facilities include a gym, and a softball and soccer field. **Graduates:** From July 1, 2015 to June 30, 2016, 316 bachelor's degrees were awarded. The most popular majors were business administration (34%), veterinary technology (18%), and education (9%). 75 companies recruited on campus in 2015-2016. In an average class, 35% graduate in 4 years or less, 41% graduate in 5 years or less, and 45% graduate in 6 years or less. Of the 2015 graduating class, 28% were enrolled in graduate school within 6 months of graduation, and 95% were employed.

SERVICES: Counseling and information services are available, as is tutoring in most subjects. There is a reader service for the blind, and remedial math, reading, and writing. **Library/Resources:** The library contains 55,690 volumes, and 1,411 audio/video tapes/CDs/DVDs, and subscribes to 236 periodicals including electronic. Computerized library services include interlibrary loans, database searching, Internet access, and Wi-Fi capability. Special learning facilities include a radio station, TV station, and media institute. **Physically Challenged Students:** All of the campus is accessible. Facilities include wheelchair ramps, elevators, special parking, specially equipped restrooms, lowered drinking fountains, and lowered telephones. **Special:** Cross-registration is available with colleges in the Western New York Consortium. Most degree programs require internships. Opportunities are provided for student-designed majors, credit by examination, pass/fail options, accelerated degrees, dual majors, and credit for work experience. There are 2 national honor societies and a freshman honors program. **Visiting:** There are regularly scheduled orientations for prospective students, including campus tours, academic program meetings, ice-breakers, and a review of policies and procedures. There are guides for informal visits, visitors may sit in on classes, and stay overnight. To schedule a visit, contact Karen McGrath at (716) 880-2200. **Campus Safety and Security:** Measures include 24-hour foot and vehicle patrol, emergency notification system, self-defense education, and security escort services. There are shuttle buses, emergency telephones, lighted pathways/sidewalks, and controlled access to dorms/residences.

REQUIREMENTS: The SAT is required. Applicants must be graduates of an accredited secondary school or hold the GED. An essay and an interview are required. AP and CLEP credits are accepted. Important factors in the admissions decision are advanced placement or honors courses, personality/intangible qualities, and leadership record. The bachelor's degree requires successful completion of 120 credit hours or 128 for elementary education and biology majors. In addition to specific course requirements for each major, students must maintain a minimum GPA of 2.0. Students must also complete a general education core curriculum of 30 required. 3 credits each in Self and Others, U.S. Colonial History, Creative Expression, Scientific Discovery, and Mathematics, 9 credits in Communication, and 6 credits in baccalaureate capstone courses. **Procedure:** Freshmen are admitted to all sessions. Entrance exams should be taken in May. There are deferred admissions and rolling admissions plans. Applications should be filed by January 15 for spring entry; May 15 for summer entry, along with a $25 fee. Notification is sent on a rolling basis. Applications are accepted online. **Transfer Students:** 205 transfer students enrolled in 2015-2016. Applicants must have a minimum GPA of 2.0 in their previous college work. An interview and recommendations are required. 30 of 120 credits required for the bachelor's degree must be completed at Medaille. **International Students:** There are 4 international students enrolled. The school actively recruits these students. They must take the TOEFL with a minimum score of 550 on the paper-based TOEFL (PBT) or 61 on the Internet-based version (iBT). They must also take the SAT.

ADMISSIONS: 60% of the 2016-2017 applicants were accepted. The SAT scores for the 2016-2017 freshman class were: Critical Reading-- 80% below 500, 17% between 500 and 599, 2% between 600 and 699, and 1% between 700 and 800. Math-- 72% below 500, 22% between 500 and 599, and 6% between 600 and 699. **Admissions Contact:** Karen McGrath, Vice President for Enrollment Management. Email: *admissionsug@medaille.edu* Web: *www.medaille.edu*

FINANCIAL AID: In 2016-2017, 100% of all full-time freshmen and 98% of continuing full-time students received some form of financial aid. 100% of all full-time freshmen and 97% of continuing full-time students received need-based aid. The average freshman award was $13,473. 15% of undergraduate students work part-time. Average annual earnings from campus work are $1500. Medaille is a member of CSS. The state aid form and the college's own financial statement are required. The FAFSA code is 002777. The deadline for filing freshman financial aid applications for fall entry is March 1.

MERCY COLLEGE D-5

www.mercy.edu

Dobbs Ferry, NY 10522 — **(877) 637-2946** / **(877) MERCY-GO**

Fax: (914) 674-7382 — **Email: admissions@mercy.edu**

Full-time: 1704 men, 3688 women	**Faculty:** 198; IIA, +$
Part-time: 751 men, 1873 women	**Ph.D.s:** 86%
Graduate: 608 men, 2671 women	**Student/Faculty:** 17 to 1
Year: semesters, summer session	**Tuition:** $18,076
Room & Board: $13,700	**Freshman Class:** 5573 applied, 3661 accepted, 938 enrolled
	CEEB CODE: 2409
Application Deadline: open	**COMPETITIVE**

Mercy College, founded in 1950, is a private institution dedicated to offering a curriculum of liberal arts and sciences as well as preprofessional and professional programs. Graduate programs provide advanced preparation in selected disciplines. Figures in the above capsule and in this profile are approximate. There are 5 undergraduate schools and 5 graduate schools. In addition to regional accreditation, Mercy has baccalaureate program accreditation with CSWE, NASAD, NCATE, ACOTE, CCNE, CAPTE, AVMA, and CAEP. The 66-acre campus is in a suburban area on Dobbs Ferry Campus, 25 miles north of New York City. Additional campus locations in the Bronx, Manhattan, and Yorktown. Including any residence halls, there are 7 buildings.

STUDENT LIFE: 93% of undergraduates are from New York. Others are from 36 states, 48 foreign countries, and Canada. 36% are White; 29% Hispanic; 21% African American; 6% race unknown; 4% Asian American; 2% two or more races; 1% American Indian/Alaska Native; 1% Foreign. **Female To Male Ratio:** 2.7:1. The average age of freshmen is 19; all undergraduates, 25. 24% do not continue beyond their first year; 38%

remain to graduate. **Housing:** 669 students can be accommodated in college housing, which includes coed dorms. On-campus housing is available on a first-come and first-served basis. Priority is given to out-of-town students. 87% of students commute. Alcohol is not permitted. Upperclassmen may keep cars.

FACULTY/CLASSROOMS: 38% of faculty are male; 62% are female. All teach undergraduates. No introductory courses are taught by graduate students. The average class size in an introductory lecture is 17 and in a regular course is 17.

PROGRAMS OF STUDY: Mercy confers B.A., B.F.A., and B.S. degrees. Associate, master's, and doctoral degrees are also awarded. Bachelor's degrees are awarded in BIOLOGICAL SCIENCE (biology/biological science), BUSINESS (accounting, banking and finance, business administration and management, business (dual major program), entrepreneurial studies, and human resources/organizational management), COMMUNICATIONS AND THE ARTS (broadcasting, communications, English, film, television and digital media, fine arts, journalism, media arts, music, music industry, music technology, and Spanish), COMPUTER AND PHYSICAL SCIENCE (computer science, digital arts/technology, information sciences and systems, and mathematics), EDUCATION (elementary education, special education, sports and wellness studies, and teaching English as a second/foreign language (TESOL/TEFOL)), HEALTH PROFESSIONS (exercise science, health science, medical laboratory technology, nursing, speech pathology/audiology, and veterinary science), SOCIAL SCIENCE (behavioral science, communication sciences & disorders, criminal justice, history, interdisciplinary studies, legal studies, liberal arts/general studies, paralegal studies, political science/government, psychology, social work, and sociology). Health professions programs is the strongest academically. Business, education, and psychology have the largest enrollments.

ACTIVITIES: There are no fraternities or sororities. There are 36 groups on campus, including veterinary club and STEM club, communications, computers, dance, drama, environmental, ethnic, film, honors, international, newspaper, political, professional, religious, social, social service, student government, and student military veteran club. Popular campus events include Veterans Day Activities, Founders Day/Alumni Weekend, Open Houses, Major League Baseball Events, Broadway Shows, Spring Fling Festival, Poetry Readings and Club Fairs. **Sports:** There are 4 intercollegiate sports for men and 6 for women, and 1 intramural sports for men and 2 for women. Facilities include a gym, soccer/baseball/softball field, swimming pools, tennis courts, a track, basketball/volleyball court, and a fitness center. **Graduates:** From July 1, 2015 to June 30, 2016, 1473 bachelor's degrees were awarded. The most popular majors were behavioral science (22%), psychology (14%), and health professions (13%). 300 companies recruited on campus in 2015-2016. In an average class, 38% graduate in 6 years or less.

SERVICES: Counseling and information services are available, as is tutoring in every subject. There is a reader service for the blind. **Library/Resources:** The 4 libraries contain 85,689 volumes, 1,616 audio/video tapes/CDs/DVDs, and subscribe to 21,126 periodicals including electronic. Computerized library services include interlibrary loans, database searching, Internet access, and Wi-Fi capability. Special learning facilities include a TV station, computer labs, center for academic excellence, STEM labs, a reference library and a digital arts center. **Physically Challenged Students:** 75% of the campus is accessible. Facilities include wheelchair ramps, elevators, special parking, specially equipped restrooms, special class scheduling, and lowered drinking fountains. **Special:** Mercy offers internships and cooperative education in each major, an on-campus employment program with a community service component, study abroad, dual majors and degrees, credit for life experience, non-degree study, and pass/fail options. There are 7 national honor societies, Phi Beta Kappa, a freshman honors program, and 14 departmental honors programs. **Visiting:** There are regularly scheduled orientations for prospective students, including spring and fall open houses and information sessions. There are guides for informal visits and visitors may sit in on classes. To schedule a visit, contact the Admissions Office. **Campus Safety and Security:** Measures include 24-hour foot and vehicle patrol, emergency notification system, self-defense education, and security escort services. There are also shuttle buses, emergency telephones, lighted pathways/sidewalks, and controlled access to dorms/residences.

REQUIREMENTS: Applicants must be graduates of an accredited secondary school or have a GED certificate. They should have completed at least 16 academic units. AP and CLEP credits are accepted. Important factors in the admissions decision are recommendations by school officials, personality/intangible qualities, and leadership record. To graduate, students must complete 120 semester hours with a minimum GPA of 2.0 overall. In total, 30 semester hours must be completed at Mercy. The Mercy College General Education Curriculum includes: 6 English credits, 3 speech credits, 6 history credits, 9 social science credits, 3 philosophy/religion credits, 3 art/music credits, 3 foreign language credits, 3 math credits, 3 computer science credits, and 3 natural science credits. **Procedure:** Freshmen are admitted fall, spring, and summer. Entrance exams should be taken between January and August of their senior year. There are deferred admissions and rolling admissions plans. Application deadlines are open. Application fee is $40. Notification is sent on a rolling basis. Applications are accepted online. **Transfer Students:** 952 transfer students enrolled in 2015-2016. Applicants must submit official transcripts from all colleges attended, as well as their high school transcript. 30 of 120 credits required for the bachelor's degree must be completed at Mercy. **International Students:** There are 91 international students enrolled. The school actively recruits these students. They must take the TOEFL with a minimum score of 550 on the paper-based TOEFL (PBT) or 79 on the Internet-based version (iBT) and the college's own test.

ADMISSIONS: 66% of the 2016-2017 applicants were accepted. **Admissions Contact:** Deirdre Whitman, Vice President for Enrollment Management. Email: *admissions@mercy.edu* Web: *www.mercy.edu*

FINANCIAL AID: In 2016-2017, 91% of all full-time freshmen and 85% of continuing full-time students received some form of financial aid. 83% of all full-time freshmen and 78% of continuing full-time students received need-based aid. The average freshman award was $14,313. Need-based scholarships or need-based grants averaged $10,734; need-based self-help aid (loans and jobs) averaged $3,425; non-need-based athletic scholarships averaged $5,326; and other non-need-based awards and non-need-based scholarships averaged $4,298. 1% of undergraduate students work part-time. The average financial indebtedness of the 2016 graduate was $17,399. The state aid form is required. The FAFSA code is 002772. The priority date for freshman financial aid applications for fall entry is February 15.

METROPOLITAN COLLEGE OF NEW YORK D-5

www.mcny.edu

New York, NY 10006 **(212) 343-1234**

Fax: (212) 343-8470
Full-time: 154 men, 467 women
Part-time: 26 men, 50 women
Graduate: 106 men, 256 women
Year: semesters, summer session
Room & Board: $9600
Application Deadline: open

Email: admissions@mcny.edu
Faculty: n/av
Ph.D.s: n/av
Student/Faculty: n/av
Tuition: see profile
Freshman Class: 257 applied, 104 accepted, 79 enrolled
CEEB CODE: 4802
VERY COMPETITIVE

Metropolitan College of New York, founded in 1964, is a private institution offering programs in business, education, emergency management, human services, healthcare, and public administration. The college operates on a 3-semester calendar, including a complete summer semester. All bachelor degree programs involve a combination of class work, and field work and may be completed in 2 years and 8 months. Most Masters degree programs can be completed in 1 year. Tuition cost varies by program contact the school. There are 2 undergraduate schools and 3 graduate schools. In addition to regional accreditation, MCNY has baccalaureate program accreditation with ACBSP and NCATE. The campus is in an urban area in New York City, NY. Including any residence halls, there is 1 building.

STUDENT LIFE: 99% of undergraduates are from New York. Others are from 4 states, 9 foreign countries, and Canada. **Female To Male Ratio:** 2.7:1. **Housing:** All students commute. Alcohol is not permitted.

FACULTY/CLASSROOMS: No introductory courses are taught by graduate students.

PROGRAMS OF STUDY: MCNY confers B.B.A., and B.P.S. degrees. Associate and master's degrees are also awarded. Bachelor's degrees are awarded in BUSINESS (business administration and management),

EDUCATION (early childhood education), HEALTH PROFESSIONS (mental health/human services), SOCIAL SCIENCE (child care/child and family studies, community services, gerontology, human services, and social work). Business management is the strongest academically. Human services has the largest enrollment.

ACTIVITIES: There are no fraternities or sororities. There are 10 groups on campus, including computers, ethnic, honors, LGBT, newspaper, professional, social, social service, and student government. Popular campus events include Career fairs, Admissions Open House, and Dean's List Ceremonies. **Sports:** There is no sports program at MCNY. **Graduates:** From July 1, 2015 to June 30, 2016, 192 bachelor's degrees were awarded. The most popular majors were human services, business, and healthcare systems management.

SERVICES: Counseling and information services are available, as is tutoring in every subject. Remedial math, reading, and writing are also available. **Library/Resources:** The library contains 32,000 volumes, 1,800 microform items, and subscribes to 3,300 periodicals including electronic. Computerized library services include interlibrary loans, database searching, Internet access, and Wi-Fi capability. **Physically Challenged Students:** All of the campus is accessible. Facilities include wheelchair ramps, elevators, specially equipped restrooms, special class scheduling, lowered drinking fountains, and lowered telephones. **Special:** Internships, which include required weekly 14-hour field sites, study abroad in 3 countries, work-study programs, B.A.-B.S. degrees, and accelerated degree programs in human services, business management, and American urban studies are offered, as well as credit by exam, and credit for life experience. **Visiting:** There are regularly scheduled orientations for prospective students. There are guides for informal visits and visitors may sit in on classes. To schedule a visit, contact the Admissions Office. **Campus Safety and Security:** Measures include 24-hour foot and vehicle patrol and emergency notification system. There are also lighted pathways/sidewalks, fire drills, and a fire escape stairwell.

REQUIREMENTS: Students must take the ETS's Accuplacer Test in reading and math. Recent high school graduates who have a satisfactory SAT score may present the SAT instead. Applicants must have graduated from an accredited secondary school. The GED is accepted. An essay and an interview are required. CLEP credits are accepted. Important factors in the admissions decision are evidence of special talent, leadership record, and personality/intangible qualities. To graduate, students must complete 120 credit hours with a minimum GPA of 2.0. The curriculum is prescribed; no electives are featured. A constructive action document based on performance in the field and mastery of course work is required each semester. **Procedure:** Freshmen are admitted to all sessions. Entrance exams should be taken in the senior year. There are deferred admissions and rolling admissions plans. Applications should be filed by December 1 for spring entry; April 1 for summer entry, along with a $30 fee. Applications are accepted online. **Transfer Students:** 45 transfer students enrolled in 2015-2016. Admission is based on current skills and abilities as measured on the entrance exam and essay. 60 of 120 credits required for the bachelor's degree must be completed at MCNY. **International Students:** There are 18 international students enrolled. The school actively recruits these students. They must take the TOEFL with a minimum score of 75 on the paper-based TOEFL (PBT) or 75 on the Internet-based version (iBT).

ADMISSIONS: 40% of the 2016-2017 applicants were accepted. **Admissions Contact:** Erica Silbiger, Director of Admissions. Email: *esilbiger@mcny.edu* Web: *www.mcny.edu*

FINANCIAL AID: In 2016-2017, 96% of all full-time freshmen received some form of financial aid, and need-based aid. The average freshman award was $14,593. Need-based scholarships or need-based grants averaged $11,181; and need-based self-help aid (loans and jobs) averaged $3,530. The FAFSA code is 009769. The deadline for filing freshman financial aid applications for fall entry is August 15.

MOLLOY COLLEGE — D-5

www.molloy.edu

Rockville Centre, NY 11570	(516) 323-4000
Fax: (516) 256-2247	**Email:** admissions@molloy.edu
Full-time: 713 men, 1966 women	**Faculty:** IIA, ++$
Part-time: 135 men, 522 women	**Ph.D.s:** 75%
Graduate: 211 men, 950 women	**Student/Faculty:** 10 to 1
Year: 4-1-4, summer session	**Tuition:** $26,850
Room & Board: $13,590	**Freshman Class:** 3277 applied, 2471 accepted, 492 enrolled
SAT CR/M/W: 520/530/510 **ACT:** 24	**CEEB CODE:** 2415
Application Deadline: open	**COMPETITIVE**

Molloy offers students a rich and multidimensional educational experience where students are encouraged to think critically and explore creatively. Combining the strengths of academic excellence and leadership with personal, compassionate mentoring, we bring out the best in every student, here and around the globe. Molloy College students develop that all-important confidence, that strong, "I will" attitude that enables them to succeed in their careers, and more importantly, to make a difference in our world. There are 2 undergraduate schools and 6 graduate schools. In addition to regional accreditation, Molloy has baccalaureate program accreditation with CSWE, NCATE, NLN, CAAHEP, and CCNE. The 30-acre campus is in a suburban area 20 miles east of New York City. Including any residence halls, there are 6 buildings.

STUDENT LIFE: 98% of undergraduates are from New York. Others are from 20 states, and 9 foreign countries. 7% are Asian American; 63% White; 2% race unknown; 14% Hispanic; 12% African American; 1% two or more races. 61% are Catholic; 13% claim no religious affiliation. **Female To Male Ratio:** 3.2:1. The average age of freshmen is 18; all undergraduates, 24. 10% do not continue beyond their first year; 70% remain to graduate. **Housing:** 258 students can be accommodated in college housing, which includes coed dorms. Priority is given to out-of-town students. 92% of students commute. Alcohol is not permitted. All students may keep cars.

FACULTY/CLASSROOMS: 31% of faculty are male; 69% are female. No introductory courses are taught by graduate students. The average class size in an introductory lecture is 17; in a laboratory is 12; and in a regular course is 17.

PROGRAMS OF STUDY: Molloy confers B.A., B.S., B.F.A. and B.S.W degrees. Associate, master's, and doctoral degrees are also awarded. Bachelor's degrees are awarded in AGRICULTURE (environmental studies), BIOLOGICAL SCIENCE (biology/biological science), BUSINESS (accounting, business administration and management, finance, and marketing), COMMUNICATIONS AND THE ARTS (art, communications, English, music, Spanish and Hispanic studies, and theatre arts), COMPUTER AND PHYSICAL SCIENCE (computer information systems, computer science, and mathematics), EDUCATION (early childhood education and music education), ENGINEERING AND ENVIRONMENTAL DESIGN (nuclear medicine technology), HEALTH PROFESSIONS (health, music therapy, nursing, and speech pathology/audiology), SOCIAL SCIENCE (criminal justice, history, interdisciplinary studies, philosophy, political science/government, psychology, social work, sociology, and theology). Nursing, education, and business are the strongest academically and have the largest enrollments are the strongest academically.

ACTIVITIES: There are no fraternities or sororities. There are 60 groups on campus, including art, band, cheerleading, chess, chorus, dance, drama, ethnic, honors, international, jazz band, literary magazine, newspaper, professional, religious, social, social service, student government, and yearbook. Popular campus events include Scavenger Hunt, Halloween Party, Relay for Life, Safe Halloween, Hats and Stockings, Stuff a Bear, Maroon Madness, Santa's Workshop, and Bunny Brunch. **Sports:** There are 7 intercollegiate sports for men and 9 for women, and 3 intramural sports for men and 3 for women. Facilities include a gym, dance studio, weight room, sports fields, basketball and tennis courts. **Graduates:** From July 1, 2015 to June 30, 2016, 775 bachelor's degrees were awarded. The most popular majors were nursing (53%), education (10%), and business (7%). In an average class, 40% graduate in 4 years or less, 65% graduate in 5 years or less, and 70% graduate in 6 years or less.

SERVICES: Counseling and information services are available, as is tutoring in every subject. There is a reader service for the blind, and remedial math, reading, and writing. **Library/Resources:** The library contains 72,697 volumes, 427 microform items, 4,947 audio/video tapes/CDs/DVDs, and subscribes to 52,928 periodicals including electronic. Computerized library services include interlibrary loans, database searching, and Internet access. Special learning facilities include an art gallery. **Physically Challenged Students:** All of the campus is accessible. Facilities include wheelchair ramps, elevators, special parking, specially equipped restrooms, special class scheduling, lowered drinking fountains, and lowered telephones. **Special:** The college offers study abroad programs, dual degree programs, and other unique internship opportunities. There are 18 national honor societies and a freshman honors program. **Visiting:** There are regularly scheduled orientations for prospective students, including an address by the president of the college, department presentations, campus tours, admissions, financial aid, and scholarship information. There are guides for informal visits and visitors may sit in on classes. To schedule a visit, contact the Admissions Office. **Campus Safety and Security:** Measures include 24-hour foot and vehicle patrol, emergency notification system, and security escort services. There are shuttle buses, emergency telephones, lighted pathways/sidewalks, and campus concerns committee.

REQUIREMENTS: The SAT or ACT is required. The ACT Optional Writing test is also required. Applicants should be graduates of a secondary school or have a GED. Preparation should include 4 units of English and social studies, 3 units of math, science, foreign language and history. An essay is required and an interview is recommended. Music students must audition and take a theory exam. A GPA of 3.0 is required. AP and CLEP credits are accepted. Important factors in the admissions decision are advanced placement or honors courses, recommendations by school officials, and extracurricular activities record. General Education requirements consist of 45 to 54 credits. A total of 128 to 137 credit hours is required for graduation. **Procedure:** Freshmen are admitted fall and spring. Entrance exams should be taken in the fall of the senior year. There are early admissions, deferred admissions, and rolling admissions plans. Application deadlines are open. Application fee is $40. Notifications are sent October 15. Applications are accepted online. **Transfer Students:** 384 transfer students enrolled in 2015-2016. A minimum college GPA of 2.0 is required, with some majors requiring a higher GPA. An interview is recommended. 30 of 128 credits required for the bachelor's degree must be completed at Molloy. **International Students:** There are 8 international students enrolled. They must take the TOEFL with a minimum score of 500 on the paper-based TOEFL (PBT).

ADMISSIONS: 75% of the 2016-2017 applicants were accepted. The SAT scores for the 2016-2017 freshman class were: Critical Reading-- 29% below 500, 58% between 500 and 599, 11% between 600 and 699, and 2% between 700 and 800. Math-- 26% below 500, 53% between 500 and 599, 19% between 600 and 699, and 2% between 700 and 800. Writing-- 39% below 500, 45% between 500 and 599, 15% between 600 and 699, and 1% between 700 and 800. The ACT scores were 14% below 12, 34% between 12 and 17, 36% between 18 and 23, 10% between 24 and 29, and 6% above 30. **Admissions Contact:** Marguerite Lane, Dean of Admissions. Email: *mlane@molloy.edu* Web: *www.molloy.edu*

FINANCIAL AID: Molloy is a member of CSS. The FAFSA code is 002775. The priority date for freshman financial aid applications for fall entry is April 15. The filing deadline for fall entry is May 1.

MONROE COLLEGE — D-5

www.monroecollege.edu

Bronx, NY 10468 — **(718) 933-6700**, **(800) 55 MONROE**

Fax: (718) 364-3552 — **Email: admissions@monroecollege.edu**

Full-time: 1410 men, 3510 women	**Faculty:** III, -$
Part-time: 155 men, 405 women	**Ph.D.s:** n/av
Graduate: n/av	**Student/Faculty:** n/av
Year: varies, summer session	**Tuition:** $14,460
Room & Board: $9200	**Freshman Class:** n/av
SAT: recommended	**CEEB CODE:** 2462
Application Deadline: August 15	**COMPETITIVE**

Monroe College, founded in 1933, offers bachelor's degrees in accounting, business management, computer information systems, criminal justice, hospitality management, and health services administration. The figures in the above capsule and in this profile are approximate. There is 1 undergraduate school. The campus in the Fordham Road section of the Bronx. Including any residence halls, there are 5 buildings.

STUDENT LIFE: 96% of undergraduates are from New York. 46% are African American; 42% Hispanic; 2% White; 1% Asian American; 1% Foreign. **Female To Male Ratio:** 2.5:1. The average age of freshmen is 23; all undergraduates, 26. **Housing:** 620 students can be accommodated in college housing, which includes single-sex and coed dorms and off-campus apartments. In addition, there are honors houses. On-campus housing is guaranteed for all 4 years. 90% of students commute. All students may keep cars.

FACULTY/CLASSROOMS: All teach undergraduates. No introductory courses are taught by graduate students. The average class size in an introductory lecture is 30.

PROGRAMS OF STUDY: Monroe confers B.S. and B.B.A. degrees. Associate and master's degrees are also awarded. Bachelor's degrees are awarded in BUSINESS (accounting, business administration and management, and hospitality management services), COMPUTER AND PHYSICAL SCIENCE (information sciences and systems), HEALTH PROFESSIONS (health care administration), SOCIAL SCIENCE (criminal justice). Business management, criminal justuce, and health services administration have the largest enrollments.

ACTIVITIES: There are no fraternities or sororities. Groups on campus include cheerleading, computers, dance, drama, honors, literary magazine, newspaper, professional, and social service. Popular campus events include talent shows, President's and Deans' List galas and cultural trips to New York City. **Sports:** There is no sports program at Monroe.

SERVICES: Counseling and information services are available, as is tutoring in every subject. There is a reader service for the blind, as well as remedial math, reading, and writing. **Library/Resources:** Computerized library services include interlibrary loans, database searching, Internet access, and Wi-Fi capability. **Physically Challenged Students:** All of the campus is accessible. Facilities include wheelchair ramps, elevators, special parking, specially equipped restrooms, special class scheduling, lowered drinking fountains, lowered telephones, and special housing. **Special:** Co-op programs are available in all degree programs. Study abroad is available for culinary students interested in studying in Italy. There is 1 national honor society, a freshman honors program, and 1 departmental honors program. **Visiting:** There are regularly scheduled orientations for prospective students, including a variety of open houses during the semester in which applicants can tour the campus and talk with faculty and/pr chairs of individual departments. There are guides for informal visits, visitors may sit in on classes, and stay overnight. **Campus Safety and Security:** Measures include 24-hour foot and vehicle patrol, self-defense education, and security escort services. There are also shuttle buses, emergency telephones, and lighted pathways/sidewalks.

REQUIREMENTS: The SAT is recommended. An application, an essay, and interview are required. Monroe requires applicants to be in the upper 50% of their class. A GPA of 70.0 is required. AP and CLEP credits are accepted. To graduate, students must have 120 credit hours and at least a 2.0 GPA. The core curriculum includes courses in writing/literature, math, liberal arts, and business or technology. **Procedure:** Freshmen are admitted fall, winter, and spring. There are early decision and rolling admissions plans. Early decision applications should be filed by February 1; regular applications, by August 15 for fall entry; January 5 for winter entry; and April 15 for spring entry. The fall 2016 application fee was $35. **Transfer Students:** Transfer students must provide an official transcript from any prior institution they have attended in addition to the application and an essay. 30 of 120 credits required for the bachelor's degree must be completed at Monroe. **International Students:** The school actively recruits these students.

Admissions Contact: Evan Jerome, Director of Admissions. Email: *admissions@monroecollege.edu* Web: *www.monroecollege.edu*

FINANCIAL AID: The state aid form, and the college's own financial statement are required. The FAFSA code is 004799. Check with the school for current application deadlines.

MOUNT SAINT MARY COLLEGE — D-4

www.msmc.edu

Newburgh, NY 12550 — **(845) 569-3255**, **(888) YES-MSMC**

Fax: (845) 562-6762 — **Email: admissions@msmc.edu**

Full-time: 507 men, 1243 women	**Faculty:** 86; IIB, +$
Part-time: 96 men, 282 women	**Ph.D.s:** 91%
Graduate: 78 men, 262 women	**Student/Faculty:** 21 to 1
Year: semesters, summer session	**Tuition:** $28,233
Room & Board: $13,828	**Freshman Class:** 3747 applied, 3368 accepted, 387 enrolled
SAT or ACT: required	**CEEB CODE:** 2423
Application Deadline: August 15	**COMPETITIVE**

Mount Saint Mary College, founded in 1959, is a private liberal arts college offering undergraduate programs leading to Bachelor of Arts and Bachelor of Science degrees, and graduate programs leading to the masters in education, nursing, and business administration. An accelerated evening program is offered for nontraditional and adult students. Figures in the above capsule and in this profile are approximate. There are 3 undergraduate schools and 3 graduate schools. In addition to regional accreditation, the Mount has baccalaureate program accreditation with NCATE, CCNE, and IACBE. The 86-acre campus is in a suburban area 58 miles north of New York City. Including any residence halls, there are 41 buildings.

STUDENT LIFE: 89% of undergraduates are from New York. Others are from 14 states. 82% are from public schools. 53% are White; 20% race unknown; 16% Hispanic; 6% African American; 2% Asian American; 1% American Indian/Alaska Native; 1% Foreign; 1% two or more races. 67% are Baptist, Christian, Episcopalian, Lutheran and Methodist; 31% Catholic. **Female To Male Ratio:** 2.6:1. The average age of freshmen is 18; all undergraduates, 22. 25% do not continue beyond their first year; 54% remain to graduate. **Housing:** 1161 students can be accommodated in college housing, which includes single-sex and coed dorms. On-campus townhouses. On-campus housing is guaranteed for all 4 years. 53% of students commute. Upperclassmen may keep cars.

FACULTY/CLASSROOMS: 37% of faculty are male; 63% are female. 94% teach undergraduates. No introductory courses are taught by graduate students. The average class size in an introductory lecture is 19; in a laboratory is 10; and in a regular course is 19.

PROGRAMS OF STUDY: The Mount confers B.A., B.S. and B.S.Ed. degrees. Master's degrees are also awarded. Bachelor's degrees are awarded in BIOLOGICAL SCIENCE (biology/biological science), BUSINESS (accounting and business administration and management), COMMUNICATIONS AND THE ARTS (English, information technology, media arts, and public relations), COMPUTER AND PHYSICAL SCIENCE (chemistry, mathematics, and science), EDUCATION (education), HEALTH PROFESSIONS (nursing), SOCIAL SCIENCE (Hispanic American studies, history, history and political science, human services, interdisciplinary studies, political science/government, psychology, social science, and sociology). Education, nursing, and business are the strongest academically and have the largest enrollments.

ACTIVITIES: There are no fraternities or sororities. There are 38 groups on campus, including art, choir, computers, dance, drama, environmental, ethnic, honors, LGBT, literary magazine, musical theater, newspaper, photography, political, professional, radio and TV, religious, social, student government, and yearbook. Popular campus events include Spring Weekend, Siblings Weekend and Holiday Formal. **Sports:** There are 10 intercollegiate sports for men and 11 for women, and 10 intramural sports for men and 10 for women. Facilities include a recreation center with basketball courts, running track, cardiovascular room, weight room, aerobics studio, indoor swimming pool, multipurpose room, all-weather, synthetic turf field, a natural grass field, and tennis courts. **Graduates:** From July 1, 2015 to June 30, 2016, 484 bachelor's degrees were awarded. The most popular majors were nursing (28%), business (20%), and psychology (13%). 60 companies recruited on campus in 2015-2016. In an average class, 1% graduate in 3 years or less, 42% graduate in 4 years or less, 52% graduate in 5 years or less, and 54% graduate in 6 years or less. Of the 2015 graduating class, 35% were enrolled in graduate school within 6 months of graduation, and 91% were employed.

SERVICES: Counseling and information services are available, as is tutoring in every subject, and remedial math, reading, and writing. **Library/Resources:** The library contains 86,692 volumes, and 6,650 audio/video tapes/CDs/DVDs, and subscribes to 62,162 periodicals including electronic. Computerized library services include interlibrary loans, database searching, Internet access, and Wi-Fi capability. Special learning facilities include a radio station, elementary school, herbarium field station, and an arboretum. **Physically Challenged Students:** 95% of the campus is accessible. Facilities include wheelchair ramps, elevators, special parking, specially equipped restrooms, and lowered telephones. Special equipment in the library and computer centers to accommodate students with low vision. **Special:** Co-op programs and internships are available in all majors. There is cross-registration with other mid-Hudson area colleges, as well as accelerated degree programs in business, accounting, and nursing, among others. There are several collaborative programs. The college also offers study abroad in more than 22 countries, a Washington semester, work-study, and dual and student-designed majors. Credit by exam and for life, military, and work experience is available for a maximum of 30 credits. There are 13 national honor societies and a freshman honors program. **Visiting:** There are regularly scheduled orientations for prospective students, including 4 open houses per year, a summer orientation program, and the Spend a Day with a Current Student program in the spring. There are guides for informal visits, visitors may sit in on classes, and stay overnight. To schedule a visit, contact the Admissions Office. **Campus Safety and Security:** Measures include 24-hour foot and vehicle patrol, emergency notification system, self-defense education, and security escort services. There are also shuttle buses, emergency telephones, lighted pathways/sidewalks, and controlled access to dorms/residences.

REQUIREMENTS: The SAT or ACT is required. Students should be graduates of an accredited secondary school. The GED is accepted. Applicants should prepare with 4 years each of English and history, and at least 3 each of math and science and 2 of foreign language. An essay and an interview are recommended. AP and CLEP credits are accepted. Important factors in the admissions decision are advanced placement or honors courses, evidence of special talent, and personality/intangible qualities. A total of 120 credit hours is required for the B.A. or B.S., with 24 to 40 in the major and a minimum GPA of 2.0. Overall requirements are higher for nursing, medical technology, and education students. All students must achieve computer literacy before graduation. **Procedure:** Freshmen are admitted to all sessions. Entrance exams should be taken by the junior year. There are deferred admissions and rolling admissions plans. Applications should be filed by August 15 for fall entry, along with a $45 fee. Notification is sent on a rolling basis. Application fees are waived if application is completed online. **Transfer Students:** 212 transfer students enrolled in 2015-2016. Applicants must have a GPA of at least 2.0 in all college work. The SAT or ACT, and an interview are recommended. 30 of 120 credits required for the bachelor's degree must be completed at the Mount. **International Students:** There are 10 international students enrolled. The school actively recruits these students. They must take the TOEFL with a minimum score of 550 on the paper-based TOEFL (PBT) or 80 on the Internet-based version (iBT). They must also take the SAT or ACT, and the college's own entrance exam. Freshman's are required to take the standard placement test.

ADMISSIONS: 90% of the 2016-2017 applicants were accepted. 25% of the current freshmen were in the top fifth of their class; 61% were in the top two fifths. **Admissions Contact:** Nancy Scaffidi, Director of Admissions. Email: *nancy.scaffidi@msmc.edu* Web: *www.msmc.edu*

FINANCIAL AID: In 2016-2017, 99% of all full-time freshmen and 95% of continuing full-time students received some form of financial aid. 86% of all full-time freshmen and 84% of continuing full-time students received need-based aid. The average freshman award was $25,691. Need-based scholarships or need-based grants averaged $8,907 ($48,939 maximum); need-based self-help aid (loans and jobs) averaged $7,613 ($37,129 maximum); and other non-need-based awards and non-need-based scholarships averaged $13,798 ($46,229 maximum). 13% of undergraduate students work part-time. Average annual earnings from campus work are $1132. The average financial indebtedness of the 2016 graduate was $26,773. The FAFSA code is 002778. The priority date for freshman financial aid applications for fall entry is February 15. The filing deadline for fall entry is March 15.

NAZARETH COLLEGE — B-3

ww.naz.edu

Rochester, NY 14618	**(585) 389-2860** **(800) 462-3944**
Fax: (585) 389-2826	**Email: admissions@naz.edu**
Full-time: 511 men, 1390 women	**Faculty:** 163; IIA, av$
Part-time: 37 men, 96 women	**Ph.D.s:** 73%
Graduate: 168 men, 621 women	**Student/Faculty:** 12 to 1
Year: semesters, summer session	**Tuition:** $32,424
Room & Board: $13,150	**Freshman Class:** 3838 applied, 2625 accepted, 423 enrolled
SAT CR/M/W: 540/540/520 **ACT:** required	**CEEB CODE:** 2511
Application Deadline: February 1	**COMPETITIVE**

Nazareth College, founded in 1924, is an independent institution offering programs in the liberal arts and sciences and preprofessional areas. Figures in the above capsule and in this profile are approximate. There are 4 undergraduate schools and 4 graduate schools. In addition to regional accreditation, Nazareth has baccalaureate program accreditation with CSWE, NASM, TEAC, ACS, CCNE, and IACBE. The 150-acre campus is in a suburban area in Pittsburgh, a suburb of Rochester. Including any residence halls, there are 29 buildings.

STUDENT LIFE: 93% of undergraduates are from New York. Others are

from 27 states, 22 foreign countries, and Canada. 88% are from public schools. 72% are White; 13% race unknown; 5% African American; 4% Hispanic; 2% Asian American; 2% Foreign; 1% American Indian/Alaska Native; 1% two or more races. **Female To Male Ratio:** 2.9:1. The average age of freshmen is 18; all undergraduates, 21. 21% do not continue beyond their first year; 68% remain to graduate. **Housing:** 1232 students can be accommodated in college housing, which includes single-sex and coed dorms and on-campus apartments. In addition, there are language houses, special-interest houses, substance-free floors, freshman experience floors, and honors floors. On-campus housing is guaranteed for all 4 years. 53% of students live on campus; of those, 88% remain on campus on weekends. All students may keep cars.

FACULTY/CLASSROOMS: 37% of faculty are male; 63% are female. 93% teach undergraduates. No introductory courses are taught by graduate students. The average class size in an introductory lecture is 21; in a laboratory is 11; and in a regular course is 19.

PROGRAMS OF STUDY: Nazareth confers B.A., B.S., B.F.A. and B.Mus. degrees. Master's and doctoral degrees are also awarded. Bachelor's degrees are awarded in BIOLOGICAL SCIENCE (biochemistry, biology/adolescence education, biology/biological science, and toxicology), BUSINESS (accounting, business administration and management, finance, international business management, and marketing and distribution), COMMUNICATIONS AND THE ARTS (art history, art, Chinese, communication rhetoric/communication, English, fine arts, French, German, information technology, Italian, literature, music, music business management, music history and appreciation, music performance, music theory and composition, musical theater, Spanish, studio art, theatre arts, and visual design), COMPUTER AND PHYSICAL SCIENCE (chemistry, chemistry/adolescence education, and mathematics), EDUCATION (art education, Asian studies, business education, elementary education, English education, foreign languages education, mathematics education, middle school education, music education, psychology education, social science education, and Spanish adolescense education), ENGINEERING AND ENVIRONMENTAL DESIGN (environmental science), HEALTH PROFESSIONS (health science, music therapy, nursing, and speech pathology/audiology), SOCIAL SCIENCE (American studies, anthropology, communication sciences & disorders, economics, history, international studies, legal studies, peace studies, philosophy, political science/government, psychology, religion, social science, social work, sociology, and women's studies). Physical therapy, and history are the strongest academically. Physical therapy, nursing, and business have the largest enrollments.

ACTIVITIES: There are no fraternities or sororities. There are 48 groups on campus, including art, band, choir, chorale, chorus, communications, computers, dance, drama, ethnic, honors, international, jazz band, LGBT, literary magazine, musical theater, newspaper, opera, orchestra, political, professional, religious, social, student government, and yearbook. Popular campus events include Springfest and Siblings Weekend, Welcome Week, Battle of the Beaks, and Family Weekend. **Sports:** There is no sports program at Nazareth. Facilities include a gym, swimming pool, soccer and lacrosse fields, outdoor turf field, tennis and racquetball courts, fitness center, sauna, stadium, and a all-weather track. **Graduates:** From July 1, 2015 to June 30, 2016, 520 bachelor's degrees were awarded. The most popular majors were education (17%), health (17%), and business (10%). 36 companies recruited on campus in 2015-2016. In an average class, 59% graduate in 4 years or less, 67% graduate in 5 years or less, and 68% graduate in 6 years or less. Of the 2015 graduating class, 49% were enrolled in graduate school within 6 months of graduation, and 72% were employed.

SERVICES: Counseling and information services are available, as is tutoring in every subject. **Library/Resources:** The library contains 237,203 volumes, 470,000 microform items, 181,114 audio/video tapes/CDs/DVDs, and subscribes to 86,321 periodicals including electronic. Computerized library services include interlibrary loans, database searching, Internet access, and Wi-Fi capability. Special learning facilities include an art gallery. **Physically Challenged Students:** 80% of the campus is accessible. Facilities include wheelchair ramps, elevators, special parking, specially equipped restrooms, special class scheduling, lowered drinking fountains, and special housing. **Special:** Nazareth offers cross-registration with members of the Rochester Area College Consortium (about 15 colleges participate in this program). Full-time students can register for courses at any of these institutions. Internships are available in any of our academic programs and are arranged through the student's academic adviser and Director of Internships. Nazareth participates in the Washington and Albany internship programs. There is study abroad in France, Spain, Italy, and Germany, and there are exchange programs in Australia, Japan, Italy, France, Peru, United Kingdom, Hungary, Wales. There are 25 national honor societies, a freshman honors program, and 13 departmental honors programs. **Visiting:** There are regularly scheduled orientations for prospective students, including individual appointments, group sessions, campus tours, open houses, and summer academic orientation. There are guides for informal visits, visitors may sit in on classes, and stay overnight. To schedule a visit, contact the Admissions Office. **Campus Safety and Security:** Measures include 24-hour foot and vehicle patrol, emergency notification system, and security escort services. There are also shuttle buses, emergency telephones, lighted pathways/sidewalks, controlled access to dorms/residences, an alarm system, and security beepers free to all students.

REQUIREMENTS: Applicants should graduate from an accredited secondary school or have a GED. A minimum of 16 academic credits is required, including 4 years of English and 3 each of social studies, foreign language, math, and science. An essay is required, as is an audition for music and theater students and a portfolio for art students. An interview is recommended. Nazareth requires applicants to be in the upper 50% of their class. A GPA of 2.8 is required. AP and CLEP credits are accepted. Important factors in the admissions decision are geographical diversity, advanced placement or honors courses, and evidence of special talent. Nazareth's new Core Curriculum is all about integration integrating the various ways that different disciplines explore Enduring Questions, engaging in three Integrative Studies courses that help you explore a question of your own, and participating in an Experiential Learning Pathway that helps you integrate what you have learned in the classroom with what is happening in the world. Additional requirements vary by major program. A total of 120 credit hours are required to graduate, with a minimum GPA of 2.0. **Procedure:** Freshmen are admitted fall and spring. Entrance exams should be taken by December of the senior year. There are early decision, early admissions, and deferred admissions plans. Early decision applications should be filed by November 1; regular applications, by February 1 for fall entry; and November 1 for spring entry, along with a $45 fee. Notification of early decision is sent December 1; regular decision, March 1. 59 early decision candidates were accepted for the 2016-2017 class. 58 applicants were on the 2016 waiting list; 6 were admitted. Applications are accepted online. **Transfer Students:** 168 transfer students enrolled in 2015-2016. Applicants must have a college GPA of 2.5 (2.75 for education and physical therapy students). Those with fewer than 30 credits must submit high school transcripts. 30 of 120 credits required for the bachelor's degree must be completed at Nazareth. **International Students:** There are 62 international students enrolled. The school actively recruits these students. They must take the TOEFL with a minimum score of 550 on the paper-based TOEFL (PBT) or 79 on the Internet-based version (iBT).

ADMISSIONS: 68% of the 2016-2017 applicants were accepted. The SAT scores for the 2016-2017 freshman class were: Critical Reading-- 29% below 500, 49% between 500 and 599, 20% between 600 and 699, and 2% between 700 and 800. Math-- 24% below 500, 49% between 500 and 599, 23% between 600 and 699, and 4% between 700 and 800. Writing-- 33% below 500, 45% between 500 and 599, 19% between 600 and 699, and 3% between 700 and 800. The ACT scores were 15% below 12, 26% between 12 and 17, 31% between 18 and 23, 14% between 24 and 29, and 14% above 30. 55% of the current freshmen were in the top fifth of their class; 81% were in the top two fifths. 6 freshmen graduated first in their class. **Admissions Contact:** Ian Mortimer, Vice President of Enrollment Management. Email: *admissions@naz.edu* Web: *ww.naz.edu*

FINANCIAL AID: In 2016-2017, 100% of all full-time freshmen and 99% of continuing full-time students received some form of financial aid. 81% of all full-time freshmen and continuing full-time students received need-based aid. The average freshman award was $25,702. Need-based scholarships or need-based grants averaged $17,253; need-based self-help aid (loans and jobs) averaged $4,991; and other non-need-based awards and non-need-based scholarships averaged $18,469. 25% of undergraduate students work part-time. Average annual earnings from campus work are $1009. The average financial indebtedness of the 2016 graduate was $28,938. Nazareth is a member of CSS. The FAFSA code is 002779. The priority date for freshman financial aid applications for fall entry is February 1.

NEW YORK INSTITUTE OF TECHNOLOGY D-5

www.nyit.edu

Old Westbury, NY 11568	(516) 686-1000 (800) 345-NYIT
Fax: (516) 686-7613	Email: admissions@nyit.edu
Full-time: 2092 men, 1167 women	Faculty: IIA, ++$
Part-time: 230 men, 121 women	Ph.D.s: 90%
Graduate: 2048 men, 2006 women	Student/Faculty: 14 to 1
Year: semesters, summer session	Tuition: $35,160
Room & Board: $13,570	Freshman Class: 10087 applied, 7317 accepted, 715 enrolled
SAT or ACT: required	CEEB CODE: 2561
Application Deadline: rolling	COMPETITIVE

New York Institute of Technology, is a global, non-profit, independent private institution of higher education, NYIT offers 90 degree programs, including undergraduate, graduate, and professional degrees, in more than 50 fields of study, including architecture and design, arts and sciences, education, engineering and computing sciences, health professions, management, and osteopathic medicine. There are 5 undergraduate schools and 2 graduate schools. In addition to regional accreditation, NYIT has baccalaureate program accreditation with AACSB, ABET, NAAB, CCNE, and CIDA. The 215-acre campus is in a suburban area 25 miles east of New York City (Old Westbury); NYIT also operates a campus in Manhattan. Including any residence halls, there are 57 buildings.

STUDENT LIFE: 90% of undergraduates are from New York. Others are from 50 states, 125 foreign countries, and Canada. 9% are Hispanic; 6% African American; 28% Foreign; 27% White; 2% two or more races; 16% Asian American; 13% race unknown. **Male To Female Ratio:** 1.3:1. The average age of freshmen is 18; all undergraduates, 22. **Housing:** 635 students can be accommodated in college housing, which includes coed dorms. On-campus housing is available on a first-come and first-served basis. 79% of students commute. Alcohol is not permitted. All students may keep cars.

FACULTY/CLASSROOMS: 62% of faculty are male; 38% are female. No introductory courses are taught by graduate students.

PROGRAMS OF STUDY: NYIT confers B.A., B.S., B.Arch., B.F.A. and B.P.S. degrees. Associate, master's, and doctoral degrees are also awarded. Bachelor's degrees are awarded in BIOLOGICAL SCIENCE (biotechnology and life science), BUSINESS (accounting, business administration and management, entrepreneurial studies, finance, hospitality management services, human resources/organizational mgmt, international business management, marketing management, and urban administration), COMMUNICATIONS AND THE ARTS (advertising, communications, English, film, television and digital media, graphic design, journalism, and telecommunications), COMPUTER AND PHYSICAL SCIENCE (chemistry, computer information technology, and computer science), ENGINEERING AND ENVIRONMENTAL DESIGN (architectural technology, architecture, computer graphics, construction management, electrical and computer engineering, electrical/electronics engineering technology, engineering management, interior design, and mechanical engineering), HEALTH PROFESSIONS (biology, health, health science, and nursing), SOCIAL SCIENCE (behavioral science, criminal justice, interdisciplinary studies, political science/government, psychology, social work, and sociology). Computer science, electrical and computer engineering, and achitectural technology have the largest enrollments.

ACTIVITIES: 3% of men belong to 1 local and 6 national fraternities; 4% of women belong to 1 local and 3 national sororities. There are 50 groups on campus, including art, cheerleading, computers, dance, drama, environmental, ethnic, film, honors, international, newspaper, political, professional, radio and TV, religious, social, social service, and student government. Popular campus events include May Fest, Relay for Life, Greek Week, and Welcome Week. **Sports:** There are 6 intercollegiate sports for men and 7 for women, and 7 intramural sports for men and 8 for women. Facilities include a recreation center, a weight room, basketball gymnasium, and outdoor tennis and basketball courts, softball, lacrosse, baseball, and soccer fields. **Graduates:** From July 1, 2015 to June 30, 2016, 993 bachelor's degrees were awarded. The most popular majors were business administration (14%), electrical and computer engineering (13%), and computer science (11%). In an average class, 25% graduate in 4 years or less, 42% graduate in 5 years or less, and 46% graduate in 6 years or less. Of the 2015 graduating class, 96% were employed within 6 months of graduation.

SERVICES: Counseling and information services are available, as is tutoring in every subject. There is remedial math, reading, and writing. **Library/Resources:** The 4 libraries contain 242,208 volumes. Computerized library services include interlibrary loans, database searching, Internet access, and Wi-Fi capability. Special learning facilities include an art gallery, radio station, TV station, motion capture lab, School of Management Simulated Trading Floor (Manhattan Campus), NYIT Auditorium on Broadway, and the Entrepreneurship and Technology Innovation Center. **Physically Challenged Students:** All of the campus is accessible. Facilities include wheelchair ramps, elevators, special parking, specially equipped restrooms, and lowered drinking fountains. **Special:** NYIT offers a semester-long study abroad programs at its campuses in Nanjing, China, Abu Dhabi, United Arab Emirates, and Vancouver, Canada. Additionally, NYIT offers semester-long exchange programs at IT University of Copenhagen, Rotterdam University (University of Applied Sciences), and Communication University of China. Other study abroad programs are available. NYIT offers the following combined programs: B.S. Life Sciences/M.S. Occupational Therapy, B.S. Life Sciences/M.S. Physician Assistant Studies, B.S. Life Sciences/Doctor of Physical Therapy, B.S. Life Sciences/Doctor of Osteopathic Medicine, B.F.A./M.A. Communication Arts, B.S./M.B.A. Accounting – CPA Track, B.S. Psychology/M.S. School Counseling. There are 14 national honor societies and 1 departmental honors program. **Visiting:** There are regularly scheduled orientations for prospective students. A number of of admissions events are held throughout the year, including fall open house, spring preview days, student for a day events, and transfer and graduate information sessions. There are guides for informal visits and visitors may sit in on classes. To schedule a visit, contact Office of Admissions. **Campus Safety and Security:** Measures include 24-hour foot and vehicle patrol, emergency notification system, and security escort services. There are shuttle buses, emergency telephones, lighted pathways/sidewalks, controlled access to dorms/residences, NYIT Alerts, and a mass text and voice messaging notification system for emergency communications and student outreach.

REQUIREMENTS: The SAT or ACT is required. Completed application for admission and $50 application fee, an essay, transcripts of all high school and previous college work, SAT or ACT scores, and two letters of recommendation. There are additional requirements for admission to the School of Architecture and Design, School of Engineering and Computing Sciences, School of Health Professions, and the B.F.A. program. AP and CLEP credits are accepted. All students take courses in NYIT's Discovery Core Curriculum, which is designed to build core competencies in the following areas: Interdisciplinary Mindset and Skills, Global Perspective/Worldview, Literacy, Ethical and Civic Engagement, Process and Nature of Science and the Arts, Critical/Analytical Thinking, and Communication. **Procedure:** Freshmen are admitted fall, spring, and summer. There are deferred admissions and rolling admissions plans. Application deadlines are open. Application fee is $50. Notification is sent on a rolling basis. Applications are accepted online. **Transfer Students:** 335 transfer students enrolled in 2015-2016. Completed application for admission and $50 application fee; official transcript(s) from all colleges attended (if less than 24 credits of college coursework have been completed, official high school transcript(s) and SAT or ACT exam scores are required); GPA, essay, and letters of recommendation are recommended and may be required for admission to specific programs. 30 of 120 credits required for the bachelor's degree must be completed at NYIT. **International Students:** There are 483 international students enrolled. The school actively recruits these students. They must take the TOEFL with a minimum score of 550 on the paper-based TOEFL (PBT) or 79 on the Internet-based version (iBT), or take the IELTS. They must also take the SAT or ACT.

ADMISSIONS: 73% of the 2016-2017 applicants were accepted. The SAT scores for the 2016-2017 freshman class were: Critical Reading-- 37% below 500, 46% between 500 and 599, 15% between 600 and 699, and 2% between 700 and 800. Math-- 21% below 500, 48% between 500 and 599, 25% between 600 and 699, and 7% between 700 and 800. The ACT scores were 1% between 12 and 17, 37% between 18 and 23, 50% between 24 and 29, and 12% above 30. **Admissions Contact:** Admissions Officer Email: *admissions@nyit.edu* Web: *www.nyit.edu*

FINANCIAL AID: In 2016-2017, 95% of all full-time freshmen and 84% of continuing full-time students received some form of financial aid. 81% of all full-time freshmen and 69% of continuing full-time students

received need-based aid. The average freshman award was $24,776. Need-based scholarships or need-based grants averaged $10,368; need-based self-help aid (loans and jobs) averaged $3,392; non-need-based athletic scholarships averaged $12,204; and other non-need-based awards and non-need-based scholarships averaged $13,307. The state aid form, and New York State residents submit Tuition Assistance Program (TAP) form are required. The FAFSA code is 002782. The priority date for freshman financial aid applications for fall entry is March 1.

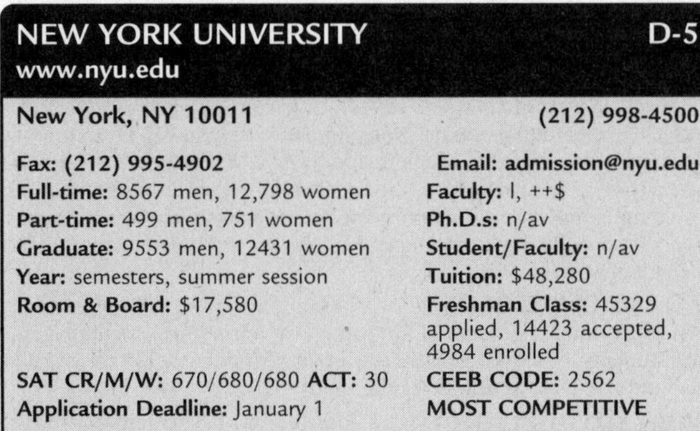

NEW YORK UNIVERSITY D-5

www.nyu.edu

New York, NY 10011 (212) 998-4500

Fax: (212) 995-4902	**Email:** admission@nyu.edu
Full-time: 8567 men, 12,798 women	**Faculty:** I, ++$
Part-time: 499 men, 751 women	**Ph.D.s:** n/av
Graduate: 9553 men, 12431 women	**Student/Faculty:** n/av
Year: semesters, summer session	**Tuition:** $48,280
Room & Board: $17,580	**Freshman Class:** 45329 applied, 14423 accepted, 4984 enrolled
SAT CR/M/W: 670/680/680 **ACT:** 30	**CEEB CODE:** 2562
Application Deadline: January 1	**MOST COMPETITIVE**

New York University, founded in 1831, is the largest private university in the United States. NYU, which is composed of 18 schools, colleges, and divisions, occupies 5 major centers in Manhattan and operates branch campus and research programs in other parts of the United States and abroad. In addition to its Manhattan locations, the University is also formally affiliated the Polytechnic Institute of NYU in Brooklyn, the second oldest school of engineering and technology in the country, and has research facilities, notably the Nelson Institute of Environmental Medicine, in Sterling Forest, near Tuxedo, New York. There are 5 undergraduate schools and 11 graduate schools. In addition to regional accreditation, NYU has baccalaureate program accreditation with AACSB, ACEJMC, ADA, CSWE, NLN, ACS, and APA. The campus is in an urban area in New York City's Greenwich Village. Including any residence halls, there are 82 buildings.

STUDENT LIFE: 70% of undergraduates are from out of state, mostly the Northeast. Students are from 50 states, 144 foreign countries, and Canada. 5% are African American; 39% White; 3% two or more races; 18% Asian American; 14% Foreign; 11% race unknown; 10% Hispanic. **Female To Male Ratio:** 1.4:1. The average age of freshmen is 18; all undergraduates, 21. 8% do not continue beyond their first year; 84% remain to graduate. **Housing:** 10774 students can be accommodated in college housing, which includes coed dorms and on-campus apartments. In addition, there are special-interest houses, fraternity houses, SAFE (Substance and Alcohol-Free Environment), First Year Residential Experience, Sophomore Residential Experience, and Explorations Learning Communities. On-campus housing is guaranteed for all 4 years. 52% of students commute. All students may keep cars.

FACULTY/CLASSROOMS: No introductory courses are taught by graduate students.

PROGRAMS OF STUDY: NYU confers B.A., B.S., B.F.A., B.S.B.E. and Mus.B. degrees. Associate, master's, and doctoral degrees are also awarded. Bachelor's degrees are awarded in AGRICULTURE (environmental studies), BIOLOGICAL SCIENCE (biochemistry, biology/biological science, cell biology, microbiology, neurosciences, and nutrition), BUSINESS (accounting, banking and finance, business administration and management, business economics, business law, finance, hotel/motel and restaurant management, human resources, industrial and labor relations, international business management, management information systems, management science, marketing management, marketing/retailing/merchandising, operations management, operations research, organizational behavior, property management, real estate, recreation and leisure services, and sports management), COMMUNICATIONS AND THE ARTS (Africana studies, American literature, animation, Arabic, art history, art history and appreciation, arts administration/management, classical languages, classics, communications, communications technology, comparative literature, creative writing, dance, design, digital communications, dramatic arts, English, English literature, film arts, fine arts, French, German, Germanic languages and literature, graphic design, Greek, Greek (classical), Greek (modern), Hebrew, information technology, instrumental performance, Italian, journalism, languages, Latin, linguistics, literature, media arts, music, music business management, music composition, music performance, music technology, music theory and composition, performing arts, photography, piano performance, Portuguese, public relations, publishing, radio/television technology, romance languages and literature, Russian, Slavic languages, Spanish, speech/debate/rhetoric, studio art, technical and business writing, theater management, vocal performance, voice, and writing), COMPUTER AND PHYSICAL SCIENCE (actuarial science, chemistry, computer engineering technology, computer mathematics, computer science, digital arts/technology, earth science, information sciences and systems, mathematics, mathematics – economics, physics, and statistics), EDUCATION (art education, Asian studies, bilingual/bicultural education, childhood education, dance education, early childhood education, education, elementary education, English education, foreign languages education, general studies, global studies, mathematics education, music education, nursing education, school psychology, science education, secondary education, social science education, social studies education, social studies secondary school education, special education, and speech correction), ENGINEERING AND ENVIRONMENTAL DESIGN (biomedical engineering, chemical engineering, civil engineering, computational sciences, computer engineering, construction management, electrical and computer engineering, electrical/electronics engineering, engineering, engineering chemistry, engineering mechanics, engineering physics, graphic arts technology, mechanical engineering, and urban design), HEALTH PROFESSIONS (art therapy, dental hygiene, environmental health science, health care administration, music therapy, nursing, nursing home administration, occupational therapy, pharmacology, physical therapy, pre-health studies, predentistry, premedicine, public health, and speech pathology/audiology), SOCIAL SCIENCE (African studies, African American studies, American studies, anthropology, applied psychology, architectural studies, area studies, Asian/American studies, Asian/Oriental studies, child care/child and family studies, classical/ancient civilization, counseling/psychology, developmental psychology, early childhood studies, East Asian studies, economics, ethnic studies, European studies, French studies, gender studies, history, humanities, humanities and social science, Iberian studies, international relations, Islamic studies, Italian studies, Japanese studies, Judaic studies, Latin American studies, law, Luso-Brazilian studies, medieval studies, Middle Eastern studies, Pacific area studies, philosophy, philosophy and religion, political science/government, psychology, public administration, religion, religious studies, Russian and Slavic studies, social science, social studies, social work, sociology, and urban studies). Business, individualized major, and theatre have the largest enrollments.

ACTIVITIES: 7% of men belong to 19 national fraternities; 5% of women belong to 12 national sororities. Groups on campus include art, bagpipe, band, cheerleading, chess, choir, chorale, chorus, computers, dance, debate, drama, environmental, ethnic, film, forensics, honors, international, jazz band, LGBT, literary magazine, marching band, musical theater, newspaper, opera, orchestra, pep band, photography, political, professional, radio and TV, religious, social, social service, student government, and symphony. Popular campus events include Spring Strawberry Festival, Grad Alley, and Career Services Fair. **Sports:** There are 10 intercollegiate sports for men and 9 for women, and 9 intramural sports for men and 9 for women. Facilities include sports and recreation facilities that house basketball, volleyball, tennis, badminton, squash, handball and racquetball courts, rooftop tennis courts, and running track, a swimming pool, a diving tank, weight-training facilities, aerobic fitness room, wrestling, judo, fencing, physical fitness, dance, and a rock-climbing wall. **Graduates:** From July 1, 2015 to June 30, 2016, 6310 bachelor's degrees were awarded. The most popular majors were social science (38%), visual and performing arts (16%), culture, education, and human development (12%). 800 companies recruited on campus in 2015-2016. In an average class, 77% graduate in 4 years or less, 82% graduate in 5 years or less, and 84% graduate in 6 years or less.

SERVICES: Counseling and information services are available, as is tutoring in every subject. There is a reader service for the blind. Sign language interpreters, scribes, research aides, and note takers for special needs. **Library/Resources:** Computerized library services include interlibrary loans, database searching, Internet access, and Wi-Fi capability. Special learning facilities include an art gallery, radio station, TV station, a speech-language-hearing clinic, a center for students with disabilities, and speaking freely (free noncredit foreign language classes). **Physically Challenged Students:** 95% of the campus is accessible. Facilities include wheelchair ramps, elevators, specially equipped restrooms, special class scheduling, lowered drinking fountains, lowered telephones, special housing, buses with hydraulic lifts, adaptive computer equipment, CART or C-print services, a CTV enlargement system, a JAWS speech synthesizer, Dragon Dictate Voice Recognition, and Kurzweil Personal Readers. **Special:** A vast array of internships is available, as well as study worldwide at NYU's 10 sites: Berlin, Buenos Aires, Florence, Ghana, London, Madrid, Paris, Prague, Shanghai, and Tel Aviv. B.A.-B.S. degree options, accelerated degrees in more than 230 majors, dual and student-designed majors, credit by exam, and pass/fail options are also available. A Washington semester is available to political science majors. There are exchange programs with several historically black colleges. There is a chapter of Phi Beta Kappa and a freshman honors program. **Visiting:** There are regularly scheduled orientations for prospective students, including campus tours and weekday information sessions by appointment. There are also 2 fall open houses. To schedule a visit, contact the Office of Undergraduate Admissions. **Campus Safety and Security:** Measures include 24-hour foot and vehicle patrol, emergency notification system, self-defense education, and security escort services. There are also shuttle buses, emergency telephones, lighted pathways/sidewalks, 24-hour security in residence halls, and a neighborhood-merchant emergency help service.

REQUIREMENTS: The SAT or ACT is required. The ACT Optional Writing test is also required. Applicants must graduate from an accredited secondary school. The GED is accepted. Students must present at least 16 Carnegie units, including 4 in English. Some majors require an audition or submission of a creative portfolio. All applicants must submit an essay and 2 letters of recommendation. Applicants can submit the SAT and 2 SAT: Subject tests; the ACT with Writing; the SAT and 2 Advanced Placement (AP) exam scores; 3 SAT: Subject tests (1 in literature or the humanities, 1 in math/science, and 1 in any non-language area); or 3 AP exam scores (1 in literature/humanities, 1 in math/science, and 1 in any nonlanguge area). AP credits are accepted. All students must complete a minimum of 128 credit hours and maintain a minimum GPA of 2.0. A course in expository writing is required. Students must complete a core liberal arts curriculum in addition to major and elective credit. **Procedure:** Freshmen are admitted fall and spring. Entrance exams should be taken by November of the senior year. There is a early decision plan. Early decision applications should be filed by November 1; regular applications, by January 1 for fall entry, along with a $70 fee. Notification of early decision is sent December 15; regular decision, April 1. 1967 early decision candidates were accepted for the 2016-2017 class. Applications are accepted online. **Transfer Students:** 607 transfer students enrolled in 2015-2016. Students must submit official college transcripts from all postsecondary institutions attended, a final high school transcript, and SAT scores. 64 of 128 credits required for the bachelor's degree must be completed at NYU. **International Students:** There are 3024 international students enrolled. The school actively recruits these students. They must take the TOEFL and the college's own test, or take the IELTS or have ESL testing. They must also take the SAT or ACT.

ADMISSIONS: 32% of the 2016-2017 applicants were accepted. The SAT scores for the 2016-2017 freshman class were: Critical Reading-- 1% below 500, 14% between 500 and 599, 50% between 600 and 699, and 35% between 700 and 800. Math-- 1% below 500, 13% between 500 and 599, 43% between 600 and 699, and 43% between 700 and 800. Writing-- 1% below 500, 10% between 500 and 599, 47% between 600 and 699, and 42% between 700 and 800. The ACT scores were 1% between 12 and 17, 10% between 18 and 23, 18% between 24 and 29, and 71% above 30. **Admissions Contact:** Joey Schmit, Director Marketing & Communications. Email: *admission@nyu.edu* Web: *www.nyu.edu*

FINANCIAL AID: The CSS/Profile and the state aid form are required. The FAFSA code is 002785. The deadline for filing freshman financial aid applications for fall entry is February 15.

NIAGARA UNIVERSITY A-3

www.niagara.edu

Niagara University, NY 14109	**(716) 286-8700** **(800) 462-2111**
Fax: (716) 286-8710	**Email: admissions@niagara.edu**
Full-time: 1153 men, 1680 women	**Faculty:** 140; IIA, av$
Part-time: 88 men, 255 women	**Ph.D.s:** n/av
Graduate: 293 men, 604 women	**Student/Faculty:** 18 to 1
Year: semesters, summer session	**Tuition:** $29,060
Room & Board: $11,950	**Freshman Class:** 3565 applied, 2348 accepted, 616 enrolled
SAT CR/M/W: 510/530/500 **ACT:** 23	**CEEB CODE:** 2558
Application Deadline: n/av	**COMPETITIVE**

Niagara University, founded in 1856 by the Vincentian fathers and brothers, is a private institution rooted in a Roman Catholic tradition. Programs offered include those in liberal arts, business, education, nursing, and travel, hotel, and restaurant administration. There are 4 undergraduate schools and 4 graduate schools. In addition to regional accreditation, Niagara has baccalaureate program accreditation with AACSB, CSWE, NCATE, ACPHA, ACS, and CCNE. The 160-acre campus is in a suburban area 4 miles north of Niagara Falls, 20 miles north of Buffalo, 90 miles from Toronto, Canada. Including any residence halls, there are 32 buildings.

STUDENT LIFE: 78% of undergraduates are from New York. Others are from 32 states, 26 foreign countries, and Canada. 71% are White. 31% are Catholic. **Female To Male Ratio:** 1.7:1. The average age of freshmen is 18; all undergraduates, 21. 16% do not continue beyond their first year; 64% remain to graduate. **Housing:** 1455 students can be accommodated in college housing, which includes single-sex and coed dorms and on-campus apartments. In addition, there are special-interest houses. On-campus housing is guaranteed for all 4 years and is available on a lottery system for upperclassmen. 52% of students live on campus. All students may keep cars.

FACULTY/CLASSROOMS: 60% of faculty are male; 40% are female. 89% teach undergraduates. No introductory courses are taught by graduate students. The average class size in an introductory lecture is 23; in a laboratory is 16; and in a regular course is 23.

PROGRAMS OF STUDY: Niagara confers B.A., B.S., B.B.A. and B.F.A. degrees. Associate, master's, and doctoral degrees are also awarded. Bachelor's degrees are awarded in AGRICULTURE (environmental studies), BIOLOGICAL SCIENCE (biochemistry, bioinformatics, biology/adolescence education, biology/biological science, and life science), BUSINESS (accounting, accounting/CPA, business administration and management, business administration marketing, business economics, finance, hotel/motel and restaurant management, human resources, international business, marketing/retailing/merchandising, sports management, tourism, and transportation management), COMMUNICATIONS AND THE ARTS (art history, communication studies, communications, dramatic arts, English, foreign language, French, Spanish, Spanish/adolescence education, theatre arts, and theater design), COMPUTER AND PHYSICAL SCIENCE (chemistry, chemistry/adolescence education, chemistry education, computer information technology, computer information systems, computer science, information sciences and systems, information science, and mathematics), EDUCATION (business education, (Education) Childhood Education, childhood education: 1-6, early childhood education, education, education of the exceptional child, elementary education, English education, foreign languages education, mathematics education, middle school education, museum studies, science education, secondary education, social studies education, social studies secondary school education, Spanish education K-12, special education, and teaching English as a second/foreign language (TESOL/TEFOL)), HEALTH PROFESSIONS (biology and nursing), SOCIAL SCIENCE (child psychology/development, criminal justice, criminology, early childhood studies, economics, history, international studies, liberal arts/general studies, philosophy, political science/government, psychology, religion, religious studies, social science, social work, and sociology). Business, social sciences, and biology are the strongest academically. Business, hospitality and tourism management have the largest enrollments.

ACTIVITIES: 4% of men belong to 1 local and 1 national fraternities; 4% of women belong to 2 national sororities. There are 81 groups on campus, including art, cheerleading, choir, dance, drama, drill team, environmental, ethnic, honors, international, literary magazine, musical theater, newspaper, pep band, political, professional, radio and TV, religious, social, social service, student government, and yearbook. Popular campus events include Orientation, CARE, and RidgeFest. **Sports:** There are 8 intercollegiate sports for men and 10 for women, and 25 intramural sports for men and 25 for women. Facilities include a 2400-seat gym, a 6-lane swimming and diving pool, exercise and weight rooms, saunas and dance areas, outdoor tennis and basketball courts, baseball and soccer fields, rugby pitch, basketball and racquetball courts, a 2100-seat hockey arena, and multipurpose courts with an indoor track. Hiking and biking trails are nearby. **Graduates:** From July 1, 2014 to June 30, 2015, 880 bachelor's degrees were awarded. The most popular majors were education (33%), business (17%), and hospitality and tourism management (14%). 299 companies recruited on campus in 2014-2015. In an average class, 3% graduate in 3 years or less, 59% graduate in 4 years or less, 64% graduate in 5 years or less, and 64% graduate in 6 years or less.

Of the 2014 graduating class, 26% were enrolled in graduate school within 6 months of graduation, and 80% were employed.

SERVICES: Counseling and information services are available, as is tutoring in most subjects. There is a reader service for the blind, remedial math and writing. Study skills development, note taking, and escort-assistance services are available, as are educational assistant services for the vision-impaired, educational/classroom assistance and machines for the hearing-impaired, and services for the learning disabled. **Library/Resources:** The library contains 165,444 volumes, 6,450 microform items, and 6,603 audio/video tapes/CDs/DVDs, and subscribes to 23,500 periodicals including electronic. Computerized library services include interlibrary loans, database searching, Internet access, and Wi-Fi capability. Special learning facilities include an art gallery, radio station, an theatre, greenhouse, nursing simulation lab, and family literacy center. **Physically Challenged Students:** 75% of the campus is accessible. Facilities include wheelchair ramps, elevators, special parking, specially equipped restrooms, special class scheduling, lowered drinking fountains, and special housing. **Special:** Niagara offers a Washington semester, a semester at the state capitol in Albany, on-campus work-study, internships in most majors with such companies as the Big 6 accounting firms and Walt Disney World, and co-op programs in all areas except nursing, education, and social work. Students may study abroad in 8 countries and cross-register through the Western New York Consortium. An accelerated degree program in business, B.A.-B.S. degrees, dual majors, non-degree study, credit for life, military, and work experience, pass/fail options, and research are also available. There is also an academic exploration program for undeclared majors. There are 19 national honor societies and a freshman honors program. **Visiting:** There are regularly scheduled orientations for prospective students, includes individual interviews and campus tours. Other arrangements can be made individually, such as to attend a class, eat in the student cafeteria, and/or speak with a faculty member. There are guides for informal visits, visitors may sit in on classes, and stay overnight. To schedule a visit, contact the Admissions Office at admissions@niagara.edu. **Campus Safety and Security:** Measures include 24-hour foot and vehicle patrol, emergency notification system, self-defense education, and security escort services. There are emergency telephones, lighted pathways/sidewalks, controlled access to dorms/residences, and a campus security advisory board.

REQUIREMENTS: The SAT or ACT is required. Applicants should be graduates of an accredited high school. The GED is accepted. The high school program should include 16 academic credits, with 4 in English and 2 each in foreign language, history, math, science, and social studies, as well as academic electives. Science, math, and computer majors should have 3 credits each in math and science. A GPA of 80.0 is required. AP and CLEP credits are accepted. Important factors in the admissions decision are advanced placement or honors courses, parents or siblings attended your school, and recommendations by school officials. To graduate, students must earn 120 to 126 credit hours and a GPA of at least 2.0; 60 to 66 such hours are required in the major, 20 in specific disciplines, and 20 in liberal arts classes. A comprehensive exam is required in some majors; a thesis is required of honor students and some majors. **Procedure:** Freshmen are admitted to all sessions. Entrance exams should be taken In the junior year or fall of the senior year. There are early decision, early admissions, deferred admissions, and rolling admissions plans. Check with the school for current application deadlines. Notification is sent on a rolling basis. Applications are accepted on-line. **Transfer Students:** 174 transfer students enrolled in 2014-2015. Applicants must have a minimum GPA of 2.0 in travel, hotel, and restaurant administration, arts and sciences, and academic exploration (except for 2.25 in business and 2.5 for nursing and education majors) and submit all high school and college transcripts. The SAT or ACT is recommended. 30 of 120 credits required for the bachelor's degree must be completed at Niagara. **International Students:** There are 302 international students enrolled. The school actively recruits these students. They must take the TOEFL with a minimum score of 550 on the paper-based TOEFL (PBT) or 79 on the Internet-based version (iBT).

ADMISSIONS: 66% of the 2015-2016 applicants were accepted. The SAT scores for the 2015-2016 freshman class were: Critical Reading-- 10% below 500, 48% between 500 and 599, 11% between 600 and 699, and 1% between 700 and 800. Math-- 32% below 500, 51% between 500 and 599, 17% between 600 and 699, and 1% between 700 and 800. Writing-- 49% below 500, 40% between 500 and 599, 10% between 600 and 699, and 1% between 700 and 800. The ACT scores were 27% below 12, 29% between 12 and 17, 26% between 18 and 23, 13% between 24 and 29, and 5% above 30. **Admissions Contact:** Harry Gong, Director of Admissions. Email: *admissions@niagara.edu* Web: *www.niagara.edu*

FINANCIAL AID: Niagara is a member of CSS. The FAFSA is required. The priority date for freshman financial aid applications for fall entry is February 15.

NYACK COLLEGE *(The complete profile is made available exclusively on our website, www.barronspac.com)*

PACE UNIVERSITY — D-5

www.pace.edu

New York, NY 10038	(212) 346-1323/(914) 773-3746 (800) 874-PACE
Fax: (212) 346-1831/(914) 773-3851	Email: infoctr@pace.edu
Full-time: 2973 men, 4718 women	**Faculty:** 475; I, av$
Part-time: 509 men, 714 women	**Ph.D.s:** 89%
Graduate: 1732 men, 2599 women	**Student/Faculty:** 16 to 1
Year: semesters, summer session	**Tuition:** $42,772
Room & Board: $15,476	**Freshman Class:** 18,463 applied, 15,466 accepted, 2032 enrolled
SAT CR/M: 550/540 **ACT:** 25	**CEEB CODE:** 2635
Application Deadline: February 15	**COMPETITIVE**

Pace University, is a private university founded in 1906, has produced thinking professionals by providing high-quality education for the professions with a firm base in liberal learning amid the advantages of the New York Metropolitan area. Pace has campuses in New York City and Westchester County, enrolling students in bachelor's, master's, and doctoral programs in its College of Health Professions, Dyson College of Arts and Sciences, Lubin School of Business, School of Education, Elizabeth Haub School of Law, and Seidenberg School of Computer Science and Information Systems. There are 5 undergraduate schools and 6 graduate schools. In addition to regional accreditation, Pace has baccalaureate program accreditation with AACSB, ABET, NCATE, CCNE, ARC-PA, and ACE. The 246-acre campus is in an urban area Pace University's lower Manhattan campus, is in the heart of the Financial District. The Pleasantville campus, is in Westchester County. NYC is just 30 miles and a quick train ride away. Including any residence halls, there are 65 buildings.

STUDENT LIFE: 57% of undergraduates are from New York. Others are from 48 states, 113 foreign countries, and Canada. 75% are from public schools. 8% are Asian American; 48% White; 4% two or more races; 4% race unknown; 13% Hispanic; 13% Foreign; 10% African American. **Female To Male Ratio:** 1.5:1. The average age of freshmen is 18; all undergraduates, 21. 23% do not continue beyond their first year; 58% remain to graduate. **Housing:** 3642 students can be accommodated in college housing, which includes coed dorms and on-campus apartments. In addition, there are honors houses, special-interest houses, and a wellness floor. 55% of students commute. Some may keep cars.

FACULTY/CLASSROOMS: 50% of faculty are male; 50% are female. 84% teach undergraduates, and 24% do research. No introductory courses are taught by graduate students. The average class size in an introductory lecture is 35; in a laboratory is 11; and in a regular course is 23.

PROGRAMS OF STUDY: Pace confers B.A., B.S., B.B.A., B.F.A. and B.S.N. degrees. Associate, master's, and doctoral degrees are also awarded. Bachelor's degrees are awarded in AGRICULTURE (environmental studies), BIOLOGICAL SCIENCE (biochemistry, biology/adolescence education, biology/biological science, and forensic science), BUSINESS (accounting, banking and finance, business administration and management, business economics, entrepreneurial studies, finance, hospitality management services, human resources, international business management, international marketing, marketing/retailing/merchandising, and sports marketing), COMMUNICATIONS AND THE ARTS (acting, advertising, art history, art, art history and appreciation, communication studies, communications, dance, English, English literature, film arts, fine arts, information technology, media management, modern language, musical theater, public relations, Spanish, stage management, theatre acting, theatre arts, theater design, theatre production, and theater management), COMPUTER AND PHYSICAL SCIENCE (chemistry, computer science, computer security and information assurance, earth science/adolescence education, information sciences and systems, mathematics, physics, and quantitative methods), EDUCA-

TION (Asian studies, education of the deaf and hearing impaired, and elementary education), ENGINEERING AND ENVIRONMENTAL DESIGN (environmental science), HEALTH PROFESSIONS (health science and nursing), SOCIAL SCIENCE (American studies, applied psychology, biopsychology, communication sciences & disorders, criminal justice, economics, forensic studies, history, Latin American studies, philosophy and religion, political science/government, psychology, social science, sociology, and women & gender studies). Accounting is the strongest academically. Finance, accounting, and nursing have the largest enrollments.

ACTIVITIES: 2% of men belong to 1 local and 11 national fraternities; 3% of women belong to 3 local and 11 national sororities. There are 83 groups on campus, including art, cheerleading, chorus, computers, dance, debate, drama, environmental, ethnic, film, honors, international, LGBT, literary magazine, musical theater, newspaper, photography, political, professional, radio and TV, religious, social, social service, student government, and yearbook. Popular campus events include Homecoming, CariCulture, and Live Love Laugh. **Sports:** There are 6 intercollegiate sports for men and 8 for women, and 9 intramural sports for men and 9 for women. Facilities include The Civic Center gym in New York City. There are football, lacrosse, soccer, softball, baseball fields, tennis courts, and a health, fitness, and recreation center on the Pleasantville campus. **Graduates:** From July 1, 2015 to June 30, 2016, 1694 bachelor's degrees were awarded. The most popular majors were nursing (9%), accounting (9%), and finance (8%). 359 companies recruited on campus in 2015-2016. In an average class, 1% graduate in 3 years or less, 36% graduate in 4 years or less, 52% graduate in 5 years or less, and 55% graduate in 6 years or less. Of the 2015 graduating class, 5% were enrolled in graduate school within 6 months of graduation, and 53% were employed.

SERVICES: Counseling and information services are available, as is tutoring in every subject. There is also remedial math, reading, and writing. All services are provided in the University's Center for Academic Excellence. **Library/Resources:** The 3 libraries contain 766,508 volumes, 53,581 microform items, 5,529 audio/video tapes/CDs/DVDs, and subscribe to 473,330 periodicals including electronic. Computerized library services include interlibrary loans, database searching, Internet access, and Wi-Fi capability. Special learning facilities include an art gallery, radio station, TV station, 2 art galleries, a performing arts center, biological research labs, an environmental center, a language lab, and computer labs. **Physically Challenged Students:** 70% of the campus is accessible. Facilities include wheelchair ramps, elevators, special parking, special class scheduling, lowered drinking fountains, and lowered telephones. There is no student parking in NYC. **Special:** Internships, study abroad, and a cooperative education program in all majors are available. Pace also offers accelerated degree programs, B.A.-B.S. degrees, dual majors, general studies degrees, and 3-2 engineering degrees with Manhattan College and Rensselaer Polytechnic Institute. Credit for life, military, and work experience, nondegree study, and pass/fail options are available. There are 25 national honor societies, a freshman honors program, and 19 departmental honors programs. **Visiting:** There are regularly scheduled orientations for prospective students, including student-for-a-day programs and overnight visits by appointment. There are guides for informal visits, visitors may sit in on classes, and stay overnight. To schedule a visit, contact the Office of Undergraduate Admission. **Campus Safety and Security:** Measures include 24-hour foot and vehicle patrol, emergency notification system, and security escort services. There are shuttle buses, emergency telephones, lighted pathways/sidewalks, and controlled access to dorms/residences, including closed circuit TV.

REQUIREMENTS: The SAT or ACT is required. Applicants should be graduates of an accredited secondary school with at least 16 academic credits, including 4 in English, 3 to 4 each in math, science, and history, and 2 to 3 in a foreign language. The GED is accepted, along with official SAT or ACT scores. An essay is required. Two letters of recommendation from a teacher or counselor who can attest to your academic potential and personal characteristics. AP and CLEP credits are accepted. Important factors in the admissions decision are advanced placement or honors courses, recommendations by school officials, and leadership record. To graduate, students must complete 128 to 133 credit hours depending on the major, including 32 to 50 in the major, with a minimum GPA of 2.0. A core curriculum with a minimum of 44 credits that includes an introductory computer science course as well as a community-based learning experience and 2 enhanced writing courses is also required. **Procedure:** Freshmen are admitted fall and spring. Entrance exams should be taken by December of the senior year. There are early admissions, deferred admissions, and rolling admissions plans. Early decision applications should be filed by November 1; regular applications, by February 15 for fall entry; and December 1 for spring entry, along with a $50 fee. Notification of early decision is sent December 1; regular decision, December 15. Applications are accepted online. **Transfer Students:** 1086 transfer students enrolled in 2015-2016. Applicants are admitted in the fall or spring. A college GPA of 2.5 is required. Grades of C or better transfer for credit. A maximum of 68 credits will be accepted from a 2-year school. Students who transfer with less than 32 credits also need to submit SAT or ACT scores. 32 of 128 credits required for the bachelor's degree must be completed at Pace. **International Students:** There are 794 international students enrolled. The school actively recruits these students. They must take the TOEFL with a minimum score of 570 on the paper-based TOEFL (PBT) or 89 on the Internet-based version (iBT) and the college's own test.

ADMISSIONS: 84% of the 2016-2017 applicants were accepted. The SAT scores for the 2016-2017 freshman class were: Critical Reading-- 21% below 500, 53% between 500 and 599, 23% between 600 and 699, and 3% between 700 and 800. Math-- 22% below 500, 53% between 500 and 599, 23% between 600 and 699, and 2% between 700 and 800. The ACT scores were 1% between 12 and 17, 38% between 18 and 23, 52% between 24 and 29, and 10% above 30. 36% of the current freshmen were in the top fifth of their class; 70% were in the top two fifths. **Admissions Contact:** Robina C. Schepp, VP Enrollment Management. Email: *infoctr@pace.edu* Web: *www.pace.edu*

FINANCIAL AID: In 2016-2017, 74% of all full-time freshmen and 70% of continuing full-time students received some form of financial aid. 74% of all full-time freshmen and 69% of continuing full-time students received need-based aid. The average freshman award was $32,826. Need-based scholarships or need-based grants averaged $28,119; need-based self-help aid (loans and jobs) averaged $8,060; non-need-based athletic scholarships averaged $9,941; and other non-need-based awards and non-need-based scholarships averaged $20,111. Average annual earnings from campus work are $2156. The average financial indebtedness of the 2016 graduate was $33,749. The FAFSA code is 002791. The priority date for freshman financial aid applications for fall entry is March 15.

PARSONS THE NEW SCHOOL FOR DESIGN *(The complete profile is made available exclusively on our website, www.barronspac.com)*

PRATT INSTITUTE — D-5

www.pratt.edu

Brooklyn, NY 11205	(718) 636-3514 (800) 331-0834
Fax: (718) 636-3670	**Email:** admissions@pratt.edu
Full-time: 941 men, 2162 women	**Faculty:** 104; IIA, +$
Part-time: 48 men, 56 women	**Ph.D.s:** 75%
Graduate: 382 men, 1009 women	**Student/Faculty:** 30 to 1
Year: semesters, summer session	**Tuition:** $46,586
Room & Board: $11,496	**Freshman Class:** 4819 applied, 3186 accepted, 703 enrolled
SAT CR/M/W: 587/570/574 **ACT:** 26	**CEEB CODE:** 2669
Application Deadline: January 5	**VERY COMPETITIVE**

Pratt Institute, founded in 1887, is a private institution offering undergraduate and graduate programs in architecture, art and design education, art history, art therapy, critical and visual studies, industrial, interior, and communication design, fine arts, design management, arts and cultural management, writing and library science. There are 4 undergraduate schools and 5 graduate schools. In addition to regional accreditation, Pratt has baccalaureate program accreditation with FIDER, NAAB, NASAD, TEAC, and ALA. The 25-acre campus is in an urban area 3 miles east of downtown Manhattan. Including any residence halls, there are 28 buildings.

STUDENT LIFE: 78% of undergraduates are from out of state, mostly the Middle Atlantic. Students are from 47 states, 82 foreign countries, and Canada. 9% are Hispanic; 5% African American; 39% White; 30% Foreign; 3% race unknown; 2% two or more races; 12% Asian American. **Female To Male Ratio:** 2.4:1. The average age of freshmen is 18; all undergraduates, 20. 15% do not continue beyond their first year; 63%

remain to graduate. **Housing:** 1700 students can be accommodated in college housing, which includes single-sex and coed dorms and on-campus apartments. In addition, there are special-interest houses, special interest communities include: healthy choices, global learning, community service, quiet floor and gender neutral. On-campus housing is guaranteed for the freshman year only, and is available on a first-come, first-served basis, and is available on a lottery system for upperclassmen. 53% of students live on campus. All students may keep cars.

FACULTY/CLASSROOMS: 58% of faculty are male; 42% are female. 76% teach undergraduates. No introductory courses are taught by graduate students. The average class size in an introductory lecture is 22; in a laboratory is 20; and in a regular course is 15.

PROGRAMS OF STUDY: Pratt confers B.Arch., B.F.A., B.I.D. and B.P.S. degrees. Associate and master's degrees are also awarded. Bachelor's degrees are awarded in COMMUNICATIONS AND THE ARTS (art history and appreciation, communications, creative writing, film arts, fine arts, industrial design, and photography), EDUCATION (art education), ENGINEERING AND ENVIRONMENTAL DESIGN (architecture, computer graphics, construction management, and interior design), SOCIAL SCIENCE (fashion design and technology). Architecture, interior design, and fine arts are the strongest academically. Architecture, communications design, and interior design have the largest enrollments.

ACTIVITIES: There are 50 groups on campus, including art, environmental, ethnic, film, honors, international, LGBT, literary magazine, martial arts, newspaper, photography, professional, radio and TV, religious, social, social service, student government, and yearbook. Popular campus events include Springfest, International Food Fair, and Holiday Ball. **Sports:** There are 6 intercollegiate sports for men and 4 for women, and 3 intramural sports for men and 1 for women. Facilities include an activities resource center containing 5 indoor tennis courts, a 200-meter indoor track, volleyball and basketball courts, a weight room, and 2 dance studios. **Graduates:** From July 1, 2015 to June 30, 2016, 615 bachelor's degrees were awarded. The most popular majors were visual and performing arts (74%), architecture (19%), and liberal arts (5%).

SERVICES: Counseling and information services are available, as is tutoring in some subjects, such as art history, English, math, science, and social science. There is a reader service for the blind. Individual tutoring and testing services are also available **Library/Resources:** The library contains 212,934 volumes, 6,384 microform items, 3,500 audio/video tapes/CDs/DVDs, and subscribes to 700 periodicals including electronic. Computerized library services include interlibrary loans, database searching, Internet access, and Wi-Fi capability. Special learning facilities include an art gallery, radio station, and a foundry and woodshop. **Physically Challenged Students:** 75% of the campus is accessible. Facilities include wheelchair ramps, elevators, special parking, specially equipped restrooms, lowered drinking fountains, and special housing. **Special:** Internships, study abroad in 4 countries Denmark, Italy, Japan, and Greece, dual degree programs, work-study programs on campus, credit for work experience, non-degree study, and pass/fail options are available. There are 4 national honor societies. **Visiting:** There are regularly scheduled orientations for prospective students, campus tour, schoolwide presentations, departmental presentations, and financial aid workshops. There are guides for informal visits and visitors may sit in on classes. To schedule a visit, contact the Office of Admissions. **Campus Safety and Security:** Measures include 24-hour foot and vehicle patrol, emergency notification system, and security escort services. There are also emergency telephones, lighted pathways/sidewalks, controlled access to dorms/residences, and orientation safety workshops.

REQUIREMENTS: The SAT or ACT is required. The ACT Optional Writing test is also required. In addition, SAT: Subject tests in writing and mathematics level I or II are recommended for architecture applicants. Applicants must be graduates of an accredited secondary school. The GED is accepted. Students should have completed 4 years of English and math, and 2 years each of science and history, and 1 of social studies. A portfolio is required. An interview is recommended but not required. A GPA of 2.8 is required. AP and CLEP credits are accepted. Important factors in the admissions decision are evidence of special talent, advanced placement or honors courses, and recommendations by school officials. The number of credits needed for graduation varies with the major, but a minimum of 132 is required, one quarter of which must be in liberal arts. Undergraduates must maintain a GPA of 2.0. All students must take 13 credits (15 for architecture majors) of liberal arts electives, 6 credits each of social sciences or philosophy, English, and cultural history, and 3 credits of science. **Procedure:** Freshmen are admitted fall and spring. Entrance exams should be taken by November of the senior year. There is a deferred admissions plan. Early decision applications should be filed by November 1; regular applications, by January 5 for fall entry; and October 1 for spring entry, along with a $50 fee. Notifications are sent April 1. 930 applicants were on the 2016 waiting list; 10 were admitted. Applications are accepted online. **Transfer Students:** 152 transfer students enrolled in 2015-2016. Applicants should provide college transcripts and recommendations. All transfer applicants without an associate degree must submit high school transcripts as well. A portfolio is required for architecture, writing, and art and design students. Applicants must have a statement of good standing from prior institution(s). 48 of 132 credits required for the bachelor's degree must be completed at Pratt. **International Students:** There are 845 international students enrolled. The school actively recruits these students. They must take the TOEFL with a minimum score of 550 on the paper-based TOEFL (PBT) or 79 on the Internet-based version (iBT) and the college's own test.

ADMISSIONS: 66% of the 2016-2017 applicants were accepted. The SAT scores for the 2016-2017 freshman class were: Critical Reading-- 11% below 500, 43% between 500 and 599, 39% between 600 and 699, and 7% between 700 and 800. Math-- 19% below 500, 39% between 500 and 599, 37% between 600 and 699, and 5% between 700 and 800. Writing-- 13% below 500, 42% between 500 and 599, 40% between 600 and 699, and 5% between 700 and 800. The ACT scores were 1% between 12 and 17, 27% between 18 and 23, 57% between 24 and 29, and 15% above 30. **Admissions Contact:** Judith Aaron, Vice President for Enrollment. Email: *jaaron@pratt.edu* Web: *www.pratt.edu*

FINANCIAL AID: In 2016-2017, 76% of all full-time freshmen received some form of financial aid. 51% of all full-time freshmen received need-based aid. The average freshman award was $17,267. 45% of undergraduate students work part-time. Average annual earnings from campus work are $2899. The average financial indebtedness of the 2016 graduate was $29,471. Pratt is a member of CSS. The state aid form and the college's own financial statement, and the parents' and students' tax returns are required. The FAFSA code is 002798. The priority date for freshman financial aid applications for fall entry is March 1. The filing deadline for fall entry is February 1.

RENSSELAER POLYTECHNIC INSTITUTE D-3
www.rpi.edu

Troy, NY 12180	(518) 276-6216 (800) 448-6562
Fax: (518) 276-4072	Email: admissions@rpi.edu
Full-time: 3984 men, 1794 women	**Faculty:** 404; I, +$
Part-time: 3 men	**Ph.D.s:** 96%
Graduate: 866 men, 372 women	**Student/Faculty:** 16 to 1
Year: semesters, summer session	**Tuition:** $49,341
Room & Board: $14,095	**Freshman Class:** 17752 applied, 7432 accepted, 1379 enrolled
SAT CR/M: 660/720 **ACT:** 30	**CEEB CODE:** 2757
Application Deadline: January 15	**MOST COMPETITIVE**

Rensselaer Polytechnic Institute, founded in 1824, is a private institution that offers bachelor's, master's and doctoral degrees in engineering, the sciences, information technology, architecture, management, and the humanities and social sciences. Institute programs serve undergraduates, graduate students, and working professionals around the world. Figures in the above capsule and in this profile are approximate. There are 5 undergraduate schools and 5 graduate schools. In addition to regional accreditation, Rensselaer has baccalaureate program accreditation with AACSB, ABET, NAAB, AAAHC, and ACS. The 297-acre campus is in a suburban area 10 miles north of Albany. Including any residence halls, there are 200 buildings.

STUDENT LIFE: 67% of undergraduates are from out of state, mostly the Northeast. Students are from 48 states, 41 foreign countries, and Canada. 70% are from public schools. 8% are Hispanic; 7% two or more races; 59% White; 3% African American; 2% race unknown; 11% Foreign; 10% Asian American. **Male To Female Ratio:** 2.2:1. The average age of freshmen is 18; all undergraduates, 20. 6% do not continue beyond their first year; 94% remain to graduate. **Housing:** 3400 students can be accommodated in college housing, which includes coed dorms, on-campus apartments, and married student housing. In addition, there are fraternity houses, sorority houses, and theme housing. On-campus housing is available on a first-come, first-served basis, and is available on a lottery system for upperclassmen. 57% of students live on campus. Upperclassmen may keep cars.

FACULTY/CLASSROOMS: 74% of faculty are male; 26% are female. No introductory courses are taught by graduate students. The average class size in an introductory lecture is 35; in a laboratory is 18; and in a regular course is 28.

PROGRAMS OF STUDY: Rensselaer confers B.S. and B.Arch. degrees. Master's and doctoral degrees are also awarded. Bachelor's degrees are awarded in BIOLOGICAL SCIENCE (biochemistry, biology/biological science, and biophysics), BUSINESS (management information systems, management science, and recreation and leisure services), COMMUNICATIONS AND THE ARTS (communications and media arts), COMPUTER AND PHYSICAL SCIENCE (applied physics, chemistry, computer science, geology, hydrogeology, mathematics, physics, and science technology), ENGINEERING AND ENVIRONMENTAL DESIGN (aeronautical engineering, architecture, biomedical engineering, chemical engineering, civil engineering, computer engineering, construction engineering, electrical/electronics engineering, engineering, engineering physics, environmental engineering, industrial engineering, materials engineering, mechanical engineering, and nuclear engineering), HEALTH PROFESSIONS (premedicine), SOCIAL SCIENCE (economics, interdisciplinary studies, philosophy, prelaw, and psychology). Engineering, sciences, and architecture are the strongest academically. General engineering, computer science, and management have the largest enrollments.

ACTIVITIES: 30% of men belong to 1 local and 31 national fraternities; 16% of women belong to 1 local and 4 national sororities. There are 229 groups on campus, including biomedical engineering society, entrepreneurship, finance, Rensselaer biotechnology students association, art, astrophysical society, band, cheerleading, chess, choir, chorale, chorus, computers, dance, drama, drill team, environmental, ethnic, film, honors, international, jazz band, LGBT, literary magazine, musical theater, orchestra, pep band, photography, political, professional, radio and TV, religious, social, social service, student government, and symphony. Popular campus events include Union Program and Activities Committees-Concerts, Comedy, Cinema, Winter Carnival, and Big Red Freakout. **Sports:** There are 12 intercollegiate sports for men and 11 for women, and 22 intramural sports for men and 21 for women. Facilities include a field house, pool, gyms, sports and recreation center, several playing fields, weight rooms, fitness center, tennis courts, handball/squash courts, artificial turf fields, an indoor track, ice hockey rink, stadium and an arena. **Graduates:** From July 1, 2015 to June 30, 2016, 1143 bachelor's degrees were awarded. The most popular majors were engineering (56%), computer science (10%), and business/marketing (7%). 370 companies recruited on campus in 2015-2016. In an average class, 63% graduate in 4 years or less, 80% graduate in 5 years or less, and 81% graduate in 6 years or less. Of the 2015 graduating class, 22% were enrolled in graduate school within 6 months of graduation, and 49% were employed.

SERVICES: Counseling and information services are available, as is tutoring in every subject. There is a reader service for the blind, and remedial math, reading, and writing, as well as a writing center and advising and learning assistance center. **Library/Resources:** The 2 libraries contain 476,510 volumes, 125,616 microform items, and 137,094 audio/video tapes/CDs/DVDs, and subscribe to 21,036 periodicals including electronic. Computerized library services include interlibrary loans, database searching, Internet access, and Wi-Fi capability. Special learning facilities include an art gallery, radio station, TV station, and an observatory. **Physically Challenged Students:** Facilities include wheelchair ramps, elevators, special parking, specially equipped restrooms, special class scheduling, lowered drinking fountains, lowered telephones, and special housing. **Special:** Rensselaer offers co-op programs, internships, study abroad/exchange program, and pass/fail options are available. Students may pursue dual and student-designed majors, a 3-2 engineering degree with more than 40 universities, 2-2 agreements, an accelerated degree program in physician-scientist, law and MBA. There are 14 national honor societies and 8 departmental honors programs. **Visiting:** There are regularly scheduled orientations for prospective students. There are guides for informal visits and visitors may sit in on classes. To schedule a visit, contact the Admissions Office. **Campus Safety and Security:** Measures include 24-hour foot and vehicle patrol, self-defense education, and security escort services. There are shuttle buses, emergency telephones, lighted pathways/sidewalks, card-access residence halls, on-campus bicycle patrol, and a student volunteer program.

REQUIREMENTS: SAT subject tests in critical reading, math and science are required for accelerated-program applicants or the ACT, which must include the optional writing component in lieu of SAT and SAT. 15 high school units are required and/or recommended, 4 each in English and math, 3 each in science (4 recommended), and social studies. AP credits are accepted. Important factors in the admissions decision are: leadership record, advanced placement or honors courses, parents or siblings attended your school, evidence of special talent, extracurricular activities record, recommendations by school officials, personality/intangible qualities, recommendations by alumni, and geographical diversity. For graduation, students must earn at least 124 credits in all majors except engineering (128 needed) and the B.Arch. Program (168 needed). The core curriculum includes 48 credits in math, science, humanities, and social sciences. Students must maintain a minimum GPA of 1.8 and must fulfill a writing requirement. **Procedure:** Freshmen are admitted fall, spring, and summer. Entrance exams should be taken in the junior or senior year. There are early decision and deferred admissions plans. Early decision applications should be filed by November 1; regular applications, by January 15 for fall entry; and November 1 for spring entry, along with a $70 fee. Notification of early decision is sent December 12; regular decision, March 12. 358 early decision candidates were accepted for the 2016-2017 class. 2203 applicants were on the 2016 waiting list; 57 were admitted. Applications are accepted online. **Transfer Students:** 148 transfer students enrolled in 2015-2016. Applicants should have completed 12 or more transferable college credits, and must be in good academic standing at the institutions they are attending or attended. 60 of 120 credits required for the bachelor's degree must be completed at Rensselaer. **International Students:** There are 614 international students enrolled. The school actively recruits these students. They must take the TOEFL with a minimum score of 570 on the paper-based TOEFL (PBT) or 88 on the Internet-based version (iBT). They must also take the SAT or ACT.

ADMISSIONS: 42% of the 2016-2017 applicants were accepted. The SAT scores for the 2016-2017 freshman class were: Critical Reading-- 1% below 500, 19% between 500 and 599, 48% between 600 and 699, and 32% between 700 and 800. Math-- 3% between 500 and 599, 33% between 600 and 699, and 64% between 700 and 800. The ACT scores were 3% between 18 and 23, 41% between 24 and 29, and 56% above 30. 89% of the current freshmen were in the top fifth of their class; 98% were in the top two fifths. 49 freshmen graduated first in their class. **Admissions Contact:** Karen S. Long, Director, Undergrad Admissions. Email: *admissions@rpi.edu* Web: *www.rpi.edu*

FINANCIAL AID: In 2016-2017, 89% of all full-time freshmen and continuing full-time students received some form of financial aid. 87% of all full-time freshmen and 79% of continuing full-time students received need-based aid. The average freshman award was $38,214. Need-based scholarships or need-based grants averaged $35,340; need-based self-help aid (loans and jobs) averaged $4,695; non-need-based athletic scholarships averaged $60,564; other non-need-based awards and non-need-based scholarships averaged $16,511; and $5,491 from other forms of aid. Rensselaer is a member of CSS. The CSS/Profile is required. The FAFSA code is 002803. The priority date for freshman financial aid applications for fall entry is February 1.

ROBERTS WESLEYAN COLLEGE B-3

www.roberts.edu

Rochester, NY 14624 (585) 594-6400 (800) 777-4792

Fax: (585) 594-6371 **Email:** admissions@roberts.edu

Full-time: 385 men, 835 women	**Faculty:** 89
Part-time: 36 men, 80 women	**Ph.D.s:** 67%
Graduate: 84 men, 342 women	**Student/Faculty:** 14 to 1
Year: semesters, summer session	**Tuition:** $28,466
Room & Board: $9840	**Freshman Class:** 697 applied, 633 accepted, 256 enrolled
SAT CR/M: 553/548 **ACT:** 24	**CEEB CODE:** 2759
Application Deadline: February 1	**COMPETITIVE**

Roberts Wesleyan College, founded in 1866 by leaders of the Free Methodist Church, is an innovative and distinctive Christian college offering excellence in liberal arts and professional programs. There are 2 undergraduate schools and 2 graduate schools. In addition to regional accreditation, Roberts has baccalaureate program accreditation with CSWE, NASAD, NASM, IACBE, CCNE, NASP, and RATE. The 75-acre campus is in a suburban area 8 miles southwest of Rochester. Including any residence halls, there are 32 buildings.

STUDENT LIFE: 89% of undergraduates are from New York. Others are from 24 states, 20 foreign countries, and Canada. 72% are White; 6% Hispanic; 4% Foreign; 3% two or more races; 2% race unknown; 11% African American; 1% Asian American. 62% are Protestant; 17% claim no religious affiliation; 16% Catholic. **Female To Male Ratio:** 2.5:1. The average age of freshmen is 19; all undergraduates, 28. 20% do not continue beyond their first year; 60% remain to graduate. **Housing:** 792 students can be accommodated in college housing, which includes single-sex dorms, on-campus apartments, and off-campus apartments. On-campus housing is guaranteed for all 4 years. 65% of students live on campus; of those, 70% remain on campus on weekends. All students may keep cars. Alcohol is not permitted.

FACULTY/CLASSROOMS: 43% of faculty are male; 57% are female. 85% teach undergraduates. No introductory courses are taught by graduate students. The average class size in an introductory lecture is 30; in a laboratory is 15; and in a regular course is 23.

PROGRAMS OF STUDY: Roberts confers B.A., and B.S. degrees. Associate and master's degrees are also awarded. Bachelor's degrees are awarded in BIOLOGICAL SCIENCE (biochemistry, biology/adolescence education, biology/biological science, biotechnology, and forensic science), BUSINESS (accounting, business administration and management, international business management, and marketing), COMMUNICATIONS AND THE ARTS (applied art, applied music, art, communications, English, graphic design, music, music performance, piano performance, Spanish, studio art, and vocal performance), COMPUTER AND PHYSICAL SCIENCE (chemistry, chemistry/adolescence education, digital arts/technology, mathematics, and physics), EDUCATION (early childhood education, elementary education, English education, mathematics education, music education, physical education, secondary education, and special education), ENGINEERING AND ENVIRONMENTAL DESIGN (biomedical equipment technology and preengineering), HEALTH PROFESSIONS (biology, nursing, pharmacy, predentistry, premedicine, prepharmacy, prephysical therapy, and preveterinary science), SOCIAL SCIENCE (biblical studies, Christian studies, criminal justice, history, humanities, interdisciplinary studies, liberal arts/general studies, philosophy, prelaw, psychology, religion, and social work). Music, education, and nursing are the strongest academically. Elementary education, nursing, and music have the largest enrollments.

ACTIVITIES: There are no fraternities or sororities. Groups on campus include band, choir, chorale, chorus, dance, drama, environmental, ethnic, honors, international, jazz band, musical theater, newspaper, opera, orchestra, pep band, photography, religious, social, social service, student government, symphony, and yearbook. Popular campus events include Winter Weekend, Spring Formal, and Talent and Variety Shows. **Sports:** There are 7 intercollegiate sports for men and 7 for women, and 6 intramural sports for men and 6 for women. Facilities include an athletic center with facilities for basketball, volleyball, tennis, badminton, track, soccer, weight lifting, walleyball, racquetball, exercise machines room, flag football, ultimate Frisbee, and swimming. **Graduates:** From July 1, 2015 to June 30, 2016, 408 bachelor's degrees were awarded. The most popular majors were nursing (20%), education (16%), and psychology (9%). In an average class, 49% graduate in 4 years or less, 61% graduate in 5 years or less, and 63% graduate in 6 years or less. Of the 2015 graduating class, 24% were enrolled in graduate school within 6 months of graduation, and 93% were employed.

SERVICES: Counseling and information services are available, as is tutoring in every subject. Note takers for the hearing impaired are available. There is a reader service for the blind, and remedial math, reading, and writing. **Library/Resources:** The library contains 144,199 volumes, 169,823 microform items, and 4,462 audio/video tapes/CDs/DVDs, and subscribes to 35,000 periodicals including electronic. Computerized library services include interlibrary loans, database searching, Internet access, and Wi-Fi capability. Special learning facilities include an art gallery. **Physically Challenged Students:** 85% of the campus is accessible. Facilities include wheelchair ramps, elevators, special parking, specially equipped restrooms, special class scheduling, lowered drinking fountains, and lowered telephones. **Special:** Students may cross-register with members of the Rochester Area Colleges consortium. Internships, study abroad in 8 countries, a Washington semester, co-op programs, B.A.-B.S. degrees, dual majors, and 3-2 engineering degrees with Clarkson University, Rensselaer Polytechnic Institute, and Rochester Institute of Technology are available. 3-4 Pharmacy with University at Buffalo. Nondegree study and credit for life, military, and work experience are also offered. The organizational management program, geared to adults, consists of 4-hour weekly sessions, with reliance on out-of-class work. There is a freshman honors program and 100 departmental honors programs. **Visiting:** There are regularly scheduled orientations for prospective students, including a campus tour, class visits, admissions overview, meetings with faculty, and a financial aid presentation. There are guides for informal visits, visitors may sit in on classes, and stay overnight. To schedule a visit, contact the Admissions Office. **Campus Safety and Security:** Measures include 24-hour foot and vehicle patrol, emergency notification system, self-defense education, and security escort services. There are emergency telephones, lighted pathways/sidewalks, controlled access to dorms/residences, and personal-safety education programs.

REQUIREMENTS: The SAT or ACT is required. Applicants must be graduates of an accredited secondary school. The GED is accepted. At least 12 academic credits are required, including 4 years of English and 2 years each of math and science. A foreign language and 3 years of social studies are recommended. The chosen major may modify requirements. An essay is required, and an interview is recommended. Roberts requires applicants to be in the upper 50% of their class. AP and CLEP credits are accepted. Important factors in the admissions decision are advanced placement or honors courses, personality/intangible qualities, and extracurricular activities record. To graduate, students must complete a minimum of 124 credit hours, with a minimum of 30 hours in the major. Required courses include first-year experience, phys ed, modern technology, world issues, speech, writing, history, Bible, and philosophy. **Procedure:** Freshmen are admitted fall, spring, and summer. There are deferred admissions and rolling admissions plans. Applications should be filed by February 1 for fall entry; December 1 for spring entry. Notification is sent on a rolling basis. Application fees are waived if application is completed online. **Transfer Students:** 101 transfer students enrolled in 2015-2016. Applicants must submit transcripts from all previous institutions attended as well as the application and a recommendation. Credit is usually accepted for courses with grade C or better. 30 of 124 credits required for the bachelor's degree must be completed at Roberts. **International Students:** There are 52 international students enrolled. The school actively recruits these students. They must take the TOEFL with a minimum score of 540 on the paper-based TOEFL (PBT) or 75 on the Internet-based version (iBT), or take the IELTS with a minimum score of 6. International students who take the SAT or ACT and score high enough do not need to take the TOEFL or IELTS.

ADMISSIONS: 91% of the 2016-2017 applicants were accepted. The SAT scores for the 2016-2017 freshman class were: Critical Reading-- 38% below 500, 46% between 500 and 599, 12% between 600 and 699, and 4% between 700 and 800. Math-- 40% below 500, 37% between 500 and 599, 21% between 600 and 699, and 2% between 700 and 800. Writing-- 55% below 500, 35% between 500 and 599, 8% between 600 and 699, and 2% between 700 and 800. The ACT scores were 23% below 12, 22% between 12 and 17, 18% between 18 and 23, 22% between 24 and 29, and 15% above 30. 42% of the current freshmen were in the top fifth of their class; 80% were in the top two fifths. 4 freshmen graduated first in their class. **Admissions Contact:** JP Anderson, Associate Vice President of UG Admissions. Email: *anderson_JP@roberts.edu* Web: *www.roberts.edu*

FINANCIAL AID: In 2016-2017, 98% of all full-time freshmen and continuing full-time students received some form of financial aid. 90% of all full-time freshmen and continuing full-time students received need-based aid. The average freshman award was $26,534. Need-based scholarships or need-based grants averaged $21,096; need-based self-help aid (loans and jobs) averaged $6,466; non-need-based athletic scholarships averaged $9,143; and other non-need-based awards and non-need-based scholarships averaged $13,502. 35% of undergraduate students work part-time. Average annual earnings from campus work are $1080. Roberts is a member of CSS. The FAFSA code is 002805. The priority date for freshman financial aid applications for fall entry is March 15. The filing deadline for fall entry is rolling.

ROCHESTER INSTITUTE OF TECHNOLOGY B-3

www.rit.edu

Rochester, NY 14623	(585) 475-6631
Fax: (585) 475-7424	**Email:** admissions@rit.edu
Full-time: 8531 men, 4212 women	**Faculty:** I, -$
Part-time: 950 men, 531 women	**Ph.D.s:** 70%
Graduate: 1959 men, 1023 women	**Student/Faculty:** 13 to 1
Year: semesters, summer session	**Tuition:** $38,568
Room & Board: $12,274	**Freshman Class:** 19824 applied, 10889 accepted, 2604 enrolled
SAT CR/M: 600/635 **ACT:** 29	**CEEB CODE:** 2760
Application Deadline: January 15	**HIGHLY COMPETITIVE**

Rochester Institute of Technology (RIT) is one of the world's leading career-oriented, technological universities. RIT offers more than 90 undergraduate programs in areas such as engineering, computing, information technology, engineering technology, business, hospitality, science, art, design, photography and film, biomedical sciences, game design and development, and the liberal arts including psychology, advertising and public relations, and public policy. Students may choose from more than 90 different minors to develop personal and professional interests that complement their academic program. Experiential education is integrated into many programs through cooperative education, internships, study abroad, and undergraduate research. As home to the National Technical Institute for the Deaf (NTID), RIT is a leader in providing access services for deaf and hard-of-hearing students. Figures in the above capsule and in this profile are approximate. There are 9 undergraduate schools and 9 graduate schools. In addition to regional accreditation, RIT has baccalaureate program accreditation with AACSB, ABET, ADA, CAHEA, CSAB, CSWE, FIDER, NASAD, and CAAHEP. The 1300-acre campus is in a suburban area 5 miles south of Rochester. Including any residence halls, there are 195 buildings.

STUDENT LIFE: 51% of undergraduates are from New York. Others are from 50 states, 107 foreign countries, and Canada. 85% are from public schools. 9% are Foreign; 70% White; 5% Asian American; 4% African American; 4% Hispanic; 1% American Indian/Alaska Native. **Male To Female Ratio:** 2.0:1. The average age of freshmen is 18; all undergraduates, 21. 8% do not continue beyond their first year; 69% remain to graduate. **Housing:** 7144 students can be accommodated in college housing, which includes single-sex and coed dorms, on-campus apartments, and married student housing. In addition, there are honors houses, special-interest houses, fraternity houses, and sorority houses. On-campus housing is guaranteed for the freshman year only, is available on a first-come, and first-served basis. 68% of students live on campus; of those, 90% remain on campus on weekends. All students may keep cars.

FACULTY/CLASSROOMS: 65% of faculty are male; 35% are female. 97% teach undergraduates, 90% do research, and 90% do both. No introductory courses are taught by graduate students. The average class size in an introductory lecture is 23; in a laboratory is 16; and in a regular course is 20.

PROGRAMS OF STUDY: RIT confers B.S. and B.F.A. degrees. Associate, master's, and doctoral degrees are also awarded. Bachelor's degrees are awarded in BIOLOGICAL SCIENCE (biochemistry, bioinformatics, biology/biological science, biotechnology, nutrition, and nutritional sciences), BUSINESS (accounting, banking and finance, business administration and management, business administration - international, business administration, management, operations, business administration marketing, business information systems, business systems analysis, finance, hospitality management services, hotel and restaurant administration, hotel/motel and restaurant management, international business, international business management, business management, management information systems, management, management science, marketing, marketing management, and tourism), COMMUNICATIONS AND THE ARTS (advertising, American Sign Language, animation, applied art, art, art and design, ceramic art and design, communication design, communications, communications technology, crafts, design, digital media, film arts, film, television and digital media, fine arts, fine/studio arts, general, glass, graphic design, graphic design & media, illustration, industrial design, information technology, journalism, media arts, metal/jewelry, photography, public relations, publishing, sculpture, studio art, studio art ceramics, studio art computer art, studio art graphic design, studio art painting, telecommunications, video, visual communication, and visual design), COMPUTER AND PHYSICAL SCIENCE (actuarial science, applied mathematics, biomedical art, chemistry, computer engineering technology, computer mathematics, computer networks & systems, computer game design/development, computer information technology, computer information systems, computer security, computer science, computer science & informatics, computer security and information assurance, digital animation & game design, information sciences and systems, information science, mathematics, mathematics - actuarial concentration, physics, polymer science, science, software engineering, statistics, and systems analysis), EDUCATION (education of the deaf and hearing impaired and museum studies), ENGINEERING AND ENVIRONMENTAL DESIGN (aerospace studies, bioengineering, biomedical engineering, chemical engineering, civil engineering technology, computer engineering, computer graphics, computer technology, electrical/electronics engineering, electrical/electronics engineering technology, engineering, engineering technology, environmental engineering technology, environmental science, furniture design, graphic arts technology, graphic and printing production, industrial engineering, interior design, manufacturing engineering, manufacturing technology, materials science, mechanical engineering, mechanical engineering technology, military science, printing technology, and woodworking), HEALTH PROFESSIONS (allied health, applied nutrition, biology, biomedical science, exercise science, medical imaging, nutrition and dietetics, nutrition and wellness, physician's assistant, predentistry, premedicine, preveterinary science, and ultrasound technology), SOCIAL SCIENCE (anthropology, criminal justice, dietetics, economics, food production/management/services, hotel, rest/tourism mangement, interpreter for the deaf, philosophy, political science/government, prelaw, psychology, public affairs, and sociology). Mechanical engineering, computer science, film & animation are the strongest academically. Engineering, information technology, and photography have the largest enrollments.

ACTIVITIES: 5% of men belong to 17 national fraternities; 5% of women belong to 12 national sororities. There are 307 groups on campus, including gospel choir club, art, band, cheerleading, chess, choir, chorale, chorus, communications, computers, dance, drama, environmental, ethnic, film, honors, international, jazz band, LGBT, literary magazine, newspaper, orchestra, pep band, photography, political, professional, radio and TV, religious, social, social service, and student government. Popular campus events include Brick City Homecoming, Freeze Fest, and Imagine RIT Festival. **Sports:** There are 11 intercollegiate sports for men and 12 for women, and 13 intramural sports for men and 13 for women. Facilities include gyms, ice rinks, swimming pools, tennis courts, a field house, athletic fields, and a student life center with racquetball courts, dance, weight training, and an indoor track. **Graduates:** From July 1, 2015 to June 30, 2016, 2483 bachelor's degrees were awarded. The most popular majors were mechanical engineering (7%), computer science (4%), and game design and development (4%). 1500 companies recruited on campus in 2015-2016. In an average class, 70% graduate in 6 years or less. Of the 2015 graduating class, 15% were enrolled in graduate school within 6 months of graduation, and 81% were employed.

SERVICES: Counseling and information services are available, as is tutoring in most subjects. There is a reader service for the blind. There are comprehensive support services for students with physical or learning disabilities, and for first-generation college students. **Library/Resources:** The library contains 422,281 volumes, 498,703 microform items, 54,935 audio/video tapes/CDs/DVDs, and subscribes to 21,208 periodicals including electronic. Computerized library services include interlibrary loans, database searching, Internet access, and Wi-Fi capability. Special learning facilities include an art gallery, radio station, TV station, a computer chip manufacturing facility, a student-operated restaurant, an electronic prepress lab, an imaging science facility, and an observatory. **Physically Challenged Students:** All of the campus is accessible. Facilities include wheelchair ramps, elevators, special parking, specially equipped restrooms, special class scheduling, lowered drinking fountains, lowered telephones, and special housing. **Special:** Experiential learning is extensive at RIT. Cooperative education is required or recommended in many programs and provides full-time paid work experience. RIT has an employer network of almost 2,200 organizations. Other forms of experiential learning include internships, undergraduate research, and study abroad. There are accelerated dual degree (BS/MS, BS/ME, BS/MBA) in many programs. Students may study abroad in 15 countries, and student-designed majors are permitted in applied arts and sciences. There is an Honors Program in general education and home colleges. There are 6 national honor societies, a freshman honors program, and 7 departmental honors programs. **Visiting:** There are regularly scheduled orientations for prospective students, including academic advising and information on housing and student services. There are guides for informal visits, visitors may sit in on classes, and stay overnight. To schedule a visit, contact the Admissions Office. **Campus Safety and Security:** Measures include 24-hour foot and vehicle patrol, emergency notification system, self-defense education, and security escort services. There are shuttle buses, emergency telephones, lighted pathways/sidewalks, and controlled access to dorms/residences.

REQUIREMENTS: The SAT or ACT is required. Applicants must be high school graduates or have a GED certificate. Applicants are required to submit an essay, and an interview is recommended. The School of Art, the School of Design, and the School for American Crafts emphasize a required portfolio of artwork. Required high school math and science credits vary by program, with 3 years in each area generally acceptable. AP and CLEP credits are accepted. Important factors in the admissions decision are advanced placement or honors courses, recommendations by school officials, and extracurricular activities record. Students must have a GPA of 2.0 and have completed a minimum of 120 semester credit hours to graduate. RIT's framework for general education provides students with courses that meet specific university approved general education learning outcomes and New York State Education Department liberal arts and sciences requirements. Students in all bachelor of science degree programs are required to complete a minimum of 60 credit hours in General Education; students in all bachelor of fine arts degree programs are required to complete a minimum of 30 credit hours in General Education. The general education framework intentionally moves through three educational phases designed to give students a strong foundation, an introduction to fundamentals of liberal arts and sciences disciplines, and the opportunity for deeper study and integrative learning through immersion in a cluster of related courses. **Procedure:** Freshmen are admitted to all sessions. Entrance exams should be taken during the junior or senior year. There are early decision and deferred admissions plans. Early decision applications should be filed by November 15; regular applications, by January 15 for fall entry, along with a $60 fee. Notification of early decision is sent December 15; regular decision, February 15. Application fees are waived if application is completed on-line. **Transfer Students:** 716 transfer students enrolled in 2015-2016. Transfer students must have a GPA of 2.8 for admission to most programs; those with fewer than 30 college credits must supply a high school transcript. Other requirements vary by program. 30 of 120 credits required for the bachelor's degree must be completed at RIT. **International Students:** There are 825 international students enrolled. The school actively recruits these students. They must take the TOEFL with a minimum score of 550 on the paper-based TOEFL (PBT) or 79 on the Internet-based version (iBT). They must also take the SAT or ACT.

ADMISSIONS: 55% of the 2016-2017 applicants were accepted. The SAT scores for the 2016-2017 freshman class were: Critical Reading-- 7% below 500, 39% between 500 and 599, 42% between 600 and 699, and 12% between 700 and 800. Math-- 2% below 500, 27% between 500 and 599, 51% between 600 and 699, and 20% between 700 and 800. The ACT scores were 7% between 18 and 23, 50% between 24 and 29, and 43% above 30. 64% of the current freshmen were in the top fifth of their class; 88% were in the top two fifths. **Admissions Contact:** Daniel Shelley, Director of Admissions. Email: *admissions@rit.edu* Web: *www.rit.edu*

FINANCIAL AID: In 2016-2017, 85% of all full-time freshmen and 89% of continuing full-time students received some form of financial aid. 81% of all full-time freshmen and 83% of continuing full-time students received need-based aid. The average freshman award was $18,900. Need-based scholarships or need-based grants averaged $16,500; and need-based self-help aid (loans and jobs) averaged $5,000. 70% of undergraduate students work part-time. Average annual earnings from campus work are $2500. The average financial indebtedness of the 2016 graduate was $23,800. The FAFSA code is 002806. The priority date for freshman financial aid applications for fall entry is March 1.

RUSSELL SAGE COLLEGE — D-3

www.sage.edu

Troy, NY 12180 — (518) 244-2217, (888) Very-Sage

Fax: (518) 244-6880	**Email:** rscadm@sage.edu
Full-time: 10 men, 772 women	**Faculty:** 61
Part-time: 9 men, 32 women	**Ph.D.s:** 90%
Graduate: n/av	**Student/Faculty:** 10 to 1
Year: semesters, summer session	**Tuition:** $28,000
Room & Board: $11,370	**Freshman Class:** n/av
SAT or ACT: required	**CEEB CODE:** 2764
Application Deadline: rolling	**COMPETITIVE**

Russell Sage College, is a comprehensive college for women. RSC offers liberal arts and professional degree programs in an environment aimed at empowering students to become women of influence in their careers and their communities. Figures in the above capsule and in this profile are approximate. There are 2 undergraduate schools and 1 graduate school. In addition to regional accreditation, Russell Sage has baccalaureate program accreditation with ADA, APTA, NASAD, NCATE, NLN, and AOTA. The 14-acre campus is in an urban area 10 miles from Albany and Schenectady. Including any residence halls, there are 38 buildings.

STUDENT LIFE: 93% of undergraduates are from New York. Others are from 16 states, and 1 foreign country. 8% are African American; 67% White; 6% Hispanic; 4% Asian American; 2% two or more races; 12% race unknown. **Female To Male Ratio:** 42.3:1. The average age of freshmen is 18; all undergraduates, 21. 10% do not continue beyond their first year; 73% remain to graduate. **Housing:** 738 students can be accommodated in college housing, which includes single-sex dorms and on-campus apartments. In addition, there are language houses and special-interest houses. On-campus housing is guaranteed for all 4 years and is available on a lottery system for upperclassmen. 52% of students commute. All students may keep cars. Alcohol is not permitted.

FACULTY/CLASSROOMS: 28% of faculty are male; 72% are female. All teach undergraduates, and do research. No introductory courses are taught by graduate students. The average class size in an introductory lecture is 19; in a laboratory is 9; and in a regular course is 16.

PROGRAMS OF STUDY: Russell Sage confers B.A. and B.S. degrees. Master's degrees are also awarded. Bachelor's degrees are awarded in BIOLOGICAL SCIENCE (biochemistry, biology/biological science, and nutrition), COMMUNICATIONS AND THE ARTS (English, musical theater, and Spanish), COMPUTER AND PHYSICAL SCIENCE (chemistry and mathematics), EDUCATION (elementary education), ENGINEERING AND ENVIRONMENTAL DESIGN (environmental science), HEALTH PROFESSIONS (art therapy, nursing, occupational therapy, and physical therapy), SOCIAL SCIENCE (applied psychology, criminal justice, forensic studies, history, interdisciplinary studies, international studies, political science/government, psychology, and sociology). Nursing, nutrition, and health sciences are the strongest academically. Health & rehabilitative sciences, education and psychology have the largest enrollments.

ACTIVITIES: There are no fraternities or sororities. There are 26 groups on campus, including choir, chorus, dance, drama, ethnic, honors, LGBT, literary magazine, musical theater, newspaper, political, religious, social, student government, and yearbook. Popular campus events include Spirit of Sage River Cruise, Rally Day, Sage Fest, and Family Weekend. **Sports:** There are 7 intercollegiate sports for men and 8 for women, and 7 intramural sports for men and 8 for women. Facilities include Neff Athletic Center, Robison Athletic Center, a weight and fitness center, swimming pool, tennis courts, a practice field, gyms, and a large multipurpose room for indoor recreation. **Graduates:** From July 1, 2015 to June 30, 2016, 212 bachelor's degrees were awarded. The most popular majors were nursing (23%), health sciences (9%), and education (9%). 20 companies recruited on campus in 2015-2016. In an average class, 65% graduate in 4 years or less, 71% graduate in 5 years or less, and 73% graduate in 6 years or less. Of the 2015 graduating class, 32% were enrolled in graduate school within 6 months of graduation, and 65% were employed.

SERVICES: Counseling and information services are available, as is tutoring in most subjects. There is remedial math, reading, and writing. **Library/Resources:** The library contains 164,946 volumes, 18,514 microform items, 6,419 audio/video tapes/CDs/DVDs, and subscribes to

65,391 periodicals including electronic. Computerized library services include interlibrary loans and database searching. **Physically Challenged Students:** 75% of the campus is accessible. Facilities include wheelchair ramps, elevators, and special parking. **Special:** Students may cross-register with the 14 area schools of the Hudson-Mohawk Association of Colleges. A theater major is offered in conjunction with Sage Theater Institute. Study abroad, internships, and work-study programs are available. RSC has several accelerated 5-year programs; 3 + 2 M.S., in Occupational Therapy, a 3-2 engineering degree with nearby Rensselaer Polytechnic Institute and our accelerated 4+3 D.P.T. program. The college confers credit for life, military, or work experience. Non-degree study, student-designed majors, dual majors, and pass/fail options are also available. There are 14 national honor societies and a freshman honors program. **Visiting:** There are regularly scheduled orientations for prospective students, including meetings with faculty, a campus tour, a financial aid session, and an admissions interview. There are guides for informal visits, visitors may sit in on classes, and stay overnight. To schedule a visit, contact Thomas Barresi at rscadm@sage.edu. **Campus Safety and Security:** Measures include 24-hour foot and vehicle patrol, self-defense education, and security escort services. There are emergency telephones, lighted pathways/sidewalks, an evening escort service, and monitored video cameras.

REQUIREMENTS: Applicants must be graduates of an accredited secondary school or have a GED. A minimum of 16 academic units are required. An essay, for applicants still in high school, is required, and an interview is recommended. AP and CLEP credits are accepted. Important factors in the admissions decision are advanced placement or honors courses, recommendations by school officials, leadership record, recommendations by alumni, parents or siblings attended your school, evidence of special talent, extracurricular activities record, and geographical diversity. A minimum of 120 credit hours is required for the baccalaureate degree. Students must complete at least half the major at Sage. Furthermore, 30 of the last 45 credits must be completed in residence (i.e. at Sage or through the Hudson Mohawk Association). Students must satisfy general education as well as major requirements and must maintain satisfactory standards of scholarship to be eligible for graduation. A Bachelor of Arts degree must include a minimum of 90 credit hours in the liberal arts. A Bachelor of Science degree must include a minimum of 60 credit hours in the liberal arts. Students must achieve a 2.2 grade point average in the major and a 2.0 overall cumulative grade point average. Some majors require a higher grade point average for graduation. The ultimate responsibility for fulfilling graduation requirements rests with the individual student. **Procedure:** Freshmen are admitted in the fall and spring. Entrance exams should be taken during spring of the junior year or fall of the senior year. There are early admissions, deferred admissions, and rolling admissions plans. Early decision applications should be filed by December 1, along with a $30 fee. Notification of early decision is sent December 15; regular decision, on a rolling basis. Applications are accepted online. **Transfer Students:** 84 transfer students enrolled in 2015-2016. Applicants must have a minimum GPA of 2.5. Interviews are strongly encouraged and may be required in some instances. 45 of 120 credits required for the bachelor's degree must be completed at Russell Sage. **International Students:** There are 4 international students enrolled. The school actively recruits these students. They must take the TOEFL. They must also take the SAT or ACT.

Admissions Contact: Elizabeth Robertson, Associate Vice President for Admissions. Email: *rscadm@sage.edu* Web: *www.sage.edu*

FINANCIAL AID: In 2016-2017, 94% of all full-time freshmen and 91% of continuing full-time students received some form of financial aid. 79% of all full-time freshmen and 74% of continuing full-time students received need-based aid. Check with the school for current application deadlines.

SARAH LAWRENCE COLLEGE D-5

www.sarahlawrence.edu

Bronxville, NY 10708	**(914) 395-2510** **(800) 888-2858**
Fax: (914) 395-2515	**Email: slcadmit@alc.edu**
Full-time: 325 men, 925 women	**Faculty:** n/av
Part-time: 15 men, 65 women	**Ph.D.s:** n/av
Graduate: 55 men, 310 women	**Student/Faculty:** n/av
Year: semesters	**Tuition:** $51,034
Room & Board: $12,354	**Freshman Class:** n/av **CEEB CODE:** 2810
Application Deadline: March 1	**HIGHLY COMPETITIVE**

Sarah Lawrence College, established in 1926, is an independent institution conferring liberal arts degrees. The academic structure is based on the British don system. Students meet biweekly with professors in tutorials and are enrolled in small seminars. While there are no formal majors, students develop individual concentrations that are usually interdisciplinary. Figures in the above capsule and in this profile are approximate. There is 1 undergraduate school and 1 graduate school. The 41-acre campus is in a suburban area 15 miles north of midtown Manhattan. Including any residence halls, there are 50 buildings.

STUDENT LIFE: 81% of undergraduates are from out of state, mostly the Middle Atlantic. Students are from 46 states, 25 foreign countries, and Canada. 65% are from public schools. 70% are White; 5% African American; 5% Asian American; 4% Hispanic; 2% Foreign; 1% American Indian/Alaska Native. **Female To Male Ratio:** 3.3:1. The average age of freshmen is 18; all undergraduates, 20. 7% do not continue beyond their first year; 72% remain to graduate. **Housing:** 965 students can be accommodated in college housing, which includes single-sex and coed dorms and on-campus apartments. French Interest House, the Perkins Art Co-op, and the Good Life House. On-campus housing is guaranteed for all 4 years. 87% of students live on campus; of those, 90% remain on campus on weekends. Upperclassmen may keep cars.

FACULTY/CLASSROOMS: 49% of faculty are male; 51% are female. All teach undergraduates, and all do research. No introductory courses are taught by graduate students. The average class size in a regular course is 11.

PROGRAMS OF STUDY: Sarah Lawrence confers B.A. degrees. Master's degrees are also awarded. Bachelor's degrees are awarded in BIOLOGICAL SCIENCE (biology/biological science), COMMUNICATIONS AND THE ARTS (art history and appreciation, classics, creative writing, dance, dramatic arts, English, film arts, fine arts, French, German, Greek, Italian, Latin, literature, music, Russian, Spanish, and visual and performing arts), COMPUTER AND PHYSICAL SCIENCE (chemistry and mathematics), HEALTH PROFESSIONS (premedicine), SOCIAL SCIENCE (anthropology, Asian/Oriental studies, economics, history, liberal arts/general studies, philosophy, political science/government, psychology, religion, Russian and Slavic studies, sociology, and women's studies).

ACTIVITIES: There are no fraternities or sororities. There are 30 groups on campus, including philosophy, human rights, art, choir, chorale, chorus, computers, dance, drama, ethnic, film, international, jazz band, LGBT, literary magazine, musical theater, newspaper, orchestra, photography, poetry, political, radio and TV, religious, social, social service, student government, and yearbook. Popular campus events include Mayfair. **Sports:** There are 5 intercollegiate sports for men and 6 for women, and 9 intramural sports for men and 9 for women. Facilities include a sports center with a gym, jogging track, swimming pool, rowing tank, multipurpose studio, squash courts, fitness center, weight room, tennis courts, and a number of open fields and lawns. Off-campus, the college has the use of a boat house, and stables.

SERVICES: Counseling and information services are available, as is tutoring in some subjects, and a reader service for the blind. **Library/Resources:** The 3 libraries contain 282,676 volumes, 24,218 microform items, 9,319 audio/video tapes/CDs/DVDs, and subscribe to 916 periodicals including electronic. Computerized library services include interlibrary loans, database searching, and Internet access. Special learning facilities include an art gallery, radio station, a library with slides of art and architecture, early childhood center, electronic music studio, music library, student-run theater, and student-run art gallery. **Physically Challenged Students:** 50% of the campus is accessible. Facilities include wheelchair ramps, elevators, special parking, specially equipped restrooms, special class scheduling, lowered drinking fountains, and lowered telephones. **Special:** Internships are available in a variety of fields, with the school offering proximity to New York City art galleries and agencies. Study abroad in many countries, work-study programs, dual concentrations, a 3-2 engineering degree with Columbia, and a general degree may be pursued. All concentrations are self-designed and can be combined. **Visiting:** There are regularly scheduled orientations for prospective students, consisting of a full day of faculty and student panels, lectures, tours, and discussion with admissions officers, offered twice per year during the fall. There are guides for informal visits, visitors may sit in on classes, and stay overnight. To schedule a visit, contact the Admissions Office. **Campus Safety and Security:** Measures include 24-hour foot and vehicle patrol, self-defense education, and security escort services. There are shuttle buses, emergency telephones, and lighted pathways/sidewalks.

REQUIREMENTS: Important academic requirements are: secondary school record, teacher recommendation(s) and essay; class rank is considered. Nonacademic requirements include character and personality qualities; extracurricular activities, talent/ability, volunteer work, and work experience. Campus interview, alumnae relations, geographical residence, and minority status are considered. AP credits are accepted. Important factors in the admissions decision are recommendations by school officials, personality/intangible qualities, and extracurricular activities record. To graduate, students must complete 120 credit hours and meet distribution requirements in 3 of 4 academic areas, including history and social sciences, creative and performing arts, natural science and math, and humanities. Students must fulfill a first-year studies requirement in one of 18 areas and meet a phys ed requirement. Students must also take 2 lecture courses, where the average class size is 40. **Procedure:** Freshmen are admitted in the fall. There are early decision, early admissions, and deferred admissions plans. Early decision applications should be filed by November 15; regular applications, by March 1 for fall entry. The fall 2016 application fee was $50. Notification of early decision is sent December 15; regular decision, April 1. Applications are accepted online. **Transfer Students:** Applicants must submit high school and college transcripts, and a statement of good standing from prior institution(s). A GPA of 3.0 is required and transfer applicants must have a minimum of 30 credits completed, or the equivalent of 2 semesters of full-time college work. Also required are a $50 application fee, Admission Information Form (in-house Form 1), essays, a graded academic paper, and 2 teacher/faculty evaluations. An interview is recommended, but not required. November 15 is the application deadline for spring entry. 60 of 120 credits required for the bachelor's degree must be completed at Sarah Lawrence. **International Students:** The school actively recruits these students. They must take the TOEFL, or SAT II: English as a second language test.

Admissions Contact: Dean of Admission. Email: *slcadmit@alc.edu* Web: *www.sarahlawrence.edu*

FINANCIAL AID: Sarah Lawrence is a member of CSS. The CSS/Profile, and non-custodial parent statement are required. The priority date for freshman financial aid applications for fall entry is February 1.

SCHOOL OF VISUAL ARTS *(The complete profile is made available exclusively on our website, www.barronspac.com)*

SIENA COLLEGE D-3

www.siena.edu

Loudonville, NY 12211 **(518) 783-2423**

Fax: (518) 783-2436	**Email:** admissions@siena.edu
Full-time: 1470 men, 1591 women	**Faculty:** 224
Part-time: 64 men, 61 women	**Ph.D.s:** 91%
Graduate: 29 men, 32 women	**Student/Faculty:** 14 to 1
Year: semesters, summer session	**Tuition:** $34,811
Room & Board: $14,105	**Freshman Class:** 764 enrolled
SAT CR/M/W: 530/550/520 **ACT:** 25	**CEEB CODE:** 2814
Application Deadline: February 15	**COMPETITIVE+**

Siena College is a private, Catholic, liberal arts college that offers 31 majors, and over 80 minors and certificates. Saints customize their education based on their interests and career goals. But that's just the beginning. They quickly realize a Siena education isn't something you get, it's something you do. Extensive study abroad programs and immersive service-learning allow for discovery and reflection. A Siena education is strengthened through a robust internship program that includes top startup companies, nonprofits, and government organizations that drive this region's growth. High-impact learning centers, caring and engaged faculty draw out the best in their students, and a Franciscan tradition of service and community define who we are and give students a lifetime advantage. There are 3 undergraduate schools and 1 graduate school. In addition to regional accreditation, Siena has baccalaureate program accreditation with AACSB, CSWE, NCATE, and ACS. The 175-acre campus is in a suburban area 2 miles north of Albany in the suburb of Loudonville, NY. Including any residence halls, there are 33 buildings.

STUDENT LIFE: 81% of undergraduates are from New York. Others are from 30 states, 17 foreign countries, and Canada. 8% are Hispanic; 79% White; 4% African American; 4% Asian American; 2% Foreign; 2% two or more races; 1% race unknown. 45% are Catholic; 24% Protestant; 24% claim no religious affiliation. **Female To Male Ratio:** 1.1:1. The average age of freshmen is 18; all undergraduates, 21. 13% do not continue beyond their first year; 77% remain to graduate. **Housing:** 2500 students can be accommodated in college housing, which includes coed dorms and on-campus apartments. On-campus housing is guaranteed for all 4 years and is available on a lottery system for upperclassmen. 83% of students live on campus. Upperclassmen may keep cars.

FACULTY/CLASSROOMS: 59% of faculty are male; 41% are female. All teach undergraduates. No introductory courses are taught by graduate students. The average class size in an introductory lecture is 21 and in a laboratory is 15.

PROGRAMS OF STUDY: Siena confers B.A. and B.S degrees. Master's degrees are also awarded. Bachelor's degrees are awarded in AGRICULTURE (environmental studies), BIOLOGICAL SCIENCE (biochemistry and biology/biological science), BUSINESS (accounting, banking and finance, business administration and management, and marketing management), COMMUNICATIONS AND THE ARTS (art/art studies, classics, English, French, Spanish, and visual and performing arts), COMPUTER AND PHYSICAL SCIENCE (actuarial science, chemistry, computer science, mathematics, and physics), ENGINEERING AND ENVIRONMENTAL DESIGN (environmental science), HEALTH PROFESSIONS (nursing), SOCIAL SCIENCE (American studies, economics, history, philosophy, political science/government, psychology, religion, social work, and sociology). Biology BA - Albany Medical College program is the strongest academically. Accounting, psychology, and biology have the largest enrollments.

ACTIVITIES: There are no fraternities or sororities. There are 80 groups on campus, including art, band, cheerleading, chess, choir, chorale, chorus, communications, computers, dance, debate, drama, environmental, ethnic, film, honors, international, jazz band, LGBT, literary magazine, musical theater, newspaper, orchestra, pep band, photography, political, professional, radio and TV, religious, social, social service, student government, and yearbook. Popular campus events include weekend movies, Charity Week, Mr. Siena, SienaFest and Family Weekend. **Sports:** There are 7 intercollegiate sports for men and 11 for women, and 9 intramural sports for men and 9 for women. Facilities include an athletic complex that offers free weights, a training facility, an indoor track, a pool, fitness equipment, life cycles, multipurpose courts, outdoor tennis courts, outdoor fields, squash courts, and racquetball courts. **Graduates:** From July 1, 2015 to June 30, 2016, 769 bachelor's degrees were awarded. The most popular majors were accounting (15%), marketing (11%), and psychology (10%). 4000 companies recruited on campus in 2015-2016. In an average class, 1% graduate in 3 years or less, 72% graduate in 4 years or less, 76% graduate in 5 years or less, and 78% graduate in 6 years or less.

SERVICES: Counseling and information services are available, as is tutoring in most subjects. There is a reader service for the blind, and remedial math and writing, and a writing center that offers free one-to-one assistance. **Library/Resources:** The library contains 369,191 volumes, 27,739 microform items, and 5,922 audio/video tapes/CDs/DVDs, and subscribes to 280 periodicals including electronic. Computerized library services include interlibrary loans, database searching, Internet access, and Wi-Fi capability. Special learning facilities include an art gallery, radio station, TV station, financial technology center, data screens, workstations, and access to financial information sources and accounting labs. **Physically Challenged Students:** 90% of the campus is accessible. Facilities include wheelchair ramps, elevators, special parking, specially equipped restrooms, special class scheduling, lowered drinking fountains, and special housing. A center that provides various resources for students with disabilities. **Special:** The College has opportunities for cross-registration through the Hudson-Mohawk Association. Domestic and international internships, study abroad in over 50 countries, a Washington semester, and work-study programs are also available. The College offers dual majors in different divisions and a B.A.-B.S. degree in math, economics, and biology as well as a 3-2 engineering degree with Rensselaer Polytechnic Institute, Catholic University, Clarkson University, Manhattan College, SUNY Binghamton, and Western New England College. We also offer a 4-1 degree in engineering with Clarkson Graduate College. A 4-4 medical program with Albany Medical College is also offered. A 4-3 law program is offered with Albany Law, Pace Law and Western New England. There are 21 national honor societies, a freshman honors program, and 13 departmental honors programs. **Visiting:** There are regularly scheduled orientations for prospective students, students may interview with an admissions counselor, tour campus, or attend a visit on the weekend. There are guides for informal visits and visitors may sit in on classes. To schedule a visit, contact Admissions Office. **Campus Safety and Security:** Measures include 24-hour foot and vehicle patrol, emergency notification system, and security escort services. There are shuttle buses, emergency telephones, lighted pathways/sidewalks, controlled access to dorms/residences. A card access system for residence halls, radio dispatch, and a 911 on-campus telephone system, are also implemented.

REQUIREMENTS: In the five core areas of math, English, science, history and language Siena likes to see a B and above. We are test optional. To be test optional we need to see 19 academic units. To be test optional for a science major we need to see the student has taken physics and pre-calculus. To be test optional for a business major we need to see four years of math. We accept either the SAT or the ACT. The essay is optional. We highly recommend an interview, however it is not required. AP and CLEP credits are accepted. Important factors in the admissions decision are advanced placement or honors courses, personality/intangible qualities, and extracurricular activities record. To graduate, students must earn 120 credits, including 30 to 39 depending on major, with at least a 2.0 GPA. At least a C-grade in every major field course used to satisfy the credit hour requirement of the major. The required core curriculum is 42 credits. **Procedure:** Freshmen are admitted in the fall and spring. Entrance exams should be taken during spring of the junior year or fall of the senior year. There are early decision, early admissions, and deferred admissions plans. Early decision applications should be filed by December 1; regular applications, by February 15 for fall entry; January 15 for spring entry; and May 1 for summer entry, along with a $50 fee. Notification of early decision is sent December 15; regular decision, March 15. 46 early decision candidates were accepted for the 2016-2017 class. 743 applicants were on the 2016 waiting list. Application fees are waived if application is completed online. **Transfer Students:** 188 transfer students enrolled in 2015-2016. Applicants must have a minimum 2.5 GPA. An interview is recommended. At least half of the major field requirements must be completed at Siena. 30 of 120 credits required for the bachelor's degree must be completed at Siena. **International Students:** There are 60 international students enrolled. The school actively recruits these students. They must take the TOEFL with a minimum score of 530 on the paper-based TOEFL (PBT) or 65 on the Internet-based version (iBT), or the IELTS.

ADMISSIONS: The SAT scores for the 2016-2017 freshman class were: Critical Reading-- 32% below 500, 44% between 500 and 599, 21% between 600 and 699, and 3% between 700 and 800. Math-- 24% below 500, 45% between 500 and 599, 26% between 600 and 699, and 6% between 700 and 800. Writing-- 39% below 500, 44% between 500 and 599, 15% between 600 and 699, and 2% between 700 and 800. The ACT scores were 4% between 12 and 17, 34% between 18 and 23, 50% between 24 and 29, and 13% above 30. 46% of the current freshmen were in the top fifth of their class; 78% were in the top two fifths. **Admissions Contact:** Katie Szalda, Director of Admissions. Email: *admissions@siena.edu* Web: *www.siena.edu*

FINANCIAL AID: In 2016-2017, 99% of all full-time freshmen and 91% of continuing full-time students received some form of financial aid. 71% of all full-time freshmen and 73% of continuing full-time students received need-based aid. The average freshman award was $30,602. Need-based scholarships or need-based grants averaged $23,060 ($20,000 maximum); need-based self-help aid (loans and jobs) averaged $3,989 ($4,500 maximum); non-need-based athletic scholarships averaged $19,883 ($49,000 maximum); and other non-need-based awards and non-need-based scholarships averaged $13,408 ($20,000 maximum). The state aid form is required. The FAFSA code is 002816. The priority date for freshman financial aid applications for fall entry is February 15. The filing deadline for fall entry is May 1.

SKIDMORE COLLEGE — D-3

www.skidmore.edu

Saratoga Springs, NY 12866	(518) 580-5570 (800) 867-6007
Fax: (518) 580-5584	Email: admissions@skidmore.edu
Full-time: 1050 men, 1587 women	Faculty: 279; IIB, +$
Part-time: 11 men, 13 women	Ph.D.s: 87%
Graduate: 3 men, 3 women	Student/Faculty: 9 to 1
Year: semesters, summer session	Tuition: $50,684
Room & Board: $13,530	Freshman Class: 9181 applied, 2670 accepted, 714 enrolled
SAT CR/M/W: 620/610/620 ACT: 29	CEEB CODE: 2815
Application Deadline: January 15	HIGHLY COMPETITIVE

Skidmore College, founded in 1903, is an independent, creative, liberal arts college, with nearly 50 majors, pre-professional offerings such as business, education, and exercise science, a popular study-abroad program, and numerous opportunities for student-faculty research and paid internships as early as year one. There is 1 undergraduate school. In addition to regional accreditation, Skidmore has baccalaureate program accreditation with CSWE, NASAD, and CAEP (Education). The 890-acre campus is in a small town in Saratoga Springs, New York, 30 miles north of Albany. Including any residence halls, there are 50 buildings.

STUDENT LIFE: 68% of undergraduates are from out of state, mostly the Northeast. Students are from 44 states, 59 Foreign countries, and Canada. 58% are from public schools. 9% are Hispanic; 64% White; 5% Asian American; 4% African American; 4% two or more races; 3% race unknown; 11% Foreign. **Female To Male Ratio:** 1.5:1. The average age of freshmen is 18; all undergraduates, 20. 9% do not continue beyond their first year; 89% remain to graduate. **Housing:** College-sponsored housing includes single-sex and coed dorms and on-campus apartments. Gender neutral wing, substance free, 24 hour quiet, women's floors, and global and multicultural communities. On-campus housing is guaranteed for all 4 years and is available on a lottery system for upperclassmen. 89% of students live on campus. All students may keep cars.

FACULTY/CLASSROOMS: 45% of faculty are male; 55% are female. All teach undergraduates and do research. No introductory courses are taught by graduate students. The average class size in an introductory lecture is 16.

PROGRAMS OF STUDY: Skidmore confers B.A. and B.S. degrees. Bachelor's degrees are awarded in AGRICULTURE (environmental studies), BIOLOGICAL SCIENCE (biology/biological science and neurosciences), BUSINESS (business administration and management and business economics), COMMUNICATIONS AND THE ARTS (art, art history and appreciation, classics, dance, dramatic arts, English, French, German, music, and Spanish), COMPUTER AND PHYSICAL SCIENCE (chemistry, computer science, geology, mathematics, and physics), EDUCATION (elementary education), HEALTH PROFESSIONS (exercise science), SOCIAL SCIENCE (American studies, anthropology, Asian/Oriental studies, economics, French studies, gender studies, history, international relations, liberal arts/general studies, philosophy, political science/government, psychology, religion, social science, social work, and sociology). Social sciences, visual & performing arts, and business/marketing have the largest enrollments.

ACTIVITIES: There are no fraternities or sororities. There are 110 groups on campus, including art, band, chorale, chorus, computers, dance, debate, drama, environmental, ethnic, film, honors, international, jazz band, LGBT, literary magazine, musical theater, newspaper, opera, orchestra, photography, political, professional, radio and TV, religious, social, social service, student government, symphony, and yearbook. Popular campus events include Martin Luther King Week, Oktoberfest, and Spring Fling. **Sports:** There are 9 intercollegiate sports for men and 10 for women. Facilities include a sports and recreation center that has a gymnasium with three basketball/volleyball courts, intramural and recreation gyms, swimming pool and diving well, racquetball courts, athletic training room, human-performance laboratory, aerobics and fitness area, weight room, tennis courts, field for field hockey, softball diamond, all-weather track, field turf playing field for soccer, lacrosse, intramurals, baseball diamond, golf driving range, barn, indoor and outdoor riding rings, hunter course, riding trails, rowing boathouse, and an ice hockey rink.**Graduates:** From July 1, 2015 to June 30, 2016, 617 bachelor's degrees were awarded. The most popular majors were social sciences (19%), business (15%), and visual and performing arts (12%). In an average class, 85% graduate in 4 years or less, 88% graduate in 5 years or less, and 89% graduate in 6 years or less.

SERVICES: Counseling and information services are available, as is tutoring in most subjects. Note takers, and books on tape are also offered. **Library/Resources:** Computerized library services include interlibrary loans, database searching, and Internet access. Special learning facilities include an art gallery, radio station, TV station, An electronic music studio, music and art studios, theater teaching facility, teaching museum, anthropology lab, and special biological habitats on campus. **Physically Challenged Students:** 98% of the campus is accessible. Facilities include wheelchair ramps, elevators, special parking, specially equipped restrooms, lowered drinking fountains, and special housing. **Special:** Skidmore offers cross-registration with the Hudson-Mohawk Consortium, individually designed internships, various study-abroad programs, a Washington semester in conjunction with American University, dual and student-designed majors, credit for life and experience, and pass/fail options, as well as a nondegree study program for senior citizens. There are cooperative programs with other schools in engineering, business administration, and health. There are 11 national honor societies, Phi Beta Kappa, and a freshman honors program. **Visiting:** There are regularly scheduled orientations for prospective students, including full-day open-house programs. There are guides for informal visits, visitors may sit in on classes, and stay overnight. To schedule a visit, contact the Admissions Office. **Campus Safety and Security:** Measures include 24-hour foot and vehicle patrol, emergency notification system, and security escort services. There are shuttle buses, emergency telephones, lighted pathways/sidewalks, controlled access to dorms/residences, special security alert system, rigorous fire response procedures, and a lock system on dorm entrances.

REQUIREMENTS: SAT subject tests are considered if submitted. Recommended High School units: 4 units each in English, math, foreign language, social studies, and science with 3 units in lab. AP and CLEP credits are accepted. Important factors in the admissions decision are advanced placement or honors courses, evidence of special talent, personality/intangible qualities, extracurricular activities record, recommendations by school officials, parents or siblings attended your school, recommendations by alumni, and geographical diversity. To graduate, students must complete 120 credits, including at least 24 at the 300 level, with a minimum GPA of 2.0 overall and in the major. B.A. candidates require 90 credits in the liberal arts to graduate, B.S. candidates require 60 credits. Students must fulfill all core curriculum, distribution, and major requirements. **Procedure:** Freshmen are admitted in the fall. Entrance exams should be taken by December of the senior year. There are early decision, early admissions, and deferred admissions plans. Early decision applications should be filed by November 15; regular applications, by January 15 for fall entry, along with a $65 fee. Notification of early decision is sent December 15; regular decision, April 1. 367 early decision candidates were accepted for the 2016-2017 class. 480 applicants were on the 2016 waiting list; 7 were admitted. Applications are accepted on-line. **Transfer Students:** 26 transfer students enrolled in 2015-2016. Transfer students must submit a high school transcript, all college transcripts, an essay or personal statement, test scores (if no 2-year degree), and a statement of good standing from prior institutions. At least one professor recommendation from the current institution and a mid-term report are also required. 60 of 120 credits required for the bachelor's degree must be completed at Skidmore. **International Students:** There are 279 international students enrolled. The school actively recruits these students. They must take the TOEFL with a minimum score of 590 on the paper-based TOEFL (PBT) or 96 on the Internet-based version (iBT). They must also take the SAT or ACT.

ADMISSIONS: 29% of the 2016-2017 applicants were accepted. The SAT scores for the 2016-2017 freshman class were: Critical Reading-- 7% below 500, 29% between 500 and 599, 47% between 600 and 699, and 16% between 700 and 800. Math-- 6% below 500, 35% between 500 and 599, 46% between 600 and 699, and 13% between 700 and 800. Writing-- 7% below 500, 26% between 500 and 599, 53% between 600 and 699, and 13% between 700 and 800. The ACT scores were 9% between 18 and 23, 56% between 24 and 29, and 35% above 30. **Admissions Contact:** Mary Lou Bates, Director of Admissions. Email: *admissions@skidmore.edu* Web: *www.skidmore.edu*

FINANCIAL AID: In 2016-2017, 39% of all full-time freshmen and 41% of continuing full-time students received some form of financial aid. 39% of all full-time freshmen and 41% of continuing full-time students received need-based aid. The average freshman award was $43,100. Need-based scholarships or need-based grants averaged $41,900; need-based self-help aid (loans and jobs) averaged $3,700; and other non-need-based awards and non-need-based scholarships averaged $12,000. The average financial indebtedness of the 2016 graduate was $25,001. Skidmore is a member of CSS. The CSS/Profile is required. The FAFSA code is 002814. The deadline for filing freshman financial aid applications for fall entry is February 1.

ST. BONAVENTURE UNIVERSITY B-4

www.sbu.edu

St. Bonaventure, NY 14778	**(716) 375-2400** **(800) 462-5050**
Fax: (716) 375-4005	**Email: admissions@sbu.edu**
Full-time: 802 men, 790 women	**Faculty:** 120
Part-time: 37 men, 31 women	**Ph.D.s:** n/av
Graduate: 148 men, 244 women	**Student/Faculty:** 11 to 1
Year: semesters, summer session	**Tuition:** $32,331
Room & Board: $11,906	**Freshman Class:** 2871 applied, 1892 accepted, 433 enrolled
SAT CR/M/W: 520/530/510 **ACT:** 24	**CEEB CODE:** 2793
Application Deadline: July 1	**COMPETITIVE**

St. Bonaventure University, founded in 1858, is a private Roman Catholic institution in the Franciscan tradition, offering programs in the arts and sciences, education, business, and journalism and mass communication. There are 4 undergraduate schools and 1 graduate school. In addition to regional accreditation, SBU has baccalaureate program accreditation with AACSB, NCATE, and CACREP. The 500-acre campus is in a small town 75 miles southeast of Buffalo. Including any residence halls, there are 36 buildings.

STUDENT LIFE: 70% of undergraduates are from New York. Others are from 37 states, 16 foreign countries, and Canada. 9% are race unknown; 7% Hispanic; 69% White; 6% African American; 4% Asian American; 3% Foreign; 2% two or more races. 42% are all other affiliations; 39% Catholic; 11% Protestant. **Female To Male Ratio:** 1.1:1. The average age of freshmen is 18; all undergraduates, 19. 18% do not continue beyond their first year; 64% remain to graduate. **Housing:** 1630 students can be accommodated in college housing, which includes single-sex and coed dorms, on-campus apartments, special-interest houses, living and learning communities. On-campus housing is guaranteed for all 4 years. 95% of students live on campus; of those, 100% remain on campus on weekends. All students may keep cars.

FACULTY/CLASSROOMS: 53% of faculty are male; 47% are female. 88% teach undergraduates. No introductory courses are taught by graduate students. The average class size in an introductory lecture is 18; in a laboratory is 13; and in a regular course is 18.

PROGRAMS OF STUDY: SBU confers B.A., B.S., B.B.A. and B.S.Ed. degrees. Master's degrees are also awarded. Bachelor's degrees are awarded in AGRICULTURE (environmental studies), BIOLOGICAL SCIENCE (biochemistry, bioinformatics, biology/biological science, and biophysics), BUSINESS (accounting, banking and finance, management information systems, management science, and marketing/retailing/merchandising), COMMUNICATIONS AND THE ARTS (art history, classical languages, communications, digital communications, dramatic arts, English, French, journalism, modern language, music, Spanish, and visual and performing arts), COMPUTER AND PHYSICAL SCIENCE (chemistry, computer science, cyber intelligence/security studies, mathematics, and physics), EDUCATION (education, elementary education, physical education, special education, and sports studies), ENGINEERING AND ENVIRONMENTAL DESIGN (engineering physics, environmental science, and industrial administration/management), SOCIAL SCIENCE (child care/child and family studies, gerontology, history, international studies, philosophy, political science/government, psychology, sociology, theological studies, and women's studies). Journalism/mass communication, biology, and accounting have the largest enrollments.

ACTIVITIES: There are no fraternities or sororities. There are 65 groups on campus, including art, band, cheerleading, choir, chorale, chorus, computers, dance, drama, environmental, ethnic, honors, international, jazz band, LGBT, literary magazine, newspaper, photography, political, professional, radio and TV, religious, social, social service, student government, and yearbook. Popular campus events include Family Weekend, and Spring and Winter Weekends. **Sports:** There are 8 intercollegiate sports for men and 8 for women, and 10 intramural sports for men and 9 for women. Facilities include a basketball arena, indoor swimming pool, golf course, weight facilities and free weights, fitness center, with strength, aerobics and conditioning areas, an indoor track, multi-use courts, and a rock climbing wall, soccer, baseball, softball, rugby, and intramural fields, and a recreation trail. **Graduates:** From July 1, 2015 to June 30, 2016, 405 bachelor's degrees were awarded. The most popular majors were business (32%), communications/journalism (15%), and biology (9%). In an average class, 1% graduate in 3 years or less, 53% graduate in 4 years or less, 63% graduate in 5 years or less, and 64% graduate in 6 years or less.

SERVICES: Counseling and information services are available, as is tutoring in most subjects, as well as remedial math. **Library/Resources:** The library contains 504,083 volumes, 15,283 microform items, 13,938 audio/video tapes/CDs/DVDs, and subscribes to 33,264 periodicals including electronic. Computerized library services include interlibrary loans, database searching, Internet access, and Wi-Fi capability. Special learning facilities include an art gallery, radio station, TV station, and observatory. **Physically Challenged Students:** 90% of the campus is accessible. Facilities include wheelchair ramps, elevators, special parking, and specially equipped restrooms. **Special:** Internships are available in business, mass communication, political science, psychology, and sociology. Study abroad is offered in 18 countries, B.A.-B.S. degrees, accelerated degree programs, dual and student-designed majors, a Washington semester with American University, with a pass/fail options. Dual admissions with George Washington University School of Medicine, Lake Erie College of Osteopathic Medicine, University at Buffalo School of Dental Medicine, Lake Erie College of Osteopathic Medicine School of Pharmacy, and SUNY-Upstate Medical are also possible. There are 15 national honor societies and a freshman honors program. **Visiting:** There are regularly scheduled orientations for prospective students, including interviews, tours, class visits, and meetings with professors. There are guides for informal visits, visitors may sit in on classes, and stay overnight. To schedule a visit, contact Christina Sutphen at csutphen@sbu.edu. **Campus Safety and Security:** Measures include 24-hour foot and vehicle patrol, emergency notification system, and security escort services. There are shuttle buses, emergency telephones, lighted pathways/sidewalks, and controlled access to dorms/residences.

REQUIREMENTS: The ACT is recommended, with a score of 24, or a satisfactory score on the SAT. Applicants must be graduates of an accredited secondary school or have a GED. 16 academic credits are required, including 4 years each of English and social studies, 3 each of math and science, and 2 of a foreign language. An essay and an interview are recommended. AP and CLEP credits are accepted. To graduate, students must complete 120 credit hours, at least 30 of them in the major, with a minimum GPA of 2.0. Students must complete general education requirements in addition to major requirements. Students in programs leading to teacher certification must have a minimum GPA of 3.0. **Procedure:** Freshmen are admitted to all sessions. Entrance exams should be taken during the spring of the junior year or the fall of the senior year. There are early admissions, deferred admissions, and rolling admissions plans. Applications should be filed by July 1 for fall entry; October 15 for spring entry. Notification is sent on a rolling basis. Applications are accepted online. **Transfer Students:** 46 transfer students enrolled in 2015-2016. Applicants must have a minimum 2.0 GPA. High school and college transcripts, essay, and a letter of recommendation are also required. 45 of 120 credits required for the bachelor's degree must be completed at SBU. **International Students:** There are 47 international students enrolled. The school actively recruits these students. They must take the TOEFL with a minimum score of 550 on the paper-based TOEFL (PBT) or 79 on the Internet-based version (iBT).

ADMISSIONS: 66% of the 2016-2017 applicants were accepted. The SAT scores for the 2016-2017 freshman class were: Critical Reading-- 40% below 500, 41% between 500 and 599, 17% between 600 and 699, and 2% between 700 and 800. Math-- 34% below 500, 43% between 500 and 599, 20% between 600 and 699, and 3% between 700 and 800. Writing-- 47% below 500, 38% between 500 and 599, 13% between 600 and 699, and 2% between 700 and 800. The ACT scores were 5% between 12 and 17, 43% between 18 and 23, 35% between 24 and 29, and 12% above 30. 41% of the current freshmen were in the top fifth of their class; 63% were in the top two fifths. 2 freshmen graduated first in their class. **Admissions Contact:** Bernard Valento, Vice President for Enrollment. Email: *admissions@sbu.edu* Web: *www.sbu.edu*

FINANCIAL AID: In 2016-2017, 99% of all full-time freshmen and 97% of continuing full-time students received some form of financial aid. 77% of all full-time freshmen and 74% of continuing full-time students received need-based aid. The average freshman award was $31,382. Need-based scholarships or need-based grants averaged $11,359; need-based self-help aid (loans and jobs) averaged $7,152; non-need-based athletic scholarships averaged $11,458; and other non-need-based awards and non-need-based scholarships averaged $17,011. 36% of undergraduate students work part-time. Average annual earnings from campus work are $936. The average financial indebtedness of the 2016 graduate was $29,501. The state aid form is required. The FAFSA code is 002817. The priority date for freshman financial aid applications for fall entry is February 15.

ST. FRANCIS COLLEGE *(The complete profile is made available exclusively on our website, www.barronspac.com)*

ST. JOHN FISHER COLLEGE — B-3

www.sjfc.edu

Rochester, NY 14618	**(585) 385-8064** **(800) 444-4640**
Fax: (585) 385-8386	**Email: admissions@sjfc.edu**
Full-time: 1048 men, 1559 women	**Faculty:** 185; IIA, +$
Part-time: 67 men, 112 women	**Ph.D.s:** 90%
Graduate: 320 men, 681 women	**Student/Faculty:** 11 to 1
Year: semesters, summer session	**Tuition:** $31,880
Room & Board: $11,740	**Freshman Class:** 4551 applied, 2937 accepted, 576 enrolled
SAT CR/M/W: 527/546/506 **ACT:** 24	**CEEB CODE:** 2798
Application Deadline: rolling	**COMPETITIVE**

St. John Fisher College is an independent, liberal arts institution in the Catholic tradition of American higher education. Guided since its inception in 1948 by the educational philosophy of the Congregation of St. Basil, the college emphasizes liberal learning for students in traditional academic disciplines, as well as for those in more directly career-oriented fields. The college welcomes qualified students, faculty, and staff regardless of religious or cultural background. There are 4 undergraduate schools and 5 graduate schools. In addition to regional accreditation, Fisher has baccalaureate program accreditation with AACSB, ACPE, NCATE, ACS, CCNE, and CAEP. The 154-acre campus is in a suburban area 6 miles southeast of Rochester. Including any residence halls, there are 26 buildings.

STUDENT LIFE: 97% of undergraduates are from New York. Others are from 22 states, 6 Foreign countries, and Canada. 84% are from public schools. 84% are White; 4% African American; 4% Asian American; 4% Hispanic; 2% two or more races; 2% race unknown. **Female To Male Ratio:** 1.6:1. The average age of freshmen is 18; all undergraduates, 21. 14% do not continue beyond their first year; 73% remain to graduate. **Housing:** 1400 students can be accommodated in college housing, which includes single-sex and coed dorms. On-campus housing is guaranteed for the freshman year only and is available on a lottery system for upperclassmen. Priority is given to out-of-town students. 50% of students commute. Upperclassmen may keep cars.

FACULTY/CLASSROOMS: 46% of faculty are male; 53% are female. 86% teach undergraduates. No introductory courses are taught by graduate students. The average class size in an introductory lecture is 22 and in a laboratory is 14.

PROGRAMS OF STUDY: Fisher confers B.A. and B.S. degrees. Master's and doctoral degrees are also awarded. Bachelor's degrees are awarded in BIOLOGICAL SCIENCE (biology/biological science), BUSINESS (accounting, business administration and management, marketing management, and sports management), COMMUNICATIONS AND THE ARTS (communications, digital communications, English, French, and Spanish), COMPUTER AND PHYSICAL SCIENCE (chemistry, computer science, mathematics, physics, and statistics), EDUCATION (elementary education, English education, foreign languages education, mathematics education, middle school education, science education, secondary education, social studies education, and special education), HEALTH PROFESSIONS (nursing), SOCIAL SCIENCE (American studies, anthropology, criminology, economics, history, interdisciplinary studies, international studies, legal studies, philosophy, political science/government, psychology, religion, and sociology). Sciences is the strongest academically. Management, nursing, and biological sciences have the largest enrollments.

ACTIVITIES: There are no fraternities or sororities. There are 70 groups on campus, including art, cheerleading, choir, chorus, computers, dance, drama, environmental, ethnic, honors, international, LGBT, literary magazine, musical theater, newspaper, pep band, photography, political, professional, radio and TV, religious, social, social service, student activities board, student government, and yearbook. Popular campus events include Spring Event, Senior Week, and TEDDI 24-hour Dance Marathon for Charity. **Sports:** There are 12 intercollegiate sports for men and 12 for women, and 4 intramural sports for men and 4 for women. Facilities include a field house, gymnasium for men's and women's basketball teams, a fitness center/weight room, and training facilities. Growney Stadium is home to the football, soccer, and lacrosse teams. Polisseni Track & Field complex features a competition track with a grass infield, and Dugan Yard baseball complex is home to the men's baseball team, a softball complex, and a grass practice field. **Graduates:** From July 1, 2015 to June 30, 2016, 729 bachelor's degrees were awarded. The most popular majors were business (24%), nursing (22%), and education (10%). In an average class, 2% graduate in 3 years or less, 65% graduate in 4 years or less, 72% graduate in 5 years or less, and 73% graduate in 6 years or less.

SERVICES: Counseling and information services are available, as is tutoring in every subject, and a reader service for the blind. Math and writing centers provide help to students at all levels, and 24 hour online tutoring, and peer tutoring is available to all students in most undergraduate subject areas. **Library/Resources:** The library contains 171,774 volumes, 52,323 microform items, 9,080 audio/video tapes/CDs/DVDs, and subscribes to 75,357 periodicals including electronic. Computerized library services include interlibrary loans, database searching, and Internet access. Special learning facilities include an art gallery, radio station, TV station, a multimedia center, "wet" and "dry" multidisciplinary science labs, animal labs, growth chambers, and athletics fitness facility. **Physically Challenged Students:** All of the campus is accessible. Facilities include wheelchair ramps, elevators, special parking, specially equipped restrooms, special class scheduling, lowered drinking fountains, lowered telephones, and accessible dorm rooms. **Special:** The college has cooperative programs and cross-registration with Rochester area colleges. The college offers internships in most majors, independent research in various majors, study abroad, accelerated degree programs in specific majors, Washington semesters, dual and student-designed majors, and degrees in interdisciplinary studies. Navy and Marine ROTC are available at the University of Rochester and Air Force and Army ROTC is available at Rochester Institute of Technology. There are 10 national honor societies, a freshman honors program, and 8 departmental honors programs. **Visiting:** There are regularly scheduled orientations for prospective students, prospective students can schedule a campus tour; an interview with a member of the admissions staff; a meeting with faculty and coaches; and lunch on campus. There are guides for informal visits, visitors may sit in on classes, and stay overnight. To schedule a visit, contact the Office of Freshman Admissions. **Campus Safety and Security:** Measures include 24-hour foot and vehicle patrol, emergency notification system, self-defense education, and security escort services, shuttle buses, emergency telephones, lighted pathways/sidewalks, controlled access to dorms/residences, and access to the residence halls is controlled by the ID card access system. Residence halls are patrolled and monitored 24 hours a day by security officers or resident advisers. All other campus facilities are locked and unlocked according to established schedules.

REQUIREMENTS: Applicants are required to submit either SAT or ACT standardized test scores for admission to the College. Applicants must be graduates of an accredited secondary school and have completed 16 academic credits including 4 years each in English and history/social studies, 3 years each in math and science, and 2 years in a foreign language. Interviews are recommended. AP and CLEP credits are accepted. Important factors in the admissions decision are advanced placement or honors courses, extracurricular activities record, and leadership record. To graduate, students must complete at least 120 credit hours, including at least 30 in the major, and maintain a 2.0 minimum GPA. The core curriculum consists of 15 courses that students must successfully complete to graduate; the core is composed of 2 tiers of study: Foundations courses and Perspectives courses. Freshmen must participate in one of the integrative learning communities. **Procedure:** Freshmen are admitted in the fall. There are early decision, deferred admissions, and rolling admissions plans. Application deadlines are open. Notification of early decision is sent January 15; regular decision, on a rolling basis. 57 early decision candidates were accepted for the 2016-2017 class. Application fees are waived if application is completed online. **Transfer Students:** 244 transfer students enrolled in 2015-2016. Applicants must have a minimum GPA of 2.0 to be considered (mean GPA is 2.8). A high school transcript is required for students with fewer than 24 college credits. Interviews are recommended. 30 of 120 credits required for the bachelor's degree must be completed at Fisher. **International Students:** There are 4 international students enrolled. They must take the TOEFL with a minimum score of 550 on the paper-based TOEFL (PBT) or 80 on the Internet-based version (iBT). They must also take the SAT or ACT. International Applicants may submit TOEFL scores or standardized entrance exams such as SAT or ACT.

ADMISSIONS: 65% of the 2016-2017 applicants were accepted. The SAT scores for the 2016-2017 freshman class were: Critical Reading-- 32% below 500, 53% between 500 and 599, 14% between 600 and 699, and 1% between 700 and 800. Math-- 23% below 500, 55% between 500 and 599, 21% between 600 and 699, and 1% between 700 and 800. Writing-- 47% below 500, 43% between 500 and 599, 9% between 600 and 699, and 1% between 700 and 800. The ACT scores were 2% between 12 and 17, 46% between 18 and 23, 45% between 24 and 29, and 7% above 30. 45% of the current freshmen were in the top fifth of their class; 83% were in the top two fifths. 6 freshmen graduated first in their class. **Admissions Contact:** Stacy Ledermann, Director of Freshman Admissions. Email: *admissions@sjfc.edu* Web: *www.sjfc.edu*

FINANCIAL AID: In 2016-2017, 100% of all full-time freshmen and 99% of continuing full-time students received some form of financial aid. 84% of all full-time freshmen and 83% of continuing full-time students received need-based aid. The average freshman award was $22,202. Need-based scholarships or need-based grants averaged $19,284 ($34,000 maximum); and need-based self-help aid (loans and jobs) averaged $4,629 ($8,000 maximum). 25% of undergraduate students work part-time. Average annual earnings from campus work are $1500. The average financial indebtedness of the 2016 graduate was $35,925. The state aid form is required. The FAFSA code is 002821. The priority date for freshman financial aid applications for fall entry is February 15.

ST. JOHN'S UNIVERSITY D-5

www.stjohns.edu

Queens, NY 11439	**(718) 990-2000** **(888) 9ST-JOHNS**
Fax: (718) 990-5686	**Email: admission@stjohns.edu**
Full-time: 5054 men, 6507 women	**Faculty:** 582; I, +$
Part-time: 2070 men, 2805 women	**Ph.D.s:** 93%
Graduate: 1763 men, 2884 women	**Student/Faculty:** 20 to 1
Year: semesters, summer session	**Tuition:** $39,460
Room & Board: $16,390	**Freshman Class:** 28590 applied, 18115 accepted, 3248 enrolled
SAT CR/M: 520/540 **ACT:** 24	**CEEB CODE:** 2799
Application Deadline: n/av	**COMPETITIVE**

St. John's University, founded in 1870 by the Vincentian Fathers, is a Catholic and Vincentian University dedicated to student success through quality academics, dynamic global studies opportunities, and a focus on social justice. The school pursue more than 100 associate, bachelor's, master's, and doctoral degree programs in the arts, business, education, law, pharmacy, the sciences, and technology. In Europe the school lets them earn up to 15 credits living and learning in three cities in one semester. About 30 percent of St. John's students take classes overseas before they graduate exceeding the national average. The Catholic and Vincentian Mission is also evident in St. John's programs like the Ozanam Scholars, which prepares undergraduates to combat poverty and injustice through teaching, service, and research. There are 5 undergraduate schools and 6 graduate schools. In addition to regional accreditation, St. John's has baccalaureate program accreditation with AACSB, ACPE, NASAD, TEAC, ABA, ARC-PA, and NAACLS. The 96-acre campus is in a suburban area. The main campus is located in a residential section of Queens. There is also a campus in Staten Island, Lower East Side of Manhattan, and Rome, Italy. Including any residence halls, there are 53 buildings.

STUDENT LIFE: 78% of undergraduates are from New York. Others are from 46 states, 127 foreign countries, and Canada. 57% are from public schools. 9% are race unknown; 44% White; 4% Foreign; 4% two or more races; 14% African American; 14% Asian American; 10% Hispanic. 45% are Catholic; 20% claim no religious affiliation; 20% Muslim, Hindu, Buddhist, Mormon, Jehovah Witness, Pentecostal, Sikh, Greek and Russian Orthodox; 13% Protestant. **Female To Male Ratio:** 1.4:1. The average age of freshmen is 18; all undergraduates, 19. 16% do not continue beyond their first year; 58% remain to graduate. **Housing:** 3537 students can be accommodated in college housing, which includes coed dorms, on-campus apartments, and off-campus apartments. Honors themed floor, international themed community that focuses on languages, and special interest housing options are available. On-campus housing is on a first-come, first-served basis, and available on a lottery system for upperclassmen. Priority is given to out-of-town students. 80% of students commute. Upperclassmen may keep cars. Alcohol is not permitted.

FACULTY/CLASSROOMS: 55% of faculty are male; 46% are female. 92% teach undergraduates. No introductory courses are taught by graduate students.

PROGRAMS OF STUDY: St. John's confers B.A., B.S., B.F.A., and B.S.Ed. degrees. Associate, master's, and doctoral degrees are also awarded. Bachelor's degrees are awarded in AGRICULTURE (environmental studies), BIOLOGICAL SCIENCE (biology/adolescence education, biology/biological science, and toxicology), BUSINESS (accounting, business administration and management, finance, hospitality management services, insurance and risk management, international business management, management science, marketing, and sports management), COMMUNICATIONS AND THE ARTS (advertising, communications, English, film, television and digital media, fine arts, French, graphic design, illustration, information technology, Italian, journalism, photography, public relations, radio/television technology, Spanish, speech/debate/rhetoric, and telecommunications), COMPUTER AND PHYSICAL SCIENCE (actuarial science, chemistry, computer science, computer security and information assurance, mathematics, physical sciences, physics secondary education, physics and mathematics, and physics), EDUCATION (education, elementary education, health information management, secondary education, social studies secondary school education, Spanish adolescense education, and special education), HEALTH PROFESSIONS (clinical science, pharmacy, physician's assistant, radiological science, and speech pathology/audiology), SOCIAL SCIENCE (anthropology, Asian/Oriental studies, criminal justice, economics, history, human services, legal studies, liberal arts/general studies, philosophy, political science/government, psychology, public administration, social studies, sociology, and theology). Pharmacy, biology, psychology, and accounting are the strongest academically. Pharmacy, biology, and psychology have the largest enrollments.

ACTIVITIES: 8% of men belong to 3 local and 17 national fraternities; 7% of women belong to 3 local and 15 national sororities. There are 148 groups on campus, including art, cheerleading, choir, chorus, computers, dance, debate, drama, environmental, ethnic, film, honors, international, jazz band, literary magazine, musical theater, newspaper, pep band, photography, political, professional, radio and TV, religious, social, social service, student government, and yearbook. Popular campus events include St. Baldrick's, Beautiful Me (EAK) Project, Blessing of Students before Finals, Founder's Week, Mass of the Holy Spirit, and Holy Days of Obligation. **Sports:** There are 7 intercollegiate sports for men and 10 for women, and 8 intramural sports for men and 4 for women. Facilities include gyms, tennis courts, weight and exercise rooms, baseball and softball diamonds, fields for football/lacrosse and soccer, basketball courts, and an outdoor track. **Graduates:** From July 1, 2015 to June 30, 2016, 1978 bachelor's degrees were awarded. The most popular majors were business/marketing (23%), communications/journalism (11%), and health professions (11%). 267 companies recruited on campus in 2015-2016. In an average class, 1% graduate in 3 years or less, 37% graduate in 4 years or less, 47% graduate in 5 years or less, and 58% graduate in 6 years or less. Of the 2015 graduating class, 37% were enrolled in graduate school within 6 months of graduation, and 68% were employed.

SERVICES: Counseling and information services are available, as is tutoring in most subjects. There is a reader service for the blind. **Library/Resources:** The 4 libraries contain 1.2 million volumes, 358,833 microform items, 3,342 audio/video tapes/CDs/DVDs, and subscribe to 87,452 periodicals including electronic. Computerized library services include interlibrary loans, database searching, Internet access, and Wi-Fi capability. Special learning facilities include an art gallery, radio station, TV station. There is also a health education resource center, model pharmacy, speech and hearing clinic, institute of Asian studies, global language and culture center, financial information lab, little theatre, math learning center and a writing center. **Physically Challenged Students:** 95% of the campus is accessible. Facilities include wheelchair ramps, elevators, special parking, specially equipped restrooms, special class scheduling, and special housing. **Special:** St. John's offers internships, cross-registration, study abroad in Europe, Central and South America, Australia, the Caribbean, Africa, and Asia, accelerated degree programs in many majors, B.A.-B.S. degrees, dual majors and combined degree programs, pass/fail options, and some credit for life, military, and work experience. There are cooperative programs in engineering with Manhattan College, optometry with SUNY College of Optometry, and a D.P.M. from New York College of Podiatric Medicine. St. John's Staten Island campus offers 3-year bachelor degree program opportunities in selected majors. There is a 6-year doctor of pharmacy program for incoming freshmen. Many dual degree programs are available. Eligible students may participate in the University Honors Program. There are 20 national honor societies, a freshman honors program, and 16 departmental honors programs. **Visiting:** There are regularly scheduled orientations for prospective students, available Monday-Sunday throughout the year; which includes information sessions with admission counselors and student-led tour of the campus. Open House and accepted students events are also available periodically throughout the calendar year. There are guides for informal visits, visitors may sit in on classes, and stay overnight. To schedule a visit, contact Corinne Gentile at (888) 9ST-JOHNS. **Campus Safety and Security:** Measures include 24-hour foot and vehicle patrol, emergency notification system, self-defense education, and security escort services. There are also shuttle buses, emergency telephones, lighted pathways/sidewalks, controlled access to dorms/residences, and a crime prevention awareness program.

REQUIREMENTS: The SAT or ACT is required. Admissions decisions are made by committee review and are based upon several criteria presentated at the time of admission. This includes high school GPA, academic curriculum, standarized test scores, resume, essay, and letters of recommendation. AP and CLEP credits are accepted. Important factors in the admissions decision are advanced placement or honors courses, leadership record, and extracurricular activities record. To graduate, students must complete at least 126 credit hours, including core courses and distribution requirements, with a minimum GPA of 2.0 overall and in the major. Other requirements vary by program. Core courses include English, theology, philosophy, Discover NY, history, scientific inquiry, and speech. Distribution requirements include a second language, fine arts, language and culture, math, philosophy, theology, and social sciences. **Procedure:** Freshmen are admitted in the fall, spring, and summer. Entrance exams should be taken late in the junior year or early in the senior year. There are early admissions, deferred admissions, and rolling admissions plans. Application deadlines are open. Notifications are sent December 1. Application fees are waived if application is completed online. **Transfer Students:** 567 transfer students enrolled in 2015-2016. Transfer applicants must present official high school and college transcripts, as well as a list of courses in progress. If the student is not currently enrolled or was out of school for one semester or more in the past, a letter of explanation is also required. 30 of 126 credits required for the bachelor's degree must be completed at St. John's. **International Students:** There are 666 international students enrolled. The school actively recruits these students. They must take the TOEFL with a minimum score of 500 on the paper-based TOEFL (PBT) or 61 on the Internet-based version (iBT).

ADMISSIONS: 63% of the 2016-2017 applicants were accepted. The SAT scores for the 2016-2017 freshman class were: Critical Reading-- 36% below 500, 45% between 500 and 599, 17% between 600 and 699, and 2% between 700 and 800. Math-- 28% below 500, 44% between 500 and 599, 22% between 600 and 699, and 5% between 700 and 800. The ACT scores were 1% between 12 and 17, 38% between 18 and 23, 50% between 24 and 29, and 11% above 30. 36% of the current freshmen were in the top fifth of their class; 67% were in the top two fifths. **Admissions Contact:** Samantha Wright, Director of Undergraduate Admission. Email: *admission@stjohns.edu* Web: *www.stjohns.edu*

FINANCIAL AID: In 2016-2017, 99% of all full-time freshmen and 96% of continuing full-time students received some form of financial aid. 70% of all full-time freshmen and 85% of continuing full-time students received need-based aid. The average freshman award was $44,756. Need-based scholarships or need-based grants averaged $8,780 ($25,980 maximum); need-based self-help aid (loans and jobs) averaged $7,723 ($16,000 maximum); non-need-based athletic scholarships averaged $30,515 ($55,850 maximum); other non-need-based awards and non-need-based scholarships averaged $4,318 ($38,630 maximum); and $16,941 from other forms of aid. 9% of undergraduate students work part-time. The average financial indebtedness of the 2016 graduate was $25,101. The FAFSA code is 002823. The priority date for freshman financial aid applications for fall entry is December 15. The filing deadline for fall entry is August 1.

ST. JOSEPH'S COLLEGE, NEW YORK/BROOKLYN CAMPUS *(The*

complete profile is made available exclusively on our website, www.barronspac.com)

ST. JOSEPH'S COLLEGE, NEW YORK/ LONG ISLAND CAMPUS E-5

St. Joseph's College, New York/Suffolk Campus
www.sjcny.edu

Patchogue, NY 11772 **(631) 687- 4500**

Fax: (631) 447- 3601 **Email:** longislandas@sjcny.edu

Full-time: 903 men, 1688 women
Part-time: 159 men, 325 women
Graduate: 199 men, 640 women
Year: semesters, summer session
Room & Board: n/app

SAT CR/M/W: 520/530/500 **ACT:** 23
Application Deadline: n/av

Faculty: 110
Ph.D.s: 75%
Student/Faculty: 24 to 1
Tuition: $25,124
Freshman Class: 1770 applied, 1272 accepted, 431 enrolled
CEEB CODE: 2841
COMPETITIVE

St. Joseph's College, founded in 1916, provides an affordable liberal arts education to a diverse group of students at its campuses at SJC Brooklyn, SJC Long Island and SJC Online. Independent and coeducational, St. Joseph's prepares students for lives of integrity, intellectual and spiritual values, social responsibility and service lives that are worthy of the College's motto, Esse non videri – "To be and not to seem." St. Joseph's challenges it's students to develop their full potential and an enthusiasm for learning. With more than 400 faculty members, the College offers a student-faculty ratio that provides individual attention in an open, supportive atmosphere. There are 2 undergraduate schools and 1 graduate school. In addition to regional accreditation, St. Joseph's College has baccalaureate program accreditation with ACEN, COAPRT, and CAEP. The 56-acre campus is in a suburban area 55 miles from midtown Manhattan. Including any residence halls, there are 9 buildings.

STUDENT LIFE: 99% of undergraduates are from New York. Others are from 13 states, 9 foreign countries, and Canada. 68% are White; 5% African American; 2% Asian American; 2% two or more races; 12% race unknown; 11% Hispanic. **Female To Male Ratio:** 2.1:1. The average age of freshmen is 19; all undergraduates, 24. 13% do not continue beyond their first year; 87% remain to graduate. **Housing:** College-sponsored housing includes Alcohol is not permitted. All students commute. All students may keep cars.

FACULTY/CLASSROOMS: 45% of faculty are male; 55% are female. All teach undergraduates. No introductory courses are taught by graduate students. The average class size in an introductory lecture is 18; in a laboratory is 15; and in a regular course is 17.

PROGRAMS OF STUDY: St. Joseph's College confers B.A., B.S., B.A./M.A., B.S./M.A., B.S./M.S., and B.S./M.B.A. degrees. Master's degrees are also awarded. Bachelor's degrees are awarded in BIOLOGICAL SCIENCE (biology/biological science), BUSINESS (accounting, business administration and management, hospitality management services, marketing management, organizational leadership and management, recreation and leisure services, and tourism), COMMUNICATIONS AND THE ARTS (English, journalism, Spanish, speech/debate/rhetoric, communication arts - speech, and studio art), COMPUTER AND PHYSICAL SCIENCE (chemistry, computer information technology, computer information systems, computer science, and mathematics), EDUCATION (education, secondary education, and special education), HEALTH PROFESSIONS (health care administration, medical technology, nursing, and public health), SOCIAL SCIENCE (child psychology/development, criminal justice, history, human services, liberal arts/general studies, philosophy and religion, political science/government, psychology, social science, and sociology). Education programs are our hallmark. Very strong accounting, biology, nursing, hospitality and tourism management, computer science, criminal justice and psychology. are the strongest academically. Child Study, business administration and organizational management. have the largest enrollments.

ACTIVITIES: There are 49 groups on campus, including campus activities board, child study club, LGBTQA, The INN and Diversity Union, art, chess, chorus, computers, dance, drama, environmental, ethnic, honors, international, musical theater, newspaper, political, professional, radio and TV, religious, social, social service, STARS, student government, and yearbook. Popular campus events include Welcome Back BBQ, Welcome Back Evening Social, Club Fair, Fall Festival, Bowl-a-thon, Charity BINGO, Spring Fling, Spring Gala, Tom DeLuca (Hypnotist), Talent Show. **Sports:** There are 9 intercollegiate sports for men and 9 for women. Facilities include multi-purpose turf field for soccer and lacrosse, softball field, baseball field, 6 full tennis courts, natatorium, and gymnasium with 2 full courts. **Graduates:** From July 1, 2015 to June 30, 2016, 774 bachelor's degrees were awarded. The most popular majors were child study/education (19%), business/marketing (10%), and speech communications (7%). 20 companies recruited on campus in 2015-2016. In an average class, 59% graduate in 4 years or less, 73% graduate in 5 years or less, and 76% graduate in 6 years or less.

SERVICES: Counseling and information services are available, as is tutoring in most subjects. There is a reader service for the blind, and remedial math, reading, and writing. **Library/Resources:** The library contains 236,309 volumes, 1,375 microform items, and 2,372 audio/video tapes/CDs/DVDs, and subscribes to 60,421 periodicals including electronic. Computerized library services include interlibrary loans, database searching, Internet access, and Wi-Fi capability. Special learning facilities include an art gallery, radio station, 3-D Printer, technology building, computer labs, and the Claire Rose Playhouse. **Physically Challenged Students:** All of the campus is accessible. Facilities include wheelchair ramps, elevators, special parking, specially equipped restrooms, special class scheduling, and lowered drinking fountains. **Special:** Study abroad in Greece, Costa Rica, France, Romania England and Spain. OCICU - Online Consortium of Independent College and Universities. There is a freshman honors program. **Visiting:** There are regularly scheduled orientations for prospective students, Acclimation to institution, programs, services, and facilities. Assistance with developing positive and realistic expectations, fostering a comfort level at the institution, opportunity to meet other new students, faculty and staff. There are guides for informal visits and visitors may sit in on classes. To schedule a visit, contact Elizabeth McGonigle in Admissions. **Campus Safety and Security:** Measures include 24-hour foot and vehicle patrol, emergency notification system, and security escort services. There are emergency telephones and lighted pathways/sidewalks.

REQUIREMENTS: The SAT or ACT is required. High School diploma is required and GED is accepted. Off-campus interview arranged with admissions representative. AP and CLEP credits are accepted. Important factors in the admissions decision are advanced placement or honors courses, leadership record, and recommendations by school officials. **Procedure:** Freshmen are admitted fall, spring, and summer. There are deferred admissions and rolling admissions plans. Application deadlines are open. Application fee is $25. Notifications are sent November 1. Applications are accepted on-line. **Transfer Students:** 582 transfer students enrolled in 2015-2016. If transferring with less than 24 credits of college level coursework, a high school transcript is required. 30 of 120 credits required for the bachelor's degree must be completed at St. Joseph's College. **International Students:** There are 11 international students enrolled. The school actively recruits these students. SAT or ACT are recommended.

ADMISSIONS: 72% of the 2016-2017 applicants were accepted. The SAT scores for the 2016-2017 freshman class were: Critical Reading-- 37% below 500, 50% between 500 and 599, 12% between 600 and 699, and 1% between 700 and 800. Math-- 32% below 500, 48% between 500 and 599, 18% between 600 and 699, and 2% between 700 and 800. Writing-- 47% below 500, 44% between 500 and 599, 8% between 600 and 699, and 1% between 700 and 800. The ACT scores were 6% between 12 and 17, 48% between 18 and 23, 43% between 24 and 29, and 3% above 30. **Admissions Contact:** Gigi Lamens, Vice President for Enrollment Management. Email: *longislandas@sjcny.edu* Web: *www.sjcny.edu*

FINANCIAL AID: In 2016-2017, 99% of all full-time freshmen and 86% of continuing full-time students received some form of financial aid. 78% of all full-time freshmen and 71% of continuing full-time students received need-based aid. The average freshman award was $19,746. Need-based scholarships or need-based grants averaged $7,593 ($19,641 maximum); need-based self-help aid (loans and jobs) averaged $3,482 ($8,000 maximum); and other non-need-based awards and non-need-based scholarships averaged $13,281 ($46,180 maximum). 7% of undergraduate students work part-time. Average annual earnings from campus work are $2116. The average financial indebtedness of the 2016 graduate was $30,881. The state aid form is required. The FAFSA code is E00505. The priority date for freshman financial aid applications for fall entry is February 25.

ST. LAWRENCE UNIVERSITY C-2

www.stlawu.edu

Canton, NY 13617	(315) 229-5261 (800) 285-1856
Fax: (315) 229-5818	Email: admissions@stlawu.edu
Full-time: 1077 men, 1325 women	**Faculty:** 176; IIB, +$
Part-time: 2 men	**Ph.D.s:** 98%
Graduate: 33 men, 60 women	**Student/Faculty:** 11 to 1
Year: semesters, summer session	**Tuition:** $51,190
Room & Board: $14,800	**Freshman Class:** 5876 applied, 2713 accepted, 680 enrolled
SAT CR/M/W: 600/605/590 **ACT:** 28	**CEEB CODE:** 2805
Application Deadline: February 1	**VERY COMPETITIVE**

St. Lawrence University, established in 1856, is a private liberal arts institution. The figures in the above capsule and in this profile are approximate. There is 1 undergraduate school and 1 graduate school. In addition to regional accreditation, St. Lawrence has baccalaureate program accreditation with ACS. The 1100-acre campus is in a small town 80 miles south of Ottawa, Canada. Including any residence halls, there are 30 buildings.

STUDENT LIFE: 59% of undergraduates are from out of state, mostly the Northeast. Students are from 40 states, 45 foreign countries, and Canada. 69% are from public schools. 83% are White; 6% Foreign; 4% Hispanic; 3% African American; 1% Asian American. **Female To Male Ratio:** 1.2:1. The average age of freshmen is 18; all undergraduates, 20. 10% do not continue beyond their first year; 79% remain to graduate. **Housing:** 2162 students can be accommodated in college housing, which includes coed on-campus apartments. In addition, there are special-interest houses, fraternity houses, sorority houses, theme cottages, women's dorms, wellness housing, and gender-neutral housing. On-campus housing is guaranteed for all 4 years. 99% of students live on campus; of those, 90% remain on campus on weekends. All students may keep cars.

FACULTY/CLASSROOMS: 55% of faculty are male; 45% are female. 99% teach undergraduates, and 99% do research. No introductory courses are taught by graduate students. The average class size in a regular course is 16.

PROGRAMS OF STUDY: St. Lawrence confers B.A. and B.S. degrees. Master's degrees are also awarded. Bachelor's degrees are awarded in AGRICULTURE (conservation and regulation and environmental studies), BIOLOGICAL SCIENCE (biochemistry, biology/biological science, biophysics, and neurosciences), BUSINESS (international economics), COMMUNICATIONS AND THE ARTS (art, art history and appreciation, communications, creative writing, dramatic arts, English, fine arts, French, German, languages, modern language, music, Spanish, studio art, and visual and performing arts), COMPUTER AND PHYSICAL SCIENCE (chemistry, computer science, geology, mathematics, and physics), ENGINEERING AND ENVIRONMENTAL DESIGN (environmental science), SOCIAL SCIENCE (African studies, anthropology, Asian/Oriental studies, Canadian studies, economics, history, interdisciplinary studies, international studies, philosophy, political science/government, psychology, religion, and sociology). Psychology, economics, and government have the largest enrollments.

ACTIVITIES: 4% of men belong to 2 national fraternities; 19% of women belong to 1 local and 3 national sororities. There are 100 groups on campus, including art, choir, chorus, computers, dance, drama, environmental, ethnic, forensics, honors, international, jazz band, LGBT, literary magazine, newspaper, orchestra, photography, political, professional, radio and TV, religious, social, social service, student government, and yearbook. Popular campus events include Moving-Up Day, 100th Night, and Candlelight Service. **Sports:** There are 16 intercollegiate sports for men and 16 for women, and 11 intramural sports for men and 11 for women. Facilities include basketball, squash, and tennis courts, a swimming pool, fitness center, field houses, an arena, artificial ice rink, golf course, riding stables, jogging and cross-country ski trails, indoor and outdoor competition tracks, soccer, baseball, and softball fields. **Graduates:** From July 1, 2015 to June 30, 2016, 585 bachelor's degrees were awarded. The most popular majors were social sciences (32%), biological/life sciences (12%), and psychology (10%). 18 companies recruited on campus in 2015-2016. In an average class, 1% graduate in 3 years or less, 78% graduate in 4 years or less, 80% graduate in 5 years or less, and 87% graduate in 6 years or less. Of the 2015 graduating class, 24% were enrolled in graduate school within 6 months of graduation, and 72% were employed.

SERVICES: Counseling and information services are available, as is tutoring in every subject, a reader service for the blind, a writing center, and science and technology counseling. **Library/Resources:** The 2 libraries contain 638,440 volumes, 594,400 microform items, 9,110 audio/video tapes/CDs/DVDs, and subscribe to 115,421 periodicals including electronic. Computerized library services include interlibrary loans, database searching, and Internet access. Special learning facilities include an art gallery, radio station, and a science field station. **Physically Challenged Students:** 75% of the campus is accessible. Facilities include wheelchair ramps, elevators, special parking, specially equipped restrooms, special class scheduling, and lowered drinking fountains. **Special:** Students may cross-register with the Associated Colleges of the St. Lawrence Valley. Internships are available through the sociology, psychology, and English departments and through a service learning program. Study-abroad in 15 countries and a Washington semester are also offered. Dual majors and student-designed majors can be arranged. Students may earn 3-2 engineering degrees in conjunction with 7 engineering schools. Non-degree study and pass/fail options are available. An Adirondack semester is also offered. There are 20 national honor societies, Phi Beta Kappa, and 17 departmental honors programs. **Visiting:** There are regularly scheduled orientations for prospective students, including interviews and tours. There are guides for informal visits, visitors may sit in on classes, and stay overnight. To schedule a visit, contact the Admissions Office. **Campus Safety and Security:** Measures include 24-hour foot and vehicle patrol, emergency notification system, self-defense education, and security escort services. There are emergency telephones, lighted pathways/sidewalks, and student patrols.

REQUIREMENTS: Applicants must be graduates of an accredited high school. 20 academic credits are recommended, including 4 years each of English, math, science and foreign language, and 2 years each of social studies, and history. Essays are required and interviews are recommended for all applicants. Submissions of standardized test scores is optional. AP credits are accepted. Important factors in the admissions decision are advanced placement or honors courses, extracurricular activities record, and recommendations by school officials. To graduate, students must maintain a minimum GPA of 2.0 and complete 120 course hours, with 29 to 43 in the major. Freshmen must take a first-year program, a 2-semester team-taught course. Requirements also include 1 course each in arts/expression, humanities, social science, math or a foreign language, 2 in natural science/science studies, and in diversity. **Procedure:** Freshmen are admitted fall and spring. Entrance exams should be taken during the spring of the junior year or the fall of the senior year. There are early decision and deferred admissions plans. Early decision applications should be filed by November 1; regular applications, by February 1 for fall entry; and December 1 for spring entry, along with a $60 fee. Notification of early decision is sent February 2; regular decision, 212 early decision candidates were accepted for the 2016-2017 class. 13 applicants were on the 2016 waiting list. Applications are accepted online. **Transfer Students:** 27 transfer students enrolled in 2015-2016. The high school transcript and SAT scores will be evaluated, but college work is more important. High school and college recommendations are required. 17 of 120 credits required for the bachelor's degree must be completed at St. Lawrence. **International Students:** There are 126 international students enrolled. The school actively recruits these students.

ADMISSIONS: 46% of the 2016-2017 applicants were accepted. The SAT scores for the 2016-2017 freshman class were: Critical Reading-- 11% below 500, 36% between 500 and 599, 42% between 600 and 699, and 11% between 700 and 800. Math-- 6% below 500, 42% between 500 and 599, 41% between 600 and 699, and 11% between 700 and 800. Writing-- 14% below 500, 35% between 500 and 599, 44% between 600 and 699, and 7% between 700 and 800. The ACT scores were 14% between 18 and 23, 58% between 24 and 29, and 26% above 30. 71% of the current freshmen were in the top fifth of their class; 91% were in the top two fifths. 14 freshmen graduated first in their class. **Admissions Contact:** Teresa Cowdrey, Vice President and Dean of Admissions and Financial Aid. Email: *admissions@stlawu.edu* Web: *www.stlwu.edu*

FINANCIAL AID: In 2016-2017, 92% of all full-time freshmen and 88% of continuing full-time students received some form of financial aid. 63% of all full-time freshmen and 66% of continuing full-time students received need-based aid. The average freshman award was $43,150. Need-based scholarships or need-based grants averaged $37,312; need-based self-help aid (loans and jobs) averaged $3,410; non-need-based athletic scholarships averaged $44,275; other non-need-based awards and non-need-based scholarships averaged $19,320; and $4,440 from other forms of aid. 33% of undergraduate students work part-time. Average annual earnings from campus work are $1100. The average financial indebtedness of the 2016 graduate was $26,756. St. Lawrence is a member of CSS. The CSS/Profile, and nocustodial profile are required. The FAFSA code is 002829. The deadline for filing freshman financial aid applications for fall entry is February 1.

ST. THOMAS AQUINAS COLLEGE D-5

www.stac.edu

Sparkill, NY 10976	(914) 398-4100 (800) 999-STAC
Fax: (914) 398-4114	Email: admissions@stac.edu
Full-time: 700 men, 710 women	**Faculty:** IIB, +$
Part-time: 350 men, 360 women	**Ph.D.s:** n/av
Graduate: 75 men, 125 women	**Student/Faculty:** n/av
Year: 4-1-4, summer session	**Tuition:** $29,600
Room & Board: $12,600	**Freshman Class:** n/av
SAT or ACT: required	**CEEB CODE:** 0807
Application Deadline: rolling	**COMPETITIVE**

St. Thomas Aquinas College, founded in 1952, is an independent liberal arts institution. Figures in above capsule and in this profile are approximate. There is 1 undergraduate school and 2 graduate schools. The 43-acre campus is in a suburban area 15 miles north of New York City. Including any residence halls, there are 12 buildings.

STUDENT LIFE: 75% of undergraduates are from New York. Others are from 6 states, 8 foreign countries, and Canada. 80% are from public schools. 9% are race unknown; 52% White; 3% Asian American; 3% Foreign; 22% Hispanic; 10% African American; 1% two or more races. 62% are Catholic; 23% Protestant. **Female To Male Ratio:** 1.1:1. The average age of freshmen is 18; all undergraduates, 23. 16% do not continue beyond their first year; 62% remain to graduate. **Housing:** 450 students can be accommodated in college housing, which includes single-sex dorms and on-campus apartments. On-campus housing is guaranteed for all 4 years. 65% of students commute. Alcohol is not permitted. All students may keep cars.

FACULTY/CLASSROOMS: 55% of faculty are male; 45% are female. 99% teach undergraduates, 50% do research, and 50% do both. No introductory courses are taught by graduate students. The average class size in an introductory lecture is 35; in a laboratory is 15; and in a regular course is 20.

PROGRAMS OF STUDY: STAC confers B.A., B.S. and B.S.E. degrees. Associate and master's degrees are also awarded. Bachelor's degrees are awarded in BUSINESS (accounting, banking and finance, business administration and management, marketing/retailing/merchandising, and recreation and leisure services), COMMUNICATIONS AND THE ARTS (communications, English, English literature, fine arts, romance languages and literature, Spanish, and visual and performing arts), COMPUTER AND PHYSICAL SCIENCE (computer information systems and mathematics), EDUCATION (art education, bilingual/bicultural education, elementary education, foreign languages education, science education, secondary education, and special education), ENGINEERING AND ENVIRONMENTAL DESIGN (commercial art), HEALTH PROFESSIONS (medical laboratory technology and premedicine), SOCIAL SCIENCE (criminal justice, history, liberal arts, sciences, general studies, humanities, parks and recreation management, philosophy, prelaw, psychology, religion, and social science). Education, business administration, and natural sciences are the strongest academically. Business administration has the largest enrollment.

ACTIVITIES: There are no fraternities or sororities. There are 15 groups on campus, including band, cheerleading, chorus, computers, dance, drama, honors, international, literary magazine, musical theater, newspaper, professional, religious, social service, student government, and yearbook. Popular campus events include trips to Broadway shows, and Halloween and Christmas mixers. **Sports:** There are 5 intercollegiate sports for men and 4 for women, and 6 intramural sports for men and 5 for women. Facilities include an auditorium, gym, weight room, baseball, basketball, bowling, cross-country, field hockey, football, golf, handball, ice hockey lacrosse, soccer, softball, track and field, and tennis courts.

SERVICES: Counseling and information services are available, as is tutoring in most subjects, as well as remedial math and writing. **Library/Resources:** The library contains 102,943 volumes, 45,900 microform items, and subscribes to 108 periodicals including electronic. Computerized library services include interlibrary loans and database searching. **Physically Challenged Students:** 90% of the campus is accessible. Facilities include wheelchair ramps, elevators, special parking, specially equipped restrooms, special class scheduling, and lowered telephones. **Special:** The college offers cross-registration with Barry University and Aquinas College and internships in business, criminal justice, commercial design, recreation and leisure, and communications. Study abroad in Europe and Asia, a 3-2 engineering degree with George Washington University and Manhattan College, and in physical therapy with New York Medical College, and work-study programs are available. Nondegree study and pass/fail options are possible. There are 7 national honor societies, Phi Beta Kappa, and a freshman honors program. **Visiting:** There are guides for informal visits, visitors may sit in on classes, and stay overnight. To schedule a visit, contact the Admissions Office. **Campus Safety and Security:** Measures include 24-hour foot and vehicle patrol and security escort services. There are emergency telephones and lighted pathways/sidewalks.

REQUIREMENTS: The SAT or ACT is required. Applicants must be graduates of an accredited secondary school or have a GED certificate. 16 Carnegie units are recommended, including 4 years of English, and social science, 2 years of math, foreign language, and science, including 2 years of lab science. A GPA of 2.2 is required. AP and CLEP credits are accepted. Important factors in the admissions decision are leadership record, extracurricular activities record, and advanced placement or honors courses. To graduate, all students must complete a total of 120 credit hours, with 36 to 54 in the major and a minimum GPA of 2.0. A core curriculum of 51 credits in liberal arts courses is required. **Procedure:** Freshmen are admitted fall and spring. Entrance exams should be taken by the spring of the junior year. There are early decision, early admissions, deferred admissions, and rolling admissions plans. Early decision applications should be filed by October 1. The fall 2016 application fee was $30. Notification is sent on a rolling basis. Applications are accepted online. **Transfer Students:** 175 transfer students enrolled in 2015-2016. Applicants must have a 2.0 GPA from the previous school. Students may enroll in the fall and spring. 30 of 120 credits required for the bachelor's degree must be completed at STAC. **International Students:** The school actively recruits these students. They must take the TOEFL.

Admissions Contact: Samantha Bazile, Director of Admissions. Email: *admissions@stac.edu* Web: *www.stac.edu*

FINANCIAL AID: STAC is a member of CSS. The FAFSA code is 002832. The deadline for filing freshman financial aid applications for fall entry is June 30.

STATE UNIVERSITY OF NEW YORK / BUFFALO STATE COLLEGE A-3

www.buffalostate.edu

Buffalo, NY 14222	(716) 878-4017
	Email: admissions@buffalostate.edu
Full-time: 3564 men, 5216 women	**Faculty:** IIA, av$
Part-time: 491 men, 551 women	**Ph.D.s:** 84%
Graduate: 566 men, 1326 women	**Student/Faculty:** 21 to 1
Year: semesters, summer session	**Tuition:** $7700 ($17,550)
Room & Board: $13,142	**Freshman Class:** 11132 applied, 4749 accepted, 1530 enrolled
SAT: required	**CEEB CODE:** 2925
Application Deadline: rolling	**COMPETITIVE**

Buffalo State College/State University of New York, established in 1871, is a public institution conferring undergraduate liberal arts degrees. Figures in the above capsule and in this profile are approximate. There are 4 undergraduate schools and 1 graduate school. In addition to regional accreditation, Buffalo State has baccalaureate program accreditation with ABET, ADA, ASLA, CSWE, FIDER, NASAD, NCATE, ACS, IACBE, NAST, and NAIT. The 127-acre campus is in an urban area in Buffalo, New York. Including any residence halls, there are 38 buildings.

STUDENT LIFE: 99% of undergraduates are from New York. Others are

from 26 states, 20 foreign countries, and Canada. 85% are from public schools. 65% are White; 5% Hispanic; 13% African American; 1% Asian American; 1% American Indian/Alaska Native; 1% Foreign. **Female To Male Ratio:** 1.5:1. The average age of freshmen is 19; all undergraduates, 25. 22% do not continue beyond their first year; 48% remain to graduate. **Housing:** 2275 students can be accommodated in college housing, which includes coed dorms, on-campus apartments, and married student housing. and international student dorm. On-campus housing is available on a first-come and first-served basis. 77% of students commute. Upperclassmen may keep cars. Alcohol is not permitted.

FACULTY/CLASSROOMS: 51% of faculty are male; 49% are female. All teach undergraduates. No introductory courses are taught by graduate students. The average class size in an introductory lecture is 34; in a laboratory is 12; and in a regular course is 18.

PROGRAMS OF STUDY: Buffalo State confers B.A., B.S., B.F.A., B.Mus., B.S.Ed. and B.Tech degrees. Master's degrees are also awarded. Bachelor's degrees are awarded in BIOLOGICAL SCIENCE (biology/biological science), BUSINESS (business administration and management and hospitality management services), COMMUNICATIONS AND THE ARTS (art, art history and appreciation, broadcasting, communications, design, dramatic arts, English, fine arts, French, journalism, music, painting, photography, printmaking, sculpture, and Spanish), COMPUTER AND PHYSICAL SCIENCE (chemistry, earth science, geology, information sciences and systems, mathematics, and physics), EDUCATION (art education, business education, elementary education, foreign languages education, industrial arts education, science education, secondary education, and special education), ENGINEERING AND ENVIRONMENTAL DESIGN (electrical/electronics engineering technology, industrial engineering technology, and mechanical engineering technology), HEALTH PROFESSIONS (health and speech pathology/audiology), SOCIAL SCIENCE (anthropology, criminal justice, dietetics, economics, geography, history, humanities, philosophy, political science/government, psychology, social work, sociology, and urban studies). Elementary education, and exceptional education are the strongest academically. Elementary education, communication, and business have the largest enrollments.

ACTIVITIES: 1% of men belong to 1 local and 9 national fraternities; 1% of women belong to 3 local and 7 national sororities. There are 75 groups on campus, including art, cheerleading, chess, choir, chorus, computers, dance, drama, ethnic, honors, international, jazz band, LGBT, literary magazine, musical theater, newspaper, orchestra, political, professional, radio and TV, religious, social, social service, and student government. Popular campus events include Commuter Daze, the Gathering, and Welcome Back Week. **Sports:** There are 8 intercollegiate sports for men and 11 for women, and 24 intramural sports for men and 24 for women. Facilities include a gym, an indoor pool, a basketball/volleyball arena, ice hockey, a game field for football, soccer, and lacrosse, a 6-lane track and field, and a softball diamond field. **Graduates:** From July 1, 2015 to June 30, 2016, 1768 bachelor's degrees were awarded. The most popular majors were elementary education (24%), business studies (13%), and social sciences (9%). 105 companies recruited on campus in 2015-2016. In an average class, 1% graduate in 3 years or less, 21% graduate in 4 years or less, 42% graduate in 5 years or less, and 48% graduate in 6 years or less. Of the 2015 graduating class, 24% were enrolled in graduate school within 6 months of graduation, and 75% were employed.

SERVICES: Counseling and information services are available, as is tutoring in every subject. There is a reader service for the blind, and remedial math, reading, and writing. Tutors for visually impaired and hearing impaired students are also available. **Library/Resources:** The library contains 618,429 volumes, 1.0 million microform items, 18,500 audio/video tapes/CDs/DVDs, and subscribes to 2,948 periodicals including electronic. Computerized library services include interlibrary loans, database searching, and Internet access. Special learning facilities include an art gallery, planetarium, radio station, TV station, a speech, language, and hearing clinic and a center for performing arts. **Physically Challenged Students:** All of the campus is accessible. Facilities include wheelchair ramps, elevators, special parking, specially equipped restrooms, special class scheduling, lowered drinking fountains, and lowered telephones. **Special:** Students may cross-register with the Western New York Consortium and exchange with 160 campus members of the National Student Exchange. Internships, Washington and Albany semesters, study abroad in 7 countries, dual majors, and a general studies degree are offered. Students may earn 3-2 engineering degrees in association with Clarkson University, and the State University of New York centers at Buffalo and Binghamton. There is a cooperative program with the Fashion Institute of Technology. Credit for life, military, and work experience, nondegree study, and pass/fail grading options are available. There is a chapter of Phi Beta Kappa, a freshman honors program, and 13 departmental honors programs. **Visiting:** There are regularly scheduled orientations for prospective students. There are guides for informal visits and visitors may sit in on classes. To schedule a visit, contact the Admissions Office. **Campus Safety and Security:** Measures include 24-hour foot and vehicle patrol, emergency notification system, self-defense education, and security escort services. There are shuttle buses, emergency telephones, lighted pathways/sidewalks, including community policing.

REQUIREMENTS: The SAT is required. Students must graduate from an accredited secondary school or have a GED. They must complete 4 years of English, 3 years each of math, science, and social studies, and 2 years of a foreign language. A portfolio is required for fine arts applicants. AP and CLEP credits are accepted. Important factors in the admissions decision are advanced placement or honors courses, evidence of special talent, and recommendations by school officials. To graduate, students must complete a 60-hour general education requirement consisting of 42 core credits in applied science and education, arts, humanities, math and science, and social science, and 18 hours of electives. Students must earn 123 credits with a minimum GPA of 2.0. The number of hours in the major varies. **Procedure:** Freshmen are admitted to all sessions. Entrance exams should be taken during the junior or senior years. There are early decision, early admissions, deferred admissions, and rolling admissions plans. Early decision applications should be filed by November 1, along with a $40 fee. Notification of early decision is sent December 15; regular decision, 57 early decision candidates were accepted for the 2016-2017 class. Applications are accepted on-line. **Transfer Students:** 1103 transfer students enrolled in 2015-2016. Transfer applicants must have a minimum GPA of 2.0. An associate degree is recommended, and a minimum of 15 credit hours must have been earned. 32 of 123 credits required for the bachelor's degree must be completed at Buffalo State. **International Students:** There are 77 international students enrolled. The school actively recruits these students. They must take the TOEFL with a minimum score of 500 on the paper-based TOEFL (PBT) or 65 on the Internet-based version (iBT). They must also take the SAT or ACT.

ADMISSIONS: 43% of the 2016-2017 applicants were accepted. The SAT scores for the 2016-2017 freshman class were: Critical Reading-- 57% below 500, 36% between 500 and 599, 7% between 600 and 699, and 1% between 700 and 800. Math-- 51% below 500, 41% between 500 and 599, and 8% between 600 and 699. 22% of the current freshmen were in the top fifth of their class; 55% were in the top two fifths. **Admissions Contact:** Carmella Thompson, Admissions Director. Email: *admissions@buffalostate.edu* Web: *www.buffalostate.edu*

FINANCIAL AID: In 2016-2017, 86% of all full-time freshmen and 80% of continuing full-time students received some form of financial aid. 71% of all full-time freshmen and 68% of continuing full-time students received need-based aid. The average financial indebtedness of the 2016 graduate was $17,657. Buffalo State is a member of CSS. The FAFSA code is 002842. The priority date for freshman financial aid applications for fall entry is March 1. The filing eadline for fall entry is May 1.

STATE UNIVERSITY OF NEW YORK / EMPIRE STATE COLLEGE

(The complete profile is made available exclusively on our website, www.barronspac.com)

STATE UNIVERSITY OF NEW YORK / SUNY COLLEGE AT OLD WESTBURY — D-5

www.oldwestbury.edu

Old Westbury, NY 11568 — **(516) 876-3200**

Fax: (516) 876-3307	**Email:** enroll@oldwestbury.edu
Full-time: 1486 men, 2070 women	**Faculty:** 145; IIB, +$
Part-time: 277 men, 325 women	**Ph.D.s:** 85%
Graduate: 86 men, 570 women	**Student/Faculty:** 25 to 1
Year: semesters, summer session	**Tuition:** $6470 ($16,320)
Room & Board: $10,390	**Freshman Class:** n/av **CEEB CODE:** 2866
Application Deadline: rolling	**COMPETITIVE**

State University of New York/College at Old Westbury, founded in 1965, is a public institution offering degree programs in the arts and sciences, business, education, fine arts, and health science. Figures in the above capsule and in this profile are approximate. There are 3 undergraduate schools and 3 graduate schools. In addition to regional accreditation, SUNY Old Westbury has baccalaureate program accreditation with NCATE and ACS. The 604-acre campus is in a suburban area 20 miles east of New York City. Including any residence halls, there are 23 buildings.

STUDENT LIFE: 97% of undergraduates are from New York. Others are from 13 states, and 9 foreign countries. 85% are from public schools. 33% are White; 30% African American; 21% Hispanic; 10% Asian American; 3% two or more races; 2% race unknown; 1% American Indian/Alaska Native; 1% Foreign. **Female To Male Ratio:** 1.6:1. The average age of freshmen is 19; all undergraduates, 24. 20% do not continue beyond their first year; 35% remain to graduate. **Housing:** 1500 students can be accommodated in college housing, which includes coed dorms. In addition, there are honors houses. On-campus housing is available on a first-come, first-served basis, and is available on a lottery system for upperclassmen. Priority is given to out-of-town students. 77% of students commute. All students may keep cars. Alcohol is not permitted.

FACULTY/CLASSROOMS: 47% of faculty are male; 53% are female. 98% teach undergraduates, 11% do research, and 11% do both. No introductory courses are taught by graduate students. The average class size in an introductory lecture is 25; in a laboratory is 20; and in a regular course is 25.

PROGRAMS OF STUDY: SUNY Old Westbury confers B.A., B.S., B.F.A. and B.P.S. degrees. Master's degrees are also awarded. Bachelor's degrees are awarded in BIOLOGICAL SCIENCE (biochemistry and biology/biological science), BUSINESS (accounting, banking and finance, business administration and management, labor studies, management information systems, and marketing/retailing/merchandising), COMMUNICATIONS AND THE ARTS (communications, media arts, Spanish, and visual and performing arts), COMPUTER AND PHYSICAL SCIENCE (chemistry, computer science, information sciences and systems, and mathematics), EDUCATION (bilingual/bicultural education, early childhood education, elementary education, foreign languages education, mathematics education, middle school education, science education, secondary education, social studies education, and special education), HEALTH PROFESSIONS (community health work and health), SOCIAL SCIENCE (American studies, criminology, history, humanities, philosophy, political science/government, psychology, religion, and sociology). Education, business, and biological sciences are the strongest academically. Psychology, accounting and biological sciences have the largest enrollments.

ACTIVITIES: 1% of men belong to 6 national fraternities; 2% of women belong to 8 national sororities. There are 60 groups on campus, including art, cheerleading, choir, chorale, computers, dance, drama, ethnic, film, honors, international, LGBT, newspaper, photography, political, professional, radio and TV, religious, social, social service, student government, and yearbook. Popular campus events include Welcome Back Festival, Wellness at Old Westbury, and Panther Pride Week. **Sports:** There are 7 intercollegiate sports for men and 7 for women, and 7 intramural sports for men and 7 for women. Facilities include a gym, and an auxiliary gym, cross-country course, playing fields, swimming pool, fitness center, weight room, jogging trails, courts for tennis, paddleball, handball, racquetball, and squash. **Graduates:** From July 1, 2015 to June 30, 2016, 864 bachelor's degrees were awarded. The most popular majors were psychology (16%), accounting (12%), and media and communications (9%). 75 companies recruited on campus in 2015-2016. In an average class, 1% graduate in 3 years or less, 21% graduate in 4 years or less, 31% graduate in 5 years or less, and 35% graduate in 6 years or less.

SERVICES: Counseling and information services are available, as is tutoring in most subjects. There is a reader service for the blind, and remedial math, reading, and writing. **Library/Resources:** The library contains 251,930 volumes, 18,864 microform items, and 1,634 audio/video tapes/CDs/DVDs, and subscribes to 2,532 periodicals including electronic. Computerized library services include interlibrary loans, database searching, Internet access, and Wi-Fi capability. Special learning facilities include an art gallery, radio station, and TV studio. **Physically Challenged Students:** 90% of the campus is accessible. Facilities include wheelchair ramps, elevators, special parking, specially equipped restrooms, special class scheduling, lowered drinking fountains, lowered telephones. limited volunteer transportation. **Special:** SUNY Old Westbury offers cross-registration with SUNY Empire State, Lirache, and colleges in Nassau and Suffolk counties, internships in teacher education, extensive study-abroad programs, a B.A.-B.S. in psychology, chemistry, industrial labor and relations, and sociology, dual majors, and a 3-2 engineering degree with SUNY at Stony Brook and SUNY Maritime College. An Accelerated B.S. in Biological Sciences/D.O. in Osteopathic Medicine (offered in collaboration with the New York College of Osteopathic Medicine). Credit for military and life experience, nondegree study, and pass/fail options are available. There are 5 national honor societies, a freshman honors program, and 6 departmental honors programs. **Visiting:** There are regularly scheduled orientations for prospective students. There are guides for informal visits. To schedule a visit, contact Enrollment Services at (516) 876-3073. **Campus Safety and Security:** Measures include 24-hour foot and vehicle patrol, emergency notification system, and security escort services. There are shuttle buses, emergency telephones, lighted pathways/sidewalks, and officers patrol dormitories.

REQUIREMENTS: The SAT is required. Applicants must be graduates of an accredited secondary school or have a GED. An essay, portfolio, and interview are also recommended. Students are evaluated according to qualifying categories of academic achievement, special knowledge and creative ability, paid work experience, and social or personal experience. AP and CLEP credits are accepted. Important factors in the admissions decision are leadership record, recommendations by school officials, and evidence of special talent. General education requirements include courses in writing and reasoning skills, creative arts, ideas and ideology, cross-cultural perspectives, U.S. society and history, physical or life science, and foreign language. A senior project or capstone course is required, based on major. To be eligible for graduation, all candidates must satisfy all college and departmental requirements for the specific degree. Students must complete a minimum of 120 credits of satisfactory work. Some departmental requirements exceed this number. Forty five of these credits must be earned in course work above the survey and the introductory levels (at or above the 3000 level). To fulfill graduation requirements, School of Education majors must have a 3.0 cumulative grade point average, School of Business majors must have a 2.5 cumulative grade point average as well as for all School of Business courses, all other students must have at least a 2.0 cumulative grade point average (GPA) for all work completed at the college. **Procedure:** Freshmen are admitted in the fall and spring. There are early decision, deferred admissions, and rolling admissions plans. Application deadlines are open. Application fee is $50. Notification is sent on a rolling basis. Applications are accepted online. **Transfer Students:** 1280 transfer students enrolled in 2015-2016. Applicants must submit official transcripts from all colleges attended. Those students with fewer than 24 college credits must also submit a high school transcript. The college requires a minimum overall GPA of 2.0. Specific academic majors may require a higher GPA. 48 of 120 credits required for the bachelor's degree must be completed at SUNY Old Westbury. **International Students:** There are 34 international students enrolled. The school actively recruits these students. They must take the TOEFL with a minimum score of 513 on the paper-based TOEFL (PBT) or 80 on the Internet-based version (iBT) and the college's own test.

Admissions Contact: Frank Pizzardi, Director of Admissions. Email: *enroll@oldwestbury.edu* Web: *www.oldwestbury.edu*

FINANCIAL AID: In 2016-2017, 69% of all full-time freshmen and 62% of continuing full-time students received some form of financial aid. 65% of all full-time freshmen and 57% of continuing full-time students received need-based aid. The average freshman award was $7,207. Need-based scholarships or need-based grants averaged $7,016; need-based self-help aid (loans and jobs) averaged $7,351; and other non-need-based awards and non-need-based scholarships averaged $1,971. Average annual earnings from campus work are $902. The average financial indebtedness of the 2016 graduate was $17,340. The college's own financial statement, and the IFAA (Institutional application), and previous year's household income are required. The FAFSA code is 007109. The deadline for filing freshman financial aid applications for fall entry is April 19.

STATE UNIVERSITY OF NEW YORK / SUNY CORTLAND C-4

www2.cortland.edu

Cortland, NY 13045	(607) 753-4711
Fax: 607-753-5598	Email: admissions@cortland.edu
Full-time: 2731 men, 3456 women	**Faculty:** 303; IIA, --$
Part-time: 49 men, 56 women	**Ph.D.s:** n/av
Graduate: 226 men, 4370 women	**Student/Faculty:** 16 to 1
Year: semesters, summer session	**Tuition:** $8106 ($17,956)
Room & Board: $12,600	**Freshman Class:** 10875 applied, 5673 accepted, 1238 enrolled
SAT CR/M: 520/545 **ACT:** 24	**CEEB CODE:** 2538
Application Deadline: rolling	**VERY COMPETITIVE**

State University of New York College at Cortland, founded in 1868, is a public institution offering academic programs leading to baccalaureate and master's degrees in liberal arts and professional studies. There are 3 undergraduate schools and 3 graduate schools. In addition to regional accreditation, SUNY Cortland has baccalaureate program accreditation with CAHEA, NCATE, and NRPA. The 191-acre campus is in a small town 18 miles north of Ithaca and 29 miles south of Syracuse.

STUDENT LIFE: 94% of undergraduates are from New York. 73% are White; 6% African American; 4% race unknown; 2% two or more races; 12% Hispanic; 1% Asian American. **Female To Male Ratio:** 2.6:1. **Housing:** 3224 students can be accommodated in college housing, which includes coed dorms and off-campus apartments. In addition, there are special-interest houses, fraternity houses, sorority houses, apartments for single students, cooperative housing, wellness housing, leadership house, transfer floor, 21 + floors, and quiet floor. All students may keep cars.

FACULTY/CLASSROOMS: All teach undergraduates, 15% do research, and 15% do both. No introductory courses are taught by graduate students.

PROGRAMS OF STUDY: SUNY Cortland confers B.A., B.S., B.S.Ed., and B.F.A. degrees. Master's degrees are also awarded. Bachelor's degrees are awarded in BIOLOGICAL SCIENCE (biology/biological science), BUSINESS (management science and sports management), COMMUNICATIONS AND THE ARTS (art, communications, English, film arts, and musical theater), COMPUTER AND PHYSICAL SCIENCE (chemistry, geochemistry, geology, geophysics and seismology, mathematics, and physics), EDUCATION (athletic training, education services, foreign languages education, health education, middle school education, physical education, recreation education, and secondary education), ENGINEERING AND ENVIRONMENTAL DESIGN (environmental science), HEALTH PROFESSIONS (health science and speech pathology/audiology), SOCIAL SCIENCE (African American studies, anthropology, economics, geography, history, human services, international studies, philosophy, political science/government, psychology, and sociology).

ACTIVITIES: There are 100 groups on campus, including art, band, cheerleading, chess, choir, chorale, chorus, computers, dance, drama, ethnic, film, honors, international, LGBT, literary magazine, Model UN, musical theater, newspaper, orchestra, political, professional, radio and TV, religious, social, social service, student government, symphony, and yearbook. Popular campus events include Cortland-Ithaca College Football Game, Winterfest, and Multicultural Festival. **Sports:** There are 11 intercollegiate sports for men and 14 for women, and 55 intramural sports for men and 55 for women. Facilities include an outdoor multipurpose stadium complex, Olympic-size pool, a gym, ice arena, gymnastics arena, wrestling and weight rooms, dance studio, handball/racquetball courts, squash courts, athletic training facility, fitness centers, swimming pool, track, baseball field, football/lacrosse/track field, soccer field, field house, and athletic fields. **Graduates:** From July 1, 2015 to June 30, 2016, 1541 bachelor's degrees were awarded. The most popular majors were education (24%), parks and recreation (21%), and social sciences (11%).

SERVICES: Counseling and information services are available, as is tutoring in some subjects. There is a reader service for the blind, and a fully staffed Academic Support and Achievement Program for writing, math, study skills, and learning strategies. Specific course tutoring is available with peer tutors. **Library/Resources:** The library contains 464,422 volumes, 8,808 microform items, and 2,378 audio/video tapes/CDs/DVDs, and subscribes to 231 periodicals including electronic. Computerized library services include interlibrary loans, database searching, Internet access, and Wi-Fi capability. Special learning facilities include an art gallery, planetarium, radio station, TV station, a greenhouse, a center for speech and hearing disorders, classrooms equipped with integrated technologies (multimedia enhanced instruction), and many specialized labs to support various program offerings. **Physically Challenged Students:** 75% of the campus is accessible. Facilities include wheelchair ramps, elevators, special parking, specially equipped restrooms, special class scheduling, lowered drinking fountains, lowered telephones, and special housing. **Special:** Cortland offers cross-registration with Tompkins Cortland Communinty College and has cooperative programs with the State University of New York College of Environmental Science and Forestry, and Centers at Binghamton and Buffalo, and Cornell and Case Western Reserve Universities. Students may study abroad in over 30 countries, and they may enroll in a Washington semester. Work-study programs are available. The college confers an individualized studies degree and allows dual majors. Students may pursue a 3-2 engineering degree in conjunction with Alfred, Case Western Reserve, and Clarkson Universities, and the State University of New York Centers at Binghamton, Buffalo, and Stony Brook. Cortland offers non-degree study opportunities. There are 19 national honor societies, Phi Beta Kappa, a freshman honors program, and 5 departmental honors programs. **Visiting:** There are regularly scheduled orientations for prospective students, consisting of Autumn Preview Days for prospective students as well as Spring Open House for accepted students. There are guides for informal visits and visitors may sit in on classes. To schedule a visit, contact The Admissions Office at admissions@cortland.edu. **Campus Safety and Security:** Measures include 24-hour foot and vehicle patrol, emergency notification system, self-defense education, and security escort services. There are shuttle buses, emergency telephones, lighted pathways/sidewalks. The university police maintain a web site with safety information and links, and a silent witness program for reporting crimes anonymously.

REQUIREMENTS: The SAT is required. Applicants must graduate from an accredited secondary school or have a GED. They must have earned 16-24 Carnegie units, 4 each in English and history, 3-4 each in math, and science (with lab), and foreign language, and 4 in social studies. Essays and recommendations are required, and in some cases auditions as well. Interviews are strongly recommended. AP and CLEP credits are accepted. Important factors in the admissions decision are advanced placement or honors courses, evidence of special talent, extracurricular activities record, recommendations by alumni, and recommendations by school officials. To graduate, undergraduates must complete 6 hours in English Composition, and at least 6 hours of writing-intensive courses, with 3 of those in the major. One course meeting the Quantitative Skills criteria must also be passed; 30 hours of courses in the General Education program must also be completed, with no more than 2 courses taken in any one of the 8 disciplines in the program. A major of 30 to 36 hours, with no more than 45 credits in discipline-specific courses must be completed. Completion of 90 credits of Liberal Arts and Science courses toward a B.A., 60 credits toward a B.S.Ed or a B.S. is required. A 2.0 GPA, both overall and in all minors and concentrations, must be maintained. Special requirements may be designated by each school of the college. **Procedure:** Freshmen are admitted in the fall and spring. Entrance exams should be taken during the spring of the junior year or fall of the senior year. There are early decision, early admissions, deferred admissions, and rolling admissions plans. Check with the school for current application deadlines. The application fee is $50. Notification is sent on a rolling basis. Applications are accepted on-line. **Transfer Students:** 654 transfer students enrolled in 2015-2016. Applicants must have a minimum GPA of 2.5. Some programs are more competitive. Interviews are encouraged. 45 of 124 credits required for the bachelor's degree must be completed at SUNY Cortland. **International Students:** The school actively recruits these students. They must take the TOEFL, the SAT I or a General Certificate of Education is acceptable in lieu of the TOEFL. They must also take the SAT or ACT.

ADMISSIONS: 52% of the 2016-2017 applicants were accepted. The SAT scores for the 2016-2017 freshman class were: Critical Reading-- 32% below 500, 55% between 500 and 599, 11% between 600 and 699, and 1% between 700 and 800. Math-- 19% below 500, 64% between 500 and 599, and 17% between 600 and 699. **Admissions Contact:** Mark Yacavone, Assistant VP, Enrollment Management. Email: *admissions@cortland.edu* Web: *www2.cortland.edu*

FINANCIAL AID: The average freshman award was $14,839. Need-based scholarships or need-based grants averaged $5,369; need-based self-help aid (loans and jobs) averaged $3,689; other non-need-based awards and non-need-based scholarships averaged $3,542; and $3,674 from other forms of aid. The average financial indebtedness of the 2016 graduate was $25,533. The FAFSA code is 002843. The priority date for freshman financial aid applications for fall entry is March 15. The deadline for filing freshman financial aid applications for fall entry is May 1.

STATE UNIVERSITY OF NEW YORK / SUNY FREDONIA A-4

www.fredonia.edu

Fredonia, NY 14063	(716) 673-3251 (800) 252-1212
Fax: (716) 673-3249	**Email:** admissions@fredonia.edu
Full-time: 1820 men, 2441 women	**Faculty:** 257; IIA, -$
Part-time: 70 men, 55 women	**Ph.D.s:** 86%
Graduate: 57 men, 169 women	**Student/Faculty:** 14 to 1
Year: semesters, summer session	**Tuition:** $8088 ($17,938)
Room & Board: $12,730	**Freshman Class:** 5381 applied, 3355 accepted, 934 enrolled
SAT CR/M: 540/540 **ACT:** 24	**CEEB CODE:** 2539
Application Deadline: rolling	**COMPETITIVE**

State University of New York at Fredonia, established in 1826, is a public institution offering undergraduate programs in the arts and sciences, business and professional curricula, teacher preparation, and the fine and performing arts. There are 5 undergraduate schools and 1 graduate school. In addition to regional accreditation, Fredonia has baccalaureate program accreditation with CSWE, NASAD, NASM, NCATE, NAST, ASHA, and CAEP. The 266-acre campus is in a small town 50 miles south of Buffalo and 45 miles north of Erie, Pennsylvania. Including any residence halls, there are 63 buildings.

STUDENT LIFE: 95% of undergraduates are from New York. Others are from 24 states, 14 foreign countries, and Canada. 92% are from public schools. 76% are White; 8% Hispanic; 7% African American; 3% Foreign; 3% two or more races; 1% Asian American; 1% American Indian/Alaska Native; 1% race unknown. **Female To Male Ratio:** 1.4:1. The average age of freshmen is 18; all undergraduates, 20. 14% do not continue beyond their first year; 65% remain to graduate. **Housing:** 2900 students can be accommodated in college housing, which includes single-sex and coed dorms and on-campus apartments. In addition, there are honors houses, special-interest houses, living space for fraternities and sororities is available in residence halls. In addition, there are special interest houses for computer and athletics students and quiet-hour centers. On-campus housing is guaranteed for the freshman year only, and is available on a first-come, first-served basis, and is available on a lottery system for upperclassmen. Priority is given to out-of-town students. 7% of students commute. All students may keep cars.

FACULTY/CLASSROOMS: 56% of faculty are male; 44% are female. All teach undergraduates, and do research. No introductory courses are taught by graduate students. The average class size in an introductory lecture is 35; in a laboratory is 16; and in a regular course is 22.

PROGRAMS OF STUDY: Fredonia confers B.A., B.F.A., B.S., B.S.Ed. and Mus.B. degrees. Master's degrees are also awarded. Bachelor's degrees are awarded in AGRICULTURE (environmental studies), BIOLOGICAL SCIENCE (biochemistry, biology/adolescence education, biology/biological science, and genetics), BUSINESS (accounting, business administration and management, business economics, finance, institutional management, and sports management), COMMUNICATIONS AND THE ARTS (acting, animation, arts administration/management, audio technology, communication studies, communications, dance, dramatic arts, drawing, English, film, television and digital media, fine arts, French, graphic design, illustration, journalism, media arts, music, music performance, music theory and composition, musical theater, painting, photography, public relations, Spanish, theatre arts, theater design, theatre production, theatre studies, and video), COMPUTER AND PHYSICAL SCIENCE (applied mathematics, chemistry, chemistry/adolescence education, computer information systems, computer science, earth science, geochemistry, geology, geoscience, mathematics, and physics), EDUCATION (early childhood education, education, elementary education, English education, foreign languages education, mathematics education, middle school education, music education, science education, secondary education, social studies education, and social studies secondary school education), ENGINEERING AND ENVIRONMENTAL DESIGN (environmental science), HEALTH PROFESSIONS (health care administration, medical laboratory technology, music therapy, predentistry, premedicine, preoptometry, and speech pathology/audiology), SOCIAL SCIENCE (American studies, early childhood studies, economics, history, interdisciplinary studies, liberal arts/general studies, philosophy, political science/government, prelaw, psychology, social work, sociology, and women's studies). Music, theatre, and visual arts are the strongest academically. STEM, arts, and business have the largest enrollments.

ACTIVITIES: 3% of men belong to 2 national fraternities; 5% of women belong to 3 national sororities. There are 170 groups on campus, including and Spectrum Entertainment Board, art, band, cheerleading, choir, chorale, chorus, communications, computers, dance, debate, drama, drill team, environmental, ethnic, film, honors, international, jazz band, LGBT, literary magazine, musical theater, newspaper, opera, orchestra, pep band, photography, political, professional, radio and TV, religious, Ski Club, social, social service, student government, and symphony. **Sports:** There are 8 intercollegiate sports for men and 9 for women, and 15 intramural sports for men and 15 for women. Facilities include a basketball arena, an ice rink, swimming pool, two gyms, weight rooms, dance studios, soccer fields, indoor and outdoor tracks, racquetball, tennis, and volleyball courts, and a soccer/lacrosse stadium. **Graduates:** From July 1, 2015 to June 30, 2016, 1031 bachelor's degrees were awarded. The most popular majors were education (15%), business administration (15%), and visual and performing arts (12%). 75 companies recruited on campus in 2015-2016. In an average class, 47% graduate in 4 years or less, 60% graduate in 5 years or less, and 62% graduate in 6 years or less.

SERVICES: Counseling and information services are available, as is tutoring in every subject, and a reader service for the blind. **Library/Resources:** The library contains 391,121 volumes, 1.1 million microform items, 26,574 audio/video tapes/CDs/DVDs, and subscribes to 1,983 periodicals including electronic. Computerized library services include interlibrary loans, database searching, Internet access, and Wi-Fi capability. Special learning facilities include an art gallery, natural history museum, planetarium, radio station, TV station, a greenhouse, child-care center, speech and audiology clinic, and the Rockefeller arts center. **Physically Challenged Students:** 85% of the campus is accessible. Facilities include wheelchair ramps, elevators, special parking, specially equipped restrooms, special class scheduling, lowered drinking fountains, lowered telephones, and special housing. **Special:** Cooperative programs are available with many other institutions. Students may cross-register with colleges in the Western New York Consortium. Fredonia offers a variety of internships, study-abroad programs in more than 60 countries, and a Washington semester. Accelerated degrees, a general studies degree, dual and student-designed majors, a 3-2 engineering degree program with 14 universities, nondegree study, and pass/fail grading options are available. There are 19 national honor societies, a freshman honors program, and 19 departmental honors programs. **Visiting:** There are regularly scheduled orientations for prospective students, including various open house programs and information sessions and tours. Visitors may sit in on classes and stay overnight. To schedule a visit, contact The Office of Admissions. **Campus Safety and Security:** Measures include 24-hour foot and vehicle patrol, emergency notification system, self-defense education, and security escort services. There are shuttle buses, emergency telephones, lighted pathways/sidewalks, controlled access to dorms/residences, and card swipe access to residence halls.

REQUIREMENTS: The SAT or ACT is required, with a satisfactory score on the SAT or 20 on the ACT. Applicants must possess a high school diploma or have a GED. 16 academic credits are recommended, including 4 credits each in English and social studies and 3 each in math, science, and a foreign language. 4 years of math and science are encouraged. Essays are required. Where applicable, an audition or portfolio is required. AP and CLEP credits are accepted. Important factors in the admissions decision are advanced placement or honors courses, leadership record, parents or siblings attended your school, evidence of special talent, personality/intangible qualities, extracurricular activities record, recommendations by alumni, geographical diversity, recommendations by school officials, and ability to finance college education. To graduate, students must complete 120 hours, including 36 to 90 or more in the major, with a 2.0 GPA. Students must also take specific courses in

English and math and complete 50 hours of general education courses, including writing, statistical/quantitative abilities, oral communication, natural and social sciences, humanities, and arts. **Procedure:** Freshmen are admitted in the fall and spring. Entrance exams should be taken Spring of the junior year or fall of the senior year. There are deferred admissions and rolling admissions plans. Application deadlines are open. Application fee is $50. Notifications are sent November 14. 48 early decision candidates were accepted for the 2016-2017 class. Application fees are waived if application is completed on-line. **Transfer Students:** 313 transfer students enrolled in 2015-2016. Applicants should have a minimum GPA of 2.0 and appropriate academic course work to be considered. 45 of 120 credits required for the bachelor's degree must be completed at Fredonia. **International Students:** There are 184 international students enrolled. The school actively recruits these students. They must take the TOEFL with a minimum score of 78 on the Internet-based version (iBT), or take the IELTS.

ADMISSIONS: 62% of the 2016-2017 applicants were accepted. The SAT scores for the 2016-2017 freshman class were: Critical Reading-- 44% below 500, 40% between 500 and 599, 13% between 600 and 699, and 3% between 700 and 800. Math-- 44% below 500, 43% between 500 and 599, 12% between 600 and 699, and 1% between 700 and 800. The ACT scores were 4% between 12 and 17, 44% between 18 and 23, 41% between 24 and 29, and 10% above 30. 30% of the current freshmen were in the top fifth of their class; 62% were in the top two fifths. 13 freshmen graduated first in their class. **Admissions Contact:** Cory Bezek, Director of Admissions. Email: *admissions@fredonia.edu* Web: *www.fredonia.edu*

FINANCIAL AID: In 2016-2017, 86% of all full-time freshmen and continuing full-time students received some form of financial aid. 86% of all full-time freshmen and continuing full-time students received need-based aid. The average freshman award was $12,060. Need-based scholarships or need-based grants averaged $6,062; need-based self-help aid (loans and jobs) averaged $5,465; and other non-need-based awards and non-need-based scholarships averaged $3,833. The average financial indebtedness of the 2016 graduate was $25,938. The state aid form, and Express TAP Application (ETA) are required. The FAFSA code is 002844. The priority date for freshman financial aid applications for fall entry is February 1.

STATE UNIVERSITY OF NEW YORK / SUNY ONEONTA D-3

www.oneonta.edu

Oneonta, NY 13820	**(607) 436-2524** **(800) 786-9123**
Fax: (607) 436-3074	**Email: admissions@oneonta.edu**
Full-time: 2294 men, 3430 women	**Faculty:** 251; IIA, --$
Part-time: 65 men, 74 women	**Ph.D.s:** 86%
Graduate: 43 men, 163 women	**Student/Faculty:** 18 to 1
Year: semesters, summer session	**Tuition:** $7870 ($17,720)
Room & Board: $11,842	**Freshman Class:** 12031 applied, 5190 accepted, 1146 enrolled
SAT CR/M: 538/563 **ACT:** 24	**CEEB CODE:** 2542
Application Deadline: open	**COMPETITIVE+**

State University of New York Oneonta, founded in 1889, offers undergraduate and graduate programs in the arts and sciences with a campus-wide emphasis on student engagement, diversity and community service. There is 1 undergraduate school and 1 graduate school. In addition to regional accreditation, SUNY Oneonta has baccalaureate program accreditation with AACSB, ADA, NASM, NCATE, ACS, and AAFCS. The 250-acre campus is in a rural area 75 miles southwest of Albany and 55 miles northeast of Binghamton. Including any residence halls, there are 36 buildings.

STUDENT LIFE: 98% of undergraduates are from New York. Others are from 25 states, and 18 foreign countries. 81% are White; 7% two or more races; 4% Hispanic; 3% African American; 2% Foreign; 2% race unknown; 1% Asian American. **Female To Male Ratio:** 1.5:1. The average age of freshmen is 18; all undergraduates, 20. 16% do not continue beyond their first year; 67% remain to graduate. **Housing:** 3557 students can be accommodated in college housing, which includes coed dorms on-campus apartments, freshman housing and special-interest groupings within residence halls. On-campus housing is guaranteed for the freshman year only, and is available on a first-come, first-served basis, and is available on a lottery system for upperclassmen. 59% of students live on campus; of those, 60% remain on campus on weekends. Upperclassmen may keep cars. Alcohol is not permitted.

FACULTY/CLASSROOMS: 50% of faculty are male; 50% are female. 96% teach undergraduates. No introductory courses are taught by graduate students. The average class size in an introductory lecture is 28; in a laboratory is 18; and in a regular course is 23.

PROGRAMS OF STUDY: SUNY Oneonta confers B.A., and B.S. degrees. Master's degrees are also awarded. Bachelor's degrees are awarded in BIOLOGICAL SCIENCE (biology/biological science), BUSINESS (accounting, business economics, and fashion merchandising), COMMUNICATIONS AND THE ARTS (art, communications, dramatic arts, English, fine arts, French, music, music business management, and Spanish), COMPUTER AND PHYSICAL SCIENCE (atmospheric sciences and meteorology, chemistry, computer science, earth science, geology, mathematics, physics, and statistics), EDUCATION (business education, elementary education, English education, foreign languages education, home economics education, mathematics education, science education, secondary education, and social science education), ENGINEERING AND ENVIRONMENTAL DESIGN (environmental science), HEALTH PROFESSIONS (predentistry and premedicine), SOCIAL SCIENCE (African studies, anthropology, child care/child and family studies, criminal justice, dietetics, economics, geography, gerontology, Hispanic American studies, history, home economics, international studies, philosophy, political science/government, prelaw, psychology, sociology, and water resources). Physical & natural sciences, business economics, and education are the strongest academically. Elementary education, adolescent education, and business have the largest enrollments.

ACTIVITIES: 1% of men belong to 5 national fraternities; 1% of women belong to 8 national sororities. There are 112 groups on campus, including academic, cultural and special-interest organizations, art, band, cheerleading, choir, chorale, chorus, computers, dance, debate, drama, environmental, ethnic, film, honors, international, jazz band, LGBT, literary magazine, musical theater, newspaper, opera, orchestra, photography, political, professional, radio and TV, religious, social, social service, student government, variety of volunteer, and yearbook. Popular campus events include Into the Streets Day of Service, OH-Fest, Battle of the Red Dragons, Red Day and Passing through the Pillars. **Sports:** There are 10 intercollegiate sports for men and 11 for women, and 13 intramural sports for men and 13 for women. Facilities include a gym, field house, dance studios, weight rooms, pool, indoor racquetball courts, tennis courts, indoor and outdoor tracks, athletic fields, and a lighted all-weather field. **Graduates:** From July 1, 2015 to June 30, 2016, 1206 bachelor's degrees were awarded. The most popular majors were education (18%), human ecology (10%), and English (9%). In an average class, 50% graduate in 4 years or less, 63% graduate in 5 years or less, and 64% graduate in 6 years or less.

SERVICES: Counseling and information services are available, as is tutoring in most subjects. There is a reader service for the blind, and remedial math, reading, and writing. Tutoring is also available in all introductory-level courses and most upper-level courses. **Library/Resources:** The library contains 482,408 volumes, 1.2 million microform items, 19,174 audio/video tapes/CDs/DVDs, and subscribes to 50,000 periodicals including electronic. Computerized library services include interlibrary loans, database searching, Internet access, and Wi-Fi capability. Special learning facilities include an art gallery, planetarium, radio station, TV station, digital planetarium, science discovery center, community service center, college camp, children's center, and off-campus biological field station. **Physically Challenged Students:** 90% of the campus is accessible. Facilities include wheelchair ramps, elevators, special parking, specially equipped restrooms, special class scheduling, and lowered drinking fountains. All academic buildings and most residence halls are accessible. **Special:** Oneonta offers limited cross-registration with Hartwick College, internships in most fields, and dual majors. Students can study abroad through eight exchange programs in Ghana, Finland, Germany, Sweden, Japan and South Korea, as well as more than 500 study abroad programs around the world through the SUNY network. A 3-1 fashion program with the Fashion Institute of Technology, 3-2 engineering degree, and other cooperative programs are offered. There are 20 national honor societies. **Visiting:** There are regularly scheduled orientations for prospective students, open houses, Friday and Saturday information sessions, individual appointments for prospective students, and Academic Exploration Day, and summer orientation sessions for admitted students. There are guides for informal visits and visitors may sit in on classes. To schedule a visit, contact the Admissions Office. **Campus Safety and Security:** Measures include 24-hour foot and vehicle patrol, emergency notification system, self-defense education, and security escort services. There are shuttle buses, emergency telephones, lighted pathways/sidewalks, and controlled access to dorms/residences.

REQUIREMENTS: The SAT or ACT is required. Applicants should be graduates of an accredited secondary school and have 19 academic credits, including 4 years each of English, social studies, mathematics and science, including lab. Three units of foreign language is required, and four units is recommended. The GED is accepted. AP and CLEP credits are accepted. Important factors in the admissions decision are advanced placement or honors courses, evidence of special talent, and leadership record. Students must complete 122 semester hours, with 30 to 36 hours in the major. A minimum GPA of 2.0 (2.5 for education majors) must be maintained. In addition, students must complete a 36-hour general education requirement including courses in math, natural sciences, social sciences, American history, Western civilization, humanities, the arts, foreign language and basic communications. Students must also pass a writing exam. **Procedure:** Freshmen are admitted in the fall and spring. Entrance exams should be taken in the spring of the junior year or the fall of the senior year. There are deferred admissions and rolling admissions plans. Application deadlines are open. Application fee is $50. Notifications are sent December 1. Applications are accepted on-line. **Transfer Students:** 465 transfer students enrolled in 2015-2016. Official transcripts of all previous college work must be submitted. A minimum of 15 semester hours of transferable credit and a GPA of 2.0 (2.5 for education majors) are required. 45 of 122 credits required for the bachelor's degree must be completed at SUNY Oneonta. **International Students:** There are 111 international students enrolled. The school actively recruits these students. They must take the TOEFL with a minimum score of 500 on the paper-based TOEFL (PBT) or 61 on the Internet-based version (iBT).

ADMISSIONS: 43% of the 2016-2017 applicants were accepted. The SAT scores for the 2016-2017 freshman class were: Critical Reading-- 23% below 500, 62% between 500 and 599, 14% between 600 and 699, and 1% between 700 and 800. Math-- 14% below 500, 59% between 500 and 599, 25% between 600 and 699, and 2% between 700 and 800. **Admissions Contact:** Rebecca Lynch, Director of Admissions. Email: *admissions@oneonta.edu* Web: *www.oneonta.edu*

FINANCIAL AID: In 2016-2017, 83% of all full-time freshmen and 66% of continuing full-time students received some form of financial aid. 42% of all full-time freshmen and 59% of continuing full-time students received need-based aid. The average freshman award was $8,818. Need-based scholarships or need-based grants averaged $6,510; need-based self-help aid (loans and jobs) averaged $3,999; and other non-need-based awards and non-need-based scholarships averaged $2,841. The average financial indebtedness of the 2016 graduate was $15,373. The state aid form is required. The FAFSA code is 002847. The priority date for freshman financial aid applications for fall entry is January 1.

STATE UNIVERSITY OF NEW YORK / SUNY PLATTSBURGH D-2

www.plattsburgh.edu

Plattsburgh, NY 12901	(518) 564-2040 (888) 673-0012
Fax: (518) 564-2045	Email: admissions@plattsburgh.edu
Full-time: 2311 men, 2875 women	**Faculty:** IIA, -$
Part-time: 159 men, 294 women	**Ph.D.s:** 81%
Graduate: 107 men, 305 women	**Student/Faculty:** 16 to 1
Year: semesters, summer session	**Tuition:** $7510 ($17,160)
Room & Board: $11,304	**Freshman Class:** n/av
SAT CR/M: 525/535 **ACT:** required	**CEEB CODE:** 2844
Application Deadline: August 1	**COMPETITIVE**

The State University of New York/SUNY Plattsburgh, founded in 1889, is a public institution offering degree programs in the liberal arts and professional programs. There are 3 undergraduate schools and 2 graduate schools. In addition to regional accreditation, SUNY Plattsburgh has baccalaureate program accreditation with AACSB, ADA, CSWE, NLN, and TEAC. The 300-acre campus is in a suburban area 150 miles north of Albany, 25 miles west of Burlington, Vermont, and 65 miles south of Montreal, Canada. Including any residence halls, there are 36 buildings.

STUDENT LIFE: 90% of undergraduates are from New York. Others are from 27 states, 67 foreign countries, and Canada. 95% are from public schools. 8% are Hispanic; 71% White; 6% African American; 6% Foreign; 4% race unknown; 2% Asian American; 2% two or more races. **Female To Male Ratio:** 1.3:1. The average age of freshmen is 18; all undergraduates, 21. 22% do not continue beyond their first year; 61% remain to graduate. **Housing:** 2682 students can be accommodated in college housing, which includes single-sex and coed dorms and on-campus apartments. In addition, there are special-interest houses, adult student halls/floors, wellness floors, and substance-free building. On-campus housing is available on a first-come, first-served basis, and is available on a lottery system for upperclassmen. 56% of students commute. All students may keep cars.

FACULTY/CLASSROOMS: 48% of faculty are male; 52% are female. All teach undergraduates, and do research. No introductory courses are taught by graduate students. The average class size in an introductory lecture is 27; in a laboratory is 17; and in a regular course is 24.

PROGRAMS OF STUDY: SUNY Plattsburgh confers B.A., B.S., B.F.A. and B.S.Ed. degrees. Master's degrees are also awarded. Bachelor's degrees are awarded in BIOLOGICAL SCIENCE (biochemistry, biology/adolescence education, biology/biological science, ecology, and nutrition), BUSINESS (accounting, business administration and management, entrepreneurial studies, finance, hotel/motel and restaurant management, international business management, management information systems, marketing/retailing/merchandising, and supply chain management), COMMUNICATIONS AND THE ARTS (art, communications, English, English literature, English Writing, French, journalism, music, public relations, and Spanish), COMPUTER AND PHYSICAL SCIENCE (chemistry, chemistry/adolescence education, computer science, geology, mathematics, and physics), EDUCATION (English education, mathematics education, Spanish adolescense education, special education, and sports and wellness studies), ENGINEERING AND ENVIRONMENTAL DESIGN (environmental science), HEALTH PROFESSIONS (cytotechnology, medical laboratory technology, medical technology, and nursing), SOCIAL SCIENCE (anthropology, Canadian studies, child care/child and family studies, communication sciences & disorders, criminal justice, economics, French studies, gender studies, geography, history, home economics, human development, interdisciplinary studies, Latin American studies, philosophy, political science/government, psychology, social work, sociology, and women's studies). Adolescence education (physics), multimedia journalism, and global supply & chain management are the strongest academically. Psychology, education, and business have the largest enrollments.

ACTIVITIES: 6% of men belong to 1 local and 11 national fraternities; 5% of women belong to 1 local and 8 national sororities. There are 120 groups on campus, including art, band, cheerleading, choir, chorale, chorus, computers, dance, debate, drama, ethnic, film, honors, international, jazz band, LGBT, literary magazine, musical theater, newspaper, orchestra, pep band, photography, political, professional, radio and TV, religious, social, social service, student government, and yearbook. Popular campus events include Volunteer Opportunities (Relay for Life, Up 'til Dawn), Family Weekend, Night of Nations, President's Gala, Plattsburgh's Best Dance Crew and Plattsburgh's Got Talent Competitions. **Sports:** There are 7 intercollegiate sports for men and 8 for women, and 9 intramural sports for men and 9 for women. Facilities include an ice arena, a gym, an indoor track, soccer and volleyball areas, an indoor swimming pool, exercise and weight rooms, an aerobics studio, racquetball courts, lighted tennis courts, softball, lacrosse, and rugby fields, and a fitness center. **Graduates:** From July 1, 2015 to June 30, 2016, 1417 bachelor's degrees were awarded. The most popular majors were business/marketing (22%), communication/journalism (10%), and education (10%). 120 companies recruited on campus in 2015-2016. In an average class, 1% graduate in 3 years or less, 40% graduate in 4 years or less, 17% graduate in 5 years or less, and 1% graduate in 6 years or less. Of the 2015 graduating class, 12% were enrolled in graduate school within 6 months of graduation, and 79% were employed.

SERVICES: Counseling and information services are available, as is tutoring in every subject. There is a reader service for the blind, and remedial math, reading, and writing. **Library/Resources:** The library contains 541,609 volumes, 723,474 microform items, and 25,698 audio/video tapes/CDs/DVDs, and subscribes to 114,144 periodicals including electronic. Computerized library services include interlibrary loans, database searching, Internet access, and Wi-Fi capability. Special learning facilities include an art gallery, planetarium, radio station, TV station, an environmental science institute, a child care center, a research institute, a teacher resource center, a speech and hearing clinic, the Alzheimer's Disease Assistance Center, auditory research labs, a virtual reality simulator, and distance learning facilities. **Physically Challenged Students:** 95% of the campus is accessible. Facilities include wheelchair ramps, elevators, special parking, specially equipped restrooms, special class scheduling, lowered drinking fountains, lowered telephones, special housing. curb cuts, and electronic doors. **Special:** The college offers cross-registration with Clinton Community College and Empire State College, internships, study abroad in 10 countries, cooperative programs in all majors, B.A.-B.S. degrees, dual and student-designed majors, an accelerated degree program in any major except nursing, and B.A./M.S.T. and B.S./MSED combined undergraduate and graduate programs. A 3-2 engineering degree is offered with SUNY Stony Brook and Binghamton, Clarkson, Syracuse, and McGill Universities, and the University of Vermont. There are 31 national honor societies and a freshman honors program. **Visiting:** There are regularly scheduled orientations for prospective students, including a group, student-led tour, and either a group or individual interview. Special overnight events for accepted freshmen include meals with students and faculty, classroom visits, discussions with faculty, and special workshops. There are guides for informal visits, visitors may sit in on classes, and stay overnight. To schedule a visit, contact the Admissions Office. **Campus Safety and Security:** Measures include 24-hour foot and vehicle patrol, emergency notification system, self-defense education, and security escort services. There are shuttle buses, emergency telephones, lighted pathways/sidewalks, controlled access to dorms/residences, bicycle patrols, combination locks on student rooms, a computerized keyless entry system for residence hall access, door viewers, and basement and ground-level security windows in residence halls.

REQUIREMENTS: The SAT or ACT is required. Applicants must have at least 12 academic credits, including 4 years of English, 5 combined years of math and science, and 3 years of social studies. An essay, portfolio, audition, and interview may be recommended in some programs. The GED is accepted. SUNY Plattsburgh requires applicants to be in the upper 50% of their class. A GPA of 78.0 is required. AP and CLEP credits are accepted. Important factors in the admissions decision are advanced placement or honors courses, recommendations by school officials, and leadership record. To graduate students must have a 2.0 GPA and complete at least 120 semester hours. Core curriculum courses total 41 to 46 credits. In addition, all students must demonstrate proficiency in writing by completion of English composition and an advanced writing requirement. Specific courses such as library research skills and computer science are offered. A comprehensive exam in some majors and a thesis in the upper-division honors program. Many majors require practicum and/or internship experience to complete a degree. **Procedure:** Freshmen are admitted fall and spring. Entrance exams should be taken during the second half of the junior year or the beginning of the senior year. There is a rolling admissions plan. Early decision applications should be filed by November 15; regular applications, by August 1 for fall entry; and November 1 for spring entry, along with a $50 fee. Notification of early decision is sent December 15; regular decision, January 15. 310 applicants were on the 2016 waiting list; 26 were admitted. Applications are accepted online. **Transfer Students:** 612 transfer students enrolled in 2015-2016. Applicants must have a minimum 2.0 GPA. Most academic programs require a 2.5 GPA or better. 36 of 120 credits required for the bachelor's degree must be completed at SUNY Plattsburgh. **International Students:** There are 308 international students enrolled. The school actively recruits these students. They must take the TOEFL with a minimum score of 450 on the paper-based TOEFL (PBT) or 45 on the Internet-based version (iBT).

ADMISSIONS: 34% of the current freshmen were in the top fifth of their class; 75% were in the top two fifths. **Admissions Contact:** Jessica Fish, Assistant Director of Admissions. Email: *jessica.fish@plattsburgh.edu* Web: *www.plattsburgh.edu*

FINANCIAL AID: In 2016-2017, 65% of all full-time freshmen received some form of financial aid. 58% of all full-time freshmen and 59% of continuing full-time students received need-based aid. The average freshman award was $11,845. Need-based scholarships or need-based grants averaged $7,093; need-based self-help aid (loans and jobs) averaged $6,510; and other non-need-based awards and non-need-based scholarships averaged $6,227. 34% of undergraduate students work part-time. Average annual earnings from campus work are $1520. The average financial indebtedness of the 2016 graduate was $26,894. The FAFSA code is 002849. The priority date for freshman financial aid applications for fall entry is February 15.

STATE UNIVERSITY OF NEW YORK / SUNY POTSDAM — D-2

www.potsdam.edu

Potsdam, NY 13676 — (315) 267-2180

Fax: (315) 267-2163	Email: admissions@potsdam.edu
Full-time: 1401 men, 1920 women	**Faculty:** 249; IIA, --$
Part-time: 49 men, 46 women	**Ph.D.s:** 67%
Graduate: 67 men, 213 women	**Student/Faculty:** 13 to 1
Year: semesters, summer session	**Tuition:** $7984 ($17,834)
Room & Board: $12,420	**Freshman Class:** 4976 applied, 3678 accepted, 344 enrolled
SAT CR/M: 610/600 **ACT:** 27	**CEEB CODE:** 2545
Application Deadline: rolling	**COMPETITIVE+**

The State University of New York at Potsdam, founded in 1816, joined the State University System in 1948. SUNY Potsdam offers over 50 programs in Arts and Sciences, 6 in The Crane School of Music and over 20 in The School of Education and Professional Studies, as well as programs in Interdisciplinary Studies. Bachelor Degrees are offered in Arts, Science, Fine Arts and Music and Master's degrees in Arts, Education, Science and Music. SUNY Potsdam offers dual degrees with a number of other Universities. There are 3 undergraduate schools and 1 graduate school. In addition to regional accreditation, SUNY Potsdam has baccalaureate program accreditation with NASM, NCATE, NAST, ICABE, and AAAHC. The 240-acre campus is in a rural area 30 miles from Massena and Ogdensburg, 140 miles northeast of Syracuse, and 80 miles from Montreal, Canada. Including any residence halls, there are 56 buildings.

STUDENT LIFE: 96% of undergraduates are from New York. Others are from 30 states, 12 foreign countries, and Canada. 85% are from public schools. 62% are White; 14% Hispanic; 11% African American; 5% race unknown; 3% two or more races; 2% Asian American; 2% American Indian/Alaska Native; 1% Foreign. **Female To Male Ratio:** 1.4:1. The average age of freshmen is 18; all undergraduates, 21. 25% do not continue beyond their first year; 52% remain to graduate. **Housing:** 2715 students can be accommodated in college housing, which includes single-sex and coed dorms, on-campus apartments, off-campus apartments, honors houses, special-interest houses, First year experience, quiet study, international house, transfer student housing, sustainability housing, and gender neutral housing. On-campus housing is guaranteed for all 4 years. 61% of students live on campus; of those, 70% remain on campus on weekends. All students may keep cars.

FACULTY/CLASSROOMS: 50% of faculty are male; 50% are female. All teach undergraduates. No introductory courses are taught by graduate students.

PROGRAMS OF STUDY: SUNY Potsdam confers B.A., B.F.A., B.M. and B.S. degrees. Master's degrees are also awarded. Bachelor's degrees are awarded in AGRICULTURE (environmental studies), BIOLOGICAL SCIENCE (biochemistry and biology/biological science), BUSINESS (business administration and management and business economics), COMMUNICATIONS AND THE ARTS (art history, art, communications, creative writing, dance, English, English literature, English writing, fine arts, French, graphic design, literature, music, music business management, music composition, music performance, Spanish, communication arts/speech, studio art, theatre arts, and visual and performing arts), COMPUTER AND PHYSICAL SCIENCE (chemistry, computer science, earth science/adolescence education, geology, mathematics, and physics), EDUCATION (early childhood education, English education, mathematics education, music education, science education, social studies education, and Spanish adolescense education), HEALTH PROFESSIONS (community health work and exercise science), SOCIAL SCIENCE (anthropology, archeology, criminal justice, economics, French studies, history, interdisciplinary studies, philosophy, political science/government, psychology, sociology, and women's studies). Psychology, business administration, and music education have the largest enrollments.

ACTIVITIES: 6% of men belong to 3 local and 2 national fraternities; 11% of women belong to 8 local and 3 national sororities. There are 87 groups on campus, including art, band, cheerleading, choir, chorale, chorus, computers, dance, drama, environmental, environmental awareness, ethnic, honors, international, jazz band, LGBT, literary magazine, musical theater, newspaper, opera, orchestra, photography, political, professional, radio and TV, religious, social, social service, student government, and symphony. Popular campus events include Welcome Weekend Carnival, Spring Fest, and Crane Candlelight Concert. **Sports:** There are 7 intercollegiate sports for men and 8 for women, and 8 intramural sports for men and 7 for women. Facilities include a climbing wall, high ropes course, a fitness center with treadmills, spin cycles, ellipticals, strength equipment, free weights a gymnasium, hockey rink, swimming pool with a diving well, a field house, with indoor track, basketball, volleyball, indoor lacrosse courts, racquetball courts, squash courts, dance studio, and physical therapy/training room, athletic fields, and courts for tennis and basketball, a track, field for softball, and modern turf field for soccer, lacrosse and intramural competition. **Graduates:** From July 1, 2015 to June 30, 2016, 806 bachelor's degrees were awarded. The most popular majors were education (14%), visual & performing arts (13%), and business administration/marketing (10%). 72 companies recruited on campus in 2015-2016. In an average class, 35% graduate in 4 years or less, 49% graduate in 5 years or less, and 52% graduate in 6 years or less. Of the 2015 graduating class, 55% were enrolled in graduate school within 6 months of graduation, and 41% were employed.

SERVICES: Counseling and information services are available, as is tutoring in every subject. There is a reader service for the blind. **Library/ Resources:** The 2 libraries contain 536,840 volumes, and 21,317 audio/ video tapes/CDs/DVDs. Computerized library services include interlibrary loans, database searching, Internet access, and Wi-Fi capability. Special learning facilities include an art gallery, natural history museum, planetarium, radio station, electronic music and recording studios, performance halls, music center, seismographic laboratory, anthropology museum, biology museum, learning & teaching excellence center, fine arts studios, and an art museum that includes the Gibson Gallery. **Physically Challenged Students:** 95% of the campus is accessible. Facilities include wheelchair ramps, elevators, special parking, specially equipped restrooms, special class scheduling, lowered drinking fountains, lowered telephones, special housing, and electric doors. **Special:** Cross-registration is offered with Clarkson University, St. Lawrence University, and SUNY Canton. 600 internships available in over 50 countries. SUNY Postdam also offers work-study opportunities, a 3-2 engineering degree with Clarkson University, study abroad, 3-2 management and accounting degrees, student-designed majors, dual majors in interdisciplinary natural science, non-degree study, and pass/fail options. Handcrafted education for students who enroll in the Honors Program or engage in Research through the UG Research and Presidential Scholars programs. There are 21 national honor societies and 6 departmental honors programs. **Visiting:** There are regularly scheduled orientations for prospective students, There are guides for informal visits and visitors may sit in on classes. To schedule a visit, contact the Admissions Office. **Campus Safety and Security:** Measures include 24-hour foot and vehicle patrol, emergency notification system, self-defense education, and security escort services. There are emergency telephones, lighted pathways/ sidewalks, controlled access to dorms/residences, bike patrol, educational programs, campus rescue squad, portable jump-start packs, vehicle lockouts, parking management, and officers trained in Narcan administration.

REQUIREMENTS: Applicants must be high school graduates in a college preparatory program or hold a GED. 4 years each of English and social studies, 3 years each of math, foreign language, and science, and 1 year of art or music recommended. An interview is important; an audition when appropriate is required. The majority of our applicants will not have to submit an SAT or ACT score. If you would like to have your scores submitted as part of your application, you must request your scores be sent directly from the testing agency. Also, you must submit an SAT or ACT score to be considered for our Mount Emmons Scholarship. Minimum scores for scholarship consideration are a 1300 on the SAT or a 29 on the ACT. AP and CLEP credits are accepted. Important factors in the admissions decision are geographical diversity, parents or siblings attended your school, and recommendations by school officials. To graduate, students must complete a major and earn at least a 2.0 in 30 hours of your major coursework (some majors have higher standards). 15 of those 30 hours must be upper division (U.D.)--level 300 or higher--and if you transfer here, at least 15 U.D. hours must be taken at SUNY Potsdam. 120 credits + 4 P.E. credits (for the B.A., B. F. A and B. S.), 120-130 credits + 4 P.E. credits (for B.M.), Thus, in order to graduate in 4 years (8 semesters) you need to take at least 16 credit hours per semester. NOTE: The college allows students to take 12 credit hours and still maintain full-time student status. This may work well for some students, However, unless classes are taken during summer or winterim sessions, a student taking less than 15 credits per semester cannot graduate in 4 years. A certain number of your 120 credits must be designated as liberal arts credits. You must complete the general education requirements. You must graduate with an overall G.P.A. of 2.0. Out of your total 120 credits, 45 of those must be designated as upper division courses (level 300 or higher). **Procedure:** Freshmen are admitted in the fall and spring. Entrance exams should be taken in the junior year or early senior year. There are early admissions, deferred admissions, and rolling admissions plans. Application deadlines are open. Application fee is $50. Notifications are sent October 1. Applications are accepted online. **Transfer Students:** 225 transfer students enrolled in 2015-2016. Applicants must have earned 12 hours of college credit. Transfers with fewer than 24 credit hours must submit a high school transcript. College transcript required and essay (required of some) or personal statement required. 30 of 124 credits required for the bachelor's degree must be completed at SUNY Potsdam. **International Students:** There are 23 international students enrolled. They must take the TOEFL with a minimum score of 550 on the paper-based TOEFL (PBT) or 79 on the Internet-based version (iBT), or take the IELTS.

ADMISSIONS: 74% of the 2016-2017 applicants were accepted. The SAT scores for the 2016-2017 freshman class were: Critical Reading-- 24% below 500, 46% between 500 and 599, 26% between 600 and 699, and 4% between 700 and 800. Math-- 25% below 500, 48% between 500 and 599, 23% between 600 and 699, and 4% between 700 and 800. The ACT scores were 2% between 12 and 17, 44% between 18 and 23, 37% between 24 and 29, and 17% above 30. **Admissions Contact:** Thomas Nesbitt, Director of Admissions. Email: *admissions@potsdam.edu* Web: *www.potsdam.edu*

FINANCIAL AID: In 2016-2017, 95% of all full-time freshmen and 88% of continuing full-time students received some form of financial aid. 81% of all full-time freshmen and 70% of continuing full-time students received need-based aid. The average freshman award was $16,496. Need-based scholarships or need-based grants averaged $8,185 ($21,153 maximum); need-based self-help aid (loans and jobs) averaged $4,019 ($9,600 maximum); and other non-need-based awards and non-need-based scholarships averaged $2,528 ($21,769 maximum). The average financial indebtedness of the 2016 graduate was $25,583. The state aid form is required. The FAFSA code is 002850. The priority date for freshman financial aid applications for fall entry is March 1. The filing deadline for fall entry is May 1.

STATE UNIVERSITY OF NEW YORK / THE COLLEGE OF ENVIRONMENTAL SCIENCE AND FORESTRY C-3

www.esf.edu

Syracuse, NY 13210	(315) 470-6600
Fax: (315) 470-6933	Email: esfinfo@esf.edu
Full-time: 918 men, 793 women	Faculty: 116
Part-time: 23 men, 19 women	Ph.D.s: n/av
Graduate: 199 men, 232 women	Student/Faculty: 13 to 1
Year: semesters	Tuition: $8103 ($17,953)
Room & Board: $15,750	Freshman Class: 1699 applied, 899 accepted, 327 enrolled
SAT CR/M: 575/590 ACT: 25	CEEB CODE: 2530
Application Deadline: February 1	VERY COMPETITIVE

SUNY College of Environmental Science and Forestry, founded in 1911, is the nation's oldest and largest college focused exclusively on the science, design, engineering, and management of our environment and natural resources. The college offers 21 undergraduate and 28 graduate degree programs, including 8 Ph.D. programs. Students also benefit from a special partnership with Syracuse University (SU) that provides access to courses, housing, and student organizations. There is 1 undergraduate school and 1 graduate school. In addition to regional accreditation, SUNY-ESF has baccalaureate program accreditation with ABET, ASLA, and SAF. The 12-acre campus is in an urban area in Syracuse, NY. Including any residence halls, there are 7 buildings.

STUDENT LIFE: 80% of undergraduates are from New York. Others are

from 27 states, and 9 foreign countries. 80% are White; 6% Hispanic; 4% Asian American; 4% race unknown; 3% two or more races; 2% Foreign; 1% African American. **Male To Female Ratio:** 1.1:1. The average age of freshmen is 18; all undergraduates, 20. 18% do not continue beyond their first year; 75% remain to graduate. **Housing:** 620 students can be accommodated in college housing, which includes single-sex and coed dorms, on-campus apartments, and off-campus apartments. In addition, there are special-interest houses, fraternity houses, sorority houses, substance-free floors, quiet floors, and learning communities. On-campus housing is guaranteed for all 4 years and is available on a lottery system for upperclassmen. 65% of students commute. Alcohol is not permitted. Upperclassmen may keep cars.

FACULTY/CLASSROOMS: 71% of faculty are male; 29% are female. All teach undergraduates, and do research. No introductory courses are taught by graduate students. The average class size in a regular course is 25.

PROGRAMS OF STUDY: SUNY-ESF confers B.S., and B.L.A. degrees. Associate, master's, and doctoral degrees are also awarded. Bachelor's degrees are awarded in AGRICULTURE (animal science, environmental studies, fishing and fisheries, forest engineering, forestry and related sciences, natural resource management, plant science, soil science, and wood science), BIOLOGICAL SCIENCE (biology/biological science, biotechnology, botany, ecology, entomology, environmental biology, microbiology, molecular biology, plant genetics, plant pathology, plant physiology, and wildlife biology), COMPUTER AND PHYSICAL SCIENCE (chemistry and polymer science), EDUCATION (environmental education), ENGINEERING AND ENVIRONMENTAL DESIGN (chemical engineering, construction management, environmental design, environmental engineering, environmental science, landscape architecture/design, paper and pulp science, paper engineering, and survey and mapping technology), HEALTH PROFESSIONS (predentistry, premedicine, and prepharmacy), SOCIAL SCIENCE (prelaw). Engineering, chemistry, and biology are the strongest academically. Biology, forest resource management, and environmental science have the largest enrollments.

ACTIVITIES: 2% of men belong to 20 national fraternities; 2% of women belong to 20 national sororities. There are 350 groups on campus, including art, bagpipe, band, cheerleading, choir, chorale, chorus, computers, dance, debate, drama, environmental, ethnic, film, honors, international, jazz band, LGBT, literary magazine, marching band, musical theater, newspaper, orchestra, pep band, photography, political, professional, radio and TV, religious, social, social service, student government, symphony, and yearbook. Popular campus events include Earth Week, Awards Banquet and December Soiree. **Sports:** There are 6 intercollegiate sports for men and 5 for women, and 15 intramural sports for men and 15 for women. Facilities include ESF has soccer, golf, cross-country, and woodsman's teams. Students can participate in all Syracuse University club teams, intramural sports, and recreational activities. **Graduates:** From July 1, 2015 to June 30, 2016, 446 bachelor's degrees were awarded. The most popular majors were biology (43%), natural resources/conservation (26%), and engineering technologies (14%). 87 companies recruited on campus in 2015-2016. In an average class, 3% graduate in 3 years or less, 59% graduate in 4 years or less, 73% graduate in 5 years or less, and 76% graduate in 6 years or less. Of the 2015 graduating class, 17% were enrolled in graduate school within 6 months of graduation, and 86% were employed.

SERVICES: Counseling and information services are available, as is tutoring in most subjects, and a reader service for the blind. **Library/Resources:** The library contains 136,438 volumes, 2,634 microform items, and 479 audio/video tapes/CDs/DVDs, and subscribes to 1,678 periodicals including electronic. Computerized library services include interlibrary loans, database searching, Internet access, and Wi-Fi capability. Special learning facilities include an art gallery, natural history museum, radio station, and TV station. **Physically Challenged Students:** 95% of the campus is accessible. Facilities include wheelchair ramps, elevators, special parking, specially equipped restrooms, lowered drinking fountains, lowered telephones, and special housing. **Special:** Cross-registration is offered with Syracuse University. Co-op programs, internships, and dual options in forest ecosystem science are available. Study abroad is available in landscape architecture and through Syracuse University. There is an Honors Program for outstanding students. There is 1 national honor society, a freshman honors program, and 8 departmental honors programs. **Visiting:** There are regularly scheduled orientations for prospective students, including a fall open house, which provides campus tours, faculty sessions, an activities fair, and student affairs presentations. There are guides for informal visits and visitors may sit in on classes. To schedule a visit, contact the Admissions Office. **Campus Safety and Security:** Measures include 24-hour foot and vehicle patrol, emergency notification system, self-defense education, and security escort services. There are shuttle buses, emergency telephones, lighted pathways/sidewalks, and controlled access to dorms/residences.

REQUIREMENTS: The SAT or ACT is required. Applicants are required to have a minimum of 3 years of math and science, including chemistry, in a college preparatory curriculum. A supplemental application form, essay and results of SAT or ACT exams are required. A campus visit, letters of recommendation, and a personal portfolio or resume are recommended. AP and CLEP credits are accepted. Important factors in the admissions decision are advanced placement or honors courses, leadership record, and extracurricular activities record. Students must complete 125 to 130 credit hours for the B.S. (160 for the B.L.A.), including 60 in the major, with a minimum 2.0 GPA. Courses in chemistry, English, math, and biology or physics are required. **Procedure:** Freshmen are admitted in the fall and spring. Entrance exams should be taken by October of the senior year. There are early decision, deferred admissions, and rolling admissions plans. Early decision applications should be filed by December 1; regular applications, by February 1 for fall entry; and November 1 for spring entry, along with a $50 fee. Notification of early decision is sent December 15; regular decision, March 1. 90 early decision candidates were accepted for the 2016-2017 class. Applications are accepted on-line. **Transfer Students:** 257 transfer students enrolled in 2015-2016. Transfer requirements vary by major. Students must successfully complete prerequisite course work and must have a 2.5 or higher GPA to be considered. 24 of 125 credits required for the bachelor's degree must be completed at SUNY-ESF. **International Students:** There are 40 international students enrolled. They must take the TOEFL with a minimum score of 550 on the paper-based TOEFL (PBT) or 79 on the Internet-based version (iBT). They must also take the SAT or ACT.

ADMISSIONS: 72% of the current freshmen were in the top fifth of their class; 95% were in the top two fifths. There was 1 National Merit finalist. **Admissions Contact:** Thomas Fletcher, Associate Director of Admissions. Email: *trfletch@esf.edu* Web: *www.esf.edu*

FINANCIAL AID: In 2016-2017, 93% of all full-time freshmen and 81% of continuing full-time students received some form of financial aid. 85% of all full-time freshmen and 72% of continuing full-time students received need-based aid. The average freshman award was $10,831. Need-based scholarships or need-based grants averaged $5,549 ($17,710 maximum); need-based self-help aid (loans and jobs) averaged $2,040 ($9,000 maximum); and other non-need-based awards and non-need-based scholarships averaged $3,342 ($24,000 maximum). 60% of undergraduate students work part-time. Average annual earnings from campus work are $1329. The average financial indebtedness of the 2016 graduate was $22,428. The state aid form is required. The FAFSA code is 002851. The priority date for freshman financial aid applications for fall entry is February 1.

STATE UNIVERSITY OF NEW YORK / UNIVERSITY AT BUFFALO — A-3

www.buffalo.edu

Buffalo, NY 14214 — **(716) 645-6900**, **(888) UB-ADMIT**

Fax: (716) 645-6411 — **Email: ubadmissions@buffalo.edu**

Full-time: 10,878 men, 7998 women
Part-time: 719 men, 816 women
Graduate: 4773 men, 4999 women
Year: semesters, summer session
Room & Board: $13,548

SAT or ACT: required
Application Deadline: rolling

Faculty: I, av$
Ph.D.s: 100%
Student/Faculty: 13 to 1
Tuition: $9574 ($26,814)
Freshman Class: 26001 applied, 15440 accepted, 4103 enrolled
CEEB CODE: 2533
COMPETITIVE+

University at Buffalo, State University of New York, established in 1846, is a public institution offering more than 300 bachelor's, master's, and doctoral degree programs. UB is a comprehensive research-extensive university and the largest campus in the State University of New York system. There are 8 undergraduate schools and 12 graduate schools. In addition to regional accreditation, UB has baccalaureate program accreditation with AACSB, ABET, ACPE, ADA, APTA, CSWE, NAAB, NASAD, ABA, ACCNE, ACOTE, CCNE, COA, LCME, TEAC, APA, ASHA, JRCNM, ACS, ACEND, CORE, ASHP, NAACLS, CEPH, PAB, ACGME, and ALA. The 1350-acre campus is in a suburban area 3 miles north of Buffalo. Including any residence halls, there are 195 buildings.

STUDENT LIFE: 97% of undergraduates are from New York. Others are from 50 states, 87 foreign countries, and Canada. 48% are White; 16% Foreign; 14% Asian American; 7% African American; 7% Hispanic; 5% race unknown; 2% two or more races; 1% American Indian/Alaska Native. **Male To Female Ratio:** 1.2:1. The average age of freshmen is 18; all undergraduates, 21. 14% do not continue beyond their first year. **Housing:** 7328 students can be accommodated in college housing, which includes coed dorms, on-campus apartments, and married student housing. In addition, there are honors houses, special-interest houses, freshmen-only housing and cultural interest housing, and special housing for disabled students. On-campus housing is guaranteed for all 4 years, and is guaranteed for the freshman year only, is available on a first-come, first-served basis, and is available on a lottery system for upperclassmen. 62% of students commute. All students may keep cars.

FACULTY/CLASSROOMS: 60% of faculty are male; 40% are female. No introductory courses are taught by graduate students.

PROGRAMS OF STUDY: UB confers B.A., B.S., B.F.A. and Mus.B. degrees. Master's and doctoral degrees are also awarded. Bachelor's degrees are awarded in AGRICULTURE (environmental studies), BIOLOGICAL SCIENCE (biochemistry, bioinformatics, biology/biological science, biophysics, and biotechnology), BUSINESS (accounting and business administration and management), COMMUNICATIONS AND THE ARTS (art history and appreciation, classics, communications, dance, English, film arts, fine arts, French, German, Italian, linguistics, media arts, music, music performance, musical theater, Spanish, studio art, and theatre arts), COMPUTER AND PHYSICAL SCIENCE (chemistry, computer science, environmental geology, geology, informatics and computer science, mathematics, mathematics – economics, physics, and statistics), EDUCATION (global studies), ENGINEERING AND ENVIRONMENTAL DESIGN (aerospace studies, architecture, biomedical engineering, chemical engineering, civil engineering, computational sciences, computer engineering, electrical/electronics engineering, engineering physics, environmental design, environmental engineering, industrial engineering, and mechanical engineering), HEALTH PROFESSIONS (biomedical science, exercise science, medical technology, nuclear medical technology, nursing, occupational therapy, pharmaceutical science, pharmacology, pharmacy, and speech pathology/audiology), SOCIAL SCIENCE (African American studies, American studies, anthropology, Asian/Oriental studies, economics, geography, geography information science, history, philosophy, political science/government, psychology, social science, and sociology). Engineering, business administration, and psychology have the largest enrollments.

ACTIVITIES: 2% of men belong to 1 local and 20 national fraternities; 2% of women belong to 14 national sororities. There are 651 groups on campus, including art, band, cheerleading, chess, choir, chorale, chorus, computers, dance, debate, drama, drill team, environmental, ethnic, film, honors, international, jazz band, LGBT, literary magazine, marching band, musical theater, newspaper, opera, orchestra, pep band, photography, political, professional, radio and TV, religious, social, social service, student government, and symphony. Popular campus events include Homecoming, Family Weekend and Fallfest. **Sports:** There are 9 intercollegiate sports for men and 9 for women, and 8 intramural sports for men and 8 for women. Facilities include badminton, baseball, basketball, boxing, crew, cricket, cross-country, gymnastics, ice hockey, lacrosse, roller hockey, rugby, skiing, soccer, Tae Kwon Do, volleyball, soccer, an indoor jogging track, a pool and diving well, tennis, weight training, wrestling rooms, dance studios, a spinning room, and frisbee. **Graduates:** From July 1, 2015 to June 30, 2016, 5379 bachelor's degrees were awarded. The most popular majors were business marketing (19%), social sciences (16%), and engineering (14%). 341 companies recruited on campus in 2015-2016. In an average class, 55% graduate in 4 years or less, 70% graduate in 5 years or less, and 74% graduate in 6 years or less. Of the 2015 graduating class, 36% were enrolled in graduate school within 6 months of graduation, and 47% were employed.

SERVICES: Counseling and information services are available, as is tutoring in most subjects, such as note-taking services, readers, tutors, text on tape, tape recorders, and extended time for tests. There is a reader service for the blind, and remedial math, reading, and writing. Peer tutoring and some computer-assisted instruction are also available. **Library/Resources:** The 12 libraries contain 4.2 million volumes, 6.2 million microform items, and 285,659 audio/video tapes/CDs/DVDs, and subscribe to 162,556 periodicals including electronic. Computerized library services include interlibrary loans, database searching, Internet access, and Wi-Fi capability. Special learning facilities include an art gallery, radio station, TV station, concert hall, anthropology research museum, School of Pharmacy and Pharmaceutical Sciences Apothecary and Historical Exhibits, Museum of Radiology and Medical Physics, Museum of Neuroanatomy, New York State Center of Excellence in Bioinformatics & Life Sciences (CBLS), Center for Computational Research (CCR), Center of Excellence for Document Analysis and Recognition (CEDAR), Center of Excellence in Materials Informatics, Buffalo Clinical and Translational Research Center (CTRC), New York State Center for Engineering Design and Industrial Innovation (NYSCEDII), Electronic Poetry Center, The Archaeological Survey, and numerous research centers. **Physically Challenged Students:** 90% of the campus is accessible. Facilities include wheelchair ramps, elevators, special parking, specially equipped restrooms, special class scheduling, lowered drinking fountains, lowered telephones, and special housing. **Special:** Students may cross-register with the Western New York Consortium. Internships are available, and students may study abroad in 29 countries. UB offers a Washington semester, work-study programs, accelerated degree programs, B.A.-B.S. degrees, dual, student-designed, and interdisciplinary majors, and credit for military experience. A 3-2 engineering degree can be pursued. Students may choose a successful/unsuccessful (S/U) grading option for selected courses. There is an early assurance of admission program to medical school for undergraduate sophomore students who possess a minimum approximate overall and science GPA of 3.75 and complete particular science courses. There are 34 national honor societies, Phi Beta Kappa, and a freshman honors program. **Visiting:** There are regularly scheduled orientations for prospective students, including the visit UB program, in which visitors tour the campus and attend an information session to learn about application procedures, admissions criteria, housing, financial aid, and scholarship programs. Visitors may sit in on classes. To schedule a visit, contact the Office of Admissions at ub-admissions@buffalo.edu. **Campus Safety and Security:** Measures include 24-hour foot and vehicle patrol, emergency notification system, self-defense education, and security escort services. There are shuttle buses, emergency telephones, lighted pathways/sidewalks, controlled access to dorms/residences, an alarm system, routine patrols, student aides in residence halls, some security cameras, blue-light phones, and a university-wide safety committee.

REQUIREMENTS: The SAT is required. Freshmen are evaluated based on secondary school performance, strength of curriculum, standardized test scores, and, in some cases, and a supplemental application. A high school diploma is required and the GED is accepted. Dance, music theatre, theatre and music applicants must audition. Architecture requires a portfolio. Academic units 17 recommended, 4 each of English and social studies, 3 each of math, science, and foreign language. AP and CLEP credits are accepted. Important factors in the admissions decision are advanced placement or honors courses, leadership record, recommendations by school officials, parents or siblings attended your school, evidence of special talent, personality/intangible qualities, extracurricular activities record, recommendations by alumni, and geographical diversity. To graduate, students must complete 120 semester hours with a minimum GPA of 2.0. General education requirements include writing skills, mathematical sciences, library skills, world civilizations, American pluralism, natural sciences, language, humanities, arts, social and behavioral sciences, and depth requirement. The total number of hours in the major varies. **Procedure:** Freshmen are admitted fall and spring. Entrance exams should be taken during the spring of the junior year or the fall of the senior year. There are early admissions and rolling admissions plans. Early decision applications should be filed by November 1, along with a $50 fee. Notifications are sent in February. 1303 applicants were on the 2016 waiting list. Applications are accepted online. **Transfer Students:** 1862 transfer students enrolled in 2015-2016. Transfer applicants with fewer than 24 credit hours must supply high school transcripts, SAT and/or ACT test scores, and the previous college academic record. It is recommended that students present a strong record of college study, with a 2.5 GPA. Entry at junior level requires a higher GPA for some programs. Credit may be awarded for military experience and other nontraditional sources. 30 of 120 credits required for the bachelor's degree must be completed at UB. **International Students:** There are 2683 international students enrolled. The school actively recruits these students. They must take the TOEFL with a minimum score of 550 on the paper-based TOEFL (PBT) or 79 on the Internet-based version (iBT). The SAT or ACT is strongly recommended.

Admissions Contact: Jose Aviles, Director of Admissions. Email: *ubadmissions@buffalo.edu* Web: *www.buffalo.edu*

FINANCIAL AID: In 2016-2017, 60% of all full-time freshmen and 55% of continuing full-time students received some form of financial aid. 46% of all full-time freshmen and 44% of continuing full-time students received need-based aid. The average freshman award was $10,577. Need-based scholarships or need-based grants averaged $7,952; need-based self-help aid (loans and jobs) averaged $3,320; non-need-based athletic scholarships averaged $16,984; and other non-need-based awards and non-need-based scholarships averaged $4,075. Average annual earnings from campus work are $950. UB is a member of CSS. The FAFSA code is 002837. The priority date for freshman financial aid applications for fall entry is March 1.

STATE UNIVERSITY OF NEW YORK / COLLEGE OF AGRICULTURE AND TECH AT COBLESKILL *(The complete profile is made available exclusively on our website, www.barronspac.com)*

STATE UNIVERSITY OF NEW YORK / MARITIME COLLEGE — D-5

www.sunymaritime.edu

Throgs Neck, NY 10465 — **(718) 409-7221** **(800) 642-1874**

Fax: (718) 409-7465 — **Email: admissions@sunymaritime.edu**

Full-time: 1326 men, 137 women	**Faculty:** 69; IIA, -$
Part-time: 97 men, 15 women	**Ph.D.s:** 49%
Graduate: 151 men, 31 women	**Student/Faculty:** 21 to 1
Year: semesters, summer session	**Tuition:** $6090 ($13,990)
Room & Board: $9930	**Freshman Class:** 1397 applied, 888 accepted, 356 enrolled
SAT CR/M: 510/550 **ACT:** 22	**CEEB CODE:** 2536
Application Deadline: September 1	**COMPETITIVE**

State University of New York/Maritime College, founded in 1874, is a public institution that prepares students for the U.S. Merchant Marine officers' license and for bachelor's degrees in engineering, naval architecture, marine environmental science, and marine transportation/business administration. Figures in the above capsule and in this profile are approximate. There is 1 undergraduate school and 1 graduate school. In addition to regional accreditation, New York Maritime has baccalaureate program accreditation with ABET. The 52-acre campus is in a suburban area on the Throgs Neck peninsula where Long Island Sound meets the East River. Including any residence halls, there are 31 buildings.

STUDENT LIFE: 65% of undergraduates are from New York. Others are from 28 states, and 20 foreign countries. 70% are from public schools. 9% are Hispanic; 71% White; 7% Foreign; 6% African American; 4% Asian American. **Male To Female Ratio:** 8.6:1. The average age of freshmen is 19; all undergraduates, 21. 23% do not continue beyond their first year; 77% remain to graduate. **Housing:** 1281 students can be accommodated in college housing, which includes single-sex and coed dorms. On-campus housing is guaranteed for all 4 years, and is available on a first-come, and first-served basis. 82% of students live on campus; of those, 25% remain on campus on weekends. Upperclassmen may keep cars. Alcohol is not permitted.

FACULTY/CLASSROOMS: 89% of faculty are male; 11% are female. 96% teach undergraduates, 20% do research, and 20% do both. No introductory courses are taught by graduate students. The average class size in an introductory lecture is 28; in a laboratory is 16; and in a regular course is 30.

PROGRAMS OF STUDY: New York Maritime confers B.E., and B.S. degrees. Associate and master's degrees are also awarded. Bachelor's degrees are awarded in BIOLOGICAL SCIENCE (marine science), BUSINESS (business administration and management and transportation management), COMPUTER AND PHYSICAL SCIENCE (atmospheric sciences and meteorology), ENGINEERING AND ENVIRONMENTAL DESIGN (electrical/electronics engineering, engineering, environmental science, marine engineering, maritime science, and naval architecture and marine engineering), SOCIAL SCIENCE (humanities). Marine operations, marine environmental science, and electrical engineering are the strongest academically. Marine transportation, marine engineering, and international transportation & trade have the largest enrollments.

ACTIVITIES: There are no fraternities or sororities. There are 30 groups on campus, including art, bagpipe, band, chorus, computers, drill team, ethnic, honors, international, jazz band, marching band, newspaper, pep band, photography, political, professional, religious, social, social service, and student government. Popular campus events include Thursdays in the TIV, Ring Dance, and Super Bowl Party. **Sports:** There are 9 intercollegiate sports for men and 9 for women, and 6 intramural sports for men and 6 for women. Facilities include an athletic center with gym, a swimming pool, exercise and weight rooms, a rifle and pistol range, and 3 handball/racquetball and squash courts, a sailing center, and football, baseball, lacrosse, and soccer fields. **Graduates:** From July 1, 2015 to June 30, 2016, 306 bachelor's degrees were awarded. The most popular majors were marine transportation (30%), international transportation and trade (18%), and naval architecture (9%). 22 companies recruited on campus in 2015-2016. In an average class, 31% graduate in 4 years or less, 47% graduate in 5 years or less, and 49% graduate in 6 years or less. Of the 2015 graduating class, 4% were enrolled in graduate school within 6 months of graduation, and 100% were employed.

SERVICES: Counseling and information services are available, as is tutoring in every subject. **Library/Resources:** The library contains 85,984 volumes, 28,400 microform items, 774 audio/video tapes/CDs/DVDs, and subscribes to 38,735 periodicals including electronic. Computerized library services include interlibrary loans, database searching, and Internet access. **Physically Challenged Students:** 81% of the campus is accessible. Facilities include wheelchair ramps, elevators, special parking, and specially equipped restrooms. **Special:** The college offers co-op programs in engineering, an accelerated degree program in marine transportation/transportation management, and internships as cadet observers aboard commercial ships. There are 2 national honor societies, a freshman honors program, and 2 departmental honors programs. **Visiting:** There are regularly scheduled orientations for prospective students, including a tour of the campus and facilities and meetings with faculty and students. There are guides for informal visits, visitors may sit in on classes, and stay overnight. To schedule a visit, contact the Admissions Office. **Campus Safety and Security:** Measures include 24-hour foot and vehicle patrol, emergency notification system, self-defense education, and security escort services. There are alsoemergency telephones, lighted pathways/sidewalks, and controlled access to dorms/residences.

REQUIREMENTS: The SAT is required. Applicants must be high school graduates or hold a GED. 16 Carnegie units are required, including 4 of English, 3-4 math, and 1 of physics or chemistry. An essay is required and an interview is recommended. AP and CLEP credits are accepted. Important factors in the admissions decision are advanced placement or honors courses, extracurricular activities record, and leadership record. Bachelor's degree candidates must earn 126 to 181 credit hours, with a GPA of 2.0 and distribution requirements vary by the major. If pursuing the U.S. Merchant Marine officers' license, all students must spend 3 summer semesters at sea acquiring hands-on experience aboard the college's training vessel. **Procedure:** Freshmen are admitted fall and spring. Entrance exams should be taken during the junior or senior year. There are early decision, early admissions, deferred admissions, and rolling admissions plans. Early decision applications should be filed by November 15; regular applications, by September 1 for fall entry, along with a $40 fee. Notification of early decision is sent December 15; regular decision, Applications are accepted online. **Transfer Students:** 77 transfer students enrolled in 2015-2016. Transfer students must have a 2.5 GPA. **International Students:** There are 94 international students enrolled. The school actively recruits these students. They must take the TOEFL, and either the SAT or ACT.

ADMISSIONS: 64% of the 2016-2017 applicants were accepted. The SAT scores for the 2016-2017 freshman class were: Critical Reading--42% below 500, 45% between 500 and 599, 11% between 600 and 699, and 2% between 700 and 800. Math-- 20% below 500, 52% between 500 and 599, 26% between 600 and 699, and 2% between 700 and 800. The ACT scores were 35% below 12, 40% between 12 and 17, 16% between 18 and 23, 4% between 24 and 29, and 5% above 30. 19% of the current freshmen were in the top fifth of their class; 52% were in the top two fifths. **Admissions Contact:** Jonathan White, Dean of Admissions. Email: *admissions@sunymaritime.edu* Web: *www.sunymaritime.edu*

FINANCIAL AID: In 2016-2017, 77% of all full-time freshmen and 80% of continuing full-time students received some form of financial aid. 44% of all full-time freshmen and 47% of continuing full-time students received need-based aid. The average financial indebtedness of the 2016 graduate was $17,345. The college's own financial statement, along with student and parent federal income tax returns are required. The FAFSA code is 002853. The priority date for freshman financial aid applications for fall entry is March 1. The filing deadline for fall entry is July 15.

STATE UNIVERSITY OF NEW YORK AT BINGHAMTON C-4
www.binghamton.edu

Binghamton, NY 13902	(607) 777-2171
Fax: (607) 777-4445	Email: admit@binghamton.edu
Full-time: 6770 men, 6415 women	**Faculty:** 724; I, -$
Part-time: 249 men, 198 women	**Ph.D.s:** 92%
Graduate: 1910 men, 1750 women	**Student/Faculty:** 20 to 1
Year: semesters, summer session	**Tuition:** $9271 ($24,351)
Room & Board: $13,590	**Freshman Class:** 32106 applied, 13023 accepted, 2747 enrolled
SAT CR/M/W: 650/670/620 **ACT:** 29	**CEEB CODE:** 2335
Application Deadline: January 15	**MOST COMPETITIVE**

Binghamton, founded in 1946, became a part of the State University of New York system in 1950 and a University Center in 1965. The university offers programs in arts and sciences, education, nursing, business, engineering and applied science, and community and public affairs. Its new pharmacy school is expected to begin enrolling students in fall 2017. There are 5 undergraduate schools and 2 graduate schools. In addition to regional accreditation, Binghamton University has baccalaureate program accreditation with AACSB, ABET, CSWE, NASM, TEAC, APA, NASPAA, and CCNE. The 930-acre campus is in a suburban area 1 mile west of Binghamton. Including any residence halls, there are 102 buildings.

STUDENT LIFE: 84% of undergraduates are from New York. Others are from 48 states, 120 foreign countries, and Canada. 90% are from public schools. 9% are Foreign; 57% White; 5% African American; 2% two or more races; 2% race unknown; 14% Asian American; 11% Hispanic. **Male To Female Ratio:** 1.1:1. The average age of freshmen is 18; all undergraduates, 20. 9% do not continue beyond their first year; 81% remain to graduate. **Housing:** 7362 students can be accommodated in college housing, which includes coed dorms, on-campus apartments, and off-campus apartments. In addition, there are special-interest houses, chemical and smoke-free housing, living learning communities, quiet living, gender inclusive housing, and family housing. On-campus housing is guaranteed for the freshman year only, and is available on a first-come, and first-served basis. 52% of students live on campus; of those, 95% remain on campus on weekends. Upperclassmen may keep cars.

FACULTY/CLASSROOMS: 58% of faculty are male; 42% are female. All teach undergraduates, and all do research. Graduate students teach 5% of introductory courses. The average class size in an introductory lecture is 55; in a laboratory is 20; and in a regular course is 33.

PROGRAMS OF STUDY: Binghamton University confers B.A., B.S. and Mus.B. degrees. Master's and doctoral degrees are also awarded. Bachelor's degrees are awarded in AGRICULTURE (environmental studies), BIOLOGICAL SCIENCE (biochemistry, biology/biological science, cell biology, environmental earth resources, evolutionary biology, molecular biology, and neurosciences), BUSINESS (accounting, business administration and management, entrepreneurial studies, finance, management information systems, management science, marketing management, and supply chain management), COMMUNICATIONS AND THE ARTS (Africana studies, Arabic, art history, art, classics, comparative literature, creative writing, dance, dramatic arts, drawing, English, English literature, film arts, French, German, Germanic languages and literature, Hebrew, Italian, Korean, Latin, linguistics, literature, music, music performance, painting, printmaking, sculpture, Spanish, speech/debate/rhetoric, studio art, theatre arts, theater design, and visual and performing arts), COMPUTER AND PHYSICAL SCIENCE (actuarial mathematics, chemistry, computer science, environmental chemistry, environmental geology, geology, information sciences and systems, mathematics, and physics), ENGINEERING AND ENVIRONMENTAL DESIGN (bioengineering, biomedical engineering, computer engineering, electrical/electronics engineering, engineering, environmental design, environmental science, industrial engineering, mechanical engineering, and systems engineering), HEALTH PROFESSIONS (nursing and pre-health studies), SOCIAL SCIENCE (anthropology, Asian/American studies, Caribbean studies, Chinese Studies, classical/ancient civilization, East Asian studies, economics, geography, history, human development, interdisciplinary studies, international studies, Japanese studies, Judaic studies, Latin American studies, medieval studies, philosophy, political science/government, psychobiology, psychology, sociology, and South Asian studies). Business administration, political science, and biology are the strongest academically. Engineering, business administration, and psychology have the largest enrollments.

ACTIVITIES: 11% of women belong to 17 national sororities. There are 373 groups on campus, including special interest groups, club sports/intramurals, art, band, cheerleading, chess, choir, chorale, chorus, communications, computers, cultural, dance, debate, drama, environmental, ethnic, film, honors, international, jazz band, LGBT, literary magazine, musical theater, newspaper, opera, orchestra, pep band, photography, political, professional, radio and TV, religious, social, social service, student government, symphony, and yearbook. Popular campus events include Spring Fling, University Fest, Shindig at the Fountain, Student Cultural Fests, Frost Fest, Welcome Week, Shabbat 1800 Dinner, Homecoming, Family Weekend, Relay for Life, University Sporting Events, Basketball Showcase, Concerts, and Comedic Shows. **Sports:** There are 11 intercollegiate sports for men and 10 for women, and 11 intramural sports for men and 11 for women. Facilities include a events center with basketball and tennis courts, track, two additional gyms equipped with swimming pools, fitness center, basketball, volleyball, racquetball and squash courts, dance and karate studios, a soccer and lacrosse complex and separate facilities for baseball, softball, track and field, tennis, and cross-country. The campus also has a nature preserve. **Graduates:** From July 1, 2015 to June 30, 2016, 3463 bachelor's degrees were awarded. The most popular majors were management (16%), psychology (12%), and engineering (10%). 239 companies recruited on campus in 2015-2016. In an average class, 5% graduate in 3 years or less, 71% graduate in 4 years or less, 81% graduate in 5 years or less, and 81% graduate in 6 years or less. Of the 2015 graduating class, 30% were enrolled in graduate school within 6 months of graduation.

SERVICES: Counseling and information services are available, as is tutoring in most subjects, alternate format reading materials for those with visual/reading disabilities, and academic success consultation/instruction sessions provided for SSD-registered students. There is a reader service for the blind, and walk-in and by appointment tutoring 7 days a week. **Library/Resources:** The 4 libraries contain 2.5 million volumes, 1.9 million microform items, and 120,055 audio/video tapes/CDs/DVDs, and subscribe to 140,509 periodicals including electronic. Computerized library services include interlibrary loans, database searching, Internet access, and Wi-Fi capability. Special learning facilities include an art gallery, radio station, TV station, theaters, art/dance studios, sculpture foundry, art museum, teaching greenhouse, information commons/workstations, public archaeology facility, child development institute, GIS core facility, biotechnology start-up suites, innovative technologies complex, analytical diagnostics laboratory, electron microscopy laboratory, innovative practice center simulation lab, collaboratory, learning studio, a public speaking lab, and centers for performing arts, learning and teaching, organized research, integrated electronics engineering, advanced microelectronics manufacturing and autonomous solar power. **Physically Challenged Students:** 95% of the campus is accessible. Facilities include wheelchair ramps, elevators, special parking, specially equipped restrooms, lowered drinking fountains, lowered telephones, and special housing. Comprehensive array of services for students with physical, learning, or other disabilities. **Special:** The university offers a number of accelerated programs (3+2 and 4+1) to earn combined bachelor's and master's degrees, access to nearly 900 study-abroad opportunities in over 100 countries, internship opportunities in New York City and other major cities, dual and interdisciplinary majors such as philosophy, politics, and law, an individualized major program in Harpur College of Arts and Sciences, pre-health programs in medicine, dentistry, optometry, veterinary medicine, podiatry, nutrition, physical and occupational therapy, and chiropractic. Early assurance programs guarantee graduate admission at partner SUNY schools (Buffalo, Upstate Medical-Syracuse, and College of Optometry). Three-semester Freshman Research Immersion Program for first-year STEM students to combine academics with real research in one of eight research streams that can yield publishable results. There are 28 national honor societies, Phi Beta Kappa, a freshman honors program, and 34 departmental honors programs. **Visiting:** There are regularly scheduled orientations for prospective students, including an information session and a student-led tour of campus. To schedule a visit, contact the Office of Undergraduate Admissions. **Campus Safety and Security:** Measures include 24-hour foot and vehicle patrol, emergency notification system, self-defense education, and security escort services. There are shuttle buses, emergency telephones, lighted pathways/sidewalks, controlled access to dorms/

residences, bike and car patrols, monitored entrance to campus with proper identification, LED vehicle speed monitoring signs, emergency text messaging/communications, and formal personal safety programs.

REQUIREMENTS: The SAT or ACT is required. The ACT Optional Writing test is also required. In addition, applicants must be graduates of an accredited secondary school or have a GED certificate and complete 16 academic credits. These include 4 units of English, 3 units of 1 foreign language or 2 units each of 2 foreign languages, 3 units of math, and 2 units each of science and social studies. Students may submit slides of artwork, request an audition for music, prepare a videotape for dance or theater, or share athletic achievements. An essay is required. Binghamton University requires that each enrolling student fulfills the graduation requirements at their high school. AP and CLEP credits are accepted. To graduate, all students must complete 124 to 128 credit hours, with 36 to 72 in the major and a minimum GPA of 2.0. General education requirements include courses in language and communication, global vision, science, aesthetic perspective, foreign language, humanities, math, social science, physical activity/wellness, and pluralism. Other requirements vary by school. **Procedure:** Freshmen are admitted in the fall and spring. Entrance exams should be taken in the spring of the junior year or the fall of the senior year. There are early admissions, deferred admissions, and rolling admissions plans. Application deadlines are open. Application fee is $50. Notification is sent on a rolling basis. 4106 applicants were on the 2016 waiting list; 276 were admitted. Applications are accepted online. **Transfer Students:** 1057 transfer students enrolled in 2015-2016. Applicants must submit college transcripts; students who wish to transfer after their first year of college must also submit their high school transcripts. 44 of 126 credits required for the bachelor's degree must be completed at Binghamton University. **International Students:** There are 998 international students enrolled. The school actively recruits these students. They must take the TOEFL with a minimum score of 560 on the paper-based TOEFL (PBT) or 83 on the Internet-based version (iBT). They must also take the SAT or ACT. If the student attends a high school in the US or a high school where the primary language of instruction is English, the SAT/ACT is required.

ADMISSIONS: 41% of the 2016-2017 applicants were accepted. The SAT scores for the 2016-2017 freshman class were: Critical Reading-- 4% below 500, 17% between 500 and 599, 58% between 600 and 699, and 21% between 700 and 800. Math-- 1% below 500, 12% between 500 and 599, 57% between 600 and 699, and 30% between 700 and 800. Writing-- 3% below 500, 17% between 500 and 599, 58% between 600 and 699, and 22% between 700 and 800. The ACT scores were 3% between 18 and 23, 50% between 24 and 29, and 48% above 30. **Admissions Contact:** Randall Edouard, Assistant Provost for Undergraduate Admission. Email: *admit@binghamton.edu* Web: *www.binghamton.edu*

FINANCIAL AID: In 2016-2017, 84% of all full-time freshmen and 68% of continuing full-time students received some form of financial aid. 63% of all full-time freshmen and 57% of continuing full-time students received need-based aid. The average freshman award was $11,426. Need-based scholarships or need-based grants averaged $4,943; need-based self-help aid (loans and jobs) averaged $2,524; non-need-based athletic scholarships averaged $507; and other non-need-based awards and non-need-based scholarships averaged $7,220. 17% of undergraduate students work part-time. Average annual earnings from campus work are $1507. The average financial indebtedness of the 2016 graduate was $20,671. The state aid form is required. The FAFSA code is 002836. The priority date for freshman financial aid applications for fall entry is February 1.

STATE UNIVERSITY OF NEW YORK AT GENESEO B-3

www.geneseo.edu

Geneseo, NY 14454 **(585) 245-5571**

Fax: (585) 245-5550
Full-time: 2177 men, 3220 women
Part-time: 63 men, 52 women
Graduate: 21 men, 69 women
Year: semesters, summer session
Room & Board: $12,264

SAT CR/M: 610/610 **ACT:** 27
Application Deadline: January 1

Email: admissions@geneseo.edu
Faculty: IIA, av$
Ph.D.s: n/av
Student/Faculty: n/av
Tuition: $8176 ($18,026)
Freshman Class: 8807 applied, 5896 accepted, 1238 enrolled
CEEB CODE: 2540
VERY COMPETITIVE+

State University of New York at Geneseo, founded in 1871, is a public institution offering liberal arts, business, accounting programs, and teaching certification. There are 2 undergraduate schools and 1 graduate school. In addition to regional accreditation, Geneseo has baccalaureate program accreditation with AACSB, NCATE, and ACS. The 220-acre campus is in a small town 30 miles south of Rochester, NY. Including any residence halls, there are 46 buildings.

STUDENT LIFE: 98% of undergraduates are from New York. Others are from 25 states, 22 foreign countries, and Canada. 75% are White; 7% Hispanic; 6% Asian American; 3% African American; 3% Foreign; 3% two or more races; 3% race unknown. 28% are Catholic; 22% claim no religious affiliation; 22% Baptist, Buddhist, Episcopal, Hindu, Lutheran, Methodist, Muslim, Presbyterian, Unitarian Universal and others. **Female To Male Ratio:** 1.5:1. The average age of freshmen is 18; all undergraduates, 20. 13% do not continue beyond their first year; 82% remain to graduate. **Housing:** 3255 students can be accommodated in college housing, which includes coed dorms and on-campus apartments. In addition, there are honors houses, special-interest houses, town houses, theme housing, and special housing for international students. On-campus housing is guaranteed for all 4 years, and is available on a first-come, and first-served basis. 54% of students live on campus; of those, 98% remain on campus on weekends. All students may keep cars.

FACULTY/CLASSROOMS: All teach undergraduates. No introductory courses are taught by graduate students.

PROGRAMS OF STUDY: Geneseo confers B.A., B.S. and B.S.Ed. degrees. Master's degrees are also awarded. Bachelor's degrees are awarded in BIOLOGICAL SCIENCE (biochemistry, biology/biological science, biophysics, and neurosciences), BUSINESS (accounting and business administration and management), COMMUNICATIONS AND THE ARTS (art history and appreciation, communications, comparative literature, English, French, music, musical theater, performing arts, Spanish, and theater design), COMPUTER AND PHYSICAL SCIENCE (applied physics, chemistry, geochemistry, geology, geophysics and seismology, mathematics, natural sciences, and physics), EDUCATION (early childhood education, elementary education, and special education), SOCIAL SCIENCE (African American studies, American studies, anthropology, economics, geography, history, international relations, philosophy, political science/government, psychology, and sociology). Biology, Psychology, and English are the strongest academically. Biology, psychology, and business administration have the largest enrollments.

ACTIVITIES: 21% of men belong to 8 local and 4 national fraternities; 30% of women belong to 8 local and 6 national sororities. There are 198 groups on campus, including art, band, cheerleading, chess, choir, chorale, chorus, computers, dance, debate, drama, environmental, ethnic, honors, international, jazz band, LGBT, literary magazine, musical theater, newspaper, orchestra, pep band, political, professional, radio and TV, religious, social, social service, student government, and symphony. Popular campus events include Siblings Weekend, Blue and White Day, Student Organization Expo, Geneseo Recognizing Excellence, Achievement and Talent Day (Great Day), Relay for Life and Weeks of Welcome. **Sports:** There are 8 intercollegiate sports for men and 12 for women, and 20 intramural sports for men and 20 for women. Facilities include an ice arena, swimming pool, gyms, squash, tennis courts, racquetball courts, an indoor jogging area, nautilus and weight rooms, an outdoor track, several playing fields, artificial turf fields for soccer, lacrosse, and field hockey. **Graduates:** From July 1, 2015 to June 30, 2016, 1251 bachelor's degrees were awarded. The most popular majors were social sciences (19%), biological/life sciences (14%), and business/marketing (14%). 43 companies recruited on campus in 2015-2016. In an average class, 71% graduate in 4 years or less, 80% graduate in 5 years or less, and 81% graduate in 6 years or less. Of the 2015 graduating class, 40% were enrolled in graduate school within 6 months of graduation, and 38% were employed.

SERVICES: Counseling and information services are available, as is tutoring in some subjects. There is a reader service for the blind. Tutoring is offered through some departments. Also a writing center and a math center are available for all students. **Library/Resources:** The library contains 335,648 volumes, 167,547 microform items, and 24,291 audio/video tapes/CDs/DVDs, and subscribes to 228,946 periodicals including electronic. Computerized library services include interlibrary loans, database searching, Internet access, and Wi-Fi capability. Special learning facilities include an art gallery, planetarium, radio station, TV station, 4 theaters, electron microscopes, integrated science center, particle accelerator, and a wave tank. **Physically Challenged Students:** 95% of the campus is accessible. Facilities include wheelchair ramps, elevators, special parking, specially equipped restrooms, special class scheduling, lowered drinking fountains, lowered telephones, and special housing. **Special:** 3-2 Engineering: Case Western Reserve, Clarkson, Columbia, and SUNY University at Buffalo, 3-4 Dentistry: SUNY University at Buffalo, 3+3 Doctorate of Physical Therapy Degree: SUNY Upstate Medical University, 4+1 MBA: Alfred University, SUNY Binghamton, Clarkson, RIT, and Union College, 3+4 Optometry: SUNY Optometry, 3+4 Osteopathic Medicine: New York Institute of Technology College of Osteopathic Medicine, Early Assurance program with SUNY Upstate for MD & College of Medicine. Cross-registration is available with the Rochester Area Colleges Consortium and all other SUNY Campuses. Geneseo offers internships, a vast study abroad program, a Washington semester, dual majors, and work-study programs. There is a chapter of Phi Beta Kappa and a freshman honors program. **Visiting:** There are regularly scheduled orientations for prospective students, Generally including a 90-minute campus tour and a 45-minute information session. Students may also elect to sit in on classes, visit faculty and coaches, or stay overnight. There are guides for informal visits, visitors may sit in on classes, and stay overnight. To schedule a visit, contact the Office of Admissions. **Campus Safety and Security:** Measures include 24-hour foot and vehicle patrol, emergency notification system, self-defense education, and security escort services. There are shuttle buses, emergency telephones, lighted pathways/sidewalks, controlled access to dorms/residences, and the police department which is open 24/7.

REQUIREMENTS: Applicants must be graduates of an accredited secondary school or have a GED certificate. They must submit either a SAT score or ACT score. A total of 20 academic units is recommended. The academic program must have 4 years each of English, math, science, social studies, and foreign language. An essay is required. A portfolio or audition for certain programs and an interview are recommended. SAT or ACT standardized test score required. Rigor of secondary school reviewed. AP and CLEP credits are accepted. Important factors in the admissions decision are advanced placement or honors courses, leadership record, evidence of special talent, extracurricular activities record, recommendations by school officials, ability to finance college education, parents or siblings attended your school, personality/intangible qualities, recommendations by alumni, and geographical diversity. To graduate, students must complete 120 credit hours with a minimum 2.0 GPA. The required core curriculum includes 2 courses each in humanities, fine arts, social sciences, and natural sciences and 1 course each in non-Western tradition, critical writing/reading, numeric and symbolic reasoning, U.S. history, and foreign language proficiency. Of the 120 total credits required to graduate, students may apply no more than 20 credits combined from Directed Studies, undergraduate teaching assistantships, EMT/EMS training, ROTC, and H&PE. The limits for each individual program are: Directed Studies 12 credits, teaching assistantships 6 credits, EMT/EMS 6 credits, ROTC 8 credits, and H&PE 10 credits of which no more than 4 credits can be from 100-level activity courses. Teaching assistantships, H&PE activity courses, and some internships and EMT/EMS courses have the S/U grading option only and, therefore, will not be counted toward students' cumulative GPA. **Procedure:** Freshmen are admitted in the fall and spring. Entrance exams should be taken during the spring of the junior year. There are early decision and deferred admissions plans. Early decision applications should be filed by November 15; regular applications, by January 1 for fall entry; and December 1 for spring entry, along with a $50 fee. Notification of early decision is sent December 15; regular decision, March 1. 184 early decision candidates were accepted for the 2016-2017 class. 2226 applicants were on the 2016 waiting list; 823 were admitted. Applications are accepted online. **Transfer Students:** 265 transfer students enrolled in 2015-2016. Applicants must provide transcripts from all previously attended colleges. A minimum 3.0 GPA is required. Students with fewer than 24 credit hours must submit SAT or ACT scores. Application for transfers admission may enroll in the fall (May 1, rolling), and spring (December 15, rolling) 30 of 120 credits required for the bachelor's degree must be completed at Geneseo. **International Students:** There are 112 international students enrolled. The school actively recruits these students. They must take the TOEFL with a minimum score of 525 on the paper-based TOEFL (PBT) or 71 on the Internet-based version (iBT), the IELTS with a minimum score of 6.5. They must also take the SAT or ACT.

ADMISSIONS: 67% of the 2016-2017 applicants were accepted. The SAT scores for the 2016-2017 freshman class were: Critical Reading-- 6% below 500, 37% between 500 and 599, 42% between 600 and 699, and 15% between 700 and 800. Math-- 5% below 500, 32% between 500 and 599, 53% between 600 and 699, and 10% between 700 and 800. The ACT scores were 12% between 18 and 23, 65% between 24 and 29, and 23% above 30. 65% of the current freshmen were in the top fifth of their class; 90% were in the top two fifths. 19 freshmen graduated first in their class. **Admissions Contact:** Kimberly Harvey, Director Of Admissions. Email: *admissions@geneseo.edu* Web: *www.geneseo.edu*

FINANCIAL AID: The average freshman award was $10,248. Need-based scholarships or need-based grants averaged $6,556; need-based self-help aid (loans and jobs) averaged $4,383; other non-need-based awards and non-need-based scholarships averaged $1,850; and $4,018 from other forms of aid. 24% of undergraduate students work part-time. Average annual earnings from campus work are $1113. The average financial indebtedness of the 2016 graduate was $22,300. Geneseo is a member of CSS. The FAFSA code is 002845. The priority date for freshman financial aid applications for fall entry is March 15. The filing deadline for fall entry is May 1.

STATE UNIVERSITY OF NEW YORK AT NEW PALTZ — D-4

www.newpaltz.edu

New Paltz, NY 12561 — **(845) 257-3200**

Fax: (845) 257-3209	**Email:** admissions@newpaltz.edu
Full-time: 1690 men, 3585 women	**Faculty:** IIA, -$
Part-time: 295 men, 560 women	**Ph.D.s:** n/av
Graduate: 490 men, 940 women	**Student/Faculty:** n/av
Year: semesters, summer session	**Tuition:** $7760 ($17,610)
Room & Board: $11,440	**Freshman Class:** n/av
SAT or ACT: required	**CEEB CODE:** 2541
Application Deadline: April 1	**COMPETITIVE**

State University of New York at New Paltz, founded in 1828, is a public institution offering undergraduate and graduate programs in the liberal arts and sciences, business, education, engineering, fine and performing arts, and the health professions. The figures in the above capsule and in this profile are approximate. There are 5 undergraduate schools and 1 graduate school. In addition to regional accreditation, SUNY New Paltz has baccalaureate program accreditation with ABET, CSAB, NASAD, NASM, and NCATE. The 216-acre campus is in a small town 100 miles north of New York City and 65 miles south of Albany. Including any residence halls, there are 53 buildings.

STUDENT LIFE: 92% of undergraduates are from New York. Others are from 28 states, 48 foreign countries, and Canada. 90% are from public schools. 8% are Hispanic; 6% African American; 58% White; 4% Foreign; 3% Asian American. **Female To Male Ratio:** 2.1:1. The average age of freshmen is 18; all undergraduates, 20. 16% do not continue beyond their first year; 59% remain to graduate. **Housing:** 2800 students can be accommodated in college housing, which includes coed dorms. In addition, there are special-interest houses. On-campus housing is guaranteed for the freshman year only, and is available on a first-come, and first-served basis. Priority is given to out-of-town students. 51% of students live on campus; of those, 90% remain on campus on weekends. Upperclassmen may keep cars.

FACULTY/CLASSROOMS: 45% of faculty are male; 55% are female. 97% teach undergraduates, and do research. Graduate students teach 1% of introductory courses. The average class size in an introductory lecture is 19; in a laboratory is 10; and in a regular course is 19.

PROGRAMS OF STUDY: SUNY New Paltz confers B.A., B.S. and B.F.A. degrees. Master's degrees are also awarded. Bachelor's degrees are awarded in BIOLOGICAL SCIENCE (biology/biological science), BUSINESS (accounting, banking and finance, business administration and management, international business management, and marketing/retailing/merchandising), COMMUNICATIONS AND THE ARTS (art history and appreciation, communications, dramatic arts, English, French, German, graphic design, journalism, metal/jewelry, music, painting, photography, sculpture, Spanish, speech/debate/rhetoric, studio art, theater design, and visual and performing arts), COMPUTER AND PHYSICAL SCIENCE (chemistry, computer science, environmental geology, geology, mathematics, and physics), EDUCATION (art education, early childhood education, elementary education, English education, foreign languages education, mathematics education, middle school education, science education, secondary education, and social studies education), ENGINEERING AND ENVIRONMENTAL DESIGN (computer engineering, electrical/electronics engineering, and woodworking), HEALTH PROFESSIONS (music therapy, nursing, and speech pathology/audiology), SOCIAL SCIENCE (African American studies, anthropology, Asian/Oriental studies, economics, geography, history, international relations, Latin American studies, liberal arts/general studies, philosophy, political science/government, psychology, social science, sociology, and women's studies). Business, computer science, and math are the strongest academically. Business, visual arts, and elementary education have the largest enrollments.

ACTIVITIES: 3% of men belong to 5 local and 5 national fraternities; 2% of women belong to 5 local and 8 national sororities. There are 136 groups on campus, including art, band, cheerleading, chess, choir, chorale, chorus, computers, dance, drama, ethnic, honors, international, jazz band, LGBT, literary magazine, musical theater, newspaper, orchestra, photography, political, professional, radio and TV, religious, social, social service, student government, and yearbook. Popular campus events include Spirit Weekend, New Paltz Summer Repertory Theater, and Rainbow Month. **Sports:** There are 9 intercollegiate sports for men and 11 for women, and 12 intramural sports for men and 9 for women. Facilities include a gym, swimming and diving teams, numerous playing fields, tennis, jogging, volleyball, basketball, softball, crew teams, riding team, and outdoor tennis courts, men's golf, lacrosse, and ice hockey. **Graduates:** From July 1, 2015 to June 30, 2016, 1592 bachelor's degrees were awarded. The most popular majors were education (21%), business and marketing (14%), and social science (11%). 135 companies recruited on campus in 2015-2016. In an average class, 36% graduate in 4 years or less, 59% graduate in 5 years or less, and 61% graduate in 6 years or less.

SERVICES: Counseling and information services are available, as is tutoring in most subjects. There is a reader service for the blind, and remedial math, reading, and writing. **Library/Resources:** The library contains 499,048 volumes, 1.2 million microform items, and 4,030 audio/video tapes/CDs/DVDs, and subscribes to 32,361 periodicals including electronic. Computerized library services include interlibrary loans, database searching, Internet access, and Wi-Fi capability. Special learning facilities include a planetarium, radio station, TV station, a greenhouse, robotics lab, electron microscope facility, speech and hearing clinic, art museum, music therapy training facility, observatory, Fournier transform mass spectrometer, honors center, electronic media center, electronic classroom, and IBM e-business virtual lab. **Physically Challenged Students:** 90% of the campus is accessible. Facilities include wheelchair ramps, elevators, special parking, specially equipped restrooms, special class scheduling, lowered drinking fountains, lowered telephones, and special housing. **Special:** There is cross-registration with the Mid-Hudson Consortium of Colleges. The university offers co-op programs and internships in most majors, work-study programs on campus and at the Children's Center of New Paltz, and opportunities for student-designed or dual majors. Students may study abroad in 18 countries. A 3-2 advanced degree in environmental biology is offered with SUNY Environmental Science and Forestry. There are 7-year medical and optometry accelerated degree programs. B.A.-B.S. degrees are offered in liberal arts and science, education, business, science and, engineering, and fine and performing arts. There are 4 national honor societies, a freshman honors program, and 6 departmental honors programs. **Visiting:** There are regularly scheduled orientations for prospective students, including daily information sessions and campus tours. Visitors may sit in on classes. To schedule a visit, contact the Admissions Office. **Campus Safety and Security:** Measures include 24-hour foot and vehicle patrol, self-defense education, and security escort services. There are emergency telephones, lighted pathways/sidewalks, bicycle patrol, locked residence halls, and a campus 911 system.

REQUIREMENTS: The SAT or ACT is required. In addition, 4 units each of English, and social studies, 3 to 4 units each of mathematics, and science including 2 units of lab science, and 2 to 4 units of foreign language are required. The GED is accepted but must be accompanied by a high school transcript and SAT or ACT scores. SUNY New Paltz requires applicants to be in the upper 50% of their class. A GPA of 3.0 is required. AP and CLEP credits are accepted. Important factors in the admissions decision are advanced placement or honors courses, recommendations by school officials, and evidence of special talent. To graduate, students must complete a minimum of 120 credits with a 2.0 GPA. The core curriculum of 16 to 17 credits includes courses in English composition, math and analytical skills, and modern world studies. The number of credits required in the major varies. Distribution requirements include courses in cultures and civilizations, American experience, social sciences, physical and biological sciences, foreign languages, and aesthetic expression, 1 writing-intensive course in the major, and 60 credits in upper-division courses. New York State Teacher Competency Exams are required of education majors. Engineering students must complete a senior project, and art majors must show their work in a senior exhibition. **Procedure:** Freshmen are admitted in the fall. Entrance exams should be taken before December 31. There are early admissions, deferred admissions, and rolling admissions plans. Applications should be filed by April 1 for fall entry. The fall 2016 application fee was $40. Notification is sent on a rolling basis. Applications are accepted on-line. **Transfer Students:** 1011 transfer students enrolled in 2015-2016. To be considered, applicants must have maintained a minimum GPA of 2.75 in all previous college work at accredited institutions. Some programs require a higher GPA for consideration. 30 of 120 credits required for the bachelor's degree must be completed at SUNY New Paltz. **International Students:** There are 219 international students enrolled. The school actively recruits these students. They must take the TOEFL with a minimum score of 550 on the paper-based TOEFL (PBT) or 80 on the Internet-based version (iBT), or take the SAT or demonstrate English Proficiency. Conditional acceptance is available to both graduate and undergraduate programs. Accepted students must take a placement test upon arrival at SUNY New Paltz. If the student is not yet proficient, he or she must take ESL courses until required proficiency is achieved.

Admissions Contact: Kimberly Lavoie, Director of Freshman/International Admissions. Email: *admissions@newpaltz.edu* Web: *www.newpaltz.edu*

FINANCIAL AID: In 2016-2017, 70% of all full-time freshmen and 75% of continuing full-time students received some form of financial aid. 55% of all full-time freshmen and 75% of continuing full-time students received need-based aid. The average freshman award was $5,500. Need-based scholarships or need-based grants averaged $2,400; need-based self-help aid (loans and jobs) averaged $2,600; and other non-need-based awards and non-need-based scholarships averaged $500. 45% of undergraduate students work part-time. Average annual earnings from campus work are $900. The average financial indebtedness of the 2016 graduate was $19,000. The FAFSA code is 002846. The deadline for filing freshman financial aid applications for fall entry is March 15.

STATE UNIVERSITY OF NEW YORK AT OSWEGO — C-3

www.oswego.edu

Oswego, NY 13126 — **(315) 312-2250**

Fax: (315) 312-3260	**Email: admiss@oswego.edu**
Full-time: 3433 men, 3435 women	**Faculty:** n/av
Part-time: 116 men, 129 women	**Ph.D.s:** 88%
Graduate: 332 men, 522 women	**Student/Faculty:** 17 to 1
Year: semesters, summer session	**Tuition:** $7961 ($17,811)
Room & Board: $13,390	**Freshman Class:** 10885 applied, 5552 accepted, 1481 enrolled
SAT CR/M: 540/560 **ACT:** 24	**CEEB CODE:** 2543
Application Deadline: January 15	**COMPETITIVE**

State University of New York at Oswego, founded in 1861, is a comprehensive institution offering more than 110 cooperative, preprofessional, and graduate programs through the College of Liberal Arts and Sciences, School of Business, School of Communication, Media and the Arts and School of Education. There are 4 undergraduate schools and 1 graduate school. In addition to regional accreditation, Oswego has baccalaureate program accreditation with AACSB, NASAD, NASM, NCATE, ACS, and NASP. The 696-acre campus is in a small town on the southeast shore of Lake Ontario, 35 miles northwest of Syracuse. Including any residence halls, there are 40 buildings.

STUDENT LIFE: 96% of undergraduates are from New York. Others are from 26 states, 15 foreign countries, and Canada. 90% are from public schools. 9% are Hispanic; 79% White; 6% African American; 2% Asian American; 2% Foreign; 2% two or more races. **Female To Male Ratio:** 1.1:1. The average age of freshmen is 18; all undergraduates, 21. 18% do not continue beyond their first year; 62% remain to graduate. **Housing:** 4600 students can be accommodated in college housing, which includes coed dorms and on-campus apartments. In addition, there are special-interest houses, resident hall living and learning communities, a freshmen-only building, upperclassmen suites and upperclassmen townhouses. On-campus housing is guaranteed for all 4 years. 65% of students live on campus; of those, 90% remain on campus on weekends. All students may keep cars.

FACULTY/CLASSROOMS: 50% of faculty are male; 50% are female. 96% teach undergraduates. No introductory courses are taught by graduate students. The average class size in an introductory lecture is 40; in a laboratory is 15; and in a regular course is 24.

PROGRAMS OF STUDY: Oswego confers B.A., B.S. and B.F.A. degrees. Master's degrees are also awarded. Bachelor's degrees are awarded in BIOLOGICAL SCIENCE (biochemistry, biology/adolescence education, biology/biological science, and zoology), BUSINESS (accounting, business administration and management, finance, human resources, insurance and risk management, management science, marketing/retailing/merchandising, operations management, and recreational facilities management), COMMUNICATIONS AND THE ARTS (art, broadcasting, communications, creative writing, dramatic arts, English, English as a second/foreign language, English Writing, film arts, French, German, graphic design, journalism, linguistics, music, musical theater, public relations, Spanish, theatre acting, theatre arts, and theatre production), COMPUTER AND PHYSICAL SCIENCE (applied mathematics, atmospheric sciences and meteorology, chemistry, computer science, earth science, earth science/adolescence education, environmental geology, geochemistry, geology, information sciences and systems, mathematics, physics, and software engineering), EDUCATION (agricultural education, business education, childhood education, elementary education, English education, foreign languages education, mathematics education, secondary education, social studies education, Spanish adolescense education, teaching English as a second/foreign language (TESOL/TEFOL), technical education, trade and industrial education, and vocational education), ENGINEERING AND ENVIRONMENTAL DESIGN (electrical and computer engineering, preengineering, and technological management), HEALTH PROFESSIONS (pre-health studies, pre-health biological studies, predentistry, premedicine, preoptometry, prephysical therapy, and preveterinary science), SOCIAL SCIENCE (American studies, anthropology, cognitive science, criminal justice, economics, family/consumer studies, French studies, history, human development, international studies, philosophy, political science/government, prelaw, psychology, sociology, women & gender studies, and women's studies). Biological sciences, chemistry, accounting and computer science are the strongest academically. Childhood/adolescence education, business administration, and biological sciences have the largest enrollments.

ACTIVITIES: 7% of men belong to 7 local and 10 national fraternities; 6% of women belong to 5 local and 7 national sororities. There are 186 groups on campus, including cheerleading and equestrian teams, ice hockey, rugby, art, band, cheerleading, choir, chorale, chorus, communications, computers, crew, dance, drama, environmental, ethnic, film, honors, international, jazz band, LGBT, literary magazine, musical theater, newspaper, opera, orchestra, pep band, photography, political, professional, radio and TV, religious, social, social service, student government, symphony, and yearbook. Popular campus events include Honors Convocations, Quest, May Day, Fall and Spring Concerts, Family & Friends Weekend, and Hockey Nights in Oswego. **Sports:** There are 12 intercollegiate sports for men and 12 for women, and 21 intramural sports for men and 21 for women. Facilities include an outdoor turf stadium for field sports, an ice hockey rink, a field house with an artificial-grass practice area, tennis courts, an outdoor track, soccer and lacrosse fields, baseball and softball fields, numerous basketball courts, racquetball and squash courts, indoor pools and diving well, fitness centers, weight rooms, a cross-country ski lodge, and a martial arts/dance studio. **Graduates:** From July 1, 2015 to June 30, 2016, 1668 bachelor's degrees were awarded. The most popular majors were education (23%), business (23%), and communications (11%). 150 companies recruited on campus in 2015-2016. In an average class, 38% graduate in 4 years or less, 54% graduate in 5 years or less, and 58% graduate in 6 years or less. Of the 2015 graduating class, 26% were enrolled in graduate school within 6 months of graduation, and 95% were employed.

SERVICES: Counseling and information services are available, as is tutoring in every subject. The Office of Learning Services provides individual and small-group tutoring. There is no cost for tutoring services. There is a reader service for the blind, and remedial math, reading, and writing. in addition, the Office of Disablility Services provides general foundation support. **Library/Resources:** The library contains 554,986 volumes, 1.6 million microform items, and 31,384 audio/video tapes/CDs/DVDs, and subscribes to 52,600 periodicals including electronic. Computerized library services include interlibrary loans, database searching, Internet access, and Wi-Fi capability. Special learning facilities include an art gallery, planetarium, radio station, TV station, and 330-acre biological Rice Creek Field Station. **Physically Challenged Students:** 85% of the campus is accessible. Facilities include wheelchair ramps, elevators, special parking, specially equipped restrooms, special class scheduling, lowered drinking fountains, lowered telephones, and special housing. **Special:** Oswego offers cross-registration with ACUSNY-Visiting Student Program. More than 1000 internships are available with business, social, cultural, and government agencies. In addition 12 departments offer co-op opportunities as well. The university also offers a Washington semester, study abroad in more than 80 programs, a 5-year accounting B.S./M.B.A. program, dual majors, B.A.-B.S. degrees in several sciences and a B.A.-B.F.A. in art, credit for military experience, nondegree study, and pass/fail options. A pre-engineering option is available. A 3-4 degree in optometry with SUNY College of Optometry, and 2+2 medical imaging/ 3+3 physical therapy with SUNY Upstate Medical Center are also possible. There are 21 national honor societies, a freshman honors program, and 9 departmental honors programs. **Visiting:** There are regularly scheduled orientations for prospective students, usually including a campus tour and a meeting/presentation with a counselor. There are guides for informal visits, visitors may sit in on classes, and stay overnight. To schedule a visit, contact the Office of Admissions. **Campus Safety and Security:** Measures include 24-hour foot and vehicle patrol, emergency notification system, self-defense education, and security escort services. There are shuttle buses, emergency telephones, lighted pathways/sidewalks, controlled access to dorms/residences, an electronic device that locates students and alerts the police when pressed.

REQUIREMENTS: The SAT or ACT is required. Applicants must be graduates of an accredited secondary school or have a GED/ TASC certificate. 18 academic units are required, preferring 4 years each of English and social studies, 7 years combined of math and science, and 2 of a foreign language. An essay and interview are strongly recommended. AP and CLEP credits are accepted. Important factors in the admissions decision are advanced placement or honors courses, extracurricular activities record, and personality/intangible qualities. To graduate, all students must complete 30 to 33 general education credits, including 9-12 in writing, mathematics, foreign language, natural science and 15 credits from areas of natural sciences, social & behavior sciences, American history, western civilization, humanities, fine & performing arts and world awareness. Students must have a minimum 2.0 GPA and complete 122 total credit hours (127 hours for technology and vocational education students). The total number of hours in the major varies from 33 to 95. **Procedure:** Freshmen are admitted in the fall and spring. Entrance exams should be taken during the spring of the junior year and fall of the senior year. There are early admissions, deferred admissions, and rolling admissions plans. Applications should be filed by January 15 for fall entry, along with a $50 fee. Notifications are sent in January. Applications are accepted online. **Transfer Students:** 690 transfer students enrolled in 2015-2016. Applicants must submit official transcripts from previously attended colleges. Students with a minimum GPA of 2.3 are encouraged to apply. SUNY associate degree holders are given preference. Secondary school records may be required for 1-year transfers. 30 of 122 credits required for the bachelor's degree must be completed at Oswego. **International Students:** There are 147 international students enrolled. The school actively recruits these students. They must take the TOEFL with a minimum score of 550 on the paper-based TOEFL (PBT) or 80 on the Internet-based version (iBT).

ADMISSIONS: 51% of the 2016-2017 applicants were accepted. The SAT scores for the 2016-2017 freshman class were: Critical Reading-- 22% below 500, 58% between 500 and 599, 18% between 600 and 699, and 2% between 700 and 800. Math-- 16% below 500, 59% between 500 and 599, 23% between 600 and 699, and 2% between 700 and 800. The ACT scores were 11% below 12, 40% between 12 and 17, 29% between 18 and 23, 15% between 24 and 29, and 5% above 30. 51% of the current freshmen were in the top fifth of their class; 80% were in the top two fifths. **Admissions Contact:** Daniel Griffin, Director of Admissions. Email: *admiss@oswego.edu* Web: *www.oswego.edu*

FINANCIAL AID: In 2016-2017, 70% of all full-time freshmen and 70% of continuing full-time students received some form of financial aid. 65% of all full-time freshmen and 66% of continuing full-time students received need-based aid. The average freshman award was $7,044. Need-based scholarships or need-based grants averaged $6,391; need-based self-help aid (loans and jobs) averaged $3,843; other non-need-based awards and non-need-based scholarships averaged $3,728; and $3,204 from other forms of aid. 65% of undergraduate students work part-time. Average annual earnings from campus work are $1500. The average financial indebtedness of the 2016 graduate was $26,611. Oswego is a member of CSS. The state aid form is required. The FAFSA code is 002848. The priority date for freshman financial aid applications for fall entry is March 1.

STATE UNIVERSITY OF NEW YORK AT PURCHASE D-5

www.purchase.edu

Purchase, NY 10577	(914) 251-6300
Fax: (914) 251-6314	**Email:** admissions@purchase.edu
Full-time: 1603 men, 2006 women	**Faculty:** 144; IIB, av$
Part-time: 97 men, 124 women	**Ph.D.s:** 100%
Graduate: 53 men, 74 women	**Student/Faculty:** 25 to 1
Year: semesters, summer session	**Tuition:** $7630 ($18,862)
Room & Board: $10,270	**Freshman Class:** n/av **CEEB CODE:** 2878
Application Deadline: August 15	**COMPETITIVE**

State University of New York at Purchase, founded in 1967, is a public institution that offers programs in visual arts, music, acting, dance, film, theater/stage design technology, natural science, social science, and humanities. The figures in the above capsule and in this capsule are approximate. There is 1 undergraduate school and 1 graduate school. In addition to regional accreditation, Purchase College SUNY has baccalaureate program accreditation with NASAD and NASM. The 500-acre campus is in a suburban area 35 miles north of midtown Manhattan. Including any residence halls, there are 40 buildings.

STUDENT LIFE: 80% of undergraduates are from New York. Others are from 43 states, 27 foreign countries, and Canada. 8% are Hispanic; 7% African American; 55% White; 3% Asian American; 2% Foreign. **Female To Male Ratio:** 1.3:1. The average age of freshmen is 18; all undergraduates, 22. 18% do not continue beyond their first year; 51% remain to graduate. **Housing:** 2600 students can be accommodated in college housing, which includes single-sex and coed dorms and on-campus apartments. In addition, there are special-interest houses, transfer student units, nontraditional-aged student units, wellness halls, presidential scholars halls, sophmore communities, conservatory halls, and learning community halls. On-campus housing is guaranteed for the freshman year only, and is available on a first-come, and first-served basis. 67% of students live on campus; of those, 75% remain on campus on weekends. All students may keep cars.

FACULTY/CLASSROOMS: 54% of faculty are male; 46% are female. All teach undergraduates. No introductory courses are taught by graduate students. The average class size in an introductory lecture is 27; in a laboratory is 12; and in a regular course is 14.

PROGRAMS OF STUDY: Purchase College SUNY confers B.A., B.S., B.A.L.A., B.F.A. and Mus.B. degrees. Master's degrees are also awarded. Bachelor's degrees are awarded in BIOLOGICAL SCIENCE (biology/biological science), COMMUNICATIONS AND THE ARTS (art history and appreciation, creative writing, dance, dramatic arts, film arts, journalism, literature, music, theater design, and visual and performing arts), COMPUTER AND PHYSICAL SCIENCE (chemistry and mathematics), ENGINEERING AND ENVIRONMENTAL DESIGN (environmental science), SOCIAL SCIENCE (anthropology, economics, ethnic studies, history, liberal arts/general studies, philosophy, political science/government, psychology, sociology, and women's studies). Biology, and journalism are the strongest academically. Visual arts, music, and liberal studies have the largest enrollments.

ACTIVITIES: There are no fraternities or sororities. There are 40 groups on campus, including art, band, cheerleading, choir, chorale, computers, dance, drama, environmental, ethnic, jazz band, literary magazine, opera, orchestra, photography, political, professional, religious, social, social service, student government, and symphony. Popular campus events include Spring Concert, Alcohol Awareness Week, and Film Programs. **Sports:** There are 7 intercollegiate sports for men and 6 for women, and 20 intramural sports for men and 20 for women. Facilities include a fitness center, pool, aerobics studio, basketball courts, raquetball courts, squash courts, tennis courts, outdoor climbing wall, soccer fields, baseball field, softball field, and bowling alley. **Graduates:** From July 1, 2015 to June 30, 2016, 499 bachelor's degrees were awarded. The most popular majors were liberal studies (28%), visual arts (23%), and music (17%). 20 companies recruited on campus in 2015-2016. In an average class, 32% graduate in 4 years or less, 44% graduate in 5 years or less, and 47% graduate in 6 years or less.

SERVICES: Counseling and information services are available, as is tutoring in every subject. There is a reader service for the blind, remedial math, reading, and writing, and drop-in sessions for math and writing. **Library/Resources:** The library contains 241,984 volumes, 257,609 microform items, and 18,273 audio/video tapes/CDs/DVDs, and subscribes to 37,153 periodicals including electronic. Computerized library services include interlibrary loans, database searching, Internet access, and Wi-Fi capability. Special learning facilities include a TV station, a listening and viewing center, science and photography labs, music practice rooms and instruments, multitrack synthesizers, music composition labs, digital video editing labs, typesetting and computer graphics labs, experimental stage, a performing arts complex, an electron microscope, and a children's center. **Physically Challenged Students:** All of the campus is accessible. Facilities include wheelchair ramps, elevators, special parking, specially equipped restrooms, note takers, extended test times, quiet rooms for tests, interpreters for the hearing impaired, readers for the visually impaired, a reading machine in the library, and special note-taking paper. **Special:** Purchase College offers cross-registration with Empire State colleges, internships with corporations, newspapers, and local agencies, and student-designed majors, dual majors, study abroad, work-study, nondegree study, and pass/fail options. There is also an arts conservatory program. **Visiting:** There are regularly scheduled orientations for prospective students, including group question and answer sessions followed by a tour of the campus. To schedule a visit, contact the Admissions Office. **Campus Safety and Security:** Measures include 24-hour foot and vehicle patrol and security escort services. There are emergency telephones and lighted pathways/sidewalks.

REQUIREMENTS: A minimum composite scores of 1100 on the SAT or 23 on the ACT are required. Applicants must be graduates of an accredited secondary school and have completed 16 academic credits and 16 Carnegie units. The GED is accepted. Visual arts students must submit an essay and portfolio and have an interview. Film students need an essay and an interview. Design technology students need a portfolio and an interview. Performing arts students must audition. AP and CLEP credits are accepted. Important factors in the admissions decision are evidence of special talent, recommendations by school officials, and personality/intangible qualities. A minimum 2.0 GPA is required with a minimum of 120 credits. Students majoring in the arts must complete a minimum of 90 professional credits and the SUNY general education curriculum. Students majoring in the liberal arts and sciences complete the general education curriculum and major requirements and must complete a senior thesis. **Procedure:** Freshmen are admitted in the fall and spring. Entrance exams should be taken by the fall of the senior year. There are early decision, early admissions, deferred admissions, and rolling admissions plans. Early decision applications should be filed by November 15; regular applications, by August 15 for fall entry; and December 1 for spring entry, along with a $30 fee. Notification of early decision is sent December 15; regular decision, on a rolling basis. 18 early decision candidates were accepted for the 2016-2017 class. Applications are accepted online. **Transfer Students:** 373 transfer students enrolled in 2015-2016. Students transferring to the School of Arts (visual or performing arts) must pass an audition or portfolio review. Transfer credit is limited; students can contact the Office of Admission to get a preliminary credit evaluation. Students transferring to programs in liberal arts and sciences must have a minimum 2.0 G.P.A. if they have completed 30 or more semester hours; if they have fewer than 30 semester hours, the high school transcript is also reviewed. Liberal arts and science transfers can transfer a maximum of 90 semester hours from 4-year colleges and 75 semester hours from 2-year colleges. 30 of 120 credits required for the bachelor's degree must be completed at Purchase College SUNY. **International Students:** There are 80 international students enrolled. The school actively recruits these students. They must take the TOEFL with a minimum score of 550 on the paper-based TOEFL (PBT) or 80 on the Internet-based version (iBT), or the IELTS or score 430 on the SAT: Verbal test.

Admissions Contact: Dennis Craig, Vice President of Admissions. Email: *dennis.craig@purchase.edu* Web: *www.purchase.edu*

FINANCIAL AID: In 2016-2017, 85% of all full-time freshmen and 69%

of continuing full-time students received some form of financial aid. 54% of all full-time freshmen and 47% of continuing full-time students received need-based aid. The average freshman award was $7,067. Need-based scholarships or need-based grants averaged $5,343 ($13,450 maximum); need-based self-help aid (loans and jobs) averaged $3,252 ($7,625 maximum); and other non-need-based awards and non-need-based scholarships averaged $3,086 ($17,625 maximum). 12% of undergraduate students work part-time. Average annual earnings from campus work are $1073. The average financial indebtedness of the 2016 graduate was $16,058. Purchase College SUNY is a member of CSS. The FAFSA code is 006791. The deadline for filing freshman financial aid applications for fall entry is February 15.

STATE UNIVERSITY OF NEW YORK POLYTECHNIC INSTITUTE C-3

www.sunypoly.edu

Utica, NY 13502 **(315) 792-7500** **(866) 2SUNYIT**

Fax: (315) 792-7837 **Email: admissions@sunyit.edu**

Full-time: 1206 men, 536 women	**Faculty:** n/av
Part-time: 130 men, 210 women	**Ph.D.s:** 85%
Graduate: 322 men, 388 women	**Student/Faculty:** 17 to 1
Year: semesters, summer session	**Tuition:** $7759 ($17,609)
Room & Board: $11,714	**Freshman Class:** 2319 applied, 1402 accepted, 347 enrolled
SAT CR/M: 541/578 **ACT:** required	**CEEB CODE:** 0755
Application Deadline: July 1	**VERY COMPETITIVE**

The State University of New York Polytechnic Institute, founded in 1966, is a public institution providing an intellectually stimulating learning environment that prepares students to fully engage in the challenges, complexities and opportunities of living in a modern technological society. There are 5 undergraduate schools and 5 graduate schools. In addition to regional accreditation, SUNY Polytechnic Institute has baccalaureate program accreditation with AACSB, ABET, CAHIIM, and CCNE. The 800-acre campus is in a suburban area the Utica site is at the western end of the Mohawk Valley. The Albany site is located at the western end of the City of Albany. Including any residence halls, there are 20 buildings.

STUDENT LIFE: 97% of undergraduates are from New York. Others are from 12 states, and 15 foreign countries. 80% are White; 7% Hispanic; 6% African American; 4% Asian American; 2% two or more races; 1% Foreign. **Male To Female Ratio:** 1.5:1. The average age of freshmen is 18; all undergraduates, 25. 26% do not continue beyond their first year; 49% remain to graduate. **Housing:** 819 students can be accommodated in college housing, which includes coed dorms, special housing for the disabled, and special housing for international students. On-campus housing is available on a first-come, first-served basis, and is available on a lottery system for upperclassmen. 62% of students commute. All students may keep cars.

FACULTY/CLASSROOMS: 60% of faculty are male; 40% are female. No introductory courses are taught by graduate students.

PROGRAMS OF STUDY: SUNY Polytechnic Institute confers B.A., B.S., B.B.A. and B.P.S. degrees. Master's and doctoral degrees are also awarded. Bachelor's degrees are awarded in BIOLOGICAL SCIENCE (biology/biological science), BUSINESS (accounting, banking and finance, business administration and management, and finance (financial planning)), COMMUNICATIONS AND THE ARTS (communications technology), COMPUTER AND PHYSICAL SCIENCE (applied computing, applied mathematics, computer science, and network & computer security), ENGINEERING AND ENVIRONMENTAL DESIGN (civil engineering, civil engineering technology, computer technology, electrical/electronics engineering, electrical/electronics engineering technology, mechanical engineering, mechanical engineering technology, nanoscale engineering, and nanoscale science), HEALTH PROFESSIONS (health, health care administration, and nursing), SOCIAL SCIENCE (interdisciplinary studies, liberal arts/general studies, psychology, and sociology). Engineering, computer science, and business have the largest enrollments.

ACTIVITIES: There are no fraternities or sororities. There are 30 groups on campus, including Black Latino African student union, West Indian African club, chess, computers, dance, drama, environmental, ethnic, international, LGBT, literary magazine, newspaper, professional, radio and TV, religious, social, student government, Veteran's, and yearbook. Popular campus events include Wildcat Weekend, Diwali and Holi Festivals, and Apocalypse Week. **Sports:** There are 6 intercollegiate sports for men and 6 for women, and 10 intramural sports for men and 10 for women. Facilities include a fitness center, fitness trail, gym with indoor track, field house, turf field, baseball, softball and soccer fields. **Graduates:** From July 1, 2015 to June 30, 2016, 425 bachelor's degrees were awarded. The most popular majors were engineering technologies (23%), business administration (21%), and nursing (18%). 68 companies recruited on campus in 2015-2016.

SERVICES: Counseling and information services are available, as is tutoring in most subjects. There is a reader service for the blind, and remedial math, reading, and writing. **Library/Resources:** The library contains 148,555 volumes, and 1,320 audio/video tapes/CDs/DVDs, and subscribes to 25,750 periodicals including electronic. Computerized library services include interlibrary loans, database searching, Internet access, and Wi-Fi capability. Special learning facilities include an art gallery, radio station, and TV station. **Physically Challenged Students:** 99% of the campus is accessible. Facilities include wheelchair ramps, elevators, special parking, specially equipped restrooms, lowered drinking fountains, and special housing. **Special:** SUNY Poly offers cross-registration with the Mohawk Valley Consortium, internships, and work study. An accelerated degree program in nursing, communications and information design, computer information science and network & computer security is possible. There is a joint partnership (1+2+1) with St. Elizabeth College of Nursing. There are 2 national honor societies. **Visiting:** There are regularly scheduled orientations for prospective students, during registration and orientation to campus. There are guides for informal visits, visitors may sit in on classes, and stay overnight. To schedule a visit, contact the Admissions Office. **Campus Safety and Security:** Measures include 24-hour foot and vehicle patrol, emergency notification system, self-defense education, and security escort services. There are emergency telephones, lighted pathways/sidewalks, controlled access to dorms/residences, and emergency call boxes.

REQUIREMENTS: The SAT or ACT is required along with official transcripts, test scores, essay, and supplemental application. AP and CLEP credits are accepted. Important factors in the admissions decision are advanced placement or honors courses, evidence of special talent, and recommendations by school officials. Students must meet general education requirements and complete 124 to 128 credit hours to graduate. **Procedure:** Freshmen are admitted in the fall and spring. Entrance exams should be taken by April of year applicant intends to enroll. There are early admissions, deferred admissions, and rolling admissions plans. Applications should be filed by July 1 for fall entry; December 1 for spring entry, along with a $50 fee. Notifications are sent January 15. Applications are accepted online. **Transfer Students:** 342 transfer students enrolled in 2015-2016. Transfer students generally must present a minimum cumulative GPA of 2.7 or better. Applicants presenting a GPA below 2.5 will be considered on an individual basis. 30 of 124 credits required for the bachelor's degree must be completed at SUNY Polytechnic Institute. **International Students:** There are 30 international students enrolled. The school actively recruits these students. They must take the TOEFL with a minimum score of 550 on the paper-based TOEFL (PBT) or 79 on the Internet-based version (iBT), or take the IELTS (International English Language Testing Service). They must also take the SAT or ACT for first-time, full-time students only.

ADMISSIONS: 60% of the 2016-2017 applicants were accepted. The SAT scores for the 2016-2017 freshman class were: Critical Reading-- 33% below 500, 43% between 500 and 599, 20% between 600 and 699, and 4% between 700 and 800. Math-- 17% below 500, 47% between 500 and 599, 28% between 600 and 699, and 8% between 700 and 800. **Admissions Contact:** Gina Liscio, Director of Admissions. Email: *admissions@sunyit.edu* Web: *www.sunypoly.edu*

FINANCIAL AID: In 2016-2017, 68% of all full-time freshmen and continuing full-time students received some form of financial aid. 55% of all full-time freshmen and 47% of continuing full-time students received need-based aid. The average freshman award was $10,882. Need-based scholarships or need-based grants averaged $8,242; and need-based self-help aid (loans and jobs) averaged $3,943. 23% of undergraduate students work part-time. The state aid form is required. The priority date for freshman financial aid applications for fall entry is March 1.

STATE UNIVERSITY OF NEW YORK SUNY ALBANY D-3

www.albany.edu

Albany, NY 12222 (518) 956-8220

Fax: (518) 442-5383 Email: ugadmissions@albany.edu

Full-time: 6271 men, 6150 women
Part-time: 368 men, 350 women
Graduate: 1651 men, 2583 women
Year: semesters, summer session
Room & Board: $12,942

Faculty: 634
Ph.D.s: 91%
Student/Faculty: 18 to 1
Tuition: $9223 ($24,303)
Freshman Class: 23799 applied, 12944 accepted, 2729 enrolled
CEEB CODE: 2532

Application Deadline: August 1
COMPETITIVE

University at Albany offers students the expansive opportunities of a major research university and an environment designed to foster academic and career success. UAlbany students choose from 120 undergraduate majors and minors and more than 125 graduate programs. Students take advantage of more than 600 study abroad opportunities in more than 50 countries through UAlbany and SUNY's networks. There are 9 undergraduate schools and 9 graduate schools. In addition to regional accreditation, University at Albany has baccalaureate program accreditation with AACSB, CSWE, TEAC, ACS, ALA, APA, CEPH, NASPAA, and PAB. The 560-acre campus is in a suburban area Five miles west of downtown Albany. Including any residence halls, there are 187 buildings.

STUDENT LIFE: 95% of undergraduates are from New York. Others are from 42 states, 53 foreign countries, and Canada. 8% are Asian American; 6% Foreign; 47% White; 3% two or more races; 3% race unknown; 17% African American; 16% Hispanic. **Female To Male Ratio:** 1.1:1. The average age of freshmen is 18.5; all undergraduates, 20.5. 16% do not continue beyond their first year; 66% remain to graduate. **Housing:** 7980 students can be accommodated in college housing, which includes coed dorms, on-campus apartments, and married student housing. In addition, there are honors houses, language houses, and special-interest houses. On-campus housing is available on a first-come, first-served basis, and is available on a lottery system for upperclassmen. Priority is given to out-of-town students. 57% of students live on campus. Alcohol is not permitted. Upperclassmen may keep cars.

FACULTY/CLASSROOMS: 61% of faculty are male; 39% are female. 93% teach undergraduates, and 75% do research. Graduate students teach 11% of introductory courses. The average class size in an introductory lecture is 65; in a laboratory is 13; and in a regular course is 35.

PROGRAMS OF STUDY: University at Albany confers B.A., and B.S. degrees. Master's and doctoral degrees are also awarded. Bachelor's degrees are awarded in AGRICULTURE (environmental studies), BIOLOGICAL SCIENCE (biochemistry, biology/biological science, and molecular biology), BUSINESS (accounting, accounting (information systems), and business administration and management), COMMUNICATIONS AND THE ARTS (art history and appreciation, Chinese, communications, English, fine arts, information technology, linguistics, music, romance languages and literature, sculpture, Spanish, studio art, studio art graphic design, and studio art painting), COMPUTER AND PHYSICAL SCIENCE (actuarial science, applied mathematics, atmospheric sciences and meteorology, chemistry, computer science, computer security and information assurance, earth science, information sciences and systems, mathematics, and physics), ENGINEERING AND ENVIRONMENTAL DESIGN (computer engineering, materials engineering, materials science, and urban design), HEALTH PROFESSIONS (predentistry and premedicine), SOCIAL SCIENCE (African American studies, anthropology, Asian/Oriental studies, Caribbean studies, criminal justice, East Asian studies, economics, geography, Hispanic American studies, history, homeland security, homeland security/emergency preparedness, interdisciplinary studies, Latin American studies, medieval studies, philosophy, political science/government, prelaw, psychology, social work, sociology, Spanish studies, women & gender studies, and women's studies). Criminal justice, accounting, and public administration & policy are the strongest academically. Business, psychology, and communication & rhetoric have the largest enrollments.

ACTIVITIES: 1% of men belong to 21 national fraternities; 2% of women belong to 1 local and 17 national sororities. There are 226 groups on campus, including chamber singers, percussion ensemble, art, band, cheerleading, chess, chorale, chorus, computers, dance, debate, drama, electronic music ensemble, environmental, ethnic, film, honors, international, jazz band, LGBT, literary magazine, marching band, musical theater, newspaper, orchestra, pep band, photography, political, professional, radio and TV, religious, social, social service, student government, symphony, and yearbook. Popular campus events include Great Danes sports, Relay for Life, and New York State Writer's Series. **Sports:** There are 8 intercollegiate sports for men and 11 for women, and 9 intramural sports for men and 8 for women. Facilities include a gym with an pool, and a ancillary gym with a quarter-mile track, football stadium, baseball, softball, soccer, field hockey, practice fields, all-weather lacrosse field, and a recreation and convocation center. **Graduates:** From July 1, 2015 to June 30, 2016, 2944 bachelor's degrees were awarded. The most popular majors were English (14%), business (12%), and psychology (11%). 140 companies recruited on campus in 2015-2016. In an average class, 56% graduate in 4 years or less, 64% graduate in 5 years or less, and 66% graduate in 6 years or less.

SERVICES: Counseling and information services are available, as is tutoring in most subjects. There is a reader service for the blind. The Excel program provides low-income and first-generation college students with a variety of mentoring, tutorial, and counseling services. **Library/Resources:** The 3 libraries contain 2.3 million volumes, 2.9 million microform items, and 13,928 audio/video tapes/CDs/DVDs, and subscribe to 97,614 periodicals including electronic. Computerized library services include interlibrary loans, database searching, Internet access, and Wi-Fi capability. Special learning facilities include an art gallery, radio station, Linear accelerator, sophisticated weather data system, national lightning detection system, interactive media center, extensive art studios, state-of-the-art electronic library, and the Northeast Regional Forensic Institute (NERFI). **Physically Challenged Students:** 99% of the campus is accessible. Facilities include wheelchair ramps, elevators, special parking, specially equipped restrooms, lowered drinking fountains, lowered telephones. disabled student services provides a broad range of personalized services to people with disabilities, including preadmission information and accessible housing information. **Special:** Cross-registration is available with Rensselaer Polytechnic Institute, Albany Law School, and Union, Siena, and Russell Sage Colleges. Internships may be arranged with state government agencies and private organizations. Study abroad in many countries, a Washington semester, B.A.-B.S. degrees, and work-study programs are offered. Dual and student-designed majors, nondegree study, and pass/fail grading options are available. There are accelerated 5-year bachelor's/master's programs in 40 fields; most arts and sciences fields may be combined with an accelerated M.B.A. A 3-2 engineering degree with 1 of 4 institutions is also possible. There are 15 national honor societies, Phi Beta Kappa, a freshman honors program, and 30 departmental honors programs. **Visiting:** There are regularly scheduled orientations for prospective students, including a 2-day summer orientation session. There are guides for informal visits and visitors may sit in on classes. To schedule a visit, contact the Undergraduate Admissions Office. **Campus Safety and Security:** Measures include 24-hour foot and vehicle patrol, emergency notification system, self-defense education, and security escort services. There are shuttle buses, emergency telephones, lighted pathways/sidewalks, controlled access to dorms/residences, 5-Quad ambulance service.

REQUIREMENTS: Applicants must be graduates of an accredited secondary school or have a GED. 18 academic credits are required, including 2 to 3 units of math, 2 units of lab sciences, and 1 unit of foreign language study. Either SAT or ACT is required. AP and CLEP credits are accepted. Important factors in the admissions decision are advanced placement or honors courses, personality/intangible qualities, and leadership record. To graduate, students must complete a total of 120 credits with a 2.0 GPA in their major and minor, including 30 to 36 credits required in the major for a B.A. degree and 30 to 42 credits for a B.S. degree. B.A. degree candidates must complete 90 credits in liberal arts courses and B.S. candidates must complete 60. The general education program at the University at Albany consists of a minimum of 30 credits of course work in the following areas: disciplinary perspectives, cultural and historical perspectives, and communication and reasoning competencies. **Procedure:** Freshmen are admitted in the fall, spring, and summer. Entrance exams should be taken by November of the senior year. There are early decision, deferred admissions, and rolling admissions plans. Early decision applications should be filed by November 15; regular applications, by August 1 for fall entry; December 1 for spring entry; and April 1 for summer entry, along with a $50 fee. Notification of early decision is sent January 1. Applications are accepted online.

Transfer Students: 1371 transfer students enrolled in 2015-2016. Admission to certain programs is competitive and based not only on a required GPA but also on completion of a certain set of prerequisite core courses. A grade average of B or better is required for applicants to the accounting, business administration, criminal justice, and social welfare programs. 30 of 120 credits required for the bachelor's degree must be completed at University at Albany. **International Students:** There are 735 international students enrolled. The school actively recruits these students. They must also take the SAT or ACT.

ADMISSIONS: 54% of the 2016-2017 applicants were accepted. The SAT scores for the 2016-2017 freshman class were: Math-- 2% between 600 and 699. **Admissions Contact:** Timothy Lee, Director of Undergraduate Admissions. Email: *ugadmissions@albany.edu* Web: *www.albany.edu*

FINANCIAL AID: In 2016-2017, 64% of all full-time freshmen and 63% of continuing full-time students received some form of financial aid. 55% of all full-time freshmen and 50% of continuing full-time students received need-based aid. The average freshman award was $10,933. Need-based scholarships or need-based grants averaged $7,679; need-based self-help aid (loans and jobs) averaged $4,847; non-need-based athletic scholarships averaged $19,384; and other non-need-based awards and non-need-based scholarships averaged $3,882. 9% of undergraduate students work part-time. The average financial indebtedness of the 2016 graduate was $25,729. The FAFSA code is 002835. The priority date for freshman financial aid applications for fall entry is March 15.

STONY BROOK UNIVERSITY/THE STATE UNIVERSITY OF NEW YORK E-5

www.stonybrook.edu

Stony Brook, NY 11794 **(631) 632-6868**

Fax: 631) 632-9898	**Email:** enroll@stonybrook.edu
Full-time: 8526 men, 7332 women	**Faculty:** 1124; I, +$
Part-time: 622 men, 546 women	**Ph.D.s:** 91%
Graduate: 3702 men, 5006 women	**Student/Faculty:** 16 to 1
Year: semesters, summer session	**Tuition:** $8999 ($26,239)
Room & Board: $12,882	**Freshman Class:** 34999 applied, 14233 accepted, 2934 enrolled
SAT CR/M/W: 620/670/620 **ACT:** 29	**CEEB CODE:** 2548
Application Deadline: January 15	**MOST COMPETITIVE**

Stony Brook University, founded in 1957, and part of the State University of New York, is a public institution offering degree programs in arts and sciences, engineering and applied sciences, business, journalism, atmospheric and marine sciences, sustainability studies, public health, nursing, health technology and management, and social work. A number of accelerated bachelor's/master's degree programs also are offered, as well as professional programs in medicine and dental medicine at the graduate level. There are 8 undergraduate schools and 11 graduate schools. In addition to regional accreditation, Stony Brook University has baccalaureate program accreditation with ABET, ADA, APTA, CSWE, NCATE, ACS, APA, PCAS, CAATE, AAMC, ACOTE, ASPT, CAPTE, ARC-PA CAAHEP, CoARC, LCME, CEPH, NAACLS, ACGME, ACEND, CCNE, ACNM, AOTCE, and APTA. The 1454-acre campus is in a suburban area on Long Island, 55 miles from New York City. Including any residence halls, there are 215 buildings.

STUDENT LIFE: 80% of undergraduates are from New York. Others are from 45 states, 128 foreign countries, and Canada. 89% are from public schools. 7% are race unknown; 6% African American; 35% White; 23% Asian American; 2% two or more races; 14% Foreign; 12% Hispanic. **Female To Male Ratio:** 1.0:1. The average age of freshmen is 18; all undergraduates, 21. 11% do not continue beyond their first year; 72% remain to graduate. **Housing:** 9912 students can be accommodated in college housing, which includes coed dorms, on-campus apartments, married student housing, honors houses, special-interest houses, and a choice of undergraduate colleges that integrate academic experience with living environments. On-campus housing is guaranteed for all 4 years. 51% of students live on campus; of those, 65% remain on campus on weekends. Alcohol is not permitted. Upperclassmen may keep cars.

FACULTY/CLASSROOMS: 58% of faculty are male; 42% are female. No introductory courses are taught by graduate students. The average class size in an introductory lecture is 37; in a laboratory is 22; and in a regular course is 32.

PROGRAMS OF STUDY: Stony Brook University confers B.A., B.S. and B.E. degrees. Master's and doctoral degrees are also awarded. Bachelor's degrees are awarded in AGRICULTURE (environmental studies), BIOLOGICAL SCIENCE (biochemistry, biology/biological science, ecology, and marine biology), BUSINESS (business administration and management), COMMUNICATIONS AND THE ARTS (art history and appreciation, comparative literature, dramatic arts, English, film arts, Germanic languages and literature, linguistics, music, Russian languages and literature, and studio art), COMPUTER AND PHYSICAL SCIENCE (applied mathematics, astronomy, atmospheric sciences and meteorology, chemistry, computer science, earth science, geology, information sciences and systems, mathematics, and physics), EDUCATION (athletic training), ENGINEERING AND ENVIRONMENTAL DESIGN (biomedical engineering, chemical engineering, computer engineering, electrical/electronics engineering, engineering and applied science, engineering chemistry, environmental design, environmental science, mechanical engineering, and technological management), HEALTH PROFESSIONS (clinical science, cytotechnology, health science, nursing, occupational therapy, pharmacology, physical therapy, and respiratory therapy), SOCIAL SCIENCE (African studies, American studies, anthropology, Asian/American studies, economics, ethnic studies, European studies, French studies, history, humanities, interdisciplinary studies, Italian studies, liberal arts/general studies, philosophy, political science/government, psychology, religion, social science, social work, sociology, Spanish studies, and women's studies). Biology, business management, economics, and applied mathematics and statistics are the strongest academically. Biology, health and psychology have the largest enrollments.

ACTIVITIES: 3% of women belong to 1 local and 13 national sororities. There are 353 groups on campus, including band, cheerleading, chess, choir, chorale, computers, dance, debate, drama, environmental, ethnic, film, forensics, honors, international, jazz band, LGBT, literary magazine, marching band, musical theater, newspaper, opera, orchestra, pep band, photography, political, professional, radio and TV, religious, social, social service, student government, and symphony. Popular campus events include Fall Fest, Opening Week Activities, and Caribbean Weekend. **Sports:** There are 9 intercollegiate sports for men and 10 for women, and 28 intramural sports for men and 28 for women. Facilities include sports complex that includes an a arena, gym, swimming pool, squash and racquetball courts, dance studio, and exercise and universal gym rooms. Outdoor facilities include stadium, softball facility, baseball facility, tennis courts, multi-sport practice facilities, basketball and handball courts, softball fields, and a multi-sport recreational area. **Graduates:** From July 1, 2015 to June 30, 2016, 3952 bachelor's degrees were awarded. The most popular majors were health sciences (12%), biology (10%), and business (8%). 468 companies recruited on campus in 2015-2016. In an average class, 2% graduate in 3 years or less, 52% graduate in 4 years or less, 69% graduate in 5 years or less, and 72% graduate in 6 years or less.

SERVICES: There is a reader service for the blind, and remedial math and writing. **Library/Resources:** The 8 libraries contain 2.2 million volumes, 3.6 million microform items, and 35,008 audio/video tapes/CDs/DVDs, and subscribe to 106,108 periodicals including electronic. Computerized library services include interlibrary loans, database searching, Internet access, and Wi-Fi capability. Special learning facilities include an art gallery, radio station, TV station, and molecular medicine and biology learning laboratories, and specialized centers for advanced computational science, physical and quantitative biology, marine sciences, planetary exploration, arts, and a state-of-the-art newsroom, affording students the opportunity to work across multiple multimedia platforms. **Physically Challenged Students:** All of the campus is accessible. Facilities include wheelchair ramps, elevators, special parking, specially equipped restrooms, special class scheduling, lowered drinking fountains, lowered telephones, and special housing. **Special:** Stony Brook offers internships including internships in the arts, business and government, with hospitals and clinics, and in legal and social agencies. The URECA Program promotes undergraduate research and creative projects, both on and off campus -- including nearby Brookhaven National Laboratory, which Stony Brook University has a role in running. A fast-track MBA program and more than thirty additional combined degree programs are available to undergraduates. Scholars for Medicine and Scholars for Dental Medicine are highly selective programs in which a small number of freshmen are admitted to eight-year combined-degree programs in medicine and dental medicine. Women in Science and Engineering, the Honors College, and University Scholars programs provide additional experiences to challenge, inspire, and sustain our most academically talented students. Students may declare double majors or pursue dual degrees. The multidisciplinary studies major is student-designed. Students have the opportunity to study at another college or university through the national student exchange program or our study-abroad programs in more than 30 countries, including China, New Zealand, France, Sweden, Taiwan, Denmark, England, Korea, Madagascar, Australia, Costa Rica, Jamaica, Tanzania, Kenya, Spain, Norway, Russia, Japan, Italy, Greece, and Germany. Cross-registration may be arranged through the Long Island Regional Advisory Council for Higher Education. There are 15 national honor societies, Phi Beta Kappa, a freshman honors program, and 36 departmental honors programs. **Visiting:** There are regularly scheduled orientations for prospective students, Informative sessions about campus life. There are guides for informal visits and visitors may sit in on classes. To schedule a visit, contact the Admissions Office. **Campus Safety and Security:** Measures include 24-hour foot and vehicle patrol, emergency notification system, self-defense education, and security escort services. There are shuttle buses, emergency telephones, lighted pathways/sidewalks, controlled access to dorms/ residences, a campus crime stoppers program, building access through use of cards, and controlled campus access after midnights.

REQUIREMENTS: The SAT is required. Applicants must be graduates of an accredited secondary school or have a GED certificate. 16 or 17 academic credits are required, including 4 years each of English and social studies, 3 or 4 of math, 3 of science (4 for engineering majors), and 2 or 3 of a foreign language. One letter of recommendation and supplemental application, including and essay are required. 3 SAT Subject tests, an essay, and an interview are recommended. AP and CLEP credits are accepted. Important factors in the admissions decision are advanced placement or honors courses, extracurricular activities record, and evidence of special talent. To graduate, students must have a minimum 2.0 GPA in 120 credit hours (B.A. and B.S.) or 128 (B.E.). The required number of hours in the major varies. At least 39 credits must be earned in upper-division courses. Students must complete at least 30 credits of general education, through which they are expected to demonstrate versatility, explore interconnectedness, pursue deeper understanding, and prepare for life-long learning. Arts and sciences majors must fulfill a foreign language requirement, unless completed through advanced high-school study. Other requirements vary by school. **Procedure:** Freshmen are admitted fall and spring. Entrance exams should be taken during the junior year or in the fall of the senior year. There is a deferred admissions plan. Applications should be filed by January 15 for fall entry; November 1 for spring entry. The fall 2016 application fee was $50. Notifications are sent April 1. 3767 applicants were on the 2016 waiting list; 110 were admitted. Applications are accepted online. **Transfer Students:** 2391 transfer students enrolled in 2015-2016. Applicants must have a minimum 2.5 GPA. An associate degree and an interview are recommended. Other requirements vary by program. Applicants who have earned fewer than 24 college credits must submit a high school transcript. 36 of 120 credits required for the bachelor's degree must be completed at Stony Brook University. **International Students:** There are 2389 international students enrolled. They must take the TOEFL with a minimum score of 550 on the paper-based TOEFL (PBT) or 80 on the Internet-based version (iBT), or take the IELTS, or the SAT critical reading.

ADMISSIONS: 41% of the 2016-2017 applicants were accepted. The SAT scores for the 2016-2017 freshman class were: Critical Reading-- 3% below 500, 30% between 500 and 599, 50% between 600 and 699, and 18% between 700 and 800. Math-- 2% below 500, 14% between 500 and 599, 50% between 600 and 699, and 34% between 700 and 800. Writing-- 5% below 500, 35% between 500 and 599, 45% between 600 and 699, and 16% between 700 and 800. The ACT scores were 3% between 18 and 23, 57% between 24 and 29, and 41% above 30. 77% of the current freshmen were in the top fifth of their class; 95% were in the top two fifths. There were 29 National Merit finalists. **Admissions Contact:** Judith Burke-Berhanan, Dean of Admissions. Email: *enroll@stonybrook.edu* Web: *www.stonybrook.edu*

FINANCIAL AID: In 2016-2017, 77% of all full-time freshmen and 67% of continuing full-time students received some form of financial aid. 49% of all full-time freshmen and 47% of continuing full-time students received need-based aid. The average freshman award was $13,800. Need-based scholarships or need-based grants averaged $9,200 ($23,300 maximum); need-based self-help aid (loans and jobs) averaged $3,700 ($6,500 maximum); non-need-based athletic scholarships averaged $22,000 ($46,000 maximum); and other non-need-based awards and non-need-based scholarships averaged $7,300 ($42,000 maximum). 14% of undergraduate students work part-time. Average annual earnings from campus work are $4000. The average financial indebtedness of the 2016 graduate was $24,700. Stony Brook University is a member of CSS. The state aid form is required. The priority date for freshman financial aid applications for fall entry is March 1.

SYRACUSE UNIVERSITY C-3

www.admissions.syr.edu

Syracuse, NY 13244 (315) 443-3611

Fax: (315) 443-4226	**Email:** admissions@syr.edu
Full-time: 6635 men, 7972 women	**Faculty:** I, av$
Part-time: 310 men, 301 women	**Ph.D.s:** 90%
Graduate: 3395 men, 3357 women	**Student/Faculty:** 15 to 1
Year: semesters, summer session	**Tuition:** $45,022
Room & Board: $15,217	**Freshman Class:** 30923 applied, 16179 accepted, 3712 enrolled
SAT or ACT: required	**CEEB CODE:** 2823
Application Deadline: January 1	**VERY COMPETITIVE**

Syracuse University, founded in 1870, is a private, coeducational, urban institution, recognized as a student-focused global research university renowned for academic rigor, richly diverse learning experiences, and a spirit of discovery. There are 9 undergraduate schools and 11 graduate schools. In addition to regional accreditation, Syracuse has baccalaureate program accreditation with AACSB, ABET, ACEJMC, CSWE, NAAB, NASAD, NASM, ACS, CIDA, CAEP, and ACEND. The 270-acre campus is in an urban area in the city of Syracuse, Central New York. Including any residence halls, there are 260 buildings.

STUDENT LIFE: 59% of undergraduates are from out of state, mostly the Northeast. Students are from 50 states, 84 foreign countries, and Canada. 66% are from public schools. 56% are White; 12% Foreign; 10% Hispanic; 8% African American; 7% Asian American; 3% two or more races; 3% race unknown; 1% American Indian/Alaska Native. 44% claim no religious affiliation; 25% Catholic; 11% Jewish. **Female To Male Ratio:** 1.1:1. The average age of freshmen is 18; all undergraduates, 20. 9% do not continue beyond their first year; 82% remain to graduate. **Housing:** 8290 students can be accommodated in college housing, which includes coed dorms and on-campus apartments. In addition, there are special-interest houses, fraternity houses, sorority houses, theme and wellness housing. On-campus housing is available on a lottery system for upperclassmen. 75% of students live on campus; of those, 85% remain on campus on weekends. Upperclassmen may keep cars.

FACULTY/CLASSROOMS: 58% of faculty are male; 42% are female. No introductory courses are taught by graduate students. The average class size in an introductory lecture is 231; in a laboratory is 18; and in a regular course is 25.

PROGRAMS OF STUDY: Syracuse confers B.A., B.S., B.Arch., B.F.A., B.I.D., B.Mus. and B.P.S. degrees. Associate, master's, and doctoral degrees are also awarded. Bachelor's degrees are awarded in BIOLOGICAL SCIENCE (biochemistry, biology/ gen science secondary education, biophysics, biotechnology, forensic science, neurosciences, nutrition, and nutritional sciences), BUSINESS (accounting, entrepreneurial studies, finance, knowledge management, management, marketing, real estate, retailing, sports management, and supply chain management), COMMUNICATIONS AND THE ARTS (acting, advertising, art history, art, art/art studies, art history and appreciation, arts/sciences planned program, broadcasting, ceramic art and design, classics, communication design, communication rhetoric/communication, dramatic arts, English, film arts, fine arts, French and Francophone studies, German studies, graphic design, illustration, industrial design, journalism & technical communications, journalism - magazine journalism, journalism - news & information, linguistics, metal/jewelry, modern language, music, music composition, music history and appreciation, music industry, music production/recording technology, musical theater, painting, percussion, photography, piano/organ, printmaking, public relations, Russian languages and literature, sculpture, stage management, strings, television & digital media production, theater design, video, voice, winds, and writing & rhetoric), COMPUTER AND PHYSICAL SCIENCE (applied mathematics, chemistry, chemistry/gen science second education, chemistry secondary education, computer science, earth science, earth science/adolescence education, energy science, inform, science, systms & tech, information sciences and systems, mathematics, physics/gen science secondary education, and physics), EDUCATION (art education, early childhood education, educational studies, elementary education, English education, health and physical education, mathematics education, music education, physical education, social studies education, Spanish education K-12, spec ed/early child dual prog, and special ed/middle level education), ENGINEERING AND ENVIRONMENTAL DESIGN (aerospace engineering, architecture, bioengineering, chemical engineering, civil engineering, computer engineering, computer graphics, engineering physics, environmental design, environmental engineering, and mechanical engineering), HEALTH PROFESSIONS (biology, electrical engineering, health science, predentistry, premedicine, and public health), SOCIAL SCIENCE (African American studies, anthropology, child care/child and family studies, classical/ancient civilization, communication sciences & disorders, economics, ethics, politics, and social policy, fashion design and technology, food science, geography, history, international relations, Italian studies, Latin American studies, legal studies, liberal arts/general studies, Middle Eastern studies, modern jewish studies, philosophy, philosophy (political thought), political science/government, prelaw, psychology, religion, religious studies, Russian and Slavic studies, social work, sociology, Spanish studies, and women & gender studies). Undergraduate degrees are offered in architecture, arts and sciences, education, engineering and computer science, sport and human dynamics, information studies, management, public communications, and visual and performing arts. Among the academically strongest degree programs are the bachelor of architecture, public communications, management, life sciences (biology, biochemistry, biophysical science, physics), sport management, drama, and recording and allied entertainment industries (The Bandier Program for Music and the Entertainment Industries). Information science/studies, architecture, and speech communications & rhetoric have the largest enrollments.

ACTIVITIES: 26% of men belong to 31 national fraternities; 36% of women belong to 24 national sororities. There are 500 groups on campus, including special interest clubs, art, band, cheerleading, chess, choir, chorale, chorus, communications, computers, dance, debate, drama, environmental, ethnic, film, forensics, honors, international, jazz band, LGBT, literary magazine, marching band, musical theater, newspaper, opera, orchestra, pep band, photography, political, professional, radio and TV, religious, social, social service, student government, symphony, and yearbook. Popular campus events include Syracuse Welcome, Winter Carnival, Senior Celebration, Dance Works, First Year Players, Block Party, University Lectures, Athletic events, Veterans Day, Martin Luther King Jr. Dinner, Latino/Hispanic Heritage Month, Asian/Pacific Heritage Month. **Sports:** There are 8 intercollegiate sports for men and 23 for women, and 17 intramural sports for men and 17 for women. Facilities include fitness centers, swimming pools, ice skating pavilion, fencing room, racquetball and squash courts, basketball courts, dance studios, volleyball facilities, table-tennis,weight rooms, tennis courts, exercise rooms, indoor track, grass playing fields, multiple outdoor artificial turf fields, an outdoor track, ropes challenge course and zip line, indoor challenge course, soccer stadium, softball stadium, football complex, athlete weight room, fitness classes, country club, golf course, boathouse/rowing facilities, and a multipurpose domed stadium for football and basketball. **Graduates:** From July 1, 2015 to June 30, 2016, 3467 bachelor's degrees were awarded. The most popular majors were communications/journalism (14%), business and marketing (14%), and social sciences (13%). 191 companies recruited on campus in 2015-2016. In an average class, 69% graduate in 4 years or less, 81% graduate in 5 years or less, and 82% graduate in 6 years or less. Of the 2015 graduating class, 18% were enrolled in graduate school within 6 months of graduation, and 65% were employed.

SERVICES: Counseling and information services are available, as is tutoring in most subjects. There is a reader service for the blind. A variety of services are offered by the Syracuse University Student Success Center including subject specific help, tutoring by academic program, and study resources. Additional services such as the writing center, the math clinic, and the physics clinic are offered by individual schools/colleges, departments, and/or honor societies. The Office of Disability Services provides additional services for those with documented disabilities. **Library/Resources:** The 3 libraries contain 3.8 million volumes, 16,260 microform items, 101,108 audio/video tapes/CDs/DVDs, and subscribe to 179,076 periodicals including electronic. Computerized library services include interlibrary loans, database searching, Internet access, and Wi-Fi capability. Special learning facilities include an art gallery, radio station, TV station, The Syracuse University Library Special Collections Research Center; the Global Collaboratory; the Syracuse Center of Excellence in Environmental and Energy Systems; Center for Science and Technology; Life Sciences Complex; Fidelity MODUS 622i flight simulator; the Dick Clark Studios; the Alan Gerry Center for Media Innovation; the Diane and Bob Miron Digital News Center; Falcone Center for Entreprenuership; Ballentine Investment Institute; Architecture studios; the Dorothea Ilgen Shaffer Art Building; Syracuse Stage; the Bernice M. Wright Child Development Laboratory; the Belfer Audio Laboratory and Archive; the Gebbie Speech/ Language, and Hearing Clinic; and Syracuse University Humanities Center. **Physically Challenged Students:** 95% of the campus is accessible. Facilities include wheelchair ramps, elevators, special parking, specially equipped restrooms, special class scheduling, lowered drinking fountains, lowered telephones, and special housing. **Special:** Co-op programs exist for aerospace engineering, bioengineering, chemical engineering, civil engineering, computer engineering, computer science, electric engineering, environmental engineering, mechanical engineering, systems and information science. Syracuse University students are encouraged to undertake internships during both the academic year and summers in the Syracuse community, across the nation and internationally. Internships can be for credit or paid, depending upon the field and degree requirements of the student's college of enrollment. The Syracuse University Career Services Office aids students in finding internships, as do individual school/college career services units. Syracuse currently operates eight overseas centers, in Beijing, Florence, Hong Kong, Istanbul, London, Madrid, Santiago (Chile), and Strasbourg (France). Through our World Partners, summer, and short-term programs, SU Abroad students have study abroad options in over 30 additional countries. SU also enrolls small cohorts of entering freshmen students in The College of Arts and Sciences to First-Semester Liberal Arts Study Abroad Programs: Discovery Florence and Discovery Strasbourg. These students begin their collegiate career at the SU Centers in Florence or Strasbourg in the fall semester. Finally, there are dozens of short term study abroad trips ranging from one to three weeks in duration, generally including travel to multiple countries. The Maxwell School of Citizenship & Public Affairs (within The College of Arts & Sciences) offers the Maxwell-Washington semester. Hundreds Syracuse University undergraduate students work on campus through the Federal Work-Study (FWS) program. FWS employers include student affairs, career services, advising, residence life, dining and catering services, universities and libraries, and academic and administrative offices across campus. There are ten dual and combined enrollment options through which a variety of major combinations may be undertaken. The College of Arts and Sciences at Syracuse University offers custom programs of study with advisor consultation and approval. There are 34 national honor societies, Phi Beta Kappa, and a freshman honors program. **Visiting:** There are regularly scheduled orientations for prospective students, Prospective students can visit Syracuse University nearly year-round. Options include daily visits which offer an information session and campus tour. See admissions.syr.edu/visit. There are guides for informal visits, visitors may sit in on classes, and stay overnight. To schedule a visit, contact Syracuse University, Office of Admissions. **Campus Safety and Security:** Measures include 24-hour foot and vehicle patrol, emergency notification system, self-defense education, and security escort services. There are shuttle buses, emergency telephones, lighted pathways/sidewalks, controlled access to dorms/residences, Campus wide video security system with central monitoring at the Department of Public Safety (DPS) Emergency Communications Center; crisis alert notification system has email, text message, voice phone, social media, campus display screens in various buildings, and outdoor emergency sirens.

REQUIREMENTS: Applicants to Syracuse University must submit the Common Application, scores for either the SAT or ACT, secondary school transcript, counselor evaluation, two academic recommendations, an essay and short written answers to questions. Applicants should have a strong college preparatory record from an accredited secondary school or have a GED equivalent. A portfolio is required for art and architecture majors, and an audition is required for music and drama majors. The SAT and ACT are not required for international applicants studying outside the U.S. who are not prospective student-athletes and not attending an American-system school. AP and CLEP credits are accepted. Portions of the liberal arts core are required by all colleges. New students are required to take a writing course. Liberal arts core courses are required in most majors: writing skills; foreign language or quantitative skills; humanities, natural sciences and mathematics, social sciences; and critical reflections on ethical and social issues. A minimum of 120 credit hours to graduate, but varies by college or major (s). Courses in recreation and physical education and computer science/information management technology are available, but are not required in most majors. Thesis required of Renee Crown Honors students, to graduate with distinction; some majors require a capstone experience. Academic requirements for majors and minors are provided in the Syracuse University course catalog. **Procedure:** Freshmen are admitted in the fall and spring. Entrance exams should be taken prior to January of the senior year for regular decision. There are early decision and deferred admissions plans. Early decision applications should be filed by November 15; regular applications, by January 1 for fall entry; and November 15 for spring entry. The fall 2016 application fee was $75. Notification of early decision is sent January 1; regular decision, March 15. 1201 early decision candidates were accepted for the 2016-2017 class. 1839 applicants were on the 2016 waiting list; 80 were admitted. Applications are accepted on-line. **Transfer Students:** 354 transfer students enrolled in 2015-2016. Online Common Application form, $75 application fee; official college academic transcripts, two academic recommendations, transfer College Report form are required. For applicants with fewer than 30 college credit hours completed, submit official SAT or ACT scores and official secondary school transcript. A portfolio is required for art and architecture applicants, and an audition for music and drama applicants. TOEFL or IELTS scores are required for students whose native language is not English. Additional requirements may apply to international students. For more information, visit the "Apply" link at admissions.syr .edu. **International Students:** There are 1869 international students enrolled. The school actively recruits these students. They must take the TOEFL with a minimum score of 550 on the paper-based TOEFL (PBT) or 85 on the Internet-based version (iBT), or take the IELTS. SAT or ACT are not required for international students who have not studied in an American-based system.

ADMISSIONS: 52% of the 2016-2017 applicants were accepted. The SAT scores for the 2016-2017 freshman class were: Critical Reading-- 13% below 500, 43% between 500 and 599, 37% between 600 and 699, and 7% between 700 and 800. Math-- 7% below 500, 34% between 500 and 599, 46% between 600 and 699, and 14% between 700 and 800. Writing-- 11% below 500, 45% between 500 and 599, 38% between 600 and 699, and 7% between 700 and 800. The ACT scores were 1% between 12 and 17, 15% between 18 and 23, 61% between 24 and 29, and 23% above 30. 61% of the current freshmen were in the top fifth of their class; 88% were in the top two fifths. **Admissions Contact:** Office of Admissions. Email: *orange@syr.edu* Web: *admissions.syr.edu*

FINANCIAL AID: In 2016-2017, 74% of all full-time freshmen and 72% of continuing full-time students received some form of financial aid. 48% of all full-time freshmen and 53% of continuing full-time students received need-based aid. The average freshman award was $36,040. Need-based scholarships or need-based grants averaged $28,517; and need-based self-help aid (loans and jobs) averaged $7,000. 45% of undergraduate students work part-time. Average annual earnings from campus work are $3000. The average financial indebtedness of the 2016 graduate was $37,753. Syracuse is a member of CSS. The CSS/Profile, and Noncustodial Profile are required. The FAFSA code is 002882. The deadline for filing freshman financial aid applications for fall entry is January 1.

THE COLLEGE AT BROCKPORT - STATE UNIVERSITY OF NEW YORK B-3

www.brockport.edu

Brockport, NY 14420	(585) 395-2751
Fax: (585) 395-5452	Email: admit@brockport.edu
Full-time: 2865 men, 3510 women	**Faculty:** 286; IIA, av$
Part-time: 289 men, 464 women	**Ph.D.s:** 76%
Graduate: 349 men, 766 women	**Student/Faculty:** 20 to 1
Year: semesters, summer session	**Tuition:** $7928 ($17,778)
Room & Board: $12,418	**Freshman Class:** 9211 applied, 5096 accepted, 1145 enrolled
SAT CR/M: 500/510 **ACT:** 23	**CEEB CODE:** 2537
Application Deadline: rolling	**COMPETITIVE**

College at Brockport, State University of New York, established in 1835, is a comprehensive public liberal arts college with offerings including 49 undergraduate majors, more than 50 masters programs, 14 nationally accredited programs, and 24 teacher certification areas. There are 5 undergraduate schools and 1 graduate school. In addition to regional accreditation, SUNY Brockport has baccalaureate program accreditation with AACSB, ABET, CSWE, NCATE, NASD, CCNE, ACS, NAST, CAAHEP, CACREP, NASPAA, COAPRT, NAADAC, and CAATE. The 464-acre campus is in a small town 16 miles west of Rochester. Including any residence halls, there are 80 buildings.

STUDENT LIFE: 98% of undergraduates are from New York. Others are from 25 states, 30 foreign countries, and Canada. 72% are White; 6% Hispanic; 6% race unknown; 3% two or more races; 2% Asian American; 11% African American; 1% Foreign. **Female To Male Ratio:** 1.4:1. The average age of freshmen is 18; all undergraduates, 22. 18% do not continue beyond their first year; 65% remain to graduate. **Housing:** 2770 students can be accommodated in college housing, which includes coed dorms and on-campus apartments. In addition, there are special-interest houses, special residence hall communities for first-year students, and academic excellence floors. On-campus housing is available on a first-come and first-served basis. 72% of students commute. All students may keep cars.

FACULTY/CLASSROOMS: 46% of faculty are male; 54% are female. 79% teach undergraduates. No introductory courses are taught by graduate students.

PROGRAMS OF STUDY: SUNY Brockport confers B.A., B.S., B.F.A. and B.S.N. degrees. Master's degrees are also awarded. Bachelor's degrees are awarded in BIOLOGICAL SCIENCE (biochemistry and biology/biological science), BUSINESS (accounting, business administration and management, finance, international business management, marketing management, recreation and leisure services, and sports management), COMMUNICATIONS AND THE ARTS (communications, dance, English, French, journalism, Spanish, studio art, and theatre acting), COMPUTER AND PHYSICAL SCIENCE (atmospheric sciences and meteorology, chemistry, computer science, earth science, geology, mathematics, and physics), EDUCATION (athletic training and physical education), ENGINEERING AND ENVIRONMENTAL DESIGN (computational sciences and environmental science), HEALTH PROFESSIONS (exercise science, health science, kinesiology, medical technology, and nursing), SOCIAL SCIENCE (African studies, African American studies, anthropology, criminal justice, history, international studies, liberal arts/general studies, philosophy, political science/government, psychology, social work, sociology, water resources, and women's studies). Nursing, health science, and business administration have the largest enrollments.

ACTIVITIES: 1% of men belong to 2 national fraternities; 1% of women belong to 2 national sororities. There are 124 groups on campus, including club sports, art, band, cheerleading, choir, chorus, computers, dance, drama, environmental, ethnic, honors, international, jazz band, LGBT, literary magazine, many academic clubs, newspaper, orchestra, political, professional, radio and TV, religious, social, social service, student government, and symphony. Popular campus events include Scholar's Day, Honors and Awards Ceremony, Diversity Conference, International Student Festival. **Sports:** There are 12 intercollegiate sports for men and 13 for women, and 20 intramural sports for men and 20 for women. Facilities include field hockey, baseball, softball fields, soccer pitch, swimming pool, six gyms, a gymnastics center, wrestling room, weight rooms, handball, squash, tennis, and racquetball courts, ice arena, special Olympics stadium, running track, basketball, and tennis courts, and personal training. **Graduates:** From July 1, 2015 to June 30, 2016, 1865 bachelor's degrees were awarded. The most popular majors were Nursing (8%), Psychology (8%), and criminal justice (7%). 170 companies recruited on campus in 2015-2016. In an average class, 3% graduate in 3 years or less, 48% graduate in 4 years or less, 65% graduate in 5 years or less, and 68% graduate in 6 years or less. Of the 2015 graduating class, 35% were enrolled in graduate school within 6 months of graduation, and 54% were employed.

SERVICES: Counseling and information services are available, as is tutoring in most subjects, and study skills. **Library/Resources:** The library contains 750,000 volumes, 18,500 microform items, and 10,600 audio/video tapes/CDs/DVDs, and subscribes to 116,000 periodicals including electronic. Computerized library services include interlibrary loans, database searching, Internet access, and Wi-Fi capability. Special learning facilities include an art gallery, planetarium, radio station, TV station, ceramic, painting, photography and sculpture studios, greenhouse, planetarium, electron microscope, nuclear magnetic resonance spectrometer, Geographic Information Systems (GIS) lab with Dopplar radar station, aquaculture ponds, environmental science deciduous woodlot, research boat, computer labs, "smart" classrooms, and a student learning center. **Physically Challenged Students:** 95% of the campus is accessible. Facilities include wheelchair ramps, elevators, special parking, specially equipped restrooms, special class scheduling, lowered drinking fountains, lowered telephones, and special housing. **Special:** Co-op programs, internships in most majors, and work-study programs in education are available, as well as an Honors College with full tuition scholarship. Brockport offers cross-registration with Rochester area colleges, a Washington semester, study abroad in over 35 countries, accelerated degree programs, and an interdisciplinary major in arts for children, emphasizing art, dance, music, and theater. Credit for military and work experience, nondegree study, and pass/fail grading options are available. An alternative general education program, Delta College, is an interdisciplinary program that emphasizes global issues and provides opportunities for work or study in other countries, as well as locally, regionally, and nationally. There are 32 national honor societies, a freshman honors program, and 5 departmental honors programs. **Visiting:** There are regularly scheduled orientations for prospective students, admissions information presentations, campus tours, and class observations. There are guides for informal visits, visitors may sit in on classes, and stay overnight. To schedule a visit, contact Undergraduate Admissions. **Campus Safety and Security:** Measures include 24-hour foot and vehicle patrol, emergency notification system, and security escort services. There are shuttle buses, emergency telephones, lighted pathways/sidewalks, controlled access to dorms/residences, a community policing program, bicycle patrols, and 24-hour locked residence halls.

REQUIREMENTS: The College at Brockport will consider many factors when reviewing admissions applications: strength of your academic program, course grades and high school average, standardized test scores (SAT and/or ACT), class rank, supplemental application information, anything additional that you supply (letters of recommendation, resume, portfolio, etc.) Most students who enter Brockport today have: the equivalent of an Advanced Regents Diploma, 4 years of English, 3 years or more of math, sciences and social studies, 3 years or more of a foreign language, additional electives as appropriate, some college-level course work, including Advanced Placement (AP), International Baccalaureate (IB), and college-affiliated programs such as Syracuse University Project Advance (SUPA). A GPA of 85.0 is required. AP and CLEP credits are accepted. Important factors in the admissions decision are advanced placement or honors courses, leadership record, and extracurricular activities record. To graduate, students must complete a minimum of 120 credits, including 30 or more credits in the major, with a 2.0 GPA. The core curriculum includes the SUNY-wide general education requirements (1 course each in math, natural sciences, social sciences, American history, Western civilization, world (non-Western) civilization, humanities, the arts, foreign language, and basic communication). All students must take courses in contemporary issues, diversity, and perspectives on women and pass the appropriate competency exams. An academic planning seminar is required of entering freshmen and recommended for incoming transfer students. **Procedure:** Freshmen are admitted in the fall and spring. Entrance exams should be taken spring of the junior year and fall of senior year. There are deferred admissions and rolling admissions plans. Application deadlines are open. Application fee is $50. Notification is sent on a rolling basis. Applications are accepted on-line. **Transfer Students:** 1420 transfer students enrolled in 2015-2016. Applicants must have a minimum GPA of 2.0 to be considered. Many departments specify pre-requisite courses and a higher GPA (nursing, social work, education). 30 of 120 credits required for the bachelor's degree must be completed at SUNY Brockport. **International Students:** There are 98 international students enrolled. The school actively recruits these students. They must take the TOEFL with a minimum score of 530 on the paper-based TOEFL (PBT) or 76 on the Internet-based version (iBT), or the IETLS, completion of ELS level 112. They must also take the SAT or ACT.

ADMISSIONS: 55% of the 2016-2017 applicants were accepted. The SAT scores for the 2016-2017 freshman class were: Critical Reading-- 49% below 500, 39% between 500 and 599, 10% between 600 and 699, and 2% between 700 and 800. Math-- 39% below 500, 46% between 500 and 599, 15% between 600 and 699, and 1% between 700 and 800. The ACT scores were 7% between 12 and 17, 50% between 18 and 23, 38% between 24 and 29, and 5% above 30. 28% of the current freshmen were in the top fifth of their class; 62% were in the top two fifths. 7 freshmen graduated first in their class. **Admissions Contact:** Megan Sarkis, Assistant Director of Admissions. Email: *admit@brockport.edu* Web: *www.brockport.edu*

FINANCIAL AID: In 2016-2017, 91% of all full-time freshmen and 83% of continuing full-time students received some form of financial aid. 70% of all full-time freshmen and 68% of continuing full-time students received need-based aid. The average freshman award was $15,437. Need-based scholarships or need-based grants averaged $7,010 ($22,105 maximum); need-based self-help aid (loans and jobs) averaged $5,249 ($9,750 maximum); and other non-need-based awards and non-need-based scholarships averaged $74,815 ($31,400 maximum). 70% of undergraduate students work part-time. Average annual earnings from campus work are $1475. The average financial indebtedness of the 2016 graduate was $29,748. The state aid form is required. The priority date for freshman financial aid applications for fall entry is March 15. The filing deadline for fall entry is January 1.

THE COLLEGE OF NEW ROCHELLE D-5

www.cnr.edu

New Rochelle, NY 10805	(914) 654-5000 (800) 933-5923
Fax: (914) 654-5464	**Email:** admissions@cnr.edu
Full-time: 25 men, 605 women	**Faculty:** IIA, +$
Part-time: 60 men, 335 women	**Ph.D.s:** n/av
Graduate: 105 men, 930 women	**Student/Faculty:** n/av
Year: semesters, summer session	**Tuition:** $33,600
Room & Board: $12,700	**Freshman Class:** n/av
SAT: required	**CEEB CODE:** 2089
Application Deadline: August 31	**VERY COMPETITIVE**

The College of New Rochelle was founded in 1904, by the Ursuline order as the first Catholic college for women in New York State. The School of Arts and Sciences offers liberal arts baccalaureate education for women only and the School of Nursing is coeducational. The School of New Resources is described in a separate profile. The figures in the above profile and in this capsule are approximate. There are 3 undergraduate schools and 1 graduate school. In addition to regional accreditation, CNR has baccalaureate program accreditation with CSWE, NLN, and CCNE. The 20-acre campus is in a suburban area 12 miles north of New York City. Including any residence halls, there are 20 buildings.

STUDENT LIFE: 87% of undergraduates are from New York. Others are from 17 states, and 10 foreign countries. 73% are from public schools. 7% are Asian American; 52% African American; 22% Hispanic; 18% White; 1% American Indian/Alaska Native; 1% Foreign. 77% are Catholic; 18% Protestant. **Female To Male Ratio:** 9.8:1. The average age of freshmen is 20; all undergraduates, 27. 29% do not continue beyond their first year; 71% remain to graduate. **Housing:** 410 students can be accommodated in college housing, which includes single-sex dorms. On-campus housing is guaranteed for all 4 years. 56% of students live on campus; of those, 50% remain on campus on weekends. All students may keep cars.

FACULTY/CLASSROOMS: 25% of faculty are male; 75% are female. All teach undergraduates, and do research. No introductory courses are taught by graduate students. The average class size in an introductory lecture is 25; in a laboratory is 10; and in a regular course is 15.

PROGRAMS OF STUDY: CNR confers B.A., B.S., B.F.A. and B.S.N. degrees. Master's degrees are also awarded. Bachelor's degrees are awarded in AGRICULTURE (environmental studies), BIOLOGICAL SCIENCE (biology/biological science), BUSINESS (business administration and management), COMMUNICATIONS AND THE ARTS (art history and appreciation, classics, communications, English, French, and Spanish), COMPUTER AND PHYSICAL SCIENCE (chemistry and mathematics), EDUCATION (art education), HEALTH PROFESSIONS (art therapy and nursing), SOCIAL SCIENCE (economics, history, international studies, philosophy, political science/government, psychology, religion, social work, sociology, and women's studies). Nursing, art, and psychology have the largest enrollments.

ACTIVITIES: There are no fraternities or sororities. There are 18 groups on campus, including art, cheerleading, choir, chorus, drama, environmental, ethnic, film, honors, international, literary magazine, musical theater, newspaper, photography, political, professional, religious, social, social service, and student government. Popular campus events include Junior Celebration, Family Weekend, and Strawberry Festival. **Sports:** There are 6 intercollegiate sports for women. Facilities include a fitness center and tennis courts. **Graduates:** From July 1, 2015 to June 30, 2016, 241 bachelor's degrees were awarded. The most popular majors were nursing (67%), psychology (9%), and commercial arts (4%). 27 companies recruited on campus in 2015-2016. In an average class, 50% graduate in 4 years or less, 51% graduate in 5 years or less, and 52% graduate in 6 years or less. Of the 2015 graduating class, 20% were enrolled in graduate school within 6 months of graduation, and 60% were employed.

SERVICES: Counseling and information services are available, as is tutoring in some subjects. There is remedial math, reading, and writing. Individual counseling and educational workshops about self-development and personal concerns are available, as are self-help materials. **Library/Resources:** The library contains 224,000 volumes, 277 microform items, 5,700 audio/video tapes/CDs/DVDs, and subscribes to 1,432 periodicals including electronic. Computerized library services include interlibrary loans, database searching, and Internet access. Special learning facilities include an art gallery, and a learning center for nursing. **Physically Challenged Students:** 50% of the campus is accessible. Facilities include wheelchair ramps, elevators, special parking, specially equipped restrooms, and special class scheduling. **Special:** CNR provides cooperative programs in all disciplines, work-study programs, dual majors, as well as interdisciplinary studies, an accelerated degree program in nursing. A Washington semester, internships, study abroad in 9 countries, non-degree study, pass/fail options, student-designed majors, and a general studies degree. There is 1 national honor society and a freshman honors program. **Visiting:** There are regularly scheduled orientations for prospective students, including several open houses providing information on admission. There are guides for informal visits, visitors may sit in on classes, and stay overnight. To schedule a visit, contact the Office of Admissions. **Campus Safety and Security:** Measures include 24-hour foot and vehicle patrol, self-defense education, and security escort services. There are shuttle buses, emergency telephones, lighted pathways/sidewalks, card access to dorms, and surveillance cameras.

REQUIREMENTS: The SAT is required, in addition to graduation from an accredited secondary school. The GED is accepted. Applicants must have completed 15 academic credits, with 4 in English, 3 each in math, science, and social studies, and 2 in a foreign language. A portfolio is required for art majors. An essay and interview are recommended. AP and CLEP credits are accepted. Important factors in the admissions decision are advanced placement or honors courses, recommendations by school officials, and leadership record. Students must complete 120 credit hours, 60 to 90 in liberal arts courses, depending on the major, meet specific course distribution requirements, and maintain a minimum GPA of 2.0 to graduate. 4 phys ed courses are also required. **Procedure:** Freshmen are admitted to all sessions. Entrance exams should be taken in the junior year or fall of the senior year. There are early decision, early admissions, deferred admissions, and rolling admissions plans. Early decision applications should be filed by November 1; regular applications, by August 31 for fall entry; and January 10 for spring entry. The fall 2016 application fee was $20. Notification of early decision is sent December 15; regular decision, on a rolling basis. **Transfer Students:** 68 transfer students enrolled in 2015-2016. Transfer students must submit a transcript from their previous college showing courses completed and a minimum GPA of 2.0. High school records and SAT scores are required. An interview is recommended. 30 of 120 credits required for the bachelor's degree must be completed at CNR. **International Students:** They must take the TOEFL, or the ESL Language Test. They must also take the SAT or ACT.

Admissions Contact: Stephanie Decker, Director of Admission. Email: *sdecker@cnr.edu* Web: *www.cnr.edu*

FINANCIAL AID: The CCS/Profile, FAFSA, FFS, or SFS, the college's own financial statement, and income documentation are required. The deadline for filing freshman financial aid applications for fall entry is February 1.

THE COLLEGE OF SAINT ROSE — D-3

www.strose.edu

Albany, NY 12203	(518) 454-5154 (800) 637-8556
Fax: (518) 454-2013	Email: admit@strose.edu
Full-time: 833 men, 1677 women	**Faculty:** 193
Part-time: 31 men, 61 women	**Ph.D.s:** 93%
Graduate: 415 men, 1194 women	**Student/Faculty:** 14 to 1
Year: semesters, summer session	**Tuition:** $30,692
Room & Board: $12,356	**Freshman Class:** 6788 applied, 5658 accepted, 641 enrolled
SAT CR/M: 520/510 **ACT:** 24	**CEEB CODE:** 2091
Application Deadline: February 1	**COMPETITIVE**

The College of Saint Rose offers students the benefits of an urban environment as well as a close-knit campus community. Saint Rose offers 43 Undergraduate Degree Programs, 6 Post-Secondary Certificate Programs, 25 Master Degree Programs, 19 Certificate of Advanced Study and, 11 dual-degree programs through its four schools: School of Arts & Humanities, School of Business, School of Education, and School of Mathematics and Sciences. Saint Rose is distinguished by its rigorous academics taught in a highly personal learning environment in state-of-the-art facilities. There are 4 undergraduate schools and 4 graduate schools. In addition to regional accreditation, College of Saint Rose has baccalaureate program accreditation with ACBSP, CSWE, NASAD, NASM, NCATE, NASP, and ASHA. The 49-acre campus is in an urban area in the Capital Region of New York state. Including any residence halls, there are 90 buildings.

STUDENT LIFE: 85% of undergraduates are from New York. Others are from 31 states, 32 foreign countries, and Canada. 7% are Hispanic; 6% two or more races; 58% White; 5% Foreign; 2% Asian American; 12% African American; 10% race unknown. **Female To Male Ratio:** 2.3:1. The average age of freshmen is 18; all undergraduates, 20. 23% do not continue beyond their first year; 60% remain to graduate. **Housing:** 1364 students can be accommodated in college housing, which includes single-sex and coed dorms and on-campus apartments. and apartments for single students. On-campus housing is guaranteed for all 4 years, and is available on a first-come, first-served basis, and is available on a lottery system for upperclassmen. 50% of students commute. Upperclassmen may keep cars.

FACULTY/CLASSROOMS: 49% of faculty are male; 51% are female. All teach undergraduates, and do research. No introductory courses are taught by graduate students. The average class size in an introductory lecture is 19; in a laboratory is 18; and in a regular course is 13.

PROGRAMS OF STUDY: College of Saint Rose confers B.A., B.S. and B.F.A. degrees. Master's degrees are also awarded. Bachelor's degrees are awarded in BIOLOGICAL SCIENCE (biochemistry, biology/adolescence education, biology/biological science, forensic psychology, and forensic science), BUSINESS (accounting and business administration and management), COMMUNICATIONS AND THE ARTS (communications, English, graphic design, information technology, music, music industry, and studio art), COMPUTER AND PHYSICAL SCIENCE (chemistry, computer science, and mathematics), EDUCATION (early childhood education, English education, mathematics education, music education, science education, social studies secondary school education, and special education), HEALTH PROFESSIONS (cytotechnology and medical technology), SOCIAL SCIENCE (communication sciences & disorders, criminal justice, history, interdisciplinary studies, law, political science/government, psychology, and social work). Communication sciences & disorders, art, and music are the strongest academically. Business administration, communications, and special education/childhood education have the largest enrollments.

ACTIVITIES: There are no fraternities or sororities. There are 40 groups on campus, including Habitat for Humanity, geology club, student events board, adventure club, band, cheerleading, chorale, dance, debate, drama, environmental, ethnic, international, jazz band, LGBT, literary magazine, musical theater, newspaper, orchestra, pep band, political, professional, radio and TV, religious, social, social service, student government, symphony, and yearbook. Popular campus events include Harvest Fest, Rose Rock Music Festival, Midnight Madnes and Dodgeball Madness. **Sports:** There are 9 intercollegiate sports for men and 10 for women, and 6 intramural sports for men and 6 for women. Facilities include basketball courts, volleyball courts, indoor pool, and fitness center, synthetic turf field lined for men's lacrosse and soccer, baseball field, softball field, and practice field. **Graduates:** From July 1, 2015 to June 30, 2016, 560 bachelor's degrees were awarded. The most popular majors were business administration (12%), communications (8%), and communication sciences & disorders (8%). 61 companies recruited on campus in 2015-2016. In an average class, 49% graduate in 4 years or less, 58% graduate in 5 years or less, and 60% graduate in 6 years or less. Of the 2015 graduating class, 21% were enrolled in graduate school within 6 months of graduation, and 79% were employed.

SERVICES: Counseling and information services are available, as is tutoring in most subjects. There is a reader service for the blind, and remedial math, reading, and writing. There is also a full-time director of disabled student services. **Library/Resources:** The 2 libraries contain 205,426 volumes, 31,339 microform items, and 5,567 audio/video tapes/CDs/DVDs, and subscribe to 46,301 periodicals including electronic. Computerized library services include interlibrary loans, database searching, Internet access, and Wi-Fi capability. Special learning facilities include an art gallery, radio station, TV station, Internship office, entrepreneurship center, TV & radio studios, music recording studio, performance venue, music/video editing computer labs, recital hall, rehearsal rooms, and labs for geology, biology, chemistry, computer science and neuro-psychology. **Physically Challenged Students:** 71% of the campus is accessible. Facilities include wheelchair ramps, elevators, special parking, specially equipped restrooms, lowered drinking fountains, lowered telephones, and special housing. **Special:** The College of Saint Rose offers cross-registration with several local colleges, internships, work-study programs, study abroad in several countries, dual and student-designed majors, non-degree study, and pass/fail options. There are 3-2 engineering degree programs with Rensselaer Polytechnic University, as well as a 6-year law program with Albany Law School, Pace University Law School, and Western New England School of Law. There are 15 national honor societies. **Visiting:** There are regularly scheduled orientations for prospective students, visits vary by month, day and time. There are guides for informal visits and visitors may sit in on classes. To schedule a visit, contact the Undergraduate Admissions office. **Campus Safety and Security:** Measures include 24-hour foot and vehicle patrol, emergency notification system, and security escort services. There are shuttle buses, emergency telephones, lighted pathways/sidewalks, and controlled access to dorms/residences.

REQUIREMENTS: Applicants must be graduates of an accredited secondary school or have a GED certificate. They should have completed college preparatory programs including 4 years of English and history, 3 years of math, and science, as well as 2 years of foreign language. All students must submit a letter of recommendation and a high school transcript. Supporting materials such as an essay, personal statement, resume and SAT/ACT scores are recommended but not required. Art students must submit portfolios, and music students must audition. AP and CLEP credits are accepted. Important factors in the admissions decision are advanced placement or honors courses, extracurricular activities record, and leadership record. To graduate, students must complete 122 credits with a minimum GPA of 2.0 overall and in the major. These requirements are higher for certain majors. At least 32 of the required 122 credits must be completed in residence. 41 credits of Liberal Education required. **Procedure:** Freshmen are admitted fall and spring. Entrance exams should be taken during junior year or the fall of senior year. There are early admissions, deferred admissions, and rolling admissions plans. Early decision applications should be filed by December 1; regular applications, by February 1 for fall entry; and December 1 for spring entry. Notification is sent on a rolling basis. Application fees are waived if application is completed online. **Transfer Students:** 249 transfer students enrolled in 2015-2016. Applicants must submit official transcripts from all colleges attended, a letter of recommendation, and a personal statement. Art majors must submit a portfolio, and music majors must audition. The minimum overall college GPA is 2.5. Students may transfer 70 credits from a two-year college and 90 credits from a four-year college. 32 of 122 credits required for the bachelor's degree must be completed at College of Saint Rose. **International Students:** There are 51 international students enrolled. The school actively recruits these students. They must take the TOEFL with a minimum score of 550 on the paper-based TOEFL (PBT) or 80 on the Internet-based version (iBT), IELTS (min. 5.5) or PTE (min. 56) also accepted. They must also take the SAT or ACT. The Test can be optional if students have alternate English proficiency (IB, A-levels, for example).

ADMISSIONS: 83% of the 2016-2017 applicants were accepted. The SAT scores for the 2016-2017 freshman class were: Critical Reading-- 38% below 500, 43% between 500 and 599, 17% between 600 and 699, and 2% between 700 and 800. Math-- 42% below 500, 42% between 500 and 599, 14% between 600 and 699, and 2% between 700 and 800. The ACT scores were 7% between 12 and 17, 44% between 18 and 23, 38% between 24 and 29, and 11% above 30. 23% of the current freshmen were in the top fifth of their class; 55% were in the top two fifths. 3 freshmen graduated first in their class. **Admissions Contact:** Kathleen Lesko, Assistant VP of Undergraduate Admissions. Email: *admit@strose.edu* Web: *www.strose.edu*

FINANCIAL AID: In 2016-2017, 99% of all full-time freshmen and 99% of continuing full-time students received some form of financial aid. 81% of all full-time freshmen and 80% of continuing full-time students received need-based aid. The average freshman award was $27,668. Need-based scholarships or need-based grants averaged $9,817; need-based self-help aid (loans and jobs) averaged $6,219; non-need-based athletic scholarships averaged $10,888; and other non-need-based awards and non-need-based scholarships averaged $19,137. 67% of undergraduate students work part-time. Average annual earnings from campus work are $2867. The average financial indebtedness of the 2016 graduate was $36,432. College of Saint Rose is a member of CSS. The priority date for freshman financial aid applications for fall entry is December 1. The filing deadline for fall entry is April 1.

TOURO COLLEGE — D-5

www.touro.edu

New York, NY 10018 — (212) 463-0400

Email: registrarinfo@touro.edu

Full-time: 1575 men, 3389 women	**Faculty:** 456
Part-time: 346 men, 726 women	**Ph.D.s:** n/av
Graduate: 1292 men, 3370 women	**Student/Faculty:** 12 to 1
Year: semesters, summer session	**Tuition:** $16,980
Room & Board: $11,970	**Freshman Class:** 2201 applied, 751 accepted, 381 enrolled
SAT CR/M/W: 555/540/535 **ACT:** recommended	**CEEB CODE:** 2902
Application Deadline: April 15	**VERY COMPETITIVE**

Touro College, founded in 1971, is a private institution offering undergraduate programs primarily through the Lander College of Arts and Sciences, the School of General Studies, and the School of Health Sciences. Campuses are in midtown Manhattan, Brooklyn, and Queens. There are 6 undergraduate schools and 8 graduate schools. In addition to regional accreditation, Touro has baccalaureate program accreditation with APTA, CAHEA, TEAC, AOTA, and ASHA. The campus is in an urban area 7th Avenue, New York, N.Y. Including any residence halls, there are 12 buildings.

STUDENT LIFE: 88% of undergraduates are from New York. Others are from 25 states, 30 foreign countries, and Canada. **Female To Male Ratio:** 2.3:1. The average age of freshmen is 20; all undergraduates, 25. 27% do not continue beyond their first year; 47% remain to graduate. **Housing:** 200 students can be accommodated in college housing, which includes single-sex on-campus apartments and off-campus apartments. men's dorm, and women's dorm. On-campus housing is available on a first-come and first-served basis. Priority is given to out-of-town students. All students may keep cars. Alcohol is not permitted.

FACULTY/CLASSROOMS: 49% of faculty are male; 51% are female. No introductory courses are taught by graduate students. The average class size in an introductory lecture is 16; in a laboratory is 12; and in a regular course is 15.

PROGRAMS OF STUDY: Touro confers B.A., B.S., B.S.N., and B.P.S. degrees. Associate, master's, and doctoral degrees are also awarded. Bachelor's degrees are awarded in BIOLOGICAL SCIENCE (biology/biological science), BUSINESS (accounting, banking and finance, business administration and management, management science, and marketing/retailing/merchandising), COMMUNICATIONS AND THE ARTS (English, Hebrew, literature, and speech/debate/rhetoric), COMPUTER AND PHYSICAL SCIENCE (chemistry, computer science, mathematics, and physics), EDUCATION (elementary education and special education), HEALTH PROFESSIONS (nursing, occupational therapy, physical therapy, predentistry, and premedicine), SOCIAL SCIENCE (economics, history, human services, interdisciplinary studies, Judaic studies, liberal arts/general studies, philosophy, political science/government, prelaw, psychology, social science, and sociology). Business/accounting, education, and health sciences are the strongest academically. Psychology, education, and business have the largest enrollments.

ACTIVITIES: There are no fraternities or sororities. There are 8 groups on campus, including dance, literary magazine, newspaper, political, religious, and student government. Popular campus events include student-sponsored lecture series, and student-faculty social events. **Sports:** There is no sports program at Touro. Facilities include baseball field, tennis courts, and basketball courts. **Graduates:** From July 1, 2015 to June 30, 2016, 1443 bachelor's degrees were awarded. The most popular majors were interdisciplinary studies and psychology (23%), health professions and related programs (17%), and business/marketing (14%). 32 companies recruited on campus in 2015-2016. In an average class, 55% graduate in 6 years or less.

SERVICES: Counseling and information services are available, as is tutoring in some subjects, such as accounting, math, English, and natural sciences. There is also remedial math, reading, and writing. **Library/Resources:** The 11 libraries contain 271,509 volumes, 14,100 microform items, and 4,054 audio/video tapes/CDs/DVDs, and subscribe to 3,163 periodicals including electronic. Computerized library services include interlibrary loans, database searching, Internet access, and Wi-Fi capability. **Physically Challenged Students:** All of the campus is accessible. Facilities include wheelchair ramps, elevators, specially equipped restrooms, lowered drinking fountains, and lowered telephones. **Special:** The college offers cross-registration with the Fashion Institute of Technology, internships for juniors and seniors, study abroad in Israel, work-study programs, interdisciplinary majors, an accelerated degree program, credit for life, military, and work experience, pass/fail options, and dual majors. Early and/or preferential admission to professional programs is also possible. There are 2 national honor societies, a freshman honors program, and 5 departmental honors programs. **Visiting:** There are guides for informal visits, visitors may sit in on classes, and stay overnight. **Campus Safety and Security:** Measures include 24-hour foot and vehicle patrol and emergency notification system. There are shuttle buses, lighted pathways/sidewalks, and controlled access to dorms/residences.

REQUIREMENTS: Applicants must be graduates of an accredited secondary school with a satisfactory average. High school diploma is required or a GED is accepted. A satisfactory SAT score is recommended. 16 required academic units includes 4 in English, 2 units each in math, science, foreign language, and history, and 4 units in academic electives. A GPA of 3.0 is required. AP and CLEP credits are accepted. Important factors in the admissions decision are advanced placement or honors courses, as well as recommendations from school officials, leadership record, parents or siblings attended the school, evidence of special talent, personality/intangible qualities, extracurricular activities record, and recommendations by alumni. To graduate, all students must complete at least 120 credit hours (varies by major), with 30 to 70 in the major; 45 of the 120 credits must be from Touro and 1/2 of the student's major has to be completed with Touro. A minimum 2.0 GPA is required, with 2.3 in the major. Specific disciplines include Judaic studies or ethnic studies. Required courses include English composition, history, literature, math, and social and natural sciences. **Procedure:** Freshmen are admitted fall, spring, and summer. Entrance exams should be taken in May of the junior year or fall of the senior year. There are early admissions, deferred admissions, and rolling admissions plans. Applications should be filed by April 15 for fall entry; December 15 for spring entry; and June 1 for summer entry, along with a $50 fee. Notification of early decision is sent December 1; regular decision, on a rolling basis. Applications are accepted online. **Transfer Students:** 900 transfer students enrolled in 2015-2016. A 2.5 GPA is required. If the student has less than 60 credits, high school documentation is also required. Transfer students may enroll in the fall, spring, and summer. 45 of 120 credits required for the bachelor's degree must be completed at Touro. **International Students:** There are 159 international students enrolled. They must take the TOEFL with a minimum score of 550 on the paper-based TOEFL (PBT) or 83 on the Internet-based version (iBT) and the college's own test, or take the IELTS. They must also take the SAT or ACT, and the college's own entrance exam, as well as in-house math and English proficiency examinations.

ADMISSIONS: 34% of the 2016-2017 applicants were accepted. The SAT scores for the 2016-2017 freshman class were: Critical Reading-- 40% below 500, 28% between 500 and 599, 20% between 600 and 699, and 12% between 700 and 800. Math-- 46% below 500, 26% between 500 and 599, 19% between 600 and 699, and 8% between 700 and 800. Writing-- 50% below 500, 29% between 500 and 599, 16% between 600 and 699, and 5% between 700 and 800. **Admissions Contact:** Admissions Director. Email: *registrarinfo@touro.edu* Web: *www.touro.edu*

FINANCIAL AID: In 2016-2017, 95% of all full-time freshmen and 93% of continuing full-time students received some form of financial aid. 95% of all full-time freshmen and 93% of continuing full-time students received need-based aid. The average freshman award was $9,788. Need-based scholarships or need-based grants averaged $3,885; need-based self-help aid (loans and jobs) averaged $2,064; other non-need-based awards and non-need-based scholarships averaged $3,369; and $3,439 from other forms of aid. The average financial indebtedness of the 2016 graduate was $17,000. The CSS/Profile is required. The FAFSA code is 010142. The priority date for freshman financial aid applications for fall entry is May 15. The filing deadline for fall entry is August 15.

UNION COLLEGE — C-3

www.union.edu

Schenectady, NY 12308 — **(518) 388-6112**

Fax: (518) 388-6986	**Email: admissions@union.edu**
Full-time: 1198 men, 1028 women	**Faculty:** IIB, ++$
Part-time: 6 men	**Ph.D.s:** 98%
Graduate: n/av	**Student/Faculty:** 10 to 1
Year: trimesters	**Tuition:** $50,013
Room & Board: $12,261	**Freshman Class:** 5996 applied, 2297 accepted, 568 enrolled
	CEEB CODE: 2920
Application Deadline: January 15	**MOST COMPETITIVE**

Union College, founded in 1795, is an independent liberal arts and engineering college. There is 1 undergraduate school. In addition to regional accreditation, Union has baccalaureate program accreditation with ABET. The 100-acre campus is in a small town 15 miles west of Albany. Including any residence halls, there are 100 buildings.

STUDENT LIFE: 66% of undergraduates are from out of state, mostly the Northeast. Students are from 40 states, 35 foreign countries, and Canada. 68% are from public schools. 73% are White; 7% Hispanic; 7% Foreign; 6% Asian American; 4% African American; 2% two or more races. **Male To Female Ratio:** 1.2:1. The average age of freshmen is 19; all undergraduates, 20. 7% do not continue beyond their first year; 93% remain to graduate. **Housing:** 1978 students can be accommodated in college housing, which includes single-sex, coed dorms, on-campus apartments, language houses, special-interest houses, fraternity houses, sorority houses, and Minerva Houses: up to 45 students live in each of seven distinct houses. On-campus housing is available on a lottery system for upperclassmen. 89% of students live on campus. Upperclassmen may keep cars.

FACULTY/CLASSROOMS: No introductory courses are taught by graduate students.

PROGRAMS OF STUDY: Union confers B.A., and B.S degrees. Bachelor's degrees are awarded in AGRICULTURE (environmental studies), BIOLOGICAL SCIENCE (biochemistry, biology/biological science, and neurosciences), COMMUNICATIONS AND THE ARTS (classics, English, fine arts, modern language, and studio art), COMPUTER AND PHYSICAL SCIENCE (astronomy, chemistry, computer science, geology, mathematics, physics, and science), ENGINEERING AND ENVIRONMENTAL DESIGN (bioengineering, computer engineering, electrical/electronics engineering, environmental science, and mechanical engineering), SOCIAL SCIENCE (American studies, anthropology, Asian/Oriental studies, Caribbean studies, economics, French studies, German area studies, history, humanities, interdisciplinary studies, liberal arts/general studies, philosophy, political science/government, psychology, religion, social science, sociology, Spanish studies, and women's studies). Chemistry, geology, and classics are the strongest academically. Economics, mechanical engineering, psychology, biology, and neuroscience have the largest enrollments.

ACTIVITIES: 37% of men belong to 13 national fraternities; 42% of women belong to 1 local and 6 national sororities. There are 101 groups on campus, including art, band, cheerleading, chess, choir, computers, dance, debate, drama, environmental, ethnic, honors, international, jazz band, LGBT, literary magazine, newspaper, orchestra, pep band, photography, political, professional, radio and TV, religious, social, social service, and student government. Popular campus events include Spring Fest, Lectures, and Concerts. **Sports:** Facilities include a field house for volleyball, recreational basketball, indoor track, intramural activities, grass fields for soccer, football, field hockey, lacrosse, intramurals, and recreation, basketball/volleyball facility, ice rink, gym, weight room, fitness center, racquetball/squash courts, aerobics room, swimming pool, outdoor tennis courts, outdoor basketball/street hockey court, and boathouse and docks. **Graduates:** From July 1, 2015 to June 30, 2016, 511 bachelor's degrees were awarded. The most popular majors were economics (14%), political science (10%), and psychology (7%). 136 companies recruited on campus in 2015-2016. In an average class, 82% graduate in 4 years or less, 87% graduate in 5 years or less, and 88% graduate in 6 years or less. Of the 2015 graduating class, 21% were enrolled in graduate school within 6 months of graduation, and 66% were employed.

SERVICES: Counseling and information services are available, as is

tutoring in most subjects. A writing center, and a language center are available. **Library/Resources:** The library contains 621,811 volumes, 831,558 microform items, 15,388 audio/video tapes/CDs/DVDs. Computerized library services include interlibrary loans, database searching, Internet access, and Wi-Fi capability. Special learning facilities include a radio station, a theater, high-tech classroom, lab center, multimedia auditorium, music center, and an art, science, and history gallery. **Physically Challenged Students:** 80% of the campus is accessible. Facilities include wheelchair ramps, elevators, special parking, specially equipped restrooms, special class scheduling, lowered drinking fountains, lowered telephones, and special housing. **Special:** Cross-registration is permitted with the Hudson Mohawk Consortium. Opportunities are provided for legislative internships in Albany and Washington, D.C., pass/fail options, B.A.-B.S. degrees, dual and student-designed majors, accelerated degree programs in law and medicine, and study abroad in 38 countries. There are 15 national honor societies, Phi Beta Kappa, a freshman honors program, and 19 departmental honors programs. **Visiting:** There are regularly scheduled orientations for prospective students, including interviews and a tour of the campus. There are guides for informal visits and visitors may sit in on classes. To schedule a visit, contact the Admissions Office. **Campus Safety and Security:** Measures include 24-hour foot and vehicle patrol, emergency notification system, self-defense education, and security escort services. There are shuttle buses, emergency telephones, lighted pathways/sidewalks, controlled access to dorms/residences, 24-hour locked residence halls, emergency medical assistance, awareness programs, a bicycle patrol, a trolley escort service, a shuttle van, and a security measures sheet.

REQUIREMENTS: Testing is optional except for combined programs. Leadership in Medicine program applicants must submit the SAT I and SAT II or the ACT; Law and Public Policy program applicants must submit the SAT I or the ACT. Applicants to these programs must complete the necessary tests no later than December of the senior year. International students are required to submit the SAT or the ACT, and the TOEFL or IELTS if English is not the first language. Applicants must submit a minimum of 16 full-year credits, distributed as follows: 4 years of English, 2 of a foreign language, 2 1/2 to 3 1/2 years of math, 2 years each of science and social studies, and the remainder in college-preparatory courses. Engineering and math majors are expected to have completed additional math and science courses beyond the minimum requirements. An essay is also required and an interview is recommended. AP credits are accepted. Important factors in the admissions decision are advanced placement or honors courses, extracurricular activities record, and recommendations by school officials. Students must complete a minimum of 36 term courses (engineering may require up to 40), requirements in the major field, degree program, or interdepartmental major, including the major field examination and/or thesis, as applicable, and attain a minimum GPA of 1.8 and 2.0 in the major (2.0 in the minor if a minor has been declared). **Procedure:** Freshmen are admitted fall, winter, and spring. Entrance exams should be taken by January of the senior year. There are early decision, early admissions, and deferred admissions plans. Early decision applications should be filed by November 15; regular applications, by January 15 for fall entry. Notification of early decision is sent December 15; regular decision, April 1. 239 early decision candidates were accepted for the 2016-2017 class. Applications are accepted on-line. **Transfer Students:** 22 transfer students enrolled in 2015-2016. A 3.0 GPA and 1 full year of college academic work is recommended. Transfer students must study at Union for at least 2 years. 18 of 36 credits required for the bachelor's degree must be completed at Union. **International Students:** There are 163 international students enrolled. The school actively recruits these students. They must take the TOEFL. Testing is optional except for combined programs. International students are required to submit the SAT or ACT.

ADMISSIONS: 38% of the 2016-2017 applicants were accepted. The SAT scores for the 2016-2017 freshman class were: Critical Reading-- 4% below 500, 25% between 500 and 599, 55% between 600 and 699, and 16% between 700 and 800. Math-- 1% below 500, 12% between 500 and 599, 53% between 600 and 699, and 34% between 700 and 800. Writing-- 4% below 500, 21% between 500 and 599, 58% between 600 and 699, and 17% between 700 and 800. **Admissions Contact:** Ann Fleming Brown, Director of Admissions. Email: brown@union.edu Web: *www.union.edu*

FINANCIAL AID: 75% of all full-time freshmen and 77% of continuing full-time students received need-based aid. Average annual earnings from campus work are $1147. Union is a member of CSS. The CSS/Profile and the state aid form, and noncustodial profile are required. The deadline for filing freshman financial aid applications for fall entry is February 1.

UNITED STATES MERCHANT MARINE ACADEMY D-5

www.usmma.edu

Kings Point, NY 11024	**(516) 726-5646** **(866) 546-4778**
Fax: (516) 773-5390	**Email: admissions@usmma.edu**
Full-time: 851 men, 136 women	**Faculty:** 120
Part-time: n/av	**Ph.D.s:** 34%
Graduate: 23 men, 2 women	**Student/Faculty:** 11 to 1
Year: trimesters	**Tuition:** see profile
Room & Board: see profile	**Freshman Class:** 2252 applied, 354 accepted, 237 enrolled
SAT CR/M: 614/643 **ACT:** required	**CEEB CODE:** 2923
Application Deadline: March 1	**HIGHLY COMPETITIVE**

United States Merchant Marine Academy, founded in 1943, is a publicly supported institution offering maritime, military, and engineering programs for the purpose of training officers for the U.S. merchant marine, the maritime industry, and the armed forces. Students make no conventional tuition and room/board payments. Required fees for freshmen are approximately $7,020; costs in subsequent years are less. There is 1 undergraduate school. In addition to regional accreditation, Kings Point has baccalaureate program accreditation with ABET. The 82-acre campus is in a suburban area 19 miles east of midtown New York City. Including any residence halls, there are 28 buildings.

STUDENT LIFE: 88% of undergraduates are from out of state, mostly the Middle Atlantic. Students are from 50 states, and 2 foreign countries. 77% are from public schools. 84% are White; 6% Hispanic; 4% Asian American; 2% African American; 2% Foreign. 48% are Catholic; 42% Protestant. **Male To Female Ratio:** 6.3:1. The average age of freshmen is 19; all undergraduates, 21. 8% do not continue beyond their first year; 92% remain to graduate. **Housing:** 930 students can be accommodated in college housing, which includes coed dorms. On-campus housing is guaranteed for all 4 years. Upperclassmen may keep cars. Alcohol is not permitted.

FACULTY/CLASSROOMS: 87% of faculty are male; 13% are female. All teach undergraduates, 25% do research, and 25% do both. No introductory courses are taught by graduate students. The average class size in an introductory lecture is 28; in a laboratory is 16; and in a regular course is 28.

PROGRAMS OF STUDY: Kings Point confers B.S. degrees. Master's degrees are also awarded. Bachelor's degrees are awarded in ENGINEERING AND ENVIRONMENTAL DESIGN (marine engineering, marine engineering/shipyard management, marine engineering systems, marine transportation, and maritime logistics & security). Marine engineering systems is the strongest academically. Logistics & intermodal transportation, marine engineering systems, and marine engineering have the largest enrollments.

ACTIVITIES: There are no fraternities or sororities. There are 51 groups on campus, including band, choir, chorus, communications, computers, dance, debate, drill team, drum and bugle corps, ethnic, marching band, newspaper, pep band, photography, professional, religious, and student government. Popular campus events include Regimental Thanksgiving and Holiday Dinners, Battle Standard Dinner, Lanier Lecture Dinners, Ring Dance, Festival of Lights, Holiday Dance, Valentines Dance, and Midshipman Appreciation Day. **Sports:** There are 14 intercollegiate sports for men and 9 for women, and 10 intramural sports for men and 10 for women. Facilities include a gymnasium with a swimming pool, basketball and racquetball courts, and outdoor track and football field. **Graduates:** From July 1, 2015 to June 30, 2016, 201 bachelor's degrees were awarded. The most popular majors were marine engineering (23%), marine transportation (22%), and logistics and intermodal transportation (21%). 78 companies recruited on campus in 2015-2016. In an average class, 77% graduate in 4 years or less and 83% graduate in 5 years or less. Of the 2015 graduating class, 100% were employed within 6 months of graduation.

SERVICES: Counseling and information services are available, as is tutoring in most subjects. **Library/Resources:** The library contains

209,217 volumes, 21,306 microform items, and 4,750 audio/video tapes/CDs/DVDs, and subscribes to 573 periodicals including electronic. Computerized library services include interlibrary loans, database searching, Internet access, and Wi-Fi capability. Special learning facilities include a planetarium, and Maritime museum. **Physically Challenged Students:** 5% of the campus is accessible. Facilities include wheelchair ramps, elevators, special parking, and specially equipped restrooms. **Special:** The college offers internships in the maritime industry and work-study programs with U.S. shipping companies. **Visiting:** There are guides for informal visits, visitors may sit in on classes, and stay overnight. To schedule a visit, contact the Admissions Office. **Campus Safety and Security:** Measures include 24-hour foot and vehicle patrol. There are lighted pathways/sidewalks.

REQUIREMENTS: The SAT or ACT is required. Candidates for admission to the academy must be nominated by a member of the U.S. Congress. They must be between the ages of 17 and 25, U.S. citizens (except by special arrangement), and in excellent physical condition. Applicants should be graduates of an accredited secondary school or have a GED equivalent. 18 academic credits are required, including 4 in English, 3 in math, 1 credit in physics or chemistry with a lab, and 10 in electives. An essay is required. AP credits are accepted. Important factors in the admissions decision are advanced placement or honors courses, leadership record, and extracurricular activities record. To graduate, students must complete a minimum of 163 credit hours according to the new curriculum with a minimum cumulative and major GPA of 2.0. The required curriculum includes courses in math, science, computer science, English, humanities, history, naval science, phys ed, and ship's medicine. Students must complete one year of sea service on U.S flag merchant ships. All students must pass resident and sea project courses, U.S. Coast Guard licensing exam and all required certificates, and the academy physical fitness test. Students must apply for and accept, if offered, a commission in the U.S. uniformed services. **Procedure:** Freshmen are admitted in the fall. Entrance exams should be taken through January for the SAT and February for ACT. There is a rolling admissions plan. Applications should be filed by March 1 for fall entry. Notifications are sent April 1. 263 applicants were on the 2016 waiting list. Applications are accepted online. **Transfer Students:** Same as for high school students, except college-level applicants must submit college transcripts and have at least a 2.5 cumulative GPA in college level work, and submit two (2) letters of recommendation from college instructors/professors. 172 credits required for the bachelor's degree must be completed at Kings Point. **International Students:** There are 15 international students enrolled. They must take the TOEFL with a minimum score of 540 on the paper-based TOEFL (PBT) or 76 on the Internet-based version (iBT). They must also take the SAT or ACT.

ADMISSIONS: 16% of the 2016-2017 applicants were accepted. The SAT scores for the 2016-2017 freshman class were: Critical Reading-- 4% below 500, 40% between 500 and 599, 45% between 600 and 699, and 11% between 700 and 800. Math-- 15% between 500 and 599, 66% between 600 and 699, and 19% between 700 and 800. The ACT scores were 2% between 12 and 17, 35% between 18 and 23, 35% between 24 and 29, and 28% above 30. 57% of the current freshmen were in the top fifth of their class; 38% were in the top two fifths. There were 13 National Merit finalists. 4 freshmen graduated first in their class. **Admissions Contact:** CPT. Robert E. Johnson, Director of Admissions and Financial Aid. Email: *admissions@usmma.edu* Web: *www.usmma.edu*

FINANCIAL AID: In 2016-2017, 14% of all full-time freshmen and 11% of continuing full-time students received some form of financial aid. 9% of all full-time freshmen and 7% of continuing full-time students received need-based aid. The average freshman award was $4,187. Need-based scholarships or need-based grants averaged $4,071 ($5,550 maximum); need-based self-help aid (loans and jobs) averaged $1,916 ($2,673 maximum); and other non-need-based awards and non-need-based scholarships averaged $3,420 ($5,446 maximum). The deadline for filing freshman financial aid applications for fall entry is May 1.

UNITED STATES MILITARY ACADEMY AT WEST POINT D-4

www.usma.edu

West Point, NY 10996	(845) 938-4041
Fax: (845) 938-8121	Email: admissions@usma.edu
Full-time: 3508 men, 881 women	Faculty: 630
Part-time: n/av	Ph.D.s: 48%
Graduate: n/av	Student/Faculty: 7 to 1
Year: semesters	Tuition: see profile
Room & Board: see profile	Freshman Class: 14829 applied, 1533 accepted, 1260 enrolled
SAT CR/M/W: 629/654/616 ACT: 28	CEEB CODE: 2924
Application Deadline: February 28	HIGHLY COMPETITIVE+

The United States Military Academy at West Point, founded in 1802, is specifically charge with educating, training, and inspiring young men and women for service as commissioned officers in the United States Army. West Point is an internationally recognized institution for academic, military and physical excellence. Career development starts on the first day; everything cadets' experience is focused on developing them as leaders committed to the values of Duty, Honor, and Country. The cadets who graduate as commissioned officers and serve the nation are our lasting legacy and are what makes West Point great. There is no tuition cost at West Point. There is 1 undergraduate school. In addition to regional accreditation, West Point has baccalaureate program accreditation with ABET and MSCHE. The 16,080-acre campus is in a small town along the lovely Hudson River, and is approximately 50 miles north of New York City. Including any residence halls, there are 906 buildings.

STUDENT LIFE: 94% of undergraduates are from out of state, mostly the Northeast. Students are from 50 states, and 33 foreign countries. 81% are from public schools. 64% are White; 12% Hispanic; 11% African American; 6% Asian American; 4% two or more races; 1% American Indian/Alaska Native; 1% Foreign; 1% race unknown. 51% are Protestant; 35% Catholic. **Male To Female Ratio:** 4.0:1. The average age of freshmen is 18; all undergraduates, 20. 8% do not continue beyond their first year; 93% remain to graduate. **Housing:** 4500 students can be accommodated in college housing, which includes coed all cadets live in cadet barracks. On-campus housing is guaranteed for all 4 years. 100% of students live on campus; of those, 20% remain on campus on weekends. Upperclassmen may keep cars.

FACULTY/CLASSROOMS: 83% of faculty are male; 17% are female. All teach undergraduates, and 40% do research. No introductory courses are taught by graduate students. The average class size in an introductory lecture is 15; in a laboratory is 15; and in a regular course is 15.

PROGRAMS OF STUDY: West Point confers B.S. degrees. Bachelor's degrees are awarded in AGRICULTURE (environmental studies), BIOLOGICAL SCIENCE (life science), BUSINESS (management science, operations research, and organizational behavior), COMMUNICATIONS AND THE ARTS (English, foreign language, and literature), COMPUTER AND PHYSICAL SCIENCE (chemistry, computer science, mathematics, and physics), ENGINEERING AND ENVIRONMENTAL DESIGN (civil engineering, electrical/electronics engineering, engineering management, engineering physics, environmental engineering, environmental science, mechanical engineering, military science, nuclear engineering, and systems engineering), HEALTH PROFESSIONS (kinesiology), SOCIAL SCIENCE (economics, geography, history, humanities, international studies, legal studies, philosophy, political science/government, sociology, and systems science). Engineering is the strongest academically. Engineering, foreign languages, and social sciences have the largest enrollments.

ACTIVITIES: There are no fraternities or sororities. There are 86 groups on campus, including art, bagpipe, band, cheerleading, chess, choir, chorus, debate, drama, drill team, drum and bugle corps, environmental, ethnic, film, honors, international, jazz band, LGBT, literary magazine, marching band, opera, pep band, photography, professional, radio and TV, religious, social, social service, student government, and yearbook. Popular campus events include Ring Weekend, 100th Night for Seniors, 500th Night for Juniors, Yearling Winter Weekend for Sophomores, and Branch Week. **Sports:** There are 16 intercollegiate sports for men and 11 for women, and 11 intramural sports for men and 11 for women.

Facilities include the Army football team, arena for basketball, rink for hockey competitions, gymnasiums, swimming pools and special purpose rooms for squash, handball, racquetball, rock climbing, wrestling and weight training. There is also a varsity indoor track, volleyball court, baseball and softball fields, indoor practice facility. **Graduates:** From July 1, 2015 to June 30, 2016, 991 bachelor's degrees were awarded. The most popular majors were engineering (27%), social sciences (19%), and foreign languages (7%). In an average class, 82% graduate in 4 years or less, 85% graduate in 5 years or less, and 85% graduate in 6 years or less. Of the 2015 graduating class, 2% were enrolled in graduate school within 6 months of graduation, and 100% were employed.

SERVICES: There is remedial reading and writing. **Library/Resources:** The library contains 460,632 volumes, 38,818 microform items, 16,104 audio/video tapes/CDs/DVDs, and subscribes to 105,252 periodicals including electronic. Computerized library services include database searching, Internet access, and Wi-Fi capability. Special learning facilities include a radio station, Combating Terrorism Center, Center for Environmental and Geographical Science, Center for Advancement of Leader Development and Organizational Learning, Center for Nation Reconstruction and Capacity Development, Cyber Research Center, Photonics Research Center, Operations Research Center, West Point Simulation Center, Center for Leadership and Diversity in STEM, US Army Space and Missile Defense Command Research and Analysis Center, and Nuclear Science and Engineering Research Center. **Physically Challenged Students:** 30% of the campus is accessible. Facilities include wheelchair ramps, elevators, special parking, and specially equipped restrooms. Disability services are only available for faculty, staff, and visitors at West Point. **Special:** AIADs - During the summers before the junior and senior years, cadets participate in Advanced Individual Academic Development in academic, military, or physical-development programs to enrich their individual development. Cadets may choose from more than 100 academic-enrichment opportunities that normally involve about three weeks of active summer participation and that might include: Operation Crossroads Africa, research work in technical laboratories throughout the United States, immersion language training in foreign countries, study at other civilian and military institutions, and numerous work-fellow positions with federal and Department of Defense agencies. Individual Advanced Study - If a cadet is an exceptional student, he or she may enroll in advanced individual study in many of the disciplines taught at West Point. These programs emphasize independent or tutorial work and are excellent preparation for graduate study. There are 17 national honor societies and 5 departmental honors programs. **Visiting:** There are regularly scheduled orientations for prospective students, candidates are escorted by a cadet, attend class, have lunch with the Corps of Cadets, and talk with cadets about all phases of West Point life. There are guides for informal visits, visitors may sit in on classes, and stay overnight. To schedule a visit, contact General Admission Information and Visits at admission-info@usma.edu. **Campus Safety and Security:** Measures include 24-hour foot and vehicle patrol, emergency notification system, and self-defense education. There are also shuttle buses, lighted pathways/sidewalks, and controlled access to dorms/residences.

REQUIREMENTS: The SAT or ACT is required. The ACT Optional Writing test is also required. Applicants must be qualified academically, physically, and medically. Candidates must be nominated for admission by members of the U.S. Congress or executive sources. West Point recommends that applicants have 4 years each of English and math, 2 years each of foreign language and lab science, such as chemistry and physics, and 1 year of U.S. history. Courses in geography, government, and economics are also suggested. An essay is required, and an interview is recommended. The GED is accepted. Applicants must be 17 to 22 years old, a U.S. citizen at the time of enrollment (except by agreement with another country), unmarried, and not pregnant or legally obligated to support children. AP credits are accepted. Important factors in the admissions decision are leadership record, extracurricular activities record, and recommendations by school officials. To graduate from West Point with a Bachelor of science degree, every First Class cadet must successfully complete the course of instruction in academic, military, and physical education, and successfully complete or validate each course in the core curriculum, including the common core courses and a core engineering sequence equivalent. In addition, they must also satisfy the requirements of at least one major, and successfully complete 40 academic courses of at least 3.0 credit hours each, and achieve a 2.00 Cumulative Quality Point Average (CQPA) in the curses above. (The CQPA is an index of cumulative performance in the academic, military science and physical education courses) also, cadets must successfully complete the Military and Physical Program at West Point, meet the height/weight standards of Army Regulation 600-9, and the physical fitness standards in Army Regulation 350-1. Cadets who are deficient in one or more of the three developmental programs for failure to maintain minimum program performance standards may be considered by the Academic Board for separation. **Procedure:** Freshmen are admitted in the fall. Entrance exams should be taken in the spring of the junior year and not later than the fall of the senior year. Applications should be filed by February 28 for fall entry. Applications are accepted on-line. **Transfer Students:** Students in college or with previous college credit may apply to West Point if they meet the basic requirements. However, those students still enter West Point as plebes (freshmen) and must complete the four-year program. **International Students:** There are 57 international students enrolled. They must take the TOEFL with a minimum score of 580 on the paper-based TOEFL (PBT) or 88 on the Internet-based version (iBT). They must also take the SAT or ACT, scoring SAT Math - 530, ACT Math - 23.

ADMISSIONS: 10% of the 2016-2017 applicants were accepted. The SAT scores for the 2016-2017 freshman class were: Critical Reading-- 3% below 500, 29% between 500 and 599, 49% between 600 and 699, and 19% between 700 and 800. Math-- 1% below 500, 23% between 500 and 599, 49% between 600 and 699, and 27% between 700 and 800. Writing-- 7% below 500, 38% between 500 and 599, 41% between 600 and 699, and 14% between 700 and 800. The ACT scores were 9% between 18 and 23, 49% between 24 and 29, and 42% above 30. 70% of the current freshmen were in the top fifth of their class; 80% were in the top two fifths. There were 115 National Merit finalists. 111 freshmen graduated first in their class. **Admissions Contact:** COL Deborah McDonald, Director of Admissions. Email: *admissions@usma.edu* Web: *www.usma.edu*

FINANCIAL AID: Check with the school for current application deadlines.

UNIVERSITY OF ROCHESTER — B-3

www.rochester.edu

Rochester, NY 14627	(585) 275-3221 (888) 822-2256
Fax: (585) 461-4595	**Email:** admit@admissions.rochester.edu
Full-time: 3133 men, 3043 women	**Faculty:** I, +$
Part-time: 60 men, 154 women	**Ph.D.s:** 94%
Graduate: 2114 men, 2273 women	**Student/Faculty:** 10 to 1
Year: semesters, summer session	**Tuition:** $50,142
Room & Board: $14,890	**Freshman Class:** 16503 applied, 5845 accepted, 1338 enrolled
SAT or ACT: recommended	**CEEB CODE:** 2928
Application Deadline: January 5	**MOST COMPETITIVE**

University of Rochester, founded in 1850, is a private research institution offering programs in the arts and sciences, engineering and applied science, nursing, medicine and dentistry, business administration, music, and education. There are 3 undergraduate schools and 6 graduate schools. In addition to regional accreditation, UR has baccalaureate program accreditation with AACSB, ABET, ACPE, ADA, NASM, NCATE, and NLNAC. The 707-acre campus is in a suburban area 2 miles south of downtown Rochester, NY. Including any residence halls, there are 192 buildings.

STUDENT LIFE: 70% of undergraduates are from out of state, mostly the Middle Atlantic. Students are from 50 states, 100 foreign countries, and Canada. 75% are from public schools. 7% are Hispanic; 7% race unknown; 5% African American; 48% White; 3% two or more races; 18% Foreign; 11% Asian American. 37% claim no religious affiliation; 19% Catholic; 13% Jewish. **Female To Male Ratio:** 1.0:1. The average age of freshmen is 18; all undergraduates, 20. 4% do not continue beyond their first year; 88% remain to graduate. **Housing:** 4112 students can be accommodated in college housing, which includes coed dorms, on-campus apartments, married student housing, language houses, special-interest houses, and fraternity houses. On-campus housing is guaranteed for all 4 years, and available on a lottery system for upperclassmen. 93% of students live on campus; of those, 90% remain on campus on weekends. Upperclassmen may keep cars.

FACULTY/CLASSROOMS: No introductory courses are taught by graduate students. The average class size in an introductory lecture is 75; in a laboratory is 20; and in a regular course is 20.

PROGRAMS OF STUDY: UR confers B.A., B.S., and B.M. degrees. Master's and doctoral degrees are also awarded. Bachelor's degrees are awarded in AGRICULTURE (environmental studies), BIOLOGICAL SCIENCE (biochemistry, biology/biological science, cell biology, ecology, microbiology, molecular biology, and neurosciences), BUSINESS (business administration and management and marketing), COMMUNICATIONS AND THE ARTS (American Sign Language, art history and appreciation, audio technology, classics, comparative literature, digital communications, English, English literature, film arts, French, German, Japanese, jazz, linguistics, media arts, music, music performance, music theory and composition, Russian, Spanish, studio art, and theatre arts), COMPUTER AND PHYSICAL SCIENCE (applied mathematics, astronomy, chemistry, computer science, geology, mathematics, optics, physics, and statistics), EDUCATION (music education), ENGINEERING AND ENVIRONMENTAL DESIGN (biomedical engineering, chemical engineering, electrical/electronics engineering, engineering and applied science, environmental science, geological engineering, mechanical engineering, and optical engineering), HEALTH PROFESSIONS (health, nursing, and public health), SOCIAL SCIENCE (African American studies, American studies, anthropology, archeology, cognitive science, East Asian studies, economics, history, interdisciplinary studies, international relations, Latin American studies, philosophy, political science/government, psychology, religion, Russian and Slavic studies, and women's studies). Biomedical engineering, optics, political science, and music are the strongest academically. Biology, economics, and engineering have the largest enrollments.

ACTIVITIES: 20% of men belong to 18 national fraternities; 20% of women belong to 15 national sororities. There are 279 groups on campus, including art, band, campus activities board, cheerleading, chess, choir, chorale, chorus, communications, computers, dance, debate, drama, drill team, environmental, ethnic, film, forensics, honors, international, jazz band, LGBT, literary magazine, marching band, musical theater, newspaper, opera, orchestra, pep band, photography, political, professional, radio and TV, religious, social, social service, student government, symphony, and yearbook. Popular campus events include Meliora Weekend, Yellowjacket Day, and Boar's Head Dinner. **Sports:** There are 10 intercollegiate sports for men and 11 for women, and 7 intramural sports for men and 7 for women. Facilities include an athletic center, stadium, field house, ice rink, courts for handball, racquetball, squash, and tennis, an indoor track, fitness center and weight room, a jogging path, and an aquatic center. **Graduates:** From July 1, 2015 to June 30, 2016, 1658 bachelor's degrees were awarded. The most popular majors were psychology, economics, and business. 1000 companies recruited on campus in 2015-2016. In an average class, 76% graduate in 4 years or less and 86% graduate in 6 years or less.

SERVICES: Counseling and information services are available, as is tutoring in most subjects. There is access to screen reading and adaptive software. **Library/Resources:** The 4 libraries contain 4.2 million volumes. Computerized library services include interlibrary loans, database searching, Internet access, and Wi-Fi capability. Special learning facilities include an art gallery, radio station, labs for nuclear structure research and laser energetics, a center for visual science, the Strong Memorial Hospital, CEK Mees observatory, Eastman School of Music, Institute of Optics. **Physically Challenged Students:** 90% of the campus is accessible. Facilities include wheelchair ramps, elevators, special parking, specially equipped restrooms, special class scheduling, lowered drinking fountains, lowered telephones, and special housing. **Special:** Cross-registration is offered with Rochester Area Colleges. Selective programs for exceptional undergraduates in medicine (REMS), engineering (GEAR), and education (GRADE) guarantee admission to professional or graduate school upon completion of the bachelor's degree. The Take Five Scholars Program allows students to stay tuition-free for a fifth year of study. Rochester offers 3-2 programs in business, human development, neuroscience, physics and astronomy, and public health. Study abroad is possible in more than 40 countries. Internships, a Washington semester, B.A.-B.S. degrees, accelerated degree programs, dual and student-designed majors, nondegree study, and pass/fail options are available. There are 8 national honor societies, Phi Beta Kappa, a freshman honors program, and 13 departmental honors programs. **Visiting:** There are regularly scheduled orientations for prospective students, group information session, campus tour, and interview (optional for seniors). There are guides for informal visits, visitors may sit in on classes, and stay overnight. To schedule a visit, contact Office of Admissions. **Campus Safety and Security:** Measures include 24-hour foot and vehicle patrol, emergency notification system, self-defense education, and security escort services. There are also shuttle buses, emergency telephones, lighted pathways/sidewalks, and controlled access to dorms/residences.

REQUIREMENTS: The SAT or ACT is recommended. Applicants should be graduates of an accredited secondary school or have a GED equivalent. An essay or personal statement and recommendations are required. An interview is recommended. An audition is required for music majors. Applicants should complete the Common Application, Coalition Application, or the Universal College Application. Admission to the College of Arts, Sciences, and Engineering is based on a holistic review process that includes a "test-flexible" philosophy. As we seek to enroll a diverse and talented class each year, our review procedures incorporate a variety of factors, including many kinds of academic records. In addition to submitting a record of courses and grades during secondary school, applicants must show evidence of preparation through examination results. A wide variety of test results can fulfill this requirement, including SAT Reasoning exams, the ACT, two or more results from SAT Subject exams, Advanced Placement, International Baccalaureate, AS- and A-level exams (in UK and Commonwealth countries), Gao Kao (China), and results from many other national secondary exams. AP credits are accepted. Important factors in the admissions decision are advanced placement or honors courses, personality/intangible qualities, and recommendations by school officials. Students focus on the humanities, social sciences, and natural sciences; one of the three areas will be their major, and they select a 3-course cluster in each of the other two. A total of 128 credit hours with a minimum GPA of 2.0 is required to graduate. Additionally, all students must satisfy a freshman writing requirement and take two upper-level courses in their major that are writing intensive. **Procedure:** Freshmen are admitted in the fall. Entrance exams should be taken by December of the senior year. There are early decision and deferred admissions plans. Early decision applications should be filed by November 1; regular applications, by January 5 for fall entry, along with a $50 fee. Notification of early decision is sent December 15; regular decision, April 1. Applications are accepted online. **Transfer Students:** 196 transfer students enrolled in 2015-2016. The most important criterion is an applicant's college record. 64 of 128 credits required for the bachelor's degree must be completed at UR. **International Students:** There are 1100 international students enrolled. The school actively recruits these students. They must take the TOEFL with a minimum score of 600 on the paper-based TOEFL (PBT) or 100 on the Internet-based version (iBT). They must also take the SAT or ACT.

ADMISSIONS: 35% of the 2016-2017 applicants were accepted. **Admissions Contact:** Jonathan Burdick, Dean of College Admissions. Email: *admit@admissions.rochester.edu* Web: *www.rochester.edu*

FINANCIAL AID: In 2016-2017, 86% of all full-time freshmen and 82% of continuing full-time students received some form of financial aid. 72% of all full-time freshmen and 74% of continuing full-time students received need-based aid. 20% of undergraduate students work part-time. Average annual earnings from campus work are $1617. UR is a member of CSS. The CSS/Profile and the state aid form are required. The FAFSA code is 002894. The priority date for freshman financial aid applications for fall entry is February 1.

UTICA COLLEGE — C-3

www.utica.edu

Utica, NY 13502	(315) 792-3006 (800) 782-8884
Fax: (315) 792-3003	**Email:** admiss@utica.edu
Full-time: 1176 men, 1582 women	**Faculty:** 143; IIB, +$
Part-time: 200 men, 592 women	**Ph.D.s:** 85%
Graduate: 647 men, 922 women	**Student/Faculty:** 11 to 1
Year: semesters, summer session	**Tuition:** $19,996
Room & Board: $10,434	**Freshman Class:** 5419 applied, 4441 accepted, 685 enrolled
SAT or ACT: recommended	**CEEB CODE:** 2931
Application Deadline: open	**COMPETITIVE**

Utica College is a private, comprehensive institution founded by Syracuse University in 1946. There are 4 undergraduate schools and 1 graduate school. In addition to regional accreditation, UC has baccalaureate program accreditation with APTA, NLN, TEAC, AOTA, and AACN. The 128-acre campus is in a suburban area 50 miles east of Syracuse. Including any residence halls, there are 18 buildings.

STUDENT LIFE: 82% of undergraduates are from New York. Others are from 47 states, 32 foreign countries, and Canada. 80% are from public schools. 66% are White; 11% African American; 8% Hispanic; 5% race unknown; 3% Asian American; 3% Foreign; 3% two or more races; 1% American Indian/Alaska Native. **Female To Male Ratio:** 1.5:1. The average age of freshmen is 18; all undergraduates, 21. 25% do not continue beyond their first year; 46% remain to graduate. **Housing:** 1034 students can be accommodated in college housing, which includes single-sex and coed dorms, special-interest houses. On-campus housing is guaranteed for all 4 years and is available on a lottery system for upperclassmen. 65% of students commute. All students may keep cars.

FACULTY/CLASSROOMS: 49% of faculty are male; 51% are female. All teach undergraduates, and do research. No introductory courses are taught by graduate students. The average class size in an introductory lecture is 23; in a laboratory is 11; and in a regular course is 17.

PROGRAMS OF STUDY: UC confers B.A., B.B.A., and B.S. degrees. Master's and doctoral degrees are also awarded. Bachelor's degrees are awarded in AGRICULTURE (animal science), BIOLOGICAL SCIENCE (biochemistry, biology/biological science, and neurosciences), BUSINESS (accounting, business administration and management, business economics, and insurance and risk management), COMMUNICATIONS AND THE ARTS (communications, English, journalism, and public relations), COMPUTER AND PHYSICAL SCIENCE (chemistry, computer science, computer security and information assurance, cyber intelligence/security studies, geoscience, mathematics, and physics), EDUCATION (education and foreign languages education), ENGINEERING AND ENVIRONMENTAL DESIGN (construction management), HEALTH PROFESSIONS (nursing, occupational therapy, physical therapy, and recreation therapy), SOCIAL SCIENCE (child psychology/development, criminal justice, economics, gerontology, history, liberal arts/general studies, philosophy, political science/government, psychobiology, psychology, social studies, and sociology). Occupational therapy, psychology, and biology are the strongest academically. Health studies, nursing, and criminal justice have the largest enrollments.

ACTIVITIES: 2% of men belong to 2 local and 3 national fraternities; 2% of women belong to 2 local and 3 national sororities. There are 86 groups on campus, including art, band, cheerleading, chess, choir, chorus, communications, computers, dance, drama, environmental, ethnic, film, honors, international, jazz band, LGBT, literary magazine, musical theater, newspaper, orchestra, pep band, photography, political, professional, radio and TV, religious, social, social service, student government, symphony, and yearbook. Popular campus events include Outdoor Concerts, Mock Elections, and Winter Weekend. **Sports:** There are 10 intercollegiate sports for men and 11 for women, and 28 intramural sports for men and 28 for women. Facilities include a gym, swimming pool, tennis, racquetball, handball, and squash courts, Nautilus and weight rooms, dance and aerobic rooms, playing fields, a stadium, and hockey facilities. **Graduates:** From July 1, 2015 to June 30, 2016, 724 bachelor's degrees were awarded. The most popular majors were health studies (47%), criminal justice (20%), and business and marketing (9%). In an average class, 30% graduate in 4 years or less, 42% graduate in 5 years or less, and 44% graduate in 6 years or less.

SERVICES: Counseling and information services are available, as is tutoring in most subjects. There is a reader service for the blind, and remedial math, reading, and writing. **Library/Resources:** The library contains 307,523 volumes, 24,458 microform items, and 2,861 audio/video tapes/CDs/DVDs, and subscribes to 413 periodicals including electronic. Computerized library services include interlibrary loans, database searching, Internet access, and Wi-Fi capability. Special learning facilities include an art gallery, radio station, TV station, an early childhood education lab, a math and writing center, stock trading room, OT, PT, nursing, and physical science labs. **Physically Challenged Students:** 85% of the campus is accessible. Facilities include wheelchair ramps, elevators, special parking, specially equipped restrooms, lowered drinking fountains. **Special:** UC offers co-op programs, internships, work-study programs in all majors, accelerated degrees, dual majors, and cross-registration with Hamilton College and the Mohawk Valley Consortium. Study abroad may be arranged in 9 countries. There is a 3-2 engineering degree with Syracuse University. There are 5 national honor societies and a freshman honors program. **Visiting:** There are regularly scheduled orientations for prospective students, including an interview, financial aid information, and a tour of the campus. There are guides for informal visits, visitors may sit in on classes, and stay overnight. To schedule a visit, contact the Admissions Office. **Campus Safety and Security:** Measures include 24-hour foot and vehicle patrol, emergency notification system, and security escort services. There are shuttle buses, emergency telephones, lighted pathways/sidewalks, and controlled access to dorms/residences.

REQUIREMENTS: The SAT or ACT, and ACT Writing Test are recommended. Graduation from an accredited secondary school or satisfactory scores on the GED are required. Recommended high school courses include 4 years of English, 3 years each of math and social studies, and 2 years each of foreign language and science. An essay and an interview are also recommended. AP and CLEP credits are accepted. Important factors in the admissions decision are advanced placement or honors courses, extracurricular activities record, and leadership record. To graduate, students must complete a total of 120 to 128 hours with a minimum 2.0 GPA. They must complete a general education requirement including basic skills and distribution requirements. **Procedure:** Freshmen are admitted fall and spring. Entrance exams should be taken during the junior year. There are early decision, early admissions, deferred admissions, and rolling admissions plans. Application deadlines are open. Application fee is $40. Notification of early decision is sent December 15; regular decision, on a rolling basis. 834 early decision candidates were accepted for the 2016-2017 class. Applications are accepted online. **Transfer Students:** 136 transfer students enrolled in 2015-2016. Applicants must have a minimum GPA of 2.0. 30 of 128 credits required for the bachelor's degree must be completed at UC. **International Students:** There are 109 international students enrolled. The school actively recruits these students. They must take the TOEFL with a minimum score of 525 on the paper-based TOEFL (PBT) or 69 on the Internet-based version (iBT) or the Comprehensive English Language Test, or take the IELTS, APIEL, or MELAB. The SAT is recommended if the student's primary language is English.

Admissions Contact: Jeffery Gates, Vice President for Enrollment Management. Email: *admiss@utica.edu* Web: *www.utica.edu*

FINANCIAL AID: In 2016-2017, 90% of all full-time freshmen and 91% of continuing full-time students received some form of financial aid. 90% of all full-time freshmen and continuing full-time students received need-based aid. The average freshman award was $14,292. Need-based scholarships or need-based grants averaged $5,486; and need-based self-help aid (loans and jobs) averaged $3,751. Average annual earnings from campus work are $1500. UC is a member of CSS. The priority date for freshman financial aid applications for fall entry is February 15. The deadline for filing freshman financial aid applications for fall entry is April 1.

VASSAR COLLEGE — D-4

www.vassar.edu

Poughkeepsie, NY 12604	(845) 437-7300 (800) 827-7270
Fax: (845) 437-7063	**Email:** admissions@vassar.edu
Full-time: 1028 men, 1377 women	**Faculty:** 275; IIB, ++$
Part-time: 5 men, 14 women	**Ph.D.s:** 87%
Graduate: n/av	**Student/Faculty:** 8 to 1
Year: semesters	**Tuition:** $53,090
Room & Board: $12,400	**Freshman Class:** 7306 applied, 1964 accepted, 660 enrolled
SAT CR/M/W: 710/700/710 **ACT:** 31	**CEEB CODE:** 2956
Application Deadline: January 1	**MOST COMPETITIVE**

Vassar College, founded in 1861, is a highly selective, residential, private college of the liberal arts and sciences. There is 1 undergraduate school. The 1000-acre campus is in a suburban area 75 miles north of New York City in the Mid-Hudson River Valley. Including any residence halls, there are 100 buildings.

STUDENT LIFE: 78% of undergraduates are from out of state, mostly the West. Students are from 49 states, 54 foreign countries, and Canada. 67% are from public schools. 7% are Foreign; 6% two or more races; 59% White; 5% African American; 11% Asian American; 11% Hispanic. **Female To Male Ratio:** 1.3:1. The average age of freshmen is 18; all undergraduates, 20. 4% do not continue beyond their first year; 92%

remain to graduate. **Housing:** 2383 students can be accommodated in college housing, which includes single-sex, coed dorms, on-campus apartments, and off-campus apartments, an all-women residence hall, and cooperative living unit. On-campus housing is guaranteed for all 4 years. 98% of students live on campus; of those, 90% remain on campus on weekends. All students may keep cars.

FACULTY/CLASSROOMS: 53% of faculty are male; 47% are female. All teach undergraduates, and do research. No introductory courses are taught by graduate students. The average class size in an introductory lecture is 21; in a laboratory is 10; and in a regular course is 17.

PROGRAMS OF STUDY: Vassar confers B.A. degrees. Master's degrees are also awarded. Bachelor's degrees are awarded in AGRICULTURE (environmental studies), BIOLOGICAL SCIENCE (biochemistry, biology/biological science, and neurosciences), COMMUNICATIONS AND THE ARTS (art history, art, Chinese, dramatic arts, English, film arts, French, German, Germanic languages and literature, Italian, Japanese, media arts, music, and Russian languages and literature), COMPUTER AND PHYSICAL SCIENCE (astronomy, chemistry, computer science, earth science, geology, mathematics, and physics), EDUCATION (education), HEALTH PROFESSIONS (premedicine), SOCIAL SCIENCE (African studies, American studies, anthropology, Asian/Oriental studies, classical/ancient civilization, cognitive science, economics, geography, Hispanic American studies, history, international studies, Judaic studies, Latin American studies, Medieval studies, philosophy, political science/government, prelaw, psychology, religion, science and society, sociology, Spanish studies, Urban studies, Victorian studies, and women's studies). Economics, political science, English, and biology have the largest enrollments.

ACTIVITIES: There are no fraternities or sororities. There are 120 groups on campus, including and an outdoors club, art, band, chess, choir, chorale, chorus, communications, computers, dance, debate, drama, environmental, ethnic, film, honors, international, jazz band, LGBT, literary magazine, musical theater, newspaper, opera, orchestra, photography, political, professional, radio and TV, religious, social, social service, student government, symphony, and yearbook. Popular campus events include Founders Day, Spring and Fall Formals, and All Parents Weekend. **Sports:** There are 12 intercollegiate sports for men and 13 for women, and 18 intramural sports for men and 18 for women. Facilities include a field house with a swimming pool, indoor tennis courts, weight and conditioning room, gyms with squash and basketball facilities, golf course, outdoor tennis courts, an all-weather track, soccer fields, turf field for field hockey and lacrosse, baseball diamond, rugby field, club and intramural fields, competition basketball gym, banked running track, and an exercise and fitness center. **Graduates:** From July 1, 2015 to June 30, 2016, 630 bachelor's degrees were awarded. The most popular majors were biology, political science, and and English (9%). 23 companies recruited on campus in 2015-2016. In an average class, 1% graduate in 3 years or less, 88% graduate in 4 years or less, 92% graduate in 5 years or less, and 93% graduate in 6 years or less. Of the 2015 graduating class, 18% were enrolled in graduate school within 6 months of graduation, and 64% were employed.

SERVICES: Counseling and information services are available, as is tutoring in most subjects. There is a reader service for the blind, and remedial math and writing. **Library/Resources:** The 3 libraries contain 1.0 million volumes, 611,076 microform items, and 23,590 audio/video tapes/CDs/DVDs, and subscribe to 4,001 periodicals including electronic. Computerized library services include interlibrary loans, database searching, Internet access, and Wi-Fi capability. Special learning facilities include an art gallery, natural history museum, radio station, studio art buildings with studios, large astronomical observatory, 3 theaters, dance theater and studios, concert halls and music practice rooms, environmental field station and ecological preserve, intercultural center, and many teaching and research-oriented lab facilities for the sciences. **Physically Challenged Students:** 70% of the campus is accessible. Facilities include wheelchair ramps, elevators, special parking, specially equipped restrooms, special class scheduling, lowered drinking fountains. There is an Office of Disability and Support Services, signage in braille, and assisted listening devices. **Special:** The school offers fieldwork/internships in all academic areas, as well as dual majors, independent/self-designed majors, and non-recorded grade options. Vassar runs study-abroad programs in 7 countries and students have access to study in 250+ other approved programs around the world, as well as domestic exchange options. A 3-2 engineering degree with Dartmouth College is offered. There is a chapter of Phi Beta Kappa. **Visiting:** There are regularly scheduled orientations for prospective students, including a campus tour, an information session, and a class visit when possible. There are guides for informal visits, visitors may sit in on classes, and stay overnight. To schedule a visit, contact the Admissions Office. **Campus Safety and Security:** Measures include 24-hour foot and vehicle patrol, emergency notification system, self-defense education, and security escort services. There are shuttle buses, emergency telephones, lighted pathways/sidewalks, and controlled access to dorms/residences.

REQUIREMENTS: The SAT or ACT is required; Optional writing tests are not required. In addition, a high school diploma or an approved alternative are also required. The high school program should typically include advanced level work with 4 years each of English, social studies, math, foreign language, and science. An essay and 2 letters of recommendation must also be submitted. AP credits are accepted. Important factors in the admissions decision are advanced placement or honors courses, recommendations by school officials, and extracurricular activities record. To graduate, students must have a total of 34 units equivalent to 120 credit hours, with a minimum GPA of 2.0. Of this total, no more than 17 units may be in a single field of concentration and 8 1/2 units must be outside the major field. Entering freshmen must take the freshman writing course. All students must meet the foreign language proficiency requirement and must take a quantitative skills course before their third year. A thesis is required in most departments. **Procedure:** Freshmen are admitted in the fall. Entrance exams should be taken as early as possible but no later than December of the senior year. There are early decision and deferred admissions plans. Early decision applications should be filed by November 15; regular applications, by January 1 for fall entry, along with a $70 fee. Notification of early decision is sent December 15; regular decision, March 30. 253 early decision candidates were accepted for the 2016-2017 class. 879 applicants were on the 2016 waiting list; 21 were admitted. Application fees are waived if application is completed online. **Transfer Students:** 10 transfer students enrolled in 2015-2016. Applicants must have a high level of achievement in both high school and college work. 17 of 34 credits required for the bachelor's degree must be completed at Vassar. **International Students:** There are 171 international students enrolled. The school actively recruits these students. They must take the TOEFL with a minimum score of 600 on the paper-based TOEFL (PBT) or 100 on the Internet-based version (iBT), or take the IELTS. They must also take the SAT or ACT.

ADMISSIONS: 27% of the 2016-2017 applicants were accepted. The SAT scores for the 2016-2017 freshman class were: Critical Reading-- 3% between 500 and 599, 33% between 600 and 699, and 64% between 700 and 800. Math-- 3% between 500 and 599, 42% between 600 and 699, and 55% between 700 and 800. Writing-- 6% between 500 and 599, 38% between 600 and 699, and 56% between 700 and 800. The ACT scores were 14% between 24 and 29, and 86% above 30. 90% of the current freshmen were in the top fifth of their class; 99% were in the top two fifths. **Admissions Contact:** J.C. Tesone, Director of Admission. Email: *admissions@vassar.edu* Web: *www.vassar.edu*

FINANCIAL AID: In 2016-2017, 65% of all full-time freshmen and 63% of continuing full-time students received some form of financial aid. 60% of all full-time freshmen and 59% of continuing full-time students received need-based aid. The average freshman award was $48,398. Need-based scholarships or need-based grants averaged $45,154 ($60,902 maximum); need-based self-help aid (loans and jobs) averaged $3,577 ($5,660 maximum); and $1,033 from other forms of aid. 65% of undergraduate students work part-time. Average annual earnings from campus work are $1367. The average financial indebtedness of the 2016 graduate was $15,091. Vassar is a member of CSS. The CSS/Profile, FFS, and the college's own financial statement are required. The FAFSA code is 002895. The priority date for freshman financial aid applications for fall entry is November 15.

VAUGHN COLLEGE OF AERONAUTICS AND TECHNOLOGY — D-5

www.vaughn.edu

Flushing, NY 11369 — **(718) 429-6600 ext 117**

Fax: (718) 779-2231
Full-time: 1190 men, 172 women
Part-time: 376 men, 61 women
Graduate: 9 men, 4 women
Year: semesters, summer session
Room & Board: $15,300

SAT CR/M: 498/547 **ACT:** 22
Application Deadline: open

Email: admitme@vaughn.edu
Faculty: 41
Ph.D.s: 54%
Student/Faculty: 15 to 1
Tuition: $21,880
Freshman Class: 723 applied, 618 accepted, 321 enrolled
CEEB CODE: 2001
COMPETITIVE

Vaughn College of Aeronautics and Technology, founded in 1932, is a private non-profit institution, offering undergraduate and masters degrees in engineering, engineering technology, management, and aviation. There is 1 undergraduate school. In addition to regional accreditation, Vaughn has baccalaureate program accreditation with ABET. The 6-acre campus is in an urban area Queens, New York, adjacent from LaGuardia Airport, 4 miles east of New York City. Including any residence halls, there are 2 buildings.

STUDENT LIFE: 89% of undergraduates are from New York. Others are from 27 states, and 20 foreign countries. 96% are from public schools. 8% are two or more races; 4% race unknown; 30% Hispanic; 25% White; 16% African American; 16% Asian American; 1% American Indian/ Alaska Native. **Male To Female Ratio:** 6.6:1. The average age of freshmen is 19; all undergraduates, 23. 20% do not continue beyond their first year; 57% remain to graduate. **Housing:** 200 students can be accommodated in college housing, which includes coed dorms, and special-interest houses. On-campus housing is available on a first-come and first-served basis. Priority is given to out-of-town students. 90% of students commute. Alcohol is not permitted. All students may keep cars.

FACULTY/CLASSROOMS: 88% of faculty are male; 12% are female. All teach undergraduates. No introductory courses are taught by graduate students. The average class size in an introductory lecture is 25; in a laboratory is 20; and in a regular course is 20.

PROGRAMS OF STUDY: Vaughn confers B.S. degrees. Associate and master's degrees are also awarded. Bachelor's degrees are awarded in BUSINESS (business administration and management), ENGINEERING AND ENVIRONMENTAL DESIGN (air traffic control, aircraft mechanics, airline piloting and navigation, aviation administration/ management, electrical/electronics engineering technology, mechanical engineering technology, and mechatronics engineering). Mechatronic engineering, mechanical engineering technology, and electronic engineering technology are the strongest academically. Aircraft operation (flight), airport management, and mechanical engineering technology have the largest enrollments.

ACTIVITIES: There are no fraternities or sororities. There are 16 groups on campus, including computers, dance, ethnic, honors, international, LGBT, professional, religious, social, social service, and student government. Popular campus events include Career and Internship Fairs, and Springfest. **Sports:** There are 4 intercollegiate sports for men and 3 for women. Facilities include a state-of-the-art fitness center. **Graduates:** From July 1, 2015 to June 30, 2016, 138 bachelor's degrees were awarded. The most popular majors were airport management (65%), electronic engineering technology (14%), and mechanical engineering technology (11%). 45 companies recruited on campus in 2015-2016. In an average class, 35% graduate in 4 years or less, 52% graduate in 5 years or less, and 57% graduate in 6 years or less.

SERVICES: Counseling and information services are available, as is tutoring in most subjects. There is remedial math, reading, and writing. **Library/Resources:** The library contains 37,455 volumes, 4,252 audio/ video tapes/CDs/DVDs, and subscribes to 80,000 periodicals including electronic. Computerized library services include interlibrary loans, database searching, and Internet access. **Physically Challenged Students:** All of the campus is accessible. Facilities include wheelchair ramps, elevators, special parking, specially equipped restrooms, special class scheduling, lowered drinking fountains, and lowered telephones. **Special:** Work-study programs are available with Vaughn College, and internships may be arranged through the career development office. B.S. degrees are offered. **Visiting:** There are regularly scheduled orientations for prospective students, scheduled prior to registration, which includes a tour and academic advisement. There are guides for informal visits and visitors may sit in on classes. To schedule a visit, contact the Admissions Office. **Campus Safety and Security:** Measures include 24-hour foot and vehicle patrol, emergency notification system, and security escort services. There are shuttle buses, lighted pathways/sidewalks, and controlled access to dorms/residences.

REQUIREMENTS: SAT or ACT scores are required for all applicants to bachelor of science degree programs. The average SAT score for the engineering program is 1160. The average SAT score for Engineering Technology, Management, and Aricraft Operations programs is 1040. AP credits are accepted. Important factors in the admissions decision are evidence of special talent, advanced placement or honors courses, and personality/intangible qualities. All students must satisfy English, math, and science requirements and fulfill appropriate licensing requirements while maintaining a GPA of at least 2.0. Students with advanced credit must complete 30 credits in residency. **Procedure:** Freshmen are admitted fall and spring. Entrance exams should be taken March 1. There is a rolling admissions plan. Application deadlines are open. The fall 2016 application fee was $40. Notification is sent on a rolling basis. **Transfer Students:** 245 transfer students enrolled in 2015-2016. A minimum 2.0 GPA is required. 30 of 134 credits required for the bachelor's degree must be completed at Vaughn. **International Students:** There are 40 international students enrolled. The school actively recruits these students. They must take the TOEFL with a minimum score of 80 on the paper-based TOEFL (PBT) or 112 on the Internet-based version (iBT), English Proficiency Certificate. They must also take the SAT. The TOEFL is accepted in place of SAT for applicants from non-English speaking countries.

ADMISSIONS: 85% of the 2016-2017 applicants were accepted. The SAT scores for the 2016-2017 freshman class were: Critical Reading-- 54% below 500, 37% between 500 and 599, 8% between 600 and 699, and 1% between 700 and 800. Math-- 25% below 500, 48% between 500 and 599, 24% between 600 and 699, and 3% between 700 and 800. The ACT scores were 16% below 12, 67% between 12 and 17, and 17% above 30. **Admissions Contact:** David Griffey, Director of Admissions. Email: *admitme@vaughn.edu* Web: *www.vaughn.edu*

FINANCIAL AID: In 2016-2017, 95% of all full-time freshmen and continuing full-time students received some form of financial aid. 80% of all full-time freshmen and continuing full-time students received need-based aid. 60% of undergraduate students work part-time. The average financial indebtedness of the 2016 graduate was $32,500. The CSS/Profile and the college's own financial statement are required. Check with the school for current application deadlines.

WAGNER COLLEGE — D-5

www.wagner.edu

Staten Island, NY 10301	(718) 390-3411 (800) 221-1010
Fax: (718) 390-3105	**Email: admissions@wagner.edu**
Full-time: 629 men, 1078 women	**Faculty:** 96
Part-time: 12 men, 22 women	**Ph.D.s:** 90%
Graduate: 149 men, 303 women	**Student/Faculty:** 15 to 1
Year: semesters, summer session	**Tuition:** $42,480
Room & Board: $13,000	**Freshman Class:** 2803 applied, 1920 accepted, 421 enrolled
SAT CR/M/W: 565/565/565 **ACT:** 25	**CEEB CODE:** 2966
Application Deadline: February 15	**COMPETITIVE+**

Wagner College, founded in 1883, is a private liberal arts institution. Figures in the above capsule and in this profile are approximate. There is 1 undergraduate school and 1 graduate school. In addition to regional accreditation, Wagner has baccalaureate program accreditation with AACSB, ACBSP, NCATE, NLN, ARC-PA, and ACS. The 105-acre campus is in a suburban area 10 miles from Manhattan. Including any residence halls, there are 19 buildings.

STUDENT LIFE: 54% of undergraduates are from out of state, mostly the Middle Atlantic. Students are from 48 states, 19 foreign countries, and Canada. 62% are from public schools. 77% are White; 6% African American; 3% Asian American; 2% Foreign; 2% two or more races; 11% race unknown; 10% Hispanic. **Female To Male Ratio:** 1.8:1. The average age of freshmen is 18; all undergraduates, 22. 17% do not continue beyond their first year; 70% remain to graduate. **Housing:** 1600 students can be accommodated in college housing, which includes coed dorms, off-campus apartments, special-interest houses, fraternity houses, sorority houses, and Greek floor. There is also an Honors building and floor, quiet floors, medical floors, and themed communities in dorms, and senior year housing. On-campus housing is guaranteed for all 4 years and is available on a lottery system for upperclassmen. 67% of students live on campus. All students may keep cars.

FACULTY/CLASSROOMS: 45% of faculty are male; 55% are female. All teach undergraduates. No introductory courses are taught by graduate students. The average class size in an introductory lecture is 21; in a laboratory is 13; and in a regular course is 19.

PROGRAMS OF STUDY: Wagner confers B.A. and B.S. degrees. Master's degrees are also awarded. Bachelor's degrees are awarded in BIOLOGICAL SCIENCE (biology/biological science and microbiology), BUSINESS (accounting and business administration and management),

COMMUNICATIONS AND THE ARTS (arts administration/management, dramatic arts, English, fine arts, music, theater design, and visual and performing arts), COMPUTER AND PHYSICAL SCIENCE (chemistry, computer science, mathematics, and physics), EDUCATION (elementary education, middle school education, and secondary education), HEALTH PROFESSIONS (nursing and physician's assistant), SOCIAL SCIENCE (anthropology, history, philosophy, political science/government, psychology, public administration, and sociology). Natural sciences, and health professions are the strongest academically. Business, nursing, and psychology have the largest enrollments.

ACTIVITIES: 10% of women belong to 1 local and 3 national sororities. There are 65 groups on campus, including art, band, cheerleading, chess, choir, chorale, chorus, communications, computers, dance, debate, drama, environmental, ethnic, honors, international, jazz band, LGBT, literary magazine, marching band, musical theater, newspaper, pep band, political, professional, religious, social, social service, student government, symphony, and yearbook. Popular campus events include Songfest, WagnerStock, Homecoming, Spring Fling Week, Fall Fest, and Family Weekend. **Sports:** There are 8 intercollegiate sports for men and 10 for women, and 5 intramural sports for men and 4 for women. Facilities include a football stadium, a gym, pool, water polo, a fitness center, track and field, basketball arena, golf, lacrosse, tennis, soccer/softball/baseball field, rugby, and men's ice hockey. **Graduates:** From July 1, 2015 to June 30, 2016, 445 bachelor's degrees were awarded. The most popular majors were nursing and physician assistants (18%), visual/performing arts (18%), and business administration (17%). 60 companies recruited on campus in 2015-2016. In an average class, 60% graduate in 4 years or less, 64% graduate in 5 years or less, and 66% graduate in 6 years or less. Of the 2015 graduating class, 20% were enrolled in graduate school within 6 months of graduation, and 79% were employed.

SERVICES: Counseling and information services are available, as is tutoring in every subject. There is also a reader service for the blind, and remedial math, reading, and writing. **Library/Resources:** The library contains 158,160 volumes, 218 microform items, 2,453 audio/video tapes/CDs/DVDs, and subscribes to 56,399 periodicals including electronic. Computerized library services include interlibrary loans, database searching, Internet access, and Wi-Fi capability. Special learning facilities include an art gallery, planetarium, and a nursing resource center. **Physically Challenged Students:** 25% of the campus is accessible. Facilities include wheelchair ramps, elevators, special parking, specially equipped restrooms, special class scheduling, and lowered drinking fountains. **Special:** Internships or field-based research is required of all majors. Students may earn B.A.-B.S. degrees in psychology. Student-designed and dual majors, credit for life experience, a Washington semester, nondegree study, and pass/fail options are available. Study abroad in most countries is possible. Learning Communities for freshmen, sophomores/juniors, and seniors. There are 11 national honor societies and a freshman honors program. **Visiting:** There are regularly scheduled orientations for prospective students, including a presentation by the Admissions Office, a tour of the campus, and meetings with faculty and staff. There are guides for informal visits, visitors may sit in on classes, and stay overnight. To schedule a visit, contact the Admissions Office at (718) 390-3411. **Campus Safety and Security:** Measures include 24-hour foot and vehicle patrol, emergency notification system, and security escort services. There are shuttle buses, emergency telephones, lighted pathways/sidewalks, controlled access to dorms/residences, ID card access into residence halls.

REQUIREMENTS: Graduation from an accredited secondary school is required, with 21 academic credits or Carnegie units, including 4 years of English, 3 years each of history and math, 2 years each of foreign language, science with 1 unit of lab, and 7 units of academic electives. An essay is required, and an interview is strongly recommended. Auditions are required for music and theater applicants. An interview is required for the Physician Assistant Program. A GPA of 3.0 is required. AP and CLEP credits are accepted. Important factors in the admissions decision are advanced placement or honors courses, recommendations by school officials, and extracurricular activities record. To graduate, students must complete 36 units with 12 to 18 in the major and a minimum GPA of 2.0. All students must take courses in English, math, and multidisciplinary studies. In addition, students must fulfill distribution requirements in physical science, life science, math and computers, history, literature, philosophy and religion, foreign culture, aesthetics, and human behavior. All students are required to enroll in Learning Communities. **Procedure:** Freshmen are admitted in the fall and spring. Entrance exams should be taken by December of the senior year. There are early decision and deferred admissions plans. Early decision applications should be filed by December 1; regular applications, by February 15 for fall entry; and November 1 for spring entry, along with a $60 fee. Notification of early decision is sent December 11; regular decision, March 1. 76 early decision candidates were accepted for the 2016-2017 class. 95 applicants were on the 2016 waiting list; 20 were admitted. Applications are accepted on-line. **Transfer Students:** 92 transfer students enrolled in 2015-2016. Transfer students should have a minimum of 30 credit hours earned with a GPA of 2.5. Applicants must submit all college and high school transcripts, a letter of recommendation, and a personal statement. An interview is recommended. SAT or ACT scores taken within the past 5 years may be submitted. 9 of 36 credits required for the bachelor's degree must be completed at Wagner. **International Students:** There are 36 international students enrolled. The school actively recruits these students. They must take the TOEFL with a minimum score of 550 on the paper-based TOEFL (PBT) or 79 on the Internet-based version (iBT).

ADMISSIONS: 68% of the 2016-2017 applicants were accepted. The SAT scores for the 2016-2017 freshman class were: Critical Reading-- 15% below 500, 49% between 500 and 599, 31% between 600 and 699, and 5% between 700 and 800. Math-- 12% below 500, 43% between 500 and 599, 38% between 600 and 699, and 7% between 700 and 800. Writing-- 20% below 500, 43% between 500 and 599, 31% between 600 and 699, and 6% between 700 and 800. The ACT scores were 6% between 12 and 17, 34% between 18 and 23, 51% between 24 and 29, and 9% above 30. 38% of the current freshmen were in the top fifth of their class; 86% were in the top two fifths. **Admissions Contact:** James Gibbons, Director of Admissions. Email: *admissions@wagner.edu* Web: *www.wagner.edu*

FINANCIAL AID: In 2016-2017, 94% of all full-time freshmen received some form of financial aid. The average freshman award was $31,362. Need-based scholarships or need-based grants averaged $16,866; need-based self-help aid (loans and jobs) averaged $4,409; non-need-based athletic scholarships averaged $17,367; and other non-need-based awards and non-need-based scholarships averaged $2,197. 19% of undergraduate students work part-time. Average annual earnings from campus work are $1004. The average financial indebtedness of the 2016 graduate was $31,850. Wagner is a member of CSS. The state aid form is required. The FAFSA code is 002899. The priority date for freshman financial aid applications for fall entry is February 15.

WEBB INSTITUTE — D-5

www.webb-institute.edu

Glen Cove, NY 11542 — **(516) 671-2213**

Fax: (516) 674-9838	**Email:** admissions@webb-institute.edu
Full-time: 75 men, 17 women	**Faculty:** 7
Part-time: n/av	**Ph.D.s:** 60%
Graduate: n/av	**Student/Faculty:** 9 to 1
Year: semesters	**Tuition:** $47,400
Room & Board: $14,400	**Freshman Class:** n/av
SAT CR/M: 700/740 **ACT:** 34	**CEEB CODE:** 2970
Application Deadline: August 16	**MOST COMPETITIVE**

Webb Institute, founded in 1889 by William Webb, is a unique, top-ranked undergraduate institution offering one academic option, a double major in Naval Architecture and Marine Engineering. It is also the only full-tuition scholarship, private undergraduate program of its kind in the country. There is 1 undergraduate school. In addition to regional accreditation, Webb has baccalaureate program accreditation with ABET. The 26-acre campus is in a suburban area 30 miles from New York City on the north shore of Long Island. Including any residence halls, there are 11 buildings.

STUDENT LIFE: 79% of undergraduates are from out of state, mostly the Northeast. Students are from 26 states, and 2 foreign countries. **Male To Female Ratio:** 4.4:1. The average age of freshmen is 18; all undergraduates, 20. 18% do not continue beyond their first year; 71% remain to graduate. **Housing:** 110 students can be accommodated in college housing, which includes single-sex and coed dorms. On-campus housing is guaranteed for all 4 years. All students may keep cars.

FACULTY/CLASSROOMS: 90% of faculty are male; 10% are female. All teach undergraduates, 50% do research, and 50% do both. No introductory courses are taught by graduate students. The average class size in an introductory lecture is 23; in a laboratory is 12; and in a regular course is 51.

PROGRAMS OF STUDY: Webb confers B.S. degrees. Bachelor's degrees are awarded in ENGINEERING AND ENVIRONMENTAL DESIGN (naval architecture and marine engineering). Naval architecture and marine engineering, have the largest enrollments.

ACTIVITIES: There are no fraternities or sororities. Groups on campus include athletic clubs, rowing, chorale, jazz band, orchestra, professional, sailing, social, student government, and yearbook. Students can participate in the North Shore Symphony Orchestra or the North Shore Community Chorus. Popular campus events include Parents Weekend, Webbstock, and Great Gatsby. **Sports:** There are 5 intercollegiate sports for men and 5 for women, and 4 intramural sports for men and 4 for women. Facilities include a gymnasium, tennis courts, basketball and vollyball court, and an athletic field. **Graduates:** The most popular majors were Naval architecture and Marine engineering (100%). Of the 2015 graduating class, 100% were employed within 6 months of graduation.

SERVICES: Counseling and information services are available, as is tutoring in most subjects. **Library/Resources:** The library contains 55,000 volumes, 1,633 microform items, and 1,851 audio/video tapes/CDs/DVDs, and subscribes to 267 periodicals including electronic. Computerized library services include interlibrary loans, database searching, Internet access, and Wi-Fi capability. **Physically Challenged Students:** 90% of the campus is accessible. Facilities include elevators and special parking. **Special:** All students are employed 2 months each year through co-op programs. **Visiting:** There are regularly scheduled orientations for prospective students, Weekend Open House in October. There are guides for informal visits, visitors may sit in on classes, and stay overnight. To schedule a visit, contact Lauren Carballo at lcarballo@webb.edu. **Campus Safety and Security:** Measures include 24-hour foot and vehicle patrol. There are emergency telephones, lighted pathways/sidewalks, Student and professional security services.

REQUIREMENTS: Applicants should be graduates of an accredited secondary school with 16 academic credits completed, including 4 each in English and math, 2 each in history and science, 1 in foreign language, and 3 in electives. 3 SAT Subject tests in writing, math level I or II, and physics or chemistry are required, as is an interview. Candidates must be U.S. citizens. Important factors in the admissions decision are advanced placement or honors courses, evidence of special talent, and personality/intangible qualities. The curriculum is prescribed, with all students taking the same courses in each of the 4 years. The Webb program has 4 practical 8-week paid work periods: freshman year, a mechanic in a shipyard; sophomore year, a cadet in the engine room of a ship, and junior and senior years, a junior engineer in a design office. All students must complete a senior seminar, thesis, and technical reports, as well as make engineering inspection visits. A total of 146 credits with a minimum passing grade of 70% is required to graduate. **Procedure:** Freshmen are admitted fall. Entrance exams should be taken by January of the senior year. There is a early decision plan. Applications should be filed by August 16 for fall entry, along with a $25 fee. **Transfer Students:** Transfers must enter as freshmen. SAT/ACT scores and an interview are required. 146 of 146 credits required for the bachelor's degree must be completed at Webb. **International Students:** There are 2 international students enrolled. They must also take the SAT or ACT, and the college's own entrance exam.

Admissions Contact: Steven P Ostendorff, Director of Admissions. Email: *admissions@webb-institute.edu* Web: *www.webb-institute.edu*

FINANCIAL AID: The CSS/Profile and the college's own financial statement are required. The FAFSA code is 002900. Check with the school for current application deadlines.

WELLS COLLEGE C-3

www.wells.edu

Aurora, NY 13026 (315) 364-3266 (800) 952-9355

Email: admissions@wells.edu

Full-time: 181 men, 377 women	**Faculty:** 34
Part-time: 7 men, 7 women	**Ph.D.s:** 91%
Graduate: n/av	**Student/Faculty:** 16 to 1
Year: semesters	**Tuition:** $37,500
Room & Board: $13,000	**Freshman Class:** 2217 applied, 1388 accepted, 168 enrolled
SAT CR/M/W: 510/500/480 **ACT:** 24	**CEEB CODE:** 2971
Application Deadline: March 1	**COMPETITIVE**

Wells College, founded in 1868, is a private liberal arts institution. There is 1 undergraduate school. The 365-acre campus is in a small town in the heart of New York's Finger Lakes, in the village of Aurora, and 30 miles north of Ithaca, 1 hour from Rochester and Syracuse, and 4 hours from New York City. Including any residence halls, there are 22 buildings.

STUDENT LIFE: 74% of undergraduates are from New York. Others are from 23 states, 5 foreign countries, and Canada. 93% are from public schools. 62% are White; 15% African American; 9% race unknown; 8% Hispanic; 4% two or more races; 2% Asian American; 1% American Indian/Alaska Native; 1% Foreign. **Female To Male Ratio:** 2.0:1. The average age of freshmen is 18; all undergraduates, 20. 30% do not continue beyond their first year; 55% remain to graduate. **Housing:** 450 students can be accommodated in college housing, which includes single-sex and coed dorms and off-campus apartments. In addition, there are special-interest houses, and additional housing for nontraditional-age students. On-campus housing is guaranteed for all 4 years. 85% of students live on campus; of those, 90% remain on campus on weekends. All students may keep cars.

FACULTY/CLASSROOMS: 44% of faculty are male; 56% are female. All teach undergraduates, and 10% do research. No introductory courses are taught by graduate students. The average class size in an introductory lecture is 25; in a laboratory is 16; and in a regular course is 14.

PROGRAMS OF STUDY: Wells confers B.A., and B.S. degrees. Bachelor's degrees are awarded in BIOLOGICAL SCIENCE (biochemistry, biology/biological science, and molecular biology), BUSINESS (business administration and management), COMMUNICATIONS AND THE ARTS (creative writing, dance, dramatic arts, English, literature, film and media studies, Spanish, theatre studies, and visual and performing arts), COMPUTER AND PHYSICAL SCIENCE (chemistry, computer science, mathematics, and physics), EDUCATION (early childhood education and elementary education), ENGINEERING AND ENVIRONMENTAL DESIGN (environmental science), SOCIAL SCIENCE (anthropology, economics, history, international studies, philosophy, political science/government, psychology, sociology, and women & gender studies). Psychology, and biology are the strongest academically. Psychology, English, biological and chemical sciences have the largest enrollments.

ACTIVITIES: There are no fraternities or sororities. There are 50 groups on campus, including campus greens, Japanese cultural club, Model UN, Spanish club, WILL (women in lifelong learning), WISA, art, band, bell ringers, choir, chorale, chorus, computers, dance, drama, environmental, ethnic, forensics, international, jazz band, LGBT, literary magazine, newspaper, orchestra, photography, political, professional, religious, social, social service, and student government. Popular campus events include Odd-Even Weekends, Spring Weekend and Senior Day. **Sports:** There are 7 intercollegiate sports for men and 9 for women, and 2 intramural sports for men and 2 for women. Facilities include complex for baseball, softball, field hockey, soccer, lacross, softball fields, pool, gymnasium for men's and women's basketball, men's and volleyball. There is also a fitness center available to students, faculty and staff, and tennis courts. **Graduates:** From July 1, 2015 to June 30, 2016, 82 bachelor's degrees were awarded. The most popular majors were psychology (17%), English (10%), and sociology/anthropology (6%). In an average class, 2% graduate in 3 years or less, 60% graduate in 4 years or less, 61% graduate in 5 years or less, and 62% graduate in 6 years or less. Of the 2015 graduating class, 15% were enrolled in graduate school within 6 months of graduation, and 37% were employed.

SERVICES: Counseling and information services are available, as is tutoring in most subjects, such as math, biology, chemistry, political science, women and gender studies, Shakespeare, Spanish, statistics, Calc 1, Calc 2, psychology, history, and international studies. There is remedial reading. Assistance is provided as needed on individual basis. Extended-time testing options are available. **Library/Resources:** The library contains 218,000 volumes, 14,882 microform items, 1,154 audio/video tapes/CDs/DVDs, and subscribes to 371 periodicals including electronic. Computerized library services include interlibrary loans, database searching, Internet access, and Wi-Fi capability. Special learning facilities include an art gallery, The Wells College archives, an education curriculum center and a walk-through art gallery, database training is available as part of the library's information literacy program. There is also a Book Arts Center containing facilities for book-binding, and letter-press and calligraphy. **Physically Challenged Students:** 43% of the campus is accessible. Facilities include wheelchair ramps, elevators, special parking, special class scheduling, and lowered telephones. **Special:** Wells offers cross-registration with Cornell University, Cayuga Community College, and

Ithaca College, internships, and accelerated degree programs in all majors. Study abroad in 20 countries is permitted. A 3-2 engineering degree is available with Columbia, Clarkson, and Cornell Universities. Students may also earn a 4+1 MBA through the University of Clarkson, and a 4+1 MEd through University of Rochester (30% tuition reduction agreement). Student-designed majors and pass/fail options are available. Work-study, B.A.-B.S. degrees, and dual majors are also available. There are 2 national honor societies and a chapter of Phi Beta Kappa. **Visiting:** There are regularly scheduled orientations for prospective students, including tours, interviews, class attendance, presentations, open houses, an overnight host program, and meetings with faculty and coaches. There are guides for informal visits, visitors may sit in on classes, and stay overnight. To schedule a visit, contact the Admissions Office. **Campus Safety and Security:** Measures include 24-hour foot and vehicle patrol, emergency notification system, self-defense education, and security escort services. There are shuttle buses, emergency telephones, lighted pathways/sidewalks, and campus safety officers are N.Y.S. licensed security guards.

REQUIREMENTS: The SAT or ACT is required. Graduation from an accredited secondary school should include 20 academic credits or Carnegie units. High school courses must include 4 years of English, 3 years each of a foreign language and math, and 2 years each of history and lab science, and 1 teacher recommendations, an essay/personal statement are required, and an interview is strongly recommended. AP and CLEP credits are accepted. Important factors in the admissions decision are recommendations by school officials, extracurricular activities record, and advanced placement or honors courses. To graduate, students must complete a total of 120 credit hours, including 33 to 63 in the major, with a minimum GPA of 2.0 overall and in the major. All students must complete 2 first-year experience courses, a comprehensive exam, 3 January intersession internships/courses, and a senior project/thesis. Distribution requirements include 4 courses in phys ed and wellness, 3 each in natural and social sciences and arts and humanities, 2 in a foreign language, and 1 in formal reasoning. **Procedure:** Freshmen are admitted in the fall. Entrance exams should be taken prior to application. There are early decision, early admissions, and deferred admissions plans. Early decision applications should be filed by December 15; regular applications, by March 1 for fall entry, along with a $40 fee. Notification of early decision is sent January 15; regular decision. Applications are accepted online. **Transfer Students:** 56 transfer students enrolled in 2015-2016. Applicants must be in good standing at the institution last attended. A minimum GPA of 2.0 is required. Wells requires official college and high school transcripts, a personal statement, standardized test scores, and a recommendation from a professor. An interview is strongly recommended. 60 of 120 credits required for the bachelor's degree must be completed at Wells. **International Students:** There are 14 international students enrolled. The school actively recruits these students. They must take the TOEFL with a minimum score of 550 on the paper-based TOEFL (PBT) or 80 on the Internet-based version (iBT). They must also take the SAT or ACT.

ADMISSIONS: 63% of the 2016-2017 applicants were accepted. The SAT scores for the 2016-2017 freshman class were: Critical Reading-- 49% below 500, 37% between 500 and 599, 12% between 600 and 699, and 2% between 700 and 800. Math-- 56% below 500, 35% between 500 and 599, 7% between 600 and 699, and 2% between 700 and 800. Writing-- 59% below 500, 32% between 500 and 599, and 9% between 600 and 699. The ACT scores were 54% between 18 and 23, 41% between 24 and 29, and 5% above 30. 3 freshmen graduated first in their class. **Admissions Contact:** Kishan Zuber, Vice President for Enrollment Services. Email: *kzuber@wells.edu* Web: *www.wells.edu*

FINANCIAL AID: In 2016-2017, 99% of all full-time freshmen received some form of financial aid. 78% of all full-time freshmen received need-based aid. The average freshman award was $18,505. Need-based scholarships or need-based grants averaged $13,645 ($21,320 maximum); need-based self-help aid (loans and jobs) averaged $4,900 ($6,600 maximum); and other non-need-based awards and non-need-based scholarships averaged $6,850 ($10,500 maximum). 82% of undergraduate students work part-time. Average annual earnings from campus work are $1600. The average financial indebtedness of the 2016 graduate was $20,355. Wells is a member of CSS. The FAFSA code is 002901. The priority date for freshman financial aid applications for fall entry is March 15.

YESHIVA UNIVERSITY — D-5

www.yu.edu

New York, NY 10033 — (212) 960-5277

Fax: (212) 960-0086
Email: yuadmit@ymail.yu.edu
Full-time: 1438 men, 1379 women
Faculty: I, +$
Part-time: 36 men, 16 women
Ph.D.s: 79%
Graduate: 1701 men, 2183 women
Student/Faculty: n/av
Year: semesters, summer session
Tuition: $36,500
Room & Board: $10,750
Freshman Class: 1898 applied, 1319 accepted, 911 enrolled
SAT CR/M/W: 619/622/610 **ACT:** 26
CEEB CODE: 2990
Application Deadline: December 1
VERY COMPETITIVE+

Yeshiva University, founded in 1886, is an independent liberal arts institution offering undergraduate programs through Yeshiva College, its undergraduate college for men, Stern College for women, and the Sy Syms School of Business. The figures in the above capsule and in this profile are approximate. There are 3 undergraduate schools and 9 graduate schools. In addition to regional accreditation, YU has baccalaureate program accreditation with CSWE. The 26-acre campus is in an urban area in New York City.

STUDENT LIFE: 44% of undergraduates are from out of state. Students are from 31 states, 16 foreign countries, and Canada. 14% are from public schools. **Female To Male Ratio:** 1.1:1. The average age of freshmen is 17; all undergraduates, 19. 8% do not continue beyond their first year; 92% remain to graduate. **Housing:** 1600 students can be accommodated in college housing, which includes single-sex dorms and off-campus apartments. On-campus housing is guaranteed for all 4 years. 85% of students live on campus. All students may keep cars. Alcohol is not permitted.

FACULTY/CLASSROOMS: 73% of faculty are male; 27% are female. 58% teach undergraduates. No introductory courses are taught by graduate students. The average class size in an introductory lecture is 38; in a laboratory is 15; and in a regular course is 18.

PROGRAMS OF STUDY: Yeshiva confers B.A., and B.S. degrees. Associate degrees are also awarded. Bachelor's degrees are awarded in BIOLOGICAL SCIENCE (biology/biological science), BUSINESS (accounting, business administration and management, and marketing/retailing/merchandising), COMMUNICATIONS AND THE ARTS (classical languages, communications, English, French, Hebrew, music, and speech/debate/rhetoric), COMPUTER AND PHYSICAL SCIENCE (chemistry, computer science, and mathematics), ENGINEERING AND ENVIRONMENTAL DESIGN (preengineering), HEALTH PROFESSIONS (health science), SOCIAL SCIENCE (economics, history, philosophy, political science/government, psychology, religion, and sociology). Liberal arts, and Jewish studies are the strongest academically. Accounting, psychology, and economics have the largest enrollments.

ACTIVITIES: There are no fraternities or sororities. There are 70 groups on campus, including art, choir, computers, drama, honors, international, jazz band, literary magazine, musical theater, newspaper, political, professional, religious, social service, student government, and yearbook. Popular campus events include Holiday and Dramatic Presentations, and Parents Day. **Sports:** There are 8 intercollegiate sports for men and 2 for women, and 5 intramural sports for men and 4 for women. Facilities include a gymnasium. **Graduates:** From July 1, 2015 to June 30, 2016, 631 bachelor's degrees were awarded. The most popular majors were busilness (27%), psychology (17%), and biology (14%).

SERVICES: There is remedial reading and writing. There is also a writing center, which helps students with composition and verbal skills. **Library/Resources:** The 7 libraries contain 900,000 volumes, 759,000 microform items, 980 audio/video tapes/CDs/DVDs, and subscribe to 7,790 periodicals including electronic. Computerized library services include interlibrary loans and database searching. Special learning facilities include an art gallery, peer tutoring program, a museum, career center, writing centers, and academic support. **Physically Challenged Students:** 95% of the campus is accessible. Facilities include wheelchair ramps and elevators. **Special:** YU offers a 3-2 degree in occupational therapy with Columbia and New York Universities; a 3-4 degree in podiatry with the New York College of Podiatric Medicine; and a 3-2 or 4-2 degree in engineering with Columbia University. Stern College students may take courses in advertising, photography, and design at the Fashion Institute of Technology. Study-abroad programs may be arranged in Israel. The school offers independent study options and an optional pass/no credit system. There are 9 national honor societies and 20 departmental honors programs. **Visiting:** There are regularly scheduled orientations for prospective students, YU holds open houses for high school students. There are guides for informal visits, visitors may sit in on classes, and stay overnight. To schedule a visit, contact the Office of Admissions. **Campus Safety and Security:** Measures include 24-hour foot and vehicle patrol and security escort services. There are also shuttle buses, emergency telephones, lighted pathways/sidewalks, ID cards, vulnerability surveys, fire drills, and alarm systems.

REQUIREMENTS: The SAT or ACT is required. Graduation from an accredited secondary school with 16 academic credits is required for admission. The GED is accepted under limited and specific circumstances. The SAT Subject test in Hebrew is recommended for placement purposes. An interview and an essay are required. A GPA of 3.3 is required. AP and CLEP credits are accepted. Important factors in the admissions decision are extracurricular activities record, personality/intangible qualities, and evidence of special talent. To graduate, students must complete a total of 128 credit hours. Under the dual program, students pursue a liberal arts or business curriculum together with courses in Hebrew language, literature, and culture. Courses in Jewish learning are geared to the student's level of preparation. **Procedure:** Freshmen are admitted to all sessions. There are early admissions, deferred admissions, and rolling admissions plans. Applications should be filed by December 1 for fall entry, along with a $70 fee. Notifications are sent February 1. **Transfer Students:** 95 of 128 credits required for the bachelor's degree must be completed at YU. **International Students:** The school actively recruits these students. They must take the TOEFL. They must also take the SAT or ACT.

ADMISSIONS: 69% of the 2016-2017 applicants were accepted. **Admissions Contact:** Michael Kranzler, Director of Undergraduate Admissions. Email: *yuadmit@ymail.yu.edu* Web: *www.yu.edu*

FINANCIAL AID: Yeshiva is a member of CSS. The CSS/Profile and the college's own financial statement are required. The FAFSA code is 002903. The priority date for freshman financial aid applications for fall entry is February 1.

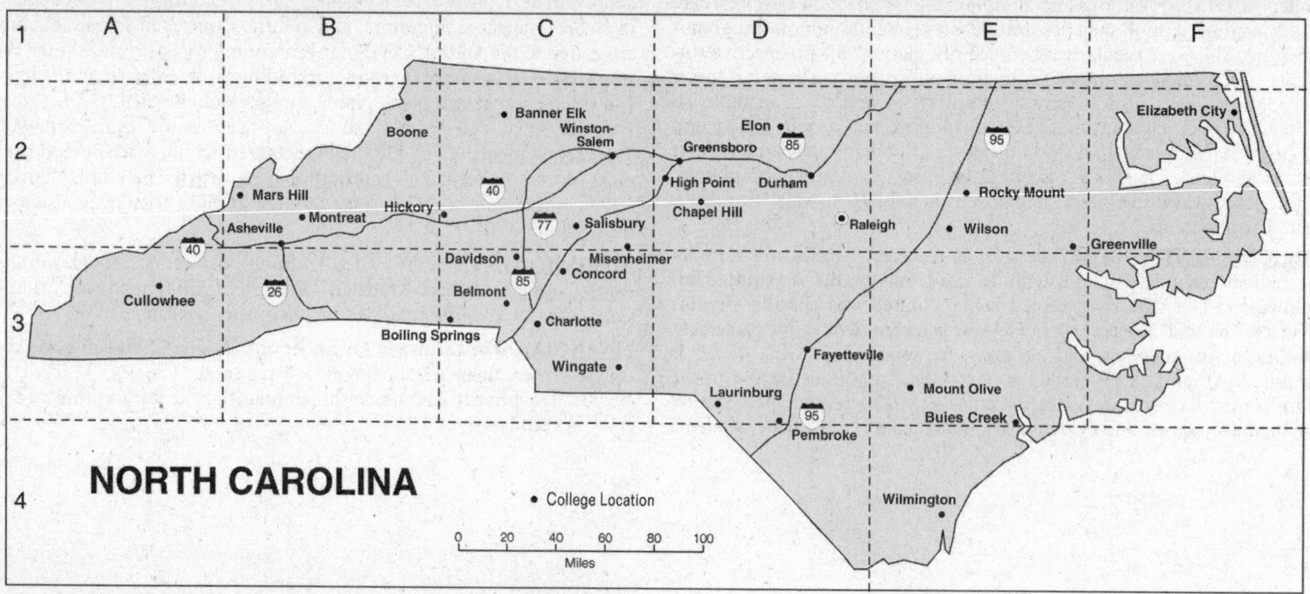

APPALACHIAN STATE UNIVERSITY B-2

www.appstate.edu

Boone, NC 28608 **(828) 262-2120**

Fax: (828) 262-3296
Email: admissions@appstate.edu
Full-time: 7097 men, 7740 women
Faculty: 814; IIA, -$
Part-time: 354 men, 521 women
Ph.D.s: 99%
Graduate: 554 men, 1323 women
Student/Faculty: 16 to 1
Year: semesters, summer session
Tuition: $7416 ($19,970)
Room & Board: $7000
Freshman Class: 12248 applied, 7744 accepted, 3028 enrolled
SAT CR/M/W: 572/581/548 **ACT:** 26
CEEB CODE: 5010
Application Deadline: March 15
VERY COMPETITIVE

Appalachian State University, founded in 1899 and is a member of the University of North Carolina system, a comprehensive university offering undergraduate and graduate programs in the arts and sciences, business, teacher education, fine and applied arts, music, and health sciences. The figures in the above capsule and in this profile are approximate. There are 8 undergraduate schools and 1 graduate school. In addition to regional accreditation, App State has baccalaureate program accreditation with AACSB, CSAB, CSWE, NASAD, NASM, NCATE, and NRPA. The 1300-acre campus is in a small town in northwestern North Carolina. Including any residence halls, there are 90 buildings.

STUDENT LIFE: 92% of undergraduates are from North Carolina. Others are from 46 states, 61 foreign countries, and Canada. 88% are from public schools. 87% are White; 4% Hispanic; 3% African American; 2% two or more races; 12% race unknown; 1% Asian American; 1% Foreign. **Female To Male Ratio:** 1.2:1. The average age of freshmen is 18; all undergraduates, 21. 12% do not continue beyond their first year; 66% remain to graduate. **Housing:** 5775 students can be accommodated in college housing, which includes single-sex and coed dorms, and sorority houses, living learning communities. On-campus housing is guaranteed for the freshman year only and is available on a lottery system for upperclassmen. 67% of students commute. All students may keep cars.

FACULTY/CLASSROOMS: 53% of faculty are male; 47% are female. 88% teach undergraduates. Graduate students teach 6% of introductory courses. The average class size in a laboratory is 22 and in a regular course is 33.

PROGRAMS OF STUDY: App State confers B.A., B.S., B.F.A., B.M., B.S.B.A., B.S.C.J., B.S.N., and B.S.W. degrees. Master's and doctoral degrees are also awarded. Bachelor's degrees are awarded in AGRICULTURE (agricultural business management and environmental studies), BIOLOGICAL SCIENCE (biology/biological science, ecology, molecular biology, and nutrition), BUSINESS (accounting, banking and finance, hospitality management services, insurance and risk management, international business management, management engineering, marketing/retailing/merchandising, and recreational facilities management), COMMUNICATIONS AND THE ARTS (advertising, apparel design, art, art and design, art/visual culture, arts administration/management, communications, dance, dramatic arts, English, French, graphic design, industrial design, journalism, languages, music business management, music performance, performing arts, photography, public relations, Spanish, and studio art), COMPUTER AND PHYSICAL SCIENCE (actuarial science, chemistry, computer science, geology, mathematics, physics, and statistics), EDUCATION (art education, athletic training, business education, computer education, drama education, education, elementary education, English education, foreign languages education, global studies, health education, mathematics education, middle school education, music education, physical education, science education, secondary education, social science education, social studies education, and special education), ENGINEERING AND ENVIRONMENTAL DESIGN (architecture, computer technology, construction management, construction technology, electrical/electronics engineering technology, engineering technology, environmental science, graphic arts technology, industrial engineering technology, and interior design), HEALTH PROFESSIONS (exercise science, health care administration, health science, music therapy, nursing, preventive/wellness health care, and speech pathology/audiology), SOCIAL SCIENCE (anthropology, area studies, child psychology/development, criminal justice, East Asian studies, economics, family/consumer studies, French studies, geography, geography information science, German area studies, history, interdisciplinary studies, Latin American studies, Middle Eastern studies, philosophy, political science/government, psychology, religion, social work, sociology, South Asian studies, Third World studies, and women's studies). Business/marketing, elementary education, and social sciences have the largest enrollments.

ACTIVITIES: 7% of men belong to 13 national fraternities; 11% of women belong to 9 national sororities. There are 289 groups on campus, including art, band, cheerleading, chess, choir, chorale, chorus, communications, computers, dance, debate, drama, drill team, environmental, ethnic, film, forensics, honors, international, jazz band, LGBT, literary magazine, marching band, musical theater, newspaper, opera, orchestra, pep band, photography, political, professional, radio and TV, religious, social, social service, student government, and symphony. Popular campus events include football and basketball games, Annual Diversity Celebration, Legends Concerts, and Greek Week. **Sports:** There are 10 intercollegiate sports for men and 10 for women, and 20 intramural sports for men and 20 for women. Facilities include a convocation center, a varsity gym, a stadium, fitness and recreation centers, facilities for football, soccer, field hockey, basketball, volleyball, wrestling, indoor and outdoor track, golf course, baseball field, tennis courts, pool, climbing wall, racquetball courts, aerobics studio, weight room, and cardio equipment. **Graduates:** From July 1, 2015 to June 30, 2016, 3435 bachelor's degrees were awarded. The most popular majors were business/marketing (20%), education (17%), and social sciences (8%). 499 companies recruited on campus in 2015-2016. In an average class, 2% graduate in 3 years or less, 44% graduate in 4 years or less, 65% graduate in 5 years or less, and 66% graduate in 6 years or less.

SERVICES: Counseling and information services are available, as is tutoring in most subjects, a reader service for the blind, and remedial math, reading, and writing. **Library/Resources:** The 2 libraries contain 937,956 volumes, 1.5 million microform items, 72,813 audio/video tapes/CDs/DVDs, subscribe to 23,861 periodicals including electronic. Computerized library services include interlibrary loans, database searching, and Internet access. Special learning facilities include an art gallery, radio station, and a dark sky observatory. **Physically Challenged Students:** All of the campus is accessible. Facilities include wheelchair ramps, elevators, special parking, specially equipped restrooms, special class scheduling, lowered drinking fountains, lowered telephones, and special housing. **Special:** App State offers dual degree in Communications with Universidad de las Americas Puebla, a private university in Mexico, a 3-2 engineering degree with Clemson and Auburn Universities, internships, work-study programs, B.A.-B.S. degrees, dual majors, and study abroad. There are 16 national honor societies, a freshman honors program, and 25 departmental honors programs. **Visiting:** There are regularly scheduled orientations for prospective students, starting at the end of May for all new students. There are guides for informal visits and visitors may sit in on classes. **Campus Safety and Security:** Measures include 24-hour foot and vehicle patrol, emergency notification system, self-defense education, and security escort services. There are also shuttle buses, emergency telephones, lighted pathways/sidewalks, and controlled access to dorms/residences.

REQUIREMENTS: The SAT or ACT is required. The ACT Optional Writing test is also required. Applicants must be graduates of an accredited secondary school, Applicants must have completed 4 course units in high school English and math, 3 in science, and 2 in foreign languages and social studies. AP and CLEP credits are accepted. Important factors in the admissions decision are advanced placement or honors courses, extracurricular activities record, and evidence of special talent. To graduate, students must complete 122 credit hours for most programs, including 60 in the major, with a minimum 2.0 GPA. General education requirements include courses in math, science, history, phys ed, English, social sciences, and humanities. **Procedure:** Freshmen are admitted in the fall, spring, and summer. Entrance exams should be taken by November 15, if possible. There are deferred admissions and rolling admissions plans. Applications should be filed by March 15 for fall entry, along with a $55 fee. 630 applicants were on the 2016 waiting list; 200 were admitted. Applications are accepted online. **Transfer Students:** 1153 transfer students enrolled in 2015-2016. Transfer students must have earned a minimum 2.0 GPA on collegiate work. They must have a minimum of 30 semester credits or else apply as a freshman. 30 of 128 credits required for the bachelor's degree must be completed at App State. **International Students:** There are 145 international students enrolled. The school actively recruits these students. The SAT or ACT may be accepted in lieu of the TOEFL.

ADMISSIONS: 63% of the 2016-2017 applicants were accepted. The SAT scores for the 2016-2017 freshman class were: Critical Reading-- 11% below 500, 55% between 500 and 599, 30% between 600 and 699, and 4% between 700 and 800. Math-- 6% below 500, 52% between 500 and 599, 38% between 600 and 699, and 4% between 700 and 800. Writing-- 22% below 500, 55% between 500 and 599, 21% between 600 and 699, and 2% between 700 and 800. The ACT scores were 3% below 12, 14% between 12 and 17, 47% between 18 and 23, 19% between 24 and 29, and 17% above 30. 45% of the current freshmen were in the top fifth of their class; 80% were in the top two fifths. **Admissions Contact:** Lloyd Scott, Director of Admissions. Email: *admissions@appstate.edu* Web: *www.appstate.edu*

FINANCIAL AID: In 2016-2017, 67% of all full-time freshmen and 64% of continuing full-time students received some form of financial aid. 47% of all full-time freshmen and 46% of continuing full-time students received need-based aid. The average freshman award was $10,345. Need-based scholarships or need-based grants averaged $7,710 ($30,679 maximum); need-based self-help aid (loans and jobs) averaged $3,292 ($6,577 maximum); non-need-based athletic scholarships averaged $10,948 ($25,727 maximum); and other non-need-based awards and non-need-based scholarships averaged $2,235 ($12,929 maximum). The average financial indebtedness of the 2016 graduate was $20,016. The FAFSA code is 002906. Check with the school for current application deadlines.

BARTON COLLEGE *(The complete profile is made available exclusively on our website, www.barronspac.com)*

BELMONT ABBEY COLLEGE — C-3

www.belmontabbeycollege.edu

Belmont, NC 28012	**(704) 461-6665** **(888) BAC-0110**
Fax: (704) 461-6220	**Email: info@BAC.edu**
Full-time: 663 men, 927 women	**Faculty:** 76; IIB
Part-time: 33 men, 83 women	**Ph.D.s:** 70%
Graduate: n/av	**Student/Faculty:** 16 to 1
Year: semesters, summer session	**Tuition:** $37,000
Room & Board: $11,156	**Freshman Class:** 1843 applied, 1185 accepted, 303 enrolled
SAT CR/M: 510/510 **ACT:** 23	**CEEB CODE:** 5055
Application Deadline: August 1	**COMPETITIVE**

Belmont Abbey College, founded by the Benedictine Monks in 1876, is a private, liberal arts college affiliated with the Roman Catholic Church. The figures in the above capsule and in this profile are approximate. There is 1 undergraduate school. In addition to regional accreditation, Belmont Abbey has baccalaureate program accreditation with NCATE. The 650-acre campus is in a suburban area 10 miles west of Charlotte, North Carolina. Including any residence halls, there are 20 buildings.

STUDENT LIFE: 70% of undergraduates are from North Carolina. Others are from 33 states, 20 foreign countries, and Canada. 35% are White; 31% race unknown; 3% Foreign; 27% African American; 2% Hispanic; 1% Asian American. 57% are Catholic; 47% claim no religious affiliation. **Female To Male Ratio:** 1.5:1. The average age of freshmen is 20; all undergraduates, 28. 37% do not continue beyond their first year; 63% remain to graduate. **Housing:** 747 students can be accommodated in college housing, which includes single-sex and coed dorms, on-campus apartments, off-campus apartments, special-interest houses, quiet residence hall, and single-occupancy housing is available for all students. On-campus housing is guaranteed for all 4 years. 82% of students live on campus. All students may keep cars.

FACULTY/CLASSROOMS: 55% of faculty are male; 45% are female. All teach undergraduates and 60% do research. No introductory courses are taught by graduate students. The average class size in an introductory lecture is 16; in a laboratory is 15; and in a regular course is 4.

PROGRAMS OF STUDY: Belmont Abbey confers B.A. and B.S. degrees. Bachelor's degrees are awarded in BIOLOGICAL SCIENCE (biology/biological science), BUSINESS (accounting, business administration and management, and sports management), COMMUNICATIONS AND THE ARTS (English), COMPUTER AND PHYSICAL SCIENCE (mathematics), EDUCATION (education and elementary education), SOCIAL SCIENCE (applied psychology, criminal justice, history, liberal arts/general studies, parks and recreation management, philosophy, political science/government, psychology, and theological studies). Psychology, elementary education, and English are the strongest academically. Business administration, education, and elementary education have the largest enrollments.

ACTIVITIES: 6% of men belong to 1 local and 2 national fraternities; 5% of women belong to 4 local sororities. There are 21 groups on campus, including a campus activities board club, ballroom dancing club, chess club, men's household club, motorsports club, art club, cheerleading, chess, choir, chorus, computers, drama, honors, international, literary magazine, newspaper, political, professional, religious, social, social service, and student government. Popular campus events include The Abbey Players, Crusader Welcome Week, President's Ball, Homecoming Festivities, Giveaway Novelties, Halloween Festival, and Crawfish Boil on the Quad. **Sports:** There are 8 intercollegiate sports for men and 8 for women. Facilities include a phys ed center with a gym. Men's sports include baseball. basketball, cross country, golf, lacrosse, soccer, tennis, track & field, wrestling and volleyball. Women's sports include basketball, cross country, golf, lacrosse, soccer, softball, tennis, track & field, and volleyball. Facilities include a wheeler center, strength & conditioning, tennis center, a country club, and a crusader field. **Graduates:** From July 1, 2015 to June 30, 2016, 379 bachelor's degrees were awarded. The most popular majors were business management (39%), education (15%), and elementary education (13%). 90 companies recruited on campus in 2015-2016. In an average class, 40% graduate in 4 years or less, 45% graduate in 5 years or less, and 46% graduate in 6 years or less. Of the 2015 graduating class, 16% were enrolled in graduate school within 6 months of graduation, and 88% were employed.

SERVICES: Counseling and information services are available, as is tutoring in some subjects, such as English, math and accounting. There is also a reader service for the blind. **Library/Resources:** The library contains 118,827 volumes, 116,173 microform items, 7,418 audio/video tapes/CDs/DVDs, and subscribes to 275 periodicals including electronic. Computerized library services include interlibrary loans, database searching, Internet access, and Wi-Fi capability. **Physically Challenged Students:** 60% of the campus is accessible. Facilities include wheelchair ramps, elevators, special parking, specially equipped restrooms, special class scheduling, and lowered drinking fountains. **Special:** Cross-registration is offered through the Charlotte Area Educational Consortium. There are internships in many majors, including required internships in educational studies, as well as on-campus work-study, accelerated degree programs, nondegree study, dual majors, and study abroad in Guatemala, Germany, and France. There are 5 national honor societies and a freshman honors program. **Visiting:** There are regularly scheduled orientations for prospective students, consisting of a campus tour and meetings with a financial aid adviser, faculty, and students. There are guides for informal visits, visitors may sit in on classes, and stay overnight. To schedule a visit, contact the Admissions Office. **Campus Safety and Security:** Measures include 24-hour foot and vehicle patrol, self-defense education, security escort services, emergency telephones, and lighted pathways/sidewalks.

REQUIREMENTS: The SAT is required. Candidates must be graduates of an accredited secondary school and a 2.0 high school GPA. A minimum of 16 academic credits must be completed, including 4 in English, 3 each in math and electives, and 2 each in foreign language, history, and science. AP and CLEP credits are accepted. Important factors in the admissions decision are advanced placement or honors courses, extracurricular activities record, and leadership record. To graduate, all students must complete a minimum of 120 credits, including 60 credits of core curriculum and 30 upper-level credits in the major. Among the core requirements are history, math, natural sciences, theology, philosophy, English, fine arts, and rhetoric. A minimum 2.0 GPA must be maintained. Honors students must submit a thesis. **Procedure:** Freshmen are admitted in the fall and spring. Entrance exams should be taken by October of the senior year. There are deferred admissions and rolling admissions plans. Applications should be filed by August 1 for fall entry, along with a $35 fee. Applications are accepted online. **Transfer Students:** 185 transfer students enrolled in 2015-2016. Students with 24 or more credit hours must submit all college transcripts, and those with fewer than 24 credit hours must also submit a high school transcript and SAT scores. All candidates must have a minimum 2.0 GPA and be eligible to return to the last college attended. An interview is recommended. 30 of 120 credits required for the bachelor's degree must be completed at Belmont Abbey. **International Students:** There are 46 international students enrolled. The school actively recruits these students. They must take the TOEFL with a minimum score of 550 on the paper-based TOEFL (PBT) or 79 on the Internet-based version (iBT). They must also take the SAT or ACT, scoring 900.

ADMISSIONS: 64% of the 2016-2017 applicants were accepted. The SAT scores for the 2016-2017 freshman class were: Critical Reading--54% below 500, 29% between 500 and 599, 13% between 600 and 699, and 3% between 700 and 800. Math-- 42% below 500, 39% between 500 and 599, 17% between 600 and 699, and 2% between 700 and 800. The ACT scores were 27% below 12, 33% between 12 and 17, 28% between 18 and 23, 4% between 24 and 29, and 7% above 30. 20% of the current freshmen were in the top fifth of their class; 46% were in the top two fifths. 3 freshmen graduated first in their class. **Admissions Contact:** Roger Jones, Director of Admissions. Email: *info@BAC.edu* Web: *www.belmontabbeycollege.edu*

FINANCIAL AID: In 2016-2017, 85% of all full-time freshmen received some form of financial aid. 90% of all full-time freshmen received need-based aid. 12% of undergraduate students work part-time. Belmont Abbey is a member of CSS. The the state aid form is required. The FAFSA code is 002910. The priority date for freshman financial aid applications for fall entry is April 1. The filing deadline for fall entry is July 1.

BENNETT COLLEGE *(The complete profile is made available exclusively on our website, www.barronspac.com)*

CABARRUS COLLEGE OF HEALTH SCIENCES *(The complete profile is made available exclusively on our website, www.barronspac.com)*

CAMPBELL UNIVERSITY — E-3

www.campbell.edu

Buies Creek, NC 27506 — **(800) 334-4111**

Fax: (910) 893-1288	**Email:** admissions@campbell.edu
Full-time: 1500 men, 1500 women	**Faculty:** n/av
Part-time: 750 men, 750 women	**Ph.D.s:** 92%
Graduate: n/av	**Student/Faculty:** n/av
Year: semesters, summer session	**Tuition:** $27,670
Room & Board: $9860	**Freshman Class:** n/av
SAT or ACT: required	**CEEB CODE:** 5100
Application Deadline: n/av	**VERY COMPETITIVE**

Campbell University, founded in 1887, is a private, nonsectarian institution offering degree programs in liberal arts and sciences, medicine, business, engineering and education. There are 7 undergraduate schools and 6 graduate schools. In addition to regional accreditation, Campbell has baccalaureate program accreditation with ACPE, CSWE, and NCATE. The 1300-acre campus is in a rural area 28 miles South of Raleigh and 30 miles North of Fayetteville. Including any residence halls, there are 84 buildings.

STUDENT LIFE: Students are from 50 states, 42 foreign countries, and Canada. 90% are from public schools. **Male To Female Ratio:** Is 1:1. The average age of freshmen is 18; all undergraduates, 20. **Housing:** 2000 students can be accommodated in college housing, which includes single-sex dorms, on-campus apartments, and fraternity houses. On-campus housing is guaranteed for all 4 years. All students may keep cars. Alcohol is not permitted.

FACULTY/CLASSROOMS: No introductory courses are taught by graduate students.

PROGRAMS OF STUDY: Campbell confers B.A., B.S., B.Applied Science., B.B.A., B.H.S., and B.S.W. degrees. Associate, master's, and doctoral degrees are also awarded. Bachelor's degrees are awarded in BIOLOGICAL SCIENCE (biochemistry and biology/biological science), BUSINESS (accounting, banking and finance, business administration and management, business administration international, business administration, management, operations, business administration marketing, business economics, international business, international business management, investments and securities, and sports management), COMMUNICATIONS AND THE ARTS (advertising, art, choral music, church music, communications, English, fine arts, French, graphic design, information technology, journalism, music, Spanish, studio art, studio art graphic design, and theatre arts), COMPUTER AND PHYSICAL SCIENCE (chemistry, computer information technology, computer information systems, computer science, information sciences and systems, and mathematics), EDUCATION (athletic training, childhood education, early childhood education, education, elementary education, English education, and middle school education), ENGINEERING AND ENVIRONMENTAL DESIGN (military science), HEALTH PROFESSIONS (biology, clinical science, exercise science, health communication, health care administration, nursing, predentistry, premedicine, preoptometry, and prepharmacy), SOCIAL SCIENCE (administration of justice, counseling/psychology, criminal justice, economics, history, homeland security, physical fitness/movement, political science/government, prelaw, psychology, religion, and social work). Health science, trust management (business), and education, are the strongest academically. Education, pharmacy, and biology have the largest enrollments.

ACTIVITIES: There are 50 groups on campus, including art, band, cheerleading, choir, chorale, chorus, computers, debate, drama, ethnic, honors, international, jazz band, literary magazine, musical theater, newspaper, orchestra, pep band, photography, political, professional, religious, social, social service, student government, and yearbook. Popular campus events include Staley Lecture Series, Spring Fling, Christmas Formals, Concerts, Plays, Homecoming, and Parents Weekend. **Sports:** Facilities include a gym for intramural sports, a gymnasium for division sports, football field, athletic complex, golf course, nature trail, NCAA track, workout facilities, tennis courts, baseball, softball, soccer fields, and an indoor pool. **Graduates:** From July 1, 2015 to June 30, 2016, 932 bachelor's degrees were awarded. The most popular majors were history (4%) and business administration (17%). 14 companies recruited on campus in 2015-2016. In an average class, 31% graduate in 4 years or less, 49% graduate in 5 years or less, and 51% graduate in 6 years or less.

Of the 2015 graduating class, 16% were enrolled in graduate school within 6 months of graduation, and 67% were employed.

SERVICES: Counseling and information services are available, as is tutoring in most subjects, and remedial math and writing. **Library/ Resources:** The 2 libraries contain 319,561 volumes, 180,914 microform items, 17,350 audio/video tapes/CDs/DVDs, and subscribe to 83,898 periodicals including electronic. Computerized library services include interlibrary loans, database searching, Internet access, and Wi-Fi capability. Special learning facilities include an art gallery, TV station, computer labs, computerized music lab, athletic learning resources center, drug information center for the school of pharmacy, pharmacy research facility, and the Lundy-Fetterman animal museum. **Physically Challenged Students:** 95% of the campus is accessible. Facilities include wheelchair ramps, elevators, special parking, specially equipped restrooms, special class scheduling, lowered drinking fountains, lowered telephones, and special housing. **Special:** Campbell offers co-op programs, internships, study abroad in 7 countries, a Washington semester, numerous apprenticeships, accelerated degrees, dual majors, and a general studies degree. There is credit for military and work experience. Cross-registration with the North Carolina Model Teacher Education Consortium is possible. There are 14 national honor societies, Phi Beta Kappa, and a freshman honors program. **Visiting:** There are regularly scheduled orientations for prospective students, including a campus tour, student panel and department visits. There are guides for informal visits, visitors may sit in on classes, and stay overnight. To schedule a visit, contact the Admissions Office. **Campus Safety and Security:** Measures include 24-hour foot and vehicle patrol, emergency notification system, self-defense education, and security escort services, emergency telephones, lighted pathways/ sidewalks, and controlled access to dorms/residences.

REQUIREMENTS: The SAT or ACT is required. Applicants should have completed 12 high school academic credits, including 4 credits of English, 3 of math, and 2 each of history or social studies, science, and foreign language. An essay, an interview, and a portfolio are recommended. An audition is required for some majors. A GPA of 2.7 is required. AP and CLEP credits are accepted. Important factors in the admissions decision are advanced placement or honors courses, leadership record, and personality/intangible qualities. To graduate, students must complete 124 credit hours with a minimum GPA of 2.0 overall and in the major. All students must take a core curriculum of 45 to 65 hours including English, math, science, social science, religion, fine arts, phys ed, and the cultural enrichment program. **Procedure:** Freshmen are admitted to all sessions. Entrance exams should be taken during the junior year or the fall of the senior year. There are deferred admissions and rolling admissions plans. Application deadlines are open. Applications are accepted online. **Transfer Students:** Applicants should have a minimum GPA of 2.5 and supply transcripts from previously attended colleges. 36 of 124 credits required for the bachelor's degree must be completed at Campbell. **International Students:** There are 153 international students enrolled. The school actively recruits these students. They must take the TOEFL with a minimum score of 500 on the paper-based TOEFL (PBT) or 63 on the Internet-based version (iBT). They must also take the SAT or ACT.

ADMISSIONS: 30 freshmen graduated first in their class. **Admissions Contact:** Jason Hall, Assistant Vice President for Admissions. Email: *admissions@campbell.edu* Web: *www.campbell.edu*

FINANCIAL AID: The FAFSA code is 002913. Check with the school for current application deadlines.

CATAWBA COLLEGE *(The complete profile is made available exclusively on our website, www.barronspac.com)*

DAVIDSON COLLEGE C-3

www.davidson.edu

Davidson, NC 28035	(704) 894-2230 (800) 768-0380
Fax: (704) 894-2016	Email: admission@davidson.edu
Full-time: 911 men, 885 women	Faculty: 177; IIB, ++$
Part-time: n/av	Ph.D.s: 97%
Graduate: n/av	Student/Faculty: 10 to 1
Year: semesters	Tuition: $46,966
Room & Board: $13,153	Freshman Class: 5382 applied, 1191 accepted, 510 enrolled
SAT CR/M/W: 680/680/670 ACT: 30	CEEB CODE: 5150
Application Deadline: January 2	MOST COMPETITIVE

Davidson College, founded in 1837, is a private liberal arts institution affiliated with the Presbyterian Church. There is 1 undergraduate school. In addition to regional accreditation, Davidson has baccalaureate program accreditation with ACS. The 665-acre campus is in a small town 19 miles North of Charlotte. Including any residence halls, there are 124 buildings.

STUDENT LIFE: 79% of undergraduates are from out of state, mostly the South. Students are from 49 states, 49 foreign countries, and Canada. 47% are from public schools. 67% are White; 7% African American; 7% Hispanic; 7% Foreign; 5% Asian American; 4% two or more races; 2% race unknown; 1% American Indian/Alaska Native. **Male To Female Ratio:** 1.0:1. The average age of freshmen is 18; all undergraduates, 20. 4% do not continue beyond their first year; 93% remain to graduate. **Housing:** 1758 students can be accommodated in college housing, which includes single-sex and coed dorms, on-campus apartments, and off-campus apartments. In addition, there are special-interest houses, and substance-free housing. On-campus housing is guaranteed for the freshman year only and on a lottery system for upperclassmen. 94% of students live on campus. All students may keep cars.

FACULTY/CLASSROOMS: 59% of faculty are male; 41% are female. All teach undergraduates and do research. No introductory courses are taught by graduate students. The average class size in an introductory lecture is 15; in a laboratory is 11; and in a regular course is 15.

PROGRAMS OF STUDY: Davidson confers A.B., and B.S. degrees. Bachelor's degrees are awarded in AGRICULTURE (environmental studies), BIOLOGICAL SCIENCE (biology/biological science), COMMUNICATIONS AND THE ARTS (Africana studies, art, Chinese, classics, dramatic arts, English, French, German, music, and Spanish), COMPUTER AND PHYSICAL SCIENCE (chemistry, mathematics, and physics), SOCIAL SCIENCE (anthropology, East Asian studies, economics, gender studies, history, interdisciplinary studies, Latin American studies, philosophy, political science/government, psychology, religion, and sociology). Biology, economics, and political science have the largest enrollments.

ACTIVITIES: 39% of men belong to 6 national fraternities; 70% of women belong to 4 local and 2 national sororities. There are 200 groups on campus, including an outing club, art, cheerleading, choir, chorale, chorus, computers, dance, drama, ethnic, honors, international, jazz band, LGBT, literary magazine, musical theater, newspaper, opera, orchestra, pep band, political, professional, radio and TV, religious, social, social service, student government, symphony, and yearbook. Popular campus events include Fall Concert, Spring Concert, and Convocations. **Sports:** There are 11 intercollegiate sports for men and 10 for women. Facilities include a basketball arena, baseball field, indoor and outdoor tennis courts, racquetball courts, asquash court, anatatorium with a diving well, Nautilus rooms, a gym, wrestling room, dance studio, golf course, cross-country course and trail, football and soccer stadium, sailing, swimming, water skiing, and canoeing. **Graduates:** From July 1, 2015 to June 30, 2016, 468 bachelor's degrees were awarded. The most popular majors were political science (13%), biology (12%), and economics (11%). 688 companies recruited on campus in 2015-2016. In an average class, 90% graduate in 4 years or less, 93% graduate in 5 years or less, and 93% graduate in 6 years or less. Of the 2015 graduating class, 13% were enrolled in graduate school within 6 months of graduation, and 72% were employed.

SERVICES: Counseling and information services are available, as is tutoring in some subjects. Tutoring is available as needed through the Student Affairs Office. There is a reader service for the blind. The Center for Teaching and Learning also provides student support. **Library/ Resources:** The 3 libraries contain 561,427 volumes, 601,821 microform items, 17,878 audio/video tapes/CDs/DVDs, and subscribe to 108,090 periodicals including electronic. Computerized library services include interlibrary loans, database searching, Internet access, and Wi-Fi capability. Special learning facilities include an art gallery, radio station, and arboretum. **Physically Challenged Students:** 90% of the campus is accessible. Facilities include wheelchair ramps, elevators, special parking, specially equipped restrooms, special class scheduling, lowered drinking fountains, and lowered telephones. **Special:** Davidson offers interdisciplinary studies programs and study abroad in 12 countries as well as through other schools' study-abroad programs. A 3-2 engineering program may be arranged with Columbia and Washington (St. Louis) Universities. Students may design their own majors and cross-register with any college in the Charlotte Area Educational Consortium. There are 15 national honor societies, Phi Beta Kappa, and 20 departmental honors programs. **Visiting:** There are guides for informal visits, visitors may sit in on classes, and stay overnight. To schedule a visit, contact the Office of Admission. **Campus Safety and Security:** Measures include 24-hour foot and vehicle patrol, emergency notification system, self-defense education, and security escort services. There are shuttle buses, emergency telephones, lighted pathways/sidewalks, and controlled access to dorms/residences.

REQUIREMENTS: The SAT or ACT is required. SAT Subject Tests are strongly recommended. At least 16 high school units are required, although 20 units are recommended. These should include 4 units of English, 3 units of math, 2 units of the same foreign language, 2 units of science, and 2 units of history/social studies. It is strongly recommended that high school students continue for the third and fourth years in science and in the same foreign language, continue math through calculus, and take additional courses in history. AP credits are accepted. Important factors in the admissions decision are advanced placement or honors courses, recommendations by school officials, and leadership record. Students must complete 32 courses, including 10 to 12 in the major, with a 2.0 GPA in order to graduate. Core curriculum requirements include courses in literature, fine arts, history, religion and philosophy, natural science, math, and social sciences. In addition, students must meet foreign language, composition, cultural diversity, and phys ed requirements. Comprehensive exams and a thesis are required in some majors. **Procedure:** Freshmen are admitted in the fall. Entrance exams should be taken by the end of the junior year. There are early decision and deferred admissions plans. Early decision applications should be filed by November 15; regular applications, by January 2 for fall entry. The fall 2016 application fee was $50. Notification of early decision is sent December 15; regular decision, April 1. 309 early decision candidates were accepted for the 2016-2017 class. Applications are accepted on-line. **Transfer Students:** 11 transfer students enrolled in 2015-2016. Applicants must have at least 1 full year of college work, generally with a 3.0 GPA. They must submit official college and high school transcripts, as well as required letters of recommendation, and be in good standing at their previous college. 16 of 32 credits required for the bachelor's degree must be completed at Davidson. **International Students:** There are 116 international students enrolled. The school actively recruits these students. They must take the TOEFL with a minimum score of 600 on the paper-based TOEFL (PBT) or 100 on the Internet-based version (iBT). They must also take the SAT or ACT.

ADMISSIONS: 22% of the 2016-2017 applicants were accepted. The SAT scores for the 2016-2017 freshman class were: Critical Reading-- 1% below 500, 13% between 500 and 599, 51% between 600 and 699, and 35% between 700 and 800. Math-- 1% below 500, 12% between 500 and 599, 47% between 600 and 699, and 40% between 700 and 800. Writing-- 1% below 500, 17% between 500 and 599, 47% between 600 and 699, and 35% between 700 and 800. The ACT scores were 2% between 18 and 23, 36% between 24 and 29, and 62% above 30. 82% of the current freshmen were in the top fifth of their class; 91% were in the top two fifths. **Admissions Contact:** Christopher J. Gruber, Dean of Admission and Financial Aid. Email: *admission@davidson.edu* Web: *www.davidson.edu*

FINANCIAL AID: In 2016-2017, 45% of all full-time freshmen received some form of financial aid. 44% of all full-time freshmen received need-based aid. The average freshman award was $37,819. Need-based scholarships or need-based grants averaged $35,003; need-based self-help aid (loans and jobs) averaged $2,816; non-need-based athletic scholarships averaged $15,616; and other non-need-based awards and non-need-based scholarships averaged $23,710. 45% of undergraduate students work part-time. The CSS/Profile, college's own financial statement, and noncustodial (divorced/separated) parent's statement; corporate tax return and/or noncustodial parent tax return are required. The FAFSA code is 002918. The deadline for filing freshman financial aid applications for fall entry is February 15.

DUKE UNIVERSITY *(The complete profile is made available exclusively on our website, www.barronspac.com)*

EAST CAROLINA UNIVERSITY — E-2

www.ecu.edu

Greenville, NC 27858 — (252) 328-6640

Fax: (252) 328-6945
Email: admis@ecu.edu
Full-time: 7637 men, 10680 women
Part-time: 1114 men, 1867 women
Graduate: 1981 men, 3668 women
Year: semesters, summer session
Room & Board: $8698
Faculty: I, --$
Ph.D.s: 81%
Student/Faculty: 18 to 1
Tuition: $8239 ($23,435)
Freshman Class: 15535 applied, 9658 accepted, 4015 enrolled
SAT CR/M/W: 510/540/490 **ACT:** 22
CEEB CODE: 5180
Application Deadline: March 15
COMPETITIVE

East Carolina University, founded in 1907, is a state-supported institution offering degree programs in the arts and sciences, business, education, fine arts and communication, health and human performance, human ecology, technology and computer science, medicine, allied health sciences, and nursing. The figures in the above capsule and in this profile are approximate. There are 11 undergraduate schools and 1 graduate school. In addition to regional accreditation, ECU has baccalaureate program accreditation with NCATE. The 400-acre campus is in an urban area in the area of Greenville, 90 miles East of Raleigh. Including any residence halls, there are 239 buildings.

STUDENT LIFE: 88% of undergraduates are from North Carolina. Others are from 42 states, 54 foreign countries, and Canada. 80% are White; 2% Asian American; 2% Hispanic; 16% African American; 1% American Indian/Alaska Native; 1% Foreign. **Female To Male Ratio:** 1.5:1. The average age of freshmen is 18; all undergraduates, 23. 22% do not continue beyond their first year; 58% remain to graduate. **Housing:** 5497 students can be accommodated in college housing, which includes single-sex and coed dorms. In addition, there are honors houses, fraternity houses, sorority houses, First-year students' floor, a leadership hall, an extended-quiet-hours floor, a substance-free hall, a nonsmoking floor, and an academic-year hall. On-campus housing is guaranteed for the freshman year only, and is available on a first-come, first-served basis. 76% of students commute. All students may keep cars. Alcohol is not permitted.

FACULTY/CLASSROOMS: 48% of faculty are male; 52% are female. No introductory courses are taught by graduate students. The average class size in an introductory lecture is 42; in a laboratory is 26; and in a regular course is 35.

PROGRAMS OF STUDY: ECU confers B.A., B.S., B.F.A., B.M., B.S.A., B.S.A.P., B.S.B.A., B.S.B.E., B.S.N., and B.S.W. degrees. Master's and doctoral degrees are also awarded. Bachelor's degrees are awarded in BIOLOGICAL SCIENCE (biochemistry, biology/biological science, and nutrition), BUSINESS (accounting, banking and finance, business administration and management, hospitality management services, management information systems, marketing management, marketing/retailing/merchandising, and recreational facilities management), COMMUNICATIONS AND THE ARTS (art, art history and appreciation, communications, dance, design, dramatic arts, English, French, German, music performance, music theory and composition, speech/debate/rhetoric, and studio art), COMPUTER AND PHYSICAL SCIENCE (applied physics, atmospheric sciences and meteorology, chemistry, computer science, geology, information sciences and systems, mathematics, and physics), EDUCATION (art education, athletic training, business education, dance education, drama education, early childhood education, education of the emotionally handicapped, education of the mentally handicapped, elementary education, English education, foreign languages education, health education, home economics education, marketing and distribution education, mathematics education, middle school education, music education, physical education, science education, social studies education, and special education), ENGINEERING AND ENVIRONMENTAL DESIGN (city/community/regional planning, construction management, electrical/electronics engineering technology, engineering, environmental engineering technology, industrial engineering technology, and interior design), HEALTH PROFESSIONS (environmental health science, exercise science, health care administration, medical records administration/services, medical technology, music therapy, nursing, occupational therapy, public health, recreation therapy, rehabilitation therapy, and speech pathology/audiology), SOCIAL

SCIENCE (African American studies, anthropology, applied social science, child care/child and family studies, clothing and textiles management/production/services, criminal justice, dietetics, economics, family and community services, geography, Hispanic American studies, history, liberal arts/general studies, parks and recreation management, philosophy, physical fitness/movement, political science/government, psychology, public history/archives, social work, sociology, and women's studies). Allied health, art, and music are the strongest academically. Elementary education, management, and communication have the largest enrollments.

ACTIVITIES: 9% of men belong to 24 national fraternities; 8% of women belong to 14 national sororities. There are 399 groups on campus, including team training, campus wellness, military, academic, art, band, cheerleading, choir, chorale, chorus, communications, computers, dance, drama, drill team, environmental, ethnic, honors, international, jazz band, LGBT, literary magazine, marching band, musical theater, newspaper, opera, orchestra, pep band, photography, political, professional, radio and TV, religious, social, social service, student government, symphony, and yearbook. Popular campus events include Barefoot on the Mall, Midnight Madness, and Pirate Palooza. **Sports:** There are 9 intercollegiate sports for men and 9 for women, and 14 intramural sports for men and 14 for women. Facilities include a stadium, arena, coliseum stadium. Sports for men include baseball, basketball, cross-country, football, golf, swimming and diving, tennis, indoor and outdoor track and field. Women's sports include basketball, cross-country, golf, soccer, fast-pitch softball, swimming and diving, tennis, indoor and outdoor track and field, and volleyball. **Graduates:** From July 1, 2015 to June 30, 2016, 4315 bachelor's degrees were awarded. The most popular majors were nursing (7%), communication (7%), and elementary education (6%). In an average class, 33% graduate in 4 years or less, 53% graduate in 5 years or less, and 58% graduate in 6 years or less.

SERVICES: Counseling and information services are available, as is tutoring in most subjects, and a reader service for the blind, and remedial math and reading. Tutoring is established by department basis. Several learning centers, and labs have established hours of operation. Meeting arrangements can be made by appointment. **Library/Resources:** The library contains 2.4 million volumes, 200,000 microform items, 439,000 audio/video tapes/CDs/DVDs, and subscribes to 73,498 periodicals including electronic. Computerized library services include interlibrary loans, database searching, and Wi-Fi capability. Special learning facilities include an art gallery, radio station, special collections, manuscripts, and rare books, music library, the Walker center, and the William E. Laupus Health Science Library, laboratories such as biomechanics, biofeedback, human performance, activity promotion, developmental motor, and visual motor. **Physically Challenged Students:** 95% of the campus is accessible. Facilities include wheelchair ramps, elevators, special parking, specially equipped restrooms, special class scheduling, lowered drinking fountains, lowered telephones, automatic doors and state-of-the art adaptive equipment. **Special:** ECU offers cooperative programs in most majors, internships, study abroad in 42 countries, a Washington semester, accelerated degrees, a B.A.-B.S. in accounting, dual majors, work-study, and a student-designed major in multidisciplinary studies. There are 18 national honor societies, Phi Beta Kappa, a freshman honors program, and 39 departmental honors programs. **Visiting:** There are regularly scheduled orientations for prospective students, including information sessions and campus tours. There are guides for informal visits. To schedule a visit, contact the Admissions Office. **Campus Safety and Security:** Measures include 24-hour foot and vehicle patrol, emergency notification system, self-defense education, and security escort services. There are also shuttle buses, emergency telephones, lighted pathways/sidewalks, controlled access to dorms/residences, residence hall doors locked, bicycle patrols & registration, motorist assistance lost and found, operation ID, the Residence Hall Liason Officer Program, on-and off campus crime prevention safety tips, Staff and Faculty Eyes (SAFE) Campus Community Watch Program, and alcohol awareness.

REQUIREMENTS: The SAT or ACT and the ACT Optional Writing test are required. Applicants must be graduates of an accredited secondary school. All degree-seeking students are required to complete 20 academic units, including 4 in English, and math, 3 in science with 1 lab course, 2 in social studies with 1 in U.S. history, and 2 units in a foreign language, 1 unit in fine arts is recommended, and 1 unit each in foreign language, natural science, and math should be taken in the senior year. Special circumstances exist for applicants with a GED. A GPA of 2.3 is required. AP and CLEP credits are accepted. To graduate, students must complete 120 to 128 semester hours with a minimum GPA of 2.0 overall and in the major. General education requirements include 12 hours of social science, 10 of humanities and fine arts, 8 of science, 6 of English, 3 of math, and 3 of health and exercise and sport science. The total must include 12 hours of writing-intensive courses and a course in cultural diversity. **Procedure:** Freshmen are admitted to all sessions. Entrance exams should be taken in the spring of the junior year or the fall of the senior year. There are deferred admissions and rolling admissions plans. Applications should be filed by March 15 for fall entry; November 1 for spring entry; and March 15 for summer entry, along with a $70 fee. Notifications are sent April 15. Applications are accepted on-line. **Transfer Students:** 1427 transfer students enrolled in 2015-2016. Applicants must submit official transcripts from high school and all colleges attended and have a satisfactory GPA in courses attempted. Applicants who will have completed less than 30 semester hours will also be required to meet the freshmen requirements. **International Students:** There are 200 international students enrolled. The school actively recruits these students. They must take the TOEFL with a minimum score of 80 on the Internet-based version (iBT), or take the IELTS. SAT or ACT scores are required if the student is receiving an athletic scholarship or if the student will graduate from a U.S. high school.

ADMISSIONS: 62% of the 2016-2017 applicants were accepted. The SAT scores for the 2016-2017 freshman class were: Critical Reading-- 49% below 500, 43% between 500 and 599, 7% between 600 and 699, and 1% between 700 and 800. Math-- 32% below 500, 55% between 500 and 599, 12% between 600 and 699, and 1% between 700 and 800. Writing-- 57% below 500, 37% between 500 and 599, and 6% between 600 and 699. The ACT scores were 18% below 12, 55% between 12 and 17, 19% between 18 and 23, 6% between 24 and 29, and 3% above 30. 35% of the current freshmen were in the top fifth of their class; 68% were in the top two fifths. **Admissions Contact:** James Coker, AssociateDirector of Undergraduate Admissions. Email: *admis@ecu.edu* Web: *www.ecu.edu*

FINANCIAL AID: In 2016-2017, 60% of all full-time freshmen and 58% of continuing full-time students received some form of financial aid. 55% of all full-time freshmen and 31% of continuing full-time students received need-based aid. The average freshman award was $9,614. Need-based scholarships or need-based grants averaged $8,031; need-based self-help aid (loans and jobs) averaged $3,834; non-need-based athletic scholarships averaged $11,120; and other non-need-based awards and non-need-based scholarships averaged $4,532. The average financial indebtedness of the 2016 graduate was $25,983. ECU is a member of CSS. The priority date for freshman financial aid applications for fall entry is March 1.

ELIZABETH CITY STATE UNIVERSITY F-2

www.ecsu.edu

Elizabeth City, NC 27909	**(252) 335-3400** **(800) 347-ECSU**
Fax: (252) 335-3537	**Email: admissions@ecsu.edu**
Full-time: 1035 men, 1474 women	**Faculty:** 113; IIB, av$
Part-time: 68 men, 183 women	**Ph.D.s:** 68%
Graduate: 29 men, 89 women	**Student/Faculty:** 16 to 1
Year: semesters, summer session	**Tuition:** $6821 ($19,175)
Room & Board: $7924	**Freshman Class:** 3925 applied, 2243 accepted, 527 enrolled
SAT or ACT: required	**CEEB CODE:** 5629
Application Deadline: August 1	**COMPETITIVE**

Elizabeth City State University, founded in 1891 as part of the University of North Carolina System, is a public institution offering undergraduate programs in liberal arts and sciences, education, and business. The figures in the above capsule and in this profile are approximate. There is 1 undergraduate school. The 829-acre campus is in a small town 55 miles from Norfolk, Virginia.

STUDENT LIFE: 90% of undergraduates are from North Carolina. Others are from 25 states. 73% are African American; 12% White. 12% are Race and ethnicity unknown. **Female To Male Ratio:** 1.5:1. 25% do not continue beyond their first year; 50% remain to graduate. **Housing:** 1019 students can be accommodated in college housing, which includes single-sex dorms and on-campus apartments, honors houses, and wellness housing. On-campus housing is guaranteed for all 4 years. 52% of students commute. All students may keep cars. Alcohol is not permitted.

FACULTY/CLASSROOMS: 50% of faculty are male; 50% are female. All teach undergraduates. No introductory courses are taught by graduate students.

PROGRAMS OF STUDY: ECSU confers B.A., B.S., and B.S.Ed. degrees. Master's degrees are also awarded. Bachelor's degrees are awarded in BIOLOGICAL SCIENCE (biology/biological science), BUSINESS (accounting and business administration and management), COMMUNICATIONS AND THE ARTS (art, English, and music), COMPUTER AND PHYSICAL SCIENCE (chemistry, computer science, geology, mathematics, and physics), EDUCATION (business education, elementary education, industrial arts education, middle school education, physical education, special education, and technical education), ENGINEERING AND ENVIRONMENTAL DESIGN (industrial engineering technology), SOCIAL SCIENCE (criminal justice, history, political science/government, psychology, social science, social work, and sociology).

ACTIVITIES: Groups on campus include band, cheerleading, choir, chorus, dance, drama, honors, international, jazz band, literary magazine, marching band, musical theater, newspaper, pep band, radio and TV, religious, social, student government, symphony, and yearbook. **Sports:** Facilities include a gym, a stadium, an all-weather track, golf, pool, weight room, tennis courts, dance and exercise studios, handball and racquetball courts, and playing fields. **Graduates:** From July 1, 2015 to June 30, 2016, 379 bachelor's degrees were awarded. The most popular majors were business/marketing (21%), education (15%), and homeland security (13%). In an average class, 33% graduate in 4 years or less, 46% graduate in 5 years or less, and 49% graduate in 6 years or less. Of the 2015 graduating class, 79% were enrolled in graduate school within 6 months of graduation.

SERVICES: In addition to vocational counseling services, tutoring is available. **Library/Resources:** The library contains 174,566 volumes, 486,884 microform items, 1,220 audio/video tapes/CDs/DVDs, and subscribes to 1,698 periodicals including electronic. Computerized library services include interlibrary loans. Special learning facilities include an art gallery, planetarium, radio station, TV station, a farm, and 639-acre educational research tract. **Physically Challenged Students:** Facilities include wheelchair ramps, elevators, special parking, specially equipped restrooms, and lowered drinking fountains. **Special:** Opportunities are provided for internships, dual majors, weekend/evening degree completion programs, work-study, and credit by exam and for military service. There are 5 national honor societies and a freshman honors program. **Visiting:** There are regularly scheduled orientations for prospective students. There are guides for informal visits. To schedule a visit, contact the Admissions Office. **Campus Safety and Security:** There are emergency telephones, and ECSU has its own police department on campus.

REQUIREMENTS: The SAT or ACT is required. Graduation from an accredited secondary school is required; the GED is accepted. Applicants should submit an academic record with 4 courses in English, 3 each in math and 2 in science, and 2 in social studies; it is recommended that applicants have at least 2 course units in foreign languages. Students must also pass the NC Competency Examination or its equivalent. AP and CLEP credits are accepted. Students must have maintained a minimum GPA of 2.0, fulfilled a major, and completed the requirements of general education courses in the fields of grammar, composition, and literature. **Procedure:** Freshmen are admitted in the fall, spring, and summer. Entrance exams should be taken as early as possible. There are early admissions and deferred admissions plans. Early decision applications should be filed by May 1; regular applications, by August 1 for fall entry; and November 1 for spring entry, along with a $30 fee. **Transfer Students:** 201 transfer students enrolled in 2015-2016. Applicants must have a minimum college GPA of 2.0 and submit high school and college transcripts. Those with fewer than 30 credit hours must meet both freshman and transfer admission requirements. 30 credits required for the bachelor's degree must be completed at ECSU. **International Students:** There are 6 international students enrolled. They must take the TOEFL or MELAB, as well as the SAT or ACT.

ADMISSIONS: 57% of the 2016-2017 applicants were accepted. The SAT scores for the 2016-2017 freshman class were: Critical Reading-- 89% below 500, 10% between 500 and 599, and 1% between 600 and 699. Math-- 83% below 500, 16% between 500 and 599, and 1% between 600 and 699. Writing-- 92% below 500 and 8% between 500 and 599. **Admissions Contact:** Bridgett Golham, Director of Admissions and Recruitment. Email: *admissions@ecsu.edu* Web: *www.ecsu.edu*

FINANCIAL AID: The college's own financial statement, and income tax forms are required. The FAFSA code is 002926. Check with the school for current application deadlines.

ELON UNIVERSITY — D-2

www.elon.edu

Elon, NC 27244	(336) 278-3566 (800) 334-8448
Fax: (336) 278-7699	Email: admissions@elon.edu
Full-time: 2390 men, 3449 women	Faculty: 385
Part-time: 73 men, 96 women	Ph.D.s: 86%
Graduate: 287 men, 444 women	Student/Faculty: 12 to 1
Year: 4-1-4, summer session	Tuition: $33,104
Room & Board: $11,495	Freshman Class: 10098 applied, 6103 accepted, 1553 enrolled
SAT CR/M/W: 594/598/599 ACT: 27	CEEB CODE: 5183
Application Deadline: January 10	VERY COMPETITIVE+

Elon University, founded in 1889 as Elon College, is a private liberal arts university. Elon's student-centered learning environment prepares students to be the ethical leaders in the world. There are 4 undergraduate schools and 5 graduate schools. In addition to regional accreditation, Elon has baccalaureate program accreditation with AACSB, ACEJMC, NCATE, CAPTE, ARC-PA, ABS, and ACS. The 646-acre campus is in a suburban area adjacent to Burlington, and 17 miles East of Greensboro. Including any residence halls, there are 215 buildings.

STUDENT LIFE: 78% of undergraduates are from out of state, mostly the Middle Atlantic. Students are from 49 states, 50 foreign countries, and Canada. 58% are from public schools. 81% are White; 6% Hispanic; 5% African American; 3% two or more races; 2% Asian American; 2% Foreign. 33% are Protestant; 29% Catholic. **Female To Male Ratio:** 1.5:1. The average age of freshmen is 18; all undergraduates, 20. 9% do not continue beyond their first year; 82% remain to graduate. **Housing:** 3873 students can be accommodated in college housing, which includes single-sex and coed dorms, on-campus apartments, off-campus apartments, honors houses, language houses, special-interest houses, fraternity houses, sorority houses, including Elon's high-tech campus encompasses seven distinct residential neighborhoods for students at various stages of their college careers. On-campus housing is guaranteed for the freshman year only and is available on a lottery system for upperclassmen. 63% of students live on campus; of those, 75% remain on campus on weekends. All students may keep cars.

FACULTY/CLASSROOMS: 51% of faculty are male; 49% are female. 91% teach undergraduates and 65% do research. No introductory courses are taught by graduate students. The average class size in an introductory lecture is 23; in a laboratory is 19; and in a regular course is 20.

PROGRAMS OF STUDY: Elon confers B.A., B.S., B.F.A., and B.S.B.A degrees. Master's and doctoral degrees are also awarded. Bachelor's degrees are awarded in AGRICULTURE (environmental studies), BIOLOGICAL SCIENCE (biochemistry, biophysics, and neurosciences), BUSINESS (accounting, business administration and management, entrepreneurial studies, finance, international business management, international economics, leadership, management, marketing, marketing management, and sports management), COMMUNICATIONS AND THE ARTS (acting, art history, art, arts administration/management, communication design, communications, creative writing, dance, dramatic arts, English, film arts, fine arts, French, German studies, human performance, journalism, literature, media arts, media management, music, music performance, music technology, musical theater, Spanish, strategic communication, theatre acting, theatre arts, theater design, theatre production, theatre studies, and writing), COMPUTER AND PHYSICAL SCIENCE (applied mathematics, chemistry, computer science, digital arts/technology, information sciences and systems, mathematics, physics, and statistics), EDUCATION (Asian studies, early childhood education, education, elementary education, foreign languages education, health education, history education, mathematics education, middle school education, music education, physical education, science education, secondary education, and special education), ENGINEERING AND ENVIRONMENTAL DESIGN (biomedical engineering, chemical engineering, computer engineering, engineering, engineering physics, environmental engineering, and environmental science), HEALTH PROFESSIONS (biology, exercise science, and public health), SOCIAL SCIENCE (African American studies, American studies, anthropology, criminal justice, economics, geography, geography information science, history, human services, international studies,

Italian studies, Judaic studies, justice and society, Latin American studies, Middle Eastern studies, peace studies, philosophy, political science/government, psychology, public administration, religious studies, sociology, and women & gender studies). Business, music theater, and biology are the strongest academically. Business, strategic communications, and psychology have the largest enrollments.

ACTIVITIES: 20% of men belong to 12 national fraternities; 39% of women belong to 13 national sororities. There are 249 groups on campus, including art, band, cheerleading, chess, choir, chorale, chorus, communications, computers, dance, debate, drama, drill team, environmental, ethnic, film, honors, international, jazz band, LGBT, literary magazine, marching band, musical theater, newspaper, orchestra, pep band, photography, political, professional, radio and TV, religious, social, social service, student government, symphony, and yearbook. Popular campus events include Family Weekend, Homecoming, Greek Week, Spring Undergraduate Research Forum (SURF Day), College Coffee, CELEBRATE, a week-long celebration of Student Achievements in Academics and in the Arts, and Festival of Holiday Lights. **Sports:** There are 7 intercollegiate sports for men and 9 for women, and 21 intramural sports for men and 21 for women. Facilities include a stadium, tennis courts, softball field, baseball stadium, a field house, and athletic fields. The athletic center has racquetball courts, aerobic rooms, a human performance lab, weight room, two-story fitness center, gyms, driving range, and an indoor swimming pool. **Graduates:** From July 1, 2015 to June 30, 2016, 1342 bachelor's degrees were awarded. The most popular majors were busines/marketing (33%), communications (19%), and psychology (6%). 316 companies recruited on campus in 2015-2016. In an average class, 77% graduate in 4 years or less, 81% graduate in 5 years or less, and 82% graduate in 6 years or less. Of the 2015 graduating class, 19% were enrolled in graduate school within 6 months of graduation, and 89% were employed.

SERVICES: Counseling and information services are available, as is tutoring in most subjects. Preparatory courses are offered, which count as elective credit toward graduation. We offer texts in alternative formats for students with print, learning, and visual disabilities. **Library/Resources:** The library contains 809,306 volumes, 285,118 microform items, 67,498 audio/video tapes/CDs/DVDs, and subscribes to 61,099 periodicals including electronic. Computerized library services include interlibrary loans, database searching, Internet access, and Wi-Fi capability. Special learning facilities include a radio station, TV station, a writing center, botanical preserve, a protected Elon Forest, art collection walk, and observatory. **Physically Challenged Students:** 85% of the campus is accessible. Facilities include wheelchair ramps, elevators, special parking, specially equipped restrooms, special class scheduling, lowered drinking fountains, lowered telephones, and special housing. **Special:** Elon offers co-op programs in most majors, dual majors, student-designed majors, cross-registration with 6 other colleges and universities in North Carolina, paid and unpaid internships, more than 100 study abroad programs, study USA programs, a Washington semester, a Los Angeles semester, a New York semester, work-study programs, pass/fail options, and 3-2 dual engineering degree programs. The month-long January term includes extensive international study opportunities as well as courses focused on domestic travel. There are 31 national honor societies, Phi Beta Kappa, a freshman honors program, and 25 departmental honors programs. **Visiting:** There are regularly scheduled orientations for prospective students, consisting of 2 weekends in spring for deposited freshmen or a spring open house for nondeposited students. There are guides for informal visits and visitors may sit in on classes. To schedule a visit, contact the Admissions Office. **Campus Safety and Security:** Measures include 24-hour foot and vehicle patrol, emergency notification system, and security escort services. There are also shuttle buses, emergency telephones, lighted pathways/sidewalks, controlled access to dorms/residences, over 200 surveillance cameras on campus, annual fire inspections through the County Fire Marshall's Office, Campus Safety and Police operates 24 hours/day 7 days/week, and Operation ID, blue light phones, panic alarms in certain buildings that call campus police, LiveSafe Application, and lighting and safety walks conducted periodically with Residence Life, SGA, and Physical Plant.

REQUIREMENTS: The SAT or ACT is required. Students must be graduates of an accredited secondary school or have a GED certificate. They should have completed 4 credits of English, 3 credits or more in math (must include algebra 1 and 2, and geometry), 2 credits or more in a foreign language, and science, including at least 1 lab science, and social studies, including U.S. history AP and CLEP credits are accepted. To graduate, students must complete 132 semester hours, including 32 to 68 in the major, with a minimum GPA of 2.0. All students must fulfill the requirements of the Core Curriculum, which includes a first-year core, experiential learning, liberal studies, and advanced studies, for a total of 59 semester hours, and must satisfactorily complete a comprehensive exam in the major. **Procedure:** Freshmen are admitted in the fall and spring. Entrance exams should be taken in the spring of the junior year and the fall of the senior year. There are early decision, early admissions, and deferred admissions plans. Early decision applications should be filed by November 1; regular applications, by January 10 for fall entry; and December 1 for spring entry, along with a $50 fee. Notification of early decision is sent December 1; regular decision, March 15. 426 early decision candidates were accepted for the 2016-2017 class. 2579 applicants were on the 2016 waiting list; 149 were admitted. Applications are accepted online. **Transfer Students:** 85 transfer students enrolled in 2015-2016. Applicants must present a high school transcript, 12 credit hours of college transferable classes in the liberal arts and sciences, and a minimum GPA of 2.7 from a two-year or four-year accredited institution. An interview is recommended. A dean's evaluation form is required from all colleges or universities attended, and the applicant must be eligible to return to that institution. 60 of 132 credits required for the bachelor's degree must be completed at Elon. **International Students:** There are 129 international students enrolled. The school actively recruits these students. They must take the TOEFL with a minimum score of 550 on the paper-based TOEFL (PBT) or 79 on the Internet-based version (iBT). They must also take the SAT or ACT, scoring 1330.

ADMISSIONS: 60% of the 2016-2017 applicants were accepted. The SAT scores for the 2016-2017 freshman class were: Critical Reading-- 7% below 500, 44% between 500 and 599, 41% between 600 and 699, and 8% between 700 and 800. Math-- 7% below 500, 39% between 500 and 599, 47% between 600 and 699, and 7% between 700 and 800. Writing-- 8% below 500, 40% between 500 and 599, 43% between 600 and 699, and 9% between 700 and 800. The ACT scores were 12% between 18 and 23, 65% between 24 and 29, and 23% above 30. 53% of the current freshmen were in the top fifth of their class; 82% were in the top two fifths. 13 freshmen graduated first in their class. **Admissions Contact:** Lisa Keegan, Dean of Admissions. Email: *admissions@elon.edu* Web: *www.elon.edu*

FINANCIAL AID: In 2016-2017, 61% of all full-time freshmen and 60% of continuing full-time students received some form of financial aid. 30% of all full-time freshmen and 29% of continuing full-time students received need-based aid. The average freshman award was $20,439. Need-based scholarships or need-based grants averaged $13,140 ($48,099 maximum); need-based self-help aid (loans and jobs) averaged $5,198 ($10,000 maximum); non-need-based athletic scholarships averaged $30,510 ($46,517 maximum); and other non-need-based awards and non-need-based scholarships averaged $7,758 ($46,976 maximum). 33% of undergraduate students work part-time. Average annual earnings from campus work are $4500. The average financial indebtedness of the 2016 graduate was $30,170. Elon is a member of CSS. The CSS/Profile and the college's own financial statement are required. The priority date for freshman financial aid applications for fall entry is February 15.

FAYETTEVILLE STATE UNIVERSITY D-3

www.uncfsu.edu

Fayetteville, NC 28301 — **(910) 672-1371** / **(800) 222-2594**

Fax: (910) 672-1414 — **Email: admissions@uncfsu.edu**

Full-time: 1297 men, 2619 women	**Faculty:** 276; IIA, av$
Part-time: 323 men, 1048 women	**Ph.D.s:** n/av
Graduate: 186 men, 587 women	**Student/Faculty:** 16 to 1
Year: semesters, summer session	**Tuition:** $9686 ($18,600)
Room & Board: $8070	**Freshman Class:** n/av
SAT or ACT: required	**CEEB CODE:** 5212
Application Deadline: August 25	**COMPETITIVE**

Fayetteville State University, founded in 1867 and part of the University of North Carolina system, it is a public institution offering degree programs in the arts and sciences, business, and teacher preparation. The figures in the above capsule and in this profile are approximate. There are 3 undergraduate schools and 1 graduate school. In addition to regional accreditation, FSU has baccalaureate program accreditation with NCATE. The 156-acre campus is in an urban area 60 miles South of Raleigh. Including any residence halls, there are 43 buildings.

STUDENT LIFE: 95% of undergraduates are from North Carolina. 76% are African American; 7% Hispanic; 20% White; 1% Asian American; 1% American Indian/Alaska Native. **Female To Male Ratio:** 2.4:1. The average age of freshmen is 19; all undergraduates, 27. 24% do not continue beyond their first year; 31% remain to graduate. **Housing:** 1298 students can be accommodated in college housing, which includes single-sex and coed dorms, on-campus apartments, and honors dorm. On-campus housing is available on a first-come, first-served basis. 71% of students commute. All students may keep cars. Alcohol is not permitted.

FACULTY/CLASSROOMS: 54% of faculty are male; 46% are female. All teach undergraduates and do research. No introductory courses are taught by graduate students. The average class size in an introductory lecture is 30; in a laboratory is 20; and in a regular course is 30.

PROGRAMS OF STUDY: FSU confers B.A. and B.S. degrees. Master's and doctoral degrees are also awarded. Bachelor's degrees are awarded in BIOLOGICAL SCIENCE (biology/biological science), BUSINESS (accounting, banking and finance, business administration and management, business economics, management information systems, and office supervision and management), COMMUNICATIONS AND THE ARTS (dramatic arts, English, Spanish, speech/debate/rhetoric, and visual and performing arts), COMPUTER AND PHYSICAL SCIENCE (chemistry, computer science, and mathematics), EDUCATION (business education, early childhood education, elementary education, health education, marketing and distribution education, middle school education, music education, secondary education, and social science education), HEALTH PROFESSIONS (medical laboratory technology and nursing), SOCIAL SCIENCE (criminal justice, economics, geography, history, political science/government, psychology, public administration, social science, social work, and sociology).

ACTIVITIES: 1% of men belong to 4 local and 4 national fraternities; 1% of women belong to 3 national sororities. There are 30 groups on campus, including band, cheerleading, choir, chorus, dance, drama, film, honors, international, jazz band, literary magazine, marching band, newspaper, pep band, political, radio and TV, religious, social service, student government, and yearbook. Popular campus events include The Lyceum, Martin Luther King Day, and Black History Month. **Sports:** There are 8 intercollegiate sports for men and 8 for women, and 7 intramural sports for men and 5 for women. Facilities include gyms, a stadium, tennis courts, bowling alley, dance studio, swimming pool, and playing fields. **Graduates:** From July 1, 2015 to June 30, 2016, 991 bachelor's degrees were awarded. The most popular majors were criminal justice (16%), psychology (16%), and business administration (14%).

SERVICES: Counseling and information services are available, as is tutoring in some subjects, and remedial math, reading, and writing. **Library/Resources:** The library contains 335,922 volumes, 1.0 million microform items, and 20,676 audio/video tapes/CDs/DVDs. Computerized library services include interlibrary loans and database searching. Special learning facilities include a planetarium and radio station. **Physically Challenged Students:** 75% of the campus is accessible. Facilities include wheelchair ramps, elevators, special parking, specially equipped restrooms, and lowered drinking fountains. **Special:** FSU offers cooperative programs in business, math, and biological and physical sciences with North Carolina State University, internships, B.A.-B.S. degrees, dual majors, 3-2 engineering degree programs, credit for military experience, and nondegree study. There are 17 national honor societies, a freshman honors program, and 7 departmental honors programs. **Visiting:** There are regularly scheduled orientations for prospective students, including a campus tour, recreational activity, placement tests, preregistration, and orientation to FSU services. There are also guides for informal visits, visitors may sit in on classes, and stay overnight. To schedule a visit, contact the Director of Enrollment Management. **Campus Safety and Security:** Measures include 24-hour foot and vehicle patrol, security escort services, and lighted pathways/sidewalks.

REQUIREMENTS: The SAT or ACT is required. Successful scores are also required on the North Carolina Competency Exam. Applicants must be graduates of an accredited secondary school or have the GED. They should have completed 4 academic units of English, 3 each of math and science with 1 lab course, and 2 of social studies; also recommended are 2 units of a foreign language and completion of 1 unit each of foreign language and math in the senior year. AP and CLEP credits are accepted. Important factors in the admissions decision are advanced placement or honors courses, recommendations by school officials, and leadership record. To graduate, students must complete 120 credit hours with a minimum GPA of 2.0 overall and in the major. The core curriculum includes 8 to 11 credits in natural science, 6 to 15 in humanities, 6 to 7 in math, 3 to 9 in social science, 3 each in critical thinking and speech, and 2 each in phys ed/health and university seminar. **Procedure:** Freshmen are admitted to all sessions. Entrance exams should be taken in November. There are early decision, early admissions, deferred admissions, and rolling admissions plans. Applications should be filed by August 25 for fall entry, along with a $35 fee. Notification is sent on a rolling basis. **Transfer Students:** 670 transfer students enrolled in 2015-2016. Applicants must submit official transcripts from all colleges attended, have a minimum GPA of 2.0, and be eligible to return to their previous institution. 33 of 120 credits required for the bachelor's degree must be completed at FSU. **International Students:** They must take the TOEFL, or other English proficiency exam administered in their country. They must also take the SAT or ACT, scoring 800.

Admissions Contact: Ulisa E. Bowles, Director of Admissions. Email: *admissions@uncfsu.edu* Web: *www.uncfsu.edu*

FINANCIAL AID: FSU is a member of CSS. The FAFSA code is 002928. Check with the school for current application deadlines.

GARDNER-WEBB UNIVERSITY C-3

www.gardner-webb.edu

Boiling Springs, NC 28017	**(704) 406-4495** **(800) 253-6472**
Fax: (704) 406-4488	**Email: admissions@gardner-webb.edu**
Full-time: 779 men, 1309 women	**Faculty:** 122; IIA, --$
Part-time: 118 men, 366 women	**Ph.D.s:** 79%
Graduate: 594 men, 1470 women	**Student/Faculty:** 13 to 1
Year: semesters, summer session	**Tuition:** $29,420
Room & Board: $9780	**Freshman Class:** 5456 applied, 2640 accepted, 434 enrolled
	CEEB CODE: 5242
Application Deadline: open	**COMPETITIVE+**

Gardner-Webb University, founded in 1905, is an independent institution affiliated with the Baptist Convention of North Carolina and offering undergraduate programs in the arts and sciences, business, education, nursing, and professional studies. The figures in the above capsule and in this profile are approximate. There are 5 undergraduate schools and 2 graduate schools. In addition to regional accreditation, Webb has baccalaureate program accreditation with ACBSP, NASM, NCATE, NLN, ATS, CHEA, CAATE, and NLNAC. The 200-acre campus is in a small town 50 miles west of Charlotte, in the Piedmont area of Western North Carolina. Including any residence halls, there are 46 buildings.

STUDENT LIFE: 78% of undergraduates are from North Carolina. Others are from 37 states, 21 foreign countries, and Canada. 70% are from public schools. 69% are White; 20% African American; 2% Hispanic; 1% Asian American. 64% are Protestant. **Female To Male Ratio:** 2.1:1. The average age of freshmen is 18; all undergraduates, 21. 26% do not continue beyond their first year; 48% remain to graduate. **Housing:** 1368 students can be accommodated in college housing, which includes single-sex dorms, on-campus apartments, and honors houses. On-campus housing is guaranteed for all 4 years. 77% of students live on campus; of those, 50% remain on campus on weekends. All students may keep cars. Alcohol is not permitted.

FACULTY/CLASSROOMS: 51% of faculty are male; 49% are female. All teach undergraduates. No introductory courses are taught by graduate students. The average class size in an introductory lecture is 25; in a laboratory is 9; and in a regular course is 18.

PROGRAMS OF STUDY: Webb confers B.A., B.S., B.F.A., B.M., and B.S.N. degrees. Associate, master's, and doctoral degrees are also awarded. Bachelor's degrees are awarded in BIOLOGICAL SCIENCE (biology/biological science), BUSINESS (accounting, business administration and management, international business management, and sports management), COMMUNICATIONS AND THE ARTS (American Sign Language, art, communications, English, French, music, and Spanish), COMPUTER AND PHYSICAL SCIENCE (chemistry, computer science, information sciences and systems, and mathematics), EDUCATION (athletic training, elementary education, foreign languages education, health education, middle school education, music education, physical education, and secondary education), ENGINEER-

ING AND ENVIRONMENTAL DESIGN (industrial administration/ management), HEALTH PROFESSIONS (health care administration, medical technology, nursing, and physician's assistant), SOCIAL SCIENCE (history, interpreter for the deaf, psychology, religion, religious music, social science, and sociology). Nursing, music, biology, and education are the strongest academically. Business, social science, education, and nursing have the largest enrollments.

ACTIVITIES: There are no fraternities or sororities. There are 65 groups on campus, including art, band, cheerleading, choir, chorale, chorus, debate, drama, drill team, film, honors, international, jazz band, literary magazine, marching band, musical theater, newspaper, opera, orchestra, pep band, photography, political, professional, radio and TV, religious, social, social service, student government, symphony, and yearbook. Popular campus events include Festival of Lights, Bulldog Madness, and Spring's Alive. **Sports:** There are 11 intercollegiate sports for men and 10 for women, and 28 intramural sports for men and 28 for women. Facilities include athletic and recreation, along with a stadium, gyms, tennis, racquetball courts, weight room, swimming pool, playing fields for softball, soccer, football, and baseball, an arena, aerobics room, and a ropes course. **Graduates:** From July 1, 2015 to June 30, 2016, 645 bachelor's degrees were awarded. The most popular majors were business administration (27%), social sciences (21%), and nursing and other health related majors (12%). In an average class, 9% graduate in 3 years or less, 37% graduate in 4 years or less, 47% graduate in 5 years or less, and 48% graduate in 6 years or less.

SERVICES: Counseling and information services are available, as is tutoring in every subject, a reader service for the blind, and remedial math, reading, and writing. **Library/Resources:** The library contains 244,133 volumes, 653,778 microform items, 12,494 audio/video tapes/ CDs/DVDs, and subscribes to 108,251 periodicals including electronic. Computerized library services include interlibrary loans, database searching, Internet access, and Wi-Fi capability. Special learning facilities include an art gallery, radio station, and observatory. **Physically Challenged Students:** All of the campus is accessible. Facilities include wheelchair ramps, elevators, special parking, specially equipped restrooms, special class scheduling, lowered drinking fountains, and special housing. **Special:** The university offers work-study programs, internships, and study abroad in 11 countries. There are 11 national honor societies, a freshman honors program, and 3 departmental honors programs. **Visiting:** There are regularly scheduled orientations for prospective students, including a campus tour, and a meeting with an admissions counselor. There are guides for informal visits, visitors may sit in on classes, and stay overnight. To schedule a visit, contact the Visit Coordinator. **Campus Safety and Security:** Measures include 24-hour foot and vehicle patrol, emergency notification system, self-defense education, security escort services, emergency telephones, lighted pathways/sidewalks, controlled access to dorms/residences, and a police foot patrol inside of dorms.

REQUIREMENTS: Candidates should be graduates of an accredited secondary school or have a GED certificate. The recommended preparatory curriculum includes 4 units of English, 3 of math, and 2 each of social science, natural science, foreign language, and electives. One standardized test, either the SAT or the ACT, are required. Webb requires applicants to be in the upper 50% of their class. A GPA of 2.5 is required. AP and CLEP credits are accepted. Important factors in the admissions decision are leadership record, extracurricular activities record, and recommendations by school officials. To graduate, students must complete 128 credit hours, including 24 to 36 in the major, with a minimum GPA of 2.0. The required core curriculum consists of 44 hours of general education, liberal arts courses. Students also receive 1 credit hour per year of Dimensions. **Procedure:** Freshmen are admitted to all sessions. Entrance exams should be taken during the junior or senior year of high school. There are deferred admissions and rolling admissions plans. Application deadlines are open. Application fee is $40. Applications are accepted online. **Transfer Students:** 114 transfer students enrolled in 2015-2016. Applicants must submit the standard application and fee, official high school and college transcripts, and SAT or ACT scores. High school transcripts and test scores are waived for applicants with 15 or more semester credits and a GPA of 2.25 and submission of a college tanscript. 32 of 128 credits required for the bachelor's degree must be completed at Webb. **International Students:** There are 67 international students enrolled. The school actively recruits these students. They must take the TOEFL with a minimum score of 500 on the paper-based TOEFL (PBT) or 61 on the Internet-based version (iBT). They must also take the SAT or ACT, scoring 870.

ADMISSIONS: 48% of the 2016-2017 applicants were accepted. 42% of the current freshmen were in the top fifth of their class; 66% were in the top two fifths. 3 freshmen graduated first in their class. **Admissions Contact:** Angela Sundell, Assistant Vice President of Admissions. Email: *admissions@gardner-webb.edu* Web: *www.gardner-webb.edu*

FINANCIAL AID: In 2016-2017, 100% of all full-time freshmen and 98% of continuing full-time students received some form of financial aid. The average freshman award was $18,540. Need-based scholarships or need-based grants averaged $7,336; need-based self-help aid (loans and jobs) averaged $4,283; non-need-based athletic scholarships averaged $15,287; and other non-need-based awards and non-need-based scholarships averaged $11,745. Average annual earnings from campus work are $1303. The average financial indebtedness of the 2016 graduate was $19,725. Webb is a member of CSS. The state aid form, and federal tax returns are required. The FAFSA code is 002929. The priority date for freshman financial aid applications for fall entry is March 1.

GREENSBORO COLLEGE *(The complete profile is made available exclusively on our website, www.barronspac.com)*

GUILFORD COLLEGE — D-2
www.guilford.edu

Greensboro, NC 27410	(336) 316-2124 (800) 992-7759
Fax: (336) 316-2954	**Email:** admission@guilford.edu
Full-time: 764 men, 796 women	**Faculty:** 104; IIB, --$
Part-time: 103 men, 146 women	**Ph.D.s:** 90%
Graduate: n/av	**Student/Faculty:** 12 to 1
Year: semesters, summer session	**Tuition:** $34,090
Room & Board: $10,000	**Freshman Class:** 3151 applied, 1959 accepted, 419 enrolled
SAT CR/M/W: 505/495/480 **ACT:** 22	**CEEB CODE:** 5261
Application Deadline: December 1	**COMPETITIVE**

Guilford's purpose is to provide a transformative, practical, and excellent liberal arts education that produces critical thinkers in an inclusive, diverse environment, guided by Quaker testimonies of community, equality, integrity, peace, and simplicity and emphasizing the creative problem-solving skills, experiences, enthusiasm, and international perspectives necessary to promote positive change in the world. There is 1 undergraduate school. In addition to regional accreditation, Guilford's has baccalaureate program accreditation with ACBSP. The 351-acre campus is in a suburban area in the western residential area of Greensboro, NC. Including any residence halls, there are 31 buildings.

STUDENT LIFE: 70% of undergraduates are from North Carolina. Others are from 39 states, and 17 foreign countries. 75% are from public schools. 57% are White; 24% African American; 7% Hispanic; 4% Asian American; 4% two or more races; 2% Foreign; 1% American Indian/ Alaska Native; 1% race unknown. 51% claim no religious affiliation; 36% Protestant. **Female To Male Ratio:** 1.1:1. The average age of freshmen is 18; all undergraduates, 20. 26% do not continue beyond their first year; 61% remain to graduate. **Housing:** 937 students can be accommodated in college housing, which includes single-sex and coed dorms, on-campus apartments, and special-interest houses. There are four houses that accommodate six to ten students and are organized around common social or academic interests. On-campus housing is guaranteed for all 4 years and is available on a lottery system for upperclassmen. 74% of students live on campus; of those, 80% remain on campus on weekends. All students may keep cars.

FACULTY/CLASSROOMS: 50% of faculty are male; 50% are female. All teach undergraduates. No introductory courses are taught by graduate students. The average class size in an introductory lecture is 15; in a laboratory is 10; and in a regular course is 15.

PROGRAMS OF STUDY: Guildford confers A.B., B.S., and B.F.A. degrees. Bachelor's degrees are awarded in AGRICULTURE (environmental studies), BIOLOGICAL SCIENCE (biology/biological science), BUSINESS (accounting, business administration and management, information & communication technology, international business management, and sports management), COMMUNICATIONS AND THE ARTS (art, dramatic arts, English, French, German, music, Spanish, theatre arts, and visual and performing arts), COMPUTER AND PHYSICAL SCIENCE (chemistry, geology, information sciences and systems, mathematics, and physics), EDUCATION (education and sports studies), ENGINEERING AND ENVIRONMENTAL DESIGN (computer technology), HEALTH PROFESSIONS (exercise science and health science), SOCIAL SCIENCE (African American studies, anthropology, community services, criminal justice, economics, forensic studies, gender studies, history, interdisciplinary studies, international studies, peace studies, philosophy, political science/government, psychology, religion, sociology, and women's studies). Biology, Health Science, Psychology, Sport Studies are the strongest academically. Business administration, psychology, and health science have the largest enrollments.

ACTIVITIES: There are no fraternities or sororities. There are 45 groups on campus, and such as Bayard Rustin Center for LGBTQA Activism, Community Aids Awareness Project, and Guilford Peace Society, poetry club, archery club, art, cheerleading, chess, choir, chorale, chorus, computers, dance, debate, drama, environmental, ethnic, film, honors, international, jazz band, literary magazine, musical theater, newspaper, pep band, photography, political, professional, radio and TV, religious, social, social service, and student government. Popular campus events include Serendipity Spring Festival, Bryan Lecture Series in the Arts, Guilford Undergraduate Symposium, Eastern Music Festival, and Holiday Choir Concerts. **Sports:** There are 9 intercollegiate sports for men and 9 for women, and 7 intramural sports for men and 7 for women. Facilities include football and track stadium, lacrosse, soccer, a field house gymnasium with multiple courts for basketball and volleyball, baseball field, cross–country course, swimming pool, intramural field, playing fields for varsity and club sports such as rugby for men and women, tennis courts, and weight and cardio room. **Graduates:** From July 1, 2015 to June 30, 2016, 430 bachelor's degrees were awarded. The most popular majors were Psychology (17%), business administration (10%), and English (7%). 90 companies recruited on campus in 2015-2016. In an average class, 44% graduate in 4 years or less and 57% graduate in 6 years or less. Of the 2015 graduating class, 17% were enrolled in graduate school within 6 months of graduation, and 83% were employed.

SERVICES: Counseling and information services are available, as is tutoring in most subjects, a reader service for the blind, and remedial math, reading, and writing. Also available are faculty tutoring for skills development, student tutoring for course-specific non–remedial writing, and the Learning Commons center is devoted to students support. **Library/Resources:** The library contains 483,434 volumes, 21,550 microform items, and 150,655 audio/video tapes/CDs/DVDs, and subscribes to 331,481 periodicals including electronic. Computerized library services include interlibrary loans, database searching, Internet access, and Wi-Fi capability. Special learning facilities include an art gallery, planetarium, radio station, Cline observatory (physics & astronomy), photography studio, outdoor sculpture studio, Guilford college farm, community garden, and Friends historical collection. **Physically Challenged Students:** 95% of the campus is accessible. Facilities include wheelchair ramps, elevators, special parking, specially equipped restrooms, special class scheduling, lowered drinking fountains, and lowered telephones. **Special:** Guilford offers many internships, a Washington semester, work-study programs, dual majors, student-designed majors, study abroad in 13 countries, B.A.-B.S. degrees, and cross-registration with members of the Greater Greensboro Consortium. Pre–professional programs that are designed specifically as preparation for graduate study. Integrated Lab chemistry research, sports management internships with national or major sports leagues, internships with senators, mayors, ACLU, Greenpeace, geology fieldwork, archaeology labs, internships. Domestic Off–campus Semester–away, Washington Semester. Formal internship agreements or partnerships: Center for Principled Problem Solving, semester abroad, Quaker Leadership Program, Bonner Center for Community Service & Learning, and the Bryan Series (brings world–class experts in their fields to address the community and meet with students). Consortia that allow open registration in seven area colleges and universities without additional fees. There are 2 national honor societies and a freshman honors program. **Visiting:** There are regularly scheduled orientations for prospective students, visits can be scheduled throughout the year. A typical visit includes an information session led by an Admission Counselor followed by a student–led tour. There are also class visits, professor meetings, and lunch buddies are available when classes are in session. There are guides for informal visits, visitors may sit in on classes, and stay overnight. To schedule a visit, contact Erin Kelly at (800) 992-7759. **Campus Safety and Security:** Measures include 24-hour foot and vehicle patrol, emergency notification system, self-defense education, security escort services, emergency telephones, lighted pathways/sidewalks, and controlled access to dorms/residences.

REQUIREMENTS: The admission committee reviews each applicant to determine academic preparedness as well as to evaluate other qualities such as leadership, creativity & school and community involvement. Coursework and grades are considered and at least four college prep courses each school year is expected. Test scores are optional, with the alternative being a portfolio of work plus a personal essay and school recommendations from a counselor and a teacher. AP and CLEP credits are accepted. Important factors in the admissions decision are advanced placement or honors courses, leadership record, and evidence of special talent. Students must fulfill requirements in fine arts, English, humanities, sciences, social sciences, and foreign language. They must take a first-year experience and an interdisciplinary capstone course, and courses in historical perspectives, intercultural studies, social justice and environmental responsibility, and diversity. A minimum GPA of 2.0 is required. 128 credit hours must be completed with at least 32 in the major. **Procedure:** Freshmen are admitted in the fall and spring. Entrance exams should be taken in the spring of the junior year or fall of the senior year. There are early decision, early admissions, deferred admissions, and rolling admissions plans. Early decision applications should be filed by November 1; regular applications, by December 1 for fall entry; and December 1 for spring entry. Notification of early decision is sent November 15; regular decision, December 15. Application fees are waived if application is completed online. **Transfer Students:** 133 transfer students enrolled in 2015-2016. Applicants for transfer must have a minimum GPA of 2.5 and must be in satisfactory academic and social standing at their current instituion. If you have earned less than 30 semester hours, you must also supply high school transcripts and either SAT/ACT scores or an academic portfolio with two writing samples. 32 of 128 credits required for the bachelor's degree must be completed at Guilford. **International Students:** There are 35 international students enrolled. The school actively recruits these students. They must take the TOEFL with a minimum score of 550 on the paper-based TOEFL (PBT) or 80 on the Internet-based version (iBT).

ADMISSIONS: 62% of the 2016-2017 applicants were accepted. 25% of the current freshmen were in the top fifth of their class; 55% were in the top two fifths. 2 freshmen graduated first in their class. **Admissions Contact:** Erin Kelly, Director of Admission. Email: *admission@guilford.edu* Web: *www.guilford.edu*

FINANCIAL AID: 27% of undergraduate students work part-time. Average annual earnings from campus work are $1500. The FAFSA code is 002931. The priority date for freshman financial aid applications for fall entry is February 1.

HIGH POINT UNIVERSITY — D-2

www.highpoint.edu

High Point, NC 27268	(336) 841-9216 (800) 345-6993
Fax: (336) 888-6382	**Email:** admiss@highpoint.edu
Full-time: 1829 men, 2679 women	**Faculty:** 301
Part-time: 11 men, 27 women	**Ph.D.s:** 78%
Graduate: 97 men, 194 women	**Student/Faculty:** 15 to 1
Year: semesters, summer session	**Tuition:** $33,405
Room & Board: $12,572	**Freshman Class:** 9683 applied, 7657 accepted, 1382 enrolled
SAT CR/M/W: 544/544/533 **ACT:** 24	**CEEB CODE:** 5293
Application Deadline: March 15	**COMPETITIVE**

High Point University combines the warmth and intimacy of a small liberal arts college with the academic offerings and amenities of a large state university. The High Point University student body is both diverse and dynamic, allowing students to interact with instructors who are well-trained career teachers, not graduate assistants. Students may earn academic credit by participating in internships or by studying abroad. High Point also offers 16 NCAA Division I athletic programs and numerous extra-curricular opportunities. There are 6 undergraduate schools and 5 graduate schools. In addition to regional accreditation, High Point has baccalaureate program accreditation with NCATE, CAATE, and CIDA. The 420-acre campus is in a suburban area 15 miles Southeast of Winston-Salem and 15 miles Southwest of Greensboro. Including any residence halls, there are 112 buildings.

STUDENT LIFE: 79% of undergraduates are from out of state, mostly

the Middle Atlantic. Students are from 47 states, 42 foreign countries, and Canada. 67% are from public schools. 75% are White; 6% African American; 6% two or more races; 5% Hispanic; 3% Foreign; 3% race unknown; 2% Asian American. 38% are Protestant; 30% unknown affiliations; 29% Catholic; 12% claim no religious affiliation. **Female To Male Ratio:** 1.5:1. The average age of freshmen is 18; all undergraduates, 19. 18% do not continue beyond their first year; 64% remain to graduate. **Housing:** 4362 students can be accommodated in college housing, which includes single-sex and coed dorms, on-campus apartments, off-campus apartments, honors houses, special-interest houses, fraternity houses, sorority houses, wellness halls, honors housing, and discipline-specific housing. On-campus housing is guaranteed for all 4 years and is guaranteed for the freshman year. 94% of students live on campus; of those, 90% remain on campus on weekends. All students may keep cars.

FACULTY/CLASSROOMS: 51% of faculty are male; 49% are female. All teach undergraduates. No introductory courses are taught by graduate students. The average class size in an introductory lecture is 23; in a laboratory is 16; and in a regular course is 20.

PROGRAMS OF STUDY: High Point confers B.A., B.S., and B.S.B.A. degrees. Master's and doctoral degrees are also awarded. Bachelor's degrees are awarded in BIOLOGICAL SCIENCE (biochemistry, biology/biological science, and neurosciences), BUSINESS (accounting (finance), business administration and management, entrepreneurial studies, international business management, marketing, and nonprofit/public organization management), COMMUNICATIONS AND THE ARTS (communications, English literature, English Writing, French, graphic design, music, Spanish, studio art, theatre arts, and visual design), COMPUTER AND PHYSICAL SCIENCE (actuarial science, chemistry, computer science, mathematics, mathematics – economics, and physics), EDUCATION (elementary education, middle school education, physical education, and special education), ENGINEERING AND ENVIRONMENTAL DESIGN (interior design), HEALTH PROFESSIONS (exercise science, human relations, predentistry, premedicine, pre-occupational therapy, prepharmacy, prephysical therapy, and preveterinary science), SOCIAL SCIENCE (criminal justice, history, international relations, philosophy, political science/government, prelaw, psychology, religion, and sociology). Business administration, communication, and exercise science have the largest enrollments.

ACTIVITIES: 19% of men belong to 9 national fraternities; 35% of women belong to 6 national sororities. There are 90 groups on campus, including art, band, cheerleading, choir, chorale, chorus, computers, dance, debate, drama, environmental, ethnic, film, honors, international, LGBT, literary magazine, musical theater, newspaper, orchestra, pep band, political, professional, radio and TV, religious, social, social service, and student government. **Sports:** There are 8 intercollegiate sports for men and 8 for women, and 9 intramural sports for men and 9 for women. Facilities include intramural fields, tennis courts, an intramural gym, recreation centers in student center and also in some residential dorms, outdoor pools, racquetball courts, a student activities center, soccer stadium, a track, and sports center. **Graduates:** From July 1, 2015 to June 30, 2016, 859 bachelor's degrees were awarded. The most popular majors were business (25%), communication (15%), and biology (7%). 131 companies recruited on campus in 2015-2016. In an average class, 60% graduate in 4 years or less, 64% graduate in 5 years or less, and 64% graduate in 6 years or less.

SERVICES: Counseling and information services are available, as is tutoring in most subjects, a reader service for the blind, and remedial math, reading, and writing. **Library/Resources:** The library contains 657,000 volumes, 66,000 microform items, 9,800 audio/video tapes/CDs/DVDs, and subscribes to 32,000 periodicals including electronic. Computerized library services include interlibrary loans, database searching, Internet access, and Wi-Fi capability. Special learning facilities include an art gallery, radio station, and TV station. **Physically Challenged Students:** 98% of the campus is accessible. Facilities include wheelchair ramps, elevators, special parking, specially equipped restrooms, special class scheduling, and lowered drinking fountains. **Special:** There is cross-registration with the University of North Carolina at Greensboro, North Carolina Agricultural and Technical State University, and Greensboro, Elon, Guilford, and Bennett Colleges. High Point also offers study abroad in many countries, the Student Career Internship Program, accelerated degree programs, unique programs in home furnishings marketing/management studies, work-study programs, student-designed majors, and a 3-2 engineering program with Vanderbilt and Virginia Tech. There are 6 national honor societies, a freshman honors program, and 13 departmental honors programs. **Visiting:** There are regularly scheduled orientations for prospective students, welcome sessions for parents and students, orientation to your major sessions, meet with success coach about scheduling, campus tours, and peer interactions throughout event. There are guides for informal visits and visitors may sit in on classes. To schedule a visit, contact the Undergraduate Admissions Office. **Campus Safety and Security:** Measures include 24-hour foot and vehicle patrol, emergency notification system, self-defense education, and security escort services. There are also shuttle buses, emergency telephones, lighted pathways/sidewalks, controlled access to dorms/residences, and 24-hour secured residence halls.

REQUIREMENTS: The ACT is required. The SAT is preferred. Applicants should be graduates of an accredited secondary school or have a GED certificate. They should have completed 15 academic units, including 4 in English, 3 each in math, science, and social studies/history, 1 unit in science lab, and at least 2 units in same spoken foreign language. AP and CLEP credits are accepted. To graduate, students must complete a minimum of 128 credit hours with a minimum GPA of 2.0. The core curriculum consists of 1 course in each of the following subject areas: English, foreign language, mathematics, ethical reasoning, as well as a First Year Seminar course, President's Seminar, and PE activity course. Distribution requirements include 2 courses in the social sciences and 1 course in each of the following areas: performing or visual arts, literature, history, religion, and natural science with laboratory. **Procedure:** Freshmen are admitted in the fall, spring, and summer. Entrance exams should be taken prior to high school graduation. There are early decision, early admissions, deferred admissions, and rolling admissions plans. Early decision applications should be filed by November 1; regular applications, by March 15 for fall entry, along with a $50 fee. Notification of early decision is sent November 28; regular decision, on a rolling basis. 452 early decision candidates were accepted for the 2016-2017 class. 237 applicants were on the 2016 waiting list; 82 were admitted. Applications are accepted online. **Transfer Students:** 59 transfer students enrolled in 2015-2016. Applicants must submit official transcripts from colleges and high schools previously attended, as well as SAT or ACT scores, if available. Generally, a minimum GPA of 2.0 is required. 32 of 128 credits required for the bachelor's degree must be completed at High Point. **International Students:** There are 143 international students enrolled. The school actively recruits these students. They must take the TOEFL with a minimum score of 79 on the Internet-based version (iBT). The SAT or ACT is required of students who wish to play on varsity athletic teams.

ADMISSIONS: 79% of the 2016-2017 applicants were accepted. The SAT scores for the 2016-2017 freshman class were: Critical Reading-- 28% below 500, 50% between 500 and 599, 21% between 600 and 699, and 1% between 700 and 800. Math-- 23% below 500, 51% between 500 and 599, 24% between 600 and 699, and 2% between 700 and 800. Writing-- 32% below 500, 48% between 500 and 599, 18% between 600 and 699, and 2% between 700 and 800. The ACT scores were 4% between 12 and 17, 47% between 18 and 23, 43% between 24 and 29, and 6% above 30. 36% of the current freshmen were in the top fifth of their class; 68% were in the top two fifths. There were 33 National Merit finalists. 13 freshmen graduated first in their class. **Admissions Contact:** Kerr Ramsay, Associate VP of Admissions Recruitment. Email: *admiss@highpoint.edu* Web: *www.highpoint.edu*

FINANCIAL AID: In 2016-2017, 83% of all full-time freshmen and 79% of continuing full-time students received some form of financial aid. 36% of all full-time freshmen and 35% of continuing full-time students received need-based aid. The average freshman award was $19,707. Need-based scholarships or need-based grants averaged $5,284 ($42,799 maximum); need-based self-help aid (loans and jobs) averaged $3,182 ($4,454 maximum); non-need-based athletic scholarships averaged $21,030 ($61,599 maximum); and other non-need-based awards and non-need-based scholarships averaged $8,550 ($45,602 maximum). 30% of undergraduate students work part-time. Average annual earnings from campus work are $1500. High Point is a member of CSS. The state aid form is required. The priority date for freshman financial aid applications for fall entry is March 1.

JOHNSON & WALES UNIVERSITY/ CHARLOTTE CAMPUS C-3

www1.jwu.edu/charlotte

Charlotte, NC 28202 (866) 598-2427

Fax: (950) 598-1111
Email: clt@admissions.jwu.edu
Full-time: 729 men, 1446 women
Faculty: 83
Part-time: 15 men, 28 women
Ph.D.s: n/av
Graduate: n/av
Student/Faculty: 23 to 1
Year: quarters, summer session
Tuition: $30,746
Room & Board: $13,242
Freshman Class: 4537 applied, 3287 accepted, 641 enrolled
CEEB CODE: 4360
Application Deadline: November 1
COMPETITIVE

Johnson & Wales University/Charlotte Campus, founded in 2004, offers degree programs in the college of business, college of culinary arts, and hospitality college. There are 3 undergraduate schools. The campus is in an urban area in the center of the New South, Charlotte. Including any residence halls, there are 6 buildings.

STUDENT LIFE: 62% of undergraduates are from out of state, mostly the South. Students are from 47 states, 22 foreign countries, and Canada. 4% are Hispanic; 39% White; 28% African American; 2% Asian American; 2% Foreign; 1% American Indian/Alaska Native. **Female To Male Ratio:** 2.0:1. The average age of freshmen is 18; all undergraduates, 21. 75% remain to graduate. **Housing:** College-sponsored housing includes coed dorms, on-campus apartments, and wellness housing are available. On-campus housing is available on a lottery system for upperclassmen. 59% of students live on campus. All students may keep cars. Alcohol is not permitted.

FACULTY/CLASSROOMS: All teach undergraduates. No introductory courses are taught by graduate students.

PROGRAMS OF STUDY: JWU confers B.S. degrees. Associate degrees are also awarded. Bachelor's degrees are awarded in BUSINESS (accounting, business administration and management, entrepreneurial studies, hospitality management services, hotel/motel and restaurant management, marketing and distribution, marketing management, marketing/retailing/merchandising, sports management, and tourism), ENGINEERING AND ENVIRONMENTAL DESIGN (food services technology), SOCIAL SCIENCE (clothing and textiles management/production/services, food production/management/services, and parks and recreation management).

ACTIVITIES: There are no fraternities or sororities. There are 36 groups on campus, including cheerleading, dance, honors, international, LGBT, newspaper, photography, religious, social, student government, and yearbook. Popular campus events include Welcome Week, Western Day, and Spring Week. **Sports:** Facilities include basketball, soccer, and volleyball for women. **Graduates:** From July 1, 2015 to June 30, 2016, 394 bachelor's degrees were awarded. The most popular majors were family and consumer sciences (55%), business/marketing (34%), and parks and recreation (11%). In an average class, 49% graduate in 6 years or less.

SERVICES: Counseling and information services are available, as is tutoring in every subject. **Library/Resources:** The library contains 28,690 volumes, 8,474 audio/video tapes/CDs/DVDs, and subscribes to 196 periodicals including electronic. Computerized library services include interlibrary loans, database searching, Internet access, and Wi-Fi capability. **Physically Challenged Students:** All of the campus is accessible. Facilities include wheelchair ramps, elevators, special parking, specially equipped restrooms, special class scheduling, lowered drinking fountains, lowered telephones, and special housing. **Special:** The university offers co-op programs, accelerated degree programs, dual majors, study abroad, and worldwide work-study opportunities in business, hospitality, technology, and culinary arts. Most majors require 11-week internships. There is a freshman honors program. **Visiting:** There are regularly scheduled orientations for prospective students, Including an introduction to the academic and social aspects of the campus experience through interactive sessions. There are guides for informal visits, visitors may sit in on classes, and stay overnight. To schedule a visit, contact the Admissions Office. **Campus Safety and Security:** Measures include 24-hour foot and vehicle patrol, self-defense education, and security escort services. There are also shuttle buses, emergency telephones, and lighted pathways/sidewalks.

REQUIREMENTS: Although SAT and ACT scores are required only for students applying for honors admissions, students with 2 who have taken these tests are encouraged to submit their scores. Requirements are 4 years of English, 3 years each of mathematics and science, and 2 years of social studies. High school diploma is required and the GED is accepted. AP and CLEP credits are accepted. Important factors in the admissions decision are advanced placement or honors courses, extracurricular activities record, parents or siblings attended your school, evidence of special talent, personality/intangible qualities, and recommendations by school officials. To graduate, students must complete 180 quarter credit hours, including at least 36 in the major, with a minimum GPA of 2.0. Required courses include English, math, history, economics, science, psychology, sociology, and professional development. **Procedure:** Freshmen are admitted to all sessions. There are deferred admissions and rolling admissions plans. Application deadlines are open. Applications are accepted online. **Transfer Students:** 98 transfer students enrolled in 2015-2016. Applicants are required to submit official high school and college transcripts and must have earned a minimum college GPA of 2.0. Students may enroll in the fall, winter, spring and summer. 45 of 180 credits required for the bachelor's degree must be completed at JWU. **International Students:** There are 46 international students enrolled. The school actively recruits these students. They must take the TOEFL with a minimum score of 550 on the paper-based TOEFL (PBT) or 80 on the Internet-based version (iBT).

ADMISSIONS: 72% of the 2016-2017 applicants were accepted. **Admissions Contact:** Joseph Campos, Director of Admissions. Email: *clt@admissions.jwu.edu* Web: *www1.jwu.edu/charlotte*

FINANCIAL AID: The average freshman award was $24,485. Need-based scholarships or need-based grants averaged $9,159; need-based self-help aid (loans and jobs) averaged $3,781; other non-need-based awards and non-need-based scholarships averaged $3,381; and $9,679 from other forms of aid. JWU is a member of CSS. The priority date for freshman financial aid applications for fall entry is March 1.

JOHNSON C. SMITH UNIVERSITY *(The complete profile is made available exclusively on our website, www.barronspac.com)*

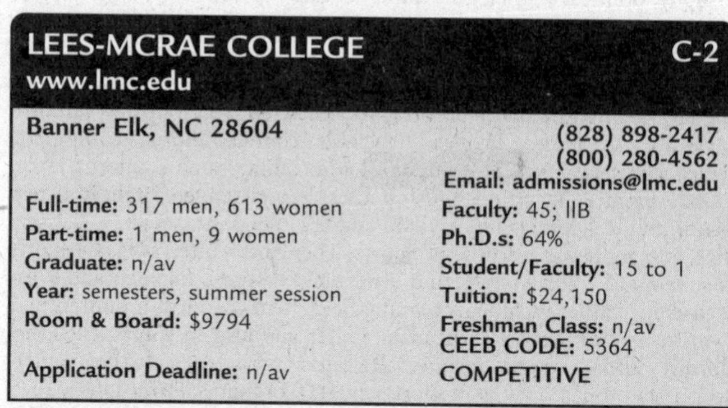

LEES-MCRAE COLLEGE C-2

www.lmc.edu

Banner Elk, NC 28604 (828) 898-2417 (800) 280-4562

Email: admissions@lmc.edu
Full-time: 317 men, 613 women
Faculty: 45; IIB
Part-time: 1 men, 9 women
Ph.D.s: 64%
Graduate: n/av
Student/Faculty: 15 to 1
Year: semesters, summer session
Tuition: $24,150
Room & Board: $9794
Freshman Class: n/av
CEEB CODE: 5364
Application Deadline: n/av
COMPETITIVE

Lees-McRae is a four-year, coeducational residential college offering diverse baccalaureate degrees, strong athletic programs and outstanding faculty. The College offers online programs and degree-completion opportunities in surrounding communities to nontraditional learners. All academic programs incorporate a broad core curriculum and field-specific career preparation and experiential learning with an emphasis in leadership and service. There is 1 undergraduate school. In addition to regional accreditation, Lees-McRae has baccalaureate program accreditation with TEAC, CAATE, and CCNE. The 460-acre campus is in a rural area 17 miles west of Boone, NC and 115 miles northwest of Charlotte, NC. Including any residence halls, there are 59 buildings.

STUDENT LIFE: 73% of undergraduates are from North Carolina. Others are from 31 states, 7 foreign countries, and Canada. **Female To Male Ratio:** 2.0:1. The average age of freshmen is 18; all undergraduates, 36. **Housing:** 704 students can be accommodated in college housing, which includes single-sex and coed dorms, on-campus apartments, honors houses, special-interest houses, substance-free, and pet-friendly houses. On-campus housing is guaranteed for all 4 years and is available on a lottery system for upperclassmen. 64% of students live on campus. All students may keep cars.

FACULTY/CLASSROOMS: 45% of faculty are male; 55% are female. All teach undergraduates. No introductory courses are taught by graduate students.

PROGRAMS OF STUDY: Lees-McRae confers B.A., B.S., B.A.A.S., and

B.F.A. degrees. Bachelor's degrees are awarded in BIOLOGICAL SCIENCE (biology/biological science and wildlife biology), BUSINESS (business administration and management and sports management), COMMUNICATIONS AND THE ARTS (art, communications, design, dramatic arts, English, musical theater, performing arts, and visual and performing arts), COMPUTER AND PHYSICAL SCIENCE (mathematics), EDUCATION (athletic training, drama education, education, and elementary education), HEALTH PROFESSIONS (premedicine and preveterinary science), SOCIAL SCIENCE (criminal justice, history, humanities, psychology, and religion). Wildlife biology, nursing, and education have the largest enrollments.

ACTIVITIES: There are no fraternities or sororities. Groups on campus include art, cheerleading, chorus, communications, dance, drama, environmental, honors, international, musical theater, photography, professional, religious, social, social service, and student government. Popular campus events include Mountain Day, and Stephenson Lecture Series. **Sports:** There are 7 intercollegiate sports for men and 8 for women. Facilities include a main gym with basketball/volleyball courts, a match field for soccer/lacrosse, practice fields, a softball field with batting cages, indoor tennis courts, outdoor tennis courts, a secondary gym for intramurals, an indoor pool, fitness center, weight room facility, and outdoor basketball court. **Graduates:** From July 1, 2015 to June 30, 2016, 221 bachelor's degrees were awarded. The most popular majors were health professions (22%), social sciences (22%), and education (19%). In an average class, 30% graduate in 4 years or less, 38% graduate in 5 years or less, and 38% graduate in 6 years or less.

SERVICES: Counseling and information services are available, as is tutoring in most subjects, and remedial math, reading, and writing. **Library/Resources:** The library contains 216,747 volumes, 7,194 microform items, and 1,488 audio/video tapes/CDs/DVDs. Computerized library services include interlibrary loans, database searching, Internet access, and Wi-Fi capability. Special learning facilities include an art gallery, an wildlife rehabilitation center, academic success center, writing center, technical theatre, and design studio. **Physically Challenged Students:** Facilities include wheelchair ramps, special parking, specially equipped restrooms, special class scheduling, and special housing. **Special:** There is a freshman honors program. **Visiting:** Regularly scheduled orientations for prospective students are available. There are guides for informal visits, visitors may sit in on classes, and stay overnight. To schedule a visit, contact Candace Silver. **Campus Safety and Security:** Measures include 24-hour foot and vehicle patrol, emergency notification system, security escort services, emergency telephones, lighted pathways/sidewalks, and controlled access to dorms/residences.

REQUIREMENTS: Applicants must have completed 18 units of secondary school academic courses, including 6 of academic electives, 4 of English, 3 of math, 2 of science (1 with lab work), and 1 each of social studies and history. AP and CLEP credits are accepted. **Procedure:** Freshmen are admitted to all sessions. There is a rolling admissions plan. Application deadlines are open. Applications are accepted on-line. **Transfer Students:** 167 transfer students enrolled in 2015-2016. Applicants must submit a college GPA of 2.0 and be in good standing at the previous or current institution. Students who have completed 24 semester hours or more must submit a dean's evaluation form; those with fewer than 24 must also submit high school transcripts 32 of 124 credits required for the bachelor's degree must be completed at Lees-McRae. **International Students:** There are 23 international students enrolled. The school actively recruits these students. They must take the TOEFL.

ADMISSIONS: The SAT scores for the 2016-2017 freshman class were: Critical Reading-- 59% below 500, 34% between 500 and 599, 6% between 600 and 699, and 1% between 700 and 800. Math-- 53% below 500, 35% between 500 and 599, and 12% between 600 and 699. **Admissions Contact:** Ginger Hansen, Vice President of Enrollment Management. Email: *admissions@lmc.edu* Web: *www.lmc.edu*

FINANCIAL AID: In 2016-2017, 88% of all full-time freshmen and 80% of continuing full-time students received some form of financial aid. Lees-McRae is a member of CSS. The FAFSA code is 002939. The priority date for freshman financial aid applications for fall entry is April 15.

LENOIR-RHYNE UNIVERSITY C-2

www.lr.edu

Hickory, NC 28603	**(828) 328-7300** **(800) 277-5721**
Fax: (828) 328-7378	**Email: admission@lr.edu**
Full-time: 569 men, 891 women	**Faculty:** 107
Part-time: 31 men, 73 women	**Ph.D.s:** 73%
Graduate: 72 men, 201 women	**Student/Faculty:** 13 to 1
Year: semesters, summer session	**Tuition:** $32,140
Room & Board: $11,060	**Freshman Class:** 3316 applied, 2882 accepted, 406 enrolled
SAT CR/M: 480/500 **ACT:** 21	**CEEB CODE:** 5363
Application Deadline: open	**COMPETITIVE**

Lenoir-Rhyne University, founded in 1891, is a private institution affiliated with the Lutheran Church, offering liberal arts programs that focus on business, education, and allied health sciences. Figures in the above capsule and in this profile are approximate. There is 1 undergraduate school and 1 graduate school. In addition to regional accreditation, Lenoir-Rhyne has baccalaureate program accreditation with NCATE and NLN. The 100-acre campus is in a suburban area 45 miles northwest of Charlotte. Including any residence halls, there are 30 buildings.

STUDENT LIFE: 70% of undergraduates are from North Carolina. Others are from 30 states, 9 foreign countries, and Canada. 89% are from public schools. 87% are White; 8% African American; 2% Asian American; 2% Hispanic; 1% Foreign. 68% are Protestant; 23% claim no religious affiliation. **Female To Male Ratio:** 1.7:1. The average age of freshmen is 18; all undergraduates, 22. 20% do not continue beyond their first year; 63% remain to graduate. **Housing:** 900 students can be accommodated in college housing, which includes single-sex and coed dorms, on-campus apartments, honors houses, special-interest houses, fraternity houses, sorority houses, hearing-impaired housing, and special interest housing. On-campus housing is guaranteed for all 4 years and is available on a lottery system for upperclassmen. 65% of students live on campus; of those, 70% remain on campus on weekends. All students may keep cars.

FACULTY/CLASSROOMS: 55% of faculty are male; 45% are female. All teach undergraduates. No introductory courses are taught by graduate students. The average class size in an introductory lecture is 26; in a laboratory is 20; and in a regular course is 20.

PROGRAMS OF STUDY: Lenoir-Rhyne confers B.A., B.S., and B.Mus.Ed. degrees. Master's degrees are also awarded. Bachelor's degrees are awarded in AGRICULTURE (environmental studies), BIOLOGICAL SCIENCE (biology/biological science), BUSINESS (accounting, business administration and management, international business management, management information systems, and sports management), COMMUNICATIONS AND THE ARTS (applied music, communications, dramatic arts, English, English as a second/foreign language, French, German, graphic design, journalism, music, music performance, piano/organ, and Spanish), COMPUTER AND PHYSICAL SCIENCE (chemistry, computer science, mathematics, and physics), EDUCATION (athletic training, Christian education, early childhood education, elementary education, English education, foreign languages education, health education, middle school education, music education, science education, and secondary education), ENGINEERING AND ENVIRONMENTAL DESIGN (preengineering), HEALTH PROFESSIONS (exercise science, medical laboratory technology, nursing, occupational therapy, predentistry, premedicine, preoptometry, and preveterinary science), SOCIAL SCIENCE (American studies, economics, history, human services, philosophy, political science/government, prelaw, psychology, religion, religious education, religious music, sociology, theological studies, and youth ministry). Business and nursing has the largest enrollment.

ACTIVITIES: 23% of men belong to 3 national fraternities; 27% of women belong to 4 national sororities. There are 50 groups on campus, including art, band, cheerleading, choir, chorus, computers, dance, debate, drama, environmental, ethnic, honors, international, jazz band, LGBT, literary magazine, musical theater, newspaper, outdoor adventure club, pep band, photography, political, professional, radio and TV, religious, social, social service, student government, symphony, and yearbook. Popular campus events include Spring Fling, Advent Candlelight Service, and Opening of School. **Sports:** There are 10 intercollegiate sports for men and 10 for women, and 14 intramural sports for men and 14 for women. Facilities include a football stadium, gym, practice fields, racquetball courts, weight rooms, swimming pool, intramural fields, baseball, softball, soccer fields, and a world class Mondotrack track.

SERVICES: Counseling and information services are available, as is tutoring in every subject, as well as remedial math and writing. Interpreters and note takers for hearing-impaired students are also available. **Library/Resources:** The library contains 145,960 volumes, 462,878 microform items, 40,379 audio/video tapes/CDs/DVDs, and subscribes to 5,376 periodicals including electronic. Computerized library services include interlibrary loans and database searching. Special learning facilities include a radio station, TV station, and observatory. **Physically Challenged Students:** All of the campus is accessible. Facilities include wheelchair ramps, elevators, special parking, specially equipped restrooms, and lowered drinking fountains. **Special:** Lenoir-Rhyne offers study abroad in more than 25 countries and with the nationally known ISEP program, a Washington semester at American University and through the Lutheran College Washington Consortium, internships in most majors, a general studies degree, work-study programs, 3-2 enginering degrees with North Carolina State, North Carolina Agricultural and Technical, and Clemson Universities and the University of North Carolina at Charlotte, pass/fail options, and auditing for most courses. In addition, the Broyhill institute for Business Leadership offers programs to promote understanding of the business community. The university offers an honors program for outstanding students. There are 12 national honor societies, a freshman honors program, and 18 departmental honors programs. **Visiting:** There are regularly scheduled orientations for prospective students, including a meeting with an admissions counselor and a student-guided tour of the campus. There are also guides for informal visits, visitors may sit in on classes, and stay overnight. To schedule a visit, contact the Enrollment Management Office. **Campus Safety and Security:** Measures include 24-hour foot and vehicle patrol, emergency notification system, self-defense education, security escort services, emergency telephones, lighted pathways/sidewalks, and controlled access to dorms/residences.

REQUIREMENTS: The SAT or ACT is required. Applicants need 16 academic credits and should have 4 units in English, 3 in math (algebra 1, geometry, and algebra 2), 2 in the same foreign language, and 1 each in American history and a lab science. An interview is recommended for all students. Music majors must also audition. AP and CLEP credits are accepted. Important factors in the admissions decision are advanced placement or honors courses, personality/intangible qualities, and leadership record. To graduate, students must complete 128 credit hours, including 56 to 57 in liberal arts courses, with a minimum GPA of 2.0. The total number of hours in a major varies by program. **Procedure:** Freshmen are admitted to all sessions. Entrance exams should be taken in the spring of the junior year and thereafter. There are early admissions, deferred admissions, and rolling admissions plans. Application deadlines are open. Application fee is $35. Notification is sent on a rolling basis. 30 applicants were on the 2016 waiting list; 5 were admitted. Applications are accepted online. **Transfer Students:** 143 transfer students enrolled in 2015-2016. Applicants with more than 30 semester hours need a 2.0 minimum GPA in general studies programs or a 2.5 minimum GPA in nursing or education programs. Those with fewer than 30 semester hours must meet freshman entrance criteria. 32 of 128 credits required for the bachelor's degree must be completed at Lenoir-Rhyne. **International Students:** There are 19 international students enrolled. The school actively recruits these students. They must take the TOEFL with a minimum score of 550 on the paper-based TOEFL (PBT) or 79 on the Internet-based version (iBT).

ADMISSIONS: 87% of the 2016-2017 applicants were accepted. The SAT scores for the 2016-2017 freshman class were: Critical Reading-- 57% below 500, 33% between 500 and 599, and 10% between 600 and 699. Math-- 46% below 500, 39% between 500 and 599, 14% between 600 and 699, and 1% between 700 and 800. The ACT scores were 74% below 12, 6% between 12 and 17, 17% between 18 and 23, 2% between 24 and 29, and 1% above 30. 42% of the current freshmen were in the top fifth of their class; 75% were in the top two fifths. **Admissions Contact:** Karen Feezor, Director of Admissions. Email: *admission@lr.edu* Web: *www.lr.edu*

FINANCIAL AID: In 2016-2017, 99% of all full-time freshmen and 92% of continuing full-time students received some form of financial aid. 40% of all full-time freshmen and 55% of continuing full-time students received need-based aid. 35% of undergraduate students work part-time. Average annual earnings from campus work are $1000. The average financial indebtedness of the 2016 graduate was $30,000. The FAFSA code is 002941. The deadline for filing freshman financial aid applications for fall entry is March 15.

LIVINGSTONE COLLEGE *(The complete profile is made available exclusively on our website, www.barronspac.com)*

MARS HILL UNIVERSITY — B-2
Mars Hill College
www.mhu.edu

Mars Hill, NC 28754 (828) 698-1201
(866) 642-4968

Fax: (828) 689-1473 — **Email:** admissions@mhu.edu
Full-time: 505 men, 605 women — **Faculty:** 80; IIB, --$
Part-time: 40 men, 100 women — **Ph.D.s:** 70%
Graduate: n/av — **Student/Faculty:** 13 to 1
Year: semesters, summer session — **Tuition:** $30,534
Room & Board: $12,154 — **Freshman Class:** n/av
SAT or ACT: required — **CEEB CODE:** 5395
Application Deadline: open — **COMPETITIVE**

Mars Hill University, founded in 1856, is a private institution affiliated with the Baptist Church offering undergraduate programs in the arts and sciences, business, education, and preprofessional studies. The figures in the above capsule and in this profile are approximate. There is 1 undergraduate school. In addition to regional accreditation, Mars Hill has baccalaureate program accreditation with CSWE, NASM, and NCATE. The 180-acre campus is in a rural area 18 miles north of Asheville. Including any residence halls, there are 47 buildings.

STUDENT LIFE: 60% of undergraduates are from North Carolina. Others are from 19 states, 20 foreign countries, and Canada. 2% are Foreign; 14% African American; 1% American Indian/Alaska Native; 1% Hispanic. 81% are Protestant; 13% claim no religious affiliation. **Female To Male Ratio:** 1.3:1. The average age of freshmen is 18; all undergraduates, 21. 20% do not continue beyond their first year; 49% remain to graduate. **Housing:** College-sponsored housing includes single-sex dorms, on-campus apartments, married student housing, and honors houses. On-campus housing is guaranteed for all 4 years. 80% of students live on campus; of those, 33% remain on campus on weekends. All students may keep cars. Alcohol is not permitted.

FACULTY/CLASSROOMS: 58% of faculty are male; 42% are female. All teach undergraduates. No introductory courses are taught by graduate students. The average class size in an introductory lecture is 20; in a laboratory is 15; and in a regular course is 15.

PROGRAMS OF STUDY: Mars Hill confers B.A., B.S., B.F.A., B.M., and B.S.W. degrees. Bachelor's degrees are awarded in BIOLOGICAL SCIENCE (biology/biological science, botany, and zoology), BUSINESS (accounting, business administration and management, fashion merchandising, and recreation and leisure services), COMMUNICATIONS AND THE ARTS (art history and appreciation, communications, dramatic arts, English, music, music performance, musical theater, performing arts, and Spanish), COMPUTER AND PHYSICAL SCIENCE (chemistry, computer science, and mathematics), EDUCATION (art education, athletic training, drama education, elementary education, mathematics education, middle school education, music education, physical education, science education, and social studies education), HEALTH PROFESSIONS (allied health, physician's assistant, predentistry, premedicine, prepharmacy, and preveterinary science), SOCIAL SCIENCE (history, international studies, political science/government, prelaw, psychology, religion, social work, and sociology). Music, education, and science are the strongest academically. Education has the largest enrollment.

ACTIVITIES: 30% of men belong to 4 local and 2 national fraternities; 12% of women belong to 4 local and 1 national sororities. There are 80 groups on campus, including art, band, cheerleading, choir, chorale, chorus, dance, drama, ethnic, honors, international, jazz band, literary magazine, marching band, musical theater, newspaper, orchestra, photography, political, professional, radio and TV, religious, social, social service, student government, and yearbook. Popular campus events include Culturefest, Spring Fling, and the Bascom Lamar Lunsford Festival. **Sports:** There are 7 intercollegiate sports for men and 6 for women, and 5 intramural sports for men and 5 for women. Facilities include a stadium, gym, swimming pool, track, baseball diamond, soccer field, an all-purpose playing field, and tennis courts.

SERVICES: Counseling and information services are available, as is tutoring in every subject, and remedial math, reading, and writing. **Library/Resources:** The library contains 98,150 volumes, 1,050 microform items, 6,180 audio/video tapes/CDs/DVDs, and subscribes to 650 periodicals including electronic. Computerized library services include interlibrary loans and database searching. Special learning facilities include an art gallery, radio station, the Southern Appalachian Center of regional history and culture, and the Rural Life Museum. **Physically Challenged Students:** 41% of the campus is accessible. Facilities include wheelchair ramps, elevators, special parking, and specially equipped restrooms. **Special:** Mars Hill offers cooperative programs with the Bowman Gray School of Medicine at Wake Forest, internships, study abroad, B.A.-B.S. degrees, dual majors, student-designed majors, and credit for life experience. The Community Life program promotes student involvement in culture and community activities. There are 4 national honor societies and a freshman honors program. **Visiting:** There are regularly scheduled orientations for prospective students, consisting of 2 days, during which a variety of special programs are offered. Individual students and their families may visit anytime throughout the year. There are guides for informal visits, visitors may sit in on classes, and stay overnight. To schedule a visit, contact the Admissions Office. **Campus Safety and Security:** Measures include 24-hour foot and vehicle patrol, self-defense education, and security escort services. There are also emergency telephones and lighted pathways/sidewalks.

REQUIREMENTS: The SAT or ACT is required. Applicants need at least 18 academic credits, including 4 in English, 3 in math, and 2 each in history, science, and foreign language. The GED is accepted. AP and CLEP credits are accepted. Important factors in the admissions decision are advanced placement or honors courses, leadership record, and extracurricular activities record. To graduate, students must complete at least 128 semester hours with a minimum GPA of 2.0. Distribution requirements include courses in fine arts, literature, American culture, foreign culture, math, natural science, social/behavioral science, ethics, and phys ed. **Procedure:** Freshmen are admitted to all sessions. There are early decision, early admissions, and rolling admissions plans. Application deadlines are open. Application fee is $25. 3 early decision candidates were accepted for the 2016-2017 class. **Transfer Students:** 66 transfer students enrolled in 2015-2016. Transfer applicants must be eligible to return to their previous college or have been out of school for at least 1 semester. They must have a minimum GPA of 2.0 for at least 30 semester credit hours. Remedial and developmental hours do not apply. 32 of 128 credits required for the bachelor's degree must be completed at Mars Hill. **International Students:** The school actively recruits these students. They must take the TOEFL.

Admissions Contact: Kristie Vance, Director of Admissisons. Email: *admissions@mhu.edu* Web: *www.mhu.edu*

FINANCIAL AID: In 2016-2017, 96% of all full-time freshmen received some form of financial aid. 35% of undergraduate students work part-time. Average annual earnings from campus work are $1000. Mars Hill is a member of CSS. The FAFSA code is 002944. The deadline for filing freshman financial aid applications for fall entry is May 1.

MEREDITH COLLEGE — D-2

www.meredith.edu

Raleigh, NC 27607	**(919) 760-8581** **(800) MEREDITH**
Fax: (919) 760-2348	**Email: admissions@meredith.edu**
Full-time: 1766 women	**Faculty:** 138; IIA, --$
Part-time: 9 men, 192 women	**Ph.D.s:** 91%
Graduate: 32 men, 263 women	**Student/Faculty:** 13 to 1
Year: semesters, summer session	**Tuition:** $34,907
Room & Board: $10,390	**Freshman Class:** 1614 applied, 1047 accepted, 1481 enrolled
SAT CR/M: 519/520 **ACT:** 21	**CEEB CODE:** 5410
Application Deadline: February 15	**COMPETITIVE**

Meredith College, founded in 1891, is a private college for women offering a comprehensive undergraduate program with a strong emphasis in the liberal arts. Graduate programs in business, music, education, and nutrition are offered to both men and women. The figures in the above capsule and in this profile are approximate. There are 6 undergraduate schools and 1 graduate school. In addition to regional accreditation, Meredith has baccalaureate program accreditation with ADA, CSWE, FIDER, NASM, and NCATE. The 225-acre campus is in an urban area in Raleigh, NC. Including any residence halls, there are 30 buildings.

STUDENT LIFE: 90% of undergraduates are from North Carolina. Others are from 36 states, and 17 foreign countries. 77% are White; 3% Asian American; 3% Hispanic; 11% African American; 1% Foreign. **Female To Male Ratio:** 54.2:1. The average age of freshmen is 18; all undergraduates, 22. 24% do not continue beyond their first year; 76% remain to graduate. **Housing:** 1150 students can be accommodated in college housing, which includes single-sex dorms, on-campus apartments, and nonsmoking halls. On-campus housing is guaranteed for all 4 years. 56% of students commute. All students may keep cars. Alcohol is not permitted.

FACULTY/CLASSROOMS: 31% of faculty are male; 69% are female. All teach undergraduates. No introductory courses are taught by graduate students. The average class size in an introductory lecture is 20; in a laboratory is 11; and in a regular course is 17.

PROGRAMS OF STUDY: Meredith confers B.A., B.S., B.M., and B.S.W. degrees. Master's degrees are also awarded. Bachelor's degrees are awarded in AGRICULTURE (environmental studies), BIOLOGICAL SCIENCE (biology/biological science and nutrition), BUSINESS (accounting, business administration and management, fashion merchandising, and international business management), COMMUNICATIONS AND THE ARTS (applied music, art, communications, dance, dramatic arts, English, fine arts, French, music, music performance, musical theater, and Spanish), COMPUTER AND PHYSICAL SCIENCE (chemistry, computer science, information sciences and systems, and mathematics), EDUCATION (music education), ENGINEERING AND ENVIRONMENTAL DESIGN (interior design), HEALTH PROFESSIONS (exercise science), SOCIAL SCIENCE (American studies, child psychology/development, economics, family/consumer studies, history, international studies, political science/government, psychology, public affairs, religion, social work, and sociology). Interior design, psychology, and biology have the largest enrollments.

ACTIVITIES: There are no fraternities or sororities. There are 91 groups on campus, including nutrition & wellness, environmental, foreign language, commuter, art, chorale, chorus, computers, dance, drama, ethnic, honors, international, LGBT, literary magazine, musical theater, newspaper, orchestra, photography, political, professional, religious, social, social service, student government, and symphony. Popular campus events include Academics and Leadership Awards Day, White Iris Ball, and Undergraduate Research Conference. **Sports:** There are 6 intercollegiate sports for women. Facilities include a indoor swimming pool, dance studio, fitness center, horseshoe pit, a putting green and driving range, softball, tennis courts, a soccer field, and a gym with basketball, volleyball, and badminton courts. **Graduates:** From July 1, 2015 to June 30, 2016, 430 bachelor's degrees were awarded. The most popular majors were psychology (10%), interior design (9%), and child development (7%). In an average class, 14% graduate in 3 years or less, 44% graduate in 4 years or less, 55% graduate in 5 years or less, and 57% graduate in 6 years or less.

SERVICES: Counseling and information services are available, as is tutoring in some subjects, such as math, writing, computer lab, French, Spanish, biology, chemistry, study skills, German, GRE prep, Praxis prep, and grammar. There is also a reader service for the blind. **Library/Resources:** The 2 libraries contain 155,165 volumes, 16,116 microform items, and 14,671 audio/video tapes/CDs/DVDs, and subscribe to 2,867 periodicals including electronic. Computerized library services include interlibrary loans, database searching, and Internet access. Special learning facilities include an art a gallery, child-care lab, greenhouse, experimental and clinical psychology labs including one on autism, an electron microscope suite, astronomy observation deck, student/faculty research labs, and language lab. **Physically Challenged Students:** 81% of the campus is accessible. Facilities include wheelchair ramps, elevators, special parking, specially equipped restrooms, special class scheduling, lowered drinking fountains, special housing, handicap lift in the swimming pool, and lowered fire alarms. **Special:** Meredith offers cooperative programs, cross-registration with Cooperating Raleigh Colleges, internships, study abroad in Europe and Asia, a Washington semester at American University, a U.N. semester at Drew University, and work-study programs on campus. Dual majors, interdisciplinary and student-designed majors, preprofessional programs, and pass/fail options are available.

Certification in social work and licensure for teaching are possible. Business administration, management, and social work majors can be completed through evening classes. There are 19 national honor societies and a freshman honors program. **Visiting:** There are regularly scheduled orientations for prospective students, students may participate in information sessions for senior students and parents, class visitation, informal conversations with students and faculty/staff, and campus tours. There are guides for informal visits, visitors may sit in on classes, and stay overnight. To schedule a visit, contact the Admissions Office. **Campus Safety and Security:** Measures include 24-hour foot and vehicle patrol, self-defense education, security escort services, emergency telephones, lighted pathways/sidewalks, controlled campus access at night, and 24-hour locked residence halls.

REQUIREMENTS: The ACT is required. The SAT is preferred. The ACT Optional Writing test is also required. Applicants must also have a minimum of 16 units of credit, including 4 in English, 3 each in math, history/social studies, and science, 2 in foreign language, and 1 elective. The student is expected to rank in the top half of her class, and grades in academic subjects are very important. An interview may be requested as part of the evaluation process. AP and CLEP credits are accepted. Important factors in the admissions decision are recommendations by school officials, advanced placement or honors courses, and evidence of special talent. To graduate, students must complete a total of 124 credit hours, including general education requirements, a major field, and electives, with a minimum GPA of 2.0. General Education is comprised of a core curriculum focusing on understanding diverse cultures, fields of knowledge that ensure breadth in the liberal arts, and across-the-curriculum threads and independent learning experiences that build competencies. Some major fields offer or require a concentration, and contract majors are possible. Electives may be used to complete a second major, a minor, teacher licensure, or to explore areas of personal, and career or pre-professional interest. **Procedure:** Freshmen are admitted in the fall and spring. Entrance exams should be taken by January of the senior year. There are early decision, deferred admissions, and rolling admissions plans. Early decision applications should be filed by October 15; regular applications, by February 15 for fall entry, along with a $40 fee. Notification of early decision is sent November 1; regular decision, on a rolling basis. 121 early decision candidates were accepted for the 2016-2017 class. Applications are accepted online. **Transfer Students:** 74 transfer students enrolled in 2015-2016. Applicants must have a minimum GPA of 2.0, be eligible to return to the last college attended, and be recommended by college officials. Those students with fewer than 30 hours of credit must also meet freshman admission requirements. 31 of 124 credits required for the bachelor's degree must be completed at Meredith. **International Students:** There are 26 international students enrolled. The school actively recruits these students. They must take the TOEFL. If English is the student's native language or primary language of instruction, the SAT should be taken instead of the TOEFL.

ADMISSIONS: 65% of the 2016-2017 applicants were accepted. The SAT scores for the 2016-2017 freshman class were: Critical Reading-- 41% below 500, 42% between 500 and 599, 16% between 600 and 699, and 1% between 700 and 800. Math-- 39% below 500, 43% between 500 and 599, 17% between 600 and 699, and 1% between 700 and 800. The ACT scores were 47% below 12, 24% between 12 and 17, 21% between 18 and 23, 5% between 24 and 29, and 6% above 30. 43% of the current freshmen were in the top fifth of their class; 72% were in the top two fifths. 5 freshmen graduated first in their class. **Admissions Contact:** Cristan Trahey Harris, Director of Admissions. Email: *admissions@meredith.edu* Web: *www.meredith.edu*

FINANCIAL AID: Meredith is a member of CSS. The FAFSA code is 002945. The priority date for freshman financial aid applications for fall entry is February 15.

METHODIST UNIVERSITY — D-3

www.methodist.edu

Fayetteville, NC 28311 — (910) 630-7027, (800) 488-7110

Fax: (910) 630-7285 — Email: admissions@methodist.edu

Full-time: 1059 men, 960 women	**Faculty:** 142
Part-time: 109 men, 152 women	**Ph.D.s:** 79%
Graduate: 83 men, 113 women	**Student/Faculty:** 13 to 1
Year: semesters, summer session	**Tuition:** $31,634
Room & Board: $11,966	**Freshman Class:** 3823 applied, 2315 accepted, 488 enrolled
SAT CR/M/W: 484/510/466 **ACT:** 21	**CEEB CODE:** 5426
Application Deadline: n/av	**COMPETITIVE**

Methodist University, founded in 1956, is a private institution affiliated with the United Methodist Church. The University offers programs in the arts and sciences, education, business, and professional training. The figures in the above capsule and in this profile are approximate. There are 4 undergraduate schools and 3 graduate schools. In addition to regional accreditation, Methodist has baccalaureate program accreditation with ACBSP, CSWE, NCATE, and CAAHEP. The 620-acre campus is in a suburban area 5 miles north of Fayetteville. Including any residence halls, there are 38 buildings.

STUDENT LIFE: 56% of undergraduates are from North Carolina. Others are from 44 states, 31 foreign countries, and Canada. 86% are from public schools. 65% are White; 6% Hispanic; 4% Foreign; 20% African American; 2% Asian American; 2% American Indian/Alaska Native. 41% are Protestant; 16% Catholic. **Male To Female Ratio:** 1.0:1. The average age of freshmen is 19; all undergraduates, 24. 33% do not continue beyond their first year; 44% remain to graduate. **Housing:** 1095 students can be accommodated in college housing, which includes single-sex dorms, on-campus apartments, honors houses, fraternity houses, sorority houses, first year experience, and health and wellness hall. On-campus housing is guaranteed for all 4 years. 57% of students live on campus; of those, 70% remain on campus on weekends. All students may keep cars. Alcohol is not permitted.

FACULTY/CLASSROOMS: 52% of faculty are male; 48% are female. All teach undergraduates. No introductory courses are taught by graduate students. The average class size in an introductory lecture is 23; in a laboratory is 20; and in a regular course is 20.

PROGRAMS OF STUDY: Methodist confers B.A., B.S., B.F.A, B.M., and B.S.W. degrees. Associate and master's degrees are also awarded. Bachelor's degrees are awarded in BIOLOGICAL SCIENCE (biology/biological science), BUSINESS (accounting, business administration and management, marketing/retailing/merchandising, organizational behavior, and sports management), COMMUNICATIONS AND THE ARTS (art, communications, creative writing, dramatic arts, English, French, music, music performance, and Spanish), COMPUTER AND PHYSICAL SCIENCE (chemistry, computer science, and mathematics), EDUCATION (art education, athletic training, elementary education, middle school education, music education, physical education, secondary education, and special education), ENGINEERING AND ENVIRONMENTAL DESIGN (computer technology), HEALTH PROFESSIONS (nursing, physician's assistant, and predentistry), SOCIAL SCIENCE (criminal justice, economics, history, international studies, political science/government, prelaw, psychology, religion, social studies, social work, and sociology). Business administration, biology, and education are the strongest academically, and have the largest enrollments.

ACTIVITIES: 6% of men belong to 1 local and 1 national fraternities; 6% of women belong to 2 local and 1 national sororities. There are 104 groups on campus, including art, band, cheerleading, choir, chorale, chorus, computers, dance, debate, drama, environmental, ethnic, forensics, honors, international, jazz band, literary magazine, marching band, musical theater, newspaper, orchestra, pep band, photography, political, professional, radio and TV, religious, social, social service, student government, and symphony. Popular campus events include Show You Care Day, Annual Woodcutting, and Spring Fest. **Sports:** There are 9 intercollegiate sports for men and 10 for women, and 7 intramural sports for men and 4 for women. Facilities include a fitness center, stadium, gym, golf course, track and field, tennis courts, and fields for baseball, softball, and soccer. **Graduates:** From July 1, 2015 to June 30, 2016, 290 bachelor's degrees were awarded. The most popular majors were business (46%), social sciences (11%), and education (7%). 180 companies recruited on campus in 2015-2016. In an average class, 1% graduate in 3 years or less, 33% graduate in 4 years or less, 38% graduate in 5 years or less, and 40% graduate in 6 years or less. Of the 2015 graduating class, 24% were enrolled in graduate school within 6 months of graduation, and 70% were employed.

SERVICES: Counseling and information services are available, as is tutoring in most subjects, a reader service for the blind, and remedial math and writing. **Library/Resources:** The library contains 181,833 volumes, 57,759 microform items, 13,412 audio/video tapes/CDs/DVDs, and subscribes to 587 periodicals including electronic. Computerized library services include interlibrary loans, database searching, Internet access, and Wi-Fi capability. Special learning facilities include an art gallery, radio station. **Physically Challenged Students:** 90% of the campus is accessible. Facilities include wheelchair ramps, elevators, special parking, specially equipped restrooms, and lowered drinking fountains. **Special:** Methodist offers internships in political science and social work, study abroad in 4 countries, a Washington semester, a general studies degree, a 3-2 engineering degree with North Carolina State University, pass/fail options, dual majors, and nondegree study. The business administration major offers concentrations in professional golf, tennis, and resort management with specialized facilities and co-op programs. There are 7 national honor societies, a freshman honors program, and 5 departmental honors programs. **Visiting:** There are regularly scheduled orientations for prospective students, 3 days prior to the first day of fall semester. There are guides for informal visits, visitors may sit in on classes, and stay overnight. To schedule a visit, contact the Admissions Office. **Campus Safety and Security:** Measures include 24-hour foot and vehicle patrol, emergency notification system, self-defense education, and security escort services. There are also shuttle buses, emergency telephones, lighted pathways/sidewalks, and controlled access to dorms/residences.

REQUIREMENTS: The SAT or ACT is required. Applicants should be graduates of an accredited secondary school or have a GED certificate. They must have 16 academic credits, including 4 in English and 3 each in history, math, and science. 2 years of foreign language are recommended. An essay and interview are also recommended. AP and CLEP credits are accepted. Important factors in the admissions decision are recommendations by school officials, evidence of special talent, and advanced placement or honors courses. To graduate, students must complete at least 124 semester hours, including core requirements, with a minimum GPA of 2.0. A liberal arts core, ranging from 36 to 62 hours, is required in all majors. **Procedure:** Freshmen are admitted in the fall, spring, and summer. There are deferred admissions and rolling admissions plans. Application deadlines are open. Application fee is $25. Applications are accepted online. **Transfer Students:** 292 transfer students enrolled in 2015-2016. Applicants must have a minimum GPA of 2.0. They must also submit a high school transcript, college transcripts, and the SAT or ACT scores. 30 of 124 credits required for the bachelor's degree must be completed at Methodist. **International Students:** There are 70 international students enrolled. The school actively recruits these students. They must take the TOEFL with a minimum score of 500 on the paper-based TOEFL (PBT) or 60 on the Internet-based version (iBT). The student may take the SAT or ACT in place of the TOEFL if English proficiency is demonstrated.

ADMISSIONS: 61% of the 2016-2017 applicants were accepted. The SAT scores for the 2016-2017 freshman class were: Critical Reading-- 59% below 500, 34% between 500 and 599, 6% between 600 and 699, and 1% between 700 and 800. Math-- 45% below 500, 40% between 500 and 599, 14% between 600 and 699, and 1% between 700 and 800. Writing-- 60% below 500, 33% between 500 and 599, 6% between 600 and 699, and 1% between 700 and 800. The ACT scores were 50% below 12, 30% between 12 and 17, 10% between 18 and 23, 6% between 24 and 29, and 4% above 30. 27% of the current freshmen were in the top fifth of their class; 54% were in the top two fifths. 4 freshmen graduated first in their class. **Admissions Contact:** Jamie Legg, Director of Admissions. Email: *admissions@methodist.edu* Web: *www.methodist.edu*

FINANCIAL AID: In 2016-2017, 92% of all full-time freshmen and continuing full-time students received some form of financial aid. 92% of all full-time freshmen and 85% of continuing full-time students received need-based aid. The average freshman award was $9,780. 60% of undergraduate students work part-time. Average annual earnings from campus work are $1000. The average financial indebtedness of the 2016 graduate was $20,026. The FAFSA code is 002946. The priority date for freshman financial aid applications for fall entry is March 15.

MONTREAT COLLEGE *(The complete profile is made available exclusively on our website, www.barronspac.com)*

NORTH CAROLINA A&T STATE UNIVERSITY *(The complete profile is made available exclusively on our website, www.barronspac.com)*

NORTH CAROLINA CENTRAL UNIVERSITY D-2
www.nccu.edu

Durham, NC 27707 **(919) 560-6298**

Fax: (919) 530-7625
Full-time: 1500 men, 2700 women
Part-time: 300 men, 800 women
Graduate: 500 men, 1300 women
Year: semesters, summer session
Room & Board: $5000
SAT or ACT: required
Application Deadline: August 1

Email: admissions@nccu.edu
Faculty: 257; IIA, -$
Ph.D.s: 75%
Student/Faculty: 16 to 1
Tuition: $5000 ($14,000)
Freshman Class: n/av
CEEB CODE: 5495
COMPETITIVE

North Carolina Central University, founded in 1910, is a publicly funded liberal arts institution in the University of North Carolina system. The figures in the above capsule and in this profile are approximate. There are 3 undergraduate schools and 2 graduate schools. In addition to regional accreditation, NCCU has baccalaureate program accreditation with NCATE and NLN. The 103-acre campus is in an urban area 2 miles from the center of Durham. Including any residence halls, there are 57 buildings.

STUDENT LIFE: 89% of undergraduates are from North Carolina. Others are from 39 states, and 17 foreign countries. 80% are African American; 3% Foreign; 14% White; 1% Asian American; 1% American Indian/Alaska Native; 1% Hispanic. **Female To Male Ratio:** 2.1:1. The average age of freshmen is 19; all undergraduates, 24. **Housing:** 2377 students can be accommodated in college housing, which includes single-sex and coed dorms and on-campus apartments, and honors houses. On-campus housing is available on a first-come, first-served basis, and on a lottery system for upperclassmen. 63% of students commute. All students may keep cars. Alcohol is not permitted.

FACULTY/CLASSROOMS: 53% of faculty are male; 47% are female. All teach undergraduates. No introductory courses are taught by graduate students.

PROGRAMS OF STUDY: NCCU confers B.A., B.S., B.B.A., B.M., B.S.N., and B.S.W. degrees. Master's degrees are also awarded. Bachelor's degrees are awarded in BIOLOGICAL SCIENCE (biology/biological science and nutrition), BUSINESS (accounting and business administration and management), COMMUNICATIONS AND THE ARTS (art, dramatic arts, English, French, jazz, music, and Spanish), COMPUTER AND PHYSICAL SCIENCE (chemistry, computer science, mathematics, and physics), EDUCATION (elementary education, health education, middle school education, and physical education), ENGINEERING AND ENVIRONMENTAL DESIGN (environmental science), HEALTH PROFESSIONS (nursing), SOCIAL SCIENCE (child care/child and family studies, child psychology/development, criminal justice, geography, history, human services, political science/government, psychology, social work, and sociology). Criminal justice and business is the strongest academically. Business, biology, and political science have the largest enrollments.

ACTIVITIES: There are 45 groups on campus, including art, band, cheerleading, chess, choir, computers, dance, drama, drill team, ethnic, honors, international, jazz band, literary magazine, marching band, newspaper, political, professional, radio and TV, religious, social, social service, student government, symphony, and yearbook. **Sports:** There are 6 intercollegiate sports for men and 5 for women. Facilities include a stadium, gym, swimming pool, handball and tennis courts, a track, bowling alley, dance studios, and a weight room. **Graduates:** From July 1, 2015 to June 30, 2016, 604 bachelor's degrees were awarded. The most popular majors were business administration (21%), education (11%), and criminal justice (9%). 297 companies recruited on campus in 2015-2016.

SERVICES: There is a reader service for the blind, and remedial math, reading, and writing. There is also assistance for students in obtaining needed documentations, registration, and appropriate individual accommodations as needed. **Library/Resources:** The 6 libraries contain 663,913 volumes, 1.2 million microform items, 10,991 audio/video tapes/CDs/DVDs, and subscribe to 6,688 periodicals including electronic. Computerized library services include database searching. Special learning facilities include an art gallery and radio station. **Physically Challenged Students:** 90% of the campus is accessible. Facilities include wheelchair ramps, elevators, special parking, specially equipped restrooms, special class scheduling, lowered drinking fountains, and lowered telephones. **Special:** NCCU offers internships, study abroad, a Washington semester, work-study programs, dual majors, and nondegree study. There are 10 national honor societies, a freshman honors program, and 10 departmental honors programs. **Visiting:** There are regularly scheduled orientations for prospective students. There are guides for informal visits, visitors may sit in on classes, and stay overnight. **Campus Safety and Security:** Measures include 24-hour foot and vehicle patrol, security escort services, emergency telephones and lighted pathways/sidewalks.

REQUIREMENTS: The SAT or ACT is required. Applicants must be graduates of an accredited secondary school or have a GED certificate. They must have completed 11 academic credits based on 4 years of English, 3 each of math and science, and 2 each of a foreign language and social studies. Music applicants must audition. AP and CLEP credits are accepted. Important factors in the admissions decision are advanced placement or honors courses, leadership record, and evidence of special talent. To graduate, students must complete 124 semester hours, including 30 in the major, with a minimum GPA of 2.0. Core requirements include courses in communications, math and natural science, social science, humanities, and health and phys ed. **Procedure:** Entrance exams should be taken in the spring of the junior year. There is a rolling admissions plan. Applications should be filed by August 1 for fall entry; November 1 for spring entry. The fall 2016 application fee was $30. Applications are accepted on-line. **Transfer Students:** 373 transfer students enrolled in 2015-2016. Applicants must have a minimum GPA of 2.0 in all college-level courses. 30 of 124 credits required for the bachelor's degree must be completed at NCCU. **International Students:** They must take the TOEFL as well as the SAT or ACT.

Admissions Contact: Nicole Gibbs, Director of Admissions. Email: *admissions@nccu.edu* Web: *www.nccu.edu*

FINANCIAL AID: In 2016-2017, 85% of all full-time freshmen and continuing full-time students received some form of financial aid. 70% of all full-time freshmen and continuing full-time students received need-based aid. The FAFSA code is 002950. The deadline for filing freshman financial aid applications for fall entry is August 1.

NORTH CAROLINA STATE UNIVERSITY D-2

www.ncsu.edu

Raleigh, NC 27695 **(919) 515-2434**

Fax: (919) 515-5039 **Email:** undergrad-admissions@ncsu.edu

Full-time: 12,859 men, 10,682 women	**Faculty:** 997; I, -$
	Ph.D.s: 98%
Part-time: 206 men, 100 women	**Student/Faculty:** 14 to 1
Graduate: 5496 men, 4412 women	**Tuition:** $8880 ($26,399)
Year: semesters, summer session	**Freshman Class:** 25938 applied, 12043 accepted, 3918 enrolled
Room & Board: $10,635	
SAT CR/M/W: 617/646/589 **ACT:** 29	**CEEB CODE:** 5496
Application Deadline: January 15	**HIGHLY COMPETITIVE+**

North Carolina State University, founded in 1887, is a member of the University of North Carolina System. Its degree programs emphasize the arts and sciences, agriculture, business, education, engineering, and preprofessional training. The figures in the above capsule and in this profile are approximate. There are 10 undergraduate schools and 10 graduate schools. In addition to regional accreditation, NC State has baccalaureate program accreditation with AACSB, ABET, CSAB, CSWE, NAAB, NASAD, NCATE, NRPA, and SAF. The 2110-acre campus is in an urban area in Raleigh, NC. Including any residence halls, there are 197 buildings.

STUDENT LIFE: 87% of undergraduates are from North Carolina. Others are from 50 states, 84 foreign countries, and Canada. 90% are from public schools. 71% are White; 6% African American; 6% Asian American; 5% Hispanic; 5% Foreign; 4% two or more races; 3% race unknown. **Male To Female Ratio:** 1.2:1. The average age of freshmen is 18; all undergraduates, 21. 6% do not continue beyond their first year; 78% remain to graduate. **Housing:** 7300 students can be accommodated in college housing, which includes single-sex and coed dorms, on-campus apartments, off-campus apartments, married student housing, honors houses, special-interest houses, fraternity houses, and sorority houses. There are also international, arts and creative living, computer theme, women in science & engineering, and first-year-experience halls. On-campus housing is guaranteed for the freshman year only, is available on a first-come, and first-served basis. 68% of students commute. All students may keep cars. Alcohol is not permitted.

FACULTY/CLASSROOMS: 70% of faculty are male; 30% are female. 67% teach undergraduates, all do research, and 67% do both. Graduate students teach 51% of introductory courses. The average class size in an introductory lecture is 41; in a laboratory is 23; and in a regular course is 35.

PROGRAMS OF STUDY: NCSU State confers B.A., B.S., B.Arch., B.E.D.A., B.L.A., and B.S.W. degrees. Associate, master's, and doctoral degrees are also awarded. Bachelor's degrees are awarded in AGRICULTURE (agricultural business management, agricultural economics, agriculture, agronomy, animal science, conservation and regulation, fishing and fisheries, forestry and related sciences, horticulture, natural resource management, poultry science, soil science, and wood science), BIOLOGICAL SCIENCE (biochemistry, biology/biological science, botany, microbiology, and zoology), BUSINESS (accounting, business administration and management, business economics, and recreation and leisure services), COMMUNICATIONS AND THE ARTS (communications, design, English, French, graphic design, industrial design, and Spanish), COMPUTER AND PHYSICAL SCIENCE (atmospheric sciences and meteorology, chemistry, computer science, earth science, geology, mathematics, physics, and statistics), EDUCATION (agricultural education, education, foreign languages education, industrial arts education, marketing and distribution education, mathematics education, middle school education, science education, secondary education, social studies education, technical education, and vocational education), ENGINEERING AND ENVIRONMENTAL DESIGN (aeronautical engineering, agricultural engineering, architecture, chemical engineering, civil engineering, computer engineering, construction management, electrical/electronics engineering, engineering, environmental design, environmental engineering, environmental science, furniture design, industrial engineering, landscape architecture/design, materials science, mechanical engineering, nuclear engineering, paper and pulp science, and textile engineering), HEALTH PROFESSIONS (medical laboratory technology, predentistry, premedicine, preveterinary science, and speech pathology/audiology), SOCIAL SCIENCE (clothing and textiles management/production/services, criminal justice, economics, food science, history, interdisciplinary studies, parks and recreation management, philosophy, political science/government, prelaw, psychology, religion, social science, social work, sociology, and textiles and clothing). Electrical engineering, chemical engineering, and architecture are the strongest academically. Business management, mechanical engineering, and electrical engineering have the largest enrollments.

ACTIVITIES: 9% of men belong to 29 national fraternities; 16% of women belong to 19 national sororities. There are 665 groups on campus, including art, bagpipe, band, cheerleading, chess, choir, chorale, chorus, communications, computers, dance, debate, drama, drill team, drum and bugle corps, environmental, ethnic, film, honors, international, jazz band, LGBT, literary magazine, marching band, musical theater, newspaper, orchestra, pep band, photography, political, professional, radio and TV, religious, social, social service, student government, symphony, and yearbook. Popular campus events include Pan African Festival, Wolfstock, and Greek Week. **Sports:** There are 42 intercollegiate sports for men and 43 for women, and 49 intramural sports for men and 50 for women. Facilities include a football stadium, sports arena, soccer stadium, a baseball stadium, a gym, tennis complex, areas for track, indoor pools, and an indoor rock-climbing wall. **Graduates:** The most popular majors were engineering (24%), business/marketing (15%), and biological/life sciences (10%). In an average class, 54% graduate in 4 years or less, 76% graduate in 5 years or less, and 78% graduate in 6 years or less. Of the 2015 graduating class, 24% were enrolled in graduate school within 6 months of graduation, and 64% were employed.

SERVICES: Counseling and information services are available, as is tutoring in most subjects, and a reader service for the blind. **Library/Resources:** The 5 libraries contain 5.1 million volumes, 5.5 million microform items, 324,053 audio/video tapes/CDs/DVDs, and subscribe to 102,734 periodicals including electronic. Computerized library services include interlibrary loans, database searching, Internet access, and Wi-Fi capability. Special learning facilities include an art gallery, radio station, TV station, nuclear reactor, phytotron, and electron microscope facilities. There is also an Materials Research Center, Integrated Manufacturing Systems Engineering Institute, Japan Center, Confucius Institute, Textile Protection and Comfort Center, and Precision Engineering Center. **Physically Challenged Students:** 78% of the campus is accessible. Facilities include wheelchair ramps, elevators, special parking, specially equipped restrooms, special class scheduling, lowered drinking fountains, lowered telephones, and special housing. **Special:** NC State offers cross-registration within the Cooperating Raleigh Colleges network, study abroad in more than 90 countries, internships, work-study programs, an accelerated degree plan, dual majors within any program, a general studies degree in education, a 3-2 engineering degree with the University of North Carolina at Asheville, student-designed multidisciplinary studies majors, credit by examination, nondegree study, and pass/fail options. There are 17 national honor societies, Phi Beta Kappa, a freshman honors program, and 44 departmental honors programs. **Visiting:** There are regularly scheduled orientations for prospective students, consisting of admissions information sessions. There are also guides for informal visits and visitors may sit in on classes. To schedule a visit, contact the Admissions Office. **Campus Safety and Security:** Measures include 24-hour foot and vehicle patrol, emergency notification system, self-defense education, and security escort services. There are also shuttle buses, emergency telephones, lighted pathways/sidewalks, controlled access to dorms/residences, bicycle patrol, and mounted police.

REQUIREMENTS: The SAT Math Subject Test is recommended. Applicants must be graduates of an accredited secondary school or have a GED certificate. They must have completed 20 academic credits, including 4 units of English, 3 each of science and math (4 of math is advised), 2 each of social studies and foreign language, and 1 of history. An essay is recommended for all applicants. A portfolio and interview are required for studio-based majors. AP and CLEP credits are accepted. Important factors in the admissions decision are advanced placement or honors courses, leadership record, and evidence of special talent. To graduate, students must complete 120 to 142 semester hours, including 60 to 70 in the major, with a minimum GPA of 2.0. Distribution requirements include 12 to 18 hours in humanities and social sciences, 6 to 8 each in math and science, 6 in English composition, and 4 in phys ed. **Procedure:** Freshmen are admitted to all sessions. Entrance exams should be taken in the spring of the junior year and the fall of the senior year. There is a deferred admissions plan. Early decision applications should be filed by October 15; regular applications, by January 15 for fall entry; October 1 for spring entry; and January 15 for summer entry, along with a $85 fee. Notification of early decision is sent January 30; regular decision, March 30. 2552 applicants were on the 2016 waiting list; 427 were admitted. Application fees are waived if application is completed online. **Transfer Students:** 1188 transfer students enrolled in 2015-2016. Applicants must have completed 30 semester hours of college-level work with a minimum GPA of 2.0. Priority is given to students who have completed 60 hours of relevant course work. An associate degree and an interview are recommended. Applicants must have math, English, and foreign language proficiency. 30 of 120 credits required for the bachelor's degree must be completed at NC State. **International Students:** There are 978 international students enrolled. The school actively recruits these students. They must take the TOEFL with a minimum score of 85 on the Internet-based version (iBT), IELTS and PTE Academic. They must also take the SAT or ACT if it is available to students in their country.

ADMISSIONS: 46% of the 2016-2017 applicants were accepted. The SAT scores for the 2016-2017 freshman class were: Critical Reading-- 4% below 500, 34% between 500 and 599, 49% between 600 and 699, and 14% between 700 and 800. Math-- 1% below 500, 21% between 500 and 599, 56% between 600 and 699, and 22% between 700 and 800. Writing-- 8% below 500, 47% between 500 and 599, 38% between 600 and 699, and 7% between 700 and 800. The ACT scores were 1% between 12 and 17, 3% between 18 and 23, 55% between 24 and 29, and 42% above 30. 79% of the current freshmen were in the top fifth of their class; 98% were in the top two fifths. 116 freshmen graduated first in their class. **Admissions Contact:** Thomas Griffin, Director of Admissions. Email: *undergrad-admissions@ncsu.edu* Web: *www.ncsu.edu*

FINANCIAL AID: In 2016-2017, 63% of all full-time freshmen and 67% of continuing full-time students received some form of financial aid. 42% of all full-time freshmen and 49% of continuing full-time students received need-based aid. The average freshman award was $12,078. Need-based scholarships or need-based grants averaged $10,820 ($49,214 maximum); need-based self-help aid (loans and jobs) averaged $8,218 ($41,517 maximum); non-need-based athletic scholarships averaged $24,022 ($40,558 maximum); and other non-need-based awards and non-need-based scholarships averaged $3,421 ($22,459 maximum). 19% of undergraduate students work part-time. Average annual earnings from campus work are $2060. The average financial indebtedness of the 2016 graduate was $16,362. The college's own financial statement is required. The deadline for filing freshman financial aid applications for fall entry is March 1.

NORTH CAROLINA WESLEYAN COLLEGE E-2

www.ncwc.edu

Rocky Mount, NC 27804	**(252) 985-5200** **(800) 488-NCWC**
Fax: (252) 985-5295	**Email: adm@ncwc.edu**
Full-time: 615 men, 515 women	**Faculty:** IIB
Part-time: 289 men, 337 women	**Ph.D.s:** 45%
Graduate: n/av	**Student/Faculty:** n/av
Year: semesters, summer session	**Tuition:** $29,350
Room & Board: $9850	**Freshman Class:** 1169 applied, 951 accepted, 288 enrolled
SAT or ACT: required	**CEEB CODE:** 5501
Application Deadline: n/av	**COMPETITIVE**

North Carolina Wesleyan College, founded in 1956, is a private liberal arts institution affiliated with the United Methodist Church. The figures in the above capsule and in this profile are approximate. There is 1 undergraduate school. In addition to regional accreditation, NCWC has baccalaureate program accreditation with NCATE. The 200-acre campus is in a suburban area 57 miles east of Raleigh. Including any residence halls, there are 18 buildings.

STUDENT LIFE: 85% of undergraduates are from North Carolina. Others are from 24 states, and 9 foreign countries. 70% are from public schools. 45% are African American; 43% White; 3% Hispanic; 1% Asian American; 1% American Indian/Alaska Native; 1% Foreign. 70% are Protestant; 16% Catholic; 14% claim no religious affiliation. **Male To Female Ratio:** 1.1:1. The average age of freshmen is 19; all undergraduates, 26. 36% do not continue beyond their first year; 26% remain to graduate. **Housing:** 504 students can be accommodated in college housing, which includes single-sex and coed dorms, off-campus apartments, single-occupancy residence halls, and smoke/substance free housing. On-campus housing is guaranteed for all 4 years. 68% of students commute. All students may keep cars.

FACULTY/CLASSROOMS: 62% of faculty are male; 38% are female. All teach undergraduates. No introductory courses are taught by graduate students. The average class size in an introductory lecture is 23; in a laboratory is 15; and in a regular course is 18.

PROGRAMS OF STUDY: NCWC confers B.A. and B.S. degrees. Bachelor's degrees are awarded in BIOLOGICAL SCIENCE (biology/biological science), BUSINESS (accounting, business administration and management, and hotel/motel and restaurant management), COMMUNICATIONS AND THE ARTS (dramatic arts and English), COMPUTER AND PHYSICAL SCIENCE (chemistry, information sciences and systems, and mathematics), EDUCATION (elementary education and middle school education), ENGINEERING AND ENVIRONMENTAL DESIGN (environmental science), HEALTH PROFESSIONS (exercise science and premedicine), SOCIAL SCIENCE (criminal justice, history, political science/government, psychology, religion, and sociology). Business administration, justice studies, and computer information systems have the largest enrollments.

ACTIVITIES: 1% of men belong to 3 national fraternities; 1% of women belong to 3 national sororities. There are 23 groups on campus, including cheerleading, chess, choir, chorus, computers, drama, ethnic, honors, international, LGBT, literary magazine, musical theater, newspaper, political, professional, religious, social, social service, and student government. Popular campus events include Spring Fling, Parents Weekend, and Alumni Homecoming. **Sports:** There are 5 intercollegiate sports for men and 5 for women, and 13 intramural sports for men and 13 for women. Facilities include a gym with areas for basketball, volleyball, soccer, tennis courts, a skeet range, and fields for intramurals and for varsity baseball, softball, and soccer. **Graduates:** From July 1, 2015 to June 30, 2016, 391 bachelor's degrees were awarded. The most popular majors were business/marketing (48%), computer and information sciences (24%), and law/legal studies (10%). In an average class, 15% graduate in 4 years or less, 23% graduate in 5 years or less, and 10% graduate in 6 years or less.

SERVICES: Counseling and information services are available, as is tutoring in most subjects, and remedial math, reading, and writing. **Library/Resources:** The library contains 65,721 volumes, 2,830 microform items, and 4,200 audio/video tapes/CDs/DVDs, and subscribes to 4,645 periodicals including electronic. Computerized library services include interlibrary loans and database searching. Special learning facilities include an art gallery, and a performing arts center. **Physically Challenged Students:** 90% of the campus is accessible. Facilities include wheelchair ramps, elevators, special parking, specially equipped restrooms, special class scheduling, lowered drinking fountains, lowered telephones, and special housing. **Special:** NCWC offers cooperative programs in all majors, internships, work-study programs through the college offices, credit for military experience, nondegree study, and pass/fail options. The B.A.-B.S. degree may be earned in all majors. There are 2 national honor societies and a freshman honors program. **Visiting:** There are regularly scheduled orientations for prospective students, including an individual campus tour, an interview, a financial aid session, and meetings with faculty and coaches. There are guides for informal visits, visitors may sit in on classes, and stay overnight. To schedule a visit, contact the Admissions Office. **Campus Safety and Security:** Measures include 24-hour foot and vehicle patrol, security escort services, emergency telephones, and lighted pathways/sidewalks.

REQUIREMENTS: The SAT or ACT is required, with a satisfactory SAT composite score or ACT score of 19 recommended. Applicants should be graduates of an accredited secondary school or have a GED. They should have completed at least 13 academic courses, including 4 in English, 3 in math, and 2 each in foreign language, social studies, and lab sciences. An essay and an interview are advised. AP and CLEP credits are accepted. Important factors in the admissions decision are advanced placement or honors courses, extracurricular activities record, and leadership record. To graduate, students must complete 124 semester hours, including 30 to 54 in the major, with a minimum GPA of 2.0. Distribution requirements consist of 6 semester hours of English composition or demonstrated proficiency; 4 each of biological and physical science; 3 each of ethics, non-Western culture, math, history, social science, psychology or sociology, religion, literature, and fine arts; 2 of phys ed; and 2 of introduction to college life. Some majors require a thesis. **Procedure:** Freshmen are admitted in the fall and spring. Entrance exams should be taken in spring of the junior year or fall or winter of the senior year. There are deferred admissions and rolling admissions plans. Application deadlines are open. Application fee is $25. Applications are accepted online. **Transfer Students:** Applicants must have a minimum GPA of 2.0 in their college courses. They must submit transcripts of all high school and college work, along with proof of high school graduation. 31 of 124 credits required for the bachelor's degree must be completed at NCWC. **International Students:** They must take the TOEFL. They must also take the SAT.

ADMISSIONS: 81% of the 2016-2017 applicants were accepted. **Admissions Contact:** Cecelia Summers, Director of Admissions. Email: *adm@ncwc.edu* Web: *www.ncwc.edu*

FINANCIAL AID: 93% of all full-time freshmen received need-based aid. The average freshman award was $8,480. Need-based scholarships or need-based grants averaged $2,917; and need-based self-help aid (loans and jobs) averaged $9,193. NCWC is a member of CSS. The FAFSA code is 002951. The priority date for freshman financial aid applications for fall entry is March 15.

PFEIFFER UNIVERSITY *(The complete profile is made available exclusively on our website, www.barronspac.com)*

QUEENS UNIVERSITY OF CHARLOTTE C-3

www.queens.edu

Charlotte, NC 28274	**(704) 337-2212** **(800) 849-0202**
Fax: (704) 337-2403	**Email: admissions@queens.edu**
Full-time: 408 men, 997 women	**Faculty:** n/av
Part-time: 66 men, 232 women	**Ph.D.s:** 79%
Graduate: 183 men, 368 women	**Student/Faculty:** 12 to 1
Year: semesters, summer session	**Tuition:** $29,045
Room & Board: $10,498	**Freshman Class:** 1949 applied, 1498 accepted, 316 enrolled
SAT CR/M/W: 520/520/510 **ACT:** 24	**CEEB CODE:** 5560
Application Deadline: rolling	**COMPETITIVE**

Queens University of Charlotte is a private, co-ed, comprehensive university with a commitment to both liberal arts and professional studies. Queens serve approximately 2,400 undergraduate and graduate students through the College of Arts and Sciences, the McColl School of Business, the Wayland H. Cato, Jr. School of Education, the James L. Knight School of Communication, Hayworth College of Graduate and Continuing Studies and the Andrew Blair College of Health which features the Presbyterian School of Nursing. The university today offers 39 undergraduate majors and 19 graduate programs. There are 5 undergraduate schools and 1 graduate school. In addition to regional accreditation, Queens has baccalaureate program accreditation with AACSB, ACBSP, NASM, NCATE, NLN, AMTA, CCNE, NASM, and SACS-COC. The 30-acre campus is in a suburban area 2 miles south of uptown Charlotte. Including any residence halls, there are 38 buildings.

STUDENT LIFE: 59% of undergraduates are from North Carolina. Others are from 36 states, 21 foreign countries, and Canada. 80% are from public schools. 59% are White; 13% African American; 12% race unknown; 6% Foreign; 4% Hispanic; 3% Asian American; 2% two or more races; 1% American Indian/Alaska Native. 17% are Protestant; 13% Catholic. **Female To Male Ratio:** 2.4:1. The average age of freshmen is 18; all undergraduates, 20. 30% do not continue beyond their first year; 52% remain to graduate. **Housing:** 916 students can be accommodated in college housing, which includes coed dorms and off-campus apartments. On-campus housing is guaranteed for all 4 years, and on a first-come, first-served basis, and is available on a lottery system for upperclassmen. 83% of students live on campus. All students may keep cars.

FACULTY/CLASSROOMS: 33% of faculty are male; 67% are female. All teach undergraduates. No introductory courses are taught by graduate students. The average class size in an introductory lecture is 15; in a laboratory is 10; and in a regular course is 15.

PROGRAMS OF STUDY: Queens confers B.A., B.B.A., B.S., B.Mus., and B.S.N. degrees. Master's degrees are also awarded. Bachelor's degrees are awarded in AGRICULTURE (environmental studies), BIOLOGICAL SCIENCE (biochemistry and biology/biological science), BUSINESS (accounting, business administration and management, finance, and sports management), COMMUNICATIONS AND THE ARTS (art, communications, creative writing, digital communications, dramatic arts, English literature, French, graphic design, music, romance languages and literature, and Spanish), COMPUTER AND PHYSICAL SCIENCE (chemistry and mathematics), EDUCATION (elementary education), ENGINEERING AND ENVIRONMENTAL DESIGN (environmental science and interior design), HEALTH PROFESSIONS (exercise science, music therapy, and nursing), SOCIAL SCIENCE (community services, history, human services, philosophy, political science/government, psychology, religion, and sociology). Liberal arts & sciences, business, and nursing are the strongest academically. Business, nursing, and communications have the largest enrollments.

ACTIVITIES: 13% of men belong to 2 national fraternities; 21% of women belong to 5 national sororities. There are 72 groups on campus, including art, cheerleading, choir, chorale, chorus, dance, drama, environmental, ethnic, honors, international, jazz band, LGBT, literary magazine, musical theater, newspaper, political, professional, religious, social, social service, student government, Triatholon club, and yearbook. Popular campus events include Casino Night, Midnight on Ice, Spring Carnival, Exam Break Breakfast, Homecoming Week, Welcome Back Week, Moravian Love Feast, Boar's Head, International Week, and Queens After Dark. **Sports:** There are 9 intercollegiate sports for men and 11 for women, and 6 intramural sports for men and 6 for women. Facilities are available for lacrosse, soccer, basketball, volleyball, a fitness center, indoor walking/jogging track, swimming pool, and advance yoga studio. **Graduates:** From July 1, 2015 to June 30, 2016, 414 bachelor's degrees were awarded. The most popular majors were health professions and related programs (30%), business (12%), and communications (11%). 325 companies recruited on campus in 2015-2016. In an average class, 44% graduate in 4 years or less, 51% graduate in 5 years or less, and 52% graduate in 6 years or less.

SERVICES: Counseling and information services are available, as is tutoring in most subjects, such as math, science, social sciences, foreign languages, nursing, and core classes. The Center for Student Success offers free individual peer tutoring, review sessions, knowledge workshops, academic success strategies, individual academic assistance and guidance, access to the writing center, and referrals to the Office of Disability Services. **Library/Resources:** The library contains 42,081 volumes, 97,670 audio/video tapes/CDs/DVDs, and subscribes to 74 periodicals including electronic. Computerized library services include interlibrary loans, database searching, Internet access, and Wi-Fi capability. Special learning facilities include an art gallery, Platiumn LEED Science Building "living" wallrare books and archival collection, photographic lab, ceramics studio, and recital hall. **Physically Challenged Students:** 70% of the campus is accessible. Facilities include wheelchair ramps, special parking, specially equipped restrooms, special class scheduling, lowered drinking fountains. **Special:** Required Internships in all majors, cross-registration with colleges of the Charlotte Area Educational Consortium, dual majors, nondegree study, and pass/fail options are available. The school offers a Washington semester. Study tours in over 14 countries (included in the cost of tuition) may be arranged through the school's John Belk International Program. There are 5 national honor societies and a freshman honors program. **Visiting:** There are regularly scheduled orientations for prospective students, including a sampling of classes, campus tours, a college overview, a question/answer segment, a meet-the-faculty session, and a scholarship/financial aid session. There are guides for informal visits and visitors may sit in on classes. To schedule a visit, contact the Undergraduate Admissions Office. **Campus Safety and Security:** Measures include 24-hour foot and vehicle patrol, emergency notification system, self-defense education, and security escort services. There are also shuttle buses, emergency telephones, lighted pathways/sidewalks, and controlled access to dorms/residences.

REQUIREMENTS: The SAT or ACT and the ACT Optional Writing test are required. Applicants should have a college preparatory background in an accredited secondary school. The GED is accepted. High school courses should include 4 years of English, 3 of math, 2 each of history or social studies and a foreign language, and 2 years of science, including 1 of lab science. An interview is recommended. An audition or portfolio is recommended for art and music students. AP and CLEP credits are accepted. Important factors in the admissions decision are recommendations by school officials, advanced placement or honors courses, and leadership record. To graduate, students must complete a total of 122 credit hours with a minimum GPA of 2.0. For the B.A., between 30 and 40 hours are required in the student's major; for the B.S., 32 are required. 2 courses in English composition, 2 in phys ed, and 1 in lab science are required. If entering freshmen do not pass the placement exams given in math and a foreign language, additional courses will be required. Some majors require a thesis or research project. **Procedure:** Freshmen are admitted in the fall, spring, and summer. Entrance exams should be taken in the junior year or as early as possible in the senior year. There are early admissions, deferred admissions, and rolling admissions plans. Application deadlines are open. Application fee is $40. Notifications are sent September 15. Application fees are waived if application is completed online. **Transfer Students:** 163 transfer students enrolled in 2015-2016. Transfer students are accepted in all but the senior class. A College GPA of 2.0 is required for all previous college-level work. 45 of 122 credits required for the bachelor's degree must be completed at Queens. **International Students:** They must take the TOEFL with a minimum score of 550 on the paper-based TOEFL (PBT). The SAT or ACT scores will be accepted by applicant.

ADMISSIONS: 77% of the 2016-2017 applicants were accepted. The SAT scores for the 2016-2017 freshman class were: Critical Reading-- 41% below 500, 44% between 500 and 599, 11% between 600 and 699, and 3% between 700 and 800. Math-- 39% below 500, 43% between 500 and 599, 17% between 600 and 699, and 1% between 700 and 800. Writing-- 45% below 500, 37% between 500 and 599, 15% between 600 and 699, and 3% between 700 and 800. The ACT scores were 22% below 12, 26% between 12 and 17, 29% between 18 and 23, 13% between 24 and 29, and 10% above 30. 32% of the current freshmen were in the top fifth of their class; 64% were in the top two fifths. **Admissions Contact:** Woody O'Cain, Assoc. Vice President, Dean of Admission. Email: *admissions@queens.edu* Web: *www.queens.edu*

FINANCIAL AID: In 2016-2017, 97% of all full-time freshmen and continuing full-time students received some form of financial aid. 58% of all full-time freshmen and continuing full-time students received need-based aid. The average freshman award was $26,550. Need-based scholarships or need-based grants averaged $9,074 ($24,446 maximum); need-based self-help aid (loans and jobs) averaged $4,763 ($8,732 maximum); non-need-based athletic scholarships averaged $9,839 ($33,800 maximum); and other non-need-based awards and non-need-based scholarships averaged $12,377 ($28,800 maximum). 15% of undergraduate students work part-time. Average annual earnings from campus work are $1700. The average financial indebtedness of the 2016 graduate was $28,507. Queens is a member of CSS. The FAFSA code is 002957. The priority date for freshman financial aid applications for fall entry is March 1.

SAINT AUGUSTINE'S UNIVERSITY D-2

www.st-aug.edu

Raleigh, NC 27610	**(919) 516-4000** **(800) 948-1126**
Fax: (919) 516-5805	**Email: admissions@st.aug.edu**
Full-time: 505 men, 705 women	**Faculty:** 87
Part-time: 50 men, 100 women	**Ph.D.s:** 59%
Graduate: n/av	**Student/Faculty:** 16 to 1
Year: semesters, summer session	**Tuition:** $17,890
Room & Board: $8158	**Freshman Class:** n/av
SAT or ACT: required	**CEEB CODE:** 5596
Application Deadline: n/av	**COMPETITIVE**

Saint Augustine's University, founded in 1867, is a historically Black Liberal Arts institution affiliated with the Episcopal Church. There is 1 undergraduate school. The 110-acre campus is in an urban area 1 mile northeast of downtown Raleigh. Including any residence halls, there are 37 buildings.

STUDENT LIFE: 51% of undergraduates are from North Carolina. Others are from 34 states, 16 foreign countries, and Canada. 99% are from public schools. 90% are African American; 9% Foreign; 1% White. 58% are Protestant; 39% claim no religious affiliation. **Female To Male Ratio:** 1.5:1. The average age of freshmen is 18; all undergraduates, 22. 38% do not continue beyond their first year; 27% remain to graduate. **Housing:** 1143 students can be accommodated in college housing, which includes single-sex dorms, and honors houses. On-campus housing is guaranteed for all 4 years. 62% of students live on campus; of those, 75% remain on campus on weekends. All students may keep cars. Alcohol is not permitted.

FACULTY/CLASSROOMS: 60% of faculty are male; 40% are female. All teach undergraduates. No introductory courses are taught by graduate students. The average class size in an introductory lecture is 22; in a laboratory is 13; and in a regular course is 14.

PROGRAMS OF STUDY: Saint Augustine's confers B.A. and B.S. degrees. Bachelor's degrees are awarded in BIOLOGICAL SCIENCE (biology/biological science), BUSINESS (accounting, business administration and management, and international business management), COMMUNICATIONS AND THE ARTS (communications, English, fine arts, French, music, music business management, Spanish, and visual and performing arts), COMPUTER AND PHYSICAL SCIENCE (applied mathematics, chemistry, computer science, information sciences and systems, and mathematics), EDUCATION (business education, education of the exceptional child, elementary education, English education, mathematics education, music education, physical education, science education, and social studies education), ENGINEERING AND ENVIRONMENTAL DESIGN (industrial administration/management and industrial engineering), HEALTH PROFESSIONS (industrial hygiene, medical laboratory technology, and premedicine), SOCIAL SCIENCE (African American studies, criminal justice, history, physical fitness/movement, political science/government, prelaw, psychology, sociology, and urban studies). Engineering, math, and premedicine are the strongest academically. Computer science, business administration, and communications have the largest enrollments.

ACTIVITIES: 6% of men belong to 5 national fraternities; 12% of women belong to 4 national sororities. There are 20 groups on campus, including band, cheerleading, chorale, dance, drama, ethnic, honors, international, newspaper, photography, professional, radio and TV, religious, social service, student government, and yearbook. Popular campus events include Opening Convocation each Semester, CIAA Tournament, and Career/Job Fairs. **Sports:** There are 5 intercollegiate sports for men and 4 for women, and 4 intramural sports for men and 3 for women. Facilities include a gym, a track, baseball fields, tennis and basketball courts. **Graduates:** From July 1, 2015 to June 30, 2016, 242 bachelor's degrees were awarded. The most popular majors were business (28%), psychology (12%), and criminal justice (8%). 25 companies recruited on campus in 2015-2016. In an average class, 1% graduate in 3 years or less, 12% graduate in 4 years or less, 25% graduate in 5 years or less, and 27% graduate in 6 years or less. Of the 2015 graduating class,

23% were enrolled in graduate school within 6 months of graduation, and 60% were employed.

SERVICES: There is remedial math, reading, and writing, in addition to help with writing and test-taking skills. **Library/Resources:** Computerized library services include database searching. Special learning facilities include a radio station. **Physically Challenged Students:** 64% of the campus is accessible. Facilities include wheelchair ramps, elevators, special parking, and specially equipped restrooms. **Special:** Students may cross-register at any of 5 area colleges, study abroad, or pursue a 3-2 engineering program with North Carolina State University. There is an accelerated degree program in organizational management for adult learners. Field experience programs, nondegree study, internships, work-study, cooperative programs, and credit for military service are offered. There is 1 national honor society and a freshman honors program. **Visiting:** There are guides for informal visits and visitors may sit in on classes. To schedule a visit, contact the Admissions Office. **Campus Safety and Security:** Measures include 24-hour foot and vehicle patrol, emergency telephones, and lighted pathways/sidewalks.

REQUIREMENTS: The SAT or ACT is required. Applicants must be graduates of an accredited secondary school with a C+ average in at least 18 academic units, including 4 in English, 3 in math, and 2 each in social studies and science. AP credits are accepted. Important factors in the admissions decision are geographical diversity, evidence of special talent, and leadership record. Students must complete at least 120 hours with a minimum 2.0 GPA for graduation. All students must complete a 50 to 55 credit core curriculum that includes courses in reading and communication, foreign language, science, math, philosophy, ethics, humanities, world civilization, psychology, and phys ed. Seniors must pass written and oral examinations in their major fields. Total credit hours required for a degree in offered majors range from 124 to 154. **Procedure:** Freshmen are admitted to all sessions. There are deferred admissions and rolling admissions plans. Check with the school for current application deadlines. The fall 2016 application fee was $25. **Transfer Students:** 43 transfer students enrolled in 2015-2016. Transfers must submit high school and college transcripts and must be eligible to reenter the last institution attended. 30 of 124 credits required for the bachelor's degree must be completed at Saint Augustine. **International Students:** There are 133 international students enrolled. The school actively recruits these students. They must take the TOEFL, as well as the SAT or ACT.

Admissions Contact: Tim Chapman, Interim Director of Admissions. Email: *admissions@st.aug.edu* Web: *www.st-aug.edu*

FINANCIAL AID: In 2016-2017, 95% of all full-time freshmen and 90% of continuing full-time students received some form of financial aid. 87% of all full-time freshmen and 80% of continuing full-time students received need-based aid. The average freshman award was $10,474. 69% of undergraduate students work part-time. Average annual earnings from campus work are $1572. The average financial indebtedness of the 2016 graduate was $12,850. SAU is a member of CSS. The deadline for filing freshman financial aid applications for fall entry is April 15.

SALEM COLLEGE — C-2

www.salem.edu

Winston-Salem, NC 27101	**(336) 721-2621** **(800) 327-2536**
Fax: (336) 917-5572	**Email: admissions@salem.edu**
Full-time: 10 men, 695 women	**Faculty:** 58; IIB, --$
Part-time: 12 men, 154 women	**Ph.D.s:** 86%
Graduate: 15 men, 226 women	**Student/Faculty:** 12 to 1
Year: 4-1-4, summer session	**Tuition:** $25,870
Room & Board: $11,824	**Freshman Class:** 387 applied, 267 accepted, 127 enrolled
SAT: required **ACT:** 28	**CEEB CODE:** 5607
Application Deadline: open	**HIGHLY COMPETITIVE**

Salem College, traces its roots back to 1772, when it began as a school for girls by the Moravians, an early Protestant denomination. Today the private college, continues the historical relationship with the church, offering a liberal arts education primarily for women. There is 1 undergraduate school and 1 graduate school. In addition to regional accreditation, Salem has baccalaureate program accreditation with NASM and NCATE. The 64-acre campus is in an urban area in the center of Old Salem, a restored 18th-century village, near downtown Winston-Salem, NC. Including any residence halls, there are 20 buildings.

STUDENT LIFE: 51% of undergraduates are from North Carolina. Others are from 23 states, and 17 foreign countries. 80% are from public schools. 65% are White; 5% Foreign; 3% Hispanic; 18% African American; 1% Asian American; 1% American Indian/Alaska Native. **Female To Male Ratio:** 29.1:1. The average age of freshmen is 18; all undergraduates, 27. 25% do not continue beyond their first year; 55% remain to graduate. **Housing:** 488 students can be accommodated in college housing, which includes single-sex dorms, on-campus apartments, and off-campus apartments. On-campus housing is guaranteed for all 4 years. 86% of students live on campus; of those, 55% remain on campus on weekends. All students may keep cars.

FACULTY/CLASSROOMS: 47% of faculty are male; 53% are female. All teach undergraduates and do research. No introductory courses are taught by graduate students. The average class size in an introductory lecture is 18; in a laboratory is 15; and in a regular course is 15.

PROGRAMS OF STUDY: Salem confers B.A., B.S., B.M., and B.S.B.A. degrees. Master's degrees are also awarded. Bachelor's degrees are awarded in BIOLOGICAL SCIENCE (biology/biological science), BUSINESS (accounting, business administration and management, and international business management), COMMUNICATIONS AND THE ARTS (art history and appreciation, arts administration/management, communications, English, French, German, music, Spanish, and studio art), COMPUTER AND PHYSICAL SCIENCE (chemistry and mathematics), ENGINEERING AND ENVIRONMENTAL DESIGN (interior design), HEALTH PROFESSIONS (medical laboratory technology), SOCIAL SCIENCE (American studies, economics, history, international relations, philosophy, psychology, religion, and sociology). Sociology, business, and communication have the largest enrollments.

ACTIVITIES: There are no fraternities or sororities. There are 41 groups on campus, including band, chorale, chorus, dance, drama, ethnic, honors, international, LGBT, literary magazine, marching band, musical theater, newspaper, orchestra at Wake Forest University, political, professional, radio and TV, religious, social, social service, student government, and yearbook. Popular campus events include Fall Fest, April Arts, and Dance Weekends. **Sports:** There are 7 intercollegiate sports for women, and 7 intramural sports for women. Facilities include multiple athletic fields, swimming pool, gyms (1 practice, 1 regular), tennis courts, dance studio, softball field, and a universal weight room. **Graduates:** From July 1, 2015 to June 30, 2016, 189 bachelor's degrees were awarded. The most popular majors were business (13%), sociology (13%), and communication (13%). In an average class, 1% graduate in 3 years or less, 52% graduate in 4 years or less, 55% graduate in 5 years or less, and 56% graduate in 6 years or less. Of the 2015 graduating class, 18% were enrolled in graduate school within 6 months of graduation, and 77% were employed.

SERVICES: Counseling and information services are available, as is tutoring in every subject. **Library/Resources:** The 2 libraries contain 135,000 volumes, 302,534 microform items, 13,553 audio/video tapes/CDs/DVDs, and subscribe to 15,000 periodicals including electronic. Computerized library services include interlibrary loans and database searching. Special learning facilities include an art gallery, radio station, and a learning lab (computer lab with multimedia capability). **Physically Challenged Students:** 75% of the campus is accessible. Facilities include special parking, specially equipped restrooms, special class scheduling, and lowered drinking fountains. Many buildings are historic, so disability access is limited to individual areas that have had recent renovations or were already accessible. **Special:** Salem offers an extensive internship program in all majors, cross-registration with Wake Forest University, and study abroad at various locations, including a summer program in Oxford, England. A Washington semester, student-designed and interdisciplinary majors, B.A.-B.S. degrees, nondegree study, and pass/fail options during the January term are also offered. A 3-2 engineering degree is available with Duke and Vanderbilt Universities. Students may participate in a model U.N. program directed by Drew University in Madison, New Jersey. Interdisciplinary majors are offered in American studies, arts management, and international relations. There are 9 national honor societies and a freshman honors program. **Visiting:** There are regularly scheduled orientations for prospective students. There are guides for informal visits, visitors may sit in on classes, and stay overnight. To schedule a visit, contact the Admissions Office. **Campus Safety and Security:** Measures include 24-hour foot and vehicle patrol, security escort services, emergency telephones, and lighted pathways/sidewalks.

REQUIREMENTS: The SAT or ACT is required. Graduation from an accredited secondary school or the GED is needed. Students must have 12 academic credits plus electives, including 4 years of high school English, 3 each of math and science, and 2 each of a foreign language and history. An essay is required for all students. Music students must audition. AP and CLEP credits are accepted. Important factors in the admissions decision are advanced placement or honors courses, leadership record, and evidence of special talent. To graduate, students must complete a total of 36 courses, or 144 semester hours, with a minimum GPA of 2.0 both cumulative and in the major. All traditional students must complete 4 January-term courses and 2 terms of phys ed. Bachelor of arts degree students must complete the following general ed courses: 3 in a modern foreign language, 3 in math/science (including at least 1 math and at least 1 lab science), 2 each in English, social science, and history, and 1 each in fine arts and philosophy/religion. **Procedure:** Freshmen are admitted in the fall and spring. Entrance exams should be taken by January of the senior year. There are early admissions, deferred admissions, and rolling admissions plans. Application deadlines are open. Application fee is $30. Applications are accepted online. **Transfer Students:** 17 transfer students enrolled in 2015-2016. Applicants must have a minimum GPA of 2.0 in all previous college work and must submit a statement of good standing from the Dean of Students of the college previously attended, 2 letters of recommendation from teachers, a high school transcript, and a transcript and catalog from each college attended. SAT or ACT scores may be required on an individual basis. An interview is recommended. 36 of 144 credits required for the bachelor's degree must be completed at Salem. **International Students:** There are 70 international students enrolled. The school actively recruits these students. They must take the TOEFL, as well as the SAT or ACT.

ADMISSIONS: 69% of the 2016-2017 applicants were accepted. 2 freshmen graduated first in their class. **Admissions Contact:** Dama E. Evans, Dean of Admissions and Financial Aid. Email: *admissions@salem.edu* Web: *www.salem.edu*

FINANCIAL AID: In 2016-2017, 73% of all full-time freshmen and 64% of continuing full-time students received some form of financial aid. 71% of all full-time freshmen and 62% of continuing full-time students received need-based aid. The average freshman award was $14,500. 66% of undergraduate students work part-time. Average annual earnings from campus work are $1600. The average financial indebtedness of the 2016 graduate was $14,500. The college's own financial statement is required. The FAFSA code is 002960. The deadline for filing freshman financial aid applications for fall entry is March 15.

SHAW UNIVERSITY — D-2

www.shawuniversity.edu

Raleigh, NC 27601	(919) 546-8275 (800) 214-6683
Fax: (919) 546-8271	Email: admissions@shawu.edu
Full-time: 870 men, 1420 women	**Faculty:** n/av
Part-time: 93 men, 189 women	**Ph.D.s:** n/av
Graduate: 94 men, 103 women	**Student/Faculty:** 26 to 1
Year: semesters, summer session	**Tuition:** $16,480
Room & Board: $8158	**Freshman Class:** 4226 applied, 2728 accepted, 601 enrolled
SAT or ACT: required	**CEEB CODE:** 5612
Application Deadline: July 30	**COMPETITIVE**

Shaw University, founded in 1865, is a private liberal arts university affiliated with the Baptist Church. The figures in the above capsule and in this profile are approximate. There is 1 undergraduate school and 1 graduate school. In addition to regional accreditation, Shaw has baccalaureate program accreditation with NCATE and CAAHEP. The 30-acre campus is in an urban area in downtown Raleigh. Including any residence halls, there are 23 buildings.

STUDENT LIFE: 73% of undergraduates are from North Carolina. Others are from 32 states, and 10 foreign countries. 94% are African American; 3% Foreign; 2% White. **Female To Male Ratio:** 1.6:1. The average age of freshmen is 24; all undergraduates, 28. **Housing:** 1293 students can be accommodated in college housing, which includes single-sex dorms. On-campus housing is available on a first-come, first-served basis. 62% of students commute. Upperclassmen may keep cars. Alcohol is not permitted.

FACULTY/CLASSROOMS: 94% teach undergraduates. No introductory courses are taught by graduate students. The average class size in a laboratory is 8 and in a regular course is 13.

PROGRAMS OF STUDY: Shaw confers B.A. and B.S. degrees. Associate and master's degrees are also awarded. Bachelor's degrees are awarded in BIOLOGICAL SCIENCE (biology/biological science), BUSINESS (accounting, business administration and management, and recreation and leisure services), COMMUNICATIONS AND THE ARTS (broadcasting, English, and visual and performing arts), COMPUTER AND PHYSICAL SCIENCE (chemistry, computer science, mathematics, and physics), EDUCATION (athletic training, elementary education, English education, mathematics education, physical education, science education, secondary education, social studies education, and special education), ENGINEERING AND ENVIRONMENTAL DESIGN (environmental science and preengineering), HEALTH PROFESSIONS (recreation therapy, rehabilitation therapy, and speech pathology/audiology), SOCIAL SCIENCE (African studies, criminal justice, gerontology, international relations, international studies, liberal arts/general studies, political science/government, psychology, public administration, religion, social work, and sociology). Business administration/management, criminal justice, and sociology have the largest enrollments.

ACTIVITIES: 4% of men belong to 4 national fraternities; 5% of women belong to 4 national sororities. There are 30 groups on campus, including band, cheerleading, choir, chorus, criminal justice and business, dance, drama, ethnic, honors, international, jazz band, marching band, musical theater, newspaper, pep band, professional, radio and TV, religious, social, social service, student government, and yearbook. Popular campus events include Career Day, Awards Day, and Religious Emphasis Week. **Sports:** There are 7 intercollegiate sports for men and 7 for women, and 5 intramural sports for men and 4 for women. **Graduates:** From July 1, 2015 to June 30, 2016, 367 bachelor's degrees were awarded. The most popular majors were business (24%), criminal justice (14%), and sociology (11%). In an average class, 26% graduate in 4 years or less, 34% graduate in 5 years or less, and 38% graduate in 6 years or less.

SERVICES: Counseling and information services are available, as is tutoring in some subjects, such as English, math, biology, chemistry, physical science, statistics, and social science. There is remedial math, reading, and writing, and peer tutoring in accounting. **Library/Resources:** The library contains 153,304 volumes, 138,950 microform items, 1,306 audio/video tapes/CDs/DVDs, and subscribes to 15,357 periodicals including electronic. Computerized library services include interlibrary loans, database searching, and Internet access. Special learning facilities include a radio station, a praxis lab, Academic Assessment and Achievement Center (AAA), and kinesiotherapy clinic. **Physically Challenged Students:** Facilities include wheelchair ramps, elevators, special parking, specially equipped restrooms, lowered drinking fountains, and labels in braille. **Special:** Shaw offers cross-registration with 4 other North Carolina colleges, internships, a work-study program, a 3-2 engineering degree with North Carolina State University and North Carolina Agrigultural and Technical State University, dual and student-designed majors, independent study, and an external degree program for working adults. There are 4 national honor societies and a freshman honors program. **Visiting:** There are regularly scheduled orientations for prospective students, consisting of parent visitation, tours, general administration, and registration. There are guides for informal visits and visitors may sit in on classes. To schedule a visit, contact the Admissions Office. **Campus Safety and Security:** Measures include 24-hour foot and vehicle patrol, self-defense education, security escort services, lighted pathways/sidewalks, and 24-hour electronic surveillance.

REQUIREMENTS: The SAT or ACT is required. Applicants must be graduates of an accredited secondary school or have a GED certificate. They should have completed 3 units of English, 2 each of math, natural science (with 1 in a lab course), and social science, and 4 of academic electives. Admission to the Teacher Education Program follows separate guidelines. AP and CLEP credits are accepted. Important factors in the admissions decision are advanced placement or honors courses, personality/intangible qualities, and recommendations by school officials. To graduate (in most majors), students must earn 120 credits, maintain a minimum GPA of 2.0, and successfully complete competency exams in math and English. The general core curriculum includes a total of 54 credits in college orientation, English, math, ethics, humanities, natural sciences, and social sciences. **Procedure:** Freshmen are admitted to all sessions. Entrance exams should be taken prior to enrollment. There are deferred admissions and rolling admissions plans. Applications should be filed by July 30 for fall entry; November 30 for spring entry. The fall 2016 application fee was $25. Applications are accepted online. **Transfer Students:** 246 transfer students enrolled in 2015-2016. Applicants must submit official transcripts from all colleges attended. Transfer credit is given only for course work of grade C or better completed at an accredited degree-granting institution. 30 of 120 credits required for the bachelor's degree must be completed at Shaw. **International Students:** There are 73 international students enrolled. The school actively recruits these students. They must take the SAT or ACT.

ADMISSIONS: 65% of the 2016-2017 applicants were accepted. **Admissions Contact:** Sandy Clifton, Interim Director of Admissions and Recruitment. Email: *admissions@shawu.edu* Web: *www.shawuniversity.edu*

FINANCIAL AID: The FAFSA code is 002962. The deadline for filing freshman financial aid applications for fall entry is open.

ST. ANDREWS UNIVERSITY *(The complete profile is made available exclusively on our website, www.barronspac.com)*

UNIVERSITY OF MOUNT OLIVE — E-3

www.umo.edu

Mount Olive, NC 28365 (919) 658-2502 (800) 653-0854

Fax: (919) 658-7180	**Email:** admissions@umo.edu
Full-time: 816 men, 1660 women	**Faculty:** 85
Part-time: 227 men, 413 women	**Ph.D.s:** 39%
Graduate: n/av	**Student/Faculty:** 29 to 1
Year: semesters, summer session	**Tuition:** $13,126
Room & Board: $5300	**Freshman Class:** 975 applied, 654 accepted, 404 enrolled
SAT or ACT: required	**CEEB CODE:** 5435
Application Deadline: n/av	**COMPETITIVE**

Mount Olive College, founded in 1951, is a private liberal arts institution affiliated with the Original Free Will Baptist Church. There is 1 undergraduate school. The 123-acre campus is in a small town 65 miles southeast of Raleigh. Including any residence halls, there are 16 buildings.

STUDENT LIFE: 92% of undergraduates are from North Carolina. Others are from 21 states, 7 foreign countries, and Canada. 93% are from public schools. 55% are White; 32% African American; 1% Asian American. **Female To Male Ratio:** 2.0:1. The average age of freshmen is 22; all undergraduates, 33. 36% do not continue beyond their first year. **Housing:** 306 students can be accommodated in college housing, which includes single-sex dorms and on-campus apartments. On-campus housing is guaranteed for the freshman year only. 90% of students commute. All students may keep cars. Alcohol is not permitted.

FACULTY/CLASSROOMS: 58% of faculty are male; 42% are female. All teach undergraduates, 14% do research, and 86% do both. No introductory courses are taught by graduate students.

PROGRAMS OF STUDY: Mount Olive confers B.A., B.S., and B.Applied Sc. degrees. Associate degrees are also awarded. Bachelor's degrees are awarded in BIOLOGICAL SCIENCE (biology/biological science), BUSINESS (accounting, business administration and management, human resources, and recreation and leisure services), COMMUNICATIONS AND THE ARTS (art, communications, English, fine arts, and music), COMPUTER AND PHYSICAL SCIENCE (computer management, information sciences and systems, and mathematics), EDUCATION (middle school education and secondary education), ENGINEERING AND ENVIRONMENTAL DESIGN (environmental science), SOCIAL SCIENCE (criminal justice, history, human services, liberal arts/general studies, ministries, psychology, and religion). Business, accounting, and psychology are the strongest academically. Business, psychology, and recreation have the largest enrollments.

ACTIVITIES: There are no fraternities or sororities. There are 20 groups on campus, including art, cheerleading, choir, chorale, chorus, drama, honors, international, literary magazine, newspaper, orchestra, pep band, photography, political, professional, religious, and student government. Popular campus events include Founders Day, Pickle Classic Weekend, and the North Carolina Pickle Festival. **Sports:** There are 6 intercollegiate sports for men and 6 for women, and 10 intramural sports for men and 8 for women. Facilities include a gym, racquetball and tennis courts, a track, wrestling/gymnastics and weight rooms, an athletic field, outdoor basketball areas, a student center, and baseball, softball, and soccer fields. **Graduates:** From July 1, 2015 to June 30, 2016, 629 bachelor's degrees were awarded. The most popular majors were business (52%), criminal justice administration (15%), and education (12%).

SERVICES: Counseling and information services are available, as is tutoring in most subjects, such as math, English, and science. There is remedial math and reading. **Library/Resources:** The 2 libraries contain 77,545 volumes, 48,735 microform items, and 2,005 audio/video tapes/CDs/DVDs, and subscribe to 5,979 periodicals including electronic. Computerized library services include interlibrary loans and database searching. Special learning facilities include an art gallery, a church archives collection. **Physically Challenged Students:** 90% of the campus is accessible. Facilities include wheelchair ramps, elevators, special parking, specially equipped restrooms, and special class scheduling. **Special:** Mount Olive offers co-op programs and internships in all majors, work-study, B.A.-B.S. degrees, dual majors, and accelerated degree programs in business, accounting, and criminal justice administration. Cross-registration with James Sprunt Community College and Wayne Community College, study abroad, and credit for life, military, and work experience are also possible. Professional degree completion programs run continuously for 55 to 57 weeks. There is 1 national honor society and a freshman honors program. **Visiting:** Regularly scheduled orientations are available for prospective students, consisting of 2 days of advising, sports, and entertainment. There are guides for informal visits and visitors may sit in on classes. To schedule a visit, contact the Admissions Office. **Campus Safety and Security:** There are lighted pathways/sidewalks, as well as evening and weekend patrols.

REQUIREMENTS: A satisfactory minimum SAT composite score or ACT score of 16 is recommended. Applicants must be graduates of an accredited secondary school or have a GED certificate. They must have completed 4 units of English, 3 units each of math and science, and 2 units of history. An essay and interview are suggested. AP and CLEP credits are accepted. To graduate, students must have completed a total of 126 credit hours, with a minimum 2.0 overall GPA in 63 credit hours for the B.A. or B.S. or in 53 hours for the B. Applied Science. Distribution requirements include 30 to 36 hours in humanities, 18 in science/math/and 12 in social science. Specific course work includes 6 hours of religion, 4 of phys ed, and 3 hours of computer competency. **Procedure:** Freshmen are admitted to all sessions. Entrance exams should be taken in the junior or senior year. There are deferred admissions and rolling admissions plans. Application deadlines are open. Application fee is $20. Notification is sent on a rolling basis. Applications are accepted online. **Transfer Students:** 548 transfer students enrolled in 2015-2016. Applicants must have a minimum GPA of 2.0 and submit an official transcript from the previous institution. An interview may be required. 32 of 126 credits required for the bachelor's degree must be completed at Mount Olive. **International Students:** The school actively recruits these students. They must take the TOEFL with a minimum score of 513 on the paper-based TOEFL (PBT) or 65 on the Internet-based version (iBT). They must also take the SAT or ACT.

ADMISSIONS: 67% of the 2016-2017 applicants were accepted. **Admissions Contact:** Tim Woodard, Director of Admissions. Email: *admissions@umo.edu* Web: *www.umo.edu*

FINANCIAL AID: In 2016-2017, 83% of all full-time freshmen and 79% of continuing full-time students received some form of financial aid. 89% of all full-time freshmen and 77% of continuing full-time students received need-based aid. The average freshman award was $8,679. Need-based scholarships or need-based grants averaged $7,351; need-based self-help aid (loans and jobs) averaged $2,210; non-need-based athletic scholarships averaged $3,689; and other non-need-based awards and non-need-based scholarships averaged $4,976. The average financial indebtedness of the 2016 graduate was $12,450. The college's own financial statement is required. The FAFSA code is 002949. The priority date for freshman financial aid applications for fall entry is March 15.

UNIVERSITY OF NORTH CAROLINA AT ASHEVILLE B-2

www.unca.edu

Asheville, NC 28804 (828) 251-6481
(800) 531-9842
Fax: (828) 251-6482 Email: admissions@unca.edu

Full-time: 1345 men, 1882 women
Part-time: 268 men, 311 women
Graduate: 14 men, 10 women
Year: semesters, summer session
Room & Board: $8746

SAT CR/M/W: 580/558/544 **ACT:** 26
Application Deadline: February 15

Faculty: 326; IIB, av$
Ph.D.s: 89%
Student/Faculty: 15 to 1
Tuition: $6977 ($23,372)
Freshman Class: 3433 applied, 2676 accepted, 666 enrolled
CEEB CODE: 5013
VERY COMPETITIVE+

University of North Carolina at Asheville is the designated public liberal arts university in the University of North Carolina system. There is 1 undergraduate school and 1 graduate school. In addition to regional accreditation, UNC Asheville has baccalaureate program accreditation with AACSB and NCATE. The 365-acre campus is in an urban area approximately 1 mile north of downtown Asheville. Including any residence halls, there are 34 buildings.

STUDENT LIFE: 89% of undergraduates are from North Carolina. Others are from 37 states, and 20 foreign countries. 88% are from public schools. 78% are White; 6% Hispanic; 4% African American; 4% two or more races; 4% race unknown; 2% Asian American; 1% American Indian/Alaska Native; 1% Foreign. **Female To Male Ratio:** 1.4:1. The average age of freshmen is 18; all undergraduates, 22. 21% do not continue beyond their first year; 62% remain to graduate. **Housing:** 1347 students can be accommodated in college housing, which includes single-sex and coed dorms, quiet dorms and wellness housing. On-campus housing is guaranteed for the freshman year only, and is available on a first-come, first-served basis. Priority is given to out-of-town students. 62% of students commute. Some may keep cars.

FACULTY/CLASSROOMS: 51% of faculty are male; 49% are female. All teach undergraduates and do research. No introductory courses are taught by graduate students. The average class size in an introductory lecture is 21; in a laboratory is 18; and in a regular course is 18.

PROGRAMS OF STUDY: UNC Asheville confers B.A., B.S., and B.F.A. degrees. Master's degrees are also awarded. Bachelor's degrees are awarded in BIOLOGICAL SCIENCE (biology/biological science), BUSINESS (accounting and business administration and management), COMMUNICATIONS AND THE ARTS (art, classics, communications, dramatic arts, English, fine arts, French, German, jazz, literature, multimedia, music, music technology, and Spanish), COMPUTER AND PHYSICAL SCIENCE (atmospheric sciences and meteorology, chemistry, computer science, mathematics, and physics), ENGINEERING AND ENVIRONMENTAL DESIGN (engineering, engineering management, environmental science, and industrial administration/management), HEALTH PROFESSIONS (health promotion), SOCIAL SCIENCE (anthropology, economics, history, history and political science, liberal arts/general studies, philosophy, political science/government, psychology, religion, sociology, and women's studies). Psychology, biology, and management have the largest enrollments.

ACTIVITIES: 3% of men belong to 2 national fraternities; 3% of women belong to 2 national sororities. There are 69 groups on campus, including art, band, cheerleading, choir, chorus, communications, computers, dance, drama, environmental, ethnic, honors, international, jazz band, LGBT, literary magazine, newspaper, pep band, political, professional, religious, social, social service, and student government. Popular campus events include Undergraduate Research Symposium, Arts Festival, and Rockypalooza. **Sports:** There are 7 intercollegiate sports for men and 8 for women, and 14 intramural sports for men and 14 for women. Facilities include a sports and health complex with weight/cardio room, basketball courts, volleyball and racquetball courts, dance and group exercise studios, indoor swimming pool, basketball arena, indoor and outdoor tracks, soccer and baseball fields, and disc golf course, mountain biking, paddling, and hiking/walking trails. **Graduates:** From July 1, 2015 to June 30, 2016, 767 bachelor's degrees were awarded. The most popular majors were psychology (11%), environmental Studies (7%), and English (6%). 649 companies recruited on campus in 2015-2016. In an average class, 2% graduate in 3 years or less, 45% graduate in 4 years or less, 60% graduate in 5 years or less, and 62% graduate in 6 years or less. Of the 2015 graduating class, 14% were enrolled in graduate school within 6 months of graduation.

SERVICES: Counseling and information services are available, as is tutoring in most subjects, and a reader service for the blind. **Library/Resources:** The library contains 821,290 volumes, 759 microform items, and 29,379 audio/video tapes/CDs/DVDs, and subscribes to 48,935 periodicals including electronic. Computerized library services include interlibrary loans, database searching, Internet access, and Wi-Fi capability. Special learning facilities include an art gallery, Bob Moog Electric Music Studio (Dr. Moog, inventor of the Moog Synthesizer, former Research Professor of Music at UNC Asheville); N.C. Center for Health & Wellness, including BodPod, Balance Lab, Biofeedback Lab, Meditation Space, Lookout Observatory for astronomical research, and Botanical Gardens. **Physically Challenged Students:** 95% of the campus is accessible. Facilities include wheelchair ramps, elevators, special parking, specially equipped restrooms, special class scheduling, lowered drinking fountains, lowered telephones, and special housing. **Special:** UNC Asheville participates in a consortium with Warren Wilson College and Mars Hill University, and there is cross-registration with a number of North Carolina universities and colleges. Study-abroad programs are available in over 50 countries. The school offers internships, dual majors, student-designed interdisciplinary majors, and a 2-2 engineering degree and 3-1 joint engineering degree with North Carolina State University. Nondegree study is available. There are 4 national honor societies, a freshman honors program, and 1 departmental honors program. **Visiting:** There are regularly scheduled orientations for prospective students, including meetings with admissions counselors, faculty, or other departments, information session for students and families, and a campus tour. Preregistration is prior to fall enrollment during the summer months. There are guides for informal visits, visitors may sit in on classes, and stay overnight. To schedule a visit, contact Nate Corbitt at (828) 350-4553. **Campus Safety and Security:** Measures include 24-hour foot and vehicle patrol, emergency notification system, self-defense education, and security escort services. There are also shuttle buses, emergency telephones, lighted pathways/sidewalks, controlled access to dorms/residences, and security cameras.

REQUIREMENTS: The SAT or ACT is required. Graduation from an accredited secondary school is required. UNC Asheville requires a minimum of 16 high school academic units, including 4 units each of English, and math (algebra I, geometry, algebra II, and a class beyond algebra II), 3 units in science (biology, physical science, and a lab course), 2 units each of social studies/history, and foreign language which needs to be a sequence (Spanish I & II, French I & II, etc). Applicants are evaluated primarily on their academic achievement record, extracurricular activities that support academic achievement, and SAT or ACT scores. A GPA of 2.5 is required. AP and CLEP credits are accepted. Important factors in the admissions decision are advanced placement or honors courses, leadership record, parents or siblings attended your school, evidence of special talent, personality/intangible qualities, extracurricular activities record, recommendations by alumni, geographical diversity, and recommendations by school officials. To graduate, students must complete a minimum of 120 credit hours, including at least 27 hours in the major and a senior capstone experience. The core curriculum requires a 3-4 hour liberal studies introductory colloquium; 12 hours of humanities; 3-4 hours of interdisciplinary arts; a minimum of 7 hours of natural science including lab; 3-4 hours of social science; up to 8 hours of foreign language; 4 hours of math; 4 hours of academic writing; and a 4-hour liberal studies senior colloquium. In addition, students are required to do intensive course work in diversity, and demonstrate competency in writing and information literacy. These courses can be taken in the major, in general education, or as electives, and need not add credit hours to the students program. **Procedure:** Freshmen are admitted in the fall and spring. Entrance exams should be taken at the end of the junior year or the beginning of the senior year. There are early admissions, deferred admissions, and rolling admissions plans. Early decision applications should be filed by November 15; regular applications, by February 15 for fall entry; and October 15 for spring entry, along with a $75 fee. Notification of early decision is sent December 15; regular decision, on a rolling basis. Applications are accepted online. **Transfer Students:** 303 transfer students enrolled in 2015-2016. Applicants under 24 years of age or with fewer than 24 semester or 36 quarter credit hours must submit high school transcripts and SAT or ACT scores. We do not need SAT scores if transferring, unless you have not received grades from present institutions (a students first semester at school and submits an application in October for spring semester). If there are no grades to submit we look at HS record and test scores. 30 of 120 credits required for the bachelor's degree must be completed at UNC Asheville. **International Students:** There are 46 international students enrolled. The school actively recruits these students. They must take the TOEFL with a minimum score of 550 on the paper-based TOEFL (PBT) or 79 on the Internet-based version (iBT). They must also take the SAT or ACT.

ADMISSIONS: 78% of the 2016-2017 applicants were accepted. The SAT scores for the 2016-2017 freshman class were: Critical Reading-- 16% below 500, 41% between 500 and 599, 34% between 600 and 699, and 8% between 700 and 800. Math-- 20% below 500, 48% between 500 and 599, 29% between 600 and 699, and 3% between 700 and 800. Writing-- 29% below 500, 47% between 500 and 599, 21% between 600 and 699, and 4% between 700 and 800. The ACT scores were 31% between 18 and 23, 54% between 24 and 29, and 14% above 30. 45% of the current freshmen were in the top fifth of their class; 80% were in the top two fifths. One freshman graduated first in the class. **Admissions Contact:** Pat McClellan, Director of Admissions and Financial Aid. Email: *admissions@unca.edu* Web: *www.unca.edu*

FINANCIAL AID: In 2016-2017, 77% of all full-time freshmen and 71% of continuing full-time students received some form of financial aid. 60% of all full-time freshmen and 58% of continuing full-time students received need-based aid. The average freshman award was $11,146. Need-based scholarships or need-based grants averaged $7,295 ($32,981 maximum); need-based self-help aid (loans and jobs) averaged $4,668 ($18,500 maximum); non-need-based athletic scholarships averaged $12,449 ($33,060 maximum); and other non-need-based awards and non-need-based scholarships averaged $3,817 ($17,500 maximum). 27% of undergraduate students work part-time. Average annual earnings from campus work are $1942. The average financial indebtedness of the 2016 graduate was $22,026. The FAFSA code is 002907. The priority date for freshman financial aid applications for fall entry is March 1.

UNIVERSITY OF NORTH CAROLINA AT CHAPEL HILL D-2

www.unc.edu

Chapel Hill, NC 27599 **(919) 962-3621**

Fax: (919) 962-3045 **Email:** unchelp@admissions.unc.edu
Full-time: 7364 men, 10505 women
Part-time: 339 men, 315 women
Graduate: 4939 men, 6007 women
Year: semesters, summer session
Room & Board: $11,218
SAT CR/M/W: 640/650/630 **ACT:** 30
Application Deadline: January 15
Faculty: 1020; I, +$
Ph.D.s: 86%
Student/Faculty: 13 to 1
Tuition: $8834 ($33,916)
Freshman Class: 34889 applied, 9400 accepted, 4228 enrolled
CEEB CODE: 5816
HIGHLY COMPETITIVE+

University of North Carolina at Chapel Hill, offers 77 bachelor's, 110 master's, 65 doctorate and seven professional degree programs through 14 schools and the College of Arts and Sciences. Every day, faculty, staff and students shape their teaching, research and public service to meet North Carolina's most pressing needs in all 100 counties. There are 9 undergraduate schools and 13 graduate schools. In addition to regional accreditation, UNC-Chapel Hill has baccalaureate program accreditation with AACSB, ACEJMC, ACPE, ADA, APTA, CSWE, NCATE, NLN, CCNE, CEPA, and URTA. The 729-acre campus is in a suburban area 25 miles west of Raleigh. Including any residence halls, there are 683 buildings.

STUDENT LIFE: 83% of undergraduates are from North Carolina. Others are from 48 states, 87 foreign countries, and Canada. 82% are from public schools. 63% are White; 10% Asian American; 8% African American; 8% Hispanic; 4% two or more races; 3% Foreign; 3% race unknown; 1% American Indian/Alaska Native. **Female To Male Ratio:** 1.3:1. The average age of freshmen is 18; all undergraduates, 20. 3% do not continue beyond their first year; 91% remain to graduate. **Housing:** 10113 students can be accommodated in college housing, which includes single-sex and coed dorms, on-campus apartments, off-campus apartments, and married student housing, honors houses, language houses, special-interest houses, fraternity houses, sorority houses, and substance-free housing. On-campus housing is guaranteed for the freshman year only and is available on a lottery system for upperclassmen. 51% of students live on campus; of those, 80% remain on campus on weekends. Upperclassmen may keep cars.

FACULTY/CLASSROOMS: 55% of faculty are male; 45% are female. 57% teach undergraduates. Graduate students teach 14% of introductory courses. The average class size in an introductory lecture is 55; in a laboratory is 30; and in a regular course is 50.

PROGRAMS OF STUDY: UNC-Chapel Hill confers B.A.Ed, B.A., B.S., B.F.A., B.S.B.A., B.S.N., B.S.Ph, B.Mus., and B.S.I.S. degrees. Master's and doctoral degrees are also awarded. Bachelor's degrees are awarded in AGRICULTURE (environmental studies), BIOLOGICAL SCIENCE (biology/biological science, biometrics and biostatistics, and nutrition), BUSINESS (business administration and management and management science), COMMUNICATIONS AND THE ARTS (art history and appreciation, classics, communications, comparative literature, dramatic arts, English, German, journalism, linguistics, music, music performance, romance languages and literature, and studio art), COMPUTER AND PHYSICAL SCIENCE (applied mathematics, applied science, chemistry, computer science, geology, information sciences and systems, mathematics, and physics), EDUCATION (elementary education and middle school education), ENGINEERING AND ENVIRONMENTAL DESIGN (biomedical engineering and environmental science), HEALTH PROFESSIONS (clinical science, dental hygiene, environmental health science, exercise science, health care administration, nursing, and radiological science), SOCIAL SCIENCE (African American studies, American studies, anthropology, archeology, Asian/Oriental studies, child care/child and family studies, economics, European studies, geography, history, interdisciplinary studies, international studies, Latin American studies, peace studies, philosophy, political science/government, psychology, public affairs, religion, Russian and Slavic studies, sociology, and women & gender studies). Business, journalism/mass communications, and information science are the strongest academically. Psychology, biology, and economics have the largest enrollments.

ACTIVITIES: 20% of men belong to 34 national fraternities; 20% of women belong to 24 national sororities. There are 796 groups on campus, including public/community service, games/e-sports, Greek alliance council, panhellenic council, academic, art, band, cheerleading, chess, choir, chorale, chorus, computers, dance, debate, drama, drill team, environmental, ethnic, film, forensics, honors, international, jazz band, LGBT, literary magazine, marching band, musical theater, newspaper, opera, orchestra, pep band, photography, political, professional, radio and TV, religious, social, social service, student government, symphony, and yearbook. Popular campus events include FallFest, Late Night with Roy, and Homecoming. **Sports:** There are 14 intercollegiate sports for men and 16 for women, and 38 intramural sports for men and 34 for women. Facilities include a football stadium, swimming pools, sports and student activities center, tennis courts, lacrosse and soccer fields, golf course, gym facilities, softball fields, and a student recreation center with aerobics, weights, and wellness programs. **Graduates:** From July 1, 2015 to June 30, 2016, 4501 bachelor's degrees were awarded. The most popular majors were biology (11%), psychology (9%), and journalism & mass communication (8%). 205 companies recruited on campus in 2015-2016. In an average class, 2% graduate in 3 years or less, 84% graduate in 4 years or less, 90% graduate in 5 years or less, and 91% graduate in 6 years or less. Of the 2015 graduating class, 24% were enrolled in graduate school within 6 months of graduation, and 67% were employed.

SERVICES: Counseling and information services are available, as is tutoring in most subjects, and a reader service for the blind. **Library/Resources:** The 13 libraries contain 9.2 million volumes, 5.3 million microform items, and 544,600 audio/video tapes/CDs/DVDs, and subscribe to 161,097 periodicals including electronic. Computerized library services include interlibrary loans, database searching, Internet access, and Wi-Fi capability. Special learning facilities include an art gallery, planetarium, radio station, TV station, a botanical garden and theater. **Physically Challenged Students:** 97% of the campus is accessible. Facilities include wheelchair ramps, elevators, special parking, lowered drinking fountains, and special housing. **Special:** Students may participate in joint programs with Duke University, North Carolina State University, and the National University of Singapore (NUS). We also have outstanding undergraduate programs in business, journalism/mass communications, information science, and nursing through our professional schools. In addition, we offer special opportunities for undergraduates to work with top scholars in First Year Seminars. Honors Carolina seminars, and Undergraduate Research, which are ranked among the best programs of their kind in the nation. There are 30 national honor societies, Phi Beta Kappa, a freshman honors program, and 48 departmental honors programs. **Visiting:** There are regularly scheduled orientations for prospective students, including campus tours and information sessions, offered twice each weekday. Visitors may sit in on classes. To schedule a visit, contact the Office of Undergraduate Admissions. **Campus Safety and Security:** Measures include 24-hour foot and vehicle patrol, emergency notification system, self-defense education, and security escort services. There are also shuttle buses, emergency telephones, lighted pathways/sidewalks, controlled access to dorms/residences, crime prevention (e.g. classes/initiatives addressing date rape, violence, larceny reduction etc.), campus-wide emergency alert system, and cellphone app/GPS-based security options.

REQUIREMENTS: The SAT or ACT is required. Applicants should present a minimum of 16 units of high school coursework within the 5 traditional academic areas (literature, math, physical and biological sciences, social sciences, and foreign languages), including 4 units of English; at least 4 units of college preparatory mathematics (2 algebra, 1 geometry, and a higher level math course for which algebra II is a prerequisite); at least 2 units of a single foreign language; 3 units in science, including at least 1 unit in a life or biological science and at least 1 in a physical science, and including at least 1 lab course; and 2 units of social science, including United States history. AP credits are accepted. To graduate, students must complete 120 credits (more for some B.S. degrees) with a 2.0 GPA. The general education requirements fall under 3 categories: Foundations, Approaches, and Connections. B.A. degree candidates must satisfy a supplemental education requirement by completing a second major or a minor, in addition to a student's major requirements 9 credit hours outside the home department of the major, or by completing a concentration outside a professional school as part of the degree requirements for graduating from that school. **Procedure:** Freshmen are admitted in the fall. Entrance exams should be taken in the junior or senior year. There are early admissions and deferred admissions plans. Early decision applications should be filed by October 15; regular applications, by January 15 for fall entry, along with a $80 fee. Notification of early decision is sent January 31; regular decision, March 31. 2024 applicants were on the 2016 waiting list; 86 were admitted. Applications are accepted on-line. **Transfer Students:** 813 transfer students enrolled in 2015-2016. Sophomore transfers need at least 30 credit hours and a minimum GPA of 2.0; junior transfers need at least 60 credit hours and a minimum GPA of 2.0. High school diploma or equivalent, meeting minimum course requirements, also required. 45 of 120 credits required for the bachelor's degree must be completed at UNC-Chapel Hill. **International Students:** There are 464 international students enrolled. The school actively recruits these students. They must take the TOEFL with a minimum score of 100 on the Internet-based version (iBT), and take the IELTS. They must also take the SAT or ACT.

ADMISSIONS: 27% of the 2016-2017 applicants were accepted. The SAT scores for the 2016-2017 freshman class were: Critical Reading-- 3% below 500, 22% between 500 and 599, 49% between 600 and 699, and 26% between 700 and 800. Math-- 2% below 500, 20% between 500 and 599, 48% between 600 and 699, and 30% between 700 and 800. Writing-- 6% below 500, 26% between 500 and 599, 45% between 600 and 699, and 23% between 700 and 800. The ACT scores were 6% between 18 and 23, 41% between 24 and 29, and 53% above 30. 88% of the current freshmen were in the top fifth of their class; 92% were in the top two fifths. 227 freshmen graduated first in their class. **Admissions Contact:** Leslie Guier, Research Specialist. Email: *unchelp@admissions.unc.edu* Web: *www.unc.edu*

FINANCIAL AID: In 2016-2017, 61% of all full-time freshmen and 60% of continuing full-time students received some form of financial aid. 39% of all full-time freshmen and 41% of continuing full-time students received need-based aid. The average freshman award was $18,861. Need-based scholarships or need-based grants averaged $17,071 ($61,074 maximum); need-based self-help aid (loans and jobs) averaged $4,669 ($13,700 maximum); non-need-based athletic scholarships averaged $21,652 ($62,319 maximum); other non-need-based awards and non-need-based scholarships averaged $5,720 ($50,575 maximum); and $10,098 from other forms of aid. 11% of undergraduate students work part-time. Average annual earnings from campus work are $1682. The average financial indebtedness of the 2016 graduate was $20,127. UNC-Chapel Hill is a member of CSS. The CSS/Profile is required. The FAFSA code is 002974. The priority date for freshman financial aid applications for fall entry is March 1.

UNIVERSITY OF NORTH CAROLINA AT CHARLOTTE C-3

www.uncc.edu

Charlotte, NC 28223 **(704) 687-5507**

Fax: (704) 687-6483
Full-time: 9972 men, 9011 women
Part-time: 1601 men, 1632 women
Graduate: 2188 men, 2834 women
Year: semesters, summer session
Room & Board: $9270

SAT CR/M/W: 530/560/520 **ACT:** 23
Application Deadline: July 1

Email: admissions@uncc.edu
Faculty: I, --$
Ph.D.s: n/av
Student/Faculty: n/av
Tuition: $6277 ($19,448)
Freshman Class: 15610 applied, 10004 accepted, 3319 enrolled
CEEB CODE: 5105
COMPETITIVE

University of North Carolina at Charlotte, founded in 1946, is the largest institution of higher education in the Charlotte region and the fourth largest of the 16 institutions within the University of North Carolina system. UNC Charlotte offers 7 colleges with 79 programs leading to Bachelor's degrees, 65 programs leading to Master's degrees and 21 programs leading to Doctoral degrees. As an urban research university, we are frequently recognized for our contributions to higher education and to the region. There is 1 graduate school. In addition to regional accreditation, UNC-Charlotte has baccalaureate program accreditation with AACSB, ABET, CSWE, NAAB, NCATE, CAAHEP, CACREP, CCNE, COA, CAATE, CAHME, CEPH, NCDPI, NASPAA, and ACS. The 1000-acre campus is in a suburban area 8 miles north of uptown Charlotte, North Carolina. Including any residence halls, there are 102 buildings.

STUDENT LIFE: 94% of undergraduates are from North Carolina. Others are from 45 states, 59 foreign countries, and Canada. 8% are Hispanic; 60% White; 6% Asian American; 4% two or more races; 3% race unknown; 2% Foreign; 17% African American. **Male To Female Ratio:** 1.0:1. The average age of freshmen is 18; all undergraduates, 21. 18% do not continue beyond their first year; 55% remain to graduate. **Housing:** 5363 students can be accommodated in college housing, which includes single-sex and coed dorms, on-campus apartments, honors houses, special-interest houses, fraternity houses, sorority houses, and learning communities. On-campus housing on a first-come, first-served basis, and on a lottery system for upperclassmen. 76% of students commute. All students may keep cars.

FACULTY/CLASSROOMS: No introductory courses are taught by graduate students.

PROGRAMS OF STUDY: UNC-Charlotte confers B.A., B.S., B.Arch., B.F.A., B.M., B.S.B.A, B.S.C.E., B.S.Cp.E, B.S.C.M., B.S.E.E., B.S.S.E., B.S.E.T., B.S.P.H., B.S.R.T., B.S.M.E., B.S.N., and B.S.W. degrees. Master's and doctoral degrees are also awarded. Bachelor's degrees are awarded in BIOLOGICAL SCIENCE (biology/biological science), BUSINESS (accounting, banking and finance, business administration and management, business economics, finance, international business management, management information systems, marketing, marketing/retailing/merchandising, real estate, and supply chain management), COMMUNICATIONS AND THE ARTS (Africana studies, art, art history and appreciation, communications, dance, English, fine arts, French, German, music, music performance, Spanish, and theatre arts), COMPUTER AND PHYSICAL SCIENCE (atmospheric sciences and meteorology, chemistry, computer science, earth science, geology, mathematics, physics, and software engineering), EDUCATION (athletic training, elementary education, English education, foreign languages education, mathematics education, middle school education, social studies education, and special education), ENGINEERING AND ENVIRONMENTAL DESIGN (architecture, civil engineering, civil engineering technology, computer engineering, construction management, electrical/electronics engineering, electrical/electronics engineering technology, engineering technology, industrial administration/management, mechanical engineering, mechanical engineering technology, and systems engineering), HEALTH PROFESSIONS (exercise science, medical technology, nursing, public health, and respiratory therapy), SOCIAL SCIENCE (anthropology, child care/child and family studies, child psychology/development, criminal justice, economics, fire control and safety technology, geography, history, international studies, Japanese studies, Latin American studies, liberal arts/general studies, philosophy, physical fitness/movement, political science/government, psychology, religious studies, social work, and sociology). Engineering, business, and education are the strongest academically. Psychology, mechanical engineering, and computer science have the largest enrollments.

ACTIVITIES: 2% of men belong to 21 national fraternities; 5% of women belong to 17 national sororities. There are 328 groups on campus, including art, cheerleading, chess, choir, chorale, chorus, communications, computers, dance, debate, drama, environmental, ethnic, film, forensics, honors, international, jazz band, LGBT, literary magazine, marching band, musical theater, newspaper, opera, pep band, photography, political, professional, radio and TV, religious, social, social service, and student government. Popular campus events include Week of Welcome, Greek Week, International Festival and Homecoming. **Sports:** There are 9 intercollegiate sports for men and 8 for women, and 16 intramural sports for men and 16 for women. Facilities include multiple basketball courts, racquetball courts, squash courts, a swimming pool, a jogging track, recreational courts, climbing wall, weight room, group fitness room, and training center. There are also 8 outdoor recreational fields along with tennis, sand volleyball, basketball courts, fitness/biking trails, and ropes courses. **Graduates:** From July 1, 2015 to June 30, 2016, 4362 bachelor's degrees were awarded. The most popular majors were business (18%), social sciences (9%), and engineering (8%). 125 companies recruited on campus in 2015-2016. In an average class, 1% graduate in 3 years or less, 26% graduate in 4 years or less, 49% graduate in 5 years or less, and 55% graduate in 6 years or less. Of the 2015 graduating class, 20% were enrolled in graduate school within 6 months of graduation, and 74% were employed.

SERVICES: Counseling and information services are available, as is tutoring in some subjects, and a reader service for the blind. **Library/Resources:** The library contains 1.2 million volumes, 2.2 million microform items, 23,002 audio/video tapes/CDs/DVDs, and subscribes to 4,872 periodicals including electronic. Computerized library services include interlibrary loans, database searching, Internet access, and Wi-Fi capability. Special learning facilities include an art gallery, radio station, TV station, NC Motorsports and Automotive Research Center, Charlotte Visualization Center, eBusiness Technology Institute, Center for Applied Geographic Information Science, Center for Precision Metrology, Center for Optoelectronics and Optical Communications, Bioinformatics Research Center, IDEAS Center, Center for Biomedical Engineering Systems, Center for Global Public Relations, Center for Professional and Applied Ethics, Multicultural Resource Center, UNC Charlotte Botanical Gardens and McMillan Greenhouse, which includes a tropical rain forest. **Physically Challenged Students:** 90% of the campus is accessible. Facilities include wheelchair ramps, elevators, special parking, specially equipped restrooms, special class scheduling, lowered drinking fountains, lowered telephones, special housing. The Disability Services Office assists students with all academic and physical accommodations. **Special:** Cross-registration is available through the Charlotte Area Educational Consortium. Also available are cooperative programs in numerous majors and internships of 1 semester arranged with public and private community organizations. There are 20 national honor societies, a freshman honors program, and 18 departmental honors programs. **Visiting:** There are regularly scheduled orientations for prospective students, including tours. There are guides for informal visits, visitors may sit in on classes, and stay overnight. To schedule a visit, contact the Undergraduate Admissions Office. **Campus Safety and Security:** Measures include 24-hour foot and vehicle patrol, emergency notification system, self-defense education, and security escort services. There are also shuttle buses, emergency telephones, and lighted pathways/sidewalks.

REQUIREMENTS: The SAT or ACT is required. Graduation from an accredited secondary school or the GED is required. The school requires 14 academic credits, including 4 years each of English, and math, 3 of science (including 1 of physical science), 2 of a foreign language, and 2 of social studies, including 1 of U.S. history. Seniors should select a challenging academic schedule that includes English, math, science, social studies or history and foreign language. A portfolio and interview are required for art and architecture students only. AP and CLEP credits are accepted. Important factors in the admissions decision are advanced placement or honors courses, leadership record, and recommendations by school officials. Students must complete a minimum of 120 credit hours with an overall minimum GPA of 2.0. Between 30 and 42 hours are required in the major with a minimum GPA of 2.0 in major and minor courses. All students must complete core requirements in the 6 interrelated areas of communication, problem solving, values, science and technology, arts, literature and ideas, and the individual, society, and culture. **Procedure:** Freshmen are admitted in the fall, spring, and summer. Entrance exams should be taken end of the junior year or by December of the senior year. There are early admissions and rolling admissions plans. Applications should be filed by July 1 for fall entry; November 15 for spring entry; and May 1 for summer entry, along with a $60 fee. Notifications are sent December 15. Applications are accepted online. **Transfer Students:** 2407 transfer students enrolled in 2015-2016. Transfer students must have a minimum GPA of 2.0 on all college courses attempted. Certain majors have limited space and require a higher GPA and/or prerequisites. Applicants with fewer than 24 hours of transferable credit must meet both transfer and freshman admissions requirements. An interview is required only for architecture students. 30 of 120 credits required for the bachelor's degree must be completed at UNC-Charlotte. **International Students:** There are 464 international students enrolled. They must take the TOEFL with a minimum score of 507 on the paper-based TOEFL (PBT) or 64 on the Internet-based version (iBT) or take the MELAB. They must also take the SAT or ACT. Students with a score of 450 or higher on the verbal part of the SAT are not required to take the TOEFL or other English Proficiency exam.

ADMISSIONS: 64% of the 2016-2017 applicants were accepted. The SAT scores for the 2016-2017 freshman class were: Critical Reading-- 26% below 500, 57% between 500 and 599, 16% between 600 and 699, and 1% between 700 and 800. Math-- 17% below 500, 57% between 500 and 599, 23% between 600 and 699, and 3% between 700 and 800. Writing-- 35% below 500, 52% between 500 and 599, 12% between 600 and 699, and 1% between 700 and 800. The ACT scores were 17% below 12, 43% between 12 and 17, 26% between 18 and 23, 8% between 24 and 29, and 6% above 30. **Admissions Contact:** Claire Kirby, Director of Admissions. Email: *admissions@uncc.edu* Web: *www.uncc.edu*

FINANCIAL AID: UNC-Charlotte is a member of CSS. The FAFSA code is 002975. The priority date for freshman financial aid applications for fall entry is March 1.

UNIVERSITY OF NORTH CAROLINA AT GREENSBORO — D-2

www.uncg.edu

Greensboro, NC 27412	(336) 334-5243
Fax: (336) 334-5051	**Email:** admissions@uncg.edu
Full-time: 4894 men, 9222 women	**Faculty:** 752; I, --$
Part-time: 645 men, 1520 women	**Ph.D.s:** 68%
Graduate: 1021 men, 2351 women	**Student/Faculty:** 18 to 1
Year: semesters, summer session	**Tuition:** $6733 ($21,595)
Room & Board: $7957	**Freshman Class:** n/av
SAT or ACT: required	**CEEB CODE:** 5913
Application Deadline: March 1	**COMPETITIVE**

University of North Carolina at Greensboro, founded in 1891, is a publicly funded liberal arts institution in the University of North Carolina system. There are 7 undergraduate schools and 8 graduate schools. In addition to regional accreditation, UNCG has baccalaureate program accreditation with AACSB, ABET, ADA, NASAD, NASM, NCATE, CACREP, CEPH, and NLNAC. The 210-acre campus is in an urban area in central Greensboro. Including any residence halls, there are 111 buildings.

STUDENT LIFE: 94% of undergraduates are from North Carolina. Others are from 48 states, 42 foreign countries, and Canada. 7% are Hispanic; 52% White; 5% Asian American; 4% two or more races; 3% Foreign; 26% African American; 2% race unknown. **Female To Male Ratio:** 2.0:1. The average age of freshmen is 18; all undergraduates, 22. 23% do not continue beyond their first year; 77% remain to graduate. **Housing:** 5402 students can be accommodated in college housing, which includes coed dorms, on-campus apartments, off-campus apartments, special-interest houses, an international house, and a residential college program. On-campus housing is guaranteed for all 4 years, is available on a first-come, first-served basis. 67% of students commute. All students may keep cars.

FACULTY/CLASSROOMS: 44% of faculty are male; 56% are female. 94% teach undergraduates, and 26% do both. Graduate students teach 19% of introductory courses. The average class size in an introductory lecture is 36; in a laboratory is 17; and in a regular course is 31.

PROGRAMS OF STUDY: UNCG confers B.A., B.F.A., B.S., B.M.,

B.S.N., and B.S.W. degrees. Master's and doctoral degrees are also awarded. Bachelor's degrees are awarded in BIOLOGICAL SCIENCE (biochemistry, biology/biological science, and nutrition), BUSINESS (accounting, apparel and accessories marketing, banking and finance, business administration and management, business economics, entrepreneurial studies, finance, hospitality management services, international business management, and marketing/retailing/merchandising), COMMUNICATIONS AND THE ARTS (art, classical languages, communications, dance, dramatic arts, English, fine arts, French, German, information technology, jazz, media arts, music, music performance, music theory and composition, and Spanish), COMPUTER AND PHYSICAL SCIENCE (chemistry, computer science, mathematics, and physics), EDUCATION (art education, dance education, drama education, early childhood education, education of the deaf and hearing impaired, elementary education, English education, foreign languages education, mathematics education, middle school education, music education, physical education, science education, social science education, social studies education, and special education), ENGINEERING AND ENVIRONMENTAL DESIGN (interior design), HEALTH PROFESSIONS (exercise science, nursing, public health, and speech pathology/audiology), SOCIAL SCIENCE (African American studies, anthropology, child care/child and family studies, economics, geography, history, human development, liberal arts/general studies, parks and recreation management, philosophy, political science/government, psychology, religion, social work, sociology, and women's studies). Business administration, biology, and psychology have the largest enrollments.

ACTIVITIES: 4% of men belong to 12 national fraternities; 4% of women belong to 9 national sororities. There are 244 groups on campus, including art, band, chess, choir, chorale, chorus, communications, dance, drama, ethnic, film, honors, international, jazz band, LGBT, literary magazine, musical theater, newspaper, opera, orchestra, pep band, photography, political, professional, radio and TV, religious, social, social service, student government, and symphony. Popular campus events include Rawkin' Welcome Week, Homecoming, SpartanFest, WinterFest. Spring Fling, and International Festival. **Sports:** There are 8 intercollegiate sports for men and 9 for women, and 12 intramural sports for men and 10 for women. Facilities include a stadium for baseball, softball and soccer, gymnasium, tennis courts, and campus recreation center. The Lake Field Campus, which includes 2 lakes for swimming, boating, and fishing. **Graduates:** From July 1, 2015 to June 30, 2016, 2549 bachelor's degrees were awarded. The most popular majors were business administration (10%), nursing (6%), and psychology (6%). In an average class, 31% graduate in 4 years or less, 51% graduate in 5 years or less, and 57% graduate in 6 years or less.

SERVICES: Counseling and information services are available, as is tutoring in most subjects, and a reader service for the blind. Tutoring services are provided by the Tutoring and Academic Skills Programs (TASP) **Library/Resources:** The 4 libraries contain 1.2 million volumes, 324,773 microform items, and 180,000 audio/video tapes/CDs/DVDs, and subscribe to 65,000 periodicals including electronic. Computerized library services include interlibrary loans, database searching, Internet access, and Wi-Fi capability. Special learning facilities include an art gallery and radio station. **Physically Challenged Students:** 95% of the campus is accessible. Facilities include wheelchair ramps, elevators, special parking, specially equipped restrooms, special class scheduling, and special housing. **Special:** Internships, and accelerated degree programs can be arranged in all majors. Cross-registration is offered with the Greater Greensboro Consortium. Students may study abroad in more than 40 countries. Dual and student-designed majors are also available. The Residential College, a 2-year program for freshmen and sophomores, offers an interdisciplinary curriculum, with faculty and students living in the same residence. Students in this program participate in independent study, community work, and workshops. Students with AP or other pre-admission college credit can complete their degree early with the UNCG in 3 accelerated degree program. There is a chapter of Phi Beta Kappa and a freshman honors program. **Visiting:** There are regularly scheduled orientations for prospective students, Spartan Orientation, Advising and Registration programs are offered by Student Affairs for new freshmen and new transfer student. Please visit:soar.uncg.edu. There are guides for informal visits. To schedule a visit, contact the Office of Undergraduate Admissions. **Campus Safety and Security:** Measures include 24-hour foot and vehicle patrol, emergency notification system, self-defense education, and security escort services. There are also shuttle buses, emergency telephones, lighted pathways/sidewalks, and controlled access to dorms/residences.

REQUIREMENTS: The SAT and the ACT Optional Writing test are required. Graduation from an accredited secondary school or the GED are also required. High school courses must include 4 credits each of English, and math, 3 credits of science, 2 credits of a foreign language, 1 credit each of U.S. history, social studies, and an elective. A portfolio or audition is required of art and music students. AP and CLEP credits are accepted. Important factors in the admissions decision are advanced placement or honors courses, leadership record, and evidence of special talent. In order to graduate, students must complete a minimum of 122 credit hours with a GPA of at least 2.0. Major requirements vary from a minimum of 12 credit hours. The general education curriculum for all students requires at least 36 to 37 credit hours chosen from specified courses in the humanities, math and physical sciences, social and behavioral sciences, and a foreign language. Students must take 36 hours at the upper-division level and earn 31 hours of resident credit. **Procedure:** Freshmen are admitted to all sessions. Entrance exams should be taken in June of the junior year or in the fall of the senior year. There is a rolling admissions plan. Applications should be filed by March 1 for fall entry; December 1 for spring entry, along with a $55 fee. Notification is sent on a rolling basis. Applications are accepted online. **Transfer Students:** 1919 transfer students enrolled in 2015-2016. Transfer students must have a minimum GPA of 2.0. Students having fewer than 30 semester hours from a regionally accredited institution must meet requirements under both transfer and freshman admissions programs. 31 of 122 credits required for the bachelor's degree must be completed at UNCG. **International Students:** There are 590 international students enrolled. They must take the TOEFL with a minimum score of 550 on the paper-based TOEFL (PBT) or 79 on the Internet-based version (iBT). Students must take the MELAB, or the IELTS. They must also take the SAT or ACT.

ADMISSIONS: 2% of the current freshmen were in the top fifth of their class; 13% were in the top two fifths. **Admissions Contact:** Christopher Keller, Director, Undergraduate Admissions. Email: *admissions@uncg.edu* Web: *www.uncg.edu*

FINANCIAL AID: In 2016-2017, 84% of all full-time freshmen and 80% of continuing full-time students received some form of financial aid. 59% of all full-time freshmen and 55% of continuing full-time students received need-based aid. The average freshman award was $11,569. Need-based scholarships or need-based grants averaged $6,623 ($18,256 maximum); need-based self-help aid (loans and jobs) averaged $3,480 ($9,500 maximum); non-need-based athletic scholarships averaged $15,765 ($33,809 maximum); and other non-need-based awards and non-need-based scholarships averaged $4,499 ($18,792 maximum). The average financial indebtedness of the 2016 graduate was $27,073. The FAFSA code is 002976. The priority date for freshman financial aid applications for fall entry is March 1.

UNIVERSITY OF NORTH CAROLINA AT PEMBROKE *(The complete profile is made available exclusively on our website, www.barronspac.com)*

UNIVERSITY OF NORTH CAROLINA AT WILMINGTON E-4

www.uncw.edu

Wilmington, NC 28403	(910) 962-3243
Fax: (910) 962-3038	Email: admissions@uncw.edu
Full-time: 4346 men, 6314 women	**Faculty:** 588; IIA, av$
Part-time: 388 men, 722 women	**Ph.D.s:** 86%
Graduate: 488 men, 813 women	**Student/Faculty:** 16 to 1
Year: semesters, summer session	**Tuition:** $6690 ($20,556)
Room & Board: $7900	**Freshman Class:** 11397 applied, 5457 accepted, 1981 enrolled
SAT CR/M/W: 592/605/561 **ACT:** 26	**CEEB CODE:** 5907
Application Deadline: February 1	**VERY COMPETITIVE**

University of North Carolina at Wilmington, founded in 1947, is a publicly funded institution offering programs in the liberal arts and sciences, education, and business. It is a part of the University of North Carolina System. The figures in the above capsule and in this profile are approximate. There are 4 undergraduate schools and 1 graduate school. In addition to regional accreditation, UNCW has baccalaureate program accreditation with NCATE and NLN. The 660-acre campus is in a suburban area 125 miles southeast of Raleigh. Including any residence halls, there are 127 buildings.

STUDENT LIFE: 82% of undergraduates are from North Carolina. Others are from 42 states, 53 foreign countries, and Canada. 86% are White; 5% Hispanic; 4% African American; 2% Asian American; 1% American Indian/Alaska Native; 1% Foreign. **Female To Male Ratio:** 1.5:1. The average age of freshmen is 18; all undergraduates, 22. 13% do not continue beyond their first year; 67% remain to graduate. **Housing:** 4143 students can be accommodated in college housing, which includes single-sex and coed dorms, on-campus apartments, honors houses, special-interest houses, fraternity houses, sorority houses, and an international student dorm. On-campus housing is guaranteed for all 4 years, and is available on a first-come, first-served basis. 61% of students commute. All students may keep cars.

FACULTY/CLASSROOMS: 53% of faculty are male; 47% are female. 96% teach undergraduates, 60% do research, and 36% do both. No introductory courses are taught by graduate students. The average class size in a regular course is 21.

PROGRAMS OF STUDY: UNCW confers B.A., B.S., B.F.A., B.S.W., and B.A. in Music. degrees. Master's and doctoral degrees are also awarded. Bachelor's degrees are awarded in BIOLOGICAL SCIENCE (biochemistry, biology/biological science, marine biology, and marine science), BUSINESS (accounting, banking and finance, business administration and management, business economics, business systems analysis, and marketing/retailing/merchandising), COMMUNICATIONS AND THE ARTS (art, art history and appreciation, communications, creative writing, dramatic arts, English, film arts, French, German, music, music performance, Spanish, speech/debate/rhetoric, studio art, and theater design), COMPUTER AND PHYSICAL SCIENCE (chemistry, computer science, geology, mathematics, physics, and statistics), EDUCATION (athletic training, early childhood education, elementary education, middle school education, music education, physical education, secondary education, and special education), ENGINEERING AND ENVIRONMENTAL DESIGN (environmental science and preengineering), HEALTH PROFESSIONS (clinical science, nursing, physical therapy, predentistry, premedicine, preoptometry, prepharmacy, prephysical therapy, prepodiatry, preveterinary science, and recreation therapy), SOCIAL SCIENCE (anthropology, criminal justice, economics, geography, German area studies, history, parks and recreation management, philosophy and religion, political science/government, prelaw, psychology, religion, social work, and sociology).

ACTIVITIES: 6% of men belong to 14 national fraternities; 4% of women belong to 13 national sororities. There are 200 groups on campus, including art, band, cheerleading, choir, chorale, chorus, computers, dance, debate, drama, environmental, ethnic, film, forensics, honors, international, jazz band, LGBT, literary magazine, musical theater, newspaper, orchestra, pep band, photography, political, professional, radio and TV, religious, social, social service, student government, and symphony. Popular campus events include Business Week, Greek Week, and Spring Week. **Sports:** There are 10 intercollegiate sports for men and 11 for women, and 47 intramural sports for men and 47 for women. Facilities include a coliseum, swimming pool and diving tank, a track and field complex, basketball, tennis, and volleyball courts. A student recreation center has basketball courts, exercise equipment and classes, indoor track, and a rock climbing wall. **Graduates:** From July 1, 2015 to June 30, 2016, 2628 bachelor's degrees were awarded. 153 companies recruited on campus in 2015-2016. In an average class, 45% graduate in 4 years or less and 67% graduate in 6 years or less.

SERVICES: Counseling and information services are available, as is tutoring in most subjects, and a reader service for the blind. There is also remedial math, reading, and writing, and a supplemental instruction program. **Library/Resources:** The library contains 1.0 million volumes, 1.0 million microform items, and 82,023 audio/video tapes/CDs/DVDs, and subscribes to 24,081 periodicals including electronic. Computerized library services include interlibrary loans, database searching, Internet access, and Wi-Fi capability. Special learning facilities include an art gallery, radio station, TV station, wildflower preserve, nature preserve, museum of world cultures, and the research vessel Cape Fear, used for a marine biology labs and for research out of the Center for Marine Science, the University's privately owned and operated research center. **Physically Challenged Students:** 98% of the campus is accessible. Facilities include wheelchair ramps, elevators, special parking, specially equipped restrooms, special class scheduling, lowered drinking fountains, lowered telephones, and special housing. **Special:** UNC Wilmington offer internships, over 500 study abroad programs in 50 different countries, mentored research, and work-study programs. Dual majors may be pursued if requirements are met, and credit is given for military experience. There is a chapter of Phi Beta Kappa and a freshman honors program. **Visiting:** There are regularly scheduled orientations for prospective students. There are guides for informal visits. To schedule a visit, contact the Admissions Office. **Campus Safety and Security:** Measures include 24-hour foot and vehicle patrol, emergency notification system, self-defense education, and security escort services. There are also shuttle buses, emergency telephones, lighted pathways/sidewalks, controlled access to dorms/residences, rape awareness defense (RAD) training, counseling services, and UNCW police.

REQUIREMENTS: The SAT or ACT as well as the ACT Optional Writing test are required. Graduation from an accredited secondary school or the GED is required for admission. High school courses must include 4 years of English, 4 years of math (algebra I, II, and geometry), and a math beyond Algebra II, 3 units of science (1 year each of biology, physical science, and a lab course), 2 years of social studies including 1 year of U.S. history and 2 years of a foreign language. AP and CLEP credits are accepted. Students may qualify for the bachelor's degree by successfully completing the university studies requirements, an approved course of study in an academic major, a minimum of 124 semester hours of credit, and a minimum quality point average of 2.0. The final 31 semester hours of course credit, including the final 15 semester hours in the major, must be completed at the University of North Carolina at Wilmington. **Procedure:** Freshmen are admitted in the fall and summer. Entrance exams should be taken during the junior or senior year. There are early admissions and deferred admissions plans. Early decision applications should be filed by November 1; regular applications, by February 1 for fall entry. The fall 2016 application fee was $60. Notification of early decision is sent January 20; regular decision, April 1. Applications are accepted online. **Transfer Students:** 1280 transfer students enrolled in 2015-2016. Transfer students must have a minimum GPA of 2.5 and be eligible to return to the institution last attended. Prior to admission, transfer applicants must have successfully completed 1 year of freshman-level English, 1 unit of college-level math and have completed at least 24 semesters or 36 quarter hours of credit. 31 of 124 credits required for the bachelor's degree must be completed at UNCW. **International Students:** There are 211 international students enrolled. The school actively recruits these students. They must take the TOEFL with a minimum score of 525 on the paper-based TOEFL (PBT) or 71 on the Internet-based version (iBT), or the IELTS (minimum score- 6.5). They must also take the SAT/ACT with acceptable scores (minimum 450 SAT writing, 20 ACT writing) if the TOEFL is not available.

ADMISSIONS: 48% of the 2016-2017 applicants were accepted. The SAT scores for the 2016-2017 freshman class were: Critical Reading-- 6% below 500, 56% between 500 and 599, 35% between 600 and 699, and 3% between 700 and 800. Math-- 4% below 500, 50% between 500 and 599, 42% between 600 and 699, and 4% between 700 and 800. Writing-- 16% below 500, 56% between 500 and 599, 26% between 600 and 699, and 2% between 700 and 800. The ACT scores were 10% below 12, 30% between 12 and 17, 39% between 18 and 23, 14% between 24 and 29, and 8% above 30. 44% of the current freshmen were in the top fifth of their class; 70% were in the top two fifths. **Admissions Contact:** Janice Rockwell, Director of Admissions. Email: *admissions@uncw.edu* Web: *www.uncw.edu*

FINANCIAL AID: In 2016-2017, 60% of all full-time freshmen and 67% of continuing full-time students received some form of financial aid. 53% of all full-time freshmen and 58% of continuing full-time students received need-based aid. The average freshman award was $8,896. Need-based scholarships or need-based grants averaged $6,692; need-based self-help aid (loans and jobs) averaged $3,121; non-need-based athletic scholarships averaged $7,219; and other non-need-based awards and non-need-based scholarships averaged $2,211. 9% of undergraduate students work part-time. Average annual earnings from campus work are $1017. The average financial indebtedness of the 2016 graduate was $16,980. The FAFSA code is 002984. The priority date for freshman financial aid applications for fall entry is March 1. The filing deadline for fall entry is December 31.

UNIVERSITY OF NORTH CAROLINA SCHOOL OF THE ARTS *(The complete profile is made available exclusively on our website, www.barronspac.com)*

WAKE FOREST UNIVERSITY C-2

www.wfu.edu

Winston-Salem, NC 27109 **(336) 758-5201**

Email: admissions@wfu.edu

Full-time: 2278 men, 2527 women
Part-time: 29 men, 32 women
Graduate: 1424 men, 1542 women
Year: semesters, summer session
Room & Board: $14,748

Faculty: 573; IIA, ++$
Ph.D.s: 87%
Student/Faculty: 10 to 1
Tuition: $49,308
Freshman Class: 13281 applied, 3903 accepted, 1284 enrolled

SAT CR/M/W: 640/665/650 **ACT:** 30
Application Deadline: January 1

CEEB CODE: 5885
MOST COMPETITIVE

Wake Forest University, established in 1834, is a private institution offering undergraduate programs in the liberal arts and sciences, education, and preprofessional fields. Figures in the above capsule and in this profile are approximate. There are 2 undergraduate schools and 6 graduate schools. In addition to regional accreditation, Wake Forest has baccalaureate program accreditation with AACSB and NCATE. The 340-acre campus is in a suburban area 4 miles northwest of Winston-Salem. Including any residence halls, there are 47 buildings.

STUDENT LIFE: 78% of undergraduates are from out of state, mostly the South. Students are from 48 states, 28 foreign countries, and Canada. 60% are from public schools. 48% are Muslim, Hindu, Buddhist, Mormon and Greek Orthodox; 40% Protestant; 25% Catholic. **Female To Male Ratio:** 1.1:1. The average age of freshmen is 19; all undergraduates, 20. 6% do not continue beyond their first year; 86% remain to graduate. **Housing:** 3380 students can be accommodated in college housing, which includes coed dorms and on-campus apartments, special-interest houses, fraternity houses, sorority houses, theme and wellness housing. On-campus housing is guaranteed for all 4 years. 77% of students live on campus; of those, 70% remain on campus on weekends. Upperclassmen may keep cars.

FACULTY/CLASSROOMS: 57% of faculty are male; 43% are female. 86% teach undergraduates, and 73% do research. No introductory courses are taught by graduate students. The average class size in a regular course is 21.

PROGRAMS OF STUDY: Wake Forest confers B.A. and B.S. degrees. Master's and doctoral degrees are also awarded. Bachelor's degrees are awarded in BIOLOGICAL SCIENCE (biology/biological science), BUSINESS (accounting, banking and finance, and business administration and management), COMMUNICATIONS AND THE ARTS (art history, art, Chinese, classics, communications, English, French, German, Greek, Japanese, Latin, music, Russian, Spanish, studio art, and theatre studies), COMPUTER AND PHYSICAL SCIENCE (chemistry, computer science, mathematics, mathematics – economics, and physics), EDUCATION (education), HEALTH PROFESSIONS (exercise science), SOCIAL SCIENCE (anthropology, economics, history, philosophy, political science/government, psychology, religion, and sociology). Business & enterprise management, psychology, and political science have the largest enrollments.

ACTIVITIES: 35% of men belong to 16 national fraternities; 57% of women belong to 11 national sororities. There are 160 groups on campus, including and environmental clubs, art, band, cheerleading, choir, chorale, chorus, computers, dance, debate, drama, drill team, environmental, ethnic, film, honors, international, jazz band, LGBT, literary magazine, marching band, newspaper, orchestra, pep band, photography, political, professional, radio and TV, religious, social, social service, student government, symphony, women's, and yearbook. Popular campus events include Project Pumpkin, Springfest and President's Ball. **Sports:** There are 8 intercollegiate sports for men and 8 for women, and 18 intramural sports for men and 15 for women. Facilities include a gym as well as many outdoor sports including tennis. **Graduates:** From July 1, 2015 to June 30, 2016, 1153 bachelor's degrees were awarded. The most popular majors were social sciences (23%), business/marketing (19%), and communication/journalism (8%). In an average class, 85% graduate in 4 years or less, 90% graduate in 5 years or less, and 88% graduate in 6 years or less. Of the 2015 graduating class, 26% were enrolled in graduate school within 6 months of graduation, and 68% were employed.

SERVICES: Counseling and information services are available, as is tutoring in some subjects, primarily in the sciences, math, and foreign languages. There is also a reader service for the blind. The Learning Assistance Center offers instructional support and skill development in writing, reading, and study strategies. **Library/Resources:** The 3 libraries contain 2.1 million volumes, 2.2 million microform items, and 38,265 audio/video tapes/CDs/DVDs, and subscribe to 51,262 periodicals including electronic. Computerized library services include interlibrary loans, database searching, Internet access, and Wi-Fi capability. Special learning facilities include an art gallery, radio station, fine arts center, anthropology museum, and laser research facility. **Physically Challenged Students:** 85% of the campus is accessible. Facilities include wheelchair ramps, elevators, special parking, specially equipped restrooms, special class scheduling, lowered drinking fountains, lowered telephones, and special housing. **Special:** Wake Forest offers cooperative programs in engineering with any other schools of engineering accredited by ABET; political science majors who minor in Latin American studies have the opportunity to pursue a 5-year cooperative B.A./M.A. program with Georgetown University. Cross-registration with Salem College is available for full-time students. Wake Forest sponsors study-abroad semester programs in 13 countries. Other special opportunities include internships, work-study programs, dual majors, and a minor in entrepreneurship and social enterprise. Students can also be certified in Spanish language translation and interpreting. An accelerated degree program may be arranged in medical technology. Interdisciplinary honors courses and the Open Curriculum program are available for selected students. Wake Forest owns residences in London, Venice, and Vienna where students and professors attend semester-long courses in a variety of disciplines. A semester-long program in Washington, D.C., is also offered. There are 11 national honor societies, Phi Beta Kappa, a freshman honors program, and 23 departmental honors programs. **Visiting:** There are regularly scheduled orientations for prospective students, including group information sessions and tours by appointment. There are guides for informal visits, visitors may sit in on classes, and stay overnight. To schedule a visit, contact the Admissions Office. **Campus Safety and Security:** Measures include 24-hour foot and vehicle patrol, emergency notification system, self-defense education, and security escort services. There are also shuttle buses, emergency telephones, and lighted pathways/sidewalks.

REQUIREMENTS: SAT Subject Tests, are considered if submitted. Graduation from an accredited secondary school or the GED is required. The school requires 16 academic credits, including 4 credits of English, 3 of math, 2 each of a foreign language, history, and social studies, and 1 of science. 1 credit each of art and music is recommended. All students must submit an essay. AP and CLEP credits are accepted. Important factors in the admissions decision are personality/intangible qualities, recommendations by school officials, leadership record, evidence of special talent, extracurricular activities record, advanced placement or honors courses, and geographical diversity. To graduate, students must complete a total of 120 credits with a minimum GPA of 2.0. The number of hours required in the major varies. All students must take 1 semester of a writing seminar, a first-year seminar, and 1 course in foreign language literature. In addition, students must complete 2 courses each in natural sciences and math, social and behavioral sciences, and history, religion, and philosophy, and 1 course each in literature and fine arts. **Procedure:** Freshmen are admitted in the fall and spring. There are early decision and deferred admissions plans. Early decision applications should be filed by November 15; regular applications, by January 1 for fall entry; and November 15 for spring entry, along with a $50 fee. Notifications are sent April 1. 532 early decision candidates were accepted for the 2016-2017 class. Applications are accepted online. **Transfer Students:** 35 transfer students enrolled in 2015-2016. Transfer students must have a minimum GPA of 2.0 on all college work attempted. An essay is required, and an interview. Also required is a statement of good standing from prior institution (s). 60 of 120 credits required for the bachelor's degree must be completed at Wake Forest. **International Students:** There are 143 international students enrolled. The school actively recruits these students. They must take the TOEFL, as well as the SAT or ACT.

ADMISSIONS: 29% of the 2016-2017 applicants were accepted. The SAT scores for the 2016-2017 freshman class were: Critical Reading-- 4% below 500, 24% between 500 and 599, 49% between 600 and 699, and 23% between 700 and 800. Math-- 2% below 500, 17% between 500 and 599, 43% between 600 and 699, and 38% between 700 and 800. Writing-- 17% between 500 and 599, 48% between 600 and 699, and 30% between 700 and 800. The ACT scores were 7% between 18 and 23, 39% between 24 and 29, and 54% above 30. 94% of the current freshmen were in the top fifth of their class; 98% were in the top two fifths. 35 freshmen graduated first in their class. **Admissions Contact:** Martha B. Allman, Director of Admissions. Email: *admissions@wfu.edu* Web: *www.wfu.edu*

FINANCIAL AID: The average freshman award was $44,598. Need-based scholarships or need-based grants averaged $42,212; need-based self-help aid (loans and jobs) averaged $9,755; non-need-based athletic scholarships averaged $29,718; other non-need-based awards and non-need-based scholarships averaged $49,236; and $8,521 from other forms of aid. The average financial indebtedness of the 2016 graduate was $36,546. Wake Forest is a member of CSS. The CSS/Profile, the state aid form, and noncustodial profile are required. The FAFSA code is 002978. The priority date for freshman financial aid applications for fall entry is February 15. The filing deadline for fall entry is March 1.

WARREN WILSON COLLEGE B-2

www.warren-wilson.edu

Asheville, NC 28815 **(828) 771-2073**

Email: admit@warren-wilson.edu

Full-time: 247 men, 397 women
Part-time: 2 men, 4 women
Graduate: 20 men, 46 women
Year: semesters, summer session
Room & Board: $10,250
SAT CR/M: 580/540 **ACT:** 26
Application Deadline: n/av

Faculty: 68
Ph.D.s: 92%
Student/Faculty: 10 to 1
Tuition: $33,970
Freshman Class: 809 applied, 678 accepted, 195 enrolled
CEEB CODE: 5886
VERY COMPETITIVE

Warren Wilson College, founded in 1894, is the country's only liberal arts college with a national student body and integrated work and service programs. Through a blend of strong academics, work and service called the Triad, our students graduate not only with a rigorous liberal arts education, but also with skills such as problem-solving and team leadership that equip them for life. It's an innovative approach to a well-rounded education that has stood the test of time. There is 1 undergraduate school and 1 graduate school. In addition to regional accreditation, Warren has baccalaureate program accreditation with CSWE. The 1135-acre campus is in a suburban area 5 miles east of Asheville, North Carolina, in the Swannanoa Valley of the Blue Ridge Mountains. Including any residence halls, there are 110 buildings.

STUDENT LIFE: 74% of undergraduates are from out of state, mostly the Middle Atlantic. Students are from 40 states, and 9 foreign countries. 74% are from public schools. 74% are White; 9% Hispanic; 5% African American; 5% race unknown; 2% American Indian/Alaska Native; 2% Foreign; 2% two or more races; 1% Asian American. **Female To Male Ratio:** 1.7:1. The average age of freshmen is 18; all undergraduates, 20. 34% do not continue beyond their first year; 52% remain to graduate. **Housing:** 820 students can be accommodated in college housing, which includes single-sex and coed dorms, special-interest houses, a wellness/substance-free dorm, and an eco-dorm. On-campus housing is guaranteed for the freshman year only, and is available on a first come, first served basis, and on a lottery system for upperclassmen. Priority is given to out-of-town students. 90% of students live on campus; of those, 95% remain on campus on weekends. Upperclassmen may keep cars.

FACULTY/CLASSROOMS: 51% of faculty are male; 49% are female. All teach undergraduates and do research. No introductory courses are taught by graduate students. The average class size in an introductory lecture is 16; in a laboratory is 15; and in a regular course is 11.

PROGRAMS OF STUDY: WWC confers B.A. and B.S. degrees. Master's degrees are also awarded. Bachelor's degrees are awarded in AGRICULTURE (environmental studies), BIOLOGICAL SCIENCE (biology/biological science), COMMUNICATIONS AND THE ARTS (art, creative writing, English, English literature, English Writing, modern language, and theatre arts), COMPUTER AND PHYSICAL SCIENCE (chemistry and mathematics), EDUCATION (global studies), HEALTH PROFESSIONS (biology), SOCIAL SCIENCE (anthropology, history, interdisciplinary studies, philosophy, political science/government, psychology, religion, social work, and sociology). Biology is the strongest academically. Environmental studies, biology, and art have the largest enrollments.

ACTIVITIES: There are no fraternities or sororities. Groups on campus include peace and social justice, art, band, choir, chorale, chorus, computers, dance, debate, drama, environmental, ethnic, film, honors, international, jazz band, LGBT, literary magazine, musical theater, newspaper, outdoor activities, photography, political, professional, religious, social, and student government. Popular campus events include Homecoming, Family Weekend, Work Day, Service Day, and Circus Day. **Sports:** There are 7 intercollegiate sports for men and 7 for women, and 5 intramural sports for men and 5 for women. Facilities include gyms, weight and fitness rooms, tennis courts, playing fields, hiking/biking trails, kayak slalom gates, alpine climbing/challenge tower, mountain bike skills area, and outdoor basketball court. **Graduates:** From July 1, 2015 to June 30, 2016, 196 bachelor's degrees were awarded. The most popular majors were environmental studies (20%), psychology (9%), and history (9%). In an average class, 40% graduate in 4 years or less, 51% graduate in 5 years or less, and 52% graduate in 6 years or less.

SERVICES: Counseling and information services are available, as is tutoring in most subjects. Tutoring is also available through the Academic Support Center and the Writing Center, as well as ESL tutoring is also available. **Library/Resources:** The library contains 403,500 volumes, and 4,400 audio/video tapes/CDs/DVDs, and subscribes to 42,000 periodicals including electronic. Computerized library services include interlibrary loans, database searching, Internet access, and Wi-Fi capability. Special learning facilities include an art gallery, an outdoor adventure learning lab, digital sound lab, GIS lab, 276-acre working farm, 5-acre garden, and 776-acre managed forest. **Physically Challenged Students:** 90% of the campus is accessible. Facilities include wheelchair ramps, elevators, special parking, specially equipped restrooms, and special housing. **Special:** Cross-registration is offered with Mars Hill College and the University of North Carolina at Asheville via the Asheville Area Educational Consortium. Students may apply for one of many internship experiences in various disciplines. Students may participate in a semester or year of study abroad in Asia, Latin America, Africa, or Europe, or in one of the College's short-term Study Abroad Courses with on-campus study and travel to places such as Chile, Costa Rica, England, Ghana, Greece, Ireland, Italy, Micronesia, New Zealand, Thailand, China, and Nicaragua. Students may choose to "double-major" by completing the requirements for more than one major program at a time. Warren Wilson College participates in the Cooperative College Program with the Nicolas School of the Environment at Duke University in a combined program of liberal arts and professional education in environmental resource management. There are 4 departmental honors programs. **Visiting:** Regularly scheduled orientations are available for prospective students. There are guides for informal visits, visitors may sit in on classes, and stay overnight. To schedule a visit, contact Monique Cote at mcote@warren-wilson.edu. **Campus Safety and Security:** Measures include 24-hour foot and vehicle patrol, emergency notification system, security escort services, emergency telephones, lighted pathways/sidewalks, and controlled access to dorms/residences.

REQUIREMENTS: The SAT or ACT is required. High school diploma and completion of a college preparatory curriculum, including the following classes is required: four years of English, Algebra I, Algebra II, Geometry, two years of laboratory sciences, and three years of social sciences. Foreign language and AP courses are strongly recommended. Applicants must submit the Common Application and official high school transcripts. Standardized test scores and the WWC writing supplement are optional. AP credits are accepted. In order to graduate, baccalaureate students must complete all the requirements of the Triad Educational Program, which includes components in academics, work, and service. All students must complete a total of 128 credit hours with a minimum GPA of 2.0. The Aims Curriculum (general education) honors a traditional Liberal Arts curriculum while embedding that curriculum in the College's distinctive mission. The curriculum includes a breadth of perspectives (Liberal Arts Disciplines), continuous writing instruction (Writing Across the Curriculum), pedagogies (Work-Learning and Service-Learning), and ethical (Values) Aims. Students work individually with an academic advisor to select courses that meet program requirements and align with their interests. Between 32 and 40 credit hours are required in the student's major, and most majors require a culminating or capstone experience. Students must have worked a minimum of 300 hours in Warren Wilson College's Work Program in order to graduate. All students must also complete a community engagement commitment, demonstrating learning in four different Points of Engagement and Growth (PEGs). Finally, each candidate for a baccalaureate degree must write a "Senior Letter" addressed to the faculty and staff of the College, which includes an evaluation of his/her experiences at the College and reflections on the college career. **Procedure:** Freshmen are admitted in the fall and winter. There are early decision, early admissions, deferred admissions, and rolling admissions plans. Early decision applications should be filed by November 15. Notification of early decision is sent December 1. Applications are accepted online. **Transfer Students:** 50 transfer students enrolled in 2015-2016. Transfer applicants must have a minimum college GPA of 2.5. Applicants must have left their previous institutions in good standing, and be eligible to return. Transfer applicants must submit the Common application, high school transcript, all college transcripts, and the Common Application's Registrar Report Form from the most recent institution. Standardized test scores and the WWC writing supplement are optional. 32 of 128 credits required for the bachelor's degree must be completed at WW. **International Students:** There are 13 international students enrolled. The school actively recruits these students. They must take the TOEFL, as well as the SAT or ACT.

ADMISSIONS: 46% of the current freshmen were in the top fifth of their class; 64% were in the top two fifths. 1 freshman graduated first in the class. **Admissions Contact:** Morning Naughton, Sr. Associate Director of Admission. Email: *admit@warren-wilson.edu* Web: *www.warren-wilson.edu*

FINANCIAL AID: 90% of undergraduate students work part-time. The FAFSA code is 002979. Check with the school for current application deadlines.

WESTERN CAROLINA UNIVERSITY — A-3

www.wcu.edu

Cullowhee, NC 28723	(828) 227-7211 (877) WCU4YOU
Fax: (828) 227-7319	Email: admiss@wcu.edu
Full-time: 3216 men, 3579 women	**Faculty:** 420; IIA, -$
Part-time: 504 men, 680 women	**Ph.D.s:** 70%
Graduate: 543 men, 1086 women	**Student/Faculty:** 16 to 1
Year: semesters, summer session	**Tuition:** $6479 ($16,076)
Room & Board: $7477	**Freshman Class:** 15234 applied, 5739 accepted, 1560 enrolled
SAT CR/M/W: 515/526/486 **ACT:** 22	**CEEB CODE:** 5897
Application Deadline: March 1	**COMPETITIVE**

Western Carolina University, founded in 1889 and part of the University of North Carolina system, is a public-funded institution offering undergraduate programs in the arts, sciences, technology, business, and humanities. There are 6 undergraduate schools and 1 graduate school. In addition to regional accreditation, WCU has baccalaureate program accreditation with AACSB, ABET, ACCE, ADA, APTA, CSWE, FIDER, NASM, NCATE, NLN, ACS, AANA, CAATE, CAAHEP, CCNE, EHAC, NAACLS, NCTE, and NASSM. The 682-acre campus is in a rural area 150 miles northeast of Atlanta, Georgia, and 50 miles west of Asheville. Including any residence halls, there are 91 buildings.

STUDENT LIFE: 93% of undergraduates are from North Carolina. Others are from 40 states, 13 foreign countries, and Canada. 95% are from public schools. 83% are White; 7% African American; 3% Hispanic; 3% two or more races; 1% Asian American; 1% American Indian/Alaska Native; 1% Foreign; 1% race unknown. **Female To Male Ratio:** 1.3:1. The average age of freshmen is 18; all undergraduates, 23. 16% do not continue beyond their first year; 48% remain to graduate. **Housing:** 4023 students can be accommodated in college housing, which includes single-sex and coed dorms, on-campus apartments, married student housing, honors houses, language houses, fraternity houses, and sorority houses. On-campus housing is guaranteed for all 4 years. 51% of students commute. All students may keep cars.

FACULTY/CLASSROOMS: 51% of faculty are male; 49% are female. 81% teach undergraduates. Graduate students teach 5% of introductory courses.

PROGRAMS OF STUDY: WCU confers B.A., B.S., B.F.A., B.M., B.S.B.A., B.S.Ed., B.S.E.E., B.S.N., and B.S.W. degrees. Master's and doctoral degrees are also awarded. Bachelor's degrees are awarded in AGRICULTURE (natural resource management), BIOLOGICAL SCIENCE (biology/biological science), BUSINESS (accounting, banking and finance, business law, entrepreneurial studies, hospitality management services, international business management, management science, marketing and distribution, and sports management), COMMUNICATIONS AND THE ARTS (art, communications, dramatic arts, English, French, German, music, Spanish, and speech/debate/rhetoric), COMPUTER AND PHYSICAL SCIENCE (chemistry, computer science, geology, and mathematics), EDUCATION (art education, early childhood education, elementary education, English education, foreign languages education, mathematics education, middle school education, music education, physical education, science education, secondary education, social science education, special education, speech correction, and teaching English as a second/foreign language (TESOL/TEFL)), ENGINEERING AND ENVIRONMENTAL DESIGN (construction management, electrical/electronics engineering, electrical/electronics engineering technology, emergency/disaster science, engineering technology, interior design, manufacturing technology, and preengineering), HEALTH PROFESSIONS (emergency medical technologies, environmental health science, health care administration, medical laboratory science, medical records administration/services, nursing, predentistry, premedicine, preoptometry, prepharmacy, prephysical therapy, preveterinary science, recreation therapy, and sports medicine), SOCIAL SCIENCE (anthropology, criminal justice, dietetics, forensic studies, geography, history, liberal arts/general studies, parks and recreation management, philosophy, political science/government, prelaw, psychology, social science, social work, and sociology). Elementary & middle school education, criminal justice, and nursing have the largest enrollments.

ACTIVITIES: 9% of men belong to 13 national fraternities; 7% of women belong to 9 national sororities. There are 150 groups on campus, including art, band, cheerleading, choir, chorale, chorus, computers, dance, debate, drama, drill team, environmental, ethnic, film, honors, international, jazz band, LGBT, literary magazine, marching band, musical theater, newspaper, pep band, photography, political, professional, radio and TV, religious, social, social service, and student government. Popular campus events include Mountain Heritage Day, Greek Week, and Fine and Performing Arts Season. **Sports:** There are 6 intercollegiate sports for men and 8 for women, and 33 intramural sports for men and 34 for women. Facilities include a football stadium, baseball diamond, track/tennis complex, intramural softball fields, intramural flag football fields, disc golf course, soccer field, gyms, field house, jogging trails, weight training room, swimming pool, golf putting green, a student recreation center with multipurpose courts, climbing wall, strength training, cardiovascular equipment, indoor track, exercise studio, and fitness assessment rooms. **Graduates:** From July 1, 2015 to June 30, 2016, 1783 bachelor's degrees were awarded. The most popular majors were criminal justice (10%), nursing (7%), and elementary and middle grades education (7%). 300 companies recruited on campus in 2015-2016. In an average class, 1% graduate in 3 years or less, 28% graduate in 4 years or less, 44% graduate in 5 years or less, and 48% graduate in 6 years or less.

SERVICES: Counseling and information services are available, as is tutoring in most subjects. There is also reader service for the blind, and remedial math, reading, and writing. **Library/Resources:** Computerized library services include interlibrary loans, database searching, Internet access, and Wi-Fi capability. Special learning facilities include an art gallery, natural history museum, radio station, TV station, the Mountain Heritage Center, the Fine and Performing Arts Center, and the Center for Applied Technology. **Physically Challenged Students:** 90% of the campus is accessible. Facilities include wheelchair ramps, elevators, special parking, specially equipped restrooms, special class scheduling, lowered drinking fountains, lowered telephones, and special housing. **Special:** WCU offers cooperative education programs in most majors, extensive internship opportunities, an accelerated degree in nursing, B.A.-B.S. degrees, dual and student designed majors, nondegree study, pass/fail options in designated courses, and credit for life experience. Study-abroad programs may be arranged in 14 countries and a Washington internship is available to a select few junior- or senior-level students each semester. A joint degree program in electrical engineering with the University of North Carolina-Charlotte is offered. There are 12 national honor societies and a freshman honors program. **Visiting:** There are regularly scheduled orientations for prospective students, consisting of 6 open houses and 8 regional tour events annually and twice-daily campus tours. There are guides for informal visits, visitors may sit in on classes, and stay overnight. To schedule a visit, contact the Admissions Office. **Campus Safety and Security:** Measures include 24-hour foot and vehicle patrol and emergency notification system. There are also shuttle buses, emergency telephones, lighted pathways/sidewalks, controlled access to dorms/residences, and crime-prevention education programs.

REQUIREMENTS: The SAT is required. Graduation from an accredited secondary school or the GED is required. High school courses must include 4 units of English, 4 units of math, 3 units of lab science, 2 of social studies, including 1 of U.S. history, and 2 units of a foreign language. 5 units of academic electives are also required. AP and CLEP credits are accepted. Important factors in the admissions decision are advanced placement or honors courses, recommendations by school officials, and evidence of special talent. In order to graduate, students must complete a total of 120 to 128 credit hours with a minimum GPA of 2.0. Between 27 and 64 hours are required in the major. All students must fulfill liberal studies requirements in writing, oral communication, wellness, social sciences, physical and biological sciences, math, humanities, history, fine and performing arts, world cultures, the freshman seminar, and 1 course in upper-level perspectives outside the major. Most degree plans include a minimum of 12 hours of free electives. **Procedure:** Freshmen are admitted in the fall, spring, and summer. Entrance exams should be taken during the spring of the junior year or the fall of the senior year. There are early decision, early admissions, and rolling admissions plans. Early decision applications should be filed by November 15; regular applications, by March 1 for fall entry; November 15 for spring entry; and April 15 for summer entry, along with a $55 fee. Notification of early decision is sent December 15; regular decision, on a rolling basis. Applications are accepted online. **Transfer Students:** 784 transfer students enrolled in 2015-2016. Transfer students must have a minimum GPA of 2.0 and meet freshman admissions requirements 32 of 128 credits required for the bachelor's degree must be completed at WCU. **International Students:** There are 81 international students enrolled. The school actively recruits these students. They must take the TOEFL with a minimum score of 550 on the paper-based TOEFL (PBT) or 79 on the Internet-based version (iBT). They must also take the SAT.

ADMISSIONS: 38% of the 2016-2017 applicants were accepted. The SAT scores for the 2016-2017 freshman class were: Critical Reading-- 43% below 500, 43% between 500 and 599, 13% between 600 and 699, and 1% between 700 and 800. Math-- 36% below 500, 47% between 500 and 599, 16% between 600 and 699, and 1% between 700 and 800. Writing-- 60% below 500, 32% between 500 and 599, 7% between 600 and 699, and 1% between 700 and 800. The ACT scores were 34% below 12, 38% between 12 and 17, 16% between 18 and 23, 6% between 24 and 29, and 6% above 30. 28% of the current freshmen were in the top fifth of their class; 62% were in the top two fifths. **Admissions Contact:** Undergraduate Admissions. Email: *admiss@wcu.edu* Web: *www.wcu.edu*

FINANCIAL AID: In 2016-2017, 66% of all full-time freshmen and continuing full-time students received some form of financial aid. 65% of all full-time freshmen and 64% of continuing full-time students received need-based aid. The average freshman award was $8,551. Need-based scholarships or need-based grants averaged $6,214; need-based self-help aid (loans and jobs) averaged $3,386; non-need-based athletic scholarships averaged $9,802; and other non-need-based awards and non-need-based scholarships averaged $3,071. 15% of undergraduate students work part-time. Average annual earnings from campus work are $4350. The average financial indebtedness of the 2016 graduate was $22,608. The college's own financial statement is required. The FAFSA code is 002981. The priority date for freshman financial aid applications for fall entry is March 15.

WILLIAM PEACE UNIVERSITY *(The complete profile is made available exclusively on our website, www.barronspac.com)*

WINGATE UNIVERSITY C-3

www.wingate.edu

Wingate, NC 28174

(704) 233-8200
(800) 755-5550
Email: admit@wingate.edu

Full-time: 809 men, 1235 women	**Faculty:** 108
Part-time: 18 men, 22 women	**Ph.D.s:** 90%
Graduate: 443 men, 666 women	**Student/Faculty:** 19 to 1
Year: semesters, summer session	**Tuition:** $29,170
Room & Board: $10,780	**Freshman Class:** 7581 applied, 5273 accepted, 625 enrolled
SAT CR/M: 510/520 **ACT:** 22	**CEEB CODE:** 5908
Application Deadline: rolling	**COMPETITIVE**

Wingate University, founded in 1896, is a private liberal arts institution. There are 5 undergraduate schools and 5 graduate schools. In addition to regional accreditation, Wingate has baccalaureate program accreditation with ACBSP, ACPE, NASM, CAATE, CSMA, and ACEN. The 330-acre campus is in a small town 25 miles east of Charlotte. Including any residence halls, there are 40 buildings.

STUDENT LIFE: 76% of undergraduates are from North Carolina. Others are from 36 states, 53 foreign countries, and Canada. 90% are from public schools. 61% are White; 15% African American; 9% race unknown; 5% two or more races; 3% Asian American; 3% Hispanic; 3% Foreign; 1% American Indian/Alaska Native. **Female To Male Ratio:** 1.5:1. The average age of freshmen is 18; all undergraduates, 20. 23% do not continue beyond their first year; 54% remain to graduate. **Housing:** 1556 students can be accommodated in college housing, which includes single-sex and coed dorms, on-campus apartments, married student housing, special-interest houses, fraternity houses, and sorority houses. On-campus housing is guaranteed for all 4 years. 75% of students live on campus; of those, 70% remain on campus on weekends. All students may keep cars.

FACULTY/CLASSROOMS: 48% of faculty are male; 52% are female. 60% teach undergraduates, 1% do research, and 2% do both. No introductory courses are taught by graduate students. The average class size in an introductory lecture is 26; in a laboratory is 24; and in a regular course is 14.

PROGRAMS OF STUDY: Wingate confers B.A., B.S., B.S.N., B.L.S., and B.M.E. degrees. Master's and doctoral degrees are also awarded. Bachelor's degrees are awarded in BIOLOGICAL SCIENCE (biology/biological science, biology (pre-physician assistant), biology/ gen science secondary education, and environmental biology), BUSINESS (accounting, finance, management, marketing, sports management, and project management), COMMUNICATIONS AND THE ARTS (church music, communication studies, communication rhetoric/communication, English, instrumental performance, journalism, music, public relations, and vocal performance), COMPUTER AND PHYSICAL SCIENCE (chemistry and mathematics), EDUCATION (athletic training, education administration, elementary education, English education, mathematics education, middle school education, music education, and reading education), ENGINEERING AND ENVIRONMENTAL DESIGN (preengineering), HEALTH PROFESSIONS (biology, exercise science, nursing, pharmacy, physical therapy, physician's assistant, predentistry, premedicine, prepharmacy, pre-physician assistant, prephysical therapy, and preveterinary science), SOCIAL SCIENCE (criminal justice, history, human services, liberal arts/general studies, parks and recreation management, political science/government, prelaw, psychology, religious studies, and sociology). Pharmacy, nursing, and biology are the strongest academically. Biology, nursing, and psychology have the largest enrollments.

ACTIVITIES: 6% of men belong to 4 national fraternities; 19% of women belong to 4 national sororities. There are 50 groups on campus, including art, band, cheerleading, choir, chorale, chorus, communications, computers, drama, environmental, ethnic, honors, international, jazz band, LGBT, literary magazine, newspaper, opera, pep band, photography, political, professional, radio and TV, religious, social, social service, and student government. Popular campus events include Spring Fling, Fall Festival at Campus Lake, and Name-band Concerts. **Sports:** There are 10 intercollegiate sports for men and 10 for women, and 13 intramural sports for men and 13 for women. Facilities include an athletic complex with indoor track, gyms, swimming pool, racquetball courts, exercise and weight rooms, tennis courts, table tennis, pool, game room, a football stadium, and baseball, soccer, and softball fields. **Graduates:** From July 1, 2015 to June 30, 2016, 366 bachelor's degrees were awarded. The most popular majors were biology (13%), education (13%), and business/marketing (12%). 50 companies recruited on campus in 2015-2016. In an average class, 44% graduate in 4 years or less, 50% graduate in 5 years or less, and 54% graduate in 6 years or less. Of the 2015 graduating class, 40% were enrolled in graduate school within 6 months of graduation, and 53% were employed.

SERVICES: Counseling and information services are available, as is tutoring in every subject. There is additional academic support available for students with learning disabilities. **Library/Resources:** The library contains 96,673 volumes, 6,856 microform items, 6,674 audio/video tapes/CDs/DVDs, and subscribes to 110 periodicals including electronic. Computerized library services include interlibrary loans, database searching, Internet access, and Wi-Fi capability. Special learning facilities include a radio station, a fine arts center, art gallery, and cadaver lab. **Physically Challenged Students:** 95% of the campus is accessible. Facilities include wheelchair ramps, elevators, special parking, specially equipped restrooms, special class scheduling, and lowered drinking fountains. **Special:** Cross-registration through the Greater Charlotte Area Consortium, in Army and Air Force ROTC programs; internships; a liberal studies degree for adult completion; B.A.-B.S. degrees; and non-degree study are available. Wingate conducts foreign study semesters in London, Denmark, and China. The school also sponsors Winternational, a semester seminar with a 10-day trip to a foreign country for which students earn academic credit at little personal cost. A new community engagement program, W'Engage, is designed for sophomores to contribute to surrounding communities and travel for 5-7 days to a U.S. destination in order to promote positive social change. Dual majors are offered in biology and education, history and education, English and education, math and education, and chemistry and business. Students can earn a B.S. in biology and Pharm.D., through a 3 + 1 program. There are 11 national honor societies and a freshman honors program. **Visiting:** There are regularly scheduled orientations for prospective students. There are guides for informal visits, visitors may sit in on classes, and stay overnight. To schedule a visit, contact the Admissions Office. **Campus Safety and Security:** Measures include 24-hour foot and vehicle patrol, emergency notification system, self-defense education, security escort services, emergency telephones, lighted pathways/sidewalks, and controlled access to dorms/residences.

REQUIREMENTS: Graduation from an accredited secondary school or the GED is required. High school curriculum should include 4 courses in English, 3 in math, 2 each in social and natural science (1 with a lab), and a foreign language. An essay and interview are recommended in some cases. The SAT or ACT is required. AP and CLEP credits are accepted. Important factors in the admissions decision are advanced placement or honors courses, leadership record, and recommendations by school officials. To graduate, students must complete a minimum of 125 credit hours with a GPA of 2.0. At least 30 hours must be completed in the student's major. All students must complete the Core Curriculum, which includes 24 hours of Global Perspectives. **Procedure:** Freshmen are admitted in the fall, spring, and summer. Entrance exams should be taken in spring of the junior year or fall of the senior year. There is a rolling admissions plan. Application deadlines are open. Application fees are waived if application is completed online. **Transfer Students:** 108 transfer students enrolled in 2015-2016. Applicants must have a minimum GPA of 2.0 and must be eligible to return to the institution last attended. The SAT or ACT is required if a student has been out of high school for less than 5 years or has fewer than 24 transferable hours. An interview may be recommended in some cases. 30 of 125 credits required for the bachelor's degree must be completed at Wingate. **International Students:** There are 93 international students enrolled. They must take the TOEFL with a minimum score of 550 on the paper-based TOEFL (PBT) or 80 on the Internet-based version (iBT). Students must also take any one of these tests the IELTS, ITEP, SAT, or ACT.

ADMISSIONS: 70% of the 2016-2017 applicants were accepted. The SAT scores for the 2016-2017 freshman class were: Critical Reading-- 41% below 500, 45% between 500 and 599, 13% between 600 and 699, and 1% between 700 and 800. Math-- 37% below 500, 45% between 500 and 599, 17% between 600 and 699, and 1% between 700 and 800. The ACT scores were 6% between 12 and 17, 57% between 18 and 23, 31% between 24 and 29, and 6% above 30. 44% of the current freshmen were in the top fifth of their class; 76% were in the top two fifths. 4 freshmen graduated first in their class. **Admissions Contact:** Gabe Hollingsworth, Director of Admissions. Email: *admit@wingate.edu* Web: *www.wingate.edu*

FINANCIAL AID: In 2016-2017, 95% of all full-time freshmen and 96% of continuing full-time students received some form of financial aid. 72% of all full-time freshmen and 82% of continuing full-time students received need-based aid. The average freshman award was $24,556. Need-based scholarships or need-based grants averaged $22,223; need-based self-help aid (loans and jobs) averaged $6,225; non-need-based athletic scholarships averaged $10,770; and other non-need-based awards and non-need-based scholarships averaged $17,350. 20% of undergraduate students work part-time. Average annual earnings from campus work are $3600. The average financial indebtedness of the 2016 graduate was $27,689. The FAFSA code is 002985. The deadline for filing freshman financial aid applications for fall entry is May 1.

WINSTON-SALEM STATE UNIVERSITY *(The complete profile is made available exclusively on our website, www.barronspac.com)*

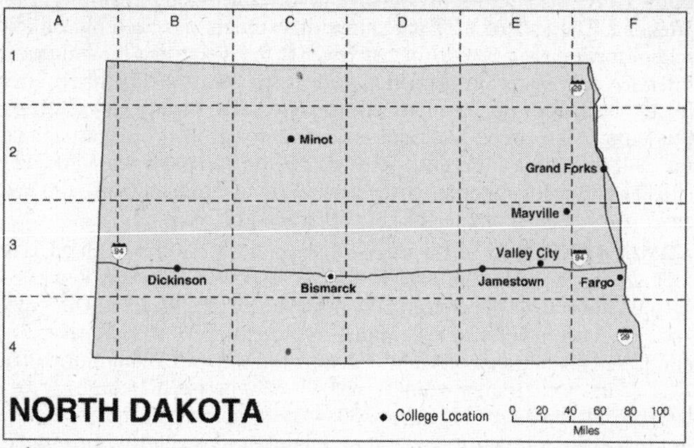

DICKINSON STATE UNIVERSITY *(The complete profile is made available exclusively on our website, www.barronspac.com)*

MAYVILLE STATE UNIVERSITY *(The complete profile is made available exclusively on our website, www.barronspac.com)*

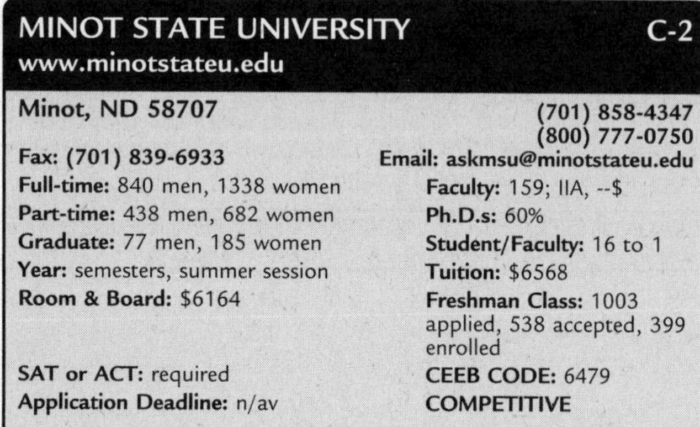

MINOT STATE UNIVERSITY C-2

www.minotstateu.edu

Minot, ND 58707 (701) 858-4347 (800) 777-0750

Fax: (701) 839-6933 **Email:** askmsu@minotstateu.edu

Full-time: 840 men, 1338 women
Part-time: 438 men, 682 women
Graduate: 77 men, 185 women
Year: semesters, summer session
Room & Board: $6164

SAT or ACT: required
Application Deadline: n/av

Faculty: 159; IIA, --$
Ph.D.s: 60%
Student/Faculty: 16 to 1
Tuition: $6568
Freshman Class: 1003 applied, 538 accepted, 399 enrolled
CEEB CODE: 6479
COMPETITIVE

Minot State University, founded in 1913, is a public institution offering undergraduate and graduate programs in arts and sciences, education, business, nursing, and human services. Figures in the above capsule and in this profile are approximate. There are 3 undergraduate schools and 1 graduate school. In addition to regional accreditation, MSU has baccalaureate program accreditation with NCATE and NLN. The 103-acre campus is in a small town. Including any residence halls, there are 21 buildings.

STUDENT LIFE: 83% of undergraduates are from North Dakota. Others are from 44 states, 18 foreign countries, and Canada. 95% are from public schools. 84% are White; 6% Foreign; 4% American Indian/Alaska Native; 3% African American; 2% Hispanic; 1% Asian American. **Female To Male Ratio:** 1.6:1. The average age of freshmen is 19; all undergraduates, 21. 36% do not continue beyond their first year; 32% remain to graduate. **Housing:** 643 students can be accommodated in college housing, which includes single-sex and coed dorms, on-campus apartments, married student housing, language houses and special-interest houses. On-campus housing is guaranteed for the freshman year only, and is available on a first-come, first-served basis, and on a lottery system for upperclassmen. 88% of students commute. All students may keep cars. Alcohol is not permitted.

FACULTY/CLASSROOMS: 49% of faculty are male; 51% are female. All teach undergraduates, and 20% do research. No introductory courses are taught by graduate students. The average class size in an introductory lecture is 60; in a laboratory is 20; and in a regular course is 16.

PROGRAMS OF STUDY: MSU confers B.A., B.S., B.A.S., B.G.S., B.S. Ed., B.S.N. and B.S.W. degrees. Associate and master's degrees are also awarded. Bachelor's degrees are awarded in BIOLOGICAL SCIENCE (biology/biological science), BUSINESS (accounting, banking and finance, international business management, management information systems, management science, and marketing/retailing/merchandising), COMMUNICATIONS AND THE ARTS (art, broadcasting, communications, English, French, German, multimedia, music, and Spanish), COMPUTER AND PHYSICAL SCIENCE (chemistry, computer science, earth science, geology, mathematics, physical sciences, physics, and radiological technology), EDUCATION (business education, drama education, education of the deaf and hearing impaired, education of the exceptional child, education of the mentally handicapped, elementary education, English education, foreign languages education, health and education science, mathematics education, music education, physical education, and science education), HEALTH PROFESSIONS (dental laboratory technology, nursing, and speech pathology/audiology), SOCIAL SCIENCE (addiction studies, criminal justice, economics, history, liberal arts/general studies, physical fitness/movement, psychology, social science, social work, and sociology). Communication disorders, special education, and elementary education are the strongest academically. Business, criminal justice, and education have the largest enrollments.

ACTIVITIES: There are no fraternities or sororities. There are 60 groups on campus, including art, band, choir, chorale, chorus, drama, ethnic, honors, international, marching band, musical theater, newspaper, orchestra, pep band, political, professional, radio and TV, religious, social service, student government, and symphony. Popular campus events include Welcome Week, Final Frenzy and Native American Awareness Week. **Sports:** There are 6 intercollegiate sports for men and 6 for women, and 4 intramural sports for men and 4 for women. Facilities include baseball, basketball, cross country, golf, track & field, wrestling, club hockey, a field house, a football stadium, and a gym. **Graduates:** From July 1, 2015 to June 30, 2016, 740 bachelor's degrees were awarded. The most popular majors were business/marketing (31%), health professions and related sciences (19%), and education (15%). 105 companies recruited on campus in 2015-2016. In an average class, 37% graduate in 6 years or less. Of the 2015 graduating class, 11% were enrolled in graduate school within 6 months of graduation, and 89% were employed.

SERVICES: Counseling and information services are available, as is tutoring in most subjects. Special services are offered for disabled students on request. **Library/Resources:** The library contains 411,678 volumes, 687,708 microform items, 12,722 audio/video tapes/CDs/DVDs, and subscribes to 802 periodicals including electronic. Computerized library services include interlibrary loans and database searching. Special learning facilities include an art gallery, natural history museum, radio station, and TV station. **Physically Challenged Students:** 99% of the campus is accessible. Facilities include wheelchair ramps, elevators, special parking, specially equipped restrooms, special class scheduling, lowered drinking fountains, lowered telephones, and special housing. **Special:** A general studies degree, independent research, internships, work-study, and unique programs of study, including student-designed majors, are available. Cross-registration through the North Dakota University System, co-op programs in all majors, and study including student-designed majors, abroad in 3 countries also are offered. Preliminary programs are available in dental hygiene, dentistry, engineering, law, medicine, and many other areas. There is a freshman honors program. **Visiting:** Regularly scheduled orientations are available for prospective students, prior to the beginning of the fall term. There are guides for informal visits and visitors may sit in on classes. To schedule a visit, contact the Enrollment Services. **Campus Safety and Security:** Measures include self-defense education, emergency telephones, and lighted pathways/sidewalks.

REQUIREMENTS: The SAT or ACT is required. Applicants must submit a high school diploma or GED certificate. Core course requirements include 4 years of English and 3 each of math, social studies, and science. AP and CLEP credits are accepted. Students must take a number of general education courses in humanities, history, communication, math, natural sciences, social and behavorial sciences, and leisure-time education. They must complete at least 128 semester hours, with 30 to 37 in the major and a minimum GPA of 2.0. **Procedure:** Freshmen are admitted to all sessions. Entrance exams should be taken any time. There are deferred admissions and rolling admissions plans. Application deadlines are open. Application fee is $35. Applications are accepted online. **Transfer Students:** 291 transfer students enrolled in 2015-2016. Transfers must submit transcripts from each college attended. 30 of 128 credits required for the bachelor's degree must be completed at MSU. **International Students:** There are 41 international students enrolled. The school actively recruits these students. They must take the TOEFL.

ADMISSIONS: 54% of the 2016-2017 applicants were accepted. **Admissions Contact:** Alexis Hendricks, Enrollment Services Representative. Email: *askmsu@minotstateu.edu* Web: *www.minotstateu.edu*

FINANCIAL AID: In 2016-2017, 67% of all full-time freshmen and 66% of continuing full-time students received some form of financial aid. 64% of all full-time freshmen and 66% of continuing full-time students received need-based aid. 1% of undergraduate students work part-time. Average annual earnings from campus work are $1260. The average financial indebtedness of the 2016 graduate was $25,117. The FAFSA code is 002994. The priority date for freshman financial aid applications for fall entry is March 15. The filing deadline for fall entry is October 15.

NORTH DAKOTA STATE UNIVERSITY F-3

www.ndsu.edu

Fargo, ND 58108	**(701) 231-8643** **(800) 488-NDSU**
Fax: (701) 231-8802	**Email: ndsu.admission@ndsu.edu**
Full-time: 5966 men, 4713 women	**Faculty:** I, --$
Part-time: 575 men, 755 women	**Ph.D.s:** n/av
Graduate: 1046 men, 1036 women	**Student/Faculty:** n/av
Year: semesters, summer session	**Tuition:** $8327 ($19,891)
Room & Board: $7918	**Freshman Class:** 5980 applied, 4759 accepted, 2503 enrolled
SAT: required **ACT:** 24	**CEEB CODE:** 6474
Application Deadline: August 1	**COMPETITIVE**

North Dakota is a student-focused, land grant, research university an economic engine that educates students, conducts primary research, creates new knowledge, and advances technology. We provide affordable access to an excellent education at a top-ranked research institution that combines teaching and research in a rich learning environment, educating future leaders who will create solutions to national and global challenges that will shape a better world. There are 8 undergraduate schools and 1 graduate school. In addition to regional accreditation, NDSU has baccalaureate program accreditation with AACSB, ABET, ACCE, ACPE, ADA, AHEA, CAHEA, CSAB, FIDER, NAAB, NASAD, NASM, NCATE, and ACS. The 258-acre campus is in an urban area 229 miles northwest of Minneapolis-St. Paul. Including any residence halls, there are 97 buildings.

STUDENT LIFE: 57% of undergraduates are from out of state, mostly the Midwest. Students are from 48 states, 69 foreign countries, and Canada. 82% are White; 3% African American; 3% two or more races; 2% Asian American; 2% Hispanic; 2% race unknown; 1% American Indian/Alaska Native. **Male To Female Ratio:** 1.2:1. The average age of freshmen is 18; all undergraduates, 21. 20% do not continue beyond their first year; 50% remain to graduate. **Housing:** 4996 students can be accommodated in college housing, which includes single-sex and coed dorms, on-campus apartments, married student housing, learning communities, and first-year student halls. On-campus housing is guaranteed for the freshman year only. 67% of students commute. All students may keep cars. Alcohol is not permitted.

FACULTY/CLASSROOMS: No introductory courses are taught by graduate students.

PROGRAMS OF STUDY: NDSU confers B.A., B.F.A., B.L.A., B.Mus., B.S., B.S.A.B.En., B.S.Arch., B.S.C.E., B.S.Cpr.E., B.S.Con.E., B.S.Cons.M., B.S.E.E., B.S.I.E.Mgt., B.S.Mfg.E., B.S.M.E., B.S.N. and B.U.S. degrees. Master's and doctoral degrees are also awarded. Bachelor's degrees are awarded in AGRICULTURE (agricultural business management, agricultural communications, agricultural economics, agricultural mechanics, agriculture, animal science, equine science, horticulture, natural resource management, plant protection (pest management), plant science, range/farm management, and soil science), BIOLOGICAL SCIENCE (biochemistry, biology/biological science, biotechnology, botany, microbiology, and nutrition), BUSINESS (accounting, business administration and management, finance, hospitality management services, hotel and restaurant administration, hotel/motel and restaurant management, management information systems, management science, marketing, recreation and leisure services, and sports management), COMMUNICATIONS AND THE ARTS (apparel design, art, communications, dramatic arts, English, French, instrumental music education, journalism/news & information, music, performing arts, public relations, Spanish, and theatre arts), COMPUTER AND PHYSICAL SCIENCE (actuarial science, chemistry, computer science, earth science, geology, mathematics, physics, radiological technology, and statistics), EDUCATION (agricultural education, athletic training, elementary education, health education, home economics education, music education, physical education, secondary education, and social science education), ENGINEERING AND ENVIRONMENTAL DESIGN (agricultural engineering, agricultural engineering technology, architecture, biomedical engineering, civil engineering, computer engineering, construction engineering, construction management, electrical/electronics engineering, emergency/disaster science, engineering management, environmental design, industrial engineering, interior design, landscape architecture/design, manufacturing engineering, and mechanical engineering), HEALTH PROFESSIONS (clinical science, health communication, nursing, pharmacy, preveterinary science, respiratory therapy, and veterinary science), SOCIAL SCIENCE (anthropology, child care/child and family studies, criminal justice, dietetics, economics, food science, history, human development, humanities, international studies, philosophy and religion, physical fitness/movement, political science/government, psychology, social science, sociology, textiles and clothing, and women & gender studies). Engineering, pharmacy, and nursing are the strongest academically. Sciences, engineering, and human development have the largest enrollments.

ACTIVITIES: 5% of men belong to 12 national fraternities; 2% of women belong to 3 national sororities. There are 300 groups on campus, including academic, leisure learning, art, band, cheerleading, choir, chorus, computers, dance, debate, drama, drill team, ethnic, forensics, honors, international, jazz band, LGBT, marching band, musical theater, newspaper, orchestra, pep band, political, professional, radio and TV, recreational, religious, social, social service, student government, and symphony. Popular campus events include International Students' Week and Multicultural Activities. **Sports:** There are 8 intercollegiate sports for men and 8 for women, and 11 intramural sports for men and 10 for women. Facilities include a sports arena, indoor and outdoor tracks, baseball and softball fields, wrestling and weight rooms, a multipurpose fitness room, volleyball, tennis, basketball, and racquetball courts, and a wellness center including aquatics facility. **Graduates:** From July 1, 2015 to June 30, 2016, 2308 bachelor's degrees were awarded. The most popular majors were business (15%), engineering (13%), health professions, and related sciences (11%). In an average class, 25% graduate in 4 years or less, 49% graduate in 5 years or less, and 56% graduate in 6 years or less.

SERVICES: Counseling and information services are available, as is tutoring in most subjects. There is a reader service for the blind, and remedial math, reading, and writing, including note takers. **Library/Resources:** The 5 libraries contain 784,978 volumes, 444,951 microform items, 2,873 audio/video tapes/CDs/DVDs, and subscribe to 5,090 periodicals including electronic. Computerized library services include interlibrary loans, database searching, Internet access, and Wi-Fi capability. Special learning facilities include an art gallery, radio station, and TV station. **Physically Challenged Students:** All of the campus is accessible. Facilities include wheelchair ramps, elevators, special parking, specially equipped restrooms, special class scheduling, lowered drinking fountains, and lowered telephones. **Special:** Special academic programs include cooperative work programs and internships. There is cross-registration with the Tri-college Consortium and all North Dakota State institutions. Student-designed and dual majors, study abroad, a B.A.-B.S. degree, nondegree study, and pass/fail options are possible. There are 22 national honor societies and a freshman honors program. **Visiting:** There are regularly scheduled orientations for prospective students, including tours of the campus, academic appointments, and meetings with admissions counselors and financial aid counselors. There are guides for informal visits and visitors may sit in on classes. To schedule a visit, contact Office of Admission. **Campus Safety and Security:** Measures include 24-hour foot and vehicle patrol, emergency notification system, self-defense education, and security escort services. There are also shuttle buses, emergency telephones, lighted pathways/sidewalks, and controlled access to dorms/residences.

REQUIREMENTS: The SAT or ACT is required. Applicants must have completed 4 units of English, and 3 each of math (algebra I or above), lab science, and social science. An additional unit from one of the core areas (English, math, lab science, social science) or from a world language (including foreign languages, Native American languages or American Sign Language) is also required. The GED is accepted, with a minimum score of 45 and no subject score lower than 40. AP and CLEP credits are accepted. Students must complete at least 122 semester credits, with at least 24 in the major, and maintain at least a 2.0 GPA. General education requirements include 10 credits in science and technology, including a 1-credit lab course, 12 credits in communication, which includes freshman English and public speaking, 6 credits each in humanities, fine arts and social and behavioral science, 3 credits in quantitative reasoning, at least 2 credits in a wellness course, and a first-year experience course. Included in these courses must be 1 course designated as a cultural diversity course and 1 designated as a global perspectives course. **Procedure:** Freshmen are admitted to all sessions. Entrance exams should be taken in the spring of the junior year or in the fall of the senior year. There are deferred admissions and rolling admissions plans. Applications should be filed by August 1 for fall entry; December 1 for spring entry; and May 1 for summer entry, along with a $35 fee. Applications are accepted on-line. **Transfer Students:** Transfer students must have a minimum GPA of 2.0; ACT or SAT scores are required if the applicant has fewer than 24 semester credits. 36 of 122 credits required for the bachelor's degree must be completed at NDSU. **International Students:** There are 1059 international students enrolled. The school actively recruits these students. They must take the TOEFL with a minimum score of 525 on the paper-based TOEFL (PBT) or 71 on the Internet-based version (iBT).

ADMISSIONS: 80% of the 2016-2017 applicants were accepted. The SAT scores for the 2016-2017 freshman class were: Critical Reading-- 26% below 500, 36% between 500 and 599, 32% between 600 and 699, and 6% between 700 and 800. Math-- 23% below 500, 26% between 500 and 599, 36% between 600 and 699, and 15% between 700 and 800. Writing-- 34% below 500, 38% between 500 and 599, 26% between 600 and 699, and 2% between 700 and 800. The ACT scores were 45% between 18 and 23, 44% between 24 and 29, and 8% above 30. There were 7 National Merit finalists. **Admissions Contact:** Merideth Sherlin, Director of Admission. Email: *ndsu.admission@ndsu.edu* Web: *www.ndsu.edu*

FINANCIAL AID: The FAFSA code is 002997. The priority date for freshman financial aid applications for fall entry is February 1.

UNIVERSITY OF JAMESTOWN — E-3

www.uj.edu

Jamestown, ND 58405	(701) 252-3467 (800) 336-2554
Fax: (701) 253-4318	**Email:** admission@uj.edu
Full-time: 480 men, 475 women	**Faculty:** 57
Part-time: n/av	**Ph.D.s:** 54%
Graduate: 71 men, 108 women	**Student/Faculty:** 13 to 1
Year: semesters, summer session	**Tuition:** $21,158
Room & Board: $7350	**Freshman Class:** 1560 applied, 894 accepted, 267 enrolled
SAT CR/M: required **ACT:** 22	**CEEB CODE:** 6318
Application Deadline: open	**COMPETITIVE**

University of Jamestown, founded in 1883, is a private, institution founded by the Presbyterian Church. It's emphases are on the liberal arts, business, arts, health science, music, religious studies, and teacher preparation. Figures in the above capsule and in this profile are approximate. There is 1 undergraduate school and 4 graduate schools. In addition to regional accreditation, Jamestown has baccalaureate program accreditation with NLN and IACBE. The 110-acre campus is in a small town in central North Dakota, 100 miles west of Fargo, and 350 miles west of Minneapolis. Including any residence halls, there are 27 buildings.

STUDENT LIFE: 55% of undergraduates are from out of state, mostly the Midwest. Students are from 31 states, 13 foreign countries, and Canada. 83% are White; 6% Foreign; 5% Hispanic; 4% African American; 1% Asian American; 1% American Indian/Alaska Native. 50% are Protestant; 27% claim no religious affiliation; 19% Catholic. **Female To Male Ratio:** 1.1:1. The average age of freshmen is 18; all undergraduates, 21. 22% do not continue beyond their first year; 52% remain to graduate. **Housing:** 744 students can be accommodated in college housing, which includes coed dorms, on-campus apartments, off-campus apartments, and married student housing. On-campus housing is guaranteed for the freshman year only, and is available on a first-come, first-served basis, and is available on a lottery system for upperclassmen. 65% of students live on campus; of those, 65% remain on campus on weekends. Alcohol is not permitted. All students may keep cars.

FACULTY/CLASSROOMS: 54% of faculty are male; 46% are female. All teach undergraduates. No introductory courses are taught by graduate students. The average class size in an introductory lecture is 26; in a laboratory is 15; and in a regular course is 20.

PROGRAMS OF STUDY: Jamestown confers B.A., B.S. and B.S.N. degrees. Master's and doctoral degrees are also awarded. Bachelor's degrees are awarded in BIOLOGICAL SCIENCE (biochemistry and biology/biological science), BUSINESS (accounting, business administration and management, and management information systems), COMMUNICATIONS AND THE ARTS (communications, English, fine arts, French, German, music, and Spanish), COMPUTER AND PHYSICAL SCIENCE (chemistry, computer science, information sciences and systems, mathematics, and radiological technology), EDUCATION (elementary education and physical education), ENGINEERING AND ENVIRONMENTAL DESIGN (graphic arts technology), HEALTH PROFESSIONS (clinical science, exercise science, and nursing), SOCIAL SCIENCE (criminal justice, history, history of science, psychology, religion, and religious education). Physical therapy, business, nursing, and physical sciences are the strongest academically. Business, nursing, exercise science, psychology, and education have the largest enrollments.

ACTIVITIES: There are no fraternities or sororities. There are 35 groups on campus, including art, band, cheerleading, choir, chorale, chorus, computers, dance, drama, environmental, film, honors, international, jazz band, literary magazine, musical theater, newspaper, orchestra, pep band, political, professional, radio and TV, religious, social, social service, and student government. Popular campus events include Jimmie Jive Week, Homecoming, and Character in Leadership Fall Conference. **Sports:** There are 10 intercollegiate sports for men and 11 for women, and 6 intramural sports for men and 6 for women. Facilities include an athletics center with a basketball court, /wrestling and volleyball practice and composition area, a football stadium with an all-weather track, a soccer field, and a sports center with a swimming pool, weight room, running track, YMCA, and basketball, handball, and racquetball courts. **Graduates:** From July 1, 2015 to June 30, 2016, 142 bachelor's degrees were awarded. The most popular majors were nursing (22%), business (13%), and elementry education and exercise science (7%). 25 companies recruited on campus in 2015-2016. In an average class, 1% graduate in 3 years or less, 30% graduate in 4 years or less, 47% graduate in 5 years or less, and 49% graduate in 6 years or less. Of the 2015 graduating class, 15% were enrolled in graduate school within 6 months of graduation, and 91% were employed.

SERVICES: Counseling and information services are available, as is tutoring in most subjects, and remedial math, reading, and writing. **Library/Resources:** The library contains 112,169 volumes, 9,000 microform items, 5,518 audio/video tapes/CDs/DVDs, and subscribes to 18,610 periodicals including electronic. Computerized library services include interlibrary loans, database searching, and Internet access. Special learning facilities include an art gallery, radio station, and TV station. **Physically Challenged Students:** 90% of the campus is accessible. Facilities include wheelchair ramps, elevators, special parking, specially equipped restrooms, special class scheduling, lowered drinking fountains, lowered telephones, and special housing. **Special:** Special academic options include co-op programs in business, nursing, computer science, and criminal justice, on-campus work-study, internships, study abroad, dual majors within any of the concentrations, and student-designed majors. There is a 3-2 engineering program with North Dakota State University. There are 5 national honor societies and 10 departmental honors programs. **Visiting:** There are regularly scheduled orientations for prospective students, including a campus tour and faculty visits. There are guides for informal visits, visitors may sit in on classes, and stay overnight. To schedule a visit, contact the Admissions Office. **Campus Safety and Security:** Measures include emergency notification system, self-defense education, security escort services, lighted pathways/sidewalks, controlled access to dorms/residences, and shuttle services.

REQUIREMENTS: The SAT or ACT is required. Requirements include graduation from an accredited secondary school. The GED is accepted. AP and CLEP credits are accepted. Important factors in the admissions decision are evidence of special talent, leadership record, and personality/intangible qualities. To graduate, students must have a minimum of 128 semester credits, at least 48 of which must be at the upper-division level, with an average of 48 semester credits in the major, and maintain at least a 2.0 GPA. **Procedure:** Freshmen are admitted to all sessions. Entrance exams should be taken before or during the fall of the senior year. There is a rolling admissions plan. Application deadlines are open. Application fees are waived if application is completed online. **Transfer Students:** 60 transfer students enrolled in 2015-2016. Applicants must have at least a 2.0 GPA and be in good standing with their previous college; Applicants are required to submit official high school and college transcripts. 35 of 128 credits required for the bachelor's degree must be completed at Jamestown. **International Students:** There are 90 international students enrolled. The school actively recruits these students. They must take the TOEFL with a minimum score of 525 on the paper-based TOEFL (PBT) or 70 on the Internet-based version (iBT) or take the MELAB.

ADMISSIONS: 57% of the 2016-2017 applicants were accepted. The SAT scores for the 2016-2017 freshman class were: Critical Reading-- 55% below 500, 28% between 500 and 599, 13% between 600 and 699, and 2% between 700 and 800. Math-- 57% below 500, 28% between 500 and 599, 11% between 600 and 699, and 2% between 700 and 800. The ACT scores were 6% between 12 and 17, 61% between 18 and 23, 28% between 24 and 29, and 4% above 30. **Admissions Contact:** Mike Heitkamp, Vice President of Enrollment. Email: *admission@uj.edu* Web: *www.uj.edu*

FINANCIAL AID: In 2016-2017, 100% of all full-time freshmen received some form of financial aid, and need-based aid. The average freshman award was $14,135. Need-based scholarships or need-based grants averaged $4,981 ($10,315 maximum); need-based self-help aid (loans and jobs) averaged $3,770 ($8,500 maximum); non-need-based athletic scholarships averaged $4,129 ($12,930 maximum); and other non-need-based awards and non-need-based scholarships averaged $9,875 ($19,930 maximum). 33% of undergraduate students work part-time. Average annual earnings from campus work are $760. The average financial indebtedness of the 2016 graduate was $22,925. The FAFSA code is 002990. The priority date for freshman financial aid applications for fall entry is March 15.

UNIVERSITY OF MARY — C-3

www.umary.edu

Bismarck, ND 58504	(701) 355-8190 (800) 288-6279
Fax: (701) 255-7687	Email: enroll@umary.edu
Full-time: 647 men, 998 women	**Faculty:** 95
Part-time: 187 men, 228 women	**Ph.D.s:** 36%
Graduate: 272 men, 451 women	**Student/Faculty:** 18 to 1
Year: semesters, summer session	**Tuition:** $16,310
Room & Board: $6870	**Freshman Class:** 1010 applied, 855 accepted, 367 enrolled
SAT: recommended **ACT:** 23	**CEEB CODE:** 6428
Application Deadline: August 15	**COMPETITIVE**

University of Mary, founded in 1959, is a private institution affiliated with the Roman Catholic Church. Undergraduate and graduate programs emphasize liberal arts, humanities, social sciences, business, health science, music, professional training, philosophy and religious studies, and teacher preparation. The figures in the above capsule and in this profile are approximate. There are 8 undergraduate schools and 4 graduate schools. In addition to regional accreditation, Mary has baccalaureate program accreditation with CAHEA, CSWE, CCNE, ACOTE, CAPTE, and CAATE. The 107-acre campus is in a suburban area 7 miles south of Bismarck. Including any residence halls, there are 13 buildings.

STUDENT LIFE: 70% of undergraduates are from North Dakota. Others are from 33 states, 23 foreign countries, and Canada. 95% are from public schools. 87% are White; 5% American Indian/Alaska Native; 3% African American; 2% Hispanic; 1% Asian American; 1% Foreign. 60% are Catholic; 30% Protestant. **Female To Male Ratio:** 1.5:1. The average age of freshmen is 18; all undergraduates, 25. 26% do not continue beyond their first year; 51% remain to graduate. **Housing:** 791 students can be accommodated in college housing, which includes single-sex dorms and on-campus apartments. On-campus housing is guaranteed for all 4 years. 61% of students commute. All students may keep cars. Alcohol is not permitted.

FACULTY/CLASSROOMS: 48% of faculty are male; 52% are female. 95% teach undergraduates, 15% do research, and 15% do both. No introductory courses are taught by graduate students. The average class size in an introductory lecture is 15; in a laboratory is 20; and in a regular course is 20.

PROGRAMS OF STUDY: Mary confers B.A., B.S., and B.Univ.Studies degrees. Master's degrees are also awarded. Bachelor's degrees are awarded in BIOLOGICAL SCIENCE (biology/biological science), BUSINESS (accounting, business administration and management, business communications, and management information systems), COMMUNICATIONS AND THE ARTS (communications, English, and music), COMPUTER AND PHYSICAL SCIENCE (information sciences and systems, mathematics, and radiological technology), EDUCATION (athletic training, early childhood education, elementary education, English education, mathematics education, music education, physical education, social science education, and special education), ENGINEERING AND ENVIRONMENTAL DESIGN (engineering and applied science), HEALTH PROFESSIONS (exercise science, nursing, occupational therapy, physical therapy, premedicine, and respiratory therapy), SOCIAL SCIENCE (addiction studies, behavioral science, criminal justice, liberal arts/general studies, ministries, pastoral studies, prelaw, psychology, social science, social work, and theological studies). Business administration, education, and nursing are the strongest academically. Business, nursing, and elementary education have the largest enrollments.

ACTIVITIES: There are no fraternities or sororities. There are 22 groups on campus, including band, cheerleading, choir, chorale, chorus, computers, drama, drill team, environmental, ethnic, forensics, jazz band, musical theater, newspaper, orchestra, pep band, photography, political, professional, radio and TV, religious, social, social service, student government, and symphony. Popular campus events include Intramural Sports and the Convocation Series. **Sports:** There are 8 intercollegiate sports for men and 7 for women, and 10 intramural sports for men and 10 for women. Facilities include an activity center housing a gym, basketball and racquetball courts, wrestling and weight rooms, a swimming pool, an indoor track, basketball/volleyball/tennis courts, and a climbing wall. There are also track/football, intramural, and softball fields, tennis courts, a fitness center, and a stadium. **Graduates:** From July 1, 2015 to June 30, 2016, 502 bachelor's degrees were awarded. The most popular majors were business (40%), nursing (19%), and education (10%). 30 companies recruited on campus in 2015-2016. In an average class, 5% graduate in 3 years or less, 39% graduate in 4 years or less, 50% graduate in 5 years or less, and 1% graduate in 6 years or less. Of the 2015 graduating class, 17% were enrolled in graduate school within 6 months of graduation, and 80% were employed.

SERVICES: Counseling and information services are available, as is tutoring in every subject, and a reader service for the blind, and remedial math, reading, and writing. **Library/Resources:** The library contains 78,137 volumes, 2 microform items, and 7,866 audio/video tapes/CDs/DVDs, and subscribes to 6,997 periodicals including electronic. Computerized library services include interlibrary loans, database searching, Internet access, and Wi-Fi capability. Special learning facilities include an art gallery and radio station. **Physically Challenged Students:** All of the campus is accessible. Facilities include wheelchair ramps, elevators, special parking, specially equipped restrooms, special class scheduling, lowered drinking fountains, lowered telephones, and special housing. **Special:** A co-op program in engineering is available as is cross-registration with the University of Minnesota. Special academic programs include internships in all fields and all programs, study abroad in France, Germany, and Spain, on-campus work-study, and a general studies degree. Dual majors include elementary education/early childhood, elementary education/special education, athletic training/biology, athletic training/phys ed, business/accounting, and business/computer information systems. There are accelerated degree programs in several majors, and a 3-2 engineering program with the University of Minnesota. There are 3 national honor societies, a freshman honors program, and 2 departmental honors programs. **Visiting:** There are regularly scheduled orientations for prospective students, including a campus tour and meetings with individual professors, coaches, students, and music instructors. There are guides for informal visits, visitors may sit in on classes, and stay overnight. To schedule a visit, contact the Admissions Office. **Campus Safety and Security:** Measures include an emergency notification system, and security escort services, emergency telephones, lighted pathways/sidewalks, and controlled access to dorms/residences.

REQUIREMENTS: The SAT or ACT and ACT Writing Test are recommended. Applicants should be graduates of an accredited secondary school; the GED is accepted. For automatic acceptance, 3 requirements must be met: a minimum 2.5 GPA; an 18 or higher score on the ACT; and rank in the upper half of the graduating class. The school's own testing can also be used to determine acceptance. A recommendation from a school counselor, teacher, or employer is requested. AP and CLEP credits are accepted. Important factors in the admissions decision are evidence of special talent, leadership record, and advanced placement or honors courses. To graduate, students must complete 128 semester hours, with 32 to 56 in the major and 44 at the 300-400 level, and have a minimum GPA of 2.0. At least 56 semester hours must be in liberal arts courses. In addition, a B.A. degree requires 16 semester hours of a foreign language or 20 semester hours of philosophy/theology, with 12 such hours at the 300-400 level. All students must take 3 courses each in humanities, math/science, philosophy/theology, and social sciences. **Procedure:** Freshmen are admitted in the fall and spring. Entrance exams should be taken in the fall of the senior year. There are early admissions, deferred admissions, and rolling admissions plans. Applications should be filed by August 15 for fall entry; December 15 for spring entry, along with a $25 fee. Applications are accepted on-line. **Transfer Students:** 259 transfer students enrolled in 2015-2016. Transfer students should have a 2.0 minimum GPA and should present a recommendation from a school counselor, instructor, or employer. 32 of 128 credits required for the bachelor's degree must be completed at Mary. **International Students:** There are 25 international students enrolled. The school actively recruits these students. They must take the TOEFL with a minimum score of 500 on the paper-based TOEFL (PBT).

ADMISSIONS: 85% of the 2016-2017 applicants were accepted. The ACT scores were 27% below 12, 33% between 12 and 17, 27% between 18 and 23, 8% between 24 and 29, and 5% above 30. 37% of the current freshmen were in the top fifth of their class; 69% were in the top two fifths. 20 freshmen graduated first in their class. **Admissions Contact:** Dave Heringer, Vice President For Enrollment. Email: *enroll@umary.edu* Web: *www.umary.edu*

FINANCIAL AID: In 2016-2017, 100% of all full-time freshmen and 85% of continuing full-time students received some form of financial aid. 85% of all full-time freshmen and 75% of continuing full-time students received need-based aid. 70% of undergraduate students work part-time. Average annual earnings from campus work are $1000. The average financial indebtedness of the 2016 graduate was $15,500. The FAFSA code is 002992. The priority date for freshman financial aid applications for fall entry is March 15. The filing deadline for fall entry is August 1.

UNIVERSITY OF NORTH DAKOTA E-2

www.und.edu

Grand Forks, ND 58202	**(701) 777 3000** **(800) CALL-UND**
Fax: (701) 777-2721	**Email: und.admissions@und.edu**
Full-time: 4745 men, 4082 women	**Faculty:** 482; I, -$
Part-time: 1626 men, 802 women	**Ph.D.s:** 94%
Graduate: 1307 men, 2086 women	**Student/Faculty:** 19 to 1
Year: semesters, summer session	**Tuition:** $8137 ($19,291)
Room & Board: $7630	**Freshman Class:** 4920 applied, 4029 accepted, 1900 enrolled
SAT: required **ACT:** 24	**CEEB CODE:** 6878
Application Deadline: July 1	**COMPETITIVE**

University of North Dakota, founded in 1883, enrolls students from every state, and more than 225 fields of study, from baccalaureate through doctoral and professional degrees, including law and medicine. In addition, UND offers more than 40 degree and graduate certificate programs through distance education. Each year, the university has more than 21,000 registrations in online academic courses and other nonacademic activities, including workforce development, conferences, professional certificates, teacher workshops, and lifelong learning courses. There are 8 undergraduate schools and 3 graduate schools. In addition to regional accreditation, UND has baccalaureate program accreditation with ABET, ADA, CSWE, NASAD, NASM, NCATE, AABI, ABET, AMTA, ATMAE, NAST, CAATE, CCNE, CAC, and COA. The 548-acre campus is in an urban area 4 hours from Minneapolis, St. Paul and 2 hours from Winnipeg, Manitoba. Including any residence halls, there are 244 buildings.

STUDENT LIFE: 63% of undergraduates are from out of state, mostly the Midwest. Students are from 50 states, 85 foreign countries, and Canada. 95% are from public schools. 80% are White; 6% Foreign; 3% Hispanic; 3% two or more races; 2% African American; 2% Asian American; 2% American Indian/Alaska Native; 2% race unknown. **Male To Female Ratio:** 1.1:1. The average age of freshmen is 18; all undergraduates, 23. 20% do not continue beyond their first year; 80% remain to graduate. **Housing:** 4267 students can be accommodated in college housing, which includes single-sex and coed dorms, on-campus apartments, married student housing, and special-interest houses. On-campus housing is guaranteed for all 4 years. 72% of students commute. All students may keep cars. Alcohol is not permitted.

FACULTY/CLASSROOMS: 52% of faculty are male; 41% are female. 70% teach undergraduates. No introductory courses are taught by graduate students. The average class size in an introductory lecture is 27; in a laboratory is 16; and in a regular course is 24.

PROGRAMS OF STUDY: UND confers B.A., B.Acc., B.B.A., B.F.A., B.G.S., B.M., B.S., B.S.A., B.S.A.T., B.S.AtSc, B.S.C.E., B.S.C.H.E., B.S.Chem., B.S.C.J.S., B.S.C.N., B.S.C.S.C.I., B.S.Cyto., B.S.D., B.S.E.E., B.S.E.D., B.S.E.G., B.S.F.W.B., B.S.G.D.T., B.S.G.E., B.S.Geol., B.S.I.T., B.S.M.E., B.S.M.L.S., B.S.N., B.S.O.S.E.H., B.S.P.A., B.S.PTE, B.S.R.T.S., B.S.R.H.S., B.S.S.W. and B.S.KIN degrees. Master's and doctoral degrees are also awarded. Bachelor's degrees are awarded in AGRICULTURE (environmental studies and fishing and fisheries), BIOLOGICAL SCIENCE (biology/biological science), BUSINESS (accounting, banking and finance, business economics, human resources, investments and securities, marketing management, and operations management), COMMUNICATIONS AND THE ARTS (Chinese, classical languages, communications, English, French, German, graphic design, music, music performance, musical theater, Norwegian, Spanish, and visual and performing arts), COMPUTER AND PHYSICAL SCIENCE (atmospheric sciences and meteorology, chemistry, computer science, geology, information sciences and systems, mathematics, natural sciences, physics, and science), EDUCATION (athletic training, business education, early childhood education, elementary education, middle school education, music education, and physical education), ENGINEERING AND ENVIRONMENTAL DESIGN (air traffic control, aviation maintenance management, chemical engineering, civil engineering, electrical/electronics engineering, geological engineering, industrial engineering technology, mechanical engineering, occupational safety and health, and petroleum/natural gas engineering), HEALTH PROFESSIONS (clinical science, cytotechnology, medical laboratory science, music therapy, nursing, and physical therapy), SOCIAL SCIENCE (American Indian studies, anthropology, criminal justice, dietetics, early childhood studies, economics, forensic studies, geography, history, interdisciplinary studies, international studies, philosophy, political science/government, psychology, public administration, religion, social science, social work, and sociology). Mulit/interdiscstudy and health professions is the strongest academically. Health professions, engineering, and business have the largest enrollments.

ACTIVITIES: 10% of men belong to 12 national fraternities; 11% of women belong to 7 national sororities. There are 275 groups on campus, including a special interest club, art, band, cheerleading, chess, choir, chorale, chorus, computers, dance, debate, departmental club, drama, drill team, ethnic, film, honors, international, jazz band, LGBT, literary magazine, marching band, musical theater, newspaper, opera, orchestra, pep band, photography, political, professional, radio and TV, religious, social, social service, student government, and symphony. Popular campus events include The Big Event-a City Wide Community Event, Athletic Events and Potato Bowl, Homecoming, Time Out and Wacipi. **Sports:** There are 9 intercollegiate sports for men and 10 for women, and 14 intramural sports for men and 14 for women. Facilities include a stadium, hockey arena, basketball center, sports/field house with racquetball and basketball courts, weight rooms and a dance studio. The wellness center houses a gymnasium, multi-activity court, cardiovascular, weight rooms, running track, and a rock-climbing wall. **Graduates:** From July 1, 2015 to June 30, 2016, 1948 bachelor's degrees were awarded. The most popular majors were psychology (6%), nursing (6%), and commercial aviation (5%). 254 companies recruited on campus in 2015-2016. In an average class, 1% graduate in 3 years or less, 23% graduate in 4 years or less, 46% graduate in 5 years or less, and 55% graduate in 6 years or less. Of the 2015 graduating class, 16% were enrolled in graduate school within 6 months of graduation, and 81% were employed.

SERVICES: Counseling and information services are available, as is tutoring in every subject, and a reader service for the blind. **Library/**

Resources: The 2 libraries contain 1.7 million volumes, 856,469 microform items, 22,034 audio/video tapes/CDs/DVDs, and subscribe to 62,508 periodicals including electronic. Computerized library services include interlibrary loans, database searching, Internet access, and Wi-Fi capability. Special learning facilities include an art gallery, natural history museum, planetarium, radio station, TV station, an entrepreneur center, atmospherium, art museum, gallery, and one stop student services. **Physically Challenged Students:** 99% of the campus is accessible. Facilities include wheelchair ramps, elevators, special parking, specially equipped restrooms, special class scheduling, lowered drinking fountains, lowered telephones, special housing. Accessible transportation, and academic and personal support services. **Special:** Special academic programs include cooperative programs, accelerated degree programs in most majors, internships in many majors, study abroad in at least 20 countries, work-study, and dual majors in all areas. Also offered are a general studies degree, honors programs, student-designed majors, B.A.-B.S. degrees, nondegree study, and pass/fail options. Alternative academic programs include the Division of Continuing Education's correspondence study, the Integrated Studies Program, which offers a means of fulfilling general education requirements by a semester of related course work, and study via telecommunications. Cross-registration with all North Dakota 2- and 4-year public institutions is possible. There are 20 national honor societies, Phi Beta Kappa, a freshman honors program, and 1 departmental honors program. **Visiting:** There are regularly scheduled orientations for prospective students, including a visit with an admissions counselor, a campus tour, an academic appointment, and an athletic appointment (if applicable). There are guides for informal visits, visitors may sit in on classes, and stay overnight. To schedule a visit, contact the Office of Admissions. **Campus Safety and Security:** Measures include 24-hour foot and vehicle patrol, emergency notification system, self-defense education, and security escort services. There are also shuttle buses, emergency telephones, lighted pathways/sidewalks, and emergency phones throughout the campus.

REQUIREMENTS: The ACT is preferred, but the SAT will be accepted. Applicants must be graduates of an accredited secondary school or have passed the GED with an average of 50. AP and CLEP credits are accepted. To graduate, students must complete at least 125 credit hours, 30 in the major, with a minimum GPA of 2.0. At least 36 credits must be numbered 300 or above, and at least 60 credits must be from a 4-year institution. Distribution requirements include 12 credits of math, science, and technology, 9 each of social sciences and arts, and humanities, and 6 of English composition. One course in social science or arts and humanities must meet the world cultures designation. **Procedure:** Freshmen are admitted to all sessions. Entrance exams should be taken in spring of the junior year or fall of the senior year. There are early decision and rolling admissions plans. Applications should be filed by July 1 for fall entry. The fall 2016 application fee was $35. Notification is sent on a rolling basis. **Transfer Students:** 706 transfer students enrolled in 2015-2016. Transfer students must have a minimum GPA of 2.0 and be in good academic standing. A higher GPA may be required in specific programs. 30 of 125 credits required for the bachelor's degree must be completed at UND. **International Students:** There are 353 international students enrolled. They must take the TOEFL, as well as the SAT or ACT.

ADMISSIONS: 82% of the 2016-2017 applicants were accepted. The ACT scores were 1% between 12 and 17, 43% between 18 and 23, 43% between 24 and 29, and 7% above 30. 32% of the current freshmen were in the top fifth of their class; 63% were in the top two fifths. 78 freshmen graduated first in their class. **Admissions Contact:** Jason Trainer, Director of Admissions. Email: *und.admissions@und.edu* Web: *www.und.edu*

FINANCIAL AID: In 2016-2017, 90% of all full-time freshmen and 80% of continuing full-time students received some form of financial aid. 41% of all full-time freshmen and 46% of continuing full-time students received need-based aid. The FAFSA code is 003005. The priority date for freshman financial aid applications for fall entry is February 1.

VALLEY CITY STATE UNIVERSITY E-3

www.vcsu.edu

Valley City, ND 58072	(701) 845-7101 (800) 532-8641
Fax: (701) 845-7299	**Email:** enrollment.services@vcsu.edu
Full-time: 379 men, 419 women	**Faculty:** 70; IIB, --$
Part-time: 167 men, 330 women	**Ph.D.s:** 51%
Graduate: 46 men, 111 women	**Student/Faculty:** 11 to 1
Year: semesters, summer session	**Tuition:** $7195 ($16,016)
Room & Board: $6072	**Freshman Class:** 372 applied, 285 accepted, 190 enrolled
ACT: 21	**CEEB CODE:** 6480
Application Deadline: open	**COMPETITIVE**

Valley City State University, founded in 1890, prepares students for life through visionary leadership and exemplary practices in teaching, learning and service. VCSU has built on that rich tradition with a student-focused, learning-centered approach, offering more than 80 degree programs. Its small, beautiful campus provides students with plentiful opportunities for close connections with fellow students, faculty and staff. One of the first "laptop universities" in the nation (each full-time student receives a laptop computer). VCSU continues its innovative use of technology with many online offerings, including several undergraduate majors and a master of education degree program. There is 1 undergraduate school. In addition to regional accreditation, VCSU has baccalaureate program accreditation with NASM, NCATE, and CAATE. The 64-acre campus is in a small town on the banks of the Sheyenne River, Valley City, and 58 miles west of Fargo, ND. Including any residence halls, there are 29 buildings.

STUDENT LIFE: 66% of undergraduates are from North Dakota. Others are from 46 states, 7 foreign countries, and Canada. 84% are White; 4% Hispanic; 3% African American; 3% two or more races; 2% Foreign; 2% race unknown; 1% Asian American; 1% American Indian/Alaska Native. **Female To Male Ratio:** 1.5:1. The average age of freshmen is 19; all undergraduates, 23. 29% do not continue beyond their first year. **Housing:** 465 students can be accommodated in college housing, which includes single-sex and coed dorms and married student housing. On-campus housing is guaranteed for all 4 years. 75% of students commute. All students may keep cars. Alcohol is not permitted.

FACULTY/CLASSROOMS: 45% of faculty are male; 55% are female. All teach undergraduates, 25% do research, and 25% do both. No introductory courses are taught by graduate students. The average class size in an introductory lecture is 40; in a laboratory is 20; and in a regular course is 25.

PROGRAMS OF STUDY: VCSU confers B.A., B.S., B.S.Ed., and B.University Studies. degrees. Master's degrees are also awarded. Bachelor's degrees are awarded in BIOLOGICAL SCIENCE (biology/biological science), BUSINESS (business administration and management, human resources, and office supervision and management), COMMUNICATIONS AND THE ARTS (art, English, music, and Spanish), COMPUTER AND PHYSICAL SCIENCE (chemistry, information sciences and systems, mathematics, and science), EDUCATION (business education, elementary education, health education, physical education, technical education, and vocational education), SOCIAL SCIENCE (history and social science). Education, business, and fisheries &wildlife science are the strongest academically. Elementary education, business, fisheries, and wildlife science have the largest enrollments.

ACTIVITIES: There are 30 groups on campus, including art, band, cheerleading, choir, chorale, chorus, computers, drama, honors, international, jazz band, musical theater, newspaper, pep band, photography, political, professional, religious, social, student government, and yearbook. Popular campus events include Sno-Daze, and Medicine Wheel Seasonal Celebrations. **Sports:** There are 6 intercollegiate sports for men and 6 for women. Facilities include a football stadium with an all-weather track, arena, indoor pool, field house, tennis and racquetball courts, a cross-country course, softball and baseball fields, golf course, weight rooms, and a fitness room. **Graduates:** From July 1, 2015 to June 30, 2016, 260 bachelor's degrees were awarded. The most popular majors were elementary edudcation (53%), business administration (8%), and fisheries & wildlife science (5%). 45 companies recruited on campus in 2015-2016. In an average class, 21% graduate in 4 years or less, 37% graduate in 5 years or less, and 45% graduate in 6 years or less.

SERVICES: Counseling and information services are available, as is tutoring in most subjects, and a reader service for the blind, and remedial math and writing. **Library/Resources:** The library contains 110,000 volumes, 250 microform items, 4,500 audio/video tapes/CDs/DVDs, and subscribes to 27,700 periodicals including electronic. Computerized library services include interlibrary loans, database searching, Internet access, and Wi-Fi capability. Special learning facilities include an art gallery and planetarium. **Physically Challenged Students:** 97% of the campus is accessible. Facilities include wheelchair ramps, elevators, special parking, specially equipped restrooms, special class scheduling, lowered drinking fountains, lowered telephones, and special housing. **Special:** VCSU offers internships, dual majors, on-campus work-study, study abroad in 2 countries, pass/fail options for some courses, and credit for life, military, and work experience. There are 6 national honor societies and 4 departmental honors programs. **Visiting:** There are regularly scheduled orientations for prospective students. There are guides for informal visits, visitors may sit in on classes, and stay overnight. To schedule a visit, contact the Office of Enrollment Services at enrollment.services@vcsu.edu. **Campus Safety and Security:** Measures include 24-hour foot and vehicle patrol, emergency notification system, self-defense education, lighted pathways/sidewalks, a night patrol, and surveillance cameras.

REQUIREMENTS: The ACT is required. Applicants must be graduates of an accredited secondary school or have a GED certificate. Core curriculum requirements include 4 units of English and 3 units each of math, lab science, and social science. AP and CLEP credits are accepted. To graduate, students must complete at least 120 semester hours with a minimum GPA of 2.0, or 2.5 for a B.S.Ed. degree. Except for those pursuing the Bachelor of University Studies degree, all students must complete the foundation studies curriculum, which includes 9 hours in communication, 6 in aesthetic engagement, 5 in global perspective, 12 in problem solving, 6 in wellness, 3 in technology, and 15 to 16 in foreign language. Students must complete 48 hours in their major if they do not have a minor, or 36 hours in their major if they have a minor. All students must complete a digital portfolio specific to their major. **Procedure:** Freshmen are admitted to all sessions. There are deferred admissions and rolling admissions plans. Application deadlines are open. Application fee is $35. Notification is sent on a rolling basis. Applications are accepted online. **Transfer Students:** Applicants must be in good academic standing, have a minimum GPA of 2.0, and be eligible to return to their previous institution. Official transcripts from all colleges attended are required. Some students may be required to submit high school transcripts and standardized test scores. 30 of 120 credits required for the bachelor's degree must be completed at VCSU. **International Students:** There are 19 international students enrolled.

ADMISSIONS: 77% of the 2016-2017 applicants were accepted. The ACT scores were 17% between 12 and 17, 57% between 18 and 23, 19% between 24 and 29, and 3% above 30. **Admissions Contact:** Charlene Stenson, Director of Enrollment Services. Email: *enrollment.services@vcsu.edu* Web: *www.vcsu.edu*

FINANCIAL AID: VCSU is a member of CSS. The FAFSA code is 003008. The priority date for freshman financial aid applications for fall entry is March 15. The filing deadline for fall entry is April 15.

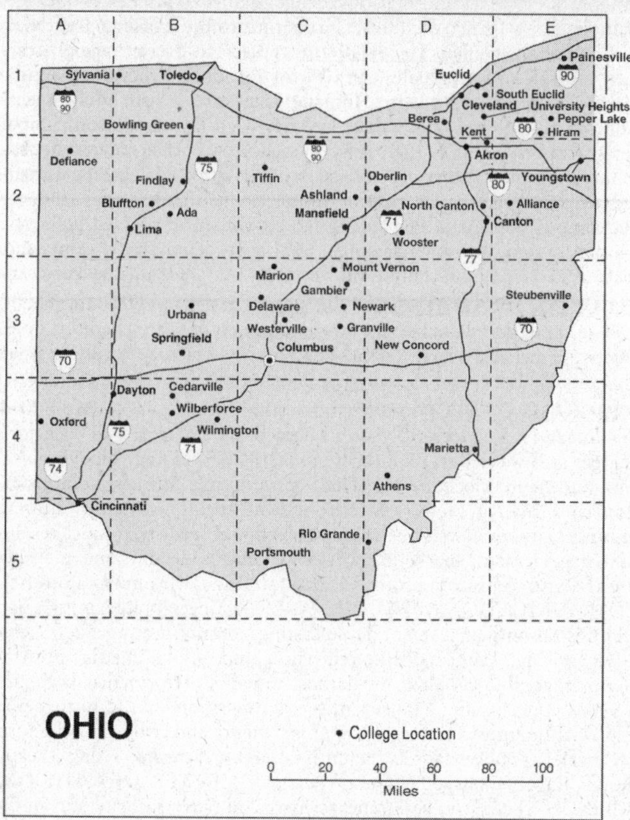

ART ACADEMY OF CINCINNATI *(The complete profile is made available exclusively on our website, www.barronspac.com)*

ASHLAND UNIVERSITY C-2
www.ashland.edu

Ashland, OH 44805 (419) 289-5052
(800) 882-1548

Fax: (419) 289-5333	Email: enrollme@ashland.edu
Full-time: 995 men, 1425 women	**Faculty:** 215
Part-time: 95 men, 270 women	**Ph.D.s:** 79%
Graduate: 1470 men, 2475 women	**Student/Faculty:** 11 to 1
Year: semesters, summer session	**Tuition:** $20,392
Room & Board: $1048	**Freshman Class:** n/av
SAT or ACT: required	**CEEB CODE:** 1021
Application Deadline: open	**COMPETITIVE**

Ashland University, founded in 1878, is a private liberal arts and sciences, institution affiliated with the Brethren Church. The University has 6 colleges: Arts & Sciences, Business & Economics, Education, Founders School for Continuing Education: Nursing, and the Ashland Theological Seminary. The figures in the above capsule and in this profile are approximate. There are 6 undergraduate schools and 3 graduate schools. In addition to regional accreditation, AU has baccalaureate program accreditation with AACSB, AHEA, CSWE, NASM, NCATE, and NLN. The 150-acre campus is in a small town midway between Cleveland and Columbus. Including any residence halls, there are 38 buildings.

STUDENT LIFE: 94% of undergraduates are from Ohio. Others are from 29 states, 13 foreign countries, and Canada. 86% are White; 8% African American; 2% Foreign; 1% Asian American; 1% American Indian/Alaska Native; 1% Hispanic. 46% claim no religious affiliation; 34% Protestant; 14% Catholic. **Female To Male Ratio:** 1.6:1. The average age of freshmen is 18; all undergraduates, 23. 42% do not continue beyond their first year; 58% remain to graduate. **Housing:** 1620 students can be accommodated in college housing, which includes single-sex and coed dorms, on-campus apartments, honors houses, fraternity houses, honors floors, sorority suites, and a resource management residence. On-campus housing is guaranteed for all 4 years. 72% of students live on campus. All students may keep cars. Alcohol is not permitted.

FACULTY/CLASSROOMS: 61% of faculty are male; 39% are female. 81% teach undergraduates. No introductory courses are taught by graduate students. The average class size in an introductory lecture is 20; in a laboratory is 11; and in a regular course is 18.

PROGRAMS OF STUDY: AU confers B.A., B.S., B.M., B.S.B.A., B.S.Ed., B.S.N. and B.S.W. degrees. Associate, master's, and doctoral degrees are also awarded. Bachelor's degrees are awarded in BIOLOGICAL SCIENCE (biology/biological science, biotechnology, and toxicology), BUSINESS (accounting, banking and finance, business administration and management, business economics, entrepreneurial studies, fashion merchandising, hotel/motel and restaurant management, management information systems, marketing/retailing/merchandising, recreational facilities management, and sports management), COMMUNICATIONS AND THE ARTS (art, broadcasting, communications, creative writing, dramatic arts, English, fine arts, French, journalism, media arts, music, musical theater, Spanish, and speech/debate/rhetoric), COMPUTER AND PHYSICAL SCIENCE (actuarial science, chemistry, chemistry education, computer science, environmental chemistry, geology, mathematics, and physics), EDUCATION (art education, athletic training, early childhood education, education administration, education of the exceptional child, elementary education, English education, foreign languages education, health education, home economics education, music education, physical education, science education, and secondary education), ENGINEERING AND ENVIRONMENTAL DESIGN (commercial art and environmental science), HEALTH PROFESSIONS (nursing, predentistry, premedicine, preoptometry, preveterinary science, and recreation therapy), SOCIAL SCIENCE (American studies, child care/child and family studies, criminal justice, economics, food science, forensic studies, history, international studies, philosophy, physical fitness/movement, political science/government, prelaw, psychology, religion, religious studies, social science, social work, sociology, and Spanish studies). Preprofessional science is the strongest academically. Business, and teacher education have the largest enrollments.

ACTIVITIES: 14% of men belong to 4 national fraternities; 22% of women belong to 5 national sororities. There are 100 groups on campus, including art, band, cheerleading, choir, chorus, dance, drama, drill team, ethnic, health club and environmental club, honors, international, jazz band, literary magazine, marching band, musical theater, newspaper, orchestra, pep band, photography, political, professional, radio and TV, religious, social, social service, student government, symphony, and yearbook. Popular campus events include Spectrum Series, Plays and Little Sibs Weekend. **Sports:** There are 10 intercollegiate sports for men and 9 for women, and 20 intramural sports for men and 20 for women. Facilities include a stadium, gym, all-weather track, field house, weight-training center, swimming pool with diving board, exercise rooms, basketball courts, handball/racquetball courts, playing fields, slow-pitch softball, a fitness center, a soccer complex, golf, quidditch, running, and snow sports. **Graduates:** Of the 2015 graduating class, 8% were enrolled in graduate school within 6 months of graduation, and 34% were employed.

SERVICES: Counseling and information services are available, as is tutoring in every subject, and a reader service for the blind. **Library/Resources:** The 2 libraries contain 270,000 volumes, 250,000 microform items, 8,800 audio/video tapes/CDs/DVDs, and subscribe to 700 periodicals including electronic. Computerized library services include interlibrary loans and database searching. Special learning facilities include an art gallery, radio station, TV station, a writing center, a media center, and theater. **Physically Challenged Students:** 5% of the campus is accessible. Facilities include wheelchair ramps, elevators, special parking, specially equipped restrooms, special class scheduling, lowered drinking fountains, lowered telephones, and special housing. **Special:** Opportunities are provided for internships, co-op programs in all business majors, work-study programs, dual majors, credit by exam, study abroad in 27 countries, a Washington semester, and pass/fail options. There are 17 national honor societies, a freshman honors program, and 10 departmental honors programs. **Visiting:** There are regularly scheduled orientations for prospective students. There are guides for informal visits, visitors may sit in on classes, and stay overnight. To schedule a visit, contact the Office of Admissions. **Campus Safety and Security:** Measures include 24-hour foot and vehicle patrol, self-defense education, and security escort services. There are emergency telephones, lighted pathways/sidewalks, controlled access to dorms/residences, encoded student identification cards, and response to reports of crime and criminal behavior.

REQUIREMENTS: The SAT or ACT is required. Applicants must be graduates of an accredited secondary school. The GED is accepted. The recommended preparatory program includes 4 units of English, 3 each of science, social studies, and math, and 2 of foreign language. An interview is recommended. A GPA of 2.5 is required. AP and CLEP credits are accepted. Important factors in the admissions decision are advanced placement or honors courses, evidence of special talent, and leadership record. To graduate, students must complete at least 128 semester hours with a minimum GPA of 2.0 overall and 2.25 in the major. All students must complete 3 semester hours of freshman studies and 44 semester hours of interdisciplinary studies, including courses in English, phys ed, religion, speech, business or economics, fine arts, humanities, science, and social science. **Procedure:** Freshmen are admitted to all sessions. Entrance exams should be taken in the spring of the junior year. There are deferred admissions and rolling admissions plans. Application deadlines are open. The fall 2016 application fee was $25. Applications are accepted online. **Transfer Students:** Official transcripts from all previous colleges, showing course credits and a minimum GPA of 2.25, must be submitted when applying for transfer. Generally, if the student has successfully completed a minimum of 1 year of college, the SAT I or ACT will not be required. 32 of 128 credits required for the bachelor's degree must be completed at AU. **International Students:** The school actively recruits these students. They must take the TOEFL.

ADMISSIONS: 13 freshmen graduated first in their class. **Admissions Contact:** Office of Admissions Email: *enrollme@ashland.edu* Web: *www.ashland.edu*

FINANCIAL AID: In 2016-2017, 99% of all full-time freshmen and 98% of continuing full-time students received some form of financial aid. 82% of all full-time freshmen and 78% of continuing full-time students received need-based aid. The average freshman award was $17,408. Need-based scholarships or need-based grants averaged $10,382 ($18,687 maximum); need-based self-help aid (loans and jobs) averaged $4,785 ($6,625 maximum); non-need-based athletic scholarships averaged $434 ($24,464 maximum); other non-need-based awards and non-need-based scholarships averaged $843 ($17,974 maximum); and $964 from other forms of aid. 30% of undergraduate students work part-time. Average annual earnings from campus work are $954. The average financial indebtedness of the 2016 graduate was $18,250. The college's own financial statement, and federal tax returns are required. The FAFSA code is 003012. The priority date for freshman financial aid applications for fall entry is March 15. The deadline for filing freshman financial aid applications for fall entry is November 15.

BALDWIN WALLACE UNIVERSITY — D-1

www.bw.edu

Berea, OH 44017	**(440) 826-6970** **(877) 292-7759**
Fax: (440) 826-3830	**Email: admission@bw.edu**
Full-time: 1404 men, 1654 women	**Faculty:** 179; IIB, av$
Part-time: 97 men, 150 women	**Ph.D.s:** 77%
Graduate: 238 men, 408 women	**Student/Faculty:** 18 to 1
Year: semesters, summer session	**Tuition:** $30,776
Room & Board: $10,330	**Freshman Class:** 4515 applied, 2697 accepted, 706 enrolled
SAT CR/M/W: 540/530/510 **ACT:** 24	**CEEB CODE:** 1050
Application Deadline: n/av	**COMPETITIVE**

Baldwin Wallace University, established in 1845, is an independent liberal arts institution that blends the hallmarks of the liberal arts with an emphasis on professional and career preparation through undergraduate and graduate degree programs. There is 1 undergraduate school and 2 graduate schools. In addition to regional accreditation, BW has baccalaureate program accreditation with NASM, NCATE, CAATE, CCNE, and ARC-PA (Provisional). The 150-acre campus is in a suburban area 14 miles southwest of Cleveland, OH. Including any residence halls, there are 79 buildings.

STUDENT LIFE: 79% of undergraduates are from Ohio. Others are from 40 states, 31 foreign countries, and Canada. 86% are from public schools. 77% are White; 5% Hispanic; 5% two or more races; 2% Asian American; 10% African American; 1% Foreign. 45% are Protestant; 32% Catholic; 15% Baha'i, Buddhist, Hindu, Mormon, Muslim, Orthodox, and Unitarian. **Female To Male Ratio:** 1.3:1. The average age of freshmen is 18; all undergraduates, 20. 20% do not continue beyond their first year; 94% remain to graduate. **Housing:** 1880 students can be accommodated in college housing, which includes coed dorms and on-campus apartments. In addition, there are honors houses, special-interest houses, fraternity houses, sorority houses, student-directed learning comm, themed housing, special housing-disabled and international students. On-campus housing is available on a first-come, first-served basis, and a lottery system for upperclassmen. 62% of students live on campus; of those, 50% remain on campus on weekends. All students may keep cars.

FACULTY/CLASSROOMS: 50% of faculty are male; 50% are female. 92% teach undergraduates. No introductory courses are taught by graduate students. The average class size in an introductory lecture is 19; in a laboratory is 14; and in a regular course is 18.

PROGRAMS OF STUDY: BW confers B.A., B.F.A., B.S., B.M., B.M.E, B.S.Ed., and B.S.N degrees. Master's degrees are also awarded. Bachelor's degrees are awarded in BIOLOGICAL SCIENCE (biology/biological science and neurosciences), BUSINESS (accounting, business administration and management, entrepreneurial studies, finance, human resources, international business, international security/conflict resolution management, marketing, organizational leadership and management, sports management, and sustainable management), COMMUNICATIONS AND THE ARTS (acting, applied music, arts administration/management, broadcasting, communication studies, creative writing, English, film, television and digital media, French, German, graphic design & media, instrumental performance, keyboard - piano concentration, music, music composition, music history and appreciation, music performance, music theory and composition, musical theater, public relations, Spanish, studio art, theatre acting, theater design, theater management, and voice), COMPUTER AND PHYSICAL SCIENCE (chemistry, computer science, computer security and information assurance, digital arts/technology, mathematics, mathematics – economics, physics, software engineering, and systems analysis), EDUCATION (art education, athletic training, early childhood education, health and physical education, middle school education, music education, physical education, science education, and specific learning disabilities), ENGINEERING AND ENVIRONMENTAL DESIGN (engineering and preengineering), HEALTH PROFESSIONS (exercise science, health care administration, health promotion, music therapy, nursing, predentistry, premedicine, prepharmacy, prephysical therapy, preveterinary science, and public health), SOCIAL SCIENCE (communication sciences & disorders, criminal justice, economics, history, industrial and organizational psychology, interdisciplinary studies, international studies, philosophy, political science/government, psychology, public administration, public history/archives, religion, and sociology). biology, psychology, business administration have the largest enrollments.

ACTIVITIES: 13% of men belong to 6 national fraternities; 24% of women belong to 5 national sororities. There are 130 groups on campus, including art, band, cheerleading, choir, chorale, chorus, computers, dance, drama, drill team, environmental, ethnic, film, forensics, honors, international, jazz band, LGBT, literary magazine, marching band, musical theater, newspaper, opera, orchestra, pep band, political, professional, radio and TV, religious, social, social service, student government, symphony, and yearbook. Popular campus events include Culture Night, Dance Marathon and April Reign. **Sports:** There are 12 intercollegiate sports for men and 11 for women, and 28 intramural sports for men and 28 for women. Facilities include a stadium with track, a gym, athletic field, baseball fields, tennis complex. The recreation center houses a track, swimming pool, dance studio, athletic training/rehab facility, wrestling/gymnastics/weight rooms, fitness complex, and facilities for basketball, racquetball, tennis, volleyball, and an area for fitness and wellness programs/activities. **Graduates:** From July 1, 2015 to June 30, 2016, 714 bachelor's degrees were awarded. The most popular majors were accounting (6%), business administration (6%), and psychology (5%). 146 companies recruited on campus in 2015-2016. In an average class, 2% graduate in 3 years or less, 54% graduate in 4 years or less, 66% graduate in 5 years or less, and 67% graduate in 6 years or less. Of the 2015 graduating class, 15% were enrolled in graduate school within 6 months of graduation, and 69% were employed.

SERVICES: Counseling and information services are available, as is tutoring in most subjects. There is also a reader service for the blind, and remedial math, reading, and writing. Software is available for students who have difficulty reading or with visual impairments, in addition to access to Learning Ally & Bookshare which both come with a downloadable reader **Library/Resources:** The 3 libraries contain 568,338 volumes, 3,000 microform items, 62,534 audio/video tapes/CDs/DVDs, and subscribe to 60,730 periodicals including electronic. Computerized library services include interlibrary loans, database searching, Internet access, and Wi-Fi capability. Special learning facilities include an art gallery, radio station, a neuroscience lab, and an observatory. **Physically Challenged Students:** 80% of the campus is accessible. Facilities include wheelchair ramps, elevators, special parking, specially equipped restrooms, special class scheduling, lowered telephones, special housing. **Special:** Special academic programs include internships that can qualify for credit, work-study programs and study abroad. There is cross-registration with 7 participating institutions within the Greater Cleveland area, as well as a 3-2 program in social work with Case Western Reserve University, 3-2 master's program in accounting, human resources, computer science/information systems, 3-2 program in engineering with Case Western Reserve and Columbia University. BW also offers the Consortium for Music Therapy, accelerated Bachelor of Science in Nursing degree, a Bachelor of Fine Arts in Acting, Associate to Bachelor (A2BW) accelerated transfer programs, interdisciplinary/student designed majors & minors, credit for life, military, work experience, and pass/fail options. The Adult, Transfer and Military Services Program offers degrees in evening and weekend formats. Pre-professional programs are available in dentistry, law, medicine, pharmacy, and veterinary. Study abroad in Argentina, Australia, Austria, China, Ecuador, England, France, Germany, Ghana, Guatemala, India, Ireland, Italy, Japan, Mexico, Morocco, Scotland, South Korea, Spain, Sweden, Switzerland and Zambia. There are 26 national honor societies and a freshman honors program. **Visiting:** There are regularly scheduled orientations for prospective students, student visits include an interview, a tour, and classroom visits. There are guides for informal visits, visitors may sit in on classes, and stay overnight. To schedule a visit, contact Libby Alsayegh at (440) 826-2222. **Campus Safety and Security:** Measures include 24-hour foot and vehicle patrol, emergency notification system, self-defense education, security escort services, emergency telephones, lighted pathways/sidewalks, controlled access to dorms/residences, and more than 100 exterior/interior security cameras.

REQUIREMENTS: The SAT or ACT is recommended. Applicants must be graduates of an accredited secondary school or have earned a GED. Applicants must have completed 16 academic credits, including 4 in English, 3 each in math, natural science, and social science, 2 in a foreign language; however, alternative distributions are considered. A teacher's recommendation is required. BW does not require students to submit test scores for admission consideration. BW requires applicants to be in the upper 50% of their class. A GPA of 2.8 is required. AP and CLEP credits are accepted. Important factors in the admissions decision are leadership record, advanced placement or honors courses, and extracurricular activities record. Traditional undergraduate baccalaureate programs at Baldwin Wallace University require at least 124 semester hours (conservatory programs may require additional hours) and at least a 2.000 GPA. The Bachelor of Arts and Sciences core requirements include coursework in the following areas: foundation courses in Mathematics, English Composition, and First-Year Experience (FYE 100), perspectives courses in Humanities, Interdisciplinary, Social Sciences and Natural Sciences, wellness courses in Health and Physical Education, extension courses in writing and quantitative reasoning, International coursework or experiences, and coursework in Diversity Studies. Completion of a minor adds depth in a particular area of study, to balance the breadth provided by distribution requirements across the Liberal Arts and Sciences. Comprehensive exams are required in some majors. **Procedure:** Freshmen are admitted in the fall and spring. Entrance exams should be taken during junior year or early in senior year. There are deferred admissions and rolling admissions plans. Application deadlines are open. Applications are accepted on-line. **Transfer Students:** 243 transfer students enrolled in 2015-2016. Students must be in good academic and social standing at prior institution(s). 45 of 124 credits required for the bachelor's degree must be completed at BW. **International Students:** There are 45 international students enrolled. The school actively recruits these students. They must take the TOEFL with a minimum score of 550 on the paper-based TOEFL (PBT) or 79 on the Internet-based version (iBT) and the college's own test, IELTS, LADO ESL Level 10 Completion. They must also take the SAT or ACT, scoring SAT critical reading - 540; ACT English - 24, can be used to replace TOEFL or IELTS if score is strong.

ADMISSIONS: 60% of the 2016-2017 applicants were accepted. The SAT scores for the 2016-2017 freshman class were: Critical Reading-- 32% below 500, 44% between 500 and 599, 19% between 600 and 699, and 5% between 700 and 800. Math-- 32% below 500, 47% between 500 and 599, 18% between 600 and 699, and 3% between 700 and 800. Writing-- 43% below 500, 41% between 500 and 599, 13% between 600 and 699, and 3% between 700 and 800. The ACT scores were 8% between 12 and 17, 38% between 18 and 23, 46% between 24 and 29, and 8% above 30. 39% of the current freshmen were in the top fifth of their class; 70% were in the top two fifths. 13 freshmen graduated first in their class. **Admissions Contact:** Scott Schulz, VP for Enrollment Management. Email: *saschulz@bw.edu* Web: *www.bw.edu*

FINANCIAL AID: In 2016-2017, 100% of all full-time freshmen and 96% of continuing full-time students received some form of financial aid. 83% of all full-time freshmen and 74% of continuing full-time students received need-based aid. The average freshman award was $28,019. Need-based scholarships or need-based grants averaged $21,561 ($30,776 maximum); need-based self-help aid (loans and jobs) averaged $6,653 ($13,400 maximum); and other non-need-based awards and non-need-based scholarships averaged $14,125 ($30,776 maximum). 31% of undergraduate students work part-time. Average annual earnings from campus work are $1352. The average financial indebtedness of the 2016 graduate was $27,275. The FAFSA code is 003014. The priority date for freshman financial aid applications for fall entry is January 1. The filing deadline for fall entry is September 1.

BLUFFTON UNIVERSITY — B-2

www.bluffton.edu

Bluffton, OH 45817	**(419) 358-3257** **(800) 488-3257**
Fax: (419) 358-3232	**Email: admissions@bluffton.edu**
Full-time: 377 men, 351 women	**Faculty:** 56
Part-time: 57 men, 80 women	**Ph.D.s:** 78%
Graduate: 23 men, 64 women	**Student/Faculty:** 13 to 1
Year: semesters, summer session	**Tuition:** $30,762
Room & Board: $10,188	**Freshman Class:** 1480 applied, 733 accepted, 208 enrolled
SAT: required **ACT:** 22	**CEEB CODE:** 1067
Application Deadline: August 15	**COMPETITIVE**

Bluffton University is a small liberal arts university with more than 40 undergraduate programs, adult degree-completion programs and master's degrees. We bring together academic quality with deep personal caring for each of our students. We bring together academic preparation with essential career/interpersonal skill training for life-success for our graduates. We bring together modest tuition with outstanding financial aid for a truly affordable private education. There is 1 undergraduate school and 1 graduate school. In addition to regional accreditation, Bluffton has baccalaureate program accreditation with ADA, CSWE, NASM, and NCATE. The 65-acre campus is in a small town Off I 75 60 miles south of Toledo, Ohio and 75 miles north of Dayton, Ohio. Including any residence halls, there are 28 buildings.

STUDENT LIFE: 87% of undergraduates are from Ohio. Others are from 18 states, 10 foreign countries, and Canada. 91% are from public schools. 83% are White; 6% African American; 4% Hispanic; 4% two or more races; 1% Asian American; 1% Foreign; 1% race unknown. 47% are Protestant; 41% unknown religion; 12% Catholic. **Female To Male Ratio:** 1.1:1. The average age of freshmen is 19; all undergraduates, 22. 31% do not continue beyond their first year; 54% remain to graduate. **Housing:** 758 students can be accommodated in college housing, which includes coed dorms, on-campus apartments. In addition, there are special-interest houses. All full-time students must live in residence halls unless commuting from the home of their parents. On-campus housing is guaranteed for all 4 years. 85% of students live on campus; of those, 60% remain on campus on weekends. All students may keep cars. Alcohol is not permitted.

FACULTY/CLASSROOMS: 56% of faculty are male; 44% are female. 97% teach undergraduates. No introductory courses are taught by graduate students. The average class size in an introductory lecture is 23; in a laboratory is 9; and in a regular course is 16.

PROGRAMS OF STUDY: Bluffton confers B.A. degrees. Master's degrees are also awarded. Bachelor's degrees are awarded in BIOLOGI-

CAL SCIENCE (biology/biological science), BUSINESS (accounting, business administration and management, human resources, information & communication technology, marketing/retailing/merchandising, organizational leadership and management, recreational facilities management, and sports management), COMMUNICATIONS AND THE ARTS (art, broadcasting, communications, creative writing, English, graphic design & media, music, public relations, and Spanish), COMPUTER AND PHYSICAL SCIENCE (chemistry, computer science, mathematics, physical sciences, and physics), EDUCATION (early childhood education, health information management, home economics education, middle school education, music education, physical education, and special education), HEALTH PROFESSIONS (nursing, premedicine, public health, and speech pathology/audiology), SOCIAL SCIENCE (biblical studies, child psychology/development, criminal justice, early childhood studies, economics, family/consumer studies, food science, history, ministries, psychology, social science, social studies, social work, sociology, and youth ministry). Social work, education, and business have the largest enrollments.

ACTIVITIES: There are no fraternities or sororities. There are 40 groups on campus, including youth ministries, student senate, art, band, cheerleading, choir, chorale, chorus, dance, drama, ethnic, honors, international, jazz band, LGBT, literary magazine, multicultural student organization, musical theater, newspaper, pep band, political, professional, radio and TV, religious, social, social service, and student government. Popular campus events include International Week, Spiritual Emphasis Weeks, and Artist Series. **Sports:** There are 7 intercollegiate sports for men and 7 for women, and 6 intramural sports for men and 6 for women. Facilities include a recreation and fitness center that includes a basketball/volleyball court, an athletic complex with baseball, softball, soccer, football stadium, and indoor sports and intramurals. **Graduates:** From July 1, 2015 to June 30, 2016, 240 bachelor's degrees were awarded. The most popular majors were business/marketing (30%), education (15%), and social work (10%). 31 companies recruited on campus in 2015-2016. In an average class, 2% graduate in 3 years or less, 48% graduate in 4 years or less, 53% graduate in 5 years or less, and 54% graduate in 6 years or less. Of the 2015 graduating class, 16% were enrolled in graduate school within 6 months of graduation, and 79% were employed.

SERVICES: Counseling and information services are available, as is tutoring in every subject. There is also a reader service for the blind, and remedial math, reading, and writing. Tutoring is available for most students, as are classes at the student's request and/or faculty designation. **Library/Resources:** The library contains 381,832 volumes, 83,822 microform items, 12,567 audio/video tapes/CDs/DVDs, and subscribes to 89,472 periodicals including electronic. Computerized library services include interlibrary loans, database searching, Internet access, and Wi-Fi capability. Special learning facilities include an art gallery, radio station, the Lion and Lamb Peace Arts Center, and a nature preserve. **Physically Challenged Students:** 75% of the campus is accessible. Facilities include wheelchair ramps, elevators, special parking, specially equipped restrooms, special class scheduling, lowered drinking fountains, lowered telephones, and special computers for visually impaired students. **Special:** Special arrangements include internships in business, recreation, social work, and education, a Washington semester through the Council for Christian Colleges and Universities, and study abroad. Student-designed majors and independent study are possible, as is credit for prior learning and for learning in voluntary service. There is an accelerated degree program in organizational management. Nondegree study and pass/fail options are offered. There are 2 national honor societies, a freshman honors program, and 14 departmental honors programs. **Visiting:** There are regularly scheduled orientations for prospective students, Personal visits are scheduled according to students' specific interests and may include obsesrving a class, visit with faculty and a tour of campus. Group visits are scheduled regularly throughout the year, and are listed on website with online registration. There are also guides for informal visits, visitors may sit in on classes, and stay overnight. To schedule a visit, contact Deanna Haan at (800) 488-3257. **Campus Safety and Security:** Measures include an emergency notification system, self-defense education, emergency telephones, lighted pathways/sidewalks, controlled access to dorms/residences, and village police cruisers who regularly patrol the campus during night hours. There are also 2 night security officers who communicate directly with village police and routinely patrol campus at night.

REQUIREMENTS: To be considered for regular admission to Bluffton University as an undergraduate student, you need to have earned a score of 920 on the SAT (critical reading plus math) or 19 on the ACT. Other admissions requirements include graduation from an accredited secondary school with a 2.3 GPA or class rank above 50%. Recommended courses include 4 units of English and 3 units each of math, science, social studies, and a foreign language. The GED is accepted. A personal campus visit and an interview are strongly recommended. Music students must audition and art students submit a portfolio. Bluffton requires applicants to be in the upper 50% of their class. AP and CLEP credits are accepted. Important factors in the admissions decision are leadership record, recommendations by school officials, and extracurricular activities record. To graduate, students must complete 124 semester hours with 40 to 60 in the major and have a minimum GPA of 2.0. The general education requirements must be met, and satisfactory achievement in departmental senior comprehensives demonstrated. Distribution requirements are approximately one third for general education requirements, including 6 hours of religion, and one third to one half for the major. **Procedure:** Freshmen are admitted in the fall and spring. Entrance exams should be taken in the spring of the junior year or fall of the senior year. There are deferred admissions and rolling admissions plans. Applications should be filed by August 15 for fall entry. Application fees are waived if application is completed online. **Transfer Students:** 29 transfer students enrolled in 2015-2016. Transfer students must have a minimum college GPA of 2.0, meet eligibility criteria from previous institutions, and have met their financial obligations at the former institution. A signed transfer recommendation must be submitted from each college attended. 30 of 124 credits required for the bachelor's degree must be completed at Bluffton. **International Students:** There are 11 international students enrolled. The school actively recruits these students. They must take the TOEFL with a minimum score of 500 on the paper-based TOEFL (PBT) or 64 on the Internet-based version (iBT). They must also take the SAT, scoring 920, and the college's own entrance exam. The SAT can substitute for the TOEFL.

ADMISSIONS: 50% of the 2016-2017 applicants were accepted. The ACT scores were 17% between 12 and 17, 57% between 18 and 23, 24% between 24 and 29, and 2% above 30. 30% of the current freshmen were in the top fifth of their class; 50% were in the top two fifths. 7 freshmen graduated first in their class. **Admissions Contact:** Robin Hopkins, Director of Undergraduate Admissions. Email: *admissions@bluffton.edu* Web: *www.bluffton.edu*

FINANCIAL AID: In 2016-2017, 88% of all full-time freshmen and 86% of continuing full-time students received some form of financial aid. 80% of all full-time freshmen and 78% of continuing full-time students received need-based aid. The average freshman award was $27,236. Need-based scholarships or need-based grants averaged $221,909 ($29,575 maximum); need-based self-help aid (loans and jobs) averaged $5,859 ($6,590 maximum); and other non-need-based awards and non-need-based scholarships averaged $15,631 ($30,312 maximum). 65% of undergraduate students work part-time. Average annual earnings from campus work are $2600. The average financial indebtedness of the 2016 graduate was $38,701. The FAFSA code is 003016. The priority date for freshman financial aid applications for fall entry is May 1. The filing deadline for fall entry is October 1.

BOWLING GREEN STATE UNIVERSITY B-1

www.bgsu.edu

Bowling Green, OH 43403	**(419) 372-2478** **(866) 246-6732**
Fax: (419) 372-6955	**Email: choosebgsu@bgsu.edu**
Full-time: 5692 men, 7492 women	**Faculty:** 655; I, --$
Part-time: 829 men, 839 women	**Ph.D.s:** 79%
Graduate: 1087 men, 1705 women	**Student/Faculty:** 20 to 1
Year: semesters, summer session	**Tuition:** $11,057 ($18,593)
Room & Board: $8690	**Freshman Class:** 14891 applied, 10957 accepted, 3545 enrolled
SAT CR/M/W: 520/520/490 **ACT:** 22	**CEEB CODE:** 1069
Application Deadline: July 15	**COMPETITIVE**

Bowling Green State University, founded in 1910, is a public institution with 7 undergraduate schools and 1 graduate school. In addition to regional accreditation, BGSU has baccalaureate program accreditation with AACSB, ACCE, ACEJMC, ADA, CSWE, NASAD, NASM, NCATE, NRPA, ACS, and NAST. The 1338-acre campus is in a small town 23 miles south of Toledo, adjacent to Interstate 75. Including any residence halls, there are 119 buildings.

STUDENT LIFE: 86% of undergraduates are from Ohio. Others are from 51 states, 85 foreign countries, and Canada. 8% are African American; 75% White; 5% Foreign; 4% Hispanic; 3% two or more races; 3% race unknown; 1% Asian American. **Female To Male Ratio:** 1.3:1. The average age of freshmen is 19; all undergraduates, 21. 24% do not continue beyond their first year; 55% remain to graduate. **Housing:** 6705 students can be accommodated in college housing, which includes single-sex and coed dorms and on-campus apartments. In addition, there are honors houses, language houses, special-interest houses, fraternity houses, sorority houses, no-alcohol wings, residential/theme communities, and gender-neutral housing. 58% of students commute. All students may keep cars.

FACULTY/CLASSROOMS: 48% of faculty are male; 52% are female. No introductory courses are taught by graduate students. The average class size in an introductory lecture is 25; in a laboratory is 17; and in a regular course is 24.

PROGRAMS OF STUDY: BGSU confers B.A., B.A.C., B.F.A., B.L.S., B.S., B.S.J., B.S.F.A., B.S.BA., B.S.Econ., B.S.AMPD., B.S.Diet., B.S.Ed., B.S.HDFS, B.S.ID., B.S.NS., B.A.HS., B.S.Comm., B.S.CJ., B.S.Gero., B.S.MLS., B.S.Nur., B.S.SW., B.Mus., B.M.Art., B.S.Tech., B.S.Arch., B.S.C.M., B.S.ECET. and B.S.ET. degrees. Master's and doctoral degrees are also awarded. Bachelor's degrees are awarded in AGRICULTURE (environmental studies), BIOLOGICAL SCIENCE (avian sciences, life science, neurosciences, and nutrition), BUSINESS (accounting, business administration and management, management information systems, marketing, sports management, and tourism), COMMUNICATIONS AND THE ARTS (apparel design, art history, art, classics, communications, creative writing, dance, design, English, English literature, film arts, fine arts, foreign language, French, German, graphic design, instrumental performance, jazz, journalism, Latin, music, music history and appreciation, music performance, music theory and composition, performing arts, romance languages and literature, Russian, Spanish, technical communication, telecommunications, theatre studies, and visual and performing arts), COMPUTER AND PHYSICAL SCIENCE (chemistry, computer science, digital arts/technology, earth science, geology, mathematics, physics, science, and statistics), EDUCATION (art education, athletic training, business education, early childhood education, education, education of the deaf and hearing impaired, education of the multiply handicapped, elementary education, foreign languages education, learner designed area of study, mathematics education, middle school education, music education, physical education, science education, secondary education, social science education, special education, and technical education), ENGINEERING AND ENVIRONMENTAL DESIGN (construction management, electrical and computer engineering, electrical/electronics engineering technology, engineering technology, environmental science, and interior design), HEALTH PROFESSIONS (biology, exercise science, health science, nursing, and public health), SOCIAL SCIENCE (African studies, American studies, architectural studies, Asian/Oriental studies, criminal justice, dietetics, economics, ethnic studies, family/consumer studies, fire services administration, geography, gerontology, history, human development, interdisciplinary studies, international studies, liberal arts/general studies, philosophy, political science/government, psychology, social science, social work, sociology, and women's studies). Biology, middle childhood education, and adolescence to young adult education have the largest enrollments.

ACTIVITIES: 12% of men belong to 22 national fraternities; 11% of women belong to 17 national sororities. There are 345 groups on campus, including art, band, cheerleading, chess, choir, chorale, chorus, communications, computers, dance, debate, drama, drill team, environmental, ethnic, film, honors, international, jazz band, LGBT, literary magazine, marching band, musical theater, newspaper, opera, pep band, photography, political, professional, radio and TV, religious, social, social service, student government, symphony, and yearbook. Popular campus events include Homecoming, Campus Fest, Move-in Weekend, and Week of Welcome. **Sports:** There are 7 intercollegiate sports for men and 11 for women, and 11 intramural sports for men and 11 for women. **Graduates:** From July 1, 2015 to June 30, 2016, 3057 bachelor's degrees were awarded. The most popular majors were individualized studies (4%), biology (4%), and psychology (4%). 1815 companies recruited on campus in 2015-2016. In an average class, 2% graduate in 3 years or less, 34% graduate in 4 years or less, 50% graduate in 5 years or less, and 53% graduate in 6 years or less.

SERVICES: Counseling and information services are available, as is tutoring in some subjects, such as writing, math and stats, and any subject that has been requested by students. There is also a reader service for the blind, and remedial math, reading, and writing. **Library/Resources:** The library contains 2.5 million volumes, 316,566 microform items, 361,922 audio/video tapes/CDs/DVDs, and subscribes to 12,326 periodicals including electronic. Computerized library services include interlibrary loans, database searching, Internet access, and Wi-Fi capability. Special learning facilities include an art gallery, planetarium, radio station, and TV station. **Physically Challenged Students:** 92% of the campus is accessible. Facilities include wheelchair ramps, elevators, special parking, specially equipped restrooms, special class scheduling, lowered drinking fountains, lowered telephones, and special housing. **Special:** Special academic programs include co-op programs in all majors with the National Student Exchange, internships, a Washington semester, work-study, and study abroad. Dual majors are available in all programs, and a B.A.-B.S. degree is offered in computer science, geology, math, psychology, statistics, scientific and technical communication, and individualized planned program. Student-designed majors, independent study, credit for experience, nondegree study, and pass/fail options are possible. There is a chapter of Phi Beta Kappa and a freshman honors program. **Visiting:** Regularly scheduled orientations are available for prospective students. There are guides for informal visits and visitors may sit in on classes. To schedule a visit, contact the Office of Admissions. **Campus Safety and Security:** Measures include 24-hour foot and vehicle patrol, emergency notification system, self-defense education, and security escort services. There are also shuttle buses, emergency telephones, lighted pathways/sidewalks, controlled access to dorms/residences, in-room safes, and campus 911.

REQUIREMENTS: The ACT is required. The SAT is recommended. AP and CLEP credits are accepted. Earn a minimum of 122 semester hours of credit and at least 30 credit hours must be BGSU courses, earn an accumulative grade point average of at least 2.0 ("C" average) for all coursework attempted, complete the BG Perspective requirements, have at least 40 hours of credit in courses numbered 3000 and above, satisfy all college requirements for a degree, and file an application for graduation. **Procedure:** Freshmen are admitted in the fall, spring, and summer. Entrance exams should be taken in the junior year. There are deferred admissions and rolling admissions plans. Applications should be filed by July 15 for fall entry; December 15 for spring entry; and May 15 for summer entry. The fall 2016 application fee was $45. Notifications are sent 8 1. Applications are accepted online. **Transfer Students:** 911 transfer students enrolled in 2015-2016. 30 of 122 credits required for the bachelor's degree must be completed at BGSU. **International Students:** There are 295 international students enrolled. The school actively recruits these students. They must take the TOEFL with a minimum score of 500 on the paper-based TOEFL (PBT) or 71 on the Internet-based version (iBT) or take the MELAB. SAT and ACT scores are considered if submitted.

ADMISSIONS: 74% of the 2016-2017 applicants were accepted. The SAT scores for the 2016-2017 freshman class were: Critical Reading-- 43% below 500, 37% between 500 and 599, 18% between 600 and 699, and 2% between 700 and 800. Math-- 38% below 500, 41% between 500 and 599, 20% between 600 and 699, and 1% between 700 and 800. Writing-- 51% below 500, 36% between 500 and 599, 11% between 600 and 699, and 2% between 700 and 800. The ACT scores were 6% between 12 and 17, 56% between 18 and 23, 33% between 24 and 29, and 5% above 30. 29% of the current freshmen were in the top fifth of their class; 58% were in the top two fifths. 41 freshmen graduated first in their class. **Admissions Contact:** Adrea Nicole Spoon, Director of Admissions. Email: *choosebgsu@bgsu.edu* Web: *www.bgsu.edu*

FINANCIAL AID: In 2016-2017, 95% of all full-time freshmen and 89% of continuing full-time students received some form of financial aid. 56% of all full-time freshmen and 54% of continuing full-time students received need-based aid. The average freshman award was $15,438. Need-based scholarships or need-based grants averaged $5,098 ($19,275 maximum); need-based self-help aid (loans and jobs) averaged $3,416 ($8,609 maximum); non-need-based athletic scholarships averaged $17,180 ($37,940 maximum); other non-need-based awards and non-need-based scholarships averaged $7,643 ($39,860 maximum); and $13,034 from other forms of aid. 15% of undergraduate students work part-time. Average annual earnings from campus work are $1952. The average financial indebtedness of the 2016 graduate was $30,328. BGSU is a member of CSS. The FAFSA code is 003018. Check with the school for current application deadlines.

CAPITAL UNIVERSITY C-3
www.capital.edu

Columbus, OH 43209	**(614) 236-6101** **(866) 544-6175**
Fax: (614) 236-6926	**Email: admission@capital.edu**
Full-time: 1007 men, 1504 women	**Faculty:** 137; IIA, av$
Part-time: 64 men, 143 women	**Ph.D.s:** 77%
Graduate: 323 men, 326 women	**Student/Faculty:** 16 to 1
Year: semesters, summer session	**Tuition:** $33,492
Room & Board: $9490	**Freshman Class:** 4287 applied, 2968 accepted, 613 enrolled
SAT CR/M/W: 537/548/537 **ACT:** 25	**CEEB CODE:** 1099
Application Deadline: May 1	**COMPETITIVE**

Capital University, established in 1830, is a private institution affiliated with the Evangelical Lutheran Church in America. Its undergraduate and graduate programs emphasize the liberal arts and sciences, music, and nursing along with professional studies such as business. There are 5 undergraduate schools and 3 graduate schools. In addition to regional accreditation, Cap has baccalaureate program accreditation with ACBSP, CSWE, NASM, NCATE, ABA, ACS, and CCNE. The 48-acre campus is in a suburban area 5 miles east of downtown Columbus. Including any residence halls, there are 24 buildings.

STUDENT LIFE: 90% of undergraduates are from Ohio. Others are from 38 states, 14 foreign countries, and Canada. 75% are White; 10% African American; 4% Hispanic; 4% two or more races; 3% race unknown; 2% Foreign; 1% Asian American; 1% American Indian/Alaska Native. 30% are Protestant; 20% Catholic; 14% claim no religious affiliation. **Female To Male Ratio:** 1.4:1. The average age of freshmen is 18; all undergraduates, 22. 25% do not continue beyond their first year; 59% remain to graduate. **Housing:** 1629 students can be accommodated in college housing, which includes coed dorms, on-campus apartments, off-campus apartments, honors houses, special-interest floors, substance-free floors, Greek organization floors, and a self-governing unit. On-campus housing is guaranteed for all 4 years and is available on a lottery system for upperclassmen. 59% of students live on campus; of those, 50% remain on campus on weekends. All students may keep cars.

FACULTY/CLASSROOMS: 46% of faculty are male; 54% are female. 87% teach undergraduates. No introductory courses are taught by graduate students. The average class size in an introductory lecture is 20; in a laboratory is 12; and in a regular course is 17.

PROGRAMS OF STUDY: Cap confers B.A., B.M., B.S.N. and B.S.W. degrees. Master's and doctoral degrees are also awarded. Bachelor's degrees are awarded in BIOLOGICAL SCIENCE (biochemistry and biology/biological science), BUSINESS (accounting and business administration and management), COMMUNICATIONS AND THE ARTS (art, communications, creative writing, dramatic arts, English, French, music, public relations, Spanish, speech/debate/rhetoric, and theatre studies), COMPUTER AND PHYSICAL SCIENCE (chemistry, computer science, and mathematics), EDUCATION (art education, athletic training, elementary education, middle school education, physical education, and secondary education), ENGINEERING AND ENVIRONMENTAL DESIGN (environmental science), HEALTH PROFESSIONS (art therapy, exercise science, nursing, predentistry, premedicine, and sports medicine), SOCIAL SCIENCE (behavioral science, criminal justice, economics, history, international relations, philosophy, physical fitness/movement, political science/government, prelaw, psychology, religion, social work, and sociology). Nursing, business, and education have the largest enrollments.

ACTIVITIES: 2% of men belong to 5 local and 5 national fraternities; 3% of women belong to 6 local and 6 national sororities. There are 63 groups on campus, including art, band, cheerleading, choir, chorale, chorus, communications, dance, debate, drama, environmental, ethnic, honors, international, jazz band, LGBT, literary magazine, musical theater, newspaper, opera, orchestra, political, professional, radio and TV, religious, social, social service, student government, and symphony. Popular campus events include Symposium on Undergraduate Scholarship, Honors Convocation, Greek Week, Martin Luther King Jr. Day of Learning, and Kids and Sibs Weekend. **Sports:** There are 10 intercollegiate sports for men and 10 for women, and 9 intramural sports for men and 9 for women. Facilities include a football stadium, a gym, tennis courts, and weight and game rooms. The recreation center offers bowling, billiards, and other game facilities. **Graduates:** From July 1, 2015 to June 30, 2016, 580 bachelor's degrees were awarded. The most popular majors were business (16%), nursing (15%), and education (13%). 27 companies recruited on campus in 2015-2016. In an average class, 51% graduate in 4 years or less, 58% graduate in 5 years or less, and 59% graduate in 6 years or less. Of the 2015 graduating class, 20% were enrolled in graduate school within 6 months of graduation, and 69% were employed.

SERVICES: Counseling and information services are available, as is tutoring in most subjects, and remedial math and writing. **Library/Resources:** The library contains 225,644 volumes, 148,096 microform items, 103,078 audio/video tapes/CDs/DVDs, and subscribes to 156,739 periodicals including electronic. Computerized library services include interlibrary loans, database searching, Internet access, and Wi-Fi capability. Special learning facilities include an art gallery, radio station, and TV station. **Physically Challenged Students:** All of the campus is accessible. Facilities include wheelchair ramps, elevators, special parking, specially equipped restrooms, and special housing. **Special:** Special academic programs include cross-registration with the Higher Education Council of Columbus, semester internships in most majors, and a Washington semester. Study abroad in 21 countries on 5 continents includes opportunities in Jamaica and at the Kodaly Institute of Music in Hungary. Also possible are a general studies degree and student-designed majors. A dual degree in engineering is offered with Case Western Reserve University and Washington University in St. Louis. Credit for life, military, and work experience may be granted, and nondegree study and pass/fail options are offered. There are 17 national honor societies and a freshman honors program. **Visiting:** There are regularly scheduled orientations for prospective students, including an interview with a counselor and a campus tour. There are guides for informal visits, visitors may sit in on classes, and stay overnight. To schedule a visit, contact the Admissions Office. **Campus Safety and Security:** Measures include 24-hour foot and vehicle patrol, emergency notification system, self-defense education, and security escort services. There are also shuttle buses, emergency telephones, lighted pathways/sidewalks, and controlled access to dorms/residences.

REQUIREMENTS: The SAT or ACT is required. Admissions requirements include graduation from an accredited secondary school with 16 academic credits, including 4 units of English, 3 each of math, science, and social science, 2 units of a foreign language, and 1 of electives; nursing applicants need chemistry. The GED is accepted. High school students must submit recommendations from their guidance counselor. An interview is recommended. Students must audition for entry to the Conservatory of Music. A GPA of 2.6 is required. AP and CLEP credits are accepted. Important factors in the admissions decision are advanced placement or honors courses, recommendations by school officials, and evidence of special talent. To graduate, all students must complete at least 124 semester hours, with a varying number of hours in the major, and maintain a minimum 2.0 GPA. The university core, 36 semester hours, must be followed in an ordered sequence throughout the 4 years; considered an assessment program, which includes specific courses in reading and writing, communication, health, art, science, social science, the humanities, ethics, and religion. **Procedure:** Freshmen are admitted in the fall, spring, and summer. Entrance exams should be taken by December of the senior year. There are deferred admissions and rolling admissions plans. Applications should be filed by May 1 for fall entry, along with a $25 fee. Notifications are sent September 30. Applications are accepted online. **Transfer Students:** 85 transfer students enrolled in 2015-2016. Transfer students must have a minimum college GPA of 2.25. The SAT or ACT is recommended, as is an interview. 30 of 124 credits required for the bachelor's degree must be completed at Cap. **International Students:** There are 42 international students enrolled. The school actively recruits these students. They must take the TOEFL with a minimum score of 500 on the paper-based TOEFL (PBT) or 61 on the Internet-based version (iBT).

ADMISSIONS: The SAT scores for the 2016-2017 freshman class were: Critical Reading-- 29% below 500, 43% between 500 and 599, 24% between 600 and 699, and 4% between 700 and 800. Math-- 34% below 500, 35% between 500 and 599, 27% between 600 and 699, and 4% between 700 and 800. Writing-- 37% below 500, 48% between 500 and 599, and 15% between 600 and 699. The ACT scores were 3% between 12 and 17, 35% between 18 and 23, 47% between 24 and 29, and 15% above 30. 37% of the current freshmen were in the top fifth of their class; 67% were in the top two fifths. 13 freshmen graduated first in their class. **Admissions Contact:** Sara Thompson, Interim Director of Admission. Email: *admission@capital.edu* Web: *www.capital.edu*

FINANCIAL AID: In 2016-2017, 99% of all full-time freshmen and 93% of continuing full-time students received some form of financial aid. 76% of all full-time freshmen and 75% of continuing full-time students received need-based aid. The average freshman award was $25,942. 33% of undergraduate students work part-time. Average annual earnings from campus work are $3400. The average financial indebtedness of the 2016 graduate was $32,496. The FAFSA code is 003023. The priority date for freshman financial aid applications for fall entry is February 28.

CASE WESTERN RESERVE UNIVERSITY D-1

www.case.edu

Cleveland, OH 44106	(216) 368-4450
Fax: (216) 368-5111	Email: admission@case.edu
Full-time: 2744 men, 2246 women	Faculty: 614; I, +$
Part-time: 84 men, 78 women	Ph.D.s: 91%
Graduate: 2934 men, 3578 women	Student/Faculty: 11 to 1
Year: semesters, summer session	Tuition: $46,006
Room & Board: $14,298	Freshman Class: 23115 applied, 8192 accepted, 1264 enrolled
SAT CR/M/W: 670/740/670 ACT: 32	CEEB CODE: 1105
Application Deadline: January 15	MOST COMPETITIVE

Case Western Reserve University, founded in 1826, is a private institution offering undergraduate, graduate, and professional programs in arts and sciences, dentistry, engineering, law, management, medicine, nursing, and social work. There are 4 undergraduate schools and 8 graduate schools. In addition to regional accreditation, CWRU has baccalaureate program accreditation with AACSB, ABET, CSAB, NASM, TEAC, and CCNC. The 267-acre campus is in an urban area 4 miles east of downtown Cleveland, OH. Including any residence halls, there are 187 buildings.

STUDENT LIFE: 60% of undergraduates are from out of state, mostly the Middle Atlantic. Students are from 47 states, 39 foreign countries, and Canada. 70% are from public schools. 6% are Hispanic; 50% White; 5% two or more races; 4% African American; 3% race unknown; 20% Asian American; 12% Foreign. **Female To Male Ratio:** 1.0:1. The average age of freshmen is 18; all undergraduates, 20. 8% do not continue beyond their first year; 82% remain to graduate. **Housing:** 4266 students can be accommodated in college housing, which includes coed dorms, on-campus apartments, special-interest houses, fraternity houses, sorority houses, recovery house, and residential colleges for first year students. On-campus housing is guaranteed for the freshman year only, and available on a first-come, first-served basis, and is available on a lottery system for upperclassmen. 80% of students live on campus; of those, 77% remain on campus on weekends. All students may keep cars.

FACULTY/CLASSROOMS: 57% of faculty are male; 43% are female. 75% teach undergraduates, 75% do research, and 75% do both. Graduate students teach 5% of introductory courses. The average class size in an introductory lecture is 35; in a laboratory is 23; and in a regular course is 29.

PROGRAMS OF STUDY: CWRU confers B.A., B.S., B.S.E., B.S. Management, and B.S.N. degrees. Master's and doctoral degrees are also awarded. Bachelor's degrees are awarded in BIOLOGICAL SCIENCE (biochemistry, biology/biological science, evolutionary biology, and nutrition), BUSINESS (accounting, business administration and management, finance, and marketing management), COMMUNICATIONS AND THE ARTS (art history, classics, comparative literature, dance, dramatic arts, English, French, German, music, Spanish, and theatre arts), COMPUTER AND PHYSICAL SCIENCE (applied mathematics, astronomy, chemistry, chemistry/chemical biology, computer science, environmental geology, geology, mathematics, natural sciences, physics, polymer science, and statistics), EDUCATION (art education, Asian studies, education, and music education), ENGINEERING AND ENVIRONMENTAL DESIGN (aerospace engineering, biomedical engineering, chemical engineering, civil engineering, computer engineering, electrical/electronics engineering, engineering, engineering physics, environmental science, materials science, mechanical engineering, and systems engineering), HEALTH PROFESSIONS (nursing and speech pathology/audiology), SOCIAL SCIENCE (American studies, anthropology, cognitive science, dietetics, economics, French studies, German area studies, gerontology, history, history of science, international studies, Japanese studies, philosophy, political science/government, psychology, religion, sociology, systems science, and women & gender studies). Engineering, biology, and management are the strongest academically. Engineering, nursing, and biology have the largest enrollments.

ACTIVITIES: 31% of men belong to 18 national fraternities; 39% of women belong to 9 national sororities. There are 218 groups on campus, including symphonic winds ensemble and percussion ensemble, art, band, cheerleading, chess, choir, chorale, chorus, communications, computers, dance, debate, drama, environmental, ethnic, film, honors, international, jazz band, LGBT, literary magazine, marching band, musical theater, newspaper, orchestra, pep band, photography, political, professional, radio, religious, social, social service, student government, symphony, and yearbook. Popular campus events include Hudson Relays, Relay-for-Life, Thwing Study Over, Snow Ball Semi-Formal, and Springfest. **Sports:** There are 10 intercollegiate sports for men and 9 for women, and 20 intramural sports for men and 20 for women. Facilities include a multipurpose courts for tennis, badminton, basketball and volleyball, an indoor running track, basketball and volleyball gym, two swimming pools, cardio room and weight rooms, racquetball and squash courts, rock climbing wall, aerobics room, auxiliary gym, and archery range. Outdoor facilities include football and soccer field/stadium, track, baseball/softball ballparks, and a throwing field. **Graduates:** From July 1, 2015 to June 30, 2016, 1137 bachelor's degrees were awarded. The most popular majors were biology (9%), biomedical engineering (9%), and mechanical engineering (8%). In an average class, 2% graduate in 3 years or less, 65% graduate in 4 years or less, 80% graduate in 5 years or less, and 82% graduate in 6 years or less.

SERVICES: Counseling and information services are available, as is tutoring in every subject, and a reader service for the blind. In addition, supplemental instruction is available in biology, chemistry, math, physics, as well as a writing resource center. **Library/Resources:** The 7 libraries contain 3.4 million volumes, 36,199 microform items, and 25,172 audio/video tapes/CDs/DVDs, and subscribe to 191,970 periodicals including electronic. Computerized library services include interlibrary loans, database searching, Internet access, and Wi-Fi capability. Special learning facilities include an art gallery, natural history museum, planetarium, and biology field station. **Physically Challenged Students:** 90% of the campus is accessible. Facilities include wheelchair ramps, elevators, special parking, specially equipped restrooms, special class scheduling, lowered drinking fountains, and lowered telephones. TDD, special testing arrangements, note-taking assistance, individualized academic counseling and planning, adaptive equipment, interpreters, and access to audiotaped text materials. **Special:** CWRU offers co-op programs with nearly 200 employers, and students may alternate classroom study with full-time employment. Cross-registration with four institutions in the Cleveland area is available, as well as internships in government, corporations, and nonprofit agencies. Students may participate in study abroad, a Washington semester, work-study programs, and accelerated-degree programs. B.A.-B.S. degrees, dual and student-designed majors, 3-2 engineering degrees, non-degree study, independent study, and pass/fail options are possible. There are extensive opportunities for undergraduates to work with faculty on research projects. Pre-professional Scholars Programs in medicine, dental medicine, social work, and law are available. Interdisciplinary majors, such as environmental geology, as well as intradisciplinary majors, such as nutritional biochemistry and metabolism, are available. There are 3 national honor societies, Phi Beta Kappa, and 16 departmental honors programs. **Visiting:** There are regularly scheduled orientations for prospective students. There are guides for informal visits, visitors may sit in on classes, and stay overnight. To schedule a visit, contact The Office of Undergraduate Admission. **Campus Safety and Security:** Measures include 24-hour foot and vehicle patrol, emergency notification system, self-defense education, and security escort services. There are also shuttle buses, emergency telephones, lighted pathways/sidewalks, controlled access to dorms/residences, property crime prevention programs, bicycle lock rental, vehicle ID etching, and equipment bolting.

REQUIREMENTS: For those students who take the ACT, the writing test is recommended. With the SAT, the essay should be taken. SAT subject tests are also recommended. Applicants must be graduates of an accredited secondary school. The GED is accepted. 16 high academic credits are required, including 4 years of English, 3 years of math (4 years for science, math, and engineering majors), 2 years of lab science (3 years for science and math majors and premedical students), 3 years of social studies (4 recommended for liberal arts students), and 2 years of foreign language (3 recommended for liberal arts students). Engineering, math, and science students should take the SAT Subject tests in math I/IC of IIC and physics and/or chemistry. An interview for is recommended for prospective students across all disciplines. AP credits are accepted. Important factors in the admissions decision are advanced placement or honors courses, recommendations by school officials, and extracurricular activities record. To graduate, students must complete a minimum of 120 semester hours, with at least 30 hours in the major, and maintain a minimum GPA of 2.0. Students must complete the SAGES (Seminar Approach to General Education and Scholarship) core curriculum and two semesters of physical education. **Procedure:** Freshmen are admitted in the fall, spring, and summer. Entrance exams should be taken by the fall of the senior year. There are early decision and deferred admissions plans. Early decision applications should be filed by November 1; regular applications, by January 15 for fall entry. Notification of early decision is sent December 15; regular decision, March 20. 143 early decision candidates were accepted for the 2016-2017 class. 4732 applicants were on the 2016 waiting list; 333 were admitted. Applications are accepted online. **Transfer Students:** 35 transfer students enrolled in 2015-2016. Transfer students should meet all high school requirements. Grades of C or better transfer for credit. 60 of 120 credits required for the bachelor's degree must be completed at CWRU. **International Students:** There are 631 international students enrolled. The school actively recruits these students. They must take the TOEFL with a minimum score of 577 on the paper-based TOEFL (PBT) or 90 on the Internet-based version (iBT), or take the International English Language Testing System. They must also take the SAT or ACT.

ADMISSIONS: 35% of the 2016-2017 applicants were accepted. The SAT scores for the 2016-2017 freshman class were: Critical Reading-- 1% below 500, 21% between 500 and 599, 42% between 600 and 699, and 36% between 700 and 800. Math-- 4% between 500 and 599, 27% between 600 and 699, and 69% between 700 and 800. Writing-- 1% below 500, 14% between 500 and 599, 51% between 600 and 699, and 34% between 700 and 800. The ACT scores were 1% between 18 and 23, 20% between 24 and 29, and 79% above 30. 90% of the current freshmen were in the top fifth of their class; 99% were in the top two fifths. 34 freshmen graduated first in their class. **Admissions Contact:** Robert McCullough, Director of Undergraduate Admissions. Email: *admission@case.edu* Web: *www.case.edu*

FINANCIAL AID: In 2016-2017, 85% of all full-time freshmen and 84% of continuing full-time students received some form of financial aid. 50% of all full-time freshmen received need-based aid. The average freshman award was $37,695. Need-based scholarships or need-based grants averaged $29,620; and need-based self-help aid (loans and jobs) averaged $5,161. 31% of undergraduate students work part-time. The average financial indebtedness of the 2016 graduate was $30,561. CWRU is a member of CSS. The CSS/Profile and the college's own financial statement are required. The FAFSA code is 003137. The priority date for freshman financial aid applications for fall entry is February 15.

CEDARVILLE UNIVERSITY — B-4

www.cedarville.edu

Cedarville, OH 45314	(937) 766-7700 (800) CEDARVILLE
Fax: (937) 766-2760	Email: admiss@cedarville.edu
Full-time: 1462 men, 1562 women	**Faculty:** 208
Part-time: 152 men, 212 women	**Ph.D.s:** 72%
Graduate: 127 men, 210 women	**Student/Faculty:** 13 to 1
Year: semesters, summer session	**Tuition:** $28,110
Room & Board: $6880	**Freshman Class:** 4092 applied, 2826 accepted, 769 enrolled
SAT CR/M/W: 600/590/570 **ACT:** 26	**CEEB CODE:** 1151
Application Deadline: open	**VERY COMPETITIVE**

Cedarville University, founded in 1887, for the Word of God and the Testimony of Jesus Christ, is recognized nationally as a baptist college with caring, authentic community, and rigorous and Christ-centered academic programs. The school has a strong graduation and retention rate, with an intentional focus on the Gospel, accredited professional and health science majors, and leading student satisfaction ratings. Cedarville University has been honored as the top-ranked Christian university granting bachelor's degrees and a best college for studying the Bible. Their academic teams regularly win or rank in the top tier of national and international competitions, and are recognized among the best universities in Ohio. There are 15 undergraduate schools and 5 graduate schools. In addition to regional accreditation, Cedarville has baccalaureate program accreditation with ABET, ACBSP, ACPE, CSWE, NASM, NCATE, CAATE, and CCNE. The 441-acre campus is in a small town 12 miles south of Springfield. Including any residence halls, there are 39 buildings.

STUDENT LIFE: 59% of undergraduates are from out of state, mostly the Midwest. Students are from 50 states, 37 foreign countries, and Canada. 48% are from public schools. 85% are White; 3% Hispanic; 3% two or more races; 3% race unknown; 2% Asian American; 2% Foreign; 1% African American; 1% American Indian/Alaska Native. **Female To Male Ratio:** 1.1:1. The average age of freshmen is 18; all undergraduates, 20. 15% do not continue beyond their first year; 72% remain to graduate. **Housing:** 2648 students can be accommodated in college housing, which includes single-sex dorms, on-campus apartments, and married student housing. On-campus housing is guaranteed for all 4 years. 75% of students live on campus; of those, 80% remain on campus on weekends. All students may keep cars. Alcohol is not permitted.

FACULTY/CLASSROOMS: 64% of faculty are male; 36% are female. 89% teach undergraduates. No introductory courses are taught by graduate students. The average class size in an introductory lecture is 28; in a laboratory is 17; and in a regular course is 25.

PROGRAMS OF STUDY: Cedarville confers B.A., B.S., B.M., B.M.E., B.S.E.E., B.S.M.E., B.S.N., and B.S.Cp.E. degrees. Master's and doctoral degrees are also awarded. Bachelor's degrees are awarded in BIOLOGICAL SCIENCE (biology/biological science, life science secondary school education, and molecular biology), BUSINESS (accounting, business administration and management, finance, international business, marketing/retailing/merchandising, and sports management), COMMUNICATIONS AND THE ARTS (broadcasting, communication rhetoric/communication, digital media, English, graphic design, industrial design, information technology, journalism, keyboard - piano concentration, linguistics, music, music composition, music performance, Spanish, studio art, technical and business writing, theatre arts, and visual design), COMPUTER AND PHYSICAL SCIENCE (chemistry, chemistry education, computer science, geology, geoscience, mathematics, physics secondary education, and physics), EDUCATION (athletic training, Christian education, early childhood education, English education, mathematics education, middle school education, music education, physical education, physical science secondary school education, science education, social studies education, Spanish education K-12, and special education), ENGINEERING AND ENVIRONMENTAL DESIGN (computer engineering, electrical/electronics engineering, environmental science, and mechanical engineering), HEALTH PROFESSIONS (allied health, exercise science, nursing, and pharmaceutical science), SOCIAL SCIENCE (biblical studies, criminal justice, economics, forensic studies, history, international studies, liberal arts/general studies, missions, political science/government, prelaw, psychology, public administration, religious education, social work, theological studies, and youth ministry). Engineering & computer science, business administration, and nursing are the strongest academically. Nursing, mechanical engineering, and early childhood education have the largest enrollments.

ACTIVITIES: There are no fraternities or sororities. There are 90 groups on campus, including art, band, cheerleading, chess, choir, chorale, chorus, dance, debate, drama, environmental, ethnic, forensics, honors, international, jazz band, musical theater, newspaper, orchestra, pep band, photography, political, professional, radio and TV, religious, social, social service, student government, and yearbook. Popular campus events include Junior and Senior Banquet, Lil' Sibs Weekend, and Campus Christmas. **Sports:** There are 8 intercollegiate sports for men and 8 for women, and 31 intramural sports for men and 31 for women. Facilities include a gym, volleyball and badminton courts, fitness center with racquetball courts, climbing wall, exercise studio, free weight room, Nautilus strength training areas and cardiovascular areas, field house with a track, basketball, volleyball, tennis, and indoor soccer courts, indoor batting cages, and training room. Outdoor facilities include tennis and sand volleyball courts, a track, soccer, baseball, softball fields, golf driving range, and intramural sports playing fields. **Graduates:** From July 1, 2015 to June 30, 2016, 678 bachelor's degrees were awarded. The most popular majors were nursing (12%), mechanical engineering (6%), and pharmaceutical sciences (4%). 422 companies recruited on campus in 2015-2016. In an average class, 3% graduate in 3 years or less, 61% graduate in 4 years or less, 70% graduate in 5 years or less, and 72% graduate in 6 years or less. Of the 2015 graduating class, 18% were enrolled in graduate school within 6 months of graduation, and 79% were employed.

SERVICES: Counseling and information services are available, as is tutoring in every subject, a reader service for the blind, and remedial math, reading, and writing. In addition to tutoring, we have academic peer coaches, tutoring labs, and mentors. **Library/Resources:** The library contains 300,524 volumes, 16,129 microform items, 10,012 audio/video tapes/CDs/DVDs, and subscribes to 10,798 periodicals including electronic. Computerized library services include interlibrary loans, database searching, Internet access, and Wi-Fi capability. Special learning facilities include a radio station, a media resource center, observatory, state-of-the-art simulation labs for nursing and pharmacy students. **Physically Challenged Students:** 90% of the campus is accessible. Facilities include wheelchair ramps, elevators, special parking, specially equipped restrooms, special class scheduling, lowered drinking fountains, lowered telephones, and special housing. We provide academic accommodations for students with disabilities as per ADAA, which includes private room, extended time, scribe, reader, CART services, alternative texts, and more. **Special:** Internships, study abroad programs, a Washington semester, dual majors, student-designed majors, B.A.-B.S. degrees in biology, chemistry, and math, and work-study programs with the college are available. Cross-registration with the Southwest Ohio Consortium for Higher Education is possible. Cooperative Learning Agreement with the International Center for Creativity for the Industrial and Innovative Design major. There are 5 national honor societies, a freshman honors program, and 1 departmental honors programs. **Visiting:** There are regularly scheduled orientations for prospective students, including campus tours, chapel services, class visits, and meetings with faculty, coaches, and admissions counselors. There are guides for informal visits, visitors may sit in on classes, and stay overnight. To schedule a visit, contact the Admissions Office. **Campus Safety and Security:** Measures include 24-hour foot and vehicle patrol, emergency notification system, self-defense education, security escort services, emergency telephones, lighted pathways/sidewalks, and controlled access to dorms/residences.

REQUIREMENTS: The SAT or ACT is required, with scores above the national average preferred. The college recommends that applicants have 4 years of English, 3 to 4 of math, and 3 each of social studies/history, math, science, and a foreign language. The GED is accepted. Recommendation from a local pastor is required. Cedarville requires applicants to be in the upper 50% of their class. AP and CLEP credits are accepted. Important factors in the admissions decision are personality/intangible qualities, recommendations by school officials, and advanced placement or honors courses. To graduate, all students must maintain a minimum GPA of 2.0 while taking 128 semester hours, with a minimum of 32 in specific disciplines, 52 in core curriculum, and 36 in major. Specific courses required include English Composition, Fundamentals of Speech, Politics and American Culture, Introduction to Humanities, and Physical Activity and the Christian life. **Procedure:** Freshmen are admitted in the fall, spring, and summer. Entrance exams should be taken by late junior year or early senior year. There are early admissions, deferred admissions, and rolling admissions plans. Application deadlines are open. Application fee is $30. Application fees are waived if application is completed online. **Transfer Students:** 100 transfer students enrolled in 2015-2016. Applicants must have a minimum college GPA of 3.0. The SAT or ACT is strongly recommended. 32 of 128 credits required for the bachelor's degree must be completed at Cedarville. **International Students:** There are 53 international students enrolled. The school actively recruits these students. They must take the TOEFL with a minimum score of 80 on the Internet-based version (iBT). They must also take the SAT or ACT, scoring 1020 SAT 22 ACT.

ADMISSIONS: 69% of the 2016-2017 applicants were accepted. The SAT scores for the 2016-2017 freshman class were: Critical Reading-- 11% below 500, 35% between 500 and 599, 40% between 600 and 699, and 14% between 700 and 800. Math-- 16% below 500, 38% between 500 and 599, 36% between 600 and 699, and 10% between 700 and 800. Writing-- 21% below 500, 41% between 500 and 599, 32% between 600 and 699, and 6% between 700 and 800. The ACT scores were 1% between 12 and 17, 25% between 18 and 23, 55% between 24 and 29, and 20% above 30. 59% of the current freshmen were in the top fifth of their class; 95% were in the top two fifths. **Admissions Contact:** Scott Van Loo, Vice President for Enrollment Management. Email: *admiss@cedarville.edu* Web: *www.cedarville.edu*

FINANCIAL AID: In 2016-2017, 99% of all full-time freshmen and 96% of continuing full-time students received some form of financial aid. 62% of all full-time freshmen and 65% of continuing full-time students received need-based aid. The average freshman award was $26,368. Need-based scholarships or need-based grants averaged $7,536 ($28,995 maximum); need-based self-help aid (loans and jobs) averaged $5,363 ($12,500 maximum); non-need-based athletic scholarships averaged $6,268 ($15,150 maximum); and other non-need-based awards and non-need-based scholarships averaged $21,298 ($57,726 maximum). 45% of undergraduate students work part-time. Average annual earnings from campus work are $2322. The average financial indebtedness of the 2016 graduate was $29,635. The college's own financial statement is required. The FAFSA code is 003025. Check with the school for current application deadlines.

CENTRAL STATE UNIVERSITY — B-4

www.centralstate.edu

Wilberforce, OH 45384	(937) 376-6348 (800) 388-CSU1
Fax: (937) 376-6648	**Email:** admissions@csu.ces.edu
Full-time: 560 men, 650 women	**Faculty:** 77
Part-time: 55 men, 70 women	**Ph.D.s:** 62%
Graduate: 30 men, 55 women	**Student/Faculty:** 16 to 1
Year: trimesters, summer session	**Tuition:** $9246 ($13,928)
Room & Board: $9318	**Freshman Class:** n/av
ACT: required	**CEEB CODE:** 1107
Application Deadline: August 1	**COMPETITIVE**

Central State University, founded in 1887, is a public institution offering programs in liberal arts, business, engineering, teacher preparation, and professional training. Figures in the above capsule and in this profile are approximate. There are 3 undergraduate schools and 1 graduate school. In addition to regional accreditation, Central State has baccalaureate program accreditation with ABET and NASM. The 60-acre campus is in a rural area 18 miles east of Dayton. Including any residence halls, there are 34 buildings.

STUDENT LIFE: 77% of undergraduates are from Ohio. Others are from 24 states, and 2 foreign countries. 96% are African American; 2% White; 1% Foreign. **Female To Male Ratio:** 1.2:1. The average age of freshmen is 18; all undergraduates, 22. 42% do not continue beyond their first year; 23% remain to graduate. **Housing:** 745 students can be accommodated in college housing, which includes single-sex dorms. On-campus housing is guaranteed for the freshman year only, and is available on a first-come, and first-served basis. 57% of students live on campus. All students may keep cars. Alcohol is not permitted.

FACULTY/CLASSROOMS: 77% of faculty are male; 23% are female. All teach undergraduates, and 75% do research. No introductory courses are taught by graduate students. The average class size in an introductory lecture is 25; in a laboratory is 20; and in a regular course is 15.

PROGRAMS OF STUDY: Central State confers B.A., B.S., B.M., B.S.Ed. and B.S.M.E. degrees. Master's degrees are also awarded. Bachelor's degrees are awarded in BIOLOGICAL SCIENCE (biology/biological science), BUSINESS (accounting, banking and finance, business administration and management, and marketing/retailing/merchandising), COMMUNICATIONS AND THE ARTS (advertising, broadcasting, English, journalism, and music), COMPUTER AND PHYSICAL SCIENCE (chemistry, computer science, and mathematics), EDUCATION (art education, elementary education, health education, music education, physical education, secondary education, and special education), ENGINEERING AND ENVIRONMENTAL DESIGN (graphic arts technology and manufacturing engineering), SOCIAL SCIENCE (economics, history, political science/government, psychology, public administration, social work, sociology, and water resources). Communication, music, and education are the strongest academically. Business administration has the largest enrollment.

ACTIVITIES: 1% of men belong to 2 national fraternities; 1% of women belong to 2 national sororities. There are 30 groups on campus, including and the entrepreneurship club, finance club, optimist club, art, band, cheerleading, choir, chorale, chorus, communications, computers, dance, drama, drill team, ethnic, honors, J'adore fashion, jazz band, marching band, pep band, political, professional, radio and TV, religious, social, and student government. Popular campus events include Career Day and May Week. **Sports:** There are 3 intercollegiate sports for men and 4 for women, and 8 intramural sports for men and 7 for women. Facilities include gyms, stadium, swimming pool, pool room, baseball diamond, tennis courts, and a weight room. **Graduates:** From July 1, 2015 to June 30, 2016, 81 bachelor's degrees were awarded. The most popular majors were education (25%), business (21%), and social sciences and history (17%). 135 companies recruited on campus in 2015-2016. In an average class, 1% graduate in 3 years or less, 9% graduate in 4 years or less, 20% graduate in 5 years or less, and 22% graduate in 6 years or less. Of the 2015 graduating class, 37% were enrolled in graduate school within 6 months of graduation, and 96% were employed.

SERVICES: Counseling and information services are available, as is tutoring in most subjects, To support academic progress, students should refer to the Student Support Services. **Library/Resources:** The library contains 179,241 volumes, 622,727 microform items, and 500 audio/video tapes/CDs/DVDs, and subscribes to 26,316 periodicals including electronic. Computerized library services include interlibrary loans and database searching. Special learning facilities include an art gallery, radio station, and the National Afro-American Museum and Cultural Center. **Physically Challenged Students:** All of the campus is accessible. Facilities include wheelchair ramps, elevators, special parking, specially equipped restrooms, lowered drinking fountains, lowered telephones. **Special:** Central State offers co-op programs in all majors, cross-registration with 15 area colleges, study abroad in 3 countries, internships, on-campus work-study programs, and B.A.-B.S. degrees. There are a freshman honors program. **Visiting:** There are regularly scheduled orientations for prospective students, SOAR is a full-day event, begins at 8:00 a.m., with registration to 3:00 p.m. There are guides for informal visits and visitors may sit in on classes. To schedule a visit, contact the Admissions Office. **Campus Safety and Security:** Measures include 24-hour foot and vehicle patrol, and lighted pathways/sidewalks.

REQUIREMENTS: The ACT is required. The SAT I is accepted. Applicants must be graduates of an accredited secondary school. The GED is accepted. Students should have completed 4 years of high school English, 3 years each of math, science, and social studies, and 2 years of the same foreign language. Ohio applicants should have a GPA of 2.0 and a minimum ACT composite score of 15 or SAT I score of 720. Criteria are higher for out-of-state applicants. AP and CLEP credits are accepted. To graduate, students must complete 186 quarter credits, with a minimum GPA of 2.0 (2.5 in education). Required university core courses include 64 credits in English composition, math, computer skills, humanities, natural sciences, social sciences, health and phys ed, and African American history. **Procedure:** Freshmen are admitted to all sessions. There are early admissions, deferred admissions, and rolling admissions plans. Applications should be filed by August 1 for fall entry; October 15 for winter entry; February 15 for spring entry; and April 15 for summer entry, along with a $15 fee. Applications are accepted on-line. **Transfer Students:** 127 transfer students enrolled in 2015-2016. Applicants should have a minimum college GPA of 2.0. Grades of C or better transfer for credit. Transfer students with fewer than 47 quarter hours must submit high school transcripts and test scores. Transfers are admitted every term. 45 of 186 credits required for the bachelor's degree must be completed at Central State. **International Students:** There are 8 international students enrolled. They must take the TOEFL, as well as the SAT or ACT, scoring 19.

Admissions Contact: Curtis Pettis, Executive Director of Administration. Email: *admissions@csu.ces.edu* Web: *www.centralstate.edu*

FINANCIAL AID: The average freshman award was $10,765. 48% of undergraduate students work part-time. Average annual earnings from campus work are $1920. The college's own financial statement is required. The FAFSA code is 003026. The deadline for filing freshman financial aid applications for fall entry is March 31.

CLEVELAND INSTITUTE OF ART — D-1

www.cia.edu

Cleveland, OH 44106	(216) 421-7418 (800) 223-4700
Fax: (216) 754-3634	**Email:** admissions@cia.edu
Full-time: 254 men, 357 women	**Faculty:** 49
Part-time: 7 men, 7 women	**Ph.D.s:** 71%
Graduate: n/av	**Student/Faculty:** 13 to 1
Year: semesters	**Tuition:** $39,585
Room & Board: $11,854	**Freshman Class:** 559 applied, 524 accepted, 179 enrolled
SAT CR/M/W: 550/520/530 **ACT:** 24	**CEEB CODE:** 1152
Application Deadline: March 1	**COMPETITIVE+**

Cleveland Institute of Art, founded in 1882, is an independent professional school of art and design offering a 4-year B.F.A. degree. There is one undergraduate school. In addition to regional accreditation, CIA has baccalaureate program accreditation with NASAD and NCA-HLC. The 5-acre campus is in an urban area 4 miles east of downtown Cleveland, adjacent to the Case Western Reserve University campus. Including any residence halls, there are 3 buildings.

STUDENT LIFE: 64% of undergraduates are from Ohio. Others are from 30 states, and 6 foreign countries. 83% are from public schools. 9% are African American; 9% Foreign; 70% White; 5% Hispanic; 4% Asian American; 3% two or more races. **Female To Male Ratio:** 1.4:1. The average age of freshmen is 19; all undergraduates, 20. 18% do not continue beyond their first year; 69% remain to graduate. **Housing:** 195 students can be accommodated in college housing, which includes single-sex and coed dorms and on-campus apartments. On-campus housing is guaranteed for the freshman year only, is available on a first-come, first-served basis, and on a lottery system for upperclassmen. Priority is given to out-of-town students. 65% of students commute. Upperclassmen may keep cars. Alcohol is not permitted.

FACULTY/CLASSROOMS: 64% of faculty are male; 36% are female. All teach undergraduates. No introductory courses are taught by graduate students. The average class size in an introductory lecture is 22; in a laboratory is 13; and in a regular course is 16.

PROGRAMS OF STUDY: CIA confers B.F.A. degrees. Bachelor's degrees are awarded in COMMUNICATIONS AND THE ARTS (animation, ceramic art and design, drawing, game design and development, glass, graphic design, illustration, industrial design, metal/jewelry, painting, photography, printmaking, and sculpture), COMPUTER AND PHYSICAL SCIENCE (biomedical art), ENGINEERING AND ENVIRONMENTAL DESIGN (interior architecture). Industrial design, painting, and illustration are the strongest academically and have the largest enrollments.

ACTIVITIES: There are 15 groups on campus, including survey student gallery. Some of the Institute's social and educational student organizations also collaborate with similar student organizations at Case Western Reserve University and the Cleveland Institute of Music, Student Activities Program Board, Student Artist Association, Student Leadership Council, art, Artists for Christ, band, ethnic, film, international, LGBT, musical theater, photography, professional, religious, social, social service, and student government. Popular campus events include Museum Trips, Annual Cookout, Spring Break, Halloween Party, Holiday Art Sale and Student Art Exhibits. **Sports:** There are 9 intramural sports for men and 8 for women. For a fee, students may use the recreation facilities of Case Western Reserve University. **Graduates:** From July 1, 2015 to June 30, 2016, 110 bachelor's degrees were awarded. The most popular majors were illustration (13%), industrial design (11%), and painting (10%). 400 companies recruited on campus in 2015-2016. In an average class, 60% graduate in 4 years or less, 67% graduate in 5 years or less, and 69% graduate in 6 years or less. Of the 2015 graduating class, 4% were enrolled in graduate school within 6 months of graduation, and 90% were employed.

SERVICES: Counseling and information services are available, as is tutoring in some subjects, such as English, art history, and academic electives, and writing and learning center staffed by peers. **Library/Resources:** The library contains 52,180 volumes, 3,264 microform items, 1,667 audio/video tapes/CDs/DVDs, and subscribes to 131 periodicals including electronic. Computerized library services include interlibrary loans, database searching, Internet access, and Wi-Fi capability. Special learning facilities include an art gallery, CIA has a movie cinema on campus. Independent museums within walking distance include: Cleveland Museum of Art, Museum of Contemporary Art, Cleveland Museum of Natural History, Dittrick Museum of Medical History, Crawford Auto-Aviation Museum, Artist Archives of Western Reserve, Cleveland Botanical Gardens, and the Children's Museum of Cleveland. **Physically Challenged Students:** 99% of the campus is accessible. Facilities include wheelchair ramps, elevators, special parking, specially equipped restrooms, lowered drinking fountains, and special housing. **Special:** Cross-registration with selected colleges in Northeast Ohio, internships for upperclassmen with business and industry, and study abroad are available. There are joint programs with Case Western Reserve University in Art Education and Biomedical Art. CIA's Cores + Connections help build the skills and confidence students say they need to seize real-world opportunities that develop in their daily lives - now and after graduation. Through courses, extracurricular projects and activities, or internships, students may connect to real-world experiences every school year. Our goal is for all students to experience an increasingly seamless transition from college to their professional lives. **Visiting:** There are regularly scheduled orientations for prospective students, consisting of a tour, interview, and classrooms visits. There are guides for informal visits and visitors may sit in on classes. To schedule a visit, contact Arlene Thomas at (216) 421-7418. **Campus Safety and Security:** Measures include emergency notification system and security escort services. There are also shuttle buses, emergency telephones, lighted pathways/sidewalks, controlled access to dorms/residences, and security officers present during building-occupied hours.

REQUIREMENTS: The SAT or ACT is required. Applicants must be graduates of an accredited secondary school. The GED is accepted. An essay and a portfolio are required. An interview is strongly recommended. AP and CLEP credits are accepted. Important factors in the admissions decision are evidence of special talent, personality/intangible qualities, and leadership record. To graduate, students must complete 129 credit hours, with 42 to 51 in the major, and must maintain a minimum GPA of 2.0. Distribution requirements call for 87 studio credits and 42 liberal arts credits. A thesis is required, which is encompassed in the B.F.A. exhibition that each student mounts in the spring of the final year. Students must receive a minimum grade of "C" in major required courses. Students must complete at least one "Engaged Practice" course- (EP courses are courses that are field-based or located off-campus. The courses focus on real-world projects and engagement with external partners). **Procedure:** Freshmen are admitted in the fall. Entrance exams should be taken Prior to students' chosen application deadline. There are early admissions and rolling admissions plans. Applications should be filed by March 1 for fall entry; November 15 for spring entry, along with a $40 fee. Notifications are sent March 15. Application fees are waived if application is completed online. **Transfer Students:** 31 transfer students enrolled in 2015-2016. Applicants must have a 2.0 GPA and must submit a portfolio. Those who have 30 to 36 credits in comparable studio courses or a strong portfolio will be reviewed by department faculty. Grades of C or better transfer for credit. 30 of 126 credits required for the bachelor's degree must be completed at CIA. **International Students:** There are 58 international students enrolled. The school actively recruits these students. They must take the TOEFL with a minimum score of 550 on the paper-based TOEFL (PBT) or 79 on the Internet-based version (iBT), or complete Level 112 at an ELS Center, or take the IELTS. They must also take the SAT or ACT.

ADMISSIONS: The SAT scores for the 2016-2017 freshman class were: Critical Reading-- 30% below 500, 37% between 500 and 599, 28% between 600 and 699, and 5% between 700 and 800. Math-- 40% below 500, 42% between 500 and 599, 16% between 600 and 699, and 2% between 700 and 800. Writing-- 35% below 500, 46% between 500 and 599, 17% between 600 and 699, and 2% between 700 and 800. The ACT scores were 6% between 12 and 17, 40% between 18 and 23, 43% between 24 and 29, and 11% above 30. 30% of the current freshmen were in the top fifth of their class; 56% were in the top two fifths. **Admissions Contact:** Jonathan Wehner, V.P., Enrollment/Dean. Email: *admissions@.cia.edu* Web: *www.cia.edu*

FINANCIAL AID: In 2016-2017, 97% of all full-time freshmen and 94% of continuing full-time students received some form of financial aid. 71% of all full-time freshmen and 78% of continuing full-time students received need-based aid. The average freshman award was $36,883. Need-based scholarships or need-based grants averaged $19,896 ($36,980 maximum); need-based self-help aid (loans and jobs) averaged $6,414 ($9,500 maximum); other non-need-based awards and non-need-based scholarships averaged $13,848 ($36,980 maximum); and $2,500 from other forms of aid. 20% of undergraduate students work part-time. Average annual earnings from campus work are $1229. The average financial indebtedness of the 2016 graduate was $30,366. The FAFSA code is 003982. The priority date for freshman financial aid applications for fall entry is December 15. The filing deadline for fall entry is March 15.

CLEVELAND INSTITUTE OF MUSIC *(The complete profile is made available exclusively on our website, www.barronspac.com)*

CLEVELAND STATE UNIVERSITY D-1

www.csuohio.com

Cleveland, OH 44115 (216) 523-7417

Email: admissions@csuohio.edu

Full-time: 4401 men, 4818 women
Part-time: 1485 men, 1729 women
Graduate: 1902 men, 2614 women
Year: semesters, summer session
Room & Board: $12,500
SAT CR/M: 510/510 **ACT:** 22
Application Deadline: August 15

Faculty: 516; I, --$
Ph.D.s: 89%
Student/Faculty: 18 to 1
Tuition: $9696 ($13,747)
Freshman Class: 11638 applied, 7359 accepted, 1914 enrolled
CEEB CODE: 1221
COMPETITIVE

Cleveland State University, founded in 1964, is a primarily commuter public institution offering undergraduate and graduate programs through the colleges of arts and sciences, business administration, education, engineering, law, urban affairs, and the school of nursing. There are 8 undergraduate schools and 8 graduate schools. In addition to regional accreditation, CSU has baccalaureate program accreditation with AACSB, ABET, CSWE, NASM, NCATE, NLN, CCNE, APA, and ASHA. The 85-acre campus is in an urban area in downtown Cleveland, Ohio. Including any residence halls, there are 45 buildings.

STUDENT LIFE: 98% of undergraduates are from Ohio. Others are from 33 states, 4 foreign countries, and Canada. 63% are White; 5% Hispanic; 5% Foreign; 4% Asian American; 3% two or more races; 2% race unknown; 17% African American. **Female To Male Ratio:** 1.2:1. The average age of freshmen is 22; all undergraduates, 24. 29% do not continue beyond their first year; 39% remain to graduate. **Housing:** 1010 students can be accommodated in college housing, which includes coed dorms, on-campus apartments, as well as law, quiet study, and first-year experience floors. On-campus housing is available on a first-come and first-served basis. 92% of students commute. All students may keep cars.

FACULTY/CLASSROOMS: 53% of faculty are male; 47% are female. No introductory courses are taught by graduate students.

PROGRAMS OF STUDY: CSU confers B.A., B.S., B.B.A., B.C.E., B.Ch.E., B.E.E., B.M., B.M.E., B.S.C.I.S., B.S.Ed., B.S.I.E., B.S.N. and B.S.T. degrees. Master's and doctoral degrees are also awarded. Bachelor's degrees are awarded in BIOLOGICAL SCIENCE (biology/biological science), BUSINESS (accounting, business economics, finance, labor studies, management information systems, management science, and marketing/retailing/merchandising), COMMUNICATIONS AND THE ARTS (art, communications, dramatic arts, English, film, television and digital media, French, linguistics, music, and Spanish), COMPUTER AND PHYSICAL SCIENCE (chemistry, computer science, geology, information sciences and systems, mathematics, and physics), EDUCATION (early childhood education, elementary education, health education, physical education, secondary education, and special education), ENGINEERING AND ENVIRONMENTAL DESIGN (chemical engineering, civil engineering, electrical/electronics engineering, electrical/electronics engineering technology, environmental science, mechanical engineering, and mechanical engineering technology), HEALTH PROFESSIONS (exercise science, health science, medical technology, nursing, occupational therapy, pharmaceutical science, physical therapy, premedicine, speech pathology/audiology, and speech therapy), SOCIAL SCIENCE (anthropology, classical/ancient civilization, criminology, economics, history, international relations, liberal arts/general studies, philosophy, political science/government, psychology, religion, social science, social studies, social work, sociology, urban studies, and women's studies). Psychology, biology, and business have the largest enrollments.

ACTIVITIES: 1% of men belong to 6 national fraternities; 1% of women belong to 3 national sororities. There are 234 groups on campus, including art, cheerleading, chess, choir, chorale, chorus, computers, dance, drama, environmental, ethnic, film, honors, international, jazz band, LGBT, literary magazine, musical theater, newspaper, opera, orchestra, pep band, photography, political, professional, radio and TV, religious, social, social service, student government, and symphony. Popular campus events include Weeks of Welcome, Homecoming, and Springfest. **Sports:** There are 8 intercollegiate sports for men and 10 for women, and 12 intramural sports for men and 8 for women. Facilities include a recreation center, complete with a gym and weight rooms, a dance studio, swimming pool, fitness trail, an indoor track, handball and squash courts, a soccer stadium, and a convocation center. **Graduates:** From July 1, 2015 to June 30, 2016, 2317 bachelor's degrees were awarded. The most popular majors were psychology (9%), health sciences (6%), and social work (4%). 84 companies recruited on campus in 2015-2016. In an average class, 16% graduate in 4 years or less, 32% graduate in 5 years or less, and 39% graduate in 6 years or less.

SERVICES: Counseling and information services are available, as is tutoring in most subjects, and remedial math, reading, and writing. **Library/Resources:** The 2 libraries contain 1.0 million volumes, 224,504 microform items, 44,367 audio/video tapes/CDs/DVDs, and subscribe to 11,923 periodicals including electronic. Computerized library services include interlibrary loans, database searching, Internet access, and Wi-Fi capability. Special learning facilities include an art gallery and radio station. **Physically Challenged Students:** All of the campus is accessible. Facilities include wheelchair ramps, elevators, special parking, specially equipped restrooms, lowered drinking fountains, and special housing. **Special:** CSU offers a developmental program for Ohio students not qualified for regular freshman admission. There are also cooperative education programs, nondegree study, work-study programs, accelerated degree programs, internships, pass/fail options, and cross-registration at other Cleveland area colleges. Student-designed and dual majors, study abroad in 10 countries, and volunteer opportunities are available, as well as a combined liberal arts and engineering degree and a 3-2 engineering degree. There are 6 national honor societies, a freshman honors program, and 38 departmental honors programs. **Visiting:** There are regularly scheduled orientations for prospective students, including general visitation days for the university (in the fall) and each of the colleges (in the spring). There are guides for informal visits, visitors may sit in on classes, and stay overnight. To schedule a visit, contact the Office of Undergraduate Admissions. **Campus Safety and Security:** Measures include 24-hour foot and vehicle patrol, emergency notification system, self-defense education, security escort services, emergency telephones, lighted pathways/sidewalks, controlled access to dorms/residences, and a campus watch organization for faculty and staff.

REQUIREMENTS: The SAT or ACT is required. In addition, a high school diploma is required or the GED is accepted. Students should have completed the following academic credits: 4 years of English, 3 of math, social studies, and science (1 must be a lab), and 2 of a foreign language. A general college-preparatory program is recommended. A GPA of 2.3 is required. AP and CLEP credits are accepted. Students must complete at least 120 semester hours with a minimum 2.0 GPA for graduation. Requirements include a core curriculum containing courses in English composition, arts and humanities, social science, natural sciences, math and logic, non-Western culture and civilization, Western culture and civilization, and human diversity and the African American experience. **Procedure:** Freshmen are admitted to all sessions. Entrance exams should be taken prior to application. There are deferred admissions and rolling admissions plans. Applications should be filed by August 15 for fall entry, along with a $30 fee. Notification is sent on a rolling basis. Applications are accepted online. **Transfer Students:** 6907 transfer students enrolled in 2015-2016. Applicants must have a minimum GPA of 2.0 and submit previous college transcripts. Transfer students entering with fewer than 24 semester hours must submit official high school transcripts and test scores if they have been out of high school less than 5 years. 30 of 120 credits required for the bachelor's degree must be completed at CSU. **International Students:** There are 575 international students enrolled. They must take the TOEFL with a minimum score of 550 on the paper-based TOEFL (PBT) or 78 on the Internet-based version (iBT).

ADMISSIONS: 63% of the 2016-2017 applicants were accepted. The SAT scores for the 2016-2017 freshman class were: Critical Reading-- 45% below 500, 37% between 500 and 599, 14% between 600 and 699, and 3% between 700 and 800. Math-- 42% below 500, 41% between 500 and 599, 14% between 600 and 699, and 3% between 700 and 800. The ACT scores were 14% between 12 and 17, 50% between 18 and 23, 32% between 24 and 29, and 4% above 30. **Admissions Contact:** Lee Furbeck, Director, Undergraduate Admissions. Email: *admissions@csuohio.edu* Web: *www.csuohio.com*

FINANCIAL AID: In 2016-2017, 74% of all full-time freshmen and 71% of continuing full-time students received some form of financial aid. 61% of all full-time freshmen and 56% of continuing full-time students received need-based aid. The average freshman award was $8,902. Need-based scholarships or need-based grants averaged $6,986; need-based self-help aid (loans and jobs) averaged $3,876; non-need-based athletic scholarships averaged $10,929; and other non-need-based awards and non-need-based scholarships averaged $5,560. The FAFSA code is 003032. The priority date for freshman financial aid applications for fall entry is February 15.

COLUMBUS COLLEGE OF ART AND DESIGN — C-3

www.ccad.edu

Columbus, OH 43215	(614) 222-3261 (877) 997-CCAD (2223)
Fax: (614) 232-8344	**Email:** admissions@ccad.edu
Full-time: 454 men, 758 women	**Faculty:** 72
Part-time: 49 men, 72 women	**Ph.D.s:** 69%
Graduate: 15 men, 16 women	**Student/Faculty:** 11 to 1
Year: semesters, summer session	**Tuition:** $29,992
Room & Board: $7740	**Freshman Class:** n/av
SAT or ACT: required	**CEEB CODE:** 1085
Application Deadline: August 15	**COMPETITIVE**

Columbus College of Art and Design, founded in 1879, is a private institution offering undergraduate and graduate programs in art and design. There are 2 undergraduate schools and 1 graduate school. In addition to regional accreditation, CCAD has baccalaureate program accreditation with NASAD and HLC-NCACS. The 9-acre campus is in an urban area in Columbus, Ohio. Including any residence halls, there are 14 buildings.

STUDENT LIFE: 73% of undergraduates are from Ohio, and Canada. 9% are African American; 9% Asian American; 7% Foreign; 69% White; 6% two or more races; 4% Hispanic; 4% race unknown. **Female To Male Ratio:** 1.6:1. The average age of freshmen is 19; all undergraduates, 21. 19% do not continue beyond their first year; 55% remain to graduate. **Housing:** 435 students can be accommodated in college housing, which includes coed dorms and on-campus apartments. On-campus housing is guaranteed for the freshman year only, and is available on a first-come, first-served basis, and on a lottery system for upperclassmen. 69% of students commute. All students may keep cars. Alcohol is not permitted.

FACULTY/CLASSROOMS: 53% of faculty are male; 47% are female. All teach undergraduates. No introductory courses are taught by graduate students. The average class size in a regular course is 19.

PROGRAMS OF STUDY: CCAD confers B.F.A. degrees. Master's degrees are also awarded. Bachelor's degrees are awarded in COMMUNICATIONS AND THE ARTS (advertising, animation, film arts, fine arts, graphic design, illustration, industrial design, and photography), ENGINEERING AND ENVIRONMENTAL DESIGN (interior design), SOCIAL SCIENCE (fashion design and technology).

ACTIVITIES: There are no fraternities or sororities. There are 27 groups on campus, including art, environmental, ethnic, film, honors, international, LGBT, literary magazine, newspaper, photography, professional, religious, social, social service, and student government. Popular campus events include Local and National International Art Exhibitions, Art Fairs, Big Boo! Halloween Party, Alumni/Family Weekend, and Welcome Fest. **Sports:** There are 4 intramural sports for men and 4 for women. Facilities include areas for soccer, basketball, dodgeball, yoga, and zumba, as well as a game room in student center, and a fitness/workout facility. **Graduates:** From July 1, 2015 to June 30, 2016, 262 bachelor's degrees were awarded. The most popular majors were advertising and graphic design (19%), media arts (16%), and fine arts (16%). In an average class, 44% graduate in 4 years or less, 54% graduate in 5 years or less, and 55% graduate in 6 years or less.

SERVICES: Counseling and information services are available, as is tutoring in most subjects, a reader service for the blind, and remedial math, reading, and writing. **Library/Resources:** The library contains 41,396 volumes, 13,475 microform items, and subscribes to 254 periodicals including electronic. Computerized library services include interlibrary loans, database searching, Internet access, and Wi-Fi capability. Special learning facilities include an art gallery. **Physically Challenged Students:** 50% of the campus is accessible. Facilities include wheelchair ramps, elevators, special parking, specially equipped restrooms, special class scheduling, lowered drinking fountains, and lowered telephones. **Special:** CCAD offers cross-registration, distance learning, double majors, ESL, domestic student exchange, internships, and study abroad.

There are a freshman honors program and 9 departmental honors programs. **Visiting:** There are regularly scheduled orientations for prospective students, including a personal interview, a portfolio review, and a tour. There are guides for informal visits. To schedule a visit, contact the Admissions Office. **Campus Safety and Security:** Measures include 24-hour foot and vehicle patrol, emergency notification system, security escort services, emergency telephones, lighted pathways/sidewalks, and controlled access to dorms/residences.

REQUIREMENTS: The SAT or ACT is required. Applicants should be graduates of an accredited secondary school or have the GED. A portfolio of artwork indicative of abilities must be submitted. An interview is advised. AP credits are accepted. Important factors in the admissions decision are recommendations by alumni, recommendations by school officials, and evidence of special talent. Students must complete a minimum of 120 credit hours in required courses, have a cumulative GPA of 2.0 or better, present an approved portfolio, and complete a minimum of 60 credit hours at CCAD in order to graduate from CCAD. Of the total credit hours, about 60 percent is studio coursework and 40 percent is liberal arts. **Procedure:** Freshmen are admitted in the fall and spring. There are early decision, early admissions, deferred admissions, and rolling admissions plans. Early decision applications should be filed by December 1; regular applications, by August 15 for fall entry, along with a $40 fee. Notification of early decision is sent December 20; regular decision, April 1. 197 early decision candidates were accepted for the 2016-2017 class. 25 applicants were on the 2016 waiting list; 4 were admitted. Applications are accepted online. **Transfer Students:** 76 transfer students enrolled in 2015-2016. Applicants must submit an acceptable portfolio of artwork as well as all high school and college transcripts. A minimum GPA of 2.0 is required. An interview is recommended. 60 of 120 credits required for the bachelor's degree must be completed at CCAD. **International Students:** There are 101 international students enrolled. The school actively recruits these students. They must take the TOEFL with a minimum score of 500 on the paper-based TOEFL (PBT) or 61 on the Internet-based version (iBT). They must also take the SAT or ACT.

ADMISSIONS: 10% of the current freshmen were in the top fifth of their class; 44% were in the top two fifths. **Admissions Contact:** Densil R.R. Porteous II, Director of Admissions. Email: *admissions@ccad.edu* Web: *www.ccad.edu*

FINANCIAL AID: In 2016-2017, 92% of all full-time freshmen and 85% of continuing full-time students received some form of financial aid. 92% of all full-time freshmen and 90% of continuing full-time students received need-based aid. The average freshman award was $19,100. Need-based scholarships or need-based grants averaged $13,200; need-based self-help aid (loans and jobs) averaged $5,400; and $500 from other forms of aid. The average financial indebtedness of the 2016 graduate was $27,000. CCAD is a member of CSS. The priority date for freshman financial aid applications for fall entry is February 15.

DEFIANCE COLLEGE — A-2
www.defiance.edu

Defiance, OH 43512	**(419) 783-2365** **(800) 520-GODC**
Fax: (419) 783-2468	**Email: admissions@defiance.edu**
Full-time: 404 men, 351 women	**Faculty:** 49; IIB
Part-time: 55 men, 147 women	**Ph.D.s:** 60%
Graduate: 37 men, 76 women	**Student/Faculty:** 15 to 1
Year: semesters, summer session	**Tuition:** $31,680
Room & Board: $9950	**Freshman Class:** 1084 applied, 937 accepted, 216 enrolled
SAT CR/M/W: required **ACT:** 22	**CEEB CODE:** 1162
Application Deadline: August 15	**COMPETITIVE**

Defiance College is an independent, coeducational institution affiliated with the United Church of Christ and home to the McMaster School for Advancing Humanity. Figures in the above capsule and in this profile are approximate. There is 1 undergraduate school and 1 graduate school. In addition to regional accreditation, Defiance has baccalaureate program accreditation with CSWE, NCATE, and IACBE. The 150-acre campus is in a small town 55 miles southwest of Toledo and 50 miles east of Fort Wayne. Including any residence halls, there are 24 buildings.

STUDENT LIFE: 85% of undergraduates are from Ohio. Others are from 15 states, and 3 foreign countries. 97% are from public schools. 86% are White; 6% African American; 4% Hispanic; 1% Asian American; 1% American Indian/Alaska Native. 23% are Protestant; 23% claim no religious affiliation; 15% Catholic. **Female To Male Ratio:** 1.2:1. The average age of freshmen is 18. 32% do not continue beyond their first year; 50% remain to graduate. **Housing:** 505 students can be accommodated in college housing, which includes single-sex and coed dorms, and on-campus apartments, as well as academic floors in the residence halls with additional academic programming and resources. On-campus housing is guaranteed for all 4 years and is available on a lottery system for upperclassmen. 66% of students live on campus; of those, 50% remain on campus on weekends. All students may keep cars.

FACULTY/CLASSROOMS: 61% of faculty are male; 39% are female. All teach undergraduates, 30% do research, and 30% do both. No introductory courses are taught by graduate students. The average class size in an introductory lecture is 22; in a laboratory is 18; and in a regular course is 16.

PROGRAMS OF STUDY: Defiance confers B.A. and B.S. degrees. Associate and master's degrees are also awarded. Bachelor's degrees are awarded in BIOLOGICAL SCIENCE (biology/biological science and ecology), BUSINESS (accounting, banking and finance, business administration and management, human resources, management science, marketing, marketing/retailing/merchandising, organizational leadership and management, and sports management), COMMUNICATIONS AND THE ARTS (art, communications, and graphic design), COMPUTER AND PHYSICAL SCIENCE (information sciences and systems and mathematics), EDUCATION (art education, athletic training, Christian education, early childhood education, elementary education, health education, mathematics education, physical education, reading education, science education, secondary education, and social studies education), ENGINEERING AND ENVIRONMENTAL DESIGN (environmental science), HEALTH PROFESSIONS (medical laboratory technology and nursing), SOCIAL SCIENCE (criminal justice, forensic studies, history, humanities, international studies, paralegal studies, physical fitness/movement, psychology, public administration, religion, and social work). Education, and sciences are the strongest academically. Business, forensic sciences, and education have the largest enrollments.

ACTIVITIES: 6% of men belong to 1 national fraternity; 6% of women belong to 2 national sororities. There are 33 groups on campus, including academic club, art, band, choir, chorale, chorus, dance, drama, ethnic, honors, international, LGBT, literary magazine, musical theater, newspaper, pep band, political, professional, religious, social, social service, student government, and yearbook. Popular campus events include Freshman Service Day, Arts on the Quad, and Thanksgiving Dinner. **Sports:** There are 9 intercollegiate sports for men and 9 for women, and 10 intramural sports for men and 10 for women. Facilities include a stadium, baseball, softball, soccer fields, cross-country course, gym, racquetball courts, indoor track, weight-lifting room, basketball courts, tennis courts, an all-weather outdoor track, and a fitness center. **Graduates:** From July 1, 2015 to June 30, 2016, 148 bachelor's degrees were awarded. The most popular majors were business adminstration (13%), criminal justice (11%), and social work (11%). 390 companies recruited on campus in 2015-2016. In an average class, 42% graduate in 4 years or less, 48% graduate in 5 years or less, and 50% graduate in 6 years or less. Of the 2015 graduating class, 10% were enrolled in graduate school within 6 months of graduation, and 92% were employed.

SERVICES: Counseling and information services are available, as is tutoring in every subject, and a reader service for the blind. **Library/Resources:** The library contains 182,812 volumes, 7,387 microform items, 3,336 audio/video tapes/CDs/DVDs, and subscribes to 7,673 periodicals including electronic. Computerized library services include interlibrary loans, database searching, Internet access, and Wi-Fi capability. Special learning facilities include an art gallery, Thoreau Wildlife Sanctuary, a greenhouse, and learning commons. **Physically Challenged Students:** 80% of the campus is accessible. Facilities include wheelchair ramps, elevators, special parking, specially equipped restrooms, special class scheduling, lowered drinking fountains, and lowered telephones. **Special:** Co-op programs and internships are available in all majors, as are B.A.-B.S. degrees and dual majors. Work study and student-designed majors are also available. The McMaster School for Advancing Humanity allows students and faculty to more closely examine global issues and how they affect the human condition. There are 1 national honor societies, a freshman honors program, and 4 departmental honors programs. **Visiting:** There are regularly scheduled orientations for prospective students, including admissions, financial aid, and special interest sessions, a campus tour, complimentary lunch, meetings with faculty, and observing a class in session. Interested applicants can also meet with a coach. There are guides for informal visits, visitors may sit in on classes, and stay overnight. To schedule a visit, contact the Office of Admission. **Campus Safety and Security:** Measures include emergency notification system and security escort services, lighted pathways/sidewalks, nighttime security guards in residence halls, security cameras in residence hall entrances, and a security guard on the grounds from dusk to dawn.

REQUIREMENTS: The ACT is required. The SAT is recommended. Applicants should be graduates of an accredited secondary school or have a GED, with 15 Carnegie units completed, including 4 in English, 3 each in math, science, and social studies, and 2 in foreign language. An essay and an interview are recommended. A GPA of 2.3 is required. AP and CLEP credits are accepted. Important factors in the admissions decision are personality/intangible qualities, advanced placement or honors courses, and leadership record. All students must fulfill general education requirements, including communication skills, arts and humanities, natural science, and social science. Freshman Seminar, fitness for Life, as well as senior assessment in the major are also required. A total of 120 semester credits, with at least 30 in the major, and a minimum GPA of 2.0 are required to graduate. Service is required in all majors; computer profiency must be demonstrated. **Procedure:** Freshmen are admitted to all sessions. Entrance exams should be taken in the spring of the junior year or the fall of the senior year. There are early admissions, deferred admissions, and rolling admissions plans. Applications should be filed by August 15 for fall entry, along with a $25 fee. Applications are accepted on-line. **Transfer Students:** 61 transfer students enrolled in 2015-2016. A high school diploma, GED certificate, or equivalent; official transcript from each college or university attended; minimum college GPA of 2.0 from the last college attended; and a record indicating good standing socially from each college or university attended are required. An interview is recommended. 30 of 120 credits required for the bachelor's degree must be completed at Defiance. **International Students:** There are 3 international students enrolled. The school actively recruits these students. They must take the TOEFL with a minimum score of 550 on the paper-based TOEFL (PBT) or 79 on the Internet-based version (iBT) or take the MELAB. They must also take the SAT or ACT, scoring 18.

ADMISSIONS: 86% of the 2016-2017 applicants were accepted. The SAT scores for the 2016-2017 freshman class were: Critical Reading--60% below 500, 32% between 500 and 599, and 8% between 600 and 699. Math-- 48% below 500, 48% between 500 and 599, and 4% between 600 and 699. Writing-- 72% below 500 and 28% between 500 and 599. The ACT scores were 42% below 12, 25% between 12 and 17, 22% between 18 and 23, 6% between 24 and 29, and 3% above 30. 22% of the current freshmen were in the top fifth of their class; 50% were in the top two fifths. 3 freshmen graduated first in their class. **Admissions Contact:** Brad Harsha, Director of Admissions. Email: *admissions@defiance.edu* Web: *www.defiance.edu*

FINANCIAL AID: The college's own financial statement is required. The FAFSA code is 003041. The deadline for filing freshman financial aid applications for fall entry is April 1.

DENISON UNIVERSITY — C-3

www.denison.edu

Granville, OH 43023	**(740) 587-6276** **(800) DENISON**
Fax: (740) 587-6306	**Email: admissions@denison.edu**
Full-time: 973 men, 1280 women	**Faculty:** 230; IIB, +$
Part-time: 14 men, 15 women	**Ph.D.s:** 100%
Graduate: n/av	**Student/Faculty:** 10 to 1
Year: semesters	**Tuition:** $47,290
Room & Board: $11,570	**Freshman Class:** 6110 applied, 2932 accepted, 632 enrolled
SAT CR/M: 647/639 **ACT:** 29	**CEEB CODE:** 1164
Application Deadline: January 15	**MOST COMPETITIVE**

Denison University, founded in 1831, is a private independent institution of liberal arts and sciences. There is 1 undergraduate school. The 960-acre campus is in a suburban area in Granville, Ohio, and 25 miles east of Columbus. Including any residence halls, there are 62 buildings.

STUDENT LIFE: 66% of undergraduates are from out of state, mostly the Midwest. Students are from 45 states, 33 foreign countries, and Canada. 68% are from public schools. 8% are Foreign; 7% African American; 66% White; 4% Asian American; 4% two or more races; 2% race unknown; 10% Hispanic. 36% are Protestant; 30% Catholic; 28% Muslim, Hindu, Buddhist, and Nondenominational. **Female To Male Ratio:** 1.3:1. The average age of freshmen is 19; all undergraduates, 21. 10% do not continue beyond their first year; 82% remain to graduate. **Housing:** 2190 students can be accommodated in college housing, which includes single-sex and coed dorms and on-campus apartments. In addition, there are honors houses, special-interest houses, first-year center, substance-free dorms, quiet dorms, all-women dorms, suite-style dorms, and apartments for juniors and seniors with high GPAs. On-campus housing is guaranteed for all 4 years and is available on a lottery system for upperclassmen. 99% of students live on campus; of those, 90% remain on campus on weekends. All students may keep cars.

FACULTY/CLASSROOMS: 55% of faculty are male; 45% are female. All teach undergraduates and do research. No introductory courses are taught by graduate students. The average class size in an introductory lecture is 18; in a laboratory is 21; and in a regular course is 19.

PROGRAMS OF STUDY: Denison confers B.A., B.F.A., and B.S. degrees. Bachelor's degrees are awarded in AGRICULTURE (environmental studies), BIOLOGICAL SCIENCE (biochemistry and biology/biological science), COMMUNICATIONS AND THE ARTS (art history and appreciation, communications, dance, dramatic arts, English, film arts, fine arts, French, German, languages, Latin, media arts, music, Spanish, speech/debate/rhetoric, and studio art), COMPUTER AND PHYSICAL SCIENCE (chemistry, computer science, geology, mathematics, and physics), EDUCATION (education and physical education), SOCIAL SCIENCE (African American studies, anthropology, classical/ancient civilization, East Asian studies, economics, history, international studies, Latin American studies, philosophy, political science/government, psychology, religion, sociology, Western European studies, and women's studies). Psychology, biology, and English are the strongest academically. Communication, biology, and economics have the largest enrollments.

ACTIVITIES: 35% of men belong to 10 national fraternities; 41% of women belong to 8 national sororities. There are 180 groups on campus, including art, cheerleading, choir, chorale, chorus, communications, computers, dance, debate, drama, environmental, ethnic, film, honors, international, jazz band, LGBT, literary magazine, musical theater, newspaper, orchestra, pep band, photography, political, professional, radio and TV, religious, social, social service, student government, and symphony. Popular campus events include Community Picnic and Fair, Gala, Academic Awards Convocation and Vail Series. **Sports:** There are 11 intercollegiate sports for men and 12 for women, and 17 intramural sports for men and 14 for women. Facilities include a stadium, aquatic center, gym, outdoor tennis courts, squash courts, track, field house with a track and tennis courts, baseball/softball fields, recreation gym with 3 volleyball/basketball courts, weight, aerobic, fitness rooms, soccer and men's lacrosse stadium, women's field hockey and lacrosse field, and multiple practice fields. **Graduates:** From July 1, 2015 to June 30, 2016, 544 bachelor's degrees were awarded. The most popular majors were economics (13%), communications (11%), and biology (10%). 138 companies recruited on campus in 2015-2016. In an average class, 81% graduate in 4 years or less, 83% graduate in 5 years or less, and 85% graduate in 6 years or less. Of the 2015 graduating class, 26% were enrolled in graduate school within 6 months of graduation, and 64% were employed.

SERVICES: Counseling and information services are available, as is tutoring in most subjects, and a reader service for the blind. A reading and writing center is available, as are study sessions for math, chemistry, and some languages, reduced course loads, special counselor services, note-taking services, oral tests, extended time for tests, untimed tests, talking books, tape recorders, and readers. **Library/Resources:** The library contains 1.3 million volumes, 128,175 microform items, 37,365 audio/video tapes/CDs/DVDs, and subscribes to 21,805 periodicals including electronic. Computerized library services include interlibrary loans, database searching, Internet access, and Wi-Fi capability. Special learning facilities include an art gallery, planetarium, radio station, TV station, an observatory, a multimedia MIX lab, a field research station in a 350-acre biological reserve, a high-resolution spectrometer, economics computer labs, and a modern languages lab. **Physically Challenged Students:** 80% of the campus is accessible. Facilities include wheelchair ramps, elevators, special parking, specially equipped restrooms, special class scheduling, lowered drinking fountains, and lowered telephones. **Special:** Work-study programs, a Washington semester, study-abroad programs in more than 35 countries, student-designed majors, a dual major in education and various other majors, a philosophy, political science, and economics interdisciplinary major, and pass/fail options are available. A 3-2 engineering program is offered with Rensselaer Polytechnic Institute and Case Western Reserve, Columbia, and Washington Universities. A May-term internship is available at more than 200 U.S. locations. A B.A.-B.S. degree, accelerated degree programs, a media technology and arts interdisciplinary major, and nondegree study are possible. There are 15 national honor societies and a chapter of Phi Beta Kappa. **Visiting:** Regularly scheduled orientations are available for prospective students, including orientation programs, class visits, tours, and interviews. There are guides for informal visits, visitors may sit in on classes, and stay overnight. To schedule a visit, contact the Admissions Office. **Campus Safety and Security:** Measures include 24-hour foot and vehicle patrol, emergency notification system, self-defense education, and security escort services, and emergency telephones, lighted pathways/sidewalks, and controlled access to dorms/residences.

REQUIREMENTS: The SAT or ACT is recommended. Denison operates under a test optional admissions policy. Applicants should have completed 19 Carnegie units, including 4 units each in English, math, and science, 3 units in foreign language, 2 units in social studies, and 1 unit each in history and academic electives. An essay is part of the application process. An interview is advised, and a portfolio or an audition is recommended for art and music majors, respectively. AP and CLEP credits are accepted. Important factors in the admissions decision are personality/intangible qualities, evidence of special talent, and advanced placement or honors courses. The General Education requirements ensure that students develop core liberal arts competencies and encounter a broad range of liberal arts inquiries-social, scientific, humanistic, and artistic-embraced by the faculty of Denison University. In addition, the requirements expose students to a diversity of perspectives that enable them to interact more effectively in an increasingly interdependent world. Thus, the General Education program seeks to accomplish three goals: Development of competencies, exposure to a broad variety of disciplines, and development of a global perspective. GENERAL EDUCATION: SUMMARY OF REQUIREMENTS: Two courses each of fine arts, sciences (one fulfilling a lab requirement), social sciences, and humanities. One interdivisional course from one of the following areas: Black Studies, East Asian Studies, Environmental Studies, International Studies, Latin American and Caribbean Studies, Queer Studies, and Women Studies. Writing Requirement, One W101 Writing Workshop, Two "W" Writing Competency courses. At a minimum, all students must complete an elementary year of Foreign Language 111-112 at the college level. Students who have studied a language in high school and who wish to continue study of that language at Denison in order to fulfill this requirement will, however, be expected to complete three semesters of that language (i.e., to pass or demonstrate proficiency in the language at the 211 level). All entering students who have studied a foreign language in high school must take the appropriate placement test during the orientation period. Language courses 111, 112, and 211 will not count toward the divisional distribution requirements, except for Latin and Greek 211 which may count toward the Humanities requirement unless used to satisfy the Foreign Language requirement. Three of these general education courses (or other courses) must fulfill one power and justice, one quantitative, and one oral communication requirement. Only one course from a single department may be used to fulfill the divisional requirements. **Procedure:** Freshmen are admitted in the fall and spring. Entrance exams should be taken by December of the senior year. There are early decision, early admissions, and deferred admissions plans. Early decision applications should be filed by December 1; regular applications, by January 15 for fall entry, along with a $40 fee. Notification of early decision is sent January 1; regular decision, April 1. 84 early decision candidates were accepted for the 2016-2017 class. 515 applicants were on the 2016 waiting list; 21 were admitted. Application fees are waived if application is completed online. **Transfer Students:** 10 transfer students enrolled in 2015-2016. A minimum GPA of 2.75 is required. SAT or ACT scores should be submitted, as well as high school and college transcripts, an essay, and a statement of good standing from previous institutions. An interview is recommended. 64 of 127 credits required for the bachelor's degree must be completed at Denison. **International Students:** There are 172 international students enrolled. The school actively recruits these students. They must take the TOEFL with a minimum score of 550 on the paper-based TOEFL (PBT) or 80 on the Internet-based version (iBT).

ADMISSIONS: 48% of the 2016-2017 applicants were accepted. The SAT scores for the 2016-2017 freshman class were: Critical Reading-- 5% below 500, 28% between 500 and 599, 51% between 600 and 699, and 16% between 700 and 800. Math-- 2% below 500, 27% between 500 and 599, 50% between 600 and 699, and 21% between 700 and 800. The ACT scores were 4% between 18 and 23, 56% between 24 and 29, and 40% above 30. 78% of the current freshmen were in the top fifth of their class; 96% were in the top two fifths. There were 25 National Merit finalists. 15 freshmen graduated first in their class. **Admissions Contact:** Mike Hills, Director of Admissions. Email: *admissions@denison.edu* Web: *www.denison.edu*

FINANCIAL AID: In 2016-2017, 97% of all full-time freshmen and 96% of continuing full-time students received some form of financial aid. 97% of all full-time freshmen and 96% of continuing full-time students received need-based aid. The average freshman award was $37,445. Need-based scholarships or need-based grants averaged $33,696; need-based self-help aid (loans and jobs) averaged $4,718; and other non-need-based awards and non-need-based scholarships averaged $22,140. 45% of undergraduate students work part-time. Average annual earnings from campus work are $2430. Denison is a member of CSS. The FAFSA code is 003042. The deadline for filing freshman financial aid applications for fall entry is February 15.

FRANCISCAN UNIVERSITY OF STEUBENVILLE — E-3

www.franciscan.edu

Steubenville, OH 43952	**(740) 283-6860** **(800) 783-6220**
Fax: (740) 284-5456	**Email: admissions@franciscan.edu**
Full-time: 779 men, 1216 women	**Faculty:** 120; IIA, -$
Part-time: 53 men, 42 women	**Ph.D.s:** 82%
Graduate: 292 men, 377 women	**Student/Faculty:** 14 to 1
Year: semesters, summer session	**Tuition:** $25,680
Room & Board: $8300	**Freshman Class:** 1760 applied, 1386 accepted, 456 enrolled
SAT CR/M/W: 590/560/570 **ACT:** 25	**CEEB CODE:** 1133
Application Deadline: n/av	**VERY COMPETITIVE**

Franciscan University of Steubenville, founded in 1946 by the Franciscan Friars, is a private liberal arts institution which embraces the call to dynamic orthodoxy and whose mission is "to educate, to evangelize, and to send forth joyful disciples," thereby restoring all things in Christ. There is 1 undergraduate school and 7 graduate schools. In addition to regional accreditation, Franciscan University has baccalaureate program accreditation with CSWE, NCATE, and CCNE. The 235-acre campus is in a small town 40 miles west of Pittsburgh. Including any residence halls, there are 25 buildings.

STUDENT LIFE: 80% of undergraduates are from out of state, mostly the Midwest. Students are from 50 states, 10 foreign countries, and Canada. 37% are from public schools. 82% are White; 2% Asian American; 2% two or more races; 2% race unknown; 11% Hispanic; 1% African American; 1% Foreign. 97% are Catholic. **Female To Male Ratio:** 1.5:1. The average age of freshmen is 18; all undergraduates, 20. 16% do not continue beyond their first year; 76% remain to graduate. **Housing:** 1394 students can be accommodated in college housing, which includes single-sex dorms, on-campus apartments, and Christian faith households in residence halls. On-campus housing is available on a first-come and first-served basis. 80% of students live on campus; of those, 80% remain on campus on weekends. Upperclassmen may keep cars.

FACULTY/CLASSROOMS: 63% of faculty are male; 37% are female. 96% teach undergraduates. No introductory courses are taught by graduate students. The average class size in an introductory lecture is 28; in a laboratory is 15; and in a regular course is 21.

PROGRAMS OF STUDY: Franciscan University confers B.A., B.S., and B.S.N. degrees. Associate and master's degrees are also awarded. Bachelor's degrees are awarded in BIOLOGICAL SCIENCE (biology/biological science), BUSINESS (accounting, business administration and management, international business management, management, and marketing management), COMMUNICATIONS AND THE ARTS (classics, communications, dramatic arts, English, French, German, and Spanish), COMPUTER AND PHYSICAL SCIENCE (chemistry, computer science, information sciences and systems, and mathematics), EDUCATION (elementary education), HEALTH PROFESSIONS (nursing), SOCIAL SCIENCE (anthropology, economics, history, humanities and social science, philosophy, political science/government, psychology, religious education, religious music, social work, sociology, and theological studies). Theology, catechetics, biology, chemistry and nursing are the strongest academically. Theology, business, nursing education, and catechetics have the largest enrollments.

ACTIVITIES: There are no fraternities or sororities. There are 35 groups on campus, including choir, chorale, chorus, computers, drama, ethnic, honors, international, literary magazine, newspaper, orchestra, political, pro-life club, professional, radio and TV, religious, social, social service, student government, and yearbook. Popular campus events include Feast of St. Francis, Pro-Life Rally, and an All-school Evangelism Events. **Sports:** There are 7 intercollegiate sports for men and 9 for women, and 8 intramural sports for men and 8 for women. Facilities include a campus athletic center, which houses basketball courts, and racquetball courts. Outdoor athletic facilities include a sand volleyball court, baseball, softball, flag football, and soccer fields. **Graduates:** From July 1, 2015 to June 30, 2016, 474 bachelor's degrees were awarded. The most popular majors were theology (20%), nursing (8%), and education (8%). 35 companies recruited on campus in 2015-2016. In an average class, 7% graduate in 3 years or less, 67% graduate in 4 years or less, 74% graduate in 5 years or less, and 76% graduate in 6 years or less. Of the 2015 graduating class, 20% were enrolled in graduate school within 6 months of graduation, and 67% were employed.

SERVICES: Counseling and information services are available, as is tutoring in most subjects, a reader service for the blind, and remedial reading and writing. Tutoring and counseling are available for learning-disabled students. Tutoring is also available for students on academic probation. **Library/Resources:** The library contains 224,280 volumes, 269 microform items, 892 audio/video tapes/CDs/DVDs, and subscribes to 399 periodicals including electronic. Computerized library services include interlibrary loans, database searching, Internet access, and Wi-Fi capability. Special learning facilities include an art gallery and radio station. **Physically Challenged Students:** 80% of the campus is accessible. Facilities include wheelchair ramps, elevators, special parking, specially equipped restrooms, special class scheduling, lowered drinking fountains, lowered telephones. **Special:** Dual majors and internships for up to 6 credit hours are available in most majors. A humanities and Catholic culture major in Western tradition and minors in human life studies, film studies, Franciscan studies, and music are offered. Study abroad is offered through our highly ranked program in Gaming, Austria, where students spend a semester studying humanities as well as traveling through Europe. There are 5 national honor societies, a freshman honors program, and 25 departmental honors programs. **Visiting:** There are regularly scheduled orientations for prospective students, including tours, interviews with professors, admissions, and financial aid officers, and class scheduling. There are guides for informal visits, visitors may sit in on classes, and stay overnight. To schedule a visit, contact Bernardo Gonzalez at bgonzalez@franciscan.edu. **Campus Safety and Security:** Measures include 24-hour foot and vehicle patrol, emergency notification system, self-defense education, and security escort services. There are also shuttle buses, emergency telephones, lighted pathways/sidewalks, and controlled access to dorms/residences.

REQUIREMENTS: Applicants should have completed 15 academic high school units, including 10 in 4 of the 5 following areas: English, foreign language, social science, math, and natural sciences. The GED is accepted. The ACT or SAT is required and an interview is recommended. A GPA of 2.4 is required. AP and CLEP credits are accepted. All students must complete core curriculum courses. Bachelor of Arts students must complete 9 credits each in theology and philosophy, 6 credits each in literature and natural science, and 3 credits each in American founding principles, Catholic traditions in fine arts, history, social science and math or economics for a total of 45 credits. In addition, they must complete a foreign language at the intermediate level. Bachelor of Science students must complete 15 credits in theology and/or philosophy, 6 credits in natural science, and 3 credits each in American founding principles, Catholic traditions in fine arts, economics, history, literature, math and social science. **Procedure:** Freshmen are admitted in the fall, spring, and summer. Entrance exams should be taken in the spring of the junior year or the fall of the senior year. There is a rolling admissions plan. Application deadlines are open. Notification is sent on a rolling basis. Applications are accepted on-line. Application fees are waived if application is completed on-line. **Transfer Students:** 122 transfer students enrolled in 2015-2016. A minimum 2.0 college GPA is required. High school and college transcripts must be submitted. An interview is recommended. 30 of 124 credits required for the bachelor's degree must be completed at Franciscan University. **International Students:** There are 17 international students enrolled. They must take the TOEFL with a minimum score of 550 on the paper-based TOEFL (PBT) or 80 on the Internet-based version (iBT).

ADMISSIONS: 79% of the 2016-2017 applicants were accepted. The SAT scores for the 2016-2017 freshman class were: Critical Reading-- 9% below 500, 42% between 500 and 599, 32% between 600 and 699, and 17% between 700 and 800. Math-- 21% below 500, 44% between 500 and 599, 28% between 600 and 699, and 7% between 700 and 800. Writing-- 18% below 500, 45% between 500 and 599, 30% between 600 and 699, and 7% between 700 and 800. The ACT scores were 32% between 18 and 23, 52% between 24 and 29, and 16% above 30. 44% of the current freshmen were in the top fifth of their class; 72% were in the top two fifths. 4 freshmen graduated first in their class. **Admissions Contact:** Christopher Krivoniak, Director of Admissions. Email: *admissions@franciscan.edu* Web: *www.franciscan.edu*

FINANCIAL AID: Check with the school for current application deadlines.

FRANKLIN UNIVERSITY *(The complete profile is made available exclusively on our website, www.barronspac.com)*

HEIDELBERG UNIVERSITY — C-2

www.heidelberg.edu

Tiffin, OH 44883 — **(419) 448-2330**

Fax: (419) 448-2334	**Email: adminfo@l.heidelberg.edu**
Full-time: 546 men, 502 women	**Faculty:** n/av
Part-time: 22 men, 40 women	**Ph.D.s:** 84%
Graduate: 56 men, 116 women	**Student/Faculty:** 16 to 1
Year: semesters, summer session	**Tuition:** $29,200
Room & Board: $10,000	**Freshman Class:** 1727 applied, 1226 accepted, 345 enrolled
SAT CR/M/W: required **ACT:** 22	**CEEB CODE:** 1292
Application Deadline: August 1	**COMPETITIVE**

Heidelberg University, founded in 1850 by the German Reformed Church, and affiliated with the United Church of Christ, is a private liberal arts institution offering undergraduate and graduate degrees. Figures in the above capsule and in this profile are approximate. There are 4 undergraduate schools and 4 graduate schools. In addition to regional accreditation, Heidelberg has baccalaureate program accreditation with NASM, CAAHEP, CAATE, and CACREP. The 110-acre campus is in a small town in Tiffin, Ohio, 90 minutes from the metropolitan areas of Columbus, Cleveland, abd Toledo. Including any residence halls, there are 7 buildings.

STUDENT LIFE: 90% of undergraduates are from Ohio. Others are from 25 states, 10 foreign countries, and Canada. 61% are from public schools. 84% are White; 3% Hispanic; 2% Foreign; 10% African American; 1% Asian American. 33% are Protestant; 22% Catholic. **Female To Male Ratio:** 1.1:1. The average age of freshmen is 18; all undergraduates, 20. 39% do not continue beyond their first year; 53% remain to graduate. **Housing:** 900 students can be accommodated in college housing, which includes single-sex and coed dorms, on-campus apartments, special-interest houses. On-campus housing is guaranteed for all 4 years, is available on a first-come, and first-served basis. Priority is given to out-of-town students. 84% of students live on campus; of those, 80% remain on campus on weekends. All students may keep cars. Alcohol is not permitted.

FACULTY/CLASSROOMS: 54% of faculty are male; 56% are female. 97% teach undergraduates. No introductory courses are taught by graduate students. The average class size in an introductory lecture is 11; in a laboratory is 15; and in a regular course is 15.

PROGRAMS OF STUDY: Heidelberg confers B.A., B.S. and B.Mus. degrees. Master's degrees are also awarded. Bachelor's degrees are awarded in BIOLOGICAL SCIENCE (biochemistry, biology/biological science, and environmental biology), BUSINESS (accounting, business administration and management, business economics, management science, and sports management), COMMUNICATIONS AND THE ARTS (communications, dramatic arts, English, German, music, public relations, and Spanish), COMPUTER AND PHYSICAL SCIENCE (chemistry, computer science, information sciences and systems, mathematics, and physics), EDUCATION (athletic training, elementary education, foreign languages education, middle school education, music education, physical education, science education, and secondary education), ENGINEERING AND ENVIRONMENTAL DESIGN (preengineering), HEALTH PROFESSIONS (predentistry and premedicine), SOCIAL SCIENCE (anthropology, criminal justice, economics, forensic studies, history, international studies, philosophy, political science/government, prelaw, psychology, public administration, religion, social science, and water resources). Business administration, education, and sciences are the strongest academically. Business administration, physical sciences, and education have the largest enrollments.

ACTIVITIES: 28% of men belong to 5 local fraternities; 18% of women belong to 4 local sororities. There are 73 groups on campus, including art, band, cheerleading, chess, choir, chorale, chorus, computers, dance, drama, drill team, environmental, ethnic, film, forensics, honors, international, jazz band, LGBT, literary magazine, musical theater, newspaper, opera, orchestra, pep band, political, professional, radio and TV, religious, social, social service, student government, symphony, and yearbook. Popular campus events include Greek Sing, Battle of the Bands, and T-Bridge. **Sports:** There are 9 intercollegiate sports for men and 9 for women, and 9 intramural sports for men and 8 for women. Facilities an wrestling arena, all-weather track, indoor courts for volleyball, basketball, racquetball, tennis, golf, a weight room and fitness area, track and field, wrestling, a sports medicine clinic, and outdoor tennis, soccer, and football facilities. A YMCA adjacent to the college provides additional recreation options. **Graduates:** From July 1, 2015 to June 30, 2016, 222 bachelor's degrees were awarded. The most popular majors were business (28%), education (18%), and political science (18%).

SERVICES: Counseling and information services are available, as is tutoring in most subjects, and remedial math and reading. **Library/Resources:** The library contains 260,055 volumes, 108,640 microform items, 8,300 audio/video tapes/CDs/DVDs, and subscribes to 829 periodicals including electronic. Computerized library services include interlibrary loans, database searching, Internet access, and Wi-Fi capability. Special learning facilities include a radio station, TV station, a media center, an anthropology museum, human cadaver lab, water quality lab, an archeology lab, a physiology lab, and a computer-assisted writing classroom. **Physically Challenged Students:** 20% of the campus is accessible. Facilities include wheelchair ramps, elevators, special parking, specially equipped restrooms, special class scheduling, and lowered drinking fountains. **Special:** Cross-registration with Terra Community College and North Central Community College and a 3-4 degree in osteropathic medicine with Lake Erie College of Osteopathic Medicine are offered. Study abroad is possible at the University of Heidelberg, Germany, Seville, Spain, and others. A Washington semester is available at American University. Dual majors in any combination, an honors program, credit for life experience, internships, and pass/fail options are possible. There are 10 national honor societies, a freshman honors program, and 15 departmental honors programs. **Visiting:** There are regularly scheduled orientations for prospective students, including coach and faculty sessions, academic overview, student panel, admissions and financial aid presentations, a tour of the college and lunch. There are guides for informal visits, visitors may sit in on classes, and stay overnight. To schedule a visit, contact the Admissions Office. **Campus Safety and Security:** Measures include 24-hour foot and vehicle patrol, emergency notification system, self-defense education, and security escort services, emergency telephones, and lighted pathways/sidewalks.

REQUIREMENTS: The SAT or ACT is required. Applicants should have completed 22 high school academic credits, including 4 years each of English and social studies, 3 each of math and science, and 2 of a foreign language. An audition is required for music majors. Recommendations and an interview are recommended. A GPA of 2.5 is required. AP and CLEP credits are accepted. Important factors in the admissions decision are recommendations by school officials, extracurricular activities record, and advanced placement or honors courses. Students must fulfill 40 semester hours of general education requirements, including English composition and public speaking, arts, languages and literature, civilization, religion and philosophy, social sciences, natural sciences, and math, and 40 semester hours each in the major and electives. Four units of health and phys ed are needed. A total of 120 semester hours with a minimum GPA of 2.0 overall and 2.5 in the major is required to graduate. **Procedure:** Freshmen are admitted to all sessions. Entrance exams should be taken by the end of the junior year or the beginning of the senior year. There are deferred admissions and rolling admissions plans. Applications should be filed by August 1 for fall entry; December 1 for spring entry; and May 1 for summer entry, along with a $25 fee. Notifications are sent September 15. Applications are accepted online. **Transfer Students:** 44 transfer students enrolled in 2015-2016. A minimum GPA of 2.0 and a character reference from the institution most recently attended are required. 30 of 120 credits required for the bachelor's degree must be completed at Heidelberg. **International Students:** There are 11 international students enrolled. The school actively recruits these students. They must take the TOEFL with a minimum score of 550 on the paper-based TOEFL (PBT) or 80 on the Internet-based version (iBT) and the college's own test.

ADMISSIONS: 71% of the 2016-2017 applicants were accepted. The SAT scores for the 2016-2017 freshman class were: Critical Reading-- 51% below 500, 35% between 500 and 599, 12% between 600 and 699, and 2% between 700 and 800. Math-- 52% below 500, 35% between 500 and 599, and 13% between 600 and 699. Writing-- 60% below 500, 30% between 500 and 599, 9% between 600 and 699, and 2% between 700 and 800. The ACT scores were 48% below 12, 24% between 12 and 17, 16% between 18 and 23, 7% between 24 and 29, and 5% above 30. 30% of the current freshmen were in the top fifth of their class; 53% were in the top two fifths. 2 freshmen graduated first in their class. **Admissions Contact:** Lindsay Sooy, VP for Enrollment and Admissions. Email: *adminfo@l.heidelberg.edu* Web: *www.heidelberg.edu*

FINANCIAL AID: In 2016-2017, 99% of all full-time freshmen and 85% of continuing full-time students received some form of financial aid. 95% of all full-time freshmen and 85% of continuing full-time students received need-based aid. 65% of undergraduate students work part-time. Average annual earnings from campus work are $850. The FAFSA code is 003048. The priority date for freshman financial aid applications for fall entry is March 1.

HIRAM COLLEGE — E-1

www.hiram.edu

Hiram, OH 44234	**(330) 569-5169** **(800) 362-5280**
Fax: (330) 569-5944	**Email: admission@hiram.edu**
Full-time: 428 men, 428 women	**Faculty:** 81
Part-time: 111 men, 123 women	**Ph.D.s:** 95%
Graduate: 11 men, 13 women	**Student/Faculty:** 10 to 1
Year: other, summer session	**Tuition:** $33,040
Room & Board: $10,190	**Freshman Class:** 2521 applied, 1366 accepted, 207 enrolled
SAT CR/M/W: required **ACT:** 22	**CEEB CODE:** 1297
Application Deadline: n/av	**COMPETITIVE**

Hiram College is a 166-year-old liberal arts college in Ohio's Western Reserve known for changing students' lives. Hiram's academic calendar, known as the Hiram Plan, is unique to the nation. The College provides students one of the country's oldest and most respected study-abroad programs and is one of 10 percent of colleges and universities to be awarded a chapter of the prestigious honor society Phi Beta Kappa. Hiram offers 32 majors and 38 minors, many of which are interdisciplinary, as well as 20 three-year undergraduate degrees, a M.A. in interdisciplinary studies and a Weekend College program. There is 1 undergraduate school. In addition to regional accreditation, Hiram has baccalaureate program accreditation with NASM, NCATE, and CCNE. The 110-acre campus is in a rural area 35 miles southeast of Cleveland. Including any residence halls, there are 39 buildings.

STUDENT LIFE: 85% of undergraduates are from Ohio. Others are from 31 states, 14 foreign countries, and Canada. 60% are White; 4% Hispanic; 3% two or more races; 2% Foreign; 15% African American; 15% race unknown; 1% Asian American. **Female To Male Ratio:** 1.0:1. The average age of freshmen is 19; all undergraduates, 23. 30% do not continue beyond their first year; 61% remain to graduate. **Housing:** 720 students can be accommodated in college housing, which includes single-sex and coed dorms, on-campus apartments, honors houses, special-interest houses, special interest housing, a entrepreneurship housing. On-campus housing is guaranteed for all 4 years and is available on a lottery system for upperclassmen. 80% of students live on campus. All students may keep cars.

FACULTY/CLASSROOMS: 43% of faculty are male; 57% are female. All teach undergraduates. No introductory courses are taught by graduate students. The average class size in an introductory lecture is 16; in a laboratory is 12; and in a regular course is 13.

PROGRAMS OF STUDY: Hiram confers B.A. and B.S.N. degrees. Master's degrees are also awarded. Bachelor's degrees are awarded in BIOLOGICAL SCIENCE (biochemistry, biology/biological science, and neurosciences), BUSINESS (accounting and management), COMMUNICATIONS AND THE ARTS (art history, art, communications, creative writing, English, French, music, Spanish, and theatre acting), COMPUTER AND PHYSICAL SCIENCE (chemistry, computer science, mathematics, and physics), EDUCATION (education), ENGINEERING AND ENVIRONMENTAL DESIGN (environmental science), HEALTH PROFESSIONS (biomedical science, exercise science, and nursing), SOCIAL SCIENCE (economics, history, philosophy, political science/government, psychology, religion, and sociology). Biomedical humanities, and creative writing are the strongest academically. Accounting and financial management, business management, and nursing have the largest enrollments.

ACTIVITIES: 1% of men belong to 1 local fraternity; 6% of women belong to 4 local sororities. There are 40 groups on campus, including art, cheerleading, choir, chorale, chorus, computers, dance, drama, drill team, environmental, ethnic, honors, international, LGBT, literary magazine, musical theater, photography, political, professional, radio and TV, religious, social, student government, and yearbook. Popular campus events include Campus Days, Springfest, Homecoming, Parents Weekend, Alumni Weekend. **Sports:** There are 7 intercollegiate sports for men and 7 for women, and 10 intramural sports for men and 10 for women. The sports center includes a gym, courts for tennis, volleyball, basketball, baseball, an elevated track, a multipurpose activity court, a pool, fitness center, weight room, an aerobics studio, racquetball courts, and a training room. Outdoor facilities include football, baseball, soccer, and softball fields, practice fields, and 3 tennis courts. **Graduates:** From July 1, 2015 to June 30, 2016, 279 bachelor's degrees were awarded. The most popular majors were accounting and financial management (17%), management (14%), and nursing (10%). In an average class, 54% graduate in 4 years or less, 60% graduate in 5 years or less, and 61% graduate in 6 years or less. Of the 2015 graduating class, 12% were enrolled in graduate school within 6 months of graduation, and 58% were employed.

SERVICES: Counseling and information services are available, as is tutoring in most subjects, and note takers are available for most classes. **Library/Resources:** The library contains 503,435 volumes, 131 microform items, 23,842 audio/video tapes/CDs/DVDs, and subscribes to 10,344 periodicals including electronic. Computerized library services include interlibrary loans, database searching, Internet access, and Wi-Fi capability. Special learning facilities include an art gallery, planetarium, radio station, and The James H. Barrow Field Station offers over 500 acres of land to support hands on research and education. **Physically Challenged Students:** 55% of the campus is accessible. Facilities include wheelchair ramps, elevators, special parking, specially equipped restrooms, and special housing. **Special:** Under the Hiran plan, students complete 12 weeks of traditional coursework, take a weeklong break and finish their academic semester with three weeks of intensive study in a single class. Unique to the nation, this plan has been described as a near-perfect approach to fostering student learning and engagement. Hiram takes yet another thoughtful approach to higher education through Hiram Connect, which links coursework, internships, study-away explorations and hands-on learning opportunities. This process, which encourages students to reflect upon their academic experiences, not only helps them determine what they want to do professionally, but who they want to be personally. Other College offerings, such as Hiram Health, which prepares health professionals as compassionate caregivers, and pathways to graduate programs at such schools as Case Western Reserve University, Washington University in St. Louis and Northeast Ohio Medical University serve Hiram students who come from throughout the United States and 20 foreign countries. Hiram College provides students with one of the country's oldest and most respected study-abroad programs. The College offers 32 majors and 38 minors, many of which are interdisciplinary, as well as 20 three-year undergraduate degrees, a M.A. in interdisciplinary studies and a Weekend College program for nontraditional students. There are 6 national honor societies, Phi Beta Kappa, and a freshman honors program. **Visiting:** There are regularly scheduled orientations for prospective students, Campus visits for prospective students consist of tours and overnights while school is in session if requested. There are guides for informal visits, visitors may sit in on classes, and stay overnight. To schedule a visit, contact Carol Agnew at AgnewCA@hiram.edu. **Campus Safety and Security:** Measures include emergency notification system, self-defense education, and security escort services, emergency telephones, lighted pathways/sidewalks, and controlled access to dorms/residences.

REQUIREMENTS: Applicants should have completed 16 academic units or the GED equivalent. An essay, portfolio, audition, and interview are recommended. AP and CLEP credits are accepted. Important factors in the admissions decision are advanced placement or honors courses, personality/intangible qualities, and extracurricular activities record. All students must complete courses in a core curriculum across a minimum of 6 disciplines; and complete at least 120 semester hours (133 for Bachelor of Science in Nursing students); and with a GPA of at least 2.0 overall and in each major and minor. A capstone project is required in all undergraduate majors. A transfer student must complete a minimum of 45 passed credit hours in residence at Hiram College, and a minimum of 50% of the major/minor coursework must be completed with Hiram College courses. **Procedure:** Freshmen are admitted in the fall and spring. Entrance exams should be taken No later than the fall of the senior year of high school. There are deferred admissions and rolling admissions plans. Application deadlines are open. Application fee is $25. Notification is sent on a rolling basis. Application fees are waived if application is completed online. **Transfer Students:** 42 transfer students enrolled in 2015-2016. Applicants should have at least a 2.5 GPA and be in good academic and social standing with the previous institution. An interview is recommended. 45 of 120 credits required for the bachelor's degree must be completed at Hiram. **International Students:** There are 23 international students enrolled. The school actively recruits these students. They must take the TOEFL with a minimum score of 500 on the paper-based TOEFL (PBT) or 61 on the Internet-based version (iBT).

ADMISSIONS: 54% of the 2016-2017 applicants were accepted. The SAT scores for the 2016-2017 freshman class were: Critical Reading-- 55% below 500, 34% between 500 and 599, 8% between 600 and 699, and 3% between 700 and 800. Math-- 63% below 500, 26% between 500 and 599, 8% between 600 and 699, and 3% between 700 and 800. Writing-- 69% below 500, 26% between 500 and 599, and 6% between 600 and 699. The ACT scores were 13% between 12 and 17, 51% between 18 and 23, 31% between 24 and 29, and 6% above 30. **Admissions Contact:** Sherman C. Dean, Director of Admissions. Email: *admission@hiram.edu* Web: *www.hiram.edu*

FINANCIAL AID: Hiram is a member of CSS. The FAFSA code is 003049. The priority date for freshman financial aid applications for fall entry is February 15.

JOHN CARROLL UNIVERSITY — D-1

www.sites.jcu.edu

University Heights, OH 44118	**(216) 397-4294** **(888) 335-6800**
Fax: (216) 397-4981	**Email: enrollment@jcu.edu**
Full-time: 1491 men, 1446 women	**Faculty:** 185; IIA, av$
Part-time: 46 men, 45 women	**Ph.D.s:** 97%
Graduate: 179 men, 318 women	**Student/Faculty:** 13 to 1
Year: semesters, summer session	**Tuition:** $38,490
Room & Board: $11,250	**Freshman Class:** 3873 applied, 3211 accepted, 799 enrolled
SAT CR/M/W: 544/549/532 **ACT:** 25	**CEEB CODE:** 1342
Application Deadline: February 1	**COMPETITIVE+**

John Carroll is a private, coeducational, Jesuit Catholic university providing programs in the liberal arts, sciences, and business at the undergraduate and master's levels. As a Jesuit Catholic university, John Carroll inspires its students to excel in learning, leadership, and service in the region and in the world. Our unique size, structure, culture, and environment make us very successful at providing an outstanding education for our students. There are 2 undergraduate schools and 2 graduate schools. In addition to regional accreditation, John Carroll has baccalaureate program accreditation with AACSB, NCATE, HLC, CACREP, and NASP. The 62-acre campus is in a suburban area in University Heights, Ohio, 10 miles east of Cleveland with easy access to the city. Including any residence halls, there are 21 buildings.

STUDENT LIFE: 65% of undergraduates are from Ohio. Others are from 34 states, 34 foreign countries, and Canada. 49% are from public schools. 86% are White; 4% African American; 4% Hispanic; 2% Asian American; 2% Foreign; 2% two or more races; 1% race unknown. 64% are Catholic; 15% Buddhist, Hindu, Muslim, Orthodox Christian, and Unitarian; 11% Protestant. **Female To Male Ratio:** 1.1:1. The average age of freshmen is 18; all undergraduates, 20. 14% do not continue beyond their first year; 77% remain to graduate. **Housing:** 1810 students can be accommodated in college housing, which includes single-sex and coed dorms, off-campus apartments, special-interest houses, wellness, and fraternity/sorority floors in residence halls. On-campus housing is available on a lottery system for upperclassmen. 57% of students live on campus. All students may keep cars.

FACULTY/CLASSROOMS: 55% of faculty are male; 45% are female. 97% teach undergraduates, 95% do research, and 95% do both. Graduate students teach 1% of introductory courses. The average class size in an introductory lecture is 19; in a laboratory is 15; and in a regular course is 19.

PROGRAMS OF STUDY: John Carroll confers B.A., B.S., B.A.Classics, B.S.B.A. and B.S.Econ. degrees. Master's degrees are also awarded. Bachelor's degrees are awarded in BIOLOGICAL SCIENCE (biochemistry, biology/biological science, cell biology, and molecular biology), BUSINESS (accounting, banking and finance, business administration and management, business (dual major program), entrepreneurial studies, finance, human resources, international business management, logistics, management information systems, and marketing/retailing/merchandising), COMMUNICATIONS AND THE ARTS (art history, art history and appreciation, classical languages, classics, communications, English, French, German, Greek, Latin, literature, modern language, Spanish, theatre arts, and theatre studies), COMPUTER AND PHYSICAL SCIENCE (chemistry, computer science, mathematics, natural sciences, and physics), EDUCATION (early childhood education, education, health information management, mathematics education, middle school education, physical education, secondary education, and sports studies), ENGINEERING AND ENVIRONMENTAL DESIGN (engineering physics and environmental science), HEALTH PROFESSIONS (exercise science, health services technology, and pre-health biological studies), SOCIAL SCIENCE (Asian/Oriental studies, criminal justice, criminology, East Asian studies, economics, European studies, gender studies, history, humanities, liberal arts/general studies, peace studies, philosophy, political science/government, psychology, religion, sociology, theological studies, and women's studies). Accounting, biology, and health and healthcare IT, education, and chemistry are the strongest academically. Communication & theatre arts, biology, and accountancy have the largest enrollments.

ACTIVITIES: 11% of men belong to 4 national fraternities; 23% of women belong to 5 national sororities. There are 110 groups on campus, including band, cheerleading, chess, choir, chorale, chorus, communications, computers, dance, debate, drama, drill team, environmental, ethnic, film, forensics, honors, international, jazz band, LGBT, literary magazine, musical theater, newspaper, pep band, photography, political, professional, radio and TV, religious, social, social service, student government, and yearbook. Popular campus events include Celebration of Scholarship, Winter Formal, Christmas Carroll Eve, Relay for Life, Carroll Fest (concert), Homecoming, Senior Week, Greek Week, Grad Fair, and Spring Concert. **Sports:** There are 12 intercollegiate sports for men and 11 for women, and 7 intramural sports for men and 6 for women. Facilities include a swimming pool and diving well, a football stadium and track, baseball stadium, soccer and softball fields, indoor track, tennis, volleyball, racquetball, and basketball courts, wrestling room, weight room, and a fitness center. Club sports include hockey, rugby, lacrosse, field hockey, crew, women's basketball, ultimate frisbee, volleyball and sailing. **Graduates:** From July 1, 2015 to June 30, 2016, 620 bachelor's degrees were awarded. The most popular majors were communications (11%), accountancy (8%), and biology (8%). In an average class, 1% graduate in 3 years or less, 66% graduate in 4 years or less, 74% graduate in 5 years or less, and 77% graduate in 6 years or less. Of the 2015 graduating class, 68% were enrolled in graduate school within 6 months of graduation.

SERVICES: Counseling and information services are available, as is tutoring in some subjects, such as accounting, biology, chemistry, economics, finance, physics, psychology. Chinese, French, German, Spanish, and Theology/Religion. There is also a reader service for the blind, and remedial writing. **Library/Resources:** The library contains 442,990 volumes, 701,000 microform items, 10,643 audio/video tapes/CDs/DVDs, and subscribes to 9,444 periodicals including electronic. Computerized library services include interlibrary loans, database searching, Internet access, and Wi-Fi capability. Special learning facilities include a radio station, TV station, a learning commons/academic resource center, various computer commons, a digital media center, on-campus radio station, modern language labs, and group study rooms. **Physically Challenged Students:** 96% of the campus is accessible. Facilities include wheelchair ramps, elevators, special parking, specially equipped restrooms, special class scheduling, lowered drinking fountains, lowered telephones, and special housing. **Special:** Cross-registration is offered with 9 area colleges, universities, and institutes. Study abroad is possible in 16 countries. Joint engineering degrees are offered with Case Western Reserve University or the University of Detroit Mercy. Other dual-degree options: after two years of study at JCU students can enter the University of Toledo College of Medicine MEDStart program, biology majors can spend 3 years at JCU and then enroll in the Bolton School of Nursing at Case Western Reserve University towards a Doctor of Nursing Practice. Work-study programs with local corporations, internships, a Washington semester, student-designed majors, dual majors, and some pass/fail options are available. We offer 32 Study Abroad programs in the following countries: Australia, China, Costa Rica, Denmark, El Salvador, France, Germany, Ghana, Ireland, Italy, Japan, South Africa, South Korea, Spain, Turkey, and United Kingdom. There are 15 national honor societies and a freshman honors program. **Visiting:** There are regularly scheduled orientations for prospective students, consisting of open houses, admission and financial aid presentations, campus and Cleveland tours, and opportunities to meet faculty, coaches, and other campus officials. There are guides for informal visits and visitors may sit in on classes. To schedule a visit, contact the Office of Admission. **Campus Safety and Security:** Measures include 24-hour foot and vehicle patrol, emergency notification system, self-defense education, and security escort services. There are also shuttle buses, emergency telephones, lighted pathways/sidewalks, and controlled access to dorms/residences.

REQUIREMENTS: The SAT or ACT is required. Applicants should be graduates of an accredited secondary school with a minimum of 16 academic credits, including 4 in English, 3 each in math and academic electives, 2 each in foreign language, science with lab, and social studies and history. An essay is part of the application process, and an interview is highly encouraged for students concerned about admissions standards. AP and CLEP credits are accepted. Important factors in the admissions decision are advanced placement or honors courses, extracurricular activities record, and personality/intangible qualities. Beginning in 2015, first-year students will participate in a new core curriculum that has a distinctive, integrative framework. In addition to courses in oral and written expression, quantitative analysis, and foreign language, students will choose 5 courses that will include at least 1 science, 1 social science and humanities, 4 of which will be linked with another course, offering multiple cross-disciplinary experiences. The core also includes student selection of: 2 philosophy courses, 2 theology and religious studies courses, 1 social justice course, and 1 arts course. A capstone course in the major, and 120 credit hours with a minimum GPA of 2.0, are required for graduation. **Procedure:** Freshmen are admitted in the fall, spring, and summer. Entrance exams should be taken in the spring of the junior year or the fall of the senior year. There are deferred admissions and rolling admissions plans. Applications should be filed by February 1 for fall entry. Notification is sent on a rolling basis. Applications are accepted online. **Transfer Students:** 76 transfer students enrolled in 2015-2016. Students must be in good standing at the time of application. The most recent term average and the cumulative average at the home school must be 2.0 or better to be considered for admission, and the cumulative average for all schools attended must be 2.0 or better. A GPA of at least 2.5 is preferred. 30 of 120 credits required for the bachelor's degree must be completed at John Carroll. **International Students:** There are 62 international students enrolled. The school actively recruits these students. They must take the TOEFL with a minimum score of 550 on the paper-based TOEFL (PBT) or 79 on the Internet-based version (iBT) and the Comprehensive English Language Test. Students may take the IELTS accepted in place of TOEFL.

ADMISSIONS: 83% of the 2016-2017 applicants were accepted. The SAT scores for the 2016-2017 freshman class were: Critical Reading-- 25% below 500, 53% between 500 and 599, 19% between 600 and 699, and 3% between 700 and 800. Math-- 22% below 500, 49% between 500 and 599, 28% between 600 and 699, and 3% between 700 and 800. Writing-- 31% below 500, 51% between 500 and 599, 15% between 600 and 699, and 3% between 700 and 800. The ACT scores were 1% between 12 and 17, 36% between 18 and 23, 51% between 24 and 29, and 12% above 30. 56% of the current freshmen were in the top fifth of their class;

32% were in the top two fifths. 35 freshmen graduated first in their class. **Admissions Contact:** Steven P. Vitatoe, Assistant Vice President for Admission. Email: *enrollment@jcu.edu* Web: *sites.jcu.edu*

FINANCIAL AID: In 2016-2017, 98% of all full-time freshmen and 85% of continuing full-time students received some form of financial aid. 82% of all full-time freshmen and 84% of continuing full-time students received need-based aid. The average freshman award was $30,761. Need-based scholarships or need-based grants averaged $24,834; need-based self-help aid (loans and jobs) averaged $4,964; and other non-need-based awards and non-need-based scholarships averaged $2,613. 31% of undergraduate students work part-time. Average annual earnings from campus work are $2484. The average financial indebtedness of the 2016 graduate was $29,137. The FAFSA code is 003050. The priority date for freshman financial aid applications for fall entry is March 15. The filing deadline for fall entry is August 1.

KENT STATE UNIVERSITY D-2
www.kent.edu

Kent, OH 44242	**(330) 672-2444** **(800) 988-KENT**
Fax: (330) 672-2499	**Email: kentadm@kent.edu**
Full-time: 8257 men, 12403 women	**Faculty:** I, --$
Part-time: 1179 men, 1768 women	**Ph.D.s:** n/av
Graduate: 2279 men, 3876 women	**Student/Faculty:** n/av
Year: semesters, summer session	**Tuition:** $10,012 ($18,376)
Room & Board: $10,720	**Freshman Class:** 15772 applied, 13369 accepted, 4334 enrolled
SAT CR/M/W: 530/530/510 **ACT:** 23	**CEEB CODE:** 1367
Application Deadline: n/av	**COMPETITIVE**

Kent State University, founded in 1910, is a public university offering degree programs in liberal and fine arts, business, health science, public health, teacher and professional training, and aviation. Figures in the above capsule and in this profile are approximate. There are 11 undergraduate schools and 11 graduate schools. In addition to regional accreditation, KSU has baccalaureate program accreditation with AACSB, ABET, ACEJMC, CAHEA, FIDER, NAAB, NASAD, NASM, NCATE, NLN, NRPA, CPME, FAA, and CACREP. The 950-acre campus is in a suburban area 45 miles southeast of Cleveland. Including any residence halls, there are 128 buildings.

STUDENT LIFE: 87% of undergraduates are from Ohio. Others are from 49 states, 75 foreign countries, and Canada. 9% are African American; 74% White; 7% Foreign; 3% Hispanic; 3% two or more races; 3% race unknown; 1% Asian American. **Female To Male Ratio:** 1.5:1. The average age of freshmen is 18; all undergraduates, 21. 19% do not continue beyond their first year; 56% remain to graduate. **Housing:** 6622 students can be accommodated in college housing, which includes single-sex and coed dorms, on-campus apartments, married student housing, honors houses and special-interest houses. On-campus housing is available on a first-come and first-served basis. 72% of students commute. All students may keep cars. Alcohol is not permitted.

FACULTY/CLASSROOMS: 45% of faculty are male; 55% are female. No introductory courses are taught by graduate students. The average class size in an introductory lecture is 35 and in a laboratory is 20.

PROGRAMS OF STUDY: KSU confers B.A., B.S., B.B.A., B.F.A, B.S.E., B.S.P.H., B.S.N., B.M. and B.I.S. degrees. Associate, master's, and doctoral degrees are also awarded. Bachelor's degrees are awarded in BIOLOGICAL SCIENCE (biology/biological science, biotechnology, botany, environmental biology, life science secondary school education, nutrition, and zoology), BUSINESS (accounting, business administration and management, business information systems, entrepreneurial studies, fashion merchandising, finance, hospitality management services, management, marketing, marketing management, sports management, and tourism), COMMUNICATIONS AND THE ARTS (advertising, American Sign Language, applied communication, art history and appreciation, classics, communication studies, crafts, dance, English, French and Francophone studies, Germanic languages and literature, journalism, language arts, languages, music, photography, public relations, recreation administration, Russian languages and literature, telecommunications systems mgmt, television & digital media production, theatre arts, visual and performing arts, and visual design), COMPUTER AND PHYSICAL SCIENCE (applied mathematics, applied science, chemistry, computer science, earth science, geology, mathematics, mathematics - actuarial concentration, and physics), EDUCATION (art education, athletic training, early childhood education, education, general studies, health education, mathematics education, middle school education, music education, physical education, physical science secondary school education, science education, social studies secondary school education, special education, and teaching English as a second/foreign language (TESOL/TEFOL)), ENGINEERING AND ENVIRONMENTAL DESIGN (aeronautical science, aerospace engineering, architecture, engineering technology, interior design, and technology and public affairs), HEALTH PROFESSIONS (community health work, exercise science, health science, medical laboratory technology, nursing, predentistry, premedicine, preosteopathy, preveterinary science, public health, and speech pathology/audiology), SOCIAL SCIENCE (African studies, American studies, anthropology, architectural studies, criminology, economics, fashion design and technology, geography, history, human development, international relations, paralegal studies, parks and recreation management, philosophy, political science/government, psychology, sociology, and Spanish studies). Nursing, psychology, and business management have the largest enrollments.

ACTIVITIES: There are 400 groups on campus, including academic, art, band, cheerleading, chess, choir, chorale, chorus, communications, computers, dance, drama, drill team, environmental, ethnic, film, honors, international, jazz band, LGBT, literary magazine, marching band, musical theater, newspaper, opera, orchestra, pep band, photography, political, professional, radio and TV, religious, social, social service, and student government. Popular campus events include Black Squirrel Festival, Folk Festival, FlashFest, and Back to School Blast-Off. **Sports:** There are 8 intercollegiate sports for men and 10 for women, and 13 intramural sports for men and 13 for women. Facilities include a gym, recreation and wellness center, football stadium, field house, fitness circuits, a golf course, bowling alley, tennis courts, basketball courts, an ice arena, a pool, weight room, soccer, lacrosse, rugby, baseball, softball, and field hockey fields, an indoor track, and outdoor track, and a wrestling room. **Graduates:** From July 1, 2015 to June 30, 2016, 4747 bachelor's degrees were awarded. The most popular majors were nursing (11%), psychology (6%), and business management (6%). In an average class, 32% graduate in 4 years or less, 51% graduate in 5 years or less, and 56% graduate in 6 years or less.

SERVICES: Counseling and information services are available, as is tutoring in some subjects. There is also a reader service for the blind, and remedial math, reading, and writing, math, writing, foreign languages, chemistry, biology, academic coaching, and study skills. **Library/Resources:** The 5 libraries contain 2.5 million volumes, 46,019 audio/video tapes/CDs/DVDs, and subscribe to 334 periodicals including electronic. Computerized library services include interlibrary loans, database searching, Internet access, and Wi-Fi capability. Special learning facilities include an art gallery, planetarium, radio station, TV station, fashion museum, and liquid crystal institute. **Physically Challenged Students:** 95% of the campus is accessible. Facilities include wheelchair ramps, elevators, special parking, specially equipped restrooms, special class scheduling, lowered drinking fountains, lowered telephones, special housing. **Special:** Cross-registration is available with the University of Akron, Cleveland State University, Youngstown State University, and Northeastern Ohio Medical University (NEOMED) for graduate students. Work-study programs and internships are offered, and co-op programs are available in several programs. Study abroad in 58 countries, semester away programs in Washington, Columbus, and New York Fashion District, an accelerated medical degree program, B.A.-B.S. degrees, dual majors, a general studies degree, an integrative studies degree, student-designed majors, credit for military education, nondegree study, and pass/fail options are also possible. The Honors College provides honors course work in all majors. Kent is a member of the National Student Exchange program. There are 37 national honor societies, including Phi Beta Kappa, and a freshman honors program. **Visiting:** There are regularly scheduled orientations for prospective students, including information sessions (financial aid, residence halls, student panel), a campus tour, and meetings with academic representatives. There are guides for informal visits. To schedule a visit, contact The Admissions Office at (800) 988-KENT. **Campus Safety and Security:** Measures include 24-hour foot and vehicle patrol, emergency notification system, self-defense education, and security escort services. There are also shuttle buses, emergency telephones, lighted pathways/sidewalks, controlled access to dorms/residences, 24-hour campus police department, overnight security guards, and a 2-key system for residence halls.

REQUIREMENTS: The ACT is required. Applicants most likely to be admitted will have at least a 2.5 cumulative GPA (on a 4.0 scale) in a solid college-preparatory program and an ACT composite score of at least 21. A GPA of 2.5 is required. AP and CLEP credits are accepted. Students are required to complete 120 credit hours, of which 39 must be upper division. Distribution requirements are encompassed in the Kent Core general education requirements, a minimum of 36 credit hours, including 9 credit hours in humanities/fine arts, 6 credit hours each in basic sciences (including one laboratory course), composition, and social sciences, 3 hours in mathematics/critical reasoning, and an additional 6 credit hours. Students must also satisfy an experiential learning requirement, a writing-intensive course requirement, and a diversity course requirement. Students must maintain an overall GPA of 2.0. **Procedure:** Freshmen are admitted in the fall, spring, and summer. Entrance exams should be taken in the spring of the junior year or the fall of the senior year. There is a rolling admissions plan. Application deadlines are open. Application fee is $40. Notification is sent on a rolling basis. Applications are accepted online. **Transfer Students:** 1077 transfer students enrolled in 2015-2016. Applicants must present a minimum GPA of 2.0 on completed college course work. For students with fewer than 24 semester hours or 36 quarter hours, a high school transcript and ACT or SAT scores are also required. 30 of 120 credits required for the bachelor's degree must be completed at KSU. **International Students:** There are 1456 international students enrolled. The school actively recruits these students. They must take the TOEFL with a minimum score of 525 on the paper-based TOEFL (PBT) or 71 on the Internet-based version (iBT) or take the MELAB, or the IELTS.

ADMISSIONS: 85% of the 2016-2017 applicants were accepted. The SAT scores for the 2016-2017 freshman class were: Critical Reading-- 63% below 500, 35% between 500 and 599, and 2% between 600 and 699. Math-- 65% below 500, 32% between 500 and 599, and 3% between 600 and 699. Writing-- 54% below 500, 41% between 500 and 599, and 5% between 600 and 699. The ACT scores were 2% between 12 and 17, 57% between 18 and 23, 35% between 24 and 29, and 6% above 30. 91 freshmen graduated first in their class. **Admissions Contact:** Nancy Dellavecchia, Director of Admissions. Email: *kentadm@kent.edu* Web: *www.kent.edu*

FINANCIAL AID: In 2016-2017, 90% of all full-time freshmen received some form of financial aid. The average freshman award was $10,556. Need-based scholarships or need-based grants averaged $5,813; need-based self-help aid (loans and jobs) averaged $4,301; non-need-based athletic scholarships averaged $18,159; and other non-need-based awards and non-need-based scholarships averaged $5,398. 16% of undergraduate students work part-time. Average annual earnings from campus work are $4860. The average financial indebtedness of the 2016 graduate was $36,538. The FAFSA code is 003051. The priority date for freshman financial aid applications for fall entry is March 1.

KENYON COLLEGE C-3

www.kenyon.edu

Gambier, OH 43022 (740) 427-5776
(800) 848-2468

Fax: (740) 427-5770 **Email:** admissions@kenyon.edu

Full-time: 760 men, 928 women	**Faculty:** 166; IIB, +$
Part-time: 10 men, 10 women	**Ph.D.s:** 99%
Graduate: n/av	**Student/Faculty:** 10 to 1
Year: semesters	**Tuition:** $51,200
Room & Board: $12,130	**Freshman Class:** 6404 applied, 1702 accepted, 517 enrolled
SAT CR/M/W: 674/658/674 **ACT:** 31	**CEEB CODE:** 1370
Application Deadline: January 15	**MOST COMPETITIVE**

Kenyon College, among the nation's finest liberal arts institutions, takes pride in its exceptionally strong academic programs, in English, the sciences, and fine arts. There is 1 undergraduate school. The 1000-acre campus is in a rural area 50 miles northeast of Columbus, OH. Including any residence halls, there are 155 buildings.

STUDENT LIFE: 85% of undergraduates are from out of state, mostly the Middle Atlantic. Students are from 50 states, 45 foreign countries, and Canada. 50% are from public schools. 8% are two or more races; 73% White; 5% Hispanic; 5% Foreign; 4% Asian American; 3% African American; 2% race unknown. **Female To Male Ratio:** 1.2:1. The average age of freshmen is 19; all undergraduates, 20. 8% do not continue beyond their first year; 90% remain to graduate. **Housing:** 1778 students can be accommodated in college housing, which includes single-sex and coed dorms, and on-campus apartments, and special-interest houses, special interest floors, including community service or social group halls, a substance-free hall, a wellness hall, an international wing, and Kosher living are also available. On-campus housing is guaranteed for all 4 years. All students may keep cars.

FACULTY/CLASSROOMS: 57% of faculty are male; 43% are female. All teach undergraduates and do research. No introductory courses are taught by graduate students. The average class size in an introductory lecture is 16 and in a regular course is 16.

PROGRAMS OF STUDY: Kenyon confers A.B. degrees. Bachelor's degrees are awarded in BIOLOGICAL SCIENCE (biochemistry, biology/biological science, molecular biology, and neurosciences), COMMUNICATIONS AND THE ARTS (art history, art, classics, dance, dramatic arts, English, film arts, French, German, Greek (classical), Latin, modern language, music, and Spanish), COMPUTER AND PHYSICAL SCIENCE (chemistry, mathematics, and physics), EDUCATION (Asian studies), SOCIAL SCIENCE (American studies, anthropology, economics, history, international studies, philosophy, political science/government, psychology, religious studies, sociology, and women & gender studies). English, economics, and psychology have the largest enrollments.

ACTIVITIES: 30% of men belong to 7 national fraternities; 33% of women belong to 4 local sororities. There are 164 groups on campus, including sports clubs, student lectureships, art, band, chess, choir, chorale, chorus, dance, debate, drama, environmental, environmental/conservation, ethnic, film, honors, international, jazz band, LGBT, literary magazine, musical theater, newspaper, opera, orchestra, pep band, photography, political, professional, radio and TV, religious, social, social service, student government, and symphony. Popular campus events include Founder's Day/Matriculation, Convocation, Summer Send-Off, Fandango, Honors Day, Family Weekend, and Martin Luther King, and Jr. Day. **Sports:** There are 11 intercollegiate sports for men and 11 for women, and 9 intramural sports for men and 9 for women. Facilities include an athletic/recreation/fitness center, football, softball, soccer fields, a pool, field house, Nautilus center and weight rooms, basketball, tennis, squash, and racquetball courts. **Graduates:** From July 1, 2015 to June 30, 2016, 480 bachelor's degrees were awarded. The most popular majors were English (13%), economics (10%), and psychology (7%). 27 companies recruited on campus in 2015-2016. In an average class, 1% graduate in 3 years or less, 89% graduate in 4 years or less, 90% graduate in 5 years or less, and 90% graduate in 6 years or less.

SERVICES: Counseling and information services are available, as is tutoring in some subjects, a reader service for the blind, and remedial writing. Peer note-taking services, oral test option, extended time on tests, use of computer for essay based tests or notes, advance syllabus access, priority registration, priority seating, permission to use digital audio recordings, digital text format and content specific tutors are also available. **Library/Resources:** The library contains 495,501 volumes, 12,167 microform items, and 30,798 audio/video tapes/CDs/DVDs, and subscribes to 8,685 periodicals including electronic. Computerized library services include interlibrary loans, database searching, Internet access, and Wi-Fi capability. Special learning facilities include an art gallery, radio station, an observatory, and an environmental center. **Physically Challenged Students:** Facilities include wheelchair ramps, elevators, special parking, specially equipped restrooms, special class scheduling, lowered drinking fountains, lowered telephones, and special housing. **Special:** Kenyon offers more than 200 off-campus study programs. The college also offers dual and student-designed majors, pass/fail options, internships, winter and/or spring break externship programs, a Washington semester consisting of apprenticeships in any of several U.S. programs, and a 3-2 engineering degree with Case Western Reserve, Washington University in St. Louis, and Rensselaer Polytechnic Institute, as well as a 3-2 environmental studies program with Duke University. 3-2 or 4-1 master's (certification) programs with The Bank Street College of Education are also possible. There is a chapter of Phi Beta Kappa and 24 departmental honors programs. **Visiting:** There are regularly scheduled orientations for prospective students, consisting of interviews with staff, a campus tour, and a class visit. Students may also request to meet with faculty and coaches. Kenyon students are also available to host a prospective student overnight in the dorm. There are guides for informal visits, visitors may sit in on classes, and stay overnight. To schedule a visit, contact the Admissions Office. **Campus Safety and Security:** Measures include 24-hour foot and vehicle patrol, emergency notification system, self-defense education, security escort services, emergency telephones, lighted pathways/sidewalks, controlled access to dorms/residences, formal safety awareness events, and student patrols.

REQUIREMENTS: The SAT or ACT is required. Applicants should be graduates of an accredited secondary school. Candidates are encouraged to exceed the minimum requirements (4 units of English and math, 3 units of science, foreign language and social studies), especially in math and science, and to take advance placement or honors work in at least 2 subjects. Kenyon recommends 4 units each of English, math, foreign language, science, and 3 units of social studies. An interview is important criteria in the admissions decision. Talent in music, theater, art, writing, and athletics is given extra consideration. AP credits are accepted. Important factors in the admissions decision are advanced placement or honors courses, evidence of special talent, and leadership record. Students are required to complete a total of 16 units, including 4 to 7 units in the major, 1 unit in each of 4 divisions representing the arts, humanities, natural sciences, and social sciences, 1 unit of foreign language, and 1/2 unit of quantitative reasoning. Students must maintain a minimum GPA of 2.0 and complete the senior exercise in their major. A thesis is required for honor students. **Procedure:** Freshmen are admitted in the fall. Entrance exams should be taken in the fall of the senior year. There are early decision, early admissions, and deferred admissions plans. Early decision applications should be filed by November 15; regular applications, by January 15 for fall entry. Notification of early decision is sent February 1; regular decision, April 1. 251 early decision candidates were accepted for the 2016-2017 class. 972 applicants were on the 2016 waiting list; 9 were admitted. Application fees are waived if application is completed online. **Transfer Students:** 13 transfer students enrolled in 2015-2016. Transfer applicants must have a minimum college GPA of 3.0 and a high school record suggesting ability and potential. In addition, Kenyon requires a letter of recommendation from a professor, the Transfer Common Application, and the Transfer Supplement. 8 of 16 credits required for the bachelor's degree must be completed at Kenyon. **International Students:** There are 78 international students enrolled. The school actively recruits these students. They must take the TOEFL with a minimum score of 600 on the paper-based TOEFL (PBT) or 100 on the Internet-based version (iBT). They must also take the SAT or ACT.

ADMISSIONS: 27% of the 2016-2017 applicants were accepted. The SAT scores for the 2016-2017 freshman class were: Critical Reading-- 2% below 500, 14% between 500 and 599, 39% between 600 and 699, and 45% between 700 and 800. Math-- 1% below 500, 20% between 500 and 599, 50% between 600 and 699, and 29% between 700 and 800. Writing-- 2% below 500, 13% between 500 and 599, 41% between 600 and 699, and 44% between 700 and 800. The ACT scores were 28% between 24 and 29, and 72% above 30. 82% of the current freshmen were in the top fifth of their class; 96% were in the top two fifths. There were 7 National Merit finalists. 7 freshmen graduated first in their class. **Admissions Contact:** Diane Anci, Interim Dean of Admissions & Financial Aid. Email: *admissions@kenyon.edu* Web: *www.kenyon.edu*

FINANCIAL AID: In 2016-2017, 42% of all full-time freshmen and continuing full-time students received some form of financial aid. 41% of all full-time freshmen and continuing full-time students received need-based aid. The average freshman award was $41,770. Need-based scholarships or need-based grants averaged $38,978; need-based self-help aid (loans and jobs) averaged $3,964; other non-need-based awards and non-need-based scholarships averaged $14,585; and $2,501 from other forms of aid. 37% of undergraduate students work part-time. Average annual earnings from campus work are $5389. The average financial indebtedness of the 2016 graduate was $26,746. Kenyon is a member of CSS. The CSS/Profile, tax returns, and non-custodial parent income tax returns are required. The FAFSA code is 003065. The deadline for filing freshman financial aid applications for fall entry is February 15.

LAKE ERIE COLLEGE *(The complete profile is made available exclusively on our website, www.barronspac.com)*

LOURDES UNIVERSITY *(The complete profile is made available exclusively on our website, www.barronspac.com)*

MALONE UNIVERSITY — D-2

www.malone.edu

Canton, OH 44709	**(330) 471-8145** **(800) 521-1146**
Fax: (330) 471-8149	**Email: admissions@malone.edu**
Full-time: 484 men, 661 women	**Faculty:** 84; IIA, --$
Part-time: 57 men, 109 women	**Ph.D.s:** 82%
Graduate: 111 men, 267 women	**Student/Faculty:** 13 to 1
Year: semesters, summer session	**Tuition:** $29,420
Room & Board: $9028	**Freshman Class:** 1762 applied, 1283 accepted, 311 enrolled
SAT CR/M: required **ACT:** 22	**CEEB CODE:** 1439
Application Deadline: n/av	**COMPETITIVE**

Malone University, founded in 1892, is a private Christian university for the arts, sciences, and professions in the liberal arts tradition. The mission of Malone University is to provide students with an education based on biblical faith in order to develop men and women in intellectual maturity, wisdom, and Christian faith who are committed to serving the church, community, and world. There are 4 undergraduate schools and 3 graduate schools. In addition to regional accreditation, Malone has baccalaureate program accreditation with ACBSP, CSWE, NASM, NCATE, CCNE, and CACREP. The 96-acre campus is in a suburban area 56 miles southeast of Cleveland. Including any residence halls, there are 22 buildings.

STUDENT LIFE: 86% of undergraduates are from Ohio. Others are from 28 states, and 6 foreign countries. 86% are from public schools. 80% are White; 3% Hispanic; 3% two or more races; 12% African American; 1% Asian American; 1% Foreign. 78% are Protestant; 13% claim no religious affiliation. **Female To Male Ratio:** 1.6:1. The average age of freshmen is 18; all undergraduates, 22. 28% do not continue beyond their first year; 57% remain to graduate. **Housing:** 1197 students can be accommodated in college housing, which includes single-sex dorms, one theme floor for mentoring freshman women by upperclass women. On-campus housing is guaranteed for the freshman year only, and on a first-come, first-served basis, and on a lottery system for upperclassmen. 63% of students live on campus; of those, 40% remain on campus on weekends. All students may keep cars. Alcohol is not permitted.

FACULTY/CLASSROOMS: 46% of faculty are male; 54% are female. 85% teach undergraduates. No introductory courses are taught by graduate students. The average class size in an introductory lecture is 26; in a laboratory is 16; and in a regular course is 18.

PROGRAMS OF STUDY: Malone confers B.A., B.S.Ed., and B.S.N. degrees. Master's degrees are also awarded. Bachelor's degrees are awarded in BIOLOGICAL SCIENCE (biochemistry, biology/biological science, life science, and zoology), BUSINESS (accounting, business administration and management, finance, marketing and distribution, and sports management), COMMUNICATIONS AND THE ARTS (art, art history and appreciation, broadcasting, communications, crafts, creative writing, English, graphic design, language arts, music, music technology, public relations, and theatre studies), COMPUTER AND PHYSICAL SCIENCE (chemistry, computer science, and mathematics), EDUCATION (Christian education, early childhood education, middle school education, music education, science education, secondary education, social studies education, and special education), ENGINEERING AND ENVIRONMENTAL DESIGN (engineering/mechanical emp/energy sys focus), HEALTH PROFESSIONS (community health work, exercise science, medical laboratory technology, nursing, and public health), SOCIAL SCIENCE (biblical studies, criminal justice, crosscultural studies, history, international studies, liberal arts/general studies, ministries, philosophy, political science/government, psychology, religious music, social work, theological studies, and youth ministry). Nursing, social work, and history are the strongest academically. Nursing, business administration, and exercise science have the largest enrollments.

ACTIVITIES: There are no fraternities or sororities. There are 50 groups on campus, including art, band, cheerleading, chess, choir, chorale, communications, computers, drama, drill team, environmental, ethnic, film, honors, international, jazz band, literary magazine, marching band, musical theater, newspaper, opera, photography, political, professional, radio and TV, religious, social, social service, and student government. Popular campus events include Little Sibs Weekend, Christmas Celebration, and Worldview Forums. **Sports:** There are 9 intercollegiate sports for men and 9 for women, and 8 intramural sports for men and 8 for women. Facilities include a gym, a wellness center with a strength room and a cardio room, an outdoor track, baseball, softball, and soccer fields, practice soccer and football fields, intramural fields, a cross-country course, and outdoor volleyball and basketball courts. **Graduates:** From July 1, 2015 to June 30, 2016, 400 bachelor's degrees were awarded. The most popular majors were business administration/management (33%), nursing and other health professions and related programs (18%), and education (12%). In an average class, 3% graduate in 3 years or less, 45% graduate in 4 years or less, 56% graduate in 5 years or less, and 57% graduate in 6 years or less.

SERVICES: Counseling and information services are available, as is tutoring in most subjects, a reader service for the blind, and remedial math, reading, and writing. There are also disability support services such as a distraction-reduced testing room. **Library/Resources:** The library contains 170,981 volumes, 471,950 microform items, 7,776 audio/video tapes/CDs/DVDs, and subscribes to 32,424 periodicals including electronic. Computerized library services include interlibrary loans, database searching, Internet access, and Wi-Fi capability. Special learning facilities include an art gallery, radio station, a writing lab, subject area tutoring, a broadcast production studio with green screen and virtual set technology available for student, and classroom use. **Physically Challenged Students:** Facilities include wheelchair ramps, elevators, special parking, specially equipped restrooms, special class scheduling, lowered drinking fountains, lowered telephones, and special housing. **Special:** Students may participate in co-op programs and internships in many majors and may cross-register within the Christian College Consortium. Malone offers study abroad in England, China, Costa Rica, Jordan, Australia, and Uganda, as well as Hollywood (Film Studies), Nashville (Contemporary Music), or Washington semesters through the Council for Christian Colleges and Universities. Approximately 20 other study abroad opportunities are available through Brethren Colleges Abroad (BCA). A liberal arts degree, dual and student-designed majors, and credit for life, military, or work experience are also available. The Malone Management Program (MGMT) offers accelerated degree- completion for students with 5 years of work experience and 40 to 88 transfer hours. MGMT offers 2 majors: Organizational Management and Health Services Management. The School of Nursing and Health Sciences offers a traditional BSN program and a degree-completion BSN program for RNs. There are 10 national honor societies and a freshman honors program. **Visiting:** There are regularly scheduled orientations for prospective students, Discover Day includes a tour of campus, a chance to meet with faculty, a community worship service, a class visit, a parent session, a student panel, an activity fair, and lunch. There are guides for informal visits, visitors may sit in on classes, and stay overnight. To schedule a visit, contact Jody Dimit at (330) 471-8147. **Campus Safety and Security:** Measures include 24-hour foot and vehicle patrol, emergency notification system, and security escort services, emergency telephones, lighted pathways/sidewalks, and controlled access to dorms/residences.

REQUIREMENTS: The ACT is preferred; the SAT is accepted. Applicants should be graduates of an accredited secondary school with a minimum GPA of 2.5. The GED is accepted. AP and CLEP credits are accepted. Important factors in the admissions decision are advanced placement or honors courses, personality/intangible qualities, and extracurricular activities record. Students must maintain a GPA of 2.0 overall and 2.25 to 2.75 in the major, depending upon the major. At least 30 hours in the major and 39 hours at the 300 or 400 level are required. To graduate, all students must complete at least 124 credit hours. The 41- to 43-credit-hour general education curriculum includes 10 hours of Faith Learning courses, 9 hours of Foundational Skills courses, 9 hours of Engaging in Human Experience courses, 7-9 hours in Engaging Cultures and Institutions courses, 3 hours in Engaging the Created Order (one course) and 3 hours in Faith in the World (one course). **Procedure:** Freshmen are admitted in the fall, spring, and summer. Entrance exams should be taken in the junior year. There are early admissions, deferred admissions, and rolling admissions plans. Application deadlines are open. Application fee is $20. Notifications are sent September 1. Application fees are waived if application is completed online. **Transfer Students:** 51 transfer students enrolled in 2015-2016. Applicants must submit official transcripts from any previously attended institution(s). Average grade in courses allowed for transfer must be 2.0 or higher (on a 4.0 scale). 30 of 124 credits required for the bachelor's degree must be completed at Malone. **International Students:** There are 7 international students enrolled. They must take the TOEFL with a minimum score of 550 on the paper-based TOEFL (PBT) or 79 on the Internet-based version (iBT). They must also take the SAT or ACT, scoring 860-SAT or 18-ACT, not required of all international students; but definitely athletes due to NCAA requirements.

ADMISSIONS: 73% of the 2016-2017 applicants were accepted. The SAT scores for the 2016-2017 freshman class were: Critical Reading-- 55% below 500, 34% between 500 and 599, and 11% between 600 and 699. Math-- 58% below 500, 32% between 500 and 599, 6% between 600 and 699, and 4% between 700 and 800. The ACT scores were 13% between 12 and 17, 55% between 18 and 23, 26% between 24 and 29, and 6% above 30. 30% of the current freshmen were in the top fifth of their class; 57% were in the top two fifths. 10 freshmen graduated first in their class. **Admissions Contact:** Linda Kurtz Hoffman, Director of Admissions. Email: *admissions@malone.edu* Web: *www.malone.edu*

FINANCIAL AID: In 2016-2017, 100% of all full-time freshmen and 96% of continuing full-time students received some form of financial aid. 84% of all full-time freshmen and 74% of continuing full-time students received need-based aid. The average freshman award was $31,097. Need-based scholarships or need-based grants averaged $10,749 ($29,029 maximum); need-based self-help aid (loans and jobs) averaged $5,749 ($10,500 maximum); non-need-based athletic scholarships averaged $11,234 ($31,906 maximum); other non-need-based awards and non-need-based scholarships averaged $13,195 ($36,076 maximum); and $11,633 from other forms of aid. 29% of undergraduate students work part-time. Average annual earnings from campus work are $1983. The average financial indebtedness of the 2016 graduate was $33,069. The FAFSA code is 003072. The priority date for freshman financial aid applications for fall entry is March 1. The filing deadline for fall entry is July 31.

MARIETTA COLLEGE D-5

www.marietta.edu

Marietta, OH 45750	**(740) 376-4600** **(800) 331-7896**
Fax: (740) 376-8888	**Email: admit@mcnet.marietta.edu**
Full-time: 816 men, 602 women	**Faculty:** 110; IIB, -$
Part-time: 27 men, 42 women	**Ph.D.s:** 92%
Graduate: 26 men, 109 women	**Student/Faculty:** 12 to 1
Year: semesters, summer session	**Tuition:** $35,090
Room & Board: $11,100	**Freshman Class:** 4157 applied, 2811 accepted, 395 enrolled
SAT CR/M/W: 539/555/517 **ACT:** 24	**CEEB CODE:** 1444
Application Deadline: April 15	**COMPETITIVE**

Marietta College, founded in 1835, is a private liberal arts college. There is 1 undergraduate school and 4 graduate schools. In addition to regional accreditation, Marietta has baccalaureate program accreditation with ABET, NASM, NCATE, CAAHEP, ACS, and ARC-PA. The 90-acre campus is in a small town 115 miles southeast of Columbus. Including any residence halls, there are 40 buildings.

STUDENT LIFE: 64% of undergraduates are from Ohio. Others are from 40 states, 15 foreign countries, and Canada. 89% are from public schools. 71% are White; 6% African American; 6% Foreign; 6% race unknown; 3% Hispanic; 1% Asian American; 1% two or more races. **Male To Female Ratio:** 1.2:1. The average age of freshmen is 18; all undergraduates, 20. 22% do not continue beyond their first year; 56% remain to graduate. **Housing:** 1276 students can be accommodated in college housing, which includes single-sex and coed dorms, on-campus apartments, honors houses, special-interest houses, fraternity houses, and sorority houses. On-campus housing is guaranteed for all 4 years. 76% of students live on campus; of those, 80% remain on campus on weekends. All students may keep cars.

FACULTY/CLASSROOMS: 51% of faculty are male; 49% are female. All teach undergraduates, 30% do research, and 30% do both. No introductory courses are taught by graduate students. The average class size in an introductory lecture is 19; in a laboratory is 13; and in a regular course is 16.

PROGRAMS OF STUDY: Marietta confers B.A., B.S., and B.F.A. degrees. Associate and master's degrees are also awarded. Bachelor's degrees are awarded in AGRICULTURE (environmental studies), BIOLOGICAL SCIENCE (biochemistry and biology/biological science),

BUSINESS (accounting, banking and finance, business administration and management, human resources, international business management, management information systems, marketing/retailing/merchandising, and sports management), COMMUNICATIONS AND THE ARTS (advertising, broadcasting, communications, dramatic arts, English, graphic design, journalism, music, public relations, Spanish, speech/debate/rhetoric, and studio art), COMPUTER AND PHYSICAL SCIENCE (applied physics, chemistry, computer science, geology, information sciences and systems, mathematics, and physics), EDUCATION (athletic training, early childhood education, and music education), ENGINEERING AND ENVIRONMENTAL DESIGN (environmental science and petroleum/natural gas engineering), HEALTH PROFESSIONS (health science and physician's assistant), SOCIAL SCIENCE (Asian/Oriental studies, economics, history, interdisciplinary studies, political science/government, and psychology). Petroleum engineering is the strongest academically. Petroleum engineering, advertising public relations, and psychology have the largest enrollments.

ACTIVITIES: 23% of men belong to 3 national fraternities; 41% of women belong to 3 national sororities. There are 80 groups on campus, including arts & humanities, Circle K, art, band, cheerleading, choir, chorale, chorus, computers, dance, debate, drama, drill team, environmental, ethnic, film, forensics, honors, international, jazz band, LGBT, literary magazine, musical theater, newspaper, orchestra, pep band, photography, political, professional, radio and TV, religious, social, social service, student government, and yearbook. Popular campus events include DooDah Day, Little Sibs Weekend, and Welcome Back Bash. **Sports:** There are 9 intercollegiate sports for men and 9 for women, and 12 intramural sports for men and 12 for women. Facilities include a stadium, a performance gym, a field house, baseball, softball, soccer fields, boat house, a cross-country course, tennis courts, and a recreational center housing a track, multipurpose and racquetball courts, an ergometer training room, cardio equipment, and a climbing wall. **Graduates:** From July 1, 2015 to June 30, 2016, 222 bachelor's degrees were awarded. The most popular majors were petroleum engineering (7%), advertising/public relations (7%), and psychology (6%). 60 companies recruited on campus in 2015-2016. In an average class, 3% graduate in 3 years or less, 46% graduate in 4 years or less, 55% graduate in 5 years or less, and 56% graduate in 6 years or less. Of the 2015 graduating class, 24% were enrolled in graduate school within 6 months of graduation, and 95% were employed.

SERVICES: Counseling and information services are available, as is tutoring in most subjects, a reader service for the blind, remedial math and writing, and a peer tutoring program. **Library/Resources:** The library contains 449,123 volumes, 146,583 microform items, and 5,031 audio/video tapes/CDs/DVDs, and subscribes to 13,557 periodicals including electronic. Computerized library services include interlibrary loans, database searching, and Internet access. Special learning facilities include an art gallery, planetarium, radio station, TV station, an observatory, a greenhouse, and a geology annex. **Physically Challenged Students:** 90% of the campus is accessible. Facilities include wheelchair ramps, elevators, special parking, specially equipped restrooms, special class scheduling, lowered drinking fountains, lowered telephones, and special housing. **Special:** There are 3-2 binary engineering programs with Case Western Reserve, Columbia, and Ohio Universities. Internships are available in many majors, and students may study abroad in numerous countries and participate in a Washington semester through American University. Work-study programs, B.A.-B.S. degrees in all majors, and student-designed majors are also available. There are 23 national honor societies, Phi Beta Kappa, a freshman honors program, and 17 departmental honors programs. **Visiting:** There are regularly scheduled orientations for prospective students, including fall and spring open houses, tours, and meetings with faculty, coaches, and financial aid representatives. There are guides for informal visits, visitors may sit in on classes, and stay overnight. To schedule a visit, contact the Office of Admissions. **Campus Safety and Security:** Measures include 24-hour foot and vehicle patrol, emergency notification system, self-defense education, and security escort services. There are also shuttle buses, emergency telephones, lighted pathways/sidewalks, and controlled access to dorms/residence.

REQUIREMENTS: The SAT or ACT is required. Students seeking admission should have completed 4 years of English and 3 of history, math, and science, and 2 years of a foreign language is also recommended. An interview is strongly recommended. AP and CLEP credits are accepted. Important factors in the admissions decision are advanced placement or honors courses, evidence of special talent, and leadership record. To graduate, students must complete at least 120 total credit hours, with general education requirements. The minimum number of hours required for a major is 36. A minimum GPA of 2.0 must be maintained. Seniors must complete a capstone project in their major. **Procedure:** Freshmen are admitted in the fall and spring. Entrance exams should be taken no later than February of the senior year. There is a rolling admissions plan. Applications should be filed by April 15 for fall entry, along with a $25 fee. Notification is sent on a rolling basis. Applications are accepted online. **Transfer Students:** 46 transfer students enrolled in 2015-2016. A minimum GPA of 2.5, a recommendation, and an essay are required. 36 of 120 credits required for the bachelor's degree must be completed at Marietta. **International Students:** There are 155 international students enrolled. The school actively recruits these students. They must take the TOEFL with a minimum score of 550 on the paper-based TOEFL (PBT) or 79 on the Internet-based version (iBT) and the college's own test, or take the IELTS. They must also take the SAT or ACT.

ADMISSIONS: 68% of the 2016-2017 applicants were accepted. The SAT scores for the 2016-2017 freshman class were: Critical Reading-- 33% below 500, 40% between 500 and 599, 25% between 600 and 699, and 2% between 700 and 800. Math-- 27% below 500, 36% between 500 and 599, 34% between 600 and 699, and 3% between 700 and 800. Writing-- 40% below 500, 42% between 500 and 599, 17% between 600 and 699, and 1% between 700 and 800. The ACT scores were 23% below 12, 27% between 12 and 17, 23% between 18 and 23, 13% between 24 and 29, and 15% above 30. 49% of the current freshmen were in the top fifth of their class; 79% were in the top two fifths. 9 freshmen graduated first in their class. **Admissions Contact:** Jason Turley, Dean of Admission. Email: *admit@mcnet.marietta.edu* Web: *www.marietta.edu*

FINANCIAL AID: In 2016-2017, 96% of all full-time freshmen and 93% of continuing full-time students received some form of financial aid. 84% of all full-time freshmen and 79% of continuing full-time students received need-based aid. The average freshman award was $27,091. Need-based scholarships or need-based grants averaged $9,561 ($19,220 maximum); need-based self-help aid (loans and jobs) averaged $3,602 ($7,500 maximum); and other non-need-based awards and non-need-based scholarships averaged $8,650 ($35,112 maximum). 30% of undergraduate students work part-time. Average annual earnings from campus work are $2000. The average financial indebtedness of the 2016 graduate was $20,911. The FAFSA code is 003073. The deadline for filing freshman financial aid applications for fall entry is March 1.

MIAMI UNIVERSITY — A-4

www.MiamiOH.edu

Oxford, OH 45056 — **(513) 529-2531**

Fax: (513) 529-1550	**Email:** admission@MiamiOH.edu
Full-time: 8100 men, 8334 women	**Faculty:** 979; I, --$
Part-time: 281 men, 266 women	**Ph.D.s:** 83%
Graduate: 826 men, 1890 women	**Student/Faculty:** 17 to 1
Year: semesters, summer session	**Tuition:** $14,736 ($32,556)
Room & Board: $12,454	**Freshman Class:** 29771 applied, 19463 accepted, 3799 enrolled
SAT CR/M: 600/640 **ACT:** 28	**CEEB CODE:** 1463
Application Deadline: February 1	**HIGHLY COMPETITIVE+**

Miami University, founded in 1809, consistently ranks among the top public universities in the nation for the quality of academic programs, faculty commitment to students, for experiences that lead to student success, and as a "Best Value." Undergraduates benefit from a well-rounded liberal arts foundation, developing skills for life and careers. More than 42 percent of students study abroad, and more than two-thirds participate in internships or field work. Undergraduate students participate with faculty and graduate students in significant research and scholarship activities. Retention and graduation rates are among the highest of NCAA Division I schools. There are 6 undergraduate schools and 1 graduate school. In addition to regional accreditation, Miami has baccalaureate program accreditation with AACSB, ABET, CSAB, CSWE, FIDER, NAAB, NASAD, NCATE, and NLN. The 2138-acre campus is in a small town in Oxford, Ohio, 35 miles north of Cincinnati, OH. Including any residence halls, there are 119 buildings.

STUDENT LIFE: 64% of undergraduates are from Ohio. Others are from 50 states, 92 foreign countries, and Canada. 71% are from public schools. 73% are White; 4% Hispanic; 3% African American; 3% two or more races; 2% Asian American; 13% Foreign. 33% are Catholic; 25% Protestant; 22% claim no religious affiliation. **Female To Male Ratio:** 1.1:1. The average age of freshmen is 18; all undergraduates, 20. 8% do not continue beyond their first year; 78% remain to graduate. **Housing:** 7786 students can be accommodated in college housing, which includes single-sex and coed dorms, on-campus apartments, off-campus apartments, married student housing, honors houses, language houses, special-interest houses, sorority houses, and international housing. On-campus housing is guaranteed for the freshman year only and is available on a lottery system for upperclassmen. 54% of students commute. All students may keep cars.

FACULTY/CLASSROOMS: 53% of faculty are male; 47% are female. All teach undergraduates. No introductory courses are taught by graduate students. The average class size in a regular course is 30.

PROGRAMS OF STUDY: Miami confers A.B., B.S., B.F.A., B.Mus., A.B.Arc., A.B.Art., A.B.The., B.I.S., B.S.Aps., B.S.Art., B.S.AT., B.S.Bus., B.S.Cj., B.S.Cs., B.S.Ed., B.S.Egr., B.S.Ff., B.S.IT., B.S.Knh., B.W.Se., and B.S.Swk degrees. Associate, master's, and doctoral degrees are also awarded. Bachelor's degrees are awarded in BIOLOGICAL SCIENCE (biochemistry, biological sciences, botany, microbiology, neurosciences, nutrition, and zoology), BUSINESS (accounting, business economics, business leadership, finance, management information systems, management science, marketing/retailing/merchandising, sports management, supply chain management, and sustainable management), COMMUNICATIONS AND THE ARTS (art, art history and appreciation, classical languages, classics, communications, dramatic arts, East Asian languages and literature, English, film arts, French, German, graphic design, journalism, linguistics, media arts, music, music performance, Russian, Spanish, speech/debate/rhetoric, and theatre arts), COMPUTER AND PHYSICAL SCIENCE (chemistry, computer science, earth science, energy science, geology, information sciences and systems, mathematics, physics, software engineering, and statistics), EDUCATION (art education, athletic training, early childhood education, elementary education, English education, foreign languages education, mathematics education, middle school education, music education, science education, secondary education, and special education), ENGINEERING AND ENVIRONMENTAL DESIGN (architectural history, architecture, bioengineering, chemical engineering, computer engineering, electrical/electronics engineering, engineering, engineering management, engineering physics, environmental science, interior design, manufacturing engineering, and mechanical engineering), HEALTH PROFESSIONS (nursing, public health, and speech pathology/audiology), SOCIAL SCIENCE (African American studies, American studies, anthropology, criminal justice, economics, family/consumer studies, geography, gerontology, history, interdisciplinary studies, international relations, international studies, Italian studies, justice and society, Latin American studies, philosophy, physical fitness/movement, political science/government, psychology, public administration, religion, social work, sociology, urban studies, and women's studies). Finance, marketing, and biology have the largest enrollments.

ACTIVITIES: 19% of men belong to 29 national fraternities; 34% of women belong to 20 national sororities. There are 548 groups on campus, including art, bagpipe, band, cheerleading, chess, choir, chorale, chorus, communications, computers, dance, debate, drama, drill team, environmental, ethnic, film, forensics, honors, international, jazz band, LGBT, literary magazine, marching band, musical theater, newspaper, opera, orchestra, pep band, photography, political, professional, radio and TV, religious, social, social service, student government, symphony, and yearbook. Popular campus events include Parents Weekend, Kidsfest Weekend, and Unity Fest. **Sports:** There are 8 intercollegiate sports for men and 10 for women, and 17 intramural sports for men and 16 for women. Facilities include a football stadium, an indoor sports center for Miami student-athlete training, an ice arena, playing fields, outdoor tennis courts, recreational sports center, indoor basketball/volleyball courts, racquetball, handball, and squash courts, floor hockey/indoor soccer court, climbing wall, equestrian stables and dressage course, aquatic center containing 3 indoor swimming pools, jogging paths, a par course, sand volleyball courts, aerobics and weight rooms, and a frisbee golf course. **Graduates:** From July 1, 2015 to June 30, 2016, 4312 bachelor's degrees were awarded. The most popular majors were finance (9%), marketing (7%), and accountancy (6%). 1705 companies recruited on campus in 2015-2016. In an average class, 1% graduate in 3 years or less, 66% graduate in 4 years or less, 77% graduate in 5 years or less, and 78% graduate in 6 years or less.

SERVICES: Counseling and information services are available, as is tutoring in most subjects, and assistance in study skills. **Library/Resources:** The 4 libraries contain 2.0 million volumes, 21,208 microform items, 194,298 audio/video tapes/CDs/DVDs, and subscribe to 26,596 periodicals including electronic. Computerized library services include interlibrary loans, database searching, Internet access, and Wi-Fi capability. Special learning facilities include an art gallery, natural history museum, radio station, and TV station. **Physically Challenged Students:** All of the campus is accessible. Facilities include wheelchair ramps, elevators, special parking, specially equipped restrooms, special class scheduling, lowered drinking fountains, lowered telephones, and special housing. **Special:** The university offers cross-registration with Cincinnati area colleges, study abroad in multiple countries, co-op programs in the School of Applied Science, internships in health and sport studies and applied science, a 3-2 engineering degree with Case Western Reserve and Columbia Universities, and a 3-2 forestry degree with Duke University. Students may pursue student-designed majors through the Western Program or interdisciplinary majors. There is a chapter of Phi Beta Kappa and a freshman honors program. **Visiting:** There are regularly scheduled orientations for prospective students, and information sessions and guided tours are available throughout the year. There are guides for informal visits and visitors may sit in on classes. To schedule a visit, contact the Office of Admissions. **Campus Safety and Security:** Measures include 24-hour foot and vehicle patrol, emergency notification system, self-defense education, and security escort services. There are also shuttle buses, emergency telephones, lighted pathways/sidewalks, and controlled access to dorms/residences.

REQUIREMENTS: Applicants must complete either the ACT or the SAT. Candidates for admission must ordinarily be graduates of accredited secondary schools or hold the GED. Students should have completed 4 units of English, 4 units of math, 3 units of science, 2 units of social studies, 2 of a foreign language, 1 unit each of history, and fine arts. An audition, a portfolio, or an interview are required for direct admission to majors in the School of Fine Arts. AP and CLEP credits are accepted. To graduate students must complete 128 semester hours, with a minimum 2.0 GPA. At least 32 semester hours must be from Miami University. Students must fulfill all requirements for the Global Miami Plan. The Global Miami plan includes 27 semester hours of foundation courses, 9 semester hours in a thematic sequence, a 3 hour capstone experience, 3 hours of Advanced Writing, and 3 hours in Intercultural Perspectives. **Procedure:** Freshmen are admitted to all sessions. There are early decision and deferred admissions plans. Early decision applications should be filed by November 15; regular applications, by February 1 for fall entry; and December 1 for spring entry. The fall 2016 application fee was $50. Notification of early decision is sent December 15; regular decision, March 15. 677 early decision candidates were accepted for the 2016-2017 class. 954 applicants were on the 2016 waiting list; 16 were admitted. Applications are accepted online. **Transfer Students:** 239 transfer students enrolled in 2015-2016. A limited number of transfer students will be accepted. A GPA of 2.00 or higher is necessary. 32 of 128 credits required for the bachelor's degree must be completed at Miami. **International Students:** There are 2259 international students enrolled. The school actively recruits these students. They must take the TOEFL with a minimum score of 550 on the paper-based TOEFL (PBT) or 80 on the Internet-based version (iBT). Students must take the MELAB, or the IELTS, or alternative proof of English language proficiency. They must also take the SAT or ACT. Standardized tests are generally not required but are recommended for international students.

ADMISSIONS: 65% of the 2016-2017 applicants were accepted. The SAT scores for the 2016-2017 freshman class were: Critical Reading-- 14% below 500, 32% between 500 and 599, 41% between 600 and 699, and 13% between 700 and 800. Math-- 4% below 500, 25% between 500 and 599, 47% between 600 and 699, and 25% between 700 and 800. The ACT scores were 5% between 18 and 23, 56% between 24 and 29, and 40% above 30. 62% of the current freshmen were in the top fifth of their class; 88% were in the top two fifths. There were 9 National Merit finalists. 56 freshmen graduated first in their class. **Admissions Contact:** Susan Schaurer, Asst. VP and Dir. of Admission. Email: *admission@MiamiOH.edu* Web: *www.MiamiOH.edu*

FINANCIAL AID: The priority date for freshman financial aid applications for fall entry is February 15.

MOUNT ST. JOSEPH UNIVERSITY A-5

www.msj.edu

Cincinnati, OH 45233 (513) 244-4531
(800) 654-9314

Fax: (513) 244-4851 **Email:** admission@mail.msj.edu

Full-time: 548 men, 675 women	**Faculty:** IIA, --$
Part-time: 114 men, 458 women	**Ph.D.s:** 71%
Graduate: 136 men, 395 women	**Student/Faculty:** 11 to 1
Year: semesters, summer session	**Tuition:** $25,800
Room & Board: $8080	**Freshman Class:** 1180 applied, 1036 accepted, 321 enrolled
SAT CR/M: required **ACT:** 22	**CEEB CODE:** 1129
Application Deadline: n/av	**COMPETITIVE**

Mount St. Joseph University, formerly College of Mount Saint Joseph, founded in 1920, is a private Catholic college offering 34 undergraduate and 5 graduate degree programs. Figures in the above capsule and in this profile are approximate. There is 1 undergraduate school and 1 graduate school. In addition to regional accreditation, the Mount has baccalaureate program accreditation with CSWE, NASM, NLN, TEAC, ABA, ACS, and CAPTE. The 92-acre campus is in a suburban area 7 miles West of downtown Cincinnati. Including any residence halls, there are 9 buildings.

STUDENT LIFE: 85% of undergraduates are from Ohio. Others are from 25 states, and 4 foreign countries. 68% are from public schools. 9% are African American; 76% White; 2% Hispanic; 2% two or more races; 10% race unknown. **Female To Male Ratio:** 1.9:1. The average age of freshmen is 19; all undergraduates, 26. 31% do not continue beyond their first year; 69% remain to graduate. **Housing:** 537 students can be accommodated in college housing, which includes coed dorms. On-campus housing is guaranteed for all 4 years. 79% of students commute. All students may keep cars.

FACULTY/CLASSROOMS: 36% of faculty are male; 65% are female. No introductory courses are taught by graduate students. The average class size in an introductory lecture is 23; in a laboratory is 19; and in a regular course is 19.

PROGRAMS OF STUDY: The Mount confers B.A., B.S., B.F.A. and B.S.N. degrees. Associate, master's, and doctoral degrees are also awarded. Bachelor's degrees are awarded in BIOLOGICAL SCIENCE (biochemistry, biology/biological science, and neurosciences), BUSINESS (accounting, business administration and management, organizational leadership and management, and sports management), COMMUNICATIONS AND THE ARTS (art history, art, communications, English, fine arts, graphic design, and music), COMPUTER AND PHYSICAL SCIENCE (chemistry and mathematics), EDUCATION (art education, athletic training, early childhood education, elementary education, general studies, health information management, middle school education, and special education), HEALTH PROFESSIONS (nursing), SOCIAL SCIENCE (criminology, history, liberal arts/general studies, paralegal studies, psychology, religion, religious education, social work, and sociology). Nursing, business administration, and sport management are the strongest academically. Business administration, nursing, and graphic design have the largest enrollments.

ACTIVITIES: There are no fraternities or sororities. There are 46 groups on campus, including art, band, cheerleading, choir, chorale, chorus, computers, dance, departmental clubs, drama, ethnic, honors, international, jazz band, LGBT, literary magazine, marching band, musical theater, newspaper, orchestra, pep band, photography, professional, religious, social, social service, and student government. Popular campus events include MLK Luncheon, Spring Formal, Homecoming Pep Rally, and Little Sibs Weekend. **Sports:** There are 10 intercollegiate sports for men and 9 for women, and 7 intramural sports for men and 7 for women. Facilities include a sports complex and field for football, soccer, lacrosse, track and field and athletic training facilities. The student center houses gyms used for basketball, volleyball, and wrestling and includes a running track, handball/racquetball courts, fitness center, athletic training center, and a wellness center. Facilities also include tennis courts, a softball field, and practice fields for soccer, lacrosse, and baseball. **Graduates:** From July 1, 2015 to June 30, 2016, 380 bachelor's degrees were awarded. The most popular majors were nursing (23%), general studies (9%), and business administration (8%). 75 companies recruited on campus in 2015-2016. In an average class, 57% graduate in 6 years or less. Of the 2015 graduating class, 17% were enrolled in graduate school within 6 months of graduation, and 82% were employed.

SERVICES: Counseling and information services are available, as is tutoring in every subject, and remedial math and writing. Peer tutoring, services to students with learning disabilities, and math and writing centers are also available. **Library/Resources:** The library contains 95,428 volumes, 340,000 microform items, 4,149 audio/video tapes/CDs/DVDs, and subscribes to 3,906 periodicals including electronic. Computerized library services include interlibrary loans, database searching, Internet access, and Wi-Fi capability. Special learning facilities include an art gallery. **Physically Challenged Students:** 95% of the campus is accessible. Facilities include wheelchair ramps, elevators, special parking, specially equipped restrooms, special class scheduling, lowered drinking fountains, lowered telephones, and special housing. Special door openings for wheelchair access, and a chairlift between levels where the science building and classroom building meet. **Special:** The University offers co-op programs in all majors, cross-registration with the Greater Cincinnati Consortium of Colleges and Universities, internships, credit for experiential learning, and study abroad in 3 countries. Also available are work-study programs, accelerated degree programs in 11 majors, dual majors, cultural immersion courses in the United States and abroad, a dual enrollment program (for transfer students), service learning, and off-campus study for RNs in area hospitals. The Mount also has a program for students with learning disabilities (Project EXCEL). There are 14 national honor societies, a freshman honors program, and 13 departmental honors programs. **Visiting:** There are regularly scheduled orientations for prospective students, including a meeting with an admissions counselor, a student-guided tour, a visit to financial aid, and a meeting with a faculty member and/or athletic coach, if requested. There are guides for informal visits, visitors may sit in on classes, and stay overnight. To schedule a visit, contact the Office of Admission. **Campus Safety and Security:** Measures include 24-hour foot and vehicle patrol, emergency notification system, and security escort services, emergency telephones, lighted pathways/sidewalks, crime prevention programs, assistance with vehicle trouble, and first aid.

REQUIREMENTS: Mount St. Joseph University conducts a comprehensive and individualized review of every candidate's credentials for admission including but not limited to the following: a college prep high school curriculum, strong GPA, standardized test scores, evidence of leadership, and extracurricular involvement. An ACT score at or above the national average is recommended. In addition, students' personal background, attributes, and individual life circumstances are taken into consideration. A GPA of 2.5 is required. AP and CLEP credits are accepted. To graduate, students must complete a minimum of 120 credits with a minimum GPA of 2.0 overall and in the major. 46-49 core curriculum total hours are required. All students must take 12-15 credit hours on the common good, and 34 credit hours of a discipline-specific core, and a capstone synthesis reflection. **Procedure:** Freshmen are admitted to all sessions. There is a rolling admissions plan. Check with the school for current application deadlines. The application fee is $25. Notification is sent on a rolling basis. Applications are accepted online. **Transfer Students:** 97 transfer students enrolled in 2015-2016. Transfer students must have a college GPA of 2.0 or better in a minimum of 12 semester or 18 quarter hours. All college hours must be presented. 30 of 120 credits required for the bachelor's degree must be completed at the Mount. **International Students:** There are 4 international students enrolled. They must also take the SAT or ACT.

ADMISSIONS: 88% of the 2016-2017 applicants were accepted. The SAT scores for the 2016-2017 freshman class were: Critical Reading-- 62% below 500, 30% between 500 and 599, 7% between 600 and 699, and 1% between 700 and 800. Math-- 61% below 500, 30% between 500 and 599, and 9% between 600 and 699. The ACT scores were 40% below 12, 29% between 12 and 17, 22% between 18 and 23, 6% between 24 and 29, and 3% above 30. 23% of the current freshmen were in the top fifth of their class; 51% were in the top two fifths. 3 freshmen graduated first in their class. **Admissions Contact:** Peggy Minnich, Director of Admission. Email: *admission@mail.msj.edu* Web: *www.msj.edu*

FINANCIAL AID: In 2016-2017, 100% of all full-time freshmen and 98% of continuing full-time students received some form of financial aid. 84% of all full-time freshmen and 81% of continuing full-time students received need-based aid. The average freshman award was $20,218. Need-based scholarships or need-based grants averaged $16,336 ($32,485 maximum); need-based self-help aid (loans and jobs) averaged $4,969 ($7,000 maximum); and other non-need-based awards and non-need-based scholarships averaged $12,022 ($27,400 maximum). 16% of undergraduate students work part-time. The FAFSA code is 003033. The priority date for freshman financial aid applications for fall entry is March 1.

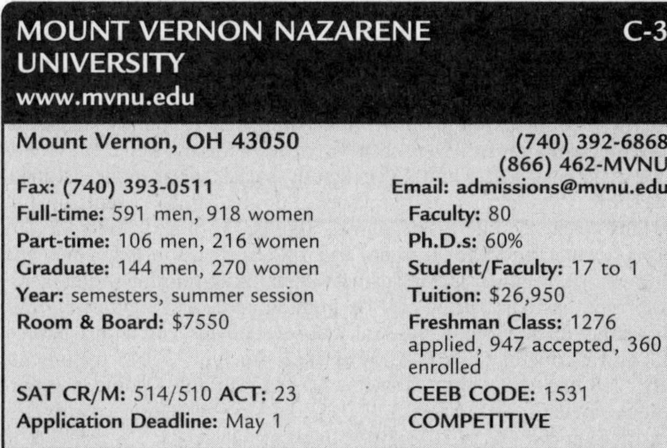

MOUNT VERNON NAZARENE UNIVERSITY C-3

www.mvnu.edu

Mount Vernon, OH 43050 (740) 392-6868
(866) 462-MVNU

Fax: (740) 393-0511 **Email:** admissions@mvnu.edu

Full-time: 591 men, 918 women	**Faculty:** 80
Part-time: 106 men, 216 women	**Ph.D.s:** 60%
Graduate: 144 men, 270 women	**Student/Faculty:** 17 to 1
Year: semesters, summer session	**Tuition:** $26,950
Room & Board: $7550	**Freshman Class:** 1276 applied, 947 accepted, 360 enrolled
SAT CR/M: 514/510 **ACT:** 23	**CEEB CODE:** 1531
Application Deadline: May 1	**COMPETITIVE**

Mount Vernon Nazarene University, founded in 1968, is a private liberal arts college affiliated with the Church of the Nazarene. Figures in the above capsule and in this profile are aproximate. There are 6 undergraduate schools and 3 graduate schools. In addition to regional accreditation, MVNU has baccalaureate program accreditation with ACBSP, CSWE, NASM, NCATE, and CCNE. The 327-acre campus is in a small town 45 miles northeast of Columbus. Including any residence halls, there are 55 buildings.

STUDENT LIFE: 92% of undergraduates are from Ohio. Others are from 30 states, and 11 foreign countries. 85% are White; 4% race unknown; 3% African American; 3% Hispanic; 3% two or more races; 1% Asian American; 1% Foreign. 52% are Protestant. **Female To Male Ratio:** 1.7:1. The average age of freshmen is 18; all undergraduates, 20. 23% do not continue beyond their first year; 58% remain to graduate. **Housing:** 1116 students can be accommodated in college housing, which includes single-sex dorms and on-campus apartments. On-campus housing is guaranteed for all 4 years, and is available on a first-come, and first-served basis. 78% of students live on campus; of those, 50% remain on campus on weekends. All students may keep cars. Alcohol is not permitted.

FACULTY/CLASSROOMS: 52% of faculty are male; 48% are female. 86% teach undergraduates. No introductory courses are taught by graduate students. The average class size in an introductory lecture is 20; in a laboratory is 18; and in a regular course is 16.

PROGRAMS OF STUDY: MVNU confers B.A., B.S., B.S.N., B.S.W., and B.B.A. degrees. Associate and master's degrees are also awarded. Bachelor's degrees are awarded in BIOLOGICAL SCIENCE (life science), BUSINESS (accounting, business administration and management, business data processing, finance, international business management, management information systems, management, marketing, and sports management), COMMUNICATIONS AND THE ARTS (art, church music, communication studies, communications, dramatic arts, English, graphic design, information technology, journalism, language arts, music, public relations, and Spanish), COMPUTER AND PHYSICAL SCIENCE (chemistry, computer networks & systems, computer science, and mathematics), EDUCATION (business education, early childhood education, English education, mathematics education, middle school education, music education, physical education, science education, social studies education, and special education), ENGINEERING AND ENVIRONMENTAL DESIGN (engineering and preengineering), HEALTH PROFESSIONS (biology, exercise science, nursing, premedicine, prepharmacy, and prephysical therapy), SOCIAL SCIENCE (biblical studies, communication sciences & disorders, criminal justice, history, ministries, missions, pastoral studies, philosophy, political science/government, prelaw, psychology, religion, religious education, religious music, social work, sociology, theological studies, and youth ministry). Biology, nursing, and education are the strongest academically. Nursing, business, and education have the largest enrollments.

ACTIVITIES: There are no fraternities or sororities. There are 49 groups on campus, including art, band, cheerleading, choir, chorale, chorus, communications, computers, drama, environmental, ethnic, honors, international, jazz band, literary magazine, musical theater, newspaper, orchestra, pep band, photography, political, professional, radio and TV, religious, social, social service, student government, symphony, and yearbook. Popular campus events include Friday Night Live, Battle of the Bands, Sonfest, Annual Luau, and all Cougars Sporting Events. **Sports:** There are 7 intercollegiate sports for men and 8 for women, and 7 intramural sports for men and 7 for women. Facilities include a main gym, intramural/practice gym, weight room, game room, fitness/exercise facility, tennis courts, intramural, soccer fields, and a baseball/softball batting facility. **Graduates:** From July 1, 2015 to June 30, 2016, 403 bachelor's degrees were awarded. The most popular majors were nursing (11%), biology (7%), and early childhood education (6%). In an average class, 51% graduate in 4 years or less, 57% graduate in 5 years or less, and 59% graduate in 6 years or less. Of the 2015 graduating class, 17% were enrolled in graduate school within 6 months of graduation, and 94% were employed.

SERVICES: Counseling and information services are available, as is tutoring in most subjects. There is also a reader service for the blind, and remedial math, reading, and writing. Students in the at-risk program are required to take University Success Strategies. **Library/Resources:** The library contains 165,069 volumes, 8 microform items, and 4,337 audio/video tapes/CDs/DVDs, and subscribes to 2,729 periodicals including electronic. Computerized library services include interlibrary loans, database searching, Internet access, and Wi-Fi capability. Special learning facilities include an art gallery, radio station, an academic support center. **Physically Challenged Students:** 95% of the campus is accessible. Facilities include wheelchair ramps, elevators, special parking, specially equipped restrooms, special class scheduling, lowered drinking fountains, lowered telephones, and special housing. **Special:** MVNU offers internships with local businesses and organizations, on-campus work-study programs, study abroad in 20 countries, dual majors, a general studies degree, and nondegree study. Cross-registration is available with Nazarene Universities, and the Council for Christian College and Universities program. There are 5 national honor societies, a freshman honors program, and 21 departmental honors programs. **Visiting:** There are regularly scheduled orientations for prospective students, MVNYou Visit Days - held throughout the year. There are guides for informal visits, visitors may sit in on classes, and stay overnight. To schedule a visit, contact the Admissions Office. **Campus Safety and Security:** Measures include 24-hour foot and vehicle patrol, emergency notification system, self-defense education, and security escort services. There are also shuttle buses, emergency telephones, lighted pathways/sidewalks, controlled access to dorms/residences, fire safety training with Student Leadership, and blood-borne pathogen seminars. Campus-wide sexual harassment training is required of all faculty, staff, and students, and there is also a campus safety and security review committee.

REQUIREMENTS: Applicants should be graduates of an accredited high school or home-school program and have ACT composite and subscores of 19 or above, or comparable SAT scores. Recommended preparatory courses include 4 units in English and 4 units each in math (algebra I and II, geometry, other), social studies, science, lab science, and 3 foreign language. An essay is required. Applicants not meeting minimum academic standards may be granted conditional admission with additional course requirements. A GPA of 2.5 is required. AP and CLEP credits are accepted. Important factors in the admissions decision are recommendations by school officials, personality/intangible qualities, and leadership record. Students must complete 120 semester hours, at least 39 in upper-division courses, and maintain a minimum GPA of 2.0. Students must also complete the 44- to 57-hour B.A. general education core requirements and the general education and major assessment programs. Additional preparatory courses may be required (0-12 hours). Students who desire two or more majors are required to complete the assessment in each major. **Procedure:** Freshmen are admitted in the fall, winter, and spring. Entrance exams should be taken in early fall. There are deferred admissions and rolling admissions plans. Applications should be filed by May 1 for fall entry; December 1 for winter entry; December 1 for spring entry; and May 15 for summer entry, along with a $25 fee. Applications are accepted on-line. **Transfer Students:** 29 transfer students enrolled in 2015-2016. Transfer students must be in good standing academically and financially. Official transcripts from all colleges attended must be submitted. 30 of 120 credits required for the bachelor's degree must be completed at MVNU. **International Students:** There are 21 international students enrolled. They must take the TOEFL with a minimum score of 550 on the paper-based TOEFL (PBT) or 80 on the Internet-based version (iBT) and the Comprehensive English Language Test. They must also take the SAT or ACT, scoring 19.

ADMISSIONS: 74% of the 2016-2017 applicants were accepted. The

SAT scores for the 2016-2017 freshman class were: Critical Reading-- 33% below 500, 40% between 500 and 599, 21% between 600 and 699, and 6% between 700 and 800. Math-- 46% below 500, 35% between 500 and 599, and 19% between 600 and 699. The ACT scores were 7% between 12 and 17, 50% between 18 and 23, 36% between 24 and 29, and 7% above 30. **Admissions Contact:** Tracy Waal, Director of Admissions. Email: *admissions@mvnu.edu* Web: *www.mvnu.edu*

FINANCIAL AID: In 2016-2017, 98% of all full-time freshmen and 92% of continuing full-time students received some form of financial aid. The average freshman award was $19,473.. 41% of undergraduate students work part-time. Average annual earnings from campus work are $1022. The average financial indebtedness of the 2016 graduate was $26,025. The FAFSA code is 007085. The priority date for freshman financial aid applications for fall entry is November 15. The filling deadline for fall entry is August 17.

MUSKINGUM UNIVERSITY D-3

www.muskingum.edu

New Concord, OH 43762	(740) 826-8137 (800) 752-6082
Fax: (740) 826-8100	Email: adminfo@muskingum.edu
Full-time: 802 men, 771 women	**Faculty:** 99; IIB, av$
Part-time: 44 men, 132 women	**Ph.D.s:** 87%
Graduate: 146 men, 395 women	**Student/Faculty:** 14 to 1
Year: semesters, summer session	**Tuition:** $25,779
Room & Board: $10,190	**Freshman Class:** 2134 applied, 1656 accepted, 438 enrolled
SAT CR/M: 491/513 **ACT:** 22	**CEEB CODE:** 1496
Application Deadline: August 1	**COMPETITIVE**

Muskingum University, founded in 1837, is a private liberal arts and sciences institution affiliated with the Presbyterian Church. Figures in the above capsule and in this profile are approximate. There is 1 undergraduate school and 1 graduate school. In addition to regional accreditation, Muskingum has baccalaureate program accreditation with NASM and NCATE. The 245-acre campus is in a small town 9 miles west of Cambridge and 50 miles east of Columbus. Including any residence halls, there are 35 buildings.

STUDENT LIFE: 86% of undergraduates are from Ohio. Others are from 28 states, and 10 foreign countries. 85% are from public schools. 87% are White; 7% African American; 3% Foreign; 2% Hispanic; 1% Asian American. 42% are Protestant; 30% claim no religious affiliation; 16% Catholic. **Female To Male Ratio:** 1.3:1. The average age of freshmen is 18; all undergraduates, 20. 33% do not continue beyond their first year; 55% remain to graduate. **Housing:** 1200 students can be accommodated in college housing, which includes single-sex and coed dorms, on-campus apartments, language houses, special-interest houses, fraternity houses, upperclassmen apartments and townhouses. On-campus housing is guaranteed for all 4 years. 87% of students live on campus; of those, 60% remain on campus on weekends. All students may keep cars.

FACULTY/CLASSROOMS: 56% of faculty are male; 44% are female. 85% teach undergraduates, 85% do research, and 85% do both. No introductory courses are taught by graduate students. The average class size in an introductory lecture is 25; in a laboratory is 16; and in a regular course is 22.

PROGRAMS OF STUDY: Muskingum confers B.A., and B.S. degrees. Master's degrees are also awarded. Bachelor's degrees are awarded in AGRICULTURE (conservation and regulation), BIOLOGICAL SCIENCE (biology/biological science, molecular biology, and neurosciences), BUSINESS (accounting, business administration and management, and international business management), COMMUNICATIONS AND THE ARTS (art, communications, digital communications, dramatic arts, English, French, German, journalism, music, Spanish, and speech/debate/rhetoric), COMPUTER AND PHYSICAL SCIENCE (chemistry, computer science, earth science, geology, mathematics, and physics), EDUCATION (Christian education, early childhood education, elementary education, foreign languages education, music education, physical education, reading education, science education, secondary education, and special education), ENGINEERING AND ENVIRONMENTAL DESIGN (engineering and environmental science), HEALTH PROFESSIONS (nursing), SOCIAL SCIENCE (American studies, criminal justice, economics, history, international relations, philosophy, political science/government, psychology, public affairs, religion, religious education, social science, and sociology). Sciences, and education are the strongest academically. Education, business, and psychology have the largest enrollments.

ACTIVITIES: 24% of men belong to 3 local and 2 national fraternities; 37% of women belong to 4 local and 2 national sororities. There are 90 groups on campus, including art, band, cheerleading, choir, chorus, computers, dance, dance team, debate, drama, environmental, ethnic, forensics, honors, international, jazz band, LGBT, literary magazine, marching band, musical theater, newspaper, orchestra, pep band, political, professional, radio and TV, religious, social, social service, student government, symphony, and yearbook. Popular campus events include Li'l Sibs Weekend and Muskiepalooza. **Sports:** There are 9 intercollegiate sports for men and 8 for women, and 8 intramural sports for men and 8 for women. Facilities include gyms, weight lifting/training rooms, aerobics room, baseball batting cage, swimming pool, walking/jogging trail, all-weather track, football, baseball, and soccer fields, and tennis, basketball, and racquetball courts. **Graduates:** From July 1, 2015 to June 30, 2016, 268 bachelor's degrees were awarded. The most popular majors were business (23%), education (21%), and biology (8%). 25 companies recruited on campus in 2015-2016. In an average class, 1% graduate in 3 years or less, 38% graduate in 4 years or less, 54% graduate in 5 years or less, and 55% graduate in 6 years or less. Of the 2015 graduating class, 15% were enrolled in graduate school within 6 months of graduation, and 93% were employed.

SERVICES: Counseling and information services are available, as is tutoring in every subject, and a reader service for the blind. The PLUS program is available for learning-disabled and disabled students. **Library/Resources:** The library contains 209,220 volumes, 171,964 microform items, 3,471 audio/video tapes/CDs/DVDs, and subscribes to 14,127 periodicals including electronic. Computerized library services include interlibrary loans, database searching, and Internet access. Special learning facilities include an art gallery, radio station, TV station, a greenhouse. **Physically Challenged Students:** 40% of the campus is accessible. Facilities include wheelchair ramps, elevators, special parking, specially equipped restrooms, and lowered drinking fountains. **Special:** Internships, both national and regional, work-study programs, study abroad in 13 countries, and a Washington semester are possible. Dual and student-designed majors, nondegree study, pass/fail options, and credit for life, military, or work experience are also available. There are 18 national honor societies. **Visiting:** There are regularly scheduled orientations for prospective students, consisting of an admission presentation, faculty panel, student panel, and class attendance. There are guides for informal visits, visitors may sit in on classes, and stay overnight. To schedule a visit, contact the Admission Office. **Campus Safety and Security:** Measures include 24-hour foot and vehicle patrol, emergency notification system, security escort services, emergency telephones, lighted pathways/sidewalks, and controlled access to dorms/residences.

REQUIREMENTS: The SAT or ACT is required. Candidates for admission must have a high school diploma or its equivalent and should have 4 years of English, 3 years of college preparatory math, and 2 years each of science, social science, and foreign language. AP and CLEP credits are accepted. Important factors in the admissions decision are advanced placement or honors courses, extracurricular activities record, and leadership record. To graduate, students must complete a minimum of 124 credit hours, including at least 30 in a major and 40 in upper-level courses. Students must maintain a GPA of at least 2.0 and must also complete the 50 to 55 credit hours of Liberal Arts Essentials, with courses in writing, speech, math, arts and humanities, religion and ethics, science, social science, American studies, and phys ed. A senior capstone experience is required in all areas. **Procedure:** Freshmen are admitted in the fall and spring. Entrance exams should be taken in the junior year or the fall of the senior year. There are deferred admissions and rolling admissions plans. Applications should be filed by August 1 for fall entry. Applications are accepted online. **Transfer Students:** 61 transfer students enrolled in 2015-2016. Applicants must submit an official college transcript and be in good academic standing at their previous institution. 32 of 124 credits required for the bachelor's degree must be completed at Muskingum. **International Students:** There are 41 international students enrolled. The school actively recruits these students. They must take the TOEFL with a minimum score of 550 on the paper-based TOEFL (PBT) or 79 on the Internet-based version (iBT). Either the SAT or the ACT is recommended.

ADMISSIONS: 78% of the 2016-2017 applicants were accepted. The

SAT scores for the 2016-2017 freshman class were: Critical Reading-- 50% below 500, 43% between 500 and 599, 5% between 600 and 699, and 2% between 700 and 800. Math-- 45% below 500, 36% between 500 and 599, 14% between 600 and 699, and 5% between 700 and 800. The ACT scores were 40% below 12, 28% between 12 and 17, 19% between 18 and 23, 6% between 24 and 29, and 6% above 30. 39% of the current freshmen were in the top fifth of their class; 59% were in the top two fifths. 11 freshmen graduated first in their class. **Admissions Contact:** Beth DaLonzo, Senior Director of Admission and Student Financial Services. Email: *adminfo@muskingum.edu* Web: *www.muskingum.edu*

FINANCIAL AID: In 2016-2017, 99% of all full-time freshmen and 98% of continuing full-time students received some form of financial aid. 84% of all full-time freshmen and 82% of continuing full-time students received need-based aid. The average freshman award was $19,518. Need-based scholarships or need-based grants averaged $15,314 ($30,500 maximum); and need-based self-help aid (loans and jobs) averaged $4,204 ($8,500 maximum). 45% of undergraduate students work part-time. Average annual earnings from campus work are $1000. The average financial indebtedness of the 2016 graduate was $34,207. Muskingum is a member of CSS. The FAFSA code is 003084. The priority date for freshman financial aid applications for fall entry is March 1.

NOTRE DAME COLLEGE D-1

www.notredamecollege.com

South Euclid, OH 44121	**(216) 373-5351** **(800) NDC-OHIO**
Fax: (216) 937-0357	**Email: admissions@ndc.edu**
Full-time: 600 men, 764 women	**Faculty:** n/av
Part-time: n/av	**Ph.D.s:** n/av
Graduate: n/av	**Student/Faculty:** n/av
Year: semesters, summer session	**Tuition:** $27,600
Room & Board: $9550	**Freshman Class:** n/av
SAT or ACT: required	**CEEB CODE:** 1566
Application Deadline: August	**VERY COMPETITIVE**

Notre Dame College, founded in 1922, is a private liberal arts and sciences college affiliated with the Roman Catholic Church. Figures in the above capsule and in this profile are approximate. There is 1 undergraduate school and 1 graduate school. In addition to regional accreditation, NDC has baccalaureate program accreditation with ADA, NCATE, CCNE, and AACN. The 53-acre campus is in a suburban area 13 miles east of Cleveland. Including any residence halls, there are 10 buildings.

STUDENT LIFE: Students are from 20 states, 12 foreign countries, and Canada. 65% are from public schools. 65% are White; 3% Hispanic; 23% African American; 1% Asian American; 1% Foreign. 55% are Catholic; 20% Baptist, and Muslim; 15% Protestant. **Female To Male Ratio:** 1.3:1. The average age of freshmen is 18; all undergraduates, 26. 34% do not continue beyond their first year; 52% remain to graduate. **Housing:** 650 students can be accommodated in college housing, which includes single-sex and coed dorms, on-campus apartments, nonsmoking floors, quiet floors, and gender specific, and underclassman dorms. On-campus housing is guaranteed for all 4 years, and is available on a lottery system for upperclassmen. 60% of students live on campus. All students may keep cars. Alcohol is not permitted.

FACULTY/CLASSROOMS: All teach undergraduates. No introductory courses are taught by graduate students. The average class size in an introductory lecture is 16.

PROGRAMS OF STUDY: NDC confers B.A. and B.S. degrees. Associate and master's degrees are also awarded. Bachelor's degrees are awarded in BIOLOGICAL SCIENCE (biology/biological science), BUSINESS (accounting, business economics, human resources, management science, and marketing/retailing/merchandising), COMMUNICATIONS AND THE ARTS (art, communications, English, graphic design, public relations, studio art, and visual and performing arts), COMPUTER AND PHYSICAL SCIENCE (chemistry, information sciences and systems, and mathematics), EDUCATION (early childhood education, elementary education, middle school education, secondary education, and special education), ENGINEERING AND ENVIRONMENTAL DESIGN (environmental science), HEALTH PROFESSIONS (nursing and physical therapy), SOCIAL SCIENCE (economics, history, ministries, political science/government, psychology, and theological studies). Business, education, and science are the strongest academically. Business administration, education, and sciences have the largest enrollments.

ACTIVITIES: There are no fraternities or sororities. There are 32 groups on campus, including indoor colorguard, indoor percussions ensemble, art, band, cheerleading, choir, chorus, computers, dance, drama, ethnic, honors, international, jazz band, LGBT, literary magazine, marching band, marching band, newspaper, pep band, political, professional, religious, social, social service, and student government. Popular campus events include Founders Weekend, Welcome Weekend, and Spring Fest Week. **Sports:** There are 11 intercollegiate sports for men and 11 for women. Facilities include a gym, pool, and fitness center.

SERVICES: Counseling and information services are available, as is tutoring in every subject. Notre Dame also offers free peer tutoring within our Dwyer Learning Center. There is also Academic Support Center for Students with Learning Differences, and remedial math, reading, and writing. **Library/Resources:** The library contains 89,292 volumes, 14,200 microform items, 1,768 audio/video tapes/CDs/DVDs, and subscribes to 300 periodicals including electronic. Computerized library services include interlibrary loans and database searching. Special learning facilities include an art gallery, and Tolerance Resource Center. There is also an Academic Support Center for Students with Learning Disabilities. **Physically Challenged Students:** 75% of the campus is accessible. Facilities include wheelchair ramps, elevators, special parking, specially equipped restrooms, lowered drinking fountains, and lowered telephones. **Special:** There is a freshman honors program. **Visiting:** There are regularly scheduled orientations for prospective students, students and their families will meet with an admissions counselor individually to discuss admissions, financial aid, and any other questions they may have. They also have the options of taking a tour of campus or meeting with a professor. There are guides for informal visits, visitors may sit in on classes, and stay overnight. To schedule a visit, contact The Admissions Office. **Campus Safety and Security:** Measures include 24-hour foot and vehicle patrol, emergency notification system, self-defense education, and security escort services. There are emergency telephones, lighted pathways/sidewalks, controlled access to dorms/residences, and 24/7 campus security that work hand in had with the South Euclid Police Department.

REQUIREMENTS: The SAT or ACT is required. Applicants should be graduates of an accredited secondary school with 15 academic credits, including 4 of English, 2 of foreign language, 1 each of math, social studies, and science, plus 5 electives. The GED is accepted. An interview is recommended. A GPA of 2.5 is required. AP and CLEP credits are accepted. To graduate, students must complete 128 semester hours with a minimum GPA of 2.0. Students must have successfully completed courses fulfilling in the General Education Requirements and those pertaining to their field of study. The following must be completed at NDC: 50% of major coursework, 50% of the last 32 credits at NDC. Have at least 45 upper-biennium courses. Have attended NDC for at least 1 semster and have completed a minimum of 32 semester credits at NDC. **Procedure:** Freshmen are admitted fall and spring. There are deferred admissions and rolling admissions plans. Application deadlines are open. Notification is sent on a rolling basis. Applications are accepted online. **Transfer Students:** Applicants must have a college GPA of at least 2.5. Perspective students must submit all college transcripts as well as high school. 32 of 128 credits required for the bachelor's degree must be completed at NDC. **International Students:** The school actively recruits these students. They must take the TOEFL, or take the ELS Proficiency Test 109.

Admissions Contact: Beth Ford, Director of Admissions/Financial Aid. Email: *admissions@ndc.edu* Web: *www.notredamecollege.com*

FINANCIAL AID: In 2016-2017, 99% of all full-time freshmen received some form of financial aid. The FAFSA code is 003085. Check with the school for current application deadlines.

OBERLIN COLLEGE D-2

www.oberlin.edu

Oberlin, OH 44074	**(440) 775-8411** **(800) 622-6243**
Fax: (440) 775-6905	**Email: college.admissions@oberlin.edu**
Full-time: 1243 men, 1626 women	**Faculty:** 372; IIB, ++$
Part-time: 12 men, 14 women	**Ph.D.s:** 96%
Graduate: 7 men, 10 women	**Student/Faculty:** 10 to 1
Year: 4-1-4	**Tuition:** $52,002
Room & Board: $14,010	**Freshman Class:** 8518 applied, 2388 accepted, 762 enrolled
SAT CR/M/W: 690/671/683 **ACT:** 30	**CEEB CODE:** 1587
Application Deadline: January 15	**MOST COMPETITIVE**

Oberlin College, is a liberal arts college of intense energy and creativity. That is built on a foundation of academic, artistic, and musical excellence. The only institution in the United States where a top-ranked liberal arts college and a world-renowned conservatory of music share a seamless student culture and campus. Noted for its sustainability initiatives and achievements, Oberlin has been recognized as one of the 'greenest' institutions in the USA and continues to challenge itself and its students to find better and more efficient ways to be environmentally responsible. Oberlin provides a world-class education to its 2900 students, the majority of whom continue on to prestigious fellowships and PhD programs. There are 2 undergraduate schools and 1 graduate school. In addition to regional accreditation, Oberlin has baccalaureate program accreditation with HLC. The 442-acre campus is in a small town 35 miles southwest of Cleveland, OH. Including any residence halls, there are 68 buildings.

STUDENT LIFE: 95% of undergraduates are from out of state, mostly the Middle Atlantic. Students are from 50 states, 42 foreign countries, and Canada. 66% are from public schools. 9% are Foreign; 8% Hispanic; 7% two or more races; 66% White; 5% African American; 4% Asian American. **Female To Male Ratio:** 1.3:1. The average age of freshmen is 18; all undergraduates, 20. 8% do not continue beyond their first year; 85% remain to graduate. **Housing:** 2700 students can be accommodated in college housing, which includes coed dorms, on-campus apartments, off-campus apartments, language houses, special-interest houses, and co-ops housing. On-campus housing is guaranteed for all 4 years. 90% of students live on campus; of those, 99% remain on campus on weekends. All students may keep cars.

FACULTY/CLASSROOMS: All teach undergraduates and do research. No introductory courses are taught by graduate students. The average class size in a laboratory is 14 and in a regular course is 20.

PROGRAMS OF STUDY: Oberlin confers B.A and B.Mus. degrees. Master's degrees are also awarded. Bachelor's degrees are awarded in AGRICULTURE (environmental studies), BIOLOGICAL SCIENCE (biochemistry, biology/biological science, and neurosciences), COMMUNICATIONS AND THE ARTS (acting, Africana studies, art history, art, art/visual culture, classics, composition, comparative literature, conducting, creative writing, dance, dramatic arts, English, film arts, fine arts, French, German, Germanic languages and literature, music, music composition, music history and appreciation, music performance, music theory and composition, painting, performing arts, photography, piano/organ, romance languages and literature, Russian, Russian languages and literature, Spanish, Spanish and Hispanic studies, strings, studio art, studio art painting, theatre acting, theater design, theatre studies, and winds), COMPUTER AND PHYSICAL SCIENCE (applied mathematics, astronomy, astronomy and physics, chemistry, computer science, geology, mathematics, and physics), EDUCATION (music education), HEALTH PROFESSIONS (biology and premedicine), SOCIAL SCIENCE (African American studies, American studies, anthropology, archeology, East Asian studies, Eastern European studies, economics, gender studies, history, humanities, international studies, Judaic studies, Latin American studies, law, Near Eastern studies, philosophy, political science/government, prelaw, psychology, religion, Russian and Slavic studies, sociology, women & gender studies, and women's studies). Sciences, art, and environmental studies are the strongest academically. Biology, politics, and economics have the largest enrollments.

ACTIVITIES: There are no fraternities or sororities. There are 175 groups on campus, including art, band, chess, choir, chorale, chorus, communications, computers, dance, debate, drama, environmental, ethnic, film, forensics, honors, international, jazz band, LGBT, literary magazine, marching band, musical theater, newspaper, opera, orchestra, photography, political, professional, radio and TV, religious, social, social service, student government, and symphony. Popular campus events include Big Parade, Earth Day, and Art Rental. **Sports:** There are 10 intercollegiate sports for men and 11 for women, and 10 intramural sports for men and 10 for women. Facilities include an all-weather multipurpose field, field house, indoor track, outdoor track, outdoor and indoor tennis courts, cross-country course, fitness trail, swimming pool, Nautilus center, free-weight room, practice/play fields, indoor space for football, soccer, and lacrosse practice, and a climbing wall. **Graduates:** From July 1, 2015 to June 30, 2016, 676 bachelor's degrees were awarded. The most popular majors were economics (7%), politics (6%), and English/environmental studies (6%). In an average class, 72% graduate in 4 years or less, 84% graduate in 5 years or less, and 85% graduate in 6 years or less. Of the 2015 graduating class, 22% were enrolled in graduate school within 6 months of graduation, and 54% were employed.

SERVICES: Counseling and information services are available, as is tutoring in every subject, and a reader service for the blind, and remedial math, reading, and writing. Computer-assisted services are also available for hearing and visually impaired students. **Library/Resources:** The 4 libraries contain 1.4 million volumes, 362,082 microform items, 115,097 audio/video tapes/CDs/DVDs, and subscribe to 181,044 periodicals including electronic. Computerized library services include interlibrary loans, database searching, Internet access, and Wi-Fi capability. Special learning facilities include an art gallery, radio station, an observatory, art museum, art library, arboretum, a conservatory of music, a music library, science library, and a learning center specializing in foreign language education. **Physically Challenged Students:** 90% of the campus is accessible. Facilities include wheelchair ramps, elevators, special parking, specially equipped restrooms, special class scheduling, lowered drinking fountains, lowered telephones, special housing, and an indoor/outdoor lift. **Special:** Internships are available through the Business Initiatives Program. Students may study abroad in 38 countries. Three-quarters of Oberlin students spend time abroad for study or service. The college offers independent and dual majors, 3-2 engineering programs with other institutions, non-degree study for special and visiting students, and a 5-year B.A.-B.Mus. double degree. Pass/no credit options are available to all students. There are 4 national honor societies, Phi Beta Kappa, and 25 departmental honors programs. **Visiting:** There are regularly scheduled orientations for prospective students, consisting of campus tour, information session, class visits, interview, and an overnight stay in the dorm. There are guides for informal visits, visitors may sit in on classes, and stay overnight. To schedule a visit, contact the Campus Visit Office at (800) 622-6243. **Campus Safety and Security:** Measures include 24-hour foot and vehicle patrol, emergency notification system, self-defense education, security escort services, emergency telephones, lighted pathways/sidewalks, controlled access to dorms/residences, full-time crime prevention officer, a 24-hour headquarters facility staffed by professional dispatchers, and an electronic card-access system in all dorms.

REQUIREMENTS: Candidates for admission should have completed 4 years each of English and math, and 3 each of science, social studies, and the same foreign language. Either the SAT or ACT is required. International students must also submit TOEFL or IELTS exam scores. AP credits are accepted. Important factors in the admissions decision are leadership record, personality/intangible qualities, and advanced placement or honors courses. Students are required to complete 32 full courses, including 2 in each of the 3 academic divisions (arts/humanities, social/behavioral sciences, natural science/math), 3 courses dealing with cultural diversity, plus 3 winter term projects. In addition, they must earn a writing and quantitative proficiency certification. **Procedure:** Freshmen are admitted in the fall. Entrance exams should be taken in the junior year or early in the senior year. There are early decision, early admissions, and deferred admissions plans. Early decision applications should be filed by November 15; regular applications, by January 15 for fall entry; and November 15 for spring entry. Notification of early decision is sent December 15; regular decision, April 1. 278 early decision candidates were accepted for the 2016-2017 class. 1700 applicants were on the 2016 waiting list; 151 were admitted. Application fees are waived if application is completed online. **Transfer Students:** 33 transfer students enrolled in 2015-2016. Applicants should submit official transcripts of all college work completed, plus a list of current courses and midterm grades. An average of B or better should be presented. A high school transcript, recommendations, and standardized test scores are also required. 16 of 32 credits required for the bachelor's degree must be completed at Oberlin. **International Students:** There are 264 international students enrolled. The school actively recruits these students. They must take the TOEFL with a minimum score of 600 on the paper-based TOEFL (PBT) or 100 on the Internet-based version (iBT), or take the IELTS. They must also take the SAT or ACT. International students whose native language is English must take the SAT or ACT Plus Writing.

ADMISSIONS: 28% of the 2016-2017 applicants were accepted. The SAT scores for the 2016-2017 freshman class were: Critical Reading-- 1% below 500, 11% between 500 and 599, 42% between 600 and 699, and 46% between 700 and 800. Math-- 2% below 500, 15% between 500 and 599, 49% between 600 and 699, and 34% between 700 and 800. Writing-- 2% below 500, 12% between 500 and 599, 46% between 600 and 699, and 40% between 700 and 800. The ACT scores were 3% between 18 and 23, 30% between 24 and 29, and 67% above 30. 84% of the current freshmen were in the top fifth of their class; 98% were in the top two fifths. **Admissions Contact:** Debra Chermonte, VP/Dean of Admissions & Financial Aid. Email: *college.admissions@oberlin.edu* Web: *www.oberlin.edu*

FINANCIAL AID: In 2016-2017, 56% of all full-time freshmen and 48% of continuing full-time students received some form of financial aid. 56% of all full-time freshmen and 48% of continuing full-time students received need-based aid. The average freshman award was $42,479. Need-based scholarships or need-based grants averaged $38,361; need-based self-help aid (loans and jobs) averaged $4,840; and other non-need-based awards and non-need-based scholarships averaged $13,130. 59% of undergraduate students work part-time. Average annual earnings from campus work are $2400. The average financial indebtedness of the 2016 graduate was $24,621. Oberlin is a member of CSS. The CSS/Profile and the college's own financial statement are required. The FAFSA code is 003086. The deadline for filing freshman financial aid applications for fall entry is February 15.

OHIO DOMINICAN UNIVERSITY C-3

www.ohiodominican.edu

Columbus, OH 43219 (614) 251-4500
(800) 955-OHIO

Fax: (614) 252-0776 Email: admissions@ohiodominican.edu

Full-time: 611 men, 780 women	**Faculty:** n/av
Part-time: 239 men, 375 women	**Ph.D.s:** 91%
Graduate: 178 men, 390 women	**Student/Faculty:** 12 to 1
Year: semesters, summer session	**Tuition:** $32,960
Room & Board: $8380	**Freshman Class:** 2652 applied, 1310 accepted
ACT: required	**CEEB CODE:** 1131
Application Deadline: open	**COMPETITIVE+**

Ohio Dominican University, founded in 1911 by the Dominican Sisters of St. Mary of the Springs, is a private liberal arts university affiliated with the Roman Catholic Church. The figures in the above capsule and in this profile are approximate. There are 2 undergraduate schools and 1 graduate school. In addition to regional accreditation, ODU has baccalaureate program accreditation with ACBSP, CSWE, and NCATE. The 98-acre campus is in an urban area 5 miles from downtown Columbus. Including any residence halls, there are 16 buildings.

STUDENT LIFE: 96% of undergraduates are from Ohio. Others are from 16 states, 12 foreign countries, and Canada. 82% are from public schools. 67% are White; 23% African American; 3% Hispanic; 3% two or more races; 2% race unknown; 1% Asian American; 1% American Indian/Alaska Native; 1% Foreign. 37% are Catholic; 34% Protestant. **Female To Male Ratio:** 1.5:1. The average age of freshmen is 18; all undergraduates, 24. 34% do not continue beyond their first year; 66% remain to graduate. **Housing:** 620 students can be accommodated in college housing, which includes single-sex, coed dorms, and honors houses. On-campus housing is available on a first-come, first-served basis. 73% of students commute. All students may keep cars. Alcohol is not permitted.

FACULTY/CLASSROOMS: 54% of faculty are male; 46% are female. All teach undergraduates. No introductory courses are taught by graduate students. The average class size in an introductory lecture is 20 and in a regular course is 20.

PROGRAMS OF STUDY: ODU confers B.A., B.S., and B.S.Ed. degrees. Associate and master's degrees are also awarded. Bachelor's degrees are awarded in AGRICULTURE (environmental studies), BIOLOGICAL SCIENCE (biology/biological science), BUSINESS (accounting, banking and finance, business administration and management, international business management, management information systems, and sports management), COMMUNICATIONS AND THE ARTS (art, communications, English, graphic design, and public relations), COMPUTER AND PHYSICAL SCIENCE (chemistry, computer science, and mathematics), EDUCATION (early childhood education, middle school education, and special education), HEALTH PROFESSIONS (exercise science), SOCIAL SCIENCE (criminal justice, economics, history, interdisciplinary studies, liberal arts/general studies, peace studies, philosophy, political science/government, psychology, social work, sociology, and theological studies). Business, education, and psychology have the largest enrollments.

ACTIVITIES: There are no fraternities or sororities. There are 40 groups on campus, including academic, art, association of resident students, band, cheerleading, choir, dance, drama, drill team, environmental, ethnic, honors, international, literary magazine, newspaper, Panther Players, pep band, political, professional, radio and TV, religious, social, social service, social work, St. Alberts Club, and student government. Popular campus events include Black History Week, International Student Week, and ODU Day in the Spring. **Sports:** There are 8 intercollegiate sports for men and 8 for women, and 5 intramural sports for men and 5 for women. Facilities include an athletic center, a gym, football stadium, baseball and softball field, soccer field, outdoor basketball courts, and outdoor tennis courts. **Graduates:** From July 1, 2015 to June 30, 2016, 338 bachelor's degrees were awarded. The most popular majors were business (41%), early childhood education (14%), and criminal justice (5%). 15 companies recruited on campus in 2015-2016. In an average class, 1% graduate in 3 years or less, 29% graduate in 4 years or less, 40% graduate in 5 years or less, and 42% graduate in 6 years or less.

SERVICES: Counseling and information services are available, as is tutoring in most subjects, and remedial math, reading, and writing. The Academic Center is a support unit designed to help all students meet their academic commitment and improve their learning skills. The staff offers workshops in study-related topics, and provides professional and peer tutoring. **Library/Resources:** The library contains 161,704 volumes, 10,878 microform items, and 4,422 audio/video tapes/CDs/DVDs, and subscribes to 13,282 periodicals including electronic. Computerized library services include interlibrary loans, database searching, Internet access, and Wi-Fi capability. Special learning facilities include an art gallery and radio station. **Physically Challenged Students:** 90% of the campus is accessible. Facilities include wheelchair ramps, elevators, special parking, specially equipped restrooms, special class scheduling, and lowered drinking fountains. **Special:** Students may cross-register with members of the Higher Education Council of Columbus Consortium, study abroad in various countries, and participate in a Washington semester. Internships are required in some majors. ODU offers dual majors and pass/fail options in some courses. Nondegree study and credit for life, military, and work experience are available. There is an accelerated degree program in business administration. There are 2 national honor societies and a freshman honors program. **Visiting:** There are regularly scheduled orientations for prospective students, including an August orientation for fall entry and a January orientation for the second semester. Individual appointments can be arranged. There are guides for informal visits, visitors may sit in on classes, and stay overnight. To schedule a visit, contact the Director of Admissions. **Campus Safety and Security:** Measures include 24-hour foot and vehicle patrol, emergency notification system, and security escort services. There are also shuttle buses, emergency telephones, and lighted pathways/sidewalks.

REQUIREMENTS: The ACT is required. Candidates for admission should have completed 4 units of English and 3 units each of a foreign language, math, science, and social studies. The freshman applicant is required to submit a completed application and transcripts of secondary courses and grades. An essay and an interview (in-state applicants) are required. AP and CLEP credits are accepted. Core curriculum requirements include 9 semester hours in arts and ideas, 6 each in English and behavioral science, 6 each in philosophy and theology, 3 each in literature, math, and science, 3 or 6 in language, 3 addressing diversity, and 4 core curriculum seminars. All students beyond the freshman year must maintain a GPA of 2.0. Students must complete 120 semester credits. Individual departments set the total hours in the major. **Procedure:** Freshmen are admitted to all sessions. There are deferred admissions and rolling admissions plans. Application deadlines are open. Application fee is $25. Applications are accepted online. **Transfer Students:** 114 transfer students enrolled in 2015-2016. A completed application, an interview, and transcripts of all college work are required of transfer applicants. 32 of 124 credits required for the bachelor's degree must be completed at ODU. **International Students:** There are 17 international students enrolled. The school actively recruits these students. They must take the TOEFL with a minimum score of 550 on the paper-based TOEFL (PBT) or 79 on the Internet-based version (iBT). They must also take the ACT.

ADMISSIONS: 49% of the 2016-2017 applicants were accepted. The SAT scores for the 2016-2017 freshman class were: Critical Reading-- 53% below 500, 28% between 500 and 599, 14% between 600 and 699, and 5% between 700 and 800. Math-- 35% below 500, 42% between 500 and 599, and 23% between 600 and 699. The ACT scores were 33% below 12, 33% between 12 and 17, 22% between 18 and 23, 7% between 24 and 29, and 4% above 30. 36% of the current freshmen were in the top fifth of their class; 68% were in the top two fifths. 7 freshmen graduated first in their class. **Admissions Contact:** Nicole Evans, Director of Admissions. Email: *admissions@ohiodominican.edu* Web: *www.ohiodominican.edu*

FINANCIAL AID: In 2016-2017, 100% of all full-time freshmen and 98% of continuing full-time students received some form of financial aid. 88% of all full-time freshmen and 87% of continuing full-time students received need-based aid. The average freshman award was $23,000. Need-based scholarships or need-based grants averaged $4,200 ($6,000 maximum); need-based self-help aid (loans and jobs) averaged $5,200 ($8,000 maximum); and other non-need-based awards and non-need-based scholarships averaged $7,000 ($13,000 maximum). 35% of undergraduate students work part-time. Average annual earnings from campus work are $1500. The FAFSA code is 003035. Check with the school for current application deadlines.

OHIO NORTHERN UNIVERSITY B-2

www.onu.edu

Ada, OH 45810	(419) 772-2529 (800) 408-4668
Fax: (419) 772-1932	Email: admissions-ug@onu.edu
Full-time: 1139 men, 1046 women	Faculty: IIB, +$
Part-time: 35 men, 14 women	Ph.D.s: 82%
Graduate: 326 men, 511 women	Student/Faculty: 12 to 1
Year: trimesters, summer session	Tuition: $33,000
Room & Board: $11,050	Freshman Class: 3337 applied, 2289 accepted, 628 enrolled
SAT CR/M/W: 570/590/555 ACT: 26	CEEB CODE: 1591
Application Deadline: August 15	VERY COMPETITIVE

Ohio Northern University, founded in 1871, is a private institution affiliated with the United Methodist Church. Undergraduate programs are offered in arts and sciences, business administration, engineering, and pharmacy. The figures in the above capsule and in this profile are approximate. The tuition cost varies by programs chosen. There are 4 undergraduate schools and 1 graduate school. In addition to regional accreditation, ONU has baccalaureate program accreditation with ABET, ACPE, NASM, NCATE, ACS, and CAAHEP. The 342-acre campus is in a small town about 75 miles South of Toledo. Including any residence halls, there are 60 buildings.

STUDENT LIFE: 86% of undergraduates are from Ohio. Others are from 42 states, 17 foreign countries, and Canada. 82% are from public schools. 95% are White; 2% African American; 1% Asian American; 1% Hispanic; 1% Foreign. 43% are Baptist, Muslim, Lutheran, and Presbyterian; 26% Catholic; 12% claim no religious affiliation. **Female To Male Ratio:** 1.0:1. The average age of freshmen is 18; all undergraduates, 20. 18% do not continue beyond their first year; 66% remain to graduate. **Housing:** 1915 students can be accommodated in college housing, which includes single-sex and coed dorms, on-campus apartments, off-campus apartments, honors houses, special-interest houses, fraternity houses, sorority houses, and theme housing. On-campus housing is guaranteed for all 4 years. 63% of students live on campus. All students may keep cars.

FACULTY/CLASSROOMS: 49% of faculty are male; 48% are female. 90% teach undergraduates. No introductory courses are taught by graduate students. The average class size in an introductory lecture is 29; in a laboratory is 14; and in a regular course is 25.

PROGRAMS OF STUDY: ONU confers B.A., B.S., B.F.A., B.M., B.S.B.A., B.S.C.E., B.S.C.P.E., B.S.E.E., B.S.M.E., B.S.M.T., and B.S.Ph. degrees. Doctoral degrees are also awarded. Bachelor's degrees are awarded in AGRICULTURE (environmental studies), BIOLOGICAL SCIENCE (biochemistry, biology/biological science, and molecular biology), BUSINESS (accounting, business administration and management, business economics, international business management, management science, and sports management), COMMUNICATIONS AND THE ARTS (broadcasting, ceramic art and design, communications, creative writing, dramatic arts, English, fine arts, French, graphic design, journalism, language arts, literature, music, music business management, music performance, music theory and composition, public relations, and Spanish), COMPUTER AND PHYSICAL SCIENCE (chemistry, computer science, mathematics, physics, and statistics), EDUCATION (athletic training, early childhood education, health education, middle school education, music education, and physical education), ENGINEERING AND ENVIRONMENTAL DESIGN (civil engineering, computer engineering, electrical/electronics engineering, mechanical engineering, and technological management), HEALTH PROFESSIONS (health, medical technology, and pharmacy), SOCIAL SCIENCE (criminal justice, history, international studies, philosophy, political science/government, psychology, religion, social studies, sociology, and youth ministry). Chemistry, engineering, and pharmacy are the strongest academically. Pharmacy, engineering, and biology have the largest enrollments.

ACTIVITIES: 14% of men belong to 8 national fraternities; 21% of women belong to 4 national sororities. There are 170 groups on campus, including art, band, cheerleading, chess, choir, chorale, chorus, computers, dance, debate, drama, drill team, ethnic, honors, international, jazz band, literary magazine, marching band, musical theater, newspaper, orchestra, pep band, political, professional, radio and TV, religious, social, social service, student government, symphony, and yearbook. Popular campus events include Tunes on the Tundra, International Week, and Little Sibs Weekend. **Sports:** There are 11 intercollegiate sports for men and 10 for women, and 12 intramural sports for men and 11 for women. Facilities include a pool, wrestling room, weight rooms, indoor/outdoor tennis courts, basketball courts, football stadium, training room, bowling lanes, a billiards room, dance room, fitness lab, indoor track, outdoor track, racquetball courts, Nautilus room, and jogging/walking path. **Graduates:** From July 1, 2015 to June 30, 2016, 434 bachelor's degrees were awarded. The most popular majors were business marketing (9%), education and visual and performing arts (14%), and public administration and social services and biology science. In an average class, 65% graduate in 6 years or less.

SERVICES: Counseling and information services are available, as is tutoring in most subjects, and a reader service for the blind, and remedial math and writing. **Library/Resources:** The 2 libraries contain 250,518 volumes, 72,067 microform items, and 10,815 audio/video tapes/CDs/DVDs, and subscribe to 1,038 periodicals including electronic. Computerized library services include interlibrary loans and database searching. Special learning facilities include an art gallery, radio station, TV station, and a pharmacy museum. **Physically Challenged Students:** 95% of the campus is accessible. Facilities include wheelchair ramps, elevators, special parking, specially equipped restrooms, special class scheduling, lowered drinking fountains, and lowered telephones. **Special:** Co-op programs are available in civil, electrical, computer, and mechanical engineering and technology, computer science, and math. Students may take internships in pharmacy, engineering, and business and may study abroad in 15 countries. B.A.-B.S. degrees and dual majors are available in arts/engineering, arts/pharmacy, and arts/business. The university also offers pass/fail options and work-study programs. There are 38 national honor societies, a freshman honors program, and 21 departmental honors programs. **Visiting:** There are regularly scheduled orientations for prospective students, including a tour, lunch, and appointments in academics, admissions, and financial aid. A meeting with a coach can also be arranged. There are guides for informal visits, visitors may sit in on classes, and stay overnight. To schedule a visit, contact the Admissions Office. **Campus Safety and Security:** Measures include 24-hour foot and vehicle patrol, self-defense education, and security escort services. There are emergency telephones and lighted pathways/sidewalks.

REQUIREMENTS: The SAT or ACT is required. The preparatory program should include 4 years of English, and 2 each of math, science, social science units are recommended, along with computer science, and visual/performing arts. ONU requires applicants to be in the upper 50% of their class. AP and CLEP credits are accepted. Important factors in the admissions decision are advanced placement or honors courses, leadership record, evidence of special talent, extracurricular activities record, and recommendations by alumni. To graduate, students must complete a minimum of 182 quarter hours, maintain a cumulative GPA of 2.0, and fulfill all departmental/college core requirements. Also, students must submit a formal application for graduation. **Procedure:** Freshmen are admitted to all sessions. Entrance exams should be taken in the spring of the junior year or the fall of the senior year. There are deferred admissions and rolling admissions plans. Applications should be filed by August 15 for fall entry. The fall 2016 application fee was $30. Notification of early decision is sent September 1; regular decision, on a rolling basis. Applications are accepted on-line. **Transfer Students:** 59 transfer students enrolled in 2015-2016. Applicants should have a minimum college GPA of 2.0 and submit official transcripts from all the schools they have attended. 45 of 182 credits required for the bachelor's degree must be completed at ONU. **International Students:** The school actively recruits these students. They must take the TOEFL or MELAB.

Admissions Contact: Deborah Miller, Director of Admissions. Email: *admissions-ug@onu.edu* Web: *www.onu.edu*

FINANCIAL AID: ONU is a member of CSS. The college's own financial statement is required. The FAFSA code is 003089. Check with the school for current application deadlines.

OHIO STATE UNIVERSITY AT COLUMBUS C-3

www.osu.edu

Columbus, OH 43210 **(614) 292-3980**

Fax: (614) 292-4818
Full-time: 21,651 men, 20,211 women
Part-time: 2117 men, 1852 women
Graduate: 6209 men, 7442women
Year: semesters, summer session
Room & Board: $11,666

SAT CR/M/W: 630/650/610 **ACT:** 29
Application Deadline: February 1

Email: askabuckeye@osu.edu
Faculty: n/av
Ph.D.s: n/av
Student/Faculty: n/av
Tuition: $10,037 ($25,757)
Freshman Class: 40240 applied, 19872 accepted, 7032 enrolled
CEEB CODE: 1152
HIGHLY COMPETITIVE+

Ohio State University at Columbus is the main campus, and is one of America's largest and most comprehensive institutions. There are 200 undergraduate majors, and 250 master's, doctoral, and professional degree programs. Ohio State is further recognized by a top-rated academic medical center and a premier cancer hospital and research center. The university's innovative prowess attains world-class status, particularly in critical areas such as cancer, infectious disease, advanced materials, and ag-bio products that feed and fuel the world. Ohio State's regional campuses include Lima, Mansfield, Marion, and Newark, and the Agricultural Technical Institute in Wooster. Founded as a federal land-grant institution in 1870, there are 15 undergraduate schools and 1 graduate school. In addition to regional accreditation, OSU has baccalaureate program accreditation with AACSB, ABET, ACPE, ADA, ASLA, CSWE, FIDER, NAAB, NASAD, and NCATE. The 1592-acre campus is in an urban area 2 miles north of downtown Columbus, OH. Including any residence halls, there are 697 buildings.

STUDENT LIFE: 83% of undergraduates are from Ohio. Others are from 50 states, 112 foreign countries, and Canada. 86% are from public schools. 69% are White; 8% Foreign; 6% African American; 6% Asian American; 4% Hispanic; 3% two or more races; 4% race unknown. **Male To Female Ratio:** 1.0:1. The average age of freshmen is 18; all undergraduates, 18. 6% do not continue beyond their first year; 94% remain to graduate. **Housing:** 11929 students can be accommodated in college housing, which includes single-sex and coed dorms, on-campus apartments, off-campus apartments, married student housing, honors houses, language houses, special-interest houses, Veterans house, international houses, language floors, and an alumnae scholarship house. On-campus housing is available on a first-come and first-served basis. 94% of students live on campus. All students may keep cars.

FACULTY/CLASSROOMS: 56% of faculty are male; 44% are female. No introductory courses are taught by graduate students.

PROGRAMS OF STUDY: Ohio State, confers B.A., B.S., B.A.E., B.F.A., B.Mus., and B.Mus.Ed. degrees. Associate, master's, and doctoral degrees are also awarded. Bachelor's degrees are awarded in AGRICULTURE (agricultural business management, agricultural economics, animal science, fishing and fisheries, forestry and related sciences, natural resource management, and plant science), BIOLOGICAL SCIENCE (avian sciences, biochemistry, biology/biological science, ecology, entomology, evolutionary biology, microbiology, molecular biology, neurosciences, nutrition, plant physiology, and zoology), BUSINESS (accounting, banking and finance, business administration and management, fashion merchandising, hospitality management services, human resources, insurance and risk management, international business management, logistics, management information systems, marketing and distribution, operations management, real estate, and transportation management), COMMUNICATIONS AND THE ARTS (Arabic, art, Chinese, classics, communications, dance, English, fine arts, French, German, Germanic languages and literature, Greek, Hebrew, industrial design, Italian, Japanese, jazz, journalism, Korean, linguistics, music, music history and appreciation, music performance, music theory and composition, piano/organ, Portuguese, Russian, Spanish, theatre arts, theater design, and visual design), COMPUTER AND PHYSICAL SCIENCE (actuarial science, astronomy, astrophysics, atmospheric sciences and meteorology, chemistry, computer science, earth science, geology, information sciences and systems, mathematics, and physics), EDUCATION (agricultural education, art education, athletic training, dance education, education, environmental education, health information management, middle school education, music education, physical education, and technical education), ENGINEERING AND ENVIRONMENTAL DESIGN (aeronautical engineering, architecture, biomedical engineering, chemical engineering, city/community/regional planning, civil engineering, computer engineering, construction management, electrical/electronics engineering, engineering physics, environmental engineering, environmental science, industrial engineering, interior design, landscape architecture/design, materials engineering, materials science, mechanical engineering, and welding engineering), HEALTH PROFESSIONS (biomedical science, dental hygiene, exercise science, health science, medical laboratory science, medical technology, nursing, occupational therapy, pharmaceutical science, physical therapy, radiograph medical technology, respiratory therapy, speech pathology/audiology, and speech therapy), SOCIAL SCIENCE (African American studies, anthropology, community services, criminal justice, criminology, economics, family/consumer resource management, family/consumer studies, French studies, geography, history, human development, human ecology, industrial and organizational psychology, international studies, Islamic studies, Judaic studies, medieval studies, philosophy, physical fitness/movement, political science/government, psychology, public affairs, social work, sociology, and women's studies). Biology, finance, and marketing have the largest enrollments.

ACTIVITIES: 7% of women belong to 1 local and 22 national sororities. There are 1216 groups on campus, including art, band, cheerleading, chess, choir, chorale, chorus, communications, computers, dance, debate, drama, environmental, ethnic, film, forensics, honors, international, jazz band, LGBT, literary magazine, marching band, musical theater, newspaper, opera, orchestra, pep band, photography, political, professional, radio and TV, religious, social, social service, student government, symphony, and yearbook. Popular campus events include Fair Festival, Community Commitment, Thanksgiving Dinner, Homecoming Parade, and Dance Marathon. **Sports:** There are 18 intercollegiate sports for men and 19 for women, and 34 intramural sports for men and 34 for women. Facilities include a football stadium, a multipurpose event center, arena, archery range, running track, sand volleyball courts, cricket field, in-line hockey rink, weight rooms, swimming pools, basketball, volleyball, and racquetball courts, field houses for tennis, volleyball, basketball, soccer, baseball and softball fields. **Graduates:** From July 1, 2015 to June 30, 2016, 10788 bachelor's degrees were awarded. The most popular majors were psychology (6%), finance (4%), and communication (4%). 1000 companies recruited on campus in 2015-2016. In an average class, 4% graduate in 3 years or less, 59% graduate in 4 years or less, 80% graduate in 5 years or less, and 83% graduate in 6 years or less.

SERVICES: Counseling and information services are available, as is tutoring in most subjects, a reader service for the blind, and remedial math, reading, and writing. **Library/Resources:** The 21 libraries contain 3.9 million volumes, 4,016,622 periodicals including electronic. Computerized library services include interlibrary loans, database searching, Internet access, and Wi-Fi capability. Special learning facilities include an art gallery, planetarium, radio station, and TV station. The Museum of Biological Diversity, the John Glenn Institute for Public Service and Public Policy, and the Cartoon Research Library. **Physically Challenged Students:** 98% of the campus is accessible. Facilities include wheelchair ramps, elevators, special parking, specially equipped restrooms, special class scheduling, lowered drinking fountains, lowered telephones, and special housing. Accessible rooms are intergrated across residential options. A campus bus system is fully lift equipped and supplemented by paratransit. Adaptive recreation facilities are also available. **Special:** Students may cross-register with all central Ohio colleges. OSU offers internships, co-op programs, extensive study abroad in about 40 countries, work-study programs, dual and student-designed majors, a general degree, an accelerated degree, credit by exam, nondegree study, and pass/fail options. There are 48 national honor societies, Phi Beta Kappa, a freshman honors program, and 15 departmental honors programs. **Visiting:** There are regularly scheduled orientations for prospective students, including campus tours, placement tests, course scheduling, and special sessions designed for parents. There are guides for informal visits, visitors may sit in on classes, and stay overnight. To schedule a visit, contact the Student Visitor Center. **Campus Safety and Security:** Measures include 24-hour foot and vehicle patrol, emergency notification system, self-defense education, and security escort services. There are also shuttle buses, emergency telephones, lighted pathways/sidewalks, including crisis action teams, and off-campus patrols in cooperation with the city police.

REQUIREMENTS: The SAT or ACT is required. Applicants must complete high school with at least 19 academic credits, including 4 in English, 3 in math, 2 each in foreign language, science, and history or social studies, and 1 in art or music. The GED is accepted. AP and CLEP credits are accepted. Important factors in the admissions decision are advanced placement or honors courses, evidence of special talent, and extracurricular activities record. To graduate, students must complete 120 or more semester hours, depending on major, including 30 to 40 in the major, with a minimum GPA of 2.0. The core curriculum consists of courses in writing skills, quantitative and logical skills, foreign language, the sciences, math, and the arts. Distribution requirements include 5 courses in arts and humanities, 4 to 5 courses in natural science, and 3 in social science. **Procedure:** Freshmen are admitted in the fall, spring, and summer. Entrance exams should be taken by October of the senior year. There is a rolling admissions plan. Applications should be filed by February 1 for fall entry; October 1 for spring entry, along with a $60 fee. Notifications are sent March 31. 304 applicants were on the 2016 waiting list; 304 were admitted. Applications are accepted online. **Transfer Students:** 3791 transfer students enrolled in 2015-2016. High school graduates with 30 hours of college credit and a minimum GPA of 2.0 are admitted for transfer. Those with fewer than 30 hours apply on a competitive basis. 30 of 120 credits required for the bachelor's degree must be completed at OSU. **International Students:** There are 3182 international students enrolled. The school actively recruits these students. They must take the TOEFL with a minimum score of 550 on the paper-based TOEFL (PBT) or 79 on the Internet-based version (iBT). They must also take the SAT or ACT.

ADMISSIONS: 49% of the 2016-2017 applicants were accepted. The SAT scores for the 2016-2017 freshman class were: Critical Reading-- 5% below 500, 30% between 500 and 599, 51% between 600 and 699, and 14% between 700 and 800. Math-- 4% below 500, 19% between 500 and 599, 56% between 600 and 699, and 21% between 700 and 800. Writing-- 7% below 500, 34% between 500 and 599, 47% between 600 and 699, and 12% between 700 and 800. The ACT scores were 2% below 12, 5% between 12 and 17, 14% between 18 and 23, 21% between 24 and 29, and 58% above 30. 89% of the current freshmen were in the top fifth of their class; 98% were in the top two fifths. 355 freshmen graduated first in their class. **Admissions Contact:** Undergraduate Admissions Email: *askabuckeye@osu.edu* Web: *www.osu.edu*

FINANCIAL AID: In 2016-2017, 90% of all full-time freshmen and 77% of continuing full-time students received some form of financial aid. 42% of all full-time freshmen and 43% of continuing full-time students received need-based aid. The average freshman award was $15,590. Need-based scholarships or need-based grants averaged $8,234 ($23,641 maximum); need-based self-help aid (loans and jobs) averaged $3,728 ($8,500 maximum); non-need-based athletic scholarships averaged $25,210 ($57,862 maximum); and other non-need-based awards and non-need-based scholarships averaged $11,472 ($44,246 maximum). The average financial indebtedness of the 2016 graduate was $27,400. The priority date for freshman financial aid applications for fall entry is February 15.

OHIO STATE UNIVERSITY AT LIMA — B-2

www.lima.osu.edu

Lima, OH 45804 — (419) 995-8396

Email: lima-askabuckeye@osu.edu

Full-time: 358 men, 466 women	**Faculty:** IIB, +$
Part-time: 73 men, 102 women	**Ph.D.s:** n/av
Graduate: 2 men, 9 women	**Student/Faculty:** n/av
Year: semesters, summer session	**Tuition:** $7140 ($22,860)
Room & Board: n/app	**Freshman Class:** 1078 applied, 1064 accepted, 349 enrolled
SAT CR/M/W: 540/545/450 **ACT:** 22	**CEEB CODE:** 1541
Application Deadline: June 1	**COMPETITIVE**

The Ohio State University at Lima, develops leaders and provides access to the resources and strength of the state's top university. Ohio State Lima students earn their degrees from the No.1 public university in the state, leveraging a big 10 quality education with the affordability of a regional campus. Offering 9 bachelors degree programs, 4 degree completion programs and access to the 200 plus Ohio State majors, our students find a unique campus spirit with a truly personalized academic experience. There is 1 undergraduate school. In addition to regional accreditation, Ohio State Lima has baccalaureate program accreditation with AACSB, ABET, ACPE, ADA, AHEA, APTA, ASLA, CSAB, CSWE, FIDER, NAAB, NASAD, NASM, and NCATE. The 562-acre campus is in a suburban area 3 miles east of Lima, OH. Including any residence halls, there are 13 buildings.

STUDENT LIFE: 100% of undergraduates are from Ohio. Others are from 5 states, and 1 foreign country. 94% are from public schools. 86% are White; 4% African American; 3% Hispanic; 3% two or more races; 2% Asian American; 2% race unknown. **Female To Male Ratio:** 1.3:1. The average age of freshmen is 18; all undergraduates, 21. 33% do not continue beyond their first year; 67% remain to graduate. All students commute. All students may keep cars. Alcohol is not permitted.

FACULTY/CLASSROOMS: 51% of faculty are male; 49% are female. No introductory courses are taught by graduate students.

PROGRAMS OF STUDY: Ohio State Lima confers B.A., B.S., and B.S.Ed. degrees. Associate and master's degrees are also awarded. Bachelor's degrees are awarded in BIOLOGICAL SCIENCE (biology/biological science), BUSINESS (business administration and management), COMMUNICATIONS AND THE ARTS (English), EDUCATION (education and health information management), HEALTH PROFESSIONS (dental hygiene and nursing), SOCIAL SCIENCE (family/consumer resource management, history, and psychology). Biology, early childhood education, and psychology have the largest enrollments.

ACTIVITIES: There are no fraternities or sororities. Groups on campus include art, choir, chorale, chorus, dance, drama, ethnic, film, honors, LGBT, literary magazine, musical theater, newspaper, professional, social, social service, and student government. Popular campus events include Welcom Back Week, Homecoming week, and Beat Michigan Week. **Sports:** There are 3 intercollegiate sports for men and 2 for women, and 5 intramural sports for men and 5 for women. Facilities include Cook Hall gymnasium (The Hanger) 634 seating; Baron's baseball field, five indoor facilities and over 70 acres of outdoor parks. **Graduates:** In an average class, 3% graduate in 3 years or less, 13% graduate in 4 years or less, 27% graduate in 5 years or less, and 32% graduate in 6 years or less.

SERVICES: **Library/Resources:** The library contains 3.9 million volumes and subscribes to 4,016,622 periodicals including electronic. Computerized library services include interlibrary loans, database searching, Internet access, and Wi-Fi capability. Special learning facilities include an art gallery, greenhouse, geology museum, nature preserve, nature trails, and observatory. **Physically Challenged Students:** 98% of the campus is accessible. Facilities include wheelchair ramps, elevators, special parking, specially equipped restrooms, and lowered drinking fountains. **Special:** Co-op programs and internships are available in some majors, and study abroad is available in some departments. Cross-registration is possible with Ohio State Main Campus and there is work-study with Ohio State. Dual and student-designed majors and nondegree study are possible, and pass/fail options are available. Co-op programs, extensive study abroad in about 40 countries, work-study programs, dual and student-designed majors, a general degree, an accelerated degree, credit by exam, nondegree study, and pass/fail options. Co-Op programs, extensive study abroad in about 40 countries, work-study programs, dual and student-designed majors, a general degree, an accelerated degree, credit by exam, nondegree study, and pass/fail options. There is a freshman honors program and 4 departmental honors programs. **Visiting:** There are regularly scheduled orientations for prospective students. There are guides for informal visits and visitors may sit in on classes. To schedule a visit, contact The Student Visitor Center at (419) 995-8539.

REQUIREMENTS: There is an open admission policy for in-state students. Applicants must complete high school and should have 4 credits in English, 3 each in math and science, 2 each in foreign language and history or social studies, and 1 in art or music. The GED is accepted. AP and CLEP credits are accepted. To graduate, all students must complete an average of 120 semester hours, with a minimum GPA of 2.0, and fulfill the general education curriculum requirements. **Procedure:** Freshmen are admitted in the fall, spring, and summer. Entrance exams should be taken October of Senior Year. There is a rolling admissions plan. Application deadlines are open. Application fee is $60. Applications are accepted online. **Transfer Students:** 93 transfer students enrolled in 2015-2016. 2.0 or 45+ quarter hours; applicants with less than 45 quarter hours are considered for admission based on college and/or high school performance where the criteria vary by hours earned. 30 of 120 credits required for the bachelor's degree must be completed at Ohio State Lima. **International Students:** There is 1 international students enrolled. They must take the TOEFL, as well asthe SAT or ACT.

ADMISSIONS: 99% of the 2016-2017 applicants were accepted. The SAT scores for the 2016-2017 freshman class were: Critical Reading-- 25% below 500, 58% between 500 and 599, and 17% between 600 and 699. Math-- 17% below 500, 58% between 500 and 599, and 24% between 600 and 699. Writing-- 58% below 500, 17% between 500 and 599, and 25% between 600 and 699. The ACT scores were 29% below 12, 32% between 12 and 17, 25% between 18 and 23, 8% between 24 and 29, and 6% above 30. 21% of the current freshmen were in the top fifth of their class; 58% were in the top two fifths. 5 freshmen graduated first in their class. **Admissions Contact:** Undergraduate Admissions. Email: *lima-askabuckeye@osu.edu* Web: *www.lima.osu.edu*

FINANCIAL AID: In 2016-2017, 94% of all full-time freshmen and 83% of continuing full-time students received some form of financial aid. 63% of all full-time freshmen and 62% of continuing full-time students received need-based aid. The average freshman award was $8,537. Need-based scholarships or need-based grants averaged $4,753 ($6,275 maximum); need-based self-help aid (loans and jobs) averaged $3,803 ($6,500 maximum); and other non-need-based awards and non-need-based scholarships averaged $4,361 ($19,287 maximum). The FAFSA code is 003090. Check with the school for current application deadlines.

OHIO STATE UNIVERSITY AT MANSFIELD C-2

www.mansfield.osu.edu

Mansfield, OH 44906 **(419) 755-4317**

Email: askabuckeye@osu.edu

Full-time: 458 men, 532 women
Part-time: 83 men, 116 women
Graduate: 10 women
Year: semesters, summer session
Room & Board: $6020

Faculty: IIB, av$
Ph.D.s: n/av
Student/Faculty: n/av
Tuition: $7140 ($22,860)
Freshman Class: 1607 applied, 1595 accepted, 522 enrolled

SAT CR/M/W: 510/550/520 **ACT:** 22
Application Deadline: June 1
CEEB CODE: 0744
COMPETITIVE

Ohio State University, founded in 1958, is a regional commuter campus of the Ohio State University system. There is 1 undergraduate school. In addition to regional accreditation, OSU Mansfield has baccalaureate program accreditation with AACSB, ABET, ACPE, ADA, AHEA, APTA, CSAB, CSWE, FIDER, NAAB, NASM, NCATE, and NCA-HLC. The 620-acre campus is in a suburban area 2 miles from Mansfield, OH. Including any residence halls, there are 29 buildings.

STUDENT LIFE: 100% of undergraduates are from Ohio. Others are from 4 states. 93% are from public schools. 79% are White; 3% Hispanic; 3% two or more races; 2% Asian American; 2% race unknown; 11% African American. **Female To Male Ratio:** 1.2:1. The average age of freshmen is 18; all undergraduates, 21. 31% do not continue beyond their first year; 69% remain to graduate. **Housing:** 197 students can be accommodated in college housing, which includes coed on-campus apartments, as well as apartments for single students. On-campus housing is guaranteed for the freshman year only, and is available on a first-come, first-served basis, and on a lottery system for upperclassmen. 83% of students commute. All students may keep cars.

FACULTY/CLASSROOMS: 60% of faculty are male; 40% are female. No introductory courses are taught by graduate students.

PROGRAMS OF STUDY: OSU Mansfield confers B.A., B.S., and B.S.Ed degrees. Associate and master's degrees are also awarded. Bachelor's degrees are awarded in BUSINESS (business administration and management), COMMUNICATIONS AND THE ARTS (English), EDUCATION (elementary education), HEALTH PROFESSIONS (nursing), SOCIAL SCIENCE (history and psychology). Psychology, biology, and English have the largest enrollments.

ACTIVITIES: There are no fraternities or sororities. Groups on campus include cheerleading, choir, drama, ethnic, LGBT, religious, social, social service, and student government. **Sports:** There are 3 intercollegiate sports for men and 3 for women, and 10 intramural sports for men and 11 for women. Facilities include a gym and a weight room. **Graduates:** In an average class, 2% graduate in 3 years or less, 19% graduate in 4 years or less, 37% graduate in 5 years or less, and 43% graduate in 6 years or less.

SERVICES: Counseling and information services are available, as is tutoring in most subjects, and remedial math, reading, and writing. **Library/Resources:** The library contains 3.9 million volumes, and subscribes to 4,016,622 periodicals including electronic. Computerized library services include interlibrary loans, database searching, Internet access, and Wi-Fi capability. Special learning facilities include a TV station. **Physically Challenged Students:** All of the campus is accessible. Facilities include wheelchair ramps, elevators, special parking, specially equipped restrooms, and lowered drinking fountains. **Special:** OSU Mansfield offers co-op programs, study abroad, internships, a general studies degree (no major), nondegree study, pass/fail options, and work-study programs. There is a freshman honors program. **Visiting:** There are regularly scheduled orientations for prospective students. There are guides for informal visits, visitors may sit in on classes, and stay overnight. To schedule a visit, contact the Student Visitor Center at (419) 755-4317.

REQUIREMENTS: There is an open admission policy for in-state students. Applicants must complete high school and should have 4 credits in English, 3 each in math and science, 2 each in foreign language and history or social studies, and 1 in art or music. The GED is accepted. AP and CLEP credits are accepted. To graduate, all students must complete 181 to 220 quarter hours, with a minimum GPA of 2.0. General education curriculum requirements must be met. **Procedure:** Freshmen are admitted in the fall, spring, and summer. Entrance exams should be taken spring of the junoir year or early fall of the senior year. There is a rolling admissions plan. Application deadlines are open. Application fee is $60. Applications are accepted online. **Transfer Students:** 109 transfer students enrolled in 2015-2016. 2.0 on 30 semester hours; applicants with less than 30 semester hours are considered for admission based on college and/or high school performance where the criteria vary by hours earned. 30 of 120 credits required for the bachelor's degree must be completed at OSU Mansfield. **International Students:** They must also take the SAT or ACT.

ADMISSIONS: 99% of the 2016-2017 applicants were accepted. The SAT scores for the 2016-2017 freshman class were: Critical Reading-- 46% below 500, 35% between 500 and 599, 16% between 600 and 699, and 3% between 700 and 800. Math-- 38% below 500, 30% between 500 and 599, 27% between 600 and 699, and 5% between 700 and 800. Writing-- 35% below 500, 51% between 500 and 599, 11% between 600 and 699, and 3% between 700 and 800. The ACT scores were 32% below 12, 28% between 12 and 17, 25% between 18 and 23, 8% between 24 and 29, and 7% above 30. 16% of the current freshmen were in the top fifth of their class; 46% were in the top two fifths. 4 freshmen graduated first in their class. **Admissions Contact:** Undergraduate Admissions. Email: *askabuckeye@osu.edu* Web: *www.mansfield.osu.edu*

FINANCIAL AID: In 2016-2017, 93% of all full-time freshmen and 82% of continuing full-time students received some form of financial aid. 73% of all full-time freshmen and 67% of continuing full-time students received need-based aid. The average freshman award was $10,921. Need-based scholarships or need-based grants averaged $5,006 ($6,275 maximum); need-based self-help aid (loans and jobs) averaged $4,364 ($7,500 maximum); and other non-need-based awards and non-need-based scholarships averaged $5,298 ($23,064 maximum). OSU Mansfield is a member of CSS. The CCS/Profile, FAFSA, FFS, or SFS are required. The FAFSA code is 003090. Check with the school for current application deadlines.

OHIO STATE UNIVERSITY AT MARION C-3

www.osu.edu

Marion, OH 43302 **(740) 389-6786**

Email: askabuckeye@osu.edu

Full-time: 418 men, 447 women
Part-time: 90 men, 128 women
Graduate: 2 women
Year: semesters, summer session
Room & Board: $6020

Faculty: IIB, +$
Ph.D.s: n/av
Student/Faculty: n/av
Tuition: $7140 ($22,860)
Freshman Class: 873 applied, 860 accepted, 388 enrolled

SAT CR/M/W: 535/555/490 **ACT:** 22
Application Deadline: June 1
CEEB CODE: 0751
COMPETITIVE

Ohio State University at Marion, founded in 1957, is a commuter campus of the Ohio State University system. Marion campus, students may earn a bachelor's degree in elementary education, English, history, business management, and psychology. In addition, students can earn 1 to 3 years of credit applicable to any other degree, including more than 170 academic programs, conferred by OSU, provided the program is completed at the main campus in Columbus. In addition to regional accreditation, OSU Marion has baccalaureate program accreditation with AACSB, ABET, ACPE, ADA, AHEA, APTA, CSAB, CSWE, FIDER, NAAB, NASM, NCATE, and NCA-HLC. The 188-acre campus is in a rural area 45 miles North of Columbus, OH. Including any residence halls, there are 16 buildings.

STUDENT LIFE: 99% of undergraduates are from Ohio. Others are from 7 states, 2 foreign countries, and Canada. 98% are from public schools. 83% are White; 4% African American; 4% Hispanic; 3% Asian American; 3% two or more races; 3% race unknown. **Female To Male Ratio:** 1.1:1. The average age of freshmen is 19; all undergraduates, 22. 36% do not continue beyond their first year; 64% remain to graduate. **Housing:** 197 students can be accommodated in college housing, which includes coed on-campus housing is available on a first-come and first-served basis. Priority is given to out-of-town students. Alcohol is not permitted. All students may keep cars.

FACULTY/CLASSROOMS: 49% of faculty are male; 51% are female. No introductory courses are taught by graduate students.

PROGRAMS OF STUDY: OSU Marion confers B.A., B.S., and B.S.Ed. degrees. Associate and master's degrees are also awarded. Bachelor's degrees are awarded in BUSINESS (business administration and management), COMMUNICATIONS AND THE ARTS (English), EDUCATION (education and elementary education), HEALTH PROFESSIONS (nursing), SOCIAL SCIENCE (history and psychology). Psychology, English, and social work have the largest enrollments.

ACTIVITIES: There are no fraternities or sororities. Groups on campus include cheerleading, choir, drama, ethnic, jazz band, LGBT, musical theater, religious, social, social service, and student government. **Sports:** There are 3 intercollegiate sports for men and 3 for women, and 10 intramural sports for men and 11 for women. Facilities include a gym, weight room, aerobic room, game room and lounge. **Graduates:** In an average class, 2% graduate in 3 years or less, 17% graduate in 4 years or less, 34% graduate in 5 years or less, and 43% graduate in 6 years or less.

SERVICES: Counseling and information services are available, as is tutoring in most subjects, remedial math, reading, and writing. **Library/Resources:** The library contains 3.9 million volumes, and subscribes to 4,016,622 periodicals including electronic. Computerized library services include interlibrary loans, database searching, Internet access, and Wi-Fi capability. Special learning facilities include an art gallery, planetarium, TV station, natural reconstructed prairie site, greenhouse, psychology lab, and early childhood education center. **Physically Challenged Students:** All of the campus is accessible. Facilities include wheelchair ramps, elevators, special parking, specially equipped restrooms, and lowered drinking fountains. **Special:** OSU Marion offers cross-registration with Ohio State University Columbus, various co-op and work-study programs, nondegree study in continuing education, and pass/fail options. There is a freshman honors program and 3 departmental honors programs. **Visiting:** There are regularly scheduled orientations for prospective students. There are guides for informal visits and visitors may sit in on classes. To schedule a visit, contact the Student Visitor Center at (740) 725-6242. **Campus Safety and Security:** Measures include emergency notification system and security escort services. There are also shuttle buses, emergency telephones, and lighted pathways/sidewalks.

REQUIREMENTS: There is an open admission policy for in-state students. Applicants must complete high school and should have 4 credits in English, 3 each in math and science, 2 each in foreign language and history or social studies, and 1 in art or music. The GED is accepted. AP and CLEP credits are accepted. To graduate, students must complete an average of 120 semester hours,with a minimum GPA of 2.0. The core curriculum consists of courses in writing skills, quantitative and logical skills, foreign language, the sciences, math, and the arts. Distribution requirements include 5 courses in arts and humanities, 4 to 5 courses in natural science, and 3 in social science. **Procedure:** Freshmen are admitted in the fall and summer. Entrance exams should be taken October of Senior Year. There is a rolling admissions plan. Application deadlines are open. Application fee is $60. Applications are accepted online. **Transfer Students:** 130 transfer students enrolled in 2015-2016. 2.0 on 30+ semester hours; applicants with less than 30 semester hours are considered for admission based on college and/or high school performance where the criteria vary by hours earned. 30 of 120 credits required for the bachelor's degree must be completed at OSU Marion. **International Students:** There are 3 international students enrolled. They must take the TOEFL, as well as the SAT or ACT.

ADMISSIONS: 99% of the 2016-2017 applicants were accepted. The SAT scores for the 2016-2017 freshman class were: Critical Reading-- 37% below 500, 42% between 500 and 599, and 21% between 600 and 699. Math-- 29% below 500, 38% between 500 and 599, 29% between 600 and 699, and 4% between 700 and 800. Writing-- 54% below 500, 38% between 500 and 599, and 8% between 600 and 699. The ACT scores were 34% below 12, 28% between 12 and 17, 20% between 18 and 23, 11% between 24 and 29, and 7% above 30. 23% of the current freshmen were in the top fifth of their class; 52% were in the top two fifths. 2 freshmen graduated first in their class. **Admissions Contact:** Undergraduate Admissions and First Year Experience, Undergraduate Admissions and First Year. Email: *askabuckeye@osu.edu* Web: *www.osu.edu*

FINANCIAL AID: In 2016-2017, 94% of all full-time freshmen and 83% of continuing full-time students received some form of financial aid. 64% of all full-time freshmen and continuing full-time students received need-based aid. The average freshman award was $9,464. Need-based scholarships or need-based grants averaged $4,712 ($6,275 maximum); need-based self-help aid (loans and jobs) averaged $3,856 ($7,500 maximum); and other non-need-based awards and non-need-based scholarships averaged $5,155 ($27,000 maximum). The CCS/Profile, FAFSA, FFS, or SFS are required. The FAFSA code is 003090. The priority date for freshman financial aid applications for fall entry is February 15.

OHIO STATE UNIVERSITY AT NEWARK C-3

www.newark.osu.edu

Newark, OH 43055	(740) 366-3321
	Email: askabuckeye@osu.edu
Full-time: 1031 men, 1023 women	**Faculty:** IIB, +$
Part-time: 194 men, 200 women	**Ph.D.s:** n/av
Graduate: 2 men, 26 women	**Student/Faculty:** n/av
Year: semesters, summer session	**Tuition:** $7140 ($22,860)
Room & Board: $10,370	**Freshman Class:** 2831 applied, 2793 accepted, 1242 enrolled
SAT CR/M/W: 510/520/490 **ACT:** 22	**CEEB CODE:** 0824
Application Deadline: June 1	**COMPETITIVE**

Ohio State University, founded in 1957, is a regional public commuter campus of the Ohio State University system. Newark campus, students may earn a bachelor's degree in elementary education, psychology, history, or English. In addition, they may earn 1 to 3 years of credit applicable to any other degree, including 219 academic programs, conferred by OSU, provided the program is completed at the main campus in Columbus. In addition to regional accreditation, OSU Newark has baccalaureate program accreditation with AACSB, ABET, ACPE, ADA, AHEA, APTA, CSAB, CSWE, FIDER, NAAB, NASM, and NCATE. The 111-acre campus is in a suburban area 40 miles East of Columbus, OH. Including any residence halls, there are 18 buildings.

STUDENT LIFE: 100% of undergraduates are from Ohio. Others are from 11 states. 92% are from public schools. 72% are White; 4% Asian American; 4% two or more races; 3% Hispanic; 3% race unknown; 13% African American. **Female To Male Ratio:** 1.0:1. The average age of freshmen is 18; all undergraduates, 20. 37% do not continue beyond their first year; 63% remain to graduate. **Housing:** 180 students can be accommodated in college housing, which includes single-sex dorms and on-campus apartments. On-campus housing is available on a first-come and first-served basis. 92% of students commute. All students may keep cars.

FACULTY/CLASSROOMS: 51% of faculty are male; 49% are female. No introductory courses are taught by graduate students.

PROGRAMS OF STUDY: OSU Newark confers B.A., B.S. and B.S.Ed. degrees. Associate and master's degrees are also awarded. Bachelor's degrees are awarded in BUSINESS (business administration and management), COMMUNICATIONS AND THE ARTS (English), EDUCATION (elementary education), HEALTH PROFESSIONS (nursing), SOCIAL SCIENCE (history and psychology). Biology, social work, and psychology have the largest enrollments.

ACTIVITIES: There are no fraternities or sororities. There are 35 groups on campus, including chorus, drama, ethnic, honors, international, LGBT, musical theater, political, professional, religious, social, social service, and student government. Popular campus events include Movies, Ice Skating, Family & Friends Day, and Halloween Boogie. **Sports:** There is no sports program at OSU Newark. Facilities include a cardio room, a weight room and gym. In addition, there is a baseball field and other outdoor areas that are utilized for intramurals. **Graduates:** In an average class, 1% graduate in 3 years or less, 11% graduate in 4 years or less, 27% graduate in 5 years or less, and 33% graduate in 6 years or less.

SERVICES: Counseling and information services are available, as is tutoring in most subjects, a reader service for the blind, and remedial math and writing. **Library/Resources:** Computerized library services include interlibrary loans, database searching, Internet access, and Wi-Fi capability. Special learning facilities include an art gallery. **Physically Challenged Students:** All of the campus is accessible. Facilities include wheelchair ramps, elevators, special parking, specially equipped restrooms, and lowered drinking fountains. **Special:** Co-op programs and internships are available in some majors, and study abroad is available in some departments. Cross-registration is possible with Central Ohio Technical College and HECC member schools, and there is work-study with Ohio State. B.A.-B.S. degrees are offered in elementary education, general business, English, history, and psychology. Dual and student-designed majors and nondegree study are possible, and pass/fail options are available. There are 4 national honor societies, a freshman honors program, and 4 departmental honors programs. **Visiting:** There are regularly scheduled orientations for prospective students. Visits include a campus tour, meeting with faculty, financial aid, and student services, a placement test, and class scheduling. There are guides for informal visits, visitors may sit in on classes, and stay overnight. To schedule a visit, contact the Student Visitor Center at (740) 366-9333. **Campus Safety and Security:** Measures include 24-hour foot and vehicle patrol, emergency notification system, self-defense education, security escort services, and emergency telephones.

REQUIREMENTS: OSU Newark follows an open admissions policy for in-state students. Applicants should be high school graduates with 4 units of English, 3 of math, 2 each of science, foreign language, and history or social studies, and 1 of visual or performing arts. OSU Newark follows an open admissions policy for Ohio resident applicants. AP and CLEP credits are accepted. To graduate, students must complete on avereage 120 semester hours, with a minimum GPA of 2.0. The core curriculum consists of courses in writing skills, quantitative and logical skills, foreign language, the sciences, math, and the arts. Distribution requirements include 5 courses in arts and humanities, 4 to 5 courses in natural science, and 3 in social science. **Procedure:** Freshmen are admitted in the fall and spring. Entrance exams should be taken October of Senior Year. There is a rolling admissions plan. Applications should be filed by June 1 for fall entry; October 1 for winter entry; and March 1 for spring entry, along with a $60 fee. Notifications are sent in November. Applications are accepted online. **Transfer Students:** 254 transfer students enrolled in 2015-2016. A GPA of 2.0 is required. 30 of 120 credits required for the bachelor's degree must be completed at OSU Newark.

ADMISSIONS: 99% of the 2016-2017 applicants were accepted. The SAT scores for the 2016-2017 freshman class were: Critical Reading--42% below 500, 45% between 500 and 599, 12% between 600 and 699, and 1% between 700 and 800. Math-- 37% below 500, 47% between 500 and 599, and 16% between 600 and 699. Writing-- 50% below 500, 39% between 500 and 599, and 11% between 600 and 699. The ACT scores were 33% below 12, 29% between 12 and 17, 24% between 18 and 23, 9% between 24 and 29, and 5% above 30. 15% of the current freshmen were in the top fifth of their class; 44% were in the top two fifths. 1 freshman graduated first in the class. **Admissions Contact:** Undergraduate Admissions. Email: *askabuckeye@osu.edu* Web: *www.newark.osu.edu*

FINANCIAL AID: In 2016-2017, 86% of all full-time freshmen and 73% of continuing full-time students received some form of financial aid. 64% of all full-time freshmen and 55% of continuing full-time students received need-based aid. The average freshman award was $9,643. Need-based scholarships or need-based grants averaged $4,930 ($12,725 maximum); need-based self-help aid (loans and jobs) averaged $3,908 ($6,500 maximum); and other non-need-based awards and non-need-based scholarships averaged $5,004 ($23,064 maximum). The FAFSA code is 003090. Check with the school for current application deadlines.

OHIO UNIVERSITY — D-4

www.ohio.edu

Athens, OH 45701 — **(740) 593-4100**

Fax: (740) 593-0560	**Email:** admissions@ohio.edu
Full-time: 8169 men, 9303 women	**Faculty:** 939; I, -$
Part-time: 1320 men, 5003 women	**Ph.D.s:** 78%
Graduate: 3039 men, 2985 women	**Student/Faculty:** 18 to 1
Year: semesters, summer session	**Tuition:** $11,748 ($21,208)
Room & Board: $11,176	**Freshman Class:** 20623 applied, 15437 accepted, 4309 enrolled
SAT CR/M/W: 550/550/520 **ACT:** 24	**CEEB CODE:** 1593
Application Deadline: December 1	**COMPETITIVE**

Ohio University, founded in 1804, is a public university offering more than 250 areas of undergraduate study. On the graduate level, the university grants master's degrees in nearly all of its major academic divisions and doctoral degrees in selected departments. The university strives to be a "home away from home" for its students, with a welcoming atmosphere and supportive professors who are both teachers and mentors. There are 9 undergraduate schools and 11 graduate schools. In addition to regional accreditation, Ohio has baccalaureate program accreditation with AACSB, ABET, ACEJMC, CSWE, NASM, NCATE, NRPA, AAFCS, ACEN, CEND, ACS, APA, ATMAE, CAAHEP, CAATE, CACREP, APTE, CCA, CNE, COAPRT, COCA, CORE, COSMA, EHAC, FEPAC, NAB, NASD, NAST, OBN, EPH, PATH, and UCIEP. The 1774-acre campus is in a small town 75 miles southeast of Columbus. Including any residence halls, there are 211 buildings.

STUDENT LIFE: 83% of undergraduates are from Ohio. Others are from 48 states, 75 foreign countries, and Canada. 82% are from public schools. 83% are White; 5% African American; 3% Hispanic; 3% two or more races; 2% Foreign; 1% Asian American; 1% race unknown. 42% are Protestant; 33% Catholic; 17% claim no religious affiliation. **Female To Male Ratio:** 1.4:1. The average age of freshmen is 19; all undergraduates, 21. 19% do not continue beyond their first year; 67% remain to graduate. **Housing:** 8100 students can be accommodated in college housing, which includes single-sex, coed dorms, honors houses, special-interest houses, fraternity houses, and sorority houses. On-campus housing is guaranteed for the freshman year only and on a lottery system for upperclassmen. 60% of students commute. Upperclassmen may keep cars.

FACULTY/CLASSROOMS: 56% of faculty are male; 44% are female. All teach undergraduates, 81% do research, and 81% do both. Graduate students teach 13% of introductory courses. The average class size in an introductory lecture is 53; in a laboratory is 20; and in a regular course is 33.

PROGRAMS OF STUDY: Ohio confers A.B., B.A., B.A.H.C.S., B.B.A., B.C.J., B.F.A., B.Mus., B.S., B.S.A., B.S.A.M., B.S.A.T., B.S.C., B.S.C.E., B.S.C.F.S., B.S.Ch.E., B.S.C.S., B.S.C.S.D., B.S.Ed., B.S.E.E., B.S.E.H., B.S.E.N.E.N.G., B.S.E.T.M, B.S.F.N.S., B.S.G.S., B.S.H., B.S.H.C.S., B.S.I.H.S., B.S.I.S.E., B.S.J., B.S.M., B.S.M.E., B.S.N., B.S.O.H.S., B.S.T.O.M., B.S.P.E., B.S.P.E.X., B.S.R.S., B.S.S., B.S.S.L.S., B.S.V.C., B.S.W., B.T.A.S., B.S.T.R.A.N.H., and B.F.A.-DA. degrees. Associate, master's, and doctoral degrees are also awarded. Bachelor's degrees are awarded in BIOLOGICAL SCIENCE (biochemistry, biology/biological science, biotechnology, botany, cell biology, customer service, ecology, environmental biology, life science, marine biology, microbiology, molecular biology, neurosciences, nutrition, wildlife biology, and zoology), BUSINESS (accounting, banking and finance, business administration and management, business economics, business law, entrepreneurial studies, fashion merchandising, finance, hotel/motel and restaurant management, international business management, management information systems, management science, management & strategic leadership, marketing management, recreation and leisure services, recreational facilities management, retailing, sports management, and tourism), COMMUNICATIONS AND THE ARTS (acting, applied communication, art history, art, audio technology, broadcasting, ceramic art and design, choral music, classics, communications, communications technology, creative writing, dance, design, digital communications, digital media, dramatic arts, English, film arts, French, German, graphic design, Greek, Greek (classical), illustration, instrumental music education, journalism, journalism - magazine journalism, journalism - news

& information, journalism - newswriting/edit, language arts, Latin, linguistics, literature, media arts, media management, modern language, multimedia, music, music composition, music history and appreciation, music performance, music theory and composition, painting, performing arts, photography, piano/organ, piano pedagogy, playwriting/screenwriting, printmaking, public relations, radio/television technology, Russian, sculpture, Spanish, speech/debate/rhetoric, stage management, sports administration, sport & lifestyle studies, studio art, telecommunications, theater design, theater management, video, visual and performing arts, vocal performance, and voice), COMPUTER AND PHYSICAL SCIENCE (actuarial science, applied mathematics, applied physics, astrophysics, atmospheric sciences and meteorology, chemistry, computer science, digital arts/technology, earth science, environmental chemistry, environmental geology, geology, geoscience, mathematics, physics, and statistics), EDUCATION (athletic training, business education, early childhood education, global studies, mathematics education, music education, nutrition education, physical education, recreation education, science education, social studies education, special education, and technical & applied studies), ENGINEERING AND ENVIRONMENTAL DESIGN (airline piloting and navigation, aviation administration/management, bioengineering, chemical engineering, civil engineering, computer engineering, electrical and computer engineering, electrical/electronics engineering, energy management technology, engineering physics, engineering technology, environmental engineering, industrial engineering, interior design, materials engineering, mechanical engineering, and technical operations management), HEALTH PROFESSIONS (applied nutrition, community health work, environmental health science, exercise science, health care administration, human biology, industrial hygiene, music therapy, nursing, nursing home administration, occupational hygiene & safety, predentistry, premedicine, prepharmacy, prephysical therapy, public health, and sports medicine), SOCIAL SCIENCE (African American studies, anthropology, Asian/American studies, child care/child and family studies, classical/ancient civilization, communication sciences & disorders, community services, criminal justice, criminology, Eastern European studies, economics, European studies, family and community services, family/consumer resource management, family/consumer studies, forensic studies, gender studies, geography, geography information science, history, human development, international studies, Latin American studies, parks and recreation management, philosophy, political science/government, prelaw, psychology, public administration, religion, social work, sociology, urban and regional studies, urban studies, women & gender studies, and women's studies). Nursing, biological sciences, and journalism have the largest enrollments.

ACTIVITIES: 11% of men belong to 20 national fraternities; 17% of women belong to 13 national sororities. There are 500 groups on campus, including art, band, cheerleading, chess, choir, chorale, chorus, computers, dance, debate, drama, environmental, ethnic, film, forensics, honors, international, jazz band, LGBT, literary magazine, marching band, musical theater, newspaper, opera, orchestra, pep band, photography, political, professional, radio and TV, religious, social, social service, student government, symphony, and yearbook. Popular campus events include Performing Arts Series, Kennedy Lecture Series, University Program Council (UPC), and Black Student Cultural Programming Board. **Sports:** There are 6 intercollegiate sports for men and 10 for women, and 25 intramural sports for men and 25 for women. Facilities include a recreation center, a football stadium, fieldhouse, convocation center (accommodating basketball, volleyball, and wrestling), an aquatic center, ice rink, tennis courts, golf course, intramural gym, running track, fitness and aerobic center, baseball and softball stadiums, soccer field, field hockey artificial turf field surrounded by a competition-size track, and 2 large outdoor recreation facilities. **Graduates:** From July 1, 2015 to June 30, 2016, 6402 bachelor's degrees were awarded. The most popular majors were nursing (40%), health administration (5%), and communication studies (4%). 356 companies recruited on campus in 2015-2016. In an average class, 48% graduate in 4 years or less, 64% graduate in 5 years or less, and 67% graduate in 6 years or less. Of the 2015 graduating class, 24% were enrolled in graduate school within 6 months of graduation, and 82% were employed.

SERVICES: Counseling and information services are available, as is tutoring in most subjects, and remedial math, reading, and writing. **Library/Resources:** The 4 libraries contain 3.5 million volumes, 1.4 million microform items, 102,671 audio/video tapes/CDs/DVDs, and subscribe to 78,172 periodicals including electronic. Computerized library services include interlibrary loans, database searching, Internet access, and Wi-Fi capability. Special learning facilities include an art gallery, radio station, TV station, a quarterly magazine, an accelerator lab, a hearing and speech and other wellness (physical & mental) clinics, integrated technology labs, specialized academic labs within buildings, land labs, recreational facilities and fields, maker space and a 3D printer. **Physically Challenged Students:** 89% of the campus is accessible. Facilities include wheelchair ramps, elevators, special parking, specially equipped restrooms, special class scheduling, lowered drinking fountains, lowered telephones, and special housing. **Special:** The University offers co-op programs in engineering and computer science, internships, study abroad, work-study programs, and an accelerated degree program for students in the Honors Tutorial College. Students may earn a B.A. - B.S. degree in most arts and sciences majors, or a general studies degree. Dual and student-designed majors, non-degree study, limited pass/fail options, and credit for life, military, or work experience are also available. There are 10 national honor societies and a freshman honors program. **Visiting:** There are regularly scheduled orientations for prospective students, include information session & campus tours, as well as special visit programs throughout the year. Visitors may sit in on classes. To schedule a visit, contact the Undergraduate Admissions. **Campus Safety and Security:** Measures include 24-hour foot and vehicle patrol, emergency notification system, self-defense education, and security escort services. There are also shuttle buses, emergency telephones, lighted pathways/sidewalks, and controlled access to dorms/residences.

REQUIREMENTS: The SAT or ACT is required. Applicants should graduate with 4 units each of English and math, 3 each of science and social studies, 2 of foreign language, and 5 academic electives (which includes 1 unit of visual/performing arts). Ohio University operates on holistic review and rolling admissions. Application, application fee, test scores, and official transcripts are required for admission. AP and CLEP credits are accepted. Important factors in the admissions decision are advanced placement or honors courses, recommendations by school officials, and extracurricular activities record. Ohio University has two sets of graduation requirements: University-wide requirements, which all students must complete, and college-level requirements, which include the requirements for completing a major or minor. In general, you must have a minimum of 120 semester hours of credit for a bachelor's degree, with all other requirements met. All baccalaureate students (except Honors Tutorial College students) also must complete Ohio University's General Education requirements. Ohio University believes that, as an educated person, you need certain intellectual skills in order to participate effectively in society. These include the following: the ability to communicate effectively through the written word and the ability to use quantitative or symbolic reasoning, broad knowledge of the major fields of learning and a capacity for evaluation and synthesis. **Procedure:** Freshmen are admitted in the fall, spring, and summer. Entrance exams should be taken in spring of the junior year or fall of the senior year. There are early admissions, deferred admissions, and rolling admissions plans. Applications should be filed by December 1 for fall entry; December 1 for spring entry; and February 1 for summer entry, along with a $50 fee. Notifications are sent September 15. Application fees are waived if application is completed online. **Transfer Students:** 545 transfer students enrolled in 2015-2016. Transfer students are evaluated individually, but must have a GPA of at least 2.0 and 20 semester hours of transferable college credit. Business and journalism majors usually require a GPA of 3.0 or higher. 30 of 120 credits required for the bachelor's degree must be completed at Ohio. **International Students:** There are 623 international students enrolled. The school actively recruits these students. They must take the TOEFL, or the IELTS.

ADMISSIONS: 75% of the 2016-2017 applicants were accepted. The SAT scores for the 2016-2017 freshman class were: Critical Reading-- 26% below 500, 45% between 500 and 599, 24% between 600 and 699, and 5% between 700 and 800. Math-- 24% below 500, 48% between 500 and 599, 24% between 600 and 699, and 4% between 700 and 800. Writing-- 36% below 500, 46% between 500 and 599, 15% between 600 and 699, and 3% between 700 and 800. The ACT scores were 1% between 12 and 17, 46% between 18 and 23, 46% between 24 and 29, and 7% above 30. 33% of the current freshmen were in the top fifth of their class; 67% were in the top two fifths. There were 6 National Merit finalists. 59 freshmen graduated first in their class. **Admissions Contact:** Candace Boeninger, Director of Admissions. Email: *admissions@ohio.edu* Web: *www.ohio.edu*

FINANCIAL AID: In 2016-2017, 90% of all full-time freshmen and 79% of continuing full-time students received some form of financial aid. 56% of all full-time freshmen and 51% of continuing full-time students received need-based aid. The average freshman award was $15,301.

Need-based scholarships or need-based grants averaged $4,494 ($12,744 maximum); need-based self-help aid (loans and jobs) averaged $4,119 ($8,330 maximum); non-need-based athletic scholarships averaged $21,557 ($45,846 maximum); and other non-need-based awards and non-need-based scholarships averaged $10,718 ($30,384 maximum). 38% of undergraduate students work part-time. Average annual earnings from campus work are $2430. The average financial indebtedness of the 2016 graduate was $28,083. The FAFSA code is 003100. The priority date for freshman financial aid applications for fall entry is March 15.

OHIO WESLEYAN UNIVERSITY C-3

www.choose.owu.edu

Delaware, OH 43015	**(740) 368-3020** **(800) 922-8953**
Fax: (740) 368-3314	**Email: owuadmit@owu.edu**
Full-time: 778 men, 846 women	**Faculty:** 134; IIB, +$
Part-time: 5 men, 10 women	**Ph.D.s:** 100%
Graduate: n/av	**Student/Faculty:** 10 to 1
Year: semesters, summer session	**Tuition:** $44,090
Room & Board: $11,770	**Freshman Class:** 3030 applied, 2823 accepted, 541 enrolled
SAT CR/M: 569/581 **ACT:** 26	**CEEB CODE:** 1594
Application Deadline: March 1	**VERY COMPETITIVE**

Ohio Wesleyan University, founded in 1842, is an independent liberal arts institution affiliated with the United Methodist Church. There is 1 undergraduate school. In addition to regional accreditation, OWU has baccalaureate program accreditation with NASM, NCATE, and ACS. The 200-acre campus is in a small town 20 miles North of Columbus. Including any residence halls, there are 55 buildings.

STUDENT LIFE: 53% of undergraduates are from Ohio. Others are from 41 states, 45 foreign countries, and Canada. 9% are African American; 69% White; 6% Foreign; 5% Hispanic; 5% two or more races; 3% Asian American; 3% race unknown. **Female To Male Ratio:** 1.1:1. The average age of freshmen is 18; all undergraduates, 20. 16% do not continue beyond their first year; 68% remain to graduate. **Housing:** 1720 students can be accommodated in college housing, which includes single-sex and coed dorms, on-campus apartments, honors houses, language houses, special-interest houses, and fraternity houses. Students are invited to submit theme proposals to run a residential house for 10 to 15 students. On-campus housing is guaranteed for all 4 years. 90% of students live on campus. All students may keep cars.

FACULTY/CLASSROOMS: 56% of faculty are male; 44% are female. All teach undergraduates and all do research. No introductory courses are taught by graduate students. The average class size in an introductory lecture is 30; in a laboratory is 19; and in a regular course is 16.

PROGRAMS OF STUDY: OWU confers B.A., B.F.A., and B.M. degrees. Bachelor's degrees are awarded in BIOLOGICAL SCIENCE (biochemistry, biology/biological science, biological sciences, botany, genetics, microbiology, neurosciences, nutrition, and zoology), BUSINESS (accounting, business administration and management, business economics, international business, and international business management), COMMUNICATIONS AND THE ARTS (art history, art, art/art studies, classics, communications, creative writing, dance, dramatic arts, English, fine arts, French, German, German studies, journalism, music, music composition, music performance, Spanish, and theatre arts), COMPUTER AND PHYSICAL SCIENCE (chemistry, computer science, earth science, geology, mathematics, and physics), EDUCATION (art education, early childhood education, education, elementary education, foreign languages education, middle school education, music education, physical education, and science education), ENGINEERING AND ENVIRONMENTAL DESIGN (environmental science), HEALTH PROFESSIONS (biology, kinesiology, predentistry, premedicine, preoccupational therapy, and preveterinary science), SOCIAL SCIENCE (African American studies, anthropology, East Asian studies, economics, geography, history, international relations, philosophy, political science/government, prelaw, psychology, public administration, religion, social science, sociology, urban studies, and women's studies). Economics & business, biological sciences, and psychology have the largest enrollments.

ACTIVITIES: 40% of men belong to 8 national fraternities; 32% of women belong to 5 national sororities. There are 100 groups on campus, including art, cheerleading, chess, choir, chorale, chorus, communications, computers, dance, drama, ethnic, honors, international, jazz band, LGBT, literary magazine, musical theater, newspaper, opera, orchestra, pep band, political, professional, radio and TV, religious, social, social service, student government, symphony, and yearbook. Popular campus events include Sagan National Colloquium Fallfest, Black Family, and Alumni Weekend Celebration. **Sports:** There are 11 intercollegiate sports for men and 11 for women, and 17 intramural sports for men and 17 for women. Facilities include a gym, football and lacrosse stadium, field hockey and soccer fields, practice fields, a weight room, indoor and outdoor tracks, handball and squash courts, indoor pool, an exercise facility, and weight resistance equipment. **Graduates:** From July 1, 2015 to June 30, 2016, 471 bachelor's degrees were awarded. The most popular majors were biological science (12%), psychology (10%), and economics management (9%). In an average class, 1% graduate in 3 years or less, 61% graduate in 4 years or less, 67% graduate in 5 years or less, and 68% graduate in 6 years or less.

SERVICES: Counseling and information services are available, as is tutoring in most subjects. Students with learning disabilities may receive special help in writing and organization and in quantitive areas. **Library/Resources:** The 2 libraries contain 498,717 volumes, 98,574 microform items, 4,789 audio/video tapes/CDs/DVDs, and subscribe to 18,478 periodicals including electronic. Computerized library services include interlibrary loans, database searching, Internet access, and Wi-Fi capability. Special learning facilities include an art gallery, radio station, and astronomical observatory. **Physically Challenged Students:** 60% of the campus is accessible. Facilities include wheelchair ramps, elevators, special parking, specially equipped restrooms, special class scheduling, lowered drinking fountains, lowered telephones, and special housing. **Special:** Cross-registration is available with members of the Great Lakes Colleges Association. Students may study abroad in 20 countries or participate in a Washington semester or a departmental internship. Students may also take dual majors in any combination, design their own majors, or pursue a 3-2 engineering degree in conjunction with 4 major universities. Nondegree study and pass/fail options are available. There are 27 national honor societies, Phi Beta Kappa, a freshman honors program, and 22 departmental honors programs. **Visiting:** There are regularly scheduled orientations for prospective students, the visit is approximately two hours and 15 minutes and includes a short presentation, a walking/riding tour of campus, and a conversation with an admission counselor. Optional class visit, meet professor or coach, and/or lunch on campus available. There are guides for informal visits, visitors may sit in on classes, and stay overnight. To schedule a visit, contact the Office of Admission. **Campus Safety and Security:** Measures include 24-hour foot and vehicle patrol, emergency notification system, self-defense education, security escort services, emergency telephones, and lighted pathways/sidewalks.

REQUIREMENTS: The SAT or ACT is required. Candidates for admission should complete a recommended 4 units of English and 3 each of math, foreign language, social studies, and science. AP credits are accepted. Important factors in the admissions decision are advanced placement or honors courses, extracurricular activities record, and recommendations by school officials. Students are required to complete at least 34 units, including 3 units each of humanities/English, social sciences, and science, 2 units of foreign languages, and 1 unit of fine or performing arts. Each unit equals a full course and 3.75 semester hours. All students must also take 8 to 12 units in the major, maintain a minimum GPA of 2.0, and satisfy the university writing skills requirements. **Procedure:** Freshmen are admitted in the fall and spring. Entrance exams should be taken in the spring of the junior year or fall of the senior year. There are early decision, early admissions, deferred admissions, and rolling admissions plans. Early decision applications should be filed by November 15; regular applications, by March 1 for fall entry. Notification of early decision is sent November 30; regular decision, on a rolling basis. 182 applicants were on the 2016 waiting list; 77 were admitted. Applications are accepted online. **Transfer Students:** 29 transfer students enrolled in 2015-2016. Applicants should have better than a 2.5 college GPA. High school and college transcripts and an essay are required, along with a statement of good standing from the previous institution. An interview is recommended. 16 of 34 credits required for the bachelor's degree must be completed at OWU. **International Students:** There are 142 international students enrolled. The school actively recruits these students. They must take the TOEFL with a minimum score of 550 on the paper-based TOEFL (PBT) or 80 on the Internet-based version (iBT), or take the IELTS. They must also take the SAT or ACT.

ADMISSIONS: 93% of the 2016-2017 applicants were accepted. The SAT scores for the 2016-2017 freshman class were: Critical Reading-- 20% below 500, 44% between 500 and 599, 26% between 600 and 699, and 10% between 700 and 800. Math-- 13% below 500, 41% between 500 and 599, 36% between 600 and 699, and 10% between 700 and 800. The ACT scores were 11% below 12, 23% between 12 and 17, 26% between 18 and 23, 19% between 24 and 29, and 25% above 30. 29% of the current freshmen were in the top fifth of their class; 42% were in the top two fifths. 20 freshmen graduated first in their class. **Admissions Contact:** Alisha Couch, Director of Admission. Email: *owuadmit@owu.edu* Web: *choose.owu.edu*

FINANCIAL AID: In 2016-2017, 97% of all full-time freshmen and 99% of continuing full-time students received some form of financial aid. 63% of all full-time freshmen and 68% of continuing full-time students received need-based aid. The average freshman award was $34,662. Need-based scholarships or need-based grants averaged $29,200; and need-based self-help aid (loans and jobs) averaged $6,422. 50% of undergraduate students work part-time. Average annual earnings from campus work are $1271. The average financial indebtedness of the 2016 graduate was $34,666. OWU is a member of CSS. The FAFSA code is 003109. The priority date for freshman financial aid applications for fall entry is December 1. The filing deadline for fall entry is May 1.

OTTERBEIN UNIVERSITY — C-3

www.otterbein.edu

Westerville, OH 43081	**(614) 823-1500** **(800) 488-8144**
Fax: (614) 823-1200	**Email: uotterb@otterbein.edu**
Full-time: 825 men, 1297 women	**Faculty:** 178; IIB, -$
Part-time: 79 men, 140 women	**Ph.D.s:** 94%
Graduate: 126 men, 338 women	**Student/Faculty:** 10 to 1
Year: trimesters, summer session	**Tuition:** $31,624
Room & Board: $10,006	**Freshman Class:** 2917 applied, 2197 accepted, 569 enrolled
SAT CR/M/W: 530/531/527 **ACT:** 23	**CEEB CODE:** 1597
Application Deadline: August 15	**COMPETITIVE**

Otterbein University, founded in 1847, is an independent institution affiliated with the United Methodist Church. The college provides a solid liberal arts education combined with professional/career preparation. Figures in the above capsule and in this profile are approximate. There is 1 undergraduate school and 3 graduate schools. In addition to regional accreditation, has baccalaureate program accreditation with NASM, NCATE, NLN, and CAAHEP. The 140-acre campus is in a suburban area 12 miles northeast of Columbus. Including any residence halls, there are 69 buildings.

STUDENT LIFE: 91% of undergraduates are from Ohio. Others are from 29 states, 28 foreign countries, and Canada. 75% are White; 6% African American; 4% two or more races; 2% Hispanic; 10% race unknown; 1% Asian American; 1% Foreign. 26% claim no religious affiliation; 22% Catholic. **Female To Male Ratio:** 1.7:1. The average age of freshmen is 18; all undergraduates, 24. 19% do not continue beyond their first year; 61% remain to graduate. **Housing:** 1183 students can be accommodated in college housing, which includes single-sex, coed dorms and on-campus apartments, honors houses, special-interest houses, fraternity houses, and sorority houses. On-campus housing is guaranteed for the freshman year only, and is available on a first-come, first-served basis, and on a lottery system for upperclassmen. Priority is given to out-of-town students. 53% of students live on campus; of those, 39% remain on campus on weekends. All students may keep cars. Alcohol is not permitted.

FACULTY/CLASSROOMS: 40% of faculty are male; 60% are female. All teach undergraduates. No introductory courses are taught by graduate students. The average class size in an introductory lecture is 10; in a laboratory is 10; and in a regular course is 10.

PROGRAMS OF STUDY: Otterbein confers B.A., B.S., B.F.A., B.M., B.Mus.Ed., B.S.E., and B.S.N. degrees. Master's and doctoral degrees are also awarded. Bachelor's degrees are awarded in AGRICULTURE (equine science), BIOLOGICAL SCIENCE (biochemistry, life science, molecular biology, and zoology), BUSINESS (accounting and business administration and management), COMMUNICATIONS AND THE ARTS (acting, art, broadcasting, communications, dance, dramatic arts, English, English literature, French, journalism, music, music performance, musical theater, public relations, Spanish, speech/debate/rhetoric, and visual and performing arts), COMPUTER AND PHYSICAL SCIENCE (actuarial science, chemistry, computer science, earth science, mathematics, and physics), EDUCATION (athletic training, early childhood education, elementary education, global studies, health education, middle school education, music education, and physical education), ENGINEERING AND ENVIRONMENTAL DESIGN (environmental science), HEALTH PROFESSIONS (biology and nursing), SOCIAL SCIENCE (economics, French studies, history, international studies, liberal arts/general studies, philosophy, political science/government, psychology, public administration, religion, sociology, and women & gender studies). Life science, chemistry, and athletic training are the strongest academically. Business, education, and communications have the largest enrollments.

ACTIVITIES: 29% of men belong to 8 local and 1 national fraternities; 30% of women belong to 6 local sororities. There are 82 groups on campus, including art, band, cheerleading, choir, chorale, chorus, communications, dance, debate, drama, drill team, equestrian, ethnic, forensics, honors, international, jazz band, LGBT, literary magazine, marching band, musical theater, newspaper, opera, orchestra, pep band, photography, political, professional, radio and TV, religious, social, social service, student government, symphony, and yearbook. Popular campus events include athletics, music and theater events, Shakespearean dramas, and British comedies, and students performing with the Westerville Symphony. **Sports:** There are 10 intercollegiate sports for men and 9 for women, and 11 intramural sports for men and 11 for women. Facilities include a basketball and volleyball center, a football stadium, soccer field, weight room, tennis courts, cross-country course, track & field, golf, softball, lacrosse, a student recreation center, and a men's wrestling program team. **Graduates:** From July 1, 2015 to June 30, 2016, 527 bachelor's degrees were awarded. The most popular majors were health professions and related programs (18%), business/marketing (12%), and education (11%). In an average class, 50% graduate in 4 years or less, 53% graduate in 5 years or less, and 61% graduate in 6 years or less. Of the 2015 graduating class, 95% were employed within 6 months of graduation.

SERVICES: Counseling and information services are available, as is tutoring in every subject, a reader service for the blind, and remedial math, reading, and writing. **Library/Resources:** The library contains 284,241 volumes, 11,978 audio/video tapes/CDs/DVDs, and subscribes to 296,219 periodicals including electronic. Computerized library services include interlibrary loans, database searching, Internet access, and Wi-Fi capability. Special learning facilities include an art gallery, planetarium, radio station, TV station, an equine facility, 2 theaters, radio station (WOBN), and a recital hall. The Austin E Knowlton Center for Equine Sciences and the Science Center. **Physically Challenged Students:** All of the campus is accessible. Facilities include wheelchair ramps, elevators, special parking, specially equipped restrooms, special class scheduling, lowered drinking fountains, lowered telephones, and special housing. There is also a Disability Services Coordinator who will assist with accommodation as well as consult with the Academic Support Center. **Special:** Students may cross-register with members of the Higher Education Council of Columbus, study abroad in 9 countries, have an internship in most majors, or participate in a Washington semester. B.A.-B.S. degrees, 3-2 engineering degrees with Case Western Reserve and Washington Universities, credit for military experience, student-designed majors, nondegree study, and limited pass/fail options are also available. There are 12 national honor societies and a freshman honors program. **Visiting:** There are regularly scheduled orientations for prospective students, which includes a conference with an admissions counselor and a campus tour. There are guides for informal visits, visitors may sit in on classes, and stay overnight. To schedule a visit, contact Mark Moffitt at mmoffitt@otterbein.edu. **Campus Safety and Security:** Measures include 24-hour foot and vehicle patrol, self-defense education, security escort services, emergency telephones, lighted pathways/sidewalks, controlled access to dorms/residences, 24-hour locked dorm facilities.

REQUIREMENTS: The SAT or ACT is required. Applicants should be graduates of an accredited secondary school. The recommended preparatory program includes 4 units of English, 3 to 4 units each of math, science, and social studies, 2 to 3 units of foreign language, and 1 to 2 units of performing arts. A high school GPA of 2.5 or better is recommended. Students who were Home-Schooled are considered for enrollment. The College also requires applicants to be in the upper 50% of their class. AP and CLEP credits are accepted. Important factors in the admissions decision are advanced placement or honors courses, evidence of special talent, and recommendations by school officials. All students must complete 126 semester hours, including 27 to 97 in the major, with a minimum GPA of 2.0. The liberal arts core includes 8 hours in English composition and literature, 8 hours each in natural and social sciences, 5 hours each in religion/philosophy, fine arts, and non-Western cultures, and 3 in phys ed. **Procedure:** Freshmen are admitted to all sessions. Entrance exams should be taken in the spring of the junior year. There are deferred admissions and rolling admissions plans. Applications should be filed by August 15 for fall entry, along with a $25 fee. Notification is sent on a rolling basis. Applications are accepted online. **Transfer Students:** 99 transfer students enrolled in 2015-2016. Applicants should present a college GPA of 2.5, and a minimum of 9 semester credits transferred. 48 of 126 credits required for the bachelor's degree must be completed at Otterbein. **International Students:** There are 70 international students enrolled. The school actively recruits these students. They must take the TOEFL with a minimum score of 523 on the paper-based TOEFL (PBT) or 69 on the Internet-based version (iBT). They must also take the SAT or ACT.

ADMISSIONS: 75% of the 2016-2017 applicants were accepted. The SAT scores for the 2016-2017 freshman class were: Critical Reading-- 35% below 500, 41% between 500 and 599, 22% between 600 and 699, and 2% between 700 and 800. Math-- 33% below 500, 43% between 500 and 599, 22% between 600 and 699, and 2% between 700 and 800. Writing-- 36% below 500, 39% between 500 and 599, 20% between 600 and 699, and 4% between 700 and 800. The ACT scores were 31% below 12, 29% between 12 and 17, 24% between 18 and 23, 9% between 24 and 29, and 7% above 30. 36% of the current freshmen were in the top fifth of their class; 59% were in the top two fifths. 16 freshmen graduated first in their class. **Admissions Contact:** Mark Moffitt, Exec. Director of Admissions. Email: *uotterb@otterbein.edu* Web: *www.otterbein.edu*

FINANCIAL AID: In 2016-2017, 94% of all full-time freshmen received some form of financial aid or need-based aid. The average freshman award was $23,489. Need-based scholarships or need-based grants averaged $18,819; need-based self-help aid (loans and jobs) averaged $5,669; and other non-need-based awards and non-need-based scholarships averaged $19,045. 28% of undergraduate students work part-time. The average financial indebtedness of the 2016 graduate was $26,583. The FAFSA code is 003110. The deadline for filing freshman financial aid applications for fall entry is April 1.

SHAWNEE STATE UNIVERSITY C-5

www.shawnee.edu

Portsmouth, OH 45662 **(740) 351-3450**

Fax: (740) 351-3111	**Email: to_ssu@shawnee.edu**
Full-time: 1431 men, 1605 women	**Faculty:** 151
Part-time: 224 men, 343 women	**Ph.D.s:** 56%
Graduate: 40 men, 129 women	**Student/Faculty:** 16 to 1
Year: semesters, summer session	**Tuition:** $7365 ($14,145)
Room & Board: $9766	**Freshman Class:** 3686 applied, 2733 accepted, 955 enrolled
SAT CR/M/W: 525/570/490 **ACT:** 21	**CEEB CODE:** 1790
Application Deadline: n/av	**COMPETITIVE**

Shawnee State University is a small, student-focused public university offering over 80 academic programs, both associate's and bachelor's degrees, and a nationally ranked Game Design program. A highly personalized, affordable, and accessible education makes the institution a best academic value. Other features include successful pre-professional preparatory programs, an undergraduate cadaver lab, unique plastics engineering technology degrees, and hands on clinical experiences. University athletics include 17 intercollegiate NAIA teams with plans to grow annually. There are 3 undergraduate schools and 1 graduate school. In addition to regional accreditation, Shawnee State has baccalaureate program accreditation with ADA, NCATE, NLN, AOTA, CoARC, OBN, OBR, ODE-DVE, CAATE, CAPTE, ODPS-DEMS, OBENHA, JRCERT, NAACLS, ODE, and USDE. The 62-acre campus is in a small town is located along the Ohio River in historic Portsmouth, Ohio. Including any residence halls, there are 42 buildings.

STUDENT LIFE: 88% of undergraduates are from Ohio. Others are from 23 states, and 21 foreign countries. 96% are from public schools. 85% are White; 5% African American; 4% race unknown; 2% two or more races; 1% Asian American; 1% American Indian/Alaska Native; 1% Hispanic; 1% Foreign. **Female To Male Ratio:** 1.2:1. The average age of freshmen is 21; all undergraduates, 23. 43% do not continue beyond their first year; 31% remain to graduate. **Housing:** 934 students can be accommodated in college housing, which includes coed on-campus apartments, honors houses, and special-interest houses. We also offer specific housing for the Game and Simulation Arts Program. On-campus housing is guaranteed for the freshman year only, and is available on a first-come, first-served basis. 76% of students commute. All students may keep cars. Alcohol is not permitted.

FACULTY/CLASSROOMS: 46% of faculty are male; 54% are female. All teach undergraduates. No introductory courses are taught by graduate students. The average class size in an introductory lecture is 17; in a laboratory is 16; and in a regular course is 16.

PROGRAMS OF STUDY: Shawnee State confers B.A., B.A.T., B.F.A., B.I.S., B.S., B.S.B., B.S.E., and B.S.N. degrees. Associate and master's degrees are also awarded. Bachelor's degrees are awarded in BIOLOGICAL SCIENCE (biology/biological science), BUSINESS (accounting, management, marketing, and sports management), COMMUNICATIONS AND THE ARTS (ceramic art and design, drawing, English, language arts, musical theater, and studio art), COMPUTER AND PHYSICAL SCIENCE (chemistry, computer engineering technology, computer game design/development, geology, inform, science, systms & tech, mathematics, natural sciences, and physics), EDUCATION (art education, athletic training, early childhood education, education, elementary education, music education, social science education, and special education), ENGINEERING AND ENVIRONMENTAL DESIGN (engineering technology, environmental engineering technology, and plastics technology), HEALTH PROFESSIONS (health administration and policy, nursing, occupational therapy, and premedicine), SOCIAL SCIENCE (history, humanities, interdisciplinary studies, international relations, legal studies, paralegal studies, philosophy and religion, political science/government, prelaw, psychology, social science, and sociology). Nursing is the strongest academically. General studies, fine arts and natural studies have the largest enrollments.

ACTIVITIES: There are 48 groups on campus, including art, cheerleading, choir, computers, drama, ethnic, honors, international, LGBT, literary magazine, marching band, musical theater, newspaper, pep band, photography, political, professional, religious, social, social service, student government, and Various Academic Clubs. Popular campus events include Weekend of Welcome, Family Weekend, Bear Runs, Fall Fest, Spring Fest, and Scare Week. **Sports:** There are 7 intercollegiate sports for men and 8 for women, and 9 intramural sports for men and 9 for women. Facilities include athletic center which offers a cardio room, weight room, four racquet courts, the Waller Gymnasium with basketball and volleyball courts, swimming pool, tennis center, and soccer field. **Graduates:** From July 1, 2015 to June 30, 2016, 422 bachelor's degrees were awarded. The most popular majors were business administration (17%), psychology (10%), and fine arts (7%). In an average class, 9% graduate in 4 years or less and 20% graduate in 6 years or less.

SERVICES: Counseling and information services are available, as is tutoring in most subjects. Free tutoring is provided for the majority of introductory courses except English or Writing. There is a reader service for the blind, and remedial math, reading, and writing. Tutoring can usually be arranged for other courses that are not introductory courses provided that the Student Success Center can secure a qualified tutor for that subject. **Library/Resources:** The library contains 136,334 volumes, 93,438 microform items, 4,460 audio/video tapes/CDs/DVDs, and subscribes to 146 periodicals including electronic. Computerized library services include interlibrary loans, database searching, Internet access, and Wi-Fi capability. Special learning facilities include an art gallery, planetarium, Shawnee State University works to make learning accessible to all students no matter their background. Shawnee State also provides a student success center, as well as advisers to provided specialized learning and assistance. **Physically Challenged Students:** All of the campus is accessible. Facilities include wheelchair ramps, elevators, special parking, specially equipped restrooms, lowered drinking fountains, and lowered telephones. **Special:** Study abroad available in several countries, internships in sports studies, business, psychology, and health management, and student-designed programs are available. Cross-registration with Miami University, a Washington semester, and 2+2 programs are also possible as well as a 3+2 program in psychology and occupational therapy. There are 3 national honor societies, a freshman honors program, and 3 departmental honors programs. **Visiting:** There are regularly scheduled orientations for prospective students, including fall and spring visitation days, which consist of small sessions with deans and faculty, orientation by student affairs offices, and tours with current college students. There are guides for informal visits and visitors may sit in on classes. To schedule a visit, contact the Office of Admissions. **Campus Safety and Security:** Measures include 24-hour foot and vehicle patrol, emergency notification system, self-defense education, security escort services, emergency telephones, lighted pathways/sidewalks, safety awareness programs such as I.C.E. and Operation Identification. The department also puts on a safety week to help educate students on a variety of safety topics.

REQUIREMENTS: Applicants must graduate from an accredited high school or have a GED. AP and CLEP credits are accepted. To graduate, students must complete a general education program of at least 34 semester hours and a senior seminar. A total of 120 to 135 semester hours including 40 hours in the major is required along with a 2.0 GPA in all course work and in the major. **Procedure:** Freshmen are admitted to all sessions. Entrance exams should be taken in late spring or early summer. There is a rolling admissions plan. Application deadlines are open. Notification is sent on a rolling basis. Applications are accepted online. **Transfer Students:** 230 transfer students enrolled in 2015-2016. A completed application and college and high school transcripts sent directly to SSU from previous institutions are required. 45 of 120 credits required for the bachelor's degree must be completed at Shawnee State. **International Students:** There are 63 international students enrolled. The school actively recruits these students. They must take the TOEFL with a minimum score of 500 on the paper-based TOEFL (PBT) or 60 on the Internet-based version (iBT) or take the MELAB, the TIBT, or IELTS.

ADMISSIONS: 74% of the 2016-2017 applicants were accepted. The SAT scores for the 2016-2017 freshman class were: Critical Reading-- 44% below 500, 34% between 500 and 599, 20% between 600 and 699, and 2% between 700 and 800. Math-- 30% below 500, 32% between 500 and 599, 34% between 600 and 699, and 4% between 700 and 800. Writing-- 55% below 500, 36% between 500 and 599, and 9% between 600 and 699. The ACT scores were 49% below 12, 26% between 12 and 17, 16% between 18 and 23, 5% between 24 and 29, and 4% above 30. 25% of the current freshmen were in the top fifth of their class; 53% were in the top two fifths. 15 freshmen graduated first in their class. **Admissions Contact:** Amanda Means, Director of Admissions. Email: *mbolter@shawnee.edu* Web: *www.shawnee.edu*

FINANCIAL AID: In 2016-2017, 91% of all full-time freshmen and 77% of continuing full-time students received some form of financial aid. 71% of all full-time freshmen and 54% of continuing full-time students received need-based aid. The average freshman award was $11,903. Need-based scholarships or need-based grants averaged $6,024 ($10,831 maximum); need-based self-help aid (loans and jobs) averaged $3,342 ($6,092 maximum); non-need-based athletic scholarships averaged $3,953 ($23,884 maximum); other non-need-based awards and non-need-based scholarships averaged $6,537 ($27,076 maximum); and $5,444 from other forms of aid. 9% of undergraduate students work part-time. Average annual earnings from campus work are $4350. The average financial indebtedness of the 2016 graduate was $24,054. Shawnee State is a member of CSS. The FAFSA code is 009942. The priority date for freshman financial aid applications for fall entry is December 1.

THE COLLEGE OF WOOSTER D-2

www.wooster.edu

Wooster, OH 44691 (330) 263-2322 (800) 877-9905

Fax: (330) 263-2621 Email: admissions@wooster.edu

Full-time: 901 men, 1082 women	**Faculty:** 169; IIB, +$
Part-time: 5 men, 15 women	**Ph.D.s:** n/av
Graduate: n/av	**Student/Faculty:** 12 to 1
Year: semesters, summer session	**Tuition:** $46,860
Room & Board: $11,040	**Freshman Class:** 5667 applied, 3296 accepted, 545 enrolled
SAT CR/M/W: 593/612/589 **ACT:** 27	**CEEB CODE:** 1134
Application Deadline: n/av	**VERY COMPETITIVE+**

The College of Wooster, founded in 1866, is America's private liberal arts college for mentored undergraduate research. There is 1 undergraduate school. In addition to regional accreditation, Wooster has baccalaureate program accreditation with NASM, NCATE, and ACS. The 240-acre campus is in a suburban area 55 miles southwest of Cleveland. Including any residence halls, there are 50 buildings.

STUDENT LIFE: 55% of undergraduates are from out of state, mostly the Midwest. Students are from 45 states, 35 foreign countries, and Canada. 64% are from public schools. 8% are African American; 67% White; 5% Asian American; 5% Hispanic; 2% race unknown; 11% Foreign; 1% American Indian/Alaska Native. 36% claim no religious affiliation; 21% Protestant; 18% Catholic. **Female To Male Ratio:** 1.2:1. The average age of freshmen is 18; all undergraduates, 20. 12% do not continue beyond their first year; 76% remain to graduate. **Housing:** 2051 students can be accommodated in college housing, which includes coed dorms, on-campus apartments, special-interest houses, fraternity houses, sorority houses, and theme housing which includes program housing, language suites, and gender neutral housing. On-campus housing is guaranteed for all 4 years. 99% of students live on campus; of those, 80% remain on campus on weekends. All students may keep cars.

FACULTY/CLASSROOMS: 54% of faculty are male; 46% are female. All teach undergraduates and do research. No introductory courses are taught by graduate students. The average class size in an introductory lecture is 15 and in a regular course is 20.

PROGRAMS OF STUDY: Wooster confers B.A., B.Mus. and B.Mus.Ed. degrees. Bachelor's degrees are awarded in BIOLOGICAL SCIENCE (biochemistry and biology/biological science), BUSINESS (accounting and business economics), COMMUNICATIONS AND THE ARTS (communications, communications technology, comparative literature, dance, dramatic arts, English, fine arts, French, German, Greek (classical), Latin, music, music theory and composition, Russian languages and literature, and Spanish), COMPUTER AND PHYSICAL SCIENCE (chemistry, computer science, geology, mathematics, and physics), ENGINEERING AND ENVIRONMENTAL DESIGN (architecture), SOCIAL SCIENCE (African American studies, anthropology, archeology, area studies, economics, history, interdisciplinary studies, international relations, Latin American studies, Middle Eastern studies, Near Eastern studies, philosophy, political science/government, psychology, religion, Russian and Slavic studies, sociology, urban studies, Western European studies, and women's studies). History, chemistry, global & international studies are the strongest academically. History, psychology, and political science have the largest enrollments.

ACTIVITIES: 14% of men belong to 4 local fraternities; 17% of women belong to 7 local sororities. Groups on campus include art, bagpipe, band, cheerleading, chess, choir, chorale, chorus, dance, debate, drama, ethnic, film, forensics, honors, international, jazz band, LGBT, literary magazine, marching band, musical theater, newspaper, orchestra, pep band, photography, political, religious, social service, student government, symphony, and yearbook. Popular campus events include Gala, Springfest, Skotoberfest, International Education Week Culture Show, WVN Carnival, Rake a Difference, Greek Week: Lip Sync, I.S. Week activities, and Scot Spirit Day. **Sports:** There are 10 intercollegiate sports for men and 11 for women, and 11 intramural sports for men and 11 for women. Facilities include a athletic and recreation center, track, multi-purpose courts, and fitness center. **Graduates:** From July 1, 2015 to June 30, 2016, 453 bachelor's degrees were awarded. The most popular majors were social sciences (26%), physical sciences (11%), and history (10%). 32 companies recruited on campus in 2015-2016. In an average class, 70% graduate in 4 years or less, 74% graduate in 5 years or less, and 76% graduate in 6 years or less. Of the 2015 graduating class, 27% were enrolled in graduate school within 6 months of graduation, and 67% were employed.

SERVICES: Counseling and information services are available, as is tutoring in every subject, a reader service for the blind, and remedial math, reading, and writing. **Library/Resources:** The 3 libraries contain 658,064 volumes, and subscribe to 1,386,697 periodicals including electronic. Computerized library services include interlibrary loans and database searching. Special learning facilities include an art gallery. **Physically Challenged Students:** 95% of the campus is accessible. Facilities include wheelchair ramps, elevators, special parking, specially equipped restrooms, special class scheduling, and lowered drinking fountains. **Special:** A 3-2 engineering degree is offered in conjunction with Case Western Reserve and Washington Universities. A B.A.-B.S. degree is offered in music/music education. Cross-registration is possible with off-campus programs of the Great Lakes Colleges Association.

Internships are available in American politics in Washington, D.C., the Ohio State Legislature, and the U.S. State Department, as well as in professional theater and economics. Student-designed majors, dual majors, study abroad in 50 countries, a Washington semester, accelerated degree programs, nondegree study, and pass/fail options for a limited number of courses are available. All seniors participate in a 2-term independent-study project in the major. The student chooses the topic and works on a one-to-one basis with a faculty mentor. A sophomore research program is available by application. There are 12 national honor societies and a chapter of Phi Beta Kappa. **Visiting:** There are regularly scheduled orientations for prospective students, including an interview, tour, class visits, and meetings with faculty and coaches. There are guides for informal visits, visitors may sit in on classes, and stay overnight. To schedule a visit, contact Melanie Schultz at melaschultz@wooster.edu. **Campus Safety and Security:** Measures include 24-hour foot and vehicle patrol, emergency notification system, security escort services, emergency telephones, lighted pathways/sidewalks, and controlled access to dorms/residences.

REQUIREMENTS: The SAT or ACT is required. Applicants should be a graduate of an accredited secondary school. The GED is accepted. Completion of a minimum of 16 high school academic credits with distribution of credits including 4 years of English, 3 years of Math, 3 years of History or Social Science, and 3 years of Natural Science with 2 units consisting of a lab, 2 in foreign language, 1 in academic electives. In addition to completion of the application, including an essay, either SAT or ACT test scores are required. A campus visit and interview are highly recommended. AP credits are accepted. Important factors in the admissions decision are advanced placement or honors courses, leadership record, personality/intangible qualities, extracurricular activities record, recommendations by school officials, parents or siblings attended your school, evidence of special talent, recommendations by alumni, and geographical diversity. 32 course credits are required for graduation, with 9 to 13 in the major and a minimum GPA of 2.0. All students must take 1 course each in critical inquiry, studies in cultural differences, religious perspectives, and quantitative reasoning and demonstrate basic writing and foreign language proficiency. 2 courses each in English, foreign languages, social science/history, natural science/math, and arts/humanities are required. **Procedure:** Freshmen are admitted in fall and winter. Entrance exams should be taken in the fall of the senior year. There are early decision, early admissions, and deferred admissions plans. Early decision applications should be filed by November 1. Notification of early decision is sent November 15; regular decision, 99 early decision candidates were accepted for the 2016-2017 class. 99 applicants were on the 2016 waiting list; 24 were admitted. Applications are accepted online. Application fees are waived if application is completed on-line. **Transfer Students:** 23 transfer students enrolled in 2015-2016. Applicants for transfer must have a minimum GPA of 2.5 and must submit either the SAT or ACT scores as well as a dean's reference, a high school transcript, and an essay or personal statement. An interview is recommended. Grades of C or better transfer for credit. Transfers are admitted every semester. 16 of 64 credits required for the bachelor's degree must be completed at Wooster. **International Students:** There are 217 international students enrolled. The school actively recruits these students. They must take the TOEFL with a minimum score of 81 on the Internet-based version (iBT), American Language Institute test. They must also take the SAT or ACT, scoring 900.

ADMISSIONS: 58% of the 2016-2017 applicants were accepted. The SAT scores for the 2016-2017 freshman class were: Critical Reading-- 13% below 500, 36% between 500 and 599, 31% between 600 and 699, and 20% between 700 and 800. Math-- 9% below 500, 30% between 500 and 599, 42% between 600 and 699, and 19% between 700 and 800. Writing-- 13% below 500, 35% between 500 and 599, 39% between 600 and 699, and 13% between 700 and 800. The ACT scores were 20% between 18 and 23, 49% between 24 and 29, and 30% above 30. 60% of the current freshmen were in the top fifth of their class; 86% were in the top two fifths. 45 freshmen graduated first in their class. **Admissions Contact:** Jennifer Winge, Dean of Admissions. Email: *admissions@wooster.edu* Web: *www.wooster.edu*

FINANCIAL AID: In 2016-2017, 99% of all full-time freshmen and 99% of continuing full-time students received some form of financial aid. 61% of all full-time freshmen and 55% of continuing full-time students received need-based aid. The average freshman award was $42,056. Need-based scholarships or need-based grants averaged $32,506; need-based self-help aid (loans and jobs) averaged $7,293; and $5,948 from other forms of aid. 42% of undergraduate students work part-time. Average annual earnings from campus work are $2000. The average financial indebtedness of the 2016 graduate was $29,650. Wooster is a member of CSS. The CSS/Profile and the college's own financial statement are required. The FAFSA code is 003037. The priority date for freshman financial aid applications for fall entry is February 15.

THE UNIVERSITY OF AKRON D-2

www.uakron.edu

Akron, OH 44325	**(330) 972-7100** **(800) 655-4884**
Fax: (330) 972-7022	**Email: admissions@uakron.edu**
Full-time: 8139 men, 7036 women	**Faculty:** 700
Part-time: 1921 men, 1941 women	**Ph.D.s:** 80%
Graduate: 1874 men, 2135 women	**Student/Faculty:** 22 to 1
Year: semesters, summer session	**Tuition:** $10,509 ($19,040)
Room & Board: $10,968	**Freshman Class:** 15166 applied, 14650 accepted, 3919 enrolled
SAT CR/M: 520/540 **ACT:** 22	**CEEB CODE:** 1829
Application Deadline: August 11	**COMPETITIVE**

The University of Akron is the public research university for northern Ohio. Home to the nation's largest academic program for polymer science and polymer engineering, The University of Akron also earned national recognition in several other undergraduate and graduate degree programs. The university offers more than 300 associate, bachelor's, master's, doctoral, and law degree programs and 100 certificate programs at sites in Summit, Wayne, Holmes, Medina and Cuyahoga counties. There are 8 undergraduate schools and 8 graduate schools. In addition to regional accreditation, UA has baccalaureate program accreditation with AACSB, ABET, ADA, CSWE, NASAD, NASM, NCATE, APA, ABA, and AAFCS. The 223-acre campus is in an urban area in downtown Akron, 40 miles South of Cleveland. Including any residence halls, there are 89 buildings.

STUDENT LIFE: 92% of undergraduates are from Ohio. Others are from 38 states, 60 foreign countries, and Canada. 74% are White; 4% two or more races; 3% Asian American; 3% race unknown; 2% Hispanic; 2% Foreign; 12% African American. **Male To Female Ratio:** 1.1:1. The average age of freshmen is 18; all undergraduates, 22. 26% do not continue beyond their first year; 40% remain to graduate. **Housing:** 2891 students can be accommodated in college housing, which includes single-sex and coed dorms and on-campus apartments. In addition, there are honors houses, special-interest houses, fraternity houses, sorority houses, private apartment-type halls, and private residence halls. On-campus housing is available on a first-come, first-served basis. Priority is given to out-of-town students. 81% of students commute. All students may keep cars. Alcohol is not permitted.

FACULTY/CLASSROOMS: 52% of faculty are male; 48% are female. 95% teach undergraduates. Graduate students teach 8% of introductory courses. The average class size in an introductory lecture is 26; in a laboratory is 24; and in a regular course is 26.

PROGRAMS OF STUDY: UA confers B.A., B.A.E., B.A.S.W., B.B.A., B.F.A., B.M., B.S., B.S.A., B.S.A.T., B.S.B.A, B.S.C.S., B.S.E., B.S.N. and B.S.T. degrees. Associate, master's, and doctoral degrees are also awarded. Bachelor's degrees are awarded in BIOLOGICAL SCIENCE (biology/biological science), BUSINESS (accounting, banking and finance, business administration and management, business communications, fashion merchandising, international business management, labor studies, management science, and marketing/retailing/merchandising), COMMUNICATIONS AND THE ARTS (art, classics, dance, English, French, media arts, music, music history and appreciation, music performance, music theory and composition, musical theater, public relations, Spanish, studio art, and theater management), COMPUTER AND PHYSICAL SCIENCE (applied mathematics, chemistry, computer science, computer security and information assurance, environmental geology, geology, geophysics and seismology, mathematics, natural sciences, physics, and statistics), EDUCATION (art education, athletic training, early childhood education, education, home economics education, middle school education, music education, physical education, special education, and technical education), ENGINEERING AND ENVIRONMENTAL DESIGN (automotive technology, biomedical engineering, chemical engineering, civil engineering, computer engineering, construction technology, electrical/electronics engineering, electrical/electronics engineering technology, emergency/disaster science, engineering, geological engineering, interior design, mechanical engineering, mechanical engineering technology, and survey and mapping technology), HEALTH PROFESSIONS (exercise science, nursing, physical therapy, respiratory therapy, and speech pathology/audiology), SOCIAL SCIENCE (anthropology, child psychology/development, criminal justice, criminology, dietetics, economics, family/consumer studies, family/juvenile justice, geography, history, interdisciplinary studies, philosophy, political science/government, psychology, social science, social work, and sociology). Engineering, nursing, and business are the strongest academically. Engineering, business, and nursing have the largest enrollments.

ACTIVITIES: 4% of men belong to 1 local and 13 national fraternities; 4% of women belong to 9 national sororities. There are 300 groups on campus, including art, band, cheerleading, chess, choir, chorale, chorus, computers, dance, drama, ethnic, honors, international, jazz band, LGBT, marching band, musical theater, newspaper, opera, orchestra, pep band, photography, political, professional, radio and TV, religious, social, social service, student government, and symphony. Popular campus events include Celebrating Akron Traditions and Zips Fest. **Sports:** There are 7 intercollegiate sports for men and 10 for women, and 19 intramural sports for men and 19 for women. Facilities include a recreation and wellness center with rock climbing wall, aerobics/dance studio, a natatorium with pool, the athletic fieldhouse and indoor varsity golf practice facility, which includes a football field, track, basketball/volleyball, arena, weight room and athletic training room, outdoor practice field, 8-lane outdoor track, outdoor soccer field, and a baseball field. **Graduates:** From July 1, 2015 to June 30, 2016, 3265 bachelor's degrees were awarded. The most popular majors were nursing (8%), business (5%), and mechanical engineering (4%). 300 companies recruited on campus in 2015-2016. In an average class, 16% graduate in 4 years or less, 34% graduate in 5 years or less, and 41% graduate in 6 years or less. Of the 2015 graduating class, 20% were enrolled in graduate school within 6 months of graduation, and 81% were employed.

SERVICES: Counseling and information services are available, as is tutoring in most subjects, a reader service for the blind, and remedial math, reading, and writing. TDDs are also available. **Library/Resources:** The 3 libraries contain 1.6 million volumes, 1.6 million microform items, 104,595 audio/video tapes/CDs/DVDs, and subscribe to 475,145 periodicals including electronic. Computerized library services include interlibrary loans, database searching, Internet access, and Wi-Fi capability. Special learning facilities include an art gallery, radio station, TV station, a nursing center, speech and hearing center, dance institute, educational media lab, and synchro hours learning classrooms. **Physically Challenged Students:** 90% of the campus is accessible. Facilities include wheelchair ramps, elevators, special parking, specially equipped restrooms, special class scheduling, lowered drinking fountains, lowered telephones, special housing. city/campus bus service, residence hall accommodations, and priority registration for disabled students. **Special:** UA offers co-op programs with local and out-of-state employers, study abroad in 22 countries, internships and work-study opportunities with community employers, a 6-year accelerated B.S.-M.D. program, B.A.-B.S. degrees in 10 majors, credit for military experience, nondegree study, and pass/fail options. There are 15 national honor societies, a freshman honors program, and 46 departmental honors programs. **Visiting:** There are regularly scheduled orientations for prospective students, including small groups for information on financial aid, student organizations, campus tours, and meetings with college faculty. There are guides for informal visits, visitors may sit in on classes, and stay overnight. To schedule a visit, contact the Office of Undergraduate Admissions. **Campus Safety and Security:** Measures include 24-hour foot and vehicle patrol, emergency notification system, self-defense education, and security escort services. There are also shuttle buses, emergency telephones, lighted pathways/sidewalks, controlled access to dorms/residences, in-room safes, and security cameras.

REQUIREMENTS: The SAT or ACT is required. Students who demonstrate outstanding college preparation through completion of a college prep curriculum may be admitted directly to a specific academic program. Criteria considered include high school GPA, test scores, class rank, and some majors/programs additional information is reviewed, such as activities, leadership, recommendations, essays, portfolios, and auditions. AP and CLEP credits are accepted. Important factors in the admissions decision are advanced placement or honors courses, leadership record, and evidence of special talent. To graduate, all students must complete at least 120 credits, with a varying number of hours in the major, and maintain a GPA of 2.0. Specific course requirements include English composition, oral communications, Western cultural traditions, math, natural science, social science, humanities, speech, cultural diversity, and phys ed. **Procedure:** Freshmen are admitted to all sessions. Entrance exams should be taken received by November 1 for scholarship consideration. There are deferred admissions and rolling admissions plans. Applications should be filed by August 11 for fall entry, along with a $45 fee. Notification is sent on a rolling basis. Applications are accepted online. **Transfer Students:** 756 transfer students enrolled in 2015-2016. Applicants should present a minimum college GPA of 2.0. There are other requirements for direct admission to specific academic programs. 32 of 120 credits required for the bachelor's degree must be completed at UA. **International Students:** There are 342 international students enrolled. The school actively recruits these students. They must take the TOEFL with a minimum score of 71 on the Internet-based version (iBT), the IELTS. The English proficiency tests are in lieu of the SAT or ACT unless they are interested in scholarships and the scholarships requires it.

ADMISSIONS: 97% of the 2016-2017 applicants were accepted. The SAT scores for the 2016-2017 freshman class were: Critical Reading--42% below 500, 38% between 500 and 599, 18% between 600 and 699, and 3% between 700 and 800. Math-- 36% below 500, 36% between 500 and 599, 23% between 600 and 699, and 5% between 700 and 800. The ACT scores were 15% between 12 and 17, 45% between 18 and 23, 33% between 24 and 29, and 7% above 30. 31% of the current freshmen were in the top fifth of their class; 57% were in the top two fifths. There were 2 National Merit finalists. **Admissions Contact:** Diane Raybuck, Director of Admissions. Email: *admissions@uakron.edu* Web: *www.uakron.edu*

FINANCIAL AID: In 2016-2017, 77% of all full-time freshmen and 73% of continuing full-time students received some form of financial aid. 58% of all full-time freshmen and 55% of continuing full-time students received need-based aid. The average freshman award was $7,696. Need-based scholarships or need-based grants averaged $4,915; need-based self-help aid (loans and jobs) averaged $3,255; non-need-based athletic scholarships averaged $4,473; and other non-need-based awards and non-need-based scholarships averaged $4,596. 11% of undergraduate students work part-time. Average annual earnings from campus work are $4800. The average financial indebtedness of the 2016 graduate was $22,453. The FAFSA code is 003123. The priority date for freshman financial aid applications for fall entry is February 1. The filing deadline for fall entry is June 30.

TIFFIN UNIVERSITY C-2

www.tiffin.edu

Tiffin, OH 44883	**(800) 968-6446** **(800) 968-6446**
Fax: (419) 443-5006	**Email: admiss@tiffin.edu**
Full-time: 968 men, 853 women	**Faculty:** 84; IIB, -$
Part-time: 222 men, 416 women	**Ph.D.s:** 60%
Graduate: 439 men, 613 women	**Student/Faculty:** 22 to 1
Year: semesters, summer session	**Tuition:** $21,510
Room & Board: $9870	**Freshman Class:** n/av **CEEB CODE:** 1817
Application Deadline: open	**COMPETITIVE**

Tiffin University, established in 1888, is a private institution emphasizing degree programs in business, arts and science, and criminal justice. Figures in the above capsule and in this profile are approximate. There are 3 undergraduate schools and 1 graduate school. In addition to regional accreditation, TU has baccalaureate program accreditation with ACBSP and ECBE. The 135-acre campus is in a small town 90 miles north of Columbus and 60 miles southeast of Toledo. Including any residence halls, there are 87 buildings.

STUDENT LIFE: 69% of undergraduates are from Ohio. Others are from 47 states, 33 foreign countries, and Canada. 43% are White; 30% race unknown; 2% Hispanic; 2% two or more races; 13% African American; 10% Foreign. **Female To Male Ratio:** 1.2:1. The average age of freshmen is 19; all undergraduates, 25. 38% do not continue beyond their first year; 45% remain to graduate. **Housing:** 1050 students can be accommodated in college housing, which includes single-sex and coed dorms, on-campus apartments, off-campus apartments, fraternity houses, sorority houses, student development housing for students who are involved in a number of activities and maintain a 3.2 GPA. On-campus housing is guaranteed for all 4 years, and is available on a first-come, and first-served basis. 30% of students commute. All students may keep cars.

FACULTY/CLASSROOMS: 53% of faculty are male; 47% are female. 88% teach undergraduates. No introductory courses are taught by graduate students. The average class size in an introductory lecture is 23; in a laboratory is 12; and in a regular course is 14.

PROGRAMS OF STUDY: TU confers B.A., B.B.A., B.S. and B.C.J. degrees. Associate and master's degrees are also awarded. Bachelor's degrees are awarded in BIOLOGICAL SCIENCE (forensic psychology and forensic science), BUSINESS (accounting, banking and finance, business administration and management, finance, marketing, marketing management, organizational leadership and management, and sports management), COMMUNICATIONS AND THE ARTS (arts administration/management, communication studies, communications, English, and music business management), COMPUTER AND PHYSICAL SCIENCE (cyber intelligence/security studies, information sciences and systems, and science), EDUCATION (English education, middle school education, and social studies education), HEALTH PROFESSIONS (exercise science and health care administration), SOCIAL SCIENCE (administration of justice , corrections, criminal justice, economics, forensic studies, history, homeland security, law enforcement and corrections, paralegal studies, and psychology). Criminal justice, and business are the strongest academically. Law enforcement, management, and forensic psychology have the largest enrollments.

ACTIVITIES: 2% of men belong to 3 local fraternities; 2% of women belong to 3 local sororities. There are 45 groups on campus, including art, band, cheerleading, choir, chorale, chorus, communications, computers, dance, drama, drill team, ethnic, honors, international, jazz band, LGBT, marching band, musical theater, newspaper, pep band, political, professional, religious, social, social service, student government, and symphony. Popular campus events include Homecoming, Springfest, Snowcoming, Late Night Breakfast, Greek Week, Drag Night, International Dinner, Athletic Events, Guest Speakers. **Sports:** There are 10 intercollegiate sports for men and 11 for women, and 10 intramural sports for men and 10 for women. Facilities include a student recreation center for volleyball and basketball, center for weight training, conditioning, and athletic training, indoor turf complex for all outdoor sports, indoor track and field complex, and 75 acre outdoor athletic complex. **Graduates:** From July 1, 2015 to June 30, 2016, 441 bachelor's degrees were awarded. The most popular majors were criminal justice/law enforcement admin (20%), business management (19%), and forensic psychology (10%). 64 companies recruited on campus in 2015-2016. In an average class, 30% graduate in 4 years or less, 42% graduate in 5 years or less, and 45% graduate in 6 years or less. Of the 2015 graduating class, 12% were enrolled in graduate school within 6 months of graduation, and 86% were employed.

SERVICES: Counseling and information services are available, as is tutoring in most subjects, a reader service for the blind, and remedial math, reading, and writing. **Library/Resources:** The library contains 41,263 volumes, 37,105 microform items, and 281 audio/video tapes/CDs/DVDs, and subscribes to 29,831 periodicals including electronic. Computerized library services include interlibrary loans, database searching, Internet access, and Wi-Fi capability. Special learning facilities include an art gallery. **Physically Challenged Students:** 90% of the campus is accessible. Facilities include wheelchair ramps, elevators, special parking, specially equipped restrooms, special class scheduling, lowered drinking fountains, and lowered telephones. **Special:** Internships are required for most majors and recommended for all students. Work-study programs, study abroad in 10 countries, and accelerated degree completion in professional studies, organizational management, and justice administration are available. There are 2 national honor societies. **Visiting:** There are regularly scheduled orientations for prospective students, consisting of placement testing, tours of the campus, lunch with advisers, and an appointment with an individual adviser to schedule fall classes. There are guides for informal visits, visitors may sit in on classes, and stay overnight. To schedule a visit, contact the Admissions Office. **Campus Safety and Security:** Measures include self-defense education, security escort services, lighted pathways/sidewalks, controlled access to dorms/residences, and in-room safes.

REQUIREMENTS: Candidates should be graduates of an accredited secondary school, with 4 units of English, 3 of math, 2 each of science and social studies, and 5 of electives. The GED is accepted. An interview is recommended. AP and CLEP credits are accepted. Important factors in the admissions decision are leadership record, recommendations by school officials, and extracurricular activities record. To graduate, all students must complete 121 semester hours, including at least 48 in the major, with a GPA of 2.0 cumulatively and 2.5 in the major. The 49-semester-hour integrated core curriculum includes courses in computer systems, speech and writing, math and statistics, economics, psychology, and sociology, history, literature, philosophy, and cultural heritage. Open electives are required to complete the degree with a minimum of 15 hours at the 200-400 level. **Procedure:** Freshmen are admitted to all sessions. Entrance exams should be taken as early as possible. There is a rolling admissions plan. Application deadlines are open. The fall 2016 application fee was $20. Notification is sent on a rolling basis. Application fees are waived if application is completed online. **Transfer Students:** 470 transfer students enrolled in 2015-2016. Applicants with 12 or more hours of credit must have a minimum college GPA of 2.0. The SAT or ACT and an interview are recommended. Official transcripts from other institutions will be reviewed to determine the number of credit hours that can be transferred. 30 of 121 credits required for the bachelor's degree must be completed at TU. **International Students:** There are 237 international students enrolled. The school actively recruits these students. They must take the TOEFL with a minimum score of 500 on the paper-based TOEFL (PBT) or 61 on the Internet-based version (iBT).

Admissions Contact: Michael Herdlick, Dean of Students. Email: *admiss@tiffin.edu* Web: *www.tiffin.edu*

FINANCIAL AID: In 2016-2017, 94% of all full-time freshmen and 88% of continuing full-time students received some form of financial aid. 94% of all full-time freshmen and 86% of continuing full-time students received need-based aid. The average freshman award was $22,469. Need-based scholarships or need-based grants averaged $13,592; need-based self-help aid (loans and jobs) averaged $5,187; non-need-based athletic scholarships averaged $8,583; and other non-need-based awards and non-need-based scholarships averaged $2,026. 24% of undergraduate students work part-time. Average annual earnings from campus work are $1733. The average financial indebtedness of the 2016 graduate was $32,331. TU is a member of CSS. The FAFSA code is 003121. The priority date for freshman financial aid applications for fall entry is January 1.

UNION INSTITUTE & UNIVERSITY *(The complete profile is made available exclusively on our website, www.barronspac.com)*

UNIVERSITY OF CINCINNATI — A-5

www.uc.edu

Cincinnati, OH 45221 — **(513) 556-1100**

Fax: (513) 556-1105	**Email: admissions@uc.edu**
Full-time: 10,939 men, 9849 women	**Faculty:** 1192; I, -$
Part-time: 1188 men, 2431 women	**Ph.D.s:** 76%
Graduate: 4328 men, 6686 women	**Student/Faculty:** 17 to 1
Year: semesters, summer session	**Tuition:** $11,010 ($26,234)
Room & Board: $10,964	**Freshman Class:** 19372 applied, 14804 accepted, 5011 enrolled
SAT CR/M/W: 570/590/550 **ACT:** 25	**CEEB CODE:** 1833
Application Deadline: March 1	**VERY COMPETITIVE**

University of Cincinnati, founded in 1819, is a state-supported institution offering undergraduate programs in art and architecture, business, engineering, health science, liberal arts and sciences, music, and technical training. There are 8 undergraduate schools and 11 graduate schools. In addition to regional accreditation, UC has baccalaureate program accreditation with AACSB, ABET, CSWE, NASAD, NASM, NCATE, and NLN. The 270-acre campus is in an urban area in downtown Cincinnati. Including any residence halls, there are 90 buildings.

STUDENT LIFE: 84% of undergraduates are from Ohio. Others are from 50 states, 118 foreign countries, and Canada. 9% are Foreign; 71% White; 7% African American; 5% race unknown; 3% Asian American; 3% Hispanic; 2% two or more races. **Female To Male Ratio:** 1.2:1. The average age of freshmen is 18; all undergraduates, 22. 14% do not continue beyond their first year. **Housing:** 5172 students can be accommodated in college housing, which includes coed dorms, on-campus apartments, and honors houses. On-campus housing is guaranteed for the freshman year only. Priority is given to out-of-town students. 81% of students commute. All students may keep cars. Alcohol is not permitted.

FACULTY/CLASSROOMS: 57% of faculty are male; 43% are female. No introductory courses are taught by graduate students.

PROGRAMS OF STUDY: UC confers B.A., B.S., B.F.A., B.M., B.S.Des., B.U.P., B.S.M.E., B.S.N., B.S.I.M., B.S.Ed., B.A.ArtHis., B.S.Ch.E., B.S.C.E., B.S.E.E., B.S.Comp.E., B.S.Aero.E., B.S.Arch., B.S.Int.Des., B.S.H.S., B.I.S., B.S.Bm.E., B.R.S.T., B.S.Mat.E., B.B.A., B.S.C.S., B.S.A.E.T., B.S.C.E.T., B.S.C.M., B.S.E.E.T., B.S.M.E.T., B.S.W., B.S.F.S.E.T., B.S.A.E., B.S.E.V.E., B.S.I.T., and B.T.A.S. degrees. Associate, master's, and doctoral degrees are also awarded. Bachelor's degrees are awarded in AGRICULTURE (environmental studies and horticulture), BIOLOGICAL SCIENCE (biochemistry, biology/biological science, and neurosciences), BUSINESS (accounting, banking and finance, business administration and management, finance, insurance, international business, management science, marketing/retailing/merchandising, operations management, organizational behavior, real estate, and sports management), COMMUNICATIONS AND THE ARTS (Arabic, art history, broadcasting, communications, communication science, comparative literature, creative writing, dance, design, digital communications, dramatic arts, English, fine arts, French, German, graphic design, Hebrew, information technology, jazz, journalism, keyboard - piano concentration, linguistics, music, music history and appreciation, music performance, music theory and composition, piano/organ, radio/TV, Spanish, speech/debate/rhetoric, theater design, visual and performing arts, and voice), COMPUTER AND PHYSICAL SCIENCE (astrophysics, chemical technology, chemistry, computer engineering technology, computer information technology, computer science, geology, information sciences and systems, mathematics, physics, and quantitative methods), EDUCATION (art education, athletic training, business education, early childhood education, elementary education, foreign languages education, guidance education, health education, health information management, industrial arts education, middle school education, music education, nutrition education, science education, secondary education, and special education), ENGINEERING AND ENVIRONMENTAL DESIGN (aeronautical engineering, architectural engineering, architectural technology, bioengineering, biomedical engineering, chemical engineering, city/community/regional planning, civil engineering, computer engineering, construction management, electrical/electronics engineering, electrical/electronics engineering technology, engineering, engineering mechanics, engineering technology, industrial administration/management, industrial engineering technology, interior design, materials engineering, mechanical engineering, mechanical engineering technology, metallurgical engineering, and nuclear engineering), HEALTH PROFESSIONS (medical laboratory technology, nuclear medical technology, nursing, predentistry, premedicine, prepharmacy, respiratory therapy, and speech pathology/audiology), SOCIAL SCIENCE (addiction studies, African American studies, anthropology, archeology, Asian/Oriental studies, classical/ancient civilization, criminal justice, dietetics, economics, fashion design and technology, geography, history, international studies, Judaic studies, Latin American studies, liberal arts/general studies, philosophy, political science/government, prelaw, psychology, social science, social work, sociology, urban studies, and women's studies). Architecture, music, and engineering are the strongest academically. Marketing, psychology, and criminal justice have the largest enrollments.

ACTIVITIES: 10% of men belong to 24 national fraternities; 11% of women belong to 15 national sororities. There are 688 groups on campus, including art, band, cheerleading, chess, choir, chorale, chorus, computers, dance, drama, environmental, ethnic, honors, international, jazz band, LGBT, literary magazine, marching band, musical theater, newspaper, opera, orchestra, pep band, photography, political, professional, radio and TV, religious, social, social service, student government, and symphony. Popular campus events include College Conservatory of Music Productions. **Sports:** There are 8 intercollegiate sports for men and 9 for women, and 14 intramural sports for men and 14 for women. The University of Cincinnati athletic and recreation facilities include a stadium, a field house, gym, indoor and outdoor tracks, climbing wall, recreation center with cardiovascular and weight equipment, swimming pools, tennis courts, and athletic fields. **Graduates:** From July 1, 2015 to June 30, 2016, 4715 bachelor's degrees were awarded. The most popular majors were business/marketing (17%), health professions and related programs (15%), and engineering (12%). In an average class, 1% graduate in 3 years or less, 31% graduate in 4 years or less, 62% graduate in 5 years or less, and 67% graduate in 6 years or less.

SERVICES: Counseling and information services are available, as is tutoring in most subjects, a reader service for the blind, and remedial math, reading, and writing. Other services offered include interpreting for the hearing impaired, and note taking for the blind. **Library/Resources:** The 13 libraries contain 4.1 million volumes, 121,446 microform items, and 409,094 audio/video tapes/CDs/DVDs, and subscribe to 167,738 periodicals including electronic. Computerized library services include interlibrary loans, database searching, Internet access, and Wi-Fi capability. Special learning facilities include an art gallery and radio station. **Physically Challenged Students:** 95% of the campus is accessible. Facilities include wheelchair ramps, elevators, special parking, specially equipped restrooms, special class scheduling, lowered drinking fountains, and lowered telephones. **Special:** The Professional Practice Program, a 5-year cooperative plan offering alternate work in academic subjects and industry, is available for students in engineering, business, arts and sciences, design, architecture, and art. Study abroad is available in 29 countries. Nondegree study is possible. There is a chapter of Phi Beta Kappa and a freshman honors program. **Visiting:** There are regularly scheduled orientations for prospective students. There are guides for informal visits, visitors may sit in on classes, and stay overnight. To schedule a visit, contact the Admissions Office. **Campus Safety and Security:** Measures include emergency notification system, self-defense education, and security escort services. There are also shuttle buses, emergency telephones, and lighted pathways/sidewalks.

REQUIREMENTS: ACT and SAT are accepted, with the ACT preferred. Applicants should be graduates of an accredited secondary school with 4 units of high school English, 3 of math, 2 each of science, social science, foreign language, and electives, and 1 of fine arts. AP and CLEP credits are accepted. Important factors in the admissions decision are extracurricular activities record, parents or siblings attended the school, and recommendations by alumni. The General Education Core has a firm foundation in UC's Academic Plan, to reaffirm liberal education as the core to preparing students as life-long learners. Our General Education course requirements are purposefully designed to strengthen four important learning outcomes or competencies throughout the student's progress toward their degree. Undergraduate courses at the University of Cincinnati promote development of four Baccalaureate Competencies: Critical Thinking, Knowledge Integration, Effective Communication, and Social Responsibility. Students must complete coursework in English Composition and Quantitative Reasoning. Students must complete at least 120 semester credit hours in order to earn a baccalaureate degree. **Procedure:** Freshmen are admitted to all sessions. Entrance exams should be taken in May of the junior year or January or March of the senior year. There is a rolling admissions plan. Applications should be filed by March 1 for fall entry, along with a $50 fee. Notifications are sent November 1. Applications are accepted on-line. **Transfer Students:** 1962 transfer students enrolled in 2015-2016. A minimum college GPA of 2.0 is required. Specific programs may have higher GPA and requirements and prerequisite courses. **International Students:** There are 1010 international students enrolled. The school actively recruits these students. They must take the TOEFL with a minimum score of 517 on the paper-based TOEFL (PBT) or 66 on the Internet-based version (iBT), or take the IELTS or SAT.

ADMISSIONS: 76% of the 2016-2017 applicants were accepted. The SAT scores for the 2016-2017 freshman class were: Critical Reading-- 20% below 500, 42% between 500 and 599, 29% between 600 and 699, and 9% between 700 and 800. Math-- 15% below 500, 36% between 500 and 599, 36% between 600 and 699, and 13% between 700 and 800. Writing-- 27% below 500, 43% between 500 and 599, 24% between 600 and 699, and 6% between 700 and 800. The ACT scores were 30% between 18 and 23, 53% between 24 and 29, and 17% above 30. 40% of the current freshmen were in the top fifth of their class; 71% were in the top two fifths. There were 55 National Merit finalists. 66 freshmen graduated first in their class. **Admissions Contact:** Tom Canepa, Assistant Vice President of Admissions. Email: *admissions@uc.edu* Web: *www.uc.edu*

FINANCIAL AID: In 2016-2017, 81% of all full-time freshmen received some form of financial aid. 46% of all full-time freshmen received need-based aid. The average freshman award was $8,558. Need-based scholarships or need-based grants averaged $6,989 ($36,022 maximum); need-based self-help aid (loans and jobs) averaged $4,193 ($12,000 maximum); non-need-based athletic scholarships averaged $14,778 ($31,497 maximum); and other non-need-based awards and non-need-based scholarships averaged $5,663 ($43,348 maximum). The average financial indebtedness of the 2016 graduate was $28,790. The FAFSA code is 003125. Check with the school for current application deadlines.

UNIVERSITY OF DAYTON B-4
www.udayton.edu

Dayton, OH 45469	**(937) 229-4411** **(800) 837-7433**
Fax: (937) 229-4729	**Email: admission@udayton.edu**
Full-time: 4135 men, 3738 women	**Faculty:** 463
Part-time: 273 men, 184 women	**Ph.D.s:** 87%
Graduate: 1237 men, 1236 women	**Student/Faculty:** 15 to 1
Year: semesters, summer session	**Tuition:** $40,940
Room & Board: $12,680	**Freshman Class:** 18665 applied, 10856 accepted, 2045 enrolled
SAT M/W: 570/555	**CEEB CODE:** 1834
Application Deadline: February 1	**COMPETITIVE**

University of Dayton, founded in 1850, is a private comprehensive institution affiliated with the Roman Catholic Church. Part of the Southwestern Ohio Council for Higher Education, it has undergraduate and graduate programs emphasizing the arts and sciences, business administration, engineering, education, health sciences, and law. There are 4 undergraduate schools and 5 graduate schools. In addition to regional accreditation, UD has baccalaureate program accreditation with AACSB, ABET, NASAD, NASM, NCATE, ABA, CAPTE, and MPAC. The 398-acre campus is in a suburban area 2 miles South of downtown Dayton. Including any residence halls, there are 59 buildings.

STUDENT LIFE: 55% of undergraduates are from out of state, mostly the Midwest. Students are from 44 states, 41 foreign countries, and Canada. 46% are from public schools. 79% are White; 4% Hispanic; 3% African American; 2% two or more races; 10% Foreign; 1% Asian American; 1% race unknown. 54% are Catholic; 12% Protestant. **Male To Female Ratio:** 1.1:1. The average age of freshmen is 18; all undergraduates, 20. 11% do not continue beyond their first year; 75% remain to graduate. **Housing:** 6600 students can be accommodated in college housing, which includes coed dorms, on-campus apartments, honors houses, special-interest houses, fraternity houses, and sorority houses. On-campus housing is available on a first-come, first-served basis, and on a lottery system for upperclassmen. 72% of students live on campus; of those, 100% remain on campus on weekends. Upperclassmen may keep cars.

FACULTY/CLASSROOMS: 58% of faculty are male; 42% are female. 88% teach undergraduates. No introductory courses are taught by graduate students. The average class size in an introductory lecture is 28; in a laboratory is 17; and in a regular course is 28.

PROGRAMS OF STUDY: UD confers B.A., B.S., B.C.E., B.Ch.E., B.E.E., B.F.A., B.G.S., B.M.E., and B.Mus. degrees. Master's and doctoral degrees are also awarded. Bachelor's degrees are awarded in BIOLOGICAL SCIENCE (biochemistry, biology/biological science, environmental biology, and nutrition), BUSINESS (accounting, accounting (finance), banking and finance, business administration and management, business economics, entrepreneurial studies, international business management, management information systems, marketing/retailing/merchandising, operations management, operations research, and sports management), COMMUNICATIONS AND THE ARTS (art, art history and appreciation, communications, dramatic arts, English, fine arts, French, German, graphic design, music, music performance, music theory and composition, photography, Spanish, theatre studies, and visual design), COMPUTER AND PHYSICAL SCIENCE (chemistry, computer science, environmental geology, geology, information sciences and systems, mathematics, mathematics – economics, physical sciences, and physics), EDUCATION (art education, early childhood education, elementary education, general studies, middle school education, music education, secondary education, and special education), ENGINEERING AND ENVIRONMENTAL DESIGN (chemical engineering, civil engineering, computer engineering, computer technology, electrical/electronics engineering, electrical/electronics engineering technology, engineering technology, industrial engineering technology, manufacturing technology, mechanical engineering, and mechanical engineering technology), HEALTH PROFESSIONS (exercise science, music therapy, pharmaceutical chemistry, pharmaceutical science, predentistry, premedicine, and prephysical therapy), SOCIAL SCIENCE (American studies, criminal justice, dietetics, early childhood studies, economics, ethics, politics, and social policy, history, international studies, liberal arts/general studies, philosophy, political science/government, psychology, religion, religious education, sociology, and women's studies). Engineering, business, and education are the strongest academically. Business/marketing and engineering/engineering technologies has the largest enrollment.

ACTIVITIES: 12% of men belong to 1 local and 8 national fraternities; 21% of women belong to 9 national sororities. There are 240 groups on campus, including art, band, cheerleading, chess, choir, chorale, chorus, computers, dance, debate, drama, drill team, environmental, ethnic, film, honors, international, jazz band, LGBT, literary magazine, marching band, musical theater, newspaper, orchestra, pep band, photography, political, professional, radio and TV, religious, social, social service, student government, symphony, and yearbook. Popular campus events include Christmas on Campus, Green Sweep, and Weekend Scene. **Sports:** There are 7 intercollegiate sports for men and 9 for women, and 25 intramural sports for men and 25 for women. Facilities include an arena, football stadium with a track, soccer field, volleyball facility, baseball stadium, softball stadium, and state-of-the-art recreational sports facility containing a gym, an aquatic center, climbing wall, racquetball courts, a fitness center, and an indoor track. Outdoor recreational facilities include outdoor basketball, sand volleyball courts, turf field, and walking/running track. **Graduates:** From July 1, 2015 to June 30, 2016, 2055 bachelor's degrees were awarded. The most popular majors were marketing (9%), communication (9%), and finance (9%). 531 companies recruited on campus in 2015-2016. In an average class, 58% graduate in 4 years or less, 74% graduate in 5 years or less, and 75% graduate in 6 years or less. Of the 2015 graduating class, 24% were enrolled in graduate school within 6 months of graduation, and 73% were employed.

SERVICES: Counseling and information services are available, as is tutoring in some subjects. Walk-in tutoring and/or Supplemental Instruction (SI) are available for many entry-level courses and some high-attrition upper level courses. Support is available for writing at all levels. **Library/Resources:** The 3 libraries contain 1.7 million volumes, 747,580 microform items, 178,881 audio/video tapes/CDs/DVDs, and subscribe to 118,311 periodicals including electronic. Computerized library services include interlibrary loans, database searching, Internet access, and Wi-Fi capability. Special learning facilities include an art gallery, radio station, TV station, UD Research Institute, Bombeck Family Learning Center, a learning teaching center, and Davis Center for Portfolio Management. **Physically Challenged Students:** Facilities include wheelchair ramps, elevators, special parking, specially equipped restrooms, special class scheduling, lowered drinking fountains, special housing. The university provides access to programs and services through the Office of Learning Resources. **Special:** Traditional co-op programs are available in the School of Engineering; however, any student in any discipline may co-op, and qualification is determined on a case-by-case basis. Internships are available in all majors. Cross-registration is available with the Southwestern Ohio Council for Higher Education. Study abroad, work-study programs, a Washington semester, accelerated degree programs, and B.A.-B.S. degrees in chemistry, math, economics, and psychology are available. For students who wish to have a dual major, almost all programs may be combined. Student-designed majors include general studies and interdisciplinary studies. An engineering curriculum agreement exists with Sinclair Community College. There is a freshman honors program. **Visiting:** There are regularly scheduled orientations for prospective students, including an admission interview, financial aid consultation, campus tour, residence hall tour, and faculty or class visit. High school seniors who have been accepted to the university may participate in an overnight visit during the winter semester. There are guides for informal visits, visitors may sit in on classes, and stay overnight. To schedule a visit, contact the Office of Admission. **Campus Safety and Security:** Measures include 24-hour foot and vehicle patrol, emergency notification system, and security escort services. There are shuttle buses, emergency telephones, lighted pathways/sidewalks, controlled access to dorms/residences, a bike patrol, electronic access control for residence hall access, about 1000 surveillance cameras, an on-campus ambulance service, automated external debrillators in residence halls and key facilities, centrally monitored fire alarm systems in all residential facilities, and fire suppression in high-density residential facilities.

REQUIREMENTS: The SAT or ACT is required. Applicants should be

graduates of an accredited secondary school with 16 units in English, math, science, social studies, and academic electives. In addition, 2 units of foreign language are required for admission to the College of Arts and Sciences. The GED is accepted. High school transcripts must be submitted. An essay or personal statement, a recommendation from the high school guidance counselor, and an interview are recommended. Music students must audition. AP and CLEP credits are accepted. Important factors in the admissions decision are personality/intangible qualities, recommendations by school officials, and leadership record. To graduate, all students must complete a minimum of 120 semester hours with at least 30 hours of residence, and maintain a minimum GPA of 2.0. The curricula must include general education requirements, including 4 classes in religious studies and philosophy as well as basic skills requirements. Departmental requirements vary. **Procedure:** Freshmen are admitted in the fall, winter, and summer. Entrance exams should be taken by December of the senior year. There are deferred admissions and rolling admissions plans. Early decision applications should be filed by November 1; regular applications, by February 1 for fall entry. Notification is sent on a rolling basis. Applications are accepted online. **Transfer Students:** 149 transfer students enrolled in 2015-2016. Attention is directed to college and high school GPA and course selection. The minimum grade point average is 2.0. The School of Education and Allied Professions requires a minimum 2.5 GPA in previous college work. Achievement of the minimum GPA does not guarantee admission. For students under 21 years of age, results of the SAT or ACT are required. All students applying to the School of Education and Allied Professions must submit SAT or ACT and Praxis I scores. 30 of 120 credits required for the bachelor's degree must be completed at UD. **International Students:** There are 751 international students enrolled. The school actively recruits these students. They must take the TOEFL with a minimum score of 523 on the paper-based TOEFL (PBT) or 70 on the Internet-based version (iBT). Students must also take either the IELTS, PTE, ELPT, or APIEL.

ADMISSIONS: 58% of the 2016-2017 applicants were accepted. The SAT scores for the 2016-2017 freshman class were: Math-- 17% below 500, 43% between 500 and 599, 34% between 600 and 699, and 6% between 700 and 800. Writing-- 23% below 500, 48% between 500 and 599, 25% between 600 and 699, and 4% between 700 and 800. The ACT scores were 21% between 18 and 23, 56% between 24 and 29, and 23% above 30. 46% of the current freshmen were in the top fifth of their class; 75% were in the top two fifths. 6 freshmen graduated first in their class. **Admissions Contact:** Robert F. Durkle, Associate VP Dean of Admission. Email: *admission@udayton.edu* Web: *www.udayton.edu*

FINANCIAL AID: In 2016-2017, 84% of all full-time freshmen and 74% of continuing full-time students received some form of financial aid. 62% of all full-time freshmen and 52% of continuing full-time students received need-based aid. The average freshman award was $28,821. Need-based scholarships or need-based grants averaged $23,610; need-based self-help aid (loans and jobs) averaged $3,722; non-need-based athletic scholarships averaged $16,351; and other non-need-based awards and non-need-based scholarships averaged $13,572. 35% of undergraduate students work part-time. Average annual earnings from campus work are $1970. The average financial indebtedness of the 2016 graduate was $21,096. UD is a member of CSS. The FAFSA code is 003127. The priority date for freshman financial aid applications for fall entry is February 1.

UNIVERSITY OF FINDLAY B-2

www.findlay.edu

Findlay, OH 45840	(419) 424-4732 (800) 548-0932
Fax: (419) 424-4822	**Email:** admissions@findlay.edu
Full-time: 1077 men, 1798 women	**Faculty:** 176
Part-time: 474 men, 655 women	**Ph.D.s:** 53%
Graduate: 679 men, 705 women	**Student/Faculty:** 16 to 1
Year: semesters, summer session	**Tuition:** $41,255
Room & Board: $9442	**Freshman Class:** 3605 applied, 2347 accepted, 820 enrolled
SAT CR/M/W: 510/530/515 **ACT:** 23	**CEEB CODE:** 1223
Application Deadline: August 1	**COMPETITIVE**

University of Findlay, founded in 1882, is a private, independent institution affiliated with the Churches of God, and General Conference, offering liberal arts and sciences and career preparation programs. Figures in the above capsule and in this profile are approximate. There are 4 undergraduate schools and 1 graduate school. In addition to regional accreditation, Findlay has baccalaureate program accreditation with NCATE. The 250-acre campus is in a small town 45 miles South of Toledo and 100 miles Northwest of Columbus. Including any residence halls, there are 55 buildings.

STUDENT LIFE: 80% of undergraduates are from Ohio. Others are from 45 states, 30 foreign countries, and Canada. 80% are from public schools. 85% are White; 6% African American; 5% Asian American; 3% Hispanic; 1% American Indian/Alaska Native. 60% are Protestant; 35% Catholic. **Female To Male Ratio:** 1.4:1. The average age of freshmen is 18; all undergraduates, 22. 25% do not continue beyond their first year; 55% remain to graduate. **Housing:** 1350 students can be accommodated in college housing, which includes single-sex dorms, on-campus apartments, honors houses, language houses, special-interest houses, fraternity houses, and sorority houses. On-campus housing is guaranteed for all 4 years. 65% of students commute. All students may keep cars. Alcohol is not permitted.

FACULTY/CLASSROOMS: 53% of faculty are male; 47% are female. All teach undergraduates. No introductory courses are taught by graduate students. The average class size in an introductory lecture is 23; in a laboratory is 15; and in a regular course is 22.

PROGRAMS OF STUDY: Findlay confers B.A.,B.S., B.S.B.M., B.S.C.J., and B.S.E.M. degrees. Associate, master's, and doctoral degrees are also awarded. Bachelor's degrees are awarded in AGRICULTURE (animal science and equine science), BIOLOGICAL SCIENCE (biology/biological science), BUSINESS (accounting, banking and finance, business administration and management, business economics, business systems analysis, hospitality management services, human resources, international business management, and marketing/retailing/merchandising), COMMUNICATIONS AND THE ARTS (art, arts administration/management, broadcasting, communications, dramatic arts, English, English as a second/foreign language, graphic design, illustration, Japanese, journalism - news & information, Spanish, studio art, and technical and business writing), COMPUTER AND PHYSICAL SCIENCE (chemistry, computer science, mathematics, and science), EDUCATION (art education, bilingual/bicultural education, education services, elementary education, foreign languages education, middle school education, physical education, and secondary education), ENGINEERING AND ENVIRONMENTAL DESIGN (environmental science, occupational safety and health, and technological management), HEALTH PROFESSIONS (health care administration, health science, nuclear medical technology, nursing, occupational therapy, physician's assistant, premedicine, and preveterinary science), SOCIAL SCIENCE (criminal justice, economics, forensic studies, history, international studies, philosophy, political science/government, prelaw, psychology, religion, religious studies, social work, and sociology). Business administration, preveterinary medicine, and education are the strongest academically. Business administration, equestrian studies, and education have the largest enrollments.

ACTIVITIES: 4% of men belong to 3 national fraternities; 1% of women belong to 2 national sororities. There are 40 groups on campus, including art, band, cheerleading, choir, chorale, chorus, computers, drama, drum and bugle corps, equestrian, ethnic, honors, international, jazz band, literary magazine, marching band, musical theater, newspaper, pep band, political, preveterinary, professional, radio and TV, religious, social, social service, and student government. Popular campus events include Family Weekend, International Night, Box, City event, and Spring Bash. **Sports:** There are 12 intercollegiate sports for men and 11 for women, and 18 intramural sports for men and 15 for women. Facilities include a fitness center, stadium, pool, aerobics area, racquetball courts, phys ed center with a gym, an ice arena, indoor track, basketball court, billards, bowling, cricket, dodgeball, Euchre Tournment, flag football, frisbee golf, floor hockey, golf, kickball, ping pong, kickball, sand-vollyball, soccer, tennis court, volleyball courts, wallyball, and wiffleball.

SERVICES: Counseling and information services are available, as is tutoring in most subjects, a reader service for the blind, and remedial math, reading, and writing. Other services include assistance with note taking, test taking, and study skills, and assistive technology per student need. **Library/Resources:** The library contains 135,000 volumes, 90,000 microform items, 1,200 audio/video tapes/CDs/DVDs, and subscribes to 2,500 periodicals including electronic. Computerized library services include interlibrary loans, database searching, Internet access, and Wi-Fi capability. Special learning facilities include an art gallery, planetarium, radio station, TV station, university-owned farm, equine facility, and emergency response training center. **Physically Challenged Students:** 90% of the campus is accessible. Facilities include wheelchair ramps, elevators, special parking, specially equipped restrooms, special class scheduling, lowered drinking fountains. **Special:** Co-op programs are available in accounting and occupational health and safety. There is cross-registration with Mount Carmel College of Nursing and Lourdes College. The field experience program provides up to 20 semester hours in field placement. Internships are available for many majors, including business, business education, communication, hazardous materials management, and theater majors. Through the College Consortium for International Studies, study abroad is possible in 16 countries. Work-study, a Washington semester, dual and student-designed majors, a general studies degree, pass/fail options, and credit for life experience are offered. Nondegree study is possible. There is a freshman honors program. **Visiting:** There are regularly scheduled orientations for prospective students, including a tour, interview, and coach/faculty visits. There are guides for informal visits, visitors may sit in on classes, and stay overnight. To schedule a visit, contact the Admissions Office. **Campus Safety and Security:** Measures include 24-hour foot and vehicle patrol, emergency notification system, self-defense education, security escort services, emergency telephones, lighted pathways/sidewalks, and an on-campus sexual assault/domestic violence advocate.

REQUIREMENTS: The SAT or ACT and the ACT Optional Writing test is also required. Applicants should have completed 16 high school credits or GED equivalents, including 4 years of English, 2 years of social studies/history, 3 to 4 math courses, and 2 to 3 science courses. A letter of recommendation and an essay are required for all applicants. AP and CLEP credits are accepted. Important factors in the admissions decision are advanced placement or honors courses, evidence of special talent, and extracurricular activities record. All students must complete 36 semester hours of general education requirements, including fine arts, humanities, natural science, math, social science, and religion or philosophy, and must take courses in wellness, computer science, and statistics. There are competency requirements in English composition and reading, and a wellness course. A total of 124 semester hours with a minimum GPA of 2.0 is required to graduate. **Procedure:** Freshmen are admitted to all sessions. Entrance exams should be taken during fall of the senior year or the spring of the junior year. There are deferred admissions and rolling admissions plans. Applications should be filed by August 1 for fall entry; December 1 for spring entry. Notification is sent on a rolling basis. Applications are accepted on-line. **Transfer Students:** 105 transfer students enrolled in 2015-2016. A minimum 2.25 GPA and eligibility to return to the current institution are required. An interview is recommended. 30 of 124 credits required for the bachelor's degree must be completed at Findlay. **International Students:** There are 800 international students enrolled. The school actively recruits these students. They must take the TOEFL.

ADMISSIONS: 65% of the 2016-2017 applicants were accepted. The SAT scores for the 2016-2017 freshman class were: Critical Reading-- 37% below 500, 45% between 500 and 599, 16% between 600 and 699, and 2% between 700 and 800. Math-- 31% below 500, 46% between 500 and 599, 21% between 600 and 699, and 2% between 700 and 800. Writing-- 36% below 500, 41% between 500 and 599, 19% between 600 and 699, and 4% between 700 and 800. The ACT scores were 16% below 12, 31% between 12 and 17, 27% between 18 and 23, 15% between 24 and 29, and 11% above 30. 54% of the current freshmen were in the top fifth of their class; 81% were in the top two fifths. **Admissions Contact:** Robin Hopkins, Director of Undergraduate Admissions. Email: *admissions@findlay.edu* Web: *www.findlay.edu*

FINANCIAL AID: In 2016-2017, 91% of all full-time freshmen received some form of financial aid. 15% of undergraduate students work part-time. Average annual earnings from campus work are $1350. The average financial indebtedness of the 2016 graduate was $31,000. Findlay is a member of CSS. The FAFSA code is 003045. The priority date for freshman financial aid applications for fall entry is April 15. The filing deadline for fall entry is September 30.

UNIVERSITY OF MOUNT UNION — E-2

www.mountunion.edu

Alliance, OH 44601 — (330) 821-5320, (800) 992-6682

Fax: (330) 823-3457 — **Email:** admission@mountunion.edu

Full-time: 1102 men, 1011 women	**Faculty:** 124
Part-time: 14 men, 13 women	**Ph.D.s:** 90%
Graduate: 49 men, 92 women	**Student/Faculty:** 14 to 1
Year: semesters, summer session	**Tuition:** $29,120
Room & Board: $9850	**Freshman Class:** 2640 applied, 2003 accepted, 699 enrolled
SAT CR/M/W: 490/510/470 **ACT:** 22	**CEEB CODE:** 1492
Application Deadline: open	**COMPETITIVE**

University of Mount Union, founded in 1846, is a private, liberal arts college affiliated with the United Methodist Church. Some figures are approximate. There is 1 undergraduate school and 1 graduate school. In addition to regional accreditation, Mount Union has baccalaureate program accreditation with ABET, NASM, NCATE, CCNE, NASPE, and COSMA. The 123-acre campus is in a suburban area 20 miles East of Canton. Including any residence halls, there are 38 buildings.

STUDENT LIFE: 82% of undergraduates are from Ohio. Others are from 29 states, 12 foreign countries, and Canada. 89% are from public schools. 79% are White; 7% African American; 5% race unknown; 3% Hispanic; 3% two or more races; 2% Foreign; 1% Asian American. 40% are Protestant; 35% claim no religious affiliation; 24% Catholic. **Male To Female Ratio:** 1.0:1. The average age of freshmen is 18; all undergraduates, 20. 21% do not continue beyond their first year; 64% remain to graduate. **Housing:** 1594 students can be accommodated in college housing, which includes single-sex and coed dorms and on-campus apartments. In addition, there are honors houses, special-interest houses, fraternity houses, and substance-free (tobacco/alcohol) houses. On-campus housing is guaranteed for the freshman year only, is available on a first-come, first-served basis, and on a lottery system for upperclassmen. 72% of students live on campus; of those, 60% remain on campus on weekends. All students may keep cars.

FACULTY/CLASSROOMS: 56% of faculty are male; 44% are female. 95% teach undergraduates. No introductory courses are taught by graduate students. The average class size in an introductory lecture is 20; in a laboratory is 15; and in a regular course is 18.

PROGRAMS OF STUDY: Mount Union confers B.A., B.S., B.Mus. and B.Mus.Ed. degrees. Master's and doctoral degrees are also awarded. Bachelor's degrees are awarded in BIOLOGICAL SCIENCE (biochemistry, biology/biological science, and environmental biology), BUSINESS (accounting, business administration and management, human resources, international business management, and sports management), COMMUNICATIONS AND THE ARTS (art, communications, creative writing, dramatic arts, English, French, German, Japanese, media arts, music, music performance, and Spanish), COMPUTER AND PHYSICAL SCIENCE (astronomy, chemistry, computer science, geology, information sciences and systems, mathematics, and physics), EDUCATION (athletic training, early childhood education, elementary education, middle school education, music education, and physical education), ENGINEERING AND ENVIRONMENTAL DESIGN (civil engineering, environmental science, and mechanical engineering), HEALTH PROFESSIONS (exercise science, health, and medical technology), SOCIAL SCIENCE (American studies, cognitive science, criminal justice, economics, history, international studies, Near Eastern studies, philosophy, political science/government, psychology, religion, social science, and sociology). Engineering, and exercise science are the strongest academically. Business, early childhood education, and sports managements have the largest enrollments.

ACTIVITIES: 25% of men belong to 4 national fraternities; 52% of women belong to 1 local and 3 national sororities. There are 80 groups on campus, including art, band, cheerleading, chess, choir, chorale, chorus, computers, dance, debate, drama, drill team, environmental, ethnic, forensics, honors, international, jazz band, LGBT, literary magazine, marching band, musical theater, newspaper, orchestra, pep band, political, professional, radio and TV, religious, social, social service, student government, and symphony. Popular campus events include Spring Fest, Greek Week and Schooler Lecture series. **Sports:** There are 11 intercollegiate sports for men and 10 for women, and 8 intramural sports for men and 8 for women. Facilities include a gym, field house, stadium, tennis courts, wellness center, exercise and aerobics rooms, and the campus center. **Graduates:** From July 1, 2015 to June 30, 2016, 452 bachelor's degrees were awarded. The most popular majors were business (13%), education (11%), and exercise science (10%). 50 companies recruited on campus in 2015-2016. In an average class, 1% graduate in 3 years or less, 54% graduate in 4 years or less, 60% graduate in 5 years or less, and 62% graduate in 6 years or less. Of the 2015 graduating class, 29% were enrolled in graduate school within 6 months of graduation, and 87% were employed.

SERVICES: Counseling and information services are available, as is tutoring in most subjects, such as general education courses and most introductory courses. There is a reader service for the blind, and remedial writing. Facilitated study groups are available for most general education courses that meet once a week. **Library/Resources:** The 2 libraries contain 302,000 volumes, 45,000 microform items, 51,000 audio/video tapes/CDs/DVDs, and subscribe to 950 periodicals including electronic. Computerized library services include interlibrary loans, database searching, Internet access, and Wi-Fi capability. Special learning facilities include an art gallery, radio station, an astronomical observatory, university theater, playhouse, nature center, and the DWOC studio (digital, written and oral communication studio). **Physically Challenged Students:** 98% of the campus is accessible. Facilities include wheelchair ramps, elevators, special parking, specially equipped restrooms, special class scheduling, lowered drinking fountains, and special housing. **Special:** Mount Union offers internships for credit in many majors, study abroad in 29 countries, co-op programs in business, work-study programs with various employers, student-designed majors, and pass/fail options. Adults in the nontraditional study program may receive credit for life, military, or work experience. There are 18 national honor societies, a freshman honors program, and 19 departmental honors programs. **Visiting:** There are regularly scheduled orientations for prospective students, including interviews, a campus tour, meetings with faculty, and classroom visits. There are guides for informal visits, visitors may sit in on classes, and stay overnight. To schedule a visit, contact the Office of Admissions. **Campus Safety and Security:** Measures include 24-hour foot and vehicle patrol, emergency notification system, self-defense education, security escort services, emergency telephones, and lighted pathways/sidewalks.

REQUIREMENTS: The ACT is required. Preference is given to high school graduates who have completed a minimum of 15 academic units, including 4 in English, 3 each in math, social science, and lab science, and 2 in foreign language. AP and CLEP credits are accepted. Important factors in the admissions decision are advanced placement or honors courses, recommendations by school officials, and personality/intangible qualities. University Requirements for all degrees, a minimum of 128 semester hours is required for all degrees, at least 48 semester hours must be completed at the University of Mount Union. The last 32 semester hours of a degree program must be pursued in residence at the university cooperative and other special programs may be excepted from this requirement. A minimum grade point average of 2.0 on a 4.0 scale must be achieved for all Mount Union and transient work attempted; Completion of a major with at least a 2.0 grade point average; Completion of a minor with at least a 2.0 grade point average; If required by the major, completion of a concentration with at least a 2.000 grade point average; Completion of the Integrative Core requirements for the degree to be earned; Demonstration of proficiency in Foreign Language and Math. General Education/Integrative Core Requirements, First Year Seminar (4 semester hours), Foundations (16 semester hours), Themes (8 semester hours), Senior Capstone (4 semester hours). **Procedure:** Freshmen are admitted in the fall and spring. Entrance exams should be taken in the spring of the junior year. There are deferred admissions and rolling admissions plans. Application deadlines are open. Notification is sent on a rolling basis. Applications are accepted on-line. **Transfer Students:** 57 transfer students enrolled in 2015-2016. Applicants must have a college GPA of 2.0 for consideration and must submit a statement of honorable dismissal and an official transcript from the last college attended. A personal statement must accompany the transfer application. 45 of 120 credits required for the bachelor's degree must be completed at Mount Union. **International Students:** There are 50 international students enrolled. The school actively recruits these students. They must take the TOEFL with a minimum score of 450 on the paper-based TOEFL (PBT) or 79 on the Internet-based version (iBT), IELTS, or certification of completion of ELS. They must also take the SAT or ACT.

ADMISSIONS: 76% of the 2016-2017 applicants were accepted. The SAT scores for the 2016-2017 freshman class were: Critical Reading-- 53% below 500, 34% between 500 and 599, 11% between 600 and 699, and 2% between 700 and 800. Math-- 50% below 500, 35% between 500 and 599, and 15% between 600 and 699. The ACT scores were 11% between 12 and 17, 52% between 18 and 23, 35% between 24 and 29, and 2% above 30. 40% of the current freshmen were in the top fifth of their class; 69% were in the top two fifths. 21 freshmen graduated first in their class. **Admissions Contact:** Michelle Sundstrom, Vice President, Enrollment Services. Email: *admission@mountunion.edu* Web: *www.mountunion.edu*

FINANCIAL AID: In 2016-2017, 98% of all full-time freshmen and 97% of continuing full-time students received some form of financial aid. 96% of all full-time freshmen and 83% of continuing full-time students received need-based aid. The average freshman award was $24,113. Need-based scholarships or need-based grants averaged $18,868 ($28,800 maximum); need-based self-help aid (loans and jobs) averaged $6,150 ($6,300 maximum); and other non-need-based awards and non-need-based scholarships averaged $13,515 ($28,800 maximum). 43% of undergraduate students work part-time. Average annual earnings from campus work are $1492. The average financial indebtedness of the 2016 graduate was $27,862. The FAFSA code is 003083. The priority date for freshman financial aid applications for fall entry is January 1. The filing deadline for fall entry is September 1.

UNIVERSITY OF RIO GRANDE & RIO GRANDE COMMUNITY COLLEGE *(The complete profile is made available exclusively on our website, www.barronspac.com)*

UNIVERSITY OF TOLEDO *(The complete profile is made available exclusively on our website, www.barronspac.com)*

URBANA UNIVERSITY — B-3

www.urbana.edu

Urbana, OH 43078	(937) 484-1356
Fax: (937) 484-1322	Email: admissions@urbana.edu
Full-time: 500 men, 420 women	**Faculty:** 55
Part-time: 191 men, 346 women	**Ph.D.s:** 74%
Graduate: 32 men, 58 women	**Student/Faculty:** 17 to 1
Year: semesters, summer session	**Tuition:** $22,012
Room & Board: $8808	**Freshman Class:** n/av
SAT or ACT: required	**CEEB CODE:** 1847
Application Deadline: open	**COMPETITIVE**

Urbana University, founded in 1850, serves more than 1800 students from around the world. Known for innovative academic programs that feature personal attention from faculty, the University offers more than 30 undergraduate programs and several graduate degrees, delivering course work in class, online, or a combination of both. Urbana University was the first college in the state to offer a nontraditional degree completion program and the second institution of higher education in Ohio to admit women. There are 3 undergraduate schools and 1 graduate school. In addition to regional accreditation, Urbana has baccalaureate program accreditation with NCATE, CCNE, and IACBE. The 128-acre campus is in a small town 40 miles West of Columbus and 50 miles North of Dayton. Including any residence halls, there are 30 buildings.

STUDENT LIFE: 90% of undergraduates are from Ohio. Others are from 5 states, and 5 foreign countries. 95% are from public schools. 79% are White; 17% African American; 1% Hispanic. **Female To Male Ratio:** 1.1:1. The average age of freshmen is 20; all undergraduates, 24. 23% do not continue beyond their first year; 35% remain to graduate. **Housing:** 500 students can be accommodated in college housing, which includes single-sex and coed dorms. In addition, there are honors houses. On-campus housing is guaranteed for all 4 years, and is guaranteed for the freshman year only, and on a lottery system for upperclassmen. Priority is given to out-of-town students. 54% of students commute. All students may keep cars.

FACULTY/CLASSROOMS: 60% of faculty are male; 40% are female. All teach undergraduates. No introductory courses are taught by graduate students. The average class size in an introductory lecture is 18; in a laboratory is 7; and in a regular course is 19.

PROGRAMS OF STUDY: Urbana confers B.A., B.S., and B.S.N. degrees.

Associate and master's degrees are also awarded. Bachelor's degrees are awarded in AGRICULTURE (agricultural business management), BUSINESS (business administration and management, business administration marketing, and sports management), COMMUNICATIONS AND THE ARTS (communications and English), COMPUTER AND PHYSICAL SCIENCE (mathematics and science), EDUCATION (early childhood education, education of the mentally handicapped, elementary education, English education, middle school education, and secondary education), HEALTH PROFESSIONS (exercise science, nursing, prehealth biological studies, and premedicine), SOCIAL SCIENCE (criminal justice, family/consumer studies, history, liberal arts/general studies, philosophy and religion, prelaw, psychology, and sociology). Business, education, and exercise science are the strongest academically. Business, education, and sport studies have the largest enrollments.

ACTIVITIES: There are no fraternities or sororities. There are 30 groups on campus, including art, band, cheerleading, choir, chorus, dance, drama, environmental, ethnic, Honor societies, honors, international, LGBT, literary magazine, marching band, musical theater, newspaper, pep band, political, professional, religious, social, social service, and student government. Popular campus events include Spring Week, Founders Day, and Activities Fair. **Sports:** There are 11 intercollegiate sports for men and 12 for women, and 6 intramural sports for men and 6 for women. Facilities include a community center with a gym, pool, handball and racquetball courts, weight room, outdoor sand volleyball court, and outdoor tennis courts.

SERVICES: Counseling and information services are available, as is tutoring in most subjects. There is remedial math, reading, and writing. Taped textbooks, reading and writing labs, and study skills seminars are also available. **Library/Resources:** The library contains 316,000 volumes, and 1,000 audio/video tapes/CDs/DVDs, and subscribes to 6,000 periodicals including electronic. Computerized library services include interlibrary loans, database searching, Internet access, and Wi-Fi capability. **Physically Challenged Students:** 70% of the campus is accessible. Facilities include wheelchair ramps, elevators, special parking, and special class scheduling. **Special:** Special academic programs include internships, cross-registration with the Southwestern Ohio Council for Higher Education, study abroad, and accelerated degree programs in teacher certification. B.A.-B.S. degrees, dual and student-designed majors, credit for life, military, and work experience, and nondegree study are also available. There are 5 national honor societies, a freshman honors program, and 3 departmental honors programs. **Visiting:** There are regularly scheduled orientations for prospective students, consisting of a campus tour, admissions, financial aid, student life, meetings with coaches, attending classes. There are guides for informal visits, visitors may sit in on classes, and stay overnight. To schedule a visit, contact the Admissions Office. **Campus Safety and Security:** Measures include 24-hour foot and vehicle patrol, emergency notification system, self-defense education, security escort services, emergency telephones, lighted pathways/sidewalks, and controlled access to dorms/residences.

REQUIREMENTS: The SAT or ACT is required. An applicant must present evidence of high school completion in the form of a high school diploma or GED Certificate. The recommended high school curriculum includes 4 units of English, 3 units of mathematics, 2 units of science, 2 units of social science and one additional unit in English, mathematics, or science, and 4 additional units from English, mathematics, science, social science, foreign language or philosophy. ACT scores are preferred. AP and CLEP credits are accepted. Important factors in the admissions decision are advanced placement or honors courses, evidence of special talent, and extracurricular activities record. To graduate, all students must complete 126 semester credits, with a minimum overall GPA of 2.0 and 2.5 in the major. Distribution requirements in a 47-49 credit core curriculum include 12 to 13 credit hours in math and science, 12 credits social sciences, 13 credits in humanities, 9 in communications, and 2-3 in health and physical education. The number of credits required per major varies. **Procedure:** Freshmen are admitted to all sessions. Entrance exams should be taken during the junior or senior year. There are deferred admissions and rolling admissions plans. Application deadlines are open. The fall 2016 application fee was $25. Applications are accepted online. **Transfer Students:** 50 transfer students enrolled in 2015-2016. Applicants must have a cumulative GPA of 2.0. 30 of 126 credits required for the bachelor's degree must be completed at Urbana. **International Students:** There are 4 international students enrolled. The school actively recruits these students. They must take the TOEFL.

Admissions Contact: Melissa Tolle, Director of Admissions. Email: *admissions@urbana.edu* Web: *www.urbana.edu*

FINANCIAL AID: The state aid form, the college's own financial statement, and the state aid form for residents are required. Check with the school for current application deadlines.

URSULINE COLLEGE *(The complete profile is made available exclusively on our website, www.barronspac.com)*

WALSH UNIVERSITY — D-2

www.walsh.edu

North Canton, OH 44720 — (330) 490-7172, (800) 362-9846

Fax: (330) 490-7165 — Email: admissions@walsh.edu

Full-time: 731 men, 1050 women	**Faculty:** 118; IIB, -$
Part-time: 124 men, 231 women	**Ph.D.s:** 65%
Graduate: 192 men, 444 women	**Student/Faculty:** 13 to 1
Year: semesters, summer session	**Tuition:** $28,770
Room & Board: $10,240	**Freshman Class:** 1693 applied, 1315 accepted, 439 enrolled
SAT CR/M: 520/520 **ACT:** 23	**CEEB CODE:** 1926
Application Deadline: August 15	**COMPETITIVE**

Walsh University was established in 1958 by the Brothers of Christian Instruction, a religious order of the Roman Catholic Church. The private institution offers undergraduate programs in liberal arts, business, communication, education, professional training, and nursing. There are 5 undergraduate schools and 5 graduate schools. In addition to regional accreditation, Walsh has baccalaureate program accreditation with CCNE and CAEP. The 143-acre campus is in a small town 20 miles South of Akron. Including any residence halls, there are 24 buildings.

STUDENT LIFE: 87% of undergraduates are from Ohio. Others are from 30 states, 31 foreign countries, and Canada. 74% are from public schools. 74% are White; 6% African American; 3% Hispanic; 2% Foreign; 2% two or more races; 12% race unknown; 1% Asian American. 42% are Catholic; 30% claim no religious affiliation; 26% Protestant. **Female To Male Ratio:** 1.6:1. The average age of freshmen is 18; all undergraduates, 24. 15% do not continue beyond their first year; 64% remain to graduate. **Housing:** 1050 students can be accommodated in college housing, which includes single-sex and coed dorms, on-campus apartments, honors houses, special-interest houses, study floors, and substance-free floors. On-campus housing is guaranteed for all 4 years. 56% of students commute. All students may keep cars.

FACULTY/CLASSROOMS: 45% of faculty are male; 55% are female. 90% teach undergraduates, 37% do research, and 20% do both. No introductory courses are taught by graduate students. The average class size in an introductory lecture is 15; in a laboratory is 14; and in a regular course is 16.

PROGRAMS OF STUDY: Walsh confers B.A., B.S., B.S.Ed., and B.S.N. degrees. Associate, master's, and doctoral degrees are also awarded. Bachelor's degrees are awarded in BIOLOGICAL SCIENCE (biochemistry, bioinformatics, and biology/biological science), BUSINESS (accounting, business administration and management, business communications, finance, international business management, and marketing management), COMMUNICATIONS AND THE ARTS (art history, communications, digital media, English, French, graphic design, music, and Spanish), COMPUTER AND PHYSICAL SCIENCE (chemistry, computer science, mathematics, and science), EDUCATION (early childhood education, education of the emotionally handicapped, education of the exceptional child, education of the mentally handicapped, education of the physically handicapped, elementary education, middle school education, museum studies, physical education, secondary education, and special education), ENGINEERING AND ENVIRONMENTAL DESIGN (environmental science), HEALTH PROFESSIONS (clinical science, exercise science, nursing, physical therapy, predentistry, premedicine, preoptometry, pre-occupational therapy, prepharmacy, prephysical therapy, and preveterinary science), SOCIAL SCIENCE (criminal justice, history, international relations, liberal arts/general studies, philosophy, political science/government, prelaw, psychology, sociology, and theological studies). Biology, nursing, and business are the strongest academically. Biology, nursing, and management have the largest enrollments.

ACTIVITIES: There are no fraternities or sororities. There are 40 groups on campus, including special interest, art, band, cheerleading, choir, chorale, chorus, dance, debate, drama, environmental, ethnic, honors, international, leadership honor societies, literary magazine, marching band, newspaper, pep band, political, professional, radio and TV, religious, social, social service, student government, and yearbook. Popular campus events include Walshfest, Spring Formal, Coffee House, and Improv. **Sports:** There are 9 intercollegiate sports for men and 9 for women, and 10 intramural sports for men and 9 for women. Facilities include gymnasiums, outdoor basketball, tennis courts, a track, softball and baseball fields, and practice and intramural fields, soccer field, game room, student exercise and weight rooms, an all-purpose artifical practice field, and football. **Graduates:** From July 1, 2015 to June 30, 2016, 541 bachelor's degrees were awarded. The most popular majors were nursing (19%), management (18%), and biology (11%). 139 companies recruited on campus in 2015-2016. In an average class, 52% graduate in 4 years or less, 62% graduate in 5 years or less, and 64% graduate in 6 years or less. Of the 2015 graduating class, 13% were enrolled in graduate school within 6 months of graduation, and 78% were employed.

SERVICES: Counseling and information services are available, as is tutoring in every subject, and remedial math, reading, and writing. One-on-one and group tutoring and a study skills course are also available. **Library/Resources:** The library contains 131,614 volumes, and 27,051 audio/video tapes/CDs/DVDs, and subscribes to 32,206 periodicals including electronic. Computerized library services include interlibrary loans, database searching, Internet access, and Wi-Fi capability. Special learning facilities include an art gallery, radio station, a child development center, corporate museum, bioinformatics lab, and a community clinic with counseling and wellness programs for the underserved. **Physically Challenged Students:** All of the campus is accessible. Facilities include wheelchair ramps, elevators, special parking, specially equipped restrooms, special class scheduling, lowered drinking fountains, lowered telephones, and special housing. **Special:** Work-study programs are available to students having financial need. Walsh offers internships for all majors; study abroad in 14 countries, with a campus outside Rome, Italy and a partner school in Kisubi, Uganda; accelerated degree programs in nursing, business and management; pre-medical, pre-dental, pre-pharmacy, pre-veterinary, pre-physical therapy, graduate programs in business, physical therapy, education, counseling, theology, and nursing; evening and continuing education programs, and credit for life experience. Reduced core for transfer students. There are 12 national honor societies, a freshman honors program, and 12 departmental honors programs. **Visiting:** There are regularly scheduled orientations for prospective students, consisting of a campus tour, a session with financial aid and admissions staff, and an opportunity to meet with faculty, coaches, and other personnel. There are guides for informal visits, visitors may sit in on classes, and stay overnight. To schedule a visit, contact the Admissions Office. **Campus Safety and Security:** Measures include 24-hour foot and vehicle patrol, emergency notification system, self-defense education, security escort services, emergency telephones, lighted pathways/sidewalks, and controlled access to dorms/residences.

REQUIREMENTS: ACT or SAT scores are not required if the applicant has a high school GPA of 3.0 or better. Test scores are required for student athletes to comply with NCAA regulations. The applicant must be a graduate of an accredited secondary school. The GED is accepted. Walsh recommends completion of 4 units of English, 3 units each of math, science, and social studies, 2 units of foreign language, and 1 unit of fine or performing arts. An essay and an interview are recommended. A GPA of 2.4 is required. AP and CLEP credits are accepted. Important factors in the admissions decision are recommendations by school officials, leadership record, and extracurricular activities record. To graduate, students must complete 125 semester hours with a minimum 2.0 GPA. The number of hours required in the major varies. A core curriculum of 37 hours is required, including courses in English, art or music, science, social science, math, humanities, theology, philosophy, service learning, diversity, and a foreign language. **Procedure:** Freshmen are admitted to all sessions. Entrance exams should be taken during the junior year. There are deferred admissions and rolling admissions plans. Applications should be filed by August 15 for fall entry; January 1 for spring entry; and April 29 for summer entry, along with a $25 fee. Notification is sent on a rolling basis. Applications are accepted online. **Transfer Students:** 103 transfer students enrolled in 2015-2016. Applicants must have a minimum GPA of 2.0 from previous colleges attended. 32 of 125 credits required for the bachelor's degree must be completed at Walsh. **International Students:** There are 93 international students enrolled. The school actively recruits these students. They must take the TOEFL with a minimum score of 500 on the paper-based TOEFL (PBT) or 61 on the Internet-based version (iBT), and take the STEP.

ADMISSIONS: 78% of the 2016-2017 applicants were accepted. The ACT scores were 8% between 12 and 17, 57% between 18 and 23, 30% between 24 and 29, and 5% above 30. 34% of the current freshmen were in the top fifth of their class; 60% were in the top two fifths. 9 freshmen graduated first in their class. **Admissions Contact:** Melissa Schoeppner, Campus Visit Coordinator. Email: *admissions@walsh.edu* Web: *www.walsh.edu*

FINANCIAL AID: In 2016-2017, 99% of all full-time freshmen and 98% of continuing full-time students received some form of financial aid. 78% of all full-time freshmen and 80% of continuing full-time students received need-based aid. The average freshman award was $27,073. Need-based scholarships or need-based grants averaged $7,746 ($19,230 maximum); need-based self-help aid (loans and jobs) averaged $4,729 ($8,500 maximum); non-need-based athletic scholarships averaged $10,764 ($38,960 maximum); and other non-need-based awards and non-need-based scholarships averaged $11,961 ($27,220 maximum). 95% of undergraduate students work part-time. Average annual earnings from campus work are $1041. The average financial indebtedness of the 2016 graduate was $27,598. Walsh is a member of CSS. The college's own financial statement is required. The FAFSA code is 003135. The priority date for freshman financial aid applications for fall entry is February 14. The filing deadline for fall entry is rolling.

WILBERFORCE UNIVERSITY B-4

www.wilberforce.edu

Wilberforce, OH 45384	(937) 376-2911 (800) 367-8568
Fax: (937) 376-4751	Email: admissions@wilberforce.edu
Full-time: 300 men, 480 women	Faculty: 46
Part-time: 10 men, 10 women	Ph.D.s: 53%
Graduate: n/av	Student/Faculty: 17 to 1
Year: semesters	Tuition: $12,560
Room & Board: $6456	Freshman Class: n/av
SAT or ACT: recommended	CEEB CODE: 1906
Application Deadline: n/av	COMPETITIVE

Wilberforce University, founded in 1856, is a private institution operated under the auspices of the African Methodist Episcopal Church; it was the first black college in America. It's programs emphasize the liberal arts, business, art and fine arts, engineering, and music. The figures in the above capsule and in this profile are approximate. There is 1 undergraduate school. The 125-acre campus is in a rural area 20 miles East of Dayton. Including any residence halls, there are 21 buildings.

STUDENT LIFE: 64% of undergraduates are from out of state, mostly the Midwest. Students are from 32 states, and 2 foreign countries. 97% are African American. **Female To Male Ratio:** 1.6:1. The average age of freshmen is 18; all undergraduates, 20. **Housing:** 775 students can be accommodated in college housing, which includes dorms, married student housing, and honors houses. On-campus housing is guaranteed for all 4 years. All students may keep cars. Alcohol is not permitted.

FACULTY/CLASSROOMS: 50% of faculty are male; 50% are female. No introductory courses are taught by graduate students. The average class size in an introductory lecture is 12 and in a regular course is 18.

PROGRAMS OF STUDY: Wilberforce confers B.A. and B.S. degrees. Master's degrees are also awarded. Bachelor's degrees are awarded in BIOLOGICAL SCIENCE (biology/biological science), BUSINESS (accounting, banking and finance, business administration and management, business economics, management science, and marketing/retailing/merchandising), COMMUNICATIONS AND THE ARTS (communications, fine arts, literature, and music), COMPUTER AND PHYSICAL SCIENCE (chemistry, computer science, information sciences and systems, mathematics, and science), ENGINEERING AND ENVIRONMENTAL DESIGN (preengineering), HEALTH PROFESSIONS (health care administration and rehabilitation therapy), SOCIAL SCIENCE (economics, liberal arts/general studies, political science/government, prelaw, psychology, social science, social work, and sociology). Business administration, accounting, and banking & finance are the strongest academically.

ACTIVITIES: 10% of men belong to 5 national fraternities; 10% of women belong to 4 national sororities. There are 30 groups on campus, including choir, computers, dance, ethnic, honors, international, literary magazine, newspaper, political, religious, social, student government, and yearbook. Popular campus events include Fall Festival and Dawn

Dance. **Sports:** There are 5 intercollegiate sports for men and 4 for women, and 4 intramural sports for men and 4 for women. Facilities include a gym, outdoor and cross-country track, softball field, basketball, volleyball, and tennis courts.

SERVICES: Counseling and information services are available, as is tutoring in most subjects, a reader service for the blind, and remedial math, reading, and writing. **Library/Resources:** The library contains 60,000 volumes, 12,000 microform items, 200 audio/video tapes/CDs/DVDs, and subscribes to 350 periodicals including electronic. **Physically Challenged Students:** 50% of the campus is accessible. Facilities include wheelchair ramps, special parking, specially equipped restrooms. There is limited elevator service in classroom buildings only. **Special:** Wilberforce offers a co-op arrangement with St. John's University School of Law and cross-registration through the Southwestern Ohio Council for Higher Education. B.A.-B.S. degrees are available in all majors, and there are dual majors in engineering along with a 3-2 engineering degree with the University of Dayton. Credit is given for the mandatory co-op education program, in which students participate in paid work experience in their chosen field. Nondegree study is possible in military science. There is 1 national honor society, Phi Beta Kappa, a freshman honors program, and 4 departmental honors programs. **Visiting:** There are regularly scheduled orientations for prospective students, guides for informal visits. To schedule a visit, contact the Office of Admissions. **Campus Safety and Security:** Measures include 24-hour foot and vehicle patrol, and controlled access to dorms/residences.

REQUIREMENTS: The SAT or ACT is recommended. Students should be graduates of an accredited secondary school and have 15 Carnegie units, including 4 units of English, 2 to 3 of math, including algebra, 2 to 3 of science, including a lab course, and 2 of social studies, including U.S. history. The GED is accepted with a score of 45 or better. SAT II: Subject tests are recommended. AP and CLEP credits are accepted. Important factors in the admissions decision are recommendations by school officials, advanced placement or honors courses, and evidence of special talent. To graduate, students must complete 126 credit hours with a minimum GPA of 2.0 and no grade in the major below a C. To fulfill the general studies requirements, all students must complete a first-year program, which includes composition and computer literacy courses, and they must also take at least 1 course from each of the following areas: humanistic traditions, music, art, religion, communication arts, literature and language, non-Western studies, behavioral sciences, economics and political science, physical sciences, and life science. 2 credits in health and phys ed and completion of 2 cooperative education experiences are also required. **Procedure:** Freshmen are admitted in the fall and spring. Entrance exams should be taken by the fall of the senior year. There are early decision, early admissions, and rolling admissions plans. Application deadlines are open. **Transfer Students:** A minimum college GPA of 2.0 is required. 30 of 126 credits required for the bachelor's degree must be completed at Wilberforce. **International Students:** They must take the TOEFL. They must also take the SAT or ACT.

Admissions Contact: Kenneth C. Christmon, Director of Admissions. Email: *admissions@wilberforce.edu* Web: *www.wilberforce.edu*

FINANCIAL AID: Wilberforce is a member of CSS. The college's own financial statement, and parent and student federal income tax returns are required. The FAFSA code is 003141. Check with the school for current application deadlines.

WILMINGTON COLLEGE — B-4

www.wilmington.edu

Wilmington, OH 45177	(937) 382-6661 (800) 341-9318
Fax: (937) 382-7077	Email: admissions@wilmington.edu
Full-time: 528 men, 631 women	Faculty: n/av
Part-time: 88 men, 148 women	Ph.D.s: 69%
Graduate: n/av	Student/Faculty: n/av
Year: semesters, summer session	Tuition: $25,000
Room & Board: $9600	Freshman Class: 1922 applied, 1603 accepted, 380 enrolled
SAT CR/M: 510/550 ACT: 21	CEEB CODE: 0909
Application Deadline: August 1	COMPETITIVE

Wilmington College, established in 1870, is a private institution sponsored by the Society of Friends. The college offers programs in the liberal arts, business, health science, teacher preparation, agricultural studies, religious studies, and athletic training. The figures in the above capsule and in this profile are approximate. There is 1 undergraduate school and 1 graduate school. In addition to regional accreditation, Wilmington has baccalaureate program accreditation with TEAC and CAAHEP. The 65-acre campus is in a small town 50 miles from Cincinnati and Columbus. Including any residence halls, there are 21 buildings.

STUDENT LIFE: 98% of undergraduates are from Ohio. Others are from 13 states, and 4 foreign countries. 67% are White; 11% African American; 1% Hispanic. 40% claim no religious affiliation; 17% Catholic. **Female To Male Ratio:** 1.3:1. The average age of freshmen is 18; all undergraduates, 21. 31% do not continue beyond their first year. **Housing:** 842 students can be accommodated in college housing, which includes single-sex and coed dorms, on-campus apartments, and fraternity houses. On-campus housing is guaranteed for all 4 years. 65% of students live on campus. All students may keep cars.

FACULTY/CLASSROOMS: 65% of faculty are male; 57% are female. All teach undergraduates. No introductory courses are taught by graduate students. The average class size in an introductory lecture is 25 and in a regular course is 19.

PROGRAMS OF STUDY: Wilmington confers B.A. and B.S. degrees. Master's degrees are also awarded. Bachelor's degrees are awarded in AGRICULTURE (agricultural business management, agronomy, animal science, equine science, and range/farm management), BIOLOGICAL SCIENCE (bacteriology, biochemistry, biology/biological science, and environmental biology), BUSINESS (accounting, business administration and management, management science, marketing and distribution, marketing management, and sports management), COMMUNICATIONS AND THE ARTS (advertising, art, communications, dramatic arts, English, journalism, music, public relations, Spanish, and speech/debate/rhetoric), COMPUTER AND PHYSICAL SCIENCE (astronomy, chemistry, computer science, geology, information sciences and systems, mathematics, and planetary and space science), EDUCATION (agricultural education, athletic training, early childhood education, education, elementary education, English education, health education, mathematics education, middle school education, physical education, science education, secondary education, social science education, and social studies education), HEALTH PROFESSIONS (premedicine and preveterinary science), SOCIAL SCIENCE (criminal justice, economics, history, liberal arts/general studies, philosophy, political science/government, prelaw, psychology, religion, social science, social work, and sociology). Chemistry, biology, and athletic training are the strongest academically. Business, agriculture, and athletic training have the largest enrollments.

ACTIVITIES: 8% of men belong to 4 local and 1 national fraternities; 8% of women belong to 4 local sororities. There are 63 groups on campus, including band, cheerleading, choir, chorale, drama, ethnic, honors, international, LGBT, literary magazine, musical theater, newspaper, orchestra, photography, political, professional, religious, social, social service, student government, and yearbook. Popular campus events include Community Day, Westheimer Peace Symposium, and Fall Fest. **Sports:** There are 11 intercollegiate sports for men and 10 for women, and 8 intramural sports for men and 8 for women. Facilities include a pool, Nautilus weight-training room, exercise room, racquetball courts, a gym, and a stadium. **Graduates:** From July 1, 2015 to June 30, 2016, 340 bachelor's degrees were awarded. The most popular majors were education (25%), business/marketing (24%), and psychology (10%).

SERVICES: Counseling and information services are available, as is tutoring in every subject, and remedial math, reading, and writing. **Library/Resources:** The library contains 110,000 volumes, 42,000 microform items, 1,400 audio/video tapes/CDs/DVDs, and subscribes to 400 periodicals including electronic. Computerized library services include interlibrary loans, database searching, Internet access, and Wi-Fi capability. Special learning facilities include an art gallery, a Peace Resource Center, Quaker museum, greenhouse, and academic farm. **Physically Challenged Students:** 20% of the campus is accessible. Facilities include wheelchair ramps, elevators, special parking, specially equipped restrooms, and special class scheduling. **Special:** Special academic programs include work-study, internships, a Washington semester, and cross-registration with the Southwest Ohio Consortium. Study abroad may be arranged in Mexico, Austria, France, and other countries. Dual majors in any subject and student-designed majors are offered. Credit for experience, nondegree study, and pass/fail options are possible. There are 5 national honor societies, a freshman honors program, and 3 departmental honors programs. **Visiting:** There are regularly scheduled orientations for prospective students, including meetings with faculty and a tour of the campus. There are guides for informal visits, visitors may sit in on classes, and stay overnight. To schedule a visit, contact the Admissions Office. **Campus Safety and Security:** Measures include 24-hour foot and vehicle patrol, security escort services, emergency telephones and lighted pathways/sidewalks.

REQUIREMENTS: The SAT or ACT is required. Applicants must be graduates of an accredited secondary school, with 4 units of English, 2 units each of math, science, and social studies, and a recommended 2 units of a foreign language, and an additional 6 units is required in other areas. The GED is accepted. An interview is recommended. An essay may be required. AP and CLEP credits are accepted. Important factors in the admissions decision are recommendations by school officials, parents or siblings attended your school, and recommendations by alumni. To graduate, students must complete 124 semester hours, with no more than 60 hours in the major, with a minimum GPA of 2.0. At least 40 hours must be in upper-division work. General education requirements include courses in English and math competence, international knowledge, basic areas of thought and expression, and personal fitness. **Procedure:** Freshmen are admitted in the fall and spring. Entrance exams should be taken as early as possible. There are deferred admissions and rolling admissions plans. Applications should be filed by August 1 for fall entry, along with a $25 fee. Notification is sent on a rolling basis. **Transfer Students:** 63 transfer students enrolled in 2015-2016. Applicants' college and high school transcripts are evaluated on an individual basis. They must have a 2.0 GPA and a completed transfer recommendation form. 30 of 124 credits required for the bachelor's degree must be completed at Wilmington. **International Students:** The school actively recruits these students. They must take the TOEFL with a minimum score of 500 on the paper-based TOEFL (PBT), The TOEFL is not required if the SAT is taken. Students who have been previously enrolled in a U.S. high school must take the SAT or ACT.

ADMISSIONS: 83% of the 2016-2017 applicants were accepted. The SAT scores for the 2016-2017 freshman class were: Critical Reading-- 61% below 500, 28% between 500 and 599, 9% between 600 and 699, and 1% between 700 and 800. Math-- 49% below 500, 35% between 500 and 599, and 16% between 600 and 699. The ACT scores were 20% below 12, 59% between 12 and 17, 10% between 18 and 23, 10% between 24 and 29, and 1% above 30. 39% of the current freshmen were in the top fifth of their class; 70% were in the top two fifths. **Admissions Contact:** Adam Lohrey, Interim Director of Admissions. Email: *admissions@wilmington.edu* Web: *www.wilmington.edu*

FINANCIAL AID: In 2016-2017, 99% of all full-time freshmen received some form of financial aid. The average freshman award was $15,604. Need-based scholarships or need-based grants averaged $10,016; need-based self-help aid (loans and jobs) averaged $4,380; and other non-need-based awards and non-need-based scholarships averaged $6,614. The FAFSA code is 003142. The priority date for freshman financial aid applications for fall entry is March 31. The filing deadline for fall entry is June 1.

WITTENBERG UNIVERSITY — B-3

www.wittenberg.edu

Springfield, OH 45501	(937) 327-6377 (877) 206-0332
Fax: (937) 327-6379	**Email:** admission@wittenberg.edu
Full-time: 838 men, 1037 women	**Faculty:** 121
Part-time: 39 men, 58 women	**Ph.D.s:** 90%
Graduate: 11 men, 17 women	**Student/Faculty:** 13 to 1
Year: semesters, summer session	**Tuition:** $38,030
Room & Board: $10,126	**Freshman Class:** 7138 applied, 6695 accepted, 603 enrolled
SAT CR/M: 560/550 **ACT:** 25	**CEEB CODE:** 1922
Application Deadline: March 15	**COMPETITIVE+**

Wittenberg University, founded in 1845, is a private liberal arts and sciences institution affiliated with the Evangelical Lutheran Church. There is 1 undergraduate school. In addition to regional accreditation, Wittenberg has baccalaureate program accreditation with NASM, NCATE, and CCNE. The 120-acre campus is in a suburban area in Springfield, Ohio off of I-70, 25 miles East of Dayton, 40 miles West of Columbus, and 75 miles North of Cincinnati. Including any residence halls, there are 26 buildings.

STUDENT LIFE: 72% of undergraduates are from Ohio. Others are from 37 states, 20 foreign countries, and Canada. 80% are from public schools. 9% are African American; 77% White; 5% two or more races; 4% Hispanic; 2% Foreign; 2% race unknown; 1% Asian American. 33% are Protestant; 23% claim no religious affiliation; 16% Catholic. **Female To Male Ratio:** 1.3:1. The average age of freshmen is 18; all undergraduates, 20. 22% do not continue beyond their first year; 64% remain to graduate. **Housing:** 1589 students can be accommodated in college housing, which includes single-sex and coed dorms, on-campus apartments, off-campus apartments, married student housing, honors houses, language houses, special-interest houses, fraternity houses, sorority houses. There is also a substance-free residence hall, and an international awareness house. On-campus housing is guaranteed for the freshman year only and is available on a lottery system for upperclassmen. 86% of students live on campus; of those, 84% remain on campus on weekends. All students may keep cars.

FACULTY/CLASSROOMS: 54% of faculty are male; 46% are female. All teach undergraduates. No introductory courses are taught by graduate students. The average class size in an introductory lecture is 25; in a laboratory is 20; and in a regular course is 18.

PROGRAMS OF STUDY: Wittenberg confers B.A., B.F.A., B.M.E., and B.S. degrees. Master's degrees are also awarded. Bachelor's degrees are awarded in BIOLOGICAL SCIENCE (biochemistry and biology/biological science), BUSINESS (accounting, business administration and management, finance, management, marketing, and sports management), COMMUNICATIONS AND THE ARTS (art, communications, dance, dramatic arts, English, fine arts, French, German, music, and Spanish), COMPUTER AND PHYSICAL SCIENCE (chemistry, computer science, geology, geology & geology oceanography, mathematics, and physics), EDUCATION (education, elementary education, foreign languages education, middle school education, music education, science education, secondary education, and special education), ENGINEERING AND ENVIRONMENTAL DESIGN (environmental science), HEALTH PROFESSIONS (exercise science), SOCIAL SCIENCE (East Asian studies, economics, history, international relations, philosophy, political science/government, psychology, religion, and sociology). Biology, communication, psychology, and business are the strongest academically. Business, education, and biology have the largest enrollments.

ACTIVITIES: 28% of men belong to 6 national fraternities; 36% of women belong to 5 national sororities. There are 100 groups on campus, including mock trail association, caving club, fishing club, outdoor club, anime club, art, band, cheerleading, choir, chorale, communications, computers, dance, debate, drama, environmental, ethnic, film, honors, international, jazz band, LGBT, literary magazine, musical theater, newspaper, opera, orchestra, pep band, photography, political, professional, radio and TV, religious, social, social service, and student government. Popular campus events include Wittenberg Series, International Festival, Wittfest, Martin Luther King, and Jr. Convocation. **Sports:** There are 11 intercollegiate sports for men and 11 for women. Facilities include a multipurpose field house, swimming pool, racquetball/handball courts, cardio fitness center, strength center, and rooms for sports medicine. There is also a gym, stadium, playing fields, baseball stadium, softball field, rugby playing field, a track, and tennis courts. **Graduates:** From July 1, 2015 to June 30, 2016, 469 bachelor's degrees were awarded. The most popular majors were education (7%), English (6%), and business (6%). In an average class, 61% graduate in 4 years or less and 68% graduate in 6 years or less. Of the 2015 graduating class, 73% were enrolled in graduate school within 6 months of graduation, and 19% were employed.

SERVICES: Counseling and information services are available, as is tutoring in most subjects, such as a math workshop, a writing center, oral communication center, and a language laboratory. **Library/Resources:** The library contains 506,072 volumes, 86,022 microform items, 20,619 audio/video tapes/CDs/DVDs, and subscribes to 14,833 periodicals including electronic. Computerized library services include interlibrary loans, database searching, Internet access, and Wi-Fi capability. Special learning facilities include an art gallery, radio station, a geology museum, an observatory, a GIS lab with supercomputer, and a parallel processing lab. **Physically Challenged Students:** 81% of the campus is accessible. Facilities include wheelchair ramps, elevators, special parking, specially equipped restrooms, special class scheduling, lowered drinking fountains, and lowered telephones. **Special:** Special academic programs include internships, cross-registration through the Southwest Ohio Consortium, a Washington semester, work-study programs, study-abroad opportunities in many countries, accelerated degree programs, dual and student-designed majors, nondegree study, and pass/fail options. A 3-2 engineering degree is offered through Washington, Columbia, and Case Western Reserve Universities and Georgia Institute of Technology. There is also a 3-2 nursing program with Johns Hopkins University and an occupational therapy program with Washington University. There are 11 national honor societies, Phi Beta Kappa, a freshman honors program, and 19 departmental honors programs. **Visiting:** There are regularly scheduled orientations for prospective students, including a tour and interview. There are guides for informal visits, visitors may sit in on classes, and stay overnight. To schedule a visit, contact Karen Hunt at (877) 206-0332. **Campus Safety and Security:** Measures include 24-hour foot and vehicle patrol, emergency notification system, self-defense education, security escort services, emergency telephones, lighted pathways/sidewalks, a bicycle patrol, and various prevention programs. City police support campus police during the evening. There is also a student Eyes and Ears Program and a campus security committee made up of students and faculty.

REQUIREMENTS: Students should have graduated from an accredited secondary school with 16 academic credits, including 4 units of English and 3 units each of foreign language, math, science, and social studies, which includes history. An essay is required and an interview advised. Art students must present a portfolio, and music students must audition. Wittenberg is test score optional. Wittenberg also has placements tests in math and language. AP credits are accepted. Important factors in the admissions decision are advanced placement or honors courses, evidence of special talent, and extracurricular activities record. To graduate, students must complete at least 126 credits and have a minimum GPA of 2.0. The required minimum GPA and number of hours in the major vary by department. All Wittenberg students complete a program of general education built on 16 learning goals. These include acquisition of foundations skills in writing, math, foreign language, speaking, research, and computing, the understanding of the different arts and sciences disciplines and their distinct methodological approaches to knowledge, and an introduction to non-Western culture, the diversity of human experience, and inter and transdisciplinary knowledge. Students achieve each general education learning goal by completing 1 to 2 courses. As part of general education, students perform 30 hours of community service. **Procedure:** Freshmen are admitted to all sessions. Entrance exams should be taken by the fall of the senior year, but as early as possible. There are early decision, early admissions, deferred admissions, and rolling admissions plans. Early decision applications should be filed by November 15; regular applications, by March 15 for fall entry; and December 1 for spring entry, along with a $40 fee. Notification of early decision is sent January 1; regular decision, on a rolling basis. 350 early decision candidates were accepted for the 2016-2017 class. Applications are accepted online. **Transfer Students:** 38 transfer students enrolled in 2015-2016. Applicants should have a minimum GPA of 2.0 at an accredited college and be in good academic and social standing. High school transcripts are required in some cases. An interview is recommended. 32 of 126 credits required for the bachelor's degree must be completed at Wittenberg. **International Students:** There are 32 international students enrolled. The school actively recruits these students. They must take the TOEFL with a minimum score of 550 on the paper-based TOEFL (PBT) or 79 on the Internet-based version (iBT), or take the SAT or ACT.

ADMISSIONS: 94% of the 2016-2017 applicants were accepted. The SAT scores for the 2016-2017 freshman class were: Critical Reading-- 27% below 500, 29% between 500 and 599, 40% between 600 and 699, and 5% between 700 and 800. Math-- 24% below 500, 35% between 500 and 599, and 40% between 600 and 699. Writing-- 27% below 500, 29% between 500 and 599, 40% between 600 and 699, and 5% between 700 and 800. The ACT scores were 1% between 12 and 17, 50% between 18 and 23, 37% between 24 and 29, and 12% above 30. 38% of the current freshmen were in the top fifth of their class; 52% were in the top two fifths. **Admissions Contact:** Karen Hunt, Executive Director of Admissions. Email: *admission@wittenberg.edu* Web: *www.wittenberg.edu*

FINANCIAL AID: In 2016-2017, 100% of all full-time freshmen and 99% of continuing full-time students received some form of financial aid. 88% of all full-time freshmen and 89% of continuing full-time students received need-based aid. The average freshman award was $35,059. Need-based scholarships or need-based grants averaged $25,997 ($40,445 maximum); and need-based self-help aid (loans and jobs) averaged $7,760 ($10,000 maximum). 45% of undergraduate students work part-time. Average annual earnings from campus work are $1500. The average financial indebtedness of the 2016 graduate was $33,520. The FAFSA code is 003143. The priority date for freshman financial aid applications for fall entry is March 1.

WRIGHT STATE UNIVERSITY B-4

www.wright.edu

Dayton, OH 45435 **(937) 775-5700**

Fax: (937) 775-4410	**Email:** admissions@wright.edu
Full-time: 4882 men, 5055 women	**Faculty:** n/av
Part-time: 1304 men, 1441 women	**Ph.D.s:** n/av
Graduate: 1969 men, 2191 women	**Student/Faculty:** n/av
Year: semesters, summer session	**Tuition:** $8354 ($16,182)
Room & Board: $8629	**Freshman Class:** 5237 applied, 5067 accepted, 2359 enrolled
SAT CR/M/W: 520/520/490 **ACT:** 22	**CEEB CODE:** 1179
Application Deadline: open	**COMPETITIVE**

Wright State University, founded in 1964, is a state-supported institution offering undergraduate programs in business and administration, education, human services, engineering, computer science, liberal arts, math and science, and nursing and health. There are 6 undergraduate schools and 8 graduate schools. In addition to regional accreditation, Wright State has baccalaureate program accreditation with AACSB, ABET, CAHEA, CSWE, NASM, NCATE, and NLN. The 557-acre campus is in a suburban area 10 miles northeast of Dayton. Including any residence halls, there are 60 buildings.

STUDENT LIFE: 90% of undergraduates are from Ohio. Others are from 49 states, 69 foreign countries, and Canada. 85% are from public schools. 68% are White; 3% Asian American; 3% Hispanic; 3% two or more races; 12% African American; 11% Foreign. **Female To Male Ratio:** 1.1:1. The average age of freshmen is 18; all undergraduates, 23. 44% do not continue beyond their first year; 40% remain to graduate. **Housing:** 3000 students can be accommodated in college housing, which includes coed dorms, on-campus apartments, married student housing, honors houses and special-interest houses. On-campus housing is available on a first-come, first-served basis, and on a lottery system for upperclassmen. 81% of students commute. All students may keep cars. Alcohol is not permitted.

FACULTY/CLASSROOMS: No introductory courses are taught by graduate students.

PROGRAMS OF STUDY: Wright State confers B.A., B.A.C.S., B.A.Mus., B.F.A., B.S., B.S.B., B.S.B.E., B.S.C.E., B.S.C.L.S., B.S.C.S., B.S.Ed., B.S.E.E., B.S.E.P., B.S.I.S.E., B.S.M.E., B.S.M.S.E., B.S.N., and B.T.A.S. degrees. Associate, master's, and doctoral degrees are also awarded. Bachelor's degrees are awarded in BIOLOGICAL SCIENCE (biology/biological science and life science), BUSINESS (accounting, banking and finance, business economics, management information systems, management science, marketing/retailing/merchandising, nonprofit/public organization management, organizational leadership and management, real estate finance, and supply chain management), COMMUNICATIONS AND THE ARTS (American Sign Language, art history, art, art history and appreciation, arts administration/management, classical languages, communications, creative writing, dance, dramatic arts, English, film arts, fine arts, French, German, Greek, guitar, instrumental performance, language arts, Latin, literature, modern language, music, music history and appreciation, music theory and composition, musical theater, organ performance, percussion, Spanish, strings, studio art, theatre acting, theater design, theatre studies, theater management, vocal performance, and winds), COMPUTER AND PHYSICAL SCIENCE (applied mathematics, chemistry, computer science, geology, geophysics and seismology, mathematics, physics, and statistics), EDUCATION (art education, athletic training, business education, childhood education, career, technical education & training, early childhood education, education, elementary education, foreign languages education, mathematics education, middle school education, music education, physical education, science education, secondary education, social science education, and special education), ENGINEERING AND ENVIRONMENTAL DESIGN (biomedical engineering, computer engineering, electrical/electronics engineering, engineering physics, environmental science, industrial engineering, materials engineering, mechanical engineering, systems engineering, and water and wastewater technology), HEALTH PROFESSIONS (clinical science, community health work, environmental health science, exercise science, medical laboratory technology, nursing, predentistry, premedicine, and rehabilitation therapy), SOCIAL SCIENCE (African American studies, anthropology, applied psychology, cognitive science, criminal justice, economics, geography, history, humanities, international relations, liberal arts/general studies, philosophy, political science/government, prelaw, psychology, religion, social work, sociology, and urban studies). Business education, theater arts, and engineering are the strongest academically. Nursing, mechanical engineering, and biological sciences have the largest enrollments.

ACTIVITIES: 3% of men belong to 11 local fraternities; 4% of women belong to 11 local sororities. There are 200 groups on campus, including band, cheerleading, chess, choir, chorale, chorus, computers, dance, drill team, ethnic, film, honors, international, jazz band, LGBT, literary magazine, newspaper, orchestra, pep band, political, professional, radio and TV, religious, social, social service, and student government. Popular campus events include Fall Fest, April Craze, Lunar New Year Celebration, and Madrigal Dinner. **Sports:** There are 7 intercollegiate sports for men and 8 for women, and 26 intramural sports for men and 23 for women. Facilities include an athletic and entertainment center with an arena, an auxiliary gym, baseball and practice fields. The student union houses a natatorium, climbing wall, weight rooms, workout center, game rooms, and playing courts. **Graduates:** From July 1, 2015 to June 30, 2016, 2374 bachelor's degrees were awarded. The most popular majors were nursing (10%), organizational leadership (8%), and psychology (7%). In an average class, 1% graduate in 3 years or less, 21% graduate in 4 years or less, 33% graduate in 5 years or less, and 38% graduate in 6 years or less.

SERVICES: Counseling and information services are available, as is tutoring in most subjects, a reader service for the blind, and remedial math, reading, and writing. **Library/Resources:** The library contains 842,026 volumes, 1.4 million microform items, 20,738 audio/video tapes/CDs/DVDs, and subscribes to 5,700 periodicals including electronic. Computerized library services include interlibrary loans, database searching, Internet access, and Wi-Fi capability. Special learning facilities include an art gallery, radio station, a TV production studio. The Department of Archives and Special Collections houses one of the most complete depositories of information on the Wright Brothers in the world. **Physically Challenged Students:** All of the campus is accessible. Facilities include wheelchair ramps, elevators, special parking, specially equipped restrooms, lowered drinking fountains, lowered telephones, and special housing. An underground tunnel system connects all academic buildings. Adaptive technology is available. **Special:** B.A.-B.S. degrees are offered in computer science, geography, urban affairs, biological sciences, chemistry, geological sciences, math, and psychology. Cross-registration with other area colleges is available through the Southwestern Ohio Council for Higher Education. Dual majors, co-op programs, internships, study abroad, work-study programs, student-designed majors, nondegree study, and credit for military experience are available. There are 3 national honor societies, a freshman honors program, and 32 departmental honors programs. **Visiting:** There are regularly scheduled orientations for prospective students, including a campus tour and information on academic and student services. There are guides for informal visits and visitors may sit in on classes. To schedule a visit, contact the Office of Undergraduate Admissions at (937) 775-5700. **Campus Safety and Security:** Measures include 24-hour foot and vehicle patrol, emergency notification system, self-defense education, and security escort services. There are also shuttle buses, emergency telephones, and lighted pathways/sidewalks.

REQUIREMENTS: The SAT or ACT is required. Applicants should be graduates of an accredited secondary school and have 4 units in English, 3 units each in math, science, and social studies, 2 units in a foreign language, and 1 unit in the arts. A portfolio is required for art majors, an audition for theater and music majors. The GED is accepted. AP and CLEP credits are accepted. To graduate, students must complete 183 quarter hours, with a minimum GPA of 2.0. All students are required to take 56 credit hours of general education courses in 4 areas: communication and math skills, the Western experience, the non-Western world, and understanding the contemporary world. **Procedure:** Freshmen are admitted to all sessions. Entrance exams should be taken in the spring of the junior year. There are deferred admissions and rolling admissions plans. Application deadlines are open. Application fee is $30. Applications are accepted online. **Transfer Students:** 2031 transfer students enrolled in 2015-2016. Applicants must have a 2.0 GPA. 45 of 183 credits required for the bachelor's degree must be completed at Wright State. **International Students:** There are 671 international students enrolled. The school actively recruits these students. They must take the TOEFL with a minimum score of 500 on the paper-based TOEFL (PBT) or 61 on the Internet-based version (iBT).

ADMISSIONS: 97% of the 2016-2017 applicants were accepted. The SAT scores for the 2016-2017 freshman class were: Critical Reading-- 40% below 500, 36% between 500 and 599, 21% between 600 and 699, and 3% between 700 and 800. Math-- 40% below 500, 39% between 500 and 599, 18% between 600 and 699, and 3% between 700 and 800. Writing-- 54% below 500, 33% between 500 and 599, 11% between 600 and 699, and 1% between 700 and 800. The ACT scores were 40% below 12, 25% between 12 and 17, 18% between 18 and 23, 9% between 24 and 29, and 8% above 30. 31% of the current freshmen were in the top fifth of their class; 57% were in the top two fifths. **Admissions Contact:** Cathy Davis, Assistant VP for Undergraduate Admission. Email: *admissions@wright.edu* Web: *www.wright.edu*

FINANCIAL AID: In 2016-2017, 83% of all full-time freshmen and 78% of continuing full-time students received some form of financial aid. 71% of all full-time freshmen and 69% of continuing full-time students received need-based aid. The average freshman award was $8,912. Need-based scholarships or need-based grants averaged $5,937; need-based self-help aid (loans and jobs) averaged $4,370; non-need-based athletic scholarships averaged $10,010; and other non-need-based awards and non-need-based scholarships averaged $3,132. 14% of undergraduate students work part-time. The average financial indebtedness of the 2016 graduate was $28,349. Wright State is a member of CSS. The FAFSA code is 003078. The priority date for freshman financial aid applications for fall entry is March 1.

XAVIER UNIVERSITY — A-5
www.xavier.edu

Cincinnati, OH 45207	**(513) 745-3301** **(877) 982-3648**
Fax: (513) 745-4319	**Email: xuadmit@xavier.edu**
Full-time: 1998 men, 2301 women	**Faculty:** 301; IIA, av$
Part-time: 119 men, 145 women	**Ph.D.s:** 76%
Graduate: 719 men, 1240 women	**Student/Faculty:** 14 to 1
Year: semesters, summer session	**Tuition:** $36,150
Room & Board: $11,730	**Freshman Class:** 10661 applied, 7631 accepted, 1150 enrolled
SAT CR/M: 530/540 **ACT:** 25	**CEEB CODE:** 1965
Application Deadline: February 1	**COMPETITIVE+**

Xavier University, founded in 1831, is a comprehensive Jesuit institution affiliated with the Roman Catholic Church. There are 3 undergraduate schools and 3 graduate schools. In addition to regional accreditation, XU has baccalaureate program accreditation with AACSB, CSWE, NASM, TEAC, ACS, CEA, ACOTE, CAHME, CACREP, CCNE, JRCERT, MACTE, APA, CAATE, and COSMA. The 175-acre campus is in an urban area 5 miles northeast of the center of Cincinnati in a residential area. Including any residence halls, there are 55 buildings.

STUDENT LIFE: 54% of undergraduates are from out of state, mostly the Midwest. Students are from 48 states, 47 foreign countries, and Canada. 41% are from public schools. 55 % are from private schools. 9% are African American; 72% White; 5% Hispanic; 5% race unknown; 4% two or more races; 3% Asian American; 3% Foreign. 63% are Catholic; 27% Protestant. **Female To Male Ratio:** 1.3:1. The average age of freshmen is 18; all undergraduates, 21. 13% do not continue beyond their first year; 72% remain to graduate. **Housing:** 2301 students can be accommodated in college housing, which includes coed dorms, on-campus apartments, off-campus apartments, honors houses, and living-learning communities. On-campus housing is guaranteed for the freshman year only, and is available on a first-come, first-served basis, and on a lottery system for upperclassmen. 50% of students commute. All students may keep cars.

FACULTY/CLASSROOMS: 45% of faculty are male; 55% are female. 82% teach undergraduates. No introductory courses are taught by graduate students. The average class size in an introductory lecture is 21; in a laboratory is 16; and in a regular course is 20.

PROGRAMS OF STUDY: XU confers B.A., B.S., Honors A.B., B.F.A.,

B.L.A., B.D.U., B.S.B.A., B.S.N., and B.S.W. degrees. Associate, master's, and doctoral degrees are also awarded. Bachelor's degrees are awarded in AGRICULTURE (agriculture), BIOLOGICAL SCIENCE (biology/biological science, biophysics, and life science), BUSINESS (accounting, banking and finance, business administration and management, business economics, business intelligence and analytics, entrepreneurial studies, human resources, international business management, management science, marketing/retailing/merchandising, purchasing/inventory management, sports management, sports marketing, and sustainable management), COMMUNICATIONS AND THE ARTS (advertising, art, classics, communication rhetoric/communication, design, digital media, English, fine arts, French, German, media arts, modern language, music, public relations, Spanish, theatre arts, and theatre studies), COMPUTER AND PHYSICAL SCIENCE (actuarial science, applied physics, chemistry, computer science, information sciences and systems, mathematics, natural sciences, physics, and radiological technology), EDUCATION (early childhood education, education, health information management, middle school education, music education, science education, and special education), ENGINEERING AND ENVIRONMENTAL DESIGN (engineering physics and environmental science), HEALTH PROFESSIONS (health administration and policy, health care administration, nursing, preallied health, and prepharmacy), SOCIAL SCIENCE (counseling/psychology, criminal justice, economics, gender studies, history, humanities, international studies, liberal arts/general studies, philosophy, political science/government, psychology, social work, sociology, theological studies, and urban ecology). Natural sciences & philosophy, politics, and public honors program are the strongest academically. Nursing, liberal arts, and biology have the largest enrollments.

ACTIVITIES: There are no fraternities or sororities. There are 163 groups on campus, including art, band, cheerleading, choir, chorale, chorus, communications, computers, dance, debate, drama, drill team, environmental, ethnic, honors, international, jazz band, LGBT, literary magazine, musical theater, newspaper, orchestra, pep band, political, professional, radio and TV, religious, social, social service, student government, and symphony. Popular campus events include Club Day, Week of Welcome, Community Action Day, Family Weekend, Spirit Celebration, Winter Week of Welcome, Winter Club Day, and Community Action Day. **Sports:** There are 8 intercollegiate sports for men and 8 for women, and 12 intramural sports for men and 12 for women. Facilities include a field house, sports center, basketball and volleyball courts, baseball and soccer fields, rifle range, and tennis courts. **Graduates:** From July 1, 2015 to June 30, 2016, 1004 bachelor's degrees were awarded. The most popular majors were liberal arts (12%), nursing (7%), and finance (7%). 428 companies recruited on campus in 2015-2016. In an average class, 1% graduate in 3 years or less, 62% graduate in 4 years or less, 71% graduate in 5 years or less, and 72% graduate in 6 years or less.

SERVICES: Counseling and information services are available, as is tutoring in every subject, a reader service for the blind, and remedial math, reading, and writing. Xavier has a Learning Assistance Center which provides individual and small group tutoring in almost all subjects and study skills assistance, a math lab, and a writing center. There is also an efficient reading and study skills course. **Library/Resources:** The library contains 915,154 volumes, 19,402 microform items, 30,797 audio/video tapes/CDs/DVDs, and subscribes to 208,232 periodicals including electronic. Computerized library services include interlibrary loans, database searching, Internet access, and Wi-Fi capability. Special learning facilities include an art gallery, radio station, TV station, an observatory and a financial trading room. **Physically Challenged Students:** 99% of the campus is accessible. Facilities include wheelchair ramps, elevators, special parking, specially equipped restrooms, special class scheduling, lowered drinking fountains, lowered telephones, and special housing. **Special:** Xavier offers internships related to some majors, cross-registration through the Greater Cincinnati Consortium, and co-op programs in business and computer science. Students may study abroad in over 100 countries through Xavier's network of program providers. A Washington semester and nondegree study are available. A 4-2 engineering degree is offered with the University of Cincinnati, and a 3-2 applied biology degree is offered with Duke University. A professional accountancy B.S.B.A and M.B.A program is also offered. There are 11 national honor societies, Phi Beta Kappa, a freshman honors program, and 2 departmental honors programs. **Visiting:** There are regularly scheduled orientations for prospective students, including an interview and a tour of the campus. There are guides for informal visits and visitors may sit in on classes. To schedule a visit, contact Office of Undergraduate Admission. **Campus Safety and Security:** Measures include 24-hour foot and vehicle patrol, emergency notification system, self-defense education, security escort services, emergency telephones, lighted pathways/sidewalks, controlled access to dorms/residences, alcohol awareness, drug awareness, sexual assault programs, security camera system for certain areas on campus. There is also a Title IX Coordinator, a Bias Advisory Response Team (BART), and a Xavier Action and Care Team (X-ACT).

REQUIREMENTS: Graduation from an accredited secondary school or satisfactory scores on the GED are required for admission. The school requires 21 academic credits, including 4 years of English, 3 each of math, social studies, and science, 2 of foreign language, and 1 of health/phys ed, plus 5 electives, one essay no fewer than 250 words, at least one recommendation from a high school counselor (preferred) or teacher, satisfactory results on the ACT or the SAT, and a resume or list of activities. AP and CLEP credits are accepted. Important factors in the admissions decision are advanced placement or honors courses, leadership record, and extracurricular activities record. To graduate, students must complete a minimum of 120 credit hours with a minimum GPA of 2.0. The total number of hours required in the major varies. All students must take core curriculum courses in English composition, cultural diversity, math, science, social science, history, theology, philosophy, a foreign language, literature, fine arts, and an ethics/religion and society focus, as well as a zero-credit first-year journey course ("GOA") that meets six times each semester for the first year and an additional first-year seminar course. **Procedure:** Freshmen are admitted i the fall, spring, and summer. Entrance exams should be taken by fall of the senior year. There are deferred admissions and rolling admissions plans. Applications should be filed by February 1 for fall entry; December 1 for spring entry; and May 10 for summer entry, along with a $35 fee. Notifications are sent April 15. 98 applicants were on the 2016 waiting list; 8 were admitted. Application fees are waived if application is completed online. **Transfer Students:** 118 transfer students enrolled in 2015-2016. Transfer students must have a minimum GPA of 2.0 in all college-level work. Students who transfer to Xavier with 30 or more semester hours are not required to submit results of the ACT or SAT tests or a counselor recommendation. 30 of 120 credits required for the bachelor's degree must be completed at XU. **International Students:** There are 96 international students enrolled. The school actively recruits these students. They must take the TOEFL with a minimum score of 550 on the paper-based TOEFL (PBT) or 79 on the Internet-based version (iBT). They must also take the SAT or ACT or TOEFL.

ADMISSIONS: 69% of the 2016-2017 applicants were accepted. The SAT scores for the 2016-2017 freshman class were: Critical Reading-- 25% below 500, 54% between 500 and 599, 17% between 600 and 699, and 4% between 700 and 800. Math-- 16% below 500, 52% between 500 and 599, 28% between 600 and 699, and 4% between 700 and 800. Writing-- 35% below 500, 43% between 500 and 599, 19% between 600 and 699, and 3% between 700 and 800. The ACT scores were 30% between 18 and 23, 55% between 24 and 29, and 15% above 30. 42% of the current freshmen were in the top fifth of their class; 74% were in the top two fifths. 11 freshmen graduated first in their class. **Admissions Contact:** Aaron Meis, Dean of Undergraduate Admissions. Email: *xuadmit@xavier.edu* Web: *www.xavier.edu*

FINANCIAL AID: In 2016-2017, 99% of all full-time freshmen and 97% of continuing full-time students received some form of financial aid. 65% of all full-time freshmen and 58% of continuing full-time students received need-based aid. The average freshman award was $18,000. Need-based scholarships or need-based grants averaged $20,543 ($40,365 maximum); need-based self-help aid (loans and jobs) averaged $4,861 ($5,900 maximum); non-need-based athletic scholarships averaged $19,303 ($40,384 maximum); other non-need-based awards and non-need-based scholarships averaged $17,198 ($37,920 maximum); and $33,114 from other forms of aid. 33% of undergraduate students work part-time. Average annual earnings from campus work are $2050. The average financial indebtedness of the 2016 graduate was $32,108. XU is a member of CSS. The FAFSA code is 003144. The priority date for freshman financial aid applications for fall entry is February 15.

YOUNGSTOWN STATE UNIVERSITY E-2

www.ysu.edu

Youngstown, OH 44555	**(330) 941-2000** **(877) 468-6978**
Fax: (330) 941-3674	**Email: enroll@ysu.edu**
Full-time: 4227 men, 4559 women	**Faculty:** 399; IIA, av$
Part-time: 1142 men, 1463 women	**Ph.D.s:** 88%
Graduate: 531 men, 829 women	**Student/Faculty:** 22 to 1
Year: semesters, summer session	**Tuition:** $8317 ($14,317)
Room & Board: $8990	**Freshman Class:** 5921 applied, 5626 accepted, 1982 enrolled
SAT CR/M/W: required **ACT:** 21	**CEEB CODE:** 1975
Application Deadline: August 1	**COMPETITIVE**

Youngstown State University, founded in 1908, is a publicly funded, primarily commuter institution offering undergraduate, graduate and doctoral programs. College include education, business, creative arts and communication, health and human services, liberal arts and social sciences, science, technology, engineering, and mathematics. There are 6 undergraduate schools and 1 graduate school. In addition to regional accreditation, YSU has baccalaureate program accreditation with AACSB, ABET, ADA, CSWE, NASAD, NASM, NCATE, NLN, ACS, ACEND, AAFS, AAFCS, CoARC, NAACLS, NAST, ETAC-ABET, and ACTFL. The 160-acre campus is in an urban area 65 miles southeast of Cleveland. Including any residence halls, there are 53 buildings.

STUDENT LIFE: 86% of undergraduates are from Ohio. Others are from 39 states, 63 foreign countries, and Canada. 75% are White; 4% Hispanic; 4% race unknown; 3% two or more races; 2% Foreign; 10% African American; 1% Asian American. **Female To Male Ratio:** 1.2:1. The average age of freshmen is 19; all undergraduates, 23. 27% do not continue beyond their first year; 31% remain to graduate. **Housing:** 1278 students can be accommodated in college housing, which includes single-sex and coed dorms, on-campus apartments, honors houses, and academic learning communities. On-campus housing is guaranteed for all 4 years, and is available on a first-come, first-served basis. 88% of students commute. All students may keep cars.

FACULTY/CLASSROOMS: 49% of faculty are male; 51% are female. All teach undergraduates. No introductory courses are taught by graduate students.

PROGRAMS OF STUDY: YSU confers B.A., B.S., B.E., B.F.A., B.G.S., B.M., B.S., B.S.A.S., B.S.B.A., B.S.Ed., B.S.N., B.S.R.C., B.S.W., and B.S.D.H. degrees. Associate, master's, and doctoral degrees are also awarded. Bachelor's degrees are awarded in AGRICULTURE (environmental studies), BIOLOGICAL SCIENCE (biochemistry, biology/biological science, and nutrition), BUSINESS (accounting, apparel and accessories marketing, banking and finance, business administration and management, business economics, fashion merchandising, hospitality management services, hotel/motel and restaurant management, human resources, management information systems, marketing management, marketing/retailing/merchandising, retailing, and supply chain management), COMMUNICATIONS AND THE ARTS (advertising, applied music, art history, art, art history and appreciation, broadcasting, communications, dance, design, digital media, dramatic arts, English, English literature, film, television and digital media, graphic design, information technology, Italian, jazz, journalism, keyboard - piano concentration, literature, media arts, music, music composition, music history and appreciation, music performance, music theory and composition, musical theater, painting, percussion, performing arts, photography, piano/organ, piano performance, printmaking, public relations, Spanish, sports media, strings, studio art, technical and business writing, telecommunications, theatre acting, theatre arts, theatre production, theatre studies, vocal performance, voice, vocal music education, and winds), COMPUTER AND PHYSICAL SCIENCE (actuarial mathematics, applied mathematics, astronomy and physics, chemistry, computer programming, computer science, digital arts/technology, geology, information sciences and systems, mathematics, physical sciences, physics, and statistics), EDUCATION (art education, childhood education, early childhood education, education, English education, general studies, health education, mathematics education, middle school education, music education, physical education, physical science secondary school education, science education, secondary education, social science education, social studies education, social studies secondary school education, Spanish adolescense education, special education, and vocational education), ENGINEERING AND ENVIRONMENTAL DESIGN (chemical engineering, civil engineering, civil engineering technology, computer technology, electrical/electronics engineering, electrical/electronics engineering technology, engineering, graphic and printing production, industrial engineering, mechanical engineering, and mechanical engineering technology), HEALTH PROFESSIONS (allied health, clinical science, dental hygiene, exercise science, nursing, nursing home administration, predentistry, premedicine, preoptometry, preosteopathy, preveterinary science, public health, and respiratory therapy), SOCIAL SCIENCE (anthropology, child care/child and family studies, criminal justice, dietetics, early childhood studies, economics, family/consumer studies, food science, forensic studies, geography, gerontology, history, Italian studies, law enforcement and corrections, philosophy, philosophy and religion, political science/government, prelaw, psychology, religion, social studies, social work, sociology, and Spanish studies). Teacher education, criminal justice, and biological sciences have the largest enrollments.

ACTIVITIES: 2% of men belong to 6 national fraternities; 3% of women belong to 5 national sororities. There are 191 groups on campus, including art, band, cheerleading, choir, chorale, chorus, computers, dance, drama, engineering, environmental, ethnic, film, forensics, honors, international, jazz band, LGBT, literary magazine, marching band, musical theater, newspaper, opera, orchestra, pep band, photography, political, professional, radio and TV, religious, social, social service, student government, and symphony. Popular campus events include Organizational Fair, Greek Sing, Homecoming and Welcome Week, Martin Luther King Jr., Breakfast, and Cinco de Mayo. **Sports:** There are 8 intercollegiate sports for men and 10 for women, and 9 intramural sports for men and 8 for women. Facilities include a student recreation and wellness center, which has more than 140 pieces of strength and conditioning equipment, a rock climbing wall, volleyball, basketball, within the multipurpose sports forum, which contains four courts. Other facilities include aerobic studios, indoor track, meditation studio. fields for football, softball, soccer, and baseball, batting cages, and a putting green. **Graduates:** From July 1, 2015 to June 30, 2016, 1632 bachelor's degrees were awarded. The most popular majors were criminal justice (6%), general studies (6%), and nursing (6%). 157 companies recruited on campus in 2015-2016. In an average class, 2% graduate in 3 years or less, 11% graduate in 4 years or less, 25% graduate in 5 years or less, and 31% graduate in 6 years or less.

SERVICES: Counseling and information services are available, as is tutoring in most subjects, reader service for the blind, and remedial math, reading, and writing. A foreign language lab is also available. **Library/Resources:** The library contains 699,998 volumes, 957,886 microform items, 33,581 audio/video tapes/CDs/DVDs, and subscribes to 42,590 periodicals including electronic. Computerized library services include interlibrary loans, database searching, Internet access, and Wi-Fi capability. Special learning facilities include an art gallery, natural history museum, planetarium, radio station, a center for historic preservation, university archives and special collections, and medical museum, art museum and a planetarium. **Physically Challenged Students:** 98% of the campus is accessible. Facilities include wheelchair ramps, elevators, special parking, specially equipped restrooms, special class scheduling, lowered drinking fountains, and special housing. **Special:** YSU offers co-op programs in a variety of majors, as well as internships, work study, dual majors, credit for military experience, nondegree study, honors degree programs, distance learning,accelerated degrees, and pass/fail options. Student-designed majors are available through the Individualized Curriculum Program, Washington Semester, study abroad in a variety of countries and cross registration opportunities and accelerated degree program, partnerships with community colleges, The English Language Institute, off-site degree programs, University honors program, 4+1 program Economics and Mathematics, combined BS/MS program in chemistry, online programs. There are 18 national honor societies and a freshman honors program. **Visiting:** There are regularly scheduled orientations for prospective students, including an official academic advising session, registration for classes, and complete overview of the university resources and services. There are guides for informal visits and visitors may sit in on classes. To schedule a visit, contact the Office of Admissions. **Campus Safety and Security:** Measures include 24-hour foot and vehicle patrol, emergency notification system, self-defense education, and security escort services. There are also shuttle buses, emergency telephones, lighted pathways/sidewalks, controlled access to dorms/residences, night security posts in dorms, and concentrated security in the parking lot and other critical areas.

REQUIREMENTS: Students who have a 2.0 H.S. GPA and a 17 or higher

ACT composite, or a SAT combined math and evidenced-based reading and writing score of 910 or higher will be admitted to the University. Students not meeting these requirements may be admitted conditionally. Students who have been out of school for 2 or more years and who are not pursuing a restricted program of study are exempt from test requirements. Graduation from an accredited secondary school or satisfactory scores on the GED are required for all applicants. High school courses recommended are 4 units of English, 4 of math, 3 of science, and 3 of social studies, 2 of foreign language, and 1 of fine or performing arts. A GPA of 2.0 is required. AP and CLEP credits are accepted. A minimum of 120 semester hours must be successfully completed to earn a bachelor's degree, with a minimum GPA of 2.0. At least 60 semester hours must be completed in courses numbered 2600 or higher; at least 48 of these 60 hours must be in courses numbered 3700 or higher. All students must fulfill core requirements including requirements in English, speech, and math. **Procedure:** Freshmen are admitted in the fall, spring, and summer. Entrance exams should be taken during spring of the junior year or fall of the senior year. There are deferred admissions and rolling admissions plans. Early decision applications should be filed by February 15; regular applications, by August 1 for fall entry; December 1 for spring entry; and April 15 for summer entry, along with a $45 fee. Notification is sent on a rolling basis. Applications are accepted online. **Transfer Students:** 976 transfer students enrolled in 2015-2016. Transfer applicants in good standing at the last institution attended with an aggregate cumulative point average of 2.0 or higher for all courses taken at other colleges or universities are admitted in good standing. Those with an aggregate cumulative point average of less than 2.0 or on probation may be considered for probationary transfer if their overall academic record, including high school grades and test scores, indicate potential success. Applicants suspended or dismissed from other institutions are not eligible for consideration (without appeal to the Office of Undergraduate Admission) until at least 1 semester has passed following the term in which the suspension occurred. 30 of 120 credits required for the bachelor's degree must be completed at YSU. **International Students:** There are 196 international students enrolled. The school actively recruits these students. They must take the TOEFL with a minimum score of 500 on the paper-based TOEFL (PBT) or 61 on the Internet-based version (iBT) or take the MELAB, with a minimum score of 80 is required.

ADMISSIONS: 95% of the 2016-2017 applicants were accepted. The SAT scores for the 2016-2017 freshman class were: Critical Reading-- 59% below 500, 29% between 500 and 599, 10% between 600 and 699, and 2% between 700 and 800. Math-- 53% below 500, 33% between 500 and 599, 12% between 600 and 699, and 2% between 700 and 800. Writing-- 70% below 500, 22% between 500 and 599, 7% between 600 and 699, and 1% between 700 and 800. The ACT scores were 18% between 12 and 17, 51% between 18 and 23, 26% between 24 and 29, and 5% above 30. 26% of the current freshmen were in the top fifth of their class; 52% were in the top two fifths. 77 freshmen graduated first in their class. **Admissions Contact:** Sue Davis, Director, Admissions. Email: *enroll@ysu.edu* Web: *www.ysu.edu*

FINANCIAL AID: In 2016-2017, 94% of all full-time freshmen and 92% of continuing full-time students received some form of financial aid. 74% of all full-time freshmen and 72% of continuing full-time students received need-based aid. The average freshman award was $10,155. 18% of undergraduate students work part-time. The average financial indebtedness of the 2016 graduate was $21,439. YSU is a member of CSS. The college's own financial statement are required. The FAFSA code is 003145. The deadline for filing freshman financial aid applications for fall entry is December 1.

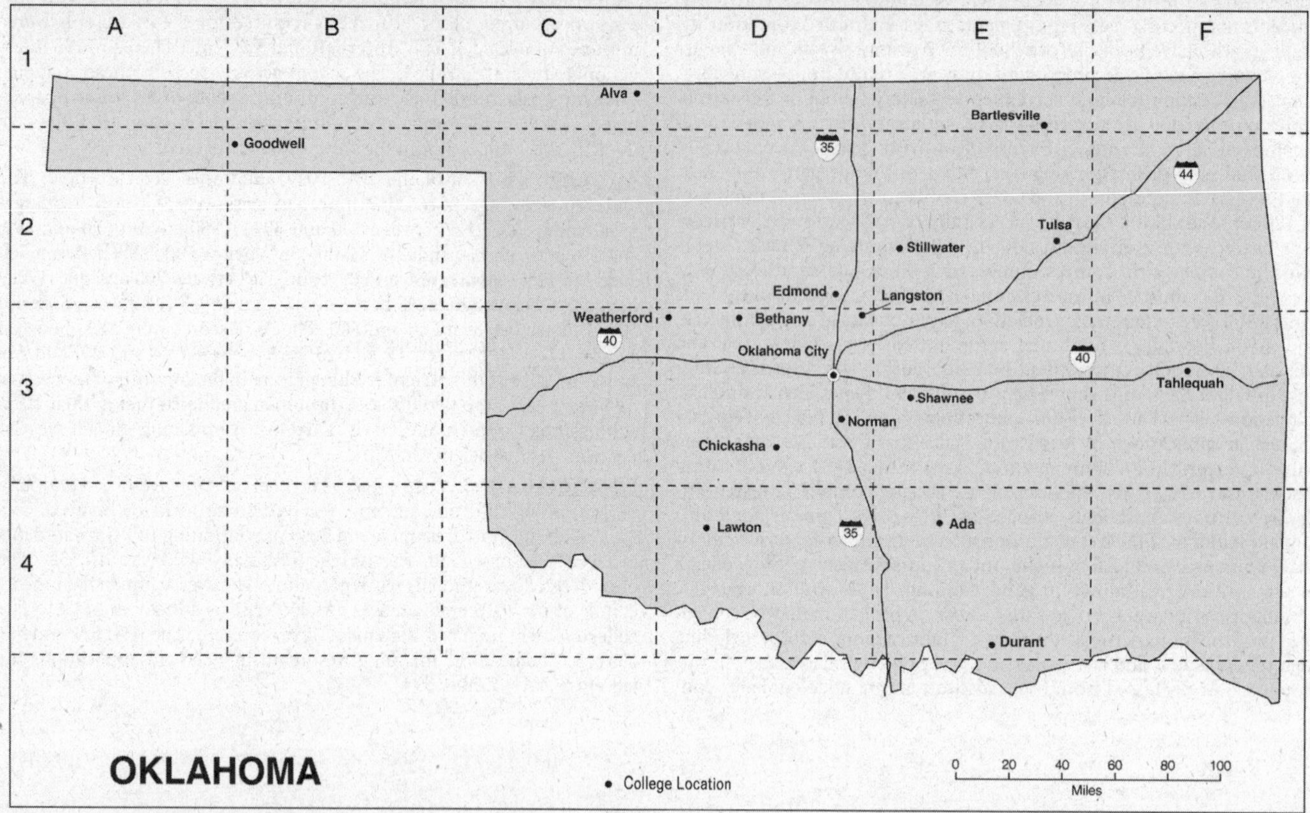

CAMERON UNIVERSITY *(The complete profile is made available exclusively on our website, www.barronspac.com)*

EAST CENTRAL UNIVERSITY — E-4
www.ecok.edu

Ada, OK 74820 — **(580) 332-8000**

Fax: (580) 559-5432
Full-time: 1213 men, 1757 women
Part-time: 226 men, 441 women
Graduate: 254 men, 537 women
Year: semesters, summer session
Room & Board: $6512
ACT: 22
Application Deadline: open

Email: scooper@ecok.edu
Faculty: n/av
Ph.D.s: 65%
Student/Faculty: 19 to 1
Tuition: $6132 ($13,512)
Freshman Class: 962 applied, 935 accepted, 605 enrolled
CEEB CODE: 6186
COMPETITIVE

East Central University, founded in 1909, is a publicly funded institution offering undergraduate programs in liberal arts and sciences, education, business, and health-related fields, and graduate programs in education, human resources, psychology. Figures in the above capsule and in this profile are approximate. There are 4 undergraduate schools and 1 graduate school. In addition to regional accreditation, ECU has baccalaureate program accreditation with ACBSP, CSWE, NASM, NCATE, and NLN. The 140-acre campus is in a small town 90 miles south of Oklahoma City.

STUDENT LIFE: 93% of undergraduates are from Oklahoma. Others are from 28 states, 32 foreign countries, and Canada. 98% are from public schools. 58% are White; 16% American Indian/Alaska Native; 9% two or more races; 6% Foreign; 4% African American; 4% Hispanic; 2% race unknown; 1% Asian American. **Female To Male Ratio:** 1.6:1. The average age of freshmen is 18; all undergraduates, 23. 33% remain to graduate. **Housing:** 1204 students can be accommodated in college housing, which includes single-sex and coed on-campus apartments and married student housing, special-interest houses, fraternity houses, sorority houses, living and learning communities: honors, athletic, music and general housing. On-campus housing is available on a first-come and first-served basis. 93% of students live on campus. Alcohol is not permitted. All students may keep cars.

FACULTY/CLASSROOMS: 51% of faculty are male; 49% are female. 97% teach undergraduates, 50% do research, and 50% do both. Graduate students teach 3% of introductory courses.

PROGRAMS OF STUDY: ECU confers B.A., B.S., B.G.S., B.S.Ed. and B.S.W. degrees. Master's degrees are also awarded. Bachelor's degrees are awarded in BIOLOGICAL SCIENCE (biology/biological science), BUSINESS (accounting, banking and finance, business administration and management, recreation and leisure services, and retailing), COMMUNICATIONS AND THE ARTS (advertising, art, communications, dramatic arts, English, music, piano/organ, speech/debate/rhetoric, and voice), COMPUTER AND PHYSICAL SCIENCE (applied mathematics, chemistry, computer science, mathematics, and physics), EDUCATION (art education, athletic training, business education, early childhood education, elementary education, English education, mathematics education, music education, physical education, and special education), ENGINEERING AND ENVIRONMENTAL DESIGN (cartography), HEALTH PROFESSIONS (environmental health science, exercise science, medical technology, and nursing), SOCIAL SCIENCE (counseling/psychology, criminal justice, family/consumer resource management, family/consumer studies, history, human services, liberal arts/general studies, Native American studies, political science/government, prelaw, psychology, social work, and sociology). Nursing, accounting, and biology have the largest enrollments.

ACTIVITIES: 2% of men belong to 1 local and 3 national fraternities; 2% of women belong to 3 national sororities. There are 88 groups on campus, including art, band, cheerleading, choir, chorale, chorus, computers, dance, debate, drama, drill team, environmental, ethnic, film, forensics, honors, international, jazz band, LGBT, literary magazine, marching band, musical theater, newspaper, nontraditional students, photography, political, professional, religious, social, social service, and student government. Popular campus events include Homecoming, concerts, plays, and movie series. **Sports:** There are 6 intercollegiate sports for men and 7 for women, and 10 intramural sports for men and 10 for women. Facilities include an indoor swimming pool, fitness/aerobics center, tennis, basketball, and racquetball courts, a weight room, football, soccer, baseball, and softball fields, indoor and outdoor tracks. **Graduates:** From July 1, 2015 to June 30, 2016, 686 bachelor's degrees were awarded. The most popular majors were business/marketing, health professions and related programs, and public administration and social sciences.

SERVICES: Counseling and information services are available, as is tutoring in every subject. There is a reader service for the blind, and remedial math, reading, and writing. Interpreters for the deaf, note taking/typing, and tape transcription are also available. **Library/ Resources:** The library contains 264,524 volumes, 355,809 microform items, and 11,302 audio/video tapes/CDs/DVDs, and subscribes to 40,969 periodicals including electronic. Computerized library services include interlibrary loans, database searching, Internet access, and Wi-Fi capability. Special learning facilities include an art gallery, and an observatory. **Physically Challenged Students:** All of the campus is accessible. Facilities include wheelchair ramps, elevators, special parking, specially equipped restrooms, special class scheduling, lowered drinking fountains, lowered telephones, and special housing. **Special:** The school offers co-op programs with the Ardmore Higher Education Center and is a member of the National Student Exchange Program. Internships are available in human resources, environmental health, political science, office technology, mass communications, and cartography. Students may participate in a work-study program with the Veterans Administration. Nondegree study, student designed majors, credit for military experience, and study abroad are available. The school offers special rates for nonresidents from approved states who wish to major in specialized fields. There are 9 national honor societies and a freshman honors program. **Visiting:** There are regularly scheduled orientations for prospective students. There are guides for informal visits. To schedule a visit, contact the Student Development Office. **Campus Safety and Security:** Measures include 24-hour foot and vehicle patrol, emergency notification system, self-defense education, security escort services, emergency telephones, and lighted pathways/sidewalks.

REQUIREMENTS: The ACT is required, with a minimum composite score of 20. The SAT will be accepted in place of the ACT. Applicants must be graduates of an accredited secondary school or have the GED. High school courses must include 4 years of English, 3 years of math, and 3 years of science (1 year must be a lab), 3 years of history and citizenship skills, and 2 years of subjects previously listed or selected from computer science, foreign language, or any Advanced Placement course except courses in the fine arts. ECU requires applicants to be in the upper 50% of their class. A GPA of 2.7 is required. AP and CLEP credits are accepted. To graduate, students must complete a minimum of 124 credit hours with a minimum GPA of 2.0. 60 hours must be from a 4-year college/university. At least 15 of his/her last semester before graduation or at least 50 percent of the hours required by the major must be earned from East Central University. All students must take 40 hours of upper-level courses, as well as 45 hours in general studies, and must meet computer proficiency requirements. **Procedure:** Freshmen are admitted to all sessions. Entrance exams should be taken during the junior or senior year of high school. Application deadlines are open. Application fee is $20. Applications are accepted online. **Transfer Students:** 312 transfer students enrolled in 2015-2016. Applicants having fewer than 24 credit hours must meet the criteria for entering freshmen. The required minimum GPA for transfer students is 2.6. 30 of 124 credits required for the bachelor's degree must be completed at ECU. **International Students:** There are 218 international students enrolled. The school actively recruits these students. They must take the TOEFL with a minimum score of 500 on the paper-based TOEFL (PBT) or 61 on the Internet-based version (iBT). They must also take the SAT or ACT.

ADMISSIONS: 97% of the 2016-2017 applicants were accepted. **Admissions Contact:** Pamla Armstrong, Registrar and Director of Admissions. Email: *bjechard@ecok.edu* Web: *www.ecok.edu*

FINANCIAL AID: The college's own financial statement, and federal tax returns are required. The FAFSA code is 003154. The priority date for freshman financial aid applications for fall entry is July 1.

LANGSTON UNIVERSITY — D-3

www.lunet.edu

Langston, OK 73050 — **(405) 466-3224**

Fax: (405) 466-3381	**Email:** admissions@langstron.edu
Full-time: 1290 men, 1920 women	**Faculty:** 105
Part-time: 290 men, 520 women	**Ph.D.s:** 50%
Graduate: 20 men, 40 women	**Student/Faculty:** 31 to 1
Year: semesters, summer session	**Tuition:** $5042 ($12,370)
Room & Board: $9272	**Freshman Class:** n/av
SAT or ACT: required	**CEEB CODE:** 6361
Application Deadline: August 10	**COMPETITIVE**

Langston University, founded in 1897, is a multiracial, public institution offering programs in liberal arts, business, allied health, and teacher preparation. The figures in above capsule and in this profile are approximate. There is 1 undergraduate school. In addition to regional accreditation, Langston has baccalaureate program accreditation with ADA, APTA, NCATE, and NLN. The 40-acre campus is in a rural area 45 miles from Oklahoma City. Including any residence halls, there are 20 buildings.

STUDENT LIFE: 66% of undergraduates are from Oklahoma. Others are from states. 98% are from public schools. 50% are White; 50% African American. **Female To Male Ratio:** 1.6:1. 65% remain to graduate. **Housing:** 676 students can be accommodated in college housing, which includes dorms and married student housing. All students may keep cars. Alcohol is not permitted.

FACULTY/CLASSROOMS: All teach undergraduates. No introductory courses are taught by graduate students.

PROGRAMS OF STUDY: Langston confers B.A., B.B.A., B.S., B.S.Ed. and B.S.N. degrees. Associate and master's degrees are also awarded. Bachelor's degrees are awarded in AGRICULTURE (agricultural economics and animal science), BIOLOGICAL SCIENCE (biology/ biological science and nutrition), BUSINESS (accounting, business administration and management, and management science), COMMUNICATIONS AND THE ARTS (dramatic arts, English, music, and speech/debate/rhetoric), COMPUTER AND PHYSICAL SCIENCE (chemistry, computer science, and mathematics), EDUCATION (business education, elementary education, home economics education, industrial arts education, mathematics education, physical education, and science education), ENGINEERING AND ENVIRONMENTAL DESIGN (industrial engineering technology), HEALTH PROFESSIONS (health care administration, medical laboratory technology, nursing, and physical therapy), SOCIAL SCIENCE (criminal justice, early childhood studies, economics, gerontology, history, home economics, psychology, social science, sociology, and urban studies).

ACTIVITIES: 25% of men belong to 4 national fraternities; 30% of women belong to 4 national sororities. There are 30 groups on campus, including band, cheerleading, choir, drama, ethnic, international, jazz band, marching band, newspaper, professional, religious, social service, student government, and yearbook. Popular campus events include Student Theater Productions, and a Performing Arts Series. **Sports:** There are 4 intercollegiate sports for men and 2 for women, and 6 intramural sports for men and 5 for women. Facilities include a gym, tennis courts, a baseball field, and a track.

SERVICES: Counseling and information services are available, as is tutoring in some subjects, and remedial math, reading, and writing. **Library/Resources:** The 6 libraries contain 110,248 volumes, 465,319 microform items, and subscribe to 80 periodicals including electronic. Computerized library services include interlibrary loans. **Physically Challenged Students:** 70% of the campus is accessible. Facilities include wheelchair ramps, elevators, special parking, specially equipped restrooms, and special class scheduling. **Special:** Work-study programs, internships, and nondegree and noncredit study are available. There are 6 national honor societies and a freshman honors program. **Visiting:** There are regularly scheduled orientations for prospective students. There are guides for informal visits, visitors may sit in on classes, and stay overnight.

REQUIREMENTS: The SAT or ACT is required. In general, test scores should place students in the upper 60 percent of Oklahoma high school seniors. Applicants should be graduates of accredited high schools with at least a C average (2.7 on a 4.0 scale) and rank in the upper 60 percent of their graduating classes. Required secondary preparation includes 4 years of English, 3 years of math, and 2 years each of lab science and history, including 1 year of American history. 4 additional academic units, including a foreign language, are strongly recommended. There are alternative admission programs for students with varying backgrounds. Langston requires applicants to be in the upper 50% of their class. A GPA of 2.7 is required. AP and CLEP credits are accepted. To graduate, students must complete a total of 124 semester hours, with a GPA of 2.0. The required general education core consists of 50 credits in English, math, computer science, biological and physical sciences, social science, and health and phys ed. 6 credits are required in American history and government, and all students must complete an internship or field experience. **Procedure:** Freshmen are admitted to all sessions. There is a rolling admissions plan. Applications should be filed by August 10 for fall entry. The fall 2016 application fee was $15. **Transfer Students:** Applicants should be in good standing and have earned at least a C average in previous college work. 30 of 124 credits required for the bachelor's degree must be completed at Langston.

Admissions Contact: Gayle T. Robertson, Director of Admissions and Enrollment Management. Email: *admissions@langstron.edu* Web: *www.lunet.edu*

FINANCIAL AID: In 2016-2017, 70% of all full-time freshmen and continuing full-time students received some form of financial aid. 65% of all full-time freshmen and 60% of continuing full-time students received need-based aid. The average freshman award was $2,800. The CSS/Profile, FFS, SFS, or FAFSA are required. The FAFSA code is 003157. The deadline for filing freshman financial aid applications for fall entry is March 1.

NORTHEASTERN STATE UNIVERSITY F-3

www.nsuok.edu

Tahlequah, OK 74464 | **(918) 456-5511, ext. 2200**

Fax: (918) 458-2342	**Email: nsuinfo@nsuok.edu**
Full-time: 2700 men, 3850 women	**Faculty:** 314
Part-time: 716 men, 1393 women	**Ph.D.s:** 72%
Graduate: 334 men, 743 women	**Student/Faculty:** 21 to 1
Year: semesters, summer session	**Tuition:** $5335 ($11,210)
Room & Board: $3280	**Freshman Class:** 1651 accepted, 1102 enrolled
ACT: 24	**CEEB CODE:** 6485
Application Deadline: open	**VERY COMPETITIVE**

Northeastern State University, founded in 1846, is a public institution offering programs in arts and sciences, professional training, teacher preparation, and business. Figures in the above capsule and in this profile are approximate. There are 4 undergraduate schools and 5 graduate schools. In addition to regional accreditation, NSU has baccalaureate program accreditation with ACBSP, ADA, ASLA, CSWE, NASM, NCATE, and NLN. The 200-acre campus is in a small town 70 miles from Tulsa. Including any residence halls, there are 51 buildings.

STUDENT LIFE: 94% of undergraduates are from Oklahoma. Others are from 34 states, 47 foreign countries, and Canada. 61% are White; 6% African American; 3% Foreign; 28% American Indian/Alaska Native; 1% Asian American; 1% Hispanic. **Female To Male Ratio:** 1.6:1. The average age of freshmen is 19; all undergraduates, 26. 30% do not continue beyond their first year. **Housing:** 1653 students can be accommodated in college housing, which includes single-sex and coed dorms, on-campus apartments, married student housing, special-interest houses. On-campus housing is available on a first-come and first-served basis. 80% of students commute. Alcohol is not permitted. All students may keep cars.

FACULTY/CLASSROOMS: 56% of faculty are male; 44% are female. 90% teach undergraduates. Graduate students teach 5% of introductory courses. The average class size in an introductory lecture is 60; in a laboratory is 24; and in a regular course is 20.

PROGRAMS OF STUDY: NSU confers B.A., B.S., B.A.Ed., B.B.A., B.S.Ed., B.S.Sci.Ed., B.S.N. and B.S.W. degrees. Master's and doctoral degrees are also awarded. Bachelor's degrees are awarded in BIOLOGICAL SCIENCE (biology/biological science), BUSINESS (accounting, banking and finance, business administration and management, and marketing/retailing/merchandising), COMMUNICATIONS AND THE ARTS (advertising, communications, English, fine arts, journalism, music, Spanish, and speech/debate/rhetoric), COMPUTER AND PHYSICAL SCIENCE (chemistry, computer science, information sciences and systems, and mathematics), EDUCATION (art education, early childhood education, elementary education, health education, industrial arts education, music education, science education, secondary education, and special education), HEALTH PROFESSIONS (medical laboratory technology and nursing), SOCIAL SCIENCE (criminal justice, geography, history, political science/government, social science, social work, and sociology). Elementary education, early childhood education, and business are the strongest academically. Administration, psychology, and criminal justice have the largest enrollments.

ACTIVITIES: 5% of men belong to 7 national fraternities; 2% of women belong to 5 national sororities. There are 80 groups on campus, including art, band, cheerleading, choir, chorus, dance, drama, drill team, ethnic, film, honors, international, jazz band, LGBT, literary magazine, marching band, musical theater, newspaper, orchestra, pep band, photography, political, professional, radio and TV, religious, social service, student government, and symphony. Popular campus events include Cherokee Seminaries, Symposium on the American Indian, and Sequoyah Institute Shows. **Sports:** There are 5 intercollegiate sports for men and 5 for women, and 16 intramural sports for men and 16 for women. Facilities include a football stadium, indoor practice facility, exercise/fitness track, baseball field, softball field, tennis courts, soccer fields, baseball field house, soccer/softball field house, basketball gymnasium and a basketball court which is used for academics. **Graduates:** From July 1, 2015 to June 30, 2016, 1404 bachelor's degrees were awarded. 254 companies recruited on campus in 2015-2016.

SERVICES: Counseling and information services are available, as is tutoring in most subjects, and remedial math, reading, and writing. **Library/Resources:** The library contains 400,000 volumes, 766,300 microform items, 8,659 audio/video tapes/CDs/DVDs, and subscribes to 15,000 periodicals including electronic. Computerized library services include interlibrary loans, database searching, Internet access, and Wi-Fi capability. Special learning facilities include a radio station. **Physically Challenged Students:** 70% of the campus is accessible. Facilities include wheelchair ramps, elevators, special parking, specially equipped restrooms, special class scheduling, lowered drinking fountains, lowered telephones, and special housing. **Special:** Internships are offered in business, mass communications, and education. There are 10 national honor societies, a freshman honors program, and 5 departmental honors programs. **Visiting:** There are regularly scheduled orientations for prospective students, including a general campus visit with highlights presented by trained tour guides. Visitors may sit in on classes and stay overnight. To schedule a visit, contact High School and College Relations. **Campus Safety and Security:** Measures include 24-hour foot and vehicle patrol, self-defense education, and security escort services. There are also shuttle buses, emergency telephones, lighted pathways/sidewalks, and a campus security police department.

REQUIREMENTS: The ACT is required, with a minimum composite score of 20. Applicants should be high school graduates or have a GED. Students should have completed 4 years of English, 3 of math, and 2 each of history and science. NSU requires applicants to be in the upper 50% of their class. A GPA of 2.7 is required. AP and CLEP credits are accepted. To graduate, students must complete at least 124 credit hours, with 24 to 50 in the major. General education requirements include 40 hours in language arts, social science, natural science, humanities, and phys ed. Freshman orientation and English proficiency are required. **Procedure:** Freshmen are admitted to all sessions. There is a rolling admissions plan. Application deadlines are open. Notification is sent on a rolling basis. **Transfer Students:** 1404 transfer students enrolled in 2015-2016. Transfer applicants must have a minimum GPA of 2.0, with 24 transfer hours completed, and be in good standing at the last institution attended. 30 of 124 credits required for the bachelor's degree must be completed at NSU. **International Students:** There are 252 international students enrolled. They must take the TOEFL.

Admissions Contact: Dawn Cain, Director of Admissions. Email: *nsuinfo@nsuok.edu* Web: *www.nsuok.edu*

FINANCIAL AID: In 2016-2017, 86% of all full-time freshmen and 85% of continuing full-time students received some form of financial aid. 67% of all full-time freshmen and 63% of continuing full-time students received need-based aid. 7% of undergraduate students work part-time. Average annual earnings from campus work are $2850. The average financial indebtedness of the 2016 graduate was $17,824. The college's own financial statement is required. The FAFSA code is 003161. The priority date for freshman financial aid applications for fall entry is March 1.

NORTHWESTERN OKLAHOMA STATE UNIVERSITY *(The complete profile is made available exclusively on our website, www.barronspac.com)*

OKLAHOMA BAPTIST UNIVERSITY E-3
www.okbu.edu

Shawnee, OK 74804	(405) 585-5120 (800) 654-3285
Fax: (405) 585-5105	**Email:** admissions@okbu.edu
Full-time: 712 men, 1097 women	**Faculty:** 127
Part-time: 52 men, 45 women	**Ph.D.s:** 74%
Graduate: 29 men, 51 women	**Student/Faculty:** 13 to 1
Year: 4-1-4, summer session	**Tuition:** $25,310
Room & Board: $7010	**Freshman Class:** 4785 applied, 3590 accepted, 556 enrolled
SAT CR/M: 540/530 **ACT:** 23	**CEEB CODE:** 6541
Application Deadline: August 1	**COMPETITIVE**

Oklahoma Baptist University, founded in 1910, is a liberal arts institution affiliated with the Southern Baptist Convention. OBU offers degrees in Christian service, business, nursing, fine arts, telecommunications, teacher education, and the traditional liberal arts areas. Figures in the above capsule and in this profile are approximate. There are 6 undergraduate schools and 1 graduate school. In addition to regional accreditation, OBU has baccalaureate program accreditation with ACBSP, NASM, NCATE, and CCNE. The 200-acre campus is in a small town Shawnee, Oklahoma, 35 miles east of Oklahoma City, 90 miles southwest of Tulsa, and 200 miles from Dallas/Forth Worth. Including any residence halls, there are 36 buildings.

STUDENT LIFE: 66% of undergraduates are from Oklahoma. Others are from 37 states, and 35 foreign countries. 79% are from public schools. 69% are White; 7% two or more races; 6% African American; 6% American Indian/Alaska Native; 4% Foreign; 4% race unknown; 3% Hispanic; 1% Asian American. 72% are Protestant; 26% claim no religious affiliation. **Female To Male Ratio:** 1.5:1. The average age of freshmen is 18; all undergraduates, 20. 21% do not continue beyond their first year; 53% remain to graduate. **Housing:** 1634 students can be accommodated in college housing, which includes single-sex dorms, on-campus apartments, and married student housing. On-campus housing is guaranteed for all 4 years. 94% of students live on campus; of those, 75% remain on campus on weekends. All students may keep cars. Alcohol is not permitted.

FACULTY/CLASSROOMS: 64% of faculty are male; 36% are female. All teach undergraduates. No introductory courses are taught by graduate students. The average class size in an introductory lecture is 25; in a laboratory is 19; and in a regular course is 15.

PROGRAMS OF STUDY: OBU confers B.A., B.S., B.B.A., B.F.A., B.M., B.M.A., B.Mus.Ed., and B.S.E. degrees. Associate and master's degrees are also awarded. Bachelor's degrees are awarded in BIOLOGICAL SCIENCE (biology/biological science, forensic science, and physiology), BUSINESS (accounting, banking and finance, business administration and management, business information systems, international business, management, marketing, recreational facilities management, and sports management), COMMUNICATIONS AND THE ARTS (applied communication, art, broadcasting, church music, communication studies, communications, conducting, congregational and youth ministries, creative writing, digital media, dramatic arts, English, fine arts, graphic design, information technology, instrumental performance, instrumental music education, journalism, journalism - news & information, English and Professional Communication, modern language, music, piano pedagogy, piano performance, recreation administration, Spanish, speech/debate/rhetoric, telecommunications, and vocal music education), COMPUTER AND PHYSICAL SCIENCE (chemistry, chemistry/forensic chemistry, computer information systems, computer science, information sciences and systems, mathematics, natural sciences, and physics), EDUCATION (early childhood education, education, elementary education, English secondary education, English education, global studies, health and physical education, music education, physical education, science education, secondary education, social studies education, special education, and spec ed/early child dual prog), HEALTH PROFESSIONS (allied health, kinesiology, nursing, physical therapy, and premedicine), SOCIAL SCIENCE (anthropology, biblical languages, biblical studies, child care/child and family studies, child psychology/development, Christian studies, community psychology, counseling/psychology, criminal justice, crosscultural studies, history, interdisciplinary studies, international relations, pastoral studies, philosophy, philosophy and religion, political science/government, prelaw, psychology, religion, religious studies, social science, family studies/soc serv/marriage family, social work, sociology, and youth ministry). Elementary education, pre-allied health and nursing have the largest enrollments.

ACTIVITIES: There are 85 groups on campus, including art, band, cheerleading, choir, chorale, chorus, computers, debate, drama, environmental, ethnic, film, honors, international, jazz band, literary magazine, marching band, musical theater, newspaper, opera, orchestra, pep band, photography, political, professional, radio and TV, religious, social, social service, student government, and yearbook. Popular campus events include Be a Bison Day, Night on the Hill, and Fall, Winter, or Spring Preview Day. **Sports:** There are 10 intercollegiate sports for men and 12 for women, and 18 intramural sports for men and 18 for women. Facilities include a sports complex houses with an arena. The recreation and wellness center, includes basketball/volleyball courts, a rock climbing wall, exercise and fitness equipment, weight rooms, a swimming pool, a walking track, an all-weather track, and football, baseball, softball, soccer, lacrosse and sand volleyball facilities. **Graduates:** From July 1, 2015 to June 30, 2016, 339 bachelor's degrees were awarded. The most popular majors were health profession & related programs (22%), education (16%), and theology/religion (12%). In an average class, 44% graduate in 4 years or less and 52% graduate in 6 years or less. Of the 2015 graduating class, 19% were enrolled in graduate school within 6 months of graduation, and 77% were employed.

SERVICES: Counseling and information services are available, as is tutoring in most subjects. There is also a reader service for the blind, and remedial math, reading, and writing. **Library/Resources:** The library contains 177,215 volumes, 179,443 microform items, and 11,000 audio/video tapes/CDs/DVDs. Computerized library services include interlibrary loans, database searching, Internet access, and Wi-Fi capability. Special learning facilities include an art gallery, planetarium, radio station, TV station, a language lab, and a Biblical research library. **Physically Challenged Students:** 95% of the campus is accessible. Facilities include wheelchair ramps, elevators, special parking, specially equipped restrooms, lowered drinking fountains, lowered telephones, and special housing. **Special:** OBU offers co-op programs in business, and a 3-2 engineering degree with Oklahoma State University. Students may study abroad in 15 countries in Europe, Central and South America, Asia, and Africa. Internships in several fields, student-designed majors, including an interdisciplinary program in humanities, and pass/fail options are available. There are 2 national honor societies and a freshman honors program. **Visiting:** There are regularly scheduled orientations for prospective students, including tours, faculty visits, and general information sessions. There are guides for informal visits, visitors may sit in on classes, and stay overnight. To schedule a visit, contact the OBU Admissions Office. **Campus Safety and Security:** Measures include 24-hour foot and vehicle patrol, emergency notification system, self-defense education, security escort services, emergency telephones, lighted pathways/sidewalks, and controlled access to dorms/residences.

REQUIREMENTS: Admission is granted to students with composite scores of 950 on the SAT or 20 on the ACT, with a 3.0 GPA. Graduation from an accredited secondary school or satisfactory scores on the GED are required for admission. The recommended high school courses should include 4 units of English, 3 units of math, and 2 units each of social studies, lab science, and a foreign language. OBU requires applicants to be in the upper 50% of their class. A GPA of 3.0 is required. AP and CLEP credits are accepted. Important factors in the admissions decision are advanced placement or honors courses, recommendations by school officials, and leadership record. To graduate, students must complete a total of 128 credit hours, including 30 to 48 hours in the major, with a 2.0 GPA. Students are also required to complete 6 credits each of English, literature, history, science, Bible, social sciences, and language; 3 each in math, fine arts, and comparative civilization; 2 each in speech, philosophy, and phys ed; and 1 in computer literacy. **Procedure:** Freshmen are admitted to all sessions. Entrance exams should be taken during the spring of the junior year. There are deferred admissions and rolling admissions plans. Applications should be filed by August 1 for fall entry; December 15 for winter entry; January 15 for spring entry; and

May 15 for summer entry. Applications are accepted online. **Transfer Students:** 93 transfer students enrolled in 2015-2016. Transfer students must have a GPA of 2.5 for all college work attempted. 32 of 128 credits required for the bachelor's degree must be completed at OBU. **International Students:** There are 77 international students enrolled. The school actively recruits these students. They must take the TOEFL with a minimum score of 550 on the paper-based TOEFL (PBT) or 61 on the Internet-based version (iBT) or take the MELAB. They must also take the SAT or ACT, scoring 20.

ADMISSIONS: 75% of the 2016-2017 applicants were accepted. The SAT scores for the 2016-2017 freshman class were: Critical Reading-- 47% below 500, 31% between 500 and 599, 16% between 600 and 699, and 6% between 700 and 800. Math-- 45% below 500, 41% between 500 and 599, 8% between 600 and 699, and 7% between 700 and 800. The ACT scores were 8% between 12 and 17, 52% between 18 and 23, 33% between 24 and 29, and 7% above 30. 49% of the current freshmen were in the top fifth of their class; 90% were in the top two fifths. **Admissions Contact:** Bruce Perkins, AVP of Enrollment Management. Email: *admissions@okbu.edu* Web: *www.okbu.edu*

FINANCIAL AID: In 2016-2017, 78% of all full-time freshmen and 72% of continuing full-time students received some form of financial aid. 62% of all full-time freshmen and continuing full-time students received need-based aid. The average freshman award was $23,031. Need-based scholarships or need-based grants averaged $8,557; and need-based self-help aid (loans and jobs) averaged $4,485. 61% of undergraduate students work part-time. Average annual earnings from campus work are $2000. The average financial indebtedness of the 2016 graduate was $24,451. The FAFSA code is 003164. The priority date for freshman financial aid applications for fall entry is April 1.

OKLAHOMA CHRISTIAN UNIVERSITY D-3

www.oc.edu

Oklahoma City, OK 73136

(405) 425-5050
(800) 877-5010

Fax: (405) 425-5069

Email: admissions@oc.edu

Full-time: 924 men, 921 women	**Faculty:** 99
Part-time: 78 men, 51 women	**Ph.D.s:** 70%
Graduate: 414 men, 182 women	**Student/Faculty:** 13 to 1
Year: semesters, summer session	**Tuition:** $20,770
Room & Board: $6880	**Freshman Class:** 2256 applied, 1372 accepted, 464 enrolled
SAT CR/M/W: 540/560/520 **ACT:** 25	**CEEB CODE:** 6086
Application Deadline: September 1	**VERY COMPETITIVE**

Oklahoma Christian University, founded in 1950, is a private, liberal arts institution affiliated with Churches of Christ. Ranked as one of the best universities in the western region of the United States Oklahoma Christian offers undergraduate programs in more than 60 fields of study, an undergraduate Honors Program, ABET accredited programs in mechanical, electrical and computer engineering, and graduate programs in accountancy, business administration, computer science, engineering, Christian ministry, divinity and theological studies. There are 5 undergraduate schools and 3 graduate schools. In addition to regional accreditation, OCU has baccalaureate program accreditation with ABET, ACBSP, NASM, NCATE, CIDA, and CCNE. The 200-acre campus is in a suburban area on the north side of Oklahoma City. Including any residence halls, there are 33 buildings.

STUDENT LIFE: 57% of undergraduates are from out of state, mostly the Midwest. Students are from 37 states, 34 foreign countries, and Canada. 9% are African American; 9% Foreign; 71% White; 6% Asian American; 6% American Indian/Alaska Native; 6% Hispanic. 28% are Protestant. **Male To Female Ratio:** 1.2:1. The average age of freshmen is 18; all undergraduates, 20. 21% do not continue beyond their first year; 47% remain to graduate. **Housing:** 1756 students can be accommodated in college housing, which includes single-sex dorms, on-campus apartments, married student housing, and honors houses. On-campus housing is guaranteed for all 4 years, is available on a first-come, and first-served basis. 82% of students live on campus. Alcohol is not permitted. All students may keep cars.

FACULTY/CLASSROOMS: 64% of faculty are male; 36% are female. All teach undergraduates, 10% do research, and 10% do both. No introductory courses are taught by graduate students. The average class size in an introductory lecture is 19; in a laboratory is 15; and in a regular course is 21.

PROGRAMS OF STUDY: OCU confers B.A., B.S., B.B.A., B.F.A., B.M.E., B.S.C.E., B.S.E., B.S.E.E., B.S.N., and B.S.M.E. degrees. Master's degrees are also awarded. Bachelor's degrees are awarded in BIOLOGICAL SCIENCE (biochemistry, biology/biological science, and forensic science), BUSINESS (accounting, banking and finance, business administration and management, business administration international, business administration, management, operations, business administration marketing, finance, international business management, marketing management, and marketing/retailing/merchandising), COMMUNICATIONS AND THE ARTS (advertising, art, broadcasting, communications, creative writing, design, English, English Writing, game design and development, instrumental performance, journalism, music, photography, public relations, Spanish, visual design, vocal performance, and writing), COMPUTER AND PHYSICAL SCIENCE (chemistry, computer game design/development, computer science, information sciences and systems, and mathematics), EDUCATION (early childhood education, elementary education, English education, mathematics education, middle school education, music education, physical education, science education, social science education, social studies education, sports and wellness studies, and teaching English as a second/foreign language (TESOL/TEFOL)), ENGINEERING AND ENVIRONMENTAL DESIGN (computer engineering, electrical and computer engineering, electrical/electronics engineering, interior design, and mechanical engineering), HEALTH PROFESSIONS (biology, medical laboratory technology, and nursing), SOCIAL SCIENCE (biblical studies, child care/child and family studies, history, history and political science, interdisciplinary studies, liberal arts/general studies, ministries, missions, prelaw, psychology, religious education, social studies, and youth ministry). Engineering programs, gaming & animation, accounting, nursing, pre-professional science programs leading to medical school, etc. are the strongest academically. Business, education, and engineering have the largest enrollments.

ACTIVITIES: 31% of men belong to 5 local fraternities; 39% of women belong to 6 local sororities. There are 56 groups on campus, including art, band, cheerleading, choir, chorale, chorus, communications, computers, debate, drama, ethnic, film, honors, international, jazz band, literary magazine, musical theater, newspaper, opera, orchestra, pep band, photography, political, professional, radio and TV, religious, social, social service, student government, symphony, and yearbook. Popular campus events include Spring Sing, Homecoming, Winter Wonderland Week, Earn Your Wings, and McGaw Lecture Series. **Sports:** There are 7 intercollegiate sports for men and 7 for women, and 10 intramural sports for men and 10 for women. Facilities include basketball courts, a swimming pool, baseball, softball, intramural football, soccer fields, a track and field facility, tennis courts, a fitness center, and an auxiliary gym. **Graduates:** From July 1, 2015 to June 30, 2016, 386 bachelor's degrees were awarded. The most popular majors were business (17%), engineering (14%), and visual and performing arts (12%). 50 companies recruited on campus in 2015-2016. In an average class, 40% graduate in 4 years or less, 51% graduate in 5 years or less, and 47% graduate in 6 years or less.

SERVICES: Counseling and information services are available, as is tutoring in some subjects, such as English, math, speech, chemistry, physics, business, education, and computer science. There is also remedial math, reading, and writing. **Library/Resources:** The library contains 195,754 volumes, 682,861 microform items, 6,775 audio/video tapes/CDs/DVDs, and subscribes to 42,000 periodicals including electronic. Computerized library services include interlibrary loans, database searching, Internet access, and Wi-Fi capability. Special learning facilities include an art gallery, radio station, TV station, journalism lab, audio visulization lab. **Physically Challenged Students:** 98% of the campus is accessible. Facilities include wheelchair ramps, elevators, special parking, specially equipped restrooms, special class scheduling, lowered drinking fountains, lowered telephones, and special housing. **Special:** OC offers a wide range of undergraduate degrees and many graduate programs in Accounting, Business, Theology, Ministry, and Engineering. Our ABET accredited engineering complements a full spectrum of majors across the arts, sciences, and humanities. Internships and practice are commonly required or offered in the nearby city. Students may study abroad in Austria, Japan, China, and Honduras. Major-minor combinations and interdisciplinary studies options help students combine fields such as business, mass communications, family life, pre-law, advertising design, speech communication, education, English, music, math and others. An interdisciplinary Honors program serves students with high ACT/SAT scores. Many chapters of disciplinary societies, such as Sigma Tau Delta or Phil Alpha Theta achieve national awards for excellence. Cross-registration can be offered with the University of Central Oklahoma. Students can apply to participate in the Best Semester programs offered by the Council for Christian Colleges and Universities. There are 8 national honor societies, a freshman honors program, and 18 departmental honors programs. **Visiting:** There are regularly scheduled orientations for prospective students, consisting of comprehensive campus overview including academic conversations. There are guides for informal visits, visitors may sit in on classes, and stay overnight. To schedule a visit, contact Daniella Rayner. **Campus Safety and Security:** Measures include 24-hour foot and vehicle patrol, emergency notification system, security escort services, emergency telephones, lighted pathways/sidewalks, controlled access to dorms/residences, and campus police.

REQUIREMENTS: High school graduates with college prep courses or satisfactory scores on the GED are required for admission. Students must also submit an ACT or SAT test score and cumulative high school GPA. An interview is required for some students not meeting minimum test score thresholds. AP and CLEP credits are accepted. To graduate, students must have a minimum of 126 credit hours, including 30 to 104 in the major, with a GPA of 2.0. All students must complete 55 hours in our general education area, which includes courses in American history, behavioral science, Bible, communication, English, fine arts, foreign language, liberal arts, literature, mathematics, music, non-western civilization, political science, science, social science, and western civilization. **Procedure:** Freshmen are admitted to all sessions. Entrance exams should be taken By August 20. There are deferred admissions and rolling admissions plans. Applications should be filed by September 1 for fall entry, along with a $25 fee. Notification is sent on a rolling basis. Application fees are waived if application is completed online. **Transfer Students:** 96 transfer students enrolled in 2015-2016. Applicants must be eligible to return to the school from which they are transferring. 30 of 126 credits required for the bachelor's degree must be completed at OC. **International Students:** There are 151 international students enrolled. The school actively recruits these students. They must take the TOEFL with a minimum score of 500 on the paper-based TOEFL (PBT) or 61 on the Internet-based version (iBT).

ADMISSIONS: 61% of the 2016-2017 applicants were accepted. The SAT scores for the 2016-2017 freshman class were: Critical Reading-- 42% below 500, 25% between 500 and 599, 26% between 600 and 699, and 7% between 700 and 800. Math-- 37% below 500, 36% between 500 and 599, 18% between 600 and 699, and 9% between 700 and 800. Writing-- 49% below 500, 33% between 500 and 599, 14% between 600 and 699, and 4% between 700 and 800. The ACT scores were 6% below 12, 4% between 12 and 17, 35% between 18 and 23, 41% between 24 and 29, and 18% above 30. 42% of the current freshmen were in the top fifth of their class; 69% were in the top two fifths. There were 7 National Merit finalists. **Admissions Contact:** Jancy Scott, Associate Director of Admissions. Email: *admissions@oc.edu* Web: *www.oc.edu*

FINANCIAL AID: In 2016-2017, 99% of all full-time freshmen and 92% of continuing full-time students received some form of financial aid. 67% of all full-time freshmen and 59% of continuing full-time students received need-based aid. The average freshman award was $24,043. Need-based scholarships or need-based grants averaged $2,964; need-based self-help aid (loans and jobs) averaged $2,752; non-need-based athletic scholarships averaged $6,956; other non-need-based awards and non-need-based scholarships averaged $6,944; and $1,764 from other forms of aid. 39% of undergraduate students work part-time. Average annual earnings from campus work are $1446. The average financial indebtedness of the 2016 graduate was $25,432. The FAFSA code is 003165. The priority date for freshman financial aid applications for fall entry is March 15. The filing deadline for fall entry is August 15.

OKLAHOMA CITY UNIVERSITY D-3

www.okcu.edu

Oklahoma City, OK 73106	**(405) 208-5055** **(800) 633-7242**
Fax: (405) 208-5916	**Email: uadmissions@okcu.edu**
Full-time: 584 men, 994 women	**Faculty:** 194
Part-time: 69 men, 134 women	**Ph.D.s:** 76%
Graduate: 598 men, 635 women	**Student/Faculty:** 11 to 1
Year: semesters, summer session	**Tuition:** $30,726
Room & Board: $9750	**Freshman Class:** 1505 applied, 1020 accepted, 297 enrolled
SAT: required **ACT:** 25	**CEEB CODE:** 6543
Application Deadline: rolling	**VERY COMPETITIVE**

Oklahoma City University, founded in 1904, is a private, comprehensive university affiliated with the United Methodist Church, offering undergraduate and graduate programs in arts and sciences, business, music and performing arts, religion and church vocations, nursing, and law. There are 7 undergraduate schools and 6 graduate schools. In addition to regional accreditation, OCU has baccalaureate program accreditation with AACSB, NASM, NCATE, NLN, AAPL, ACEN, and Oklahoma Commission for Teacher Preparation. The 104-acre campus is in an urban area within Oklahoma City. Including any residence halls, there are 37 buildings.

STUDENT LIFE: 53% of undergraduates are from Oklahoma. Others are from 46 states, 41 foreign countries, and Canada. 88% are from public schools. 8% are Hispanic; 8% two or more races; 61% White; 5% African American; 2% Asian American; 2% American Indian/Alaska Native; 13% Foreign. 54% are Protestant; 29% claim no religious affiliation; 13% Catholic. **Female To Male Ratio:** 1.4:1. The average age of freshmen is 18.3; all undergraduates, 22.3. 20% do not continue beyond their first year; 60% remain to graduate. **Housing:** 1270 students can be accommodated in college housing, which includes single-sex and coed dorms, on-campus apartments, and married student housing. In addition, there are honors houses, special-interest houses, fraternity houses, and learning communities. On-campus housing is guaranteed for all 4 years. 53% of students live on campus. All students may keep cars. Alcohol is not permitted.

FACULTY/CLASSROOMS: 52% of faculty are male; 48% are female. 80% teach undergraduates. No introductory courses are taught by graduate students. The average class size in an introductory lecture is 16 and in a laboratory is 13.

PROGRAMS OF STUDY: OCU confers B.A., B.S., B.F.A., B.M., B.Perf.Arts, B.S.B., B.B.A., B.M., B.M.E., and B.S.N. degrees. Master's and doctoral degrees are also awarded. Bachelor's degrees are awarded in AGRICULTURE (environmental studies), BIOLOGICAL SCIENCE (biochemistry and cell biology), BUSINESS (accounting, banking and finance, business administration and management, management science, and marketing), COMMUNICATIONS AND THE ARTS (acting, advertising, art, broadcasting, church music, communications, dance, English, film arts, French, guitar, instrumental performance, instrumental music education, instrumental music education, music, music composition, photography, piano/organ, piano pedagogy, piano performance, public relations, Spanish, studio art, theatre acting, theatre arts, theater design, theatre production, and vocal performance), COMPUTER AND PHYSICAL SCIENCE (chemistry, mathematics, physics, science, and software engineering), EDUCATION (early childhood education, education, elementary education, music education, and secondary education), HEALTH PROFESSIONS (biology, biomedical science, exercise science, health care administration, nursing, pre-health studies, and premedicine), SOCIAL SCIENCE (addiction studies, behavioral science, economics, history, humanities, liberal arts/general studies, philosophy, philosophy and religion, political science/government, prelaw, psychology, religion, religious education, and sociology). Nursing, business, and performing arts are the strongest academically. Sciences, performing arts, and liberal arts have the largest enrollments.

ACTIVITIES: 25% of men belong to 3 national fraternities; 14% of women belong to 4 national sororities. There are 87 groups on campus, including art, band, cheerleading, choir, chorus, computers, dance, debate, drama, environmental, ethnic, film, honors, international, jazz band, LGBT, literary magazine, musical theater, newspaper, opera, orchestra, pep band, photography, political, professional, radio and TV, religious, social, social service, student government, symphony, and yearbook. Popular campus events include Midnight Breakfast, Movie Night, Oozeball, Homecoming, and Relay for Life. **Sports:** There are 9 intercollegiate sports for men and 11 for women, and 7 intramural sports for men and 7 for women. Facilities include a baseball, softball, and soccer fields, a wellness and activity center which houses basketball, volleyball, and wrestling. **Graduates:** From July 1, 2015 to June 30, 2016, 594 bachelor's degrees were awarded. The most popular majors were liberal arts and sciences (34%), nursing (30%), and business (9%). 102 companies recruited on campus in 2015-2016. In an average class, 49% graduate in 4 years or less, 58% graduate in 5 years or less, and 59% graduate in 6 years or less.

SERVICES: Counseling and information services are available, as is tutoring in most subjects. There is a reader service for the blind, and remedial math, reading, and writing. Also available are writing and learning enhancement centers and a math lab. **Library/Resources:** The 2 libraries contain 327,229 volumes, 635,725 microform items, 16,618 audio/video tapes/CDs/DVDs, and subscribe to 10,976 periodicals including electronic. Computerized library services include interlibrary loans, database searching, Internet access, and Wi-Fi capability. Special learning facilities include an art gallery, radio station, and TV station. **Physically Challenged Students:** 98% of the campus is accessible. Facilities include wheelchair ramps, elevators, special parking, specially equipped restrooms, lowered drinking fountains, and lowered telephones. **Special:** OCU offers internships, a Washington semester, work-study programs, a general studies degree, dual and student-designed majors, credit for life experience, and study-abroad programs in many countries. B.A.-B.S. degrees and an accelerated degree program in nursing and law are also available. There are 8 national honor societies, a freshman honors program, and 10 departmental honors programs. **Visiting:** There are regularly scheduled orientations for prospective students, consisting of informational presentations, and a campus tour. There are guides for informal visits and visitors may sit in on classes. To schedule a visit, contact Tasha Casey-Loveless. **Campus Safety and Security:** Measures include 24-hour foot and vehicle patrol, emergency notification system, security escort services, emergency telephones, lighted pathways/sidewalks, controlled access to dorms/residences, and inner-campus bicycle patrol.

REQUIREMENTS: Graduation from an accredited secondary school or satisfactory scores on the GED is required for admission. High school courses must include 4 units of English, 2-3 units each of science (at least one should be lab), one unit of world history, one unit of state history and civics, one unit of US History, 2 units math, and 2 units of a foreign language. We look for a 3.0 unweighted GPA and 22 on the ACT or 1020 on the SAT. Additionally, we review the essay, letter of recommendation, and application materials. Dance and arts management, music, and theatre all require an audition. Studio art and photography require portfolio review. A GPA of 3.0 is required. AP and CLEP credits are accepted. Important factors in the admissions decision are evidence of special talent, advanced placement or honors courses, and leadership record. To graduate, students must complete a total of 124 credit hours, including 30 to 80 in the major, with a minimum GPA of 2.0. Students must complete their last 15 hours, including the last 6 in the major, at OCU with a minimum GPA of 2.0. All students must take 43 hours in the core curriculum as specified by their college or department. **Procedure:** Freshmen are admitted to all sessions. Entrance exams should be taken by February of the senior year. There are deferred admissions and rolling admissions plans. Application deadlines are open. The fall 2016 application fee was $55. Notification is sent on a rolling basis. Applications are accepted online. **Transfer Students:** 252 transfer students enrolled in 2015-2016. Applicants must submit a transcript from each college attended and must have a minimum cumulative GPA of 2.0 from an accredited institution. Applicants having fewer than 29 credit hours must submit a high school transcript and ACT or SAT scores. The application also requires an essay and recommendation from their Dean of Students. 30 of 124 credits required for the bachelor's degree must be completed at OCU. **International Students:** There are 13 international students enrolled. The school actively recruits these students. They must take the TOEFL with a minimum score of 550 on the paper-based TOEFL (PBT) or 80 on the Internet-based version (iBT), or take the IELTS.

ADMISSIONS: 68% of the 2016-2017 applicants were accepted. The ACT scores were 13% below 12, 20% between 12 and 17, 32% between 18 and 23, 12% between 24 and 29, and 23% above 30. 56% of the current freshmen were in the top fifth of their class; 82% were in the top two fifths. There were 4 National Merit finalists. 14 freshmen graduated first in their class. **Admissions Contact:** Michelle Cook, Director of Admissions Operations. Email: *uadmissions@okcu.edu* Web: *www.okcu.edu*

FINANCIAL AID: In 2016-2017, 97% of all full-time freshmen and 80% of continuing full-time students received some form of financial aid. 82% of all full-time freshmen and 58% of continuing full-time students received need-based aid. The average freshman award was $26,609. Need-based scholarships or need-based grants averaged $16,681 ($38,836 maximum); need-based self-help aid (loans and jobs) averaged $2,348 ($12,000 maximum); non-need-based athletic scholarships averaged $7,398 ($20,000 maximum); and other non-need-based awards and non-need-based scholarships averaged $19,120 ($44,851 maximum). 31% of undergraduate students work part-time. Average annual earnings from campus work are $2749. The average financial indebtedness of the 2016 graduate was $24,237. OCU is a member of CSS. The FAFSA code is 003166. The priority date for freshman financial aid applications for fall entry is March 1. The filing deadline for fall entry is June 30.

OKLAHOMA PANHANDLE STATE UNIVERSITY *(The complete profile is made available exclusively on our website, www.barronspac.com)*

OKLAHOMA STATE UNIVERSITY — E-2

www.okstate.edu

Stillwater, OK 74078	**(405) 744-5000** **(800) 223-5019**
Fax: (405) 744-7092	**Email: admissions@okstate.edu**
Full-time: 9171 men, 8903 women	**Faculty:** 808; I, --$
Part-time: 1330 men, 1177 women	**Ph.D.s:** 91%
Graduate: 2651 men, 2186 women	**Student/Faculty:** 20 to 1
Year: semesters, summer session	**Tuition:** $8320 ($22,442)
Room & Board: $8860	**Freshman Class:** 12259 applied, 9188 accepted, 4057 enrolled
SAT CR/M: required **ACT:** 25	**CEEB CODE:** 6546
Application Deadline: n/av	**VERY COMPETITIVE**

Oklahoma State University, founded in 1890, is a publicly funded land-grant institution, offering undergraduate programs in agricultural sciences and natural resources, arts and sciences, business, education, engineering, architecture, technology, and human environmental resources. Figures in the above capsule and in this profile are approximate. There are 6 undergraduate schools and 1 graduate school. In addition to regional accreditation, OSU has baccalaureate program accreditation with AACSB, ABET, ACEJMC, ADA, AHEA, ASLA, FIDER, NAAB, NASM, NCATE, NRPA, SAF, ACS, APA, ASLHA, and NAACLS. The 840-acre campus is in a small town 65 miles north of Oklahoma City.

STUDENT LIFE: 74% of undergraduates are from Oklahoma. Others are from 48 states, 128 foreign countries, and Canada. 70% are White; 7% Foreign; 6% two or more races; 5% American Indian/Alaska Native; 4% African American; 4% Hispanic; 2% Asian American; 1% race unknown. **Male To Female Ratio:** 1.1:1. The average age of freshmen is 18; all undergraduates, 22. 21% do not continue beyond their first year; 79% remain to graduate. **Housing:** College-sponsored housing includes single-sex and coed dorms, on-campus apartments, off-campus apartments, and married student housing. In addition, there are honors houses, language houses, special-interest houses, fraternity houses, sorority houses, theme and wellness housing. On-campus housing is guaranteed for the freshman year only, and is available on a first-come, and first-served basis. 55% of students commute. All students may keep cars. Alcohol is not permitted.

FACULTY/CLASSROOMS: 63% of faculty are male; 37% are female. Graduate students teach 19% of introductory courses. The average class size in an introductory lecture is 30 and in a laboratory is 21.

PROGRAMS OF STUDY: OSU confers B.A., B.S., B.Arch.,B.E.N., B.F.A., B.Land.Arch., B.M., B.S.A.E, B.S.A.G., B.S.B.A., B.S.B.E., B.S.C.H., B.S.C.P., B.S.C.V., B.S.E.E., B.S.E.T., B.S.I.E., B.S.M.E., and B.U.S. degrees. Master's and doctoral degrees are also awarded. Bachelor's degrees are awarded in AGRICULTURE (agricultural business management, agricultural communications, agricultural economics, animal science, horticulture, natural resource management, plant science, and soil science), BIOLOGICAL SCIENCE (biochemistry, biology/biological science, botany, cell biology, entomology, microbiology, molecular biology, nutrition, physiology, and zoology), BUSINESS (accounting, banking and finance, business administration and management, entrepreneurial studies, hotel/motel and restaurant management, international business management, management information systems, marketing/retailing/merchandising, and recreation and leisure services), COMMUNICATIONS AND THE ARTS (art, broadcasting, design, dramatic arts, English, French, German, journalism, music, Russian languages and literature, and Spanish), COMPUTER AND PHYSICAL SCIENCE (chemistry, computer science, geology, mathematics, physics, and statistics), EDUCATION (agricultural education, athletic training, education, elementary education, health education, music education, physical education, secondary education, and vocational education), ENGINEERING AND ENVIRONMENTAL DESIGN (aerospace studies, architectural engineering, architecture, bioengineering, chemical engineering, civil engineering, computer engineering, construction management, construction technology, electrical/electronics engineering, electrical/electronics engineering technology, environmental science, industrial administration/management, industrial engineering, landscape architecture/design, mechanical engineering, and mechanical engineering technology), HEALTH PROFESSIONS (speech pathology/audiology), SOCIAL SCIENCE (American studies, child care/child and family studies, economics, fire control and safety technology, food science, geography, history, human development, liberal arts/general studies, philosophy, political science/government, psychology, and sociology).

ACTIVITIES: There are 400 groups on campus, including art, band, cheerleading, choir, chorale, chorus, computers, dance, drama, environmental, ethnic, honors, international, jazz band, LGBT, literary magazine, marching band, musical theater, newspaper, opera, orchestra, pep band, political, professional, radio and TV, religious, social, social service, student government, and symphony. Popular campus events include Freshmen Follies, Salsa Ball, and African Night. **Sports:** There are 8 intercollegiate sports for men and 8 for women. Facilities include a recreation center, with basketball-volleyball courts, a multipurpose court, weight and fitness equipment, cardio-theater, indoor climbing wall, golf practice area including golf simulators, a jogging track, indoor and outdoor swimming pools, and racquetball-handball courts. **Graduates:** From July 1, 2015 to June 30, 2016, 4102 bachelor's degrees were awarded. The most popular majors were business/marketing (26%), engineering (10%), and agriculture (8%). In an average class, 2% graduate in 3 years or less, 32% graduate in 4 years or less, 55% graduate in 5 years or less, and 61% graduate in 6 years or less.

SERVICES: Counseling and information services are available, as is tutoring in most subjects, and a reader service for the blind, and remedial math, reading, and writing. Academic assessment and minority programs are also available. **Library/Resources:** The 5 libraries contain 3.5 million volumes, 4.6 million microform items, and 445,551 audio/video tapes/CDs/DVDs. Computerized library services include interlibrary loans, database searching, Internet access, and Wi-Fi capability. Special learning facilities include an art gallery and radio station. **Physically Challenged Students:** 99% of the campus is accessible. Facilities include wheelchair ramps, elevators, special parking, specially equipped restrooms, special class scheduling, lowered drinking fountains, lowered telephones, and special housing. **Special:** OSU offers cross-registration with Northern Oklahoma College and Tulsa Community College, a Washington semester, and an internship program. A B.A.-B.S. degree, dual majors, an individualized university studies degree, multidisciplinary majors in biosystems engineering and in cell and molecular biology, nondegree study, and pass/fail options are available. Students may study abroad in several countries. The school also sponsors Semester at Sea, a 1-semester program of study on a ship traveling to ports throughout the world. There is a freshman honors program. **Visiting:** There are regularly scheduled orientations for prospective students, including personal meetings and tours. Appointments are scheduled with other campus departments, as needed, to assist prospective students. There are guides for informal visits, visitors may sit in on classes, and stay overnight. To schedule a visit, contact the Undergraduate Admissions Office. **Campus Safety and Security:** Measures include 24-hour foot and vehicle patrol, emergency notification system, self-defense education, and security escort services. There are also shuttle buses, emergency telephones, lighted pathways/sidewalks, and controlled access to dorms/residences.

REQUIREMENTS: Freshman applicants must have a cumulative high school GPA of 3.0 and rank in the upper third of their graduating class; or achieve at least a 24 composite score on the ACT or 1090 on the SAT; or have a 3.0 GPA in the required 15 curricular units, which include 4 years of English, 3 of math (algebra I and above), 2 each of history and lab science, 1 of citizenship skills, and 3 more from any of the above or computer science or foreign language, along with an ACT score of 21 or SAT 980. OSU requires applicants to be in the upper 33% of their class. AP and CLEP credits are accepted. Important factors in the admissions decision are advanced placement or honors courses, evidence of special talent, and recommendations by school officials. To graduate, students must have a minimum GPA of 2.0 and at least 120 hours, including a minimum of 30 hours in the major for most programs. A higher GPA may be required in some majors. All students must take a minimum of 40 credit hours of core courses, including 6 each of English, humanities, analytical and quantitative thought, natural sciences, and social and behavioral sciences, 3 each of American history and government, and 1 each of scientific investigation and international studies. **Procedure:** Freshmen are admitted in the fall, spring, and summer. Entrance exams should be taken during the junior or senior year. There is a rolling admissions plan. Application deadlines are open. Application fee is $40. Applications are accepted online. **Transfer Students:** 1655 transfer students enrolled in 2015-2016. Applicants must submit official transcripts from all colleges attended. Students having fewer than 24 credit hours must also meet the requirements for entering freshmen and have a 2.25 GPA. Students that have earned 24-59 hours of college credit must achieve a minimum transfer GPA of 2.25 or higher in all college-level course work attempted. Students that have earned 60 or more hours of college credit must achieve a minimum transfer GPA of 2.0 or higher in all college-level course work attempted. 30 of 120 credits required for the bachelor's degree must be completed at OSU. **International Students:** There are 757 international students enrolled. The school actively recruits these students. They must take the TOEFL with a minimum score of 500 on the paper-based TOEFL (PBT) or 61 on the Internet-based version (iBT). They must also take the SAT or ACT.

ADMISSIONS: 75% of the 2016-2017 applicants were accepted. The SAT scores for the 2016-2017 freshman class were: Critical Reading-- 28% below 500, 45% between 500 and 599, 23% between 600 and 699, and 4% between 700 and 800. Math-- 21% below 500, 45% between 500 and 599, 29% between 600 and 699, and 6% between 700 and 800. 48% of the current freshmen were in the top fifth of their class; 78% were in the top two fifths. There were 16 National Merit finalists. **Admissions Contact:** Christine Crenshaw, Director Undergraduate Admissions. Email: *admissions@okstate.edu* Web: *www.okstate.edu*

FINANCIAL AID: In 2016-2017, 51% of all full-time freshmen and 50% of continuing full-time students received some form of financial aid. 51% of all full-time freshmen and 50% of continuing full-time students received need-based aid. The average freshman award was $13,284. Need-based scholarships or need-based grants averaged $7,006; need-based self-help aid (loans and jobs) averaged $3,324; non-need-based athletic scholarships averaged $12,820; other non-need-based awards and non-need-based scholarships averaged $3,237; and $6,461 from other forms of aid. The average financial indebtedness of the 2016 graduate was $22,591. The college's own financial statement is required. The FAFSA code is 003170. The priority date for freshman financial aid applications for fall entry is February 1. The filing deadline for fall entry is rolling.

OKLAHOMA WESLEYAN UNIVERSITY — E-1

www.okwu.edu

Bartlesville, OK 74006	(918) 335-6219 (866) 222-8226
Fax: (918) 335-6229	**Email:** admissions@okwu.edu
Full-time: 278 men, 290 women	**Faculty:** 31
Part-time: 163 men, 328 women	**Ph.D.s:** 48%
Graduate: n/av	**Student/Faculty:** 18 to 1
Year: semesters, summer session	**Tuition:** $25,070
Room & Board: $8136	**Freshman Class:** n/av
SAT or ACT: recommended	**CEEB CODE:** 6135
Application Deadline: n/av	**COMPETITIVE**

Oklahoma Wesleyan University, founded in 1909, is a private liberal arts institution affiliated with the Wesleyan Church. Figures in the above capsule and in this profile are approximate. There are 5 undergraduate schools and 1 graduate school. In addition to regional accreditation, OWU has baccalaureate program accreditation with NCATE, CCNE, and IACBE. The 101-acre campus is in a suburban area 40 miles north of Tulsa. Including any residence halls, there are 15 buildings.

STUDENT LIFE: 73% of undergraduates are from Oklahoma. Others are from 33 states, and 9 foreign countries. 80% are from public schools. 83% are White; 2% African American; 2% Hispanic; 2% Foreign; 1% Asian American. 74% are Protestant; 23% claim no religious affiliation. **Female To Male Ratio:** 1.4:1. The average age of freshmen is 18; all undergraduates, 26. 20% do not continue beyond their first year; 60% remain to graduate. **Housing:** 315 students can be accommodated in college housing, which includes single-sex dorms. In addition, there are honors houses. On-campus housing is guaranteed for all 4 years. 69% of students commute. All students may keep cars. Alcohol is not permitted.

FACULTY/CLASSROOMS: 65% of faculty are male; 35% are female. All teach undergraduates. No introductory courses are taught by graduate students. The average class size in an introductory lecture is 20; in a laboratory is 20; and in a regular course is 20.

PROGRAMS OF STUDY: OWU confers B.A., and B.S. degrees. Associate and master's degrees are also awarded. Bachelor's degrees are awarded in BIOLOGICAL SCIENCE (biology/biological science), BUSINESS (accounting, business administration and management, and human resources), COMMUNICATIONS AND THE ARTS (communications, English, and music), COMPUTER AND PHYSICAL SCIENCE (chemistry, mathematics, and science), EDUCATION (business education, elementary education, English education, mathematics education, middle school education, music education, physical education, science education, secondary education, and social studies education), HEALTH PROFESSIONS (predentistry and premedicine), SOCIAL SCIENCE (behavioral science, history, liberal arts/general studies, pastoral studies, political science/government, prelaw, religion, religious music, social studies, sociology, and youth ministry). Business, and education are the strongest academically, and have the largest enrollments.

ACTIVITIES: There are no fraternities or sororities. There are 10 groups on campus, including band, cheerleading, choir, chorale, chorus, computers, drama, ethnic, honors, international, musical theater, photography, political, professional, religious, social service, and student government. Popular campus events include Spiritual Emphasis Week and Youth Conference. **Sports:** There are 7 intercollegiate sports for men and 7 for women, and 10 intramural sports for men and 10 for women. Facilities include a indoor gym and athletic field. **Graduates:** The most popular majors were business/marketing (99%), biological/life science (18%), and parks/recreation (10%).

SERVICES: Counseling and information services are available, as is tutoring in most subjects, and remedial math, reading, and writing. **Library/Resources:** The library contains 120,000 volumes, 20,000 microform items, and 500 audio/video tapes/CDs/DVDs, and subscribes to 18,000 periodicals including electronic. Computerized library services include interlibrary loans and database searching. **Physically Challenged Students:** 73% of the campus is accessible. Facilities include wheelchair ramps, elevators, special parking, and specially equipped restrooms. **Special:** OWU offers cross-registration with Tri-County Tech, a Washington semester, a co-op program, internships, a general studies degree, credit for life experience, and an accelerated degree program in business and the B.S.N. **Visiting:** There are regularly scheduled orientations for prospective students. There are guides for informal visits, visitors may sit in on classes, and stay overnight. To schedule a visit, contact the Enrollment Services Office. **Campus Safety and Security:** There are lighted pathways/sidewalks, an evening patrol by a security guard.

REQUIREMENTS: The SAT or ACT is recommended. Graduation from an accredited secondary school or satisfactory scores on the GED are required for admission. 18 academic credits must be completed, including 4 credits of English and 2 credits each of history, math, science, and social studies. AP and CLEP credits are accepted. To graduate, students must complete a total of 126 credit hours with a minimum GPA of 2.0. About 40 hours are required in the major. All students must take 9 hours of religion and a writing proficiency exam. **Procedure:** Freshmen are admitted to all sessions. Entrance exams should be taken during the senior year. There is a rolling admissions plan. Application deadlines are open. Application fee is $25. Applications are accepted online. **Transfer Students:** 54 transfer students enrolled in 2015-2016. Applicants must have a minimum GPA of 2.0. 24 of 126 credits required for the bachelor's degree must be completed at OWU. **International Students:** There are 16 international students enrolled. They must take the TOEFL or MELAB.

Admissions Contact: Audrey Kelleher, Associate Vice President for Enrollment. Email: *admissions@okwu.edu* Web: *www.okwu.edu*

FINANCIAL AID: In 2016-2017, 98% of all full-time freshmen and continuing full-time students received some form of financial aid. 90% of all full-time freshmen and continuing full-time students received need-based aid. 60% of undergraduate students work part-time. The average financial indebtedness of the 2016 graduate was $20,000. The college's own financial statement is required. The FAFSA code is 003151. The deadline for filing freshman financial aid applications for fall entry is open.

ORAL ROBERTS UNIVERSITY — E-2

www.oru.edu

Tulsa, OK 74171	(918) 495-6161 (800) 678-8876
Fax: (918) 495-6166	Email: admissions@oru.edu
Full-time: 1078 men, 1435 women	Faculty: 135
Part-time: 211 men, 333 women	Ph.D.s: 3%
Graduate: 278 men, 279 women	Student/Faculty: 14 to 1
Year: semesters, summer session	Tuition: $25,676
Room & Board: $8640	Freshman Class: 2378 applied, 522 accepted, 437 enrolled
SAT CR/M: 503/505 ACT: 22	CEEB CODE: 6552
Application Deadline: rolling	COMPETITIVE

Oral Roberts University, founded in 1963, is a private, Christian University, offering more than 60 undergraduate, 13 master's and 2 doctoral degree programs. There are 6 undergraduate schools and 3 graduate schools. In addition to regional accreditation, ORU has baccalaureate program accreditation with ABET, ACBSP, CSWE, NASM, NCATE, CCNE, ATS, and OCTP. The 263-acre campus is in an urban area in Tulsa, Oklahoma. Including any residence halls, there are 29 buildings.

STUDENT LIFE: 51% of undergraduates are from out of state, mostly the Midwest. Students are from 50 states, 83 foreign countries, and Canada. 75% are from public schools. 5% are Hispanic; 5% Foreign; 42% White; 2% American Indian/Alaska Native; 2% two or more races; 11% African American; 1% Asian American. 98% are Protestant. **Female To Male Ratio:** 1.3:1. The average age of freshmen is 19; all undergraduates, 21. 8% do not continue beyond their first year; 54% remain to graduate. **Housing:** 2218 students can be accommodated in college housing, which includes single-sex honors wings of several dorms, men's dorms, and women's dorms. On-campus housing is available on a first-come and first-served basis. 66% of students live on campus. All students may keep cars. Alcohol is not permitted.

FACULTY/CLASSROOMS: 56% of faculty are male; 44% are female. And 84% do research. No introductory courses are taught by graduate students. The average class size in an introductory lecture is 30; in a laboratory is 20; and in a regular course is 20.

PROGRAMS OF STUDY: ORU confers B.A., B.S., B.M., B.Mus.Ed., B.S.E., B.S.N. and B.S.W. degrees. Master's and doctoral degrees are also awarded. Bachelor's degrees are awarded in BIOLOGICAL SCIENCE (biology/biological science), BUSINESS (accounting, banking and finance, business administration and management, international business management, management information systems, management science, marketing/retailing/merchandising, organizational behavior, and recreation and leisure services), COMMUNICATIONS AND THE ARTS (applied art, broadcasting, communications, dance, dramatic arts, English, English literature, film arts, French, German, literature, music, music performance, music theory and composition, Spanish, speech/debate/rhetoric, and studio art), COMPUTER AND PHYSICAL SCIENCE (chemistry, computer science, mathematics, and physics), EDUCATION (art education, business education, drama education, early childhood education, elementary education, English education, foreign languages education, health education, mathematics education, music education, physical education, recreation education, science education, social studies education, and special education), ENGINEERING AND ENVIRONMENTAL DESIGN (bioengineering, commercial art, computer engineering, electrical/electronics engineering, engineering, engineering management, mechanical engineering, and preengineering), HEALTH PROFESSIONS (biomedical science, health science, medical laboratory technology, nursing, optometry, predentistry, and premedicine), SOCIAL SCIENCE (biblical studies, history, international relations, international studies, liberal arts/general studies, ministries, philosophy, political science/government, prelaw, psychology, religion, religious education, religious music, and social work). All science programs, and music & theology are the strongest academically. Nursing, media, business, psychology, Ministry and leadership have the largest enrollments.

ACTIVITIES: There are no fraternities or sororities. There are 40 groups on campus, including art, band, cheerleading, choir, chorale, chorus, Community Outreach and Summer Mission, computers, dance, debate, drama, environmental, ethnic, honors, international, jazz band, musical theater, newspaper, opera, pep band, photography, political, professional, radio and TV, religious, social, social service, student government, symphony, and yearbook. **Sports:** There are 8 intercollegiate sports for men and 8 for women, and 20 intramural sports for men and 20 for women. Facilities include an physical fitness center, track, tennis, racquetball, squash, volleyball, basketball courts, baseball and soccer fields. **Graduates:** From July 1, 2015 to June 30, 2016, 592 bachelor's degrees were awarded. The most popular majors were business marketing (22%), theology and religious vocations (13%), and communication/journalism (11%). In an average class, 55% graduate in 6 years or less.

SERVICES: Counseling and information services are available, as is tutoring in most subjects, and a reader service for the blind, and remedial math, reading, and writing. **Library/Resources:** The library contains 487,000 volumes, 50,000 microform items, 18,000 audio/video tapes/CDs/DVDs, and subscribes to 65 periodicals including electronic. Computerized library services include interlibrary loans, database searching, Internet access, and Wi-Fi capability. Special learning facilities include a natural history museum, radio station, and a TV production studio.

Physically Challenged Students: 90% of the campus is accessible. Facilities include wheelchair ramps, elevators, special parking, specially equipped restrooms, special class scheduling, lowered drinking fountains, lowered telephones, and special housing. **Special:** ORU offers combined B.A.-B.S. degrees, internships, 3-2 programs, a Washington semester, work-study programs, dual and student-designed majors, study abroad in 5 countries, independent study, nondegree study, an accelerated degree in business and education, and a liberal arts degree. An honors program/leadership academy is also offered. There are 4 national honor societies, a freshman honors program, and 12 departmental honors programs. **Visiting:** There are regularly scheduled orientations for prospective students, College Weekend, which consists of visiting classes, meeting with faculty and staff, attending chapel services, and attending student life events. Visitors may sit in on classes and stay overnight. To schedule a visit, contact the Admissions Office. **Campus Safety and Security:** Measures include 24-hour foot and vehicle patrol, emergency notification system, self-defense education, and security escort services. There are also shuttle buses, lighted pathways/sidewalks, and controlled access to dorms/residences.

REQUIREMENTS: The SAT or ACT is required. Students should be graduates of an accredited secondary school or hold a GED. High school preparation should include 4 years of English, 2 years each of math, including algebra and geometry or 2 years of algebra, foreign language, social studies, and science, including lab science, and 4 of academic electives. A recommendation from the student's minister is required. An academic recommendation and an interview are recommended. A GPA of 2.6 is required. AP and CLEP credits are accepted. A minimum of 128 credit hours, with a minimum of 30 hours in the major, and a 2.0 GPA are required to graduate. All students must complete specific courses in the Bible, theology, and English, plus 12 hours in social sciences, 11 in biological or physical, and mathematical sciences, 6 to 7 in a modern foreign language, 3 in communication arts, and 2 in fine arts, and 1 physical activity course is required per semester, along with regular, semiweekly chapel attendance. A senior paper must be completed in most majors. Some other courses may be required such as history, humanities, philosophy, and government. **Procedure:** Freshmen are admitted to all sessions. Entrance exams should be taken The last semester of the junior year or during senior year. There are deferred admissions and rolling admissions plans. Application deadlines are open. Application fee is $35. Applications are accepted online. **Transfer Students:** 209 transfer students enrolled in 2015-2016. An official transcript showing honorable dismissal from each previous institution is required. 30 of 128 credits required for the bachelor's degree must be completed at ORU. **International Students:** There are 167 international students enrolled. They must take the TOEFL with a minimum score of 500 on the paper-based TOEFL (PBT) or 61 on the Internet-based version (iBT). They must also take the SAT or ACT.

ADMISSIONS: 22% of the 2016-2017 applicants were accepted. The SAT scores for the 2016-2017 freshman class were: Critical Reading-- 47% below 500, 40% between 500 and 599, 10% between 600 and 699, and 3% between 700 and 800. Math-- 49% below 500, 35% between 500 and 599, 15% between 600 and 699, and 1% between 700 and 800. The ACT scores were 16% between 12 and 17, 54% between 18 and 23, 24% between 24 and 29, and 6% above 30. There were 7 National Merit finalists. 21 freshmen graduated first in their class. **Admissions Contact:** Cal Easterling, Ph.D.,Dean of Institutional Effectiveness. Email: *admissions@oru.edu* Web: *www.oru.edu*

FINANCIAL AID: In 2016-2017, 75% of all full-time freshmen and 69% of continuing full-time students received some form of financial aid. 74% of all full-time freshmen and 66% of continuing full-time students received need-based aid. The average freshman award was $24,735. Need-based scholarships or need-based grants averaged $17,314; need-based self-help aid (loans and jobs) averaged $7,927; non-need-based athletic scholarships averaged $21,104; other non-need-based awards and non-need-based scholarships averaged $7,077; and $12,154 from other forms of aid. 8% of undergraduate students work part-time. The average financial indebtedness of the 2016 graduate was $32,799. The FAFSA code is 003985. The priority date for freshman financial aid applications for fall entry is March 15. The filing deadline for fall entry is rolling.

SOUTHEASTERN OKLAHOMA STATE UNIVERSITY E-4

www.se.edu

Durant, OK 74701 **(580) 745-2060**

Fax: (580) 745-7502
Full-time: 1268 men, 1435 women
Part-time: 295 men, 465 women
Graduate: 183 men, 153 women
Year: semesters, summer session
Room & Board: $6030

ACT: 21
Application Deadline: open

Email: admissions@sosu.edu
Faculty: 142; IIA, --$
Ph.D.s: 72%
Student/Faculty: 17 to 1
Tuition: $5845 ($12,019)
Freshman Class: 980 applied, 771 accepted, 507 enrolled
CEEB CODE: 6657
COMPETITIVE

Southeastern Oklahoma State University, founded in 1909, is a public institution offering programs in the arts and sciences, business, education, music, and technology to a primarily commuter student body. Figures in the above capsule and in this profile are approximate. There are 3 undergraduate schools and one graduate school. In addition to regional accreditation, Southeastern has baccalaureate program accreditation with AACSB, ACBSP, NASM, and NCATE. The 268-acre campus is in a rural area 90 miles north of Dallas. Including any residence halls, there are 46 buildings.

STUDENT LIFE: 74% of undergraduates are from Oklahoma. Others are from 39 states, 25 foreign countries, and Canada. 99% are from public schools. 60% are White; 54% African American; 30% American Indian/Alaska Native; 3% Hispanic; 1% Asian American; 1% Foreign. **Female To Male Ratio:** 1.2:1. The average age of freshmen is 19; all undergraduates, 25. 42% do not continue beyond their first year; 40% remain to graduate. **Housing:** 648 students can be accommodated in college housing, which includes single-sex and coed dorms and on-campus apartments. On-campus housing is guaranteed for all 4 years. 84% of students commute. All students may keep cars. Alcohol is not permitted.

FACULTY/CLASSROOMS: 62% of faculty are male; 38% are female. All teach undergraduates, and 10% do research. No introductory courses are taught by graduate students. The average class size in an introductory lecture is 28; in a laboratory is 18; and in a regular course is 23.

PROGRAMS OF STUDY: Southeastern confers B.A., B.S., B.A.A.S., B.B.A., B.G.S., B.M. and B.M.Ed. degrees. Master's degrees are also awarded. Bachelor's degrees are awarded in AGRICULTURE (conservation and regulation and environmental studies), BIOLOGICAL SCIENCE (biology/biological science and biotechnology), BUSINESS (accounting, business administration and management, recreation and leisure services, and secretarial studies/office management), COMMUNICATIONS AND THE ARTS (art, communications, dramatic arts, English, fine arts, music, and speech/debate/rhetoric), COMPUTER AND PHYSICAL SCIENCE (chemistry, computer science, information sciences and systems, mathematics, and physics), EDUCATION (art education, business education, early childhood education, education of the mentally handicapped, elementary education, mathematics education, music education, physical education, science education, secondary education, and social studies education), ENGINEERING AND ENVIRONMENTAL DESIGN (aviation administration/management and occupational safety and health), HEALTH PROFESSIONS (medical laboratory technology), SOCIAL SCIENCE (criminal justice, economics, gerontology, history, political science/government, psychology, social science, and sociology). Chemistry, history, and music are the strongest academically. Occupational safety & health, elementary education, and criminal justice have the largest enrollments.

ACTIVITIES: 1% of men belong to 2 national fraternities; 5% of women belong to 2 national sororities. There are 70 groups on campus, including art, band, cheerleading, chess, choir, chorale, chorus, communications, computers, dance, debate, drama, drill team, environmental, ethnic, forensics, honors, international, jazz band, literary magazine, marching band, musical theater, newspaper, opera, pep band, photography, political, professional, religious, social, social service, student government, and yearbook. Popular campus events include Parents Day, Candlelighting, and Springfest. **Sports:** There are 6 intercollegiate sports for men and 6 for women, and 2 intramural sports for men and 1 for women. Facilities include a football stadium, gym, baseball and softball fields, track, tennis courts, playing fields, and a swimming pool. **Gradu-**

ates: From July 1, 2015 to June 30, 2016, 668 bachelor's degrees were awarded. The most popular majors were engineering technologies, business/marketing, and education, and liberal arts. 130 companies recruited on campus in 2015-2016. In an average class, 77% graduate in 4 years or less and 81% graduate in 5 years or less.

SERVICES: Counseling and information services are available, as is tutoring in every subject, and a reader service for the blind, and remedial math, reading, and writing. There is also tutoring in study skills for students in need. **Library/Resources:** The library contains 306,071 volumes, 591,277 microform items, 9,254 audio/video tapes/CDs/DVDs, and subscribes to 841 periodicals including electronic. Computerized library services include interlibrary loans, database searching, and Internet access. **Physically Challenged Students:** 90% of the campus is accessible. Facilities include wheelchair ramps, elevators, special parking, specially equipped restrooms, special class scheduling, lowered drinking fountains, lowered telephones, and special housing. **Special:** Internships, study abroad, credit for military experience, pass/fail options in some courses, and nondegree study are available. There are 15 national honor societies and 9 departmental honors programs. **Visiting:** There are guides for informal visits and visitors may sit in on classes. To schedule a visit, contact the Admissions and Recruitment Services. **Campus Safety and Security:** Measures include 24-hour foot and vehicle patrol, emergency notification system, self-defense education, security escort services, lighted pathways/sidewalks, in room safes, and safety training.

REQUIREMENTS: The ACT is required. Applicants should be graduates of an accredited secondary school or have earned a GED. High school courses must include 4 years of English, 3 of math, 3 of science with lab, and history, 1 of citizenship skills (from the subjects of economics, geography, government, or non-Western culture), and 3 additional units of subjects previously listed or of computer science or foreign language. Southeastern requires applicants to be in the upper 50% of their class. AP and CLEP credits are accepted. Important factors in the admissions decision are advanced placement or honors courses, evidence of special talent, personality/intangible qualities, and geographical diversity. A total of 124 credit hours with a minimum GPA of 2.0 (2.5 for teacher education majors) is required for graduation. All students must complete 41 semester hours of general education requirements, including English, American history, government, humanities, arts, social and lab sciences, math, communications, and health education, and 3 hours of computer science. **Procedure:** Freshmen are admitted to all sessions. Entrance exams should be taken by the fall of the senior year. There is a rolling admissions plan. Application deadlines are open. Application fee is $20. Notification is sent on a rolling basis. Applications are accepted online. **Transfer Students:** 414 transfer students enrolled in 2015-2016. Out-of-state applicants must have a 2.0 GPA. In-state applicants must have a 1.7 GPA with 24 to 36 credit hours earned, 1.8 with 37 to 72 hours, and 2.0 with 73 or more hours. 30 of 124 credits required for the bachelor's degree must be completed at Southeastern. **International Students:** There are 39 international students enrolled. They must take the TOEFL with a minimum score of 500 on the paper-based TOEFL (PBT) or 61 on the Internet-based version (iBT). They must also take the SAT or ACT.

ADMISSIONS: 79% of the 2016-2017 applicants were accepted. The SAT scores for the 2016-2017 freshman class were: 30% of the current freshmen were in the top fifth of their class; 59% were in the top two fifths. 28 freshmen graduated first in their class. **Admissions Contact:** Kristie Luke, Associate Dean of Admissions and Records/Registrar. Email: *admissions@sosu.edu* Web: *www.se.edu*

FINANCIAL AID: In 2016-2017, 78% of all full-time freshmen and 56% of continuing full-time students received some form of financial aid. 56% of all full-time freshmen and 67% of continuing full-time students received need-based aid. The average freshman award was $10,410. Need-based scholarships or need-based grants averaged $1,786; need-based self-help aid (loans and jobs) averaged $1,213; non-need-based athletic scholarships averaged $2,235; and other non-need-based awards and non-need-based scholarships averaged $1,311. 45% of undergraduate students work part-time. Average annual earnings from campus work are $1200. The average financial indebtedness of the 2016 graduate was $19,368. Southeastern is a member of CSS. The college's own financial statement is required. The FAFSA code is 003179. The priority date for freshman financial aid applications for fall entry is March 1.

SOUTHERN NAZARENE UNIVERSITY *(The complete profile is made available exclusively on our website, www.barronspac.com)*

SOUTHWESTERN OKLAHOMA STATE UNIVERSITY — D-3

www.swosu.edu

Weatherford, OK 73096 — **(580) 774-3782**

Fax: (580) 774-7131
Email: admissions@swosu.edu

Full-time: 1622 men, 2053 women
Part-time: 271 men, 600 women
Graduate: 305 men, 503 women
Year: semesters, summer session
Room & Board: $5400
ACT: 21
Application Deadline: n/av

Faculty: 180; IIA, --$
Ph.D.s: 65%
Student/Faculty: 20 to 1
Tuition: $6390 ($13,140)
Freshman Class: 2124 applied, 2037 accepted, 947 enrolled
CEEB CODE: 6673
COMPETITIVE

Southwestern Oklahoma State University is known for its quality academic programs and its friendly service to students, alumni, and friends. Located in the center of western Oklahoma, students may take classes on the main campus located in Weatherford and on the branch campus located in Sayre. Students may complete associate, bachelor's, master's, and doctoral degrees while attending either the traditional on-campus classes or participating in distance learning opportunities provided through state-of-the-art technology. There are 3 undergraduate schools and 2 graduate schools. In addition to regional accreditation, SWOSU has baccalaureate program accreditation with ABET, ABHES, ACPE, NASM, NCATE, ACS, ACOTE, IACBE, AMTA, JRCERT, ACEN, ATMAE, CAAHIM, and CAPTE. The 292-acre campus is in a small town 70 miles west of Oklahoma City. Including any residence halls, there are 69 buildings.

STUDENT LIFE: 87% of undergraduates are from Oklahoma. Others are from 33 states, 31 foreign countries, and Canada. 65% are White; 9% Hispanic; 8% two or more races; 5% Foreign; 4% African American; 4% American Indian/Alaska Native; 3% race unknown; 2% Asian American. **Female To Male Ratio:** 1.4:1. The average age of freshmen is 19; all undergraduates, 23. 34% do not continue beyond their first year; 33% remain to graduate. **Housing:** 1156 students can be accommodated in college housing, which includes single-sex dorms and married student housing. On-campus housing is available on a first-come and first-served basis. 78% of students commute. All students may keep cars. Alcohol is not permitted.

FACULTY/CLASSROOMS: 43% of faculty are male; 57% are female. 93% teach undergraduates. No introductory courses are taught by graduate students. The average class size in a laboratory is 18 and in a regular course is 18.

PROGRAMS OF STUDY: SWOSU confers B.A., B.S., B.A.Ed., B.F.A., B.B.A., B.M., B.M.Ed., B.S.Ed., and B.S.N. degrees. Associate, master's, and doctoral degrees are also awarded. Bachelor's degrees are awarded in BIOLOGICAL SCIENCE (biology/biological science, environmental biology, and microbiology), BUSINESS (accounting, business administration and management, entrepreneurial studies, finance, management, marketing/retailing/merchandising, organizational leadership and management, and sports management), COMMUNICATIONS AND THE ARTS (art, communications, English, graphic design, music, and Spanish), COMPUTER AND PHYSICAL SCIENCE (chemistry, computer science, industrial technology, mathematics, natural sciences, and radiological technology), EDUCATION (art education, early childhood education, education administration, elementary education, English education, health information management, health and physical education, history education, mathematics education, music education, reading education, school psychology, science education, secondary education, social science education, and special education), ENGINEERING AND ENVIRONMENTAL DESIGN (engineering physics, engineering technology, fire protection science, and instructional design), HEALTH PROFESSIONS (biomedical science, exercise science, health care administration, health science, medical laboratory technology, medical records administration/services, music therapy, nursing, occupational therapy, pharmacy, and physical therapy assistant), SOCIAL SCIENCE (American Indian studies, counseling/psychology, criminal justice, history, interdisciplinary studies, law enforcement and corrections, parks and recreation management, political science/government, and psychology). Pharmacy, chemistry, biological sciences, and majors related to health care are the strongest academically. Health sciences, nursing, and pharmacy have the largest enrollments.

ACTIVITIES: 3% of men belong to 2 local and 2 national fraternities; 4% of women belong to 3 local sororities. There are 72 groups on campus, including art, band, cheerleading, choir, chorale, chorus, computers, drama, drill team, ethnic, honors, international, jazz band, LGBT, literary magazine, marching band, musical theater, newspaper, opera, orchestra, pep band, political, professional, religious, social, social service, student government, symphony, and yearbook. Popular campus events include Fall Homecoming, Bull dog Blitz Talent Show, Tough Enough to Wear Teal 5k Fund-raiser. **Sports:** There are 5 intercollegiate sports for men and 7 for women, and 5 intramural sports for men and 4 for women. Facilities include Athletic facilities include a football stadium, basketball and volleyball center, baseball, softball, and soccer fields, golf facility, strength and conditioning center, rock wall, basketball courts, indoor running track, weight room, indoor pool, outdoor track, tennis courts, rodeo arena, ropes course, soccer practice field, sand volleyball courts, and outdoor basketball courts. **Graduates:** From July 1, 2015 to June 30, 2016, 698 bachelor's degrees were awarded. The most popular majors were Nursing (26%), Health Sciences (8%), and Accounting (4%). 127 companies recruited on campus in 2015-2016. In an average class, 33% graduate in 6 years or less.

SERVICES: Counseling and information services are available, as is tutoring in some subjects, such as mathematics, writing, psychology, physics, biological sciences, chemistry, language, and social sciences. There is also remedial math, reading, and writing, and a student development center offers counseling and tutoring on an individual basis. **Library/Resources:** The library contains 301,353 volumes, 422,414 microform items, and 4,423 audio/video tapes/CDs/DVDs, and subscribes to 288 periodicals including electronic. Computerized library services include interlibrary loans, database searching, Internet access, and Wi-Fi capability. **Physically Challenged Students:** 98% of the campus is accessible. Facilities include wheelchair ramps, elevators, special parking, specially equipped restrooms, special class scheduling, lowered drinking fountains, and lowered telephones. **Special:** More than 40 percent of SWOSU students participate in some form of practicum, internship, field experience, co-op, service learning, or clinical assignment by the spring of the senior year. Assignments include a variety of local and state businesses, manufacturers, schools, health care entities, and government agencies, as well as national placements such as NASA. Recent Study Abroad opportunities include England, Spain, Italy, France,Jordan, South Korea, Taiwan, Costa Ric There are 4 national honor societies and a freshman honors program. **Visiting:** There are regularly scheduled orientations for prospective students. New Student Orientation includes an Orientation Session prior to the beginning of the fall semester, Mass Orientation, a one-hour freshman orientation, and planned activities during the first few weeks of the fall semester. There are guides for informal visits, visitors may sit in on classes, and stay overnight. To schedule a visit, contact Todd Boyd, Director at (580) 774-3782. **Campus Safety and Security:** Measures include 24-hour foot and vehicle patrol, emergency notification system, self-defense education, emergency telephones, and lighted pathways/sidewalks.

REQUIREMENTS: The ACT is required. Applicants must also meet one of the following requirements: a minimum of 20 on the ACT; rank in the top 50 percent of high school class with a 2.7 GPA; or have a 2.7 GPA in a 15-unit core high school curriculum that includes 4 credits in English; 3 each in mathematics, history, and lab science; and 2 additional units in one of the previously listed subjects, computer science, or foreign language. Open admission is available at the Sayre campus. A GPA of 2.7 is required. AP and CLEP credits are accepted. To graduate, students must complete a minimum of 120 semester hours with a minimum GPA of 2.0. (Some degree programs may require more semester hours and/or higher GPA.) Each student must complete 40 semester hours in general education courses, including 6 hours in written communication; 3 each in mathematics, U.S. history, American government; 7-8 in science; 6 in humanities; 3-4 in human, cultural and social diversity; and elective hours to bring the total to 40. Additionally, each student must demonstrate computer proficiency with through a course at high school or SWOSU or through a SWOSU computer proficiency exam. **Procedure:** Freshmen are admitted to all sessions. Entrance exams should be taken during the senior year. There is a rolling admissions plan. Application deadlines are open. Application fee is $15. Notification is sent on a rolling basis. Application fees are waived if application is completed online. **Transfer Students:** 549 transfer students enrolled in 2015-2016. Applicants must have a minimum college GPA of 1.7 for 30 hours attempted or fewer and 2.0 GPA for 31 or more hours attempted. 30 of 120 credits required for the bachelor's degree must be completed at SWOSU. **International Students:** There are 241 international students enrolled. The school actively recruits these students. They must take the TOEFL with a minimum score of 500 on the paper-based TOEFL (PBT) or 61 on the Internet-based version (iBT). They must also take the SAT or ACT.

ADMISSIONS: 96% of the 2016-2017 applicants were accepted. The ACT scores were 19% between 12 and 17, 52% between 18 and 23, 24% between 24 and 29, and 5% above 30. 40% of the current freshmen were in the top fifth of their class; 68% were in the top two fifths. 108 freshmen graduated first in their class. **Admissions Contact:** Todd Boyd, Director of Enrollment Management. Email: *admissions@swosu.edu* Web: *www.swosu.edu*

FINANCIAL AID: In 2016-2017, 79% of all full-time freshmen and 73% of continuing full-time students received some form of financial aid. The college's own financial statement is required. The FAFSA code is 003181. The priority date for freshman financial aid applications for fall entry is March 1.

ST. GREGORY'S UNIVERSITY *(The complete profile is made available exclusively on our website, www.barronspac.com)*

UNIVERSITY OF CENTRAL OKLAHOMA D-2

www.uco.edu

Edmond, OK 73034	**(405) 974-2631** **(800) 254-4215**
Fax: 405-974-3930	**Email: 4ucoinfo@uco.edu**
Full-time: 4482 men, 6204 women	**Faculty:** 487; IIA, -$
Part-time: 1804 men, 2577 women	**Ph.D.s:** 78%
Graduate: 573 men, 1270 women	**Student/Faculty:** 22 to 1
Year: semesters, summer session	**Tuition:** $6096 ($14,971)
Room & Board: $7390	**Freshman Class:** 5122 applied, 3581 accepted, 2420 enrolled
ACT: 21	**CEEB CODE:** 6091
Application Deadline: August 16	**COMPETITIVE**

University of Central Oklahoma, founded in 1890, is a state-supported institution offering undergraduate and graduate programs in the liberal arts and sciences, education, business, and fine arts. There are 5 undergraduate schools and 1 graduate school. In addition to regional accreditation, UCO has baccalaureate program accreditation with ABET, ABFSE, ACBSP, ADA, NASAD, NASM, NCATE, NLN, PGA, ABFSE, and ASHA. The 210-acre campus is in a suburban area North of Oklahoma City. Including any residence halls, there are 53 buildings.

STUDENT LIFE: 89% of undergraduates are from Oklahoma. Others are from 40 states, 68 foreign countries, and Canada. 83% are from public schools. 57% are White; 9% African American; 9% Hispanic; 9% two or more races; 8% Foreign; 4% American Indian/Alaska Native; 3% Asian American; 2% race unknown. **Female To Male Ratio:** 1.5:1. The average age of freshmen is 19; all undergraduates, 23. 38% do not continue beyond their first year; 39% remain to graduate. **Housing:** 1875 students can be accommodated in college housing, which includes single-sex and coed dorms, on-campus apartments, married student housing, fraternity houses and sorority houses. On-campus housing is available on a first-come, first-served basis, and is available on a lottery system for upperclassmen. 91% of students commute. Alcohol is not permitted. All students may keep cars.

FACULTY/CLASSROOMS: 50% of faculty are male; 50% are female. Graduate students teach 2% of introductory courses. The average class size in an introductory lecture is 31 and in a laboratory is 26.

PROGRAMS OF STUDY: UCO confers B.A., B.S., B.A.Ed., B.B.A., B.F.A., B.F.A.Ed., B.M.Ed., B.Mus., B.A.T., and B.S.Ed. degrees. Bachelor's degrees are awarded in BIOLOGICAL SCIENCE (biology/biological science, forensic psychology, forensic science, and nutrition), BUSINESS (accounting, banking and finance, business administration and management, fashion merchandising, finance, funeral home services, human resources, insurance, management information systems, and marketing/retailing/merchandising), COMMUNICATIONS AND THE ARTS (advertising, art history, art, broadcasting, communications, creative writing, dance, English, English as a second/foreign language, French, German, graphic design, journalism, music, photography, piano performance, public relations, Spanish, theatre acting, theatre arts, theater design, and theatre studies), COMPUTER AND PHYSICAL SCIENCE (actuarial science, applied mathematics, chemistry, computer science, and mathematics), EDUCATION (art education, athletic training, bilingual/bicultural education, dance education, early childhood education, elementary education, English education, foreign languages education, general studies, mathematics education, museum studies, music education, physical education, science education, secondary education, social studies education, and special education), ENGINEERING AND ENVIRONMENTAL DESIGN (biomedical engineering, electrical/electronics engineering, engineering, engineering physics, and interior design), HEALTH PROFESSIONS (allied health, art therapy, community health work, exercise science, industrial hygiene, nursing, predentistry, premedicine, preoptometry, and speech pathology/audiology), SOCIAL SCIENCE (addiction studies, child psychology/development, criminal justice, economics, family/consumer studies, forensic studies, geography, gerontology, history, humanities, legal studies, liberal arts/general studies, philosophy, physical fitness/movement, political science/government, psychology, public administration, and sociology). Nursing, speech/language pathology, and educational leadership are the strongest academically. Nursing, biology, and psychology have the largest enrollments.

ACTIVITIES: 3% of men belong to 11 national fraternities; 5% of women belong to 8 national sororities. There are 240 groups on campus, including art, band, cheerleading, chess, choir, chorus, communications, computers, dance, debate, drama, drum and bugle corps, ethnic, film, forensics, honors, international, jazz band, LGBT, marching band, musical theater, newspaper, orchestra, pep band, photography, political, professional, radio and TV, religious, social, social service, student government, symphony, and yearbook. Popular campus events include Homecoming, Earth Day, May Day, The Big Event, Winterglow, International Festival, Big Pink Volleyball, and Miss UCO. **Sports:** There are 5 intercollegiate sports for men and 9 for women, and 17 intramural sports for men and 17 for women. Facilities include a field house with a gym, a swimming pool, a track, a weight room, a stadium with a track and a softball field, and a wellness center with basketball courts, aerobic classes, cardiovascular equipment, weights, and various classes. **Graduates:** From July 1, 2015 to June 30, 2016, 2578 bachelor's degrees were awarded. The most popular majors were general studies (14%), psychology (5%), and nursing (4%). 68 companies recruited on campus in 2015-2016. In an average class, 1% graduate in 3 years or less, 14% graduate in 4 years or less, 30% graduate in 5 years or less, and 39% graduate in 6 years or less.

SERVICES: Counseling and information services are available, as is tutoring in some subjects, such as English, math, reading, and writing. There is also a reader service for the blind, and remedial math. **Library/Resources:** The library contains 922,614 volumes, 161,698 microform items, 30,206 audio/video tapes/CDs/DVDs, and subscribes to 29,549 periodicals including electronic. Computerized library services include interlibrary loans, database searching, Internet access, and Wi-Fi capability. Special learning facilities include an art gallery, radio station, and TV station. **Physically Challenged Students:** All of the campus is accessible. Facilities include wheelchair ramps, elevators, special parking, specially equipped restrooms, special class scheduling, and lowered drinking fountains. **Special:** There is cross-registration with the Downtown Consortium. Opportunities are provided for internships, B.A.-B.S. degrees, dual majors, a general studies degree, credit by exam, nondegree study, and credit for military experience. Work-study programs may be arranged through the Federal College Work-Study Program. There are 6 national honor societies. **Visiting:** There are regularly scheduled orientations for prospective students, including a brief tour, a question-and-answer period, and access to an information booth. There are guides for informal visits. To schedule a visit, contact Gina Hickey at ghickey@uco.edu. **Campus Safety and Security:** Measures include 24-hour foot and vehicle patrol, emergency notification system, security escort services, emergency telephones, lighted pathways/sidewalks, controlled access to dorms/residences, and crime and terrorism tip line.

REQUIREMENTS: Minimum composite ACT of 20 or a 2.7 non-weighted, cumulative GPA and class ranking in the upper 50% of graduating class. Graduation from an accredited secondary school is required and a GED is accepted. The applicant's academic record should include 4 units of English; 3 units of math (first-year algebra and beyond); 3 units of lab science; and 3 units of history, of which 1 year must be in American history. Applicants must have a 2.7 GPA in the core curriculum courses. UCO requires applicants to be in the upper 50% of their class. AP and CLEP credits are accepted. Important factors in the admissions decision are evidence of special talent, extracurricular activities record, and leadership record. Students must complete 124 semester hours with a 2.0 GPA. Students must take 40 hours of upper division courses with at least 15 hours from the major. 10 hours of major course work must be earned from UCO. Students must also complete a maximum of 12 semester hours in general education requirements, including physical education. 60 hours must be earned from a bachelor's granting university. **Procedure:** Freshmen are admitted to all sessions. Entrance exams should be taken within 30 days of submitting the application. There are deferred admissions and rolling admissions plans. Application deadlines are open. Application fee is $90. Applications are accepted online. **Transfer Students:** 1401 transfer students enrolled in 2015-2016. Applicants must submit official transcripts from all previously attended colleges and have a minimum GPA of 1.7 if the student has 30 or less credit hours or a 2.0 GPA for students with 31 or more credit hours. Students who have completed fewer than 24 hours of transferable credit must meet the requirements for entering freshmen. Out of state students must have a minimum 2.0 GPA. 30 of 124 credits required for the bachelor's degree must be completed at UCO. **International Students:** There are 1075 international students enrolled. The school actively recruits these students. They must take the TOEFL with a minimum score of 500 on the paper-based TOEFL (PBT) or 61 on the Internet-based version (iBT). They must also take the ACT.

ADMISSIONS: 70% of the 2016-2017 applicants were accepted. The ACT scores were 11% between 12 and 17, 61% between 18 and 23, 25% between 24 and 29, and 3% above 30. 21% of the current freshmen were in the top fifth of their class; 59% were in the top two fifths. **Admissions Contact:** Dallas Caldwell, Director of Undergraduate Admissions. Email: *4ucoinfo@uco.edu* Web: *www.uco.edu*

FINANCIAL AID: In 2016-2017, 85% of all full-time freshmen and 58% of continuing full-time students received some form of financial aid. 58% of all full-time freshmen and 63% of continuing full-time students received need-based aid. The average freshman award was $6,867. Need-based scholarships or need-based grants averaged $6,867; and need-based self-help aid (loans and jobs) averaged $5,244. 8% of undergraduate students work part-time. Average annual earnings from campus work are $7133. The average financial indebtedness of the 2016 graduate was $22,665. The CSS/Profile, FFS, and the college's own financial statement are required. The FAFSA code is 003152. The deadline for filing freshman financial aid applications for fall entry is May 31.

UNIVERSITY OF OKLAHOMA — D-3

www.ou.edu

Norman, OK 73019	(405) 325-2252 (800) 234-6868
Fax: (405) 325-7124	**Email:** admrec@ou.edu
Full-time: 9327 men, 9097 women	**Faculty:** 1176
Part-time: 1729 men, 1475 women	**Ph.D.s:** 74%
Graduate: 3128 men, 3181 women	**Student/Faculty:** 18 to 1
Year: semesters, summer session	**Tuition:** $8631 ($22,953)
Room & Board: $10,280	**Freshman Class:** 14389 applied, 10195 accepted, 4198 enrolled
SAT CR/M: 580/600 **ACT:** 26	**CEEB CODE:** 6879
Application Deadline: February 1	**VERY COMPETITIVE**

University of Oklahoma, founded in 1890, is a comprehensive research university offering 155 different majors for undergraduate study. There are 13 undergraduate schools and 13 graduate schools. In addition to regional accreditation, UO has baccalaureate program accreditation with AACSB, ABET, ACCE, ACEJMC, CSWE, NAAB, NASM, NCATE, NAST, EAC, and AAM. The 3337-acre campus is in a suburban area 20 miles south of Oklahoma City. Including any residence halls, there are 297 buildings.

STUDENT LIFE: 65% of undergraduates are from Oklahoma. Others are from 50 states, 125 foreign countries, and Canada. 61% are White; 9% Hispanic; 8% two or more races; 6% Asian American; 5% African American; 5% Foreign; 4% American Indian/Alaska Native; 2% race unknown. **Male To Female Ratio:** 1.0:1. The average age of freshmen is 18; all undergraduates, 22. 10% do not continue beyond their first year; 66% remain to graduate. **Housing:** 5962 students can be accommodated in college housing, which includes single-sex and coed dorms, on-campus apartments, and married student housing. In addition, there are honors houses, International floors, honors house, cultural housing, national merit, scholastic and quiet lifestyle floor. On-campus housing is guaranteed for the freshman year only, is available on a first-come, and first-served basis. 77% of students commute. All students may keep cars. Alcohol is not permitted.

FACULTY/CLASSROOMS: 61% of faculty are male; 39% are female. Graduate students teach 30% of introductory courses. The average class size in an introductory lecture is 42; in a laboratory is 21; and in a regular course is 38.

PROGRAMS OF STUDY: UO confers B.A., B.S., B.Arch., B.B.A., B.F.A., B.Int.Des., B.Mus.Arts, B.Mus.Ed., and B.Mus. degrees. Master's and doctoral degrees are also awarded. Bachelor's degrees are awarded in AGRICULTURE (environmental studies), BIOLOGICAL SCIENCE (biochemistry, botany, microbiology, and zoology), BUSINESS (accounting, business administration and management, business economics, finance, human resources, international business, management information systems, marketing, and organizational behavior), COMMUNICATIONS AND THE ARTS (advertising, Arabic, art, art history and appreciation, arts/sciences planned program, broadcasting, Chinese, classics, communications, dance, dramatic arts, English, film arts, French, German, Italian, journalism, language arts, languages, linguistics, literature, music, music performance, musical theater, Russian languages and literature, Spanish, video, and visual communication), COMPUTER AND PHYSICAL SCIENCE (astronomy, astrophysics, atmospheric sciences and meteorology, chemistry, computer science, geology, information sciences and systems, mathematics, and physics), EDUCATION (early childhood education, elementary education, foreign languages education, mathematics education, music education, science education, social studies education, special education, and world language education), ENGINEERING AND ENVIRONMENTAL DESIGN (aeronautical engineering, architectural engineering, architecture, aviation administration/management, biomedical engineering, chemical engineering, civil engineering, computer engineering, construction management, electrical/electronics engineering, engineering physics, environmental design, environmental engineering, environmental science, geological engineering, geophysical engineering, industrial engineering, interior design, mechanical engineering, and petroleum/natural gas engineering), HEALTH PROFESSIONS (exercise science and human relations), SOCIAL SCIENCE (African American studies, anthropology, area studies, criminal justice, economics, geography, geography information science, history, history of science, humanities, international studies, Judaic studies, liberal arts/general studies, Native American studies, philosophy, political science/government, psychology, public administration, religion, social work, sociology, women's studies, and world cultural studies). Chemistry, finance & accounting, and meteorology are the strongest academically. Biology, health & exercise science and psychology have the largest enrollments.

ACTIVITIES: 24% of men belong to 28 national fraternities; 33% of women belong to 18 national sororities. There are 478 groups on campus, including art, band, cheerleading, chess, choir, chorale, chorus, computers, dance, debate, drama, drill team, environmental, ethnic, film, forensics, honors, international, jazz band, LGBT, literary magazine, marching band, musical theater, newspaper, opera, orchestra, pep band, photography, political, professional, radio and TV, religious, social, social service, student government, symphony, and yearbook. Popular campus events include Homecoming, Eve of Nations, Pink and Black Ball, and CAC Soonerthon. **Sports:** There are 10 intercollegiate sports for men and 11 for women, and 27 intramural sports for men and 27 for women. Facilities include a golf course, field house, arena, gymnastics center, tennis courts, swimming pool complex, fitness center, football stadium, track and field facilities, baseball, soccer, softball fields and an indoor rowing facility. **Graduates:** From July 1, 2015 to June 30, 2016, 4148 bachelor's degrees were awarded. The most popular majors were finance (4%), accounting (4%), and psychology (3%). 1710 companies recruited on campus in 2015-2016. In an average class, 2% graduate in 3 years or less, 41% graduate in 4 years or less, 63% graduate in 5 years or less, and 66% graduate in 6 years or less.

SERVICES: Counseling and information services are available, as is tutoring in some subjects, also a reader service for the blind, and remedial math, reading, and writing. There are also volunteer note takers, interpreter, and real-time reporting services for the deaf or hearing impaired, and alternative testing services. **Library/Resources:** The 6 libraries contain 5.4 million volumes, 3.6 million microform items, 13,194 audio/video tapes/CDs/DVDs, and subscribe to 201,117 periodicals including electronic. Computerized library services include interlibrary loans, database searching, Internet access, and Wi-Fi capability. Special learning facilities include an art gallery, natural history museum, radio station, TV station, an observatory. **Physically Challenged Students:** 95% of the campus is accessible. Facilities include wheelchair ramps, elevators, special parking, specially equipped restrooms, special class scheduling, lowered drinking fountains, lowered telephones, special housing. **Special:** Co-op programs are available in Arts and Sciences, and Business, and Engineering. A variety of voluntary and required internships are available in more than 50 fields of study. OU offers study abroad in over 50 countries, work-study programs, a Washington semester, a general studies degree, dual and student-designed majors, nondegree study, pass/fail options, and credit for life experience. B.A.-B.S. degrees are offered in many subjects and an accelerated degree is offered in 15 majors. The interdisciplinary major in Letters combines the classics, history, philosophy, and languages. There are 17 national honor societies, Phi Beta Kappa, and a freshman honors program. **Visiting:** There are regularly scheduled orientations for prospective students, consisting of sessions tailored to individual needs and interests. There are guides for informal visits and visitors may sit in on classes. To schedule a visit, contact Admissions & Recruitment. **Campus Safety and Security:** Measures include 24-hour foot and vehicle patrol, emergency notification system, self-defense education, and security escort services. There are also shuttle buses, emergency telephones, lighted pathways/sidewalks, controlled access to dorms/residences, a bicycle patrol, and safe ride program.

REQUIREMENTS: Applicants will be considered for admission using a holistic review and selection process which considers several factors that predict academic success (i.e. high school grade point average, high school course rigor, academic engagement, writing ability, leadership and ACT/SAT scores). Students must have a total of 15 curricular units, including 4 units of English, 3 units of math, 3 units of lab science, 3 unit of history and citizenship, and 2 elective units from areas previously mentioned or computer science or foreign language. Some alternative admission opportunities are available, but limited. AP and CLEP credits are accepted. To graduate, students must have a minimum 2.0 GPA, depending on the major, and complete a minimum of 120 semester hours, the last 30 hours of which must be in residence. The number of hours required in the major varies. A 40-hour general education core includes courses in arts and humanities, oral and symbolic communication, natural science, and social science. All students must take 6 hours each of English composition, American history and government, and general education requirements. Seniors must take a 3-credit-hour capstone experience course integrating their undergraduate studies, and it must include writing. **Procedure:** Freshmen are admitted to all sessions. Entrance exams should be taken during the junior year or the first part of the senior year. There is a rolling admissions plan. Applications should be filed by February 1 for fall entry; November 1 for spring entry; and March 1 for summer entry, along with a $40 fee. Notification is sent on a rolling basis. 1621 applicants were on the 2016 waiting list; 172 were admitted. Applications are accepted online. **Transfer Students:** 1135 transfer students enrolled in 2015-2016. Applicants with 60 or more semester hours attempted must have a minimum GPA of 2.00. The College of Architecture, College of Atmospheric and Geographic Sciences, College of Business, College of Earth and Energy and College of Fine Arts require a 2.50. The College of Education and College of Journalism and Mass Communication require a 2.75. Nonresident Engineering applicants must have a minimum GPA of 3.00. The Applicants with fewer than 24 semester hours of college-level work must also meet freshman admission requirements. Applicants must be in good standing at the last institution attended. 30 of 120 credits required for the bachelor's degree must be completed at UO. **International Students:** There are 848 international students enrolled. The school actively recruits these students. They must take the TOEFL with a minimum score of 79 on the Internet-based version (iBT).

ADMISSIONS: 71% of the 2016-2017 applicants were accepted. The SAT scores for the 2016-2017 freshman class were: Critical Reading-- 14% below 500, 41% between 500 and 599, 27% between 600 and 699, and 18% between 700 and 800. Math-- 10% below 500, 37% between 500 and 599, 34% between 600 and 699, and 19% between 700 and 800. The ACT scores were 25% between 18 and 23, 52% between 24 and 29, and 23% above 30. 57% of the current freshmen were in the top fifth of their class; 84% were in the top two fifths. There were 278 National Merit finalists. 316 freshmen graduated first in their class. **Admissions Contact:** Jeffrey Blahnik, Director of Admissions and Recruitment. Email: *admrec@ou.edu* Web: *www.ou.edu*

FINANCIAL AID: 14% of undergraduate students work part-time.

Average annual earnings from campus work are $6400. The average financial indebtedness of the 2016 graduate was $28,231. UO is a member of CSS. The FAFSA code is 003184. The priority date for freshman financial aid applications for fall entry is December 15. The filing deadline for fall entry is March 1.

UNIVERSITY OF SCIENCE AND ARTS OF OKLAHOMA D-3

www.usao.edu

Chickasha, OK 73018 (405) 574-1367 (800) 933-8726

Fax: (405) 574-1220 Email: usao-admissions@usao.edu

Full-time: 276 men, 514 women	**Faculty:** 55; IIB
Part-time: 26 men, 29 women	**Ph.D.s:** 85%
Graduate: n/av	**Student/Faculty:** 12 to 1
Year: trimesters, summer session	**Tuition:** $5670 ($15,210)
Room & Board: $5470	**Freshman Class:** 567 applied, 383 accepted, 170 enrolled
ACT: 24	**CEEB CODE:** 6544
Application Deadline: September 1	**VERY COMPETITIVE**

University of Science and Arts of Oklahoma, founded in 1908, is Oklahoma's only publicly funded liberal arts college, providing interdisciplinary learning opportunities. There is 1 undergraduate school and 5 graduate schools. In addition to regional accreditation, USAO has baccalaureate program accreditation with NASM, NCATE, and CED. The 75-acre campus is in a small town 40 miles southwest of Oklahoma City. Including any residence halls, there are 14 buildings.

STUDENT LIFE: 86% of undergraduates are from Oklahoma. Others are from 24 states, 19 foreign countries, and Canada. 95% are from public schools. 70% are White; 6% Foreign; 5% Hispanic; 4% African American; 13% American Indian/Alaska Native; 1% Asian American. **Female To Male Ratio:** 1.8:1. The average age of freshmen is 18; all undergraduates, 23. **Housing:** College-sponsored housing includes coed dorms and on-campus apartments. On-campus housing is guaranteed for the freshman year only, and is available on a first-come, and first-served basis. Priority is given to out-of-town students. 53% of students commute. All students may keep cars.

FACULTY/CLASSROOMS: 49% of faculty are male; 51% are female. All teach undergraduates, 55% do research, and 55% do both. No introductory courses are taught by graduate students. The average class size in an introductory lecture is 20; in a laboratory is 20; and in a regular course is 17.

PROGRAMS OF STUDY: USAO confers B.A., B.S., and B.F.A. degrees. Bachelor's degrees are awarded in BIOLOGICAL SCIENCE (biology/biological science), BUSINESS (business administration and management), COMMUNICATIONS AND THE ARTS (art, communications, dramatic arts, English, fine arts, and music), COMPUTER AND PHYSICAL SCIENCE (chemistry, mathematics, natural sciences, and physics), EDUCATION (early childhood education, education of the deaf and hearing impaired, elementary education, and physical education), HEALTH PROFESSIONS (speech pathology/audiology), SOCIAL SCIENCE (American Indian studies, economics, history, political science/government, psychology, and sociology). Humanities, and physical science are the strongest academically. Business administration, psychology and art have the largest enrollments.

ACTIVITIES: 2% of men belong to 1 national fraternity; 13% of women belong to 1 national sorority. There are 45 groups on campus, including art, band, cheerleading, choir, chorale, computers, dance, drama, drill team, ethnic, honors, jazz band, LGBT, musical theater, pep band, political, professional, religious, social, social service, and student government. Popular campus events include Montmartre Art Festival/Droverstock, Festival of Arts and Ideas, and Drover Difference Day. **Sports:** There are 5 intercollegiate sports for men and 5 for women, and 5 intramural sports for men and 5 for women. Facilities include a field house, a gym, a ballpark with baseball and softball fields, a soccer field, tennis courts, weight room, a fitness center, indoor pool, outdoor pool, and volleyball courts. **Graduates:** From July 1, 2015 to June 30, 2016, 183 bachelor's degrees were awarded. The most popular majors were business marketing, education, and history. 15 companies recruited on campus in 2015-2016. In an average class, 6% graduate in 3 years or less, 28% graduate in 4 years or less, 38% graduate in 5 years or less, and 41% graduate in 6 years or less. Of the 2015 graduating class, 46% were enrolled in graduate school within 6 months of graduation.

SERVICES: Counseling and information services are available, as is tutoring in some subjects, such as math, writing, and reading. There are also tutors and interpreters are available for hearing-impaired students. **Library/Resources:** The library contains 69,605 volumes, 214 microform items, and 3,562 audio/video tapes/CDs/DVDs, and subscribes to 55,000 periodicals including electronic. Computerized library services include interlibrary loans, database searching, and Internet access. Special learning facilities include an art gallery, TV station, a commercial art computer lab, a child development center, a herbarium, art gallery and a speech pathology clinic. **Physically Challenged Students:** 95% of the campus is accessible. Facilities include wheelchair ramps, elevators, special parking, specially equipped restrooms, special class scheduling, lowered drinking fountains, lowered telephones, and special housing. **Special:** USAO offers dual majors, accelerated degree programs in all majors through year-round study, work-study programs, internship placement in community institutions, a tutorial scholars program for student-designed majors, an interdisciplinary studies program, and a limited number of pass/fail options. There are 7 national honor societies, a freshman honors program, and 1 departmental honors program. **Visiting:** There are guides for informal visits, visitors may sit in on classes, and stay overnight. To schedule a visit, contact the Admissions Office. **Campus Safety and Security:** Measures include 24-hour foot and vehicle patrol, emergency notification system, security escort services, lighted pathways/sidewalks, and security cameras near housing and parking lots.

REQUIREMENTS: Applicants must meet one of the following 3 options: (1) have a minimum score of 24 on the ACT or 1090 on the SAT AND (3.0 GPA or top 50% of HS class); (2) have a high school GPA of 3.0 and be in the top 25% of their high school class; or (3) have a minimum GPA of 3.0 in their HS core courses and a minimum score of 22 on the ACT or 1020 on the SAT. USAO requires applicants to be in the upper 50% of their class. A GPA of 3.0 is required. AP and CLEP credits are accepted. Important factors in the admissions decision are evidence of special talent, leadership record, and personality/intangible qualities. To graduate, students must complete a total of 124 credit hours with a minimum GPA of 2.0. **Procedure:** Freshmen are admitted to all sessions. Entrance exams should be taken by May of the preceding spring. There is a rolling admissions plan. Applications should be filed by September 1 for fall entry, along with a $40 fee. Notification is sent on a rolling basis. Applications are accepted online. **Transfer Students:** 87 transfer students enrolled in 2015-2016. Applicants must have a minimum GPA of 2.0. Those students with fewer than 30 college-level credit hours must submit a high school transcript or GED and ACT scores. 30 of 124 credits required for the bachelor's degree must be completed at USAO. **International Students:** There are 63 international students enrolled. The school actively recruits these students. They must take the TOEFL with a minimum score of 500 on the paper-based TOEFL (PBT) or 61 on the Internet-based version (iBT). They must also take the SAT or ACT.

ADMISSIONS: 68% of the 2016-2017 applicants were accepted. The ACT scores were 18% below 12, 29% between 12 and 17, 28% between 18 and 23, 16% between 24 and 29, and 9% above 30. 57% of the current freshmen were in the top fifth of their class; 85% were in the top two fifths. **Admissions Contact:** Sarah Crevar, Assistant Director of Admissions. Email: *usao-admissions@usao.edu* Web: *www.usao.edu*

FINANCIAL AID: In 2016-2017, 74% of all full-time freshmen and 62% of continuing full-time students received some form of financial aid. 74% of all full-time freshmen and 62% of continuing full-time students received need-based aid. The average freshman award was $10,779. Need-based scholarships or need-based grants averaged $8,911; need-based self-help aid (loans and jobs) averaged $3,321; non-need-based athletic scholarships averaged $10,463; other non-need-based awards and non-need-based scholarships averaged $2,727; and $3,132 from other forms of aid. The average financial indebtedness of the 2016 graduate was $20,074. The college's own financial statement, and International Student's Certification of Finances are required. The FAFSA code is 003167. The priority date for freshman financial aid applications for fall entry is March 1. The filing deadline for fall entry is rolling.

UNIVERSITY OF TULSA E-2

www.utulsa.edu

Tulsa, OK 74104	(918) 631-2307 (800) 331-3050
Fax: (918) 631-5003	**Email:** admission@utulsa.edu
Full-time: 1856 men, 1403 women	**Faculty:** 318; IIA, ++$
Part-time: 77 men, 70 women	**Ph.D.s:** 95%
Graduate: 669 men, 488 women	**Student/Faculty:** 11 to 1
Year: semesters, summer session	**Tuition:** $41,509
Room & Board: $11,116	**Freshman Class:** 8089 applied, 2990 accepted, 717 enrolled
SAT CR/M/W: 620/620/590 **ACT:** 30	**CEEB CODE:** 6883
Application Deadline: n/av	**HIGHLY COMPETITIVE+**

University of Tulsa, was founded in 1894, and is a private comprehensive institution offering over 60 undergraduate major areas of study through its programs in liberal arts and social sciences, engineering and natural sciences, business and finance, and health sciences. A number of interdisciplinary programs are also available and students are encouraged to participate in individual research, scholarship, and creative endeavors beginning in their freshman year. The University also offers a number of combined undergraduate/graduate degree programs which allow interested and qualified students to earn an undergraduate and graduate degree in less time than would normally be required to earn both degrees separately. There are 4 undergraduate schools and 2 graduate schools. In addition to regional accreditation, TU has baccalaureate program accreditation with AACSB, ABET, CSAB, NASM, TEAC, CED, NLNAC, and CAATE. The 209-acre campus is in an urban area in the city of Tulsa. Including any residence halls, there are 95 buildings.

STUDENT LIFE: 58% of undergraduates are from Oklahoma. Others are from 48 states, 72 foreign countries, and Canada. 67% are from public schools. 55% are White; 23% Foreign; 5% Hispanic; 4% African American; 4% Asian American; 4% American Indian/Alaska Native; 4% race unknown; 1% two or more races. 37% are Protestant; 35% claim no religious affiliation; 15% Catholic. **Male To Female Ratio:** 1.3:1. The average age of freshmen is 18; all undergraduates, 21. 13% do not continue beyond their first year; 73% remain to graduate. **Housing:** 2809 students can be accommodated in college housing, which includes single-sex and coed dorms, on-campus apartments, off-campus apartments, and married student housing. In addition, there are honors houses, language houses, special-interest houses, fraternity houses, and sorority houses. On-campus housing is guaranteed for the freshman year only, and on a first-come, first-served basis, and is available on a lottery system for upperclassmen. 69% of students live on campus; of those, 91% remain on campus on weekends. All students may keep cars.

FACULTY/CLASSROOMS: 67% of faculty are male; 33% are female. 92% teach undergraduates, 98% do research, and 92% do both. Graduate students teach 6% of introductory courses. The average class size in an introductory lecture is 21; in a laboratory is 18; and in a regular course is 21.

PROGRAMS OF STUDY: UT confers B.A., B.F.A., B.A.D.E., B.M., B.M.E., B.S., B.S.A.M., B.S.A.T., B.S.B., B.S.B.A., B.S.Ch.E., B.S.C., B.S.C.S., B.S.D.E., B.S.S.P., B.S.E.C.E., B.S.I.T., B.S.E.E., B.S.E.P., B.S.E.S.S., B.S.G.S., B.S.I.B.L., B.S.M.E., B.S.N., B.S.P.E., B.S.E.P., B.S.B.G., and B.S.G.P. degrees. Master's and doctoral degrees are also awarded. Bachelor's degrees are awarded in AGRICULTURE (environmental studies), BIOLOGICAL SCIENCE (biochemistry and biology/biological science), BUSINESS (accounting, accounting (finance), accounting (information systems), banking and finance, business administration and management, business (dual major program), business administration/international, international business management, management information systems, management science, marketing/retailing/merchandising, organizational behavior, and sports management), COMMUNICATIONS AND THE ARTS (art history, art, arts administration/management, communications, creative writing, English, film arts, French, game design and development, game programming, German, music, music performance, musical theater, piano/organ, Spanish, theatre arts, visual and performing arts, and voice), COMPUTER AND PHYSICAL SCIENCE (applied mathematics, chemistry, computer game design/development, computer science, geology, geophysics and seismology, geoscience, information sciences and systems, mathematics, and physics), EDUCATION (athletic training, education, education of the deaf and hearing impaired, elementary education, and music education), ENGINEERING AND ENVIRONMENTAL DESIGN (chemical engineering, computer engineering, electrical/electronics engineering, energy management technology, engineering physics, mechanical engineering, and petroleum/natural gas engineering), HEALTH PROFESSIONS (allied health, biology, exercise science, nursing, premedicine, and speech pathology/audiology), SOCIAL SCIENCE (anthropology, archeology, Chinese Studies, communication sciences & disorders, economics, history, philosophy, political science/government, prelaw, psychology, religion, Russian and Slavic studies, sociology, women & gender studies, and women's studies). Petroleum engineering, mechanical engineering, and English are the strongest academically. Petroleum engineering, psychology, and finance have the largest enrollments.

ACTIVITIES: 19% of men belong to 7 national fraternities; 21% of women belong to 9 national sororities. There are 178 groups on campus, including art, band, cheerleading, chess, choir, chorale, chorus, communications, computers, dance, debate, drama, drill team, environmental, ethnic, film, forensics, honors, international, jazz band, LGBT, literary magazine, marching band, musical theater, newspaper, orchestra, pep band, photography, political, professional, radio and TV, religious, social, social service, student government, symphony, and yearbook. Popular campus events include Homecoming, Springfest, Hurrican Thursdays, and International Education Week. **Sports:** There are 7 intercollegiate sports for men and 10 for women, and 22 intramural sports for men and 22 for women. Facilities include a stadium, basketball arena, a gym, athletic field, indoor racquetball courts, basketball and tennis courts, handball court, weight room, dance studio, student fitness center, soccer fields, softball field, track, multi-purpose recreational field, and outdoor track. **Graduates:** From July 1, 2015 to June 30, 2016, 770 bachelor's degrees were awarded. The most popular majors were petroleum engineering (10%), finance (7%), and psychology (5%). 248 companies recruited on campus in 2015-2016. In an average class, 58% graduate in 4 years or less, 71% graduate in 5 years or less, and 73% graduate in 6 years or less. Of the 2015 graduating class, 31% were enrolled in graduate school within 6 months of graduation, and 62% were employed.

SERVICES: Counseling and information services are available, as is tutoring in most subjects, and a reader service for the blind. Special labs are available to students in need of assistance in math and writing. **Library/Resources:** The 2 libraries contain 1.6 million volumes, 2.6 million microform items, 163,836 audio/video tapes/CDs/DVDs, and subscribe to 59,347 periodicals including electronic. Computerized library services include interlibrary loans, database searching, Internet access, and Wi-Fi capability. Special learning facilities include an art gallery, natural history museum, radio station, and TV station. **Physically Challenged Students:** 96% of the campus is accessible. Facilities include wheelchair ramps, elevators, special parking, specially equipped restrooms, special class scheduling, lowered drinking fountains, lowered telephones, and special housing. **Special:** Internships are available in the Tulsa area during the school year and in cities throughout the world during the summer. Students are encouraged to participate in study abroad, with more than 60 study-abroad programs in countries across the entire globe available. TU offers B.A.-B.S. degrees, combined bachelors/master's degree programs in a variety majors, dual and student-designed majors, accelerated degree programs, non-degree study, work-study programs, and pass/fail options. There are 34 national honor societies, Phi Beta Kappa, and a freshman honors program. **Visiting:** There are regularly scheduled orientations for prospective students, one hour walking tour of campus; an admission presentation and interview; appointments with relevant faculty members; classroom visits; lunch with current students. There are guides for informal visits, visitors may sit in on classes, and stay overnight. To schedule a visit, contact the Office of Admission. **Campus Safety and Security:** Measures include 24-hour foot and vehicle patrol, emergency notification system, self-defense education, and security escort services. There are also shuttle buses, emergency telephones, lighted pathways/sidewalks, and controlled access to dorms/residences.

REQUIREMENTS: The SAT or ACT is required. Graduation from an accredited secondary school or satisfactory scores on the GED are also required for admission. The school recommends a minimum of 18 academic credits, including 4 years of English, 4 years of math, 3 years of science and social studies (including history), 2 years of a single foreign language and one year of fine arts and humanities. Computer competency is also expected. An essay and an interview are highly recommended. An audition or a portfolio is required for students applying for music, theater, or art scholarships. AP credits are accepted. Important factors in the admissions decision are advanced placement or honors courses, leadership record, and extracurricular activities record. To graduate, students must complete 124 to 134 credit hours, including 24 to 51 in the major, with a minimum GPA determined by the major. Freshmen in liberal arts and business administration must complete a First Seminar. All students must complete the core curriculum, which includes 2 writing courses and at least 1 course in math. All students must also complete the general curriculum, which requires 25 credit hours in 3 categories (aesthetic inquiry and creative expression, historical and social interpretation, and scientific investigation). A foreign language requirement of 2 years for liberal arts and sciences students and 1 year for business majors must be completed. **Procedure:** Freshmen are admitted in the fall and spring. Entrance exams should be taken during spring of the junior year or fall of the senior year. There are early admissions, deferred admissions, and rolling admissions plans. Application deadlines are open. Application fee is $50. Notification is sent on a rolling basis. Applications are accepted online. **Transfer Students:** 129 transfer students enrolled in 2015-2016. Transfer students must submit official transcripts from all colleges attended and should have a minimum GPA of 2.75 for all college and high school work. Applicants with fewer than 30 credit hours must submit ACT or SAT scores. Those with fewer than 60 credit hours must submit an official high school transcript. Applicants 25 years of age or older are exempt from submitting ACT or SAT scores unless requested to do so by the Admission Office. 45 of 126 credits required for the bachelor's degree must be completed at UT. **International Students:** There are 824 international students enrolled. The school actively recruits these students. They must take the TOEFL with a minimum score of 525 on the paper-based TOEFL (PBT) or 70 on the Internet-based version (iBT), a minimum IELTS score of 6.0.

ADMISSIONS: 37% of the 2016-2017 applicants were accepted. The SAT scores for the 2016-2017 freshman class were: Critical Reading-- 14% below 500, 25% between 500 and 599, 33% between 600 and 699, and 28% between 700 and 800. Math-- 11% below 500, 27% between 500 and 599, 37% between 600 and 699, and 25% between 700 and 800. Writing-- 22% below 500, 32% between 500 and 599, 30% between 600 and 699, and 16% between 700 and 800. The ACT scores were 10% between 18 and 23, 37% between 24 and 29, and 53% above 30. 86% of the current freshmen were in the top fifth of their class; 97% were in the top two fifths. There were 32 National Merit finalists. 23 freshmen graduated first in their class. **Admissions Contact:** Casey Reed, Dean of Admission. Email: *admission@utulsa.edu* Web: *www.utulsa.edu*

FINANCIAL AID: In 2016-2017, 93% of all full-time freshmen and 86% of continuing full-time students received some form of financial aid. 34% of all full-time freshmen and 27% of continuing full-time students received need-based aid. The average freshman award was $29,598. Need-based scholarships or need-based grants averaged $5,904 ($8,005 maximum); need-based self-help aid (loans and jobs) averaged $4,852 ($7,600 maximum); non-need-based athletic scholarships averaged $37,778 ($58,566 maximum); and other non-need-based awards and non-need-based scholarships averaged $24,925 ($52,187 maximum). 26% of undergraduate students work part-time. Average annual earnings from campus work are $5100. The average financial indebtedness of the 2016 graduate was $28,842. The FAFSA code is 003185. The priority date for freshman financial aid applications for fall entry is March 1.

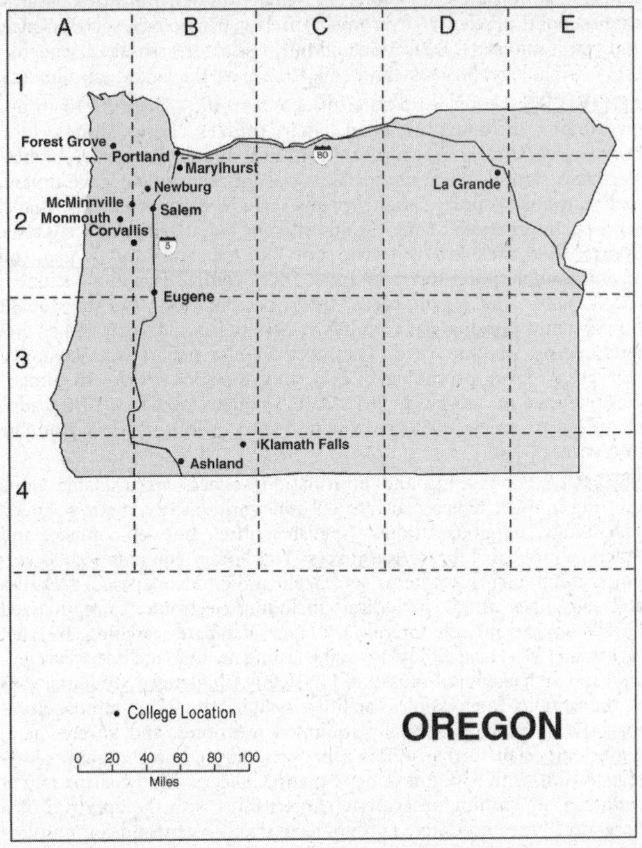

ART INSTITUTE OF PORTLAND *(The complete profile is made available exclusively on our website, www.barronspac.com)*

CONCORDIA UNIVERSITY B-1

www.cu-portland.edu

Portland, OR 97211	**(503) 280-8501** **(800) 321-9371**
Fax: (503) 280-8531	**Email: admission@cu-portland.edu**
Full-time: 369 men, 706 women	**Faculty:** 40
Part-time: 44 men, 138 women	**Ph.D.s:** 57%
Graduate: 1271 men, 4907 women	**Student/Faculty:** 20 to 1
Year: semesters, summer session	**Tuition:** $28,510
Room & Board: $8010	**Freshman Class:** 804 applied, 532 accepted, 201 enrolled
SAT CR/M: 500/500 **ACT:** required	**CEEB CODE:** 4079
Application Deadline: open	**COMPETITIVE**

Concordia University, founded in 1905, is a private liberal arts institution affiliated with the Lutheran Church Missouri Synod and is 1 of 10 institutions of the Concordia University System. There are 4 undergraduate schools and 3 graduate schools. In addition to regional accreditation, Concordia has baccalaureate program accreditation with NWCCU. The 24-acre campus is in an urban area in Portland. Including any residence halls, there are 20 buildings.

STUDENT LIFE: 65% of undergraduates are from Oregon. Others are from 14 states, 18 foreign countries, and Canada. 75% are White; 4% African American; 4% Hispanic; 3% Asian American; 2% American Indian/Alaska Native; 1% Foreign. 59% are Protestant; 30% claim no religious affiliation. **Female To Male Ratio:** 3.4:1. The average age of freshmen is 19; all undergraduates, 25. 25% do not continue beyond their first year; 45% remain to graduate. **Housing:** 500 students can be accommodated in college housing, which includes single-sex and coed dorms, on-campus apartments, and married student housing. On-campus housing is guaranteed for the freshman year only, and is available on a first-come, first-served basis, and is available on a lottery system for upperclassmen. 59% of students live on campus; of those, 95% remain on campus on weekends. Alcohol is not permitted. All students may keep cars.

FACULTY/CLASSROOMS: 67% of faculty are male; 33% are female. All teach undergraduates, and 5% do research. No introductory courses are taught by graduate students. The average class size in an introductory lecture is 19; in a laboratory is 19; and in a regular course is 17.

PROGRAMS OF STUDY: Concordia confers B.A. and B.S. degrees. Associate, master's, and doctoral degrees are also awarded. Bachelor's degrees are awarded in BIOLOGICAL SCIENCE (biology/biological science), BUSINESS (business administration and management), COMMUNICATIONS AND THE ARTS (English), COMPUTER AND PHYSICAL SCIENCE (chemistry), EDUCATION (early childhood education, elementary education, and secondary education), ENGINEERING AND ENVIRONMENTAL DESIGN (environmental science), HEALTH PROFESSIONS (health care administration, nursing, and premedicine), SOCIAL SCIENCE (humanities, psychology, social work, theological studies, and youth ministry). Nursing, biology, and business administration are the strongest academically. Nursing, business, and education have the largest enrollments.

ACTIVITIES: There are no fraternities or sororities. There are 14 groups on campus, including handbell choir, brass ensemble, cheerleading, choir, chorus, communications, drama, environmental, honors, international, literary magazine, newspaper, orchestra, professional, religious, social, social service, and student government. **Sports:** There are 6 intercollegiate sports for men and 7 for women, and 10 intramural sports for men and 10 for women. Facilities include a weight room, 1200-seat gym, and baseball/soccer stadium. **Graduates:** From July 1, 2015 to June 30, 2016, 219 bachelor's degrees were awarded. The most popular majors were business administration (36%), education (34%), and nursing . 35 companies recruited on campus in 2015-2016. In an average class, 30% graduate in 4 years or less, 39% graduate in 5 years or less, and 43% graduate in 6 years or less.

SERVICES: Counseling and information services are available, as is tutoring in most subjects. There is remedial math, reading, and writing. There is also student-supported individual help and media resources. **Library/Resources:** The library contains 70,000 volumes, 56,706 microform items, and 2,888 audio/video tapes/CDs/DVDs, and subscribes to 424 periodicals including electronic. Computerized library services include interlibrary loans, database searching, and Internet access. **Physically Challenged Students:** 80% of the campus is accessible. Facilities include wheelchair ramps, elevators, special parking, specially equipped restrooms, special class scheduling, and lowered telephones. **Special:** Cross-registration may be arranged through the Concordia University System and with Oregon Independent. There is a dual enrollment program with Portland Community College. There are also internships, study abroad in more than 20 countries, and an accelerated degree program in business, health care administration, and social work. There is 1 national honor society, a freshman honors program, and 1 departmental honors program. **Visiting:** There are regularly scheduled orientations for prospective students, including class visitations and meetings with program deans and faculty. There are guides for informal visits, visitors may sit in on classes, and stay overnight. To schedule a visit, contact Office of Admission. **Campus Safety and Security:** Measures include 24-hour foot and vehicle patrol, self-defense education, and security escort services. There are emergency telephones, lighted pathways/sidewalks, controlled access to dorms/residences, and emergency cell phone available 24 hours.

REQUIREMENTS: The SAT or ACT is required, with satisfactory SAT verbal scores recommended. Graduation from an accredited secondary school or satisfactory scores on the GED are required. The school recommends that high school courses include 4 units of English, 3 units each of social studies, math, and science, 2 units of a foreign language, and 1 unit of art and music. An interview is recommended. AP and CLEP credits are accepted. Important factors in the admissions decision are recommendations by school officials, leadership record, and personality/intangible qualities. To graduate, students must complete a total of 124 semester hours with a minimum GPA of 2.0. General education requirements total 48 semester hours. All students must take freshman composition and courses in math, phys ed, humanities, religion, science, writing, fine arts, and social sciences. In the major, 45 hours of 300-400 level courses must be taken. **Procedure:** Freshmen are admitted fall, spring, and summer. Entrance exams should be taken during the junior year or early in the senior year. There is a rolling admissions plan. Early decision applications should be filed by March 1. Notification is sent on a rolling basis. Applications are accepted on-line. **Transfer Students:** 141 transfer students enrolled in 2015-2016. Transfer students must have a minimum GPA of 2.0. 45 of 124 credits required for the bachelor's degree must be completed at Concordia. **International Students:** There are 15 international students enrolled. The school actively recruits these students. They must take the TOEFL. They must also take the SAT or ACT.

ADMISSIONS: 66% of the 2016-2017 applicants were accepted. The ACT scores were 40% below 12, 35% between 12 and 17, 16% between 18 and 23, 9% between 24 and 29, and 2% above 30. 42% of the current freshmen were in the top fifth of their class; 69% were in the top two fifths. **Admissions Contact:** Office of Admission Email: *admission@cu-portland.edu* Web: *www.cu-portland.edu*

FINANCIAL AID: The average freshman award was $13,000. The FAFSA code is 003191. Check with the school for current application deadlines.

CORBAN UNIVERSITY — B-2

www.corban.edu

Salem, OR 97317	(503) 375-8180 (800) 845-3005
Fax: (503) 375-7042	Email: admissions@corban.edu
Full-time: 347 men, 599 women	**Faculty:** 45
Part-time: 24 men, 25 women	**Ph.D.s:** 68%
Graduate: 68 men, 98 women	**Student/Faculty:** 15 to 1
Year: semesters, summer session	**Tuition:** $29,640
Room & Board: $9580	**Freshman Class:** 3108 applied, 949 accepted, 275 enrolled
SAT CR/M/W: 540/510/525 **ACT:** 24	**CEEB CODE:** 4956
Application Deadline: August 1	**COMPETITIVE**

Corban University is a Christian university offering degrees in biblical-theological studies, business administration, education, humanities, math, phys ed, social sciences, psychology, intercultural studies, and youth work. There are 5 undergraduate schools and 4 graduate schools. The 142-acre campus is in a suburban area in Salem, Oregon. Including any residence halls, there are 28 buildings.

STUDENT LIFE: 53% of undergraduates are from Oregon. Others are from 29 states, 11 foreign countries, and Canada. 60% are from public schools. 78% are White; 7% race unknown; 5% two or more races; 4% Hispanic; 2% Asian American; 2% Foreign; 1% African American; 1% American Indian/Alaska Native. 96% are Protestant. **Female To Male Ratio:** 1.6:1. The average age of freshmen is 18; all undergraduates, 20. 24% do not continue beyond their first year; 53% remain to graduate. **Housing:** 547 students can be accommodated in college housing, which includes single-sex married student housing, men's dorms, women's dorms, and apartments for single students. On-campus housing is guaranteed for the freshman year only, and is available on a first-come, first-served basis. 59% of students live on campus; of those, 90% remain on campus on weekends. Alcohol is not permitted. All students may keep cars.

FACULTY/CLASSROOMS: 76% of faculty are male; 24% are female. 90% teach undergraduates, and 10% do research. No introductory courses are taught by graduate students. The average class size in a regular course is 15.

PROGRAMS OF STUDY: Corban confers B.A. and B.S. degrees. Associate, master's, and doctoral degrees are also awarded. Bachelor's degrees are awarded in BUSINESS (accounting, business administration and management, marketing, marketing management, and sports management), COMMUNICATIONS AND THE ARTS (communications, creative writing, English, journalism, music, and music performance), COMPUTER AND PHYSICAL SCIENCE (information sciences and systems and mathematics), EDUCATION (business education, education, elementary education, mathematics education, music education, physical education, social studies education, and sports and wellness studies), HEALTH PROFESSIONS (exercise science, health care administration, health science, predentistry, premedicine, preoptometry, prepharmacy, prephysical therapy, and preveterinary science), SOCIAL SCIENCE (biblical studies, counseling/psychology, criminal justice, crosscultural studies, history, humanities, interdisciplinary studies, ministries, pastoral studies, political science/government, prelaw, psychology, social science, and youth ministry). Education and business are the strongest academically. Psychology, business, and education have the largest enrollments.

ACTIVITIES: There are no fraternities or sororities. There are 16 groups on campus, including art, band, choir, chorale, chorus, drama, film, honors, jazz band, literary magazine, musical theater, newspaper, orchestra, radio station, religious, social, social service, student government, and yearbook. Popular campus events include sports weekends, chapel services, International Fair, various student led activities and contests. **Sports:** There are 6 intercollegiate sports for men and 7 for women, and 12 intramural sports for men and 12 for women. Facilities include a sports center with a gym, soccer fields, baseball fields and the student fitness center. **Graduates:** From July 1, 2015 to June 30, 2016, 194 bachelor's degrees were awarded. The most popular majors were business/marketing (25%), psychology (22%), and education (10%). 10 companies recruited on campus in 2015-2016. In an average class, 10% graduate in 3 years or less, 49% graduate in 4 years or less, and 53% graduate in 6 years or less.

SERVICES: Counseling and information services are available, as is tutoring in most subjects such as US and world history, math, sciences, psychology, religious studies, English/writing, business, music, and others as needed. **Library/Resources:** The library contains 85,000 volumes, 2,000 microform items, and 3,000 audio/video tapes/CDs/DVDs, and subscribes to 552 periodicals including electronic. Computerized library services include interlibrary loans, database searching, Internet access, and Wi-Fi capability. Special learning facilities include an art gallery, and archaeological museum. **Physically Challenged Students:** 95% of the campus is accessible. Facilities include wheelchair ramps, elevators, special parking, specially equipped restrooms, and lowered telephones. **Special:** Corban offers a pre-seminary co-op program, cross-registration with Oregon Independent Colleges, study abroad in 4 countries, a Washington semester, internships with the approval of a program adviser, accelerated programs in management and communication and in family studies, and student-designed majors with adviser approval. Also, Corban offers a Fast-Track B.S./M.Div. degree and AMBEX Study Abroad in Germany. There is a freshman honors program. **Visiting:** There are regularly scheduled orientations for prospective students, including a campus tour, classroom visit, and activities with the student body. There are guides for informal visits, visitors may sit in on classes, and stay overnight. To schedule a visit, contact the Admissions Office. **Campus Safety and Security:** Measures include 24-hour foot and vehicle patrol, emergency notification system, self-defense education, and security escort services. There are emergency telephones, lighted pathways/sidewalks, controlled access to dorms/residences, 24 hour emergency response not patrol, threat assessment, safety planning, emergency planning, self-defense education mentoring, events and mass gatherings, travel security planning, crisis management, executive protection, bomb threats, intellectual property protection, personal protection best practices, loss prevention, security risk assessment, access management, crime prevention through environmental design, Clery compliance and reporting, media relations, money transport, armed and unarmed security, environmental security, business continuity, counterterrorism, intelligence gathering, security management, and internal investigations.

REQUIREMENTS: The SAT or ACT is required. Admissions requirements (recommended) consist of 14 units of 4 in English, 3 each in math and social studies, and 2 each in social studies and science. Corban University requires a Statement of Faith Essay. AP and CLEP credits are accepted. Important factors in the admissions decision are recommendations by school officials, leadership record, personality/intangible qualities, extracurricular activities record, and recommendations by alumni. To graduate, students must complete 128 credits with 40 to 74 in the major. The minimum required GPA is 2.0 for most programs; the education major requires a 3.0 GPA. The general education core consists of 68 credits. Courses must be taken in Bible, humanities, social sciences, math, science, and phys ed. **Procedure:** Freshmen are admitted fall and spring. There is a rolling admissions plan. Applications should be filed by August 1 for fall entry; December 1 for spring entry, along with a $40 fee. Notification is sent on a rolling basis. Applications are accepted on-line. **Transfer Students:** 63 transfer students enrolled in 2015-2016. Transfer applicants are required to have a minimum 2.0 cumulative college GPA and submit the college transcript and 3 references. Transfer students may enroll in the fall, and spring. 30 of 128 credits required for the bachelor's degree must be completed at Corban. **International Students:** There are 23 international students enrolled. The school actively recruits these students. They must take the TOEFL with a minimum score of 500 on the paper-based TOEFL (PBT) or 61 on the Internet-based version (iBT). They must also take the SAT or ACT.

ADMISSIONS: 31% of the 2016-2017 applicants were accepted. The SAT scores for the 2016-2017 freshman class were: Critical Reading-- 29% below 500, 41% between 500 and 599, 25% between 600 and 699, and 5% between 700 and 800. Math-- 40% below 500, 44% between 500 and 599, 14% between 600 and 699, and 3% between 700 and 800. Writing-- 43% below 500, 35% between 500 and 599, 19% between 600 and 699, and 3% between 700 and 800. 27% of the current freshmen were in the top fifth of their class; 41% were in the top two fifths. There was 1 National Merit finalist. 15 freshmen graduated first in their class. **Admissions Contact:** Chris Vetter, Associate Provost of Enrollment Services. Email: *admissions@corban.edu* Web: *www.corban.edu*

FINANCIAL AID: In 2016-2017, 99% of all full-time freshmen and 84% of continuing full-time students received some form of financial aid. 80% of all full-time freshmen and 83% of continuing full-time students received need-based aid. The average freshman award was $20,775. Need-based scholarships or need-based grants averaged $17,989; need-based self-help aid (loans and jobs) averaged $3,821; non-need-based athletic scholarships averaged $12,116; other non-need-based awards and non-need-based scholarships averaged $4,085; and $8,374 from other forms of aid. 37% of undergraduate students work part-time. Average annual earnings from campus work are $1721. The average financial indebtedness of the 2016 graduate was $27,325. The FAFSA code is 001339. The priority date for freshman financial aid applications for fall entry is February 1.

EASTERN OREGON UNIVERSITY D-2

www.eou.edu

La Grande, OR 97850	(541) 962-3393 (800) 452-8639
Fax: (541) 962-3418	Email: admissions@eou.edu
Full-time: 642 men, 1097 women	Faculty: 96
Part-time: 390 men, 636 women	Ph.D.s: 88%
Graduate: 109 men, 251 women	Student/Faculty: 18 to 1
Year: n/av	Tuition: $8073 ($17,520)
Room & Board: $9642	Freshman Class: 994 applied, 967 accepted, 325 enrolled
SAT: required ACT: 21	CEEB CODE: 4300
Application Deadline: September 1	COMPETITIVE

Founded in 1929, Eastern Oregon University prepares students for the world beyond college with high-quality liberal arts and professional programs. As one of the best values in higher education today, EOU offers small classes, flexible programs, and low tuition to help graduates get ahead with an education personalized to meet their goals. Classes are available when and where students need them at the university's main campus in La Grande, online from almost anywhere in the world, and onsite at centers across the state of Oregon. The figures in the above capsule and in this profile are approximate. There are 3 undergraduate schools and 1 graduate school. In addition to regional accreditation, Eastern has baccalaureate program accreditation with NCATE, IACBE, and TSPC. The 121-acre campus is in a rural area 260 miles east of Portland. Including any residence halls, there are 13 buildings.

STUDENT LIFE: 72% of undergraduates are from Oregon. Others are from 42 states, 25 foreign countries, and Canada. 96% are from public schools. 82% are White; 5% Foreign; 4% Asian American; 3% Hispanic; 1% African American; 1% American Indian/Alaska Native. **Female To Male Ratio:** 1.7:1. The average age of freshmen is 19; all undergraduates, 29. 32% do not continue beyond their first year; 37% remain to graduate. **Housing:** 436 students can be accommodated in college housing, which includes single-sex and coed dorms and married student housing, a wellness floor, and an academic focus floor. On-campus housing is available on a first-come, first-served basis. 89% of students commute. All students may keep cars.

FACULTY/CLASSROOMS: 57% of faculty are male; 43% are female. All teach undergraduates, and all do research. No introductory courses are taught by graduate students. The average class size in an introductory lecture is 60; in a laboratory is 20; and in a regular course is 35.

PROGRAMS OF STUDY: Eastern confers B.A. and B.S degrees. Master's degrees are also awarded. Bachelor's degrees are awarded in AGRICULTURE (agricultural business management, agricultural economics, forestry and related sciences, range/farm management, and soil science), BIOLOGICAL SCIENCE (biology/biological science), BUSINESS (accounting and business administration and management), COMMUNICATIONS AND THE ARTS (art, dramatic arts, English, and music), COMPUTER AND PHYSICAL SCIENCE (chemistry, computer science, mathematics, and physics), EDUCATION (education and physical education), HEALTH PROFESSIONS (health and nursing), SOCIAL SCIENCE (anthropology, history, liberal arts/general studies, psychology, and sociology). Sciences is the strongest academically. Business and education have the largest enrollments.

ACTIVITIES: There are no fraternities or sororities. There are 44 groups on campus, including art, band, cheerleading, choir, chorale, chorus, communications, computers, dance, drama, ethnic, international, jazz band, literary magazine, musical theater, newspaper, orchestra, photography, professional, radio and TV, religious, social, student government, and symphony. Popular campus events include Casino Night, Spring Fling, and Spring Symposium. **Sports:** There are 6 intercollegiate sports for men and 6 for women, and 6 intramural sports for men and 6 for women. Facilities include racquetball courts, a weight room, 3 gyms, a swimming pool, aerobics facilities, a track, and indoor and outdoor tennis courts. **Graduates:** From July 1, 2015 to June 30, 2016, 703 bachelor's degrees were awarded. The most popular majors were business/marketing (31%), liberal arts and general studies (24%), and social science (7%). 30 companies recruited on campus in 2015-2016. In an average class, 20% graduate in 4 years or less, 45% graduate in 5 years or less, and 37% graduate in 6 years or less.

SERVICES: Counseling and information services are available, as is tutoring in most subjects. There is a reader service for the blind, and remedial math, reading, and writing. **Library/Resources:** The library contains 346,285 volumes, 316,320 microform items, and 37,995 audio/video tapes/CDs/DVDs, and subscribes to 996 periodicals including electronic. Computerized library services include interlibrary loans, database searching, Internet access, and Wi-Fi capability. Special learning facilities include an art gallery, natural history museum, radio station, and a learning center that provides one-on-one tutoring in math and writing for all students. Computer lab facilities are available to students in multiple locations across campus. **Physically Challenged Students:** 80% of the campus is accessible. Facilities include wheelchair ramps, elevators, special parking, and specially equipped restrooms. **Special:** There are cooperative and 3-2 engineering degree programs with Oregon State University. The university offers internships, work-study with federal agencies, accelerated degree program, student-designed and dual majors, study abroad in 8 countries, a general studies degree, B.A.-B.S. degrees, a multidisciplinary degree, numerous preprofessional programs, credit by exam and for life/military/work experience, external degrees, and pass/fail options. The university also serves students with course-work via telecommunications and video, and with a weekend University. There are 6 national honor societies, Phi Beta Kappa, and 6 departmental honors programs. **Visiting:** There are regularly scheduled orientations for prospective students, including a campus tour, academic advising, and information sessions on financial aid and residence life. There are guides for informal visits, visitors may sit in on classes, and stay overnight. To schedule a visit, contact Admissions/New Student Programs at admissions@eou.edu. **Campus Safety and Security:** Measures include 24-hour foot and vehicle patrol and security escort services. There are emergency telephones and lighted pathways/sidewalks.

REQUIREMENTS: The SAT or ACT is required. A GED is accepted. Applicants must complete 15-16 academic credit units, 4 units of English, 3 each of math, social studies, and science with 1 unit of lab, and 2 of foreign language. AP and CLEP credits are accepted. Important factors in the admissions decision are extracurricular activities record and geographical diversity. Students must complete 180 credit hours, including 60 hours of general education courses that include 15 hours each of social science, natural science, humanities, art-language, and logic, with a GPA of at least 2.0. They must demonstrate computer competency and pass a writing proficiency exam. A senior capstone experience is required. **Procedure:** Freshmen are admitted to all sessions. Entrance exams should be taken in the senior year. There are deferred admissions and rolling admissions plans. Applications should be filed by September 1 for fall entry, along with a $50 fee. Notifications are sent February 1. **Transfer Students:** 378 transfer students enrolled in 2015-2016. Applicants must have 30 credits of transferable academic work with a GPA of 2.25. Transfer Student may enroll in the fall, winter, spring, and summer. 45 of 180 credits required for the bachelor's degree must be completed at Eastern. **International Students:** There are 92 international students enrolled. They must take the TOEFL or MELAB, and the University of Michigan Language Test for placement.

ADMISSIONS: 97% of the 2016-2017 applicants were accepted. The SAT scores for the 2016-2017 freshman class were: Critical Reading--61% below 500, 31% between 500 and 599, and 7% between 600 and 699. Math-- 65% below 500, 27% between 500 and 599, and 7% between 600 and 699. Writing-- 77% below 500, 19% between 500 and 599, and 4% between 600 and 699. The ACT scores were 25% between 12 and 17, 58% between 18 and 23, and 17% between 24 and 29. **Admissions Contact:** Sherri Edvalson, Director of Admissions. Email: *admissions@eou.edu* Web: *www.eou.edu*

FINANCIAL AID: The average freshman award was $9,287. Need-based scholarships or need-based grants averaged $6,609; need-based self-help aid (loans and jobs) averaged $3,198; non-need-based athletic scholarships averaged $3,213; other non-need-based awards and non-need-based scholarships averaged $3,033; and $1,759 from other forms of aid. Eastern is a member of CSS. The FAFSA code is 003193. The priority date for freshman financial aid applications for fall entry is January 1. The deadline for filing freshman financial aid applications for fall entry is March 1.

GEORGE FOX UNIVERSITY B-2

www.georgefox.edu

Newberg, OR 97132 (503) 554-2240 (800) 765-4369
Fax: (503) 554-3110 Email: admissions@georgefox.edu

Full-time: 1003 men, 1247 women	**Faculty:** 110; IIA, -$
Part-time: 87 men, 159 women	**Ph.D.s:** 75%
Graduate: 514 men, 615 women	**Student/Faculty:** 14 to 1
Year: semesters, summer session	**Tuition:** $32,786
Room & Board: $10,152	**Freshman Class:** 2777 applied, 2122 accepted, 608 enrolled
SAT CR/M/W: 540/545/528 **ACT:** 23	**CEEB CODE:** 4325
Application Deadline: February 1	**COMPETITIVE**

George Fox University, founded in 1891, is a Christian university of the humanities, sciences, and professional studies. It offers bachelor's degrees in more than 40 majors, adult degree programs, 6 seminary degrees, and 13 master's and doctoral degrees at its main campus, and at teaching centers in Portland and Salem, Oregon. There are 6 undergraduate schools and 4 graduate schools. In addition to regional accreditation, George Fox has baccalaureate program accreditation with ABET, ACBSP, CSWE, NASM, NCATE, CAATE, and CCNE. The 85-acre campus is in a small town in Newberg, Oregon, and 23 miles southwest of Portland. Including any residence halls, there are 80 buildings.

STUDENT LIFE: 65% of undergraduates are from Oregon. Others are from 27 states, 17 foreign countries, and Canada. 72% are from public schools. 71% are White; 8% race unknown; 5% Hispanic; 5% Foreign; 4% Asian American; 4% two or more races; 2% African American; 1% American Indian/Alaska Native. 82% are Protestant; 14% claim no religious affiliation. **Female To Male Ratio:** 1.3:1. The average age of freshmen is 18; all undergraduates, 21. 18% do not continue beyond their first year; 62% remain to graduate. **Housing:** 1211 students can be accommodated in college housing, which includes single-sex and coed on-campus apartments. In addition, there are special-interest houses, smoke-free and drug-free housing, and theme housing. On-campus housing is available on a first-come, first-served basis, and is available on a lottery system for upperclassmen. 54% of students live on campus. Alcohol is not permitted. All students may keep cars.

FACULTY/CLASSROOMS: 55% of faculty are male; 45% are female. 64% teach undergraduates. No introductory courses are taught by graduate students. The average class size in an introductory lecture is 36; in a laboratory is 17; and in a regular course is 20.

PROGRAMS OF STUDY: George Fox confers B.A., B.S., B.S.A.T. and B.S.W. degrees. Master's and doctoral degrees are also awarded. Bachelor's degrees are awarded in BIOLOGICAL SCIENCE (biology/biological science), BUSINESS (accounting, business administration and management, business communications, management information systems, management science, and organizational leadership and management), COMMUNICATIONS AND THE ARTS (art, communications, creative writing, dramatic arts, film arts, literature, multimedia, music, and Spanish), COMPUTER AND PHYSICAL SCIENCE (chemistry, computer science, information sciences and systems, and mathematics), EDUCATION (athletic training, elementary education, and music education), ENGINEERING AND ENVIRONMENTAL DESIGN (engineering and applied science), HEALTH PROFESSIONS (allied health, exercise science, health, health care administration, nursing, predentistry, premedicine, and preveterinary science), SOCIAL SCIENCE (behavioral science, biblical studies, cognitive science, economics, family/consumer studies, history, international studies, ministries, philosophy, political science/government, prelaw, psychology, religion, social science, social work, and sociology). Nursing and engineering are the strongest academically. Business, engineering, and nursing have the largest enrollments.

ACTIVITIES: There are no fraternities or sororities. There are 20 groups on campus, including art, band, choir, chorale, chorus, computers, debate, drama, ethnic, film, forensics, honors, international, jazz band, literary magazine, musical theater, newspaper, orchestra, outdoor club, pep band, political, professional, radio and TV, religious, social, social service, student government, symphony, and yearbook. Popular campus events include Serve Day, Juniors Abroad, and Cultural Celebration Week. **Sports:** There are 7 intercollegiate sports for men and 8 for women, and 7 intramural sports for men and 7 for women. Facilities include an all-weather track, a fitness center, tennis and handball/racquetball courts, a climbing wall, a 2500-seat gym, and baseball, softball, and soccer fields. **Graduates:** From July 1, 2015 to June 30, 2016, 589 bachelor's degrees were awarded. The most popular majors were interdisciplinary studies (9%), visual and performing arts/healh professions and related programs/engineering (7%), psychology/area, ethnic, and and gender studies (6%). 275 companies recruited on campus in 2015-2016. In an average class, 2% graduate in 3 years or less, 50% graduate in 4 years or less, 62% graduate in 5 years or less, and 64% graduate in 6 years or less.

SERVICES: Counseling and information services are available, as is tutoring in most subjects. There is a reader service for the blind, and remedial math, reading, and writing. **Library/Resources:** The 2 libraries contain 174,988 volumes, 210,708 microform items, and 5,372 audio/video tapes/CDs/DVDs, and subscribe to 60,000 periodicals including electronic. Computerized library services include interlibrary loans, database searching, Internet access, and Wi-Fi capability. Special learning facilities include an art gallery, radio station, a television production studio, a pottery kiln, physical therapy, and nursing, and engineering labs. **Physically Challenged Students:** All of the campus is accessible. Facilities include wheelchair ramps, elevators, special parking, specially equipped restrooms, special class scheduling, lowered drinking fountains, lowered telephones, and special housing. **Special:** Half of George Fox students participate in study abroad programs, which include a three-week faculty-led, subsidized trip in the spring of a student's junior year. The university offers a dual-degree 3/2 program through its applied science major, enabling students to pursue engineering in a discipline such as chemical, environmental, or aerospace engineering. Students can complete a semester at the Contemporary Music Center in Martha's Vineyard or the Los Angeles Film Studies Center. George Fox offers internships with area companies, study abroad, and a Washington semester through the Council of Christian Colleges and Universities. Work-study programs, accelerated degrees, dual and student-designed interdisciplinary majors, and pass/fail options in upper-division courses outside of the major also are offered. There are 3 national honor societies, a freshman honors program, and 1 departmental honors program. **Visiting:** There are regularly scheduled orientations for prospective students, including observation of classes and talking with professors. There are guides for informal visits, visitors may sit in on classes, and stay overnight. To schedule a visit, contact the Office of Admissions. **Campus Safety and Security:** Measures include 24-hour foot and vehicle patrol, emergency notification system, self-defense education, and security escort services. There are emergency telephones, lighted pathways/sidewalks, controlled access to dorms/residences, parking lot cameras, and video surveillance of key buildings.

REQUIREMENTS: The SAT or ACT is required. Applicants need 16 academic credits or 14 Carnegie units, including 4 units of English, 3 units of social studies, 2 units each of a foreign language, math, history, and science with lab, and 1 unit of health and physical education. An essay and 2 personal recommendations are required; a portfolio, audition, and interview are recommended in certain majors. AP and CLEP credits are accepted. Important factors in the admissions decision are advanced placement or honors courses, extracurricular activities record, and leadership record. To graduate, students must have a minimum 2.0 GPA and complete 126 semester hours, including 15 hours of sciences, 11 hours of humanities, 10 hours of Bible and religion, 6 hours each of communication and global and cultural understanding, 3 hours of health and human performance, and a 3 hour senior capstone. Majors require a minimum of 36 hours. A thesis is required in biology, chemistry, and social and behavioral sciences. **Procedure:** Freshmen are admitted fall and spring. Entrance exams should be taken in fall or winter. There are early admissions, deferred admissions, and rolling admissions plans. Applications should be filed by February 1 for fall entry; December 1 for spring entry, along with a $40 fee. Notification is sent on a rolling basis. Applications are accepted on-line. **Transfer Students:** 107 transfer students enrolled in 2015-2016. Transfers must have a minimum 2.6 GPA and 16 semester hours from their previous college. An essay and two personal recommendations are required. 30 of 126 credits required for the bachelor's degree must be completed at George Fox. **International Students:** There are 150 international students enrolled. The school actively recruits these students. They must take the TOEFL with a minimum score of 550 on the paper-based TOEFL (PBT) or 80 on the Internet-based version (iBT), and the college's own test.

ADMISSIONS: 76% of the 2016-2017 applicants were accepted. The SAT scores for the 2016-2017 freshman class were: Critical Reading-- 30% below 500, 42% between 500 and 599, 22% between 600 and 699, and 6% between 700 and 800. Math-- 29% below 500, 42% between 500 and 599, 22% between 600 and 699, and 6% between 700 and 800. Writing-- 38% below 500, 41% between 500 and 599, 19% between 600 and 699, and 3% between 700 and 800. 36 freshmen graduated first in their class. **Admissions Contact:** Lindsay Knox, Director of Undergraduate Admissions. Email: *admissions@georgefox.edu* Web: *www.georgefox.edu*

FINANCIAL AID: In 2016-2017, 100% of all full-time freshmen and 75% of continuing full-time students received some form of financial aid. 84% of all full-time freshmen and 75% of continuing full-time students received need-based aid. The average freshman award was $27,919. Need-based scholarships or need-based grants averaged $7,896; need-based self-help aid (loans and jobs) averaged $4,685; other non-need-based awards and non-need-based scholarships averaged $11,561; and $2,872 from other forms of aid. The average financial indebtedness of the 2016 graduate was $25,143. George Fox is a member of CSS. The state aid form is required. The FAFSA code is 003194. The priority date for freshman financial aid applications for fall entry is February 1.

LEWIS & CLARK COLLEGE — B-1

www.lclark.edu

Portland, OR 97219	**(503) 768-7040** **(800) 444-4111**
Fax: (503) 768-7055	**Email: admissions@lclark.edu**
Full-time: 808 men, 1294 women	**Faculty:** 153
Part-time: 15 men, 17 women	**Ph.D.s:** 92%
Graduate: 423 men, 862 women	**Student/Faculty:** 11 to 1
Year: semesters, summer session	**Tuition:** $46,894
Room & Board: $11,540	**Freshman Class:** 7796 applied, 4284 accepted, 506 enrolled
SAT or ACT: required	**CEEB CODE:** 4384
Application Deadline: January 15	**HIGHLY COMPETITIVE+**

Lewis and Clark College, founded in 1867, is a private, independent liberal arts and sciences institution with a global reach. There is 1 undergraduate school and 2 graduate schools. In addition to regional accreditation, L & C has baccalaureate program accreditation with NCATE, ABA, CACREP, and COAMFTE. The 137-acre campus is in a suburban area 6 miles south of downtown Portland. Including any residence halls, there are 58 buildings.

STUDENT LIFE: 89% of undergraduates are from out of state, mostly the West. Students are from 46 states, 75 foreign countries, and Canada. 77% are from public schools. 62% are White; 11% Hispanic; 7% Foreign; 6% Asian American; 5% race unknown; 4% two or more races; 3% African American; 1% American Indian/Alaska Native. **Female To Male Ratio:** 1.7:1. The average age of freshmen is 18; all undergraduates, 20. 15% do not continue beyond their first year; 79% remain to graduate.

Housing: 1394 students can be accommodated in college housing, which includes single-sex and coed dorms and on-campus apartments. In addition, there are special-interest houses and theme communities. On-campus housing is available on a lottery system for upperclassmen. 69% of students live on campus; of those, 95% remain on campus on weekends. Upperclassmen may keep cars.

FACULTY/CLASSROOMS: 45% of faculty are male; 55% are female. All teach undergraduates and do research. No introductory courses are taught by graduate students. The average class size in a regular course is 20.

PROGRAMS OF STUDY: L & C confers B.A. degrees. Master's and doctoral degrees are also awarded. Bachelor's degrees are awarded in AGRICULTURE (environmental studies), BIOLOGICAL SCIENCE (biochemistry and biology/biological science), COMMUNICATIONS AND THE ARTS (art history and appreciation, classics, communications, dramatic arts, English, fine arts, languages, music, and studio art), COMPUTER AND PHYSICAL SCIENCE (chemistry, computer mathematics, computer science, mathematics, and physics), SOCIAL SCIENCE (anthropology, East Asian studies, economics, French studies, German area studies, Hispanic American studies, history, interdisciplinary studies, international relations, philosophy, political science/government, psychology, religion, and sociology). Psychology, biology, and sociology/anthropology have the largest enrollments.

ACTIVITIES: There are no fraternities or sororities. There are 110 groups on campus, including art, band, choir, chorale, chorus, college outdoors club, computers, dance, debate, drama, ethnic, forensics, honors, international, jazz band, LGBT, literary magazine, newspaper, orchestra, photography, political, professional, radio and TV, religious, social, social service, student government, and symphony. Popular campus events include Gender Studies Symposium, International Affairs Symposium, Environmental Studies Symposium, Day of Service, and Alternative Breaks. **Sports:** There are 9 intercollegiate sports for men and 10 for women, and 19 intramural sports for men and 19 for women. Facilities include a gym with 3 full courts that serves basketball, volleyball, and indoor practice facilities for several intercollegiate teams, and a weigh-room. The field features a state-of-the art Astro-Turf Game Day 3D Synthetic Surface. The Zehntbauer Swimming Pavilion, houses an eight-lane, 25-yard pool with one, and three-meter diving boards. The pavilion, with its fully automatic Colorado timing system, has been the site of an NAIA National Swimming Championship meet. **Graduates:** From July 1, 2015 to June 30, 2016, 464 bachelor's degrees were awarded. The most popular majors were social sciences (24%), psychology (13%), and biological/life science (11%). 100 companies recruited on campus in 2015-2016. In an average class, 74% graduate in 4 years or less, 78% graduate in 5 years or less, and 79% graduate in 6 years or less.

SERVICES: Counseling and information services are available, as is tutoring in most subjects. There is a reader service for the blind. There are mentors, note takers, books on tape, and math and writing skills centers. **Library/Resources:** The 2 libraries contain 586,144 volumes, 1.5 million microform items, and 23,851 audio/video tapes/CDs/DVDs, and subscribe to 42,560 periodicals including electronic. Computerized library services include interlibrary loans, database searching, Internet access, and Wi-Fi capability. Special learning facilities include an art gallery, radio station, telescope, research astronomical observatory, language lab, greenhouse, and adaptive technology lab. **Physically Challenged Students:** 80% of the campus is accessible. Facilities include wheelchair ramps, elevators, special parking, specially equipped restrooms, lowered drinking fountains, and lowered telephones. **Special:** L & C offers internships; study-abroad programs in 60 countries; semesters in Washington and New York City; dual and student-designed majors; and cross-registration with schools that are a part of the Oregon Independent College Association; A 3-2 engineering program is available with Columbia University, Washington University, and the University of Southern California. There are 5 national honor societies and a chapter of Phi Beta Kappa. **Visiting:** There are regularly scheduled orientations for prospective students, information session and campus tours daily; class visits, interviews, special-interest appointments available, and 4 open house events. Visitors may sit in on classes and stay overnight. To schedule a visit, contact the Office of Admissions. **Campus Safety and Security:** Measures include 24-hour foot and vehicle patrol, emergency notification system, self-defense education, and security escort services. There are shuttle buses, emergency telephones, lighted pathways/sidewalks, and controlled access to dorms/residences card key locks in all residence halls.

REQUIREMENTS: When admitting new students, our admissions staff look for individuals from diverse backgrounds, with diverse talents and interests, students who will not only meet the rigorous academic challenges of a Lewis & Clark education, but will also take full advantage of the opportunities for individual achievement and growth offered here. Students high school course load (grades 9-12) should include a minimum of: 4 years each of English and math, 3-4 years of history and social sciences, 2-3 years of a foreign language, 3 years of lab sciences, and 1 year of creative arts. Advanced Placement, International Baccalaureate, or honors courses are viewed as further evidence of serious preparation for college-level studies. Successful candidates have taken some of these advanced courses if they are offered at their schools. We look not only at your performance in a challenging curriculum, and the following criteria as well: SAT or ACT scores (unless applying through the Portfolio Path), counselor report (first-year students only), teacher recommendation, personal essay, leadership, community service and work experience, and extracurricular involvements, and expressed interest in the College or personal interview (interviews are optional, not required). The committee weighs all of these factors to make a prediction about an applicant's potential for academic success at Lewis & Clark. We want to make sure that any student who has the opportunity to enroll at the College will have the tools they need to flourish in and enjoy our academic program. The committee also looks for students who will contribute to our community as musicians, leaders, athletes, or community service participants, just to name a few, while they are succeeding academically. AP credits are accepted. To graduate, students must complete a total of 128 semester hours with a GPA of at least 2.0. A third of the student's credits generally falls in the major program, a third in electives, and a third in general requirements, which include a required first-year course, 12 hours in scientific and quantitative reasoning, 8 hours in international studies, 3 semesters of a foreign language, 2 semesters of phys ed, and 1 course in creative arts. Certain majors require a thesis or a senior project/recital. **Procedure:** Freshmen are admitted in the fall and spring. Entrance exams should be taken during spring of the junior year or fall of the senior year. There is an early decision plan. Early decision applications should be filed by November 1; regular applications, by January 15 for fall entry. Notification of early decision is sent December 15; regular decision, April 1. 57 early decision candidates were accepted for the 2016-2017 class. 404 applicants were on the 2016 waiting list; 61 were admitted. Applications are accepted on-line. Application fees are waived if application is completed on-line. **Transfer Students:** 51 transfer students enrolled in 2015-2016. Applicants must submit high school and college transcripts, and 2 essays. SAT or ACT scores are required for transfers with fewer than 2 years of transferable credit (60 semester units). 60 of 128 credits required for the bachelor's degree must be completed at L & C. **International Students:** There are 104 international students enrolled. The school actively recruits these students. They must take the TOEFL with a minimum score of 575 on the paper-based TOEFL (PBT) or 91 on the Internet-based version (iBT) or take either the MELAB, ELPT, or IB English. They must also take the SAT or ACT, ECPE, FCE, CAE, CPE, or IELTS.

ADMISSIONS: 55% of the 2016-2017 applicants were accepted. **Admissions Contact:** Erica Johnson, Director of Admissions. Email: *admissions@lclark.edu* Web: *www.lclark.edu*

FINANCIAL AID: In 2016-2017, 93% of all full-time freshmen and 93% of continuing full-time students received some form of financial aid. 54% of all full-time freshmen and 56% of continuing full-time students received need-based aid. The average freshman award was $34,552. Need-based scholarships or need-based grants averaged $31,827; need-based self-help aid (loans and jobs) averaged $9,373; and other non-need-based awards and non-need-based scholarships averaged $15,647. The average financial indebtedness of the 2016 graduate was $29,913. The CSS/Profile is required. The FAFSA code is 003197. The priority date for freshman financial aid applications for fall entry is February 15.

LINFIELD COLLEGE — B-2

www.linfield.edu

McMinnville, OR 97128 — (503) 883-2213, (800) 640-2287

Fax: (503) 883-2472 — Email: admission@linfield.edu

Full-time: 603 men, 999 women	**Faculty:** 119; IIB, av$
Part-time: 17 men, 13 women	**Ph.D.s:** 93%
Graduate: n/av	**Student/Faculty:** 14 to 1
Year: 4-1-4, summer session	**Tuition:** $40,105
Room & Board: $11,905	**Freshman Class:** 2296 applied, 1854 accepted, 393 enrolled
SAT CR/M/W: 520/520/510 **ACT:** 24	**CEEB CODE:** 4387
Application Deadline: February 1	**COMPETITIVE**

Linfield College is dedicated exclusively to undergraduate education and is home to a vibrant community of engaged students. There are 3 undergraduate schools. In addition to regional accreditation, Linfield College has baccalaureate program accreditation with NASM, CCNE, CAATE, NAEYC, and ACS. The 189-acre campus is in a small town 40 miles southwest of Portland, Oregon. Including any residence halls, there are 79 buildings.

STUDENT LIFE: 53% of undergraduates are from Oregon. Others are from 24 states, and 23 foreign countries. 90% are from public schools. 59% are White; 20% two or more races; 6% Hispanic; 5% Asian American; 4% Foreign; 3% race unknown; 2% African American; 1% American Indian/Alaska Native. **Female To Male Ratio:** 1.6:1. The average age of freshmen is 18; all undergraduates, 20. 15% do not continue beyond their first year; 68% remain to graduate. **Housing:** 1376 students can be accommodated in college housing, which includes single-sex and coed dorms and on-campus apartments. In addition, there are special-interest houses. On-campus housing is guaranteed for all 4 years. 77% of students live on campus; of those, 80% remain on campus on weekends. All students may keep cars.

FACULTY/CLASSROOMS: 50% of faculty are male; 50% are female. All teach undergraduates, and all do research. No introductory courses are taught by graduate students. The average class size in an introductory lecture is 19; in a laboratory is 16; and in a regular course is 15.

PROGRAMS OF STUDY: Linfield College confers B.A., B.S., and B.S.N. degrees. Bachelor's degrees are awarded in AGRICULTURE (environmental studies), BIOLOGICAL SCIENCE (biochemistry and biology/biological science), BUSINESS (accounting, banking and finance, business administration and management, international business management, and marketing management), COMMUNICATIONS AND THE ARTS (art, communications, creative writing, dramatic arts, English, French, French and Francophone studies, German, Japanese, journalism, literature, music, Spanish, studio art, and theatre arts), COMPUTER AND PHYSICAL SCIENCE (applied physics, chemistry, computer science, mathematics, and physics), EDUCATION (athletic training, elementary education, health education, music education, and physical education), HEALTH PROFESSIONS (exercise science and nursing), SOCIAL SCIENCE (African studies, anthropology, crosscultural studies, economics, German area studies, history, international relations, Japanese studies, Latin American studies, philosophy, political science/government, psychology, religion, and sociology). Nursing, accounting, and exercise science are the strongest academically. Nursing, psychology, exercise science, and elementary education have the largest enrollments.

ACTIVITIES: 26% of men belong to 1 local and 3 national fraternities; 30% of women belong to 1 local and 3 national sororities. There are 85 groups on campus, including ultimate frisbee, the Hawaiian club, art, ASL, band, cheerleading, choir, chorale, chorus, computers, dance, debate, drama, environmental, ethnic, forensics, honors, international, jazz band, LGBT, literary magazine, musical theater, newspaper, opera, orchestra, pep band, photography, political, professional, radio and TV, religious, social, social service, student government, and symphony. Popular campus events include Wildstock (outdoor fair, including music and activities booths), Luau, Hispanic Heritage Day and Homecoming. **Sports:** There are 9 intercollegiate sports for men and 10 for women, and 6 intramural sports for men and 6 for women. Facilities include a football stadium with turf field, all-weather track, soccer field with lights, indoor complex with 2,200-seat gym, 3 basketball courts, 25-yard swimming pool, 2 racquetball courts, 6,000-square-foot weight room, baseball stadium with turf infield and lights, softball stadium with lights, field house with 3 tennis courts and 4 hitting cages, wellness trail, bike co-op, and a campus garden. **Graduates:** From July 1, 2015 to June 30, 2016, 320 bachelor's degrees were awarded. The most popular majors were business/marketing (22%), psychology (8%), and biology (7%). 210 companies recruited on campus in 2015-2016. In an average class, 1% graduate in 3 years or less, 57% graduate in 4 years or less, 69% graduate in 5 years or less, and 70% graduate in 6 years or less. Of the 2015 graduating class, 13% were enrolled in graduate school within 6 months of graduation, and 57% were employed.

SERVICES: Counseling and information services are available, as is tutoring in every subject. There is a reader service for the blind. Linfield speaking center, and a writing lab. **Library/Resources:** The library contains 189,314 volumes, 17,491 microform items, and 39,154 audio/video tapes/CDs/DVDs, and subscribes to 991 periodicals including electronic. Computerized library services include interlibrary loans, database searching, Internet access, and Wi-Fi capability. Special learning facilities include an art gallery, radio station, Linfield Center for the Northwest,

Delkin Recital Hall, Ford Theatre, Linfield Research Institute, Linfield Anthropology Museum, Writing Center, Career Development Center, Speaking Center, Academic Advising Office, Multimedia Studio, and Science and Computer Labs. **Physically Challenged Students:** 85% of the campus is accessible. Facilities include wheelchair ramps, elevators, special parking, specially equipped restrooms, special class scheduling, lowered drinking fountains, lowered telephones, and special housing. **Special:** Linfield is highly ranked among U.S. undergraduate schools for participation in study abroad. Through Linfield's January Term and Semester Abroad programs, students study in 30 locations around the globe in China, Africa, Europe, and Southeast Asia. During the past five years, almost 700 students completed internships off campus, many in the industry of their choice. Some students intern abroad through the IE3 Global Internships program, and others take advantage of off-campus work-study programs that target literacy and disadvantaged youth. Education is personalized, and student-designed majors are available. Last year more than 50 students collaborated on research projects with their professors, and many presented papers at professional conferences. In addition to Linfield's campus-based programs, online degrees and certificates are available, including accelerated degrees. Students may also choose a 3-2 engineering degree as part of a collaboration with the University of Southern California and Oregon and Washington State Universities. Students partner with more than 100 community-based organizations for service learning, sponsored through Linfield's Community Engagement and Service Office. Many outreach projects lead to job opportunities. New students are introduced to college with rich immersion experiences that include First CLAS (Community, Leadership, Action, and Service); iFocus (for those interested in the sciences); SOIL (sustainability); and AHA (arts & humanities). In addition, all new students participate in a Colloquium and Inquiry Seminars. Many also choose to get to know their faculty through the "Take a Professor to Lunch" program. There are 19 national honor societies and 13 departmental honors programs. **Visiting:** There are regularly scheduled orientations for prospective students, tours, and interviews. There are guides for informal visits and visitors may sit in on classes. To schedule a visit, contact Office of Admission. **Campus Safety and Security:** Measures include 24-hour foot and vehicle patrol, emergency notification system, self-defense education, and security escort services. There are emergency telephones, lighted pathways/sidewalks, and controlled access to dorms/residences.

REQUIREMENTS: The SAT or ACT is required. Linfield recommends that applicants have 4 years each of English and math, 3 to 4 years each of natural science and social studies, and 2 to 4 years of a foreign language. An essay is required, and an interview is recommended. The GED is accepted. AP and CLEP credits are accepted. Important factors in the admissions decision are advanced placement or honors courses, evidence of special talent, and recommendations by school officials. Core requirements include courses from the sciences, literature, fine arts, religion or philosophy, the social sciences, history, and quantitative reasoning. An inquiry seminar in critical thinking and writing is also required. Students also take courses in American pluralism and global diversity. 3 credits of activity courses in phys ed, music, or community service are required. Students must maintain 2.0 cumulative GPA and complete 125 semester credit hours, including 35 to 45 in the major. **Procedure:** Freshmen are admitted fall and spring. Entrance exams should be taken during the fall of the senior year of high school. There are early admissions and deferred admissions plans. Applications should be filed by February 1 for fall entry; December 1 for spring entry. Notifications are sent April 1. Applications are accepted on-line. Application fees are waived if application is completed on-line. **Transfer Students:** 69 transfer students enrolled in 2015-2016. Applicants from regionally accredited community colleges, 4-year colleges, and universities with at least a B average/3.0 GPA at their previous institution(s) are most likely to succeed. Consistent academic progress, leadership and liklihood of contribution to the Linfield community are also considered. 30 of 125 credits required for the bachelor's degree must be completed at Linfield College. **International Students:** There are 66 international students enrolled. The school actively recruits these students. They must take the TOEFL with a minimum score of 550 on the paper-based TOEFL (PBT) or 80 on the Internet-based version (iBT) or take the MELAB, One or more of these exams are required: EIKEN, IELTS, MELAB, SAT Critical Reading, ACT English, TOEFL, or TOEIC. For international students whose first language is English, the SAT or ACT is required.

ADMISSIONS: 81% of the 2016-2017 applicants were accepted. The SAT scores for the 2016-2017 freshman class were: Critical Reading-- 39% below 500, 37% between 500 and 599, 21% between 600 and 699, and 3% between 700 and 800. Math-- 39% below 500, 44% between 500 and 599, 15% between 600 and 699, and 2% between 700 and 800. Writing-- 43% below 500, 40% between 500 and 599, 15% between 600 and 699, and 2% between 700 and 800. The ACT scores were 9% between 12 and 17, 40% between 18 and 23, 41% between 24 and 29, and 9% above 30. 51% of the current freshmen were in the top fifth of their class; 87% were in the top two fifths. 17 freshmen graduated first in their class. **Admissions Contact:** Lisa Knodle-Bragiel, Director of Admission. Email: *admission@linfield.edu* Web: *www.linfield.edu*

FINANCIAL AID: In 2016-2017, 99% of all full-time freshmen and 98% of continuing full-time students received some form of financial aid. 80% of all full-time freshmen and 76% of continuing full-time students received need-based aid. The average freshman award was $32,052. Need-based scholarships or need-based grants averaged $28,872; need-based self-help aid (loans and jobs) averaged $6,073; and other non-need-based awards and non-need-based scholarships averaged $19,324. 10% of undergraduate students work part-time. Average annual earnings from campus work are $1393. The average financial indebtedness of the 2016 graduate was $23,665. Linfield College is a member of CSS. The FAFSA code is 003198. The priority date for freshman financial aid applications for fall entry is February 1.

MARYLHURST UNIVERSITY *(The complete profile is made available exclusively on our website, www.barronspac.com)*

NORTHWEST CHRISTIAN UNIVERSITY B-2

www.nwcu.edu

Eugene, OR 97401	**(541) 684-7201** **(877) 463-6622**
Fax: (541) 684-7317	**Email: admissions@nwcu.edu**
Full-time: n/av	**Faculty:** 19
Part-time: n/av	**Ph.D.s:** 47%
Graduate: n/av	**Student/Faculty:** 12 to 1
Year: trimesters, summer session	**Tuition:** $27,930
Room & Board: $8650	**Freshman Class:** 179 applied, 114 accepted, 50 enrolled
SAT or ACT: required	**CEEB CODE:** 4543
Application Deadline: n/av	**COMPETITIVE**

Northwest Christian University, founded in 1895, is a private institution affiliated with the Christian Church offering programs in the arts and sciences, business, education, and ministries. Figures in the above capsule and in this profile are approximate. There is 1 undergraduate school. In addition to regional accreditation, NCU has baccalaureate program accreditation with IACBE, NCCU, Board of Licensed Professional Counselors & Therap, and Teachers Standards & Practices Commission. The 8-acre campus is in an urban area at the south end of the Willamette Valley, near McKenzie and Willamette rivers, about 50 miles east of the Oregon Coast. Including any residence halls, there are 14 buildings.

STUDENT LIFE: 92% of undergraduates are from Oregon. Others are from 8 states. 94% are from public schools. 70% are White; 1% African American; 1% Asian American; 1% Hispanic. 64% claim no religious affiliation; 35% Protestant. The average age of freshmen is 18; all undergraduates, 30. 38% do not continue beyond their first year; 38% remain to graduate. **Housing:** 213 students can be accommodated in college housing, which includes single-sex and coed dorms and off-campus apartments. On-campus housing is guaranteed for the freshman year only. 73% of students commute. Alcohol is not permitted. All students may keep cars.

FACULTY/CLASSROOMS: 40% of faculty are male; 60% are female. All teach undergraduates. No introductory courses are taught by graduate students. The average class size in an introductory lecture is 40 and in a regular course is 25.

PROGRAMS OF STUDY: NCU confers B.A. and B.S. degrees. Associate and master's degrees are also awarded. Bachelor's degrees are awarded in BUSINESS (accounting, business administration and management, and management information systems), COMMUNICATIONS AND THE ARTS (communications and music), COMPUTER AND PHYSICAL SCIENCE (computer science), EDUCATION (education and elementary education), HEALTH PROFESSIONS (exercise science and health care administration), SOCIAL SCIENCE (human services, humanities, interdisciplinary studies, international studies, ministries, psychology, and social science). Business administration, and elementary education are the strongest academically. Accounting, business administration, and exercise science have the largest enrollments.

ACTIVITIES: There are no fraternities or sororities. There are 15 groups on campus, including cheerleading, choir, chorale, debate, drama, forensics, literary magazine, musical theater, newspaper, religious, social service, student government, and yearbook. Popular campus events include Annual Musical, Spirit Week, and Wellness Week. **Sports:** There is 1 intercollegiate sports for men and 2 for women, and 4 intramural sports for men and 4 for women. Facilities include an event center with a basketball court, fitness rooms, locker rooms, and softball practice area. **Graduates:** From July 1, 2015 to June 30, 2016, 103 bachelor's degrees were awarded. The most popular majors were management (51%), teacher education (27%), and psychology (6%). In an average class, 30% graduate in 4 years or less, and 38% graduate in 5 years or less. Of the 2015 graduating class, 13% were enrolled in graduate school within 6 months of graduation, and 72% were employed.

SERVICES: Counseling and information services are available, as is tutoring in most subjects. There is remedial math, reading, and writing. **Library/Resources:** The library contains 60,250 volumes, 766 microform items, and 10,367 audio/video tapes/CDs/DVDs, and subscribes to 261 periodicals including electronic. Computerized library services include interlibrary loans, database searching, and Internet access. **Physically Challenged Students:** 60% of the campus is accessible. Facilities include wheelchair ramps, elevators, special parking, specially equipped restrooms, special class scheduling, lowered drinking fountains, and lowered telephones. **Special:** NCC offers internships, study abroad in 4 countries, a Washington semester, work study, accelerated degree programs, and student-designed majors. **Visiting:** There are regularly scheduled orientations for prospective students. There are guides for informal visits, visitors may sit in on classes, and stay overnight. To schedule a visit, contact the Admissions Office. **Campus Safety and Security:** Measures include 24-hour foot and vehicle patrol and security escort services. There are emergency telephones and lighted pathways/sidewalks.

REQUIREMENTS: The SAT or ACT is required. Students are required to submit a completed admission application, high school transcripts, and 2 references. An interview is recommended. A GPA of 2.5 is required. AP and CLEP credits are accepted. Important factors in the admissions decision are advanced placement or honors courses, recommendations by school officials, and extracurricular activities record. To graduate, students must complete 124-186 quarter credits with at least 40 in the major and a minimum GPA of 2.0. The core curriculum consists of 55-86 credit hours in humanities, social sciences, math and science, and Bible; a 1-credit-hour chapel for every term enrolled is also required as are 3 service credits. **Procedure:** Freshmen are admitted fall and spring. There are early admissions, deferred admissions, and rolling admissions plans. Check with the school for current application deadlines. Notification is sent on a rolling basis. Applications are accepted on-line. **Transfer Students:** 55 transfer students enrolled in 2015-2016. Students are required to submit a completed application, official transcripts from each college or university attended, an academic reference, and official high school transcripts if they have fewer than 36 transferable credits. 30 of 124 credits required for the bachelor's degree must be completed at Northwest Christian University. **International Students:** They must take the TOEFL.

ADMISSIONS: 64% of the 2016-2017 applicants were accepted. 36% of the current freshmen were in the top fifth of their class; 67% were in the top two fifths. **Admissions Contact:** Randy Jones, Dean of Admissions. Email: *admissions@nwcu.edu* Web: *www.nwcu.edu*

FINANCIAL AID: In 2016-2017, 100% of all full-time freshmen and 100% of continuing full-time students received some form of financial aid. NCU is a member of CSS. The college's own financial statement is required. The FAFSA code is 003208. Check with the school for current application deadlines.

OREGON INSTITUTE OF TECHNOLOGY B-4
www.oit.edu

Klamath Falls, OR 97601	(541) 885-1150
Fax: (541) 885-1115	Email: oit@oit.edu
Full-time: 1115 men, 840 women	Faculty: 107
Part-time: 560 men, 555 women	Ph.D.s: 31%
Graduate: 15 men, no women	Student/Faculty: 18 to 1
Year: trimesters, summer session	Tuition: $3946 ($10,726)
Room & Board: $5160	Freshman Class: n/av
SAT or ACT: required	CEEB CODE: 4587
Application Deadline: June 1	COMPETITIVE

Oregon Institute of Technology, the only public institute of technology in the Pacific Northwest, provides degree programs in engineering and health technologies, management, communications, and applied sciences that prepare students to be effective participants in their professional, public, and international communities. Figures in the above capsule and in this profile are approximate. There are 3 undergraduate schools and 1 graduate school. In addition to regional accreditation, OIT has baccalaureate program accreditation with ABET and NLN. The 173-acre campus is in a small town 60 miles east of Medford in south central Oregon. Including any residence halls, there are 12 buildings.

STUDENT LIFE: 85% of undergraduates are from Oregon. Others are from 35 states, and 17 foreign countries. 95% are from public schools. 80% are White; 5% Asian American; 4% Hispanic; 2% American Indian/Alaska Native; 1% African American; 1% Foreign. **Male To Female Ratio:** 1.2:1. The average age of freshmen is 23; all undergraduates, 26. 26% do not continue beyond their first year; 29% remain to graduate. **Housing:** 500 students can be accommodated in college housing, which includes single-sex and coed dorms. On-campus housing is guaranteed for all 4 years. 82% of students commute. All students may keep cars.

FACULTY/CLASSROOMS: 77% of faculty are male; 23% are female. All teach undergraduates. No introductory courses are taught by graduate students. The average class size in an introductory lecture is 30; in a laboratory is 18; and in a regular course is 30.

PROGRAMS OF STUDY: OIT confers B.S. degrees. Associate and master's degrees are also awarded. Bachelor's degrees are awarded in BUSINESS (management information systems), ENGINEERING AND ENVIRONMENTAL DESIGN (civil engineering, computer technology, electrical/electronics engineering technology, engineering technology, environmental science, industrial administration/management, laser electro-optics technology, manufacturing technology, mechanical engineering technology, and surveying engineering), HEALTH PROFESSIONS (dental hygiene, health science, radiograph medical technology, and ultrasound technology), SOCIAL SCIENCE (industrial and organizational psychology). Engineering technology programs have the largest enrollment.

ACTIVITIES: 3% of men belong to 1 local and 1 national fraternities; 3% of women belong to 1 local and 1 national sororities. There are 37 groups on campus, including cheerleading, communications, computers, ethnic, honors, international, newspaper, outdoor club, pep band, professional, radio and TV, religious, social, and student government. Popular campus events include Tech Challenge, Family Weekend Tech Fest, and a Skills Contest for Business and Math Students. **Sports:** There are 4 intercollegiate sports for men and 6 for women. Facilities include a 3000-seat stadium, a 2066-seat gym, football, baseball, and softball fields, free weights and aerobics areas, an indoor swimming pool, a track, and tennis, volleyball, basketball, and badminton courts. **Graduates:** 76 companies recruited on campus in 2015-2016. Of the 2015 graduating class, 11% were enrolled in graduate school within 6 months of graduation, and 86% were employed.

SERVICES: Counseling and information services are available, as is tutoring in some subjects, such as math, sciences, and computers There is a reader service for the blind, and remedial math, reading, and writing. **Library/Resources:** The library contains 145,988 volumes, 158,278 microform items, and 2,069 audio/video tapes/CDs/DVDs, and subscribes to 1,815 periodicals including electronic. Computerized library services include interlibrary loans and database searching. Special learning facilities include an art gallery and radio station. **Physically Challenged Students:** 90% of the campus is accessible. Facilities include wheelchair ramps, elevators, special parking, specially equipped restrooms, and special class scheduling. **Special:** Cross-registration with Klamath Community College, internships in all majors, and co-op programs in all engineering technologies are available. OIT also offers advanced degree programs in software engineering technology and vascular imaging. There are 2 national honor societies. **Visiting:** There are regularly scheduled orientations for prospective students, including tours and meetings with admissions counselors, faculty, and students. There are guides for informal visits, visitors may sit in on classes, and stay overnight. To schedule a visit, contact the Admissions Office. **Campus Safety and Security:** Measures include 24-hour foot and vehicle patrol and security escort services. There are lighted pathways/sidewalks.

REQUIREMENTS: A composite score of 1000 on the SAT I or 21 on the ACT is required for applicants who do not meet the minimum GPA requirement. Applicants must have 14 academic units, including 4 years of English, 3 each of math and social sciences, and 2 each of science and a foreign language. The GED is accepted. Applications are accepted on disk. AP and CLEP credits are accepted. General education requirements include 12 hours in social science and 9 hours each in communication, business, and humanities. Students also must take 9 hours in English composition and technical report writing. Completion of about 200 quarter hours, with a minimum GPA of 2.0, is required to graduate. **Procedure:** Freshmen are admitted to all sessions. The SAT I or ACT should be taken during the senior year, and placement tests just prior to registration. There are early admissions and rolling admissions plans. Applications should be filed by June 1 for fall entry; December 1 for winter entry; March 1 for spring entry; and June 1 for summer entry. The fall 2016 application fee was $50. Notification is sent on a rolling basis. **Transfer Students:** 168 transfer students enrolled in 2015-2016. Applicants must have a minimum GPA of 2.0 and at least 24 quarter credit hours; students with fewer credit hours must submit high school transcripts or GED scores. An associate degree is recommended. 45 of 190 credits required for the bachelor's degree must be completed at OIT. **International Students:** There are 29 international students enrolled. The school actively recruits these students. They must take the TOEFL.

Admissions Contact: Palmer Muntz, Director of Admissions. Email: *oit@oit.edu* Web: *www.oit.edu*

FINANCIAL AID: In 2016-2017, 85% of all full-time freshmen and 60% of continuing full-time students received some form of financial aid. 80% of all full-time freshmen and 75% of continuing full-time students received need-based aid. The average freshman award was $9,700. 40% of undergraduate students work part-time. Average annual earnings from campus work are $1200. The average financial indebtedness of the 2016 graduate was $22,629. The FAFSA code is 003211. The deadline for filing freshman financial aid applications for fall entry is May 1.

OREGON STATE UNIVERSITY B-2

www.oregonstate.edu

Corvallis, OR 97331

(541) 737-4411
(800) 291-4192
Email: osuadmit@oregonstate.edu

Full-time: 10,261 men, 8591 women	**Faculty:** 1175; I, -$
Part-time: 3361 men, 3114 women	**Ph.D.s:** 86%
Graduate: 2560 men, 2467 women	**Student/Faculty:** 16 to 1
Year: quarters, summer session	**Tuition:** $10,366 ($28,846)
Room & Board: $12,153	**Freshman Class:** 14595 applied, 11308 accepted, 3814 enrolled
SAT CR/M/W: 550/560/530 **ACT:** 25	**CEEB CODE:** 4586
Application Deadline: September 1	**VERY COMPETITIVE**

Oregon State University is one of only two American universities that are designated a land, sea, sun, and space grant institution. Since the 1860s, states have selected a university for the unique role of land-grant institution. This role entails providing students of all economic backgrounds access to instruction and research in agriculture, science, and engineering, as well as the traditional liberal arts. The sea, sun, and space grants reflect national recognition of expertise and research leadership in marine, environmental, and space sciences and technologies. The university has an intense focus on science and technology; the majority of students major in a STEM field. Among the most popular undergraduate majors are Computer Science, Business Administration, Mechanical Engineering, Kinesiology, and Human Development and Family Sciences. There are 12 undergraduate schools and 12 graduate schools. In addition to regional accreditation, Oregon State has baccalaureate program accreditation with AACSB, ABET, ACCE, ACPE, AHEA, CSAB, NASM, NCATE, and SAF. The 400-acre campus is in a small town 90 miles south of Portland, and an hour from the Cascades or the Pacific Coast. Including any residence halls, there are 203 buildings.

STUDENT LIFE: 72% of undergraduates are from Oregon. Others are from 50 states, 75 foreign countries, and Canada. 65% are White; 9% Hispanic; 8% Asian American; 7% Foreign; 7% two or more races; 2% race unknown; 1% African American; 1% American Indian/Alaska Native. **Male To Female Ratio:** 1.1:1. The average age of freshmen is 19; all undergraduates, 23. 17% do not continue beyond their first year; 63% remain to graduate. **Housing:** 5069 students can be accommodated in college housing, which includes coed dorms and married student housing. In addition, there are honors houses, special-interest houses, fraternity houses, sorority houses, housing for international students and housing for entrepreneurship majors. On-campus housing is guaranteed for the freshman year only, and is available on a first-come, first-served basis. 83% of students commute. Alcohol is not permitted. All students may keep cars.

FACULTY/CLASSROOMS: 57% of faculty are male; 43% are female. No introductory courses are taught by graduate students. The average class size in an introductory lecture is 60; in a laboratory is 26; and in a regular course is 38.

PROGRAMS OF STUDY: Oregon State confers B.A., B.S., and B.F.A. degrees. Master's and doctoral degrees are also awarded. Bachelor's degrees are awarded in AGRICULTURE (agricultural business management, agriculture, agronomy, animal science, fishing and fisheries, forest engineering, forestry and related sciences, horticulture, natural resource management, range/farm management, and soil science), BIOLOGICAL SCIENCE (biochemistry, biology/biological science, biotechnology, botany, ecology, microbiology, molecular biology, nutrition, wildlife biology, and zoology), BUSINESS (accounting, business administration and management, business systems analysis, environment & natnl resource economics, finance, hospitality management services, management science, marketing, marketing/retailing/merchandising, and recreation/leisure (adventure leadership), COMMUNICATIONS AND THE ARTS (apparel design, applied art, art, digital communications, English, French, German, graphic design, music, Spanish, speech/debate/rhetoric, and visual and performing arts), COMPUTER AND PHYSICAL SCIENCE (chemistry, computer science, earth science, mathematics, medical physics, and physics), EDUCATION (education), ENGINEERING AND ENVIRONMENTAL DESIGN (agricultural engineering, bioengineering, bioresource engineering, chemical engineering, civil engineering, computer engineering, construction management, electrical/electronics engineering, engineering/mechanical emp/energy sys focus, environmental engineering, environmental science, industrial engineering, interior design, manufacturing engineering, mechanical engineering, and nuclear engineering), HEALTH PROFESSIONS (biomedical science, kinesiology, predentistry, premedicine, preoptometry, prepharmacy, prephysical therapy, prepodiatry, and public health), SOCIAL SCIENCE (American studies, anthropology, economics, ethnic studies, food science, history, human development, international studies, liberal arts/general studies, parks and recreation management, philosophy, political science/government, psychology, religious studies, social science, sociology, and women's studies). Engineering, agricultural sciences, and forestry are the strongest academically. Computer science, business administration, and mechanical engineering have the largest enrollments.

ACTIVITIES: 11% of men belong to 24 national fraternities; 16% of women belong to 20 national sororities. There are 360 groups on campus, including adventure club, art, band, cheerleading, chess, choir, chorale, chorus, communications, computers, dance, debate, drama, drill team, drum and bugle corps, environmental, ethnic, film, forensics, honors, international, jazz band, LGBT, literary magazine, marching band, musical theater, newspaper, orchestra, pep band, photography, political, professional, radio and TV, religious, social, social service, student government, student sustainability initiative, symphony, and yearbook. Popular campus events include Connect Week, Dads Weekend, Civil War, Moms Weekend, Battle of the Bands and Bard in the Quad. **Sports:** There are 7 intercollegiate sports for men and 10 for women, and 19 intramural sports for men and 17 for women. Dixon Recreation Center is one of the main social hubs of activity on campus. It houses two cardio rooms, two weight rooms, two gyms, six racquetball courts, three squash courts, three multipurpose rooms, a 42ft-tall climbing wall, 1/10 mile indoor track, 25-yard pool, a dive well, a hot tub, three sand volleyball courts, and the Adventure Leadership Institute. There is a fieldhouse with indoor multipurpose court, turf field, and rock-climbing wall. There are multiple artificial and natural turf fields around campus, tennis courts, and basketball courts. **Graduates:** From July 1, 2015 to June 30, 2016, 5084 bachelor's degrees were awarded. The most popular majors were human development and family sciences (7%), computer science (6%), and exercise and sport science (4%). In an average class, 33% graduate in 4 years or less, 57% graduate in 5 years or less, and 63% graduate in 6 years or less.

SERVICES: Counseling and information services are available, as is tutoring in most subjects. There is a reader service for the blind, and remedial math, reading, and writing. Facilities include a communication skills center and a math sciences learning center. **Library/Resources:** The 4 libraries contain 2.0 million volumes, 2.2 million microform items, and 27,256 audio/video tapes/CDs/DVDs, and subscribe to 107,975 periodicals including electronic. Computerized library services include interlibrary loans, database searching, Internet access, and Wi-Fi capability. Special learning facilities include an art gallery, natural history museum, radio station, TV station, an arboretum, a wave research lab, a research farm, research vessel, and the Linus Pauling Collection. **Physically Challenged Students:** 92% of the campus is accessible. Facilities include wheelchair ramps, elevators, special parking, specially equipped restrooms, special class scheduling, lowered drinking fountains, and lowered telephones. **Special:** Oregon State University offers a double degree in Education, where a student has a primary degree in any field and then also earns an Education degree. With the Education degree the student also earns an Oregon teaching license. The university began a new program in the fall of 2012 offering a double degree in sustainability where students take an additional 36 credits beyond their primary degree. The Sustainability degree is interdisciplinary, drawing on courses from many disciplines in the university. OSU has a list of over 200 approved study abroad programs in 77 different countries. There are 14 national honor societies and a freshman honors program. **Visiting:** There are regularly scheduled orientations for prospective students. There are guides for informal visits, visitors may sit in on classes, and stay overnight. To schedule a visit, contact the Visitor Center at (541) 737-2626. **Campus Safety and Security:** Measures include 24-hour foot and vehicle patrol, emergency notification system, and security escort services. There are shuttle buses, emergency telephones, lighted pathways/sidewalks, and controlled access to dorms/residences.

REQUIREMENTS: The SAT or ACT is required. Applicants should be high school graduates or hold the GED. Required high school preparation includes 4 years of English; 3 years of math, including algebra II; 3 years of science; 3 years of social science; and 2 years of foreign language. Some subject requirements may be fulfilled by test scores. AP and CLEP credits are accepted. To graduate, students must complete at least 180 quarter credits with a GPA of 2.0. The required core curriculum includes writing, mathematics, speech, physical science, biological science, culture, difference and power, technology and society, global issues, and fitness. Students must also take a writing-intensive course in their major field and meet additional distribution requirements. **Procedure:** Freshmen are admitted to all sessions. Entrance exams should be taken during the junior or senior year. There are early admissions, deferred admissions, and rolling admissions plans. Early decision applications should be filed by February 1; regular applications, by September 1 for fall entry; December 12 for winter entry; March 6 for spring entry; and June 26 for summer entry, along with a $60 fee. Notification of early decision is sent March 15; regular decision. Applications are accepted on-line. **Transfer Students:** 1998 transfer students enrolled in 2015-2016. Applicants must present a GPA of at least 2.25 in previous college work. Students should have completed at least 36 hours of college credit. Must have a C- or better on English Composition and College Algebra. Transfer students must show two years of foreign language in high school or two semesters of foreign language. Either SAT I or ACT scores must be submitted. 45 of 180 credits required for the bachelor's degree must be completed at Oregon State. **International Students:** There are 1974 international students enrolled. The school actively recruits these students. They must take the TOEFL with a minimum score of 80 on the Internet-based version (iBT).

ADMISSIONS: 77% of the 2016-2017 applicants were accepted. The SAT scores for the 2016-2017 freshman class were: Critical Reading-- 26% below 500, 41% between 500 and 599, 26% between 600 and 699, and 7% between 700 and 800. Math-- 25% below 500, 40% between 500 and 599, 27% between 600 and 699, and 8% between 700 and 800. Writing-- 35% below 500, 42% between 500 and 599, 20% between 600 and 699, and 3% between 700 and 800. The ACT scores were 4% between 12 and 17, 35% between 18 and 23, 44% between 24 and 29, and 17% above 30. 50% of the current freshmen were in the top fifth of their class; 82% were in the top two fifths. 181 freshmen graduated first in their class. **Admissions Contact:** Noah Buckley, Director of Admissions. Email: *osuadmit@oregonstate.edu* Web: *www.oregonstate.edu*

FINANCIAL AID: In 2016-2017, 77% of all full-time freshmen and 69% of continuing full-time students received some form of financial aid. 58% of all full-time freshmen and 56% of continuing full-time students received need-based aid. The average freshman award was $11,453. Need-based scholarships or need-based grants averaged $7,265 ($25,237 maximum); need-based self-help aid (loans and jobs) averaged $4,122 ($17,100 maximum); non-need-based athletic scholarships averaged $29,349 ($43,574 maximum); and other non-need-based awards and non-need-based scholarships averaged $4,338 ($18,000 maximum). 22% of undergraduate students work part-time. Average annual earnings from campus work are $2800. The average financial indebtedness of the 2016 graduate was $26,400. Oregon State is a member of CSS. The FAFSA code is 003210. The priority date for freshman financial aid applications for fall entry is February 28.

PACIFIC NORTHWEST COLLEGE OF ART *(The complete profile is made available exclusively on our website, www.barronspac.com)*

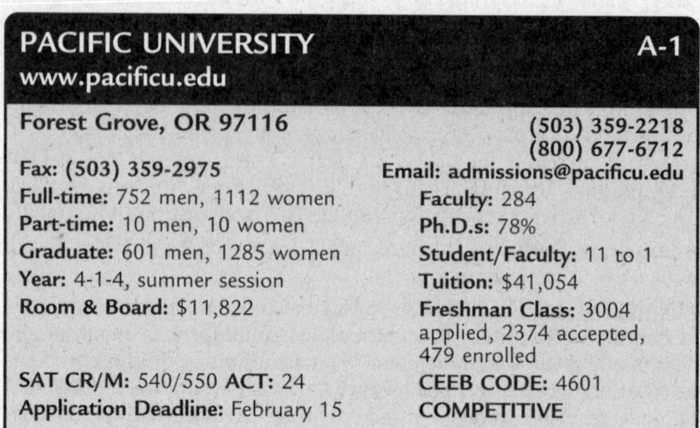

PACIFIC UNIVERSITY — A-1
www.pacificu.edu

Forest Grove, OR 97116 — (503) 359-2218, (800) 677-6712

Fax: (503) 359-2975	**Email:** admissions@pacificu.edu
Full-time: 752 men, 1112 women	**Faculty:** 284
Part-time: 10 men, 10 women	**Ph.D.s:** 78%
Graduate: 601 men, 1285 women	**Student/Faculty:** 11 to 1
Year: 4-1-4, summer session	**Tuition:** $41,054
Room & Board: $11,822	**Freshman Class:** 3004 applied, 2374 accepted, 479 enrolled
SAT CR/M: 540/550 **ACT:** 24	**CEEB CODE:** 4601
Application Deadline: February 15	**COMPETITIVE**

Pacific University, founded in Forest Grove in 1849, is an independent institution affiliated with the Congregational Church (United Church of Christ) offering degree programs in liberal arts, science, business, education, and health professions. The figures in the above capsule and in this profile are approximate. There are 4 undergraduate schools. In addition to regional accreditation, Pacific has baccalaureate program accreditation with NASM. The 55-acre campus is in a small town 25 miles west of Portland. Including any residence halls, there are 18 buildings.

STUDENT LIFE: 50% of undergraduates are from out of state, mostly the West. Students are from 31 states, 7 foreign countries, and Canada. 91% are from public schools. 64% are White; 2% Hispanic; 2% Foreign; 18% Asian American; 1% African American; 1% American Indian/Alaska Native. **Female To Male Ratio:** 1.8:1. The average age of freshmen is 18; all undergraduates, 21. 22% do not continue beyond their first year; 54% remain to graduate. **Housing:** 680 students can be accommodated in college housing, which includes single-sex and coed dorms and off-campus apartments. In addition, there are special-interest houses, We also offer women's floor and apartments for singles. On-campus housing is guaranteed for the freshman year only, and is available on a first-come, first-served basis, is available on a lottery system for upperclassmen. 50% of students commute. All students may keep cars.

FACULTY/CLASSROOMS: 52% of faculty are male; 48% are female. All teach undergraduates, and all do research. No introductory courses are taught by graduate students. The average class size in an introductory lecture is 35; in a laboratory is 20; and in a regular course is 19.

PROGRAMS OF STUDY: Pacific confers B.A., B.S. and B.M. degrees. Master's and doctoral degrees are also awarded. Bachelor's degrees are awarded in BIOLOGICAL SCIENCE (biology/biological science), BUSINESS (business administration and management), COMMUNICATIONS AND THE ARTS (creative writing, dramatic arts, Japanese, literature, music, and Spanish), COMPUTER AND PHYSICAL SCIENCE (chemistry, computer science, mathematics, and physics), SOCIAL SCIENCE (economics, history, humanities, philosophy, political science/government, psychology, social work, and sociology). Natural sciences, literature, and creative writing are the strongest academically. Business administration, English, and psychology have the largest enrollments.

ACTIVITIES: 6% of men belong to 3 local fraternities; 9% of women belong to 3 local sororities. There are 35 groups on campus, including art, band, cheerleading, choir, chorale, chorus, computers, dance, debate, drama, ethnic, film, forensics, honors, international, jazz band, LGBT, literary magazine, newspaper, orchestra, pep band, photography, political, professional, radio and TV, religious, social, social service, student government, and symphony. Popular campus events include Hawaiian Club Luau, International Club Banquet, and Japan Day. **Sports:** There are 8 intercollegiate sports for men and 8 for women, and 10 intramural sports for men and 10 for women. Facilities include a gym, various courts, a sauna, weight and wrestling rooms, a dance studio, outdoor playing fields, a field house, and racquetball courts. **Graduates:** From July 1, 2015 to June 30, 2016, 379 bachelor's degrees were awarded. The most popular majors were health professions and related programs (41%), psychology (15%), and engineering (8%). 10 companies recruited on campus in 2015-2016. In an average class, 44% graduate in 4 years or less, 57% graduate in 5 years or less, and 63% graduate in 6 years or less. Of the 2015 graduating class, 82% were employed within 6 months of graduation.

SERVICES: Counseling and information services are available, as is tutoring in most subjects. There is a reader service for the blind. **Library/ Resources:** The library contains 152,060 volumes, 76,609 microform items, and 3,708 audio/video tapes/CDs/DVDs, and subscribes to 945 periodicals including electronic. Computerized library services include interlibrary loans and database searching. Special learning facilities include an art gallery, radio station, and a museum of the history of Pacific University. **Physically Challenged Students:** 80% of the campus is accessible. Facilities include wheelchair ramps, elevators, special parking, specially equipped restrooms, lowered drinking fountains, and special housing. **Special:** Cross-registration is available with Oregon Independent Colleges and Oregon Graduate Institute of Science and Technology (OGIST). The university also offers cooperative programs with Washington University in St. Louis, OGIST, and Oregon School of Arts and Crafts, as well as study abroad in 13 countries. Full-time, semester-long internships, including one in Washington D.C., are possible. Dual majors, a general studies degree in humanities, nondegree study, 3-2 engineering programs with Washington University in St. Louis and OGIST, and an interdisciplinary program in peace and conflict studies are available. There are 2 national honor societies, a freshman honors program, and 1 departmental honors program. **Visiting:** There are regularly scheduled orientations for prospective students, a campus tour, classroom visitations, and meetings with faculty and coaches. There are guides for informal visits, visitors may sit in on classes, and stay overnight. To schedule a visit, contact the Admissions Office. **Campus Safety and Security:** Measures include 24-hour foot and vehicle patrol, emergency notification system, and security escort services. There are emergency telephones, lighted pathways/sidewalks, and controlled access to dorms/residences.

REQUIREMENTS: The SAT or ACT is required. Applicants are expected to be high school graduates or to hold the GED. A personal essay is required, and an interview is recommended. On-line applications are available on Pacific's web pages. 21 high school units are recommended: 4 each in English and academic electives, 3 each in math, science (of these units, 1 must be with lab), and social studies, 2 in foreign language, and 1 in history. AP and CLEP credits are accepted. Important factors in the admissions decision are advanced placement or honors courses, recommendations by school officials, and extracurricular activities record. All students take a core curriculum that includes a first-year seminar and courses in writing, foreign language, social and natural sciences, art, and cross-cultural studies. A cumulative GPA of 2.0 in 124 semester hours is required for graduation. 34 to 64 hours are required in the major, depending on the discipline. **Procedure:** Freshmen are admitted fall and spring. There are deferred admissions and rolling admissions plans. Applications should be filed by February 15 for fall entry, along with a $40 fee. Applications are accepted on-line. **Transfer Students:** 118 transfer students enrolled in 2015-2016. Transfer applicants must present at least a 2.75 GPA in previous college work; those with fewer than 30 semester hours or 45 quarter hours must also submit SAT I or ACT test scores and high school transcripts. A personal interview is strongly recommended. Application for admission is in the fall, August 15, and spring January 15. 30 of 124 credits required for the bachelor's degree must be completed at Pacific. **International Students:** There are 48 international students enrolled. The school actively recruits these students.

ADMISSIONS: 79% of the 2016-2017 applicants were accepted. The SAT scores for the 2016-2017 freshman class were: Critical Reading-- 28% below 500, 48% between 500 and 599, 20% between 600 and 699, and 3% between 700 and 800. Math-- 21% below 500, 52% between 500 and 599, 25% between 600 and 699, and 2% between 700 and 800. The ACT scores were 5% between 12 and 17, 42% between 18 and 23, 46% between 24 and 29, and 7% above 30. 18 freshmen graduated first in their class. **Admissions Contact:** Beth Woodward, Director of Admissions. Email: *admissions@pacificu.edu* Web: *www.pacificu.edu*

FINANCIAL AID: In 2016-2017, 87% of all full-time freshmen received some form of financial aid. 84% of all full-time freshmen received need-based aid. The average freshman award was $33,920. Need-based scholarships or need-based grants averaged $11,440; need-based self-help aid (loans and jobs) averaged $6,195; non-need-based athletic scholarships averaged $19,599; and other non-need-based awards and non-need-based scholarships averaged $4,341. 54% of undergraduate students work part-time. Average annual earnings from campus work are $823. The average financial indebtedness of the 2016 graduate was $22,163. Pacific is a member of CSS. The FAFSA code is 003212. The priority date for freshman financial aid applications for fall entry is March 1. The deadline for filing freshman financial aid applications for fall entry is rolling.

PORTLAND STATE UNIVERSITY — B-1

www.pdx.edu

Portland, OR 97207	503-725-5504 (800) 547-8887
Fax: 503-725-5525	Email: mtrifi@pdx.edu
Full-time: 6935 men, 7582 women	**Faculty:** I, --$
Part-time: 4074 men, 4579 women	**Ph.D.s:** n/av
Graduate: 2237 men, 3324 women	**Student/Faculty:** 18 to 1
Year: quarters, summer session	**Tuition:** $8424 ($15,852)
Room & Board: $11,019	**Freshman Class:** n/av
SAT CR/M: 520/510 **ACT:** 22	**CEEB CODE:** 4610
Application Deadline: open	**COMPETITIVE**

Portland State University, was founded in 1946, as a public research university. It is a nationally acclaimed leader in sustainability and community-based learning. Portland State offers more than 220 undergraduate, master's, and doctoral degree options, as well as graduate certificates and continuing education programs. Figures in the above capsule and in this profile are approximate. There are 8 undergraduate schools. In addition to regional accreditation, PSU has baccalaureate program accreditation with AACSB, ABET, ASLA, CSWE, NASAD, NASM, NCATE, CACREP, ABE, and ASLHA. The 50-acre campus is in an urban area in the center of Portland. Including any residence halls, there are 56 buildings.

STUDENT LIFE: 89% of undergraduates are from Oregon. Others are from states, and Canada. 65% are White; 8% Hispanic; 7% Asian American; 7% Foreign; 4% two or more races; 4% race unknown; 3% African American; 2% American Indian/Alaska Native. **Female To Male Ratio:** 1.2:1. The average age of all undergraduates is 27. 26% do not continue beyond their first year; 74% remain to graduate. **Housing:** 1729 students can be accommodated in college housing, which includes coed dorms, on-campus apartments, and off-campus apartments. First year experience. On-campus housing is available on a first-come and first-served basis. Priority is given to out-of-town students. 93% of students commute. All students may keep cars.

FACULTY/CLASSROOMS: 50% of faculty are male; 50% are female. No introductory courses are taught by graduate students.

PROGRAMS OF STUDY: PSU confers B.A., B.S. and B.M. degrees. Master's and doctoral degrees are also awarded. Bachelor's degrees are awarded in BIOLOGICAL SCIENCE (biochemistry and biology/biological science), BUSINESS (accounting, business administration and management, management science, marketing/retailing/merchandising, and personnel management), COMMUNICATIONS AND THE ARTS (advertising, art history and appreciation, Chinese, dramatic arts, English, fine arts, French, German, Japanese, languages, music, Russian, Spanish, and speech/debate/rhetoric), COMPUTER AND PHYSICAL SCIENCE (chemistry, computer science, geology, information sciences and systems, mathematics, and physics), EDUCATION (health education), ENGINEERING AND ENVIRONMENTAL DESIGN (architecture, civil engineering, computer engineering, electrical/electronics engineering, and environmental science), SOCIAL SCIENCE (anthropology, child care/child and family studies, community services, economics, geography, history, international studies, law enforcement and corrections, liberal arts/general studies, philosophy, political science/government, psychology, social work, sociology, and women's studies). Electrical engineering, environmental science, and physics are the strongest academically. Psychology, business administration, and art have the largest enrollments.

ACTIVITIES: There are 246 groups on campus, including students with disabilities, art, band, cheerleading, chess, choir, chorale, chorus, communications, computers, dance, debate, drama, drill team, environmental, ethnic, film, forensics, honors, international, jazz band, LGBT, literary magazine, musical theater, newspaper, opera, orchestra, outdoor, pep band, photography, political, professional, radio and TV, religious, social, social service, student government, and symphony. Popular campus events include Portland State of Mind, International Student Cultural Night, Friends of Chamber Music and LunchBox Theater. **Sports:** There are 6 intercollegiate sports for men and 9 for women, and 6 intramural sports for men and 6 for women. Facilities include Rec Center, a practice field, an all-weather tennis facility, gyms, circuit training and weight rooms, a golf putting green, running track, and racquetball, handball, and squash courts. Nearby Civic Stadium and Duniway Park provide football, baseball, and track and field facilities. **Graduates:** From July 1, 2015 to June 30, 2016, 4320 bachelor's degrees were awarded. The most popular majors were social sciences/general (7%), business administration/management (6%), and psychology/general (6%). In an average class, 11% graduate in 4 years or less, 30% graduate in 5 years or less, and 40% graduate in 6 years or less.

SERVICES: Counseling and information services are available, as is tutoring in most subjects. There is a reader service for the blind, and remedial math and writing. Student Support Services, provides assistance to students who are low-income, who have a physical disability, or whose parents did not graduate from college. **Library/Resources:** Computerized library services include interlibrary loans, database searching, and Internet access. Special learning facilities include an art gallery, radio station, a multicultural center and a Native American center. **Physically Challenged Students:** 95% of the campus is accessible. Facilities include wheelchair ramps, elevators, special parking, specially equipped restrooms, special class scheduling, lowered drinking fountains, lowered telephones, and special housing. **Special:** Students may study abroad in 59 countries. Numerous internships, co-op programs, a Washington semester, and work-study programs are available. Most undergraduate programs may be taken on an accelerated basis, and students in all programs may undertake dual majors or design their own majors. A general studies program is available in arts and letters, science, or social science. Nondegree study and pass/fail grading options are possible. Students may enroll for 7 or fewer credits per term without formal admission. There are 8 national honor societies and a freshman honors program. **Visiting:** There are regularly scheduled orientations for prospective students, including daily campus tours led by student guides and opportunities for prospective students to meet with faculty, staff, and advisers. There are guides for informal visits, visitors may sit in on classes, and stay overnight. To schedule a visit, contact Campus Tour Coordinator at (503) 725-5555. **Campus Safety and Security:** Measures include 24-hour foot and vehicle patrol, emergency notification system, self-defense education, and security escort services. There are emergency telephones, lighted pathways/sidewalks, A campus watch newsletter, information lectures, and community liaison.

REQUIREMENTS: The SAT or ACT is required. A minimum GPA of 3.0 is required. Various combination of test scores and GPA may qualify for admissions under special action by admissions commitee. Applicants should be high school graduates or have earned the GED. Secondary preparation should include 4 years of English, 3 years of math, and 2 years each of science and foreign language and social studies and 1 year of history. In addition, one unit of laboratory science is recommended. A GPA of 3.0 is required. AP and CLEP credits are accepted. All students must complete at least 180 quarter credits with a 2.0 GPA in all courses in the major, and in all residence work. Other requirements and the number of hours that must be completed in the major vary by degree program. Freshmen must complete 3 5-credit freshman inquiry courses, sophomores, 3 4-credit courses from different interdisciplinary programs or general education clusters, juniors and seniors, 1 interdisciplinary program or general education cluster (4 3-credit courses), and seniors must complete a Senior Capstone. A thesis is required in the honors program only. **Procedure:** Freshmen are admitted to all sessions. Entrance exams should be taken as early as possible. There are deferred admissions and rolling admissions plans. Application deadlines are open. Application fee is $50. Notification is sent on a rolling basis. Applications are accepted on-line. **Transfer Students:** 2827 transfer students enrolled in 2015-2016. Applicants who are Oregon residents must have earned at least a 2.0 GPA in 30 college credits; those with 12 to 30 credits must meet freshman admission requirements and have a 2.0 GPA in all college work attempted. Nonresident applicants must have at least a 2.25 GPA in 30 hours of college work; those with 12 to 30 hours must meet freshman requirements and have a 2.5 GPA in all college work attempted. 45 of 180 credits required for the bachelor's degree must be completed at PSU. **International Students:** There are 880 international students enrolled. The school actively recruits these students. They must take the TOEFL and the college's own test, Only the international TOEFL exam or the PSU institutional TOEFL exam will be accepted.

ADMISSIONS: The SAT scores for the 2016-2017 freshman class were: Critical Reading-- 39% below 500, 39% between 500 and 599, 19% between 600 and 699, and 3% between 700 and 800. Math-- 42% below 500, 4% between 500 and 599, 16% between 600 and 699, and 1% between 700 and 800. Writing-- 50% below 500, 36% between 500 and 599, 13% between 600 and 699, and 1% between 700 and 800. The ACT scores were 38% below 12, 26% between 12 and 17, 20% between 18 and 23, 10% between 24 and 29, and 6% above 30. **Admissions Contact:** Dana Tasson, Ececutive Director of Student Affairs. Email: *mtrifi@pdx.edu* Web: *www.pdx.edu*

FINANCIAL AID: In 2016-2017, 73% of all full-time freshmen and 87% of continuing full-time students received some form of financial aid. 58% of all full-time freshmen and 77% of continuing full-time students received need-based aid. The average freshman award was $11,540. Need-based scholarships or need-based grants averaged $5,350 ($18,500 maximum); need-based self-help aid (loans and jobs) averaged $6,916 ($27,661 maximum); non-need-based athletic scholarships averaged $14,168 ($28,610 maximum); and other non-need-based awards and non-need-based scholarships averaged $3,589 ($33,152 maximum). 80% of undergraduate students work part-time. Average annual earnings from campus work are $1716. The college's own financial statement is required. The FAFSA code is 003216. Check with the school for current application deadlines.

REED COLLEGE B-1

www.reed.edu

Portland, OR 97202	(503) 777-7511 (800) 547-4750
Fax: (503) 777-7553	**Email:** admission@reed.edu
Full-time: 620 men, 750 women	**Faculty:** 153; IIB, +$
Part-time: 1 man, 5 women	**Ph.D.s:** 96%
Graduate: 8 men, 9 women	**Student/Faculty:** 9 to 1
Year: semesters	**Tuition:** $52,150
Room & Board: $13,150	**Freshman Class:** 3956 applied, 1532 accepted, 347 enrolled
SAT CR/M/W: 715/670/685 **ACT:** 31	**CEEB CODE:** 4654
Application Deadline: January 15	**MOST COMPETITIVE**

Reed College, founded in 1908, is a private, nonsectarian institution offering programs in liberal arts and sciences and emphasizing instruction through small, conference-style classes. Figures in the above capsule and in this profile are approximate. There is 1 undergraduate school and 1 graduate school. In addition to regional accreditation, Reed has baccalaureate program accreditation with ACS. The 116-acre campus is in an urban area in Portland, Oregon. Including any residence halls, there are 43 buildings.

STUDENT LIFE: 92% of undergraduates are from out of state, mostly the Southwest. Students are from 47 states, 45 foreign countries, and Canada. 56% are from public schools. 59% are White; 11% Hispanic; 8% Asian American; 8% race unknown; 7% Foreign; 3% African American; 3% two or more races; 1% American Indian/Alaska Native. **Female To Male Ratio:** 1.2:1. The average age of freshmen is 18; all undergraduates, 20. **Housing:** 946 students can be accommodated in college housing, which includes coed dorms, on-campus apartments, and off-campus apartments. In addition, there are language houses, special-interest houses, quiet, substance-free, cooperative housing, theme and wellness housing, and no-smoking dorms. On-campus housing is guaranteed for the freshman year only, is available on a first-come, first-served basis, and is available on a lottery system for upperclassmen. 67% of students live on campus; of those, 95% remain on campus on weekends. Alcohol is not permitted. All students may keep cars.

FACULTY/CLASSROOMS: 56% of faculty are male; 44% are female. All teach undergraduates, and all do research. No introductory courses are taught by graduate students.

PROGRAMS OF STUDY: Reed confers B.A. degrees. Master's degrees are also awarded. Bachelor's degrees are awarded in AGRICULTURE (environmental studies), BIOLOGICAL SCIENCE (biochemistry and biology/biological science), COMMUNICATIONS AND THE ARTS (art, Chinese, classics, dramatic arts, English literature, Germanic languages and literature, linguistics, literature, music, and Russian languages and literature), COMPUTER AND PHYSICAL SCIENCE (chemical physics, chemistry, mathematics, mathematics – economics, and physics), SOCIAL SCIENCE (American studies, anthropology, economics, French studies, history, international political science, philosophy, political science/government, psychology, religion, sociology, and Spanish studies). English, biology, and psychology have the largest enrollments.

ACTIVITIES: There are no fraternities or sororities. There are 104 groups on campus, including model UN, art, chess, choir, chorus, computers, dance, debate, drama, environmental, ethnic, international, jazz band, LGBT, literary magazine, musical theater, newspaper, orchestra, photography, radio club, religious, social service, student government, and symphony. Popular campus events include Performing Arts Festival, Campus Clean Up Day (Canyon Day), and Reed Arts Week (RAW). **Sports:** There are 7 intramural sports for men and 6 for women. Facilities include a sports center that houses 2 gyms, an indoor pool, squash and racquetball courts, saunas, a weight room, an exercise room, and a dance studio. Outdoor facilities include tennis courts, a track, and areas for soccer, rugby, volleyball, and baseball. **Graduates:** From July 1, 2015 to June 30, 2016, 314 bachelor's degrees were awarded. The most popular majors were social sciences (15%), biological/life sciences, and physical sciences (13%), and visual and performing arts (10%). 110 companies recruited on campus in 2015-2016. In an average class, 70% graduate in 4 years or less, 80% graduate in 5 years or less, and 82% graduate in 6 years or less.

SERVICES: Counseling and information services are available, as is tutoring in every subject. There is a reader service for the blind, and remedial math, reading, and writing. **Library/Resources:** The 2 libraries contain 629,871 volumes, 180,996 microform items, and 31,456 audio/video tapes/CDs/DVDs, and subscribe to 17,169 periodicals including electronic. Computerized library services include interlibrary loans, database searching, Internet access, and Wi-Fi capability. Special learning facilities include an art gallery, a research reactor, and centers for bio science, math, quantitative skills, science, and writing. **Physically Challenged Students:** Facilities include wheelchair ramps, elevators, special parking, specially equipped restrooms, special class scheduling, lowered drinking fountains, lowered telephones, and special housing. **Special:** Cross-registration is available through the Oregon Independent Colleges organization and Pacific Northwest College of Art. 3-2 programs are available for computer science with University of Washington and for engineering with CalTech, Columbia University, and Rensselaer Polytechnic Institute. Also available are combined programs with the Pacific Northwest College of Art for Visual Arts. Study abroad in 18 countries, a domestic exchange program with Howard University in Washington, D.C., Sarah Lawrence College, and Sea Education Association (SEA), accelerated degree programs, dual majors, student-designed majors, numerous interdisciplinary majors, nondegree study, and pass/fail options are also offered. There is a chapter of Phi Beta Kappa. **Visiting:** There are regularly scheduled orientations for prospective students, including an information session, campus tour, and an admission interview. Visitors may sit in on classes and stay overnight. To schedule a visit, contact the Office of Admission. **Campus Safety and Security:** Measures include 24-hour foot and vehicle patrol, emergency notification system, self-defense education, and security escort services. There are shuttle buses, emergency telephones, lighted pathways/sidewalks, and controlled access to dorms/residences.

REQUIREMENTS: The results of either the SAT or ACT are required, and SAT Subject tests are recommended. Reed strongly recommends that applicants have 4 years of English, 3-4 of math, 3 each of science and foreign language, and 3-4 of social studies. An essay is required, and an interview is recommended. The GED is accepted. AP credits are accepted. Important factors in the admissions decision are advanced placement or honors courses, personality/intangible qualities, and evidence of special talent. All students are required to maintain a C average while fulfilling 120 semester hours of credit. The liberal arts program also requires a year-long humanities course and year-long senior research project, in addition to distribution requirements in literature, philosophy, religion, the arts, history, social sciences, psychology, natural sciences, mathematics, logic, or foreign language or linguistics. Students are also required to take 6 quarters of phys ed. **Procedure:** Freshmen are admitted fall. Entrance exams should be taken no later than December of application year. There are early decision and deferred admissions plans. Early decision applications should be filed by November 15; regular applications, by January 15 for fall entry, along with a $50 fee. Notification of early decision is sent February 1; regular decision, April 1. 114 early decision candidates were accepted for the 2016-2017 class. 437 applicants were on the 2016 waiting list. Applications are accepted on-line. **Transfer Students:** 32 transfer students enrolled in 2015-2016. Transfer students must submit their High school transcripts, college transcripts, an essay or personal statement, all standardized test scores, and a statement of good standing from prior institution(s). An interview is also recommended. Student may enroll fall March 1. Notification is sent May 15, and must reply by June 1. 60 of 120 credits required for the bachelor's degree must be completed at Reed. **International Students:** There are 92 international students enrolled. The school actively recruits these students. They must take the TOEFL with a minimum score of 600 on the paper-based TOEFL (PBT) or 100 on the Internet-based version (iBT). They must also take the SAT or ACT.

ADMISSIONS: 39% of the 2016-2017 applicants were accepted. The SAT scores for the 2016-2017 freshman class were: Critical Reading-- 5% between 500 and 599, 36% between 600 and 699, and 59% between 700 and 800. Math-- 1% below 500, 12% between 500 and 599, 50% between 600 and 699, and 37% between 700 and 800. Writing-- 1% below 500, 8% between 500 and 599, 50% between 600 and 699, and 41% between 700 and 800. The ACT scores were 1% between 18 and 23, 25% between 24 and 29, and 74% above 30. 84% of the current freshmen were in the top fifth of their class; 94% were in the top two fifths. 13 freshmen graduated first in their class. **Admissions Contact:** Keith Todd, Dean of Admission. Email: *admission@reed.edu* Web: *www.reed.edu*

FINANCIAL AID: In 2016-2017, 53% of all full-time freshmen received some form of financial aid. 50% of all full-time freshmen received need-based aid. The average freshman award was $40,911. Need-based scholarships or need-based grants averaged $38,279; need-based self-help aid (loans and jobs) averaged $4,168; and other non-need-based awards and non-need-based scholarships averaged $3,449. 39% of undergraduate students work part-time. The average financial indebtedness of the 2016 graduate was $19,010. Reed is a member of CSS. The CSS/Profile, the college's own financial statement, and parent and student federal tax forms are required. The FAFSA code is 003217. The deadline for filing freshman financial aid applications for fall entry is February 1.

SOUTHERN OREGON UNIVERSITY B-4

www.sou.edu

Ashland, OR 97520 **(541) 552-6411**

Fax: (541) 552-8403	**Email:** admissions@sou.edu
Full-time: 1551 men, 2086 women	**Faculty:** 199
Part-time: 759 men, 1048 women	**Ph.D.s:** 93%
Graduate: 234 men, 508 women	**Student/Faculty:** 21 to 1
Year: quarters, summer session	**Tuition:** $7720 ($21,296)
Room & Board: $11,397	**Freshman Class:** 2209 applied, 2064 accepted, 629 enrolled
SAT CR/M/W: 525/505/490 **ACT:** 23	**CEEB CODE:** 4702
Application Deadline: September 9	**COMPETITIVE**

Southern Oregon University (SOU), founded in 1926, is a public comprehensive university providing undergraduate and graduate programs in humanities, science, business, fine and performing arts, social sciences, and teacher education. Figures in the above capsule and in this profile are approximate. There are 3 undergraduate schools and 1 graduate school. In addition to regional accreditation, Southern has baccalaureate program accreditation with ACBSP, NASM, NCATE, ACS, and CACREP. The 175-acre campus is in a small town 10 miles southeast of Medford, Oregon. Including any residence halls, there are 40 buildings.

STUDENT LIFE: 71% of undergraduates are from Oregon. Others are from 44 states, 17 foreign countries, and Canada. 85% are from public schools. 64% are White; 15% race unknown; 10% Hispanic; 4% two or more races; 2% African American; 2% Asian American; 2% Foreign; 1% American Indian/Alaska Native. **Female To Male Ratio:** 1.4:1. The average age of freshmen is 19; all undergraduates, 24. 30% do not continue beyond their first year; 40% remain to graduate. **Housing:** 1300 students can be accommodated in college housing, which includes single-sex and coed dorms, on-campus apartments, off-campus apartments, and married student housing. In addition, there are special-interest houses, 24-hour and 12-hour quiet halls, a wellness hall, a freshman hall, a smoke-

and incense-free hall, and an age 21-plus hall. On-campus housing is guaranteed for the freshman year only and is available on a first-come, first-served basis. 74% of students commute. All students may keep cars.

FACULTY/CLASSROOMS: 55% of faculty are male; 45% are female. All teach undergraduates. No introductory courses are taught by graduate students. The average class size in a regular course is 25.

PROGRAMS OF STUDY: Southern confers B.A., B.S., and B.F.A. degrees. Master's degrees are also awarded. Bachelor's degrees are awarded in AGRICULTURE (environmental studies and natural resource management), BIOLOGICAL SCIENCE (biology/biological science), BUSINESS (accounting, business administration and management, business (dual major program), hospitality management services, hotel and restaurant administration, marketing, and marketing/retailing/merchandising), COMMUNICATIONS AND THE ARTS (art history, art, communications, digital media, dramatic arts, English, English Writing, film, television and digital media, fine arts, foreign language, graphic design, graphic design & media, languages, music, music business management, music composition, music performance, Spanish, studio art, theatre arts, theatre production, theatre studies, visual and performing arts, and writing), COMPUTER AND PHYSICAL SCIENCE (chemistry, computer mathematics, computer programming, computer information systems, computer science, digital arts/technology, mathematics, mathematics – economics, and science), EDUCATION (early childhood education, education, elementary education, English education, environmental education, physical education, and recreation education), ENGINEERING AND ENVIRONMENTAL DESIGN (environmental science and preengineering), HEALTH PROFESSIONS (biology, biomedical science, health, mental health/human services, nursing, premedicine, prepharmacy, prephysical therapy, and sports medicine), SOCIAL SCIENCE (American Indian studies, anthropology, criminal justice, criminology, economics, gender studies, geography, history, human services, interdisciplinary studies, international studies, liberal arts/general studies, Native American studies, philosophy, political science/government, prelaw, psychology, social science, sociology, and women & gender studies). Fine & performing arts, psychology, and criminology/criminal justice are the strongest academically. Business, psychology, and communication have the largest enrollments.

ACTIVITIES: There are no fraternities or sororities. There are 125 groups on campus, including art, band, cheerleading, chess, choir, chorale, chorus, communications, computers, dance, drama, environmental, ethnic, film, forensics, honors, international, jazz band, LGBT, literary magazine, musical theater, newspaper, pep band, photography, political, professional, radio and TV, religious, social, social service, student government, and symphony. Popular campus events include Raider Orientation, Convocation, Southern Oregon Arts and Research Symposium, Commencement Weekend, International Week, and One World Series. **Sports:** There are 6 intercollegiate sports for men and 7 for women, and 11 intramural sports for men and 7 for women. Facilities include an indoor swimming pool, 6 racquetball courts, 12 tennis courts, 4 gyms, a climbing-wall gym, a dance studio, wrestling and weight rooms, sauna, football stadium, an all-weather track, and a student fitness and recreations center. **Graduates:** From July 1, 2015 to June 30, 2016, 838 bachelor's degrees were awarded. The most popular majors were business/marketing (17%), visual and performing arts (13%), and psychology (10%). 25 companies recruited on campus in 2015-2016. In an average class, 2% graduate in 3 years or less, 16% graduate in 4 years or less, 28% graduate in 5 years or less, and 32% graduate in 6 years or less.

SERVICES: Counseling and information services are available, as is tutoring in some subjects, such as all levels of math and writing. There is a reader service for the blind, and remedial math and writing. **Library/Resources:** The library contains 336,000 volumes, 807,000 microform items, and 90,000 audio/video tapes/CDs/DVDs, and subscribes to 4,300 periodicals including electronic. Computerized library services include interlibrary loans, database searching, Internet access, and Wi-Fi capability. Special learning facilities include a radio station, TV station, a center for the visual arts, an art museum, art galleries, a wildlife forensics lab, a music recital hall, 2 theaters, a greenhouse, and an ecology center. **Physically Challenged Students:** 95% of the campus is accessible. Facilities include wheelchair ramps, elevators, special parking, specially equipped restrooms, special class scheduling, lowered drinking fountains, lowered telephones, and special housing. **Special:** Cross-registration through the National Student and Western Student Exchanges, study abroad in 23 countries, internships, and federal work-study are all available. Accelerated degrees in business, communication, computer science, economics, geography, math, political science, foreign languages and literature, and sociology, dual majors in business and chemistry, physics, math, or music, and in math and computer science, and interdisciplinary majors in environmental or international studies are all offered. There are 13 national honor societies, a freshman honors program, and 10 departmental honors programs. **Visiting:** There are regularly scheduled orientations for prospective students, which includes tour of the campus, residence halls, and a meeting with an admissions representative. Appointments with faculty and class visits can be arranged. There are guides for informal visits, visitors may sit in on classes, and stay overnight. To schedule a visit, contact the Admissions Office. **Campus Safety and Security:** Measures include 24-hour foot and vehicle patrol, emergency notification system, self-defense education, and security escort services. There are emergency telephones, lighted pathways/sidewalks, and controlled access to dorms/residences.

REQUIREMENTS: A satisfactory score on the SAT is needed if the high school GPA is less than 2.75. Applicants need 14 academic credits, including 4 years of English, 3 each of math and social studies, 2 of science with 1 unit of lab, and 2 years of 1 foreign language. The GED is accepted. AP and CLEP credits are accepted. Students need a minimum GPA of 2.0 earned over 180 quarter hours, with 50 to 100 in the major and at least 60 in upper-division coursework. Competency must be demonstrated through coursework in writing and research. General education requirements include a yearlong course in speaking, writing, and critical thinking and both lower- and upper-division courses in arts and letters, natural sciences, social sciences, and quantitative reasoning. There is a required senior capstone experience. **Procedure:** Freshmen are admitted to all sessions. Entrance exams should be taken during junior or senior year. There are early admissions, deferred admissions, and rolling admissions plans. Application deadlines are open. Application fee is $50. Notification of early decision is sent March 15; regular decision, October 9. Applications are accepted on-line. **Transfer Students:** 540 transfer students enrolled in 2015-2016. Transfer students need a minimum GPA of 2.25 and at least 36 quarter credits. 45 of 180 credits required for the bachelor's degree must be completed at Southern. **International Students:** There are 166 international students enrolled. The school actively recruits these students. They must take the TOEFL with a minimum score of 520 on the paper-based TOEFL (PBT) or 68 on the Internet-based version (iBT).

ADMISSIONS: 93% of the 2016-2017 applicants were accepted. The SAT scores for the 2016-2017 freshman class were: Critical Reading-- 39% below 500, 38% between 500 and 599, 19% between 600 and 699, and 3% between 700 and 800. Math-- 47% below 500, 40% between 500 and 599, and 12% between 600 and 699. Writing-- 52% below 500, 38% between 500 and 599, and 9% between 600 and 699. **Admissions Contact:** Kelly Moutsatson, Director of Admissions. Email: *admissions@sou.edu* Web: *www.sou.edu*

FINANCIAL AID: In 2016-2017, 88% of all full-time freshmen and 81% of continuing full-time students received some form of financial aid. 88% of all full-time freshmen and 51% of continuing full-time students received need-based aid. The average freshman award was $8,560. Need-based scholarships or need-based grants averaged $6,728; need-based self-help aid (loans and jobs) averaged $3,260; non-need-based athletic scholarships averaged $2,869; other non-need-based awards and non-need-based scholarships averaged $3,047; and $3,560 from other forms of aid. 50% of undergraduate students work part-time. The average financial indebtedness of the 2016 graduate was $30,936. The FAFSA code is 003219. The priority date for freshman financial aid applications for fall entry is March 1.

UNIVERSITY OF OREGON — B-2

www.uoregon.edu

Eugene, OR 97403 — (541) 346-3201, (800) 232-3825

Fax: (541) 346-5815
Email: uoadmit@uoregon.edu
Full-time: 8479 men, 9849 women
Faculty: 1114; I, -$
Part-time: 846 men, 873 women
Ph.D.s: 90%
Graduate: 1725 men, 1836 women
Student/Faculty: 17 to 1
Year: quarters, summer session
Tuition: $10,762 ($33,442)
Room & Board: $12,210
Freshman Class: 21821 applied, 16992 accepted, 4041 enrolled
SAT CR/M/W: 550/550/540 **ACT:** 25
CEEB CODE: 4846
Application Deadline: January 15
COMPETITIVE

University of Oregon, founded in 1876. The university is a comprehensive public research university encompassing the humanities & arts, natural & social sciences, and the professions. We strive for excellence in teaching, artistic expression, and the generation, dissemination, preservation, and application of knowledge. There are 7 undergraduate schools and 9 graduate schools. In addition to regional accreditation, UO has baccalaureate program accreditation with AACSB, ACEJMC, ASLA, FIDER, NAAB, NASM, ACS, APA, and ASLA. The 295-acre campus is in a suburban area 110 miles south of Portland. Including any residence halls, there are 80 buildings.

STUDENT LIFE: 52% of undergraduates are from Oregon. 59% are White; 13% Foreign; 11% Hispanic; 7% two or more races; 6% Asian American; 2% African American; 1% American Indian/Alaska Native; 1% race unknown. **Female To Male Ratio:** 1.1:1. The average age of freshmen is 19; all undergraduates, 21. 13% do not continue beyond their first year; 72% remain to graduate. **Housing:** 4714 students can be accommodated in college housing, which includes single-sex and coed dorms, on-campus apartments, off-campus apartments, and married student housing, gender-inclusive hall, quiet hall, and a wellness hall. On-campus housing is available on a first-come, first-served basis. 81% of students commute. All students may keep cars.

FACULTY/CLASSROOMS: 53% of faculty are male; 47% are female. 96% teach undergraduates. Graduate students teach 28% of introductory courses. The average class size in an introductory lecture is 41; in a laboratory is 21; and in a regular course is 44.

PROGRAMS OF STUDY: UO confers B.A., B.S., B.Arch., B.Ed., B.F.A., B.I.Arch., B.L.A., B.Mus., and B.Mme degrees. Master's and doctoral degrees are also awarded. Bachelor's degrees are awarded in AGRICULTURE (environmental studies), BIOLOGICAL SCIENCE (biochemistry, biology/biological science, marine biology, and physiology), BUSINESS (accounting and business administration and management), COMMUNICATIONS AND THE ARTS (advertising, art, art history and appreciation, ceramic art and design, Chinese, classics, communications, communication science, comparative literature, creative writing, dance, design, digital communications, dramatic arts, English, fiber/textiles/weaving, film arts, fine arts, folklore and mythology, French, German, Greek, Italian, Japanese, jazz, journalism, Latin, linguistics, metal/jewelry, music, music performance, music theory and composition, painting, photography, printmaking, public relations, romance languages and literature, Russian, sculpture, Spanish, and theatre arts), COMPUTER AND PHYSICAL SCIENCE (chemistry, computer science, digital arts/technology, geology, mathematics, physics, and science), EDUCATION (education and music education), ENGINEERING AND ENVIRONMENTAL DESIGN (architecture, environmental science, and landscape architecture/design), HEALTH PROFESSIONS (speech pathology/audiology), SOCIAL SCIENCE (anthropology, Asian/Oriental studies, classical/ancient civilization, economics, ethnic studies, family and community services, geography, history, humanities, international studies, Judaic studies, Latin American studies, medieval studies, philosophy, political science/government, psychology, public administration, religion, social science, sociology, and women's studies). Pre-business administration, psychology, and human physiology have the largest enrollments.

ACTIVITIES: 14% of men belong to 18 national fraternities; 22% of women belong to 1 local and 11 national sororities. There are 250 groups on campus, including art, band, cheerleading, chess, choir, chorale, chorus, communications, computers, dance, debate, drama, drill team, environmental, ethnic, film, forensics, honors, international, jazz band, LGBT, literary magazine, marching band, musical theater, newspaper, pep band, photography, political, professional, radio and TV, religious, social, social service, and student government. Popular campus events include University Day, Family Weekends, and Convocation. **Sports:** There are 7 intercollegiate sports for men and 11 for women, and 15 intramural sports for men and 15 for women. Facilities include a football stadium, basketball arena, track and field complex, a softball field and complex, baseball stadium, tennis courts, soccer, and lacrosse. Student Recreation Center is 110,000 square feet of fitness space, exercise and yoga studios, cycling studio, an additional 3-court gym (more capacity for basketball, volleyball and badminton), 12-lane lap pool (used for lap swimming, water polo, water aerobics, instructional classes), 3-lane recreational pool (water volleyball, basketball instructional classes). **Graduates:** From July 1, 2015 to June 30, 2016, 4661 bachelor's degrees were awarded. The most popular majors were business administration (12%), general social science (9%), and economics (7%). In an average class, 2% graduate in 3 years or less, 50% graduate in 4 years or less, 68% graduate in 5 years or less, and 72% graduate in 6 years or less.

SERVICES: Counseling and information services are available, as is tutoring in some subjects. There is a reader service for the blind, and remedial math, reading, and writing. Private tutoring is available for many courses. Math and writing labs offer free drop-in support. **Library/Resources:** The 5 libraries contain 2.9 million volumes, 3.0 million microform items, and 114,281 audio/video tapes/CDs/DVDs, and subscribe to 106,750 periodicals including electronic. Computerized library services include interlibrary loans, database searching, Internet access, and Wi-Fi capability. Special learning facilities include an art gallery, natural history museum, radio station, TV station, an art museum, a natural and cultural history museum, centers for sports marketing, entrepreneurship, a green chemistry lab, and a longhouse. **Physically Challenged Students:** 95% of the campus is accessible. Facilities include wheelchair ramps, elevators, special parking, specially equipped restrooms, and lowered drinking fountains. An adviser is available for students with disabilities. Other accommodations are made upon request. **Special:** Matriculation agreements with more than 30 Oregon and Washington community colleges, dual enrollment with Lane and Southwestern Oregon Community Colleges, study abroad in more than 90 countries, pre-engineering in conjunction with Lane Community College, and a 3-2 engineering degree with Oregon State University are available. In addition, numerous internship opportunities, dual majors, and pass/fail options are available. There are 21 national honor societies, Phi Beta Kappa, and 48 departmental honors programs. **Visiting:** There are regularly scheduled orientations for prospective students, including IntroDUCKtion, a 2-day program scheduled for late July that includes both advising and Web-based registration. There are guides for informal visits and visitors may sit in on classes. **Campus Safety and Security:** Measures include 24-hour foot and vehicle patrol, emergency notification system, self-defense education, and security escort services. There are shuttle buses, emergency telephones, lighted pathways/sidewalks, and controlled access to dorms/residences. The university has a campuswide emergency management program, campus emergency operations, and mitigation plans.

REQUIREMENTS: The SAT or ACT is required. Standard freshman admission requirements include graduation from a standard or regionally accredited high school, and C- or higher in 15 college preparatory courses. Applications are evaluated based on strength of academic coursework, grades earned, grade trends, senior year courseload, standardized test scores, academic motivation as demonstrated in the application essay, academic potential, special talents, extracurricular activities, including community service or the need to work to assist your family, and ability to enhance the diversity of the university. AP and CLEP credits are accepted. For graduation, at least 180 quarter credits are required of all students, with a minimum GPA of 2.0 and a minimum of 62 credits upper division. A minimum of 36 credits must be in the major, including 24 in upper-division work. Basic courses vary by major, but all students must complete 12 to 16 credits each in the areas of arts and letters, social science, and science, as well as 2 courses in written English and 2 courses in multicultural studies. A bachelor of science requires one year college-level or equivalent mathematics or computer science or combination of the two. A bachelor of arts requires two years college level or equivalent of a second language. **Procedure:** Freshmen are admitted to all sessions. 2/15 is latest date scores accepted for fall term admission. There is a rolling admissions plan. Applications should be filed by January 15 for fall entry; October 15 for winter entry; February 1 for spring entry; and March 1 for summer entry, along with a $65 fee. Notifications are sent April 1. 444 applicants were on the 2016 waiting list; 388 were admitted. Applications are accepted on-line. Application fees are waived if application is completed on-line. **Transfer Students:** 1181 transfer students enrolled in 2015-2016. If transfer students have completed 35 or fewer transferable quarter credits (23 semester credits), they must meet admission requirements for both freshmen and transfer students; admission will be based on both high school and college work. If transfer students have completed 36 or more quarter credits (24 of which must be graded), admission will be based on college-level coursework only. Transfer students must be eligible to return to their most recent institution and have completed 1 college-level composition course and 1 college-level mathematics course with grades of C- or better, P (pass), or S (satisfactory); earned a minimum GPA of 2.25 if they are Oregon residents or 2.5 if they are nonresidents; and demonstrate second-language proficiency. 45 of 180 credits required for the bachelor's degree must be completed at UO. **International Students:** There are 2428 international students enrolled. The school actively recruits these students. They must take the TOEFL with a minimum score of 500 on the paper-based TOEFL (PBT) or 61 on the Internet-based version (iBT). SAT/ACT scores not required for international students except when applying to architecture program or honors college.

ADMISSIONS: 78% of the 2016-2017 applicants were accepted. The SAT scores for the 2016-2017 freshman class were: Critical Reading-- 26% below 500, 41% between 500 and 599, 28% between 600 and 699, and 6% between 700 and 800. Math-- 27% below 500, 42% between 500 and 599, 27% between 600 and 699, and 4% between 700 and 800. Writing-- 30% below 500, 43% between 500 and 599, 23% between 600 and 699, and 4% between 700 and 800. The ACT scores were 5% between 12 and 17, 34% between 18 and 23, 50% between 24 and 29, and 12% above 30. 51% of the current freshmen were in the top fifth of their class; 82% were in the top two fifths. There were 8 National Merit finalists. **Admissions Contact:** Jim Rawlins, Assistant VP, Director of Admissions. Email: *uoadmit@uoregon.edu* Web: *www.uoregon.edu*

FINANCIAL AID: 13% of undergraduate students work part-time. Average annual earnings from campus work are $3295. The average financial indebtedness of the 2016 graduate was $25,542. The FAFSA code is 003223. The priority date for freshman financial aid applications for fall entry is March 1.

UNIVERSITY OF PORTLAND B-1

www.up.edu

Portland, OR 97203	(503) 943-7147 (888) 627-5601
Fax: (503) 943-7315	Email: admissio@up.edu
Full-time: 1522 men, 2176 women	**Faculty:** 214; IIA, -$
Part-time: 20 men, 23 women	**Ph.D.s:** 92%
Graduate: 197 men, 312 women	**Student/Faculty:** 14 to 1
Year: semesters, summer session	**Tuition:** $40,250
Room & Board: $11,902	**Freshman Class:** 11202 applied, 6939 accepted, 941 enrolled
SAT CR/M: 590/600 **ACT:** required	**CEEB CODE:** 4847
Application Deadline: February 1	**VERY COMPETITIVE**

University of Portland, founded in 1901, is an independent institution affiliated with the Roman Catholic Church. It offers degree programs in the arts and sciences, business administration, education, engineering, and nursing. The figures in the above capsule are approximate. There are 5 undergraduate schools and 1 graduate school. In addition to regional accreditation, UP has baccalaureate program accreditation with AACSB, ABET, CSWE, NASM, NCATE, CCNE, and NAST. The 155-acre campus is in an urban area 4 miles north of downtown Portland. Including any residence halls, there are 30 buildings.

STUDENT LIFE: 71% of undergraduates are from out of state, mostly the Northwest. Students are from 44 states, 37 foreign countries, and Canada. 67% are from public schools. 62% are White; 12% Asian American; 12% Hispanic; 8% two or more races; 3% Foreign; 2% race unknown; 1% African American; 1% American Indian/Alaska Native. 45% are Catholic; 18% claim no religious affiliation. **Female To Male Ratio:** 1.4:1. The average age of freshmen is 19; all undergraduates, 20. 10% do not continue beyond their first year; 79% remain to graduate. **Housing:** 2100 students can be accommodated in college housing, which includes single-sex and coed dorms and on-campus apartments. In addition, there are honors houses, language houses, special-interest houses, university-owned rental houses, coed dorms, women's dorms, and theme housing. On-campus housing is guaranteed for the freshman year only and is available on a lottery system for upperclassmen. 57% of students live on campus; of those, 85% remain on campus on weekends. Upperclassmen may keep cars.

FACULTY/CLASSROOMS: 56% of faculty are male; 44% are female. All teach undergraduates. No introductory courses are taught by graduate students. The average class size in an introductory lecture is 25; in a laboratory is 20; and in a regular course is 20.

PROGRAMS OF STUDY: UP confers B.A., B.S., B.A.Ed., B.B.A., B.M.Ed., B.S.C.E., B.S.E.E., B.S.E.M., B.S.E.S., B.S.M.E., and B.S.N. degrees. Master's and doctoral degrees are also awarded. Bachelor's degrees are awarded in BIOLOGICAL SCIENCE (biology/biological science), BUSINESS (accounting, banking and finance, entrepreneurial studies, international business management, marketing/retailing/merchandising, and operations management), COMMUNICATIONS AND THE ARTS (communications, dramatic arts, English, music, and Spanish), COMPUTER AND PHYSICAL SCIENCE (chemistry, computer science, mathematics, and physics), EDUCATION (elementary education and secondary education), ENGINEERING AND ENVIRONMENTAL DESIGN (civil engineering, electrical/electronics engineering, engineering, environmental science, and mechanical engineering), HEALTH PROFESSIONS (nursing), SOCIAL SCIENCE (economics, French studies, German area studies, history, interdisciplinary studies, philosophy, political science/government, psychology, social work, sociology, and theological studies). Engineering, nursing, and biology are the strongest academically. Nursing, biology, and mechanical engineering have the largest enrollments.

ACTIVITIES: There are no fraternities or sororities. There are 62 groups on campus, including art, band, cheerleading, choir, chorale, chorus, computers, dance, debate, drama, environmental, ethnic, film, honors, international, jazz band, LGBT, literary magazine, musical theater, newspaper, orchestra, pep band, photography, political, professional, radio station, religious, social, social service, student government, symphony, and yearbook. Popular campus events include Dance of the Decade, International Night, Pilotpalooza, and Luau. **Sports:** There are 6 intercollegiate sports for men and 6 for women, and 20 intramural sports for men and 20 for women. Facilities include 72,000-square foot cardio machine loft, a weight training area, 3 studios for exercise/spin classes, 3 gymnasiums, a rock wall, a suspended track, and an outdoor pursuits office and bike shop. Rental equipment is available for biking and camping activities. **Graduates:** From July 1, 2015 to June 30, 2016, 854 bachelor's degrees were awarded. The most popular majors were health professions and related programs (20%), business/marketing (15%), and engineering (14%). 85 companies recruited on campus in 2015-2016. In an average class, 75% graduate in 4 years or less, 81% graduate in 5 years or less, and 80% graduate in 6 years or less. Of the 2015 graduating class, 12% were enrolled in graduate school within 6 months of graduation.

SERVICES: Counseling and information services are available, as is tutoring in most subjects. The faculty is available for individual assistance. **Library/Resources:** The library contains 220,340 volumes, 41,624 microform items, and 15,002 audio/video tapes/CDs/DVDs, and subscribes to 6,830 periodicals including electronic. Computerized library services include interlibrary loans, database searching, Internet access, and Wi-Fi capability. Special learning facilities include an art gallery. **Physically Challenged Students:** All of the campus is accessible. Facilities include wheelchair ramps, elevators, special parking, specially equipped restrooms, special class scheduling, lowered drinking fountains, and lowered telephones. **Special:** UP offers internships through individual departments, cross-registration with members of the Oregon Independent College Association, dual and interdisciplinary majors, including engineering chemistry and organizational communications, work-study programs, and pass/fail options. Study abroad may be arranged in Japan, Mexico, Australia, Chile, and several European countries. There are 9 national honor societies and a freshman honors program. **Visiting:** There are regularly scheduled orientations for prospective students, including a campus tour, class attendance, and a meeting with an admissions counselor. There are guides for informal visits, visitors may sit in on classes, and stay overnight. To schedule a visit, contact the Office of Admissions. **Campus Safety and Security:** Measures include 24-hour foot and vehicle patrol, emergency notification system, self-defense education, and security escort services. There are shuttle buses, emergency telephones, lighted pathways/sidewalks, and controlled access to dorms/residences.

REQUIREMENTS: The SAT or ACT is required, with a minimum score of 550 on each section of the SAT or a composite of 19 on the ACT. Graduation from an accredited secondary school or satisfactory scores on the GED are required. The high school curriculum should include 3-4 units in English composition, 2-3 units in math, 2 each in social studies, science, and history, and 7 in academic electives. 2 essays are required, as is a letter of recommendation from the high school counselor or principal. Applicants for fall 2017, the ACT with or without writing is accepted. UP requires applicants to be in the upper 50% of their class. A GPA of 3.0 is required. AP and CLEP credits are accepted. Important factors in the admissions decision are advanced placement or honors courses, leadership record, recommendations by school officials, parents or siblings attended your school, evidence of special talent, personality/intangible qualities, extracurricular activities record, and geographical diversity. To graduate, students must complete 120 credit hours, including at least 24 upper-division classes in the major, with a minimum GPA of 2.0. Required courses include 9 hours each of philosophy and theology, 6 each of science, social sciences, and electives, and

3 each of fine arts, history, math, and literature. Some majors may require a comprehensive exam and/or thesis. **Procedure:** Freshmen are admitted to all sessions. Entrance exams should be taken preferably before February 1 but no later than June 1 of the senior year. There are deferred admissions and rolling admissions plans. Applications should be filed by February 1 for fall entry, along with a $50 fee. Notification is sent on a rolling basis. 3031 applicants were on the 2016 waiting list. Applications are accepted on-line. **Transfer Students:** 81 transfer students enrolled in 2015-2016. Applicants with 26 or more credits must have a minimum GPA of 2.5 and be in good standing at their previous school. Students with fewer credits may need to meet freshman requirements. 30 of 120 credits required for the bachelor's degree must be completed at UP. **International Students:** There are 115 international students enrolled. The school actively recruits these students. They must take the TOEFL with a minimum score of 71 on the Internet-based version (iBT).

ADMISSIONS: 62% of the 2016-2017 applicants were accepted. The SAT scores for the 2016-2017 freshman class were: Critical Reading-- 10% below 500, 43% between 500 and 599, 32% between 600 and 699, and 15% between 700 and 800. Math-- 8% below 500, 35% between 500 and 599, 47% between 600 and 699, and 9% between 700 and 800. **Admissions Contact:** Jason McDonald, Dean of Admissions. Email: *admissio@up.edu* Web: *www.up.edu*

FINANCIAL AID: In 2016-2017, 97% of all full-time freshmen and 94% of continuing full-time students received some form of financial aid. 67% of all full-time freshmen and 64% of continuing full-time students received need-based aid. The average freshman award was $29,487. Need-based scholarships or need-based grants averaged $23,025; need-based self-help aid (loans and jobs) averaged $4,382; non-need-based athletic scholarships averaged $23,189; other non-need-based awards and non-need-based scholarships averaged $17,079; and $3,632 from other forms of aid. The average financial indebtedness of the 2016 graduate was $36,221. The FAFSA code is 003224. The priority date for freshman financial aid applications for fall entry is February 1.

WARNER PACIFIC COLLEGE B-1

www.warnerpacific.edu

Portland, OR 97215 (503) 517-1024
(800) 8041510

Fax: (503) 517-1540 Email: admissions@warnerpacific.edu

Full-time: 532 men, 956 women	**Faculty:** 34
Part-time: 19 men, 43 women	**Ph.D.s:** 50%
Graduate: 49 men, 80 women	**Student/Faculty:** 14 to 1
Year: semesters, summer session	**Tuition:** $25,560
Room & Board: $8230	**Freshman Class:** n/av
SAT or ACT: required	**CEEB CODE:** 4595
Application Deadline: open	**COMPETITIVE**

Warner Pacific College, founded in 1937, is a private Christian liberal arts college affiliated with the Church of God. Figures in the above capsule and in this profile are approximate. Tuition cost varies by programs chosen by student. There is 1 undergraduate school and 1 graduate school. The 14-acre campus is in an urban area 5 miles east of downtown Portland. Including any residence halls, there are 10 buildings.

STUDENT LIFE: 71% of undergraduates are from Oregon. Others are from 18 states, 3 foreign countries, and Canada. 78% are from public schools. 78% are White; 7% Foreign; 5% African American; 5% Hispanic; 3% Asian American; 1% American Indian/Alaska Native. 51% claim no religious affiliation; 42% Protestant. **Female To Male Ratio:** 1.8:1. The average age of freshmen is 27; all undergraduates, 31. 25% do not continue beyond their first year; 45% remain to graduate. **Housing:** 288 students can be accommodated in college housing, which includes single-sex dorms, on-campus apartments, and married student housing. On-campus housing is guaranteed for all 4 years, is available on a first-come, first-served basis, and is available on a lottery system for upperclassmen. Priority is given to out-of-town students. 54% of students live on campus. Alcohol is not permitted. All students may keep cars.

FACULTY/CLASSROOMS: 62% of faculty are male; 38% are female. All teach undergraduates, and 40% do research. No introductory courses are taught by graduate students. The average class size in an introductory lecture is 15; in a laboratory is 10; and in a regular course is 15.

PROGRAMS OF STUDY: Warner Pacific confers B.A. and B.S degrees. Associate degrees are also awarded. Bachelor's degrees are awarded in BIOLOGICAL SCIENCE (biology/biological science), BUSINESS (business administration and management), COMMUNICATIONS AND THE ARTS (English and music), EDUCATION (music education and physical education), SOCIAL SCIENCE (American studies, history, human development, liberal arts/general studies, ministries, religious music, social science, and sociology). Biological science, and business administration are the strongest academically. Business administration, human development, and education have the largest enrollments.

ACTIVITIES: There are no fraternities or sororities. There are 11 groups on campus, including spiritual growth groups, art, band, Bible study, choir, chorale, chorus, dance, debate, drama, environmental, ethnic, international, jazz band, literary magazine, newspaper, orchestra, professional, religious, social, social service, student government, and yearbook. Popular campus events include Winter Banquet and Spring Banquet. **Sports:** There are 5 intercollegiate sports for men and 6 for women, and 2 intramural sports for men and 2 for women. Facilities include men's and women's basketball, cross country, soccer, outdoor track and field, golf, wrestling, women's volleyball, weight-training room, a gym, and hiking trails. **Graduates:** From July 1, 2015 to June 30, 2016, 149 bachelor's degrees were awarded. The most popular majors were business (35%), human development (30%), and education (10%). In an average class, 2% graduate in 3 years or less, 29% graduate in 4 years or less, 8% graduate in 5 years or less, and 2% graduate in 6 years or less.

SERVICES: Counseling and information services are available, as is tutoring in most subjects. There is remedial math, reading, and writing, and testing and study skills workshops. **Library/Resources:** The library contains 67,948 volumes, 2,093 microform items, and 2,899 audio/video tapes/CDs/DVDs, and subscribes to 27,038 periodicals including electronic. Computerized library services include interlibrary loans, database searching, and Internet access. **Physically Challenged Students:** 75% of the campus is accessible. Facilities include wheelchair ramps, elevators, special parking, specially equipped restrooms, special class scheduling, and lowered drinking fountains. **Special:** Warner Pacific offers cross-registration through OICA, a Washington semester, a co-op nursing program, 27 majors, accelerated degree programs in human development and business administration, and study abroad in Latin America, the Middle East, and Russia. Internships, work-study programs, double majors, individualized majors, independent study credit for life and military experience, and pass/fail options are available. **Visiting:** There are regularly scheduled orientations for prospective students, including 2 campus preview days, 2 Knight Life visit weekends, academic fairs, and scholarship days. There are guides for informal visits, visitors may sit in on classes, and stay overnight. To schedule a visit, contact the Office of Enrollment. **Campus Safety and Security:** Measures include 24-hour foot and vehicle patrol, emergency notification system, self-defense education, and security escort services. There are emergency telephones, lighted pathways/sidewalks, and controlled access to dorms/residences.

REQUIREMENTS: The SAT or ACT is required. Applicants must be graduates of an accredited secondary school. The GED is accepted. High school preparation should include 4 years of English, 3 of social studies, and 2 each of math and lab science. AP and CLEP credits are accepted. Important factors in the admissions decision are evidence of special talent, leadership record, and advanced placement or honors courses. To graduate, students must complete 124 credits with a minimum GPA of 2.0. All students must take a core curriculum of 42 credits, consisting of 15 hours in humanities, 9 in communication, 7 to 9 in religion, 6 in social science, 4 in fine arts, and 3 each in science and health and phys ed. **Procedure:** Freshmen are admitted to all sessions. Entrance exams should be taken no later than the early fall of the senior year. There is a rolling admissions plan. Application deadlines are open. Application fee is $50. Applications are accepted on-line. **Transfer Students:** 170 transfer students enrolled in 2015-2016. Applicants must provide transcripts from their previous college. A minimum GPA of 2.0 is required. 30 of 124 credits required for the bachelor's degree must be completed at Warner Pacific. **International Students:** There are 12 international students enrolled. The school actively recruits these students. They must take the TOEFL and the college's own test.

Admissions Contact: Shannon Mackey, Exec. Director of Enrollment Management. Email: *admissions@warnerpacific.edu* Web: *www.warnerpacific.edu*

FINANCIAL AID: In 2016-2017, 98% of all full-time freshmen and 98% of continuing full-time students received some form of financial aid. 97% of all full-time freshmen and 97% of continuing full-time students

received need-based aid. The average freshman award was $15,003. 5% of undergraduate students work part-time. Average annual earnings from campus work are $2000. The average financial indebtedness of the 2016 graduate was $27,000. Warner Pacific is a member of CSS. The FAFSA code is 003225. Check with the school for current application deadlines.

WESTERN OREGON UNIVERSITY *(The complete profile is made available exclusively on our website, www.barronspac.com)*

WILLAMETTE UNIVERSITY — B-2

www.willamette.edu

Salem, OR 97301	**(503) 370-6303** **(877) 542-2787**
Fax: (503) 375-5363	**Email: libarts@willamette.edu**
Full-time: 826 men, 1092 women	**Faculty:** 217; IIA, +$
Part-time: 7 men, 13 women	**Ph.D.s:** 95%
Graduate: 302 men, 277 women	**Student/Faculty:** 10 to 1
Year: semesters	**Tuition:** $50,217
Room & Board: $11,600	**Freshman Class:** 6332 applied, 4935 accepted, 521 enrolled
SAT CR/M/W: 610/605/600 **ACT:** 28	**CEEB CODE:** 4954
Application Deadline: February 1	**VERY COMPETITIVE+**

Willamette University, founded in 1842, is an independent liberal arts institution affiliated with the Methodist Church. Figures in the above capsule and in this profile are approximate. There is 1 undergraduate school and 2 graduate schools. In addition to regional accreditation, Willamette has baccalaureate program accreditation with NASM. The 72-acre campus is in an urban area 50 minutes south of Portland. Including any residence halls, there are 45 buildings.

STUDENT LIFE: 73% of undergraduates are from out of state, mostly the West. Students are from 42 states, 19 foreign countries, and Canada. 69% are from public schools. 63% are White; 10% Hispanic; 8% two or more races; 7% Asian American; 5% race unknown; 2% African American; 1% American Indian/Alaska Native; 1% Foreign. 50% claim no religious affiliation; 27% Protestant; 12% Catholic. **Female To Male Ratio:** 1.2:1. The average age of freshmen is 18; all undergraduates, 20. 12% do not continue beyond their first year; 78% remain to graduate. **Housing:** 1493 students can be accommodated in college housing, which includes coed dorms and on-campus apartments. In addition, there are special-interest houses, fraternity houses, sorority houses, 24-hour quiet-hour dorm (intensive study) and substance-free options, and apartments for single students. On-campus housing is guaranteed for the freshman year only and is available on a lottery system for upperclassmen. 64% of students live on campus. All students may keep cars.

FACULTY/CLASSROOMS: 54% of faculty are male; 46% are female. All teach undergraduates, and all do research. No introductory courses are taught by graduate students. The average class size in an introductory lecture is 30; in a laboratory is 14; and in a regular course is 16.

PROGRAMS OF STUDY: Willamette confers B.A. and B.M. degrees. Master's and doctoral degrees are also awarded. Bachelor's degrees are awarded in BIOLOGICAL SCIENCE (biology/biological science), COMMUNICATIONS AND THE ARTS (art history and appreciation, comparative literature, dramatic arts, English, French, German, music, music performance, music theory and composition, Spanish, speech/debate/rhetoric, and studio art), COMPUTER AND PHYSICAL SCIENCE (chemistry, computer science, mathematics, physics, and science), EDUCATION (music education), ENGINEERING AND ENVIRONMENTAL DESIGN (environmental science), HEALTH PROFESSIONS (exercise science), SOCIAL SCIENCE (American studies, anthropology, Asian/Oriental studies, classical/ancient civilization, economics, history, humanities, international studies, Japanese studies, Latin American studies, philosophy, political science/government, psychology, religion, sociology, and women's studies). Politics, biology, and economics have the largest enrollments.

ACTIVITIES: 18% of men belong to 5 national fraternities; 12% of women belong to 3 national sororities. There are 105 groups on campus, including art, band, cheerleading, choir, chorale, chorus, computers, dance, debate, drama, ethnic, film, forensics, honors, international, jazz band, LGBT, literary magazine, musical theater, newspaper, orchestra, pep band, photography, political, professional, religious, social, social service, student government, symphony, and yearbook. Popular campus events include Lu'au, Black Tie Affair, and Wulapalooza. **Sports:** There are 10 intercollegiate sports for men and 10 for women, and 10 intramural sports for men and 10 for women. Facilities include a phys ed and recreation center, a 4000-seat football stadium, 3000-seat indoor gym, 1200-seat auditorium, a baseball stadium, soccer field, an all-weather track, a mini-Olympic-size indoor swimming pool, a outdoor swimming pool, 3 indoor and 10 outdoor tennis courts, handball/racquetball courts, weight training facilities. **Graduates:** From July 1, 2015 to June 30, 2016, 502 bachelor's degrees were awarded. The most popular majors were social sciences (29%), biological/life sciences (12%), and English (10%). 109 companies recruited on campus in 2015-2016. In an average class, 69% graduate in 4 years or less, 75% graduate in 5 years or less, and 78% graduate in 6 years or less. Of the 2015 graduating class, 20% were enrolled in graduate school within 6 months of graduation, and 70% were employed.

SERVICES: Counseling and information services are available, as is tutoring in most subjects. There is a reader service for the blind. Therapists are available for students on an individual needs basis, including braille services and readers. **Library/Resources:** The 2 libraries contain 403,135 volumes, 290,140 microform items, and 13,425 audio/video tapes/CDs/DVDs, and subscribe to 26,430 periodicals including electronic. Computerized library services include interlibrary loans, database searching, and Internet access. Special learning facilities include an art gallery, natural history museum, botanical and Japanese gardens, a multimedia center, and "smart" classrooms. **Physically Challenged Students:** 90% of the campus is accessible. Facilities include wheelchair ramps, elevators, special parking, specially equipped restrooms, special class scheduling, lowered drinking fountains, and lowered telephones. **Special:** Willamette offers internships with the state and city governments, a Chicago semester, a Washington semester, and a 3-2 engineering degree with Washington University, University of Southern California, and Columbia University. Nondegree study, B.A.-B.S. degrees, dual majors, work-study programs with numerous employers in the Salem area and at the university, and credit/no-credit options are also available. Study abroad programs are available in 14 countries. There are 3-2 degrees in management, forestry, and computer science. There are 7 national honor societies and a chapter of Phi Beta Kappa. **Visiting:** There are regularly scheduled orientations for prospective students, consisting of fall and spring campus preview days, tours, and faculty and student presentations. There are guides for informal visits, visitors may sit in on classes, and stay overnight. To schedule a visit, contact Associate Director of Admissions. **Campus Safety and Security:** Measures include 24-hour foot and vehicle patrol, emergency notification system, self-defense education, and security escort services. There are emergency telephones, lighted pathways/sidewalks, formal programs and education, and a weekly published campus safety report.

REQUIREMENTS: The SAT or ACT is required. The ACT Optional Writing test is also required. Graduation from an accredited secondary school or satisfactory scores on the GED are required. Institutional preferences recommend 4 units each of English, math, science, foreign language, social studies, academic electives, and visual/performing arts. 2 essays are required, and an interview is recommended. Portfolios or auditions are recommended for art and music students. AP credits are accepted. Important factors in the admissions decision are advanced placement or honors courses, recommendations by school officials, parents or siblings attended your school, evidence of special talent, personality/intangible qualities, extracurricular activities record, and geographical diversity. To graduate, students must complete a total of 124 semester hours, including a minimum of 32 in the major, with a minimum GPA of 2.0. All students must complete general education requirements in fine arts, humanities, literature, foreign language, interdisciplinary courses, natural sciences, and social sciences, and meet math and English proficiency levels. Freshmen are required to take a World Views seminar. Seniors are required to complete a senior thesis or other project in their major. **Procedure:** Freshmen are admitted fall and spring. Entrance exams should be taken December 1. There are early admissions and deferred admissions plans. Applications should be filed by February 1 for fall entry; November 1 for spring entry, along with a $50 fee. Notifications are sent April 1. 168 applicants were on the 2016 waiting list; 53 were admitted. Applications are accepted on-line. Application fees are waived if application is completed on-line. **Transfer Students:** 39 transfer students enrolled in 2015-2016. Transfer students must submit transcripts for all college and high school courses. A Transfer Reference (recommendation form) and essay are required. SAT/ACT required for applicants with less than 2 years transferable coursework. Students may enroll in the fall, February 1, and spring, November 1. 60 of 124 credits required for the bachelor's degree must be completed at Willamette. **International Students:** There are 27 international students enrolled. The school actively recruits these students. They must take the TOEFL with a minimum score of 560 on the paper-based TOEFL (PBT) or 83 on the Internet-based version (iBT), and also take the ELPT (English Language Placement Test), and the SAT or ACT.

ADMISSIONS: 78% of the 2016-2017 applicants were accepted. The SAT scores for the 2016-2017 freshman class were: Critical Reading-- 6% below 500, 36% between 500 and 599, 40% between 600 and 699, and 18% between 700 and 800. Math-- 8% below 500, 36% between 500 and 599, 45% between 600 and 699, and 10% between 700 and 800. Writing-- 10% below 500, 35% between 500 and 599, 44% between 600 and 699, and 11% between 700 and 800. The ACT scores were 14% between 18 and 23, 59% between 24 and 29, and 28% above 30. 38 freshmen graduated first in their class. **Admissions Contact:** Michael Beseda, Vice President, Enrollment & Communication. Email: *libarts@willamette.edu* Web: *www.willamette.edu*

FINANCIAL AID: In 2016-2017, 84% of all full-time freshmen and 66% of continuing full-time students received some form of financial aid. 84% of all full-time freshmen and 65% of continuing full-time students received need-based aid. The average freshman award was $35,204. Need-based scholarships or need-based grants averaged $29,199; need-based self-help aid (loans and jobs) averaged $5,529; non-need-based athletic scholarships averaged $19,925; and other non-need-based awards and non-need-based scholarships averaged $3,742. The average financial indebtedness of the 2016 graduate was $26,936. Willamette is a member of CSS. The FAFSA code is 003227. The priority date for freshman financial aid applications for fall entry is February 1.

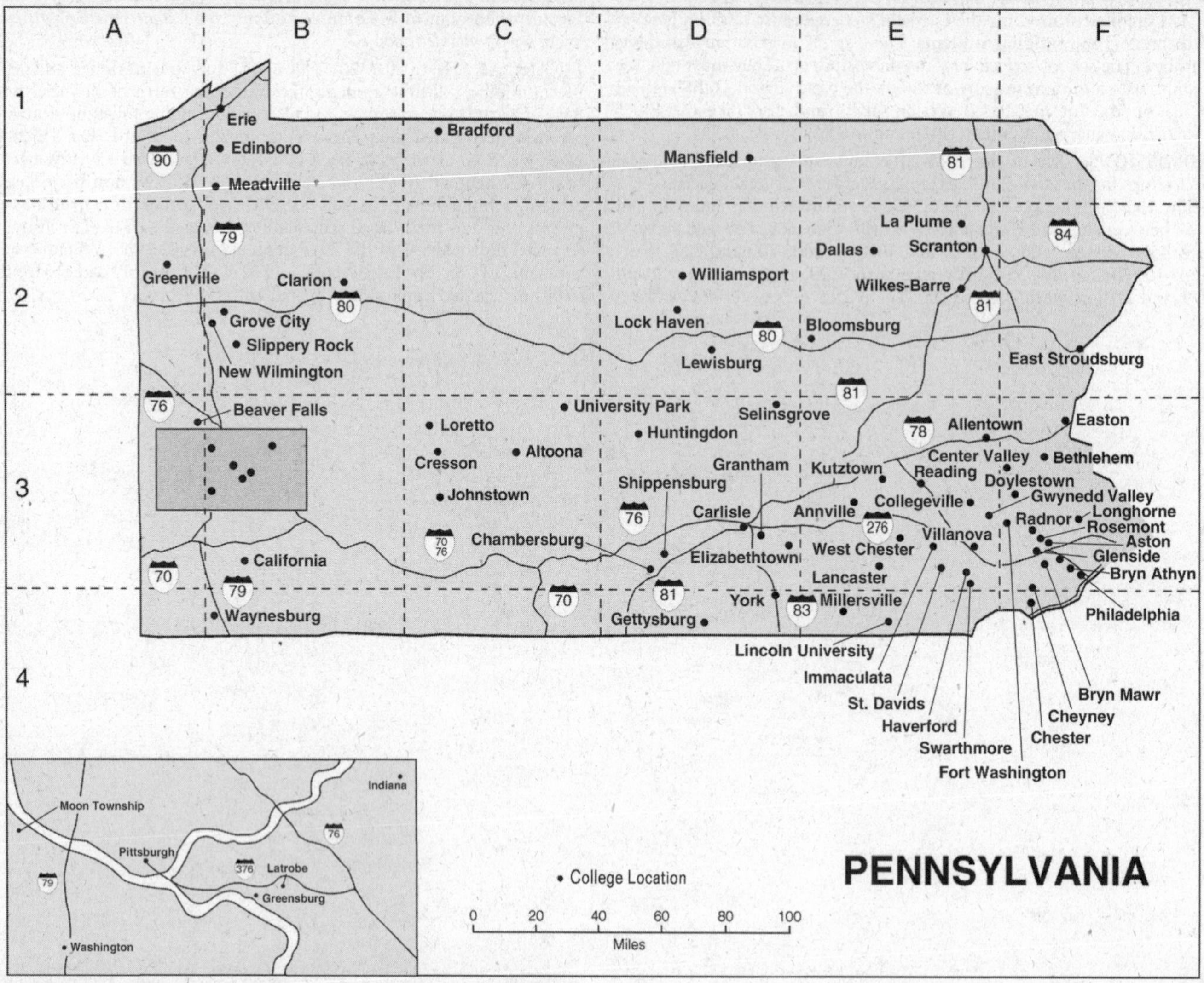

A B C D E F
1 2 3 4
Erie
Edinboro
Meadville
Bradford
Mansfield
Greenville
Clarion
Grove City
Slippery Rock
New Wilmington
Williamsport
Lock Haven
Lewisburg
Bloomsburg
La Plume
Dallas
Scranton
Wilkes-Barre
East Stroudsburg
Beaver Falls
Loretto
Cresson
Altoona
Johnstown
University Park
Huntingdon
Selinsgrove
Allentown
Easton
Center Valley
Bethlehem
Kutztown
Reading
Doylestown
Gwynedd Valley
Grantham
Shippensburg
Carlisle
Annville
Collegeville
Radnor
Longhorne
Rosemont
Aston
Glenside
Bryn Athyn
Chambersburg
Elizabethtown
West Chester
Villanova
California
Waynesburg
York
Lancaster
Millersville
Gettysburg
Philadelphia
Lincoln University
Immaculata
St. Davids
Haverford
Swarthmore
Fort Washington
Bryn Mawr
Cheyney
Chester
Moon Township
Indiana
Pittsburgh
Latrobe
Greensburg
Washington
• College Location
0 20 40 60 80 100
Miles
PENNSYLVANIA

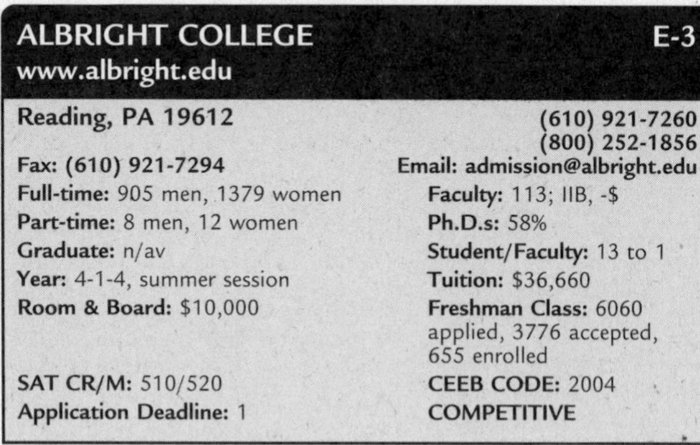

ALBRIGHT COLLEGE E-3
www.albright.edu

Reading, PA 19612 (610) 921-7260
(800) 252-1856
Fax: (610) 921-7294 Email: admission@albright.edu

Full-time: 905 men, 1379 women
Part-time: 8 men, 12 women
Graduate: n/av
Year: 4-1-4, summer session
Room & Board: $10,000

SAT CR/M: 510/520
Application Deadline: 1

Faculty: 113; IIB, -$
Ph.D.s: 58%
Student/Faculty: 13 to 1
Tuition: $36,660
Freshman Class: 6060 applied, 3776 accepted, 655 enrolled
CEEB CODE: 2004
COMPETITIVE

Founded in 1856, Albright College educates creative, curious students to become adaptable, global citizens who discover and reach their full potential. The College's flexible interdisciplinary curriculum encourages students to combine majors and disciplines to create individualized academic programs. Close faculty mentorship, numerous experiential learning options, and a diverse, supportive and nurturing community of scholars and learners help students exceed their own expectations and graduate with a commitment to a lifetime of service and learning. There is 1 undergraduate school and 1 graduate school. In addition to regional accreditation, Albright has baccalaureate program accreditation with Committee on Professional Training of the American. The 118-acre campus is in a suburban area 55 miles west of Philadelphia. Including any residence halls, there are 47 buildings.

STUDENT LIFE: 60% of undergraduates are from Pennsylvania. Others are from 30 states, and 14 foreign countries. 84% are from public schools. 61% are White; 4% Foreign; 3% Asian American; 2% two or more races; 18% African American; 10% Hispanic; 1% race unknown. 52% claim no religious affiliation; 23% unknown religious affiliation; 22% Catholic. **Female To Male Ratio:** 1.5:1. The average age of freshmen is 18; all undergraduates, 20. 25% do not continue beyond their first year; 62% remain to graduate. **Housing:** 1192 students can be accommodated in college housing, which includes single-sex and coed dorms, honors houses, special-interest houses, and theme housing. On-campus housing is guaranteed for the freshman year only. 69% of students live on campus; of those, 80% remain on campus on weekends. All students may keep cars.

FACULTY/CLASSROOMS: 46% of faculty are male; 54% are female. All teach undergraduates. No introductory courses are taught by graduate students. The average class size in an introductory lecture is 25; in a laboratory is 15; and in a regular course is 18.

PROGRAMS OF STUDY: Albright confers B.A., and B.S. degrees. Master's degrees are also awarded. Bachelor's degrees are awarded in BIOLOGICAL SCIENCE (biochemistry and biology/biological science), BUSINESS (accounting, business administration and management, and fashion merchandising), COMMUNICATIONS AND THE ARTS (art, communications, digital communications, dramatic arts, English, French, music business management, and Spanish), COMPUTER AND PHYSICAL SCIENCE (chemistry, computer science, information sciences and systems, mathematics, and physics), EDUCATION (elementary education, secondary education, and special education), ENGINEERING AND ENVIRONMENTAL DESIGN (environmental science), SOCIAL SCIENCE (American studies, child care/child and family studies, criminal justice, economics, history, Latin American studies, philosophy, political science/government, psychobiology, psychology, religion, sociology, textiles and clothing, and women's studies). Visual & performing arts, business, and social sciences have the largest enrollments.

ACTIVITIES: 15% of men belong to 4 national fraternities; 22% of women belong to 3 national sororities. There are 72 groups on campus, including band, cheerleading, chess, choir, chorus, computers, dance, debate, drama, environmental, ethnic, film, honors, international, jazz band, LGBT, literary magazine, musical theater, newspaper, orchestra, pep band, photography, political, professional, radio and TV, religious, social, social service, student government, and yearbook. **Sports:** There are 11 intercollegiate sports for men and 12 for women, and 5 intramural sports for men and 3 for women. Facilities include a stadium, gymnasium, baseball, softball, and soccer fields, fitness center, weight room, indoor track, bowling alley, a swimming pool, spin bikes, and racquetball courts. **Graduates:** From July 1, 2015 to June 30, 2016, 353 bachelor's degrees were awarded. The most popular majors were visual and performing arts (18%), social sciences (16%), and business/marketing (16%). 25 companies recruited on campus in 2015-2016. In an average class, 54% graduate in 6 years or less. Of the 2015 graduating class, 28% were enrolled in graduate school within 6 months of graduation, and 61% were employed.

SERVICES: Counseling and information services are available, as is tutoring in most subjects. An academic learning center, a writing center, and an ESL program are available. **Library/Resources:** The library contains 224,174 volumes, 13,967 microform items, 5,730 audio/video tapes/CDs/DVDs, and subscribes to 37,520 periodicals including electronic. Computerized library services include interlibrary loans, database searching, Internet access, and Wi-Fi capability. Special learning facilities include an art gallery, radio station, a center for business, civic and global leadership, a radio station, satellite dish for foreign language program, transmission and scanning electron microscopes, Holocaust resource center, center for excellence in local government, center for cultural ecology, center for Latin American studies, and an Albright community garden. **Physically Challenged Students:** 75% of the campus is accessible. Facilities include wheelchair ramps, elevators, special parking, specially equipped restrooms, and special class scheduling. **Special:** The school offers credit and noncredit internships, a Washington center, an accelerated degree program for working adults, cross-registration, dual majors, and student-designed majors. Study abroad may be arranged in any country. There are 11 national honor societies and a freshman honors program. **Visiting:** There are regularly scheduled orientations for prospective students, including an interview with a counselor and a tour of the campus with a currently enrolled student. There are guides for informal visits, visitors may sit in on classes, and stay overnight. To schedule a visit, contact the Admissions Office. **Campus Safety and Security:** Measures include 24-hour foot and vehicle patrol, emergency notification system, self-defense education, and security escort services. There are shuttle buses, emergency telephones, lighted pathways/sidewalks, controlled access to dorms/residences, comprehensive crisis action plan, and a bicycle patrol.

REQUIREMENTS: Graduation from an accredited secondary school or satisfactory scores on the GED are required for admission. Students must have a total of 16 Carnegie units, including 4 years of English, 3 in both math and science with 1 lab, 2 years each of a foreign language and social studies, and 1 year of both history and visual/performing arts. An essay is required, and an interview recommended. Submission of test scores is optional for admission. Students applying test optional must complete an on-campus admission interview. AP and CLEP credits are accepted. Important factors in the admissions decision are advanced placement or honors courses, leadership record, and recommendations by school officials. To graduate, students must complete 32 courses, including 13-14 in the major, with minimum cumulative and major GPAs of 2.0. General Studies requirements include a First Year Seminar, English Composition, Foreign Language, Foundations courses from the Humanities, Social Sciences, Natural Sciences, Fine Arts and Quantitative Skills, Connections courses and a capstone Synthesis course. Students must also fulfill the Cultural Experience requirement by attending cultural events on campus. **Procedure:** Freshmen are admitted in the fall, spring, and summer. Entrance exams should be taken during the spring of the junior year or the fall of the senior year. There are early admissions, deferred admissions, and rolling admissions plans. Application deadlines are open. Application fee is $35. Applications are accepted on-line. **Transfer Students:** 20 transfer students enrolled in 2015-2016. Transfer students must have a minimum GPA of 2.5 and be in good standing. 64 of 128 credits required for the bachelor's degree must be completed at Albright. **International Students:** There are 72 international students enrolled. The school actively recruits these students. They must take the TOEFL with a minimum score of 520 on the paper-based TOEFL (PBT) or 68 on the Internet-based version (iBT) or take the MELAB. SAT or ACT considered if submitted.

ADMISSIONS: 62% of the 2016-2017 applicants were accepted. The SAT scores for the 2016-2017 freshman class were: Critical Reading-- 42% below 500, 43% between 500 and 599, 14% between 600 and 699, and 1% between 700 and 800. Math-- 36% below 500, 48% between 500 and 599, 14% between 600 and 699, and 2% between 700 and 800. 49% of the current freshmen were in the top fifth of their class; 69% were in the top two fifths. 4 freshmen graduated first in their class. **Admissions Contact:** Paul Cramer, Vice President of Enrollment Management. Email: *admission@albright.edu* Web: *www.albright.edu*

FINANCIAL AID: In 2016-2017, 94% of all full-time freshmen and 90% of continuing full-time students received some form of financial aid. 94% of all full-time freshmen and 90% of continuing full-time students received need-based aid. The average freshman award was $35,065. Need-based scholarships or need-based grants averaged $34,162; need-based self-help aid (loans and jobs) averaged $6,434; and other non-need-based awards and non-need-based scholarships averaged $23,572. 40% of undergraduate students work part-time. Average annual earnings from campus work are $1825. The average financial indebtedness of the 2016 graduate was $38,196. Albright is a member of CSS. The FAFSA code is 003229. The priority date for freshman financial aid applications for fall entry is March 1.

ALLEGHENY COLLEGE — B-1

www.allegheny.edu

Meadville, PA 16335	(814) 332-4351 (800) 521-5293
Fax: (814) 337-0431	Email: admissions@allegheny.edu
Full-time: 890 men, 979 women	**Faculty:** 167; IIB, +$
Part-time: 19 men, 32 women	**Ph.D.s:** 92%
Graduate: n/av	**Student/Faculty:** 11 to 1
Year: semesters	**Tuition:** $44,250
Room & Board: $11,170	**Freshman Class:** 4724 applied, 3201 accepted, 551 enrolled
SAT CR/M/W: 600/590/572 **ACT:** 26	**CEEB CODE:** 2006
Application Deadline: February 15	**VERY COMPETITIVE**

Allegheny College is the premier college for students with "unusual combinations" of interests, skills, and talents. It is one of the nation's oldest and most dynamic liberal arts institutions. For more than 200 years, Allegheny has prepared graduates for extraordinary outcomes through its academic rigor and commitment to experiential learning, including undergraduate research. The 565-acre campus is in a suburban area 90 miles north of Pittsburgh, 35 miles south of Erie. Including any residence halls, there are 39 buildings.

STUDENT LIFE: 50% of undergraduates are from out of state, mostly the Middle Atlantic. Students are from 43 states, 51 foreign countries, and Canada. 84% are from public schools. 8% are Hispanic; 71% White; 7% African American; 4% Foreign; 4% two or more races; 3% Asian American; 3% race unknown. 41% claim no religious affiliation; 24% Catholic; 20% Protestant; 12% Buddhist, Hindu, Muslim and other Christian. **Female To Male Ratio:** 1.1:1. The average age of freshmen is 19; all undergraduates, 20. 17% do not continue beyond their first year; 83% remain to graduate. **Housing:** 1886 students can be accommodated in college housing, which includes single-sex and coed dorms, on-campus apartments, and off-campus apartments. In addition, there are language houses, special-interest houses, fraternity houses, wellness community, quiet study floors, townhouses, ADA accessible, gender neutral, living and learning residential communities. On-campus housing is guaranteed for all 4 years and is available on a lottery system for upperclassmen. 96% of students live on campus; of those, 80% remain on campus on weekends. All students may keep cars.

FACULTY/CLASSROOMS: 50% of faculty are male; 50% are female. All teach undergraduates, 83% do research, and 83% do both. No introductory courses are taught by graduate students. The average class size in an introductory lecture is 18; in a laboratory is 16; and in a regular course is 16.

PROGRAMS OF STUDY: Allegheny confers B.A., and B.S. degrees. Bachelor's degrees are awarded in AGRICULTURE (environmental studies), BIOLOGICAL SCIENCE (biochemistry, biology/biological science, and neurosciences), COMMUNICATIONS AND THE ARTS (art, art history and appreciation, communications, dramatic arts, English, French, German, music, Spanish, and studio art), COMPUTER AND PHYSICAL SCIENCE (chemistry, computer science, environmental geology, geology, mathematics, physics, and software engineering), ENGINEERING AND ENVIRONMENTAL DESIGN (environmental science), HEALTH PROFESSIONS (public health), SOCIAL SCIENCE (economics, history, international studies, philosophy, political science/government, psychology, religion, and women & gender studies). Physical & biological sciences, economics, environmental science, psychology, and international studies are the strongest academically. Biology, economics, and psychology have the largest enrollments.

ACTIVITIES: 25% of men belong to 6 national fraternities; 27% of women belong to 5 national sororities. There are 121 groups on campus, including coffee house, Model UN, music ensembles, outdoor programs, student programming board, academic, art, band, cheerleading, chess, choir, chorale, chorus, computers, dance, debate, drama, environmental, ethnic, honors, international, jazz band, LGBT, literary magazine, musical theater, newspaper, opera, orchestra, political, professional, radio and TV, religious, social, social service, student government, symphony, and yearbook. Popular campus events include Homecoming, Orchesis Dance Performance, Make A Difference Day, Springfest, Black Heritage Month, Celebrate Asia, International Month, Wingfest, Relay For Life, Coming Out Week, and Athletic Talent Show. **Sports:** There are 10 intercollegiate sports for men and 11 for women, and 3 intramural sports for men and 3 for women. Facilities include a sports and fitness center that includes a training track, weight rooms, cardio machines, multipurpose indoor courts (volleyball, basketball, tennis, badminton, putting green, batting cage), a natatorium, a dance studio, racquetball courts. An outdoor sports complex has a stadium, cross-country course, tennis courts, baseball, softball, soccer, rugby fields, field for shot put, discus and hammer throw, and a competition track. In addition, there are 80 wooded acres for mountain biking, hiking, and cross-country skiing. **Graduates:** From July 1, 2015 to June 30, 2016, 451 bachelor's degrees were awarded. The most popular majors were biology (14%), economics (11%), and psychology (10%). 82 companies recruited on campus in 2015-2016. In an average class, 68% graduate in 4 years or less, 74% graduate in 5 years or less, and 76% graduate in 6 years or less. Of the 2015 graduating class, 29% were enrolled in graduate school within 6 months of graduation, and 52% were employed.

SERVICES: Counseling and information services are available, as is tutoring in some subjects, such as biology, chemistry, economics, geology, mathematics, modern languages, physics, and psychology. Other support services and resources are available such as study strategies, test taking strategies, time management, organization skills, speech consultation, a learning center, writing consultants, academic advising, note-taking scribe services, tape recorders, and books on tape. **Library/Resources:** The library contains 1.0 million volumes, 133,500 microform items, 147,200 audio/video tapes/CDs/DVDs, and subscribes to 20,676 periodicals including electronic. Computerized library services include interlibrary loans, database searching, Internet access, and Wi-Fi capability. Special learning facilities include an art gallery, planetarium, radio station, TV station, an observatory, experimental research reserve, art studio, protected forest, dance studio, geographic information systems learning laboratory, language learning center, science complex, seismographic network station, center for political participation, theater and communication arts center, living and learning residential communities, environmental roof garden, center for environmental science. There is also Allegheny Gateway which connects classroom learning to real-world experience, creek connections, and augmented reality sandbox. **Physically Challenged Students:** 50% of the campus is accessible. Facilities include wheelchair ramps, elevators, special parking, specially equipped restrooms, special class scheduling, lowered drinking fountains, and special housing. Reasonable accommodations are made for special needs. **Special:** Allegheny offers domestic off campus semesters in 7 programs such as New York Arts, Oak Ridge Science Center, Philadelphia Center, Washington semester, Duke Marine Lab NC, Ecosystems Center MA, Newberry Seminar Research in the Humanities IL. Internships, double majors, independent study, student-designed majors, study abroad in 16 countries, and a work study program. A 3-2 engineering degree is available with Case Western Reserve, Columbia, Duke, University of Pittsburgh, and Washington University. Accelerated masters in public policy & management, occupational therapy, and physician assistant. Accelerated doctorates in nursing. Preprofessional programs, graduate school partnerships, and an experiential learning term are also available. There are 14 national honor societies, Phi Beta Kappa, and 12 departmental honors programs. **Visiting:** There are regularly scheduled orientations for prospective students, consisting of tours, panels, presentations on academic programs, student life, admissions, and financial aid. There are guides for informal visits, visitors may sit in on classes, and stay overnight. To schedule a visit, contact the Office of Admissions. **Campus Safety and Security:** Measures include 24-hour foot and vehicle patrol, emergency notification system, self-defense education, and security escort services. There are shuttle buses, emergency telephones, lighted pathways/sidewalks, controlled access to dorms/residences, TTY phones, emergency medical dispatching, motorist assistance, property engraving, on-campus sworn police officers, compliance program, and CCTV cameras.

REQUIREMENTS: The SAT or ACT is optional but will be considered if submitted. Graduation from an accredited secondary school is required for admission. The GED is accepted. Students must have 16 Carnegie units, including 4 years of English, 3 years each of math, science, and social studies, and 2 years of a foreign language. An essay is required, and an interview is recommended. A college prep program and 2 letters of recommendation (1 from a guidance counselor, 1 from a teacher) are required. AP and CLEP credits are accepted. Important factors in the admissions decision are advanced placement or honors courses, extracurricular activities record, and leadership record. To graduate, students must complete 128 credit hours with a minimum GPA of 2.0 in both the major and a minor. Between 40 and 64 hours are required in the major, including the junior seminar and senior research project. The major and minor must be from different divisions or interdivisional areas of study. All students must fulfill liberal arts studies requirements of 4 credit hours in each of 8 specified areas of inquiry. Additional required courses include freshman first seminar, freshman second seminar, and a sophomore writing and speaking seminar. All graduating seniors must complete an independent research project and an oral defense of the project. **Procedure:** Freshmen are admitted in the fall and spring. Entrance exams should be taken by January of the senior year. There are early decision, early admissions, and deferred admissions plans. Early decision applications should be filed by November 1; regular applications, by February 15 for fall entry; and November 1 for spring entry. Notification of early decision is sent November 15; regular decision, March 15. 87 early decision candidates were accepted for the 2016-2017 class. 333 applicants were on the 2016 waiting list; 20 were admitted. Application fees are waived if application is completed online. **Transfer Students:** 31 transfer students enrolled in 2015-2016. Transfer applicants must submit a transcript of all college courses, a high school transcript, college official's report from prior institutions, essay/personal statement, a letter describing reasons for transfer, and one recommendation from college official. A minimum GPA of 2.5 from college and high school is required, with 3.0 from college recommended. An interview is also recommended. 64 of 128 credits required for the bachelor's degree must be completed at Allegheny. **International Students:** There are 133 international students enrolled. The school actively recruits these students. SAT or ACT can be submitted in place of TOEFL if the applicant is native English speaking.

ADMISSIONS: 68% of the 2016-2017 applicants were accepted. The SAT scores for the 2016-2017 freshman class were: Critical Reading-- 11% below 500, 35% between 500 and 599, 41% between 600 and 699, and 13% between 700 and 800. Math-- 9% below 500, 43% between 500 and 599, 40% between 600 and 699, and 8% between 700 and 800. Writing-- 21% below 500, 38% between 500 and 599, 34% between 600 and 699, and 7% between 700 and 800. The ACT scores were 2% between 12 and 17, 22% between 18 and 23, 55% between 24 and 29, and 21% above 30. 59% of the current freshmen were in the top fifth of their class; 83% were in the top two fifths. 14 freshmen graduated first in their class. **Admissions Contact:** Cornell B. LeSane, II, V.P. of Enrollment & Dean of Admissions. Email: *admissions@allegheny.edu* Web: *www.allegheny.edu/admissions*

FINANCIAL AID: In 2016-2017, 100% of all full-time freshmen and 99% of continuing full-time students received some form of financial aid. 81% of all full-time freshmen and 71% of continuing full-time students received need-based aid. The average freshman award was $40,200. Need-based scholarships or need-based grants averaged $35,455 ($55,392 maximum); need-based self-help aid (loans and jobs) averaged $5,528 ($10,000 maximum); other non-need-based awards and non-need-based scholarships averaged $22,434 ($50,420 maximum); and

$38,316 from other forms of aid. 70% of undergraduate students work part-time. Average annual earnings from campus work are $1400. The FAFSA code is 003230. The priority date for freshman financial aid applications for fall entry is February 15.

ALVERNIA UNIVERSITY E-3

www.alvernia.edu

Reading, PA 19607	**(610) 796-3005** **(888) ALVERNIA**
Fax: (610) 796-8336	**Email: admissions@alvernia.edu**
Full-time: 521 men, 1243 women	**Faculty:** 107; IIB, -$
Part-time: 102 men, 311 women	**Ph.D.s:** 66%
Graduate: 153 men, 307 women	**Student/Faculty:** 12 to 1
Year: semesters, summer session	**Tuition:** $32,470
Room & Board: $11,430	**Freshman Class:** 1670 applied, 1240 accepted, 401 enrolled
SAT CR/M/W: 495/500/475 **ACT:** 22	**CEEB CODE:** 2431
Application Deadline: October 1	**COMPETITIVE**

Alvernia College, established in 1958, is a Roman Catholic liberal arts institution. The figures in the above capsule and in this profile are approximate. There are 2 undergraduate schools and 1 graduate school. In addition to regional accreditation, Alvernia has baccalaureate program accreditation with APTA, CSWE, NCATE, NLN, ACOTE, and CCNE. The 121-acre campus is in a suburban area 3 miles southwest of Reading. Including any residence halls, there are 20 buildings.

STUDENT LIFE: 83% of undergraduates are from Pennsylvania. Others are from 18 states, and 4 foreign countries. 71% are White; 7% Hispanic; 5% race unknown; 2% two or more races; 14% African American; 1% Asian American. 56% are Hindu, Muslim, and Buddist; 38% Catholic. **Female To Male Ratio:** 2.4:1. The average age of freshmen is 18; all undergraduates, 25. 29% do not continue beyond their first year; 51% remain to graduate. **Housing:** 964 students can be accommodated in college housing, which includes single-sex and coed dorms and on-campus apartments, honors houses, theme, and townhouses. On-campus housing is guaranteed for the freshman year only, and is available on a first-come, first-served basis. Priority is given to out-of-town students. 57% of students commute. All students may keep cars.

FACULTY/CLASSROOMS: 46% of faculty are male; 54% are female. 93% teach undergraduates. No introductory courses are taught by graduate students. The average class size in an introductory lecture is 19; in a laboratory is 18; and in a regular course is 19.

PROGRAMS OF STUDY: Alvernia confers B.A., B.S., B.S.N. and B.S.W. degrees. Associate, master's, and doctoral degrees are also awarded. Bachelor's degrees are awarded in BIOLOGICAL SCIENCE (biochemistry, biology/biological science, and forensic science), BUSINESS (accounting, business administration and management, human resources, marketing and distribution, and sports management), COMMUNICATIONS AND THE ARTS (communications, English, and theatre arts), COMPUTER AND PHYSICAL SCIENCE (chemistry, mathematics, and science), EDUCATION (athletic training, elementary education, middle school education, and secondary education), HEALTH PROFESSIONS (health science and nursing), SOCIAL SCIENCE (behavioral science, criminal justice, history, liberal arts/general studies, philosophy, political science/government, psychology, social work, and theological studies). Biology, chemistry, and occupational therapy are the strongest academically. Criminal justice, nursing, and business have the largest enrollments.

ACTIVITIES: There are no fraternities or sororities. There are 35 groups on campus, including band, cheerleading, chorale, chorus, computers, dance, drama, ethnic, honors, international, literary magazine, musical theater, newspaper, political, professional, religious, social, social service, and student government. Popular campus events include Christmas on Campus, Spring Fling, and Club Fair. **Sports:** There are 9 intercollegiate sports for men and 11 for women, and 8 intramural sports for men and 8 for women. Facilities include a gym, physical fitness and recreation center, playing fields, and outdoor tennis, basketball, and volleyball courts. **Graduates:** From July 1, 2015 to June 30, 2016, 469 bachelor's degrees were awarded. The most popular majors were health professions and related programs (36%), business/marketing (16%), and homeland security (14%). 67 companies recruited on campus in 2015-2016. In an average class, 38% graduate in 4 years or less, 48% graduate in 5 years or less, and 51% graduate in 6 years or less.

SERVICES: Counseling and information services are available, as is tutoring in every subject, and remedial math, reading, writing, math, and science tutorial lab. **Library/Resources:** The library contains 89,361 volumes, and 2,140 audio/video tapes/CDs/DVDs, and subscribes to 41,005 periodicals including electronic. Computerized library services include interlibrary loans, database searching, Internet access, and Wi-Fi capability. Special learning facilities include an art gallery. **Physically Challenged Students:** 75% of the campus is accessible. Facilities include wheelchair ramps, elevators, special parking, specially equipped restrooms, special class scheduling, lowered drinking fountains, lowered telephones, and special housing. **Special:** The college offers co-op programs in business and sports management, internships, cross-registration with Kutztown University, Pennsylvania State University, Albright College, and Reading area community colleges, a Washington semester, dual and student-designed majors, and practicums in psychology, criminal justice, education, addiction studies, social work, athletic training, and occupational therapy. There are 13 national honor societies, a freshman honors program, and 10 departmental honors programs. **Visiting:** There are regularly scheduled orientations for prospective students, including faculty displays, lunch, tours of the campus, and the opportunity to interact with current students. There are guides for informal visits, visitors may sit in on classes, and stay overnight. To schedule a visit, contact the Admissions Office. **Campus Safety and Security:** Measures include 24-hour foot and vehicle patrol and security escort services. There are shuttle buses, emergency telephones, lighted pathways/sidewalks, controlled access to dorms/residences, and photo ID cards must be carried by students.

REQUIREMENTS: The SAT or ACT is required. All applicants must be graduates of an accredited secondary school or have a GED certificate. They should have completed at least 16 academic units, including 4 each in English and math, 3 in social studies, 2 in science and foreign language, and 1 in academic electives. An interview is required for nursing applicants and strongly recommended for all others. A GPA of 2.0 is required. AP and CLEP credits are accepted. Important factors in the admissions decision are advanced placement or honors courses, personality/intangible qualities, extracurricular activities record, recommendations by alumni, parents or siblings attended your school, and evidence of special talent. To graduate, all students must complete at least 123 credit hours with a minimum GPA of 2.0 overall and in the major (2.5 for elementary education and nursing majors). Requirements include 54 to 55 credits in a liberal arts core, consisting of theology and philosophy, social science, communications, literature, fine arts, math, and science. All students also must perform 40 clock hours of service to others before graduation, complete course work in college success skills and in human diversity, and demonstrate computer proficiency. **Procedure:** Freshmen are admitted in the fall and spring. Entrance exams should be taken in the spring of the junior year or fall of the senior year. There are deferred admissions and rolling admissions plans. Application deadlines are open. Application fee is $25. Notification is sent on a rolling basis. Applications are accepted on-line. **Transfer Students:** 90 transfer students enrolled in 2015-2016. Applicants must have a college GPA of 2.0 or better. Student may enroll in the fall, spring, and summer. High school and college transcript(s), and an essay are required. 45 of 123 credits required for the bachelor's degree must be completed at Alvernia. **International Students:** There are 4 international students enrolled. They must take the TOEFL with a minimum score of 550 on the paper-based TOEFL (PBT) or 75 on the Internet-based version (iBT). They must also take the SAT or ACT.

ADMISSIONS: 74% of the 2016-2017 applicants were accepted. The SAT scores for the 2016-2017 freshman class were: Critical Reading-- 52% below 500, 41% between 500 and 599, and 7% between 600 and 699. Math-- 47% below 500, 45% between 500 and 599, and 8% between 600 and 699. Writing-- 58% below 500, 35% between 500 and 599, and 7% between 600 and 699. The ACT scores were 12% between 12 and 17, 56% between 18 and 23, 31% between 24 and 29, and 1% above 30. **Admissions Contact:** Dan Hartman, Director of Undergraduate Admssions. Email: *admissions@alvernia.edu* Web: *www.alvernia.edu*

FINANCIAL AID: In 2016-2017, 87% of all full-time freshmen and 85% of continuing full-time students received some form of financial aid. 87% of all full-time freshmen and 83% of continuing full-time students received need-based aid. The average freshman award was $22,775. Need-based scholarships or need-based grants averaged $18,979; need-based self-help aid (loans and jobs) averaged $4,465; other non-need-based awards and non-need-based scholarships averaged $3,206; and $15,108 from other forms of aid. Alvernia is a member of CSS. The state aid form, and the noncustodial parent's statement, if applicable are required. The FAFSA code is 003233. Check with the school for current application deadlines.

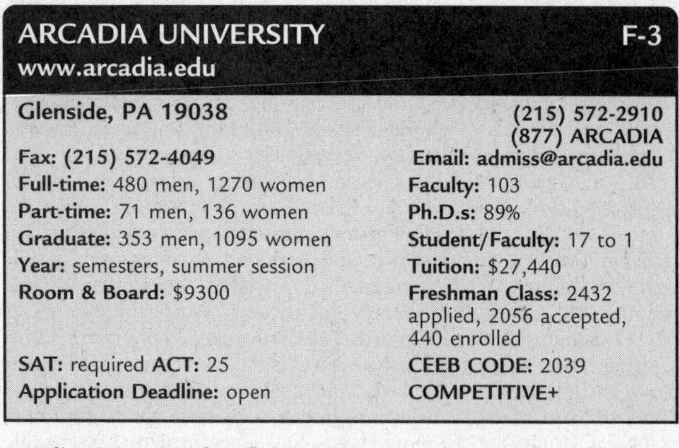

ARCADIA UNIVERSITY F-3
www.arcadia.edu

Glenside, PA 19038	(215) 572-2910 (877) ARCADIA
Fax: (215) 572-4049	Email: admiss@arcadia.edu
Full-time: 480 men, 1270 women	**Faculty:** 103
Part-time: 71 men, 136 women	**Ph.D.s:** 89%
Graduate: 353 men, 1095 women	**Student/Faculty:** 17 to 1
Year: semesters, summer session	**Tuition:** $27,440
Room & Board: $9300	**Freshman Class:** 2432 applied, 2056 accepted, 440 enrolled
SAT: required **ACT:** 25	**CEEB CODE:** 2039
Application Deadline: open	**COMPETITIVE+**

Arcadia University, founded in 1853, is a private institution offering undergraduate and graduate degrees in the fine arts, sciences, business, education, and pre-professional fields. There is 1 undergraduate school. In addition to regional accreditation, has baccalaureate program accreditation with ACBSP, APTA, CAHEA, and NASAD. The 76-acre campus is in a suburban area 10 miles north of Philadelphia. Including any residence halls, there are 21 buildings.

STUDENT LIFE: 68% of undergraduates are from Pennsylvania. Others are from 24 states, and 12 foreign countries. 70% are from public schools. 9% are African American; 70% White; 2% Asian American; 2% Hispanic; 1% Foreign. 77% claim no religious affiliation; 13% Catholic. **Female To Male Ratio:** 2.8:1. The average age of freshmen is 18; all undergraduates, 22. 19% do not continue beyond their first year; 64% remain to graduate. **Housing:** 1284 students can be accommodated in college housing, which includes single-sex and coed dorms, on-campus apartments, and off-campus apartments. There is a living and learning community in Grey Towers Castle. On-campus housing is guaranteed for all 4 years. 68% of students live on campus. Upperclassmen may keep cars.

FACULTY/CLASSROOMS: 44% of faculty are male; 56% are female. All teach undergraduates, and do research. No introductory courses are taught by graduate students. The average class size in an introductory lecture is 28; in a laboratory is 20; and in a regular course is 16.

PROGRAMS OF STUDY: Arcadia confers B.A., B.S. and B.F.A. degrees. Master's and doctoral degrees are also awarded. Bachelor's degrees are awarded in BIOLOGICAL SCIENCE (biology/biological science), BUSINESS (accounting, banking and finance, business administration and management, international business management, marketing/retailing/merchandising, and personnel management), COMMUNICATIONS AND THE ARTS (art history and appreciation, communications, dramatic arts, English, fine arts, graphic design, illustration, photography, and theater design), COMPUTER AND PHYSICAL SCIENCE (chemistry, computer science, mathematics, and science), EDUCATION (art education, early childhood education, elementary education, music education, secondary education, and special education), ENGINEERING AND ENVIRONMENTAL DESIGN (engineering, environmental science, and interior design), HEALTH PROFESSIONS (art therapy, health care administration, predentistry, premedicine, preoptometry, and preveterinary science), SOCIAL SCIENCE (criminal justice, history, international studies, liberal arts/general studies, philosophy, political science/government, prelaw, psychobiology, psychology, and sociology). Biology, psychology, and math are the strongest academically. Fine arts, business, and education have the largest enrollments.

ACTIVITIES: There are no fraternities or sororities. There are 40 groups on campus, including art, cheerleading, choir, chorale, chorus, communications, computers, dance, drama, ethnic, honors, international, LGBT, literary magazine, musical theater, newspaper, photography, political, professional, radio and TV, religious, social, social service, student government, and yearbook. Popular campus events include Mr. Beaver Contest, Woodstock Weekend, and International Festival. **Sports:** There are 6 intercollegiate sports for men and 9 for women, and 5 intramural sports for men and 5 for women. Facilities include a softball field, outdoor tennis and basketball courts, field hockey and soccer/lacrosse fields. There are also an athletic and recreation center with a gym for basketball and volleyball, a track, pool, aerobics and dance studio, and fitness and training rooms. **Graduates:** From July 1, 2015 to June 30, 2016, 381 bachelor's degrees were awarded. The most popular majors were business (15%), education (15%), and psychology (11%).

SERVICES: Counseling and information services are available, as is tutoring in every subject. There is a reader service for the blind, and remedial math, reading, and writing. **Library/Resources:** The library contains 148,271 volumes, 50,301 microform items, and 3,236 audio/video tapes/CDs/DVDs, and subscribes to 7,832 periodicals including electronic. Computerized library services include interlibrary loans, database searching, Internet access, and Wi-Fi capability. Special learning facilities include an art gallery, radio station, an observatory, theater, computer graphics and communication labs, and multimedia classrooms. **Physically Challenged Students:** 70% of the campus is accessible. Facilities include wheelchair ramps, elevators, special parking, specially equipped restrooms, special class scheduling, lowered drinking fountains, and lowered telephones. **Special:** Internships are encouraged in all majors. There are study-abroad programs in 13 countries and co-op programs in business, computer science, chemistry, actuarial science, and accounting. There is a 3+2 engineering program with Columbia University or Washington University in St. Louis, as well as a 3+4 optometry program with Salus University. Arcadia also offers work study, student-designed majors, and credit by exam. There are 13 national honor societies and a freshman honors program. **Visiting:** There are regularly scheduled orientations for prospective students, including personal interviews, open houses, and opportunities to dine on campus and to meet with faculty, financial aid officers, and current students. There are guides for informal visits, visitors may sit in on classes, and stay overnight. To schedule a visit, contact the Office of Enrollment Management. **Campus Safety and Security:** Measures include 24-hour foot and vehicle patrol, self-defense education, and security escort services. There are shuttle buses, emergency telephones, lighted pathways/sidewalks, alarmed doors, night receptionists, and card access to residence halls.

REQUIREMENTS: The SAT is required. The ACT and ACT Writing Test are recommended. Applicants must be graduates of an accredited secondary school or have a GED. A total of 16 academic credits is required, including 4 years of English, 3 each of math and social studies, and 2 each of a foreign language and science. An essay is required. All art and illustration majors (except art education) must submit a portfolio. AP and CLEP credits are accepted. Important factors in the admissions decision are advanced placement or honors courses, recommendations by school officials, and extracurricular activities record. Students must take English composition, math, and 2 semesters each of a lab science and a foreign language. They must also fulfill 24 credits of distribution requirements in the arts, humanities, and social sciences; core courses in American pluralism and non-Western cultures; and a final project or thesis. 128 credit hours are required to graduate, including 40 to 52 in the major, with a minimum GPA of 2.0. **Procedure:** Freshmen are admitted fall and spring. Entrance exams should be taken during orientation. There are early decision, early admissions, deferred admissions, and rolling admissions plans. Application deadlines are open. Application fee is $30. Notification of early decision is sent December 1; regular decision, on a rolling basis. 12 early decision candidates were accepted for the 2016-2017 class. Applications are accepted on-line. **Transfer Students:** 167 transfer students enrolled in 2015-2016. Applicants must have a GPA of 2.5. Art majors must submit a portfolio. The SAT or the ACT is required if the student has earned less than 1 year of college credit. An interview is encouraged. 32 of 128 credits required for the bachelor's degree must be completed at Arcadia. **International Students:** There are 41 international students enrolled. The school actively recruits these students. They must take the TOEFL, or take the IELTS.

ADMISSIONS: 85% of the 2016-2017 applicants were accepted. 51% of the current freshmen were in the top fifth of their class; 86% were in the top two fifths. 4 freshmen graduated first in their class. **Admissions Contact:** Office of Enrollment Management Email: *admiss@arcadia.edu* Web: *www.arcadia.edu*

FINANCIAL AID: In 2016-2017, 99% of all full-time freshmen and 94% of continuing full-time students received some form of financial aid. 77% of all full-time freshmen received need-based aid. 30% of undergraduate students work part-time. Average annual earnings from campus work are $709. The average financial indebtedness of the 2016 graduate was $31,923. The college's own financial statement, the PHEAA, and parent and student tax returns are required. The FAFSA code is 003235. The priority date for freshman financial aid applications for fall entry is March 1.

BLOOMSBURG UNIVERSITY OF PENNSYLVANIA *(The complete profile is made available exclusively on our website, www.barronspac.com)*

BRYN ATHYN COLLEGE F-3
www.brynathyn.edu

Bryn Athyn, PA 19009 **(267) 502-6044**

Fax: (267) 502-2593 **Email:** admissions@brynathyn.edu
Full-time: 106 men, 150 women
Part-time: 6 men, 5 women
Graduate: 12 men, 5 women
Year: trimesters
Room & Board: $11,538
Faculty: 32
Ph.D.s: 56%
Student/Faculty: 8 to 1
Tuition: $19,932
Freshman Class: 396 applied, 207 accepted, 80 enrolled
SAT CR/M/W: 510/510/470 **ACT:** 22
Application Deadline: February 1
CEEB CODE: 2002
COMPETITIVE

Bryn Athyn College of the New Church, founded in 1877, is a small private, coeducational, independent, liberal arts institution affiliated with the General Church of the New Jerusalem. Figures in the above capsule and in this profile are approximate. There is 1 undergraduate school and 1 graduate school. The 130-acre campus is in a suburban area in Bryn Athyn, PA, just 14 miles north of center city Philadelphia. Including any residence halls, there are 13 buildings.

STUDENT LIFE: 71% of undergraduates are from Pennsylvania. Others are from 16 states, 11 foreign countries, and Canada. 39% are from public schools. 8% are African American; 67% White; 3% Asian American; 2% Hispanic; 19% Foreign.. **Female To Male Ratio:** 1.3:1. The average age of freshmen is 18; all undergraduates, 21. 9% do not continue beyond their first year; 91% remain to graduate. **Housing:** 210 students can be accommodated in college housing, which includes single-sex dorms, on-campus apartments, and off-campus apartments. Upperclassmen can choose to live in one of our apartment-style residences, cottages or suites. On-campus housing is guaranteed for all 4 years. 60% of students live on campus; of those, 100% remain on campus on weekends. All students may keep cars. Alcohol is not permitted.

FACULTY/CLASSROOMS: 50% of faculty are male; 50% are female. All teach undergraduates, 24% do research, and 24% do both. No introductory courses are taught by graduate students. The average class size in a regular course is 12.

PROGRAMS OF STUDY: BA confers B.A. and B.S. degrees. Associate and master's degrees are also awarded. Bachelor's degrees are awarded in BIOLOGICAL SCIENCE (biology/biological science), COMMUNICATIONS AND THE ARTS (dance, English, and fine arts), EDUCATION (education), HEALTH PROFESSIONS (nursing), SOCIAL SCIENCE (anthropology, history, interdisciplinary studies, philosophy, political science/government, psychology, religion, religious studies, and sociology). Interdisciplinary studies, history, and education have the largest enrollments.

ACTIVITIES: There are no fraternities or sororities. There are 18 groups on campus, including college games club, business club, psychology club, chorale, chorus, dance, drama, international, newspaper, outing club, social, social service, and student government. Popular campus events include Charter Day, Service Day, and Alumni Weekend. **Sports:** There are 6 intercollegiate sports for men and 5 for women. Facilities include a gym, an open air ice hockey/skating rink, tennis courts, athletic fields, a fitness center, cross country, soccer, lacrosse, volleyball, basketball, golf, and a dance studio. **Graduates:** From July 1, 2015 to June 30, 2016, 29 bachelor's degrees were awarded. The most popular majors were interdisciplinary studies (28%), elementary education (24%), and religion and history (14%). Of the 2015 graduating class, 17% were enrolled in graduate school within 6 months of graduation, and 57% were employed.

SERVICES: Counseling and information services are available, as is tutoring in most subjects. **Library/Resources:** The 2 libraries contain 144,475 volumes, 3,593 microform items, 2,017 audio/video tapes/CDs/DVDs, and subscribe to 8,497 periodicals including electronic. Computerized library services include interlibrary loans, database searching, Internet access, and Wi-Fi capability. **Physically Challenged Students:** 90% of the campus is accessible. Facilities include wheelchair ramps, elevators, special parking, specially equipped restrooms, lowered drinking fountains, and special housing. **Special:** Cross-registration is available with Holy Family University, co-op programs, internships, B.A.-B.S. degrees, student-designed majors, non-degree study, and study-abroad opportunities are also available. **Visiting:** There are regularly scheduled orientations for prospective students, consisting of touring the campus, attending chapel, and visiting classes. There are guides for informal visits, visitors may sit in on classes, and stay overnight. To schedule a visit, contact Angella Irwin at (267) 502-6044. **Campus Safety and Security:** Measures include 24-hour foot and vehicle patrol. There are emergency telephones, lighted pathways/sidewalks, and controlled access to dorms/residences.

REQUIREMENTS: SAT or ACT scores must reflect promise of success in college work. Applicants must complete an essay and also be graduates of an accredited secondary school or achieve satisfactory scores on the GED. An interview is recommended. AP and CLEP credits are accepted. Important factors in the admissions decision are recommendations by school officials, personality/intangible qualities, and advanced placement or honors courses. To graduate, students must complete a total of 130 credit hours with a minimum GPA of 2.0 and must satisfy the Core Program. All students must take required courses in religion, writing, philosophy, and physical education. Some majors require a comprehensive project, exam, or thesis. **Procedure:** Freshmen are admitted in the fall, winter, and spring. Entrance exams should be taken by the fall of senior year. There are deferred admissions and rolling admissions plans. Application deadlines are open. Notification is sent on a rolling basis. Applications are accepted online. **Transfer Students:** 20 transfer students enrolled in 2015-2016. Transfer students with less than 30 credits must supply SAT or ACT scores, high school transcript, transcripts from all colleges attended, and a letter of recommendation. An interview is recommended. Transfers with 30+ credits need not supply SAT/ACT and high school transcript. 60 of 130 credits required for the bachelor's degree must be completed at BA. **International Students:** There are 38 international students enrolled. They must take the TOEFL with a minimum score of 520 on the paper-based TOEFL (PBT) or 70 on the Internet-based version (iBT). They must also take the SAT or ACT.

ADMISSIONS: 52% of the 2016-2017 applicants were accepted. The SAT scores for the 2016-2017 freshman class were: Critical Reading-- 44% below 500, 27% between 500 and 599, 25% between 600 and 699, and 4% between 700 and 800. Math-- 44% below 500, 35% between 500 and 599, 18% between 600 and 699, and 3% between 700 and 800. Writing-- 56% below 500, 26% between 500 and 599, 12% between 600 and 699, and 6% between 700 and 800. The ACT scores were 11% below 12, 56% between 12 and 17, 11% between 18 and 23, and 22% above 30. **Admissions Contact:** Angella Irwin, Admissions Counselor. Email: *admissions@brynathyn.edu* Web: *www.brynathyn.edu*

FINANCIAL AID: In 2016-2017, 98% of all full-time freshmen received some form of financial aid. 98% of all full-time freshmen received need-based aid. The average freshman award was $17,130. Need-based scholarships or need-based grants averaged $9,656; need-based self-help aid (loans and jobs) averaged $4,718; and other non-need-based awards and non-need-based scholarships averaged $4,868. 59% of undergraduate students work part-time. Average annual earnings from campus work are $1850. The average financial indebtedness of the 2016 graduate was $17,988. The priority date for freshman financial aid applications for fall entry is February 15.

BRYN MAWR COLLEGE F-3
www.brynmawr.edu

Bryn Mawr, PA 19010 **(610) 526-5152** **(800) 262-1885**

Fax: (610) 526-7471 **Email:** admissions@brynmawr.edu
Full-time: 1291 women
Part-time: 17 women
Graduate: 80 men, 321 women
Year: semesters, summer session
Room & Board: $14,350
Faculty: 161; IIA, ++$
Ph.D.s: 93%
Student/Faculty: 8 to 1
Tuition: $45,540
Freshman Class: 2706 applied, 1095 accepted, 351 enrolled
SAT CR/M/W: 660/650/670 **ACT:** 29
Application Deadline: January 15
CEEB CODE: 2049
MOST COMPETITIVE

Bryn Mawr College, founded in 1885, is an independent liberal arts institution, primarily for women. The graduate school of social work and research, the graduate school of the arts and sciences, and the postbaccalaureate premedical programs are coed. There is 1 undergraduate school and 2 graduate schools. The 135-acre campus is in a suburban area 11 miles west of Philadelphia. Including any residence halls, there are 40 buildings.

STUDENT LIFE: 81% of undergraduates are from out of state, mostly the Middle Atlantic. Students are from 44 states, 57 foreign countries, and Canada. 64% are from public schools. 9% are Hispanic; 9% race unknown; 5% African American; 5% two or more races; 36% White; 25% Foreign; 12% Asian American. **Female To Male Ratio:** 20.4:1. The average age of freshmen is 18; all undergraduates, 20. 9% do not continue beyond their first year; 82% remain to graduate. **Housing:** 1247 students can be accommodated in college housing, which includes single-sex and coed dorms and off-campus apartments. In addition, there are language houses, and special-interest houses. Foreign language houses are available to students studying Chinese, French, German, Hebrew, Italian, Russian or Spanish. Coed housing is available, as is special housing available for non-traditional-aged students, Co-ops, such as a Vegan house, are available. On-campus housing is guaranteed for all 4 years. 91% of students live on campus; of those, 90% remain on campus on weekends. Upperclassmen may keep cars.

FACULTY/CLASSROOMS: 43% of faculty are male; 57% are female. All teach undergraduates, and do research. No introductory courses are taught by graduate students. The average class size in an introductory lecture is 25; in a laboratory is 15; and in a regular course is 16.

PROGRAMS OF STUDY: Bryn Mawr confers A.B. degrees. Master's and doctoral degrees are also awarded. Bachelor's degrees are awarded in BIOLOGICAL SCIENCE (biology/biological science), COMMUNICATIONS AND THE ARTS (art history and appreciation, classical languages, classics, comparative literature, English, fine arts, French, German, Greek, Italian, Latin, linguistics, music, romance languages and literature, Russian, and Spanish), COMPUTER AND PHYSICAL SCIENCE (astronomy, chemistry, computer science, geology, mathematics, and physics), SOCIAL SCIENCE (anthropology, archeology, East Asian studies, economics, history, international studies, philosophy, political science/government, psychology, religion, sociology, and urban studies). English, psychology, and math have the largest enrollments.

ACTIVITIES: There are no fraternities or sororities. There are 100 groups on campus, including art, business, chess, choir, chorale, chorus, computers, dance, drama, environmental, ethnic, forensics, honors, international, LGBT, literary magazine, musical theater, orchestra, photography, political, professional, religious, social, social service, and student government. Popular campus events include May Day, Lantern Night, and Fall Frolic. **Sports:** There are 12 intercollegiate sports for women, and 10 intramural sports for women. Facilities include playing fields with access to an indoor track, a gym with pool and diving well, basketball, badminton, and volleyball courts, a gymnastics room and dance studio, a weight-training and fitness room, a auditorium, and student center. **Graduates:** From July 1, 2015 to June 30, 2016, 333 bachelor's degrees were awarded. The most popular majors were mathematics (13%), psychology (10%), and English (10%). 175 companies recruited on campus in 2015-2016. In an average class, 2% graduate in 3 years or less, 78% graduate in 4 years or less, 84% graduate in 5 years or less, and 84% graduate in 6 years or less. Of the 2015 graduating class, 19% were enrolled in graduate school within 6 months of graduation, and 35% were employed.

SERVICES: Counseling and information services are available, as is tutoring in every subject. There is a reader service for the blind. **Library/Resources:** The 4 libraries contain 951,791 volumes, 18,726 microform items, 10,352 audio/video tapes/CDs/DVDs, and subscribe to 102,519 periodicals including electronic. Computerized library services include interlibrary loans, database searching, Internet access, and Wi-Fi capability. Special learning facilities include an art gallery, an archeological museum, and a language learning center with audio, video, and computer technology. **Physically Challenged Students:** Facilities include wheelchair ramps, elevators, special parking, specially equipped restrooms, special class scheduling, lowered drinking fountains, lowered telephones, and special housing. **Special:** Students may cross-register with Haverford and Swarthmore Colleges and the University of Pennsylvania. Bryn Mawr sponsors more than 100 grants and internships for summer study in a wide range of disciplines and sponsors/co-sponsors study abroad in 27 countries. Student-designed and dual majors are possible. Pass/fail options, work-study programs, a 3-2 degree in engineering with the California Institute of Technology, and a 3-2 degree in city and regional planning with the University of Pennsylvania are offered as well. **Visiting:** There are regularly scheduled orientations for prospective students, including student-guided campus tours and interviews can be arranged. There are guides for informal visits, visitors may sit in on classes, and stay overnight. To schedule a visit, contact the Office of Admissions. **Campus Safety and Security:** Measures include 24-hour foot and vehicle patrol, emergency notification system, self-defense education, and security escort services. There are shuttle buses, emergency telephones, lighted pathways/sidewalks, controlled access to dorms/residences, bicycle registration, and personal safety education (road safety, car maintenance).

REQUIREMENTS: Requirements for admission are 4 years of English, 3 years of math (2 of algebra and 1 of geometry), 3 years of a foreign language or 2 years of 2 languages, and 1 year each of science and history. Most applicants have taken at least 3 lab science courses and trigonometry. An essay is required. An interview is strongly recommended. Submission of standardized test scores (SAT or ACT) is optional for US citizens and US permanent residents. Non-US citizens and Non-US permanent residents are required to submit standardized test scores (SAT I or ACT) as well as either the TOEFL or IELTS if their primary language is not English and/or their language of instruction over the past four years has not been English. AP credits are accepted. Important factors in the admissions decision are advanced placement or honors courses, evidence of special talent, and extracurricular activities record. To graduate, students must complete 128 semester hours, with 40 to 60 in the major and a minimum GPA of 2.0. All students must complete 2 courses each in the social sciences, humanities, and natural sciences or math, including 1 lab science. Additional required courses include 1 college seminar and 1 quantitative skills course. Students must be able to demonstrate proficiency in 1 foreign language. **Procedure:** Freshmen are admitted in the fall. Entrance exams should be taken in the spring of the junior year or the fall of the senior year. There are early decision and deferred admissions plans. Early decision applications should be filed by November 15; regular applications, by January 15 for fall entry, along with a $50 fee. Notification of early decision is sent December 15; regular decision, in April. 118 early decision candidates were accepted for the 2016-2017 class. 696 applicants were on the 2016 waiting list; 33 were admitted. Application fees are waived if application is completed online. **Transfer Students:** 46 transfer students enrolled in 2015-2016. Applicants for transfer must be in good academic standing at their current institutions. An official SAT score report or ACT score report (for international students only), 2 professor recommendations, a school official's report, high school transcripts, college transcripts, and the Bryn Mawr Supplement to the College Application for Transfers must be submitted. 96 of 128 credits required for the bachelor's degree must be completed at Bryn Mawr. **International Students:** There are 377 international students enrolled. The school actively recruits these students. They must take the TOEFL with a minimum score of 600 on the paper-based TOEFL (PBT) or 90 on the Internet-based version (iBT), or a score of 7 or above on the IELTS. They must also take the SAT or ACT.

ADMISSIONS: 40% of the 2016-2017 applicants were accepted. The SAT scores for the 2016-2017 freshman class were: Critical Reading-- 2% below 500, 20% between 500 and 599, 47% between 600 and 699, and 31% between 700 and 800. Math-- 1% below 500, 24% between 500 and 599, 41% between 600 and 699, and 34% between 700 and 800. Writing-- 2% below 500, 13% between 500 and 599, 51% between 600 and 699, and 35% between 700 and 800. The ACT scores were 3% below 12, 6% between 12 and 17, 14% between 18 and 23, 25% between 24 and 29, and 52% above 30. 83% of the current freshmen were in the top fifth of their class; 96% were in the top two fifths. 5 freshmen graduated first in their class. **Admissions Contact:** Peaches Valdes, Director of Admissions. Email: *admissions@brynmawr.edu* Web: *www.brynmawr.edu*

FINANCIAL AID: In 2016-2017, 75% of all full-time freshmen and 75% of continuing full-time students received some form of financial aid. 50% of all full-time freshmen and 52% of continuing full-time students received need-based aid. The average freshman award was $42,724. Need-based scholarships or need-based grants averaged $36,525; and need-based self-help aid (loans and jobs) averaged $5,490. 63% of undergraduate students work part-time. Average annual earnings from campus work are $2000. The average financial indebtedness of the 2016 graduate was $24,675. Bryn Mawr is a member of CSS. The CSS/Profile, the prior year's tax returns, noncustodial parent statement, and the business/farm supplement are required. The FAFSA code is 003237. The filing deadline for freshman financial aid applications for fall entry is March 1.

BUCKNELL UNIVERSITY D-2
www.bucknell.edu

Lewisburg, PA 17837 **(570) 577-3000**

Fax: (570) 577-3538	**Email:** admissions@bucknell.edu
Full-time: 1743 men, 1787 women	**Faculty:** 378
Part-time: 15 men, 26 women	**Ph.D.s:** 97%
Graduate: 28 men, 27 women	**Student/Faculty:** 9 to 1
Year: semesters, summer session	**Tuition:** $51,960
Room & Board: $12,656	**Freshman Class:** 10487 applied, 3138 accepted, 950 enrolled
SAT CR/M/W: 640/660/650 **ACT:** 30	**CEEB CODE:** 2050
Application Deadline: January 15	**MOST COMPETITIVE**

Bucknell University, established in 1846, is a private independent institution offering undergraduate and graduate programs in arts, music, education, humanities, management, engineering, sciences, and social sciences. There are 3 undergraduate schools and 1 graduate school. In addition to regional accreditation, Bucknell has baccalaureate program accreditation with AACSB, ABET, NASM, CAC, and ACS. The 450-acre campus is in a small town 75 miles north of Harrisburg. Including any residence halls, there are 133 buildings.

STUDENT LIFE: 79% of undergraduates are from out of state, mostly the Middle Atlantic. Students are from 45 states, 46 foreign countries, and Canada. 64% are from public schools. 76% are White; 6% Hispanic; 6% Foreign; 5% Asian American; 4% African American; 4% two or more races. 39% are Catholic; 25% Protestant; 15% claim no religious affiliation; 12% Muslims, Buddhists, Hindu, Mormon and unknown. **Female To Male Ratio:** 1.0:1. The average age of freshmen is 18; all undergraduates, 20. 8% do not continue beyond their first year; 88% remain to graduate. **Housing:** 3289 students can be accommodated in college housing, which includes single-sex and coed dorms and on-campus apartments. In addition, there are special-interest houses, fraternity houses, sustainable living, and substance-free housing. There are also 7 residential colleges for the first year (arts, discovery, environmental, humanities, global, science and technology, languages and cultures and social justice). On-campus housing is guaranteed for all 4 years and is available on a lottery system for upperclassmen. 92% of students live on campus; of those, 85% remain on campus on weekends. Upperclassmen may keep cars.

FACULTY/CLASSROOMS: 59% of faculty are male; 41% are female. All teach undergraduates, and do research. No introductory courses are taught by graduate students. The average class size in an introductory lecture is 22; in a laboratory is 14; and in a regular course is 18.

PROGRAMS OF STUDY: Bucknell confers B.A., B.S., B.S.B.A., B.E.V.E., B.S.B.E., B.S.C.E., B.S.C.M., B.S.C.S., B.S.E.D., B.S.E.E., B.S.M.E., B.C.E.N. and B.M.U.S. degrees. Master's degrees are also awarded. Bachelor's degrees are awarded in AGRICULTURE (animal science), BIOLOGICAL SCIENCE (biochemistry, biology/biological science, cell biology, and neurosciences), BUSINESS (accounting, business administration and management, international finance, and marketing), COMMUNICATIONS AND THE ARTS (art, art history and appreciation, classics, dramatic arts, English, fine arts, French, German, linguistics, music, music history and appreciation, music performance, music theory and composition, Russian, Spanish, visual and performing arts, and voice), COMPUTER AND PHYSICAL SCIENCE (applied mathematics, chemistry, computer science, geology, mathematics, physics, and quantitative methods), EDUCATION (early childhood education, education, and music education), ENGINEERING AND ENVIRONMENTAL DESIGN (biomedical engineering, chemical engineering, civil engineering, computer engineering, electrical/electronics engineering, engineering, environmental engineering, environmental science, and mechanical engineering), SOCIAL SCIENCE (anthropology, East Asian studies, economics, geography, history, humanities, interdisciplinary studies, international relations, Latin American studies, philosophy, political science/government, psychology, religion, sociology, and women's studies). Humanities, biology, and engineering are the strongest academically. Economics, biology, and mechanical engineering have the largest enrollments.

ACTIVITIES: 39% of men belong to 9 national fraternities; 46% of women belong to 9 national sororities. There are 150 groups on campus, including art, band, cheerleading, chess, choir, chorale, chorus, communications, computers, dance, debate, drama, environmental, ethnic, film, forensics, honors, international, jazz band, LGBT, literary magazine, musical theater, newspaper, opera, orchestra, pep band, photography, political, professional, radio station club, religious, social, social service, student government, symphony, and yearbook. Popular campus events include Celebration for the Arts, Chrysalis Ball, Family Weekend, Christy's (a capella concert) and Christmas Candlelight Service. **Sports:** There are 13 intercollegiate sports for men and 14 for women, and 16 intramural sports for men and 16 for women. Facilities include an athletic and recreation center with a pool, a fitness center, basketball, 8-lane track, hockey, lacrosse fields, baseball fields, and recreational fields for soccer, softball, and other activities. There is a field house with track, tennis, squash, and racquetball courts, climbing wall, dance studio, an 18-holde golf course with training facility, tennis courts, and a high-ropes course. **Graduates:** From July 1, 2015 to June 30, 2016, 851 bachelor's degrees were awarded. The most popular majors were economics (9%), psychology (7%), and biology (7%). 1063 companies recruited on campus in 2015-2016. In an average class, 84% graduate in 4 years or less, 88% graduate in 5 years or less, and 88% graduate in 6 years or less. Of the 2015 graduating class, 18% were enrolled in graduate school within 6 months of graduation, and 75% were employed.

SERVICES: Counseling and information services are available, as is tutoring in some subjects, such as biology, chemistry, physics, math, and writing across the curriculum. **Library/Resources:** The library contains 1.1 million volumes, 9,989 microform items, 13,491 audio/video tapes/CDs/DVDs, and subscribes to 52,399 periodicals including electronic. Computerized library services include interlibrary loans, database searching, Internet access, and Wi-Fi capability. Special learning facilities include an art gallery, an outdoor natural area, greenhouse, primate facility, observatory, photography lab, race and gender resource center, library resources training lab, electronic classroom, multimedia lab, conference center, performing arts center, and multicultural, writing, craft, environmental, public policy and poetry centers, herbarium, and engineering structural test lab. **Physically Challenged Students:** 80% of the campus is accessible. Facilities include wheelchair ramps, elevators, special parking, specially equipped restrooms, special class scheduling, lowered drinking fountains, lowered telephones, and special housing. **Special:** Bucknell offers internships, service learning, study abroad in more than 60 countries, a Washington semester, 5-year dual degree programs in arts & sciences and engineering and business management and engineering as well as dual and student-designed majors. Interdisciplinary majors include Africana studies, animal behavior, cell biology & biochemistry, interdisciplinary studies in economics & mathematics, Italian studies, neuroscience and women's and gender studies. Academic centers include the Bucknell Center for the Study of Sustainability and the Environment, the Bucknell Institute for Public Policy, the Center for the Study of Race, Ethnicity and Gender, the Griot Institute for Africana Studies, the Institute for Leadership in Technology and Management and the Stadler Center for Poetry. The Residential College program offers an academically focused, residential experience for first year students. Undergraduate research opportunities are available across the College of Arts & Sciences, School of Management and College of Engineering. There are 26 national honor societies, Phi Beta Kappa, a freshman honors program, and 55 departmental honors programs. **Visiting:** There are regularly scheduled orientations for prospective students, with several activities available. There are guides for informal visits and visitors may sit in on classes. To schedule a visit, contact the Admissions Office. **Campus Safety and Security:** Measures include 24-hour foot and vehicle patrol, emergency notification system, self-defense education, and security escort services. There are shuttle buses, emergency telephones, lighted pathways/sidewalks, controlled access to dorms/residences, campus safety alerts, and intrusion alarms in residence halls.

REQUIREMENTS: The SAT or ACT is required. The ACT Optional Writing test is also required. Applicants must graduate from an accredited secondary school or have a GED. 16 units must be earned, including 4 in English, 3 in math, and 2 each in history, science, social studies, and a foreign language. One additional elective is also required. An essay is required, and a campus visit is recommended. Music applicants are required to audition. A portfolio is recommended for art applicants. AP and CLEP credits are accepted. Important factors in the admissions decision are advanced placement or honors courses, evidence of special talent, and extracurricular activities record. **Procedure:** Freshmen are admitted in the fall. Entrance exams should be taken before January 1. There are early decision and deferred admissions plans. Early decision applications should be filed by November 15; regular applications, by January 15 for fall entry, along with a $40 fee. Notification of early decision is sent December 15; regular decision, April 1. 421 early decision candidates were accepted for the 2016-2017 class. 2592 applicants were on the 2016 waiting list; 65 were admitted. Applications are accepted on-line. **Transfer Students:** 23 transfer students enrolled in 2015-2016. Transfer students must have a minimum GPA of 2.5 in courses comparable to those offered at Bucknell. The SAT or ACT is required. A minimum of 16 credit hours must have been earned; 32 are recommended. Students are accepted on a space-available basis. 48 of 128 credits required for the bachelor's degree must be completed at Bucknell. **International Students:** There are 221 international students enrolled. The school actively recruits these students. They must take the TOEFL with a minimum score of 600 on the paper-based TOEFL (PBT) or 100 on the Internet-based version (iBT). They must also take the SAT or ACT.

ADMISSIONS: 30% of the 2016-2017 applicants were accepted. The SAT scores for the 2016-2017 freshman class were: Critical Reading-- 3% below 500, 23% between 500 and 599, 55% between 600 and 699, and 20% between 700 and 800. Math-- 1% below 500, 16% between 500 and 599, 55% between 600 and 699, and 29% between 700 and 800. Writing-- 3% below 500, 21% between 500 and 599, 55% between 600 and 699, and 21% between 700 and 800. The ACT scores were 1% between 18 and 23, 40% between 24 and 29, and 59% above 30. 81% of the current freshmen were in the top fifth of their class; 95% were in the top two fifths. There were 3 National Merit finalists. 14 freshmen graduated first in their class. **Admissions Contact:** Robert G. Springall, Dean of Admissions. Email: *admissions@bucknell.edu* Web: *www.bucknell.edu*

FINANCIAL AID: In 2016-2017, 55% of all full-time freshmen and 60% of continuing full-time students received some form of financial aid. 36% of all full-time freshmen and 52% of continuing full-time students received need-based aid. The average freshman award was $35,500. Need-based scholarships or need-based grants averaged $29,200 ($64,616 maximum); need-based self-help aid (loans and jobs) averaged $4,200 ($7,300 maximum); non-need-based athletic scholarships averaged $37,635 ($64,616 maximum); and other non-need-based awards and non-need-based scholarships averaged $13,676 ($51,960 maximum). 35% of undergraduate students work part-time. Average annual earnings from campus work are $1500. The average financial indebtedness of the 2016 graduate was $22,600. Bucknell is a member of CSS. The CSS/Profile, and noncustodial parent's statement are required. The FAFSA code is 003238. The deadline for filing freshman financial aid applications for fall entry is January 15.

CABRINI UNIVERSITY *(The complete profile is made available exclusively on our website, www.barronspac.com)*

CAIRN UNIVERSITY F-3

www.cairn.edu

Langhorne, PA 19047	**(215) 752-5800** **(800) 366-0049**
Fax: (215) 702-4248	**Email: admissions@cairn.edu**
Full-time: 316 men, 387 women	**Faculty:** 38; IIB, --$
Part-time: 21 men, 20 women	**Ph.D.s:** 70%
Graduate: 145 men, 153 women	**Student/Faculty:** 18 to 1
Year: semesters, summer session	**Tuition:** $26,493
Room & Board: $9803	**Freshman Class:** 338 applied, 331 accepted, 147 enrolled
SAT CR/M/W: 510/500/490 **ACT:** 22	**CEEB CODE:** 2661
Application Deadline: open	**COMPETITIVE**

Cairn University, formerly Philadelphia Biblical University, was founded in 1913, and is a Christian liberal arts institution. There are 6 undergraduate schools and 4 graduate schools. In addition to regional accreditation, Cairn University has baccalaureate program accreditation with CSWE, NASM, ABHE, IACBE, and ACSI. The 115-acre campus is in a suburban area 30 miles north of Philadelphia. Including any residence halls, there are 26 buildings.

STUDENT LIFE: 55% of undergraduates are from Pennsylvania. Others are from 31 states, 28 foreign countries, and Canada. 47% are from public schools. 7% are Hispanic; 68% White; 4% Asian American; 4% Foreign; 15% African American; 1% two or more races; 1% race unknown. 100% are Protestant. **Female To Male Ratio:** 1.2:1. The average age of freshmen is 18; all undergraduates, 22. 26% do not continue beyond their first year; 63% remain to graduate. **Housing:** 645 students can be accommodated in college housing, which includes single-sex dorms, on-campus apartments, and married student housing. On-campus housing is guaranteed for all 4 years. 66% of students live on campus. All students may keep cars. Alcohol is not permitted.

FACULTY/CLASSROOMS: 57% of faculty are male; 43% are female. 87% teach undergraduates. No introductory courses are taught by graduate students. The average class size in an introductory lecture is 18 and in a regular course is 17.

PROGRAMS OF STUDY: Cairn University confers B.A., B.S., B.S Bible, B.Mus., B.S.BusAdmin, B.S.Ed. B.S.W., and B.S. Youth & Family degrees. Master's degrees are also awarded. Bachelor's degrees are awarded in BUSINESS (accounting and business administration and management), COMMUNICATIONS AND THE ARTS (English, music, music composition, and music performance), EDUCATION (education, education administration, and music education), SOCIAL SCIENCE (biblical studies, history, liberal arts/general studies, psychology, social work, and youth ministry). Biblical studies is the strongest academically. Teacher education, and social work have the largest enrollments.

ACTIVITIES: There are no fraternities or sororities. There are 21 groups on campus, including art, band, choir, chorale, chorus, drama, honors, international, musical theater, newspaper, opera, orchestra, professional, religious, social, social service, student government, symphony, and yearbook. Popular campus events include Homecoming, Hoedown, and Christmas Celebration. **Sports:** There are 6 intercollegiate sports for men and 6 for women, and 17 intramural sports for men and 17 for women. Facilities include a gym, baseball diamond, soccer, hockey, softball fields, sand volleyball court, tennis courts, fitness circuit, and weight room. **Graduates:** From July 1, 2015 to June 30, 2016, 228 bachelor's degrees were awarded. The most popular majors were Bible (60%), teacher education (15%), and business (8%). 284 companies recruited on campus in 2015-2016. In an average class, 16% graduate in 4 years or less, 55% graduate in 5 years or less, and 58% graduate in 6 years or less. Of the 2015 graduating class, 38% were enrolled in graduate school within 6 months of graduation, and 80% were employed.

SERVICES: Counseling and information services are available, as is tutoring in most subjects. **Library/Resources:** The library contains 122,140 volumes, 63,817 microform items, 6,990 audio/video tapes/CDs/DVDs, and subscribes to 50,709 periodicals including electronic. Computerized library services include interlibrary loans, database searching, Internet access, and Wi-Fi capability. **Physically Challenged Students:** 99% of the campus is accessible. Facilities include wheelchair ramps, elevators, special parking, specially equipped restrooms, lowered drinking fountains, and special housing. **Special:** Cairn University offers an accelerated degree program in Biblical studies, along with multiple internship and study abroad opportunities in the traditional undergraduate programs. There are double degree programs in social work, music, education, and business administration. There is 1 national honor society and a freshman honors program. **Visiting:** There are regularly scheduled orientations for prospective students, Class and chapel visits, a meal in the dining room, and an interview with a counselor. There are guides for informal visits, visitors may sit in on classes, and stay overnight. To schedule a visit, contact Kristina O'Connell at (215) 702-4235. **Campus Safety and Security:** Measures include 24-hour foot and vehicle patrol, emergency notification system, and security escort services. There are shuttle buses, emergency telephones, lighted pathways/sidewalks, and controlled access to dorms/residences.

REQUIREMENTS: The SAT or ACT is required. AP and CLEP credits are accepted. Students must complete 30 credits in Biblical Studies. At least 121 credits, with a minimum GPA of 2.0, is required. Approximately 30% of the students are enrolled in dual degree programs and receive the BS in Bible degree plus a baccalaureate or masters in their professional area. **Procedure:** Freshmen are admitted fall and spring. Entrance exams should be taken Junior or senior year of high school. There are deferred admissions and rolling admissions plans. Application deadlines are open. Application fee is $25. Notification is sent on a rolling basis. Applications are accepted online. **Transfer Students:** 68 transfer students enrolled in 2015-2016. Transfers must submit an application, a pastor's reference, college transcripts, and a health form. SAT scores and high school transcripts are also required if the student has fewer than 30 college credit hours. 60 of 121 credits required for the bachelor's degree must be completed at Cairn University. **International Students:** There are 14 international students enrolled. The school actively recruits these students. They must take the TOEFL with a minimum score of 520 on the paper-based TOEFL (PBT) or 68 on the Internet-based version (iBT).

ADMISSIONS: 98% of the 2016-2017 applicants were accepted. The SAT scores for the 2016-2017 freshman class were: Critical Reading-- 38% below 500, 44% between 500 and 599, 15% between 600 and 699, and 3% between 700 and 800. Math-- 48% below 500, 39% between 500 and 599, 14% between 600 and 699, and 3% between 700 and 800. Writing-- 51% below 500, 29% between 500 and 599, 16% between 600 and 699, and 3% between 700 and 800. The ACT scores were 15% between 12 and 17, 59% between 18 and 23, 19% between 24 and 29, and 7% above 30. 29% of the current freshmen were in the top fifth of their class; 56% were in the top two fifths. **Admissions Contact:** Rebecca Lippert, Director of Undergraduate Admissions. Email: *admissions@cairn.edu* Web: *www.cairn.edu*

FINANCIAL AID: In 2016-2017, 85% of all full-time freshmen and 80% of continuing full-time students received some form of financial aid. 85% of all full-time freshmen and 79% of continuing full-time students received need-based aid. The average freshman award was $23,175. Need-based scholarships or need-based grants averaged $18,778; need-based self-help aid (loans and jobs) averaged $4,871; and other non-need-based awards and non-need-based scholarships averaged $13,011. 55% of undergraduate students work part-time. The average financial indebtedness of the 2016 graduate was $31,166. The FAFSA code is 003351. Check with the school for current application deadlines.

CALIFORNIA UNIVERSITY OF PENNSYLVANIA *(The complete profile is made available exclusively on our website, www.barronspac.com)*

CARLOW UNIVERSITY *(The complete profile is made available exclusively on our website, www.barronspac.com)*

CARNEGIE MELLON UNIVERSITY — B-3
www.cmu.edu

Pittsburgh, PA 15213 — **(412) 268-2000**

Fax: (412) 268-7838	**Email:** admissions@andrew.cmu.edu
Full-time: 3404 men, 3035 women	**Faculty:** I, +$
Part-time: 133 men, 101 women	**Ph.D.s:** 90%
Graduate: 4689 men, 2599 women	**Student/Faculty:** 13 to 1
Year: semesters, summer session	**Tuition:** $52,310
Room & Board: $13,270	**Freshman Class:** n/av
SAT or ACT: required	**CEEB CODE:** 2074
Application Deadline: n/av	**MOST COMPETITIVE**

Carnegie Mellon University, established in 1900, is a private institution offering undergraduate programs in liberal arts and science and technology. There are 6 undergraduate schools and 7 graduate schools. In addition to regional accreditation, Carnegie Mellon has baccalaureate program accreditation with AACSB, ABET, NAAB, NASM, and NASPAA. The 148-acre campus is in an urban area 4 miles from downtown Pittsburgh. Including any residence halls, there are 158 buildings.

STUDENT LIFE: 85% of undergraduates are from out of state, mostly the Middle Atlantic. Students are from 50 states, 69 foreign countries, and Canada. 8% are Hispanic; 5% race unknown; 4% African American; 4% two or more races; 29% White; 26% Asian American; 23% Foreign. **Male To Female Ratio:** 1.4:1. The average age of freshmen is 18; all undergraduates, 20. 2% do not continue beyond their first year; 88% remain to graduate. **Housing:** 4058 students can be accommodated in college housing, which includes coed dorms, on-campus apartments, and off-campus apartments. In addition, there are special-interest houses, fraternity houses, sorority houses, wellness housing, theme housing, and block housing. On-campus housing is guaranteed for all 4 years. 61% of students live on campus. All students may keep cars. Alcohol is not permitted.

FACULTY/CLASSROOMS: 72% of faculty are male; 28% are female. No introductory courses are taught by graduate students.

PROGRAMS OF STUDY: Carnegie Mellon confers B.A., B.S., B.H.A., B.Arch., B.C.S.A., B.Design, B.F.A., and B.S.A. degrees. Master's and doctoral degrees are also awarded. Bachelor's degrees are awarded in BIOLOGICAL SCIENCE (biochemistry, biology/biological science, and neurosciences), BUSINESS (business administration and management, business economics, marketing/retailing/merchandising, and policy analysis and management), COMMUNICATIONS AND THE ARTS (acting, art, communications, creative writing, design, dramatic arts, English, fine arts, French, German, journalism, languages, linguistics, music, music composition, music performance, Spanish, and technical communication), COMPUTER AND PHYSICAL SCIENCE (chemistry, computer programming, computer science, information sciences and systems, mathematics, physics, and statistics), EDUCATION (music education), ENGINEERING AND ENVIRONMENTAL DESIGN (architecture, chemical engineering, civil engineering, computer engineering, electrical/electronics engineering, engineering, materials engineering, and mechanical engineering), SOCIAL SCIENCE (Chinese Studies, economics, Hispanic American studies, history, international political science, Japanese studies, philosophy, political science/government, psychology, public administration, Russian and Slavic studies, social science, and urban studies). Engineering, and computer science have the largest enrollments.

ACTIVITIES: 17% of men belong to 16 national fraternities; 14% of women belong to 11 national sororities. There are 357 groups on campus, including art, bagpipe, band, cheerleading, chess, choir, chorale, chorus, computers, dance, debate, drama, ethnic, film, honors, international, LGBT, literary magazine, marching band, musical theater, newspaper, orchestra, pep band, photography, political, professional, radio station, religious, social, social service, student government, symphony, and yearbook. Popular campus events include Spring Carnival, International Festival and Jill Watson Festival Across the Arts. **Sports:** There are 9 intercollegiate sports for men and 9 for women, and 38 intramural sports for men and 38 for women. Facilities include a gym, a football stadium with track, athletic fields, tennis and racquetball courts, and a pool. **Graduates:** From July 1, 2015 to June 30, 2016, 1483 bachelor's degrees were awarded. The most popular majors were computer science (12%), electrical and computer engineering (9%), and mechanical engineering (8%). In an average class, 85% graduate in 5 years or less and 88% graduate in 6 years or less. Of the 2015 graduating class, 22% were enrolled in graduate school within 6 months of graduation, and 59% were employed.

SERVICES: Counseling and information services are available, as is tutoring in most subjects. There is a reader service for the blind. **Library/Resources:** The 3 libraries contain 1.1 million volumes, 1.2 million microform items, 43,936 audio/video tapes/CDs/DVDs, and subscribe to 140,006 periodicals including electronic. Computerized library services include interlibrary loans, database searching, Internet access, and Wi-Fi capability. Special learning facilities include an art gallery. **Physically Challenged Students:** 95% of the campus is accessible. Facilities include wheelchair ramps, elevators, special parking, specially equipped restrooms, special class scheduling, lowered drinking fountains, lowered telephones, and special housing. **Special:** Students may cross-register with other Pittsburgh Council of Higher Education institutions. Also available are internships, work-study programs, study abroad in 45+ countries, a Washington semester, accelerated degrees, B.A.-B.S. degrees, co-op programs, dual majors, independent study, double major, distance learning, liberal arts/career combination and limited student-designed majors. There are 18 national honor societies, Phi Beta Kappa, and a freshman honors program. **Visiting:** There are regularly scheduled orientations for prospective students, consisting of Saturday group sessions in September, October, November, and January. There are guides for informal visits, visitors may sit in on classes, and stay overnight. To schedule a visit, contact the Admissions Office at undergraduate-admissions@andrew.cmu.edu. **Campus Safety and Security:** Measures include 24-hour foot and vehicle patrol, emergency notification system, self-defense education, and security escort services. There are also shuttle buses, emergency telephones, lighted pathways/sidewalks, controlled access to dorms/residences, and safewalk program.

REQUIREMENTS: The SAT or ACT is required. SAT Subject tests are not required for drama, design, art, or music applicants. All other applicants must take appropriate tests, preferably by November, but no later than December. Applicants must graduate from an accredited secondary school or have a GED and must have completed 4 years of English. All other preferred Carnegie credits vary by college and program. Essays are required and interviews are recommended. Art and design applicants must submit a portfolio. Drama and music applicants must audition. AP credits are accepted. Requirements vary considerably across colleges and programs. **Procedure:** Freshmen are admitted in the fall. Entrance exams should be taken be received by Jan 1 (Dec 1 for college of fine arts). There are early decision, early admissions, and deferred admissions plans. Early decision applications should be filed by November 1, along with a $75 fee. Notification of early decision is sent December 15; regular decision, April 15. 326 early decision candidates were accepted for the 2016-2017 class. 2835 applicants were on the 2016 waiting list; 4 were admitted. Applications are accepted on-line. **Transfer Students:** 20 transfer students enrolled in 2015-2016. Applicants must submit secondary school and college transcripts (including school catalogs with course descriptions so that Carnegie Mellon can evaluate transferable credits). **International Students:** There are 1449 international students enrolled. The school actively recruits these students. They must take the TOEFL with a minimum score of 600 on the paper-based TOEFL (PBT) or 100 on the Internet-based version (iBT), and take the International English Language Testing System (IELTS). They must also take the SAT or ACT.

ADMISSIONS: 24% of the 2016-2017 applicants were accepted. The SAT scores for the 2016-2017 freshman class were: Critical Reading-- 1% below 500, 6% between 500 and 599, 41% between 600 and 699, and 52% between 700 and 800. Math-- 1% below 500, 3% between 500 and 599, 17% between 600 and 699, and 79% between 700 and 800. Writing-- 6% between 500 and 599, 32% between 600 and 699, and 62% between 700 and 800. The ACT scores were 1% between 18 and 23, 13% between 24 and 29, and 86% above 30. 92% of the current freshmen were in the top fifth of their class; 99% were in the top two fifths. **Admissions Contact:** Michael Steidel, Dean of Admissions. Email: *admissions@andrew.cmu.edu* Web: *www.cmu.edu*

FINANCIAL AID: In 2016-2017, 46% of all full-time freshmen and 42% of continuing full-time students received some form of financial aid. 45% of all full-time freshmen and 41% of continuing full-time students received need-based aid. The average freshman award was $36,002. Need-based scholarships or need-based grants averaged $31,926; need-based self-help aid (loans and jobs) averaged $6,334; and other non-need-based awards and non-need-based scholarships averaged $13,140. Carnegie Mellon is a member of CSS. The CSS/Profile, the college's own financial statement, noncustodial profile, and parent and student federal tax returns, and W-2 forms are required. The FAFSA code is 003242. The deadline for filing freshman financial aid applications for fall entry is February 15.

CEDAR CREST COLLEGE E-3

www.cedarcrest.edu

Allentown, PA 18104	(610) 740-3780 (800) 360-1222
Fax: (610) 606-4647	**Email:** admissions@cedarcrest.edu
Full-time: 74 men, 700 women	**Faculty:** 76; IIB, -$
Part-time: 64 men, 549 women	**Ph.D.s:** 71%
Graduate: 20 men, 183 women	**Student/Faculty:** 10 to 1
Year: semesters, summer session	**Tuition:** $35,950
Room & Board: $10,765	**Freshman Class:** 1063 applied, 625 accepted, 141 enrolled
SAT CR/M/W: required **ACT:** 22	**CEEB CODE:** 2079
Application Deadline: open	**COMPETITIVE**

Cedar Crest College, founded in 1867, was one of the first women's colleges in the nation. Today it remains an independent, comprehensive liberal arts college for women that combines excellence in scholarship and undergraduate education with an extensive School of Adult and Graduate Education (SAGE) program and growing graduate programs that serve women and men in the surrounding region. Figures in the above capsule and in this profile are approximate. There is 1 undergraduate school and 1 graduate school. In addition to regional accreditation, Cedar Crest has baccalaureate program accreditation with ACBSP, CSWE, NLNAC, and FEPAC. The 84-acre campus is in a suburban area 55 miles north of Philadelphia and 90 miles west of New York City. Including any residence halls, there are 20 buildings.

STUDENT LIFE: 67% of undergraduates are from Pennsylvania. Others are from 21 states, and 27 foreign countries. 95% are from public schools. 9% are African American; 69% White; 4% race unknown; 3% Asian American; 12% Hispanic; 1% Foreign; 1% two or more races. **Female To Male Ratio:** 9.1:1. The average age of freshmen is 18; all undergraduates, 28. 33% do not continue beyond their first year; 60% remain to graduate. **Housing:** 550 students can be accommodated in college housing, which includes single-sex dorms. smoke-free floors, and living learning communities. On-campus housing is guaranteed for all 4 years. 78% of students commute. All students may keep cars.

FACULTY/CLASSROOMS: 32% of faculty are male; 68% are female. All teach undergraduates. No introductory courses are taught by graduate students. The average class size in an introductory lecture is 20; in a laboratory is 13; and in a regular course is 14.

PROGRAMS OF STUDY: Cedar Crest confers B.A. and B.S degrees. Master's degrees are also awarded. Bachelor's degrees are awarded in BIOLOGICAL SCIENCE (biochemistry, biology/biological science, environmental biology, genetics, neurosciences, and nutrition), BUSINESS (accounting, business administration and management, and marketing/retailing/merchandising), COMMUNICATIONS AND THE ARTS (art, communications, dance, dramatic arts, English, fine arts, and music), COMPUTER AND PHYSICAL SCIENCE (chemistry, computer science, information sciences and systems, mathematics, and science), EDUCATION (early childhood education, education, and elementary education), HEALTH PROFESSIONS (nuclear medical technology and nursing), SOCIAL SCIENCE (criminal justice, history, industrial and organizational psychology, political science/government, psychology, social work, and Spanish studies). Sciences, and nursing are the strongest academically. Nursing, social work, and business have the largest enrollments.

ACTIVITIES: There are no fraternities or sororities. There are 51 groups on campus, including art, band, cheerleading, choir, chorus, computers, dance, drama, ethnic, forensics, honors, international, LGBT, literary magazine, musical theater, newspaper, political, professional, radio and TV, religious, social, social service, student government, and yearbook. Popular campus events include Student Faculty Frolic, Midnight Breakfast, and Ring Ceremony. **Sports:** There are 8 intercollegiate sports for women, and 4 intramural sports for women. Facilities include tennis courts, softball, field hockey, soccer, and lacrosse fields, a cross-country course, a gym with basketball, volleyball, and badminton courts, dance and aerobics studios, weight training, a swimming pool, and a fitness center. **Graduates:** From July 1, 2015 to June 30, 2016, 268 bachelor's degrees were awarded. The most popular majors were nursing (35%), psychology (15%), and business administration (6%). 11 companies recruited on campus in 2015-2016. In an average class, 51% graduate in 4 years or less, 57% graduate in 5 years or less, and 60% graduate in 6 years or less. Of the 2015 graduating class, 7% were enrolled in graduate school within 6 months of graduation, and 70% were employed.

SERVICES: Counseling and information services are available, as is tutoring in most subjects. There is remedial math and writing. Computer software skills program for underprepared students. **Library/Resources:** Computerized library services include interlibrary loans, database searching, Internet access, and Wi-Fi capability. Special learning facilities include an art gallery, radio station, an arboretum, theaters, and a sculpture garden. **Physically Challenged Students:** 35% of the campus is accessible. Facilities include wheelchair ramps, elevators, special parking, specially equipped restrooms, special class scheduling, lowered drinking fountains, and lowered telephones. **Special:** Cross-registration is available through the Lehigh Valley Association of Independent Colleges and Online Consortium. Also available are internships, work-study programs, an accelerated degree program in business, and B.A.-B.S. degrees in math, biology, and psychology. Dual majors, student-designed majors, pass/fail options, and credit for life, military, and work experience are offered. There are 15 national honor societies, a freshman honors program, and 1 departmental honors program. **Visiting:** There are regularly scheduled orientations for prospective students. There are guides for informal visits, visitors may sit in on classes, and stay overnight. To schedule a visit, contact the Admissions Office at admissions@cedarcrest.edu. **Campus Safety and Security:** Measures include 24-hour foot and vehicle patrol, emergency notification system, self-defense education, and security escort services. There are emergency telephones, lighted pathways/sidewalks. Residence halls are equipped with fire/intrusion alarms, which are monitored 24 hours a day. A keyless access system is in place, and exterior doors are locked 24 hours a day.

REQUIREMENTS: The SAT is required. Applicants must be graduates of an accredited secondary school. The GED is accepted. Students should have completed 16 high school academic credits, including 4 years of English, 3 of math, 2 each of science, history, and foreign language, and 1 each of art, music, and social studies. An essay is required. Cedar Crest requires applicants to be in the upper 50% of their class. A GPA of 2.0 is required. AP and CLEP credits are accepted. Important factors in the admissions decision are advanced placement or honors courses, leadership record, and evidence of special talent. To graduate, students must complete 120 credit hours (122 for nursing) with a minimum GPA of 2.0 (some majors have higher requirements). Distribution requirements include 7 credits in natural sciences, 6 each in writing, mathematics and logic, humanities, the arts, and social sciences, and 3 each in global studies and ethics. A major capstone experience is required. **Procedure:** Freshmen are admitted in the fall and spring. Entrance exams should be taken in the junior year or early in the senior year. There are deferred admissions and rolling admissions plans. Application deadlines are open, and accepted online. **Transfer Students:** 49 transfer students enrolled in 2015-2016. Applicants should have a minimum college GPA of 2.0. An interview is recommended. 30 of 120 credits required for the bachelor's degree must be completed at Cedar Crest. **International Students:** There are 16 international students enrolled. The school actively recruits these students. They must take the TOEFL with a minimum score of 550 on the paper-based TOEFL (PBT) or 61 on the Internet-based version (iBT).

ADMISSIONS: 59% of the 2016-2017 applicants were accepted. The SAT scores for the 2016-2017 freshman class were: Critical Reading-- 64% below 500, 30% between 500 and 599, and 6% between 600 and 699. Math-- 57% below 500, 38% between 500 and 599, and 5% between 600 and 699. Writing-- 70% below 500, 23% between 500 and 599, and 7% between 600 and 699. 55% of the current freshmen were in the top fifth of their class; 92% were in the top two fifths. **Admissions Contact:** Jonathan Squire, Associate Director of Admissions. Email: *admissions@cedarcrest.edu* Web: *www.cedarcrest.edu*

FINANCIAL AID: In 2016-2017, 97% of all full-time freshmen and 99% of continuing full-time students received some form of financial aid. 94% of all full-time freshmen and 95% of continuing full-time students received need-based aid. The average freshman award was $31,302. Need-based scholarships or need-based grants averaged $27,930; need-based self-help aid (loans and jobs) averaged $3,761; and other non-need-based awards and non-need-based scholarships averaged $3,364. 53% of undergraduate students work part-time. Average annual earnings from campus work are $1500. The average financial indebtedness of the 2016 graduate was $27,200. Cedar Crest is a member of CSS. The FAFSA code is 003243. The deadline for filing freshman financial aid applications for fall entry is May 1.

CHATHAM UNIVERSITY B-3

www.chatham.edu

Pittsburgh, PA 15232 **(412) 365-1139** **(800) 837-1290**

Fax: (412) 365-1609 **Email: admission@chatham.edu**

Full-time: 151 men, 594 women	**Faculty:** 42; IIA, --$
Part-time: 42 men, 215 women	**Ph.D.s:** 93%
Graduate: 227 men, 881 women	**Student/Faculty:** 13 to 1
Year: 4-1-4, summer session	**Tuition:** $35,475
Room & Board: $11,042	**Freshman Class:** 1916 applied, 1015 accepted, 194 enrolled
SAT CR/M/W: 550/530/520 **ACT:** 24	**CEEB CODE:** 2081
Application Deadline: August 1	**COMPETITIVE**

Chatham University, founded in 1869, is a private university composed of the Falk School of Sustainability, the School of Health Sciences, the School of Arts, Science and Business, and the College for Continuing and Professional Studies. Chatham offers undergraduate and graduate degrees in more than 60 programs, on campus and online. There are 4 undergraduate schools and 3 graduate schools. In addition to regional accreditation, Chatham has baccalaureate program accreditation with ACS. The 427-acre campus is in an urban area 5 miles east of downtown Pittsburgh. Including any residence halls, there are 62 buildings.

STUDENT LIFE: 79% of undergraduates are from Pennsylvania. Others are from 47 states, 26 foreign countries, and Canada. 96% are from public schools. 8% are African American; 7% Foreign; 59% White; 4% Hispanic; 2% Asian American; 19% race unknown; 1% two or more races. **Female To Male Ratio:** 4.0:1. The average age of freshmen is 19; all undergraduates, 22. 19% do not continue beyond their first year; 81% remain to graduate. **Housing:** 635 students can be accommodated in college housing, which includes single-sex and coed dorms, on-campus apartments, and off-campus apartments. In addition, there are special-interest houses, and a intercultural residence hall. On-campus housing is available on a lottery system for upperclassmen. 57% of students live on campus; of those, 75% remain on campus on weekends. Upperclassmen may keep cars.

FACULTY/CLASSROOMS: 33% of faculty are male; 67% are female. All teach undergraduates. No introductory courses are taught by graduate students. The average class size in an introductory lecture is 12; in a laboratory is 13; and in a regular course is 12.

PROGRAMS OF STUDY: Chatham confers B.A., B.S., B.S.N., B.F.A., B.I.A., and B.S.W. degrees. Master's and doctoral degrees are also awarded. Bachelor's degrees are awarded in AGRICULTURE (environmental studies), BIOLOGICAL SCIENCE (biochemistry and biology/biological science), BUSINESS (accounting, business administration and management, business economics, international business management, management information systems, management, marketing, marketing management, and sustainable management), COMMUNICATIONS AND THE ARTS (art history and appreciation, arts administration/management, communications, creative writing, English, English literature, film, television and digital media, media arts, music, Spanish, theatre studies, and visual and performing arts), COMPUTER AND PHYSICAL SCIENCE (chemistry, mathematics, and physics), EDUCATION (early childhood education, education, and elementary education), ENGINEERING AND ENVIRONMENTAL DESIGN (environmental science, interior architecture, and interior design), HEALTH PROFESSIONS (exercise science, nursing, and physical therapy), SOCIAL SCIENCE (criminology, crosscultural studies, cultural studies/critical theory & analysis, economics, forensic studies, history, interdisciplinary studies, international relations, international studies, political science/government, psychology, public affairs, social work, and women's studies). Biology, sustainability, business, and psychology are the strongest academically. Biology, nursing, and psychology have the largest enrollments.

ACTIVITIES: There are no fraternities or sororities. There are 43 groups on campus, including art, cheerleading, choir, dance, drama, environmental, ethnic, film, forensics, honors, international, LGBT, literary magazine, newspaper, pep band, photography, political, professional, religious, social, and student government. Popular campus events include Battle of the Classes, Song Contest, Harvest Fun Fest, Halloween Dinner and Mocktails, Thanksgiving Dinner, Candlelight, Eggnog & Holiday Ball, Airband & Senior Skits, Spring Formal, Step Afrika, and Diversity Dialogues. **Sports:** There are 6 intercollegiate sports for men and 9 for women, and 8 intramural sports for men and 8 for women. Facilities include The AFC is a 4 level athletic and fitness center on campus. On the bottom level there is an eight-lane competition swimming pool, whirlpool/sauna/steam room, 2 regulation squash courts, and rock-climbing wall, and a varsity athletic training room. The next level has a smart classroom, dance studio, and weight room which contains treadmills, elliptical machines, bikes, free weights, and circuit strength machines. The dance and aerobics studio is a multi-function space that houses Pilates, martial arts, aerobic classes, and dance courses. The third level is the gymnasium, which seats 600 spectators for athletic events and up to 1,000 for other event. The fourth level gives access to a three-lane walking track and is the home of McCrady Café- which is open for athletic events. There is also an out-door turf field which is used for soccer. **Graduates:** From July 1, 2015 to June 30, 2016, 180 bachelor's degrees were awarded. The most popular majors were nursing (30%), biology (10%), and psychology (6%). 55 companies recruited on campus in 2015-2016. In an average class, 6% graduate in 3 years or less, 48% graduate in 4 years or less, 51% graduate in 5 years or less, and 52% graduate in 6 years or less. Of the 2015 graduating class, 17% were enrolled in graduate school within 6 months of graduation.

SERVICES: Counseling and information services are available, as is tutoring in every subject. There is a reader service for the blind, and remedial math, reading, and writing. One-on-one and group tutoring are available by both students and professional specialists, and there is also computer-aided tutoring and an organized study group. **Library/Resources:** The library contains 96,883 volumes, 22,434 microform items, and 1,854 audio/video tapes/CDs/DVDs, and subscribes to 443,403 periodicals including electronic. Computerized library services include interlibrary loans, database searching, Internet access, and Wi-Fi capability. Special learning facilities include an art gallery, theaters, a media center, and an arboretum. **Physically Challenged Students:** 50% of the campus is accessible. Facilities include wheelchair ramps, elevators, special parking, specially equipped restrooms, special class scheduling, lowered drinking fountains, lowered telephones, and special housing. **Special:** Chatham offers a study-abroad program in 12 countries, cross-registration with other Pittsburgh Council on Higher Education institutions, co-op programs in all majors, internships in the public and private sectors, and a Washington semester in conjunction with American University and the Public Leadership Education Network.

Accelerated degree programs, work-study, combined B.A.-B.S. degrees, multidisciplinary majors, and dual and student-designed majors are available. There are 3-2 engineering degrees with Carnegie Mellon and Penn State Universities and the University of Pittsburgh, dual degree programs, and an accelerated Master's program with Carnegie Mellon's Heinz School. There are 7 national honor societies, Phi Beta Kappa, and a freshman honors program. **Visiting:** There are regularly scheduled orientations for prospective students, including campus tours, student and faculty panels, financial aid presentations, and athletic coach meetings. There are guides for informal visits, visitors may sit in on classes, and stay overnight. To schedule a visit, contact Todd Pilipovich at (800)837-1290. **Campus Safety and Security:** Measures include 24-hour foot and vehicle patrol, emergency notification system, self-defense education, and security escort services. There are shuttle buses, emergency telephones, lighted pathways/sidewalks, and controlled access to dorms/residences.

REQUIREMENTS: Applicants who choose not to submit the SAT or ACT will be required to submit a graded writing sample and resume or list of curricular and cocurricular activities. Applicants will also have the option to submit a portfolio or special project or activity. These materials may also be applied toward Chatham's scholarship review process upon acceptance. AP and CLEP credits are accepted. Important factors in the admissions decision are recommendations by school officials, leadership record, and extracurricular activities record. To graduate, students must complete 120 credit hours, including a general education curriculum of 7 courses and a senior tutorial, with a minimum GPA of 2.0. Students must also demonstrate proficiencies in writing, math, and computer literacy. **Procedure:** Freshmen are admitted fall and spring. Entrance exams should be taken by fall of the senior year. There are deferred admissions and rolling admissions plans. Applications should be filed by August 1 for fall entry, along with a $35 fee. Notification is sent on a rolling basis. Applications are accepted on-line. Application fees are waived if application is completed on-line. **Transfer Students:** 108 transfer students enrolled in 2015-2016. Applicants must present college transcripts 45 of 120 credits required for the bachelor's degree must be completed at Chatham. **International Students:** There are 59 international students enrolled. The school actively recruits these students. They must take the TOEFL with a minimum score of 550 on the paper-based TOEFL (PBT) or 79 on the Internet-based version (iBT) or take the MELAB, or take the IELTS. The SAT is required if no TOEFL score are available.

ADMISSIONS: 53% of the 2016-2017 applicants were accepted. The SAT scores for the 2016-2017 freshman class were: Critical Reading-- 32% below 500, 36% between 500 and 599, 27% between 600 and 699, and 5% between 700 and 800. Math-- 33% below 500, 49% between 500 and 599, 17% between 600 and 699, and 1% between 700 and 800. Writing-- 38% below 500, 44% between 500 and 599, 15% between 600 and 699, and 3% between 700 and 800. The ACT scores were 3% between 12 and 17, 42% between 18 and 23, 48% between 24 and 29, and 7% above 30. 42% of the current freshmen were in the top fifth of their class; 81% were in the top two fifths. 4 freshmen graduated first in their class. **Admissions Contact:** Amy Becher, Vice President for Enrollment Management. Email: *admission@chatham.edu* Web: *www.chatham.edu*

FINANCIAL AID: In 2016-2017, 100% of all full-time freshmen and 99% of continuing full-time students received some form of financial aid. 69% of all full-time freshmen and 99% of continuing full-time students received need-based aid. The average freshman award was $29,123. Need-based scholarships or need-based grants averaged $9,515; need-based self-help aid (loans and jobs) averaged $4,392; and other non-need-based awards and non-need-based scholarships averaged $16,394. Average annual earnings from campus work are $2200. The average financial indebtedness of the 2016 graduate was $28,518. The FAFSA code is 003244. The priority date for freshman financial aid applications for fall entry is March 1.

CHESTNUT HILL COLLEGE *(The complete profile is made available exclusively on our website, www.barronspac.com)*

CHEYNEY UNIVERSITY OF PENNSYLVANIA *(The complete profile is made available exclusively on our website, www.barronspac.com)*

CLARION UNIVERSITY OF PENNSYLVANIA *(The complete profile is made available exclusively on our website, www.barronspac.com)*

CURTIS INSTITUTE OF MUSIC *(The complete profile is made available exclusively on our website, www.barronspac.com)*

DELAWARE VALLEY UNIVERSITY F-3

www.devalcol.edu

Doylestown, PA 18901	(215) 489-2372 (800) 2-DEL-VAL
Fax: (215) 230-2968	**Email:** admitme@devalcol.edu
Full-time: 700 men, 900 women	**Faculty:** 79; IIB, av$
Part-time: 209 men, 191 women	**Ph.D.s:** 62%
Graduate: 27 men, 43 women	**Student/Faculty:** 20 to 1
Year: semesters, summer session	**Tuition:** $36,750
Room & Board: $13,046	**Freshman Class:** 1476 applied, 1164 accepted, 451 enrolled
ACT: 22 **SAT:** required	**CEEB CODE:** 2510
Application Deadline: open	**COMPETITIVE**

Delaware Valley University, founded in 1896, is a private institution offering undergraduate programs in specialized fields of agriculture, business administration, English, the sciences, math, criminal justice administration, and secondary education. The college also offers graduate programs in educational leadership, and in food and agribusiness. Figures in the above capsule and in this profile are approximate. There is 1 undergraduate school. The 550-acre campus is in a suburban area 20 miles north of Philadelphia. Including any residence halls, there are 36 buildings.

STUDENT LIFE: 67% of undergraduates are from Pennsylvania. Others are from 22 states, 1 foreign country, and Canada. 85% are from public schools. 80% are White; 4% African American; 1% Hispanic. 35% are Catholic; 32% Protestant; 16% claim no religious affiliation; 14% Buddhist, and Seventh-day Adventist. **Female To Male Ratio:** 1.2:1. The average age of freshmen is 18; all undergraduates, 21. 26% do not continue beyond their first year; 75% remain to graduate. **Housing:** 960 students can be accommodated in college housing, which includes single-sex and coed dorms, and honors houses. On-campus housing is available on a first-come, first-served basis, and on a lottery system for upperclassmen. 63% of students live on campus; of those, 65% remain on campus on weekends. Upperclassmen may keep cars.

FACULTY/CLASSROOMS: 66% of faculty are male; 34% are female. All teach undergraduates. No introductory courses are taught by graduate students. The average class size in an introductory lecture is 24; in a laboratory is 21; and in a regular course is 20.

PROGRAMS OF STUDY: DelVal confers B.A. and B.S. degrees. Associate and master's degrees are also awarded. Bachelor's degrees are awarded in AGRICULTURE (agronomy, animal science, dairy science, equine science, horticulture, and wildlife management), BIOLOGICAL SCIENCE (biology/biological science and zoology), BUSINESS (accounting, business administration and management, marketing/retailing/merchandising, and sports management), COMMUNICATIONS AND THE ARTS (English), COMPUTER AND PHYSICAL SCIENCE (chemistry and computer science), EDUCATION (secondary education), ENGINEERING AND ENVIRONMENTAL DESIGN (environmental science and food services technology), SOCIAL SCIENCE (criminal justice, food production/management/services, and food science). Physical & biological science, and animal science are the strongest academically. Business administration, and animal science have the largest enrollments.

ACTIVITIES: 4% of men belong to 5 national fraternities; 5% of women belong to 3 national sororities. There are 40 groups on campus, including habitat for humanity, block and bridle, bowling, colleges against cancer club, landscape nursery club, rock climbing club, ski and outdoor club, animal service club, art, band, cheerleading, chess, choir, chorale, chorus, computers, dance, drama, ethnic, honors, international, jazz band, literary magazine, newspaper, pep band, photography, professional, radio and TV, religious, social, social service, student government, symphony, and yearbook. Popular campus events include A-Day, Parents Day, and Family Weekend. **Sports:** There are 8 intercollegiate sports for men and 7 for women, and 9 intramural sports for men and 9 for women. Facilities include 2 gyms, tennis courts, outdoor playing courts and fields, a football stadium, a running track, a small lake, a video game room, picnic areas, nature walks, lacrosse, ultimate frisbee, wrestling, riding trails, and indoor and outdoor equine facilities. **Graduates:** From July 1, 2015 to June 30, 2016, 281 bachelor's degrees were awarded. The most popular majors were business administration (30%), animal science (22%), and ornamental horticulture (10%). 310 companies recruited on campus in 2015-2016. In an average class, 44% graduate in 4 years or less, 54% graduate in 5 years or less, and 57% graduate in 6 years or less. Of the 2015 graduating class, 24% were enrolled in graduate school within 6 months of graduation, and 80% were employed.

SERVICES: Counseling and information services are available, as is tutoring in most subjects. There is a reader service for the blind, and remedial math, reading, and writing. **Library/Resources:** The library contains 70,000 volumes, 162,914 microform items, and subscribes to 728 periodicals including electronic. Computerized library services include interlibrary loans, database searching, Internet access, and Wi-Fi capability. Special learning facilities include a radio station, TV station, a dairy science center, a livestock farm, horse facilities, an apiary, a small animal lab, a tissue culture lab, an arboretum, and greenhouses. **Physically Challenged Students:** 85% of the campus is accessible. Facilities include wheelchair ramps, elevators, special parking, specially equipped restrooms, special class scheduling, and lowered drinking fountains. **Special:** DelVal offers a specialized methods and techniques program that enables students to learn lab techniques and gain experience in the practical aspects of their majors. There is a zoo science major that prepares students for careers in zoo management and animal conservation. There are co-op programs in all majors, dual majors, study abroad in England, internships, and work-study programs in a wide variety of employment and research settings. Cross-registration is available with Rutgers University and Middle Bucks Technical Institute. Nondegree study and pass/fail options are also available. There are 3 national honor societies, a freshman honors program, and 2 departmental honors programs. **Visiting:** There are regularly scheduled orientations for prospective students, consisting of a student panel, meetings with department chairs, and general information sessions. There are guides for informal visits, visitors may sit in on classes, and stay overnight. To schedule a visit, contact the Admissions Department. **Campus Safety and Security:** Measures include 24-hour foot and vehicle patrol, self-defense education, and security escort services. There are also shuttle buses, emergency telephones, and lighted pathways/sidewalks.

REQUIREMENTS: The SAT or ACT is required. Applicants must be graduates of accredited secondary schools or have earned a GED. The college requires 15 academic units, including 6 in electives, 3 in English, and 2 each in math, science, and social studies. An interview is recommended. DelVal requires applicants to be in the upper 50% of their class. AP and CLEP credits are accepted. Important factors in the admissions decision are leadership record, personality/intangible qualities, and extracurricular activities record. The bachelor's degree requires completion of at least 128 credits, including 48 in the major, with a minimum GPA of 2.0. The core curriculum consists of 48 credits of liberal arts courses, including cultural enrichment, phys ed, and an introduction to computers. Students must also fulfill employment program requirements. **Procedure:** Freshmen are admitted in the fall and spring. Entrance exams should be taken in the junior or senior year. There are deferred admissions and rolling admissions plans. Application deadlines are open. Application fee is $35. Applications are accepted online. **Transfer Students:** 109 transfer students enrolled in 2015-2016. Applicants must have a minimum GPA of 2.0 and must submit SAT scores. An interview is recommended. 60 of 130 credits required for the bachelor's degree must be completed at DelVal. **International Students:** There is 1 international student enrolled. They must take the TOEFL. They must also take the SAT or ACT.

ADMISSIONS: 79% of the 2016-2017 applicants were accepted. The ACT scores were 38% below 12, 25% between 12 and 17, 25% between 18 and 23, and 13% between 24 and 29. 25% of the current freshmen were in the top fifth of their class; 49% were in the top two fifths. 1 freshman graduated first in their class. **Admissions Contact:** Thomas O'Connor, Director of Admissions. Email: *admitme@devalcol.edu* Web: *www.devalcol.edu*

FINANCIAL AID: In 2016-2017, 98% of all full-time freshmen received some form of financial aid. 78% of all full-time freshmen received need-based aid. 20% of undergraduate students work part-time. Average annual earnings from campus work are $1600. The FAFSA code is 003252. The deadline for filing freshman financial aid applications for fall entry is April 1.

DESALES UNIVERSITY F-3
www.desales.edu

Center Valley, PA 18034	**(610) 282-1100** **(877) 337-2537**
Fax: (610) 282-0131	**Email: admiss@desales.edu**
Full-time: 760 men, 1024 women	**Faculty:** 100; IIA, -$
Part-time: 189 men, 408 women	**Ph.D.s:** 84%
Graduate: 309 men, 498 women	**Student/Faculty:** 16 to 1
Year: semesters, summer session	**Tuition:** $32,350
Room & Board: $11,620	**Freshman Class:** 2658 applied, 2117 accepted, 406 enrolled
SAT: required	**CEEB CODE:** 2021
Application Deadline: August 1	**COMPETITIVE**

DeSales University, is a medium-sized, private, four-year Catholic university with a Salesian mission administered by the Oblates of St. Francis de Sales. Our priority is to give our students a quality, broad-based liberal arts and career-centered education. Students are exposed to Catholic teachings but are also afforded the luxury of exploring in an atmosphere of intellectual freedom. There is 1 undergraduate school. In addition to regional accreditation, DSU has baccalaureate program accreditation with ACBSP, NLN, ARC-PA, CAPTE, and ACEN. The 480-acre campus is in a suburban area in Lehigh County, Pennsylvania, 50 miles north of Philadelphia. Including any residence halls, there are 33 buildings.

STUDENT LIFE: 68% of undergraduates are from Pennsylvania. Others are from 18 states, and 5 foreign countries. 93% are White; 8% Hispanic; 6% race unknown; 3% African American; 3% Asian American; 1% American Indian/Alaska Native. **Female To Male Ratio:** 1.5:1. The average age of freshmen is 18. 15% do not continue beyond their first year; 70% remain to graduate. **Housing:** 1192 students can be accommodated in college housing, which includes single-sex dorms and on-campus apartments. In addition, there are special-interest houses. On-campus housing is guaranteed for all 4 years, and is available on a first-come, first-served basis, and is available on a lottery system for upperclassmen. 65% of students live on campus. All students may keep cars.

FACULTY/CLASSROOMS: 42% of faculty are male; 58% are female. 85% teach undergraduates, and 85% do research. No introductory courses are taught by graduate students.

PROGRAMS OF STUDY: DSU confers B.A., B.S. and B.S.N. degrees. Master's and doctoral degrees are also awarded. Bachelor's degrees are awarded in BIOLOGICAL SCIENCE (biochemistry and biology/biological science), BUSINESS (accounting, business administration and management, finance, human resources, management information systems, marketing/retailing/merchandising, and sports management), COMMUNICATIONS AND THE ARTS (communications, dance, dramatic arts, English, film arts, media arts, performing arts, radio/television technology, Spanish, theatre acting, theater design, theatre production, and theater management), COMPUTER AND PHYSICAL SCIENCE (chemistry, computer game design/development, computer science, and mathematics), EDUCATION (early childhood education and elementary education), HEALTH PROFESSIONS (exercise science, nursing, pharmaceutical science, physical therapy, and physician's assistant), SOCIAL SCIENCE (criminal justice, history, liberal arts/general studies, philosophy, political science/government, psychology, and theological studies). Physician assistant, physical thearpy, and theatre are the strongest academically. Biology, physician assistant, and nursing have the largest enrollments.

ACTIVITIES: There are no fraternities or sororities. There are 50 groups on campus, including band, cheerleading, choir, chorale, chorus, communications, computers, dance, debate, drama, ethnic, film, honors, international, literary magazine, marching band, musical theater, newspaper, pep band, political, professional, radio and TV, religious, social, social service, student government, and yearbook. **Sports:** There are 7 intercollegiate sports for men and 7 for women, and 9 intramural sports for men and 9 for women. Facilities include areas for soccer, baseball, softball, tennis, basketball, lacrosse, track, cross country, volleyball, and a sports and recreation facility that has a fitness center and multipurpose athletic courts. Club sports include ice hockey, rugby, swimming, tennis and volleyball. **Graduates:** From July 1, 2015 to June 30, 2016, 557 bachelor's degrees were awarded. The most popular majors were business (23%), health professions and related fields (23%), and visual and performing arts (11%). In an average class, 64% graduate in 4 years or less, 69% graduate in 5 years or less, and 70% graduate in 6 years or less.

SERVICES: Counseling and information services are available, as is tutoring in most subjects. There is a reader service for the blind, and remedial math, reading, and writing. The Academic Resource Center (ARC) provides services (including tutoring) for students. **Library/Resources:** The library contains 388,812 volumes, 373,050 microform items, 4,464 audio/video tapes/CDs/DVDs, and subscribes to 23,000 periodicals including electronic. Computerized library services include interlibrary loans, database searching, Internet access, and Wi-Fi capability. Special learning facilities include a radio station, TV station. There is also state-of-the-science simulation laboratories to replicate clinical scenarios specific to adult, pediatric, and birthing care. The green architecture design is consistent with the Leadership in Energy and Environmental Design (LEED) certification standards of the U.S. Green Building Council. State-of-the-art teaching and research laboratories in chemistry, biology, biotechnology, environmental, and human performance. An arts center is home to Act 1 events, and an American and international film library also has reference works relating to film, television, and media. Our total volumes 388,812 consists of 168,812 paper volumes and 120,000 electronic books. **Physically Challenged Students:** 99% of the campus is accessible. Facilities include wheelchair ramps, elevators, special parking, specially equipped restrooms, special class scheduling, lowered drinking fountains, lowered telephones, and special housing. **Special:** Students may cross-register with schools in the Lehigh Valley Association of Independent Colleges (LVAIC). Internships are strongly encouraged in all majors, and study abroad in seven countries is possible. Dual majors, a Washington semester, pass/fail options, accelerated degree programs, and credit for life, military, and work experience are offered. 5 Year BA/MACJ, 4 1/2 Year BS/MBA, and 5 Year Medical Studies/Physician Assistant Programs. There are 11 national honor societies and a freshman honors program. **Visiting:** There are regularly scheduled orientations for prospective students, including meetings with faculty advisers and social activities. There are guides for informal visits, visitors may sit in on classes, and stay overnight. To schedule a visit, contact Mr. Derrick Wetzel at (610) 282-4443. **Campus Safety and Security:** Measures include 24-hour foot and vehicle patrol, emergency notification system, self-defense education, and security escort services. There are emergency telephones, lighted pathways/sidewalks, and controlled access to dorms/residences.

REQUIREMENTS: The SAT is required. Applicants must be graduates of an accredited secondary school. The GED is accepted. Applicants should have completed 17 college preparatory courses including 4 years each of English, history, and math, 3 years of science, and 2 years of foreign language. The school will accept an essay but strongly recommends an interview. For theater students, a performance appraisal is required. For dance students an audition is required. AP and CLEP credits are accepted. Important factors in the admissions decision are advanced placement or honors courses, leadership record, recommendations by school officials, and evidence of special talent. For graduation, students must complete a minimum of 120 credit hours including a maximum of 48 in the major with a minimum GPA of 2.0 overall and in the major. Liberal arts distribution requirements consist of 12 to 16 courses including cultural literacy, modes of thinking, and Christian values and theology, as well as 3 courses in phys ed (one-credit courses). Internships are strongly encouraged for most majors. **Procedure:** Freshmen are admitted in the fall and spring. Entrance exams should be taken during the junior or senior year. There are deferred admissions and rolling admissions plans. Applications should be filed by August 1 for fall entry, along with a $30 fee. Notification is sent on a rolling basis. Applications are accepted online. **Transfer Students:** 72 transfer students enrolled in 2015-2016. Applicants for transfer should have completed a minimum of 24 college credit hours with a GPA of 2.5. An interview is recommended. 45 of 120 credits required for the bachelor's degree must be completed at DSU. **International Students:** The school actively recruits these students. They must take the TOEFL with a minimum score of 550 on the paper-based TOEFL (PBT) or 100 on the Internet-based version (iBT). The SAT, ACT or the IELTS must also be taken.

ADMISSIONS: 80% of the 2016-2017 applicants were accepted. The SAT scores for the 2016-2017 freshman class were: Critical Reading-- 44% below 500, 37% between 500 and 599, 15% between 600 and 699, and 5% between 700 and 800. Math-- 46% below 500, 36% between 500 and 599, 15% between 600 and 699, and 3% between 700 and 800. Writing-- 48% below 500, 34% between 500 and 599, 15% between 600 and 699, and 3% between 700 and 800. **Admissions Contact:** Mary Birkhead, Dean of Enrollment Management. Email: *admiss@desales.edu* Web: *www.desales.edu*

FINANCIAL AID: In 2016-2017, 86% of all full-time freshmen and 79% of continuing full-time students received some form of financial aid. 86% of all full-time freshmen and 76% of continuing full-time students received need-based aid. The average freshman award was $25,787. Need-based scholarships or need-based grants averaged $20,398; need-based self-help aid (loans and jobs) averaged $5,097; and other non-need-based awards and non-need-based scholarships averaged $13,014. The average financial indebtedness of the 2016 graduate was $25,875. DSU is a member of CSS. The state aid form and the college's own financial statement are required. The FAFSA code is 003986. The deadline for filing freshman financial aid applications for fall entry is February 1.

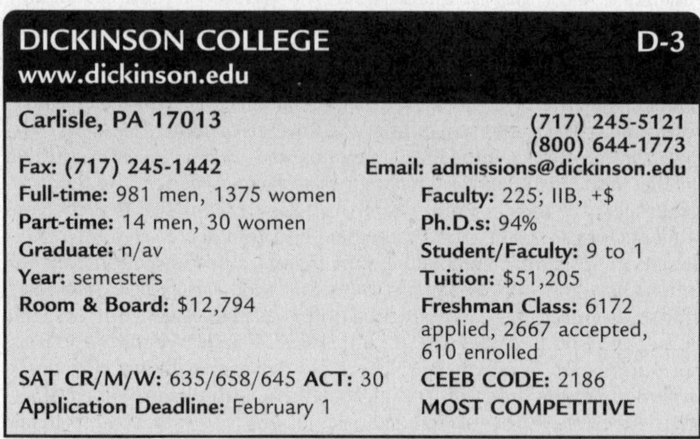

DICKINSON COLLEGE D-3
www.dickinson.edu

Carlisle, PA 17013 (717) 245-5121 (800) 644-1773

Fax: (717) 245-1442 Email: admissions@dickinson.edu

Full-time: 981 men, 1375 women	**Faculty:** 225; IIB, +$
Part-time: 14 men, 30 women	**Ph.D.s:** 94%
Graduate: n/av	**Student/Faculty:** 9 to 1
Year: semesters	**Tuition:** $51,205
Room & Board: $12,794	**Freshman Class:** 6172 applied, 2667 accepted, 610 enrolled
SAT CR/M/W: 635/658/645 **ACT:** 30	**CEEB CODE:** 2186
Application Deadline: February 1	**MOST COMPETITIVE**

Dickinson College, founded in 1783, is a nationally recognized liberal-arts institution. Devoted to its revolutionary roots, the college maintains the mission of founder Benjamin Rush to provide a useful education in the liberal arts and sciences. The college is a leader among educational institutions committed to environmental sustainability and green initiatives. There is 1 undergraduate school. In addition to regional accreditation, Dickinson has baccalaureate program accreditation with ACS, Pa Department of Education, and University Senate of the United Methodist Church. The 112-acre campus is in a suburban area about 20 miles west of Harrisburg, PA, and 2 hours from Washington, D.C., and the area grants access to all major East Coast cities. Including any residence halls, there are 138 buildings.

STUDENT LIFE: 78% of undergraduates are from out of state, mostly the Middle Atlantic. Students are from 43 states, 46 foreign countries, and Canada. 56% are from public schools. 7% are Hispanic; 69% White; 5% African American; 4% two or more races; 3% Asian American; 10% Foreign; 1% race unknown. 27% are Protestant; 23% claim no religious affiliation; 22% Catholic; 11% Jewish. **Female To Male Ratio:** 1.4:1. The average age of freshmen is 18; all undergraduates, 20. 8% do not continue beyond their first year; 85% remain to graduate. **Housing:** 2108 students can be accommodated in college housing, which includes coed dorms and on-campus apartments. In addition, there are language houses, special-interest houses, fraternity houses, sorority houses, arts, environmental, learning communities, multicultural and wellness housing. On-campus housing is guaranteed for all 4 years and is available on a lottery system for upperclassmen. 94% of students live on campus; of those, 85% remain on campus on weekends. Upperclassmen may keep cars.

FACULTY/CLASSROOMS: 51% of faculty are male; 49% are female. All teach undergraduates, and do research. No introductory courses are taught by graduate students. The average class size in an introductory lecture is 35 and in a laboratory is 21.

PROGRAMS OF STUDY: Dickinson confers B.A. and B.S. degrees. Bachelor's degrees are awarded in AGRICULTURE (environmental studies), BIOLOGICAL SCIENCE (biochemistry, biology/biological science, and neurosciences), BUSINESS (international business management), COMMUNICATIONS AND THE ARTS (art history, classical languages, dance, English, French, German, Greek, Latin, music, Russian, Spanish, and theatre arts), COMPUTER AND PHYSICAL SCIENCE (chemistry, computer science, earth science, mathematics, and physics), EDUCATION (educational studies), ENGINEERING AND ENVIRONMENTAL DESIGN (environmental science), SOCIAL SCIENCE (African studies, American studies, anthropology, archeology, classical/ancient civilization, East Asian studies, economics, history, international studies, Italian studies, Judaic studies, Latin American studies, law, medieval studies, Middle Eastern studies, philosophy, political science/government, psychology, public affairs, religion, sociology, and women's studies). International education/foreign languages, sciences, and sustainability education & preprofessional programs are the strongest academically. International business & management/international studies, political science, and economics have the largest enrollments.

ACTIVITIES: 17% of men belong to 5 national fraternities; 27% of women belong to 1 local and 4 national sororities. There are 111 groups on campus, including art, band, cheerleading, chess, choir, chorale, chorus, computers, dance, debate, drama, environmental, ethnic, film, honors, international, jazz band, LGBT, literary magazine, musical theater, newspaper, orchestra, photography, political, professional, radio station, religious, social, social service, student government, symphony, and yearbook. Popular campus events include Public Affairs Symposium and Clarke Forum Events. **Sports:** There are 12 intercollegiate sports for men and 13 for women, and 9 intramural sports for men and 9 for women. Facilities include a fitness center that has strength training equipment, cardio machines and five international squash courts, basketball, volleyball, and racquetball courts, a track, indoor rock-climbing wall, swimming pool with diving well, a dance studio, multi-purpose indoor training area for sports teams and fitness classes, and tennis courts. Turf fields are available for varsity football, field hockey, lacrosse, softball, baseball, and soccer. There is also a golf simulator, and jogging and bicycle trails. **Graduates:** From July 1, 2015 to June 30, 2016, 527 bachelor's degrees were awarded. The most popular majors were social sciences (23%), biological science (13%), and business/marketing (11%). 15 companies recruited on campus in 2015-2016. In an average class, 80% graduate in 4 years or less, 84% graduate in 5 years or less, and 84% graduate in 6 years or less. Of the 2015 graduating class, 39% were enrolled in graduate school within 6 months of graduation, and 74% were employed.

SERVICES: Counseling and information services are available, as is tutoring in every subject. Services are provided as necessary on a case-by-case basis. There is a reader service for the blind. **Library/Resources:** The library contains 539,648 volumes, 168,703 microform items, and 140,079 audio/video tapes/CDs/DVDs, and subscribes to 6,565 periodicals including electronic. Computerized library services include interlibrary loans, database searching, Internet access, and Wi-Fi capability. Special learning facilities include an art gallery, planetarium, fiber-optic and satellite telecommunications networks, a telescope observatory, scanning electron microscope, research-quality greenhouse and an archival collection. **Physically Challenged Students:** 69% of the campus is accessible. Facilities include wheelchair ramps, elevators, special parking, specially equipped restrooms, special class scheduling, lowered drinking fountains, lowered telephones, and special housing. **Special:** Students may cross-register with Central Pennsylvania Consortium Colleges. Instruction in 13 languages is available. Internships are available on and off campus. Dickinson now sponsors more than 40 programs on six continents in 24 countries. These options include academic year programs, semester programs, summer programs, globally-integrated courses that include a January international field experience and specialized programs which combine domestic study with international study. A Washington semester, work-study, and accelerated degree programs are available, as are dual majors, student-designed majors, non-degree study, pass/fail options, and a 3-3 law degree with the Dickinson School of Law of Pennsylvania State University. There are 3-2 engineering degrees offered with Case Western Reserve University, Rensselaer Polytechnic Institute, the University of Pennsylvania and with Columbia University. Graduate school agreements are currently in place for: Medicine/Health programs with The Johns Hopkins University School of Nursing; Jefferson School of Population Health at the Jefferson Medical College; Law with The Pennsylvania State University Dickinson School of Law (3-3 Program); Business with The Thunderbird School of Global Management; William E. Simon Graduate School of Business Administration at The University of Rochester; Engineering with Rensselaer Polytechnic Institute (3-2 Program) and Case Western Reserve University (3-2 Program); Columbia University (3-2 Program); International Graduate Education with The Network of Autonomous Schools of the Lombardy Region (Italy); University of Bremen (Bremen, Germany); University of East Anglia (Norwich, England); University of Maine; University of Malaga (Malaga, Spain), and the University of Queensland (Queensland, Australia). There are 16 national honor societies, Phi Beta Kappa, and 36 departmental honors programs. **Visiting:** There are regularly scheduled orientations for prospective students, prospective students can participate in campus tours, individual interviews, group information sessions, class visits, overnight stays in residence halls, and open houses. There are guides for informal visits, visitors may sit in on classes, and stay overnight. To schedule a visit, contact the Admissions Office. **Campus Safety and Security:** Measures include 24-hour foot and vehicle patrol, emergency notification system, self-defense education, and security escort services. There are shuttle buses, emergency telephones, lighted pathways/sidewalks, controlled access to dorms/residences, electronic access to residence halls, and required electronic access for on-campus administrative and academic buildings.

REQUIREMENTS: The SAT and ACT Subject Tests are optional submissions. The GED is accepted. Applicants should have completed 16 academic credits, including 4 years of English, 3 each of math and science, of those, 2 must be lab, 2-3 of foreign language, 2 each of social studies, and academic electives. An essay is required, and an interview is recommended. AP credits are accepted. Important factors in the admissions decision are advanced placement or honors courses, evidence of special talent, personality/intangible qualities, extracurricular activities record, leadership record, and geographical diversity. To graduate, students must complete 32 courses with a minimum GPA of 2.0. The school requires 1 course each in the arts, humanities, social sciences, sustainability, and lab sciences. Also required are 3 courses of cross-cultural studies (including foreign language, comparative civilizations, and U.S. diversity), a first-year seminar, phys ed, and the completion of a major averaging 9 to 15 courses. Writing in the discipline and quantitative reasoning courses are also required. **Procedure:** Freshmen are admitted fall. Entrance exams should be taken in the spring of the junior year or the fall of the senior year. There are early decision, early admissions, and deferred admissions plans. Early decision applications should be filed by November 15; regular applications, by February 1 for fall entry, along with a $65 fee. Notification of early decision is sent December 15; regular decision, March 20. 314 early decision candidates were accepted for the 2016-2017 class. 238 applicants were on the 2016 waiting list; 29 were admitted. Applications are accepted on-line. **Transfer Students:** 10 transfer students enrolled in 2015-2016. Applicants for transfer must have at least a 2.0 cumulative GPA and must submit secondary school and college transcripts and 1 professor recommendation in addition to the standard application for admission. 16 of 32 credits required for the bachelor's degree must be completed at Dickinson. **International Students:** There are 227 international students enrolled. The school actively recruits these students. They must take the TOEFL with a minimum score of 90 on the Internet-based version (iBT), or take the IELTS.

ADMISSIONS: 43% of the 2016-2017 applicants were accepted. The SAT scores for the 2016-2017 freshman class were: Critical Reading-- 2% below 500, 24% between 500 and 599, 54% between 600 and 699, and 20% between 700 and 800. Math-- 1% below 500, 20% between 500 and 599, 51% between 600 and 699, and 28% between 700 and 800. Writing-- 3% below 500, 20% between 500 and 599, 53% between 600 and 699, and 23% between 700 and 800. The ACT scores were 3% between 18 and 23, 50% between 24 and 29, and 48% above 30. **Admissions Contact:** Catherine McDonald Davenport, Dean of Admissions. Email: *admissions@dickinson.edu* Web: *www.dickinson.edu*

FINANCIAL AID: In 2016-2017, 81% of all full-time freshmen and 74% of continuing full-time students received some form of financial aid. 56% of all full-time freshmen and 54% of continuing full-time students received need-based aid. The average freshman award was $45,673. Need-based scholarships or need-based grants averaged $40,828; need-based self-help aid (loans and jobs) averaged $5,191; other non-need-based awards and non-need-based scholarships averaged $9,474; and $3,549 from other forms of aid. 49% of undergraduate students work part-time. Average annual earnings from campus work are $1217. The average financial indebtedness of the 2016 graduate was $26,908. Dickinson is a member of CSS. The CSS/Profile state aid form, and noncustodial parent statement are required. The FAFSA code is 003253. The priority date for freshman financial aid applications for fall entry is November 15. The deadline for fall entry is February 1.

DREXEL UNIVERSITY F-3
www.drexel.edu

Philadelphia, PA 19104	(215) 895-2000 (800) 2 DREXEL
Fax: (215) 895-5939	Email: enroll@drexel.edu
Full-time: 7486 men, 5810 women	Faculty: n/av
Part-time: 681 men, 1522 women	Ph.D.s: 86%
Graduate: 3270 men, 5463 women	Student/Faculty: 12 to 1
Year: quarters, summer session	Tuition: $51,065
Room & Board: $14,367	Freshman Class: 28535 applied, 21298 accepted, 2324 enrolled
SAT CR/M/W: 580/620/580 ACT: 27	CEEB CODE: 2149
Application Deadline: January 15	VERY COMPETITIVE+

Drexel is a comprehensive national research university ranked among the top 100 in the United States. The University has built its global reputation on core achievements that include: leadership in experiential learning through its cooperative education program; a history of academic technology firsts; and recognition as a model of best practices in translational research initiatives. Founded in 1891 in Philadelphia, Drexel now engages with students and communities around the world via three Philadelphia campuses and other regional sites, Drexel University Sacramento, The Academy of Natural Sciences of Drexel University and international research partnerships in several countries around the globe. Drexel Online is one of the oldest and most successful providers of online degree programs. There are 15 undergraduate schools and 12 graduate schools. In addition to regional accreditation, Drexel has baccalaureate program accreditation with AACSB, ABET, ACCE, ADA, NAAB, and NASAD. The 96-acre campus is in an urban area in the University City neighborhood of Philadelphia. Including any residence halls, there are 111 buildings.

STUDENT LIFE: 53% of undergraduates are from out of state, mostly the Middle Atlantic. Students are from 48 states, 115 foreign countries, and Canada. 6% are African American; 6% Hispanic; 52% White; 4% two or more races; 2% race unknown; 16% Asian American; 14% Foreign. **Female To Male Ratio:** 1.1:1. The average age of freshmen is 18; all undergraduates, 22. 11% do not continue beyond their first year; 70% remain to graduate. **Housing:** College-sponsored housing includes coed dorms, on-campus apartments, and off-campus apartments, fraternity houses, sorority houses, honors floors in residence halls, and international student housing. On-campus housing is guaranteed for the freshman year only, and is available on a first-come, first-served basis, and is available on a lottery system for upperclassmen. 80% of students commute. All students may keep cars.

FACULTY/CLASSROOMS: 50% of faculty are male; 50% are female. No introductory courses are taught by graduate students.

PROGRAMS OF STUDY: Drexel confers B.S.B.A., B.A.C.S., B.S.S.M., B.S.I.S., B.S.A.E., B.S.I., B.S.E.T., B.S.C.S., BSc.MGT, B.Arch, B.S.M.E., B.S.I.T., B.S.ClSc, B.S., B.S.C.A., B.S.Civ, B.S.S.E., B.S.Ch.E, B.A., B.S.B.E., B.S.Ee.E., B.S.C.A.E., B.S.N., B.S.ECON, B.S.Ma.E., B.S.C.E., B.S.E., B.S.E.E., B.S.B.A.E., B.A.Econ, B.S.Pr.Mt., B.S.M.S.E. and B.S.H.M. degrees. Master's and doctoral degrees are also awarded. Bachelor's degrees are awarded in AGRICULTURE (environmental studies), BIOLOGICAL SCIENCE (biology/biological science and nutrition), BUSINESS (accounting, business administration and management, business economics, business intelligence and analytics, entrepreneurial studies, fashion merchandising, hotel/motel and restaurant management, international business, management information systems, marketing/retailing/merchandising, organizational leadership and management, and sports management), COMMUNICATIONS AND THE ARTS (animation, art history, communications, dance, design, English, film arts, graphic design, media arts, music industry, photography, television & digital media production, and video), COMPUTER AND PHYSICAL SCIENCE (chemistry, computer engineering technology, computer game design/development, computer science, computer security and information assurance, digital arts/technology, geoscience, information sciences and systems, mathematics, physics, science, software engineering, and web technology), EDUCATION (education and elementary education), ENGINEERING AND ENVIRONMENTAL DESIGN (architectural engineering, architecture, biomedical engineering, chemical engineering, civil engineering, computer engineering, construction management, electrical/electronics engineering, engineering, engineering technology, environmental engineering, environmental science, interior design, materials engineering, materials science and engineering, and mechanical engineering), HEALTH PROFESSIONS (health services administration, health science, nursing, premedicine, and public health), SOCIAL SCIENCE (anthropology, criminal justice, criminology, culinary arts, economics, fashion design and technology, history, international studies, legal studies, philosophy, political science/government, psychology, and sociology). Engineering, business, and design arts are the strongest academically. Nursing, mechanical engineering, and finance have the largest enrollments.

ACTIVITIES: 12% of men belong to 21 national fraternities; 11% of women belong to 14 national sororities. There are 250 groups on campus, including art, band, cheerleading, chess, choir, chorus, communications, computers, dance, drama, environmental, ethnic, film, forensics, honors, international, jazz band, LGBT, literary magazine, musical theater, newspaper, orchestra, pep band, photography, political, professional, radio and TV, religious, social, social service, student government, and yearbook. Popular campus events include Musical, Cultural, and Art Events. **Sports:** There are 10 intercollegiate sports for men and 10 for women, and 11 intramural sports for men and 11 for women. Facilities include an athletic center with gyms, squash courts, a swimming pool and diving well, exercise rooms, wrestling room, a recreation center, exercise studios, climbing wall, indoor track; and an armory with 3 multipurpose courts. **Graduates:** From July 1, 2015 to June 30, 2016, 3657 bachelor's degrees were awarded. The most popular majors were nursing (4%), mechanical engineering (3%), and finance (3%). In an average class, 70% graduate in 6 years or less. Of the 2015 graduating class, 13% were enrolled in graduate school within 6 months of graduation, and 82% were employed.

SERVICES: Counseling and information services are available, as is tutoring in most subjects. There is remedial math, reading, and writing. **Library/Resources:** The 2 libraries contain 551,548 volumes, 18,133 microform items, 10,287 audio/video tapes/CDs/DVDs, and subscribe to 36,584 periodicals including electronic. Computerized library services include interlibrary loans, database searching, Internet access, and Wi-Fi capability. Special learning facilities include an art gallery, natural history museum, radio station, and TV station. **Physically Challenged Students:** 98% of the campus is accessible. Facilities include wheelchair ramps, elevators, special parking, specially equipped restrooms, special class scheduling, lowered drinking fountains, and special housing. **Special:** Cooperative education enables students to alternate full-time classroom study and 6-month full-time employment periods with university-approved employers. As part of its global initiatives, Drexel offers study abroad and co-op abroad experiences as well as global classrooms and a global engagement certificate. As part of its commitment to community engagement, all freshmen enroll in an introductory civic engagement course that combines classroom study with community service. Undergraduate research and research co-ops allow students to work with faculty, post-docs, and graduate students on state-of-the art projects that contribute to academic research, scholarship, and creative work. Drexel offers several disciplinary or interdisciplinary bachelor's-master's accelerated degree programs as well as minors, and concentrations. Drexel offers a Custom-designed major that enables students to pursue an individualized course of study not readily available through an existing major. The program of study incorporates an early intensive research experience and cooperative education as part of its degree requirements and culminates in an original, interdisciplinary senior-year project. There is 1 national honor society and a freshman honors program. **Visiting:** There are regularly scheduled orientations for prospective students, consisting of a 2-day program for new freshmen and their parents in late July. There are guides for informal visits, visitors may sit in on classes, and stay overnight. To schedule a visit, contact Drexel Admissions. **Campus Safety and Security:** Measures include 24-hour foot and vehicle patrol, emergency notification system, self-defense education, and security escort services. There are shuttle buses, emergency telephones, lighted pathways/sidewalks, and controlled access to dorms/residences, and residential and commuter safety and security programs.

REQUIREMENTS: The SAT is required. Applicants must be graduates of an accredited secondary school. The GED is accepted. AP and CLEP credits are accepted. The graduation requirements for Drexel undergraduate programs require the completion of between 180 and 192 quarter credits depending on the major with a 2.0 cumulative grade point average. The successful completion of co-op terms is required of students with programs of study that include cooperative education experience(s). **Procedure:** Freshmen are admitted fall. There are early decision, early admissions, and deferred admissions plans. Early decision applications should be filed by November 1; regular applications, by January 15 for fall entry, along with a $50 fee. Notification of early decision is sent December 15; regular decision, April 1. Application fees are waived if application is completed online. **Transfer Students:** 845 transfer students enrolled in 2015-2016. Applicants must have a minimum GPA of 2.5. Other requirements vary among the individual colleges within the university. 45 of 180 credits required for the bachelor's degree must be completed at Drexel. **International Students:** There are 2328 international students enrolled. The school actively recruits these students. They must take the TOEFL with a minimum score of 79 on the Internet-based version (iBT), or take the IELTS.

ADMISSIONS: 75% of the 2016-2017 applicants were accepted. The SAT scores for the 2016-2017 freshman class were: Critical Reading-- 11% below 500, 43% between 500 and 599, 37% between 600 and 699, and 10% between 700 and 800. Math-- 6% below 500, 35% between 500 and 599, 44% between 600 and 699, and 15% between 700 and 800. Writing-- 17% below 500, 45% between 500 and 599, 30% between 600 and 699, and 8% between 700 and 800. The ACT scores were 20% between 18 and 23, 55% between 24 and 29, and 25% above 30. 58% of the current freshmen were in the top fifth of their class; 85% were in the top two fifths. **Admissions Contact:** Evelyn Thimba, Freshman & International Admissions. Email: *ekt38@drexel.edu* Web: *www.drexel.edu*

FINANCIAL AID: In 2016-2017, 99% of all full-time freshmen and 92% of continuing full-time students received some form of financial aid. 69% of all full-time freshmen and 54% of continuing full-time students received need-based aid. The average freshman award was $42,995. Need-based scholarships or need-based grants averaged $33,006; need-based self-help aid (loans and jobs) averaged $9,096; non-need-based athletic scholarships averaged $32,568; and other non-need-based awards and non-need-based scholarships averaged $14,619. 71% of undergraduate students work part-time. Drexel is a member of CSS. The CSS/Profile is required. The FAFSA code is 003256. The priority date for freshman financial aid applications for fall entry is February 15.

DUQUESNE UNIVERSITY — B-3

www.duq.edu

Pittsburgh, PA 15282	**(412) 396-6222 (800) 456-0590**
Fax: (412) 396-5644	**Email: admissions@duq.edu**
Full-time: 2165 men, 3686 women	**Faculty:** 467; I, --$
Part-time: 111 men, 137 women	**Ph.D.s:** 94%
Graduate: 1252 men, 2052 women	**Student/Faculty:** 14 to 1
Year: semesters, summer session	**Tuition:** $35,062
Room & Board: $11,760	**Freshman Class:** 7655 applied, 5660 accepted, 1556 enrolled
SAT CR/M/W: 560/570/550 **ACT:** 26	**CEEB CODE:** 2196
Application Deadline: July 1	**VERY COMPETITIVE**

Duquesne University, founded in 1878 by the Spiritan Congregation, is a private Roman Catholic institution offering degrees in liberal arts, sciences, music, business, nursing, pharmacy, health sciences, education, leadership and biomedical engineering. There are 9 undergraduate schools and 9 graduate schools. In addition to regional accreditation, Duquesne has baccalaureate program accreditation with AACSB, NASM, NCATE, AMTA, APA, and CAATE. The 50-acre campus is in an urban area on a private, self-contained campus in the center of Pittsburgh. Including any residence halls, there are 46 buildings.

STUDENT LIFE: 74% of undergraduates are from Pennsylvania. Others are from 46 states, 44 foreign countries, and Canada. 79% are White; 6% Foreign; 5% African American; 3% Asian American; 3% Hispanic; 2% two or more races; 2% race unknown. 46% are Catholic; 29% claim no religious affiliation; 16% Protestant. **Female To Male Ratio:** 1.7:1. The average age of freshmen is 18; all undergraduates, 20. 13% do not continue beyond their first year; 72% remain to graduate. **Housing:** 3748 students can be accommodated in college housing, which includes single-sex and coed dorms and on-campus apartments. In addition, there are honors houses, special-interest houses, fraternity and sorority wings, international wings, and club wings. On-campus housing is available on a first-come, first-served basis, and is available on a lottery system for upperclassmen. 57% of students live on campus; of those, 70% remain on campus on weekends. All students may keep cars.

FACULTY/CLASSROOMS: 49% of faculty are male; 51% are female. 95% teach undergraduates. No introductory courses are taught by graduate students. The average class size in an introductory lecture is 25; in a laboratory is 20; and in a regular course is 27.

PROGRAMS OF STUDY: Duquesne confers B.A., B.S., B.M., B.S.A.T., B.S.B.A., B.S.Ed., B.S.H.M.S., B.S.H.S.,and B.S.N. degrees. Master's and doctoral degrees are also awarded. Bachelor's degrees are awarded in BIOLOGICAL SCIENCE (biochemistry, biology/adolescence education, and biology/biological science), BUSINESS (accounting, banking and finance, business administration and management, business communications, business economics, entrepreneurial studies, international business management, management information systems, management science, marketing/retailing/merchandising, nonprofit/public organization management, sports marketing, and supply chain management), COMMUNICATIONS AND THE ARTS (advertising, art history and appreciation, classical languages, communications, dramatic arts, English, Greek (classical), journalism, Latin, modern language, multimedia, music business management, music performance, music technology, public relations, Spanish, and speech/debate/rhetoric), COMPUTER AND PHYSICAL SCIENCE (chemistry, chemistry/adolescence education, computer science, mathematics, and physics), EDUCATION (athletic training, early childhood education, education, English education, foreign languages education, health information management, mathematics education, middle school education, music education, physical science secondary school education, and social studies education), ENGINEERING AND ENVIRONMENTAL DESIGN (biomedical engineering, computer technology, and environmental science), HEALTH PROFESSIONS (health care administration, health science, music therapy, nursing, occupational therapy, pharmaceutical science, pharmacy, physical therapy, physician's assistant, and speech pathology/audiology), SOCIAL SCIENCE (behavioral science, classical/ancient civilization, economics, history, humanities, international relations, liberal arts/ general studies, philosophy, political science/government, psychology, sociology, theological studies, and women & gender studies). Pharmacy, nursing, and psychology have the largest enrollments.

ACTIVITIES: 15% of men belong to 1 local and 9 national fraternities; 22% of women belong to 10 national sororities. There are 200 groups on campus, including art, band, cheerleading, chess, choir, chorale, chorus, computers, dance, debate, drama, drill team, environmental, ethnic, film, forensics, honors, international, jazz band, LGBT, literary magazine, marching band, musical theater, newspaper, opera, orchestra, pep band, photography, political, professional, radio and TV, religious, social, social service, student government, symphony, and yearbook. Popular campus events include Orientation, Carnival, International Student Organization Week, Christmas Ball, Family Weekend, Greek Week, Trivia Nights, Multi-Cultural Unity Banquet, Commuter Family Day, Spotlight Musical Theater Shows, DUQ 'n Roll and Battle of the Bands. **Sports:** There are 6 intercollegiate sports for men and 11 for women, and 6 intramural sports for men and 6 for women. Facilities include athletic buildings that have aerobics space, cardio machines, multipurpose courts, walking/running track, free weight rooms, racquetball courts, basketball courts, athletic training room, and weight training. An athletic field house football, soccer, and lacrosse. There is also a swimming pool, tennis court, outdoor basketball/ deck hockey court. **Graduates:** From July 1, 2015 to June 30, 2016, 1484 bachelor's degrees were awarded. The most popular majors were nursing (17%), biology (8%), and accounting (5%). 136 companies recruited on campus in 2015-2016. In an average class, 63% graduate in 4 years or less, 71% graduate in 5 years or less, and 72% graduate in 6 years or less.

SERVICES: Counseling and information services are available, as is tutoring in every subject. There is a reader service for the blind, and remedial math, reading, and writing. **Library/Resources:** The 2 libraries contain 648,583 volumes, 245,493 microform items, 89,089 audio/video tapes/CDs/DVDs, and subscribe to 117,936 periodicals including electronic. Computerized library services include interlibrary loans, database searching, Internet access, and Wi-Fi capability. Special learning facilities include an art gallery, radio station, TV station, 235 multimedia-enhanced teaching facilities, and 25 labs. **Physically Challenged Students:** 95% of the campus is accessible. Facilities include wheelchair ramps, elevators, special parking, specially equipped restrooms, special class scheduling, lowered drinking fountains, and special housing. **Special:** The university offers cross-registration through the Pittsburgh Council on Higher Education, internships, study abroad in 23 countries, and a Washington semester. Also available are B.A.-B.S. degrees, accelerated degree programs, dual and student-designed majors, a 3-2 engineering program with Case Western Reserve University and University of Pittsburgh, the nation's first dual degree in biomedical engineering and nursing (BME-BSN), a 3-3 law degree and a 3-2 business degree, pass/fail options, and credit evaluation for life, military, and work experience. There are 26 national honor societies, a freshman honors program, and 60 departmental honors programs. **Visiting:** There are regularly scheduled orientations for prospective students, consisting of a campus tour and individual interviews with counselors and professors. There are guides for informal visits and visitors may sit in on classes. To schedule a visit, contact Robbyn Snyder at (412) 396-6222. **Campus Safety and Security:** Measures include 24-hour foot and vehicle patrol, emergency notification system, self-defense education, and security escort services. There are shuttle buses, emergency telephones, lighted pathways/sidewalks, controlled access to dorms/residences, and security cameras throughout campus that monitor exterior areas 24 hours a day.

REQUIREMENTS: Business, liberal arts, and music applicants select meeting criteria and can choose to apply as standardized test-optional candidates. Students should have either a high school diploma or the GED. Applicants are required to have 16 academic credits, including 4 each in English and academic electives, and 8 combined in social studies, language, math, and science. An essay, letter of recommendation, and interview are recommended. An audition is required for music majors. 40 hours shadowing for physical therapy (prior to enrollment). A GPA of 3.0 is required. AP and CLEP credits are accepted. Important factors in the admissions decision are advanced placement or honors courses, recommendations by school officials, and extracurricular activities record. To graduate, students are required to complete at least 120 credit hours, including a specified number in the major (varies by program), with a minimum 2.0 GPA. General requirements vary by department, but there is a 33 credit liberal arts core curriculum. **Procedure:** Freshmen are admitted in the fall, spring, and summer. Entrance exams should be taken during the spring of the junior year or the fall of the senior year. There are early decision, early admissions, deferred admissions, and rolling admissions plans. Early decision applications should be filed by November 1; regular applications, by July 1 for fall entry; December 1 for spring entry; and April 1 for summer entry, along with a $50 fee. Notification of early decision is sent December 15; regular decision, on a rolling basis. 72 early decision candidates were accepted for the 2016-2017 class. Application fees are waived if application is completed online. **Transfer Students:** 208 transfer students enrolled in 2015-2016. Applicants must submit complete high school and college transcripts. Students should have a minimum GPA of 2.5 for the university, but some schools require a higher average. A minimum of 12 credits earned is required, and an interview is recommended. 30 of 120 credits required for the bachelor's degree must be completed at Duquesne. **International Students:** There are 205 international students enrolled. The school actively recruits these students. They must take the college's own test, and students are required to sit for ENG language placement tests as part of their arrival program.

ADMISSIONS: 74% of the 2016-2017 applicants were accepted. The SAT scores for the 2016-2017 freshman class were: Critical Reading-- 9% below 500, 60% between 500 and 599, 28% between 600 and 699, and 3% between 700 and 800. Math-- 11% below 500, 52% between 500 and 599, 32% between 600 and 699, and 5% between 700 and 800. Writing-- 20% below 500, 56% between 500 and 599, 23% between 600 and 699, and 1% between 700 and 800. The ACT scores were 16% between 18 and 23, 64% between 24 and 29, and 20% above 30. 48% of the current freshmen were in the top fifth of their class; 78% were in the top two fifths. 20 freshmen graduated first in their class. **Admissions Contact:** Debra Zugates, Director, Admissions. Email: *admissions@duq.edu* Web: *www.duq.edu*

FINANCIAL AID: 13% of undergraduate students work part-time. The college's own financial statement is required. The FAFSA code is 003258. The deadline for filing freshman financial aid applications for fall entry is May 1.

EAST STROUDSBURG UNIVERSITY F-2

www.esu.edu

East Stroudsburg, PA 18301	(570) 422-3542 (877) 230-5547
Fax: (570) 422-3933	Email: undergrads@esu.edu
Full-time: 2442 men, 3200 women	Faculty: 247
Part-time: 223 men, 294 women	Ph.D.s: 91%
Graduate: 231 men, 440 women	Student/Faculty: 22 to 1
Year: semesters, summer session	Tuition: $9944 ($21,036)
Room & Board: $8390	Freshman Class: 7447 applied, 5419 accepted, 1307 enrolled
SAT CR/M/W: required ACT: 21	CEEB CODE: 2650
Application Deadline: May 1	COMPETITIVE

East Stroudsburg University of Pennsylvania is a comprehensive public university offering 56 undergraduate and 24 graduate degree programs. It includes five academic colleges: Arts and Sciences, Business and Management, Education, Health Sciences, and University College. The highest enrolled academic programs are business management, biology, psychology, exercise science and criminal justice. ESU is a member of Pennsylvania's State System of Higher Education with its main campus in East Stroudsburg, Pennysylvania, and additional offerings at the ESU Lehigh Valley Center and Northampton Community College, both in Bethlehem, Pa. There are 5 undergraduate schools and 1 graduate school. In addition to regional accreditation, East Stroudsburg has baccalaureate program accreditation with ABET, ACBSP, CSWE, NCATE, NRPA, ACPHA, COSMA, CAAHEP, CAATE, CEPH, and ACEN. The 258-acre campus is in a small town 90 minutes from New York City and 2 hours northeast of Philadelphia. Including any residence halls, there are 66 buildings.

STUDENT LIFE: 78% of undergraduates are from Pennsylvania. Others are from 32 states, 44 foreign countries, and Canada. 89% are from public schools. 65% are White; 4% two or more races; 2% Asian American; 2% race unknown; 15% African American; 11% Hispanic; 1% Foreign. **Female To Male Ratio:** 1.4:1. The average age of freshmen is 18; all undergraduates, 25. 26% do not continue beyond their first year; 55% remain to graduate. **Housing:** 2943 students can be accommodated in college housing, which includes coed dorms and on-campus apartments, honors houses, special-interest houses, and honors floors. On-campus housing is guaranteed for all 4 years. 54% of students commute. Alcohol is not permitted. Upperclassmen may keep cars.

FACULTY/CLASSROOMS: 50% of faculty are male; 50% are female. 86% teach undergraduates. No introductory courses are taught by graduate students. The average class size in an introductory lecture is 48; in a laboratory is 16; and in a regular course is 35.

PROGRAMS OF STUDY: East Stroudsburg confers B.A., B.S. and B.F.A. degrees. Associate, master's, and doctoral degrees are also awarded. Bachelor's degrees are awarded in BIOLOGICAL SCIENCE (biochemistry, biotechnology, and marine science), BUSINESS (business management, recreation and leisure services, and sports management), COMMUNICATIONS AND THE ARTS (art and design, communication studies, digital media technologies, English, fine arts, integrated art and design, Spanish, and theatre arts), COMPUTER AND PHYSICAL SCIENCE (chemistry, computer security, computer science, earth & space science, mathematics, physics, and science), EDUCATION (athletic training, early childhood education, environmental education, health education, middle school education, physical ed teacher education, special ed/early child dual prog, and special ed / middle level education), ENGINEERING AND ENVIRONMENTAL DESIGN (chemical biotechnology), HEALTH PROFESSIONS (biology, communicative disorders, exercise science, medical laboratory technology, nursing, public health, and rehabilitative and human services), SOCIAL SCIENCE (criminal justice, economics, history, hotel, rest/tourism management, interdisciplinary studies, philosophy, political science/government, psychology, social work, and sociology). Biology, business, and health sciences are the strongest academically. Biological sciences, business management, and exercise science have the largest enrollments.

ACTIVITIES: 5% of men belong to 7 national fraternities; 4% of women belong to 1 local and 5 national sororities. There are 148 groups on campus, including art, band, cheerleading, choir, chorus, clubs for most majors, communications, computers, dance, debate, drama, environmental, ethnic, honors, international, jazz band, LGBT, literary magazine, marching band, musical theater, newspaper, orchestra, pep band, political, professional, radio and TV, religious, social, social service, and student government. Popular campus events include New Student Convocation, Welcome Week, Family Weekend, Homecoming, Diversity Week, African-American History Month, Women's History Month, Drag Show, Greek Week, Community on the Quad, and many Ethnic Festivals. **Sports:** There are 8 intercollegiate sports for men and 12 for women, and 12 intramural sports for men and 8 for women. Facilities include a field house arena with a wrestling room, a natatorium and batting cages, turf fields lined for football, soccer, field hockey, lacrosse, a softball field, baseball field with batting cages, and outdoor tennis courts. Additional recreational facilties include an arena for basketball, volleyball, tennis, elevated track, group fitness studio, boxing zone, fitness center, racquetball courts, indoor cycling studio, and a personal training assessment office, and locker rooms. **Graduates:** From July 1, 2015 to June 30, 2016, 1350 bachelor's degrees were awarded. The most popular majors were business management (11%), psychology (8%), and biology (6%). 140 companies recruited on campus in 2015-2016. In an average class, 31% graduate in 4 years or less, 51% graduate in 5 years or less, and 55% graduate in 6 years or less.

SERVICES: Counseling and information services are available, as is tutoring in every subject. There is remedial math, reading, and writing. **Library/Resources:** The library contains 2.0 million volumes, 1.4 million microform items, 7,765 audio/video tapes/CDs/DVDs, and subscribes to 110,988 periodicals including electronic. Computerized library services include interlibrary loans, database searching, Internet access, and Wi-Fi capability. Special learning facilities include an art gallery, natural history museum, planetarium, radio station, TV station, student newspaper, 3D Design Lab, Northeast Wildlife DNA Lab, Northeast Infectious Disease Diagnostic Lab, College of Education CREATE Lab, Human Performance Lab, Biomechanics Lab, Speech and Hearing Center, and Business Accelerator/Entrepreneur Club. **Physically Challenged Students:** 65% of the campus is accessible. Facilities include wheelchair ramps, elevators, special parking, specially equipped restrooms, special class scheduling, lowered drinking fountains, lowered telephones, and special housing. **Special:** Internships are offered in most programs, as are dual majors and interdisciplinary majors. Our Extended Learning Program is designed to meet the academic needs of society by extending undergraduate and graduate programs to student populations who would otherwise not have access to ESU. Offerings are primarily scheduled at times and locations convenient for working adults. Also offered is a 3-2 engineering degree with Pennsylvania State University, and a transfer program in podiatry. Non-degree study, and study abroad opportunities are also available for students. There are 27 national honor societies and a freshman honors program. **Visiting:** There are regularly scheduled orientations for prospective students, meetings with orientaton leaders, administration, faculty, tours of planetarium & museum, and residence life. There are guides for informal visits and visitors may sit in on classes. To schedule a visit, contact Jeff Jones at jjones@esu.edu. **Campus Safety and Security:** Measures include 24-hour foot and vehicle patrol, emergency notification system, self-defense education, and security escort services. There are shuttle buses, emergency telephones, lighted pathways/sidewalks, controlled access to dorms/residences, controlled building access.

REQUIREMENTS: ESU recommends that students have college prep high school curriculum including: 4 years of language arts/literacy, 3 years of math (Algebra 1, geometry & algebra II, or probability/stats in their junior year); Math based science is recommended for seniors along with; 3 years of science (biology & chemistry 1 with lab); one inquiry-based science such as physics, engineering, environmental or earth science. 3 years of social studies (civics, US History, world history, geography or economics) ESU requires SAT or ACT test scores. ESU super scores SAT with the highest critical reading and math scores. The essay is optional. ESU does not conduct interviews as part of the application process, but would gladly speak with a student requesting further information. If you have received a GED we will accept that as proof of high school graduation. AP and CLEP credits are accepted. All students must maintain a GPA of at least 2.0 while taking at least 120 semester hours (including 27 to 60 hours in the major), and complete the general education requirements and competencies requirements. **Procedure:** Freshmen are admitted fall and spring. Entrance exams should be taken junior year and again in senior year. There is a rolling admissions plan. Applications should be filed by May 1 for fall entry; November 15 for spring entry, along with a $25 fee. Notifications are sent October 1. Applications are accepted online. **Transfer Students:** 609 transfer students enrolled in 2015-2016. A minimum of 12 college credits with a GPA of 2.0 or higher is required for consideration. Applicants with fewer than 12 college-level credits completed at the time of application are considered freshme in the application process, and will be evaluated using a combination of their official college GPA, high school record, and SAT/ACT scores. Although a 2.0 GPA is required for general admission consideration, "Special Admission Programs" have higher admission criteria. 30 of 120 credits required for the bachelor's degree must be completed at East Stroudsburg. **International Students:** There are 40 international students currently enrolled.

ADMISSIONS: 73% of the 2016-2017 applicants were accepted. The SAT scores for the 2016-2017 freshman class were: Critical Reading--68% below 500, 28% between 500 and 599, and 4% between 600 and 699. Math-- 65% below 500, 30% between 500 and 599, and 5% between 600 and 699. Writing-- 75% below 500, 22% between 500 and 599, 2% between 600 and 699, and 1% between 700 and 800. The ACT scores were 11% between 12 and 17, 57% between 18 and 23, 28% between 24 and 29, and 4% above 30. 18% of the current freshmen were in the top fifth of their class; 45% were in the top two fifths. 3 freshmen graduated first in their class. **Admissions Contact:** Jeff Jones, Director, Admissions Office. Email: *jjones@esu.edu* Web: *www.esu.edu*

FINANCIAL AID: In 2016-2017, 73% of all full-time freshmen and 51% of continuing full-time students received some form of financial aid. 52% of all full-time freshmen and 35% of continuing full-time students received need-based aid. The average freshman award was $6,969. Need-based scholarships or need-based grants averaged $5,149; and need-based self-help aid (loans and jobs) averaged $3,245. East Stroudsburg is a member of CSS. The FAFSA code is 003320. Check with the school for current application deadlines.

EASTERN UNIVERSITY — E-3

www.eastern.edu

St. Davids, PA 19087	**(610) 341-5800** **(800) 452-0996**
Fax: (610) 341-1723	**Email: ugadm@eastern.edu**
Full-time: 590 men, 1402 women	**Faculty:** IIA, --$
Part-time: 99 men, 311 women	**Ph.D.s:** 77%
Graduate: 479 men, 881 women	**Student/Faculty:** 11 to 1
Year: semesters, summer session	**Tuition:** $29,600
Room & Board: $9940	**Freshman Class:** 1711 applied, 1156 accepted, 330 enrolled
SAT CR/M/W: 524/516/513 **ACT:** 22	**CEEB CODE:** 2220
Application Deadline: n/av	**COMPETITIVE**

Eastern University, founded in 1932, is a private liberal arts institution affiliated with the American Baptist Church, offering undergraduate and graduate programs. There are 4 undergraduate schools and 2 graduate schools. In addition to regional accreditation, Eastern has baccalaureate program accreditation with CSWE, CCNE, CAATE, and CAAHEP. The 114-acre campus is in a suburban area 20 miles northwest of Philadelphia. Including any residence halls, there are 23 buildings.

STUDENT LIFE: 56% of undergraduates are from Pennsylvania. Others are from 41 states, 41 foreign countries, and Canada. 6% are race unknown; 51% White; 22% African American; 2% Asian American; 2% Foreign; 16% Hispanic. 59% are unknown denominations; 32% Protestant. **Female To Male Ratio:** 2.2:1. The average age of freshmen is 18; all undergraduates, 21. 22% do not continue beyond their first year; 62% remain to graduate. **Housing:** 1242 students can be accommodated in college housing, which includes single-sex and coed dorms and on-campus apartments, and apartment living by application. On-campus housing is guaranteed for all 4 years. 75% of students live on campus; of those, 70% remain on campus on weekends. Alcohol is not permitted. Upperclassmen may keep cars.

FACULTY/CLASSROOMS: 54% of faculty are male; 46% are female. No introductory courses are taught by graduate students.

PROGRAMS OF STUDY: Eastern confers B.A., B.S., B.S.N., and B.S.W. degrees. Associate, master's, and doctoral degrees are also awarded. Bachelor's degrees are awarded in BIOLOGICAL SCIENCE (biochemistry and biology/biological science), BUSINESS (accounting, business administration and management, entrepreneurial studies, marketing/retailing/merchandising, and organizational leadership and management), COMMUNICATIONS AND THE ARTS (communications, dance, English, music, and Spanish), COMPUTER AND PHYSICAL SCIENCE (chemistry and mathematics), EDUCATION (athletic training, early childhood education, and middle school education), ENGINEERING AND ENVIRONMENTAL DESIGN (environmental science), HEALTH PROFESSIONS (exercise science and nursing), SOCIAL SCIENCE (biblical studies, criminal justice, history, missions, philosophy, political science/government, psychology, social work, sociology, theological studies, and youth ministry). Youth Ministry, education, and social work are the strongest academically. Social work, early childhood education, and psychology have the largest enrollments.

ACTIVITIES: There are no fraternities or sororities. There are 53 groups on campus, including cheerleading, choir, chorale, chorus, communications, computers, dance, drama, ethnic, honors, international, literary magazine, musical theater, newspaper, political, professional, radio and TV, religious, social, social service, student government, and yearbook. Popular campus events include Welcome Back Bash/Club Fair, Homecoming, and Concerts. **Sports:** There are 7 intercollegiate sports for men and 9 for women, and 4 intramural sports for men and 4 for women. Facilities include a gym, soccer pitch, baseball, field hockey, softball field, weight room, outdoor track, tennis courts, health fitness trail, outdoor pool, and basketball and volleyball courts. **Graduates:** From July 1, 2015 to June 30, 2016, 497 bachelor's degrees were awarded. The most popular majors were early childhood education (18%), business administration (8%), and psychology (7%). In an average class, 53% graduate in 4 years or less and 9% graduate in 5 years or less. Of the 2015 graduating class, 21% were enrolled in graduate school within 6 months of graduation, and 71% were employed.

SERVICES: Counseling and information services are available, as is tutoring in every subject. There is a reader service for the blind, and remedial math, reading, and writing. **Library/Resources:** The 4 libraries contain 277,660 volumes, 868,506 microform items, 19,366 audio/video tapes/CDs/DVDs, and subscribe to 108,376 periodicals including electronic. Computerized library services include interlibrary loans, database searching, Internet access, and Wi-Fi capability. Special learning facilities include a planetarium, radio station, and an observatory. **Physically Challenged Students:** 75% of the campus is accessible. Facilities include wheelchair ramps, elevators, special parking, specially equipped restrooms, special class scheduling, lowered drinking fountains, lowered telephones, and special housing. **Special:** The college offers cross-registration with Cabrini and Rosemont Colleges, Valley Forge Military Academy, and Villanova University, internships, a Washington semester in the American studies program, and student-designed majors. Also available are accelerated degree programs in organizational management and management of information systems, credit for experience, nondegree study, and pass/fail options. There is a different calendar for the organizational management program. There are 10 national honor societies, a freshman honors program, and 1 departmental honors program. **Visiting:** There are regularly scheduled orientations for prospective students. There are guides for informal visits, visitors may sit in on classes, and stay overnight. To schedule a visit, contact Admissions Office. **Campus Safety and Security:** Measures include 24-hour foot and vehicle patrol, emergency notification system, self-defense education, and security escort services. There are shuttle buses, emergency telephones, lighted pathways/sidewalks, and controlled access to dorms/residences.

REQUIREMENTS: The SAT or ACT is required. AP and CLEP credits are accepted. Important factors in the admissions decision are advanced placement or honors courses, recommendations by school officials, and geographical diversity. To graduate, all students must complete at least 127 credit hours with a minimum 2.0 GPA. The required hours in the major vary. Students must take courses in the Old and New Testament, humanities, social sciences, non-Western heritage, natural sciences, college writing, Living and Learning in Community, Heritage of Western Thought and Civilization, Science Technology and Values, and Justice in a Pluralistic Society and complete a capstone. **Procedure:** Freshmen are admitted in the fall and spring. Entrance exams should be taken as early as possible. There are early admissions, deferred admissions, and rolling admissions plans. Application deadlines are open. Application fee is $35. Notification is sent on a rolling basis. Application fees are waived if application is completed online. **Transfer Students:** 86 transfer students enrolled in 2015-2016. Applicants should have a 2.0 GPA with more than 24 credits, and a 2.5 GPA with fewer than 24 credits. Candidates must be in good standing at their previous institution. 32 of 127 credits required for the bachelor's degree must be completed at Eastern. **International Students:** There are 55 international students enrolled. The school actively recruits these students. They must take the TOEFL with a minimum score of 79 on the Internet-based version (iBT).

ADMISSIONS: 44% of the current freshmen were in the top fifth of their class; 69% were in the top two fifths. 2 freshmen graduated first in their class. **Admissions Contact:** Michael Dziedziak, Executive Director of Enrollment Management. Email: *ugadm@eastern.edu* Web: *www.eastern.edu*

FINANCIAL AID: In 2016-2017, 86% of all full-time freshmen and 92% of continuing full-time students received some form of financial aid. 67% of all full-time freshmen and 78% of continuing full-time students received need-based aid. The average freshman award was $30,641. Need-based scholarships or need-based grants averaged $6,969 ($22,396 maximum); need-based self-help aid (loans and jobs) averaged $4,324 ($5,948 maximum); other non-need-based awards and non-need-based scholarships averaged $13,506 ($33,000 maximum); and $10,929 from other forms of aid. 63% of undergraduate students work part-time. Average annual earnings from campus work are $1200. The average financial indebtedness of the 2016 graduate was $32,284. Eastern is a member of CSS. The FAFSA code is 003259. Check with the school for current application deadlines.

EDINBORO UNIVERSITY *(The complete profile is made available exclusively on our website, www.barronspac.com)*

ELIZABETHTOWN COLLEGE D-3

www.etown.edu

Elizabethtown, PA 17022 **(717) 361-1400**

Fax: (717) 361-1365	**Email: admissions@etown.edu**
Full-time: 655 men, 1052 women	**Faculty:** 129; IIB, +$
Part-time: 18 men, 12 women	**Ph.D.s:** 94%
Graduate: 2 men, 45 women	**Student/Faculty:** 13 to 1
Year: semesters, summer session	**Tuition:** $43,490
Room & Board: $10,560	**Freshman Class:** n/av
SAT or ACT: required	**CEEB CODE:** 2225
Application Deadline: n/av	**COMPETITIVE**

Elizabethtown College is a community of learners which educates students intellectually, socially, aesthetically and ethically for lives of service and leadership as citizens of the world. We offer more than four dozen degrees in liberal arts, fine and performing arts, science and engineering, business, communications and education. Through personal attention, creative inspiration and academic challenge, Elizabethtown students are encouraged to expand their intellectual curiosity. Elizabethtown links classroom instruction with experiential learning through five Signature Learning Experiences (SLEs) including internships, community-based learning, cross-cultural experiences, supervised research and a capstone course/project/portfolio. During their time at Elizabethtown, each student is guaranteed the opportunity to experience at least two of five SLEs, which supplement classroom learning. When combined, SLEs prepare our students for lives of purpose and are hallmarks of the "Elizabethtown Experience." Embedded in an ever changing global context, Elizabethtown promotes the developmental, collaborative and complex nature of learning. In seeking to 'Educate for Service,' we believe students perform no greater service than when they share their knowledge and creativity with theirs. Challenged to take responsibility for their education, our students embark on a journey of self-transformation that involves intellectual, social and personal growth. Students are encouraged to develop and challenge their own values, while seeking to understand and appreciate alternative perspectives. The impact of an Elizabethtown College education is long lasting and far reaching. Students acquire new habits of mind and heart some in the course of the undergraduate experience, others as they grow beyond college. There are 2 undergraduate schools. In addition to regional accreditation, E-town has baccalaureate program accreditation with ABET, ACBSP, CSWE, NASM, ACOTE, ACS, and ACBSP. The 204-acre campus is in a small town in Lancaster County, PA. It is 10 minutes from Hershey and 25 minutes from Lancaster and Harrisburg. Including any residence halls, there are 54 buildings.

STUDENT LIFE: 64% of undergraduates are from Pennsylvania. Others are from 30 states, 26 foreign countries, and Canada. 84% are from public schools. 85% are White; 4% Hispanic; 3% African American; 3% Asian American; 3% Foreign; 2% two or more races. 34% are Protestant; 27% Catholic. **Female To Male Ratio:** 1.6:1. The average age of freshmen is 18; all undergraduates, 20. 13% do not continue beyond their first year; 74% remain to graduate. **Housing:** 1494 students can be accommodated in college housing, which includes coed dorms, on-campus apartments, off-campus apartments, honors houses, special-interest houses, substance free, and quiet study. On-campus housing is guaranteed for all 4 years. 85% of students live on campus; of those, 85% remain on campus on weekends. All students may keep cars.

FACULTY/CLASSROOMS: 48% of faculty are male; 52% are female. All teach and do research. No introductory courses are taught by graduate students. The average class size in an introductory lecture is 20 and in a laboratory is 19.

PROGRAMS OF STUDY: E-town confers B.A., B.S., B.S.W. and B.Mus. degrees. Master's degrees are also awarded. Bachelor's degrees are awarded in AGRICULTURE (forestry and related sciences), BIOLOGICAL SCIENCE (biochemistry, biology/adolescence education, biology/biological science, and biotechnology), BUSINESS (accounting, business administration and management, business economics, business systems analysis, international business management, and marketing management), COMMUNICATIONS AND THE ARTS (art history and appreciation, communications, dramatic arts, English, English literature, English Writing, fine arts, French, German, Japanese, modern language, music, performing arts, Spanish, and studio art), COMPUTER AND PHYSICAL SCIENCE (actuarial science, applied mathematics, chemistry, chemistry/adolescence education, computer science, earth science/adolescence education, information sciences and systems, mathematics, and physics), EDUCATION (art education, early childhood education, education, elementary education, English education, mathematics education, music education, science education, secondary education, social studies education, and social studies secondary school education), ENGINEERING AND ENVIRONMENTAL DESIGN (computer engineering, electrical/electronics engineering, engineering, environmental science, industrial engineering, mechanical engineering, and preengineering), HEALTH PROFESSIONS (music therapy, occupational therapy, predentistry, premedicine, and prephysical therapy), SOCIAL SCIENCE (criminal justice, economics, history, legal studies, philosophy, political science/government, psychology, public administration, religion, social work, and sociology). Business administration, occupational therapy, and biology have the largest enrollments.

ACTIVITIES: There are no fraternities or sororities. There are 84 groups on campus, including art, band, cheerleading, choir, chorale, chorus, computers, dance, drama, environmental, ethnic, forensics, honors, international, jazz band, LGBT, literary magazine, musical theater, newspaper, orchestra, photography, political, professional, radio and TV, religious, social, social service, student government, and yearbook. Popular campus events include Scholarship and Creative Arts Day, Martin Luther King Celebration Week, Hispanic Heritage Month, and Into the Streets. **Sports:** There are 11 intercollegiate sports for men and 11 for women, and 10 intramural sports for men and 10 for women. Facilities include a soccer stadium, gymnasium, pool, track and field complex, fitness center, racquetball, and tennis courts, sand volleyball courts and baseball, softball, lacrosse, and field hockey fields. **Graduates:** From July 1, 2015 to June 30, 2016, 409 bachelor's degrees were awarded. The most popular majors were business administration (16%), biology (11%), and health and occupational therapy (9%). 175 companies recruited on campus in 2015-2016. In an average class, 68% graduate in 4 years or less, 74% graduate in 5 years or less, and 74% graduate in 6 years or less. Of the 2015 graduating class, 25% were enrolled in graduate school within 6 months of graduation, and 60% were employed.

SERVICES: Counseling and information services are available, as is tutoring in most subjects. Workshops and individual help with study skills as well as assistive technology are also available. **Library/Resources:** The library contains 264,124 volumes, 24,304 microform items, and 9,104 audio/video tapes/CDs/DVDs, and subscribes to 50,588 periodicals including electronic. Computerized library services include interlibrary loans, database searching, Internet access, and Wi-Fi capability. Special learning facilities include an art gallery, radio station, TV station, the Young Center for Anabaptist and Pietist Studies, a nationally unique academic research facility, and mineral gallery. **Physically Challenged Students:** 75% of the campus is accessible. Facilities include wheelchair ramps, elevators, special parking, specially equipped restrooms, special class scheduling, lowered drinking fountains, lowered telephones, and special housing. **Special:** Students can participate in short-term, semester-long, and year-long study-abroad experiences in 26 different locations worldwide. Also available are work-study programs, internships, a Washington semester, and dual majors. There are two 5-year cooperative programs where the student will participate in two 7-month co-op rotations, one in engineering and one in business, a 3-3 allied health degree and a 3-3 physical therapy degree with Thomas Jefferson University and Widener University, a Premedical Primary Care Program with Penn State University College of Medicine, Biotechnology (B.S.) and Molecular Medicine (M.S.) with Drexel University College of Medicine, a 3-4 B.S. in biology/D.M.D. program with Temple University, a Cardiovascular Invasive Specialty program with Lancaster General College of Nursing and Health Sciences, a D.O program with Philadelphia College of Osteopathic Medicine, a 3-3 and 3-4 D.O. with Lake Erie College of Osteopathic Medicine, and a 3-3 and 3-4 Doctor of Pharmaceutical with Lake Erie College of Osteopathic Medicine. There are 20 national honor societies, a freshman honors program, and 19 departmental honors programs. **Visiting:** There are regularly scheduled orientations for prospective students, including 5 open houses and weekday appointments throughout the year. Special academic department days are also hosted. There are guides for informal visits, visitors may sit in on classes, and stay overnight. To schedule a visit, contact the Admissions Office. **Campus Safety and Security:** Measures include 24-hour foot and vehicle patrol, emergency notification system, self-defense education, and security escort services. There are shuttle buses, emergency telephones, lighted pathways/sidewalks, controlled access to dorms/residences, and a crime prevention program.

REQUIREMENTS: The SAT or ACT is required. Recommended composite scores for the SAT range from 1030 to 1230; for the ACT, 21 to 27. Applicants must be graduates of an accredited secondary school or have earned a GED. The college encourages completion of 18 academic credits, based on 4 years of English, 3 of math, 2 each of lab science, social studies, and consecutive foreign language, and 5 additional college preparatory units. An audition is required for music majors and an interview is required for occupational therapy majors. AP credits are accepted. Important factors in the admissions decision are advanced placement or honors courses, recommendations by school officials, and extracurricular activities record. The core curriculum includes a first-year seminar and courses in math, language, creative expression, western cultural heritage, non-western cultural heritage, the natural and social sciences, and humanities. Distribution requirements include 40 hours in 8 areas of understanding. Students must complete a minimum of 125 credit hours and maintain a GPA of 2.0 overall and in their major. Additional requirements are dependent on the enrolled major. **Procedure:** Freshmen are admitted to all sessions. Entrance exams should be taken in the spring of the junior year or fall of the senior year. There are deferred admissions and rolling admissions plans. Application deadlines are open. Application fee is $30. 51 applicants were on the 2016 waiting list; 2 were admitted. Application fees are waived if application is completed on-line. **Transfer Students:** 25 transfer students enrolled in 2015-2016. Applicants should present a minimum GPA of 3.0 in at least 15 credit hours earned from a community college, or 2.5 from a 4-year institution. 30 of 125 credits required for the bachelor's degree must be completed at E-town. **International Students:** There are 55 international students enrolled. The school actively recruits these students. They must take the TOEFL with a minimum score of 500 on the paper-based TOEFL (PBT) or 61 on the Internet-based version (iBT). They must also take the SAT or ACT.

ADMISSIONS: 55% of the current freshmen were in the top fifth of their class; 78% were in the top two fifths. There were 13 National Merit finalists. 8 freshmen graduated first in their class. **Admissions Contact:** George Walter, Interim Vice President for Enrollment. Email: *admissions@etown.edu* Web: *www.etown.edu*

FINANCIAL AID: In 2016-2017, 99% of all full-time freshmen and 98% of continuing full-time students received some form of financial aid. 79% of all full-time freshmen and 74% of continuing full-time students received need-based aid. The average freshman award was $32,839. Need-based scholarships or need-based grants averaged $29,302 ($37,093 maximum); and need-based self-help aid (loans and jobs) averaged $4,711 ($6,000 maximum). 58% of undergraduate students work part-time. Average annual earnings from campus work are $1428. E-town is a member of CSS. The college's own financial statement, and family federal tax returns are required. The FAFSA code is 003262. The deadline for filing freshman financial aid applications for fall entry is March 15.

ELIZABETHTOWN COLLEGE SCHOOL OF CONTINUING AND PROFESSIONAL STUDIES
www.etowndegrees.com

Elizabethtown, PA 17022 (717) 361-3750

Fax: (717) 361-1466
Email: randazzob@etown.edu
Full-time: n/av
Faculty: n/av
Part-time: 106 men, 240 women
Ph.D.s: n/av
Graduate: 33 men, 43 women
Student/Faculty: n/av
Year: other, summer session
Tuition: $18,900
Room & Board: n/app
Freshman Class: n/av
CEEB CODE: 2225
Application Deadline: n/av
COMPETITIVE

Elizabethtown College School of Continuing and Professional Studies, offers more than four dozen degrees in liberal arts, fine and performing arts, science and engineering, business,communications and education. Through personal attention, creative inspiration and academic challenge, Elizabethtown students are encouraged to expand their intellectual curiosity. They also are given an opportunity to be a bigger part of the world through experiential learning-collaborative research with caring faculty mentors, study-abroad and civic engagement opportunities, and internships. Figures in the above capsule and in this profile are approximate. There is 1 undergraduate school. The 201-acre campus is in a small town 10 minutes from Hershey and 25 minutes from Lancaster and Harrisburg. Including any residence halls, there are 52 buildings.

STUDENT LIFE: 98% of undergraduates are from Pennsylvania. Others are from 3 states, and 2 foreign countries. 9% are African American; 85% White; 5% Hispanic; 1% Asian American. **Female To Male Ratio:** 2.0:1. The average age of all undergraduates is 37. **Housing:** College-sponsored housing includes All students commute. All students may keep cars.

FACULTY/CLASSROOMS: 63% of faculty are male; 37% are female. All teach undergraduates. No introductory courses are taught by graduate students. The average class size in an introductory lecture is 20.

PROGRAMS OF STUDY: Elizabethtown College confers B.A., B.S. and B.P.S. degrees. Associate and master's degrees are also awarded. Bachelor's degrees are awarded in BUSINESS (accounting, business administration and management, human resources, and marketing/retailing/merchandising), COMMUNICATIONS AND THE ARTS (communications and information technology), SOCIAL SCIENCE (addiction studies, behavioral science, criminal justice, human services, public administration, and religion). Business administration, accounting, and human services have the largest enrollments.

ACTIVITIES: There are no fraternities or sororities. **Sports:** There is no sports program at Elizabethtown College. **Graduates:** From July 1, 2015 to June 30, 2016, 128 bachelor's degrees were awarded. The most popular majors were business administration (38%), accounting (17%), and corporate communications (12%).

SERVICES: **Library/Resources:** The library contains 262,101 volumes, 24,078 microform items, and 9,750 audio/video tapes/CDs/DVDs, and subscribes to 96,260 periodicals including electronic. Computerized library services include interlibrary loans, database searching, Internet access, and Wi-Fi capability. Special learning facilities include an art gallery, TV station, the Young Center for Anabaptist and Pietist Studies, a nationally unique academic research facility, and mineral gallery. **Physically Challenged Students:** 75% of the campus is accessible. Facilities include wheelchair ramps, elevators, special parking, specially equipped restrooms, special class scheduling, lowered drinking fountains, and lowered telephones. **Campus Safety and Security:** Measures include 24-hour foot and vehicle patrol, emergency notification system, self-defense education, and security escort services. There are shuttle buses, emergency telephones, lighted pathways/sidewalks, controlled access to dorms/residences, and crime prevention programs.

REQUIREMENTS: **Procedure:** Freshmen are admitted to all sessions. There is a rolling admissions plan. Application deadlines are open. Applications are accepted on-line. **Transfer Students:** 65 transfer students enrolled in 2015-2016.

Admissions Contact: Barbara Randazzo, Asst. Dean of Enrollment Management. Email: *randazzob@etown.edu* Web: *www.etowndegrees.com*

FINANCIAL AID: Check with the school for current application deadlines.

FRANKLIN AND MARSHALL COLLEGE E-3
www.fandm.edu

Lancaster, PA 17604 (717) 291-3953
(877) 678-9111

Fax: (717) 291-4389
Email: admission@fandm.edu
Full-time: 1046 men, 1179 women
Faculty: 234; IIB, +$
Part-time: 16 men, 14 women
Ph.D.s: 94%
Graduate: n/av
Student/Faculty: 9 to 1
Year: semesters, summer session
Tuition: $50,400
Room & Board: $12,770
Freshman Class: 7146 applied, 2305 accepted, 592 enrolled
SAT CR/M: required **ACT:** 30
CEEB CODE: 2261
Application Deadline: January 15
HIGHLY COMPETITIVE

Franklin and Marshall College, founded in 1787, is a private liberal arts institution. There is 1 undergraduate school. The 209-acre campus is in a suburban area 60 miles west of Philadelphia. Including any residence halls, there are 45 buildings.

STUDENT LIFE: 73% of undergraduates are from out of state, mostly the Middle Atlantic. Students are from 43 states, 54 foreign countries, and Canada. 62% are from public schools. 8% are Hispanic; 6% African American; 6% race unknown; 59% White; 5% Asian American; 2% two or more races; 14% Foreign. **Female To Male Ratio:** 1.1:1. The average age of freshmen is 18; all undergraduates, 20. 9% do not continue beyond their first year; 87% remain to graduate. **Housing:** 2367 students can be accommodated in college housing, which includes single-sex and coed dorms, on-campus apartments, and off-campus apartments. In addition, there are language houses, special-interest houses, an arts house, international living center, and a community outreach house. On-campus housing is guaranteed for all 4 years, and is available on a lottery system for upperclassmen. 99% of students live on campus. Upperclassmen may keep cars.

FACULTY/CLASSROOMS: 52% of faculty are male; 48% are female. All teach undergraduates and do research. No introductory courses are taught by graduate students. The average class size in an introductory lecture is 23; in a laboratory is 19; and in a regular course is 17.

PROGRAMS OF STUDY: F & M confers B.A. degrees. Bachelor's degrees are awarded in AGRICULTURE (environmental studies), BIOLOGICAL SCIENCE (biochemistry, biology/biological science, and neurosciences), BUSINESS (business administration and management), COMMUNICATIONS AND THE ARTS (art history and appreciation, classics, dramatic arts, English, fine arts, French, German, Greek, Latin, music, Spanish, and studio art), COMPUTER AND PHYSICAL SCIENCE (astronomy, astrophysics, chemistry, geology, mathematics, and physics), ENGINEERING AND ENVIRONMENTAL DESIGN (environmental science), SOCIAL SCIENCE (African studies, American studies, anthropology, economics, history, interdisciplinary studies, philosophy, political science/government, psychology, religion, and sociology). Chemistry, geosciences, and psychology are the strongest academically. Government, business, and organizations & society have the largest enrollments.

ACTIVITIES: 20% of men belong to 7 national fraternities; 30% of women belong to 3 national sororities. There are 120 groups on campus, including a student-run club/restaurant, art, band, Ben's underground, cheerleading, chess, choir, chorale, chorus, communications, computers, dance, debate, drama, environmental, ethnic, film, forensics, honors, international, jazz band, LGBT, literary magazine, musical theater, newspaper, opera, orchestra, photography, political, professional, radio and TV, religious, social, social service, student government, symphony, and yearbook. Popular campus events include Spring Arts Weekend. **Sports:** There are 13 intercollegiate sports for men and 13 for women, and 12 intramural sports for men and 12 for women. Facilities include a gym, squash courts, wrestling room, playing fields, all-weather track, wellness/aerobic center, strength training center, and tennis courts. A sports center features a fitness center, multipurpose courts, jogging tracks, and an Olympic-size pool. **Graduates:** From July 1, 2015 to June 30, 2016, 553 bachelor's degrees were awarded. The most popular majors were business, organizations, and society (12%), government (11%), and English(7%). In an average class, 81% graduate in 4 years or less, 86% graduate in 5 years or less, and 87% graduate in 6 years or less.

SERVICES: Counseling and information services are available, as is tutoring in every subject. **Library/Resources:** The 2 libraries contain

588,333 volumes, 22,924 microform items, and 8,722 audio/video tapes/CDs/DVDs, subscribe to 2,366 periodicals including electronic. Computerized library services include interlibrary loans, database searching, Internet access, and Wi-Fi capability. Special learning facilities include an art gallery, natural history museum, planetarium, radio station, academic technology services, writing center, and student newspaper. **Physically Challenged Students:** 80% of the campus is accessible. Facilities include wheelchair ramps, elevators, special parking, specially equipped restrooms, special class scheduling, lowered drinking fountains, lowered telephones, and special housing. **Special:** There is a 3-2 degree program in forestry and environmental studies with Duke University as well as 3-2 degree programs in engineering with the Pennsylvania State University College of Engineering, Columbia University, Rensselaer Polytechnic Institute, Case Western Reserve, and Washington University at St. Louis. Cross-registration is possible with the Lancaster Theological Seminary, the Central Pennsylvania Consortium, and Millersville University allows students to study at nearby Dickinson College or Gettysburg College. Students may also study architecture and urban planning at Columbia University, studio art at the School of Visual Arts in New York City, theater in Connecticut, oceanography in Massachusetts, and American studies at American University. There are study-abroad programs in England, France, Germany, Greece, Italy, Denmark, India, Japan, and other countries. There are internships for credit, joint majors, many minors, dual majors, student-designed majors, independent study, interdisciplinary studies, optional first-year seminars, collaborative projects, pass/fail options, and nondegree study. There are 12 national honor societies and a chapter of Phi Beta Kappa. **Visiting:** There are regularly scheduled orientations for prospective students, including a campus tour, an interview, and a class visit. There are guides for informal visits and visitors may sit in on classes. To schedule a visit, contact the Admission Office at admission@fandm.edu. **Campus Safety and Security:** Measures include 24-hour foot and vehicle patrol, emergency notification system, self-defense education, and security escort services. There are shuttle buses, emergency telephones, lighted pathways/sidewalks, controlled access to dorms/residences, regular fire safety drills are held in residence halls and academic buildings and residence hall access requires a fob.

REQUIREMENTS: Standardized tests are optional for students; if this option is selected, 2 recent graded writing samples are required. Applicants must be graduates of accredited secondary schools. Recommended college preparatory study includes 4 years each of English, and math, 3-4 of foreign language, 3 each of lab science and history/social studies, and 1-2 courses in art or music. All students must also submit their high school transcripts, recommendations from a teacher and a counselor, and a personal essay. An interview is recommended. AP and CLEP credits are accepted. Important factors in the admissions decision are advanced placement or honors courses, recommendations by school officials, and extracurricular activities record. General education requirements proceed from 2 connections courses and a distribution requirement to a major. Students must take at least 1 course in arts, humanities, social science, non-Western cultures, and 1 natural science (including a lab) and a second lab course or natural science in perspective course. 3 semesters of language study are required. The bachelor's degree requires completion of 32 courses, including a minimum of 8 in the major, with a minimum GPA of 2.0. **Procedure:** Freshmen are admitted fall and spring. Entrance exams should be taken by December of the senior year. There are early decision and deferred admissions plans. Early decision applications should be filed by November 15; regular applications, by January 15 for fall entry, along with a $60 fee. Notification of early decision is sent December 15; regular decision, April 1. 340 early decision candidates were accepted for the 2016-2017 class. 1944 applicants were on the 2016 waiting list; 59 were admitted. Applications are accepted online. **Transfer Students:** 21 transfer students enrolled in 2015-2016. An interview, SAT or ACT scores, college and secondary school transcripts, a dean's form, recommendations from 2 professors, and a letter explaining the reason for transfer are also required. 16 of 32 credits required for the bachelor's degree must be completed at F & M. **International Students:** There are 313 international students enrolled. The school actively recruits these students. They must take the TOEFL as well as the SAT or ACT.

ADMISSIONS: 32% of the 2016-2017 applicants were accepted. The SAT scores for the 2016-2017 freshman class were: Critical Reading-- 4% below 500, 29% between 500 and 599, 51% between 600 and 699, and 17% between 700 and 800. Math-- 11% between 500 and 599, 52% between 600 and 699, and 37% between 700 and 800. The ACT scores were 56% between 24 and 29, and 44% above 30. **Admissions Contact:** Eric Maguire, Vice President for Enrollment Management and Dean of Admissions. Email: *admission@fandm.edu* Web: *www.fandm.edu*

FINANCIAL AID: In 2016-2017, 51% of all full-time freshmen and 53% of continuing full-time students received some form of financial aid. 50% of all full-time freshmen and 51% of continuing full-time students received need-based aid. The average freshman award was $47,424. Need-based scholarships or need-based grants averaged $43,342; and need-based self-help aid (loans and jobs) averaged $4,564. The average financial indebtedness of the 2016 graduate was $26,162. F & M is a member of CSS. The CSS/Profile, the college's own financial statement, business/farm supplement, and noncustodial parents statement are required. The FAFSA code is 003265. The deadline for filing freshman financial aid applications for fall entry is February 15.

GANNON UNIVERSITY — B-1

www.gannon.edu

Erie, PA 16541	(814) 871-7408 (800) 426-6668 Email: admissions@gannon.edu
Full-time: 1108 men, 1373 women	**Faculty:** 200; IIA, -$
Part-time: 245 men, 372 women	**Ph.D.s:** 78%
Graduate: 608 men, 637 women	**Student/Faculty:** 12 to 1
Year: semesters, summer session	**Tuition:** $30,042
Room & Board: $11,990	**Freshman Class:** 4710 applied, 3662 accepted, 626 enrolled
SAT CR/M: 500/520 **ACT:** 23	**CEEB CODE:** 2270
Application Deadline: open	**COMPETITIVE**

Gannon University, is a Catholic, Diocesan university dedicated to excellence in teaching, scholarship and service. Our faculty and staff prepare students to be global citizens through programs grounded in the liberal arts and sciences and professional specializations. Inspired by the Catholic Intellectual Tradition, we offer a comprehensive, values-centered learning experience that emphasizes faith, leadership, inclusiveness and social responsibility. There are 3 undergraduate schools and 1 graduate school. In addition to regional accreditation, Gannon has baccalaureate program accreditation with ABET, ACBSP, APTA, CSWE, ACOTE, ARC-PA, CoARC, CAAHEP, CCNE, PDE, FLDOE, and JRCERT. The 52-acre campus is in an urban area downtown Erie, Pennsylvania, 128 miles north of Pittsburgh, 99 miles east of Cleveland, and 106 miles southwest of Buffalo. Including any residence halls, there are 52 buildings.

STUDENT LIFE: 70% of undergraduates are from Pennsylvania. Others are from 30 states, 39 foreign countries, and Canada. 8% are Foreign; 74% White; 6% race unknown; 4% African American; 3% Hispanic; 2% Asian American; 2% two or more races. 48% claim no religious affiliation; 32% Catholic; 12% Protestant. **Female To Male Ratio:** 1.2:1. The average age of freshmen is 18; all undergraduates, 20. 22% do not continue beyond their first year; 78% remain to graduate. **Housing:** 1433 students can be accommodated in college housing, which includes coed dorms, on-campus apartments, off-campus apartments, honors houses, special-interest houses, fraternity houses, and sorority houses. On-campus housing is guaranteed for the freshman year only. Priority is given to out-of-town students. 63% of students commute. Upperclassmen may keep cars.

FACULTY/CLASSROOMS: 53% of faculty are male; 47% are female. 76% teach undergraduates. Graduate students teach 1% of introductory courses. The average class size in an introductory lecture is 21 and in a laboratory is 20.

PROGRAMS OF STUDY: Gannon confers B.A., B.S., B.S.E., B.S.M., B.S.B.A., and B.S.N. degrees. Associate, master's, and doctoral degrees are also awarded. Bachelor's degrees are awarded in BIOLOGICAL SCIENCE (bioinformatics, biology/adolescence education, biology/biological science, and nutrition), BUSINESS (accounting, banking and finance, business administration and management, entrepreneurial studies, funeral home services, insurance and risk management, international business management, management science, marketing/retailing/merchandising, sports management, and supply chain management), COMMUNICATIONS AND THE ARTS (advertising, communications, dramatic arts, English, foreign language, and journalism), COMPUTER AND PHYSICAL SCIENCE (chemistry, computer science, information sciences and systems, mathematics, science, and software engineering), EDUCATION (early childhood education, English education, health information management, mathematics education, middle school education, social studies education, and special education), ENGINEERING AND ENVIRONMENTAL DESIGN (biomedical engineering, chemical engineering, computer engineering, electrical/electronics engineering, environmental engineering, environmental science, and mechanical engineering), HEALTH PROFESSIONS (health science, kinesiology, medical technology, nursing, nutrition and wellness, occupational therapy, physical therapy, physician's assistant, predentistry, premedicine, preoptometry, prepodiatry, preveterinary science, and respiratory therapy), SOCIAL SCIENCE (criminal justice, forensic studies, history, interdisciplinary studies, international studies, philosophy, political science/government, psychology, social work, and theological studies). Health professions is the strongest academically. Nursing, physician's assistant, and biology have the largest enrollments.

ACTIVITIES: 15% of men belong to 7 national fraternities; 12% of women belong to 5 national sororities. There are 91 groups on campus, including Phi Eta Sigma, and Lambda Sigma, sports clubs, fraternities and sororities, Relay for Life, activities programming board, art, band, cheerleading, choir, chorus, computers, dance, drama, environmental, ethnic, honors, international, literary magazine, newspaper, pep band, professional, radio and TV, religious, social, social service, and student government. Popular campus events include Family Weekend, GIVE Day, Home Coming Weekend, Day of Caring, Springtopia, Hunger and Homelessness Week, Take Back the Night, and Greek Week, Relay for Life, Dance Marathon, and Preview GU. **Sports:** There are 9 intercollegiate sports for men and 11 for women, and 26 intramural sports for men and 26 for women. Facilities include a multi-purpose athletic field, varsity basketball and volleyball, recreation and wellness center, swimming pool, an indoor turf field, basketball courts, racquetball courts, indoor running track, human performance laboratory, and weight machines and cardio equipment. **Graduates:** From July 1, 2015 to June 30, 2016, 563 bachelor's degrees were awarded. The most popular majors were health sciences (15%), nursing (13%), and sports and exercise science (10%). 8 companies recruited on campus in 2015-2016. In an average class, 47% graduate in 4 years or less, 62% graduate in 5 years or less, and 64% graduate in 6 years or less.

SERVICES: Counseling and information services are available, as is tutoring in most subjects. There is a reader service for the blind, and remedial math, reading, and writing. A STEM Center, Writing and Research Center, Speech Communication Center, and Academic Advising Center are also available. **Library/Resources:** The library contains 220,582 volumes, 79 microform items, and 4,165 audio/video tapes/CDs/DVDs, and subscribes to 53,030 periodicals including electronic. Computerized library services include interlibrary loans, database searching, Internet access, and Wi-Fi capability. Special learning facilities include an art gallery, radio station, an environaut research vessel, patient simulation center, human performance center, and archaeology museum. **Physically Challenged Students:** 70% of the campus is accessible. Facilities include wheelchair ramps, elevators, special parking, specially equipped restrooms, special class scheduling, lowered drinking fountains, and special housing. **Special:** The university offers co-op programs, dual majors, summer internships, pass/fail options, work-study programs, a general studies program, pre-med programs in medicine, optometry, podiatry, veterinary, and pharmacy. Gannon University also has various affiliations with other colleges and universities such as Charleston School of Pharmacy, LECOM, PCOM, PCO, Ross University School of Medicine, and Duquesne with their law school. In addition, our institution also offers study abroad including semester exchange, summer programs, and short-term faculty led courses in over 18 countries. Gannon provides students with numerous service and experiential learning opportunities. There are 15 national honor societies, a freshman honors program, and 11 departmental honors programs. **Visiting:** There are regularly scheduled orientations for prospective students, consisting of open houses in the fall and spring. Students may talk with faculty, tour the campus, meet with financial aid advisors, and sit in on a variety of presentations. There are guides for informal visits and visitors may stay overnight. To schedule a visit, contact Kristin Manczka at (814) 871-7407. **Campus Safety and Security:** Measures include 24-hour foot and vehicle patrol, emergency notification system, and security escort services. There are shuttle buses, emergency telephones, lighted pathways/sidewalks, controlled access to dorms/residences, security cameras in buildings and outside of campus facilities, card access systems to all residential halls, fire alarm systems in all buildings, fire suppression systems in all residential halls, and card access in educational buildings for after hour access.

REQUIREMENTS: The SAT or ACT is required. Candidates should have completed 16 academic units including 4 in English and 12 in social sciences, foreign languages, math, and science, depending on the degree sought. Specific courses in math and science are required for some majors in health sciences and engineering. Essays are required for some programs and encouraged for the general population. The same is true for letters of recommendation. Credits may be earned for those that complete AP exams and IB exams. Gannon accepts the GED in replacement of a high school diploma with appropriate scores earned overall and in each subject matter. AP and CLEP credits are accepted. Important factors in the admissions decision are advanced placement or honors courses, leadership record, recommendations by school officials, parents or siblings attended your school, personality/intangible qualities, and extracurricular activities record. Students must complete at least 128 hours of academic work. Each academic program has specific course requirements. Students must have a cumulative GPA of at least 2.0 overall and in the area of concentration. **Procedure:** Freshmen are admitted in the fall, spring, and summer. Entrance exams should be taken at the end of the junior year or the beginning of the senior year. There are deferred admissions and rolling admissions plans. Application deadlines are open. Application fee is $25. Notification is sent on a rolling basis. 303 applicants were on the 2016 waiting list; 40 were admitted. Application fees are waived if application is completed online. **Transfer Students:** 104 transfer students enrolled in 2015-2016. Transfer students should be in good standing at their previous institution with at least a 2.0 GPA. They must submit a clearance from the college most recently attended as well as transcripts from all institutions. A high school transcript is required from transfer students with fewer than 30 credits, or for those pursuing a health related field. Some health profession programs offer limited seating. 40 of 128 credits required for the bachelor's degree must be completed at Gannon. **International Students:** There are 237 international students enrolled. The school actively recruits these students. They must take the TOEFL with a minimum score of 550 on the paper-based TOEFL (PBT) or 79 on the Internet-based version (iBT).

ADMISSIONS: 78% of the 2016-2017 applicants were accepted. The SAT scores for the 2016-2017 freshman class were: Critical Reading-- 44% below 500, 42% between 500 and 599, 12% between 600 and 699, and 2% between 700 and 800. Math-- 37% below 500, 46% between 500 and 599, 16% between 600 and 699, and 1% between 700 and 800. The ACT scores were 9% between 12 and 17, 44% between 18 and 23, 42% between 24 and 29, and 5% above 30. 40% of the current freshmen were in the top fifth of their class; 74% were in the top two fifths. 10 freshmen graduated first in their class. **Admissions Contact:** Patricia Maughn, Coordinator, Admissions Inquiries. Email: *admissions@gannon.edu* Web: *www.gannon.edu*

FINANCIAL AID: In 2016-2017, 99% of all full-time freshmen and 98% of continuing full-time students received some form of financial aid. 82% of all full-time freshmen and 76% of continuing full-time students received need-based aid. The average freshman award was $25,699. Need-based scholarships or need-based grants averaged $22,430; need-based self-help aid (loans and jobs) averaged $3,934; non-need-based athletic scholarships averaged $10,423; and other non-need-based awards and non-need-based scholarships averaged $16,559. 27% of undergraduate students work part-time. Average annual earnings from campus work are $1582. The average financial indebtedness of the 2016 graduate was $27,092. Gannon is a member of CSS. The FAFSA code is 003266. The priority date for freshman financial aid applications for fall entry is March 15.

GENEVA COLLEGE — A-3

www.geneva.edu

Beaver Falls, PA 15010	(724) 847-6500 (800) 847-8255
Fax: (724) 847-6776	**Email:** admissions@geneva.edu
Full-time: 650 men, 653 women	**Faculty:** 65; IIB, --$
Part-time: 67 men, 88 women	**Ph.D.s:** 78%
Graduate: 66 men, 139 women	**Student/Faculty:** 13 to 1
Year: semesters, summer session	**Tuition:** $25,680
Room & Board: $9770	**Freshman Class:** 1587 applied, 1120 accepted, 289 enrolled
SAT CR/M/W: 530/540/500 **ACT:** 25	**CEEB CODE:** 2273
Application Deadline: open	**COMPETITIVE**

Geneva College, founded in 1848, is a private institution affiliated with the Reformed Presbyterian Church of North America. The college offers undergraduate programs in the arts and sciences, business, education, health science, biblical and religious studies, engineering, and preprofessional training. In addition to the above figures, there are 440 nontraditional undergraduates. There is 1 undergraduate school. In addition to regional accreditation, Geneva has baccalaureate program accreditation with ABET and ACBSP. The 50-acre campus is in a small town 35 miles northwest of Pittsburgh. Including any residence halls, there are 30 buildings.

STUDENT LIFE: 75% of undergraduates are from Pennsylvania. Others are from 36 states, 11 foreign countries, and Canada. 87% are from public schools. 9% are African American; 82% White; 3% two or more races; 3% race unknown; 2% Hispanic; 1% Asian American; 1% Foreign. 79% are Protestant; 13% and unknown denomination. **Female To Male Ratio:** 1.1:1. The average age of freshmen is 18; all undergraduates, 23. 19% do not continue beyond their first year; 57% remain to graduate. **Housing:** 942 students can be accommodated in college housing, which includes single-sex dorms, on-campus apartments, and off-campus apartments. A Discipleship house is available for those interested in structural growth opportunities. On-campus housing is guaranteed for all 4 years. 60% of students live on campus; of those, 70% remain on campus on weekends. Alcohol is not permitted. All students may keep cars.

FACULTY/CLASSROOMS: 64% of faculty are male; 36% are female. 76% teach undergraduates. No introductory courses are taught by graduate students. The average class size in an introductory lecture is 128; in a laboratory is 14; and in a regular course is 20.

PROGRAMS OF STUDY: Geneva confers B.A., B.S., B.S.B.A., B.S.E., B.S.Ed. and B.P.S. degrees. Associate and master's degrees are also awarded. Bachelor's degrees are awarded in BIOLOGICAL SCIENCE (biology/biological science), BUSINESS (accounting and business administration and management), COMMUNICATIONS AND THE ARTS (applied music, broadcasting, communications, creative writing, English, languages, music, music business management, Spanish, and speech/debate/rhetoric), COMPUTER AND PHYSICAL SCIENCE (applied mathematics, chemistry, computer science, and physics), EDUCATION (early childhood education, education, elementary education, mathematics education, and music education), ENGINEERING AND ENVIRONMENTAL DESIGN (aviation administration/management, chemical engineering, and engineering), HEALTH PROFESSIONS (speech pathology/audiology), SOCIAL SCIENCE (biblical studies, counseling/psychology, history, human services, interdisciplinary studies, ministries, philosophy, political science/government, psychology, and sociology). Engineering, business administration, and education are the strongest academically. Engineering, business, and elementary education have the largest enrollments.

ACTIVITIES: There are no fraternities or sororities. There are 50 groups on campus, including band, cheerleading, chess, choir, chorale, chorus, computers, drama, ethnic, forensics, honors, international, literary magazine, marching band, newspaper, photography, political, professional, radio club, religious, social, social service, student government, and yearbook. Popular campus events include International Day, Fall Fest, The Big Event, and Homecoming. **Sports:** There are 7 intercollegiate sports for men and 7 for women, and 6 intramural sports for men and 5 for women. Facilities include a seat stadium, a field house, gym, practice gym, track, athletic fields, racquetball, and tennis courts, weight training rooms, and soccer/track complex. **Graduates:** From July 1, 2015 to June 30, 2016, 407 bachelor's degrees were awarded. The most popular majors were engineering, general (14%), human services, general (11%), business administration and management, and general (10%). In an average class, 39% graduate in 3 years or less, 50% graduate in 4 years or less, 52% graduate in 5 years or less, and 52% graduate in 6 years or less.

SERVICES: Counseling and information services are available, as is tutoring in most subjects. There is remedial math, reading, and writing. **Library/Resources:** The library contains 167,206 volumes, 198,624 microform items, 12,901 audio/video tapes/CDs/DVDs, and subscribes to 879 periodicals including electronic. Computerized library services include interlibrary loans, database searching, and Internet access. Special learning facilities include a TV station, an observatory. **Physically Challenged Students:** 90% of the campus is accessible. Facilities include wheelchair ramps, elevators, special parking, specially equipped restrooms, special class scheduling, lowered drinking fountains, and lowered telephones. **Special:** Cross-registration is offered in conjunction with Pennsylvania State University/Beaver Campus and Community College of Beaver County. There are accelerated degree programs in human resources and community ministry. Off-campus study includes programs at the Philadelphia Center for Urban Theological Studies, a Washington semester, a summer program at AuSable, Institute of Environmental Studies in Michigan, art studies in Pittsburgh, CCCU music program in Martha's Vineyard, film studies in Los Angeles, and study abroad in Costa Rica, Egypt, China, England, Russia, and Israel. Geneva also offers internships, independent study, and credit by proficiency exam. Nondegree study is available through adult education programs. There are 7 national honor societies, a freshman honors program, and 1 departmental honors program. **Visiting:** There are regularly scheduled orientations for prospective students, including class visits, a campus tour, meetings with faculty, admissions, and financial aid counselors, and meetings with coaches. There are guides for informal visits, visitors may sit in on classes, and stay overnight. To schedule a visit, contact Campus Visit Coordinator. **Campus Safety and Security:** Measures include 24-hour foot and vehicle patrol and security escort services. There are emergency telephones, lighted pathways/sidewalks, and off-duty city policemen on campus daily.

REQUIREMENTS: The SAT or ACT is required. Applicants must be graduates of an accredited secondary school or have earned a GED. Geneva requires 16 academic units, based on 4 each of English and electives, 3 of social studies, 2 each of math and foreign language, and 1 of science. An essay is required and an interview is recommended. A GPA of 2.5 is required. AP and CLEP credits are accepted. Important factors in the admissions decision are recommendations by school officials, advanced placement or honors courses, and leadership record. The core curriculum includes 12 hours of humanities, 9 each of biblical studies and social science, 8 to 10 of natural science, 6 of communications, 2 of phys ed, and the 1-hour Freshman Experience course. Students must also fulfill a chapel requirement per semester. To graduate, students must complete 120 to 138 semester hours, including those required for a major, with a minimum GPA of 2.0 in the major. **Procedure:** Freshmen are admitted to all sessions. Entrance exams should be taken during the junior or senior year. There are deferred admissions and rolling admissions plans. Application deadlines are open. Application fee is $25. Notification is sent on a rolling basis. Applications are accepted on-line. **Transfer Students:** 52 transfer students enrolled in 2015-2016. Applicants must have a GPA of 2.0 from college, and complete 48 semester hours at Geneva, including 15 in a chosen major, have a high school diploma or GED, and take the SAT I/ACT if less than 3 years out of high school. Letters of recommendation are required. 48 of 120 credits required for the bachelor's degree must be completed at Geneva. **International Students:** There are 21 international students enrolled. The school actively recruits these students. They must take the TOEFL with a minimum score of 550 on the paper-based TOEFL (PBT) or 80 on the Internet-based version (iBT) and the college's own test. They must also take the SAT or ACT.

ADMISSIONS: 71% of the 2016-2017 applicants were accepted. The SAT scores for the 2016-2017 freshman class were: Critical Reading-- 32% below 500, 43% between 500 and 599, 21% between 600 and 699, and 4% between 700 and 800. Math-- 36% below 500, 34% between 500 and 599, 24% between 600 and 699, and 6% between 700 and 800. Writing-- 47% below 500, 34% between 500 and 599, 15% between 600 and 699, and 3% between 700 and 800. The ACT scores were 9% between 12 and 17, 34% between 18 and 23, 41% between 24 and 29, and 16% above 30. 3 freshmen graduated first in their class. **Admissions Contact:** Roger Blevins, Assistant Director of Admissions. Email: *admissions@geneva.edu* Web: *www.geneva.edu*

FINANCIAL AID: In 2016-2017, 93% of all full-time freshmen and 96% of continuing full-time students received some form of financial aid. 80% of all full-time freshmen and 84% of continuing full-time students received need-based aid. The average freshman award was $21,573. Need-based scholarships or need-based grants averaged $16,892 ($25,680 maximum); need-based self-help aid (loans and jobs) averaged $5,593 ($7,500 maximum); and other non-need-based awards and non-need-based scholarships averaged $11,299 ($15,000 maximum). 68% of undergraduate students work part-time. Average annual earnings from campus work are $2000. The average financial indebtedness of the 2016 graduate was $32,900. Geneva is a member of CSS. The state aid form is required. The FAFSA code is 003267. The priority date for freshman financial aid applications for fall entry is March 15. The filing deadline for fall entry is April 15.

GETTYSBURG COLLEGE D-4
www.gettysburg.edu

Gettysburg, PA 17325 (717) 337-6100
(800) 431-0803
Fax: (717) 337-6145 Email: admiss@gettysburg.edu

Full-time: 1112 men, 1259 women	**Faculty:** 223; IIB, +$
Part-time: 5 men, 8 women	**Ph.D.s:** 96%
Graduate: n/av	**Student/Faculty:** 10 to 1
Year: semesters	**Tuition:** $50,860
Room & Board: $12,140	**Freshman Class:** 6386 applied, 2540 accepted, 699 enrolled
ACT: required	**CEEB CODE:** 2275
Application Deadline: January 15	**HIGHLY COMPETITIVE**

Gettysburg College, founded in 1832. The college offers programs in the liberal arts, and sciences. There is 1 undergraduate school. The 200-acre campus is in a suburban area 30 miles south of Harrisburg, 55 miles from Baltimore, MD, and 80 miles from Washington, D.C. Including any residence halls, there are 81 buildings.

STUDENT LIFE: 75% of undergraduates are from out of state, mostly the Middle Atlantic. Students are from 32 states, 36 foreign countries, and Canada. 65% are from public schools. 76% are White; 6% Hispanic; 6% Foreign; 3% African American; 3% two or more races; 2% Asian American; 2% race unknown. 32% are Catholic. **Female To Male Ratio:** 1.1:1. The average age of freshmen is 18; all undergraduates, 20. 10% do not continue beyond their first year; 86% remain to graduate. **Housing:** 2389 students can be accommodated in college housing, which includes single-sex and coed dorms, on-campus apartments, and off-campus apartments. In addition, there are honors houses, language houses, special-interest houses, fraternity houses, and theme housing. On-campus housing is guaranteed for all 4 years and is available on a lottery system for upperclassmen. Upperclassmen may keep cars.

FACULTY/CLASSROOMS: 59% of faculty are male; 41% are female. All teach undergraduates, and do research. No introductory courses are taught by graduate students. The average class size in an introductory lecture is 19; in a laboratory is 15; and in a regular course is 18.

PROGRAMS OF STUDY: Gettysburg confers B.A., B.S. and B.M.(Performance and Music) degrees. Bachelor's degrees are awarded in BIOLOGICAL SCIENCE (biochemistry and biology/biological science), BUSINESS (business administration and management), COMMUNICATIONS AND THE ARTS (art history and appreciation, classics, dramatic arts, English, French, German, Greek, Latin, music, Spanish, and studio art), COMPUTER AND PHYSICAL SCIENCE (chemistry, computer science, mathematics, mathematics – economics, and physics), EDUCATION (elementary education, foreign languages education, music education, science education, and secondary education), ENGINEERING AND ENVIRONMENTAL DESIGN (environmental science), HEALTH PROFESSIONS (health science, predentistry, and premedicine), SOCIAL SCIENCE (anthropology, Caribbean studies, economics, gender studies, history, international relations, Islamic studies, Japanese studies, Judaic studies, Latin American studies, Middle Eastern studies, philosophy, political science/government, prelaw, psychology, religion, sociology, and women's studies). Sciences, psychology, and history are the strongest academically. Management, political science, and psychology have the largest enrollments.

ACTIVITIES: 31% of men belong to 9 national fraternities; 33% of women belong to 7 national sororities. There are 120 groups on campus, including art, band, cheerleading, choir, chorale, chorus, communications, computers, dance, drama, environmental, ethnic, film, honors, international, jazz band, LGBT, literary magazine, marching band, musical theater, newspaper, opera, orchestra, outdoor recreation program, pep band, photography, political, professional, radio and TV, religious, social, social service, student government, symphony, and yearbook. Popular campus events include Thanksgiving Dinner, Oceanfest, Snowball, and Springfest. **Sports:** There are 11 intercollegiate sports for men and 11 for women, and 10 intramural sports for men and 10 for women. Facilities include John F. Jaeger Center for Athletics, recreation, and fitness, a natatorium, rock walls, basketball courts, indoor and outdoor tennis courts, several tracks and fields, 2 outdoor turf fields, a field house, and athletic training. **Graduates:** From July 1, 2015 to June 30, 2016, 756 bachelor's degrees were awarded. The most popular majors were English (8%), psychology (8%), and political science (7%). 160 companies recruited on campus in 2015-2016. In an average class, 80% graduate in 4 years or less, 84% graduate in 5 years or less, and 87% graduate in 6 years or less. Of the 2015 graduating class, 20% were enrolled in graduate school within 6 months of graduation, and 78% were employed.

SERVICES: Counseling and information services are available, as is tutoring in most subjects. **Library/Resources:** The library contains 412,379 volumes, 71,368 microform items, 69,530 audio/video tapes/CDs/DVDs, and subscribes to 61,435 periodicals including electronic. Computerized library services include interlibrary loans, database searching, Internet access, and Wi-Fi capability. Special learning facilities include an art gallery, planetarium, radio station, TV station, electron microscopes, spectrometers, an optics lab, plasma physics lab, greenhouse, observatory, child study lab, fine and performing arts facilities, and a state-of-the-art athletic facility. **Physically Challenged Students:** 90% of the campus is accessible. Facilities include wheelchair ramps, elevators, special parking, specially equipped restrooms, special class scheduling, lowered drinking fountains, and special housing. **Special:** The college offers an extensive global education (study abroad) program and has special centers worldwide. There are summer internships and a Washington semester with American University. Cross-registration is possible with members of the Central Pennsylvania Consortium. There is a United Nations semester at Drew University, and a 3-2 engineering program with Columbia University, Rensselaer Polytechnic, and Washington University in St. Louis. There are also joint programs in optometry with the Pennsylvania College of Optometry, and forestry and environmental studies with Duke University. The college offers double majors, student-designed majors, and B.A.-B.S. degrees in biology, chemistry, physics, biochemistry, and molecular biology, environmental studies and health and exercise sciences. Education certification is also available. There are 29 national honor societies and a chapter of Phi Beta Kappa. **Visiting:** There are regularly scheduled orientations for prospective students, including interviews, tours, day visits, open houses, and group information sessions. There are guides for informal visits and visitors may sit in on classes. To schedule a visit, contact The Admissions Office at (717) 337-6100. **Campus Safety and Security:** Measures include 24-hour foot and vehicle patrol, emergency notification system, self-defense education, and security escort services. There are emergency telephones, lighted pathways/sidewalks, and controlled access to dorms/residences.

REQUIREMENTS: The ACT is required. An essay is required. Students planning to major in music must audition and art students can submit a portfolio. An interview and SAT Subject tests are recommended. AP credits are accepted. Important factors in the admissions decision are evidence of special talent, recommendations by school officials, and advanced placement or honors courses. All students must complete 32 courses including a concentration in a major field of study culminating with a capstone experience; 1 course each in the arts, humanities, social sciences, quantitative reasoning, diversity: non-western culture; first-year writing; 2 courses in natural sciences and in a foreign language. The minimum GPA is 2.0. **Procedure:** Freshmen are admitted in the fall and spring. Entrance exams should be taken by the January testing date of the senior year. There are early decision and deferred admissions plans. Early decision applications should be filed by November 15; regular applications, by January 15 for fall entry, along with a $60 fee. Notification of early decision is sent December 15; regular decision, April 1. 301 early decision candidates were accepted for the 2016-2017 class. 768 applicants were on the 2016 waiting list. Applications are accepted on-line. **Transfer Students:** 17 transfer students enrolled in 2015-2016. Transfer applicants must have a GPA of at least 2.5. An interview is recommended. The high school record, test scores, college official's report and transcript from college(s) attended are also required. 16 of 32 credits required for the bachelor's degree must be completed at Gettysburg. **International Students:** There are 164 international students enrolled. The school actively recruits these students. They must take the TOEFL. They must also take the SAT or ACT.

ADMISSIONS: 40% of the 2016-2017 applicants were accepted. The SAT scores for the 2016-2017 freshman class were: Critical Reading-- 25% between 500 and 599, 59% between 600 and 699, and 16% between 700 and 800. Math-- 19% between 500 and 599, 64% between 600 and 699, and 17% between 700 and 800. 82% of the current freshmen were in the top fifth of their class; 98% were in the top two fifths. **Admissions Contact:** Gail Sweezey, Director of Admissions. Email: *admiss@gettysburg.edu* Web: *www.gettysburg.edu*

FINANCIAL AID: In 2016-2017, 53% of all full-time freshmen and 60%

of continuing full-time students received some form of financial aid. 52% of all full-time freshmen and 59% of continuing full-time students received need-based aid. The average freshman award was $38,146. 46% of undergraduate students work part-time. Average annual earnings from campus work are $1500. The average financial indebtedness of the 2016 graduate was $30,544. Gettysburg is a member of CSS. The CSS/Profile is required. The deadline for filing freshman financial aid applications for fall entry is February 1.

GROVE CITY COLLEGE — B-2

www.gcc.edu

Grove City, PA 16127 (724) 458-2100

Fax: (724) 458-3395	**Email:** admissions@gcc.edu
Full-time: 1172 men, 1162 women	**Faculty:** 153
Part-time: 32 men, 26 women	**Ph.D.s:** 84%
Graduate: n/av	**Student/Faculty:** 15 to 1
Year: semesters, summer session	**Tuition:** $16,630
Room & Board: $9062	**Freshman Class:** 1517 applied, 1251 accepted, 583 enrolled
SAT CR/M: 595/590 **ACT:** 26	**CEEB CODE:** 2277
Application Deadline: February 1	**VERY COMPETITIVE**

Grove City College, founded in 1876, is a private, liberal arts and science Christian college. Everything we do is founded on three essential pillars: A rich academic tradition, an amazing value and a Christ-centered community. There are 2 undergraduate schools. In addition to regional accreditation, Grove City has baccalaureate program accreditation with ABET, ACBSP, CAAHEP, and ACS. The 180-acre campus is in a small town 60 miles north of Pittsburgh, PA. Including any residence halls, there are 30 buildings.

STUDENT LIFE: 54% of undergraduates are from Pennsylvania. Others are from 45 states, and 13 foreign countries. 60% are from public schools. 92% are White; 3% two or more races; 2% Asian American; 2% Hispanic; 1% Foreign. 67% claim no religious affiliation; 25% Protestant. **Male To Female Ratio:** 1.0:1. The average age of freshmen is 18; all undergraduates, 20. 6% do not continue beyond their first year; 83% remain to graduate. **Housing:** 2333 students can be accommodated in college housing, which includes single-sex dorms and on-campus apartments. On-campus housing is guaranteed for all 4 years and is available on a lottery system for upperclassmen. 96% of students live on campus; of those, 85% remain on campus on weekends. Alcohol is not permitted. Upperclassmen may keep cars.

FACULTY/CLASSROOMS: 61% of faculty are male; 39% are female. All teach undergraduates, 30% do research, and 30% do both. No introductory courses are taught by graduate students. The average class size in an introductory lecture is 21; in a laboratory is 21; and in a regular course is 22.

PROGRAMS OF STUDY: Grove City confers B.A., B.S., B.Mus., B.S.E.E., and B.S.M.E. degrees. Bachelor's degrees are awarded in BIOLOGICAL SCIENCE (biochemistry, biology/biological science, biology/gen science secondary education, and molecular biology), BUSINESS (accounting, business administration and management, business economics, entrepreneurial studies, finance, international business, and marketing management), COMMUNICATIONS AND THE ARTS (communication studies, English, French, music, music business management, music performance, and Spanish), COMPUTER AND PHYSICAL SCIENCE (chemistry, chemistry/gen science second education, chemistry secondary education, computer information systems, computer science, mathematics, physics/gen science secondary education, physics secondary education, physics/computer, and physics), EDUCATION (early childhood education, English secondary education, English comm secondary education, French studies K-12 education, mathematics education, middle school education, music education, social studies secondary school education, Spanish education K-12, and special education), ENGINEERING AND ENVIRONMENTAL DESIGN (electrical and computer engineering, industrial administration/management, and mechanical engineering), HEALTH PROFESSIONS (exercise science and health science), SOCIAL SCIENCE (biblical studies, economics, history, philosophy, political science/government, psychology, religious music, and sociology). Engineering, computer science, and biology are the strongest academically. Mechanical engineering, biology, and communication studies have the largest enrollments.

ACTIVITIES: 17% of men belong to 10 local fraternities; 21% of women belong to 8 local sororities. There are 230 groups on campus, including art, band, cheerleading, chess, choir, chorale, chorus, communications, computers, dance, debate, drama, drill team, environmental, ethnic, film, forensics, honors, international, jazz band, literary magazine, marching band, musical theater, newspaper, opera, orchestra, pep band, photography, political, professional, radio and TV, religious, social, social service, student government, symphony, and yearbook. Popular campus events include Family Weekend, Christmas Candlelight Service, Homecoming, and President's Gala. **Sports:** There are 10 intercollegiate sports for men and 11 for women, and 10 intramural sports for men and 10 for women. Facilities include a field house, indoor pools, running track, basketball courts, volleyball, tennis racquetball, a bowling alley, 2 fitness rooms, tennis courts, and a turf football stadium with an all-weather track, baseball, soccer, and softball fields, and 3 intramural fields. **Graduates:** From July 1, 2015 to June 30, 2016, 585 bachelor's degrees were awarded. The most popular majors were biology (8%), mechanical engineering (7%), and communication studies (6%). 344 companies recruited on campus in 2015-2016. In an average class, 1% graduate in 3 years or less, 77% graduate in 4 years or less, 82% graduate in 5 years or less, and 83% graduate in 6 years or less. Of the 2015 graduating class, 13% were enrolled in graduate school within 6 months of graduation.

SERVICES: Counseling and information services are available, as is tutoring in most subjects. A student peer tutoring program is available for a small fee. EduWizards online tutoring is available at no cost to students for a select group of math and science courses. **Library/Resources:** The library contains 164,800 volumes, 4,000 microform items, 3,850 audio/video tapes/CDs/DVDs, and subscribes to 124,800 periodicals including electronic. Computerized library services include interlibrary loans, database searching, Internet access, and Wi-Fi capability. Special learning facilities include an art gallery, radio station, TV station, and research grade observatory. **Physically Challenged Students:** 10% of the campus is accessible. Facilities include wheelchair ramps, elevators, special parking, specially equipped restrooms, special class scheduling, lowered drinking fountains, and special housing. **Special:** The college offers domestic and international travel courses, study abroad, accelerated and double major degrees, semester and summer internships, and a Washington, DC semester. There are 18 national honor societies and 15 departmental honors programs. **Visiting:** There are regularly scheduled orientations for prospective students, Daily interviews and tours; high school visitation days: 5 in the fall and 2 in the spring. There are various department-specific open houses throughout the year as well. There are guides for informal visits, visitors may sit in on classes, and stay overnight. To schedule a visit, contact Admissions Office. **Campus Safety and Security:** Measures include 24-hour foot and vehicle patrol, emergency notification system, and security escort services. There are emergency telephones, lighted pathways/sidewalks, controlled access to dorms/residences, an emergency response program with public warning siren, and cell phone call/text message system.

REQUIREMENTS: The SAT or ACT is required. An academic or college preparatory curriculum is highly recommended, including 4 units of English, 3 units each of math, science, and a foreign language, and 2 units of history. One essay is required of all applicants, and an audition is required of music students. An interview is highly recommended. AP and CLEP credits are accepted. Important factors in the admissions decision are extracurricular activities record, personality/intangible qualities, and parents or siblings attended your school. Students are required to complete a minimum of 128 credit hours. All students must complete the 40-46 semester-hour general education curriculum, which includes 15 hours of humanities, 3 hour writing course, 8 hours of natural science, 3 hours of science, social science, faith, and technology, and 6 hours of quantitative and logical reasoning. Specific courses required include 2 hours of physical/wellness education and 2 years demonstrated proficiency in a foreign language. A minimum GPA of 2.0 is required. **Procedure:** Freshmen are admitted fall and spring. Entrance exams should be taken spring of the junior year or the fall of the senior year. There are early decision, early admissions, and deferred admissions plans. Early decision applications should be filed by November 15; regular applications, by February 1 for fall entry; and December 15 for spring entry, along with a $50 fee. Notification of early decision is sent December 15; regular decision, March 1. 255 early decision candidates were accepted for the 2016-2017 class. 52 applicants were on the 2016 waiting list; 2 were admitted. Application fees are waived if application is completed online. **Transfer Students:** 45 transfer students enrolled in 2015-2016. Either the SAT or the ACT is required as well as two letters of recommendation, official high school and college transcripts, and an essay. An interview is highly recommended. 64 of 128 credits required for the bachelor's degree must be completed at Grove City. **International Students:** There are 23 international students enrolled. The school actively recruits these students. They must take the TOEFL with a minimum score of 550 on the paper-based TOEFL (PBT) or 79 on the Internet-based version (iBT). If the TOEFL is not available, either the SAT or the ACT is required.

ADMISSIONS: 82% of the 2016-2017 applicants were accepted. The SAT scores for the 2016-2017 freshman class were: Critical Reading-- 11% below 500, 42% between 500 and 599, 34% between 600 and 699, and 13% between 700 and 800. Math-- 12% below 500, 40% between 500 and 599, 38% between 600 and 699, and 10% between 700 and 800. The ACT scores were 1% between 12 and 17, 26% between 18 and 23, 51% between 24 and 29, and 22% above 30. 61% of the current freshmen were in the top fifth of their class; 79% were in the top two fifths. There were 5 National Merit finalists. 31 freshmen graduated first in their class. **Admissions Contact:** Sarah E. Gibbs, Director of Admissions. Email: *admissions@gcc.edu* Web: *www.gcc.edu*

FINANCIAL AID: In 2016-2017, 81% of all full-time freshmen and 78% of continuing full-time students received some form of financial aid. 51% of all full-time freshmen and 44% of continuing full-time students received need-based aid. The average freshman award was $13,885. Need-based scholarships or need-based grants averaged $5,299; need-based self-help aid (loans and jobs) averaged $11,815; and other non-need-based awards and non-need-based scholarships averaged $5,706. 43% of undergraduate students work part-time. Average annual earnings from campus work are $1100. The average financial indebtedness of the 2016 graduate was $37,655. The college's own financial statement is required. The FAFSA code is G03269. The deadline for filing freshman financial aid applications for fall entry is April 15.

GWYNEDD MERCY UNIVERSITY *(The complete profile is made available exclusively on our website, www.barronspac.com)*

HAVERFORD COLLEGE — E-4

www.haverford.edu

Haverford, PA 19041 — **(610) 896-1350**

Fax: (610) 896-1338	**Email:** admission@haverford.edu
Full-time: 613 men, 655 women	**Faculty:** 131; IIB, ++$
Part-time: n/av	**Ph.D.s:** 96%
Graduate: n/av	**Student/Faculty:** 9 to 1
Year: semesters	**Tuition:** $51,024
Room & Board: $15,466	**Freshman Class:** 4066 applied, 870 accepted, 349 enrolled
SAT CR/M/W: 710/710/710 **ACT:** 33	**CEEB CODE:** 2289
Application Deadline: January 15	**MOST COMPETITIVE**

Haverford College, founded in 1833, is a private liberal arts college. There is 1 undergraduate school. The 200-acre campus is in a suburban area 8 miles west of Philadelphia, PA. Including any residence halls, there are 87 buildings.

STUDENT LIFE: 89% of undergraduates are from out of state, mostly the Middle Atlantic. Students are from 41 states, 37 foreign countries, and Canada. 54% are from public schools. 9% are Foreign; 8% Hispanic; 7% African American; 60% White; 4% two or more races; 3% race unknown; 17% Asian American. **Female To Male Ratio:** 1.1:1. The average age of freshmen is 18; all undergraduates, 20. 3% do not continue beyond their first year; 90% remain to graduate. **Housing:** 1236 students can be accommodated in college housing, which includes coed dorms and on-campus apartments. In addition, there are language houses, and special-interest houses. Haverford students may live at Bryn Mawr College through a dorm exchange program. On-campus housing is guaranteed for all 4 years and is available on a lottery system for upperclassmen. 99% of students live on campus; of those, 90% remain on campus on weekends. Upperclassmen may keep cars.

FACULTY/CLASSROOMS: 52% of faculty are male; 48% are female. All teach undergraduates, 80% do research, and 80% do both. No introductory courses are taught by graduate students. The average class size in a regular course is 20.

PROGRAMS OF STUDY: Haverford confers B.A. and B.S. degrees. Bachelor's degrees are awarded in BIOLOGICAL SCIENCE (biology/biological science), COMMUNICATIONS AND THE ARTS (art history and appreciation, classics, comparative literature, English, fine arts, French, German, Greek, Italian, Latin, linguistics, music, romance languages and literature, Russian, Spanish, and visual and performing arts), COMPUTER AND PHYSICAL SCIENCE (astronomy, astrophysics, chemistry, computer science, geology, information sciences and systems, mathematics, and physics), SOCIAL SCIENCE (anthropology, archeology, East Asian studies, economics, history, interdisciplinary studies, liberal arts/general studies, philosophy, political science/government, psychology, religion, sociology, and urban studies). Natural Sciences is the strongest academically. English, biology, and psychology have the largest enrollments.

ACTIVITIES: There are no fraternities or sororities. There are 145 groups on campus, including art, chess, choir, chorale, communications, computers, dance, debate, drama, environmental, ethnic, film, international, LGBT, literary magazine, musical theater, newspaper, photography, political, religious, social, social service, student government, and yearbook. Popular campus events include Haverfest, Snowball, and Haverford vs Swarthmore Athletic Events. **Sports:** There are 11 intercollegiate sports for men and 13 for women, and 3 intramural sports for men and 3 for women. Facilities include an athletic center with basketball, volleyball and fitness center, exercise equipment, multipurpose room for dance, martial arts, recreational activities, international squash courts, sports medicine, and a conference/AV room. **Graduates:** From July 1, 2015 to June 30, 2016, 304 bachelor's degrees were awarded. The most popular majors were biology (12%), psychology (9%), and English (7%). 275 companies recruited on campus in 2015-2016. In an average class, 86% graduate in 4 years or less, 89% graduate in 5 years or less, and 90% graduate in 6 years or less. Of the 2015 graduating class, 18% were enrolled in graduate school within 6 months of graduation, and 60% were employed.

SERVICES: Counseling and information services are available, as is tutoring in every subject. There is a reader service for the blind. **Library/Resources:** The 4 libraries contain 592,984 volumes, 8,039 microform items, and 16,280 audio/video tapes/CDs/DVDs, and subscribe to 14,775 periodicals including electronic. Computerized library services include interlibrary loans, database searching, Internet access, and Wi-Fi capability. Special learning facilities include an art gallery, planetarium, an observatory, and an arboretum. **Physically Challenged Students:** 60% of the campus is accessible. Facilities include wheelchair ramps, elevators, special parking, specially equipped restrooms, special class scheduling, lowered drinking fountains, and lowered telephones. **Special:** Haverford offers internship programs, cross-registration with Bryn Mawr and Swarthmore Colleges, study abroad in 38 countries, dual majors, and student-designed majors. Pass/fail options are limited to 4 in 4 years. Haverford offers a 3-2 program in engineering with the California Institute of Technology and a 4-1 program in engineering with the University of Pennsylvania. **Visiting:** There are guides for informal visits, visitors may sit in on classes, and stay overnight. To schedule a visit, contact the Admissions Office. **Campus Safety and Security:** Measures include 24-hour foot and vehicle patrol, emergency notification system, self-defense education, and security escort services. There are shuttle buses, emergency telephones, lighted pathways/sidewalks, controlled access to dorms/residences, and a fire safety program.

REQUIREMENTS: First-year applicants must take the SAT or the ACT before the deadline for the decision plan chosen. Candidates for admission must be graduates of an accredited secondary school and have taken 4 courses in English, 3 each in a foreign language and math, 2 in social studies, and 1 each in science. The GED is accepted. An essay is required, and an interview is recommended. AP credits are accepted. Important factors in the admissions decision are advanced placement or honors courses, leadership record, and recommendations by school officials. All students must take a minimum of 32 course credits, including freshman writing and 3 courses each in social science, natural science, and the humanities. Students must also take 3 semesters of phys ed and demonstrate proficiency in a foreign language. Students must take a minimum of 6 courses in the major and 6 in related fields. Each major includes a capstone experience. **Procedure:** Freshmen are admitted fall. Entrance exams should be taken by February 1. There are early decision, early admissions, and deferred admissions plans. Early decision applications should be filed by November 15; regular applications, by January 15 for fall entry. The fall 2016 application fee was $65. Notification of early decision is sent December 15; regular decision, April 1. 173 early decision candidates were accepted for the 2016-2017 class. 412 applicants were on the 2016 waiting list; 26 were admitted. Applications are accepted on-line. **Transfer Students:** 9 transfer students enrolled in 2015-2016. Transfer students must be able to enter the sophomore or junior class. Admission depends mainly on the strength of college grades. A minimum GPA of 3.0 is necessary and the SAT is recommended. The equivalent of 1 year of courses must have been earned. A liberal arts curriculum is also recommended. 64 of 128 credits required for the bachelor's degree must be completed at Haverford. **International Students:** There are 115 international students enrolled. The school actively recruits these students. They must take the TOEFL with a minimum score of 600 on the paper-based TOEFL (PBT) or 100 on the Internet-based version (iBT). They must also take the SAT or ACT.

ADMISSIONS: 21% of the 2016-2017 applicants were accepted. The SAT scores for the 2016-2017 freshman class were: Critical Reading-- 6% between 500 and 599, 34% between 600 and 699, and 60% between 700 and 800. Math-- 7% between 500 and 599, 32% between 600 and 699, and 61% between 700 and 800. Writing-- 3% between 500 and 599, 38% between 600 and 699, and 59% between 700 and 800. The ACT scores were 12% between 24 and 29, and 88% above 30. 98% of the current freshmen were in the top fifth of their class; 100% were in the top two fifths. **Admissions Contact:** Jess Lord, Dean of Admission & Financial Aid. Email: *admission@haverford.edu* Web: *www.haverford.edu*

FINANCIAL AID: In 2016-2017, 46% of all full-time freshmen and 50% of continuing full-time students received some form of financial aid. 45% of all full-time freshmen and 49% of continuing full-time students received need-based aid. The average freshman award was $49,928. Need-based scholarships or need-based grants averaged $46,398; and need-based self-help aid (loans and jobs) averaged $2,931. 64% of undergraduate students work part-time. The average financial indebtedness of the 2016 graduate was $18,932. Haverford is a member of CSS. The CSS/Profile is required. The FAFSA code is 003274. The deadline for filing freshman financial aid applications for fall entry is February 1.

HOLY FAMILY UNIVERSITY *(The complete profile is made available exclusively on our website, www.barronspac.com)*

IMMACULATA UNIVERSITY — E-4

Immaculata College
www.immaculata.edu

Immaculata, PA 19345	**(610) 647-4400** **(877) 42-TODAY**
Fax: (610) 640-0836	**Email: admiss@immaculata.edu**
Full-time: 283 men, 660 women	**Faculty:** 96; IIA
Part-time: 109 men, 503 women	**Ph.D.s:** 85%
Graduate: 236 men, 819 women	**Student/Faculty:** 10 to 1
Year: semesters, summer session	**Tuition:** $26,500
Room & Board: $12,500	**Freshman Class:** 1584 applied, 1304 accepted, 217 enrolled
	CEEB CODE: 2320
Application Deadline: n/av	**COMPETITIVE**

Immaculata University, founded in 1920, is a private, Catholic, comprehensive, coeducational university that offers associate, bachelor's, master's and doctoral degrees. Immaculata awards more than 60 majors, minors, and pre-professional certifications, including accelerated and online career-oriented programs. Figures in the above capsule and in this profile are approximate. There are 2 undergraduate schools and 1 graduate school. In addition to regional accreditation, Immaculata has baccalaureate program accreditation with ACBSP, AHEA, NASM, NLN, CCNE, and CAATE. The 400-acre campus is in a suburban area 20 miles west of Philadelphia. Including any residence halls, there are 22 buildings.

STUDENT LIFE: 74% of undergraduates are from Pennsylvania. Others are from states. 57% are from public schools. 76% are White; 6% Hispanic; 2% Asian American; 2% two or more races; 13% African American; 1% Foreign; 1% race unknown. 59% are Catholic; 19% Protestant; 15% Islamic. **Female To Male Ratio:** 3.2:1. The average age of freshmen is 18. 20% do not continue beyond their first year; 63% remain to graduate. **Housing:** 568 students can be accommodated in college housing, which includes single-sex and coed dorms and on-campus apartments. On-campus housing is guaranteed for all 4 years. 53% of students live on campus. All students may keep cars. Alcohol is not permitted

FACULTY/CLASSROOMS: 21% of faculty are male; 79% are female. No introductory courses are taught by graduate students.

PROGRAMS OF STUDY: Immaculata confers B.A., B.S., B.Mus., and B.S.N. degrees. Associate, master's, and doctoral degrees are also awarded. Bachelor's degrees are awarded in BIOLOGICAL SCIENCE (biology/biological science), BUSINESS (accounting, business administration and management, fashion merchandising, finance, human resources/organizational mgmt, and marketing management), COMMUNICATIONS AND THE ARTS (communications, digital media, English, music, and Spanish), COMPUTER AND PHYSICAL SCIENCE (chemistry, chemistry secondary education, information sciences and systems, and mathematics), EDUCATION (athletic training, early childhood education, elementary education, English secondary education, foreign languages education, mathematics education, middle school education, music education, science education, secondary education, and social studies secondary school education), HEALTH PROFESSIONS (allied health, exercise science, music therapy, nursing, premedicine, pre-occupational therapy, and prephysical therapy), SOCIAL SCIENCE (biopsychology, criminology, dietetics, economics, history, international relations, political science/government, prelaw, psychology, social science, social work, sociology, and theological studies). Healthcare professions, education, and business are the strongest academically. Nursing, exercise science, and business management have the largest enrollments.

ACTIVITIES: There are 40 groups on campus, including gaming, fashion group, sign language, art, band, cheerleading, choir, chorale, chorus, computers, dance, debate, drama, environmental, ethnic, honors, international, jazz band, literary magazine, newspaper, orchestra, photography, political, professional, religious, social, social service, student government, and wellness. Popular campus events include Rose Arbor Dinner, Senior Ball, Carol Night, Amethyst Day, Family Week, Block Party, and Beyond the Campus. **Sports:** There are 9 intercollegiate sports for men and 10 for women. Facilities include a stadium housing a multi-sport, synthetic turf field, baseball stadium, outdoor basketball courts, full indoor gymnasium, indoor training facility with turf surface, athletic training facility, hard-court tennis courts, indoor swimming pool, and fitness center (weights, exercise equipment). **Graduates:** From July 1, 2015 to June 30, 2016, 613 bachelor's degrees were awarded. The most popular majors were health professions (51%), exercise science (6%), and Psychology (4%). In an average class, 55% graduate in 4 years or less, 60% graduate in 5 years or less, and 62% graduate in 6 years or less.

SERVICES: Counseling and information services are available, as is tutoring in most subjects. There is also remedial math and writing. **Library/Resources:** The library contains 120,000 volumes, 10,000 audio/video tapes/CDs/DVDs, and subscribes to 250 periodicals including electronic. Computerized library services include interlibrary loans, database searching, Internet access, and Wi-Fi capability. **Physically Challenged Students:** All of the campus is accessible. Facilities include wheelchair ramps, elevators, special parking, specially equipped restrooms, special class scheduling, lowered drinking fountains, lowered telephones, and special housing. **Special:** All academic departments offer opportunities for internships, and some majors require internships. Students may also study abroad. Immaculata offers accelerated degree programs in 10 areas: Cybersecurity Emergency, Planning and Management Organizational, Behavior Health Care Management, Nursing (RN to BSN), Marketing Management, Human Resource Management, Finance Business Management and Business Administration. Immaculata also offers dual-majors, non-degree study, and pass/fail options for students. There are 21 national honor societies, Phi Beta Kappa, and a freshman honors program. **Visiting:** There are regularly scheduled orientations for prospective students, campus tour, information session, and class visit. There are guides for informal visits, visitors may sit in on classes, and stay overnight. To schedule a visit, contact Office of Admissions. **Campus Safety and Security:** Measures include 24-hour foot and vehicle patrol, emergency notification system, self-defense education, and security escort services. There are emergency telephones, lighted pathways/sidewalks, controlled access to dorms/residences, and security cameras.

REQUIREMENTS: Candidates for admission should be graduates of an accredited secondary school with a minimum of 16 academic courses including 4 in English, 2 each in social studies, a foreign language, math, and science, and 4 more in college preparatory courses. The GED is accepted. An essay and letter of recommendation are required for all applicants. An audition is required for music students. AP and CLEP credits are accepted. Important factors in the admissions decision are advanced placement or honors courses, recommendations by school officials, and extracurricular activities record. To graduate, all students must complete the Liberal Arts Core requirements for the university which include 42-54 credits in humanities, social sciences, sciences, foreign language, and theology. Students in the College of Undergraduate Studies must take a minimum of 128 credits, including 36 to 52 in the major. 2 credits of phys ed are also required. Immaculata requires a minimum GPA of 2.0 to graduate. Undergraduates requires the completion a capstone project or culminating learning experience. Internships are required for several majors, including dietetics, music therapy, communications, and education. **Procedure:** Freshmen are admitted in the fall and spring. Entrance exams should be taken junior year or fall of senior year. There are deferred admissions and rolling admissions plans. Application deadlines are open. Application fee is $35. Applications are accepted on-line. Application fees are waived if application is completed online. **Transfer Students:** 54 transfer students enrolled in 2015-2016. In addition, to high school credentials, transfer applicants must present college transcripts. Courses in which the student has achieved a C or better are accepted if they are comparable to Immaculata's courses up to a maximum of 64 credits for the College of Undergraduate Studies or 72 credits for the College of Lifelong Learning. Students must have a minimum GPA of 2.0. **International Students:** The school actively recruits these students. They must take the TOEFL with a minimum score of 513 on the paper-based TOEFL (PBT) or 65 on the Internet-based version (iBT). They must also take the SAT or ACT.

ADMISSIONS: 82% of the 2016-2017 applicants were accepted. **Admissions Contact:** Nicola Di Fronzo-Heitzer, Ed.D, Director of Admissions. Email: *admiss@immaculata.edu* Web: *www.immaculata.edu*

FINANCIAL AID: In 2016-2017, 100% of all full-time freshmen and 99% of continuing full-time students received some form of financial aid. 75% of all full-time freshmen and 70% of continuing full-time students received need-based aid. The average freshman award was $28,463. Need-based scholarships or need-based grants averaged $8,835; need-based self-help aid (loans and jobs) averaged $5,888; and other non-need-based awards and non-need-based scholarships averaged $16,136. 35% of undergraduate students work part-time. Average annual earnings from campus work are $1005. Immaculata is a member of CSS. The FAFSA code is 003276. The priority date for freshman financial aid applications for fall entry is October 1. The filing deadline for fall entry is April 15.

INDIANA UNIVERSITY OF PENNSYLVANIA *(The complete profile is made available exclusively on our website, www.barronspac.com)*

JUNIATA COLLEGE — D-3

www.juniata.edu

Huntingdon, PA 16652	**(814) 641-3420** **(877) JUNIATA**
Fax: (814) 641-3100	**Email: admissions@juniata.edu**
Full-time: 658 men, 841 women	**Faculty:** 99; IIB, +$
Part-time: 28 men, 42 women	**Ph.D.s:** 95%
Graduate: 2 men, 3 women	**Student/Faculty:** 13 to 1
Year: semesters, summer session	**Tuition:** $38,630
Room & Board: $10,710	**Freshman Class:** 2207 applied, 1637 accepted, 423 enrolled
SAT CR/M: 570/580 **ACT:** recommended	**CEEB CODE:** 2341
Application Deadline: June 15	**VERY COMPETITIVE**

Juniata College, founded in 1876, is an independent liberal arts college. Figures in the above capsule and in this profile are approximate. In addition to regional accreditation, Juniata has baccalaureate program accreditation with CSWE and ACS. The 110-acre campus is in a small town 31 miles south of State College, in the heart of rural Pennsylvania. Including any residence halls, there are 43 buildings.

STUDENT LIFE: 59% of undergraduates are from Pennsylvania. Others are from 32 states, 44 foreign countries, and Canada. 78% are from public schools. 72% are White; 7% race unknown; 4% Hispanic; 3% African American; 2% Asian American; 2% two or more races; 10% Foreign. 56% are Protestant; 32% Catholic. **Female To Male Ratio:** 1.2:1. The average age of freshmen is 18; all undergraduates, 20. 12% do not continue beyond their first year; 88% remain to graduate. **Housing:** 1274 students can be accommodated in college housing, which includes single-sex and coed dorms, on-campus apartments, off-campus apartments, special-interest houses, and international housing. On-campus housing is guaranteed for all 4 years. 82% of students live on campus; of those, 75% remain on campus on weekends. All students may keep cars.

FACULTY/CLASSROOMS: 59% of faculty are male; 41% are female. All teach undergraduates. No introductory courses are taught by graduate students. The average class size in an introductory lecture is 19.

PROGRAMS OF STUDY: Juniata confers B.A. and B.S. degrees. Master's degrees are also awarded. Bachelor's degrees are awarded in AGRICULTURE (environmental studies), BIOLOGICAL SCIENCE (biochemistry and biology/biological science), BUSINESS (accounting, banking and finance, business administration and management, human resources, international business management, and marketing/retailing/merchandising), COMMUNICATIONS AND THE ARTS (art history and appreciation, communications, digital communications, dramatic arts, English, French, German, Russian, Spanish, and studio art), COMPUTER AND PHYSICAL SCIENCE (chemistry, computer science, geology, information sciences and systems, mathematics, and physics), EDUCATION (early childhood education, elementary education, English education, foreign languages education, mathematics education, museum studies, science education, secondary education, social studies education, and special education), ENGINEERING AND ENVIRONMENTAL DESIGN (engineering physics and environmental science), SOCIAL SCIENCE (anthropology, economics, history, international studies, peace studies, philosophy, political science/government, psychology, public administration, social work, sociology, and theological studies). Biology, psychology, and business are the strongest academically. Biology, business, and environmental studies/science have the largest enrollments.

ACTIVITIES: There are no fraternities or sororities. There are 96 groups on campus, including art, band, cheerleading, chess, choir, chorale, chorus, computers, dance, drama, environmental, ethnic, honors, international, jazz band, LGBT, literary magazine, musical theater, newspaper, orchestra, outing and Model UN club, photography, political, professional, radio and TV, religious, social, social service, student government, and symphony. Popular campus events include Mountain Day, Madrigal Dinner and Dance, Spring Fest, and Relay for Life. **Sports:** There are 9 intercollegiate sports for men and 10 for women, and 6 intramural sports for men and 6 for women. Facilities include gyms, swimming pool, fitness center, racquetball courts, multipurpose fitness/dance room, varsity football field and stadium, baseball, soccer, softball, and hockey fields, an outdoor running track, tennis courts, and an outdoor basketball court. **Graduates:** From July 1, 2015 to June 30, 2016, 326 bachelor's degrees were awarded. The most popular majors were biology/prehealth (15%), business/accounting (12%), and psychology (10%). 122 companies recruited on campus in 2015-2016. In an average class, 72% graduate in 4 years or less, 71% graduate in 5 years or less, and 78% graduate in 6 years or less. Of the 2015 graduating class, 39% were enrolled in graduate school within 6 months of graduation, and 61% were employed.

SERVICES: Counseling and information services are available, as is tutoring in most subjects. There is a reader service for the blind. Juniata also offers courses and workshops in study, reading, and writing skills. JC offers temporary assistance to those with mobility challenges as a result of accident, injury or surgery. **Library/Resources:** The library contains 505,000 volumes, 400 microform items, 2,800 audio/video tapes/CDs/DVDs, and subscribes to 11,000 periodicals including electronic. Computerized library services include interlibrary loans, database searching, Internet access, and Wi-Fi capability. Special learning facilities include an art gallery, radio station, observatory, an environmental studies field station, a nature preserve, an early childhood education center, and a ceramics studio. **Physically Challenged Students:** 75% of the campus is accessible. Facilities include wheelchair ramps, elevators, special parking, specially equipped restrooms, lowered drinking fountains, and wide doors. **Special:** Juniata offers cooperative programs in marine science, cytogenetics, cytotechnology, marine biology, biotechnology, nursing, medical technology, diagnostic imaging, occupational and physical therapy, dentistry, medicine, optometry, and podiatry.

Internships, study abroad in 26 countries, Washington and Philadelphia semesters, and nondegree study are also offered. There are 3-2 engineering degrees with Columbia, Clarkson, Washington, and Pennsylvania State Universities, a 3-3 law program with Duquesne University, and various preprofessional programs, including optometry, chiropractic, medicine, dentistry, pharmacy, physician assistant, and podiatry. With the assistance of faculty advisers, most students design their own majors to meet their individual goals. There are 15 national honor societies, a freshman honors program, and 16 departmental honors programs. **Visiting:** There are regularly scheduled orientations for prospective students, including a campus tour, interviews, attending classes, and meeting with faculty, coaches, and members of the financial planning staff. There are guides for informal visits, visitors may sit in on classes, and stay overnight. To schedule a visit, contact Pam Zilch, Campus Visit Coordinator at (814) 641-3428. **Campus Safety and Security:** Measures include 24-hour foot and vehicle patrol, emergency notification system, self-defense education, and security escort services. There are emergency telephones, awareness programs, fire safety training, weather alerts, terror alerts, an emergency operation plan, a firearms storage vault, vehicle lockout service, identification processing, and evacuation mapping.

REQUIREMENTS: The SAT or ACT is recommended. Candidates for admission should be graduates of an accredited secondary school and have completed 16 academic credits, including 4 in English, 2 in a foreign language, and a combination of 10 in math, social studies, and lab science. The GED is accepted, and homeschoolers are encouraged to apply. An essay is required, and an interview is recommended. A GPA of 3.0 is required. AP credits are accepted. Important factors in the admissions decision are advanced placement or honors courses, leadership record, and recommendations by school officials. Students are required to complete a minimum of 120 credit hours, including courses in fine arts, international studies, social sciences, humanities, and natural sciences, as well as 4 communications-based courses, 2 cultural analysis courses, a math and statistics course, and the college writing seminar. The total number of hours required for the program of emphasis varies from 45 to 60; majors do not exist as such, and students must develop a program of emphasis and complete it to obtain their degree. Students must have a minimum GPA of 2.0. **Procedure:** Freshmen are admitted in the fall and spring. Entrance exams should be taken by the January test date of the year of admission for fall entry. There are early decision, deferred admissions, and rolling admissions plans. Early decision applications should be filed by November 15; regular applications, by June 15 for fall entry; and December 1 for spring entry. Notification of early decision is sent December 23; regular decision, on a rolling basis. 79 early decision candidates were accepted for the 2016-2017 class. 40 applicants were on the 2016 waiting list; 8 were admitted. Application fees are waived if application is completed online. **Transfer Students:** 23 transfer students enrolled in 2015-2016. A GPA of 2.5 is required. Applicants must submit a high school transcript, a college transcript, and an essay. SAT scores are required of some students. 30 of 120 credits required for the bachelor's degree must be completed at Juniata. **International Students:** There are 155 international students enrolled. The school actively recruits these students. They must take the TOEFL with a minimum score of 550 on the paper-based TOEFL (PBT) or 79 on the Internet-based version (iBT).

ADMISSIONS: 74% of the 2016-2017 applicants were accepted. The SAT scores for the 2016-2017 freshman class were: Critical Reading-- 15% below 500, 45% between 500 and 599, 31% between 600 and 699, and 10% between 700 and 800. Math-- 14% below 500, 48% between 500 and 599, 32% between 600 and 699, and 6% between 700 and 800. 59% of the current freshmen were in the top fifth of their class; 89% were in the top two fifths. There were 9 National Merit finalists. 6 freshmen graduated first in their class. **Admissions Contact:** Michelle Bartol, Office of Enrollment. Email: *admissions@juniata.edu* Web: *www.juniata.edu*

FINANCIAL AID: In 2016-2017, 100% of all full-time freshmen and continuing full-time students received some form of financial aid. 86% of all full-time freshmen and 81% of continuing full-time students received need-based aid. The average freshman award was $31,877. Need-based scholarships or need-based grants averaged $26,934 ($44,750 maximum); and need-based self-help aid (loans and jobs) averaged $4,558 ($11,000 maximum). 53% of undergraduate students work part-time. Average annual earnings from campus work are $680. The average financial indebtedness of the 2016 graduate was $33,421. The FAFSA code is 003279. The priority date for freshman financial aid applications for fall entry is February 15.

KEYSTONE COLLEGE *(The complete profile is made available exclusively on our website, www.barronspac.com)*

KING'S COLLEGE — E-2

www.kings.edu

Wilkes Barre, PA 18711	**(570) 208-5858** **(888) 546-4772**
Fax: (570) 208-5971	**Email: admissions@kings.edu**
Full-time: 1022 men, 885 women	**Faculty:** 126; IIB, av$
Part-time: 65 men, 110 women	**Ph.D.s:** 88%
Graduate: 92 men, 246 women	**Student/Faculty:** 15 to 1
Year: semesters, summer session	**Tuition:** $34,720
Room & Board: $12,138	**Freshman Class:** 3852 applied, 2731 accepted, 570 enrolled
SAT CR/M/W: 520/530/500 **ACT:** 23	**CEEB CODE:** 2353
Application Deadline: n/av	**COMPETITIVE**

King's College, founded in 1946, is a private institution affiliated with the Roman Catholic Church. The college offers 37 undergraduate majors plus master's degree programs in health care administration, education with a concentration in reading, curriculum and instruction, and special education. A 5-year physician assistant program is also offered. In addition, King's College offers a 3-2 engineering degree with the University of Notre Dame. There is 1 undergraduate school and 1 graduate school. In addition to regional accreditation, King's has baccalaureate program accreditation with AACSB, NCATE, ACS, ARC-PA, and CAATE. The 48-acre campus is in an urban area in northeastern Pennsylvania 19 miles south of Scranton. Including any residence halls, there are 30 buildings.

STUDENT LIFE: 65% of undergraduates are from Pennsylvania. Others are from 20 states, and 4 foreign countries. 71% are from public schools. 74% are White; 7% Hispanic; 6% Foreign; 5% race unknown; 3% African American; 2% Asian American; 2% two or more races. 42% are Catholic. **Female To Male Ratio:** 1.1:1. The average age of freshmen is 19; all undergraduates, 20. 23% do not continue beyond their first year; 65% remain to graduate. **Housing:** 1076 students can be accommodated in college housing, which includes single-sex and coed dorms and on-campus apartments. On-campus housing is guaranteed for all 4 years. 50% of students commute. All students may keep cars.

FACULTY/CLASSROOMS: 51% of faculty are male; 49% are female. 93% teach undergraduates. No introductory courses are taught by graduate students. The average class size in an introductory lecture is 20; in a laboratory is 14; and in a regular course is 17.

PROGRAMS OF STUDY: King's confers B.A., B.S., and B.S.B.A degrees. Master's degrees are also awarded. Bachelor's degrees are awarded in AGRICULTURE (environmental studies), BIOLOGICAL SCIENCE (biology/biological science and neurosciences), BUSINESS (accounting, banking and finance, business administration and management, international business management, marketing/retailing/merchandising, and personnel management), COMMUNICATIONS AND THE ARTS (communications, dramatic arts, English, French, and Spanish), COMPUTER AND PHYSICAL SCIENCE (chemistry, computer science, information sciences and systems, mathematics, physics, and science), EDUCATION (early childhood education, elementary education, foreign languages education, middle school education, science education, secondary education, and special education), ENGINEERING AND ENVIRONMENTAL DESIGN (civil engineering and mechanical engineering), HEALTH PROFESSIONS (exercise science, medical laboratory technology, physician's assistant, predentistry, premedicine, and sports medicine), SOCIAL SCIENCE (criminal justice, economics, history, philosophy, political science/government, prelaw, psychology, sociology, and theological studies). Physician assistant, accounting, and engineering are the strongest academically. Physician assistant, criminal justice, and accounting have the largest enrollments.

ACTIVITIES: There are no fraternities or sororities. There are 50 groups on campus, including art, cheerleading, choir, chorale, chorus, communications, computers, dance, drama, environmental, ethnic, film, honors, international, literary magazine, musical theater, newspaper, photography, political, professional, radio and TV, religious, social, social service, student government, and yearbook. Popular campus events include All College Ball, Student Activities Fair, and Spring Fling. **Sports:** There are 12 intercollegiate sports for men and 11 for women, and 5 intramural sports for men and 5 for women. Facilities include a phys ed center, multipurpose courts, fitness center, wrestling room, racquetball courts, swimming pool, multipurpose area, gym, free weight area, an outdoor athletic complex with a field house, a multi-purpose turf for football, field hockey, soccer, and women's and men's lacrosse, and grass soccer and field hockey fields as well as baseball and softball field, and an 8-lane NCAA standard track. **Graduates:** From July 1, 2015 to June 30, 2016, 415 bachelor's degrees were awarded. The most popular majors were criminal justice (11%), medical studies (9%), and accounting (9%). 43 companies recruited on campus in 2015-2016. In an average class, 60% graduate in 4 years or less, 65% graduate in 5 years or less, and 65% graduate in 6 years or less. Of the 2015 graduating class, 29% were enrolled in graduate school within 6 months of graduation, and 70% were employed.

SERVICES: Counseling and information services are available, as is tutoring in every subject. The academic skills center provides a writing center, learning skills workshops, a tutoring program, and learning disability services. **Library/Resources:** The library contains 185,069 volumes, 13,985 microform items, 3,019 audio/video tapes/CDs/DVDs, and subscribes to 15,165 periodicals including electronic. Computerized library services include interlibrary loans, database searching, Internet access, and Wi-Fi capability. Special learning facilities include an art gallery, radio station, a TV studio. **Physically Challenged Students:** 99% of the campus is accessible. Facilities include wheelchair ramps, elevators, special parking, specially equipped restrooms, special class scheduling, lowered drinking fountains, lowered telephones, and special housing. **Special:** King's College offers a 3-2 engineering degree with the University of Notre Dame. The Experiential Learning Program provides internship opportunities in all majors with a variety of employers. King's also offers an accelerated degree program in Healthcare Administration, dual majors, and credit for life experience. Student-designed majors are available through the King's honors program. Cross-registrations with Wilkes University and College Misericordia are also offered. In addition, King's offers study-abroad through affiliation agreements with 20 overseas institutions of higher education as well as numerous summer study abroad opportunities, including short-term faculty-led study abroad programs. There are 11 national honor societies and a freshman honors program. **Visiting:** There are regularly scheduled orientations for prospective students, consisting of interviews, financial aid presentations, faculty one-on-one meetings, and campus tours. There are guides for informal visits, visitors may sit in on classes, and stay overnight. To schedule a visit, contact the Admissions Office. **Campus Safety and Security:** Measures include 24-hour foot and vehicle patrol, emergency notification system, self-defense education, and security escort services. There are shuttle buses, emergency telephones, lighted pathways/sidewalks, and controlled access to dorms/residences.

REQUIREMENTS: The SAT is recommended. King's requires 16 academic credits, although 24 are recommended, including 4 in English, 3 each in science, math, and social studies, and 2 in foreign language. AP and CLEP credits are accepted. Important factors in the admissions decision are extracurricular activities record, recommendations by school officials, and leadership record. All students must earn a minimum of 120 credits and maintain a GPA of 2.0. The core requirements represent between 52 and 59 credits. The major comprises a maximum of 60 credits, of which up to 40 can be specified in the major department, with the balance designated for related fields. **Procedure:** Freshmen are admitted in the fall, spring, and summer. Entrance exams should be taken so that scores are received by April 1. There are deferred admissions and rolling admissions plans. Application deadlines are open. Application fee is $30. Notification is sent on a rolling basis. Application fees are waived if application is completed online. **Transfer Students:** 71 transfer students enrolled in 2015-2016. Applicants must present a minimum GPA of 2.0 to 3.0. Students must have earned at least 12 credit hours at another college. An interview is recommended. 60 of 120 credits required for the bachelor's degree must be completed at King's. **International Students:** There are 122 international students enrolled. The school actively recruits these students. They must take the TOEFL with a minimum score of 530 on the paper-based TOEFL (PBT) or 71 on the Internet-based version (iBT). They must also take the SAT or ACT.

ADMISSIONS: 71% of the 2016-2017 applicants were accepted. The SAT scores for the 2016-2017 freshman class were: Critical Reading-- 39% below 500, 46% between 500 and 599, 14% between 600 and 699, and 1% between 700 and 800. Math-- 31% below 500, 47% between 500 and 599, 20% between 600 and 699, and 1% between 700 and 800. Writing-- 47% below 500, 43% between 500 and 599, and 10% between 600 and 699. The ACT scores were 7% between 12 and 17, 48% between 18 and 23, 42% between 24 and 29, and 3% above 30. 35% of the current freshmen were in the top fifth of their class; 62% were in the top two fifths. **Admissions Contact:** James Anderson, Director of Admissions. Email: *admissions@kings.edu* Web: *www.kings.edu*

FINANCIAL AID: In 2016-2017, 91% of all full-time freshmen and 93% of continuing full-time students received some form of financial aid. 80% of all full-time freshmen and 79% of continuing full-time students received need-based aid. The average freshman award was $24,586. Need-based scholarships or need-based grants averaged $21,070 ($33,620 maximum); need-based self-help aid (loans and jobs) averaged $4,160 ($7,000 maximum); and other non-need-based awards and non-need-based scholarships averaged $12,350 ($33,620 maximum). 47% of undergraduate students work part-time. Average annual earnings from campus work are $1500. The average financial indebtedness of the 2016 graduate was $33,482. King's is a member of CSS. The FAFSA code is 003282. The priority date for freshman financial aid applications for fall entry is February 15.

KUTZTOWN UNIVERSITY OF PENNSYLVANIA *(The complete profile is made available exclusively on our website, www.barronspac.com)*

LA ROCHE COLLEGE *(The complete profile is made available exclusively on our website, www.barronspac.com)*

LA SALLE UNIVERSITY — F-3

www.lasalle.edu

Philadelphia, PA 19141	**(215) 951-1500** **(800) 328-1910**
Fax: (215) 951-1656	**Email: admiss@lasalle.edu**
Full-time: 1343 men, 2011 women	**Faculty:** IIA, +$
Part-time: 137 men, 456 women	**Ph.D.s:** 84%
Graduate: 486 men, 1242 women	**Student/Faculty:** 12 to 1
Year: semesters, summer session	**Tuition:** $41,100
Room & Board: $13,060	**Freshman Class:** 5601 applied, 4381 accepted, 708 enrolled
SAT CR/M: 520/510 **ACT:** 21	**CEEB CODE:** 2363
Application Deadline: April 1	**COMPETITIVE**

La Salle University, is inspired by St. John Baptist de La Salle, the patron saint of teachers, and shaped by Lasallian and Catholic values. The La Salle University experience prepares students for a lifetime of personal development, service and success. La Salle provides excellence in teaching and learning, personal attention, a sense of community and a global perspective. La Salle University puts theory into practice by guiding each student's intellectual and spiritual development. Thanks to a creative and practical education, La Salle graduates go on to make a difference for the greater good. Figures in the above capsule and in this profile are approximate. There are 3 undergraduate schools and 22 graduate schools. In addition to regional accreditation, La Salle has baccalaureate program accreditation with AACSB, CSWE, NLN, CCNE, CAA-ASHA, APA, COA, CACREP, ACEND, AACTE, PDE, ACS, COAMFTE, and AAMFT. The 133-acre campus is in an urban area 8 miles northwest of Center City, Philadelphia. Including any residence halls, there are 58 buildings.

STUDENT LIFE: 66% of undergraduates are from Pennsylvania. Others are from 35 states, 29 foreign countries, and Canada. 50% are from public schools. 55% are White; 17% African American. 66% are Catholic; 21% Christian. **Female To Male Ratio:** 1.9:1. The average age of freshmen is 18; all undergraduates, 21. 22% do not continue beyond their first year; 63% remain to graduate. **Housing:** 1868 students can be accommodated in college housing, which includes single-sex and coed dorms and on-campus apartments. In addition, there are honors houses, special-interest houses. Townhouses are owned and operated by La Salle University. On-campus housing is guaranteed for all 4 years, and is available on a first-come, first-served basis, and is available on a lottery system for upperclassmen. 56% of students live on campus; of those, 70% remain on campus on weekends. Upperclassmen may keep cars.

FACULTY/CLASSROOMS: 49% of faculty are male; 51% are female. No introductory courses are taught by graduate students. The average class size in an introductory lecture is 23 and in a laboratory is 14.

PROGRAMS OF STUDY: La Salle confers B.A., B.S., B.S.N. and B.S.W. degrees. Associate, master's, and doctoral degrees are also awarded. Bachelor's degrees are awarded in BIOLOGICAL SCIENCE (biochemistry, biology/biological science, and nutrition), BUSINESS (accounting, banking and finance, business administration and management, business intelligence and analytics, international economics, management information systems, marketing/retailing/merchandising, and organizational behavior), COMMUNICATIONS AND THE ARTS (classical languages, communications, English, fine arts, French, German, Italian, multimedia, music, Russian, and Spanish), COMPUTER AND PHYSICAL SCIENCE (chemistry, computer science, geology, information sciences and systems, mathematics, and science), EDUCATION (elementary education, foreign languages education, science education, secondary education, social studies education, and special education), ENGINEERING AND ENVIRONMENTAL DESIGN (computer graphics and environmental science), HEALTH PROFESSIONS (nursing, preallied health, predentistry, premedicine, and speech pathology/audiology), SOCIAL SCIENCE (criminal justice, economics, history, philosophy, political science/government, prelaw, psychology, public administration, religion, social work, and sociology). Accounting, education, speech-language and hearing, and biology are the strongest academically. Nursing, communication, and psychology have the largest enrollments.

ACTIVITIES: 6% of men belong to 1 local and 4 national fraternities; 18% of women belong to 1 local and 3 national sororities. There are 121 groups on campus, including art, band, cheerleading, choir, chorus, computers, dance, drama, drill team, environmental, ethnic, film, forensics, honors, international, jazz band, LGBT, literary magazine, musical theater, newspaper, orchestra, pep band, photography, political, professional, radio and TV, religious, social, social service, student government, and yearbook. **Sports:** There are 9 intercollegiate sports for men and 11 for women, and 5 intramural sports for men and 5 for women. Facilities include a fitness center, 4000-seat arena, 6000-seat lighted stadium and track, swimming pool, wrestling rooms, sauna, and basketball, volleyball and tennis, and squash courts. **Graduates:** From July 1, 2014 to June 30, 2015, 933 bachelor's degrees were awarded. The most popular majors were nursing (23%), marketing (8%), and communication (7%). In an average class, 55% graduate in 4 years or less, 62% graduate in 5 years or less, and 63% graduate in 6 years or less.

SERVICES: Counseling and information services are available, as is tutoring in most subjects. There is a reader service for the blind, and remedial writing. A writing center is also available. **Library/Resources:** The library contains 422,600 volumes, 7,154 microform items, and 17,207 audio/video tapes/CDs/DVDs, and subscribes to 123,437 periodicals including electronic. Computerized library services include interlibrary loans, database searching, Internet access, and Wi-Fi capability. Special learning facilities include an art gallery, radio station, TV station, La Salle University Art Museum: a collection of European and American since the Middle Ages. In addition to paintings, the museum has a collection of Old Master prints and drawings from the 19th and 20th centuries. Collections include: illustrated rare Bibles, Japanese prints, Indian miniatures, African tribal art, pre-Columbian pottery and ancient Greek cotta pottery. La Salle 56 is a cable television station housed in the University's Communication Center. **Physically Challenged Students:** 95% of the campus is accessible. Facilities include wheelchair ramps, elevators, special parking, specially equipped restrooms, special class scheduling, lowered drinking fountains, and special housing. **Special:** Cross-registration is offered in conjunction with Chestnut Hill College, and there is a 2-2 program in allied health with Thomas Jefferson University. La Salle also offers travel study courses, study abroad in Ireland, Austrailia, Rome, Mexico and more, co-op programs, work-study programs, internships in most majors, dual majors, an university-honors program for gifted students, as well as a business scholars co-op program. An integrated science, business, and technology program is offered. La Salle offers a 4-year BS/MBA in Accounting, a 5-year BA/BS/MS in Computer Science, a 5-year BA/MA in History, and a 5-year BS/MA in Speech Language Hearing Science. There are 16 national honor societies, Phi Beta Kappa, a freshman honors program, and 2 departmental honors programs. **Visiting:** There are regularly scheduled orientations for prospective students, group Information sessions and tours are scheduled 5 days a week. Two Open Houses in the fall. In addition, we have opportunities for prospective student to sit in on classes for the day. There are guides for informal visits and visitors may sit in on classes. To schedule a visit, contact Office of Undergraduate Admissions at (215) 951-1500. **Campus Safety and Security:** Measures include 24-hour foot and vehicle patrol, emergency notification system, and security escort services. There are shuttle buses, emergency telephones, lighted pathways/sidewalks, controlled access to dorms/residences, magnetic card access to residence facilities.

REQUIREMENTS: The SAT is required. The ACT is recommended. In addition, the SAT: Subject Test in math is recommended. Applicants must be graduates of accredited secondary schools or have earned a GED. La Salle requires 16 academic units, based on 4 years of English, 3 of math, 2 of foreign language, and 1 of history, with the remaining 5 units in academic electives; science and math majors must have an additional one-half unit of math. An essay is required, and an interview is recommended. AP and CLEP credits are accepted. Important factors in the admissions decision are advanced placement or honors courses, leadership record, and recommendations by school officials. All courses in the core may be counted towards any minor or major barring exclusions by the academic departments sponsoring the minor or major. To complete the core requirements, most School of Arts and Sciences majors must complete a maximum of 19 courses, School of Business Administration majors, a maximum of 16 courses, and School of Nursing majors, a maximum of 15 courses. A major feature of the Core is the Doubles program. All students will be required to enroll in a "Double" during the freshman year. Doubles are thematically linked core courses in different disciplines. In the Doubles program students will explore some or all of the topics in these courses under the guidance of two professors. A sense of academic and social community forms more readily in Doubles courses than in traditional courses because students take both courses with the same small group of students. The First Year Odyssey" refers to the one credit program which introduces students to La Salle University and the city of Philadelphia through activities such as field trips and campus wide programs. Students participate in the First Year Odyssey as part of designated courses or in special First Year Odyssey sections. "Understanding at Home and Abroad" refers to fostering the Christian Brothers' ideals of community, social justice, and compassionate understanding across barriers dividing human beings. Students are required to enroll in one course in the Academic Bulletin designated by the symbol of a "house" (H Understanding at Home) and one course designated by the symbol of a "plane" (Q Understanding Abroad). Some students may fulfill the Understanding at Home or Understanding Abroad requirement through an independent project with the approval of the Department Chair and the Core Director. Faculty and Staff will mentor a limited number of such projects. **Procedure:** Freshmen are admitted fall and spring. Entrance exams should be taken before January of the senior year. There are early admissions, deferred admissions, and rolling admissions plans. Applications should be filed by April 1 for fall entry; December 15 for spring entry. Notifications are sent December 15. Applications are accepted on-line. Application fees are waived if application is completed on-line. **Transfer Students:** 116 transfer students enrolled in 2014-2015. Minimum cumulative GPA of 2.5 (2.75 preferred) required for consideration. Individual programs may have higher GPA requirements. Nursing program applicants must have minimum GPA of 3.0 as well as science GPA of 3.0. Education program applicants should have 3.0 cumulative GPA. Speech, Language and Hearing program applicants should have minimum cumulative GPA of 3.2 (3.4 preferred) for consideration. 50 of 120 credits required for the bachelor's degree must be completed at La Salle. **International Students:** There are 92 international students enrolled. The school actively recruits these students. They must take the TOEFL with a minimum score of 540 on the paper-based TOEFL (PBT) or 80 on the Internet-based version (iBT), and the IELTS.

ADMISSIONS: 78% of the 2015-2016 applicants were accepted. The SAT scores for the 2015-2016 freshman class were: Critical Reading-- 38% below 500, 47% between 500 and 599, 14% between 600 and 699, and 1% between 700 and 800. Math-- 39% below 500, 44% between 500 and 599, 15% between 600 and 699, and 2% between 700 and 800. The ACT scores were 40% below 12, 40% between 12 and 17, 15% between 18 and 23, 3% between 24 and 29, and 2% above 30. 30% of the current freshmen were in the top fifth of their class; 59% were in the top two fifths. 1 freshman graduated first in the class. **Admissions Contact:** James Plunkett, Executive Director of Admission. Email: *admiss@lasalle .edu* Web: *www.lasalle.edu*

FINANCIAL AID: In 2015-2016, 99% of all full-time freshmen and 96% of continuing full-time students received some form of financial aid. 83% of all full-time freshmen and 79% of continuing full-time students received need-based aid. The average freshman award was $33,489. Need-based scholarships or need-based grants averaged $28,394 ($54,660 maximum); need-based self-help aid (loans and jobs) averaged $3,975 ($6,550 maximum); non-need-based athletic scholarships averaged $10,494 ($24,293 maximum); and other non-need-based awards and non-need-based scholarships averaged $7,585 ($25,254 maximum). 27% of undergraduate students work part-time. Average annual earnings from campus work are $1575. The average financial indebtedness of the

2015 graduate was $34,479. The FAFSA is required. The deadline for filing freshman financial aid applications for fall entry is February 15.

LAFAYETTE COLLEGE F-3

www.lafayette.edu

Easton, PA 18042 (610) 330-5100

Fax: (610) 330-5355 Email: admissions@lafayette.edu

Full-time: 1227 men, 1278 women	**Faculty:** 229; IIB, ++$
Part-time: 21 men, 24 women	**Ph.D.s:** 98%
Graduate: n/av	**Student/Faculty:** 10 to 1
Year: semesters, summer session	**Tuition:** $48,885
Room & Board: $14,470	**Freshman Class:** 8123 applied, 2298 accepted, 649 enrolled
SAT CR/M/W: 626/662/637 **ACT:** 29	**CEEB CODE:** 2361
Application Deadline: January 15	**MOST COMPETITIVE**

Lafayette College, founded in 1826, is a highly selective private, exclusively undergraduate college, emphasizing the liberal arts, sciences, and engineering. There is 1 undergraduate school. In addition to regional accreditation, Lafayette has baccalaureate program accreditation with ABET and ACS. The 342-acre campus is in a suburban area 70 miles west of New York City, off Interstate 78 and US 22. Including any residence halls, there are 81 buildings.

STUDENT LIFE: 82% of undergraduates are from out of state, mostly the Middle Atlantic. Students are from 45 states, 59 foreign countries, and Canada. 60% are from public schools. 65% are White; 6% Hispanic; 6% race unknown; 5% African American; 4% Asian American; 2% two or more races; 10% Foreign. 27% are Catholic; 22% claim no religious affiliation; 17% Protestant. **Female To Male Ratio:** 1.0:1. The average age of freshmen is 18; all undergraduates, 20. 5% do not continue beyond their first year; 89% remain to graduate. **Housing:** 2308 students can be accommodated in college housing, which includes single-sex and coed dorms, on-campus apartments, and off-campus apartments. In addition, there are honors houses, special-interest houses, fraternity houses, sorority houses, diversity-oriented houses, arts houses, a black cultural center, language and special-interest floors. On-campus housing is guaranteed for all 4 years. 93% of students live on campus; of those, 98% remain on campus on weekends. Upperclassmen may keep cars.

FACULTY/CLASSROOMS: 63% of faculty are male; 37% are female. All teach undergraduates and do research. No introductory courses are taught by graduate students. The average class size in a laboratory is 12 and in a regular course is 17.

PROGRAMS OF STUDY: Lafayette confers A.B. and B.S. degrees. Bachelor's degrees are awarded in BIOLOGICAL SCIENCE (biochemistry, biology/biological science, and neurosciences), BUSINESS (business economics and international economics), COMMUNICATIONS AND THE ARTS (art, English, French, German, music, and Spanish), COMPUTER AND PHYSICAL SCIENCE (chemistry, computer science, geology, mathematics, and physics), ENGINEERING AND ENVIRONMENTAL DESIGN (chemical engineering, civil engineering, electrical/electronics engineering, engineering, and mechanical engineering), SOCIAL SCIENCE (African studies, American studies, anthropology, Asian/Oriental studies, economics, history, interdisciplinary studies, international relations, philosophy, political science/government, prelaw, psychology, religion, Russian and Slavic studies, and sociology). Social sciences, engineering, and biological life sciences are the strongest academically. Mechanical engineering, economics and biology have the largest enrollments.

ACTIVITIES: 23% of men belong to 3 national fraternities; 34% of women belong to 6 national sororities. There are 250 groups on campus, including art, band, cheerleading, chess, choir, chorale, chorus, computers, dance, debate, drama, environmental, ethnic, film, forensics, honors, international, jazz band, LGBT, literary magazine, musical theater, newspaper, orchestra, pep band, photography, political, professional, radio and TV, religious, social, social service, and student government. Popular campus events include 1,000 Nights, Block pARTy, Rivalry Week, Earth Day, International Extravaganza, and Presidential Ball. **Sports:** There are 11 intercollegiate sports for men and 11 for women, and 18 intramural sports for men and 18 for women. Facilities include a stadium, sports center, arena, field house, varsity house, a natatorium, fitness center, exercise rooms, weight training room, outdoor track, indoor track, climbing wall, racquet courts, multipurpose courts, and athletic complex for outdoor track lacrosse, field hockey, soccer, and baseball. **Graduates:** From July 1, 2015 to June 30, 2016, 591 bachelor's degrees were awarded. The most popular majors were social sciences (35%), engineering (18%), and biological life sciences (9%). 89 companies recruited on campus in 2015-2016. In an average class, 85% graduate in 4 years or less, 88% graduate in 5 years or less, and 89% graduate in 6 years or less.

SERVICES: Counseling and information services are available, as is tutoring in most subjects, most 100-level and many 200-level classes. **Library/Resources:** The 2 libraries contain 510,000 volumes, 120,000 microform items, and subscribe to 2,600 periodicals including electronic. Computerized library services include interlibrary loans, database searching, Internet access, and Wi-Fi capability. Special learning facilities include an art gallery, radio station, a geological museum, foreign languages lab, and calculus lab. **Physically Challenged Students:** 95% of the campus is accessible. Facilities include wheelchair ramps, elevators, special parking, specially equipped restrooms, special class scheduling, lowered drinking fountains, and lowered telephones. **Special:** Cross-registration is available through the Lehigh Valley Association of Independent Colleges, internships in all academic departments, study abroad in 3 countries as well as through other individually arranged plans, a Washington semester at American University, and work-study programs with area employers are possible. An accelerated degree plan in all majors, dual and student-designed majors, 5-year dual-degree programs, and pass/fail options in any non major subject also are available. There are 12 national honor societies, Phi Beta Kappa, and 24 departmental honors programs. **Visiting:** There are regularly scheduled orientations for prospective students, student visits include student/faculty panel discussions, tours, and departmental open houses. There are guides for informal visits, visitors may sit in on classes, and stay overnight. To schedule a visit, contact Ed Bianchi at (610) 330-5100. **Campus Safety and Security:** Measures include 24-hour foot and vehicle patrol, emergency notification system, self-defense education, and security escort services. There are shuttle buses, emergency telephones, lighted pathways/sidewalks, controlled access to dorms/residences, advisors in all residence halls, and residence hall lock down from 8 p.m. to 7 a.m.

REQUIREMENTS: The SAT or ACT is required. The ACT Optional Writing test is also required. Applicants should have taken 4 years of English, 3 of math (4 for science or engineering majors), 2 each of a foreign language and lab science (with physics and chemistry for science or engineering students), and at least an additional 5 units in academic subjects. An essay is required and an interview recommended. Evaluations from the secondary school counselor and a teacher are required. The GED is accepted. AP credits are accepted. Important factors in the admissions decision are advanced placement or honors courses, leadership record, evidence of special talent, extracurricular activities record, ability to finance college education, parents or siblings attended your school, personality/intangible qualities, and geographical diversity. To graduate, students must maintain a GPA of 2.0, and take a minimum of 32 to 36 courses (36 for engineering). The common course of study, designed to build a background in the liberal arts and sciences includes interdisciplinary seminars, a course in humanities, social science, natural science with a lab, and quantitative reasoning. Students must take 2 courses dealing with global and multicultural issues, and must demonstrate elementary proficiency in a foreign language (typically 2 courses). A Science and Technology in a Social Context requirement can be met by taking two classes designated as STSC outside of the student's home division. Finally, students must take one course that explores values in society and four writing intensive courses. **Procedure:** Freshmen are admitted in the fall. Entrance exams should be taken by January of the senior year. There are early decision, early admissions, and deferred admissions plans. Early decision applications should be filed by November 15; regular applications, by January 15 for fall entry, along with a $65 fee. Notification of early decision is sent December 15; regular decision, April 1. 336 early decision candidates were accepted for the 2016-2017 class. 444 applicants were on the 2016 waiting list; 5 were admitted. Application fees are waived if application is completed on-line. **Transfer Students:** 10 transfer students enrolled in 2015-2016. Acceptance usually depends on college-level performance and achievements. An interview is required if the student lives within 200 miles of the college. No minimum GPA is required, and neither the SAT nor the ACT is needed. The number of credit hours required varies with the program, but usually enough for freshman status with advanced standing is needed. Typically, Lafayette will enroll about 15 transfers in the fall and about 5 in the spring of each year, 16 of 32 credits required for the bachelor's degree must be completed at Lafayette. **International Students:** There are 264 international students enrolled. The school actively recruits these students. They must take the TOEFL with a minimum score of 513 on the paper-based TOEFL (PBT) or 80 on the Internet-based version (iBT) and the Comprehensive English Language Test. They must also take the SAT or ACT.

ADMISSIONS: 28% of the 2016-2017 applicants were accepted. The SAT scores for the 2016-2017 freshman class were: Critical Reading-- 4% below 500, 29% between 500 and 599, 51% between 600 and 699, and 17% between 700 and 800. Math-- 17% between 500 and 599, 52% between 600 and 699, and 31% between 700 and 800. Writing-- 4% below 500, 22% between 500 and 599, 52% between 600 and 699, and 22% between 700 and 800. The ACT scores were 4% between 18 and 23, 44% between 24 and 29, and 52% above 30. 91% of the current freshmen were in the top fifth of their class; 99% were in the top two fifths. 9 freshmen graduated first in their class. **Admissions Contact:** Matt Hyde, Dean of Admissions. Email: *hydem@lafayette.edu* Web: *www.lafayette.edu*

FINANCIAL AID: In 2016-2017, 66% of all full-time freshmen and 57% of continuing full-time students received some form of financial aid. 43% of all full-time freshmen and 34% of continuing full-time students received need-based aid. The average freshman award was $40,162. Need-based scholarships or need-based grants averaged $39,349 ($66,015 maximum); need-based self-help aid (loans and jobs) averaged $4,315 ($7,000 maximum); non-need-based athletic scholarships averaged $37,571 ($65,077 maximum); other non-need-based awards and non-need-based scholarships averaged $12,050 ($61,250 maximum); and $8,746 from other forms of aid. 44% of undergraduate students work part-time. Average annual earnings from campus work are $1648. The average financial indebtedness of the 2016 graduate was $29,324. Lafayette is a member of CSS. The CSS/Profile, the college's own financial statement, the business/farm supplement, and divorce/separation parent statement (if applicable) are required. The FAFSA code is 003284. The priority date for freshman financial aid applications for fall entry is January 15. The filing deadline for fall entry is March 1.

LEBANON VALLEY COLLEGE E-3

www.lvc.edu

Annville, PA 17003	**(717) 867-6181** **(866) LVC-4ADM**
Fax: (717) 867-6026	**Email: admission@lvc.edu**
Full-time: 743 men, 860 women	**Faculty:** 108; IIB, av$
Part-time: 60 men, 53 women	**Ph.D.s:** 88%
Graduate: 68 men, 123 women	**Student/Faculty:** 11 to 1
Year: semesters, summer session	**Tuition:** $40,550
Room & Board: $10,980	**Freshman Class:** 3329 applied, 2413 accepted, 456 enrolled
SAT CR/M/W: 540/565/530 **ACT:** 22	**CEEB CODE:** 2364
Application Deadline: March 1	**COMPETITIVE**

Lebanon Valley College, founded in 1866, is a private institution that offers 34 major fields of study, where students can develop their own individualized major. LVC offers graduate programs in physical therapy, business, music education, and science education. Figures in the above capsule and in this profile are approximate. There is 1 undergraduate school. In addition to regional accreditation, LVC has baccalaureate program accreditation with NASM and CAPTE. The 340-acre campus is in a small town 6 miles east of Hershey, PA. Including any residence halls, there are 53 buildings.

STUDENT LIFE: 79% of undergraduates are from Pennsylvania. Others are from 23 states, 3 foreign countries, and Canada. 94% are from public schools. 92% are White; 2% African American; 2% Asian American; 2% Hispanic. **Female To Male Ratio:** 1.2:1. The average age of freshmen is 18; all undergraduates, 20. 14% do not continue beyond their first year; 71% remain to graduate. **Housing:** 1292 students can be accommodated in college housing, which includes coed dorms and on-campus apartments. In addition, there are special-interest houses, theme and wellness housing, and other small houses. On-campus housing is guaranteed for all 4 years. 80% of students live on campus; of those, 60% remain on campus on weekends. All students may keep cars.

FACULTY/CLASSROOMS: 63% of faculty are male; 37% are female. 90% teach undergraduates. No introductory courses are taught by graduate students. The average class size in an introductory lecture is 23; in a laboratory is 14; and in a regular course is 19.

PROGRAMS OF STUDY: LVC confers B.A., B.S., B.M., B.S.Ch. and B.S.Med.Tech. degrees. Associate, master's, and doctoral degrees are also awarded. Bachelor's degrees are awarded in BIOLOGICAL SCIENCE (biochemistry and biology/biological science), BUSINESS (accounting and business administration and management), COMMUNICATIONS AND THE ARTS (art history, art, audio technology, communications technology, digital communications, English, French, German, music, music business management, and Spanish), COMPUTER AND PHYSICAL SCIENCE (actuarial science, chemistry, computer science, mathematics, and physics), EDUCATION (early childhood education, elementary education, music education, and special education), HEALTH PROFESSIONS (biology, health, health care administration, medical laboratory technology, and physical therapy), SOCIAL SCIENCE (American studies, criminal justice, economics, French studies, history, philosophy, political science/government, psychobiology, psychology, religion, religious studies, sociology, and Spanish studies). Actuarial science, natural sciences, and education are the strongest academically. Education, business, and natural sciences have the largest enrollments.

ACTIVITIES: 9% of women belong to 1 local and 3 national sororities. There are 85 groups on campus, including and music ensembles., art, band, cheerleading, choir, chorus, concert band, dance, drama, ethnic, honors, international, jazz band, LGBT, literary magazine, marching band, musical theater, newspaper, orchestra, political, professional, radio and TV, religious, social, social service, student government, and symphony. Popular campus events include Christmas at the Valley, Valley Festival, and Dutchmen Day. **Sports:** There are 12 intercollegiate sports for men and 11 for women, and 12 intramural sports for men and 12 for women. Facilities include a 3000-seat stadium, a sports center, more than 60 acres of athletic fields, indoor and outdoor tracks, a 1660 seat gym, playing courts for basketball, handball, squash, and tennis, a 500-seat baseball grandstand, and a football field. Including golf, swimming, ice hockey, lacrosse, volleyball and track and field. **Graduates:** From July 1, 2015 to June 30, 2016, 416 bachelor's degrees were awarded. The most popular majors were business/marketing (13%), health professions and related programs (10%), and social science (9%). 65 companies recruited on campus in 2015-2016. In an average class, 68% graduate in 4 years or less, 75% graduate in 5 years or less, and 74% graduate in 6 years or less. Of the 2015 graduating class, 26% were enrolled in graduate school within 6 months of graduation, and 82% were employed.

SERVICES: Counseling and information services are available, as is tutoring in every subject. There is a reader service for the blind. **Library/Resources:** The library contains 203,335 volumes, 15,485 microform items, and 17,827 audio/video tapes/CDs/DVDs, and subscribes to 792 periodicals including electronic. Computerized library services include interlibrary loans, database searching, Internet access, and Wi-Fi capability. Special learning facilities include an art gallery and radio station. **Physically Challenged Students:** 80% of the campus is accessible. Facilities include wheelchair ramps, elevators, special parking, specially equipped restrooms, special class scheduling, lowered drinking fountains, lowered telephones, and special housing. **Special:** Study abroad opportunities are available in Argentina, Australia, England, France, Italy, Germany, Greece, Sweden, Spain, the Netherlands, and New Zealand. There are also 2 off-campus domestic programs in Philadelphia and Washingtgon, D.C. There are 3-2 degree programs in engineering with Penn State University and Case Western Reserve, and in forestry with Duke University. There is also a 2-2 degree program in allied health sciences with Thomas Jefferson University. LVC offers internships in a number of areas. There are 6 national honor societies and 11 departmental honors programs. **Visiting:** There are regularly scheduled orientations for prospective students, visiting students can take tours, and schedule interviews and meetings with professors. There are guides for informal visits and visitors may sit in on classes. To schedule a visit, contact the Director of Admission. **Campus Safety and Security:** Measures include 24-hour foot and vehicle patrol, self-defense education, and security escort services. There are emergency telephones and lighted pathways/sidewalks.

REQUIREMENTS: The SAT is required. The ACT Optional Writing test is also required. Applicants must be graduates of an accredited secondary school or have earned a GED. LVC requires 16 academic units or 16 Carnegie units, including 4 in English, 3 each in math and social studies, and 3 in science with 2 lab units recommended, 2-3 units of foreign language, and 2 in history. An interview is recommended. Students applying as music majors must audition. AP and CLEP credits are accepted. Important factors in the admissions decision are advanced placement or honors courses, leadership record, evidence of special talent, personality/intangible qualities, extracurricular activities record, parents or siblings attended your school, recommendations by alumni, geographical diversity, and recommendations by school officials. The general education program consists of course work in these areas: communications, liberal studies, foreign studies, social diversity studies, and disciplinary perspectives. Students are required to complete 3 writing process courses, and be proficient in computer applications and modes of information access and retrieval. To graduate, students must complete at least 120 credit hours, 2 units of phys ed, and the requirements for the major with a minimum cumulative GPA of 2.0. **Procedure:** Freshmen are admitted fall and spring. There is a rolling admissions plan. Application deadlines are open. Application fee is $30. Notifications are sent December 1. Applications are accepted on-line. **Transfer Students:** 48 transfer students enrolled in 2015-2016. Requirements for transfer applicants include a minimum GPA of 2.0, SAT scores, and an interview. 30 of 120 credits required for the bachelor's degree must be completed at LVC. **International Students:** There are 9 international students enrolled. They must take the TOEFL with a minimum score of 550 on the paper-based TOEFL (PBT) or 80 on the Internet-based version (iBT).

ADMISSIONS: 72% of the 2016-2017 applicants were accepted. The SAT scores for the 2016-2017 freshman class were: Critical Reading-- 32% below 500, 45% between 500 and 599, 21% between 600 and 699, and 2% between 700 and 800. Math-- 23% below 500, 42% between 500 and 599, 29% between 600 and 699, and 6% between 700 and 800. Writing-- 36% below 500, 44% between 500 and 599, 17% between 600 and 699, and 3% between 700 and 800. The ACT scores were 4% between 12 and 17, 42% between 18 and 23, 45% between 24 and 29, and 8% above 30. 54% of the current freshmen were in the top fifth of their class; 75% were in the top two fifths. 9 freshmen graduated first in their class. **Admissions Contact:** Susan Jones, Director of Admission. Email: *admission@lvc.edu* Web: *www.lvc.edu*

FINANCIAL AID: In 2016-2017, 99% of all full-time freshmen and 98% of continuing full-time students received some form of financial aid. 85% of all full-time freshmen and 80% of continuing full-time students received need-based aid. The average freshman award was $35,546. Need-based scholarships or need-based grants averaged $25,445; need-based self-help aid (loans and jobs) averaged $5,342; other non-need-based awards and non-need-based scholarships averaged $3,984; and $15,022 from other forms of aid. 48% of undergraduate students work part-time. Average annual earnings from campus work are $1071. The average financial indebtedness of the 2016 graduate was $27,319. LVC is a member of CSS. The college's own financial statement is required. The FAFSA code is 003288. The priority date for freshman financial aid applications for fall entry is March 1.

LEHIGH UNIVERSITY — F-3

www.lehigh.edu

Bethlehem, PA 18015 — **(610) 758-3100**

Fax: (610) 758-4361
Email: admissions@lehigh.edu

Full-time: 2766 men, 2235 women
Part-time: 51 men, 23 women
Graduate: 1085 men, 894 women
Year: semesters, summer session
Room & Board: $12,280

Faculty: 465; I, +$
Ph.D.s: 96%
Student/Faculty: 10 to 1
Tuition: $46,230
Freshman Class: 12843 applied, 3905 accepted, 1261 enrolled

SAT CR/M: 630/690 **ACT:** 31
Application Deadline: January 1

CEEB CODE: 2365
MOST COMPETITIVE

Lehigh University, founded in 1865, is a private research university offering both undergraduate and graduate programs in liberal arts, sciences, business, education, and engineering. Our students experience interesting, independent research, and work closely with faculty who offer their time and attention to hands-on projects, internships, and innovative studies. There are 3 undergraduate schools and 4 graduate schools. In addition to regional accreditation, Lehigh has baccalaureate program accreditation with AACSB, ABET, and NCATE. The 2355-acre campus is in a suburban area 50 miles north of Philadelphia and 75 miles southwest of New York City. Including any residence halls, there are 169 buildings.

STUDENT LIFE: 73% of undergraduates are from out of state, mostly the Middle Atlantic. Students are from 49 states, 60 foreign countries, and Canada. 65% are White. **Male To Female Ratio:** 1.2:1. The average age of freshmen is 18; all undergraduates, 20. 5% do not continue beyond their first year; 88% remain to graduate. **Housing:** 3347 students can be accommodated in college housing, which includes coed dorms, on-campus apartments, and married student housing. In addition, there are special-interest houses, fraternity houses, sorority houses, substance free housing, and an ROTC house. On-campus housing is guaranteed for the freshman year only, and is available on a first-come, first-served basis, and on a lottery system for upperclassmen. 67% of students live on campus; of those, 85% remain on campus on weekends. Upperclassmen may keep cars.

FACULTY/CLASSROOMS: 64% of faculty are male; 36% are female. All teach undergraduates and do research. No introductory courses are taught by graduate students. The average class size in a regular course is 29.

PROGRAMS OF STUDY: Lehigh confers B.A., and B.S. degrees. Master's and doctoral degrees are also awarded. Bachelor's degrees are awarded in AGRICULTURE (environmental studies), BIOLOGICAL SCIENCE (biochemistry, biology/biological science, and molecular biology), BUSINESS (accounting, business economics, business information systems, finance, marketing, management & strategic leadership, and supply chain management), COMMUNICATIONS AND THE ARTS (art, art history and appreciation, Chinese, classics, design, English, French, German, journalism, music, music theory and composition, Spanish, and theater design), COMPUTER AND PHYSICAL SCIENCE (applied mathematics, applied science, astronomy, astrophysics, chemistry, computer science, earth science, mathematics, physics, science technology, and statistics), ENGINEERING AND ENVIRONMENTAL DESIGN (architecture, bioengineering, chemical engineering, civil engineering, computer engineering, electrical/electronics engineering, engineering mechanics, engineering physics, environmental engineering, environmental science, industrial engineering, materials science and engineering, and mechanical engineering), HEALTH PROFESSIONS (pharmaceutical chemistry, predentistry, premedicine, and preoptometry), SOCIAL SCIENCE (African studies, anthropology, Asian/Oriental studies, behavioral science, classical/ancient civilization, cognitive science, economics, (Social Science) Global Studies, history, interdisciplinary studies, international relations, philosophy, political science/government, psychology, religion, sociology, and women's studies). Finance, mechanical engineering, and accounting have the largest enrollments.

ACTIVITIES: 40% of men belong to 20 national fraternities; 45% of women belong to 11 national sororities. There are 150 groups on campus, including art, band, cheerleading, chess, choir, chorale, chorus, computers, dance, debate, drama, environmental, ethnic, honors, international, jazz band, LGBT, literary magazine, marching band, musical theater, newspaper, orchestra, pep band, photography, political, professional, radio and TV, religious, social, social service, student government, symphony, and yearbook. Popular campus events include Spirit Week, Spring Fling, International Week, Move Out Collection Drive, and Great South Side Sale. **Sports:** There are 12 intercollegiate sports for men and 13 for women, and 11 intramural sports for men and 11 for women. Facilities include a stadium, arena, gym, cross-country course, field house with basketball and tennis courts, swimming pools, a track, indoor squash and racquetball courts, playing fields including astro-turf for field hockey, football, lacrosse, and soccer, weight rooms. There is also a fitness center, climbing wall, indoor tennis center, and golf range (driving/chipping/putting). **Graduates:** From July 1, 2014 to June 30, 2015, 1232 bachelor's degrees were awarded. The most popular majors were finance (12%), mechanical engineering (8%), and accounting (7%). 235 companies recruited on campus in 2014-2015. In an average class, 1% graduate in 3 years or less, 74% graduate in 4 years or less, 85% graduate in 5 years or less, and 88% graduate in 6 years or less. Of the 2014 graduating class, 23% were enrolled in graduate school within 6 months of graduation, and 69% were employed.

SERVICES: Counseling and information services are available, as is tutoring in most subjects, such as calculus, physics, English, accounting, finance, and economics. There is a reader service for the blind. Tutoring is available upon request. Also, there are special programs for students with learning disabilities and English as a Second Language. **Library/Resources:** The 2 libraries contain 1.1 million volumes, 575,007 microform items, 10,847 audio/video tapes/CDs/DVDs, and subscribe to 54,991 periodicals including electronic. Computerized library services include interlibrary loans, database searching, Internet access, and Wi-Fi capability. Special learning facilities include an art gallery, radio station, TV station, special collections/rare book reading room, digital media studio, financial services lab, and international multimedia resource center. **Physically Challenged Students:** Facilities include wheelchair ramps, elevators, special parking, specially equipped restrooms, special class scheduling, lowered drinking fountains, lowered telephones, and special housing. **Special:** Lehigh offers many interdisciplinary programs including Integrated Product Development, Computer Science and Business, Integrated Business and Engineering, Integrated Degree in Engineering, Arts and Sciences, Global Citizenship, Lehigh Earth Observatory, and South Mountain College, Lehigh's residential academic program. The university offers co-op programs, cross-registration with the Lehigh Valley Association of Independent Colleges, many combinations of dual majors, study abroad programs in 40 countries, internships, a Washington semester, work-study, a 7-year BA/MD program with Drexel University College of Medicine, a 7-year BA/OD program with SUNY Optometry and a 7-year BA/DMD program with the School of Dental Medicine at the University of Pennsylvania. There are 18 national honor societies, Phi Beta Kappa, and a freshman honors program. **Visiting:** There are regularly scheduled orientations for prospective students, including group information sessions and tours, as well as special events and open houses. There are guides for informal visits, visitors may sit in on classes, and stay overnight. To schedule a visit, contact the Office of Admissions. **Campus Safety and Security:** Measures include 24-hour foot and vehicle patrol, emergency notification system, self-defense education, and security escort services. There are shuttle buses, emergency telephones, lighted pathways/sidewalks, controlled access to dorms/residences, LU-alert text messaging system, emergency preparedness presentations, and emergence safety app.

REQUIREMENTS: The SAT or ACT is required. The ACT Optional Writing test is also required. Candidates for admission should have completed 4 years of English, 3 years of math and electives, and 2 years each of a foreign language, science, and social science. Most students present 4 years each of science, math, and English. Opportunities for an on-campus interview are made available to prospective students but are not required. Interviews are by appointment only. AP credits are accepted. Important factors in the admissions decision are advanced placement or honors courses, recommendations by school officials, evidence of special talent, and extracurricular activities record. Graduation requirements vary by degree sought, but all students must complete 2 semesters of English, at least 30 credits in the chosen major, and a minimum of 121 credit hours. Students must also maintain a minimum GPA of 2.0. **Procedure:** Freshmen are admitted in the fall and spring. Entrance exams should be taken by the January test date. There are early decision, early admissions, and deferred admissions plans. Early decision applications should be filed by November 15; regular applications, by January 1 for fall entry; and November 1 for spring entry. The fall 2015 application fee was $70. Notification of early decision is sent December 15; regular decision, April 1. 582 early decision candidates were accepted for the 2015-2016 class. 1847 applicants were on the 2015 waiting list. Applications are accepted online. **Transfer Students:** 26 transfer students enrolled in 2014-2015. Transfer candidates should have a minimum GPA of 3.25 and submit high school and college transcripts, an essay, and a statement of good standing from previous institutions. 30 of 121 credits required for the bachelor's degree must be completed at Lehigh. **International Students:** There are 418 international students enrolled. The school actively recruits these students. They must take the TOEFL with a minimum score of 570 on the paper-based TOEFL (PBT) or 90 on the Internet-based version (iBT). They must also take the SAT or ACT.

ADMISSIONS: 30% of the 2015-2016 applicants were accepted. The SAT scores for the 2015-2016 freshman class were: Critical Reading-- 2% below 500, 26% between 500 and 599, 56% between 600 and 699, and 17% between 700 and 800. Math-- 1% below 500, 12% between 500 and 599, 42% between 600 and 699, and 46% between 700 and 800. 84% of the current freshmen were in the top fifth of their class; 96% were in the top two fifths. 15 freshmen graduated first in their class. **Admissions Contact:** Bruce Bunnick, Director of Admissions. Email: *admissions@lehigh.edu* Web: *www.lehigh.edu*

FINANCIAL AID: In 2015-2016, 40% of all full-time freshmen and 39% of continuing full-time students received some form of financial aid. 38% of all full-time freshmen and 39% of continuing full-time students received need-based aid. The average freshman award was $39,778. Need-based scholarships or need-based grants averaged $34,998; need-based self-help aid (loans and jobs) averaged $5,252; non-need-based athletic scholarships averaged $37,245; and other non-need-based awards and non-need-based scholarships averaged $13,129. 32% of undergraduate students work part-time. Average annual earnings from campus work are $1212. The average financial indebtedness of the 2015 graduate was $34,940. Lehigh is a member of CSS. The CSS/Profile, FAFSA, noncustodial profile, and business/farm supplement are required. The deadline for filing freshman financial aid applications for fall entry is February 15.

LOCK HAVEN UNIVERSITY OF PENNSYLVANIA *(The complete profile is made available exclusively on our website, www.barronspac.com)*

LYCOMING COLLEGE D-2

www.lycoming.edu

Williamsport, PA 17701 (570) 321-4026
(800) 345-3920

Fax: (570) 321-4317
Email: admissions@lycoming.edu

Full-time: 598 men, 647 women
Part-time: 13 men, 14 women
Graduate: n/av
Year: semesters, summer session
Room & Board: $11,418
Faculty: 89; IIB, av$
Ph.D.s: 96%
Student/Faculty: 14 to 1
Tuition: $37,162
Freshman Class: 1876 applied, 1305 accepted, 343 enrolled
SAT CR/M/W: 510/520/480 **ACT:** 22
Application Deadline: August 1
CEEB CODE: 2372
COMPETITIVE

Lycoming College, established in 1812, is a private, residential, liberal arts institution affiliated with the United Methodist Church. There is 1 undergraduate school. In addition to regional accreditation, Lycoming has baccalaureate program accreditation with AACSB. The 35-acre campus is in a small town in north central Pennsylvania. Including any residence halls, there are 25 buildings.

STUDENT LIFE: 61% of undergraduates are from Pennsylvania. Others are from 28 states, 26 foreign countries, and Canada. 9% are Hispanic; 67% White; 5% Foreign; 5% race unknown; 3% two or more races; 10% African American; 1% Asian American. 23% are Protestant; 16% Catholic. **Female To Male Ratio:** 1.1:1. The average age of freshmen is 18; all undergraduates, 20. 21% do not continue beyond their first year; 72% remain to graduate. **Housing:** 1147 students can be accommodated in college housing, which includes single-sex and coed dorms, on-campus apartments, and off-campus apartments. In addition, there are special-interest houses, nonsmoking and Greek floors, special housing for disabled students, wellness housing, and living and learning communities. On-campus housing is guaranteed for all 4 years. 88% of students live on campus; of those, 75% remain on campus on weekends. All students may keep cars.

FACULTY/CLASSROOMS: 57% of faculty are male; 43% are female. All teach undergraduates. No introductory courses are taught by graduate students. The average class size in an introductory lecture is 18 and in a laboratory is 18.

PROGRAMS OF STUDY: Lycoming confers B.A., and B.S. degrees. Bachelor's degrees are awarded in BIOLOGICAL SCIENCE (biology/biological science), BUSINESS (accounting and business administration and management), COMMUNICATIONS AND THE ARTS (art, art history and appreciation, communications, comparative literature, creative writing, digital communications, dramatic arts, English, French, German, literature, music, Spanish, studio art, and theatre acting), COMPUTER AND PHYSICAL SCIENCE (actuarial mathematics, astronomy, astrophysics, chemistry, mathematics, and physics), SOCIAL SCIENCE (American studies, anthropology, archeology, criminal justice, criminology, economics, history, international studies, philosophy, political science/government, psychology, religion, sociology, and women & gender studies). Archaeology, creative writing, and astrophysics are the strongest academically. Business, psychology, and biology have the largest enrollments.

ACTIVITIES: 11% of men belong to 5 national fraternities; 19% of women belong to 3 local and 2 national sororities. There are 66 groups on campus, including art, band, cheerleading, choir, chorus, computers, dance, drama, environmental, ethnic, film, honors, international, jazz band, LGBT, literary magazine, musical theater, newspaper, orchestra, pep band, photography, political, professional, radio and TV, religious, social, social service, student government, and yearbook. Popular campus events include Campus Carnival, Annual Christmas Candlelight Service, and Choir Concert. **Sports:** There are 9 intercollegiate sports for men and 8 for women, and 7 intramural sports for men and 5 for women. Facilities include an outdoor softball, football, soccer, and lacrosse complex, indoor basketball courts, weight and exercise rooms, indoor pool, and intramural fields. **Graduates:** From July 1, 2015 to June 30, 2016, 262 bachelor's degrees were awarded. The most popular majors were business/marketing (21%), social sciences (15%), and psychology (12%). 15 companies recruited on campus in 2015-2016. In an average class, 59% graduate in 4 years or less, 69% graduate in 5 years or less, and 72% graduate in 6 years or less.

SERVICES: Counseling and information services are available, as is tutoring in every subject, and remedial math, reading, and writing. **Library/Resources:** The library contains 342,951 volumes, 199,856 microform items, and 1,387 audio/video tapes/CDs/DVDs, and subscribes to 35,916 periodicals including electronic. Computerized library services include interlibrary loans, database searching, Internet access, and Wi-Fi capability. Special learning facilities include an art gallery, planetarium, radio station, TV station, Lynn Science Center, and art gallery. **Physically Challenged Students:** 85% of the campus is accessible. Facilities include wheelchair ramps, elevators, special parking, specially equipped restrooms, special class scheduling, lowered drinking fountains, lowered telephones, and special housing. **Special:** Cooperative programs are available with the Ohio and Pennsylvania Colleges of Podiatric Medicine, Pennsylvania College of Optometry, and Penn State, Duke, and Binghamton Universities. Cross-registration is available with the Pennsylvania College of Technology. More than 200 internships, including teacher programs, study abroad in 7 countries, and a Washington semester at American University are available. Lycoming offers work-study programs, dual and student-designed majors, and an accelerated degree program in conjunction with the college's Scholar Program in optometry, podiatric medicine, and dentistry. Nondegree study and pass/fail grading options are available. There are 22 national honor societies, a freshman honors program, and 35 departmental honors programs. **Visiting:** There are regularly scheduled orientations for prospective students, consisting of a student-guided tour of campus and an interview with an admissions counselor. Meetings with professors and coaches and attending a class are possible upon request. There are guides for informal visits, visitors may sit in on classes, and stay overnight. To schedule a visit, contact Barb Carlin at admissions@lycoming.edu. **Campus Safety and Security:** Measures include 24-hour foot and vehicle patrol, emergency notification system, self-defense education, and security escort services. There are emergency telephones, lighted pathways/sidewalks, and controlled access to dorms/residences.

REQUIREMENTS: The SAT or ACT is recommended. Applicants must graduate from an accredited secondary school or have a GED. They must have earned 16 academic units including a minimum of 4 years of English, 3 each of math and social studies, and 2 each of lab science, a foreign language, and academic electives. 2 personal letters of recommendation are also required. Admissions interview is recommended. Portfolios and auditions may be required for students seeking scholarships in the arts. A GPA of 2.3 is required. AP and CLEP credits are accepted. Important factors in the admissions decision are advanced placement or honors courses, leadership record, and evidence of special talent. To graduate, students must complete 128 credits with a minimum overall GPA of 2.0 and a minimum GPA of 2.0 within the major (with an exception of one accounting major that requires 150 credits). Distribution requirements include 4 courses in humanities and 2 each in math (unless exempted on the basis of placement), fine arts, natural science, and social science, one in English composition, global diversity, and domestic diversity. Foreign language requirements include a course numbered 101 (unless exempted on the basis of placement) and a course numbered above 101 in the same language. (If English is a second language, another writing intensive course or an English course above 107 would meet the foreign language requirement.) Students must also complete 3 writing intensive courses (1 in major, 1 outside the major, and 1 additional). Regardless of major, students complete the first-year seminar and an enhanced academic experience. The Enhanced Academic Experience (EAE) provides students with the opportunity to reach their greatest potential by fulfilling an in-depth academic experience outside of the requirements of their major. This added-value experience ensures academic excellence by requiring that students expand their horizons beyond the distribution and major requirements. **Procedure:** Freshmen are admitted in the fall and spring. Entrance exams should be taken during the junior year or by January of the senior year. There are early decision, early admissions, deferred admissions, and rolling admissions plans. Early decision applications should be filed by November 1; regular applications, by August 1 for fall entry; and December 1 for spring entry. Notification of early decision is sent November 15; regular decision, on a rolling basis. 16 early decision candidates were accepted for the 2016-2017 class. 76 applicants were on the 2016 waiting list; 52 were admitted. Application fees are waived if application is completed on-line. **Transfer Students:** 31 transfer students enrolled in 2015-2016. Applicants must submit appropriate transcripts and have a minimum GPA of 2.0 in transferable courses. Students who have completed 24 transferable semester hours are not required to submit SAT I or ACT results. 32 of 128 credits required for the bachelor's degree must be completed at Lycoming. **International Students:** There are 59 international students enrolled. The school actively recruits these students. They must take the TOEFL with a minimum score of 525 on the paper-based TOEFL (PBT) or 70 on the Internet-based version (iBT). Students must also take the IELTS.

ADMISSIONS: 70% of the 2016-2017 applicants were accepted. The SAT scores for the 2016-2017 freshman class were: Critical Reading-- 39% below 500, 50% between 500 and 599, 10% between 600 and 699, and 2% between 700 and 800. Math-- 38% below 500, 48% between 500 and 599, 13% between 600 and 699, and 1% between 700 and 800. Writing-- 56% below 500, 35% between 500 and 599, and 8% between 600 and 699. The ACT scores were 5% between 12 and 17, 61% between 18 and 23, 30% between 24 and 29, and 4% above 30. 34% of the current freshmen were in the top fifth of their class; 61% were in the top two fifths. 1 freshman graduated first in the class. **Admissions Contact:** Mike Konopski, VP for Enrollment Management. Email: *admissions@lycoming.edu* Web: *www.lycoming.edu*

FINANCIAL AID: In 2016-2017, 100% of all full-time freshmen and continuing full-time students received some form of financial aid. 83% of all full-time freshmen and 86% of continuing full-time students received need-based aid. The average freshman award was $39,438. Need-based scholarships or need-based grants averaged $16,766 ($33,688 maximum); need-based self-help aid (loans and jobs) averaged $3,710 ($8,500 maximum); and other non-need-based awards and non-need-based scholarships averaged $25,557 ($51,877 maximum). 52% of undergraduate students work part-time. Average annual earnings from campus work are $1548. Lycoming is a member of CSS. The FAFSA code is 003293. The deadline for filing freshman financial aid applications for fall entry is May 1.

MANSFIELD UNIVERSITY *(The complete profile is made available exclusively on our website, www.barronspac.com)*

MARYWOOD UNIVERSITY — E-2

www.marywood.edu

Scranton, PA 18509 — **(570) 348-6234** / **(866) 279-9663**

Fax: (570) 961-4763 — **Email: yourfuture@marywood.edu**

Full-time: 556 men, 1209 women
Part-time: 41 men, 137 women
Graduate: 267 men, 810 women
Year: semesters, summer session
Room & Board: $13,900

Faculty: IIA, -$
Ph.D.s: 87%
Student/Faculty: 11 to 1
Tuition: $33,000
Freshman Class: 2230 applied, 1513 accepted, 331 enrolled

SAT CR/M/W: 515/523/508 **ACT:** recommended
CEEB CODE: 2407
Application Deadline: open
COMPETITIVE

Marywood University, founded in 1915, is a comprehensive, Catholic university with 99 undergraduate, graduate and doctoral degree programs. Established by the Sisters, Servants of the Immaculate Heart of Mary, Marywood University offered the region's first doctoral degree program and is a leading provider of graduate education in the region, with 36 master's degree programs and 37 certificate offerings. Marywood University has eight divisions and includes four Colleges and four Schools: The Insalaco College of Creative and Performing Arts, The Reap College of Education and Human Development, The College of Health and Human Services, The Munley College of Liberal Arts and Sciences,

The School of Architecture, The School of Business and Global Innovation, The School of Social Work and the Center for Interdisciplinary Studies. Committed to enriching human lives through ethical and religious values and a tradition of service, and motivated by a pioneering, progressive spirit, Marywood provides a framework for educational excellence that enables students to develop fully as persons and to master professional and leadership skills necessary for meeting human needs. There are 7 undergraduate schools and 7 graduate schools. In addition to regional accreditation, Marywood has baccalaureate program accreditation with ACBSP, ADA, CSWE, NASAD, NASM, NCATE, NLN, AATA, AMTA, APA, ACEN, ARC-PA, ASHA, CAATE, and CACREP. The 123-acre campus is in a suburban area 120 miles west of New York City and 115 miles north of Philadelphia. Including any residence halls, there are 33 buildings.

STUDENT LIFE: 67% of undergraduates are from Pennsylvania. Others are from 18 states, and 20 foreign countries. 74% are White; 6% Hispanic; 3% Foreign; 2% African American; 2% Asian American; 2% two or more races; 10% race unknown. **Female To Male Ratio:** 2.5:1. The average age of freshmen is 19; all undergraduates, 21. 16% do not continue beyond their first year; 67% remain to graduate. **Housing:** 934 students can be accommodated in college housing, which includes single-sex and coed dorms and on-campus apartments, themed, and special interest housing. On-campus housing is guaranteed for all 4 years. 63% of students commute. All students may keep cars. Alcohol is not permitted

FACULTY/CLASSROOMS: 43% of faculty are male; 57% are female. No introductory courses are taught by graduate students.

PROGRAMS OF STUDY: Marywood confers B.A., B.Arch., B.E.D.A., B.S., B.B.A., B.F.A., B.M., B.S.N. and B.S.W. degrees. Master's and doctoral degrees are also awarded. Bachelor's degrees are awarded in BIOLOGICAL SCIENCE (biology/biological science and biotechnology), BUSINESS (accounting, banking and finance, business administration and management, hospitality management services, information & communication technology, international business management, marketing/retailing/merchandising, and retailing), COMMUNICATIONS AND THE ARTS (advertising, arts administration/management, broadcasting, ceramic art and design, communications, digital communications, dramatic arts, English, French, graphic design, illustration, music business management, music performance, musical theater, painting, photography, sculpture, Spanish, studio art, and theater management), COMPUTER AND PHYSICAL SCIENCE (information sciences and systems, mathematics, and science), EDUCATION (art education, athletic training, dance education, early childhood education, education of the deaf and hearing impaired, elementary education, English education, foreign languages education, mathematics education, music education, physical education, science education, secondary education, social science education, and special education), ENGINEERING AND ENVIRONMENTAL DESIGN (architecture, aviation administration/management, environmental design, environmental science, and interior design), HEALTH PROFESSIONS (art therapy, health care administration, health science, medical technology, music therapy, nursing, physician's assistant, premedicine, preosteopathy, and speech pathology/audiology), SOCIAL SCIENCE (clinical psychology, communication sciences & disorders, criminal justice, dietetics, family/consumer studies, gerontology, history, industrial and organizational psychology, philosophy, physical fitness/movement, political science/government, prelaw, psychology, religion, social science, and social work). Architecture, Pre-physician assistant, and communication sciences & disorders are the strongest academically. Pre-physician assistant, nursing, and communication sciences & disorders have the largest enrollments.

ACTIVITIES: There are no fraternities; 31% of women belong to 2 local sororities. There are 60 groups on campus, including art, band, cheerleading, choir, chorus, dance, drama, environmental, ethnic, film, honors, international, jazz band, LGBT, literary magazine, musical theater, newspaper, orchestra, photography, political, professional, radio and TV, religious, social, social service, student government, symphony, and volunteers in action. Popular campus events include Spring Fling, Homecoming formal, Flapjack Fest, and Midnight Madness. **Sports:** There are 9 intercollegiate sports for men and 11 for women. Facilities include a fitness center, climbing wall, elevated running track, dance/aerobics studio, arena and high tech athletic training areas, swimming pool with diving boards. Outdoor facilities include a multipurpose turf field, tennis courts, sand volleyball court, basketball courts, and three grass fields. **Graduates:** From July 1, 2015 to June 30, 2016, 396 bachelor's degrees were awarded. The most popular majors were health professions and related programs (30%), business, management, marketing & related support services (14%), architecture, and interior architecture (10%). 89 companies recruited on campus in 2015-2016. In an average class, 4% graduate in 3 years or less, 47% graduate in 4 years or less, 66% graduate in 5 years or less, and 67% graduate in 6 years or less.

SERVICES: Counseling and information services are available, as is tutoring in most subjects. There is also a reader service for the blind, and a writing center available for students. **Library/Resources:** The library contains 220,273 volumes, 25,040 audio/video tapes/CDs/DVDs, and subscribes to 31,928 periodicals including electronic. Computerized library services include interlibrary loans, database searching, Internet access, and Wi-Fi capability. Special learning facilities include an art gallery, radio station, an academic excellence center, a student counseling center, a human physiology lab, human development (counseling, psychology) laboratories, biotechnology lab, a communication sciences and disorders clinic, a nutrition and dietetics lab, an assistive technology center, an outpatient mental health clinic, multiple "smart" classrooms, multiple computer labs, a center for architectural studies studios, a television studio and editing suites, an art center (including ceramic, painting, drawing/foundation, sculpture, glass, metal, clay, wood, photography, fabric, jewelry, and printmaking studios), a visual arts center (including graphic design and interior architecture computer labs), 2 art exhibit galleries, the Maslow Collection of Contemporary Art and Maslow Study Gallery), a theater, and a black box theater. **Physically Challenged Students:** 95% of the campus is accessible. Facilities include wheelchair ramps, elevators, special parking, specially equipped restrooms, special class scheduling, and lowered drinking fountains. **Special:** Marywood offers cross-registration with the University of Scranton, internships, and study abroad (Argentina, Austria, Brazil, China, England, France, Greece Ireland, Italy, Japan, New Zealand, Portugal, South Africa, South Korea, Spain, Taiwan, Turkey, and Wales). Also offered are accelerated degree programs in dietetics and social work, dual majors, and student-designed majors. Students may earn credit for life, military and work experience. There are 20 national honor societies, a freshman honors program, and 18 departmental honors programs. **Visiting:** There are regularly scheduled orientations for prospective students, including a presentation/overview of Marywood University, talking with academic department faculty members and meeting and talking with current students. There are guides for informal visits, visitors may sit in on classes, and stay overnight. To schedule a visit, contact the Office of University Admissions. **Campus Safety and Security:** Measures include 24-hour foot and vehicle patrol, emergency notification system, self-defense education, and security escort services. There are emergency telephones, lighted pathways/sidewalks, controlled access to dorms/residences, night security in dorms, card access to dorm floors, and transportation on request.

REQUIREMENTS: The SAT is required. The ACT is recommended. Applicants are expected to be graduates of an accredited secondary school or have the GED. A minimum of 17 academic credits is required, including 4 in English, 3 each in social studies and science (1 as lab), 2 in math and 6 academic electives. A letter of support is required in selected majors, as is a portfolio or an audition where appropriate. A personal interview is strongly recommended. AP and CLEP credits are accepted. Important factors in the admissions decision are advanced placement or honors courses, leadership record, and recommendations by school officials. To graduate, students must complete a liberal arts core consisting of religious studies, philosophy, math, science, history, social science, literature, writing, foreign language and fine arts. Additional course requirements include a fist-year experience course for new undergraduate students who have not transferred from another post-secondary institution and one course with a global studies perspective. **Procedure:** Freshmen are admitted in the fall and spring. Entrance exams should be taken in the junior and senior year before graduation. There are deferred admissions and rolling admissions plans. Application deadlines are open. Application fee is $35. Notification of early decision is sent September 1; regular decision. Application fees are waived if application is completed online. **Transfer Students:** 132 transfer students enrolled in 2015-2016. SAT or ACT scores are required of transfer applicants who have earned fewer then 12 college credits; both secondary school and college transcripts are required. Transfer students are required to have earned a minimum GPA of 2.25 at the college most recently attended (3.0 minimum for some majors). A grade of C is the minimum requirement for transfer of academic credit. The SAT is required for nursing transfer students. 42 of 120 credits required for the bachelor's degree must be completed at Marywood. **International Students:** There are 81 international students enrolled. The school actively recruits these students. They must take the TOEFL with a minimum score of 71 on the Internet-based version (iBT), or take the IELTS score band of 5.5 minimum. They must also take the SAT or ACT, scoring 19 ACT/900 SAT.

ADMISSIONS: 68% of the 2016-2017 applicants were accepted. The SAT scores for the 2016-2017 freshman class were: Critical Reading-- 39% below 500, 49% between 500 and 599, and 12% between 600 and 699. Math-- 34% below 500, 53% between 500 and 599, 12% between 600 and 699, and 1% between 700 and 800. Writing-- 43% below 500, 47% between 500 and 599, and 10% between 600 and 699. 2 freshmen graduated first in their class. **Admissions Contact:** Christian DiGregorio, Director of University Admissions. Email: *yourfuture@marywood.edu* Web: *www.marywood.edu*

FINANCIAL AID: In 2016-2017, 90% of all full-time freshmen and 83% of continuing full-time students received some form of financial aid. 85% of all full-time freshmen and 80% of continuing full-time students received need-based aid. The average freshman award was $26,371. Need-based scholarships or need-based grants averaged $21,467; need-based self-help aid (loans and jobs) averaged $4,695; other non-need-based awards and non-need-based scholarships averaged $3,637; and $1,114 from other forms of aid. Average annual earnings from campus work are $1948. The average financial indebtedness of the 2016 graduate was $28,330. The state aid form is required. The FAFSA code is 003296. The priority date for freshman financial aid applications for fall entry is February 15.

MERCYHURST UNIVERSITY B-1

www.mercyhurst.edu

Erie, PA 16546 **(814) 824-2202** **(800) 825-1926**

Fax: (814) 824-3634 **Email: admissions@mercyhurst.edu**

Full-time: 1390 men, 1988 women
Part-time: 129 men, 333 women
Graduate: 140 men, 140 women
Year: semesters, summer session
Room & Board: $13,000

Faculty: IIB, -$
Ph.D.s: 60%
Student/Faculty: n/av
Tuition: $34,420
Freshman Class: 3000 applied, 1900 accepted, 650 enrolled

SAT CR/M/W: 550/530/510 **ACT:** 23
Application Deadline: September 1

CEEB CODE: 2410
COMPETITIVE

Mercyhurst University, established in 1926, is a private, nonprofit institution affiliated with the Roman Catholic Church. The university offers undergraduate degrees in the arts, business, health science, liberal arts, religious studies, and teacher preparation, as well as a degree-directed program for the learning disabled. There is 1 undergraduate school and 1 graduate school. In addition to regional accreditation, Mercyhurst has baccalaureate program accreditation with ADA and CSWE. The 88-acre campus is in a suburban area within Erie, PA. Including any residence halls, there are 44 buildings.

STUDENT LIFE: 60% of undergraduates are from Pennsylvania. Others are from 37 states, 14 foreign countries, and Canada. 76% are from public schools. 91% are White; 4% African American; 3% Foreign; 1% Asian American; 1% Hispanic. 53% are Catholic; 21% Protestant; 18% claim no religious affiliation. **Female To Male Ratio:** 1.5:1. The average age of freshmen is 18; all undergraduates, 26. 20% do not continue beyond their first year; 62% remain to graduate. **Housing:** 1718 students can be accommodated in college housing, which includes single-sex and coed dorms, on-campus apartments, and married student housing. On-campus housing is guaranteed for all 4 years. 65% of students live on campus; of those, 91% remain on campus on weekends. Upperclassmen may keep cars.

FACULTY/CLASSROOMS: 57% of faculty are male; 43% are female. All teach undergraduates, and 30% do research. No introductory courses are taught by graduate students. The average class size in an introductory lecture is 35; in a laboratory is 12; and in a regular course is 25.

PROGRAMS OF STUDY: Mercyhurst University confers B.A., B.S., B.F.A. and B.M. degrees. Associate, master's, and doctoral degrees are also awarded. Bachelor's degrees are awarded in BIOLOGICAL SCIENCE (biochemistry and biology/biological science), BUSINESS (accounting, banking and finance, business administration and management, fashion merchandising, hotel/motel and restaurant management, insurance and risk management, management information systems, and marketing/retailing/merchandising), COMMUNICATIONS AND THE ARTS (advertising, broadcasting, communications, dance, English, graphic design, journalism, languages, music, musical theater, public relations, and studio art), COMPUTER AND PHYSICAL SCIENCE (chemistry, earth science, geology, mathematics, web services, and web technology), EDUCATION (art education, athletic training, business education, early childhood education, elementary education, home economics education, mathematics education, music education, science education, secondary education, social science education, and special education), ENGINEERING AND ENVIRONMENTAL DESIGN (environmental science and interior design), HEALTH PROFESSIONS (art therapy, medical laboratory technology, predentistry, premedicine, preosteopathy, prepharmacy, preveterinary science, and sports medicine), SOCIAL SCIENCE (anthropology, archeology, criminal justice, family/consumer studies, forensic studies, history, philosophy, political science/government, prelaw, psychology, religion, religious education, social work, and sociology). Applied forensic science, intelligence studies, and sports medicine are the strongest academically. Business, education, and sports medicine have the largest enrollments.

ACTIVITIES: There are no fraternities or sororities. There are 93 groups on campus, including art, band, cheerleading, choir, chorus, communications, computers, dance, debate, drama, ethnic, film, honors, international, jazz band, LGBT, literary magazine, musical theater, newspaper, opera, orchestra, pep band, photography, political, professional, radio and TV, religious, social, social service, and student government. Popular campus events include Activities Day, Parents Weekend, and Winter and Spring Formals. **Sports:** There are 13 intercollegiate sports for men and 12 for women, and 9 intramural sports for men and 9 for women. Facilities include indoor crew tanks, football, field hockey, lacrosse, soccer fields, an ice hockey rink/arena, Nautilus facilities, free-weight room, baseball/softball complex, training room, and a basketball arena. **Graduates:** From July 1, 2015 to June 30, 2016, 800 bachelor's degrees were awarded. 100 companies recruited on campus in 2015-2016.

SERVICES: Counseling and information services are available, as is tutoring in every subject, and remedial math, reading, and writing. **Library/Resources:** The library contains 165,644 volumes, 50,631 microform items, 9,309 audio/video tapes/CDs/DVDs, and subscribes to 848 periodicals including electronic. Computerized library services include interlibrary loans and database searching. Special learning facilities include an art gallery, planetarium, radio station, TV station, Northwestern Pennsylvania historical archives, and archeological institute. **Physically Challenged Students:** 90% of the campus is accessible. Facilities include wheelchair ramps, elevators, special parking, specially equipped restrooms, and lowered drinking fountains. **Special:** There are 7 national honor societies, a freshman honors program, and 4 departmental honors programs. **Visiting:** There are regularly scheduled orientations for prospective students, including tours, class visits, faculty meetings, and interviews with financial aid and admissions counselors. There are guides for informal visits, visitors may sit in on classes, and stay overnight. To schedule a visit, contact the Admissions Office. **Campus Safety and Security:** Measures include 24-hour foot and vehicle patrol, emergency notification system, and self-defense education. There are also shuttle buses, emergency telephones, lighted pathways/sidewalks, controlled access to dorms/residences, and 24-hour security camera surveillance system.

REQUIREMENTS: The SAT or ACT is required. Applicants must graduate from an accredited secondary school or have a GED. 16 academic credits are required, including 4 years of English, 3 each of math and social studies, and 2 each of history, science, and a foreign language. Interviews are recommended. Art applicants must submit portfolios; auditions are required of music and dance applicants. AP and CLEP credits are accepted. Important factors in the admissions decision are recommendations by alumni, evidence of special talent, and personality/intangible qualities. To graduate, students must complete the core curriculum, which includes English, math, science, religion, philosophy, history, and a computer course. Distribution requirements include American history, cultural appreciation, human behavior, and ethics. A minimum GPA of 2.0 is required, with a 2.5 in the major, and a minimum total of 123 credit hours. The number of credit hours in the major varies, with a minimum of 30. A thesis is necessary for history and English majors. **Procedure:** Freshmen are admitted to all sessions. Entrance exams should be taken during the spring of the junior year. There are deferred admissions and rolling admissions plans. Applications should be filed by September 1 for fall entry. Notification is sent on a rolling basis. Applications are accepted online. **Transfer Students:** 90 transfer students enrolled in 2015-2016. A minimum GPA of 2.5 on previous college work is required 45 of 121 credits required for the bachelor's degree must be completed at Mercyhurst. **International Students:** There are 250 international students enrolled. The school actively recruits these students. They must take the TOEFL, and either the SAT or ACT.

ADMISSIONS: 63% of the 2016-2017 applicants were accepted. The ACT scores were 21% below 12, 46% between 12 and 17, and 33% between 18 and 23. 79% were in the top two fifths. 20 freshmen graduated first in their class. **Admissions Contact:** Christian Beyer, Director of Admissions. Email: *cbeyer@mercyhurst.edu* Web: *www.mercyhurst.edu*

FINANCIAL AID: In 2016-2017, 95% of all full-time freshmen received some form of financial aid. 76% of all full-time freshmen received need-based aid. The average freshman award was $18,000. Need-based scholarships or need-based grants averaged $12,000. 60% of undergraduate students work part-time. Average annual earnings from campus work are $1200. The average financial indebtedness of the 2016 graduate was $27,000. Mercyhurst is a member of CSS. The FAFSA code is 003297. The priority date for freshman financial aid applications for fall entry is May 1. The filing deadline for fall entry is August 1.

MESSIAH COLLEGE — D-3

www.messiah.edu

Mechanicsburg, PA 17055	(717) 691-6000 (800) 233-4220
Fax: (717) 796-5374	**Email:** admiss@messiah.edu
Full-time: 1050 men, 1598 women	**Faculty:** 171; IIB, av$
Part-time: 42 men, 98 women	**Ph.D.s:** 81%
Graduate: 133 men, 384 women	**Student/Faculty:** 13 to 1
Year: semesters, summer session	**Tuition:** $33,180
Room & Board: $9920	**Freshman Class:** 2472 applied, 1977 accepted, 696 enrolled
SAT CR/M/W: 560/560/530 **ACT:** 25	**CEEB CODE:** 2411
Application Deadline: open	**COMPETITIVE+**

Messiah College, founded in 1909, is a private Christian college of the liberal and applied arts and sciences. The college is committed to the evangelical spirit rooted in the Anabaptist, Pietist, and Wesleyan traditions. There are 4 undergraduate schools and 1 graduate school. In addition to regional accreditation, Messiah has baccalaureate program accreditation with ABET, ACBSP, ADA, CSWE, NASAD, NASM, CAAHEP, CCNE, and ACEND. The 471-acre campus is in a small town 12 miles southwest of Harrisburg. Including any residence halls, there are 53 buildings.

STUDENT LIFE: 63% of undergraduates are from Pennsylvania. Others are from 38 states, 29 foreign countries, and Canada. 74% are from public schools. 81% are White; 4% Hispanic; 5% Foreign; 3% two or more races; 2% African American; 2% Asian American; 1% race unknown. 90% are Protestant. **Female To Male Ratio:** 1.6:1. The average age of freshmen is 19; all undergraduates, 21. 15% do not continue beyond their first year; 76% remain to graduate. **Housing:** 2383 students can be accommodated in college housing, which includes single-sex and coed dorms, on-campus apartments, off-campus apartments, and special-interest houses. On-campus housing is guaranteed for all 4 years. 86% of students live on campus; of those, 70% remain on campus on weekends. Upperclassmen may keep cars. Alcohol is not permitted.

FACULTY/CLASSROOMS: 50% of faculty are male; 50% are female, 92% teach undergraduates. No introductory courses are taught by graduate students. The average class size in an introductory lecture is 27; in a laboratory is 18; and in a regular course is 24.

PROGRAMS OF STUDY: Messiah confers B.A., B.S., B.M., B.S.E., B.S.N., B.S.W., and B.F.A. degrees. Master's and doctoral degrees are also awarded. Bachelor's degrees are awarded in BIOLOGICAL SCIENCE (biochemistry, biology/adolescence education, biology/biological science, molecular biology, and nutrition), BUSINESS (accounting, business administration and management, international business management, management information systems, marketing/retailing/merchandising, sports management, and sustainable management), COMMUNICATIONS AND THE ARTS (art history and appreciation, arts administration/management, communications, dance, dramatic arts, English, film, television and digital media, French, German, journalism, media arts, media management, music, music business management, music ministry, music performance, musical theater, public relations, Spanish, studio art, and theater management), COMPUTER AND PHYSICAL SCIENCE (applied science, chemistry, chemistry/adolescence education, computer science, digital arts/technology, mathematics, and physics), EDUCATION (art education, athletic training, early childhood education, elementary education, English education, environmental education, foreign languages education, mathematics education, music education, physical education, recreation education, science education, social studies education, and Spanish adolescense education), ENGINEERING AND ENVIRONMENTAL DESIGN (engineering and environmental science), HEALTH PROFESSIONS (exercise science, nursing, and pre-health studies), SOCIAL SCIENCE (biblical studies, biopsychology, child care/child and family studies, Chinese Studies, criminal justice, dietetics, economics, ethnic studies, family/consumer studies, history, human development, interdisciplinary studies, ministries, peace studies, philosophy, political science/government, psychology, social work, sociology, Spanish studies, and theological studies). Engineering, nursing, and business administration have the largest enrollments.

ACTIVITIES: There are no fraternities or sororities. There are 81 groups on campus, including art, band, choir, chorale, chorus, dance, debate, drama, environmental, ethnic, film, honors, international, jazz band, literary magazine, musical theater, newspaper, orchestra, pep band, political, professional, radio and TV, religious, social, social service, student government, symphony, and yearbook. Popular campus events include Cultural Series, Traveling Music Ensembles, and Theater Productions. **Sports:** There are 10 intercollegiate sports for men and 10 for women, and 5 intramural sports for men and 5 for women. Facilities include indoor and outdoor tracks, a pool with separate diving well, wrestling and gymnastics areas, a weight room, numerous playing fields, and courts for racquetball, basketball, and tennis. The campus center provides additional recreational facilities. **Graduates:** From July 1, 2015 to June 30, 2016, 652 bachelor's degrees were awarded. The most popular majors were nursing (8%), psychology (6%), and business administration (6%). 558 companies recruited on campus in 2015-2016. In an average class, 72% graduate in 4 years or less, 76% graduate in 5 years or less, and 76% graduate in 6 years or less. Of the 2015 graduating class, 14% were enrolled in graduate school within 6 months of graduation, and 81% were employed.

SERVICES: Counseling and information services are available, as is tutoring in most subjects. There is a reader service for the blind, and remedial math, reading, and writing. **Library/Resources:** The library contains 254,862 volumes, 6 microform items, 20,583 audio/video tapes/CDs/DVDs, and subscribes to 107,565 periodicals including electronic. Computerized library services include interlibrary loans, database searching, Internet access, and Wi-Fi capability. Special learning facilities include an art gallery, natural history museum, and radio station. **Physically Challenged Students:** 80% of the campus is accessible. Facilities include wheelchair ramps, elevators, special parking, specially equipped restrooms, special class scheduling, lowered drinking fountains, and special housing. **Special:** Off-campus study is available through over 30 carefully selected programs on every continent (except Antarctica) and in a variety of major metropolitan cities around the world, including Paris, London, and Barcelona, and in such diverse counties as Chile, China, India, and Lithuania. Off-campus options within the United States include the Contemporary Music Center in Nashville, the American Studies Program in Washington DC, the AuSable Institute of Environmental Studies, Los Angeles Film Studies, Oregon Extension, and others. Students may also spend a semester or year at any of 12 other Christian Consortium Colleges in a student exchange program. Numerous internships, practicum, and service opportunities are also available both domestically and around the globe, with an average of over 600 students traveling around the world each year through Messiah College. There are 7 national honor societies, a freshman honors program, and 17 departmental honors programs. **Visiting:** There are regularly scheduled orientations for prospective students, including a campus tour, academic and career advising, and a financial aid information session. There are guides for informal visits, visitors may sit in on classes, and stay overnight. To schedule a visit, contact the Admissions Office. **Campus Safety and Security:** Measures include 24-hour foot and vehicle patrol, emergency notification system, self-defense education, and security escort services. There are emergency telephones, lighted pathways/sidewalks, controlled access to dorms/residences, and text messaging alert system.

REQUIREMENTS: The SAT or ACT is required. Applicants must have graduated from an accredited high school or the equivalent. Secondary preparation of students who enroll usually includes 4 units in English, 2 or 3 in math, 2 or 3 in natural science, 2 or more in both social studies and foreign languages, and 4 in academic electives. Students who enroll are usually in the top one third of their class and have a B average or better. A campus visit with an information session is recommended. Potential music majors must audition. AP and CLEP credits are accepted. Important factors in the admissions decision are advanced placement or honors courses, recommendations by school officials, and leadership record. All students must complete at least 123 credits with a minimum GPA of 2.0. The last 30 credits must be taken at Messiah College and a minimum of 12 credits must be in the major. **Procedure:** Freshmen are admitted fall and spring. Entrance exams should be taken in the spring of the junior year. There are early admissions and rolling admissions plans. Application deadlines are open. Application fee is $20. Notification is sent on a rolling basis. Applications are accepted online. **Transfer Students:** 81 transfer students enrolled in 2015-2016. Transfer applicants should have earned a 2.5 GPA in at least 12 college credits. The college prefers that applicants also have composite SAT or ACT scores and that they seek a campus visit. Students with fewer than 30 credits in college should submit a high school transcript as well. 30 of 123 credits required for the bachelor's degree must be completed at Messiah. **International Students:** There are 143 international students enrolled. The school actively recruits these students. They must take the TOEFL, and either the SAT or ACT.

ADMISSIONS: 80% of the 2016-2017 applicants were accepted. The SAT scores for the 2016-2017 freshman class were: Critical Reading-- 23% below 500, 44% between 500 and 599, 27% between 600 and 699, and 6% between 700 and 800. Math-- 20% below 500, 44% between 500 and 599, 29% between 600 and 699, and 8% between 700 and 800. Writing-- 29% below 500, 45% between 500 and 599, 20% between 600 and 699, and 5% between 700 and 800. The ACT scores were 24% below 12, 26% between 12 and 17, 36% between 18 and 23, 14% between 24 and 29, and 20% above 30. 53% of the current freshmen were in the top fifth of their class; 79% were in the top two fifths. There were 2 National Merit finalists. 9 freshmen graduated first in their class. **Admissions Contact:** John Chopka, Vice President for Enrollment Management. Email: *admiss@messiah.edu* Web: *www.messiah.edu*

FINANCIAL AID: In 2016-2017, 100% of all full-time freshmen and 99% of continuing full-time students received some form of financial aid. 63% of all full-time freshmen and 64% of continuing full-time students received need-based aid. The average freshman award was $15,056. 58% of undergraduate students work part-time. Average annual earnings from campus work are $2175. The average financial indebtedness of the 2016 graduate was $34,301. Messiah is a member of CSS. The FAFSA code is 003298. The priority date for freshman financial aid applications for fall entry is April 1.

MILLERSVILLE UNIVERSITY OF PENNSYLVANIA — E-4

www.millersville.edu

Millersville, PA 17551 — **(717) 871-4625**

Fax: (717) 871-2147	**Email:** admissions@millersville.edu
Full-time: 2654 men, 3288 women	**Faculty:** 292
Part-time: 442 men, 596 women	**Ph.D.s:** 98%
Graduate: 233 men, 714 women	**Student/Faculty:** 20 to 1
Year: 4-1-4, summer session	**Tuition:** $11,494 ($20,854)
Room & Board: $12,288	**Freshman Class:** 6861 applied, 4767 accepted, 1327 enrolled
SAT CR/M/W: 510/510/490 **ACT:** 22	**CEEB CODE:** 2656
Application Deadline: rolling	**COMPETITIVE**

Millersville University of Pennsylvania, founded in 1855 as a teaching college, and is one of the most highly regarded universities in the northeast region of the United States. Millersville recognizes excellence in teaching and learning as its reason for being, and is committed to offering students a high quality, comprehensive university experience of exceptional value. MU mission is to provide diverse, dynamic, meaningful experiences to inspire learners to grow both intellectually and personally to enable them to contribute positively to local and global communities. Millersville is one of 14 comprehensive universities within the PA State System of Higher Education and is committed to providing rigorous academic programs through nationally recognized teacher education programs, strong science and technology programs, ample service learning opportunities and a strong liberal arts-based curriculum. With more than 55 majors to choose from, students select Millersville for its academic reputation and array of academic programs that are supported by state-of-the-art science and industrial technology laboratories, art studios, writing and language laboratories. The University emphasizes holistic development by complimenting academic programs with countless co-curricular opportunities such as intercollegiate (NCAA Division II) and intramural athletics, and the University's emphasis on community engagement and civic responsibility. There are 3 undergraduate schools and 1 graduate school. In addition to regional accreditation, Millersville, MU has baccalaureate program accreditation with ABET, ACBSP, CSWE, NASAD, NASM, NCATE, NLN, AACTE, ACEN, ACS, ATMAE, CAEP, CoARC, ITEEA, and NASP. The 250-acre campus is in a small town 5 miles southwest of Lancaster. Including any residence halls, there are 89 buildings.

STUDENT LIFE: 94% of undergraduates are from Pennsylvania. Others are from 34 states, 61 foreign countries, and Canada. 9% are African American; 9% Hispanic; 75% White; 3% Asian American; 2% two or more races; 1% Foreign; 1% race unknown. **Female To Male Ratio:** 1.4:1. The average age of freshmen is 18; all undergraduates, 21. 23% do not continue beyond their first year; 77% remain to graduate. **Housing:** 2225 students can be accommodated in college housing, which includes coed dorms, on-campus apartments, and off-campus apartments. In addition, there are honors houses, special-interest houses, apartments for single students, housing for disabled students, housing for international students, theme housing, wellness housing, and academic interest housing for several subject areas. University-affiliated apartments and dormitories for single students adjacent to campus are available. On-campus housing is available on a first-come, first-served basis, and is available on a lottery system for upperclassmen. 69% of students commute. All students may keep cars. Alcohol is not permitted.

FACULTY/CLASSROOMS: 49% of faculty are male; 51% are female. 93% teach undergraduates. No introductory courses are taught by graduate students. The average class size in an introductory lecture is 28; in a laboratory is 20; and in a regular course is 27.

PROGRAMS OF STUDY: MU confers B.A., B.Des., B.S., B.F.A., B.S.Ed. and B.S.N. degrees. Associate, master's, and doctoral degrees are also awarded. Bachelor's degrees are awarded in AGRICULTURE (animal science and environmental studies), BIOLOGICAL SCIENCE (biochemistry, biology/biological science, biotechnology, botany, environmental biology, and marine biology), BUSINESS (accounting, business administration and management, business administration - international, business administration marketing, finance, and international business), COMMUNICATIONS AND THE ARTS (art, broadcasting, communication studies, English, English as a second/foreign language, English literature, English Writing, film, television and digital media, French, German, graphic communications, graphic design, journalism, linguistics, music, music technology, public relations, Spanish, communication arts - speech, and theatre acting), COMPUTER AND PHYSICAL SCIENCE (actuarial science, applied mathematics, atmospheric sciences and meteorology, chemistry, computer science, earth science, environmental chemistry, environmental geology, geology, mathematics, oceanography, physics & physical oceanography, physics, polymer science, quantitative methods, and statistics), EDUCATION (art education, athletic training, early childhood education, elementary education, English education, general studies, global studies, mathematics education, middle school education, music education, science education, social studies education, special education, and technical education), ENGINEERING AND ENVIRONMENTAL DESIGN (construction technology, engineering, industrial engineering technology, manufacturing technology, nuclear medicine technology, and occupational safety and health), HEALTH PROFESSIONS (allied health, biology, medical technology, nursing, pre-optometry, prepharmacy, prepodiatry, and respiratory therapy), SOCIAL SCIENCE (anthropology, archeology, criminology, economics, geography, history, interdisciplinary studies, international studies, philosophy, political science/government, psychology, social studies, social work, and sociology). Applied engineering technology is the strongest academically. Business administration, biology, and psychology have the largest enrollments.

ACTIVITIES: 3% of men belong to 9 national fraternities; 4% of women belong to 9 national sororities. There are 205 groups on campus, including art, band, cheerleading, choir, chorale, chorus, communications, computers, dance, drama, environmental, ethnic, film, honors, jazz band, LGBT, literary magazine, marching band, musical theater, newspaper, orchestra, political, professional, radio and TV, religious, social, social service, student government, and symphony. Popular campus events include Organization Outbreak, Homecoming, Superfest, Into the Streets, Spring Concert, PrideFest, Wellness Fair/Breast-A-Ville, and Greek Week. **Sports:** There are 7 intercollegiate sports for men and 12 for women, and 22 intramural sports for men and 22 for women. Facilities include a football stadium, pools, gyms, fitness centers, dance studio, ropes course, wrestling and weight rooms, basketball, volleyball, tennis, badminton courts, indoor and outdoor running track, baseball, and softball stadiums, a golf course, frisbee, and walking/jogging routes. **Graduates:** From July 1, 2015 to June 30, 2016, 1458 bachelor's degrees were awarded. The most popular majors were business administration (13%), speech communication (8%), and psychology (8%). 243 companies recruited on campus in 2015-2016. In an average class, 37% graduate in 4 years or less, 58% graduate in 5 years or less, and 61% graduate in 6 years or less.

SERVICES: Counseling and information services are available, as is tutoring in most subjects. There is a reader service for the blind, and remedial math and writing. Every effort is made to tailor tutoring services to individual needs. **Library/Resources:** The library contains 322,704 volumes, 81,177 microform items, 4,759 audio/video tapes/CDs/DVDs, and subscribes to 377,017 periodicals including electronic. Computerized library services include interlibrary loans, database searching, Internet access, and Wi-Fi capability. Special learning facilities include an art gallery, radio station, TV station, a recording studio, teleconferencing center, weather information center, foreign language lab, 2 performing arts centers - Winter and Ware, Atmospheric Research and Aerostat Facility, Center for Disaster Research & Education, Foucault Pendulum, Chincoteague Bay Field Station at the Marine Science Consortium, Servicemembers Opportunity Colleges Consortium (SOCC), Aircraft flight simulators, safety engineering and training modules. **Physically Challenged Students:** 85% of the campus is accessible. Facilities include wheelchair ramps, elevators, special parking, specially equipped restrooms, special class scheduling, lowered drinking fountains, lowered telephones, and special housing. **Special:** Numerous co-ops and internship programs, including student teaching opportunities, are available. Millersville has formal agreements, e.g. cross-registration, with the following institutions: West Chester University, Shippensburg University, Kutztown University, Franklin and Marshall College, Harrisburg Area Commuity College, Reading Area Community College, Lancaster Theological Seminary, Chincoteague Bay Field Station at the Marine Science Consortium, and Servicemembers Opportunity Colleges Consortium (SOCC), as well as 3-2 and 4-2 programs with Penn State University, the University of Southern California, and the University of Delaware. Study abroad is offered in Australia, Chile, China, France, Germany, Japan, South Africa, Spain, and United Kingdom. Dual majors, student-designed majors, and accelerated degrees are possible in most disciplines. There are 18 national honor societies, a freshman honors program, and 16 departmental honors programs. **Visiting:** There are regularly scheduled orientations for prospective students, campus info sessions and tours are offered to prospective students on a daily basis. Opportunities include department sessions, admissions info sessions and tours, or transfer student info sessions, as well as open houses and special group visits. There are guides for informal visits and visitors may sit in on classes. To schedule a visit, contact the Office of Admissions. **Campus Safety and Security:** Measures include 24-hour foot and vehicle patrol, emergency notification system, self-defense education, and security escort services. There are shuttle buses, emergency telephones, lighted pathways/sidewalks, controlled access to dorms/residences, student patrols, crime awareness programs, timely warning alerts, and LiveSafe app, and a Threat Assessment Team (online incident report).

REQUIREMENTS: The SAT is required. To be considered for admission to Millersville University, one must be a graduate of an approved secondary school or hold a GED high school equivalency diploma. Traditional students applying directly from high school must have completed a college preparatory curriculum. Generally, the student's academic program should include 4 units of academic English in addition to 3 units or more of academic mathematics, science, and social science course work. Also required are satisfactory scores on the SAT or ACT. Finally, auditions are required for music majors, portfolios are required for art majors, and an associate degree in Nursing or Diploma and RN license required for nursing program. MU requires applicants to be in the upper 40% of their class. A GPA of 2.0 is required. AP and CLEP credits are accepted. Important factors in the admissions decision are advanced placement or honors courses, extracurricular activities record, and leadership record. All students must complete at least 120 hours, demonstrating proficiency in mathematics and English and maintaining a minimum of 2.0 GPA. Students must complete the general education program and complete specific courses in physical education, fundamentals of speech, writing, and cultural diversity and community. **Procedure:** Freshmen are admitted to all sessions. Entrance exams should be taken during spring of the junior year. There are early admissions, deferred admissions, and rolling admissions plans. Application deadlines are open. Application fee is $50. Notification is sent on a rolling basis. 547 applicants were on the 2016 waiting list; 97 were admitted. Application fees are waived if application is completed online. **Transfer Students:** 618 transfer students enrolled in 2015-2016. All transfer applicants must submit college transcript, essay or personal statement, and a statement of good standing. Some are required to submit a high school transcript and standardized test scores. The review is based on course selection and performance at your previous college. Preference is given to students with a 2.5 GPA or higher. Preference is also given to graduates of in-state community colleges and students transferring from other PA State System of Higher Education Schools. 30 of 120 credits required for the bachelor's degree must be completed at MU. **International Students:** There are 42 international students enrolled. The school actively recruits these students. They must take the TOEFL with a minimum score of 550 on the paper-based TOEFL (PBT) or 70 on the Internet-based version (iBT). MU will accept IELTS (Minimum score of 6). Students must also take the SAT or ACT.

ADMISSIONS: 69% of the 2016-2017 applicants were accepted. The SAT scores for the 2016-2017 freshman class were: Critical Reading-- 43% below 500, 43% between 500 and 599, 12% between 600 and 699, and 2% between 700 and 800. Math-- 42% below 500, 43% between 500 and 599, 13% between 600 and 699, and 2% between 700 and 800. Writing-- 56% below 500, 37% between 500 and 599, and 7% between 600 and 699. The ACT scores were 14% between 12 and 17, 52% between 18 and 23, 30% between 24 and 29, and 4% above 30. 17% of the current freshmen were in the top fifth of their class; 38% were in the top two fifths. 4 freshmen graduated first in their class. **Admissions Contact:** Katy Ferrier, Director of Admissions. Email: *admissions@millersville.edu* Web: *www.millersville.edu*

FINANCIAL AID: In 2016-2017, 86% of all full-time freshmen and 84% of continuing full-time students received some form of financial aid. 65% of all full-time freshmen and 64% of continuing full-time students received need-based aid. The average freshman award was $14,819. Need-based scholarships or need-based grants averaged $5,327 ($14,467 maximum); need-based self-help aid (loans and jobs) averaged $3,214 ($5,860 maximum); non-need-based athletic scholarships averaged $2,552 ($20,000 maximum); and other non-need-based awards and non-need-based scholarships averaged $7,000 ($34,934 maximum). Average annual earnings from campus work are $1770. The average financial indebtedness of the 2016 graduate was $29,481. The FAFSA code is 003325. The priority date for freshman financial aid applications for fall entry is March 15.

MISERICORDIA UNIVERSITY — E-2

www.misericordia.edu

Dallas, PA 18612 — **(570) 674-6400**, **(866) 262-6363**

Fax: (570) 675-2441 — **Email: admiss@misericordia.edu**

Full-time: 589 men, 1052 women	**Faculty:** 112; IIB, av$
Part-time: 129 men, 425 women	**Ph.D.s:** 77%
Graduate: 173 men, 511 women	**Student/Faculty:** 15 to 1
Year: semesters, summer session	**Tuition:** $30,690
Room & Board: $13,150	**Freshman Class:** 1823 applied, 1357 accepted, 423 enrolled
SAT CR/M: 520/530 **ACT:** 24	**CEEB CODE:** 2087
Application Deadline: n/av	**COMPETITIVE**

Misericordia University, founded in 1924, by the Sisters of Mercy, is a private liberal arts institution affiliated with the Roman Catholic Church and offers professional programs in health-related fields. There are 3 undergraduate schools. In addition to regional accreditation, Misericordia has baccalaureate program accreditation with APTA, ASLA, CAHEA,

CSWE, ACOTE, CCNE, JRCERT, and IACBE. The 120-acre campus is in a suburban area 9 miles north of Wilkes-Barre, PA. Including any residence halls, there are 22 buildings.

STUDENT LIFE: 75% of undergraduates are from Pennsylvania. Others are from 27 states, and 1 foreign countries. 88% are from public schools. 87% are White; 3% African American; 3% Hispanic; 2% two or more races; 2% race unknown; 1% Asian American; 1% American Indian/Alaska Native; 1% Foreign. 47% are Catholic; 20% Protestant; 17% claim no religious affiliation; 14% Christian, Buddhist, and Hindu. **Female To Male Ratio:** 2.2:1. The average age of freshmen is 18; all undergraduates, 24. 15% do not continue beyond their first year; 71% remain to graduate. **Housing:** 993 students can be accommodated in college housing, which includes coed dorms, and special-interest houses. On-campus housing is guaranteed for the freshman year only, and is available on a first-come, first-served basis, and on a lottery system for upperclassmen. 56% of students live on campus; of those, 50% remain on campus on weekends. Upperclassmen may keep cars.

FACULTY/CLASSROOMS: 43% of faculty are male; 57% are female. 82% teach undergraduates, 10% do research, and 10% do both. No introductory courses are taught by graduate students. The average class size in an introductory lecture is 20; in a laboratory is 14; and in a regular course is 19.

PROGRAMS OF STUDY: Misericordia confers B.A., B.S., B.S.N. and B.S.W. degrees. Master's and doctoral degrees are also awarded. Bachelor's degrees are awarded in BIOLOGICAL SCIENCE (biochemistry and biology/biological science), BUSINESS (accounting, business administration and management, and sports management), COMMUNICATIONS AND THE ARTS (communications and English), COMPUTER AND PHYSICAL SCIENCE (chemistry, computer science, information sciences and systems, and mathematics), EDUCATION (early childhood education and middle school education), HEALTH PROFESSIONS (health care administration, medical laboratory technology, nursing, occupational therapy, physical therapy, radiograph medical technology, and speech therapy), SOCIAL SCIENCE (history, liberal arts/general studies, philosophy, psychology, and social work). Occupational therapy, physical therapy, and speech language pathology are the strongest academically. Nursing, business, and occupational therapy have the largest enrollments.

ACTIVITIES: There are no fraternities or sororities. There are 41 groups on campus, including art, cheerleading, choir, chorale, chorus, drama, environmental, ethnic, honors, international, literary magazine, musical theater, newspaper, political, professional, radio and TV, religious, social service, and student government. Popular campus events include Winter Snowball Dance, Homecoming, and Spring Fest. **Sports:** There are 11 intercollegiate sports for men and 11 for women, and 14 intramural sports for men and 14 for women. Facilities include a softball field, six tennis courts, basketball, volleyball, swim teams, indoor track, racquetball courts, fitness center, aerobic/dance studio, hockey, football, soccer, field hockey, track & field, baseball and lacrosse teams. **Graduates:** From July 1, 2015 to June 30, 2016, 534 bachelor's degrees were awarded. The most popular majors were business (14%), nursing (12%), and psychology (6%). In an average class, 64% graduate in 4 years or less, 71% graduate in 5 years or less, and 72% graduate in 6 years or less. Of the 2015 graduating class, 21% were enrolled in graduate school within 6 months of graduation, and 85% were employed.

SERVICES: Counseling and information services are available, as is tutoring in every subject. There is a reader service for the blind. Services for students with disabilities are provided through the Alternative Learners Program. **Library/Resources:** The library contains 80,036 volumes, 4,219 microform items, 8,153 audio/video tapes/CDs/DVDs, and subscribes to 178 periodicals including electronic. Computerized library services include interlibrary loans, database searching, Internet access, and Wi-Fi capability. Special learning facilities include an art gallery and radio station. **Physically Challenged Students:** 95% of the campus is accessible. Facilities include wheelchair ramps, elevators, special parking, specially equipped restrooms, special class scheduling, and lowered drinking fountains. **Special:** Students may cross-register with King's College and Wilkes University. The college offers internships, work-study programs, study abroad, an accelerated degree program in Business, Govt Law and National Security, Applied Behavioral Science, and Nursing for adult students, and a student-designed major. Credit may be granted for life, military, and work experience through prior learning assessment. Nondegree study is also available. The college offers an alternative learner's project, which accepts a limited number of learning disabled students each year. There are 10 national honor societies, a freshman honors program, and 3 departmental honors programs. **Visiting:** There are regularly scheduled orientations for prospective students, meetings with admissions and financial aid counselors, a tour of the campus, and optional meetings with faculty and coaches. There are guides for informal visits, visitors may sit in on classes, and stay overnight. To schedule a visit, contact Glenn Bozinski at (570) 675-6264. **Campus Safety and Security:** Measures include 24-hour foot and vehicle patrol, emergency notification system, and security escort services. There are also shuttle buses, emergency telephones, lighted pathways/sidewalks, and controlled access to dorms/residences.

REQUIREMENTS: The SAT is required. Applicants must graduate from an accredited secondary school or have a GED. 16 Carnegie units must be earned, and students must complete 3 years each in English, math, history, and science, and 2 to 3 years in social studies. Requires applicants to be in the upper 50% of their class. A GPA of 2.0 is required. AP and CLEP credits are accepted. Important factors in the admissions decision are extracurricular activities record, advanced placement or honors courses, and leadership record. To graduate, students must earn a minimum of 120 credits. The required core curriculum includes courses in behavioral science, English literature, fine arts, history, math, philosophy, religious studies, and natural science. Within the core curriculum, students must complete 1 Unviersity Writing Seminar, and 2 additional courses that are writing intensive. A minimum GPA of 2.0 is required. **Procedure:** Freshmen are admitted in the fall and spring. Entrance exams should be taken during the junior year. There are deferred admissions and rolling admissions plans. Application deadlines are open. Application fee is $35. Applications are accepted on-ine. **Transfer Students:** 125 transfer students enrolled in 2015-2016. Applicants must have a minimum GPA of 2.0. Requirements may be higher for selected majors. 30 of 120 credits required for the bachelor's degree must be completed at Misericordia. **International Students:** There are 3 international students enrolled. The school actively recruits these students. They must take the TOEFL with a minimum score of 500 on the paper-based TOEFL (PBT) or 75 on the Internet-based version (iBT).

ADMISSIONS: 74% of the 2016-2017 applicants were accepted. The SAT scores for the 2016-2017 freshman class were: Critical Reading-- 35% below 500, 50% between 500 and 599, 14% between 600 and 699, and 1% between 700 and 800. Math-- 29% below 500, 50% between 500 and 599, 18% between 600 and 699, and 1% between 700 and 800. The ACT scores were 4% between 12 and 17, 42% between 18 and 23, 48% between 24 and 29, and 6% above 30. 40% of the current freshmen were in the top fifth of their class; 69% were in the top two fifths. 3 freshmen graduated first in their class. **Admissions Contact:** Glenn Bozinski, Director of Admissions. Email: *admiss@misericordia.edu* Web: *www.misericordia.edu*

FINANCIAL AID: In 2016-2017, 100% of all full-time freshmen and 99% of continuing full-time students received some form of financial aid. 71% of all full-time freshmen and 70% of continuing full-time students received need-based aid. The average freshman award was $31,521. Need-based scholarships or need-based grants averaged $7,522 ($29,150 maximum); need-based self-help aid (loans and jobs) averaged $3,741 ($8,300 maximum); other non-need-based awards and non-need-based scholarships averaged $15,094 ($39,150 maximum); and $7,435 from other forms of aid. The average financial indebtedness of the 2016 graduate was $35,140. is a member of CSS. The college's own financial statement is required. The FAFSA code is 003247. The priority date for freshman financial aid applications for fall entry is March 1. The filing deadline for fall entry is May 1.

MOORE COLLEGE OF ART AND DESIGN *(The complete profile is made available exclusively on our website, www.barronspac.com)*

MORAVIAN COLLEGE *(The complete profile is made available exclusively on our website, www.barronspac.com)*

MOUNT ALOYSIUS COLLEGE C-3

www.mtaloy.edu

Cresson, PA 16630 (814) 886-6383
(888) 823-2220
Fax: (814) 886-6441 Email: admissions@mtaloy.edu

Full-time: 385 men, 881 women
Part-time: 78 men, 267 women
Graduate: 11 men, 27 women
Year: semesters, summer session
Room & Board: $9186
SAT or ACT: required
Application Deadline: August 3
Faculty: 68
Ph.D.s: 44%
Student/Faculty: 18 to 1
Tuition: $20,790
Freshman Class: 1189 applied, 850 accepted, 338 enrolled
CEEB CODE: 2420
COMPETITIVE

Mount Aloysius College is a comprehensive, private, Catholic, coeducational, liberal arts and sciences based institution offering undergraduate and graduate education emphasizing career preparation and Mercy values. There are 3 undergraduate schools and 1 graduate school. In addition to regional accreditation, Mount Aloysius has baccalaureate program accreditation with APTA, NLN, CAPTE, CAAHEP, and NAACLS. The 220-acre campus is in a small town in the southern Allegheny Mountains between Altoona and Johnstown. Including any residence halls, there are 14 buildings.

STUDENT LIFE: 90% of undergraduates are from Pennsylvania. Others are from 20 states, 15 foreign countries, and Canada. 80% are from public schools. 94% are White; 3% African American; 1% Asian American; 1% Hispanic; 1% Foreign. 40% are Catholic; 35% Protestant. **Female To Male Ratio:** 2.5:1. The average age of freshmen is 19; all undergraduates, 25. 30% do not continue beyond their first year; 60% remain to graduate. **Housing:** 545 students can be accommodated in college housing, which includes single-sex and coed dorms, on-campus apartments, and off-campus apartments. In addition, there are special-interest houses, and a Christian living community. On-campus housing is guaranteed for all 4 years, and is available on a first-come, first-served basis. Priority is given to out-of-town students. 60% of students commute. Alcohol is not permitted. All students may keep cars.

FACULTY/CLASSROOMS: 39% of faculty are male; 61% are female. All teach undergraduates and do research. No introductory courses are taught by graduate students. The average class size in an introductory lecture is 17; in a laboratory is 12; and in a regular course is 17.

PROGRAMS OF STUDY: Mount Aloysius College confers B.A., and B.S. degrees. Associate and master's degrees are also awarded. Bachelor's degrees are awarded in BIOLOGICAL SCIENCE (biology/biological science, biotechnology, and environmental biology), BUSINESS (accounting, business administration and management, business economics, entrepreneurial studies, human resources, management information systems, management science, marketing management, nonprofit/public organization management, organizational leadership and management, and small business management), COMMUNICATIONS AND THE ARTS (American Sign Language, choral music, English, and voice), COMPUTER AND PHYSICAL SCIENCE (computer security and information assurance, information sciences and systems, radiological technology, science, and web technology), EDUCATION (childhood education, early childhood education, education, elementary education, English education, middle school education, science education, secondary education, and social studies education), ENGINEERING AND ENVIRONMENTAL DESIGN (computational sciences and environmental science), HEALTH PROFESSIONS (allied health, chiropractic, health care administration, medical laboratory technology, medical technology, nuclear medical technology, nursing, nursing home administration, occupational therapy, physical therapy, physical therapy assistant, physician's assistant, preallied health, predentistry, premedicine, preoptometry, preosteopathy, prepharmacy, prephysical therapy, prepodiatry, preventive/wellness health care, preveterinary science, radiation therapy, radiograph medical technology, radiological science, and ultrasound technology), SOCIAL SCIENCE (behavioral science, child care/child and family studies, community psychology, criminal justice, criminology, history, humanities, humanities and social science, interpreter for the deaf, law enforcement and corrections, liberal arts/general studies, paralegal studies, political science/government, prelaw, psychology, public administration, religion, social studies, and women's studies). Nursing, medical imaging, and allied health sciences are the strongest academically. Nursing, medical imaging, and business have the largest enrollments.

ACTIVITIES: There are no fraternities or sororities. There are 100 groups on campus, including art, band, campus ministry (community service organization) basically cheerleading, choir, chorale, chorus, computers, dance, drama, environmental, ethnic, forensics, honors, international, musical theater, newspaper, photography, political, professional, religious, social, social service, student government, and yearbook. Popular campus events include Madrigal Dinner, Heritage days, Mountie Madness, and Christmas at MAC. **Sports:** There are 6 intercollegiate sports for men and 8 for women, and 13 intramural sports for men and 12 for women. Facilities include an athletic convocation and wellness center with floating gym floor, an auxillary gym, and 2 weight-and-exercise rooms. **Graduates:** From July 1, 2015 to June 30, 2016, 176 bachelor's degrees were awarded. The most popular majors were nursing (28%), business administration (14%), and criminology (10%). 200 companies recruited on campus in 2015-2016. In an average class, 27% graduate in 3 years or less, 45% graduate in 4 years or less, 50% graduate in 5 years or less, and 51% graduate in 6 years or less. Of the 2015 graduating class, 22% were enrolled in graduate school within 6 months of graduation, and 97% were employed.

SERVICES: Counseling and information services are available, as is tutoring in every subject, and remedial math, reading, and writing. **Library/Resources:** The library contains 77,186 volumes, 4,680 microform items, 2,431 audio/video tapes/CDs/DVDs, and subscribes to 275 periodicals including electronic. Computerized library services include interlibrary loans, database searching, Internet access, and Wi-Fi capability. Special learning facilities include an art gallery. **Physically Challenged Students:** All of the campus is accessible. Facilities include wheelchair ramps, elevators, special parking, specially equipped restrooms, special class scheduling, lowered drinking fountains, lowered telephones, and special housing. **Special:** The Professional Studies curriculum provides a student-designed course of study, with an emphasis in behavior and social science, humanities, math/science/computer science, or prelaw. B.A.-B.S. degrees are offered, as are internships in nursing, business, criminology, and student teaching. Our education department offers Early Level Pre K-4/Middle Level 4-8, and secondary education. There are 3 national honor societies, a freshman honors program, and 1 departmental honors program. **Visiting:** There are regularly scheduled orientations for prospective students. There are guides for informal visits, visitors may sit in on classes, and stay overnight. To schedule a visit, contact the Admissions Office. **Campus Safety and Security:** Measures include 24-hour foot and vehicle patrol, emergency notification system, self-defense education, and security escort services. There are also shuttle buses, emergency telephones, lighted pathways/sidewalks, and controlled access to dorms/residences.

REQUIREMENTS: The SAT or ACT is required. Applicants must graduate from an accredited high school or have the GED. A placement test and any necessary developmental studies classes may need to be taken. Science classes and an interview are required of some allied health programs. AP and CLEP credits are accepted. Important factors in the admissions decision are recommendations by school officials, advanced placement or honors courses, and leadership record. Baccalaureate-level students are required during their final semester of study to complete 2 3-credit courses designed to integrate and synthesize scientific, behavioral, and moral concepts. Students in allied health programs must complete an approved clinical experience. Courses in research writing and speech are also required. A total of 120 credits is required with an overall 2.0 GPA, including a C average in all core courses. **Procedure:** Freshmen are admitted in the fall and spring. Entrance exams should be taken as early as possible. There is a rolling admissions plan. Applications should be filed by August 3 for fall entry, along with a $30 fee. Notifications are sent in weekly. 7 applicants were on the 2016 waiting list. Applications are accepted on-line. **Transfer Students:** 250 transfer students enrolled in 2015-2016. Transfer students must have a 2.0 GPA. Only courses with a C or better will be considered for transfer; all other requirements are the same as for freshmen. 30 of 120 credits required for the bachelor's degree must be completed at Mount Aloysius College. **International Students:** There are 23 international students enrolled. The school actively recruits these students. They must take the TOEFL with a minimum score of 500 on the paper-based TOEFL (PBT) or 61 on the Internet-based version (iBT) and the Comprehensive English Language Test. They must also take the SAT or ACT, and the New Jersey Basic Skills Test.

ADMISSIONS: 71% of the 2016-2017 applicants were accepted. 5 freshmen graduated first in their class. **Admissions Contact:** Francis Crouse, Vice President for Enrollment Management. Email: *admissions@mtaloy.edu* Web: *www.mtaloy.edu*

FINANCIAL AID: In 2016-2017, 94% of all full-time freshmen and 95% of continuing full-time students received some form of financial aid. 85% of all full-time freshmen and 86% of continuing full-time students received need-based aid. The average freshman award was $11,000. Need-based scholarships or need-based grants averaged $3,000 ($5,000 maximum); need-based self-help aid (loans and jobs) averaged $3,000 ($5,000 maximum); and other non-need-based awards and non-need-based scholarships averaged $3,000 ($7,000 maximum). 65% of undergraduate students work part-time. Average annual earnings from campus work are $750. The average financial indebtedness of the 2016 graduate was $17,125. Mount Aloysius College is a member of CSS. The FAFSA code is 003302. The priority date for freshman financial aid applications for fall entry is April 1. The filing deadline for fall entry is May 1.

MUHLENBERG COLLEGE E-3

www.muhlenberg.edu

Allentown, PA 18104 **(484) 664-3200**

Fax: (484) 664-3234	**Email:** admissions@muhlenberg.edu
Full-time: 924 men, 1383 women	**Faculty:** 177; IIB, +$
Part-time: 37 men, 53 women	**Ph.D.s:** 85%
Graduate: n/av	**Student/Faculty:** 11 to 1
Year: semesters, summer session	**Tuition:** $45,875
Room & Board: $10,770	**Freshman Class:** 5015 applied, 2426 accepted, 582 enrolled
SAT CR/M/W: 605/613/604 **ACT:** 28	**CEEB CODE:** 2424
Application Deadline: February 15	**VERY COMPETITIVE+**

Muhlenberg College founded in 1848, is an independent, undergraduate, coeducational institution related to the Evangelical Lutheran Church in America, offering liberal arts education in the Judeo-Christian humanistic tradition, Muhlenberg is committed to the highest standards of academic integrity and excellence. Muhlenberg offers programs in the humanities, the natural and social sciences, and in professional areas such as business, education, pre-medical, pre-theological, and pre-law studies. Flexibility is provided through course options and opportunities for independent study, research and internships, and through a plan for self-designed majors. The college stives to keep its curriculum vital and current with the rapidly changing intellectual world. There is 1 undergraduate school. The 82-acre campus is in a suburban area 50 miles north of Philadelphia and 90 miles west of New York City. Including any residence halls, there are 102 buildings.

STUDENT LIFE: 73% of undergraduates are from out of state, mostly the Middle Atlantic. Students are from 31 states, 18 foreign countries, and Canada. 74% are from public schools. 75% are White; 7% Hispanic; 7% race unknown; 3% African American; 3% Asian American; 3% Foreign; 2% two or more races. 30% are Catholic; 29% Jewish; 13% claim no religious affiliation. **Female To Male Ratio:** 1.5:1. The average age of freshmen is 18; all undergraduates, 21. 7% do not continue beyond their first year; 85% remain to graduate. **Housing:** 2006 students can be accommodated in college housing, which includes single-sex and coed dorms, on-campus apartments, and off-campus apartments. In addition, there are language houses, special-interest houses, fraternity houses, and college-owned houses in the surrounding community. On-campus housing is guaranteed for all 4 years. 92% of students live on campus; of those, 80% remain on campus on weekends. Upperclassmen may keep cars.

FACULTY/CLASSROOMS: 50% of faculty are male; 50% are female. All teach undergraduates, 84% do research, and teach. No introductory courses are taught by graduate students. The average class size in an introductory lecture is 26; in a laboratory is 16; and in a regular course is 19.

PROGRAMS OF STUDY: Berg confers B.A. and B.S. degrees. Associate degrees are also awarded. Bachelor's degrees are awarded in BIOLOGICAL SCIENCE (biochemistry, biology/biological science, and neurosciences), BUSINESS (accounting, banking and finance, and business administration and management), COMMUNICATIONS AND THE ARTS (art, communications, dance, dramatic arts, English, film arts, French, German, music, and Spanish), COMPUTER AND PHYSICAL SCIENCE (chemistry, computer science, mathematics, natural sciences, physical sciences, and physics), ENGINEERING AND ENVIRONMENTAL DESIGN (environmental science), SOCIAL SCIENCE (American studies, anthropology, economics, German area studies, history, international studies, philosophy, political science/government, psychology, religion, Russian and Slavic studies, and sociology). Biology, theatre, and psychology are the strongest academically. Biology, business administration, and psychology have the largest enrollments.

ACTIVITIES: 14% of men belong to 4 national fraternities; 17% of women belong to 1 local and 4 national sororities. There are 126 groups on campus, including and step team, art, band, cheerleading, chess, choir, chorale, chorus, computers, dance, drama, environmental, ethnic, film, honors, human rights, international, jazz band, LGBT, literary magazine, musical theater, newspaper, opera, orchestra, pep band, photography, political, professional, radio and TV, religious, social, social service, student government, and yearbook. Popular campus events include Spring Fling Weekend, Candlelight Carols, and Jefferson Field Day. **Sports:** There are 11 intercollegiate sports for men and 11 for women, and 13 intramural sports for men and 13 for women. Facilities include a sports center, which has a swimming pool, racquetball, squash courts, and wrestling, weight training rooms. There is also a multipurpose field house with indoor tennis courts, running track, basketball and tennis courts, as well as a large aerobic fitness center and weight room, outdoor volleyball, and a football/lacrosse/field hockey stadium. **Graduates:** From July 1, 2015 to June 30, 2016, 614 bachelor's degrees were awarded. The most popular majors were psychology (12%), business administration (10%), and theatre (9%). 74 companies recruited on campus in 2015-2016. In an average class, 2% graduate in 3 years or less, 83% graduate in 4 years or less, 85% graduate in 5 years or less, and 85% graduate in 6 years or less. Of the 2015 graduating class, 35% were enrolled in graduate school within 6 months of graduation, and 62% were employed.

SERVICES: Counseling and information services are available, as is tutoring in every subject, and a reader service for the blind, and a writing center. **Library/Resources:** Computerized library services include interlibrary loans, database searching, Internet access, and Wi-Fi capability. Special learning facilities include an art gallery, natural history museum, radio station, TV station, and The Raker Wildlife Preserve & Graver Arboretum. **Physically Challenged Students:** 95% of the campus is accessible. Facilities include wheelchair ramps, elevators, special parking, specially equipped restrooms, special class scheduling, lowered drinking fountains, lowered telephones, and special housing. **Special:** Students may cross-register with Lehigh, Lafayette, Cedar Crest, Moravian, and Allentown Colleges. Internships, work-study programs, B.A-B.S. degrees, study abroad in Asia, Australia, Latin America, Russia, and Europe, and a Washington semester are available. Dual majors and student-designed majors may be pursued. A 3-2 engineering degree is available in cooperation with Columbia and Washington Universities, a 4-4 assured admission medical program is offered with Drexel University College of Medicine, a 3-4 dental program is offered with University of Pennsylvania, and a 3-2 forestry degree is offered in cooperation with Duke University. An army ROTC program is also available. Nondegree study and a pass/fail grading option are also offered. There are 14 national honor societies, Phi Beta Kappa, a freshman honors program, and 8 departmental honors programs. **Visiting:** There are regularly scheduled orientations for prospective students, consisting of a tour of the campus and a personal interview. There are 2 open houses in the fall and 1 in the spring. There are guides for informal visits, visitors may sit in on classes, and stay overnight. **Campus Safety and Security:** Measures include 24-hour foot and vehicle patrol, self-defense education, and security escort services. There are shuttle buses, emergency telephones, and lighted pathways/sidewalks.

REQUIREMENTS: Applicants must graduate from an accredited secondary school or have a GED. 16 Carnegie units are required, and students must complete 4 courses in English, 3 in math, and 2 each in history, science, and a foreign language. All students must submit essays. Interviews are recommended and required for those who do not submit SAT scores. AP and CLEP credits are accepted. Important factors in the admissions decision are geographical diversity, evidence of special talent, personality/intangible qualities, parents or siblings of the applicant attended the school, extracurricular activities record, recommendations by alumni, recommendations by school officials, ability to finance college education, leadership record, and advanced placement or honors courses. The Muhlenberg curriculum is designed to engage students in thoughtful deliberation, critical analysis, and creative thinking. Students will complete a diverse set of general academic requirements and a major in their chosen field of specialization. They will earn no fewer than 34 course units with a cumulative grade point average of not less than 2.0. Skills are acquired through courses emphasizing writing, critical thinking, and language proficiency. Required courses include a First Year Seminar, writing-intensive courses, two semesters of foreign language, and a course in logic or mathematical reasoning. A breadth of knowledge is achieved through study in each of the four academic divisions: Arts (one required), Humanities (three required), Social Sciences (two required), and Natural Sciences (two required). Further, the curriculum encourages students to move between different disciplines in order to learn what sets them apart and how to bring them together. Required courses include a two-course cluster focused on related subject matter approached from different disciplinary angles or points of view, two courses in human difference and global engagement, and a culminating undergraduate experience specified by the major. Students may choose from a wide variety of majors, from accounting to sociology (40 majors in all, plus a self-designed major option). The major provides an in-depth study in the selected field and preparation for work, graduate, or professional school. Majors vary in the number of units required from nine to fifteen, but all students must earn a grade point average of not less than 2.0. A significant percentage of Muhlenberg seniors graduate with double majors, and many majors offer departmental honors programs, senior portfolios, recitals, and mentored research opportunities. **Procedure:** Freshmen are admitted in the fall and spring. Entrance exams should be taken during the spring of the junior year or the fall of the senior year. There are early decision and deferred admissions plans. Early decision applications should be filed by February 1; regular applications, by February 15 for fall entry, along with a $50 fee. Notifications are sent March 15. 354 early decision candidates were accepted for the 2016-2017 class. 314 applicants were on the 2016 waiting list; 41 were admitted. Applications are accepted on-line. **Transfer Students:** 12 transfer students enrolled in 2015-2016. A minimum college GPA of 2.5 and an interview are required. 17 of 34 credits required for the bachelor's degree must be completed at Berg. **International Students:** There are 62 international students enrolled. The school actively recruits these students. They must take the TOEFL with a minimum score of 550 on the paper-based TOEFL (PBT).

ADMISSIONS: 48% of the 2016-2017 applicants were accepted. The SAT scores for the 2016-2017 freshman class were: Critical Reading-- 7% below 500, 39% between 500 and 599, 40% between 600 and 699, and 13% between 700 and 800. Math-- 10% below 500, 32% between 500 and 599, 52% between 600 and 699, and 10% between 700 and 800. Writing-- 13% below 500, 42% between 500 and 599, 36% between 600 and 699, and 8% between 700 and 800. The ACT scores were 9% between 18 and 23, 60% between 24 and 29, and 31% above 30. **Admissions Contact:** Christopher Hooker-Haring, Dean of Admissions. Email: *admissions@muhlenberg.edu* Web: *www.muhlenberg.edu*

FINANCIAL AID: In 2016-2017, 89% of all full-time freshmen and continuing full-time students received some form of financial aid. 52% of all full-time freshmen and 56% of continuing full-time students received need-based aid. The average freshman award was $28,883. Need-based scholarships or need-based grants averaged $26,247 ($56,646 maximum); need-based self-help aid (loans and jobs) averaged $5,150 ($9,300 maximum); and other non-need-based awards and non-need-based scholarships averaged $16,134 ($44,000 maximum). 20% of undergraduate students work part-time. Average annual earnings from campus work are $1000. The average financial indebtedness of the 2016 graduate was $23,279. Berg is a member of CSS. The CSS/Profile, the college's own financial statement, parent and student tax returns, and W-2 forms are required. The FAFSA code is 003304. The deadline for filing freshman financial aid applications for fall entry is February 15.

NEUMANN UNIVERSITY *(The complete profile is made available exclusively on our website, www.barronspac.com)*

PEIRCE COLLEGE *(The complete profile is made available exclusively on our website, www.barronspac.com)*

PENN STATE ERIE/THE BEHREND COLLEGE — B-1

www.psbehrend.psu.edu

Erie, PA 16563 — **(814) 898-6000**, **(866) 374-3378**

Fax: (814) 898-6044 — **Email: behrend.admissions@psu.edu**

Full-time: 2473 men, 1358 women	**Faculty:** 204
Part-time: 103 men, 81 women	**Ph.D.s:** 61%
Graduate: 81 men, 26 women	**Student/Faculty:** 16 to 1
Year: semesters, summer session	**Tuition:** $11,000 ($16,000)
Room & Board: $6230	**Freshman Class:** 2590 applied, 2092 accepted, 854 enrolled
SAT or ACT: required	**CEEB CODE:** 2660
Application Deadline: open	**COMPETITIVE**

Penn State Erie/The Behrend College, founded in 1948, offers 34 baccalaureate programs as well as the first 2 years of most Penn State University Park baccalaureate programs. It offers courses in business, humanities, social sciences, science, engineering technology, and engineering. Figures in the above capsule and in this profile are approximate. There are 5 undergraduate schools and 1 graduate school. In addition to regional accreditation, Penn State Erie has baccalaureate program accreditation with AACSB, ABET, and NLN. The 840-acre campus is in a suburban area 5 miles east of Erie. Including any residence halls, there are 45 buildings.

STUDENT LIFE: 92% of undergraduates are from Pennsylvania. Others are from 28 states, 23 foreign countries, and Canada. 86% are White; 5% African American; 3% Hispanic; 2% Asian American; 2% Foreign. **Male To Female Ratio:** 1.8:1. The average age of freshmen is 18; all undergraduates, 22. 9% do not continue beyond their first year; 61% remain to graduate. **Housing:** 1650 students can be accommodated in college housing, which includes single-sex and coed dorms, on-campus apartments, honors houses, and special-interest houses. On-campus housing is guaranteed for the freshman year only, is on a first-come, first-served basis, and is available on a lottery system for upperclassmen. 53% of students commute. All students may keep cars. Alcohol is not permitted.

FACULTY/CLASSROOMS: 70% of faculty are male; 30% are female. All teach undergraduates and do research. No introductory courses are taught by graduate students. The average class size in an introductory lecture is 35; in a laboratory is 18; and in a regular course is 29.

PROGRAMS OF STUDY: Penn State Erie confers B.A., B.S. and B.F.A. degrees. Associate and master's degrees are also awarded. Bachelor's degrees are awarded in BIOLOGICAL SCIENCE (biology/biological science), BUSINESS (accounting, banking and finance, business administration and management, business economics, management information systems, and marketing management), COMMUNICATIONS AND THE ARTS (communications and English), COMPUTER AND PHYSICAL SCIENCE (chemistry, computer science, mathematics, physics, and science), ENGINEERING AND ENVIRONMENTAL DESIGN (computer engineering, engineering, engineering technology, mechanical engineering technology, and plastics technology), SOCIAL SCIENCE (economics, history, political science/government, and psychology). Management information systems, psychology, and math are the strongest academically. Engineering, business, and psychology have the largest enrollments.

ACTIVITIES: 5% of men belong to 3 national fraternities; 16% of women belong to 3 national sororities. There are 80 groups on campus, including band, cheerleading, chess, choir, computers, dance, drama, ethnic, honors, international, jazz band, LGBT, literary magazine, newspaper, pep band, political, professional, radio and TV, religious, social, social service, student government, and yearbook. Popular campus events include Speaker Series, Parents Events, and Black Cultural Awareness Month. **Sports:** There are 10 intercollegiate sports for men and 11 for women, and 18 intramural sports for men and 18 for women. Facilities include an athletic center with indoor track, pool, tennis courts, weight room, fitness trail, basketball courts, baseball, softball, and soccer fields.

SERVICES: Counseling and information services are available, as is tutoring in every subject. There is a reader service for the blind, and remedial math, reading, and writing. **Library/Resources:** Computerized library services include interlibrary loans, database searching, Internet access, and Wi-Fi capability. Special learning facilities include a radio station, engineering workstation labs, media labs, and an observatory. **Physically Challenged Students:** 90% of the campus is accessible. Facilities include wheelchair ramps, elevators, special parking, specially equipped restrooms, special class scheduling, lowered drinking fountains, and lowered telephones. **Special:** Internships, study abroad in 14 countries, work-study programs, and accelerated degree programs are available. In addition, a B.A.-B.S. degree in psychology, a 3-2 engineering degree with Edinboro University, dual majors, a general studies degree, and student-designed majors in business and general arts and sciences are offered. Nondegree study and up to 12 credits of pass/fail options are possible. There are 4 national honor societies and a freshman honors program. **Visiting:** There are regularly scheduled orientations for prospective students, including meetings with a counselor and faculty, a campus tour, and a class visit. There are guides for informal visits, visitors may sit in on classes, and stay overnight. To schedule a visit, contact the Admissions Office. **Campus Safety and Security:** Measures include 24-hour foot and vehicle patrol, self-defense education, and security escort services. There are emergency telephones and lighted pathways/sidewalks.

REQUIREMENTS: The SAT or ACT is required. Candidates for admission must have 15 academic credits or 15 Carnegie units, including 5 in social studies, 4 in English, 3 each in math and science, and 2 in foreign language. The GED is accepted. AP and CLEP credits are accepted. All baccalaureate degree candidates must take 46 general education credits, including 27 in arts, humanities, natural science, and social and behavioral sciences including a cultural diversity course, 15 in quantification and communication skills including a writing intensive course, and 3 in health, phys ed, and a freshman seminar. All students must complete a minimum of 120 credit hours with a minimum GPA of 2.0. Further requirements vary by degree program. **Procedure:** Freshmen are admitted to all sessions. Entrance exams should be taken during the junior year. There are deferred admissions and rolling admissions plans. Application deadlines are open. Application fee is $50. Notification is sent on a rolling basis. Applications are accepted on-line. **Transfer Students:** Transfer candidates need a minimum GPA of 2.4, good academic standing, and 18 or more credits from a regionally accredited institution at the college level. 36 of 120 credits required for the bachelor's degree must be completed at Penn State Erie. **International Students:** There are 32 international students enrolled. The school actively recruits these students. They must take the TOEFL.

ADMISSIONS: 81% of the 2016-2017 applicants were accepted. 25% of the current freshmen were in the top fifth of their class; 40% were in the top two fifths. 12 freshmen graduated first in their class. **Admissions Contact:** Andrea Konkol, Associate Director of Admissions. Email: *amkonkol.admissions@psu.edu* Web: *www.psbehrend.psu.edu*

FINANCIAL AID: The priority date for freshman financial aid applications for fall entry is February 15.

PENN STATE UNIVERSITY/ALTOONA C-3

www.altoona.psu.edu

Altoona, PA 16601	(814) 949-5466 (800) 848-9843 Email: aaadmit@psu.edu
Full-time: 1948 men, 1803 women	**Faculty:** 122
Part-time: 109 men, 172 women	**Ph.D.s:** n/av
Graduate: 3 women	**Student/Faculty:** 31 to 1
Year: semesters, summer session	**Tuition:** $13,658 ($21,392)
Room & Board: $10,926	**Freshman Class:** n/av
SAT or ACT: required	**CEEB CODE:** 2660
Application Deadline: open	**COMPETITIVE**

Penn State Altoona, founded in 1939, offers 18 baccalaureate degree programs, 8 associate degrees, and 19 minors. Figures in the above capsule and in this profile are approximate. There are 17 undergraduate schools and 1 graduate school. In addition to regional accreditation, Altoona has baccalaureate program accreditation with ABET, NASAD, NCATE, and NRPA. The 150-acre campus is in a suburban area. Including any residence halls, there are 33 buildings.

STUDENT LIFE: 85% of undergraduates are from Pennsylvania. Others are from 28 states, 20 foreign countries, and Canada. 84% are White; 7% African American; 3% Hispanic; 2% Asian American; 1% American Indian/Alaska Native; 1% Foreign. **Male To Female Ratio:** 1.0:1. The average age of freshmen is 18; all undergraduates, 22. 12% do not continue beyond their first year; 65% remain to graduate. **Housing:** 900 students can be accommodated in college housing, which includes single-sex and coed dorms, honors houses, special-interest houses, and alcohol-free and substance-free housing. On-campus housing is available on a first-come, and first-served basis, and is available on a lottery system for upperclassmen. 78% of students commute. Alcohol is not permitted. All students may keep cars.

FACULTY/CLASSROOMS: No introductory courses are taught by graduate students. The average class size in an introductory lecture is 50; in a laboratory is 24; and in a regular course is 28.

PROGRAMS OF STUDY: Altoona confers B.A. and B.S. degrees. Associate and master's degrees are also awarded. Bachelor's degrees are awarded in AGRICULTURE (environmental studies), BIOLOGICAL SCIENCE (biology/biological science), BUSINESS (business administration and management), COMMUNICATIONS AND THE ARTS (communications, English, and visual and performing arts), COMPUTER AND PHYSICAL SCIENCE (mathematics and science), EDUCATION (elementary education), ENGINEERING AND ENVIRONMENTAL DESIGN (electromechanical technology), HEALTH PROFESSIONS (nursing), SOCIAL SCIENCE (criminal justice, history, human development, and liberal arts/general studies). Engineering, and education are the strongest academically. Business, criminal justice, and elementary education have the largest enrollments.

ACTIVITIES: There are 70 groups on campus, including horticulture, STEP team, cheerleading, choir, communications, dance, drama, ethnic, honors, international, jazz band, LGBT, literary magazine, martial arts, newspaper, pep band, political, professional, religious, social, social service, student government, and yearbook. Popular campus events include Distinguished Speaker Series, Hoops Hysteria, and Black History and Women's History Month events. **Sports:** There are 6 intercollegiate sports for men and 6 for women. Facilities include a gym, an indoor pool, racquetball courts, weight room, fitness loft, tennis, outdoor track, sand volleyball courts, baseball, softball, and soccer fields. **Graduates:** From July 1, 2015 to June 30, 2016, 350 bachelor's degrees were awarded. The most popular majors were business (15%), criminal justice (14%), and elementary education (13%). In an average class, 38% graduate in 4 years or less, 64% graduate in 5 years or less, and 65% graduate in 6 years or less.

SERVICES: Counseling and information services are available, as is tutoring in most subject, and remedial math, reading, and writing. **Library/Resources:** The library contains 90,000 audio/video tapes/CDs/DVDs, and subscribes to 500 periodicals including electronic. Computerized library services include interlibrary loans, database searching, Internet access, and Wi-Fi capability. Special learning facilities include an art gallery, Pic-Tel teleconferencing, 5 state-of-the-art engineering labs, and CAD/CAM computer lab facilities. **Physically Challenged Students:** 95% of the campus is accessible. Facilities include wheelchair ramps, elevators, special parking, specially equipped restrooms, special class scheduling, lowered drinking fountains, and lowered telephones. **Special:** Internships, study abroad in 5 countries, work-study programs, B.A.-B.S. degrees, accelerated degree programs, and dual and student-designed majors are available. There is an integrative arts major, which allows students to pursue interest across artistic boundaries. There is a chapter of Phi Beta Kappa and a freshman honors program. **Visiting:** There are regularly scheduled orientations for prospective students, including campus tours and meetings with academic counselors and faculty. There are guides for informal visits, visitors may sit in on classes, and stay overnight. To schedule a visit, contact the Admissions Office - Altoona campus. **Campus Safety and Security:** Measures include 24-hour foot and vehicle patrol, emergency notification system, self-defense education, and security escort services. There are shuttle buses, emergency telephones, and lighted pathways/sidewalks.

REQUIREMENTS: The SAT or ACT is required. Applicants should have 15 academic or Carnegie units, including 4 in English, 3 each in math, science, and social studies, and 2 in foreign language (required for some majors). The GED is accepted. Applications are accepted on computer disk and on-line at the school's web site. AP and CLEP credits are accepted. To graduate, students must complete a minimum of 120 credit hours with a minimum GPA of 2.0. They must complete 46 general education credits, including 27 in arts, humanities, natural science, and social and behavioral sciences and 15 in quantification and communication skills. **Procedure:** Freshmen are admitted to all sessions. Entrance exams should be taken during the junior year. There are deferred admissions and rolling admissions plans. Application deadlines are open. The fall 2016 application fee was $50. Notification is sent on a rolling basis. Applications are accepted online. **Transfer Students:** 100 transfer students enrolled in 2015-2016. High school and college transcripts are required, as is good academic standing. The minimum GPA varies by major. 36 of 120 credits required for the bachelor's degree must be completed at Altoona. **International Students:** There are 8 international students enrolled. The school actively recruits these students. They must take the TOEFL, and the SAT or ACT.

Admissions Contact: Richard Shaffer, Director of Admissions. Email: *aaadmit@psu.edu* Web: *www.altoona.psu.edu*

FINANCIAL AID: The deadline for filing freshman financial aid applications for fall entry is February 15.

PENNSYLVANIA COLLEGE OF TECHNOLOGY *(The complete profile is made available exclusively on our website, www.barronspac.com)*

PENNSYLVANIA STATE UNIVERSITY - UNIVERSITY PARK C-3

www.psu.edu

University Park, PA 16802 **(814) 865-5471**

Fax: (814) 863-7590
Full-time: 21,204 men, 18,679 women
Part-time: 644 men, 364 women
Graduate: 3468 men, 2856 women
Year: semesters, summer session
Room & Board: $11,860

SAT CR/M: 580/610 **ACT:** 27
Application Deadline: November 30

Email: admissions@psu.edu
Faculty: n/av
Ph.D.s: 81%
Student/Faculty: 16 to 1
Tuition: $17,900 ($32,382)
Freshman Class: 52974 applied, 29878 accepted, 8501 enrolled
CEEB CODE: 2660
HIGHLY COMPETITIVE

Pennsylvania State University-University Park, founded in 1855, is a public institution that is the oldest and largest of 24 campuses in the Penn State system. The university offers undergraduate and graduate degrees in agricultural sciences, arts and agricultural, business, earth and mineral sciences, education, engineering, health and human development, liberal arts, science, communications, information sciences and technology, and nursing. Penn State also offers graduate and first professional degrees in medicine and law. There are 14 undergraduate schools and one graduate school. In addition to regional accreditation, Penn State has baccalaureate program accreditation with AACSB, ABET, ACEJMC, APTA, ASLA, NAAB, NASAD, NASM, and SAF. The 8556-acre campus is in a suburban area 90 miles west of Harrisburg, PA. Including any residence halls, there are 933 buildings.

STUDENT LIFE: 60% of undergraduates are from Pennsylvania. Others are from 50 states, 130 foreign countries, and Canada. 64% are White; 6% Asian American; 6% Hispanic; 4% African American; 3% two or more races; 2% race unknown; 15% Foreign. **Male To Female Ratio:** 1.2:1. The average age of freshmen is 18; all undergraduates, 20. 7% do not continue beyond their first year; 86% remain to graduate. **Housing:** 13728 students can be accommodated in college housing, which includes single-sex and coed dorms, on-campus apartments, and married student housing. In addition, there are honors houses, language houses, special-interest houses, fraternity houses, and sorority houses. On-campus housing is guaranteed for the freshman year only and is available on a lottery system for upperclassmen. 65% of students commute. Upperclassmen may keep cars.

FACULTY/CLASSROOMS: 62% of faculty are male; 38% are female. No introductory courses are taught by graduate students.

PROGRAMS OF STUDY: Penn State confers B.A., B.S., B.A.E., B.Arch., B.Des., B.Eled., B.F.A., B.Hum., B.L.A., B.M., B.M.A., B.M.E., B.Ph., and B.Sosc. degrees. Associate, master's, and doctoral degrees are also awarded. Bachelor's degrees are awarded in AGRICULTURE (agricultural business management, agricultural sciences, agriculture, animal science, environmental studies, forestry and related sciences, natural resources, natural resource management, plant science, and turfgrass and landscape management), BIOLOGICAL SCIENCE (biochemistry, biology/biological science, biological sciences, biotechnology, forensic science, microbiology, nutrition, and toxicology), BUSINESS (accounting, business administration and management, business administration marketing, entrepreneurial studies, finance, hospitality management services, labor studies, management information systems, marketing management, and supply chain management), COMMUNICATIONS AND THE ARTS (acting, advertising, art, art/art studies, classical languages, communication science, comparative literature, design, English literature, French, Germanic languages and literature, graphic design, journalism, journalism & technical communications, film and media studies, music, music performance, Russian languages and literature, speech/debate/rhetoric, theater design, and visual and performing arts), COMPUTER AND PHYSICAL SCIENCE (astronomy, atmospheric sciences and meteorology, chemistry, computer information systems, geology, information science, mathematics, physics, science technology, and statistics), EDUCATION (agricultural education, art education, Asian studies, athletic training, early childhood education, educational media, elementary education, foreign languages education, music education, secondary education, and special education), ENGINEERING AND ENVIRONMENTAL DESIGN (aerospace engineering, architectural engineering, architecture, bioengineering, biomedical engineering, chemical engineering, civil engineering, computer engineering, electrical/electronics engineering, engineering, engineering science, geological engineering, industrial engineering, landscape architecture, landscape architecture/design, materials science, mechanical engineering, mining and mineral engineering, nuclear engineering, and petroleum/natural gas engineering), HEALTH PROFESSIONS (biomedical science, environmental health science, health care administration, kinesiology, nuclear medical technology, nursing, premedicine, preveterinary science, rehabilitation therapy, and veterinary science), SOCIAL SCIENCE (African American studies, anthropology, archeology, Chinese Studies, criminal justice, economics, food science, geography information science, history, homeland security/emergency preparedness, human development & family studies, international relations, Italian studies, Japanese studies, Judaic studies, Latin American studies, liberal arts, sciences, general studies, humanities, medieval studies, parks and recreation management, philosophy, political science/government, psychology, sociology, Spanish studies, and women's studies). Business & marketing, engineering, and communications & journalism. have the largest enrollments.

ACTIVITIES: 17% of men belong to 1 local and 55 national fraternities; 20% of women belong to 27 national sororities. There are 1038 groups on campus, including art, band, cheerleading, chess, choir, chorale, chorus, computers, dance, debate, drama, drill team, environmental, ethnic, film, forensics, honors, international, jazz band, LGBT, literary magazine, marching band, musical theater, newspaper, opera, orchestra, pep band, photography, political, professional, radio and TV, religious, social, social service, student government, symphony, and yearbook. Popular campus events include Late Night Penn State, Dance Marathon, Penn State football, and Distinguished Speaker Series. **Sports:** There are 15 intercollegiate sports for men and 14 for women, and 25 intramural sports for men and 25 for women. Facilities include a football stadium, baseball field, basketball center, golf courses, ice skating pavilion, indoor track/multipurpose field, outdoor track, soccer field, indoor and outdoor swimming pools, bowling lanes, tennis center, fitness facilities, environmental center, recreation center (fishing, swimming, canoeing, sailing, and kayaking), rifle range, and facilities for gymnastics, volleyball, field hockey, lacrosse, fencing, wrestling, softball field, and ice skating arena. **Graduates:** From July 1, 2015 to June 30, 2016, 10984 bachelor's degrees were awarded. The most popular majors were business/marketing (17%), engineering (17%), and communications/journalism (8%). 540 companies recruited on campus in 2015-2016. In an average class, 65% graduate in 4 years or less, 83% graduate in 5 years or less, and 86% graduate in 6 years or less. Of the 2015 graduating class, 19% were enrolled in graduate school within 6 months of graduation, and 44% were employed.

SERVICES: Counseling and information services are available, as is tutoring in most subjects. There is a reader service for the blind, and remedial math, reading, and writing. **Library/Resources:** The 28 libraries contain 8.1 million volumes, 4.7 million microform items, and 116,394 audio/video tapes/CDs/DVDs, and subscribe to 205,782 periodicals including electronic. Computerized library services include interlibrary loans, database searching, Internet access, and Wi-Fi capability. Special learning facilities include an art gallery, planetarium, six major museums at University Park house, significant research, and educational collections in the fields of agriculture, anthropology, entomology, earth and mineral sciences, and fine arts. **Physically Challenged Students:** 95% of the campus is accessible. Facilities include wheelchair ramps, elevators, special parking, specially equipped restrooms, special class scheduling, lowered drinking fountains, lowered telephones, and special housing.

Reasonable accommodations are available to provide access to all campus services, programs, and activities. **Special:** Co-op programs, internships, study-abroad in more than 50 countries, and work-study programs are available. Dual majors and student-designed majors are possible. Accelerated degree programs and a 3-2 engineering degree are also offered. Integrated Bachelors/Masters degrees in several areas such as engineering, accounting, computer science, meteorology, and labor studies and employment relations. There are 39 national honor societies and a freshman honors program. **Visiting:** Visitors may sit in on classes and stay overnight. To schedule a visit, contact Undergraduate Admissions Office. **Campus Safety and Security:** Measures include 24-hour foot and vehicle patrol, emergency notification system, self-defense education, and security escort services. There are shuttle buses, emergency telephones, lighted pathways/sidewalks, and controlled access to dorms/residences.

REQUIREMENTS: Applicants are required to submit SAT or ACT scores. Admissions decisions for first-year students are made on the basis of several combined factors. Approximately two thirds of the decision for each student is based upon the high school GPA. The remaining one third of the decision is based on factors, which may include standardized critical reading and math test scores, class rank, personal statement, and activities list. AP and CLEP credits are accepted. The typical baccalaureate Penn State academic program requires the completion of between 120 and 130 credits. The General Education requirements are common to all degree programs and compose about one third of the course work (45 credits). All students must also complete a Writing-Across-The-Curriculum course (3 credits), a first-year seminar (1 credit), United States Culture (3 credits), and International Cultures (3 credits) as part of their degree program. **Procedure:** Freshmen are admitted fall, spring, and summer. Entrance exams should be taken in the junior year. There are early admissions, deferred admissions, and rolling admissions plans. Applications should be filed by November 30 for fall entry, along with a $65 fee. Notification is sent on a rolling basis. Applications are accepted online. **Transfer Students:** 338 transfer students enrolled in 2015-2016. Each academic college has its own criteria for transfer admission. See http:/admissions.psu.edu/info/future/transfer/requirements/. Transfer applicants need a minimum GPA of 2.0 and good academic standing. 36 of 120 credits required for the bachelor's degree must be completed at Penn State. **International Students:** There are 4813 international students enrolled. The school actively recruits these students. They must take the TOEFL with a minimum score of 550 on the paper-based TOEFL (PBT) or 80 on the Internet-based version (iBT), or take the IELTS. They must also take the SAT or ACT.

ADMISSIONS: 56% of the 2016-2017 applicants were accepted. The SAT scores for the 2016-2017 freshman class were: Critical Reading-- 13% below 500, 47% between 500 and 599, 33% between 600 and 699, and 7% between 700 and 800. Math-- 7% below 500, 34% between 500 and 599, 44% between 600 and 699, and 15% between 700 and 800. The ACT scores were 14% between 18 and 23, 63% between 24 and 29, and 23% above 30. **Admissions Contact:** Clark Brigger, Exec Director Undergraduate Admissions. Email: *admissions@psu.edu* Web: *www.psu.edu*

FINANCIAL AID: The FAFSA code is 003329. The priority date for freshman financial aid applications for fall entry is February 15.

PHILADELPHIA UNIVERSITY F-3

www.philau.edu

Philadelphia, PA 19144	**(215) 951-2700**
	(800) 951-7287
Fax: (215) 951-2907	**Email: admissions@philau.edu**
Full-time: 825 men, 1618 women	**Faculty:** 123
Part-time: 97 men, 248 women	**Ph.D.s:** 83%
Graduate: 310 men, 608 women	**Student/Faculty:** 13 to 1
Year: semesters, summer session	**Tuition:** $37,800
Room & Board: $12,570	**Freshman Class:** 4129 applied, 2651 accepted, 527 enrolled
SAT CR/M/W: 535/545/520 **ACT:** 24	**CEEB CODE:** 2666
Application Deadline: rolling	**COMPETITIVE**

Philadelphia University, founded in 1884, is a private institution offering preprofessional programs in architecture, design, business, sciences, textiles, fashion, and health. Figures in the above capsule and in this profile are approximate. Tuition cost varies by program. There are 6 undergraduate schools and 1 graduate school. In addition to regional accreditation, PhilaU has baccalaureate program accreditation with ABET, FIDER, NAAB, NASAD, and ACS. The 100-acre campus is in a suburban area in the section of East Falls, 15 minutes from Center City Philadelphia. Including any residence halls, there are 56 buildings.

STUDENT LIFE: 59% of undergraduates are from Pennsylvania. Others are from 37 states, 24 foreign countries, and Canada. 65% are from public schools. 72% are White; 6% Hispanic; 3% Asian American; 10% African American. 18% claim no religious affiliation **Female To Male Ratio:** 2.0:1. The average age of freshmen is 18; all undergraduates, 23. 20% do not continue beyond their first year; 56% remain to graduate. **Housing:** 1265 students can be accommodated in college housing, which includes single-sex and coed dorms, on-campus apartments, off-campus apartments, and town houses. On-campus housing is guaranteed for the freshman year only, is available on a first-come, first-served basis, and on a lottery system for upperclassmen. Priority is given to out-of-town students. 50% of students commute. Upperclassmen may keep cars.

FACULTY/CLASSROOMS: 58% of faculty are male; 42% are female. All teach undergraduates, 50% do research, and teach. No introductory courses are taught by graduate students. The average class size in an introductory lecture is 25; in a laboratory is 14; and in a regular course is 17.

PROGRAMS OF STUDY: PhilaU confers B.S., and B.Arch. degrees. Associate, master's, and doctoral degrees are also awarded. Bachelor's degrees are awarded in BIOLOGICAL SCIENCE (biochemistry and biology/biological science), BUSINESS (accounting, banking and finance, fashion merchandising, international business management, management information systems, management science, and marketing/retailing/merchandising), COMMUNICATIONS AND THE ARTS (graphic design and industrial design), COMPUTER AND PHYSICAL SCIENCE (chemistry, digital arts/technology, and science and management), ENGINEERING AND ENVIRONMENTAL DESIGN (architecture, engineering, environmental science, industrial engineering, interior design, landscape architecture/design, textile engineering, and textile technology), HEALTH PROFESSIONS (physician's assistant and premedicine), SOCIAL SCIENCE (biopsychology, fashion design and technology, and psychology). Physician's assistant, architecture, and engineering are the strongest academically. Architecture, fashion merchandising, and fashion design have the largest enrollments.

ACTIVITIES: 1% of men belong to 1 national fraternity; 1% of women belong to 1 national sorority. There are 30 groups on campus, including cheerleading, choir, dance, drama, ethnic, honors, international, LGBT, newspaper, professional, religious, social, social service, and student government. Popular campus events include Annual Fashion Show and Design Competition, Welcome Week, and Spring Weekend. **Sports:** There are 6 intercollegiate sports for men and 8 for women, and 13 intramural sports for men and 13 for women. Facilities include gyms, basketball, fitness center, tennis courts, athletic fields, soccer, softball, track, rowing, cross country, golf, volleyball, lacrosse, cheerleading, group exercise, and a student recreation center and wellness room. **Graduates:** From July 1, 2015 to June 30, 2016, 648 bachelor's degrees were awarded. The most popular majors were business/marketing (28%), architecture (18%), and health professions & related programs (17%). 70 companies recruited on campus in 2015-2016. In an average class, 43% graduate in 4 years or less, 58% graduate in 5 years or less, and 65% graduate in 6 years or less. Of the 2015 graduating class, 19% were enrolled in graduate school within 6 months of graduation, and 71% were employed.

SERVICES: Counseling and information services are available, as is tutoring in every subject. There is a reader service for the blind, and remedial math, reading, and writing. There are also study skills workshops, course-related workshops, math review sessions, writing review sessions, time management and stress reduction workshops are also available. **Library/Resources:** The library contains 109,235 volumes, 125,000 microform items, 50,630 audio/video tapes/CDs/DVDs, and subscribes to 1,011 periodicals including electronic. Computerized library services include interlibrary loans and database searching. Special learning facilities include an art gallery, TV station, the Design Center at Philadelphia University, and the Kanbar Campus Center for sustainability, energy efficiency, and design. **Physically Challenged Students:** 85% of the campus is accessible. Facilities include wheelchair ramps, elevators, special parking, specially equipped restrooms, special class scheduling, lowered drinking fountains, and lowered telephones. **Special:** Internships in all academic majors, study abroad, a dual major in international business, an accelerated business administration degree program, and an integrated major in business and science are available. There is a freshman honors program. **Visiting:** There are regularly scheduled orientations for prospective students, including an interview and a campus tour. There are guides for informal visits, visitors may sit in on classes, and stay overnight. To schedule a visit, contact the Admissions Office. **Campus Safety and Security:** Measures include 24-hour foot and vehicle patrol, self-defense education, and security escort services. There are shuttle buses, emergency telephones, and lighted pathways/sidewalks.

REQUIREMENTS: The SAT or ACT is required. Applicants should be high school graduates or have earned the GED. Recommended secondary preparation includes 4 years each of English and history, 3 years of math which must include algebra II and geometry, and 3 years of science and 2 years of social studies, and 1 year of history. Potential science majors are strongly urged to take 4 years of math and science. A GPA of 2.5 is required. AP and CLEP credits are accepted. Important factors in the admissions decision are evidence of special talent and extracurricular activities record. All students are required to complete 60-credit residency with courses in math, science, social science, computer literacy, English, history, and the humanities. A total of 121 to 146 credits is required with an overall GPA of 2.0 **Procedure:** Freshmen are admitted in the fall and spring. There are deferred admissions and rolling admissions plans. Application deadlines are open. Application fee is $40. Notifications are sent November 1. Applications are accepted online. **Transfer Students:** 207 transfer students enrolled in 2015-2016. A 2.5 GPA is usually required, and previously attended college transcripts. An interview is recommended. 60 of 121 credits required for the bachelor's degree must be completed at PhilaU. **International Students:** There are 14 international students enrolled. The school actively recruits these students. They must take the TOEFL with a minimum score of 500 on the paper-based TOEFL (PBT), and the English placement test.

ADMISSIONS: 64% of the 2016-2017 applicants were accepted. The SAT scores for the 2016-2017 freshman class were: Critical Reading-- 31% below 500, 51% between 500 and 599, and 17% between 600 and 699. Math-- 28% below 500, 46% between 500 and 599, 23% between 600 and 699, and 3% between 700 and 800. Writing-- 34% below 500, 47% between 500 and 599, 15% between 600 and 699, and 1% between 700 and 800. The ACT scores were 3% between 12 and 17, 51% between 18 and 23, 40% between 24 and 29, and 6% above 30. 31% of the current freshmen were in the top fifth of their class; 65% were in the top two fifths. **Admissions Contact:** Greg Potts, Director of Admissions. Email: *admissions@philau.edu* Web: *www.philau.edu*

FINANCIAL AID: In 2016-2017, 78% of all full-time freshmen and 71% of continuing full-time students received some form of financial aid. 78% of all full-time freshmen and 69% of continuing full-time students received need-based aid. The average freshman award was $32,021. Need-based scholarships or need-based grants averaged $27,568; need-based self-help aid (loans and jobs) averaged $5,430; non-need-based athletic scholarships averaged $9,750; other non-need-based awards and non-need-based scholarships averaged $12,760; and $3,741 from other forms of aid. 28% of undergraduate students work part-time. Average annual earnings from campus work are $1067. The average financial indebtedness of the 2016 graduate was $39,938. The FAFSA code is 003354. The priority date for freshman financial aid applications for fall entry is March 1.

POINT PARK UNIVERSITY — B-3

www.pointpark.edu

Pittsburgh, PA 15222 — **(412) 392-3430**

Fax: (412) 392-3902	**Email: enroll@pointpark.edu**
Full-time: 1070 men, 1481 women	**Faculty:** n/av
Part-time: 313 men, 362 women	**Ph.D.s:** 75%
Graduate: 273 men, 342 women	**Student/Faculty:** 19 to 1
Year: semesters, summer session	**Tuition:** $28,250
Room & Board: $13,020	**Freshman Class:** 3237 applied, 2393 accepted, 548 enrolled
SAT or ACT: required	**CEEB CODE:** 2676
Application Deadline: open	**COMPETITIVE**

Point Park University, is a comprehensive, master's-level institute with a strong liberal arts tradition. Point Park currently enrolls students in 82 undergraduate programs and 17 graduate programs offered through its school of arts and sciences, school of business, school of communication, and conservatory of performing arts. Figures in the above capsule and in this profile are approximate. There are 4 undergraduate schools and 4 graduate schools. In addition to regional accreditation, Point Park has baccalaureate program accreditation with ABET, IACBE, and NASD. The campus is in an urban area in Downtown Pittsburgh. Including any residence halls, there are 15 buildings.

STUDENT LIFE: 79% of undergraduates are from Pennsylvania. Others are from 49 states, 25 foreign countries, and Canada. 72% are White; 4% two or more races; 3% Hispanic; 3% Foreign; 16% African American; 1% Asian American; 1% race unknown. **Female To Male Ratio:** 1.3:1. The average age of freshmen is 18; all undergraduates, 24. 26% do not continue beyond their first year; 50% remain to graduate. **Housing:** 1022 students can be accommodated in college housing, which includes single-sex and coed dorms and on-campus apartments. There are also living and learning communities. On-campus housing is available on a first-come and first-served basis. 70% of students commute. Some may keep cars.

FACULTY/CLASSROOMS: No introductory courses are taught by graduate students.

PROGRAMS OF STUDY: Point Park confers B.A., B.S. and B.F.A. degrees. Associate and master's degrees are also awarded. Bachelor's degrees are awarded in AGRICULTURE (environmental studies), BIOLOGICAL SCIENCE (biology/biological science, biotechnology, and forensic science), BUSINESS (accounting, business administration and management, finance, funeral home services, human resources, management science, organizational leadership and management, and sports management), COMMUNICATIONS AND THE ARTS (advertising, applied art, arts administration/management, broadcasting, communications, dance, dramatic arts, English, film arts, journalism, media arts, performing arts, photography, public relations, theatre arts, and video), COMPUTER AND PHYSICAL SCIENCE (computer science, digital arts/technology, earth science, and information sciences and systems), EDUCATION (childhood education, dance education, drama education, early childhood education, education, elementary education, secondary education, and special education), ENGINEERING AND ENVIRONMENTAL DESIGN (civil engineering, civil engineering technology, electrical/electronics engineering, electrical/electronics engineering technology, engineering management, engineering technology, environmental science, mechanical engineering, mechanical engineering technology, and systems engineering), HEALTH PROFESSIONS (environmental health science, health care administration, pre-health studies, premedicine, and respiratory therapy), SOCIAL SCIENCE (behavioral science, criminal justice, early childhood studies, history, international studies, law enforcement and corrections, legal studies, liberal arts/general studies, paralegal studies, political science/government, psychology, and public administration). Business, dance, and theater have the largest enrollments.

ACTIVITIES: There are no fraternities or sororities. There are 34 groups on campus, including choir, chorale, computers, dance, drama, ethnic, film, honors, international, LGBT, literary magazine, musical theater, newspaper, photography, political, professional, radio and TV, religious, social, social service, and student government. **Sports:** There are 5 intercollegiate sports for men and 6 for women, and 8 intramural sports for men and 8 for women. Facilities include an auditorium, gymnasium, racquetball, training and fitness, and a recreation center. **Graduates:** From July 1, 2015 to June 30, 2016, 719 bachelor's degrees were awarded. The most popular majors were business management (12%), theatre arts (9%), and dance (9%). In an average class, 50% graduate in 6 years or less.

SERVICES: Counseling and information services are available, as is tutoring in some subjects. Learning-disabled services available on case-by-case basis. There is also a reader service for the blind, and remedial math, reading, and writing. **Library/Resources:** The library contains 82,565 volumes, 16,275 microform items, 6,831 audio/video tapes/CDs/DVDs, and subscribes to 77,064 periodicals including electronic. Computerized library services include interlibrary loans, database searching, Internet access, and Wi-Fi capability. Special learning facilities include an art gallery, radio station, TV station, natural sciences labs, engineering technology, forensic crime scene house, computer newsrooms, MAC and PC multimedia labs, black/white and color photography darkrooms, digital photography lab, radio station, TV studio/newsroom, cinema production and editing suites, performance and dance studios, performing arts center/theaters, and art galleries. **Physically Challenged Students:** 95% of the campus is accessible. Facilities include wheelchair ramps, elevators, specially equipped restrooms, special class scheduling, lowered drinking fountains, lowered telephones, and special housing. **Special:** Cross-registration is available through the Pittsburgh Council on Higher Education. The university offers internships, work study, dual and student-designed majors, credit by exam and for life/military/work experience, and nondegree study. Capstone programs are available for students with associate degrees. Accelerated degree programs are available. There are 2 national honor societies and a freshman honors program. **Visiting:** There are regularly scheduled orientations for prospective students. There are guides for informal visits and visitors may sit in on classes. To schedule a visit, contact the Office of Admissions. **Campus Safety and Security:** Measures include 24-hour foot and vehicle patrol, emergency notification system, self-defense education, and security escort services. There are shuttle buses, emergency telephones, and lighted pathways/sidewalks.

REQUIREMENTS: The SAT or ACT is required. Students should have completed 12 academic credits or 16 Carnegie units consisting of 4 in English, 3 in history, science, and math, and 2 years of foreign language. The GED is accepted. Theater and dance students must audition, and an interview is requested for all candidates. AP and CLEP credits are accepted. All majors leading to a baccalaureate degree require a minimum of 120 credits. Most programs require 42 core curriculum credits, with at least 30 completed in residence. A 2.0 GPA is required. **Procedure:** Freshmen are admitted to all sessions. Entrance exams should be taken in the junior or senior year. There are deferred admissions and rolling admissions plans. Application deadlines are open. Application fee is $40. Notification is sent on a rolling basis. Application fees are waived if application is completed online. **Transfer Students:** 446 transfer students enrolled in 2015-2016. Applicants must have completed 12 credit hours with at least a 2.0 GPA. The SAT or ACT and an interview are recommended. 30 of 120 credits required for the bachelor's degree must be completed at Point Park. **International Students:** There are 101 international students enrolled. The school actively recruits these students. They must take the TOEFL with a minimum score of 500 on the paper-based TOEFL (PBT) or 61 on the Internet-based version (iBT). Students whose native language is English may submit SAT scores.

ADMISSIONS: 74% of the 2016-2017 applicants were accepted. The SAT scores for the 2016-2017 freshman class were: Critical Reading-- 45% below 500, 39% between 500 and 599, 14% between 600 and 699, and 2% between 700 and 800. Math-- 57% below 500, 34% between 500 and 599, 8% between 600 and 699, and 1% between 700 and 800. Writing-- 52% below 500, 35% between 500 and 599, 12% between 600 and 699, and 2% between 700 and 800. The ACT scores were 34% below 12, 22% between 12 and 17, 25% between 18 and 23, 20% between 24 and 29, and 6% above 30. **Admissions Contact:** Joell Minford, Director, Undergraduate Admissions. Email: *enroll@pointpark.edu* Web: *www.pointpark.edu*

FINANCIAL AID: In 2016-2017, 99% of all full-time freshmen and continuing full-time students received some form of financial aid. 75% of all full-time freshmen and 76% of continuing full-time students received need-based aid. The average freshman award was $29,218. Need-based scholarships or need-based grants averaged $5,664 ($16,000 maximum); need-based self-help aid (loans and jobs) averaged $5,788 ($7,000 maximum); non-need-based athletic scholarships averaged $5,335 ($14,000 maximum); and other non-need-based awards and non-need-based scholarships averaged $11,086 ($31,540 maximum). 16% of undergraduate students work part-time. Average annual earnings from campus work are $2173. The average financial indebtedness of the 2016 graduate was $21,838. The FAFSA code is 003357. The priority date for freshman financial aid applications for fall entry is March 15. The filing deadline for fall entry is August 15.

ROBERT MORRIS UNIVERSITY — A-3

www.rmu.edu

Moon Township, PA 15108 — **(800) 762-0097**

Fax: (412) 397-2425	**Email:** admissionsoffice@rmu.edu
Full-time: 2339 men, 1601 women	**Faculty:** 200; IIA, ++$
Part-time: 184 men, 260 women	**Ph.D.s:** 92%
Graduate: 336 men, 479 women	**Student/Faculty:** 15 to 1
Year: semesters, summer session	**Tuition:** $27,394
Room & Board: $10,910	**Freshman Class:** 6123 applied, 4664 accepted, 888 enrolled
SAT CR/M/W: 517/535/494 **ACT:** 22	**CEEB CODE:** 2769
Application Deadline: May 1	**COMPETITIVE**

Robert Morris University, founded in 1921, is a private institution offering 49 undergraduate degree programs and 35 master's and doctoral degree programs, many of which are available fully online. There are 5 undergraduate schools and 5 graduate schools. In addition to regional accreditation, RMU has baccalaureate program accreditation with AACSB, ABET, TEAC, CCNE, Society of Actuaries, and JRC on Educational Programs in Nuclear Medicine. The 230-acre campus is in a suburban area 17 miles southwest of downtown Pittsburgh. Including any residence halls, there are 32 buildings.

STUDENT LIFE: 83% of undergraduates are from Pennsylvania. Others are from 48 states, 39 foreign countries, and Canada. 90% are from public schools. 9% are Foreign; 75% White; 6% African American; 4% race unknown; 3% two or more races; 2% Hispanic; 1% Asian American. 41% are Catholic; 35% Protestant. **Male To Female Ratio:** 1.2:1. The average age of freshmen is 18; all undergraduates, 22. 14% do not continue beyond their first year; 63% remain to graduate. **Housing:** 2015 students can be accommodated in college housing, which includes single-sex, and coed dorms and on-campus apartments. On-campus housing is guaranteed for the freshman year only, and is available on a first-come, and first-served basis. 54% of students commute. All students may keep cars. Alcohol is not permitted.

FACULTY/CLASSROOMS: 46% of faculty are male; 44% are female. 99% teach undergraduates, 80% do research, and teach. No introductory courses are taught by graduate students. The average class size in an introductory lecture is 22; in a laboratory is 12; and in a regular course is 22.

PROGRAMS OF STUDY: RMU confers B.A., B.S., B.F.A., B.S.B.A., and B.S.N. degrees. Master's and doctoral degrees are also awarded. Bachelor's degrees are awarded in BIOLOGICAL SCIENCE (biology/biological science), BUSINESS (accounting, banking and finance, business administration and management, hospitality management services, marketing/retailing/merchandising, organizational behavior, and sports management), COMMUNICATIONS AND THE ARTS (communications, English, media arts, and television & digital media production), COMPUTER AND PHYSICAL SCIENCE (actuarial science, applied mathematics, and information sciences and systems), EDUCATION (business education and elementary education), ENGINEERING AND ENVIRONMENTAL DESIGN (engineering, environmental science, and manufacturing engineering), HEALTH PROFESSIONS (health care administration, nuclear medical technology, and nursing), SOCIAL SCIENCE (economics, history, psychology, social science, and sociology). Actuarial science, and engineering are the strongest academically. Accounting, nursing, and engineering have the largest enrollments.

ACTIVITIES: 10% of men belong to 8 national fraternities; 16% of women belong to 6 national sororities. There are 131 groups on campus, including band, cheerleading, chess, choir, chorale, chorus, computers, dance, drama, environmental, ethnic, film, honors, international, jazz band, LGBT, literary magazine, marching band, musical theater, newspaper, orchestra, pep band, photography, political, professional, radio and TV, religious, social, social service, student government, and yearbook. Popular campus events include Homecoming, Prom and Dances. **Sports:** There are 6 intercollegiate sports for men and 9 for women, and 11 intramural sports for men and 11 for women. Facilities include a field house, gym, health club, and athletic fields. The RMU Island Sports Center has hockey rinks, golf dome, health club, and an 8-lane track. **Graduates:** From July 1, 2015 to June 30, 2016, 955 bachelor's degrees were awarded. The most popular majors were management (11%), accounting (11%), and communications (9%). 140 companies recruited on campus in 2015-2016. In an average class, 46% graduate in 4 years or less, 61% graduate in 5 years or less, and 61% graduate in 6 years or less. Of the 2015 graduating class, 7% were enrolled in graduate school within 6 months of graduation, and 85% were employed.

SERVICES: Counseling and information services are available, as is tutoring in most subjects. There is also a reader service for the blind, and remedial math, reading, and writing. **Library/Resources:** The library contains 106,862 volumes, 7,054 microform items, and 3,210 audio/video tapes/CDs/DVDs, and subscribes to 242 periodicals including electronic. Computerized library services include interlibrary loans, database searching, Internet access, and Wi-Fi capability. Special learning facilities include an art gallery, radio station, TV station, and a manufacturing lab for engineering. Nursing students also learn to care for patients in a nursing laboratory, where bedside computers and patient simulators assist in developing clinical decision-making skills. **Physically Challenged Students:** 75% of the campus is accessible. Facilities include wheelchair ramps, elevators, special parking, specially equipped restrooms, special class scheduling, lowered drinking fountains, lowered telephones, and special housing. **Special:** The university offers internship programs in most majors, cross-registration with the 9 colleges of the Pittsburgh Council of Higher Education, work-study programs, study abroad in 12 countries, and non-degree study. Credit by exam and pass/fail options are available. There are 9 national honor societies, a freshman honors program, and 1 departmental honors program. **Visiting:** There are regularly scheduled orientations for prospective students, consisting of placement testing, orientation, and academic advising. There are guides for informal visits, visitors may sit in on classes, and stay overnight. To schedule a visit, contact the Admissions Office. **Campus Safety and Security:** Measures include 24-hour foot and vehicle patrol, emergency notification system, and security escort services. There are shuttle buses, emergency telephones, lighted pathways/sidewalks, and controlled access to dorms/residences.

REQUIREMENTS: The SAT is required. Applicants should be graduates of an accredited secondary school or hold a GED diploma. They must have completed 16 Carnegie units, including 4 in English and social studies, 3 in math and 2 in science. An interview is required for some and recommended for all others. AP and CLEP credits are accepted. Important factors in the admissions decision are advanced placement or honors courses, leadership record, and personality/intangible qualities. All candidates must complete 126 to 135 credit hours, including 24 to 31 in the major, with a 2.0 GPA overall and a 2.5 in the major. A core curriculum varies with each major and consists of humanities, communication skills, social sciences, computing, and math. All students must demonstrate competency in computer software applications. **Procedure:** Freshmen are admitted in the fall, spring, and summer. Entrance exams should be taken by fall or late winter of the senior year. There are deferred admissions and rolling admissions plans. Applications should be filed by May 1 for fall entry; December 1 for spring entry, along with a $30 fee. Notification is sent on a rolling basis. 111 applicants were on the 2016 waiting list; 27 were admitted. Application fees are waived if application is completed online. **Transfer Students:** 347 transfer students enrolled in 2015-2016. Students must have a minimum 2.0 GPA in nondevelopmental academic courses. Those with fewer than 30 earned credits must also submit an official high school transcript and test results of the SAT or ACT. An interview is recommended. 30 of 126 credits required for the bachelor's degree must be completed at RMU. **International Students:** There are 543 international students enrolled. The school actively recruits these students. They must take the TOEFL with a minimum score of 500 on the paper-based TOEFL (PBT) or 61 on the Internet-based version (iBT).

ADMISSIONS: 76% of the 2016-2017 applicants were accepted. The SAT scores for the 2016-2017 freshman class were: Critical Reading-- 42% below 500, 44% between 500 and 599, 12% between 600 and 699, and 2% between 700 and 800. Math-- 36% below 500, 44% between 500 and 599, 17% between 600 and 699, and 3% between 700 and 800. Writing-- 56% below 500, 35% between 500 and 599, 8% between 600 and 699, and 1% between 700 and 800. 12 freshmen graduated first in their class. **Admissions Contact:** Kellie Laurenzi, Associate Vice President of Admissions. Email: *admissionsoffice@rmu.edu* Web: *www.rmu.edu*

FINANCIAL AID: In 2016-2017, 99% of all full-time freshmen and 90% of continuing full-time students received some form of financial aid. 99% of all full-time freshmen and 95% of continuing full-time students received need-based aid. The average freshman award was $24,242. Need-based scholarships or need-based grants averaged $18,623; need-based self-help aid (loans and jobs) averaged $6,394; and non-need-based athletic scholarships averaged $4,989. 100% of undergraduate students work part-time. The average financial indebtedness of the 2016 graduate was $37,531. RMU is a member of CSS. The FAFSA code is 003359. The deadline for filing freshman financial aid applications for fall entry is May 1.

ROSEMONT COLLEGE F-4

www.rosemont.edu

Rosemont, PA 19010	(610) 527-0200 (800) 331-0708
Fax: (610) 520-4399	**Email:** admissions@rosemont.edu
Full-time: 155 men, 299 women	**Faculty:** 28
Part-time: 30 men, 45 women	**Ph.D.s:** 90%
Graduate: 68 men, 290 women	**Student/Faculty:** 10 to 1
Year: semesters, summer session	**Tuition:** $19,480
Room & Board: $11,500	**Freshman Class:** 875 applied, 619 accepted, 135 enrolled
SAT CR/M/W: required **ACT:** 23	**CEEB CODE:** 2763
Application Deadline: August 1	**COMPETITIVE**

Rosemont College, founded in 1921, is an independent coeducational liberal arts and sciences college affiliated with the Roman Catholic Church. Accelerated degree and graduate programs are offered in the school of graduate and professional studies. There are 2 undergraduate schools and 1 graduate school. The 56-acre campus is in a suburban area 11 miles west of Philadelphia. Including any residence halls, there are 15 buildings.

STUDENT LIFE: 75% of undergraduates are from Pennsylvania. Others are from 18 states, and 14 foreign countries. 6% are Hispanic; 5% Asian American; 40% African American; 4% two or more races; 4% race unknown; 39% White; 2% Foreign. 60% are Catholic; 17% Protestant. **Female To Male Ratio:** 2.5:1. The average age of freshmen is 18; all undergraduates, 23. 8% do not continue beyond their first year; 72% remain to graduate. **Housing:** 373 students can be accommodated in college housing, which includes single-sex, and coed dorms, honors houses and special-interest houses. On-campus housing is guaranteed for all 4 years. 75% of students live on campus; of those, 60% remain on campus on weekends. All students may keep cars.

FACULTY/CLASSROOMS: 41% of faculty are male; 59% are female. All teach undergraduates, 70% do research, and teach. No introductory courses are taught by graduate students. The average class size in an introductory lecture is 20; in a laboratory is 10; and in a regular course is 12.

PROGRAMS OF STUDY: Rosemont confers B.A., B.F.A., and B.S. degrees. Master's degrees are also awarded. Bachelor's degrees are awarded in BIOLOGICAL SCIENCE (biochemistry and biology/biological science), BUSINESS (accounting and business administration and management), COMMUNICATIONS AND THE ARTS (communications, creative writing, English, fine arts, French, German, and Spanish), COMPUTER AND PHYSICAL SCIENCE (chemistry and mathematics), EDUCATION (art education, education, foreign languages education, and secondary education), ENGINEERING AND ENVIRONMENTAL DESIGN (environmental science), HEALTH PROFESSIONS (predentistry and premedicine), SOCIAL SCIENCE (economics, history, humanities, Italian studies, liberal arts/general studies, philosophy, political science/government, prelaw, psychology, religion, social science, sociology, and women's studies). Biology & chemstry, and liberal arts are the strongest academically. Biology, psychology, and business have the largest enrollments.

ACTIVITIES: There are no fraternities or sororities. There are 23 groups on campus, including art, band, choir, chorus, dance, drama, ethnic, honors, international, jazz band, LGBT, literary magazine, marching band, musical theater, newspaper, orchestra, photography, political, professional, religious, social service, student government, symphony, and yearbook. Popular campus events include Oktoberfest, Founders Day, International/Multi-Cultural Festival, and Petaltones Concert. **Sports:** There are 6 intercollegiate sports for men and 7 for women. Facilities include hockey, softball, tennis, treadmills, weight equipment, an auditorium, and indoor basketball, badminton, and volleyball courts. **Graduates:** From July 1, 2015 to June 30, 2016, 118 bachelor's degrees were awarded. The most popular majors were business (24%), education (14%), and biology (6%). 18 companies recruited on campus in 2015-2016. In an average class, 74% graduate in 4 years or less and 77% graduate in 5 years or less. Of the 2015 graduating class, 20% were enrolled in graduate school within 6 months of graduation, and 60% were employed.

SERVICES: Counseling and information services are available, as is tutoring in every subject. There is a reader service for the blind, and remedial reading and writing. **Library/Resources:** The library contains 165,600 volumes, 22,900 microform items, 3,485 audio/video tapes/CDs/DVDs, and subscribes to 16,370 periodicals including electronic. Computerized library services include interlibrary loans, database searching, Internet access, and Wi-Fi capability. Special learning facilities include an art gallery. **Physically Challenged Students:** 20% of the campus is accessible. Facilities include wheelchair ramps, elevators, special parking, specially equipped restrooms, special class scheduling, lowered drinking fountains, and lowered telephones. **Special:** Cross-registration opportunities are available with Villanova, Arcadia, Eastern, Holy Family, Immaculata, and Neumann Universities; Cabrini, Gwynedd-Mercy, and Chestnut Hill Colleges; and the Art Institute International Exchange Program. There is a joint admission program with Temple University School of Dentistry and Drexel University College of Medicine. Internships, study abroad, a Washington semester, dual and student-designed majors, and accelerated degree programs are also available. There are 6 national honor societies and a freshman honors program. **Visiting:**

There are regularly scheduled orientations for prospective students, including a campus tour and meetings with financial aid advisers, faculty, and student life representatives. There are guides for informal visits, visitors may sit in on classes, and stay overnight. To schedule a visit, contact Cecelia Samar at (610) 527-0200 x2966. **Campus Safety and Security:** Measures include 24-hour foot and vehicle patrol, emergency notification system, self-defense education, and security escort services. There are also shuttle buses, emergency telephones, lighted pathways/sidewalks, controlled access to dorms/residences, and electronically operated residence hall entrances activated by security cards.

REQUIREMENTS: The SAT is required. A GED is accepted. Applicants must complete 16 academic units, including 4 in English and 2 each in foreign language, history, math, and science. An interview is recommended. A GPA of 2.0 is required. AP and CLEP credits are accepted. Important factors in the admissions decision are advanced placement or honors courses, leadership record, and recommendations by school officials. General education requirements, major requirements, internship, study abroad, service learning. All majors have a comprehensive examination or senior project. 120 minimum credit hours for most majors. **Procedure:** Freshmen are admitted in the fall and spring. Entrance exams should be taken before January of the senior year. There are deferred admissions and rolling admissions plans. Applications should be filed by August 1 for fall entry. Notification is sent on a rolling basis. Applications are accepted online. **Transfer Students:** 27 transfer students enrolled in 2015-2016. Transfer applicants should submit transcripts from each college attended, a letter of good standing from the dean at the last college attended, and catalogs from the colleges from which the student wishes to transfer credits. Students with fewer than 30 credits are required to submit high school transcripts and SAT scores. The minimum GPA is 2.0. An interview is recommended. 30 of 120 credits required for the bachelor's degree must be completed at Rosemont. **International Students:** There are 11 international students enrolled. The school actively recruits these students. They must take the TOEFL with a minimum score of 550 on the paper-based TOEFL (PBT) or 61 on the Internet-based version (iBT). They must also take the SAT. One exam is also required.

ADMISSIONS: 71% of the 2016-2017 applicants were accepted. The SAT scores for the 2016-2017 freshman class were: Critical Reading-- 67% below 500, 26% between 500 and 599, 5% between 600 and 699, and 2% between 700 and 800. Math-- 74% below 500, 18% between 500 and 599, 6% between 600 and 699, and 2% between 700 and 800. Writing-- 74% below 500, 21% between 500 and 599, 3% between 600 and 699, and 2% between 700 and 800. The ACT scores were 17% between 24 and 29, and 83% above 30. **Admissions Contact:** Dennis J. Murphy, Vice President for Enrollment Management. Email: *admissions@rosemont.edu* Web: *www.rosemont.edu*

FINANCIAL AID: In 2016-2017, 99% of all full-time freshmen and 95% of continuing full-time students received some form of financial aid. 93% of all full-time freshmen and 86% of continuing full-time students received need-based aid. 27% of undergraduate students work part-time. Average annual earnings from campus work are $1000. The FAFSA code is 003360. The priority date for freshman financial aid applications for fall entry is February 15. The filing deadline for fall entry is March 15.

SAINT FRANCIS UNIVERSITY *(The complete profile is made available exclusively on our website, www.barronspac.com)*

SAINT JOSEPH'S UNIVERSITY — F-3

www.sju.edu

Philadelphia, PA 19131	**(610) 660-1300** **(888) BE-A-HAWK**
Fax: (610) 660-1314	**Email: admit@sju.edu**
Full-time: 2125 men, 2531 women	**Faculty:** 270; IIA, ++$
Part-time: 295 men, 426 women	**Ph.D.s:** 91%
Graduate: 1144 men, 1894 women	**Student/Faculty:** 17 to 1
Year: semesters, summer session	**Tuition:** $43,020
Room & Board: $14,524	**Freshman Class:** 8876 applied, 6934 accepted, 1262 enrolled
SAT CR/M: 560/570 **ACT:** 26	**CEEB CODE:** 2801
Application Deadline: February 1	**VERY COMPETITIVE**

Saint Joseph's University, founded by the Society of Jesus in 1851, advances the professional and personal ambitions of men and women by providing a demanding, yet supportive, educational experience. Saint Joseph's has two principal academic colleges – the College of Arts and Sciences, and the Erivan K. Haub School of Business. Saint Joseph's University offers over 55 undergraduate majors, 50 minors, and over 30-degree completion and certificate programs including online options. Graduate programs include over 40 areas of study with many programs offering both campus-based and online options. There are 2 undergraduate schools and 2 graduate schools. In addition to regional accreditation, Saint Joseph's has baccalaureate program accreditation with AACSB. The 113-acre campus is in a suburban area on the western edge of Philadelphia and eastern Montgomery County. Including any residence halls, there are 81 buildings.

STUDENT LIFE: 54% of undergraduates are from out of state, mostly the Middle Atlantic. Students are from 43 states, 44 foreign countries, and Canada. 78% are White; 6% African American; 6% Hispanic; 3% Asian American; 2% Foreign; 2% two or more races; 2% race unknown. 75% are Catholic; 17% Protestant. **Female To Male Ratio:** 1.4:1. The average age of freshmen is 18; all undergraduates, 21. 9% do not continue beyond their first year; 80% remain to graduate. **Housing:** 2938 students can be accommodated in college housing, which includes single-sex, and coed dorms, on-campus apartments, off-campus apartments, honors houses, special-interest houses, and special interest floors. On-campus housing is available on a lottery system for upperclassmen. 55% of students live on campus. Some may keep cars.

FACULTY/CLASSROOMS: 55% of faculty are male; 45% are female. No introductory courses are taught by graduate students. The average class size in an introductory lecture is 29; in a laboratory is 17; and in a regular course is 25.

PROGRAMS OF STUDY: Saint Joseph's confers B.A. and B.S. degrees. Associate, master's, and doctoral degrees are also awarded. Bachelor's degrees are awarded in BIOLOGICAL SCIENCE (biochemistry and biology/biological science), BUSINESS (accounting, business administration and management, entrepreneurial studies, finance, human resources, insurance and risk management, international business management, investments and securities, management information systems, marketing management, marketing/retailing/merchandising, organizational leadership and management, and sports marketing), COMMUNICATIONS AND THE ARTS (art, art/art studies, communications, English, French, German, Italian, Latin, music, Spanish, and theatre arts), COMPUTER AND PHYSICAL SCIENCE (actuarial science, chemistry, computer science, information sciences and systems, mathematics, and physics), EDUCATION (art education, Asian studies, early childhood education, elementary education, and special education), ENGINEERING AND ENVIRONMENTAL DESIGN (environmental science), HEALTH PROFESSIONS (health care administration and health science), SOCIAL SCIENCE (criminal justice, economics, European studies, French studies, history, international relations, liberal arts/general studies, philosophy, political science/government, psychology, public administration, religious studies, sociology, and theological studies). Biology, and accounting are the strongest academically. Food marketing, finance, and biology have the largest enrollments.

ACTIVITIES: 6% of men belong to 3 national fraternities; 15% of women belong to 5 national sororities. There are 100 groups on campus, including band, cheerleading, choir, chorale, dance, debate, drama, environmental, ethnic, film, forensics, honors, international, jazz band, LGBT, literary magazine, musical theater, newspaper, orchestra, pep band, political, professional, radio and TV, religious, social, social service, and student government. Popular campus events include Community Day, Spring Concert, and Hawk-A-Palooza. **Sports:** There are 10 intercollegiate sports for men and 10 for women, and 16 intramural sports for men and 16 for women. Saint Joseph's University students are encouraged to participate in intercollegiate, club, and intramural activities as well as in recreational, and fitness. **Graduates:** From July 1, 2015 to June 30, 2016, 937 bachelor's degrees were awarded. The most popular majors were food marketing (10%), marketing (9%), and finance (9%). 424 companies recruited on campus in 2015-2016. In an average class, 72% graduate in 4 years or less, 79% graduate in 5 years or less, and 80% graduate in 6 years or less. Of the 2015 graduating class, 12% were enrolled in graduate school within 6 months of graduation, and 81% were employed.

SERVICES: Counseling and information services are available, as is tutoring in most subjects. There is also a reader service for the blind, as well as study, and life skills workshops, supplemental instruction, a writing center, and other support services to help with student needs. **Library/Resources:** The library contains 260,000 volumes, 860,581 microform items, 2,576 audio/video tapes/CDs/DVDs, and subscribes to 79,725 periodicals including electronic. Computerized library services include interlibrary loans, database searching, Internet access, and Wi-Fi capability. Special learning facilities include an art gallery, radio station, an instructional media center, foreign language labs, Mandeville Hall Wall Street Trading Room, Claver Honors House, and Post Learning Commons. **Physically Challenged Students:** 85% of the campus is accessible. Facilities include wheelchair ramps, elevators, special parking, specially equipped restrooms, special class scheduling, lowered drinking fountains, lowered telephones, and special housing. There is also automatic eye doors, curb cuts, a specially equipped van for wheelchairs, a pool lift, and a bell system at major road crossings. **Special:** The University offers internships, a Washington semester, 5-year combined Bachelors/Masters degree programs, dual majors, minor concentrations, and study abroad, and co-op programs for business majors. There are 23 national honor societies, Phi Beta Kappa, a freshman honors program, and 16 departmental honors programs. **Visiting:** Regularly scheduled orientations for prospective students, consisting of open houses, tours, and information sessions. There are also guides for informal visits and visitors may sit in on classes. To schedule a visit, contact the Admissions Office. **Campus Safety and Security:** Measures include 24-hour foot and vehicle patrol, emergency notification system, and security escort services. There are shuttle buses, emergency telephones, lighted pathways/sidewalks, controlled access to dorms/residences, a bicycle patrol, public safety orientation/education, emergency preparedness awareness training, active shooter training, building evacuation drills, fire extinguisher use training, and close circuit television cameras and monitoring, CPR/AED/First Aid certification of Public Safety Personnel is also available as is, defensive driver's training, public safety presentations, traffic and parking lot access controls, crime and safety bulletins, and hiring of local law enforcement to patrol communities around campus.

REQUIREMENTS: Submission of the SAT and ACT standardized test scores is optional for admission. Academic information, recommendations, and the record of extracurricular involvement and evidence of special talent, leadership and service will be reviewed. A variety of factors are considered during the application process including, but not limited to strength of high school, rigor of academic curriculum, and overall academic achievement and community involvement. AP and CLEP credits are accepted. Important factors in the admissions decision are advanced placement or honors courses, recommendations by school officials, and extracurricular activities record. The General Education Program (GEP) consists of 6 signature core courses; up to 10 variable courses (AP and transfer credits may be accepted), 3 integrative learning courses, and 3 overlay courses focusing on the areas of diversity/globalization, ethics, and writing-intensive. **Procedure:** Freshmen are admitted fall and spring. Entrance exams should be taken in the spring of the junior year and/or the fall of the senior year. There are early admissions and deferred admissions plans. Applications should be filed by February 1 for fall entry; December 15 for spring entry, along with a $50 fee. Notifications are sent March 15. 206 applicants were on the waiting list; 4 were admitted. Application fees are waived if application is completed online. **Transfer Students:** 73 transfer students enrolled in 2015-2016. Transfer students requirements include a minimum of 12 transferable credits. Typically, students with a 2.5 cumulative GPA or higher are considered for admission. Transfer applicants must submit high school and college transcripts. 60 of 120 credits required for the bachelor's degree must be completed at Saint Joseph's. **International Students:** There are 109 international students enrolled. The school actively recruits these students. They must take the TOEFL with a minimum score of 550 on the paper-based TOEFL (PBT) or 80 on the Internet-based version (iBT). They must also take the SAT or ACT, scoring 450.

ADMISSIONS: 78% of the 2016-2017 applicants were accepted. The SAT scores for the 2016-2017 freshman class were: Critical Reading-- 15% below 500, 49% between 500 and 599, 32% between 600 and 699, and 4% between 700 and 800. Math-- 11% below 500, 51% between 500 and 599, 34% between 600 and 699, and 4% between 700 and 800. The ACT scores were 29% between 18 and 23, 55% between 24 and 29, and 16% above 30. 44% of the current freshmen were in the top fifth of their class; 74% were in the top two fifths. 4 freshmen graduated first in their class. **Admissions Contact:** Maureen Mathis, Assistant Provost. Email: *admit@sju.edu* Web: *www.sju.edu*

FINANCIAL AID: In 2016-2017, 97% of all full-time freshmen and 93% of continuing full-time students received some form of financial aid. The average freshman award was $30,985. Average annual earnings from campus work was $1500. Saint Joseph's is a member of CSS. The FAFSA code is 003367. The priority date for freshman financial aid applications for fall entry is February 15. The filing deadline for fall entry is May 1.

SAINT VINCENT COLLEGE — B-3

www.stvincent.edu

Latrobe, PA 15650	**(724) 532-6600** **(800) 782-5549**
Fax: (724) 805-2953	**Email: admission@stvincent.edu**
Full-time: 821 men, 765 women	**Faculty:** 101; IIB, av$
Part-time: 34 men, 26 women	**Ph.D.s:** 89%
Graduate: 90 men, 100 women	**Student/Faculty:** 16 to 1
Year: semesters, summer session	**Tuition:** $33,814
Room & Board: $10,812	**Freshman Class:** 2256 applied, 1486 accepted, 393 enrolled
SAT CR/M/W: 520/520/500 **ACT:** 23	**CEEB CODE:** 2808
Application Deadline: May 1	**COMPETITIVE**

Saint Vincent College, founded in 1846, is a private Catholic college of liberal arts and sciences sponsored by Benedictine Monks. Figures in the above capsule and in this profile are approximate. There are 4 undergraduate schools and 3 graduate schools. In addition to regional accreditation, Saint Vincent has baccalaureate program accreditation with ACBSP and MSCHE. The 200-acre campus is in a suburban area 35 miles east of Pittsburgh. Including any residence halls, there are 26 buildings.

STUDENT LIFE: 82% of undergraduates are from Pennsylvania. Others are from 27 states, 9 foreign countries, and Canada. 85% are White; 5% African American; 4% race unknown; 3% Hispanic; 2% Asian American; 1% Foreign; 1% two or more races. 57% are Catholic; 20% Protestant; 11% unknown denominations. **Male To Female Ratio:** 1.1:1. The average age of freshmen is 18; all undergraduates, 20. 15% do not continue beyond their first year; 70% remain to graduate. **Housing:** 1283 students can be accommodated in college housing, which includes coed dorms and on-campus apartments. On-campus housing is guaranteed for the freshman year only, and is available on a first-come, first-served basis, and on a lottery system for upperclassmen. 72% of students live on campus. All students may keep cars.

FACULTY/CLASSROOMS: 62% of faculty are male; 38% are female. All teach undergraduates and do research. No introductory courses are taught by graduate students. The average class size in an introductory lecture is 20; in a laboratory is 20; and in a regular course is 25.

PROGRAMS OF STUDY: Saint Vincent confers B.A., and B.S. degrees. Master's and doctoral degrees are also awarded. Bachelor's degrees are awarded in BIOLOGICAL SCIENCE (biochemistry, bioinformatics, and biology/biological science), BUSINESS (accounting, banking and finance, business administration and management, international business management, and marketing/retailing/merchandising), COMMUNICATIONS AND THE ARTS (art, art history and appreciation, arts administration/management, communications, English, fine arts, French, music, music performance, Spanish, studio art, and visual and performing arts), COMPUTER AND PHYSICAL SCIENCE (chemistry, computer science, mathematics, and physics), EDUCATION (art education, business education, early childhood education, middle school education, psychology education, and science education), ENGINEERING AND ENVIRONMENTAL DESIGN (engineering and environmental science), HEALTH PROFESSIONS (occupational therapy, physical therapy, physician's assistant, predentistry, premedicine, prepharmacy, and preveterinary science), SOCIAL SCIENCE (anthropology, economics, history, liberal arts/general studies, philosophy, political science/government, prelaw, psychology, public affairs, sociology, and theological studies). Biology, economics, and psychology are the strongest academically. Biology, psychology, and criminology have the largest enrollments.

ACTIVITIES: There are no fraternities or sororities. There are 63 groups on campus, including art, band, cheerleading, choir, chorus, dance, drama, environmental, ethnic, honors, international, literary magazine, marching band, musical theater, newspaper, pep band, political, professional, radio and TV, religious, social, social service, student government, and yearbook. Popular campus events include Founders' Day,

Threshold Lecture Series, and Pittsburgh Steelers Training Camp. **Sports:** There are 10 intercollegiate sports for men and 10 for women, and 9 intramural sports for men and 9 for women. Facilities include a gym, basketball, volleyball, a weight and exercise room, an indoor pool, tennis, baseball, soccer, football, and a student union, and game room area. **Graduates:** From July 1, 2015 to June 30, 2016, 305 bachelor's degrees were awarded. The most popular majors were biology (15%), communication (10%), and psychology (8%). 58 companies recruited on campus in 2015-2016. In an average class, 2% graduate in 3 years or less, 65% graduate in 4 years or less, 71% graduate in 5 years or less, and 73% graduate in 6 years or less.

SERVICES: Counseling and information services are available, as is tutoring in most subjects. The Opportunity Office provides individual counseling and a study skills class for first-year students. **Library/Resources:** The library contains 289,773 volumes, 99,261 microform items, 7,626 audio/video tapes/CDs/DVDs, and subscribes to 287 periodicals including electronic. Computerized library services include interlibrary loans, database searching, Internet access, and Wi-Fi capability. Special learning facilities include an art gallery, planetarium, radio station, TV station, an observatory, a radio telescope, a small-business development center, a nature reserve, and the Fred Rogers archives. **Physically Challenged Students:** 95% of the campus is accessible. Facilities include wheelchair ramps, elevators, special parking, specially equipped restrooms, lowered drinking fountains, special housing, and lowered computer desks. **Special:** There is cross-registration with Seton Hill University, co-op programs, internships, study abroad in Europe and Asia, a work-study program, double majors, a general studies degree, credit by exam and for life/military/work experience, nondegree study, and pass/fail options. There is a 3-2 engineering option with Pennsylvania State University, the University of Pittsburgh, and the Catholic University of America. The college offers teacher certificate courses in early childhood (K-12) and secondary education. There are 16 national honor societies, a freshman honors program, and 13 departmental honors programs. **Visiting:** There are regularly scheduled orientations for prospective students, consisting of a general information session, an informal meeting with faculty, and campus tours. There are guides for informal visits, visitors may sit in on classes, and stay overnight. To schedule a visit, contact the Admission Office. **Campus Safety and Security:** Measures include 24-hour foot and vehicle patrol, emergency notification system, and security escort services. There are emergency telephones, lighted pathways/sidewalks, and controlled access to dorms/residences.

REQUIREMENTS: The SAT or ACT is required. Applicants must complete 16 academic credits (20 recommended), including 4 of English, 3 each of social studies and math, and 1 of science with a lab, (3 science and lab recommended). Also recommended are two credits of foreign language. Art students must submit a portfolio, and music must audition. An essay is required. A GED is accepted. AP and CLEP credits are accepted. To graduate, students must complete 124 credit hours with a minimum GPA of 2.0. All students are required to take a language and rhetoric, first theology, and first philosophy. The core curriculum includes 9 hours each of social science, theology, and English, 8 of natural sciences, 6 hours each of history, philosophy, and foreign language, and 3/4 of math. All students complete a first-year seminar experience. Total number of hours in major varies depending on the program. The majority of majors require a culminating activity, such as a thesis, research project, or capstone course/seminar. **Procedure:** Freshmen are admitted in the fall and spring. Entrance exams should be taken at the end of the junior year or the beginning of the senior year. There are early admissions, deferred admissions, and rolling admissions plans. Applications should be filed by May 1 for fall entry; January 1 for spring entry. The fall 2016 application fee was $25. Applications are accepted online. **Transfer Students:** 42 transfer students enrolled in 2015-2016. Transfer applicants must submit transcripts from postsecondary schools attended and a catalog describing courses taken, plus secondary school transcript(s). 34 of 124 credits required for the bachelor's degree must be completed at Saint Vincent. **International Students:** There are 11 international students enrolled. The school actively recruits these students. They must take the TOEFL with a minimum score of 550 on the paper-based TOEFL (PBT), an also the SAT or ACT.

ADMISSIONS: 66% of the 2016-2017 applicants were accepted. The SAT scores for the 2016-2017 freshman class were: Critical Reading-- 37% below 500, 41% between 500 and 599, 17% between 600 and 699, and 5% between 700 and 800. Math-- 38% below 500, 41% between 500 and 599, 19% between 600 and 699, and 2% between 700 and 800. Writing-- 50% below 500, 34% between 500 and 599, 14% between 600 and 699, and 2% between 700 and 800. The ACT scores were 9% between 12 and 17, 47% between 18 and 23, 37% between 24 and 29, and 7% above 30. 43% of the current freshmen were in the top fifth of their class; 70% were in the top two fifths. **Admissions Contact:** Admission and Financial Aid Office Email: *admission@stvincent.edu* Web: *www.stvincent.edu*

FINANCIAL AID: In 2016-2017, 100% of all full-time freshmen and 93% of continuing full-time students received some form of financial aid. 70% of all full-time freshmen and 62% of continuing full-time students received need-based aid. The average freshman award was $35,980. Need-based scholarships or need-based grants averaged $7,071 ($13,693 maximum); need-based self-help aid (loans and jobs) averaged $5,165 ($7,820 maximum); and other non-need-based awards and non-need-based scholarships averaged $25,396 ($47,927 maximum). 29% of undergraduate students work part-time. Average annual earnings from campus work are $1700. The average financial indebtedness of the 2016 graduate was $38,493. The FAFSA code is 003368. The priority date for freshman financial aid applications for fall entry is May 1.

SETON HILL UNIVERSITY — B-4

www.setonhill.edu

Greensburg, PA 15601	**(724) 838-4255** **(800) 826-6234**
Fax: (724) 830-1294	**Email: admit@setonhill.edu**
Full-time: 519 men, 964 women	**Faculty:** 101; IIB, av$
Part-time: 41 men, 82 women	**Ph.D.s:** 43%
Graduate: 100 men, 229 women	**Student/Faculty:** 12 to 1
Year: 4-1-4, summer session	**Tuition:** $33,362
Room & Board: $13,610	**Freshman Class:** 2206 applied, 1612 accepted, 363 enrolled
SAT or ACT: recommended	**CEEB CODE:** 2812
Application Deadline: August 15	**COMPETITIVE**

Seton Hill University, founded in 1885, is a private university affiliated with the Roman Catholic Church that offers programs in liberal arts and career preparation. There is 1 undergraduate school and 1 graduate school. In addition to regional accreditation, Seton Hill has baccalaureate program accreditation with ADA, CSWE, NASM, ARC-PA, AAMFT, ACEND, CODA, IACBE, NAEYC, AATA, and AMTA. The 200-acre campus is in a small town in Greenburg, PA, just 35 miles east of Pittsburgh. Including any residence halls, there are 19 buildings.

STUDENT LIFE: 74% of undergraduates are from Pennsylvania. Others are from 36 states, 15 foreign countries, and Canada. 80% are White; 8% African American; 3% Hispanic; 3% Foreign; 3% two or more races; 2% race unknown; 1% Asian American. **Female To Male Ratio:** 1.9:1. The average age of freshmen is 18; all undergraduates, 21. 21% do not continue beyond their first year; 57% remain to graduate. **Housing:** 750 students can be accommodated in college housing, which includes single-sex and coed dorms, as well as honors houses. On-campus housing is guaranteed for all 4 years. 54% of students commute. All students may keep cars. Alcohol is not permitted.

FACULTY/CLASSROOMS: 47% of faculty are male; 53% are female. 87% teach undergraduates, and 60% do research. No introductory courses are taught by graduate students. The average class size in an introductory lecture is 25; in a laboratory is 16; and in a regular course is 17.

PROGRAMS OF STUDY: Seton Hill confers B.A., B.S., B.F.A., B.Mus., B.S.Med.Tech. and B.S.W. degrees. Master's degrees are also awarded. Bachelor's degrees are awarded in BIOLOGICAL SCIENCE (biochemistry and biology/biological science), BUSINESS (accounting, business administration and management, business economics, entrepreneurial studies, human resources, international business management, management information systems, marketing/retailing/merchandising, personnel management, sports management, and tourism), COMMUNICATIONS AND THE ARTS (art and design, art history and appreciation, arts administration/management, communications, creative writing, dance, dramatic arts, English, English Writing, fine arts, graphic design, journalism, music, music theory and composition, musical theater, performing arts, Spanish, studio art, theatre arts, theater design, and theater management), COMPUTER AND PHYSICAL SCIENCE (actuarial science, chemistry, computer science, mathematics, and physics), EDUCATION (art education, early childhood education, elementary education, English education, foreign languages education, home economics education, mathematics education, music education, science education, secondary education, social science education, and special education), ENGINEERING AND ENVIRONMENTAL DESIGN (engineering), HEALTH PROFESSIONS (art therapy, biology, dental education, medical laboratory technology, music therapy, pharmacy, physician's assistant, predentistry, premedicine, preosteopathy, and preveterinary science), SOCIAL SCIENCE (child care/child and family studies, criminal justice, dietetics, economics, family/consumer resource management, family/consumer studies, food production/management/services, forensic studies, gender studies, history, human services, international studies, liberal arts/general studies, philosophy, political science/government, prelaw, psychology, religion, religious music, social work, sociology, and women & gender studies). Sciences, education, and fine arts are the strongest academically. Psychology, art, and business have the largest enrollments.

ACTIVITIES: There are no fraternities or sororities. There are 40 groups on campus, including best buddies club, entrepreneur's, make-a-wish club, respect life club, animal service club, art, bagpipe, band, cheerleading, choir, chorale, chorus, dance, drama, environmental, ethnic, honors, international, jazz band, LGBT, literary magazine, marching band, musical theater, newspaper, orchestra, pep band, political, professional, religious, social, social service, student government, and symphony. Popular campus events include Christmas on the Hill, Family Weekend, President's Reception, Battle of the Building, and Midnight Breakfast. **Sports:** There are 10 intercollegiate sports for men and 12 for women. Facilities include gyms, fitness center, aerobics room, swimming pool, field house with weight and training rooms, natural grass playing fields, and a football stadium. **Graduates:** From July 1, 2015 to June 30, 2016, 324 bachelor's degrees were awarded. The most popular majors were business/marketing (20%), visual/performing arts (11%), and health Professions and related programs (10%). In an average class, 43% graduate in 4 years or less, 55% graduate in 5 years or less, and 57% graduate in 6 years or less.

SERVICES: Counseling and information services are available, as is tutoring in most subjects. There is also a reader service for the blind, and remedial math and writing. **Library/Resources:** The library contains 123,538 volumes, 5,403 microform items, and 6,684 audio/video tapes/CDs/DVDs, and subscribes to 423 periodicals including electronic. Computerized library services include interlibrary loans, database searching, and Internet access. Special learning facilities include an art gallery, TV station, a nursery school that functions as a laboratory for students, a performing arts center, a visual arts center, and a technology wing. **Physically Challenged Students:** 95% of the campus is accessible. Facilities include wheelchair ramps, elevators, special parking, specially equipped restrooms, special class scheduling, lowered drinking fountains, and lowered telephones. **Special:** There are cooperative programs in all majors and cross-registration with St. Vincent College, the University of Pittsburgh at Greensburg, and Westmoreland County Community College. Internships are encouraged. Seton Hill offers study abroad, a Washington semester, work-study, dual and student-designed majors, accelerated degree programs, a 3-2 engineering program with Pennsylvania State University and Georgia Institute of Technology, a 2-2 nursing program with Catholic University of America, a 3-2 or 3-1 medical technology program with area hospitals, credit by exam and for life/military/work experience, nondegree study, and pass/fail options. There are 5 national honor societies and a freshman honors program. **Visiting:** There are regularly scheduled orientations for prospective students, consisting of an introduction, an address by the president or dean, an open reception with faculty, a financial aid session, a student panel, and a campus tour. There are guides for informal visits, visitors may sit in on classes, and stay overnight. To schedule a visit, contact the Campus Visit Coordinator. **Campus Safety and Security:** Measures include 24-hour foot and vehicle patrol, emergency notification system, self-defense education, and security escort services. There are also shuttle buses, emergency telephones, and lighted pathways/sidewalks.

REQUIREMENTS: Two graded writing samples are accepted in place of SAT or ACT scores. A total of 15 Carnegie units is required, including 4 each of English and electives, 2 each of math, social studies, and foreign language, and 1 of a lab science, and 4 academic electives. Art students must submit a portfolio; music and theater students must audition. An interview is recommended. The GED is accepted with supporting recommendations. AP and CLEP credits are accepted. Important factors in the admissions decision are advanced placement or honors courses, evidence of special talent, personality/intangible qualities, extracurricular activities record, leadership record, and recommendations by alumni. The core curriculum requires 6 credits in Western cultures, 6 credits in writing, and 3 each in theology, philosophy/senior seminar, math, computer science, science, college-level foreign language, U.S. cultures, non-Western cultures, and artistic expression. A total of 120 credit hours with a minimum GPA of 2.0 is required for graduation. **Procedure:** Freshmen are admitted in the fall and spring. Entrance exams should be taken in spring of the junior year or fall of the senior year. There are deferred admissions and rolling admissions plans. Applications should be filed by August 15 for fall entry, along with a $35 fee. Notification is sent on a rolling basis. Applications are accepted online. **Transfer Students:** 58 transfer students enrolled in 2015-2016. Applicants must submit college transcripts and have a GPA of at least 2.0. An interview is recommended, as are supporting letters. 48 of 120 credits required for the bachelor's degree must be completed at Seton Hill. **International Students:** There are 39 international students enrolled. The school actively recruits these students. They must take the TOEFL with a minimum score of 550 on the paper-based TOEFL (PBT) or 79 on the Internet-based version (iBT).

ADMISSIONS: 73% of the 2016-2017 applicants were accepted. The SAT scores for the 2016-2017 freshman class were: Critical Reading--37% below 500, 42% between 500 and 599, 16% between 600 and 699, and 5% between 700 and 800. Math-- 36% below 500, 45% between 500 and 599, 17% between 600 and 699, and 2% between 700 and 800. Writing-- 43% below 500, 39% between 500 and 599, 15% between 600 and 699, and 3% between 700 and 800. The ACT scores were 7% between 12 and 17, 42% between 18 and 23, 41% between 24 and 29, and 10% above 30. 56% of the current freshmen were in the top fifth of their class; 81% were in the top two fifths. **Admissions Contact:** Ashley Zullo, Director of Admissions. Email: *admit@setonhill.edu* Web: *www.setonhill.edu*

FINANCIAL AID: In 2016-2017, 86% of all full-time freshmen and 84% of continuing full-time students received some form of financial aid. 86% of all full-time freshmen and 83% of continuing full-time students received need-based aid. The average freshman award was $25,298. Need-based scholarships or need-based grants averaged $20,878; need-based self-help aid (loans and jobs) averaged $5,777; non-need-based athletic scholarships averaged $12,088; and other non-need-based awards and non-need-based scholarships averaged $15,028. 30% of undergraduate students work part-time. Average annual earnings from campus work are $1300. The average financial indebtedness of the 2016 graduate was $38,414. The college's own financial statement is required. The FAFSA code is 003362. The priority date for freshman financial aid applications for fall entry is April 30. The filing deadline for fall entry is August 1.

SHIPPENSBURG UNIVERSITY OF PENNSYLVANIA D-3
www.ship.edu

Shippensburg, PA 17257 **(717) 477-1231**

Fax: (717) 477-4016 **Email: admiss@ship.edu**
Full-time: 2802 men, 2743 women
Part-time: 181 men, 186 women
Graduate: 450 men, 627 women
Year: semesters, summer session
Room & Board: $11,756
SAT: required **ACT:** 21
Application Deadline: n/av
Faculty: n/av
Ph.D.s: n/av
Student/Faculty: n/av
Tuition: $11,452 ($19,542)
Freshman Class: 5799 applied, 5121 accepted, 1381 enrolled
CEEB CODE: 2657
COMPETITIVE

Shippensburg University, founded in 1871, is a public university that is part of the Pennsylvania State System of Higher Education offering undergraduate and graduate degree programs in the college of arts and sciences, college of business, and college of education and human services. There are 4 undergraduate schools and 1 graduate school. In addition to regional accreditation, Ship has baccalaureate program accreditation with AACSB, ABET, ACEJMC, CSWE, NCATE, ACS, ACJS, CACREP, and IACS. The 200-acre campus is in a rural area 40 miles southwest of Harrisburg. Including any residence halls, there are 51 buildings.

STUDENT LIFE: 92% of undergraduates are from Pennsylvania. Others are from 24 states, 18 foreign countries, and Canada. 89% are from public schools. 77% are White; 5% Hispanic; 3% two or more races; 2% Asian American; 2% Foreign; 10% African American; 1% race unknown. **Female To Male Ratio:** 1.0:1. The average age of freshmen is 18; all undergraduates, 21. 25% do not continue beyond their first year; 56% remain to graduate. **Housing:** 2105 students can be accommodated in college housing, which includes coed dorms, on-campus apartments, and off-campus apartments, and living learning communities provide the opportunity to live together with those who have similar academic, personal, or social interests. Academic Communities include: Biology First-year Interest Group, Computer Science & Engineering Deck, Future Educators, Grove StartUp for Business majors, Honors Program, and Discover SU for first-year exploratory majors. Interest Communities include the following: ROTC/Vets, Engaging Services through Action, Healthy Living Community, Shippensburg Leadership Academy and Transformations for incoming transfer students. On-campus housing is guaranteed for the freshman year only and is available on a lottery system for upperclassmen. 67% of students commute. All students may keep cars. Alcohol is not permitted.

FACULTY/CLASSROOMS: 56% of faculty are male; 44% are female. 93% teach undergraduates and 39% do both. No introductory courses are taught by graduate students.

PROGRAMS OF STUDY: Ship confers B.A., B.S., B.S.B.A., B.S.Ed. and B.S.W. degrees. Master's and doctoral degrees are also awarded. Bachelor's degrees are awarded in BIOLOGICAL SCIENCE (biology/biological science), BUSINESS (accounting, business administration and management, entrepreneurial studies, finance, management information systems, marketing management, supply chain management, and professional studies), COMMUNICATIONS AND THE ARTS (art, communications, English, French, journalism, Spanish, and speech/debate/rhetoric), COMPUTER AND PHYSICAL SCIENCE (applied physics, chemistry, computer science, earth science, geoenvironmental studies, mathematics, physics, and software engineering), EDUCATION (art education, early childhood education, elementary education, English education, foreign languages education, mathematics education, middle school education, secondary education, social studies education, and special education), ENGINEERING AND ENVIRONMENTAL DESIGN (computer engineering, electrical/electronics engineering, and environmental science), HEALTH PROFESSIONS (exercise science, health care administration, and pre-health biological studies), SOCIAL SCIENCE (criminal justice, economics, geography, history, interdisciplinary studies, international studies, political science/government, psychology, public administration, social work, and sociology). Psychology, criminal justice, and accounting have the largest enrollments.

ACTIVITIES: 8% of men belong to 11 national fraternities; 9% of women belong to 8 national sororities. There are 111 groups on campus, including BigBrother/Big Sister, activities program board, art, band, cheerleading, choir, chorale, chorus, computers, dance, debate, drama, environmental, ethnic, honors, international, jazz band, LGBT, literary magazine, marching band, musical theater, newspaper, orchestra, pep band, photography, political, professional, radio and TV, religious, social, social service, student government, Vet's club, and yearbook. Popular campus events include Planetarium Shows, Senior Olympics, and Summer Music Festival. **Sports:** There are 8 intercollegiate sports for men and 10 for women, and 6 intramural sports for men and 6 for women. Facilities include a stadium for football, track-and-field, baseball, softball, tennis, soccer, field hockey, lacrosse, basketball, volleyball, wrestling, and a swimming pool. **Graduates:** From July 1, 2015 to June 30, 2016, 1203 bachelor's degrees were awarded. The most popular majors were management (10%), psychology (9%), and criminal justice (7%). In an average class, 41% graduate in 4 years or less, 54% graduate in 5 years or less, and 56% graduate in 6 years or less.

SERVICES: Counseling and information services are available, as is tutoring in most subjects, including most general education courses, and writing. There is remedial math, reading, and writing, as well as individual meetings with learning specialists who are available to help students interested in developing individual strategies and group study. **Library/Resources:** The library contains 357,662 volumes, 1.2 million microform items, 69,280 audio/video tapes/CDs/DVDs, and subscribes to 55,245 periodicals including electronic. Computerized library services include interlibrary loans, database searching, Internet access, and Wi-Fi capability. Special learning facilities include an art gallery, planetarium, radio station, TV station, a closed-circuit television, fashion archives center, vertebrate museum, women's center, on-campus elementary school, electron microscope, greenhouse, and herbarium. **Physically Challenged Students:** 92% of the campus is accessible. Facilities include wheelchair ramps, elevators, special parking, special class scheduling, lowered drinking fountains, and lowered telephones. Enlarged printing, extended time for tests, alternative testing sites, classroom accessibility, note taking, reader and scribe services for exams, books in alternate format, and priority scheduling. The tech room in the library has the following software: Kurzweil 3000 (firefly), ReadWrite Gold, JAWS, and Zoom Text. All resident halls are ADA compliant. **Special:** There are 22 national honor societies, a freshman honors program, and 1 departmental honors program. **Visiting:** There are regularly scheduled orientations for prospective students, including daily academic group meetings, campus tours, and 5 weekend open house programs per year. There are guides for informal visits and visitors may sit in on classes. To schedule a visit, contact the Admissions Office. **Campus Safety and Security:** Measures include 24-hour foot and vehicle patrol, emergency notification system, self-defense education, and security escort services. There are also shuttle buses, emergency telephones, lighted pathways/sidewalks, and controlled access to dorms/residences, residence halls are equipped with an automatic heat/smoke detection sprinkler system monitored 24 hours a day by police. The system also includes strobe lights to notify students who are hearing impaired. All exterior doors to residence hall doors are locked 24 hours a day and require card access for entry. There are security cameras at the main entrance to residence halls, computer labs, and academic buildings, as well as many exterior cameras covering parking lots and other campus areas. A text emergency message system has also been implemented to notify students, faculty, and staff of impending or active emergency situations. Additional cameras are in place, and card swipes are used to gain floor entry into the residence halls.

REQUIREMENTS: The SAT is required. Applicants are urged to pursue a typical college preparatory program, which should include 4 units of English, 3 units each of social sciences, math, lab science, and foreign language. A GED is accepted. AP and CLEP credits are accepted. Important factors in the admissions decision are advanced placement or honors courses, recommendations by school officials, and evidence of special talent. General education courses include English composition, oral communications, math, and history, as well as courses in logic and numbers for rational thinking, linguistic, literary, artistic, and cultural traditions, lab science, biological and physical science, political, economic, and geographic sciences, and social and behavioral sciences. The core curriculum varies for degree programs. Most degree programs require 120 credit hours, with 22 to 30 hours in the major, and a 2.0 minimum GPA for graduation. **Procedure:** Freshmen are admitted to all sessions. Entrance exams should be taken in the junior year and senior year. There are early admissions, deferred admissions, and rolling admissions plans. Application deadlines are open. The fall 2016 application fee was $45. Notification is sent on a rolling basis. Application fees are waived if application is completed online. **Transfer Students:** 451 transfer students enrolled in 2015-2016. Applicants must provide high school and college transcripts, and SAT or ACT scores if they have fewer than 30 college credits. 30 of 120 credits required for the bachelor's degree must be completed at Ship. **International Students:** There are 40 international students enrolled. They must take the TOEFL with a minimum score of 500 on the paper-based TOEFL (PBT) or 66 on the Internet-based version (iBT). Students whose native language is English must submit SAT scores instead of the TOEFL.

ADMISSIONS: 88% of the 2016-2017 applicants were accepted. The SAT scores for the 2016-2017 freshman class were: Critical Reading-- 56% below 500, 35% between 500 and 599, 8% between 600 and 699, and 1% between 700 and 800. Math-- 51% below 500, 40% between 500 and 599, and 9% between 600 and 699. Writing-- 67% below 500, 27% between 500 and 599, and 6% between 600 and 699. The ACT scores were 18% between 12 and 17, 57% between 18 and 23, 24% between 24 and 29, and 1% above 30. 18% of the current freshmen were in the top fifth of their class; 44% were in the top two fifths. 3 freshmen graduated first in their class. **Admissions Contact:** Dr. Jennifer A. Haughie, Assistant VP for Enrollment & Dean of Admmissions. Email: *admiss@ship.edu* Web: *www.ship.edu*

FINANCIAL AID: In 2016-2017, 93% of all full-time freshmen and 88% of continuing full-time students received some form of financial aid. 75% of all full-time freshmen and 67% of continuing full-time students received need-based aid. The average freshman award was $15,760. Need-based scholarships or need-based grants averaged $6,599 ($25,065 maximum); need-based self-help aid (loans and jobs) averaged $10,021

($30,054 maximum); non-need-based athletic scholarships averaged $2,637 ($8,550 maximum); and other non-need-based awards and non-need-based scholarships averaged $9,899 ($37,949 maximum). 11% of undergraduate students work part-time. Average annual earnings from campus work are $2041. The average financial indebtedness of the 2016 graduate was $33,673. Ship is a member of CSS. The FAFSA code is 003326. The deadline for filing freshman financial aid applications for fall entry is May 1.

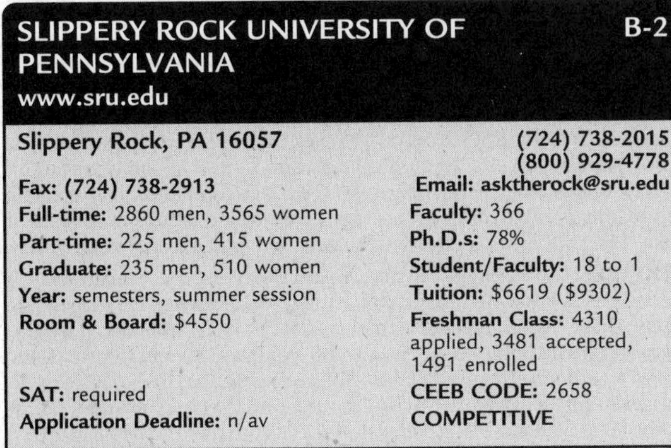

SLIPPERY ROCK UNIVERSITY OF PENNSYLVANIA B-2

www.sru.edu

Slippery Rock, PA 16057 (724) 738-2015 (800) 929-4778

Fax: (724) 738-2913 **Email:** asktherock@sru.edu

Full-time: 2860 men, 3565 women **Faculty:** 366

Part-time: 225 men, 415 women **Ph.D.s:** 78%

Graduate: 235 men, 510 women **Student/Faculty:** 18 to 1

Year: semesters, summer session **Tuition:** $6619 ($9302)

Room & Board: $4550 **Freshman Class:** 4310 applied, 3481 accepted, 1491 enrolled

SAT: required **CEEB CODE:** 2658

Application Deadline: n/av **COMPETITIVE**

Slippery Rock University of Pennsylvania, founded in 1889, is a public institution that is part of the Pennsylvania State System of Higher Education. It offers programs in business, information, social sciences, education, health, environment, science, humanities, and fine and performing arts. There are 4 undergraduate schools and 1 graduate school. In addition to regional accreditation, The Rock has baccalaureate program accreditation with ACBSP, APTA, CSWE, NASAD, NASM, NCATE, NLN, NRPA, and CAAHEP. The 600-acre campus is in a small town 50 miles north of Pittsburgh. Including any residence halls, there are 60 buildings.

STUDENT LIFE: 96% of undergraduates are from Pennsylvania. Others are from 35 states, 47 foreign countries, and Canada. 70% are from public schools. 87% are White; 4% African American; 2% Foreign; 1% Asian American; 1% Hispanic. **Female To Male Ratio:** 1.4:1. The average age of freshmen is 18; all undergraduates, 22. 22% do not continue beyond their first year; 49% remain to graduate. **Housing:** 2810 students can be accommodated in college housing, which includes single-sex and coed dorms, on-campus apartments, off-campus apartments, and married student housing. In addition, there are honors houses, language houses, special-interest houses, fraternity houses, and sorority houses. On-campus housing is guaranteed for the freshman year only, and is available on a first-come, and first-served basis. 62% of students commute. Alcohol is not permitted. All students may keep cars.

FACULTY/CLASSROOMS: 53% of faculty are male; 47% are female. All teach undergraduates. No introductory courses are taught by graduate students. The average class size in an introductory lecture is 33; in a laboratory is 20; and in a regular course is 25.

PROGRAMS OF STUDY: The Rock confers B.A., B.S., B.F.A., B.Mus., B.Mus.Ed., B.S.B.A., B.S.Ed., and B.S.N. degrees. Master's and doctoral degrees are also awarded. Bachelor's degrees are awarded in BIOLOGICAL SCIENCE (biology/biological science), BUSINESS (accounting, business administration and management, international business management, and marketing/retailing/merchandising), COMMUNICATIONS AND THE ARTS (communications, dance, English, fine arts, French, German, music, and Spanish), COMPUTER AND PHYSICAL SCIENCE (chemistry, computer science, earth science, geology, information sciences and systems, mathematics, and physics), EDUCATION (early childhood education, elementary education, foreign languages education, health education, music education, science education, secondary education, and special education), HEALTH PROFESSIONS (community health work, medical laboratory technology, and nursing), SOCIAL SCIENCE (anthropology, economics, geography, history, parks and recreation management, philosophy, political science/government, psychology, public administration, social science, social work, and sociology). Business, education, and health science areas have the largest enrollments.

ACTIVITIES: 7% of men belong to 11 national fraternities; 6% of women belong to 9 national sororities. There are 100 groups on campus, including art, band, cheerleading, chess, choir, chorale, chorus, communications, computers, dance, drama, ethnic, film, honors, international, jazz band, LGBT, literary magazine, marching band, musical theater, newspaper, orchestra, pep band, photography, political, professional, radio and TV, religious, social, social service, student government, symphony, and yearbook. Popular campus events include Spring Weekend. **Sports:** There are 12 intercollegiate sports for men and 12 for women, and 7 intramural sports for men and 7 for women. Facilities include a field house, a gym, and a fitness center. **Graduates:** From July 1, 2015 to June 30, 2016, 1190 bachelor's degrees were awarded. The most popular majors were education (23%), marketing (15%), and parks and recreation (13%). 260 companies recruited on campus in 2015-2016. In an average class, 24% graduate in 4 years or less, 46% graduate in 5 years or less, and 49% graduate in 6 years or less. Of the 2015 graduating class, 12% were enrolled in graduate school within 6 months of graduation, and 81% were employed.

SERVICES: Counseling and information services are available, as is tutoring in some subjects. There is also a reader service for the blind, and remedial math and writing. **Library/Resources:** The library contains 502,974 volumes, 1.5 million microform items, 22,707 audio/video tapes/CDs/DVDs, and subscribes to 1,300 periodicals including electronic. Computerized library services include interlibrary loans, database searching, and Internet access. Special learning facilities include an art gallery, natural history museum, planetarium, radio station, TV station, and a wellness center. **Physically Challenged Students:** 80% of the campus is accessible. Facilities include wheelchair ramps, elevators, special parking, specially equipped restrooms, special class scheduling, lowered drinking fountains, lowered telephones, and special housing. **Special:** Study abroad is available in 16 countries. Internships are offered in most majors, and international internships are available in Scotland and England. There is a 3-2 engineering program with Pennsylvania State University. The dual major is an option, and credit is given for military experience. Pass/fail options also are available. There are 26 national honor societies, a freshman honors program, and 33 departmental honors programs. **Visiting:** There are regularly scheduled orientations for prospective students, including a meeting with faculty, an information fair, and a campus tour. There are guides for informal visits, visitors may sit in on classes, and stay overnight. To schedule a visit, contact the Admissions Office. **Campus Safety and Security:** Measures include 24-hour foot and vehicle patrol, self-defense education, and security escort services. There are also shuttle buses, emergency telephones, lighted pathways/sidewalks. The university maintains its own police department, having the same powers as municipal police.

REQUIREMENTS: The SAT is required. The ACT is recommended. Students should graduate from an accredited secondary school or have a GED. A total of 16 academic credits is required. The recommended college preparatory program includes 4 years of English and social studies, 3 each of science and math, and 2 of a foreign language. An interview is recommended. AP and CLEP credits are accepted. Important factors in the admissions decision are advanced placement or honors courses, extracurricular activities record, and evidence of special talent. B.A. students must demonstrate proficiency in a foreign language, and all must complete 42 to 53 credits in a 7-part liberal studies program, including basic competencies, arts, cultural diversity/global perspective, human institutions, science and math, natural experience, and modern age. Specific requirements include public speaking, college writing, algebra, and phys ed. A minimum of 120 credit hours, with at least 30 in the major, is required for graduation. **Procedure:** Freshmen are admitted in the fall, spring, and summer. Entrance exams should be taken in the junior year or fall of the senior year. There are deferred admissions and rolling admissions plans. Check with the school for current application deadlines. The fall 2016 application fee was $25. Notification is sent on a rolling basis. Applications are accepted on-line. **Transfer Students:** 559 transfer students enrolled in 2015-2016. Applicants should have completed at least 24 credit hours with a GPA of 2.5. The SAT I or ACT, as well as an interview, are recommended. 36 of 120 credits required for the bachelor's degree must be completed at The Rock. **International Students:** There are 130 international students enrolled. The school actively recruits these students. They must take the TOEFL.

ADMISSIONS: 81% of the 2016-2017 applicants were accepted. 10 freshmen graduated first in their class. **Admissions Contact:** Jim Barrett, Director of Admissions. Email: *asktherock@sru.edu* Web: *www.sru.edu*

FINANCIAL AID: In 2016-2017, 64% of all full-time freshmen and 58% of continuing full-time students received some form of financial aid.

51% of all full-time freshmen and 43% of continuing full-time students received need-based aid. The average freshman award was $6,074. Need-based scholarships or need-based grants averaged $2,907; need-based self-help aid (loans and jobs) averaged $2,437; non-need-based athletic scholarships averaged $2,507; and other non-need-based awards and non-need-based scholarships averaged $3,590. 30% of undergraduate students work part-time. Average annual earnings from campus work are $1000. The average financial indebtedness of the 2016 graduate was $19,195. The Rock is a member of CSS. The FAFSA code is 003327. The priority date for freshman financial aid applications for fall entry is May 1.

SUSQUEHANNA UNIVERSITY D-3

www.susqu.edu

Selinsgrove, PA 17870	**(570) 372-4260** **(800) 326-9672**
Fax: (570) 372-2722	**Email: suadmiss@susqu.edu**
Full-time: 951 men, 1163 women	**Faculty:** 133; IIB, av$
Part-time: 42 men, 40 women	**Ph.D.s:** 90%
Graduate: n/av	**Student/Faculty:** 12 to 1
Year: semesters, summer session	**Tuition:** $43,720
Room & Board: $11,620	**Freshman Class:** 5343 applied, 4488 accepted, 637 enrolled
SAT or ACT: recommended	**CEEB CODE:** 2820
Application Deadline: February 15	**VERY COMPETITIVE**

Susquehanna University, founded in 1858, is an independent, residential institution affiliated with the Lutheran Church. It offers programs through schools of arts and sciences, and business. There are 2 undergraduate schools. In addition to regional accreditation, S.U. has baccalaureate program accreditation with AACSB, NASM, and ACS. The 325-acre campus is in a small town 50 miles north of Harrisburg. Including any residence halls, there are 92 buildings.

STUDENT LIFE: 52% of undergraduates are from Pennsylvania. Others are from 34 states, 22 foreign countries, and Canada. 83% are from public schools. 78% are White; 7% African American; 6% Hispanic; 3% two or more races; 2% Asian American; 2% Foreign; 2% race unknown. 33% are Protestant; 26% Catholic; 20% Buddhist, Muslim, Hindu, Mormon, and Eastern Orthodox, and unknown; 17% claim no religious affiliation. **Female To Male Ratio:** 1.2:1. The average age of freshmen is 18; all undergraduates, 20. 17% do not continue beyond their first year; 74% remain to graduate. **Housing:** 2016 students can be accommodated in college housing, which includes coed dorms, on-campus apartments, off-campus apartments, honors houses, special-interest houses, fraternity houses, and sorority houses. On-campus housing is guaranteed for all 4 years and is available on a lottery system for upperclassmen. 91% of students live on campus; of those, 85% remain on campus on weekends. All students may keep cars.

FACULTY/CLASSROOMS: 54% of faculty are male; 46% are female. All teach undergraduates and do research. No introductory courses are taught by graduate students. The average class size in a laboratory is 19 and in a regular course is 19.

PROGRAMS OF STUDY: SU confers B.A., B.S., and B.M. degrees. Bachelor's degrees are awarded in BIOLOGICAL SCIENCE (biochemistry, biology/biological science, and ecology), BUSINESS (accounting, business administration and management, finance, and marketing), COMMUNICATIONS AND THE ARTS (art history and appreciation, communications, English, French, German, graphic design, Italian, music, music performance, Spanish, studio art, theatre arts, and visual and performing arts), COMPUTER AND PHYSICAL SCIENCE (chemistry, computer science, earth science, mathematics, and physics), EDUCATION (early childhood education and music education), ENGINEERING AND ENVIRONMENTAL DESIGN (environmental science), HEALTH PROFESSIONS (biomedical science), SOCIAL SCIENCE (anthropology, economics, history, international studies, liberal arts/general studies, philosophy, political science/government, psychology, religion, and sociology). Business, communications, and biology have the largest enrollments.

ACTIVITIES: 20% of men belong to 6 national fraternities; 15% of women belong to 5 national sororities. There are 156 groups on campus, including academic clubs. Asian student coalition, Big Brothers/Big Sisters, black student union, equestrian, Habitat for Humanity, Hispanic organization for student awareness, honor societies, national organization of women, student awareness of the value of the environment, art, band, cheerleading, chess, choir, chorale, chorus, communications, computers, dance, drama, environmental, ethnic, film, international, jazz band, LGBT, literary magazine, musical theater, newspaper, opera, orchestra, outdoors club, pep band, photography, political, professional, radio and TV, religious, social, social service, student government, and yearbook. Popular campus events include Thanksgiving Dinner, Spring Weekend, Candlelight Christmas Service, Homecomimg Semi-Formal Ball, Annual Concert and Fall Frenzy. **Sports:** There are 11 intercollegiate sports for men and 12 for women, and 6 intramural sports for men and 6 for women. Facilities include a field house with indoor track, tennis, basketball, football, soccer, baseball, lacrosse, rugby, hockey, a pool, racquetball, weight training, and a fitness center. **Graduates:** From July 1, 2015 to June 30, 2016, 513 bachelor's degrees were awarded. The most popular majors were business/admin (23%), communications (15%), and biological/life sciences (11%). 65 companies recruited on campus in 2015-2016. In an average class, 67% graduate in 4 years or less, 71% graduate in 5 years or less, and 74% graduate in 6 years or less.

SERVICES: Counseling and information services are available, as is tutoring in some subjects, such as writing, math, foreign languages, and study skills. Academic departments also provide tutoring. **Library/Resources:** The library contains 429,437 volumes, 299 microform items, 157,979 audio/video tapes/CDs/DVDs, and subscribes to 79,727 periodicals including electronic. Computerized library services include interlibrary loans, database searching, Internet access, and Wi-Fi capability. Special learning facilities include an art gallery, radio station, multimedia classrooms, video studios, a campus wide telecommunications network, satellite dishes and distribution system for foreign-language broadcasts, video conferencing facility, an ecological field station, an observatory, a child development center, and an electronic music lab. **Physically Challenged Students:** 95% of the campus is accessible. Facilities include wheelchair ramps, elevators, special parking, specially equipped restrooms, special class scheduling, lowered drinking fountains, and lowered telephones. **Special:** 78% of Susquehanna students get professional experience before graduation in the form of internships and research opportunities. The Global Opportunities program places students in short-term or semester-long study with programs in 75 countries on 6 continents. The School of Business offers a semester in London specifically for junior business majors. The university offers dual and student-designed majors, work-study programs, credit by examination, non-degree study, and pass/fail options. The B.A., B.S. and B.M. degree is available in 42 majors. In addition, the university offers a 2-2 program in allied health with Thomas Jefferson University, and a 3-2 program in dentistry with Temple University. Highly motivated students have the option of earning their baccalaureate degree in three years. There are 23 national honor societies and a freshman honors program. **Visiting:** There are regularly scheduled orientations for prospective students, as well as visiting days they can attend with parents held in the spring, fall, and summer. These events include sessions with faculty, admissions, financial aid, placement staff, and tours of the campus. There are guides for informal visits, visitors may sit in on classes, and stay overnight. To schedule a visit, contact Philip M. Betz at (570) 372-4260. **Campus Safety and Security:** Measures include 24-hour foot and vehicle patrol, emergency notification system, self-defense education, and security escort services. There are also emergency telephones, lighted pathways/sidewalks, controlled access to dorms/residences, and closed circuit TV cameras in common exterior areas on campus.

REQUIREMENTS: Applicants must submit either the Susquehanna Application or Common Application, along with an official high school transcript, school report, and SAT/ACT scores or a writing sample under our Test Score Optional plan. Students should be graduates of an accredited high school. Academic preparation should include 4 years of English and math, 3 to 4 years of science, and 2 to 3 years each of social studies and foreign language. In addition, 1 unit of art or music is recommended. An essay is required, as are, for relevant fields, a music audition or writing or graphic design portfolio. An interview is recommended. AP and CLEP credits are accepted. Important factors in the admissions decision are advanced placement or honors courses, evidence of special talent, and recommendations by school officials. The Central Curriculum is at the heart of a Susquehanna education. The diverse courses in the Central Curriculum comprise 40 percent of the graduation requirement, and are divided into five complementary sections: Richness of Thought, Natural World, Human Interactions, Intellectual Skills, and Connections. All students at Susquehanna are required to participate in a unique, nationally recognized cross-cultural program, and global opportunities. Students study in the U.S. or abroad, for at least two weeks or as long as a semester, in a culture different other than their own. They take a reflection course after their return to campus. **Procedure:** Freshmen are admitted in the fall and spring. Entrance exams should be taken by January of the senior year. There are early decision, early admissions, deferred admissions, and rolling admissions plans. Early decision applications should be filed by November 15; regular applications, by February 15 for fall entry; and January 1 for spring entry. Notification of early decision is sent December 1; regular decision, November 1. 89 early decision candidates were accepted for the 2016-2017 class. Applications are accepted online. Application fees are waived if application is completed online. **Transfer Students:** 16 transfer students enrolled in 2015-2016. Applicants must submit high school and college transcripts, test scores, and a recommendation from a dean. An interview is strongly recommended. A music audition or writing portfolio is required for relevant fields. 65 of 130 credits required for the bachelor's degree must be completed at SU. **International Students:** There are 45 international students enrolled. The school actively recruits these students. They must take the TOEFL with a minimum score of 550 on the paper-based TOEFL (PBT) or 80 on the Internet-based version (iBT), or take the IELTS.

ADMISSIONS: 84% of the 2016-2017 applicants were accepted. The SAT scores for the 2016-2017 freshman class were: Critical Reading-- 21% below 500, 47% between 500 and 599, 27% between 600 and 699, and 5% between 700 and 800. Math-- 20% below 500, 51% between 500 and 599, 26% between 600 and 699, and 3% between 700 and 800. The ACT scores were 33% between 18 and 23, 61% between 24 and 29, and 6% above 30. 43% of the current freshmen were in the top fifth of their class; 74% were in the top two fifths. 3 freshmen graduated first in their class. **Admissions Contact:** Philip M. Betz, Director of Admissions. Email: *suadmiss@susqu.edu* Web: *www.susqu.edu*

FINANCIAL AID: In 2016-2017, 99% of all full-time freshmen and continuing full-time students received some form of financial aid. 80% of all full-time freshmen and 84% of continuing full-time students received need-based aid. The average freshman award was $35,083. Need-based scholarships or need-based grants averaged $29,891 ($48,903 maximum); need-based self-help aid (loans and jobs) averaged $4,276 ($15,950 maximum); and other non-need-based awards and non-need-based scholarships averaged $37,740 ($43,160 maximum). 49% of undergraduate students work part-time. Average annual earnings from campus work are $1158. The average financial indebtedness of the 2016 graduate was $36,883. SU is a member of CSS. The CSS/Profile, and prior year federal tax return for parents and students are required. The FAFSA code is 003369. The priority date for freshman financial aid applications for fall entry is March 1. The filing deadline for fall entry is May 1.

SWARTHMORE COLLEGE E-3

www.swarthmore.edu

Swarthmore, PA 19081	**(610) 328-8300** **(800) 667-3110**
Fax: (610) 328-8580	**Email: admissions@swarthmore.edu**
Full-time: 783 men, 798 women	**Faculty:** 183
Part-time: n/av	**Ph.D.s:** 98%
Graduate: n/av	**Student/Faculty:** 8 to 1
Year: semesters	**Tuition:** $49,104
Room & Board: $14,446	**Freshman Class:** 7818 applied, 976 accepted, 407 enrolled
SAT CR/M/W: 730/720/720 **ACT:** 32	**CEEB CODE:** 2821
Application Deadline: January 1	**MOST COMPETITIVE**

Swarthmore College, a highly selective college of liberal arts and engineering, has empowered students to pursue their academic curiosity with purpose for over 150 years. Swarthmore's world-class faculty collaborates with students on joint research projects, which helps students call on their diverse backgrounds to envision themselves as scholars and leaders and doers. The Honors Program brims with intellectual exploration, celebrating the free and critical exchange of ideas through small-group interactions. Swarthmore's financial aid program ensures affordability without loans. International applicants are admitted on a need-aware basis, and are eligible for financial aid. There is 1 undergraduate school. In addition to regional accreditation, Swarthmore has baccalaureate program accreditation with ABET. The 425-acre campus is in a suburban area Swarthmore, Pennsylvania, 11 miles southwest of Philadelphia. Including any residence halls, there are 56 buildings.

STUDENT LIFE: 87% of undergraduates are from out of state, mostly the Middle Atlantic. Students are from 50 states, 70 foreign countries, and Canada. 59% are from public schools. 42% are White; 17% Asian American; 13% Hispanic; 11% Foreign; 8% two or more races; 6% African American; 3% race unknown; 1% American Indian/Alaska Native. **Female To Male Ratio:** 1.0:1. The average age of freshmen is 18; all undergraduates, 20. 4% do not continue beyond their first year; 93% remain to graduate. **Housing:** 1429 students can be accommodated in college housing, which includes single-sex and coed dorms, gender neutral housing (students of any gender may share rooms and/or bathrooms). On-campus housing is guaranteed for all 4 years. 95% of students live on campus; of those, 100% remain on campus on weekends. Upperclassmen may keep cars.

FACULTY/CLASSROOMS: 57% of faculty are male; 43% are female. All teach undergraduates and do research. No introductory courses are taught by graduate students. The average class size in a laboratory is 12 and in a regular course is 16.

PROGRAMS OF STUDY: Swarthmore confers B.A. and B.S. degrees. Bachelor's degrees are awarded in BIOLOGICAL SCIENCE (biochemistry, biology/biological science, and neurosciences), COMMUNICATIONS AND THE ARTS (art, art history and appreciation, Chinese, classics, comparative literature, dance, dramatic arts, English literature, film arts, French, German, Greek, Latin, linguistics, literature, media arts, music, Russian, Spanish, and theatre arts), COMPUTER AND PHYSICAL SCIENCE (astronomy, astrophysics, chemical physics, chemistry, computer science, mathematics, and physics), EDUCATION (education), ENGINEERING AND ENVIRONMENTAL DESIGN (engineering), SOCIAL SCIENCE (anthropology, Asian/Oriental studies, Chinese Studies, classical/ancient civilization, economics, gender studies, German area studies, history, Japanese studies, medieval studies, peace studies, philosophy, political science/government, psychobiology, psychology, religion, and sociology). Economics, biology, computer science, psychology, and political science have the largest enrollments.

ACTIVITIES: 6% of women belong to 1 national sorority. There are 150 groups on campus, including cappella groups, drama board, band, chess, choir, chorus, club sports, computers, dance, debate, drama, environmental, ethnic, film, honors, international, jazz band, LGBT, literary magazine, musical theater, newspaper, orchestra, photography, political, radio and TV, religious, social, social service, student government, and yearbook. Popular campus events include Large Scale Event, Worthstock, and the Crum Regatta. **Sports:** There are 10 intercollegiate sports for men and 12 for women, and 7 intramural sports for men and 7 for women. Facilities include space to support wellness, fitness weights, and cardio training, yoga, pilates, basketball, tennis, badminton, volleyball, baseball, softball, and a banked tartan track. Another complex includes fields for tennis, facilities for lacrosse, field hockey, soccer, Rugby and ultimate frisbee, baseball, multipurpose fields, track, and swimming pool. There is also a sports medicine department, a fully equipped athletic training room, running trails, and cross country interval training. **Graduates:** From July 1, 2015 to June 30, 2016, 397 bachelor's degrees were awarded. The most popular majors were social sciences (24%), biology/life sciences, political science (13%), computer and informatin sciences, and visual & performing arts (13%). 50 companies recruited on campus in 2015-2016. In an average class, 89% graduate in 4 years or less, 83% graduate in 5 years or less, and 93% graduate in 6 years or less. Of the 2015 graduating class, 21% were enrolled in graduate school within 6 months of graduation, and 39% were employed.

SERVICES: Counseling and information services are available, as is tutoring in most subjects, and a reader service for the blind. The campus writing center, student academic mentors, science associates, and math associates provide academic support to students. **Library/Resources:** The 7 libraries contain 100,000 volumes, 40,000 microform items, 50,000 audio/video tapes/CDs/DVDs, and subscribe to 75,000 periodicals including electronic. Computerized library services include interlibrary loans, database searching, Internet access, and Wi-Fi capability. Special learning facilities include an art gallery, and radio station. The College's LEED-certified integrated science center includes an observatory, robotics and solar energy labs. Arts resources include two galleries, one of which is curated by students, a dance studios, a cinema, and theater. Research facilities include a music and dance library, a science library, the Friends Historical Library, and the Swarthmore Peace Collection.

Students interested in community-based learning are supported by the Lang Center for Civic and Social Responsibility. **Physically Challenged Students:** 85% of the campus is accessible. Facilities include wheelchair ramps, elevators, special parking, specially equipped restrooms, special class scheduling, lowered drinking fountains, lowered telephones, and special housing. **Special:** Special educational opportunities at the college include the honors program which features small groups of students working closely with faculty and peers; an emphasis on independent learning; and a final examination by outside scholars. Swarthmore offers an engineering major and a program leading toward Teacher Certification. Students may cross-register for courses at Bryn Mawr and Haverford Colleges and the University of Pennsylvania. Cooperative exchange programs are available with Tufts University and Harvey Mudd, Pomona, Mills, and Middlebury colleges. The Off-Campus Study Office supports students who wish to study abroad, where opportunities are widely available and off campus study is encouraged. There are 3 national honor societies, Phi Beta Kappa, and 31 departmental honors programs. **Visiting:** There are regularly scheduled orientations for prospective students, tours, information sessions, and interviews are offered throughout the year. There are guides for informal visits, visitors may sit in on classes, and stay overnight. To schedule a visit, contact the Admissions Office. **Campus Safety and Security:** Measures include 24-hour foot and vehicle patrol, emergency notification system, self-defense education, and security escort services. There are also shuttle buses, emergency telephones, lighted pathways/sidewalks, and controlled access to dorms/residences.

REQUIREMENTS: Swarthmore does not require a specific high school curriculum. We do, however, recommend the inclusion of 4 years of English, 3 years each of mathematics, sciences, history, and social studies, 1 or 2 foreign languages, and coursework in art and music. Applicants are required to submit scores for either the SAT and any two SAT Subject tests, or the ACT with writing, or the SAT and the ACT (with or without writing). Two essays are required. Interviews are recommended, though not required for first-year applicants. AP credits are accepted. Important factors in the admissions decision are parents or siblings attended your school, evidence of special talent, recommendations by alumni, geographical diversity, extracurricular activities record, leadership record, advanced placement or honors courses, personality/intangible qualities, and recommendations by school officials. In order to graduate, students must complete 3 courses in each of 3 divisions consisting of humanities, natural sciences and engineering, and social sciences. Concurrent with distribution and/or major requirements, there is a requirement of 3 writing courses and a science laboratory. Students must demonstrate foreign language competency and fulfill a physical education requirement including a swimming test. Each major has a culminating experience, which may be a thesis, project, or comprehensive exam. **Procedure:** Freshmen are admitted in the fall. Entrance exams should be taken in spring of the junior year or fall of the senior year. There are early decision and deferred admissions plans. Early decision applications should be filed by November 15; regular applications, by January 1 for fall entry, along with a $60 fee. Notification of early decision is sent December 15; regular decision, April 1. 202 early decision candidates were accepted for the 2016-2017 class. Applications are accepted online. **Transfer Students:** 7 transfer students enrolled in 2015-2016. Applicants for transfer must present both secondary and college transcripts, an essay or personal statement, and an official statement of good standing from the tertiary institution. Application closing date is fall, April 1, and notification date is May 15. 16 of 32 credits required for the bachelor's degree must be completed at Swarthmore. **International Students:** There are 130 international students enrolled. The school actively recruits these students. They must submit scores for either the SAT and any 2 SAT subject tests, and the ACT with writing.

ADMISSIONS: 12% of the 2016-2017 applicants were accepted. The SAT scores for the 2016-2017 freshman class were: Critical Reading-- 4% between 500 and 599, 33% between 600 and 699, and 62% between 700 and 800. Math-- 3% between 500 and 599, 34% between 600 and 699, and 62% between 700 and 800. Writing-- 4% between 500 and 599, 29% between 600 and 699, and 67% between 700 and 800. The ACT scores were 22% between 24 and 29, and 78% above 30. 88% of the current freshmen were in the top fifth of their class; 99% were in the top two fifths. 30 freshmen graduated first in their class. **Admissions Contact:** Joseph J.T. Duck, Director of Admissions. Email: *admissions@swarthmore.edu* Web: *www.swarthmore.edu*

FINANCIAL AID: In 2016-2017, 52% of all full-time freshmen and 50% of continuing full-time students received some form of financial aid. 52% of all full-time freshmen and 50% of continuing full-time students received need-based aid. The average freshman award was $47,676. Need-based scholarships or need-based grants averaged $46,053; and need-based self-help aid (loans and jobs) averaged $1,623. 81% of undergraduate students work part-time. Average annual earnings from campus work are $1890. Swarthmore is a member of CSS. The CSS/Profile, state aid form, college's own financial statement, federal tax returns, W-2 statements, and noncustodial are required. The FAFSA code is 003370. The priority date for freshman financial aid applications for fall entry is February 15. The filing deadline for fall entry is rolling.

TEMPLE UNIVERSITY F-3

www.temple.edu

Philadelphia, PA 19122

(215) 204-8556
(888) 340-2222
Email: tuadm@temple.edu

Full-time: 12,116 men, 12,800 women
Part-time: 1749 men, 1578 women
Graduate: 4204 men, 5174 women
Year: semesters, summer session
Room & Board: $10,296

SAT CR/M/W: 558/571/553 **ACT:** 24
Application Deadline: March 1

Faculty: 1343; 1, av$
Ph.D.s: 76%
Student/Faculty: 18 to 1
Tuition: $14,096 ($24,122)
Freshman Class: 18813 applied, 12016 accepted, 4390 enrolled
CEEB CODE: 2906
VERY COMPETITIVE

Temple University, founded in 1888, is part of the Commonwealth System of Higher Education in Pennsylvania. It offers programs in the liberal arts, science and technology, health professions and social work, education, engineering, art, business and management, environmental design, media and communication, music and dance, theater, film and media arts, and tourism & hospitality. Temple has 9 campuses, including 1 in Rome and 1 in Tokyo. There are 11 undergraduate schools. In addition to regional accreditation, Temple has baccalaureate program accreditation with AACSB, ABET, ACEJMC, ACPE, ADA, APTA, ASLA, CSWE, NAAB, NASAD, NASM, NRPA, TEAC, ACS, APA-COA AOTA NATA, CAAHEP, COAPRT, ABA, ASHA, NASP, CAHIIM CAATE, AMTA, U/RTA, PDE, UCEA, NAST, CAHME, CCNE CEPH, NASD, APMA, and LCME. The 330-acre campus is in an urban area approximately 1.5 miles from downtown Philadelphia. Including any residence halls, there are 211 buildings.

STUDENT LIFE: 79% of undergraduates are from Pennsylvania. Others are from 50 states, 96 foreign countries, and Canada. 9% are race unknown; 6% Foreign; 56% White; 5% Hispanic; 2% two or more races; 12% African American; 10% Asian American. **Female To Male Ratio:** 1.1:1. The average age of freshmen is 18; all undergraduates, 22. 11% do not continue beyond their first year; 66% remain to graduate. **Housing:** 5506 students can be accommodated in college housing, which includes coed dorms, on-campus apartments, off-campus apartments, honors houses, special-interest houses, and living-learning communities. On-campus housing is guaranteed for the freshman year only. 86% of students commute. Alcohol is not permitted. All students may keep cars.

FACULTY/CLASSROOMS: 61% of faculty are male; 39% are female. No introductory courses are taught by graduate students.

PROGRAMS OF STUDY: Temple confers B.A., B.F.A., B.B.A., B.MUS, B.S., B.S.BioE, B.S.Arch, B.S.A.T., B.S.C.E., B.S. Ed., B.S.E.E., B.S.E.T., B.S.M.E., B.S.N., and B.S.W. degrees. Associate, master's, and doctoral degrees are also awarded. Bachelor's degrees are awarded in AGRICULTURE (environmental studies and horticulture), BIOLOGICAL SCIENCE (biochemistry, biology/adolescence education, biology/biological science, and biophysics), BUSINESS (accounting, banking and finance, business administration and management, entrepreneurial studies, finance, international business management, management information systems, marketing/retailing/merchandising, real estate, sports management, and tourism), COMMUNICATIONS AND THE ARTS (advertising, art, art history and appreciation, broadcasting, ceramic art and design, classics, communications, dance, English, fiber/textiles/weaving, film arts, French, German, glass, graphic design, Italian, jazz, journalism, linguistics, media arts, metal/jewelry, music, music composition, music history and appreciation, music performance, music theory and composition, painting, performing arts, photography, piano/organ, printmaking, public relations, sculpture, Spanish, speech/debate/rhetoric, telecommunications, theater design, theater management, and visual and performing arts), COMPUTER AND PHYSICAL SCIENCE (actuarial science, applied mathematics, chemistry, chemistry/adolescence education, computer science, earth science / adolescence education, geology, information sciences and systems, mathematics, mathematics/computational, mathematics – economics, and physics), EDUCATION (art education, athletic training, career, technical education & training, early childhood education, elementary education, health information management, mathematics education, music education, physical education, secondary education, and technical education), ENGINEERING AND ENVIRONMENTAL DESIGN (architecture, city/community/regional planning, civil engineering, construction management, electrical/electronics engineering, engineering, engineering technology, environmental science, landscape architecture/design, and mechanical engineering), HEALTH PROFESSIONS (music therapy, nursing, predentistry, premedicine, public health, recreation therapy, and speech therapy), SOCIAL SCIENCE (African American studies, American studies, anthropology, Asian/Oriental studies, criminal justice, economics, geography, history, Latin American studies, legal studies, philosophy, physical fitness/movement, political science/government, prelaw, psychology, religion, social science, social work, sociology, and women's studies). Art, journalism, and business are the strongest academically. Biology, psychology, and accounting have the largest enrollments.

ACTIVITIES: 4% of men belong to 19 national fraternities; 4% of women belong to 15 national sororities. There are 329 groups on campus, including art, band, cheerleading, chess, choir, chorale, chorus, communications, computers, dance, debate, drama, drill team, environmental, ethnic, film, forensics, honors, international, jazz band, LGBT, literary magazine, marching band, musical theater, newspaper, opera, orchestra, pep band, photography, political, professional, radio and TV, religious, social, social service, student government, symphony, and yearbook. Popular campus events include Homecoming, Cherry & White Day. **Sports:** There are 12 intercollegiate sports for men and 13 for women, and 14 intramural sports for men and 14 for women. Facilities include a climbing wall, fitness mezzanine, cardio machines, selectorized machines, and areas designated for circuit training and light weight, stretch/abs/core, basketball, football, volleyball, gymnastics, fencing, basketball, field hockey and women's lacrosse, tennis, baseball, softball stadium, and soccer. **Graduates:** From July 1, 2015 to June 30, 2016, 6080 bachelor's degrees were awarded. The most popular majors were business/marketing (20%), visual and performing arts (11%), and communication/journalism (11%). In an average class, 38% graduate in 4 years or less, 61% graduate in 5 years or less, and 66% graduate in 6 years or less.

SERVICES: Counseling and information services are available, as is tutoring in most subjects. There is also a reader service for the blind, and remedial math, reading, and writing. **Library/Resources:** The 14 libraries contain 4.1 million volumes, 3.4 million microform items, 45,385 audio/video tapes/CDs/DVDs, and subscribe to 67,942 periodicals including electronic. Computerized library services include interlibrary loans, database searching, Internet access, and Wi-Fi capability. Special learning facilities include an art gallery, planetarium, radio station, and TV station. **Physically Challenged Students:** All of the campus is accessible. Facilities include wheelchair ramps, elevators, special parking, specially equipped restrooms, special class scheduling, lowered drinking fountains, lowered telephones, and special housing. Additional services may be arranged through the Disabled Student Services Office. **Special:** Temple offers co-op programs in business/marketing, computer/information sciences, and engineering, internships, study abroad in 15 countries, an extern program in which participating students receive 2 or 3 academic credits, dual majors, distance learning, dual enrollment, ESL, domestic exchange, independent study, and a teacher certification program. There are 3 national honor societies, Phi Beta Kappa, and a freshman honors program. **Visiting:** There are regularly scheduled orientations for prospective students as well as guides for informal visits, and visitors may sit in on classes. To schedule a visit, contact the Office of Undergraduate Admissions. **Campus Safety and Security:** Measures include 24-hour foot and vehicle patrol, emergency notification system, self-defense education, and security escort services. There are also shuttle buses, emergency telephones, lighted pathways/sidewalks, controlled access to dorms/residences, 24-hour security in residence halls.

REQUIREMENTS: The SAT or ACT is required. Applicants should complete 16 academic credits/carnegie units, including 4 years of English, 3 of math, 2 each of social studies, foreign language, and science, including 1 of lab science, and 1 each of history and an academic elective. A GED is accepted. A portfolio and audition are required in relevant fields. AP and CLEP credits are accepted. Important factors in the admissions decision are advanced placement or honors courses, parents or siblings attended your school, evidence of special talent, and recommendations by school officials. The required core curriculum includes nine areas of learning and a total of eleven courses. Areas include: Analytical Reading & Writing, Quantitative Literacy, Mosaic I and Mosaic II, Arts, Human Behavior, Race & Diversity, World Society, Science & Technology, and U.S. Society. All GenEd courses must be completed with a grade of C- or higher to satisfy a GenEd requirement. **Procedure:** Freshmen are admitted in the fall and spring. Entrance exams should be taken by March of the junior year or April of the senior year. There is a rolling admissions plan. Applications should be filed by March 1 for fall entry; November 15 for spring entry. The fall 2016 application fee was $55. Notification is sent on a rolling basis. Applications are accepted on-line. **Transfer Students:** 3847 transfer students enrolled in 2015-2016. Applicants must have earned at least 15 college credit hours with at least a 2.5 GPA and must submit official high school and college transcripts. 30 of 124 credits required for the bachelor's degree must be completed at Temple. **International Students:** There are 1022 international students enrolled. The school actively recruits these students. They must take the TOEFL with a minimum score of 550 on the paper-based TOEFL (PBT) or 79 on the Internet-based version (iBT). They must also take the SAT or ACT.

ADMISSIONS: 64% of the 2016-2017 applicants were accepted. The SAT scores for the 2016-2017 freshman class were: Critical Reading-- 22% below 500, 48% between 500 and 599, 25% between 600 and 699, and 5% between 700 and 800. Math-- 17% below 500, 46% between 500 and 599, 30% between 600 and 699, and 7% between 700 and 800. Writing-- 24% below 500, 46% between 500 and 599, 25% between 600 and 699, and 5% between 700 and 800. The ACT scores were 16% below 12, 27% between 12 and 17, 28% between 18 and 23, 12% between 24 and 29, and 17% above 30. 42% of the current freshmen were in the top fifth of their class; 77% were in the top two fifths. 13 freshmen graduated first in their class. **Admissions Contact:** Karin Mormando, Director of Undergraduate Admissions. Email: *tuadm@temple.edu* Web: *www.temple.edu*

FINANCIAL AID: The average freshman award was $15,200. Need-based scholarships or need-based grants averaged $6,193; need-based self-help aid (loans and jobs) averaged $3,518; non-need-based athletic scholarships averaged $17,929; and other non-need-based awards and non-need-based scholarships averaged $5,192. The average financial indebtedness of the 2016 graduate was $34,382. The college's own financial statement, and the PHEAA (Pennsylvania residents) is required. The FAFSA code is 003371. The priority date for freshman financial aid applications for fall entry is March 1.

THE LINCOLN UNIVERSITY *(The complete profile is made available exclusively on our website, www.barronspac.com)*

THIEL COLLEGE — A-2
www.thiel.edu

Greenville, PA 16125	**(724) 589-2182** **(800) 24-THIEL**
Fax: (724) 589-2683	**Email: slazowski@thiel.edu**
Full-time: 492 men, 377 women	**Faculty:** 60
Part-time: 14 men, 11 women	**Ph.D.s:** 79%
Graduate: n/av	**Student/Faculty:** 10 to 1
Year: semesters, summer session	**Tuition:** $29,890
Room & Board: $11,700	**Freshman Class:** 2035 applied, 1511 accepted, 279 enrolled
SAT: required **ACT:** 21	**CEEB CODE:** 2910
Application Deadline: n/av	**COMPETITIVE**

Thiel College, founded in 1866, is a private independent college affiliated with the Lutheran Church. It offers programs in liberal arts, business, engineering, religion, teacher preparation, and professional programs. There is 1 undergraduate school. The 135-acre campus is in a rural area 75 miles north of Pittsburgh and 75 miles southeast of Cleveland. Including any residence halls, there are 52 buildings.

STUDENT LIFE: 66% of undergraduates are from Pennsylvania. Others

are from 21 states, and 6 foreign countries. 90% are from public schools. 60% are White; 5% Foreign; 2% Hispanic; 2% two or more races; 14% African American; 1% Asian American. 46% are Protestant; 25% Catholic; 22% claim no religious affiliation. **Male To Female Ratio:** 1.3:1. The average age of freshmen is 18; all undergraduates, 20. 30% do not continue beyond their first year; 35% remain to graduate. **Housing:** 1129 students can be accommodated in college housing, which includes single-sex, coed dorms and on-campus apartments, special-interest houses, fraternity houses, sorority houses, and living-learning centers. On-campus housing is guaranteed for all 4 years. 90% of students live on campus; of those, 75% remain on campus on weekends. All students may keep cars.

FACULTY/CLASSROOMS: 52% of faculty are male; 48% are female. All teach undergraduates. No introductory courses are taught by graduate students. The average class size in an introductory lecture is 25; in a laboratory is 15; and in a regular course is 15.

PROGRAMS OF STUDY: Thiel confers B.A., and B.S. degrees. Associate degrees are also awarded. Bachelor's degrees are awarded in BIOLOGICAL SCIENCE (biology/biological science and neurosciences), BUSINESS (accounting, business administration and management, electronic business, international business management, and management information systems), COMMUNICATIONS AND THE ARTS (art, communications, English, and media arts), COMPUTER AND PHYSICAL SCIENCE (actuarial science, chemistry, computer science, mathematics, physics, and web services), EDUCATION (secondary education and special education), ENGINEERING AND ENVIRONMENTAL DESIGN (environmental science and preengineering), HEALTH PROFESSIONS (cytotechnology, medical laboratory technology, predentistry, premedicine, prepharmacy, preveterinary science, and speech pathology/audiology), SOCIAL SCIENCE (criminal justice, history, philosophy, political science/government, prelaw, psychology, religion, religious education, and sociology). Engineering, biology, and chemistry are the strongest academically. Business administration, psychology and biology have the largest enrollments.

ACTIVITIES: 20% of men belong to 4 national fraternities; 26% of women belong to 4 national sororities. There are 40 groups on campus, including art, band, cheerleading, choir, chorus, computers, dance, drama, drill team, ethnic, forensics, honors, international, LGBT, literary magazine, marching band, musical theater, newspaper, pep band, political, professional, radio and TV, religious, social, social service, student government, symphony, and yearbook. Popular campus events include Spring Weekend, Greek Week, and Theatrical Productions. **Sports:** There are 10 intercollegiate sports for men and 9 for women, and 4 intramural sports for men and 3 for women. Facilities include a gym, basketball and handball courts, playing fields, fitness center, tennis courts, and a football stadium. **Graduates:** From July 1, 2015 to June 30, 2016, 202 bachelor's degrees were awarded. The most popular majors were business (24%), psychology (13%), and biology (11%). 49 companies recruited on campus in 2015-2016. In an average class, 32% graduate in 4 years or less, 46% graduate in 5 years or less, and 41% graduate in 6 years or less. Of the 2015 graduating class, 29% were enrolled in graduate school within 6 months of graduation, and 67% were employed.

SERVICES: Counseling and information services are available, as is tutoring in most subjects, and remedial math. **Library/Resources:** The library contains 347,312 volumes, 89,530 microform items, and subscribes to 26 periodicals including electronic. Computerized library services include interlibrary loans, database searching, Internet access, and Wi-Fi capability. Special learning facilities include an art gallery, radio station, and a wildlife sanctuary. **Physically Challenged Students:** 75% of the campus is accessible. Facilities include wheelchair ramps, elevators, special parking, specially equipped restrooms, special class scheduling, and lowered drinking fountains. **Special:** Students may spend a semester at Argonne National Laboratories, the Art Institute of Pittsburgh, or Drew University. Special programs include a UN semester, a Washington semester, an Appalachian semester, study at Pittsburgh Institute of Mortuary Science, and a forestry and environmental management semester at Duke University. There is a 3-2 engineering program with Case Western Reserve University and the University of Pittsburgh. Internships, study abroad, work-study, dual majors, nondegree study, cooperative programs in all majors, credit by examination, and credit for life, military, and work experience are also available. There are 11 national honor societies, a freshman honors program, and 10 departmental honors programs. **Visiting:** There are regularly scheduled orientations for prospective students, including orientation sessions for students enrolling in the fall and monthly sessions beginning in February. There are guides for informal visits, visitors may sit in on classes, and stay overnight. To schedule a visit, contact Stephen Lazowski at slazowski@thiel.edu. **Campus Safety and Security:** Measures include 24-hour foot and vehicle patrol, emergency notification system, and security escort services. There are shuttle buses, emergency telephones, lighted pathways/sidewalks, and controlled access to dorms/residences.

REQUIREMENTS: The SAT or ACT is required. The ACT Optional Writing test is also required. Applicants should be high school graduates who have completed 16 academic units, including 4 years of English, 3 of social science, and 2 each of foreign language, math, and science. The GED is accepted. An essay and an interview are recommended. A GPA of 2.0 is required. AP and CLEP credits are accepted. Important factors in the admissions decision are advanced placement or honors courses, evidence of special talent, and leadership record. To graduate, students must complete a total of 124 credit hours, with 35 to 55 in the major and a minimum GPA of 2.0. Requirements include 3 hours of composition, 3 hours of presentation, 10 to 12 hours of quantitative/scientific reasoning, 3 hours each of religion, humanities, social science, and math/sciences, and 4 hours for physical well-being. Math must be quantitative reasoning or higher. Some majors require a comprehensive exam or thesis. **Procedure:** Freshmen are admitted to all sessions. Entrance exams should be taken by May 1. There are deferred admissions and rolling admissions plans. Check with the school for current application deadlines. Notification is sent on a rolling basis. Applications are accepted online. **Transfer Students:** 36 transfer students enrolled in 2015-2016. Applicants should meet the same criteria as entering freshmen and should submit official transcripts, statements of good standing, financial aid transcripts, and transfer forms from all colleges previously attended. Students must have a 2.0 GPA to transfer. 30 of 124 credits required for the bachelor's degree must be completed at Thiel. **International Students:** There are 41 international students enrolled. The school actively recruits these students. They must take the TOEFL with a minimum score of 503 on the paper-based TOEFL (PBT) or 62 on the Internet-based version (iBT), or take the MELAB.

ADMISSIONS: 74% of the 2016-2017 applicants were accepted. **Admissions Contact:** Stephen Lazowski, Vice President for Enrollment Management. Email: *slazowski@thiel.edu* Web: *www.thiel.edu*

FINANCIAL AID: In 2016-2017, 98% of all full-time freshmen and continuing full-time students received some form of financial aid. 98% of all full-time freshmen and continuing full-time students received need-based aid. The average freshman award was $26,874. Need-based scholarships or need-based grants averaged $22,896; need-based self-help aid (loans and jobs) averaged $4,435; and other non-need-based awards and non-need-based scholarships averaged $16,182. 39% of undergraduate students work part-time. Average annual earnings from campus work are $1500. The average financial indebtedness of the 2016 graduate was $33,500. The CCS/Profile, FFS, or SFS, are required, and the FAFSA is perferred. The FAFSA code is 003376. The deadline for filing freshman financial aid applications for fall entry is May 1.

UNIVERSITY OF PENNSYLVANIA — F-3

www.upenn.edu

Philadelphia, PA 19104	(215) 898-7507
Fax: (215) 898-9670	Email: info@admissions.upenn.edu
Full-time: 4703 men, 4704 women	Faculty: 1456
Part-time: 169 men, 136 women	Ph.D.s: 100%
Graduate: 5455 men, 6191 women	Student/Faculty: 6 to 1
Year: semesters, summer session	Tuition: $49,536
Room & Board: $13,990	Freshman Class: 35866 applied, 3718 accepted, 2425 enrolled
SAT or ACT: required	CEEB CODE: 2926
Application Deadline: January 1	MOST COMPETITIVE

University of Pennsylvania, founded in 1740, is a member of the Ivy League. Penn's 4 undergraduate schools include the college of engineering, college of nursing, and the Wharton school. Students are able to pursue interdisciplinary study within the schools and across the University's 12 graduate schools, and are engaged in learning in our 165 research centers. In addition to regional accreditation, Penn has baccalaureate program accreditation with AACSB, ABET, CCNE, and ACNM.

The 302-acre campus is in an urban area in Philadelphia. Including any residence halls, there are 187 buildings.

STUDENT LIFE: 82% of undergraduates are from out of state, mostly the Middle Atlantic. Students are from 50 states, 103 foreign countries, and Canada. 59% are from public schools. 46% are White; 19% Asian American; 11% Foreign; 10% Hispanic; 7% African American; 4% two or more races; 4% race unknown. 29% claim no religious affiliation; 26% Protestant; 19% Catholic; 19% Jewish. **Female To Male Ratio:** 1.1:1. The average age of freshmen is 18; all undergraduates, 20. 2% do not continue beyond their first year; 96% remain to graduate. **Housing:** 6850 students can be accommodated in college housing, which includes coed dorms, on-campus apartments, off-campus apartments, and married student housing. In addition, there are language houses, special-interest houses, and fraternity houses. There are over 40 academic residence programs, including the areas of: arts, entrepreneurship, politics, law & society, international studies, media, visual arts, and women in science. On-campus housing is guaranteed for the freshman year only, and is available on a first-come, first-served basis, on a lottery system for upperclassmen. All students may keep cars.

FACULTY/CLASSROOMS: 63% of faculty are male; 37% are female. All teach undergraduates, and do research. No introductory courses are taught by graduate students.

PROGRAMS OF STUDY: Penn confers B.A., B.S., B.Applied Sc., B.B.A., B.F.A., B.S.E., and B.S.N. degrees. Associate, master's, and doctoral degrees are also awarded. Bachelor's degrees are awarded in AGRICULTURE (environmental studies), BIOLOGICAL SCIENCE (biochemistry, biology/biological science, and biophysics), BUSINESS (accounting, business administration and management, entrepreneurial studies, human resources, insurance and risk management, logistics, management information systems, marketing/retailing/merchandising, operations management, real estate, retailing, and transportation management), COMMUNICATIONS AND THE ARTS (art history and appreciation, classics, communications, comparative literature, design, dramatic arts, English, fine arts, folklore and mythology, French, German, linguistics, music, Russian, and visual and performing arts), COMPUTER AND PHYSICAL SCIENCE (actuarial science, applied science, chemistry, computer science, digital arts/technology, geology, information sciences and systems, mathematics, physics, science technology, and statistics), EDUCATION (elementary education), ENGINEERING AND ENVIRONMENTAL DESIGN (architecture, bioengineering, chemical engineering, civil engineering, computer engineering, electrical/electronics engineering, and materials engineering), HEALTH PROFESSIONS (health, health care administration, and nursing), SOCIAL SCIENCE (African studies, African American studies, American studies, anthropology, Asian/Oriental studies, cognitive science, economics, gender studies, Hispanic American studies, history, history of science, international relations, international studies, Italian studies, Judaic studies, Latin American studies, law, Middle Eastern studies, Near Eastern studies, philosophy, political science/government, psychology, public administration, religion, sociology, South Asian studies, urban studies, and women's studies). Finance, economics, and nursing have the largest enrollments.

ACTIVITIES: 30% of men belong to 36 national fraternities; 17% of women belong to 13 national sororities. There are 450 groups on campus, including art, band, cheerleading, chess, choir, chorale, chorus, computers, dance, debate, drama, environmental, ethnic, film, forensics, honors, international, jazz band, LGBT, literary magazine, marching band, musical theater, newspaper, opera, orchestra, pep band, photography, political, professional, radio and TV, religious, social, social service, student government, and symphony. **Sports:** There are 17 intercollegiate sports for men and 16 for women, and 11 intramural sports for men and 11 for women. Facilities include gyms, swimming pool, squash courts, indoor and outdoor tennis courts, playing fields, an indoor ice rink, rowing tanks, saunas, weight rooms, exercise facilities, a boathouse, and a stadium. **Graduates:** From July 1, 2015 to June 30, 2016, 2848 bachelor's degrees were awarded. The most popular majors were finance (14%), nursing (6%), and economics (5%). 601 companies recruited on campus in 2015-2016. In an average class, 88% graduate in 4 years or less and 96% graduate in 6 years or less. Of the 2015 graduating class, 20% were enrolled in graduate school within 6 months of graduation, and 60% were employed.

SERVICES: Counseling and information services are available, as is tutoring in most subjects. There is also a reader service for the blind. The WHEEL academic support program is available in all residences. **Library/Resources:** The 15 libraries contain 5.9 million volumes, 4.2 million microform items, 121,233 audio/video tapes/CDs/DVDs, and subscribe to 98,145 periodicals including electronic. Computerized library services include interlibrary loans, database searching, Internet access, and Wi-Fi capability. Special learning facilities include an art gallery, natural history museum, planetarium, radio station, TV station, museum of archaeology and anthropology, institute of contemporary art, arboretum, theater, astronomical observatory, animal research center, equine sports medicine and imaging center, women's center, undergraduate research center, wind tunnel, Cyclotron facility, Marshak dairy, Arthur Ross gallery, galleries in Van Pelt Library, galleries in Inn@ Penn, Charles Addams Gallery, gallery in architectural archives, Kelly Writer's House, ENIAC Museum, Hillel Foundation, center for advanced Judaic studies, LRSM material testing equipment. **Physically Challenged Students:** 93% of the campus is accessible. Facilities include wheelchair ramps, elevators, special parking, specially equipped restrooms, special class scheduling, lowered drinking fountains, lowered telephones, and special housing. **Special:** Cross-registration is permitted with Haverford, Swarthmore, and Bryn Mawr Colleges and through the Quaker Consortium. Opportunities are provided for internships, a Washington semester, accelerated degree programs, joint degree programs, preprofessional programs, B.A.-B.S. degrees, dual and student-designed majors, credit by exam, limited pass/fail options, and study abroad in 39 countries. Through the "one university" concept, students in one undergraduate school may study in any of the other three. There are 11 national honor societies, a freshman honors program, and 27 departmental honors programs. **Visiting:** There are regularly scheduled orientations for prospective students, including an information session by the Admissions Office and a tour of the campus led by current students. There are guides for informal visits, visitors may sit in on classes, and stay overnight. To schedule a visit, contact the Admissions Office. **Campus Safety and Security:** Measures include 24-hour foot and vehicle patrol, emergency notification system, self-defense education, and security escort services. There are also shuttle buses, emergency telephones, lighted pathways/sidewalks, controlled access to dorms/residences, a bicycle patrol, police officers, victim support and special services. Students together against acquaintance rape, student walking escort, and security guard personnel, and many on public patrol.

REQUIREMENTS: The SAT or ACT is required as graduation from an accredited secondary school. Recommended preparation includes 4 years of high school English, 3 or 4 each of a foreign language and math, and 3 each of history and social science. An essay is required. A portfolio is recommended for prospective art majors. AP credits are accepted. The bachelor's degree requires completion of 32 to 40 course units, depending on the student's major, with 12 to 18 of these units in the major and a GPA of 2.0. **Procedure:** Freshmen are admitted in the fall. Entrance exams should be taken by December of the senior year. There are early decision and deferred admissions plans. Early decision applications should be filed by November 1; regular applications, by January 1 for fall entry, along with a $75 fee. Notification of early decision is sent December 15; regular decision, April 1. 1299 early decision candidates were accepted for the 2016-2017 class. 1600 applicants were on the 2016 waiting list; 136 were admitted. Applications are accepted online. **Transfer Students:** 170 transfer students enrolled in 2015-2016. Applicants must provide college and high school transcripts, essays, and 2 recommendations. SAT or ACT scores are required for transfer students. 16 of 32 credits required for the bachelor's degree must be completed at Penn. **International Students:** There are 1077 international students enrolled. The school actively recruits these students. They must take the TOEFL, and SAT; Subject tests as well as or the ACT with writing.

ADMISSIONS: 10% of the 2016-2017 applicants were accepted. The SAT scores for the 2016-2017 freshman class were: Critical Reading-- 5% between 500 and 599, 31% between 600 and 699, and 64% between 700 and 800. Math-- 2% between 500 and 599, 24% between 600 and 699, and 74% between 700 and 800. Writing-- 3% between 500 and 599, 22% between 600 and 699, and 75% between 700 and 800.; 100% were in the top two fifths. **Admissions Contact:** Email: *info@admissions.upenn.edu* Web: *www.upenn.edu*

FINANCIAL AID: In 2016-2017, 50% of all full-time freshmen and 47% of continuing full-time students received some form of financial aid. 50% of all full-time freshmen and 47% of continuing full-time students received need-based aid. The average freshman award was $41,713. Need-based scholarships or need-based grants averaged $39,459; and need-based self-help aid (loans and jobs) averaged $2,890. 44% of undergraduate students work part-time. Average annual earnings from campus work are $1835. The average financial indebtedness of the 2016 graduate was $19,798. Penn is a member of CSS. The CSS/Profile, the college's own financial statement, and parents' and student's most recently completed income tax returns are required. The FAFSA code is 003378. The priority date for freshman financial aid applications for fall entry is February 15.

UNIVERSITY OF PITTSBURGH B-3

www.pitt.edu

Pittsburgh, PA 15260 (412) 624-PITT

Fax: (412) 648-4138 Email: oafa@pitt.edu

Full-time: 8729 men, 9434 women
Part-time: 502 men, 458 women
Graduate: 4236 men, 5305 women
Year: semesters, summer session
Room & Board: $10,950

SAT CR/M/W: 630/650/620 **ACT:** 29
Application Deadline: open

Faculty: n/av
Ph.D.s: 94%
Student/Faculty: 15 to 1
Tuition: $18,618 ($29,888)
Freshman Class: 29,175 applied, 16165 accepted, 3954 enrolled
CEEB CODE: 2927
HIGHLY COMPETITIVE+

University of Pittsburgh, founded in 1787, is a state-related, public research university with programs in arts and sciences, education, engineering, law, social work, business, health and rehabilitation sciences, nursing, pharmacy, dental medicine, public health, medicine, information sciences, and public and international affairs. There are 9 undergraduate schools and 6 graduate schools. In addition to regional accreditation, Pitt has baccalaureate program accreditation with AACSB, ABET, ADA, and CSWE. The 145-acre campus is in a suburban area 3 miles east of downtown Pittsburgh. Including any residence halls, there are 131 buildings.

STUDENT LIFE: 69% of undergraduates are from Pennsylvania. Others are from 50 states, 49 foreign countries, and Canada. 73% are White; 5% African American; 4% Foreign; 4% two or more races; 3% Hispanic; 10% Asian American; 1% race unknown. **Female To Male Ratio:** 1.1:1. The average age of all undergraduates is 21. 8% do not continue beyond their first year; 82% remain to graduate. **Housing:** 7916 students can be accommodated in college housing, which includes single-sex and coed dorms, on-campus apartments, and off-campus apartments. In addition, there are honors houses, language houses, special-interest houses, fraternity houses, sorority houses, emerging leaders, engineering, nursing, business, international living, and health sciences houses. On-campus housing is guaranteed for the freshman year only, and is available on a first-come, first-served basis, and on a lottery system for upperclassmen. 57% of students commute. All students may keep cars.

FACULTY/CLASSROOMS: 56% of faculty are male; 44% are female. No introductory courses are taught by graduate students.

PROGRAMS OF STUDY: Pitt confers B.A., B.S., B.A.S.W., B.Phil., B.S.B.A., B.S.E., B.S.N. and B.S.P.S. degrees. Master's and doctoral degrees are also awarded. Bachelor's degrees are awarded in AGRICULTURE (environmental studies), BIOLOGICAL SCIENCE (bioinformatics, biology/biological science, ecology, microbiology, molecular biology, and neurosciences), BUSINESS (accounting, business (dual major program), business information systems, economics – statistics, finance, global/general management, human resources, international business management, marketing/retailing/merchandising, and supply chain management), COMMUNICATIONS AND THE ARTS (Africana studies, Chinese, classics, communication rhetoric/communication, communication science, creative writing, English literature, film arts, French, German studies, Germanic languages and literature, Italian, Japanese, linguistics, media arts, music, Polish, Russian, Slavic languages, Spanish, studio art, and theatre arts), COMPUTER AND PHYSICAL SCIENCE (actuarial mathematics, applied mathematics, astronomy, chemistry, computer science, geology, information sciences and systems, mathematics, mathematics – economics, natural sciences, physics, and statistics), EDUCATION (athletic training, health information management, and health and physical education), ENGINEERING AND ENVIRONMENTAL DESIGN (bioengineering, chemical engineering, civil engineering, computer engineering, electrical/electronics engineering, engineering physics, engineering science, environmental science, industrial engineering, materials engineering, materials science, and mechanical engineering), HEALTH PROFESSIONS (dental hygiene, emergency medical technologies, health services technology, nursing, pharmaceutical science, and rehabilitation therapy), SOCIAL SCIENCE (administration of justice , anthropology, applied psychology, architectural studies, economics, history, history of philosophy, humanities, interdisciplinary studies, international studies, legal studies, liberal arts/general studies, philosophy, political science/government, psychology, public administration, public affairs, religion, social science, social work, sociology, urban studies, and women's studies). Psychology, biological Sciences, and nursing have the largest enrollments.

ACTIVITIES: 10% of men belong to 24 national fraternities; 9% of women belong to 18 national sororities. There are 570 groups on campus, including art, band, cheerleading, chess, choir, chorale, chorus, communications, dance, debate, drama, ethnic, film, honors, international, jazz band, LGBT, literary magazine, marching band, musical theater, newspaper, pep band, political, professional, radio and TV, religious, social, social service, student government, and symphony. Popular campus events include Lantern Night, Fall Fest, and Bigelow Bash. **Sports:** There are 8 intercollegiate sports for men and 9 for women, and 15 intramural sports for men and 14 for women. Facilities include basketball courts, a fitness center, a field house with volleyball, gymnastics training center, baseball stadium, soccer stadium, and a softball stadium, billiard tables, table tennis, video games, and televisions in the student union. **Graduates:** From July 1, 2015 to June 30, 2016, 4521 bachelor's degrees were awarded. The most popular majors were psychology (7%), finance (6%), and nursing (5%). 978 companies recruited on campus in 2015-2016. In an average class, 82% graduate in 6 years or less.

SERVICES: Counseling and information services are available, as is tutoring in some subjects, such as many lower-level undergraduate science, and humanities courses. There is also remedial math and writing. **Library/Resources:** The 16 libraries contain 7.4 million volumes, 5.5 million microform items, and subscribes to 336,416 periodicals including electronic. Computerized library services include interlibrary loans, database searching, Internet access, and Wi-Fi capability. Special learning facilities include an art gallery, radio station, TV station, international classrooms, Cathedral of Learning, an observatory, music hall, and a natural history museum. **Physically Challenged Students:** 90% of the campus is accessible. Facilities include wheelchair ramps, elevators, special parking, specially equipped restrooms, lowered drinking fountains, lowered telephones, and special housing. **Special:** Students may cross-register with 9 neighboring colleges and universities. Internships, unlimited study abroad, work-study programs, a dual major in business and any other subject in arts and sciences, and student-designed majors are available. There is a 5-year joint degree in arts and sciences/engineering. There are co-op programs in engineering, computer science, and chemistry. An accelerated second degree B.S.N. program is available as well as a 3-2 engineering degree. There are 23 national honor societies, Phi Beta Kappa, and a freshman honors program. **Visiting:** There are regularly scheduled orientations for prospective students, including information sessions, student-guided tours, and class attendance. There are guides for informal visits and visitors may sit in on classes. To schedule a visit, contact the Office of Admissions. **Campus Safety and Security:** Measures include 24-hour foot and vehicle patrol, emergency notification system, self-defense education, and security escort services. There are shuttle buses, emergency telephones, lighted pathways/sidewalks, and controlled access to dorms/residences.

REQUIREMENTS: The SAT or ACT is required, as is the ACT Optional Writing test is also required. Applicants for admission to the Kenneth P. Dietrich School of Arts and Sciences must be graduates of an accredited secondary school. Students must have 17 high school academic credits, including 4 units of English, 3-4 each of math and lab science, 2-3 of social studies, plus 3-5 units in academic electives. Pitt recommends that the student have 3 or more years of a single foreign language. An essay is recommended if the student is seeking scholarship consideration. AP and CLEP credits are accepted. Important factors in the admissions decision are advanced placement or honors courses, leadership record, and evidence of special talent. All students in the Kenneth P. Dietrich School of Arts and Sciences must take a minimum of 120 credits. Skills and general education requirements vary but include course work in the humanities, social and natural sciences, and foreign culture. A 2.0 GPA are required. Students must earn their last 30 credits while enrolled in arts and sciences and earn at least half of the credits for their majors. Requirements for other schools may vary. **Procedure:** Freshmen are admitted to all sessions. Entrance exams should be taken preferably by January for September admission. There are deferred admissions and rolling admissions plans. Application deadlines are open. Application fee is $45. Notification is sent on a rolling basis. 2382 applicants were on the 2016 waiting list; 170 were admitted. Applications are accepted online. **Transfer Students:** 753 transfer students enrolled in 2015-2016. Applicants for transfer to the Kenneth P. Dietrich School of Arts and Sciences must supply transcripts of all secondary school and college course work and have a minimum GPA of 3.0. An interview is recommended. Grades of C or better transfer for credit. Application deadlines vary by school. 30 of 120 credits required for the bachelor's degree must be completed at Pitt. **International Students:** There are 696 international students enrolled. The school actively recruits these students. They must take the TOEFL with a minimum score of 600 on the paper-based TOEFL (PBT) or 100 on the Internet-based version (iBT), or take the IELTS. They must also take the SAT or ACT.

ADMISSIONS: 55% of the 2016-2017 applicants were accepted. The SAT scores for the 2016-2017 freshman class were: Critical Reading-- 2% below 500, 28% between 500 and 599, 50% between 600 and 699, and 20% between 700 and 800. Math-- 1% below 500, 20% between 500 and 599, 53% between 600 and 699, and 26% between 700 and 800. Writing-- 3% below 500, 34% between 500 and 599, 47% between 600 and 699, and 16% between 700 and 800. The ACT scores were 6% below 12, 3% between 12 and 17, 21% between 18 and 23, 22% between 24 and 29, and 53% above 30. 79% of the current freshmen were in the top fifth of their class; 97% were in the top two fifths. **Admissions Contact:** Marc L. Harding, Chief Enrollment Officer. Email: *oafa@pitt.edu* Web: *www.pitt.edu*

FINANCIAL AID: In 2016-2017, 63% of all full-time freshmen and 58% of continuing full-time students received some form of financial aid. 54% of all full-time freshmen and 53% of continuing full-time students received need-based aid. The average freshman award was $15,648. Need-based scholarships or need-based grants averaged $9,239; need-based self-help aid (loans and jobs) averaged $7,122; and non-need-based athletic scholarships averaged $13,130. The average financial indebtedness of the 2016 graduate was $38,045. The FAFSA code is 008815. The priority date for freshman financial aid applications for fall entry is March 1.

UNIVERSITY OF PITTSBURGH AT BRADFORD — C-1

www.upb.pitt.edu

Bradford, PA 16701 — (814) 362-7555, (800) 872-1787

Fax: (814) 362-7578 — **Email:** admissions@upb.pitt.edu

Full-time: 635 men, 725 women	**Faculty:** 75
Part-time: 42 men, 74 women	**Ph.D.s:** 72%
Graduate: n/av	**Student/Faculty:** 17 to 1
Year: semesters, summer session	**Tuition:** $13,608 ($24,680)
Room & Board: $8794	**Freshman Class:** 2502 applied, 477 accepted, 398 enrolled
SAT CR/M/W: 520/520/460 **ACT:** 21	**CEEB CODE:** 2935
Application Deadline: n/av	**COMPETITIVE**

University of Pittsburgh at Bradford, established in 1963, is a public, state-related college for students who want to earn a world-renowned education in a personalized environment. There is 1 undergraduate school. In addition to regional accreditation, Pitt-Bradford has baccalaureate program accreditation with NLN and CAATE. The 317-acre campus is in a small town 160 miles northeast of Pittsburgh and 80 miles south of Buffalo. Including any residence halls, there are 32 buildings.

STUDENT LIFE: 78% of undergraduates are from Pennsylvania. Others are from 24 states, 19 foreign countries, and Canada. 86% are from public schools. 7% are race unknown; 67% White; 5% Hispanic; 3% Foreign; 2% Asian American; 2% two or more races; 12% African American. 51% are Protestant; 23% Catholic; 16% claim no religious affiliation. **Female To Male Ratio:** 1.2:1. The average age of freshmen is 18; all undergraduates, 21. 35% do not continue beyond their first year; 52% remain to graduate. **Housing:** 1047 students can be accommodated in college housing, which includes single-sex and coed on-campus apartments. On-campus housing is available on a first-come and first-served basis. 69% of students live on campus; of those, 33% remain on campus on weekends. All students may keep cars.

FACULTY/CLASSROOMS: 51% of faculty are male; 49% are female. All teach undergraduates. No introductory courses are taught by graduate students. The average class size in an introductory lecture is 21; in a laboratory is 13; and in a regular course is 18.

PROGRAMS OF STUDY: Pitt-Bradford confers B.A., B.S., and B.S.N. degrees. Associate degrees are also awarded. Bachelor's degrees are awarded in AGRICULTURE (environmental studies), BIOLOGICAL SCIENCE (biology/biological science), BUSINESS (accounting, business administration and management, hospitality management services, and sports management), COMMUNICATIONS AND THE ARTS (communications, English, and public relations), COMPUTER AND PHYSICAL SCIENCE (applied mathematics, chemistry, mathematics, and physical sciences), EDUCATION (athletic training, business education, elementary education, English education, environmental education, health education, mathematics education, science education, and social studies education), ENGINEERING AND ENVIRONMENTAL DESIGN (engineering), HEALTH PROFESSIONS (nursing, radiological science, and sports medicine), SOCIAL SCIENCE (criminal justice, economics, history, human development, interdisciplinary studies, liberal arts/general studies, psychology, social science, and sociology). Engineering, nursing, and biology are the strongest academically. Criminal justice, business management, and biology have the largest enrollments.

ACTIVITIES: 5% of men belong to 5 local fraternities; 5% of women belong to 4 local sororities. There are 60 groups on campus, including art, cheerleading, choir, chorale, computers, dance, drama, environmental, ethnic, honors, international, LGBT, literary magazine, newspaper, pep band, political, professional, radio and TV, religious, social, social service, and student government. Popular campus events include Winter Weekend, Spring Fling, and Alumni Weekend. **Sports:** There are 6 intercollegiate sports for men and 7 for women, and 15 intramural sports for men and 15 for women. Facilities include a sport and fitness center that includes basketball, volleyball, and general recreation, fitness center with physical conditioning equipment, an exercise arts studio for dance, martial arts, and aerobics. There is also an auxiliary gym for recreated and intramurals, phys ed classes, and a swimming pool. Outdoor facilities include a softball field, baseball field, tennis courts, handball courts, basketball courts, football/softball fields, and a volleyball court. **Graduates:** From July 1, 2015 to June 30, 2016, 264 bachelor's degrees were awarded. The most popular majors were biology (13%), sports medicine (10%), and business management (9%). 56 companies recruited on campus in 2015-2016. In an average class, 34% graduate in 4 years or less, 50% graduate in 5 years or less, and 53% graduate in 6 years or less. Of the 2015 graduating class, 30% were enrolled in graduate school within 6 months of graduation, and 80% were employed.

SERVICES: Counseling and information services are available, as is tutoring in most subjects, and remedial math, reading, and writing. **Library/Resources:** The library contains 105,300 volumes, 14,125 microform items, 3,874 audio/video tapes/CDs/DVDs, and subscribes to 91 periodicals including electronic. Computerized library services include interlibrary loans, database searching, and Internet access. Special learning facilities include an art gallery, radio station, a crime scene investigation house, a nursing suite with computerized mannequins, a psychology lab, a human performance lab, and athletic training facilities. **Physically Challenged Students:** 99% of the campus is accessible. Facilities include elevators, special parking, specially equipped restrooms, lowered drinking fountains, lowered telephones, and special housing. **Special:** Students may cross-register with colleges in the University of Pittsburgh system. Internships are required or strongly recommended for all majors. The school offers study abroad, dual majors, nondegree study, and a 3-2 engineering degree with the University of Pittsburgh (Oakland campus). Interdisciplinary majors are offered in human relations combining anthropology, psychology, and sociology; social sciences, combining anthropology, economics, history, political science, and sociology; and in interdisciplinary arts, combining art, music, and theater. Professional preparation is available in many areas including premedicine, prelaw, preveterinary science, prepharmacy, and predentistry. Teacher certification is also offered. There are 7 national honor societies. **Visiting:** There are regularly scheduled orientations for prospective students, programs throughout the year, offering a workshop with admissions representatives on academics, admissions, guidance, standardized tests, the application process, and financial aid. Tours led by students, a financial aid presentation, and a special campus event are also offered. There are guides for informal visits and visitors may sit in on classes. To schedule a visit, contact Alexander Nazemetz at (800) 872-1787. **Campus Safety and Security:** Measures include 24-hour foot and vehicle patrol, emergency notification system, and security escort services. There are shuttle buses, emergency telephones, and lighted pathways/sidewalks.

REQUIREMENTS: The SAT or ACT is required. Students must be graduates of an accredited secondary school with 16 Carnegie units, including 4 in English, 3 in history or social studies, and 3 each in science and math. The GED is accepted. Also used in the admissions decision are standardized test scores, rank in class, extracurricular activities, and recommendations. An essay is strongly recommended, as is an interview. A GPA of 2.0 is required. AP and CLEP credits are accepted. Important factors in the admissions decision are advanced placement or honors courses, extracurricular activities record, and leadership record. To graduate, students must complete a minimum of 120 credits with 30 to 76 in the major, and maintan a minimum GPA of 2.0. At least 30 should be upper-level courses. The core curriculum varies from 12 to 30 credits and distribution requirements from 56 to 59. English, math competency, and phys ed courses are required. **Procedure:** Freshmen are admitted in the fall, spring, and summer. Entrance exams should be taken during the junior year or the fall of the senior year. There are deferred admissions and rolling admissions plans. Application deadlines are open. Application fee is $45. Notifications are sent October 16. Applications are accepted online. **Transfer Students:** 106 transfer students enrolled in 2015-2016. A GPA of 2.0 or higher is required. 30 of 120 credits required for the bachelor's degree must be completed at Pitt-Bradford. **International Students:** There are 48 international students enrolled. They must take the TOEFL with a minimum score of 550 on the paper-based TOEFL (PBT) or 80 on the Internet-based version (iBT), or the IELTS, scoring 6.5.

ADMISSIONS: 19% of the 2016-2017 applicants were accepted. The SAT scores for the 2016-2017 freshman class were: Critical Reading-- 35% below 500, 49% between 500 and 599, 14% between 600 and 699, and 2% between 700 and 800. Math-- 34% below 500, 49% between 500 and 599, 14% between 600 and 699, and 3% between 700 and 800. Writing-- 72% below 500, 25% between 500 and 599, and 3% between 600 and 699. The ACT scores were 16% between 12 and 17, 59% between 18 and 23, 23% between 24 and 29, and 2% above 30. 25% of the current freshmen were in the top fifth of their class; 50% were in the top two fifths. 3 freshmen graduated first in their class. **Admissions Contact:** Alexander P. Nazemetz, Director of Admissions. Email: *admissions@upb.pitt.edu* Web: *www.upb.pitt.edu*

FINANCIAL AID: In 2016-2017, 92% of all full-time freshmen and 93% of continuing full-time students received some form of financial aid. 80% of all full-time freshmen and 76% of continuing full-time students received need-based aid. The average freshman award was $16,385. Need-based scholarships or need-based grants averaged $9,712 ($14,825 maximum); need-based self-help aid (loans and jobs) averaged $6,670 ($7,510 maximum); and other non-need-based awards and non-need-based scholarships averaged $5,530 ($20,700 maximum). 12% of undergraduate students work part-time. Average annual earnings from campus work are $1980. The average financial indebtedness of the 2016 graduate was $35,987. The FAFSA code is 008816. The priority date for freshman financial aid applications for fall entry is March 1.

UNIVERSITY OF PITTSBURGH AT GREENSBURG — B-3

www.upg.pitt.edu

Greensburg, PA 15601 — (724) 836-9880

Fax: (724) 836-7160	**Email:** upgadmit@pitt.edu
Full-time: 798 men, 840 women	**Faculty:** 89
Part-time: 79 men, 78 women	**Ph.D.s:** 84%
Graduate: n/av	**Student/Faculty:** 18 to 1
Year: semesters, summer session	**Tuition:** $13,382 ($24,198)
Room & Board: $9750	**Freshman Class:** 1568 applied, 1405 accepted, 424 enrolled
SAT: required	**CEEB CODE:** 2936
Application Deadline: open	**COMPETITIVE**

University of Pittsburgh at Greensburg, established in 1963, is a public state-related institution, offering undergraduate majors that can be completed at Pitt-Greensburg, as well as relocation programs that can begin at Greensburg and be completed at another Pitt campus. Figures in the above capsule and in this profile are approximate. There is 1 undergraduate school. The 219-acre campus is in a suburban area 33 miles southeast of Pittsburgh. Including any residence halls, there are 25 buildings.

STUDENT LIFE: 99% of undergraduates are from Pennsylvania. Others are from 5 states, 1 foreign country, and Canada. 94% are White; 3% African American; 2% Asian American; 1% Hispanic; 1% Foreign. **Female To Male Ratio:** 1.0:1. The average age of freshmen is 18; all undergraduates, 21. 25% do not continue beyond their first year; 55% remain to graduate. **Housing:** 585 students can be accommodated in college housing, which includes coed dorms, on-campus apartments, and special-interest houses. On-campus housing is available on a first-come and first-served basis. 68% of students commute. All students may keep cars. Alcohol is not permitted.

FACULTY/CLASSROOMS: 52% of faculty are male; 48% are female. All teach undergraduates, and 50% do research. No introductory courses are taught by graduate students. The average class size in an introductory lecture is 30; in a laboratory is 15; and in a regular course is 25.

PROGRAMS OF STUDY: Pitt-Greensburg confers B.A., and B.S. degrees. Bachelor's degrees are awarded in BIOLOGICAL SCIENCE (biology/biological science), BUSINESS (accounting and management science), COMMUNICATIONS AND THE ARTS (communications, creative writing, and English literature), COMPUTER AND PHYSICAL SCIENCE (applied mathematics and natural sciences), SOCIAL SCIENCE (American studies, anthropology, humanities, political science/government, psychology, and social science). Management, and psychology are the strongest academically. Management and administration of justice has the largest enrollment.

ACTIVITIES: There are no fraternities or sororities. There are 44 groups on campus, including academic club, band, cheerleading, chess, choir, chorale, chorus, computers, dance, debate, drama, ethnic, honors, literary magazine, newspaper, pep band, political, religious, social, social service, and student government. Popular campus events include La Cultura Study (a different historically significant era each year), St. Clair History Lecture, and Westmoreland Forum. **Sports:** There are 6 intercollegiate sports for men and 6 for women, and 8 intramural sports for men and 8 for women. Facilities include a gym, a weight room, playing fields, tennis, and racquetball courts. **Graduates:** From July 1, 2015 to June 30, 2016, 212 bachelor's degrees were awarded. The most popular majors were management (23%), psychology (21%), and accounting (15%). 5 companies recruited on campus in 2015-2016. In an average class, 27% graduate in 4 years or less, 52% graduate in 5 years or less, and 2% graduate in 6 years or less. Of the 2015 graduating class, 23% were enrolled in graduate school within 6 months of graduation, and 56% were employed.

SERVICES: Counseling and information services are available, as is tutoring in most subjects. There is remedial math, reading, and writing. **Library/Resources:** The library contains 75,000 volumes, 9,458 microform items, and 1,280 audio/video tapes/CDs/DVDs. Computerized library services include interlibrary loans, database searching, Internet access, and Wi-Fi capability. **Physically Challenged Students:** 95% of the campus is accessible. Facilities include wheelchair ramps, elevators, special parking, specially equipped restrooms, special class scheduling, lowered drinking fountains, lowered telephones, and special housing. **Special:** Pitt-Greensburg offers cross-registration with the Pittsburgh and Johnstown campuses of the university system and with Seton Hill College and Westmoreland County Community College. Internships are available in all majors and required for English writing and criminology. Double majors, student-designed majors, a Washington semester, nondegree study, and pass/fail options are available. There are 2 national honor societies and a chapter of Phi Beta Kappa. **Visiting:** There are regularly scheduled orientations for prospective students, including open house, preview day, and junior jump start, weekday visits that include campus tours and information sessions. There are guides for informal visits and visitors may sit in on classes. To schedule a visit, contact the Admissions Office. **Campus Safety and Security:** Measures include 24-hour foot and vehicle patrol and security escort services. There are also emergency telephones and lighted pathways/sidewalks.

REQUIREMENTS: The SAT is required. Students must be graduates of an accredited secondary school. The GED is also accepted. Students must complete 15 college-preparatory high school units, including 4 each of English and academic electives, 3 of a single foreign language (recommended), 2 of math, and 1 each of history and a lab science; additional units in all but English are recommended. An essay is optional; an interview is recommended. Students must also submit scores from the SAT or ACT (including the Writing test). GPA and class rank are also considered heavily. Pitt-Greensburg requires applicants to be in the upper 60% of their class. A GPA of 2.0 is required. AP and CLEP credits are accepted. Important factors in the admissions decision are advanced placement or honors courses, recommendations by school officials, and leadership record. To graduate, students must complete 120 to 126 hours, with 24 to 36 in the major, and maintain a minimum GPA of 2.0. General education requirements include 15 credits each in humanities, social sciences, and natural sciences, 6 to 15 in writing courses, 3 each in speech and critical reasoning, and 2 to 3 in math. **Procedure:** Freshmen are admitted in the fall and spring. Entrance exams should be taken by November. There are deferred admissions and rolling admissions plans. Application deadlines are open. The fall 2016 application fee was $35. Applications are accepted online. **Transfer Students:** 139 transfer students enrolled in 2015-2016. Applicants must have a minimum GPA of 2.0 and at least 12 college credits. 30 of 120 credits required for the bachelor's degree must be completed at Pitt-Greensburg. **International Students:** They must take the TOEFL.

ADMISSIONS: 90% of the 2016-2017 applicants were accepted. 22% of the current freshmen were in the top fifth of their class; 60% were in the top two fifths. **Admissions Contact:** Heather Kabala, Director of Admissions. Email: *upgadmit@pitt.edu* Web: *www.hlk3@pitt.edu*

FINANCIAL AID: In 2016-2017, 85% of all full-time freshmen and continuing full-time students received some form of financial aid. 67% of all full-time freshmen and continuing full-time students received need-based aid. The average freshman award was $7,200. Need-based scholarships or need-based grants averaged $4,000 ($9,050 maximum); need-based self-help aid (loans and jobs) averaged $5,700 ($5,700 maximum); and other non-need-based awards and non-need-based scholarships averaged $3,000 ($5,000 maximum). 10% of undergraduate students work part-time. Average annual earnings from campus work are $2250. The average financial indebtedness of the 2016 graduate was $17,000. The college's own financial statement is required. The priority date for freshman financial aid applications for fall entry is March 1. The filing deadline for fall entry is April 1.

UNIVERSITY OF PITTSBURGH AT JOHNSTOWN — C-3

www.upj.pitt.edu

Johnstown, PA 15904	**(814) 269-7050** **(800) 765-4875**
Fax: (814) 269-7044	**Email: upjadmit@pitt.edu**
Full-time: 1528 men, 1295 women	**Faculty:** n/av
Part-time: 60 men, 49 women	**Ph.D.s:** 68%
Graduate: n/av	**Student/Faculty:** n/av
Year: semesters, summer session	**Tuition:** $12,892 ($23,288)
Room & Board: $9200	**Freshman Class:** 1570 applied, 1419 accepted, 772 enrolled
SAT CR/M/W: 505/520/500 **ACT:** required	**CEEB CODE:** 2934
Application Deadline: n/av	**COMPETITIVE**

University of Pittsburgh at Johnstown is a public institution offering programs in arts and sciences, education, engineering technology, and nursing. There is 1 undergraduate school. In addition to regional accreditation, UPJ has baccalaureate program accreditation with ABET. The 650-acre campus is in a suburban area 70 miles east of Pittsburgh. Including any residence halls, there are 35 buildings.

STUDENT LIFE: 98% of undergraduates are from Pennsylvania. Others are from 14 states, and 12 foreign countries. 88% are White; 3% African American; 1% Asian American; 1% Hispanic. **Male To Female Ratio:** 1.2:1. The average age of freshmen is 18; all undergraduates, 20. 27% do not continue beyond their first year; 55% remain to graduate. **Housing:** 1700 students can be accommodated in college housing, which includes coed dorms, on-campus apartments, off-campus apartments, special-interest houses, and clubs and organizations that provide housing. On-campus housing is guaranteed for all 4 years. 56% of students live on campus; of those, 65% remain on campus on weekends. All students may keep cars.

FACULTY/CLASSROOMS: 63% of faculty are male; 37% are female. All teach undergraduates. No introductory courses are taught by graduate students. The average class size in an introductory lecture is 25; in a laboratory is 18; and in a regular course is 25.

PROGRAMS OF STUDY: UPJ confers B.A., and B.S. degrees. Associate degrees are also awarded. Bachelor's degrees are awarded in AGRICULTURE (environmental studies), BIOLOGICAL SCIENCE (biology/biological science), BUSINESS (accounting, banking and finance, business administration and management, and business economics), COMMUNICATIONS AND THE ARTS (communications, creative writing, dramatic arts, English, and journalism), COMPUTER AND PHYSICAL SCIENCE (chemistry, computer science, geology, and mathematics), EDUCATION (elementary education, English education, mathematics education, science education, secondary education, and social science education), ENGINEERING AND ENVIRONMENTAL DESIGN (civil engineering technology, computer engineering, electrical/electronics engineering technology, and mechanical engineering technology), HEALTH PROFESSIONS (medical laboratory technology and nursing), SOCIAL SCIENCE (American studies, criminal justice, economics, geography, history, humanities, political science/government, psychology, social science, and sociology). Business, education, and biology have the largest enrollments.

ACTIVITIES: 7% of men belong to 5 national fraternities; 7% of women belong to 3 national sororities. There are 85 groups on campus, including band, cheerleading, choir, chorus, computers, dance, drama, environmental, ethnic, honors, LGBT, literary magazine, musical theater, newspaper, political, professional, radio and TV, religious, social, social service, student government, symphony, and yearbook. Popular campus events include Spring Concert, Pitt Fest, and Sephia Fashion Show. **Sports:** There are 7 intercollegiate sports for men and 7 for women, and 11 intramural sports for men and 11 for women. Facilities include a gym, pool, dance studio, weight room, cross-country track, basketball courts, and a nature area. **Graduates:** From July 1, 2015 to June 30, 2016, 494 bachelor's degrees were awarded. The most popular majors were business marketing (27%), education (16%), and engineering technologies (10%). In an average class, 63% graduate in 6 years or less.

SERVICES: Counseling and information services are available, as is tutoring in most subjects. There is also a reader service for the blind and remedial math. **Library/Resources:** Computerized library services include interlibrary loans, database searching, and Internet access. Special learning facilities include an art gallery, radio station, and TV station. **Physically Challenged Students:** 80% of the campus is accessible. Facilities include elevators, special parking, specially equipped restrooms, special class scheduling, lowered drinking fountains, lowered telephones, and special housing. **Special:** Students may cross-register with schools in the Pittsburgh Council for Higher Education, and internships are available both on and off campus. The school offers study abroad, work-study programs, accelerated degree programs, dual majors, student-designed majors, nondegree study, and pass/fail options. There are 10 national honor societies. **Visiting:** There are regularly scheduled orientations for prospective students, including 5 programs held on saturdays in the fall, 2 saturdays in the spring, 3 fridays in the spring, and 4 fridays in the summer. There are guides for informal visits, visitors may sit in on classes, and stay overnight. To schedule a visit, contact the Admissions Office. **Campus Safety and Security:** Measures include 24-hour foot and vehicle patrol, emergency notification system, self-defense education, and security escort services. There are also shuttle buses, emergency telephones, and lighted pathways/sidewalks.

REQUIREMENTS: The SAT or ACT is required. Applicants must be graduates of an accredited secondary school. The GED is accepted. For first time freshman admission, 15 academic credits are required, including 4 of English, 3 of math (2 of algebra, 1 of geometry preferred), 2 of foreign language, 1 to 2 of lab science, 1 of social science, and electives. Engineering students must have completed chemistry, physics, and trigonometry. An interview is recommended, and an essay is highly recommended. AP credits are accepted. Important factors in the admissions decision are advanced placement or honors courses, leadership record, and recommendations by school officials. To graduate, students must complete 120 to 139 credits, with 30 to 36 credits in the major and a minimum GPA of 2.0. The school requires a core set of general education courses to include 12 credits each in humanities, natural sciences, and social sciences. **Procedure:** Freshmen are admitted to all sessions. Entrance exams should be taken between April and June of the junior year or by November of the senior year. There are early admissions, deferred admissions, and rolling admissions plans. Application deadlines are open. Application fee is $45. Notification is sent on a rolling basis. **Transfer Students:** 84 transfer students enrolled in 2015-2016. Students wishing to transfer must have a minimum GPA of 2.5 and at least 15 credit hours earned. The SAT or ACT is required. Grades of C or better transfer for credit. 30 of 120 credits required for the bachelor's degree must be completed at UPJ. **International Students:** They must take the

TOEFL with a minimum score of 550 on the paper-based TOEFL (PBT) or 80 on the Internet-based version (iBT). The SAT may be required for some students.

ADMISSIONS: 90% of the 2016-2017 applicants were accepted. The SAT scores for the 2016-2017 freshman class were: Critical Reading-- 50% below 500, 41% between 500 and 599, 8% between 600 and 699, and 1% between 700 and 800. Math-- 41% below 500, 43% between 500 and 599, 15% between 600 and 699, and 1% between 700 and 800. Writing-- 55% below 500, 38% between 500 and 599, 6% between 600 and 699, and 1% between 700 and 800. The ACT scores were 52% below 12, 36% between 12 and 17, 10% between 18 and 23, 1% between 24 and 29, and 1% above 30. 35% of the current freshmen were in the top fifth of their class; 73% were in the top two fifths. **Admissions Contact:** Therese Grimes, Director of Admissions. Email: *upjadmit@pitt.edu* Web: *www.upj.pitt.edu*

FINANCIAL AID: In 2016-2017, 85% of all full-time freshmen and 84% of continuing full-time students received some form of financial aid. 54% of all full-time freshmen and 55% of continuing full-time students received need-based aid. The average freshman award was $12,574. Need-based scholarships or need-based grants averaged $6,362; need-based self-help aid (loans and jobs) averaged $5,429; non-need-based athletic scholarships averaged $4,863; and other non-need-based awards and non-need-based scholarships averaged $4,984. The average financial indebtedness of the 2016 graduate was $26,526. The deadline for filing freshman financial aid applications for fall entry is April 1.

UNIVERSITY OF SCRANTON — E-2

www.scranton.edu

Scranton, PA 18510	**(570) 941-7540** **(888) SCRANTON**
Fax: (570) 941-5928	**Email: admissions@scranton.edu**
Full-time: 1735 men, 2112 women	**Faculty:** IIA, +$
Part-time: 88 men, 106 women	**Ph.D.s:** 85%
Graduate: 755 men, 1102 women	**Student/Faculty:** n/av
Year: semesters, summer session	**Tuition:** $41,044
Room & Board: $13,918	**Freshman Class:** 9672 applied, 6655 accepted, 971 enrolled
SAT or ACT: required	**CEEB CODE:** 2929
Application Deadline: March 1	**VERY COMPETITIVE**

University of Scranton, founded in 1888, is a private institution operated by the Jesuit order of the Roman Catholic Church. It offers programs in business, behavioral sciences, education, health science, humanities, math, science, and social science. Figures in the above capsule and in this profile are approximate. There are 4 undergraduate schools and 1 graduate school. In addition to regional accreditation, the University has baccalaureate program accreditation with AACSB, ABET, APTA, CSAB, NCATE, NLN, ACOTE, CCNE, and CACREP. The 58-acre campus is in an urban area 125 miles north of Philadelphia. Including any residence halls, there are 67 buildings.

STUDENT LIFE: 60% of undergraduates are from out of state, mostly the Middle Atlantic. Students are from 24 states, and 12 foreign countries. 81% are White; 7% Hispanic; 6% race unknown; 3% Asian American; 2% African American; 2% two or more races. 75% are Catholic. **Female To Male Ratio:** 1.3:1. The average age of freshmen is 19; all undergraduates, 21. 12% do not continue beyond their first year; 83% remain to graduate. **Housing:** 2647 students can be accommodated in college housing, which includes single-sex and coed dorms, on-campus apartments, off-campus apartments, and special-interest houses. On-campus housing is guaranteed for all 4 years. 64% of students live on campus; of those, 80% remain on campus on weekends. Upperclassmen may keep cars.

FACULTY/CLASSROOMS: 59% of faculty are male; 41% are female. No introductory courses are taught by graduate students. The average class size in a regular course is 20.

PROGRAMS OF STUDY: Scranton confers B.A., and B.S., degrees. Associate, master's, and doctoral degrees are also awarded. Bachelor's degrees are awarded in BIOLOGICAL SCIENCE (biochemistry, biology/biological science, biomathematics, biophysics, and neurosciences), BUSINESS (accounting, banking and finance, business administration and management, business economics, electronic business, human resources, information & communication technology, international business management, marketing/retailing/merchandising, and operations management), COMMUNICATIONS AND THE ARTS (communications, English, French, German, Greek, Latin, Spanish, and theatre arts), COMPUTER AND PHYSICAL SCIENCE (chemistry, computer science, information sciences and systems, mathematics, and physics), EDUCATION (early childhood education, elementary education, and secondary education), ENGINEERING AND ENVIRONMENTAL DESIGN (computer engineering, electrical/electronics engineering, and environmental science), HEALTH PROFESSIONS (community health work, exercise science, health care administration, medical laboratory technology, nursing, and occupational therapy), SOCIAL SCIENCE (criminal justice, economics, forensic studies, history, human services, international studies, philosophy, political science/government, psychology, sociology, theological studies, and women's studies). Chemistry, biology, and nursing are the strongest academically. Biology, communication, and nursing have the largest enrollments.

ACTIVITIES: There are no fraternities or sororities. There are 80 groups on campus, including art, band, cheerleading, chess, choir, chorale, chorus, communications, computers, dance, debate, drama, environmental, ethnic, film, forensics, honors, international, jazz band, literary magazine, musical theater, newspaper, orchestra, photography, political, professional, radio and TV, religious, social, social service, student government, symphony, and yearbook. Popular campus events include Spring Fest, Senior Formal, Royal Ball, Shamrockin' Eve, IGNITE Leadershop Conference, and Relay for Life. **Sports:** There are 9 intercollegiate sports for men and 9 for women, and 20 intramural sports for men and 19 for women. Facilities include a gym, basketball courts, wrestling and weight, handball/racquetball and tennis, sand volleyball, soccer/lacrosse field, softball field, swimming pool, physical therapy room, a multipurpose gym, a fitness center, sauna and steamroom, and dance aerobics. **Graduates:** From July 1, 2015 to June 30, 2016, 902 bachelor's degrees were awarded. The most popular majors were business/marketing (21%), health professions/related sciences (15%), and biological/life sciences (11%). In an average class, 73% graduate in 4 years or less, 79% graduate in 5 years or less, and 80% graduate in 6 years or less. Of the 2015 graduating class, 55% were enrolled in graduate school within 6 months of graduation, and 40% were employed.

SERVICES: Counseling and information services are available, as is tutoring in most subjects. There is also a reader service for the blind, as well as time management, organizational skills, learning strategies, writing labs, math labs, and study skills. **Library/Resources:** The library contains 486,650 volumes, 26,241 microform items, and 21,285 audio/video tapes/CDs/DVDs, and subscribes to 75,198 periodicals including electronic. Computerized library services include interlibrary loans, database searching, Internet access, and Wi-Fi capability. Special learning facilities include a radio station, Hope Horn Gallery in Hyland Hall for paintings and sculpture, the Royal Theater and a studio theater in the McDade Center for Literary and Performing Arts for University Players productions, television studio and broadcast FM-radio station, performance hall in the Houlihan-McLean Center, and the Institute of Molecular Biology and Medicine offering proteomics, and genomics and PCR equipment. **Physically Challenged Students:** All of the campus is accessible. Facilities include wheelchair ramps, elevators, special parking, specially equipped restrooms, special class scheduling, lowered drinking fountains, lowered telephones, and special housing. **Special:** Honors, Business Leadership Honors & Special Jesuit Liberal Arts Honors Programs, first-year experience courses, service learning, faculty/student research, independent study, internships, study abroad in over 60 countries, cross registration, IB/AP/College Credit and Washington Center. The university also offers dual, student-designed, and interdisciplinary majors, including chemistry-business, chemistry-computers, electronics-business, and international language-business, credit by exam and for life/military/work experience, work-study, nondegree study, and pass/fail options. There are 32 national honor societies. **Visiting:** There are regularly scheduled orientations for prospective students, group information sessions and tours that are available most weekdays and Saturdays throughout the year. There are also personal appointments available with admissions counselors by appointment. There are guides for informal visits and visitors may sit in on classes. To schedule a visit, contact the Office of Admissions. **Campus Safety and Security:** Measures include 24-hour foot and vehicle patrol, emergency notification system, self-defense education, and security escort services. There are also emergency telephones, lighted pathways/sidewalks, and controlled access to dorms/residences.

REQUIREMENTS: The SAT or ACT is required. Applicants should be

graduates of an accredited secondary school, in some cases a GED may be accepted. Student should have completed 18 academic or Carnegie units, including 4 years of high school English, 3 each of math, science, history, and social studies, and 2 of foreign language, and 2 letters of reference/recommendation are required. Essays are required. AP and CLEP credits are accepted. Important factors in the admissions decision are advanced placement or honors courses, leadership record, and extracurricular activities record. Students take general education requirements according to their area of study. All are required to take philosophy/theology, phys ed, English composition, speech, and computer literacy. The minimum GPA is 2.0, although some majors require a higher GPA. **Procedure:** Freshmen are admitted in the fall and spring. Entrance exams should be taken by fall of the senior year. There are deferred admissions and rolling admissions plans. Applications should be filed by March 1 for fall entry; December 15 for spring entry; and May 1 for summer entry. Notifications are sent December 15. 1087 applicants were on the 2016 waiting list; 57 were admitted. Applications are accepted online. **Transfer Students:** 89 transfer students enrolled in 2015-2016. Applicants should have earned a GPA of at least 2.5. 60 of 130 credits required for the bachelor's degree must be completed at the University. **International Students:** There are 40 international students enrolled. The school actively recruits these students. They must take the TOEFL with a minimum score of 500 on the paper-based TOEFL (PBT) or 61 on the Internet-based version (iBT).

ADMISSIONS: 69% of the 2016-2017 applicants were accepted. The SAT scores for the 2016-2017 freshman class were: Critical Reading-- 15% below 500, 56% between 500 and 599, 25% between 600 and 699, and 4% between 700 and 800. Math-- 12% below 500, 51% between 500 and 599, 31% between 600 and 699, and 5% between 700 and 800. 11 freshmen graduated first in their class. **Admissions Contact:** Joseph M. Roback, Associate Vice Provost for Admissions and Enrollment. Email: *admissions@scranton.edu* Web: *www.scranton.edu*

FINANCIAL AID: In 2016-2017, 90% of all full-time freshmen and 89% of continuing full-time students received some form of financial aid. 69% of all full-time freshmen and 66% of continuing full-time students received need-based aid. The average freshman award was $25,338. Scranton is a member of CSS. The FAFSA code is 003384. The priority date for freshman financial aid applications for fall entry is February 15.

UNIVERSITY OF THE ARTS *(The complete profile is made available exclusively on our website, www.barronspac.com)*

UNIVERSITY OF THE SCIENCES F-3

www.usciences.edu

Philadelphia, PA 19104	**(215) 596-8815** **(888) 996-8747**
Fax: (215) 596-8821	**Email: admit@usciences.edu**
Full-time: 927 men, 1474 women	**Faculty:** 182
Part-time: 12 men, 25 women	**Ph.D.s:** 84%
Graduate: 146 men, 196 women	**Student/Faculty:** 10 to 1
Year: semesters, summer session	**Tuition:** $38,850
Room & Board: $15,188	**Freshman Class:** 4099 applied, 2500 accepted, 440 enrolled
SAT CR/M/W: 557/603/567 **ACT:** 25	**CEEB CODE:** 2663
Application Deadline: n/av	**VERY COMPETITIVE**

University of the Sciences, the institution was established in 1821, as America's first pharmacy college, The Philadelphia College of Pharmacy. Today, USciences continues to build on that esteemed reputation and is home to 25 undergraduate and 25 graduate programs. Our students have enrolled in our premier programs in the health sciences, ranging from pharmacy to pre-med to healthcare business, and health policy. There are 5 undergraduate schools and 4 graduate schools. In addition to regional accreditation, Usciences has baccalaureate program accreditation with ACBSP, ACPE, APTA, ACOTE, ACS, ARC-PA, CAPTE, and NAACLS. The 35-acre campus is in an urban area in the heart of University City. Including any residence halls, there are 23 buildings.

STUDENT LIFE: 58% of undergraduates are from out of state, mostly the Middle Atlantic. Students are from 40 states, 19 foreign countries, and Canada. 7% are race unknown; 5% African American; 46% White; 36% Asian American; 2% Hispanic; 2% Foreign; 2% two or more races. **Female To Male Ratio:** 1.6:1. The average age of freshmen is 18; all undergraduates, 21. 12% do not continue beyond their first year; 80% remain to graduate. **Housing:** 768 students can be accommodated in college housing, which includes coed dorms, on-campus apartments, and honors houses. On-campus housing is available on a first come, first served basis, and on a lottery system for upperclassmen. Priority is given to out of town students. 71% of students commute. Upperclassmen may keep cars. Alcohol is not permitted.

FACULTY/CLASSROOMS: 46% of faculty are male; 54% are female. 99% teach undergraduates. No introductory courses are taught by graduate students. The average class size in an introductory lecture is 100; in a laboratory is 28; and in a regular course is 25.

PROGRAMS OF STUDY: Usciences confers B.S., and B.S.H.S. degrees. Master's and doctoral degrees are also awarded. Bachelor's degrees are awarded in BIOLOGICAL SCIENCE (biochemistry, bioinformatics, biology/biological science, microbiology, and toxicology), BUSINESS (marketing management and recreational facilities management), COMPUTER AND PHYSICAL SCIENCE (chemistry, computer science, and physics), ENGINEERING AND ENVIRONMENTAL DESIGN (environmental science), HEALTH PROFESSIONS (health science, medical technology, mental health/human services, occupational therapy, pharmaceutical chemistry, pharmaceutical science, pharmacology, pharmacy, physical therapy, and physician's assistant), SOCIAL SCIENCE (humanities and social science, interdisciplinary studies, and psychology). Pharmacy, physical therapy, and physician assistant studies are the strongest academically. Pharmacy, physical therapy, and biology have the largest enrollments.

ACTIVITIES: 7% of women belong to 3 local and 5 national sororities. There are 83 groups on campus, including drama, band, cheerleading, chess, chorale, chorus, computers, dance, drama, ethnic, honors, international, LGBT, literary magazine, martial arts, musical theater, newspaper, orchestra, political, professional, religious, social, social service, and student government. Popular campus events include Student Appreciation Weekend, Founder's Day, Usciences Scholarly Day, and Convocation. **Sports:** There are 6 intercollegiate sports for men and 7 for women, and 5 intramural sports for men and 5 for women. Facilities include an indoor track, gym, baseball, basketball, cross country, golf, volleyball, rifle range, field hockey, tennis courts, softball field, and a jogging path. **Graduates:** From July 1, 2015 to June 30, 2016, 453 bachelor's degrees were awarded. The most popular majors were pharmacy (41%), physical therapy/occup. and health science (32%), and biology (5%). 150 companies recruited on campus in 2015-2016. In an average class, 65% graduate in 4 years or less, 79% graduate in 5 years or less, and 80% graduate in 6 years or less. Of the 2015 graduating class, 14% were enrolled in graduate school within 6 months of graduation, and 74% were employed.

SERVICES: Counseling and information services are available, as is tutoring in every subject, and remedial math and writing. **Library/Resources:** The library contains 82,380 volumes, 24,485 microform items, and 1,790 audio/video tapes/CDs/DVDs, and subscribes to 22,634 periodicals including electronic. Computerized library services include interlibrary loans, database searching, Internet access, and Wi-Fi capability. **Physically Challenged Students:** 90% of the campus is accessible. Facilities include wheelchair ramps, elevators, special parking, specially equipped restrooms, and special class scheduling. **Special:** USciences offers 5- and 6-year integrated professional programs in occupational therapy, physical therapy, and physician's assistant studies. Internships are required in all health science disciplines. Study abroad is available in Asia, Africa, and Europe through the NYU study abroad program. A 1-year undeclared major program is offered, a program of curriculum, and advisement to prepare students to enter medical school. Students may elect dual majors or a minor in communications, economics, psychology, sociology, math, physics, computer science, biochemistry, biology, chemistry, forensic science, humanities, math, microbiology, social sciences, and writing. There are 5 national honor societies. **Visiting:** There are regularly scheduled orientations for prospective students. Student visits consist of summer open houses for rising seniors, campus day visits, campus tours, and meetings with faculty members. There are guides for informal visits and visitors may sit in on classes. To schedule a visit, contact the Admission Office. **Campus Safety and Security:** Measures include 24-hour foot and vehicle patrol, self-defense education, and security escort services. There are also shuttle buses, emergency telephones, lighted pathways/sidewalks, controlled access to dorms/residences, required key and student identification for dorm entry, and ID access only to campus buildings in the evenings.

REQUIREMENTS: The SAT or ACT is required. Applicants must be high school graduates or hold the GED. Minimum academic requirements include 4 credits in English, 1 credit each in American history and social science, and 4 credits in academic electives, math requirements include 2 years of algebra and 1 year of geometry. The university strongly recommends an additional year of higher-level math, such as pre-calculus or calculus. In addition, 3 science credits are required, and the university strongly recommends that students have 1 credit each in biology, chemistry, and physics. A strong background in English, science, and math is recommended. USciences requires applicants to be in the upper 50% of their class. AP and CLEP credits are accepted. Important factors in the admissions decision are extracurricular activities record, leadership record, and advanced placement or honors courses. Total credits required for graduation range from 120 to 210 depending on the major, with a 2.0 GPA for BS majors, and higher minimum GPA for professional programs and other specific programs. The core curriculum consists of 38 credits including 16 credits of natural science, 6 each of math, social sciences, communication, and an intellectual heritage sequence, 3 of literature, world culture, history, and advanced social sciences, and 1 of phys ed, along with 3 of electives. Students must pass a writing proficiency exam and demonstrate proficiency in computer applications. **Procedure:** Freshmen are admitted fall. Entrance exams should be taken by the end of the junior year or the fall of the senior year. There are early admissions, deferred admissions, and rolling admissions plans. Application deadlines are open. Application fee is $45. Notification is sent on a rolling basis. Applications are accepted on-line. Application fees are waived if application is completed online. **Transfer Students:** 117 transfer students enrolled in 2015-2016. To be considered, pharmacy and physical therapy applicants must present a minimum GPA of 3.0. All other majors must have at least a 2.7 GPA. All applicants must meet high school requirements as well. 51 credits required for the bachelor's degree must be completed at Usciences. **International Students:** There are 38 international students enrolled. They must take the TOEFL with a minimum score of 550 on the paper-based TOEFL (PBT) or 80 on the Internet-based version (iBT), and the college's own test. They must also take the SAT or ACT, scoring 1000.

ADMISSIONS: 61% of the 2016-2017 applicants were accepted. The SAT scores for the 2016-2017 freshman class were: Critical Reading-- 15% below 500, 61% between 500 and 599, 21% between 600 and 699, and 3% between 700 and 800. Math-- 6% below 500, 43% between 500 and 599, 40% between 600 and 699, and 11% between 700 and 800. Writing-- 16% below 500, 52% between 500 and 599, 26% between 600 and 699, and 6% between 700 and 800. The ACT scores were 3% below 12, 34% between 12 and 17, 31% between 18 and 23, 16% between 24 and 29, and 16% above 30. 71% of the current freshmen were in the top fifth of their class; 93% were in the top two fifths. 3 freshmen graduated first in their class. **Admissions Contact:** Dianna Collins, Executive Director of Admission and Enrollment Services. Email: *admit@usciences .edu* Web: *www.usciences.edu*

FINANCIAL AID: The FAFSA code is 003353. The priority date for freshman financial aid applications for fall entry is March 15. The filing deadline for fall entry is open.

URSINUS COLLEGE — E-3

www.ursinus.edu

Collegeville, PA 19426 — **(610) 409-3200**

Fax: (610) 409-3197	**Email: admission@ursinus.edu**
Full-time: 721 men, 821 women	**Faculty:** 121; IIB, av$
Part-time: 7 men, 7 women	**Ph.D.s:** 93%
Graduate: n/av	**Student/Faculty:** 11 to 1
Year: semesters	**Tuition:** $49,370
Room & Board: $12,320	**Freshman Class:** 2491 applied, 2053 accepted, 382 enrolled
SAT CR/M/W: 580/580/560 **ACT:** 26	**CEEB CODE:** 2931
Application Deadline: February 1	**VERY COMPETITIVE**

The mission of Ursinus College is to enable students to become independent, responsible, and thoughtful individuals through a program of liberal education, and prepares them to live creatively and usefully, and provide leadership for their society in an interdependent world. There is 1 undergraduate school. In addition to regional accreditation, Ursinus has baccalaureate program accreditation with ACS. The 170-acre campus is in a suburban area 25 miles west of Philadelphia. Including any residence halls, there are 65 buildings.

STUDENT LIFE: 56% of undergraduates are from Pennsylvania. Others are from 33 states, and 9 foreign countries. 67% are from public schools. 74% are White; 6% African American; 6% Hispanic; 4% Asian American; 3% Foreign; 3% two or more races; 3% race unknown; 1% American Indian/Alaska Native. **Female To Male Ratio:** 1.1:1. The average age of freshmen is 18; all undergraduates, 20. 12% do not continue beyond their first year; 79% remain to graduate. **Housing:** 1576 students can be accommodated in college housing, which includes single-sex and coed dorms, on-campus apartments, and off-campus apartments, and special-interest houses. On-campus housing is guaranteed for all 4 years. 95% of students live on campus; of those, 90% remain on campus on weekends. Upperclassmen may keep cars.

FACULTY/CLASSROOMS: 41% of faculty are male; 59% are female. All teach undergraduates and do research. No introductory courses are taught by graduate students.

PROGRAMS OF STUDY: Ursinus confers B.A., and B.S., degrees. Bachelor's degrees are awarded in BIOLOGICAL SCIENCE (biochemistry, biology/biological science, and neurosciences), BUSINESS (business economics), COMMUNICATIONS AND THE ARTS (art history, art, communications, dance, dramatic arts, English, French, German, music, and Spanish), COMPUTER AND PHYSICAL SCIENCE (chemistry, computer science, mathematics, and physics), ENGINEERING AND ENVIRONMENTAL DESIGN (environmental science), HEALTH PROFESSIONS (exercise science), SOCIAL SCIENCE (American studies, anthropology, East Asian studies, economics, history, international relations, philosophy, political science/government, psychology, religious studies, and sociology). Biology, chemistry, and history are the strongest academically. Biology, applied economics, and health & exercise physiology have the largest enrollments.

ACTIVITIES: 19% of men belong to 5 local and 4 national fraternities; 25% of women belong to 4 local and 1 national sororities. There are 100 groups on campus, including art, band, cheerleading, chess, choir, chorale, chorus, computers, dance, debate, drama, environmental, ethnic, film, forensics, honors, international, jazz band, LGBT, literary magazine, newspaper, pep band, photography, political, professional, radio and TV, religious, social, social service, student government, and yearbook. Popular campus events include Air Band Competition, Relay for Life, and Family Day. **Sports:** There are 12 intercollegiate sports for men and 13 for women. Facilities include a fitness center and weight room, indoor track, indoor tennis courts, a dance studio, basketball courts, wrestling room, swimming pool, squash, racquetball courts, and a gymnastics space. Outdoor athletic and recreational facilities include turf fields for football, soccer, lacrosse, track & field, field hockey, baseball, softball, cross-country, and tennis courts. **Graduates:** From July 1, 2015 to June 30, 2016, 367 bachelor's degrees were awarded. The most popular majors were biology/life sciences (31%), social sciences (20%), and psychology (10%). In an average class, 73% graduate in 4 years or less, 78% graduate in 5 years or less, and 78% graduate in 6 years or less.

SERVICES: Counseling and information services are available, as is tutoring in every subject, and a reader service for the blind. The college also provides appropriate services as-needed, including group tutoring is also available. **Library/Resources:** The library contains 387,800 volumes, 300 microform items, and 24,800 audio/video tapes/CDs/DVDs, and subscribes to 21,500 periodicals including electronic. Computerized library services include interlibrary loans, database searching, Internet access, and Wi-Fi capability. Special learning facilities include an art gallery, planetarium, radio station, TV station, and an observatory. **Physically Challenged Students:** 95% of the campus is accessible. Facilities include wheelchair ramps, elevators, special parking, specially equipped restrooms, special class scheduling, lowered drinking fountains, lowered telephones, and special housing. **Special:** The college offers study abroad, student-designed majors, internships, a Washington semester, dual majors, and a 3-2 engineering degree with Columbia University. There are 16 national honor societies, Phi Beta Kappa, and 29 departmental honors programs. **Visiting:** There are regularly scheduled orientations for prospective students, including a campus interview and a tour. There are guides for informal visits, visitors may sit in on classes, and stay overnight. To schedule a visit, contact Office of Admission. **Campus Safety and Security:** Measures include 24-hour foot and vehicle patrol, emergency notification system, self-defense education, and security escort services. There are also emergency telephones and lighted pathways/sidewalks.

REQUIREMENTS: The SAT or ACT, and ACT Writing Test, and SAT Subject Tests are recommended. Applicants should prepare with 16 academic credits, including 4 years of English, 3 of math, 2 of foreign language, and 1 each of science and social studies. An interview is recommended. Following are the exceptions for which applicants must submit testing results: students applying for our Early Assurance program to medical school in cooperation with the Drexel University School of Medicine are required to submit SAT Reasoning Test (preferred) or ACT score results. To be considered for the Early Assurance program, applicants must meet the November 15 submission deadline and achieve at least a minimal SAT Critical Reading and Mathematics combined score of 1300 with no subset less than 560 (the Writing section of the SAT test is not included); or an ACT composite score of 31. Homeschooled students and students who attend schools that provide narrative comments in lieu of grades are required to submit results from one or more standardized tests (SAT Reasoning Test, SAT Subject Tests, or ACT). AP credits are accepted. Important factors in the admissions decision are advanced placement or honors courses, recommendations by school officials, and leadership record. All students must fulfill requirements in the common intellectual experience, math or logic, foreign language, humanities, social science, natural science plus a lab, and an independent learning experience. A total of 128 semester hours, with 32 to 40 in the major, is required, as is a GPA of at least 2.0. A new core curriculum is under development for implementation beginning with the fall 2017 incoming first year students. **Procedure:** Freshmen are admitted in the fall and spring. Entrance exams should be taken in the junior or senior year. There are early decision, deferred admissions, and rolling admissions plans. Early decision applications should be filed by December 1; regular applications, by February 1 for fall entry; and December 1 for spring entry. Applications are accepted online. **Transfer Students:** Transfer applicants must submit transcripts from all institutions attended. 64 of 128 credits required for the bachelor's degree must be completed at Ursinus. **International Students:** There are 40 international students enrolled. The school actively recruits these students. They must take the TOEFL with a minimum score of 80 on the Internet-based version (iBT). They must also take the SAT.

ADMISSIONS: 82% of the 2016-2017 applicants were accepted. 42% of the current freshmen were in the top fifth of their class; 79% were in the top two fifths. **Admissions Contact:** Scott Myers, Director of Admission. Email: *smyer@ursinus.edu* Web: *www.ursinus.edu*

FINANCIAL AID: In 2016-2017, 99% of all full-time freshmen received some form of financial aid. Ursinus is a member of CSS. The CSS/Profile is required. The FAFSA code is 003385. The deadline for filing freshman financial aid applications for fall entry is February 15.

VILLANOVA UNIVERSITY — E-3

www.villanova.edu

Villanova, PA 19085 — **(610) 519-4000**

Fax: (610) 519-6450	**Email: gotovu@villanova.edu**
Full-time: 3055 men, 3435 women	**Faculty:** IIA, ++$
Part-time: 218 men, 291 women	**Ph.D.s:** 84%
Graduate: 1917 men, 1926 women	**Student/Faculty:** 12 to 1
Year: semesters, summer session	**Tuition:** $49,430
Room & Board: $13,093	**Freshman Class:** 17272 applied, 7514 accepted, 1678 enrolled
SAT CR/M/W: 650/670/650 **ACT:** 31	**CEEB CODE:** 2959
Application Deadline: January 15	**MOST COMPETITIVE**

Villanova University, founded in 1842, is an Augustinian Catholic institution whose intellectual tradition has been the cornerstone of an academic community that teaches students to think critically, act compassionately and succeed while serving others. The University's six colleges include the College of Liberal Arts and Sciences, the Villanova School of Business, the College of Engineering, the College of Nursing, the College of Professional Studies and the Villanova University Charles Widger School of Law. As students grow intellectually, Villanova prepares them to become ethical leaders who create positive change everywhere life takes them. There are 4 undergraduate schools and 6 graduate schools. In addition to regional accreditation, Villanova has baccalaureate program accreditation with AACSB, ABET, NLN, and ABA. The 260-acre campus is in a suburban area 12 miles west of Philadelphia. Including any residence halls, there are 69 buildings.

STUDENT LIFE: 78% of undergraduates are from out of state, mostly the Middle Atlantic. Students are from 45 states, 49 foreign countries, and Canada. 52% are from public schools. 74% are White; 7% Asian American; 7% Hispanic; 5% African American; 2% Foreign; 2% two or more races; 2% race unknown. 70% are Catholic; 12% Protestant. **Female To Male Ratio:** 1.1:1. The average age of freshmen is 18; all undergraduates, 21. 5% do not continue beyond their first year; 90% remain to graduate. **Housing:** 4500 students can be accommodated in college housing, which includes single-sex and coed dorms and on-campus apartments. In addition, there are honors houses, learning communities for freshmen, a special sophomore residence hall, a service learning community, and a 24-hour quiet study hall. On-campus housing is available on a lottery system for upperclassmen. 66% of students live on campus; of those, 85% remain on campus on weekends. Upperclassmen may keep cars.

FACULTY/CLASSROOMS: 60% of faculty are male; 40% are female. 90% teach undergraduates, 74% do research, and 74% do both. Graduate students teach 1% of introductory courses. The average class size in a regular course is 22.

PROGRAMS OF STUDY: Villanova confers B.A., B.S., B.B.A., B.S.N. and B.I.S. degrees. Associate, master's, and doctoral degrees are also awarded. Bachelor's degrees are awarded in AGRICULTURE (environmental studies), BIOLOGICAL SCIENCE (biochemistry and biology/biological science), BUSINESS (accounting, banking and finance, business administration and management, business economics, finance, international business management, management information systems, management, marketing/retailing/merchandising, and real estate), COMMUNICATIONS AND THE ARTS (art history and appreciation, classics, communications, English, French, Italian, and Spanish), COMPUTER AND PHYSICAL SCIENCE (astronomy, astrophysics, chemistry, computer science, information sciences and systems, mathematics, physics, science, and statistics), EDUCATION (secondary education), ENGINEERING AND ENVIRONMENTAL DESIGN (chemical engineering, civil engineering, computer engineering, electrical/electronics engineering, environmental science, and mechanical engineering), HEALTH PROFESSIONS (nursing), SOCIAL SCIENCE (behavioral science, cognitive science, criminal justice, crosscultural studies, economics, gender studies, geography, history, humanities, interdisciplinary studies, Latin American studies, liberal arts/general studies, philosophy, political science/government, psychology, religion, sociology, and theological studies). Nursing, engineering, and business have the largest enrollments.

ACTIVITIES: 15% of men belong to 13 national fraternities; 39% of women belong to 14 national sororities. There are 265 groups on campus, including day of service, multicultural, service and advocacy, art, band, cheerleading, choir, chorale, chorus, communications, computers, dance, debate, drama, drill team, environmental, ethnic, film, forensics, honors, international, jazz band, LGBT, literary magazine, marching band, musical theater, newspaper, pep band, photography, political, professional, radio and TV, religious, social, social service, student government, university service blue key ambassadors, special olympics, and yearbook. Popular campus events include Special Olympics, Hoops Mania, and Diwahni, Diwali, and Holi. **Sports:** There are 11 intercollegiate sports for men and 13 for women, and 11 intramural sports for men and 11 for women. Facilities include an outdoor track, swimming pool, weight rooms, field house, basketball, and volleyball courts, softball field, soccer fields, tennis courts, football stadium, and soccer complex. **Graduates:** From July 1, 2015 to June 30, 2016, 1770 bachelor's degrees were awarded. The most popular majors were business/marketing (31%), social sciences (12%), and engineering (11%). 260 companies recruited on campus in 2015-2016. In an average class, 86% graduate in 4 years or less, 90% graduate in 5 years or less, and 90% graduate in 6 years or less.

SERVICES: Counseling and information services are available, as is tutoring in some subjects, and a reader service for the blind. Tutoring is open to all students, and is not particular to students with disabilities. Some tutoring is offered through individual departments and colleges for first, and second year courses. There is also a writing center and math center for all students. Study skills and academic coaching is available to all students. **Library/Resources:** The 2 libraries contain 940,000 volumes, 10,000 microform items, 5,700 audio/video tapes/CDs/DVDs, and subscribe to 12,000 periodicals including electronic. Computerized library services include interlibrary loans, database searching, Internet access, and Wi-Fi capability. Special learning facilities include an art gallery, radio station, TV station, and an observatory. **Physically Challenged Students:** 90% of the campus is accessible. Facilities include wheelchair ramps, elevators, special parking, specially equipped restrooms, special class scheduling, lowered drinking fountains, and lowered telephones. There is also a specially equipped van for campus transportation, and proximity card readers for several buildings with automatic doors. **Special:** Internships are available for each college in the Philadelphia, area as well as in New York City, and Washington D.C. Students may study abroad worldwide. Villanova offers a Washington semester, an accelerated degree program in biology for allied health program, dual majors, a general studies degree, and credit by exam. There are 36 national honor societies, Phi Beta Kappa, and a freshman honors program. **Visiting:** There are regularly scheduled orientations for prospective students, consisting of group admission presentations, and campus tours are conducted throughout the year. There are guides for informal visits and visitors may sit in on classes. To schedule a visit, contact the Office of University Admission. **Campus Safety and Security:** Measures include 24-hour foot and vehicle patrol, emergency notification system, self-defense education, and security escort services. There are also shuttle buses, emergency telephones, lighted pathways/sidewalks, and controlled access to dorms/residences.

REQUIREMENTS: The SAT or ACT is required as is the ACT Optional Writing test is also required. Applicants must be graduates of an accredited secondary school, and should have completed 16 academic units. The specific courses required vary according to college. A GED is accepted. An essay is required. AP and CLEP credits are accepted. Important factors in the admissions decision are leadership record, advanced placement or honors courses, and evidence of special talent. All students are required to take core courses in humanities, Augustine and culture, social science, religious studies, natural sciences, philosophy, and math. Students must complete a minimum of 122 credit hours and achieve at least a 2.0 overall G.P.A. **Procedure:** Freshmen are admitted in the fall. Entrance exams should be taken by December of the senior year. There is a deferred admissions plan. Early decision applications should be filed by November 1; regular applications, by January 15 for fall entry. The fall 2016 application fee was $80. Notification of early decision is sent December 20; regular decision, April 1. 2677 applicants were on the 2016 waiting list; 26 were admitted. Applications are accepted on-line. **Transfer Students:** 182 transfer students enrolled in 2015-2016. 60 of 122 credits required for the bachelor's degree must be completed at Villanova. **International Students:** There are 111 international students enrolled. The school actively recruits these students. They must take the TOEFL with a minimum score of 550 on the paper-based TOEFL (PBT) or 85 on the Internet-based version (iBT). They must also take the SAT or ACT.

ADMISSIONS: The SAT scores for the 2016-2017 freshman class were: Critical Reading-- 3% below 500, 19% between 500 and 599, 52% between 600 and 699, and 25% between 700 and 800. Math-- 2% below 500, 15% between 500 and 599, 47% between 600 and 699, and 36% between 700 and 800. Writing-- 4% below 500, 20% between 500 and 599, 50% between 600 and 699, and 25% between 700 and 800. The ACT scores were 2% between 18 and 23, 23% between 24 and 29, and 75% above 30. **Admissions Contact:** Michael Gaynor, Director of Admission. Email: *gotovu@villanova.edu* Web: *www.villanova.edu*

FINANCIAL AID: In 2016-2017, 48% of all full-time freshmen and 47% of continuing full-time students received some form of financial aid. 44% of all full-time freshmen and continuing full-time students received need-based aid. The average freshman award was $35,801. Need-based scholarships or need-based grants averaged $31,433; need-based self-help aid (loans and jobs) averaged $5,922; non-need-based athletic scholarships averaged $44,836; and other non-need-based awards and non-need-based scholarships averaged $14,527. Villanova is a member of CSS. The CSS/Profile, state aid form, the college's own financial statement, and parent and student federal income tax returns and W2s are required. The FAFSA code is 003388. The priority date for freshman financial aid applications for fall entry is January 15. The filing deadline for fall entry is February 7.

WASHINGTON & JEFFERSON COLLEGE A-3

www.washjeff.edu

Washington, PA 15301 (724) 223-6025
(888) 926-3529

Fax: (724) 223-6534 **Email:** admission@washjeff.edu

Full-time: 709 men, 677 women	**Faculty:** 111; IIB, av$
Part-time: 5 men, 5 women	**Ph.D.s:** 95%
Graduate: 5 men, 5 women	**Student/Faculty:** 11 to 1
Year: 4-1-4, summer session	**Tuition:** $44,900
Room & Board: $11,612	**Freshman Class:** 7155 applied, 3258 accepted, 429 enrolled
SAT CR/M: 583/587 **ACT:** 26	**CEEB CODE:** 2967
Application Deadline: March 1	**VERY COMPETITIVE**

Washington & Jefferson College, founded in 1781, is a highly selective, residential, private liberal arts and sciences college. There is 1 undergraduate school and 1 graduate school. In addition to regional accreditation, W & J has baccalaureate program accreditation with ACS. The 60-acre campus is in a small town 27 miles southwest of Pittsburgh, PA. Including any residence halls, there are 53 buildings.

STUDENT LIFE: 73% of undergraduates are from Pennsylvania. Others are from 35 states, 29 foreign countries, and Canada. 84% are from public schools. 77% are White; 5% African American; 5% Foreign; 5% race unknown; 3% Hispanic; 3% two or more races; 2% Asian American. **Male To Female Ratio:** 1.0:1. The average age of freshmen is 18; all undergraduates, 19. 14% do not continue beyond their first year; 76% remain to graduate. **Housing:** 1396 students can be accommodated in college housing, which includes single-sex and coed dorms and on-campus apartments. In addition, there are special-interest houses, fraternity houses, sorority houses, on-campus suites, special housing for international students, wellness housing, green house, pet housing, quiet house, STEM house, and living learning community. On-campus housing is guaranteed for all 4 years. 95% of students live on campus; of those, 85% remain on campus on weekends. All students may keep cars.

FACULTY/CLASSROOMS: 55% of faculty are male; 45% are female. All teach undergraduates, and do research. No introductory courses are taught by graduate students. The average class size in an introductory lecture is 16; in a laboratory is 14; and in a regular course is 16.

PROGRAMS OF STUDY: W&J confers B.A. degrees. Master's degrees are also awarded. Bachelor's degrees are awarded in AGRICULTURE (environmental studies), BIOLOGICAL SCIENCE (biochemistry, biology/biological science, biophysics, cell biology, and neurosciences), BUSINESS (accounting, business administration and management, and international business management), COMMUNICATIONS AND THE ARTS (communication rhetoric/communication, English, French, German, music, Spanish, and studio art), COMPUTER AND PHYSICAL SCIENCE (chemistry, computer information technology, mathematics, and physics), EDUCATION (art education and education), ENGINEERING AND ENVIRONMENTAL DESIGN (environmental science), SOCIAL SCIENCE (economics, history, interdisciplinary studies, international studies, philosophy, political science/government, psychology, public affairs, and sociology). Biology, chemistry, and political science are the strongest academically. Business/accounting, psychology, and economics have the largest enrollments.

ACTIVITIES: 28% of men belong to 6 national fraternities; 29% of women belong to 4 national sororities. There are 81 groups on campus, including investment, yoga and zumba., young entrepreneurs society, art, band, cheerleading, choir, chorale, chorus, computers, dance, debate, drama, environmental, equestrian, ethnic, film, honors, international, jazz band, LGBT, literary magazine, musical theater, newspaper, pep band, photography, political, professional, radio and TV, religious, social, social service, student government, and yearbook. Popular campus events include International Week, Street Fair, Holiday Kick-off Week, Family Weekend, Welcome Week/Involvement Expo and the Spring Concert. **Sports:** There are 12 intercollegiate sports for men and 12 for women, and 19 intramural sports for men and 19 for women. Facilities include indoor track lanes, indoor multi-sport courts, yoga and exercise rooms, batting cages, a pole-vault pen, swimming and diving pools, an all-weather track, weight room, football, baseball, softball, soccer/lacrosse fields, basketball, volleyball, squash, racquetball, tennis courts, and fitness center. **Graduates:** From July 1, 2015 to June 30, 2016, 297 bachelor's degrees were awarded. The most popular majors were business administration/accounting (28%), psychology (10%), and economics (5%). 32 companies recruited on campus in 2015-2016. In an average class, 1% graduate in 3 years or less, 70% graduate in 4 years or less, 70% graduate in 5 years or less, and 76% graduate in 6 years or less. Of the 2015 graduating class, 38% were enrolled in graduate school within 6 months of graduation, and 85% were employed.

SERVICES: Counseling and information services are available, as is tutoring in most subjects, such as accounting, biology, chemistry, computing and information studies, economics, math (general and probability & statistics), modern languages (Chinese, French, German, Russian, Spanish), physics, psychology and writing. **Library/Resources:** The 4 libraries contain 190,358 volumes, 15,684 microform items, 5,726 audio/video tapes/CDs/DVDs, and subscribe to 46,670 periodicals including electronic. Computerized library services include interlibrary loans, database searching, Internet access, and Wi-Fi capability. Special learning facilities include an art gallery, radio station, biological field station, microplate reader, cell culture labs, isolator lab, X-ray diffraction unit, neuropsychology lab, atomic absorption unit, nuclear magnetic resonance lab, refrigerated centrifuge, global learning unit, language lab, spectrometers, and a laser, scanning confocal microscope facility. **Physically Challenged Students:** 90% of the campus is accessible. Facilities include wheelchair ramps, elevators, special parking, specially equipped restrooms, special class scheduling, lowered drinking fountains, and special housing. **Special:** The college offers semester-long off-campus study in Australia, Austria, Canada, Chile, China, Costa Rica, Ecuador and the Galapagos Islands, Egypt, France, Germany, Greece, Hong Kong, Ireland, Italy, Japan, Netherlands, Russia, South Africa, South Korea, Spain, United Kingdom and the United States. Internships as well as in all majors, are available dual and student-designed majors, credit by exam, and pass/fail options. Concentrations are offered in American studies, computational science, conflict and resolution studies, entrepreneurship, graphic design, professional writing and Russian area studies. Special programs are offered in education, biological physics, engineering, prelaw, ROTC and pre-health professions. The college also offers emphasis in economic development, entrepreneurship, film studies, financial economics, human resource management, public relations, rhetoric, theatre and thematic emphasis, computer science, digital media, interaction design, web and mobile technologies, and an emphasis in Big Data available to CIS majors. Students can take electives in Arabic, Chinese, earth and space science, physical activity and wellness, Russian, and interdisciplinary courses. There is a 3-3 law program with Duquesne University and the University of Pittsburgh, medicine program with Temple University School of Medicine, optometry program with Pennsylvania College of Optometry at Salus University, a physician assistant program, physical therapy program and an occupational therapy program at Chatham University. In addition, there is a 3-2 engineering program with Case Western Reserve University, Washington University and Columbia University. There is also a 3-4 program known as the Integrated Program in Human Health with the Sidney Kimmel Medical College at Thomas Jefferson University. A Washington semester is available with American University. W&J's proprietary Magellan Project provides financial support for students who wish to pursue summer internships or independent study abroad, making these opportunities available to every student. There are 22 national honor societies, Phi Beta Kappa, a freshman honors program, and 18 departmental honors programs. **Visiting:** There are regularly scheduled orientations for prospective students, student visits that include a general session, departmental meetings, preprofessional meetings, a financial aid meeting, and class scheduling. There are guides for informal visits, visitors may sit in on classes, and stay overnight. To schedule a visit, contact Hannah Aloia at (724) 223-6025. **Campus Safety and Security:** Measures include 24-hour foot and vehicle patrol, emergency notification system, self-defense education, and security escort services. There are emergency telephones, lighted pathways/sidewalks, controlled access to dorms/residences, and blue light emergency phones, and security cameras monitored 24/7.

REQUIREMENTS: The SAT or ACT is recommended. Applicants must complete 15 academic credits or Carnegie units, including 3 credits of English and math, 2 of foreign language, 1 of history, social science, or nautural science and 6 or more academic courses from the aforementioned areas. An essay is required and interviews are recommended. A GED is accepted. AP credits are accepted. Important factors in the admissions decision are advanced placement or honors courses, evidence of special talent, and personality/intangible qualities. Students must complete the general education requirement of at least 8 courses in 4 divisions. Other requirements include phys ed, first-year seminar, freshman composition, foreign language, cultural diversity, oral communication, quantitative reasoning, academic skills, and 8 to 10 elective courses. A total of 34 courses, with 8 to 10 courses in the major, is required for graduation, as is a 2.0 GPA. **Procedure:** Freshmen are admitted in the fall, winter, and spring. Entrance exams should be taken junior or senior year. There are early decision, early admissions, deferred admissions, and rolling admissions plans. Early decision applications should be filed by December 1; regular applications, by March 1 for fall entry; December 15 for winter entry; and January 15 for spring entry, along with a $25 fee. Notification of early decision is sent December 15; regular decision, April 1. 11 early decision candidates were accepted for the 2016-2017 class. 12 applicants were on the 2016 waiting list; 2 were admitted. Applications are accepted on-line. Application fees are waived if application is completed on-line. **Transfer Students:** 10 transfer students enrolled in 2015-2016. Transfer students are required to submit an official high school transcript with standardized test results from the SAT or ACT unless they are applying score optional. 64 of 136 credits required for the bachelor's degree must be completed at W & J. **International Students:** There are 69 international students enrolled. The school actively recruits these students. They must take the TOEFL with a minimum score of 563 on the paper-based TOEFL (PBT) or 85 on the Internet-based version (iBT).

ADMISSIONS: 46% of the 2016-2017 applicants were accepted. The SAT scores for the 2016-2017 freshman class were: Critical Reading-- 8% below 500, 52% between 500 and 599, 32% between 600 and 699, and 8% between 700 and 800. Math-- 9% below 500, 47% between 500 and 599, 39% between 600 and 699, and 5% between 700 and 800. The ACT scores were 1% between 12 and 17, 22% between 18 and 23, 55% between 24 and 29, and 22% above 30. 48% of the current freshmen were in the top fifth of their class; 80% were in the top two fifths. 10 freshmen graduated first in their class. **Admissions Contact:** Robert J. Gould, Vice President for Enrollment. Email: *admission@washjeff.edu* Web: *www.washjeff.edu*

FINANCIAL AID: In 2016-2017, 100% of all full-time freshmen and 99% of continuing full-time students received some form of financial aid. 72% of all full-time freshmen and 71% of continuing full-time students received need-based aid. The average freshman award was $35,900. Need-based scholarships or need-based grants averaged $6,821; need-based self-help aid (loans and jobs) averaged $3,231; and other non-need-based awards and non-need-based scholarships averaged $25,848. 44% of undergraduate students work part-time. Average annual earnings from campus work are $1100. The average financial indebtedness of the 2016 graduate was $27,248. The FAFSA code is 003389. The priority date for freshman financial aid applications for fall entry is February 15.

WAYNESBURG UNIVERSITY — B-4

www.waynesburg.edu

Waynesburg, PA 15370	**(724) 852-3216** **(800) 225-7393**
Fax: (724) 627-8124	**Email: admissions@waynesburg.edu**
Full-time: 558 men, 774 women	**Faculty:** 71; IIB, -$
Part-time: 11 men, 57 women	**Ph.D.s:** 67%
Graduate: 156 men, 249 women	**Student/Faculty:** 13 to 1
Year: semesters, summer session	**Tuition:** $22,800
Room & Board: $9490	**Freshman Class:** 1478 applied, 1385 accepted, 401 enrolled
SAT CR/M/W: required **ACT:** 22	**CEEB CODE:** 2969
Application Deadline: open	**COMPETITIVE**

Waynesburg University, founded in 1849 by the Cumberland Presbyterian Church, is a private, comprehensive Christian university offering doctoral, graduate and undergraduate programs in more than 70 academic concentrations. The University has three adult centers located in the Pittsburgh region. The University is a member of the Council for Christian Colleges and Universities and is 1 of only 27 schools in the country to offer the Bonner Scholarship that affords local, regional and international opportunities to touch the lives of others through service. There is 1 undergraduate school and 1 graduate school. In addition to regional accreditation, Waynesburg has baccalaureate program accreditation with TEAC, CCNE, CACREP, and IACBE. The 30-acre campus is in a small town in Waynesburg, 50 miles south of Pittsburgh. Including any residence halls, there are 40 buildings.

STUDENT LIFE: 83% of undergraduates are from Pennsylvania. Others

are from 32 states, and 2 foreign countries. 90% are from public schools. 90% are White; 5% African American; 2% two or more races; 1% Asian American; 1% Hispanic; 1% race unknown. 64% are Protestant; 19% Catholic; 16% 14 % Unknown, Agnostic, and Jehovah Witness. **Female To Male Ratio:** 1.5:1. The average age of freshmen is 18; all undergraduates, 21. 23% do not continue beyond their first year; 60% remain to graduate. **Housing:** 1045 students can be accommodated in college housing, which includes single-sex dorms. On-campus housing is guaranteed for all 4 years. 74% of students live on campus; of those, 54% remain on campus on weekends. Upperclassmen may keep cars. Alcohol is not permitted.

FACULTY/CLASSROOMS: 46% of faculty are male; 54% are female. No introductory courses are taught by graduate students. The average class size in a regular course is 17.

PROGRAMS OF STUDY: Waynesburg confers B.A., B.S., B.M.L., B.S.B.A., B.S.M.B. and B.S.N. degrees. Master's and doctoral degrees are also awarded. Bachelor's degrees are awarded in BIOLOGICAL SCIENCE (biology/biological science, forensic science, and marine biology), BUSINESS (accounting, entrepreneurial studies, finance, international business management, management science, and marketing/retailing/merchandising), COMMUNICATIONS AND THE ARTS (advertising, art, arts administration/management, broadcasting, communication rhetoric/communication, creative writing, English, graphic design, literature, multimedia, and public relations), COMPUTER AND PHYSICAL SCIENCE (chemistry, computer science, information sciences and systems, and mathematics), EDUCATION (athletic training, early childhood education, elementary education, middle school education, and special education), ENGINEERING AND ENVIRONMENTAL DESIGN (engineering and environmental science), HEALTH PROFESSIONS (exercise science, nursing, predentistry, premedicine, prephysical therapy, and preveterinary science), SOCIAL SCIENCE (biblical studies, criminal justice, history, human services, ministries, prelaw, psychology, social science, and sociology). Nursing, business, and communication are the strongest academically. Nursing, business, and criminal justice have the largest enrollments.

ACTIVITIES: There are no fraternities or sororities. There are 51 groups on campus, including band, cheerleading, choir, chorale, chorus, drama, environmental, ethnic, film, honors, jazz band, literary magazine, marching band, musical theater, newspaper, orchestra, pep band, photography, professional, radio and TV, religious, social, social service, student government, and yearbook. Popular campus events include Spring Weekend Formal, VIP Forum, and Fine Arts Series. **Sports:** There are 9 intercollegiate sports for men and 9 for women, and 7 intramural sports for men and 7 for women. Facilities include a stadium, gym, arena, fitness center, basketball and racquetball courts, wrestling and weight rooms, golf driving net, 3 all-weather tennis courts, and table tennis and billiards tables. **Graduates:** From July 1, 2015 to June 30, 2016, 345 bachelor's degrees were awarded. The most popular majors were registered nurse (25%), business administration (13%), and communication (11%). In an average class, 53% graduate in 4 years or less, 59% graduate in 5 years or less, and 60% graduate in 6 years or less.

SERVICES: Counseling and information services are available, as is tutoring in every subject, and remedial writing. **Library/Resources:** The library contains 219,782 volumes, and 7,083 audio/video tapes/CDs/DVDs. Computerized library services include interlibrary loans, database searching, and Internet access. Special learning facilities include an art gallery, natural history museum, radio station, and a TV station. **Physically Challenged Students:** 98% of the campus is accessible. Facilities include wheelchair ramps, elevators, special parking, specially equipped restrooms, special class scheduling, lowered drinking fountains, and special housing. **Special:** The college offers internships, an accelerated degree program in marketing and business management, dual majors, a student-designed interdisciplinary major, credit for experience, nondegree study, and pass/fail options. There is a 3-2 engineering degree program with Penn State University and a 3-1 in marine biology with Florida Institute of Technology or University of North Carolina Wilmington. A variety of study abroad experiences are available in countries around the world. There are 18 national honor societies and a freshman honors program. **Visiting:** There are regularly scheduled orientations for prospective students, including visits with faculty, students, administrators, and financial aid officers, and a tour of the campus. There are guides for informal visits, visitors may sit in on classes, and stay overnight. To schedule a visit, contact the Admissions Office. **Campus Safety and Security:** Measures include 24-hour foot and vehicle patrol, emergency notification system, and security escort services. There are emergency telephones, lighted pathways/sidewalks, and 24-hour security access.

REQUIREMENTS: The SAT or ACT is required. Applicants must be graduates of an accredited secondary school or have a GED certificate, and have completed 16 academic credits, including 4 in English, 3 in math, and 2 in sciences, history, or social studies. A GPA of 2.8 is required. AP and CLEP credits are accepted. Important factors in the admissions decision are advanced placement or honors courses, recommendations by school officials, and extracurricular activities record. To graduate, students must complete a minimum of 124 semester hours, including at least 30 in the major, with a minimum 2.0 GPA. Requirements include 15 credits of humanities and social and behavioral sciences, 8 of natural and physical sciences, 6 each of English and literature/arts, 3 credits each in math and computer science and 1 each of life skills, service learning, and Fiat Lux. Students must also pass an English usage and written competency test as well as a math test. **Procedure:** Freshmen are admitted in the fall, spring, and summer. Entrance exams should be taken in April of the junior year or December of the senior year. There is a rolling admissions plan. Application deadlines are open. Application fee is $20. Applications are accepted on-line. **Transfer Students:** 27 transfer students enrolled in 2015-2016. Students must submit a high school transcript and complete transcripts from all colleges previously attended. 45 of 124 credits required for the bachelor's degree must be completed at Waynesburg. **International Students:** There are 3 international students enrolled. The school actively recruits these students. They must take the TOEFL with a minimum score of 80 on the Internet-based version (iBT).

Admissions Contact: Jacquelin Palko, Director of Admissions. Email: *admissions@waynesburg.edu* Web: *www.waynesburg.edu*

FINANCIAL AID: In 2016-2017, 100% of all full-time freshmen and continuing full-time students received some form of financial aid. 90% of all full-time freshmen and continuing full-time students received need-based aid. The average freshman award was $21,500. Need-based scholarships or need-based grants averaged $1,600 ($9,500 maximum); need-based self-help aid (loans and jobs) averaged $7,000 ($11,000 maximum); and other non-need-based awards and non-need-based scholarships averaged $9,000 ($32,290 maximum). 24% of undergraduate students work part-time. Average annual earnings from campus work are $1500. The average financial indebtedness of the 2016 graduate was $30,000. The deadline for filing freshman financial aid applications for fall entry is rolling.

WEST CHESTER UNIVERSITY OF PENNSYLVANIA — E-3

www.wcupa.edu

West Chester, PA 19383	**(610) 436-3411** **(877) 315-2165**
Fax: (610) 436-2907	**Email: ugadmiss@wcupa.edu**
Full-time: 5149 men, 7675 women	**Faculty:** n/av
Part-time: 711 men, 863 women	**Ph.D.s:** n/av
Graduate: 783 men, 1825 women	**Student/Faculty:** n/av
Year: semesters, summer session	**Tuition:** $9720 ($20,812)
Room & Board: $8736	**Freshman Class:** 12609 applied, 8127 accepted, 2454 enrolled
SAT CR/M/W: 540/540/530 **ACT:** 24	**CEEB CODE:** 2959
Application Deadline: open	**COMPETITIVE**

West Chester University, founded in 1871, as a leading comprehensive university that excels in teacher education, business, health, natural and social sciences, music, and the arts. WCU is committed to high quality education at every level, and offers more than 180 undergraduate and graduate programs, through in-class instruction, hybrid models, and online options. There are 6 undergraduate schools and 5 graduate schools. In addition to regional accreditation, West Chester University has baccalaureate program accreditation with AACSB, ABET, CSWE, NASAD, NASM, NCATE, ACCME, ACS, AOSA, ASHA, CAAHEP, CAATE, CACREP, CADE, CCNE, CEPH, CoARC, FEPAC, EHAC, IRA, MSCHE, NAST, OAKE, and PDE. The 409-acre campus is in a suburban area 25 miles west of Philadelphia. Including any residence halls, there are 115 buildings.

STUDENT LIFE: 88% of undergraduates are from Pennsylvania. Others

are from 29 states, 70 foreign countries, and Canada. 85% are from public schools. 77% are White; 6% Hispanic; 3% two or more races; 2% Asian American; 11% African American; 1% race unknown. **Female To Male Ratio:** 1.6:1. The average age of freshmen is 18; all undergraduates, 21. 14% do not continue beyond their first year; 70% remain to graduate. **Housing:** 5146 students can be accommodated in college housing, which includes coed dorms and on-campus apartments. In addition, there are special-interest houses, international student sections, and housing for disabled students. On-campus housing is available on a first-come, first-served basis, and is available on a lottery system for upperclassmen. 60% of students commute. Alcohol is not permitted. Upperclassmen may keep cars.

FACULTY/CLASSROOMS: No introductory courses are taught by graduate students.

PROGRAMS OF STUDY: West Chester confers B.A., B.S., B.F.A., B.Mus., B.S.Ed., B.S.N. and B.S.W. degrees. Master's and doctoral degrees are also awarded. Bachelor's degrees are awarded in BIOLOGICAL SCIENCE (biology ecology and field biology, biochemistry, biology/biological science, biology/ gen science secondary education, cell biology, cell & molecular biology, environmental biology, marine science, microbiology, molecular biology, and nutrition), BUSINESS (accounting, banking and finance, business administration and management, business administration - international, business administration marketing, business economics, international business, business management, and marketing management), COMMUNICATIONS AND THE ARTS (applied music, art, communication studies, communications, dance, dramatic arts, English, English literature, English Writing, French, German, German studies, Germanic languages and literature, jazz, keyboard - piano concentration, Latin, literature, music, music history and appreciation, music performance, music theory and composition, musical theater, performing arts, piano performance, Russian, Russian languages and literature, Spanish, studio art, theatre arts, theater design, theatre production, theatre studies, theater management, visual and performing arts, vocal performance, voice, and vocal music education), COMPUTER AND PHYSICAL SCIENCE (actuarial mathematics, chemistry, chemistry/chemical biology, chemistry education, chemistry/ forensic chemistry, chemistry/gen science second education, chemistry secondary education, computer science, earth science, earth & space science, geoenvironmental studies, geology, geoscience, mathematics, mathematics - actuarial concentration, mathematics/computational, physics, and statistics), EDUCATION (athletic training, childhood education, early childhood education, elementary education, English secondary education, English education, health education, health and physical education, mathematics education, middle school education, music education, physical education, science education, secondary education, social studies education, special education, spec ed/early child dual prog, and special education/middle level education), ENGINEERING AND ENVIRONMENTAL DESIGN (engineering physics and urban planning technology), HEALTH PROFESSIONS (environmental health science, exercise science, health, health science, medical technology, nursing, pharmaceutical science, predentistry, premedicine, prephysical therapy, public health, respiratory therapy, speech pathology/ audiology, and sports medicine), SOCIAL SCIENCE (American studies, anthropology, communication sciences & disorders, criminal justice, dietetics, early childhood studies, economics, government, forensic studies, French studies, geography, history, international relations, liberal arts/general studies, liberal arts, sciences, general studies, humanities, philosophy, philosophy and religion, political science/government, prelaw, psychology, Russian and Slavic studies, social work, sociology, Spanish studies, women & gender studies, and women's studies). Premedical is the strongest academically. Psychology, PK-4 early grades prep, and criminal justice have the largest enrollments.

ACTIVITIES: 14% of men belong to 16 national fraternities; 19% of women belong to 18 national sororities. There are 293 groups on campus, including art, band, cheerleading, chess, choir, chorale, chorus, communications, computers, dance, debate, drama, drill team, drum and bugle corps, environmental, ethnic, film, forensics, honors, international, jazz band, LGBT, literary magazine, marching band, musical theater, newspaper, opera, orchestra, pep band, photography, political, professional, radio and TV, religious, social, social service, student government, symphony, and yearbook. Popular campus events include Martin Luther King Day, University Festival, Student Involvement Fair, Homecoming, Greek Week, and Spring Weekend. **Sports:** There are 10 intercollegiate sports for men and 14 for women, and 16 intramural sports for men and 16 for women. Facilities include a field house, multi-gyms, swimming pools and diving well, several practice and game fields, softball complex, tennis courts, basketball, baseball stadium, field hockey/lacrosse complex, fitness centers, fi mile track, climbing wall, and recreational outdoor (ROPE) course. **Graduates:** From July 1, 2015 to June 30, 2016, 3407 bachelor's degrees were awarded. The most popular majors were psychology (7%), liberal studies (6%), and finance (6%). 170 companies recruited on campus in 2015-2016. In an average class, 50% graduate in 4 years or less, 69% graduate in 5 years or less, and 70% graduate in 6 years or less.

SERVICES: Counseling and information services are available, as is tutoring in some subjects. There is a reader service for the blind, and remedial math, reading, and writing. **Library/Resources:** The library contains 1.5 million volumes, 768,407 microform items, and 61,094 audio/video tapes/CDs/DVDs, and subscribes to 100,390 periodicals including electronic. Computerized library services include interlibrary loans, database searching, Internet access, and Wi-Fi capability. Special learning facilities include an art gallery, planetarium, radio station, TV station, art gallery, radio station, TV station, planetarium, observatory, an herbarium, a speech and hearing clinic, an autism clinic, a center for government and community affairs, a 151-acre natural area for environmental studies, mineral museum, music library, fully-equipped food preparation laboratory for nutrition, and dietetics programs, nursing skills laboratory, athletic training rooms, HEAT (Heat Illness Evaluation Avoidance and Treatment) Institute, dance studio, and poetry center. There is also an outdoor classroom & native plant & ornithology, microsoft demonstration and application center. The entire campus forest is designated an Arboretum Level II by ArbNet. **Physically Challenged Students:** 95% of the campus is accessible. Facilities include wheelchair ramps, elevators, special parking, specially equipped restrooms, special class scheduling, lowered drinking fountains, and lowered telephones. **Special:** There is cross-registration with Cheyney University and a 3-2 engineering program with Pennsylvania State University and Philadelphia University. The university offers some accelerated degree programs, a Washington semester, some student-designed majors, credit by examination for life, military, and work experience, and pass/fail options. Students arrange study-abroad programs through a third party, and several faculty-led study programs. There are 35 national honor societies and a freshman honors program. **Visiting:** There are regularly scheduled orientations for prospective students, campus tours are offered daily, some include an information session. We also host preview days for prospective students. They include faculty presentations, sessions on financial aid, tours of campus and interactions with administrative staff. There are guides for informal visits and visitors may sit in on classes. To schedule a visit, contact the Office of Admissions. **Campus Safety and Security:** Measures include 24-hour foot and vehicle patrol, emergency notification system, self-defense education, and security escort services. There are shuttle buses, emergency telephones, lighted pathways/sidewalks, controlled access to dorms/residences, bike patrol, card access/security alarms in all resident halls, security officers are posted in residence halls overnight, crime prevention programming, and alcohol-free alternative events.

REQUIREMENTS: A college preparatory curriculum in high school, standardized test scores from the SAT or ACT, and a personal statement are required. An interview is required for premedical, pharmaceutical product development, and respiratory care programs. An audition is required for music applicants, and portfolio for art applicants. Specific course prerequisites depend on major selection. Additional documentation is required of candidates for the summer academic development program. The GED is acceptable. West Chester University requires applicants to be in the upper 40% of their class. A GPA of 3.0 is required. AP and CLEP credits are accepted. All students must satisfy requirements in English composition, math, and interdisciplinary study. Distribution requirements include 6 hours each of science, behavioral and social science, and humanities, and 3 hours in the arts. A total of 120 (126 or 124 for some degrees) credit hours and a 2.0 GPA are required. **Procedure:** Freshmen are admitted fall and spring. Entrance exams should be taken in spring of the junior year or fall of the senior year. There is a rolling admissions plan. Application deadlines are open. Application fee is $45. Notification is sent on a rolling basis. 749 applicants were on the 2016 waiting list. Applications are accepted on-line. **Transfer Students:** 1457 transfer students enrolled in 2015-2016. Applicants must submit official copies of college transcripts for every institution attended. In some cases students will be required to submit a midterm progress report. If a transfer applicant has completed less than 24 credits they must submit a high school transcript and standardized test scores if they have been out of high school for less than 3 years. Audition is required for music applicants, portfolio for art applicants, and interview for Pre-Med, pharmaceutical product development, and respiratory care. 30 of 120 credits required for the bachelor's degree must be completed at West Chester University. **International Students:** There are 60 international students enrolled. The school actively recruits these students. They must take the TOEFL with a minimum score of 550 on the paper-based TOEFL (PBT) or 80 on the Internet-based version (iBT) and the college's own test, passing ELS language school's level 112 or the IELTS. The SAT is recommended.

ADMISSIONS: 64% of the 2016-2017 applicants were accepted. The SAT scores for the 2016-2017 freshman class were: Critical Reading-- 34% below 500, 51% between 500 and 599, 13% between 600 and 699, and 2% between 700 and 800. Math-- 30% below 500, 52% between 500 and 599, 17% between 600 and 699, and 1% between 700 and 800. Writing-- 39% below 500, 48% between 500 and 599, 12% between 600 and 699, and 1% between 700 and 800. The ACT scores were 5% between 12 and 17, 50% between 18 and 23, 41% between 24 and 29, and 4% above 30. 22% of the current freshmen were in the top fifth of their class; 40% were in the top two fifths. 1 freshman graduated first in the class. **Admissions Contact:** Marsha Haug, Executive Director of Admissions. Email: *ugadmiss@wcupa.edu* Web: *www.wcupa.edu/admissions*

FINANCIAL AID: In 2016-2017, 80% of all full-time freshmen and 75% of continuing full-time students received some form of financial aid. 60% of all full-time freshmen and 56% of continuing full-time students received need-based aid. The average freshman award was $7,378. Need-based scholarships or need-based grants averaged $6,472 ($26,029 maximum); need-based self-help aid (loans and jobs) averaged $3,074 ($11,500 maximum); non-need-based athletic scholarships averaged $3,109 ($8,000 maximum); and other non-need-based awards and non-need-based scholarships averaged $4,586. 7% of undergraduate students work part-time. Average annual earnings from campus work are $3500. The average financial indebtedness of the 2016 graduate was $33,814. West Chester University is a member of CSS. The FAFSA code is 003328. The priority date for freshman financial aid applications for fall entry is February 15.

WESTMINSTER COLLEGE — B-2

www.westminster.edu

New Wilmington, PA 16172 — (800) 748-4753, (801) 832-3300

Fax: (724) 946-6171 — Email: admissions@westminstercollege.edu

Full-time: 510 men, 905 women	**Faculty:** 100; IIB, --$
Part-time: 20 men, 34 women	**Ph.D.s:** 83%
Graduate: 43 men, 86 women	**Student/Faculty:** 14 to 1
Year: semesters, summer session	**Tuition:** $31,228
Room & Board: $7952	**Freshman Class:** 1302 applied, 1006 accepted, 359 enrolled
SAT: required **ACT:** 24	**CEEB CODE:** 2975
Application Deadline: open	**COMPETITIVE+**

Westminster College, founded in 1852, is a private liberal arts institution related to the Presbyterian Church. Figures in the above capsule and in this profile are approximate. There is 1 undergraduate school. In addition to regional accreditation, Westminster has baccalaureate program accreditation with NASM. The 350-acre campus is in a rural area 60 miles north of Pittsburgh. Including any residence halls, there are 25 buildings.

STUDENT LIFE: 79% of undergraduates are from Pennsylvania. Others are from 23 states, and 1 foreign country. 90% are from public schools. 97% are White; 2% African American; 1% Asian American. 56% are Protestant; 34% Catholic. **Female To Male Ratio:** 1.8:1. The average age of freshmen is 18; all undergraduates, 20. 11% do not continue beyond their first year; 76% remain to graduate. **Housing:** 1098 students can be accommodated in college housing, which includes single-sex dorms and on-campus apartments. In addition, there are fraternity houses, and some residence hall floors have 24-hour weekend visitation. On-campus housing is guaranteed for all 4 years. 90% of students live on campus; of those, 70% remain on campus on weekends. All students may keep cars. Alcohol is not permitted.

FACULTY/CLASSROOMS: 53% of faculty are male; 47% are female. All teach undergraduates. No introductory courses are taught by graduate students. The average class size in an introductory lecture is 20; in a laboratory is 20; and in a regular course is 22.

PROGRAMS OF STUDY: Westminster confers B.A., B.S., and B.M. degrees. Master's degrees are also awarded. Bachelor's degrees are awarded in BIOLOGICAL SCIENCE (biology/biological science and molecular biology), BUSINESS (accounting, banking and finance, business administration and management, international business management, and marketing/retailing/merchandising), COMMUNICATIONS AND THE ARTS (art, broadcasting, communications, dramatic arts, English, fine arts, French, German, Latin, music, music performance, music theory and composition, public relations, and Spanish), COMPUTER AND PHYSICAL SCIENCE (chemistry, computer science, mathematics, and physics), EDUCATION (Christian education, elementary education, guidance education, music education, and secondary education), HEALTH PROFESSIONS (predentistry and premedicine), SOCIAL SCIENCE (criminal justice, economics, history, international relations, philosophy, political science/government, prelaw, psychology, religion, religious music, social science, and sociology). Sciences, business, and education are the strongest academically and have the largest enrollments.

ACTIVITIES: 33% of men belong to 5 national fraternities; 34% of women belong to 5 national sororities. There are 60 groups on campus, including band, cheerleading, choir, chorale, chorus, communications, dance, debate, drama, drill team, ethnic, forensics, honors, jazz band, LGBT, literary magazine, marching band, musical theater, newspaper, orchestra, pep band, political, radio and TV, religious, social, social service, student government, and symphony. Popular campus events include Mock Conventions, Mardi Gras, and Volleyrock. **Sports:** There are 9 intercollegiate sports for men and 9 for women, and 7 intramural sports for men and 6 for women. Facilities include a natatorium, racquetball, tennis, and basketball courts, an all-weather track, and weight, and aerobics rooms. **Graduates:** From July 1, 2015 to June 30, 2016, 222 bachelor's degrees were awarded. The most popular majors were elementary education (21%), business administration (16%), and social sciences and history (13%). In an average class, 74% graduate in 4 years or less, 75% graduate in 5 years or less, and 76% graduate in 6 years or less. Of the 2015 graduating class, 90% were employed within 6 months of graduation.

SERVICES: Counseling and information services are available, as is tutoring in most subjects. There is a reader service for the blind, as well as remedial math, reading, and writing. **Library/Resources:** The 2 libraries contain 283,070 volumes, 9,737 microform items, and 14,251 audio/video tapes/CDs/DVDs, and subscribe to 848 periodicals including electronic. Computerized library services include interlibrary loans, database searching, Internet access, and Wi-Fi capability. Special learning facilities include an art gallery, planetarium, radio station, TV station, electron microscope labs in the science center, and a graphics computer center. **Physically Challenged Students:** 50% of the campus is accessible. Facilities include wheelchair ramps, elevators, special parking, specially equipped restrooms, and special class scheduling. **Special:** The college offers internships, study abroad in many countries, a Washington semester, various dual and student-designed majors, a 3-2 engineering degree with Case Western Reserve, Pennsylvania State, and Washington Universities, London study at Regent's College, a 3-3 J.D. program with Duquesne, and nondegree study. There are 12 national honor societies and a freshman honors program. **Visiting:** There are regularly scheduled orientations for prospective students, consisting of an introduction, student panel, financial aid workshop, a campus tour, a faculty fair, lunch and a tour of residence hall. There are 2 visitation days in the fall and 2 in the spring. There are guides for informal visits, visitors may sit in on classes, and stay overnight. To schedule a visit, contact the Office of Admissions. **Campus Safety and Security:** Measures include 24-hour foot and vehicle patrol, self-defense education, and security escort services. There are also shuttle buses, emergency telephones, and lighted pathways/sidewalks.

REQUIREMENTS: The SAT or ACT is required, with a minimum recommended composite score of 900 on the SAT or 20 on the ACT. Applicants must be graduates of an accredited secondary school and have a minimum of 16 academic credits, including 4 units in English, 3 in math, and 2 each in foreign language, science, and social studies. The GED will be considered with a minimum composite score of 270. A portfolio, audition, and interview are recommended. An essay is required. Applications are accepted on-line. Westminster requires applicants to be in the upper 50% of their class. A GPA of 2.5 is required. AP and CLEP credits are accepted. Important factors in the admissions decision are advanced placement or honors courses, leadership record, and recommendations by school officials. First-year students are required to take Inquiry I and II, as well as writing and a speech course. Students must fulfill a distribution requirement by taking a course in one of each of the intellectual perspectives: visual and performing arts, quantitative reasoning, social thought and tradition, humanity and culture, scientific discovery, foreign language, and religious and philosophical thought. A capstone experience in their major and community service are also required. Students must complete 132 semester hours with a minimum of 84 outside their majors, and have a minimum of 2.0 GPA in all courses. Majors require between 32 and 60 hours of coursework. **Procedure:** Freshmen are admitted in the fall, winter, and spring. Entrance exams should be taken during the junior year. There are deferred admissions and rolling admissions plans. Early decision applications should be filed by November 15, along with a $35 fee. Notification of early decision is sent December 1; regular decision, December 1. Applications are accepted on-line. **Transfer Students:** 11 transfer students enrolled in 2015-2016. Applicants must have a college GPA of 2.0 or better. 60 of 132 credits required for the bachelor's degree must be completed at Westminster. **International Students:** There are 2 international students enrolled. They must take the TOEFL or MELAB, or the SAT for students who come from a country where English is the spoken language. They must also take the SAT or ACT, scoring 900.

ADMISSIONS: 77% of the 2016-2017 applicants were accepted. The ACT scores were 73% below 12, 13% between 12 and 17, 8% between 18 and 23, 2% between 24 and 29, and 3% above 30. 48% of the current freshmen were in the top fifth of their class; 80% were in the top two fifths. 8 freshmen graduated first in their class. **Admissions Contact:** Dawn Chapman, Associate Director of Admissions. Email: *chapmadm@westminster.edu* Web: *www.westminster.edu*

FINANCIAL AID: In 2016-2017, 98% of all full-time freshmen and 97% of continuing full-time students received some form of financial aid. 81% of all full-time freshmen and 78% of continuing full-time students received need-based aid. The average freshman award was $16,427. 40% of undergraduate students work part-time. Average annual earnings from campus work are $1650. The average financial indebtedness of the 2016 graduate was $20,386. Westminster is a member of CSS. The college's own financial statement is required. The FAFSA code is 003392. The deadline for filing freshman financial aid applications for fall entry is May 1.

WIDENER UNIVERSITY — F-4
www.widener.edu

Chester, PA 19013 — (610) 499-4126, (888) WIDENER
Fax: (610) 499-4676 — Email: admissions.office@widener.edu

Full-time: 1372 men, 1582 women	**Faculty:** 223; IIA, +$
Part-time: 208 men, 392 women	**Ph.D.s:** 90%
Graduate: 847 men, 1817 women	**Student/Faculty:** 12 to 1
Year: semesters, summer session	**Tuition:** $41,224
Room & Board: $13,092	**Freshman Class:** 5421 applied, 3692 accepted, 846 enrolled
SAT CR/M: 504/523	**CEEB CODE:** 2642
Application Deadline: February 15	**COMPETITIVE**

Widener University, founded in 1821, is a private liberal arts institution offering undergraduate programs in the arts and sciences, business administration, engineering, nursing, and hospitality management. There are campuses in Harrisburg and Wilmington, Delaware. Figures in the above capsule and in this profile are approximate. There are 6 undergraduate schools and 7 graduate schools. In addition to regional accreditation, Widener has baccalaureate program accreditation with AACSB, ABET, APTA, CSWE, NCATE, ABA, and CCNE. The 105-acre campus is in a suburban area 12 miles south of Philadelphia. Including any residence halls, there are 90 buildings.

STUDENT LIFE: 60% of undergraduates are from Pennsylvania. Others are from 34 states and 15 foreign countries. 66% are White; 16% African American. **Female To Male Ratio:** 1.6:1. The average age of freshmen is 18; all undergraduates, 22. 22% do not continue beyond their first year; 56% remain to graduate. **Housing:** 1700 students can be accommodated in college housing, which includes single-sex and coed dorms and on-campus apartments. In addition, there are honors houses, special-interest houses, fraternity houses, sorority houses, substance-free housing, affinity housing, wellness housing, and quiet/study wings. On-campus housing is guaranteed for all 4 years and is available on a lottery system for upperclassmen. 52% of students commute. All students may keep cars.

FACULTY/CLASSROOMS: 47% of faculty are male; 53% are female. 77% teach undergraduates. No introductory courses are taught by graduate students. The average class size in an introductory lecture is 30; in a laboratory is 14; and in a regular course is 24.

PROGRAMS OF STUDY: Widener confers B.A., B.S., B.S.B., B.S.C.E., B.S.Ch.E., B.S.E.E., B.S. in H.M., B.S.M.E., B.S.N. and B.S.W. degrees. Associate, master's, and doctoral degrees are also awarded. Bachelor's degrees are awarded in BIOLOGICAL SCIENCE (biochemistry and biology/biological science), BUSINESS (accounting, business administration and management, business economics, finance, hospitality management services, international business management, and management information systems), COMMUNICATIONS AND THE ARTS (art, communications, creative writing, English, fine arts, French, media arts, modern language, and Spanish), COMPUTER AND PHYSICAL SCIENCE (chemistry, computer science, information sciences and systems, mathematics, physics, and science), EDUCATION (early childhood education, elementary education, mathematics education, science education, and special education), ENGINEERING AND ENVIRONMENTAL DESIGN (biomedical engineering, chemical engineering, civil engineering, electrical/electronics engineering, engineering, environmental science, mechanical engineering, and preengineering), HEALTH PROFESSIONS (nursing and prephysical therapy), SOCIAL SCIENCE (anthropology, behavioral science, criminal justice, economics, gender studies, history, humanities, international relations, political science/government, psychology, social work, sociology, and women's studies). Computer science, biology, and psychology are the strongest academically. Nursing, psychology, and management have the largest enrollments.

ACTIVITIES: 10% of men belong to 6 national fraternities; 9% of women belong to 5 national sororities. There are 106 groups on campus, including art, cheerleading, chess, choir, chorale, chorus, computers, dance, drama, environmental, environmental, ethnic, film, honors, international, jazz band, LGBT, literary magazine, musical theater, pep band, photography, political, professional, radio and TV, religious, social, social service, student government, and yearbook. Popular campus events include Greek Week, Hundredth Night, and Honors Week. **Sports:** There are 10 intercollegiate sports for men and 10 for women, and 7 intramural sports for men and 7 for women. Facilities include a stadium, basketball gym, field house, ice hockey, men's hockey, a pool, ski and snowboard, weight training and exercise room, tennis courts, outdoor game and practice fields, Rugby, and all-weather championship track. **Graduates:** From July 1, 2014 to June 30, 2015, 682 bachelor's degrees were awarded. The most popular majors were nursing/health professions (26%), business/marketing (19%), and engineering (15%). In an average class, 40% graduate in 4 years or less, 54% graduate in 5 years or less, and 56% graduate in 6 years or less. Of the 2014 graduating class, 17% were enrolled in graduate school within 6 months of graduation, and 72% were employed.

SERVICES: Counseling and information services are available, as is tutoring in every subject, and a reader service for the blind. Academic support is offered as needed for all students. **Library/Resources:** Computerized library services include interlibrary loans, database searching, and Internet access. Special learning facilities include an art gallery, radio station, TV station, and a child development center. **Physically Challenged Students:** All of the campus is accessible. Facilities include wheelchair ramps, elevators, special parking, specially equipped restrooms, special class scheduling, lowered drinking fountains, and lowered telephones. **Special:** Widener offers internships, study abroad in 12 countries, a Washington semester, accelerated degree programs, dual, student-designed, and interdisciplinary majors, including chemistry management, nondegree study, and pass/fail options. Co-op programs are available in business administration, computer science, and engineering and are required in hospitality management. There are 26 national honor societies, a freshman honors program, and 8 departmental honors programs. **Visiting:** There are regularly scheduled orientations for prospective students. There are guides for informal visits, visitors may sit in on classes, and stay overnight. To schedule a visit, contact the Office of Admissions. **Campus Safety and Security:** Measures include 24-hour foot and vehicle patrol, emergency notification system, self-defense education, and security escort services. There are also shuttle buses, emergency telephones, lighted pathways/sidewalks, controlled access to dorms/residences, residence hall briefings on personal safety, housing security, enforcement procedures, and bike patrols.

REQUIREMENTS: The SAT is required. Applicants must be graduates of an accredited secondary school and have completed 4 units each of English and social studies, 3 units each of math and science, and 1 unit each of art, history, and music. The GED is accepted under limited circumstances. An interview is recommended. A GPA of 3.0 is required. AP credits are accepted. Important factors in the admissions decision are advanced placement or honors courses, recommendations by school officials, and extracurricular activities record. All students must complete 12 credits each in humanities, social sciences, and science/math, and 1 credit in phys ed. For graduation, students must have 121 credit hours and a GPA of 2.0. Hours in the major vary by program. There is a university-wide writing requirement for all students. **Procedure:** Freshmen are admitted in the fall and spring. Entrance exams should be taken in the junior year and November or December of the senior year. There are early admissions, deferred admissions, and rolling admissions plans. Applications should be filed by February 15 for fall entry; January 3 for spring entry, along with a $35 fee. Notification of early decision is sent December 15; regular decision, February 15. 20 applicants were on the 2015 waiting list. Applications are accepted online. **Transfer Students:** 92 transfer students enrolled in 2014-2015. Applicants must have at least 12 college credits with a minimum GPA of 2.0 (2.5 for nursing students). An associate's degree and an interview are recommended. 45 of 121 credits required for the bachelor's degree must be completed at Widener. **International Students:** There are 139 international students enrolled. The school actively recruits these students. They must take the TOEFL.

ADMISSIONS: 68% of the 2015-2016 applicants were accepted. The SAT scores for the 2015-2016 freshman class were: Critical Reading-- 47% below 500, 43% between 500 and 599, 9% between 600 and 699, and 1% between 700 and 800. Math-- 39% below 500, 45% between 500 and 599, 14% between 600 and 699, and 2% between 700 and 800. The ACT scores were 7% between 12 and 17, 57% between 18 and 23, 33% between 24 and 29, and 3% above 30. **Admissions Contact:** Jason Britton, Director of Admissions. Email: *admissions.office@widener.edu* Web: *www.widener.edu*

FINANCIAL AID: Widener is a member of CSS. The FAFSA is required. The deadline for filing freshman financial aid applications for fall entry is February 15.

WILKES UNIVERSITY — E-2

www.wilkes.edu

Wilkes Barre, PA 18766	(570) 408-4400 (800) WILKESU
Fax: (570) 408-4904	**Email:** admissions@wilkes.edu
Full-time: 1184 men, 1070 women	**Faculty:** IIA, +$
Part-time: 77 men, 90 women	**Ph.D.s:** 90%
Graduate: 703 men, 1929 women	**Student/Faculty:** 15 to 1
Year: semesters, summer session	**Tuition:** $32,356
Room & Board: $13,266	**Freshman Class:** 3164 applied, 2586 accepted, 584 enrolled
SAT CR/M/W: 520/530/500 **ACT:** required	**CEEB CODE:** 2977
Application Deadline: open	**COMPETITIVE**

Wilkes University, founded in 1933, is an independent comprehensive university offering undergraduate programs in 40 fields, including the arts and sciences, business, and engineering. There are 7 undergraduate schools and 1 graduate school. In addition to regional accreditation, Wilkes has baccalaureate program accreditation with ABET, ACBSP, ACPE, and CCNE. The 27-acre campus is in an urban area 120 miles west of New York City. Including any residence halls, there are 54 buildings.

STUDENT LIFE: 82% of undergraduates are from Pennsylvania. Others are from 23 states, and 8 foreign countries. 80% are from public schools. 8% are Foreign; 72% White; 6% Hispanic; 4% African American; 4% two or more races; 3% Asian American; 3% race unknown. **Female To Male Ratio:** 1.6:1. The average age of freshmen is 18; all undergraduates, 21. 23% do not continue beyond their first year; 59% remain to graduate. **Housing:** 1129 students can be accommodated in college housing, which includes single-sex and coed dorms and on-campus apartments. On-campus housing is guaranteed for all 4 years and is available on a lottery system for upperclassmen. 59% of students commute. All students may keep cars. Alcohol is not permitted.

FACULTY/CLASSROOMS: 54% of faculty are male; 46% are female. No introductory courses are taught by graduate students. The average class size in an introductory lecture is 22; in a laboratory is 15; and in a regular course is 18.

PROGRAMS OF STUDY: Wilkes confers B.A., B.S., B.F.A. and B.B.A. degrees. Master's and doctoral degrees are also awarded. Bachelor's degrees are awarded in BIOLOGICAL SCIENCE (biochemistry, biology/biological science, and neurosciences), BUSINESS (accounting, business administration and management, entrepreneurial studies, marketing and distribution, and sports management), COMMUNICATIONS AND THE ARTS (communications, dramatic arts, English, media arts, musical theater, and Spanish), COMPUTER AND PHYSICAL SCIENCE (chemistry, computer science, earth science, information sciences and systems, mathematics, and physics), EDUCATION (elementary education and middle school education), ENGINEERING AND ENVIRONMENTAL DESIGN (electrical/electronics engineering, engineering and applied science, engineering management, environmental engineering, and mechanical engineering), HEALTH PROFESSIONS (medical technology, nursing, and prepharmacy), SOCIAL SCIENCE (criminology, history, international studies, liberal arts/general studies, philosophy, political science/government, psychology, public administration, and sociology). Pre-pharmacy, biology, and engineering are the strongest academically. Nursing, biology, and mechanical engineering have the largest enrollments.

ACTIVITIES: There are no fraternities or sororities. There are 80 groups on campus, including art, band, cheerleading, choir, chorus, computers, dance, debate, drama, environmental, ethnic, honors, international, jazz band, LGBT, literary magazine, marching band, musical theater, newspaper, orchestra, pep band, political, professional, radio and TV, religious, social, social service, and student government. Popular campus events include Casino Night, Junior-Senior Dinner Dance, and Winter Weekend. **Sports:** There are 10 intercollegiate sports for men and 10 for women. Facilities include tennis courts, a stadium, gym, game room, weight and exercise rooms, and an indoor recreation and athletic center. **Graduates:** From July 1, 2015 to June 30, 2016, 474 bachelor's degrees were awarded. The most popular majors were business (16%), nursing (14%), and engineering (14%). In an average class, 47% graduate in 4 years or less, 58% graduate in 5 years or less, and 59% graduate in 6 years or less. Of the 2015 graduating class, 22% were enrolled in graduate school within 6 months of graduation, and 73% were employed.

SERVICES: Counseling and information services are available, as is tutoring in every subject, and remedial math, reading, and writing. The Learning Center also provides individual tutoring, group study sessions, and small-group supplemental instruction seminars. **Library/Resources:** The library contains 178,000 volumes, 19,500 microform items, and 1,760 audio/video tapes/CDs/DVDs. Computerized library services include interlibrary loans, database searching, Internet access, and Wi-Fi capability. Special learning facilities include an art gallery, radio station, and TV station. **Physically Challenged Students:** All of the campus is accessible. Facilities include wheelchair ramps, elevators, special parking, specially equipped restrooms, special class scheduling, lowered drinking fountains, and lowered telephones. **Special:** Wilkes offers cooperative education, cross-registration with King's College and Misericordia University, internships, and study abroad. Dual majors in all disciplines, credit for military experience, and nondegree study are also offered. There are 19 national honor societies and a freshman honors program. **Visiting:** There are regularly scheduled orientations for prospective students, including a general orientation session, a tour of the campus, and a meeting with faculty from the department of the student's intended major. There are guides for informal visits, visitors may sit in on classes, and stay overnight. To schedule a visit, contact Admissions Office. **Campus Safety and Security:** Measures include 24-hour foot and vehicle patrol, emergency notification system, and security escort services. There are also shuttle buses, emergency telephones, lighted pathways/sidewalks, controlled access to dorms/residences, personal alarm devices for students who wish to carry one, and engraving of personal belongings.

REQUIREMENTS: The SAT or ACT is required. Applicants must be graduates of an accredited secondary school or have the GED. Secondary-school preparation should include 4 years of English, 3 years each of math and social studies, and 2 years of science. Theater majors must audition. Wilkes requires applicants to be in the upper 50% of their class. A GPA of 2.5 is required. AP and CLEP credits are accepted. Important factors in the admissions decision are recommendations by school officials, advanced placement or honors courses, and leadership record. To graduate, all students must complete at least 120 credit hours, with a minimum of 30 in the major, and a cumulative GPA of at least 2.0 overall and in the major. Students must demonstrate competency in written communication, computer literacy, oral communication, and qualitative reasoning. General education requirements consist of 12 to 15 credits in humanities, 9 to 12 in sciences, 6 to 9 in social sciences, and 3 in fine arts. **Procedure:** Freshmen are admitted in the fall, spring, and summer. Entrance exams should be taken before the second semester of the senior year in high school. There are early admissions, deferred admissions, and rolling admissions plans. Application deadlines are open. Application fee is $40. Notification is sent on a rolling basis. Applications are accepted online. **Transfer Students:** 173 transfer students enrolled in 2015-2016. Applicants must have a minimum college GPA of 2.0 and at least 30 earned credits. A GPA of 2.5 is required for engineering majors. Students with fewer than 30 credits must submit official high school transcripts and SAT or ACT scores. An interview is recommended. 60 of 120 credits required for the bachelor's degree must be completed at Wilkes. **International Students:** There are 203 international students enrolled. The school actively recruits these students. They must take the TOEFL with a minimum score of 500 on the paper-based TOEFL (PBT) or 60 on the Internet-based version (iBT). They must also take the SAT or ACT.

ADMISSIONS: 82% of the 2016-2017 applicants were accepted. The SAT scores for the 2016-2017 freshman class were: Critical Reading-- 40% below 500, 43% between 500 and 599, 15% between 600 and 699, and 2% between 700 and 800. Math-- 33% below 500, 42% between 500 and 599, 22% between 600 and 699, and 3% between 700 and 800. Writing-- 48% below 500, 39% between 500 and 599, 12% between 600 and 699, and 1% between 700 and 800. 43% of the current freshmen were in the top fifth of their class; 70% were in the top two fifths. **Admissions Contact:** Melanie Wade, Vice President for Enrollment Services. Email: *admissions@wilkes.edu* Web: *www.wilkes.edu*

FINANCIAL AID: In 2016-2017, 97% of all full-time freshmen and 90% of continuing full-time students received some form of financial aid. 30% of undergraduate students work part-time. Average annual earnings from campus work are $800. The average financial indebtedness of the 2016 graduate was $38,049. The FAFSA code is 003394. The deadline for filing freshman financial aid applications for fall entry is March 1.

WILSON COLLEGE — D-3

www.wilson.edu

Chambersburg, PA 17201	(717) 262-2002 (800) 421-8402
Fax: (717) 262-2546	**Email:** admissions@wilson.edu
Full-time: 38 men, 327 women	**Faculty:** 40
Part-time: 50 men, 192 women	**Ph.D.s:** 78%
Graduate: 32 men, 120 women	**Student/Faculty:** 9 to 1
Year: 4-1-4, summer session	**Tuition:** $24,392
Room & Board: $11,190	**Freshman Class:** 677 applied, 589 accepted, 191 enrolled
SAT: required **ACT:** 21	**CEEB CODE:** 2979
Application Deadline: August 1	**COMPETITIVE**

Wilson College, founded in 1869, is a private, coeducational liberal arts college offering bachelor's degrees in 29 majors and master's degrees in education, humanities, fine arts, management, accountancy and nursing. Wilson is committed to providing an affordable education that offers value to its students beyond graduation. Wilson College prepares all of its graduates for fulfilling lives and professions, ethical leadership, and humane stewardship of our communities and our world. There is 1 undergraduate school and 1 graduate school. In addition to regional accreditation, Wilson has baccalaureate program accreditation with AVMA. The 300-acre campus is in a small town 55 miles south of Harrisburg, 76 miles west of Baltimore, 90 miles west of Washington, D.C. Including any residence halls, there are 34 buildings.

STUDENT LIFE: 83% of undergraduates are from Pennsylvania. Others are from 19 states, 21 foreign countries, and Canada. 91% are from public schools. 85% are White; 5% African American; 5% Foreign; 3% Hispanic; 1% Asian American; 1% American Indian/Alaska Native. 51% claim no religious affiliation; 31% Protestant; 11% Catholic. **Female To Male Ratio:** 5.3:1. The average age of freshmen is 18; all undergraduates, 30. 33% do not continue beyond their first year; 48% remain to graduate. **Housing:** 473 students can be accommodated in college housing, which includes single-sex and coed dorms and on-campus apartments. There is also single-parent housing for students with children. On-campus housing is guaranteed for all 4 years. 59% of students commute. All students may keep cars.

FACULTY/CLASSROOMS: 47% of faculty are male; 53% are female. All teach undergraduates. No introductory courses are taught by graduate students. The average class size in an introductory lecture is 20; in a laboratory is 14; and in a regular course is 14.

PROGRAMS OF STUDY: Wilson confers B.A. and B.S. degrees. Associate and master's degrees are also awarded. Bachelor's degrees are awarded in AGRICULTURE (animal science, environmental studies, and equine science), BIOLOGICAL SCIENCE (biochemistry, biology/biological science, biology/gen sci/envir sci second ed, and biology/ gen science secondary education), BUSINESS (accounting, business administration and management, business economics, and sports management), COMMUNICATIONS AND THE ARTS (art, communications, creative writing, English, English writing, fine arts, French, graphic design, graphic design & media, languages, Spanish, and studio art), COMPUTER AND PHYSICAL SCIENCE (actuarial mathematics, chemistry, chemistry/gen science second education, chemistry secondary education, and mathematics), EDUCATION (childhood education, early childhood education, elementary education, English secondary education, English comm secondary education, English education, foreign languages education, global studies, health and physical education, mathematics education, middle school education, physical education, secondary education, social science education, social studies education, social studies secondary school education, and special education), ENGINEERING AND ENVIRONMENTAL DESIGN (environmental science), HEALTH PROFESSIONS (biology, exercise science, nursing, pre-health studies, pre-health biological studies, predentistry, premedicine, preoptometry, pre-occupational therapy, preosteopathy, prepharmacy, pre-physician assistant, prephysical therapy, prepodiatry, preveterinary science, and veterinary science), SOCIAL SCIENCE (economics, history, international relations, international studies, law, liberal arts/general studies, liberal arts, sciences, general studies, humanities, philosophy, philosophy and religion, political science/government, prelaw, psychobiology, psychology, religion, sociology, and therapeutic riding). Biology, and veterinary medical technology are the strongest academically. Business & economics, education, and veterinary medical technology have the largest enrollments.

ACTIVITIES: There are no fraternities or sororities. There are 28 groups on campus, including art, cheerleading, choir, chorale, dance, drama, environmental, equestrian, ethnic, honors, international, LGBT, literary magazine, newspaper, photography, political, professional, radio and TV, religious, social, social service, student government, and yearbook. Popular campus events include May Weekend, Thanksgiving, Christmas, Arts Day, Senior Research Day, and Muhibbah International Dinners. **Sports:** There are 5 intercollegiate sports for men and 5 for women, and 3 intramural sports for men and 3 for women. Facilities include a gym, field house, a pool, an archery range, hockey field, softball field, tennis courts, bowling alley, an equestrian center (indoor and outdoor arena), soccer field, and a fitness center. **Graduates:** From July 1, 2015 to June 30, 2016, 95 bachelor's degrees were awarded. The most popular majors were veterinary medical (21%), elementary education (13%), and business economics (10%). In an average class, 58% graduate in 4 years or less, 59% graduate in 5 years or less, and 62% graduate in 6 years or less.

SERVICES: Counseling and information services are available, as is tutoring in every subject, and remedial math, reading, and writing. Including study skills workshops, and time management workshops are also available. **Library/Resources:** The library contains 175,000 volumes, 10,933 microform items, 2,007 audio/video tapes/CDs/DVDs, and subscribes to 293 periodicals including electronic. Computerized library services include interlibrary loans, database searching, Internet access, and Wi-Fi capability. Special learning facilities include an art gallery, natural history museum, radio station, a veterinary technology center, transmission electron microscope, classics collection, center for sustainable living with USDA-certified organic farm, and an on-campus equestrian center and stables. **Physically Challenged Students:** 55% of the campus is accessible. Facilities include wheelchair ramps, elevators, special parking, specially equipped restrooms, special class scheduling, and special housing. **Special:** Cross-registration is available with Shippensburg University and Gettysburg College. Wilson offers internships, a Washington semester, student-designed majors, B.A.-B.S. degree in psychology and sociology credit by exam, pass/fail options, and credit for noncollegiate learning. Students may participate in study-abroad programs sponsored by other colleges. Army ROTC is available through Shippensburg University There are 2 national honor societies, Phi Beta Kappa, and a freshman honors program. **Visiting:** There are regularly scheduled orientations for prospective students, campus tour, meetings with faculty, students, or administration, and an interview with an admissions counselor and financial aid. There are guides for informal visits, visitors may sit in on classes, and stay overnight. To schedule a visit, contact the Office of Admissions. **Campus Safety and Security:** Measures include 24-hour foot and vehicle patrol, emergency notification system, and security escort services. There are also shuttle buses, emergency telephones, lighted pathways/sidewalks, and controlled access to dorms/residences.

REQUIREMENTS: Wilson is test-optional for applicants with a 3.0 unweighted GPA who have completed a college prep curriculum including 4 years each of English and social studies/history, 3 years of math, and 2 of science with a lab, and 1 year of foreign language. A graded English paper and at least one academic reference are required, with an interview is recommended. Wilson requires applicants to be in the upper 50% of their class. AP and CLEP credits are accepted. Important factors in the admissions decision are personality/intangible qualities, advanced placement or honors courses, and leadership record. To graduate, students must complete a minimum of 120 credits, with a minimum GPA of 2.0. At least half of the credits must be outside any single discipline. **Procedure:** Freshmen are admitted in the fall and spring. Entrance exams should be taken in the spring of the junior year. There are deferred admissions and rolling admissions plans. Applications should be filed by August 1 for fall entry; December 1 for spring entry. Notification is sent on a rolling basis. Applications are accepted online. **Transfer Students:** 22 transfer students enrolled in 2015-2016. Applicants must have a college GPA of at least 2.0. The SAT I or ACT may be waived after discussion with the Admissions Office. 73 of 120 credits required for the bachelor's degree must be completed at Wilson. **International Students:** There are 32 international students enrolled. The school actively recruits these students. They must take the TOEFL with a minimum score of 500 on the paper-based TOEFL (PBT) or 61 on the Internet-based version (iBT), or take either the IELTS, or STEP.

ADMISSIONS: 87% of the 2016-2017 applicants were accepted. The SAT scores for the 2016-2017 freshman class were: Critical Reading-- 59% below 500, 36% between 500 and 599, 4% between 600 and 699, and 1% between 700 and 800. Math-- 60% below 500, 30% between 500 and 599, and 9% between 600 and 699. Writing-- 70% below 500, 25% between 500 and 599, and 3% between 600 and 699. The ACT scores were 33% between 12 and 17, 33% between 18 and 23, and 42% between 24 and 29. 35% of the current freshmen were in the top fifth of their class; 74% were in the top two fifths. 3 freshmen graduated first in their class. **Admissions Contact:** Michael Montana, Director of Admissions. Email: *admissions@wilson.edu* Web: *www.wilson.edu*

FINANCIAL AID: In 2016-2017, 99% of all full-time freshmen and continuing full-time students received some form of financial aid. 77% of all full-time freshmen and 71% of continuing full-time students received need-based aid. The average freshman award was $15,469. Need-based scholarships or need-based grants averaged $12,411; need-based self-help aid (loans and jobs) averaged $3,855; and other non-need-based awards and non-need-based scholarships averaged $11,381. 40% of undergraduate students work part-time. Average annual earnings from campus work are $2000. The average financial indebtedness of the 2016 graduate was $32,957. The college's own financial statement is required. The FAFSA code is 003396. The priority date for freshman financial aid applications for fall entry is April 30.

YORK COLLEGE OF PENNSYLVANIA — D-4

www.ycp.edu

York, PA 17403	**(717) 849-1600** **(800) 455-8018**
Fax: (717) 849-1607	**Email: admissions@ycp.edu**
Full-time: 1834 men, 2238 women	**Faculty:** 173; IIA, +$
Part-time: 176 men, 173 women	**Ph.D.s:** 87%
Graduate: 75 men, 126 women	**Student/Faculty:** 16 to 1
Year: semesters, summer session	**Tuition:** $18,780
Room & Board: $10,460	**Freshman Class:** 13235 applied, 5694 accepted, 896 enrolled
SAT CR/M/W: 520/535/500 **ACT:** 23	**CEEB CODE:** 2991
Application Deadline: September 15	**COMPETITIVE**

York College of Pennsylvania, founded in 1787, is a private institution offering undergraduate programs in the liberal arts and sciences, as well as professional programs. Figures in the above capsule and in this profile are approximate. There is 1 undergraduate school. In addition to regional accreditation, YCP has baccalaureate program accreditation with ABET, ACBSP, NASM, NLN, NRPA, CoARC, CCNE, CANRPE, and CANAEP. The 190-acre campus is in a suburban area 45 miles north of Baltimore. Including any residence halls, there are 46 buildings.

STUDENT LIFE: 58% of undergraduates are from Pennsylvania. Others are from 32 states, and 7 foreign countries. 85% are from public schools. 83% are White; 5% African American; 5% Hispanic; 3% two or more races; 3% race unknown; 1% Asian American. 36% claim no religious affiliation; 25% Protestant; 24% Catholic; 13% unknown denominations, and Muslim. **Female To Male Ratio:** 1.2:1. The average age of freshmen is 18; all undergraduates, 21. 25% do not continue beyond their first year; 58% remain to graduate. **Housing:** 2575 students can be accommodated in college housing, which includes single-sex and coed dorms and on-campus apartments, special-interest houses, fraternity houses, and sorority houses. On-campus housing is guaranteed for the freshman year only, and is available on a first-come, and first-served basis. 57% of students live on campus; of those, 65% remain on campus on weekends. All students may keep cars. Alcohol is not permitted.

FACULTY/CLASSROOMS: 57% of faculty are male; 43% are female. All teach undergraduates. No introductory courses are taught by graduate students. The average class size in an introductory lecture is 22; in a laboratory is 17; and in a regular course is 19.

PROGRAMS OF STUDY: YCP confers B.A. and B.S. degrees. Associate, master's, and doctoral degrees are also awarded. Bachelor's degrees are awarded in BIOLOGICAL SCIENCE (biology/biological science), BUSINESS (accounting, banking and finance, business administration and management, entrepreneurial studies, management information systems, marketing/retailing/merchandising, recreation and leisure services, and sports management), COMMUNICATIONS AND THE ARTS (broadcasting, communications, creative writing, dramatic arts, English, English literature, fine arts, graphic design, music, music technology, public relations, and Spanish), COMPUTER AND PHYSICAL SCIENCE (chemistry, computer science, and mathematics), EDUCATION (education, elementary education, English education, mathematics education, music education, science education, secondary education, social studies education, and special education), ENGINEERING AND ENVIRONMENTAL DESIGN (computer engineering, electrical/electronics engineering, engineering, engineering management, and mechanical engineering), HEALTH PROFESSIONS (medical laboratory science, nuclear medical technology, nursing, and respiratory therapy), SOCIAL SCIENCE (behavioral science, criminal justice, economics, history, humanities, parks and recreation management, philosophy, political science/government, psychology, and sociology). Electrical, computer, and mechanical engineering are the strongest academically. Nursing, education, and criminal justice have the largest enrollments.

ACTIVITIES: 4% of men belong to 8 national fraternities; 6% of women belong to 6 national sororities. There are 80 groups on campus, including band, cheerleading, chess, choir, chorale, chorus, computers, debate, drama, environmental, ethnic, forensics, honors, international, jazz band, LGBT, literary magazine, musical theater, newspaper, orchestra, photography, political, professional, radio and TV, religious, social, social service, student government, and symphony. Popular campus events include Fall Weekend, Spring Weekend, and Spartalooza. **Sports:** There are 10 intercollegiate sports for men and 10 for women, and 10 intramural sports for men and 10 for women. Facilities include gyms, a track, swimming pool, game room, fitness center, weight training rooms, tennis courts, soccer, hockey, baseball, softball, and athletic/intramural fields. **Graduates:** From July 1, 2015 to June 30, 2016, 936 bachelor's degrees were awarded. The most popular majors were business administration (18%), nursing (14%), and criminal justice (13%). In an average class, 37% graduate in 4 years or less, 55% graduate in 5 years or less, and 61% graduate in 6 years or less.

SERVICES: Counseling and information services are available, as is tutoring in most subjects, and remedial math and writing. There is also an education learning resource center. **Library/Resources:** The library contains 300,000 volumes, 500,000 microform items, 11,000 audio/video tapes/CDs/DVDs, and subscribes to 1,500 periodicals including electronic. Computerized library services include interlibrary loans, database searching, and Internet access. Special learning facilities include an art gallery, radio station, TV station, a telecommunications center, Abraham Lincoln artifacts collection, rare books collection, oral history room, and a nursing education center. **Physically Challenged Students:** 90% of the campus is accessible. Facilities include wheelchair ramps, elevators, special parking, specially equipped restrooms, special class scheduling, lowered drinking fountains, and lowered telephones. **Special:** YCP offers internships for upper-division students and a co-op program in mechanical engineering. Study abroad is offered in England, Mexico, Japan, Puerto Rico, Korea, and other countries. Dual majors in any combination, nondegree study, and pass/fail options are available. There are 6 national honor societies. **Visiting:** There are regularly scheduled orientations for prospective students, including 2 open houses in October/November; 1 junior open house in April; and 2 spring orientation programs in April/May, featuring a general orientation, academic and support services sessions, and campus tours. There are guides for informal visits and visitors may sit in on classes. To schedule a visit, contact the Admissions Office. **Campus Safety and Security:** Measures include 24-hour foot and vehicle patrol, emergency notification system, and security escort services. There are also shuttle buses, emergency telephones, lighted pathways/sidewalks, safety seminars, crime prevention speakers, a desk monitor in residence halls, and a personal property engraving program.

REQUIREMENTS: The SAT or ACT is required, as is the ACT Optional Writing test. Applicants must be graduates of an accredited secondary school or have a GED certificate. 15 academic credits are required, including 4 units in English, 3 or 4 in math, 3 in science, 2 in foreign language, and 3 in social studies. Music students must audition. A GPA of 2.5 is required. AP and CLEP credits are accepted. Important factors in the admissions decision are advanced placement or honors courses, leadership record, personality/intangible qualities, and extracurricular activities record. To graduate, all students must complete at least 124 credit hours, with 60 to 80 in the major. The required core curriculum consists of English Composition, Writing about Literature, Human Communications, Critical Thinking and Problem Solving in Mathematics, Information Literacy, and physical education. Distribution requirements include 6 credits in fine arts and humanities, 6 in social and behavioral sciences, 6 to 8 in laboratory sciences, 6 in American civilization/government and Western civilization, and 6 in international studies/foreign language. A minimum GPA of 2.0 is required. **Procedure:** Freshmen are admitted in the fall and spring. Entrance exams should be taken in the spring of the junior year or the fall of the senior year. There are deferred admissions and rolling admissions plans. Application deadlines are open. Notification is sent on a rolling basis. Application fees are waived if application is completed online. **Transfer Students:** 171 transfer students enrolled in 2015-2016. Applicants must have a minimum GPA of 2.0 from a regionally accredited institution. Students with fewer than 30 credit hours must submit a high school transcript. An interview is recommended. 30 of 124 credits required for the bachelor's degree must be completed at YCP. **International Students:** There are 14 international students enrolled. They must take the TOEFL with a minimum score of 530 on the paper-based TOEFL (PBT) or 72 on the Internet-based version (iBT). They must also take the SAT or ACT or take the IELTS with a score of 6.

ADMISSIONS: 43% of the 2016-2017 applicants were accepted. The SAT scores for the 2016-2017 freshman class were: Critical Reading-- 37% below 500, 48% between 500 and 599, 13% between 600 and 699, and 1% between 700 and 800. Math-- 30% below 500, 49% between 500 and 599, 19% between 600 and 699, and 1% between 700 and 800. Writing-- 50% below 500, 39% between 500 and 599, and 11% between 600 and 699. The ACT scores were 5% between 12 and 17, 57% between 18 and 23, 36% between 24 and 29, and 3% above 30. 4 freshmen graduated first in their class. **Admissions Contact:** Ines Ramirez, Director of Admissions. Email: *admissions@ycp.edu* Web: *www.ycp.edu*

FINANCIAL AID: In 2016-2017, 90% of all full-time freshmen and 83% of continuing full-time students received some form of financial aid. 74% of all full-time freshmen and 58% of continuing full-time students received need-based aid. The average freshman award was $14,604. Need-based scholarships or need-based grants averaged $5,219 ($15,100 maximum); need-based self-help aid (loans and jobs) averaged $6,231 ($5,700 maximum); other non-need-based awards and non-need-based scholarships averaged $6,350 ($27,340 maximum); and $5,681 from other forms of aid. 20% of undergraduate students work part-time. Average annual earnings from campus work are $1500. The average financial indebtedness of the 2016 graduate was $39,334. YCP is a member of CSS. The FAFSA code is 003399. The priority date for freshman financial aid applications for fall entry is March 1.

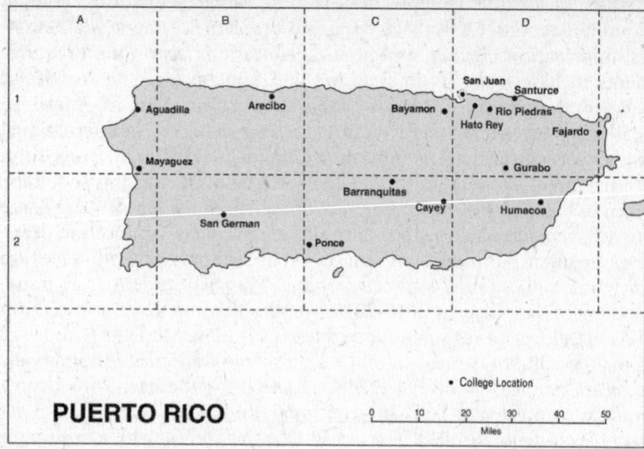

BAYAMON CENTRAL UNIVERSITY *(The complete profile is made available exclusively on our website, www.barronspac.com)*

CARIBBEAN UNIVERSITY *(The complete profile is made available exclusively on our website, www.barronspac.com)*

CONSERVATORY OF MUSIC OF PUERTO RICO *(The complete profile is made available exclusively on our website, www.barronspac.com)*

ESCUELA DE ARTES PLASTICAS DE PUERTO RICO *(The complete profile is made available exclusively on our website, www.barronspac.com)*

INTER-AMERICAN UNIVERSITY OF PUERTO RICO PONCE *(The complete profile is made available exclusively on our website, www.barronspac.com)*

INTER-AMERICAN UNIVERSITY OF PUERTO RICO-AGUADILLA CAMPUS *(The complete profile is made available exclusively on our website, www.barronspac.com)*

INTER-AMERICAN UNIVERSITY OF PUERTO RICO-ARECIBO CAMPUS *(The complete profile is made available exclusively on our website, www.barronspac.com)*

INTER-AMERICAN UNIVERSITY OF PUERTO RICO-BARRANQUITAS *(The complete profile is made available exclusively on our website, www.barronspac.com)*

INTER-AMERICAN UNIVERSITY OF PUERTO RICO-BAYAMON *(The complete profile is made available exclusively on our website, www.barronspac.com)*

INTER-AMERICAN UNIVERSITY OF PUERTO RICO-FAJARDO CAMPUS *(The complete profile is made available exclusively on our website, www.barronspac.com)*

INTER-AMERICAN UNIVERSITY OF PUERTO RICO-METROPOLITAN CAMPUS *(The complete profile is made available exclusively on our website, www.barronspac.com)*

INTER-AMERICAN UNIVERSITY OF PUERTO RICO-SAN GERMÁN *(The complete profile is made available exclusively on our website, www.barronspac.com)*

PONTIFICAL CATHOLIC UNIVERSITY OF PUERTO RICO *(The complete profile is made available exclusively on our website, www.barronspac.com)*

UNIVERSIDAD ADVENTISTA DE LAS ANTILLAS *(The complete profile is made available exclusively on our website, www.barronspac.com)*

UNIVERSIDAD DEL TURABO *(The complete profile is made available exclusively on our website, www.barronspac.com)*

UNIVERSIDAD METROPOLITANA *(The complete profile is made available exclusively on our website, www.barronspac.com)*

UNIVERSIDAD POLITECNICA DE PUERTO RICO, HATO REY CAMPUS *(The complete profile is made available exclusively on our website, www.barronspac.com)*

UNIVERSITY OF PUERTO RICO, AT ARECIBO *(The complete profile is made available exclusively on our website, www.barronspac.com)*

UNIVERSITY OF PUERTO RICO, AT BAYAMON *(The complete profile is made available exclusively on our website, www.barronspac.com)*

UNIVERSITY OF PUERTO RICO, AT CAYEY *(The complete profile is made available exclusively on our website, www.barronspac.com)*

UNIVERSITY OF PUERTO RICO, AT HUMACAO *(The complete profile is made available exclusively on our website, www.barronspac.com)*

UNIVERSITY OF PUERTO RICO, AT MAYAGUEZ *(The complete profile is made available exclusively on our website, www.barronspac.com)*

UNIVERSITY OF PUERTO RICO-RIO PIEDRAS CAMPUS *(The complete profile is made available exclusively on our website, www.barronspac.com)*

UNIVERSITY OF THE SACRED HEART *(The complete profile is made available exclusively on our website, www.barronspac.com)*

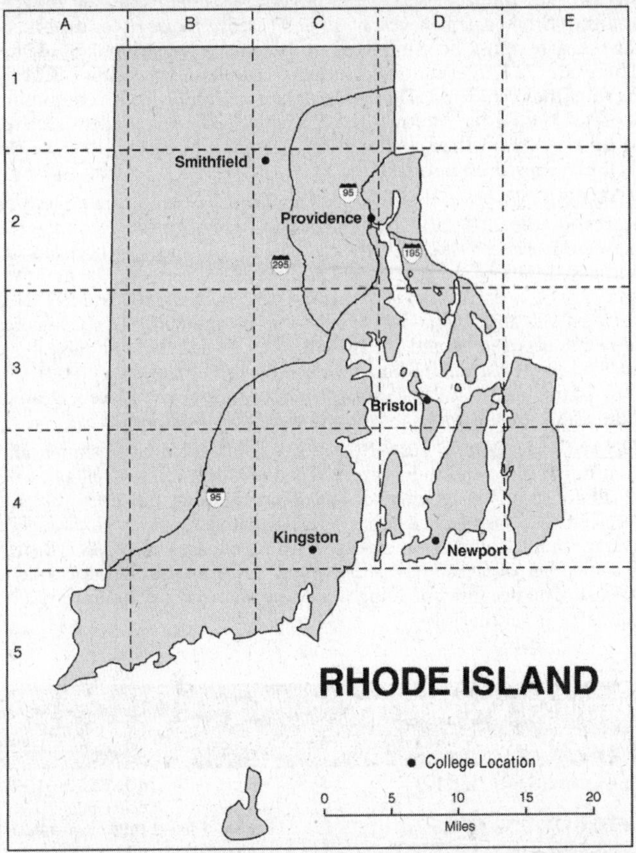

BROWN UNIVERSITY C-2

www.brown.edu

Providence, RI 02912 **(401) 863-2378**

Fax: (401) 863-9300
Email: admission@brown.edu
Full-time: 3133 men, 3423 women
Faculty: 770; I, ++$
Part-time: 10 men, 14 women
Ph.D.s: 100%
Graduate: 1206 men, 1049 women
Student/Faculty: 9 to 1
Year: semesters, summer session
Tuition: $51,366
Room & Board: $1320
Freshman Class: 32390 applied, 3015 accepted, 1684 enrolled
SAT CR/M/W: 740/750/740 **ACT:** 33
CEEB CODE: 3094
Application Deadline: January 1
MOST COMPETITIVE

Brown University is the seventh-oldest college in the United States founded in 1764. The college is an independent Ivy League institution comprised of undergraduate and graduate programs, plus the Alpert Medical School, School of Public Health, School of Engineering, and School of Professional Studies. There is 1 undergraduate school and 2 graduate schools. In addition to regional accreditation, Brown has baccalaureate program accreditation with ABET. The 154-acre campus is in an urban area 45 miles south of Boston, MA. Including any residence halls, there are 240 buildings.

STUDENT LIFE: 95% of undergraduates are from out of state, mostly the Northeast. Students are from 50 states, 81 foreign countries, and Canada. 70% are from public schools. 43% are White; 14% Asian American; 12% Hispanic; 11% Foreign; 7% African American; 6% two or more races; 6% race unknown; 1% American Indian/Alaska Native. **Female To Male Ratio:** 1.0:1. The average age of freshmen is 18; all undergraduates, 20. 2% do not continue beyond their first year; 96% remain to graduate. **Housing:** 4858 students can be accommodated in college housing, which includes single-sex and coed dorms, on-campus apartments, off-campus apartments, and married student housing. In addition, there are language houses, special-interest houses, fraternity houses, sorority houses, international house, technology house, environmental studies house, and cooperatives. On-campus housing is guaranteed for all 4 years and is available on a lottery system for upperclassmen. 76% of students live on campus; of those, 85% remain on campus on weekends. Upperclassmen may keep cars.

FACULTY/CLASSROOMS: 66% of faculty are male; 34% are female. All teach undergraduates and do research. Graduate students teach 5% of introductory courses.

PROGRAMS OF STUDY: Brown confers A.B. and Sc.B. degrees. Master's and doctoral degrees are also awarded. Bachelor's degrees are awarded in AGRICULTURE (environmental studies), BIOLOGICAL SCIENCE (biology ecology and field biology, biochemistry, biology/biological science, biology and society, biological sciences, biomathematics, biophysics, ecology, coastal enviornmental studies, environmental biology, human biology, health, and society, marine biology, molecular biology, and neurosciences), BUSINESS (business economics, economics – statistics, entrepreneurial studies, and organizational leadership and management), COMMUNICATIONS AND THE ARTS (Africana studies, American literature, art history, art, art history and appreciation, classics, comparative literature, creative writing, English, English literature, French language and literature, French and Francophone studies, German studies, Germanic languages and literature, Italian, linguistics, media arts, music, music composition, musicology/ethnomusicology, performing arts, Portuguese, Russian languages and literature, theatre arts, visual and performing arts, and visual arts), COMPUTER AND PHYSICAL SCIENCE (applied mathematics, astronomy, astronomy and physics, astrophysics, chemical physics, chemistry, computer mathematics, computer science, earth & space science, environmental geology, geochemistry, geology, geoscience, mathematics, mathematics/computational, mathematics – economics, mathematics/theoretical, physics and mathematics, physics, physics with astrophysics option, planetary and space science, and statistics), EDUCATION (education and latino and latina studies), ENGINEERING AND ENVIRONMENTAL DESIGN (architectural history, architecture, bioengineering, biomedical engineering, chemical engineering, computational sciences, computer engineering, computer graphics, engineering, engineering physics, environmental engineering, environmental science, history of architecture / urban development, materials engineering, materials science, materials science and engineering, and mechanical engineering), HEALTH PROFESSIONS (biology, biomedical science, community health work, electrical engineering, human biology, and public health), SOCIAL SCIENCE (African studies, African American studies, American Indian studies, American studies, anthropology, archeology, architectural studies, Asian/American studies, classical/ancient civilization, classical and near eastern civilization, cognitive science, developmental psychology, East Asian studies, economics, ethnic studies, feminist, gender, sexuality studies, French studies, gender studies, German area studies, Hispanic American studies, history, human development, international relations, international studies, Italian studies, Judaic studies, Latin American studies, Luso-Brazilian studies, medieval studies, Middle Eastern studies, Native American studies, philosophy, political science/government, psychology, public administration, religion, religious studies, Russian and Slavic studies, Sanskrit and Indian studies, science and society, sociology, South Asian studies, Third World studies, urban studies, women & gender studies, and women's studies). Applied mathematics, computer science, creative writing, economics, and engineering are the strongest academically. Economics, biology, and computer science have the largest enrollments.

ACTIVITIES: 12% of men belong to 11 national fraternities; 9% of women belong to 4 national sororities. There are 400 groups on campus, including ethnic groups, volunteer, art, band, cheerleading, chess, choir, chorale, chorus, computers, dance, debate, drama, environmental, ethnic, film, honors, international, jazz band, LGBT, literary magazine, marching band, musical theater, newspaper, opera, orchestra, pep band, photography, political, professional, public service, radio and TV, religious, social, social service, student government, symphony, and yearbook. Popular campus events include Commencement, Spring Weekend, Family Weekend, and Student of Color Heritage Series. **Sports:** There are 17 intercollegiate sports for men and 21 for women, and 19 intramural sports for men and 19 for women. Facilities include a pool, 6-lane track, hockey rink, playing fields, weight-training rooms, facilities for wrestling, and courts for squash, handball, racquetball, tennis, basketball, and volleyball. **Graduates:** From July 1, 2015 to June

30, 2016, 1591 bachelor's degrees were awarded. The most popular majors were economics (8%), computer science (6%), and biology (6%). 238 companies recruited on campus in 2015-2016. In an average class, 83% graduate in 4 years or less, 94% graduate in 5 years or less, and 96% graduate in 6 years or less. Of the 2015 graduating class, 20% were enrolled in graduate school within 6 months of graduation, and 69% were employed.

SERVICES: Counseling and information services are available, as is tutoring in most subjects, and a reader service for the blind. Other services include class note taking, books on tape, diagnostic testing services, oral tests, tutors, and untimed tests. **Library/Resources:** The 6 libraries contain 4.4 million volumes, 2.0 million microform items, 100,000 audio/video tapes/CDs/DVDs, and subscribe to 106,301 periodicals including electronic. Computerized library services include interlibrary loans, database searching, Internet access, and Wi-Fi capability. Special learning facilities include an art gallery, radio station, TV station, List Art Center, Haffenreffer Museum of Anthropology, Language Resource Center, Child Language Lab, Infant Research Lab, Educational Technology Center, Center for Information Technology, Forbes Center for Culture and Media Studies, John Nicholas Brown Center, John Hay Library, Joukowsky Institute for Archaeology & the Ancient World, Center for Creative Arts, Ann Mary Brown Library, Brown Design Workshop, Digital Scholarship Lab, Microelectronics processing facility, Electron Microscope Central Facility, Nanotools facilities, two virtual reality spaces: The YURT, and The Cave. **Physically Challenged Students:** Facilities include wheelchair ramps, elevators, special parking, specially equipped restrooms, special class scheduling, lowered drinking fountains, lowered telephones, and special housing. **Special:** Students may cross-register with Rhode Island School of Design (RISD) or study abroad in any of 120 programs in 11 countries. A combined A.B. - S.C.B. degree is possible in any major field with five years of study. Dual and student-designed majors and community internships are available. Students may pursue five year programs in the arts or sciences, or the eight year program in the Liberal Medical Education continuum, or the five year Brown/RISD dual degree program. Undergraduates study abroad in regions across the world. There are 3 national honor societies and a chapter of Phi Beta Kappa. **Visiting:** There are regularly scheduled orientations for prospective students, as well as group information sessions There are guides for informal visits and visitors may sit in on classes. To schedule a visit, contact the receptionist at admission@brown.edu. **Campus Safety and Security:** Measures include 24-hour foot and vehicle patrol, emergency notification system, self-defense education, and security escort services. There are also shuttle buses, emergency telephones, lighted pathways/sidewalks, controlled access to dorms/residences, SafeWALK, and SafeRIDE programs.

REQUIREMENTS: The SAT or ACT is required. Applicants must be graduates of accredited high schools or have completed an appropriate home school curriculum. Preparation is expected to include courses in English, foreign language, math, lab science, the arts (music or art), and history. A personal essay is required, as are two teacher recommendations. They may submit the SAT with or without essay, or they may submit the ACT with Writing recommended. (Applicants should check the Admission Office website for the current policy regarding SAT Subject Tests.) The high school transcript is the central criterion for admission. AP credits are accepted. Important factors in the admissions decision are advanced placement or honors courses, evidence of special talent, and personality/intangible qualities. Undergraduates at Brown design individualized programs of study across multiple departments. A strong advising network helps students engage fully with the Brown curriculum. To graduate, students must pass 30 courses in eight semesters, including 8 to 21 courses in the major. Students must also demonstrate writing proficiency throughout their time at Brown. With the exception of required courses specific to each major, there are no separate distribution requirements nor is there a core curriculum shared by all Brown undergraduates. Most students will complete a Capstone Project or Thesis by the time they graduate. **Procedure:** Freshmen are admitted in the fall. Entrance exams should be taken In the junior or early in the senior year. There are early decision and deferred admissions plans. Early decision applications should be filed by November 1; regular applications, by January 1 for fall entry, along with a $75 fee. Notification of early decision is sent December 15; regular decision, March 31. 669 early decision candidates were accepted for the 2016-2017 class. Application fees are waived if application is completed online. **Transfer Students:** 51 transfer students enrolled in 2015-2016. Transfer applicants must submit high school and college transcripts, two recommendations from college professors, scores on the ACT or on the SAT and any two SAT Subject tests, a letter of good standing from their original institution, and a personal essay. 15 of 30 credits required for the bachelor's degree must be completed at Brown. **International Students:** There are 744 international students enrolled. The school actively recruits these students. They must take the TOEFL with a minimum score of 100 on the Internet-based version (iBT), If a student receives at least a 600 on their SAT Critical Reading, they need not take the TOEFL. They must also take the ACT.

ADMISSIONS: 9% of the 2016-2017 applicants were accepted. The SAT scores for the 2016-2017 freshman class were: Critical Reading-- 5% between 500 and 599, 24% between 600 and 699, and 71% between 700 and 800. Math-- 4% between 500 and 599, 23% between 600 and 699, and 73% between 700 and 800. Writing-- 6% between 500 and 599, 21% between 600 and 699, and 73% between 700 and 800. The ACT scores were 1% between 18 and 23, 16% between 24 and 29, and 83% above 30. 97% of the current freshmen were in the top fifth of their class; 100% were in the top two fifths. **Admissions Contact:** Logan Powell, Dean of Admission. Email: *admission@brown.edu* Web: *www.brown.edu*

FINANCIAL AID: In 2016-2017, 45% of all full-time freshmen and continuing full-time students received some form of financial aid. 43% of all full-time freshmen and 44% of continuing full-time students received need-based aid. The average freshman award was $45,071.. The average financial indebtedness of the 2016 graduate was $22,197. Brown is a member of CSS. The CSS/Profile is required. The FAFSA code is 003401. The deadline for filing freshman financial aid applications for fall entry is February 1.

BRYANT UNIVERSITY — C-2

www.bryant.edu

Smithfield, RI 02917	**(401) 232-6100** **(800) 622-7001**
Fax: (401) 232-6741	**Email: admission@bryant.edu**
Full-time: 2046 men, 1355 women	**Faculty:** 162; IIB, ++$
Part-time: 38 men, 23 women	**Ph.D.s:** 79%
Graduate: 123 men, 113 women	**Student/Faculty:** 21 to 1
Year: semesters, summer session	**Tuition:** $40,962
Room & Board: $14,684	**Freshman Class:** 6013 applied, 4603 accepted, 890 enrolled
SAT CR/M/W: 550/585/545 **ACT:** 25	**CEEB CODE:** 3095
Application Deadline: n/av	**VERY COMPETITIVE**

Throughout its 150-year history, Bryant University has earned a distinguished reputation for innovative academic programs and technology that are marketplace driven and highly attuned to the emerging needs of industry and society. Bryant's close-knit, student-centered community of scholars delivers challenging academic programs that integrate business and the arts and sciences, with an emphasis on real-world application and a global perspective. Abundant co-curricular opportunities, service learning programs, internships, and practicums allow students to put theory into practice while building character and leadership skills. There are 2 undergraduate schools and 3 graduate schools. In addition to regional accreditation, Bryant has baccalaureate program accreditation with AACSB and AAC+U. The 435-acre campus is in a suburban area 10 miles northwest of Providence, 45 miles southwest of Boston, 190 miles from New York City. Including any residence halls, there are 55 buildings.

STUDENT LIFE: 86% of undergraduates are from out of state, mostly the Northeast. Students are from 35 states, 53 foreign countries, and Canada. 71% are from public schools. 74% are White; 7% Hispanic; 7% Foreign; 4% African American; 4% Asian American; 2% race unknown; 1% American Indian/Alaska Native; 1% two or more races. **Male To Female Ratio:** 1.5:1. The average age of freshmen is 18; all undergraduates, 20. 10% do not continue beyond their first year; 77% remain to graduate. **Housing:** 2882 students can be accommodated in college housing, which includes single-sex and coed dorms and on-campus apartments. In addition, there are honors houses, special-interest houses, and gender neutral housing. On-campus housing is guaranteed for all 4 years and is available on a lottery system for upperclassmen. 80% of students live on campus; of those, 85% remain on campus on weekends. All students may keep cars.

FACULTY/CLASSROOMS: 57% of faculty are male; 43% are female.

94% teach undergraduates, 55% do research, and 55% do both. No introductory courses are taught by graduate students. The average class size in an introductory lecture is 26; in a laboratory is 12; and in a regular course is 24.

PROGRAMS OF STUDY: Bryant confers B.A, B.S., B.S.B.A., B.S.I.B. and B.Sc.I.T. degrees. Master's degrees are also awarded. Bachelor's degrees are awarded in AGRICULTURE (conservation and regulation, environmental studies, natural resource/environmental economics, natural resources, and natural resource management), BIOLOGICAL SCIENCE (biology ecology and field biology, biochemistry, biology/biological science, biology (pre-physician assistant), biological sciences, cell biology, cell & molecular biology, ecology, environmental biology, environmental earth resources, forensic science, microbiology, molecular biology, and wildlife conservation biology), BUSINESS (accounting, accounting (finance), accounting (information systems), applied economics / management, applied management, banking and finance, business administration w/legal studies, business administration and management, business administration - international, business administration marketing, business communications, business data processing, business economics, business information systems, business intelligence and analytics, business law, business leadership, business statistics, business systems analysis, economics/ statistics, entrepreneurial studies, environment & national resource economics, finance, financial institutions management, financial services, finance (financial planning), global/general management, global management, human resources, industrial and labor relations, human resources/organizational management, institutional management, information & communication technology, insurance, international accounting, international business, insurance and risk management, international business information systems, international business management, international economics, investments and securities, international entrepreneurial management, international finance, international marketing, international supply and value chain management, labor studies, leadership, logistics, business management, management information systems, management, management science, marketing, management & strategic leadership, marketing and distribution, marketing management, marketing/retailing/merchandising, nonprofit/public organization management, operations research, organizational behavior, organizational leadership and management, personal financial planning, retailing, sports management, sports marketing, supply chain management, sustainable management, and professional program in accounting), COMMUNICATIONS AND THE ARTS (American literature, applied communication, applied speech communication, art and design, art/visual culture, Chinese, communication design, communication studies, communications, communication rhetoric/communication, communication science, comparative literature, design and environmental analysis, English, English literature, foreign language, French, French and Francophone studies, information technology, intermedia/multimedia, languages, literature, modern language, public relations, romance languages and literature, Spanish, Spanish and Hispanic studies, speech/debate/rhetoric, communication arts/speech, sports administration, sport & lifestyle studies, sports communication, sports media, strategic communication, visual communication, and visual design), COMPUTER AND PHYSICAL SCIENCE (actuarial science, actuarial mathematics, applied computing, applied geoscience, applied mathematics, applied science, chemistry / chemical biology, clinical laboratory science, computer management, computer information technology, computer information systems, computer science, computer science & informatics, earth science, geoenvironmental studies, inform, science, systms & tech, information sciences and systems, information science, informatics and computer science, mathematics, mathematics - actuarial concentration, mathematics/computational, mathematics/economics, quantitative methods, science of earth systems, science of natural and environmental systems, statistics, sustainable energy, and sustainable energy science), EDUCATION (general studies, global studies, sports and wellness studies, and sports studies), ENGINEERING AND ENVIRONMENTAL DESIGN (computational sciences, computer technology, environmental design, and environmental science), HEALTH PROFESSIONS (biology, medical science, pre-health studies, pre-health biological studies, pre-medicine, and pre-physician assistant), SOCIAL SCIENCE (American studies, applied psychology, applied social science, Chinese Studies, community services, cultural studies/critical theory & analysis, economics, government, feminist, gender, sexuality studies, forensic studies, French studies, gender studies, history, history and political science, humanities, humanities and social science, Iberian studies, international political science, international relations, international studies, law, legal studies, liberal arts/general studies, liberal arts, sciences, general studies, humanities, philosophy (history/contemporary thought), philosophy (political thought), political science/government, prelaw, psychology, public administration, public affairs, social science, sociology, Spanish studies, water resources, women & gender studies, and women's studies). Accounting, actuarial math, applied analytics, and international business are the strongest academically. Finance, marketing, accounting have the largest enrollments.

ACTIVITIES: 5% of men belong to 4 national fraternities; 11% of women belong to 4 national sororities. There are 111 groups on campus, including art, band, cheerleading, chess, choir, chorale, chorus, communications, computers, dance, debate, drama, drill team, environmental, ethnic, film, forensics, honors, international, jazz band, LGBT, literary magazine, musical theater, newspaper, orchestra, pep band, photography, political, professional, radio and TV, religious, social, social service, student government, and yearbook. Popular campus events include Student Arts & Speaker Series, Black History Month, Women's Summit, Research & Engagement Day, World Trade Day, Reunion @ Homecoming, Family & Friends Weekend, and Festival of Lights. **Sports:** There are 18 intercollegiate sports for men and 19 for women, and 15 intramural sports for men and 15 for women. Facilities include a wellness fitness center, a stadium, a gym, track & turf complex, softball, tennis complex, multipurpose athletic center, and weight room.**Graduates:** From July 1, 2015 to June 30, 2016, 783 bachelor's degrees were awarded. The most popular majors were business/marketing (79%), mathematics and statistics (5%), and communications/journalism (5%). 150 companies recruited on campus in 2015-2016. In an average class, 77% graduate in 4 years or less, 80% graduate in 5 years or less, and 80% graduate in 6 years or less. Of the 2015 graduating class, 18% were enrolled in graduate school within 6 months of graduation, and 80% were employed.

SERVICES: Counseling and information services are available, as is tutoring in most subjects. The Academic Center for Excellence offers tutoring for all currently enrolled students at Bryant and is certified by the College Reading and Learning Association. **Library/Resources:** The library contains 184,831 volumes, 14,451 microform items, 3,642 audio/video tapes/CDs/DVDs, and subscribes to 371,285 periodicals including electronic. Computerized library services include interlibrary loans, database searching, Internet access, and Wi-Fi capability. Special learning facilities include a radio station, TV station, George E. Bello Center for Information and Technology, C.V. Star Financial Markets Center, Stepan Grand Hall, Cerce Multi Media Wall; Douglas and Judith Krupp Library, Mahre Periodical Center; Koffler Technology Center and Communications Complex, Janikies Memorial Auditiorium; Koffler Rotunda multimedia student exhibition space; John H. Chafee Center for International Business; Center for Global and Regional Economic Studies; Intercultural Center; Gertrude Meth Hochberg Women's Center; Ronald K. and Kati C. Machtley Interfaith Center; Center for Student Invovlement. **Physically Challenged Students:** 90% of the campus is accessible. Facilities include wheelchair ramps, elevators, special parking, specially equipped restrooms, special class scheduling, lowered drinking fountains, lowered telephones, and special housing. **Special:** First-Year Gateway: 10 credits includes Global Foundations of Character & Leadership, Global Foundations of Organizations and Business, a writing course, and during winter session a 72 hour intensive course, IDEA (Innovation and Design Experience for All) experiential learning generating creative solutions to a real-world situation, plus cocurrcular programs with Student Life. Honors Program culminating in a Senior Capstone Project, an interdisciplinary topic of personal interest and aligned to future career or study. Sophomore International Experience (3 credit pre-travel class work plus travel abraod during winter and summer sessions). Study Abroad (semester length via nine providers in over 54 countries). Exchange Programs for semester or year in Japan, Great Britain, and Spain. Service Learning through student organizations and/or coursework in Sociology, Mangement, Literary & Cultural Studies, and/or History, volunteering in community service, learning, reflecting, and devising solutions in classroom and in service. Academic Internships, 3 credits for professional work experience with faculty advisor. Practicum, 6 to 9 credits for professional work experience culminating in a major research project. European Studay Abroad (EUSA) A ten week summer program providing a living, learning and professional working experience in Dublin. The program includes a supervised internship (3 credits); a course taught in Dublin by a Bryant professor (3 credits) and opportunities to explore Dublin, as well as travel in

Europe. Internship and housing is provided. The Washington Center, a full-time internship and seminar program offered during the fall, spring and summer semesters in DC. Eligible students can earn 9 to 15 credits for one semester by living, learning and working in DC. The internship placement, seminar program, one evening course and housing is provided. Work Study: Bryant University provides part-time employment opportunities for work-study eligible students to assist them in meeting the cost of education. Army ROTC. There are 10 national honor societies, a freshman honors program, and 13 departmental honors programs. **Visiting:** There are regularly scheduled orientations for prospective students, student-guided tours, admissions staff information sessions, day with class, and interviews offered. There are guides for informal visits, visitors may sit in on classes, and stay overnight. To schedule a visit, contact the Office of Admission at (800) 622-7001. **Campus Safety and Security:** Measures include 24-hour foot and vehicle patrol, emergency notification system, self-defense education, and security escort services. There are also shuttle buses, emergency telephones, lighted pathways/sidewalks, controlled access to dorms/residences, and one vehicular entrance monitored by an Entry Control Station.

REQUIREMENTS: Accredited high school diploma or GED. High school general college prepatory program. Academic units: 4 English, 4 Math, 2 Lab Science, 2 Foreign Language, 2 History. Very important: rigor of high school record, GPA. Important: class rank, standardized test scores, application essay, recommendations. AP and CLEP credits are accepted. Students must complete 122-125 credits. First-Year Gateway: 10 credits includes Global Foundations of Character & Leadership, Global Foundations of Organizations and Business, Writing Workshop, and during winter session a 72 hour intensive course, IDEA (Innovation and Design Experience for All) experiential learning generating creative solutions to a real-world situation. Upper Level Gateway: a culminating course across all disciplines. Liberal Arts Core: includes Literary Studies, Micro and Macro-Economics, Mathematics, and Statistics courses. Liberal Arts Distribution: includes two social science, two laboratory science, history, and literature courses. Business Core: includes accounting, finance, information technology, management, and marketing courses. Cross college minors: College of Arts & Sciences majors must minor in a College of Business field, and College of Business majors must minor in a College of Arts & Sciences field. All majors include a senior capstone course, a senior research seminar, and/or a senior practicum combining classroom and work experience related to the major. **Procedure:** Freshmen are admitted in the fall and spring. Entrance exams should be taken by the fall. There are early decision, early admissions, and deferred admissions plans. Early decision applications should be filed by November 15. The fall 2016 application fee was $50. Notification of early decision is sent December 17; regular decision, 116 early decision candidates were accepted for the 2016-2017 class. 383 applicants were on the 2016 waiting list; 95 were admitted. Applications are accepted on-line. **Transfer Students:** 92 transfer students enrolled in 2015-2016. Your high school transcript, college transcript, and personal essay are required, as well as list of course numbers not included on college transcript that the applicant expects to complete before enrollment. 30 credits required for the bachelor's degree must be completed at Bryant. **International Students:** There are 247 international students enrolled. The school actively recruits these students. They must take the TOEFL with a minimum score of 550 on the paper-based TOEFL (PBT) or 80 on the Internet-based version (iBT).

ADMISSIONS: 77% of the 2016-2017 applicants were accepted. The SAT scores for the 2016-2017 freshman class were: Critical Reading-- 18% below 500, 59% between 500 and 599, 20% between 600 and 699, and 3% between 700 and 800. Math-- 8% below 500, 48% between 500 and 599, 37% between 600 and 699, and 7% between 700 and 800. Writing-- 22% below 500, 53% between 500 and 599, 23% between 600 and 699, and 2% between 700 and 800. The ACT scores were 3% below 12, 23% between 12 and 17, 45% between 18 and 23, 16% between 24 and 29, and 13% above 30. 43% of the current freshmen were in the top fifth of their class; 77% were in the top two fifths. 1 freshman graduated first in the class. **Admissions Contact:** Michelle Beauregard, Director of Admission. Email: *admission@bryant.edu* Web: *www.bryant.edu*

FINANCIAL AID: The average freshman award was $23,109. Need-based scholarships or need-based grants averaged $11,816; need-based self-help aid (loans and jobs) averaged $5,005; non-need-based athletic scholarships averaged $17,835; other non-need-based awards and non-need-based scholarships averaged $3,862; and $12,412 from other forms of aid. The average financial indebtedness of the 2016 graduate was $44,580. Bryant is a member of CSS. The FAFSA code is 003402. Check with the school for current application deadlines.

JOHNSON & WALES UNIVERSITY/ PROVIDENCE CAMPUS C-2

www.jwu.edu/providence

Providence, RI 02903 (401) 598-1000

Email: admissions.pvd@jwu.edu

Full-time: 3290 men, 4855 women
Part-time: 218 men, 355 women
Graduate: 295 men, 441 women
Year: trimesters, summer session
Room & Board: $12,672

Faculty: 294
Ph.D.s: 25%
Student/Faculty: 20 to 1
Tuition: $29,576
Freshman Class: 11971 applied, 9807 accepted, 2006 enrolled
CEEB CODE: 3465

Application Deadline: n/av
COMPETITIVE

Johnson & Wales University/Providence Campus, founded in 1914, is the largest of the JWU campuses and offers more than 50 majors in business, hospitality, culinary arts, technology, and graduate programs. There are 4 undergraduate schools and 2 graduate schools. The 166-acre campus is in a small town in Providence, 45 minutes from Boston, Cape Cod, and Newport and 3 hours from New York. Including any residence halls, there are 38 buildings.

STUDENT LIFE: 81% of undergraduates are from out of state, mostly the Northeast. Students are from 50 states, 91 foreign countries, and Canada. 8% are two or more races; 56% White; 4% race unknown; 11% African American; 11% Hispanic; 10% Foreign; 1% Asian American. **Female To Male Ratio:** 1.5:1. The average age of freshmen is 18; all undergraduates, 21. **Housing:** 3748 students can be accommodated in college housing, which includes coed dorms and on-campus apartments, apartments for single students, and wellness housing. On-campus housing is available on a lottery system for upperclassmen. 56% of students commute. All students may keep cars. Alcohol is not permitted.

FACULTY/CLASSROOMS: 56% of faculty are male; 44% are female. 95% teach undergraduates. No introductory courses are taught by graduate students.

PROGRAMS OF STUDY: JWU confers B.S. degrees. Associate, master's, and doctoral degrees are also awarded. Bachelor's degrees are awarded in AGRICULTURE (equine science), BUSINESS (accounting, business administration and management, entrepreneurial studies, fashion merchandising, hospitality management services, hotel/motel and restaurant management, international business management, management information systems, marketing and distribution, marketing management, marketing/retailing/merchandising, office supervision and management, recreation and leisure services, recreational facilities management, retailing, secretarial studies/office management, small business management, sports management, tourism, and transportation and travel marketing), COMMUNICATIONS AND THE ARTS (advertising), COMPUTER AND PHYSICAL SCIENCE (computer management, computer science, information sciences and systems, systems analysis, and web services), EDUCATION (marketing and distribution education), ENGINEERING AND ENVIRONMENTAL DESIGN (electrical/electronics engineering, food services technology, and technological management), SOCIAL SCIENCE (clothing and textiles management/production/services, criminal justice, food production/management/services, paralegal studies, parks and recreation management, and systems science). Culinary arts, hotel/restaurant management, and marketing are the strongest academically. Culinary arts, hotel/restaurant management, and sports entertainment event management have the largest enrollments.

ACTIVITIES: 2% of men belong to 9 national fraternities; 2% of women belong to 7 national sororities. There are 100 groups on campus, including cheerleading, computers, dance, debate, drama, environmental, ethnic, honors, international, LGBT, Multicultural clubs, musical theater, newspaper, pep band, political, professional, religious, social, social service, student government, and yearbook. **Sports:** There are 8 intercollegiate sports for men and 6 for women, and 7 intramural sports for men and 4 for women. Facilities include exercise machines, numerous programs, weight management, personal exercise, wellness programs, body composition analysis, strength training, physical fitness testing, nutritional analysis, physical fitness assessments, life saving, and stress relief days. **Graduates:** From July 1, 2015 to June 30, 2016, 1944 bachelor's degrees were awarded. The most popular majors were business/marketing (39%), family and consumer sciences (25%), and parks and recreation (11%). In an average class, 54% graduate in 6 years or less.

SERVICES: Counseling and information services are available, as is tutoring in every subject. Workshops in stress and time management, and wellness and learning centers are available. **Library/Resources:** The 2 libraries contain 108,706 volumes, 439,822 microform items, and 3,832 audio/video tapes/CDs/DVDs, and subscribe to 26,160 periodicals including electronic. Computerized library services include interlibrary loans, database searching, Internet access, and Wi-Fi capability. **Physically Challenged Students:** All of the campus is accessible. Facilities include wheelchair ramps, elevators, special parking, specially equipped restrooms, special class scheduling, lowered drinking fountains, lowered telephones, and special housing. **Special:** The university offers 11-week internships in most majors, study abroad in 19 countries, work-study programs, accelerated degree programs, and dual majors. Students have the opportunity to receive hands-on experience through 2 JWU programs: Summer Work Experience (SWEP) and Cooperative Education. There is 1 national honor society, a freshman honors program, and 5 departmental honors programs. **Visiting:** There are regularly scheduled orientations for prospective students, including tours conducted by JWU students. These tours include an introduction to the academic and social aspects of the campus experience through interactive sessions. There are guides for informal visits, visitors may sit in on classes, and stay overnight. To schedule a visit, contact the Admissions Office. **Campus Safety and Security:** Measures include 24-hour foot and vehicle patrol, emergency notification system, and security escort services. There are also shuttle buses, emergency telephones, lighted pathways/sidewalks, controlled access to dorms/residences 24-hour dorm coverage, phone hot line for campus emergencies, and crime alerts in the student weekly newspaper.

REQUIREMENTS: Although SAT and ACT scores are required only for students applying for honors admissions, students who have taken these tests are encouraged to submit their scores. GED is accepted. Applicants must complete 4 years of English, 3 years each of mathematics and science, and 2 years of social studies. AP and CLEP credits are accepted. Important factors in the admissions decision are advanced placement or honors courses, extracurricular activities record, evidence of special talent, personality/intangible qualities, recommendations by alumni, and by school officials. To graduate, students must complete 180 quarter credit hours, including at least 36 in the major, with a minimum GPA of 2.0. Required classes include English, math, history, economics, science, psychology, sociology, and professional development. **Procedure:** There are deferred admissions and rolling admissions plans. Application deadlines are open. **Transfer Students:** 472 transfer students enrolled in 2015-2016. Applicants are required to submit official high school and college transcripts and must have earned a minimum college GPA of 2.0. Students may enroll in the fall, winter, spring and summer. 45 of 180 credits required for the bachelor's degree must be completed at JWU. **International Students:** There are 949 international students enrolled. The school actively recruits these students.

ADMISSIONS: 82% of the 2016-2017 applicants were accepted. **Admissions Contact:** Kim Medina, Director of Admissions. Email: *admissions.pvd@jwu.edu* Web: *www.jwu.edu/providence*

FINANCIAL AID: The average freshman award was $23,037. Need-based scholarships or need-based grants averaged $6,048; need-based self-help aid (loans and jobs) averaged $4,303; other non-need-based awards and non-need-based scholarships averaged $3,395; and $9,619 from other forms of aid. The FAFSA code is 003404. Check with the school for current application deadlines.

PROVIDENCE COLLEGE C-2

www.providence.edu

Providence, RI 02918 **(401) 865-2535** **(800) 721-6444**
Fax: (401) 865-2826 **Email: pcadmiss@providence.edu**

Full-time: 1703 men, 2208 women	**Faculty:** 296; IIA, +$
Part-time: 137 men, 153 women	**Ph.D.s:** 94%
Graduate: 211 men, 323 women	**Student/Faculty:** 8 to 1
Year: semesters, summer session	**Tuition:** $45,400
Room & Board: $13,390	**Freshman Class:** 10217 applied, 5802 accepted, 1034 enrolled
SAT CR/M/W: 570/580/580 **ACT:** 25	**CEEB CODE:** 3693
Application Deadline: January 15	**VERY COMPETITIVE**

Providence College is a primarily undergraduate, liberal arts, independent, not-for-profit, Catholic institution of higher education. Committed to fostering academic excellence rooted in the arts and sciences, the college provides a variety of opportunities for intellectual, social and spiritual growth in a supportive environment. There are 4 undergraduate schools and 3 graduate schools. In addition to regional accreditation, PC has baccalaureate program accreditation with AACSB, CSWE, NASM, and ACS. The 105-acre campus is in a suburban area 50 miles south of Boston. Including any residence halls, there are 46 buildings.

STUDENT LIFE: 85% of undergraduates are from out of state, mostly the Northeast. Students are from 40 states, 30 foreign countries, and Canada. 8% are Hispanic; 78% White; 5% race unknown; 4% African American; 2% Foreign; 2% two or more races; 1% Asian American. 68% are Catholic; 16% claim no religious affiliation. **Female To Male Ratio:** 1.3:1. The average age of freshmen is 18; all undergraduates, 21. 10% do not continue beyond their first year; 85% remain to graduate. **Housing:** 2975 students can be accommodated in college housing, which includes single-sex and coed dorms and on-campus apartments. Housing is for freshman and sophomore years only. On-campus housing is available on a first-come, first-served basis, and on a lottery system for upperclassmen. 71% of students live on campus; of those, 90% remain on campus on weekends. Upperclassmen may keep cars.

FACULTY/CLASSROOMS: 55% of faculty are male; 45% are female. 93% teach undergraduates. No introductory courses are taught by graduate students. The average class size in an introductory lecture is 20; in a laboratory is 18; and in a regular course is 21.

PROGRAMS OF STUDY: PC confers B.A., and B.S., degrees. Associate and master's degrees are also awarded. Bachelor's degrees are awarded in BIOLOGICAL SCIENCE (biochemistry and biology/biological science), BUSINESS (accounting, business administration and management, business economics, finance, management & strategic leadership, marketing management, organizational leadership and management, and professional studies), COMMUNICATIONS AND THE ARTS (art history, dramatic arts, English, French, German, Italian, music, painting, photography, printmaking, sculpture, Spanish, studio art, and theatre arts), COMPUTER AND PHYSICAL SCIENCE (applied physics, chemistry, computer science, and mathematics), EDUCATION (elementary education, English education, foreign languages education, global studies, mathematics education, music education, secondary education, social studies education, and special education), ENGINEERING AND ENVIRONMENTAL DESIGN (preengineering), HEALTH PROFESSIONS (health administration and policy), SOCIAL SCIENCE (American studies, community services, economics, fire science, history, humanities, liberal arts/general studies, philosophy, political science/government, psychology, social science, social work, sociology, theological studies, and women's studies). Biology, business, and chemistry are the strongest academically. Marketing, finance, and biology have the largest enrollments.

ACTIVITIES: There are no fraternities or sororities. There are 120 groups on campus, including intramural sports, art, band, cheerleading, chess, chorale, dance, debate, drama, environmental, ethnic, film, honors, international, jazz band, LGBT, literary magazine, mock trial club, musical theater, newspaper, pep band, political, professional, radio and TV, religious, social, social service, student government, and yearbook. Popular campus events include Late Night Madness, Clam Jam, and Provapalooza. **Sports:** There are 7 intercollegiate sports for men and 10 for women, and 20 intramural sports for men and 20 for women.

Facilities include an ice arena, indoor track, tennis courts, basketball courts, volleyball court, a pool, intercollegiate strength and conditioning facilities, softball field, an outdoor track, outdoor artificial fields, and an outdoor grass field. **Graduates:** From July 1, 2015 to June 30, 2016, 993 bachelor's degrees were awarded. The most popular majors were marketing (10%), finance (10%), and biology (8%). In an average class, 79% graduate in 4 years or less, 83% graduate in 5 years or less, and 85% graduate in 6 years or less. Of the 2015 graduating class, 24% were enrolled in graduate school within 6 months of graduation, and 70% were employed.

SERVICES: Counseling and information services are available, as is tutoring in most subjects, and assistance with time management and study skills **Library/Resources:** The library contains 1.5 million volumes, 10,965 microform items, and 3,126 audio/video tapes/CDs/DVDs, and subscribes to 52,631 periodicals including electronic. Computerized library services include interlibrary loans, database searching, Internet access, and Wi-Fi capability. Special learning facilities include an art gallery, radio station, TV station, theater, center for the arts, science center complex, center for the humanities, a community learning space, and computer and language labs. **Physically Challenged Students:** 90% of the campus is accessible. Facilities include wheelchair ramps, elevators, special parking, specially equipped restrooms, lowered drinking fountains, and special housing. **Special:** Providence College offers internships in a variety of fields, including politics, broadcasting, journalism and business. Study abroad is available to students in every major. PC approves over 350 study abroad program options in more than 50 different countries. Also available are student-designed majors, a 3-2 engineering program with Columbia University or Washington University in St. Louis, non-degree study, a Washington semester, work-study, B.A.-B.S. degrees and pass/fail options. There are 21 national honor societies, a freshman honors program, and 16 departmental honors programs. **Visiting:** There are regularly scheduled orientations for prospective students, including campus tours and information sessions. Visitors may also sit in on classes. To schedule a visit, contact The Admissions Office. **Campus Safety and Security:** Measures include 24-hour foot and vehicle patrol, emergency notification system, self-defense education, and security escort services. There are shuttle buses, emergency telephones, lighted pathways/sidewalks, and controlled access to dorms/residences.

REQUIREMENTS: Applicants must be graduates of an accredited secondary school. An unweighted GPA of 3.25 in a rigorous curriculum is recommended. High school preparation should include 4 years of English, 4 years of math, 3 years of 1 foreign language, 3 years of science with at least 2 years of lab science, 2 years of history/social studies, and 2 other academic subjects. An essay and 2 academic letters of recommendation are required. Submission of standardized tests is optional. AP and CLEP credits are accepted. Important factors in the admissions decision are advanced placement or honors courses, extracurricular activities record, and personality/intangible qualities. To graduate, all students must complete at least 120 credit hours including all requirements for the student's major, and maintain an overall and major GPA of at least 2.0. Students must also meet all core requirements, including 16 credits in Development of Western Civilization, 6 credits in theology, 6 credits in philosophy (3 in ethics and 3 in a non-ethics philosophy course), 3 credits each in natural science, social science, fine arts and quantitative reasoning. Courses in the major or elective courses must include two intensive writing courses, as well as courses which address oral communication skills, diversity and civic engagement, and a set of two linked courses outside the major. **Procedure:** Freshmen are admitted in the fall and spring. Entrance exams should be taken by February 15. There are early decision, early admissions, and deferred admissions plans. Early decision applications should be filed by December 1; regular applications, by January 15 for fall entry; and December 1 for spring entry, along with a $65 fee. Notifications are sent April 1. 171 early decision candidates were accepted for the 2016-2017 class. 2430 applicants were on the 2016 waiting list; 158 were admitted. Applications are accepted online. **Transfer Students:** 57 transfer students enrolled in 2015-2016. Students must complete the Common Application and forms for Transfer students, and submit a final official high school transcript, college transcript (s), essay, statement of good standing from prior institution (s) and a minimum college grade point average of 3.0 on a 4.0 scale. Submission of standardized tests is optional. Class Syllabi should be sent to syllabi@providence.edu for transfer credit evaluation. Transfer student policies listed here apply to our traditional undergraduate day school only. However, we also have a School of Continuing Education that enrolls transfer students and they are included in our above transfer student totals. The School of Continuing Education has a variety of different transfer credit policies and requirements. If applying to our School of Continuing Education program, please contact them directly for guidelines. 60 of 120 credits required for the bachelor's degree must be completed at PC. **International Students:** There are 88 international students enrolled. The school actively recruits these students. They must take the TOEFL with a minimum score of 90 on the Internet-based version (iBT), and take the IELTS.

ADMISSIONS: 57% of the 2016-2017 applicants were accepted. The SAT scores for the 2016-2017 freshman class were: Critical Reading-- 15% below 500, 52% between 500 and 599, 29% between 600 and 699, and 4% between 700 and 800. Math-- 13% below 500, 46% between 500 and 599, 36% between 600 and 699, and 5% between 700 and 800. Writing-- 15% below 500, 45% between 500 and 599, 34% between 600 and 699, and 6% between 700 and 800. The ACT scores were 1% between 12 and 17, 29% between 18 and 23, 55% between 24 and 29, and 15% above 30. 62% of the current freshmen were in the top fifth of their class; 90% were in the top two fifths. 13 freshmen graduated first in their class. **Admissions Contact:** Raul A. Fonts, Dean of Admission. Email: *pcadmiss@providence.edu* Web: *www.providence.edu*

FINANCIAL AID: In 2016-2017, 77% of all full-time freshmen and 78% of continuing full-time students received some form of financial aid. 77% of all full-time freshmen and 78% of continuing full-time students received need-based aid. The average freshman award was $28,504. Need-based scholarships or need-based grants averaged $26,300 ($52,185 maximum); need-based self-help aid (loans and jobs) averaged $5,980 ($10,800 maximum); non-need-based athletic scholarships averaged $35,581 ($65,265 maximum); and other non-need-based awards and non-need-based scholarships averaged $20,388 ($44,520 maximum). 31% of undergraduate students work part-time. Average annual earnings from campus work are $950. The average financial indebtedness of the 2016 graduate was $37,740. PC is a member of CSS. The CSS/Profile is required. The FAFSA code is 003406. The deadline for filing freshman financial aid applications for fall entry is February 1.

RHODE ISLAND COLLEGE *(The complete profile is made available exclusively on our website, www.barronspac.com)*

RHODE ISLAND SCHOOL OF DESIGN *(The complete profile is made available exclusively on our website, www.barronspac.com)*

ROGER WILLIAMS UNIVERSITY D-3

www.rwu.edu

Bristol, RI 02809	**(401) 254-3500** **(800) 458-7144**
Fax: (401) 254-3557	**Email: admit@rwu.edu**
Full-time: 1977 men, 2053 women	**Faculty:** 207; IIB, ++$
Part-time: 306 men, 274 women	**Ph.D.s:** 90%
Graduate: 131 men, 143 women	**Student/Faculty:** 19 to 1
Year: semesters, summer session	**Tuition:** $31,750
Room & Board: $14,546	**Freshman Class:** 9913 applied, 7727 accepted, 1152 enrolled
SAT CR/M/W: 545/570/555 **ACT:** 25	**CEEB CODE:** 3729
Application Deadline: February 1	**COMPETITIVE+**

Roger Williams University, founded in 1956, is a leading independent, coeducational university with programs in arts and sciences, professional studies, architecture, and law. Offering 43 majors and a plethora of co-curricular activities as well as study abroad options, RWU is dedicated to the success of students, commitment to a set of core values, the pursuit of affordable excellence and to providing a relevant, world-class education above all else. There are 8 undergraduate schools and 6 graduate schools. In addition to regional accreditation, RWU has baccalaureate program accreditation with AACSB, ABET, ACCE, NAAB, NASDTEC, ABA, and NASDTEC. The 140-acre campus is in a small town 18 miles southeast of Providence. Including any residence halls, there are 42 buildings.

STUDENT LIFE: 81% of undergraduates are from out of state, mostly the Northeast. Students are from 44 states, 62 foreign countries, and

Canada. 72% are White; 12% race unknown; 5% Hispanic; 5% Foreign; 2% African American; 2% Asian American; 2% two or more races; 1% American Indian/Alaska Native. **Female To Male Ratio:** 1.0:1. The average age of freshmen is 18; all undergraduates, 22. 21% do not continue beyond their first year; 62% remain to graduate. **Housing:** 3050 students can be accommodated in college housing, which includes single-sex and coed dorms, on-campus apartments, off-campus apartments, and married student housing, honors houses, special-interest houses, and academic major living learning communities. On-campus housing is guaranteed for the freshman year only and on a lottery system for upperclassmen. 67% of students live on campus; of those, 70% remain on campus on weekends. Upperclassmen may keep cars.

FACULTY/CLASSROOMS: 57% of faculty are male; 43% are female. All teach undergraduates. No introductory courses are taught by graduate students.

PROGRAMS OF STUDY: RWU confers B.A., B.S., B.Arch., B.F.A. and B.G.S degrees. Associate and master's degrees are also awarded. Bachelor's degrees are awarded in BIOLOGICAL SCIENCE (biochemistry, biology/biological science, and marine biology), BUSINESS (accounting, banking and finance, business administration and management, business law, international business management, management science, and marketing/retailing/merchandising), COMMUNICATIONS AND THE ARTS (art history and appreciation, communications, creative writing, dance, dramatic arts, English, graphic design, historic preservation, journalism, languages, media arts, music, theatre arts, and visual and performing arts), COMPUTER AND PHYSICAL SCIENCE (chemistry, computer science, computer security and information assurance, mathematics, web services, and web technology), EDUCATION (education, elementary education, and secondary education), ENGINEERING AND ENVIRONMENTAL DESIGN (architecture, construction management, engineering, environmental science, industrial engineering technology, and technological management), HEALTH PROFESSIONS (health care administration), SOCIAL SCIENCE (American studies, anthropology, community services, criminal justice, economics, history, humanities, international relations, legal studies, paralegal studies, philosophy, political science/government, psychology, public administration, social science, and sociology). Architecture, and engineering are the strongest academically. Architecture, psychology, and criminal justice have the largest enrollments.

ACTIVITIES: There are no fraternities or sororities. There are 70 groups on campus, including art, band, cheerleading, chess, choir, chorale, chorus, communications, computers, dance, drama, environmental, ethnic, film, honors, international, jazz band, LGBT, literary magazine, musical theater, newspaper, orchestra, photography, political, professional, radio and TV, religious, social service, student government, and yearbook. Popular campus events include Spring Weekend, International Dinner, and Campus Entertainment Network. **Sports:** There are 11 intercollegiate sports for men and 11 for women, and 17 intramural sports for men and 16 for women. Facilities include a fitness center, aquatic center, dance studios, racquetball/squash courts squash court, sailing and kayaking, soccer and lacrosse, softball and baseball, outdoor tennis, volleyball, and basketball courts. **Graduates:** From July 1, 2015 to June 30, 2016, 884 bachelor's degrees were awarded. The most popular majors were business/marketing (24%), architecture (10%), and justice studies (9%). 80 companies recruited on campus in 2015-2016. In an average class, 50% graduate in 4 years or less, 58% graduate in 5 years or less, and 62% graduate in 6 years or less. Of the 2015 graduating class, 13% were enrolled in graduate school within 6 months of graduation.

SERVICES: Counseling and information services are available, as is tutoring in every subject, a reader service for the blind, and remedial math, reading, and writing. **Library/Resources:** The 3 libraries contain 499,355 volumes, 140,689 microform items, 5,347 audio/video tapes/CDs/DVDs, and subscribe to 50,391 periodicals including electronic. Computerized library services include interlibrary loans, database searching, Internet access, and Wi-Fi capability. Special learning facilities include an art gallery, radio station, RWU Marine and Natural Sciences building is home to a marine biology wet-lab and shellfish hatchery. The University also accesses an 80 acre field site on nearby Prudence Island, which includes Jenny's Creek Salt Marsh and the Oyster Nursey Pond. **Physically Challenged Students:** Facilities include wheelchair ramps, elevators, special parking, specially equipped restrooms, special class scheduling, lowered drinking fountains, and lowered telephones. **Special:** RWU offers co-op programs, internships, accelerated degree programs, study abroad in 30 countries, work-study, individualized majors, and dual majors. There are 16 national honor societies and a freshman honors program. **Visiting:** There are regularly scheduled orientations for prospective students. There are guides for informal visits and visitors may sit in on classes. To schedule a visit, contact the Office of Admission. **Campus Safety and Security:** Measures include 24-hour foot and vehicle patrol, emergency notification system, and security escort services. There are shuttle buses, emergency telephones, lighted pathways/sidewalks, and controlled access to dorms/residences.

REQUIREMENTS: Applicants should be graduates of an accredited secondary school with a minimum GPA of 2.0. The GED is accepted. Students should have 4 years of English, 3 years of math, 3 years of social sciences, 3 years of natural sciences (of which 2 must be lab units), 2 years of history and 4 to 6 electives, for a total of 16 Carnegie units. Art and architecture students must submit portfolios. An essay is required, and an interview is recommended. See admission requirements for individual colleges. AP and CLEP credits are accepted. Important factors in the admissions decision are recommendations by school officials, leadership record, and advanced placement or honors courses. All students must: earn a minimum cumulative grade point average (GPA) of 2.0 in order to graduate. Each college or school may also require a minimum GPA in the major. Successfully complete a minimum of 30 credits of course work in a major, all University Core Curriculum requirements and the Service Learning Requirement. Complete 45 of the last 60 credits at RWU or at an RWU Semester Abroad program. All financial obligations must be satisfied. **Procedure:** Freshmen are admitted fall and spring. Entrance exams should be taken September or October of the senior year. There are early admissions, deferred admissions, and rolling admissions plans. Applications should be filed by February 1 for fall entry, along with a $50 fee. Notification of early decision is sent December 15; regular decision, March 15. 164 applicants were on the 2016 waiting list; 56 were admitted. Applications are accepted online. **Transfer Students:** 184 transfer students enrolled in 2015-2016. Applicants need a minimum college GPA of 2.5, college transcripts, an essay or personal statement and a statement of good standing from the prior institution. 45 of 120 credits required for the bachelor's degree must be completed at RWU. **International Students:** There are 229 international students enrolled. The school actively recruits these students. They must take the TOEFL with a minimum score of 85 on the Internet-based version (iBT) and the college's own test. SAT scores are required for all education majors.

ADMISSIONS: 78% of the 2016-2017 applicants were accepted. 44% of the current freshmen were in the top fifth of their class; 81% were in the top two fifths. **Admissions Contact:** Amanda Marsili, Director of Admissions Operations. Email: *admit@rwu.edu* Web: *www.rwu.edu*

FINANCIAL AID: In 2016-2017, 66% of all full-time freshmen and continuing full-time students received some form of financial aid. 50% of all full-time freshmen and 40% of continuing full-time students received need-based aid. The average freshman award was $20,071. Need-based scholarships or need-based grants averaged $14,310; need-based self-help aid (loans and jobs) averaged $5,761; and other non-need-based awards and non-need-based scholarships averaged $11,831. 35% of undergraduate students work part-time. Average annual earnings from campus work are $2000. RWU is a member of CSS. The CSS/Profile is required. The FAFSA code is 003410. The priority date for freshman financial aid applications for fall entry is February 1. The filing deadline for fall entry is February 1.

SALVE REGINA UNIVERSITY D-4

www.salve.edu

Newport, RI 02840	**(401) 341-2908** **(888) GO-SALVE**
Fax: (401) 848-2823	**Email: sruadmis@salve.edu**
Full-time: 608 men, 1367 women	**Faculty:** 125; IIA, av$
Part-time: 25 men, 124 women	**Ph.D.s:** 84%
Graduate: 225 men, 397 women	**Student/Faculty:** 16 to 1
Year: semesters, summer session	**Tuition:** $37,820
Room & Board: $13,650	**Freshman Class:** 4803 applied, 3526 accepted, 554 enrolled
SAT CR/M/W: 550/540/550 **ACT:** 24	**CEEB CODE:** 3759
Application Deadline: February 1	**COMPETITIVE**

Salve Regina University, founded in 1934 and sponsored by the Sisters of Mercy, is an independent institution affiliated with the Roman Catholic Church. The university offers programs in liberal arts, business, health science, and professional training. There is 1 undergraduate school and 1 graduate school. In addition to regional accreditation, Salve has baccalaureate program accreditation with CSWE, NASAD, IACBE, CORE, and AACN. The 80-acre campus is in a suburban area is 35 south of Providence and 60 miles south of Boston with an off-site location in Warwick, Rhode Island. Including any residence halls, there are 51 buildings.

STUDENT LIFE: 79% of undergraduates are from out of state, mostly the Northeast. Students are from 33 states, 17 foreign countries, and Canada. 72% are from public schools. 81% are White; 7% race unknown; 6% Hispanic; 2% African American; 2% two or more races; 1% Asian American; 1% Foreign. **Female To Male Ratio:** 2.2:1. The average age of freshmen is 18; all undergraduates, 21. 16% do not continue beyond their first year; 70% remain to graduate. **Housing:** 1274 students can be accommodated in college housing, which includes single-sex and coed dorms, on-campus apartments, and off-campus apartments, language houses, special-interest houses, and living/learning dorms. On-campus housing is available on a first-come, first-served basis, and on a lottery system for upperclassmen. 60% of students live on campus; of those, 75% remain on campus on weekends. Upperclassmen may keep cars.

FACULTY/CLASSROOMS: 42% of faculty are male; 58% are female. All teach undergraduates, 50% do research, and 50% do both. No introductory courses are taught by graduate students. The average class size in an introductory lecture is 22; in a laboratory is 17; and in a regular course is 18.

PROGRAMS OF STUDY: Salve confers B.A., B.S. and B.A.S. degrees. Associate, master's, and doctoral degrees are also awarded. Bachelor's degrees are awarded in BIOLOGICAL SCIENCE (biology/biological science and environmental biology), BUSINESS (accounting, business administration and management, finance, international business management, management science, and marketing and distribution), COMMUNICATIONS AND THE ARTS (art history and appreciation, communications, communications technology, dramatic arts, English, French, historic preservation, media arts, music, Spanish, and studio art), COMPUTER AND PHYSICAL SCIENCE (chemistry and mathematics), EDUCATION (early childhood education, elementary education, secondary education, and special education), HEALTH PROFESSIONS (health administration and policy and nursing), SOCIAL SCIENCE (American studies, criminal justice, economics, history, international studies, liberal arts/general studies, philosophy, political science/government, psychology, religion, social work, and sociology). Social work, nursing, administration of justice, business and accounting. are the strongest academically. Business, administration of justice, and teacher education have the largest enrollments.

ACTIVITIES: There are no fraternities or sororities. There are 42 groups on campus, including art, band, cheerleading, choir, chorus, computers, dance, drama, environmental, ethnic, film, honors, international, jazz band, LGBT, literary magazine, musical theater, newspaper, outdoor clubs, pep band, photography, political, professional, radio and TV, religious, social, social service, student government, and yearbook. Popular campus events include September Welcome-Back Weekend, Octoberfest Weekend, and New Year's Eve Ball. **Sports:** There are 8 intercollegiate sports for men and 10 for women, and 8 intramural sports for men and 9 for women. Facilities include a recreation center, tennis courts, outdoor basketball courts, weight room, fitness center, soccer, baseball, and softball fields. **Graduates:** From July 1, 2015 to June 30, 2016, 481 bachelor's degrees were awarded. The most popular majors were nursing (17%), administration of justice (10%), and business administration (9%). In an average class, 1% graduate in 3 years or less, 67% graduate in 4 years or less, 3% graduate in 5 years or less, and 1% graduate in 6 years or less. Of the 2015 graduating class, 20% were enrolled in graduate school within 6 months of graduation, and 85% were employed.

SERVICES: Counseling and information services are available, as is tutoring in most subjects. There is remedial math, reading, and writing. There also is a writing center and a computer-based tutorial program. **Library/Resources:** The library contains 158,092 volumes, 46,067 microform items, 64,829 audio/video tapes/CDs/DVDs, and subscribes to 1,041 periodicals including electronic. Computerized library services include interlibrary loans, database searching, Internet access, and Wi-Fi capability. Special learning facilities include an art gallery, radio station, biology, chemistry and nursing labs, graphic design and studio art facilities, information systems and computer labs. **Physically Challenged Students:** 75% of the campus is accessible. Facilities include wheelchair ramps, elevators, special parking, specially equipped restrooms, special class scheduling, lowered drinking fountains, and lowered telephones. **Special:** Salve offers internships in most academic disciplines as well as work-study programs on campus. Study abroad in 18 countries, a Washington semester, B.A.-B.S. degrees in biology, business, and economics, dual majors in many programs, and accelerated degree programs in administration of justice, business, international relations, holistic counseling leadership, and rehabilitation counseling are available. A liberal studies degree, credit for life, military, and work experience, non degree study, and pass/fail options are also offered. There are 15 national honor societies, a freshman honors program, and 10 departmental honors programs. **Visiting:** There are regularly scheduled orientations for prospective students, including information sessions led by an admissions professional with question/answer sessions and a student-led campus tour. There are guides for informal visits, visitors may sit in on classes, and stay overnight. To schedule a visit, contact the Admissions Office. **Campus Safety and Security:** Measures include 24-hour foot and vehicle patrol, emergency notification system, self-defense education, and security escort services. There are shuttle buses, emergency telephones, lighted pathways/sidewalks, and controlled access to dorms/residences.

REQUIREMENTS: Applicants must be high school graduates or hold a GED. Students should have 16 Carnegie units, consisting of 4 in English, 3 in math including algebra and geometry, 2 each in science and foreign language, and 1 in history, and 4 in electives. An essay is required. The submission of standardized test scores is optional at Salve Regina unless you are considering a major in education or nursing. Students who decide not to submit scores will not be at any disadvantage during the admission process. AP and CLEP credits are accepted. Important factors in the admissions decision are advanced placement or honors courses, recommendations by school officials, and leadership record. To graduate, students must have 120 credit hours including approximately 36 in the major and must maintain a minimum GPA of 2.0. Distribution requirements include 9 credit hours in social science, 6 each in religious studies, science, English, and a foreign language, and 3 each in visual and performing arts, philosophy, and math. **Procedure:** Freshmen are admitted in the fall and spring. Entrance exams should be taken as early as possible. There are early admissions and deferred admissions plans. Applications should be filed by February 1 for fall entry; December 1 for spring entry, along with a $50 fee. Notifications are sent December 25. 40 applicants were on the 2016 waiting list. Applications are accepted online. **Transfer Students:** 31 transfer students enrolled in 2015-2016. Applicants must have a college GPA of 2.7 or better and follow the regular admissions process. 36 of 120 credits required for the bachelor's degree must be completed at Salve. **International Students:** There are 29 international students enrolled. The school actively recruits these students. They must take the TOEFL with a minimum score of 550 on the paper-based TOEFL (PBT) or 80 on the Internet-based version (iBT). The submission of standardized test scores is optional unless you are considering a major in education or nursing.

ADMISSIONS: 73% of the 2016-2017 applicants were accepted. The SAT scores for the 2016-2017 freshman class were: Critical Reading-- 17% below 500, 59% between 500 and 599, 22% between 600 and 699, and 2% between 700 and 800. Math-- 18% below 500, 60% between 500 and 599, 21% between 600 and 699, and 1% between 700 and 800. Writing-- 20% below 500, 57% between 500 and 599, 22% between 600 and 699, and 1% between 700 and 800. The ACT scores were 40% between 18 and 23, 56% between 24 and 29, and 4% above 30. 36% of the current freshmen were in the top fifth of their class; 70% were in the top two fifths. 2 freshmen graduated first in their class. **Admissions Contact:** Colleen Emerson, MBA, Dean of Admissions. Email: *sruadmis@salve.edu* Web: *www.salve.edu*

FINANCIAL AID: In 2016-2017, 98% of all full-time freshmen and 96% of continuing full-time students received some form of financial aid. 78% of all full-time freshmen and 79% of continuing full-time students received need-based aid. 24% of undergraduate students work part-time. Average annual earnings from campus work are $1745. The average financial indebtedness of the 2016 graduate was $29,192. Salve is a member of CSS. The FAFSA code is 003411. The priority date for freshman financial aid applications for fall entry is March 1.

UNIVERSITY OF RHODE ISLAND C-4

www.uri.edu

Kingston, RI 02881 (401) 874-1000

Fax: (401) 874-5523 Email: admission@uri.edu

Full-time: 5562 men, 6913 women
Part-time: 948 men, 1378 women
Graduate: 1221 men, 1812 women
Year: semesters, summer session
Room & Board: $12,022

Faculty: I
Ph.D.s: n/av
Student/Faculty: 16 to 1
Tuition: $12,884 ($28,874)
Freshman Class: 21797 applied, 15485 accepted, 3489 enrolled

SAT CR/M/W: 540/550/530 **ACT:** 24
Application Deadline: February 1

CEEB CODE: 3919
COMPETITIVE

University of Rhode Island, founded in 1892, is a land-grant, sea-grant, and urban-grant institution offering programs in liberal arts, business, engineering, human services, nursing, and pharmacy. The university has strong marine and environmental programs. There are satellite campuses in Providence, West Greenwich, and Narragansett. URI is small enough to be friendly, intimate, safe, and student-centered, with more than 100 undergraduate and 80 graduate degree programs, plus more than 100 student clubs and activities spark creativity and inspire our students' pioneering spirit. There are 9 undergraduate schools and 3 graduate schools. In addition to regional accreditation, URI has baccalaureate program accreditation with AACSB, ABET, ACPE, ADA, ASLA, NASM, NCATE, and NLN. The 1245-acre campus is in a small town 6 miles from Rhode Island's coastal beaches and easy driving distances from Providence, Boston, and New York. Including any residence halls, there are 324 buildings.

STUDENT LIFE: 54% of undergraduates are from Rhode Island. Others are from 44 states, 62 foreign countries, and Canada. 71% are White; 7% race unknown; 5% African American; 3% Asian American; 2% Foreign; 2% two or more races; 10% Hispanic. **Female To Male Ratio:** 1.3:1. The average age of freshmen is 18; all undergraduates, 21. 17% do not continue beyond their first year; 63% remain to graduate. **Housing:** 6946 students can be accommodated in college housing, which includes single-sex and coed dorms, on-campus apartments, off-campus apartments, and married student housing. In addition, there are language houses, special-interest houses, fraternity houses, sorority houses, first year focused residence halls, and living learning communities by academic college and program. On-campus housing is guaranteed for the freshman year only and is available on a lottery system for upperclassmen. 58% of students commute. All students may keep cars.

FACULTY/CLASSROOMS: No introductory courses are taught by graduate students.

PROGRAMS OF STUDY: URI confers B.B., B.F.A., B.I.S., B.L.A., B.M., and B.S. degrees. Master's and doctoral degrees are also awarded. Bachelor's degrees are awarded in AGRICULTURE (animal science & technology, aquaculture & fishery technology, environmental studies, environmental horticulture & turf mgmt, and plant science), BIOLOGICAL SCIENCE (biological sciences, cell & molecular biology, marine affairs, marine biology, microbiology, and wildlife conservation biology), BUSINESS (accounting, business administration and management, business administration - international, business institutions, entrepreneurial studies, environment & national resource economics, finance, management information systems, marketing, supply chain management, and sustainable management), COMMUNICATIONS AND THE ARTS (Africana studies, applied communication, art history, art, Chinese, communication studies, English, film, television and digital media, French, German, Hebrew, Italian, journalism, music, Portuguese, public relations, Spanish, theatre arts, and writing & rhetoric), COMPUTER AND PHYSICAL SCIENCE (chemistry, chemistry/forensic chemistry, computer science, geology & geology oceanography, physics & physical oceanography, physics, and statistics), EDUCATION (classical studies, elementary education, and secondary education), ENGINEERING AND ENVIRONMENTAL DESIGN (biomedical engineering, chemical engineering, civil engineering, computer engineering, electrical and computer engineering, environmental science, industry & systems engineering, landscape architecture, mechanical engineering, ocean engineering, textile marketing, textile, and fashion merchandising & design), HEALTH PROFESSIONS (biology, communicative disorders, health services administration, human studies, kinesiology, medical laboratory science, nursing, nutrition and dietetics, and pharmaceutical science), SOCIAL SCIENCE (anthropology, criminal justice, criminology, economics, gender studies, history, human development & family studies, Latin American studies, philosophy, political science/government, psychology, and sociology). Pharmacy, engineering, and biology are the strongest academically. Nursing, kinesiology, and psychology have the largest enrollments.

ACTIVITIES: 15% of men belong to 15 national fraternities; 22% of women belong to 9 national sororities. There are 100 groups on campus, including music ensembles, band, cheerleading, chess, choir, chorale, chorus, computers, concert band, dance, drama, ethnic, honors, international, jazz band, LGBT, literary magazine, marching band, musical theater, newspaper, pep band, photography, political, professional, radio and TV, religious, social, social service, student government, and yearbook. Popular campus events include First Night, Welcome Week, and Wintefest. **Sports:** Facilities include a stadium, pools, a multipurpose field house with a fitness center, and courts for basketball, tennis, and volleyball. There are also outdoor tennis courts, an all-weather track, and varsity and practice fields. **Graduates:** From July 1, 2015 to June 30, 2016, 3233 bachelor's degrees were awarded. The most popular majors were nursing (7%), communication studies (6%), and psychology (6%). In an average class, 42% graduate in 4 years or less, 17% graduate in 5 years or less, and 63% graduate in 6 years or less.

SERVICES: Counseling and information services are available, as is tutoring in some subjects, such as ELS and popular freshman courses, including math, physics, chemistry, and biology. There is a reader service for the blind, and remedial math, reading, and writing. **Library/Resources:** The 3 libraries contain 1.8 million volumes, 1.7 million microform items, 1,200 audio/video tapes/CDs/DVDs, and subscribe to 248,194 periodicals including electronic. Computerized library services include interlibrary loans, database searching, Internet access, and Wi-Fi capability. Special learning facilities include an art gallery, planetarium, radio station, TV station, a historic textile collection, and an early childhood education center. **Physically Challenged Students:** Facilities include wheelchair ramps, elevators, special parking, specially equipped restrooms, special class scheduling, lowered drinking fountains, lowered telephones, and special housing. **Special:** Cross-registration is available with Rhode Island College and Community College of Rhode Island. URI also offers a Washington semester as well as semester-long internships with businesses and state agencies, study abroad in 40 countries, a B.A.-B.S. degree in German and engineering and in languages and business, a general studies degree, dual majors, pass/fail options, and credit for life, military, and work experience. The College of Engineering offers co-op programs and an international internship. There are 30 national honor societies, including Phi Beta Kappa, and a freshman honors program. **Visiting:** There are regularly scheduled orientations for prospective students, including campus tours and information sessions, and visitors may sit in on classes. To schedule a visit, contact the Admission Office. **Campus Safety and Security:** Measures include 24-hour foot and vehicle patrol, emergency notification system, self-defense education, and security escort services. There are also shuttle buses, emergency telephones, lighted pathways/sidewalks, and controlled access to dorms/residences.

REQUIREMENTS: The SAT or ACT is required. Applicants should be high school graduates, having completed 18 courses, including 4 of English, 3 to 4 of math, and 2 each of science (chemistry and physics for engineering majors), foreign language, and history or social studies. Remaining units should be college preparatory. Music majors must audition. AP and CLEP credits are accepted. Important factors in the admissions decision are evidence of special talent, personality/intangible qualities, extracurricular activities record, recommendations by alumni, geographical diversity, and recommendations by school officials. To graduate, the student must earn 120 to 150 credit hours, at least 30 in the major, with a GPA of 2.0. Distribution requirements include 6 credits each in English communication, fine arts and literature, foreign language or culture, letters, natural science, and social sciences, as well as 3 credits in math and quantitative reasoning. **Procedure:** Freshmen are admitted in the fall and spring. Entrance exams should be taken during the spring of the junior year or fall of the senior year. There are early admissions, deferred admissions, and rolling admissions plans. Applications should be filed by February 1 for fall entry; December 1 for spring entry, along with a $65 fee. Notification is sent on a rolling basis. 1020 applicants were on the 2016 waiting list; 2 were admitted. Applications are accepted online. **Transfer Students:** 531 transfer students enrolled in 2015-2016. Applicants must submit transcripts from high school and all colleges or universities attended. A minimum GPA of 2.5 is required; many programs require higher. An essay or personal statement is required and a statement of good standing from prior institutions. 24 of 120 credits required for the bachelor's degree must be completed at URI. **International Students:** There are 160 international students enrolled. The school actively recruits these students. They must take the TOEFL with a minimum score of 550 on the paper-based TOEFL (PBT) or 79 on the Internet-based version (iBT), or the English proficiency test administered by the American Consulate. They must also take the SAT or ACT.

ADMISSIONS: 71% of the 2016-2017 applicants were accepted. The SAT scores for the 2016-2017 freshman class were: Critical Reading-- 25% below 500, 52% between 500 and 599, 21% between 600 and 699, and 2% between 700 and 800. Math-- 22% below 500, 50% between 500 and 599, 25% between 600 and 699, and 3% between 700 and 800. Writing-- 29% below 500, 50% between 500 and 599, 20% between 600 and 699, and 1% between 700 and 800. The ACT scores were 6% between 12 and 17, 32% between 18 and 23, 56% between 24 and 29, and 6% above 30. 47% of the current freshmen were in the top fifth of their class; 85% were in the top two fifths. **Admissions Contact:** Cynthia Bonn, Dean of Admissions. Email: *admission@uri.edu* Web: *www.uri.edu*

FINANCIAL AID: In 2016-2017, 73% of all full-time freshmen and 78% of continuing full-time students received some form of financial aid. 70% of all full-time freshmen and 74% of continuing full-time students received need-based aid. The average freshman award was $16,577. Need-based scholarships or need-based grants averaged $10,594 ($19,515 maximum); need-based self-help aid (loans and jobs) averaged $6,147 ($6,700 maximum); and non-need-based athletic scholarships averaged $944 ($46,997 maximum). 23% of undergraduate students work part-time. Average annual earnings from campus work are $1620. The average financial indebtedness of the 2016 graduate was $23,554. The FAFSA code is 003414. The priority date for freshman financial aid applications for fall entry is March 1.

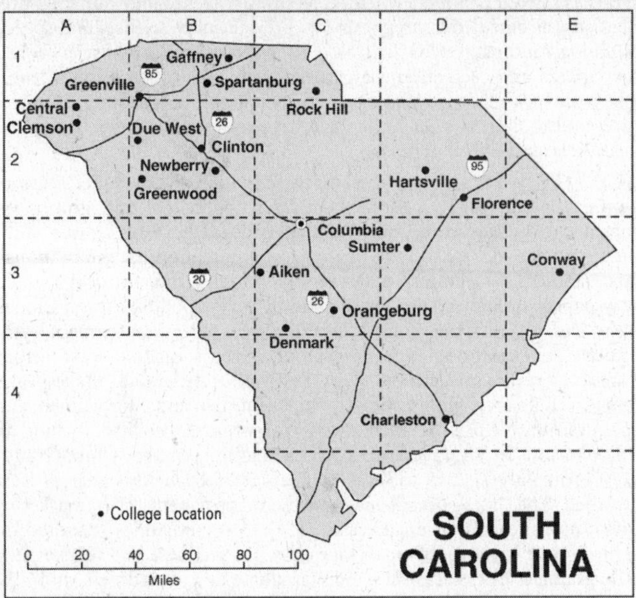

ALLEN UNIVERSITY *(The complete profile is made available exclusively on our website, www.barronspac.com)*

BENEDICT COLLEGE *(The complete profile is made available exclusively on our website, www.barronspac.com)*

CHARLESTON SOUTHERN UNIVERSITY D-4

www.csuniv.edu

Charleston, SC 29423 **(843) 863-7050**
(800) 947-7474
Fax: (843) 863-7070 **Email: enroll@csuniv.edu**

Full-time: 805 men, 1205 women	**Faculty:** 93
Part-time: 160 men, 320 women	**Ph.D.s:** 71%
Graduate: 100 men, 140 women	**Student/Faculty:** 16 to 1
Year: semesters, summer session	**Tuition:** $23,400
Room & Board: $9000	**Freshman Class:** n/av
SAT or ACT: recommended	**CEEB CODE:** 5079
Application Deadline: August 15	**COMPETITIVE**

Charleston Southern University, founded in 1964, is a private liberal arts institution affiliated with the South Carolina Baptist Convention. The figures in the above capsule and in this profile are approximate. There are 5 undergraduate schools and 3 graduate schools. In addition to regional accreditation, CSU has baccalaureate program accreditation with NASDTEC, NASM, NCATE, AMTA, and NLNAC. The 300-acre campus is in a suburban area in Charleston, South Carolina. Including any residence halls, there are 16 buildings.

STUDENT LIFE: 81% of undergraduates are from South Carolina. Others are from 26 states, 21 foreign countries, and Canada. 85% are from public schools. 60% are White; 5% Hispanic; 3% Foreign; 27% African American; 1% Asian American. 50% claim no religious affiliation; 42% Protestant. **Female To Male Ratio:** 1.6:1. The average age of freshmen is 18; all undergraduates, 25. 28% do not continue beyond their first year; 31% remain to graduate. **Housing:** 1250 students can be accommodated in college housing, which includes single-sex dorms and married student housing. On-campus housing is guaranteed for the freshman year only, and is available on a first-come, and first-served basis. 56% of students commute. All students may keep cars. Alcohol is not permitted.

FACULTY/CLASSROOMS: 55% of faculty are male; 45% are female. All teach undergraduates. No introductory courses are taught by graduate students. The average class size in an introductory lecture is 40; in a laboratory is 15; and in a regular course is 25.

PROGRAMS OF STUDY: CSU confers B.A., B.S., and B.Tech. degrees. Associate and master's degrees are also awarded. Bachelor's degrees are awarded in BIOLOGICAL SCIENCE (biochemistry and biology/biological science), BUSINESS (business administration and management), COMMUNICATIONS AND THE ARTS (dramatic arts, English, fine arts, music, Spanish, and speech/debate/rhetoric), COMPUTER AND PHYSICAL SCIENCE (chemistry, computer science, geology, mathematics, and natural sciences), EDUCATION (early childhood education, elementary education, music education, physical education, and science education), ENGINEERING AND ENVIRONMENTAL DESIGN (environmental science), HEALTH PROFESSIONS (music therapy and nursing), SOCIAL SCIENCE (criminal justice, economics, geography, history, humanities, political science/government, psychology, religion, religious music, social science, sociology, and youth ministry).

ACTIVITIES: There are no fraternities or sororities. There are 20 groups on campus, including sociology club, psychology club, art, band, cheerleading, choir, chorus, drama, health promotions club, honors, international, jazz band, literary magazine, marching band, newspaper, radio and TV, religious, social service, student government, and yearbook. **Sports:** There are 9 intercollegiate sports for men and 9 for women, and 4 intramural sports for men and 4 for women. Facilities include a gym, tennis courts, softball, track and field, football and soccer fields, baseball diamond, training and weight rooms, a 3-hole golf course with driving range, and a wellness center. **Graduates:** From July 1, 2015 to June 30, 2016, 275 bachelor's degrees were awarded. The most popular majors were business administration (21%), education (14%), and psychology/social science (9%). 30 companies recruited on campus in 2015-2016. In an average class, 31% graduate in 4 years or less. Of the 2015 graduating class, 27% were enrolled in graduate school within 6 months of graduation, and 63% were employed.

SERVICES: Counseling and information services are available, as is tutoring in most subjects, and remedial math, reading, and writing. **Library/Resources:** The library contains 212,666 volumes, 212,539 microform items, 7,527 audio/video tapes/CDs/DVDs, and subscribes to 9,788 periodicals including electronic. Computerized library services include database searching. Special learning facilities include a radio station, an earthquake education center and a field physics laboratory. **Physically Challenged Students:** All of the campus is accessible. Facilities include wheelchair ramps, elevators, special parking, specially equipped restrooms, and lowered drinking fountains. **Special:** CSU offers internships, cross-registration through the Trident Area Consortium, work-study programs, dual majors, and nondegree study. Nonmajor preprofessional programs are available in dentistry, engineering, law, medicine, and ministry. There are 5 national honor societies, a freshman honors program, and 100 departmental honors programs. **Visiting:** There are regularly scheduled orientations for prospective students, consisting of orientation for students, orientation for parents, placement testing for students, a tour, and lunch. There are guides for informal visits and visitors may sit in on classes. To schedule a visit, contact the Office of Enrollment Services. **Campus Safety and Security:** Measures include 24-hour foot and vehicle patrol, security escort services, emergency telephones and lighted pathways/sidewalks.

REQUIREMENTS: The SAT or ACT is recommended. Applicants must be graduates of an accredited secondary school. The GED is accepted. Character references are preferred. An English proficiency exam is required for all entering students. AP and CLEP credits are accepted. Important factors in the admissions decision are evidence of special talent, leadership record, and advanced placement or honors courses. To graduate, students must complete 125 credit hours, including all core curriculum, major, and minor requirements, with a GPA of 2.0. At least 45 hours must be in the major. Core courses include 24 hours of communications and fine arts, 11 of natural science/math, and 9 of social studies. **Procedure:** Freshmen are admitted to all sessions. Entrance exams should be taken any time before filing for admission. There is a rolling admissions plan. Applications should be filed by August 15 for fall entry. The fall 2016 application fee was $25. Applications are accepted online. **Transfer Students:** 278 transfer students enrolled in 2015-2016. Applicants must submit official transcripts from all previous colleges attended. Accepted transfers must take an English proficiency exam. 30 of 125 credits required for the bachelor's degree must be completed at CSU. **International Students:** There are 69 international students enrolled. They must take the TOEFL, as well as the SAT or ACT.

ADMISSIONS: 1 freshman graduated first in the class. **Admissions Con-**

tact: Cheryl Burton, Director of Enrollment Services. Email: *enroll@csuniv.edu* Web: *www.csuniv.edu*

FINANCIAL AID: In 2016-2017, 95% of all full-time freshmen received some form of financial aid. 95% of all full-time freshmen received need-based aid. 26% of undergraduate students work part-time. CSU is a member of CSS. The CSS/Profile is required. The FAFSA code is 003419. The deadline for filing freshman financial aid applications for fall entry is May 1.

CLAFLIN UNIVERSITY *(The complete profile is made available exclusively on our website, www.barronspac.com)*

CLEMSON UNIVERSITY — A-2

www.clemson.edu

Clemson, SC 29634 — **(864) 656-2287**

Fax: (864) 656-0622	**Email:** cuadmissions@clemson.edu
Full-time: 9311 men, 8572 women	**Faculty:** I, -$
Part-time: 414 men, 302 women	**Ph.D.s:** 88%
Graduate: 2481 men, 2326 women	**Student/Faculty:** 18 to 1
Year: semesters, summer session	**Tuition:** $14,708 ($34,590)
Room & Board: $9144	**Freshman Class:** 16282 applied, 10224 accepted, 3386 enrolled
SAT CR/M/W: 611/641 **ACT:** 28	**CEEB CODE:** 5111
Application Deadline: December 1	**HIGHLY COMPETITIVE**

Clemson University, founded in 1889, is a public institution with programs in agriculture, architecture, commerce and industry, education, engineering, forest and recreation resources, liberal arts, nursing, and sciences. Figures in the above capsule, and in this profile are approximate. There are 5 undergraduate schools and 1 graduate school. In addition to regional accreditation, Clemson has baccalaureate program accreditation with AACSB, ABET, CSAB, NAAB, NCATE, NLN, and NRPA. The 1400-acre campus is in a small town 32 miles west of Greenville. Including any residence halls, there are 587 buildings.

STUDENT LIFE: 69% of undergraduates are from South Carolina. Others are from 50 states, 96 foreign countries, and Canada. 81% are from public schools. 78% are White; 6% African American; 4% Foreign; 2% Asian American; 2% Hispanic. **Male To Female Ratio:** 1.1:1. The average age of freshmen is 18; all undergraduates, 21. 10% do not continue beyond their first year; 80% remain to graduate. **Housing:** 6448 students can be accommodated in college housing, which includes single-sex and coed dorms, on-campus apartments, and honors houses, special-interest houses, fraternity houses, sorority houses, and living-learning communities. On-campus housing is guaranteed for the freshman year only and is available on a lottery system for upperclassmen. All students may keep cars.

FACULTY/CLASSROOMS: 66% of faculty are male; 34% are female. 99% teach undergraduates, 73% do research, and 72% do both. Graduate students teach 18% of introductory courses. The average class size in an introductory lecture is 45; in a laboratory is 19; and in a regular course is 29.

PROGRAMS OF STUDY: Clemson confers B.A., B.S., B.F.A., and B.L.A. degrees. Master's and doctoral degrees are also awarded. Bachelor's degrees are awarded in AGRICULTURE (agriculture, animal science, forestry production and processing, forestry and related sciences, horticulture, and soil science), BIOLOGICAL SCIENCE (biochemistry, biology/biological science, and microbiology), BUSINESS (accounting, banking and finance, business administration and management, management science, and marketing/retailing/merchandising), COMMUNICATIONS AND THE ARTS (communications, design, English, fine arts, French, German, modern language, and Spanish), COMPUTER AND PHYSICAL SCIENCE (chemistry, computer science, geology, information sciences and systems, mathematics, and physics), EDUCATION (agricultural education, early childhood education, elementary education, industrial arts education, secondary education, and special education), ENGINEERING AND ENVIRONMENTAL DESIGN (agricultural engineering, ceramic engineering, chemical engineering, civil engineering, computer engineering, construction management, electrical/electronics engineering, graphic arts technology, industrial administration/management, industrial engineering, landscape architecture/design, mechanical engineering, and textile technology), HEALTH PROFESSIONS (medical laboratory technology, nursing, predentistry, premedicine, prepharmacy, preveterinary science, and speech pathology/audiology), SOCIAL SCIENCE (economics, food science, history, parks and recreation management, philosophy, political science/government, prelaw, psychology, and sociology). Engineering, architecture, and biological sciences are the strongest academically. Marketing has the largest enrollment.

ACTIVITIES: 18% of men belong to 18 national fraternities; 24% of women belong to 17 national sororities. There are 350 groups on campus, including art, bagpipe, band, cheerleading, choir, chorus, computers, dance, debate, drama, drill team, ethnic, honors, international, jazz band, LGBT, literary magazine, marching band, musical theater, newspaper, orchestra, pep band, photography, political, professional, radio and TV, religious, social, social service, student government, symphony, and yearbook. Popular campus events include First Friday Parade, Tigerama, Welcome Back Festival, and Annual Shakespeare. **Sports:** There are 10 intercollegiate sports for men and 9 for women, and 45 intramural sports for men and 45 for women. Facilities include an indoor tennis facility, recreation center, stadium, and coliseum. **Graduates:** From July 1, 2015 to June 30, 2016, 3075 bachelor's degrees were awarded. The most popular majors were management (6%), marketing (6%), and mechanical engineering (5%). 340 companies recruited on campus in 2015-2016. In an average class, 1% graduate in 3 years or less, 40% graduate in 4 years or less, 68% graduate in 5 years or less, and 72% graduate in 6 years or less.

SERVICES: Counseling and information services are available, as is tutoring in most subjects, and is a reader service for the blind. Other services include textbooks, testing modifications, library assistance, interpreters, note takers, and letters to faculty members. **Library/Resources:** The 3 libraries contain 1.2 million volumes, 1.2 million microform items, 140,000 audio/video tapes/CDs/DVDs, and subscribe to 11,400 periodicals including electronic. Computerized library services include interlibrary loans, database searching, Internet access, and Wi-Fi capability. Special learning facilities include an art gallery, natural history museum, planetarium, radio station, TV station, a geology museum, experimental forest, research park, and state botanical gardens. **Physically Challenged Students:** 75% of the campus is accessible. Facilities include wheelchair ramps, elevators, special parking, specially equipped restrooms, special class scheduling, lowered drinking fountains, lowered telephones, and special housing. **Special:** Co-op programs are available in all majors except nursing. Work-study programs and study abroad in 39 countries are offered. There are 24 national honor societies, Phi Beta Kappa, a freshman honors program, and 40 departmental honors programs. **Visiting:** There are regularly scheduled orientations for prospective students, including a series of 2-day summer programs of advisement, student services presentations, and registration for the fall semester. There are guides for informal visits and visitors may sit in on classes. To schedule a visit, contact the Visitors Center. **Campus Safety and Security:** Measures include 24-hour foot and vehicle patrol, emergency notification system, self-defense education, and security escort services. There are also shuttle buses, emergency telephones, lighted pathways/sidewalks, electronic card access to residence halls, and outdoor surveillance cameras.

REQUIREMENTS: The SAT or ACT is required, as is the ACT Optional Writing test. Applicants should be graduates of an accredited secondary school. The GED is accepted. AP and CLEP credits are accepted. Important factors in the admissions decision are advanced placement or honors courses, parents or siblings attended your school, and evidence of special talent. To graduate, students must complete 120 to 157 credit hours, including 89 to 108 hours in the major, with a GPA of 2.0. Courses are required in English, humanities, math, science, and social science. **Procedure:** Freshmen are admitted in the fall, spring, and summer. Entrance exams should be taken during spring of the junior year or fall of the senior year. Applications should be filed by December 1 for fall entry, along with a $70 fee. Notifications are sent February 15. Applications are accepted online. **Transfer Students:** 980 transfer students enrolled in 2015-2016. Transfer applicants must have completed at least 30 semester hours with approximately a 2.5 GPA. 37 of 120 credits required for the bachelor's degree must be completed at Clemson. **International Students:** There are 160 international students enrolled. The school actively recruits these students. They must take the TOEFL with a minimum score of 550 on the paper-based TOEFL (PBT). They must also take the SAT or ACT.

ADMISSIONS: 63% of the 2016-2017 applicants were accepted. The

SAT scores for the 2016-2017 freshman class were: Critical Reading-- 8% below 500, 41% between 500 and 599, 42% between 600 and 699, and 9% between 700 and 800. Math-- 4% below 500, 25% between 500 and 599, 54% between 600 and 699, and 17% between 700 and 800. Writing-- 24% below 500, 49% between 500 and 599, 23% between 600 and 699, and 2% between 700 and 800. The ACT scores were 8% below 12, 15% between 12 and 17, 31% between 18 and 23, 15% between 24 and 29, and 31% above 30. 69% of the current freshmen were in the top fifth of their class; 97% were in the top two fifths. There were 24 National Merit finalists. 179 freshmen graduated first in their class. **Admissions Contact:** Robert S. Barkley, Director of Admissions. Email: *cuadmissions@clemson.edu* Web: *www.clemson.edu*

FINANCIAL AID: The average freshman award was $9,147. Need-based scholarships or need-based grants averaged $4,680 ($7,500 maximum); need-based self-help aid (loans and jobs) averaged $4,113 ($7,125 maximum); non-need-based athletic scholarships averaged $17,653 ($25,390 maximum); and other non-need-based awards and non-need-based scholarships averaged $6,971 ($26,990 maximum). 57% of undergraduate students work part-time. Average annual earnings from campus work are $3353. The average financial indebtedness of the 2016 graduate was $14,382. The FAFSA code is 003425. The priority date for freshman financial aid applications for fall entry is March 1.

COASTAL CAROLINA UNIVERSITY E-3

www.coastal.edu

Conway, SC 29528
(843) 349-2170
(800) 277-7000
Fax: (843) 349-6436
Email: admissions@coastal.edu

Full-time: 4220 men, 4644 women
Part-time: 375 men, 508 women
Graduate: 220 men, 512 women
Year: semesters, summer session
Room & Board: $8890
SAT CR/M: 500/510 **ACT:** 22
Application Deadline: August 1

Faculty: 423; IIA, --$
Ph.D.s: 76%
Student/Faculty: 20 to 1
Tuition: $10,876 ($25,120)
Freshman Class: 17768 applied, 10871 accepted, 2249 enrolled
CEEB CODE: 5837
COMPETITIVE

Coastal Carolina University, established in 1954, is a public liberal arts institution offering undergraduate programs through the colleges of business, science, education, humanities, fine arts and university college. Graduate programs are offered through the colleges of business, education, humanities and fine arts, and science. There are 5 undergraduate schools and 4 graduate schools. In addition to regional accreditation, Coastal Carolina has baccalaureate program accreditation with AACSB, ABET, NASAD, NASM, and NCATE. The 633-acre campus is in a suburban area 9 miles west of Myrtle Beach. Including any residence halls, there are 115 buildings.

STUDENT LIFE: 51% of undergraduates are from out of state, mostly the Northeast. Students are from 48 states, 65 foreign countries, and Canada. 92% are from public schools. 68% are White; 5% two or more races; 4% Hispanic; 20% African American; 1% Asian American; 1% Foreign; 1% race unknown. **Female To Male Ratio:** 1.2:1. The average age of freshmen is 18; all undergraduates, 21. 31% do not continue beyond their first year; 42% remain to graduate. **Housing:** 4700 students can be accommodated in college housing, which includes coed dorms, off-campus apartments, honors houses and special-interest houses. On-campus housing is available on a first-come, first-served basis, and is available on a lottery system for upperclassmen. 58% of students commute. All students may keep cars. Alcohol is not permitted.

FACULTY/CLASSROOMS: 51% of faculty are male; 49% are female. 95% teach undergraduates, 50% do research, and 50% do both. No introductory courses are taught by graduate students. The average class size in an introductory lecture is 23; in a laboratory is 20; and in a regular course is 18.

PROGRAMS OF STUDY: Coastal Carolina confers B.A., B.F.A., B.S., B.S.N., B.A.Ed., B.A.I.S., B.S.B.A., B.S.Ed., B.S.I.S. and B.S.P.E. degrees. Master's and doctoral degrees are also awarded. Bachelor's degrees are awarded in BIOLOGICAL SCIENCE (biochemistry, biology/biological science, and marine science), BUSINESS (accounting, banking and finance, business administration and management, information & communication technology, marketing/retailing/merchandising, sports management, and tourism), COMMUNICATIONS AND THE ARTS (communications, dramatic arts, English, fine arts, graphic design, music, musical theater, Spanish, and studio art), COMPUTER AND PHYSICAL SCIENCE (chemistry, computer science, information sciences and systems, mathematics, and physics), EDUCATION (early childhood education, elementary education, middle school education, physical education, and special education), HEALTH PROFESSIONS (exercise science, health, health care administration, and nursing), SOCIAL SCIENCE (economics, history, interdisciplinary studies, philosophy, political science/government, psychology, and sociology). Accounting, finance, and management are the strongest academically. Marine science, management, and exercise & sport science have the largest enrollments.

ACTIVITIES: 3% of men belong to 10 national fraternities; 5% of women belong to 8 national sororities. There are 219 groups on campus, including art, band, cheerleading, chess, choir, chorale, chorus, computers, dance, drama, environmental, ethnic, honors, international, jazz band, LGBT, literary magazine, marching band, musical theater, newspaper, pep band, political, professional, radio and TV, religious, social, social service, and student government. Popular campus events include CINO Day, Cultural Celebration, Club Recruitment Day, and Homecoming. **Sports:** There are 8 intercollegiate sports for men and 10 for women, and 13 intramural sports for men and 13 for women. Facilities include a gym, football stadium, baseball, soccer, and softball fields, tennis, basketball, volleyball, and racquetball courts, an indoor swimming pool, an aerobic dance room, weight rooms, and a track. **Graduates:** From July 1, 2015 to June 30, 2016, 1581 bachelor's degrees were awarded. The most popular majors were management (8%), communication (8%), and interdisciplinary studies (8%). 237 companies recruited on campus in 2015-2016. In an average class, 27% graduate in 4 years or less, 39% graduate in 5 years or less, and 42% graduate in 6 years or less.

SERVICES: Counseling and information services are available, as is tutoring in some subjects, such as English, foreign languages, math and statistics. There is also a reader service for the blind. **Library/Resources:** The library contains 116,080 volumes, 1,226 microform items, 5,867 audio/video tapes/CDs/DVDs, and subscribes to 11,366 periodicals including electronic. Computerized library services include interlibrary loans, database searching, Internet access, and Wi-Fi capability. Special learning facilities include an art gallery, radio station, a marine science research center. **Physically Challenged Students:** 95% of the campus is accessible. Facilities include wheelchair ramps, elevators, special parking, specially equipped restrooms, special class scheduling, lowered drinking fountains, and special housing. **Special:** Internships are offered in most majors, as well as study abroad in 15 countries. Interdisciplinary studies and a 3-2 engineering degree with Clemson University are available. There are 16 national honor societies and a freshman honors program. **Visiting:** There are regularly scheduled orientations for prospective students, including sessions for academic requirements, housing, financial aid, and student life, parents' orientation, tours, cookouts, and entertainment. Visitors may sit in on classes. To schedule a visit, contact Holley Aufdemorte in Admissions. **Campus Safety and Security:** Measures include 24-hour foot and vehicle patrol, emergency notification system, self-defense education, and security escort services. There are also shuttle buses, emergency telephones, and lighted pathways/sidewalks.

REQUIREMENTS: The SAT or ACT is required. Graduation from an accredited secondary or homeschool program is required; a GED will be accepted with appropriate scores. Applicants are required to submit complete specific high school credits, including 4 years of college prep English, 4 units of mathematics (algebra ll required), 3 units of lab science, 3 units of social sciences (U.S. history required), 2 units of the same foreign language, 1 advanced electives (from computer science, math, additional science, foreign language, social science, humanities, and arts), 1 unit of visual/performing arts, and 1 unit of physical education or ROTC. An interview is recommended. AP and CLEP credits are accepted. Important factors in the admissions decision are advanced placement or honors courses, recommendations by school officials, and evidence of special talent. Students must successfully complete a minimum of 120 credits, varying with major department requirements, and must maintain a minimum GPA of 2.0. A 4-year core curriculum of 34 to 41 hours is required for proficiency in the broad areas of writing, library research, a foreign language, and computer usage. **Procedure:** Freshmen are admitted to all sessions. Entrance exams should be taken in spring of the junior year or fall of the senior year. There are deferred admissions and rolling admissions plans. Applications should be filed by

August 1 for fall entry; December 1 for spring entry, along with a $45 fee. Notification is sent on a rolling basis. Application fees are waived if application is completed online. **Transfer Students:** 761 transfer students enrolled in 2015-2016. A minimum GPA of 2.0 is required. Transfers with fewer than 30 hours earned must also meet freshman admission requirements. Students must submit college transcripts and be eligible to return to the last institution attended. 30 of 120 credits required for the bachelor's degree must be completed at Coastal Carolina. **International Students:** There are 174 international students enrolled. They must take the TOEFL with a minimum score of 527 on the paper-based TOEFL (PBT) or 71 on the Internet-based version (iBT). They must also take the SAT or ACT.

ADMISSIONS: 61% of the 2016-2017 applicants were accepted. The SAT scores for the 2016-2017 freshman class were: Critical Reading-- 50% below 500, 40% between 500 and 599, 9% between 600 and 699, and 1% between 700 and 800. Math-- 42% below 500, 47% between 500 and 599, 10% between 600 and 699, and 1% between 700 and 800. The ACT scores were 1% between 12 and 17, 65% between 18 and 23, 31% between 24 and 29, and 3% above 30. 33% of the current freshmen were in the top fifth of their class; 69% were in the top two fifths. **Admissions Contact:** Amanda Craddock, Director of Admissions. Email: *admissions@coastal.edu* Web: *www.coastal.edu*

FINANCIAL AID: In 2016-2017, 93% of all full-time freshmen and 87% of continuing full-time students received some form of financial aid. 64% of all full-time freshmen and 59% of continuing full-time students received need-based aid. The average freshman award was $20,169. Need-based scholarships or need-based grants averaged $3,571; need-based self-help aid (loans and jobs) averaged $3,381; non-need-based athletic scholarships averaged $8,496; other non-need-based awards and non-need-based scholarships averaged $3,297; and $8,015 from other forms of aid. 19% of undergraduate students work part-time. Average annual earnings from campus work are $3000. The average financial indebtedness of the 2016 graduate was $35,882. The college's own financial statement is required. The FAFSA code is 003451. The priority date for freshman financial aid applications for fall entry is March 1.

COKER COLLEGE *(The complete profile is made available exclusively on our website, www.barronspac.com)*

COLLEGE OF CHARLESTON D-4

www.cofc.edu

Charleston, SC 29424 **(843) 953-5670**

Fax: (843) 953-6322	**Email:** admissions@cofc.edu
Full-time: 3404 men, 6120 women	**Faculty:** 553; IIA, av$
Part-time: 391 men, 460 women	**Ph.D.s:** 91%
Graduate: 224 men, 695 women	**Student/Faculty:** 17 to 1
Year: semesters, summer session	**Tuition:** $11,386 ($29,544)
Room & Board: $11,313	**Freshman Class:** 10828 applied, 9110 accepted, 2349 enrolled
SAT CR/M: 550/540 **ACT:** 24	**CEEB CODE:** 5113
Application Deadline: April 1	**COMPETITIVE**

College of Charleston is a nationally recognized public liberal arts and sciences university. Founded in 1770, the College is among the nation's top universities for quality education, student life and affordability. The College offers the distinctive combination of a beautiful and historic campus, modern facilities and cutting-edge programs. The City of Charleston, is world-renowned for its history, culture, architecture and coastal environment, as well as experiences in business, science, teaching, the humanities, languages and the arts. At the same time, students and faculty are engaged with the community in partnerships to improve education, enhance the business environment and enrich the overall quality of life in the region. There are 7 undergraduate schools and 1 graduate school. In addition to regional accreditation, C of C has baccalaureate program accreditation with AACSB, ABET, NASM, NCATE, NAST, CAATE, and NCTE. The 52-acre campus is in an urban area in the historic city center of Charleston. Including any residence halls, there are 146 buildings.

STUDENT LIFE: 67% of undergraduates are from South Carolina. Others are from 51 states, 62 foreign countries, and Canada. 74% are from public schools. 8% are African American; 79% White; 5% Hispanic; 4% two or more races; 2% Asian American; 1% Foreign; 1% race unknown. **Female To Male Ratio:** 1.8:1. The average age of freshmen is 18; all undergraduates, 21. 21% do not continue beyond their first year; 79% remain to graduate. **Housing:** 3374 students can be accommodated in college housing, which includes single-sex and coed dorms, on-campus apartments, honors houses, language houses, special-interest houses, fraternity houses, and sorority houses. There are also restored historic Charleston houses used as residence halls, some with kitchen facilities in suites. On-campus housing is available on a first-come and first-served basis. 67% of students commute. Some may keep cars.

FACULTY/CLASSROOMS: 50% of faculty are male; 50% are female. 97% teach undergraduates. No introductory courses are taught by graduate students. The average class size in an introductory lecture is 29; in a laboratory is 19; and in a regular course is 21.

PROGRAMS OF STUDY: Charleston confers B.A., B.S., A.B. and B.P.S degrees. Master's degrees are also awarded. Bachelor's degrees are awarded in BIOLOGICAL SCIENCE (biochemistry, biology/biological science, and marine biology), BUSINESS (accounting, business administration and management, finance, hospitality management services, international business management, marketing, supply chain management, and professional studies), COMMUNICATIONS AND THE ARTS (art history, arts administration/management, classics, communications, dance, English, German, historic preservation, music, Spanish, studio art, and theatre arts), COMPUTER AND PHYSICAL SCIENCE (astronomy, astrophysics, chemistry, computer information systems, computer science, data processing, geology, mathematics, and physics), EDUCATION (athletic training, early childhood education, elementary education, foreign languages education, middle school education, physical education, secondary education, and special education), HEALTH PROFESSIONS (exercise science and public health), SOCIAL SCIENCE (African American studies, anthropology, archeology, economics, French studies, history, international studies, Judaic studies, Latin American studies, philosophy, political science/government, psychology, religious studies, sociology, urban studies, and women's studies). Business, biology, and psychology have the largest enrollments.

ACTIVITIES: 19% of men belong to 14 national fraternities; 25% of women belong to 13 national sororities. There are 200 groups on campus, including art, band, cheerleading, chess, choir, chorale, chorus, communications, computers, dance, drama, ethnic, film, forensics, honors, international, jazz band, LGBT, literary magazine, musical theater, newspaper, opera, orchestra, pep band, political, professional, radio and TV, religious, social, social service, student government, and symphony. Popular campus events include Pep Supper, Homecoming Spirit Cup Competition, Georgestock, Welcome Week, and Cougarpalooza. **Sports:** There are 7 intercollegiate sports for men and 12 for women, and 30 intramural sports for men and 30 for women. Facilities include strength and conditioning areas, practice area, sports medicine facility, tennis, sailing, golf, basketball courts, volleyball courts, racquetball/squash courts, running track, cardio machines, and resistance training equipment. **Graduates:** From July 1, 2015 to June 30, 2016, 2507 bachelor's degrees were awarded. The most popular majors were business administration (9%), communication (8%), and biology (7%). 169 companies recruited on campus in 2015-2016. In an average class, 55% graduate in 4 years or less, 65% graduate in 5 years or less, and 67% graduate in 6 years or less. Of the 2015 graduating class, 14% were enrolled in graduate school within 6 months of graduation, and 52% were employed.

SERVICES: Counseling and information services are available, as is tutoring in most subjects. There is also walk-in tutoring labs for Spanish, math, accounting, writing, and natural sciences. Appointment tutoring for other foreign languages, psychology, computer science, music theory, finance, economics, and additional courses with demonstrated need. There is also a reader service for the blind, and remedial math, reading, and writing, as well as study strategies appointments, supplemental instruction, peer coaching, and assistance with oral presentations. **Library/Resources:** The 4 libraries contain 1.2 million volumes, 33,000 microform items, 12,718 audio/video tapes/CDs/DVDs, and subscribe to 70,830 periodicals including electronic. Computerized library services include interlibrary loans, database searching, Internet access, and Wi-Fi capability. Special learning facilities include an art gallery, natural history museum, radio station, iCat program (accelerator), center for supply chain management, natural history museum, observatory, marine science laboratory, communications museum, early childhood development center, bronze sculpture foundry, sailing center, African-American history and culture research center, center for entrepreneurship, real estate center, English Language Institute, Halsey Institute of Contemporary Art, Riley Center for Livable Communities, and a S.C. Space Grant Consortium. **Physically Challenged Students:** 70% of the campus is accessible. Facilities include wheelchair ramps, elevators, special parking, specially equipped restrooms, special class scheduling, lowered drinking fountains, and lowered telephones. **Special:** Cross-registration is possible with the Medical University of South Carolina and Trident Technical College. Co-op programs and internships in all majors, a Washington semester, study abroad in 36 countries, work-study programs, B.A.-B.S. degrees, and dual majors are offered. A 2-2 program in allied health, biometry or nursing is offered with the Medical University of South Carolina. The college's 3-week Maymester session offers unconventional courses and programs using alternative methods of instruction. There is an interdisciplinary honors program available to talented students. There are 15 national honor societies, a freshman honors program, and 3 departmental honors programs. **Visiting:** There are regularly scheduled orientations for prospective students, Prospective student visits typically consist of a campus tour and an information session. These visits are available most weekdays, and some Saturdays throughout the academic year and in the summer. We also host several "open house" programs. Visitors may sit in on classes. To schedule a visit, contact the Admissions Office at (843) 953-5670. **Campus Safety and Security:** Measures include 24-hour foot and vehicle patrol, emergency notification system, self-defense education, security escort services, emergency telephones, lighted pathways/sidewalks, and controlled access to dorms/residences.

REQUIREMENTS: The SAT or ACT is required. The admissions committee carefully weighs the student's academic preparation (which includes grades, rank in class, and rigor of courses taken), SAT /ACT results, personal statements and essays, leadership qualification, and special talents. Applicants should have completed the following high school units: 4 units of English, 4 units of math, 3 units of lab science, 3 units of foreign language, 2 units of social studies, 1 unit of history (2 recommended), 3 units of academic electives. 1 unit of computer science (advanced math, computer science or a combination of the two will fulfill this) and 1 unit of fine arts are recommended. The GED is accepted. AP and CLEP credits are accepted. In order to graduate with a BA or a BS degree, a student must satisfy the liberal arts and sciences general education requirement, select and complete the requirements for at least one academic major program with a minimum grade point average of 2.0 in all major courses, and complete elective coursework such that the total credit hours reach a minimum of 122 with a minimum grade point average of 2.0 in all courses taken at the College. All students, regardless of major, must satisfy General Education requirements by completing approved courses distributed across seven areas: Writing, Foreign Languages, History, Humanities, Natural Science, Mathematics or Logic, and Social Science. All students entering the College of Charleston with less than one year of college experience are also required to complete a First Year Experience by selecting a First Year Seminar course or two courses organized into a Learning Community. As required by South Carolina statute, all degree-seeking students must complete instruction in the essentials of the Declaration of Independence, Federalist Papers, and the Constitution and achieve satisfactory performance on an accompanying examination. **Procedure:** Freshmen are admitted in the fall and spring. Entrance exams should be taken by March 1; by June 1 for state scholarship consideration. There are early admissions and deferred admissions plans. Early decision applications should be filed by November 1; regular applications, by April 1 for fall entry; and November 1 for spring entry, along with a $50 fee. Notification of early decision is sent January 1; regular decision, April 1. Application fees are waived if application is completed online. **Transfer Students:** 712 transfer students enrolled in 2015-2016. Applicants must have 24 hours and must have a 2.6 GPA for in-state residents and 3.0 for out-of-state residents. 30 of 122 credits required for the bachelor's degree must be completed at C of C. **International Students:** There are 116 international students enrolled. The school actively recruits these students. They must take the TOEFL with a minimum score of 550 on the paper-based TOEFL (PBT) or 80 on the Internet-based version (iBT), IELTS, or take the ITEP. They must also take the SAT or ACT, scoring SAT/ACT Reading 500/18 and ACT English 20.

ADMISSIONS: 84% of the 2016-2017 applicants were accepted. The SAT scores for the 2016-2017 freshman class were: Critical Reading-- 24% below 500, 49% between 500 and 599, 22% between 600 and 699, and 5% between 700 and 800. Math-- 24% below 500, 54% between 500 and 599, 20% between 600 and 699, and 2% between 700 and 800. The ACT scores were 2% between 12 and 17, 39% between 18 and 23, 48% between 24 and 29, and 11% above 30. 41% of the current freshmen were in the top fifth of their class; 77% were in the top two fifths. There were 7 National Merit finalists. 15 freshmen graduated first in their class. **Admissions Contact:** Mackenzie Chasteen, Director, Recruitment and Enrollment. Email: *admissions@cofc.edu* Web: *www.cofc.edu*

FINANCIAL AID: In 2016-2017, 47% of all full-time freshmen received some form of financial aid. 35% of all full-time freshmen received need-based aid. The average freshman award was $13,290. Need-based scholarships or need-based grants averaged $3,317; need-based self-help aid (loans and jobs) averaged $2,959; non-need-based athletic scholarships averaged $19,438; and other non-need-based awards and non-need-based scholarships averaged $10,240. The average financial indebtedness of the 2016 graduate was $25,644. The FAFSA code is 003428. The priority date for freshman financial aid applications for fall entry is March 1. The filing deadline for fall entry is June 1.

COLUMBIA COLLEGE — C-3

www.columbia.edu

Columbia, SC 29203 (803) 786-3871, (800) 277-1301

Fax: (803) 786-3674 **Email: admissions-ugrad@sc.edu**

Full-time: 6 men, 978 women	**Faculty:** n/av
Part-time: 24 men, 231 women	**Ph.D.s:** 80%
Graduate: 17 men, 255 women	**Student/Faculty:** 11 to 1
Year: semesters, summer session	**Tuition:** $28,900
Room & Board: $7650	**Freshman Class:** 1097 applied, 833 accepted, 271 enrolled
SAT CR/M: 500/500 **ACT:** recommended	**CEEB CODE:** 5117
Application Deadline: August 1	**COMPETITIVE**

Columbia College, founded in 1854, is a private primarily women's liberal arts college affiliated with the United Methodist Church. Figures in the above capsule and in this profile are approximate. There is 1 undergraduate school and 1 graduate school. In addition to regional accreditation, Columbia has baccalaureate program accreditation with CSWE, NASAD, NASDTEC, NASM, NCATE, and CASE. The 53-acre campus is in an urban area in the northern section of Columbia. Including any residence halls, there are 26 buildings.

STUDENT LIFE: 90% of undergraduates are from South Carolina. Others are from 23 states, and 10 foreign countries. 52% are White; 39% African American; 2% Hispanic; 1% Asian American; 1% Foreign. 84% are Protestant; 17% claim no religious affiliation. **Female To Male Ratio:** 31.1:1. The average age of freshmen is 18; all undergraduates, 23. 30% do not continue beyond their first year; 70% remain to graduate. **Housing:** 650 students can be accommodated in college housing, which includes single-sex dorms, and honors houses. On-campus housing is guaranteed for all 4 years. 63% of students live on campus. Alcohol is not permitted. All students may keep cars.

FACULTY/CLASSROOMS: 36% of faculty are male; 64% are female. 95% teach undergraduates. No introductory courses are taught by graduate students. The average class size in an introductory lecture is 20 and in a laboratory is 20.

PROGRAMS OF STUDY: Columbia confers B.A., B.F.A., and B.Mus. degrees. Master's degrees are also awarded. Bachelor's degrees are awarded in BIOLOGICAL SCIENCE (biology/biological science), BUSINESS (accounting and business administration and management), COMMUNICATIONS AND THE ARTS (communications, dance, English, French, languages, music, music performance, performing arts, piano/organ, Spanish, and studio art), COMPUTER AND PHYSICAL SCIENCE (chemistry, information sciences and systems, and mathematics), EDUCATION (Christian education, dance education, early childhood education, elementary education, music education, special education, and speech correction), HEALTH PROFESSIONS (medical laboratory technology), SOCIAL SCIENCE (history, political science/government, psychology, public affairs, religion, religious music, social work, and sociology). Education, sciences, and performing arts have the largest enrollments.

ACTIVITIES: There are no fraternities or sororities. There are 57 groups on campus, including women interested in sustainability and the environment (WISE), art, band, choir, chorus, computers, dance, drama, equestrian club, ethnic, honors, international, literary magazine, musical theater, newspaper, opera, photography, political, professional, radio and TV, religious, social, social service, and student government. Popular campus events include Fine Arts Series, Follies, Christmas Tree Lighting, Commencement Bibles, Dad's Night, Mom's Day, Surcies, and Ludy Bowl. **Sports:** There are 4 intercollegiate sports for women, and 4 intramural sports for women. Facilities include an athletic field, basketball, golf, soccer, softball, volleyball, lacrosse, tennis courts, pool, fitness lab, cross country, track and field, and a dance studio.

SERVICES: Columbia counseling and information services are available, as is peer tutoring and remedial instruction in some subjects. **Library/Resources:** The library contains 170,000 volumes, 8,353 microform items, 29,834 audio/video tapes/CDs/DVDs, and subscribes to 633 periodicals including electronic. Computerized library services include interlibrary loans, database searching, Internet access, and Wi-Fi capability. Special learning facilities include an art gallery, radio station, women's leadership center, and a science and technology center. **Physically Challenged Students:** 90% of the campus is accessible. Facilities include wheelchair ramps, elevators, special parking, specially equipped restrooms, and special class scheduling. **Special:** The Center for Contractual Studies allows qualified students to pursue individualized programs through independent study, practicums, and a senior project. The college also offers internships, study abroad, a Washington semester, dual majors, and credit for life, military, and work experience. Nondegree study and pass/fail options are available. There is a freshman honors program. **Visiting:** There are regularly scheduled orientations for prospective students, consisting of meetings with faculty advisers, classroom visits, campus tours, lunch, and student life and financial aid presentations. There are guides for informal visits and visitors may sit in on classes. To schedule a visit, contact the Admissions Office. **Campus Safety and Security:** Measures include 24-hour foot and vehicle patrol, emergency notification system, self-defense education, security escort services, emergency telephones, and lighted pathways/sidewalks.

REQUIREMENTS: The SAT is required. The ACT is recommended. Applicants must be graduates of an accredited secondary school or have earned a GED. They should complete 16 Carnegie units, including 4 years of English, 3 of math, and 2 each of foreign language and lab science, as well as courses in history and social studies. An essay and an interview are recommended, as is a portfolio or an audition for fine or performing arts students. AP and CLEP credits are accepted. Important factors in the admissions decision are recommendations by school officials, advanced placement or honors courses, and leadership record. To graduate, students must complete 127 semester hours, with a minimum GPA of 2.5 in the major and 2.0 overall. General education requirements for the B.A. degree include 15 hours of communication skills, 12 of social science, 9 of aesthetics, 8 of natural science, 6 of religion, and 3 each of math and phys ed. Students also must satisfy proficiency requirements in English and math. **Procedure:** Freshmen are admitted to all sessions. Entrance exams should be taken near the end of the junior year or by December of the senior year. There is a rolling admissions plan. Applications should be filed by August 1 for fall entry. The fall 2016 application fee was $25. Applications are accepted on-line. **Transfer Students:** 118 transfer students enrolled in 2015-2016. An interview is recommended for transfer students. Applicants with fewer than 24 semester hours must present ACT or SAT scores and high school transcripts. Grades of C or better transfer for credit. 30 of 127 credits required for the bachelor's degree must be completed at Columbia. **International Students:** There are 13 international students enrolled. The school actively recruits these students. They must take the TOEFL.

ADMISSIONS: 76% of the 2016-2017 applicants were accepted. The SAT scores for the 2016-2017 freshman class were: Critical Reading-- 49% below 500, 32% between 500 and 599, 16% between 600 and 699, and 3% between 700 and 800. Math-- 50% below 500, 36% between 500 and 599, 13% between 600 and 699, and 1% between 700 and 800. **Admissions Contact:** Julie A. King, Director of Admissions. Email: *admissions-ugrad@sc.edu* Web: *www.columbia.edu*

FINANCIAL AID: The FAFSA code is 003430. Check with the school for current application deadlines.

CONVERSE COLLEGE — B-1
www.converse.edu

Spartanburg, SC 29302 — **(864) 596-9040**, **(800) 766-1125**

Fax: (864) 596-9225	**Email: admissions@converse.edu**
Full-time: 608 women	**Faculty:** 76; IIB, --$
Part-time: 82 women	**Ph.D.s:** 89%
Graduate: 120 men, 411 women	**Student/Faculty:** 11 to 1
Year: 4-1-4, summer session	**Tuition:** $16,500
Room & Board: $9995	**Freshman Class:** 1383 applied, 710 accepted, 183 enrolled
SAT CR/M: 530/520 **ACT:** 23	**CEEB CODE:** 5121
Application Deadline: August 1	**COMPETITIVE**

Converse College, founded in 1889, is a private women's liberal arts college. Men are admitted to the graduate programs. Figures in the above capsule and in this profile are approximate. There are 3 undergraduate schools and 2 graduate schools. In addition to regional accreditation, has baccalaureate program accreditation with NASAD, NASM, and NCATE. The 72-acre campus is in an urban area 80 miles southwest of Charlotte. Including any residence halls, there are 27 buildings.

STUDENT LIFE: 65% of undergraduates are from South Carolina. Others are from 27 states, 11 foreign countries, and Canada. 70% are from public schools. 8% are African American; 45% White; 3% Hispanic; 1% Asian American; 1% Foreign. **Female To Male Ratio:** 9.2:1. The average age of freshmen is 18; all undergraduates, 20. 26% do not continue beyond their first year; 54% remain to graduate. **Housing:** 700 students can be accommodated in college housing, which includes single-sex dorms and on-campus apartments. There is a special residence hall for students enrolled in the South Carolina Institute of Leadership for Women, in addition to a wellness dorm. On-campus housing is guaranteed for all 4 years. 85% of students live on campus; of those, 50% remain on campus on weekends. All students may keep cars. Alcohol is not permitted.

FACULTY/CLASSROOMS: 46% of faculty are male; 54% are female. All teach undergraduates, 50% do research, and 50% do both. No introductory courses are taught by graduate students. The average class size in an introductory lecture is 20; in a laboratory is 15; and in a regular course is 11.

PROGRAMS OF STUDY: Converse confers B.A., B.S., B.F.A., and B.Mus. degrees. Master's degrees are also awarded. Bachelor's degrees are awarded in BIOLOGICAL SCIENCE (biology/biological science), BUSINESS (accounting and business administration and management), COMMUNICATIONS AND THE ARTS (English, fine arts, French, languages, modern language, music, and Spanish), COMPUTER AND PHYSICAL SCIENCE (chemistry, computer science, and mathematics), EDUCATION (art education, early childhood education, elementary education, foreign languages education, music education, science education, and secondary education), ENGINEERING AND ENVIRONMENTAL DESIGN (interior design), HEALTH PROFESSIONS (art therapy, predentistry, and premedicine), SOCIAL SCIENCE (economics, history, political science/government, prelaw, psychology, and religion). English, politics, and biology are the strongest academically. Music, education, and business have the largest enrollments.

ACTIVITIES: There are no fraternities or sororities. There are 50 groups on campus, including art, cheerleading, choir, chorale, chorus, computers, dance, debate, drama, ethnic, honors, international, LGBT, literary magazine, musical theater, newspaper, opera, orchestra, photography, political, professional, religious, social service, student government, symphony, and yearbook. Popular campus events include Founders Day, May Day, and Family Weekend. **Sports:** There are 9 intercollegiate sports for women, and 6 intramural sports for women. Facilities include an athletic field, a field house with training, and weight rooms, a gym, pool, dance studio, tennis courts, and a bowling alley. **Graduates:** From July 1, 2015 to June 30, 2016, 153 bachelor's degrees were awarded. The most popular majors were psychology (10%), biology (8%), and music (5%). 140 companies recruited on campus in 2015-2016. In an average class, 1% graduate in 3 years or less, 48% graduate in 4 years or less, 53% graduate in 5 years or less, and 54% graduate in 6 years or less. Of the 2015 graduating class, 31% were enrolled in graduate school within 6 months of graduation, and 63% were employed.

SERVICES: Counseling and information services are available, as is

tutoring in most subjects, and a reader service for the blind. **Library/ Resources:** The library contains 150,000 volumes, 310 microform items, 12,000 audio/video tapes/CDs/DVDs, and subscribes to 700 periodicals including electronic. Computerized library services include interlibrary loans and database searching. Special learning facilities include an art gallery and natural history museum. **Physically Challenged Students:** 75% of the campus is accessible. Facilities include wheelchair ramps, elevators, special parking, and specially equipped restrooms. **Special:** There are co-op programs and cross-registration with Wofford College. Internships, study abroad, a work-study program, accelerated degree programs, B.A.-B.S. degrees in business, economics, sociology, biology, and chemistry, and dual and student-designed majors are offered. There are 10 national honor societies, a freshman honors program, and 100 departmental honors programs. **Visiting:** There are regularly scheduled orientations for prospective students, consisting of faculty meetings, panel discussions, campus tours, tours of Spartanburg, and private interview sessions. There are guides for informal visits, visitors may sit in on classes, and stay overnight. To schedule a visit, contact the Admissions Office. **Campus Safety and Security:** Measures include 24-hour foot and vehicle patrol, self-defense education, security escort services, emergency telephones and lighted pathways/sidewalks.

REQUIREMENTS: The SAT or ACT is recommended. Applicants should be graduates of an accredited secondary school, having completed 20 Carnegie units, including 4 years of English, 3 of math, 2 each of foreign language, science, and social studies, and 1 of history. The GED is accepted. An interview is recommended for all students and an audition is recommended for music students. AP and CLEP credits are accepted. Important factors in the admissions decision are advanced placement or honors courses, recommendations by school officials, and leadership record. To graduate, students must complete 120 semester hours, including 52 hours across the liberal arts discipline, with a minimum GPA of 2.0. Courses in ideas and culture, computer literacy, public speaking, and phys ed are required. **Procedure:** Freshmen are admitted to all sessions. Entrance exams should be taken by the senior year of high school. There are deferred admissions and rolling admissions plans. Applications should be filed by August 1 for fall entry. **Transfer Students:** 16 transfer students enrolled in 2015-2016. Transfer applicants should have a minimum GPA of 2.0. 42 of 120 credits required for the bachelor's degree must be completed at Converse. **International Students:** There are 14 international students enrolled. The school actively recruits these students. They must take the TOEFL.

ADMISSIONS: 51% of the 2016-2017 applicants were accepted. The SAT scores for the 2016-2017 freshman class were: Critical Reading-- 29% below 500, 43% between 500 and 599, 25% between 600 and 699, and 3% between 700 and 800. Math-- 35% below 500, 50% between 500 and 599, 14% between 600 and 699, and 1% between 700 and 800. The ACT scores were 32% below 12, 25% between 12 and 17, 25% between 18 and 23, 13% between 24 and 29, and 6% above 30. 5 freshmen graduated first in their class. **Admissions Contact:** April Lewis, Director of Admissions. Email: *admissions@converse.edu* Web: *www.converse.edu*

FINANCIAL AID: The FAFSA code is 003431. The deadline for filing freshman financial aid applications for fall entry is March 15.

ERSKINE COLLEGE B-2

www.erskine.edu

Due West, SC 29639	(864) 379-8830 (800) 241-8721
Fax: (864) 379-2167	**Email:** admissions@erskine.edu
Full-time: 250 men, 291 women	**Faculty:** 41
Part-time: 9 men, 3 women	**Ph.D.s:** 85%
Graduate: n/av	**Student/Faculty:** 11 to 1
Year: 4-1-4, summer session	**Tuition:** $34,560
Room & Board: $10,900	**Freshman Class:** 500 applied, 373 accepted, 144 enrolled
SAT CR/M: 531/543 **ACT:** required	**CEEB CODE:** 5188
Application Deadline: open	**COMPETITIVE**

Erskine College, founded in 1839, is a private liberal arts college affiliated with the Associate Reformed Presbyterian Church. The figures in the above capsule and in this profile are approximate. There is 1 undergraduate school and 1 graduate school. In addition to regional accreditation, Erskine has baccalaureate program accreditation with NCATE, CAATE, and ATS. The 85-acre campus is in a rural area in Abbeville County, 90 miles west of Columbia. Including any residence halls, there are 30 buildings.

STUDENT LIFE: 76% of undergraduates are from South Carolina. Others are from 19 states, 8 foreign countries, and Canada. 85% are from public schools. 8% are African American; 72% White; 4% Foreign; 2% Hispanic; 1% Asian American. **Female To Male Ratio:** 1.1:1. The average age of freshmen is 18; all undergraduates, 20. 23% do not continue beyond their first year; 69% remain to graduate. **Housing:** 654 students can be accommodated in college housing, which includes single-sex dorms. On-campus housing is guaranteed for all 4 years. 89% of students live on campus; of those, 50% remain on campus on weekends. All students may keep cars. Alcohol is not permitted.

FACULTY/CLASSROOMS: 61% of faculty are male; 39% are female. All teach undergraduates. No introductory courses are taught by graduate students. The average class size in an introductory lecture is 22; in a laboratory is 25; and in a regular course is 14.

PROGRAMS OF STUDY: Erskine confers A.B. and B.S. degrees. Master's and doctoral degrees are also awarded. Bachelor's degrees are awarded in BIOLOGICAL SCIENCE (biology/biological science), BUSINESS (business administration and management and sports management), COMMUNICATIONS AND THE ARTS (art, English, music, and visual and performing arts), COMPUTER AND PHYSICAL SCIENCE (chemistry, mathematics, natural sciences, and physics), EDUCATION (athletic training, Christian education, early childhood education, elementary education, foreign languages education, physical education, and special education), SOCIAL SCIENCE (American studies, behavioral science, history, philosophy, psychology, religion, and social studies). Mathematics, chemistry, philosophy, and Spanish are the strongest academically. Business administration, and biology have the largest enrollments.

ACTIVITIES: There are no fraternities or sororities. There are 51 groups on campus, including art, cheerleading, choir, chorale, chorus, computers, dance, drama, ethnic, honors, jazz band, literary magazine, newspaper, pep band, political, professional, radio and TV, religious, social, social service, student government, and yearbook. Popular campus events include Spring Fling, Back to School Bash, and Freshman Follies. **Sports:** There are 6 intercollegiate sports for men and 8 for women. Facilities include a physical activities center, gyms, racquetball courts, soccer and baseball fields, tennis and basketball courts, an outdoor pavilion, an outdoor pool, sand volleyball courts, a weight room, a dance/ aerobics studio, and a climbing wall. **Graduates:** From July 1, 2015 to June 30, 2016, 141 bachelor's degrees were awarded. The most popular majors were biology (21%), business (20%), and education (13%). In an average class, 63% graduate in 5 years or less and 69% graduate in 6 years or less.

SERVICES: Counseling and information services are available, as is tutoring in every subject, and a reader service for the blind. **Library/ Resources:** The library contains 217,947 volumes, 63,064 microform items, 2,979 audio/video tapes/CDs/DVDs, and subscribes to 1,125 periodicals including electronic. Computerized library services include interlibrary loans, database searching, Internet access, and Wi-Fi capability. Special learning facilities include an art gallery and radio station. **Physically Challenged Students:** 75% of the campus is accessible. Facilities include wheelchair ramps, elevators, special parking, specially equipped restrooms, and special class scheduling. **Special:** Externships are available during the January term. Study abroad in 5 countries, 3-2 engineering degrees with Clemson University, the University of Tennessee at Knoxville, and Medical University of South Carolina, and pass/fail options are offered. There are 7 national honor societies and 10 departmental honors programs. **Visiting:** There are guides for informal visits, visitors may sit in on classes, and stay overnight. To schedule a visit, contact the Admissions Office. **Campus Safety and Security:** Measures include emergency notification system, security escort services, and lighted pathways/sidewalks.

REQUIREMENTS: Grades from college preparatory courses are weighed twice as heavily as the SAT or ACT scores. Applicants must be graduates of an accredited secondary school. The GED is accepted. Applicants should have a minimum of 14 high school academic credits, including 4 credits of English and 2 credits each of math, science, and history. AP and CLEP credits are accepted. Important factors in the admissions decision are advanced placement or honors courses, recommendations by school officials, and extracurricular activities record. Students must complete 124 semester hours with an average of 27 credits in a major and a minimum GPA of 2.0. A basic curriculum of arts and letters, humanities, natural science and math, social sciences, and phys ed is required. Attendance at 17 convocations per semester is also required. **Procedure:** Freshmen are admitted to all sessions. Entrance exams should be taken in the spring of the junior year or the fall of the senior year. There are deferred admissions and rolling admissions plans. Application deadlines are open. The fall 2016 application fee was $25. Notification is sent on a rolling basis. Applications are accepted online. **Transfer Students:** 17 transfer students enrolled in 2015-2016. Transfer applicants should have a minimum GPA of 2.0. An interview is recommended. 60 of 124 credits required for the bachelor's degree must be completed at Erskine. **International Students:** There are 20 international students enrolled. They must take the TOEFL, as well as the SAT.

ADMISSIONS: 75% of the 2016-2017 applicants were accepted. The SAT scores for the 2016-2017 freshman class were: Critical Reading-- 40% below 500, 36% between 500 and 599, 19% between 600 and 699, and 5% between 700 and 800. Math-- 37% below 500, 35% between 500 and 599, 23% between 600 and 699, and 5% between 700 and 800. 65% of the current freshmen were in the top fifth of their class; 87% were in the top two fifths. **Admissions Contact:** Buck Brown, Director of Admissions. Email: *brown@erskine.edu* Web: *www.erskine.edu*

FINANCIAL AID: The college's own financial statement is required. The FAFSA code is 003432. The deadline for filing freshman financial aid applications for fall entry is April 1.

FRANCIS MARION UNIVERSITY *(The complete profile is made available exclusively on our website, www.barronspac.com)*

FURMAN UNIVERSITY — B-1

www.furman.edu

Greenville, SC 29613 — (864) 294-2034

Fax: (864) 294-2018
Email: admission@furman.edu

Full-time: 1131 men, 1492 women	**Faculty:** 234; IIB, +$
Part-time: 55 men, 53 women	**Ph.D.s:** 96%
Graduate: 30 men, 123 women	**Student/Faculty:** 11 to 1
Year: semesters, summer session	**Tuition:** $46,012
Room & Board: $12,080	**Freshman Class:** 5143 applied, 3268 accepted, 671 enrolled
SAT CR/M/W: 610/610/610 **ACT:** 28	**CEEB CODE:** 5222
Application Deadline: January 15	**VERY COMPETITIVE+**

Furman University, founded in 1826, is an independent liberal arts institution offering undergraduate and graduate programs. Figures in the above capsule and in this profile are approximate. There is 1 undergraduate school. In addition to regional accreditation, Furman has baccalaureate program accreditation with NASM and NCATE. The 750-acre campus is in a suburban area 5 miles north of Greenville. Including any residence halls, there are 69 buildings.

STUDENT LIFE: 73% of undergraduates are from out of state, mostly the South. Students are from 45 states, 53 foreign countries, and Canada. 58% are from public schools. 80% are White; 6% African American; 6% Foreign; 4% Hispanic; 2% Asian American; 2% two or more races; 2% race unknown. 73% are Protestant; 15% Catholic. **Female To Male Ratio:** 1.4:1. The average age of freshmen is 18; all undergraduates, 20. 11% do not continue beyond their first year; 84% remain to graduate. **Housing:** 2480 students can be accommodated in college housing, which includes single-sex and coed dorms, on-campus apartments, language houses, special-interest houses, small houses, lakeside cabins, an eco-cottage, and a healthy living dorm section. On-campus housing is guaranteed for all 4 years and is available on a lottery system for upperclassmen. 96% of students live on campus; of those, 75% remain on campus on weekends. All students may keep cars.

FACULTY/CLASSROOMS: 65% of faculty are male; 35% are female. All teach undergraduates. No introductory courses are taught by graduate students. The average class size in an introductory lecture is 19; in a laboratory is 10; and in a regular course is 16.

PROGRAMS OF STUDY: Furman confers B.A., B.S., B.L.A., and B.M. degrees. Master's degrees are also awarded. Bachelor's degrees are awarded in BIOLOGICAL SCIENCE (biology/biological science and neurosciences), BUSINESS (accounting and business administration and management), COMMUNICATIONS AND THE ARTS (art, classics, communications, dramatic arts, English, French, German, Greek, Latin, music, music performance, music theory and composition, and Spanish), COMPUTER AND PHYSICAL SCIENCE (chemistry, computer science, information sciences and systems, mathematics, and physics), EDUCATION (education, elementary education, and music education), ENGINEERING AND ENVIRONMENTAL DESIGN (environmental science and preengineering), HEALTH PROFESSIONS (exercise science and health science), SOCIAL SCIENCE (Asian/Oriental studies, economics, history, philosophy, political science/government, psychology, religion, religious music, sociology, and urban studies). Chemistry, health sciences, biology, and music are the strongest academically. Political science, health sciences, and business administration have the largest enrollments.

ACTIVITIES: 33% of men belong to 7 national fraternities; 58% of women belong to 7 national sororities. There are 150 groups on campus, including art, band, cheerleading, chess, choir, chorale, chorus, computers, dance, debate, drama, drill team, environmental, ethnic, film, forensics, honors, international, jazz band, LGBT, literary magazine, marching band, musical theater, newspaper, opera, orchestra, pep band, photography, political, professional, radio and TV, religious, social, social service, student government, symphony, and yearbook. Popular campus events include Beach Weekend and Mountain Weekend. **Sports:** There are 9 intercollegiate sports for men and 9 for women, and 20 intramural sports for men and 20 for women. Facilities include a football stadium, an arena, gym, pool, golf course, a tennis center with indoor and outdoor courts, a soccer stadium, 12 playing fields, a varsity softball field, and a baseball stadium. The Physical Activities Center includes a multi-level fitness center and pool. **Graduates:** From July 1, 2015 to June 30, 2016, 660 bachelor's degrees were awarded. The most popular majors were business administration (11%), political science (11%), and health sciences (9%). 14 companies recruited on campus in 2015-2016. In an average class, 1% graduate in 3 years or less, 80% graduate in 4 years or less, 83% graduate in 5 years or less, and 84% graduate in 6 years or less. Of the 2015 graduating class, 34% were enrolled in graduate school within 6 months of graduation, and 61% were employed.

SERVICES: Counseling and information services are available, as is tutoring in every subject, and a reader service for the blind. **Library/Resources:** The 3 libraries contain 621,903 volumes, 862,324 microform items, 9,550 audio/video tapes/CDs/DVDs, and subscribe to 179,800 periodicals including electronic. Computerized library services include interlibrary loans, database searching, Internet access, and Wi-Fi capability. Special learning facilities include an art gallery, planetarium, radio station, an observatory, and cable TV with on-campus broadcasting. **Physically Challenged Students:** 99% of the campus is accessible. Facilities include wheelchair ramps, elevators, special parking, specially equipped restrooms, special class scheduling, lowered drinking fountains, lowered telephones, and special housing. **Special:** A 3-2 engineering degree is offered with the Georgia Institute of Technology, Clemson, North Carolina State, and Auburn and Washington Universities. Internships, study abroad in at least 17 countries, a Washington semester with an internship in a government agency or political organization, and work-study programs are offered. B.A.-B.S. degrees, dual majors, interdisciplinary majors such as computer science-math, math-economics, and computing-business, and student-designed majors are available. A bachelor of general studies degree is granted in the evening division. Nondegree study and pass/fail options are possible. Furman features student/faculty research programs. There are 20 national honor societies and a chapter of Phi Beta Kappa. **Visiting:** There are regularly scheduled orientations for prospective students, consisting of an individual or group session with an admissions officer and a campus tour. There are guides for informal visits, visitors may sit in on classes, and stay overnight. To schedule a visit, contact the Admissions Office at admissions@furman.edu. **Campus Safety and Security:** Measures include 24-hour foot and vehicle patrol, emergency notification system, self-defense education, and security escort services. There are also shuttle buses, emergency telephones, lighted pathways/sidewalks, and controlled access to dorms/residences.

REQUIREMENTS: The SAT or ACT and ACT Writing Test are recommended. Applicants must be high school graduates or hold a GED. Students should have earned at least 20 units in high school, including 4 of English, 3 each of history, math, and science, and 2 each of social studies and foreign language. A portfolio or an audition, where appropriate, is required. AP credits are accepted. Important factors in the admissions decision are advanced placement or honors courses, evidence of special talent, personality/intangible qualities, extracurricular activities record, leadership record, and parents or siblings attended your school. Students must complete 1 to 3 courses in foreign languages, 4 empirical studies classes, 2 natural world, 2 human and social behavior, 3 courses in human culture, 2 courses in global awareness, 1 course in math and formal reasoning, 1 course in ultimate questions, and 1 course in body and mind. To graduate students must complete 128 credit hours, including 24 to 44 in the major, with a GPA of 2.0. **Procedure:** Freshmen are admitted in the fall. Entrance exams should be taken by late junior or early senior year. There are early decision and early admissions plans. Early decision applications should be filed by November 1; regular applications, by January 15 for fall entry, along with a $50 fee. Notification of early decision is sent November 15; regular decision, March 1. 119 early decision candidates were accepted for the 2016-2017 class. 51 applicants were on the 2016 waiting list; 14 were admitted. Applications are accepted online. **Transfer Students:** 27 transfer students enrolled in 2015-2016. Applicants should complete at least 1 year elsewhere before seeking admission. 64 of 128 credits required for the bachelor's degree must be completed at Furman. **International Students:** There are 158 international students enrolled. The school actively recruits these students. They must take the TOEFL.

ADMISSIONS: 64% of the 2016-2017 applicants were accepted. The SAT scores for the 2016-2017 freshman class were: Critical Reading-- 9% below 500, 36% between 500 and 599, 42% between 600 and 699, and 13% between 700 and 800. Math-- 7% below 500, 35% between 500 and 599, 45% between 600 and 699, and 13% between 700 and 800. Writing-- 10% below 500, 35% between 500 and 599, 43% between 600 and 699, and 12% between 700 and 800. The ACT scores were 1% between 12 and 17, 16% between 18 and 23, 63% between 24 and 29, and 21% above 30. 63% of the current freshmen were in the top fifth of their class; 87% were in the top two fifths. **Admissions Contact:** Brad Pochard, Dean of Admission. Email: *admission@furman.edu* Web: *www.furman.edu*

FINANCIAL AID: In 2016-2017, 97% of all full-time freshmen and 93% of continuing full-time students received some form of financial aid. 52% of all full-time freshmen and 43% of continuing full-time students received need-based aid. The average freshman award was $34,803. 47% of undergraduate students work part-time. Average annual earnings from campus work are $2400. The average financial indebtedness of the 2016 graduate was $32,594. Furman is a member of CSS. The CSS/Profile and the state aid form are required. The FAFSA code is 003434. The deadline for filing freshman financial aid applications for fall entry is January 15.

LANDER UNIVERSITY — B-2
www.lander.edu

Greenwood, SC 29649	**(864) 388-8307** **(888) 4LANDER**
Fax: (864) 388-8125	**Email: admissions@lander.edu**
Full-time: 735 men, 1361 women	**Faculty:** 130
Part-time: 75 men, 192 women	**Ph.D.s:** 63%
Graduate: 6 men, 42 women	**Student/Faculty:** 14 to 1
Year: semesters, summer session	**Tuition:** $22,194 ($40,740)
Room & Board: $21,800	**Freshman Class:** 2230 applied, 946 accepted, 433 enrolled
SAT CR/M: 470/500 **ACT:** 21	**CEEB CODE:** 5363
Application Deadline: open	**COMPETITIVE**

Lander University, founded in 1872, is a state-supported institution offering undergraduate programs in liberal arts, science and math, business, education, nursing, and phys ed and exercise studies. The figures in the above capsule and in this profile are approximate. There are 10 undergraduate schools and 1 graduate school. In addition to regional accreditation, Lander has baccalaureate program accreditation with AACSB, NASAD, NASM, NCATE, and CCSACS. The 100-acre campus is in a small town in the city of Greenwood, 75 miles west of Columbia. Including any residence halls, there are 6 buildings.

STUDENT LIFE: 92% of undergraduates are from South Carolina. Others are from 23 states, 21 foreign countries, and Canada. 67% are White; 3% Foreign; 24% African American; 1% Asian American; 1% American Indian/Alaska Native; 1% Hispanic. **Female To Male Ratio:** 2.0:1. The average age of freshmen is 19; all undergraduates, 26. 38% do not continue beyond their first year; 62% remain to graduate. **Housing:** 1082 students can be accommodated in college housing, which includes single-sex and coed dorms, on-campus apartments, and off-campus apartments. On-campus housing is available on a first-come and first-served basis. 68% of students commute. All students may keep cars. Alcohol is not permitted.

FACULTY/CLASSROOMS: 47% of faculty are male; 53% are female. All teach undergraduates. No introductory courses are taught by graduate students. The average class size in a regular course is 22.

PROGRAMS OF STUDY: Lander confers B.A., B.S., and B.M.Ed. degrees. Master's degrees are also awarded. Bachelor's degrees are awarded in BIOLOGICAL SCIENCE (biology/biological science), BUSINESS (business administration and management), COMMUNICATIONS AND THE ARTS (communications, dramatic arts, English, music, Spanish, speech/debate/rhetoric, and visual and performing arts), COMPUTER AND PHYSICAL SCIENCE (chemistry, computer science, and mathematics), EDUCATION (early childhood education, elementary education, music education, physical education, and special education), ENGINEERING AND ENVIRONMENTAL DESIGN (environmental science), HEALTH PROFESSIONS (exercise science, nursing, and sports medicine), SOCIAL SCIENCE (history, interdisciplinary studies, political science/government, psychology, and sociology). Premedical, and dual engineering are the strongest academically. Business administration, education, and behavioral science have the largest enrollments.

ACTIVITIES: 11% of men belong to 5 national fraternities; 12% of women belong to 5 national sororities. There are 65 groups on campus, including art, band, cheerleading, choir, chorale, chorus, computers, dance, drama, ethnic, honors, international, jazz band, literary magazine, musical theater, newspaper, orchestra, pep band, political, professional, religious, social, social service, and student government. Popular campus events include The Greenwood Performing Arts Series. **Sports:** There are 5 intercollegiate sports for men and 6 for women, and 11 intramural sports for men and 11 for women. Facilities include a gym, basketball courts, weight room, softball field, soccer and tennis courts, golf, softball, volleyball teams, equestrian, ultimate disc, rugby, indoor pool, and an indoor suspended track. **Graduates:** From July 1, 2015 to June 30, 2016, 485 bachelor's degrees were awarded. The most popular majors were business (23%), education (14%), and social and political sciences (13%). 20 companies recruited on campus in 2015-2016. In an average class, 2% graduate in 3 years or less, 28% graduate in 4 years or less, 39% graduate in 5 years or less, and 40% graduate in 6 years or less.

SERVICES: Counseling and information services are available, as is tutoring in most subjects, and a reader service for the blind, and remedial math, reading, and writing. **Library/Resources:** The library contains 174,624 volumes, 157,707 microform items, 2,592 audio/video tapes/CDs/DVDs, and subscribes to 656 periodicals including electronic. Computerized library services include interlibrary loans, database searching, and Internet access. Special learning facilities include an art gallery, and a media center. **Physically Challenged Students:** All of the campus is accessible. Facilities include wheelchair ramps, elevators, special parking, specially equipped restrooms, special class scheduling, lowered drinking fountains, and lowered telephones. **Special:** Lander offers internships, co-op and work-study programs, accelerated degrees, B.A.-B.S. degrees, dual engineering degree's with Clemson University, student-designed majors in interdisciplinary studies, credit for military experience, and nondegree study. Students in the Honors International Program study abroad in England for 1 semester during their sophomore year. There are 7 national honor societies and a freshman honors program. **Visiting:** There are regularly scheduled orientations for prospective students, consisting of open houses. There are guides for informal visits and visitors may sit in on classes. To schedule a visit, contact the Admissions Office. **Campus Safety and Security:** Measures include 24-hour foot and vehicle patrol, emergency notification system, self-defense education, security escort services, emergency telephones, lighted pathways/sidewalks, and controlled access to dorms/residences.

REQUIREMENTS: The SAT or ACT is required. Applicants must be high school graduates with 20 credits, including 4 each of English and academic electives, and 3 each of math and lab science, 2 each of foreign language and social studies, and 1 each of American history and phys ed or ROTC. An interview and a portfolio or an audition, if appropriate, are recommended. AP and CLEP credits are accepted. To graduate, students must complete 125 semester hours, including 36 in the major, with a GPA of 2.0. **Procedure:** Freshmen are admitted to all sessions. Entrance exams should be taken in the junior year. There are early admissions, deferred admissions, and rolling admissions plans. Application deadlines are open. The fall 2016 application fee was $35. Notification is sent on a rolling basis. Applications are accepted on-line. **Transfer Students:** 203 transfer students enrolled in 2015-2016. Applicants must have a minimum college GPA of 2.0, otherwise they may be considered on the strength of military or work experience. Transcripts from every school attended should be submitted. Students under 21 with fewer than 30 semester credits must submit high school transcripts and SAT or ACT results as well. An interview is recommended. 30 of 125 credits required for the bachelor's degree must be completed at Lander. **International Students:** The school actively recruits these students. They must take the TOEFL with a minimum score of 550 on the paper-based TOEFL (PBT). They must also take the SAT or ACT.

ADMISSIONS: 42% of the 2016-2017 applicants were accepted. The SAT scores for the 2016-2017 freshman class were: Critical Reading-- 59% below 500, 32% between 500 and 599, and 8% between 600 and 699. Math-- 47% below 500, 38% between 500 and 599, 14% between 600 and 699, and 1% between 700 and 800. The ACT scores were 47% below 12, 32% between 12 and 17, 15% between 18 and 23, 4% between 24 and 29, and 2% above 30. 33% of the current freshmen were in the top fifth of their class; 69% were in the top two fifths. 5 freshmen graduated first in their class. **Admissions Contact:** Brooks Schadell, Director of Admissions. Email: *admissions@lander.edu* Web: *www.lander.edu*

FINANCIAL AID: The FAFSA code is 003435. Check with the school for current application deadlines.

LIMESTONE COLLEGE B-1

www.limestone.edu

Gaffney, SC 29340 | (864) 489-7151 | (800) 795-7151

Fax: (864) 487-8706 | Email: admissions@limestone.edu

Full-time: 771 men, 456 women	**Faculty:** 81; IIA
Part-time: 14 men, 5 women	**Ph.D.s:** 79%
Graduate: 32 men, 42 women	**Student/Faculty:** 14 to 1
Year: semesters, summer session	**Tuition:** $23,900
Room & Board: $8200	**Freshman Class:** 3196 applied, 1653 accepted, 526 enrolled
SAT CR/M: 500/510 **ACT:** 21	**CEEB CODE:** 5366
Application Deadline: August 23	**COMPETITIVE**

Limestone College, founded in 1845, is an independent, accredited, coeducational, Christian non-denominational, four-year liberal arts College offering programs in the arts, sciences, business, and teacher preparation. Its programs lead to the Bachelor of Arts, Bachelor of Fine Arts, Bachelor of Science, Bachelor of Social Work, Associate of Arts, and Associate of Science degrees. At the graduate level, a Master of Business Administration is offered. There is 1 undergraduate school and 1 graduate school. In addition to regional accreditation, has baccalaureate program accreditation with CSWE, NASM, NCATE, and CAATE. The 125-acre campus is in a suburban area 50 miles south of Charlotte, NC and 25 miles north of Spartanburg, SC. Including any residence halls, there are 33 buildings.

STUDENT LIFE: 58% of undergraduates are from South Carolina. Others are from 36 states, 31 foreign countries, and Canada. 9% are Foreign; 48% White; 4% Hispanic; 34% African American; 3% two or more races; 1% race unknown. **Male To Female Ratio:** 1.6:1. The average age of freshmen is 18; all undergraduates, 19. 45% do not continue beyond their first year; 66% remain to graduate. **Housing:** 823 students can be accommodated in college housing, which includes single-sex dorms, on-campus apartments, and off-campus apartments. CELP. On-campus housing is guaranteed for the freshman year only, and is available on a first-come, and first-served basis. 58% of students live on campus; of those, 55% remain on campus on weekends. All students may keep cars. Alcohol is not permitted.

FACULTY/CLASSROOMS: 51% of faculty are male; 49% are female. All teach undergraduates, 20% do research, and 20% do both. No introductory courses are taught by graduate students. The average class size in an introductory lecture is 22; in a laboratory is 16; and in a regular course is 14.

PROGRAMS OF STUDY: Limestone confers B.A., B.S., B.F.A. and B.S.W. degrees. Associate and master's degrees are also awarded. Bachelor's degrees are awarded in BIOLOGICAL SCIENCE (biology/biological science), BUSINESS (accounting, business administration and management, business economics, electronic business, finance, human resources, management science, marketing, marketing and distribution, personnel management, and sports management), COMMUNICATIONS AND THE ARTS (communications, English, English Writing, graphic design, jazz, music, musical theater, studio art, and theatre arts), COMPUTER AND PHYSICAL SCIENCE (chemistry, computer programming, computer information technology, computer science, computer security and information assurance, information sciences and systems, mathematics, web services, and web technology), EDUCATION (athletic training, early childhood education, elementary education, English education, mathematics education, music education, and physical education), ENGINEERING AND ENVIRONMENTAL DESIGN (computer technology), HEALTH PROFESSIONS (health care administration), SOCIAL SCIENCE (child care/child and family studies, criminal justice, economics, history, liberal arts/general studies, physical fitness/movement, prelaw, psychology, and social work). Business administration, sport management, and criminal justice have the largest enrollments.

ACTIVITIES: 3% of women belong to 1 local sororities. There are 32 groups on campus, including art, band, cheerleading, choir, chorus, computers, dance, drama, environmental, honors, international, jazz band, LGBT, literary magazine, marching band, musical theater, pep band, professional, religious, social, social service, student government, and symphony. Popular campus events include Christmas on Campus and Homecoming. **Sports:** There are 13 intercollegiate sports for men and 12 for women, and 28 intramural sports for men and 28 for women. Facilities include a basketball gym with six goals, indoor swimming pool, fieldhouse, tennis courts, lacrosse, soccer and field hockey, football practice field, additional practice fields, and athletic weight room. **Graduates:** From July 1, 2015 to June 30, 2016, 142 bachelor's degrees were awarded. The most popular majors were business administration (16%), PE-strength and conditioning (11%), and sport management (10%). In an average class, 20% graduate in 4 years or less and 42% graduate in 6 years or less. Of the 2015 graduating class, 19% were enrolled in graduate school within 6 months of graduation.

SERVICES: Counseling and information services are available, as is tutoring in every subject, and remedial math, reading, and writing. Special assistance is also available to students with documented learning disabilities through the Program for Alternative Learning Styles. **Library/Resources:** The library contains 77,342 volumes, 2,924 microform items, and 4,032 audio/video tapes/CDs/DVDs, and subscribes to 277,823 periodicals including electronic. Computerized library services include interlibrary loans, database searching, Internet access, and Wi-Fi capability. **Physically Challenged Students:** 75% of the campus is accessible. Facilities include wheelchair ramps, elevators, special parking, specially equipped restrooms, special class scheduling, lowered drinking fountains, and special housing. Individual accommodations are made on an as-needed basis. **Special:** The College offers senior internships in public and private organizations for 3 to 6 semester credit hours, as well as a work-study program, on- and off-campus evening courses, and courses on the Internet. The College confers a liberal studies degree and may grant credit for military experience. Double majors are possible; however, granting of 2 baccalaureate degrees requires an additional 31 semester hours. There are 5 national honor societies and a freshman honors program. **Visiting:** There are regularly scheduled orientations for prospective students, a tour of the campus facility. presentations, Academic Fair, and Q & A session. There are guides for informal visits, visitors may sit in on classes, and stay overnight. To schedule a visit, contact Jennifer Ledbetter at (864) 488-4552. **Campus Safety and Security:** Measures include 24-hour foot and vehicle patrol, emergency notification system, security escort services, emergency telephones, lighted pathways/sidewalks, and controlled access to dorms/residences.

REQUIREMENTS: SAT combined score (critical reading and math) of 910 or ACT combined score (English and math) of 19, are required. The College recommends that students present 4 units of English, 3 each of math and social science, and 2 of lab science. The GED is accepted. An interview is recommended. AP and CLEP credits are accepted. Important factors in the admissions decision are advanced placement or honors courses, leadership record, and evidence of special talent. To graduate a student must complete a minimum of 123 credit hours for a baccalaureate degree or 62 credit hours for an associate degree with a minimum overall GPA of 2.0, including within their major. **Procedure:**

Freshmen are admitted in the fall and spring. Entrance exams should be taken during fall of the senior year of high school. There are deferred admissions and rolling admissions plans. Application deadlines are open. Application fee is $25. Notification is sent on a rolling basis. Application fees are waived if application is completed online. **Transfer Students:** 95 transfer students enrolled in 2015-2016. Applicants must have a minimum GPA of 2.0 and be in good standing at their previous school. 31 of 123 credits required for the bachelor's degree must be completed at Limestone. **International Students:** There are 112 international students enrolled. The school actively recruits these students. They must take the TOEFL with a minimum score of 500 on the paper-based TOEFL (PBT) or 75 on the Internet-based version (iBT). They must also take the SAT or ACT, scoring 910.

ADMISSIONS: 52% of the 2016-2017 applicants were accepted. The SAT scores for the 2016-2017 freshman class were: Critical Reading--60% below 500, 31% between 500 and 599, 8% between 600 and 699, and 0% between 700 and 800. Math-- 39% below 500, 51% between 500 and 599, and 9% between 600 and 699. The ACT scores were 75% between 18 and 23, 19% between 24 and 29, and 4% above 30. 18% of the current freshmen were in the top fifth of their class; 38% were in the top two fifths. 1 freshman graduated first in the class. **Admissions Contact:** Travis McDowell, Director of Admissions. Email: *admissions@limestone.edu* Web: *www.limestone.edu*

FINANCIAL AID: In 2016-2017, 92% of all full-time freshmen and 94% of continuing full-time students received some form of financial aid. 92% of all full-time freshmen and 93% of continuing full-time students received need-based aid. The average freshman award was $16,675. Need-based scholarships or need-based grants averaged $5,660 ($9,825 maximum); need-based self-help aid (loans and jobs) averaged $6,575 ($12,500 maximum); non-need-based athletic scholarships averaged $6,985 ($25,600 maximum); other non-need-based awards and non-need-based scholarships averaged $4,875 ($28,800 maximum); and $1,650 from other forms of aid. 31% of undergraduate students work part-time. Average annual earnings from campus work are $1650. The average financial indebtedness of the 2016 graduate was $30,950. is a member of CSS. The FAFSA code is 003436. The priority date for freshman financial aid applications for fall entry is February 1. The filing deadline for fall entry is June 30.

MORRIS COLLEGE *(The complete profile is made available exclusively on our website, www.barronspac.com)*

NEWBERRY COLLEGE B-2
www.newberry.edu

Newberry, SC 29108 (803) 321-5127 (800) 845-4955

Fax: (803) 321-5138 **Email:** admissions@newberry.edu

Full-time: 435 men, 325 women	**Faculty:** 46; IIB
Part-time: 10 men, 25 women	**Ph.D.s:** 70%
Graduate: n/av	**Student/Faculty:** 16 to 1
Year: semesters, summer session	**Tuition:** $27,000
Room & Board: $9550	**Freshman Class:** n/av
SAT or ACT: required	**CEEB CODE:** 5493
Application Deadline: open	**COMPETITIVE**

Newberry College, founded in 1856, is a private liberal arts institution affiliated with the Evangelical Lutheran Church in America. Figures in the above capsule and in this profile are approximate. There is 1 undergraduate school. In addition to regional accreditation, Newberry has baccalaureate program accreditation with NASM, NCATE, and AVMA. The 90-acre campus is in a small town 40 miles northwest of Columbia. Including any residence halls, there are 22 buildings.

STUDENT LIFE: 84% of undergraduates are from South Carolina. Others are from 13 states, 8 foreign countries, and Canada. 90% are from public schools. 71% are White; 26% African American; 1% Hispanic; 1% Foreign. 80% are Protestant; 12% claim no religious affiliation. **Male To Female Ratio:** 1.3:1. The average age of freshmen is 18; all undergraduates, 20. 49% do not continue beyond their first year; 47% remain to graduate. **Housing:** 622 students can be accommodated in college housing, which includes single-sex and coed dorms, and honors houses. On-campus housing is guaranteed for all 4 years. 77% of students live on campus; of those, 66% remain on campus on weekends. All students may keep cars.

FACULTY/CLASSROOMS: 58% of faculty are male; 41% are female. All teach undergraduates. No introductory courses are taught by graduate students. The average class size in an introductory lecture is 30; in a laboratory is 30; and in a regular course is 25.

PROGRAMS OF STUDY: Newberry confers B.A., B.S., B.M., and B.M.E. degrees. Bachelor's degrees are awarded in BIOLOGICAL SCIENCE (biology/biological science), BUSINESS (business administration and management), COMMUNICATIONS AND THE ARTS (applied music, art, communications, dramatic arts, English, French, German, languages, music, music performance, music theory and composition, and Spanish), COMPUTER AND PHYSICAL SCIENCE (chemistry, computer science, and mathematics), EDUCATION (early childhood education, elementary education, music education, and physical education), HEALTH PROFESSIONS (veterinary science), SOCIAL SCIENCE (history, philosophy, political science/government, psychology, religion, and sociology). Education, and natural sciences are the strongest academically. Business administration, education, and physical education have the largest enrollments.

ACTIVITIES: 11% of men belong to 6 national fraternities; 13% of women belong to 3 national sororities. There are 50 groups on campus, including band, cheerleading, choir, chorale, chorus, computers, dance, drama, ethnic, honors, international, jazz band, literary magazine, marching band, musical theater, newspaper, orchestra, pep band, political, professional, radio and TV, religious, social, social service, student government, and yearbook. Popular campus events include Fall Fling and Spring Fling. **Sports:** There are 8 intercollegiate sports for men and 9 for women, and 6 intramural sports for men and 5 for women. Facilities include a stadium, a phys ed complex with a basketball arena and racquetball courts, an outdoor pool, tennis courts, and baseball, softball, cross country, lacrosse, golf, field hockey, volleyball, wrestling and soccer fields. **Graduates:** The most popular majors were business and management (16%), education (13%), and social sciences and history (9%). 124 companies recruited on campus in 2015-2016. Of the 2015 graduating class, 20% were enrolled in graduate school within 6 months of graduation, and 60% were employed.

SERVICES: Counseling and information services are available, as is tutoring in most subjects, and remedial math, reading, and writing. **Library/Resources:** The 2 libraries contain 79,464 volumes, 7,153 microform items, 1,217 audio/video tapes/CDs/DVDs, and subscribe to 258 periodicals including electronic. Computerized library services include interlibrary loans, database searching, and Internet access. Special learning facilities include a radio station, TV station, an herbarium. **Physically Challenged Students:** 90% of the campus is accessible. Facilities include wheelchair ramps, elevators, special parking, specially equipped restrooms, and special class scheduling. **Special:** Internships, dual and student-designed majors, study abroad, a Washington semester, work-study programs, independent study, and cooperative education are offered. A 3-2 engineering degree program with Clemson University, a 3-2 forestry program with Duke University, a 3-3 cytotechnology program, and a 3-1 medical technology program are available. Nondegree study is possible. There are 3 national honor societies, a freshman honors program, and 3 departmental honors programs. **Visiting:** There are regularly scheduled orientations for prospective students, including a campus tour, informational sessions, and meetings with faculty, staff, and students. There are guides for informal visits, visitors may sit in on classes, and stay overnight. To schedule a visit, contact the Admissions Office. **Campus Safety and Security:** Measures include 24-hour foot and vehicle patrol, emergency notification system, and security escort services, emergency telephones, lighted pathways/sidewalks, and controlled access to dorms/residences.

REQUIREMENTS: The SAT or ACT is required. Applicants should have completed 18 high school academic units, including 4 of English, 3 each of math and social science (1 of U.S. history), 2 each of lab science and a foreign language, and 1 elective. The GED is accepted. An essay is recommended. A GPA of 2.0 is required. AP and CLEP credits are accepted. Important factors in the admissions decision are leadership record, evidence of special talent, and recommendations by school officials. To graduate, students must complete 126 semester hours, with a minimum GPA of 2.0. Core curriculum requirements include 10 to 11 hours of math and natural science, 9 each of communication skills, humanities or fine arts, and history or social sciences, up to 6 of foreign language, 3 of religion, and 2 of phys ed. There is also a 24-event fine arts and lectures requirement. All students must fulfill Communications Across the Curriculum writing projects. **Procedure:** Freshmen are admitted to all sessions. Entrance exams should be taken in the spring of the junior year or the fall of the senior year. There are deferred admissions and rolling admissions plans. Application deadlines are open. The fall 2016 application fee was $30. **Transfer Students:** 57 transfer students enrolled in 2015-2016. Applicants must be eligible to return to their previous school. A 2.0 minimum GPA is recommended. 32 of 126 credits required for the bachelor's degree must be completed at Newberry. **International Students:** There are 8 international students enrolled. The school actively recruits these students. They must take the TOEFL and the college's own test. They must also take the SAT or ACT, scoring 900.

Admissions Contact: Joel Vander Horst, Director of Admissions. Email: *admissions@newberry.edu* Web: *www.newberry.edu*

FINANCIAL AID: In 2016-2017, 91% of all full-time freshmen and 96% of continuing full-time students received some form of financial aid. 63% of all full-time freshmen and 65% of continuing full-time students received need-based aid. The average freshman award was $12,450. 12% of undergraduate students work part-time. Average annual earnings from campus work are $625. The average financial indebtedness of the 2016 graduate was $3,135. Newberry is a member of CSS. The FAFSA code is 003440. The priority date for freshman financial aid applications for fall entry is March 30. The filing deadline for fall entry is May 15.

NORTH GREENVILLE UNIVERSITY
www.ngu.edu

Tigerville, SC 29688

(864) 977-7001
(800) 468-6642
Email: admissions@ngu.edu

Full-time: 1163 men, 1046 women
Part-time: 75 men, 197 women
Graduate: 115 men, 95 women
Year: semesters, summer session
Room & Board: $9640

Faculty: 137
Ph.D.s: 50%
Student/Faculty: 14 to 1
Tuition: $16,290
Freshman Class: 1593 applied, 919 accepted, 531 enrolled

SAT CR/M/W: 562/552/528 **ACT:** 24
Application Deadline: open

CEEB CODE: 005498
COMPETITIVE+

North Greenville University, founded in 1892, is a public university offering the Master of Christian Ministry, the Master of Business Administration, the Master of Education, the Master of Arts in Teaching, and the Doctor of Ministry. July 2014 an undergraduate online degree program offering business administration, elementary studies, Christian Ministries, criminal justice & legal studies, general studies, and psychology. NGU mission is to offer a quality education in a biblically sound, Christ-center environment. There are 7 undergraduate schools and 2 graduate schools. In addition to regional accreditation, NGU has baccalaureate program accreditation with NASM, NCATE, and NLN. The 315-acre campus is in a rural area in Tigerville in the foothills of the Blue Ridge Mountains, 18 miles north of Greenville. Including any residence halls, there are 100 buildings.

STUDENT LIFE: 66% of undergraduates are from South Carolina. Others are from 35 states, and Canada. 79% are White; 7% African American; 7% race unknown; 3% Hispanic; 3% two or more races. 87% are Protestant; 12% claim no religious affiliation. **Male To Female Ratio:** 1.0:1. The average age of freshmen is 18; all undergraduates, 20. **Housing:** 1550 students can be accommodated in college housing, which includes single-sex dorms. On-campus housing is guaranteed for all 4 years, and is available on a first-come, and first-served basis. Priority is given to out-of-town students. 65% of students live on campus; of those, 30% remain on campus on weekends. All students may keep cars.

FACULTY/CLASSROOMS: 57% of faculty are male; 43% are female. All teach undergraduates. No introductory courses are taught by graduate students. The average class size in an introductory lecture is 30; in a laboratory is 20; and in a regular course is 20.

PROGRAMS OF STUDY: NGU confers B.A. and B.S. degrees. Master's and doctoral degrees are also awarded. Bachelor's degrees are awarded in BIOLOGICAL SCIENCE (biological sciences), BUSINESS (accounting, international business information systems, marketing, and sports management), COMMUNICATIONS AND THE ARTS (broadcasting, music performance, Spanish, studio art, and theatre arts), COMPUTER AND PHYSICAL SCIENCE (mathematics), EDUCATION (education, English secondary education, mathematics education, music education, outdoor leadership/education, and social studies education), HEALTH PROFESSIONS (health promotion), SOCIAL SCIENCE (Christian studies, history and political science, psychology, and youth ministry). Business, sport management, biology, education, and Christian studies are the strongest academically. Business, education, and biology have the largest enrollments.

ACTIVITIES: There are no fraternities or sororities. There are 16 groups on campus, including art, band, cheerleading, choir, chorale, chorus, computers, debate, drama, honors, jazz band, literary magazine, marching band, musical theater, newspaper, orchestra, political, professional, social, social service, student government, and yearbook. Popular campus events include Homecoming, and the Miss NGU pagent. **Sports:** There are 10 intercollegiate sports for men and 10 for women. Facilities include a gym, baseball and softball fields, football and soccer/lacrosse stadiums, practice fields, an athletic weight training facility, tennis courts, and all-weather track. **Graduates:** From July 1, 2015 to June 30, 2016, 378 bachelor's degrees were awarded. The most popular majors were education (12%), health promotion & wellness (8%), and business administration (7%). In an average class, 42% graduate in 4 years or less, 55% graduate in 5 years or less, and 56% graduate in 6 years or less. Of the 2015 graduating class, 27% were enrolled in graduate school within 6 months of graduation, and 66% were employed.

SERVICES: Counseling and information services are available, as is tutoring in most subjects. and remedial math, reading, and writing. **Library/Resources:** The library contains 67,637 volumes, and 4,548 audio/video tapes/CDs/DVDs. Computerized library services include interlibrary loans, database searching, Internet access, and Wi-Fi capability. **Physically Challenged Students:** 90% of the campus is accessible. Facilities include wheelchair ramps, elevators, special parking, specially equipped restrooms, and lowered drinking fountains. **Special:** There is a freshman honors program. **Visiting:** There are guides for informal visits, visitors may sit in on classes, and stay overnight. **Campus Safety and Security:** Measures include 24-hour foot and vehicle patrol, self-defense education, security escort services, lighted pathways/sidewalks, and controlled access to dorms/residences.

REQUIREMENTS: The SAT or ACT is required. A GPA of 2.5 is required. AP and CLEP credits are accepted. Important factors in the admissions decision are advanced placement or honors courses, leadership record, and personality/intangible qualities. Students at North Greenville University will experience a general education curriculum that seeks to develop persons who can apply Biblical truths and principles to learning and life, and students who will be good stewards of a Christian mind and body given to us by God. Students are exposed to courses in the liberal arts, fine arts, the social and behavioral sciences, and the natural and logical sciences. Such a curriculum will enable students to develop a broad knowledge of civilization, literature, religious traditions, and the human condition needed for successful interaction with individuals and institutions. Specific general education requirements may be found listed within each major, each of which requires a minimum of thirty-eight general education hours. **Procedure:** Freshmen are admitted to all sessions. There are early admissions, deferred admissions, and rolling admissions plans. Application deadlines are open. Application fee is $30. Applications are accepted online. **Transfer Students:** 179 transfer students enrolled in 2015-2016. 30 of 120 credits required for the bachelor's degree must be completed at NGU. **International Students:** There are 12 international students enrolled. They must take the TOEFL with a minimum score of 550 on the paper-based TOEFL (PBT) or 80 on the Internet-based version (iBT). They must also take the SAT or ACT.

ADMISSIONS: 58% of the 2016-2017 applicants were accepted. The SAT scores for the 2016-2017 freshman class were: Critical Reading-- 15% below 500, 60% between 500 and 599, 21% between 600 and 699, and 4% between 700 and 800. Math-- 21% below 500, 54% between 500 and 599, 22% between 600 and 699, and 3% between 700 and 800. Writing-- 20% below 500, 53% between 500 and 599, 21% between 600 and 699, and 6% between 700 and 800. The ACT scores were 4% between 12 and 17, 42% between 18 and 23, 45% between 24 and 29, and 9% above 30. 24% of the current freshmen were in the top fifth of their class; 75% were in the top two fifths. **Admissions Contact:** Ms. Keli Sewell, Vice President for Enrollment Services. Email: *admissions@ngu.edu* Web: *www.ngu.edu*

FINANCIAL AID: In 2016-2017, 75% of all full-time freshmen and 53% of continuing full-time students received some form of financial aid. 73% of all full-time freshmen and 53% of continuing full-time students received need-based aid. The average freshman award was $5,074. Need-based scholarships or need-based grants averaged $5,074; need-based self-help aid (loans and jobs) averaged $5,074; non-need-based athletic scholarships averaged $8,654; and other non-need-based awards and non-need-based scholarships averaged $7,576. Average annual earnings from campus work are $1000. The average financial indebtedness of the 2016 graduate was $2,000. NGU is a member of CSS. The state aid form is required. The FAFSA code is 003441. The priority date for freshman financial aid applications for fall entry is March 1.

PRESBYTERIAN COLLEGE B-2

www.presby.edu

Clinton, SC 29325	(864) 833-8194 (800) 960-7583
Fax: (864) 833-8195	**Email:** admissions@presby.edu
Full-time: 476 men, 520 women	**Faculty:** 77
Part-time: 17 men, 50 women	**Ph.D.s:** 97%
Graduate: 96 men, 194 women	**Student/Faculty:** 13 to 1
Year: semesters, summer session	**Tuition:** $37,142
Room & Board: $10,044	**Freshman Class:** 2636 applied, 1577 accepted, 287 enrolled
SAT CR/M: 550/540 **ACT:** 25	**CEEB CODE:** 5540
Application Deadline: February 1	**VERY COMPETITIVE**

Presbyterian College, founded in 1880, is a private liberal arts institution affiliated with the Presbyterian Church. PC also has a graduate school of pharmacy that offers a doctorate in pharmacy (PharmD). There is 1 undergraduate school and 1 graduate school. In addition to regional accreditation, PC has baccalaureate program accreditation with ACPE, NASM, NCATE, SACSCOC, ASBMB, and CAEP. The 240-acre campus is in a small town 40 miles south of Greenville. Including any residence halls, there are 71 buildings.

STUDENT LIFE: 66% of undergraduates are from South Carolina. Others are from 28 states, 20 foreign countries, and Canada. 8% are Foreign; 72% White; 3% Hispanic; 2% two or more races; 13% African American; 1% Asian American; 1% race unknown. 73% are Protestant; 16% claim no religious affiliation. **Female To Male Ratio:** 1.3:1. The average age of freshmen is 18; all undergraduates, 20. 18% do not continue beyond their first year; 70% remain to graduate. **Housing:** 1151 students can be accommodated in college housing, which includes single-sex and coed dorms, on-campus apartments, off-campus apartments, special-interest houses, fraternity houses. Carol International House serves as housing for international students and students with an interest in studying abroad or experiencing international cultures. On-campus housing is guaranteed for all 4 years. 99% of students live on campus; of those, 75% remain on campus on weekends. All students may keep cars.

FACULTY/CLASSROOMS: 59% of faculty are male; 41% are female. All teach undergraduates and do research. No introductory courses are taught by graduate students. The average class size in an introductory lecture is 20; in a laboratory is 15; and in a regular course is 15.

PROGRAMS OF STUDY: PC confers B.A. and B.S. degrees. Doctoral degrees are also awarded. Bachelor's degrees are awarded in BIOLOGICAL SCIENCE (biochemistry and biology/biological science), BUSINESS (business administration and management and business economics), COMMUNICATIONS AND THE ARTS (art, art history and appreciation, creative writing, dramatic arts, English, French, modern language, music, and Spanish), COMPUTER AND PHYSICAL SCIENCE (chemistry, mathematics, medical physics, and physics), EDUCATION (early childhood education, elementary education, and middle school education), HEALTH PROFESSIONS (pharmacy), SOCIAL SCIENCE (history, international studies, philosophy and religion, political science/government, psychology, religion, religious education, and sociology). Arts and humanities, social sciences, and natural sciences are the strongest academically. Business administration, biology, and psychology have the largest enrollments.

ACTIVITIES: 38% of men belong to 6 national fraternities; 50% of women belong to 3 national sororities. There are 80 groups on campus, including art, bagpipe, band, cheerleading, choir, chorale, chorus, computers, dance, drama, environmental, ethnic, film, honors, international, jazz band, LGBT, literary magazine, newspaper, orchestra, pep band, photography, political, professional, religious, social, social service, student government, symphony, and yearbook. Popular campus events include Week of Welcome, First Weekend Stadium Dance, Scotoberfest, College-wide Thanksgiving Lunch, Annual Christmas Concert, MLK Day of Service, Greek Week, and Spring Fling. **Sports:** There are 7 intercollegiate sports for men and 8 for women, and 10 intramural sports for men and 10 for women. Facilities include a football stadium, basketball, tennis and volleyball, weight rooms, a stadium, baseball complex and softball complex, lacrosse field, and a golf course. There is also an outdoor recreation program and intramurals that includes basketball, billiards, dodgeball, flag, football, giant kickball, sand volleyball, soccer, co-ed softball, table tennis and ultimate Frisbee. **Graduates:** From July 1, 2015 to June 30, 2016, 226 bachelor's degrees were awarded. The most popular majors were business administration (23%), psychology (14%), and biology (11%). 80 companies recruited on campus in 2015-2016. In an average class, 62% graduate in 4 years or less, 68% graduate in 5 years or less, and 70% graduate in 6 years or less. Of the 2015 graduating class, 30% were enrolled in graduate school within 6 months of graduation, and 65% were employed.

SERVICES: Counseling and information services are available, as is tutoring in every subject, and a reader service for the blind. **Library/Resources:** The library contains 122,528 volumes, 1,146 microform items, 10,832 audio/video tapes/CDs/DVDs, and subscribes to 16,642 periodicals including electronic. Computerized library services include interlibrary loans, database searching, Internet access, and Wi-Fi capability. The special learning facilities includes an art gallery. **Physically Challenged Students:** 95% of the campus is accessible. Facilities include wheelchair ramps, elevators, special parking, specially equipped restrooms, lowered drinking fountains, and special housing. **Special:** Educational internships, study abroad and a Washington semester are available. Dual majors, work-study programs, B.A.-B.S. degrees, and a 3-2 engineering degree with Auburn University, Clemson University, Georgia Institute of Technology, University of South Carolina and Vanderbilt University are offered. There is a forestry environmental studies program with Duke University. Credit for military experience, auditing courses, and pass/fail options are also possible. There are 12 national honor societies, a freshman honors program, and 16 departmental honors programs. **Visiting:** There are regularly scheduled orientations for prospective students, Academics, student activity, financial aid information, tour, and lunch. There are guides for informal visits, visitors may sit in on classes, and stay overnight. To schedule a visit, contact Brian J. Fortman at (800) 960-7583. **Campus Safety and Security:** Measures include 24-hour foot and vehicle patrol, emergency notification system, and security escort services. There are shuttle buses, emergency telephones, lighted pathways/sidewalks, controlled access to dorms/residences, 24-hour key card dorm locks.

REQUIREMENTS: Applicants must be graduates of an accredited secondary school with 18 academic credits, including 4 years of English, 3 of math, and 2 or more each of foreign language, history, science, and social studies. The GED is accepted. For music scholarships, an audition is required. Depending on high school GPA, some students will be required to submit either SAT or ACT scores. The SAT and ACT scores above do not reflect the entire incoming freshman class, rather they include scores from all freshmen with a GPA below 3.25, and scores from freshmen with a GPA at or above 3.25 that did not apply as a test-optional student. AP and CLEP credits are accepted. Important factors in the admissions decision are advanced placement or honors courses, evidence of special talent, and leadership record. To graduate, students must complete a minimum of 122 semester hours with a minimum GPA of 2.0. Distribution requirements include 8 hours of natural science, 6 hours each of English, History, social science, and Religion, 4 to 6 hours of intercultural/internship experience, 3 hours each of Mathematics and Fine Arts, 2 to 3 hours, 1 hour of freshman experience and 1 to 3 hours of senior capstone courses (specific to the major), and a minimum of 3 hours (intermediate level) of a foreign language. **Procedure:** Freshmen are admitted to all sessions. Entrance exams should be taken Spring of the junior year or fall of senior year. There are early decision, early admissions, and deferred admissions plans. Early decision applications should be filed by November 1; regular applications, by February 1 for fall entry; and December 1 for spring entry. Notification of early decision is sent December 1; regular decision, March 15. 46 early decision candidates were accepted for the 2016-2017 class. Application fees are waived if application is completed online. **Transfer Students:** 30 transfer students enrolled in 2015-2016. Transfer students are admitted based on the academic record of all colleges or universities a student has attended, their high school record, and scores from the SAT or ACT. For additional information, see pages 11 & 12 of the 2016-17 Presbyterian College Catalog. 48 of 122 credits required for the bachelor's degree must be completed at PC. **International Students:** There are 88 international students enrolled. The school actively recruits these students. They must take the TOEFL with a minimum score of 550 on the paper-based TOEFL (PBT) or 80 on the Internet-based version (iBT). They must also take the SAT or ACT.

ADMISSIONS: 60% of the 2016-2017 applicants were accepted. The SAT scores for the 2016-2017 freshman class were: Critical Reading--21% below 500, 52% between 500 and 599, 21% between 600 and 699, and 6% between 700 and 800. Math-- 20% below 500, 48% between 500 and 599, 26% between 600 and 699, and 6% between 700 and 800. The ACT scores were % below 12, 3% between 12 and 17, 33% between 18 and 23, 46% between 24 and 29, and 18% above 30. 53% of the current freshmen were in the top fifth of their class; 81% were in the top two fifths. 8 freshmen graduated first in their class. **Admissions Contact:** Suzanne M. Petrusch, VP for Enrollment Management & Marketing. Email: *admissions@presby.edu* Web: *www.presby.edu*

FINANCIAL AID: In 2016-2017, 100% of all full-time freshmen and 99% of continuing full-time students received some form of financial aid. 76% of all full-time freshmen and 66% of continuing full-time students received need-based aid. The average freshman award was $33,838. Need-based scholarships or need-based grants averaged $5,219 ($12,908 maximum); need-based self-help aid (loans and jobs) averaged $2,321 ($5,057 maximum); non-need-based athletic scholarships averaged $16,530 ($27,886 maximum); other non-need-based awards and non-need-based scholarships averaged $11,929 ($29,318 maximum); and $940 from other forms of aid. 34% of undergraduate students work part-time. Average annual earnings from campus work are $1880. The average financial indebtedness of the 2016 graduate was $42,809. The FAFSA code is 003445. The priority date for freshman financial aid applications for fall entry is February 15. The filing deadline for fall entry is May 15.

SOUTH CAROLINA STATE UNIVERSITY *(The complete profile is made available exclusively on our website, www.barronspac.com)*

SOUTHERN WESLEYAN UNIVERSITY *(The complete profile is made available exclusively on our website, www.barronspac.com)*

THE CITADEL, THE MILITARY COLLEGE OF SOUTH CAROLINA D-4

www.citadel.edu

Charleston, SC 29409	(843) 953-5230 (800) 868-1842
Fax: (843) 953-7036	**Email:** admissions@citadel.edu
Full-time: 2353 men, 164 women	**Faculty:** IIA, av$
Part-time: 129 men, 89 women	**Ph.D.s:** 92%
Graduate: 370 men, 493 women	**Student/Faculty:** 14 to 1
Year: semesters, summer session	**Tuition:** $27,838 ($48,916)
Room & Board: $7501	**Freshman Class:** 2765 applied, 2116 accepted, 645 enrolled
SAT CR/M: 538/549 **ACT:** 23	**CEEB CODE:** 5108
Application Deadline: n/av	**COMPETITIVE**

The Citadel, The Military College of South Carolina, established in 1842 by the South Carolina legislature, is a liberal arts military college supported by the state and offers degrees in the humanities, business, math, science, engineering, and education. Tuition figures for students in the Corps of Cadets include charges for lab fees, athletic fees, most books, school supplies, uniforms, alterations, and laundry and dry cleaning. There are 5 undergraduate schools and 1 graduate school. In addition to regional accreditation, The Citadel has baccalaureate program accreditation with AACSB, ABET, NCATE, and ACS. The 300-acre campus is in a suburban area in Charleston, SC. Including any residence halls, there are 69 buildings.

STUDENT LIFE: 58% of undergraduates are from South Carolina. Others are from 43 states, and 12 foreign countries. 8% are African American; 79% White; 6% Hispanic; 2% Asian American; 1% American Indian/Alaska Native; 1% Foreign; 1% two or more races. **Male To Female Ratio:** 3.8:1. The average age of freshmen is 18; all undergraduates, 20. 15% do not continue beyond their first year; 85% remain to graduate. **Housing:** 2135 students can be accommodated in college housing, which includes coed dorms. All cadets live in barracks. On-campus housing is guaranteed for all 4 years. Upperclassmen may keep cars. Alcohol is not permitted.

FACULTY/CLASSROOMS: 65% of faculty are male; 35% are female. All teach undergraduates and do research. No introductory courses are taught by graduate students. The average class size in an introductory lecture is 25 and in a regular course is 20.

PROGRAMS OF STUDY: The Citadel confers B.A., B.S., B.S.B.A., B.S.C.E. and B.S.E.E. degrees. Master's degrees are also awarded. Bachelor's degrees are awarded in BIOLOGICAL SCIENCE (biology/biological science), BUSINESS (business administration and management), COMMUNICATIONS AND THE ARTS (English, French, German, and Spanish), COMPUTER AND PHYSICAL SCIENCE (chemistry, computer science, mathematics, and physics), EDUCATION (health education, physical education, and secondary education), ENGINEERING AND ENVIRONMENTAL DESIGN (civil engineering and electrical/electronics engineering), SOCIAL SCIENCE (criminal justice, history, political science/government, and psychology). Engineering is the strongest academically. Business administration has the largest enrollment.

ACTIVITIES: There are no fraternities or sororities. There are 100 groups on campus, including bagpipe, band, cheerleading, choir, chorale, debate, drill team, ethnic, honors, literary magazine, marching band, newspaper, pep band, political, professional, religious, student government, and yearbook. Popular campus events include Parents Weekend, Corps Day, and parades most Friday afternoons during fall and spring semesters. **Sports:** There are 8 intercollegiate sports for men and 6 for women, and 24 intramural sports for men and 24 for women. Facilities include a stadium, field house, golf driving range, baseball batting tunnel, weight and wrestling rooms, tennis courts, an all-weather track, and playing fields. The boating center is on campus and The Citadel Beach House is within a half-hour drive of the college. **Graduates:** From July 1, 2015 to June 30, 2016, 523 bachelor's degrees were awarded. The most popular majors were business/marketing (25%), engineering (17%), and criminal justice (14%). 145 companies recruited on campus in 2015-2016. In an average class, 60% graduate in 4 years or less, 68% graduate in 5 years or less, and 66% graduate in 6 years or less. Of the 2015 graduating class, 90% were employed within 6 months of graduation.

SERVICES: Counseling and information services are available, as is tutoring in every subject. **Library/Resources:** The library contains 193,992 volumes, 1.2 million microform items, 5,538 audio/video tapes/CDs/DVDs, and subscribes to 1,260 periodicals including electronic. Computerized library services include interlibrary loans, database searching, Internet access, and Wi-Fi capability. **Physically Challenged Students:** 80% of the campus is accessible. Facilities include wheelchair ramps, elevators, special parking, and specially equipped restrooms. **Special:** Work-study programs, internships, dual majors, independent study, and study abroad are available. Qualified students may enroll in a separate honors program. There is a teacher certification program. There are 8 national honor societies, Phi Beta Kappa, a freshman honors program, and 1 departmental honors program. **Visiting:** There are regularly scheduled orientations for prospective students, including an interview with an admissions counselor and a campus tour guided by a cadet. There are guides for informal visits, visitors may sit in on classes, and stay overnight. To schedule a visit, contact the Admissions Office. **Campus Safety and Security:** Measures include 24-hour foot and vehicle patrol, emergency notification system, security escort services, emergency telephones, lighted pathways/sidewalks, and controlled access to dorms/residences.

REQUIREMENTS: The SAT or ACT is required. High school diploma is required and GED is accepted. Applicants must be between 17 and 22, unmarried, and must meet certain physical requirements. High school preparation should include 4 units in English; 4 in math, 3 in lab science: biology, chemistry, or physics, 2 each in foreign language and social science, 1 academic elective, 1 in visual/perfoming arts, 1 in phys ed or ROTC, and 1 in American history. AP and CLEP credits are accepted. Important factors in the admissions decision are advanced placement or honors courses, extracurricular activities record, and leadership record. To graduate, students must complete 121 to 139 credit hours, depending on the major, with an overall GPA of 2.0 (2.5 for education and health, exercise, and sport science majors). The required core curriculum for all majors includes study in 5 areas: English, history, math, science, social sciences, computer literacy, and foreign languages. Specific course requirements include 8 semesters of ROTC, 4 of English and science, 2 of math and history, and 1 of social science. In addition, cadets must satisfy disciplinary requirements and observe the honor system. **Procedure:** Freshmen are admitted in the fall. Entrance exams should be taken by February of the senior year. There is a rolling admissions plan. Application deadlines are open. The fall 2016 application fee was $40. Notification is sent on a rolling basis. Applications are accepted online. **Transfer Students:** 117 transfer students enrolled in 2015-2016. Applicants must meet freshmen entrance requirements and submit official transcripts from high school and all previous colleges attended. Transfer students must have completed a minimum of 2 semesters as full-time students (minimum 12 hours each semester) and maintained a GPA of 2.0. A full year of course work, including half the required hours in the major, must be completed at The Citadel. A statement of good standing from prior institutions and an interview are required. **International Students:** There are 26 international students enrolled. They must take the TOEFL with a minimum score of 550 on the paper-based TOEFL (PBT) or 80 on the Internet-based version (iBT).

ADMISSIONS: 77% of the 2016-2017 applicants were accepted. The SAT scores for the 2016-2017 freshman class were: Critical Reading-- 36% below 500, 46% between 500 and 599, 15% between 600 and 699, and 3% between 700 and 800. Math-- 23% below 500, 51% between 500 and 599, 23% between 600 and 699, and 3% between 700 and 800. The ACT scores were 22% below 12, 35% between 12 and 17, 27% between 18 and 23, 7% between 24 and 29, and 9% above 30. 30% of the current freshmen were in the top fifth of their class; 59% were in the top two fifths. **Admissions Contact:** Lt. Col. John Powell, Director of Admissions. Email: *admissions@citadel.edu* Web: *www.citadel.edu*

FINANCIAL AID: In 2016-2017, 84% of all full-time freshmen and 78% of continuing full-time students received some form of financial aid. 61% of all full-time freshmen and 46% of continuing full-time students received need-based aid. 2% of undergraduate students work part-time. Average annual earnings from campus work are $1325. The average financial indebtedness of the 2016 graduate was $33,998. The FAFSA code is 003423. The priority date for freshman financial aid applications for fall entry is March 1.

UNIVERSITY OF SOUTH CAROLINA AIKEN — C-3

www.usca.edu

Aiken, SC 29801	**(803) 641-3366**
	(888) WOW-USCA
Fax: (803) 641-3727	**Email: admit@usca.edu**
Full-time: 914 men, 1580 women	**Faculty:** 149
Part-time: 301 men, 444 women	**Ph.D.s:** 75%
Graduate: 42 men, 140 women	**Student/Faculty:** 17 to 1
Year: semesters, summer session	**Tuition:** $9602 ($18,926)
Room & Board: $7110	**Freshman Class:** 2103 applied, 1448 accepted, 635 enrolled
SAT CR/M/W: required **ACT:** 21	**CEEB CODE:** 5840
Application Deadline: August 1	**COMPETITIVE**

The University of South Carolina Aiken, founded in 1961 is a comprehensive liberal arts institution committed to active learning through teaching, faculty and student scholarship, research, creative activities and service. The university offers degrees in the arts and sciences and in the professional disciplines of business, education, and nursing. There are 5 undergraduate schools and 2 graduate schools. In addition to regional accreditation, USCA has baccalaureate program accreditation with AACSB, ABET, NASM, NCATE, and CCNE. The 453-acre campus is in a suburban area 14 miles east of Augusta, Georgia. Including any residence halls, there are 25 buildings.

STUDENT LIFE: 86% of undergraduates are from South Carolina. Others are from 29 states, and 24 foreign countries. 91% are from public schools. 61% are White; 4% Hispanic; 3% Foreign; 3% two or more races; 25% African American; 2% race unknown; 1% Asian American. **Female To Male Ratio:** 1.7:1. The average age of freshmen is 18; all undergraduates, 22. 34% do not continue beyond their first year; 43% remain to graduate. **Housing:** 950 students can be accommodated in college housing, which includes coed dorms and on-campus apartments. On-campus housing on a first-come, first-served basis, and is available on a lottery system for upperclassmen. 71% of students commute. All students may keep cars.

FACULTY/CLASSROOMS: 48% of faculty are male; 52% are female. All teach undergraduates. No introductory courses are taught by graduate students. The average class size in an introductory lecture is 17 and in a laboratory is 15.

PROGRAMS OF STUDY: USCA confers B.A., B.S., B.S.(in Business Administration), B.A.Ed, B.S.Ed, B.A.Spec.Ed, B.A.I.S, B.S.N. and B.S.I.S. degrees. Master's degrees are also awarded. Bachelor's degrees are awarded in BIOLOGICAL SCIENCE (biology/biological science), BUSINESS (business administration and management), COMMUNICATIONS AND THE ARTS (communications, English, and fine arts), COMPUTER AND PHYSICAL SCIENCE (applied mathematics, chemistry, and computer mathematics), EDUCATION (early childhood education, elementary education, middle school education, music education, secondary education, and special education), HEALTH PROFESSIONS (exercise science and nursing), SOCIAL SCIENCE (history, interdisciplinary studies, political science/government, psychology, and sociology). Special education, early childhood education, and nursing are the strongest academically. Business, exercise & sports science, and nursing have the largest enrollments.

ACTIVITIES: There are 78 groups on campus, including veterans, band, cheerleading, choir, chorus, computers, dance, drama, ethnic, honors, international, jazz band, LGBT, literary magazine, musical theater, newspaper, nontraditional students, pep band, photography, political, professional, religious, social, social service, and student government. Popular campus events include Waterfest, Homecoming, Greek Life Recruitment Week, Dance Marathon, and Relay for Life. **Sports:** There are 5 intercollegiate sports for men and 6 for women, and 6 intramural sports for men and 6 for women. Facilities include an activities center, baseball stadium, a soccer/intramural/softball field, tennis courts, and a wellness/exercise center. **Graduates:** From July 1, 2015 to June 30, 2016, 516 bachelor's degrees were awarded. The most popular majors were business (23%), nursing (13%), and education (12%). 296 companies recruited on campus in 2015-2016. In an average class, 24% graduate in 4 years or less, 35% graduate in 5 years or less, and 43% graduate in 6 years or less.

SERVICES: Counseling and information services are available, as is tutoring in most subjects, and a reader service for the blind. Individual subject tutoring is also available upon request. **Library/Resources:** The library contains 174,413 volumes, 79,876 microform items, and 309,706 audio/video tapes/CDs/DVDs, and subscribes to 30,188 periodicals including electronic. Computerized library services include interlibrary loans, database searching, Internet access, and Wi-Fi capability. Special learning facilities include an art gallery, planetarium, a science education center, and a language lab. **Physically Challenged Students:** All of the campus is accessible. Facilities include wheelchair ramps, elevators, special parking, specially equipped restrooms, lowered drinking fountains, and lowered telephones. **Special:** Cross-registration is permitted with other schools in the University of South Carolina system. Co-op programs,internships, study abroad, student-designed majors, and work-study programs are offered. B.A.-B.S. degrees in Interdisciplinary Studies, nondegree study, and pass/fail options are possible. There are 13 national honor societies, a freshman honors program, and 10 departmental honors programs. **Visiting:** There are regularly scheduled orientations for prospective students, including regularly scheduled 3-day orientations for prospective students. There are guides for informal visits and visitors may sit in on classes. To schedule a visit, contact the Admissions Office at admit@usca.edu. **Campus Safety and Security:** Measures include 24-hour foot and vehicle patrol, emergency notification system, self-defense education, security escort services, emergency telephones, lighted pathways/sidewalks, and controlled access to dorms/residences.

REQUIREMENTS: The SAT is required. The ACT and ACT Writing Test are recommended. Admission is based on a combination of an applicant's scores on college entrance exams and high school GPA. Applicants are required to submit 21 academic credits, including 4 years of high school English, 3 units of math, 3 units of social studies, 2 units of foreign language, 3 units of a lab science, 1 of US history, and 1 year of phys ed or ROTC, and 4 electives from 3 different areas such as computer science, English, fine arts, foreign language, humanities, certain lab sciences, a math above algebra II, and social science. It is strongly suggested that 1 be in computer science programming. AP and CLEP credits are accepted. Important factors in the admissions decision are advanced placement or honors courses, recommendations by school officials, and leadership record. Students must complete a minimum of 120 credit hours, with at least a 2.0 GPA. USC Aiken has a strong liberal arts emphasis. General education requirements include courses in English, math, applied speech, natural science, social and behavioral sciences, humanities, non-western studies course, and history. In addition, students must complete a critical inquiry course, a prescribed number of writing intensive courses and inter-curricular enrichment events. **Procedure:** Freshmen are admitted to all sessions. Entrance exams should be taken by the fall of the senior year. There are early admissions, deferred admissions, and rolling admissions plans. Applications should be filed by August 1 for fall entry; December 1 for spring entry. The fall 2016 application fee was $45. Notification is sent on a rolling basis. Applications are accepted on-line. **Transfer Students:** The college GPA is considered. A high school transcript is required of applicants with fewer than 30 semester hours. 30 of 120 credits required for the bachelor's degree must be completed at USCA. **International Students:** There are 96 international students enrolled. They must take the TOEFL with a minimum score of 550 on the paper-based TOEFL (PBT) or 80 on the Internet-based version (iBT). They must also take the SAT or ACT.

ADMISSIONS: 69% of the 2016-2017 applicants were accepted. The SAT scores for the 2016-2017 freshman class were: Critical Reading-- 57% below 500, 33% between 500 and 599, and 10% between 600 and 699. Math-- 55% below 500, 34% between 500 and 599, and 11% between 600 and 699. Writing-- 68% below 500, 27% between 500 and 599, and 5% between 600 and 699. The ACT scores were 38% below 12, 27% between 12 and 17, 20% between 18 and 23, 10% between 24 and 29, and 5% above 30. 33% of the current freshmen were in the top fifth of their class; 67% were in the top two fifths. 9 freshmen graduated first in their class. **Admissions Contact:** Jamie Williams, Director of Admissions. Email: *admit@usca.edu* Web: *www.usca.edu*

FINANCIAL AID: The FAFSA code is 003449. The priority date for freshman financial aid applications for fall entry is February 15. The filing deadline for fall entry is March 15.

UNIVERSITY OF SOUTH CAROLINA AT COLUMBIA — C-3

www.sc.edu

Columbia, SC 29208	**(803) 777-7700** **(800) 868-5872**
Fax: (803) 777-0101	**Email: admissions-ugrad@sc.edu**
Full-time: 9849 men, 11797 women	**Faculty:** 854
Part-time: 898 men, 819 women	**Ph.D.s:** 84%
Graduate: 3268 men, 4657 women	**Student/Faculty:** 25 to 1
Year: semesters, summer session	**Tuition:** $10,816 ($28,528)
Room & Board: $8909	**Freshman Class:** 23429 applied, 14199 accepted, 4625 enrolled
SAT CR/M: 590/610 **ACT:** 27	**CEEB CODE:** 5818
Application Deadline: December 1	**VERY COMPETITIVE+**

The University of South Carolina at Columbia, founded in 1801, is a publicly assisted institution serving the entire state of South Carolina. In addition to the main campus at Columbia, there are 3 senior campuses at Aiken, Beaufort, and Upstate, and 4 regional campuses at Lancaster, Salkehatchie, Sumter, and Union. There are 11 undergraduate schools and 12 graduate schools. In addition to regional accreditation, USC has baccalaureate program accreditation with AACSB, ABET, ACEJMC, ACPE, CSAB, NASM, NCATE, and NLN. The 444-acre campus is in an urban area in the downtown area of Columbia. Including any residence halls, there are 181 buildings.

STUDENT LIFE: 65% of undergraduates are from South Carolina. Others are from 50 states, 115 foreign countries, and Canada. 77% are White; 4% Hispanic; 3% Asian American; 3% two or more races; 2% Foreign; 11% African American. **Female To Male Ratio:** 1.2:1. The average age of freshmen is 18; all undergraduates, 21. 13% do not continue beyond their first year; 72% remain to graduate. **Housing:** 6838 students can be accommodated in college housing, which includes single-sex and coed dorms, on-campus apartments, married student housing, honors houses, language houses, special-interest houses, fraternity houses, sorority houses, wellness, residential college, and environmentally housing. On-campus housing is guaranteed for the freshman year only and is available on a lottery system for upperclassmen. 64% of students commute. All students may keep cars.

FACULTY/CLASSROOMS: 59% of faculty are male; 41% are female. All teach undergraduates all do research, and 61% do both. No introductory courses are taught by graduate students. The average class size in an introductory lecture is 30; in a laboratory is 23; and in a regular course is 29.

PROGRAMS OF STUDY: USC confers B.A., B.A.I.S., B.A.I.S., B.A.J.M.C., B.F.A., B.M., B.S., B.S.B.A., B.S.C., B.S.C.S., B.S.E., B.S.I.S., B.S.N., B.S.P.E., B.S.W. and BarSc. degrees. Associate, master's, and doctoral degrees are also awarded. Bachelor's degrees are awarded in BIOLOGICAL SCIENCE (biology/biological science and marine science), BUSINESS (accounting, banking and finance, business administration and management, business economics, hotel/motel and restaurant management, insurance, management science, marketing/retailing/merchandising, office supervision and management, real estate, retailing, and sports management), COMMUNICATIONS AND THE ARTS (advertising, art history and appreciation, broadcasting, classics, communications, comparative literature, dance, dramatic arts, English, fine arts, French, German, journalism, media arts, music, public relations, Russian, Spanish, speech/debate/rhetoric, and studio art), COMPUTER AND PHYSICAL SCIENCE (chemistry, computer science, geology, geophysics and seismology, mathematics, physics, and statistics), EDUCATION (art education, early childhood education, elementary education, middle school education, music education, and physical education), ENGINEERING AND ENVIRONMENTAL DESIGN (biomedical engineering, chemical engineering, civil engineering, computer engineering, electrical/electronics engineering, environmental science, and mechanical engineering), HEALTH PROFESSIONS (exercise science, nursing, and public health), SOCIAL SCIENCE (African American studies, anthropology, criminal justice, economics, European studies, experimental psychology, geography, history, interdisciplinary studies, Latin American studies, philosophy, political science/government, psychology, religion, social work, sociology, and women's studies). Engineering, business, and nursing are the strongest academically. Biology, nursing, and experimental psychology have the largest enrollments.

ACTIVITIES: 13% of men belong to 22 national fraternities; 28% of women belong to 16 national sororities. There are 387 groups on campus, including art, band, cheerleading, chess, choir, chorale, chorus, computers, dance, debate, drama, drill team, ethnic, film, forensics, honors, international, jazz band, LGBT, literary magazine, marching band, musical theater, newspaper, opera, orchestra, pep band, photography, political, professional, radio and TV, religious, social, social service, student government, symphony, and yearbook. Popular campus events include First-Year Reading Experience, Civil Rights Tour, Parents Weekend, Alternative Spring and Fall Break Trips, Homecoming Week, and Carolina Cares. **Sports:** There are 9 intercollegiate sports for men and 11 for women, and 29 intramural sports for men and 29 for women. Facilities include football and soccer stadiums, a basketball coliseum, a field house, a volleyball and basketball practice facility, baseball, softball, and practice fields, and an all-weather track. There is also a recreation center with badminton, basketball, handball/racquetball, an aquatics center, climbing wall, and a weight room. **Graduates:** From July 1, 2015 to June 30, 2016, 7162 bachelor's degrees were awarded. The most popular majors were experimental psychology (6%), integrated IT (6%), and biology (5%). 900 companies recruited on campus in 2015-2016. In an average class, 56% graduate in 4 years or less, 70% graduate in 5 years or less, and 72% graduate in 6 years or less. Of the 2015 graduating class, 23% were enrolled in graduate school within 6 months of graduation.

SERVICES: Counseling and information services are available, as is tutoring in every subject, and a reader service for the blind. **Library/Resources:** The 7 libraries contain 4.5 million volumes, and 5.5 million microform items. Computerized library services include interlibrary loans, database searching, Internet access, and Wi-Fi capability. Special learning facilities include an art gallery, natural history museum, planetarium, radio station, and a TV station. **Physically Challenged Students:** 85% of the campus is accessible. Facilities include wheelchair ramps, elevators, special parking, specially equipped restrooms, special class scheduling, lowered drinking fountains, special housing. Listening devices, sign language interpreting, and adapted transportation and computers. **Special:** USC transmits live interactive televised instruction to more than 20 locations in the state. Cross-registration is offered with the National Technological University in Engineering and through the National Student Exchange. Internships in many fields, study abroad in many countries through the Byrnes International Center, co-op programs, and work-study programs are available. Double majors through the colleges of humanities and social sciences and science and math, student-designed majors, an interdisciplinary studies degree, and a 3-2 engineering degree with the College of Charleston are offered. Credit for military experience, nondegree study, and pass/fail options also are possible.

There are 28 national honor societies, Phi Beta Kappa, and a freshman honors program. **Visiting:** There are regularly scheduled orientations for prospective students, students take placement tests, are advised and register for classes. There are guides for informal visits. To schedule a visit, contact the USC Visitor's Center. **Campus Safety and Security:** Measures include 24-hour foot and vehicle patrol, emergency notification system, self-defense education, and security escort services. There are shuttle buses, emergency telephones, lighted pathways/sidewalks, controlled access to dorms/residences, and all police officers have state wide police authority.

REQUIREMENTS: Admission as a freshman into the University is primarily based upon a combination of grades earned in specific high-school courses and official SAT or ACT scores. Additional factors may be taken into consideration, such as extraordinary personal circumstances, special talents, outstanding extracurricular activities, and evidence of leadership. A GPA of 2.0 is required. AP and CLEP credits are accepted. All students must maintain a GPA of 2.0 in 120 semester hours including 24 in their major. Distribution requirements include 6 hours in English, 6 in numerical/analytical reasoning, 12 in liberal arts, 7 in natural sciences, and foreign language demonstrated proficiency. **Procedure:** Freshmen are admitted to all sessions. Entrance exams should be taken during spring of the junior year and fall of the senior year, if necessary. There is a rolling admissions plan. Applications should be filed by December 1 for fall entry; November 1 for spring entry; and May 1 for summer entry, along with a $50 fee. Applications are accepted online. **Transfer Students:** 1961 transfer students enrolled in 2015-2016. Cumulative GPA of 2.25 from all regionally accredited colleges (remedial courses are not included in the GPA computation). Must meet freshman requirements if the student has attempted fewer than 30 semester hours. Transfer requirements are higher for certain majors consult http:/www.sc.edu/admissions/transrequire.php for current information. 30 of 120 credits required for the bachelor's degree must be completed at USC. **International Students:** There are 390 international students enrolled. The school actively recruits these students. They must take the TOEFL with a minimum score of 550 on the paper-based TOEFL (PBT) or 77 on the Internet-based version (iBT). The SAT and ACT are recommended.

ADMISSIONS: 61% of the 2016-2017 applicants were accepted. The SAT scores for the 2016-2017 freshman class were: Critical Reading-- 10% below 500, 45% between 500 and 599, 36% between 600 and 699, and 10% between 700 and 800. Math-- 5% below 500, 37% between 500 and 599, 48% between 600 and 699, and 11% between 700 and 800. The ACT scores were 3% below 12, 17% between 12 and 17, 29% between 18 and 23, 22% between 24 and 29, and 29% above 30. 57% of the current freshmen were in the top fifth of their class; 88% were in the top two fifths. There were 47 National Merit finalists. 66 freshmen graduated first in their class. **Admissions Contact:** R. Scott Verzyl, Associate Vice President for Enrollment. Email: *admissions-ugrad@sc.edu* Web: *www.sc.edu*

FINANCIAL AID: In 2016-2017, 96% of all full-time freshmen and 87% of continuing full-time students received some form of financial aid. 47% of all full-time freshmen and 46% of continuing full-time students received need-based aid. The average freshman award was $13,526. Need-based scholarships or need-based grants averaged $7,116 ($27,912 maximum); need-based self-help aid (loans and jobs) averaged $2,358 ($15,500 maximum); non-need-based athletic scholarships averaged $11,747; and other non-need-based awards and non-need-based scholarships averaged $5,304. 15% of undergraduate students work part-time. Average annual earnings from campus work are $2396. USC is a member of CSS. The deadline for filing freshman financial aid applications for fall entry is April 15.

UNIVERSITY OF SOUTH CAROLINA UPSTATE *(The complete profile is made available exclusively on our website, www.barronspac.com)*

VOORHEES COLLEGE — C-3

www.voorhees.edu

Denmark, SC 29042 — **(803) 780-1023**

Fax: (803) 780-1430 — **Email:** admissions@voorhees.edu

Full-time: 185 men, 222 women	**Faculty:** 30
Part-time: 4 men, 4 women	**Ph.D.s:** 43%
Graduate: n/av	**Student/Faculty:** 7 to 1
Year: semesters, summer session	**Tuition:** $12,630
Room & Board: $7346	**Freshman Class:** n/av
SAT or ACT: recommended	**CEEB CODE:** 5863
Application Deadline: n/av	**COMPETITIVE**

Voorhees College, founded in 1897, is a historically black liberal arts college affiliated with the Protestant Episcopal Church. There is 1 undergraduate school. In addition to regional accreditation, Voorhees has baccalaureate program accreditation with ACBSP. The 342-acre campus is in a small town 50 miles south of Columbia. Including any residence halls, there are 26 buildings.

STUDENT LIFE: 70% of undergraduates are from South Carolina. Others are from 17 states, and 1 foreign country. 80% are from public schools. 93% are African American; 2% White; 2% race unknown; 1% Hispanic; 1% Foreign. 90% are Protestant. **Female To Male Ratio:** 1.2:1. The average age of freshmen is 18; all undergraduates, 22. 40% remain to graduate. **Housing:** 537 students can be accommodated in college housing, which includes single-sex and coed dorms. On-campus housing is guaranteed for all 4 years. 72% of students live on campus; of those, 50% remain on campus on weekends. All students may keep cars. Alcohol is not permitted.

FACULTY/CLASSROOMS: 58% of faculty are male; 42% are female. All teach undergraduates. No introductory courses are taught by graduate students. The average class size in an introductory lecture is 30; in a laboratory is 20; and in a regular course is 25.

PROGRAMS OF STUDY: Voorhees confers B.A. and B.S. degrees. Bachelor's degrees are awarded in BIOLOGICAL SCIENCE (biology/biological science), BUSINESS (accounting, business administration and management, organizational leadership and management, and recreation and leisure services), COMMUNICATIONS AND THE ARTS (communications and English), COMPUTER AND PHYSICAL SCIENCE (computer science and mathematics), HEALTH PROFESSIONS (health), SOCIAL SCIENCE (criminal justice and sociology). Biology, and business administration are the strongest academically. Biology, business administration and sports management have the largest enrollments.

ACTIVITIES: 20% of men belong to 4 national fraternities; 20% of women belong to 4 national sororities. There are 20 groups on campus, including cheerleading, choir, chorus, computers, honors, newspaper, pep band, political, professional, radio and TV, religious, social, student government, and yearbook. Popular campus events include Career Awareness Week, Black History Month, Religious Emphasis Week, National Women's History Month, Business Week, National Library Week, Founders Day Week. **Sports:** There are 4 intercollegiate sports for men and 4 for women, and 4 intramural sports for men and 4 for women. Facilities include a gym, swimming pool, tennis and basketball courts, baseball and softball fields, track field, a weight room, a dance studio, and a student center. **Graduates:** From July 1, 2015 to June 30, 2016, 70 bachelor's degrees were awarded. The most popular majors were criminal justice (19%), sports management (14%), biology, and child development and health and recreation (10%). In an average class, 44% graduate in 4 years or less, 46% graduate in 5 years or less, and 10% graduate in 6 years or less.

SERVICES: Counseling and information services are available, as is tutoring in most subjects, and remedial math, reading, and writing. **Library/Resources:** The library contains 309,479 volumes, 26,110 microform items, 298 audio/video tapes/CDs/DVDs, and subscribes to 14,522 periodicals including electronic. Computerized library services include interlibrary loans, database searching, Internet access, and Wi-Fi capability. Special learning facilities include a radio station, an academic success center and a writing center. **Physically Challenged Students:** 90% of the campus is accessible. Facilities include wheelchair ramps, elevators, special parking, specially equipped restrooms, and lowered drinking fountains. **Special:** Voorhees offers cooperative education, internships in some programs, work-study, an evening/saturday program, off-campus summer study, dual majors, credit by exam, and a degree completion program. Cross-registration with Denmark Technical College and interdisciplinary majors, such as health and recreation, are possible. There are 3 national honor societies and 1 departmental honors program. **Visiting:** There are regularly scheduled orientations for prospective students, consisting of senior visitation days held January through April. There are guides for informal visits, visitors may sit in on classes, and stay overnight. To schedule a visit, contact Adrian West. **Campus Safety and Security:** Measures include 24-hour foot and vehicle patrol, emergency notification system, and lighted pathways/sidewalks.

REQUIREMENTS: The SAT or ACT is recommended, with a satisfactory minimum score of 600 on the SAT or 16 on the ACT. Applicants must be high school graduates or hold a GED. Students should have earned 24 academic credits in high school, including 4 units of English, 4 units of math, 3 units of science, 1 unit of foreign language (optional), and 1 each of history, social studies, economics/government, 1 unit of physical education, 1 unit of computer science/keyboarding and 7 electives. A campus visit are advised. AP and CLEP credits are accepted. Important factors in the admissions decision are advanced placement or honors courses, recommendations by school officials, and recommendations by alumni. To graduate, students must earn at least 122 credit hours, with at least 30 in the major, and have a minimum GPA of 2.0. The 50-hour general education requirement includes 12 hours of English/speech, 5 hours of humanities, 3 hours of foreign language, 1 hour of freshmen orientation, 2 hours of physical fitness, 12 hours of economics and history and 15 hours of mathematics, science and technology. A number of free electives and a senior seminar are also required. An English proficiency exam and an exit exam must be passed. **Procedure:** Freshmen are admitted to all sessions. Entrance exams should be taken in the senior year. There are deferred admissions and rolling admissions plans. Applications should be filed by December 16 for spring entry, along with a $25 fee. Notification of early decision is sent August 16; regular decision, December 16. **Transfer Students:** 20 transfer students enrolled in 2015-2016. Transfer students must submit complete records, including a confidential report from each college attended. The confidential report form is provided by the Office of Admission and Recruitment. Students with fewer than 30 semester hours must submit their high school record with rank in class and GPA. The SAT is recommended; a satisfactory composite score is expected. An interview is advised. **International Students:** There are 3 international students enrolled. They must take the TOEFL, as well as the SAT or ACT.

Admissions Contact: Diondra Smalls, Director of Admissions and Recruitment. Email: *admissions@voorhees.edu* Web: *www.voorhees.edu*

FINANCIAL AID: The average freshman award was $14,315. Need-based self-help aid (loans and jobs) averaged $5,500. Voorhees is a member of CSS. The college's own financial statement, and SAR are required. The FAFSA code is 003455. The priority date for freshman financial aid applications for fall entry is April 16.

WINTHROP UNIVERSITY — C-1

www.winthrop.edu

Rock Hill, SC 29733	(803) 323-2191 (800) 946-8476
Fax: (803) 323-2137	**Email:** admissions@winthrop.edu
Full-time: 1413 men, 3125 women	**Faculty:** 280; IIA, -$
Part-time: 179 men, 367 women	**Ph.D.s:** 76%
Graduate: 251 men, 767 women	**Student/Faculty:** 14 to 1
Year: semesters, summer session	**Tuition:** $14,510 ($28,090)
Room & Board: $8572	**Freshman Class:** 4940 applied, 3384 accepted, 1072 enrolled
SAT CR/M: 521/509 **ACT:** 23	**CEEB CODE:** 5910
Application Deadline: May 1	**COMPETITIVE**

Winthrop University, nationally recognized for quality and value is a public, comprehensive institution, blending liberal arts, professional programs, global awareness and civic engagement. Students who attend Winthrop develop the integrity that makes them stand out as leaders in their communities and in their chosen professions. There are 4 undergraduate schools and 4 graduate schools. In addition to regional accreditation, Winthrop has baccalaureate program accreditation with AACSB, ABET, ACEJMC, CSAB, CSWE, NASAD, NASM, NCATE, and CIDA. The 445-acre campus is in a small town 23 miles south of Charlotte, NC. Including any residence halls, there are 75 buildings.

STUDENT LIFE: 91% of undergraduates are from South Carolina. Others are from 40 states, 36 foreign countries, and Canada. 58% are White; 5% Hispanic; 30% African American; 3% two or more races; 2% Foreign; 1% Asian American. **Female To Male Ratio:** 2.3:1. The average age of freshmen is 18; all undergraduates, 21. 27% do not continue beyond their first year; 74% remain to graduate. **Housing:** 2513 students can be accommodated in college housing, which includes single-sex and coed dorms and on-campus apartments. In addition, there are honors houses, special-interest houses, fraternity houses, sorority houses, and independent housing. On-campus housing is available on a first-come and first-served basis. 53% of students live on campus; of those, 50% remain on campus on weekends. All students may keep cars.

FACULTY/CLASSROOMS: 38% of faculty are male; 62% are female. All teach undergraduates. No introductory courses are taught by graduate students. The average class size in an introductory lecture is 30 and in a laboratory is 15.

PROGRAMS OF STUDY: Winthrop confers B.A., B.S., B.F.A., B.M., B.M.E. and B.S.W. degrees. Master's degrees are also awarded. Bachelor's degrees are awarded in AGRICULTURE (environmental studies), BIOLOGICAL SCIENCE (biology/biological science and nutrition), BUSINESS (business administration and management, electronic business, and sports management), COMMUNICATIONS AND THE ARTS (art, art history and appreciation, communications, dance, English, English literature, fine arts, French, German, modern language, music, music performance, public relations, Spanish, technical and business writing, and theatre arts), COMPUTER AND PHYSICAL SCIENCE (chemistry, computer science, and mathematics), EDUCATION (athletic training, early childhood education, elementary education, middle school education, music education, physical education, secondary education, special education, and sports and wellness studies), ENGINEERING AND ENVIRONMENTAL DESIGN (environmental science and interior design), HEALTH PROFESSIONS (exercise science and medical laboratory technology), SOCIAL SCIENCE (economics, history, philosophy, philosophy and religion, political science/government, psychology, religion, social work, sociology, and Spanish studies). Business administration, biology, psychology, and fine arts have the largest enrollments.

ACTIVITIES: 9% of women belong to 9 national sororities. There are 160 groups on campus, including art, band, cheerleading, chess, choir, chorale, chorus, computers, dance, drama, environmental, ethnic, honors, international, jazz band, LGBT, literary magazine, musical theater, newspaper, opera, pep band, political, professional, radio and TV, religious, social, social service, and student government. Popular campus events include Welcome Week, Convocation and Picnic, Basketball Game Tailgaiting, Homecoming Talent Show, and Movies at DiGiorgio Campus Center. **Sports:** There are 7 intercollegiate sports for men and 9 for women, and 16 intramural sports for men and 16 for women. Facilities include athletics and recreational fields, ropes course, a golf course, tennis complex, a track & field stadium, soccer field, climbing wall, raquetball courts, a pool, basketball courts, weight room, cardio room, and aerobic/activity rooms. **Graduates:** From July 1, 2015 to June 30, 2016, 968 bachelor's degrees were awarded. The most popular majors were business administration (21%), psychology (10%), and biology (7%). 149 companies recruited on campus in 2015-2016. In an average class, 33% graduate in 4 years or less, 18% graduate in 5 years or less, and 53% graduate in 6 years or less. Of the 2015 graduating class, 25% were enrolled in graduate school within 6 months of graduation, and 46% were employed.

SERVICES: Counseling and information services are available, as is tutoring in some subjects, such as math and writing, as well as the subjects tutoring program within residence halls. There is also a reader service for the blind. Academic Success Center focuses on helping students achieve academic excellence and earn their college degree. This program provides tutoring opportunities and tools so students can excel in their classes. **Library/Resources:** The library contains 454,562 volumes, 1.2 million microform items, 15,277 audio/video tapes/CDs/DVDs, and subscribes to 40,755 periodicals including electronic. Computerized library services include interlibrary loans, database searching, Internet access, and Wi-Fi capability. Special learning facilities include an art gallery, radio station, TV station, an audio recording studio, an early childhood lab school, the MIDI lab, the Instructional Technology Center, Johnson Theatre, Mathematics Tutorial Center, the Writing Center, Academic Success Center and the Conservatory of Music. **Physically Challenged Students:** 95% of the campus is accessible. Facilities include wheelchair ramps, elevators, special parking, specially equipped restrooms, special class scheduling, lowered drinking fountains, lowered telephones, and special housing. **Special:** Cross-registration is permitted with the Charlotte Area Educational Consortium. Internships in Business, Education, Visual and Performing Arts and Arts and Sciences. Study abroad in 20 countries and on-campus work-study programs are offered. Interdisciplinary majors such as science communication, nondegree study, and pass/fail options are possible. There are 15 national honor societies, Phi Beta Kappa, a freshman honors program, and 24 departmental honors programs. **Visiting:** There are regularly scheduled orientations for prospective students. There are guides for informal visits, visitors may sit in on classes, and stay overnight. To schedule a visit, contact the Admissions Office at (803) 323-2191. **Campus Safety and Security:** Measures include 24-hour foot and vehicle patrol, emergency notification system, self-defense education, security escort services, emergency telephones, lighted pathways/sidewalks, and controlled access to dorms/residences.

REQUIREMENTS: The SAT or ACT is required. Graduation from an accredited secondary school is required; a GED will be accepted. Applicants must have successfully completed 4 credits in high school English, 3 in math, 3 in lab science, 2 each in social studies and foreign language, 1 in United States history, and 4 in Electives that must be taken from at least three different fields selected from among Computer Science, English, Fine Arts, Foreign Languages, Humanities, Laboratory Science (excluding earth science, general physical science,general environmental science, or other introductory science courses for which biology and/or chemistry is not a prerequisite), Mathematics above the level of Algebra II, and Social Sciences. It is suggested that one unit be in Computer Science which includes programming (not just keyboarding) and one unit in Fine Arts (i.e. appreciation of, history, or performance). A GPA of 3.0 is required. AP and CLEP credits are accepted. Important factors in the admissions decision are advanced placement or honors courses, evidence of special talent, and geographical diversity. Students must complete a minimum of 120 semester hours, including a 38 to 53 hour general education distribution requirement, and maintain a minimum GPA of 2.0. Specific courses in writing, oral communication, computer information systems, critical issues, and the American Constitution are required. **Procedure:** Freshmen are admitted to all sessions. Entrance exams should be taken December of senior year. There are deferred admissions and rolling admissions plans. Applications should be filed by May 1 for fall entry; January 2 for spring entry. The fall 2016 application fee was $40. Notification is sent on a rolling basis. Applications are accepted online. **Transfer Students:** 357 transfer students enrolled in 2015-2016. Applicants must be eligible to return to the previous institution and submit college transcripts. 30 of 120 credits required for the bachelor's degree must be completed at Winthrop. **International Students:** There are 81 international students enrolled. The school actively recruits these students. They must take the TOEFL with a minimum score of 520 on the paper-based TOEFL (PBT) or 68 on the Internet-based version (iBT). They must also take the SAT or ACT.

ADMISSIONS: 69% of the 2016-2017 applicants were accepted. The SAT scores for the 2016-2017 freshman class were: Critical Reading-- 37% below 500, 40% between 500 and 599, 19% between 600 and 699, and 2% between 700 and 800. Math-- 44% below 500, 38% between 500 and 599, 13% between 600 and 699, and 1% between 700 and 800. The ACT scores were 7% between 12 and 17, 53% between 18 and 23, 35% between 24 and 29, and 5% above 30. **Admissions Contact:** Deborah Barber, Director of Admissions. Email: *admissions@winthrop.edu* Web: *www.winthrop.edu*

FINANCIAL AID: 18% of undergraduate students work part-time. Average annual earnings from campus work are $1600. Winthrop is a member of CSS. The FAFSA code is 003456. The priority date for freshman financial aid applications for fall entry is March 1.

WOFFORD COLLEGE — B-1

www.wofford.edu

Spartanburg, SC 29303 — **(864) 597-4130**

Fax: (864) 597-4147	**Email: admission@wofford.edu**
Full-time: 800 men, 749 women	**Faculty:** 130; IIB, av$
Part-time: 17 men, 18 women	**Ph.D.s:** 90%
Graduate: n/av	**Student/Faculty:** 11 to 1
Year: 4-1-4, summer session	**Tuition:** $38,705
Room & Board: $11,180	**Freshman Class:** 2718 applied, 1870 accepted, 415 enrolled
SAT CR/M: 585/597 **ACT:** 26	**CEEB CODE:** 5912
Application Deadline: February 1	**VERY COMPETITIVE**

Wofford College, founded in 1854, is a private four-year institution affiliated with the United Methodist Church, offering programs in liberal arts and preprofessional studies. It is especially known for leadership in studies abroad, service learning, and its innovative apartment-style housing, known as "The Wofford Village." There is 1 undergraduate school. In addition to regional accreditation, Wofford has baccalaureate program accreditation with NASDTEC. The 170-acre campus is in an urban area 70 miles southwest of Charlotte. Including any residence halls, there are 72 buildings.

STUDENT LIFE: 56% of undergraduates are from South Carolina. Others are from 37 states, and 12 foreign countries. 67% are from public schools. 80% are White; 8% African American; 3% Asian American; 3% Hispanic; 3% two or more races; 2% Foreign; 1% race unknown. 67% are Protestant; 18% Unknown Religious affiliation; 12% Catholic. **Male To Female Ratio:** 1.1:1. The average age of freshmen is 18; all undergraduates, 20. 10% do not continue beyond their first year; 82% remain to graduate. **Housing:** 1479 students can be accommodated in college housing, which includes coed dorms and on-campus apartments. On-campus housing is guaranteed for all 4 years. 94% of students live on campus; of those, 80% remain on campus on weekends. All students may keep cars.

FACULTY/CLASSROOMS: 60% of faculty are male; 40% are female. All teach undergraduates, 30% do research, and 30% do both. No introductory courses are taught by graduate students. The average class size in an introductory lecture is 21; in a laboratory is 21; and in a regular course is 17.

PROGRAMS OF STUDY: Wofford confers B.A. and B.S. degrees. Bachelor's degrees are awarded in AGRICULTURE (environmental studies), BIOLOGICAL SCIENCE (biology/biological science), BUSINESS (accounting, banking and finance, business economics, and finance), COMMUNICATIONS AND THE ARTS (art history, Chinese, creative writing, dramatic arts, English, French, German, Spanish, studio art, and theatre arts), COMPUTER AND PHYSICAL SCIENCE (applied mathematics, chemistry, computer science, mathematics, and physics), SOCIAL SCIENCE (African American studies, crosscultural studies, economics, gender studies, history, humanities, Latin American studies, philosophy, political science/government, psychology, religion, and sociology). Biology, foreign languages, and finance/accounting are the strongest academically. Biology, business economics, and Spanish have the largest enrollments.

ACTIVITIES: 43% of men belong to 8 national fraternities; 55% of women belong to 4 national sororities. There are 98 groups on campus, including and the interfaith youth core, band, cheerleading, choir, chorale, chorus, college bowl team, computers, dance, drama, environmental, ethnic, international, jazz band, LGBT, literary magazine, newspaper, orchestra, pep band, photography, political, professional, religious, social, social service, student government, and yearbook. Popular campus events Phi Beta Kappa Day, Honors Day, Novel Experience, Winter Lighting. **Sports:** There are 9 intercollegiate sports for men and 8 for women, and 10 intramural sports for men and 10 for women. Facilities include a stadium, arena, tennis complex, soccer and baseball fields, a wellness and athletic center built to the specifications of the Carolina Panthers, sand volleyball court and basketball court. **Graduates:** From July 1, 2015 to June 30, 2016, 374 bachelor's degrees were awarded. The most popular majors were business/marketing (26%), biological/life sciences (18%), and foreign languages (12%). 25 companies recruited on campus in 2015-2016. In an average class, 78% graduate in 4 years or less, 81% graduate in 5 years or less, and 82% graduate in 6 years or less.

SERVICES: Counseling and information services are available, as is tutoring in every subject, and a reader service for the blind. **Library/Resources:** The library contains 184,715 volumes, 21,150 microform items, 3,866 audio/video tapes/CDs/DVDs, and subscribes to 47,528 periodicals including electronic. Computerized library services include interlibrary loans, database searching, Internet access, and Wi-Fi capability. Special learning facilities include an art gallery, International studies center with simultaneous translation capabilities, arboretum, greenhouse, the Goodall environmental studies center at Glendale Shoals, Montgomery Music Building, and The Space in The Mungo Center that houses several programs: The Space to: Prepare (houses the Career Services office, the Sophomore Experience and the Institute); The Space to: Impact a competitive four-year program teaching design thinking, entrepreneurship, project management & the consultative approach to problem solving; The Space to: Launch (supports students in the concept, development & launch of a business idea); The Space to: Consult (student consulting group providing business & organizations strategies to improve performance); The Space to: Explore (helps make the Wofford liberal arts degree global-ready by providing internship & travel opportunities). **Physically Challenged Students:** 95% of the campus is accessible. Facilities include wheelchair ramps, elevators, special parking, specially equipped restrooms, special class scheduling, lowered drinking fountains, and lowered telephones. **Special:** Special academic programs include study abroad in 70 countries, a Washington semester, and a concentration in Latin American and Caribbean studies. In addition, students can major or minor in multiple fields or complete interdisciplinary, humanities, or intercultural studies majors. The January interim allows students to concentrate on a single study project, internship, or travel experience. There are 9 national honor societies and a chapter of Phi Beta Kappa. **Visiting:** There are regularly scheduled orientations for prospective students, information sessions are offered Mon-Fri at 10:00am and 2:00pm. A visit consists of an information session with an admission counselor and campus tour. There are guides for informal visits, visitors may sit in on classes, and stay overnight. To schedule a visit, contact the Director of Admission. **Campus Safety and Security:** Measures include 24-hour foot and vehicle patrol, emergency notification system, self-defense education, and security escort services. There are emergency telephones, lighted pathways/sidewalks, and controlled access to dorms/residences.

REQUIREMENTS: The SAT or ACT is required, as well as the ACT Optional Writing test are required. Applicants must be graduates of an accredited secondary school. The GED is accepted. Students should have completed 4 years each of high school English and math, 3 of lab science, and 3 each of a foreign language and social studies. An essay is required and an interview is strongly recommended. AP and CLEP credits are accepted. Important factors in the admissions decision are advanced placement or honors courses, leadership record, and personality/intangible qualities. To graduate, students must complete 124 credits, with 24 to 40 credits in the major and a minimum GPA of 2.0. General education requirements include 3 credits each of history, philosophy, religion, mathematics and cultures & peoples; 3-4 credits of fine arts; 4-10 credits of foreign languages; 4-16 credits of natural sciences, 6 credits of English; and 2 credits of phys ed. Students must complete 4 interim projects, and a freshman humanities seminar. **Procedure:** Freshmen are admitted to all sessions. Entrance exams should be taken in the spring of the junior year or fall of the senior year. There are early decision, early admissions, and deferred admissions plans. Early decision applications should be filed by November 1; regular applications, by February 1 for fall entry, along with a $35 fee. Notification of early decision is sent December 1; regular decision, March 15. 1155 early decision candidates were accepted for the 2016-2017 class. 52 applicants were on the 2016 waiting list; 52 were admitted. Applications are accepted online. **Transfer Students:** 19 transfer students enrolled in 2015-2016. Transfers should have a minimum GPA of 2.5 from a 4-year college or 3.0 from a 2-year college, or they may submit ACT or SAT scores. An interview is recommended. 30 of 124 credits required for the bachelor's degree must be completed at Wofford. **International Students:** There are 28 international students enrolled. They must take the TOEFL with a minimum score of 550 on the paper-based TOEFL (PBT) or 80 on the Internet-based version (iBT). They must also take the SAT or ACT.

ADMISSIONS: 69% of the 2016-2017 applicants were accepted. The SAT scores for the 2016-2017 freshman class were: Critical Reading--12% below 500, 40% between 500 and 599, 42% between 600 and 699, and 6% between 700 and 800. Math-- 11% below 500, 35% between 500 and 599, 42% between 600 and 699, and 11% between 700 and 800. Writing-- 21% below 500, 38% between 500 and 599, 37% between 600 and 699, and 4% between 700 and 800. The ACT scores were 3% below 12, 15% between 12 and 17, 27% between 18 and 23, 23% between 24 and 29, and 32% above 30. 69% of the current freshmen were in the top fifth of their class; 96% were in the top two fifths. 7 freshmen graduated first in their class. **Admissions Contact:** John W. Birney, Director of Admission. Email: *admission@wofford.edu* Web: *www.wofford.edu*

FINANCIAL AID: In 2016-2017, 93% of all full-time freshmen and 94% of continuing full-time students received some form of financial aid. 65% of all full-time freshmen and 58% of continuing full-time students received need-based aid. The average freshman award was $27,649. Need-based scholarships or need-based grants averaged $28,257; need-based self-help aid (loans and jobs) averaged $3,312; non-need-based athletic scholarships averaged $21,855; and other non-need-based awards and non-need-based scholarships averaged $14,262. 19% of undergraduate students work part-time. Average annual earnings from campus work are $1014. The average financial indebtedness of the 2016 graduate was $24,721. Wofford is a member of CSS. The FAFSA code is 003457. The deadline for filing freshman financial aid applications for fall entry is March 15.

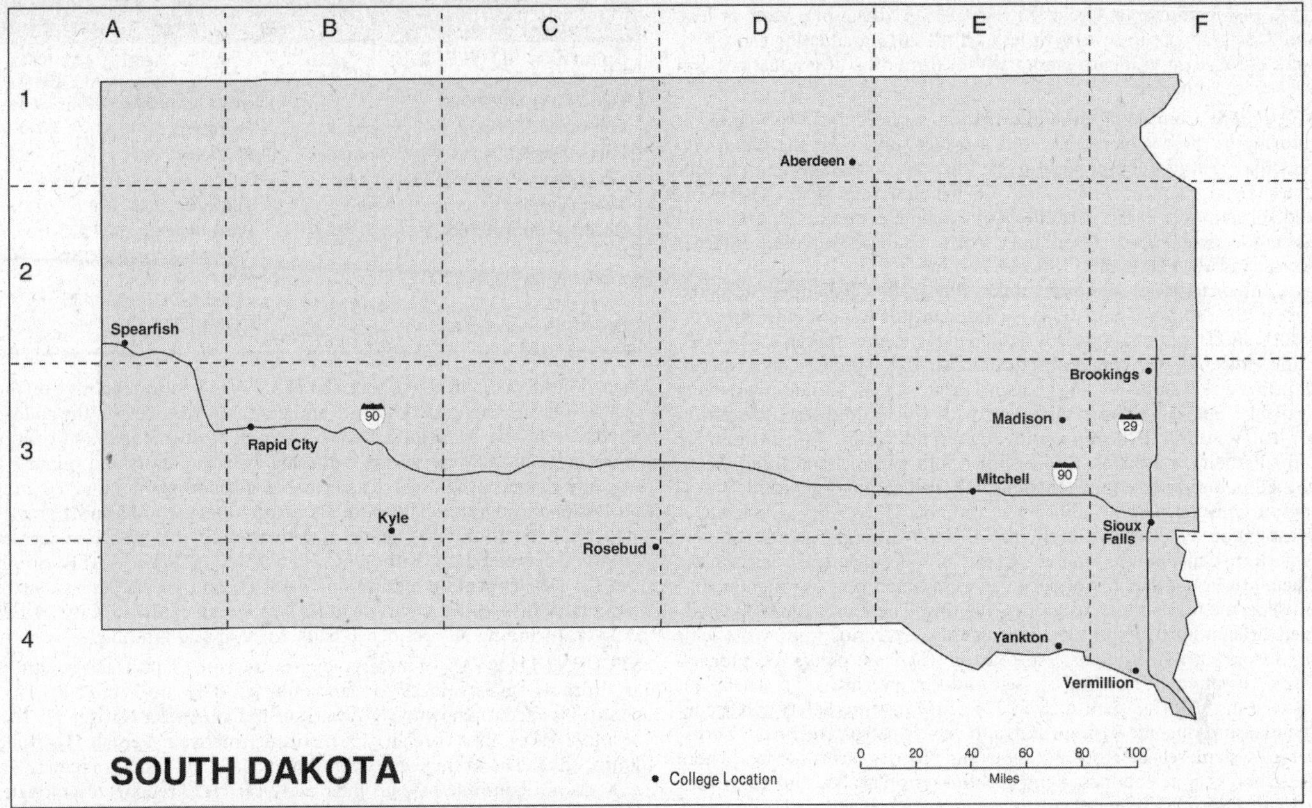

AUGUSTANA UNIVERSITY F-3
www.augie.edu

Sioux Falls, SD 57197	(605) 274-5516 (800) 727-2844
Fax: (605) 274-5518	Email: admission@augie.edu
Full-time: 627 men, 947 women	Faculty: 130; IIB, -$
Part-time: 52 men, 39 women	Ph.D.s: 86%
Graduate: 49 men, 223 women	Student/Faculty: 11 to 1
Year: 4-1-4, summer session	Tuition: $30,944
Room & Board: $7480	Freshman Class: 1464 applied, 1012 accepted, 424 enrolled
ACT: 26	CEEB CODE: 6015
Application Deadline: n/av	VERY COMPETITIVE

Augustana University, founded in 1860, is a comprehensive liberal arts and professional university of the Lutheran church. There is 1 undergraduate school and 1 graduate school. In addition to regional accreditation, Augusta has baccalaureate program accreditation with NASM, NCATE, NCA, DECA, CED, CCNE, CAATE, ACS, SDBN, and NAACLS. The 100-acre campus is in an urban area in Sioux Falls, SD. Including any residence halls, there are 47 buildings.

STUDENT LIFE: 51% of undergraduates are from South Dakota. Others are from 35 states, and 38 foreign countries. 85% are from public schools. 9% are Foreign; 85% White; 3% Hispanic; 2% African American; 2% two or more races; 1% Asian American; 1% American Indian/Alaska Native. 58% are Protestant; 21% Catholic. **Female To Male Ratio:** 1.7:1. The average age of freshmen is 18; all undergraduates, 20. 16% do not continue beyond their first year; 71% remain to graduate. **Housing:** 1225 students can be accommodated in college housing, which includes coed dorms, on-campus apartments, off-campus apartments, and married student housing. In addition, there are special-interest houses, and theme houses. On-campus housing is guaranteed for all 4 years, is guaranteed for the freshman year only, and is available on a first-come, first-served basis. 72% of students live on campus; of those, 70% remain on campus on weekends. Alcohol is not permitted. All students may keep cars.

FACULTY/CLASSROOMS: 46% of faculty are male; 54% are female. 94% teach undergraduates, and all do research. No introductory courses are taught by graduate students. The average class size in an introductory lecture is 32; in a laboratory is 18; and in a regular course is 20.

PROGRAMS OF STUDY: August confers B.A. and B.S. degrees. Master's degrees are also awarded. Bachelor's degrees are awarded in BIOLOGICAL SCIENCE (biochemistry and biology/biological science), BUSINESS (accounting, business administration and management, business communications, and sports management), COMMUNICATIONS AND THE ARTS (American Sign Language, art, classics, communications, dramatic arts, English, French, German, journalism, modern language, music, Spanish, and theatre arts), COMPUTER AND PHYSICAL SCIENCE (chemical physics, chemistry, computer science, information sciences and systems, mathematics, and physics), EDUCATION (athletic training, drama education, elementary education, health education, middle school education, music education, physical education, social studies education, and special education), ENGINEERING AND ENVIRONMENTAL DESIGN (engineering physics), HEALTH PROFESSIONS (exercise science, medical laboratory science, and nursing), SOCIAL SCIENCE (American studies, anthropology, economics, history, interdisciplinary studies, international studies, philosophy, philosophy and religion, physical fitness/movement, political science/government, psychology, religion, and sociology). Nursing, biology, and business are the strongest academically. Nursing, biology, and education have the largest enrollments.

ACTIVITIES: There are no fraternities or sororities. There are 80 groups on campus, including art, band, cheerleading, chess, choir, chorale, chorus, computers, dance, drama, drill team, environmental, ethnic, honors, international, jazz band, LGBT, literary magazine, musical theater, newspaper, opera, orchestra, pep band, photography, political, professional, religious, social, social service, student government, symphony, and yearbook. Popular campus events include Christmas at Augustana, Viking Days, Boe Forum on Public Affairs, and Semester Shutdown. **Sports:** There are 9 intercollegiate sports for men and 10 for women, and 55 intramural sports for men and 55 for women. Facilities include an athletic facility, 2 practice gyms, football complex with stadium, softball and baseball complexes, soccer, baseball and softball fields, a pool, weight/cardio work-out room, and a health, phys ed, and recreation center. **Graduates:** From July 1, 2015 to June 30, 2016, 344 bachelor's degrees were awarded. The most popular majors were business/

marketing (16%), education (16%), and nursing/health professions (15%). 85 companies recruited on campus in 2015-2016. In an average class, 54% graduate in 4 years or less, 69% graduate in 5 years or less, and 71% graduate in 6 years or less. Of the 2015 graduating class, 21% were enrolled in graduate school within 6 months of graduation, and 99% were employed.

SERVICES: Counseling and information services are available, as is tutoring in most subjects. There is a reader service for the blind, and remedial writing. **Library/Resources:** The library contains 234,700 volumes, 7,950 microform items, and 7,800 audio/video tapes/CDs/DVDs, and subscribes to 6,450 periodicals including electronic. Computerized library services include interlibrary loans, database searching, Internet access, and Wi-Fi capability. Special learning facilities include an art gallery, and a center for Western studies. **Physically Challenged Students:** 75% of the campus is accessible. Facilities include wheelchair ramps, elevators, special parking, specially equipped restrooms, special class scheduling, lowered drinking fountains, lowered telephones, and special housing. Arkenstone reader, Dragon Dictate, TTYs, and doorbell lights available. **Special:** Cross-registration with Upper Midwest Association for Intercultural Education and Higher Education Consortium for Urban Affairs is available. Internships (both national and local), study abroad in unlimited countries, and a 3-2 engineering degree with Washington University in St. Louis and Columbia University are offered. A Washington semester with Lutheran College Washington Consortium or American University is offered. Credit for life experience is possible. There are 12 national honor societies, a freshman honors program, and 21 departmental honors programs. **Visiting:** There are regularly scheduled orientations for prospective students, a campus tour, visits with professors, current students, and coaches. There are guides for informal visits, visitors may sit in on classes, and stay overnight. To schedule a visit, contact Alexis Fredin at (605) 274-5516. **Campus Safety and Security:** Measures include 24-hour foot and vehicle patrol, emergency notification system, self-defense education, and security escort services. There are emergency telephones, lighted pathways/sidewalks, and controlled access to dorms/residences.

REQUIREMENTS: Applicants may present either ACT or SAT scores. Applicants should have completed 4 years of high school English, math, and science, 2 years of a foreign language, and 3 years of history. An essay, a transcript, and a recommendation are required. AP and CLEP credits are accepted. Important factors in the admissions decision are advanced placement or honors courses, extracurricular activities record, leadership record, and personality/intangible qualities. Students must complete 124 semester hours with a minimum GPA of 2.0. General education requirements total 59 semester hours, including component courses in writing for graduation. **Procedure:** Freshmen are admitted to all sessions. Entrance exams should be taken in the spring of the junior year or early fall of the senior. There are deferred admissions and rolling admissions plans. Application deadlines are open. Notification is sent on a rolling basis. Applications are accepted on-line. **Transfer Students:** 49 transfer students enrolled in 2015-2016. Applicants must have a 2.25 GPA in previous college work. 30 of 124 credits required for the bachelor's degree must be completed at Augusta. **International Students:** There are 153 international students enrolled. The school actively recruits these students. They must take the TOEFL with a minimum score of 550 on the paper-based TOEFL (PBT) or 79 on the Internet-based version (iBT). They must also take the SAT or ACT, scoring 20.

ADMISSIONS: 69% of the 2016-2017 applicants were accepted. The ACT scores were 29% between 18 and 23, 53% between 24 and 29, and 18% above 30. **Admissions Contact:** Nancy L. Davidson, Vice President of Enrollment. Email: *admission@augie.edu* Web: *www.augie.edu*

FINANCIAL AID: In 2016-2017, 100% of all full-time freshmen and 100% of continuing full-time students received some form of financial aid. 66% of all full-time freshmen and 58% of continuing full-time students received need-based aid. The average freshman award was $28,520. Need-based scholarships or need-based grants averaged $25,013; need-based self-help aid (loans and jobs) averaged $5,499; non-need-based athletic scholarships averaged $10,836; and other non-need-based awards and non-need-based scholarships averaged $18,052. 26% of undergraduate students work part-time. Average annual earnings from campus work are $1416. The average financial indebtedness of the 2016 graduate was $26,876. The FAFSA code is 003458. The priority date for freshman financial aid applications for fall entry is March 1.

BLACK HILLS STATE UNIVERSITY — A-2

www.bhsu.edu

Spearfish, SD 57799	**(605) 642-6343** **(800) ALL-BHSU**
Fax: (605) 642-6022	**Email: admissions@bhsu.edu**
Full-time: 859 men, 1420 women	**Faculty:** 231
Part-time: 601 men, 1140 women	**Ph.D.s:** n/av
Graduate: 113 men, 356 women	**Student/Faculty:** 20 to 1
Year: semesters, summer session	**Tuition:** $9204 ($12,120)
Room & Board: $6695	**Freshman Class:** 1355 applied, 1267 accepted, 507 enrolled
ACT: 21	**CEEB CODE:** 003459
Application Deadline: n/av	**COMPETITIVE**

Black Hills State University, founded in 1883, is a comprehensive public institution offering undergraduate and graduate programs in the college of education and behavioral sciences, college of liberal arts, and college of business and natural sciences, offering over 80 majors and minors, 5 master's degree programs, 4 associate degree programs, and 20 pre-professional programs. There are 3 undergraduate schools and 1 graduate school. In addition to regional accreditation, BHSU has baccalaureate program accreditation with AACSB, NASM, NCATE, CAEP, South Dakota Department of Education, AASCU, and ACU. The 123-acre campus is in a small town 45 miles northwest of Rapid City, South Dakota. Including any residence halls, there are 20 buildings.

STUDENT LIFE: 74% of undergraduates are from South Dakota. Others are from 44 states, and 29 foreign countries. 82% are White; 4% Hispanic; 4% race unknown; 3% American Indian/Alaska Native; 3% two or more races; 2% Foreign; 1% African American. **Female To Male Ratio:** 1.9:1. The average age of freshmen is 19; all undergraduates, 24. 37% do not continue beyond their first year; 31% remain to graduate. **Housing:** 840 students can be accommodated in college housing, which includes single-sex and coed dorms, on-campus apartments, and married student housing. On-campus housing is guaranteed for the freshman year only. 79% of students commute. Alcohol is not permitted. All students may keep cars.

FACULTY/CLASSROOMS: 95% teach undergraduates. No introductory courses are taught by graduate students.

PROGRAMS OF STUDY: BHSU confers B.A., B.G.S., B.A.T.S., B.S., and B.S.Ed degrees. Associate and master's degrees are also awarded. Bachelor's degrees are awarded in BIOLOGICAL SCIENCE (biology/adolescence education and biology/biological science), BUSINESS (accounting, business administration and management, business administration, mgmt, operations, business administration marketing, entrepreneurial studies, human resources, human resources/organizational mgmt, tourism, and professional program in accounting), COMMUNICATIONS AND THE ARTS (art, art/art studies, communication studies, communications, English, graphic communications management, graphic design, English and Professional Communication, music, Spanish, speech/debate/rhetoric, and communication arts - speech), COMPUTER AND PHYSICAL SCIENCE (applied science, chemistry, chemistry/adolescence education, industrial technology, mathematics, physical sciences, and science), EDUCATION (business education, early childhood education, elementary education, English education, general studies, mathematics education, outdoor leadership/education, physical education, reading education, science education, social science education, Spanish education K-12, and special education), ENGINEERING AND ENVIRONMENTAL DESIGN (construction technology and manufacturing technology), HEALTH PROFESSIONS (biology and exercise science), SOCIAL SCIENCE (economics, history, history and political science, human services, Native American studies, political science/government, psychology, social science, and sociology). Elementary education, biology, and business administration are the strongest academically and have the largest enrollments.

ACTIVITIES: Groups on campus include art, band, cheerleading, choir, chorale, chorus, computers, dance, debate, drama, drill team, environmental, ethnic, forensics, honors, international, jazz band, LGBT, musical theater, newspaper, pep band, photography, political, professional, radio and TV, religious, social, social service, student government, and yearbook. Popular campus events include Swarm Week. **Sports:** There are 5 intercollegiate sports for men and 7 for women. Facilities include a stadium, gymnasium with basketball and volleyball courts, tennis courts, swimming pools, indoor and outdoor tracks, golf course, and a baseball and softball complex.

SERVICES: Counseling and information services are available, as is tutoring in most subjects. There is remedial math, reading, and writing. **Library/Resources:** Computerized library services include interlibrary loans, database searching, Internet access, and Wi-Fi capability. Special learning facilities include an art gallery, radio station, TV station, a gymnasium, and theater. **Physically Challenged Students:** Facilities include wheelchair ramps, elevators, special parking, specially equipped restrooms, lowered drinking fountains, and special housing. **Special:** There is a Phi Beta Kappa and a freshman honors program. **Visiting:** There are regularly scheduled orientations for prospective students, consisting of open houses, receptions, and green and gold days. There are guides for informal visits, visitors may sit in on classes, and stay overnight. To schedule a visit, contact Beth Oaks at Beth.Oaks@BHSU.edu. **Campus Safety and Security:** Measures include 24-hour foot and vehicle patrol, emergency notification system, and security escort services. There are lighted pathways/sidewalks and controlled access to dorms/residences.

REQUIREMENTS: To be admitted to Black Hills State University, you must have the following credentials: ACT Composite Score of 18 or above or Rank in the top 60 percent of your graduating class or high school GPA of 2.60 on a 4.00 scale. All baccalaureate or general studies students under 24 years of age, including students transferring with fewer than 24 credit hours, must meet the following minimum high school course requirements with an overall grade point average of "C" or higher: 4 years of English, or an ACT English subtest score of 18 or above, or an Advanced Placement Language and Composition or Literature and Composition score of 3 or above. 3 years of Advanced Math (algebra and above) or an ACT mathematics subtest score of 20 or above; or an Advanced Placement Calculus AB or Calculus BC score of 3 or above. 3 years of Laboratory Science (biology, chemistry, or physics, or approved physical science or earth science), or an ACT science reasoning subtest score of 17 or above, or an Advanced Placement Biology, Chemistry, or Physics B score of 3 or above. 3 years of Social Sciences, or an ACT social studies subtest score of 17 or above, or an Advanced Placement Microeconomics, Macroeconomics, Comparative or United States Government and Policies, European or United States History, or Psychology score of 3 or above. 1 year of Fine Arts. Applications received from students with deficiencies will be reviewed on an individual basis. A GPA of 2.0 is required. AP and CLEP credits are accepted. Depending on Catalog year, 120/128 minimum hours (baccalaureate degrees) (150 minimum semester hours for Professional Accountancy). Depending on Catalog year, 60/64 minimum hours (associate degrees). All major, minor, and professional education requirements must be met. 2.0 minimum institutional and cumulative grade point average (non-teaching degrees). 2.6 minimum cumulative grade point average (teaching degrees). 2.6 minimum grade point average in teaching major, teaching minor and professional education core (teaching degrees). 36 minimum upper-division hours (courses numbered 300/400) (baccalaureate degrees). System and institutional general education requirements must be met. Must take and pass the CAAP Proficiency Exam. Must take exit examination for each major (baccalaureate degrees). No more than 16 hours of internship will be counted toward a major or a degree. No more than 32 hours can be earned by special examinations, correspondence, extension courses from other colleges and/or non-collegiate courses, other than military courses. No more than 6 hours will be accepted toward graduation or final GPA for participation in the following activities: physical education activities, wind ensemble, choir, small ensembles, jazz ensemble, forensics, theatre, yearbook or newspaper unless such participation is a requirement for a major or minor. Depending on Catalog year, a minimum of 30/32 hours (baccalaureate degrees) and 15/16 semester hours (associate degrees) must be earned from Black Hills State University. Depending on Catalog year, 15/16 hours (baccalaureate degrees) of the last 30/32 hours and 6/8 hours (associate degrees) of the last 15/16 hours preceding the completion of a degree must be earned from Black Hills State University. Minimum number of credit hours in the major or minor that must be completed from Black Hills State University: 50 percent. Composite majors do not need to complete a minor. Degree-seeking students may complete requirements for a minor at any regental university that has been approved to grant that minor. This minor will be recorded on the transcript in conjunction with a degree/major at that university or a degree/major at any other regental university. A minor will only be recorded on the transcript in conjunction with a degree and major. Non-teaching regular majors must complete a minor or a second major. Bachelor of Arts candidates must complete twelve hours of a foreign language (Minimum of 4 courses of Beginning I & II and Intermediate I & II). Remedial courses (courses numbered below 100) will not be counted toward graduation. Coursework taken for graduate credit will not apply toward a baccalaureate degree. In addition to the BHSU cumulative GPA requirement, transfer students must have a BHSU and transfer combined GPA of 2.0 for non-teaching programs and 2.6 for teaching programs. **Procedure:** Freshmen are admitted to all sessions. Entrance exams should be taken during the senior year of high school. There are early admissions and rolling admissions plans. Application deadlines are open. Application fee is $20. Applications are accepted online. **Transfer Students:** 313 transfer students enrolled in 2015-2016. Transfer to Baccalaureate Program-Students who are under the age of 24 at the start of the term and who are transferring into baccalaureate degree programs with fewer than 24 transfer credit hours may be required to fulfill the baccalaureate degree admission requirements. Students with 24 or more transfer credit hours with a cumulative GPA of at least 2.0 may transfer into baccalaureate degree programs. Specific degree programs may include additional admissions requirements. If students are applying for federal financial aid, they must meet federal guidelines for transfer students. Transfer to Associate Degree Program-Students who are under the age of 24 at the start of the term and who are transferring into associate degree programs with fewer than 12 transfer credit hours must meet the associate degree admission requirements. Students with 12 or more transfer credit hours with a cumulative GPA of at least 2.0 may transfer into associate degree programs. Specific degree programs may include additional admissions requirements. Non-Regental Accredited Colleges or Universities–Transfer students may be accepted from other non-Regental universities outside of the SD system; preferential consideration will be given to applicants from institutions which are accredited by their respective regional accrediting association. Non-Accredited Colleges–BHSU is not required to accept credits from a non-accredited college or university. The university may admit the applicant on a provisional basis and provide a means for the evaluation of some or all of the credits. Credits from colleges or universities that are not accredited by a regional accrediting association may be considered for transfer, subject to all other provisions of these guidelines and any conditions for validation which may be set by BHSU. Students on Suspension/Probation–Transfer student who have not maintained a cumulative grade point average of 2.00 may appeal for admissions. If admitted, such students are on academic probation. If the last institution attended was outside the Regental system, and the transfer applicant left under academic suspension, the applicant will not be considered for admission during the period of suspension or, if suspended for an indefinite period, until one semester has passed since the last date of attendance at the previous school. Students on academic suspension from a Regental university will not be allowed to register for any coursework at any Regental university except when an appeal has been approved by the Regental university from which the student is pursuing a degree. An approved appeal granted by one Regental university will be honored by all Regental universities. Application Procedure: Transfer applicants should submit a completed admission application, a $20 non-refundable application fee, a current complete official transcript sent directly from each college, schools or institution attended since high school, and an official high school transcript. The application fee is not charged to students who transfer from other South Dakota Regental schools. Applicant who are 21 years of age or younger must submit Enhanced ACT (or SAT-I) results. Applicants who are over 21 need to submit their scores if they have taken the test within the last five years. Students transferring from a degree-seeking program at one Regental university to a degree-seeking program at BHSU are required to apply for admission. Note: Transfer students applying for federal financial aid must meet federal guidelines for transfer students. **International Students:** The school actively recruits these students. They must take the TOEFL. They must also take the ACT, scoring 18.

ADMISSIONS: 94% of the 2016-2017 applicants were accepted. **Admissions Contact:** Admissions Officer, Enrollment Services Center. Email: *admissions@bhsu.edu* Web: *www.bhsu.edu*

FINANCIAL AID: The FAFSA code is 003459. Check with the school for current application deadlines.

DAKOTA STATE UNIVERSITY E-3

www.dsu.edu

Madison, SD 57042 (605) 256-5139
(888) DSU-9988

Fax: (605) 256-5020 **Email: admissions@dsu.edu**

Full-time: n/av **Faculty:** IIB, av$
Part-time: n/av **Ph.D.s:** n/av
Graduate: n/av **Student/Faculty:** n/av
Year: semesters, summer session **Tuition:** $8286 ($10,286)
Room & Board: $5525 **Freshman Class:** 600 accepted, 360 enrolled
SAT or ACT: required **CEEB CODE:** 6247
Application Deadline: open **COMPETITIVE**

Dakota State University, founded in 1881, is a public institution offering undergraduate programs through the Colleges of Business and Information Systems, Education, and Arts and Sciences. There are 3 undergraduate schools and 1 graduate school. In addition to regional accreditation, DSU has baccalaureate program accreditation with ACBSP, AHEA, NCATE, AHIMA, and CoARC. The 56-acre campus is in a rural area 45 miles northwest of Sioux Falls. Including any residence halls, there are 22 buildings.

STUDENT LIFE: **Housing:** 659 students can be accommodated in college housing, which includes single-sex and coed dorms and on-campus apartments. On-campus housing is guaranteed for the freshman year only, is available on a first-come, first-served basis, and is available on a lottery system for upperclassmen. Alcohol is not permitted. All students may keep cars.

FACULTY/CLASSROOMS: No introductory courses are taught by graduate students.

PROGRAMS OF STUDY: DSU confers B.S., B.B.A., B.G.S., and B.S.Ed. degrees. Associate, master's, and doctoral degrees are also awarded. Bachelor's degrees are awarded in BIOLOGICAL SCIENCE (biology/biological science), BUSINESS (business administration and management), COMMUNICATIONS AND THE ARTS (communications technology, English, and information technology), COMPUTER AND PHYSICAL SCIENCE (computer programming, computer game design/development, computer science, computer security and information assurance, digital arts/technology, information sciences and systems, mathematics, and physical sciences), EDUCATION (business education, computer education, elementary education, English education, health education, health information management, marketing and distribution education, mathematics education, and secondary education), ENGINEERING AND ENVIRONMENTAL DESIGN (computer graphics), HEALTH PROFESSIONS (medical records administration/services, premedicine, and respiratory therapy).

ACTIVITIES: There are no fraternities or sororities. There are 36 groups on campus, including art, band, cheerleading, choir, chorale, chorus, computers, dance, drama, ethnic, honors, international, literary magazine, musical theater, newspaper, pep band, political, professional, radio and TV, religious, social, and student government. Popular campus events include Homecoming, Convocation and Frost Bites Week. **Sports:** There are 6 intercollegiate sports for men and 6 for women, and 3 intramural sports for men and 3 for women. Facilities include courts for basketball and racquetball, a football field, a weight room, and a swimming pool. **Graduates:** From July 1, 2015 to June 30, 2016, 145 bachelor's degrees were awarded. 25 companies recruited on campus in 2015-2016. In an average class, 24% graduate in 4 years or less, 42% graduate in 5 years or less, and 15% graduate in 6 years or less. Of the 2015 graduating class, 1% were enrolled in graduate school within 6 months of graduation, and 96% were employed.

SERVICES: Counseling and information services are available, as is tutoring in every subject. There is a reader service for the blind, and remedial math, reading, and writing. **Library/Resources:** The library contains 177,454 volumes, 3,669 microform items, and 3,426 audio/video tapes/CDs/DVDs, and subscribes to 350 periodicals including electronic. Computerized library services include interlibrary loans, database searching, Internet access, and Wi-Fi capability. Special learning facilities include an art gallery, natural history museum, and radio station. **Physically Challenged Students:** 80% of the campus is accessible. Facilities include wheelchair ramps, elevators, special parking, specially equipped restrooms, special class scheduling, and lowered drinking fountains. **Special:** The university offers co-op programs with South Dakota State University, internships, study abroad in London, and on-campus work-study programs. Also available are the general studies degree, a 3-2 engineering degree with the University of Minnesota/Twin Cities, credit for life, military, and work experience, nondegree study, and pass/fail options. There are 2 national honor societies and a freshman honors program. **Visiting:** There are regularly scheduled orientations for prospective students, including general information and academic sessions, a campus tour, and financial aid information. There are guides for informal visits, visitors may sit in on classes, and stay overnight. To schedule a visit, contact the Admissions Office. **Campus Safety and Security:** Measures include self-defense education and security escort services. There are emergency telephones, lighted pathways/sidewalks, controlled access to dorms/residences, and foot patrol.

REQUIREMENTS: The SAT or ACT is required, with a minimum composite score of 18 on the ACT. Applicants must be graduates of an accredited secondary school or have a GED certificate, and have completed 4 years of English, 3 years each of math, science, and social studies, and 1/2 year each of computer science and the fine arts. AP and CLEP credits are accepted. All students seeking a bachelor's degree are required to complete 30 credit hours of general education coursework (math, English, science, humanities) as well as 11 credit hours of institutional specific coursework (information technology and personal health). Associate's degree-seeking students are required to complete 18 credit hours of general education coursework as well as 6 credit hours of institutional specific coursework. Graduates must have a 2.0 GPA. A general education assessment exam and exit assessment are required of all students. **Procedure:** Freshmen are admitted to all sessions. Entrance exams should be taken before students register for classes. There is a rolling admissions plan. Application deadlines are open. Application fee is $20. Notification is sent on a rolling basis. Applications are accepted on-line. **Transfer Students:** 67 transfer students enrolled in 2015-2016. Transfer applicants must have a minimum 2.0 GPA. 32 of 128 credits required for the bachelor's degree must be completed at DSU. **International Students:** There are 120 international students enrolled. The school actively recruits these students. They must take the TOEFL.

ADMISSIONS: 9 freshmen graduated first in their class. **Admissions Contact:** Amy Crissinger, Director of Admission. Email: *admissions@dsu.edu* Web: *www.dsu.edu*

FINANCIAL AID: In 2016-2017, 88% of continuing full-time students received some form of financial aid. The average freshman award was $5,836. 50% of undergraduate students work part-time. Average annual earnings from campus work are $1405. The average financial indebtedness of the 2016 graduate was $16,588. The FAFSA code is 003463. The deadline for filing freshman financial aid applications for fall entry is March 1.

DAKOTA WESLEYAN UNIVERSITY E-3

www.dwu.edu

Mitchell, SD 57301 (605) 995-2661
(800) 333-8506

Fax: (605) 995-2699 **Email: admissionsk@dwu.edu**

Full-time: 328 men, 400 women **Faculty:** 51; IIB
Part-time: 7 men, 21 women **Ph.D.s:** 68%
Graduate: 13 men, 19 women **Student/Faculty:** 14 to 1
Year: semesters, summer session **Tuition:** $26,050
Room & Board: $6800 **Freshman Class:** n/av
SAT: required **ACT:** 21 **CEEB CODE:** 6155
Application Deadline: August 25 **COMPETITIVE**

Dakota Wesleyan University, founded in 1885, is a private liberal arts institution affiliated with the United Methodist Church. The figures in the above capsule and in this profile are approximate. Tuition cost is based on 12-16 credit hours. There are 3 undergraduate schools. In addition to regional accreditation, DWU has baccalaureate program accreditation with NLN and CAAHEP. The 50-acre campus is in a small town 70 miles west of Sioux Falls. Including any residence halls, there are 18 buildings.

STUDENT LIFE: 69% of undergraduates are from South Dakota. Others are from 27 states, 3 foreign countries, and Canada. 99% are from public schools. 86% are White; 4% Hispanic; 3% American Indian/Alaska Native; 1% African American; 1% Asian American; 1% Foreign. 50% are Protestant; 24% Catholic. **Female To Male Ratio:** 1.3:1. The average age of freshmen is 19; all undergraduates, 23. 32% do not continue beyond their first year. **Housing:** 385 students can be accommodated in college housing, which includes single-sex and coed dorms and on-campus apartments. In addition, there are honors houses. On-campus housing is guaranteed for the freshman year only, and is available on a first-come, first-served basis. 60% of students commute. Alcohol is not permitted. All students may keep cars.

FACULTY/CLASSROOMS: 45% of faculty are male; 55% are female. All teach undergraduates. No introductory courses are taught by graduate students. The average class size in an introductory lecture is 20; in a laboratory is 17; and in a regular course is 17.

PROGRAMS OF STUDY: DWU confers B.A. degrees. Associate and master's degrees are also awarded. Bachelor's degrees are awarded in AGRICULTURE (wildlife management), BIOLOGICAL SCIENCE (biology/biological science), BUSINESS (accounting, business administration and management, and sports management), COMMUNICATIONS AND THE ARTS (art, communications, dramatic arts, English, multimedia, and music), COMPUTER AND PHYSICAL SCIENCE (mathematics), EDUCATION (athletic training, elementary education, physical education, special education, and sports and wellness studies), HEALTH PROFESSIONS (nursing), SOCIAL SCIENCE (behavioral science, criminal justice, history, human services, philosophy and religion, psychology, public administration, and sociology). Biochemistry is the strongest academically. Nursing and business have the largest enrollments.

ACTIVITIES: There are no fraternities or sororities. There are 30 groups on campus, including brass and woodwind ensembles, bell choir, academic, art, band, cheerleading, choir, chorale, chorus, dance, drama, drill team, ethnic, forensics, honors, international, literary magazine, musical theater, newspaper, political, professional, religious, social, social service, student government, and yearbook. Popular campus events include Spring Week, and Family Life Conference. **Sports:** There are 7 intercollegiate sports for men and 6 for women, and 3 intramural sports for men and 3 for women. Facilities include a wellness center with a double gym, cardio, weight training, and cybex rooms. City facilities include a stadium, auditorium/arena, baseball stadium, softball field, and a outdoor track. **Graduates:** From July 1, 2015 to June 30, 2016, 128 bachelor's degrees were awarded. The most popular majors were business administration (27%), elementary education (17%), and criminal justice (10%). Of the 2015 graduating class, 95% were enrolled in graduate school within 6 months of graduation, and 98% were employed.

SERVICES: Counseling and information services are available, as is tutoring in every subject. There is a reader service for the blind, and remedial math, reading, and writing. **Library/Resources:** The library contains 62,500 volumes, 72,500 microform items, and 3,700 audio/video tapes/CDs/DVDs, and subscribes to 620 periodicals including electronic. Computerized library services include interlibrary loans, database searching, and Internet access. **Physically Challenged Students:** 80% of the campus is accessible. Facilities include wheelchair ramps, elevators, special parking, specially equipped restrooms, special class scheduling, lowered drinking fountains, and lowered telephones. **Special:** DWU offers internships, study abroad on a limited basis, work-study programs, a general studies degree, dual majors, student-designed minors, credit for experience, and credit/no credit options. There are 4 national honor societies and a freshman honors program. **Visiting:** There are regularly scheduled orientations for prospective students, including a campus tour and meetings with faculty and students, during April and June. There are guides for informal visits, visitors may sit in on classes, and stay overnight. To schedule a visit, contact Mateya Berg at maberg@dwu.edu. **Campus Safety and Security:** Measures include self-defense education and security escort services. There are emergency telephones, lighted pathways/sidewalks, Safety and security personnel trained in first aid and self-defense, 20-hour foot and vehicle patrol, and pamphlets and posters.

REQUIREMENTS: The SAT or ACT is required. Applicants must be graduates of an accredited secondary school or have a GED certificate. An interview is recommended. AP and CLEP credits are accepted. Important factors in the admissions decision are advanced placement or honors courses, extracurricular activities record, and parents or siblings attended your school. To graduate, students must complete a total of 125 credit hours, including 30 or more in the major, and at least 42 in upper-level courses, with a minimum 2.0 GPA. General education requirements include 6 hours of communication, literature and the arts, and social, psychological, and political thought, 3 to 5 of physical science, 3 to 4 each of math and cultural awareness, 3 each of history and philosophy/theology, and 2 of physical activities; students must demonstrate basic skills in reading, writing, and math. All new freshmen must take Forum and Advising courses. **Procedure:** Freshmen are admitted fall, spring, and summer. Entrance exams should be taken during the senior year. There is a rolling admissions plan. Applications should be filed by August 25 for fall entry; January 2 for spring entry; and June 4 for summer entry, along with a $25 fee. Notifications are sent September 1. Applications are accepted on-line. **Transfer Students:** 107 transfer students enrolled in 2015-2016. Students must submit official transcripts from all previous colleges attended. DWU will accept credits from regionally accredited institutions, but half the credits for the student's major must be completed at DWU. 30 of 125 credits required for the bachelor's degree must be completed at DWU. **International Students:** There are 15 international students enrolled. The school actively recruits these students. They must take the TOEFL with a minimum score of 500 on the paper-based TOEFL (PBT) or 71 on the Internet-based version (iBT) or take the MELAB. They must also take the SAT or ACT, scoring 18.

ADMISSIONS: The ACT scores were 26% above 30. **Admissions Contact:** Amy Novak, Vice President for Enrollment Management. Email: *admissionsk@dwu.edu* Web: *www.dwu.edu*

FINANCIAL AID: In 2016-2017, 100% of all full-time freshmen and continuing full-time students received some form of financial aid. 99% of all full-time freshmen and continuing full-time students received need-based aid. The average freshman award was $23,000. DWU is a member of CSS. The FAFSA code is 003461. The priority date for freshman financial aid applications for fall entry is April 15. The deadline for filing freshman financial aid applications for fall entry is August 30.

MOUNT MARTY COLLEGE — E-4

www.mtmc.edu

Yankton, SD 57078	**(605) 668-1545** **(800) 658-4552**
Fax: (605) 668-1607	**Email: mmcadmit@mtmc.edu**
Full-time: 215 men, 500 women	**Faculty:** 35; IIB, --$
Part-time: 76 men, 301 women	**Ph.D.s:** 64%
Graduate: 50 men, 50 women	**Student/Faculty:** 10 to 1
Year: semesters, summer session	**Tuition:** $25,280
Room & Board: $7692	**Freshman Class:** 397 accepted, 190 enrolled
ACT: required	**CEEB CODE:** 6416
Application Deadline: open	**COMPETITIVE**

Mount Marty College is a private, Catholic Benedictine, liberal, coeducational, arts college, open to students of all faiths and backgrounds. Mount Marty prepares students for a contemporary world of work, service to the human community, and personal growth. The figures in the above capsule and in this profile are approximate. There are 2 undergraduate schools and 3 graduate schools. In addition to regional accreditation, Mount Marty has baccalaureate program accreditation with ADA and NLN. The 80-acre campus is in a small town in Yankton, 60 miles northwest of Sioux City, Iowa, and 80 miles southwest of Sioux Falls. Including any residence halls, there are 11 buildings.

STUDENT LIFE: 60% of undergraduates are from South Dakota. Others are from 25 states, and 5 foreign countries. 79% are from public schools. 94% are White; 3% Hispanic; 1% African American; 1% Asian American; 1% American Indian/Alaska Native. 42% are Catholic; 36% claim no religious affiliation. **Female To Male Ratio:** 2.5:1. The average age of freshmen is 19; all undergraduates, 26. 22% do not continue beyond their first year; 61% remain to graduate. **Housing:** College-sponsored housing includes single-sex dorms. On-campus housing is guaranteed for all 4 years. 75% of students live on campus; of those, 60% remain on campus on weekends. Alcohol is not permitted. All students may keep cars.

FACULTY/CLASSROOMS: 54% of faculty are male; 46% are female. All teach undergraduates. No introductory courses are taught by graduate students. The average class size in an introductory lecture is 30; in a laboratory is 15; and in a regular course is 20.

PROGRAMS OF STUDY: Mount Marty confers B.A., B.S., and B.S.N. degrees. Associate and master's degrees are also awarded. Bachelor's degrees are awarded in BIOLOGICAL SCIENCE (biology/biological science), BUSINESS (accounting and business administration and management), COMMUNICATIONS AND THE ARTS (English, journalism, and music), COMPUTER AND PHYSICAL SCIENCE (chemistry, computer science, mathematics, and radiological technology), EDUCATION (athletic training, elementary education, physical education, secondary education, and special education), ENGINEERING AND ENVIRONMENTAL DESIGN (environmental science), HEALTH PROFESSIONS (health care administration, medical technology, and nursing), SOCIAL SCIENCE (behavioral science, criminal justice, food production/management/services, history, religion, and social science). Nursing, business, and teacher education are the strongest academically.

ACTIVITIES: There are no fraternities or sororities. There are 50 groups on campus, including business, dentistry, martial arts, nursing, pool, psychology, art, band, choir, chorus, theatre, computers, drama, ethnic, forensics, honors, jazz band, literary magazine, musical theater, newspaper, pep band, photography, political, professional, religious, social, social service, and student government. Popular campus events include Blue & Gold Days, Formal Dances, Benedictine Lecture Series, Bowling, Carmike Movie Night, Ice Skating, Yoga, Zumba, Family Weekend, and Homecoming. **Sports:** There are 6 intercollegiate sports for men and 6 for women, and 4 intramural sports for men and 4 for women. Facilities include volleyball and basketball courts, a jogging track, 2 racquetball courts, weight and training rooms, a stadium, an indoor gym, and a auditorium. **Graduates:** The most popular majors were health professions (28%), business (23%), and education (15%). In an average class, 30% graduate in 4 years or less, 41% graduate in 5 years or less, and 44% graduate in 6 years or less. Of the 2015 graduating class, 5% were enrolled in graduate school within 6 months of graduation, and 96% were employed.

SERVICES: Counseling and information services are available, as is tutoring in most subjects. There is remedial math, reading, and writing. **Library/Resources:** The library contains 79,228 volumes, 11,624 microform items, and 8,465 audio/video tapes/CDs/DVDs, and subscribes to 439 periodicals including electronic. Computerized library services include interlibrary loans, database searching, Internet access, and Wi-Fi capability. Special learning facilities include an art gallery. **Physically Challenged Students:** All of the campus is accessible. Facilities include wheelchair ramps, elevators, special parking, specially equipped restrooms, special class scheduling, lowered drinking fountains, and lowered telephones. **Special:** Mount Marty offers co-op programs, internships, student-designed majors in selected studies, an accelerated degree program in business administration, credit for work, life, and military experience, and pass/fail options. There are 8 national honor societies, a freshman honors program, and 7 departmental honors programs. **Visiting:** There are regularly scheduled orientations for prospective students, including campus tours, faculty appointments, and admission and financial aid information. There are guides for informal visits, visitors may sit in on classes, and stay overnight. To schedule a visit, contact the Director of Admissions. **Campus Safety and Security:** Measures include 24-hour foot and vehicle patrol and security escort services. There are emergency telephones and lighted pathways/sidewalks.

REQUIREMENTS: The ACT is required. Applicants must be graduates of an accredited secondary school or have a GED certificate. An audition and an interview are recommended. AP and CLEP credits are accepted. To graduate, all students must complete at least 128 credit hours, with a minimum GPA of 2.0. General education requirements include 10 credit hours in religious studies/philosophy, 9 in humanities, 6 in English, 4 each in math, natural science, and lab science, and 3 in speech. **Procedure:** Freshmen are admitted fall, spring, and summer. Entrance exams should be taken by October of the senior year. There are deferred admissions and rolling admissions plans. Application deadlines are open. The fall 2016 application fee was $25. Notification is sent on a rolling basis. Applications are accepted on-line. **Transfer Students:** 60 transfer students enrolled in 2015-2016. Transfer students with fewer than 28 semester hours must submit high school and college transcripts. A minimum GPA of 2.0 and at least 64 credit hours are required. An interview is recommended. 32 of 128 credits required for the bachelor's degree must be completed at Mount Marty. **International Students:** There are 5 international students enrolled. The school actively recruits these students. They must take the TOEFL.

ADMISSIONS: The ACT scores were 10% below 12, 50% between 12 and 17, 30% between 18 and 23, 5% between 24 and 29, and 5% above 30. 10% of the current freshmen were in the top fifth of their class; 56% were in the top two fifths. 5 freshmen graduated first in their class. **Admissions Contact:** Jill Paulson, Director of Admissions. Email: *mmcadmit@mtmc.edu* Web: *www.mtmc.edu*

FINANCIAL AID: In 2016-2017, 99% of all full-time freshmen and 99% of continuing full-time students received some form of financial aid. 84% of all full-time freshmen and 84% of continuing full-time students received need-based aid. The average freshman award was $12,343. 60% of undergraduate students work part-time. Average annual earnings from campus work are $1500. The average financial indebtedness of the 2016 graduate was $17,407. The FAFSA code is 003465. The deadline for filing freshman financial aid applications for fall entry is March 1.

NORTHERN STATE UNIVERSITY — D-1

www.northern.edu

Aberdeen, SD 57401	(605) 626-2544 (800) 678-5330
Fax: (605) 626-2587	Email: admissions@northern.edu
Full-time: 666 men, 811 women	**Faculty:** 90
Part-time: 597 men, 927 women	**Ph.D.s:** 86%
Graduate: 121 men, 409 women	**Student/Faculty:** 21 to 1
Year: semesters, summer session	**Tuition:** $7563 ($10,042)
Room & Board: $6942	**Freshman Class:** 1379 applied, 1143 accepted, 363 enrolled
ACT: 22	**CEEB CODE:** 6487
Application Deadline: September 1	COMPETITIVE

Northern State University, established in 1901, is a state-supported institution offering undergraduate and graduate programs in the liberal arts and sciences, business, and education. Distance-delivery technology is a core mission in all programs, especially all levels of teacher preparation. There are 4 undergraduate schools and 1 graduate school. In addition to regional accreditation, NSU has baccalaureate program accreditation with NASM and NCATE. The 72-acre campus is in an urban area one-half mile south of Aberdeen's city center. Including any residence halls, there are 21 buildings.

STUDENT LIFE: 77% of undergraduates are from South Dakota. Others are from 41 states, 36 foreign countries, and Canada. 87% are White; 3% Hispanic; 2% African American; 2% American Indian/Alaska Native; 2% race unknown. **Female To Male Ratio:** 1.6:1. The average age of freshmen is 18; all undergraduates, 22. 30% do not continue beyond their first year; 70% remain to graduate. **Housing:** 850 students can be accommodated in college housing, which includes coed dorms, on-campus apartments, married student housing, and learning communities. On-campus housing is guaranteed for all 4 years. 59% of students commute. Alcohol is not permitted. All students may keep cars.

FACULTY/CLASSROOMS: 50% of faculty are male; 50% are female. All teach undergraduates, and all do research. No introductory courses are taught by graduate students. The average class size in an introductory lecture is 25 and in a laboratory is 18.

PROGRAMS OF STUDY: NSU confers B.A., B.S., B.M.E., B.G.S. and B.S.Ed. degrees. Associate and master's degrees are also awarded. Bachelor's degrees are awarded in BIOLOGICAL SCIENCE (biology/biological science), BUSINESS (accounting, banking and finance, business administration and management, business economics, international business management, marketing/retailing/merchandising, and personnel management), COMMUNICATIONS AND THE ARTS (English, fine arts, French, German, music, and Spanish), COMPUTER AND PHYSICAL SCIENCE (chemistry and mathematics), EDUCATION (art education, business education, early childhood education, elementary education, foreign languages education, health education, middle school education, music education, physical education, science education, secondary education, and special education), ENGINEERING AND ENVIRONMENTAL DESIGN (environmental science), HEALTH PROFESSIONS (medical laboratory technology, predentistry, premedicine, and speech pathology/audiology), SOCIAL SCIENCE (community services, criminal justice, economics, history, human services, physical fitness/movement, political science/government, prelaw, psychology, social science, and sociology). Business and education are the strongest academically.

ACTIVITIES: There are no fraternities or sororities. There are 100 groups on campus, including art, band, cheerleading, chess, choir, chorale, chorus, computers, dance, debate, drama, drill team, drum and bugle corps, environmental, ethnic, forensics, honors, international, jazz band, LGBT, literary magazine, marching band, musical theater, newspaper, orchestra, pep band, photography, political, professional, radio and TV, religious, social, social service, student government, and symphony. Popular campus events include Gypsy Day, Gypsy Week, and I Hate Winter Weekend. **Sports:** There are 6 intercollegiate sports for men and 7 for women, and 11 intramural sports for men and 11 for women. Facilities include a sports complex, football stadium and an all-weather track, a 160-meter track, an Olympic-size pool, weight room, 3 racquetball courts, human performance lab, 2 basketball courts, and arena. **Graduates:** From July 1, 2015 to June 30, 2016, 300 bachelor's degrees were awarded. The most popular majors were business (33%), education (20%), and social sciences (10%). 37 companies recruited on campus in 2015-2016. Of the 2015 graduating class, 33% were enrolled in graduate school within 6 months of graduation, and 99% were employed.

SERVICES: Counseling and information services are available, as is tutoring in most subjects. There is remedial math, reading, and writing. There is an educational media center, a math lab, reading and writing centers, an ASL interpreter for the deaf, and a speech, language, and hearing clinic. **Library/Resources:** The library contains 179,721 volumes, 381,874 microform items, and 10,092 audio/video tapes/CDs/DVDs, and subscribes to 45,379 periodicals including electronic. Computerized library services include interlibrary loans, database searching, Internet access, and Wi-Fi capability. Special learning facilities include an art gallery, radio station, TV station, and a fine arts center. **Physically Challenged Students:** 90% of the campus is accessible. Facilities include wheelchair ramps, elevators, special parking, specially equipped restrooms, lowered drinking fountains. **Special:** Opportunities are provided for internships, a Washington semester, work-study programs, a B.A.-B.S. degree, dual majors, a general studies degree, credit by exam, and nondegree study. Study abroad and a co-op program in international business are available. Technology proficiency certification is available with a diverse selection of certifications. There are 4 national honor societies, Phi Beta Kappa, a freshman honors program, and 4 departmental honors programs. **Visiting:** There are regularly scheduled orientations for prospective students, consisting of a welcome presentation, registration, refreshments, an academic visit, a campus tour, lunch, a financial aid presentation, a student panel, and a cost and scholarship presentation. There are guides for informal visits, visitors may sit in on classes, and stay overnight. To schedule a visit, contact the Admissions Office. **Campus Safety and Security:** Measures include emergency notification system, self-defense education, and security escort services. There are emergency telephones, lighted pathways/sidewalks, and controlled access to dorms/residences.

REQUIREMENTS: Minimum ACT composite score of 18 required, or students must earn a high school GPA of at least 2.6 on a 4.0 scale, or rank in the top 60% of their graduating class. Graduation from an accredited secondary school is required; a GED will be accepted. Applicants should submit a minimum academic record distributed as follows: 4 years of English, 3 each of math, science, and social studies, and one year of fine arts. A GPA of 2.0 is required. AP and CLEP credits are accepted. Important factors in the admissions decision are evidence of special talent, advanced placement or honors courses, and extracurricular activities record. Students must complete a minimum of 120 semester hours, with 27 to 36 in the major, and must maintain a 2.0 minimum GPA. The core curriculum consists of courses in English, history, fine arts, science, math, and psychology. In addition, there are specific course requirements. All students must pass a comprehensive exam. **Procedure:** Freshmen are admitted fall, spring, and summer. Entrance exams should be taken during the summer before the senior year. There are early admissions, deferred admissions, and rolling admissions plans. Applications should be filed by September 1 for fall entry, along with a $20 fee. Notification is sent on a rolling basis. **Transfer Students:** 119 transfer students enrolled in 2015-2016. Applicants must submit official transcripts from all previous colleges attended. D grades do not transfer. If the applicant has not maintained a C average, an ACT score that places the applicant in the upper 50% of college-bound freshmen may be submitted for consideration. 24 of 120 credits required for the bachelor's degree must be completed at NSU. **International Students:** There are 107 international students enrolled. The school actively recruits these students. They must take the TOEFL with a minimum score of 525 on the paper-based TOEFL (PBT) or 61 on the Internet-based version (iBT).

ADMISSIONS: 83% of the 2016-2017 applicants were accepted. The SAT scores for the 2016-2017 freshman class were: Critical Reading-- 58% below 500, 30% between 500 and 599, 8% between 600 and 699, and 4% between 700 and 800. Math-- 47% below 500, 38% between 500 and 599, 12% between 600 and 699, and 3% between 700 and 800. The ACT scores were 42% below 12, 26% between 12 and 17, 15% between 18 and 23, 14% between 24 and 29, and 3% above 30. **Admissions Contact:** JoEllen Lindner, VP Student Affairs & Enrollment Management. Email: *admissions@northern.edu* Web: *www.northern.edu*

FINANCIAL AID: In 2016-2017, 95% of all full-time freshmen and 90% of continuing full-time students received some form of financial aid. NSU is a member of CSS. The CCS/Profile, FAFSA, FFS, or SFS are required. The FAFSA code is 003466. The priority date for freshman financial aid applications for fall entry is March 1.

OGLALA LAKOTA COLLEGE *(The complete profile is made available exclusively on our website, www.barronspac.com)*

PRESENTATION COLLEGE *(The complete profile is made available exclusively on our website, www.barronspac.com)*

SINTE GLESKA UNIVERSITY *(The complete profile is made available exclusively on our website, www.barronspac.com)*

SOUTH DAKOTA SCHOOL OF MINES AND TECHNOLOGY — B-3

www.sdsmt.edu

Rapid City, SD 57701	**(605) 394-2414** **(877) 877-6044**
Fax: (605) 394-1979	**Email: admissions@sdsmt.edu**
Full-time: 1350 men, 370 women	**Faculty:** 143
Part-time: 223 men, 158 women	**Ph.D.s:** 88%
Graduate: 243 men, 80 women	**Student/Faculty:** 13 to 1
Year: semesters, summer session	**Tuition:** $11,493
Room & Board: $7152	**Freshman Class:** 1127 applied, 991 accepted, 454 enrolled
SAT CR/M/W: 560/600/500 **ACT:** 26	**CEEB CODE:** 6652
Application Deadline: August 15	**VERY COMPETITIVE**

South Dakota School of Mines and Technology, founded in 1885, is a public university offering undergraduate and graduate programs in engineering, science, and mathematics. Figures in the above capsule and in this profile are approximate. There is 1 undergraduate school and 1 graduate school. In addition to regional accreditation, SDSM&T has baccalaureate program accreditation with ABET, CSAB, and ACS. The 120-acre campus is in a suburban area 350 miles northeast of Denver, CO. Including any residence halls, there are 21 buildings.

STUDENT LIFE: 55% of undergraduates are from South Dakota. Others are from 45 states, 39 foreign countries, and Canada. 82% are White; 6% Foreign; 3% Hispanic; 3% two or more races; 2% American Indian/Alaska Native; 1% African American; 1% Asian American; 1% race unknown. **Male To Female Ratio:** 3.0:1. The average age of freshmen is 19; all undergraduates, 22. 20% do not continue beyond their first year; 55% remain to graduate. **Housing:** 671 students can be accommodated in college housing, which includes single-sex and coed dorms and off-campus apartments. In addition, there are fraternity houses and sorority houses. On-campus housing is available on a first-come, first-served basis. 67% of students commute. Alcohol is not permitted. All students may keep cars.

FACULTY/CLASSROOMS: 76% of faculty are male; 24% are female. All teach undergraduates, and 31% do research. Graduate students teach 4% of introductory courses. The average class size in an introductory lecture is 38; in a laboratory is 17; and in a regular course is 21.

PROGRAMS OF STUDY: SDSM&T confers B.S. degrees. Associate, master's, and doctoral degrees are also awarded. Bachelor's degrees are awarded in COMPUTER AND PHYSICAL SCIENCE (chemistry, computer science, geology, mathematics, and physics), ENGINEERING AND ENVIRONMENTAL DESIGN (chemical engineering, civil engineering, computer engineering, electrical/electronics engineering, environmental engineering, geological engineering, industrial engineering, mechanical engineering, metallurgical engineering, and mining and mineral engineering), SOCIAL SCIENCE (interdisciplinary studies). Engineering is the strongest academically. Mechanical engineering, civil engineering, and electrical engineering have the largest enrollments.

ACTIVITIES: 8% of men belong to 4 national fraternities; 9% of women belong to 2 national sororities. There are 135 groups on campus, including professional, ski club, biking, art, band, cheerleading, choir, chorale, chorus, circle k, computers, dance, drama, drill team, environmental, ethnic, film, honors, international, jazz band, LGBT, newspaper, orchestra, pep band, political, professional, radio and TV, religious, social, social service, and student government. Popular campus events include M-Week, Christmas Chorale Concert, International Cultural Exposition, and Engineers Week. **Sports:** There are 7 intercollegiate sports for men and 6 for women, and 10 intramural sports for men and 10 for women. Facilities include a football field, a track, a gym, a sand volleyball court, a swimming pool, squash/racquetball courts, weight room, and wellness center. **Graduates:** From July 1, 2015 to June 30, 2016, 376 bachelor's degrees were awarded. The most popular majors were mechanical engineering (15%), civil engineering (7%), and electrical engineering (6%). 176 companies recruited on campus in 2015-2016. In an average class, 20% graduate in 4 years or less, 46% graduate in 5 years or less, and 55% graduate in 6 years or less. Of the 2015 graduating class, 26% were enrolled in graduate school within 6 months of graduation, and 83% were employed.

SERVICES: Counseling and information services are available, as is tutoring in most subjects. There is a reader service for the blind, and remedial math. **Library/Resources:** The library contains 172,180 volumes, 18,958 microform items, and 10,357 audio/video tapes/CDs/DVDs, and subscribes to 7,364 periodicals including electronic. Computerized library services include interlibrary loans, database searching, Internet access, and Wi-Fi capability. Special learning facilities include an art gallery, natural history museum, planetarium, radio station, a Geology and Paleontology Museum, and a Apex Gallery. **Physically Challenged Students:** 81% of the campus is accessible. Facilities include wheelchair ramps, elevators, special parking, specially equipped restrooms, special class scheduling, lowered drinking fountains, and special housing. ADA lab with specialized workstations, software, and hardware to aid students with visual, auditory, and mobility impairments and dyslexia. **Special:** Opportunities are provided for study abroad, co-op programs, internships, dual degrees, undergraduate research experiences, interdisciplinary design teams, credit by exam, and nondegree study. There are 5 national honor societies and a chapter of Phi Beta Kappa. **Visiting:** There are regularly scheduled orientations for prospective students, including a campus tour, discussions, training, and a meal. There are guides for informal visits, visitors may sit in on classes, and stay overnight. To schedule a visit, contact the Admissions Office. **Campus Safety and Security:** Measures include 24-hour foot and vehicle patrol, emergency notification system, self-defense education, and security escort services. There are emergency telephones, lighted pathways/sidewalks, and controlled access to dorms/residences.

REQUIREMENTS: The SAT is accepted, the ACT is preferred, with a minimum composite score of 920 (420 critical reading/writing and 500 math) on the SAT, or a minimum composite score of 18 on the ACT. Graduation from an accredited secondary school is required. A GED is accepted. Applicants must submit high school credits, distributed as follows: 4 years of English, 3 each of math, lab science, and social studies, and 1/2 year each of fine arts and computer science. AP and CLEP credits are accepted. Students must complete 120 credits for the science major or 130 credits for the engineering major, and maintain a minimum GPA of 2.0. Included in these requirements are 16 credit hours each of math at a level of calculus and above, basic science, and humanities/social science (for engineering, 3 credits must be at the 300 or above level). State regents mandated distribution requirements include 6 credits each of written communications, social sciences, arts/humanities, science, and cultural diversity, 3 credits each of speech communications and math, and 2 credits of information technology literacy, plus completion of an exam. **Procedure:** Freshmen are admitted fall, spring, and summer. Entrance exams should be taken preferably in October and December. There is a rolling admissions plan. Application deadlines are open. The fall 2016 application fee was $20. Notification is sent on a rolling basis. Applications are accepted on-line. **Transfer Students:** 103 transfer students enrolled in 2015-2016. Transfer students must submit an official transcript from their high school or GED and their previous college(s)and must have maintained a minimum GPA 2.75 or higher. 30 of 130 credits required for the bachelor's degree must be completed at SDSM&T. **International Students:** There are 35 international students enrolled. The school actively recruits these students. They must take the TOEFL with a minimum score of 520 on the paper-based TOEFL (PBT) or 68 on the Internet-based version (iBT), or take the IELTS. They must also take the ACT. TOEFL's may be submitted in place of SAT or ACT's.

ADMISSIONS: 88% of the 2016-2017 applicants were accepted. The SAT scores for the 2016-2017 freshman class were: Critical Reading-- 31% below 500, 40% between 500 and 599, 22% between 600 and 699, and 7% between 700 and 800. Math-- 12% below 500, 40% between 500 and 599, 29% between 600 and 699, and 19% between 700 and 800. Writing-- 42% below 500, 40% between 500 and 599, 16% between 600 and 699, and 2% between 700 and 800. The ACT scores were 4% below 12, 17% between 12 and 17, 35% between 18 and 23, 20% between 24 and 29, and 24% above 30. 39% of the current freshmen were in the top fifth of their class; 65% were in the top two fifths. There were 6 National Merit finalists. 24 freshmen graduated first in their class. **Admissions Contact:** Office of Admissions Email: *admissions@sdsmt.edu* Web: *www.sdsmt.edu*

FINANCIAL AID: In 2016-2017, 60% of all full-time freshmen and 56% of continuing full-time students received some form of financial aid. 44% of all full-time freshmen and 34% of continuing full-time students received need-based aid. The average freshman award was $13,258. Need-based scholarships or need-based grants averaged $4,115; need-based self-help aid (loans and jobs) averaged $3,646; non-need-based athletic scholarships averaged $3,868; and other non-need-based awards and non-need-based scholarships averaged $2,799. 16% of undergraduate students work part-time. Average annual earnings from campus work are $1286. The average financial indebtedness of the 2016 graduate was $18,331. The FAFSA code is 003470. The deadline for filing freshman financial aid applications for fall entry is March 15.

SOUTH DAKOTA STATE UNIVERSITY F-3

www.sdstate.edu

Brookings, SD 57007 **(605) 688-4121**
(800) 952-3541

Fax: (605) 688-6891 **Email: sdsu.admissions@sdstate.edu**

Full-time: 4222 men, 4337 women	**Faculty:** n/av
Part-time: 915 men, 1533 women	**Ph.D.s:** 439%
Graduate: 720 men, 862 women	**Student/Faculty:** 17 to 1
Year: semesters, summer session	**Tuition:** $8172 ($11,053)
Room & Board: $7462	**Freshman Class:** 5060 applied, 4640 accepted, 2222 enrolled
ACT: required	**CEEB CODE:** 6653
Application Deadline: open	**COMPETITIVE**

South Dakota State University, founded in 1881, is a public land-grant institution. There are 9 undergraduate schools and one graduate school. In addition to regional accreditation, SDSU has baccalaureate program accreditation with ABET, ACCE, ACEJMC, NASM, ACEND, ASABE, ASBMB, AABI, CAATE, CoAES, CCNE, CIDA, CAEP, NAACLS, and SRM. The 261-acre campus is in a small town 50 miles north of Sioux Falls, 200 miles west of Minneapolis. Including any residence halls, there are 17 buildings.

STUDENT LIFE: Students are from 50 states, 81 foreign countries, and Canada. 88% are White; 4% Foreign; 2% African American; 2% Hispanic; 2% two or more races; 1% Asian American; 1% American Indian/Alaska Native. **Female To Male Ratio:** 1.1:1. **Housing:** 4359 students can be accommodated in college housing, which includes coed dorms, on-campus apartments, and married student housing. In addition, there are honors houses, special-interest houses, fraternity houses, sorority houses, and living learning communities. On-campus housing is available on a first-come, first-served basis. All students may keep cars.

FACULTY/CLASSROOMS: 50% of faculty are male; 50% are female. No introductory courses are taught by graduate students.

PROGRAMS OF STUDY: SDSU confers B.A., B.G.S., B.S., B.S.Ed., B.F.A., B.M.E., and B.L.A degrees. Associate, master's, and doctoral degrees are also awarded. Bachelor's degrees are awarded in AGRICULTURE (agricultural business management, agricultural communications, agricultural economics, agriculture, agronomy, animal science, dairy science, fish and game management, forestry and related sciences, horticulture, natural resource management, plant science, and range/farm management), BIOLOGICAL SCIENCE (biochemistry, biology/biological science, biotechnology, ecology, environmental biology, microbiology, nutrition, and wildlife biology), BUSINESS (apparel and accessories marketing, entrepreneurial studies, and hotel/motel and restaurant management), COMMUNICATIONS AND THE ARTS (art, communications, dramatic arts, English, German, graphic design, journalism, music, and Spanish), COMPUTER AND PHYSICAL SCIENCE (chemistry, computer science, geoscience, mathematics, physics, and software engineering), EDUCATION (agricultural education, art education, athletic training, early childhood education, education, health education, home economics education, music education, physical education, secondary education, technical education, and vocational education), ENGINEERING AND ENVIRONMENTAL DESIGN (agricultural engineering, agricultural engineering technology, architecture, aviation administration/management, aviation maintenance management, civil engineering, construction management, electrical/electronics engineering, electrical/electronics engineering technology, engineering, engineering physics, engineering technology, environmental engineering, industrial administration/management, interior design, landscape architecture/design, manufacturing technology, and mechanical engineering), HEALTH PROFESSIONS (clinical science, exercise science, medical laboratory science, nursing, pharmaceutical science, and pharmacy), SOCIAL SCIENCE (consumer services, early childhood studies, economics, family/consumer resource management, family/consumer studies, food production/management/services, food science, French studies, geography, history, human development, liberal arts/general studies, parks and recreation management, philosophy and religion, political science/government, psychology, rural sociology, safety management, and sociology).

ACTIVITIES: 4% of men belong to 8 national fraternities; 3% of women belong to 4 national sororities. There are 200 groups on campus, including water polo, bowling, cheer, cricket, frisbee, hockey, human-powered vehicle team, karate, rock climbing, rodeo, wrestling, art, badminton, band, cheerleading, chess, choir, chorale, chorus, computers, dance, debate, drama, drill team, environmental, ethnic, film, forensics, honors, international, jazz band, LGBT, literary magazine, marching band, musical theater, newspaper, opera, orchestra, pep band, photography, political, professional, radio and TV, religious, social, social service, student government, and symphony. Popular campus events include Little International, Engineering Exploration Days, Capers, Cavorts, and Hobo Days. **Sports:** There are 11 intercollegiate sports for men and 12 for women, and 16 intramural sports for men and 17 for women. Facilities include a physical education complex, an intramural building, outdoor track, lighted tennis courts, a wellness center, and intramural football and softball fields, soccer fields, and rugby fields. **Graduates:** From July 1, 2015 to June 30, 2016, 1910 bachelor's degrees were awarded. The most popular majors were health professions and related programs (24%), agriculture (15%), and social sciences (7%).

SERVICES: Counseling and information services are available, as is tutoring in most subjects, such as accounting, biology, chemistry, economics, physics, and history. There is a reader service for the blind, and remedial math, reading, and writing. **Library/Resources:** The library contains 956,114 volumes, 156,803 microform items, and 4,354 audio/video tapes/CDs/DVDs, and subscribes to 37,000 periodicals including electronic. Computerized library services include interlibrary loans, database searching, Internet access, and Wi-Fi capability. Special learning facilities include an art gallery, radio station, McCrory Gardens Education and Visitor Center which includes an Arboretum, Agricultural Heritage Museum, Northern Plains Biostress Laboratory, Animal Disease Research, and Diagnostic Laboratory. **Physically Challenged Students:** 99% of the campus is accessible. Facilities include wheelchair ramps, elevators, special parking, specially equipped restrooms, special class scheduling, lowered drinking fountains, lowered telephones, and special housing. All academic programs can be made accessible. **Special:** Co-op programs in elementary education and social work, internships, work-study programs, B.A.-B.S. degrees, and interdisciplinary majors including agricultural journalism, environmental management, and wildlife and fisheries science, are available. SDSU offers cross-registration with Dakota State University, Black Hills State University, the University of South Dakota, Northern State University and South Dakota School of Mines and Technology. Opportunities are provided for dual majors, study abroad in more than 50 countries, credit by examination, student-designed majors, credit for military experience, nondegree study, a general studies degree, and pass/fail options. There are 32 national honor societies and a freshman honors program. **Visiting:** There are regularly scheduled orientations for prospective students, and student orientation sessions which are offered each June. Students become acquainted with the university and student resources. They also meet with an academic adviser and register for fall semester classes. Information is sent to all admitted students. There are guides for informal visits, visitors may sit in on classes, and stay overnight. To schedule a visit, contact the Admissions Office at SDSU_Admissions@sdstate.edu.

Campus Safety and Security: Measures include 24-hour foot and vehicle patrol, emergency notification system, self-defense education, and security escort services. There are emergency telephones, lighted pathways/sidewalks, and controlled access to dorms/residences.

REQUIREMENTS: The ACT is required. Students must have an 18 ACT composite score, or be in the top 60% of their class, or have a 2.6 GPA in required classes. Graduation from an accredited secondary school is required. A GED will be accepted. Applicants must submit 4 years of English, 3 years of advanced math-algebra 1 and higher, 3 years of laboratory science, and 3 of social science, and 1 year of fine arts, and basic computer skills (students should have basic keyboarding, word processing, spreadsheet, and Internet skills) SDSU requires applicants to be in the upper 60% of their class. AP and CLEP credits are accepted. Important factors in the admissions decision are advanced placement or honors courses, evidence of special talent, and extracurricular activities record. Students must complete at least 120 semester credit hours for the baccalaureate degree (see individual professional college requirements) and 60 semester credit hours for the associate degree. Remedial course credits are not counted as meeting degree requirements. A Cumulative Grade Point Average (CGPA) of 2.0 required for grauduation. **Procedure:** Freshmen are admitted to all sessions. Entrance exams should be taken by spring of the junior year. There is a rolling admissions plan. Application deadlines are open. Application fee is $20. Notification is sent on a rolling basis. Applications are accepted on-line. **Transfer Students:** To be eligible for transfer, students must have been in good standing at the previous college and must have maintained a minimum GPA of 2.0 to 2.5, depending on the student's major. 30 of 120 credits required for the bachelor's degree must be completed at SDSU. **International Students:** The school actively recruits these students. They must take the TOEFL with a minimum score of 500 on the paper-based TOEFL (PBT) or 61 on the Internet-based version (iBT).

ADMISSIONS: 92% of the 2016-2017 applicants were accepted. The SAT scores for the 2016-2017 freshman class were: Critical Reading-- 60% below 500, 23% between 500 and 599, 14% between 600 and 699, and 3% between 700 and 800. Math-- 30% below 500, 46% between 500 and 599, 21% between 600 and 699, and 3% between 700 and 800. The ACT scores were 7% between 12 and 17, 47% between 18 and 23, 40% between 24 and 29, and 6% above 30. **Admissions Contact:** Tracy Welsh, Director. Email: *sdsu.admissions@sdstate.edu* Web: *www.sdstate.edu*

FINANCIAL AID: SDSU is a member of CSS. The FAFSA code is 003471. The priority date for freshman financial aid applications for fall entry is March 20.

UNIVERSITY OF SIOUX FALLS — F-3

www.usiouxfalls.edu

Sioux Falls, SD 57105 — **(605) 331-6600** / **(800) 888-1047**

Fax: (605) 331-6615	**Email: admissions@usiouxfalls.edu**
Full-time: 402 men, 603 women	**Faculty:** 60; IIB, --$
Part-time: 81 men, 99 women	**Ph.D.s:** 75%
Graduate: 93 men, 165 women	**Student/Faculty:** 14 to 1
Year: 4-1-4, summer session	**Tuition:** $27,160
Room & Board: $7140	**Freshman Class:** 1733 applied, 1596 accepted, 278 enrolled
SAT CR/M: 510/490 **ACT:** 23	**CEEB CODE:** 6651
Application Deadline: June 1	**COMPETITIVE**

University of Sioux Falls, founded in 1883, is a private liberal arts institution affiliated with the American Baptist Churches. It offers more than 40 undergraduate majors and on-line adult and graduate programs. In addition to regional accreditation, USF has baccalaureate program accreditation with CSWE and NCATE. The 40-acre campus is in a suburban area in Sioux Falls, 240 miles from Minneapolis/St. Paul, and 560 miles from Chicago, IL. Including any residence halls, there are 15 buildings.

STUDENT LIFE: 67% of undergraduates are from South Dakota. Others are from 28 states, 5 foreign countries, and Canada. 95% are from public schools. 94% are White; 2% African American; 1% Asian American; 1% American Indian/Alaska Native; 1% Hispanic; 1% Foreign. 42% are Luthern, Baptist, Methodist, Presbyterian, Evangelical, and reformed;

11% Catholic. **Female To Male Ratio:** 1.5:1. The average age of freshmen is 18; all undergraduates, 22. 32% do not continue beyond their first year; 68% remain to graduate. **Housing:** 350 students can be accommodated in college housing, which includes single-sex and coed dorms, on-campus apartments, and married student housing. On-campus housing is guaranteed for the freshman year only, and is available on a first-come, first-served basis, and is available on a lottery system for upperclassmen. Priority is given to out-of-town students. 53% of students commute. Alcohol is not permitted. All students may keep cars.

FACULTY/CLASSROOMS: 35% of faculty are male; 62% are female. All teach undergraduates, and 60% do research. No introductory courses are taught by graduate students. The average class size in an introductory lecture is 40; in a laboratory is 15; and in a regular course is 20.

PROGRAMS OF STUDY: USF confers B.A. and B.S. degrees. Associate and master's degrees are also awarded. Bachelor's degrees are awarded in BIOLOGICAL SCIENCE (biology/biological science), BUSINESS (accounting, business administration and management, business economics, and marketing/retailing/merchandising), COMMUNICATIONS AND THE ARTS (communications, English, fine arts, music, and speech/debate/rhetoric), COMPUTER AND PHYSICAL SCIENCE (chemistry, computer science, mathematics, and natural sciences), EDUCATION (art education, early childhood education, elementary education, middle school education, music education, science education, and secondary education), HEALTH PROFESSIONS (medical laboratory technology, nursing, and premedicine), SOCIAL SCIENCE (history, humanities, philosophy, political science/government, prelaw, psychology, religion, social science, social work, and sociology). Business, and elementary education are the strongest academically, and have the largest enrollment.

ACTIVITIES: There are no fraternities or sororities. There are 35 groups on campus, including art, band, cheerleading, choir, chorale, chorus, computers, dance, drama, ethnic, honors, international, jazz band, musical theater, newspaper, opera, orchestra, pep band, photography, political, professional, religious, social, social service, and student government. Popular campus events include Spring Formal and Madrigals. **Sports:** There are 9 intercollegiate sports for men and 9 for women. Facilities include a student lounge, 160-meter running track, volleyball, tennis, badminton, racquetball, and basketball courts, aerobics facilities, exercise machines, whirlpool, and a 700-seat gym. **Graduates:** From July 1, 2015 to June 30, 2016, 229 bachelor's degrees were awarded. Of the 2015 graduating class, 97% were employed within 6 months of graduation.

SERVICES: Counseling and information services are available, as is tutoring in most subjects. There is remedial math, reading, and writing. **Library/Resources:** The library contains 78,000 volumes, and 4,600 audio/video tapes/CDs/DVDs, and subscribes to 450 periodicals including electronic. Computerized library services include interlibrary loans and database searching. Special learning facilities include a TV station. **Physically Challenged Students:** 54% of the campus is accessible. Facilities include wheelchair ramps, elevators, special parking, specially equipped restrooms, special class scheduling, lowered drinking fountains, and lowered telephones. **Special:** There are co-op programs with Augustana College, the Center for Public Higher Education, Dakota State University, and the North American Baptist Seminary. USF offers internships, study abroad in Japan, Central America, and China, an American Studies Program in Washington, D.C., and a January interim. Also available are on-campus work-study programs, B.A.-B.S. degrees, dual and student-designed interdisciplinary majors, a general studies degree, a 3-2 engineering degree, credit for life and work experience, and pass/fail options. There are 3 national honor societies, a freshman honors program, and 2 departmental honors programs. **Visiting:** There are regularly scheduled orientations for prospective students, including meetings with faculty and staff, attendance at class, a campus tour, and a financial aid session. There are guides for informal visits, visitors may sit in on classes, and stay overnight. To schedule a visit, contact the Admissions Office. **Campus Safety and Security:** Measures include self-defense education and security escort services. There are emergency telephones and lighted pathways/sidewalks.

REQUIREMENTS: A minimum score for the critical reading and math section of the SAT is 1050 the ACT is 22. Applicants must be graduates of an accredited secondary school or have a GED certificate. Students should have completed 4 years of English, 3 years each of math and science with lab, 2 years of social studies, 2 years recommended of foreign language, and 3 years of academic electives. USF requires applicants to be in the upper 50% of their class. A GPA of 2.5 is required. AP and CLEP credits are accepted. Important factors in the admissions decision are advanced placement or honors courses, evidence of special talent, and leadership record. To graduate, all students must complete a minimum of 128 credit hours, with 64 hours in the major. Required courses include phys ed, computer science, religion, history, English, science, economics, political science, psychology, math, social science, cross-cultural experience, speech, and fine arts. A writing proficiency test and a minimum 2.0 GPA are also required. **Procedure:** Freshmen are admitted to all sessions. Entrance exams should be taken during the junior or senior year of high school. There are early admissions and rolling admissions plans. Application deadlines are open. Application fee is $25. Applications are accepted on-line. **Transfer Students:** 100 transfer students enrolled in 2015-2016. Transfer students must meet freshman admission requirements and have completed at least 24 hours of college courses with a minimum 2.0 GPA. The SAT or the ACT and an interview are recommended. Transfers may enroll in the fall, spring, and summer. 30 of 128 credits required for the bachelor's degree must be completed at USF. **International Students:** The school actively recruits these students. They must take the TOEFL. They must also take the ACT if the examination is available to the student.

ADMISSIONS: 92% of the 2016-2017 applicants were accepted. The SAT scores for the 2016-2017 freshman class were: Critical Reading-- 55% below 500, 40% between 500 and 599, and 5% between 600 and 699. Math-- 40% below 500, 50% between 500 and 599, and 10% between 600 and 699. The ACT scores were 5% between 12 and 17, 50% between 18 and 23, 40% between 24 and 29, and 5% above 30. There was 1 National Merit finalist. **Admissions Contact:** Ben Weins, Associate Director of Admissions. Email: *admissions@usiouxfalls.edu* Web: *www.usiouxfalls.edu*

FINANCIAL AID: In 2016-2017, 100% of all full-time freshmen received some form of financial aid. 100% of all full-time freshmen received need-based aid. The average freshman award was $19,904. Need-based scholarships or need-based grants averaged $15,411; need-based self-help aid (loans and jobs) averaged $4,456; non-need-based athletic scholarships averaged $4,315; other non-need-based awards and non-need-based scholarships averaged $14,012; and $12,361 from other forms of aid. USF is a member of CSS. The FFS and CCS/Profile, or FAFSA, or SFS are required. The FAFSA code is 003469. The priority date for freshman financial aid applications for fall entry is March 1.

UNIVERSITY OF SOUTH DAKOTA F-4

www.usd.edu

Vermillion, SD 57069	**(605) 677-5434** **(877) COYOTES**
Fax: (605) 677-6323	**Email: admission@usd.edu**
Full-time: 1927 men, 2805 women	**Faculty:** 383
Part-time: 895 men, 2006 women	**Ph.D.s:** 85%
Graduate: 1125 men, 1477 women	**Student/Faculty:** 17 to 1
Year: semesters, summer session	**Tuition:** $8938 ($11,336)
Room & Board: $7171	**Freshman Class:** 3606 applied, 3469 accepted, 1342 enrolled
SAT CR/M: 509/527 **ACT:** 23	**CEEB CODE:** 6681
Application Deadline: open	**COMPETITIVE**

University of South Dakota, founded in 1862, is a public institution with undergraduate programs in arts and sciences, education, fine arts, business, and health sciences and professional schools of law, medicine, audiology and physcial therapy. Figures in the above capsule and in this profile are approximate. There are 6 undergraduate schools and 7 graduate schools. In addition to regional accreditation, USD has baccalaureate program accreditation with AACSB, APTA, CSWE, NASAD, NASM, NCATE, and NLN. The 284-acre campus is in a small town between Sioux City, Iowa, and Sioux Falls. Including any residence halls, there are 69 buildings.

STUDENT LIFE: 69% of undergraduates are from South Dakota. Others are from 48 states, 27 foreign countries, and Canada. 86% are White; 3% Hispanic; 3% two or more races; 2% African American; 2% American Indian/Alaska Native; 1% Asian American; 1% Foreign; 1% race unknown. **Female To Male Ratio:** 1.6:1. The average age of freshmen is 18; all undergraduates, 22. 25% do not continue beyond their first year; 56% remain to graduate. **Housing:** 2218 students can be accommodated in college housing, which includes single-sex and coed dorms, on-campus apartments, and married student housing. In addition, there are fraternity houses and sorority houses. On-campus housing is guaranteed for the freshman year only, is available on a first-come, first-served basis. 72% of students commute. Alcohol is not permitted. All students may keep cars.

FACULTY/CLASSROOMS: 50% of faculty are male; 50% are female. 95% teach undergraduates, and 95% do research. Graduate students teach 8% of introductory courses. The average class size in an introductory lecture is 29; in a laboratory is 19; and in a regular course is 23.

PROGRAMS OF STUDY: USD confers B.A., B.S., B.B.A., B.F.A., B.G.S., B.M., B.S.Ed, B.S.N., and B.S.R. degrees. Associate, master's, and doctoral degrees are also awarded. Bachelor's degrees are awarded in BIOLOGICAL SCIENCE (biology/biological science), BUSINESS (accounting, banking and finance, finance, human resources, management science, recreation and leisure services, and sports management), COMMUNICATIONS AND THE ARTS (art, communication studies, communications technology, dramatic arts, English, German, journalism, media management, music, music performance, Spanish, and theatre studies), COMPUTER AND PHYSICAL SCIENCE (chemistry, computer science, earth science, mathematics, and physics), EDUCATION (art education, education, elementary education, journalism education, music education, physical education, secondary education, and special education), HEALTH PROFESSIONS (dental hygiene, exercise science, health care administration, health science, medical technology, nursing, and speech pathology/audiology), SOCIAL SCIENCE (addiction studies, American Indian studies, anthropology, criminal justice, economics, French studies, history, international studies, liberal arts/general studies, philosophy, political science/government, psychology, social work, sociology, and women & gender studies). Business, biology, and chemistry are the strongest academically. Business, psychology, and biology have the largest enrollments.

ACTIVITIES: 18% of men belong to 7 national fraternities; 11% of women belong to 8 national sororities. There are 140 groups on campus, including art, band, cheerleading, chess, choir, chorale, chorus, computers, dance, debate, drama, drill team, ethnic, forensics, honors, international, jazz band, LGBT, literary magazine, marching band, musical theater, newspaper, opera, orchestra, pep band, photography, political, professional, radio and TV, religious, social, social service, student government, and symphony. Popular campus events include Dakota Days, Strollers (a variety production), and Rockfest. **Sports:** There are 7 intercollegiate sports for men and 10 for women, and 12 intramural sports for men and 12 for women. Facilities include a Wellness Center, an indoor football field, 5 basketball courts, a 25-meter swimming pool, an 8-lane, 200-meter track, a fitness center, a fitness room, batting cages, and racquetball, volleyball, and tennis courts. Outdoor areas include a softball complex, soccer fields, flag football fields, and tennis courts. **Graduates:** From July 1, 2015 to June 30, 2016, 1055 bachelor's degrees were awarded. The most popular majors were health professions (21%), business/marketing (15%), and education (11%). 72 companies recruited on campus in 2015-2016. In an average class, 2% graduate in 3 years or less, 32% graduate in 4 years or less, 50% graduate in 5 years or less, and 56% graduate in 6 years or less. Of the 2015 graduating class, 30% were enrolled in graduate school within 6 months of graduation, and 60% were employed.

SERVICES: Counseling and information services are available, as is tutoring in most subjects. There is a reader service for the blind, and remedial math, reading, and writing. There is an academic advising and testing center. **Library/Resources:** The library contains 863,292 volumes, 740,454 microform items, and 15,185 audio/video tapes/CDs/DVDs, and subscribes to 64,575 periodicals including electronic. Computerized library services include interlibrary loans, database searching, Internet access, and Wi-Fi capability. Special learning facilities include an art gallery, natural history museum, radio station, TV station, music museum, historical study center, institutes of American Indian studies, social science research, child welfare training, business and governmental research bureaus, centers for speech and hearing, international studies, fine arts, and telecommunications, natural sciences field station, and archeology and human factors labs. **Physically Challenged Students:** 95% of the campus is accessible. Facilities include wheelchair ramps, elevators, special parking, specially equipped restrooms, special class scheduling, lowered drinking fountains, and lowered telephones. **Special:** USD offers internships, study abroad in 7 countries, and work-study programs. B.A.-B.S. degrees in 34 majors, a student-designed liberal studies major, dual majors, nondegree study, and pass/fail options are available. The Arts Outreach program provides arts activities and noncredit classes. There are 16 national honor societies, Phi Beta Kappa, a freshman honors program, and 19 departmental honors programs. **Visiting:** There are regularly scheduled orientations for prospective students, student visits include an introductory session with an admission counselor, academic department visits, a campus tour with a student guide, and any other requested units. There are guides for informal visits, visitors may sit in on classes, and stay overnight. **Campus Safety and Security:** Measures include 24-hour foot and vehicle patrol, emergency notification system, self-defense education, and security escort services. There are shuttle buses, emergency telephones, and lighted pathways/sidewalks.

REQUIREMENTS: The ACT is required. Applicants must have earned a 2.0 GPA in 4 years of English, 3 years each of lab science, math, and social studies, and 2 semesters of fine arts. They must also rank in the top 60% of their graduation class, have an ACT score of 18, or have a high school GPA of 2.6. AP and CLEP credits are accepted. Students must complete 132 hours with a minimum GPA of 2.0. At least 32 hours must be at the 300/400 level. All students should complete 9 hours of interdisciplinary course-work, 6 hours each in composition, humanities, social science, natural science, and multicultural diversity, 1 hour each in fine arts, and a computer literacy course. **Procedure:** Freshmen are admitted fall, spring, and summer. There are deferred admissions and rolling admissions plans. Application deadlines are open. Application fee is $20. Applications are accepted on-line. **Transfer Students:** 635 transfer students enrolled in 2015-2016. Applicants should have a minimum college GPA of 2.0 and be in good standing at their previous school. 32 of 130 credits required for the bachelor's degree must be completed at USD. **International Students:** There are 91 international students enrolled. The school actively recruits these students. They must take the TOEFL with a minimum score of 550 on the paper-based TOEFL (PBT).

ADMISSIONS: 96% of the 2016-2017 applicants were accepted. The SAT scores for the 2016-2017 freshman class were: Critical Reading-- 46% below 500, 34% between 500 and 599, 18% between 600 and 699, and 2% between 700 and 800. Math-- 39% below 500, 32% between 500 and 599, 25% between 600 and 699, and 4% between 700 and 800. The ACT scores were 24% below 12, 31% between 12 and 17, 26% between 18 and 23, 11% between 24 and 29, and 8% above 30. 31% of the current freshmen were in the top fifth of their class; 60% were in the top two fifths. 66 freshmen graduated first in their class. **Admissions Contact:** Travis Vlasman, Dean of Enrollment. Email: *admission@usd.edu* Web: *www.usd.edu*

FINANCIAL AID: In 2016-2017, 95% of all full-time freshmen and 88% of continuing full-time students received some form of financial aid. 59% of all full-time freshmen and 62% of continuing full-time students received need-based aid. The average freshman award was $10,479. Need-based scholarships or need-based grants averaged $1,389 ($14,150 maximum); need-based self-help aid (loans and jobs) averaged $2,148 ($10,150 maximum); non-need-based athletic scholarships averaged $609 ($18,818 maximum); and other non-need-based awards and non-need-based scholarships averaged $2,992 ($19,856 maximum). 15% of undergraduate students work part-time. The average financial indebtedness of the 2016 graduate was $26,629. The FAFSA code is 003474. The priority date for freshman financial aid applications for fall entry is March 15.

TENNESSEE

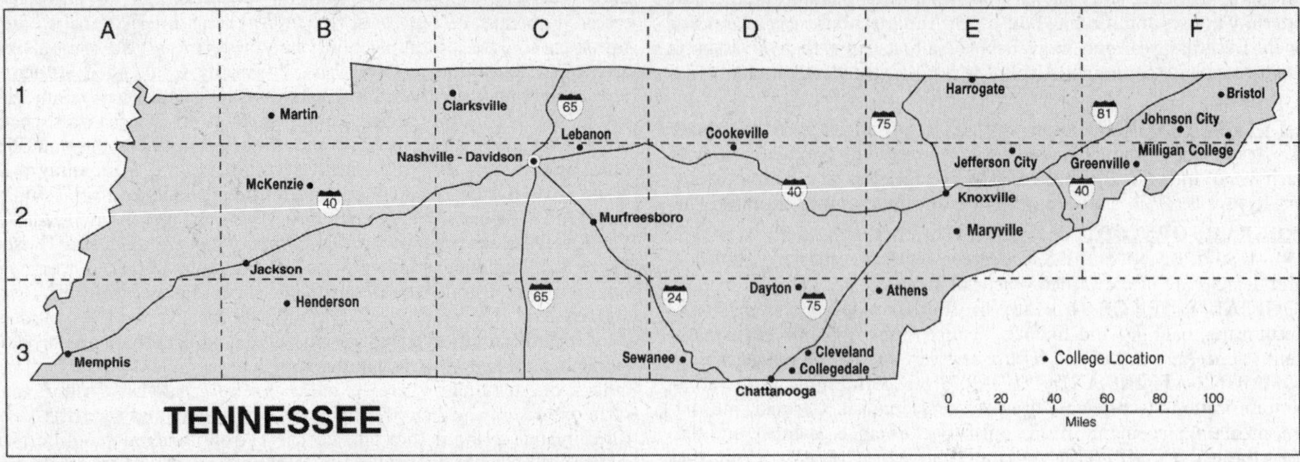

AQUINAS COLLEGE C-2

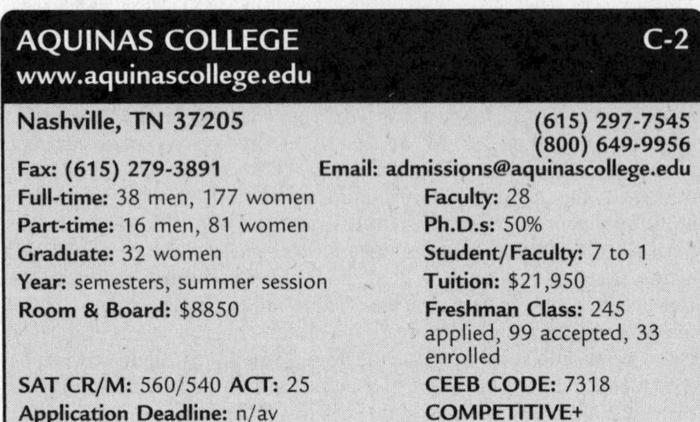

www.aquinascollege.edu

Nashville, TN 37205	**(615) 297-7545** **(800) 649-9956**
Fax: (615) 279-3891	**Email: admissions@aquinascollege.edu**
Full-time: 38 men, 177 women	**Faculty:** 28
Part-time: 16 men, 81 women	**Ph.D.s:** 50%
Graduate: 32 women	**Student/Faculty:** 7 to 1
Year: semesters, summer session	**Tuition:** $21,950
Room & Board: $8850	**Freshman Class:** 245 applied, 99 accepted, 33 enrolled
SAT CR/M: 560/540 **ACT:** 25	**CEEB CODE:** 7318
Application Deadline: n/av	**COMPETITIVE+**

Aquinas College is a Catholic community of learning in the Dominican Tradition with Christ at its center. The College directs all its efforts to the intellectual, moral, spiritual, and professional formation of the human person in wisdom. Students are formed individually and in Christian community so that the harmonious integration between faith and reason can permeate every dimension of their lives. Immersed in exploring the relationship between human civilization and the message of salvation, the college community embraces the Dominican imperative to preach the Gospel, serve others, and engage culture in truth and charity. There are 4 undergraduate schools. In addition to regional accreditation, has baccalaureate program accreditation with ACEN. The 83-acre campus is in an urban area in the western section of metropolitan Nashville, four miles from downtown. Including any residence halls, there are 8 buildings.

STUDENT LIFE: 67% of undergraduates are from Tennessee. Others are from 29 states, 6 foreign countries, and Canada. 76% are White; 6% African American; 4% Hispanic; 4% Foreign; 4% two or more races; 4% race unknown; 2% Asian American; 1% American Indian/Alaska Native. 60% are Catholic. **Female To Male Ratio:** 5.4:1. The average age of freshmen is 18; all undergraduates, 25. 17% do not continue beyond their first year; 83% remain to graduate. **Housing:** 190 students can be accommodated in college housing, which includes single-sex dorms. On-campus housing is guaranteed for the freshman year only, and is available on a first-come, and first-served basis. Priority is given to out-of-town students. 78% of students commute. All students may keep cars. Alcohol is not permitted.

FACULTY/CLASSROOMS: 31% of faculty are male; 69% are female. All teach undergraduates. No introductory courses are taught by graduate students. The average class size in an introductory lecture is 12; in a laboratory is 8; and in a regular course is 12.

PROGRAMS OF STUDY: Aquinas confers B.A., B.B.A., B.S. and B.S.N. degrees. Associate and master's degrees are also awarded. Bachelor's degrees are awarded in BUSINESS (business administration and management, finance, and marketing management), COMMUNICATIONS AND THE ARTS (English), COMPUTER AND PHYSICAL SCIENCE (mathematics), EDUCATION (elementary education and secondary education), HEALTH PROFESSIONS (nursing), SOCIAL SCIENCE (history, interdisciplinary studies, liberal arts/general studies, philosophy, psychology, and theological studies). Nursing, education, and management have the largest enrollments.

ACTIVITIES: There are no fraternities or sororities. There are 11 groups on campus, including Synaxis of St. John, Socratic club, house life, literary magazine, professional, religious, social, and social service. Popular campus events include House Competitions and Lectures, Fall Fest, Spring Fling, and St. Thomas Aquinas Day. **Sports:** There is no sports program at Aquinas. Facilities include softball, basketball, tennis and volleyball. Students frequently initiate House competitions, including Capture the Flag and other less-formalized sporting activities. **Graduates:** From July 1, 2015 to June 30, 2016, 25 bachelor's degrees were awarded. The most popular majors were nursing (48%), education (20%), and English (12%).

SERVICES: Counseling and information services are available, as is tutoring in some subjects, such as nursing, theology, philosophy, math, writing, and biology. There is remedial math and writing. Write Reason writing center is available to all students for assistance with writing assignments for any course. **Library/Resources:** The library contains 129,919 volumes, 140,602 microform items, 2,251 audio/video tapes/CDs/DVDs, and subscribes to 18,724 periodicals including electronic. Computerized library services include interlibrary loans, database searching, Internet access, and Wi-Fi capability. **Physically Challenged Students:** 75% of the campus is accessible. Facilities include wheelchair ramps, special parking, specially equipped restrooms, special class scheduling, and lowered drinking fountains. **Special:** The RN-BSN program is offered in an accelerated format. Also, students of the School of Business must complete an internship as a component of their program of study. A study abroad program (in Bracciano, Italy) is also available. There are 3 national honor societies. **Visiting:** There are regularly scheduled orientations for prospective students, including campus tours and information on admissions, financial aid, student life, and degree programs. There are guides for informal visits and visitors may sit in on classes. To schedule a visit, contact Connie Hansom at admissions@aquinascollege.edu. **Campus Safety and Security:** Measures include 24-hour foot and vehicle patrol, emergency notification system, self-defense education, security escort services, lighted pathways/sidewalks, and controlled access to dorms/residences.

REQUIREMENTS: The SAT or ACT is required. The GED is accepted. A GPA of 2.4 is required. AP and CLEP credits are accepted. Courses in theology and philosophy are required in every undergraduate curriculum. **Procedure:** Freshmen are admitted to all sessions. There is a rolling admissions plan. Application deadlines are open. Application fees are waived if application is completed online. **Transfer Students:** 84 transfer students enrolled in 2015-2016. Transfer applicants must have a 2.4 GPA in previous college work. Transfer students with less than 30 semester hours of college-level course work must also submit their high school transcripts and SAT/ACT scores. 30 of 120 credits required for the bachelor's degree must be completed at Aquinas. **International Students:** There are 11 international students enrolled. They must take the TOEFL with a minimum score of 80 on the Internet-based version (iBT), International English Language Testing System (IELTS). They must also take the SAT or ACT, scoring 21.

ADMISSIONS: 40% of the 2016-2017 applicants were accepted. The

SAT scores for the 2016-2017 freshman class were: Critical Reading-- 21% below 500, 42% between 500 and 599, 16% between 600 and 699, and 21% between 700 and 800. Math-- 26% below 500, 37% between 500 and 599, 32% between 600 and 699, and 5% between 700 and 800. The ACT scores were 48% between 18 and 23, 39% between 24 and 29, and 13% above 30. **Admissions Contact:** Connie Hansom, Director of Admissions. Email: *admissions@aquinascollege.edu* Web: *www.aquinascollege.edu*

FINANCIAL AID: Aquinas is a member of CSS. The FAFSA code is 003477. The deadline for filing freshman financial aid applications for fall entry is February 15.

AUSTIN PEAY STATE UNIVERSITY C-1

www.apsu.edu

Clarksville, TN 37044	**(931) 221-7661** **(800) 844-2778**
Fax: (931) 221-6168	**Email: admissions@apsu.edu**
Full-time: 2834 men, 4122 women	**Faculty:** 370; IIA, --$
Part-time: 1166 men, 1391 women	**Ph.D.s:** n/av
Graduate: 242 men, 589 women	**Student/Faculty:** 18 to 1
Year: semesters, summer session	**Tuition:** $7689 ($22,929)
Room & Board: $8708	**Freshman Class:** 6272 applied, 5570 accepted, 1963 enrolled
ACT: 22	**CEEB CODE:** 1028
Application Deadline: August 8	**COMPETITIVE**

Austin Peay State University, established in 1927, is a public institution offering undergraduate degrees in the liberal arts and sciences and professional preparation. Figures in the above capsule and in this profile are aproximate. There are 6 undergraduate schools and 1 graduate school. In addition to regional accreditation, APSU has baccalaureate program accreditation with ABET, CSWE, NASAD, NASM, NCATE, NLN, ACS, NAACLS, and JRCERT. The 182-acre campus is in an urban area 47 miles from Nashville. Including any residence halls, there are 82 buildings.

STUDENT LIFE: 89% of undergraduates are from Tennessee. Others are from 43 states, 17 foreign countries, and Canada. 62% are White; 6% Hispanic; 6% two or more races; 3% race unknown; 21% African American; 2% Asian American. **Female To Male Ratio:** 1.4:1. The average age of freshmen is 19; all undergraduates, 24. 29% do not continue beyond their first year; 39% remain to graduate. **Housing:** 1817 students can be accommodated in college housing, which includes single-sex and coed dorms, on-campus apartments, married student housing, and honors houses. On-campus housing is available on a first-come and first-served basis. 83% of students commute. All students may keep cars. Alcohol is not permitted.

FACULTY/CLASSROOMS: 45% of faculty are male; 55% are female. All teach undergraduates. No introductory courses are taught by graduate students. The average class size in an introductory lecture is 24; in a laboratory is 20; and in a regular course is 19.

PROGRAMS OF STUDY: APSU confers B.A., B.S., B.B.A., B.F.A., B.P.S., and B.S.N. degrees. Associate and master's degrees are also awarded. Bachelor's degrees are awarded in AGRICULTURE (agriculture), BIOLOGICAL SCIENCE (biology/biological science), BUSINESS (accounting, business administration and management, finance, marketing, and professional studies), COMMUNICATIONS AND THE ARTS (art, communications, English, foreign language, languages, music, and theatre/dance), COMPUTER AND PHYSICAL SCIENCE (chemistry, computer science, geoscience, mathematics, physics, and radiological technology), EDUCATION (general studies, health education, and special education), ENGINEERING AND ENVIRONMENTAL DESIGN (engineering technology), HEALTH PROFESSIONS (medical laboratory science, nursing, and radiological science), SOCIAL SCIENCE (criminal justice, history, interdisciplinary studies, liberal arts/general studies, philosophy and religion, political science/government, psychology, public administration, social work, and sociology). Biology, nursing, and physics are the strongest academically. Business, health & human performance, and nursing have the largest enrollments.

ACTIVITIES: 8% of men belong to 11 national fraternities; 9% of women belong to 9 national sororities. There are 182 groups on campus, including art, band, cheerleading, choir, chorus, debate, drama, ethnic, honors, international, jazz band, LGBT, literary magazine, marching band, newspaper, orchestra, pep band, political, professional, radio and TV, religious, social, social service, student government, and yearbook. Popular campus events include Graduation, Parents Day and Mud Bowl. **Sports:** There are 6 intercollegiate sports for men and 9 for women, and 14 intramural sports for men and 14 for women. Facilities include the recreation complex which houses multipurpose courts, fully-enclosed racquetball courts, an indoor track, climbing area, fitness studios, indoor cycling studio, fitness center and outdoor recreation fields. **Graduates:** From July 1, 2015 to June 30, 2016, 1558 bachelor's degrees were awarded. The most popular majors were health and human performance (13%), general business (11%), and nursing (8%). In an average class, 3% graduate in 3 years or less, 19% graduate in 4 years or less, 35% graduate in 5 years or less, and 39% graduate in 6 years or less.

SERVICES: Counseling and information services are available, as is tutoring in some subjects, such as sciences, math, English, and history. There is also a reader service for the blind, as well as help with academic, learning, and test-taking problems. **Library/Resources:** The library contains 219,393 volumes, 668,958 microform items, 7,378 audio/video tapes/CDs/DVDs, and subscribes to 54,392 periodicals including electronic. Computerized library services include interlibrary loans, database searching, and Internet access. Special learning facilities include an art gallery, radio station, and TV station. **Physically Challenged Students:** 90% of the campus is accessible. Facilities include wheelchair ramps, elevators, special parking, specially equipped restrooms, special class scheduling, lowered drinking fountains, and lowered telephones. **Special:** APSU offers cooperative programs in nuclear medicine with Vanderbilt University and a pre-engineering (2-year transfer) program in which a student will earn a degree in physics and an engineering degree from one of Tennessee's colleges of engineering. Credit may be granted for military experience. Pass/fail grading options and work-study programs are available. There are 20 national honor societies and a freshman honors program. **Visiting:** There are regularly scheduled orientations for prospective students, as are guides for informal visits. To schedule a visit, contact the Admissions Office. **Campus Safety and Security:** Measures include 24-hour foot and vehicle patrol, emergency notification system, self-defense education, and security escort services. There are also shuttle buses, emergency telephones, lighted pathways/sidewalks, and controlled access to dorms/residences.

REQUIREMENTS: Applicants must be graduates of an accredited secondary school or have a GED. 14 academic units are required, including 4 units of English, 3 units of mathematics, 2 units each of natural/physical science, and a foreign language, and 1 unit each of visual and/or performing arts, social studies, and U.S. history. Applicants who do not meet these requirements may be considered for admission. A GPA of 2.8 is required. AP and CLEP credits are accepted. To graduate, students must earn a minimum of 120 semester hours, of which 39 hours are in upper division courses, earn a cumulative GPA of 2.0, complete a Common General Education Core, and complete the First Year Experience Course. **Procedure:** Freshmen are admitted in the fall, spring, and summer. There is a rolling admissions plan. Applications should be filed by August 8 for fall entry; December 14 for spring entry; and May 21 for summer entry. The fall 2016 application fee was $25. Applications are accepted online. **Transfer Students:** 913 transfer students enrolled in 2015-2016. Applicants must have a 2.0 GPA and be in good standing with the last institution attended. Grades of D or better will be considered for credit. Application deadlines are the same as those for freshmen. Transfer students having attended only non-regionally accredited institutions are considered new students. 30 of 120 credits required for the bachelor's degree must be completed at APSU. **International Students:** There are 40 international students enrolled. They must take the TOEFL with a minimum score of 500 on the paper-based TOEFL (PBT) or 61 on the Internet-based version (iBT).

ADMISSIONS: 89% of the 2016-2017 applicants were accepted. The SAT scores for the 2016-2017 freshman class were: The ACT scores were 12% between 12 and 17, 61% between 18 and 23, 24% between 24 and 29, and 3% above 30. 29% of the current freshmen were in the top fifth of their class; 57% were in the top two fifths. **Admissions Contact:** Amy Corlew, Director of Admissions. Email: *admissions@apsu.edu* Web: *www.apsu.edu*

FINANCIAL AID: In 2016-2017, 99% of all full-time freshmen and 97% of continuing full-time students received some form of financial aid. 65% of all full-time freshmen and 75% of continuing full-time students received need-based aid. The FAFSA code is 003478. The priority date for freshman financial aid applications for fall entry is October 1. The filing deadline for fall entry is August 8.

BELMONT UNIVERSITY C-2

www.belmont.edu

Nashville, TN 37212 | (615) 460-6785 | (800) 56E-NROL

Fax: (615) 460-5434 | Email: buadmission@belmont.edu

Full-time: 2143 men, 3496 women	**Faculty:** 302; IIA, +$
Part-time: 144 men, 200 women	**Ph.D.s:** 87%
Graduate: 485 men, 882 women	**Student/Faculty:** 14 to 1
Year: semesters, summer session	**Tuition:** $30,000
Room & Board: $10,970	**Freshman Class:** 6145 applied, 4934 accepted, 1387 enrolled
SAT CR/M: 580/570 **ACT:** 26	**CEEB CODE:** 1058
Application Deadline: August 1	**VERY COMPETITIVE**

Belmont University, founded in 1890, is a private, Christian liberal arts university. Figures in the above capsule and in this profile are approximate. There are 7 undergraduate schools and 6 graduate schools. In addition to regional accreditation, Belmont has baccalaureate program accreditation with AACSB, ABET, CSWE, NASAD, NASM, NCATE, NLN, MACTE, and NASAD. The 69-acre campus is in an urban area in Nashville, TN. Including any residence halls, there are 37 buildings.

STUDENT LIFE: 69% of undergraduates are from out of state, mostly the South. Students are from 50 states, 30 foreign countries, and Canada. 80% are White; 5% African American; 5% Hispanic; 4% race unknown; 3% two or more races; 2% Asian American; 1% Foreign. **Female To Male Ratio:** 1.7:1. The average age of freshmen is 18; all undergraduates, 21. 17% do not continue beyond their first year; 69% remain to graduate. **Housing:** College-sponsored housing includes single-sex dorms and on-campus apartments. On-campus housing is guaranteed for the freshman year only, and is available on a first-come, and first-served basis. 55% of students live on campus. All students may keep cars. Alcohol is not permitted.

FACULTY/CLASSROOMS: 49% of faculty are male; 51% are female. No introductory courses are taught by graduate students. The average class size in a regular course is 20.

PROGRAMS OF STUDY: Belmont confers B.A., B.S., B.B.A., B.F.A., B.M., B.S.W., and B.S.N. degrees. Master's and doctoral degrees are also awarded. Bachelor's degrees are awarded in BIOLOGICAL SCIENCE (biochemistry, biology/biological science, environmental biology, and neurosciences), BUSINESS (accounting, business administration and management, entrepreneurial studies, finance, international business management, international economics, management science, and marketing/retailing/merchandising), COMMUNICATIONS AND THE ARTS (art history, art/art studies, audio technology, church music, communications, design, English, French, German, journalism, multimedia, music, music business management, music performance, music theory and composition, musical theater, public relations, Spanish, studio art, theatre arts, theater design, and visual and performing arts), COMPUTER AND PHYSICAL SCIENCE (applied mathematics, chemistry, computer science, mathematics, medical physics, physics, and web technology), EDUCATION (art education, early childhood education, elementary education, middle school education, and physical education), ENGINEERING AND ENVIRONMENTAL DESIGN (engineering physics), HEALTH PROFESSIONS (exercise science, medical technology, nursing, and pharmaceutical science), SOCIAL SCIENCE (Asian/Oriental studies, biblical languages, biblical studies, Christian studies, economics, food production/management/services, history, liberal arts/general studies, ministries, philosophy, political science/government, psychology, religion, social work, and sociology). Music, business, and humanities are the strongest academically. Music business management, nursing, and audio engineering technology have the largest enrollments.

ACTIVITIES: There are 73 groups on campus, including art, band, cheerleading, choir, chorale, chorus, computers, dance, debate, drama, environmental, ethnic, film, forensics, honors, international, jazz band, LGBT, literary magazine, marching band, musical theater, newspaper, orchestra, pep band, photography, political, professional, radio and TV, religious, social, social service, student government, and symphony. **Sports:** There are 7 intercollegiate sports for men and 7 for women, and 8 intramural sports for men and 8 for women. Facilities include an arena with basketball courts, an athletic training facility, and golf course. The E.S. Rose Park allows the University to lease space for athletics. **Graduates:** From July 1, 2015 to June 30, 2016, 1285 bachelor's degrees were awarded. The most popular majors were music business, nursing, and audion engineering technology. 113 companies recruited on campus in 2015-2016. In an average class, 58% graduate in 4 years or less, 69% graduate in 5 years or less, and 69% graduate in 6 years or less. Of the 2015 graduating class, 8% were enrolled in graduate school within 6 months of graduation, and 92% were employed.

SERVICES: Counseling and information services are available, as is tutoring in some subjects, and writing and computer labs. **Library/Resources:** The 2 libraries contain 232,140 volumes, 29,999 microform items, 34,506 audio/video tapes/CDs/DVDs, and subscribe to 788 periodicals including electronic. Computerized library services include interlibrary loans, database searching, and Internet access. Special learning facilities include an art gallery, radio station, TV station, including a 19th century antebellum mansion. **Physically Challenged Students:** 98% of the campus is accessible. Facilities include wheelchair ramps, elevators, special parking, specially equipped restrooms, special class scheduling, and lowered drinking fountains. **Special:** Belmont offers study abroad, student-designed majors, and dual majors in math, physics, and chemistry. Dual degree programs are available with Auburn University and the University of Tennessee at Knoxville. Programs require 3 years of study at Belmont followed by 2 years at the other institution. There are 11 national honor societies, a freshman honors program, and 1 departmental honors program. **Visiting:** There are regularly scheduled orientations for prospective students, consisting of a 2-day program in summer and a 4-day program right before classes begin. There are guides for informal visits, visitors may sit in on classes, and stay overnight. To schedule a visit, contact the Admissions Office at buadmissions@belmont.edu. **Campus Safety and Security:** Measures include 24-hour foot and vehicle patrol, emergency notification system, self-defense education, and security escort services. There are also shuttle buses, emergency telephones, lighted pathways/sidewalks, and controlled access to dorms/residences.

REQUIREMENTS: The university expects a composite score of at least 21 on the ACT and 1000 on the SAT. Applicants should be high school graduates or hold the GED. Secondary preparation should include 4 units of English, 3 of math, and 2 each of a foreign language, history, science, and social studies. Potential music majors must audition. AP and CLEP credits are accepted. Important factors in the admissions decision are advanced placement or honors courses, recommendations by school officials, and evidence of special talent. All students must complete at least 128 hours with a C average, including 22 to 24 hours in the major field. B.A. candidates are required to pursue a minor field. All programs except the B.B.A. require a core curriculum, which includes courses in language and literature, humanities (including religion), social sciences, science, math, and phys ed. **Procedure:** Freshmen are admitted in the fall, spring, and summer. Entrance exams should be taken during the junior or senior year. There are early admissions and rolling admissions plans. Applications should be filed by August 1 for fall entry; December 1 for spring entry, along with a $50 fee. Notification is sent on a rolling basis. Applications are accepted online. **Transfer Students:** 466 transfer students enrolled in 2015-2016. Applicants should present an above average GPA in previous college work and be able to meet freshman entrance requirements. Those with fewer than 64 credit hours must also submit SAT or ACT scores. 32 of 128 credits required for the bachelor's degree must be completed at Belmont. **International Students:** There are 73 international students enrolled. The school actively recruits these students. They must take the TOEFL with a minimum score of 550 on the paper-based TOEFL (PBT) or 80 on the Internet-based version (iBT).

ADMISSIONS: 80% of the 2016-2017 applicants were accepted. The SAT scores for the 2016-2017 freshman class were: Critical Reading-- 13% below 500, 47% between 500 and 599, 34% between 600 and 699, and 6% between 700 and 800. Math-- 18% below 500, 46% between 500 and 599, 31% between 600 and 699, and 5% between 700 and 800. The ACT scores were 29% between 18 and 23, 54% between 24 and 29, and 17% above 30. 58% of the current freshmen were in the top fifth of their class; 89% were in the top two fifths. **Admissions Contact:** Angela Sheed, Director, Institutional Research. Email: *buadmission@belmont.edu* Web: *www.belmont.edu*

FINANCIAL AID: 70% of all full-time freshmen and 70% of continuing full-time students received need-based aid. The average financial indebtedness of the 2016 graduate was $28,477. The FAFSA code is 003479. The deadline for filing freshman financial aid applications for fall entry is March 1.

BETHEL UNIVERSITY B-2
www.bethelu.edu

McKenzie, TN 38201 (731) 352-4030

Fax: (731) 352-4069 Email: undergraqd-admission@bethel.edu

Full-time: 738 men, 996 women	**Faculty:** 80
Part-time: 147 men, 351 women	**Ph.D.s:** 35%
Graduate: 190 men, 309 women	**Student/Faculty:** 16 to 1
Year: semesters, summer session	**Tuition:** $24,738
Room & Board: n/app	**Freshman Class:** 598 applied, 317 accepted, 198 enrolled
	CEEB CODE: 1063
Application Deadline: August 30	**COMPETITIVE**

Bethel University, established in 1842, is a private institution affiliated with the Cumberland Presbyterian Church. The three colleges of Bethel University offer undergraduate degrees through a variety of traditional and nontraditional programs. The figures in the above capsule and in this profile are approximate. There are 3 undergraduate schools and 1 graduate school. The 100-acre campus is in a small town in McKenzie, Tenn, and 120 miles northeast of Memphis. Including any residence halls, there are 18 buildings.

STUDENT LIFE: 89% of undergraduates are from Tennessee. Others are from 26 states, 25 foreign countries, and Canada. 99% are from public schools. 49% are White; 33% African American; 2% Foreign; 1% Hispanic. 72% are Protestant. **Female To Male Ratio:** 1.5:1. The average age of freshmen is 26; all undergraduates, 31. 38% do not continue beyond their first year; 37% remain to graduate. **Housing:** 530 students can be accommodated in college housing, which includes single-sex and coed dorms and on-campus apartments. On-campus housing is available on a first-come and first-served basis. 75% of students commute. All students may keep cars. Alcohol is not permitted.

FACULTY/CLASSROOMS: 54% of faculty are male; 46% are female. All teach undergraduates. No introductory courses are taught by graduate students. The average class size in an introductory lecture is 25; in a laboratory is 15; and in a regular course is 12.

PROGRAMS OF STUDY: Bethel confers B.A., B.S., and B.S.N. degrees. Master's degrees are also awarded. Bachelor's degrees are awarded in BIOLOGICAL SCIENCE (biology/biological science), BUSINESS (business administration and management and management science), COMMUNICATIONS AND THE ARTS (English, music, music business management, and theater management), COMPUTER AND PHYSICAL SCIENCE (chemistry and mathematics), EDUCATION (education of the exceptional child, music education, and physical education), HEALTH PROFESSIONS (nursing and premedicine), SOCIAL SCIENCE (child psychology/development, history, human services, psychology, and sociology). Education, physicians assistant studies, and nursing are the strongest academically. Education, and organizational management have the largest enrollments.

ACTIVITIES: 25% of men belong to 5 local fraternities; 25% of women belong to 5 local sororities. There are 25 groups on campus, including art, band, cheerleading, choir, chorale, chorus, drama, honors, marching band, musical theater, pep band, political, professional, religious, social, social service, student government, and yearbook. **Sports:** There are 12 intercollegiate sports for men and 12 for women, and 9 intramural sports for men and 8 for women. Facilities include a gym with a indoor pool, weight room, field house, health and fitness complex, football, soccer, tennis courts, track, and baseball fields. **Graduates:** From July 1, 2015 to June 30, 2016, 388 bachelor's degrees were awarded. The most popular majors were management and organizational development (66%), business management (14%), and nursing (9%). In an average class, 16% graduate in 3 years or less, 35% graduate in 4 years or less, 37% graduate in 5 years or less, and 37% graduate in 6 years or less.

SERVICES: Counseling and information services are available, as is tutoring in every subject, and remedial math, reading, and writing. Tutoring is available free of charge to students. **Library/Resources:** The library contains 79,164 volumes, 185 microform items, 2,166 audio/video tapes/CDs/DVDs, and subscribes to 1,208 periodicals including electronic. Computerized library services include interlibrary loans, database searching, Internet access, and Wi-Fi capability. **Physically Challenged Students:** 75% of the campus is accessible. Facilities include wheelchair ramps, elevators, special parking, specially equipped restrooms, special class scheduling, and lowered drinking fountains. **Special:** Bethel offers evening classes for adults, in-service training for teachers, off-site classes, an accelerated degree program in organizational management, student-designed majors, internships, work-study, non-degree study, a pass/fail option, and portfolio credit for prior learning and work experience. There is 1 national honor society, a freshman honors program, and 11 departmental honors programs. **Visiting:** There are regularly scheduled orientations for prospective students, including about the college, dorms, and the lap-top program; they meet advisers, register for classes, and meet with the financial aid and business office. There are guides for informal visits, visitors may sit in on classes, and stay overnight. To schedule a visit, contact the Admissions Office. **Campus Safety and Security:** Measures include 24-hour foot and vehicle patrol, self-defense education, security escort services, lighted pathways/sidewalks, controlled access to dorms/residences, and security cameras in some buildings.

REQUIREMENTS: Applicants must graduate from an accredited secondary school. Those ranking in the upper half of their class or scoring a satisfactory score on the SAT or ACT are granted regular acceptance. Other applicants may be admitted conditionally. Other factors in the admission procedure are standardized test scores, an interview, evidence of special talent, and personality. Open admission is available for the nontraditional bachelor of science in the Management and Organizational Development program. Admission for all other programs is competitive. Bethel requires applicants to be in the upper 50% of their class. A GPA of 2.0 is required. AP and CLEP credits are accepted. Important factors in the admissions decision are advanced placement or honors courses, leadership record, and evidence of special talent. Requirements for graduation include courses in English, history, lab science, math, phys ed, and religion. Students must complete 128 to 132 hours with a minimum GPA of 2.0. A thesis is required in some majors. **Procedure:** Freshmen are admitted to all sessions. Entrance exams should be taken prior to enrollment, preferably by fall of the senior year. There is a rolling admissions plan. Applications should be filed by August 30 for fall entry; January 10 for spring entry; and June 5 for summer entry, along with a $30 fee. Notification is sent on a rolling basis. Applications are accepted on-line. **Transfer Students:** 56 transfer students enrolled in 2015-2016. Applicants must meet the GPA requirements for the number of hours they previously earned. Up to 68 hours may be transferred from community or junior colleges. Students with fewer than 12 semester hours must submit high school transcripts and ACT or SAT scores. 32 of 128 credits required for the bachelor's degree must be completed at Bethel. **International Students:** There are 55 international students enrolled. The school actively recruits these students. They must also take the SAT or ACT, scoring 860.

ADMISSIONS: 53% of the 2016-2017 applicants were accepted. **Admissions Contact:** Bret Hyder, Director of Admissions. Email: *undergraqd-admission@bethel.edu* Web: *www.bethelu.edu*

FINANCIAL AID: In 2016-2017, 95% of all full-time freshmen and 90% of continuing full-time students received some form of financial aid. 67% of all full-time freshmen and 51% of continuing full-time students received need-based aid. 14% of undergraduate students work part-time. Average annual earnings from campus work are $1187. The college's own financial statement is required. The FAFSA code is 003480. The deadline for filing freshman financial aid applications for fall entry is March 15.

BRYAN COLLEGE D-3
www.bryan.edu

Dayton, TN 37321 (423) 939-9574 (800) 277-9522

Fax: (423) 775-7199 Email: info@bryan.edu

Full-time: 453 men, 521 women	**Faculty:** n/av
Part-time: 17 men, 20 women	**Ph.D.s:** 81%
Graduate: 48 men, 24 women	**Student/Faculty:** 14 to 1
Year: semesters, summer session	**Tuition:** $24,450
Room & Board: $6990	**Freshman Class:** 459 applied, 344 accepted, 192 enrolled
SAT or ACT: required	**CEEB CODE:** 1908
Application Deadline: open	**COMPETITIVE**

Bryan College, founded in 1930, is a private, Christian institution that is evangelical and interdenominational. Its emphases are on the liberal arts, business, health science, fine arts, Bible and religious studies, music, and teacher preparation. Figures in the above capsule and in this profile are approximate. There is 1 undergraduate school and 1 graduate school. The 128-acre campus is in a small town in Dayton, Tenn., 35 minutes north of Chattanooga. Including any residence halls, there are 28 buildings.

STUDENT LIFE: 55% of undergraduates are from out of state, mostly the South. Students are from 41 states, 9 foreign countries, and Canada. 89% are White; 4% African American; 2% Hispanic; 2% Foreign; 1% Asian American. 99% are Protestant. **Female To Male Ratio:** 1.1:1. The average age of freshmen is 18; all undergraduates, 20. 24% do not continue beyond their first year; 56% remain to graduate. **Housing:** 615 students can be accommodated in college housing, which includes single-sex dorms and married student housing. On-campus housing is guaranteed for all 4 years. 58% of students live on campus; of those, 75% remain on campus on weekends. Alcohol is not permitted. All students may keep cars.

FACULTY/CLASSROOMS: 81% of faculty are male; 18% are female. All teach undergraduates. No introductory courses are taught by graduate students. The average class size in an introductory lecture is 27; in a laboratory is 13; and in a regular course is 16.

PROGRAMS OF STUDY: Bryan confers B.A. and B.S. degrees. Associate and master's degrees are also awarded. Bachelor's degrees are awarded in BIOLOGICAL SCIENCE (biology/biological science), BUSINESS (business administration and management), COMMUNICATIONS AND THE ARTS (communications, creative writing, English, music, Spanish, and theatre arts), COMPUTER AND PHYSICAL SCIENCE (computer science and mathematics), EDUCATION (elementary education, physical education, and science education), HEALTH PROFESSIONS (exercise science), SOCIAL SCIENCE (Christian studies, history, liberal arts/general studies, psychology, and religion). Communication studies, and business administration have the largest enrollments.

ACTIVITIES: There are no fraternities or sororities. There are 17 groups on campus, including art, choir, chorale, computers, drama, honors, international, literary magazine, musical theater, newspaper, orchestra, pep band, photography, religious, social, social service, student government, and yearbook. Popular campus events include Fine Arts Series. **Sports:** There are 3 intercollegiate sports for men and 4 for women, and 6 intramural sports for men and 6 for women. Facilities include a gym, soccer fields, baseball field, outdoor swimming pool, and tennis courts. **Graduates:** From July 1, 2015 to June 30, 2016, 213 bachelor's degrees were awarded. The most popular majors were business/marketing (56%), communication/journalism (15%), and education (5%). In an average class, 45% graduate in 4 years or less, 52% graduate in 5 years or less, and 53% graduate in 6 years or less.

SERVICES: Counseling and information services are available, as is tutoring in some subjects, and remedial math, reading, and writing. **Library/Resources:** The library contains 150,000 volumes, 13,489 microform items, 3,015 audio/video tapes/CDs/DVDs, and subscribes to 10,000 periodicals including electronic. Computerized library services include interlibrary loans, database searching, Internet access, and Wi-Fi capability. **Physically Challenged Students:** All of the campus is accessible. Facilities include wheelchair ramps, elevators, special parking, specially equipped restrooms, and lowered drinking fountains. **Special:** Special academic programs include practicum's in business and psychology, and psychology internships. An American Studies Program in Washington and a study-abroad Latin American Studies Program are offered through the Christian College Coalition. There is a freshman honors program. **Visiting:** There are regularly scheduled orientations for prospective students, consisting of college visitation weekends, which include a tour of the campus, sitting in on classes and chapel, meeting with professors in the area of academic interest, staying with current students in residence halls, and eating meals in the dining room. There are guides for informal visits, visitors may sit in on classes, and stay overnight. **Campus Safety and Security:** Measures include self-defense education, security escort services, and lighted pathways/sidewalks.

REQUIREMENTS: The SAT or ACT and the ACT Optional Writing test are required. Clear admission is granted to applicants who have graduated from an approved high school and who have a minimum GPA of 2.5 with a minimum composite score of 18 on the ACT or 860 on the SAT; clear admission is also granted to applicants with a minimum GPA of 2.0 and a composite score of 20 on the ACT or 920 on the SAT. The high school record should include a minimum of 18 academic credits with a recommended distribution of 4 units of English, 3 each of math, science, and social science/humanities, and 2 of a foreign language. The GED is also accepted. References are required, and an interview is recommended. AP and CLEP credits are accepted. To graduate, students must complete 124 semester hours, with a minimum of 30 in the major, and maintain a GPA of at least 2.0. Distributions requirements include 16 semester hours in Bible, 9 in communications, 7 each in personal development and natural science, and 6 each in the humanities and social science. Specific courses that must be taken include 7 semester hours in science, 6 hours each in freshman English, foreign language, and history of Western civilization, and 3 each in speech, general psychology, introduction to literature, fine arts, and phys ed. In addition, math and English proficiency must be met, and a comprehensive exam in the major is also required. **Procedure:** Freshmen are admitted in the fall and spring. Entrance exams should be taken before the fall of the senior year in high school. There are deferred admissions and rolling admissions plans. Application deadlines are open. Application fee is $30. Applications are accepted on-line. **Transfer Students:** 59 transfer students enrolled in 2015-2016. Applicants need a minimum GPA of 2.0. Transcripts and test scores must be submitted as well as a personal statement or essay. 30 of 124 credits required for the bachelor's degree must be completed at Bryan. **International Students:** There are 9 international students enrolled. They must take the TOEFL, as well as the SAT or ACT.

ADMISSIONS: 75% of the 2016-2017 applicants were accepted. **Admissions Contact:** Joshua Hood, Director of Admissions. Email: *info@bryan.edu* Web: *www.bryan.edu*

FINANCIAL AID: In 2016-2017, 95% of all full-time freshmen received some form of financial aid. 95% of all full-time freshmen received need-based aid. The average freshman award was $17,870. Need-based scholarships or need-based grants averaged $11,374; need-based self-help aid (loans and jobs) averaged $3,734; non-need-based athletic scholarships averaged $6,699; and other non-need-based awards and non-need-based scholarships averaged $5,307. 55% of undergraduate students work part-time. Average annual earnings from campus work are $1500. The average financial indebtedness of the 2016 graduate was $14,976. The college's own financial statement is required. The FAFSA code is 003536. The priority date for freshman financial aid applications for fall entry is February 15.

CARSON-NEWMAN UNIVERSITY — E-2

www.cn.edu

Jefferson City, TN 37760	**(865) 471-3223** **(800) 678-9061**
Fax: (865) 471-4817	**Email: admitme@cn.edu**
Full-time: 735 men, 838 women	**Faculty:** IIB
Part-time: 33 men, 40 women	**Ph.D.s:** 77%
Graduate: 105 men, 216 women	**Student/Faculty:** 12 to 1
Year: semesters, summer session	**Tuition:** $26,360
Room & Board: $7800	**Freshman Class:** 2917 applied, 1913 accepted, 453 enrolled
SAT CR/M: 455/520 **ACT:** 23	**CEEB CODE:** 1102
Application Deadline: August 1	**COMPETITIVE**

Carson-Newman, founded in 1851, is a private liberal arts college affiliated with the Tennessee Baptist Convention. Figures in the above capsule and in this profile are approximate. There is 1 undergraduate school and 2 graduate schools. In addition to regional accreditation, Carson-Newman has baccalaureate program accreditation with ADA, AHEA, NASAD, NASM, NCATE, and NLN. The 100-acre campus is in a small town 27 miles northeast of Knoxville, TN. Including any residence halls, there are 27 buildings.

STUDENT LIFE: 86% of undergraduates are from Tennessee. Others are from 29 states, 17 foreign countries, and Canada. 92% are from public schools. 81% are White; 3% Foreign; 2% Hispanic; 2% two or more races; 2% race unknown; 10% African American. 84% are Protestant. **Female To Male Ratio:** 1.3:1. The average age of freshmen is 18; all undergraduates, 22. 25% do not continue beyond their first year; 60% remain to graduate. **Housing:** 1430 students can be accommodated in college housing, which includes single-sex dorms, on-campus apartments, married student housing, and honors houses. On-campus housing is guaranteed for all 4 years. 50% of students commute. All students may keep cars. Alcohol is not permitted

FACULTY/CLASSROOMS: 53% of faculty are male; 47% are female. All teach undergraduates, and 40% do research. No introductory courses are taught by graduate students. The average class size in an introductory lecture is 25; in a laboratory is 16; and in a regular course is 17.

PROGRAMS OF STUDY: Carson-Newman confers B.A., B.S., B.M., B.S.M. and B.S.N. degrees. Associate and master's degrees are also awarded. Bachelor's degrees are awarded in BIOLOGICAL SCIENCE (biology/biological science), BUSINESS (accounting, business administration and management, and business economics), COMMUNICATIONS AND THE ARTS (communications, English, fine arts, French, languages, music, and Spanish), EDUCATION (art education, early childhood education, elementary education, foreign languages education, health education, home economics education, middle school education, music education, science education, and secondary education), HEALTH PROFESSIONS (nursing and physical therapy), SOCIAL SCIENCE (economics, history, philosophy, psychology, religion, social science, and sociology). Nursing, music, and biology are the strongest academically. Nursing, business, and education have the largest enrollments.

ACTIVITIES: 20% of men belong to 2 local and 1 national fraternities; 20% of women belong to 2 local and 1 national sororities. There are 55 groups on campus, including art, band, cheerleading, chess, choir, chorale, chorus, computers, dance, debate, drama, drill team, ethnic, film, forensics, honors, international, jazz band, literary magazine, marching band, musical theater, newspaper, orchestra, pep band, photography, political, professional, radio and TV, religious, social, social service, student government, and yearbook. Popular campus events include Spring Fest, Fall Formal, and Honors Convocation. **Sports:** There are 9 intercollegiate sports for men and 8 for women, and 40 intramural sports for men and 40 for women. Facilities include a football stadium, soccer, baseball, softball, and intramural fields, a pool and a student center with racquetball courts, gyms, a weight room, and pool. **Graduates:** From July 1, 2015 to June 30, 2016, 340 bachelor's degrees were awarded. The most popular majors were education (22%), health professions and related programs (18%), and business/marketing (18%). In an average class, 41% graduate in 4 years or less, 54% graduate in 5 years or less, and 55% graduate in 6 years or less.

SERVICES: Counseling and information services are available, as is tutoring in most subjects, and remedial math, reading, and writing. **Library/Resources:** The library contains 300,000 volumes, 221,960 microform items, 15,000 audio/video tapes/CDs/DVDs, and subscribes to 2,000 periodicals including electronic. Computerized library services include interlibrary loans, database searching, and Internet access. Special learning facilities include an art gallery, natural history museum, radio station, and TV station. **Physically Challenged Students:** 10% of the campus is accessible. Facilities include wheelchair ramps, elevators, special parking, and special class scheduling. **Special:** The college offers internships, study in England, France, Japan, Hong Kong, and Spain, a Washington semester, on-campus work-study programs, B.A.-B.S. degrees, dual majors, a general studies degree, student-designed majors, and pass/fail options. Students may receive credit for life, military, or work experience. There is 1 national honor society, a freshman honors program, and 16 departmental honors programs. **Visiting:** There are regularly scheduled orientations for prospective students, including information sessions, meetings with advisers, and preregistration. There are guides for informal visits, visitors may sit in on classes, and stay overnight. To schedule a visit, contact the Admissions Office. **Campus Safety and Security:** Measures include 24-hour foot and vehicle patrol, self-defense education, security escort services, and lighted pathways/sidewalks.

REQUIREMENTS: Students must have a minimum composite score of 19 on the ACT or a satisfactory score on the SAT. Applicants should be graduates of an accredited secondary school. The GED is accepted. 20 academic credits are required, including 4 units of English and 2 units each of history, math, science, and social studies. An essay, a portfolio, an audition, and an interview are recommended. AP and CLEP credits are accepted. Important factors in the admissions decision are advanced placement or honors courses, leadership record, and parents or siblings attended your school. All students must complete 128 credit hours, including Composition I and II, Survey of Old Testament, Survey of New Testament, 15 hours in English and communications, 9 in social sciences, 6 each in religion, humanities, and science, and 3 each in history, literature, and math. The major requires 40 to 48 hours. Students must achieve a minimum GPA of 2.0. **Procedure:** Freshmen are admitted to all sessions. Entrance exams should be taken in the fall of the senior year or the spring of the junior year. There are deferred admissions and rolling admissions plans. Applications should be filed by August 1 for fall entry; December 15 for spring entry; and April 15 for summer entry, along with a $25 fee. Applications are accepted on-line. **Transfer Students:** 102 transfer students enrolled in 2015-2016. Transfer students should have a minimum GPA of 2.0. Either the SAT or the ACT is required if the student has fewer than 32 hours of college credit. An interview is recommended. 32 of 128 credits required for the bachelor's degree must be completed at Carson-Newman. **International Students:** There are 55 international students enrolled. The school actively recruits these students. They must take the TOEFL, or score 4 on the APIEL, and must also take English proficiency and math placement exams.

ADMISSIONS: 66% of the 2016-2017 applicants were accepted. The ACT scores were 35% below 12, 30% between 12 and 17, 20% between 18 and 23, 7% between 24 and 29, and 8% above 30. There were 3 National Merit finalists. 10 freshmen graduated first in their class. **Admissions Contact:** Kate Amburn, Assistant Director of Admissions. Email: *kamburn@cn.edu* Web: *www.cn.edu*

FINANCIAL AID: Carson-Newman is a member of CSS. The college's own financial statement is required. The FAFSA code is 003481. The deadline for filing freshman financial aid applications for fall entry is March 1.

CHRISTIAN BROTHERS UNIVERSITY A-3

www.cbu.edu

Memphis, TN 38104	**(901) 321-4208** **(800) 288-7576**
Fax: (901) 321-3202	**Email: admissions@cbu.edu**
Full-time: 564 men, 631 women	**Faculty:** 94
Part-time: 52 men, 104 women	**Ph.D.s:** 87%
Graduate: 222 men, 255 women	**Student/Faculty:** 13 to 1
Year: semesters, summer session	**Tuition:** $28,600
Room & Board: $3070	**Freshman Class:** 1853 applied, 889 accepted, 290 enrolled
ACT: 25	**CEEB CODE:** 1121
Application Deadline: August 1	**VERY COMPETITIVE**

Christian Brothers University, founded in 1871, is a private Catholic university providing undergraduate educational opportunities in the arts, business, engineering, the sciences, and teacher education, and specialized graduate programs. There are 4 undergraduate schools and 4 graduate schools. In addition to regional accreditation, CBU has baccalaureate program accreditation with ABET, NCATE, and CCNE. The 75-acre campus is in an urban area in Memphis, about 4 miles east of downtown. Including any residence halls, there are 23 buildings.

STUDENT LIFE: 79% of undergraduates are from Tennessee. Others are from 23 states, 26 foreign countries, and Canada. 70% are from public schools. 5% are Asian American; 48% White; 30% African American; 2% Hispanic; 2% Foreign. 50% are Protestant; 41% Buddhist, Muslim and unknown; 29% claim no religious affiliation; 21% Catholic. **Female To Male Ratio:** 1.2:1. The average age of freshmen is 18; all undergraduates, 23. 26% do not continue beyond their first year; 56% remain to graduate. **Housing:** 576 students can be accommodated in college housing, which includes single-sex and coed dorms, on-campus apartments, quiet floors in residence halls, and a living/learning community dorm. On-campus housing is available on a first-come, first-served basis, and on a lottery system for upperclassmen. Priority is given to out-of-town students. 67% of students live on campus; of those, 50% remain on campus on weekends. All students may keep cars.

FACULTY/CLASSROOMS: 56% of faculty are male; 44% are female. 83% teach undergraduates. No introductory courses are taught by graduate students. The average class size in an introductory lecture is 17; in a laboratory is 12; and in a regular course is 17.

PROGRAMS OF STUDY: CBU confers B.A., B.F.A., and B.S. degrees. Master's degrees are also awarded. Bachelor's degrees are awarded in BIOLOGICAL SCIENCE (biochemistry and biology/biological science), BUSINESS (accounting and business administration and management), COMMUNICATIONS AND THE ARTS (English and studio art), COMPUTER AND PHYSICAL SCIENCE (chemistry, computer science, mathematics, natural sciences, and physics), EDUCATION (early childhood education and special education), ENGINEERING AND ENVI-

RONMENTAL DESIGN (chemical engineering, civil engineering, electrical/electronics engineering, engineering management, engineering physics, and mechanical engineering), HEALTH PROFESSIONS (biomedical science), SOCIAL SCIENCE (applied psychology, history, liberal arts/general studies, philosophy and religion, and psychology). Engineering, and biology are the strongest academically. Psychology, business, and electrical have the largest enrollments.

ACTIVITIES: 25% of men belong to 5 national fraternities; 19% of women belong to 6 national sororities. There are 37 groups on campus, including art, chess, chorale, chorus, computers, drama, ethnic, honors, international, LGBT, literary magazine, musical theater, political, professional, religious, social, social service, student government, and yearbook. Popular campus events include Bacchus, Sofapalooza, and Up Til Dawn. **Sports:** There are 5 intercollegiate sports for men and 6 for women, and 10 intramural sports for men and 10 for women. Facilities include a swimming pool, gym, batting cage, jogging track, basketball/volleyball and handball/racquetball courts, baseball and soccer fields, tennis courts, cross-country, and weight-training facilities. **Graduates:** From July 1, 2015 to June 30, 2016, 257 bachelor's degrees were awarded. The most popular majors were business (41%), psychology (15%), and engineering (15%). In an average class, 39% graduate in 4 years or less, 54% graduate in 5 years or less, and 55% graduate in 6 years or less.

SERVICES: Counseling and information services are available, as is tutoring in most subjects, and centers for math and writing. **Library/Resources:** The library contains 165,796 volumes, 61,523 microform items, and 2,004 audio/video tapes/CDs/DVDs. Computerized library services include interlibrary loans, database searching, Internet access, and Wi-Fi capability. Special learning facilities include an art gallery. **Physically Challenged Students:** 90% of the campus is accessible. Facilities include wheelchair ramps, elevators, special parking, specially equipped restrooms, lowered drinking fountains, and lowered telephones. **Special:** Special academic programs include on-campus work-study, study abroad in 4 countries, and internships for all juniors and seniors. There is cross-registration with the Greater Memphis Consortium, Rhodes College, and the University of Memphis. An accelerated degree program is available to all business and psychology majors through the professional studies program, and a general studies degree is offered. Up to 36 hours of nondegree study is possible, as are dual majors, an honors program, and pass/fail options. Numerous teacher licensure programs are also offered. There are 9 national honor societies and a freshman honors program. **Visiting:** There are regularly scheduled orientations for prospective students, including attendance at classes, meetings with professors and students, a campus tour, and meetings with admissions and financial aid representatives. There are guides for informal visits, visitors may sit in on classes, and stay overnight. To schedule a visit, contact the Dean of Admissions. **Campus Safety and Security:** Measures include 24-hour foot and vehicle patrol, emergency notification system, security escort services, emergency telephones, lighted pathways/sidewalks, and controlled access to dorms/residences.

REQUIREMENTS: The ACT is required, with a score of 21, and a high school GPA of at least 2.5. Other admissions requirements include graduation from an accredited secondary school, with a college-preparatory curriculum recommended. The GED is also accepted. An interview is advised. ACT scores between 18 and 20 with a high school GPA of 3.0 or better are considered. AP and CLEP credits are accepted. Important factors in the admissions decision are advanced placement or honors courses, leadership record, and recommendations by school officials. In addition to meeting degree requirements for a particular major, a student at CBU is required to have a broad understanding of self, others, and the contemporary world. The graduate of CBU shall have cultivated, through the arts and sciences, the necessary skills of inquiry, reasoning, and communication, and shall have developed an awareness of the religious dimension of human existence. All students take a broad range of courses; common requirements are 9 hours of English, 3 hours of math, 4 hours of natural, and physical sciences, 6 hours of religious studies, 3 hours of moral values, and 6 hours of social science/history for a total of 31 general education hours. Students must take a minimum of 30 hours of general education courses. **Procedure:** Freshmen are admitted to all sessions. Entrance exams should be taken by the end of the junior year. There are deferred admissions and rolling admissions plans. Applications should be filed by August 1 for fall entry; December 1 for spring entry; and May 1 for summer entry, along with a $25 fee. Notifications are sent December 1. Applications are accepted on-line. **Transfer Students:** 41 transfer students enrolled in 2015-2016. Transfer students should have a minimum GPA of 2.5 and be in good academic and disciplinary standing. 35 of 122 credits required for the bachelor's degree must be completed at CBU. **International Students:** There are 35 international students enrolled. The school actively recruits these students. They must take the TOEFL with a minimum score of 500 on the paper-based TOEFL (PBT).

ADMISSIONS: 48% of the 2016-2017 applicants were accepted. The SAT scores for the 2016-2017 freshman class were: The ACT scores were 4% below 12, 42% between 12 and 17, 28% between 18 and 23, 11% between 24 and 29, and 15% above 30. 68% of the current freshmen were in the top fifth of their class; 84% were in the top two fifths. 4 freshmen graduated first in their class. **Admissions Contact:** Kristi Forman, Director of Admissions. Email: *admissions@cbu.edu* Web: *www.cbu.edu*

FINANCIAL AID: In 2016-2017, 95% of all full-time freshmen received some form of financial aid. The average freshman award was $21,283. Need-based scholarships or need-based grants averaged $24,188; and non-need-based athletic scholarships averaged $8,937. 91% of undergraduate students work part-time. Average annual earnings from campus work are $2400. The average financial indebtedness of the 2016 graduate was $29,207. The FAFSA code is 003482. Check with the school for current application deadlines.

CUMBERLAND UNIVERSITY — C-2

www.cumberland.edu

Lebanon, TN 37087 — **(615) 547-1246** **(800) 467-0562**

Fax: (615) 444-2569 — **Email: admissions@cumberland.edu**

Full-time: 461 women — **Faculty:** n/av
Part-time: 69 men, 93 women — **Ph.D.s:** 49%
Graduate: 82 men, 185 women — **Student/Faculty:** n/av
Year: semesters, summer session — **Tuition:** $20,160
Room & Board: $7550 — **Freshman Class:** 602 applied, 367 accepted, 212 enrolled
SAT: recommended **ACT:** 21 — **CEEB CODE:** 1146
Application Deadline: open — **COMPETITIVE**

Cumberland University, founded in 1842, is a private institution offering undergraduate and graduate degrees in business, education, and social sciences. The figures in the above capsule and in this profile are approximate. There is 1 undergraduate school and 4 graduate schools. In addition to regional accreditation, Cumberland has baccalaureate program accreditation with AACSB and NLN. The 44-acre campus is in a small town 28 miles east of Nashville. Including any residence halls, there are 17 buildings.

STUDENT LIFE: 87% of undergraduates are from Tennessee. Others are from 29 states, 29 foreign countries, and Canada. 89% are from public schools. 72% are White; 3% Foreign; 2% Hispanic; 14% African American; 1% Asian American; 1% American Indian/Alaska Native. **Female To Male Ratio:** 4.9:1. The average age of freshmen is 18; all undergraduates, 22. 44% do not continue beyond their first year; 35% remain to graduate. **Housing:** 400 students can be accommodated in college housing, which includes single-sex dorms. On-campus housing is available on a first-come and first-served basis. 62% of students commute. All students may keep cars. Alcohol is not permitted.

FACULTY/CLASSROOMS: 52% of faculty are male; 48% are female. 82% teach undergraduates. No introductory courses are taught by graduate students. The average class size in an introductory lecture is 20; in a laboratory is 20; and in a regular course is 20.

PROGRAMS OF STUDY: Cumberland confers B.A., B.S., B.B.A., and B.S.N. degrees. Associate and master's degrees are also awarded. Bachelor's degrees are awarded in BIOLOGICAL SCIENCE (biology/biological science), BUSINESS (accounting, business administration and management, management science, marketing management, and recreation and leisure services), COMMUNICATIONS AND THE ARTS (English, fine arts, and music), COMPUTER AND PHYSICAL SCIENCE (mathematics), EDUCATION (elementary education, middle school education, music education, physical education, secondary education, and special education), HEALTH PROFESSIONS (nursing), SOCIAL SCIENCE (American studies, criminal justice, history, political science/government, psychology, social science, and sociology). Business, education, and nursing have the largest enrollments.

ACTIVITIES: 17% of men belong to 3 national fraternities; 7% of

women belong to 2 national sororities. There are 15 groups on campus, including art, band, cheerleading, chorale, chorus, computers, dance, drama, honors, international, jazz band, marching band, musical theater, newspaper, pep band, political, professional, religious, social, social service, and student government. Popular campus events include Fall Frolic, Halloween at CU, and Fall and Spring Preview Days. **Sports:** There are 9 intercollegiate sports for men and 8 for women, and 4 intramural sports for men and 5 for women. Facilities include a gym, field house, weight room, baseball and soccer fields, tennis courts, outdoor volleyball courts, football field, and softball field. **Graduates:** From July 1, 2015 to June 30, 2016, 154 bachelor's degrees were awarded. The most popular majors were nursing (45%), education (27%), and business administration (17%). In an average class, 10% graduate in 4 years or less, 20% graduate in 5 years or less, and 5% graduate in 6 years or less.

SERVICES: Counseling and information services are available, as is tutoring in most subjects, and remedial math, reading, and writing. **Library/Resources:** The library contains 37,056 volumes, 590 microform items, 1,260 audio/video tapes/CDs/DVDs, and subscribes to 357 periodicals including electronic. Computerized library services include interlibrary loans, database searching, and Internet access. Special learning facilities include an art gallery and natural history museum. **Physically Challenged Students:** All of the campus is accessible. Facilities include wheelchair ramps, special parking, and lowered telephones. **Special:** Internships with local businesses and with the state legislature are available. Nondegree study, pass/fail options, and an accelerated degree program in general business are offered. There are 13 national honor societies, a freshman honors program, and 5 departmental honors programs. **Visiting:** There are regularly scheduled orientations for prospective students, consisting of campus tours, testing, information sessions pertaining to college life, and academic advising. A parent orientation is provided in conjunction with student orientation programs. There are guides for informal visits and visitors may sit in on classes. To schedule a visit, contact the Admissions Office. **Campus Safety and Security:** Measures include 24-hour foot and vehicle patrol and emergency notification system, emergency telephones, lighted pathways/sidewalks, and controlled access to dorms/residences.

REQUIREMENTS: The SAT and ACT Writing Test are recommended. A minimum composite ACT score of 19 and a GPA of 2.5 are expected. Applicants must be high school graduates or have earned the GED with a composite 50 score. AP and CLEP credits are accepted. To graduate, students must complete 120 to 132 (depending on major) semester hours, including a 41-hour core curriculum, and maintain a GPA of 2.0. **Procedure:** Freshmen are admitted in the fall, spring, and summer. Entrance exams should be taken during spring of the junior year or fall of the senior year. There is a rolling admissions plan. Application deadlines are open. Application fee is $25. Applications are accepted online. **Transfer Students:** 131 transfer students enrolled in 2015-2016. Transfer applicants should have a GPA of at least 2.0. 33 of 120 credits required for the bachelor's degree must be completed at Cumberland. **International Students:** There are 40 international students enrolled. The school actively recruits these students. They must take the TOEFL with a minimum score of 500 on the paper-based TOEFL (PBT), as well as the SAT or ACT, scoring 18.

ADMISSIONS: 61% of the 2016-2017 applicants were accepted. The SAT scores for the 2016-2017 freshman class were: Critical Reading-- 65% below 500, 30% between 500 and 599, and 5% between 700 and 800. Math-- 50% below 500 and 50% between 500 and 599. Writing-- 88% between 500 and 599 and 12% between 600 and 699. The ACT scores were 44% below 12, 33% between 12 and 17, 10% between 18 and 23, 11% between 24 and 29, and 2% above 30. 38% of the current freshmen were in the top fifth of their class; 73% were in the top two fifths. **Admissions Contact:** Tyler Ragland, Admissions Representative. Email: *admissions@cumberland.edu* Web: *www.cumberland.edu*

FINANCIAL AID: In 2016-2017, 95% of all full-time freshmen and 95% of continuing full-time students received some form of financial aid. 33% of all full-time freshmen and 33% of continuing full-time students received need-based aid. The average freshman award was $6,133. Need-based scholarships or need-based grants averaged $5,191 ($9,972 maximum); need-based self-help aid (loans and jobs) averaged $2,800 ($11,500 maximum); non-need-based athletic scholarships averaged $7,899 ($20,020 maximum); and other non-need-based awards and non-need-based scholarships averaged $3,212 ($14,710 maximum). Average annual earnings from campus work are $1000. The college's own financial statement is required. The FAFSA code is 003485. The priority date for freshman financial aid applications for fall entry is February 1. The filing deadline for fall entry is July 15.

EAST TENNESSEE STATE UNIVERSITY F-1

www.etsu.edu

Johnson City, TN 37614	(423) 439-4213 (800) 462-3878
Fax: (423) 439-4630	**Email:** gozetsu@etsu.edu
Full-time: 3400 men, 4550 women	**Faculty:** 350; IIA, --$
Part-time: 650 men, 980 women	**Ph.D.s:** 75%
Graduate: 620 men, 1225 women	**Student/Faculty:** 23 to 1
Year: semesters, summer session	**Tuition:** $8994 ($13,145)
Room & Board: $5000	**Freshman Class:** n/av
SAT or ACT: required	**CEEB CODE:** 1198
Application Deadline: open	**COMPETITIVE**

East Tennessee State University, founded in 1911, is a public institution that is part of the State University and Community College System of Tennessee. ETSU's undergraduate and graduate programs stress the liberal arts, business, art, fine arts, professional training, music, teacher preparation, technical studies, and health science. The figures in the above capsule and in this profile are approximate. There are 6 undergraduate schools and 2 graduate schools. In addition to regional accreditation, ETSU has baccalaureate program accreditation with AACSB, ABET, ACEJMC, ADA, CSAB, CSWE, NASAD, NASM, NCATE, NLN, ACS, CAAHEP, and NEHSPAC. The 366-acre campus is in a small town 90 miles northeast of Knoxville, TN. Including any residence halls, there are 68 buildings.

STUDENT LIFE: 89% of undergraduates are from Tennessee. Others are from 38 states, 46 foreign countries, and Canada. 97% are from public schools. 91% are White; 4% African American; 1% Asian American; 1% American Indian/Alaska Native; 1% Hispanic; 1% Foreign. **Female To Male Ratio:** 1.4:1. The average age of freshmen is 19; all undergraduates, 23. 33% do not continue beyond their first year; 38% remain to graduate. **Housing:** 2478 students can be accommodated in college housing, which includes single-sex and coed dorms, on-campus apartments, and married student housing. On-campus housing is available on a first-come and first-served basis. 79% of students commute. All students may keep cars. Alcohol is not permitted.

FACULTY/CLASSROOMS: 55% of faculty are male; 45% are female. 85% teach undergraduates. No introductory courses are taught by graduate students. The average class size in an introductory lecture is 30; in a laboratory is 15; and in a regular course is 25.

PROGRAMS OF STUDY: ETSU confers B.A., B.S., B.A.S., B.B.A., B.F.A., B.G.S., B.M., B.S.D.H., B.S.Ed., B.S.E.H., B.S.M.T., B.S.N., and B.S.W. degrees. Associate, master's, and doctoral degrees are also awarded. Bachelor's degrees are awarded in BIOLOGICAL SCIENCE (biology/biological science), BUSINESS (accounting, management science, and marketing/retailing/merchandising), COMMUNICATIONS AND THE ARTS (art, communications, English, fine arts, music, and speech/debate/rhetoric), COMPUTER AND PHYSICAL SCIENCE (chemistry, computer science, information sciences and systems, mathematics, and physics), EDUCATION (foreign languages education, physical education, and special education), ENGINEERING AND ENVIRONMENTAL DESIGN (engineering technology and survey and mapping technology), HEALTH PROFESSIONS (allied health, dental hygiene, environmental health science, health science, nursing, and public health), SOCIAL SCIENCE (child psychology/development, criminal justice, economics, geography, history, human development, interdisciplinary studies, liberal arts/general studies, philosophy, political science/government, psychology, social work, and sociology). Engineering technology, computer science, and nursing have the largest enrollments.

ACTIVITIES: 4% of men belong to 8 national fraternities; 4% of women belong to 1 local and 6 national sororities. There are 200 groups on campus, including art, band, cheerleading, choir, chorale, chorus, computers, dance, drama, drill team, ethnic, forensics, honors, international, jazz band, LGBT, literary magazine, newspaper, pep band, photography, political, professional, radio and TV, religious, social, social service, and student government. Popular campus events include Leadership Retreat, National Clean Up for Hunger, and Winter Cruise. **Sports:** There are 6 intercollegiate sports for men and 8 for women, and 8 intramural sports for men and 8 for women. Facilities include a gym and a domed stadium which includes a basketball arena, tennis and handball/racquetball courts, a track, and weight and training rooms. **Graduates:** From July 1, 2015 to June 30, 2016, 1499 bachelor's degrees were awarded. The most popular majors were nursing (8%), psychology (6%), and finance and elementary education (5%). 200 companies recruited on campus in 2015-2016. In an average class, 12% graduate in 4 years or less, 29% graduate in 5 years or less, and 38% graduate in 6 years or less.

SERVICES: Counseling and information services are available, as is tutoring in most subjects, and a reader service for the blind, and remedial math, reading, and writing. **Library/Resources:** The library contains 1.1 million volumes, 1.7 million microform items, and 23,658 audio/video tapes/CDs/DVDs, and subscribes to 3,714 periodicals including electronic. Computerized library services include interlibrary loans, database searching, and Internet access. Special learning facilities include an art gallery, planetarium, radio station, TV station, a regional art and history museum. **Physically Challenged Students:** 75% of the campus is accessible. Facilities include wheelchair ramps, elevators, special parking, specially equipped restrooms, special class scheduling, lowered drinking fountains, lowered telephones, and special housing. Adaptive computer equipment. **Special:** Special academic programs include cooperative education programs, cross-registration with Milligan College, internships in political science, applied human sciences, and management,and dual majors study abroad in Scotland, England, France, and Spain, and B.A.-B.S. degrees and dual majors in most arts and sciences undergraduate majors. A general studies degree is offered. Credit for military experience may be granted, and nondegree study and pass/fail options are possible. There are 19 national honor societies, a freshman honors program, and 12 departmental honors programs. **Visiting:** There are regularly scheduled orientations for prospective students, including 5; 2-day orientation programs held during spring and summer for new students admitted to fall term. There are guides for informal visits, visitors may sit in on classes, and stay overnight. To schedule a visit, contact the Admissions Office. **Campus Safety and Security:** Measures include 24-hour foot and vehicle patrol, self-defense education, and security escort services. There are also shuttle buses, emergency telephones, lighted pathways/sidewalks, and engravers available to identify personal property.

REQUIREMENTS: Students must have a minimum composite score of 890 on the SAT I or a minimum score of 19 on the ACT. Other admissions requirements include graduation from an accredited secondary school, with 20 Carnegie units and 14 academic credits, including 4 of English, 3 of math, 2 each of a foreign language and science, and 1 each of history, social studies, and art. In-state students who pass the Tennessee State Proficiency Test are eligible to apply for admission. Applicants whose ACT/SAT I is below a certain score must complete the Academic Assessment Placement Program (AAPP) test battery before registration for classes. The GED is also accepted. AP and CLEP credits are accepted. All students must complete 120 semester hours, with 30 to 60 in the major, and maintain a minimum GPA of 2.0. Distribution requirements, which total 46 semester hours, include English, American history, phys ed, natural science, social and behavioral science, the humanities, analysis, and a 3-hour computer literacy course. An exit exam is also required. **Procedure:** Freshmen are admitted to all sessions. Entrance exams should be taken during the junior and/or senior year. There is a rolling admissions plan. Application deadlines are open. The fall 2016 application fee was $15. Notification is sent on a rolling basis. Applications are accepted online. **Transfer Students:** 857 transfer students enrolled in 2015-2016. Transfer students must have a minimum GPA of 2.0 in 12 or more semester credit hours of course work from a regionally accredited institution. Transfer students must also satisfy high school unit requirements if deficiencies exist. 34 of 120 credits required for the bachelor's degree must be completed at ETSU. **International Students:** There are 99 international students enrolled. They must take the TOEFL with a minimum score of 500 on the paper-based TOEFL (PBT) or 61 on the Internet-based version (iBT). They must also take the SAT or ACT, scoring 19.

Admissions Contact: Brian Henley, Director of Admissions. Email: *howardJ@etsu.edu* Web: *www.etsu.edu*

FINANCIAL AID: In 2016-2017, 74% of all full-time freshmen and 75% of continuing full-time students received some form of financial aid. 55% of all full-time freshmen and 55% of continuing full-time students received need-based aid. The average freshman award was $7,407. Need-based scholarships or need-based grants averaged $5,002; need-based self-help aid (loans and jobs) averaged $2,992; and other non-need-based awards and non-need-based scholarships averaged $1,760. 28% of undergraduate students work part-time. Average annual earnings from campus work are $2119. The average financial indebtedness of the 2016 graduate was $17,668. The FAFSA code is 003487. The priority date for freshman financial aid applications for fall entry is April 15. The filing deadline for fall entry is July 1.

FISK UNIVERSITY *(The complete profile is made available exclusively on our website, www.barronspac.com)*

FREED-HARDEMAN UNIVERSITY B-3

www.fhu.edu

Henderson, TN 38340	(731) 989-6651 (800) 630-3480
Fax: (731) 989-6047	Email: admissions@fhu.edu
Full-time: 614 men, 752 women	Faculty: 90; IIA, --$
Part-time: 51 men, 62 women	Ph.D.s: 69%
Graduate: 197 men, 335 women	Student/Faculty: 15 to 1
Year: semesters, summer session	Tuition: $21,500
Room & Board: $7950	Freshman Class: n/av
ACT: 23	CEEB CODE: 1230
Application Deadline: open	COMPETITIVE

Freed-Hardeman University, founded in 1869, is a private, liberal arts institution associated with Church of Christ. Figures in the above capsule and in this profile are approximate. There are 6 undergraduate schools and 4 graduate schools. In addition to regional accreditation, FHU has baccalaureate program accreditation with ACBSP, CSWE, and NCATE. The 120-acre campus is in a small town in Henderson, 85 miles east of Memphis. Including any residence halls, there are 39 buildings.

STUDENT LIFE: 52% of undergraduates are from out of state, mostly the South. Students are from 33 states, 20 foreign countries, and Canada. 75% are from public schools. 91% are White; 4% African American; 3% Foreign; 1% Asian American; 1% Hispanic. 99% are Protestant. **Female To Male Ratio:** 1.3:1. The average age of freshmen is 19; all undergraduates, 21. 26% do not continue beyond their first year; 57% remain to graduate. **Housing:** College-sponsored housing includes single-sex dorms, on-campus apartments, and student teacher houses. On-campus housing is guaranteed for all 4 years. 75% of students live on campus; of those, 55% remain on campus on weekends. All students may keep cars. Alcohol is not permitted.

FACULTY/CLASSROOMS: 68% of faculty are male; 32% are female. 91% teach undergraduates. No introductory courses are taught by graduate students. The average class size in a laboratory is 22 and in a regular course is 20.

PROGRAMS OF STUDY: FHU confers B.A., B.S., B.B.A., and B.S.W. degrees. Associate and master's degrees are also awarded. Bachelor's degrees are awarded in BIOLOGICAL SCIENCE (biochemistry and biology/biological science), BUSINESS (accounting, banking and finance, and business administration and management), COMMUNICATIONS AND THE ARTS (art, broadcasting, communications, dramatic arts, English, fine arts, journalism, public relations, and speech/debate/rhetoric), COMPUTER AND PHYSICAL SCIENCE (chemistry, computer programming, computer science, information sciences and systems, mathematics, and physical sciences), EDUCATION (art education, early childhood education, elementary education, health education, middle school education, music education, physical education, science education, secondary education, and special education), ENGINEERING AND ENVIRONMENTAL DESIGN (preengineering), HEALTH PROFESSIONS (predentistry, premedicine, preoptometry, prepharmacy, and preveterinary science), SOCIAL SCIENCE (biblical studies, child care/child and family studies, criminal justice, family/consumer studies, history, ministries, psychology, and social work). Premedicine, preengineering, and business are the strongest academically. Business, Bible, and elementary education have the largest enrollments.

ACTIVITIES: There are no fraternities or sororities. There are 52 groups on campus, including art, band, cheerleading, choir, chorus, communications, computers, drama, drum and bugle corps, ethnic, honors, international, jazz band, musical theater, newspaper, orchestra, pep band, photography, political, professional, radio and TV, religious, social, social service, student government, and yearbook. Popular campus events include Makin' Music and Annual Bible Lectureship. **Sports:** There are 3 intercollegiate sports for men and 4 for women, and 7 intramural sports for men and 7 for women. Facilities include a swimming pool, gyms, playing fields, tennis courts, a walking track, weight room, racquetball courts, and a game room.

SERVICES: Counseling and information services are available, as is

tutoring in most subjects, and remedial math, reading, and writing. **Library/Resources:** The library contains 175,748 volumes, 240,000 microform items, and 43,000 audio/video tapes/CDs/DVDs, and subscribes to 1,650 periodicals including electronic. Computerized library services include interlibrary loans, database searching, and Internet access. Special learning facilities include an art gallery, radio station, TV station, an undergraduate research center. **Physically Challenged Students:** 70% of the campus is accessible. Facilities include wheelchair ramps, elevators, special parking, specially equipped restrooms, special class scheduling, lowered drinking fountains, and lowered telephones. **Special:** FHU offers study abroad in Belgium and Italy, a B.A.-B.S. degree in Bible, biology, communication, and arts and humanities, co-op programs, a dual major, field practicum opportunities in several majors, student-designed majors, 3-2 engineering degrees with 6 universities, and nondegree study. There are 4 national honor societies, a freshman honors program, and 13 departmental honors programs. **Visiting:** There are regularly scheduled orientations for prospective students, including an orientation during the 5 days prior to classes beginning in the fall. There are guides for informal visits, visitors may sit in on classes, and stay overnight. **Campus Safety and Security:** Measures include 24-hour foot and vehicle patrol, emergency notification system, security escort services, and lighted pathways/sidewalks.

REQUIREMENTS: Students must have a minimum composite score of 19 on the ACT. Candidates for admission should be graduates of an accredited secondary school. An interview is recommended. AP and CLEP credits are accepted. Important factors in the admissions decision are personality/intangible qualities, recommendations by school officials, and leadership record. To graduate, students must complete 132 semester hours, including 44 in upper-division courses in Bible, skills, humanities, and science, plus 3 hours of speech communication and 2 hours of phys ed. The major requires a minimum of 30 semester hours, including 15 upper-division hours. Students must maintain a GPA of 2.0. All students must demonstrate, by approved tests or criteria, basic competence in reading, writing, oral communication, math, and computers. **Procedure:** Freshmen are admitted in the fall, spring, and summer. Entrance exams should be taken in early fall or summer before senior year. There are early admissions and rolling admissions plans. Application deadlines are open. Applications are accepted online. **Transfer Students:** Applicants should have a minimum college GPA of 2.0. Those with fewer than 30 college credits must also submit a high school transcript and ACT or SAT scores. 33 of 132 credits required for the bachelor's degree must be completed at FHU. **International Students:** They must take the TOEFL with a minimum score of 500 on the paper-based TOEFL (PBT) or 61 on the Internet-based version (iBT). They must also take the ACT, scoring 19.

ADMISSIONS: The ACT scores were 30% below 12, 27% between 12 and 17, 21% between 18 and 23, 10% between 24 and 29, and 12% above 30. **Admissions Contact:** Joe Askew, Director of Admissions. Email: *admissions@fhu.edu* Web: *www.fhu.edu*

FINANCIAL AID: The FAFSA code is 003492. Check with the school for current application deadlines.

KING UNIVERSITY — F-1

www.king.edu

Bristol, TN 37620	**(423) 652-4861** **(800) 362-0014**
Fax: (423) 652-4727	**Email: admissions@king.edu**
Full-time: 784 men, 1460 women	**Faculty:** IIA
Part-time: 80 men, 143 women	**Ph.D.s:** 63%
Graduate: 140 men, 313 women	**Student/Faculty:** n/av
Year: semesters, summer session	**Tuition:** $26,480
Room & Board: $8180	**Freshman Class:** 371 applied, 240 accepted, 114 enrolled
SAT or ACT: required	**CEEB CODE:** 1371
Application Deadline: open	**COMPETITIVE**

King University is a Presbyterian, doctoral-level, comprehensive university offering more than 90 majors, minors, pre-professional degrees and concentrations in fields such as business, digital media, nursing, forensic science, education, and humanities. A number of off-campus learning opportunities and travel destinations are also available. King has seven academic schools of learning: arts and sciences, applied science and technology, behavioral and health sciences, business and economics, education, and nursing, and Peeke School of Christian Mission. Figures in the above capsule and in this profile are approximate. In addition to regional accreditation, King has baccalaureate program accreditation with CCNE and CAATE. The 135-acre campus is in a small town 2 miles east of Bristol, Virginia. Including any residence halls, there are 20 buildings.

STUDENT LIFE: 63% of undergraduates are from Tennessee. Others are from 38 states, 33 foreign countries, and Canada. 83% are from public schools. 79% are White; 6% African American; 6% race unknown; 3% Hispanic; 3% Foreign; 1% Asian American; 1% American Indian/Alaska Native; 1% two or more races. 57% are Muslim and unknown; 38% Protestant. **Female To Male Ratio:** 1.9:1. The average age of freshmen is 18.5; all undergraduates, 29.5. 26% do not continue beyond their first year; 55% remain to graduate. **Housing:** 490 students can be accommodated in college housing, which includes single-sex dorms, and honors houses. On-campus housing is guaranteed for all 4 years, is available on a first-come, and first-served basis. 58% of students commute. All students may keep cars. Alcohol is not permitted.

FACULTY/CLASSROOMS: No introductory courses are taught by graduate students. The average class size in an introductory lecture is 13; in a laboratory is 11; and in a regular course is 11.

PROGRAMS OF STUDY: King confers B.A., B.B.A., B.S., and B.S.W. degrees. Associate, master's, and doctoral degrees are also awarded. Bachelor's degrees are awarded in BIOLOGICAL SCIENCE (biochemistry, bioinformatics, biology/adolescence education, biology/biological science, biology/ gen science secondary education, cell & molecular biology, forensic science, and neurosciences), BUSINESS (business administration and management, business administration marketing, business economics, and sports management), COMMUNICATIONS AND THE ARTS (arts administration/management, communications, digital media, English, English literature, English Writing, French, information technology, instrumental music education, music, photography, Spanish, technical communication, theatre arts, theater management, and vocal music education), COMPUTER AND PHYSICAL SCIENCE (applied science, chemistry, chemistry/adolescence education, chemistry secondary education, digital arts/technology, mathematics, and physics), EDUCATION (athletic training, elementary education, English secondary education, general studies, health information management, history education, learner designed area of study, mathematics education, music education, physical education, social studies education, and Spanish adolescense education), HEALTH PROFESSIONS (health care administration, human biology, and nursing), SOCIAL SCIENCE (biblical studies, criminal justice, history, interdisciplinary studies, international relations, philosophy, psychology, religious studies, social work, and youth ministry). Nursing, business, and natural sciences are the strongest academically. Nursing, business, and information technology have the largest enrollments.

ACTIVITIES: There are no fraternities or sororities. There are 15 groups on campus, including band, cheerleading, choir, chorale, chorus, dance, drama, environmental, honors, international, jazz band, musical theater, newspaper, pep band, political, professional, religious, social, social service, student government, and yearbook. Popular campus events include Fall Ball and Dogwood Ball. **Sports:** There are 11 intercollegiate sports for men and 14 for women, and 6 intramural sports for men and 6 for women. Facilities include basketball & volleyball, acrobatics and tumbling, wrestling, weight room, cardiovascular space, racquetball court, soccer, outdoor baseball field, softball field and tennis courts. **Graduates:** From July 1, 2015 to June 30, 2016, 895 bachelor's degrees were awarded. The most popular majors were nursing (39%), business (28%), and information technology (6%). 25 companies recruited on campus in 2015-2016. In an average class, 2% graduate in 3 years or less, 39% graduate in 4 years or less, 53% graduate in 5 years or less, and 55% graduate in 6 years or less. Of the 2015 graduating class, 21% were enrolled in graduate school within 6 months of graduation, and 71% were employed.

SERVICES: Counseling and information services are available, as is tutoring in every subject, and a reader service for the blind. The Academic Center for Excellence (ACE) houses a writing center, math center, and speaking center. 24-hour online tutoring in all subjects and an online writing center are also available to all students. **Library/Resources:** The 3 libraries contain 199,734 volumes, 12,465 microform items, and 5,720 audio/video tapes/CDs/DVDs, and subscribe to 268 periodicals including electronic. Computerized library services include interlibrary loans, database searching, Internet access, and Wi-Fi capability. Special learning facilities include an art gallery, an observatory. **Physically Challenged Students:** 60% of the campus is accessible. Facilities include wheelchair ramps, elevators, special parking, specially equipped restrooms, special class scheduling, lowered drinking fountains, lowered telephones, and special housing. **Special:** King offers cooperative education, internships, dual majors, and an accelerated degree in all programs, as well as a pharmacy dual degree program, interdisciplinary and student-designed majors. King also offers a first-year experience program with a Discover Washington DC component, and a transfer experience. King offers a Washington semester, and work-study programs. Nondegree study and pass/fail options for special students are available. There is 1 national honor society, a freshman honors program, and 1 departmental honors program. **Visiting:** There are regularly scheduled orientations for prospective students, including a campus tour; sessions on admission, athletics, financial aid, academics/meeting with faculty; lunch. There are guides for informal visits, visitors may sit in on classes, and stay overnight. To schedule a visit, contact Tom VerDow at admissions@king.edu. **Campus Safety and Security:** Measures include 24-hour foot and vehicle patrol, emergency notification system, self-defense education, security escort services, emergency telephones, lighted pathways/sidewalks, and controlled access to dorms/residences.

REQUIREMENTS: The SAT or ACT is required. Graduation from an accredited or recognized secondary institution is required (GED is accepted), with a minimum of 16 academic units, distributed as follows: 4 of English; 2 of algebra (Algebra I and II); 1 of geometry; 2 of foreign language; 2 of history and social studies; 1 of natural science; and 4 of other academic electives. A GPA of 3.0 is required. AP and CLEP credits are accepted. Students must complete a minimum of 124 semester credit hours with 32 to 76 in the major. The minimum 48 semester hours of core curriculum include courses in English, history, math, Bible, humanities, science, social science, and physical education. Students must have a minimum GPA of 2.0 in most majors (may vary according to field of study). A comprehensive exam in the student's major area of concentration is required. **Procedure:** Freshmen are admitted in the fall, spring, and summer. Entrance exams should be taken by May 1. There are deferred admissions and rolling admissions plans. Application deadlines are open. The fall 2016 application fee was $25. Applications are accepted online. **Transfer Students:** 1017 transfer students enrolled in 2015-2016. Transfer applicants should have a minimum 2.0 GPA and 30 semester hours earned. If fewer hours have been completed, a 3.0 high school GPA and a minimum ACT composite score of 22 or SAT score of 1000 are required. 48 of 124 credits required for the bachelor's degree must be completed at King. **International Students:** There are 72 international students enrolled. The school actively recruits these students. They must take the TOEFL with a minimum score of 600 on the paper-based TOEFL (PBT) or 100 on the Internet-based version (iBT). They must also take the SAT or ACT, scoring 1000/22.

ADMISSIONS: 16% of the current freshmen were in the top fifth of their class; 32% were in the top two fifths. 4 freshmen graduated first in their class. **Admissions Contact:** Tom VerDow, Director of Undergraduate Enrollment. Email: *admissions@king.edu* Web: *www.king.edu*

FINANCIAL AID: In 2016-2017, 99% of all full-time freshmen received some form of financial aid. 77% of all full-time freshmen and 85% of continuing full-time students received need-based aid. The average freshman award was $270,276. Need-based scholarships or need-based grants averaged $14,236; need-based self-help aid (loans and jobs) averaged $2,896; non-need-based athletic scholarships averaged $1,602; other non-need-based awards and non-need-based scholarships averaged $2,732; and $408 from other forms of aid. 46% of undergraduate students work part-time. Average annual earnings from campus work are $1072. The average financial indebtedness of the 2016 graduate was $21,091. The college's own financial statement is required. The FAFSA code is 003496. The priority date for freshman financial aid applications for fall entry is March 1. The filing deadline for fall entry is rolling.

LANE COLLEGE — B-2
www.lanecollege.edu

Jackson, TN 38301	(731) 426-7533 (800) 960-7533
Fax: (731) 426-7559	**Email:** admissions@lanecollege.edu
Full-time: 750 men, 750 women	**Faculty:** 50
Part-time: n/av	**Ph.D.s:** 60%
Graduate: n/av	**Student/Faculty:** 19 to 1
Year: semesters, summer session	**Tuition:** $9930
Room & Board: $6620	**Freshman Class:** n/av
ACT: required	**CEEB CODE:** 1395
Application Deadline: August 1	**COMPETITIVE**

Lane College, founded in 1882, is a private, co-educational, liberal arts institution affiliated with the Christian Methodist Episcopal Church. Figures in the above capsule and in this profile are approximate. There is 1 undergraduate school. The 55-acre campus is in a small town in Jackson, 79 miles from Memphis, 122 miles from Nashville.

STUDENT LIFE: 57% of undergraduates are from Tennessee. Others are from 30 states, and 1 foreign country. 85% are from public schools. 99% are African American; 1% Hispanic. 95% are Protestant. **Male To Female Ratio:** Is 1:1. The average age of freshmen is 19; all undergraduates, 21. 20% do not continue beyond their first year; 65% remain to graduate. **Housing:** 638 students can be accommodated in college housing, which includes single-sex dorms and on-campus apartments. On-campus housing is guaranteed for all 4 years. 63% of students live on campus; of those, 40% remain on campus on weekends. All students may keep cars. Alcohol is not permitted.

FACULTY/CLASSROOMS: 72% of faculty are male; 28% are female. All teach undergraduates. No introductory courses are taught by graduate students. The average class size in an introductory lecture is 25; in a laboratory is 16; and in a regular course is 16.

PROGRAMS OF STUDY: Lane confers B.A. and B.S. degrees. Bachelor's degrees are awarded in BIOLOGICAL SCIENCE (biology/biological science), BUSINESS (business administration and management), COMMUNICATIONS AND THE ARTS (communications, English, French, and music), COMPUTER AND PHYSICAL SCIENCE (chemistry, computer science, mathematics, and physics), EDUCATION (physical education), SOCIAL SCIENCE (criminal justice, history, interdisciplinary studies, religion, and sociology). Business, education, and criminal justice are the strongest academically. Education, business, and sociology have the largest enrollments.

ACTIVITIES: 3% of men belong to 2 local and 2 national fraternities; 9% of women belong to 4 local and 4 national sororities. There are 21 groups on campus, including band, cheerleading, chess, choir, chorus, computers, debate, drama, honors, marching band, newspaper, pep band, religious, social, social service, student government, and yearbook. Popular campus events include Founders Day, Fine Arts Week, and Religious Emphasis Week. **Sports:** There are 6 intercollegiate sports for men and 6 for women, and 4 intramural sports for men and 4 for women. Facilities include a swimming pool, a multipurpose/weight room, gym, off-campus football and baseball fields, a campus recreation center, dance floor, and billiards. **Graduates:** From July 1, 2015 to June 30, 2016, 88 bachelor's degrees were awarded. The most popular majors were interdisciplinary studies (23%), computer science (14%), and criminal justice (12%). 31 companies recruited on campus in 2015-2016. In an average class, 39% graduate in 4 years or less, 54% graduate in 5 years or less, and 61% graduate in 6 years or less. Of the 2015 graduating class, 32% were enrolled in graduate school within 6 months of graduation, and 63% were employed.

SERVICES: Counseling and information services are available, as is tutoring in most subjects. The writing center provides tutoring in writing and the mathematics. Student Support Services provides tutoring in English, math, reading, computer science, computer literacy, test-taking, and study skills. **Library/Resources:** The library contains 98,619 volumes, 53,125 microform items, 820 audio/video tapes/CDs/DVDs, and subscribes to 226 periodicals including electronic. Computerized library services include interlibrary loans, database searching, and Internet access. **Physically Challenged Students:** 70% of the campus is accessible. Facilities include wheelchair ramps, elevators, special parking, and specially equipped restrooms. **Special:** Cooperative programs are available in engineering with Tennessee State University School of Engineering and Technology. The College also offers work-study programs, dual majors, student-designed majors, and nondegree study. Internships are available in many fields in various corporations, universities, and federal agencies. There is also a cooperative agreement with Milwaukee Area Technical College. There are 2 national honor societies. **Visiting:** There are regularly scheduled orientations for prospective students, including meetings on financial aid, residential life, rules and regulations of the college, course requirements, and registration. There are guides for informal visits, visitors may sit in on classes, and stay overnight. To schedule a visit, contact the Office of Recruitment/Admissions. **Campus Safety and Security:** Measures include 24-hour foot and vehicle patrol, security escort services, emergency telephones, lighted pathways/sidewalks, a security guard at the entrance to the campus, and camera surveillance in parking lots and dorms.

REQUIREMENTS: The ACT is required, with a minimum composite score of 17. Graduation from an accredited secondary school is required;

a GED will be accepted. Applicants' academic record must include 16 credits, including 4 credits in English, and 2 credits each in math, science, and social studies. An additional 2 credits in a foreign language is recommended. An interview is recommended. AP and CLEP credits are accepted. Important factors in the admissions decision are evidence of special talent, recommendations by school officials, and ability to finance college education. Students must complete a minimum of 124 semester hours with a 2.0 GPA. 50 to 69 hours are required in the general studies curriculum, which includes courses in art, music, personal finance, foreign language, speech, composition, literature, history, sociology, math, physical science, biology, computer literacy, foundations of education, religion, and phys ed. The ETS Academic Profile is also required. ETS Major Field Tests are given as exit exams by major. **Procedure:** Freshmen are admitted to all sessions. Entrance exams should be taken by October of the senior year. There are early decision, early admissions, and rolling admissions plans. Applications should be filed by August 1 for fall entry; November 15 for spring entry; and May 15 for summer entry. Notification is sent on a rolling basis. 137 early decision candidates were accepted for the 2016-2017 class. Applications are accepted online. **Transfer Students:** 103 transfer students enrolled in 2015-2016. Applicants must submit transcripts from previous colleges attended and be in good standing at the time of application. Students having an associate degree will be given credit for a maximum of 68 semester hours in general education courses with a grade of C or higher. 31 of 124 credits required for the bachelor's degree must be completed at Lane. **International Students:** There are 1 international students enrolled. The school actively recruits these students. They must take the TOEFL. They must also take the ACT, scoring 13.

Admissions Contact: Monica Scott, Director of Admissions. Email: *admissions@lanecollege.edu* Web: *www.lanecollege.edu*

FINANCIAL AID: The average freshman award was $9,318. 39% of undergraduate students work part-time. Average annual earnings from campus work are $971. The average financial indebtedness of the 2016 graduate was $19,275. The CCS/Profile, FAFSA, FFS, and the SFS are required. The FAFSA code is 003499. The deadline for filing freshman financial aid applications for fall entry is March 31.

LEE UNIVERSITY — D-3

www.leeuniversity.edu

Cleveland, TN 37320 — (423) 614-8500, (800) 533-9930

Fax: (423) 614-8533 — Email: admissions@leeuniversity.edu

Full-time: 1544 men, 2222 women	**Faculty:** 158; IIB, -$
Part-time: 195 men, 155 women	**Ph.D.s:** 73%
Graduate: 251 men, 231 women	**Student/Faculty:** 17 to 1
Year: semesters, summer session	**Tuition:** $15,000
Room & Board: $7045	**Freshman Class:** 1745 applied, 1554 accepted, 756 enrolled
SAT CR/M: 520/480 **ACT:** 24	**CEEB CODE:** 1401
Application Deadline: September 1	**COMPETITIVE**

Lee University, founded in 1918, is a private liberal arts institution affiliated with the Church of God. Figures in the above capsule and in this profile are approximate. There are 5 undergraduate schools and 5 graduate schools. In addition to regional accreditation, Lee has baccalaureate program accreditation with ACBSP, NASM, and NCATE. The 120-acre campus is in a suburban area 20 miles north of Chattanooga. Including any residence halls, there are 50 buildings.

STUDENT LIFE: 55% of undergraduates are from out of state, mostly the South. Students are from 49 states, 54 foreign countries, and Canada. 83% are White; 6% Foreign; 5% African American; 4% Hispanic; 2% Asian American. **Female To Male Ratio:** 1.3:1. The average age of freshmen is 18; all undergraduates, 23. **Housing:** 1870 students can be accommodated in college housing, which includes single-sex and coed dorms, on-campus apartments, off-campus apartments, married student housing, and apartments for single students. On-campus housing is guaranteed for the freshman year only, and is available on a first-come, and first-served basis. 56% of students commute. Alcohol is not permitted. All students may keep cars.

FACULTY/CLASSROOMS: 63% of faculty are male; 37% are female. All teach undergraduates, 20% do research, and 20% do both. No introductory courses are taught by graduate students. The average class size in an introductory lecture is 25; in a laboratory is 15; and in a regular course is 28.

PROGRAMS OF STUDY: Lee confers B.A., B.S., B.C.M., B.M. and B.M.E. degrees. Master's degrees are also awarded. Bachelor's degrees are awarded in BIOLOGICAL SCIENCE (biochemistry and biology/biological science), BUSINESS (accounting and business administration and management), COMMUNICATIONS AND THE ARTS (communications, dramatic arts, English, French, music, music business management, music performance, public relations, Spanish, and telecommunications), COMPUTER AND PHYSICAL SCIENCE (chemistry, information sciences and systems, mathematics, and science), EDUCATION (athletic training, business education, elementary education, health education, mathematics education, middle school education, music education, physical education, and special education), HEALTH PROFESSIONS (health care administration, health science, and medical laboratory technology), SOCIAL SCIENCE (anthropology, biblical studies, crosscultural studies, history, human development, humanities, interdisciplinary studies, ministries, political science/government, psychology, religious music, sociology, and youth ministry). Business administration, communication, and human development are the strongest academically. Education, business, and psychology have the largest enrollments.

ACTIVITIES: 10% of men belong to 5 local fraternities; 10% of women belong to 5 local sororities. There are 95 groups on campus, including art, band, cheerleading, choir, chorale, chorus, computers, debate, drama, ethnic, honors, international, jazz band, literary magazine, musical theater, newspaper, opera, orchestra, pep band, photography, political, professional, religious, social, social service, student government, symphony, and yearbook. Popular campus events include Lee Day, Parade of Favorites, and Dorm Wars. **Sports:** There are 6 intercollegiate sports for men and 6 for women, and 11 intramural sports for men and 11 for women. Facilities include an arena, recreation complex, softball field, tennis center, soccer field, baseball field, and a playing field. **Graduates:** From July 1, 2015 to June 30, 2016, 781 bachelor's degrees were awarded. The most popular majors were education, and theology and religious studies (18%), psychology, and business/marketing (9%), and health professions and related programs (7%). In an average class, 1% graduate in 3 years or less, 29% graduate in 4 years or less, 44% graduate in 5 years or less, and 49% graduate in 6 years or less.

SERVICES: Counseling and information services are available, as is tutoring in every subject, and a reader service for the blind, and remedial math, reading, and writing. **Library/Resources:** The 2 libraries contain 271,897 volumes, 51,385 microform items, 1,671 audio/video tapes/CDs/DVDs, and subscribe to 34,881 periodicals including electronic. Computerized library services include interlibrary loans, database searching, Internet access, and Wi-Fi capability. **Physically Challenged Students:** 73% of the campus is accessible. Facilities include wheelchair ramps, elevators, special parking, specially equipped restrooms, special class scheduling, lowered drinking fountains, and lowered telephones. **Special:** Lee offers internships, cross-registration with the Coalition for Christian Colleges and Universities, study abroad in 25 countries, a Washington semester, numerous work-study programs, an accelerated degree program in Christian leadership, dual and student-designed majors, nondegree study, and limited pass/fail options. Every student completes a minor in religion. There are 16 national honor societies, a freshman honors program, and 6 departmental honors programs. **Visiting:** There are regularly scheduled orientations for prospective students, a complete campus tour upon request. There are guides for informal visits and visitors may sit in on classes. To schedule a visit, contact the Admissions Office. **Campus Safety and Security:** Measures include 24-hour foot and vehicle patrol, emergency notification system, and security escort services. There are shuttle buses, emergency telephones, and lighted pathways/sidewalks.

REQUIREMENTS: The SAT or ACT is recommended. Students must be graduates of accredited secondary schools. The GED is accepted. A portfolio is recommended. 13 High school units are required, 14 recommended, includes 4 units in English, 3 in math 2 each in science, social studies and 1 each in foreign language and history, recommended 1 in computer science. Students with 16 college semester hours, 24 for TN residents, are not required to provide test scores. A GPA of 2.0 is required. AP and CLEP credits are accepted. Important factors in the admissions decision are advanced placement or honors courses, leadership record, personality/intangible qualities, parents or siblings attended your school, evidence of special talent, extracurricular activities record, geographical diversity, and recommendations by school officials. All students must complete a minimum of 130 credit hours, including a core curriculum and 36 hours in the major, with a 2.0 GPA (2.5 for education majors). A Global Perspectives seminar and cross-cultural experience are required, in addition to a major field test the last semester before graduation in all fields except preprofessional science and teacher licensure. **Procedure:** Freshmen are admitted in the fall and spring. Entrance exams should be taken prior to registration. There are early admissions, deferred admissions, and rolling admissions plans. Early decision applications should be filed by January 1; regular applications, by September 1 for fall entry, along with a $25 fee. Notifications are sent September 1. Applications are accepted on-line. **Transfer Students:** 232 transfer students enrolled in 2015-2016. Transfer students must take the SAT or the ACT unless they have 16 credit hours with a GPA of 2.0 or better. Students must have official transcripts from all prior colleges. 30 of 130 credits required for the bachelor's degree must be completed at Lee. **International Students:** There are 208 international students enrolled. The school actively recruits these students. They must take the TOEFL, as well as the SAT or ACT.

ADMISSIONS: 89% of the 2016-2017 applicants were accepted. The SAT scores for the 2016-2017 freshman class were: Critical Reading-- 39% below 500, 38% between 500 and 599, 21% between 600 and 699, and 2% between 700 and 800. Math-- 46% below 500, 40% between 500 and 599, 11% between 600 and 699, and 2% between 700 and 800. 43% of the current freshmen were in the top fifth of their class; 68% were in the top two fifths. **Admissions Contact:** Phil Cook, Vice President for Enrollment. Email: *admissions@leeuniversity.edu* Web: *www.leeuniversity.edu*

FINANCIAL AID: In 2016-2017, 89% of all full-time freshmen and 61% of continuing full-time students received some form of financial aid. 89% of all full-time freshmen and 61% of continuing full-time students received need-based aid. The average freshman award was $12,763. Need-based scholarships or need-based grants averaged $10,615; need-based self-help aid (loans and jobs) averaged $3,565; non-need-based athletic scholarships averaged $9,134; other non-need-based awards and non-need-based scholarships averaged $8,465; and $3,528 from other forms of aid. The average financial indebtedness of the 2016 graduate was $32,162. The college's own financial statement is required. The FAFSA code is 003500. The priority date for freshman financial aid applications for fall entry is March 15. The filing deadline for fall entry is rolling.

LEMOYNE-OWEN COLLEGE — A-3

www.loc.edu

Memphis, TN 38126 — **(901) 435-1528**, **(800) 737-7778**

Fax: (901) 942-6233 — **Email: admissions@loc.edu**

Full-time: 300 men, 340 women	**Faculty:** 45
Part-time: 65 men, 80 women	**Ph.D.s:** 80%
Graduate: n/av	**Student/Faculty:** 14 to 1
Year: semesters, summer session	**Tuition:** $10,880
Room & Board: $6100	**Freshman Class:** n/av
SAT or ACT: required	**CEEB CODE:** 1403
Application Deadline: n/av	**COMPETITIVE**

LeMoyne-Owen College, established in 1862, is a private, liberal arts college affiliated with the United Church of Christ and the Tennessee Baptist, Missionary and Educational Convention, offering degrees in the liberal arts and sciences and business administration. The figures in the above capsule and in this profile are approximate. There is 1 undergraduate school. In addition to regional accreditation, LOC has baccalaureate program accreditation with NCATE. The 15-acre campus is in an urban area in Memphis. Including any residence halls, there are 18 buildings.

STUDENT LIFE: 87% of undergraduates are from Tennessee. Others are from 17 states, and 10 foreign countries. 95% are from public schools. 97% are African American; 1% White; 1% Hispanic; 1% Foreign. 87% are Protestant. **Female To Male Ratio:** 1.2:1. The average age of freshmen is 18; all undergraduates, 26. **Housing:** 336 students can be accommodated in college housing, which includes single-sex dorms. On-campus housing is available on a first-come and first-served basis. Priority is given to out-of-town students. 80% of students commute. Alcohol is not permitted. All students may keep cars.

FACULTY/CLASSROOMS: All teach undergraduates, and 40% do research. No introductory courses are taught by graduate students. The average class size in an introductory lecture is 15; in a laboratory is 15; and in a regular course is 12.

PROGRAMS OF STUDY: LOC confers B.A., B.S., and B.B.A. degrees. Associate degrees are also awarded. Bachelor's degrees are awarded in BIOLOGICAL SCIENCE (biology/biological science), BUSINESS (accounting and business administration and management), COMMUNICATIONS AND THE ARTS (art, English, information technology, language arts, and music), COMPUTER AND PHYSICAL SCIENCE (chemistry, computer science, mathematics, natural sciences, and science), EDUCATION (early childhood education, education, and special education), SOCIAL SCIENCE (criminal justice, history, humanities, interdisciplinary studies, political science/government, social science, social work, sociology, and urban studies). Business, biology, and education are the strongest academically. Business, and biology have the largest enrollments.

ACTIVITIES: 8% of men belong to 4 national fraternities; 5% of women belong to 4 national sororities. There are 15 groups on campus, including cheerleading, choir, chorus, community outreach, drama, ethnic, newspaper, professional, religious, social service, and student government. Popular campus events include Homecoming and Black History Month. **Sports:** There are 4 intercollegiate sports for men and 5 for women. Facilities include a gym, a pool, and other phys ed installations. **Graduates:** From July 1, 2015 to June 30, 2016, 118 bachelor's degrees were awarded. The most popular majors were business management (37%), liberal studies (12%), and education (12%).

SERVICES: Counseling and information services are available, as is tutoring in every subject. There is also remedial math, reading, and writing. **Library/Resources:** The library contains 90,000 volumes, 1,000 audio/video tapes/CDs/DVDs, and subscribes to 300 periodicals including electronic. Computerized library services include interlibrary loans, database searching, Internet access, and Wi-Fi capability. Special learning facilities include an art gallery. **Physically Challenged Students:** All of the campus is accessible. Facilities include wheelchair ramps, elevators, special parking, and special class scheduling. **Special:** Students may cross-register with other institutions of the Greater Memphis Consortium. The college offers a work-study program, dual and student-designed majors, internships, nondegree study, and a pass/fail grading option. There is 1 national honor society, a freshman honors program, and 1 departmental honors program. **Visiting:** Regularly scheduled orientations are available for prospective students. There are guides for informal visits and visitors may sit in on classes.. **Campus Safety and Security:** Measures include 24-hour foot and vehicle patrol, security escort service, emergency telephones and lighted pathways/sidewalks.

REQUIREMENTS: The SAT or ACT is required. Applicants must graduate from an accredited secondary school, having completed 20 high school units. The college recommends 4 years of English, 2 each of math, science, and social studies, and 1 of a foreign language. Applicants must submit 2 letters of recommendation. Students 23 or older may be admitted to the division of lifelong learning, which accepts the GED. A GPA of 2.0 is required. AP and CLEP credits are accepted. Important factors in the admissions decision are advanced placement or honors courses, evidence of special talent, and parents or siblings attended your school. Successfully complete at least 120 semester hours of course work with a minimum cumulative GPA of 2.0. The last 30 of these credit hours must have been earned in residence at LeMoyne-Owen, and must include at least three credit hours in Core II courses at LeMoyne-Owen College. Only courses completed with a grade of A, B, C, D or P can be credited toward the degree. Earned at least 45 credit hours in 300 and 400 numbered courses at the junior/senior level. Completed the General and Liberal Arts Education Core Requirements with a minimum grade of C in all Core I and six of the Core II courses. Met the specific course requirements for a major concentration area with a minimum grade of C in all courses required for the major including cognate courses. Submitted a formal application for the degree and completed the College exit interview. All recent high school graduates must participate in the Freshman Year Experience Program. **Procedure:** Freshmen are admitted to all sessions. Entrance exams should be taken in the spring of the junior year. There are early admissions, deferred admissions, and rolling admissions plans. Applications should be filed by November 1 for spring entry; March 1 for summer entry, along with a $25 fee. Notifications are sent July 1. **Transfer Students:** 122 transfer students enrolled in 2015-2016. Applicants should have a GPA of 2.0 and must submit 2 copies of official transcripts plus a statement of good standing from the previous college attended. Students with fewer than 28 college credit hours must also submit a high school transcript and, if below age 21, ACT or SAT I scores. 30 of 120 credits required for the bachelor's degree must be completed at LOC. **International Students:** They must take the TOEFL, as well as the ACT.

Admissions Contact: Delphia Harris, Director of Admissions. Email: *admissions@loc.edu* Web: *www.loc.edu*

FINANCIAL AID: In 2016-2017, 90% of all full-time freshmen and continuing full-time students received some form of financial aid. 80% of all full-time freshmen and 90% of continuing full-time students received need-based aid. 90% of undergraduate students work part-time. Average annual earnings from campus work are $2880. LOC is a member of CSS. The college's own financial statement is required. The FAFSA code is 003501. The priority date for freshman financial aid applications for fall entry is May 1.

LINCOLN MEMORIAL UNIVERSITY E-1

www.lmunet.edu

Harrogate, TN 37752 (423) 869-6280
(800) 325-0900
Fax: (423) 869-6370 Email: admissions@lmunet.edu

Full-time: 350 men, 1000 women	**Faculty:** n/av
Part-time: 84 men, 220 women	**Ph.D.s:** n/av
Graduate: 408 men, 1078 women	**Student/Faculty:** 12 to 1
Year: semesters, summer session	**Tuition:** $20,520
Room & Board: $7550	**Freshman Class:** 1350 applied, 494 accepted, 184 enrolled
SAT or ACT: required	**CEEB CODE:** 1408
Application Deadline: open	**COMPETITIVE**

Lincoln Memorial University, founded in 1897, is an independent institution offering degree programs in the arts and sciences, business, education, and preprofessional training. The figures in the above capsule and in this profile are approximate. There are 4 undergraduate schools and 2 graduate schools. In addition to regional accreditation, LMU has baccalaureate program accreditation with CAHEA and NLN. The 1000-acre campus is in a rural area 55 miles north of Knoxville. Including any residence halls, there are 32 buildings.

STUDENT LIFE: 67% of undergraduates are from Tennessee. Others are from 25 states, 22 foreign countries, and Canada. 89% are from public schools. 94% are White; 4% Foreign; 2% African American. **Female To Male Ratio:** 2.7:1. The average age of freshmen is 19; all undergraduates, 23. 20% do not continue beyond their first year; 50% remain to graduate. **Housing:** 500 students can be accommodated in college housing, which includes single-sex and coed dorms, on-campus apartments, and married student housing. On-campus housing is guaranteed for the freshman year only, and is available on a first-come, and first-served basis. Priority is given to out-of-town students. 70% of students commute. All students may keep cars. Alcohol is not permitted.

FACULTY/CLASSROOMS: 49% of faculty are male; 51% are female. 80% teach undergraduates. No introductory courses are taught by graduate students. The average class size in an introductory lecture is 20; in a laboratory is 25; and in a regular course is 20.

PROGRAMS OF STUDY: LMU confers B.A., B.S., B.B.A., B.S.N. and B.S.W. degrees. Associate and master's degrees are also awarded. Bachelor's degrees are awarded in AGRICULTURE (wildlife management), BIOLOGICAL SCIENCE (biology/biological science), BUSINESS (accounting and business administration and management), COMMUNICATIONS AND THE ARTS (broadcasting, communications, English, and fine arts), COMPUTER AND PHYSICAL SCIENCE (chemistry, information sciences and systems, and mathematics), EDUCATION (athletic training, business education, early childhood education, elementary education, health education, middle school education, science education, and secondary education), ENGINEERING AND ENVIRONMENTAL DESIGN (environmental science), HEALTH PROFESSIONS (medical laboratory technology, nursing, predentistry, premedicine, and veterinary science), SOCIAL SCIENCE (history, prelaw, psychology, social science, and social work). Nursing, business, and education have the largest enrollments.

ACTIVITIES: There are 26 groups on campus, including art, cheerleading, choir, chorus, computers, drama, drill team, honors, international, literary magazine, newspaper, photography, radio and TV, religious, social service, student government, and yearbook. Popular campus events include Lincoln Day. **Sports:** There are 6 intercollegiate sports for men and 6 for women, and 4 intramural sports for men and 4 for women. Facilities include an arena, a gym, golf complex, soccer complex, tennis complex, and playing fileds. **Graduates:** From July 1, 2015 to June 30, 2016, 145 bachelor's degrees were awarded. The most popular majors were nursing (30%), elementary education (27%), and business (26%). In an average class, 42% graduate in 4 years or less.

SERVICES: Counseling and information services are available, as is tutoring in most subjects, and remedial math, reading, and writing. **Library/Resources:** The library contains 200,000 volumes, 160,506 microform items, 254 audio/video tapes/CDs/DVDs, and subscribes to 893 periodicals including electronic. Computerized library services include interlibrary loans, database searching, and Internet access. Special learning facilities include a radio station, TV station, and the Lincoln Museum. **Physically Challenged Students:** 60% of the campus is accessible. Facilities include wheelchair ramps, elevators, special parking, and special class scheduling. **Special:** LMU offers pass/fail options and credit for life, military, and work experience. Some internships are available. **Visiting:** There are regularly scheduled orientations for prospective students, including introductory sessions for both students and their parents and opportunities for advising, and registration sessions. There are guides for informal visits, visitors may sit in on classes, and stay overnight. To schedule a visit, contact the Office of Admissions and Recruitment. **Campus Safety and Security:** Measures include 24-hour foot and vehicle patrol, and lighted pathways/sidewalks.

REQUIREMENTS: Applicants must score 19 on the ACT or satisfactorily on the SAT, or graduate with a GPA of at least 2.3. Candidates for admission should be graduates of accredited secondary schools or have the GED. Students should have completed 4 years of English, 2 each of math and science, and 1 each of history and social studies. LMU requires applicants to be in the upper 50% of their class. AP and CLEP credits are accepted. Important factors in the admissions decision are recommendations by school officials, personality/intangible qualities, and leadership record. To graduate, all students must complete at least 128 semester credit hours, including the general studies requirements of the declared major and a minimum of 30 hours of in the major. Students must achieve a minimum GPA of 2.0. **Procedure:** Freshmen are admitted fall, spring, and summer. Entrance exams should be taken in the spring of the junior year. There are early admissions, deferred admissions, and rolling admissions plans. Application deadlines are open. The fall 2016 application fee was $25. **Transfer Students:** Transfer students who have completed 12 or more semester credit hours of potentially transferable course work at a regionally accredited college or university will be considered for transfer admissions. Students with fewer that 12 semester credit hours are subject to freshman admission procedures. Official transcripts from all colleges and universities must be submitted. 32 of 128 credits required for the bachelor's degree must be completed at LMU. **International Students:** There are 48 international students enrolled. They must take the TOEFL.

ADMISSIONS: 37% of the 2016-2017 applicants were accepted. **Admissions Contact:** Carla Brandon, Assistant Director of Admissions. Email: *admissions@lmunet.edu* Web: *www.lmunet.edu*

FINANCIAL AID: LMU is a member of CSS. The CCS/Profile, FAFSA, FFS, or SFS are required. The FAFSA code is 003502. Check with the school for current application deadlines.

LIPSCOMB UNIVERSITY C-2

www.lipscomb.edu

Nashville, TN 37204 (615) 966-6150
(877) 582-4766
Fax: (615) 966-1804 Email: admissions@lipscomb.edu

Full-time: 1028 men, 1628 women	**Faculty:** 166; IIA, +$
Part-time: 115 men, 215 women	**Ph.D.s:** 83%
Graduate: 577 men, 1069 women	**Student/Faculty:** 15 to 1
Year: semesters, summer session	**Tuition:** $29,756
Room & Board: $11,540	**Freshman Class:** 3464 applied, 2108 accepted, 636 enrolled
SAT CR/M: 570/570 **ACT:** 25	**CEEB CODE:** 1161
Application Deadline: open	**VERY COMPETITIVE**

Lipscomb University is a private coeducational institution whose principal focus is undergraduate education in the liberal arts and sciences, combined with a number of undergraduate professional and preprofessional fields, master's and doctoral degree programs. Its primary mission is to integrate Christian faith and practice with academic excellence. This mission is carried out not only in the classroom but also by involvement in numerous services to the church and the larger community. There are 10 undergraduate schools and 16 graduate schools. In addition to regional accreditation, Lipscomb has baccalaureate program accreditation with ABET, ACBSP, ACPE, ADA, CSWE, NASM, NCATE, NLN, CAAHEP, ACS, and ATS. The 89-acre campus is in a suburban area 2 miles south of downtown Nashville. Including any residence halls, there are 48 buildings.

STUDENT LIFE: 65% of undergraduates are from Tennessee. Others are from 44 states, 43 foreign countries, and Canada. 56% are from public schools. 77% are White; 7% African American; 7% Hispanic; 3% Asian American; 2% Foreign; 2% two or more races; 2% race unknown. 76% are Protestant. **Female To Male Ratio:** 1.6:1. The average age of freshmen is 19; all undergraduates, 22. 17% do not continue beyond their first year; 55% remain to graduate. **Housing:** 1500 students can be accommodated in college housing, which includes single-sex dorms and on-campus apartments. On-campus housing is guaranteed for the freshman year only, and is available on a first-come, and first-served basis. 50% of students commute. All students may keep cars. Alcohol is not permitted.

FACULTY/CLASSROOMS: 69% teach undergraduates, and 2% do research. No introductory courses are taught by graduate students.

PROGRAMS OF STUDY: Lipscomb confers B.A., B.S., B.B.A., B.F.A., B.M., B.S.N., B.S.W. and B.P.S. degrees. Associate, master's, and doctoral degrees are also awarded. Bachelor's degrees are awarded in AGRICULTURE (conservation and regulation), BIOLOGICAL SCIENCE (biochemistry, biology/adolescence education, biology/biological science, biophysics, and molecular biology), BUSINESS (accounting, business administration and management, entrepreneurial studies, fashion merchandising, finance, human resources/organizational management, international business management, management information systems, marketing management, marketing/retailing/merchandising, sports management, supply chain management, and sustainable management), COMMUNICATIONS AND THE ARTS (acting, art, communications, English, French, German, graphic design, journalism, music, music composition, music ministry, music performance, musical theater, Spanish, studio art, theatre arts, and visual and performing arts), COMPUTER AND PHYSICAL SCIENCE (applied mathematics, chemistry, chemistry/adolescence education, computer science, mathematics, physics, software engineering, and web services), EDUCATION (art education, drama education, early childhood education, education, elementary education, English education, foreign languages education, health education, mathematics education, middle school education, music education, and physical education), ENGINEERING AND ENVIRONMENTAL DESIGN (civil engineering, computer engineering, electrical/electronics engineering, environmental science, mechanical engineering, and preengineering), HEALTH PROFESSIONS (art therapy, exercise science, medical technology, nursing, predentistry, premedicine, preoptometry, prepharmacy, prephysical therapy, and preveterinary science), SOCIAL SCIENCE (American studies, biblical languages, biblical studies, dietetics, economics, European studies, family/consumer studies, food production/management/services, history, interdisciplinary studies, international studies, legal studies, liberal arts/general studies, missions, philosophy, political science/government, prelaw, psychology, social work, textiles and clothing, urban studies, and youth ministry). Biology, education, and engineering are the strongest academically. Business, biology, and nursing have the largest enrollments.

ACTIVITIES: 16% of men belong to 6 local fraternities; 17% of women belong to 7 local sororities. There are 55 groups on campus, including art, band, cheerleading, choir, chorale, chorus, computers, drama, environmental, ethnic, honors, international, jazz band, musical theater, newspaper, orchestra, pep band, photography, political, professional, radio and TV, religious, social, social service, student government, and yearbook. Popular campus events include Singarama, Annual Service Day, International Square Fair, StompFest, Anteater's Ball, Paint the Herd, and Battle of the Boulevard. **Sports:** There are 7 intercollegiate sports for men and 8 for women, and 13 intramural sports for men and 13 for women. Facilities include a basketball/multi-purpose court, racquetball courts, jogging course, and weight, aerobics, spinning, and recreation rooms for both men and women. **Graduates:** From July 1, 2015 to June 30, 2016, 565 bachelor's degrees were awarded. The most popular majors were business administration and marketing (23%), health professions and related programs (10%), and biological/life sciences (9%). 70 companies recruited on campus in 2015-2016. In an average class, 48% graduate in 4 years or less, 56% graduate in 5 years or less, and 58% graduate in 6 years or less. Of the 2015 graduating class, 30% were enrolled in graduate school within 6 months of graduation, and 60% were employed.

SERVICES: Counseling and information services are available, as is tutoring in some subjects, and a reader service for the blind, and remedial math, reading, and writing. **Library/Resources:** The library contains 184,759 volumes, 401,791 microform items, 5,740 audio/video tapes/CDs/DVDs, and subscribes to 825 periodicals including electronic. Computerized library services include interlibrary loans, database searching, Internet access, and Wi-Fi capability. Special learning facilities include an art gallery, radio station, and a multimedia production studio. **Physically Challenged Students:** All of the campus is accessible. Facilities include wheelchair ramps, elevators, special parking, specially equipped restrooms, special class scheduling, and lowered drinking fountains. **Special:** Some majors require an internship. There are study-abroad options through Lipscomb programs in Austria, Chile, and England, as well as a cooperative with the Council for Christian Colleges & Universities (CCCU) that allows students to choose from multiple countries. Several degree programs can be completed in an accelerated three-year format. A B.A.-B.S. option is available in music, and a B.F.A. option is available in art and theatre. Students can pursue an integrated studies major that allows them to custom design a course of study to match their personal and professional interests and goals. Dual bachelor's/master's degree options are available in accounting, biology, and information technology. There are also 5 national honor societies and a freshman honors program. **Visiting:** Regularly scheduled orientations are available for prospective students. There are guides for informal visits, visitors may sit in on classes, and stay overnight. To schedule a visit, contact Dana Anderson at (615) 966-1776. **Campus Safety and Security:** Measures include 24-hour foot and vehicle patrol, emergency notification system, self-defense education, and security escort services. There are also shuttle buses, emergency telephones, lighted pathways/sidewalks, controlled access to dorms/residences, and residence hall security systems.

REQUIREMENTS: The SAT or ACT is required. Candidates for admission should be graduates of accredited secondary schools. The GED is accepted. 14 academic units are required. Students should have completed 4 units of English and 2 units each of history, math, and science. 2 units of a foreign language are highly recommended. 2 additional units from the areas of English, foreign language, history, math, science, and social studies are also required. AP and CLEP credits are accepted. All students must take 18 hours of Bible/theology courses. Other general education requirements include Lipscomb Seminar (freshman seminar class), 6 semester hours each in communications, humanities, science, history, and social science, 3 in math, 2 physical education, and 2 service learning experiences. Students must complete a total of 126 semester hours and have a minimum GPA of 2.0. At least 25% of credit hours must be earned at Lipscomb. Students are required to take and pass a proficiency test of basic computer concepts. **Procedure:** Freshmen are admitted to all sessions. There is a rolling admissions plan. Application deadlines are open. Application fee is $50. Applications are accepted online. **Transfer Students:** 155 transfer students enrolled in 2015-2016. College transcripts, an interview, and a statement of good standing from prior institutions are required. 32 of 126 credits required for the bachelor's degree must be completed at Lipscomb. **International Students:** There are 79 international students enrolled. The school actively recruits these students. They must take the TOEFL with a minimum score of 550 on the paper-based TOEFL (PBT) or 80 on the Internet-based version (iBT) or take the MELAB. They must also take the SAT or ACT.

ADMISSIONS: 61% of the 2016-2017 applicants were accepted. The SAT scores for the 2016-2017 freshman class were: Critical Reading-- 22% below 500, 36% between 500 and 599, 35% between 600 and 699, and 8% between 700 and 800. Math-- 27% below 500, 35% between 500 and 599, 31% between 600 and 699, and 8% between 700 and 800. The ACT scores were 1% between 12 and 17, 34% between 18 and 23, 48% between 24 and 29, and 17% above 30. 48% of the current freshmen were in the top fifth of their class; 74% were in the top two fifths. There were 4 National Merit finalists. 13 freshmen graduated first in their class. **Admissions Contact:** Johnathan Akin, Senior Director of Admissions. Email: *admissions@lipscomb.edu* Web: *www.lipscomb.edu*

FINANCIAL AID: In 2016-2017, 99% of all full-time freshmen and 90%

of continuing full-time students received some form of financial aid. Average annual earnings from campus work are $3500. The FAFSA code is 003486. The priority date for freshman financial aid applications for fall entry is January 31.

MARYVILLE COLLEGE E-2

www.maryvillecollege.edu

Maryville, TN 37804	**(865) 981-8206** **(800) 597-2687**
Fax: (865) 981-8005	**Email: admissions@maryvillecollege.edu**
Full-time: 518 men, 644 women	**Faculty:** 78; IIB, --$
Part-time: 8 men, 6 women	**Ph.D.s:** 91%
Graduate: n/av	**Student/Faculty:** 15 to 1
Year: 4-1-4, summer session	**Tuition:** $33,542
Room & Board: $10,868	**Freshman Class:** 1584 applied, 1203 accepted, 317 enrolled
SAT CR/M/W: 537/535/528 **ACT:** 24	**CEEB CODE:** 1454
Application Deadline: March 1	**COMPETITIVE**

Maryville College, founded in 1819, is a private liberal arts college affiliated with the Presbyterian Church. Figures in the above capsule and in this profile are approximate. There is 1 undergraduate school. In addition to regional accreditation, Maryville has baccalaureate program accreditation with NASM. The 350-acre campus is in a suburban area 15 miles south of Knoxville. Including any residence halls, there are 22 buildings.

STUDENT LIFE: 76% of undergraduates are from Tennessee. Others are from 32 states, 20 foreign countries, and Canada. 87% are from public schools. 85% are White; 6% African American; 4% Foreign; 2% Hispanic; 1% Asian American; 1% American Indian/Alaska Native. 64% are Protestant. **Female To Male Ratio:** 1.2:1. The average age of freshmen is 18; all undergraduates, 21. 28% do not continue beyond their first year; 52% remain to graduate. **Housing:** 802 students can be accommodated in college housing, which includes single-sex and coed dorms, on-campus apartments, and off-campus apartments. In addition, there are language houses and special-interest houses. On-campus housing is guaranteed for all 4 years. 69% of students live on campus; of those, 50% remain on campus on weekends. All students may keep cars.

FACULTY/CLASSROOMS: 45% of faculty are male; 55% are female. All teach undergraduates, and all do research. No introductory courses are taught by graduate students. The average class size in an introductory lecture is 28; in a laboratory is 15; and in a regular course is 16.

PROGRAMS OF STUDY: Maryville confers B.A. and B.Mus. degrees. Bachelor's degrees are awarded in AGRICULTURE (environmental studies), BIOLOGICAL SCIENCE (biochemistry and biology/biological science), BUSINESS (business administration and management and recreation and leisure services), COMMUNICATIONS AND THE ARTS (American Sign Language, art, art history and appreciation, creative writing, dramatic arts, English, English as a second/foreign language, music, music performance, and Spanish), COMPUTER AND PHYSICAL SCIENCE (chemical physics, chemistry, computer science, and mathematics), EDUCATION (elementary education, music education, physical education, science education, and secondary education), ENGINEERING AND ENVIRONMENTAL DESIGN (engineering and preengineering), HEALTH PROFESSIONS (nursing, predentistry, and premedicine), SOCIAL SCIENCE (economics, history, international relations, interpreter for the deaf, political science/government, prelaw, psychology, religion, social science, and sociology). Biology, chemistry, and English are the strongest academically. Business, biology, and psychology have the largest enrollments.

ACTIVITIES: There are no fraternities or sororities. There are 53 groups on campus, including art, band, cheerleading, choir, chorus, computers, dance, drama, equestrian and gospel music, ethnic, honors, international, jazz band, LGBT, literary magazine, musical theater, newspaper, orchestra, pep band, photography, political, professional, radio and TV, religious, social service, student government, and symphony. Popular campus events include Dogwood Arts Festival, Blister-in-the-Sun, and Spring Fling. **Sports:** There are 7 intercollegiate sports for men and 7 for women, and 12 intramural sports for men and 11 for women. Facilities include a phys ed building with an indoor pool, tennis and racquetball courts, a weight room, and football, soccer, baseball, and softball fields, and an off-campus equestrian arena. **Graduates:** From July 1, 2015 to June 30, 2016, 201 bachelor's degrees were awarded. The most popular majors were business/commerce (16%), child development (11%), and psychology (6%). 80 companies recruited on campus in 2015-2016. In an average class, 45% graduate in 4 years or less, 50% graduate in 5 years or less, and 52% graduate in 6 years or less. Of the 2015 graduating class, 28% were enrolled in graduate school within 6 months of graduation, and 67% were employed.

SERVICES: Counseling and information services are available, as is tutoring in every subject, and a reader service for the blind, and remedial math. There are sign language interpreters for deaf students. **Library/Resources:** The 2 libraries contain 133,686 volumes, 8,263 microform items, and subscribe to 16,525 periodicals including electronic. Computerized library services include interlibrary loans, database searching, Internet access, and Wi-Fi capability. Special learning facilities include an art gallery, radio station, a greenhouse, and college woods. **Physically Challenged Students:** 75% of the campus is accessible. Facilities include wheelchair ramps, elevators, special parking, specially equipped restrooms, special class scheduling, lowered drinking fountains, lowered telephones, and special housing. **Special:** Maryville offers cross-registration with the University of Tennessee and Vanderbilt University, internships, study abroad in 9 countries, a Washington semester, accelerated degree programs, a B.A.-B.S. degree in engineering, and dual and student-designed majors. There are 3-2 engineering degrees offered with regional universities. Nondegree study and pass/fail options are possible. There are 6 national honor societies, a freshman honors program, and 100 departmental honors programs. **Visiting:** There are regularly scheduled orientations for prospective students, including an overnight in a residence hall, class attendance, meeting with students and faculty, a campus tour, and an interview. There are guides for informal visits, visitors may sit in on classes, and stay overnight. To schedule a visit, contact the Admissions Office. **Campus Safety and Security:** Measures include 24-hour foot and vehicle patrol, security escort services, and lighted pathways/sidewalks.

REQUIREMENTS: The SAT or ACT is required. Candidates should be graduates of accredited secondary schools or have the GED. They should also have 15 academic credits with 4 years of English, 3 each of math and science, 2 years of foreign language, and 2 of history or social studies. An essay, portfolio, audition, and interview are all recommended. AP and CLEP credits are accepted. Important factors in the admissions decision are advanced placement or honors courses, extracurricular activities record, and leadership record. Each degree has its own general education requirements, which include humanities and a foreign language. Students must complete at least 128 total credit hours, including 48 in the major, and must maintain a minimum 2.0 GPA. A year-long freshman seminar and orientation are required in addition to a senior thesis in all majors and senior comprehensive exams. **Procedure:** Freshmen are admitted in the fall, spring, and summer. Entrance exams should be taken by October of the senior year. There are early decision, early admissions, and deferred admissions plans. Early decision applications should be filed by November 15; regular applications, by March 1 for fall entry; November 1 for spring entry; and May 1 for summer entry. Notification of early decision is sent December 1; regular decision, April 1. 84 early decision candidates were accepted for the 2016-2017 class. Applications are accepted on-line. **Transfer Students:** 53 transfer students enrolled in 2015-2016. Transfer applicants must have a minimum GPA of 2.0 and a recommended 15 credit hours earned. An interview is also recommended. 45 of 128 credits required for the bachelor's degree must be completed at Maryville. **International Students:** There are 44 international students enrolled. The school actively recruits these students. They must take the TOEFL with a minimum score of 525 on the paper-based TOEFL (PBT) or 74 on the Internet-based version (iBT), an IELTS score of 6, a STEP test grade pre-One, or a Michigan Test score of 80.

ADMISSIONS: 76% of the 2016-2017 applicants were accepted. The SAT scores for the 2016-2017 freshman class were: Critical Reading-- 35% below 500, 34% between 500 and 599, 27% between 600 and 699, and 4% between 700 and 800. Math-- 34% below 500, 42% between 500 and 599, 23% between 600 and 699, and 1% between 700 and 800. Writing-- 35% below 500, 37% between 500 and 599, 25% between 600 and 699, and 3% between 700 and 800. The ACT scores were 20% below 12, 26% between 12 and 17, 23% between 18 and 23, 16% between 24 and 29, and 15% above 30. 52% of the current freshmen were in the top fifth of their class; 80% were in the top two fifths. 5 freshmen graduated first in their class. **Admissions Contact:** Doug Carter, Assistant Director of

Admissions. Email: *admissions@maryvillecollege.edu* Web: *www.maryvillecollege.edu*

FINANCIAL AID: In 2016-2017, 100% of all full-time freshmen received some form of financial aid. 97% of all full-time freshmen received need-based aid. The average freshman award was $26,518. Need-based scholarships or need-based grants averaged $17,728 ($36,610 maximum); need-based self-help aid (loans and jobs) averaged $2,859 ($7,500 maximum); and other non-need-based awards and non-need-based scholarships averaged $1,947 ($23,000 maximum). 49% of undergraduate students work part-time. Average annual earnings from campus work are $1559. The average financial indebtedness of the 2016 graduate was $14,344. Maryville is a member of CSS. The FAFSA code is 003505. The priority date for freshman financial aid applications for fall entry is March 1.

MEMPHIS COLLEGE OF ART A-3

www.mca.edu

Memphis, TN 38104	(901) 272-5151 (800) 727-1088
Fax: (901) 272-5158	**Email:** info@mca.edu
Full-time: 123 men, 220 women	**Faculty:** 26
Part-time: 13 men, 21 women	**Ph.D.s:** 85%
Graduate: 17 men, 39 women	**Student/Faculty:** 11 to 1
Year: semesters, summer session	**Tuition:** $31,000
Room & Board: $8750	**Freshman Class:** 239 applied, 219 accepted, 94 enrolled
SAT: required **ACT:** 22	**CEEB CODE:** 1511
Application Deadline: August 3	**COMPETITIVE**

Memphis College of Art, established in 1936, is a private, independent institution offering degree programs in fine arts and design arts, drawing, painting, photography, printmaking, sculpture, metals, graphic design, illustration, animation, sequential narrative, and digital cinema. The figures in the above capsule and in this profile are approximate. There is 1 undergraduate school and 1 graduate school. In addition to regional accreditation, MCA has baccalaureate program accreditation with NASAD. The 200-acre campus is in an urban area Memphis, Tennessee. Including any residence halls, there are 6 buildings.

STUDENT LIFE: 60% of undergraduates are from out of state, mostly the South. Students are from 25 states, and 4 foreign countries. 69% are from public schools. 64% are White; 6% Hispanic; 2% Asian American; 2% Foreign; 19% African American. **Female To Male Ratio:** 1.8:1. The average age of freshmen is 18; all undergraduates, 23. 24% do not continue beyond their first year; 46% remain to graduate. **Housing:** 165 students can be accommodated in college housing, which includes single-sex on-campus apartments and off-campus apartments. On-campus housing is available on a first-come and first-served basis. Priority is given to out-of-town students. 56% of students commute. All students may keep cars. Alcohol is not permitted.

FACULTY/CLASSROOMS: 56% of faculty are male; 44% are female. 97% teach undergraduates. No introductory courses are taught by graduate students. The average class size in an introductory lecture is 20 and in a regular course is 17.

PROGRAMS OF STUDY: MCA confers B.F.A. degrees. Master's degrees are also awarded. Bachelor's degrees are awarded in COMMUNICATIONS AND THE ARTS (animation, applied art, design, drawing, film arts, fine arts, graphic design, illustration, metal/jewelry, painting, photography, and studio art), COMPUTER AND PHYSICAL SCIENCE (digital arts/technology).

ACTIVITIES: There are no fraternities or sororities. There are 5 groups on campus, including art, ethnic, photography, and student government. Popular campus events include Holiday Bazaar, Gallery Openings, and Community Dinners. **Sports:** There is no sports program at MCA. Facilities include football, soccer, bicycling, a public golf, playing fields, and a volleyball court. **Graduates:** From July 1, 2015 to June 30, 2016, 53 bachelor's degrees were awarded. The most popular majors were fine arts (38%), design arts (38%), and digital media (13%). 25 companies recruited on campus in 2015-2016. In an average class, 46% graduate in 6 years or less.

SERVICES: Counseling and information services are available, as is tutoring in some subjects, and remedial writing. Academic Counseling is available for weekly individual sessions. **Library/Resources:** The library contains 18,000 volumes, and subscribes to 120 periodicals including electronic. Computerized library services include interlibrary loans and Internet access. Special learning facilities include an art gallery, and a sound & lighting studios. **Physically Challenged Students:** All of the campus is accessible. Facilities include wheelchair ramps, elevators, special parking, specially equipped restrooms, lowered drinking fountains, lowered telephones, and special housing. **Special:** Special academic programs include off-campus internships for juniors and seniors in advertising agencies, design firms, or other educational situations; on- and off-campus work-study; and study abroad in Europe, Canada, Japan, Italy, or Ireland. There are mobility programs with the Association of Independent Colleges of Art and Design (AICAD), and the Memphis Area Consortium. **Visiting:** There are regularly scheduled orientations for prospective students. There are guides for informal visits and visitors may sit in on classes. To schedule a visit, contact the Admissions Office. **Campus Safety and Security:** Measures include 24-hour foot and vehicle patrol, emergency notification system, and security escort services. There are shuttle buses, lighted pathways/sidewalks, card access to campus building and some housing. 24/7 security staff, chaperone, shuttle service, and 24/7 security contact phone number.

REQUIREMENTS: The SAT or ACT is required. Test scores are used for admissions and placement purposes. Other admissions requirements include a completed application form, high school transcripts (GED is accepted), and a portfolio. An interview is recommended. A GPA of 2.0 is required. AP and CLEP credits are accepted. Important factors in the admissions decision are evidence of special talent, advanced placement or honors courses, and extracurricular activities record. Students must complete 120 credit hours, including 33 in the major, with a minimum GPA of 2.0. Distribution requirements comprise 45 credits in liberal studies, including 12 in art history, 6 in English, and 3 each in literature, social sciences, and natural science or math; 30 credits in elective studio art; and 21 credits in foundation classes, including drawing, 2-D and 3-D design, digital foundations, color foundations, and idea, process, and criticism. **Procedure:** Freshmen are admitted in the fall and spring. There is a rolling admissions plan. Applications should be filed by August 3 for fall entry, along with a $25 fee. Applications are accepted online. **Transfer Students:** 33 transfer students enrolled in 2015-2016. Applicants must submit official college transcripts and a portfolio. 48 of 120 credits required for the bachelor's degree must be completed at MCA. **International Students:** There are 12 international students enrolled. The school actively recruits these students. They must take the TOEFL, as well as the SAT or ACT.

ADMISSIONS: 92% of the 2016-2017 applicants were accepted. The ACT scores were 23% below 12, 39% between 12 and 17, 23% between 18 and 23, 13% between 24 and 29, and 3% above 30. **Admissions Contact:** Annette Moore, Dean of Admissions. Email: *info@mca.edu* Web: *www.mca.edu*

FINANCIAL AID: In 2016-2017, 97% of all full-time freshmen and 92% of continuing full-time students received some form of financial aid. 52% of all full-time freshmen and 47% of continuing full-time students received need-based aid. 40% of undergraduate students work part-time. Average annual earnings from campus work are $325. The average financial indebtedness of the 2016 graduate was $34,360. MCA is a member of CSS. The FAFSA code is 003507. The priority date for freshman financial aid applications for fall entry is March 1. The filing deadline for fall entry is rolling.

MIDDLE TENNESSEE STATE UNIVERSITY C-2

www.mtsu.edu

Murfreesboro, TN 37132	(615) 898-2111 (800) 433-MTSU
Fax: (615) 898-5478	**Email:** admissions@mtsu.edu
Full-time: 9204 men, 9708 women	**Faculty:** n/av
Part-time: 1577 men, 1810 women	**Ph.D.s:** 68%
Graduate: 963 men, 1926 women	**Student/Faculty:** n/av
Year: semesters, summer session	**Tuition:** $4000 ($11,900)
Room & Board: $4650	**Freshman Class:** 9431 applied, 6616 accepted, 1758 enrolled
SAT: required **ACT:** 22	**CEEB CODE:** 1466
Application Deadline: July 1	**COMPETITIVE**

Middle Tennessee State University, founded in 1911, is a comprehensive public university that offers undergraduate and graduate programs reflecting an emphasis on research, creative arts, and public and professional service activities. The figures in the above capsule and in this profile are approximate. There are 7 undergraduate schools and 1 graduate school. In addition to regional accreditation, MTSU has baccalaureate program accreditation with AACSB, ABET, ACEJMC, ADA, CSAB, CSWE, FIDER, NASAD, NASM, NCATE, NLN, NRPA, ACS, NAIT, AAFCS, CAA, NASP, and CACREP. The 500-acre campus is in an urban area 32 miles southeast of Nashville, TN. Including any residence halls, there are 159 buildings.

STUDENT LIFE: 93% of undergraduates are from Tennessee. Others are from 47 states, 70 foreign countries, and Canada. 80% are White; 3% Asian American; 2% Hispanic; 14% African American. 45% are Protestant; 43% claim no religious affiliation. **Female To Male Ratio:** 1.1:1. The average age of freshmen is 18; all undergraduates, 19. **Housing:** 3294 students can be accommodated in college housing, which includes single-sex and coed dorms, on-campus apartments, married student housing, honors houses, fraternity houses, sorority houses, first year experience program, and various learning community programs. On-campus housing is available on a first-come and first-served basis. 85% of students commute. All students may keep cars. Alcohol is not permitted.

FACULTY/CLASSROOMS: 53% of faculty are male; 47% are female. No introductory courses are taught by graduate students. The average class size in an introductory lecture is 24; in a laboratory is 18; and in a regular course is 23.

PROGRAMS OF STUDY: MTSU confers B.A., B.S., B.B.A., B.F.A., B.Mus., B.S.N., B.S.W., and B.U.S. degrees. Master's and doctoral degrees are also awarded. Bachelor's degrees are awarded in AGRICULTURE (agricultural business management, animal science, and plant science), BIOLOGICAL SCIENCE (biology/biological science and nutrition), BUSINESS (accounting, banking and finance, business administration and management, entrepreneurial studies, marketing/retailing/merchandising, office supervision and management, and recreation and leisure services), COMMUNICATIONS AND THE ARTS (communications, English, French, German, graphic design, music, music business management, public relations, Spanish, and studio art), COMPUTER AND PHYSICAL SCIENCE (chemistry, computer science, information sciences and systems, mathematics, physics, and science), EDUCATION (art education, athletic training, business education, early childhood education, health education, physical education, and special education), ENGINEERING AND ENVIRONMENTAL DESIGN (engineering technology, environmental science, industrial engineering technology, and interior design), HEALTH PROFESSIONS (health science and nursing), SOCIAL SCIENCE (anthropology, criminal justice, economics, family/consumer studies, geography, history, interdisciplinary studies, international relations, philosophy, political science/government, prelaw, psychology, public administration, social work, sociology, and textiles and clothing). Nursing, and science are the strongest academically. Recording industry has the largest enrollment.

ACTIVITIES: 9% of men belong to 16 national fraternities; 11% of women belong to 1 local and 11 national sororities. There are 153 groups on campus, including art, band, cheerleading, chess, choir, chorale, chorus, computers, dance, debate, drama, drill team, ethnic, film, honors, international, jazz band, LGBT, literary magazine, marching band, musical theater, newspaper, pep band, photography, political, professional, radio and TV, religious, social, social service, student government, and symphony. Popular campus events include Founders Day, Family Day, and African American History Month. **Sports:** There are 8 intercollegiate sports for men and 9 for women, and 13 intramural sports for men and 13 for women. Facilities include an athletic center with a stadium, a gym, soccer/track complex, tennis courts, baseball and softball fields, and a recreation center with courts, an indoor track, indoor and outdoor pools, a rock-climbing wall, and a sand volleyball court. **Graduates:** From July 1, 2015 to June 30, 2016, 3629 bachelor's degrees were awarded. The most popular majors were business/marketing (20%), visual and performing arts (11%), and interdisciplinary studies (10%).

SERVICES: Counseling and information services are available, as is tutoring in most subjects, and a reader service for the blind, and remedial math, reading, and writing. **Library/Resources:** The library contains 702,764 volumes, 1.3 million microform items, and subscribes to 3,798 periodicals including electronic. Computerized library services include interlibrary loans, database searching, and Internet access. Special learning facilities include an art gallery, planetarium, radio station, TV station, and numerous research centers. **Physically Challenged Students:** All of the campus is accessible. Facilities include wheelchair ramps, elevators, special parking, specially equipped restrooms, special class scheduling, lowered drinking fountains, and lowered telephones. **Special:** MTSU offers co-op programs in aerospace, computer science, math, engineering technology, and industrial studies, cross-registration with Tennessee State University, internships, study abroad, work-study, double majors, a general studies degree, student-designed majors, nondegree study, and pass/fail options. Credit for life, military, and work experience may be granted. There are 2 national honor societies, a freshman honors program, and 25 departmental honors programs. **Visiting:** There are regularly scheduled orientations for prospective students, including campus tours and meeting with a departmental adviser. There are guides for informal visits and visitors may sit in on classes. To schedule a visit, contact the Office of Admissions. **Campus Safety and Security:** Measures include 24-hour foot and vehicle patrol, self-defense education, and security escort services. There are also shuttle buses, emergency telephones, and lighted pathways/sidewalks.

REQUIREMENTS: Applicants must have a minimum composite score of 22 on the ACT if the GPA is less than 3.0. A high school diploma is required, the GED is accepted. The number of academic credits required is 14, including 4 years of English, 3 of math, 2 each of a foreign language and science, and 1 each of social studies, U.S. history, and visual and/or performance arts, with an additional unit of math, language, or art recommended. AP and CLEP credits are accepted. To graduate, a total of at least 132 hours, including at least 48 of upper-level courses, is needed with a minimum overall GPA of 2.0. All students must complete the general studies requirements, including 9 hours each of natural science/math and humanities, 6 each of English composition, and history, 2 each of phys ed., arts/fine arts, social science, demonstrate computer literacy. A major field test and general studies exam are required. **Procedure:** Freshmen are admitted to all sessions. Entrance exams should be taken in the first half of the senior year. There are deferred admissions and rolling admissions plans. Applications should be filed by July 1 for fall entry, along with a $25 fee. Notification is sent on a rolling basis. Applications are accepted online. **Transfer Students:** Applicants must have a minimum 2.0 GPA and submit official transcripts from all previous colleges attended. If transferring fewer than 9 semester hours, they must also meet freshman admission requirements. 24 of 120 credits required for the bachelor's degree must be completed at MTSU. **International Students:** There are 124 international students enrolled. The school actively recruits these students. They must take the TOEFL or MELAB. They must also take the SAT or ACT, scoring 20.

ADMISSIONS: 70% of the 2016-2017 applicants were accepted. The ACT scores were 32% below 12, 35% between 12 and 17, 20% between 18 and 23, 7% between 24 and 29, and 5% above 30. There were 2 National Merit finalists. 31 freshmen graduated first in their class. **Admissions Contact:** Linda Elaine Olsen, Director of Admissions. Email: *admissions@mtsu.edu* Web: *www.mtsu.edu*

FINANCIAL AID: In 2016-2017, 35% of all full-time freshmen and 52% of continuing full-time students received some form of financial aid. 19% of all full-time freshmen and 29% of continuing full-time students received need-based aid. The average freshman award was $6,265. Need-based scholarships or need-based grants averaged $2,295 ($6,150 maximum); need-based self-help aid (loans and jobs) averaged $1,589 ($10,500 maximum); non-need-based athletic scholarships averaged $11,180 ($9,500 maximum); and other non-need-based awards and non-need-based scholarships averaged $4,057 ($5,000 maximum). 84% of undergraduate students work part-time. Average annual earnings from campus work are $3200. The average financial indebtedness of the 2016 graduate was $19,800. The FAFSA code is 003510. Check with the school for current application deadlines.

MILLIGAN COLLEGE F-1
www.milligan.edu

Milligan College, TN 37682 (423) 461-8757 (800) 262-8337

Fax: (423) 461-8982 — **Email:** operations@milligan.edu

Full-time: 307 men, 455 women	**Faculty:** 68; IIB, --$
Part-time: 46 men, 77 women	**Ph.D.s:** 75%
Graduate: 132 men, 183 women	**Student/Faculty:** 13 to 1
Year: semesters, summer session	**Tuition:** $30,350
Room & Board: $6700	**Freshman Class:** 528 applied, 513 accepted, 253 enrolled
SAT CR/M/W: 530/530/500 **ACT:** 24	**CEEB CODE:** 1469
Application Deadline: August 1	**COMPETITIVE**

Milligan College, founded in 1866, is a private institution affiliated with the Christian Church, that offers degree programs stress the liberal arts and professional studies. The figures in the above capsule and in this profile are approximate. There are 5 undergraduate schools and 5 graduate schools. In addition to regional accreditation, Milligan has baccalaureate program accreditation with NCATE, ACOTE, CCNE, and ATS. The 235-acre campus is in a suburban area 4 miles south of Johnson City. Including any residence halls, there are 50 buildings.

STUDENT LIFE: 63% of undergraduates are from Tennessee. Others are from 33 states, 15 foreign countries, and Canada. 80% are from public schools. 85% are White; 4% Hispanic; 4% Foreign; 3% African American; 2% two or more races; 1% Asian American. 83% are Protestant. **Female To Male Ratio:** 1.5:1. The average age of freshmen is 18; all undergraduates, 24. 20% do not continue beyond their first year; 54% remain to graduate. **Housing:** 643 students can be accommodated in college housing, which includes single-sex dorms, on-campus apartments, and married student housing. On-campus housing is guaranteed for all 4 years. 70% of students live on campus; of those, 85% remain on campus on weekends. All students may keep cars. Alcohol is not permitted.

FACULTY/CLASSROOMS: 49% of faculty are male; 51% are female. 96% teach undergraduates. No introductory courses are taught by graduate students. The average class size in an introductory lecture is 50; in a laboratory is 15; and in a regular course is 15.

PROGRAMS OF STUDY: Milligan confers B.A., B.S., B.S.W., and B.S.N. degrees. Master's and doctoral degrees are also awarded. Bachelor's degrees are awarded in BIOLOGICAL SCIENCE (biology/biological science), BUSINESS (accounting, business administration w/legal studies, and business administration and management), COMMUNICATIONS AND THE ARTS (art, communications, English, fine arts, music, photography, and piano performance), COMPUTER AND PHYSICAL SCIENCE (chemistry, computer information systems, computer science, information sciences and systems, and mathematics), EDUCATION (early childhood education, mathematics education, music education, and special education), ENGINEERING AND ENVIRONMENTAL DESIGN (engineering), HEALTH PROFESSIONS (allied health, exercise science, nursing, pre-health studies, premedicine, and prepharmacy), SOCIAL SCIENCE (biblical studies, history, humanities, liberal arts, sciences, general studies, humanities, psychology, religious music, social work, sociology, and youth ministry). Engineering, and nursing are the strongest academically. Business, psychology, and nursing have the largest enrollments.

ACTIVITIES: There are no fraternities or sororities. There are 40 groups on campus, including art, band, cheerleading, choir, chorus, computers, dance, drama, ethnic, film, honors, international, jazz band, literary magazine, musical theater, newspaper, orchestra, pep band, photography, political, professional, radio and TV, religious, social, social service, student government, symphony, and yearbook. Popular campus events include Wonderful Wednesday, Campus Theater Productions, and Faculty Auction. **Sports:** There are 6 intercollegiate sports for men and 6 for women, and 7 intramural sports for men and 7 for women. Facilities include a swimming pool, basketball court, stadium, gym, tennis courts, baseball, softball, soccer fields, and a Wellness Center with workout rooms and exercise equipment. **Graduates:** From July 1, 2015 to June 30, 2016, 204 bachelor's degrees were awarded. The most popular majors were business administration (16%), nursing (15%), and human performance and exercise science (10%). In an average class, 55% graduate in 4 years or less, 57% graduate in 5 years or less, and 63% graduate in 6 years or less.

SERVICES: Counseling and information services are available, as is tutoring in most subjects, and a remedial math, reading, and writing. **Library/Resources:** The 2 libraries contain 395,323 volumes, 3,497 microform items, 3,894 audio/video tapes/CDs/DVDs, and subscribe to 33,622 periodicals including electronic. Computerized library services include interlibrary loans, database searching, Internet access, and Wi-Fi capability. Special learning facilities include an art gallery, radio station, TV station, editing rooms, theater, prop shop, and darkroom. **Physically Challenged Students:** 80% of the campus is accessible. Facilities include wheelchair ramps, elevators, special parking, specially equipped restrooms, and lowered drinking fountains. **Special:** Milligan offers a Washington semester, study abroad in England, Australia, China, Costa Rica, Egypt, Russia, and Uganda, co-op programs and internships in several majors, work-study, nondegree study, and dual majors. 3 credits are offered for students participating in the annual summer tour of Europe. There are 5 national honor societies and a freshman honors program.

Visiting: There are regularly scheduled orientations for prospective students, consisting of 1-day open houses that include a campus tour, a financial aid workshop, a meal in the cafeteria, and the opportunity to meet faculty and to learn about student life. There are new student orientation weekends in April, June, and August. There are guides for informal visits, visitors may sit in on classes, and stay overnight. To schedule a visit, contact the Campus Visits Coordinator at REBooher@milligan.edu. **Campus Safety and Security:** Measures include 24-hour foot and vehicle patrol and emergency notification system. There are emergency telephones, lighted pathways/sidewalks, controlled access to dorms/residences, and evening vehicle patrol.

REQUIREMENTS: The SAT or ACT is required. Students must be graduates of an accredited secondary school, with 18 Carnegie units and 18 academic credits, including courses in English, math, science, history and social studies, and speech, music, or art, along with 2 years of a foreign language. Music students must audition. The GED is accepted. Other factors in the admission decision include character, recommendations by school officials, advanced placement, dual enrollment, or honor courses, ability, preparation, and Christian commitment. AP and CLEP credits are accepted. Important factors in the admissions decision are leadership record, recommendations by school officials, and personality/intangible qualities. Students must complete at least 128 semester hours, including 24 to 62 in the major, and 59 to 71 in the general education core, with a minimum GPA of 2.0. Required disciplines include 24 credit hours of humanities, 9 of Bible studies, 8 of lab science, 6 of social science, 3 each of math, speech, and ethnic studies, 2 of phys ed, and 1 of introduction to college; B.A. candidates must also complete 6 to 12 in foreign language. All students must demonstrate computer literacy and attend all required chapel/convocation sessions. Measures of Academic Proficiency and Progress and an exam in the major are also required. **Procedure:** Freshmen are admitted in the fall, spring, and summer. Entrance exams should be taken beginning in the spring of the junior year. There are deferred admissions and rolling admissions plans. Applications should be filed by August 1 for fall entry; December 15 for spring entry, along with a $30 fee. Notification is sent on a rolling basis. Applications are accepted on-line. **Transfer Students:** 70 transfer students enrolled in 2015-2016. A minimum GPA of 2.5 is preferred. Applicants must submit transcripts of all previous college work. Church or Character Reference, and Academic Reference. 45 of 128 credits required for the bachelor's degree must be completed at Milligan. **International Students:** There are 29 international students enrolled. They must take the TOEFL with a minimum score of 79 on the Internet-based version (iBT). They must also take the SAT or ACT.

ADMISSIONS: 97% of the 2016-2017 applicants were accepted. **Admissions Contact:** Jacqui Potter, Operations Manager. Email: *operations@milligan.edu* Web: *www.milligan.edu*

FINANCIAL AID: In 2016-2017, 99% of all full-time freshmen and 96% of continuing full-time students received some form of financial aid. 56% of all full-time freshmen and 62% of continuing full-time students received need-based aid. The average freshman award was $23,571.. 38% of undergraduate students work part-time. Average annual earnings from campus work are $1649. The average financial indebtedness of the 2016 graduate was $27,146. The college's own financial statement is required. The FAFSA code is 003511. The priority date for freshman financial aid applications for fall entry is March 1.

RHODES COLLEGE — A-3

www.rhodes.edu

Memphis, TN 38112	(901) 843-3700 (800) 844-5969
Fax: (901) 843-3631	Email: adminfo@rhodes.edu
Full-time: 846 men, 1170 women	Faculty: 174; IIB, av$
Part-time: 6 men, 9 women	Ph.D.s: 92%
Graduate: 13 men, 10 women	Student/Faculty: 11 to 1
Year: semesters, summer session	Tuition: $41,572
Room & Board: $10,328	Freshman Class: 3382 applied, 2029 accepted, 507 enrolled
SAT CR/M/W: 630/630/620 ACT: 28	CEEB CODE: 1730
Application Deadline: January 15	HIGHLY COMPETITIVE

Rhodes College, founded in 1848, is a private, church-affiliated institution of arts and sciences, with a campus in a Gothic architectural style. 13 of its buildings have been listed on the National Register of Historic Places. There is 1 undergraduate school and 1 graduate school. The 100-acre campus is in an urban area Memphis, TN. Including any residence halls, there are 45 buildings.

STUDENT LIFE: 74% of undergraduates are from out of state, mostly the South. Students are from 47 states, and 15 foreign countries. 53% are from public schools. 75% are White; 6% African American; 6% Asian American; 4% Hispanic; 3% Foreign; 3% two or more races; 2% race unknown; 1% American Indian/Alaska Native. **Female To Male Ratio:** 1.4:1. The average age of freshmen is 18; all undergraduates, 20. 11% do not continue beyond their first year; 80% remain to graduate. **Housing:** 1488 students can be accommodated in college housing, which includes single-sex and coed dorms and on-campus apartments, and learning communities. On-campus housing is guaranteed for the freshman year only and is available on a lottery system for upperclassmen. 71% of students live on campus; of those, 90% remain on campus on weekends. All students may keep cars.

FACULTY/CLASSROOMS: 52% of faculty are male; 48% are female. All teach undergraduates and do research. No introductory courses are taught by graduate students. The average class size in an introductory lecture is 14; in a laboratory is 14; and in a regular course is 14.

PROGRAMS OF STUDY: Rhodes confers B.A. and B.S. degrees. Master's degrees are also awarded. Bachelor's degrees are awarded in AGRICULTURE (environmental studies), BIOLOGICAL SCIENCE (biochemistry, biology/biological science, molecular biology, and neurosciences), BUSINESS (business administration and management), COMMUNICATIONS AND THE ARTS (art, English, French, German, music, Spanish, and theatre arts), COMPUTER AND PHYSICAL SCIENCE (chemistry, computer science, mathematics, and physics), ENGINEERING AND ENVIRONMENTAL DESIGN (environmental science), SOCIAL SCIENCE (anthropology, classical/ancient civilization, economics, history, interdisciplinary studies, international studies, Latin American studies, philosophy, political science/government, psychology, religion, Russian and Slavic studies, sociology, and urban studies). Business administration, biology, psychology and English are the strongest academically and have the largest enrollments.

ACTIVITIES: 35% of men belong to 8 national fraternities; 65% of women belong to 7 national sororities. There are 103 groups on campus, including Black Student Association, Contents Under Pressure (comedy improv troupe), Mock Trial Team, Model UN, art, cheerleading, chess, choir, chorale, chorus, computers, dance, debate, drama, environmental, ethnic, Honor Council, honors, international, LGBT, literary magazine, musical theater, newspaper, orchestra, pep band, photography, political, professional, religious, social, social service, student government, symphony, and yearbook. Popular campus events include Rites of Spring, All-Sing, and Hunger for Homeless. **Sports:** There are 11 intercollegiate sports for men and 12 for women, and 16 intramural sports for men and 16 for women. Facilities include a campus life center, which includes a performance gym, a multi-use gym, racquetball, and squash courts, a fitness center, and an indoor jogging track. Outdoor facilities include a pool, tennis courts, soccer fields, football field, track, and baseball and softball fields. **Graduates:** From July 1, 2015 to June 30, 2016, 433 bachelor's degrees were awarded. The most popular majors were business (15%), english, and psychology (9%), biology, and and history (8%). 100 companies recruited on campus in 2015-2016. In an average class, 76% graduate in 4 years or less, 80% graduate in 5 years or less, and 80% graduate in 6 years or less.

SERVICES: Counseling and information services are available, as is tutoring in some subjects, such as math, writing, modern languages, biology, chemistry, economics, business, computer science and physics. There is also a reader service for the blind. **Library/Resources:** The library contains 304,512 volumes, 110,513 microform items, 14,017 audio/video tapes/CDs/DVDs, and subscribes to 7,355 periodicals including electronic. Computerized library services include interlibrary loans, database searching, Internet access, and Wi-Fi capability. Special learning facilities include an art gallery, an art gallery, MRI, electron microscopes, astronomical observatory, GIS and archeology labs, and a modern languages lab. **Physically Challenged Students:** 90% of the campus is accessible. Facilities include wheelchair ramps, elevators, special parking, specially equipped restrooms, special class scheduling, lowered drinking fountains, lowered telephones, and an infrared hearing system in 1 of the auditoriums. **Special:** More than half of Rhodes students have an internship experience, in which off-campus work and significant academic work are combined for credit. Study abroad in 11 countries, a Washington semester, cross-registration with Memphis College of Art and Christian Brothers University, and a science semester at Oak Ridge National Laboratory are offered. A 3-2 engineering degree with Washington University is available. The B.A.-B.S. degree and dual majors are offered in any combination, and student-designed majors can be arranged. Nondegree study and pass/fail options are possible. There are 20 national honor societies and a chapter of Phi Beta Kappa. **Visiting:** There are regularly scheduled orientations for prospective students, including class visits, meetings with students and faculty, tours, and an overnight stay with students if desired. Interviews also are available. There are guides for informal visits, visitors may sit in on classes, and stay overnight. To schedule a visit, contact the Admissions Office. **Campus Safety and Security:** Measures include 24-hour foot and vehicle patrol, emergency notification system, self-defense education, security escort services, emergency telephones, lighted pathways/sidewalks, controlled access to dorms/residences, 24/7 staffed guard house, electronic readers on all gate entrances and residential dorms, security cameras monitored 24 hours a day, a fenced campus, and a city service billed to student accounts.

REQUIREMENTS: The SAT or ACT is required. Graduation from an accredited secondary school is required, with 16 or more academic credits, including 4 years of English, 3 of math, and 2 each of a foreign language, science, and social studies/history. The GED is accepted. An essay is required; an interview is recommended. AP credits are accepted. Important factors in the admissions decision are advanced placement or honors courses, recommendations by school officials, and extracurricular activities record. To graduate, students must complete 128 credit hours with a variable number of hours in the major, and maintain a minimum GPA of 2.0. There is a basic degree requirement in 12 foundation areas. Students must complete 3 courses examining questions of meaning and value, 2 courses in writing, 1 course in each of literature, art, math, natural science, human interaction and contemporary institutions, and cultural perspective. Students must further demonstrate intermediate proficiency with a second language, engage in 1 for-credit activity broadening connections between the classroom and the world, participate in three half-semesters of physical education, and complete a senior seminar in the major. **Procedure:** Freshmen are admitted in the fall and spring. Entrance exams should be taken prior to December of the senior year. There are early decision, early admissions, and deferred admissions plans. Early decision applications should be filed by November 1; regular applications, by January 15 for fall entry; and December 1 for spring entry. Notification of early decision is sent December 1; regular decision, April 1. 75 early decision candidates were accepted for the 2016-2017 class. 738 applicants were on the 2016 waiting list; 52 were admitted. Applications are accepted online. **Transfer Students:** 15 transfer students enrolled in 2015-2016. Applicants must submit all high school and college transcripts, as well as SAT or ACT scores, and must be in good standing at the last institution they attended. 64 of 128 credits required for the bachelor's degree must be completed at Rhodes. **International Students:** There are 47 international students enrolled. The school actively recruits these students. They must take the TOEFL with a minimum score of 550 on the paper-based TOEFL (PBT) or 80 on the Internet-based version (iBT). They must also take the SAT or ACT.

ADMISSIONS: 60% of the 2016-2017 applicants were accepted. The SAT scores for the 2016-2017 freshman class were: Critical Reading-- 3% below 500, 20% between 500 and 599, 53% between 600 and 699, and 24% between 700 and 800. Math-- 2% below 500, 22% between 500 and 599, 56% between 600 and 699, and 20% between 700 and 800. The ACT scores were 4% between 12 and 17, 22% between 18 and 23, 24% between 24 and 29, and 46% above 30. **Admissions Contact:** Carey Thompson, VP of Enrollment and Communications. Email: *adminfo@rhodes.edu* Web: *www.rhodes.edu*

FINANCIAL AID: In 2016-2017, 95% of all full-time freshmen and 93% of continuing full-time students received some form of financial aid. 52% of all full-time freshmen and 41% of continuing full-time students received need-based aid. The average freshman award was $34,061. 26% of undergraduate students work part-time. Average annual earnings from campus work are $2000. The average financial indebtedness of the 2016 graduate was $27,077. Rhodes is a member of CSS. The CSS/Profile is required. The FAFSA code is 003519. The deadline for filing freshman financial aid applications for fall entry is March 1.

SEWANEE: THE UNIVERSITY OF THE SOUTH D-3

www.sewanee.edu

Sewanee, TN 37383	(931) 598-1238 (800) 522-2234
Fax: (931) 538-3248	**Email:** admiss@sewanee.edu
Full-time: 814 men, 904 women	**Faculty:** IIB, +$
Part-time: 6 men, 7 women	**Ph.D.s:** n/av
Graduate: 50 men, 34 women	**Student/Faculty:** n/av
Year: semesters, summer session	**Tuition:** $42,400
Room & Board: $12,100	**Freshman Class:** 4423 applied, 1930 accepted, 514 enrolled
SAT CR/M/W: 630/620/610 **ACT:** 29	**CEEB CODE:** 1842
Application Deadline: February 1	**MOST COMPETITIVE**

Sewanee: The University of the South, founded in 1857, is an independent liberal arts institution affiliated with the Episcopal Church. Figures in the above capsule and in this profile are approximate. There is 1 undergraduate school and 2 graduate schools. In addition to regional accreditation, Sewanee has baccalaureate program accreditation with SACSCOC. The 13000-acre campus is in a small town 45 miles northwest of Chattanooga. Including any residence halls, there are 102 buildings.

STUDENT LIFE: 79% of undergraduates are from out of state, mostly the South. Students are from 48 states, and 26 foreign countries. 46% are from public schools. 82% are White; 6% Hispanic; 4% African American; 3% Foreign; 3% two or more races; 2% Asian American. **Female To Male Ratio:** 1.1:1. The average age of freshmen is 18; all undergraduates, 20. 12% do not continue beyond their first year; 82% remain to graduate. **Housing:** 1739 students can be accommodated in college housing, which includes single-sex and coed dorms, on-campus apartments, and married student housing. In addition, there are language houses, special-interest houses, fraternity houses, sorority houses, and substance-free housing, community engagement house, and first year program. On-campus housing is guaranteed for all 4 years. 99% of students live on campus; of those, 98% remain on campus on weekends. All students may keep cars.

FACULTY/CLASSROOMS: All teach undergraduates. No introductory courses are taught by graduate students.

PROGRAMS OF STUDY: Sewanee confers B.A. and B.S. degrees. Master's and doctoral degrees are also awarded. Bachelor's degrees are awarded in AGRICULTURE (environmental studies, forestry and related sciences, and natural resources), BIOLOGICAL SCIENCE (biochemistry, biology/biological science, ecology, and environmental biology), COMMUNICATIONS AND THE ARTS (art history, classical languages, English, fine arts, French, German, Greek, Latin, music, Russian, Spanish, and theatre arts), COMPUTER AND PHYSICAL SCIENCE (chemistry, computer science, geology, mathematics, and physics), SOCIAL SCIENCE (American studies, anthropology, Asian/Oriental studies, economics, French studies, history, international studies, medieval studies, philosophy, political science/government, psychology, religion, and women's studies). English, economics/pre-business, natural resources and the environment, international and global studies are the strongest academically. Economics, English, and psychology have the largest enrollments.

ACTIVITIES: There are 95 groups on campus including art, cheerleading, chess, choir, chorale, chorus, communications, computers, dance, drama, environmental, ethnic, film, honors, international, jazz band, LGBT, literary magazine, musical theater, newspaper, orchestra, pep band, photography, political, professional, radio and TV, religious, social, social service, student government, symphony, and yearbook. Popular campus events include Tennessee Williams Theatre Festival, perpetual motion student dance performances, Sewaneroo Music Festival, and Sewanee Monologues. **Sports:** There are 11 intercollegiate sports for men and 13 for women, and 13 intramural sports for men and 12 for women. Facilities include a sport and fitness center with multipurpose volleyball and basketball courts, an indoor pool with a diving well, indoor track, batting cage, racquetball, squash courts, indoor and outdoor tennis courts, dance and fitness studios, a climbing wall, golf course, multiweather track, an equestrian center and stables, playing fields, and areas for rappelling, mountain biking, caving, hiking, and rock climbing. The school loans out equipment and provides students the chance to develop as outdoor trip leaders, with backpacking, bouldering, canoeing, caving, cycling, hiking, and kayaking. The SOP offers sport climbing,**Graduates:** From July 1, 2015 to June 30, 2016, 397 bachelor's degrees were awarded. The most popular majors were economics (18%), English (12%), and psychology (11%). 26 companies recruited on campus in 2015-2016. In an average class, 79% graduate in 4 years or less, 82% graduate in 5 years or less, and 82% graduate in 6 years or less.

SERVICES: Counseling and information services are available, as is tutoring in most subjects, and a reader service for the blind, and study skills training is also offered. **Library/Resources:** The library contains 784,306 volumes, 333,359 microform items, and 133,429 audio/video tapes/CDs/DVDs. Computerized library services include interlibrary loans, database searching, Internet access, and Wi-Fi capability. Special learning facilities include an art gallery, radio station, an observatory, materials analysis lab with an electron scanning microscope, rare books collection, archives, and a music listening room and library, as well as 13,000 acres for study and reflection. **Physically Challenged Students:** 90% of the campus is accessible. Facilities include wheelchair ramps, elevators, special parking, specially equipped restrooms, special class scheduling, lowered drinking fountains, special housing. Special administrative services, and a telecommunications device for the deaf are available. **Special:** Sewanee offers internships in economics and public affairs, study abroad more than 60 countries, a Washington semester, and student-designed majors. Peace Corps, medical, law, and veterinary preparation are available. A 3-2 engineering degree is offered with Columbia, Washington, and Vanderbilt Universities. A 3/2 forestry degree is offered with Duke University. There are 10 national honor societies and a chapter of Phi Beta Kappa. **Visiting:** There are regularly scheduled orientations for prospective students, include a tour, an interview, class visits, and a meeting with an admission counselor. There are guides for informal visits, visitors may sit in on classes, and stay overnight. To schedule a visit, contact the Office of Admission. **Campus Safety and Security:** Measures include 24-hour foot and vehicle patrol, emergency notification system, self-defense education, and security escort services. There are also shuttle buses, emergency telephones, lighted pathways/sidewalks, and controlled access to dorms/residences.

REQUIREMENTS: Candidates for admission should have 15 secondary school academic credits, including 4 years of English, 3 of math, and 2 each of lab science, a foreign language, and history or social science. An essay and 2 letters of recommendation are required and an interview is recommended. AP credits are accepted. Important factors in the admissions decision are advanced placement or honors courses, leadership record, and evidence of special talent. To graduate, students must complete at least 32 full courses (128 semester hours) with a minimum GPA of 2.0. Comprehensive exams in the major field of study are required. Students must complete a general education curriculum that encourages intellectual curiosity and exposure to significant traditions and ways of seeing the world that our disciplines and interdisciplinary programs present. **Procedure:** Freshmen are admitted in the fall. Entrance exams should be taken by December of the senior year. There are early decision, early admissions, and deferred admissions plans. Early decision applications should be filed by November 15; regular applications, by February 1 for fall entry. Notification of early decision is sent December 15; regular decision, April 1. 146 early decision candidates were accepted for the 2016-2017 class. 120 applicants were on the 2016 waiting list; 25 were admitted. Application fees are waived if application is completed online. **Transfer Students:** 21 transfer students enrolled in 2015-2016. Applicants should have a cumulative college GPA of 3.0 or above on a 4.0 scale. They must submit official transcripts from high school and all previous colleges attended, a letter of recommendation from a college instructor, and a statement of good standing from their current college. An interview is recommended. 64 of 128 credits required for the bachelor's degree must be completed at Sewanee. **International Students:** There are 50 international students enrolled. The school actively recruits these students. They must take the TOEFL with a minimum score of 577 on the paper-based TOEFL (PBT) or 90 on the Internet-based version (iBT).

ADMISSIONS: 44% of the 2016-2017 applicants were accepted. The SAT scores for the 2016-2017 freshman class were: Critical Reading-- 4% below 500, 24% between 500 and 599, 56% between 600 and 699, and 16% between 700 and 800. Math-- 5% below 500, 33% between 500 and 599, 46% between 600 and 699, and 16% between 700 and 800. Writing-- 5% below 500, 35% between 500 and 599, 44% between 600 and 699, and 16% between 700 and 800. The ACT scores were 5% between

18 and 23, 59% between 24 and 29, and 36% above 30. **Admissions Contact:** Lee Ann Backlund, Dean of Admission and Financial Aid. Email: *admiss@sewanee.edu* Web: *www.sewanee.edu*

FINANCIAL AID: In 2016-2017, 90% of all full-time freshmen and 82% of continuing full-time students received some form of financial aid. 48% of all full-time freshmen and 46% of continuing full-time students received need-based aid. The average freshman award was $28,539. Need-based scholarships or need-based grants averaged $15,973 ($57,750 maximum); need-based self-help aid (loans and jobs) averaged $1,959 ($12,493 maximum); other non-need-based awards and non-need-based scholarships averaged $8,275 ($56,650 maximum); and $2,332 from other forms of aid. 32% of undergraduate students work part-time. Average annual earnings from campus work are $1500. The average financial indebtedness of the 2016 graduate was $24,431. Sewanee is a member of CSS. The CSS/Profile is required. The FAFSA code is 003534. The deadline for filing freshman financial aid applications for fall entry is February 1.

SOUTHERN ADVENTIST UNIVERSITY D-3
www.southern.edu

Collegedale, TN 37315	**(423) 236-2835** **(800) 768-8437**
Fax: (423) 236-1835	**Email: admissions@southern.edu**
Full-time: 985 men, 1172 women	**Faculty:** 132
Part-time: 130 men, 190 women	**Ph.D.s:** 64%
Graduate: 56 men, 107 women	**Student/Faculty:** 16 to 1
Year: semesters, summer session	**Tuition:** $21,150
Room & Board: $6450	**Freshman Class:** 1513 applied, 1074 accepted, 603 enrolled
SAT: recommended **ACT:** 22	**CEEB CODE:** 1727
Application Deadline: open	**COMPETITIVE**

Southern Adventist University, founded in 1892, is a private liberal arts institution affiliated with the Seventh-day Adventist Church. Figures in the above capsule and in this profile are approximate. There are 9 undergraduate schools. In addition to regional accreditation, Southern has baccalaureate program accreditation with CSWE, NASM, NCATE, and NLN. The 1000-acre campus is in a small town 18 miles southeast of Chattanooga. Including any residence halls, there are 17 buildings.

STUDENT LIFE: 78% of undergraduates are from out of state, mostly the South. Students are from 46 states, 42 foreign countries, and Canada. 16% are from public schools. 63% are White; 6% Foreign; 5% Asian American; 15% Hispanic; 11% African American. 97% are Protestant. **Female To Male Ratio:** 1.3:1. The average age of freshmen is 19; all undergraduates, 21. 31% do not continue beyond their first year; 45% remain to graduate. **Housing:** 1837 students can be accommodated in college housing, which includes single-sex dorms, on-campus apartments, and married student housing. On-campus housing is guaranteed for all 4 years. 65% of students live on campus; of those, 70% remain on campus on weekends. All students may keep cars. Alcohol is not permitted.

FACULTY/CLASSROOMS: 60% of faculty are male; 40% are female. 98% teach undergraduates. No introductory courses are taught by graduate students. The average class size in an introductory lecture is 40; in a laboratory is 25; and in a regular course is 13.

PROGRAMS OF STUDY: Southern confers B.A., B.S., B.B.A., B.F.A., B.Mus., and B.S.W. degrees. Associate and master's degrees are also awarded. Bachelor's degrees are awarded in BIOLOGICAL SCIENCE (biology/biological science), BUSINESS (accounting, banking and finance, business administration and management, entrepreneurial studies, international business management, marketing/retailing/merchandising, and nonprofit/public organization management), COMMUNICATIONS AND THE ARTS (animation, art, broadcasting, communications, English, film arts, fine arts, graphic design, journalism, music, and public relations), COMPUTER AND PHYSICAL SCIENCE (chemistry, computer management, computer science, information sciences and systems, mathematics, physics, and web services), EDUCATION (elementary education, music education, physical education, and recreation education), HEALTH PROFESSIONS (health care administration, health science, medical technology, and nursing), SOCIAL SCIENCE (behavioral science, history, international studies, psychology, public administration, religious education, social work, and theological studies). Business, nursing, and education are the strongest academically, and have the largest enrollments.

ACTIVITIES: There are no fraternities or sororities. There are 30 groups on campus, including band, choir, chorus, drama, ethnic, honors, international, jazz band, newspaper, orchestra, professional, radio and TV, religious, social, student government, symphony, and yearbook. Popular campus events include Alumni Weekend, Strawberry Festival, and Week of Spiritual Emphasis. **Sports:** There are 10 intramural sports for men and 10 for women. Facilities include a field house, tennis courts, athletic fields, a pool, racquetball courts, track, soccer fields, gym, weight rooms, and a golf course. **Graduates:** From July 1, 2015 to June 30, 2016, 371 bachelor's degrees were awarded. The most popular majors were nursing (21%), business (15%), and education (8%). In an average class, 22% graduate in 4 years or less, 36% graduate in 5 years or less, and 48% graduate in 6 years or less. Of the 2015 graduating class, 15% were enrolled in graduate school within 6 months of graduation, and 41% were employed.

SERVICES: Counseling and information services are available, as is tutoring in most subjects, and a remedial math, reading, and writing. **Library/Resources:** The library contains 166,905 volumes, 410,551 microform items, 6,600 audio/video tapes/CDs/DVDs, and subscribes to 2,123 periodicals including electronic. Computerized library services include interlibrary loans, database searching, Internet access, and Wi-Fi capability. Special learning facilities include an art gallery and radio station. **Physically Challenged Students:** 70% of the campus is accessible. Facilities include wheelchair ramps, elevators, special parking, specially equipped restrooms, and special class scheduling. **Special:** Internships are available in long-term care, nursing, and journalism. A social work practicum, an accelerated degree program in nursing, and study abroad in Austria, Spain, Argentina, Italy, Germany, Mexico, and France are offered. The B.A.-B.S. degree and dual majors in any combination including business administration and automotive service and business administration and public relations, and interdisciplinary student-designed majors are available. Credit may be granted for 4 years of military experience. Pass/fail options are possible only for phys ed activity classes. There are paraprofessional and pre-professional programs in dentistry and medicine, law, and various other health-related fields. There are 9 national honor societies. **Visiting:** There are regularly scheduled orientations for prospective students, visiting students can take a tour of the campus and dorms, schedule appointments with academic departments, and interview with an admissions officer. There are guides for informal visits, visitors may sit in on classes, and stay overnight. To schedule a visit, contact the Admissions Office. **Campus Safety and Security:** Measures include 24-hour foot and vehicle patrol, emergency notification system, security escort services, emergency telephones and lighted pathways/sidewalks.

REQUIREMENTS: The ACT is required. The SAT is recommended. Applicants must have a minimum composite score of 22 on the ACT. Students must graduate from an accredited secondary school with 14 academic credits, including 4 units of English and 2 each of a foreign language, math, science, social studies, and history. The GED is accepted. An essay must be submitted if home schooled. AP and CLEP credits are accepted. Important factors in the admissions decision are advanced placement or honors courses, recommendations by school officials, and leadership record. Students must complete 124 semester hours with at least 30 in the major, and maintain a minimum GPA of 2.0. General education requirements include 12 semester hours of religion, 6 of history, language, literature, and fine arts, 6 to 9 of English and natural science, 5 of behavioral, family, and health science, 3 each of activity skills, computer competencies, oral communication, and of political and economic systems, and up to 3 of math, depending on the ACT scores. **Procedure:** Freshmen are admitted in the fall, spring, and summer. Entrance exams should be taken at least prior to admission. There is a rolling admissions plan. Application deadlines are open. Application fee is $25. Notification is sent on a rolling basis. Applications are accepted online. **Transfer Students:** 165 transfer students enrolled in 2015-2016. Transfer applicants must have a cumulative GPA of at least 2.0 and a minimum ACT composite score of 18. 2 letters of recommendation are also required. 30 of 124 credits required for the bachelor's degree must be completed at Southern. **International Students:** There are 110 international students enrolled. The school actively recruits these students. They must take the TOEFL with a minimum score of 550 on the paper-based TOEFL (PBT) or 79 on the Internet-based version (iBT) or take the MELAB. They must also take the ACT, scoring 18.

ADMISSIONS: 71% of the 2016-2017 applicants were accepted. The

ACT scores were 34% below 12, 27% between 12 and 17, 21% between 18 and 23, 10% between 24 and 29, and 8% above 30. There were 2 National Merit finalists. **Admissions Contact:** Ryan Herman, Director of Admissions. Email: *admissions@southern.edu* Web: *www.southern.edu*

FINANCIAL AID: In 2016-2017, 93% of all full-time freshmen and 90% of continuing full-time students received some form of financial aid. 77% of all full-time freshmen and 76% of continuing full-time students received need-based aid. The average freshman award was $20,130. Need-based scholarships or need-based grants averaged $4,697 ($10,000 maximum); need-based self-help aid (loans and jobs) averaged $3,740 ($5,800 maximum); and other non-need-based awards and non-need-based scholarships averaged $2,290 ($16,205 maximum). 43% of undergraduate students work part-time. Average annual earnings from campus work are $3000. The average financial indebtedness of the 2016 graduate was $17,524. The FAFSA code is 003518. The priority date for freshman financial aid applications for fall entry is March 1.

TENNESSEE STATE UNIVERSITY C-2

www.tnstate.edu

Nashville, TN 37209	(615) 963-5101
Fax: (615) 963-5108	**Email: recruitment@tnstate.edu**
Full-time: n/av	**Faculty:** 434; IIA
Part-time: n/av	**Ph.D.s:** 73%
Graduate: n/av	**Student/Faculty:** 17 to 1
Year: semesters, summer session	**Tuition:** $7299 ($20,016)
Room & Board: $7124	**Freshman Class:** 6069 applied, 3799 accepted, 1509 enrolled
SAT: required **ACT:** 18	**CEEB CODE:** 1803
Application Deadline: August 1	**COMPETITIVE**

Tennessee State University, founded in 1912, is led by its defining mission of teaching, research and service which is evident through the university's motto, "Think. Work. Serve." TSU is among the nation's prominent Historically Black Colleges and Universities and offers unparalleled research and service opportunities for students, scholars, and business partners from around the globe. As Nashville's only public comprehensive, urban, co-educational, land-grant university, offers two associate's, 38 bachelor's, 24 master's and seven doctoral degrees. Founded in 1912, Tennessee State University is led by its defining mission of teaching, research and service which is evident through the university's motto, "Think. Work. Serve." TSU is among the nation's prominent Historically Black Colleges and Universities and offers unparalleled research and service opportunities for students, scholars, and business partners from around the globe. There are 8 undergraduate schools and 1 graduate school. In addition to regional accreditation, TSU has baccalaureate program accreditation with AACSB, ABET, AHEA, CSWE, NASAD, NASM, NCATE, NLN, AAFCS, APA, ASLHA, AUPHA, NAACLS, and NASPAA. The 450-acre campus is in an urban area in Nashville. Including any residence halls, there are 66 buildings.

STUDENT LIFE: 77% of undergraduates are from Tennessee. Others are from 44 states, 38 foreign countries, and Canada. 90% are from public schools. 70% are African American; 25% White. The average age of freshmen is 18; all undergraduates, 25. **Housing:** 3225 students can be accommodated in college housing, which includes single-sex and coed dorms, off-campus apartments, and honors houses. On-campus housing is guaranteed for all 4 years. 58% of students commute. All students may keep cars. Alcohol is not permitted.

FACULTY/CLASSROOMS: 55% of faculty are male; 45% are female. 90% teach undergraduates, 85% do research, and 85% do both. No introductory courses are taught by graduate students. The average class size in an introductory lecture is 30; in a laboratory is 35; and in a regular course is 30.

PROGRAMS OF STUDY: TSU confers B.A., B.S., B.B.A., and B.S.N. degrees. Associate, master's, and doctoral degrees are also awarded. Bachelor's degrees are awarded in AGRICULTURE (agriculture), BIOLOGICAL SCIENCE (biology/biological science), BUSINESS (accounting, business administration and management, business economics, and hotel/motel and restaurant management), COMMUNICATIONS AND THE ARTS (art, dramatic arts, English, languages, music, and speech/debate/rhetoric), COMPUTER AND PHYSICAL SCIENCE (chemistry, computer science, mathematics, and physics), EDUCATION (early childhood education, health education, and special education), ENGINEERING AND ENVIRONMENTAL DESIGN (aeronautical technology, architectural engineering, civil engineering, electrical/electronics engineering, and mechanical engineering), HEALTH PROFESSIONS (dental hygiene, health care administration, medical records administration/services, medical technology, nursing, occupational therapy, physical therapy, respiratory therapy, and speech pathology/audiology), SOCIAL SCIENCE (African studies, criminal justice, family/consumer studies, history, interdisciplinary studies, political science/government, psychology, social work, and sociology). Engineering, allied health professions, and nursing are the strongest academically and have the largest enrollments.

ACTIVITIES: 1% of men belong to 4 national fraternities; 2% of women belong to 4 national sororities. There are 63 groups on campus, including band, cheerleading, choir, chorale, computers, dance, drama, forensics, honors, jazz band, literary magazine, marching band, newspaper, pep band, professional, radio and TV, religious, social, social service, and student government. Popular campus events include Miss TSU Pageant and Inauguration, Greek Show, and Christmas Tree Lighting Ceremony. **Sports:** There are 8 intercollegiate sports for men and 7 for women. Facilities include swimming, handball, and basketball, softball, track and field, and golf. **Graduates:** From July 1, 2015 to June 30, 2016, 988 bachelor's degrees were awarded. The most popular majors were arts and sciences (14%), business administration (12%), and biology (7%). 250 companies recruited on campus in 2015-2016. In an average class, 9% graduate in 3 years or less, 13% graduate in 4 years or less, and 5% graduate in 5 years or less. Of the 2015 graduating class, 7% were enrolled in graduate school within 6 months of graduation.

SERVICES: Counseling and information services are available, as is tutoring in some subjects, and a reader service for the blind, and remedial math, reading, and writing. In the writing clinic, math lab, and reading room, provides individualized assistance for students needs. **Library/Resources:** The 2 libraries contain 420,000 volumes, 1,500 microform items, 5,125 audio/video tapes/CDs/DVDs, and subscribe to 1,775 periodicals including electronic. Computerized library services include interlibrary loans, database searching, and Internet access. Special learning facilities include an art gallery, radio station, Hiram Van Gordon Memorial Gallery, exhibitions, and lectures. **Physically Challenged Students:** 90% of the campus is accessible. Facilities include wheelchair ramps, elevators, special parking, specially equipped restrooms, and lowered drinking fountains. **Special:** Opportunities are provided for co-op programs in business and engineering, cross-registration with Middle Tennessee State University and Meharry Medical College, a B.A.-B.S. degree in interdisciplinary studies, credit by exam, and nondegree study. There are 19 national honor societies, a freshman honors program, and 5 departmental honors programs. **Visiting:** There are guides for informal visits, visitors may sit in on classes, and stay overnight. To schedule a visit, contact the Recruiting Staff. **Campus Safety and Security:** Measures include 24-hour foot and vehicle patrol, shuttle buses, emergency telephones, and lighted pathways/sidewalks.

REQUIREMENTS: Students must have a minimum score of 890 on the SAT or 19 on the ACT. Graduation from an accredited secondary school is required; the GED is accepted. Applicants should have 4 credits in English, 3 in math, 2 each in science and a foreign language, and 1 each in history, social studies, and art. AP and CLEP credits are accepted. To graduate, students must complete at least 120 semester hours, with 25% in the major, and maintain a minimum GPA of 2.0. Additional requirements include demonstration of proficiency in English composition, completion of a senior project, and courses in English, math, social sciences, American history, humanities, and natural sciences. **Procedure:** Freshmen are admitted to all sessions. Entrance exams should be taken in the junior year. There is an early admissions plan. Applications should be filed by August 1 for fall entry; December 1 for spring entry; and May 1 for summer entry. The fall 2016 application fee was $15. **Transfer Students:** 631 transfer students enrolled in 2015-2016. Applicants must submit official transcripts from all previous colleges attended. Students from other than Tennessee colleges must have maintained a minimum GPA of 2.0. The GPA requirements for students transferring from Tennessee colleges vary according to the number of semester hours being submitted for transfer credit. 30 of 120 credits required for the bachelor's degree must be completed at TSU. **International Students:** There are 63 international students enrolled. They must take the TOEFL, as well as the SAT or ACT.

ADMISSIONS: 63% of the 2016-2017 applicants were accepted. The

ACT scores were 77% below 12, 17% between 12 and 17, 5% between 18 and 23, 1% between 24 and 29, and 1% above 30. **Admissions Contact:** John Cade, Dean of Admissions and Records. Email: *recruitment@tnstate.edu* Web: *www.tnstate.edu*

FINANCIAL AID: In 2016-2017, 74% of all full-time freshmen and 79% of continuing full-time students received some form of financial aid. 71% of all full-time freshmen and 69% of continuing full-time students received need-based aid. The average freshman award was $5,316. Need-based scholarships or need-based grants averaged $6,288 ($6,581 maximum); need-based self-help aid (loans and jobs) averaged $4,680 ($6,375 maximum); non-need-based athletic scholarships averaged $5,894 ($19,075 maximum); and other non-need-based awards and non-need-based scholarships averaged $146 ($1,000 maximum). The FAFSA code is 003522. The deadline for filing freshman financial aid applications for fall entry is April 1.

TENNESSEE TECHNOLOGICAL UNIVERSITY D-2

www.tntech.edu

Cookeville, TN 38505 **(931) 372-3888**
(800) 255-8881
Fax: (931) 372-6250 **Email: admissions@tntech.edu**

Full-time: 3902 men, 3269 women	**Faculty:** 381
Part-time: 412 men, 477 women	**Ph.D.s:** 83%
Graduate: 708 men, 1553 women	**Student/Faculty:** 18 to 1
Year: semesters, summer session	**Tuition:** $8300 ($16,500)
Room & Board: $8750	**Freshman Class:** 3254 accepted, 1661 enrolled
ACT: 23	**CEEB CODE:** 1804
Application Deadline: August 1	**COMPETITIVE**

Tennessee Technological University, founded in 1915, is a public institution and member of the state university and community college system of Tennessee, offering undergraduate and graduate programs in the liberal arts, business, engineering, agriculture studies, art and fine arts, music, professional training, teacher preparation, nursing, home economics, and crafts. The figures in the above capsule and in this profile are approximate. There are 8 undergraduate schools and 5 graduate schools. In addition to regional accreditation, Tennessee Tech has baccalaureate program accreditation with AACSB, ABET, NASAD, NASM, NCATE, NLN, and AAFCS. The 235-acre campus is in a small town 78 miles east of Nashville. Including any residence halls, there are 97 buildings.

STUDENT LIFE: 86% of undergraduates are from Tennessee. Others are from 33 states, 55 foreign countries, and Canada. 79% are White; 4% African American; 2% Hispanic; 11% Foreign; 1% Asian American. 55% claim no religious affiliation. **Female To Male Ratio:** 1.1:1. The average age of freshmen is 19; all undergraduates, 22. 27% do not continue beyond their first year; 44% remain to graduate. **Housing:** College-sponsored housing includes single-sex and coed dorms, on-campus apartments, married student housing, honors houses, special-interest houses, and private room dorms for upper class students. On-campus housing is guaranteed for all 4 years. 75% of students commute. All students may keep cars. Alcohol is not permitted.

FACULTY/CLASSROOMS: 64% of faculty are male; 36% are female. 99% teach undergraduates, 73% do research, and 70% do both. Graduate students teach 5% of introductory courses. The average class size in an introductory lecture is 27; in a laboratory is 30; and in a regular course is 26.

PROGRAMS OF STUDY: Tennessee Tech confers B.A., B.S., B.F.A., B.M., B.S.Agr., B.S.B.A., B.S.C.E., B.S.Ch.E., B.S.Ed., B.S.E.E., B.S.H.E., B.S.I.E., B.S.Ind.Tech., B.S.M.E., and B.S.N. degrees. Master's and doctoral degrees are also awarded. Bachelor's degrees are awarded in AGRICULTURE (agricultural economics, agriculture, animal science, fish and game management, plant science, soil science, and wildlife management), BIOLOGICAL SCIENCE (biochemistry and biology/biological science), BUSINESS (accounting, banking and finance, business administration and management, management science, and marketing/retailing/merchandising), COMMUNICATIONS AND THE ARTS (English, fine arts, French, German, journalism, Spanish, and technical and business writing), COMPUTER AND PHYSICAL SCIENCE (chemistry, computer science, geology, mathematics, physics, and web technology), EDUCATION (agricultural education, art education, home economics education, music education, physical education, secondary education, and special education), ENGINEERING AND ENVIRONMENTAL DESIGN (chemical engineering, civil engineering, electrical/electronics engineering, engineering, environmental engineering, industrial engineering, industrial engineering technology, manufacturing engineering, and mechanical engineering), HEALTH PROFESSIONS (nursing), SOCIAL SCIENCE (child care/child and family studies, economics, history, human ecology, political science/government, psychology, and sociology). Engineering, business, and education are the strongest academically. Mechanical engineering, multidisciplinary studies, and exercise science have the largest enrollments.

ACTIVITIES: 10% of men belong to 13 national fraternities; 10% of women belong to 9 national sororities. There are 178 groups on campus, including art, band, cheerleading, chess, choir, chorale, chorus, communications, computers, dance, debate, drama, drill team, ethnic, forensics, honors, international, jazz band, LGBT, literary magazine, marching band, musical theater, newspaper, opera, orchestra, pep band, photography, political, professional, radio and TV, religious, social, social service, student government, symphony, and yearbook. Popular campus events include Intramural Events, Greek Week, and Parents Day. **Sports:** There are 7 intercollegiate sports for men and 9 for women, and 10 intramural sports for men and 8 for women. Facilities include volleyball, basketball, indoor tennis courts, a fitness center with a pool, handball courts, weight room, turf practice field, a strength center, baseball, football, cross country, soccer, and golf. **Graduates:** From July 1, 2015 to June 30, 2016, 1354 bachelor's degrees were awarded. The most popular majors were business (22%), education (20%), and engineering (13%). 475 companies recruited on campus in 2015-2016. In an average class, 1% graduate in 3 years or less, 17% graduate in 4 years or less, 36% graduate in 5 years or less, and 45% graduate in 6 years or less. Of the 2015 graduating class, 10% were enrolled in graduate school within 6 months of graduation, and 80% were employed.

SERVICES: Counseling and information services are available, as is tutoring in some subjects, and a reader service for the blind, and remedial math, reading, and writing. **Library/Resources:** The library contains 353,000 volumes, 100,005 microform items, 38,000 audio/video tapes/CDs/DVDs, and subscribes to 30,050 periodicals including electronic. Computerized library services include interlibrary loans, database searching, and Internet access. Special learning facilities include an art gallery, radio station, TV station, and Angelo & Jennette Volpe Library. **Physically Challenged Students:** 95% of the campus is accessible. Facilities include wheelchair ramps, elevators, special parking, specially equipped restrooms, special class scheduling, lowered drinking fountains, lowered telephones, and special housing. **Special:** Co-op programs in most academic areas, internships in community-based programs, study abroad, a Washington semester, multidisciplinary majors and work-study programs are available. Accelerated degree programs are offered in all specified majors with 3 calendar years of continuous studies. A B.A.-B.S. degree is available, as are dual majors in all areas. Credit may be granted for military experience, and nondegree study and pass/fail options are offered. There are 29 national honor societies and a freshman honors program. **Visiting:** There are regularly scheduled orientations for prospective students, including visits either morning or afternoon each weekday and meetings with an admission officer, faculty member in student's major, and a campus tour. There are guides for informal visits and visitors may sit in on classes. To schedule a visit, contact the Admissions Office. **Campus Safety and Security:** Measures include 24-hour foot and vehicle patrol, self-defense education, security escort services, emergency telephones, lighted pathways/sidewalks, and student safety organization.

REQUIREMENTS: The ACT is required, with a minimum composite score of 19. Other admissions requirements include graduation from an accredited secondary school with 14 academic credits, including 4 of English, 3 of math, 2 each in science and a single foreign language, 1 in American history, 1 in world history, ancient history, modern history, world geography or European history, and 1 in music/art. The GED is also accepted. AP and CLEP credits are accepted. Students must complete 120 semester hours, with a variable number of hours in the major, and maintain a minimum GPA of 2.0. 9 semester hours of English, 8 of a lab science, 6 of American history, 6 each of social sciences and humanities, and 3 hours each of math and speech. **Procedure:** Freshmen are admitted to all sessions. Entrance exams should be taken during the senior year. There are deferred admissions and rolling admissions plans. Applications should be filed by August 1 for fall entry; December 1 for spring entry; and May 1 for summer entry, along with a $15 fee. Applications are accepted online. **Transfer Students:** 755 transfer students enrolled in 2015-2016. Transfer students should have a minimum of 12 credit hours earned; the minimum GPA depends on the number of credit hours accumulated. Official transcripts must be submitted, and the ACT is required, depending on age (for applicants 21 or older it is not required). If an applicant has fewer than 12 credit hours, admissions requirements are the same as for freshmen. 30 of 120 credits required for the bachelor's degree must be completed at Tennessee Tech. **International Students:** There are 209 international students enrolled. The school actively recruits these students. They must take the TOEFL with a minimum score of 500 on the paper-based TOEFL (PBT) or 61 on the Internet-based version (iBT) and the college's own test. They must also take the SAT or ACT.

ADMISSIONS: The SAT scores for the 2016-2017 freshman class were: Critical Reading-- 38% below 500, 30% between 500 and 599, 28% between 600 and 699, and 4% between 700 and 800. Math-- 26% below 500, 38% between 500 and 599, 6% between 600 and 699, and 30% between 700 and 800. Writing-- 42% below 500, 35% between 500 and 599, 21% between 600 and 699, and 2% between 700 and 800. 48% of the current freshmen were in the top fifth of their class; 80% were in the top two fifths. There were 4 National Merit finalists. **Admissions Contact:** Alexis Pope, Associate Director of Admissions. Email: *admissions@tntech.edu* Web: *www.tntech.edu*

FINANCIAL AID: In 2016-2017, 91% of all full-time freshmen and 89% of continuing full-time students received some form of financial aid. 87% of all full-time freshmen and 83% of continuing full-time students received need-based aid. The average freshman award was $8,120. Need-based scholarships or need-based grants averaged $3,922; need-based self-help aid (loans and jobs) averaged $2,405; non-need-based athletic scholarships averaged $13,681; and other non-need-based awards and non-need-based scholarships averaged $5,271. The average financial indebtedness of the 2016 graduate was $14,478. The deadline for filing freshman financial aid applications for fall entry is December 15.

TENNESSEE WESLEYAN UNIVERSITY E-3

Tennessee Wesleyan College
www.tnwesleyan.edu

Athens, TN 37303	**(423) 746-7504** **(800) PICK-TWU**
Fax: (423) 744-9968	**Email: admissions@tnwesleyan.edu**
Full-time: 341 men, 570 women	**Faculty:** 57; IIB
Part-time: 37 men, 67 women	**Ph.D.s:** 57%
Graduate: 9 men, 13 women	**Student/Faculty:** 12 to 1
Year: semesters, summer session	**Tuition:** $23,000
Room & Board: $7540	**Freshman Class:** n/av
SAT or ACT: required	**CEEB CODE:** 1805
Application Deadline: August	**COMPETITIVE**

Tennessee Wesleyan University, founded in 1857, is a private institution affiliated with the United Methodist Church. Its undergraduate programs stress the liberal arts, teacher preparation, business, and nursing. The figures in the above capsule and in this profile are approximate. In addition to regional accreditation, TWU has baccalaureate program accreditation with CCNE. The 40-acre campus is in a small town 55 miles south of Knoxville. Including any residence halls, there are 21 buildings.

STUDENT LIFE: 82% of undergraduates are from Tennessee. Others are from 24 states, 30 foreign countries, and Canada. 86% are from public schools. 50% are White; 43% race unknown; 4% African American; 2% two or more races; 1% Hispanic. 47% are Baptist, Church of Christ, Church of God, Lutheran, Presbyterian, and Pentecostal. **Female To Male Ratio:** 1.7:1. The average age of freshmen is 18; all undergraduates, 23. 33% do not continue beyond their first year; 67% remain to graduate. **Housing:** 415 students can be accommodated in college housing, which includes single-sex and coed dorms and on-campus apartments. On-campus housing is guaranteed for all 4 years. 65% of students commute. All students may keep cars. Alcohol is not permitted.

FACULTY/CLASSROOMS: 54% of faculty are male; 46% are female. All teach undergraduates. No introductory courses are taught by graduate students. The average class size in an introductory lecture is 13; in a laboratory is 20; and in a regular course is 12.

PROGRAMS OF STUDY: TWU confers B.A., B.S., B.Mus.Ed., and B.S.N. degrees. Master's degrees are also awarded. Bachelor's degrees are awarded in BIOLOGICAL SCIENCE (biology/ gen science secondary education), BUSINESS (accounting (finance), business administration and management, business administration - international, business administration, operations, business administration marketing, business information systems, finance, human resources, and sports management), COMMUNICATIONS AND THE ARTS (communication studies, creative writing, English, fine arts, fine/studio arts, general, human performance, and music), COMPUTER AND PHYSICAL SCIENCE (chemistry, chemistry/forensic chemistry, chemistry/general science second education, chemistry secondary education, computer information systems, mathematics, and physics/gen science secondary education), EDUCATION (early childhood education, education, elementary education, English secondary education, music education, physical education, secondary education, and special education), HEALTH PROFESSIONS (biology, health science, nursing, and prephysical therapy), SOCIAL SCIENCE (behavioral science, criminal justice, history, human services, legal studies, philosophy and religion, psychology, religion, religious music, social work, and sociology). Business administration, natural sciences, nursing, and health and human performance are the strongest academically and have the largest enrollments.

ACTIVITIES: 6% of men belong to 1 local fraternity; 10% of women belong to 1 local and 1 national sororities. There are 24 groups on campus, including art, band, cheerleading, choir, chorale, computers, drama, ethnic, honors, international, literary magazine, musical theater, newspaper, professional, religious, social, social service, and student government. Popular campus events include Skiing Trips, and the Annual Spring Dodge Ball Tournament. **Sports:** There are 7 intercollegiate sports for men and 8 for women. Facilities include a soccer/lacrosse stadium, a gym, fitness center, baseball field, tennis, and the YMCA adjacent to campus, which students may use for a fee. **Graduates:** From July 1, 2015 to June 30, 2016, 241 bachelor's degrees were awarded. The most popular majors were business admininstration (37%), nursing (25%), and behavioral science (10%). In an average class, 37% graduate in 4 years or less, 8% graduate in 5 years or less, and 44% graduate in 6 years or less.

SERVICES: Counseling and information services are available, as is tutoring in most subjects, and remedial math and writing. Testing accommodations for learning disabled students are offered in the Academic Success Center. **Library/Resources:** The library contains 52,369 volumes, 2,550 microform items, and 597 audio/video tapes/CDs/DVDs, and subscribes to 82 periodicals including electronic. Computerized library services include interlibrary loans, database searching, Internet access, and Wi-Fi capability. Special learning facilities include an art gallery, an education technology lab. **Physically Challenged Students:** Facilities include wheelchair ramps, elevators, special parking, specially equipped restrooms, and special class scheduling. **Special:** The university offers for credit internships in most majors, study abroad, an accelerated degree program, B.A.-B.S. degrees, and dual and student-designed majors. Students in natural science programs may take summer courses offered by the Gulf Coast Research Laboratory of the University of Southern Mississippi Institute of Marine Sciences. TWU also holds an ambassadorial agreement with the University of St. Augustine for health sciences. There are 5 national honor societies, a freshman honors program, and 4 departmental honors programs. **Visiting:** There are regularly scheduled orientations for prospective students, Information sessions, advisement, financial arrangements. There are guides for informal visits, visitors may sit in on classes, and stay overnight. To schedule a visit, contact the Office of Admissions. **Campus Safety and Security:** Measures include 24-hour foot and vehicle patrol, emergency notification system, self-defense education, and security escort services. There are lighted pathways/sidewalks and controlled access to dorms/residences.

REQUIREMENTS: The SAT is recommended. The ACT is preferred. Other admission requirements include graduation from an accredited secondary school, with 10 academic credits, including 4 units in English, 2 each in math and science, and 1 each in social studies and history, and a foreign language is recommended. The GED is also accepted in lieu of a high school diploma and test scores. AP and CLEP credits are accepted. Important factors in the admissions decision are advanced placement or honors courses, recommendations by school officials, evidence of special talent, personality/intangible qualities, extracurricular activities record, and recommendations by alumni. Students must complete at least 120 semester hours of academic work, of which 30 hours must be at the 300-400 level and must maintain a minimum GPA of 2.0. Some majors may require more than 120 hours to complete. Distribution of requirements include: Written Word - 6 s.h. total (Composition I & II); Spoken Word - 6 s.h. total (Choose from French, Spanish, English and Speech); Artist's Expression - 6 s.h. total (Choose two from two separate disciplines: Art, Communication, Literature, Music or Theatre); Western Heritage - 9 s.h. total (Choose from Religion; History or Philosophy; Religion, History or Philosophy); Cultural Diversity - 6 s.h. total (Choose two from two separate disciplines: Art, History, Literature, Music, Philosophy, Religion or Theatre); Scientific Perspectives - 9 s.h. total (Choose from Math or Statistics; Biology, Chemistry or Physics; and Mathematics, Statistics, Biology, Chemistry, or Physics); Societal Perspectives - 6 s.h. (Choose two from two separate disciplines: Criminal Justice, Economics, Education, Political Science, Psychology, Sociology, or Social Work. B.A. degree candidates must demonstrate knowledge of at least one modern language (12 hour of a language at a university level). Internships are also required for human services students, and all students must take an exit exam. **Procedure:** Freshmen are admitted in the fall, spring, and summer. Entrance exams should be taken by July of the year they wish to enter the college. There is a rolling admissions plan. Check with the school for current application deadlines. The application fee is $25. Notification is sent on a rolling basis. Applications are accepted on-line. **Transfer Students:** 205 transfer students enrolled in 2015-2016. Transfer students must have a minimum GPA of 2.0; an associate degree is recommended. 15 of 120 credits required for the bachelor's degree must be completed at TWU. **International Students:** There are 68 international students enrolled. They must take the TOEFL with a minimum score of 550 on the paper-based TOEFL (PBT) or 79 on the Internet-based version (iBT). They must also take the SAT or ACT, scoring 18 or 870.

Admissions Contact: Michelle Boyd/Debbie Hahn, Office Coordinator. Email: *admissions@tnwesleyan.edu* Web: *www.tnwesleyan.edu*

FINANCIAL AID: In 2016-2017, 100% of all full-time freshmen and 94% of continuing full-time students received some form of financial aid. 88% of all full-time freshmen and 85% of continuing full-time students received need-based aid. The average freshman award was $6,588. Need-based scholarships or need-based grants averaged $4,602 ($5,815 maximum); need-based self-help aid (loans and jobs) averaged $3,130 ($3,500 maximum); and non-need-based athletic scholarships averaged $12,898 ($20,000 maximum). 10% of undergraduate students work part-time. Average annual earnings from campus work are $1305. The average financial indebtedness of the 2016 graduate was $31,000. The college's own financial statement is required. The FAFSA code is 003525. The priority date for freshman financial aid applications for fall entry is March 1.

THE UNIVERSITY OF TENNESSEE AT CHATTANOOGA — D-3

www.utc.edu

Chattanooga, TN 37403 — (423) 425-4662

Fax: (423) 425-4157	**Email:** info@utc.edu
Full-time: 3790 men, 4973 women	**Faculty:** IIA, -$
Part-time: 630 men, 691 women	**Ph.D.s:** 75%
Graduate: 597 men, 707 women	**Student/Faculty:** 18 to 1
Year: semesters, summer session	**Tuition:** $8356 ($24,474)
Room & Board: $8388	**Freshman Class:** n/av
SAT CR/M: 510/510 **ACT:** 23	**CEEB CODE:** 1831
Application Deadline: May 1	**COMPETITIVE**

The University of Tennessee at Chattanooga, founded in 1886, is a public institution, and part of the state's university system, offering programs in liberal and fine arts, business, engineering, health science, and teacher preparation. There are 5 undergraduate schools and 1 graduate school. In addition to regional accreditation, UTC has baccalaureate program accreditation with AACSB, ABET, ACEJMC, AHEA, APTA, CSWE, NASAD, NASM, NCATE, NLN, CCNE, CAPTE, and CACREP. The 418-acre campus is in an urban area 120 miles north of Atlanta. Including any residence halls, there are 85 buildings.

STUDENT LIFE: 94% of undergraduates are from Tennessee. Others are from 43 states, 36 foreign countries, and Canada. 75% are from public schools. 75% are White; 6% two or more races; 3% Hispanic; 2% Asian American; 11% African American; 1% Foreign; 1% race unknown. **Female To Male Ratio:** 1.3:1. The average age of freshmen is 18; all undergraduates, 22. 29% do not continue beyond their first year; 71% remain to graduate. **Housing:** 3146 students can be accommodated in college housing, which includes coed on-campus apartments, language houses, special-interest houses, and theme housing. On-campus housing is guaranteed for the freshman year only, and is available on a first-come, first-served basis. 70% of students commute. All students may keep cars. Alcohol is not permitted.

FACULTY/CLASSROOMS: 52% of faculty are male; 48% are female. 95% teach undergraduates, 2% do research, and 2% do both. Graduate students teach 1% of introductory courses. The average class size in an introductory lecture is 25 and in a laboratory is 10.

PROGRAMS OF STUDY: UTC confers B.A., B.S., B.F.A., B.M., B.S.E., B.S.E.E., B.S.M.E., B.S.N., B.S.W., B.S.ChE., and B.S.C.E. degrees. Master's and doctoral degrees are also awarded. Bachelor's degrees are awarded in BIOLOGICAL SCIENCE (biology/biological science), BUSINESS (business administration and management and recreation and leisure services), COMMUNICATIONS AND THE ARTS (art, communications, dramatic arts, English, fine arts, French, Greek, Latin, music, and Spanish), COMPUTER AND PHYSICAL SCIENCE (applied mathematics, chemistry, computer science, geology, mathematics, and physics), EDUCATION (art education, early childhood education, education, education of the exceptional child, English education, music education, secondary education, and special education), ENGINEERING AND ENVIRONMENTAL DESIGN (chemical engineering, civil engineering, construction management, electrical/electronics engineering, engineering, engineering management, environmental engineering, environmental science, industrial engineering, interior design, mechanical engineering, and nuclear engineering), HEALTH PROFESSIONS (medical laboratory technology, nursing, and rehabilitation therapy), SOCIAL SCIENCE (criminal justice, economics, history, humanities, paralegal studies, philosophy, political science/government, psychology, social work, and sociology). Education, physical therapy, and engineering are the strongest academically. Business, health & human performance, and biology have the largest enrollments.

ACTIVITIES: 8% of men belong to 11 national fraternities; 18% of women belong to 9 national sororities. There are 130 groups on campus, including band, cheerleading, chess, choir, chorale, chorus, communications, computers, dance, debate, drama, drill team, environmental, ethnic, film, honors, international, jazz band, LGBT, literary magazine, marching band, musical theater, newspaper, opera, orchestra, pep band, photography, political, professional, radio and TV, religious, social, social service, student government, and symphony. Popular campus events include Homecoming, and Welcome Week. **Sports:** There are 7 intercollegiate sports for men and 8 for women, and 9 intramural sports for men and 10 for women. Facilities include an aquatic and recreation center, an arena, tennis and racquet center, swimming pool, sport fields, and a soccer field. **Graduates:** From July 1, 2015 to June 30, 2016, 1883 bachelor's degrees were awarded. The most popular majors were business marketing (18%), education (10%), and health and human performance (9%). 24 companies recruited on campus in 2015-2016. In an average class, 22% graduate in 4 years or less, 39% graduate in 5 years or less, and 44% graduate in 6 years or less.

SERVICES: Counseling and information services are available, as is tutoring in most subjects, and a reader service for the blind, and remedial math, reading, and writing. **Library/Resources:** The library contains 634,306 volumes, 78 microform items, and 21,853 audio/video tapes/CDs/DVDs, and subscribes to 55,988 periodicals including electronic. Computerized library services include interlibrary loans, database searching, Internet access, and Wi-Fi capability. Special learning facilities include an art gallery, radio station, an observatory, and challenger center. **Physically Challenged Students:** 95% of the campus is accessible. Facilities include wheelchair ramps, elevators, special parking, specially equipped restrooms, special class scheduling, lowered drinking fountains, and lowered telephones. **Special:** Cooperative programs are offered in accounting, business systems, chemistry, communications, engineering, environmental studies, nursing, and psychology. UTC offers internships, study abroad in England, work-study and accelerated degree programs, B.A.-B.S. degrees, dual majors, interdisciplinary majors, including theater and speech, 3-2 engineering degrees, and non-degree study. Credit is given for life, military, or work experience. There are 33 national honor societies, a freshman honors program, and 29 departmental honors programs. **Visiting:** There are regularly scheduled orientations for prospective students. There are guides for informal visits, visitors may sit in on classes, and stay overnight. To schedule a visit, contact the Admissions Office. **Campus Safety and Security:** Measures include 24-hour foot and vehicle patrol, emergency notification system, self-defense education, and security escort services. There are also shuttle buses, emergency telephones, lighted pathways/sidewalks, and controlled access to dorms/residences.

REQUIREMENTS: The SAT or ACT is required. Secondary school credits should include 4 each in English, and math, 3 in science with lab, 2 each in foreign language and history, 1 in visual performing arts. The GED is accepted. AP and CLEP credits are accepted. Important factors in the admissions decision are advanced placement or honors courses, personality/intangible qualities, evidence of special talent, and extracurricular activities record. All students must complete at least 120 semester hours and maintain a minimum GPA of 2.0. General education requirements include 9 hours in humanities and fine arts, 6 hours in English and math, 8 hours in natural sciences, 9 hours in cultures and civilizations, and 6 hours in behavioral and social sciences. Students must complete at least 25% of the minimum credit hours under the direction of UTC faculty, complete 60 credit hours at an accredited senior institution, complete the last 24 credit hours at UTC, and complete at least 39 credit hours at the senior (300-400) level. They must also complete a minimum 12 hours at the senior level in the UTC major department or program offering the degree and also complete the senior exit exam. Other requirements vary by major. **Procedure:** Freshmen are admitted in the fall and spring. Entrance exams should be taken in spring of the junior year. There are deferred admissions and rolling admissions plans. Applications should be filed by May 1 for fall entry; November 1 for spring entry; and April 15 for summer entry, along with a $30 fee. Applications are accepted on-line. Application fees are waived if application is completed on-line. **Transfer Students:** 804 transfer students enrolled in 2015-2016. Transfer students must have pursued courses appropriate to the curriculum at UTC, be eligible to return to their previous institution, and meet UTC's continuation standards. 24 of 120 credits required for the bachelor's degree must be completed at UTC. **International Students:** There are 78 international students enrolled. The school actively recruits these students. They must take the TOEFL with a minimum score of 500 on the paper-based TOEFL (PBT) or 61 on the Internet-based version (iBT). They must also take the SAT or ACT.

ADMISSIONS: The SAT scores for the 2016-2017 freshman class were: Critical Reading-- 40% below 500, 40% between 500 and 599, 18% between 600 and 699, and 2% between 700 and 800. Math-- 38% below 500, 43% between 500 and 599, 17% between 600 and 699, and 2% between 700 and 800. The ACT scores were 1% between 12 and 17, 55% between 18 and 23, 38% between 24 and 29, and 6% above 30. **Admissions Contact:** Lee Pierce, Director of Admissions. Email: *info@utc.edu* Web: *www.utc.edu*

FINANCIAL AID: In 2016-2017, 57% of all full-time freshmen received some form of financial aid. 74% of all full-time freshmen received need-based aid. The average freshman award was $10,611. Need-based scholarships or need-based grants averaged $8,558; need-based self-help aid (loans and jobs) averaged $3,375; non-need-based athletic scholarships averaged $20,681; other non-need-based awards and non-need-based scholarships averaged $3,293; and $3,107 from other forms of aid. The average financial indebtedness of the 2016 graduate was $21,420. The FAFSA code is 003529. The priority date for freshman financial aid applications for fall entry is April 1.

THE UNIVERSITY OF TENNESSEE AT KNOXVILLE E-2

www.utk.edu

Knoxville, TN 37996 (865) 974-2184

Email: admissions@utk.edu

Full-time: 10,136 men, 10,042 women
Part-time: 668 men, 550 women
Graduate: 3983 men, 4582 women
Year: semesters, summer session
Room & Board: $9926

SAT CR/M: 575/585 **ACT:** 27
Application Deadline: December 1

Faculty: 1324; I, av$
Ph.D.s: 85%
Student/Faculty: 17 to 1
Tuition: $12,186 ($30,636)
Freshman Class: 15442 applied, 11555 accepted, 4701 enrolled
CEEB CODE: 1843
VERY COMPETITIVE

The University of Tennessee at Knoxville, founded in 1794. There are 9 undergraduate schools and 11 graduate schools. In addition to regional accreditation, UT Knoxville has baccalaureate program accreditation with AACSB, ABET, ACEJMC, ACPE, ADA, ASLA, CAHEA, CSWE, FIDER, NAAB, NASAD, NASM, NCATE, NLN, NRPA, SAF, AAFCS, ABA, ACS, AVMA, and CCNE. The figures in the above capsule and in this profile are approximate. The 560-acre campus is in an urban area in Knoxville. and is just minutes from the Great Smoky Mountains National Park. Including any residence halls, there are 236 buildings.

STUDENT LIFE: 90% of undergraduates are from Tennessee. Others are from 50 states, 113 foreign countries, and Canada. 81% are White; 7% African American; 4% Asian American; 3% Hispanic; 3% two or more races; 2% race unknown. **Female To Male Ratio:** 1.0:1. The average age of freshmen is 18; all undergraduates, 21. 15% do not continue beyond their first year; 85% remain to graduate. **Housing:** 7312 students can be accommodated in college housing, which includes single-sex and coed dorms, on-campus apartments, honors houses, special-interest houses, fraternity houses, sorority houses, and theme housing. On-campus housing is guaranteed for the freshman year only, and is available on a first-come, first-served basis. 63% of students commute. All students may keep cars. Alcohol is not permitted.

FACULTY/CLASSROOMS: 58% of faculty are male; 42% are female. 76% teach undergraduates. No introductory courses are taught by graduate students.

PROGRAMS OF STUDY: UT Knoxville confers B.A., B.S., B.Arch., B.F.A., B.M., B.S.ArtEd., B.S.Ag.E., BSAN, BSFS, B.S.F., B.S.P.S., BSID, B.S.C., B.S.B.A., B.A.C., B.S.H.S., B.S.Ed., B.S.Ch.E., B.S.C.E., BSCOME, B.S.C.S., B.S.E.E., B.S.I.E., B.S.A.E., BSBME, B.S.M.E., B.S.N., and B.S.S.W. degrees. Master's and doctoral degrees are also awarded. Bachelor's degrees are awarded in AGRICULTURE (agricultural economics, agriculture, animal science, forestry and related sciences, natural resources, plant science, and soil science), BIOLOGICAL SCIENCE (biology/biological science, nutrition, and wildlife biology), BUSINESS (accounting, business systems analysis, finance, hotel/motel and restaurant management, human resources, logistics, management science, retailing, and sports management), COMMUNICATIONS AND THE ARTS (advertising, art history, art, classics, communications, English, French, German, graphic design, Italian, journalism, music, public relations, Russian, studio art, and theatre arts), COMPUTER AND PHYSICAL SCIENCE (chemistry, computer science, geology, mathematics, physics, and statistics), EDUCATION (education, health information management, marketing and distribution education, recreation education, and special education), ENGINEERING AND ENVIRONMENTAL DESIGN (aerospace studies, architecture, biomedical engineering, chemical engineering, civil engineering, computer engineering, electrical/electronics engineering, environmental science, industrial engineering, interior design, materials engineering, mechanical engineering, and nuclear engineering), HEALTH PROFESSIONS (clinical science, dental hygiene, medical technology, nursing, predentistry, premedicine, prepharmacy, and preveterinary science), SOCIAL SCIENCE (anthropology, child care/child and family studies, economics, food science, geography, Hispanic American studies, history, interdisciplinary studies, philosophy, political science/government, psychology, public administration, religion, social work, and sociology). Engineering, business, and nursing are the strongest academically. Logistics, accounting, and psychology have the largest enrollments.

ACTIVITIES: 16% of men belong to 24 national fraternities; 25% of women belong to 18 national sororities. There are 296 groups on campus, including art, band, cheerleading, chess, choir, chorale, chorus, computers, dance, debate, drama, environmental, ethnic, film, honors, international, jazz band, LGBT, literary magazine, marching band, musical theater, newspaper, opera, orchestra, pep band, photography, political, professional, radio and TV, religious, social, social service, student government, symphony, and yearbook. Popular campus events include All-Sing, Torch Night, International Festival, Volapalooza, Vol Night Long, Dance Marathon, Carnius, Football and Basketball Games. **Sports:** There are 9 intercollegiate sports for men and 11 for women, and 50 intramural sports for men and 50 for women. Facilities include a basketball arena and facility, a track, indoor and outdoor pools, a baseball stadium, and softball and soccer fields. The Recreation Center has multi-purpose gym courts, raised running/jogging/walking track, a stretching and fitness areas (with cardio equipment, selectorized equipment and free weights), cycling studio, group exercise studios, and racquetball courts. The Sports Bubble has indoor soccer, floor hockey, roller blading, volleyball, basketball, and fencing club. RecSports has multi-purpose court areas, a small weight room, racquetball courts, quash courts, a multi-purpose gym area with a climbing wall and bouldering, tennis courts, and sand volleyball. **Graduates:** From July 1, 2015 to June 30, 2016, 4771 bachelor's degrees were awarded. The most popular majors were business/marketing (19%), engineering (10%), and social sciences (9%). 527 companies recruited on campus in 2015-2016. In an average class, 36% graduate in 4 years or less, 62% graduate in 5 years or less, and 66% graduate in 6 years or less. Of the 2015 graduating class, 12% were enrolled in graduate school within 6 months of graduation, and 86% were employed.

SERVICES: Counseling and information services are available, as is tutoring in some subjects, and a reader service for the blind. There is also supplemental instruction in math and chemistry, as well as tutoring in English, math, chemistry and most lower division courses. **Library/Resources:** The 5 libraries contain 3.1 million volumes, 4.7 million microform items, and 80,122 audio/video tapes/CDs/DVDs, and subscribe to 58,765 periodicals including electronic. Computerized library services include interlibrary loans, database searching, Internet access, and Wi-Fi capability. Special learning facilities include an art gallery, natural history museum, radio station, the Scripps Laboratory, an emergent communications technology facility with workstations and facilities to conduct focus-group research. Communications students also get hands-on media experience at WUTK, a student-run radio station and UTTV, and a television production facility on campus. Business students have access to a finance laboratory with real-time stock quotes from the world's financial markets, and the Anderson Center for Entrepreneurship and Innovation, a learning environment for those interested in starting and growing new businesses. The Clarence Brown Theatre produces plays and musicals featuring nationally renowned guest artists. Home to the Clarence Brown Theatre Professional Company, the University Company, and the undergraduate performance group, the theatre also provides students with space to rehearse and perform experimental stage plays. The University of Tennessee is one of only twenty-seven universities nationwide that is affiliated with the League of Resident Theatres (LORT). This professional theatre affiliation allows students regular opportunities to work alongside professional actors, directors, designers, and production artists. Campus is also home to the McClung Museum of Natural History and Culture, which is accredited by the American Association of Museums. The McClung Museum is one of only thirteen AAM-accredited museums in Tennessee, which puts it in the top four percent of museums nationwide. The Ewing Gallery of Art and Architecture emphasizes historic and current trends in art and architecture and supports creative works by students in these areas. The Commons in Hodges Library is a learning environment designed to meet the changing needs of students with the latest technological advances in a private yet collaborative workspace. The Commons provides its users with the tools, information, and adaptability they need to be successful learners and teachers in the 21st century. The Humanities and Social Sciences Building is one of the first higher-education facilities in the country to transform its classrooms into student-centric collaborative teaching and learning centers. **Physically Challenged Students:** 95% of the campus is accessible. Facilities include wheelchair ramps, elevators, special parking, specially equipped restrooms, special class scheduling, lowered drinking fountains, lowered telephones, and special housing. **Special:** Students can design a wide variety of interdisciplinary majors through the College of Arts and Sciences. Honors programs exist within several colleges. University-wide honors programs include the Baker Scholars, Haslam Scholars and Chancellor's Honors Programs. The university offers many dual graduate and professional degrees that include law and business, public administration and law, business and engineering, and recreation and sport management and business. New graduate programs include a master's in landscape architecture, a master's in public health, a master's in business analytics, a doctorate in energy science and engineering, a doctorate of nursing practice, and a doctorate in social work. Study-abroad programs are offered in more than fifty-nine countries. There are 27 national honor societies, including Phi Beta Kappa, and a freshman honors program. **Visiting:** There are regularly scheduled orientations for prospective students, including 2 open houses yearly where prospective students can meet with faculty, administrators, and students to discuss admissions, housing, financial aid, and student activities. There are guides for informal visits and visitors may sit in on classes. **Campus Safety and Security:** Measures include 24-hour foot and vehicle patrol, emergency notification system, self-defense education, and security escort services. There are also shuttle buses, emergency telephones, lighted pathways/sidewalks, and campus safety educational programs.

REQUIREMENTS: The ACT or SAT is accepted. Applicants should be high school graduates or have the GED. Required secondary school courses include 4 credits in English, and math, 3 in science with lab, and 2 in foreign language, 1 each in history, social studies, and visual/performing arts. AP and CLEP credits are accepted. Important factors in the admissions decision are advanced placement or honors courses, evidence of special talent, leadership record, parents or siblings attended your school, extracurricular activities record, and geographical diversity. All students must complete at least 120 credits with a minimum 2.0 GPA. Students must take 3 courses in communicating through writing: 2 courses in oral communication, quantitative reasoning, natural sciences, arts and humanities, social sciences, and cultures and civilizations, including 8 courses to develop broadening perspectives. **Procedure:** Freshmen are admitted to all sessions. Entrance exams should be taken in spring of the junior yearor fall of the senior year. Applications should be filed by December 1 for fall entry; November 1 for spring entry; and December 1 for summer entry, along with a $40 fee. Notifications are sent March 31. 2051 applicants were on the 2016 waiting list; 19 were admitted. Applications are accepted on-line. **Transfer Students:** 1265 transfer students enrolled in 2015-2016. Transfer applicants should present a minimum 2.0 GPA in previous college work, although many specific programs have higher requirements. Transfer applicants must have completed a minimum of 15 transferable college credits by the date they apply. 30 of 120 credits required for the bachelor's degree must be completed at UT Knoxville. **International Students:** There are 385 international students enrolled. The school actively recruits these students. They must take the TOEFL with a minimum score of 523 on the paper-based TOEFL (PBT) or 70 on the Internet-based version (iBT). Students must take the Comprehensive English Language Test, and the college's own test. They can also take either the ILETS, SAT or ACT.

ADMISSIONS: 75% of the 2016-2017 applicants were accepted. The SAT scores for the 2016-2017 freshman class were: Critical Reading-- 15% below 500, 47% between 500 and 599, 29% between 600 and 699, and 10% between 700 and 800. Math-- 14% below 500, 44% between 500 and 599, 32% between 600 and 699, and 10% between 700 and 800. There were 20 National Merit finalists. **Admissions Contact:** Tom Broadhead, Director of Admissions. Email: *admissions@utk.edu* Web: *www.utk.edu*

FINANCIAL AID: In 2016-2017, 51% of all full-time freshmen received some form of financial aid, and need-based aid. The average freshman award was $13,793. Need-based scholarships or need-based grants averaged $11,207; need-based self-help aid (loans and jobs) averaged $5,219; non-need-based athletic scholarships averaged $15,303; other non-need-based awards and non-need-based scholarships averaged $5,093; and $5,042 from other forms of aid. The average financial indebtedness of the 2016 graduate was $23,870. The FAFSA code is 003530. The priority date for freshman financial aid applications for fall entry is March 1.

THE UNIVERSITY OF TENNESSEE AT MARTIN B-1

www.utm.edu

Martin, TN 38238	**(731) 587-7020** **(800) 829-8861**
Fax: (731) 587-7029	**Email: admitme@utm.edu**
Full-time: 2437 men, 3301 women	**Faculty:** 295; IIA, --$
Part-time: 345 men, 594 women	**Ph.D.s:** 73%
Graduate: 107 men, 258 women	**Student/Faculty:** 17 to 1
Year: semesters, summer session	**Tuition:** $8024 ($21,968)
Room & Board: $5786	**Freshman Class:** 3526 applied, 2586 accepted, 1181 enrolled
ACT: 22	**CEEB CODE:** 1844
Application Deadline: August 1	**COMPETITIVE**

University of Tennessee at Martin, founded in 1900, is a primary campus in the University of Tennessee System and known for providing high-quality undergraduate and graduate academic programs. Today's status as a comprehensive public university, UT Martin remains committed to preparing students for success in the global economy. UT Martin serves students by offering more than 100 different areas of study at the undergraduate and graduate levels. Figures in the above capsule and in this profile are approximate. There are 5 undergraduate schools and 4 graduate schools. In addition to regional accreditation, UT Martin has baccalaureate program accreditation with AACSB, ABET, ACEJMC, ADA,

AHEA, CSWE, NASM, NCATE, NLN, and ACS. The 250-acre campus is in a rural area 125 miles northeast of Memphis and 150 miles northwest of Nashville. Including any residence halls, there are 49 buildings.

STUDENT LIFE: 93% of undergraduates are from Tennessee. Others are from 38 states, 19 foreign countries, and Canada. 91% are from public schools. 77% are White; 3% Foreign; 2% Hispanic; 2% two or more races; 15% African American; 1% Asian American. 73% are Protestant. **Female To Male Ratio:** 1.4:1. The average age of freshmen is 19; all undergraduates, 23. 29% do not continue beyond their first year; 47% remain to graduate. **Housing:** 2382 students can be accommodated in college housing, which includes single-sex and coed dorms, on-campus apartments, married student housing, honors houses and special-interest houses. On-campus housing is guaranteed for all 4 years, and is available on a first-come, and first-served basis. 70% of students commute. Alcohol is not permitted. All students may keep cars.

FACULTY/CLASSROOMS: 56% of faculty are male; 44% are female. All teach undergraduates, 84% do research, and 84% do both. No introductory courses are taught by graduate students. The average class size in an introductory lecture is 23; in a laboratory is 16; and in a regular course is 17.

PROGRAMS OF STUDY: UT Martin confers B.A., B.S., B.A.Mus., B.F.A., B.Mus., B.S.Agri., B.S.Bus.Admn., B.S.Chem., B.S.Crim.Just., B.S.Ed., B.S.Eng., B.S.Fam.C.S., B.S.Health/HP., B.S.N.R.M., B.S.N., B.S.S.W., and B.U.S. degrees. Master's degrees are also awarded. Bachelor's degrees are awarded in AGRICULTURE (agricultural business management, agriculture, animal science, natural resource management, and plant science), BIOLOGICAL SCIENCE (biology/biological science and nutrition), BUSINESS (accounting, business administration and management, business economics, management science, and marketing/retailing/merchandising), COMMUNICATIONS AND THE ARTS (communications, English, fine arts, French, music, performing arts, and Spanish), COMPUTER AND PHYSICAL SCIENCE (chemistry, computer science, geology, information sciences and systems, and mathematics), EDUCATION (education administration, elementary education, secondary education, and special education), ENGINEERING AND ENVIRONMENTAL DESIGN (engineering), HEALTH PROFESSIONS (health science and nursing), SOCIAL SCIENCE (child care/child and family studies, criminal justice, economics, geography, history, international studies, philosophy, political science/government, psychology, public administration, social work, and sociology). Preprofessional health programs, biology, and engineering are the strongest academically. Agriculture, health & human performance, and integrated studies have the largest enrollments.

ACTIVITIES: 5% of men belong to 12 national fraternities; 10% of women belong to 1 local and 9 national sororities. There are 175 groups on campus, including art, band, cheerleading, choir, chorale, chorus, computers, dance, drama, drill team, environmental, ethnic, film, honors, international, jazz band, LGBT, literary magazine, marching band, musical theater, newspaper, opera, pep band, photography, political, professional, radio and TV, religious, social, social service, student government, and yearbook. Popular campus events include Greekfest, Homecoming, and Pyramid. **Sports:** There are 7 intercollegiate sports for men and 10 for women, and 11 intramural sports for men and 11 for women. Facilities include swimming pool, racquetball courts, a running/walking track, weight room, basketball, volleyball, badminton, a 1.5 mile fitness track, tennis courts, a soccer field, and playing fields. **Graduates:** From July 1, 2015 to June 30, 2016, 1224 bachelor's degrees were awarded. The most popular majors were business/marketing (18%), interdisciplinary studies (13%), and education (12%). 62 companies recruited on campus in 2015-2016. In an average class, 21% graduate in 4 years or less, 40% graduate in 5 years or less, and 46% graduate in 6 years or less. Of the 2015 graduating class, 25% were enrolled in graduate school within 6 months of graduation, and 68% were employed.

SERVICES: Counseling and information services are available, as is tutoring in some subjects, such as astronomy, biology, chemistry, computer science, English, French, geography, geology, German, history, Japanese, math, psychology, and Spanish. **Library/Resources:** The library contains 379,072 volumes, 709,966 microform items, and 17,122 audio/video tapes/CDs/DVDs. Computerized library services include interlibrary loans, database searching, Internet access, and Wi-Fi capability. Special learning facilities include a natural history museum, radio station, TV station, a teacher resource center, agriculture and natural resources teaching and demonstration complex, teaching/research facility at Reelfoot Lake State resort, and a center for global studies and international education. **Physically Challenged Students:** All of the campus is accessible. Facilities include wheelchair ramps, elevators, special parking, specially equipped restrooms, special class scheduling, lowered drinking fountains, lowered telephones, and special housing. **Special:** UTM offers co-op programs in engineering, agriculture, computer science, business, and chemistry, for-credit internships, cross-registration through the Gulf Coast consortium, study abroad, B.A.-B.S. degrees, dual and student-designed majors, and pass/fail options. There are 11 national honor societies, a freshman honors program, and 6 departmental honors programs. **Visiting:** There are regularly scheduled orientations for prospective students, Campus visits include Summer Orientation and Registration (SOAR); 4 sessions conducted for students and parents that include information sessions and class registration. There are guides for informal visits, visitors may sit in on classes, and stay overnight. To schedule a visit, contact the Admissions Office. **Campus Safety and Security:** Measures include 24-hour foot and vehicle patrol, emergency notification system, and self-defense education. There are emergency telephones, lighted pathways/sidewalks, bicycle patrol, security cameras in residence halls, auto dialer alert system, text messaging alert system, and severe weather siren alert system.

REQUIREMENTS: Students should have a minimum composite score of 21 on the ACT, with a minimum 2.50 GPA, or 18 with a minimum 2.85 GPA. Candidates for admission should be graduates of an accredited secondary school with 14 academic credits. The GED is accepted with a score of 500. Secondary school units should include 4 of English, 3 of math, 2 of a foreign language, and 1 each of science, history, social studies, and fine and performing arts. AP and CLEP credits are accepted. The number of credit hours required for graduation ranges from 120 to 134 (based on degree). All students must have at least a 2.0 GPA. Specific courses and major requirements vary by the program selected. There is a 1 year or 30 hour UTM residency requirement. The general education core curriculum is 38 hours; English and communications courses are required. Major field and general education tests are required. **Procedure:** Freshmen are admitted to all sessions. Entrance exams should be taken by the spring of the junior year. There are deferred admissions and rolling admissions plans. Applications should be filed by August 1 for fall entry, along with a $30 fee. Notification is sent on a rolling basis. Applications are accepted on-line. **Transfer Students:** 543 transfer students enrolled in 2015-2016. Transfer students should have a minimum GPA of 2.0. 30 of 120 credits required for the bachelor's degree must be completed at UT Martin. **International Students:** There are 140 international students enrolled. The school actively recruits these students. They must take the TOEFL with a minimum score of 500 on the paper-based TOEFL (PBT) or 61 on the Internet-based version (iBT), and a writing proficiency exam.

ADMISSIONS: 73% of the 2016-2017 applicants were accepted. The ACT scores were 34% below 12, 28% between 12 and 17, 19% between 18 and 23, 6% between 24 and 29, and 12% above 30. 49% of the current freshmen were in the top fifth of their class; 80% were in the top two fifths. 21 freshmen graduated first in their class. **Admissions Contact:** Emily Sparks, Admissions. Email: *admitme@utm.edu* Web: *www.utm.edu*

FINANCIAL AID: In 2016-2017, 78% of all full-time freshmen and 75% of continuing full-time students received some form of financial aid. 52% of all full-time freshmen and 54% of continuing full-time students received need-based aid. The average freshman award was $13,655. Need-based scholarships or need-based grants averaged $6,695 ($10,039 maximum); need-based self-help aid (loans and jobs) averaged $3,376; non-need-based athletic scholarships averaged $10,506; and other non-need-based awards and non-need-based scholarships averaged $2,046 ($2,956 maximum). 39% of undergraduate students work part-time. Average annual earnings from campus work are $2147. The average financial indebtedness of the 2016 graduate was $27,147. The FAFSA code is 003531. The priority date for freshman financial aid applications for fall entry is March 1.

TREVECCA NAZARENE UNIVERSITY C-2

www.trevecca.edu

Nashville, TN 37210

(615) 248-1320
(888) 210-4TNU

Fax: (615) 248-7406

Email: admissions@trevecca.edu

Full-time: 505 men, 671 women	**Faculty:** IIA, --$
Part-time: 237 men, 264 women	**Ph.D.s:** 90%
Graduate: 295 men, 634 women	**Student/Faculty:** 18 to 1
Year: semesters, summer session	**Tuition:** $23,126
Room & Board: $8060	**Freshman Class:** 1029 applied, 752 accepted, 320 enrolled
SAT CR/M: 530/520 **ACT:** 23	**CEEB CODE:** 1809
Application Deadline: August 1	**COMPETITIVE**

Trevecca Nazarene University, founded in 1901, is a private institution affiliated with the Church of the Nazarene, and offers programs in liberal arts and sciences and a number of professional content areas. The university also provides a variety of nontraditional continuing education professional programs at the undergraduate and graduate levels. There are 4 undergraduate schools and 4 graduate schools. In addition to regional accreditation, TNU has baccalaureate program accreditation with NASM, NCATE, CCNE, and ARC-PA. The 80-acre campus is in an urban area. Including any residence halls, there are 26 buildings.

STUDENT LIFE: 62% of undergraduates are from Tennessee. Others are from 42 states, 15 foreign countries, and Canada. 71% are White; 11% race unknown; 9% African American; 4% Hispanic; 3% two or more races; 1% Asian American; 1% American Indian/Alaska Native; 1% Foreign. 51% are Protestant; 15% claim no religious affiliation. **Female To Male Ratio:** 1.5:1. The average age of freshmen is 19; all undergraduates, 26. 21% do not continue beyond their first year; 51% remain to graduate. **Housing:** 759 students can be accommodated in college housing, which includes single-sex dorms, on-campus apartments, off-campus apartments, and married student housing. On-campus housing is guaranteed for all 4 years. 53% of students commute. All students may keep cars. Alcohol is not permitted.

FACULTY/CLASSROOMS: 63% of faculty are male; 37% are female. No introductory courses are taught by graduate students.

PROGRAMS OF STUDY: TNU confers B.A., B.S., B.B.A., B.S.N., and B.S.S.W. degrees. Associate, master's, and doctoral degrees are also awarded. Bachelor's degrees are awarded in BIOLOGICAL SCIENCE (biology/biological science), BUSINESS (accounting, business administration and management, business administration - international, electronic business, management science, marketing, marketing/retailing/ merchandising, and sports management), COMMUNICATIONS AND THE ARTS (communication studies, digital communications, dramatic arts, English, journalism, music, and music business management), COMPUTER AND PHYSICAL SCIENCE (chemistry, chemistry/ adolescence education, computer information technology, information sciences and systems, mathematics, physics, and science), EDUCATION (business education, drama education, early childhood education, education, English education, mathematics education, music education, physical education, science education, secondary education, and special education), HEALTH PROFESSIONS (biology, exercise science, and nursing), SOCIAL SCIENCE (behavioral science, criminal justice, history, pastoral studies, political science/government, psychology, religion, social work, and sociology). Management & human relations, religion, and biology have the largest enrollments.

ACTIVITIES: There are no fraternities or sororities. There are 23 groups on campus, including art, band, cheerleading, choir, chorale, chorus, drama, environmental, forensics, honors, international, jazz band, literary magazine, marching band, musical theater, newspaper, orchestra, pep band, professional, religious, social service, student government, symphony, and yearbook. Popular campus events include Drama Productions and Athletic Events. **Sports:** There are 6 intercollegiate sports for men and 7 for women, and 10 intramural sports for men and 10 for women. Facilities include a gym, a jogging track, handball, racquetball, and tennis courts, exercise and weight rooms, and playing fields. **Graduates:** From July 1, 2015 to June 30, 2016, 353 bachelor's degrees were awarded. The most popular majors were business/management (42%), religion/christian ministry (6%), and psychology (5%). In an average class, 39% graduate in 4 years or less, 49% graduate in 5 years or less, and 51% graduate in 6 years or less.

SERVICES: Counseling and information services are available, as is tutoring in every subject, and a reader service for the blind, and remedial math, reading, and writing. An academic enrichment program for students scoring below 19 on the ACT provides tutoring in math, reading, writing, and study skills. **Library/Resources:** The library contains 183,605 volumes. Computerized library services include interlibrary loans, database searching, Internet access, and Wi-Fi capability. **Physically Challenged Students:** Facilities include wheelchair ramps, elevators, special parking, specially equipped restrooms, special class scheduling, and lowered drinking fountains. **Special:** Trevecca offers students cross registration with other Nazarene colleges and universities in the United States, including internships, practicums, Washington semester, and study abroad through the Council of Christian Colleges & Universities. Trevecca also offers an adult degree-completion programs leading to bachelor degrees. A 3-2 nursing program is offered with Belmont University. There is 1 national honor society. **Visiting:** There are regularly scheduled orientations for prospective students, including a tour and meetings with admissions and financial aid personnel and faculty. There are guides for informal visits, visitors may sit in on classes, and stay overnight. To schedule a visit, contact the Admissions Office. **Campus Safety and Security:** Measures include 24-hour foot and vehicle patrol and emergency notification system. There are lighted pathways/ sidewalks.

REQUIREMENTS: The SAT is required. The ACT is preferred, with a composite score of at least 18. Candidates should have completed at least 15 academic secondary credits, including 4 units in English, 2 each in math, foreign language, and social science, and 1 in natural science. A GED of at least 45 is also accepted. The teacher education program has special admission requirements. AP and CLEP credits are accepted. To graduate, students must complete at least 120 semester hours with a minimum 2.0 GPA. The required 54-hour general education curriculum includes courses in English, communications, religion and philosophy, fine arts, history and social science (including foreign language), science, math, financial stewardship and health & wellness. **Procedure:** Freshmen are admitted in the fall, spring, and summer. Entrance exams should be taken in the junior or senior year. There are deferred admissions and rolling admissions plans. Applications should be filed by August 1 for fall entry, along with a $25 fee. Application fees are waived if application is completed online. **Transfer Students:** 87 transfer students enrolled in 2015-2016. Transfer applicants must present official transcripts and recommendations from a regionally accredited institution. 30 of 120 credits required for the bachelor's degree must be completed at TNU. **International Students:** There are 18 international students enrolled. They must take the TOEFL with a minimum score of 500 on the paper-based TOEFL (PBT) or 61 on the Internet-based version (iBT). They must also take the SAT or ACT.

ADMISSIONS: 73% of the 2016-2017 applicants were accepted. The SAT scores for the 2016-2017 freshman class were: Critical Reading-- 31% below 500, 44% between 500 and 599, 15% between 600 and 699, and 10% between 700 and 800. Math-- 37% below 500, 41% between 500 and 599, 18% between 600 and 699, and 4% between 700 and 800. The ACT scores were 28% below 12, 29% between 12 and 17, 22% between 18 and 23, 8% between 24 and 29, and 13% above 30. **Admissions Contact:** Melinda Miller, Director Undergraduate Admissions. Email: *admissions@trevecca.edu* Web: *www.trevecca.edu*

FINANCIAL AID: In 2016-2017, 94% of all full-time freshmen received some form of financial aid. The FAFSA code is 003526. The priority date for freshman financial aid applications for fall entry is February 1.

TUSCULUM COLLEGE F-2

www.tusculum.edu

Greeneville, TN 37743	**(423) 636-7300** **(800) 729-0256**
Fax: (423) 638-7166	**Email: admissions@tusculum.edu**
Full-time: 696 men, 721 women	**Faculty:** 72
Part-time: 54 men, 114 women	**Ph.D.s:** 64%
Graduate: 69 men, 142 women	**Student/Faculty:** 15 to 1
Year: semesters, summer session	**Tuition:** $23,125
Room & Board: $8500	**Freshman Class:** 2238 applied, 1665 accepted, 324 enrolled
SAT CR/M: required **ACT:** 21	**CEEB CODE:** 1812
Application Deadline: open	**COMPETITIVE**

Tusculum College, a civic arts institution chartered in 1794, is the oldest college in Tennessee and the oldest coeducational college affiliated with the Presbyterian Church. The figures in the above capsule and in this profile are approximate. There are 4 undergraduate schools and 1 graduate school. In addition to regional accreditation, Tusculum has baccalaureate program accreditation with CAATE. The 164-acre campus is in a small town in Greenville, 30 miles south of Johnson City. Tusculum has sites in Knoxville, Morristown and Kingsport. Including any residence halls, there are 49 buildings.

STUDENT LIFE: 73% of undergraduates are from Tennessee. Others are from 28 states, 22 foreign countries, and Canada. 97% are from public schools. 74% are White; 4% race unknown; 3% Hispanic; 3% Foreign; 2% two or more races; 14% African American. **Female To Male Ratio:** 1.2:1. The average age of freshmen is 19; all undergraduates, 25. 32% do not continue beyond their first year; 41% remain to graduate. **Housing:**

780 students can be accommodated in college housing, which includes single-sex and coed dorms and on-campus apartments, honors houses, smoke-free housing, and theme housing. On-campus housing is guaranteed for all 4 years. 50% of students commute. All students may keep cars. Alcohol is not permitted.

FACULTY/CLASSROOMS: 51% of faculty are male; 49% are female. 88% teach undergraduates, 30% do research, and 27% do both. No introductory courses are taught by graduate students. The average class size in an introductory lecture is 16; in a laboratory is 18; and in a regular course is 14.

PROGRAMS OF STUDY: Tusculum confers B.A. and B.S. degrees. Associate and master's degrees are also awarded. Bachelor's degrees are awarded in BIOLOGICAL SCIENCE (biology/biological science), BUSINESS (management science, small business management, and sports management), COMMUNICATIONS AND THE ARTS (art and design, design, English, and fine arts), COMPUTER AND PHYSICAL SCIENCE (chemistry, computer science, information sciences and systems, and mathematics), EDUCATION (athletic training, early childhood education, education, elementary education, middle school education, museum studies, physical education, and special education), ENGINEERING AND ENVIRONMENTAL DESIGN (environmental science), HEALTH PROFESSIONS (medical technology, nursing, premedicine, and sports medicine), SOCIAL SCIENCE (criminal justice, history, political science/government, and psychology). Business, biology, and psychology are the strongest academically. business, education, and nursing have the largest enrollments.

ACTIVITIES: There are no fraternities or sororities. There are 21 groups on campus, including art, band, cheerleading, chorale, dance, drama, environmental, ethnic, HerStory, honors, international, jazz band, marching band, musical theater, newspaper, pep band, photography, political, professional, radio and TV, religious, social service, student government, and yearbook. Popular campus events include McCormick Day, Opening Convocation, Old Oak Festival, and Honors Convocation. **Sports:** There are 9 intercollegiate sports for men and 9 for women, and 12 intramural sports for men and 13 for women. Facilities include a gym/pool complex, tennis courts, football, soccer, softball, baseball fields, basketball, cheerleading, cross crountry, golf, and volleyball. **Graduates:** From July 1, 2015 to June 30, 2016, 394 bachelor's degrees were awarded. The most popular majors were business (47%), psychology (12%), and education (11%). 50 companies recruited on campus in 2015-2016. In an average class, 18% graduate in 4 years or less, 36% graduate in 5 years or less, and 41% graduate in 6 years or less. Of the 2015 graduating class, 10% were enrolled in graduate school within 6 months of graduation, and 71% were employed.

SERVICES: Counseling and information services are available, as is tutoring in most subjects, and a reader service for the blind, and remedial math, reading, and writing. Math and English tutoring are available through the College Learning Center. **Library/Resources:** The 2 libraries contain 48,290 volumes, 131,453 microform items, 435 audio/video tapes/CDs/DVDs, and subscribe to 50,000 periodicals including electronic. Computerized library services include interlibrary loans, database searching, Internet access, and Wi-Fi capability. Special learning facilities include an art gallery, radio station, and TV station, the President Andrew Johnson Museum, the Doak House Museum, and the Museum Studies Program, and the Allison Gallery. **Physically Challenged Students:** 60% of the campus is accessible. Facilities include wheelchair ramps, elevators, special parking, specially equipped restrooms, special class scheduling, lowered drinking fountains, lowered telephones, and special housing. Classes and activities are scheduled in accessible areas. **Special:** Each semester is divided into 2 8-week blocks, with options to take 2 or more courses per block and a semester-long course. Internships, practicums, and student-teaching opportunities are offered in business administration, professional and special education, psychology, biology, chemistry, and criminal justice. Fully online programs are management and the masters of education in human resource development. Study abroad, independent majors, non-degree study, work-study programs, student-designed majors, and pass/fail options are available. There is an accelerated evening program for working adults. There is 1 national honor society and a freshman honors program. **Visiting:** There are regularly scheduled orientations for prospective students, including a fall and spring open house during which students are given campus tours, financial aid information, and application materials. There are guides for informal visits, visitors may sit in on classes, and stay overnight. To schedule a visit, contact Melissa Ripley in Admissions. **Campus Safety and Security:** Measures include 24-hour foot and vehicle patrol, emergency notification system, security escort services, emergency telephones, lighted pathways/sidewalks, and controlled access to dorms/residences.

REQUIREMENTS: The SAT or ACT is required. Applicants should be high school graduates or have the GED. Secondary school preparation should include 4 units of English, 2 units each of foreign language, math, and science, and 1 unit of history. A personal essay is also required and an interview may be necessary. Tusculum requires applicants to be in the upper 50% of their class. AP and CLEP credits are accepted. Important factors in the admissions decision are advanced placement or honors courses, leadership record, and evidence of special talent. All students must complete at least 120 hours, a minimum GPA of 2.0 overall and 2.25 in the major. Specific degree programs have varying requirements. B.S. and B.A. candidates must take a core curriculum consisting of courses in English, art and humanities, history, civic studies, natural sciences, math, and religion, and fulfill the requirements of a major. **Procedure:** Freshmen are admitted to all sessions. Entrance exams should be taken in the spring of the junior year. There are deferred admissions and rolling admissions plans. Application deadlines are open. Applications are accepted online. **Transfer Students:** 56 transfer students enrolled in 2015-2016. Transfer applicants should present at least a 2.0 GPA in previous college work. Tusculum recommends that applicants also submit SAT or ACT scores. 30 of 120 credits required for the bachelor's degree must be completed at Tusculum. **International Students:** There are 58 international students enrolled. They must take the TOEFL with a minimum score of 540 on the paper-based TOEFL (PBT) or 207 on the Internet-based version (iBT). They must also take the SAT or ACT.

ADMISSIONS: 74% of the 2016-2017 applicants were accepted. The SAT scores for the 2016-2017 freshman class were: Critical Reading-- 68% below 500, 29% between 500 and 599, and 3% between 600 and 699. Math-- 56% below 500, 37% between 500 and 599, and 7% between 600 and 699. The ACT scores were 19% between 12 and 17, 62% between 18 and 23, 18% between 24 and 29, and 1% above 30. **Admissions Contact:** Melissa Ripley, Executive Director of Enrollment Managem. Email: *admissions@tusculum.edu* Web: *www.tusculum.edu*

FINANCIAL AID: In 2016-2017, 97% of all full-time freshmen received some form of financial aid. 79% of all full-time freshmen received need-based aid. The average freshman award was $21,282. Need-based scholarships or need-based grants averaged $10,882 ($22,625 maximum); need-based self-help aid (loans and jobs) averaged $3,304 ($3,500 maximum); non-need-based athletic scholarships averaged $8,625 ($29,625 maximum); and other non-need-based awards and non-need-based scholarships averaged $8,680 ($25,195 maximum). 19% of undergraduate students work part-time. Average annual earnings from campus work are $956. The average financial indebtedness of the 2016 graduate was $28,455. The FAFSA code is 003527. The priority date for freshman financial aid applications for fall entry is January 1.

UNION UNIVERSITY — B-2

www.uu.edu

Jackson, TN 38305	**(731) 661-5009** **(800) 33-UNION**
Fax: (731) 338-6466	**Email: admissions@uu.edu**
Full-time: 803 men, 1369 women	**Faculty:** 239
Part-time: 303 men, 354 women	**Ph.D.s:** 80%
Graduate: 428 men, 739 women	**Student/Faculty:** 11 to 1
Year: 4-1-4, summer session	**Tuition:** $28,190
Room & Board: $5780	**Freshman Class:** 1930 applied, 1432 accepted, 452 enrolled
SAT CR/M: 590/590 **ACT:** 25	**CEEB CODE:** 1826
Application Deadline: August 15	**VERY COMPETITIVE**

Union University, founded in 1823, is a private, institution affiliated with the Southern Baptist Convention, and offers programs in arts and sciences, education, business, and nursing. The figures in the above capsule and in this profile are approximate. There are 5 undergraduate schools and 3 graduate schools. In addition to regional accreditation, Union has baccalaureate program accreditation with AACSB, ABET, CSWE, NASAD, NASM, NCATE, NLN, ACS, CCNE, and CAAHEP. The 360-acre campus is in a suburban area 80 miles east of Memphis. Including any residence halls, there are 40 buildings.

STUDENT LIFE: 69% of undergraduates are from Tennessee. Others are from 44 states, 35 foreign countries, and Canada. 75% are from public schools. 75% are White; 5% race unknown; 2% Hispanic; 14% African American; 1% Asian American. 94% are Protestant. **Female To Male Ratio:** 1.6:1. The average age of freshmen is 18; all undergraduates, 20. 7% do not continue beyond their first year; 64% remain to graduate. **Housing:** 1180 students can be accommodated in college housing, which includes single-sex dorms, on-campus apartments, and married student housing. On-campus housing is guaranteed for all 4 years. 65% of students live on campus; of those, 40% remain on campus on weekends. All students may keep cars. Alcohol is not permitted.

FACULTY/CLASSROOMS: 53% of faculty are male; 47% are female. All teach undergraduates and 25% do research. No introductory courses are taught by graduate students. The average class size in an introductory lecture is 25; in a laboratory is 18; and in a regular course is 15.

PROGRAMS OF STUDY: Union confers B.A., B.S., B.M., B.S.B.A., B.S.M.T., and B.S.N. degrees. Associate, master's, and doctoral degrees are also awarded. Bachelor's degrees are awarded in BIOLOGICAL SCIENCE (biology/biological science), BUSINESS (accounting, banking and finance, business administration and management, management science, marketing management, marketing/retailing/merchandising, and sports management), COMMUNICATIONS AND THE ARTS (advertising, art, broadcasting, communications, dramatic arts, English, English as a second/foreign language, English literature, French, graphic design, Greek, journalism, music, music performance, music theory and composition, piano/organ, public relations, Spanish, and voice), COMPUTER AND PHYSICAL SCIENCE (chemistry, computer science, mathematics, physical chemistry, physical sciences, and physics), EDUCATION (education, elementary education, middle school education, music education, physical education, secondary education, special education, and teaching English as a second/foreign language (TESOL/TEFOL)), ENGINEERING AND ENVIRONMENTAL DESIGN (preengineering), HEALTH PROFESSIONS (medical laboratory technology, nursing, predentistry, premedicine, prepharmacy, and sports medicine), SOCIAL SCIENCE (biblical languages, biblical studies, Christian studies, economics, family and community services, history, ministries, missions, pastoral studies, philosophy, political science/government, prelaw, psychology, religion, religious music, social work, sociology, and youth ministry). Business, nursing, and education have the largest enrollments.

ACTIVITIES: 27% of men belong to 3 national fraternities; 23% of women belong to 3 national sororities. There are 73 groups on campus, including art, band, cheerleading, choir, chorus, computers, debate, drama, ethnic, film, honors, international, jazz band, literary magazine, musical theater, newspaper, opera, orchestra, photography, political, professional, religious, social, social service, student government, and symphony. Popular campus events include Campus Day, Parents Weekend, and Variety Show. **Sports:** There are 5 intercollegiate sports for men and 5 for women, and 12 intramural sports for men and 12 for women. Facilities include racquetball courts, a student recreation center, an indoor swimming pool, a wellness center, gyms, soccer fields, baseball and softball complexes. **Graduates:** From July 1, 2015 to June 30, 2016, 640 bachelor's degrees were awarded. The most popular majors were business/marketing (26%), health professions and related science (20%), and education (15%). 47 companies recruited on campus in 2015-2016. In an average class, 4% graduate in 3 years or less, 47% graduate in 4 years or less, 59% graduate in 5 years or less, and 60% graduate in 6 years or less. Of the 2015 graduating class, 40% were enrolled in graduate school within 6 months of graduation, and 78% were employed.

SERVICES: Counseling and information services are available, as is tutoring in most subjects. There is also assistance with study skills, time management, note taking, reading comprehension, and writing. **Library/Resources:** The 2 libraries contain 146,055 volumes, 479,357 microform items, and 11,088 audio/video tapes/CDs/DVDs, and subscribe to 705 periodicals including electronic. Computerized library services include interlibrary loans, database searching, and Internet access. Special learning facilities include an art gallery, a radio and TV lab facilities. **Physically Challenged Students:** 98% of the campus is accessible. Facilities include wheelchair ramps, elevators, special parking, specially equipped restrooms, special class scheduling, lowered drinking fountains, lowered telephones, and special housing. **Special:** Cooperative and accelerated degree programs are available in business department majors. Cross-registration with Freed-Hardeman Universities, internships, study abroad in 7 countries, a Washington semester, work-study programs, composite majors in religion and church ministry, religion and Greek, and religion and philosophy, dual and student-designed majors, 3-2 engineering degrees, and nondegree study are also offered. There are 15 national honor societies, a freshman honors program, and 14 departmental honors programs. **Visiting:** There are regularly scheduled orientations for prospective students, including campus tours, class visits, and appointments with counselors. There are guides for informal visits, visitors may sit in on classes, and stay overnight. To schedule a visit, contact Robbie Graves at (731) 661-5590. **Campus Safety and Security:** Measures include 24-hour foot and vehicle patrol, emergency notification system, self-defense education, security escort services, emergency telephones and lighted pathways/sidewalks.

REQUIREMENTS: A minimum composite score of 20 on the ACT or 820 on the SAT I is recommended. Candidates must be graduates of an accredited secondary school or have the GED. A minimum of 20 academic credits is required, including at least 14 in English, math, foreign language, and social and natural sciences. An interview is also recommended. Union requires applicants to be in the upper 50% of their class. AP and CLEP credits are accepted. Important factors in the admissions decision are leadership record, advanced placement or honors courses, and recommendations by school officials. All students must complete 128 credit hours, with at least 30 in the major, and maintain a minimum overall GPA of 2.0. The general core requirements are 8 credit hours of lab sciences, 6 each of history, composition, literature, and religion, 3 each of math, oral communication, social sciences/humanities, and fine arts, and 2 of phys ed. Students must pass comprehensive exams in each course and at completion of the major. **Procedure:** Freshmen are admitted to all sessions. Entrance exams should be taken in the spring of the junior year. There are early decision, early admissions, deferred admissions, and rolling admissions plans. Applications should be filed by August 15 for fall entry, along with a $35 fee. 14 early decision candidates were accepted for the 2016-2017 class. Applications are accepted on-line. **Transfer Students:** 145 transfer students enrolled in 2015-2016. Candidates must have a minimum GPA of 2.0 in more than 12 semester hours and submit a student transfer form from the last institution attended. 32 of 128 credits required for the bachelor's degree must be completed at Union. **International Students:** There are 40 international students enrolled. The school actively recruits these students. If the TOEFL has not been taken, the ACT or the SAT is required.

ADMISSIONS: 74% of the 2016-2017 applicants were accepted. The SAT scores for the 2016-2017 freshman class were: Critical Reading-- 13% below 500, 23% between 500 and 599, 30% between 600 and 699, and 23% between 700 and 800. Math-- 13% below 500, 35% between 500 and 599, 36% between 600 and 699, and 10% between 700 and 800. The ACT scores were 16% below 12, 21% between 12 and 17, 22% between 18 and 23, 12% between 24 and 29, and 29% above 30. 66% of the current freshmen were in the top fifth of their class; 89% were in the top two fifths. There were 6 National Merit finalists. 44 freshmen graduated first in their class. **Admissions Contact:** Ted Wingo, Assistant Director of Undergraduate Admissions. Email: *admissions@uu.edu* Web: *www.uu.edu*

FINANCIAL AID: 65% of all full-time freshmen and 63% of continuing full-time students received need-based aid. 35% of undergraduate students work part-time. Average annual earnings from campus work are $1000. The college's own financial statement is required. The FAFSA code is 003528. Check with the school for current application deadlines.

UNIVERSITY OF MEMPHIS — A-3

www.memphis.edu

Memphis, TN 38152 — **(800) 669-2678**

Email: admissions@memphis.edu

Full-time: 5070 men, 7253 women	**Faculty:** I, --$
Part-time: 1350 men, 2415 women	**Ph.D.s:** 80%
Graduate: 1611 men, 2206 women	**Student/Faculty:** 16 to 1
Year: semesters, summer session	**Tuition:** $9125 ($23,684)
Room & Board: $9153	**Freshman Class:** 6798 applied, 4243 accepted, 2252 enrolled
SAT CR/M/W: 515/515/500 **ACT:** 23	**CEEB CODE:** 1459
Application Deadline: July 1	**COMPETITIVE**

University of Memphis, founded in 1912, is a public metropolitan research university and part of the Tennessee Board of Regents. There are 7 undergraduate schools and 4 graduate schools. In addition to regional accreditation, U of M has baccalaureate program accreditation with AACSB, ABET, ACEJMC, ADA, ASLA, CAHEA, CSWE, FIDER, NASAD, NASM, NCATE, NLN, AAFCS, ACS, APA, CACREPCCNE, NASPAA, NASPE, and NAST. The 1607-acre campus is in an urban area in Memphis. Including any residence halls, there are 239 buildings.

STUDENT LIFE: 65% of undergraduates are from out of state, mostly the South. Students are from 44 states, 54 foreign countries, and Canada. 55% are White; 39% African American; 3% Hispanic; 2% Asian American; 2% two or more races. **Female To Male Ratio:** 1.5:1. The average age of freshmen is 19; all undergraduates, 24. **Housing:** 2557 students can be accommodated in college housing, which includes single-sex and coed dorms, on-campus apartments, married student housing, special-interest houses, fraternity houses, sorority houses, family housing, and cooperative housing. On-campus housing is guaranteed for all 4 years. 87% of students commute. All students may keep cars. Alcohol is not permitted.

FACULTY/CLASSROOMS: 53% of faculty are male; 47% are female. No introductory courses are taught by graduate students.

PROGRAMS OF STUDY: U of M confers B.A., B.S., B.B.A., B.F.A., B.L.S., B.M., B.P.S., B.S.B.E., B.S.C.E., B.S.Ch., B.S.C.P., B.S.Ed., B.S.E.E., B.S.E.T., B.S.M.E., and B.S.N. degrees. Master's and doctoral degrees are also awarded. Bachelor's degrees are awarded in BIOLOGICAL SCIENCE (biology/biological science and microbiology), BUSINESS (accounting, banking and finance, business economics, hospitality management services, international business management, logistics, management information systems, management science, marketing management, and recreation and leisure services), COMMUNICATIONS AND THE ARTS (art, art history and appreciation, communications, dramatic arts, English, journalism, languages, music, and music business management), COMPUTER AND PHYSICAL SCIENCE (chemistry, computer science, earth science, mathematics, and physics), EDUCATION (physical education and special education), ENGINEERING AND ENVIRONMENTAL DESIGN (architecture, biomedical engineering, civil engineering, computer engineering, computer technology, electrical/electronics engineering, electrical/electronics engineering technology, engineering technology, manufacturing engineering, and mechanical engineering), HEALTH PROFESSIONS (health science and nursing), SOCIAL SCIENCE (African American studies, anthropology, criminal justice, criminology, economics, geography, history, human development, interdisciplinary studies, international studies, liberal arts/general studies, philosophy, political science/government, psychology, social work, and sociology). Nursing, professional studies, and psychology have the largest enrollments.

ACTIVITIES: 8% of men belong to 14 national fraternities; 7% of women belong to 11 national sororities. There are 140 groups on campus, including art, band, cheerleading, chess, choir, chorale, chorus, computers, dance, drama, drill team, environmental, ethnic, honors, international, jazz band, LGBT, literary magazine, marching band, musical theater, newspaper, opera, orchestra, pep band, photography, political, professional, religious, social, social service, student government, and symphony. Popular campus events include Black History Month, Step Shows by Greek organizations, and International Night. **Sports:** There are 9 intercollegiate sports for men and 9 for women, and 10 intramural sports for men and 10 for women. Facilities include a gym, football stadium, baseball field, swimming pools, track, weight room, tennis, handball, and racquetball courts. **Graduates:** From July 1, 2015 to June 30, 2016, 2991 bachelor's degrees were awarded. The most popular majors were professional studies (9%), nursing (8%), and psychology (6%). In an average class, 13% graduate in 4 years or less, 34% graduate in 5 years or less, and 40% graduate in 6 years or less.

SERVICES: Counseling and information services are available, as is tutoring in most subjects, and a reader service for the blind, remedial math, reading, and writing. **Library/Resources:** Computerized library services include interlibrary loans, database searching, Internet access, and Wi-Fi capability. Special learning facilities include an art gallery, an earthquake research center, a center for electron microscopy, Chucalissa Indian Village and Museum, a speech and hearing center, and a center for humanities. There is also a Institute for Intelligent Systems, Institute of Egyptian Art and Archaeology, Ecological Research Center, and Biological Station. **Physically Challenged Students:** 95% of the campus is accessible. Facilities include wheelchair ramps, elevators, special parking, specially equipped restrooms, special class scheduling, lowered drinking fountains, lowered telephones, special housing, and transportation service when needed. **Special:** The university offers co-op programs, dual enrollment, internships, study abroad and domestic student exchange, accelerated degree programs, double and student-designed majors, independent study, distance learning, an external degree program, preprofessional and professional studies programs, teacher certification, ESL, nondegree study, and pass/fail options. Students may receive credit for life, military, and work experience. There are 20 national honor societies, a freshman honors program, and 17 departmental honors programs. **Visiting:** There are regularly scheduled orientations for prospective students, including daily campus tour programs Monday-Friday and the first Saturday of the month. There are guides for informal visits, visitors may sit in on classes, and stay overnight. To schedule a visit, contact Recruitment and Orientation Services at (800) 669-2678. **Campus Safety and Security:** Measures include 24-hour foot and vehicle patrol, emergency notification system, and security escort services. There are also shuttle buses, emergency telephones, lighted pathways/sidewalks, controlled access to dorms/residences, digital video cameras, a computerized entry system, a gated parking lot, parking lot with security towers, campus safety forums, and a personal safety program.

REQUIREMENTS: The SAT or ACT is required, with a minimum acceptable composite score of 20. Candidates for admission should be graduates of an accredited secondary school and have 15 academic credits or 20 Carnegie units. The GED is accepted. Academic preparation should include 4 units in English, 3 in math, 2 each in science (1 must be lab), social studies, and foreign language, 1 each in history, and visual and performing arts. An interview is required for University College applicants, a portfolio is required for art program applicants, and an audition is required for music applicants. AP and CLEP credits are accepted. Important factors in the admissions decision are advanced placement or honors courses, parents or siblings attended your school, personality/intangible qualities, and recommendations by school officials. To graduate, students must complete a minimum of 120 credit hours with a GPA of 2.0 and demonstrate proficiency in computer skills. Requirements include 9 hours of humanities and fine arts with at least 1 literature course, 8 hours of natural science, 6 of English composition, 6 of social and behavioral science, 6 of U.S. history, 3 each of math, and 3 of oral communication. **Procedure:** Freshmen are admitted in the fall, spring, and summer. Entrance exams should be taken in the spring of the junior year or October of the senior year. There are deferred admissions and rolling admissions plans. Applications should be filed by July 1 for fall entry; December 1 for spring entry; and May 1 for summer entry, along with a $25 fee. Notification is sent on a rolling basis. Applications are accepted online. **Transfer Students:** 1454 transfer students enrolled in 2015-2016. Applicants must have honorable dismissal from the last institution attended and have a cumulative GPA that meets the required minimum established by the Tennessee State Board of Regents. 30 of 120 credits required for the bachelor's degree must be completed at U of M. **International Students:** There are 133 international students enrolled. The school actively recruits these students. They must take the TOEFL with a minimum score of 500 on the paper-based TOEFL (PBT) or 61 on the Internet-based version (iBT). They must also take the SAT or ACT.

ADMISSIONS: 62% of the 2016-2017 applicants were accepted. The SAT scores for the 2016-2017 freshman class were: Critical Reading-- 38% below 500, 45% between 500 and 599, 12% between 600 and 699, and 6% between 700 and 800. Math-- 37% below 500, 44% between 500 and 599, 13% between 600 and 699, and 4% between 700 and 800. Writing-- 52% below 500, 31% between 500 and 599, 13% between 600 and 699, and 4% between 700 and 800. **Admissions Contact:** Dr. Justin Lawhead, Interim Associate & VP Dean of Students. Email: *admissions@memphis.edu* Web: *www.memphis.edu*

FINANCIAL AID: In 2016-2017, 72% of all full-time freshmen and 68% of continuing full-time students received some form of financial aid. 72% of all full-time freshmen and 68% of continuing full-time students received need-based aid. The average freshman award was $10,415. Need-based scholarships or need-based grants averaged $6,519; need-based self-help aid (loans and jobs) averaged $3,367; non-need-based athletic scholarships averaged $14,687; other non-need-based awards and non-need-based scholarships averaged $7,855; and $3,342 from other forms of aid. The FAFSA code is 003509. The priority date for freshman financial aid applications for fall entry is March 1. The filing deadline for fall entry is May 1.

VANDERBILT UNIVERSITY C-2
www.vanderbilt.edu

Nashville, TN 37203	**(615) 322-2561** **(800) 288-0432**
Fax: (615) 343-7765	**Email: admissions@vanderbilt.edu**
Full-time: 3369 men, 3448 women	**Faculty:** I, ++$
Part-time: 32 men, 22 women	**Ph.D.s:** 96%
Graduate: 2334 men, 3382 women	**Student/Faculty:** 8 to 1
Year: semesters, summer session	**Tuition:** $45,610
Room & Board: $14,962	**Freshman Class:** 32442 applied, 3487 accepted, 1601 enrolled
SAT or ACT: required	**CEEB CODE:** 1871
Application Deadline: January 1	**MOST COMPETITIVE**

Vanderbilt University, founded in 1873, has a combination of excellent academic rigor, a vibrant campus life, attracts exceptionally talented students from around the world, are constantly immersed in the multidisciplinary research and teaching that are at the heart of the Vanderbilt community, over 50 percent of undergraduates participate in research. There are 4 undergraduate schools and 8 graduate schools. In addition to regional accreditation, Vanderbilt has baccalaureate program accreditation with AACSB, ABET, CAHEA, and NCATE. The 330-acre campus is in an urban area in Nashville. Including any residence halls, there are 227 buildings.

STUDENT LIFE: 90% of undergraduates are from out of state, mostly the South. Students are from 51 states, 90 foreign countries, and Canada. 65% are from public schools. 9% are African American; 9% Hispanic; 7% Foreign; 51% White; 5% two or more races; 5% race unknown; 12% Asian American. **Female To Male Ratio:** 1.2:1. The average age of freshmen is 18; all undergraduates, 19. 3% do not continue beyond their first year; 93% remain to graduate. **Housing:** 6039 students can be accommodated in college housing, which includes single-sex and coed dorms, on-campus apartments, married student housing, language houses, special-interest houses, fraternity houses, and sorority houses. On-campus housing is guaranteed for the freshman year only, is available on a first-come, first-served basis, and on a lottery system for upperclassmen. Priority is given to out-of-town students. 92% of students live on campus. Upperclassmen may keep cars.

FACULTY/CLASSROOMS: 60% of faculty are male; 39% are female. No introductory courses are taught by graduate students. The average class size in an introductory lecture is 20; in a laboratory is 31; and in a regular course is 19.

PROGRAMS OF STUDY: Vanderbilt confers B.A., B.S., B.E., and B.Mu. degrees. Master's and doctoral degrees are also awarded. Bachelor's degrees are awarded in AGRICULTURE (environmental studies), BIOLOGICAL SCIENCE (biochemistry, biology/biological science, ecology, molecular biology, and neurosciences), COMMUNICATIONS AND THE ARTS (art history, art, classical languages, classics, communications, composition, English, French, German, media arts, music performance, music theory and composition, Russian, Spanish, and theatre arts), COMPUTER AND PHYSICAL SCIENCE (chemistry, computer science, earth science, mathematics, and physics), EDUCATION (Asian studies, early childhood education, education, elementary education, latino and latina studies, music education, secondary education, and special education), ENGINEERING AND ENVIRONMENTAL DESIGN (bioengineering, biomedical engineering, chemical engineering, civil engineering, computer engineering, electrical/electronics engineering, engineering and applied science, and mechanical engineering), HEALTH PROFESSIONS (medicine and health & society), SOCIAL SCIENCE (African American studies, American studies, anthropology, child psychology/development, cognitive science, East Asian studies, economics, European studies, history, human development, interdisciplinary studies, Italian studies, Judaic studies, Latin American studies, philosophy, political science/government, psychology, public affairs, religious studies, sociology, and women & gender studies). Social science, engineering, and education have the largest enrollments.

ACTIVITIES: 35% of men belong to 18 national fraternities; 53% of women belong to 15 national sororities. There are 771 groups on campus, including art, band, cheerleading, chess, choir, chorale, chorus, computers, dance, debate, drama, drill team, environmental, ethnic, film, honors, international, jazz band, LGBT, literary magazine, marching band, musical theater, newspaper, opera, orchestra, pep band, photography, political, professional, radio and TV, religious, social, social service, student government, symphony, and yearbook. Popular campus events include Rites of Spring, International Lens Film Series, Diwali Festival, and IMPACT Speakers Series. **Sports:** There are 6 intercollegiate sports for men and 9 for women, and 32 intramural sports for men and 31 for women. Facilities include a gym, pool, football and intramural fields, tennis, basketball and racquetball courts, a indoor track, and a climbing wall. **Graduates:** From July 1, 2015 to June 30, 2016, 1723 bachelor's degrees were awarded. The most popular majors were social sciences (28%), engineering (15%), and interdisciplinary studies (5%). 205 companies recruited on campus in 2015-2016. In an average class, 87% graduate in 4 years or less, 91% graduate in 5 years or less, and 92% graduate in 6 years or less.

SERVICES: Counseling and information services are available, as is tutoring in most subjects, and a reader service for the blind. **Library/Resources:** The 9 libraries contain 4.6 million volumes, 3.1 million microform items, and 64,912 audio/video tapes/CDs/DVDs, and subscribe to 95,722 periodicals including electronic. Computerized library services include interlibrary loans, database searching, Internet access, and Wi-Fi capability. Special learning facilities include an art gallery, radio station, TV station, 2 observatories, and the TV news archive. **Physically Challenged Students:** 90% of the campus is accessible. Facilities include wheelchair ramps, elevators, special parking, specially equipped restrooms, special class scheduling, lowered drinking fountains, and lowered telephones. **Special:** Vanderbilt offers honors programs, teacher licensure, accelerated degree programs, and the opportunity to double major and/or add one or more minors. Vanderbilt offers more than 140 study abroad programs in over 40 countries where students can study for a semester, an academic year, a summer, or the month of May. In each of the four undergraduate schools, students can apply to programs that allow them to earn both a bachelor's and a master's degree in five years. The School of Engineering offers a Three-Two program with certain liberal arts colleges as well as a Dual Degree Program with Fisk University. There are 6 national honor societies, Phi Beta Kappa, a freshman honors program, and 21 departmental honors programs. **Visiting:** There are regularly scheduled orientations for prospective students, including group information sessions and campus tours available Monday through Saturday during the academic year and Monday through Friday during the summer. Schedules vary, so visitors must call in advance. There are guides for informal visits, visitors may sit in on classes, and stay overnight. To schedule a visit, contact the Office of Undergraduate Admissions. **Campus Safety and Security:** Measures include 24-hour foot and vehicle patrol, emergency notification system, self-defense education, and security escort services. There are also shuttle buses, emergency telephones, lighted pathways/sidewalks, a bicycle patrol, and student dorm monitors.

REQUIREMENTS: The SAT or ACT is required. Requirements for first-year applicants: all required parts of either the Common Application or the Universal College Application, $50 nonrefundable application fee, or fee waiver for qualified students, an official high school transcript, counselor letter of recommendation, and an official SAT or ACT scores (SAT code: 1871 / ACT code: 4036), and if applicable, TOEFL, IELTS, or Pearson. Applicants to the Blair School of Music must complete an additional application, which includes a prescreening audition video. Please visit the Blair website for details. AP credits are accepted. Important factors in the admissions decision are advanced placement or honors courses, extracurricular activities record, and evidence of special talent. Graduation requirements vary with the student's program of study but include a minimum of 120 hours (at least 60 of which must have been earned at Vanderbilt) and a minimum cumulative grade point average of 2.0. A degree candidate must also have a 2.0 cumulative grade point average in his or her major. **Procedure:** Freshmen are admitted fall. Entrance exams should be taken Spring of the junior year or the fall of the senior year. There are early decision and deferred admissions plans. Early decision applications should be filed by November 1; regular applications, by January 1 for fall entry, along with a $50 fee. Notification of early decision is sent December 15; regular decision, April 1. 865 early decision candidates were accepted for the 2016-2017 class. Applications are accepted on-line. **Transfer Students:** 218 transfer students enrolled in 2015-2016. To be a transfer student, a minimum of 12 hours of college credit must have been earned. Requirements for transfer applicants: all required parts of either the Common Application Transfer Application or the Universal College Application Transfer Application, $50 nonrefundable application fee, or fee waiver for qualified students, an official high school transcript, official college transcript(s) (from each institution attended), transfer college report (from the institution you are transferring from), two academic teacher letters of recommendation (we prefer that at least one letter is from a college professor/instructor), and an official SAT or ACT scores (SAT code: 1871 / ACT code: 4036), and if applicable, TOEFL, IELTS, or Pearson. 60 of 120 credits required for the bachelor's degree must be completed at Vanderbilt. **International Students:** There are 491 international students enrolled. The school actively recruits these students. They must take the TOEFL, as well as the SAT or ACT.

ADMISSIONS: 11% of the 2016-2017 applicants were accepted. The SAT scores for the 2016-2017 freshman class were: Critical Reading-- 1% below 500, 3% between 500 and 599, 16% between 600 and 699, and 80% between 700 and 800. Math-- 1% below 500, 3% between 500 and 599, 14% between 600 and 699, and 82% between 700 and 800. Writing-- 2% below 500, 3% between 500 and 599, 26% between 600 and 699, and 69% between 700 and 800. The ACT scores were 1% between 12 and 17, 2% between 18 and 23, 7% between 24 and 29, and 91% above 30. 95% of the current freshmen were in the top fifth of their class; 98% were in the top two fifths. There were 231 National Merit finalists. 95 freshmen graduated first in their class. **Admissions Contact:** Linda Forceno, Assoc. Institutional Research Analyst. Email: *admissions@vanderbilt.edu* Web: *www.vanderbilt.edu*

FINANCIAL AID: In 2016-2017, 69% of all full-time freshmen and 66% of continuing full-time students received some form of financial aid. 53% of all full-time freshmen and 49% of continuing full-time students received need-based aid. The average freshman award was $47,712. Need-based scholarships or need-based grants averaged $42,430; need-based self-help aid (loans and jobs) averaged $2,508; non-need-based athletic scholarships averaged $52,777; and other non-need-based awards and non-need-based scholarships averaged $21,873. The average financial indebtedness of the 2016 graduate was $24,122. The CSS/Profile and tax return information are required. The FAFSA code is 003535. The priority date for freshman financial aid applications for fall entry is February 2.

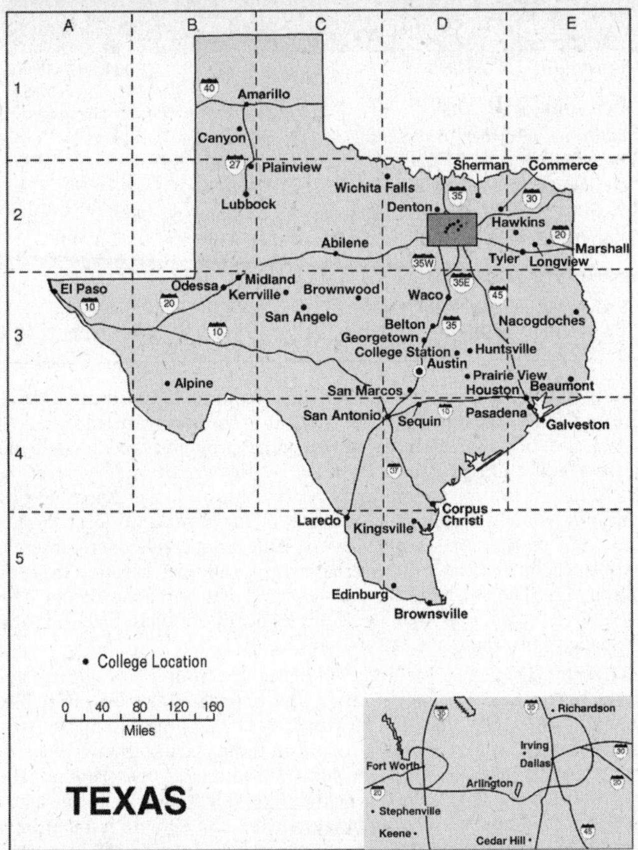

ABILENE CHRISTIAN UNIVERSITY — C-2

www.acu.edu

Abilene, TX 79699 — (325) 674-2650, (800) 460-6228

Fax: (325) 674-2130 — **Email:** info@admissions.acu.edu

Full-time: 1475 men, 2087 women
Part-time: 83 men, 113 women
Graduate: 434 men, 718 women
Year: semesters, summer session
Room & Board: $9730
Faculty: 238; IIA, -$
Ph.D.s: 80%
Student/Faculty: 14 to 1
Tuition: $32,070
Freshman Class: 10252 applied, 5217 accepted, 1047 enrolled
SAT CR/M/W: 526/525/502 **ACT:** 24
CEEB CODE: 6001
Application Deadline: February 15
COMPETITIVE+

Abilene Christian University, is a selective four-year private Christian university, that provides exceptional academics in a Christ-centered community. It includes the colleges of Arts and Sciences, Biblical Studies, Business Administration, Education and Human Services, Graduate and Professional Studies, and Honors; the Graduate School of Theology, and the schools of Information Technology and Computing, Nursing, and Social Work. ACU is affiliated with the Churches of Christ and is one of the largest private universities in the Southwest. There are 8 undergraduate schools and 7 graduate schools. In addition to regional accreditation, ACU has baccalaureate program accreditation with AACSB, ABET, ACEJMC, CSWE, FIDER, NASM, TEAC, ACEND, and CCNE. The 250-acre campus is in a small town 180 miles west of the Dallas-Fort Worth metroplex. Including any residence halls, there are 52 buildings.

STUDENT LIFE: 84% of undergraduates are from Texas. Others are from 43 states, 37 foreign countries, and Canada. 67% are from public schools. 9% are African American; 64% White; 5% two or more races; 4% Foreign; 16% Hispanic; 1% Asian American; 1% race unknown. 61% are Protestant. **Female To Male Ratio:** 1.5:1. The average age of freshmen is 18; all undergraduates, 20. 23% do not continue beyond their first year; 60% remain to graduate. **Housing:** 2013 students can be accommodated in college housing, which includes single-sex dorms, on-campus apartments, and married student housing. On-campus housing is available on a first-come, first-served basis, and on a lottery system for upperclassmen. 51% of students commute. All students may keep cars. Alcohol is not permitted.

FACULTY/CLASSROOMS: 62% of faculty are male; 38% are female. 90% teach undergraduates, 14% do research, and 14% do both. Graduate students teach 1% of introductory courses. The average class size in an introductory lecture is 34; in a laboratory is 16; and in a regular course is 23.

PROGRAMS OF STUDY: ACU confers B.A., B.S., B.B.A., B.F.A., B.M., B.S.E. and B.S.N. degrees. Associate, master's, and doctoral degrees are also awarded. Bachelor's degrees are awarded in AGRICULTURE (agricultural business management and animal science), BIOLOGICAL SCIENCE (biochemistry, biology/biological science, biology/ gen science secondary education, and nutrition), BUSINESS (accounting, finance, information & communication technology, management science, and marketing/retailing/merchandising), COMMUNICATIONS AND THE ARTS (advertising, art, communications, dramatic arts, English, fine arts, graphic design, journalism, multimedia, music, piano performance, public relations, Spanish, and vocal performance), COMPUTER AND PHYSICAL SCIENCE (chemistry, computer game design/development, computer science, information sciences and systems, mathematics, mathematics/computational, and physics), EDUCATION (computer education, English secondary education, English education, foreign languages education, global studies, journalism education, mathematics education, middle school education, music education, secondary education, and special education), ENGINEERING AND ENVIRONMENTAL DESIGN (engineering, environmental science, and interior design), HEALTH PROFESSIONS (kinesiology and nursing), SOCIAL SCIENCE (biblical studies, child care/child and family studies, communication sciences & disorders, criminal justice, history, liberal arts/general studies, ministries, political science/government, psychology, social work, and sociology). Accounting, biology, and engineering are the strongest academically. Management, biology, and kinesiology have the largest enrollments.

ACTIVITIES: 28% of men belong to 7 local fraternities; 34% of women belong to 6 local sororities. There are 100 groups on campus, including art, band, cheerleading, chess, choir, chorale, chorus, computers, dance, debate, drama, environmental, ethnic, film, forensics, honors, international, jazz band, LGBT, literary magazine, marching band, musical theater, newspaper, opera, orchestra, photography, political, professional, radio and TV, religious, social, social service, student government, and symphony. Popular campus events include Freshman Follies, Homecoming Carnival & Parade, Sing Song Festival, and Summit Bible Lectures. **Sports:** There are 7 intercollegiate sports for men and 7 for women, and 7 intramural sports for men and 7 for women. Facilities include the student recreation and wellness center with a pool fitness center, indoor track, group exercise studios, bouldering wall, gyms, and racquetball courts; a coliseum, track/soccer stadium, baseball and softball stadiums, tennis center, and a disc golf course. **Graduates:** From July 1, 2015 to June 30, 2016, 757 bachelor's degrees were awarded. The most popular majors were nursing (6%), accounting (6%), and psychology (6%). 272 companies recruited on campus in 2015-2016. In an average class, 3% graduate in 3 years or less, 47% graduate in 4 years or less, 59% graduate in 5 years or less, and 60% graduate in 6 years or less. Of the 2015 graduating class, 31% were enrolled in graduate school within 6 months of graduation, and 49% were employed.

SERVICES: There is a reader service for the blind, and remedial math and writing. A sign language interpreter is available. **Library/Resources:** The library contains 554,415 volumes, 1.2 million microform items, 65,805 audio/video tapes/CDs/DVDs, and subscribes to 24,753 periodicals including electronic. Computerized library services include interlibrary loans, database searching, Internet access, and Wi-Fi capability. Special learning facilities include an art gallery, planetarium, radio station, TV station, a learning commons, writing center, speaking center, AT&T learning studio, maker lab, center for Christian service and leadership, a converged media newsroom, center for speech and language disorders, a farm, and center for restoration studies. **Physically Challenged Students:** 95% of the campus is accessible. Facilities include wheelchair ramps, elevators, special parking, specially equipped restrooms, special class scheduling, and lowered drinking fountains. **Special:** ACU offers a Health Professions Cooperative Degree. ACU offers cross-registration with Hardin-Simmons and McMurry Universities and study abroad in 3 countries; England, Uruguay, and Germany. Double majors are available. Internships are possible in most majors, as are B.A.-B.S. degrees in biology, bio-chemistry, communication, convergence journalism and mathematics. Student designed majors (interdisciplinary studies) are available. There are 17 national honor societies and a freshman honors program. **Visiting:** There are regularly scheduled orientations for prospective students, consisting of academic department, attend chapel, financial aid and admission information, and special interest sessions. There are guides for informal visits and visitors may sit in on classes. To schedule a visit, contact the Director of Campus Visits. **Campus Safety and Security:** Measures include 24-hour foot and vehicle patrol, emergency notification system, self-defense education, and security escort services. There are shuttle buses, emergency telephones, lighted pathways/sidewalks, controlled access to dorms/residences, and fire safety discussions.

REQUIREMENTS: Satisfactory SAT or ACT score, with at least one writing score. Applicants must be graduates of an accredited secondary school or have the GED and have completed 12 academic credits, including 4 in English, 3 each in math and science, and 2 years of the same foreign language. Art majors need to submit a portfolio, and music and theater majors must audition. ACU requires applicants to be in the upper 50% of their class. AP and CLEP credits are accepted. Important factors in the admissions decision are leadership record, recommendations by alumni, and advanced placement or honors courses. To graduate, students must complete courses in Bible (15 hours), English, communication, science, mathematics, social science, kinesiology (2 hours), including historical literacy and cultural awareness. 33 semester hours of advanced work must be taken and a minimum 2.0 GPA maintained. A minimum of 128 credit hours is needed (more in some programs) and 30 to 64 hours of that is in the major, 18 of which must be upper division. **Procedure:** Freshmen are admitted to all sessions. Entrance exams should be taken by February of the senior year. There is an early admissions plan. Applications should be filed by February 15 for fall entry, along with a $50 fee. Notification of early decision is sent November 1; regular decision. Application fees are waived if application is completed online. **Transfer Students:** 113 transfer students enrolled in 2015-2016. Transfer students are evaluated for admission on the basis of their college GPA. Entrance exam scores and high school transcripts will be reviewed for students with GPA's below 2.5. 40 of 128 credits required for the bachelor's degree must be completed at ACU. **International Students:** There are 147 international students enrolled. The school actively recruits these students. They must take the TOEFL with a minimum score of 400 on the paper-based TOEFL (PBT) or 80 on the Internet-based version (iBT). They must also take the SAT or ACT.

ADMISSIONS: 51% of the 2016-2017 applicants were accepted. The SAT scores for the 2016-2017 freshman class were: Critical Reading-- 36% below 500, 42% between 500 and 599, 18% between 600 and 699, and 4% between 700 and 800. Math-- 38% below 500, 40% between 500 and 599, 20% between 600 and 699, and 2% between 700 and 800. Writing-- 50% below 500, 35% between 500 and 599, 14% between 600 and 699, and 1% between 700 and 800. The ACT scores were 5% between 12 and 17, 41% between 18 and 23, 42% between 24 and 29, and 12% above 30. 46% of the current freshmen were in the top fifth of their class; 75% were in the top two fifths. There were 3 National Merit finalists. 10 freshmen graduated first in their class. **Admissions Contact:** Tamara Long, Dean of Admissions. Email: *info@admissions.acu.edu* Web: *www.acu.edu*

FINANCIAL AID: In 2016-2017, 100% of all full-time freshmen and 97% of continuing full-time students received some form of financial aid. 76% of all full-time freshmen and 65% of continuing full-time students received need-based aid. The average freshman award was $13,933. Need-based scholarships or need-based grants averaged $21,787; need-based self-help aid (loans and jobs) averaged $3,487; non-need-based athletic scholarships averaged $22,528; and other non-need-based awards and non-need-based scholarships averaged $12,817. 28% of undergraduate students work part-time. Average annual earnings from campus work are $4800. The FAFSA code is 003537. The deadline for filing freshman financial aid applications for fall entry is March 1.

ANGELO STATE UNIVERSITY *(The complete profile is made available exclusively on our website, www.barronspac.com)*

AUSTIN COLLEGE D-2
www.austincollege.edu

Sherman, TX 75090 (903) 813-3000
(800) 442-5363
Fax: (903) 813-3198 **Email:** admission@austincollege.edu
Full-time: 616 men, 655 women
Part-time: 2 men, 5 women
Graduate: 10 men, 13 women
Year: 4-1-4, summer session
Room & Board: $11,035
SAT CR/M: 601/604 **ACT:** 26
Application Deadline: March 1
Faculty: 123; IIB, av$
Ph.D.s: 95%
Student/Faculty: 12 to 1
Tuition: $34,840
Freshman Class: 3044 applied, 1657 accepted, 357 enrolled
CEEB CODE: 6016
VERY COMPETITIVE

Austin College is a private, residential, co-educational institution dedicated to educating undergraduate students in the liberal arts and sciences while also offering select pre-professional programs and a graduate teacher education program. Founded by the Presbyterian Church in 1849, Austin College continues its relationship with the church and its commitment to a heritage that values personal growth, justice, community, and service. An Austin College education emphasizes academic excellence, intellectual and personal integrity, and participation in community life. There is 1 undergraduate school and 1 graduate school. The 70-acre campus is in a rural area 60 miles north of Dallas. Including any residence halls, there are 34 buildings.

STUDENT LIFE: 91% of undergraduates are from Texas. Others are from 32 states, 17 foreign countries, and Canada. 85% are from public schools. 56% are White; 20% Hispanic; 14% Asian American; 7% African American; 3% Foreign; 1% American Indian/Alaska Native; 1% two or more races; 1% race unknown. 44% are Protestant; 18% claim no religious affiliation; 17% Catholic. **Female To Male Ratio:** 1.1:1. The average age of freshmen is 18; all undergraduates, 20. 13% do not continue beyond their first year; 68% remain to graduate. **Housing:** 1072 students can be accommodated in college housing, which includes single-sex, coed dorms and on-campus apartments, language houses, and a suite-style residence hall. On-campus housing is available on a lottery system for upperclassmen. 81% of students live on campus; of those, 35% remain on campus on weekends. All students may keep cars.

FACULTY/CLASSROOMS: 63% of faculty are male; 37% are female. All teach undergraduates and do research. No introductory courses are taught by graduate students. The average class size in an introductory lecture is 19; in a laboratory is 16; and in a regular course is 20.

PROGRAMS OF STUDY: AC confers B.A. degrees. Master's degrees are also awarded. Bachelor's degrees are awarded in AGRICULTURE (natural resources), BIOLOGICAL SCIENCE (biochemistry and biology/biological science), BUSINESS (business administration and management and international economics), COMMUNICATIONS AND THE ARTS (art history, art, classical languages, classics, communications, East Asian languages and literature, English, French, German, Latin, music, and Spanish), COMPUTER AND PHYSICAL SCIENCE (chemistry, computer science, mathematics, and physics), SOCIAL SCIENCE (American studies, economics, history, interdisciplinary studies, international studies, Latin American studies, philosophy, political science/government, psychology, religion, sociology, and women & gender studies). Biology, psychology, and political science are the strongest academically. Business administration has the largest enrollment.

ACTIVITIES: 20% of men belong to 10 local fraternities; 11% of women belong to 5 local sororities. There are 55 groups on campus, including art, cheerleading, choir, chorale, chorus, communications, dance, drama, ethnic, film, honors, international, jazz band, LGBT, literary magazine, Model UN and International Student organizations, musical theater, newspaper, orchestra, pep band, photography, political, professional, religious, social, social service, student government, symphony, and yearbook. Popular campus events include Christmas Pops, Kangapalooza (spring concert), Great Day of Service, Film Series and Diwali Dinner. **Sports:** There are 7 intercollegiate sports for men and 7 for women, and 8 intramural sports for men and 8 for women. Facilities include an athletic/recreation complex that includes 2 gyms, a natatorium, and a fitness pavilion, tennis stadium, and soccer and baseball fields. **Graduates:** From July 1, 2015 to June 30, 2016, 246 bachelor's degrees were awarded. The most popular majors were business administration (17%), psychology (14%), and biology (10%). 43 companies recruited on campus in 2015-2016. In an average class, 67% graduate in 4 years or less, 73% graduate in 5 years or less, and 77% graduate in 6 years or less. Of the 2015 graduating class, 44% were enrolled in graduate school within 6 months of graduation, and 47% were employed.

SERVICES: Counseling and information services are available, as is tutoring in some subjects, such as introductory-level courses. Individual and group assistance to strengthen reading, writing, and study skills are available. **Library/Resources:** The library contains 227,019 volumes, 120,808 microform items, 6,393 audio/video tapes/CDs/DVDs, and subscribes to 5,727 periodicals including electronic. Computerized library services include interlibrary loans, database searching, Internet access, and Wi-Fi capability. **Physically Challenged Students:** All of the campus is accessible. Facilities include wheelchair ramps, elevators, special parking, specially equipped restrooms, special class scheduling, and lowered drinking fountains. **Special:** AC offers study abroad in 58 countries, internships during January and summer terms, and fall, spring, and summer internships in Washington, D.C. Work-study, accelerated degree programs in all majors, and dual and student-designed majors are available. There is a 3-2 engineering degree program in conjunction with the University of Texas at Dallas and Washington University in St. Louis, as well as cooperative agreements with Columbia University and Texas A&M University. There are 14 national honor societies and a chapter of Phi Beta Kappa. **Visiting:** There are regularly scheduled orientations for prospective students, 1-day and 2-day preview programs held for high school juniors, seniors and parents. Individual appointments may be made as well. There are guides for informal visits, visitors may sit in on classes, and stay overnight. To schedule a visit, contact the Admissions Office. **Campus Safety and Security:** Measures include 24-hour foot and vehicle patrol, emergency notification system, self-defense education, security escort services, emergency telephones, and lighted pathways/sidewalks.

REQUIREMENTS: The SAT or ACT is required. Applicants must be graduates of an accredited secondary school, home school, or have a GED. The minimum recommended academic requirements are 4 credits in English, 3 each in math and science, 2 each in social studies and foreign language, and 1 in art/music/theater. An essay and recommendation are required. AP and CLEP credits are accepted. Important factors in the admissions decision are advanced placement or honors courses, leadership record, and extracurricular activities record. Core requirements for graduation include completion of the Foundation Dimension, the Breadth Dimension, and 1 course in Lifetime Sports. To graduate, students must have a minimum 2.0 GPA and a total of 34 course credits (136 semester hours). Students must demonstrate an ability in a modern or classical language other than their own, quantitative competency with an approved course or test, and the required skills in written communication with approved course work. A minor or a 2nd major is required. **Procedure:** Freshmen are admitted fall and summer. Entrance exams should be taken by the junior year or the fall of the senior year. There are deferred admissions and rolling admissions plans. Applications should be filed by March 1 for fall entry. Notifications are sent April 1. 12 applicants were on the 2016 waiting list; 6 were admitted. Applications are accepted online. **Transfer Students:** 46 transfer students enrolled in 2015-2016. Applicants must have a minimum 3.0 GPA, submit official college transcripts and 2 recommendations, and be in good standing at most recently attended schools. Students with fewer than 30 credit hours must submit SAT or ACT scores and their high school transcript or GED. 17 of 34 credits required for the bachelor's degree must be completed at AC. **International Students:** There are 39 international students enrolled. The school actively recruits these students. They must take the TOEFL with a minimum score of 550 on the paper-based TOEFL (PBT) or 80 on the Internet-based version (iBT). They must also take the SAT or ACT.

ADMISSIONS: 54% of the 2016-2017 applicants were accepted. The SAT scores for the 2016-2017 freshman class were: Critical Reading-- 14% below 500, 30% between 500 and 599, 42% between 600 and 699, and 14% between 700 and 800. Math-- 8% below 500, 34% between 500 and 599, 41% between 600 and 699, and 17% between 700 and 800. Writing-- 15% below 500, 40% between 500 and 599, 34% between 600 and 699, and 11% between 700 and 800. The ACT scores were 13% below 12, 20% between 12 and 17, 55% between 18 and 23, 12% between 24 and 29, and 20% above 30. 72% of the current freshmen were in the top fifth of their class; 96% were in the top two fifths. **Admissions Contact:** Nan Davis, VP for Institutional Enrollment. Email: *admission@austincollege.edu* Web: *www.austincollege.edu*

FINANCIAL AID: In 2016-2017, 93% of all full-time freshmen and 96% of continuing full-time students received some form of financial aid. 68% of all full-time freshmen and 61% of continuing full-time students received need-based aid. 30% of undergraduate students work part-time. Average annual earnings from campus work are $1700. The average financial indebtedness of the 2016 graduate was $34,744. AC is a member of CSS. The FAFSA code is 003543. The priority date for freshman financial aid applications for fall entry is March 1. The filing deadline for fall entry is April 1.

BAYLOR UNIVERSITY — D-3
www.baylor.edu

Waco, TX 76798 (254) 710-3435
(800) BAYLOR-U
Email: admissions@baylor.edu

Full-time: 8185 men, 5924 women	**Faculty:** I, -$
Part-time: 128 men, 111 women	**Ph.D.s:** 83%
Graduate: 1205 men, 1406 women	**Student/Faculty:** 15 to 1
Year: semesters, summer session	**Tuition:** $42,006
Room & Board: $11,754	**Freshman Class:** n/av
SAT or ACT: required	**CEEB CODE:** 6032
Application Deadline: February 1	**HIGHLY COMPETITIVE**

Baylor University in Waco, Texas, is a private Christian university and a nationally ranked research institution. Chartered in 1845 by the Republic of Texas, Baylor is the oldest, continually operating university in the state. Its offerings include undergraduate programs in liberal arts and sciences, business, computer science, education, engineering, health and human services, music, nursing, social work, and an honors college. There are 9 undergraduate schools and 10 graduate schools. In addition to regional accreditation, Baylor has baccalaureate program accreditation with AACSB, ABET, ACEJMC, ADA, APTA, CSWE, FIDER, NASM, NCATE, NAST, and ACS. The 1000-acre campus is in a small town 100 miles south of Dallas/Fort Worth. Including any residence halls, there are 127 buildings.

STUDENT LIFE: 71% of undergraduates are from Texas. Others are from 50 states, 71 foreign countries, and Canada. 7% are African American; 64% White; 6% Asian American; 5% two or more races; 3% Foreign; 15% Hispanic. 17% are Catholic. **Male To Female Ratio:** 1.3:1. The average age of freshmen is 19; all undergraduates, 20. 11% do not continue beyond their first year; 73% remain to graduate. **Housing:** 5395 students can be accommodated in college housing, which includes single-sex and coed dorms, on-campus apartments, off-campus apartments, married student housing, honors houses, language houses, special-interest houses, and living-learning centers. On-campus housing is guaranteed for the freshman year only, is available on a first-come, and first-served basis. 65% of students commute. All students may keep cars. Alcohol is not permitted.

FACULTY/CLASSROOMS: 58% of faculty are male; 42% are female. No introductory courses are taught by graduate students. The average class size in a regular course is 27.

PROGRAMS OF STUDY: Baylor confers B.A., B.B.A., B.F.A., B.M., B.M.E., B.S., B.S.Av.Sc., B.S.C., B.S.C.S., B.S.E., B.S.E.C.E., B.S.Ed., B.S.F.C.S., B.S.I., B.S.M.E., B.S.N., B.S.P.H. and B.S.W. degrees. Master's and doctoral degrees are also awarded. Bachelor's degrees are awarded in BIOLOGICAL SCIENCE (biochemistry, bioinformatics, biology/biological science, life science, neurosciences, and nutrition), BUSINESS (accounting, apparel and accessories marketing, apparel and textiles, banking and finance, business administration and management, business economics, business statistics, business systems analysis, entrepreneurial studies, fashion merchandising, human resources, insurance, international business management, management information systems, marketing/retailing/merchandising, personnel management, real estate, and sports marketing), COMMUNICATIONS AND THE ARTS (acting, apparel design, applied music, art history, art, art history and appreciation, broadcasting, choral music, classics, communications, creative writing, dramatic arts, English, French, German, Greek (classical), journalism, languages, Latin, literature, music, music history and appreciation, music performance, music theory and composition, performing arts, Russian, Spanish, speech/debate/rhetoric, studio art, telecommunications, theater design, and theatre studies), COMPUTER AND PHYSICAL SCIENCE (applied mathematics, chemistry, computer science, earth science, geology, geophysics and seismology, information sciences and systems, mathematics, and physics), EDUCATION (art education, athletic training, business education, computer education, drama education, elementary education, English education, foreign languages education, health education, home economics education, journalism education, mathematics education, museum studies, music education, physical education, reading education, recreation education, science education, secondary education, social science education, social studies education, and special education), ENGINEERING AND ENVIRONMENTAL DESIGN (airline piloting and navigation, computer engineering, electrical/electronics engineering, engineering, environmental science, interior design, and mechanical engineering), HEALTH PROFESSIONS (health science, medical laboratory technology, nursing, optometry, predentistry, premedicine, speech pathology/audiology, and speech therapy), SOCIAL SCIENCE (American studies, anthropology, area studies, Asian/Oriental studies, biblical languages, child care/child and family studies, dietetics, economics, family/consumer studies, fashion design and technology, forensic studies, history, interdisciplinary studies, international public service, Latin American studies, Middle Eastern studies, philosophy, physical fitness/movement, political science/government, psychology, public administration, religion, religious education, religious music, Russian and Slavic studies, social work, sociology, and urban studies). Pre-business (accounting, marketing, finance), biology/pre-biology, and biochemistry have the largest enrollments.

ACTIVITIES: 16% of men belong to 2 local and 19 national fraternities; 31% of women belong to 1 local and 17 national sororities. There are 316 groups on campus, including academic (language, discipline specific), art, band, cheerleading, chess, choir, chorale, chorus, computers, dance, debate, drama, environmental, ethnic, film, forensics, honors, international, jazz band, literary magazine, marching band, musical theater, newspaper, opera, orchestra, pep band, photography, political, professional, radio and TV, religious, social, social service, Sport Clubs (non-NCAA athletics), student government, symphony, and yearbook. Popular campus events include Dia del Oso (Day of the Bear), Campus Sing and Pigskin Review. **Sports:** There are 20 intercollegiate sports for men and 19 for women, and 23 intramural sports for men and 23 for women. Facilities include a football stadium, athletic facilities, an indoor football practice facility, softball stadium, baseball stadium, soccer complex, outdoor and indoor tennis facilities, a basketball practice facility and a center for basketball and volleyball. Close by students have access to gyms, intramural fields, tennis courts, a marina, and a student life center that offers a 53-feet-tall climbing rock plus a separate bouldering area, a fitness center, aerobics room, racquetball/squash courts, basketball courts, an indoor pool, an indoor walking/jogging track, and an outdoor sand volleyball court. **Graduates:** From July 1, 2015 to June 30, 2016, 3062 bachelor's degrees were awarded. The most popular majors were biology (8%), nursing (7%), and psychology (5%). In an average class, 2% graduate in 3 years or less, 58% graduate in 4 years or less, 72% graduate in 5 years or less, and 73% graduate in 6 years or less.

SERVICES: Counseling and information services are available, as is tutoring in some subjects. There is a reader service for the blind. **Library/Resources:** The 7 libraries contain 2.3 million volumes, 2.3 million microform items, 199,530 audio/video tapes/CDs/DVDs, and subscribe to 90,381 periodicals including electronic. Computerized library services include interlibrary loans, database searching, Internet access, and Wi-Fi capability. Special learning facilities include an art gallery, natural history museum, radio station, TV station, a speech/hearing clinic. **Physically Challenged Students:** 95% of the campus is accessible. Facilities include wheelchair ramps, elevators, special parking, specially equipped restrooms, and lowered drinking fountains. **Special:** Baylor offers internships in each school, study abroad and student exchange in more than 30 countries, and pass/fail options. There are also honors and university scholars programs and faculty exchange with 4 schools in China and 1 each in Japan, Thailand, and Russia. There are 36 national honor societies, a chapter of Phi Beta Kappa, and a freshman honors program. **Visiting:** There are regularly scheduled orientations for prospective students, including day-and-a-half sessions in June and a Welcome Week in August. There are guides for informal visits, visitors may sit in on classes, and stay overnight. To schedule a visit, contact Campus Visitation Program. **Campus Safety and Security:** Measures include 24-hour foot and vehicle patrol, emergency notification system, and security escort services. There are shuttle buses, emergency telephones, lighted pathways/sidewalks, and controlled access to dorms/residences.

REQUIREMENTS: The SAT or ACT is required. Applicants must be graduates of an accredited secondary school. An interview is recommended. Baylor requires applicants to be in the upper 50% of their class. AP and CLEP credits are accepted. All degree programs require a minimum of 124 hours and a 2.0 GPA to graduate. Basic requirements for the B.A. degree include 18 semester hours of social science, 12 each of English and science, 6 to 9 of fine arts, 6 of religion, 4 of phys ed, 3 to 16 of foreign language, 3 of math, and 2 semesters of chapel forum. Requirements for other degrees vary. **Procedure:** Freshmen are admitted in the fall, spring, and summer. Entrance exams should be taken in spring of the junior year or fall of the senior year. There are early admissions and deferred admissions plans. Early decision applications should be filed by November 1; regular applications, by February 1 for fall entry. Notification of early decision is sent January 15; regular decision, April 10. 912 applicants were on the 2016 waiting list; 351 were admitted. Applications are accepted on-line. Application fees are waived if application is completed online. **Transfer Students:** 430 transfer students enrolled in 2015-2016. Transfer students should begin studies no later than the end of the sophomore year because of the 60-semester-hour residence requirement for a bachelor's degree. Students with fewer than 30 credit hours earned must meet the entrance requirements for freshmen. 60 of 124 credits required for the bachelor's degree must be completed at Baylor. **International Students:** There are 665 international students enrolled. The school actively recruits these students. They must take the TOEFL with a minimum score of 540 on the paper-based TOEFL (PBT) or 76 on the Internet-based version (iBT).

ADMISSIONS: 40% of the 2016-2017 applicants were accepted. The SAT scores for the 2016-2017 freshman class were: Critical Reading-- 7% below 500, 42% between 500 and 599, 39% between 600 and 699, and 12% between 700 and 800. Math-- 3% below 500, 37% between 500 and 599, 45% between 600 and 699, and 15% between 700 and 800. Writing-- 12% below 500, 46% between 500 and 599, 33% between 600 and 699, and 8% between 700 and 800. The ACT scores were 9% between 18 and 23, 57% between 24 and 29, and 34% above 30. There were 75 National Merit finalists. **Admissions Contact:** Jessica King Gereghty, Assistant VP of Undergraduate Admissions. Email: *admissions@baylor.edu* Web: *www.baylor.edu*

FINANCIAL AID: The FAFSA code is 003545. The priority date for freshman financial aid applications for fall entry is February 15. The filing deadline for fall entry is May 1.

CONCORDIA UNIVERSITY TEXAS D-3

www.concordia.edu

Austin, TX 78705	**(512) 486-2000** **(800) 865-4282**
Fax: (512) 486-1350	**Email: admissions@concordia.edu**
Full-time: 350 men, 410 women	**Faculty:** n/av
Part-time: 85 men, 185 women	**Ph.D.s:** 74%
Graduate: 20 men, 70 women	**Student/Faculty:** 18 to 1
Year: semesters, summer session	**Tuition:** $29,460
Room & Board: $10,750	**Freshman Class:** 728 applied, 532 accepted, 194 enrolled
SAT or ACT: required	**CEEB CODE:** 6127
Application Deadline: August 15	**COMPETITIVE**

Concordia University, founded in 1926, is a private college affiliated with the Lutheran Church-Missouri Synod. It offers undergraduate programs in liberal arts, behavioral science, business, communication, education, environmental science, and church music. The figures in the above capsule and in this profile are approximate. There are 4 undergraduate schools. In addition to regional accreditation, Concordia has baccalaureate program accreditation with SACSCOC. The 389-acre campus is in an urban area in Northwest Austin,TX. Including any residence halls, there are 20 buildings.

STUDENT LIFE: 93% of undergraduates are from Texas. Others are from 21 states, and 13 foreign countries. 89% are from public schools. 9% are African American; 63% White; 16% Hispanic; 1% Asian American. 78% are Protestant; 16% Catholic. **Female To Male Ratio:** 1.5:1. The average age of freshmen is 19; all undergraduates, 25. 40% do not continue beyond their first year; 35% remain to graduate. **Housing:** 245 students can be accommodated in college housing, which includes single-sex, coed dorms, and residence halls. On-campus housing is guaranteed for the freshman year only, and is available on a first-come, and first-served basis. 68% of students commute. All students may keep cars.

FACULTY/CLASSROOMS: 69% of faculty are male; 31% are female. All

teach undergraduates. No introductory courses are taught by graduate students. The average class size in a laboratory is 16 and in a regular course is 21.

PROGRAMS OF STUDY: Concordia confers B.A. degrees. Associate and master's degrees are also awarded. Bachelor's degrees are awarded in BUSINESS (accounting and business administration and management), COMMUNICATIONS AND THE ARTS (communications, English, music, and Spanish), COMPUTER AND PHYSICAL SCIENCE (computer science), EDUCATION (elementary education and secondary education), ENGINEERING AND ENVIRONMENTAL DESIGN (environmental science), SOCIAL SCIENCE (behavioral science, history, liberal arts/general studies, Mexican-American/Chicano studies, and religious music). Education is the strongest academically. Business management, education, and communication have the largest enrollments.

ACTIVITIES: There are no fraternities or sororities. There are 9 groups on campus, including band, choir, chorus, dance, drama, ethnic, religious, social, and student government. Popular campus events include Fall Festival Weekend, Parents Day, and Founders Day. **Sports:** There are 6 intercollegiate sports for men and 5 for women, and 10 intramural sports for men and 9 for women. Facilities include an activities center, gym, auditorium, baseball field, beach volleyball court, and tennis courts. **Graduates:** From July 1, 2015 to June 30, 2016, 151 bachelor's degrees were awarded. The most popular majors were business/marketing (44%), education (12%), and social sciences (9%). In an average class, 20% graduate in 4 years or less and 30% graduate in 5 years or less.

SERVICES: Counseling and information services are available, as is tutoring in most subjects. **Library/Resources:** The library contains 56,146 volumes, 8,504 microform items, 3,213 audio/video tapes/CDs/DVDs, and subscribes to 514 periodicals including electronic. Computerized library services include interlibrary loans and database searching. Special learning facilities include a TV station. **Physically Challenged Students:** 75% of the campus is accessible. Facilities include wheelchair ramps, elevators, special parking, specially equipped restrooms, and lowered drinking fountains. **Special:** Concordia offers internships in communications, behavioral science, business, environmental science, and Mexican-American studies, study abroad in Mexico, an accelerated degree program in business management, dual majors, credit for prior experiential learning, nondegree study, pass/fail options, and a preseminary program. There is 1 national honor society. **Visiting:** There are regularly scheduled orientations for prospective students, consisting of placement exams, scheduling and registration of classes, and information sessions for parents with faculty and administrators. There are guides for informal visits, visitors may sit in on classes, and stay overnight. To schedule a visit, contact the Admissions Office. **Campus Safety and Security:** Measures include 24-hour foot and vehicle patrol and security escort services. There are lighted pathways/sidewalks.

REQUIREMENTS: The recommended minimum composite score is 860 on the SAT I or 17 on the ACT. Applicants must be graduates of an accredited secondary school or have the GED. AP and CLEP credits are accepted. To graduate, all students must complete 12 hours each of English, social/behavioral science, and religion, 6 to 8 hours of natural science, and 3 hours each of fine arts, math, phys ed, and speech. Students must earn 128 semester hours, including 39 upper-level hours and 33 to 48 hours in the major. A minimum 2.0 GPA is required, plus a 2.25 GPA in the major. **Procedure:** Freshmen are admitted fall, spring, and summer. There are early admissions, deferred admissions, and rolling admissions plans. Applications should be filed by August 15 for fall entry. The fall 2016 application fee was $25. **Transfer Students:** 71 transfer students enrolled in 2015-2016. Transfer students with fewer than 18 hours earned must meet freshman admissions requirements and submit high school and college transcripts; those with 18 or more hours earned must be in good standing at the previously attended college with a minimum 2.5 GPA. 45 of 128 credits required for the bachelor's degree must be completed at Concordia. **International Students:** The school actively recruits these students. They must take the TOEFL.

ADMISSIONS: 73% of the 2016-2017 applicants were accepted. **Admissions Contact:** Dr. Michael Mogavero, Vice President of Enrollment Services. Email: *admissions@concordia.edu* Web: *www.concordia.edu*

FINANCIAL AID: In 2016-2017, 80% of all full-time freshmen received some form of financial aid, and received need-based aid. The average freshman award was $16,678. Need-based scholarships or need-based grants averaged $10,250; need-based self-help aid (loans and jobs) averaged $3,034; and other non-need-based awards and non-need-based scholarships averaged $6,896. The average financial indebtedness of the 2016 graduate was $15,084. The college's own financial statement is required. The FAFSA code is 003557. The priority date for freshman financial aid applications for fall entry is May 1. The filing deadline for fall entry is rolling.

DALLAS BAPTIST UNIVERSITY — D-2

www.dbu.edu

Dallas, TX 75211	**(214) 333-5360** **(800) 460-1328**
Fax: (214) 333-5447	**Email: admiss@dbu.edu**
Full-time: 1037 men, 1371 women	**Faculty:** 95
Part-time: 301 men, 514 women	**Ph.D.s:** 83%
Graduate: 741 men, 1192 women	**Student/Faculty:** 12 to 1
Year: 4-1-4, summer session	**Tuition:** $26,180
Room & Board: $7533	**Freshman Class:** 3259 applied, 1405 accepted, 527 enrolled
SAT CR/M: 563/555 **ACT:** 22	**CEEB CODE:** 6159
Application Deadline: n/av	**COMPETITIVE**

Dallas Baptist University is a Christ-centered comprehensive, liberal arts university offering 7 Associate, 72 Bachelor, 55 Accelerated Bachelor/Master, 29 Master, 62 Dual Master, and 2 Doctoral degree programs. DBU integrates faith and academic learning, giving students freedom to explore their faith in the classroom and the encouragement to live out their faith as servant leaders in the world. With online, weekend and evening classes at locations throughout the Dallas/Fort Worth Metroplex, DBU offers working adults the convenience and flexibility they need to complete their degree. There are 7 undergraduate schools and 29 graduate schools. In addition to regional accreditation, DBU has baccalaureate program accreditation with ACBSP, NASM, TEA, and CEA. The 293-acre campus is in a suburban area 13 miles from downtown Dallas and 29 miles from downtown Fort Worth. Including any residence halls, there are 47 buildings.

STUDENT LIFE: 83% of undergraduates are from Texas. Others are from 40 states, 41 foreign countries, and Canada. 9% are Foreign; 58% White; 2% Asian American; 16% Hispanic; 14% African American; 1% American Indian/Alaska Native. 93% are Protestant. **Female To Male Ratio:** 1.5:1. The average age of freshmen is 18; all undergraduates, 24. 23% do not continue beyond their first year; 58% remain to graduate. **Housing:** 2137 students can be accommodated in college housing, which includes single-sex dorms, on-campus apartments, and off-campus apartments. On-campus housing is available on a first-come and first-served basis. 60% of students live on campus; of those, 80% remain on campus on weekends. All students may keep cars. Alcohol is not permitted.

FACULTY/CLASSROOMS: 58% of faculty are male; 42% are female. 74% teach undergraduates. No introductory courses are taught by graduate students. The average class size in a regular course is 11.

PROGRAMS OF STUDY: DBU confers B.A., B.S., B.A.S., B.B.A., B.B.S., B.M., B.M.E., and B.M.A. degrees. Associate, master's, and doctoral degrees are also awarded. Bachelor's degrees are awarded in BIOLOGICAL SCIENCE (biology/biological science and cell biology), BUSINESS (accounting, business administration and management, business administration - international, entrepreneurial studies, finance, hospitality management services, human resources/organizational mgmt, international business, management information systems, marketing, and sports management), COMMUNICATIONS AND THE ARTS (applied music, art, broadcasting, choral music, church music, communication design , communications, English, film, television and digital media, fine arts, graphic design, keyboard - piano concentration, music, music business management, music performance, music theory and composition, piano performance, public relations, and vocal performance), COMPUTER AND PHYSICAL SCIENCE (computer science, mathematics, natural sciences, and science), EDUCATION (Christian education, early childhood education, education, elementary education, English education, middle school education, physical education, reading education, science education, and secondary education), ENGINEERING AND ENVIRONMENTAL DESIGN (environmental science), HEALTH PROFESSIONS (biology and health care administration), SOCIAL SCIENCE (biblical studies, Christian studies, counseling/psychology, criminal justice, cultural studies/critical theory & analysis, East Asian studies, European studies, history, interdisciplinary studies, liberal arts/general studies, ministries, philosophy, physical fitness/movement, political science/government, psychology, religion, religious education, religious studies, religious music, sociology, and youth ministry). biology, pre-med, pre-nursing, and business are the strongest academically. Business administration/management, education, and psychology have the largest enrollments.

ACTIVITIES: 13% of men belong to 4 local fraternities; 21% of women belong to 6 local sororities. There are 48 groups on campus, including community outreach, art, cheerleading, choir, chorale, chorus, communications, dance, drama, drill team, ethnic, honors, international, leadership/mission work, musical theater, opera, pep band, political, professional, religious, social, social service, student government, and yearbook. Popular campus events include All Night Party, Battle at the Burg, Mr. Big Chief, Christmas Tree Lighting, Family Weekend, Great Pumpkin Chase, Homecoming, Red Rally, Sadie Hawkins, Singled Out, Welcome Week, Winter Ball, and SWAT. **Sports:** There are 11 intercollegiate sports for men and 9 for women, and 8 intramural sports for men and 7 for women. Facilities include a fitness center, tennis courts, baseball field, ballpark, baseball clubhouse, baseball field house, batting cages, soccer field, putting green, golf hitting facility, 3 pools, sand volleyball courts, indoor/outdoor basketball courts, ping pong, billiards, and foosball tables, intramural fields, and athletic training center. **Graduates:** From July 1, 2015 to June 30, 2016, 734 bachelor's degrees were awarded. The most popular majors were multi/interdisciplinary studies (13%), business administration & management (13%), and psychology (10%). 206 companies recruited on campus in 2015-2016. In an average class, 45% graduate in 4 years or less, 50% graduate in 5 years or less, and 58% graduate in 6 years or less.

SERVICES: Counseling and information services are available, as is tutoring in most subjects, such as math, science, writing, English, computer science, chemistry, Spanish, music, accounting, and Greek. There is also a reader service for the blind, and remedial math. **Library/Resources:** The 3 libraries contain 297,708 volumes, 521,772 microform items, 7,986 audio/video tapes/CDs/DVDs, and subscribe to 39,400 periodicals including electronic. Computerized library services include interlibrary loans, database searching, Internet access, and Wi-Fi capability. **Physically Challenged Students:** 90% of the campus is accessible. Facilities include wheelchair ramps, elevators, special parking, specially equipped restrooms, special class scheduling, lowered drinking fountains, lowered telephones, and special housing. **Special:** Study abroad programs are available in Brisbane, Australia; San Jose, Costa Rica; Oxford, England; Jerusalem, Israel; and Mukono; Uganda. National Culture-Shaping Programs include American Studies Program in Washington, D.C. Contemporary Music Center in Nashville, Tennessee; and the L.A. Film Studies Center in Los Angeles, California. There are 8 national honor societies and a freshman honors program. **Visiting:** There are regularly scheduled orientations for prospective students, Patriot Preview days each fall, spring, and summer semesters provide parents and students information about life at DBU. Campus tours, visits with faculty and administration, information about admissions, financial aid, and campus life are included. There are guides for informal visits and visitors may sit in on classes. To schedule a visit, contact the Undergraduate Admissions Office. **Campus Safety and Security:** Measures include 24-hour foot and vehicle patrol, emergency notification system, self-defense education, and security escort services. There are also shuttle buses, emergency telephones, lighted pathways/sidewalks, and controlled access to dorms/residences.

REQUIREMENTS: The ACT Optional Writing test is also required. Applicants must be graduates, or expect to graduate, from an accredited secondary school, home school, or have a GED. A composite SAT score of at least 1020 (Critical Reading and Math sections) or a composite ACT score of at least 21 is required, along with a minimum high school GPA of 2.5. An essay is required, and an interview is encouraged. Recommended high school courses should include 4 years each of English and history/social studies, 3 years of math, 2 years of science (including 1 year Lab Science), and 2 to 3 years of a foreign language. DBU requires applicants to be in the upper 50% of their class. AP and CLEP credits are accepted. Important factors in the admissions decision are leadership record, personality/intangible qualities, and extracurricular activities record. To graduate with a bachelor degree, students must have a minimum GPA of 2.0 and complete a minimum of 120 credit hours, including 24 hours in the major and 42 upper-level hours. At least 12 credit hours in the major program must be completed at DBU, including 9 upper-level credits. Students must complete a minimum of 25% of credit hours in residence at DBU; complete 30 of the last 36 credit hours with courses offered by DBU; and complete the General Studies requirements including English, history, religion, fine arts, computer science, math, kinesiology, natural science, and social science. Chapel attendance is required. **Procedure:** Freshmen are admitted to all sessions. Entrance exams should be taken during the spring of the junior year or the fall of the senior year. There are deferred admissions and rolling admissions plans. Application deadlines are open. Application fee is $25. Applications are accepted on-line. Application fees are waived if application is completed on-line. **Transfer Students:** 476 transfer students enrolled in 2015-2016. Applicants must submit an essay along with their application and fee and transcripts of all previous college work. Applicants should have a cumulative GPA of 2.5 or higher on all previous college work. Students with fewer than 30 credit hours must furnish high school transcripts and ACT or SAT scores. 30 of 120 credits required for the bachelor's degree must be completed at DBU. **International Students:** There are 169 international students enrolled. The school actively recruits these students. They must take the TOEFL with a minimum score of 525 on the paper-based TOEFL (PBT) or 71 on the Internet-based version (iBT), or the IELTS, PTE, CAE, or complete the DBU intensive English program.

ADMISSIONS: 43% of the 2016-2017 applicants were accepted. The SAT scores for the 2016-2017 freshman class were: Critical Reading-- 18% below 500, 51% between 500 and 599, 28% between 600 and 699, and 4% between 700 and 800. Math-- 17% below 500, 60% between 500 and 599, 23% between 600 and 699, and 1% between 700 and 800. The ACT scores were 10% between 12 and 17, 60% between 18 and 23, 25% between 24 and 29, and 4% above 30. 4 freshmen graduated first in their class. **Admissions Contact:** Bobby Soto, Director of Admissions. Email: *admiss@dbu.edu* Web: *www.dbu.edu*

FINANCIAL AID: In 2016-2017, 98% of all full-time freshmen and 88% of continuing full-time students received some form of financial aid. 50% of all full-time freshmen and 49% of continuing full-time students received need-based aid. The average freshman award was $20,236. Need-based scholarships or need-based grants averaged $6,529 ($12,861 maximum); need-based self-help aid (loans and jobs) averaged $3,511 ($7,000 maximum); non-need-based athletic scholarships averaged $18,244 ($36,450 maximum); other non-need-based awards and non-need-based scholarships averaged $8,981 ($28,764 maximum); and $9,476 from other forms of aid. 22% of undergraduate students work part-time. Average annual earnings from campus work are $3600. The average financial indebtedness of the 2016 graduate was $25,654. The college's own financial statement is required. The FAFSA code is 003560. The priority date for freshman financial aid applications for fall entry is March 1.

EAST TEXAS BAPTIST UNIVERSITY — E-2

www.etbu.edu

Marshall, TX 75670	(903) 923-2000 (800) 804-ETBU
Fax: (903) 923-2001	**Email:** admissions@etbu.edu
Full-time: 512 men, 584 women	**Faculty:** 73
Part-time: 54 men, 83 women	**Ph.D.s:** 84%
Graduate: 34 men, 41 women	**Student/Faculty:** 15 to 1
Year: semesters, summer session	**Tuition:** $23,700
Room & Board: $9434	**Freshman Class:** 843 applied, 807 accepted, 342 enrolled
SAT CR/M: 490/510 **ACT:** 21	**CEEB CODE:** 6187
Application Deadline: August 17	**COMPETITIVE**

East Texas Baptist University, established in 1912, provides a Christ-centered education that emphasizes the integration of faith and learning. The ETBU experience is known for "Embracing Faith, Engaging Minds, and Empowering Leaders." There are 7 undergraduate schools and 4 graduate schools. In addition to regional accreditation, ETBU has baccalaureate program accreditation with NASM, CCNE, and CAATE. The 250-acre campus is in a small town 40 miles west of Shreveport, Louisiana (location of Shreveport Regional Airport), 23 miles east of Longview, Texas, and 61 miles east of Tyler, Texas. Including any residence halls, there are 27 buildings.

STUDENT LIFE: 91% of undergraduates are from Texas. Others are from 17 states, 12 foreign countries, and Canada. 73% are from public schools. 63% are White; 21% African American; 2% Foreign; 2% two or more races; 10% Hispanic; 1% race unknown. 73% are Protestant; 21% claim no religious affiliation. **Female To Male Ratio:** 1.2:1. The average age of freshmen is 18; all undergraduates, 20. 48% do not continue beyond their first year; 46% remain to graduate. **Housing:** 1079 students can be accommodated in college housing, which includes single-sex dorms, on-campus apartments, and married student housing. On-campus housing is guaranteed for the freshman year only, and is available on a first-come, first-served basis, and is available on a lottery system for upperclassmen. 85% of students live on campus; of those, 75% remain on campus on weekends. All students may keep cars. Alcohol is not permitted.

FACULTY/CLASSROOMS: 56% of faculty are male; 44% are female. 97% teach undergraduates, 25% do research, and 25% do both. No introductory courses are taught by graduate students. The average class size in an introductory lecture is 21; in a laboratory is 12; and in a regular course is 18.

PROGRAMS OF STUDY: ETBU confers B.A., B.S., B.A.S., B.M., B.S.E., and B.S.N. degrees. Master's degrees are also awarded. Bachelor's degrees are awarded in BIOLOGICAL SCIENCE (biology/biological science), BUSINESS (business administration and management and business administration marketing), COMMUNICATIONS AND THE ARTS (communications, English, English literature, English writing, music, music performance, piano/organ, piano performance, Spanish, speech/debate/rhetoric, theatre arts, visual and performing arts, vocal performance, and voice), COMPUTER AND PHYSICAL SCIENCE (chemistry and mathematics), EDUCATION (athletic training, drama education, early childhood education, education, elementary education, English education, foreign languages education, general studies, history education, mathematics education, music education, physical education, science education, secondary education, social studies education, social studies secondary school education, speech correction, and university studies), HEALTH PROFESSIONS (biology, exercise science, health science, kinesiology, and nursing), SOCIAL SCIENCE (biblical studies, child psychology/development, counseling/psychology, criminal justice, history, interdisciplinary studies, international studies, ministries, missions, pastoral studies, physical fitness/movement, political science/government, psychology, religion, religious education, religious music, sociology, and youth ministry). Nursing, athletic training, and business are the strongest academically. Nursing, business administration, and teacher education have the largest enrollments.

ACTIVITIES: There are 29 groups on campus, including band, cheerleading, choir, chorale, chorus, communications, dance, debate, drama, drill team, ethnic, honors, international, jazz band, literary magazine, marching band, musical theater, newspaper, opera, orchestra, pep band, photography, political, professional, religious, social, social service, student government, symphony, and yearbook. Popular campus events include Tiger Camp, Family Weekend, Connexus, Christmas on the Hill, Homecoming, Miss ETBU, Tiger Football Tailgates, Chill on the Hill, Fall Formal, 2k in Color, ETBU Cares, Bonfire, Tigers Serve Days, and athletic games. **Sports:** There are 7 intercollegiate sports for men and 7 for women, and 8 intramural sports for men and 6 for women. Facilities include a baseball field, tennis courts, weight room, soccer field, softball field, intramural field, practice gym, football practice fields, and football field and stadium. **Graduates:** From July 1, 2015 to June 30, 2016, 174 bachelor's degrees were awarded. The most popular majors were interdisciplinary studies (19%), education (18%), and business (15%). 44 companies recruited on campus in 2015-2016. In an average class, 5% graduate in 3 years or less, 19% graduate in 4 years or less, 37% graduate in 5 years or less, and 46% graduate in 6 years or less. Of the 2015 graduating class, 36% were enrolled in graduate school within 6 months of graduation, and 87% were employed.

SERVICES: Counseling and information services are available, as is tutoring in most subjects. There is also remedial math, reading, and writing. **Library/Resources:** The library contains 5.6 million volumes, 10,000 microform items, 307,542 audio/video tapes/CDs/DVDs, and subscribes to 42,777 periodicals including electronic. Computerized library services include interlibrary loans, database searching, Internet access, and Wi-Fi capability. **Physically Challenged Students:** 95% of the campus is accessible. Facilities include wheelchair ramps, elevators, special parking, specially equipped restrooms, special class scheduling, lowered drinking fountains, lowered telephones, and special housing. **Special:** ETBU students have the opportunity to study in many different national and international arenas through service-learning courses in a variety of disciplines. In addition, through the Council for Christian College & Universities, ETBU provides semester abroad programs in Washington D. C., Oxford, Australia, and Uganda as well as other US and international locations. ETBU also has exchange partnerships with Hong Kong Baptist University, Jana Dlugosza University, and Lanzhou University of Technology. Internships are offered in business, religion, education, biology, communication, psychology, and sociology. Students also may take advantage of undergraduate majors like religion and business that provide for the completion of both undergraduate and graduate degrees in 5 years. East Texas Baptist University is a member of the Council for Christian Colleges & Universities (CCCU). There are 8 national honor societies, a freshman honors program, and 13 departmental honors programs. **Visiting:** There are regularly scheduled orientations for prospective students, including campus tours, meals, scholarship interviews/testing, faculty visits, class visits, sports/entertainment, and financial aid seminars. There are guides for informal visits, visitors may sit in on classes, and stay overnight. To schedule a visit, contact Alicia Earle at (903) 923-2000. **Campus Safety and Security:** Measures include 24-hour foot and vehicle patrol, emergency notification system, self-defense education, security escort services, emergency telephones, lighted pathways/sidewalks, controlled access to dorms/residences, and security partnership with the local police department, and the Marshall Police Department for campus security.

REQUIREMENTS: Applicants must be graduates of an accredited secondary school or have the GED, and must have composite scores of at least 18 on the ACT or 860 on the SAT (critical reading and math), or rank in the top 30% of their graduating class. Students not meeting these requirements may be admitted conditionally for 1 term or semester. ETBU requires applicants to be in the upper 30% of their class. AP and CLEP credits are accepted. To graduate, students must complete general education requirements and maintain a minimum GPA of 2.0. A total of 120 to 130 semester hours, with at least 30 in the major, is required. **Procedure:** Freshmen are admitted in the fall, spring, and summer. Entrance exams should be taken in the first semester of the senior year. There are deferred admissions and rolling admissions plans. Applications should be filed by August 17 for fall entry; January 15 for spring entry, along with a $25 fee. Applications are accepted online. **Transfer Students:** 135 transfer students enrolled in 2015-2016. Transfer students must have a minimum GPA of 2.0 and be eligible to return to the last college attended. 33 of 120 credits required for the bachelor's degree must be completed at ETBU. **International Students:** There are 14 international students enrolled. The school actively recruits these students. They must take the TOEFL with a minimum score of 500 on the paper-based TOEFL (PBT) or 61 on the Internet-based version (iBT). They must also take the SAT or ACT, scoring 18.

ADMISSIONS: 96% of the 2016-2017 applicants were accepted. The SAT scores for the 2016-2017 freshman class were: Critical Reading--61% below 500, 27% between 500 and 599, 11% between 600 and 699, and 1% between 700 and 800. Math-- 41% below 500, 45% between 500 and 599, 13% between 600 and 699, and 1% between 700 and 800. The ACT scores were 15% between 12 and 17, 66% between 18 and 23, and 19% between 24 and 29. 36% of the current freshmen were in the top fifth of their class; 63% were in the top two fifths. 5 freshmen graduated first in their class. **Admissions Contact:** Vince Blankenship, VP for Enrollment Management & Marketing. Email: *admissions@etbu.edu* Web: *www.etbu.edu*

FINANCIAL AID: In 2016-2017, 99% of all full-time freshmen and continuing full-time students received some form of financial aid. 75% of all full-time freshmen and 77% of continuing full-time students received need-based aid. The average freshman award was $26,076. Need-based scholarships or need-based grants averaged $6,070 ($14,775 maximum); need-based self-help aid (loans and jobs) averaged $3,561 ($5,820 maximum); and other non-need-based awards and non-need-based scholarships averaged $19,549 ($35,910 maximum). 22% of undergraduate students work part-time. Average annual earnings from campus work are $5710. The average financial indebtedness of the 2016 graduate was $35,716. The college's own financial statement is required. The FAFSA code is 003564. The priority date for freshman financial aid applications for fall entry is June 1.

HARDIN-SIMMONS UNIVERSITY C-2
www.hsutx.edu

Abilene, TX 79698 (325) 670-1206
(877) 464-7889
Fax: (325) 670-1527 Email: enroll@hsutx.edu

Full-time: 776 men, 992 women	**Faculty:** 120; IIA, --$
Part-time: 91 men, 171 women	**Ph.D.s:** 77%
Graduate: 184 men, 221 women	**Student/Faculty:** 12 to 1
Year: semesters, summer session	**Tuition:** $25,830
Room & Board: $8136	**Freshman Class:** 1757 applied, 635 accepted, 465 enrolled
SAT CR/M/W: 510/520/510 **ACT:** 22	**CEEB CODE:** 6268
Application Deadline: open	**COMPETITIVE**

Hardin-Simmons University, founded in 1891, is a private liberal arts institution affiliated with the Baptist General Convention of Texas. HSU offers "The HSU Commitment" that means your tuition rate will not increased while you are enrolled as a full-time undergraduate student during consecutive fall/spring semesters and making satisfactory progress toward a degree. The figures in the above capsule and in this capsule are approximate. There are 7 undergraduate schools and 1 graduate school. In addition to regional accreditation, HSU has baccalaureate program accreditation with ACBSP, CSWE, NASM, CCNE, CAPTE, CCSACS, and SACS. The 220-acre campus is in an urban area 150 miles west of Fort Worth. Including any residence halls, there are 41 buildings.

STUDENT LIFE: 96% of undergraduates are from Texas. Others are from 23 states, 19 foreign countries, and Canada. 88% are from public schools. 74% are White; 5% African American; 2% Foreign; 10% Hispanic; 1% Asian American; 1% American Indian/Alaska Native. 66% are Protestant; 13% claim no religious affiliation. **Female To Male Ratio:** 1.3:1. The average age of freshmen is 18; all undergraduates, 21. 34% do not continue beyond their first year; 49% remain to graduate. **Housing:** 1111 students can be accommodated in college housing, which includes single-sex dorms, off-campus apartments, and married student housing. On-campus housing is available on a first-come and first-served basis. 56% of students commute. All students may keep cars. Alcohol is not permitted.

FACULTY/CLASSROOMS: 64% of faculty are male; 39% are female. 87% teach undergraduates. No introductory courses are taught by graduate students. The average class size in an introductory lecture is 23; in a laboratory is 15; and in a regular course is 17.

PROGRAMS OF STUDY: HSU confers B.A., B.S., B.B.A., B.B.S., B.F.A., B.Mus., and B.S.N. degrees. Master's and doctoral degrees are also awarded. Bachelor's degrees are awarded in AGRICULTURE (agricultural business management, agriculture, and animal science), BIOLOGICAL SCIENCE (biochemistry, biology/biological science, and molecular biology), BUSINESS (accounting, banking and finance, business administration and management, finance, management science, and marketing management), COMMUNICATIONS AND THE ARTS (art, broadcasting, communications, dramatic arts, English, graphic design, music, music business management, music history and appreciation, music performance, music theory and composition, piano/organ, public relations, radio/television technology, Spanish, speech/debate/rhetoric, strings, theatre studies, and voice), COMPUTER AND PHYSICAL SCIENCE (chemistry, computer science, geology, mathematics, and physics), EDUCATION (art education, athletic training, business education, computer education, drama education, early childhood education, education, elementary education, English education, foreign languages education, mathematics education, middle school education, music education, physical education, reading education, science education, secondary education, and social studies education), ENGINEERING AND ENVIRONMENTAL DESIGN (environmental science), HEALTH PROFESSIONS (exercise science, health science, nursing, predentistry, premedicine, and speech pathology/audiology), SOCIAL SCIENCE (biblical studies, corrections, criminal justice, economics, history, legal studies, ministries, missions, philosophy, political science/government, prelaw, psychology, religious studies, religious music, social work, sociology, theological studies, and youth ministry). English, speech pathology, and music are the strongest academically. Education, biology, and nursing have the largest enrollments.

ACTIVITIES: 5% of men belong to 4 local fraternities; 16% of women belong to 4 local sororities. There are 57 groups on campus, including art, band, cheerleading, choir, chorale, computers, debate, drama, drill team, ethnic, honors, international, literary magazine, marching band, musical theater, newspaper, opera, orchestra, pep band, photography, political, professional, radio and TV, religious, social, social service, student government, and symphony. Popular campus events include Western Heritage Day, All-School SING, Cowboy Fridays, and Founders Day. **Sports:** There are 6 intercollegiate sports for men and 6 for women, and 17 intramural sports for men and 17 for women. Facilities include a rodeo arena, 2 running ovals, a practice field, football stadium, soccer field, softball and baseball fields, outdoor and indoor swimming pools, 6 bowling alleys, a fitness course, 4 basketball, 4 racquetball, 8 tennis, and 8 badminton/paddleball courts, and a Nautilus weight-lifting room. **Graduates:** From July 1, 2015 to June 30, 2016, 383 bachelor's degrees were awarded. The most popular majors were education (18%), business/marketing (13%), and communication/journalism (9%). 9 companies recruited on campus in 2015-2016. In an average class, 2% graduate in 3 years or less, 27% graduate in 4 years or less, 45% graduate in 5 years or less, and 49% graduate in 6 years or less.

SERVICES: Counseling and information services are available, as is tutoring in most subjects, and remedial math, reading, and writing. **Library/Resources:** The 2 libraries contain 443,979 volumes, 23,734 microform items, 12,013 audio/video tapes/CDs/DVDs, and subscribe to 33,942 periodicals including electronic. Computerized library services include interlibrary loans, database searching, Internet access, and Wi-Fi capability. Special learning facilities include an art gallery, radio station, an observatory. **Physically Challenged Students:** All of the campus is accessible. Facilities include wheelchair ramps, elevators, special parking, specially equipped restrooms, special class scheduling, lowered drinking fountains, lowered telephones, and special housing. **Special:** Cross-registration may be arranged with Abilene Christian and McMurry Universities. HSU offers cooperative programs, internships, dual majors, credit by exam, nondegree study, and pass/fail options. Students may study abroad in England, Austria, China, Spain, Italy and Israel, where HSU is involved in an ongoing archeological excavation of early Christian sites. There are 9 national honor societies and a freshman honors program. **Visiting:** There are regularly scheduled orientations for prospective students, including Cowboy Fridays, plus Fall and Winter preview and Spring Round-Up. There are guides for informal visits and visitors may sit in on classes. To schedule a visit, contact the Visitor Coordinator. **Campus Safety and Security:** Measures include 24-hour foot and vehicle patrol. There are emergency telephones and lighted pathways/sidewalks.

REQUIREMENTS: The ACT Optional Writing test is required, as is the SAT score with a minimum of 1390 and a minimum on the ACT score of 20. Graduation from an accredited secondary school is required; a GED will be accepted. Applicants should submit an academic record of at least 16 units, distributed as follows: 3 units of English, 2 units each of math, science, and social studies, and 7 units of electives, with a GPA of 2.0 or above. 3 letters of recommendation are also required. HSU requires applicants to be in the upper 75% of their class. AP and CLEP credits are accepted. To graduate, students must complete a minimum of 124 semester hours with a minimum 2.0 GPA. A minimum of 18 to 30 hours are required in the major (18 must be advanced and 12 of the advanced must be from HSU). 42 hours in upper-division courses are required. Core courses that must be taken include 12 to 18 hours of social science, 9 of English, 7 of natural science (from 2 separate fields and 1 requiring a lab), 6 each of Bible and humanities (3 of fine arts and 3 of non-fine arts), 3 to 6 each of math, 3 to 4 of phys ed, 3 of oral communication, and computer science. All students must satisfy chapel attendance requirements and must demonstrate proficiency in written English. **Procedure:** Freshmen are admitted to all sessions. There are deferred admissions and rolling admissions plans. Application deadlines are open. Application fee is $50. Notification is sent on a rolling basis. Applications are accepted online. **Transfer Students:** 155 transfer students enrolled in 2015-2016. Applicants must submit official transcripts from all previous colleges. Students may petition to transfer up to 2 D grades if the overall GPA is 2.0 or higher. Students transferring from a 2-year college may receive credit for up to 66 semester hours of transferable courses. Applicants with fewer than 24 semester hours must submit a high school transcript and official report of ACT or SAT scores. Students ineligible to continue at another institution are not eligible for regular admission to HSU. 31 of 124 credits required for the bachelor's degree must be completed at HSU. **International Students:** There are 16 international students enrolled. The school actively recruits these students. They must take the TOEFL with a minimum score of 550 on the paper-based TOEFL (PBT). They must also take the SAT or ACT.

ADMISSIONS: 36% of the 2016-2017 applicants were accepted. The

SAT scores for the 2016-2017 freshman class were: Critical Reading-- 43% below 500, 35% between 500 and 599, 20% between 600 and 699, and 2% between 700 and 800. Math-- 38% below 500, 44% between 500 and 599, 17% between 600 and 699, and 1% between 700 and 800. Writing-- 43% below 500, 45% between 500 and 599, 11% between 600 and 699, and 1% between 700 and 800. The ACT scores were 39% below 12, 25% between 12 and 17, 24% between 18 and 23, 6% between 24 and 29, and 6% above 30. 44% of the current freshmen were in the top fifth of their class; 71% were in the top two fifths. 10 freshmen graduated first in their class. **Admissions Contact:** Vicki House, Director of Admissions and Recruiting. Email: *enroll@hsutx.edu* Web: *www.hsutx.edu*

FINANCIAL AID: In 2016-2017, 72% of all full-time freshmen and 69% of continuing full-time students received some form of financial aid. 56% of all full-time freshmen and 52% of continuing full-time students received need-based aid. The average freshman award was $17,609. Need-based scholarships or need-based grants averaged $5,439 ($7,808 maximum); need-based self-help aid (loans and jobs) averaged $3,550 ($5,900 maximum); and other non-need-based awards and non-need-based scholarships averaged $10,062 ($25,272 maximum). 21% of undergraduate students work part-time. Average annual earnings from campus work are $2400. The average financial indebtedness of the 2016 graduate was $31,934. The priority date for freshman financial aid applications for fall entry is March 15. The filing deadline for fall entry is open.

HOUSTON BAPTIST UNIVERSITY — E-3

www.hbu.edu

Houston, TX 77074	**(281) 649-3211** **(800) 969-3210**
Fax: (281) 649-3217	**Email: admissions@hbu.edu**
Full-time: 839 men, 1298 women	**Faculty:** 118
Part-time: 111 men, 199 women	**Ph.D.s:** 69%
Graduate: 238 men, 602 women	**Student/Faculty:** 15 to 1
Year: semesters, summer session	**Tuition:** $28,800
Room & Board: $7650	**Freshman Class:** 6519 applied, 4562 accepted, 615 enrolled
SAT CR/M/W: 530/540/520 **ACT:** 22	**CEEB CODE:** 6282
Application Deadline: open	**COMPETITIVE**

Houston Baptist University, founded in 1960, is a private institution affiliated with the Baptist General Convention of Texas, and offering undergraduate programs in nursing, arts and science, music, and business administration. There are 8 undergraduate schools and 5 graduate schools. In addition to regional accreditation, HBU has baccalaureate program accreditation with ACBSP and NLN. The 100-acre campus is in an urban area in southwest Houston. Including any residence halls, there are 29 buildings.

STUDENT LIFE: 95% of undergraduates are from Texas. Others are from 32 states, 27 foreign countries, and Canada. 6% are race unknown; 4% Foreign; 4% two or more races; 28% White; 24% African American; 23% Hispanic; 11% Asian American. 49% are Protestant; 31% claim no religious affiliation; 11% Catholic. **Female To Male Ratio:** 1.8:1. The average age of freshmen is 19; all undergraduates, 21. 30% do not continue beyond their first year; 70% remain to graduate. **Housing:** 568 students can be accommodated in college housing, which includes single-sex dorms and on-campus apartments. On-campus housing is available on a first-come, first-served basis, and is available on a lottery system for upperclassmen. Priority is given to out-of-town students. 61% of students commute. score of 20. All students may keep cars. Alcohol is not permitted.

FACULTY/CLASSROOMS: 45% of faculty are male; 55% are female. 94% teach undergraduates. No introductory courses are taught by graduate students. The average class size in a laboratory is 14 and in a regular course is 10.

PROGRAMS OF STUDY: HBU confers B.A., B.S., B.B.A., B.M., and B.S.N. degrees. Master's degrees are also awarded. Bachelor's degrees are awarded in BIOLOGICAL SCIENCE (biology/biological science and molecular biology), BUSINESS (accounting, banking and finance, business administration and management, and entrepreneurial studies), COMMUNICATIONS AND THE ARTS (art, communications, English, French, music, music performance, music theory and composition, and Spanish), COMPUTER AND PHYSICAL SCIENCE (chemistry, information sciences and systems, mathematics, and physics), EDUCATION (art education, early childhood education, elementary education, mathematics education, music education, physical education, reading education, secondary education, special education, and teaching English as a second/foreign language (TESOL/TEFOL)), HEALTH PROFESSIONS (nursing), SOCIAL SCIENCE (biblical languages, Christian studies, economics, history, liberal arts/general studies, physical fitness/movement, political science/government, psychology, religious music, and sociology). Premedical studies, health professions, nursing are the strongest academically. Biology, nursing, and business administration have the largest enrollments.

ACTIVITIES: 3% of men belong to 1 local and 1 national fraternities; 5% of women belong to 3 national sororities. There are 51 groups on campus, including art, band, cheerleading, choir, chorale, chorus, computers, debate, drama, ethnic, forensics, honors, international, jazz band, newspaper, opera, pep band, photography, political, professional, radio and TV, religious, social service, student government, and symphony. Popular campus events include Welcome Days for New Students, Husky Fest Fall Festival, and Winter Formal. **Sports:** There are 6 intercollegiate sports for men and 7 for women, and 12 intramural sports for men and 12 for women. Facilities include volleyball, basketball, and tennis courts, an indoor track, softball, baseball, and soccer fields, and areas for track. **Graduates:** From July 1, 2015 to June 30, 2016, 365 bachelor's degrees were awarded. The most popular majors were nursing (21%), biology (10%), and psychology (8%). In an average class, 24% graduate in 4 years or less, 40% graduate in 5 years or less, and 44% graduate in 6 years or less.

SERVICES: Counseling and information services are available, as is tutoring in most subjects, remedial math and writing. **Library/ Resources:** The library contains 235,026 volumes, 98,065 microform items, 9,591 audio/video tapes/CDs/DVDs, and subscribes to 29,992 periodicals including electronic. Computerized library services include interlibrary loans, database searching, Internet access, and Wi-Fi capability. Special learning facilities include an art gallery, radio station, TV station, a Museum of American Architecture and Decorative Arts, Dunham Family Bible in America Museum, Museum of Southern History, and Morris Cultural Arts Center. **Physically Challenged Students:** 90% of the campus is accessible. Facilities include wheelchair ramps, elevators, special parking, specially equipped restrooms, lowered drinking fountains, lowered telephones, and special housing. **Special:** HBU offers internships through its academic colleges, B.A.-B.S. degrees, and dual majors in most areas, work-study programs, credit for military experience, and pass/fail options. There is a freshman honors program. **Visiting:** There are guides for informal visits, visitors may sit in on classes, and stay overnight. To schedule a visit, contact the Office of Admissions. **Campus Safety and Security:** Measures include 24-hour foot and vehicle patrol, emergency notification system, security escort services, emergency telephones and lighted pathways/sidewalks.

REQUIREMENTS: The ACT Optional Writing test is required, along with a satisfactory score on the SAT or an ACT composite score of 20. One counselor or teacher written recommendation, and an official high school transcript or GED scores are also required. AP and CLEP credits are accepted. Important factors in the admissions decision are recommendations by school officials, personality/intangible qualities, and advanced placement or honors courses. To graduate, students must complete a minimum of 130 semester hours, including at least 48 semester hours of upper-level courses and 24 to 36 hours in the major. They must complete courses in Christianity, written and oral communications, math, lab science, computer, kinetics, social and behavioral sciences, humanities, and fine arts. No grade below "C" within majors and program requirements and a cumulative GPA of 2.0 is required. Proficiency is required in reading, computer, communication, and math. Spiritual Life Program participation is also a graduation requirement. **Procedure:** Freshmen are admitted to all sessions. Entrance exams should be taken in the fall of the senior year. There are early decision and rolling admissions plans. Application deadlines are open. Application fee is $25. Applications are accepted online. **Transfer Students:** 334 transfer students enrolled in 2015-2016. Applicants with fewer than 30 semester hours earned must submit high school and college transcripts and SAT or ACT scores. All students must have a minimum 2.0 GPA and submit all previous college transcripts. 32 of 130 credits required for the bachelor's degree must be completed at HBU. **International Students:** There are 110 international students enrolled. They must take the TOEFL with a minimum score of 550 on the paper-based TOEFL (PBT) or 80 on the Internet-based version (iBT), or the IELTS.

ADMISSIONS: The SAT scores for the 2016-2017 freshman class were: Critical Reading-- 37% below 500, 38% between 500 and 599, 22% between 600 and 699, and 3% between 700 and 800. Math-- 35% below 500, 41% between 500 and 599, 22% between 600 and 699, and 2% between 700 and 800. Writing-- 39% below 500, 40% between 500 and 599, 17% between 600 and 699, and 4% between 700 and 800. The ACT scores were 40% below 12, 30% between 12 and 17, 16% between 18 and 23, 8% between 24 and 29, and 6% above 30. 38% of the current freshmen were in the top fifth of their class; 67% were in the top two fifths. **Admissions Contact:** Eduardo Borges, Director of Admissions. Email: *admissions@hbu.edu* Web: *www.hbu.edu*

FINANCIAL AID: In 2016-2017, 90% of all full-time freshmen and 79% of continuing full-time students received some form of financial aid. 27% of all full-time freshmen and continuing full-time students received need-based aid. The average freshman award was $14,957. Need-based scholarships or need-based grants averaged $9,941 ($22,941 maximum); need-based self-help aid (loans and jobs) averaged $5,352 ($9,000 maximum); non-need-based athletic scholarships averaged $13,994 ($25,671 maximum); and other non-need-based awards and non-need-based scholarships averaged $7,613 ($23,203 maximum). 100% of undergraduate students work part-time. Average annual earnings from campus work are $867. The average financial indebtedness of the 2016 graduate was $23,000. The college's own financial statement is required. The FAFSA code is 003576. The priority date for freshman financial aid applications for fall entry is March 1. The filing deadline for fall entry is April 15.

HOWARD PAYNE UNIVERSITY C-3

www.hputx.edu

Brownwood, TX 76801	(325) 649-8020 (800) 880-4478
Fax: (325) 649-8901	**Email:** pgrambling@hputx.edu
Full-time: 516 men, 435 women	**Faculty:** 84
Part-time: 53 men, 59 women	**Ph.D.s:** 49%
Graduate: 58 men, 26 women	**Student/Faculty:** 10 to 1
Year: semesters, summer session	**Tuition:** $26,630
Room & Board: $7690	**Freshman Class:** 1076 applied, 763 accepted, 478 enrolled
SAT: required **ACT:** 21	**CEEB CODE:** 6278
Application Deadline: March 15	**COMPETITIVE**

Howard Payne University, founded in 1889, and affiliated with the Baptist General Convention of Texas, offers undergraduate programs in the arts and sciences, business administration, education, Christianity, music, and social sciences. The figures in the above capsule and in this profile are approximate. There are 6 undergraduate schools. In addition to regional accreditation, HPU has baccalaureate program accreditation with CSWE, NASM, IACBE, and SACSCC. The 29-acre campus is in a rural area 150 miles from Dallas, 77 miles from Abilene. Including any residence halls, there are 31 buildings.

STUDENT LIFE: 96% of undergraduates are from Texas. Others are from 18 states, and 2 foreign countries. 93% are from public schools. 74% are White; 6% African American; 14% Hispanic; 1% Asian American; 1% American Indian/Alaska Native; 1% Foreign. 85% are Protestant. **Male To Female Ratio:** 1.2:1. The average age of freshmen is 18; all undergraduates, 22. 40% do not continue beyond their first year; 33% remain to graduate. **Housing:** 764 students can be accommodated in college housing, which includes single-sex dorms, on-campus apartments, and married student housing. On-campus housing is available on a lottery system for upperclassmen. 59% of students live on campus; of those, 50% remain on campus on weekends. All students may keep cars. Alcohol is not permitted.

FACULTY/CLASSROOMS: 64% of faculty are male; 36% are female. All teach undergraduates. No introductory courses are taught by graduate students. The average class size in an introductory lecture is 22; in a laboratory is 20; and in a regular course is 18.

PROGRAMS OF STUDY: HPU confers B.A., B.S., B.A.A.S., B.B.A., and B.M. degrees. Associate degrees are also awarded. Bachelor's degrees are awarded in BIOLOGICAL SCIENCE (biology/biological science), BUSINESS (accounting and business administration and management), COMMUNICATIONS AND THE ARTS (art, communications, dramatic arts, English, multimedia, music, and Spanish), COMPUTER AND PHYSICAL SCIENCE (chemistry, computer science, and mathematics), EDUCATION (athletic training, elementary education, secondary education, and teaching English as a second/foreign language (TESOL/TEFOL)), ENGINEERING AND ENVIRONMENTAL DESIGN (occupational safety and health), HEALTH PROFESSIONS (exercise science), SOCIAL SCIENCE (Christian studies, history, liberal arts/general studies, political science/government, psychology, social work, and sociology). Biology, chemistry, and political science are the strongest academically. Business management, elementary education, and exercise & sports science have the largest enrollments.

ACTIVITIES: 14% of men belong to 5 local fraternities; 17% of women belong to 6 local sororities. There are 33 groups on campus, including art, band, cheerleading, choir, chorus, drama, drill team, ethnic, honors, jazz band, literary magazine, marching band, musical theater, newspaper, photography, professional, radio and TV, religious, social, social service, student government, and yearbook. Popular campus events include S.W.A.R.M. Day, Spring Street Party, Spring Sing, Paynt Rave, Impact Day, Meet the Greeks, Family Weekend, Christian Concerts, HPU Feast, and College Preview Weekends. **Sports:** There are 5 intercollegiate sports for men and 5 for women, and 5 intramural sports for men and 5 for women. Facilities include a stadium, an auditorium, basketball and volleyball courts, an indoor walking track, free weights & exercise equipment, tennis, football and non tackle, golf, soccer, tennis and table tennis, baseball and softball. **Graduates:** From July 1, 2015 to June 30, 2016, 240 bachelor's degrees were awarded. The most popular majors were business/marketing (20%), education (19%), and Theology and religious vocations (9%). In an average class, 2% graduate in 3 years or less, 23% graduate in 4 years or less, 34% graduate in 5 years or less, and 46% graduate in 6 years or less. Of the 2015 graduating class, 20% were enrolled in graduate school within 6 months of graduation.

SERVICES: Counseling and information services are available, as is tutoring in some subjects, and remedial math, reading, and writing. A writing lab and computer lab are also available for English, math, and computer science. **Library/Resources:** The library contains 118,825 volumes, 271,542 microform items, and subscribes to 30,598 periodicals including electronic. Computerized library services include interlibrary loans, database searching, Internet access, and Wi-Fi capability. Special learning facilities include a radio station, a children's literature center, audio production facility, TV production studio, and video editing facility, an art center, and a center for social justice. **Physically Challenged Students:** 90% of the campus is accessible. Facilities include wheelchair ramps, elevators, special parking, specially equipped restrooms, special class scheduling, and lowered drinking fountains. **Special:** Cross-registration is offered with several hospitals, and internships are available in many fields. HPU offers credit for experience for B.A.A.S. candidates only, study abroad in Israel and England, pass/fail options, and work-study programs. Special programs include the Douglas MacArthur Academy of Freedom, an interdisciplinary honors program in the social sciences, a chemistry honors program, and a provisional program for underprepared students. There are 4 national honor societies, a freshman honors program, and 1 departmental honors program. **Visiting:** There are regularly scheduled orientations for prospective students, including college preview weekends in the fall and spring. There are guides for informal visits, visitors may sit in on classes, and stay overnight. To schedule a visit, contact the Enrollment Services Office. **Campus Safety and Security:** There are emergency telephones, lighted pathways/sidewalks, 12-hour foot patrols, 2 security seminars for the entire campus, and 24-hour telephone availability with on-duty officers carrying cell phones.

REQUIREMENTS: The SAT or ACT is required. Applicants must be graduates of an accredited secondary school or have a GED. It is recommended that they have completed 4 units each in English, math, science with 3 units of lab, 3 units of social studies, and 2 units of foreign language and history, .5 in computer science, 1 unit in visual/performing arts, and 4.5 in any academic electives. Graduates of high schools or home study programs that are not accredited by a regional or state accrediting agency will have their work reviewed by the admissions committee on an individual basis. An interview may be required by the admissions committee for select applicants. Audition required for the music program. A GPA of 3.0 is required. AP and CLEP credits are accepted. Important factors in the admissions decision are leadership record, recommendations by school officials, and personality/intangible qualities. To graduate, students must complete a minimum of 128 credit hours, 49 in general education courses, 30 to 36 in the major, and 18 to 24 in a minor, plus electives. A minimum 2.0 GPA is required. The general education core includes Bible, English, social science, computer science, fine arts, phys ed, lab science, speech, and math courses. Requirements for students not obtaining the B.A. or B.S. vary. All students must complete 6 semester credits of chapel/convocation attendance. **Procedure:** Freshmen are admitted to all sessions. Entrance exams should be taken during the senior year. There are early admissions and rolling admissions plans. Applications should be filed by March 15 for fall entry, along with a $25 fee. Notifications are sent October 15. **Transfer Students:** 67 transfer students enrolled in 2015-2016. Transfer students must be able to return to the university they are leaving and submit official transcripts from all previously attended colleges/universities. Students younger than 21 with fewer than 12 semester hours must submit the SAT or ACT scores. The same GPA per number of hours attempted is required of transfers as for continuing HPU students. 32 of 128 credits required for the bachelor's degree must be completed at HPU. **International Students:** There are 11 international students enrolled. The school actively recruits these students. They must take the TOEFL with a minimum score of 79 on the Internet-based version (iBT). A TOEFL score is not required for International students entering the English as a Second Language (ESL) pro. Students must score 19 on the ACT or 830 on the SAT for unconditional admission; otherwise, a provisional program may be available.

ADMISSIONS: 71% of the 2016-2017 applicants were accepted. The SAT scores for the 2016-2017 freshman class were: Critical Reading-- 62% below 500, 28% between 500 and 599, 8% between 600 and 699, and 2% between 700 and 800. Math-- 58% below 500, 34% between 500 and 599, and 8% between 600 and 699. The ACT scores were 20% between 12 and 17, 56% between 18 and 23, 20% between 24 and 29, and 4% above 30. 32% of the current freshmen were in the top fifth of their class; 60% were in the top two fifths. 4 freshmen graduated first in their class. **Admissions Contact:** PJ Grambling, Director of Admission. Email: *pgrambling@hputx.edu* Web: *www.hputx.edu*

FINANCIAL AID: The average freshman award was $19,529. Need-based scholarships or need-based grants averaged $17,215; need-based self-help aid (loans and jobs) averaged $5,817; other non-need-based awards and non-need-based scholarships averaged $3,412; and $13,487 from other forms of aid. 65% of undergraduate students work part-time. Average annual earnings from campus work are $2000. The FAFSA code is 003575. The deadline for filing freshman financial aid applications for fall entry is March 1.

HUSTON-TILLOTSON UNIVERSITY *(The complete profile is made available exclusively on our website, www.barronspac.com)*

JARVIS CHRISTIAN COLLEGE *(The complete profile is made available exclusively on our website, www.barronspac.com)*

LAMAR UNIVERSITY *(The complete profile is made available exclusively on our website, www.barronspac.com)*

LETOURNEAU UNIVERSITY — E-2

www.letu.edu

Longview, TX 75607	(903) 233-3000 (800) 759-8811
Fax: (903) 233-3411	Email: admissions@letu.edu
Full-time: 831 men, 367 women	**Faculty:** n/av
Part-time: 431 men, 624 women	**Ph.D.s:** 76%
Graduate: 65 men, 403 women	**Student/Faculty:** 14 to 1
Year: semesters, summer session	**Tuition:** $28,480
Room & Board: $9770	**Freshman Class:** 1842 applied, 814 accepted, 286 enrolled **CEEB CODE:** 6365
Application Deadline: n/av	**VERY COMPETITIVE**

LeTourneau University is a Christ-centered, interdenominational university with a wide array of undergraduate and graduate degree programs in the College of Engineering, Business and Technology, the College of Aviation & Aeronautical Science, the College of College of Education, Arts and Sciences, and the College of Health Sciences & Professional Studies. Students are also enrolled in a robust suite of online programs, as well as the university's innovative hybrid programs in Dallas and Houston. LETU offers more than 90 programs that prepare students for success in aviation, biblical studies, business, communication, criminal justice, education, engineering, nursing, human services, kinesiology, liberal arts, psychology and science. Graduate programs in business administration, counseling, education, engineering, health care administration, marriage and family therapy, psychology and strategic leadership. Committed to its core mission, LeTourneau University is where educators engage learners to nurture Christian virtue, to develop competency and ingenuity in their professional fields, to integrate faith and work, and to serve the local and global community. The university is also led by its vision: claiming every workplace in every nation as their mission field, LeTourneau University graduates are professionals of ingenuity and Christ-like character who see life's work as a holy calling with eternal impact. In every lab, airplane and classroom, LETU builds on the legacy of our university founder, the legendary entrepreneur and inventor R.G. LeTourneau, by preparing students for a lifetime spent fusing their faith with their work and ingeniously approaching their careers to make a practical impact with innovative solutions to global challenges. LETU students benefit from small classes and outstanding faculty dedicated to providing personal attention and hands-on, collaborative learning opportunities to apply knowledge in practical and powerful ways. All freshman engineering students build their own 3D printers. Engineering students are building human-powered water pumps for farmers in Senegal and designing livable shelters for the homeless in Haiti. Biology students are researching ways to improve wheelchair functionality in rough-terrain environments. Our aviation program is a past recipient of the Loening Trophy, which recognizes the most outstanding collegiate aviation program in the nation. LETU is where excellent career preparation and Christian convictions collide. Students graduate with hands-on skills that employers demand. Our placement rates prove it. They carry their incredible ingenuity and faith into countless nations and workplaces including John Deere, American Airlines, US Steel, Boeing, Apple, Garmin, Google and countless classrooms, mission fields, and more. There are 8 undergraduate schools and 1 graduate school. In addition to regional accreditation, LeTourneau has baccalaureate program accreditation with ABET and BON. The 162-acre campus is in a small town 60 miles west of Shreveport, Louisiana, and 120 miles east of the Dallas/Fort Worth metroplex.

STUDENT LIFE: 69% of undergraduates are from Texas. Others are from 50 states, 30 foreign countries, and Canada. 57% are White; 14% African American; 10% Hispanic; 7% race unknown; 5% two or more races; 4% Foreign; 2% Asian American; 1% American Indian/Alaska Native. **Female To Male Ratio:** 1.1:1. The average age of freshmen is 19; all undergraduates, 26. **Housing:** College-sponsored housing includes single-sex dorms, on-campus apartments, married student housing, and special-interest houses. On-campus housing is guaranteed for all 4 years. 70% of students live on campus. All students may keep cars. Alcohol is not permitted.

FACULTY/CLASSROOMS: 65% of faculty are male; 35% are female. No introductory courses are taught by graduate students.

PROGRAMS OF STUDY: LeTourneau confers B.A., B.S. and B.B.A. degrees. Associate and master's degrees are also awarded. Bachelor's degrees are awarded in BIOLOGICAL SCIENCE (biology/biological science), BUSINESS (accounting, business administration and management, management information systems, marketing management, and marketing/retailing/merchandising), COMMUNICATIONS AND THE ARTS (English), COMPUTER AND PHYSICAL SCIENCE (chemistry, computer mathematics, computer science, and mathematics), EDUCATION (business education, elementary education, physical education, science education, and secondary education), ENGINEERING AND ENVIRONMENTAL DESIGN (aeronautical science, aeronautical technology, computer engineering, computer technology, electrical/electronics engineering, engineering, engineering technology, industrial administration/management, mechanical engineering, and welding engineering), HEALTH PROFESSIONS (health, nursing, premedicine, and preveterinary science), SOCIAL SCIENCE (biblical studies, history, interdisciplinary studies, prelaw, psychology, and public administration).

ACTIVITIES: There are no fraternities or sororities. Groups on campus include chorale, drama, film, honors, international, jazz band, religious, student government, and yearbook. **Sports:** There are 6 intercollegiate sports for men and 7 for women. **Graduates:** From July 1, 2015 to June 30, 2016, 428 bachelor's degrees were awarded. The most popular majors were business (25%), engineering (24%), and education (10%).

SERVICES: Counseling and information services are available, as is

tutoring in every subject. and remedial math and writing. **Library/Resources:** Computerized library services include interlibrary loans, database searching, Internet access, and Wi-Fi capability. **Physically Challenged Students:** Facilities include wheelchair ramps, elevators, special parking, specially equipped restrooms, special class scheduling, lowered drinking fountains, lowered telephones, special housing, and automated doors. **Special:** There is a freshman honors program. **Visiting:** There are regularly scheduled orientations for prospective students, visits are individualized and may include touring the school, attending classes, special events, or chapel, meeting with faculty and financial aid personnel, and staying in a dorm. There are guides for informal visits, visitors may sit in on classes, and stay overnight. **Campus Safety and Security:** Measures include 24-hour foot and vehicle patrol, emergency notification system, self-defense education, security escort services, lighted pathways/sidewalks, and controlled access to dorms/residences.

REQUIREMENTS: AP and CLEP credits are accepted. **Procedure:** Freshmen are admitted in the fall, spring, and summer. There are deferred admissions and rolling admissions plans. Application deadlines are open. Applications are accepted online. **Transfer Students:** 193 transfer students enrolled in 2015-2016. **International Students:** The school actively recruits these students. They must take the TOEFL with a minimum score of 525 on the paper-based TOEFL (PBT) or 80 on the Internet-based version (iBT).

ADMISSIONS: 44% of the 2016-2017 applicants were accepted. The SAT scores for the 2016-2017 freshman class were: Critical Reading-- 21% below 500, 41% between 500 and 599, 29% between 600 and 699, and 10% between 700 and 800. Math-- 16% below 500, 41% between 500 and 599, 33% between 600 and 699, and 11% between 700 and 800. Writing-- 34% below 500, 40% between 500 and 599, 22% between 600 and 699, and 3% between 700 and 800. The ACT scores were 5% between 12 and 17, 33% between 18 and 23, 43% between 24 and 29, and 20% above 30. **Admissions Contact:** Mike VanBrocklin, Director of Admissions. Email: *admissions@letu.edu* Web: *www.letu.edu*

FINANCIAL AID: LeTourneau is a member of CSS. The FAFSA code is 003584. Check with the school for current application deadlines.

LUBBOCK CHRISTIAN UNIVERSITY B-2

www.lcu.edu

Lubbock, TX 79407 | (806) 720-7155
(800) 933-7601

Fax: 806-720-7162 | **Email:** admissions@lcu.edu
Full-time: 525 men, 742 women | **Faculty:** 86
Part-time: 63 men, 141 women | **Ph.D.s:** 72%
Graduate: 91 men, 350 women | **Student/Faculty:** 12 to 1
Year: semesters, summer session | **Tuition:** $21,166
Room & Board: $7260 | **Freshman Class:** 815 applied, 812 accepted, 320 enrolled
SAT CR/M/W: 560/506/453 **ACT:** 22 | **CEEB CODE:** 6378
Application Deadline: August 15 | **COMPETITIVE**

Lubbock Christian University, founded in 1957 is affiliated with the Churches of Christ. LCU offers undergraduate degrees in liberal arts and professional studies, and graduate degrees in Biblical studies and education, behavioral sciences, and nursing. There are 4 undergraduate schools and 2 graduate schools. In addition to regional accreditation, LCU has baccalaureate program accreditation with CSWE, ACEN, and Texas Education Agency Educator Cert. and Standard. The 65-acre campus is in a suburban area 350 miles from Dallas and 325 miles from Albuquerque. Including any residence halls, there are 37 buildings.

STUDENT LIFE: 90% of undergraduates are from Texas. Others are from 34 states, 20 foreign countries, and Canada. 83% are from public schools. 68% are White; 6% African American; 22% Hispanic; 2% Foreign; 1% Asian American; 1% American Indian/Alaska Native. 53% are Protestant; 12% Catholic. **Female To Male Ratio:** 1.8:1. The average age of freshmen is 18; all undergraduates, 23. 35% do not continue beyond their first year; 65% remain to graduate. **Housing:** 589 students can be accommodated in college housing, which includes single-sex dorms, on-campus apartments, and married student housing. On-campus housing is guaranteed for the freshman year only, and is available on a first-come, and first-served basis. 63% of students commute. All students may keep cars. Alcohol is not permitted.

FACULTY/CLASSROOMS: 52% of faculty are male; 48% are female. All teach undergraduates. No introductory courses are taught by graduate students. The average class size in an introductory lecture is 17; in a laboratory is 13; and in a regular course is 13.

PROGRAMS OF STUDY: LCU confers B.A., B.S., B.B.A., B.F.A., B.M., B.S.I.S., B.S.N. and B.S.W. degrees. Associate and master's degrees are also awarded. Bachelor's degrees are awarded in AGRICULTURE (animal science and natural resource management), BIOLOGICAL SCIENCE (biochemistry and biology/biological science), BUSINESS (accounting, banking and finance, business administration and management, finance, marketing, organizational leadership and management, personal financial planning, and sports management), COMMUNICATIONS AND THE ARTS (communications, communications technology, literature, music, music business management, and theatre arts), COMPUTER AND PHYSICAL SCIENCE (chemistry, digital arts/technology, information sciences and systems, and mathematics), EDUCATION (art education, athletic training, early childhood education, elementary education, middle school education, music education, physical education, secondary education, and Spanish education K-12), ENGINEERING AND ENVIRONMENTAL DESIGN (engineering), HEALTH PROFESSIONS (exercise science, health promotion, medical technology, music therapy, nursing, premedicine, prepharmacy, prephysical therapy, and sports psychology), SOCIAL SCIENCE (biblical studies, criminal justice, economics, family/consumer studies, history, humanities, ministries, missions, physical fitness/movement, prelaw, psychology, social work, and youth ministry). Education, nursing, and business are the strongest academically. Early childhood education, nursing, and secondary education have the largest enrollments.

ACTIVITIES: 19% of men belong to 3 local fraternities; 17% of women belong to 4 local sororities. There are 32 groups on campus, including art, band, cheerleading, choir, chorus, drama, ethnic, honors, international, jazz band, musical theater, newspaper, pep band, political, professional, radio and TV, religious, social, social service, student government, symphony, and yearbook. Popular campus events include Master Follies, Family Weekend, and Spiritual Renewal Week. **Sports:** There are 5 intercollegiate sports for men and 5 for women, and 7 intramural sports for men and 8 for women. Facilities include a recreation center for intramural and phys ed activities with an indoor track, a rock wall, basketball courts, volleyball, futsball, ping pong, and a fitness center. **Graduates:** From July 1, 2015 to June 30, 2016, 378 bachelor's degrees were awarded. The most popular majors were nursing (23%), early childhood education (8%), and psychology (5%). In an average class, 2% graduate in 3 years or less, 29% graduate in 4 years or less, 36% graduate in 5 years or less, and 39% graduate in 6 years or less. Of the 2015 graduating class, 10% were enrolled in graduate school within 6 months of graduation.

SERVICES: Counseling and information services are available, as is tutoring in every subject, a reader service for the blind, and remedial math, reading, and writing. **Library/Resources:** The library contains 125,715 volumes, 47 audio/video tapes/CDs/DVDs, and subscribes to 256 periodicals including electronic. Computerized library services include interlibrary loans, database searching, Internet access, and Wi-Fi capability. Special learning facilities include an art gallery and radio station. **Physically Challenged Students:** Facilities include wheelchair ramps, elevators, special parking, specially equipped restrooms, special class scheduling, and lowered drinking fountains. **Special:** LCU offers co-op programs in engineering, medical technology, and criminal justice, internships in several fields, and cross-registration with Texas Tech University and other regional schools. A general studies degree, nondegree study, and pass/fail options are also available. A 3-2 engineering degree with Texas Tech University is offered. There are 3 national honor societies, a freshman honors program, and 1 departmental honors program. **Visiting:** There are regularly scheduled orientations for prospective students. There are guides for informal visits, visitors may sit in on classes, and stay overnight. To schedule a visit, contact LCU Admissions. **Campus Safety and Security:** Measures include 24-hour foot and vehicle patrol, emergency notification system, security escort services, lighted pathways/sidewalks, and controlled access to dorms/residences.

REQUIREMENTS: Applicants must be graduates of an accredited secondary school or have a GED certificate. Unconditional admission is granted to freshmen who score 18 or higher on the ACT or 860 or higher on the SAT and who meet all other admission requirements. AP and CLEP credits are accepted. Important factors in the admissions decision are personality/intangible qualities, parents or siblings attended your school, and geographical diversity. To graduate, students must complete 120 credit hours, including at least 39 in upper-division courses, 18 in the major, and 15 in residence after achieving senior status, with a minimum GPA of 2.25 overall and 2.5 in the major. All students must fulfill general education and biblical studies course requirements, including courses in English, math, history, science, communication, computer science, and exercise science. The core curriculum totals 45 hours. **Procedure:** Freshmen are admitted in the fall, spring, and summer. Entrance exams should be taken before registration. There is a rolling admissions plan. Applications should be filed by August 15 for fall entry, along with a $25 fee. Applications are accepted online. **Transfer Students:** 190 transfer students enrolled in 2015-2016. Transfer students with fewer than 16 hours of college credit must meet freshman admission requirements. All transfers must submit an official transcript from previously attended colleges or universities and be in good academic standing. Only courses with a grade of C or above are transferred from another institution. 30 of 126 credits required for the bachelor's degree must be completed at LCU. **International Students:** There are 39 international students enrolled. They must take the TOEFL with a minimum score of 525 on the paper-based TOEFL (PBT) or 71 on the Internet-based version (iBT), or take the MELAB. They must also take the SAT or ACT, scoring 18.

ADMISSIONS: 100% of the 2016-2017 applicants were accepted. The SAT scores for the 2016-2017 freshman class were: Critical Reading-- 53% below 500, 27% between 500 and 599, 15% between 600 and 699, and 11% between 700 and 800. Math-- 57% below 500, 27% between 500 and 599, 11% between 600 and 699, and 5% between 700 and 800. Writing-- 66% below 500 and 33% between 600 and 699. The ACT scores were 10% between 12 and 17, 48% between 18 and 23, 38% between 24 and 29, and 4% above 30. 32% of the current freshmen were in the top fifth of their class; 57% were in the top two fifths. 11 freshmen graduated first in their class. **Admissions Contact:** Chris Hayes, Director of Recruiting. Email: *admissions@lcu.edu* Web: *www.lcu.edu*

FINANCIAL AID: In 2016-2017, 74% of all full-time freshmen and 72% of continuing full-time students received some form of financial aid. 73% of all full-time freshmen and 69% of continuing full-time students received need-based aid. The average freshman award was $14,608. Need-based scholarships or need-based grants averaged $10,699; need-based self-help aid (loans and jobs) averaged $4,481; non-need-based athletic scholarships averaged $14,394; and other non-need-based awards and non-need-based scholarships averaged $5,893. 15% of undergraduate students work part-time. Average annual earnings from campus work are $1241. The average financial indebtedness of the 2016 graduate was $25,761. The college's own financial statement is required. The FAFSA code is 003586. The priority date for freshman financial aid applications for fall entry is June 1.

MCMURRY UNIVERSITY *(The complete profile is made available exclusively on our website, www.barronspac.com)*

MIDWESTERN STATE UNIVERSITY D-2

www.mwsu.edu

Wichita Falls, TX 76308	(940) 397-4334 (800) 842-1922
Fax: (940) 397-4672	**Email:** admissions@mwsu.edu
Full-time: 1745 men, 2310 women	**Faculty:** 236
Part-time: 498 men, 724 women	**Ph.D.s:** 68%
Graduate: 264 men, 472 women	**Student/Faculty:** 18 to 1
Year: semesters, summer session	**Tuition:** $9560
Room & Board: $8012	**Freshman Class:** 2854 applied, 2169 accepted, 826 enrolled
SAT CR/M/W: 495/500/465 **ACT:** 22	**CEEB CODE:** 6408
Application Deadline: August 7	**COMPETITIVE**

Midwestern State University, founded in 1922, is a public liberal arts institution offering courses in business administration, education, fine arts, health sciences, humanities, math and science, political science and public administration, and social and behavioral sciences. The figres in the above capsule and in this profile are approximate. There are 6 undergraduate schools and 5 graduate schools. In addition to regional accreditation, MSU has baccalaureate program accreditation with ABET, ACBSP, ADA, NASM, NCATE, and NLN. The 172-acre campus is in an urban area 135 miles northwest of Dallas. Including any residence halls, there are 31 buildings.

STUDENT LIFE: 92% of undergraduates are from Texas. Others are from 50 states, 40 foreign countries, and Canada. 9% are Hispanic; 67% White; 5% Foreign; 4% Asian American; 13% African American; 1% American Indian/Alaska Native. **Female To Male Ratio:** 1.4:1. The average age of freshmen is 18; all undergraduates, 24. 28% do not continue beyond their first year; 30% remain to graduate. **Housing:** 733 students can be accommodated in college housing, which includes single-sex and coed dorms, on-campus apartments, off-campus apartments, married student housing, honors houses, and theme housing. On-campus housing is guaranteed for the freshman year only, is available on a first-come, and first-served basis. Priority is given to out-of-town students. 72% of students commute. All students may keep cars. Alcohol is not permitted.

FACULTY/CLASSROOMS: 50% of faculty are male; 50% are female. All teach undergraduates. Graduate students teach 10% of introductory courses. The average class size in an introductory lecture is 25; in a laboratory is 20; and in a regular course is 25.

PROGRAMS OF STUDY: MSU confers B.A., B.S., B.A.A.S., B.B.A., B.F.A., B.M., B.S.C.J., B.S.D.H., B.S.I.S., B.S.M.T., B.S.N., B.S.R.C., B.S.R.S. and B.S.W. degrees. Associate and master's degrees are also awarded. Bachelor's degrees are awarded in BIOLOGICAL SCIENCE (biology/biological science), BUSINESS (accounting, banking and finance, business administration and management, business economics, international economics, management science, and marketing/retailing/merchandising), COMMUNICATIONS AND THE ARTS (communications, dramatic arts, English, fine arts, music, and Spanish), COMPUTER AND PHYSICAL SCIENCE (chemical technology, chemistry, computer science, geology, information sciences and systems, and mathematics), EDUCATION (music education and physical education), ENGINEERING AND ENVIRONMENTAL DESIGN (engineering technology, environmental science, manufacturing engineering, and preengineering), HEALTH PROFESSIONS (dental hygiene, health care administration, health science, medical laboratory technology, nursing, predentistry, premedicine, prepharmacy, preveterinary science, radiological science, and respiratory therapy), SOCIAL SCIENCE (criminal justice, economics, history, humanities, interdisciplinary studies, political science/government, prelaw, psychology, social work, and sociology). Business, and nursing have the largest enrollments.

ACTIVITIES: 8% of men belong to 6 national fraternities; 10% of women belong to 6 national sororities. There are 102 groups on campus, including art, band, cheerleading, choir, chorale, chorus, computers, dance, drama, environmental, ethnic, honors, international, jazz band, literary magazine, marching band, newspaper, pep band, political, professional, radio and TV, religious, social, social service, student government, and symphony. Popular campus events include Family Day, Spirit Days, and College Day Preview. **Sports:** There are 4 intercollegiate sports for men and 4 for women, and 18 intramural sports for men and 21 for women. Facilities include a gym, soccer stadium, tennis courts, an indoor swimming pool, a sand volleyball court, and a walking track. **Graduates:** From July 1, 2015 to June 30, 2016, 993 bachelor's degrees were awarded. The most popular majors were health professions and related sciences (32%), business/marketing (17%), and interdisciplinary studies (13%). In an average class, 10% graduate in 4 years or less, 22% graduate in 5 years or less, and 44% graduate in 6 years or less.

SERVICES: Counseling and information services are available, as is tutoring in some subjects, such as algebra, sciences, and history. There is also a reader service for the blind, as well as remedial math, reading, and writing. **Library/Resources:** The library contains 241,000 volumes, 158,000 microform items, and 6,757 audio/video tapes/CDs/DVDs, and subscribes to 1,100 periodicals including electronic. Computerized library services include interlibrary loans and database searching. Special learning facilities include an art gallery, planetarium, radio station, TV station, greenhouse, and TTVN studio. **Physically Challenged Students:** 99% of the campus is accessible. Facilities include wheelchair ramps, elevators, special parking, specially equipped restrooms, special class scheduling, lowered drinking fountains, lowered telephones, and special housing. **Special:** An exchange program with the Monterrey Institute of Technology, internships with local firms and agencies, and study abroad in London are available. Dual majors, co-op programs in all majors, a general studies degree, credit for military experience, and nondegree study up to 12 hours are also offered. There are 23 national honor societies and a freshman honors program. **Visiting:** There are regularly scheduled orientations for prospective students, consisting of a college day preview each February, which introduces high school juniors, seniors, and their parents to the campus and faculty. There are also daily tours. There are guides for informal visits, visitors may sit in on classes, and stay overnight. To schedule a visit, contact the Admissions Office. **Campus Safety and Security:** Measures include 24-hour foot and vehicle patrol, self-defense education, lighted pathways/sidewalks, and seminars on safety and living on campus.

REQUIREMENTS: The minimum required composite score on the SAT or ACT is dependent on class rank. For students in the top quarter of the class, there is no minimum requirement. High school credits should include 4 years each of English, math, social studies, and science, and 2 o foreign language, 6 units of electives, other speech .5, and P.E. 1 unit. The GED is accepted. AP and CLEP credits are accepted. All students must earn a minimum GPA of 2.0 while taking 120 semester hours, 24 in the major. Distribution requirements include 7 to 10 hours from natural science, 6 hours from a list of humanities classes, 6 from social science, and additional phys ed requirements. **Procedure:** Freshmen are admitted to all sessions. Entrance exams should be taken before applying for admission. There are early decision and rolling admissions plans. Applications should be filed by August 7 for fall entry; December 15 for spring entry; and May 15 for summer entry, along with a $25 fee. Notifications are sent September 1. Applications are accepted online. **Transfer Students:** 554 transfer students enrolled in 2015-2016. Transfer students with fewer than 18 semester hours must meet beginning freshman criteria. A minimum GPA of a 2.0, college transcripts, and a statement of good standing from prior institutions are required. Student may enroll in the fall, spring, and summer. 31 of 120 credits required for the bachelor's degree must be completed at MSU. **International Students:** The school actively recruits these students. They must take the TOEFL with a minimum score of 530 on the paper-based TOEFL (PBT). They must also take the SAT or ACT.

ADMISSIONS: 76% of the 2016-2017 applicants were accepted. The SAT scores for the 2016-2017 freshman class were: Critical Reading-- 55% below 500, 36% between 500 and 599, and 8% between 600 and 699. Math-- 45% below 500, 44% between 500 and 599, and 11% between 600 and 699. Writing-- 68% below 500, 26% between 500 and 599, 5% between 600 and 699, and 1% between 700 and 800. The ACT scores were 8% between 12 and 17, 62% between 18 and 23, 27% between 24 and 29, and 3% above 30. 29% of the current freshmen were in the top fifth of their class; 60% were in the top two fifths. **Admissions Contact:** Mark McClendon, Director Institutional Research. Email: *admissions@mwsu.edu* Web: *www.mwsu.edu*

FINANCIAL AID: In 2016-2017, 45% of all full-time freshmen and 49% of continuing full-time students received some form of financial aid. 38% of all full-time freshmen and 44% of continuing full-time students received need-based aid. The average freshman award was $10,632. Need-based scholarships or need-based grants averaged $8,369; need-based self-help aid (loans and jobs) averaged $5,223; non-need-based athletic scholarships averaged $6,632; other non-need-based awards and non-need-based scholarships averaged $5,177; and $2,033 from other forms of aid. The average financial indebtedness of the 2016 graduate was $28,867. MSU is a member of CSS. The college's own financial statement is required. The FAFSA code is 003592. The priority date for freshman financial aid applications for fall entry is March 1.

OUR LADY OF THE LAKE UNIVERSITY *(The complete profile is made available exclusively on our website, www.barronspac.com)*

PAUL QUINN COLLEGE *(The complete profile is made available exclusively on our website, www.barronspac.com)*

PRAIRIE VIEW A&M UNIVERSITY *(The complete profile is made available exclusively on our website, www.barronspac.com)*

RICE UNIVERSITY E-3

William Marsh Rice University
www.rice.edu

Houston, TX 77251 **(713) 348-7423**
(800) 527-OWLS
Fax: (713) 348-5952 **Email: admission@rice.edu**

Full-time: 1998 men, 1795 women
Part-time: 27 men, 19 women
Graduate: 598 men, 308 women
Year: semesters, summer session
Room & Board: $13,750
Faculty: 665; I, ++$
Ph.D.s: 97%
Student/Faculty: 6 to 1
Tuition: $43,918
Freshman Class: 17951 applied, 2865 accepted, 969 enrolled
SAT CR/M/W: 720/755/725 **ACT:** 34
Application Deadline: n/av
CEEB CODE: 6609
MOST COMPETITIVE

Rice University, founded in 1912, is a comprehensive research university offering more than 50 undergraduate and graduate programs through its schools of engineering, natural sciences, humanities, social sciences, music, and architecture. The school of business offers graduate degrees and an undergraduate minor. There are 6 undergraduate schools and 7 graduate schools. In addition to regional accreditation, Rice University has baccalaureate program accreditation with AACSB, ABET, and NAAB. The 295-acre campus is in an urban area 3 miles southwest of downtown Houston. Including any residence halls, there are 75 buildings.

STUDENT LIFE: 55% of undergraduates are from Texas. Others are from 50 states, 44 foreign countries, and Canada. 7% are African American; 6% Foreign; 48% White; 21% Asian American; 12% Hispanic; 1% American Indian/Alaska Native. 33% are Protestant; 32% claim no religious affiliation; 18% Catholic; 13% Hindu, Muslim, and unknown denomination. **Male To Female Ratio:** 1.2:1. The average age of freshmen is 19; all undergraduates, 20. 3% do not continue beyond their first year; 93% remain to graduate. **Housing:** 2080 students can be accommodated in college housing, which includes coed dorms. On-campus housing is available on a lottery system for upperclassmen. 72% of students live on campus; of those, 95% remain on campus on weekends. All students may keep cars.

FACULTY/CLASSROOMS: 69% of faculty are male; 31% are female. All teach undergraduates and do research. No introductory courses are taught by graduate students. The average class size in a regular course is 14.

PROGRAMS OF STUDY: Rice University confers B.A., B.S., B.Arch., B.F.A., B.Mus., and B.S.E degrees. Master's and doctoral degrees are also awarded. Bachelor's degrees are awarded in BIOLOGICAL SCIENCE (biology/biological science), BUSINESS (management science), COMMUNICATIONS AND THE ARTS (art history and appreciation, classics, English, linguistics, music, music history and appreciation, music performance, music theory and composition, and visual and performing arts), COMPUTER AND PHYSICAL SCIENCE (applied mathematics, chemistry, computer science, earth science, geology, geophysics and seismology, mathematics, physics, and statistics), ENGINEERING AND ENVIRONMENTAL DESIGN (architectural engineering, architecture, bioengineering, chemical engineering, civil engineering, electrical/electronics engineering, environmental engineering, and mechanical engineering), HEALTH PROFESSIONS (exercise science), SOCIAL SCIENCE (anthropology, Asian/Oriental studies, classical/ancient civilization, cognitive science, economics, French studies, German area studies, Hispanic American studies, history, medieval studies, philosophy, political science/government, psychology, public affairs, religion, sociology, and women's studies). Biochemistry & cell biology, mechanical engineering, and political science have the largest enrollments.

ACTIVITIES: There are no fraternities or sororities. There are 225 groups on campus, including art, band, cheerleading, chess, choir, chorale, chorus, computers, dance, debate, drama, environmental, ethnic, film, forensics, honors, international, jazz band, LGBT, literary magazine, marching band, musical theater, newspaper, opera, orchestra, pep band, photography, political, professional, radio and TV, religious, social, social service, student government, symphony, and yearbook. Popular campus events include Baker Shakespeare Festival, Annual Biking Relay Race, Archi Arts, and a Costume Ball. **Sports:** There are 19 intercollegiate sports for men and 18 for women, and 14 intramural sports for men and 13 for women. Facilities include a recreation center with a pool, indoor and outdoor basketball courts, an indoor soccer and hockey arena, racquetball courts, squash courts, a weight and cardio workout room, and multipurpose rooms for group fitness and dance classes, a 5000-seat gym, a pool, a track stadium, fields for soccer, lacrosse, and rugby, courts for tennis, squash, racquetball, volleyball, and basketball. **Graduates:** From July 1, 2015 to June 30, 2016, 1038 bachelor's degrees were awarded. The most popular majors were engineering (18%), social sciences (15%), and biological/life sciences (8%). In an average class, 82% graduate in 4 years or less, 92% graduate in 5 years or less, and 93% graduate in 6 years or less. Of the 2015 graduating class, 43% were enrolled in graduate school within 6 months of graduation, and 49% were employed.

SERVICES: Counseling and information services are available, as is tutoring in every subject. **Library/Resources:** The library contains 2.6 million volumes, 3.3 million microform items, 62,279 audio/video tapes/CDs/DVDs, and subscribes to 72,352 periodicals including electronic. Computerized library services include interlibrary loans, database searching, Internet access, and Wi-Fi capability. Special learning facilities include an art gallery, radio station, TV station, a media center, and an observatory. **Physically Challenged Students:** 90% of the campus is accessible. Facilities include wheelchair ramps, elevators, special parking, specially equipped restrooms, special class scheduling, lowered drinking fountains, lowered telephones, special housing, and a stair lift. **Special:** An 8-year guaranteed medical school program with the Baylor College of Medicine; a 5-year joint degree program for the B.S.E./M.S.E. in engineering; a 5-year joint degree for the B.S.E./M.B.A. in engineering and business; and a 3-2 engineering degree are possible, as are cross-registration, internships, study abroad, work-study, dual majors, and student-designed majors. There are 10 national honor societies, Phi Beta Kappa, and 9 departmental honors programs. **Visiting:** There are regularly scheduled orientations for prospective students, consisting of information sessions and tours available year-round. There are guides for informal visits, visitors may sit in on classes, and stay overnight. To schedule a visit, contact the Office of Admissions. **Campus Safety and Security:** Measures include 24-hour foot and vehicle patrol, emergency notification system, self-defense education, and security escort services. There are also shuttle buses, emergency telephones, lighted pathways/sidewalks, controlled access to dorms/residences, a campus police department, and a variety of outreach programs.

REQUIREMENTS: Official high school transcript(s), 1 counselor recommendation, and 1 teacher recommendation are required. To satisfy the testing requirement, students must submit either (a) the SAT plus 2 SAT Subject Tests or (b) the ACT with the Writing Test. Music students must arrange an audition. Architecture students must submit a portfolio. An interview is recommended but not required. Candidates should have completed 16 college preparatory units, including 4 years of English, 3 of math, or academic electives, and 2 each of social studies, foreign language, and lab science. AP credits are accepted. All students must complete at least 120 credits, with a 1.67 overall GPA and a 2.0 GPA in the major field. Distribution requirements include 12 credit/semester hours in natural sciences, social sciences, or humanities, depending on the major, and additional courses in these fields to meet distribution requirements. All students take 2 semesters of phys ed. At least 48 semester hours in upper-level courses are required. **Procedure:** Freshmen are admitted in the fall. Entrance exams should be taken no later than December of the senior year. There is a early decision plan. Early decision applications should be filed by November 1, along with a $65 fee. Notification of early decision is sent December 15; regular decision, April 1. 220 early decision candidates were accepted for the 2016-2017 class. 1659 applicants were on the 2016 waiting list; 127 were admitted. Applications are accepted online. **Transfer Students:** 42 transfer students enrolled in 2015-2016. Transfer applicants should present at least a 3.2 GPA in previous college work, SAT scores, 2 college teacher recommendations, high school and college transcripts, and a letter from the dean of their current college. 60 of 120 credits required for the bachelor's degree must be completed at Rice University. **International Students:** There are 220 international students enrolled. The school actively recruits these students. They must take the TOEFL with a minimum score of 600 on the paper-based TOEFL (PBT) or 90 on the Internet-based version (iBT). They must also take the SAT or ACT.

ADMISSIONS: 16% of the 2016-2017 applicants were accepted. The SAT scores for the 2016-2017 freshman class were: Critical Reading-- 2% below 500, 5% between 500 and 599, 24% between 600 and 699, and 69% between 700 and 800. Math-- 1% below 500, 4% between 500 and 599, 16% between 600 and 699, and 79% between 700 and 800. Writing-- 3% below 500, 5% between 500 and 599, 26% between 600 and 699, and 66% between 700 and 800. The ACT scores were 2% between 18 and 23, 9% between 24 and 29, and 90% above 30. **Admissions Contact:** Julie M. Browning, Dean for Undergraduate Enrollment. Email: *admission@rice.edu* Web: *www.rice.edu*

FINANCIAL AID: In 2016-2017, 60% of all full-time freshmen and continuing full-time students received some form of financial aid. 35% of all full-time freshmen and 37% of continuing full-time students received need-based aid. The average freshman award was $40,885. Need-based scholarships or need-based grants averaged $36,568; need-based self-help aid (loans and jobs) averaged $3,310; non-need-based athletic scholarships averaged $43,705; other non-need-based awards and non-need-based scholarships averaged $2,675; and $24,208 from other forms of aid. The average financial indebtedness of the 2016 graduate was $11,108. Rice University is a member of CSS. The CSS/Profile, and the parents' and student's tax returns are required. The FAFSA code is 003604. The priority date for freshman financial aid applications for fall entry is February 15.

SAM HOUSTON STATE UNIVERSITY D-3

www.shsu.edu

Huntsville, TX 77341 (936) 294-1845 (866) 232-7528

Fax: (936) 294-3758 **Email:** admissions@shsu.edu

Full-time: 5429 men, 7010 women
Part-time: 1041 men, 1515 women
Graduate: 911 men, 1711 women
Year: semesters, summer session
Room & Board: $8680
SAT or ACT: required
Application Deadline: August 1

Faculty: 582; IIA, av$
Ph.D.s: 95%
Student/Faculty: 20 to 1
Tuition: $10,112 ($18,583)
Freshman Class: 7070 applied, 5473 accepted, 2069 enrolled
CEEB CODE: 6643
COMPETITIVE

Sam Houston University, founded in 1879, is a public institution offering programs in fine arts and mass communication, applied sciences, business administration, criminal justice, education, and humanities and social sciences. Figures in the above capsule and in this profile are approximate. There are 6 undergraduate schools and 6 graduate schools. In addition to regional accreditation, Sam Houston State has baccalaureate program accreditation with AACSB, ABET, ADA, NASM, and NCATE. The 1256-acre campus is in a small town 70 miles north of Houston. Including any residence halls, there are 228 buildings.

STUDENT LIFE: 98% of undergraduates are from Texas. Others are from 48 states, 59 foreign countries, and Canada. 71% are White; 14% African American; 12% Hispanic; 1% Asian American; 1% American Indian/Alaska Native; 1% Foreign. **Female To Male Ratio:** 1.4:1. The average age of freshmen is 18; all undergraduates, 22. 31% do not continue beyond their first year; 40% remain to graduate. **Housing:** 3293 students can be accommodated in college housing, which includes single-sex and coed dorms, on-campus apartments, off-campus apartments, honors houses, special-interest houses, fraternity houses, and sorority houses. On-campus housing is guaranteed for all 4 years. 73% of students commute. All students may keep cars.

FACULTY/CLASSROOMS: 53% of faculty are male; 47% are female. All teach undergraduates and do research. Graduate students teach 5% of introductory courses.

PROGRAMS OF STUDY: Sam Houston State confers B.A., B.S., B.A.A.S., B.B.A., B.F.A., and B.M. degrees. Master's and doctoral degrees are also awarded. Bachelor's degrees are awarded in AGRICULTURE (agriculture, animal science, and horticulture), BIOLOGICAL SCIENCE (biology/biological science), BUSINESS (accounting, banking and finance, business administration and management, and marketing/retailing/merchandising), COMMUNICATIONS AND THE ARTS (art, dance, dramatic arts, English, French, German, graphic design, journalism, music, music performance, music theory and composition, musical theater, photography, Spanish, and speech/debate/rhetoric), COMPUTER AND PHYSICAL SCIENCE (chemistry, computer science, geology, mathematics, and physics), EDUCATION (physical education), ENGINEERING AND ENVIRONMENTAL DESIGN (environmental science), HEALTH PROFESSIONS (health, medical technology, and music therapy), SOCIAL SCIENCE (criminal justice, economics, geography, history, law enforcement and corrections, philosophy, physical fitness/movement, political science/government, psychology, and sociology). Criminal justice, general business, and psychology have the largest enrollments.

ACTIVITIES: 9% of men belong to 15 local fraternities; 5% of women belong to 13 local sororities. There are 235 groups on campus, including art, band, cheerleading, choir, chorale, chorus, computers, dance, drama, drill team, environmental, ethnic, film, forensics, honors, international, jazz band, LGBT, marching band, musical theater, newspaper, orchestra, pep band, photography, political, professional, radio and TV, religious, social, social service, student government, and symphony. Popular campus events include Organization Fair, Greek Week, and Welcome Week. **Sports:** There are 7 intercollegiate sports for men and 7 for women, and 13 intramural sports for men and 13 for women. Facilities include a stadium, a gym, basketball courts, racquetball courts, swimming pools, and weight rooms. **Graduates:** From July 1, 2015 to June 30, 2016, 3188 bachelor's degrees were awarded. The most popular majors were business/marketing (25%), homeland security (16%), and interdisciplinary studies (13%). 34 companies recruited on campus in 2015-2016. In an average class, 17% graduate in 4 years or less and 41% graduate in 6 years or less.

SERVICES: Counseling and information services are available, as is tutoring in every subject, a reader service for the blind, and remedial math, reading, and writing. **Library/Resources:** The library contains 1.3 million volumes, 3,744 audio/video tapes/CDs/DVDs, and subscribes to 7,175 periodicals including electronic. Computerized library services include interlibrary loans, database searching, Internet access, and Wi-Fi capability. Special learning facilities include a planetarium, radio station, TV station, the Sam Houston Museum. **Physically Challenged Students:** 90% of the campus is accessible. Facilities include wheelchair ramps, elevators, special parking, specially equipped restrooms, lowered drinking fountains, closed-circuit television (CCTV), computer workstations with large print and speech output capabilities, and telecommunication devices for the disabled. **Special:** Work-study programs with the university, study abroad in 6 countries, second degrees, and B.A.-B.S. degrees are available. There are 10 national honor societies and a freshman honors program. **Visiting:** There are regularly scheduled orientations for prospective students, including a tour of the campus, dorms, and departments. There are guides for informal visits. To schedule a visit, contact the Visitor Center. **Campus Safety and Security:** Measures include 24-hour foot and vehicle patrol, emergency notification system, security escort service, emergency telephones, and lighted pathways/sidewalks.

REQUIREMENTS: The SAT or ACT is required. Applicants must have secondary school credits as follows: 4 of English, 2 each of math, history, and science, 1 1/2 of phys ed, and a half credit each of social studies and health education. The GED is accepted. AP and CLEP credits are accepted. All students must maintain a GPA of 2.0 while taking 128 semester hours, including 30 in the major. The core curriculum includes 15 hours of social and behavioral sciences, 9 hours of humanities and visual and performing arts, 8 hours of natural sciences, 6 hours of communication, 4 hours of an institutionally designated option, and 3 hours of math. **Procedure:** Freshmen are admitted in the fall, spring, and summer. There are early admissions and rolling admissions plans. Applications should be filed by August 1 for fall entry. The fall 2016 application fee was $40. Notification is sent on a rolling basis. **Transfer Students:** 2153 transfer students enrolled in 2015-2016. Transfer applicants must present a 2.0 GPA on all previous college work. 42 of 128 credits required for the bachelor's degree must be completed at Sam Houston State. **International Students:** There are 105 international students enrolled. The school actively recruits these students. They must take the TOEFL with a minimum score of 550 on the paper-based TOEFL (PBT). They must also take the SAT or ACT.

ADMISSIONS: 77% of the 2016-2017 applicants were accepted. 32% of the current freshmen were in the top fifth of their class; 67% were in the top two fifths. 10 freshmen graduated first in their class. **Admissions Contact:** Donna Artho, Assistant VP Effectiveness. Email: *admissions@shsu.edu* Web: *www.shsu.edu*

FINANCIAL AID: In 2016-2017, 61% of continuing full-time students received some form of financial aid. 5% of undergraduate students work part-time. The average financial indebtedness of the 2016 graduate was $19,188. The FAFSA code is 003606. The priority date for freshman financial aid applications for fall entry is March 31. The filing deadline for fall entry is May 31.

SCHREINER UNIVERSITY *(The complete profile is made available exclusively on our website, www.barronspac.com)*

SOUTHERN METHODIST UNIVERSITY D-2

www.smu.edu

Dallas, TX 75275	**(214) 768-2058** **(800) 323-0672**
Fax: (214) 768-0103	**Email: ugadmission@smu.edu**
Full-time: 3132 men, 3162 women	**Faculty:** I, av$
Part-time: 113 men, 80 women	**Ph.D.s:** 82%
Graduate: 2724 men, 2262 women	**Student/Faculty:** n/av
Year: semesters, summer session	**Tuition:** $50,358
Room & Board: $16,125	**Freshman Class:** n/av
SAT CR/M/W: 650/670/640 **ACT:** 30	**CEEB CODE:** 6660
Application Deadline: January 15	**MOST COMPETITIVE**

Southern Methodist University, founded in 1911, is a private nonsectarian institution affiliated with the United Methodist Church. SMU offers undergraduate and graduate programs in humanities and sciences, business, arts, education, engineering and applied sciences. There are 5 undergraduate schools and 7 graduate schools. In addition to regional accreditation, SMU has baccalaureate program accreditation with AACSB, ABET, NASAD, NASM, ACS, NASD, and NAST. The 234-acre campus is in an urban area 5 miles north of downtown Dallas. Including any residence halls, there are 101 buildings.

STUDENT LIFE: 54% of undergraduates are from out of state, mostly the Southwest. Students are from 48 states, 70 foreign countries, and Canada. 46% are from public schools. 6% are African American; 6% Asian American; 58% White; 3% two or more races; 15% Foreign; 10% Hispanic; 1% race unknown. 27% are Protestant; 21% Catholic. **Male To Female Ratio:** 1.1:1. The average age of freshmen is 18; all undergraduates, 20. 10% do not continue beyond their first year; 79% remain to graduate. **Housing:** 3727 students can be accommodated in college housing, which includes coed dorms, on-campus apartments, and married student housing. In addition, there are honors houses, special-interest houses, fraternity houses, sorority houses, and living-learning communities with some classes taught in residence hall classrooms. On-campus housing is available on a first-come and first-served basis. 54% of students live on campus; of those, 85% remain on campus on weekends. All students may keep cars. Alcohol is not permitted.

FACULTY/CLASSROOMS: 59% of faculty are male; 41% are female. No introductory courses are taught by graduate students.

PROGRAMS OF STUDY: SMU confers B.A., B.S., B.B.A., B.F.A., B.M., B.S.C.P.E., B.S.C.E., B.S.E.E., B.S.Env.E. and B.S.M.E. degrees. Master's and doctoral degrees are also awarded. Bachelor's degrees are awarded in AGRICULTURE (environmental studies), BIOLOGICAL SCIENCE (biochemistry and biology/biological science), BUSINESS (accounting, business administration and management, economics – statistics, finance, finance (financial planning), insurance and risk management, management science, marketing/retailing/merchandising, real estate, and real estate finance), COMMUNICATIONS AND THE ARTS (advertising, art history and appreciation, broadcasting, communications, creative writing, dance, dramatic arts, English, film arts, fine/studio arts, general, French, German, journalism, languages, media arts, music performance, music theory and composition, performing arts, piano/organ, public relations, Spanish, sports administration, and studio art), COMPUTER AND PHYSICAL SCIENCE (chemistry, computer science, environmental geology, geology, geophysics and seismology, mathematics, physics, and statistics), EDUCATION (health education and music education), ENGINEERING AND ENVIRONMENTAL DESIGN (civil engineering, computer engineering, electrical/electronics engineering, environmental engineering, environmental science, and mechanical engineering), HEALTH PROFESSIONS (music therapy), SOCIAL SCIENCE (African American studies, anthropology, economics, history, humanities, Iberian studies, international relations, international studies, Italian studies, Latin American studies, liberal arts/general studies, medieval studies, Mexican-American/Chicano studies, philosophy, physical fitness/movement, political science/government, psychology, public affairs, religion, and sociology). Finance, mechanical engineering, and economics & finance applications have the largest enrollments.

ACTIVITIES: 28% of men belong to 15 national fraternities; 37% of women belong to 14 national sororities. There are 180 groups on campus, including art, band, cheerleading, choir, chorale, chorus, computers, dance, debate, drama, drill team, ethnic, forensics, honors, international, jazz band, LGBT, literary magazine, marching band, musical theater, opera, orchestra, pep band, photography, political, professional, religious, social, social service, student government, and symphony. Popular campus events include Celebration of Lights and Community Service Day. **Sports:** There are 6 intercollegiate sports for men and 11 for women, and 20 intramural sports for men and 20 for women. Facilities include a gym & weight rooms, a dance studio, indoor and outdoor jogging tracks, indoor and outdoor pools, an outdoor stadium, indoor stadium, and courts for basketball, volleyball, tennis, badminton, and racquetball. **Graduates:** From July 1, 2015 to June 30, 2016, 1723 bachelor's degrees were awarded. The most popular majors were economics (10%), finance (9%), and accounting (6%). In an average class, 3% graduate in 3 years or less, 68% graduate in 4 years or less, 78% graduate in 5 years or less, and 79% graduate in 6 years or less.

SERVICES: Counseling and information services are available, as is tutoring in most subjects, a reader service for the blind, and remedial reading and writing. The Learning Enhancement Center provides study skills workshops, note-taking techniques, and time management skills seminars. **Library/Resources:** The 8 libraries contain 3.1 million volumes, 2.0 million microform items, 58,145 audio/video tapes/CDs/

DVDs, and subscribe to 29,852 periodicals including electronic. Computerized library services include interlibrary loans, database searching, Internet access, and Wi-Fi capability. Special learning facilities include an art gallery, natural history museum, and TV station. Meadows Museum houses one of the finest Spanish art collections outside Spain; SMU's engineering school is the nation's first to host a Lockheed Martin Skunk Works Lab modeled after the California research facility; performance facilities include theatres with classical thrust stage, proscenium stage and black box area; journalism complex includes digital newsroom and TV studio. **Physically Challenged Students:** 95% of the campus is accessible. Facilities include wheelchair ramps, elevators, special parking, specially equipped restrooms, special class scheduling, lowered drinking fountains, lowered telephones, and automatic doors. **Special:** SMU offers a co-op program in engineering, work-study programs, B.A.-B.S. degrees, study abroad in 50 countries with 150 programs, dual majors in any combination, student-designed majors, numerous internships, and interdisciplinary majors, including economics with finance applications and economics with systems analysis. A 3-2 advanced degree in business is available, as are evening degree programs in humanities and social sciences, and teacher certification programs. There are 30 national honor societies, Phi Beta Kappa, and a freshman honors program. **Visiting:** There are regularly scheduled orientations for prospective students, including information about academic studies, financial aid sessions, discussions with current students, lunch with faculty and students, and a tour of the campus. There is also a Spring Fest visitation in March for high school sophomores & juniors. There are guides for informal visits, visitors may sit in on classes, and stay overnight. To schedule a visit, contact the Undergraduate Admissions Office. **Campus Safety and Security:** Measures include 24-hour foot and vehicle patrol, emergency notification system, self-defense education, and security escort services. There are also shuttle buses, emergency telephones, lighted pathways/sidewalks, controlled access to dorms/residences. Card-key devices, issued to all students living in residence halls, must be used to enter these buildings.

REQUIREMENTS: Applicants should graduate from an accredited high school with a minimum of 15 academic credits: 4 in English, 3 in higher math, including algebra I, II, and plane geometry, 3 each in natural science and social science, and 2 in a foreign language. Home School Certificate applicants may qualify with the SAT or ACT and 3 SAT Subject Tests in math, literature, and science. Performing arts majors must audition. AP and CLEP credits are accepted. Important factors in the admissions decision are advanced placement or honors courses, leadership record, and recommendations by school officials. Basic requirements consist of 122 semester hours, including the major requirements for one of SMU's over 100 majors, as well as the University Curriculum (UC), which consists of three, main course-based components: Foundations, Pillars and Capstone. The Foundations emphasize reading and writing, quantitative reasoning, applied critical thinking, and wellness. The five UC Pillars cover the natural sciences, the arts and humanities, and the social and behavioral sciences. The Capstone completes each student's general education. In addition to the three core components, there are eight proficiencies and experiences that can be satisfied through coursework or out-of-class activities. **Procedure:** Freshmen are admitted to all sessions. Entrance exams should be taken by December of the senior year. There are early decision, deferred admissions, and rolling admissions plans. Early decision applications should be filed by November 1; regular applications, by January 15 for fall entry, along with a $60 fee. Notification of early decision is sent April 1; regular decision, on a rolling basis. 261 early decision candidates were accepted for the 2016-2017 class. 862 applicants were on the 2016 waiting list; 40 were admitted. Applications are accepted online. **Transfer Students:** 288 transfer students enrolled in 2015-2016. A minimum 2.5 GPA is generally required for transfer, but specific requirements vary according to the program of study. Candidates must demonstrate math proficiency. A foreign language requirement may be met through high school or college work. 60 of 122 credits required for the bachelor's degree must be completed at SMU. **International Students:** There are 532 international students enrolled. The school actively recruits these students. They must take the TOEFL with a minimum score of 550 on the paper-based TOEFL (PBT) or 80 on the Internet-based version (iBT), or the IELTS, with a minimum score of 6.5.

ADMISSIONS: 49% of the 2016-2017 applicants were accepted. 70% of the current freshmen were in the top fifth of their class; 91% were in the top two fifths. **Admissions Contact:** Byron Lewis, Interim Dean, Undergraduate Admission. Email: *ugadmission@smu.edu* Web: *www.smu.edu*

FINANCIAL AID: In 2016-2017, 73% of all full-time freshmen received some form of financial aid. 25% of all full-time freshmen received need-based aid. The average freshman award was $41,801. Need-based scholarships or need-based grants averaged $20,909; need-based self-help aid (loans and jobs) averaged $6,672; non-need-based athletic scholarships averaged $50,753; and other non-need-based awards and non-need-based scholarships averaged $21,192. The average financial indebtedness of the 2016 graduate was $30,826. SMU is a member of CSS. The CSS/Profile is required. The FAFSA code is 003613. The priority date for freshman financial aid applications for fall entry is February 15.

SOUTHWESTERN ADVENTIST UNIVERSITY *(The complete profile is made available exclusively on our website, www.barronspac.com)*

SOUTHWESTERN UNIVERSITY D-3

www.southwestern.edu/admission

Georgetown, TX 78626	**(512) 863-1200** **(800) 252-3166**
Fax: (512) 863-9601	**Email: admission@southwestern.edu**
Full-time: 619 men, 845 women	**Faculty:** 110; IIB, av$
Part-time: 14 men, 11 women	**Ph.D.s:** 100%
Graduate: n/av	**Student/Faculty:** 12 to 1
Year: semesters, summer session	**Tuition:** $39,060
Room & Board: $11,660	**Freshman Class:** 3773 applied, 1699 accepted, 381 enrolled
SAT CR/M: 590/580 **ACT:** 26	**CEEB CODE:** 6674
Application Deadline: February 1	**VERY COMPETITIVE**

Southwestern University, founded in 1840, is a private, national liberal arts institution affiliated with the United Methodist Church. There are 2 undergraduate schools. In addition to regional accreditation, Southwestern has baccalaureate program accreditation with NASM, SACS, University Senate of United Methodist Church, and Texas Education Agency. The 700-acre campus is in a suburban area 28 miles north of Austin. Including any residence halls, there are 36 buildings.

STUDENT LIFE: 89% of undergraduates are from Texas. Others are from 35 states, 14 foreign countries, and Canada. 81% are from public schools. 62% are White; 6% African American; 4% Asian American; 4% two or more races; 21% Hispanic; 2% Foreign; 1% race unknown. 58% are Protestant. **Female To Male Ratio:** 1.4:1. The average age of freshmen is 18; all undergraduates, 20. 15% do not continue beyond their first year; 75% remain to graduate. **Housing:** 1119 students can be accommodated in college housing, which includes single-sex, coed dorms and on-campus apartments, and fraternity houses. On-campus housing is available on a first-come, first-served basis, and on a lottery system for upperclassmen. 72% of students live on campus; of those, 80% remain on campus on weekends. All students may keep cars.

FACULTY/CLASSROOMS: 46% of faculty are male; 54% are female. All teach undergraduates and do research. No introductory courses are taught by graduate students. The average class size in an introductory lecture is 20 and in a laboratory is 18.

PROGRAMS OF STUDY: Southwestern confers B.A., B.S., B.F.A., B.S.Ed and B.M. degrees. Bachelor's degrees are awarded in AGRICULTURE (environmental studies), BIOLOGICAL SCIENCE (biochemistry and biology/biological science), BUSINESS (business administration and management), COMMUNICATIONS AND THE ARTS (art history, art, classics, communications, dramatic arts, English, French, German, Greek, Latin, music, and Spanish), COMPUTER AND PHYSICAL SCIENCE (applied science, chemistry, computer science, mathematics, mathematics/computational, and physics), EDUCATION (education), HEALTH PROFESSIONS (exercise science), SOCIAL SCIENCE (anthropology, economics, history, international studies, Latin American studies, philosophy, political science/government, psychology, religion, sociology, and women's studies). psychology, business, and communication have the largest enrollments.

ACTIVITIES: 22% of men belong to 4 national fraternities; 21% of women belong to 5 national sororities. There are 99 groups on campus, including art, band, cheerleading, choir, chorale, chorus, communications, computers, dance, debate, drama, environmental, ethnic, film, honors, international, jazz band, LGBT, literary magazine, musical theater, newspaper, opera, orchestra, political, professional, radio and TV, religious, social, social service, student government, and symphony. Popular campus events include Homecoming, Sing, Sound Wave Musical Festival, and Brown Symposium. **Sports:** There are 10 intercollegiate sports for men and 10 for women, and 20 intramural sports for men and 20 for women. Facilities include a recreation center, a performance gym, indoor jogging track, racquetball & handball courts, indoor swimming pool, weight room and fitness area. Outdoor facilities include baseball, softball, soccer and lacrosse fields, tennis courts, recreational fields, an athletic field house with locker room, weight room, athletic training center, football practice fields, outdoor track and field complex, and sand volleyball. **Graduates:** From July 1, 2015 to June 30, 2016, 307 bachelor's degrees were awarded. The most popular majors were psychology (10%), business (10%), and communication studies (9%). 100 companies recruited on campus in 2015-2016. In an average class, 2% graduate in 3 years or less, 67% graduate in 4 years or less, 72% graduate in 5 years or less, and 73% graduate in 6 years or less.

SERVICES: Counseling and information services are available, as is tutoring in every subject, a reader service for the blind, and remedial writing. **Library/Resources:** The library contains 301,487 volumes, 63,906 microform items, and 20,949 audio/video tapes/CDs/DVDs, and subscribes to 4,405 periodicals including electronic. Computerized library services include interlibrary loans, database searching, Internet access, and Wi-Fi capability. Special learning facilities include an art gallery, radio station, and observatory. **Physically Challenged Students:** 90% of the campus is accessible. Facilities include wheelchair ramps, elevators, special parking, specially equipped restrooms, special class scheduling, lowered drinking fountains, lowered telephones, and special housing. **Special:** Students may study abroad in a multitude of countries. The university offers a Fall London semester, Washington semester, dual, student-designed, and independent majors, and internships in government, fine arts, psychology, sociology, science, and other fields, including those in the New York Arts Program. An Applied Physics major allows students to spend several years at Southwestern, then finish their SU degree with a year's qualifying engineering coursework at another university. There are 7 national honor societies, Phi Beta Kappa, and 21 departmental honors programs. **Visiting:** There are regularly scheduled orientations for prospective students, including 3 or 4 group overnight options and individually arranged visits throughout the year. All visits typically include tours, faculty appointments and interview, and may also include an overnight on campus and class visit. There are guides for informal visits, visitors may sit in on classes, and stay overnight. To schedule a visit, contact the Admission's Office. **Campus Safety and Security:** Measures include 24-hour foot and vehicle patrol, emergency notification system, self-defense education, and security escort services. There are emergency telephones, lighted pathways/sidewalks, and controlled access to dorms/residences.

REQUIREMENTS: The SAT or ACT is recommended. Applicants should be graduates of an accredited high school or have the GED. Secondary preparation should include, at a minimum, 4 years each of English and math, 3 each of science and social science or history, 2 of a foreign language, and 1 of an academic elective. An essay, an SAT or ACT score and a counselor recommendation are required, and an interview is recommended. AP and CLEP credits are accepted. Important factors in the admissions decision are advanced placement or honors courses and leadership record. All degrees require a 2.0 or higher GPA in 127 or more credits. Each requires a first year seminar, 2 fitness and recreational activity credits, at least 1 course (3-4 credits) tagged for each of social justice, intercultural perspectives, math or computer science, fine arts performance, fine arts lecture, and natural science with lab. 2 tagged courses in both humanities and social science are required, as is 3rd semester proficiency in a foreign language. Major requirements vary, but require a minimum of 30 credits, including a capstone. **Procedure:** Freshmen are admitted in the fall. Entrance exams should be taken In the fall or early spring of the senior year. There are early admissions and deferred admissions plans. Applications should be filed by February 1 for fall entry. Notifications are sent April 15. 31 applicants were on the 2016 waiting list; 5 were admitted. Applications are accepted on-line. **Transfer Students:** 59 transfer students enrolled in 2015-2016. Preference is given to students having a 3.0 in all college work. 64 of 127 credits required for the bachelor's degree must be completed at Southwestern. **International Students:** There are 33 international students enrolled. The school actively recruits these students. They must take the TOEFL with a minimum score of 570 on the paper-based TOEFL (PBT) or 88 on the Internet-based version (iBT), or take the IELTS. They must also take the SAT or ACT.

ADMISSIONS: 45% of the 2016-2017 applicants were accepted. The SAT scores for the 2016-2017 freshman class were: Critical Reading-- 13% below 500, 40% between 500 and 599, 35% between 600 and 699, and 12% between 700 and 800. Math-- 13% below 500, 48% between 500 and 599, 31% between 600 and 699, and 7% between 700 and 800. The ACT scores were 1% between 12 and 17, 30% between 18 and 23, 49% between 24 and 29, and 21% above 30. 65% of the current freshmen were in the top fifth of their class; 88% were in the top two fifths. There were 4 National Merit finalists. 4 freshmen graduated first in their class. **Admissions Contact:** Bob Baldwin, Director of Admission. Email: *admission@southwestern.edu* Web: *www.southwestern.edu*

FINANCIAL AID: In 2016-2017, 99% of all full-time freshmen and 98% of continuing full-time students received some form of financial aid. 67% of all full-time freshmen and 61% of continuing full-time students received need-based aid. The average freshman award was $34,640. Need-based scholarships or need-based grants averaged $30,100; need-based self-help aid (loans and jobs) averaged $4,951; and other non-need-based awards and non-need-based scholarships averaged $20,581. 42% of undergraduate students work part-time. Average annual earnings from campus work are $1261. The average financial indebtedness of the 2016 graduate was $33,093. Southwestern is a member of CSS. The FAFSA code is 003620. The deadline for filing freshman financial aid applications for fall entry is March 1.

ST. EDWARD'S UNIVERSITY — D-3

www.stedwards.edu

Austin, TX 78704	(512) 448-8500 (800) 555-0164
Fax: (512) 464-8877	**Email:** seu.admit@stedwards.edu
Full-time: 1426 men, 2184 women	**Faculty:** n/av
Part-time: 166 men, 280 women	**Ph.D.s:** 82%
Graduate: 178 men, 367 women	**Student/Faculty:** n/av
Year: semesters, summer session	**Tuition:** $40,928
Room & Board: $12,172	**Freshman Class:** 6046 applied, 4468 accepted, 864 enrolled
SAT CR/M/W: 560/540/540 **ACT:** 25	**CEEB CODE:** 6619
Application Deadline: May 1	**VERY COMPETITIVE**

St. Edward's University is an independent, Catholic, liberal arts university where students are part of a small yet diverse community that provides a global perspective. Students learn to think critically and creatively, make ethical decisions, solve problems rationally, and lead effectively. Through hands-on service projects and internships, students develop a deeper understanding of their role in the world and gain the confidence to excel and make a difference in the community. St. Edward's was founded by the Congregation of Holy Cross in 1885. There are 6 undergraduate schools and 4 graduate schools. In addition to regional accreditation, SEU has baccalaureate program accreditation with CSWE. The 160-acre campus is in an urban area in Austin. Including any residence halls, there are 57 buildings.

STUDENT LIFE: 13% of undergraduates are from out of state, mostly the West. Students are from 49 states, 54 foreign countries, and Canada. 74% are from public schools. 8% are Foreign; 41% Hispanic; 4% African American; 37% White; 3% Asian American; 3% two or more races; 2% race unknown. 43% are Muslim, Buddhist, Christian, Hindu, Mormon, and unknown; 27% Catholic; 15% Protestant. **Female To Male Ratio:** 1.6:1. The average age of freshmen is 18; all undergraduates, 22. 19% do not continue beyond their first year; 64% remain to graduate. **Housing:** 1448 students can be accommodated in college housing, which includes coed dorms, on-campus apartments, off-campus apartments, and 6 living learning communities. On-campus housing is guaranteed for the freshman year only, is available on a first-come, first-served basis, and on a lottery system for upperclassmen. 63% of students commute. All students may keep cars.

FACULTY/CLASSROOMS: 47% of faculty are male; 53% are female. No introductory courses are taught by graduate students.

PROGRAMS OF STUDY: St.E confers B.A., B.S., B.B.A., B.F.A. and B.L.S. degrees. Master's degrees are also awarded. Bachelor's degrees are awarded in BIOLOGICAL SCIENCE (biochemistry, bioinformatics, biology/biological science, and biology/ gen science secondary education), BUSINESS (accounting, accounting (information systems), banking and finance, business administration and management, entrepreneurial studies, international business management, and marketing management), COMMUNICATIONS AND THE ARTS (acting, art, communications, digital communications, English literature, English Writing, French, game design and development, graphic design, photography, Spanish, and theatre arts), COMPUTER AND PHYSICAL SCIENCE (chemistry, chemistry/gen science second education, computer information technology, computer science, environmental chemistry, information sciences and systems, and mathematics), EDUCATION (art education, athletic training, drama education, English education, foreign languages education, global studies, mathematics education, physical education, physical science secondary school education, science education, social studies education, and special education), ENGINEERING AND ENVIRONMENTAL DESIGN (environmental design, policy and planning, environmental science, and preengineering), HEALTH PROFESSIONS (human studies, medical laboratory science, predentistry, premedicine, and prephysical therapy), SOCIAL SCIENCE (criminal justice, criminology, economics, forensic studies, history, interdisciplinary studies, international relations, liberal arts/general studies, philosophy, physical fitness/movement, political science/government, prelaw, psychology, religion, social work, and sociology). Psychology, biology, and communication have the largest enrollments.

ACTIVITIES: St, E has no fraternities or sororities. There are 142 groups on campus, including art, cheerleading, choir, chorale, chorus, computers, dance, debate, drama, drill team, environmental, ethnic, film, forensics, honors, international, jazz band, LGBT, literary magazine, musical theater, newspaper, orchestra, pep band, photography, political, professional, radio and TV, religious, social, social service, and student government. Popular campus events include Welcome Barbecue, Halloween Block Party, Homecoming, Involvement Fair, Hillfest, Casino Night, Leadershape, Festival of Lights, MAC Lead, End of Year Party, Anchors, Legacy Walk, and Medallion Ceremony. **Sports:** There are 6 intercollegiate sports for men and 7 for women, and 10 intramural sports for men and 10 for women. Facilities include gyms, baseball and softball fields, soccer field, tennis, basketball, racquetball/handball, and volleyball courts, indoor pool, fitness center, sand volleyball courts, recreation multipurpose field, and a fitness studio. **Graduates:** From July 1, 2015 to June 30, 2016, 847 bachelor's degrees were awarded. The most popular majors were communication (9%), psychology (9%), and global studies (6%). 200 companies recruited on campus in 2015-2016. In an average class, 3% graduate in 3 years or less, 50% graduate in 4 years or less, 61% graduate in 5 years or less, and 64% graduate in 6 years or less.

SERVICES: Counseling and information services are available, as is tutoring in some subjects, such as accounting, biology, business, computer, chemistry, economics, French, math, physics, psychology, and Spanish. There is also a reader service for the blind, and remedial math, reading, and writing. **Library/Resources:** The library contains 438,089 volumes, and 19,668 audio/video tapes/CDs/DVDs, and subscribes to 2,601 periodicals including electronic. Computerized library services include interlibrary loans, database searching, Internet access, and Wi-Fi capability. Special learning facilities include an art gallery, radio station, fine arts facility with photography laboratory, 60 Global Digital Classrooms in the Munday Library and throughout campus, Mary Moody Northen Theatre, Our Lady Queen of Peace Chapel, interdisciplinary research laboratory at Wild Basin Wilderness Preserve, partner campus in Angers, France at Universite Catholique de l'Ouest, and 21 international partner universities. **Physically Challenged Students:** 93% of the campus is accessible. Facilities include wheelchair ramps, elevators, special parking, specially equipped restrooms, special class scheduling, lowered drinking fountains, lowered telephones, and special housing. **Special:** Internships and study abroad in a variety of countries through the ISEP, SEU, and other university programs are available. Student-designed majors, nondegree study, and pass/fail options also are possible. A flexible program for working adults is offered through New College. There are 13 national honor societies and a freshman honors program. **Visiting:** There are regularly scheduled orientations for prospective students, including a tour, financial aid session, academic session, class visits, and entertainment. There are guides for informal visits, visitors may sit in on classes, and stay overnight. To schedule a visit, contact Lisa Furler at (512) 448-8500. **Campus Safety and Security:** Measures include 24-hour foot and vehicle patrol, emergency notification system, self-defense education, security escort services, emergency telephones, lighted pathways/sidewalks, and controlled access to dorms/residences.

REQUIREMENTS: The SAT or ACT is required. Successful applicants should be in the top half of their graduating class with testing at or above a combined evidenced based reading and writing and math score of 1080 on the SAT, or a composite score, not including writing, of 21 on the ACT. The GED is accepted. An interview is recommended. An essay is required. AP and CLEP credits are accepted. Important factors in the admissions decision are advanced placement or honors courses, extracurricular activities record, and leadership record. All students must maintain a minimum GPA of 2.0 while taking 120 semester hours, including 36 to 81 in the major. The core curriculum includes courses from Foundational Skills, Cultural Foundations, and Foundations for Values and Decisions. In the required capstone class, seniors identify a problem in society, research it, present their solutions orally and in writing, and perform a civic engagement activity that supports their position. **Procedure:** Freshmen are admitted in the fall and spring. Entrance exams should be taken in spring of the junior year or in summer or fall of the senior year. There are deferred admissions and rolling admissions plans. Early decision applications should be filed by February 1; regular applications, by May 1 for fall entry; November 15 for spring entry; and May 1 for summer entry, along with a $50 fee. Notification is sent on a rolling basis. 985 applicants were on the 2016 waiting list; 137 were admitted. Applications are accepted on-line. **Transfer Students:** 300 transfer students enrolled in 2015-2016. Transfer applicants must have a minimum GPA of 2.5. 30 of 120 credits required for the bachelor's degree must be completed at SEU. **International Students:** There are 312 international students enrolled. The school actively recruits these students. They must take the TOEFL with a minimum score of 500 on the paper-based TOEFL (PBT) or 61 on the Internet-based version (iBT), or IELTS; IB (English Higher Level) and AP (English or English Literature) may be submitted. They must also take the SAT or ACT, which may take the place of TOEFL or IELTS.

ADMISSIONS: 74% of the 2016-2017 applicants were accepted. The SAT scores for the 2016-2017 freshman class were: Critical Reading-- 19% below 500, 49% between 500 and 599, 27% between 600 and 699, and 5% between 700 and 800. Math-- 21% below 500, 56% between 500 and 599, 20% between 600 and 699, and 3% between 700 and 800. Writing-- 31% below 500, 47% between 500 and 599, 20% between 600 and 699, and 2% between 700 and 800. The ACT scores were 1% between 12 and 17, 34% between 18 and 23, 57% between 24 and 29, and 8% above 30. 52% of the current freshmen were in the top fifth of their class; 79% were in the top two fifths. 3 freshmen graduated first in their class. **Admissions Contact:** Tracy Manier, Associate Vice President and Dean of Admission. Email: *seu.admit@stedwards.edu* Web: *www.stedwards.edu*

FINANCIAL AID: In 2016-2017, 85% of all full-time freshmen and 91% of continuing full-time students received some form of financial aid. 74% of all full-time freshmen and 84% of continuing full-time students received need-based aid. The average freshman award was $33,812. Need-based scholarships or need-based grants averaged $20,893; need-based self-help aid (loans and jobs) averaged $3,729; non-need-based athletic scholarships averaged $20,483; and other non-need-based awards and non-need-based scholarships averaged $18,294. 33% of undergraduate students work part-time. Average annual earnings from campus work are $2022. The average financial indebtedness of the 2016 graduate was $36,123. SEU is a member of CSS. The FAFSA code is 003621. The priority date for freshman financial aid applications for fall entry is February 1.

ST. MARY'S UNIVERSITY D-4

www.stmarytx.edu

San Antonio, TX 78228 — **(210) 436-3126** **(800) FOR-STMU**

Fax: (210) 431-6742 — **Email: uadm@stmarytx.edu**

Full-time: 1000 men, 1284 women — **Faculty:** 162; IIA, +$

Part-time: 50 men, 57 women — **Ph.D.s:** 93%

Graduate: 777 men, 698 women — **Student/Faculty:** 12 to 1

Year: semesters, summer session — **Tuition:** $28,200

Room & Board: $9300 — **Freshman Class:** 5147 applied, 2997 accepted, 596 enrolled

SAT CR/M/W: 510/530/490 **ACT:** 22 — **CEEB CODE:** 6637

Application Deadline: open — **COMPETITIVE**

Saint Mary's University, established in 1852, is a private Roman Catholic institution in the Marianist tradition, offering undergraduate programs in humanities and social sciences, business and administration, and science, engineering, and technology. Figures in the above capsule and in this profile are approximate. There are 3 undergraduate schools and 2 graduate schools. In addition to regional accreditation, St. Mary's has baccalaureate program accreditation with AACSB and ABET. The 135-acre campus is in a suburban area 5 miles northwest of downtown San Antonio. Including any residence halls, there are 45 buildings.

STUDENT LIFE: 7% of undergraduates are from out of state, mostly the Southwest. Students are from 32 states, 36 foreign countries, and Canada. 68% are from public schools. 72% are Hispanic; 5% Foreign; 4% African American; 3% Asian American; 3% race unknown; 14% White. 41% are Catholic; 15% Baptist, Buddhist, Eastern Orthodox, Episcopal and Hindu. **Female To Male Ratio:** 1.1:1. The average age of freshmen is 18; all undergraduates, 21. 27% do not continue beyond their first year; 64% remain to graduate. **Housing:** 1454 students can be accommodated in college housing, which includes coed dorms. theme housing. On-campus housing is guaranteed for the freshman year only, and is available on a first-come, and first-served basis. Priority is given to out-of-town students. 58% of students live on campus; of those, 80% remain on campus on weekends. All students may keep cars.

FACULTY/CLASSROOMS: 63% of faculty are male; 37% are female. 75% teach undergraduates. No introductory courses are taught by graduate students. The average class size in an introductory lecture is 30; in a laboratory is 60; and in a regular course is 25.

PROGRAMS OF STUDY: St. Mary's confers B.A., B.S. and B.B.A. degrees. Master's and doctoral degrees are also awarded. Bachelor's degrees are awarded in BIOLOGICAL SCIENCE (biochemistry and biology/biological science), BUSINESS (accounting, banking and finance, business administration and management, human resources, international business management, and marketing/retailing/merchandising), COMMUNICATIONS AND THE ARTS (communications, English, French, German, music, Spanish, and speech/debate/rhetoric), COMPUTER AND PHYSICAL SCIENCE (chemistry, computer science, earth science, mathematics, and physics), EDUCATION (business education, elementary education, science education, and secondary education), ENGINEERING AND ENVIRONMENTAL DESIGN (computer engineering, electrical/electronics engineering, engineering, environmental science, industrial engineering, and mechanical engineering), HEALTH PROFESSIONS (predentistry and premedicine), SOCIAL SCIENCE (criminal justice, economics, history, international relations, international studies, Latin American studies, philosophy, political science/government, prelaw, psychology, sociology, and theological studies). Biology, accounting, and political science are the strongest academically. Biology, business, and political science have the largest enrollments.

ACTIVITIES: 15% of men belong to 1 local and 4 national fraternities; 13% of women belong to 1 local and 3 national sororities. There are 55 groups on campus, including art, band, cheerleading, choir, chorale, dance, drama, ethnic, honors, international, jazz band, newspaper, pep band, photography, political, professional, religious, social, social service, and student government. Popular campus events include Campus Ministry Retreat, Hunger Awareness Week, Fiesta Oyster Bake, President's Peace Commision, and Lin Great Speaker. **Sports:** There are 5 intercollegiate sports for men and 5 for women, and 28 intramural sports for men and 28 for women. Facilities include a gym, weight room, tennis, handball, basketball courts, pools, tracks, dance movement studio, baseball and softball stadium, batting cages, soccer field and sports arena. **Graduates:** From July 1, 2015 to June 30, 2016, 513 bachelor's degrees were awarded. The most popular majors were psychology (7%), criminal justice (6%), and political science (6%). 30 companies recruited on campus in 2015-2016. In an average class, 33% graduate in 4 years or less, 53% graduate in 5 years or less, and 55% graduate in 6 years or less.

SERVICES: Counseling and information services are available, as is tutoring in most subjects, such as biology, chemistry, physics, psychology, languages, math, writing, accounting, statistics, English, and engineering. There is also remedial math, reading, and writing, biochemistry, organic chemistry, programming, macro/micro economics, philosphy, and electronics. **Library/Resources:** The 2 libraries contain 222,220 volumes, 367,294 microform items, and 5,741 audio/video tapes/CDs/DVDs, and subscribe to 36,954 periodicals including electronic. Computerized library services include interlibrary loans, database searching, Internet access, and Wi-Fi capability. Special learning facilities include an art gallery, natural history museum, the learning assistance center is a learner-oriented service that provides academic support and instructional resources. **Physically Challenged Students:** 80% of the campus is accessible. Facilities include wheelchair ramps, elevators, special parking, specially equipped restrooms, special class scheduling, lowered drinking fountains, and special housing. **Special:** St. Mary's offers cooperative programs and internships in all majors, depending on the student's needs. Students may cross-register at any of the United Colleges of San Antonio, spend a semester in Washington, D.C., or study in England, Austria, or Mexico. Dual majors are possible in computer science and engineering and public justice and sociology, political science, or psychology. Accelerated degree programs are offered in law, (J.D./M.B.A.) and dentistry (B.A. in combined science and dentistry). Required theology courses may be taken on a pass/fail basis. There are 10 national honor societies, a freshman honors program, and 3 departmental honors programs. **Visiting:** Regularly scheduled orientations are available for prospective students, consisting of a campus tour, admissions/financial aid session, overnight stay, student only activities, parent only activities, and placement testing. There are guides for informal visits, visitors may sit in on classes, and stay overnight. To schedule a visit, contact Undergraduate Admissions Office at (800) 367-7868. **Campus Safety and Security:** Measures include 24-hour foot and vehicle patrol, emergency notification system, self-defense education, and security escort services, emergency telephones, lighted pathways/sidewalks, controlled access to dorms/residences, and a crime prevention awareness program each semester.

REQUIREMENTS: All applicants must be high school graduates or have the GED, rank in the upper half of their graduating classes, and score in the 50th percentile on SAT I or ACT. Secondary school preparation should include 4 units of English, 3 each of math and academic electives, and 3 each of social science, natural science, and foreign language. Potential science and engineering majors should have 4 units of math and 3 of lab science, including chemistry or physics. AP and CLEP credits are accepted. Important factors in the admissions decision are leadership record, advanced placement or honors courses, and personality/intangible qualities. All students must complete at least 128 semester hours, 24 to 30 in the major, with a minimum 2.0 GPA. Core curriculum requirements include courses in fine arts, English, foreign language, speech, natural science, math, social science, philosophy, and theology. Students must also take computer science, demonstrate computer literacy, and take interdisciplinary electives. 128 hours includes CORE, Major and Minor (if applicable), and elective requirements. 6 advanced writing, intensive courses in major. **Procedure:** Freshmen are admitted in the fall and spring. Entrance exams should be taken by the fall of the senior year. There are early admissions, deferred admissions, and rolling admissions plans. Application deadlines are open. The fall 2016 application fee was $30. Notification is sent on a rolling basis. Applications are accepted online. **Transfer Students:** 124 transfer students enrolled in 2015-2016. Prospective transfer students possessing the aptitude and motivation to succeed at St. Mary's are encouraged to apply for admission. To be considered for admission, a minimum cumulative grade point average of 2.5 (on a 4.0 scale) in all academic work attempted and good standing at the college or university last attended are required. Applicants in good standing with the last institution attended and who present a grade point average between 2.0 and 2.49 (on a 4.0 scale) may be considered for probationary admission. (Developmental or technical course work is not considered in the evaluation of the academic GPA.) Possession of the minimum grade point average for consideration does not imply admissibility to St. Mary's University. The merits of each application are considered on a case-by-case basis. Academic credits ordinarily will be accepted in transfer from another college if the grade(s) earned is/are at least C (2.0 on a 4.0 scale). The school(s) must be accredited by one of the six regional accrediting associations. 45 of 126 credits required for the bachelor's degree must be completed at St. Mary's. **International Students:** There are 117 international students enrolled. The school actively recruits these students. They must take the TOEFL with a minimum score of 550 on the paper-based TOEFL (PBT) or 80 on the Internet-based version (iBT), International English Language-Testing System (IELTS). They must also take the SAT or ACT.

ADMISSIONS: 58% of the 2016-2017 applicants were accepted. The SAT scores for the 2016-2017 freshman class were: Critical Reading-- 43% below 500, 42% between 500 and 599, 12% between 600 and 699, and 2% between 700 and 800. Math-- 31% below 500, 51% between 500 and 599, 17% between 600 and 699, and 1% between 700 and 800. Writing-- 52% below 500, 38% between 500 and 599, 9% between 600 and 699, and 1% between 700 and 800. The ACT scores were 25% below 12, 42% between 12 and 17, 21% between 18 and 23, 6% between 24 and 29, and 6% above 30. 3 freshmen graduated first in their class. **Admissions Contact:** Nelson Delgado, Acting Director of Undergrad Admissions. Email: *uadm@stmarytx.edu* Web: *www.stmarytx.edu*

FINANCIAL AID: St. Mary's is a member of CSS. The CSS/Profile is required. The deadline for filing freshman financial aid applications for fall entry is April 1.

STEPHEN F. AUSTIN STATE UNIVERSITY *(The complete profile is made available exclusively on our website, www.barronspac.com)*

SUL ROSS STATE UNIVERSITY *(The complete profile is made available exclusively on our website, www.barronspac.com)*

TARLETON STATE UNIVERSITY *(The complete profile is made available exclusively on our website, www.barronspac.com)*

TEXAS A&M UNIVERSITY D-3

www.tamu.edu

College Station, TX 77843	(979) 845-3741
Fax: (979) 847-8737	**Email:** admissions@tamu.edu
Full-time: 22,826 men, 22,004 women	**Faculty:** 1917
	Ph.D.s: 88%
Part-time: 3315 men, 2602 women	**Student/Faculty:** 23 to 1
Graduate: 8145 men, 6657 women	**Tuition:** $10,153 ($30,331)
Year: semesters, summer session	**Freshman Class:** 34781 applied, 23362 accepted, 10142 enrolled
Room & Board: $10,368	
SAT CR/M/W: 590/610/550 **ACT:** 27	**CEEB CODE:** 6003
Application Deadline: December 1	**VERY COMPETITIVE+**

Texas A&M University, founded in 1876, is part of the Texas A&M University system. Undergraduate degrees are offered in agriculture and life sciences, architecture, business administration, education, engineering, geosciences, liberal arts, science, and biomedical science. There are 15 undergraduate schools and 17 graduate schools. In addition to regional accreditation, Texas A&M has baccalaureate program accreditation with AACSB, ABET, ACCE, ACEJMC, ADA, ASLA, CSAB, NAAB, NCATE, and SAF. The 11492-acre campus is in an urban area 90 miles northwest of Houston. Including any residence halls, there are 796 buildings.

STUDENT LIFE: 94% of undergraduates are from Texas. Others are from 50 states, 132 foreign countries, and Canada. 8% are Foreign; 7% Asian American; 59% White; 4% African American; 20% Hispanic; 2% two or more races; 1% race unknown. **Male To Female Ratio:** 1.1:1. The average age of freshmen is 18; all undergraduates, 21. 4% do not continue beyond their first year; 46% remain to graduate. **Housing:** 11079 students can be accommodated in college housing, which includes single-sex and coed dorms, on-campus apartments, off-campus apartments, married student housing, honors houses, fraternity houses, and sorority houses. On-campus housing is available on a first-come and first-served basis. 76% of students commute. All students may keep cars.

FACULTY/CLASSROOMS: 64% of faculty are male; 36% are female. 57% teach undergraduates, 59% do research, and 35% do both. Graduate students teach 9% of introductory courses. The average class size in an introductory lecture is 67; in a laboratory is 36; and in a regular course is 41.

PROGRAMS OF STUDY: Texas A&M confers B.A., B.S., B.B.A., B.Ed., B.L.A. and B.S.N. degrees. Master's and doctoral degrees are also awarded. Bachelor's degrees are awarded in AGRICULTURE (agricultural business management, agricultural communications, agricultural economics, agricultural sciences, agronomy, animal science, food technology for companion animals, horticulture, plant science, poultry science, range/farm management, and wildlife science), BIOLOGICAL SCIENCE (biochemistry, biology/biological science, ecology, entomology, genetics, marine biology, marine science, microbiology, molecular biology, nutrition, and zoology), BUSINESS (accounting, business administration and management, business systems analysis, finance, human resources, management information systems, management science, marketing and distribution, recreational facilities management, and supply chain management), COMMUNICATIONS AND THE ARTS (communications, English, French, German, modern language, music, performing arts, Russian, Spanish, speech/debate/rhetoric, telecommunications, and theatre acting), COMPUTER AND PHYSICAL SCIENCE (applied mathematics, chemistry, computer science, geology, geophysics and seismology, mathematics, and physics), EDUCATION (agricultural education, elementary education, physical education, and secondary education), ENGINEERING AND ENVIRONMENTAL DESIGN (aerospace engineering, bioengineering, biomedical engineering, chemical engineering, civil engineering, computer engineering, electrical/electronics engineering, engineering technology, environmental design, environmental science, geological engineering, industrial engineering technology, landscape architecture, landscape architecture/design, manufacturing technology, marine engineering, marine engineering systems, marine transportation, maritime science, mechanical engineering, nuclear engineering, ocean engineering, petroleum/natural gas engineering, and technological management), HEALTH PROFESSIONS (biomedical science, community health work, dental hygiene, health, nursing, public health, and radiological science), SOCIAL SCIENCE (anthropology, economics, forensic studies, geography, history, international studies, philosophy, political science/government, psychology, sociology, Spanish studies, and urban and regional studies). Biomedical science, business administration, and engineering are the strongest academically. Biomedical science, engineering, and business administration have the largest enrollments.

ACTIVITIES: 7% of men belong to 2 local and 30 national fraternities; 16% of women belong to 28 national sororities. There are 1111 groups on campus, including campus services, community/volunteer service, enthusiasts/special interest, healthy living, military, recreation, spirit and tradition (60), academic, art, band, cheerleading, chess, choir, chorale, chorus, computers, dance, debate, drill team, drum and bugle corps, environmental, ethnic, film, honors, international, literary magazine, marching band, newspaper, orchestra, photography, political, professional, radio and TV, religious, social, social service, student government, and symphony. Popular campus events include Midnight Yell Practice, Silver Taps and Muster. **Sports:** There are 8 intercollegiate sports for men and 10 for women, and 11 intramural sports for men and 11 for women. Facilities include a coliseum, a natatorium, basketball/volleyball courts, handball/racquetball courts, badminton, weight and activity rooms, jogging trails, tennis courts, a squash court, golf course, auditorium/arena, driving range, flag football fields, soccer fields, outdoor basketball courts, and walking trails. Intercollegiate athletic facilities include a football stadium, indoor basketball and volleyball coliseum, a baseball stadium, softball complex, soccer complex, a natatorium, track-and-field complex, tennis center, and physical strength and conditioning lab. **Graduates:** From July 1, 2015 to June 30, 2016, 10329 bachelor's degrees were awarded. The most popular majors were business/marketing (19%), engineering (17%), and agriculture (8%). 4400 companies recruited on campus in 2015-2016. In an average class, 53% graduate in 4 years or less, 76% graduate in 5 years or less, and 78% graduate in 6 years or less.

SERVICES: Counseling and information services are available, as is tutoring in most subjects, a reader service for the blind, and remedial math, reading, and writing. Workshops in time management, basic study techniques, and test-taking skills are also available. **Library/Resources:** The 14 libraries contain 5.6 million volumes, 6.5 million microform items, and 956,695 audio/video tapes/CDs/DVDs, subscribe to 134,626 periodicals including electronic. Computerized library services include interlibrary loans, database searching, Internet access, and Wi-Fi capability. Special learning facilities include an art gallery, radio station, TV station, a weather station, observatory, cyclotron, wind tunnel, visualization lab, nuclear reactor, ocean wave pool, and the Bush Museum and Library. **Physically Challenged Students:** 85% of the campus is accessible. Facilities include wheelchair ramps, elevators, special parking, specially equipped restrooms, special class scheduling, lowered drinking fountains, and lowered telephones. **Special:** The university offers extensive opportunities through the Career Center and Study Abroad Office. B.A.- B.S. degrees, study abroad in 12 countries, internships, a Washington semester, credit for military experience, nondegree study, co-op programs, dual majors, and pass/fail options are available. A 5-year graduate business/liberal arts program is offered, as well as a 3-2 engineering degree with Sam Houston State University. There are 25 national honor societies, Phi Beta Kappa, and a freshman honors program. **Visiting:** There are regularly scheduled orientations for prospective students, new-student conferences are held for students to meet with academic advisers to select courses, become acquainted with student life activities, and tour the campus. There are guides for informal visits and visitors may sit in on classes. To schedule a visit, contact the Aggieland Visitor Center at (979) 845-5851. **Campus Safety and Security:** Measures include 24-hour foot and vehicle patrol, emergency notification system, self-defense education, and security escort services. There are shuttle buses, emergency telephones, lighted pathways/sidewalks, a security awareness committee, and crime-watch and safety tip lines. Crime bulletins are available on the university police web site.

REQUIREMENTS: The SAT or ACT is required as is the ACT Optional Writing test. Secondary school graduation is a condition of freshman admission. Required high school courses include 4 credits in English, 3 1/2 credits in math, 3 credits in science (2 from biology, chemistry, or physics), 2 credits of social studies and the same foreign language, and 1 of history. AP and CLEP credits are accepted. Important factors in the admissions decision are leadership record, evidence of special talent, and extracurricular activities record. To graduate, students must complete at least 128 credit hours, including 30 to 33 in the major. Students must complete a core curriculum of 48 hours in 8 subject areas, including courses in American history and government, phys ed, computers, foreign language, speech and writing skills, math/logical reasoning, science, humanities, and social science. Requirements in the major vary. **Procedure:** Freshmen are admitted in the fall and spring. Entrance exams should be taken during the spring of the junior year or by December of the senior year. There is a rolling admissions plan. Applications should be filed by December 1 for fall entry; October 15 for spring entry, along with a $75 fee. Notifications are sent March 31. Applications are accepted on-line. **Transfer Students:** 11626 transfer students enrolled in 2015-2016. Applicants must submit transcripts from previously attended colleges. Requirements vary, depending on how many semester hours were attempted and the grades for those hours. Transfer applicants must submit high school transcripts and, if they have fewer than 12 graded semester hours, SAT or ACT scores. 30 of 128 credits required for the bachelor's degree must be completed at Texas A&M. **International Students:** There are 678 international students enrolled. They must take the TOEFL with a minimum score of 600 on the paper-based TOEFL (PBT) or 100 on the Internet-based version (iBT). The SAT or ACT is required for graduates of U.S. high schools only.

ADMISSIONS: 67% of the 2016-2017 applicants were accepted. The SAT scores for the 2016-2017 freshman class were: Critical Reading--18% below 500, 38% between 500 and 599, 34% between 600 and 699, and 10% between 700 and 800. Math-- 11% below 500, 33% between 500 and 599, 41% between 600 and 699, and 15% between 700 and 800. Writing-- 26% below 500, 43% between 500 and 599, 26% between 600 and 699, and 5% between 700 and 800. The ACT scores were 1% between 12 and 17, 17% between 18 and 23, 49% between 24 and 29, and 33% above 30. 82% of the current freshmen were in the top fifth of their class; 97% were in the top two fifths. There were 150 National Merit finalists. 371 freshmen graduated first in their class. **Admissions Contact:** Admissions Counseling Email: *admissions@tamu.edu* Web: *www.tamu.edu*

FINANCIAL AID: In 2016-2017, 72% of all full-time freshmen and 60% of continuing full-time students received some form of financial aid. 49% of all full-time freshmen and 48% of continuing full-time students received need-based aid. The average freshman award was $7,873. Need-based scholarships or need-based grants averaged $4,066 ($15,000 maximum); need-based self-help aid (loans and jobs) averaged $2,901 ($14,500 maximum); non-need-based athletic scholarships averaged $5,140 ($17,500 maximum); and other non-need-based awards and non-need-based scholarships averaged $5,410 ($39,500 maximum). 19% of undergraduate students work part-time. Average annual earnings from campus work are $3045. The average financial indebtedness of the 2016 graduate was $23,055. The FAFSA code is 003632. The priority date for freshman financial aid applications for fall entry is March 15.

TEXAS A&M UNIVERSITY AT COMMERCE D-2

www.tamu.edu

Commerce, TX 75429 **(903) 886-5072**

Fax: (903) 468-8685	**Email:** admissions@tamuc.edu
Full-time: 1547 men, 2470 women	**Faculty:** 206
Part-time: 438 men, 730 women	**Ph.D.s:** 65%
Graduate: 1416 men, 2420 women	**Student/Faculty:** 19 to 1
Year: semesters, summer session	**Tuition:** $5126 ($13,466)
Room & Board: $5370	**Freshman Class:** 7195 applied, 3413 accepted, 1080 enrolled
SAT: required **ACT:** 21	**CEEB CODE:** 6205
Application Deadline: August 15	**COMPETITIVE**

Texas A&M University at Commerce, founded in 1889, offers undergraduate and graduate programs in business and technology, arts and sciences, and education. The figures in the above capsule and in this profile are approximate. There are 3 undergraduate schools and 1 graduate school. In addition to regional accreditation, TAMU-C has baccalaureate program accreditation with AACSB, CSWE, NASM, and NCATE. The 1883-acre campus is in a small town 65 miles northeast of Dallas. Including any residence halls, there are 121 buildings.

STUDENT LIFE: 97% of undergraduates are from Texas. Others are from 30 states, 21 foreign countries, and Canada. 98% are from public schools. 9% are Hispanic; 65% White; 6% Foreign; 2% Asian American; 17% African American; 1% American Indian/Alaska Native. **Female To Male Ratio:** 1.7:1. The average age of freshmen is 19; all undergraduates, 25. 42% do not continue beyond their first year; 57% remain to graduate. **Housing:** 1910 students can be accommodated in college housing, which includes single-sex, coed dorms, on-campus apartments, off-campus apartments, and married student housing, honors houses, special-interest houses, fraternity houses, sorority houses, women's dorms, and theme housing. On-campus housing is guaranteed for the freshman year only, is available on a first-come, and first-served basis. 71% of students commute. All students may keep cars. Alcohol is not permitted.

FACULTY/CLASSROOMS: 53% of faculty are male; 47% are female. 77% teach undergraduates, 46% do research, and 37% do both. Graduate students teach 21% of introductory courses. The average class size in an introductory lecture is 30; in a laboratory is 20; and in a regular course is 25.

PROGRAMS OF STUDY: TAMU-C confers B.A., B.S., B.A.C.J., B.B.A., B.F.A., B.G.S., B.M., B.M.Ed., B.S.C.J., B.S.Lib.Sci., and B.S.W. degrees. Master's and doctoral degrees are also awarded. Bachelor's degrees are awarded in AGRICULTURE (agricultural economics, agriculture, animal science, and wildlife management), BIOLOGICAL SCIENCE (biology/biological science and botany), BUSINESS (accounting, banking and finance, business administration and management, and marketing/retailing/merchandising), COMMUNICATIONS AND THE ARTS (advertising, broadcasting, dramatic arts, English, fine arts, French, German, journalism, languages, music, photography, printmaking, and Spanish), COMPUTER AND PHYSICAL SCIENCE (chemistry, computer science, earth science, geology, mathematics, and physics), EDUCATION (agricultural education, business education, early childhood education, elementary education, guidance education, health education, industrial arts education, music education, science education, and secondary education), ENGINEERING AND ENVIRONMENTAL DESIGN (engineering technology and preengineering), HEALTH PROFESSIONS (predentistry, premedicine, and prepharmacy), SOCIAL SCIENCE (anthropology, criminal justice, economics, geography, history, political science/government, prelaw, psychology, religion, social work, and sociology). Education, computer science, and business administration are the strongest academically and have the largest enrollments are the strongest academically.

ACTIVITIES: 15% of men belong to 9 national fraternities; 12% of women belong to 7 national sororities. There are 96 groups on campus, including art, band, cheerleading, chess, choir, chorale, chorus, dance, drama, ethnic, film, honors, international, jazz band, LGBT, literary magazine, marching band, musical theater, newspaper, orchestra, pep band, photography, political, professional, radio and TV, religious, social, social service, and student government. Popular campus events include Sam Rayburn Symposium, Christmas Feast of Carols, and Spring Fest. **Sports:** There are 5 intercollegiate sports for men and 5 for women, and 7 intramural sports for men. Facilities include an auditorium, a stadium, a gym, handball and racquetball courts, a bowling alley, swimming pool, weight room, tennis courts, a field house, and intramural fields. **Graduates:** From July 1, 2015 to June 30, 2016, 1476 bachelor's degrees were awarded. The most popular majors were interdisciplinary studies (32%), business/marketing (16%), and psychology (5%). 55 companies recruited on campus in 2015-2016.

SERVICES: Counseling and information services are available, as is tutoring in some subjects, such as math and writing There is also remedial math, reading, and writing. **Library/Resources:** The library contains 1.2 million volumes, 1.2 million microform items, and subscribes to 16,222 periodicals including electronic. Computerized library services include interlibrary loans, database searching, Internet access, and Wi-Fi capability. Special learning facilities include a planetarium, radio station, TV station, performing arts center, and a teaching farm. **Physically Challenged Students:** All of the campus is accessible. Facilities include wheelchair ramps, elevators, special parking, and specially equipped restrooms. **Special:** TAMU-C offers co-op programs with E-Systems Inc.

and numerous other firms, cross-registration by independent arrangement, study abroad in England, and work-study programs. B.A.-B.S. degrees, second degrees, dual majors, a general studies degree, credit for life experience, internships, nondegree study, and pass/fail options are also available. There are 18 national honor societies, a freshman honors program, and 26 departmental honors programs. **Visiting:** There are regularly scheduled orientations for prospective students. There are guides for informal visits and visitors may sit in on classes. To schedule a visit, contact the Admissions Office. **Campus Safety and Security:** Measures include 24-hour foot and vehicle patrol, self-defense education, and security escort services, emergency telephones, lighted pathways/sidewalks, a victim assistance officer, a police service for special and social events, crime and date-rape prevention presentations, and motorist assistance.

REQUIREMENTS: The SAT or ACT is required, with a minimum recommended composite score of 800 or 20, respectively. Applicants need not be graduates of an accredited secondary school, although high school graduation is required. The GED is also accepted. AP and CLEP credits are accepted. To graduate, all students must earn a GPA of 2.0 while taking at least 126 semester hours, including 24 hours in the major. Distribution requirements include 24 in culture courses such as American history and foreign languages, 12 each in English composition, math, and speech skills, 8 in sciences, 6 in upper-division courses, and 4 in phys ed. **Procedure:** Freshmen are admitted to all sessions. Entrance exams should be taken prior to enrollment. There are deferred admissions and rolling admissions plans. Applications should be filed by August 15 for fall entry, along with a $25 fee. Notification is sent on a rolling basis. **Transfer Students:** 1175 transfer students enrolled in 2015-2016. Applicants must have a college GPA of 2.0 with a minimum of 21 credit hours. The SAT or ACT is not required. College transcripts and a statement of good standing from the prior institution are required. 30 of 126 credits required for the bachelor's degree must be completed at TAMU-C. **International Students:** There are 61 international students enrolled. They must take the TOEFL, and either the SAT or ACT.

ADMISSIONS: 47% of the 2016-2017 applicants were accepted. 42% of the current freshmen were in the top fifth of their class; 72% were in the top two fifths. **Admissions Contact:** Jody Tod Hunter, Interim Director of Admissions. Email: *admissions@tamuc.edu* Web: *www.tamu.edu*

FINANCIAL AID: The average freshman award was $12,250. Need-based scholarships or need-based grants averaged $10,903; need-based self-help aid (loans and jobs) averaged $3,520; non-need-based athletic scholarships averaged $4,393; other non-need-based awards and non-need-based scholarships averaged $3,459; and $2,145 from other forms of aid. The college's own financial statement is required. The FAFSA code is 003565. The deadline for filing freshman financial aid applications for fall entry is October 1.

TEXAS A&M UNIVERSITY AT CORPUS CHRISTI *(The complete profile is made available exclusively on our website, www.barronspac.com)*

TEXAS A&M UNIVERSITY AT GALVESTON E-4

www.tamug.edu

Galveston, TX 77553	**(409) 740-4414** **(877) 322-4443**
Fax: (409) 740-4731	**Email: seaaggie@tamug.edu**
Full-time: 863 men, 592 women	**Faculty:** 114
Part-time: 61 men, 49 women	**Ph.D.s:** 40%
Graduate: 12 men, 37 women	**Student/Faculty:** 13 to 1
Year: semesters, summer session	**Tuition:** $7920 ($11,850)
Room & Board: $8000	**Freshman Class:** 1068 applied, 917 accepted, 444 enrolled
SAT CR/M: 520/540 **ACT:** 23	**CEEB CODE:** 6835
Application Deadline: open	**COMPETITIVE**

Texas A&M University at Galveston, founded in 1962, is a public institution that offers marine and maritime-related programs. It is part of the Texas A&M University system. The figures in the above capsule and in this profile are approximate. There are 9 undergraduate schools and 1 graduate school. In addition to regional accreditation, TAMUG has baccalaureate program accreditation with ABET. The 120-acre campus is in a suburban area 50 miles south of Houston, Texas on the Gulf of Mexico. Including any residence halls, there are 14 buildings.

STUDENT LIFE: 81% of undergraduates are from Texas. Others are from 43 states, and 8 foreign countries. 94% are from public schools. 9% are Hispanic; 85% White; 1% African American; 1% Asian American; 1% American Indian/Alaska Native; 1% Foreign. **Male To Female Ratio:** 1.4:1. The average age of freshmen is 18; all undergraduates, 20. 28% do not continue beyond their first year; 52% remain to graduate. **Housing:** 650 students can be accommodated in college housing, which includes coed dorms. On-campus housing is guaranteed for the freshman year only, and is available on a first-come, and first-served basis. 58% of students commute. All students may keep cars. Alcohol is not permitted.

FACULTY/CLASSROOMS: 65% of faculty are male; 35% are female. All teach undergraduates. No introductory courses are taught by graduate students. The average class size in an introductory lecture is 48; in a laboratory is 14; and in a regular course is 24.

PROGRAMS OF STUDY: Galveston confers B.A. and B.S. degrees. Master's degrees are also awarded. Bachelor's degrees are awarded in AGRICULTURE (environmental studies, fishing and fisheries, and natural resource management), BIOLOGICAL SCIENCE (biology/biological science, environmental biology, marine biology, and marine science), BUSINESS (international business management, recreation and leisure services, and transportation management), COMPUTER AND PHYSICAL SCIENCE (earth science, geoscience, hydrology, natural sciences, oceanography, and science and management), ENGINEERING AND ENVIRONMENTAL DESIGN (civil engineering, electrical/electronics engineering technology, electromechanical technology, environmental science, land use management and reclamation, marine engineering, maritime science, mechanical engineering technology, naval architecture and marine engineering, ocean engineering, systems engineering, and transportation engineering), SOCIAL SCIENCE (archeology, geography, humanities and social science, liberal arts/general studies, and water resources). Marine systems engineering is the strongest academically. Marine biology has the largest enrollment.

ACTIVITIES: There are no fraternities or sororities. There are 39 groups on campus, including chorale, drama, ethnic, international, literary magazine, newspaper, political, professional, religious, social, social service, student government, and yearbook. Popular campus events include Springfest, Mardi Grass, and Maritime Ball. **Sports:** There are 2 intercollegiate sports for men and 1 for women, and 6 intramural sports for men and 5 for women. Facilities include tennis courts, a volleyball court, a swimming pool, and a basketball court. **Graduates:** From July 1, 2015 to June 30, 2016, 250 bachelor's degrees were awarded. The most popular majors were marine biology (30%), maritime administration (20%), and marine transportation (10%). 87 companies recruited on campus in 2015-2016. In an average class, 1% graduate in 3 years or less, 25% graduate in 4 years or less, 35% graduate in 5 years or less, and 52% graduate in 6 years or less. Of the 2015 graduating class, 30% were enrolled in graduate school within 6 months of graduation, and 90% were employed.

SERVICES: Counseling and information services are available, as is tutoring in most subjects, a reader service for the blind, and remedial math, reading, and writing. **Library/Resources:** The library contains 43,000 volumes, 52,984 microform items, and subscribes to 970 periodicals including electronic. Computerized library services include interlibrary loans and database searching. **Physically Challenged Students:** 85% of the campus is accessible. Facilities include wheelchair ramps, elevators, special parking, specially equipped restrooms, special class scheduling, and lowered drinking fountains. **Special:** TAMUG offers dual majors in all majors, dual degrees, internships in marine biology and oceanography, a summer semester at sea, and credit for military service. Students may challenge any course for credit by exam. A pass/fail option is available for electives taken by juniors or seniors who have a minimum 2.5 GPA. Selected majors may earn a ship's officer license with a degree program. **Visiting:** There are regularly scheduled orientations for prospective students, including campus tours conducted Monday and Friday at 10 a.m. There are guides for informal visits and visitors may sit in on classes. To schedule a visit, contact the Student Relations Department at (409) 740-4422. **Campus Safety and Security:** Measures include 24-hour foot and vehicle patrol, emergency notification system, and security escort services. There are shuttle buses and lighted pathways/sidewalks.

REQUIREMENTS: Acceptable test scores depend on high school rank, with minimum composite scores of 1000 for the SAT I and 24 for the ACT. Applicants must be graduates of an accredited high school or hold a GED. A minimum of 16 academic credits is required, including 4 units of English, 3.5 units of math, 2.5 units of either history or social studies,

2 units each of a foreign language and science, and the rest in electives. AP and CLEP credits are accepted. Important factors in the admissions decision are leadership record, extracurricular activities record, and recommendations by school officials. Depending on the major, students must complete 130 to 160 credit hours with a GPA of 2.0 overall as well as in the major. The required core curriculum includes courses in math, political science, American history, and macroeconomics. Distribution requirements include 6 credits each in English, calculus, humanities and social sciences; 8 credits in science; and 12 credits in citizenship. Students must also complete a 2-semester sequence of a foreign language and 1 computer language course. Total number of hours in the major is 36. **Procedure:** Freshmen are admitted to all sessions. Entrance exams should be taken late in the junior year or early in the senior year. There are early decision, early admissions, deferred admissions, and rolling admissions plans. Application deadlines are open. Application fee is $45. Notification is sent on a rolling basis. 350 early decision candidates were accepted for the 2016-2017 class. Applications are accepted online. **Transfer Students:** 109 transfer students enrolled in 2015-2016. Applicants must have a cumulative 2.0 GPA in a minimum of 24 completed credit hours as well as a 2.0 GPA in each of the last 2 terms attended. 30 of 130 credits required for the bachelor's degree must be completed at Galveston. **International Students:** There are 13 international students enrolled. They must take the TOEFL, the college's own test, as well as the SAT or ACT.

ADMISSIONS: 86% of the 2016-2017 applicants were accepted. The SAT scores for the 2016-2017 freshman class were: Critical Reading-- 30% below 500, 55% between 500 and 599, 14% between 600 and 699, and 1% between 700 and 800. Math-- 30% below 500, 55% between 500 and 599, 14% between 600 and 699, and 1% between 700 and 800. The ACT scores were 20% below 12, 30% between 12 and 17, 40% between 18 and 23, 7% between 24 and 29, and 3% above 30. 30% of the current freshmen were in the top fifth of their class; 65% were in the top two fifths. There was 1 National Merit finalist. 2 freshmen graduated first in their class. **Admissions Contact:** Sarah Trombley, Director of Admissions. Email: *seaaggie@tamug.edu* Web: *www.tamug.edu*

FINANCIAL AID: In 2016-2017, 85% of continuing full-time students received some form of financial aid. 65% of all full-time freshmen and 85% of continuing full-time students received need-based aid. 65% of undergraduate students work part-time. Average annual earnings from campus work are $1400. The average financial indebtedness of the 2016 graduate was $8,600. The deadline for filing freshman financial aid applications for fall entry is April 1.

TEXAS A&M UNIVERSITY AT KINGSVILLE *(The complete profile is made available exclusively on our website, www.barronspac.com)*

TEXAS CHRISTIAN UNIVERSITY — D-2

www.tcu.edu

Fort Worth, TX 76129	**(817) 257-7490** **(800) TCU-FROG**
Fax: (817) 257-7268	**Email: frogmail@tcu.edu**
Full-time: 3388 men, 5220 women	**Faculty:** 630; I, -$
Part-time: 141 men, 142 women	**Ph.D.s:** 85%
Graduate: 662 men, 841 women	**Student/Faculty:** 14 to 1
Year: semesters, summer session	**Tuition:** $42,670
Room & Board: $12,000	**Freshman Class:** 19972 applied, 7506 accepted, 1888 enrolled
SAT or ACT: required	**CEEB CODE:** 6820
Application Deadline: February 15	**HIGHLY COMPETITIVE**

Texas Christian University, founded in 1873, is a private university affiliated with the Christian Church (Disciples of Christ). TCU is a teaching and research institution offering undergraduate programs in arts, sciences, business, education, fine arts, communications, nursing, and engineering. There are 8 undergraduate schools and 8 graduate schools. In addition to regional accreditation, TCU has baccalaureate program accreditation with AACSB, ABET, ACEJMC, CSWE, NASAD, NASM, ACS, ASHA, CAATE, CIDA, COA, AACN, ACEND, CCNE, BON, TEA, NAEYC, SACS CASI, UCIEP, NASD, SAIS, TANS, and AAIEP. The 289-acre campus is in a suburban area 5 miles southwest of downtown Fort Worth. Including any residence halls, there are 125 buildings.

STUDENT LIFE: 51% of undergraduates are from Texas. Others are from 49 states, 72 foreign countries, and Canada. 57% are from public schools. 72% are White; 5% African American; 5% Foreign; 3% Asian American; 2% race unknown; 12% Hispanic; 1% American Indian/Alaska Native. 48% are Protestant; 25% Catholic; 15% claim no religious affiliation. **Female To Male Ratio:** 1.5:1. The average age of freshmen is 18; all undergraduates, 20. 9% do not continue beyond their first year; 77% remain to graduate. **Housing:** 4267 students can be accommodated in college housing, which includes single-sex and coed dorms, on-campus apartments, honors houses, language houses, fraternity houses, and sorority houses. On-campus housing is available on a lottery system for upperclassmen. 51% of students commute. All students may keep cars.

FACULTY/CLASSROOMS: 51% of faculty are male; 49% are female. All teach undergraduates, and all do research. No introductory courses are taught by graduate students. The average class size in an introductory lecture is 31 and in a laboratory is 21.

PROGRAMS OF STUDY: TCU confers B.A., B.B.A., B.F.A., B.G.S., B.Mus., B.S., B.S.Ed., B.S.N., B.S.W., B.C.J., B.Mus.Ed., B.S.Ath.Trng. and B.C.S. degrees. Master's and doctoral degrees are also awarded. Bachelor's degrees are awarded in AGRICULTURE (ranch management), BIOLOGICAL SCIENCE (biochemistry, biology/biological science, neurosciences, and nutrition), BUSINESS (accounting, business information systems, entrepreneurial studies, fashion merchandising, finance, international accounting, international business information systems, international economics, international entrepreneurial management, international finance, international real estate finance, international marketing, international supply and value chain management, marketing, real estate finance, supply chain management, and professional program in accounting), COMMUNICATIONS AND THE ARTS (art history, ballet, ballet modern dance, church music, communications, English, film, television and digital media, French, German, graphic design, instrumental performance, instrumental music education, journalism, keyboard - piano concentration, modern dance, music, music theory and composition, musical theater, organ performance, photography, piano pedagogy, printmaking, sculpture, Spanish, sports media, strategic communication, strings, studio art, studio art ceramics, studio art painting, theatre acting, theatre arts, theater design, theatre production, theatre studies, vocal performance, vocal music education, and writing), COMPUTER AND PHYSICAL SCIENCE (applied geoscience, astronomy and physics, chemistry, combined science, computer information technology, computer science, geology, mathematics, mathematics - actuarial concentration, and physics), EDUCATION (art education, athletic training, bilingual early childhood education, early childhood education, educational studies, general studies, middle school education, physical education, and secondary education), ENGINEERING AND ENVIRONMENTAL DESIGN (electrical/electronics engineering, engineering, engineering/ele emphasis/energy sys focus, engineering/mechanical emp/energy sys focus, environmental science, interior design, and mechanical engineering), HEALTH PROFESSIONS (habilitation of the deaf, health, movement science, nursing, pre-health studies, speech pathology/audiology, and sports psychology), SOCIAL SCIENCE (anthropology, child psychology/development, criminal justice, dietetics, economics, food production/management/services, geography, history, international political science, philosophy, political science/government, psychology, religion, social work, and sociology). General business, nursing, and biology have the largest enrollments.

ACTIVITIES: 41% of men belong to 19 national fraternities; 58% of women belong to 1 local and 19 national sororities. There are 256 groups on campus, including art, band, cheerleading, choir, chorale, chorus, communications, computers, dance, debate, drama, drill team, environmental, ethnic, film, forensics, honors, international, jazz band, LGBT, literary magazine, marching band, musical theater, newspaper, opera, orchestra, pep band, photography, political, professional, radio and TV, religious, social, social service, student government, symphony, and yearbook. Popular campus events include Frog Camp, Frogs First Weekend, Family Weekend, Second Year Pinning, Homecoming, Christmas Tree Lighting, Carols by Candlelight, and Senior Fiesta. **Sports:** There are 8 intercollegiate sports for men and 11 for women, and 19 intramural sports for men and 19 for women. Facilities include a recreation facility which has a natatorium, outdoor swimming pool, racquetball courts, squash court, track, two multi-use gymnasiums sports, weight training, a cardiovascular fitness area, multi-purpose exercise studios, and a climbing wall. **Graduates:** From July 1, 2015 to June 30, 2016, 2061 bachelor's degrees were awarded. The most popular majors were nursing (9%), communication studies (6%), and strategic communication (5%).

In an average class, 1% graduate in 3 years or less, 63% graduate in 4 years or less, 76% graduate in 5 years or less, and 77% graduate in 6 years or less. Of the 2015 graduating class, 28% were enrolled in graduate school within 6 months of graduation, and 75% were employed.

SERVICES: **Library/Resources:** The library contains 1.4 million volumes, 511,411 microform items, 68,829 audio/video tapes/CDs/DVDs, and subscribes to 730,255 periodicals including electronic. Computerized library services include interlibrary loans, database searching, Internet access, and Wi-Fi capability. Special learning facilities include an art gallery, natural history museum, radio station, TV station, an observatory, speech and hearing clinic, energy institute, behavioral research institute, laboratory schools, and other centers within each college. **Physically Challenged Students:** All of the campus is accessible. Facilities include wheelchair ramps, elevators, special parking, specially equipped restrooms, lowered drinking fountains, and lowered telephones. **Special:** A general studies degree and a combined B.A.-B.S. degree in numerous majors are offered. TCU also accepts credit by exam and credit for life, military, and work experience. Accelerated programs are available in education and nursing. Internships are available in almost all major areas. The university also offers a Washington semester and study abroad in approximately 25 countries. TCU has a student-designed major, Interdisciplinary Inquiry, available on the BA, or BS degree. There are 36 national honor societies, Phi Beta Kappa, and a freshman honors program. **Visiting:** There are regularly scheduled orientations for prospective students, including student-led campus tours, group information sessions, optional personal interviews, and departmental visits. There are guides for informal visits, visitors may sit in on classes, and stay overnight. To schedule a visit, contact the Admissions Office. **Campus Safety and Security:** Measures include 24-hour foot and vehicle patrol, emergency notification system, self-defense education, and security escort services. There are also shuttle buses, emergency telephones, lighted pathways/sidewalks, controlled access to dorms/residences, bike patrol, and video monitoring of most parking lots.

REQUIREMENTS: Either the SAT or the ACT is required for admission. Candidates should be graduates of an accredited secondary school and have completed at least 17 Carnegie units, including 4 years of English, 3 years each of math, science, and social studies, and 2 years each of the same foreign language and of academic electives. TCU also requires an essay, a counselor's recommendation and a teacher's recommendation. A personal interview is optional. AP and CLEP credits are accepted. Important factors in the admissions decision are advanced placement or honors courses, leadership record, and extracurricular activities record. TCU requires completion of the TCU Core Curriculum Requirements, which are divided into the Essential Competencies Curriculum (12 hours plus 6 hours Writing Emphasis); Human Experiences and Endeavors Curriculum (27 hours; the Heritage, Mission, Vision and Values Curriculum (18 hours). Courses in the TCU Core Curriculum may overlay with other requirements of the student's degree program. The overlay feature provides the flexibility for core requirement to be satisfied in a range between 39 and 63 hours. At least 124 semester hours of credit (58 of which must be in residence) with a 2.0 GPA, 42 hours of upper division work, at least 30 hours in residence, and a major or concentration. **Procedure:** Freshmen are admitted in the fall, spring, and summer. Entrance exams should be taken during or before the fall semester of the senior year. There are early decision, early admissions, and deferred admissions plans. Early decision applications should be filed by November 1; regular applications, by February 15 for fall entry, along with a $50 fee. Notification of early decision is sent December 5; regular decision, April 1. 310 early decision candidates were accepted for the 2016-2017 class. 2302 applicants were on the 2016 waiting list; 436 were admitted. Applications are accepted online. **Transfer Students:** 434 transfer students enrolled in 2015-2016. The recommended GPA is 2.7 and a minimum GPA of 2.0 is required. Applicants must complete an application form and submit official transcripts from each college attended. If fewer than 24 semester hours of transferable work have been completed at the time of application, SAT or ACT scores and secondary school transcripts are required. 58 of 124 credits required for the bachelor's degree must be completed at TCU. **International Students:** There are 418 international students enrolled. The school actively recruits these students. They must take the TOEFL with a minimum score of 550 on the paper-based TOEFL (PBT) or 80 on the Internet-based version (iBT), or take the SAT, ACT, or IELTS. The SAT or ACT is required for freshmen whose high school was taught in English or who want to be considered for scholarship.

ADMISSIONS: 38% of the 2016-2017 applicants were accepted. The SAT scores for the 2016-2017 freshman class were: 67% of the current freshmen were in the top fifth of their class; 93% were in the top two fifths. **Admissions Contact:** Heath Einstein, Dean of Admissions. Email: *frogmail@tcu.edu* Web: *www.tcu.edu*

FINANCIAL AID: In 2016-2017, 78% of all full-time freshmen and 68% of continuing full-time students received some form of financial aid. 38% of all full-time freshmen and continuing full-time students received need-based aid. The average freshman award was $30,126. Need-based scholarships or need-based grants averaged $19,238 ($57,716 maximum); need-based self-help aid (loans and jobs) averaged $2,918 ($9,000 maximum); non-need-based athletic scholarships averaged $37,415 ($73,771 maximum); and other non-need-based awards and non-need-based scholarships averaged $16,515 ($60,516 maximum). 22% of undergraduate students work part-time. Average annual earnings from campus work are $1830. The average financial indebtedness of the 2016 graduate was $36,550. TCU is a member of CSS. The CSS/Profile is required. The FAFSA code is 003636. The priority date for freshman financial aid applications for fall entry is February 15.

TEXAS LUTHERAN UNIVERSITY — D-4

www.tlu.edu

Seguin, TX 78155 — **(830) 372-8050**, **(800) 771-8521**

Fax: (830) 372-8096	**Email:** admissions@tlu.edu
Full-time: 600 men, 613 women	**Faculty:** 82
Part-time: 25 men, 45 women	**Ph.D.s:** 84%
Graduate: 7 men, 9 women	**Student/Faculty:** 16 to 1
Year: semesters, summer session	**Tuition:** $28,900
Room & Board: $9720	**Freshman Class:** 2131 applied, 908 accepted, 377 enrolled
SAT CR/M/W: 490/500/460 **ACT:** 21	**CEEB CODE:** 6823
Application Deadline: August 1	**COMPETITIVE**

Texas Lutheran University, founded in 1891, is an exclusively undergraduate university of the liberal arts, sciences, and professional studies. The university's mission is to prepare students academically, spiritually, and socially for lives of leadership and service. There is 1 undergraduate school and 1 graduate school. In addition to regional accreditation, TLU has baccalaureate program accreditation with ACBSP, NASM, TEAC, and CAATE. The 184-acre campus is in a small town 37 miles east of San Antonio and 50 miles south of Austin. Including any residence halls, there are 37 buildings.

STUDENT LIFE: 98% of undergraduates are from Texas. Others are from 15 states, 11 foreign countries, and Canada. 54% are White; 32% Hispanic; 9% African American; 2% race unknown; 1% Asian American; 1% American Indian/Alaska Native; 1% Foreign; 1% two or more races. 48% are Protestant; 33% claim no religious affiliation; 16% Catholic. **Female To Male Ratio:** 1.1:1. The average age of freshmen is 18; all undergraduates, 21. 32% do not continue beyond their first year; 52% remain to graduate. **Housing:** 952 students can be accommodated in college housing, which includes single-sex and coed dorms, on-campus apartments, and married student housing. On-campus housing is guaranteed for all 4 years, and is available on a first-come, and first-served basis. 58% of students live on campus; of those, 70% remain on campus on weekends. All students may keep cars.

FACULTY/CLASSROOMS: 48% of faculty are male; 52% are female. All teach undergraduates. No introductory courses are taught by graduate students. The average class size in an introductory lecture is 20; in a laboratory is 20; and in a regular course is 12.

PROGRAMS OF STUDY: TLU confers B.A., B.S., B.B.A., B.S.N., and B.M.MAacy degrees. Master's degrees are also awarded. Bachelor's degrees are awarded in BIOLOGICAL SCIENCE (biochemistry and biology/biological science), BUSINESS (accounting and business administration and management), COMMUNICATIONS AND THE ARTS (art, communications, dramatic arts, English, music, and Spanish), COMPUTER AND PHYSICAL SCIENCE (applied science, chemistry, computer science, information sciences and systems, mathematics, and physics), EDUCATION (athletic training, education, and physical education), HEALTH PROFESSIONS (nursing), SOCIAL SCIENCE (economics, history, international studies, philosophy, political science/government, psychology, sociology, and theological studies). Business, biology, and psychology are the strongest academically. Business, education, and kinesiology have the largest enrollments.

ACTIVITIES: 7% of men belong to 3 local fraternities; 11% of women belong to 5 local sororities. There are 47 groups on campus, including art, band, cheerleading, choir, chorus, computers, dance, drama, environmental, ethnic, forensics, honors, international, jazz band, LGBT, literary magazine, musical theater, newspaper, orchestra, pep band, political, professional, religious, science club, social, social service, student government, and symphony. Popular campus events include Christmas Vespers, Spring Fling and Student Academic Symposium. **Sports:** There are 8 intercollegiate sports for men and 8 for women, and 14 intramural sports for men and 14 for women. Facilities include a football and track stadium, a gym, fitness center, swimming pool, softball, baseball, and soccer fields, intramural/recreation fields, golf practice greens, a walking track, practice gym, sand volleyball courts, tennis courts, and racquetball courts. **Graduates:** From July 1, 2015 to June 30, 2016, 323 bachelor's degrees were awarded. The most popular majors were business administration (16%), kinesiology (11%), and education (9%). 29 companies recruited on campus in 2015-2016. In an average class, 30% graduate in 4 years or less, 49% graduate in 5 years or less, and 52% graduate in 6 years or less.

SERVICES: Counseling and information services are available, as is tutoring in most subjects, and a reader service for the blind. Assistance with writing assignments is also available. **Library/Resources:** The library contains 162,832 volumes, 117,629 microform items, 2,833 audio/video tapes/CDs/DVDs, and subscribes to 126,205 periodicals including electronic. Computerized library services include interlibrary loans, database searching, Internet access, and Wi-Fi capability. **Physically Challenged Students:** 90% of the campus is accessible. Facilities include wheelchair ramps, elevators, special parking, specially equipped restrooms, special class scheduling, lowered drinking fountains, and special housing. **Special:** Internships are available in most majors. Study abroad in all countries affiliated with ISEP, Augsburg College, Central College, Equador Exchange, and Kansai Gaidai, a Washington semester with American University, and work-study programs are available. The college offers student-designed majors and dual majors. There is a 3-2 engineering program with Texas A&M, Baylor University and Southern Methodist University There are 11 national honor societies, a freshman honors program, and 20 departmental honors programs. **Visiting:** There are regularly scheduled orientations for prospective students, including a campus tour, classroom visits, a financial aid presentation, a study abroad session, an athlete session, and a student panel. There are guides for informal visits, visitors may sit in on classes, and stay overnight. To schedule a visit, contact the Admissions Office. **Campus Safety and Security:** Measures include 24-hour foot and vehicle patrol, self-defense education, security escort services, lighted pathways/sidewalks, and coded locks in residence halls.

REQUIREMENTS: The SAT or ACT is required. Applicants must have 16 Carnegie units, including a recommended 4 years in English, 3 each of social studies, math, and science, and 2 in foreign language. The GED is accepted. A GPA of 2.5 is required. AP and CLEP credits are accepted. Important factors in the admissions decision are advanced placement or honors courses, recommendations by school officials, and extracurricular activities record. All students must complete 124 semester hours, including 24 to 54 in their major, with a 2.0 GPA. Between 45 and 49 hours of distribution courses are required. A senior seminar, project, or concert is required in all majors. **Procedure:** Freshmen are admitted fall, spring, and summer. Entrance exams should be taken in the spring of the junior year or the summer before the senior year. There are early decision and early admissions plans. Early decision applications should be filed by December 15; regular applications, by August 1 for fall entry, along with a $300 fee. Applications are accepted online. **Transfer Students:** 53 transfer students enrolled in 2015-2016. Applicants for transfer must have a GPA of at least 2.25 and be in good academic standing. 33 of 124 credits required for the bachelor's degree must be completed at TLU. **International Students:** There are 8 international students enrolled. The school actively recruits these students. They must take the TOEFL with a minimum score of 550 on the paper-based TOEFL (PBT) or 79 on the Internet-based version (iBT). They must also take the SAT or ACT, scoring 960.

ADMISSIONS: 43% of the 2016-2017 applicants were accepted. The SAT scores for the 2016-2017 freshman class were: Critical Reading-- 55% below 500, 35% between 500 and 599, and 10% between 600 and 699. Math-- 52% below 500, 36% between 500 and 599, and 11% between 600 and 699. Writing-- 72% below 500, 24% between 500 and 599, and 3% between 600 and 699. The ACT scores were 13% between 12 and 17, 64% between 18 and 23, 22% between 24 and 29, and 1% above 30. 36% of the current freshmen were in the top fifth of their class; 62% were in the top two fifths. **Admissions Contact:** Adam Navarro-Jusino, Director of Admissions. Email: *admissions@tlu.edu* Web: *www.tlu.edu*

FINANCIAL AID: In 2016-2017, 99% of all full-time freshmen and 97% of continuing full-time students received some form of financial aid. 93% of all full-time freshmen and 97% of continuing full-time students received need-based aid. The average freshman award was $28,790. Need-based scholarships or need-based grants averaged $19,482 ($28,910 maximum); need-based self-help aid (loans and jobs) averaged $5,319 ($5,500 maximum); and other non-need-based awards and non-need-based scholarships averaged $7,181 ($34,000 maximum). The average financial indebtedness of the 2016 graduate was $27,424. The state aid form, and TASFA is required. The FAFSA code is 003641. The priority date for freshman financial aid applications for fall entry is March 1.

TEXAS SOUTHERN UNIVERSITY *(The complete profile is made available exclusively on our website, www.barronspac.com)*

TEXAS STATE UNIVERSITY — D-3

www.txstate.edu

San Marcos, TX 78666 — (512) 245-2364

Fax: (512) 245-8044	**Email:** admissions@txstate.edu
Full-time: 11,896 men, 16,284 women	**Faculty:** 971; IIA, -$
	Ph.D.s: 77%
Part-time: 2780 men, 3284 women	**Student/Faculty:** 20 to 1
Graduate: 1647 men, 2917 women	**Tuition:** $10,218 ($22,458)
Year: semesters, summer session	**Freshman Class:** 21524 applied, 15239 accepted, 5732 enrolled
Room & Board: $9132	
SAT CR/M/W: 510/510/480 **ACT:** 23	**CEEB CODE:** 6667
Application Deadline: May 1	**COMPETITIVE**

Texas State University, founded in 1899, and part of the Texas State University System. Texas State offers programs in general studies, applied arts, business, education, fine arts, health professions, liberal arts, science, engineering and technology. Texas State offers 98 Bachelor degrees, 90 Master degrees, 11 Doctoral degrees and 1 Special Professional degree. There are 8 undergraduate schools and 1 graduate school. In addition to regional accreditation, Texas State has baccalaureate program accreditation with AACSB, ABET, ACCE, ACEJMC, ADA, AHEA, CSAB, CSWE, FIDER, NASM, NRPA, NAACLS, CAAHEP, and Texas State Board for Education Certification/TEA. The 495-acre campus is in a suburban area 30 miles south of Austin and 45 miles northeast of San Antonio. Including any residence halls, there are 313 buildings.

STUDENT LIFE: 98% of undergraduates are from Texas. Others are from 48 states, 46 foreign countries, and Canada. 98% are from public schools. 47% are White; 4% two or more races; 36% Hispanic; 2% Asian American; 10% African American; 1% Foreign. **Female To Male Ratio:** 1.4:1. The average age of freshmen is 19; all undergraduates, 22. 24% do not continue beyond their first year; 54% remain to graduate. **Housing:** 6926 students can be accommodated in college housing, which includes single-sex and coed dorms, on-campus apartments, and married student housing. In addition, there are honors houses, special-interest houses, special residences for international students, single parents, upper-division students, and freshmen experience. On-campus housing is guaranteed for the freshman year only, and is available on a first-come, and first-served basis. 81% of students commute. All students may keep cars.

FACULTY/CLASSROOMS: 48% of faculty are male; 52% are female. 74% teach undergraduates, 30% do research, and 28% do both. Graduate students teach 8% of introductory courses. The average class size in an introductory lecture is 39; in a laboratory is 21; and in a regular course is 36.

PROGRAMS OF STUDY: Texas State confers B.A., B.A.A.S., B.A.I.S., B.B.A., B.E.S.S., B.F.A., B.G.S., B.H.A., B.H.W.P., B.M., B.P.A., B.S., B.S.A.G., B.S.C.D., B.S.C.L.S., B.S.C.J., B.S.F.C.S., B.S.H.I.M., B.S.N, B.S.R.A., B.S.R.C., B.S.R.T., B.S.T. and B.S.W. degrees. Master's and doctoral degrees are also awarded. Bachelor's degrees are awarded in AGRI-

CULTURE (agricultural business management, agriculture, and animal science), BIOLOGICAL SCIENCE (biochemistry, biology/biological science, marine biology, microbiology, nutrition, physiology, wildlife biology, and zoology), BUSINESS (accounting, banking and finance, business administration and management, business economics, fashion merchandising, finance, management science, marketing/retailing/merchandising, recreational facilities management, and tourism), COMMUNICATIONS AND THE ARTS (advertising, applied art, art, art history and appreciation, audio technology, broadcasting, communication design , communication studies, communications, dance, digital media, dramatic arts, English, French, German, jazz, journalism, music, music performance, musical theater, photography, public relations, Spanish, studio art, and theatre arts), COMPUTER AND PHYSICAL SCIENCE (applied mathematics, chemistry, computer information systems, computer science, mathematics, and physics), EDUCATION (athletic training, education, health education, health information management, physical education, special education, and technical education), ENGINEERING AND ENVIRONMENTAL DESIGN (cartography, city/community/regional planning, construction management, construction technology, electrical/electronics engineering, engineering technology, environmental science, industrial engineering, industrial engineering technology, interior design, land use management and reclamation, manufacturing engineering, manufacturing technology, urban planning technology, and water and wastewater technology), HEALTH PROFESSIONS (allied health, clinical science, exercise science, health and physical activity, health care administration, medical records administration/services, nursing, radiation therapy, respiratory therapy, and speech pathology/audiology), SOCIAL SCIENCE (American studies, anthropology, Asian/Oriental studies, child care/child and family studies, communication sciences & disorders, corrections, criminal justice, economics, European studies, family/consumer studies, geography, history, interdisciplinary studies, international relations, international studies, law enforcement and corrections, liberal arts/general studies, Middle Eastern studies, philosophy, political science/government, psychology, public administration, social work, and sociology). Geography, anthropology, education, and nursing are the strongest academically. Education, business, and psychology have the largest enrollments.

ACTIVITIES: 5% of men belong to 6 local and 15 national fraternities; 5% of women belong to 12 national sororities. There are 388 groups on campus, including art, band, cheerleading, chess, choir, chorale, chorus, communications, computers, dance, debate, drama, drill team, ethnic, film, honors, international, jazz band, LGBT, literary magazine, marching band, musical theater, newspaper, opera, orchestra, pep band, photography, political, professional, radio and TV, religious, social, social service, student government, symphony, and yearbook. Popular campus events include Unversity Common Experience, Welcome Week, Trade Up Days, Moonlight Breakfast, Philosophy Dialogues Series, Encore Series of Music and Theatrical Performances. **Sports:** There are 5 intercollegiate sports for men and 7 for women, and 10 intramural sports for men and 10 for women. Facilities include a gym, baseball, and softball stadium, tennis courts, a spring-fed pool, and aquatic sports center. A student recreation center has basketball and volleyball courts, racquetball courts, an indoor jogging/walking track, weight-lifting equipment, exercise machines, and rooms for fitness, dance, and aerobics. Intramural fields include softball, soccer, and lacross. There is also a separate walking/running track from those used by the NCAA athletes. **Graduates:** From July 1, 2015 to June 30, 2016, 6470 bachelor's degrees were awarded. The most popular majors were business/marketing (18%), interdisciplinary studies in education (9%), and parks and recreation (8%). 889 companies recruited on campus in 2015-2016. In an average class, 2% graduate in 3 years or less, 27% graduate in 4 years or less, 48% graduate in 5 years or less, and 54% graduate in 6 years or less. Of the 2015 graduating class, 22% were enrolled in graduate school within 6 months of graduation, and 83% were employed.

SERVICES: Counseling and information services are available, as is tutoring in most subjects, such as any core curriculum subjects and other advanced science and mathematics courses. There is also a reader service for the blind, and remedial math, reading, and writing. Tutoring is available for all core curriculum classes. **Library/Resources:** The library contains 4.3 million volumes, 1.9 million microform items, and 112,360 audio/video tapes/CDs/DVDs, and subscribes to 34,564 periodicals including electronic. Computerized library services include interlibrary loans, database searching, Internet access, and Wi-Fi capability. Special learning facilities include an art gallery, planetarium, radio station, recording studio, 17 inch telescope, clean room for manufacturing micro chips, anthropology forensics laboratory, and special collections library in southwest writing and photography. **Physically Challenged Students:** 90% of the campus is accessible. Facilities include wheelchair ramps, elevators, special parking, specially equipped restrooms, special class scheduling, lowered drinking fountains, lowered telephones, special housing, curb cuts, pay TTY text telephones, adaptive computer technology, sign language interpreter, and reading recorder services for the visually impaired. **Special:** Co-op programs in medicine, dentistry, engineering, architecture, law, pharmacy, nursing, occupational therapy, and veterinary medicine, internships in many departments not exclusive of education and business, study abroad in 26 countries, and Washington semesters are available. Dual majors, credit for life experience, and non-degree study also are possible. Two summer sessions are offered in most programs. A 3-2 engineering degree is possible with the University of Texas, Texas A&M, Texas Tech University, and University of Texas at San Antonio. There are 24 national honor societies, a freshman honors program, and 1 departmental honors program. **Visiting:** There are regularly scheduled orientations for prospective students, a 2-day event, with registration required. First-time freshmen parents may attend. Students receive registration instructions, academic advising, and information concerning Texas State's academic policies, procedures, and student services. Time is allotted to register for classes. There are guides for informal visits and visitors may sit in on classes. To schedule a visit, contact the Admissions Office. **Campus Safety and Security:** Measures include 24-hour foot and vehicle patrol, emergency notification system, self-defense education, and security escort services. There are shuttle buses, emergency telephones, lighted pathways/sidewalks, and controlled access to dorms/residences.

REQUIREMENTS: The ACT Optional Writing test is required. Minimum test scores are determined by high school class rank. Applicants need 26 academic credits, including 4 units in English, 4 in math, 4 in science (2 with labs), 3 in social studies, 2 in foreign language, 1 in fine arts and 8 in academic electives. The GED is accepted; applicants with a GED are treated as though they were in the 4th quarter of their graduating class which requires an SAT (math and verbal) of 1270 or and ACT of 29. AP and CLEP credits are accepted. Important factors in the admissions decision are advanced placement or honors courses, leadership record, and extracurricular activities record. All students must earn a minimum GPA of 2.0 while taking at least 120 semester hours, including 30 SCH in their major. The core curriculum includes basic skills, language and communication, mathematics, history and political science, natural science, social science, philosophy, international perspectives, literature, fine arts, and physical fitness. **Procedure:** Freshmen are admitted in the fall, spring, and summer. Entrance exams should be taken at the end of the junior year. There is a rolling admissions plan. Applications should be filed by May 1 for fall entry; December 1 for spring entry; and May 1 for summer entry, along with a $75 fee. Notifications are sent September 1. Applications are accepted on-line. Application fees are waived if application is completed on-line. **Transfer Students:** 5354 transfer students enrolled in 2015-2016. Transfer students with 29 or fewer credits must meet freshman requirements; those with 30 or more credits must submit official transcripts to verify a minimum 2.25 GPA and good standing at their previous institution. 30 of 120 credits required for the bachelor's degree must be completed at Texas State. **International Students:** There are 187 international students enrolled. They must take the TOEFL with a minimum score of 550 on the paper-based TOEFL (PBT) or 78 on the Internet-based version (iBT). They must also take the SAT or ACT.

ADMISSIONS: 71% of the 2016-2017 applicants were accepted. The SAT scores for the 2016-2017 freshman class were: Critical Reading-- 44% below 500, 42% between 500 and 599, 12% between 600 and 699, and 2% between 700 and 800. Math-- 41% below 500, 46% between 500 and 599, 12% between 600 and 699, and 1% between 700 and 800. Writing-- 56% below 500, 36% between 500 and 599, 7% between 600 and 699, and 1% between 700 and 800. The ACT scores were 3% between 12 and 17, 56% between 18 and 23, 36% between 24 and 29, and 5% above 30. 40% of the current freshmen were in the top fifth of their class; 82% were in the top two fifths. 24 freshmen graduated first in their class. **Admissions Contact:** Stephanie Anderson, Assistant VP for Enrollment Management. Email: *admissions@txstate.edu* Web: *www.txstate.edu*

FINANCIAL AID: In 2016-2017, 84% of all full-time freshmen and 71% of continuing full-time students received some form of financial aid. 59% of all full-time freshmen and 54% of continuing full-time students received need-based aid. The average freshman award was $12,474. Need-based scholarships or need-based grants averaged $8,111 ($12,815 maximum); need-based self-help aid (loans and jobs) averaged $3,423

($8,100 maximum); non-need-based athletic scholarships averaged $10,860 ($21,820 maximum); and other non-need-based awards and non-need-based scholarships averaged $13,739 ($34,430 maximum). 56% of undergraduate students work part-time. Average annual earnings from campus work are $5676. The average financial indebtedness of the 2016 graduate was $25,246. The FAFSA code is 003615. The priority date for freshman financial aid applications for fall entry is April 1. The filing deadline for fall entry is March 15.

TEXAS TECH UNIVERSITY B-2

www.ttu.edu

Lubbock, TX 79409 **(806) 742-1480**

Fax: (806) 742-0062
Email: admissions@ttu.edu
Full-time: 14,545 men, 12,082 women
Faculty: 1572; I, --$
Ph.D.s: 83%
Part-time: 1892 men, 1444 women
Student/Faculty: 17 to 1
Graduate: 3177 men, 3411 women
Tuition: $10,231 ($22,471)
Year: semesters, summer session
Freshman Class: 23311 applied, 14592 accepted, 4762 enrolled
Room & Board: $8505
SAT CR/M/W: 540/560/520 **ACT:** 24
CEEB CODE: 6827
Application Deadline: August 1
COMPETITIVE+

Texas Tech University, founded in 1923, is a large, comprehensive public university offering undergraduate and graduate programs in a variety of professional fields. The figures in the above capsule and in this profile are approximate. There are 11 undergraduate schools and 1 graduate school. In addition to regional accreditation, Texas Tech has baccalaureate program accreditation with AACSB, ABET, ASLA, CSWE, NAAB, NASAD, NASM, and NCATE. The 1839-acre campus is in an urban area in Lubbock, TX. Including any residence halls, there are 161 buildings.

STUDENT LIFE: 92% of undergraduates are from Texas. Others are from 49 states, 111 foreign countries, and Canada. 87% are from public schools. 9% are Foreign; 7% African American; 58% White; 22% Hispanic; 2% Asian American; 2% two or more races. **Male To Female Ratio:** 1.2:1. The average age of freshmen is 18; all undergraduates, 21. 16% do not continue beyond their first year; 60% remain to graduate. **Housing:** 7750 students can be accommodated in college housing, which includes single-sex coed dorms and on-campus apartments, honors houses, special-interest houses, learning communities, and an international community. On-campus housing is guaranteed for the freshman year only, and is available on a first-come, and first-served basis. 76% of students commute. All students may keep cars. Alcohol is not permitted.

FACULTY/CLASSROOMS: 56% of faculty are male; 44% are female. All teach undergraduates. No introductory courses are taught by graduate students. The average class size in an introductory lecture is 48 and in a laboratory is 22.

PROGRAMS OF STUDY: Texas Tech confers B.A., B.A.AS, B.B.A., B.F.A., B.G.S., B.I.D., B.L.A., B.M., B.S., B.S.ARCH, B.S.CE, B.S.CHE, B.S.EE, B.S.ENEGR., B.S.FCS, B.S.IE, B.S.INECO, B.S.ME, B.S.PE, and B.S.RHIM degrees. Master's and doctoral degrees are also awarded. Bachelor's degrees are awarded in AGRICULTURE (agricultural business management, agricultural communications, agricultural economics, agriculture, animal science, conservation and regulation, environmental studies, natural resource management, and plant science), BIOLOGICAL SCIENCE (biochemistry, cell & molecular biology, microbiology, nutrition, and zoology), BUSINESS (accounting, finance, hotel/motel and restaurant management, international business, international economics, management information systems, management, marketing, personal financial planning, retailing, sports management, and supply chain management), COMMUNICATIONS AND THE ARTS (advertising, apparel design, art, arts/sciences planned program, classics, communication studies, dance, English, French, German, information technology, journalism, languages, literature, media management, music, public relations, Spanish, technical communication, television & digital media production, theatre arts, and winds), COMPUTER AND PHYSICAL SCIENCE (chemistry, computer science, energy science, geoscience, mathematics, and physics), EDUCATION (early childhood education, general studies, global studies, and university studies), ENGINEERING AND ENVIRONMENTAL DESIGN (architecture, chemical engineering, civil engineering, computer engineering, construction engineering, electrical/electronics engineering, environmental engineering, industrial engineering, interior design, landscape architecture, mechanical engineering, and petroleum/natural gas engineering), HEALTH PROFESSIONS (biology, human studies, kinesiology, and nutrition and dietetics), SOCIAL SCIENCE (addiction studies, anthropology, economics, family/consumer studies, food science, geography, history, human development & family studies, Latin American studies, liberal arts/general studies, philosophy, political science/government, psychology, Russian and Slavic studies, social work, and sociology). business, agriculture, music, and personal financial planning are the strongest academically. kinesiology, biology, and psychology have the largest enrollments.

ACTIVITIES: 6% of men belong to 35 national fraternities; 13% of women belong to 23 national sororities. There are 500 groups on campus, including art, band, cheerleading, chess, choir, chorale, chorus, communications, computers, dance, debate, drama, drill team, drum and bugle corps, environmental, ethnic, film, forensics, honors, international, jazz band, LGBT, literary magazine, marching band, musical theater, newspaper, opera, orchestra, pep band, photography, political, professional, radio and TV, religious, social, social service, student government, symphony, and yearbook. Popular campus events include Carol of Lights, Madrigal Dinner, Homecoming Week, Arbor Day, RaiderGate, and Diversity Week. **Sports:** There are 8 intercollegiate sports for men and 9 for women, and 13 intramural sports for men and 12 for women. Facilities include athletic training center, a student recreation center which includes basketball courts, rock wall, free-wight room, workout space, tennis courts, turf field complex, bike shop/rental program. There is also an indoor aquatic center, and outdoor leisure pool featuring a lazy river, lap pool, hot tub, diving well, water basketball, volleyball courts, wading pools and fountains. **Graduates:** From July 1, 2015 to June 30, 2016, 5203 bachelor's degrees were awarded. The most popular majors were exercise & sport science (6%), multidisciplinary studies (5%), and marketing (5%). 740 companies recruited on campus in 2015-2016. In an average class, 3% graduate in 3 years or less, 34% graduate in 4 years or less, 55% graduate in 5 years or less, and 60% graduate in 6 years or less.

SERVICES: Counseling and information services are available, as is tutoring in some subjects, such as accounting, biology, chemistry, computer science, economics, engineering, English, foreign language, history, math, physics, political science, and statistics. There is also a reader service for the blind, and remedial math, reading, and writing. The Learning Center offers academic coaching on topics such as time management, note taking, stress management, plus computer lab, study area and class presentations. The Student Disability Services office provides in-class accommodations based on the documented needs of each student. **Library/Resources:** The 5 libraries contain 2.9 million volumes, 2.5 million microform items, 92,126 audio/video tapes/CDs/DVDs, and subscribe to 155,013 periodicals including electronic. Computerized library services include interlibrary loans, database searching, Internet access, and Wi-Fi capability. Special learning facilities include an art gallery, natural history museum, planetarium, radio station, TV station, museum, observatory, national ranching heritage center, special collections library, archaeological dig/state park, international cultural center, fiber and biopolymer research institute, arid and semi-arid land studies center, child development research center, institutes for environmental and human health, Vietnam center, planetarium, National Wind Institute, Burkhart Center for Autism Education and Research, innovation hub. **Physically Challenged Students:** All of the campus is accessible. Facilities include wheelchair ramps, elevators, special parking, specially equipped restrooms, special class scheduling, lowered drinking fountains, lowered telephones, and special housing. **Special:** Texas Tech offers many bachelor-to-masters accelerated degree programs, internships, study abroad in over 70 countries, dual degrees, dual majors, extended studies, and pass/fail options. We also offer in accelerated program, cooperative education, independent study, and student design program. There are 32 national honor societies, Phi Beta Kappa, and a freshman honors program. **Visiting:** There are regularly scheduled orientations for prospective students, including summer orientation conferences offering new students an opportunity to meet with advisers, register early for the fall semester, and get acquainted with the campus. There are guides for informal visits. To schedule a visit, contact Visitor Center at (806)742-1299. **Campus Safety and Security:** Measures include 24-hour foot and vehicle patrol and emergency notification system. There are also shuttle buses, emergency telephones, lighted pathways/sidewalks, controlled access to dorms/residences, crime prevention programs, Operation ID, and bike registration.

REQUIREMENTS: The SAT or ACT is required. Applicants should be

graduates of an accredited high school or have the GED. The university requires 4 credits in English, 3-4 in math, and 3-4 in science with laboratory sciences, and 2 in foreign language, 3-3.5 in social studies and history, 5-6 in academic electives, 1 each in visual performing art, and physical education, recommended .5 in speech and economics. AP and CLEP credits are accepted. Important factors in the admissions decision are advanced placement or honors courses, recommendations by school officials, and extracurricular activities record. All students seeking a bachelor's degree must meet the requirements of the core curriculum. A minimum of 120 credits hours is required, depending on the degree program. A minimum GPA of 2.0 is required. The last 30 hours and 25% of all credit hours must be from Texas Tech. **Procedure:** Freshmen are admitted in the fall, spring, and summer. Entrance exams should be taken before registering for classes. Applications should be filed by August 1 for fall entry; November 1 for spring entry; and May 1 for summer entry, along with a $75 fee. Notification is sent on a rolling basis. Application fees are waived if application is completed online. **Transfer Students:** 3068 transfer students enrolled in 2015-2016. If a student has any transferable credits, then they must apply as a transfer student. Twelve credit hours are required to be considered a full transfer, and if a student has fewer than twelve transferable credit hours, then they are evaluated by both high school and college coursework for admission. A transfer student is considered assured admit if they have a 2.5 GPA with 12-23 hours, or if they have a 2.25 GPA with 24+ hours. 30 of 120 credits required for the bachelor's degree must be completed at Texas Tech. **International Students:** There are 688 international students enrolled. The school actively recruits these students. They must take the TOEFL with a minimum score of 550 on the paper-based TOEFL (PBT) or 79 on the Internet-based version (iBT), or IELTS, Cambridge Exam, PTE Academic, or an ELS Intensive Program. They must also take the SAT or ACT, scoring 1270.

ADMISSIONS: 63% of the 2016-2017 applicants were accepted. The SAT scores for the 2016-2017 freshman class were: Critical Reading-- 21% below 500, 54% between 500 and 599, 22% between 600 and 699, and 3% between 700 and 800. Math-- 14% below 500, 54% between 500 and 599, 28% between 600 and 699, and 4% between 700 and 800. Writing-- 37% below 500, 48% between 500 and 599, 14% between 600 and 699, and 1% between 700 and 800. The ACT scores were 1% between 12 and 17, 39% between 18 and 23, 54% between 24 and 29, and 9% above 30. 41% of the current freshmen were in the top fifth of their class; 79% were in the top two fifths. There were 15 National Merit finalists. 139 freshmen graduated first in their class. **Admissions Contact:** Jamie Hansard, Executive Director/Undergrad Admissions. Email: *admissions@ttu.edu* Web: *www.ttu.edu*

FINANCIAL AID: The FAFSA code is 003644. The priority date for freshman financial aid applications for fall entry is March 15.

TEXAS WESLEYAN UNIVERSITY D-2

www.txwes.edu

Fort Worth, TX 76105	**(817) 531-4422** **(800) 580-8980**
Fax: (817) 531-7515	**Email: admissions@txwes.edu**
Full-time: 744 men, 744 women	**Faculty:** 123; IIA, av$
Part-time: 189 men, 232 women	**Ph.D.s:** 89%
Graduate: 243 men, 467 women	**Student/Faculty:** 13 to 1
Year: semesters, summer session	**Tuition:** $26,050
Room & Board: $9084	**Freshman Class:** 2959 applied, 1218 accepted, 301 enrolled
SAT CR/M/W: 501/504/463 **ACT:** 21	**CEEB CODE:** 6828
Application Deadline: open	**COMPETITIVE**

Texas Wesleyan University, founded in 1890, is a liberal arts institution affiliated with the United Methodist Church. There are 4 undergraduate schools and 3 graduate schools. In addition to regional accreditation, Texas Wesleyan has baccalaureate program accreditation with AACSB, ACBSP, NASM, and CAATE. The 79-acre campus is in an urban area 2 miles east of downtown Fort Worth. Including any residence halls, there are 38 buildings.

STUDENT LIFE: 80% of undergraduates are from Texas. Others are from 28 states, 50 foreign countries, and Canada. 88% are from public schools. 36% are White; 28% Hispanic; 22% Foreign; 15% African American; 8% Asian American; 7% race unknown; 3% two or more races; 1% American Indian/Alaska Native. 44% claim no religious affiliation; 41% Protestant; 12% Catholic. **Female To Male Ratio:** 1.2:1. The average age of freshmen is 18; all undergraduates, 23. 49% do not continue beyond their first year; 51% remain to graduate. **Housing:** 541 students can be accommodated in college housing, which includes single-sex and coed dorms and on-campus apartments. On-campus housing is available on a first-come and first-served basis. 71% of students commute. All students may keep cars. Alcohol is not permitted.

FACULTY/CLASSROOMS: 43% of faculty are male; 57% are female. 86% teach undergraduates. No introductory courses are taught by graduate students. The average class size in an introductory lecture is 16 and in a laboratory is 12.

PROGRAMS OF STUDY: Texas Wesleyan confers B.A., B.A.A.S., B.B.A., B.M., B.S., B.S.A.T. and B.S.H.S. degrees. Master's and doctoral degrees are also awarded. Bachelor's degrees are awarded in BIOLOGICAL SCIENCE (biochemistry, biology/adolescence education, and biology/biological science), BUSINESS (accounting, business administration and management, business economics, marketing management, and marketing/retailing/merchandising), COMMUNICATIONS AND THE ARTS (dramatic arts, English, journalism, music, Spanish, and theater design), COMPUTER AND PHYSICAL SCIENCE (chemistry and computer science), EDUCATION (athletic training, education, elementary education, foreign languages education, mathematics education, physical education, social science education, social studies education, and teaching English as a second/foreign language (TESOL/TEFOL)), HEALTH PROFESSIONS (biology, biomedical science, and exercise science), SOCIAL SCIENCE (criminal justice, history, industrial and organizational psychology, interdisciplinary studies, paralegal studies, political science/government, prelaw, psychology, religion, religious education, and sociology). General business, criminal justice and liberal studies have the largest enrollments.

ACTIVITIES: 5% of men belong to 1 local and 3 national fraternities; 4% of women belong to 1 local and 2 national sororities. There are 34 groups on campus, including art, band, cheerleading, choir, chorale, computers, drama, ethnic, forensics, honors, international, jazz band, LGBT, literary magazine, musical theater, newspaper, opera, political, professional, radio and TV, religious, social, social service, and student government. Popular campus events include We Are Wesleyan Concert, RAM JAM and University College Day. **Sports:** There are 9 intercollegiate sports for men and 10 for women, and 7 intramural sports for men and 7 for women. Facilities include an athletic center, tennis courts, off-campus baseball park, softball and soccer fields. **Graduates:** From July 1, 2015 to June 30, 2016, 331 bachelor's degrees were awarded. The most popular majors were liberal studies (12%), psychology (11%), and general business (9%). 72 companies recruited on campus in 2015-2016. In an average class, 1% graduate in 3 years or less, 19% graduate in 4 years or less, 32% graduate in 5 years or less, and 35% graduate in 6 years or less. Of the 2015 graduating class, 5% were enrolled in graduate school within 6 months of graduation, and 87% were employed.

SERVICES: Counseling and information services are available, as is tutoring in most subjects, and a remedial math, reading, and writing. **Library/Resources:** The library contains 175,506 volumes, 170 microform items, 6,720 audio/video tapes/CDs/DVDs, and subscribes to 1,499 periodicals including electronic. Computerized library services include interlibrary loans, database searching, Internet access, and Wi-Fi capability. Special learning facilities include an art gallery, radio station, and a theater. **Physically Challenged Students:** Facilities include wheelchair ramps, elevators, special parking, specially equipped restrooms, special class scheduling, and lowered telephones. **Special:** Study abroad is offered in more than 25 countries. A 3-2 engineering degree is offered in conjunction with a number of universities. Pass/fail options are available, as are B.A.-B.S. degrees and internships in sports management, business, psychology, mass communication, and sociology. A predentistry program is available. There are 15 national honor societies and 10 departmental honors programs. **Visiting:** There are regularly scheduled orientations for prospective students. There are guides for informal visits, visitors may sit in on classes, and stay overnight. To schedule a visit, contact the Office of Admissions. **Campus Safety and Security:** Measures include 24-hour foot and vehicle patrol, emergency notification system, self-defense education, and security escort services. There are emergency telephones, lighted pathways/sidewalks, controlled access to dorms/residences, and residence hall programs.

REQUIREMENTS: Applicants must be graduates of an accredited secondary school or have a GED equivalent, with satisfactory scores of 19

ACT composite score or 920 SAT combined score in critical reading and math only. AP and CLEP credits are accepted. Important factors in the admissions decision are leadership record, extracurricular activities record, and recommendations by alumni. A minimum GPA of 2.0 and a minimum of 124 credit hours are required to graduate. All students must complete a general education requirement of 51 credits, including courses in writing, literature, religion, lab science, history, math, political or economic systems, fine arts, humanities, phys ed, and social science, philosophy, or psychology. The total number of hours in the major varies. **Procedure:** Freshmen are admitted to all sessions. Entrance exams should be taken as early as possible. There is a rolling admissions plan. Application deadlines are open. Applications are accepted online. **Transfer Students:** 340 transfer students enrolled in 2015-2016. Applicants with fewer than 30 credit hours must submit a high school transcript and the results of either the SAT or the ACT. A minimum GPA of 2.0 is required. 45 of 124 credits required for the bachelor's degree must be completed at Texas Wesleyan. **International Students:** There are 253 international students enrolled. The school actively recruits these students. They must take the TOEFL with a minimum score of 520 on the paper-based TOEFL (PBT) or 68 on the Internet-based version (iBT). an IELTS score of at least 6.0. The score must be less than 2 years old.

ADMISSIONS: 41% of the 2016-2017 applicants were accepted. The SAT scores for the 2016-2017 freshman class were: Critical Reading-- 50% below 500, 42% between 500 and 599, 7% between 600 and 699, and 1% between 700 and 800. Math-- 46% below 500, 48% between 500 and 599, and 6% between 600 and 699. Writing-- 74% below 500, 22% between 500 and 599, and 4% between 600 and 699. The ACT scores were 3% between 12 and 17, 77% between 18 and 23, 18% between 24 and 29, and 2% above 30. 28% of the current freshmen were in the top fifth of their class; 58% were in the top two fifths. **Admissions Contact:** Djuana Young, Associate Vice President for Enrollment. Email: *admissions@txwes.edu* Web: *www.txwes.edu*

FINANCIAL AID: In 2016-2017, 99% of all full-time freshmen and 84% of continuing full-time students received some form of financial aid. 53% of all full-time freshmen and 60% of continuing full-time students received need-based aid. The average freshman award was $21,919. Need-based scholarships or need-based grants averaged $19,963; need-based self-help aid (loans and jobs) averaged $6,343; non-need-based athletic scholarships averaged $11,836; and other non-need-based awards and non-need-based scholarships averaged $11,231. 13% of undergraduate students work part-time. Average annual earnings from campus work are $3232. The average financial indebtedness of the 2016 graduate was $33,090. The college's own financial statement is required. The FAFSA code is 003645. The deadline for filing freshman financial aid applications for fall entry is March 1.

TEXAS WOMAN'S UNIVERSITY *(The complete profile is made available exclusively on our website, www.barronspac.com)*

TRINITY UNIVERSITY D-4

www.trinity.edu

San Antonio, TX 78212 **(210) 999-7207**

Email: admissions@trinity.edu

Full-time: 1055 men, 1195 women
Part-time: 26 men, 18 women
Graduate: 75 men, 93 women
Year: semesters, summer session
Room & Board: $12,754

Faculty: 264; IIA, ++$
Ph.D.s: 98%
Student/Faculty: 9 to 1
Tuition: $39,560
Freshman Class: 7255 applied, 2950 accepted, 662 enrolled

SAT CR/M/W: 640/630/610 **ACT:** 29
Application Deadline: February 1
CEEB CODE: 6831
HIGHLY COMPETITIVE+

Trinity University is known for its challenging and supportive academic environment, personalized attention from outstanding faculty, large school resources, post-graduate preparation, and vibrant campus life. Trinity encourages students to discover, grow, and become global citizens engaged with the community and the world. There is 1 undergraduate school and 1 graduate school. In addition to regional accreditation, Trinity has baccalaureate program accreditation with AACSB, ABET, NCATE, and CAHME. The 117-acre campus is in an urban area 3 miles north of downtown San Antonio. Including any residence halls, there are 45 buildings.

STUDENT LIFE: 72% of undergraduates are from Texas. Others are from 48 states, 44 foreign countries, and Canada. 57% are from public schools. 7% are Foreign; 6% Asian American; 55% White; 5% two or more races; 4% African American; 21% Hispanic; 2% race unknown. 27% are Protestant; 21% Catholic; 13% claim no religious affiliation. **Female To Male Ratio:** 1.1:1. The average age of freshmen is 18; all undergraduates, 20. 11% do not continue beyond their first year; 77% remain to graduate. **Housing:** 1814 students can be accommodated in college housing, which includes coed dorms, language houses and special-interest houses. On-campus housing is guaranteed for all 4 years. 77% of students live on campus. All students may keep cars.

FACULTY/CLASSROOMS: 58% of faculty are male; 42% are female. All teach and do research. No introductory courses are taught by graduate students. The average class size in an introductory lecture is 21; in a laboratory is 25; and in a regular course is 22.

PROGRAMS OF STUDY: Trinity confers B.A., B.S. and B.M. degrees. Master's degrees are also awarded. Bachelor's degrees are awarded in AGRICULTURE (environmental studies), BIOLOGICAL SCIENCE (biochemistry, biology/biological science, and neurosciences), BUSINESS (accounting, business administration and management, business intelligence and analytics, and finance), COMMUNICATIONS AND THE ARTS (art history, art, Chinese, classics, communications, dramatic arts, English, French, German, Greek, Latin, music, Russian, Spanish, and theatre studies), COMPUTER AND PHYSICAL SCIENCE (chemistry, computer science, geoscience, mathematics, and physics), ENGINEERING AND ENVIRONMENTAL DESIGN (engineering and applied science), SOCIAL SCIENCE (anthropology, Chinese Studies, economics, history, international relations, philosophy, political science/government, psychology, religion, sociology, and urban studies). Business administration, communication, and engineering science have the largest enrollments.

ACTIVITIES: 19% of men belong to 6 local fraternities; 31% of women belong to 7 local sororities. There are 135 groups on campus, including art, band, cheerleading, chess, choir, chorale, chorus, communications, computers, dance, debate, drama, drill team, environmental, ethnic, film, forensics, honors, international, jazz band, LGBT, literary magazine, musical theater, newspaper, opera, orchestra, pep band, photography, political, professional, radio and TV, religious, social, social service, student government, symphony, wind ensemble and gaming, and yearbook. Popular campus events include TigerFest Gala, Chocolate Festival, and Trinity Spotlight. **Sports:** There are 9 intercollegiate sports for men and 9 for women, and 14 intramural sports for men and 14 for women. Facilities include football, soccer and basketball, arenas for water polo and sand volleyball as well as. In addition, there are competition facilities for football, soccer, basketball, volleyball, and tennis, students enjoy access to weight rooms, racquetball courts, tennis courts, and indoor and outdoor pools. **Graduates:** From July 1, 2015 to June 30, 2016, 479 bachelor's degrees were awarded. The most popular majors were business administration (7%), economics (6%), and communication (6%). 81 companies recruited on campus in 2015-2016. In an average class, 68% graduate in 4 years or less, 76% graduate in 5 years or less, and 77% graduate in 6 years or less. Of the 2015 graduating class, 35% were enrolled in graduate school within 6 months of graduation, and 55% were employed.

SERVICES: Counseling and information services are available, as is tutoring in most subjects. **Library/Resources:** The library contains 819,196 volumes, 40,000 microform items, 36,649 audio/video tapes/CDs/DVDs, and subscribes to 2,196 periodicals including electronic. Computerized library services include interlibrary loans, database searching, Internet access, and Wi-Fi capability. Special learning facilities include an art gallery, radio station, and TV station. **Physically Challenged Students:** Facilities include wheelchair ramps, elevators, special parking, specially equipped restrooms, special class scheduling, lowered drinking fountains, lowered telephones, and special housing. Accommodations for students with disabilities are determined through the office of Disability Services for Students. **Special:** The university offers student-designed interdisciplinary majors, double majors, significant opportunities for undergraduate research in the humanities and sciences, an entrepreneurship minor and program, a robust business curriculum, study abroad in 35 countries, and internship experiences outside the normal classroom for credit, as well as teacher certification. There are 21 national honor societies, Phi Beta Kappa, and 14 departmental honors programs.

Visiting: There are regularly scheduled orientations for prospective students, campus tour, information session, and meetings with current students, faculty, or staff. There are guides for informal visits, visitors may sit in on classes, and stay overnight. To schedule a visit, contact the Admissions Office. **Campus Safety and Security:** Measures include 24-hour foot and vehicle patrol, emergency notification system, self-defense education, security escort services, emergency telephones, lighted pathways/sidewalks, controlled access to dorms/residences, and shuttle carts.

REQUIREMENTS: Applicants are expected to have completed 4 years of English, 3 of math, 3 each of lab science and social studies, and 2 foreign language. A personal essay, standardized test scores, an official high school transcript, high school counselor recommendation, and teacher evaluation are required. A campus visit is also recommended. AP credits are accepted. Important factors in the admissions decision are advanced placement or honors courses, recommendations by school officials, and extracurricular activities record. To graduate, students must satisfy the Pathways curriculum, complete at least one major, the residency requirements, and complete a minimum of 124 credit hours (129 for B.S. in engineering science and 141 for a B.M. in performance and composition). Students must complete at least six of the Curricular Requirements and 30 hours in upper-division courses. A minimum 2.0 GPA is required. **Procedure:** Freshmen are admitted in the fall, spring, and summer. Entrance exams should be taken late in the junior year or early in the senior year. There are early decision, early admissions, and deferred admissions plans. Early decision applications should be filed by November 1; regular applications, by February 1 for fall entry; and November 15 for spring entry. Notification of early decision is sent December 15; regular decision, April 1. 52 early decision candidates were accepted for the 2016-2017 class. 469 applicants were on the 2016 waiting list; 31 were admitted. Application fees are waived if application is completed online. **Transfer Students:** 25 transfer students enrolled in 2015-2016. Transcripts for all colleges attended or attending, high school transcripts, an essay, standardized test scores, and a statement of good standing from the prior institution are required. An interview and visit to campus is recommended. 62 of 124 credits required for the bachelor's degree must be completed at Trinity. **International Students:** There are 164 international students enrolled. The school actively recruits these students. They must take the TOEFL and either the SAT or ACT.

ADMISSIONS: 41% of the 2016-2017 applicants were accepted. The SAT scores for the 2016-2017 freshman class were: Critical Reading-- 3% below 500, 29% between 500 and 599, 48% between 600 and 699, and 21% between 700 and 800. Math-- 1% below 500, 30% between 500 and 599, 52% between 600 and 699, and 18% between 700 and 800. Writing-- 6% below 500, 35% between 500 and 599, 45% between 600 and 699, and 14% between 700 and 800. The ACT scores were 2% between 18 and 23, 51% between 24 and 29, and 47% above 30. 69% of the current freshmen were in the top fifth of their class; 89% were in the top two fifths. There were 9 National Merit finalists. 13 freshmen graduated first in their class. **Admissions Contact:** Office of Admissions Email: *admissions@trinity.edu* Web: *www.trinity.edu*

FINANCIAL AID: In 2016-2017, 98% of all full-time freshmen and 91% of continuing full-time students received some form of financial aid. 45% of all full-time freshmen and 40% of continuing full-time students received need-based aid. The average freshman award was $29,156. Need-based scholarships or need-based grants averaged $6,417; need-based self-help aid (loans and jobs) averaged $1,477; other non-need-based awards and non-need-based scholarships averaged $18,063; and $2,474 from other forms of aid. The average financial indebtedness of the 2016 graduate was $38,605. Trinity is a member of CSS. The CSS/Profile is required. The priority date for freshman financial aid applications for fall entry is February 15.

UNIVERSITY OF DALLAS D-2

www.udallas.edu

Irving, TX 75062	**(972) 721-5266** **(800) 628-6999**
Fax: (972) 721-5017	**Email: crusader@udallas.edu**
Full-time: 641 men, 739 women	**Faculty:** 81; I, av$
Part-time: 15 men, 9 women	**Ph.D.s:** 88%
Graduate: 731 men, 489 women	**Student/Faculty:** 11 to 1
Year: semesters, summer session	**Tuition:** $34,430
Room & Board: $11,070	**Freshman Class:** 1426 applied, 1212 accepted, 353 enrolled
SAT CR/M/W: 615/595/595 **ACT:** 27	**CEEB CODE:** 6868
Application Deadline: March 1	**VERY COMPETITIVE+**

University of Dallas, founded in 1955, is a private Catholic liberal arts institution. The university includes four schools: Constantin College of Liberal Arts (undergraduates), Braniff Graduate School of Liberal Arts, Satish and Yasmin Gupta College of Business and School of Ministry. There are 4 undergraduate schools and 3 graduate schools. In addition to regional accreditation, UD has baccalaureate program accreditation with AACSB and IACBE. The 750-acre campus is in an urban area Irving, Texas, 10 miles west of Dallas, 30 miles east of Fort Worth. Including any residence halls, there are 33 buildings.

STUDENT LIFE: 52% of undergraduates are from out of state, mostly the Mid-West. Students are from 50 states, 15 foreign countries, and Canada. 45% are from public schools. 69% are White; 4% Asian American; 3% Foreign; 3% two or more races; 2% race unknown; 17% Hispanic; 1% African American. 84% are Catholic. **Male To Female Ratio:** 1.1:1. The average age of freshmen is 18; all undergraduates, 20. 20% do not continue beyond their first year; 73% remain to graduate. **Housing:** 838 students can be accommodated in college housing, which includes single-sex and coed dorms and on-campus apartments. On-campus housing is guaranteed for the freshman year only, and is available on a first-come, and first-served basis. 65% of students live on campus; of those, 90% remain on campus on weekends. All students may keep cars.

FACULTY/CLASSROOMS: 64% of faculty are male; 36% are female. 90% teach undergraduates. No introductory courses are taught by graduate students. The average class size in an introductory lecture is 22; in a laboratory is 16; and in a regular course is 19.

PROGRAMS OF STUDY: UD confers B.A., and B.S. degrees. Master's and doctoral degrees are also awarded. Bachelor's degrees are awarded in BIOLOGICAL SCIENCE (biochemistry and biology/biological science), BUSINESS (business administration and management), COMMUNICATIONS AND THE ARTS (art history and appreciation, ceramic art and design, classics, dramatic arts, English, French, German, painting, printmaking, sculpture, and Spanish), COMPUTER AND PHYSICAL SCIENCE (chemistry, computer science, mathematics, and physics), EDUCATION (art education, education, and elementary education), ENGINEERING AND ENVIRONMENTAL DESIGN (electrical/electronics engineering technology), HEALTH PROFESSIONS (nursing), SOCIAL SCIENCE (economics, history, pastoral studies, philosophy, political science/government, psychology, and theological studies). Biology, classics, and English are the strongest academically. Business, biology, and English have the largest enrollments.

ACTIVITIES: There are no fraternities or sororities. There are 50 groups on campus, including intramural sports, ultimate, art, chess, choir, chorale, chorus, club Rugby, computers, dance, debate, drama, ethnic, film, honors, international, literary magazine, musical theater, newspaper, opera, photography, political, professional, religious, social, social service, student government, symphony, and yearbook. Popular campus events include Charity Week, Groundhog Celebration, Lazy Faire, Mallapalooza, Winter Cotillion, Battle of the Bands, Alumni and Family Weekend, TGIT and Spring Formal. **Sports:** There are 7 intercollegiate sports for men and 8 for women, and 6 intramural sports for men and 3 for women. Facilities include an athletic center with a gym, weight room, aerobics equipment,an outdoor pool and tennis courts, soccer field, baseball field, multipurpose field, and jogging trails. **Graduates:** From July 1, 2015 to June 30, 2016, 310 bachelor's degrees were awarded. The most popular majors were social science (16%), business (14%), and English (12%). 26 companies recruited on campus in 2015-2016. In an average class, 66% graduate in 4 years or less and 73% graduate in 6 years or less. Of the 2015 graduating class, 21% were enrolled in graduate school within 6 months of graduation.

SERVICES: Counseling and information services are available, as is tutoring in most subjects, and remedial math and writing. There are also writing and math labs, an academic success office, and department sponsored tutoring in nearly every subject. **Library/Resources:** The library contains 364,691 volumes, 4,526 microform items, 432 audio/video tapes/CDs/DVDs, and subscribes to 64,000 periodicals including electronic. Computerized library services include interlibrary loans, database searching, Internet access, and Wi-Fi capability. Special learning facilities include an art gallery, an 80-seat theater, a performance lab and an observatory. **Physically Challenged Students:** 70% of the campus is accessible. Facilities include wheelchair ramps, elevators, special parking, specially equipped restrooms, special class scheduling, and lowered drinking fountains. **Special:** UD offers internships in field experience or an off-campus research semester. The majority of students participate in the Rome Program, a semester-long experience on the UD Rome campus, and summer programs are available in Rome, as well. 3-2 electrical engineering degree (UT-Arlington) and 3-2 nursing degree (Texas Woman's University) are available. There are myriad opportunities for on-campus work-study programs. B.A.-B.S. degrees and double majors are available, as well. 33 concentrations are offered to combine with any major. There are 5 national honor societies, Phi Beta Kappa, and 4 departmental honors programs. **Visiting:** There are regularly scheduled orientations for prospective students, including a campus tour, meeting with admission counselor, scholarship competition, tour of residence halls, sitting in on classes, lunch with students in the cafeteria, mass and one-on-one meetings with professors. There are guides for informal visits, visitors may sit in on classes, and stay overnight. To schedule a visit, contact the Office of Admission. **Campus Safety and Security:** Measures include 24-hour foot and vehicle patrol, emergency notification system, self-defense education, and security escort services. There are emergency telephones, lighted pathways/sidewalks, and controlled access to dorms/residences.

REQUIREMENTS: The SAT or ACT is required. The university seeks high school students who have pursued a curriculum of college preparatory courses including English, social science, math, science, and a foreign language. Applicants pursuing a discipline in the sciences should have 4 years of math. Depth in a foreign language is advised. Although the university is flexible in its admission requests, applicants should be in the upper third of their graduating class and should present satisfactory SAT or ACT scores. AP and CLEP credits are accepted. Important factors in the admissions decision are leadership record, extracurricular activities record, and advanced placement or honors courses. To graduate with a B.A., students must complete at least 120 credits, including 38 in advanced credits, which included 12 in the major, with a 2.0 GPA. Completion of the 60-credit-hour Core curriculum as well as major requirements is required. To graduate with a B.S degree, students must complete the above requirements for a B.A. plus 12 additional hours in the major. Seniors must pass a comprehensive exam, write a thesis or complete a research or capstone project in their major. **Procedure:** Freshmen are admitted in the fall and spring. Entrance exams should be taken During the junior year or by the fall of the senior year. There are early admissions, deferred admissions, and rolling admissions plans. Early decision applications should be filed by November 1; regular applications, by March 1 for fall entry; and December 1 for spring entry, along with a $50 fee. Notification is sent on a rolling basis. Applications are accepted on-line. **Transfer Students:** 38 transfer students enrolled in 2015-2016. Applicants must have a minimum 2.5 GPA from an accredited college or university. Official transcripts from all previous colleges attended, a writing sample, a personal statement, and an academic letter of recommendation are required. Students with fewer than 30 transferable credits must also submit SAT or ACT scores and an official high school transcript. 60 of 120 credits required for the bachelor's degree must be completed at UD. **International Students:** There are 34 international students enrolled. The school actively recruits these students. They must take the TOEFL with a minimum score of 79 on the Internet-based version (iBT). The SAT or ACT scores may be submitted in place of the TOEFL.

ADMISSIONS: 85% of the 2016-2017 applicants were accepted. The SAT scores for the 2016-2017 freshman class were: Critical Reading-- 7% below 500, 36% between 500 and 599, 39% between 600 and 699, and 18% between 700 and 800. Math-- 12% below 500, 44% between 500 and 599, 29% between 600 and 699, and 15% between 700 and 800. Writing-- 13% below 500, 40% between 500 and 599, 30% between 600 and 699, and 17% between 700 and 800. The ACT scores were 4% below 12, 22% between 12 and 17, 29% between 18 and 23, 14% between 24 and 29, and 31% above 30. 68% of the current freshmen were in the top fifth of their class; 80% were in the top two fifths. There were 14 National Merit finalists. **Admissions Contact:** Elizabeth Griffin Smith, Director of Admission. Email: *crusader@udallas.edu* Web: *www.udallas.edu*

FINANCIAL AID: In 2016-2017, 96% of all full-time freshmen and 94% of continuing full-time students received some form of financial aid. 68% of all full-time freshmen and 58% of continuing full-time students received need-based aid. The average freshman award was $26,613. Need-based scholarships or need-based grants averaged $22,328; need-based self-help aid (loans and jobs) averaged $5,208; and other non-need-based awards and non-need-based scholarships averaged $14,168. 15% of undergraduate students work part-time. Average annual earnings from campus work are $1650. The average financial indebtedness of the 2016 graduate was $31,446. The priority date for freshman financial aid applications for fall entry is January 15.

UNIVERSITY OF HOUSTON — E-3

www.uh.edu

Houston, TX 77004 — **(713) 743-1010**

Email: admissions@uh.edu

Full-time: 12,929 men, 12,865 women	**Faculty:** 973
	Ph.D.s: 85%
Part-time: 5411 men, 4666 women	**Student/Faculty:** 26 to 1
Graduate: 3911 men, 3992 women	**Tuition:** $11,653 ($26,893)
Year: semesters, summer session	**Freshman Class:** 19860 applied, 11627 accepted, 4463 enrolled
Room & Board: $9830	
SAT CR/M: 561/585 **ACT:** 25	**CEEB CODE:** 6870
Application Deadline: June 30	**VERY COMPETITIVE**

University of Houston is a Carnegie-designated Tier One public research university that serves the globally competitive Houston and Gulf Coast Region by providing world-class faculty, experiential learning and strategic industry partnerships. There are 10 undergraduate schools and 4 graduate schools. In addition to regional accreditation, UH has baccalaureate program accreditation with AACSB, ABET, ACCE, ACPE, NAAB, NASM, NCATE, ACS, CSAC, and ACCE. The 594-acre campus is in an urban area 3 miles from downtown Houston, Texas. Including any residence halls, there are 161 buildings.

STUDENT LIFE: 94% of undergraduates are from Texas. Others are from 47 states, 114 foreign countries, and Canada. 92% are from public schools. 9% are Foreign; 3% two or more races; 29% Hispanic; 27% White; 21% Asian American; 10% African American; 1% race unknown. **Male To Female Ratio:** 1.0:1. The average age of freshmen is 18; all undergraduates, 22. 15% do not continue beyond their first year; 51% remain to graduate. **Housing:** 8008 students can be accommodated in college housing, which includes coed dorms, on-campus apartments, off-campus apartments, married student housing, honors houses, special-interest houses, fraternity houses, and sorority houses. On-campus housing is available on a first-come and first-served basis. 81% of students commute. All students may keep cars.

FACULTY/CLASSROOMS: 62% of faculty are male; 38% are female. 56% teach undergraduates. Graduate students teach 19% of introductory courses. The average class size in an introductory lecture is 77; in a laboratory is 27; and in a regular course is 4.

PROGRAMS OF STUDY: UH confers B.A., B.S., B.A.C.Y., B.Arch., B.B.A., B.F.A., B.M., B.S.C.E., B.S.Ch.E., B.S.C.P.E., B.S.E.E., B.S.I.E., B.S.M.E., B.S.B.E., BSN, and B.S.P.E.T.E. degrees. Master's and doctoral degrees are also awarded. Bachelor's degrees are awarded in BIOLOGICAL SCIENCE (biology/biological science), BUSINESS (accounting, hotel/motel and restaurant management, management information systems, marketing and distribution, and supply chain management), COMMUNICATIONS AND THE ARTS (American Sign Language, applied music, art, Chinese, communications, dance, English, French, industrial design, Spanish, and studio art), COMPUTER AND PHYSICAL SCIENCE (chemistry, geology, mathematics, and physics), ENGINEERING AND ENVIRONMENTAL DESIGN (architecture, biomedical engineering, chemical engineering, civil engineering, computer engineering, construction management, electrical/electronics engineering, environmental design, environmental science, industrial engineering, mechanical engineering, mechanical engineering technology, and petroleum/natural gas engineering), HEALTH PROFESSIONS (health and pharmaceutical science), SOCIAL SCIENCE (anthropology, interdisciplinary studies, Italian studies, liberal arts/general studies, and philosophy). Business, and engineering are the strongest academically. Biology, exploratory studies, and exercise science have the largest enrollments.

ACTIVITIES: 4% of men belong to 27 national fraternities; 4% of women belong to 23 national sororities. There are 491 groups on campus, including art, band, cheerleading, chess, choir, chorale, chorus, computers, dance, debate, drama, drill team, environmental, ethnic, film, forensics, honors, international, jazz band, LGBT, literary magazine, marching band, musical theater, newspaper, opera, orchestra, pep band, photography, political, professional, radio and TV, religious, social, social service, student government, symphony, and yearbook. Popular campus events include Frontier Fiesta, Homecoming and Cat's Back. **Sports:** There are 7 intercollegiate sports for men and 10 for women, and 31 intramural sports for men and 31 for women. Facilities include The Department of Intercollegiate Athletics offers eight athletics facilities for more than 400 student-athletes in which to train and compete TDECU Stadium (football); Schroeder Park (baseball); Cougar Softball Stadium; Hofheinz Pavilion and the Guy V. Lewis Development Facility (men's and women's basketball); Yeoman Fieldhouse within the Athletics/Alumni Center (Athletics administrative offices, volleyball, indoor men's and women's track); Carl Lewis Track and Soccer Complex - Tom Tellez Track & Yokubaitis Field (women's soccer, men's and women's outdoor track); John E. Hoff Tennis Courts (women's tennis) and football practice fields. Athletics partners with the University for its Swimming & Diving program to train and compete in the Campus Recreation and Wellness Center Natatorium. Hofheinz Pavilion, Cougar Softball Stadium and Schroeder Park (baseball) are equipped for NCAA postseason events. **Graduates:** From July 1, 2015 to June 30, 2016, 6802 bachelor's degrees were awarded. The most popular majors were business/marketing (28%), engineering (7%), and psychology (6%). 486 companies recruited on campus in 2015-2016. In an average class, 23% graduate in 4 years or less, 43% graduate in 5 years or less, and 51% graduate in 6 years or less.

SERVICES: Counseling and information services are available, as is tutoring in most subjects. There is a reader service for the blind, and remedial math, reading, and writing. Accommodation assistance for students taking exams, tutors assisting with course work, and other accommodations are available. **Library/Resources:** The 5 libraries contain 3.8 million volumes, 160,968 microform items, and 35,523 audio/video tapes/CDs/DVDs, and subscribe to 148,769 periodicals including electronic. Computerized library services include interlibrary loans, database searching, Internet access, and Wi-Fi capability. Special learning facilities include an art gallery, radio station, TV station, an observatory. **Physically Challenged Students:** 98% of the campus is accessible. Facilities include wheelchair ramps, elevators, special parking, specially equipped restrooms, special class scheduling, lowered drinking fountains, lowered telephones, special housing. **Special:** Many colleges at the University of Houston offer internships and cooperative education opportunities in areas such as business, engineering, government/policy, education, hospitality, research, healthcare/health education, communications/media, sports, and science, math and technology. UH also offers a 3-2 program with the School of Nursing at the University of Texas Health Science Center and a 3-3 program with the University of Houston Law Center. Dual degree and accelerated degrees are offered in the disciplines of business, computer science, global retailing and human resource development, health, hospitality, and political science. Learning Abroad programs include Faculty-Led programs, such as those offered through the Department of Modern and Classical Languages to China and France, and through the African American Studies Program to Africa; Bauer Study Abroad Programs to Chile and India; Affiliated Programs through organizations such as International Studies Abroad (ISA), and the University Study Abroad Consortium (USAC), which have established programs all over the world; Reciprocal Exchange Studies; and Service Learning or Internships abroad. There are 18 national honor societies, Phi Beta Kappa, a freshman honors program, and 12 departmental honors programs. **Visiting:** There are regularly scheduled orientations for prospective students, consisting of a tour, information sessions that help with the transition from high school to college and have scheduled time with an academic advisor. There are guides for informal visits and visitors may stay overnight. To schedule a visit, contact the Office of Admission. **Campus Safety and Security:** Measures include 24-hour foot and vehicle patrol, emergency notification system, self-defense education, and security escort services. There are shuttle buses, emergency telephones, lighted pathways/sidewalks, controlled access to dorms/residences, Community dialogues, and assistance with disabled vehicles.

REQUIREMENTS: The SAT or ACT is required. Automatic enrollment granted to applicants who rank in top-tenth of secondary school class and submit a completed application by August 1st. All other students are reviewed using a holistic review process. AP and CLEP credits are accepted. Important factors in the admissions decision are evidence of special talent, recommendations by school officials, and advanced placement or honors courses. To graduate, student must complete 120 semester credit hours, including at least 36 in advance-level courses, with a minimum GPA of 2.0. Core Curriculum requires each student complete 42 hours of coursework from select courses under 10 different component areas such as math, history, creative arts and the sciences. **Procedure:** Freshmen are admitted to all sessions. Entrance exams should be taken priority deadline of November 15. There is a rolling admissions plan. Applications should be filed by June 30 for fall entry; December 1 for spring entry; and April 1 for summer entry, along with a $75 fee. Applications are accepted on-line. **Transfer Students:** 5243 transfer students enrolled in 2015-2016. Applicants must be eligible to return to their last college. A 2.0 GPA is required for students with 30 or more semester hours of college credit, a 2.5 GPA for those with 15 to 29. 30 of 120 credits required for the bachelor's degree must be completed at UH. **International Students:** There are 1322 international students enrolled. The school actively recruits these students. They must take the TOEFL with a minimum score of 550 on the paper-based TOEFL (PBT) or 79 on the Internet-based version (iBT). They must also take the SAT or ACT.

ADMISSIONS: 59% of the 2016-2017 applicants were accepted. The SAT scores for the 2016-2017 freshman class were: Critical Reading-- 20% below 500, 48% between 500 and 599, 26% between 600 and 699, and 6% between 700 and 800. Math-- 12% below 500, 44% between 500 and 599, 36% between 600 and 699, and 8% between 700 and 800. The ACT scores were 2% between 12 and 17, 30% between 18 and 23, 53% between 24 and 29, and 15% above 30. 56% of the current freshmen were in the top fifth of their class. There were 27 National Merit finalists. 37 freshmen graduated first in their class. **Admissions Contact:** Mara Affre, Associate Vice President for Enrollment Services. Email: *admissions@uh.edu* Web: *www.uh.edu*

FINANCIAL AID: In 2016-2017, 84% of all full-time freshmen and 74% of continuing full-time students received some form of financial aid. 55% of all full-time freshmen and 55% of continuing full-time students received need-based aid. The average freshman award was $12,916. Need-based scholarships or need-based grants averaged $9,094 ($22,864 maximum); need-based self-help aid (loans and jobs) averaged $3,577 ($7,500 maximum); non-need-based athletic scholarships averaged $17,102 ($32,990 maximum); and other non-need-based awards and non-need-based scholarships averaged $7,234 ($51,000 maximum). 8% of undergraduate students work part-time. Average annual earnings from campus work are $6129. The average financial indebtedness of the 2016 graduate was $23,665. The priority date for freshman financial aid applications for fall entry is March 15.

UNIVERSITY OF HOUSTON-DOWNTOWN *(The complete profile is made available exclusively on our website, www.barronspac.com)*

UNIVERSITY OF MARY HARDIN-BAYLOR D-3

www.umhb.edu

Belton, TX 76513	**(254) 295-4513** **(800) 727-8642**
Fax: (254) 295-5049	**Email: admission@umhb.edu**
Full-time: 1099 men, 1897 women	**Faculty:** n/av
Part-time: 110 men, 172 women	**Ph.D.s:** 78%
Graduate: 290 men, 338 women	**Student/Faculty:** 19 to 1
Year: semesters, summer session	**Tuition:** $26,650
Room & Board: $7300	**Freshman Class:** 8954 applied, 7056 accepted, 750 enrolled
SAT CR/M/W: 520/525/475 **ACT:** 24	**CEEB CODE:** 6396
Application Deadline: rolling	**COMPETITIVE+**

University of Mary Hardin-Baylor, founded in 1845, is a private facility affiliated with the Baptist General Convention of Texas. It offers undergraduate degrees in liberal arts, fine arts, music, business, education, nursing, and social work, as well as masters degrees in business, information systems, education, psychology/counseling, and nursing, and doctorates in educational administration, physical therapy and nurse practitioner. There are 7 undergraduate schools and 7 graduate schools. In addition to regional accreditation, UMHB has baccalaureate program accreditation with CSWE, BCAT, CAATE, CCNE, and TEA. The 170-acre campus is in a small town in central Texas halfway between San Antonio and Dallas/Fort Worth. Including any residence halls, there are 71 buildings.

STUDENT LIFE: 97% of undergraduates are from Texas. Others are from 36 states, 31 foreign countries, and Canada. 56% are White; 21% Hispanic; 15% African American; 3% two or more races; 2% Asian American; 2% race unknown; 1% American Indian/Alaska Native; 1% Foreign. 17% claim no religious affiliation; 14% Catholic. **Female To Male Ratio:** 1.6:1. The average age of freshmen is 18; all undergraduates,

22. 29% do not continue beyond their first year; 48% remain to graduate. **Housing:** 1924 students can be accommodated in college housing, which includes single-sex dorms and on-campus apartments. On-campus housing is guaranteed for all 4 years. 57% of students live on campus. All students may keep cars. Alcohol is not permitted.

FACULTY/CLASSROOMS: 44% of faculty are male; 56% are female. No introductory courses are taught by graduate students. The average class size in an introductory lecture is 25; in a laboratory is 20; and in a regular course is 17.

PROGRAMS OF STUDY: UMHB confers B.A., B.S., B.B.A., B.C.M., B.F.A., B.G.S., B.M., B.S.N., and B.S.W. degrees. Master's and doctoral degrees are also awarded. Bachelor's degrees are awarded in BIOLOGICAL SCIENCE (biology/adolescence education and biology/biological science), BUSINESS (accounting, business administration and management, finance, international business, marketing/retailing/merchandising, and sports management), COMMUNICATIONS AND THE ARTS (art, church music, communications, English, journalism, multimedia, music, music performance, performing arts, Spanish, speech/debate/rhetoric, and visual design), COMPUTER AND PHYSICAL SCIENCE (chemistry, chemistry/adolescence education, clinical laboratory science, computer science, information sciences and systems, and mathematics), EDUCATION (art education, early childhood education, elementary education, English education, foreign languages education, mathematics education, middle school education, music education, physical education, reading education, science education, secondary education, social studies education, and special education), ENGINEERING AND ENVIRONMENTAL DESIGN (computer graphics and engineering science), HEALTH PROFESSIONS (exercise science and nursing), SOCIAL SCIENCE (biblical studies, Christian studies, criminal justice, economics, history, ministries, political science/government, psychology, religion, social work, and sociology). Nursing, business, and education are the strongest academically and have the largest enrollments.

ACTIVITIES: There are no fraternities or sororities. There are 59 groups on campus, including art, band, cheerleading, chess, choir, chorale, chorus, computers, debate, drama, drill team, ethnic, film, honors, international, jazz band, literary magazine, musical theater, newspaper, opera, orchestra, pep band, photography, political, professional, religious, social service, student government, and yearbook. Popular campus events include Miss UMHB Pageants, Mr. Crusader Knights, Play Day, and Easter Pageant. **Sports:** There are 6 intercollegiate sports for men and 6 for women, and 21 intramural sports for men and 21 for women. Facilities include a football stadium, with training facility and practice fields, a tennis center, and soccer fields, and a campus recreation center housing a pool, basketball courts, and cardio and weight equipment. **Graduates:** From July 1, 2015 to June 30, 2016, 622 bachelor's degrees were awarded. The most popular majors were health professions and related programs (25%), business/marketing (17%), and education (10%). In an average class, 31% graduate in 4 years or less, 44% graduate in 5 years or less, and 48% graduate in 6 years or less.

SERVICES: Counseling and information services are available, as is tutoring in most subjects. There is a reader service for the blind, and remedial math, reading, and writing. Academic counselors and software for the blind are also available. **Library/Resources:** The library contains 209,656 volumes, 3,697 microform items, and 8,479 audio/video tapes/CDs/DVDs, and subscribes to 140,934 periodicals including electronic. Computerized library services include interlibrary loans, database searching, Internet access, and Wi-Fi capability. Special learning facilities include an art gallery, a nature walk. **Physically Challenged Students:** 85% of the campus is accessible. Facilities include wheelchair ramps, elevators, special parking, specially equipped restrooms, special class scheduling, lowered drinking fountains, lowered telephones, and special housing. **Special:** Study abroad in 5 countries, internships, a work-study program, dual majors, a professional studies degree, an applied science bachelor's degree, post-baccalaureate certification in education, and a 5-year B.B.A./M.B.A. accounting specialization are offered. There are 7 national honor societies and a freshman honors program. **Visiting:** There are regularly scheduled orientations for prospective students, consisting of campus tours and visits with counselors to discuss admissions, financial aid, housing, and degree plans. There are guides for informal visits, visitors may sit in on classes, and stay overnight. To schedule a visit, contact the Admissions Office at admissions@umhb.edu. **Campus Safety and Security:** Measures include 24-hour foot and vehicle patrol, emergency notification system, self-defense education, security escort services, emergency telephones, lighted pathways/sidewalks, and a campus police force.

REQUIREMENTS: Students who rank in the top half of their high school graduating class must score a minimum of 950 on the SAT or 20 on the ACT. Those who graduate in the lower half of their class must score a minimum of 990 on the SAT or 21 on the ACT. There is no minimum test score for students who rank in the top 10% of their high school graduating class. All students should be graduates of an accredited high school and have 24 units of credit, including 4 in English, 3 in math, 3 in social science, 2 in foreign language, and 3 1/2 in social studies. AP and CLEP credits are accepted. Important factors in the admissions decision are leadership record, advanced placement or honors courses, parents or siblings attended your school, evidence of special talent, personality/intangible qualities, extracurricular activities record, recommendations by alumni, geographical diversity, and recommendations by school officials. To graduate all students must complete at least 124 credits, including at least 24 in the major field and at least 36 upper-level credits, with a 2.0 GPA. Requirements include 6 credits each in English, social sciences, religion, and electives, 3 each in math and communication, an additional 3 to 4 in math, lab science, or foreign language, and a 1-credit Success in Academics course. There is a chapel attendance requirement for full-time students and a residency requirement of 31 hours. **Procedure:** Freshmen are admitted fall, spring, and summer. Entrance exams should be taken by the fall of the senior year. There is a rolling admissions plan. Application deadlines are open. Application fee is $35. Notification is sent on a rolling basis. Applications are accepted online. **Transfer Students:** 247 transfer students enrolled in 2015-2016. Applicants must present at least a 2.0 GPA, be in good standing at their previous institutions, and submit all college transcripts. Those with fewer than 12 transferable credits must also meet freshman requirements. 31 of 124 credits required for the bachelor's degree must be completed at UMHB. **International Students:** There are 36 international students enrolled. The school actively recruits these students. They must take the TOEFL with a minimum score of 40 on the Internet-based version (iBT).

ADMISSIONS: 79% of the 2016-2017 applicants were accepted. The SAT scores for the 2016-2017 freshman class were: Critical Reading--44% below 500, 43% between 500 and 599, 11% between 600 and 699, and 2% between 700 and 800. Math-- 40% below 500, 46% between 500 and 599, 13% between 600 and 699, and 1% between 700 and 800. Writing-- 61% below 500, 32% between 500 and 599, 6% between 600 and 699, and 1% between 700 and 800. The ACT scores were 5% between 12 and 17, 50% between 18 and 23, 38% between 24 and 29, and 7% above 30. **Admissions Contact:** Dr. Brent Burks, Director of Admissions & Recruiting. Email: *admission@umhb.edu* Web: *www.umhb.edu*

FINANCIAL AID: In 2016-2017, 96% of all full-time freshmen and 69% of continuing full-time students received some form of financial aid. 69% of all full-time freshmen and 50% of continuing full-time students received need-based aid. The average freshman award was $24,903. Need-based scholarships or need-based grants averaged $15,420; need-based self-help aid (loans and jobs) averaged $4,087; and other non-need-based awards and non-need-based scholarships averaged $7,889. 15% of undergraduate students work part-time. Average annual earnings from campus work are $2800. The average financial indebtedness of the 2016 graduate was $24,380. The priority date for freshman financial aid applications for fall entry is March 1. The filing deadline for fall entry is September 1.

UNIVERSITY OF NORTH TEXAS D-2

www.unt.edu

Denton, TX 76203 — **(940) 565-2681** **(800) UNT-8211**

Fax: (940) 565-2408 — **Email: unt.freshman@unt.edu**

Full-time: 11,976 men, 13,504 women
Part-time: 2966 men, 2725 women
Graduate: 2844 men, 3926 women
Year: semesters, summer session
Room & Board: $8769

Faculty: 1034; I, -$
Ph.D.s: 80%
Student/Faculty: 25 to 1
Tuition: $10,519 ($22,759)
Freshman Class: 16253 applied, 11391 accepted, 4661 enrolled

SAT CR/M/W: 545/550/520 **ACT:** 23 — **CEEB CODE:** 6481
Application Deadline: August 1 — **COMPETITIVE**

University of North Texas, is a student-focused public research university, offering a breadth of disciplines from engineering to visual arts. UNT offers 97 bachelor's, 88 master's and 40 doctoral degree programs. UNT's mission as a university is to develop new knowledge and solutions while giving rise to the next generation of engineers, scientists, artists, educators and business leaders. UNT also is a top draw for transfer students, leading the state and ranking fourth nationally among public universities for its transfer student enrollment. The figures in the profile are approximate, and the total average cost in the capsule is for the 2016 attendance and it covers tuition, fee, room and board, and other expenses. There are 12 undergraduate schools and 1 graduate school. In addition to regional accreditation, UNT has baccalaureate program accreditation with AACSB, ABET, ACCE, ACEJMC, CSAB, CSWE, FIDER, NASM, NCATE, and NRPA. The 875-acre campus is in a suburban area 35 miles north of Dallas/Fort Worth. Including any residence halls, there are 166 buildings.

STUDENT LIFE: 90% of undergraduates are from Texas. Others are from 50 states, 131 foreign countries, and Canada. 48% are White; 22% Hispanic; 12% African American; 6% Asian American; 6% Foreign; 4% two or more races; 1% American Indian/Alaska Native; 1% race unknown. **Female To Male Ratio:** 1.1:1. The average age of freshmen is 18; all undergraduates, 23. 20% do not continue beyond their first year; 53% remain to graduate. **Housing:** 6208 students can be accommodated in college housing, which includes single-sex and coed dorms, on-campus apartments, off-campus apartments, and married student housing. In addition, there are honors houses, special-interest houses, fraternity houses, sorority houses, theme and wellness housing available. On-campus housing is available on a first-come and first-served basis. 84% of students commute. All students may keep cars.

FACULTY/CLASSROOMS: 55% of faculty are male; 45% are female. 80% teach undergraduates. Graduate students teach 34% of introductory courses. The average class size in an introductory lecture is 52 and in a laboratory is 51.

PROGRAMS OF STUDY: UNT confers B.A., B.A.A.S., B.B.A., B.F.A., B.M., B.S., B.S.B.C., B.S.Bio, B.S.Chem., B.S.Eco., B.S.E.P., B.S.E.T., B.S.Math., B.S.M.T., B.S.Phy. and B.S.W. degrees. Master's and doctoral degrees are also awarded. Bachelor's degrees are awarded in BIOLOGICAL SCIENCE (biochemistry and biology/biological science), BUSINESS (accounting, banking and finance, business administration and management, electronic business, entrepreneurial studies, hospitality management services, human resources, insurance, investments and securities, logistics, management information systems, management science, marketing/retailing/merchandising, operations management, organizational behavior, organizational leadership and management, purchasing/inventory management, real estate, and recreation and leisure services), COMMUNICATIONS AND THE ARTS (applied art, art, art history and appreciation, broadcasting, choral music, communications, dance, design, dramatic arts, English, French, German, jazz, journalism, music, music history and appreciation, music performance, music theory and composition, musical theater, performing arts, radio/television technology, Spanish, studio art, telecommunications, theater design, theater management, and visual and performing arts), COMPUTER AND PHYSICAL SCIENCE (chemistry, computer science, information sciences and systems, mathematics, and physics), ENGINEERING AND ENVIRONMENTAL DESIGN (aviation administration/management, commercial art, computer engineering, construction engineering, electrical/electronics engineering, electrical/electronics engineering technology, emergency/disaster science, engineering physics, engineering technology, interior design, manufacturing engineering, mechanical engineering, mechanical engineering technology, and nuclear engineering technology), HEALTH PROFESSIONS (cytotechnology, health, medical laboratory technology, rehabilitation therapy, and speech pathology/audiology), SOCIAL SCIENCE (anthropology, applied psychology, child care/child and family studies, criminal justice, economics, fashion design and technology, geography, history, home furnishings and equipment management/production/services, human services, interdisciplinary studies, international studies, liberal arts/general studies, philosophy, physical fitness/movement, political science/government, psychology, social science, social work, and sociology). Jazz studies, public administration, and accounting are the strongest academically. Biology, psychology, and interdisciplinary studies have the largest enrollments.

ACTIVITIES: 5% of men belong to 25 national fraternities; 6% of women belong to 16 national sororities. There are 440 groups on campus, including band, cheerleading, chess, choir, chorale, chorus, computers, dance, debate, drama, ethnic, film, honors, international, jazz band, LGBT, literary magazine, marching band, musical theater, newspaper, opera, orchestra, pep band, photography, political, professional, radio and TV, religious, social, social service, student government, and symphony. Popular campus events include Howdy Week , Taste of North Texas, Union Day and Earth Day. **Sports:** There are 6 intercollegiate sports for men and 10 for women, and 23 intramural sports for men and 20 for women. Facilities include a football stadium, a weight-training building, tennis courts, indoor swimming pools, gyms, handball and racquetball courts, gymnastics equipment, intramural fields, and a recreational sports complex. **Graduates:** From July 1, 2015 to June 30, 2016, 6519 bachelor's degrees were awarded. The most popular majors were integrative studies (9%), applied arts and sciences (5%), and psychology (4%). 628 companies recruited on campus in 2015-2016. In an average class, 31% graduate in 4 years or less, 49% graduate in 5 years or less, and 53% graduate in 6 years or less.

SERVICES: Counseling and information services are available, as is tutoring in most subjects, a reader service for the blind, and remedial math, reading, and writing. **Library/Resources:** The 6 libraries contain 3.8 million volumes, 3.4 million microform items, 232,620 audio/video tapes/CDs/DVDs, and subscribe to 133,889 periodicals including electronic. Computerized library services include interlibrary loans, database searching, Internet access, and Wi-Fi capability. Special learning facilities include an art gallery, planetarium, radio station, TV station, an observatory, and a TV and film production unit. **Physically Challenged Students:** 90% of the campus is accessible. Facilities include wheelchair ramps, elevators, special parking, specially equipped restrooms, special class scheduling, lowered drinking fountains, lowered telephones, and dorm rooms adapted for disabled students. **Special:** UNT offers co-op programs, internships, and work-study programs with the university. Students may study abroad in several locations. An accelerated degree program in math and science allows Texas high school students to obtain 2 years of college credit during their last 2 years in high school. Dual degrees, a general studies degree, and pass/fail options are also offered. There are 42 national honor societies and a freshman honors program. **Visiting:** There are regularly scheduled orientations for prospective students, including 3-day, 2-night sessions throughout the summer. There are guides for informal visits, visitors may sit in on classes, and stay overnight. **Campus Safety and Security:** Measures include 24-hour foot and vehicle patrol, emergency notification system, self-defense education, and security escort services. There are shuttle buses, emergency telephones, lighted pathways/sidewalks, and controlled access to dorms/residences. There is also a crime prevention program, sexual assault information services, and a full-time crime prevention officer on duty.

REQUIREMENTS: The SAT or ACT is required. Applicants must be graduates of an accredited high school and submit a high school transcript. The required minimum score for entrance exams is determined by high school class rank. 26 high school academic units are required such as 4 each in English, math, science with labs, 2 units each in social studies, foreign language, and history, and 1 unit each in computer science, and visual/ performing arts, and 3.5 unites in academic electives. Others could be .5 in health, 1.5 in P.E. and .5 speech. AP and CLEP credits are accepted. All students must complete at least 120 semester hours, including a minimum of 42 hours in the major, with a 2.0 GPA. The core requirements include English, natural science, U.S. history, political science, visual/performing arts, and humanities. Proficiency in English composition must be demonstrated. **Procedure:** Freshmen are admitted in the fall, spring, and summer. Entrance exams should be taken at least 2 months before admissions deadlines. There are early admissions, deferred admissions, and rolling admissions plans. Applications should be filed by August 1 for fall entry; December 3 for spring entry; and May 12 for summer entry, along with a $75 fee. Notification is sent on a rolling basis. Applications are accepted online. **Transfer Students:** 4037 transfer students enrolled in 2015-2016. Applicants with fewer than 30 hours from an accredited college must have a 2.5 GPA and meet freshman entrance requirements. Applicants with at least 30 but no more than 44 transferable hours must have a 2.3 GPA; those with more than 44 hours must have a 2.0 GPA. Students may enroll in the fall, spring, and summer. 30 of 120 credits required for the bachelor's degree must be completed at UNT. **International Students:** There are 1895 international students enrolled. The school actively recruits these students. They must take the TOEFL with a minimum score of 550 on the paper-based TOEFL (PBT) or 79 on the Internet-based version (iBT), or take the MELAB, or any one of these tests the ECPE, FCE, CAE, CPE, IELTS, or ELPT. U.S. high school graduates who are not U.S. citizens may take either the SAT I or ACT instead of the TOEFL.

ADMISSIONS: 70% of the 2016-2017 applicants were accepted. The

SAT scores for the 2016-2017 freshman class were: Critical Reading-- 29% below 500, 46% between 500 and 599, 21% between 600 and 699, and 4% between 700 and 800. Math-- 24% below 500, 49% between 500 and 599, 21% between 600 and 699, and 6% between 700 and 800. Writing-- 38% below 500, 41% between 500 and 599, 14% between 600 and 699, and 3% between 700 and 800. The ACT scores were 6% between 12 and 17, 47% between 18 and 23, 40% between 24 and 29, and 7% above 30. 40% of the current freshmen were in the top fifth of their class; 75% were in the top two fifths. **Admissions Contact:** Dr. Rebecca Lothringer, Director of Undergraduate Admissions. Email: *unt.freshman@unt.edu* Web: *www.unt.edu*

FINANCIAL AID: The priority date for freshman financial aid applications for fall entry is March 15.

UNIVERSITY OF ST. THOMAS - HOUSTON E-3

www.stthom.edu

Houston, TX 77006	(713) 525-3500
Fax: (713) 525-3558	**Email:** admissions@stthom.edu
Full-time: 469 men, 922 women	**Faculty:** 127; IIA, ++$
Part-time: 248 men, 175 women	**Ph.D.s:** 91%
Graduate: 459 men, 1039 women	**Student/Faculty:** 10 to 1
Year: semesters, summer session	**Tuition:** $31,520
Room & Board: $8500	**Freshman Class:** 795 applied, 628 accepted, 227 enrolled
SAT CR/M/W: 530/560/526 **ACT:** 23	**CEEB CODE:** 6880
Application Deadline: May 1	**VERY COMPETITIVE**

Committed to educating leaders of faith and character, the University of St. Thomas in Houston offers a Catholic liberal arts education for a lifetime of opportunities. Liberal arts degrees provide invaluable training to a range of careers including business, teaching and health. UST offers 33 undergraduate and 15 graduate degree programs. There are 4 undergraduate schools and 6 graduate schools. In addition to regional accreditation, UST has baccalaureate program accreditation with AACSB, TEAC, ATS, and CCNE. The 23-acre campus is in an urban area 3 miles from Downtown Houston. Including any residence halls, there are 65 buildings.

STUDENT LIFE: 97% of undergraduates are from Texas. Others are from 26 states, 60 foreign countries, and Canada. 74% are from public schools. 6% are African American; 37% Hispanic; 30% White; 3% two or more races; 2% race unknown; 12% Asian American; 10% Foreign. 50% are Catholic; 28% Buddhist, Muslim, Hindu, Orthodox, Unitarian, Baptist, Methodist, Episcolapian, and Mormon. **Female To Male Ratio:** 1.8:1. The average age of freshmen is 18; all undergraduates, 25. 12% do not continue beyond their first year; 52% remain to graduate. **Housing:** 382 students can be accommodated in college housing, which includes single-sex, coed dorms and on-campus apartments, special-interest houses. Residents are grouped by classification and gender. On-campus housing is available on a first-come and first-served basis. Priority is given to out-of-town students. 78% of students commute. All students may keep cars.

FACULTY/CLASSROOMS: 55% of faculty are male; 45% are female. 70% teach undergraduates. No introductory courses are taught by graduate students. The average class size in an introductory lecture is 18 and in a laboratory is 16.

PROGRAMS OF STUDY: UST confers B.A., B.F.A., B.S., B.S.N., B.B.A., and B.I.B. degrees. Master's and doctoral degrees are also awarded. Bachelor's degrees are awarded in AGRICULTURE (environmental studies), BIOLOGICAL SCIENCE (biochemistry, bioinformatics, and biology/biological science), BUSINESS (accounting, banking and finance, business administration and management, finance, international business management, marketing, and marketing/retailing/merchandising), COMMUNICATIONS AND THE ARTS (communications, dramatic arts, English, French, music, Spanish, and studio art), COMPUTER AND PHYSICAL SCIENCE (applied mathematics, chemistry, computer science, mathematics, and physics), EDUCATION (business education, education, music education, and nursing education), ENGINEERING AND ENVIRONMENTAL DESIGN (environmental science), HEALTH PROFESSIONS (nursing), SOCIAL SCIENCE (economics, history, international studies, liberal arts/general studies, philosophy, political science/government, psychology, religion, and theological studies). Biology is the strongest academically. Biology, finance, and education have the largest enrollments.

ACTIVITIES: There are no fraternities or sororities. There are 103 groups on campus, including art, cheerleading, choir, communications, dance, drama, environmental, ethnic, film, forensics, honors, international, jazz band, literary magazine, musical theater, newspaper, orchestra, political, professional, religious, social, social service, and student government. Popular campus events include Research Symposium, Mass of Holy Spirit, Mass of St. Thomas Aquinas, Family and Alumni Weekend, President's Day of Service, and Deck the Mall. **Sports:** There are 3 intercollegiate sports for men and 4 for women, and 12 intramural sports for men and 12 for women. Facilities include a gym, racquetball courts, weight room, fitness room, dance room, swimming pool, tennis courts, and sand volleyball court. Outdoor facilities include playing fields, batting cages, pitching machine, half basketball court, and soccer goals. **Graduates:** From July 1, 2015 to June 30, 2016, 323 bachelor's degrees were awarded. The most popular majors were finance (11%), nursing (9%), and psychology (7%). In an average class, 34% graduate in 4 years or less, 48% graduate in 5 years or less, and 52% graduate in 6 years or less.

SERVICES: Counseling and information services are available, as is tutoring in most subjects, and remedial math, reading, and writing. Kurzweil Educational software is available for the visually impaired. **Library/Resources:** The 4 libraries contain 264,427 volumes, 2,177 microform items, 2,177 audio/video tapes/CDs/DVDs, and subscribe to 78,433 periodicals including electronic. Computerized library services include interlibrary loans, database searching, Internet access, and Wi-Fi capability. Special learning facilities include an art gallery, a meditation garden. **Physically Challenged Students:** 90% of the campus is accessible. Facilities include wheelchair ramps, elevators, special parking, specially equipped restrooms, lowered drinking fountains, lowered telephones, special housing. **Special:** UST has a cooperative 3-2 engineering program with the University of Houston, Texas A&M University, University of Notre Dame and Catholic University of America. Internships in the major field of study and study abroad in 11 countries are also available. Dual and joint majors and 5 year joint bachelor's and master's degree programs, combining BBA/MBA are available. There are 24 national honor societies, a freshman honors program, and 1 departmental honors programs. **Visiting:** There are regularly scheduled orientations for prospective students, tours, class visitations, introductions to faculty, administrative members, and currently enrolled students, financial aid sessions and social activities. There are guides for informal visits, visitors may sit in on classes, and stay overnight. To schedule a visit, contact the Admissions Counselor at (713) 525-3500. **Campus Safety and Security:** Measures include 24-hour foot and vehicle patrol, emergency notification system, self-defense education, and security escort services. There are also shuttle buses, emergency telephones, lighted pathways/sidewalks, controlled access to dorms/residences, fire suppression system, fire extinguishers, smoke detectors, fire drills, and IP security cameras.

REQUIREMENTS: The SAT or ACT and the ACT Optional Writing test are required. In addition, applicants must graduate from an accredited secondary school, home school program or successfully complete the GED. Additionally, applicants should have competitive grades (mimimum high school GPA of 2.80 on a 4.0 scale) in a minimum of 18 college preparatory high school units: including 4 units of English, 3 units of social science, 3 units of mathematics, 3 units of science, 2 units of the same classical or modern language other than English, and 3 units of electives in college preparatory classes. Applicants should also have competitive official SAT or ACT scores and competitive class rank if high school ranks graduates. If appropriate, applicants should submit official transcripts of home school coursework. Home schooled students may also need to submit course descriptions, reading lists, or other information if requested. UST requires applicants to be in the upper 50% of their class. A GPA of 2.5 is required. AP and CLEP credits are accepted. Important factors in the admissions decision are advanced placement or honors courses, recommendations by school officials, and extracurricular activities record. To graduate, students must complete the core curriculum and 30 to 48 hours in their selected majors. In some cases, students need to complete special projects according to the requirements of specific majors. Students must have a minimum 2.0 GPA in a total of 126 credit hours, including 36 hours of upper-division credits and the final 36 hours competed in residence at the University. **Procedure:** Freshmen are admitted in the fall, spring, and summer. Entrance exams should be taken as early as possible. There are early admissions and deferred admissions plans. Early decision applications should be filed by December 1; regular applications, by May 1 for fall entry; December 1 for spring entry; and May 1 for summer entry. Notification of early decision is sent 12 15; regular decision, on a rolling basis. Application fees are waived if application is completed online. **Transfer Students:** 244 transfer students enrolled in 2015-2016. Transfer students must have a minimum 2.50 GPA college GPA a minimum high school GPA of 2.80 and have a high school diploma or GED. 36 of 126 credits required for the bachelor's degree must be completed at UST. **International Students:** There are 145 international students enrolled. The school actively recruits these students. They must take the TOEFL with a minimum score of 550 on the paper-based TOEFL (PBT) or 79 on the Internet-based version (iBT). They must also take the SAT or ACT, scoring 23.

ADMISSIONS: 79% of the 2016-2017 applicants were accepted. The SAT scores for the 2016-2017 freshman class were: Critical Reading-- 27% below 500, 46% between 500 and 599, 20% between 600 and 699, and 7% between 700 and 800. Math-- 23% below 500, 43% between 500 and 599, 29% between 600 and 699, and 6% between 700 and 800. Writing-- 33% below 500, 50% between 500 and 599, 13% between 600 and 699, and 4% between 700 and 800. The ACT scores were 12% below 12, 30% between 12 and 17, 30% between 18 and 23, 7% between 24 and 29, and 22% above 30. 47% of the current freshmen were in the top fifth of their class; 75% were in the top two fifths. 3 freshmen graduated first in their class. **Admissions Contact:** Arthur Ortiz, Assistant Vice President for Enrollment. Email: *admissions@stthom.edu* Web: *www.stthom.edu*

FINANCIAL AID: In 2016-2017, 91% of all full-time freshmen and 84% of continuing full-time students received some form of financial aid. 72% of all full-time freshmen and 60% of continuing full-time students received need-based aid. The average freshman award was $22,540. Need-based scholarships or need-based grants averaged $18,997; need-based self-help aid (loans and jobs) averaged $5,371; non-need-based athletic scholarships averaged $4,654; and other non-need-based awards and non-need-based scholarships averaged $11,794. 17% of undergraduate students work part-time. Average annual earnings from campus work are $2367. The average financial indebtedness of the 2016 graduate was $36,497. The priority date for freshman financial aid applications for fall entry is April 15.

UNIVERSITY OF TEXAS AT ARLINGTON *(The complete profile is made available exclusively on our website, www.barronspac.com)*

UNIVERSITY OF TEXAS AT AUSTIN D-3

www.utexas.edu

Austin, TX 78712 **(512) 471-3833**

Fax: (512) 471-8950

Full-time: 17839 men, 19244 women
Part-time: 1553 men, 1319 women
Graduate: 6403 men, 5828 women
Year: semesters, summer session
Room & Board: $15,042

SAT: required **ACT:** 26
Application Deadline: February 1

Faculty: 2599; I, +$
Ph.D.s: 84%
Student/Faculty: 17 to 1
Tuition: $11,060 ($21,066)
Freshman Class: 35431 applied, 16563 accepted, 8092 enrolled
CEEB CODE: 6882
HIGHLY COMPETITIVE

University of Texas at Austin, founded in 1883, is a major research institution within the University of Texas System and provides a broad range of degree programs. The figures in the above capsule and in this profile are approximate. There are 18 undergraduate schools and 15 graduate schools. In addition to regional accreditation, UT has baccalaureate program accreditation with AACSB, ABET, ACEJMC, ACPE, ADA, CSWE, FIDER, NAAB, NASAD, and NASM. The 431-acre campus is in an urban area near downtown Austin, just off the interstate. Including any residence halls, there are 120 buildings.

STUDENT LIFE: 92% of undergraduates are from Texas. Others are from 50 states, 127 foreign countries, and Canada. 47% are White; 4% African American; 3% two or more races; 19% Hispanic; 16% Asian American; 10% Foreign; 1% race unknown. 11% are unknown denomination. **Female To Male Ratio:** 1.0:1. The average age of freshmen is 18; all undergraduates, 21. 7% do not continue beyond their first year; 93% remain to graduate. **Housing:** 6815 students can be accommodated in college housing, which includes single-sex, coed dorms, off-campus apartments, married student housing, honors houses, and living learning centers are for freshmen. On-campus housing is available on a first-come and first-served basis. 80% of students commute. All students may keep cars.

FACULTY/CLASSROOMS: 64% of faculty are male; 36% are female. All teach undergraduates and do research. No introductory courses are taught by graduate students.

PROGRAMS OF STUDY: UT confers B.A., B.S., B.Arch., B.B.A., B.F.A., B.M., B.J. and B.S.W. degrees. Master's and doctoral degrees are also awarded. Bachelor's degrees are awarded in BIOLOGICAL SCIENCE (biochemistry, biology/biological science, microbiology, molecular biology, and nutrition), BUSINESS (accounting, banking and finance, business administration and management, management information systems, management science, and marketing management), COMMUNICATIONS AND THE ARTS (advertising, applied music, Arabic, art history and appreciation, classics, creative writing, dance, design, dramatic arts, English, film arts, French, German, Greek, Hebrew, Italian, journalism, Latin, linguistics, music, music theory and composition, Portuguese, public relations, Russian, Scandinavian languages, Slavic languages, Spanish, speech/debate/rhetoric, studio art, and visual and performing arts), COMPUTER AND PHYSICAL SCIENCE (astronomy, chemistry, computer science, geology, geophysics and seismology, mathematics, and physics), ENGINEERING AND ENVIRONMENTAL DESIGN (aerospace studies, architectural engineering, architecture, biomedical engineering, chemical engineering, civil engineering, electrical/electronics engineering, geophysical engineering, interior design, landscape architecture/design, mechanical engineering, and petroleum/natural gas engineering), HEALTH PROFESSIONS (medical technology, nursing, pharmacy, and speech pathology/audiology), SOCIAL SCIENCE (American studies, anthropology, archeology, Asian/Oriental studies, child care/child and family studies, classical/ancient civilization, dietetics, Eastern European studies, economics, ethnic studies, geography, history, human ecology, humanities, Islamic studies, Judaic studies, Latin American studies, liberal arts/general studies, Middle Eastern studies, philosophy, physical fitness/movement, political science/government, psychology, religion, Russian and Slavic studies, social work, sociology, textiles and clothing, and urban studies). Biological sciences, electrical & computer engineering, and government have the largest enrollments.

ACTIVITIES: 13% of men belong to 27 national fraternities; 18% of women belong to 23 national sororities. There are 100 groups on campus, including art, band, cheerleading, chess, choir, chorale, chorus, computers, dance, drama, ethnic, film, forensics, honors, international, LGBT, literary magazine, marching band, musical theater, newspaper, orchestra, photography, political, professional, radio and TV, religious, social, social service, student government, symphony, and yearbook. Popular campus events include Gone to Texas (welcome for new students), Cinco de Mayo, and Texas Revue (talent show). **Sports:** There are 8 intercollegiate sports for men and 10 for women, and 45 intramural sports for men and 45 for women. Facilities include a football stadium, basketball center, volleyball arena, baseball stadium, and swimming facility. There is also multipurpose indoor recreational/athletic facilities of various sizes available for basketball, volleyball, racquetball, swimming, weight training, and related activities, outdoor facilities covering nearly 40 acres are available for swimming, tennis, basketball, racquetball, and various field sports. There is also a softball stadium, track, and soccer stadium. **Graduates:** From July 1, 2015 to June 30, 2016, 8821 bachelor's degrees were awarded. The most popular majors were social sciences (12%), business/marketing (12%), and education (12%). In an average class, 52% graduate in 4 years or less, 76% graduate in 5 years or less, and 79% graduate in 6 years or less.

SERVICES: Counseling and information services are available, as is tutoring in most subjects, a reader service for the blind, and remedial math, reading, and writing. **Library/Resources:** The 17 libraries contain 10.2 million volumes, 6.7 million microform items, 14.1 million audio/video tapes/CDs/DVDs, and subscribe to 103,589 periodicals including electronic. Computerized library services include interlibrary loans, database searching, Internet access, and Wi-Fi capability. Special learning facilities include an art gallery, natural history museum, radio station, TV station, an observatory, marine science institute, fusion reactor, and Lyndon Baines Johnson Library and Museum, and the Texas Memorial Museum collection. **Physically Challenged Students:** 98% of the campus is accessible. Facilities include wheelchair ramps, elevators, special parking, specially equipped restrooms, lowered drinking fountains, lowered telephones. ‘specially equipped reading rooms, a speech and hearing center, academic accommodations specific to the student's disability, and interpreters for the hearing impaired. **Special:** Cooperative programs are available in most engineering courses, microbiology, chemistry, computer science, geology, and actuarial studies. Cross-registration is provided in pharmacy with the University of Texas at San Antonio. Internships, study abroad, B.A.-B.S. degrees, dual majors, student-designed majors for humanities students, and pass/fail options are offered. There are approximate 450 study abroad programs, and 78 countries where study abroad is offered. There are 45 national honor societies, Phi Beta Kappa, a freshman honors program, and 50 departmental honors programs. **Visiting:** There are regularly scheduled orientations for prospective students. There are guides for informal visits and visitors may sit in on classes. To schedule a visit, contact the Office of Admissions. **Campus Safety and Security:** Measures include 24-hour foot and vehicle patrol, self-defense education, and security escort services. There are also shuttle buses, emergency telephones, lighted pathways/sidewalks, There is also a crime prevention unit and closed-circuit TV covering some parking areas and offices.

REQUIREMENTS: All students graduating in the top 10% of their class from an accredited Texas high school are eligible for admission. Applicants not meeting that requirement are reviewed based on SAT or ACT scores, class rank, writing samples, and related factors; consideration may be given to socioeconomic and geographic information. In addition, applicants need 15 1/2 academic credits, including 4 in English, 3 each in math and social studies, 2 each in science and foreign language, and 1 1/2 in electives. An audition is required for applied music majors. The GED is accepted, with supportive information. Home-schooled students are required to submit the results of either the SAT: Subject tests or AP exams in English, math, and a third subject of the student's choosing. AP and CLEP credits are accepted. Important factors in the admissions decision are leadership record, evidence of special talent, extracurricular activities record, and geographical diversity. All students must maintain a GPA of 2.0 while satisfactorily completing 120 to 167 semester hours. Distribution requirements include 6 hours each in American government, American history, natural science, and courses containing a substantial writing component (with at least 3 hours being upper-division), 3 hours each in math, social science, English composition, literature, and humanities/fine arts, plus 3 additional hours in either math, natural science, computer science, or social science, and a fourth semester proficiency in a single foreign language. **Procedure:** Freshmen are admitted in the fall, spring, and summer. Entrance exams should be taken in the junior year or early in the senior year. There are deferred admissions and rolling admissions plans. Early decision applications should be filed by December 1; regular applications, by February 1 for fall entry; October 1 for spring entry; and February 1 for summer entry, along with a $75 fee. Notifications are sent November 15. 321 applicants were on the 2016 waiting list; 34 were admitted. Applications are accepted online. **Transfer Students:** 2639 transfer students enrolled in 2015-2016. Applicants must have at least 24 transferable hours (30 for business). 60 of 120 credits required for the bachelor's degree must be completed at UT. **International Students:** There are 1189 international students enrolled. They must take the TOEFL with a minimum score of 550 on the paper-based TOEFL (PBT) or 79 on the Internet-based version (iBT). They must also take the SAT or ACT.

ADMISSIONS: 47% of the 2016-2017 applicants were accepted. The ACT scores were 10% below 12, 16% between 12 and 17, 26% between 18 and 23, 18% between 24 and 29, and 30% above 30. 88% of the current freshmen were in the top fifth of their class; 98% were in the top two fifths. **Admissions Contact:** Susan Kearns, Director of Admission. Web: *www.utexas.edu*

FINANCIAL AID: In 2016-2017, 50% of all full-time freshmen and 49% of continuing full-time students received some form of financial aid. 50% of all full-time freshmen and 49% of continuing full-time students received need-based aid. The average freshman award was $13,669. Need-based scholarships or need-based grants averaged $9,204; need-based self-help aid (loans and jobs) averaged $3,663; other non-need-based awards and non-need-based scholarships averaged $6,031; and $3,601 from other forms of aid. The average financial indebtedness of the 2016 graduate was $26,097. UT is a member of CSS. The college's own financial statement is required. The priority date for freshman financial aid applications for fall entry is March 31.

UNIVERSITY OF TEXAS AT DALLAS D-2

www.utdallas.edu

Richardson, TX 75080 (972) 883-2270

Fax: (972) 883-2599
Email: interest@utdallas.edu
Full-time: 8148 men, 6176 women
Faculty: 515; I, ++$
Part-time: 1769 men, 1258 women
Ph.D.s: 93%
Graduate: 5364 men, 4077 women
Student/Faculty: 21 to 1
Year: semesters, summer session
Tuition: $12,162 ($33,654)
Room & Board: $10,668
Freshman Class: 12687 applied, 8626 accepted, 3232 enrolled
SAT CR/M/W: 610/650/580 **ACT:** 28
CEEB CODE: 6897
Application Deadline: July 1
VERY COMPETITIVE+

University of Texas at Dallas, founded in 1969 as part of the University of Texas system, offers undergraduate and graduate programs in the liberal arts and sciences, business, engineering, computer science, cognitive science, and neuroscience. There are 8 undergraduate schools and 8 graduate schools. In addition to regional accreditation, UTD has baccalaureate program accreditation with AACSB, ABET, ACS, and NASPAA. The 550-acre campus is in a suburban area 18 miles north of downtown Dallas. Including any residence halls, there are 154 buildings.

STUDENT LIFE: 93% of undergraduates are from Texas. Others are from 47 states, 75 foreign countries, and Canada. 93% are from public schools. 5% are African American; 31% White; 3% two or more races; 23% Foreign; 22% Asian American; 2% race unknown; 14% Hispanic. **Male To Female Ratio:** 1.3:1. The average age of freshmen is 18; all undergraduates, 22. 13% do not continue beyond their first year; 68% remain to graduate. **Housing:** 6154 students can be accommodated in college housing, which includes coed dorms, on-campus apartments, married student housing, and privately owned campus apartments. Students can also request to be assigned to a living learning group. On-campus housing is available on a first-come and first-served basis. 73% of students commute. All students may keep cars.

FACULTY/CLASSROOMS: 65% of faculty are male; 35% are female. 34% teach undergraduates, 18% do research, and 24% do both. Graduate students teach 9% of introductory courses. The average class size in an introductory lecture is 44; in a laboratory is 36; and in a regular course is 43.

PROGRAMS OF STUDY: UTD confers B.A., B.S., B.S.EE. and B.S.TE. degrees. Master's and doctoral degrees are also awarded. Bachelor's degrees are awarded in BIOLOGICAL SCIENCE (biochemistry, biology/biological science, molecular biology, and neurosciences), BUSINESS (accounting, banking and finance, business administration and management, international business management, and marketing management), COMMUNICATIONS AND THE ARTS (fine arts, literature, media arts, telecommunications, telecommunications engineering technology, and visual and performing arts), COMPUTER AND PHYSICAL SCIENCE (actuarial science, chemistry, computer science, geoscience, information sciences and systems, mathematics, physics, and software engineering), ENGINEERING AND ENVIRONMENTAL DESIGN (biomedical engineering, computer engineering, electrical/electronics engineering, and mechanical engineering), HEALTH PROFESSIONS (speech pathology/audiology), SOCIAL SCIENCE (American studies, child psychology/development, cognitive science, criminology, economics, geography, history, humanities, interdisciplinary studies, international public service, political science/government, psychology, public administration, and sociology). Electrical engineering, biological sciences, and arts are the strongest academically. Business administration, biology, and computer science have the largest enrollments.

ACTIVITIES: 2% of men belong to 12 national fraternities; 3% of women belong to 8 national sororities. There are 355 groups on campus, including art, band, cheerleading, chess, choir, chorale, chorus, computers, dance, debate, drama, drill team, environmental, ethnic, film, forensics, honors, international, jazz band, LGBT, literary magazine, musical theater, newspaper, opera, orchestra, pep band, photography, political, professional, radio and TV, religious, social, social service, and student government. Popular campus events include Welcome Week, Homecoming, Holiday Sing, Oozeball and Green Lecture Series. **Sports:** There are 6 intercollegiate sports for men and 7 for women, and 21 intramural sports for men and 19 for women. Facilities include racquetball courts, squash courts, tennis courts, indoor and outdoor basketball courts, a sand volleyball court, gravel track, soccer fields, softball fields, a junior pool/natatorium, gym, basketball court, and weight room. **Graduates:** From July 1, 2015 to June 30, 2016, 3083 bachelor's degrees were awarded. The most popular majors were accounting (8%), biology (7%), and business administration (6%). 1055 companies recruited on campus in 2015-2016. In an average class, 6% graduate in 3 years or less, 51% graduate in 4 years or less, 64% graduate in 5 years or less, and 68% graduate in 6 years or less. Of the 2015 graduating class, 8% were enrolled in graduate school within 6 months of graduation, and 84% were employed.

SERVICES: Counseling and information services are available, as is tutoring in most subjects, a reader service for the blind, and remedial math, reading, and writing. **Library/Resources:** The library contains 3.2 million volumes, 642,850 microform items, 13,420 audio/video tapes/ CDs/DVDs, and subscribes to 264,849 periodicals including electronic. Computerized library services include interlibrary loans, database searching, and Internet access. Special learning facilities include an art gallery, radio station, TV station, a center for communications disorders, a rare books library, and special library collections on aviation history, geophysics, philatelic research, and botanicals. **Physically Challenged Students:** All of the campus is accessible. Facilities include wheelchair ramps, elevators, special parking, specially equipped restrooms, lowered drinking fountains, and lowered telephones. **Special:** Cross-registration is available with other University of Texas campuses. Accelerated degree programs and B.A.-B.S. degrees are offered in several majors, as is a 3-2 engineering degree. Co-op programs, internships, work-study programs with several major corporations, dual majors, student-designed majors and Washington semester are also possible. In addition, students may study abroad in Europe, Asia, Mexico and New Zealand. There are 5 national honor societies, a freshman honors program, and 16 departmental honors programs. **Visiting:** There are regularly scheduled orientations for prospective students, including meetings with faculty and an admissions counselor, and a campus tour. There are guides for informal visits and visitors may sit in on classes. To schedule a visit, contact the Office of Enrollment Services. **Campus Safety and Security:** Measures include 24-hour foot and vehicle patrol, emergency notification system, self-defense education, security escort services, emergency telephones, lighted pathways/sidewalks, controlled access to dorms/residences, campus crime watch bulletins, bicycle patrols, crime prevention programs, ID engraving, and a police liaison who works with students on security issues.

REQUIREMENTS: The SAT or ACT, and the ACT Optional Writing test are required. Applicants should be graduates of an accredited secondary school. In-state students who rank in the top 10% of their class gain automatic admission to UTD. Credentials for other students must include completion of 4 units of English, 3.5 of math, 3 each of social science and lab science, 2 of a foreign language, and course work in fine arts and electives, with health and phys ed courses recommended. AP and CLEP credits are accepted. Important factors in the admissions decision are advanced placement or honors courses, leadership record, and evidence of special talent. To graduate, students must complete at least 120 credit hours, including 30 in the major and 51 in upper-division courses, with a minimum GPA of 2.0. Core courses include 15 credits in social science (with 6 each in U.S./Texas government and U.S./Texas history), 9 in natural science, and 6 each in communications, math, and humanities/fine arts. Magna and summa cum laude graduates must complete a thesis. **Procedure:** Freshmen are admitted to all sessions. Entrance exams should be taken at the end of the junior year or beginning of the senior year. There are deferred admissions and rolling admissions plans. Applications should be filed by July 1 for fall entry; November 1 for spring entry; and April 1 for summer entry, along with a $50 fee. Applications are accepted online. **Transfer Students:** 2005 transfer students enrolled in 2015-2016. Sophomore applicants must present a GPA of 3.0 and 12 credits in the general education core. Upper-division applicants should have a GPA of 2.5 and be in good standing at the last school attended. 30 of 120 credits required for the bachelor's degree must be completed at UTD. **International Students:** There are 628 international students enrolled. They must take the TOEFL with a minimum score of 550 on the paper-based TOEFL (PBT) or 80 on the Internet-based version (iBT). They must also take the SAT or ACT.

ADMISSIONS: 68% of the 2016-2017 applicants were accepted. The SAT scores for the 2016-2017 freshman class were: Critical Reading-- 9% below 500, 35% between 500 and 599, 38% between 600 and 699, and 18% between 700 and 800. Math-- 3% below 500, 24% between 500 and 599, 44% between 600 and 699, and 29% between 700 and 800. Writing-- 16% below 500, 39% between 500 and 599, 32% between 600 and 699, and 13% between 700 and 800. The ACT scores were 13% between 18 and 23, 47% between 24 and 29, and 39% above 30. 54% of the current freshmen were in the top fifth of their class; 81% were in the top two fifths. There were 119 National Merit finalists. 42 freshmen graduated first in their class. **Admissions Contact:** Wray Weldon, Assistant Provost, Enrollment Management. Email: *interest@utdallas.edu* Web: *www.utdallas.edu*

FINANCIAL AID: In 2016-2017, 52% of all full-time freshmen and 53% of continuing full-time students received some form of financial aid. 49% of all full-time freshmen and 48% of continuing full-time students received need-based aid. The average freshman award was $15,325. Need-based scholarships or need-based grants averaged $11,085; need-based self-help aid (loans and jobs) averaged $4,761; and other non-need-based awards and non-need-based scholarships averaged $13,459. 11% of undergraduate students work part-time. Average annual earnings from campus work are $6985. The average financial indebtedness of the 2016 graduate was $21,174. The FAFSA code is 009741. The priority date for freshman financial aid applications for fall entry is March 31. The filing deadline for fall entry is April 15.

UNIVERSITY OF TEXAS AT EL PASO *(The complete profile is made available exclusively on our website, www.barronspac.com)*

UNIVERSITY OF TEXAS RIO GRANDE VALLEY *(The complete profile is made available exclusively on our website, www.barronspac.com)*

UNIVERSITY OF TEXAS AT SAN ANTONIO — D-4

www.utsa.edu

San Antonio, TX 78249	**(210) 458-4536** **(800) 669-0919**
Fax: (210) 458-7857	**Email: onestop@utsa.edu**
Full-time: 10,455 men, 9578 women	**Faculty:** 784; I, --$
Part-time: 2359 men, 1950 women	**Ph.D.s:** 74%
Graduate: 1909 men, 2372 women	**Student/Faculty:** 23 to 1
Year: semesters, summer session	**Tuition:** $9361 ($20,674)
Room & Board: $10,796	**Freshman Class:** 13988 applied, 8671 accepted, 3689 enrolled
SAT CR/M: 500/530 **ACT:** 22	**CEEB CODE:** 6919
Application Deadline: July 1	**COMPETITIVE**

University of Texas at San Antonio is dedicated to the advancement of knowledge through research and discovery, teaching and learning, community engagement and public service. As an institution of access and excellence, UTSA embraces multicultural traditions, and serves as a center for intellectual and creative resources as well as a catalyst for socioeconomic development and the commercialization of intellectual property for Texas, the nation and the world. Figures in the above capsule and in this profile are approximate. There are 9 undergraduate schools and 7 graduate schools. In addition to regional accreditation, UTSA has baccalaureate program accreditation with AACSB, ABET, NASAD, NASM, NASPAA, CIDA, and ACS. The 725-acre campus is in a suburban area approximately 18 miles northwest of downtown San Antonio. Including any residence halls, there are 121 buildings.

STUDENT LIFE: 98% of undergraduates are from Texas. Others are from 50 states, 96 foreign countries, and Canada. 9% are African American; 6% Foreign; 5% Asian American; 47% Hispanic; 3% two or more races; 29% White; 1% race unknown. **Male To Female Ratio:** 1.1:1. The average age of freshmen is 18; all undergraduates, 23. 37% do not continue beyond their first year; 34% remain to graduate. **Housing:** 4298 students can be accommodated in college housing, which includes single-sex and coed dorms and on-campus apartments. On-campus housing is available on a first-come and first-served basis. 95% of students commute. All students may keep cars.

FACULTY/CLASSROOMS: 58% of faculty are male; 42% are female. 81% teach undergraduates. Graduate students teach 13% of introductory courses. The average class size in an introductory lecture is 55 and in a laboratory is 21.

PROGRAMS OF STUDY: UTSA confers B.A., B.S., B.A.A.S., B.B.A., B.F.A., B.M., B.S.C.E., B.S.E.E., B.P.A. and B.S.M.E. degrees. Master's and doctoral degrees are also awarded. Bachelor's degrees are awarded in BIOLOGICAL SCIENCE (biochemistry and biology/biological science), BUSINESS (accounting, business administration and management, business statistics, finance, human resources, management science, and marketing management), COMMUNICATIONS AND THE ARTS (art, art history and appreciation, classics, communications, English, modern language, music, and Spanish), COMPUTER AND PHYSICAL SCIENCE (actuarial science, actuarial mathematics, chemistry, computer science, computer security and information assurance, geology, information sciences and systems, mathematics, physics, and statistics), EDUCATION (childhood education, early childhood education, and education), ENGINEERING AND ENVIRONMENTAL DESIGN (architecture, biomedical engineering, civil engineering, computer engineering, construction management, electrical/electronics engineering, engineering, environmental science, interior design, and mechanical engineering), HEALTH PROFESSIONS (health), SOCIAL SCIENCE (American studies, anthropology, child care/child and family studies, criminal justice, economics, geography, history, humanities, interdisciplinary studies, Mexican-American/Chicano studies, philosophy, philosophy and religion, political science/government, public administration, sociology, and women's studies). Honors college, business, engineering, and sciences are the strongest academically. Business, biology, and psychology have the largest enrollments.

ACTIVITIES: 3% of men belong to 12 national fraternities; 3% of women belong to 10 national sororities. There are 217 groups on campus, including art, band, cheerleading, chess, choir, chorale, chorus, computers, dance, debate, drama, environmental, ethnic, film, forensics, honors, international, jazz band, LGBT, marching band, newspaper, orchestra, pep band, political, professional, religious, social, social service, student government, and symphony. Popular campus events include Fiesta UTSA, Best Fest, and Rowdy Rampage Fireworks Spectacular. **Sports:** There are 7 intercollegiate sports for men and 8 for women, and 26 intramural sports for men and 26 for women. Facilities include numerous gyms, including those for basketball, volleyball, badminton, indoor soccer, and inline hockey. There are also weight rooms, a track, tennis center, cardio room, dance studios, racquetball courts, wallyball courts, a rock wall, an indoor 1/6-mile track, a climbing wall, a swimming pool, sand volleyball courts, an outdoor basketball court, outdoor multipurpose fields, and a Frisbee golf course. **Graduates:** From July 1, 2015 to June 30, 2016, 4371 bachelor's degrees were awarded. The most popular majors were business/marketing (25%), interdisciplinary studies (9%), and biological/life sciences (7%). 111 companies recruited on campus in 2015-2016. In an average class, 11% graduate in 4 years or less, 20% graduate in 5 years or less, and 31% graduate in 6 years or less.

SERVICES: Counseling and information services are available, as is tutoring in some subjects, a reader service for the blind, and remedial math, reading, and writing. **Library/Resources:** The 3 libraries contain 1.9 million volumes, 2.9 million microform items, 3.6 million audio/video tapes/CDs/DVDs, and subscribe to 70,467 periodicals including electronic. Computerized library services include interlibrary loans, database searching, Internet access, and Wi-Fi capability. Special learning facilities include an art gallery, the institute of Texan cultures. **Physically Challenged Students:** All of the campus is accessible. Facilities include wheelchair ramps, elevators, special parking, specially equipped restrooms, special class scheduling, lowered drinking fountains, lowered telephones, and special housing. **Special:** UTSA offers a wide variety of programs to enrich educational opportunities for students. Programs such as University College, ROTC and the Honors College are designed to provide opportunities for research, service and leadership. There are also programs for Pre-Professional Studies (Pre-Med and Pre-Law), internships and a newly offered degree in Multidisciplinary Studies where students have an opportunity to choose three focus areas. There are 40 national honor societies, a freshman honors program, and 17 departmental honors programs. **Visiting:** There are regularly scheduled orientations for prospective students. There are guides for informal visits. To schedule a visit, contact the Visitor Center. **Campus Safety and Security:** Measures include 24-hour foot and vehicle patrol, emergency notification system, self-defense education, and security escort services. There are shuttle buses, emergency telephones, lighted pathways/sidewalks, and controlled access to dorms/residences.

REQUIREMENTS: Admission is based on a formula derived from high school class rank and SAT or ACT scores. Applicants must be graduates of accredited high schools or have earned the GED. AP and CLEP credits are accepted. In order to receive a bachelor's degree from UTSA, a student must meet these minimum requirements: Complete a minimum of 120 semester credit hours, at least 39 of which must be upper-division level. Complete the University Core Curriculum requirements outlined in this chapter. Complete at least one course in the University Core Curriculum designated as a Q-course to satisfy the Quantitative Scholarship requirement. Complete the major and support work requirements and the free elective requirements for the desired degree. Free electives refer to any semester credit hours accepted by UTSA in transfer or awarded by UTSA that, for degree purposes, are not applied to Core Curriculum, major, minor, or support work requirements. Meet all requirements for a degree as put forth by the Texas State Education Code, including the following: Meet the minimum UTSA residence requirements. Achieve an overall 2.0 grade point average in all work attempted at UTSA and a 2.0 grade point average in all work included in the major. Be in good academic standing at UTSA. Apply formally for the degree before the deadline in the Office of the Registrar. **Procedure:** Freshmen are admitted to all sessions. Entrance exams should be taken in the spring of the junior year. There is a rolling admissions plan. Applications should be filed by July 1 for fall entry; November 15 for spring entry; and May 2 for summer entry, along with a $60 fee. Notification is sent on a rolling basis. Applications are accepted online. **Transfer Students:** 2463 transfer students enrolled in 2015-2016. Admissions requirements for transfer students with 30+ hours completed at time of application (work in progress is not considered) must: Have at least a cumulative 2.25 GPA on a 4.0 scale in all transferable college coursework from a regionally accredited institutions Submit your official transcripts from EACH college or university attended, including Dual Credit work Be eligible to return to most recent institution (includes academic and disciplinary actions)* Note: When calculating the cumulative grade point average for admission, all attempted work is considered. Repeated courses are NOT excluded. A student currently on suspension at a previous institution will not be considered for admission. 30 of 120 credits required for the bachelor's degree must be completed at UTSA. **International Students:** There are 1104 international students enrolled. The school actively recruits these students. They must take the TOEFL with a minimum score of 500 on the paper-based TOEFL (PBT) or 61 on the Internet-based version (iBT), or take the IELTS, with a minimum score of 5. They must also take the SAT or ACT.

ADMISSIONS: 62% of the 2016-2017 applicants were accepted. The SAT scores for the 2016-2017 freshman class were: Critical Reading-- 49% below 500, 36% between 500 and 599, 13% between 600 and 699, and 2% between 700 and 800. Math-- 35% below 500, 45% between 500 and 599, 18% between 600 and 699, and 2% between 700 and 800. The ACT scores were 38% below 12, 29% between 12 and 17, 21% between 18 and 23, 7% between 24 and 29, and 5% above 30. 23 freshmen graduated first in their class. **Admissions Contact:** George Norton, Director of Admissions. Email: *george.norton@utsa.edu* Web: *www.utsa.edu*

FINANCIAL AID: In 2016-2017, 46% of all full-time freshmen and 53% of continuing full-time students received some form of financial aid. 45% of all full-time freshmen and 52% of continuing full-time students received need-based aid. The average freshman award was $10,434. Need-based scholarships or need-based grants averaged $7,557; need-based self-help aid (loans and jobs) averaged $3,301; non-need-based athletic scholarships averaged $8,557; and other non-need-based awards and non-need-based scholarships averaged $1,518. 7% of undergraduate students work part-time. Average annual earnings from campus work are $5855. The average financial indebtedness of the 2016 graduate was $25,140. The college's own financial statement is required. The FAFSA code is 010115. The priority date for freshman financial aid applications for fall entry is March 15. The filing deadline for fall entry is June 30.

UNIVERSITY OF THE INCARNATE WORD *(The complete profile is made available exclusively on our website, www.barronspac.com)*

WAYLAND BAPTIST UNIVERSITY *(The complete profile is made available exclusively on our website, www.barronspac.com)*

WEST TEXAS A&M UNIVERSITY B-1

www.wtamu.edu

Canyon, TX 79016	**(806) 651-2020** **(800) 99-WTAMU**
Fax: (806) 651-5285	**Email: admissions@wtamu.edu**
Full-time: 2487 men, 3036 women	**Faculty:** 210; IIA, -$
Part-time: 637 men, 748 women	**Ph.D.s:** 70%
Graduate: 509 men, 964 women	**Student/Faculty:** 21 to 1
Year: semesters, summer session	**Tuition:** $6970 ($7870)
Room & Board: $6508	**Freshman Class:** 1665 applied, 1204 accepted, 801 enrolled
SAT: required **ACT:** 21	**CEEB CODE:** 6938
Application Deadline: open	**COMPETITIVE**

West Texas A&M University, founded in 1910, and a member of the Texas A&M University System, is a public institution offering programs in the liberal arts and sciences, fine arts, agriculture, nursing, and education. There are 4 undergraduate schools and 1 graduate school. In addition to regional accreditation, WTAMU has baccalaureate program accreditation with ACBSP, CSWE, NASM, and CCNE. The 135-acre campus is in a small town 17 miles south of Amarillo. Including any residence halls, there are 82 buildings.

STUDENT LIFE: 89% of undergraduates are from Texas. Others are from 39 states, 26 foreign countries, and Canada. 93% are from public schools. 76% are White; 4% African American; 4% Foreign; 14% Hispanic; 1% Asian American; 1% American Indian/Alaska Native. **Female To Male Ratio:** 1.3:1. The average age of freshmen is 18; all undergraduates, 24. 36% do not continue beyond their first year; 66% remain to graduate. **Housing:** 1520 students can be accommodated in college housing, which includes single-sex and coed dorms, special-interest houses, sorority units within the residence halls, and an honors hall. On-campus housing is guaranteed for all 4 years. 82% of students commute. All students may keep cars. Alcohol is not permitted.

FACULTY/CLASSROOMS: 56% of faculty are male; 44% are female. 95% teach undergraduates, 47% do research, and 47% do both. Graduate students teach 16% of introductory courses. The average class size in an introductory lecture is 28; in a laboratory is 23; and in a regular course is 26.

PROGRAMS OF STUDY: WTAMU confers B.A., B.S., B.A.A.S., B.B.A., B.F.A., B.G.S., B.M., B.S.M.T. and B.S.N. degrees. Master's and doctoral degrees are also awarded. Bachelor's degrees are awarded in AGRICULTURE (agricultural business management, agricultural economics, agriculture, animal science, plant protection (pest management), plant science, and soil science), BIOLOGICAL SCIENCE (biology/biological science, biotechnology, and wildlife biology), BUSINESS (accounting, banking and finance, business administration and management, business economics, management science, and marketing/retailing/merchandising), COMMUNICATIONS AND THE ARTS (applied art, art, broadcasting, dance, dramatic arts, English, graphic design, music, music theory and composition, musical theater, performing arts, public relations, publishing, Spanish, speech/debate/rhetoric, and studio art), COMPUTER AND PHYSICAL SCIENCE (chemistry, computer science, geology, information sciences and systems, mathematics, and physics), EDUCATION (art education, athletic training, business education, drama education, English education, foreign languages education, mathematics education, music education, physical education, reading education, science education, social studies education, and special education), ENGINEERING AND ENVIRONMENTAL DESIGN (emergency/disaster science, engineering technology, environmental science, mechanical engineering, and preengineering), HEALTH PROFESSIONS (allied health, exercise science, medical technology, music therapy, nursing, predentistry, premedicine, prepharmacy, preveterinary science, and speech pathology/audiology), SOCIAL SCIENCE (criminal justice, economics, geography, history, interdisciplinary studies, liberal arts/general studies, political science/government, prelaw, psychology, public administration, social science, social work, and sociology). Education and music is the strongest academically. Education has the largest enrollment.

ACTIVITIES: 4% of men belong to 1 local and 4 national fraternities; 4% of women belong to 2 local and 3 national sororities. There are 97 groups on campus, including academic club, art, band, cheerleading, choir, chorale, chorus, computers, dance, debate, drama, ethnic, film, forensics, honors, international, jazz band, literary magazine, marching band, musical theater, newspaper, opera, orchestra, photography, political, professional, radio and TV, religious, social, social service, student government, and symphony. Popular campus events include Workathon, RHA Mud Pull, and Buffalo Branding. **Sports:** There are 6 intercollegiate sports for men and 6 for women, and 39 intramural sports for men and 39 for women. Facilities include a swimming pool, bowling alley, weight-training rooms, stadium, event center, handball, racquetball, tennis, badminton, basketball, and volleyball courts, a flag football field, and softball fields. **Graduates:** From July 1, 2015 to June 30, 2016, 980 bachelor's degrees were awarded. The most popular majors were general studies (23%), business (19%), and nursing/interdisciplinary studies (10%). 299 companies recruited on campus in 2015-2016. In an average class, 1% graduate in 3 years or less, 14% graduate in 4 years or less, 28% graduate in 5 years or less, and 32% graduate in 6 years or less. Of the 2015 graduating class, 40% were enrolled in graduate school within 6 months of graduation.

SERVICES: Counseling and information services are available, as is tutoring in most subjects, a reader service for the blind, and remedial math, reading, and writing. **Library/Resources:** The 2 libraries contain 1.1 million volumes, 1.3 million microform items, 1,555 audio/video tapes/CDs/DVDs, and subscribe to 16,973 periodicals including electronic. Computerized library services include interlibrary loans, database searching, Internet access, and Wi-Fi capability. Special learning facilities include an art gallery, natural history museum, radio station, an alternative energy institute, an electronic learning center, a communications disorders center, and a nursing learning center. **Physically Challenged Students:** All of the campus is accessible. Facilities include wheelchair ramps, elevators, special parking, specially equipped restrooms, special class scheduling, lowered drinking fountains, lowered telephones, and special housing. **Special:** West Texas A&M University, offers work-study programs, a Washington semester, internships, co-op programs, credit by exam, B.A.-B.S. degrees, a general studies degree, interdisciplinary studies in elementary/secondary education fields, nondegree study, and pass/fail options. There are 12 national honor societies, a freshman honors program, and 14 departmental honors programs. **Visiting:** There are regularly scheduled orientations for prospective students, including a tour of campus, admissions and financial services sessions, selection of a major, and a visit with faculty. There are guides for informal visits, visitors may sit in on classes, and stay overnight. To schedule a visit, contact the Admissions Office. **Campus Safety and Security:** Measures include 24-hour foot and vehicle patrol, self-defense education, and security escort services. There are also shuttle buses, emergency telephones, lighted pathways/sidewalks, and shuttle buses provided by city transport.

REQUIREMENTS: Applicants should have graduated from an accredited secondary school or have a GED. Admission requires graduation in the top 50% of the student's high school class or a minimum composite score of 20 on the ACT or 950 on the SAT I. WTAMU requires applicants to be in the upper 50% of their class. AP and CLEP credits are accepted. A general education requirement of 46 hours includes courses in analytic reasoning and communication skills, cultural heritage, English, computer literacy, math, science, history, political science, humanities, and sports and exercise sciences. Additional core requirements vary according to major. A minimum 2.0 GPA and 127 credit hours, including at least 36 of advanced work, up to a maximum of 60, 30 of which must be at WTAMU, are required to graduate. At least 33 hours must be earned in residence at WTAMU, including at least 24 of the last 30 hours counted toward a degree. **Procedure:** Freshmen are admitted to all sessions. Entrance exams should be taken in the fall of the senior year. There are deferred admissions and rolling admissions plans. Application deadlines are open. Application fee is $25. Applications are accepted online. **Transfer Students:** 799 transfer students enrolled in 2015-2016. A 2.0 GPA is generally required for transfer students. 30 of 127 credits required for the bachelor's degree must be completed at WTAMU. **International Students:** The school actively recruits these students. They must take the TOEFL as well as the SAT or ACT, scoring 950.

ADMISSIONS: 72% of the 2016-2017 applicants were accepted. The ACT scores were 49% below 12, 28% between 12 and 17, 15% between 18 and 23, 5% between 24 and 29, and 2% above 30. 44% of the current freshmen were in the top fifth of their class; 82% were in the top two fifths. There was 1 National Merit finalist. 27 freshmen graduated first in their class. **Admissions Contact:** Joseph Stiles, Director of Admissions. Email: *jstiles@wtamu.edu* Web: *www.wtamu.edu*

FINANCIAL AID: In 2016-2017, 51% of all full-time freshmen and 47%

of continuing full-time students received some form of financial aid. 39% of all full-time freshmen and 45% of continuing full-time students received need-based aid. The average freshman award was $5,958. Need-based scholarships or need-based grants averaged $3,282 ($4,562 maximum); need-based self-help aid (loans and jobs) averaged $1,376 ($2,160 maximum); and $260 from other forms of aid. 4% of undergraduate students work part-time. Average annual earnings from campus work are $1405. The FAFSA code is 003665. The priority date for freshman financial aid applications for fall entry is April 15. The filing deadline for fall entry is May 1.

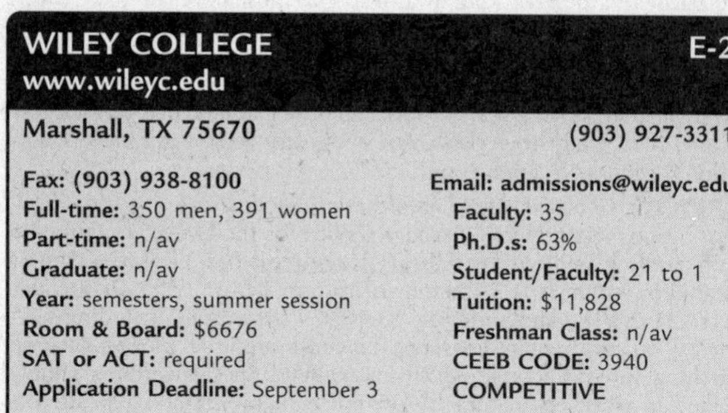

WILEY COLLEGE E-2
www.wileyc.edu

Marshall, TX 75670 (903) 927-3311

Fax: (903) 938-8100
Email: admissions@wileyc.edu

Full-time: 350 men, 391 women	**Faculty:** 35
Part-time: n/av	**Ph.D.s:** 63%
Graduate: n/av	**Student/Faculty:** 21 to 1
Year: semesters, summer session	**Tuition:** $11,828
Room & Board: $6676	**Freshman Class:** n/av
SAT or ACT: required	**CEEB CODE:** 3940
Application Deadline: September 3	**COMPETITIVE**

Wiley College, founded in 1873 is affiliated with the United Methodist Church and offers programs in the liberal arts, sciences, and teacher training. The figures in the above capsule and in this profile are approximate. There are 3 undergraduate schools. The 70-acre campus is in a small town on the west side of Marshall, Texas. Including any residence halls, there are 17 buildings.

STUDENT LIFE: **Female To Male Ratio:** 1.1:1. **Housing:** College-sponsored housing includes Jack Ingram Hall and the Haywood L. Strickland Living-learning center.

FACULTY/CLASSROOMS: All teach undergraduates. No introductory courses are taught by graduate students.

PROGRAMS OF STUDY: Wiley confers B.A., B.S., and B.B.A. degrees. Bachelor's degrees are awarded in BIOLOGICAL SCIENCE (biology/biological science), BUSINESS (business administration and management, hotel/motel and restaurant management, and office supervision and management), COMMUNICATIONS AND THE ARTS (communications, English, music, music performance, and Spanish), COMPUTER AND PHYSICAL SCIENCE (chemistry, computer science, mathematics, and physics), EDUCATION (business education, elementary education, English education, mathematics education, music education, physical education, secondary education, social science education, and special education), SOCIAL SCIENCE (history, liberal arts/general studies, philosophy, religion, social science, and sociology).

ACTIVITIES: There are no fraternities or sororities. Groups on campus include cheerleading, choir, and religious. **Sports:** There is no sports program at Wiley. Facilities include a basketball arena, a wellness center, baseball, soccer, track & field, cross-country, and volleyball.

SERVICES: **Library/Resources:** The library contains 80,000 volumes, and subscribes to 298 periodicals including electronic.

REQUIREMENTS: Applicants must be graduates of an accredited secondary school or have scored at least 40 on the GED. A letter of recommendation from a high school counselor or teacher is required. Core requirements include courses in education, English, humanities, history, religion, science, and math. 2 credits in phys ed and 3 in computer science are required. A 2.0 GPA and 124 semester hours are needed to graduate. **Procedure:** There are early decision and early admissions plans. Applications should be filed by September 3 for fall entry, along with a $50 fee. **Transfer Students:** Transfer applicants must be in good standing at their last college, and official transcripts. 30 of 124 credits required for the bachelor's degree must be completed at Wiley. **International Students:** They must take the TOEFL.

Admissions Contact: Bishop B. Curry, Director of Admissions. Email: *admissions@wileyc.edu* Web: *www.wileyc.edu*

FINANCIAL AID: The FAFSA code is 003669. Check with the school for current application deadlines.

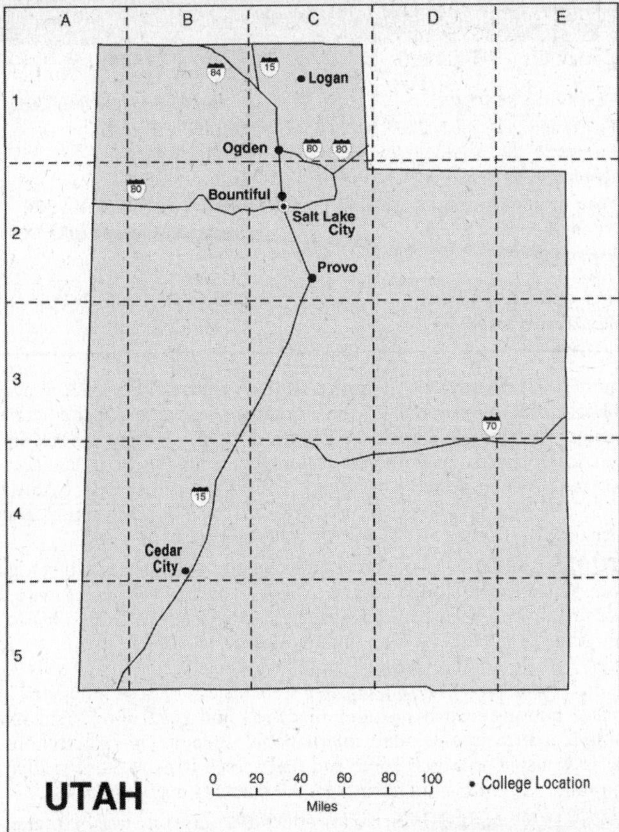

BRIGHAM YOUNG UNIVERSITY C-2
www.byu.edu

Provo, UT 84602	(801) 422-4636 (801) 422-4104
Fax: (801) 422-0005	**Email:** ugrad@byu.edu
Full-time: 14524 men, 13488 women	**Faculty:** n/av
Part-time: 1600 men, 1367 women	**Ph.D.s:** 92%
Graduate: 2023 men, 1238 women	**Student/Faculty:** 20 to 1
Year: semesters, summer session	**Tuition:** $5300
Room & Board: $7448	**Freshman Class:** 13376 applied, 6427 accepted, 5127 enrolled
SAT or ACT: required	**CEEB CODE:** 4019
Application Deadline: February 15	**HIGHLY COMPETITIVE**

Brigham Young University, founded in 1875, is a private university affiliated with the Church of Jesus Christ of Latter-day Saints. The university follows a semester calendar with spring and summer terms. Tuition figures in this profile are for members of the church. Students who are not members of the Church of Jesus Christ of Latter-day Saints pay twice the tuition amount listed. Living costs are identical for members and nonmembers. There are 10 undergraduate schools and 1 graduate school. In addition to regional accreditation, BYU has baccalaureate program accreditation with AACSB, ABET, ACCE, ACEJMC, ADA, ASLA, CSAB, CSWE, NASAD, NASDTEC, NASM, NCATE, NLN, NRPA, AAMFT, APA, ASHA, CAAMEP, CAAHEP, CCNE, NASD, NAACLS, and NASO. The 557-acre campus is in a suburban area 45 miles south of Salt Lake City. Including any residence halls, there are 330 buildings.

STUDENT LIFE: 71% of undergraduates are from out of state, mostly the West. Students are from 50 states, 121 foreign countries, and Canada. 83% are White; 6% Hispanic; 4% Foreign; 4% two or more races; 2% Asian American; 1% African American; 1% race unknown. **Male To Female Ratio:** 1.1:1. The average age of freshmen is 19; all undergraduates, 22. 11% do not continue beyond their first year; 77% remain to graduate. **Housing:** 6302 students can be accommodated in college housing, which includes single-sex dorms, on-campus apartments, and married student housing. In addition, there are honors houses, language houses, special-interest houses, and family housing contracts for 1324 student family residences. On-campus housing is available on a first-come and first-served basis. 80% of students commute. All students may keep cars. Alcohol is not permitted.

FACULTY/CLASSROOMS: 67% of faculty are male; 33% are female. No introductory courses are taught by graduate students.

PROGRAMS OF STUDY: BYU confers B.A., B.S., B.F.A., B.G.S., B.M. and B.Mus. degrees. Master's and doctoral degrees are also awarded. Bachelor's degrees are awarded in AGRICULTURE (agricultural business management, environmental studies, plant science, and wildlife management), BIOLOGICAL SCIENCE (biochemistry, bioinformatics, biology/biological science, biophysics, biotechnology, botany, microbiology, molecular biology, neurosciences, nutrition, physiology, plant genetics, and plant physiology), BUSINESS (accounting, business administration and management, management information systems, management science, marketing management, recreation and leisure services, and tourism), COMMUNICATIONS AND THE ARTS (advertising, animation, art, art history and appreciation, audio technology, Chinese, classical languages, classics, communications, comparative literature, dance, dramatic arts, English, fine arts, French, German, graphic design, Greek, illustration, industrial design, Italian, Japanese, jazz, Korean, Latin, linguistics, literature, media arts, music, music performance, music technology, music theory and composition, musical theater, performing arts, photography, Portuguese, public relations, Russian, Spanish, studio art, and visual and performing arts), COMPUTER AND PHYSICAL SCIENCE (actuarial science, astronomy, chemistry, computer science, geology, information sciences and systems, mathematics, physics, and statistics), EDUCATION (art education, dance education, drama education, early childhood education, elementary education, English education, home economics education, mathematics education, music education, science education, social science education, special education, and technical education), ENGINEERING AND ENVIRONMENTAL DESIGN (chemical engineering, city/community/regional planning, civil engineering, computer engineering, construction management, electrical/electronics engineering, electrical/electronics engineering technology, environmental design, food services technology, landscape architecture/design, manufacturing engineering, manufacturing technology, and mechanical engineering), HEALTH PROFESSIONS (clinical science, exercise science, health science, nursing, and speech pathology/audiology), SOCIAL SCIENCE (American studies, anthropology, archeology, Asian/American studies, Asian/Oriental studies, classical/ancient civilization, dietetics, economics, family/consumer studies, food science, geography, history, human development, humanities, international relations, Latin American studies, Middle Eastern studies, Near Eastern studies, philosophy, political science/government, psychology, social work, and sociology). Engineering, accounting and business are the strongest academically. Business, communications, and exercise science have the largest enrollments.

ACTIVITIES: There are no fraternities or sororities. There are 390 groups on campus, including art, band, cheerleading, chess, choir, chorale, chorus, computers, dance, debate, drama, drill team, environmental, ethnic, film, honors, international, jazz band, literary magazine, marching band, musical theater, newspaper, opera, orchestra, pep band, photography, political, professional, radio and TV, religious, social, social service, student government, and symphony. Popular campus events include Fall and Spring Fling, and Preference Dances. **Sports:** There are 10 intercollegiate sports for men and 11 for women, and 34 intramural sports for men and 32 for women. Facilities include tennis and racquetball courts, pools, gyms, tracks, fields, and a strength and conditioning complex. **Graduates:** From July 1, 2015 to June 30, 2016, 6457 bachelor's degrees were awarded. The most popular majors were business marketing (13%), biological/life sciences (12%), and education (9%). 430 companies recruited on campus in 2015-2016. In an average class, 31% graduate in 4 years or less and 77% graduate in 6 years or less.

SERVICES: Counseling and information services are available, as is tutoring in most subjects, a reader service for the blind, and remedial math, reading, and writing. **Library/Resources:** The 2 libraries contain 4.0 million volumes, 3.5 million microform items, 304,688 audio/video tapes/CDs/DVDs, and subscribe to 198,871 periodicals including electronic. Computerized library services include interlibrary loans, database searching, Internet access, and Wi-Fi capability. Special learning facilities include an art gallery, natural history museum, planetarium, radio station, TV station, an archeological museum, an earth science museum, reading and writing labs, and math, language, and computer labs. **Physically Challenged Students:** 97% of the campus is accessible. Facilities include wheelchair ramps, elevators, special parking, specially equipped restrooms, special class scheduling, lowered drinking fountains, lowered telephones, and special housing. **Special:** Brigham Young offers cooperative programs, national and international internships, study abroad in 55 countries, a Washington semester, dual majors, nondegree study, and credit for life and work experience. There are 22 national honor societies, including Phi Beta Kappa, a freshman honors program, and 100 departmental honors programs. **Visiting:** There are regularly scheduled orientations for prospective students, including a campus tour, visits with the prospective major's department and advisement center, and an interview with a school relations counselor. There are guides for informal visits and visitors may sit in on classes. To schedule a visit, contact the Admissions Office. **Campus Safety and Security:** Measures include 24-hour foot and vehicle patrol, emergency notification system, self-defense education, and security escort services. There are emergency telephones, lighted pathways/sidewalks, bicycle patrol, academic building security officers from 7 p.m. to 2 a.m., and night time limited access to dorms.

REQUIREMENTS: The SAT or ACT is required. Applicants must be graduates of an accredited secondary school. The GED is accepted. The school recommends that applicants complete 4 years of English, 3 years of math, and 2 courses in foreign language, lab science, history, and literature or writing. Essays and letters of recommendation are required with the application. AP and CLEP credits are accepted. Important factors in the admissions decision are advanced placement or honors courses, recommendations by school officials, and evidence of special talent. To graduate, students must complete 120 semester hours with a minimum GPA of 2.0. All students must take a total of 14 semester hours of religion and 2 hours of phys ed. There are general education requirements in English, advanced writing, foreign language or math, arts and letters, natural sciences, social sciences, and American heritage. **Procedure:** Freshmen are admitted to all sessions. Entrance exams should be taken by December of the senior year. There are early admissions, deferred admissions, and rolling admissions plans. Applications should be filed by February 15 for fall entry; October 1 for winter entry; February 15 for spring entry; and February 15 for summer entry, along with a $35 fee. Applications are accepted online. **Transfer Students:** 795 transfer students enrolled in 2015-2016. For applicants, primary consideration will be given to basic general education subjects (English, math, history, and foreign languages) and major subjects. The GPA from those subjects must be near 3.5 to be competitive for admission. 30 credits required for the bachelor's degree must be completed at BYU. **International Students:** There are 943 international students enrolled. They must take the TOEFL with a minimum score of 550 on the paper-based TOEFL (PBT) or 80 on the Internet-based version (iBT). They must also take the SAT or ACT.

ADMISSIONS: 48% of the 2016-2017 applicants were accepted. The SAT scores for the 2016-2017 freshman class were: Critical Reading-- 6% below 500, 29% between 500 and 599, 45% between 600 and 699, and 21% between 700 and 800. Math-- 4% below 500, 27% between 500 and 599, 49% between 600 and 699, and 21% between 700 and 800. Writing-- 9% below 500, 35% between 500 and 599, 44% between 600 and 699, and 11% between 700 and 800. The ACT scores were 7% between 18 and 23, 52% between 24 and 29, and 41% above 30. 80% of the current freshmen were in the top fifth of their class. **Admissions Contact:** Director of Admissions Office. Email: *ugrad@byu.edu* Web: *www.byu.edu*

FINANCIAL AID: In 2016-2017, 63% of all full-time freshmen and 69% of continuing full-time students received some form of financial aid. 19% of all full-time freshmen and 42% of continuing full-time students received need-based aid. The average freshman award was $6,902. Need-based scholarships or need-based grants averaged $4,908; need-based self-help aid (loans and jobs) averaged $3,241; non-need-based athletic scholarships averaged $6,590; other non-need-based awards and non-need-based scholarships averaged $3,910; and $5,678 from other forms of aid. 54% of undergraduate students work part-time. Average annual earnings from campus work are $6390. The FAFSA code is 003670. The deadline for filing freshman financial aid applications for fall entry is June 30.

SOUTHERN UTAH UNIVERSITY — B-4

www.suu.edu

Cedar City, UT 84720 — (435) 586-7740

Fax: (435) 865-8223 — Email: adminfo@suu.edu

Full-time: 2428 men, 2703 women	**Faculty:** 283; IIA
Part-time: 720 men, 1102 women	**Ph.D.s:** 69%
Graduate: 283 men, 420 women	**Student/Faculty:** n/av
Year: semesters, summer session	**Tuition:** $6138 ($18,596)
Room & Board: $6890	**Freshman Class:** 8268 applied, 5046 accepted, 1195 enrolled
SAT or ACT: required	**CEEB CODE:** 4092
Application Deadline: May 1	**COMPETITIVE**

Southern Utah University, founded in 1897, is part of the Utah System of Higher Education and offers undergraduate degrees in arts and letters, science, education, and business. There are 7 undergraduate schools and 4 graduate schools. In addition to regional accreditation, SUU has baccalaureate program accreditation with AACSB, ABET, ACBSP, NASAD, NASM, TEAC, NASD, CCNE, and AACN. The 133-acre campus is in a small town Cedar City, Utah, 170 miles north of Las Vegas.

STUDENT LIFE: 74% of undergraduates are from Utah. Others are from 50 states, 28 foreign countries, and Canada. 79% are White; 6% race unknown; 5% Hispanic; 5% Foreign; 2% Asian American; 1% African American; 1% American Indian/Alaska Native; 1% two or more races. **Female To Male Ratio:** 1.2:1. The average age of freshmen is 23; all undergraduates, 24. **Housing:** 599 students can be accommodated in college housing, which includes single-sex and coed dorms and on-campus apartments, including international students. On-campus housing is available on a first-come and first-served basis. 90% of students commute. Alcohol is not permitted. All students may keep cars.

FACULTY/CLASSROOMS: No introductory courses are taught by graduate students.

PROGRAMS OF STUDY: SUU confers B.A., B.F.A., B.M.U., B.S.N., B.S. and B.I.S. degrees. Associate and master's degrees are also awarded. Bachelor's degrees are awarded in Business, science, and education are the strongest academically. Education, business, and psychology have the largest enrollments.

ACTIVITIES: Groups on campus include art, band, cheerleading, choir, chorus, communications, computers, dance, drama, ethnic, film, honors, international, jazz band, LGBT, literary magazine, musical theater, newspaper, opera, pep band, political, professional, radio and TV, religious, social, social service, student government, and symphony. Popular campus events include Homecoming, Founders Day, Dances, and Service Programs. **Sports:** Facilities include a stadium for football and track and field, a baseball field, recreation grounds, a special events facility for basketball, volleyball, and gymnastics, tennis and racquetball courts, and large, all-weather practice areas. **Graduates:** From July 1, 2015 to June 30, 2016, 954 bachelor's degrees were awarded. The most popular majors were education (21%), business/marketing (12%), and psychology (8%).

SERVICES: Counseling and information services are available, as is tutoring in most subjects, a reader service for the blind, and remedial math, reading, and writing. **Library/Resources:** The library contains 289,486 volumes, 28,525 microform items, 10,821 audio/video tapes/CDs/DVDs, and subscribes to 749 periodicals including electronic. Computerized library services include interlibrary loans, database searching, and Internet access. Special learning facilities include an art gallery, natural history museum, planetarium, radio station, and TV station. **Physically Challenged Students:** Facilities include wheelchair ramps, elevators, special parking, specially equipped restrooms, special class scheduling, lowered drinking fountains, lowered telephones, and special housing. **Special:** SUU offers co-op programs with Weber State University, work-study programs, study abroad, dual majors, student-designed majors leading to a B.I.S. degree, and internships with government officials in Washington, D.C. Other programs offered include distance learning, ESL, independent study, liberal arts/career combinations, a teacher certification program, and weekend college. **Visiting:** There are regularly scheduled orientations for prospective students, including campus tours, which can be arranged by appointment. There are guides for informal visits, visitors may sit in on classes, and stay overnight. To schedule a visit, contact the Admissions Welcome Center. **Campus**

Safety and Security: Measures include self-defense education and security escort services. There are emergency telephones and lighted pathways/sidewalks.

REQUIREMENTS: The SAT is required. The ACT is recommended. Applicants should be graduates of an accredited secondary school or have a GED, and should have completed 4 years of English, (composition and literature emphasis), 3 of math, at least 2 of which are elementary algebra or beyond, 3 each of biological/physical sciences (1 with a lab) and social studies including U.S. history/government, and 2 years of a foreign language. AP and CLEP credits are accepted. To graduate, all students must complete at least 122 credit hours with a minimum 2.0 GPA. Students must satisfy general education, major, minor, and basic skills requirements, including 4 courses each in social and physical sciences, 2 each in English, fine arts, and humanities, 1 each in math, phys ed, and communications, and a course in either history, political science, or economics to fulfill the U.S. government requirement. Other courses required for graduation include computer literacy and philosophy. **Procedure:** Freshmen are admitted in the fall, spring, and summer. There are deferred admissions and rolling admissions plans. Applications should be filed by May 1 for fall entry; December 1 for spring entry. The fall 2016 application fee was $50. Applications are accepted online. **Transfer Students:** 330 transfer students enrolled in 2015-2016. Applicants must submit transcripts from previously attended colleges and have a minimum 2.0 GPA in college courses and a 2.0 high school GPA. ACT scores as well as high school transcripts are required from students who have not completed English or math courses at another institution or who have not completed a minimum of 24 credit hours at an institution of higher education. 30 of 120 credits required for the bachelor's degree must be completed at SUU. **International Students:** There are 287 international students enrolled. The school actively recruits these students. They must take the TOEFL with a minimum score of 525 on the paper-based TOEFL (PBT) or 71 on the Internet-based version (iBT), or take the IELTS.

ADMISSIONS: 61% of the 2016-2017 applicants were accepted. The SAT scores for the 2016-2017 freshman class were: Critical Reading-- 39% below 500, 43% between 500 and 599, 16% between 600 and 699, and 2% between 700 and 800. Math-- 44% below 500, 42% between 500 and 599, 11% between 600 and 699, and 3% between 700 and 800. Writing-- 50% below 500, 36% between 500 and 599, 12% between 600 and 699, and 2% between 700 and 800. **Admissions Contact:** Christine Proctor, Associate Director of Admissions. Email: *adminfo@suu.edu* Web: *www.suu.edu*

FINANCIAL AID: The college's own financial statement is required. The FAFSA code is 003678. The priority date for freshman financial aid applications for fall entry is December 1.

THE UNIVERSITY OF UTAH — C-2

www.utah.edu

Salt Lake City, UT 84112	**(801) 581-8761** **(800) 685-8856**
Fax: (801) 585-7864	**Email: admissions@utah.edu**
Full-time: 9350 men, 7847 women	**Faculty:** 1271
Part-time: 3597 men, 2995 women	**Ph.D.s:** 84%
Graduate: 4387 men, 3684 women	**Student/Faculty:** 16 to 1
Year: semesters, summer session	**Tuition:** $8518 ($27,039)
Room & Board: $9406	**Freshman Class:** 14308 applied, 10934 accepted, 3601 enrolled
SAT CR/M/W: 570/590/560 **ACT:** 25	**CEEB CODE:** 4853
Application Deadline: April 1	**VERY COMPETITIVE**

The University of Utah, founded in 1850, is part of the Utah System of Higher Education and offers graduate and undergraduate programs. Step one: Imagine. Step two: Do. Imagine what you want to accomplish, then really making it happen. Imagine designing and publishing a video game before earning your diploma, starting a business while studying business, and doing all this in a setting that begs you to get out and do something. Imagine, then Do. Opportunity awaits and all things are possible at a place we call Imagine U The University of Utah. There are 13 undergraduate schools and 16 graduate schools. In addition to regional accreditation, U of U has baccalaureate program accreditation with AACSB, ABET, ACEJMC, ACPE, ADA, APTA, CAHEA, CSWE, NAAB, NRPA, TEAC, CCNE, and PAB. The 1534-acre campus is in an urban area in Salt Lake City. Including any residence halls, there are 298 buildings.

STUDENT LIFE: 72% of undergraduates are from Utah. Others are from 50 states, 87 foreign countries, and Canada. 95% are from public schools. 69% are White; 6% Asian American; 5% Foreign; 5% two or more races; 2% race unknown; 12% Hispanic; 1% African American. **Male To Female Ratio:** 1.2:1. The average age of freshmen is 18; all undergraduates, 23. 11% do not continue beyond their first year; 65% remain to graduate. **Housing:** 5251 students can be accommodated in college housing, which includes single-sex and coed dorms, on-campus apartments, off-campus apartments, and married student housing. In addition, there are honors houses, special-interest houses, sorority houses, theme houses, and 24-hour quiet housing. On-campus housing is available on a first-come and first-served basis. 85% of students commute. All students may keep cars. Alcohol is not permitted.

FACULTY/CLASSROOMS: 59% of faculty are male; 41% are female. 86% teach undergraduates, 71% do research, and 59% do both. Graduate students teach 22% of introductory courses. The average class size in an introductory lecture is 53 and in a laboratory is 20.

PROGRAMS OF STUDY: The university confers B.A., B.F.A., B.Mus., B.S., B.S.W., and B.U.S. degrees. Master's and doctoral degrees are also awarded. Bachelor's degrees are awarded in AGRICULTURE (environmental studies), BIOLOGICAL SCIENCE (biology/biological science and biology/ gen science secondary education), BUSINESS (accounting, business administration and management, entrepreneurial studies, finance, management information systems, management science, marketing management, marketing/retailing/merchandising, operations management, and recreation and leisure services), COMMUNICATIONS AND THE ARTS (art history, art, ballet, ballet modern dance, Chinese, classics, communications, comparative literature, design, English, film arts, film, television and digital media, French, German, Hebrew, Japanese, linguistics, modern dance, music, Russian, Spanish, theatre arts, and writing), COMPUTER AND PHYSICAL SCIENCE (applied mathematics, atmospheric sciences and meteorology, chemistry, computer science, earth science, environmental geology, geology, geophysics and seismology, geoscience, information sciences and systems, mathematics, physics secondary education, and physics), EDUCATION (art education, athletic training, elementary education, English education, French studies K-12 education, health education, history education, mathematics education, social science education, special education, and teaching English as a second/foreign language (TESOL/TEFOL)), ENGINEERING AND ENVIRONMENTAL DESIGN (biomedical engineering, chemical engineering, civil engineering, computer engineering, electrical/electronics engineering, engineering, geological engineering, materials engineering, materials science, mechanical engineering, metallurgical engineering, mining and mineral engineering, and urban planning technology), HEALTH PROFESSIONS (exercise science, health administration and policy, medical laboratory science, medical laboratory technology, medical science, nursing, and speech pathology/audiology), SOCIAL SCIENCE (anthropology, architectural studies, Asian/Oriental studies, behavioral science, consumer services, economics, ethnic studies, family/consumer studies, gender studies, geography, history, international studies, Latin American studies, Middle Eastern studies, parks and recreation management, peace studies, philosophy, political science/government, psychology, religious studies, social science, social work, sociology, and urban studies). Business, biology, and computer science have the largest enrollments.

ACTIVITIES: 6% of men belong to 10 national fraternities; 8% of women belong to 7 national sororities. There are 605 groups on campus, including art, band, cheerleading, chess, choir, chorale, chorus, computers, dance, debate, drama, drill team, drum and bugle corps, environmental, ethnic, film, forensics, honors, international, jazz band, LGBT, marching band, musical theater, newspaper, opera, orchestra, pep band, photography, political, professional, radio and TV, religious, social, social service, student government, and symphony. Popular campus events include Redfest, Plazafest, and Welcome Week. **Sports:** There are 15 intercollegiate sports for men and 16 for women, and 11 intramural sports for men and 11 for women. Facilities include a stadium, basketball arena, indoor gyms, indoor tennis courts, sand volleyball court, indoor swimming pools, gymnastics room, weight rooms, handball/racquetball/squash courts, indoor track, outdoor track, disc golf course, outdoor playing fields, and a bowling alley. **Graduates:** From July 1, 2015 to June 30, 2016, 5182 bachelor's degrees were awarded. The most popular majors were communication (7%), psychology (7%), and economics

(5%). 230 companies recruited on campus in 2015-2016. In an average class, 29% graduate in 4 years or less, 53% graduate in 5 years or less, and 65% graduate in 6 years or less.

SERVICES: Counseling and information services are available, as is tutoring in most subjects, a reader service for the blind, and remedial math. There are also support services for the deaf, including readers, scribes, tutors, and interpreters. The on-campus Center for Disability Services directs students to on-campus services for people with disabilities and provides a supportive environment so they can achieve their academic goals. **Library/Resources:** The 3 libraries contain 3.7 million volumes, 3.0 million microform items, 94,200 audio/video tapes/CDs/DVDs, and subscribe to 11,400 periodicals including electronic. Computerized library services include interlibrary loans, database searching, Internet access, and Wi-Fi capability. Special learning facilities include an art gallery, natural history museum, radio station, TV station, and an arboretum. **Physically Challenged Students:** 90% of the campus is accessible. Facilities include wheelchair ramps, elevators, special parking, specially equipped restrooms, special class scheduling, lowered drinking fountains, lowered telephones, and special housing. **Special:** The university offers numerous opportunities for cross-registration through the Western Undergraduate Exchange (WUE) as part of the Western Interstate Commission for Higher Education (WICHE), study abroad in more than 60 countries, internships, work-study, accelerated degree programs, and BS/MS combined degrees in Information systems, chemistry, math, nursing, mining engineering, and geological engineering. Also available are the Washington semester, student-designed and dual majors, credit for military experience, nondegree study, and pass/fail options. There are 44 national honor societies, Phi Beta Kappa, a freshman honors program, and 52 departmental honors programs. **Visiting:** There are regularly scheduled orientations for prospective students, including an information session with an admissions counselor to discuss academic and student involvement opportunities, scholarships, financial aid, admissions requirements, and deadlines, along with a campus tour and tour of residence halls. If time permits, prospective students are encouraged to meet with academic advisers on various majors, visit classrooms, and stay overnight in a residence hall. There are guides for informal visits, visitors may sit in on classes, and stay overnight. To schedule a visit, contact the Office of Admissions (Welcome Center). **Campus Safety and Security:** Measures include 24-hour foot and vehicle patrol, emergency notification system, self-defense education, and security escort services. There are also shuttle buses, emergency telephones, lighted pathways/sidewalks, and controlled access to dorms/residences.

REQUIREMENTS: Most applicants submit the ACT but the SAT is accepted. Applicants must be graduates of an accredited secondary school or have the GED. Academic credits required include 4 years each of English and electives, 2 years each of foreign language and math, 3 years of biological and/or physical science, and 1 year of history. AP and CLEP credits are accepted. To graduate, all students must satisfy requirements in the general education and intellectual exploration programs. General education requirements include 1 course each in American institutions and lower-division writing; 2 in quantitative reasoning; and 2 each in fine arts, humanities, physical/life science, applied science, social/behavioral science, excluding the major area. Additionally, students must take 2 quantitative intensive courses and 1 course each in diversity, international, and upper-division communication/writing. Students must complete at least 122 credit hours. A minimum 2.0 GPA is required. **Procedure:** Freshmen are admitted in the fall, spring, and summer. Entrance exams should be taken in the junior year of high school. There are deferred admissions and rolling admissions plans. Applications should be filed by April 1 for fall entry; November 1 for spring entry; and March 15 for summer entry, along with a $45 fee. Notification is sent on a rolling basis. Application fees are waived if application is completed online. **Transfer Students:** 2870 transfer students enrolled in 2015-2016. Transfer students must have completed at least 45 quarter (30 semester) hours with a minimum 2.6 GPA. 30 of 122 credits required for the bachelor's degree must be completed at the university. **International Students:** There are 1030 international students enrolled. They must take the TOEFL with a minimum score of 550 on the paper-based TOEFL (PBT) or 80 on the Internet-based version (iBT). They must also take the SAT or ACT.

ADMISSIONS: 76% of the 2016-2017 applicants were accepted. The SAT scores for the 2016-2017 freshman class were: Critical Reading-- 19% below 500, 41% between 500 and 599, 29% between 600 and 699, and 11% between 700 and 800. Math-- 11% below 500, 40% between 500 and 599, 35% between 600 and 699, and 14% between 700 and 800. Writing-- 24% below 500, 41% between 500 and 599, 28% between 600 and 699, and 7% between 700 and 800. The ACT scores were 4% between 12 and 17, 34% between 18 and 23, 43% between 24 and 29, and 19% above 30. 55% of the current freshmen were in the top fifth of their class; 80% were in the top two fifths. 20 freshmen graduated first in their class. **Admissions Contact:** Matthew Lopez, Director of Admissions. Email: *admissions@utah.edu* Web: *admissions.utah.edu*

FINANCIAL AID: In 2016-2017, 79% of all full-time freshmen and 55% of continuing full-time students received some form of financial aid. 46% of all full-time freshmen and continuing full-time students received need-based aid. The average freshman award was $19,868. Need-based scholarships or need-based grants averaged $8,212 ($15,532 maximum); need-based self-help aid (loans and jobs) averaged $7,892 ($40,512 maximum); non-need-based athletic scholarships averaged $26,114 ($41,688 maximum); and other non-need-based awards and non-need-based scholarships averaged $7,260 ($46,000 maximum). 21% of undergraduate students work part-time. Average annual earnings from campus work are $9913. The average financial indebtedness of the 2016 graduate was $34,066. The FAFSA code is 003675. The priority date for freshman financial aid applications for fall entry is March 15.

UTAH STATE UNIVERSITY C-1

www.usu.edu

Logan, UT 84322	**(435) 797-1079** **(800) 488-8108**
Fax: (435) 797-3708	**Email: admit@usu.edu**
Full-time: 8293 men, 8698 women	**Faculty:** 894; I, --$
Part-time: 3326 men, 4521 women	**Ph.D.s:** 78%
Graduate: 1467 men, 1813 women	**Student/Faculty:** 22 to 1
Year: semesters, summer session	**Tuition:** $6866 ($19,772)
Room & Board: $5870	**Freshman Class:** n/av
SAT CR/M: 550/550 **ACT:** 24	**CEEB CODE:** 4857
Application Deadline: April 1	**COMPETITIVE**

Utah State University, founded in 1888, is a public institution that offers degree programs in the liberal arts and sciences, agriculture and natural resources, engineering, business, education, fine arts, music, family life, and the sciences. The figures in the above capsule and in this profile are approximate. There are 8 undergraduate schools and 1 graduate school. In addition to regional accreditation, USU has baccalaureate program accreditation with AACSB, ABET, ADA, AHEA, ASLA, CSWE, FIDER, NASM, NCATE, NRPA, and SAF. The 332-acre campus is in a small town 86 miles north of Salt Lake City. Including any residence halls, there are 104 buildings.

STUDENT LIFE: 74% of undergraduates are from Utah. Others are from 50 states, 87 foreign countries, and Canada. 81% are White; 6% Hispanic; 5% race unknown; 2% American Indian/Alaska Native; 2% Foreign; 2% two or more races; 1% African American; 1% Asian American. **Female To Male Ratio:** 1.1:1. The average age of freshmen is 19; all undergraduates, 23. 29% do not continue beyond their first year; 49% remain to graduate. **Housing:** 3640 students can be accommodated in college housing, which includes single-sex dorms, on-campus apartments, and married student housing. In addition, there are honors houses, special-interest houses, fraternity houses, and sorority houses. On-campus housing is available on a first-come and first-served basis. All students may keep cars. Alcohol is not permitted.

FACULTY/CLASSROOMS: 61% of faculty are male; 39% are female. Graduate students teach 5% of introductory courses. The average class size in an introductory lecture is 35; in a laboratory is 20; and in a regular course is 25.

PROGRAMS OF STUDY: USU confers B.A., B.S., B.F.A., B.I.D., B.L.A. and B.M. degrees. Associate, master's, and doctoral degrees are also awarded. Bachelor's degrees are awarded in AGRICULTURE (agricultural business management, agricultural economics, animal science, dairy science, forestry and related sciences, international agriculture, natural resource management, plant science, range/farm management, soil science, and wildlife management), BIOLOGICAL SCIENCE (biochemistry, biology/biological science, and microbiology), BUSINESS (accounting, banking and finance, business administration and management, business economics, fashion merchandising, international business management, management information systems, marketing/retailing/merchandising, and personnel management), COMMUNICA-

TIONS AND THE ARTS (dance, dramatic arts, English, fine arts, French, German, journalism, music, and Spanish), COMPUTER AND PHYSICAL SCIENCE (chemistry, computer science, earth science, geology, information sciences and systems, mathematics, physics, and statistics), EDUCATION (agricultural education, art education, business education, early childhood education, elementary education, foreign languages education, health education, home economics education, industrial arts education, mathematics education, music education, physical education, science education, secondary education, and special education), ENGINEERING AND ENVIRONMENTAL DESIGN (agricultural engineering, civil engineering, electrical/electronics engineering, engineering, environmental science, industrial engineering, industrial engineering technology, interior design, landscape architecture/design, and mechanical engineering), HEALTH PROFESSIONS (medical laboratory technology, music therapy, predentistry, premedicine, public health, speech pathology/audiology, and veterinary science), SOCIAL SCIENCE (American studies, child care/child and family studies, economics, food science, geography, history, home economics, human development, international relations, liberal arts/general studies, parks and recreation management, philosophy, political science/government, prelaw, psychology, social work, and sociology). Natural resources, engineering, and special education are the strongest academically. Humanities, business, and education have the largest enrollments.

ACTIVITIES: 4% of men belong to 1 local and 6 national fraternities; 4% of women belong to 1 local and 3 national sororities. There are 230 groups on campus, including art, bagpipe, band, cheerleading, choir, chorale, chorus, computers, dance, drama, drill team, environmental, ethnic, film, honors, international, jazz band, LGBT, literary magazine, marching band, musical theater, newspaper, opera, orchestra, pep band, photography, political, professional, radio and TV, religious, social, social service, student government, and symphony. Popular campus events include Festival of the American West, Halloween Howl, Homecoming, and A-Day. **Sports:** There are 7 intercollegiate sports for men and 9 for women, and 18 intramural sports for men and 18 for women. Facilities include gyms, indoor and outdoor tennis courts, swimming pools, a student recreation center including climbing walls, a field house, and golf and skiing areas. There is also a campus stadium, and auditorium. **Graduates:** From July 1, 2015 to June 30, 2016, 3810 bachelor's degrees were awarded. The most popular majors were communicative disorders and deaf education (10%), economics (8%), and business administration (4%). 235 companies recruited on campus in 2015-2016. In an average class, 49% graduate in 6 years or less.

SERVICES: Counseling and information services are available, as is tutoring in most subjects, a reader service for the blind, and remedial math, reading, and writing. There is also a writing lab and a tutor room. **Library/Resources:** The 3 libraries contain 2.6 million volumes, 2.7 million microform items, 17,863 audio/video tapes/CDs/DVDs, and subscribe to 60,903 periodicals including electronic. Computerized library services include interlibrary loans, database searching, Internet access, and Wi-Fi capability. Special learning facilities include an art gallery, natural history museum, radio station, a laboratory school, historical farm, fine arts center, and a developmental center for people who are disabled. **Physically Challenged Students:** 99% of the campus is accessible. Facilities include wheelchair ramps, elevators, special parking, specially equipped restrooms, special class scheduling, lowered drinking fountains, lowered telephones, special phones to receive calls from the deaf, and a disability resource center. **Special:** Internships are available in most departments through the Cooperative Education Program. The National Student Exchange Program allows students to cross-register in designated institutions and programs, and the International Student Exchange Program enables students to study abroad. There is also cross-registration with the University of the Americas of Mexico. A general studies degree and student-designed majors are available. Nondegree study, work-study programs, co-op programs, B.A.-B.S. degrees, pass/fail options, and credit for military experience are offered. There are 12 national honor societies, a freshman honors program, and 36 departmental honors programs. **Visiting:** There are regularly scheduled orientations for prospective students, consisting of a campus tour, including a meeting with an academic adviser, lunch, and a housing tour. There are guides for informal visits, visitors may sit in on classes, and stay overnight. To schedule a visit, contact the Admissions Office. **Campus Safety and Security:** Measures include 24-hour foot and vehicle patrol, emergency notification system, self-defense education, and security escort services. There are also shuttle buses, emergency telephones, lighted pathways/sidewalks, and campus police.

REQUIREMENTS: USU requires that either the SAT or ACT be provided. The ACT has been the preferred choice, but either is accepted. In addition, students should graduate from an accredited secondary school with 15 academic units, including 4 in English, 3 each in math and science, and 1 in social sciences. GED equivalency is accepted, provided ACT scores are 19 or higher. Students not meeting entrance requirements may be considered for admission on a provisional basis. A GPA of 2.7 is required. AP and CLEP credits are accepted. Important factors in the admissions decision are evidence of special talent, parents or siblings attended your school, and recommendations by school officials. The core curriculum of 30 semester credits includes at least 6 of writing; the total number of credits required for graduation is 120. Students must maintain a minimum GPA of 2.5. The number of credits required in the major varies, but there is a minimum of 40 in major classes. **Procedure:** Freshmen are admitted to all sessions. Entrance exams should be taken in the spring of the junior year. There are deferred admissions and rolling admissions plans. Applications should be filed by April 1 for fall entry; October 1 for spring entry; and April 1 for summer entry, along with a $50 fee. Applications are accepted on-line. **Transfer Students:** 1712 transfer students enrolled in 2015-2016. A minimum 2.2 GPA, higher for some majors, is required for transfer students. Those applicants with fewer than 45 credits must also submit ACT scores. 30 of 120 credits required for the bachelor's degree must be completed at USU. **International Students:** There are 307 international students enrolled. They must take the TOEFL with a minimum score of 525 on the paper-based TOEFL (PBT) or 71 on the Internet-based version (iBT) or take the MELAB. The TOEFL is preferred.

ADMISSIONS: The SAT scores for the 2016-2017 freshman class were: Critical Reading-- 27% below 500, 41% between 500 and 599, 26% between 600 and 699, and 6% between 700 and 800. Math-- 27% below 500, 43% between 500 and 599, 24% between 600 and 699, and 6% between 700 and 800. The ACT scores were 10% between 12 and 17, 40% between 18 and 23, 36% between 24 and 29, and 14% above 30. **Admissions Contact:** Katie Nielsen, Director of Admissions Office. Email: *admit@usu.edu* Web: *www.usu.edu*

FINANCIAL AID: The FAFSA code is 003677. The priority date for freshman financial aid applications for fall entry is March 1.

WEBER STATE UNIVERSITY — C-1

www.weber.edu

Ogden, UT 84408 — **(801) 626-7670**

Fax: (801) 626-6747	**Email: admissions@weber.edu**
Full-time: 5302 men, 5656 women	**Faculty:** 496; IIA, -$
Part-time: 6435 men, 7816 women	**Ph.D.s:** 68%
Graduate: 292 men, 248 women	**Student/Faculty:** 21 to 1
Year: semesters, summer session	**Tuition:** $5321 ($14,235)
Room & Board: $5400	**Freshman Class:** 5692 applied, 5692 accepted, 1745 enrolled
ACT: 21	**CEEB CODE:** 4941
Application Deadline: August 21	**COMPETITIVE**

Weber State University provides associate, baccalaureate and master degree programs in liberal arts, sciences, technical and professional fields. Encouraging freedom of expression and valuing diversity, the university provides excellent educational experiences for students through extensive personal contact among faculty, staff and students in and out of the classroom. Through academic programs, research, artistic expression, public service and community-based learning, the university serves as an educational, cultural and economic leader for the region. There are 8 undergraduate schools and 11 graduate schools. In addition to regional accreditation, WSU has baccalaureate program accreditation with AACSB, ABET, ACCE, ADA, CSWE, NASAD, NASM, NCATE, NLN, TEAC, ACEN, ACS, AUPHA, CAAHEP, CAATE, CAHIM, CARC, CEA, CIDA, CODA, NAACLS, NAEYC, NCFR, and NKBA. The 504-acre campus is in an urban area on the foothills of the Wasatch Mountains, 33 miles north of Salt Lake City. Including any residence halls, there are 100 buildings.

STUDENT LIFE: 90% of undergraduates are from Utah. Others are from 49 states, 56 foreign countries, and Canada. 99% are from public schools. 48% are White; 36% race unknown; 2% Asian American; 2% Foreign; 2% two or more races; 10% Hispanic; 1% African American.

Female To Male Ratio: 1.1:1. The average age of freshmen is 20; all undergraduates, 25. 41% do not continue beyond their first year. **Housing:** 1001 students can be accommodated in college housing, which includes single-sex dorms, on-campus apartments, and married student housing. On-campus housing is available on a first-come and first-served basis. 96% of students commute. All students may keep cars. Alcohol is not permitted.

FACULTY/CLASSROOMS: 52% of faculty are male; 48% are female. All teach undergraduates. No introductory courses are taught by graduate students. The average class size in an introductory lecture is 18; in a laboratory is 18; and in a regular course is 21.

PROGRAMS OF STUDY: WSU confers B.A., B.S., B.F.A., B.I.S., B.M., and B.M.E. degrees. Associate and master's degrees are also awarded. Bachelor's degrees are awarded in BIOLOGICAL SCIENCE (biology/biological science, botany, microbiology, and zoology), BUSINESS (accounting, banking and finance, business administration and management, business economics, finance, human resources, international economics, management information systems, marketing management, personnel management, purchasing/inventory management, and supply chain management), COMMUNICATIONS AND THE ARTS (advertising, art, communications, creative writing, dance, dramatic arts, English, fine arts, French, German, graphic design, instrumental performance, instrumental music education, journalism, media arts, music, music performance, musical theater, photography, piano/organ, public relations, Spanish, strings, technical and business writing, theatre arts, visual and performing arts, visual design, and voice), COMPUTER AND PHYSICAL SCIENCE (applied mathematics, chemistry, chemistry education, computer networks & systems, computer programming, computer science, computer security and information assurance, earth science, earth science / adolescence education, geology, information sciences and systems, mathematics, and physics), EDUCATION (art education, athletic training, business education, early childhood education, education, elementary education, English education, foreign languages education, health education, health information management, history education, mathematics education, music education, physical education, physical science secondary school education, psychology education, science education, secondary education, social science education, special education, and teaching English as a second/foreign language (TESOL/TEFOL)), ENGINEERING AND ENVIRONMENTAL DESIGN (automotive technology, computer engineering, construction management, electrical/electronics engineering, electrical/electronics engineering technology, environmental science, interior design, manufacturing engineering, manufacturing technology, mechanical engineering technology, plastics engineering, plastics technology, and welding engineering), HEALTH PROFESSIONS (cardiac sonography, clinical science, dental hygiene, health care administration, health promotion, health services administration, health services technology, medical laboratory science, nuclear medicine, nursing, radiation therapy, radiograph medical technology, radiological science, radiologic imaging modalities, respiratory therapy, and vascular sonography), SOCIAL SCIENCE (anthropology, child care/child and family studies, criminal justice, early childhood studies, economics, family/consumer studies, geography, gerontology, history, interdisciplinary studies, law enforcement and corrections, liberal arts/general studies, philosophy, political science/government, psychology, public history/archives, social work, and sociology). Nursing, criminal justice, education, and business administration are the strongest academically. Nursing, health sciences, computer science, and business administration have the largest enrollments.

ACTIVITIES: There are 222 groups on campus, including art, band, cheerleading, chess, choir, chorale, chorus, communications, computers, dance, debate, drama, drill team, drum and bugle corps, environmental, ethnic, film, forensics, honors, international, jazz band, LGBT, literary magazine, marching band, musical theater, newspaper, opera, orchestra, pep band, photography, political, professional, radio and TV, religious, social, social service, student government, symphony, and The Latter-day Saint Student Association (LDSSA) is established by the Ogden Institute of Religion to help students attending a Weber State University have a balanced secular and spiritual educational experience during their years of formal education. Popular campus events include Homecoming, Graduation, and Back to School Block Party. **Sports:** There are 6 intercollegiate sports for men and 8 for women, and 9 intramural sports for men and 9 for women. Facilities include an indoor track, a strength-training center, indoor basketball and volleyball courts, group fitness areas, a pool, racquetball and tennis courts, stadium, events center, performing arts center, an ice skating rink, outdoor playing fields, and a climbing wall. **Graduates:** From July 1, 2015 to June 30, 2016, 2509 bachelor's degrees were awarded. The most popular majors were nursing (14%), technical sales (4%), and criminal justice (4%). In an average class, 13% graduate in 4 years or less, 27% graduate in 5 years or less, and 35% graduate in 6 years or less.

SERVICES: Counseling and information services are available, as is tutoring in every subject. There is a reader service for the blind, and remedial math, reading, and writing. Translators are offered for the hearing impaired. **Library/Resources:** The library contains 534,760 volumes, 635,432 microform items, 24,915 audio/video tapes/CDs/DVDs, and subscribes to 450 periodicals including electronic. Computerized library services include interlibrary loans, database searching, Internet access, and Wi-Fi capability. Special learning facilities include an art gallery, natural history museum, planetarium, radio station, TV station, and crime lab. **Physically Challenged Students:** 99% of the campus is accessible. Facilities include wheelchair ramps, elevators, special parking, specially equipped restrooms, special class scheduling, lowered drinking fountains, lowered telephones, and special housing. **Special:** Weber State University offers co-op programs and internships in many majors, a Washington semester, study abroad in Mexico and England, work-study programs with community businesses, B.A.-B.S. degrees, dual majors in many combinations, student-designed majors resulting in a B.I.S. degree, a general studies degree, credit for military experience, non-degree study, and pass/fail options. There are 20 national honor societies, a freshman honors program, and 17 departmental honors programs. **Visiting:** There are regularly scheduled orientations for prospective students. There are guides for informal visits, visitors may sit in on classes, and stay overnight. **Campus Safety and Security:** Measures include 24-hour foot and vehicle patrol, emergency notification system, self-defense education, and security escort services. There are also shuttle buses, emergency telephones, lighted pathways/sidewalks, and controlled access to dorms/residences.

REQUIREMENTS: The ACT is recommended. Applicants must be graduates of an accredited secondary school or have a GED. Other requirements vary by department. Out-of-state residents must have a minimum high school GPA of 2.0. AP and CLEP credits are accepted. To graduate, students must demonstrate math competency and complete courses in government/history, English, humanities, math, biological/physical sciences, and social sciences. For a bachelor's degree, a student must complete at least 120 semester credit hours, with 45 at the upper-division level, and a minimum GPA of 2.0 are required. Hours in the major and distribution requirements vary with the degree. **Procedure:** Freshmen are admitted to all sessions. Entrance exams should be taken junior or senior year of high school. There are early admissions, deferred admissions, and rolling admissions plans. Applications should be filed by August 21 for fall entry, along with a $30 fee. Applications are accepted on-line. **Transfer Students:** 591 transfer students enrolled in 2015-2016. Transfer students must submit official transcripts from previously attended colleges or universities and have a minimum GPA of 2.0. 30 of 120 credits required for the bachelor's degree must be completed at WSU. **International Students:** There are 333 international students enrolled. The school actively recruits these students.

ADMISSIONS: 100% of the 2016-2017 applicants were accepted. The ACT scores were 23% between 12 and 17, 49% between 18 and 23, 24% between 24 and 29, and 3% above 30. **Admissions Contact:** Scott Teichert, Director of Admissions. Email: *admissions@weber.edu* Web: *www.weber.edu*

FINANCIAL AID: In 2016-2017, 55% of all full-time freshmen and 70% of continuing full-time students received some form of financial aid. 47% of all full-time freshmen and 54% of continuing full-time students received need-based aid. The average freshman award was $2,856. Need-based scholarships or need-based grants averaged $2,333; need-based self-help aid (loans and jobs) averaged $1,457; non-need-based athletic scholarships averaged $2,707; and other non-need-based awards and non-need-based scholarships averaged $1,952. 41% of undergraduate students work part-time. Average annual earnings from campus work are $8514. The average financial indebtedness of the 2016 graduate was $18,545. The college's own financial statement is required. The FAFSA code is 003680. The deadline for filing freshman financial aid applications for fall entry is March 1.

WESTMINSTER COLLEGE C-2
www.westminstercollege.edu

Salt Lake City, UT 84105 (801) 832-2200
(800) 748-4753
Fax: (801) 832-3101 Email: admission@westminstercollege.edu

Full-time: 872 men, 1141 women	**Faculty:** 154
Part-time: 58 men, 56 women	**Ph.D.s:** 93%
Graduate: 247 men, 318 women	**Student/Faculty:** 13 to 1
Year: 4-1-4, summer session	**Tuition:** $32,104
Room & Board: $8974	**Freshman Class:** 1938 applied, 1820 accepted, 434 enrolled
SAT CR/M: 540/540 **ACT:** required	**CEEB CODE:** 4948
Application Deadline: August 15	**COMPETITIVE+**

Westminster is private, independent, and comprehensive college in Salt Lake City, Utah. Students experience the liberal arts blended with professional programs in an atmosphere dedicated to civic engagement. With the goal of enabling its graduates to live vibrant, just, and successful lives, Westminster provides transformational learning experiences for both undergraduate and graduate students in a truly student-centered environment. Faculty focus on teaching, learning, and developing distinctive, innovative programs, while students thrive on Westminster's urban Sugar House campus within minutes of the Rocky Mountains. There are 4 undergraduate schools and 4 graduate schools. In addition to regional accreditation, Westminister has baccalaureate program accreditation with ACBSP, TEAC, AABI, CEPH, CCNE, and COA. The 27-acre campus is in an urban area 6 miles southeast of downtown Salt Lake City. Including any residence halls, there are 31 buildings.

STUDENT LIFE: 77% of undergraduates are from Utah. Others are from 42 states, 15 foreign countries, and Canada. 73% are from public schools. 71% are White; 5% Foreign; 4% two or more races; 4% race unknown; 3% Asian American; 2% African American; 10% Hispanic. **Female To Male Ratio:** 1.3:1. The average age of freshmen is 18; all undergraduates, 22. 79% remain to graduate. **Housing:** 809 students can be accommodated in college housing, which includes coed dorms and on-campus apartments. There are also themed living floors. On-campus housing is available on a first-come, first-served basis, and is available on a lottery system for upperclassmen. 68% of students commute. All students may keep cars.

FACULTY/CLASSROOMS: 49% of faculty are male; 51% are female. All teach undergraduates. No introductory courses are taught by graduate students.

PROGRAMS OF STUDY: Westminster confers B.A., B.S., and B.F.A. degrees. Master's degrees are also awarded. Bachelor's degrees are awarded in AGRICULTURE (environmental studies), BIOLOGICAL SCIENCE (biology/biological science and neurosciences), BUSINESS (accounting, banking and finance, business administration and management, international business management, investments and securities, and marketing/retailing/merchandising), COMMUNICATIONS AND THE ARTS (art, arts administration/management, communications, dramatic arts, English, fine arts, and music), COMPUTER AND PHYSICAL SCIENCE (chemistry, computer science, information sciences and systems, mathematics, and physics), EDUCATION (early childhood education, elementary education, and special education), ENGINEERING AND ENVIRONMENTAL DESIGN (aviation administration/management and aviation computer technology), HEALTH PROFESSIONS (nursing), SOCIAL SCIENCE (criminal justice, economics, gender studies, history, homeland security, philosophy, political science/government, prelaw, psychology, social science, sociology, and Spanish studies). Nursing, business, and biologica/life science, are the strongest and have the largest enrollments are the strongest academically.

ACTIVITIES: There are no fraternities or sororities. There are 40 groups on campus, including art, choir, chorale, chorus, dance, debate, drama, environmental, ethnic, film, honors, jazz band, LGBT, literary magazine, musical theater, newspaper, orchestra, photography, political, professional, religious, social service, student government, and symphony. Popular campus events include Westminster Welcome Week, Griffin Swoop Ins, Pizza Tasting, Halloween Dance, Documentary Film and Lecture Series, Homecoming Week, and Late Night Breakfast. **Sports:** There are 8 intercollegiate sports for men and 9 for women, and 9 intramural sports for men and 9 for women. Facilities include an elevated soccer/lacrosse field, health and wellness recreation center, basketball/volleyball, and multipurpose courts, a weight room, lap pool, racquetball courts, dance studio, two floors of cardio equipment, climbing wall, and training rooms. **Graduates:** From July 1, 2015 to June 30, 2016, 509 bachelor's degrees were awarded. The most popular majors were business (25%), health professions (24%), and biological/life sciences (8%). 60 companies recruited on campus in 2015-2016. In an average class, 45% graduate in 4 years or less, 60% graduate in 5 years or less, and 62% graduate in 6 years or less.

SERVICES: Counseling and information services are available, as is tutoring in most subjects, a reader service for the blind, and remedial math, reading, and writing. **Library/Resources:** The library contains 462,759 volumes, 128,054 microform items, 159,539 audio/video tapes/CDs/DVDs, and subscribes to 323,137 periodicals including electronic. Computerized library services include interlibrary loans, database searching, Internet access, and Wi-Fi capability. **Physically Challenged Students:** 90% of the campus is accessible. Facilities include wheelchair ramps, elevators, special parking, specially equipped restrooms, lowered drinking fountains, and special housing. **Special:** The college offers internships in every major, study abroad, dual and student-designed majors, an accelerated degree, work-study, independent study, weekend college, and freshman seminar courses. A 3-2 engineering degree with USC in Los Angeles or Washington University in St. Louis, Missouri, is also possible. There is 1 national honor society, a freshman honors program, and 1 departmental honors program. **Visiting:** There are regularly scheduled orientations for prospective students, including a welcome program, lunch, various workshops, a campus tour, and meetings with faculty. There are guides for informal visits, visitors may sit in on classes, and stay overnight. To schedule a visit, contact Darlene Dilley at admission@westminstercollege.edu. **Campus Safety and Security:** Measures include 24-hour foot and vehicle patrol, emergency notification system, and security escort services. There are also also emergency telephones, lighted pathways/sidewalks, and controlled access to dorms/residences.

REQUIREMENTS: The SAT or ACT is required. Applicants must be graduates of an accredited secondary school or have a GED certificate. College preparatory work should include 4 units of English, 3 of science, 2 each of math, foreign language, social studies, and electives, and 1 of history. An interview is recommended. AP and CLEP credits are accepted. Important factors in the admissions decision are evidence of special talent, extracurricular activities record, and advanced placement or honors courses. To be eligible for a bachelor's degree, students must satisfy the following requirements: complete a minimum of 124 semester credit hours, 30 of which must be upper division courses numbered 300 or above from a four-year institution, fulfill all WCore (liberal education) requirements, maintain an overall grade point average of 2.0 or above, meet all course requirements and grade point average requirements in the major, complete the last 36 credit hours in residency, and maintain good academic standing. **Procedure:** Freshmen are admitted to all sessions. Entrance exams should be taken in the junior or senior year of high school. There are deferred admissions and rolling admissions plans. Applications should be filed by August 15 for fall entry. The fall 2016 application fee was $50. Notifications are sent September 1. Applications are accepted online. **Transfer Students:** 161 transfer students enrolled in 2015-2016. Transfer students are recommended to have a minimum 2.5 GPA and be in good standing at all previously attended institutions. They must provide college transcripts and submit an essay. An interview is recommended. Some students may need to present standardized test scores and high school transcripts. 36 of 124 credits required for the bachelor's degree must be completed at Westminster. **International Students:** There are 94 international students enrolled. The school actively recruits these students. They must take the TOEFL with a minimum score of 550 on the paper-based TOEFL (PBT) or 79 on the Internet-based version (iBT). They must also take the SAT or ACT.

ADMISSIONS: 94% of the 2016-2017 applicants were accepted. The SAT scores for the 2016-2017 freshman class were: Critical Reading-- 22% below 500, 45% between 500 and 599, 28% between 600 and 699, and 4% between 700 and 800. Math-- 21% below 500, 48% between 500 and 599, 24% between 600 and 699, and 4% between 700 and 800. The ACT scores were 1% between 12 and 17, 42% between 18 and 23, 44% between 24 and 29, and 12% above 30. 40% of the current freshmen were in the top fifth of their class; 72% were in the top two fifths. 10 freshmen graduated first in their class. **Admissions Contact:** Darlene Dilley, Interim Chief Enrollment Officer. Email: *admission@westminstercollege.edu* Web: *www.westminstercollege.edu*

FINANCIAL AID: In 2016-2017, 99% of all full-time freshmen and 98%

of continuing full-time students received some form of financial aid. 68% of all full-time freshmen and 59% of continuing full-time students received need-based aid. The average freshman award was $28,357. Need-based scholarships or need-based grants averaged $19,781 ($40,243 maximum); need-based self-help aid (loans and jobs) averaged $5,680 ($12,000 maximum); non-need-based athletic scholarships averaged $6,493 ($32,104 maximum); and other non-need-based awards and non-need-based scholarships averaged $15,636 ($32,404 maximum). 28% of undergraduate students work part-time. Average annual earnings from campus work are $2500. The average financial indebtedness of the 2016 graduate was $30,442. is a member of CSS. The FAFSA code is 003681. The priority date for freshman financial aid applications for fall entry is March 1. The filing deadline for fall entry is rolling.

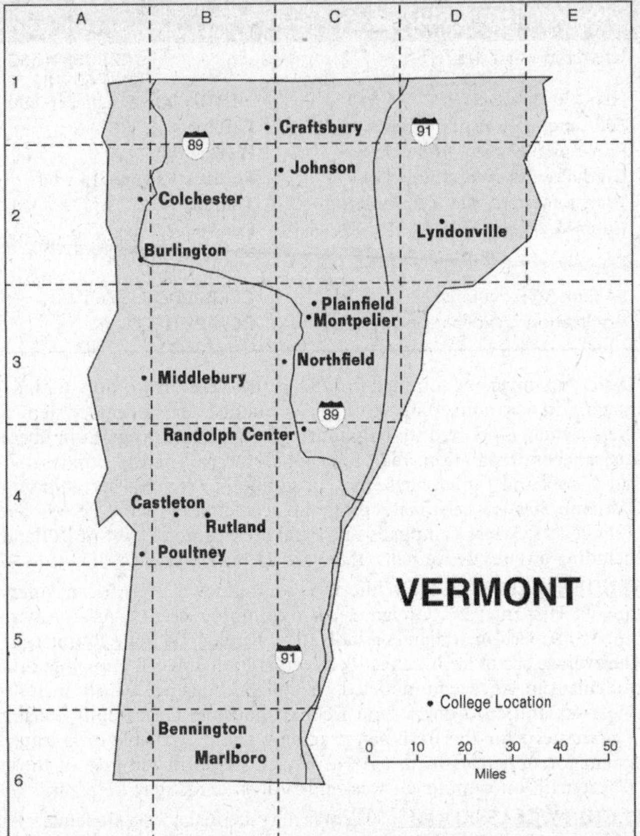

BENNINGTON COLLEGE A-6

www.bennington.edu

Bennington, VT 05201 (802) 440-4312 (800) 833-6845

Fax: (802) 440-4320 Email: hnbui@bennington.edu

Full-time: 244 men, 440 women	**Faculty:** 64
Part-time: 1 men, 3 women	**Ph.D.s:** 70%
Graduate: 27 men, 111 women	**Student/Faculty:** 11 to 1
Year: other	**Tuition:** $49,440
Room & Board: $14,520	**Freshman Class:** 1236 applied, 779 accepted, 197 enrolled
SAT CR/M/W: 690/610/660 **ACT:** 29	**CEEB CODE:** 3080
Application Deadline: January 3	**MOST COMPETITIVE**

Bennington College, founded in 1932, is a private liberal arts institution characterized by cross-disciplinary learning, a close working relationship between student and teacher, a self-directed academic planning process, and a connection to the world through its winter internship term. Figures in the above capsule and in this profile are approximate. There are 4 undergraduate schools and 4 graduate schools. The 440-acre campus is in a small town in the southwestern corner of Vermont, 160 miles north of New York City and 150 miles west of Boston. Including any residence halls, there are 70 buildings.

STUDENT LIFE: 96% of undergraduates are from out of state, mostly the Middle Atlantic. Students are from 46 states, 35 foreign countries, and Canada. 57% are from public schools. 77% are White; 7% Foreign; 5% Hispanic; 4% race unknown; 3% two or more races; 2% African American; 2% Asian American. **Female To Male Ratio:** 2.0:1. The average age of freshmen is 18; all undergraduates, 20. 17% do not continue beyond their first year; 64% remain to graduate. **Housing:** 661 students can be accommodated in college housing, which includes coed dorms, on-campus apartments, and off-campus apartments. In addition, there are special-interest houses. On-campus housing is guaranteed for all 4 years. 95% of students live on campus; of those, 75% remain on campus on weekends. All students may keep cars.

FACULTY/CLASSROOMS: 51% of faculty are male; 49% are female. All teach undergraduates, and all do research. No introductory courses are taught by graduate students. The average class size in an introductory lecture is 16; in a laboratory is 15; and in a regular course is 10.

PROGRAMS OF STUDY: Bennington confers B.A. degrees. Master's degrees are also awarded. Bachelor's degrees are awarded in AGRICULTURE (environmental studies), BIOLOGICAL SCIENCE (biology/biological science, botany, ecology, environmental biology, evolutionary biology, and zoology), COMMUNICATIONS AND THE ARTS (American literature, animation, art, ceramic art and design, Chinese, comparative literature, creative writing, dance, design, digital communications, dramatic arts, drawing, English, English literature, film arts, fine arts, French, Germanic languages and literature, illustration, Italian, Japanese, jazz, journalism, languages, literature, multimedia, music, music performance, music theory and composition, painting, performing arts, photography, piano/organ, playwriting/screenwriting, printmaking, sculpture, Spanish, strings, studio art, theater design, video, visual and performing arts, and voice), COMPUTER AND PHYSICAL SCIENCE (astronomy, chemistry, computer science, digital arts/technology, mathematics, physical sciences, physics, and science), EDUCATION (drama education, early childhood education, education, elementary education, foreign languages education, mathematics education, middle school education, and secondary education), ENGINEERING AND ENVIRONMENTAL DESIGN (architecture and environmental science), HEALTH PROFESSIONS (premedicine), SOCIAL SCIENCE (American studies, anthropology, child psychology/development, European studies, fashion design and technology, history, humanities, humanities and social science, interdisciplinary studies, international relations, international studies, Judaic studies, Latin American studies, liberal arts/general studies, philosophy, political science/government, prelaw, psychology, social psychology, social science, sociology, and women's studies). Literature, languages, and visual & performing arts are the strongest academically. Literature and interdisciplinary studies have the largest enrollments.

ACTIVITIES: There are no fraternities or sororities. There are 37 groups on campus, including campus activities board, student educational policies committee, student endowment for the arts, sustainability committee, art, chess, choir, chorale, chorus, computers, dance, debate, drama, environmental, ethnic, film, international, jazz band, LGBT, literary magazine, musical theater, newspaper, opera, outing club, photography, political, radio and TV, religious, social, social service, student government, and symphony. Popular campus events include Sunfest, Faculty Concerts, and Student-Work Performances. **Sports:** There are 2 intercollegiate sports for men and 2 for women, and 15 intramural sports for men and 15 for women. Facilities include a recreation barn (includes aerobic room, free weights, weight training equipment, yoga and martial arts equipment, cardiovascular machines), rock climbing wall, dance studio, tennis courts, soccer field, and basketball court. Swimming, horseback riding, rock climbing, canoeing, caving, snowshoeing, whitewater rafting, and skiing facilities are available in the surrounding area. **Graduates:** From July 1, 2015 to June 30, 2016, 151 bachelor's degrees were awarded. The most popular majors were visual and performing arts (46%), social sciences (10%), and English language and literature (10%). In an average class, 59% graduate in 4 years or less, 63% graduate in 5 years or less, and 64% graduate in 6 years or less.

SERVICES: Counseling and information services are available, as is tutoring in some subjects. There is remedial writing. Tutoring for learning disabilities is available in the town of Bennington at a cost to the student. **Library/Resources:** The 2 libraries contain 125,000 volumes, 6,000 audio/video tapes/CDs/DVDs, and subscribe to 14,500 periodicals including electronic. Computerized library services include interlibrary loans, database searching, Internet access, and Wi-Fi capability. Special learning facilities include an art gallery, radio station, a center for the advancement of Public Action with unique tiered symposium space for U.N.-style dialogue and web-casting, observatory, greenhouse, digital arts lab, art gallery, architecture, drawing, painting, printmaking, and sculpture studios, ceramics studio and kilns, photography darkrooms, film and video editing studio, several fully equipped theaters, dance studios, scripts library, costume shop, electronic music and sound recording studios, music practice rooms and music library, student-run cafe and bar, and 440 acres of forest, ponds, wetlands, and fields for recreation and scientific study. **Physically Challenged Students:** 80% of the campus is accessible. Facilities include wheelchair ramps, elevators, special parking, specially equipped restrooms, lowered drinking fountains, and special housing. **Special:** 7-week work/internships (during January and February) are required each year in residence. Cross-registration with Williams College, Southern Vermont College, and Massachusetts College of Liberal Arts is possible. In addition, study abroad, dual, and student-designed majors are offered. Students receive narrative evaluations with the option of letter grades. **Visiting:** There are regularly scheduled orientations for prospective students, including a tour of campus, classes, lunch in the dining hall, and meeting with an admissions counselor. Overnight visits are also possible during the term. There are guides for informal visits, visitors may sit in on classes, and stay overnight. To schedule a visit, contact the Admissions Office. **Campus Safety and Security:** Measures include 24-hour foot and vehicle patrol, emergency notification system, and security escort services. There are shuttle buses, emergency telephones, and lighted pathways/sidewalks.

REQUIREMENTS: Bennington admits students who have demonstrated a passion for learning and academic excellence. The Common Application as well as the Bennington Supplement are required. Submission of standardized test scores is optional. A majority of applicants are interviewed in person or by phone. A minimum of 128 credit hours is required to graduate. Students must also complete a Field Work Term (job/internship) for each year in residence. Students programs must reflect breadth and depth in curricular choices, and their academic plan process must be approved by a faculty committee. **Procedure:** Freshmen are admitted fall and spring. Entrance exams should be taken during the spring of the junior year or the fall of the senior year. There are early decision, early admissions, and deferred admissions plans. Early decision applications should be filed by November 15; regular applications, by January 3 for fall entry; and November 15 for spring entry, along with a $60 fee. Notification of early decision is sent December 20; regular decision, April 1. 21 early decision candidates were accepted for the 2016-2017 class. 152 applicants were on the 2016 waiting list; 27 were admitted. Applications are accepted on-line. **Transfer Students:** 15 transfer students enrolled in 2015-2016. Applicants must submit the common application for transfer students, including essays, secondary school reports, college transcripts, and recommendations from 2 faculty members at the college from which they are transferring. They must also interview with a member of the admissions staff. Submission of SAT or ACT scores is optional. 64 of 128 credits required for the bachelor's degree must be completed at Bennington. **International Students:** There are 48 international students enrolled. The school actively recruits these students. They must take the TOEFL with a minimum score of 577 on the paper-based TOEFL (PBT) or 90 on the Internet-based version (iBT); a band score of 7 or more on the Academic Module of the IELTS exam is also acceptable.

ADMISSIONS: 63% of the 2016-2017 applicants were accepted. The SAT scores for the 2016-2017 freshman class were: Critical Reading-- 13% between 500 and 599, 46% between 600 and 699, and 41% between 700 and 800. Math-- 2% below 500, 38% between 500 and 599, 48% between 600 and 699, and 13% between 700 and 800. Writing-- 2% below 500, 21% between 500 and 599, 51% between 600 and 699, and 27% between 700 and 800. The ACT scores were 5% below 12, 23% between 18 and 23, 23% between 24 and 29, and 50% above 30. 56% of the current freshmen were in the top fifth of their class; 84% were in the top two fifths. **Admissions Contact:** Bui Hung, Vice President Dean. Email: *hnbui@bennington.edu* Web: *www.bennington.edu*

FINANCIAL AID: In 2016-2017, 95% of all full-time freshmen and 90% of continuing full-time students received some form of financial aid. 58% of all full-time freshmen and 63% of continuing full-time students received need-based aid. The average freshman award was $33,336. Need-based scholarships or need-based grants averaged $23,448; need-based self-help aid (loans and jobs) averaged $4,696; and other non-need-based awards and non-need-based scholarships averaged $13,019. 20% of undergraduate students work part-time. Average annual earnings from campus work are $2214. The average financial indebtedness of the 2016 graduate was $25,716. Bennington is a member of CSS. The CSS/Profile, the college's own financial statement, and student and parent tax returns and W-2s are required. The FAFSA code is 003682. The priority date for freshman financial aid applications for fall entry is February 1.

CASTLETON UNIVERSITY B-4

www.castleton.edu

Castleton, VT 05735 (802) 468-1352
(800) 639-8521

Fax: (802) 468-5237
Email: info@castleton.edu
Full-time: 859 men, 861 women
Part-time: 97 men, 168 women
Graduate: 49 men, 150 women
Year: semesters, summer session
Room & Board: $9414
Faculty: 102
Ph.D.s: 99%
Student/Faculty: 14 to 1
Tuition: $10,772 ($25,436)
Freshman Class: 2397 applied, 1868 accepted, 382 enrolled
SAT or ACT: required
Application Deadline: open
CEEB CODE: 3765
COMPETITIVE

Castleton University, founded in 1787, is the oldest institution of higher learning in Vermont. As part of the Vermont State Colleges system, it offers a state-supported undergraduate and graduate program in liberal arts, teacher preparation, and professional studies. There is 1 undergraduate school and 1 graduate school. In addition to regional accreditation, Castleton has baccalaureate program accreditation with CSWE and NLN. The 165-acre campus is in a rural area 12 miles west of Rutland. Including any residence halls, there are 24 buildings.

STUDENT LIFE: 85% are White; 6% race unknown; 2% African American; 2% Hispanic; 2% Foreign; 2% two or more races; 1% Asian American; 1% American Indian/Alaska Native. **Female To Male Ratio:** 1.2:1. The average age of freshmen is 18; all undergraduates, 21. **Housing:** 1100 students can be accommodated in college housing, which includes single-sex and coed dorms and wellness housing. On-campus housing is guaranteed for the freshman year only and is available on a lottery system for upperclassmen. 54% of students live on campus; of those, 70% remain on campus on weekends. All students may keep cars.

FACULTY/CLASSROOMS: 50% of faculty are male; 50% are female. All teach undergraduates, 50% do research, and 50% do both. No introductory courses are taught by graduate students. The average class size in an introductory lecture is 25; in a laboratory is 14; and in a regular course is 18.

PROGRAMS OF STUDY: Castleton confers B.A., B.S., B.M., and B.S.W. degrees. Associate and master's degrees are also awarded. Bachelor's degrees are awarded in BIOLOGICAL SCIENCE (biology/biological science and ecology), BUSINESS (business administration and management and sports management), COMMUNICATIONS AND THE ARTS (art, communications, English, literature, music, Spanish, and theatre arts), COMPUTER AND PHYSICAL SCIENCE (chemistry, computer science, geology, mathematics, and natural sciences), EDUCATION (athletic training, education, global studies, health education, music education, and physical education), ENGINEERING AND ENVIRONMENTAL DESIGN (environmental science), HEALTH PROFESSIONS (exercise science, health science, and nursing), SOCIAL SCIENCE (criminal justice, economics, history, liberal arts/general studies, philosophy, political science/government, psychology, social science, social work, sociology, and women & gender studies). Business, nursing, and teacher preparation have the largest enrollments.

ACTIVITIES: There are no fraternities or sororities. There are 40 groups on campus, including art, band, cheerleading, choir, chorale, chorus, computers, dance, drama, drill team, environmental, ethnic, film, honors, international, jazz band, LGBT, literary magazine, marching band, musical theater, newspaper, pep band, photography, political, professional, radio and TV, religious, social, social service, and student government. Popular campus events include Spring, Winter, and Alumni Weekends. **Sports:** There are 10 intercollegiate sports for men and 10 for women, and 10 intramural sports for men and 10 for women. Facilities include gymnasiums, a swimming pool, racquetball courts, 3 fitness centers, recreation gym, an ice hockey rink, outdoor skating facility, multipurpose turf field, baseball and softball fields, athletic training rooms, a rock climbing wall, hiking, running, and X-C skiing. **Graduates:** From July 1, 2015 to June 30, 2016, 372 bachelor's degrees were awarded. The most popular majors were health professions and related programs (20%), business/marketing (13%), and communication/journalism (10%). 63 companies recruited on campus in 2015-2016. In an average class, 34% graduate in 4 years or less, 47% graduate in 5 years or less, and 51% graduate in 6 years or less.

SERVICES: Counseling and information services are available, as is

tutoring in every subject. There is a reader service for the blind, and remedial math, reading, and writing. **Library/Resources:** The library contains 272,223 volumes, 626,965 microform items, and 22,349 audio/video tapes/CDs/DVDs, and subscribes to 67,896 periodicals including electronic. Computerized library services include interlibrary loans, database searching, Internet access, and Wi-Fi capability. Special learning facilities include an art gallery, radio station, TV studio, observatory, and theater. **Physically Challenged Students:** 95% of the campus is accessible. Facilities include wheelchair ramps, elevators, special parking, specially equipped restrooms, special class scheduling, lowered drinking fountains, and lowered telephones. **Special:** Cross-registration with other Vermont State Colleges, co-op programs, internships, study abroad, and work-study programs are available. In addition, B.A.-B.S. degrees, dual majors, student-designed majors in history, math, and social sciences, credit for life experience, nondegree study, and pass/fail options are offered. There are 8 national honor societies, a freshman honors program, and 4 departmental honors programs. **Visiting:** There are regularly scheduled orientations for prospective students, including meetings with admissions counselors, faculty, and coaches as well as a campus tour. There are guides for informal visits and visitors may sit in on classes. To schedule a visit, contact the Admissions Office. **Campus Safety and Security:** Measures include 24-hour foot and vehicle patrol, emergency notification system, self-defense education, and security escort services. There are emergency telephones, lighted pathways/sidewalks, and controlled access to dorms/residences.

REQUIREMENTS: The SAT or ACT is required. The college requires that candidates have 4 years of English, and 3 years each of math, social studies or history, and sciences (two of which must be a lab). The college recommends 2 years of a foreign language. The GED is accepted. An interview is recommended. AP and CLEP credits are accepted. Important factors in the admissions decision are advanced placement or honors courses, leadership record, and recommendations by school officials. All students must maintain a GPA of 2.0 while taking 122 semester hours, including 30 or more in their major. Distribution requirements include 3 courses each in literature and the arts, 2 each in math and natural sciences, and 1 each in foreign cultures, history, philosophy and psychology, and social analysis. Specific courses include computers, communication, and an introduction to liberal arts. **Procedure:** Freshmen are admitted fall and spring. Entrance exams should be taken during the spring of the junior year or fall of the senior year. There are early admissions, deferred admissions, and rolling admissions plans. Application deadlines are open. Application fee is $40. Applications are accepted on-line. **Transfer Students:** 183 transfer students enrolled in 2015-2016. All transfer applicants must have a 2.0 GPA and submit both previous college transcripts and an essay/personal statement. Some transfer applicants will be asked to submit high school transripts, standardized test scores, and a statement of good standing from the prior institution. An interview may also be required of some transfer students. 30 of 122 credits required for the bachelor's degree must be completed at Castleton. **International Students:** There are 27 international students enrolled. The school actively recruits these students. They must take the TOEFL with a minimum score of 550 on the paper-based TOEFL (PBT) or 80 on the Internet-based version (iBT). They must also take the SAT or ACT.

ADMISSIONS: 78% of the 2016-2017 applicants were accepted. 3 freshmen graduated first in their class. **Admissions Contact:** Maurice Ouimet, Dean of Enrollment. Email: *info@castleton.edu* Web: *www.castleton.edu*

FINANCIAL AID: Castleton is a member of CSS. The FAFSA code is 003683. The deadline for filing freshman financial aid applications for fall entry is April 1.

CHAMPLAIN COLLEGE — A-2

www.champlain.edu

Burlington, VT 05402 — **(802) 865-5740** / **(800) 570-5858**

Fax: (802) 860-2767 — **Email: admission@champlain.edu**

Full-time: 1339 men, 830 women	**Faculty:** 100
Part-time: 31 men, 11 women	**Ph.D.s:** 68%
Graduate: 256 men, 350 women	**Student/Faculty:** 24 to 1
Year: semesters, summer session	**Tuition:** $38,660
Room & Board: $14,472	**Freshman Class:** 5587 applied, 3697 accepted, 554 enrolled
SAT CR/M/W: 570/560/540 **ACT:** 26	**CEEB CODE:** 3291
Application Deadline: February 1	**COMPETITIVE+**

Champlain College, founded in 1878, is a leading private college, with additional campuses in Montreal, Quebec, and Dublin, Ireland. Our career-driven approach to education prepares students for their professional life beginning with their very first semester. Students choose from more than 80 subject areas, including undergraduate majors, minors, specializations, graduate degrees, and certificate programs. Champlain also boasts over 50 student clubs and organizations, exceptional study abroad opportunities, and a strong internship program. There is 1 undergraduate school and 5 graduate schools. In addition to regional accreditation, Champlain has baccalaureate program accreditation with CSWE, ASCLD, and JRCERT. The 22-acre campus is in an urban area just up the hill from the city's downtown area and Lake Champlain, and at the edge of Vermont's Green Mountains and within sight of New York's Adirondack Mountains. Including any residence halls, there are 49 buildings.

STUDENT LIFE: 78% of undergraduates are from out of state, mostly the Northeast. Students are from 46 states, 26 foreign countries, and Canada. 71% are White; 4% Hispanic; 3% two or more races; 2% African American; 2% Asian American; 16% race unknown; 1% Foreign. **Male To Female Ratio:** 1.4:1. The average age of freshmen is 18; all undergraduates, 20. 21% do not continue beyond their first year. **Housing:** 1418 students can be accommodated in college housing, which includes single-sex and coed dorms and off-campus apartments. In addition, there are special-interest houses, including international student housing, and sophmore housing. On-campus housing is guaranteed for the freshman year only, is available on a first-come, first-served basis, and is available on a lottery system for upperclassmen. 64% of students live on campus; of those, 90% remain on campus on weekends. Alcohol is not permitted. No one may keep cars.

FACULTY/CLASSROOMS: 57% of faculty are male; 43% are female. All teach undergraduates. No introductory courses are taught by graduate students. The average class size in a laboratory is 8 and in a regular course is 16.

PROGRAMS OF STUDY: Champlain confers B.S., B.F.A., B.S.W., and B.S.B.A. degrees. Associate and master's degrees are also awarded. Bachelor's degrees are awarded in AGRICULTURE (environmental studies), BUSINESS (accounting, business administration and management, finance, international business management, management science, marketing, and marketing management), COMMUNICATIONS AND THE ARTS (advertising, broadcasting, communications, communications technology, film arts, fine arts, game design and development, game art, game programming, graphic design, graphic design & media, information technology, media arts, multimedia, public relations, and writing), COMPUTER AND PHYSICAL SCIENCE (computer game design/development, computer information technology, computer science, computer security and information assurance, cyber intelligence/security studies, information sciences and systems, radiological technology, and web services), EDUCATION (early childhood education, elementary education, health information management, middle school education, and secondary education), ENGINEERING AND ENVIRONMENTAL DESIGN (computational sciences), SOCIAL SCIENCE (criminal justice, forensic studies, legal studies, liberal arts/general studies, psychology, and social work). Game design & programming, graphic design, and digital media are the strongest academically. Game design & programming, graphic design, and business administration have the largest enrollments.

ACTIVITIES: There are no fraternities or sororities. There are 50 groups on campus, including art, chess, chorale, computers, dance, debate, drama, environmental, ethnic, forensics, honors, international, LGBT, literary magazine, musical theater, newspaper, photography, professional, radio and TV, religious, ski and ride, sailing, social, social service, and student government. Popular campus events include Skiing, Snowboarding Trips, and Spring Meltdown. **Sports:** There are 16 intramural sports for men and 16 for women. Facilities include a wellness and fitness center, a gym, and game centers. **Graduates:** From July 1, 2015 to June 30, 2016, 516 bachelor's degrees were awarded. The most popular majors were business administration (8%), communication (7%), and graphic design & digital media (6%). 980 companies recruited on campus in 2015-2016. In an average class, 50% graduate in 4 years or less, 61% graduate in 5 years or less, and 58% graduate in 6 years or less. Of the 2015 graduating class, 4% were enrolled in graduate school within 6 months of graduation, and 87% were employed.

SERVICES: Counseling and information services are available, as is tutoring in some subjects, such as math, accounting, and writing. Peer tutoring is available. **Library/Resources:** The library contains 260,381 volumes, and 835 audio/video tapes/CDs/DVDs, and subscribes to 55,221 periodicals including electronic. Computerized library services include interlibrary loans, database searching, Internet access, and Wi-Fi capability. Special learning facilities include an art gallery, and radio station. Champlain College offers on-campus learning centers in studio-like environments in which students across majors work on professional projects that put Champlain students' classroom knowledge to the test through practical application on real projects. These Centers include CCM (Center for Communications and Creative Media), EMC (Emergent Media Center), BYOBiz (Build Your Own Business), LCDI (Leahy Center for Digital Investigation) and the Publishing Initiative. There is a video production studio, broadcasting studio, several multimedia and graphic design studios, and game design and production studio. **Physically Challenged Students:** 79% of the campus is accessible. Facilities include wheelchair ramps, elevators, special parking, specially equipped restrooms, special class scheduling, lowered drinking fountains, and lowered telephones. **Special:** Champlain College offers Bachelor of Science (BS) degrees in various fields of study in the areas of business, communication and creative media, education, human studies, and computer and information technology. We also offer the Bachelor of Social Work degree (BSW), the Bachelor of Fine Arts (BFA) degrees in creative media, filmmaking and graphic design, and the Bachelor of Business Administration (BSBA). The College also offers study abroad opportunities with campuses in Dublin, Ireland, and Montreal, Canada in addition to global partnerships with institutions around the world. The courses offered at the Champlain Abroad campuses fit across majors with a variety of professional, liberal arts, and interdisciplinary options that provide students with an understanding of culture and global perspective. Located in Burlington, Vermont, the College is accredited by the New England Association of Schools and Colleges (NEASC), which allows the credit transfer process to be seamless! We also prioritize creating internship opportunities! As a professionally focused institution, Champlain emphasizes the value of getting as much time in the field as possible. We go to great lengths to create the best options for our students to do so. If you have the drive, we will work with you extensively to help you find or create an internship that will give you a chance to really dig into the work of your profession, build up your professional portfolio, and capture impressive credentials for your resume. Champlain has established close ties with the local business community, and Champlain students are the interns of choice at numerous businesses in and around Vermont. The College has developed a relationship with other area schools that allows students to take classes at their campuses as part of their regular class load. Champlain students can register for select classroom courses offered during the academic year at St. Michaels's College or Burlington College. The agreement does not apply to summer session or online courses. The College maintains guaranteed admissions arrangements with NYU's School of Continuing and Professional Studies and the Vermont Law School. Students who meet the G.P.A. and other admission requirements of the programs are guaranteed admission into one of 14 Masters programs offered through NYU including an M.S. in Management and Systems and an M.S. in Global Affairs or into the J.D. program at Vermont Law School. An additional agreement with Clarkson University for a 4+1 graduate program allows students to complete the M.B.A. or M.S. in Management in one additional year. Through a special agreement with the prestigious Thunderbird School of Global Management, Champlain students may be able to pursue a Certificate of Advanced Global Studies during the fall of the fourth year, and upon successful completion, have those credits apply toward one of Thunderbird's masters programs. Students are also eligible for a 15% reduction in price per credit hour for certain Thunderbird Master's programs. **Visiting:** There are regularly scheduled orientations for prospective students, including a group information session followed by a tour. Personal interviews are also available with an admissions counselor. There are guides for informal visits and visitors may sit in on classes. To schedule a visit, contact the Admissions Office at admission@champlain.edu. **Campus Safety and Security:** Measures include 24-hour foot and vehicle patrol, emergency notification system, self-defense education, and security escort services. There are shuttle buses, emergency telephones, lighted pathways/sidewalks, and controlled access to dorms/residences.

REQUIREMENTS: The SAT or ACT is required. Applicants must be graduates of an accredited high school or the equivalent. AP and CLEP credits are accepted. Important factors in the admissions decision are extracurricular activities record, recommendations by school officials, and advanced placement or honors courses. Traditional Student: a GPA of 2.0 and 120 credits are required for Baccalaureate degrees. Students must take between 40 and 60 hours in the major. Every undergraduate takes Champlain's Core Curriculum, a four-year course of interdisciplinary study that cultivates the intellectual leadership prized by a complex economy and a rapidly changing world. All undergraduate students also participate in LEAD (Life Experience and Action Dimension), a four-year program designed to help develop life skills that are practical, meaningful, and useful and that will serve graduates throughout their entire lifetime. CPS Student: adult undergraduate students complete a professionally focused general education curriculum intentionally designed to support courses in the major. **Procedure:** Freshmen are admitted fall and spring. Entrance exams should be taken prior to applying. There are early decision and deferred admissions plans. Early decision applications should be filed by November 15; regular applications, by February 1 for fall entry and December 1 for spring entry. Notification of early decision is sent December 15; regular decision, March 15. 380 early decision candidates were accepted for the 2016-2017 class. 146 applicants were on the 2016 waiting list; 4 were admitted. Applications are accepted on-line. **Transfer Students:** 67 transfer students enrolled in 2015-2016. High school and college transcripts are required. 45 of 120 credits required for the bachelor's degree must be completed at Champlain. **International Students:** There are 33 international students enrolled. The school actively recruits these students. They must take the TOEFL with a minimum score of 550 on the paper-based TOEFL (PBT) or 79 on the Internet-based version (iBT). The SAT or ACT is required for students whose high school was conducted in English.

ADMISSIONS: 66% of the 2016-2017 applicants were accepted. The SAT scores for the 2016-2017 freshman class were: Critical Reading-- 16% below 500, 43% between 500 and 599, 32% between 600 and 699, and 9% between 700 and 800. Math-- 20% below 500, 43% between 500 and 599, 33% between 600 and 699, and 4% between 700 and 800. Writing-- 26% below 500, 46% between 500 and 599, 23% between 600 and 699, and 4% between 700 and 800. The ACT scores were 10% below 12, 20% between 12 and 17, 28% between 18 and 23, 14% between 24 and 29, and 28% above 30. **Admissions Contact:** Chris Perlongo, Director of Admissions. Email: *admission@champlain.edu* Web: *www.champlain.edu*

FINANCIAL AID: In 2016-2017, 97% of all full-time freshmen and 99% of continuing full-time students received some form of financial aid. 71% of all full-time freshmen and 72% of continuing full-time students received need-based aid. The average freshman award was $28,795. Need-based scholarships or need-based grants averaged $9,510 ($45,386 maximum); need-based self-help aid (loans and jobs) averaged $4,830 ($10,000 maximum); and other non-need-based awards and non-need-based scholarships averaged $11,730 ($43,086 maximum). 25% of undergraduate students work part-time. Average annual earnings from campus work are $1200. The average financial indebtedness of the 2016 graduate was $26,003. The FAFSA code is 003684. The priority date for freshman financial aid applications for fall entry is February 15.

COLLEGE OF ST JOSEPH *(The complete profile is made available exclusively on our website, www.barronspac.com)*

GODDARD COLLEGE — C-3

www.goddard.edu

Plainfield, VT 05667	**(802) 454-8311** **(800) 906-8312**
Fax: (802) 454-1029	**Email: admissions@goddard.edu**
Full-time: 73 men, 136 women	**Faculty:** 16
Part-time: n/av	**Ph.D.s:** 87%
Graduate: 108 men, 274 women	**Student/Faculty:** n/av
Year: semesters	**Tuition:** $15,476
Room & Board: $1564	**Freshman Class:** n/av **CEEB CODE:** 3416
Application Deadline: open	**VERY COMPETITIVE**

Goddard College, founded in 1863, is a private college that stresses progressive, individualized education for personal and community transformation based on John Dewey's learning-by-engagement philosophy. There is 1 undergraduate school and 1 graduate school. The 200-acre campus is in a rural area 10 miles from Montpelier, and 45 miles from Burlington, Vermont. Including any residence halls, there are 28 buildings.

STUDENT LIFE: 85% of undergraduates are from out of state, mostly

the Northeast. 73% are White; 6% Hispanic; 4% two or more races; 2% African American; 13% race unknown; 1% Asian American; 1% American Indian/Alaska Native. **Female To Male Ratio:** 2.3:1. The average age of freshmen is 32; all undergraduates, 34. **Housing:** 175 students can be accommodated in college housing, which includes single-sex and coed dorms. In addition, there are special-interest houses, a family-friendly dorm, and substance-free (i.e. no perfumes, etc.) dorm. 100% of students commute. All students may keep cars.

FACULTY/CLASSROOMS: 23% of faculty are male; 77% are female. No introductory courses are taught by graduate students.

PROGRAMS OF STUDY: Goddard confers B.A. and B.F.A. degrees. Master's degrees are also awarded. Bachelor's degrees are awarded in AGRICULTURE (environmental studies), BIOLOGICAL SCIENCE (nutrition), BUSINESS (sustainable management), COMMUNICATIONS AND THE ARTS (applied art, art, comparative literature, creative writing, dramatic arts, English, English writing, fine arts, folklore and mythology, intermedia/multimedia, literature, media arts, photography, playwriting/screenwriting, and visual and performing arts), EDUCATION (art education, collaborative education, early childhood education, education, elementary education, English education, health education, learner designed area of study, middle school education, and secondary education), HEALTH PROFESSIONS (health, health promotion, and health science), SOCIAL SCIENCE (addiction studies, clinical psychology, counseling/psychology, crosscultural studies, cultural studies/critical theory & analysis, ethics, politics, and social policy, history, human development, human ecology, humanities and social science, industrial and organizational psychology, interdisciplinary studies, justice and society, liberal arts/general studies, psychology, social psychology, social science, and women & gender studies). Creative writing, individualized studies, and BA-to-MA Fast Track in psychology are the strongest academically. Psychology and creative writing have the largest enrollments.

ACTIVITIES: There are no fraternities or sororities. There are 9 groups on campus, including art, drama, environmental, literary magazine, radio and TV, and student government. **Sports:** There is no sports program at Goddard. Facilities include a workout room and hiking trails. **Graduates:** From July 1, 2015 to June 30, 2016, 92 bachelor's degrees were awarded.

SERVICES: There is remedial writing. **Library/Resources:** The library contains 173,000 volumes, 400 audio/video tapes/CDs/DVDs, and subscribes to 10,000 periodicals including electronic. Computerized library services include interlibrary loans, database searching, Internet access, and Wi-Fi capability. Special learning facilities include a radio station. **Physically Challenged Students:** 60% of the campus is accessible. Facilities include wheelchair ramps, elevators, special parking, and specially equipped restrooms. **Special:** The BA/MA Fast Track in Psychology saves students a semester toward earning an MA while completing their bachelor's degree. All programs entail students designing their own studies. The B.A. in Sustainability, B.A. in Education, B.A. in Health Arts & Sciences, and B.F.A. in Creative Writing are upper-division programs requiring 60 prior credits. The main undergraduate program encompasses both lower and upper divisions. **Visiting:** There are regularly scheduled orientations for prospective students, one Discover Goddard Day held each fall and spring, one visiting day during every residency, and individual meetings by appointment. There are guides for informal visits and visitors may sit in on classes. To schedule a visit, contact respective admissions counselor for the program. **Campus Safety and Security:** Measures include 24-hour foot and vehicle patrol. There are lighted pathways/sidewalks and controlled access to dorms/residences.

REQUIREMENTS: Goddard admits students who can contribute to its learning community and who will thrive in a self-directed degree program. The admission decision is based on the application, essays, letters of recommendation, transcripts, samples of the student's creative or academic work, and an interview. Standardized test scores are unhelpful, not required. Homeschooled students are welcome to apply. AP and CLEP credits are accepted. Important factors in the admissions decision are personality/intangible qualities, recommendations by alumni, and evidence of special talent. Students come to campus for eight days at the beginning of each semester, then study independently the rest of the term, at home or elsewhere. Collaborating with a faculty advisor, students design and carry out programs of study specifically tailored to their own personal and professional interests and goals. Assessment takes the form of narrative evaluations rather than letter grades; students must pass comprehensive reviews of performance and progress. There are no declared majors, but in the last semester of enrollment, all students must complete a culminating senior study or project that may be multidisciplinary and requires extensive foundational work comparable to a major. A total of 120 credits is required to graduate. Students must conduct, or transfer in, substantive studies in the arts, humanities, social sciences, natural sciences, and quantitative reasoning. **Procedure:** Freshmen are admitted to all sessions. There are deferred admissions and rolling admissions plans. Check with the school for current application deadlines. The application fee is $65. Notification is sent on a rolling basis. Applications are accepted on-line. **Transfer Students:** Official transcripts from previous institutions, writing samples, an essay, letters of recommendation, and an interview are required. 45 of 120 credits required for the bachelor's degree must be completed at Goddard. **International Students:** There are 2 international students enrolled.

Admissions Contact: Admissions Office Email: *admissions@goddard.edu* Web: *www.goddard.edu*

FINANCIAL AID: The average freshman award was $9,515. Need-based scholarships or need-based grants averaged $5,662; and need-based self-help aid (loans and jobs) averaged $3,853. The average financial indebtedness of the 2016 graduate was $25,856. The FAFSA code is 003686. Check with the school for current application deadlines.

GREEN MOUNTAIN COLLEGE *(The complete profile is made available exclusively on our website, www.barronspac.com)*

JOHNSON STATE COLLEGE — B-2

www.jsc.edu

Johnson, VT 05656	(802) 635-1219 (800) 635-2356
Fax: (802) 635-1230	**Email:** Patrick.Rogers@jsc.edu
Full-time: 505 men, 610 women	**Faculty:** 62; IIB, --$
Part-time: 105 men, 320 women	**Ph.D.s:** 90%
Graduate: 60 men, 170 women	**Student/Faculty:** 19 to 1
Year: semesters, summer session	**Tuition:** $11,056 ($23,752)
Room & Board: $9696	**Freshman Class:** 1333 applied, 1093 accepted, 410 enrolled
SAT CR/M: 500/500 **ACT:** required	**CEEB CODE:** 3766
Application Deadline: n/av	**COMPETITIVE**

Johnson State College, founded in 1828, is a public liberal arts and science college offering more than 30 academic and professional degree programs. The figures in the above capsule and in this profile are approximate. There is 1 undergraduate school and 1 graduate school. In addition to regional accreditation, Johnson State has baccalaureate program accreditation with NEASC. The 350-acre campus is in a small town in the heart of the Green Mountains, 1 hour from Burlington, and 3.5 hours from Boston. Including any residence halls, there are 14 buildings.

STUDENT LIFE: 63% of undergraduates are from Vermont. Others are from 23 states, 6 foreign countries, and Canada. 90% are White; 5% African American; 2% American Indian/Alaska Native; 2% Hispanic; 1% Foreign. **Female To Male Ratio:** 1.6:1. The average age of freshmen is 19; all undergraduates, 21. 30% do not continue beyond their first year; 45% remain to graduate. **Housing:** 549 students can be accommodated in college housing, which includes coed dorms, on-campus apartments, and married student housing. In addition, there are special-interest houses and alcohol-free residence hall. On-campus housing is guaranteed for all 4 years. 57% of students live on campus. Alcohol is not permitted. All students may keep cars.

FACULTY/CLASSROOMS: 58% of faculty are male; 42% are female. All teach undergraduates. No introductory courses are taught by graduate students.

PROGRAMS OF STUDY: Johnson State confers B.A., B.S. and B.F.A. A.A., A.S., M.A. and M.F.A. degrees. Associate and master's degrees are also awarded. Bachelor's degrees are awarded in AGRICULTURE (natural resource management), BIOLOGICAL SCIENCE (biology/biological science and cell biology), BUSINESS (business administration and management, business systems analysis, hospitality management services, recreational facilities management, small business management, and tourism), COMMUNICATIONS AND THE ARTS (art, creative writing, English, fine arts, jazz, journalism, music, music business management, music history and appreciation, music performance, performing arts, studio art, theater design, theater management, visual and performing arts, and writing), COMPUTER AND PHYSICAL SCIENCE (mathematics), EDUCATION (art education, athletic training, education, elementary education, English education, environmental education, mathematics education, middle school education, music education, physical education, recreation education, science education, and secondary education), ENGINEERING AND ENVIRONMENTAL DESIGN (environmental science), HEALTH PROFESSIONS (allied health, health science, and premedicine), SOCIAL SCIENCE (anthropology, behavioral science, history, humanities, liberal arts/general studies, physical fitness/movement, political science/government, prelaw, psychology, and sociology). Environmental science, elementary/secondary/middle school education, and wellness & alternative medicine have the largest enrollments.

ACTIVITIES: There are no fraternities or sororities. There are 35 groups on campus, including ski & snowboard club, finance & investment club, hospitality, humans vs zombies, leadership, Magic the Gathering club, art, band, choir, chorale, chorus, dance, debate, drama, environmental, jazz band, LGBT, literary magazine, musical theater, newspaper, outdoor, photography, political, professional, radio and TV, religious, social, social service, and student government. Popular campus events include Winter Carnival and Coffee House (weekly live entertainment). **Sports:** There are 6 intercollegiate sports for men and 6 for women, and 20 intramural sports for men and 20 for women. Facilities include a 7000-square-foot multiuse facility with health monitoring and exercise equipment, 2 gyms, state-of-the-art weight room, 25-yard indoor pool, 700-seat varsity basketball court, 2 racquetball courts, 26-foot indoor climbing and bouldering wall, and 1 squash court. **Graduates:** The most popular majors were business, education, and behavioral sciences.

SERVICES: Counseling and information services are available, as is tutoring in most subjects. There is a reader service for the blind, and remedial math, reading, and writing. The Academic Support Services Department provides accommodations for students with a documented learning disability. **Library/Resources:** The library contains 111,000 volumes, 180,158 microform items, and 7,200 audio/video tapes/CDs/DVDs, and subscribes to 42,884 periodicals including electronic. Computerized library services include interlibrary loans, database searching, Internet access, and Wi-Fi capability. Special learning facilities include an art gallery and radio station. **Physically Challenged Students:** 60% of the campus is accessible. Facilities include wheelchair ramps, elevators, special parking, specially equipped restrooms, special class scheduling, and lowered drinking fountains. **Special:** All students are encouraged to complete an internship. Through the National Student Exchange Program, students may study at another institution or abroad for a semester or a year. Co-op programs are offered in business, tourism, hospitality management, and education, and cross-registration is available with other Vermont state colleges. There is 1 national honor society. **Visiting:** There are regularly scheduled orientations for prospective students, including a campus tour and an admission interview. Students may request to meet with a faculty member. There are guides for informal visits and visitors may sit in on classes. To schedule a visit, contact the Admissions Office. **Campus Safety and Security:** Measures include 24-hour foot and vehicle patrol, self-defense education, and security escort services. There are shuttle buses, emergency telephones, and lighted pathways/sidewalks.

REQUIREMENTS: The SAT or ACT is required. Successful candidates for admission have generally completed a college preparatory curriculum consisting of 4 years of English, 3 of math (2 of algebra, 1 of geometry), 3 of social sciences, and 2 of science (including 1 lab science). An official high school transcript or GED test score must be submitted with the application. In addition, 1 letter of recommendation, preferably from a guidance counselor, and SAT or ACT scores should be sent with the application or under separate cover. A GPA of 2.3 is required. AP and CLEP credits are accepted. Important factors in the admissions decision are advanced placement or honors courses, recommendations by school officials, and extracurricular activities record. The bachelor's degree requires completion of at least 120 credit hours of course-work (not including basic skills credits), with a minimum cumulative GPA of 2.0. In addition, students must complete the general education core curriculum and an approved major as well as take a writing proficiency exam. **Procedure:** Freshmen are admitted fall and spring. There are deferred admissions and rolling admissions plans. Applications should be filed by December 1 for spring entry, along with a $38 fee. Applications are accepted on-line. **Transfer Students:** A GPA of at least 2.0 is required. 30 of 120 credits required for the bachelor's degree must be completed at Johnson State. **International Students:** They must take the TOEFL with a minimum score of 500 on the paper-based TOEFL (PBT) or 80 on the Internet-based version (iBT). They must also take the SAT or ACT.

ADMISSIONS: 82% of the 2016-2017 applicants were accepted. **Admissions Contact:** Patrick Rogers, Director of Admissions. Email: *Patrick.Rogers@jsc.edu* Web: *www.jsc.edu*

FINANCIAL AID: Johnson State is a member of CSS. The FAFSA code is 003688. The priority date for freshman financial aid applications for fall entry is November 1. The deadline for filing freshman financial aid applications for fall entry is March 1.

LYNDON STATE COLLEGE D-2

www.lyndonstate.edu

Lyndonville, VT 05851	**(802) 626-6413** **(800) 225-1998**
Fax: (802) 626-6335	**Email: nolan.atkins@lyndonstate.edu**
Full-time: 560 men, 570 women	**Faculty:** 56
Part-time: 70 men, 230 women	**Ph.D.s:** 60%
Graduate: 1 men, 5 women	**Student/Faculty:** 20 to 1
Year: semesters, summer session	**Tuition:** $11,018 ($22,418)
Room & Board: $9696	**Freshman Class:** n/av
SAT or ACT: required	**CEEB CODE:** 3767
Application Deadline: open	**COMPETITIVE**

Lyndon State College, founded in 1911 as a teachers' college, became a liberal arts school in 1962, and offers undergraduate and graduate courses. The figures in the above capsule and in this profile are approximate. There is 1 undergraduate school and 1 graduate school. In addition to regional accreditation, LSC has baccalaureate program accreditation with NRPA. The 175-acre campus is in a small town in northeastern Vermont, 184 miles north of Boston. Including any residence halls, there are 17 buildings.

STUDENT LIFE: 60% of undergraduates are from Vermont. Others are from 24 states, 12 foreign countries, and Canada. 99% are White. **Female To Male Ratio:** 1.3:1. The average age of freshmen is 18; all undergraduates, 24. 33% do not continue beyond their first year; 41% remain to graduate. **Housing:** 600 students can be accommodated in college housing, which includes single-sex and coed dorms. In addition, there are special-interest houses. On-campus housing is available on a first-come, first-served basis. Priority is given to out-of-town students. 56% of students commute. All students may keep cars.

FACULTY/CLASSROOMS: 66% of faculty are male; 34% are female. All teach undergraduates. No introductory courses are taught by graduate students. The average class size in an introductory lecture is 20; in a laboratory is 16; and in a regular course is 16.

PROGRAMS OF STUDY: LSC confers B.A., and B.S. degrees. Associate and master's degrees are also awarded. Bachelor's degrees are awarded in BUSINESS (accounting, business administration and management, recreation and leisure services, and sports management), COMMUNICATIONS AND THE ARTS (communications, English, graphic design, journalism, multimedia, and radio/television technology), COMPUTER AND PHYSICAL SCIENCE (atmospheric sciences and meteorology, mathematics, natural sciences, and science), EDUCATION (early childhood education, elementary education, English education, physical education, recreation education, and science education), SOCIAL SCIENCE (human services, interdisciplinary studies, psychology, and social science). Meteorology, natural science, and math are the strongest academically. Education, communications, and business have the largest enrollments.

ACTIVITIES: There are no fraternities or sororities. There are 22 groups on campus, including snowmobile club, anime, flight club, LAN party club and Lyndon sports broadcasting club, weightlifting, capella club, cheerleading, choir, chorale, chorus, communications, dance, drama, film, honors, international, jazz band, LGBT, literary magazine, newspaper, photography, political, professional, radio and TV, religious, social, social service, student government, and yearbook. Popular campus events include Family Weekend, Alumni Weekend, and a Concert Series. **Sports:** There are 5 intercollegiate sports for men and 5 for women, and 12 intramural sports for men and 12 for women. Facilities include a fitness center, which includes a wide variety of cardiovascular, selectorized and free weight equipment, racquetball courts, an auxiliary gym, and an

Olympic-size pool, outdoor tennis courts, ice hockey, cross-country ski trails and running trails, and softball, soccer, basketball, and rugby fields. **Graduates:** The most popular majors were psychology/human services (19%), business (10%), and education (10%). In an average class, 21% graduate in 4 years or less, 35% graduate in 5 years or less, and 41% graduate in 6 years or less.

SERVICES: Counseling and information services are available, as is tutoring in every subject. There is remedial math, reading, and writing. A math lab and a writing center are available for student use. **Library/Resources:** The library contains 100,000 volumes, and 3,600 audio/video tapes/CDs/DVDs, and subscribes to 48,000 periodicals including electronic. Computerized library services include interlibrary loans, database searching, and Internet access. Special learning facilities include an art gallery, radio station, TV station, a founder's museum, and meteorology lab. **Physically Challenged Students:** 70% of the campus is accessible. Facilities include wheelchair ramps, elevators, special parking, specially equipped restrooms, and lowered drinking fountains. **Special:** Cooperative programs in a variety of businesses, including local ski areas, social agencies, and radio and TV stations, internships in recreation programs and communications, and study abroad in Nova Scotia and England are available. B.A.-B.S. degrees, work-study, a general studies degree, dual and student-designed majors, a 3-2 engineering degree with Norwich University in Vermont, credit for life experience, nondegree study, cross-registration, work study, accelerated degree programs, and pass/fail options also are offered. There is 1 national honor society, a freshman honors program, and 1 departmental honors program. **Visiting:** There are regularly scheduled orientations for prospective students, including a tour, an information session, and faculty presentations. There are guides for informal visits, visitors may sit in on classes, and stay overnight. To schedule a visit, contact the Admissions Office. **Campus Safety and Security:** Measures include 24-hour foot and vehicle patrol, self-defense education, and security escort services. There are emergency telephones, lighted pathways/sidewalks. There is a security and safety service on campus as well as a 24-hour emergency rescue squad.

REQUIREMENTS: The SAT or ACT is required. LSC recommends that applicants have 4 years of English and 2 each of math, foreign language, history, and science. An essay is required, as is a recommendation from the high school principal or guidance counselor. An interview is recommended. The GED is accepted. AP and CLEP credits are accepted. Important factors in the admissions decision are advanced placement or honors courses, recommendations by school officials, and leadership record. All students must maintain a minimum GPA of 2.0 while taking 122 semester hours, including 42 hours in liberal arts. Distribution requirements include 28 credits in arts, humanities, math and science, and social and behavioral sciences. Required courses include freshman English and college algebra. **Procedure:** Freshmen are admitted fall and spring. There are early decision, early admissions, deferred admissions, and rolling admissions plans. Application deadlines are open. Application fee is $32. Notification of early decision is sent December 1; regular decision, on a rolling basis. Applications are accepted on-line. **Transfer Students:** 115 transfer students enrolled in 2015-2016. Interviews are recommended for transfer students. An official transcript from each college attended is required. 30 of 122 credits required for the bachelor's degree must be completed at LSC. **International Students:** There are 10 international students enrolled. They must take the TOEFL.

ADMISSIONS: 4 freshmen graduated first in their class. **Admissions Contact:** Nolan Atkins, Interim Dean. Email: *nolan.atkins@lyndonstate.edu* Web: *www.lyndonstate.edu*

FINANCIAL AID: In 2016-2017, 89% of all full-time freshmen received some form of financial aid. 89% of all full-time freshmen and 75% of continuing full-time students received need-based aid. The average freshman award was $8,079. Need-based scholarships or need-based grants averaged $3,879 ($5,000 maximum); need-based self-help aid (loans and jobs) averaged $3,817 ($4,625 maximum); and other non-need-based awards and non-need-based scholarships averaged $3,860 ($5,646 maximum). Average annual earnings from campus work are $1262. The average financial indebtedness of the 2016 graduate was $18,084. LSC is a member of CSS. The FAFSA code is 003689. The priority date for freshman financial aid applications for fall entry is January 1. The deadline for filing freshman financial aid applications for fall entry is February 15.

MARLBORO COLLEGE B-6

www.marlboro.edu

Marlboro, VT 05344	(802) 258-9261 (800) 343-0049
Fax: (802) 258-9300	Email: blawler@marlboro.edu
Full-time: 88 men, 102 women	Faculty: 38
Part-time: 1 man, 1 woman	Ph.D.s: 77%
Graduate: 31 men, 39 women	Student/Faculty: 5 to 1
Year: semesters	Tuition: $40,030
Room & Board: $10,802	Freshman Class: 144 applied, 136 accepted, 35 enrolled
SAT CR/M/W: 670/555/620 ACT: 25	CEEB CODE: 3509
Application Deadline: January 15	VERY COMPETITIVE+

Marlboro College, established in 1946, is a small, private institution offering degrees in the liberal and fine arts and humanities and employing self-designed programs of study. The figures in the above capsule and in this profile are approximate. There is 1 undergraduate school and 1 graduate school. The 300-acre campus is in a rural area in the southern Vermont town of Marlboro, approximately 9 miles west of Brattleboro, and just 1 1/2 hours from Albany and Hartford. Including any residence halls, there are 36 buildings.

STUDENT LIFE: 88% of undergraduates are from out of state, mostly the Northeast. Students are from 37 states, 4 foreign countries, and Canada. 70% are from public schools. 78% are White; 8% race unknown; 4% two or more races; 3% African American; 3% Hispanic; 2% Asian American; 1% American Indian/Alaska Native; 1% Foreign. **Female To Male Ratio:** 1.2:1. The average age of freshmen is 19; all undergraduates, 21. 28% do not continue beyond their first year; 48% remain to graduate. **Housing:** 266 students can be accommodated in college housing, which includes single-sex and coed dorms, on-campus apartments, and married student housing, residence halls, alcohol-free & smoke-free dorms, theme housing, wellness housing, and cottages. On-campus housing is guaranteed for all 4 years, and is available on a first-come, first-served basis. 78% of students live on campus; of those, 90% remain on campus on weekends. All students may keep cars.

FACULTY/CLASSROOMS: 62% of faculty are male; 38% are female. All teach undergraduates. No introductory courses are taught by graduate students. The average class size in a laboratory is 8 and in a regular course is 8.

PROGRAMS OF STUDY: Marlboro confers B.A. and B.S. degrees. Master's degrees are also awarded. Bachelor's degrees are awarded in AGRICULTURE (environmental studies), BIOLOGICAL SCIENCE (biochemistry, biology/biological science, botany, and microbiology), COMMUNICATIONS AND THE ARTS (art history and appreciation, creative writing, dance, dramatic arts, English, fine arts, French, German, Greek, Italian, languages, Latin, linguistics, music, photography, Russian, Spanish, and theatre studies), COMPUTER AND PHYSICAL SCIENCE (chemistry, computer science, mathematics, and physics), HEALTH PROFESSIONS (premedicine), SOCIAL SCIENCE (anthropology, economics, history, interdisciplinary studies, international studies, liberal arts, sciences, general studies, humanities, philosophy, political science/government, prelaw, psychology, religion, social science, and sociology). Sciences, humanities, and world studies are the strongest academically. Literature, biology, and sociology have the largest enrollment.

ACTIVITIES: There are no fraternities or sororities. There are 25 groups on campus, including art, chess, chorus, communications, computers, dance, drama, environmental, ethnic, film, international, jazz band, LGBT, literary magazine, musical theater, newspaper, photography, political, professional, religious, social, social service, and student government. Popular campus events include Green-up Day, Creativity Lecture Series, and Visiting Writers Series. **Sports:** There is 1 intercollegiate sports for men and 1 for women, and 1 intramural sports for men and 1 for women. Facilities include a soccer field, volleyball court, cross-country trails, basketball court, weight room, climbing wall, field trips for canoeing, white-water rafting, hiking, and skiing. **Graduates:** From July 1, 2015 to June 30, 2016, 44 bachelor's degrees were awarded. The most popular majors were film/video studies, literature, and psychology. In an average class, 66% graduate in 6 years or less. Of the 2015 graduating class, 76% were employed within 6 months of graduation.

SERVICES: Counseling and information services are available, as is

tutoring in some subjects, such as writing and languages, math, and organic chemistry. **Library/Resources:** The library contains 75,000 volumes, 5,799 microform items, and 2,990 audio/video tapes/CDs/DVDs, and subscribes to 188 periodicals including electronic. Computerized library services include interlibrary loans, database searching, Internet access, and Wi-Fi capability. Special learning facilities include an art gallery, and observatory. **Physically Challenged Students:** 90% of the campus is accessible. Facilities include wheelchair ramps, elevators, special parking, specially equipped restrooms, and special class scheduling. **Special:** Marlboro offers a variety of internships, cross-registration with Huron University in London, and study abroad in many countries, including China, Cambodia, Thailand, New Zealand, Hungary, and Mexico. The World Studies Program combines liberal arts with international studies, including 5 to 8 months of internship work in another culture. Accelerated and B.A.-B.S. degree programs are available. Students may pursue dual majors. Majors reflect an integrated course of study designed by students and their faculty advisers during the junior year. **Visiting:** There are regularly scheduled orientations for prospective students, which include a campus tour, visit with admissions staff, optional class visit, optional interview. There are guides for informal visits, visitors may sit in on classes, and stay overnight. To schedule a visit, contact the Office of Admissions. **Campus Safety and Security:** Measures include self-defense education.

REQUIREMENTS: Applicants typically graduate from an accredited secondary school or have a GED. They are encouraged to earn 14 Carnegie units and complete 4 years of English, 3 years each of math, and science, 2 years each of history, social studies, and a foreign language. Supplementary essays and analytical writing samples are required. Interviews are required. Standardized test scores (SAT, ACT, etc.) are not required, but may be submitted. It is encouraged to submit scores if a student feels it will strengthen their application. Any additional materials a student wishes to submit, such as an art portfolio or writing project, are encouraged and will be accepted and reviewed. AP and CLEP credits are accepted. Important factors in the admissions decision are personality/intangible qualities, leadership record, and extracurricular activities record. To graduate, students must complete a Plan of Concentration, a writing requirement, and a freshman seminar. A minimum GPA of 2.0 is required. Students must earn 120 credits, with 50 credits in the major, and complete a thesis and an oral exam. **Procedure:** Freshmen are admitted fall and spring. Entrance exams should be taken by October before entry. There are early decision, early admissions, deferred admissions, and rolling admissions plans. Early decision applications should be filed by November 15; regular applications, by January 15 for fall entry; and December 15 for spring entry, along with a $50 fee. Notification of early decision is sent December 1; regular decision, May 1. Applications are accepted on-line. Application fees are waived if application is completed on-line. **Transfer Students:** 15 transfer students enrolled in 2015-2016. Transfers must have a minimum GPA of 2.0. All high school and college transcripts are required. An essay and interview are also required. Students may apply for admissions fall and spring. 42 of 120 credits required for the bachelor's degree must be completed at Marlboro. **International Students:** There are 6 international students enrolled. The school actively recruits these students. They must take the TOEFL.

ADMISSIONS: 94% of the 2016-2017 applicants were accepted. The SAT scores for the 2016-2017 freshman class were: Critical Reading-- 8% below 500, 25% between 500 and 599, 17% between 600 and 699, and 50% between 700 and 800. Math-- 17% below 500, 58% between 500 and 599, 17% between 600 and 699, and 8% between 700 and 800. Writing-- 8% below 500, 17% between 500 and 599, 67% between 600 and 699, and 8% between 700 and 800. The ACT scores were 35% between 12 and 17, 29% between 18 and 23, 29% between 24 and 29, and 7% above 30. 46% of the current freshmen were in the top fifth of their class; 82% were in the top two fifths. 2 freshmen graduated first in their class. **Admissions Contact:** Brigid Lawler, Director of Admissions. Email: *blawler@marlboro.edu* Web: *www.marlboro.edu*

FINANCIAL AID: In 2016-2017, 85% of all full-time freshmen and 85% of continuing full-time students received some form of financial aid. 68% of all full-time freshmen and 80% of continuing full-time students received need-based aid. The average freshman award was $33,928. Need-based scholarships or need-based grants averaged $15,969; need-based self-help aid (loans and jobs) averaged $29,231; other non-need-based awards and non-need-based scholarships averaged $13,000; and $34,912 from other forms of aid. 68% of undergraduate students work part-time. Average annual earnings from campus work are $1118. Marlboro is a member of CSS. The CSS/Profile is required. The FAFSA code is 003690. The priority date for freshman financial aid applications for fall entry is March 1.

MIDDLEBURY COLLEGE — A-3

www.middlebury.edu

Middlebury, VT 05753 — **(802) 443-3000**

Fax: (802) 443-2065	**Email: admissions@middlebury.edu**
Full-time: 1208 men, 1298 women	**Faculty:** IIB, ++$
Part-time: 9 men, 17 women	**Ph.D.s:** n/av
Graduate: 1 man, 25 women	**Student/Faculty:** n/av
Year: 4-1-4	**Tuition:** $50,063
Room & Board: $14,269	**Freshman Class:** 8819 applied, 1423 accepted, 606 enrolled
SAT CR/M/W: 705/700/710 **ACT:** 32	**CEEB CODE:** 3526
Application Deadline: January 1	**MOST COMPETITIVE**

Middlebury College, founded in 1800, is a small, private liberal arts institution offering degree programs in languages, humanities, and social and natural sciences. Figures in the above capsule and in this profile are approximate. There is 1 undergraduate school and 3 graduate schools. The 355-acre campus is in a small town 35 miles south of Burlington. Including any residence halls, there are 115 buildings.

STUDENT LIFE: 95% of undergraduates are from out of state, mostly the Northeast. Students are from 52 states, 69 foreign countries, and Canada. 9% are Hispanic; 7% Asian American; 64% White; 5% two or more races; 3% African American; 10% Foreign; 1% race unknown. **Female To Male Ratio:** 1.1:1. The average age of freshmen is 18; all undergraduates, 20. 6% do not continue beyond their first year; 94% remain to graduate. **Housing:** 2546 students can be accommodated in college housing, which includes single-sex and coed dorms, on-campus apartments, and married student housing. In addition, there are language houses, special-interest houses, and coed social, multicultural, and environmental houses. On-campus housing is guaranteed for all 4 years and is available on a lottery system for upperclassmen. 96% of students live on campus. All students may keep cars.

FACULTY/CLASSROOMS: All teach undergraduates. No introductory courses are taught by graduate students. The average class size in an introductory lecture is 18 and in a regular course is 18.

PROGRAMS OF STUDY: Midd confers A.B. degrees. Master's and doctoral degrees are also awarded. Bachelor's degrees are awarded in AGRICULTURE (environmental studies), BIOLOGICAL SCIENCE (biochemistry, biology/biological science, molecular biology, and neurosciences), BUSINESS (international economics), COMMUNICATIONS AND THE ARTS (Arabic, Chinese, classics, comparative literature, dance, dramatic arts, English, film arts, French, German, Italian, Japanese, music, Russian, Spanish, and studio art), COMPUTER AND PHYSICAL SCIENCE (chemistry, computer science, geology, mathematics, and physics), EDUCATION (museum studies), ENGINEERING AND ENVIRONMENTAL DESIGN (architectural history), SOCIAL SCIENCE (African American studies, American studies, anthropology, East Asian studies, economics, European studies, geography, history, Latin American studies, liberal arts/general studies, Middle Eastern studies, philosophy, political science/government, psychology, religion, Russian and Slavic studies, sociology, South Asian studies, and women's studies). Foreign languages, international studies, and sciences are the strongest academically. Economics, environmental studies, and political science have the largest enrollments.

ACTIVITIES: There are no fraternities or sororities. There are 178 groups on campus, including art, band, cheerleading, chess, choir, chorus, communications, computers, dance, debate, drama, environmental, ethnic, film, honors, international, jazz band, LGBT, literary magazine, Middlebury Mountain Club, musical theater, newspaper, orchestra, pep band, photography, political, professional, radio and TV, religious, social, social service, student government, and yearbook. Popular campus events include Winter Carnival, Student Concert Series, and Clifford Symposium. **Sports:** There are 12 intercollegiate sports for men and 11 for women, and 16 intramural sports for men and 16 for women. Middlebury's well-maintained playing fields and outstanding athletic facilities rank among the best in the country. Facilities include a 3,500-

seat football and lacrosse complex, baseball and softball fields, 18-hole golf course, 3.5-km cross country trail, 2,200-seat hockey arena, Olympic-size natatorium, squash courts, tennis courts, climbing wall, gymnasium, 6,500-square-foot fitness center, astro-turf fields, and all-weather outdoor track. **Graduates:** From July 1, 2015 to June 30, 2016, 651 bachelor's degrees were awarded. The most popular majors were economics (20%), political science (6%), and environmental studies (6%). In an average class, 85% graduate in 4 years or less, 93% graduate in 5 years or less, and 93% graduate in 6 years or less. Of the 2015 graduating class, 12% were enrolled in graduate school within 6 months of graduation, and 55% were employed.

SERVICES: Counseling and information services are available, as is tutoring in every subject. There is a reader service for the blind. **Library/Resources:** The 2 libraries contain 970,734 volumes, 620 microform items, and 74,487 audio/video tapes/CDs/DVDs, and subscribe to 181,350 periodicals including electronic. Computerized library services include interlibrary loans, database searching, Internet access, and Wi-Fi capability. Special learning facilities include an art gallery, planetarium, and radio station. **Physically Challenged Students:** 65% of the campus is accessible. Facilities include wheelchair ramps, elevators, special parking, specially equipped restrooms, special class scheduling, lowered drinking fountains, lowered telephones, and special housing. **Special:** In addition to extensive study abroad opportunities, Middlebury College offers pre-professional combined programs as well as Washington semester, Maritime studies, and exchange programs with Spelman and Swarthmore Colleges and the Association of Vermont Independent Colleges. Other opportunities include a semester at Woods Hole Marine Biological Laboratory and dual-degree engineering programs with Dartmouth and Columbia. There is a chapter of Phi Beta Kappa and 38 departmental honors programs. **Visiting:** There are regularly scheduled orientations for prospective students, including campus tours and a group or individual interview. There are guides for informal visits and visitors may sit in on classes. To schedule a visit, contact the Admissions Office. **Campus Safety and Security:** Measures include 24-hour foot and vehicle patrol, emergency notification system, self-defense education, and security escort services. There are shuttle buses, emergency telephones, lighted pathways/sidewalks, controlled access to dorms/residences, a paid student patrol, a ski patrol at the Snow Bowl, and a special events staff.

REQUIREMENTS: The SAT or ACT is required. AP credits are accepted. Important factors in the admissions decision are leadership record, advanced placement or honors courses, evidence of special talent, personality/intangible qualities, extracurricular activities record, geographical diversity, recommendations by school officials, and parents or siblings attended your school. Candidates for the Bachelor of Arts degree must complete 36 courses. At least 18 of these courses must be Middlebury courses. Courses taken at Middlebury summer language schools or at the Middlebury Schools Abroad will count in the 18-course total and the grades will count in the undergraduate grade point average. **Procedure:** Freshmen are admitted fall and spring. Entrance exams should be taken by December of the senior year. There are early decision, early admissions, and deferred admissions plans. Early decision applications should be filed by November 1; regular applications, by January 1 for fall entry, along with a $65 fee. Notification of early decision is sent January 1; regular decision, March 30. 398 early decision candidates were accepted for the 2016-2017 class. 565 applicants were on the 2016 waiting list; 7 were admitted. Applications are accepted on-line. **Transfer Students:** 11 transfer students enrolled in 2015-2016. Transfer students must have the strongest academic record possible through high school and a minimum 3.0 average in college. 18 of 36 credits required for the bachelor's degree must be completed at Midd. **International Students:** There are 252 international students enrolled. The school actively recruits these students. They must take the TOEFL. They must also take the SAT or ACT and fulfill the same requirements as first-year applicants.

ADMISSIONS: 16% of the 2016-2017 applicants were accepted. The SAT scores for the 2016-2017 freshman class were: Critical Reading-- 9% between 500 and 599, 38% between 600 and 699, and 53% between 700 and 800. Math-- 10% between 500 and 599, 40% between 600 and 699, and 50% between 700 and 800. Writing-- 8% between 500 and 599, 35% between 600 and 699, and 57% between 700 and 800. The ACT scores were 1% between 18 and 23, 22% between 24 and 29, and 77% above 30. **Admissions Contact:** Greg Buckles, Dean of Admissions. Email: *admissions@middlebury.edu* Web: *www.middlebury.edu*

FINANCIAL AID: Midd is a member of CSS. The CSS/Profile, federal tax forms, and non-custodial profile are required. The FAFSA code is 003691. The priority date for freshman financial aid applications for fall entry is November 15. The deadline for filing freshman financial aid applications for fall entry is February 1.

NORWICH UNIVERSITY — C-3

www.norwich.edu

Northfield, VT 05663	**(802) 485-2001** **(800) 468-6679**
Fax: (802) 485-2032	**Email: nuadm@norwich.edu**
Full-time: 1360 men, 502 women	**Faculty:** 117; IIA, -$
Part-time: 34 men, 7 women	**Ph.D.s:** 85%
Graduate: 537 men, 211 women	**Student/Faculty:** 16 to 1
Year: semesters, summer session	**Tuition:** $21,000
Room & Board: $7374	**Freshman Class:** 1899 applied, 1470 accepted, 578 enrolled
SAT: required **ACT:** 22	**CEEB CODE:** 3669
Application Deadline: n/av	**COMPETITIVE**

Norwich University, founded in 1819, is the oldest private military college in the country and the birthplace of the Reserve Officers' Training Corps (ROTC). Norwich is a coeducational a four-year university where students choose either a military or civilian lifestyle. Norwich offers both undergraduate and graduate programs. There are 6 undergraduate schools and 2 graduate schools. In addition to regional accreditation, Norwich has baccalaureate program accreditation with ABET, ACBSP, NLN, and CAAHEP. The 1125-acre campus is in a rural area 11 miles south of Montpelier. Including any residence halls, there are 36 buildings.

STUDENT LIFE: 80% of undergraduates are from out of state, mostly the Northeast. Students are from 39 states, 13 foreign countries, and Canada. 82% are White; 3% African American; 3% Hispanic; 2% Asian American; 2% Foreign. **Male To Female Ratio:** 2.7:1. The average age of freshmen is 18; all undergraduates, 21. 25% do not continue beyond their first year; 52% remain to graduate. **Housing:** 1598 students can be accommodated in college housing, which includes single-sex and coed dorms. On-campus housing is guaranteed for the freshman year only and is available on a lottery system for upperclassmen. Priority is given to out-of-town students. 83% of students live on campus; of those, 85% remain on campus on weekends. Alcohol is not permitted. Upperclassmen may keep cars.

FACULTY/CLASSROOMS: 74% of faculty are male; 26% are female. 82% teach undergraduates, 82% do research, and 82% do both. No introductory courses are taught by graduate students. The average class size in an introductory lecture is 20; in a laboratory is 13; and in a regular course is 18.

PROGRAMS OF STUDY: Norwich confers B.A., B.S., and B.Arch. degrees. Associate degrees are also awarded. Bachelor's degrees are awarded in BIOLOGICAL SCIENCE (biochemistry and biology/biological science), BUSINESS (accounting, business administration and management, and business economics), COMMUNICATIONS AND THE ARTS (communications and English), COMPUTER AND PHYSICAL SCIENCE (chemistry, computer science, computer security and information assurance, geology, information sciences and systems, mathematics, and physics), EDUCATION (physical education), ENGINEERING AND ENVIRONMENTAL DESIGN (architecture, civil engineering, computer engineering, electrical/electronics engineering, environmental science, mechanical engineering, and military science), HEALTH PROFESSIONS (medical laboratory technology, nursing, and sports medicine), SOCIAL SCIENCE (criminal justice, history, international studies, liberal arts/general studies, peace studies, political science/government, and psychology). Engineering and architecture are the strongest academically. Criminal justice and nursing have the largest enrollments.

ACTIVITIES: There are no fraternities or sororities. There are 75 groups on campus, including band, cheerleading, chess, choir, chorus, communications, computers, drama, drill team, ethnic, honors, international, jazz band, literary magazine, marching band, musical theater, newspaper, orchestra, pep band, photography, political, professional, radio and TV, religious, social service, and student government. Popular campus events include Regimental Ball, Winter Carnival, and Junior Weekend.

Sports: There are 12 intercollegiate sports for men and 7 for women, and 8 intramural sports for men and 8 for women. Facilities include an ice hockey arena, a field house with an indoor track, indoor swimming pool, aerobics room, weight and wrestling rooms, playing fields and an outdoor track, basketball arena, and a hockey arena. **Graduates:** From July 1, 2015 to June 30, 2016, 269 bachelor's degrees were awarded. The most popular majors were criminal justice (18%), management (12%), and nursing/civil engineering (7%). 25 companies recruited on campus in 2015-2016. In an average class, 37% graduate in 4 years or less, 49% graduate in 5 years or less, and 52% graduate in 6 years or less.

SERVICES: Counseling and information services are available, as is tutoring in most subjects. There is remedial math, reading, and writing. **Library/Resources:** The library contains 245,931 volumes, 90,435 microform items, and 2,872 audio/video tapes/CDs/DVDs, and subscribes to 815 periodicals including electronic. Computerized library services include interlibrary loans, database searching, Internet access, and Wi-Fi capability. Special learning facilities include an art gallery, natural history museum, radio station, a greenhouse, and 5 computer labs. **Physically Challenged Students:** Facilities include wheelchair ramps, elevators, special parking, specially equipped restrooms, and lowered drinking fountains. **Special:** Norwich offers internships, a Washington semester, work-study on-and-off-campus for service organizations and criminal justice programs, a B.A.-B.S. degree in communiations, and study abroad in 15 countries through other schools and organizations and through the Vermont Overseas Studies Program. International studies majors must study abroad in a country whose language they are studying. There are 5 national honor societies, Phi Beta Kappa, and 5 departmental honors programs. **Visiting:** There are regularly scheduled orientations for prospective students, including meetings with representatives from admissions, financial aid, academic offices, including Dean of Students or Commandant's Office, athletics (if desired), and a campus tour. There are guides for informal visits, visitors may sit in on classes, and stay overnight. To schedule a visit, contact the Admissions, Main Office. **Campus Safety and Security:** Measures include 24-hour foot and vehicle patrol. There are lighted pathways/sidewalks.

REQUIREMENTS: The SAT or ACT is required. Applicants should graduate from an accredited secondary school with 18 academic credits or achieve the GED equivalent. AP and CLEP credits are accepted. Important factors in the admissions decision are leadership record, extracurricular activities record, and evidence of special talent. The total number of required credits and courses vary by program. All students are required to complete 3 credit hours in history and English 101-102, and 2 semesters in phys ed. A 2.0 GPA is required to graduate. **Procedure:** Freshmen are admitted fall and spring. Entrance exams should be taken starting with spring of the junior year. There is a rolling admissions plan. Application deadlines are open. Application fee is $35. 60 early decision candidates were accepted for the 2016-2017 class. Applications are accepted on-line. **Transfer Students:** 91 transfer students enrolled in 2015-2016. Transfer students should present a 2.0 GPA and meet all standards for entering freshmen. 60 of 116 credits required for the bachelor's degree must be completed at Norwich. **International Students:** There are 39 international students enrolled. They must take the TOEFL.

ADMISSIONS: 77% of the 2016-2017 applicants were accepted. The ACT scores were 40% below 12, 28% between 12 and 17, 20% between 18 and 23, 7% between 24 and 29, and 5% above 30. 30% of the current freshmen were in the top fifth of their class; 58% were in the top two fifths. 3 freshmen graduated first in their class. **Admissions Contact:** Karen McGarth, Dean of Enrollment Management. Email: *nuadm@norwich.edu* Web: *www.norwich.edu*

FINANCIAL AID: In 2016-2017, 97% of all full-time freshmen and 96% of continuing full-time students received some form of financial aid. 90% of all full-time freshmen and 89% of continuing full-time students received need-based aid. 50% of undergraduate students work part-time. Average annual earnings from campus work are $990. The average financial indebtedness of the 2016 graduate was $26,072. Norwich is a member of CSS. The CSS/Profile is required. The FAFSA code is 003692. The priority date for freshman financial aid applications for fall entry is March 1.

SAINT MICHAEL'S COLLEGE — A-2

www.smcvt.edu

Colchester, VT 05439 — **(802) 654-3000**, **(800) 762-8000**

Fax: (802) 654-2906 — **Email: admission@smcvt.edu**

Full-time: 894 men, 1077 women
Part-time: 15 men, 11 women
Graduate: 71 men, 299 women
Year: semesters, summer session
Room & Board: $10,975
SAT CR/M/W: 590/580/580 **ACT:** 26
Application Deadline: February 1

Faculty: 147; IIB, +$
Ph.D.s: 91%
Student/Faculty: 13 to 1
Tuition: $40,750
Freshman Class: 4767 applied, 3621 accepted, 478 enrolled
CEEB CODE: 3757
VERY COMPETITIVE+

Saint Michael's College, founded in 1904 by the Society of Saint Edmund. We are a selective Catholic liberal arts college. There is 1 undergraduate school and 1 graduate school. In addition to regional accreditation, Saint Michael's has baccalaureate program accreditation with ACS, ROPA, and CELPA. The 440-acre campus is in a suburban area 2 miles east of Burlington, Vermont. Including any residence halls, there are 52 buildings.

STUDENT LIFE: 83% of undergraduates are from out of state, mostly the Northeast. Students are from 33 states, 46 foreign countries, and Canada. 69% are from public schools. 85% are White; 4% Hispanic; 3% African American; 3% Foreign; 2% Asian American; 2% two or more races; 2% race unknown. 46% are Catholic; 34% claim no religious affiliation. **Female To Male Ratio:** 1.4:1. The average age of freshmen is 18; all undergraduates, 20. 13% do not continue beyond their first year; 76% remain to graduate. **Housing:** 2077 students can be accommodated in college housing, which includes single-sex and coed dorms and on-campus apartments. In addition, there are honors houses, special-interest houses, theme housing, substance-free housing, and ambassador housing (opportunity to live with international students). On-campus housing is guaranteed for all 4 years. 95% of students live on campus; of those, 90% remain on campus on weekends. All students may keep cars.

FACULTY/CLASSROOMS: 57% of faculty are male; 43% are female. All teach undergraduates, and all do research. No introductory courses are taught by graduate students. The average class size in an introductory lecture is 24; in a laboratory is 18; and in a regular course is 19.

PROGRAMS OF STUDY: Saint Michael's confers B.A. and B.S. degrees. Master's degrees are also awarded. Bachelor's degrees are awarded in AGRICULTURE (environmental studies), BIOLOGICAL SCIENCE (biochemistry, biology/biological science, and neurosciences), BUSINESS (accounting and business administration and management), COMMUNICATIONS AND THE ARTS (dramatic arts, English, fine arts, French, journalism, music, and Spanish), COMPUTER AND PHYSICAL SCIENCE (chemistry, computer science, information sciences and systems, mathematics, physical sciences, and physics), EDUCATION (art education, elementary education, foreign languages education, science education, and secondary education), ENGINEERING AND ENVIRONMENTAL DESIGN (preengineering), HEALTH PROFESSIONS (preallied health and prepharmacy), SOCIAL SCIENCE (American studies, anthropology, economics, gender studies, history, international relations, philosophy, political science/government, prelaw, psychology, religion, and sociology). Biology, mathematics, and history are the strongest academically. Business administration, biology, and psychology have the largest enrollments.

ACTIVITIES: There are no fraternities or sororities. There are 50 groups on campus, including mobilization of volunteer efforts club, cycling, skiing, wilderness program, art, band, choir, chorale, chorus, communications, dance, drama, environmental, ethnic, film, fire and rescue, honors, international, jazz band, LGBT, literary magazine, musical theater, newspaper, photography, political, professional, radio and TV, religious, social, social service, student government, and yearbook. Popular campus events include Family Weekend, Homecoming, Martin Luther King, Jr. Convocation, Research Symposium, and Jib Fest. **Sports:** There are 10 intercollegiate sports for men and 11 for women, and 15 intramural sports for men and 15 for women. Facilities include a gym and field house with basketball, volleyball, tennis, and badminton courts, multipurpose courts, a swimming pool, fitness center, training room, weight room, climbing wall, pool, table tennis, suspended track, soccer, racquetball and squash courts, field hockey, lacrosse, baseball, and softball fields. **Graduates:** From July 1, 2015 to June 30, 2016, 468 bachelor's degrees were awarded. The most popular majors were social sciences (24%), business administration and accounting (22%), and biological/life sciences (12%). 72 companies recruited on campus in 2015-2016. In an average class, 73% graduate in 4 years or less, 74% graduate in 5 years or less, and 76% graduate in 6 years or less. Of the 2015 graduating class, 13% were enrolled in graduate school within 6 months of graduation, and 70% were employed.

SERVICES: Counseling and information services are available, as is tutoring in every subject. Tutoring can be arranged on an individual basis. The following are available: peer tutoring, writing center, quantitative skills, study skills, and research help. **Library/Resources:** The library contains 469,578 volumes, 137,000 microform items, and 12,984 audio/video tapes/CDs/DVDs, and subscribes to 13,000 periodicals including electronic. Computerized library services include interlibrary loans, database searching, Internet access, and Wi-Fi capability. Special learning facilities include an art gallery, radio station, an observatory, the Maker Space, and McCarthy Arts Center. **Physically Challenged Students:** 75% of the campus is accessible. Facilities include wheelchair ramps, elevators, special parking, specially equipped restrooms, special class scheduling, lowered drinking fountains, lowered telephones, and special housing. Other accommodations are provided on an individual basis. **Special:** A variety of special academic programs and enriching academic experiences are available at Saint Michael's College. During the most recent academic year over 40% of our graduates participated in a "for credit" internship, most of which were associated with the student's major. On-campus work-study opportunities are available in departments and offices throughout the College. Students can choose from more than 100 study abroad programs in countries spanning the globe. There are also opportunities for semester-long domestic "study away" programs including a Washington semester with American University. Student-designed majors may be pursued and nearly 20% of our most recent graduating class completed a double major. During the last four years an average of nearly 40% of the graduating classes participated in "for credit" study abroad experiences including summer and winter sessions as well as short-term faculty-led programs. The college offers a 3-2 engineering degree program in cooperation with Clarkson University and the University of Vermont and a 4+1 graduate business program is available with Clarkson University. A B.S./Pharm.D. degree is also available with the Albany College of Pharmacy and Health Services. Non-degree study and pass/fail grading options are offered on a limited basis. Independent research and undergraduate research opportunities with faculty are available through most departments. There are 11 national honor societies, Phi Beta Kappa, a freshman honors program, and 1 departmental honors programs. **Visiting:** There are regularly scheduled orientations for prospective students. A campus visit begins with a group information session led by an admission counselor, which includes information about admission criteria and financial aid. It is followed by a student-led tour. Informational interviews are also available. There are guides for informal visits, visitors may sit in on classes, and stay overnight. To schedule a visit, contact the Admissions Office. **Campus Safety and Security:** Measures include 24-hour foot and vehicle patrol, emergency notification system, self-defense education, and security escort services. There are shuttle buses, emergency telephones, lighted pathways/sidewalks, controlled access to dorms/residences. There is also a campus fire, and rescue squad.

REQUIREMENTS: The SAT or ACT and ACT Writing Test are recommended. Applicants must graduate from an accredited secondary school or have a GED. They must complete 16 Carnegie units. The college requires 4 credits in English, 3 to 4 credits in math and science, and 3 credits each in history, social studies, and a foreign language. An essay is required and an interview is recommended. Stanardized tests are optional. There are three application deadlines: Early Action 1- November 1, Early Action 2- December 1, Regular Decision- February 1. AP and CLEP credits are accepted. Important factors in the admissions decision are advanced placement or honors courses, evidence of special talent, and recommendations by school officials. To earn the degree of Bachelor of Arts or the degree of Bachelor of Science a student must: Complete a minimum of 128 credit hours (equivalent to 32 full-courses). Complete the degree requirements of one of the established majors or a self-designated major approved by the Curriculum and Education Policy Committee. Complete the Liberal Studies Curriculum requirements (see below). Achieve a minimum cumulative quality point average of 2.0 and a minimum of a 2.0 average in courses taken in the major. Complete a minimum of twenty-four of the last thirty-two credits at Saint Michael's. Transfer students, must earn a minimum of sixty-four credits at Saint Michael's College. The Liberal Studies Curriculum (LSC) is fulfilled through specific course requirement options and courses within the student's major field. Areas of study within the LSC include: Fundamental Philosophical Questions, Study of Christian Traditions and Thought, Ethical Decision Making, Global Issues that Impact the Common Good, Historical Studies, Literary Studies, Processes of Scientific Reasoning, Quantitative Reasoning, Second Language (depending on placement), Social and Institutional Dimensions of Human Behavior, Artistic Experience, Experiential Learning, and Oral and Written Communication. **Procedure:** Freshmen are admitted fall and spring. Entrance exams should be taken in the fall of the senior year. There are early admissions and deferred admissions plans. Applications should be filed by February 1 for fall entry; December 1 for winter entry; and November 1 for spring entry, along with a $50 fee. Notifications are sent April 1. 45 applicants were on the 2016 waiting list. Applications are accepted on-line. **Transfer Students:** 22 transfer students enrolled in 2015-2016. Transfer applicants must have a minimum GPA of 3.0; generally. The SAT is optional. An interview is recommended. 64 of 128 credits required for the bachelor's degree must be completed at Saint Michael's. **International Students:** There are 63 international students enrolled. The school actively recruits these students. They must take the TOEFL with a minimum score of 550 on the paper-based TOEFL (PBT) or 79 on the Internet-based version (iBT) and the college's own test. The SAT or ACT is optional for international students but recommended. The TOEFL may be used in place of the SAT.

ADMISSIONS: 76% of the 2016-2017 applicants were accepted. The SAT scores for the 2016-2017 freshman class were: Critical Reading-- 8% below 500, 36% between 500 and 599, 45% between 600 and 699, and 10% between 700 and 800. Math-- 4% below 500, 41% between 500 and 599, 43% between 600 and 699, and 11% between 700 and 800. Writing-- 6% below 500, 36% between 500 and 599, 44% between 600 and 699, and 14% between 700 and 800. The ACT scores were 2% between 12 and 17, 18% between 18 and 23, 65% between 24 and 29, and 15% above 30. 50% of the current freshmen were in the top fifth of their class; 74% were in the top two fifths. 5 freshmen graduated first in their class. **Admissions Contact:** Jacqueline Murphy, Director of Office of Admission. Email: *admission@smcvt.edu* Web: *www.smcvt.edu*

FINANCIAL AID: In 2016-2017, 99% of all full-time freshmen and 98% of continuing full-time students received some form of financial aid. 64% of all full-time freshmen and 64% of continuing full-time students received need-based aid. The average freshman award was $30,000. Need-based scholarships or need-based grants averaged $22,340 ($40,425 maximum); need-based self-help aid (loans and jobs) averaged $6,370 ($13,250 maximum); non-need-based athletic scholarships averaged $52,095 ($51,725 maximum); and other non-need-based awards and non-need-based scholarships averaged $17,140 ($40,425 maximum). 39% of undergraduate students work part-time. Average annual earnings from campus work are $1750. The average financial indebtedness of the 2016 graduate was $26,841. Saint Michael's is a member of CSS. The FAFSA code is 003694. The deadline for filing freshman financial aid applications for fall entry is February 1.

SOUTHERN VERMONT COLLEGE *(The complete profile is made available exclusively on our website, www.barronspac.com)*

STERLING COLLEGE — B-1
www.sterlingcollege.edu

Craftsbury Common, VT 05827 — **(802) 586-7711** **(800) 648-3591**

Fax: (802) 586-2596 — **Email:** admission@sterlingcollege.edu

Full-time: 57 men, 46 women	**Faculty:** 14
Part-time: 1 man, 1 woman	**Ph.D.s:** 29%
Graduate: n/av	**Student/Faculty:** 7 to 1
Year: semesters, summer session	**Tuition:** $32,790
Room & Board: $9104	**Freshman Class:** 97 applied, 74 accepted, 30 enrolled
SAT or ACT: required	**CEEB CODE:** 3752
Application Deadline: February 15	**VERY COMPETITIVE**

Sterling College is a small and progressive liberal arts college in northern

Vermont. Our small size, our environmental focus, and our commitment to grassroots sustainability all make us unique. We offer a liberal arts education through the lens of ecology. There is 1 undergraduate school. The 430-acre campus is in a rural area 40 miles north of Montpelier and 60 miles from Burlington. Including any residence halls, there are 16 buildings.

STUDENT LIFE: 82% of undergraduates are from out of state, mostly the Northeast. Students are from 22 states. 70% are White; 2% Hispanic. **Male To Female Ratio:** 1.2:1. The average age of freshmen is 19; all undergraduates, 21. 33% do not continue beyond their first year; 60% remain to graduate. **Housing:** 90 students can be accommodated in college housing, which includes coed dorms. On-campus housing is guaranteed for all 4 years. 77% of students live on campus. All students may keep cars.

FACULTY/CLASSROOMS: 50% of faculty are male; 50% are female. All teach undergraduates, 25% do research, and 25% do both. No introductory courses are taught by graduate students. The average class size in an introductory lecture is 12; in a laboratory is 12; and in a regular course is 12.

PROGRAMS OF STUDY: Sterling confers B.A. degrees. Bachelor's degrees are awarded in AGRICULTURE (agriculture), BIOLOGICAL SCIENCE (ecology), SOCIAL SCIENCE (humanities and social science). Ecology, sustainable agriculture, and sustainable food systems are the strongest academically. Sustainable agriculture, sustainable food systems, and ecology have the largest enrollments.

ACTIVITIES: There are no fraternities or sororities. Groups on campus include veterans, diversity, folk music, art, environmental, LGBT, photography, social, social and environmental justice, student government, and yearbook. Popular campus events include All-College Work Days, Earth Day, and Annual Wood Projects Show. **Sports:** There are 2 intercollegiate sports for men and 2 for women, and 1 intramural sports for men and 1 for women. Facilities include a climbing tower, nature trails on campus, and nationally recognized cross-country ski trails managed by a nearby sports center. There is a soccer field and access to a gym at a local high school. **Graduates:** From July 1, 2015 to June 30, 2016, 27 bachelor's degrees were awarded. 30 companies recruited on campus in 2015-2016. In an average class, 40% graduate in 4 years or less, 52% graduate in 5 years or less, and 56% graduate in 6 years or less. Of the 2015 graduating class, 30% were employed within 6 months of graduation.

SERVICES: Counseling and information services are available, as is tutoring in every subject. There is remedial math. Students seek assistance directly from faculty or teacher assistants. In addition, there is a learning support coordinator as well as a writing center. **Library/Resources:** The 2 libraries contain 13,630 volumes, and 600 audio/video tapes/CDs/DVDs, and subscribe to 127 periodicals including electronic. Computerized library services include interlibrary loans, database searching, Internet access, and Wi-Fi capability. Special learning facilities include an art gallery, a woodshop, darkroom, managed woodlot, organic garden, working livestock farm, greenhouse, blacksmith shop, sugar house, sugar bush, and a 300-acre boreal forest/wetland research area. **Physically Challenged Students:** Facilities include wheelchair ramps and specially equipped restrooms. **Special:** Internships are required. Study abroad, work study, and student-designed majors are available. We are the only federally recognized Work College in the Northeast; all students, regardless of financial aid, must work on campus. **Visiting:** There are regularly scheduled orientations for prospective students, including a student-led campus tour, an interview with admissions, and a meal in the dining hall. Weekend Open Houses offer a more comprehensive view of the college. There are 2 open houses per year. Monday Visit Days are similar to open houses, but students may sit in on classes. There are guides for informal visits, visitors may sit in on classes, and stay overnight. To schedule a visit, contact Tim Patterson at tpatterson@sterlingcollege.edu. **Campus Safety and Security:** Measures include emergency notification system.

REQUIREMENTS: Well-written essays, quality of the interview, and the comments provided by references are equal to the value of high school and college transcripts. Home-schooled students are strongly encouraged to contact the admissions office to discuss their particular needs and interests. AP credits are accepted. Important factors in the admissions decision are advanced placement or honors courses, recommendations by school officials, and leadership record. Candidates for the Bachelor of Arts degree must earn a minimum of 120 credits with a minimum cumulative Q.P.A. of 2.0 and pass the Mathematics Competency requirement. Candidates must also complete all required Core Courses, complete six credits each of Natural Science, Social Science, and Humanities electives, including a minimum of four credits emphasizing textual analysis and written critical response, and complete an approved major. All resident students must receive a satisfactory grade in the College's Work Program during their final semester of academic enrollment. Non-resident students must receive a satisfactory grade in their final semester of record in the College's Work Program. **Procedure:** Freshmen are admitted fall and spring. There are early decision, early admissions, and deferred admissions plans. Early decision applications should be filed by November 15; regular applications, by February 15 for fall entry, along with a $35 fee. Notification of early decision is sent December 15; regular decision, April 1. One early decision candidate was accepted for the 2016-2017 class. Applications are accepted on-line. **Transfer Students:** 15 transfer students enrolled in 2015-2016. In addition to the standard application, transfer students must provide copies of college transcripts. They may begin in the spring semester. 30 of 120 credits required for the bachelor's degree must be completed at Sterling. **International Students:** There are 4 international students enrolled. The school actively recruits these students. They must take the TOEFL with a minimum score of 500 on the paper-based TOEFL (PBT).

ADMISSIONS: 76% of the 2016-2017 applicants were accepted. 20% of the current freshmen were in the top fifth of their class; 40% were in the top two fifths. **Admissions Contact:** Tim Patterson, Director of Admission. Email: *admission@sterlingcollege.edu* Web: *www.sterlingcollege.edu*

FINANCIAL AID: In 2016-2017, 100% of all full-time freshmen and 100% of continuing full-time students received some form of financial aid. 90% of all full-time freshmen and 95% of continuing full-time students received need-based aid. The average freshman award was $22,000. Need-based scholarships or need-based grants averaged $15,000 ($35,000 maximum); need-based self-help aid (loans and jobs) averaged $10,000 ($30,000 maximum); and other non-need-based awards and non-need-based scholarships averaged $10,000 ($20,000 maximum). 100% of undergraduate students work part-time. Average annual earnings from campus work are $1500. The FAFSA code is 014991. The priority date for freshman financial aid applications for fall entry is March 1. The deadline for filing freshman financial aid applications for fall entry is April 1.

UNIVERSITY OF VERMONT — A-2

www.uvm.edu

Burlington, VT 05401 — **(802) 656-3370**

Fax: (802) 656-8611	**Email: admissions@uvm.edu**
Full-time: 4381 men, 5802 women	**Faculty:** I, -$
Part-time: 428 men, 548 women	**Ph.D.s:** 84%
Graduate: 787 men, 1159 women	**Student/Faculty:** 16 to 1
Year: semesters, summer session	**Tuition:** $17,300 ($40,364)
Room & Board: $11,578	**Freshman Class:** 24234 applied, 17793 accepted, 2310 enrolled
SAT CR/M/W: 592/595/591 **ACT:** 27	**CEEB CODE:** 3920
Application Deadline: January 15	**HIGHLY COMPETITIVE**

University of Vermont, established in 1791, is a public, land-grant, comprehensive institution with a dual focus on teaching and research. Its undergraduate and graduate offerings include the liberal arts, business administration, engineering, math, natural resources, agricultural studies, fine arts, teacher preparation, social services, environmental studies, and health sciences, including nursing. There are 7 undergraduate schools and 2 graduate schools. In addition to regional accreditation, UVM has baccalaureate program accreditation with AACSB, ABET, APTA, ASLA, CAHEA, CSWE, NCATE, and CCNE. The 460-acre campus is in a suburban area 90 miles south of Montreal, and 200 miles north of Boston. Including any residence halls, there are 115 buildings.

STUDENT LIFE: 69% of undergraduates are from out of state, mostly the Northeast. Students are from 48 states, 50 foreign countries, and Canada. 88% are White; 4% Hispanic; 3% Foreign; 2% Asian American; 1% African American. 40% claim no religious affiliation **Female To Male Ratio:** 1.3:1. The average age of freshmen is 18; all undergraduates, 20. 13% do not continue beyond their first year; 75% remain to graduate. **Housing:** 5500 students can be accommodated in college housing, which includes coed dorms, on-campus apartments, off-campus apartments, married student housing, honors houses, language houses, special-interest houses, fraternity houses, and sorority houses. In addition, the living/learning center provides an integrated, theme-based academic, and residential option. On-campus housing is guaranteed for all 4 years and is available on a lottery system for upperclassmen. 50% of students commute. Upperclassmen may keep cars.

FACULTY/CLASSROOMS: 58% of faculty are male; 42% are female. Graduate students teach 2% of introductory courses. The average class size in a regular course is 31.

PROGRAMS OF STUDY: UVM confers B.A., B.S., B.Mus., B.S.A.E., B.S.B.A., B.S.Ed., B.S.C.E., B.S.C.S., B.S.E.E., B.S.E.M., B.S.M., B.S.M.E., and B.S.M.S. degrees. Master's and doctoral degrees are also awarded. Bachelor's degrees are awarded in AGRICULTURE (agriculture, animal science, environmental studies, fishing and fisheries, forestry and related sciences, horticulture, natural resource management, and plant science), BIOLOGICAL SCIENCE (biochemistry, biology/biological science, botany, genetics, microbiology, molecular biology, neurosciences, nutrition, wildlife biology, and zoology), BUSINESS (business administration and management, entrepreneurial studies, and international economics), COMMUNICATIONS AND THE ARTS (art, art history and appreciation, Chinese, classics, communications, dramatic arts, English, film arts, French, German, Greek, Japanese, Latin, linguistics, music, Russian, and Spanish), COMPUTER AND PHYSICAL SCIENCE (chemistry, computer science, geology, information sciences and systems, mathematics, physics, and statistics), EDUCATION (art education, athletic training, early childhood education, education, elementary education, English education, foreign languages education, mathematics education, middle school education, music education, physical education, science education, secondary education, social studies education, and special education), ENGINEERING AND ENVIRONMENTAL DESIGN (civil engineering, electrical/electronics engineering, engineering, engineering management, environmental engineering, environmental science, landscape architecture/design, and mechanical engineering), HEALTH PROFESSIONS (biomedical science, exercise science, medical laboratory science, nuclear medical technology, nursing, radiation therapy, and speech pathology/audiology), SOCIAL SCIENCE (anthropology, area studies, Asian/Oriental studies, child care/child and family studies, dietetics, economics, ethnic studies, European studies, food science, gender studies, geography, history, human development, Italian studies, Latin American studies, parks and recreation management, philosophy, political science/government, psychology, religion, Russian and Slavic studies, social work, and sociology). Business administration, psychology, and biology/biological science have the largest enrollments.

ACTIVITIES: 6% of men belong to 9 national fraternities; 6% of women belong to 6 national sororities. There are 170 groups on campus, including outing club, art, band, cheerleading, chess, choir, chorale, chorus, communications, community service, computers, dance, debate, drama, environmental, ethnic, honors, international, jazz band, LGBT, literary magazine, musical theater, newspaper, orchestra, pep band, photography, political, professional, radio and TV, religious, social, social service, and student government. Popular campus events include Winterfest, Community Serve-a-thon, and Sugar on Snow day. **Sports:** There are 8 intercollegiate sports for men and 10 for women, and 24 intramural sports for men and 24 for women. Facilities include a gym, an ice hockey stadium, turffield, a field house, soccer and baseball fields, fitness center, indoor and outdoor tracks, a natatorium, indoor tennis courts, racquetball court, and dance studio. **Graduates:** From July 1, 2015 to June 30, 2016, 2319 bachelor's degrees were awarded. The most popular majors were business (8%), psychology (5%), and English (4%). 170 companies recruited on campus in 2015-2016. In an average class, 62% graduate in 4 years or less, 75% graduate in 5 years or less, and 75% graduate in 6 years or less. Of the 2015 graduating class, 24% were enrolled in graduate school within 6 months of graduation, and 85% were employed.

SERVICES: Counseling and information services are available, as is tutoring in most subjects. There is a reader service for the blind. There is also supplemental instruction, note-taking and test-taking seminars, time management instruction, outreach programs, exam proctoring, and writing tutors, as well as support for ESL students. **Library/Resources:** The 2 libraries contain 2.5 million volumes, 2.0 million microform items, and 55,310 audio/video tapes/CDs/DVDs, and subscribe to 30,000 periodicals including electronic. Computerized library services include interlibrary loans, database searching, Internet access, and Wi-Fi capability. Special learning facilities include an art gallery, radio station, TV station, a health care center (the University of Vermont Medical Center), 4 research farms, the Fleming Museum, geology museum, 9 natural areas, lakeshore science center, and aquatic research vessel. **Physically Challenged Students:** 90% of the campus is accessible. Facilities include wheelchair ramps, elevators, special parking, specially equipped restrooms, special class scheduling, lowered drinking fountains, and lowered telephones. First-priority routes in poor weather, a TTY phone system for hearing-impaired students, and closed-caption video decoders are available. **Special:** Special academic programs include co-op programs, internships in every discipline, study abroad in 110 countries, a Washington semester, work-study, an accelerated degree program in computer science,secondary education, and public administration, RN-BS-MS, dual majors, and student-designed majors. In addition, a 3-4 veterinary medicine degree is offered with Tufts University. There are 25 national honor societies, Phi Beta Kappa, a freshman honors program, and 14 departmental honors programs. **Visiting:** There are regularly scheduled orientations for prospective students, group information sessions and tours most weekdays and many Saturdays year round. Visitors may sit in on classes. To schedule a visit, contact the Admissions Office. **Campus Safety and Security:** Measures include 24-hour foot and vehicle patrol, emergency notification system, self-defense education, and security escort services. There are shuttle buses, emergency telephones, lighted pathways/sidewalks, controlled access to dorms/residences, bike registration, identification of property, and 18 fully certified police officers.

REQUIREMENTS: The SAT or ACT is required. The ACT Optional Writing test is also required. Graduation from an accredited secondary school with 16 Carnegie units. Required high school course-work includes 4 years of English, 3 years each of social science and math, including algebra I and II and geometry, and 2 years each of the same foreign language and science (one of which must be a lab science). Some academic units require additional course-work. An essay must be submitted. The GED is also accepted. AP and CLEP credits are accepted. Important factors in the admissions decision are advanced placement or honors courses, extracurricular activities record, and recommendations by school officials. Degree requirements vary among the individual colleges, but all require at least a 2.0 GPA and 122 credit hours to graduate. Most students must enroll in at least 30 distribution credits (approximately 10 courses) in the arts, humanities, social sciences, languages, literature, math, and the sciences. All academic units require 2 courses in Race and Culture. **Procedure:** Freshmen are admitted fall and spring. Entrance exams should be taken by November of the senior year. There are early admissions and deferred admissions plans. Early decision applications should be filed by November 1; regular applications, by January 15 for fall entry; and November 1 for spring entry, along with a $55 fee. Notification of early decision is sent December 15; regular decision, March 15. 3094 applicants were on the 2016 waiting list; 103 were admitted. Applications are accepted on-line. **Transfer Students:** 600 transfer students enrolled in 2015-2016. Successful transfer students have a cumulative grade point average of at least 2.8 in credited courses and meet the same entrance requirements as first-year applicants. Considerations include the college and high school records, the major indicated, and availability of space at UVM. 30 of 122 credits required for the bachelor's degree must be completed at UVM. **International Students:** There are 268 international students enrolled. The school actively recruits these students. They must take the TOEFL with a minimum score of 90 on the Internet-based version (iBT), or take the IELTS. They must also take the SAT or ACT.

ADMISSIONS: 73% of the 2016-2017 applicants were accepted. The SAT scores for the 2016-2017 freshman class were: Critical Reading-- 8% below 500, 42% between 500 and 599, 41% between 600 and 699, and 9% between 700 and 800. Math-- 8% below 500, 42% between 500 and 599, 41% between 600 and 699, and 9% between 700 and 800. Writing-- 10% below 500, 42% between 500 and 599, 41% between 600 and 699, and 7% between 700 and 800. The ACT scores were 5% below 12, 12% between 12 and 17, 29% between 18 and 23, 23% between 24 and 29, and 31% above 30. 55% of the current freshmen were in the top fifth of their class; 88% were in the top two fifths. There were 2 National Merit finalists. **Admissions Contact:** Dr. Beth A. Wiser, Director of Admission. Email: *admissions@uvm.edu* Web: *www.uvm.edu*

FINANCIAL AID: In 2016-2017, 94% of all full-time freshmen and 84% of continuing full-time students received some form of financial aid. 62% of all full-time freshmen and 56% of continuing full-time students received need-based aid. The average freshman award was $18,810. Need-based scholarships or need-based grants averaged $16,621 ($52,299 maximum). The average financial indebtedness of the 2016 graduate was $25,783. The FAFSA code is 003696. The priority date for freshman financial aid applications for fall entry is February 10.

VERMONT TECHNICAL COLLEGE C-4
www.vtc.edu

Randolph Center, VT 05061 **(802) 728-1000**

Email: admissions@vtc.edu

Full-time: 655 men, 378 women	**Faculty:** 71; III, -$
Part-time: 165 men, 158 women	**Ph.D.s:** 54%
Graduate: n/av	**Student/Faculty:** 15 to 1
Year: semesters	**Tuition:** $13,850 ($16,034)
Room & Board: $9988	**Freshman Class:** 757 applied, 528 accepted, 314 enrolled
SAT or ACT: required	**CEEB CODE:** 3941
Application Deadline: n/av	**COMPETITIVE**

Vermont Tech College is the only public institution of higher learning in Vermont whose mission is applied education. Vermont Tech takes an optimistic, rooted and personal approach to education to support students in gaining the confidence and practical skills necessary to not only see their potential, but to experience it. Our academic programs encompass a wide range of engineering technology, agricultural, health, and business fields that are vital to producing the knowledgeable workers needed most by employers in the state and in the region. The figures in the above capsule and in this profile are approximate. There are 5 undergraduate schools. In addition to regional accreditation, VTC has baccalaureate program accreditation with ABET, NLNAC, AVMA, and CODA. The 544-acre campus is in a rural area in Randolph Center, VT. Including any residence halls, there are 19 buildings.

STUDENT LIFE: 60% of undergraduates are from Vermont. Others are from 12 states, and 2 foreign countries. 90% are from public schools. 94% are White; 2% Asian American; 2% Hispanic; 1% African American; 1% American Indian/Alaska Native. **Male To Female Ratio:** 1.5:1. The average age of freshmen is 25; all undergraduates, 26. 25% do not continue beyond their first year; 55% remain to graduate. **Housing:** 550 students can be accommodated in college housing, which includes single-sex and coed dorms. On-campus housing is guaranteed for all 4 years. 60% of students commute. All students may keep cars.

FACULTY/CLASSROOMS: 58% of faculty are male; 42% are female. All teach undergraduates. No introductory courses are taught by graduate students. The average class size in an introductory lecture is 28; in a laboratory is 16; and in a regular course is 32.

PROGRAMS OF STUDY: VTC confers B.S. degrees. Associate degrees are also awarded. Bachelor's degrees are awarded in COMPUTER AND PHYSICAL SCIENCE (information sciences and systems and software engineering), EDUCATION (business education), ENGINEERING AND ENVIRONMENTAL DESIGN (architectural engineering, computer engineering, and electromechanical technology). Electromechanical engineering technology is the strongest academically. Architectural engineering technology and business have the largest enrollments.

ACTIVITIES: There are no fraternities or sororities. Groups on campus include chess, computers, drama, ethnic, international, LGBT, photography, professional, radio and TV, religious, social, social service, and student government. Popular campus events include Harvest Days, Winter Carnival, and Spring Fling. **Sports:** There are 6 intercollegiate sports for men and 5 for women, and 21 intramural sports for men and 21 for women. Facilities include a double-court gym, racquetball courts, swimming pool, fitness center, outdoor soccer, baseball, and softball fields, trails for cross-country skiing, and a downhill ski run. **Graduates:** From July 1, 2015 to June 30, 2016, 64 bachelor's degrees were awarded. The most popular majors were business (37%) and electromechanical engineering (25%). 45 companies recruited on campus in 2015-2016. In an average class, 50% graduate in 4 years or less, 55% graduate in 5 years or less, and 59% graduate in 6 years or less. Of the 2015 graduating class, 97% were employed within 6 months of graduation.

SERVICES: Counseling and information services are available, as is tutoring in every subject. **Library/Resources:** The library contains 59,480 volumes, 5,920 microform items, and 4,122 audio/video tapes/CDs/DVDs, and subscribes to 348 periodicals including electronic. Computerized library services include interlibrary loans, database searching, and Internet access. Special learning facilities include a radio station, and the Vermont Interactive Technologies, and Anaerobic Digester. **Physically Challenged Students:** All of the campus is accessible. Facilities include wheelchair ramps, elevators, special parking, specially equipped restrooms, special class scheduling, lowered drinking fountains, and lowered telephones. **Special:** Cross-registration, internships, work-study programs, and dual majors are offered. There are 2 national honor societies, a freshman honors program, and 2 departmental honors programs. **Visiting:** There are regularly scheduled orientations for prospective students. There are guides for informal visits, visitors may sit in on classes, and stay overnight. To schedule a visit, contact the Admissions Office. **Campus Safety and Security:** Measures include 24-hour foot and vehicle patrol, self-defense education, and security escort services. There are emergency telephones and lighted pathways/sidewalks.

REQUIREMENTS: The SAT or ACT is required. AP and CLEP credits are accepted. To graduate, students must complete 120 to 130 credit hours with a minimum GPA of 2.0. Required courses include English, technical communications, math, and computer. **Procedure:** Freshmen are admitted fall and spring. There is a rolling admissions plan. Application deadlines are open. Application fee is $32. Applications are accepted on-line. **Transfer Students:** 251 transfer students enrolled in 2015-2016. Transcripts are required from all colleges attended. 50 of 120 credits required for the bachelor's degree must be completed at VTC. **International Students:** There are 2 international students enrolled. They must take the TOEFL. They must also take the SAT or ACT, and the college's own entrance exam.

ADMISSIONS: 70% of the 2016-2017 applicants were accepted. 23% of the current freshmen were in the top fifth of their class; 70% were in the top two fifths. **Admissions Contact:** Dwight Cross, Assistant Dean of Enrollment. Email: *admissions@vtc.edu* Web: *www.vtc.edu*

FINANCIAL AID: In 2016-2017, 77% of all full-time freshmen and 90% of continuing full-time students received some form of financial aid. 63% of all full-time freshmen and 73% of continuing full-time students received need-based aid. The average freshman award was $12,400. Need-based scholarships or need-based grants averaged $4,000 ($13,200 maximum); need-based self-help aid (loans and jobs) averaged $2,750 ($5,025 maximum); and other non-need-based awards and non-need-based scholarships averaged $5,650 ($37,800 maximum). 26% of undergraduate students work part-time. Average annual earnings from campus work are $800. The average financial indebtedness of the 2016 graduate was $12,000. The FAFSA code is 003698. The deadline for filing freshman financial aid applications for fall entry is March 1.

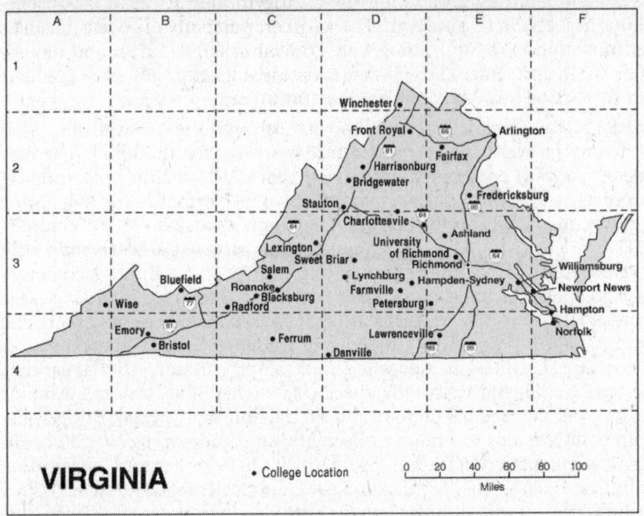

AVERETT UNIVERSITY *(The complete profile is made available exclusively on our website, www.barronspac.com)*

BLUEFIELD COLLEGE — B-3

www.bluefield.edu

Bluefield, VA 24605	**(276) 326-4339** **(800) 872-0175**
Fax: (276) 326-4288	**Email: admissions@bluefield.edu**
Full-time: 287 men, 405 women	**Faculty:** 33; IIB
Part-time: 27 men, 57 women	**Ph.D.s:** 61%
Graduate: n/av	**Student/Faculty:** 21 to 1
Year: semesters, summer session	**Tuition:** $24,570
Room & Board: $9550	**Freshman Class:** 731 applied, 358 accepted, 110 enrolled
SAT: required **ACT:** 21	**CEEB CODE:** 1523
Application Deadline: August 31	**COMPETITIVE+**

Bluefield College is a Christ-centered liberal arts college in covenant with the Baptist General Association of Virginia. We offer a challenging academic experience within a diverse Christian environment. Our academic and co-curricular programs transform students' lives by integrating liberal arts with career-oriented studies and service to God and the global community. We are committed to graduating students who think critically, communicate effectively, and adapt readily to a changing world. Figures in the above capsule and in this profile are approximate. There is 1 undergraduate school. In addition to regional accreditation, BC has baccalaureate program accreditation with TEAC and SCHEV. The 82-acre campus is in a small town 100 miles west of Roanoke on the Virginia-West Virginia state line. Including any residence halls, there are 26 buildings.

STUDENT LIFE: 80% of undergraduates are from Virginia. Others are from 19 states, and 2 foreign countries. 79% are White; 18% African American; 1% Asian American; 1% American Indian/Alaska Native; 1% Foreign. **Female To Male Ratio:** 1.5:1. **Housing:** 330 students can be accommodated in college housing, which includes single-sex dorms, on-campus apartments, and married student housing. On-campus housing is available on a lottery system for upperclassmen. 65% of students live on campus; of those, 60% remain on campus on weekends. All students may keep cars. Alcohol is not permitted.

FACULTY/CLASSROOMS: 70% of faculty are male; 30% are female. All teach undergraduates, 30% do research, and 30% do both. No introductory courses are taught by graduate students. The average class size in an introductory lecture is 17; in a laboratory is 12; and in a regular course is 10.

PROGRAMS OF STUDY: BC confers B.A., B.S., and M.A. degrees. Bachelor's degrees are awarded in BIOLOGICAL SCIENCE (biology/biological science), BUSINESS (business administration and management), COMMUNICATIONS AND THE ARTS (communications, English, fine arts, and music), COMPUTER AND PHYSICAL SCIENCE (chemistry and mathematics), EDUCATION (middle school education and secondary education), HEALTH PROFESSIONS (exercise science), SOCIAL SCIENCE (Christian studies, criminal justice, history, interdisciplinary studies, psychology, religion, and social studies). Business, teacher education, and biology are the strongest academically. Business, organizational management & development, and criminal justice have the largest enrollments.

ACTIVITIES: 5% of men belong to 2 local fraternities; 10% of women belong to 2 local sororities. There are 15 groups on campus, including art, cheerleading, choir, chorale, communications, dance, drama, honors, literary magazine, musical theater, newspaper, orchestra, professional, religious, social, and student government. Popular campus events include Homecoming and Mud Pig Day. **Sports:** There are 6 intramural sports for men and 6 for women. Facilities include a gym with game courts, excercise facility, student activities center, a game room, tennis courts, and a sand volleyball court. **Graduates:** From July 1, 2015 to June 30, 2016, 246 bachelor's degrees were awarded. 4 companies recruited on campus in 2015-2016. In an average class, 1% graduate in 3 years or less, 47% graduate in 4 years or less, 50% graduate in 5 years or less, and 55% graduate in 6 years or less. Of the 2015 graduating class, 16% were enrolled in graduate school within 6 months of graduation.

SERVICES: Counseling and information services are available, as is tutoring in most subjects, and remedial math and writing. **Library/Resources:** The library contains 47,000 volumes, 3,477 audio/video tapes/CDs/DVDs, and subscribes to 70,000 periodicals including electronic. Computerized library services include interlibrary loans, database searching, and Internet access. **Physically Challenged Students:** 95% of the campus is accessible. Facilities include wheelchair ramps, elevators, special parking, specially equipped restrooms, and lowered drinking fountains. **Special:** The college offers credit for life/military/work experience, nondegree study through the Fine Arts Community School, study abroad in England, an accelerated degree program in organizational management and development and in criminal justice, and internships in criminal justice, psychology, and recreation. There are 4 national honor societies, a freshman honors program, and 7 departmental honors programs. **Visiting:** There are regularly scheduled orientations for prospective students, including campus tours, opportunities to develop class schedules, and financial aid workshops. Visitors may sit in on classes and stay overnight. To schedule a visit, contact the Admissions Office. **Campus Safety and Security:** Measures include 24-hour foot and vehicle patrol, emergency notification system, security escort services, lighted pathways/sidewalks and controlled access to dorms/residences.

REQUIREMENTS: The SAT or ACT is required. Applicants must be graduates of an accredited secondary school or have a GED certificate, and have completed 4 years of English, 2 of social sciences, 1 of science, and 5 of electives. AP and CLEP credits are accepted. Important factors in the admissions decision are leadership record, advanced placement or honors courses, and recommendations by school officials. To graduate, students must have completed a minimum of 126 semester hours, including a liberal arts requirement of 51 to 53 hours, with 30 to 45 hours in the major, and a minimum 2.0 GPA. Other requirements vary per program. All graduates must demonstrate computer proficiency by testing, passing computer courses, or having components in required courses. **Procedure:** Freshmen are admitted to all sessions. Entrance exams should be taken early in the senior year. There are deferred admissions and rolling admissions plans. Applications should be filed by August 31 for fall entry, along with a $30 fee. Notification is sent on a rolling basis. Applications are accepted online. **Transfer Students:** 337 transfer students enrolled in 2015-2016. Prospective students must submit transcripts of all academic work, a financial aid transcript, and SAT or ACT scores if they have fewer than 30 hours of college level work. 32 of 126 credits required for the bachelor's degree must be completed at BC. **International Students:** There are 2 international students enrolled. The school actively recruits these students. They must take the TOEFL.

ADMISSIONS: 49% of the 2016-2017 applicants were accepted. The ACT scores were 57% below 12, 20% between 12 and 17, 13% between 18 and 23, 3% between 24 and 29, and 7% above 30. 38% of the current freshmen were in the top fifth of their class; 64% were in the top two fifths. **Admissions Contact:** Evan Sherman, Director of Admissions. Email: *esherman@bluefield.edu* Web: *www.bluefield.edu*

FINANCIAL AID: The college's own financial statement is required. The FAFSA code is 003703. The deadline for filing freshman financial aid applications for fall entry is March 10.

BRIDGEWATER COLLEGE D-2

www.bridgewater.edu

Bridgewater, VA 22812 **(540) 828-5469** **(800) 759-8328**

Fax: (540) 828-5481 **Email: admissions@bridgewater.edu**

Full-time: 873 men, 1003 women	**Faculty:** 115; IIB, --$
Part-time: 3 men, 3 women	**Ph.D.s:** 80%
Graduate: n/av	**Student/Faculty:** 16 to 1
Year: 4-1-4, summer session	**Tuition:** $32,590
Room & Board: $11,920	**Freshman Class:** 7486 applied, 3949 accepted, 600 enrolled
SAT CR/M/W: 500/510/480 **ACT:** 24	**CEEB CODE:** 5069
Application Deadline: May 1	**COMPETITIVE**

Bridgewater College, founded in 1880, is a private liberal arts institution affiliated with the Church of the Brethren. There is 1 undergraduate school. In addition to regional accreditation, Bridgewater has baccalaureate program accreditation with CAATE. The 300-acre campus is in a small town 2 hours southwest of Washington D.C., and 8 miles south of Harrisonburg, Virginia. Including any residence halls, there are 44 buildings.

STUDENT LIFE: 73% of undergraduates are from Virginia. Others are from 28 states, 17 foreign countries, and Canada. 92% are from public schools. 68% are White; 6% Hispanic; 6% two or more races; 5% race unknown; 13% African American; 1% Asian American; 1% Foreign. 53% are Protestant; 29% claim no religious affiliation. **Female To Male Ratio:** 1.1:1. The average age of freshmen is 18; all undergraduates, 20. 22% do not continue beyond their first year; 66% remain to graduate. **Housing:** 1522 students can be accommodated in college housing, which includes single-sex and coed dorms, on-campus apartments, and honors houses. 82% of students live on campus; of those, 60% remain on campus on weekends. Alcohol is not permitted. All students may keep cars.

FACULTY/CLASSROOMS: 52% of faculty are male; 48% are female. All teach undergraduates, 50% do research, and 50% do both. No introductory courses are taught by graduate students. The average class size in an introductory lecture is 22; in a laboratory is 14; and in a regular course is 17.

PROGRAMS OF STUDY: Bridgewater confers B.A., B.S., and B.G.S. degrees. Bachelor's degrees are awarded in BIOLOGICAL SCIENCE (biochemistry, biology/biological science, and nutritional sciences), BUSINESS (business administration and management and management information systems), COMMUNICATIONS AND THE ARTS (art, communications, English, French, music, and Spanish), COMPUTER AND PHYSICAL SCIENCE (applied chemistry, applied physics, chemistry, computer science, mathematics, physics and mathematics, and physics), EDUCATION (athletic training, global studies, and health and physical education), ENGINEERING AND ENVIRONMENTAL DESIGN (environmental science), HEALTH PROFESSIONS (exercise science), SOCIAL SCIENCE (economics, family/consumer studies, history, history and political science, liberal arts/general studies, philosophy and religion, political science/government, psychology, and sociology). Biology, chemistry, and English are the strongest academically. Business administration, biology, and health/exercise science have the largest enrollments.

ACTIVITIES: There are no fraternities or sororities. There are 79 groups on campus, including band, cheerleading, choir, chorale, chorus, communications, computers, dance, drama, environmental, ethnic, honors, international, jazz band, LGBT, literary magazine, newspaper, pep band, political, professional, radio and TV, religious, social, social service, student government, and yearbook. Popular campus events include Homecoming, Welcome Week Activities, and Spring Fest. **Sports:** There are 9 intercollegiate sports for men and 11 for women, and 24 intramural sports for men and 24 for women. Facilities include a gym, football stadium, swimming pool, tennis courts, an all-weather track, playing fields for baseball, lacrosse, softball, football, field hockey, and soccer, fitness center with basketball, volleyball, racquetball courts, indoor track, cardiac and weight-training center, aerobics/dance rooms, and an equestrian center. **Graduates:** From July 1, 2015 to June 30, 2016, 422 bachelor's degrees were awarded. The most popular majors were business administration (19%), health and exercise science (13%), and biology (11%). In an average class, 58% graduate in 4 years or less, 65% graduate in 5 years or less, and 66% graduate in 6 years or less.

SERVICES: Counseling and information services are available, as is tutoring in every subject, and a reader service for the blind. The academic support center provides services that assist students in their development of skills necessary for effective performance in a learning environment. **Library/Resources:** The library contains 133,901 volumes, 5,096 microform items, 5,892 audio/video tapes/CDs/DVDs, and subscribes to 51,812 periodicals including electronic. Computerized library services include interlibrary loans, database searching, Internet access, and Wi-Fi capability. Special learning facilities include an art gallery and radio station. **Physically Challenged Students:** 95% of the campus is accessible. Facilities include wheelchair ramps, elevators, special parking, specially equipped restrooms, special class scheduling, lowered drinking fountains, lowered telephones, and special housing. **Special:** Bridgewater offers internships to junior and seniors; study abroad in over 50 countries; participation in the Smithsonian-Mason Semester for Conservation Studies; and a teacher certification program in elementary and secondary education. Interdisciplinary majors include environmental science, history and political science, global studies, liberal studies, nutrition and wellness, philosophy and religion, and physics and math. Dual-degree programs are offered in engineering with George Washington University (3-2) and Virginia Tech (3-2), in physical therapy with Shenandoah University (3-4), and in nursing with Vanderbilt University (3-2). There are 9 national honor societies, a freshman honors program, and 16 departmental honors programs. **Visiting:** There are regularly scheduled orientations for prospective students, Information on academic programs, student services, housing options, student organizations, intercollegiate athletics, financial aid and campus events. Also includes placement tests and assistance with pre-registration from faculty advisors. There are guides for informal visits and visitors may sit in on classes. To schedule a visit, contact the Admissions Office. **Campus Safety and Security:** Measures include 24-hour foot and vehicle patrol, emergency notification system, self-defense education, security escort services, emergency telephones, lighted pathways/sidewalks, and controlled access to dorms/residences.

REQUIREMENTS: The SAT or ACT is required, with the SAT preferred, and an interview is recommended. Applicants must be graduates of an accredited secondary school or have a GED certificate, and have completed 17 units, including 4 in English, 3 in math, 3 in science, 3 in history and social studies, and 4 electives. AP and CLEP credits are accepted. Important factors in the admissions decision are advanced placement or honors courses, recommendations by school officials, and leadership record. To graduate, all students must complete a minimum of 123 credit hours, with a minimum of 48 credit hours chosen from junior/senior level courses. A major consists of 32 to 54 credit hours. A minimum 2.0 GPA is required, overall and in the major. The BA and BS degrees are awarded as defined by the chosen major. Students must complete a course in Critical Inquiry in the Liberal Arts and an e-senior portfolio requirement. Other general education requirements include core skill courses in writing, oral communication, math, and exercise science, courses for a global society in world languages, world cultures, and global dynamics, courses across the disciplines in fine arts and music, literature, history, philosophy or religion, social sciences, and natural and physical sciences, and courses integrating skills of writing intensive, ethical reasoning, and experiential learning. A minimum of 33 credit hours with 30 of the last 33 credits hours earned in residence at the college. **Procedure:** Freshmen are admitted in the fall and spring. Entrance exams should be taken in spring of the junior year or fall of the senior year. There are deferred admissions and rolling admissions plans. Applications should be filed by May 1 for fall entry; January 1 for spring entry. 67 applicants were on the 2016 waiting list; 8 were admitted. Application fees are waived if application is completed online. **Transfer Students:** 55 transfer students enrolled in 2015-2016. A degree from an accredited high school and a 2.2 GPA in all undergraduate work are required. 33 of 123 credits required for the bachelor's degree must be completed at Bridgewater. **International Students:** There are 25 international students enrolled. The school actively recruits these students. They must take the TOEFL with a minimum score of 550 on the paper-based TOEFL (PBT) or 79 on the Internet-based version (iBT), The SAT may replace the TOEFL. Most international students take the SAT rather than TOEFL. They must also take the ACT.

ADMISSIONS: 53% of the 2016-2017 applicants were accepted. The

SAT scores for the 2016-2017 freshman class were: Critical Reading-- 45% below 500, 42% between 500 and 599, 11% between 600 and 699, and 2% between 700 and 800. Math-- 44% below 500, 43% between 500 and 599, 11% between 600 and 699, and 2% between 700 and 800. Writing-- 60% below 500, 32% between 500 and 599, 7% between 600 and 699, and 1% between 700 and 800. The ACT scores were 4% between 12 and 17, 44% between 18 and 23, 44% between 24 and 29, and 8% above 30. 33% of the current freshmen were in the top fifth of their class; 64% were in the top two fifths. 7 freshmen graduated first in their class. **Admissions Contact:** Jarret L. Smith, Director of Admissions. Email: *admissions@bridgewater.edu* Web: *www.bridgewater.edu*

FINANCIAL AID: In 2016-2017, 100% of all full-time freshmen and continuing full-time students received some form of financial aid. 86% of all full-time freshmen and 81% of continuing full-time students received need-based aid. The average freshman award was $31,579. Need-based scholarships or need-based grants averaged $28,113 ($38,215 maximum); need-based self-help aid (loans and jobs) averaged $4,704 ($7,500 maximum); and other non-need-based awards and non-need-based scholarships averaged $21,809 ($35,200 maximum). 24% of undergraduate students work part-time. Average annual earnings from campus work are $791. The average financial indebtedness of the 2016 graduate was $34,035. Bridgewater is a member of CSS. The state aid form is required. The FAFSA code is 003704. The priority date for freshman financial aid applications for fall entry is March 1.

CHRISTENDOM COLLEGE D-2

www.christendom.edu

Front Royal, VA 22630	**(540) 636-2900** **(800) 877-5456**
Fax: (540) 636-1655	**Email: admissions@christendom.edu**
Full-time: 177 men, 255 women	**Faculty:** 32
Part-time: 1 man	**Ph.D.s:** 65%
Graduate: n/av	**Student/Faculty:** 15 to 1
Year: semesters	**Tuition:** $23,900
Room & Board: $8700	**Freshman Class:** 228 applied, 211 accepted, 104 enrolled
SAT CR/M/W: 632/570/616 **ACT:** 25	**CEEB CODE:** 5691
Application Deadline: March 1	**VERY COMPETITIVE**

Christendom College, founded in 1977, is a private liberal arts institution affiliated with the Roman Catholic Church. Figures in the above capsule and in this profile are approximate. There is 1 undergraduate school and 1 graduate school. In addition to regional accreditation, Christendom has baccalaureate program accreditation with SACS. The 120-acre campus is in a rural area 65 miles west of Washington, D.C. Including any residence halls, there are 21 buildings.

STUDENT LIFE: 74% of undergraduates are from out of state, mostly the Middle Atlantic. Students are from 43 states, 2 foreign countries, and Canada. 91% are White; 4% Hispanic; 2% Asian American; 2% Foreign; 1% African American. 100% are Catholic. **Female To Male Ratio:** 1.4:1. The average age of freshmen is 18; all undergraduates, 20. 7% do not continue beyond their first year; 70% remain to graduate. **Housing:** College-sponsored housing includes single-sex dorms and on-campus apartments. On-campus housing is guaranteed for all 4 years. 95% of students live on campus; of those, 100% remain on campus on weekends. All students may keep cars. Alcohol is not permitted.

FACULTY/CLASSROOMS: 79% of faculty are male; 21% are female. All teach undergraduates. No introductory courses are taught by graduate students. The average class size in an introductory lecture is 22 and in a regular course is 20.

PROGRAMS OF STUDY: Christendom confers B.A. degrees. Associate and master's degrees are also awarded. Bachelor's degrees are awarded in COMMUNICATIONS AND THE ARTS (English), SOCIAL SCIENCE (classical/ancient civilization, history, philosophy, political science/government, and theological studies). Philosophy is the strongest academically, and has the largest enrollment.

ACTIVITIES: There are no fraternities or sororities. There are 15 groups on campus, including chess, choir, chorale, computers, debate, drama, film, literary magazine, musical theater, newspaper, photography, political, professional, radio and TV, religious, social, social service, student government, and yearbook. Popular campus events include Christmas Dinner Dance, Coffee House, and St. Patrick's Day. **Sports:** There are 4 intercollegiate sports for men and 3 for women, and 7 intramural sports for men and 7 for women. Facilities include indoor basketball and volleyball courts, racquetball courts, playing fields, table games, a recreation center, and an outdoor swimming pool. **Graduates:** From July 1, 2015 to June 30, 2016, 69 bachelor's degrees were awarded. 8 companies recruited on campus in 2015-2016. In an average class, 70% graduate in 4 years or less and 70% graduate in 6 years or less. Of the 2015 graduating class, 12% were enrolled in graduate school within 6 months of graduation, and 80% were employed.

SERVICES: **Library/Resources:** The library contains 90,000 volumes, 860 microform items, and 1,345 audio/video tapes/CDs/DVDs, subscribes to 279 periodicals including electronic. Computerized library services include interlibrary loans and database searching. Special learning facilities include a radio station, and a writing center. **Physically Challenged Students:** 60% of the campus is accessible. Facilities include wheelchair ramps, elevators, special parking, and specially equipped restrooms. **Special:** Christendom offers summer internships in Washington, D.C. for political science students and also sponsors a semester in Rome during the junior year. Students may pursue dual majors. There is a work-study program with the college. There are 5 departmental honors programs. **Visiting:** There are guides for informal visits, visitors may sit in on classes, and stay overnight. To schedule a visit, contact the Admissions Counselor. **Campus Safety and Security:** Measures include 24-hour foot and vehicle patrol, security escort services, emergency telephones, and lighted pathways/sidewalks.

REQUIREMENTS: The SAT or ACT is required, the SAT is preferred. A minimum composite score of 1500 on the newest SAT or 21 on the ACT is required. Applicants need not be graduates of an accredited secondary school. GED certificates are accepted. Essays and letters of recommendation are required. A campus visit and a meeting with the Admissions Director are highly recommended. Christendom requires applicants to be in the upper 50% of their class. A GPA of 3.0 is required. AP credits are accepted. To graduate, all students must complete a total of 126 credit hours, including a 30-hour major and an 86-credit core curriculum, which includes 18 hours each in theology and philosophy. A minimum 2.0 GPA is required. All students must demonstrate proficiency in a foreign language and complete a thesis. **Procedure:** Freshmen are admitted in the fall and spring. Entrance exams should be taken in the spring of the junior year or fall of the senior year. There is an early admissions plan. Early decision applications should be filed by December 1; regular applications, by March 1 for fall entry; and January 2 for spring entry, along with a $25 fee. Notification of early decision is sent December 15; regular decision, April 1. Applications are accepted on-line. **Transfer Students:** 9 transfer students enrolled in 2015-2016. Students must have a minimum 2.0 GPA and meet all other applicable standard admissions requirements. The SAT or ACT is recommended. 36 of 126 credits required for the bachelor's degree must be completed at Christendom. **International Students:** There are 7 international students enrolled. They must take the TOEFL.

ADMISSIONS: 93% of the 2016-2017 applicants were accepted. The SAT scores for the 2016-2017 freshman class were: Critical Reading-- 5% below 500, 33% between 500 and 599, 33% between 600 and 699, and 29% between 700 and 800. Math-- 20% below 500, 46% between 500 and 599, 24% between 600 and 699, and 10% between 700 and 800. Writing-- 11% below 500, 24% between 500 and 599, 43% between 600 and 699, and 22% between 700 and 800. The ACT scores were 3% below 12, 28% between 12 and 17, 50% between 18 and 23, 12% between 24 and 29, and 7% above 30. 40% of the current freshmen were in the top fifth of their class; 85% were in the top two fifths. **Admissions Contact:** Samuel J. Phillips, Director of Admissions. Email: *admissions@christendom.edu* Web: *www.christendom.edu*

FINANCIAL AID: In 2016-2017, 69% of all full-time freshmen and 56% of continuing full-time students received some form of financial aid. 56% of all full-time freshmen and 54% of continuing full-time students received need-based aid. The average freshman award was $17,236. Need-based scholarships or need-based grants averaged $6,270; need-based self-help aid (loans and jobs) averaged $7,530; and other non-need-based awards and non-need-based scholarships averaged $8,183. 40% of undergraduate students work part-time. Average annual earnings from campus work are $2000. The average financial indebtedness of the 2016 graduate was $28,084. The college's own financial statement is required. Check with the school for current application deadlines.

CHRISTOPHER NEWPORT UNIVERSITY F-3

www.cnu.edu

Newport News, VA 23606
(757) 594-7015
(800) 333-4268
Fax: (757) 594-7333
Email: admit@cnu.edu

Full-time: 2100 men, 2756 women
Part-time: 44 men, 30 women
Graduate: 38 men, 74 women
Year: semesters, summer session
Room & Board: $10,914

SAT CR/M: 583/575 **ACT:** 26
Application Deadline: February 1

Faculty: 275; IIB, +$
Ph.D.s: 89%
Student/Faculty: 18 to 1
Tuition: $13,054 ($24,680)
Freshman Class: 7532 applied, 4682 accepted, 1228 enrolled
CEEB CODE: 5128
VERY COMPETITIVE+

Christopher Newport University is a public school offering a private school experience - great teaching, small classes and a safe, vibrant campus. A "student-first, teaching-first" community, Christopher Newport is dedicated to the ideals of scholarship, leadership and service. We celebrate the values inherent in the liberal arts and sciences and live as a community of honor, transforming hearts and minds. Christopher Newport has more than doubled the size of its freshman class, increased the SAT average by more than 200 points, dramatically enhanced the number of faculty and seen applications increase by more than 700 percent. There are 4 undergraduate schools and 1 graduate school. In addition to regional accreditation, CNU has baccalaureate program accreditation with AACSB, ABET, CSWE, NASM, NAST, and ACS. The 260-acre campus is in a suburban area in the heart of Newport News, Virginia. Three hours south of Washington, D.C. Including any residence halls, there are 49 buildings.

STUDENT LIFE: 92% of undergraduates are from Virginia. Others are from 31 states, 36 foreign countries, and Canada. 8% are African American; 75% White; 5% Hispanic; 5% two or more races; 4% race unknown; 3% Asian American. **Female To Male Ratio:** 1.3:1. The average age of freshmen is 18; all undergraduates, 20. 14% do not continue beyond their first year; 75% remain to graduate. **Housing:** 3805 students can be accommodated in college housing, which includes coed dorms and on-campus apartments. In addition, there are special-interest houses, fraternity houses, sorority houses, and learning communities. On-campus housing is available on a lottery system for upperclassmen. 78% of students live on campus; of those, 75% remain on campus on weekends. Alcohol is not permitted. All students may keep cars.

FACULTY/CLASSROOMS: 55% of faculty are male; 45% are female. No introductory courses are taught by graduate students.

PROGRAMS OF STUDY: CNU confers B.A., B.S., B.M., B.S.B.A. and B.S.I.S. degrees. Master's degrees are also awarded. Bachelor's degrees are awarded in AGRICULTURE (environmental studies), BIOLOGICAL SCIENCE (biochemistry, biology/biological science, cell & molecular biology, environmental biology, and neurosciences), BUSINESS (accounting, business administration and management, finance, integrative studies, management, and marketing), COMMUNICATIONS AND THE ARTS (communications, English, fine arts, French, German, music, Spanish, and theatre arts), COMPUTER AND PHYSICAL SCIENCE (applied mathematics, applied physics, chemistry, computer science, information science, mathematics, and mathematics/computational), ENGINEERING AND ENVIRONMENTAL DESIGN (computer engineering and electrical and computer engineering), HEALTH PROFESSIONS (predentistry, premedicine, prepharmacy, prephysical therapy, and preveterinary science), SOCIAL SCIENCE (American studies, economics, history, interdisciplinary studies, philosophy, political science/government, prelaw, psychology, social work, and sociology). Psychology, biology and communications have the largest enrollments.

ACTIVITIES: 24% of men belong to 8 national fraternities; 33% of women belong to 9 national sororities. There are 200 groups on campus, including class council, REACH alternative breaks, residence hall association, student diversity and equality council, student honor council, art, band, campus activities board, cheerleading, choir, chorale, chorus, communications, computers, dance, drama, environmental, ethnic, film, honors, international, jazz band, LGBT, literary magazine, marching band, musical theater, newspaper, opera, orchestra, pep band, photography, political, professional, radio and TV, religious, social, social service, student government, and symphony. Popular campus events include Campus Tie Dye, Candelight Ceremony, Captain's Ball, Club Fair, Day of Service, FallFest, Family Weekend, Ferguson Center for the Arts Concerts - Performances, Food 4 Thought, Glow in the Dar-Capella, and Spectrum Drag Ball. **Sports:** There are 12 intercollegiate sports for men and 12 for women, and 9 intramural sports for men and 9 for women. Facilities include The Freeman Center is home to Christopher Newport University's volleyball, men's and women's basketball and indoor track and field programs. Opened in 2000, The Freeman Center can seat up to 2.500 fans for basketball and volleyball contests and plays host to thousands of collegiate and high school track and field athletes annually. There is a 200-meter indoor track, 5 basketball courts (2 housed in a separate Auxiliary gymnasium) and a 13,500 square foot fitness pavilion with state of the art fitness equipment. CNU has a football stadium which includes a 400-meter track, 12 outdoor tennis courts, individual state of the art fields for soccer, field hockey/lacrosse, baseball and softball. **Graduates:** From July 1, 2015 to June 30, 2016, 1192 bachelor's degrees were awarded. The most popular majors were communications (13%), psychology (12%), cell, and molecular & phys biology (7%). 1027 companies recruited on campus in 2015-2016. In an average class, 2% graduate in 3 years or less, 63% graduate in 4 years or less, 73% graduate in 5 years or less, and 75% graduate in 6 years or less.

SERVICES: Counseling and information services are available, as is tutoring in most subjects. **Library/Resources:** The library contains 590,565 volumes, 199,488 microform items, and 15,110 audio/video tapes/CDs/DVDs, and subscribes to 65,279 periodicals including electronic. Computerized library services include interlibrary loans, database searching, Internet access, and Wi-Fi capability. Special learning facilities include an art gallery, radio station, TV station, and the Ferguson Center for the Arts. **Physically Challenged Students:** 96% of the campus is accessible. Facilities include wheelchair ramps, elevators, special parking, specially equipped restrooms, special class scheduling, lowered drinking fountains, and special housing. **Special:** CNU offers cross-registration, dual majors, a student-designed interdisciplinary studies major, internships, and study abroad. Special course offerings: Honors Program, the President's Leadership Program and Freshman Learning Communities. There are 31 national honor societies and a freshman honors program. **Visiting:** There are regularly scheduled orientations for prospective students, information sessions and walking campus tours are available Monday through Friday at 10 a.m. & 2 p.m.; Saturday information session and tour at 11 a.m. Special on and off campus events and receptions as scheduled annually. Visitors may sit in on classes and stay overnight. To schedule a visit, contact Kimberly McDaniel at (757) 594-7334. **Campus Safety and Security:** Measures include 24-hour foot and vehicle patrol, emergency notification system, self-defense education, and security escort services. There are emergency telephones, lighted pathways/sidewalks, controlled access to dorms/residences, campus police department, and a full time communication center for emergency radio and telephone communications.

REQUIREMENTS: CNU requires Virginia's Advanced Studies Diploma (ASD) or similar college preparatory diploma from an accredited high school with a satisfactory score on the SAT verbal and math or ACT composite. The GED is not accepted in lieu of a final high school transcript for freshman admission, as GED recipients do not meet ASD requirements. A total of 24 academic credits are recommended, including 4 units of English, 4 each of social science, math, and science and either 3 units of 1 foreign language (preferred) or 2 years of 2 foreign languages. An essay and a personal statement are required. SAT or ACT scores are not required for students with a 3.5 or higher high school GPA in a rigorous curriculum that includes college level work. Letters of recommendation and interviews are strongly recommended but not required. AP and CLEP credits are accepted. Important factors in the admissions decision are recommendations by school officials, extracurricular activities record, and evidence of special talent. To graduate, all students must fulfill the liberal learning core, including mathematics, second language literacy, written communication (with minimum grades of C- or better), logical reasoning, economic modeling and analysis, civic and democratic engagement, global and multicultural perspectives, creative expressions, science lecture with laboratory, western traditions, two writing intensive designated courses, with a minimum of 120 semester hours and with 45 credits in residence, and 30 of the last 36 credit hours, including last 12 credit hours within the major in residence. In addition, students must complete all requirements specific to the major, present an overall and an 'in-major' GPA of at least 2.0, and enroll in at least one CNU course during the semester of the degree conferral. **Procedure:** Freshmen are admitted fall and spring. Entrance exams should be taken before the senior year. There are early decision, early admissions, and deferred admissions plans. Early decision applications should be filed by November 15; regular applications, by February 1 for fall entry; and November 1 for spring entry. The fall 2016 application fee was $65. Notification of early decision is sent December 15; regular decision, March 15. 373 early decision candidates were accepted for the 2016-2017 class. 385 applicants were on the 2016 waiting list; 244 were admitted. Applications are accepted on-line. Application fees are waived if application is completed on-line. **Transfer Students:** 188 transfer students enrolled in 2015-2016. Applicants must present a minimum 3.0 GPA, and be academically eligible to return to the most recently attended college or university. All transfer applicants must submit official college and high school transcripts. SAT or ACT scores are recommended if high school graduation is within the last five years. In addition, transfer applicants must submit the Transfer College Report certified from each college or university attended. 45 of 120 credits required for the bachelor's degree must be completed at CNU. **International Students:** There are 19 international students enrolled. The school actively recruits these students. They must take the TOEFL with a minimum score of 530 on the paper-based TOEFL (PBT) or 71 on the Internet-based version (iBT), or take the IELTS, or the iTep. They must also take the SAT or ACT.

ADMISSIONS: 62% of the 2016-2017 applicants were accepted. The SAT scores for the 2016-2017 freshman class were: Critical Reading-- 10% below 500, 47% between 500 and 599, 37% between 600 and 699, and 6% between 700 and 800. Math-- 11% below 500, 51% between 500 and 599, 34% between 600 and 699, and 4% between 700 and 800. The ACT scores were 1% between 12 and 17, 25% between 18 and 23, 61% between 24 and 29, and 13% above 30. 43% of the current freshmen were in the top fifth of their class; 75% were in the top two fifths. **Admissions Contact:** Robert J. Lange III, Dean of Admission. Email: *admit@cnu.edu* Web: *www.cnu.edu*

FINANCIAL AID: In 2016-2017, 76% of all full-time freshmen and 70% of continuing full-time students received some form of financial aid. 40% of all full-time freshmen and 40% of continuing full-time students received need-based aid. The average freshman award was $12,748. Need-based scholarships or need-based grants averaged $6,954 ($7,980 maximum); need-based self-help aid (loans and jobs) averaged $3,338 ($4,500 maximum); and other non-need-based awards and non-need-based scholarships averaged $9,000 ($35,930 maximum). 32% of undergraduate students work part-time. Average annual earnings from campus work are $1849. The average financial indebtedness of the 2016 graduate was $30,451. The FAFSA code is 003706. The priority date for freshman financial aid applications for fall entry is March 1. The deadline for filing freshman financial aid applications for fall entry is June 30.

COLLEGE OF WILLIAM & MARY E-3

www.wm.edu

Williamsburg, VA 23187	**(757) 221-4223** n/av
Fax: (757) 221-1242	**Email: admission@wm.edu**
Full-time: 2631 men, 3578 women	**Faculty:** I, -$
Part-time: 18 men, 21 women	**Ph.D.s:** n/av
Graduate: 1182 men, 1159 women	**Student/Faculty:** n/av
Year: semesters, summer session	**Tuition:** n/av
Room & Board: n/app	**Freshman Class:** n/av **CEEB CODE:** 5115
Application Deadline: January 1	**MOST COMPETITIVE**

College of William & Mary, founded by Royal Charter in 1693, is the second-oldest college in the country. It has a long history of liberal arts education and a growing research and science curriculum that demonstrates a strong commitment to undergraduate research. The figures in the above capsule and in this profile are approximate. There are 2 undergraduate schools and 5 graduate schools. In addition to regional accreditation, William & Mary has baccalaureate program accreditation with AACSB and NCATE. The 1200-acre campus is in a small town 50 miles southeast of Richmond. Including any residence halls, there are 173 buildings.

STUDENT LIFE: 66% of undergraduates are from Virginia. Others are from 50 states, 79 foreign countries, and Canada. 9% are Hispanic; 8% Asian American; 7% African American; 6% Foreign; 6% race unknown; 59% White; 5% two or more races. **Female To Male Ratio:** 1.2:1. The average age of freshmen is 18; all undergraduates, 20. 5% do not continue beyond their first year. **Housing:** 5000 students can be accommodated in college housing, which includes coed dorms, on-campus apartments, honors houses, language houses, special-interest houses, fraternity houses, sorority houses, smoke-free, substance free, multicultural housing, and an Africana house. On-campus housing is guaranteed for the freshman year only and is available on a lottery system for upperclassmen. 73% of students live on campus; of those, 80% remain on campus on weekends. Upperclassmen may keep cars.

FACULTY/CLASSROOMS: No introductory courses are taught by graduate students.

PROGRAMS OF STUDY: William & Mary confers B.A., B.S. and B.B.A. degrees. Master's and doctoral degrees are also awarded. Bachelor's degrees are awarded in BIOLOGICAL SCIENCE (neurosciences), BUSINESS (accounting, banking and finance, business administration and management, business intelligence and analytics, entrepreneurial studies, and marketing management), COMMUNICATIONS AND THE ARTS (Africana studies, art history, art, Chinese, English, French, German, linguistics, music, and theatre arts), COMPUTER AND PHYSICAL SCIENCE (chemistry, computer science, geology, mathematics, and physics), HEALTH PROFESSIONS (biology, health science, and kinesiology), SOCIAL SCIENCE (American studies, anthropology, classical/ancient civilization, economics, gender studies, history, interdisciplinary studies, international relations, Latin American studies, medieval studies, philosophy, political science/government, psychology, public affairs, religion, sociology, Spanish studies, and women's studies). Biology, government, and kinesiology & health sciences have the largest enrollments.

ACTIVITIES: 26% of men belong to 15 national fraternities; 36% of women belong to 12 national sororities. There are 475 groups on campus, including art, band, cheerleading, chess, choir, chorale, chorus, computers, dance, debate, drama, drill team, environmental, ethnic, film, honors, international, jazz band, LGBT, literary magazine, musical theater, newspaper, opera, orchestra, pep band, photography, political, professional, radio and TV, religious, social, social service, student government, symphony, and yearbook. Popular campus events include Yule Log Ceremony, Raft Debate and Senior Walk Across Campus (Commencement). **Sports:** There are 11 intercollegiate sports for men and 12 for women, and 28 intramural sports for men and 26 for women. Facilities include a football stadium, a basketball arena, baseball facility, field for lacrosse and soccer, tennis courts, hockey field, a pool, a basketball court, volleyball courts, strength training center, a recreation center, a gymnasium with pool, a fitness room, weight rooms, racquetball courts, and squash courts. **Graduates:** From July 1, 2015 to June 30, 2016, 1631 bachelor's degrees were awarded. The most popular majors were business administration (27%), psychology (9%), and economics (8%). 78 companies recruited on campus in 2015-2016.

SERVICES: Counseling and information services are available, as is tutoring in most subjects, and a reader service for the blind. **Library/Resources:** The 5 libraries contain 2.1 million volumes, 1.3 million microform items, 38,544 audio/video tapes/CDs/DVDs, and subscribe to 150,399 periodicals including electronic. Computerized library services include interlibrary loans, database searching, Internet access, and Wi-Fi capability. Special learning facilities include an art gallery, radio station, An anthropology museum, an art studio, a greenhouse, the Center for Archaeological Research, and the Omohundro Institute of Early American History and Culture. **Physically Challenged Students:** 95% of the campus is accessible. Facilities include wheelchair ramps, elevators, special parking, specially equipped restrooms, special class scheduling, lowered drinking fountains. Modified recreational facilities, braille signage, Kurzweil reader, and a special learning lab for the visually impaired. Individual accommodations are made on a case-by-case basis. **Special:** William and Mary has various special academic programs available to students: Study abroad in 23 countries around the world. Work-study programs with various employers including campus departments and off-campus community agencies. Washington Program which is open to students in all majors and disciplines. Accelerated degree program in Computer Science and Public Policy with an option whereby a small number of current W&M undergraduates will be able to earn both a Bachelor's degree and a Master degree in a total of five years of coursework; Student Self-designed majors in Interdisciplinary Studies. A Combined Degree Program in engineering with Columbia University; a Joint Degree programme with the University of St Andrews in Scotland; The Department Honors programs administered by the Roy R. Charles Center; Internships for credit; and the opportunity to double major across the curriculum. There are 16 national honor societies, Phi Beta Kappa, a freshman honors program, and 27 departmental honors programs. **Visiting:** There are regularly scheduled orientations for prospective students, group information session followed by a student-led tour. Visitors may sit in on classes. To schedule a visit, contact the Office of Admissions. **Campus Safety and Security:** Measures include 24-hour foot and vehicle patrol, emergency notification system, self-defense education, and security escort services. There are also shuttle buses, emergency telephones, lighted pathways/sidewalks, controlled access to dorms/residences, and crime prevention programs.

REQUIREMENTS: The Common Application, William & Mary Supplement to the Common Application, Secondary School Report form complete with a high school transcript and counselor letter of recommendation, Midyear School Report form, and official report of standardized test scores (SAT and/or ACT), application fee, or a fee waiver request. AP and CLEP credits are accepted. Important factors in the admissions decision are advanced placement or honors courses, extracurricular activities record, leadership record, evidence of special talent, personality/intangible qualities, and geographical diversity. The College Curriculum (COLL), adopted in Fall 2015, requires a "big ideas" course, a writing-intensive seminar, three integrative sophomore/junior-level courses, an experience beyond the college, and a capstone course. To graduate, students must complete the COLL courses and demonstrate proficiencies in foreign language and mathematics; other proficiencies, such as digital information literacy, writing, and other forms of communication, are built into COLL courses. Distribution requirements include courses in Arts, Letters, and Values, Cultures, Societies, and the Individual and Natural World and Quantitative Reasoning. Students must complete 120 credit hours, with 33 to 48 in the major, a minimum 2.0 GPA cumulatively and in the major, and a minimum of 60 credit hours in residence at the College. **Procedure:** Freshmen are admitted in the fall. Entrance exams should be taken in spring of the junior year or fall of the senior year. There are early decision and deferred admissions plans. Early decision applications should be filed by November 1; regular applications, by January 1 for fall entry; and November 1 for spring entry. The fall 2016 application fee was $70. Notification of early decision is sent December 1; regular decision, April 1. 519 early decision candidates were accepted for the 2016-2017 class. 4115 applicants were on the 2016 waiting list; 154 were admitted. Applications are accepted online. **Transfer Students:** 189 transfer students enrolled in 2015-2016. William & Mary recommends that students interested in transferring to the College take challenging courses in the liberal arts and sciences. Typically, competitive transfer applicants have a GPA of 3.5 or higher at their current institution. Additional application requirements include: official transcripts from all colleges and universities attended, official high school transcript or copy of GED certificate, and if you have completed less than a full year of college coursework when you apply, you must submit SAT or ACT scores. If you have been out of high school for more than five years, SAT or ACT scores are not required. Test scores listed on the high school transcript will be accepted. Midterm grades are due November 22 for students applying for Spring and March 28 for students applying for the Fall. Student must use the Midterm Report form to submit current grades. 60 of 120 credits required for the bachelor's degree must be completed at William & Mary. **International Students:** There are 376 international students enrolled. The school actively recruits these students. They must take the TOEFL with a minimum score of 600 on the paper-based TOEFL (PBT) or 100 on the Internet-based version (iBT), or take the IELTS. They must also take the SAT or ACT. SAT II: Subject tests are considered if they are submitted.

ADMISSIONS: 95% of the current freshmen were in the top fifth of their class; 99% were in the top two fifths. **Admissions Contact:** Deborah Basket, Associate Dean. Email: *admission@wm.edu* Web: *www.wm.edu*

FINANCIAL AID: The college's own financial statement, and the CSS Profile is required for early decision enrollees. The FAFSA code is 003705. The deadline for filing freshman financial aid applications for fall entry is March 1.

EASTERN MENNONITE UNIVERSITY D-2

www.emu.edu

Harrisonburg, VA 22802 — (540) 432-4118, (800) 368-2665

Fax: (540) 432-4444 — **Email:** admiss@emu.edu

Full-time: 388 men, 699 women	**Faculty:** 89; IIa
Part-time: 44 men, 90 women	**Ph.D.s:** 79%
Graduate: 177 men, 375 women	**Student/Faculty:** 10 to 1
Year: semesters, summer session	**Tuition:** $32,300
Room & Board: $10,250	**Freshman Class:** 1762 applied, 1098 accepted, 257 enrolled
SAT CR/M: 505/503 **ACT:** 22	**CEEB CODE:** 5181
Application Deadline: n/av	**COMPETITIVE**

Eastern Mennonite University, founded in 1917, is a private Christian liberal arts university affiliated with the Mennonite Church. The university offers programs in the arts and sciences, education, biology, and nursing. EMU also offers master's degrees in several areas. EMU's Lancaster site provides some programs in Lancaster, Pennsylvania. There is 1 undergraduate school and 6 graduate schools. In addition to regional accreditation, EMU has baccalaureate program accreditation with ACPE, CSWE, NCATE, and NLN. The 97-acre campus is in the small town of Harrisonburg. 110 miles southwest of Washington, D.C. Including any residence halls, there are 46 buildings.

STUDENT LIFE: 56% of undergraduates are from Virginia. Others are from 33 states, 38 foreign countries, and Canada. 58% are from public schools. 8% are Hispanic; 71% White; 3% Asian American; 3% Foreign; 10% African American. 91% are Protestant; 13% claim no religious affiliation. **Female To Male Ratio:** 1.9:1. The average age of freshmen is 18; all undergraduates, 25. 27% do not continue beyond their first year; 61% remain to graduate. **Housing:** 667 students can be accommodated in college housing, which includes single-sex and coed dorms, on-campus apartments, off-campus apartments, married student housing, and an intentional community. On-campus housing is guaranteed for all 4 years. 63% of students live on campus. All students may keep cars. Alcohol is not permitted.

FACULTY/CLASSROOMS: 58% of faculty are male; 42% are female. 75% teach undergraduates, 38% do research, and 35% do both. No introductory courses are taught by graduate students. The average class size in an introductory lecture is 40; in a laboratory is 17; and in a regular course is 18.

PROGRAMS OF STUDY: EMU confers B.A., and B.S., degrees. Associate and master's degrees are also awarded. Bachelor's degrees are awarded in BIOLOGICAL SCIENCE (biochemistry and biology/biological science), BUSINESS (accounting, business administration and management, international business management, and recreational facilities management), COMMUNICATIONS AND THE ARTS (art, communications, congregational and youth ministries, digital media, English, music, outdoor ministry & adventure leadership, photography, Spanish, theatre arts, and writing), COMPUTER AND PHYSICAL SCIENCE (chemistry, clinical laboratory science, computer science, and mathematics), EDUCATION (early childhood education, elementary education, health and physical education, physical education, secondary education, and special education), ENGINEERING AND ENVIRONMENTAL DESIGN (environmental science and preengineering), HEALTH PROFESSIONS (medical laboratory technology, nursing, predentistry, premedicine, pre-occupational therapy, preosteopathy, prepharmacy, pre-physician assistant, and prephysical therapy), SOCIAL SCIENCE (biblical studies, economics, history, liberal arts/general studies, ministries, peace studies, philosophy, psychology, religion, social science, social work, sociology, and theological studies). Biology/pre-med, education, and nursing are the strongest academically. Business, education, and nursing have the largest enrollments.

ACTIVITIES: There are no fraternities or sororities. There are 37 groups on campus, including art, chess, choir, chorale, chorus, computers, dance, drama, environmental, ethnic, film, honors, international, jazz band, literary magazine, musical theater, newspaper, orchestra, pep band, photography, political, professional, radio and TV, religious, social, social service, student government, student women's association and peace fellowship, and yearbook. Popular campus events include Spring Fling, Fall Festival, and Multicultural Week. **Sports:** There are 7 intercollegiate sports for men and 8 for women, and 15 intramural sports for men and 15 for women. Facilities include a fitness center, aerobics room, indoor track, climbing wall, varsity court, courts for team practice, playing field, tennis courts, baseball, softball, and soccer fields, a outdoor track, basketball and sand volleyball courts. **Graduates:** From July 1, 2015 to June 30, 2016, 360 bachelor's degrees were awarded. The most popular majors were nursing (36%), business (14%), and education (6%). 46 companies recruited on campus in 2015-2016. In an average class, 50% graduate in 4 years or less, 58% graduate in 5 years or less, and 61% graduate in 6 years or less.

SERVICES: Counseling and information services are available, as is tutoring in most subjects, and a reader service for the blind, and remedial reading and writing. EMU owns technology, such as the ability to burn textbooks onto CD's, for visually impaired students and those with other special learning needs. Technology for the hearing impaired is be provided as needed. **Library/Resources:** The library contains 340,838 volumes, 63,490 microform items, 32,240 audio/video tapes/CDs/DVDs, and subscribes to 86,373 periodicals including electronic. Computerized library services include interlibrary loans, database searching, Internet access, and Wi-Fi capability. Special learning facilities include an art gallery, natural history museum, planetarium, radio station, an arboretum and greenhouse, nursing laboratory, and cadaver laboratory. **Physically Challenged Students:** 75% of the campus is accessible. Facilities include wheelchair ramps, elevators, special parking, specially equipped restrooms, special class scheduling, lowered drinking fountains, special housing. Newer buildings on campus have accessible telephones. **Special:** EMU offers study-abroad programs each semester and during the summer at a variety of locations around the world. Students may also choose to study 1 or 2 semesters in Washington, D.C. There are internships in a variety of majors, dual majors, a student-designed major, and a 2 year general studies degree. There is 1 national honor society and a freshman honors program. **Visiting:** There are regularly scheduled orientations for prospective students, an address by the president, a financial aid seminar, a review of general education, the opportunity to sit in on classes, meet with professors and admissions representatives, sleep in residence halls, and eat in the cafeteria. There are guides for informal visits, visitors may sit in on classes, and stay overnight. To schedule a visit, contact Admissions Office. **Campus Safety and Security:** Measures include emergency notification system, self-defense education, security escort services, emergency telephones, lighted pathways/sidewalks, controlled access to dorms/residences, and a 12-hour foot or vehicle watchman.

REQUIREMENTS: SAT and/or ACT scores are required for admission. The minimum SAT score is 900 (reading and math), the minimum ACT score, composite, is a 19. Applicants must be graduates of an accredited secondary school or have a GED certificate. The university recommends that students have completed 4 credits of English, 3 each of math, science, and social studies, 2 or more of foreign language and chemistry for nursing majors. A GPA of 2.6 is required. AP and CLEP credits are accepted. Important factors in the admissions decision are leadership record, extracurricular activities record, and recommendations by school officials. To graduate, students must complete interdisciplinary core courses, courses in Bible and religion, cross-cultural study, writing, speech, and math, a major (minors are optional), and a variety of electives for a minimum of 128 semester hours. A minimum cumulative GPA of 2.0 is required while some majors require a higher GPA in the major or overall. **Procedure:** Freshmen are admitted in the fall and spring. Entrance exams should be taken in the spring of the junior year or the fall of the senior year. There are deferred admissions and rolling admissions plans. Application deadlines are open. The fall 2016 application fee was $25. Applications are accepted online. **Transfer Students:** 77 transfer students enrolled in 2015-2016. Transfer students must have a minimum college GPA of 2.0. 63 of 128 credits required for the bachelor's degree must be completed at EMU. **International Students:** There are 60 international students enrolled. The school actively recruits these students. They must take the TOEFL with a minimum score of 500 on the paper-based TOEFL (PBT) or 61 on the Internet-based version (iBT). They must also take the SAT or ACT, scoring 900 SAT.

ADMISSIONS: 62% of the 2016-2017 applicants were accepted. The SAT scores for the 2016-2017 freshman class were: Critical Reading-- 41% below 500, 26% between 500 and 599, 13% between 600 and 699, and 1% between 700 and 800. Math-- 43% below 500, 25% between 500 and 599, 11% between 600 and 699, and 2% between 700 and 800. The ACT scores were 6% between 12 and 17, 16% between 18 and 23, 9% between 24 and 29, and 4% above 30. 36% of the current freshmen were in the top fifth of their class; 65% were in the top two fifths. **Admissions Contact:** Matt Ruth, Director of Undergraduate Admissions. Email: *admiss@emu.edu* Web: *www.emu.edu*

FINANCIAL AID: EMU is a member of CSS. The state aid form is required. The FAFSA code is 003708. The deadline for filing freshman financial aid applications for fall entry is April 15.

EMORY AND HENRY COLLEGE B-4

www.ehc.edu

Emory, VA 24327	(276) 944-6133 (800) 848-5493
Fax: (276) 944-6935	**Email:** admission@ehc.edu
Full-time: 464 men, 410 women	**Faculty:** 72; IIB, --$
Part-time: 12 men, 11 women	**Ph.D.s:** n/av
Graduate: 14 men, 34 women	**Student/Faculty:** 10 to 1
Year: semesters, summer session	**Tuition:** $30,900
Room & Board: $10,510	**Freshman Class:** n/av
SAT or ACT: required	**CEEB CODE:** 5185
Application Deadline: April 15	**COMPETITIVE**

Emory and Henry College, founded in 1836, is a private liberal arts institution affiliated with the United Methodist Church. Figures in the above capsule and in this profile are approximate. There is 1 undergraduate school. In addition to regional accreditation, E and H has baccalaureate program accreditation with CAAHEP. The 331-acre campus is in a rural area in Emory, Southwest Virginia.

STUDENT LIFE: 64% of undergraduates are from Virginia. Others are from 26 states, 5 foreign countries, and Canada. 99% are from public schools. 80% are White; 10% African American; 1% Asian American; 1% Hispanic; 1% Foreign. **Male To Female Ratio:** 1.1:1. The average age of freshmen is 18; all undergraduates, 20. **Housing:** College-sponsored housing includes single-sex and coed dorms, on-campus apartments, off-campus apartments, honors houses, and special-interest houses. On-campus housing is guaranteed for all 4 years. 77% of students live on campus; of those, 50% remain on campus on weekends. All students may keep cars. Alcohol is not permitted.

FACULTY/CLASSROOMS: 59% of faculty are male; 41% are female. All teach undergraduates. No introductory courses are taught by graduate students. The average class size in an introductory lecture is 25; in a laboratory is 13; and in a regular course is 22.

PROGRAMS OF STUDY: E and H confers B.A. and B.S. degrees. Master's degrees are also awarded. Bachelor's degrees are awarded in BIOLOGICAL SCIENCE (biology/biological science), BUSINESS (business administration and management), COMMUNICATIONS AND THE ARTS (art, communications, creative writing, dramatic arts, English literature, journalism, literature, modern language, music performance, and music theory and composition), COMPUTER AND PHYSICAL SCIENCE (chemistry, computer management, computer science, mathematics, and physics), EDUCATION (English education, mathematics education, and physical education), ENGINEERING AND ENVIRONMENTAL DESIGN (environmental science), SOCIAL SCIENCE (community services, East Asian studies, economics, European studies, geography, history, interdisciplinary studies, international studies, Middle Eastern studies, philosophy, political science/government, psychology, public affairs, religion, and sociology).

ACTIVITIES: 15% of men belong to 9 local fraternities; 30% of women belong to 6 local sororities. There are 50 groups on campus, including art, band, cheerleading, choir, chorus, dance, debate, drama, ethnic, international, LGBT, literary magazine, musical theater, newspaper, opera, pep band, photography, political, professional, radio and TV, religious, social, social service, student government, and yearbook. Popular campus events include Homecoming, Founder's Day, Martin Luther King Junior Day, Fall Formals, Parents Day, Greek Air Band, and the Literary Festival. **Sports:** Facilities include a gym, pool, racquetball court, outdoor volleyball courts, tennis courts, a weight room, dance room, golf course, baseball and football fields, and a horseshoe area.

SERVICES: Counseling and information services are available, as is tutoring in most subjects, and a reader service for the blind, and remedial math and writing. **Library/Resources:** The library contains 271,209 volumes, 207,000 microform items, and 7,950 audio/video tapes/CDs/DVDs, and subscribes to 352 periodicals including electronic. Computerized library services include interlibrary loans, database searching, and

Internet access. Special learning facilities include an art gallery, radio station, and TV station. **Physically Challenged Students:** 50% of the campus is accessible. Facilities include wheelchair ramps, elevators, special parking, specially equipped restrooms, special class scheduling, lowered drinking fountains, and special housing. **Special:** A cooperative program in medical technology and 2-2, 4-1, and 3-2 engineering degrees are available. Dual and student-designed majors, an interdisciplinary English major, combined B.A.-B.S. degrees, internships, a Washington Semester, work-study, nondegree study, and pass/fail options are also available. There are 10 national honor societies and 8 departmental honors programs. **Visiting:**Regularly scheduled orientations are available for prospective students, including a program for students to meet faculty and staff and to attend education sessions on college life. There are guides for informal visits, visitors may sit in on classes, and stay overnight. To schedule a visit, contact the Admissions Office. **Campus Safety and Security:** Measures include 24-hour foot and vehicle patrol, self-defense education, security escort services, and lighted pathways/sidewalks.

REQUIREMENTS: The SAT or ACT is required. In addition, applicants should be high school graduates. High school courses required include 4 years of English, 3 or more units of math including algebra I, algebra II, and geometry, 2 or more units of lab science, 2 units of a single foreign language, and 2 or more units of social studies and history. One additional unit in fine arts is strongly recommended. A personal essay is required. AP credits are accepted. Important factors in the admissions decision are advanced placement or honors courses, recommendations by school officials, and evidence of special talent. All students must complete a general studies curriculum covering Western traditions, great books, religion, ethical values inquiry, and global studies and must demonstrate proficiency in oral skills. Specific courses include a first-year writing course, 1 each from 3 disciplines, including social sciences, humanities and arts, and natural sciences, and according to major, either a foreign language or quantitative methods. A total of 120 semester hours for a B.A. or 124 for a B.S., with a GPA of 2.0, is required for graduation. The total number of hours in the major varies. **Procedure:** Freshmen are admitted in the fall, spring, and summer. Entrance exams should be taken in November of the senior year. There are early decision, deferred admissions, and rolling admissions plans. Early decision applications should be filed by November 1; regular applications, by April 15 for fall entry, along with a $30 fee. Applications are accepted online. **Transfer Students:** 64 transfer students enrolled in 2015-2016. Transfers must have at least a 2.5 GPA in previous college work. Those with at least 24 credits may be admitted without high school data; those with fewer than 24 credits must meet freshman admission standards. 33 of 120 credits required for the bachelor's degree must be completed at E and H. **International Students:** There are 5 international students enrolled. The school actively recruits these students. They must take the TOEFL.

Admissions Contact: Dave Voskuil, Vice President of Enrollment Management. Email: *dvoskuil@ehc.edu* Web: *www.ehc.edu*

FINANCIAL AID: The state aid form and the college's own financial statement are required. The FAFSA code is 003709. The priority date for freshman financial aid applications for fall entry is April 1. The filing deadline for fall entry is August 1.

FERRUM COLLEGE — C-4

www.ferrum.edu

Ferrum, VA 24088	**(540) 365-4290** **(800) 868-9797**
Fax: (540) 365-4266	**Email: admissions@ferrum.edu**
Full-time: 680 men, 534 women	**Faculty:** 69
Part-time: 13 men, 13 women	**Ph.D.s:** 68%
Graduate: n/av	**Student/Faculty:** 18 to 1
Year: semesters	**Tuition:** $29,680
Room & Board: $9970	**Freshman Class:** 2009 applied, 1570 accepted, 546 enrolled **CEEB CODE:** 5213
Application Deadline: open	**COMPETITIVE**

Ferrum College, founded in 1913, is a private, primarily residential, 4-year institution offering both professional and liberal arts majors. The figures in the above capsule and in this profile are approximate. There is 1 undergraduate school. In addition to regional accreditation, Ferrum has baccalaureate program accreditation with CSWE and SACS. The 700-acre campus is in a rural area in the Blue Ridge Mountains of southwestern Virginia. Including any residence halls, there are 54 buildings.

STUDENT LIFE: 86% of undergraduates are from Virginia. Others are from 24 states, and 5 foreign countries. 59% are White; 25% African American; 2% Hispanic; 1% Asian American; 1% American Indian/Alaska Native; 1% Foreign. 29% claim no religious affiliation. **Male To Female Ratio:** 1.3:1. The average age of freshmen is 18; all undergraduates, 21. 40% do not continue beyond their first year; 35% remain to graduate. **Housing:** 1300 students can be accommodated in college housing, which includes single-sex and coed dorms, on-campus apartments, off-campus apartments, and married student housing. theme housing by floors. On-campus housing is guaranteed for all 4 years. 86% of students live on campus; of those, 50% remain on campus on weekends. All students may keep cars.

FACULTY/CLASSROOMS: 57% of faculty are male; 43% are female. All teach undergraduates, and all do research. No introductory courses are taught by graduate students. The average class size in an introductory lecture is 20; in a laboratory is 15; and in a regular course is 13.

PROGRAMS OF STUDY: Ferrum confers B.A., B.S., B.F.A., and B.S.W. degrees. Bachelor's degrees are awarded in AGRICULTURE (agriculture and horticulture), BIOLOGICAL SCIENCE (biology/biological science), BUSINESS (accounting, business administration and management, recreation and leisure services, and sports management), COMMUNICATIONS AND THE ARTS (art, dramatic arts, English, performing arts, Russian, and Spanish), COMPUTER AND PHYSICAL SCIENCE (chemistry, information sciences and systems, and mathematics), EDUCATION (physical education), ENGINEERING AND ENVIRONMENTAL DESIGN (environmental science), HEALTH PROFESSIONS (health science), SOCIAL SCIENCE (criminal justice, history, international studies, liberal arts/general studies, philosophy, political science/government, psychology, religion, social studies, and social work). Chemistry, biology, and environmental science are the strongest academically. Business administration, criminal justice, and liberal arts/teacher education have the largest enrollments.

ACTIVITIES: 6% of men belong to 2 local fraternities; 9% of women belong to 3 local sororities. There are 63 groups on campus, including art, cheerleading, choir, chorale, chorus, communications, computers, dance, drama, environmental, ethnic, film, honors, international, jazz band, LGBT, literary magazine, musical theater, newspaper, photography, political, professional, radio and TV, religious, social, social service, and student government. Popular campus events include Spring Fling, Blue Ridge Folklife Festival, Relay for Life, and Snow Ball. **Sports:** There are 7 intercollegiate sports for men and 7 for women, and 13 intramural sports for men and 13 for women. Facilities include a gym, field house, tennis courts, weight room, an indoor pool, outdoor volleyball court, football stadium, soccer field, baseball field, women's softball field, recreation center (with indoor basketball courts, racquetball courts, and universal weights), and hiking/mountain biking trails. **Graduates:** From July 1, 2015 to June 30, 2016, 157 bachelor's degrees were awarded. The most popular majors were business administration (22%), criminal justice (11%), and parks and recreation (10%). 45 companies recruited on campus in 2015-2016. In an average class, 17% graduate in 4 years or less, 27% graduate in 5 years or less, and 29% graduate in 6 years or less. Of the 2015 graduating class, 13% were enrolled in graduate school within 6 months of graduation, and 100% were employed.

SERVICES: Counseling and information services are available, as is tutoring in most subjects, and remedial math, reading, and writing. College skills classes, individual assistance for study strategies, and subject-specific tutoring by professors and students are also available. **Library/Resources:** The library contains 219,774 volumes, 7,578 microform items, 2,285 audio/video tapes/CDs/DVDs, and subscribes to 21,014 periodicals including electronic. Computerized library services include interlibrary loans, database searching, Internet access, and Wi-Fi capability. Special learning facilities include an art gallery, radio station, a folklife museum, and a living history museum. **Physically Challenged Students:** 75% of the campus is accessible. Facilities include wheelchair ramps, elevators, special parking, specially equipped restrooms, special class scheduling, and lowered drinking fountains. **Special:** The college encourages internships, and some majors require internships. Study abroad, work-study programs, dual majors, an accelerated degree program in social work, and B.A.-B.S. degrees are offered. A liberal studies degree and nondegree study are available. There are 6 national honor societies, a freshman honors program, and 33 departmental honors programs. **Visiting:** There are regularly scheduled orientations for prospective students, including faculty information sessions, parent-to-parent and student-to-student sessions, and tours of the campus and residence halls. There are guides for informal visits, visitors may sit in on classes, and stay overnight. To schedule a visit, contact the Director of Admissions. **Campus Safety and Security:** Measures include 24-hour foot and vehicle patrol, self-defense education, and security escort services. There are emergency telephones, lighted pathways/sidewalks, and controlled access to dorms/residences.

REQUIREMENTS: Applicants must be graduates of an accredited secondary school or receive a GED certificate. Applicants should complete 18 high school academic credits. The Admissions Committee considers courses taken, grades, extracurricular activities, SAT or ACT scores, and recommendations. Personal interviews may be required for students lacking appropriate GPA or standardized test scores. AP and CLEP credits are accepted. Important factors in the admissions decision are advanced placement or honors courses, leadership record, and evidence of special talent. To graduate, students must complete at least 121 semester hours with a minimum GPA of 2.0. There are 37 hours of distribution requirements, including social sciences, natural sciences, English, religion/philosophy, math, literature, fine arts, and phys ed. A major may require up to 57 semester hours, and 30 hours of the total must be in upper-level courses. **Procedure:** Freshmen are admitted to all sessions. There are deferred admissions and rolling admissions plans. Application deadlines are open. Application fee is $25. Notification is sent on a rolling basis. Applications are accepted online. **Transfer Students:** 73 transfer students enrolled in 2015-2016. Applicants for transfer must be in good academic standing at their current schools. 32 of 127 credits required for the bachelor's degree must be completed at Ferrum. **International Students:** There are 9 international students enrolled. The school actively recruits these students. They must take the TOEFL, as well as the SAT or ACT.

ADMISSIONS: 78% of the 2016-2017 applicants were accepted. 13% of the current freshmen were in the top fifth of their class; 33% were in the top two fifths. **Admissions Contact:** Jason Byrd, Dean of Admissions. Email: *admissions@ferrum.edu* Web: *www.ferrum.edu*

FINANCIAL AID: The state aid form is required. The FAFSA code is 003711. The deadline for filing freshman financial aid applications for fall entry is April 1.

GEORGE MASON UNIVERSITY — E-2

www.gmu.edu

Fairfax, VA 22030 — **(703) 993-2400**

Fax: (703) 993-4622	**Email:** admissions@gmu.edu
Full-time: 7147 men, 8042 women	**Faculty:** 1041; I, av$
Part-time: 2203 men, 2310 women	**Ph.D.s:** 90%
Graduate: 5117 men, 7248 women	**Student/Faculty:** 15 to 1
Year: semesters, summer session	**Tuition:** $8024 ($24,008)
Room & Board: $7700	**Freshman Class:** 13732 applied, 8691 accepted, 2656 enrolled
SAT CR/M: 560/570 **ACT:** 25	**CEEB CODE:** 5827
Application Deadline: January 15	**VERY COMPETITIVE**

George Mason University, founded in 1972, is an entrepreneurial public institution with national distinction in a range of academic fields. The university has undergraduate and graduate degree programs in engineering, information technology, biotechnology, and health care. The figures in the above capsule and in this profile are approximate. There are 8 undergraduate schools and 11 graduate schools. In addition to regional accreditation, Mason has baccalaureate program accreditation with AACSB, ABET, CSAB, CSWE, NASM, NCATE, ACS, CAAHEP, and CCNE. The 806-acre campus is in a suburban area in the Greater Washington Metropolitan area, 21 miles southwest of Washington, D.C. Including any residence halls, there are 115 buildings.

STUDENT LIFE: 88% of undergraduates are from Virginia. Others are from 50 states, 131 foreign countries, and Canada. 86% are from public schools. 9% are African American; 9% Hispanic; 7% Foreign; 59% White; 16% Asian American. **Female To Male Ratio:** 1.2:1. The average age of freshmen is 18; all undergraduates, 23. 15% do not continue beyond their first year; 69% remain to graduate. **Housing:** 5057 students can be accommodated in college housing, which includes single-sex and coed dorms, on-campus apartments, off-campus apartments, honors houses and special-interest houses. On-campus housing is guaranteed for all 4 years, is available on a first-come, and first-served basis. 74% of students commute. All students may keep cars.

FACULTY/CLASSROOMS: 55% of faculty are male; 45% are female. 84% teach undergraduates. Graduate students teach 12% of introductory courses. The average class size in an introductory lecture is 43; in a laboratory is 23; and in a regular course is 25.

PROGRAMS OF STUDY: Mason confers B.A., B.S., B.F.A., B.I.S., B.S.E.D., and B.S.N. degrees. Master's and doctoral degrees are also awarded. Bachelor's degrees are awarded in AGRICULTURE (environmental studies), BIOLOGICAL SCIENCE (biology/biological science and neurosciences), BUSINESS (accounting, banking and finance, business administration and management, marketing/retailing/merchandising, operations management, and tourism), COMMUNICATIONS AND THE ARTS (art history and appreciation, communications, communications technology, dance, dramatic arts, English, film arts, French, music, Spanish, video, and visual and performing arts), COMPUTER AND PHYSICAL SCIENCE (astronomy, chemistry, computer science, earth science, geology, information sciences and systems, mathematics, physics, science and management, and software engineering), EDUCATION (athletic training and physical education), ENGINEERING AND ENVIRONMENTAL DESIGN (civil engineering, computational sciences, computer engineering, electrical/electronics engineering, industrial engineering, and systems engineering), HEALTH PROFESSIONS (community health work, health science, medical technology, and nursing), SOCIAL SCIENCE (anthropology, criminal justice, economics, geography, history, interdisciplinary studies, international relations, Latin American studies, parks and recreation management, philosophy, political science/government, psychology, public administration, religion, Russian and Slavic studies, social work, and sociology). Accounting, biology, and psychology have the largest enrollments.

ACTIVITIES: 7% of men belong to 23 national fraternities; 6% of women belong to 15 national sororities. There are 255 groups on campus, including art, band, cheerleading, chess, choir, chorale, chorus, computers, dance, drama, environmental, ethnic, film, forensics, honors, international, jazz band, LGBT, literary magazine, musical theater, newspaper, opera, orchestra, pep band, photography, political, professional, radio and TV, religious, social, social service, student government, symphony, and yearbook. Popular campus events include Welcome Week, Mason Day, and Patriot Day. **Sports:** There are 11 intercollegiate sports for men and 11 for women, and 11 intramural sports for men and 11 for women. Facilities include an arena for basketball, and indoor soccer. A sports and recreation complex includes a track, basketball, handball/racquetball, tennis, volleyball courts, baseball and softball diamonds, batting cages, a weight room, and a golf and archery net, outdoor track, and playing fields. The aquatic and fitness center offers a cardio and weight training equipment, a recreational pool, competition pool, and diving well. **Graduates:** From July 1, 2015 to June 30, 2016, 4009 bachelor's degrees were awarded. The most popular majors were business/marketing (22%), social sciences (14%), and English (9%). 546 companies recruited on campus in 2015-2016. In an average class, 2% graduate in 3 years or less, 39% graduate in 4 years or less, 58% graduate in 5 years or less, and 63% graduate in 6 years or less.

SERVICES: Counseling and information services are available, as is tutoring in most subjects, and a reader service for the blind. Additional tutoring is offered for a fee. **Library/Resources:** The 5 libraries contain 1.9 million volumes, 3.2 million microform items, 43,289 audio/video tapes/CDs/DVDs, and subscribe to 56,433 periodicals including electronic. Computerized library services include interlibrary loans, database searching, Internet access, and Wi-Fi capability. Special learning facilities include an art gallery, radio station, TV station, an astronomy observatory, and the Smithsonian Conservation and Research Center. **Physically Challenged Students:** 95% of the campus is accessible. Facilities include wheelchair ramps, elevators, special parking, specially equipped restrooms, special class scheduling, lowered drinking fountains, lowered telephones, special housing. Special arrangements can be made for testing, readers, note takers, and interpreters. **Special:** Mason offers internships through academic departments and on-campus work-study programs. Also available are dual and student-designed majors, accelerated degrees, non-degree study, and pass/fail options. New Century College is an integrated program of study that emphasizes collaboration, experimental learning, and self-reflection. Mason also offers the Smithsonian Semester, a 16-credit resident program in conservation studies at the Smithsonian Conservation and Research Center in Front Royal, Virginia. There are 4 national honor societies, a freshman honors program, and 1 departmental honors program. **Visiting:** There are regularly scheduled orientations for prospective students, including campus tours and an information session. There are guides for informal visits and visitors may sit in on classes. To schedule a visit, contact the Admissions Office. **Campus Safety and Security:** Measures include 24-hour foot and vehicle patrol, emergency notification system, self-defense education, and security escort services. There are also shuttle buses, lighted pathways/sidewalks, controlled access to dorms/residences, Security call boxes located throughout the campus.

REQUIREMENTS: The ACT is recommended. A score-optional review of applications allows applicants to be considered for admission without submitting test scores. Applicants must be graduates of an accredited secondary school or have a GED certificate. A minimum high school GPA of 3.5 is recommended. A minimum of 18 academic credits is required, including 4 years of English, 3 each of math, science, lab science, social studies, and academic electives, and 2 of foreign language. An written personal statement is required. AP and CLEP credits are accepted. Important factors in the admissions decision are advanced placement or honors courses, evidence of special talent, and recommendations by school officials. To graduate, all students must complete a core of study that includes 6 credits written communication, 3 to 4 credits information technology, 4 credits lab science, 3 credits each oral communication, quantitative reasoning, literature, arts, Western civilization/world history, social and behavioral science, natural science, and global understanding, and 1 to 6 credits synthesis as well as at least 45 hours of upper-division work. Hours in the major vary. A minimum 2.0 GPA is required and a total of 120 to 133 credit hours must be completed. **Procedure:** Freshmen are admitted in the fall, spring, and summer. Entrance exams should be taken during the spring of the junior year. There is a deferred admissions plan. Applications should be filed by January 15 for fall entry; October 15 for spring entry. The fall 2016 application fee was $75. Notifications are sent April 1. Applications are accepted online. **Transfer Students:** 2600 transfer students enrolled in 2015-2016. Applicants must have a minimum 2.0 GPA and generally have completed 30 or more transferable credits from an accredited college or university. Official transcripts (including high school if 30 credits or less have been completed) are required. SAT or ACT scores must be submitted if 30 credits or less have been completed unless applicant graduated from high school more than 5 years before application. 30 of 120 credits required for the bachelor's degree must be completed at Mason. **International Students:** There are 488 international students enrolled. The school actively recruits these students. They must take the TOEFL with a minimum score of 570 on the paper-based TOEFL (PBT) or 88 on the Internet-based version (iBT). They must also take the SAT or ACT.

ADMISSIONS: 63% of the 2016-2017 applicants were accepted. The SAT scores for the 2016-2017 freshman class were: Critical Reading-- 15% below 500, 52% between 500 and 599, 28% between 600 and 699, and 6% between 700 and 800. Math-- 12% below 500, 49% between 500 and 599, 34% between 600 and 699, and 5% between 700 and 800. The ACT scores were 4% below 12, 30% between 12 and 17, 37% between 18 and 23, 15% between 24 and 29, and 14% above 30. 44% of the current freshmen were in the top fifth of their class; 83% were in the top two fifths. **Admissions Contact:** Andrew Flagel, Dean of Undergraduate Admissions. Email: *admissions@gmu.edu* Web: *www.gmu.edu*

FINANCIAL AID: In 2016-2017, 67% of all full-time freshmen and 61% of continuing full-time students received some form of financial aid. 43% of all full-time freshmen and 44% of continuing full-time students received need-based aid. The average freshman award was $12,012. Need-based scholarships or need-based grants averaged $7,182 ($24,800 maximum); need-based self-help aid (loans and jobs) averaged $3,660 ($8,500 maximum); non-need-based athletic scholarships averaged $16,156 ($36,533 maximum); and other non-need-based awards and non-need-based scholarships averaged $5,940 ($33,540 maximum). The average financial indebtedness of the 2016 graduate was $19,582. The FAFSA code is 003749. The priority date for freshman financial aid applications for fall entry is March 1.

HAMPDEN-SYDNEY COLLEGE D-3

www.hsc.edu

Hampden-Sydney, VA 23943	**(434) 223-6120** **(800) 755-0733**
Fax: (434) 223-6346	**Email: hsapp@hsc.edu**
Full-time: 1025 men, 2 women	**Faculty:** 87; IIB, av$
Part-time: n/av	**Ph.D.s:** 89%
Graduate: n/av	**Student/Faculty:** 10 to 1
Year: semesters, summer session	**Tuition:** $42,962
Room & Board: $13,286	**Freshman Class:** 3683 applied, 2018 accepted, 305 enrolled
SAT CR/M/W: 563/553/526 **ACT:** 25	**CEEB CODE:** 5291
Application Deadline: March 1	**COMPETITIVE+**

Hampden-Sydney College, founded in 1775, is a private men's liberal arts institution affiliated with the Presbyterian Church. There is 1 undergraduate school. The 1340-acre campus is in a rural area 60 miles southwest of Richmond. Including any residence halls, there are 117 buildings.

STUDENT LIFE: 68% of undergraduates are from Virginia. Others are from 27 states, and 9 foreign countries. 66% are from public schools. 84% are White; 5% African American; 4% Hispanic; 4% two or more races; 2% race unknown; 1% Asian American; 1% Foreign. 64% are Protestant; 18% claim no religious affiliation; 16% Catholic. **Male To Female Ratio:** 512.5:1. The average age of freshmen is 18; all undergraduates, 20. 20% do not continue beyond their first year; 66% remain to graduate. **Housing:** 1122 students can be accommodated in college housing, which includes single-sex dorms, on-campus apartments, off-campus apartments, and married student housing. In addition, there are honors houses, language houses, special-interest houses, fraternity houses, minority student house, substance-free house, and foreign & LGBT inclusion house. On-campus housing is guaranteed for all 4 years. 95% of students live on campus; of those, 60% remain on campus on weekends. All students may keep cars.

FACULTY/CLASSROOMS: 72% of faculty are male; 28% are female. All teach undergraduates, and do research. No introductory courses are taught by graduate students. The average class size in an introductory lecture is 13; in a laboratory is 13; and in a regular course is 14.

PROGRAMS OF STUDY: Hampden-Sydney confers B.A. and B.S. degrees. Bachelor's degrees are awarded in BIOLOGICAL SCIENCE (biology/biological science), BUSINESS (business economics), COMMUNICATIONS AND THE ARTS (classics, English, fine arts, French, German, Greek, Latin, Spanish, theatre arts, and visual and performing arts), COMPUTER AND PHYSICAL SCIENCE (applied mathematics, chemistry, computer science, mathematics, and physics), SOCIAL SCIENCE (economics, history, humanities, philosophy, political science/government, psychology, and religion). Sciences, economics, and rhetoric are the strongest academically. Economics & business, economics, and biology have the largest enrollments.

ACTIVITIES: 34% of men belong to 10 national fraternities. There are no sororities. There are 83 groups on campus, including etc., mountain climbing, art, band, chess, choir, chorale, chorus, computers, debate, drama, environmental, ethnic, honors, international, LGBT, literary magazine, newspaper, photography, political, professional, radio and TV, religious, social, social service, student government, Union Philanthropic Literary Society: facilitates lively discussion and debate about current events; Outsiders: hosts trips such as white-water kayaking, and yearbook. Popular campus events include Greek Week, Macon Week, and Midwinters CAC events. **Sports:** There are 11 intercollegiate sports for men, and 12 intramural sports for men. Facilities include a field house with indoor basketball courts, outdoor basektball courts, racquetball/handball courts, an outdoor track, a pool, squash courts, weight room, gym, tennis courts, a beach volleyball court, and many playing fields. Snyder Hall also includes an Athletic Hall of Fame. **Graduates:** From July 1, 2015 to June 30, 2016, 213 bachelor's degrees were awarded. The most popular majors were economics (18%), economics & business (16%), and history (13%). 50 companies recruited on campus in 2015-2016. In an average class, 60% graduate in 4 years or less, 64% graduate in 5 years or less, and 65% graduate in 6 years or less. Of the 2015 graduating class, 10% were enrolled in graduate school within 6 months of graduation, and 35% were employed.

SERVICES: Counseling and information services are available, as is tutoring in every subject. **Library/Resources:** The library contains

274,361 volumes, 6,841 microform items, 7,549 audio/video tapes/CDs/DVDs, and subscribes to 52 periodicals including electronic. Computerized library services include interlibrary loans, database searching, Internet access, and Wi-Fi capability. Special learning facilities include an art gallery, planetarium, radio station, an international communications center, college history museum, and observatory, men's studies, Wilson Center for Leadership, and Energy Research Laboratory. **Physically Challenged Students:** 80% of the campus is accessible. Facilities include wheelchair ramps, elevators, special parking, specially equipped restrooms, special class scheduling, and lowered telephones. **Special:** The college offers co-op programs with Longwood, Randolph-Macon, Randolph College, Hollins, and Mary Baldwin Colleges and Washington and Lee University. Cross-registration with Longwood College, internships, study abroad, a 3-2 engineering program with the University of Virginia, dual-degree program in Physics and Engineering from Hampden-Sydney College and Old Dominion University, Eastern Virginia Medical School Joint program, The George Washington University School of Medicine Early Selection program, the VCU-MCV early selection program, Duke University Fuqua School of Business Early Admission program - Master of Management Studies, The UVA Darden School of Business preferred consideration program - Master of Business Administration, Washington semester, work-study programs, B.A.-B.S. degree, and dual majors are available. There is a public service concentration in all majors. There are 15 national honor societies, Phi Beta Kappa, a freshman honors program, and 10 departmental honors programs. **Visiting:** There are regularly scheduled orientations for prospective students, consisting of lectures, information sessions, tours, lunch, and an athletic event. There are guides for informal visits, visitors may sit in on classes, and stay overnight. To schedule a visit, contact Mary Brooks at (434) 223-6123. **Campus Safety and Security:** Measures include 24-hour foot and vehicle patrol, emergency notification system, and self-defense education, emergency telephones, lighted pathways/sidewalks, controlled access to dorms/residences, a fire department on campus, a first responder unit for emergency medical assistance, and all dorm phone lines are hooked into 911.

REQUIREMENTS: The ACT is required. The school recommends the SAT. Applicants must be graduates of an accredited secondary school and have completed 16 high school academic credits, including 4 of English, 3 of math, 2 each of foreign language and science, and 1 of social studies. An essay is required and an interview is recommended. The GED is accepted. AP credits are accepted. Important factors in the admissions decision are advanced placement or honors courses, recommendations by school officials, and leadership record. To graduate, students must complete 120 credit hours with a minimum GPA of 2.0. Distribution requirements include 7 courses in humanities, 4 in math and natural sciences, and 3 in social sciences. All students must also take rhetoric and foreign language and pass a rhetoric exam. **Procedure:** Freshmen are admitted in the fall and spring. Entrance exams should be taken during the junior or senior year of high school. There are early decision and early admissions plans. Early decision applications should be filed by November 15; regular applications, by March 1 for fall entry; and December 1 for spring entry, along with a $30 fee. Notification of early decision is sent December 15; regular decision, April 15. 64 early decision candidates were accepted for the 2016-2017 class. Applications are accepted online. Application fees are waived if application is completed on-line. **Transfer Students:** 15 transfer students enrolled in 2015-2016. Applicants must have a minimum GPA of 2.5 and must take either the SAT or the ACT. An interview is recommended. 60 of 120 credits required for the bachelor's degree must be completed at Hampden-Sydney. **International Students:** There are 13 international students enrolled. They must take the TOEFL with a minimum score of 114 on the Internet-based version (iBT). They must also take the SAT or ACT.

ADMISSIONS: 55% of the 2016-2017 applicants were accepted. The SAT scores for the 2016-2017 freshman class were: Critical Reading-- 25% below 500, 45% between 500 and 599, 21% between 600 and 699, and 9% between 700 and 800. Math-- 22% below 500, 46% between 500 and 599, 27% between 600 and 699, and 5% between 700 and 800. Writing-- 38% below 500, 44% between 500 and 599, 17% between 600 and 699, and 1% between 700 and 800. The ACT scores were 40% between 18 and 23, 41% between 24 and 29, and 15% above 30. 28% of the current freshmen were in the top fifth of their class; 85% were in the top two fifths. **Admissions Contact:** Anita H. Garland, Dean of Admissions. Email: *hsapp@hsc.edu* Web: *www.hsc.edu*

FINANCIAL AID: In 2016-2017, 99% of all full-time freshmen and continuing full-time students received some form of financial aid. 70% of all full-time freshmen and 63% of continuing full-time students received need-based aid. The average freshman award was $35,474. Need-based scholarships or need-based grants averaged $28,626 ($39,000 maximum); need-based self-help aid (loans and jobs) averaged $4,559 ($11,000 maximum); and other non-need-based awards and non-need-based scholarships averaged $19,993 ($56,710 maximum). 22% of undergraduate students work part-time. Average annual earnings from campus work are $1380. The average financial indebtedness of the 2016 graduate was $25,364. The FAFSA code is 223713. The deadline for filing freshman financial aid applications for fall entry is March 1.

HAMPTON UNIVERSITY *(The complete profile is made available exclusively on our website, www.barronspac.com)*

HOLLINS UNIVERSITY — C-3

www.hollins.edu

Roanoke, VA 24020 — **(540) 362-6401**, **(800) 456-9595**

Fax: (540) 362-6218 — **Email: huadm@hollins.edu**

Full-time: 1 men, 643 women	**Faculty:** n/av
Part-time: 10 women	**Ph.D.s:** n/av
Graduate: 30 men, 143 women	**Student/Faculty:** n/av
Year: 4-1-4	**Tuition:** $36,835
Room & Board: $12,800	**Freshman Class:** 2901 applied, 1737 accepted, 224 enrolled
SAT CR/M/W: 575/525/555 **ACT:** 26	**CEEB CODE:** 5294
Application Deadline: February 1	**VERY COMPETITIVE**

Hollins University, formerly Hollins College, founded in 1842 is Virginia's first chartered women's college, offering a broad liberal arts curriculum. The figures in the above capsule and in this profile are approximate. There is 1 undergraduate school and 1 graduate school. In addition to regional accreditation, Hollins has baccalaureate program accreditation with TEAC. The 475-acre campus is in a suburban area in Roanoke County. Including any residence halls, there are 73 buildings.

STUDENT LIFE: 52% of undergraduates are from out of state, mostly the South. Students are from 38 states, and 21 foreign countries. 84% are from public schools. 65% are White; 12% African American; 7% Hispanic; 5% Foreign; 5% two or more races; 4% race unknown; 2% Asian American; 1% American Indian/Alaska Native. **Female To Male Ratio:** 25.7:1. The average age of freshmen is 19; all undergraduates, 21. 31% do not continue beyond their first year; 53% remain to graduate. **Housing:** 688 students can be accommodated in college housing, which includes single-sex dorms, on-campus apartments, language houses, special-interest houses, women's dorm, international housing, theme and wellness housing. On-campus housing is guaranteed for all 4 years. 84% of students live on campus; of those, 50% remain on campus on weekends. All students may keep cars.

FACULTY/CLASSROOMS: All teach undergraduates. Graduate students teach 1% of introductory courses. The average class size in an introductory lecture is 11; in a laboratory is 11; and in a regular course is 14.

PROGRAMS OF STUDY: Hollins confers B.A., B.S., and B.A./B.F.A. degrees. Master's degrees are also awarded. Bachelor's degrees are awarded in AGRICULTURE (environmental studies), BIOLOGICAL SCIENCE (biology/biological science), BUSINESS (business administration and management), COMMUNICATIONS AND THE ARTS (art history and appreciation, classical languages, communications, dance, English, film arts, French, music, Spanish, studio art, and theatre arts), COMPUTER AND PHYSICAL SCIENCE (chemistry and mathematics), EDUCATION (classical studies), ENGINEERING AND ENVIRONMENTAL DESIGN (environmental science), SOCIAL SCIENCE (economics, gender studies, history, interdisciplinary studies, international studies, philosophy, political science/government, psychology, religion, and sociology). Art history, classical studies, and biology are the strongest academically. English/creative writing, psychology, and biology have the largest enrollments.

ACTIVITIES: There are no fraternities or sororities. There are 36 groups on campus, including art, choir, chorale, dance, drama, environmental, ethnic, film, honors, international, LGBT, literary magazine, musical theater, political, religious, social, social service, and student government. Popular campus events include Day of Service, Tinker Day, Ring Night, Founder's Day, Holiday Tea, Dance & Theatre Productions, and Women's History Month. **Sports:** There are 9 intercollegiate sports for women. Facilities include a swimming center, fitness center, weight rooms, a gym, an auxilary gym, an equestrian center, jogging loop, outdoor tennis courts, playing fields, a putting green, an exercise studio, 2 training rooms, 2 saunas, and a climbing wall. **Graduates:** From July 1, 2015 to June 30, 2016, 123 bachelor's degrees were awarded. The most popular majors were English/creative writing (18%), biology (11%), and psychology (10%). 4 companies recruited on campus in 2015-2016. In an average class, 50% graduate in 4 years or less, 57% graduate in 5 years or less, and 57% graduate in 6 years or less. Of the 2015 graduating class, 29% were enrolled in graduate school within 6 months of graduation, and 68% were employed.

SERVICES: Counseling and information services are available, as is tutoring in most subjects, and a reader service for the blind, and remedial writing. There is also a writing center and a quantitative reasoning center. **Library/Resources:** The library contains 626,085 volumes, 12,985 microform items, 13,796 audio/video tapes/CDs/DVDs, and subscribes to 38,349 periodicals including electronic. Computerized library services include interlibrary loans, database searching, Internet access, and Wi-Fi capability. Special learning facilities include an art gallery. **Physically Challenged Students:** 42% of the campus is accessible. Facilities include wheelchair ramps, elevators, special parking, specially equipped restrooms, special class scheduling, lowered drinking fountains, and special housing. **Special:** Hollins offers internships during the January term, dual majors, student-designed majors, accelerated degrees, and study abroad in 16 countries. There is cross-registration with the Virginia Seven College Exchange and Roanoke College. A Washington Semester is availalbe through The American University. There is also a domestic student exchange program. There are 17 national honor societies, Phi Beta Kappa, a freshman honors program, and 20 departmental honors programs. **Visiting:** There are regularly scheduled orientations for prospective students, includes 2 open houses for Seniors, 1 in October and 1 in November. Sophomores and Juniors are invited to Spring Visit Days in March and May. Admitted students are invited to campus in April. There are guides for informal visits, visitors may sit in on classes, and stay overnight. To schedule a visit, contact Rena Musyt at (540) 362-6401. **Campus Safety and Security:** Measures include 24-hour foot and vehicle patrol, emergency notification system, self-defense education, and security escort services, emergency telephones, lighted pathways/sidewalks, and emergency buttons located along walkways and in labs.

REQUIREMENTS: The SAT or ACT is required. Applicants must be graduates of an accredited secondary school. With proper documentation, the GED and home-schooled students are accepted. Applicants should complete 16 high school academic credits, 4 credits of English and 3 credits each of math, science, and social studies, and 2 of foreign language. Official high school transcripts and letters of recommendation are required. An essay is also required, and an interview is recommended. AP credits are accepted. Important factors in the admissions decision are advanced placement or honors courses, personality/intangible qualities, and leadership record. To graduate, students must complete 128 credits for the B.A., 140 credits for the B.S., and 150 credits for the B.A./B.F.A., plus 4 short terms. At least 32 hours in the major and a 2.0 GPA are required. All students must fulfill Hollins' general education program (Education Through Skills and Perspectives). Students are also required to take 2 semesters of phys ed or participate in a varsity sport. A thesis is required for some majors. **Procedure:** Freshmen are admitted in the fall and spring. Entrance exams should be taken by January of the senior year. There are early decision, deferred admissions, and rolling admissions plans. Early decision applications should be filed by November 1; regular applications, by February 1 for fall entry; and December 1 for spring entry. Notification of early decision is sent November 15; regular decision, November 1. 6 early decision candidates were accepted for the 2016-2017 class. Applications are accepted on-line. **Transfer Students:** 17 transfer students enrolled in 2015-2016. Applicants for transfer should have a minimum college GPA of 2.5. Other criteria are the same as for entering freshmen, such as high school transcript, all college transcripts, an essay or personal statement, and a statement of good standing from prior institution(s). Students may enroll in the fall, rolling and spring, rolling. 64 of 128 credits required for the bachelor's degree must be completed at Hollins. **International Students:** There are 30 international students enrolled. The school actively recruits these students. They must take the TOEFL with a minimum score of 550 on the paper-based TOEFL (PBT) or 79 on the Internet-based version (iBT), SAT scores may be submitted in lieu of the TOEFL; however, if SAT scores are low the TOEFL may also be required. They must also take the SAT or ACT. Students whose native language is not English must score 550 on the TOEFL (79 on the iBT).

ADMISSIONS: 60% of the 2016-2017 applicants were accepted. The SAT scores for the 2016-2017 freshman class were: Critical Reading-- 13% below 500, 44% between 500 and 599, 32% between 600 and 699, and 11% between 700 and 800. Math-- 30% below 500, 46% between 500 and 599, 23% between 600 and 699, and 1% between 700 and 800. Writing-- 27% below 500, 46% between 500 and 599, 21% between 600 and 699, and 3% between 700 and 800. The ACT scores were 1% between 12 and 17, 31% between 18 and 23, 54% between 24 and 29, and 14% above 30. 52% of the current freshmen were in the top fifth of their class; 84% were in the top two fifths. **Admissions Contact:** Ashkey Browning, Director of Admissions. Email: *huadm@hollins.edu* Web: *www.hollins.edu*

FINANCIAL AID: In 2016-2017, 100% of all full-time freshmen and 99% of continuing full-time students received some form of financial aid. 60% of all full-time freshmen and 64% of continuing full-time students received need-based aid. The average freshman award was $37,844. Need-based scholarships or need-based grants averaged $5,093 ($9,815 maximum); need-based self-help aid (loans and jobs) averaged $4,340 ($8,000 maximum); and other non-need-based awards and non-need-based scholarships averaged $30,364 ($52,910 maximum). The average financial indebtedness of the 2016 graduate was $34,414. The state aid form is required. The FAFSA code is 003715. The priority date for freshman financial aid applications for fall entry is January 1.

JAMES MADISON UNIVERSITY — D-2

www.jmu.edu

Harrisonburg, VA 22807 — **(540) 568-5681**

Fax: (540) 568-3332	**Email:** admissions@jmu.edu
Full-time: 6999 men, 10,330 women	**Faculty:** 840; IIA, av$
Part-time: 400 men, 378 women	**Ph.D.s:** 78%
Graduate: 559 men, 1261 women	**Student/Faculty:** 20 to 1
Year: semesters, summer session	**Tuition:** $10,066 ($25,200)
Room & Board: $9018	**Freshman Class:** 22648 applied, 14392 accepted, 4325 enrolled
SAT CR/M/W: 570/580/565 **ACT:** required	**CEEB CODE:** 5392
Application Deadline: January 15	**VERY COMPETITIVE**

James Madison University, founded in 1908, is a public institution with programs in science and math, business, education, arts and letters, visual and performing arts, and integrated science and technology. The figures in the above capsule and in this profile are approximate. There are 7 undergraduate schools and 1 graduate school. In addition to regional accreditation, JMU has baccalaureate program accreditation with AACSB, ABET, ADA, AHEA, CSWE, FIDER, NASAD, NASM, NCATE, ACS, AOTA, APA, CACREP, and NAST. The 712-acre campus is in a small town 123 miles southwest of Washington, D.C. Including any residence halls, there are 111 buildings.

STUDENT LIFE: 71% of undergraduates are from Virginia. Others are from 45 states, 55 foreign countries, and Canada. 81% are White; 6% Asian American; 4% African American; 3% Hispanic; 1% Foreign; 1% two or more races. 32% are Catholic; 26% Protestant; 23% claim no religious affiliation. **Female To Male Ratio:** 1.5:1. The average age of freshmen is 18; all undergraduates, 21. 8% do not continue beyond their first year; 81% remain to graduate. **Housing:** 6100 students can be accommodated in college housing, which includes coed dorms and off-campus apartments. In addition, there are honors houses, special-interest houses, fraternity houses, sorority houses, substance-free and international communities, and learning communities for education, health, psychology, community service, biology, ecology, wellness housing, special housing for disabled students, and theme housing. On-campus housing is guaranteed for the freshman year only. 64% of students commute. Upperclassmen may keep cars.

FACULTY/CLASSROOMS: 52% of faculty are male; 48% are female. 92% teach undergraduates. Graduate students teach 1% of introductory courses. The average class size in an introductory lecture is 39; in a laboratory is 22; and in a regular course is 31.

PROGRAMS OF STUDY: JMU confers B.A., B.S., B.B.A., B.F.A., B.I.S.,

B.M., B.S.N., and B.S.W. degrees. Master's and doctoral degrees are also awarded. Bachelor's degrees are awarded in BIOLOGICAL SCIENCE (biology/biological science and biotechnology), BUSINESS (accounting, banking and finance, business administration and management, business economics, hospitality management services, international business management, marketing/retailing/merchandising, recreation and leisure services, and tourism), COMMUNICATIONS AND THE ARTS (art, art history and appreciation, communications, communications technology, dance, dramatic arts, English, fine arts, media arts, modern language, music, and speech/debate/rhetoric), COMPUTER AND PHYSICAL SCIENCE (chemistry, computer science, geology, information sciences and systems, mathematics, physics, quantitative methods, science technology, and statistics), EDUCATION (athletic training), ENGINEERING AND ENVIRONMENTAL DESIGN (engineering), HEALTH PROFESSIONS (health care administration, health science, nursing, and speech pathology/audiology), SOCIAL SCIENCE (anthropology, criminal justice, dietetics, economics, geography, history, international studies, liberal arts/general studies, philosophy, physical fitness/movement, political science/government, psychology, public administration, religion, social science, social work, and sociology). Interdisciplinary liberal studies, health science, and kinesiology have the largest enrollments.

ACTIVITIES: 12% of men belong to 15 national fraternities; 12% of women belong to 9 national sororities. There are 298 groups on campus, including art, band, cheerleading, chess, choir, chorale, chorus, computers, dance, drama, environmental, ethnic, honors, international, jazz band, LGBT, literary magazine, marching band, musical theater, newspaper, opera, orchestra, pep band, photography, political, professional, radio and TV, religious, social, social service, student government, symphony, and yearbook. Popular campus events include Madison Symposium, James Madison Week, and International Week. **Sports:** There are 6 intercollegiate sports for men and 12 for women, and 10 intramural sports for men and 10 for women. Facilities include a stadium, convocation center, all-weather track, a gym, natatorium, tennis courts, baseball, soccer, and softball fields. A recreation center houses a fitness center, racquetball courts, basketball gyms, an indoor track, a pool, and a climbing wall. **Graduates:** From July 1, 2015 to June 30, 2016, 4096 bachelor's degrees were awarded. The most popular majors were health professions and related programs (15%), business/marketing (14%), and communication/journalism (9%). 194 companies recruited on campus in 2015-2016. In an average class, 64% graduate in 4 years or less, 80% graduate in 5 years or less, and 81% graduate in 6 years or less. Of the 2015 graduating class, 27% were enrolled in graduate school within 6 months of graduation, and 46% were employed.

SERVICES: Counseling and information services are available, as is tutoring in every subject, and a reader service for the blind. Support is also available in time management, organization, test preparation, and test taking. **Library/Resources:** The 3 libraries contain 645,740 volumes, 1.1 million microform items, 42,676 audio/video tapes/CDs/DVDs, and subscribe to 12,662 periodicals including electronic. Computerized library services include interlibrary loans, database searching, and Internet access. Special learning facilities include an art gallery, planetarium, radio station, an arboretum, a music library, CISAT library services, a mineral museum, and science on a sphere. **Physically Challenged Students:** 90% of the campus is accessible. Facilities include wheelchair ramps, elevators, special parking, specially equipped restrooms, special class scheduling, lowered drinking fountains, lowered telephones, and special housing. **Special:** JMU offers internships, work-study programs, a Washington semester, and study abroad in London, Antwerp, Florence, and Salamanca. There is a combined program in forestry with Virginia Tech. An individualized study degree, nondegree study, pass/fail options, and credit for life, military, and work experience are available. There are 28 national honor societies, Phi Beta Kappa, a freshman honors program, and 82 departmental honors programs. **Visiting:** There are regularly scheduled orientations for prospective students, including daily campus tours during the week and on Saturdays, and tours following group conferences with admissions counselors. There are guides for informal visits. To schedule a visit, contact the Admissions Office. **Campus Safety and Security:** Measures include 24-hour foot and vehicle patrol, emergency notification system, self-defense education, security escort services, emergency telephones, lighted pathways/sidewalks, controlled access to dorms/residences. There are public bus transportation routes through the campus.

REQUIREMENTS: The SAT or ACT is required. Applicants must be graduates of an accredited secondary school. They must show solid achievement in 4 or more academic courses each year of high school including some honors or advanced course work. A personal statement is optional. Art students must present a portfolio. Theater, dance, and music students must audition. Nursing students must apply to the nursing department in addition to applying for undergraduate admission. AP credits are accepted. Important factors in the admissions decision are advanced placement or honors courses, recommendations by school officials, and extracurricular activities record. To graduate, students must complete a minimum of 120 credit hours, with a GPA of at least 2.0., meet the general education requirements and the requirements of their major, have been enrolled at JMU a minimum of two regular semesters, and have earned a minimum of 30 credit hours at JMU during that period of enrollment. **Procedure:** Freshmen are admitted in the fall. Entrance exams should be taken in the spring of the junior year or the fall of the senior year. There are early admissions and deferred admissions plans. Early decision applications should be filed by November 1; regular applications, by January 15 for fall entry, along with a $50 fee. Notification of early decision is sent January 15; regular decision, April 1. 1431 applicants were on the 2016 waiting list; 7 were admitted. Applications are accepted online. **Transfer Students:** 621 transfer students enrolled in 2015-2016. Applicants must have a minimum GPA of 2.0 and must submit a complete application, official college transcripts, and secondary school records or a copy of their GED. A one-page personal statement is optional. If applicants have fewer than 30 credit hours completed at the time of application, they must submit SAT scores unless they are 25 years old or older. 30 of 120 credits required for the bachelor's degree must be completed at JMU. **International Students:** There are 272 international students enrolled. The school actively recruits these students. They must take the TOEFL with a minimum score of 550 on the paper-based TOEFL (PBT) or 81 on the Internet-based version (iBT).

ADMISSIONS: 64% of the 2016-2017 applicants were accepted. The SAT scores for the 2016-2017 freshman class were: Critical Reading-- 13% below 500, 52% between 500 and 599, 31% between 600 and 699, and 4% between 700 and 800. Math-- 10% below 500, 47% between 500 and 599, 39% between 600 and 699, and 4% between 700 and 800. Writing-- 14% below 500, 51% between 500 and 599, 31% between 600 and 699, and 4% between 700 and 800. 21 freshmen graduated first in their class. **Admissions Contact:** Adam Anderson, Associate Dean of Admissions. Email: *admissions@jmu.edu* Web: *www.jmu.edu*

FINANCIAL AID: In 2016-2017, 32% of all full-time freshmen and 33% of continuing full-time students received some form of financial aid. 35% of all full-time freshmen and 31% of continuing full-time students received need-based aid. The average freshman award was $9,509. Need-based scholarships or need-based grants averaged $7,560; need-based self-help aid (loans and jobs) averaged $4,736; non-need-based athletic scholarships averaged $18,500; other non-need-based awards and non-need-based scholarships averaged $4,695; and $3,384 from other forms of aid. 20% of undergraduate students work part-time. Average annual earnings from campus work are $1885. The average financial indebtedness of the 2016 graduate was $23,562. The FAFSA code is 003721. The deadline for filing freshman financial aid applications for fall entry is March 1.

LIBERTY UNIVERSITY D-3

www.liberty.edu

Lynchburg, VA 24502	**(434) 582-7307** **(800) 543-5317**
Fax: (434) 582-2421	**Email:** admissions@liberty.edu
Full-time: 2800 men, 3300 women	**Faculty:** 200
Part-time: 110 men, 120 women	**Ph.D.s:** 67%
Graduate: n/av	**Student/Faculty:** 31 to 1
Year: semesters, summer session	**Tuition:** $14,000
Room & Board: $5401	**Freshman Class:** n/av
SAT or ACT: required	**CEEB CODE:** 5385
Application Deadline: n/av	**COMPETITIVE**

Liberty University, founded in 1971, is a private liberal arts institution affiliated with the Baptist Church. The figures in the above capsule and in this profile are approximate. There are 6 undergraduate schools and 5 graduate schools. In addition to regional accreditation, Liberty has baccalaureate program accreditation with NASM and NLN. The 160-acre campus is in a suburban area 45 miles east of Roanoke. Including any residence halls, there are 73 buildings.

STUDENT LIFE: 60% of undergraduates are from out of state, mostly the Middle Atlantic. Students are from 48 states, 76 foreign countries, and Canada. 78% are White; 4% Asian American; 3% Hispanic; 11% African American; 1% American Indian/Alaska Native. 89% are Protestant. **Female To Male Ratio:** 1.2:1. The average age of freshmen is 19; all undergraduates, 21. **Housing:** 4303 students can be accommodated in college housing, which includes single-sex dorms and on-campus apartments. On-campus housing is guaranteed for all 4 years. 64% of students live on campus; of those, 90% remain on campus on weekends. All students may keep cars. Alcohol is not permitted.

FACULTY/CLASSROOMS: 67% of faculty are male; 33% are female. 90% teach undergraduates. No introductory courses are taught by graduate students. The average class size in an introductory lecture is 43; in a laboratory is 22; and in a regular course is 23.

PROGRAMS OF STUDY: Liberty confers B.A., B.S., B.M., and B.S.N. degrees. Associate, master's, and doctoral degrees are also awarded. Bachelor's degrees are awarded in BIOLOGICAL SCIENCE (biology/biological science), BUSINESS (accounting, business administration and management, management information systems, and sports management), COMMUNICATIONS AND THE ARTS (communications, English, English as a second/foreign language, music, and Spanish), COMPUTER AND PHYSICAL SCIENCE (computer science and mathematics), EDUCATION (athletic training, elementary education, and physical education), HEALTH PROFESSIONS (community health work, exercise science, and nursing), SOCIAL SCIENCE (family/consumer studies, history, interdisciplinary studies, international studies, liberal arts/general studies, political science/government, psychology, religion, and social science). Education, psychology, and business are the strongest academically. Business, psychology, and education have the largest enrollments.

ACTIVITIES: There are no fraternities or sororities. There are 40 groups on campus, including band, cheerleading, choir, chorale, chorus, communications, computers, debate, drama, drill team, ethnic, honors, international, marching band, musical theater, newspaper, opera, orchestra, pep band, political, professional, radio and TV, religious, social service, student government, and yearbook. Popular campus events include Super Conference and Missions Emphasis Week. **Sports:** There are 9 intercollegiate sports for men and 8 for women, and 16 intramural sports for men and 16 for women. Facilities include a football stadium, basketball arena/convention center, baseball and soccer fields, a track complex and a tennis center. **Graduates:** From July 1, 2015 to June 30, 2016, 945 bachelor's degrees were awarded. The most popular majors were psychology (17%), business (16%), and religion (14%).

SERVICES: Counseling and information services are available, as is tutoring in every subject, and remedial math, reading, and writing. **Library/Resources:** The library contains 211,092 volumes, 95,329 microform items, 7,149 audio/video tapes/CDs/DVDs, and subscribes to 10,806 periodicals including electronic. Computerized library services include interlibrary loans, database searching, and Internet access. Special learning facilities include a radio station and TV station. **Physically Challenged Students:** 90% of the campus is accessible. Facilities include wheelchair ramps, elevators, special parking, specially equipped restrooms, special class scheduling, lowered drinking fountains, lowered telephones, and special housing. **Special:** Liberty offers internships, B.A.-B.S. degrees, and student-designed majors in interdisciplinary and general studies. There are 8 national honor societies, Phi Beta Kappa, and a freshman honors program. **Visiting:** There are regularly scheduled orientations for prospective students, including College for a Weekend, a 2-day program offering a chance to attend classes and special meetings. There are guides for informal visits, visitors may sit in on classes, and stay overnight. To schedule a visit, contact the Visitor's Center. **Campus Safety and Security:** Measures include 24-hour foot and vehicle patrol, self-defense education, and security escort services. There are shuttle buses and lighted pathways/sidewalks.

REQUIREMENTS: The SAT or ACT is required. Applicants must have completed 16 high school academic credits. The GED is accepted. An essay is required. AP and CLEP credits are accepted. Important factors in the admissions decision are ability to finance college education, recommendations by school officials, and advanced placement or honors courses. Students must complete 120 to 123 credit hours to graduate, with a minimum GPA of 2.0. with few exceptions, by major, all must complete 18 hours of foundational studies in English, math, speech communications, and general education. An additional 42 credits of investigative studies are required; these vary according to the degree sought, either B.A. or B.S., but include English, natural sciences, history, arts, music, languages, government, social sciences, philosophy, theology, Bible studies, and integrated studies. **Procedure:** Freshmen are admitted to all sessions. Entrance exams should be taken during the junior year. There are early decision, early admissions, deferred admissions, and rolling admissions plans. Application deadlines are open. Application fee is $35. Notification is sent on a rolling basis. Applications are accepted online. **Transfer Students:** 743 transfer students enrolled in 2015-2016. Applicants for transfer must have a GPA of 2.0. If transferring fewer than 60 hours, a high school transcript and test scores are required. 30 of 120 credits required for the bachelor's degree must be completed at Liberty. **International Students:** There are 238 international students enrolled. The school actively recruits these students. They must take the TOEFL or MELAB, as well as the SAT or ACT.

ADMISSIONS: There were 5 National Merit finalists. **Admissions Contact:** David Hart, Associate Director of Admissions. Email: *admissions@liberty.edu* Web: *www.liberty.edu*

FINANCIAL AID: In 2016-2017, 98% of all full-time freshmen and 88% of continuing full-time students received some form of financial aid. 64% of all full-time freshmen and continuing full-time students received need-based aid. The average freshman award was $8,506. Need-based scholarships or need-based grants averaged $1,800 ($4,000 maximum); need-based self-help aid (loans and jobs) averaged $3,725 ($3,940 maximum); non-need-based athletic scholarships averaged $8,172 ($18,850 maximum); and other non-need-based awards and non-need-based scholarships averaged $4,667 ($15,220 maximum). 15% of undergraduate students work part-time. Average annual earnings from campus work are $2500. The average financial indebtedness of the 2016 graduate was $15,619. The FAFSA code is 010392. The deadline for filing freshman financial aid applications for fall entry is March 1.

LONGWOOD UNIVERSITY D-3

www.longwood.edu

Farmville, VA 23909	**(434) 395-2060** **(800) 281-4677**
Fax: (434) 395-2332	**Email: admissions@longwood.edu**
Full-time: 1283 men, 2635 women	**Faculty:** 238; IIA, --$
Part-time: 166 men, 291 women	**Ph.D.s:** 77%
Graduate: 77 men, 430 women	**Student/Faculty:** 18 to 1
Year: semesters, summer session	**Tuition:** $22,184 ($36,614)
Room & Board: n/app	**Freshman Class:** 4055 applied, 3299 accepted, 1111 enrolled
SAT CR/M: 500/500 **ACT:** 21	**CEEB CODE:** 5368
Application Deadline: March 1	**COMPETITIVE**

Longwood University, founded in 1839, is a state-supported institution with programs in liberal arts, business, and teacher preparation. The figures in the above capsule are approximate and include tuition, and fees for 15 credit hours, and room and board on a 14 meal/week plan. There are 3 undergraduate schools and 1 graduate school. In addition to regional accreditation, Longwood has baccalaureate program accreditation with AACSB, CSWE, NASM, NCATE, and NRPA. The 160-acre campus is in a small town 60 miles west of Richmond and 60 miles south of Charlottesville. Including any residence halls, there are 44 buildings.

STUDENT LIFE: 94% of undergraduates are from Virginia. Others are from 39 states, 23 foreign countries, and Canada. 93% are from public schools. 9% are African American; 76% White; 4% Hispanic; 4% race unknown; 3% two or more races; 1% Asian American; 1% Foreign. **Female To Male Ratio:** 2.2:1. The average age of freshmen is 18; all undergraduates, 20. 20% do not continue beyond their first year; 66% remain to graduate. **Housing:** College-sponsored housing includes single-sex and coed dorms, off-campus apartments, honors houses, substance-free dorm, international studies, fraternity/sorority, and ecology floors. On-campus housing is guaranteed for the freshman year only, and is available on a first-come, first-served basis, and on a lottery system for upperclassmen. 74% of students live on campus; of those, 60% remain on campus on weekends. Upperclassmen may keep cars.

FACULTY/CLASSROOMS: 45% of faculty are male; 55% are female. All teach undergraduates, 50% do research, and 50% do both. No introductory courses are taught by graduate students. The average class size in an introductory lecture is 21 and in a regular course is 21.

PROGRAMS OF STUDY: Longwood confers B.A., B.S., B.F.A., B.M., and B.S.B.A. degrees. Master's degrees are also awarded. Bachelor's degrees are awarded in BIOLOGICAL SCIENCE (biology/biological science), BUSINESS (business administration and management), COMMUNICATIONS AND THE ARTS (art, communications, English, modern language, music, and visual and performing arts), COMPUTER AND PHYSICAL SCIENCE (chemistry, computer science, mathematics, and physics), EDUCATION (art education, athletic training, elementary education, music education, physical education, and special education), HEALTH PROFESSIONS (community health work, nursing, and recreation therapy), SOCIAL SCIENCE (anthropology, criminal justice, criminology, economics, history, liberal arts/general studies, political science/government, psychology, social work, and sociology). Natural sciences, and secondary education are the strongest academically. Business, biology, and elementary education have the largest enrollments.

ACTIVITIES: 22% of men belong to 12 national fraternities; 22% of women belong to 10 national sororities. There are 176 groups on campus, including art, band, cheerleading, chess, choir, chorus, computers, dance, drama, ethnic, honors, international, jazz band, LGBT, musical theater, newspaper, pep band, photography, political, professional, radio and TV, religious, social, social service, and student government. Popular campus events include Spring Weekend, and Oktoberfest. **Sports:** There are 6 intercollegiate sports for men and 8 for women, and 14 intramural sports for men and 16 for women. Facilities include a golf course, a weight training facility, gym, racquetball courts, tennis courts, pools, bowling alley, outdoor sand volleyball courts, fitness trail, a frisbee golf course, outdoor basketball courts, and soccer, baseball, and softball fields. **Graduates:** In an average class, 1% graduate in 3 years or less, 40% graduate in 4 years or less, 56% graduate in 5 years or less, and 59% graduate in 6 years or less.

SERVICES: Counseling and information services are available, as is tutoring in some subjects, such as learning strategies, study skills, organizational skills and time management. There is a reader service for the blind, and remedial writing. There is also assistance in study skills, learning strategies, advocacy training, and compensatory strategy instruction. **Library/Resources:** The library contains 362,151 volumes, 667,409 microform items, and 23,331 audio/video tapes/CDs/DVDs. Computerized library services include interlibrary loans, database searching, Internet access, and Wi-Fi capability. Special learning facilities include an art gallery, radio station, a greenhouse, language lab, 6 computer labs, and a psychology lab. **Physically Challenged Students:** Facilities include wheelchair ramps, elevators, special parking, special class scheduling, lowered drinking fountains, lowered telephones, and special housing. The campus is mostly accessible with continuous monitoring for accessibility. **Special:** Longwood offers internships or directed research projects in all majors, study abroad in 15 countries, and B.A.-B.S. degrees in many majors. Cross-registration is possible with Hampden-Sydney College, as are 3-2 engineering degrees with several regional universities. Also, there is a 3-3 preprofessional program in physical therapy with University of Virginia, Old Dominion, and Virginia Commonwealth Universities. There are 10 national honor societies and a freshman honors program. **Visiting:** There are regularly scheduled orientations for prospective students, including informational and tour programs, and open houses September - December and March - May. Visitors may sit in on classes and stay overnight. To schedule a visit, contact the Admissions Office. **Campus Safety and Security:** Measures include 24-hour foot and vehicle patrol, emergency notification system, self-defense education, and security escort services. There are also shuttle buses, emergency telephones, lighted pathways/sidewalks, electronic card key entry controlled access to dorms/residences, and surveillance cameras.

REQUIREMENTS: The SAT or ACT is required. Applicants must be graduates of an accredited secondary school; the GED is accepted. Students should complete 4 years of high school English, 2 years each of foreign language and 3 years science (including 2 lab courses), 2 years of history, and algebra I, II, and geometry. A personal statement is required. An audition is required for music students. AP and CLEP credits are accepted. Important factors in the admissions decision are advanced placement or honors courses, leadership record, and evidence of special talent. To graduate, students must complete 120 to 145 credits, including 36 to 77 in the major, with a minimum GPA of 2.0 overall. A 41-hour general education core curriculum, 4 intensive writing courses, a phys ed course, and 30 upper-level credit hours are also required. **Procedure:** Freshmen are admitted to all sessions. Entrance exams should be taken in the fall of the senior year. There are early admissions and rolling admissions plans. Early decision applications should be filed by December 1; regular applications, by March 1 for fall entry; October 15 for winter entry; October 15 for spring entry; and March 1 for summer entry, along with a $50 fee. Notification is sent on a rolling basis. Applications are accepted online. **Transfer Students:** 214 transfer students enrolled in 2015-2016. Applicants for transfer must have a GPA of at least 2.5 in all college course work attempted. Other criteria are the same as for entering freshmen. 30 of 120 credits required for the bachelor's degree must be completed at Longwood. **International Students:** The school actively recruits these students. They must take the TOEFL with a minimum score of 550 on the paper-based TOEFL (PBT) or 79 on the Internet-based version (iBT). They must also take the SAT or ACT.

ADMISSIONS: 81% of the 2016-2017 applicants were accepted. The SAT scores for the 2016-2017 freshman class were: Critical Reading-- 43% below 500, 44% between 500 and 599, 10% between 600 and 699, and 1% between 700 and 800. Math-- 44% below 500, 45% between 500 and 599, and 9% between 600 and 699. **Admissions Contact:** Johnice Brown, Associate Director/Undergrad Admission. Email: *admissions@longwood.edu* Web: *www.longwood.edu*

FINANCIAL AID: The FAFSA code is 003719. The priority date for freshman financial aid applications for fall entry is March 1.

LYNCHBURG COLLEGE D-3

www.lynchburg.edu

Lynchburg, VA 24501 **(800) 426-8101**

Fax: (434) 544-8653
Email: admissions@lynchburg.edu
Full-time: 767 men, 1171 women
Faculty: IIA, -$
Part-time: 54 men, 87 women
Ph.D.s: 85%
Graduate: 184 men, 457 women
Student/Faculty: 11 to 1
Year: semesters, summer session
Tuition: $36,620
Room & Board: $10,120
Freshman Class: 5223 applied, 3331 accepted, 521 enrolled
SAT CR/M: 500/510 **ACT:** 22
CEEB CODE: 5372
Application Deadline: open
COMPETITIVE

Lynchburg College, established in 1903, is a private institution affiliated with the Christian Church (Disciples of Christ). LC offers bachelor's degrees in 40 majors, master's degrees in 16 programs, and 3 doctoral degrees (physical therapy, medical science/physician assistant & leadership studies). The mission of Lynchburg College is to develop students with strong character and balanced perspectives and to prepare them for engagement in a global society and for effective leadership in the civic, professional, and spiritual dimensions of life. There are 6 undergraduate schools and 1 graduate school. In addition to regional accreditation, L.C. has baccalaureate program accreditation with ACBSP, NASM, CCNE, CAAHEP, and CACREP. The 264-acre campus is in a suburban area 180 miles southwest of Washington, D.C., and 120 west of Richmond. Including any residence halls, there are 40 buildings.

STUDENT LIFE: 69% of undergraduates are from Virginia. Others are from 37 states, 15 foreign countries, and Canada. 72% are White; 5% Hispanic; 4% two or more races; 3% Foreign; 3% race unknown; 12% African American; 1% Asian American. **Female To Male Ratio:** 1.7:1. The average age of freshmen is 18; all undergraduates, 20. 19% do not continue beyond their first year; 56% remain to graduate. **Housing:** 1800 students can be accommodated in college housing, which includes single-sex and coed dorms, on-campus apartments, honors houses, language houses, special-interest houses, fraternity houses, and sorority houses. On-campus housing is guaranteed for all 4 years. 75% of students live on campus. Upperclassmen may keep cars.

FACULTY/CLASSROOMS: 45% of faculty are male; 55% are female. 93% teach undergraduates. No introductory courses are taught by graduate students. The average class size in a regular course is 17.

PROGRAMS OF STUDY: Lynchburg confers B.A. and B.S. degrees. Master's and doctoral degrees are also awarded. Bachelor's degrees are awarded in AGRICULTURE (environmental studies), BIOLOGICAL SCIENCE (biology/biological science), BUSINESS (accounting, business administration and management, human resources, management science, marketing/retailing/merchandising, and sports management), COMMUNICATIONS AND THE ARTS (art, communications, English, French, music, Spanish, and theatre arts), COMPUTER AND PHYSICAL SCIENCE (chemistry, computer science, mathematics, and physics), EDUCATION (athletic training, education, elementary education, and music education), ENGINEERING AND ENVIRONMENTAL DESIGN (environmental science), HEALTH PROFESSIONS (biomedical science, exercise science, health promotion, and nursing), SOCIAL SCIENCE (criminology, economics, history, international relations, liberal arts/general studies, philosophy, physical fitness/movement, political science/government, psychology, religion, and sociology). Nursing, exercise physiology and criminology have the largest enrollments.

ACTIVITIES: 10% of men belong to 5 national fraternities; 14% of women belong to 5 national sororities. There are 80 groups on campus, including art, cheerleading, choir, chorus, communications, computers, dance, drama, environmental, ethnic, honors, international, jazz band, LGBT, literary magazine, musical theater, newspaper, orchestra, political, professional, religious, social, social service, and student government. Popular campus events include Homecoming, Turkey Bowl and Campus Days. **Sports:** There are 10 intercollegiate sports for men and 11 for women, and 12 intramural sports for men and 12 for women. Facilities include fields for soccer, field hockey & lacrosse, weight room, exercise physiology lab, field house, athletic fields, ropes course, and hiking trails. **Graduates:** From July 1, 2015 to June 30, 2016, 482 bachelor's degrees were awarded. The most popular majors were nursing (9%), communication studies (8%), and elementary education (7%). In an average class, 1% graduate in 3 years or less, 47% graduate in 4 years or less, 55% graduate in 5 years or less, and 56% graduate in 6 years or less.

SERVICES: Counseling and information services are available, as is tutoring in most freshman and sophomore subjects, some upperclass subjects, and in math and writing. **Library/Resources:** The library contains 465,878 volumes, 466,605 microform items, 6,629 audio/video tapes/CDs/DVDs, and subscribes to 139 periodicals including electronic. Computerized library services include interlibrary loans, database searching, Internet access, and Wi-Fi capability. Special learning facilities include an art gallery, Belk astronomical observatory, Claytor nature center (470 acre farm used for science classes), a theatre, and 2 cadaver labs. **Physically Challenged Students:** 95% of the campus is accessible. Facilities include wheelchair ramps, elevators, special parking, specially equipped restrooms, special class scheduling, lowered drinking fountains, lowered telephones, and special housing. **Special:** Students may cross-register with Randolph College as part of the Tri-College Consortium, and they may also study abroad in 20 countries. More than half of our graduates complete an external internship. A 3-2 engineering degree is available in cooperation with Old Dominion University and the University of Virginia. There are 14 national honor societies and a freshman honors program. **Visiting:** There are regularly scheduled orientations for prospective students, including individual appointments. There are guides for informal visits, visitors may sit in on classes, and stay overnight. To schedule a visit, contact the Admissions Office. **Campus Safety and Security:** Measures include 24-hour foot and vehicle patrol, emergency notification system, security escort services, emergency telephones, lighted pathways/sidewalks, controlled access to dorms/residences, and residence halls locked 24 hours a day, and only accessible by scanning an ID card.

REQUIREMENTS: The ACT is required. SAT: Subject Tests are recommended. GED's are reviewed on a case-by-case basis. Applicants should have earned between 16 to 20 academic high school credits in English, math and social science, lab science, and foreign language. A GPA of 2.0 is required. AP and CLEP credits are accepted. Important factors in the admissions decision are advanced placement or honors courses, leadership record, and recommendations by school officials. The 51 hour core includes foreign language, fine arts, written composition, history, lab science, literature, math, oral communications, philosophy, religious studies, social science, and wellness. A senior symposium is also required, as is a senior project/thesis in some programs. Students must complete 124 credit hours to graduate, with a minimum 2.0 GPA, and 30 to 69 hours in their major. **Procedure:** Freshmen are admitted in the fall, spring, and summer. Entrance exams should be taken Junior year and in the first semester of the senior year. There are early decision, deferred admissions, and rolling admissions plans. Early decision applications should be filed by November 15, along with a $30 fee. Notification of early decision is sent December 15; regular decision. Application fees are waived if application is completed online. **Transfer Students:** 72 transfer students enrolled in 2015-2016. Transfer students must have a minimum GPA of 2.0 to be considered, and must be in good academic and social standing. The SAT or ACT is not required for transfer students. An interview is recommended. 48 of 124 credits required for the bachelor's degree must be completed at L.C. **International Students:** There are 57 international students enrolled. The school actively recruits these students. They must take the TOEFL with a minimum score of 550 on the paper-based TOEFL (PBT) or 78 on the Internet-based version (iBT). They must also take the SAT or ACT.

ADMISSIONS: 64% of the 2016-2017 applicants were accepted. The SAT scores for the 2016-2017 freshman class were: Critical Reading-- 45% below 500, 39% between 500 and 599, 15% between 600 and 699, and 1% between 700 and 800. Math-- 44% below 500, 42% between 500 and 599, 13% between 600 and 699, and 1% between 700 and 800. The ACT scores were 14% between 12 and 17, 49% between 18 and 23, 35% between 24 and 29, and 2% above 30. **Admissions Contact:** Sharon Walters-Bower, Director of Admissions. Email: *admissions@lynchburg.edu* Web: *www.lynchburg.edu*

FINANCIAL AID: In 2016-2017, 80% of all full-time freshmen and 76% of continuing full-time students received some form of financial aid. 80% of all full-time freshmen and 75% of continuing full-time students received need-based aid. The average freshman award was $28,414. Need-based scholarships or need-based grants averaged $25,614; need-based self-help aid (loans and jobs) averaged $3,842; and other non-need-based awards and non-need-based scholarships averaged $19,222. 35% of undergraduate students work part-time. Average annual earnings from campus work are $2000. The average financial indebtedness of the 2016 graduate was $35,000. Lynchburg College is a member of CSS. The state aid form is required. The FAFSA code is 003720. The deadline for filing freshman financial aid applications for fall entry is March 1.

MARY BALDWIN UNIVERSITY — D-2

www.marybaldwin.edu

Staunton, VA 24401	**(540) 887-7211** **(800) 468-2262**
Fax: (540) 887-7292	**Email: admit@marybaldwin.edu**
Full-time: 40 men, 826 women	**Faculty:** 59; IIB, -$
Part-time: 61 men, 383 women	**Ph.D.s:** 88%
Graduate: 79 men, 359 women	**Student/Faculty:** 10 to 1
Year: 4-1-4, summer session	**Tuition:** $30,635
Room & Board: $9230	**Freshman Class:** 2771 applied, 2757 accepted, 264 enrolled
SAT CR/M/W: 500/460/470 **ACT:** 22	**CEEB CODE:** 5397
Application Deadline: April 15	**COMPETITIVE**

A belief in student potential and in the transformative power of the liberal arts and sciences has guided Mary Baldwin University since its founding as Augusta Female Seminary in 1842. At MBU, students find the skills and the inspiration to become the architects of their lives. Resilient. Confident in their strengths. Ready for a lifetime of taking charge. Mary Baldwin students experience the proven advantages of a close-knit women's college combined with the opportunities and access of a multifaceted, coed university, preparing them to lead both on the job and around the world. The President's Higher Education Community Service Honor Roll recognizes Mary Baldwin as one of the top service-oriented institutions in the nation. The University's four academic colleges: the College of Arts and Sciences, the College of Business and Professional Studies, the College of Education, and the Murphy Deming College of Health Sciences, and Mary Baldwin College for Women. Master's degrees in education and undergraduate degrees through Baldwin Online and Adult Programs are available on campus, online, and at locations throughout the state. Master's and doctoral programs in the health sciences debuted in 2014 in a state-of-the-art facility on a branch campus in nearby Fishersville, Virginia. In the same spirit of innovation that has propelled the institution for 175 years, new fast-track residential programs and in-demand graduate programs for women and men are slated to begin in 2017. There are 4 undergraduate schools and 4 graduate schools. In addition to regional accreditation, MBU has baccalaureate program accreditation with CSWE, TEAC, and SACS. The 58-acre campus is in a small town in downtown Staunton. Including any residence halls, there are 40 buildings.

STUDENT LIFE: 75% of undergraduates are from Virginia. Others are from 40 states, and 7 foreign countries. 89% are from public schools. 57% are White; 22% African American; 7% Hispanic; 5% race unknown; 4% two or more races; 2% Asian American; 2% Foreign; 1% American Indian/Alaska Native. 78% are Unknown denomination. **Female To**

Male Ratio: 8.7:1. The average age of freshmen is 18; all undergraduates, 24. 35% do not continue beyond their first year; 45% remain to graduate. **Housing:** 775 students can be accommodated in college housing, which includes single-sex dorms, on-campus apartments, honors houses, special-interest houses, and lofts and suites. On-campus housing is guaranteed for all 4 years and is available on a lottery system for upperclassmen. 85% of students live on campus; of those, 70% remain on campus on weekends. All students may keep cars.

FACULTY/CLASSROOMS: 28% of faculty are male; 72% are female. 87% teach undergraduates. No introductory courses are taught by graduate students. The average class size in an introductory lecture is 21; in a laboratory is 12; and in a regular course is 18.

PROGRAMS OF STUDY: MBU confers B.A., B.S., and B.S.W. degrees. Master's and doctoral degrees are also awarded. Bachelor's degrees are awarded in BIOLOGICAL SCIENCE (biology/biological science), BUSINESS (business administration and management, international economics, and marketing management), COMMUNICATIONS AND THE ARTS (art, art history and appreciation, arts administration/management, English, performing arts, and studio art), COMPUTER AND PHYSICAL SCIENCE (applied mathematics, chemistry, mathematics, and physics), EDUCATION (education), HEALTH PROFESSIONS (clinical science, health care administration, and nursing), SOCIAL SCIENCE (American studies, Asian/Oriental studies, criminal justice, economics, history, international relations, philosophy, political science/government, psychology, social work, and sociology). Psychology, business, biology, and education are the strongest academically. Business, social work, liberal arts, and educational studies have the largest enrollments.

ACTIVITIES: There are no fraternities or sororities. There are 50 groups on campus, including academic honor societies, event planning, civic engagement, leadership, wellness, art, choir, chorale, chorus, dance, drama, drill team, drum and bugle corps, environmental, ethnic, film, hiking, honors, international, LGBT, literary magazine, marching band, musical theater, orchestra, photography, political, professional, religious, social, social service, student government, and yearbook. Popular campus events include Apple Day, Junior Dads, Family Weekend, Signature Ball, Halloween pumpkin carving, Las Posadas, Kwanzaa, International Festival, and Capstone Festival. **Sports:** There are 7 intercollegiate sports for women, and 6 intramural sports for women. Facilities include a physical activities center which has a main gym for basketball, volleyball practice and competition, a studio used for dance, fencing, and aerobics and other group fitness classes, a cardio and weight room, a climbing wall, and racquetball courts. Surrounding facilities include a track, tennis courts, and fields for softball, soccer, field hockey, and lacrosse. **Graduates:** From July 1, 2015 to June 30, 2016, 270 bachelor's degrees were awarded. The most popular majors were psychology (12%), business (12%), and social work (7%). 17 companies recruited on campus in 2015-2016. In an average class, 1% graduate in 3 years or less, 37% graduate in 4 years or less, 44% graduate in 5 years or less, and 45% graduate in 6 years or less. Of the 2015 graduating class, 20% were enrolled in graduate school within 6 months of graduation, and 84% were employed.

SERVICES: Counseling and information services are available, as is tutoring in most subjects, a reader service for the blind, and remedial math and writing. **Library/Resources:** The library contains 280,000 volumes, 31,540 audio/video tapes/CDs/DVDs, and subscribes to 28,325 periodicals including electronic. Computerized library services include interlibrary loans, database searching, Internet access, and Wi-Fi capability. Special learning facilities include an art gallery, the Staunton Military Academy/Virginia Women's Institute for Leadership Museum, dedicated to preserving local military history while inspiring future service members. In addition, the Spencer Center for Civic and Global Engagement at the heart of campus provides connections to local and regional service organizations, coordinates study abroad and international visitors, and offers meeting and event space. **Physically Challenged Students:** 30% of the campus is accessible. Facilities include wheelchair ramps, elevators, special parking, and specially equipped restrooms. **Special:** Study abroad locations vary from year to year, and can include: Costa Rica, Mexico, Japan, China, England, South Korea, Italy, Bermuda, Wales, The Netherlands, France, and Peru; cadets in the Virginia Women's Institute for Leadership are eligible for special study opportunities in India and at Norwich University in Connecticut. Dual-degree programs in education (BA/MAT and BA/MEd) and Shakespeare studies (BA/MLitt) through Mary Baldwin; 3-2 program in engineering (BS/MS) in partnership with the University of Virginia; 3-2 program in nursing (BS/MSN) with Vanderbilt University. Virginia State Teacher Licensure via the College of Education in undergraduate, Master of Arts in Teaching, and post-baccalaureate teacher Licensure programs. MBC and six other private colleges in Virginia (Hampden-Sydney College, Hollins University, Randolph-Macon College, Randolph College, and Washington and Lee University) form a consortium through which students may attend another of the participating colleges for a semester or a year. An agreement with the Virginia Community College System provides that a student with a transfer-oriented degree may qualify for guaranteed admission. Minor in public history through a partnership with the nearby Woodrow Wilson Presidential Library. Accelerated degree program, double majors, and student-designed major. Non-degree study, pass/fail grading options. There are 18 national honor societies, Phi Beta Kappa, a freshman honors program, and 29 departmental honors programs. **Visiting:** There are regularly scheduled orientations for prospective students, a tour, an interview, meet faculty, attend class, eat in dining hall, student events, athletic tours and other activities as requested or available. There are guides for informal visits, visitors may sit in on classes, and stay overnight. To schedule a visit, contact the MBu Admissions Office. **Campus Safety and Security:** Measures include 24-hour foot and vehicle patrol, emergency notification system, self-defense education, and security escort services. There are also shuttle buses, emergency telephones, lighted pathways/sidewalks, controlled access to dorms/residences, 24-hour locked residence halls, video surveillance in all-night computer labs and access areas, as well as video surveillance in the Program for the Exceptionally Gifted Center.

REQUIREMENTS: Applicants must graduate from an accredited secondary school, have a GED, or meet state equivalency requirements for homeschooling. A minimum of 16 academic units are required, including 4 in English, 3 in math, 2 to 3 in social studies, and 2 each in a foreign language, and science. Either the SAT or the ACT (not both) is required. Essays and interviews are recommended. A GPA of 2.0 is required. AP and CLEP credits are accepted. Important factors in the admissions decision are extracurricular activities record, leadership record, and advanced placement or honors courses. To graduate, students must complete a minimum of 126 semester hours, including at least 18 in the major. The Common Curriculum, which is organized by three learning outcomes (understanding of the liberal arts and sciences, understanding of the self in relationship to the broader community, and the capacity to make a positive difference in the world), includes 6 hours or more each in natural sciences, social sciences, arts, and humanities and history, 6 hours each in courses focused on writing, quantitative reasoning, and diverse cultures in a global context (foreign language, cross-cultural studies, and/or study abroad), 3 hours each in courses emphasizing oral communication, role of race and ethnicity, role of gender, and research and information literacy, 2 hours of health and physical education, and 1 hour of community involvement credit. Additional requirements for the Bachelor of Science (offered in biology, business, chemistry, economics, mathematics, physics, policy analysis, psychology) are 6 semester hours in mathematics at the 200-level or above, three hours emphasizing quantitative reasoning/data analysis, and at least two 200-level lab science courses. All graduates must complete a senior requirement for a minimum of 3 and a maximum of 6 semester hours of credit. The purpose of the senior requirement is to serve as a context within which students may establish themselves as capable of independent scholarship on a significant level. **Procedure:** Freshmen are admitted in the fall and spring. Entrance exams should be taken in the junior or senior year. There are early admissions, deferred admissions, and rolling admissions plans. Applications should be filed by April 15 for fall entry; December 15 for spring entry. Application fees are waived if application is completed online. **Transfer Students:** 31 transfer students enrolled in 2015-2016. Transfer applicants must have at least a 2.0 GPA at the institution where they are currently enrolled. 66 of 126 credits required for the bachelor's degree must be completed at MBU. **International Students:** There are 45 international students enrolled. The school actively recruits these students. They must take the TOEFL with a minimum score of 500 on the paper-based TOEFL (PBT) or 61 on the Internet-based version (iBT).

ADMISSIONS: The SAT scores for the 2016-2017 freshman class were: Critical Reading-- 48% below 500, 34% between 500 and 599, 14% between 600 and 699, and 4% between 700 and 800. Math-- 61% below 500, 30% between 500 and 599, 7% between 600 and 699, and 2% between 700 and 800. Writing-- 57% below 500, 26% between 500 and 599, 16% between 600 and 699, and 1% between 700 and 800. The ACT scores were 18% between 12 and 17, 44% between 18 and 23, 35% between 24 and 29, and 3% above 30. 39% of the current freshmen were in the top fifth of their class; 61% were in the top two fifths. **Admissions Contact:** Amber Wilkins, Interim Director of Admissions. Email: *admit@marybaldwin.edu* Web: *www.marybaldwin.edu*

FINANCIAL AID: In 2016-2017, 92% of all full-time freshmen and 90% of continuing full-time students received some form of financial aid. 90% of all full-time freshmen and 88% of continuing full-time students received need-based aid. The average freshman award was $22,529. Need-based scholarships or need-based grants averaged $7,592 ($20,322 maximum); need-based self-help aid (loans and jobs) averaged $9,780 ($19,900 maximum); and other non-need-based awards and non-need-based scholarships averaged $15,716 ($29,595 maximum). 20% of undergraduate students work part-time. Average annual earnings from campus work are $1400. The average financial indebtedness of the 2016 graduate was $30,340. The state aid form is required. The FAFSA code is 003723. The priority date for freshman financial aid applications for fall entry is February 15. The filing deadline for fall entry is May 1.

MARYMOUNT UNIVERSITY *(The complete profile is made available exclusively on our website, www.barronspac.com)*

NORFOLK STATE UNIVERSITY *(The complete profile is made available exclusively on our website, www.barronspac.com)*

OLD DOMINION UNIVERSITY F-4

www.odu.edu

Norfolk, VA 23529	**(757) 683-3648** **(800) 348-7926**
Fax: (757) 683-3255	**Email: admissions@odu.edu**
Full-time: 7042 men, 8161 women	**Faculty:** 635; I, --$
Part-time: 1980 men, 2610 women	**Ph.D.s:** 80%
Graduate: 1834 men, 2695 women	**Student/Faculty:** 24 to 1
Year: semesters, summer session	**Tuition:** $10,864 ($27,026)
Room & Board: $10,864	**Freshman Class:** 11352 applied, 9608 accepted, 2756 enrolled
SAT CR/M: 510/500 **ACT:** 21	**CEEB CODE:** 5126
Application Deadline: February 1	**COMPETITIVE**

Old Dominion University is Virginia's forward-focused public doctoral research university, established in 1930 as the Norfolk Division of the College of William & Mary. Today, we are one of the largest universities in Virginia, offering 73 bachelors, 43 masters, 22 doctoral degrees and 2 education specialist programs through its colleges of Arts and Letters, Business, Continuing Education and Professional Studies, Education, Engineering and Technology, Health Sciences, Sciences and Honors College. There are 6 undergraduate schools and 6 graduate schools. In addition to regional accreditation, ODU has baccalaureate program accreditation with AACSB, ABET, ADA, NASAD, NASM, NCATE, NRPA, CCNE, COAES, EHAC, NAACLS, and NAST. The 251-acre campus is in an urban area in Norfolk. Minutes from Virginia Beach, and three hours from Washington, DC. Including any residence halls, there are 143 buildings.

STUDENT LIFE: 93% of undergraduates are from Virginia. Others are from 45 states, 79 foreign countries, and Canada. 93% are from public schools. 9% are Hispanic; 7% two or more races; 5% Asian American; 44% White; 31% African American; 3% race unknown; 2% Foreign. **Female To Male Ratio:** 1.2:1. The average age of freshmen is 19; all undergraduates, 22. 22% do not continue beyond their first year; 51% remain to graduate. **Housing:** 4823 students can be accommodated in college housing, which includes single-sex and coed dorms, on-campus apartments, honors houses, special-interest houses, and living learning communities. On-campus housing is guaranteed for the freshman year only, and is available on a first-come, first-served basis, and on a lottery system for upperclassmen. 77% of students commute. Upperclassmen may keep cars.

FACULTY/CLASSROOMS: 56% of faculty are male; 44% are female. 76% teach undergraduates, and 3% do research. No introductory courses are taught by graduate students. The average class size in an introductory lecture is 33; in a laboratory is 21; and in a regular course is 31.

PROGRAMS OF STUDY: ODU confers B.A., B.S., B.F.A., B.M., B.S.B.A., B.S.C.E., B.S.C.O.M.E., B.S.C.S., B.S.D.H., B.S.E.E., B.S.E.H., B.S.E.T., B.S.H.S., B.S.M.&S.E., B.S.M.E., B.S.M.T., B.S.N., and B.S.N.M.T. degrees. Master's and doctoral degrees are also awarded. Bachelor's degrees are awarded in BIOLOGICAL SCIENCE (biochemistry, biology/adolescence education, biology/biological science, and marine biology), BUSINESS (accounting, business administration and management, business intelligence and analytics, electronic business, fashion merchandising, finance, financial services, insurance, international business management, management information systems, marketing management, real estate, recreation and leisure services, sports management, supply chain management, and professional studies), COMMUNICATIONS AND THE ARTS (acting, art history and appreciation, communications, creative writing, dance, dramatic arts, drawing, English, film arts, fine arts, French, German, graphic design, journalism, linguistics, literature, music, music business management, music performance, music theory and composition, performing arts, printmaking, Spanish, studio art, studio art fibers, studio art painting, theater design, and writing), COMPUTER AND PHYSICAL SCIENCE (chemistry, chemistry/adolescence education, computer science, earth science, earth science / adolescence education, geology, information sciences and systems, mathematics, oceanography, physics, and statistics), EDUCATION (art education, dance education, drama education, elementary education, English education, foreign languages education, mathematics education, music education, physical education, science education, secondary education, social studies education, Spanish adolescense education, and special education), ENGINEERING AND ENVIRONMENTAL DESIGN (civil engineering, civil engineering technology, computer engineering, electrical/electronics engineering, electrical/electronics engineering technology, engineering technology, mechanical engineering, and mechanical engineering technology), HEALTH PROFESSIONS (cytotechnology, dental hygiene, environmental health science, health administration and policy, health science, medical technology, nuclear medical technology, nursing, ophthalmic technology, public health, and speech pathology/audiology), SOCIAL SCIENCE (African studies, African American studies, Asian/Oriental studies, criminal justice, economics, geography, geography information science, history, human services, interdisciplinary studies, international studies, philosophy, political science/government, psychology, religious studies, sociology, and women's studies). Criminal justice, accounting, and speech pathology are the strongest academically. Biology, psychology, and nursing have the largest enrollments.

ACTIVITIES: 9% of men belong to 21 national fraternities; 7% of women belong to 11 national sororities. There are 286 groups on campus, including art, band, cheerleading, chess, choir, chorale, chorus, communications, computers, dance, debate, drama, drill team, environmental, ethnic, film, forensics, honors, international, jazz band, LGBT, marching band, musical theater, newspaper, pep band, political, professional, radio and TV, religious, social, and student government. Popular campus events include Unity Fest, Exam Jam, Homecoming, Greek Week, and Relay for Life. **Sports:** There are 9 intercollegiate sports for men and 9 for women, and 11 intramural sports for men and 11 for women. Facilities include a tennis center with indoor and outdoor courts, baseball stadium, basketball arena, varsity soccer game field, soccer practice field, practice gym, wrestling practice room, field stadium for field hockey and lacrosse, practice football fields, football stadium, golf course, sailing centers, a water area for varsity rowing, and a swimming pool. **Graduates:** From July 1, 2015 to June 30, 2016, 4003 bachelor's degrees were awarded. The most popular majors were psychology (8%), criminology (7%), and health services (6%). 350 companies recruited on campus in 2015-2016. In an average class, 1% graduate in 3 years or less, 26% graduate in 4 years or less, 45% graduate in 5 years or less, and 51% graduate in 6 years or less.

SERVICES: Counseling and information services are available, as is tutoring in some subjects, such as English, sciences, math, and remedial writing. **Library/Resources:** The 3 libraries contain 1.3 million volumes, 1.9 million microform items, 55,869 audio/video tapes/CDs/DVDs, and subscribe to 21,717 periodicals including electronic. Computerized library services include interlibrary loans, database searching, Internet access, and Wi-Fi capability. Special learning facilities include an art gallery, planetarium, radio station, a music library and composers collections, university special collections and archives, an art library, and a digital library. **Physically Challenged Students:** All of the campus is accessible. Facilities include wheelchair ramps, elevators, special parking, specially equipped restrooms, special class scheduling, lowered drinking fountains, and special housing. **Special:** Old Dominion offers cross-registration with schools in the Tidewater Consortium program. There are co-op programs, guaranteed internships, study abroad in 70 countries, and a work-study program. An interdisciplinary program, dual majors, combined degree programs, non-degree study, pass/fail options, and credit for military and life experience are available. There are 26 national honor societies and a freshman honors program. **Visiting:** There are regularly scheduled orientations for prospective students, consisting of academic advising, tours, college presentations, and registration. There are guides for informal visits and visitors may sit in on classes. To schedule a visit, contact the Admissions Office. **Campus Safety and Security:** Measures include 24-hour foot and vehicle patrol, emergency notification system, self-defense education, and security escort services. There are also shuttle buses, emergency telephones, lighted pathways/sidewalks, controlled access to dorms/residences, and a bicycle patrol.

REQUIREMENTS: The SAT or ACT is required. Applicants must be graduates of an accredited secondary school. The GED is accepted. Applicants should have completed 4 years of math and 3 years each of English, foreign languages, science, and social science. An essay and recommendation are required. A list of extracurricular activities is required. AP and CLEP credits are accepted. Important factors in the admissions decision are advanced placement or honors courses, recommendations by school officials, and leadership record. At least 120 credits, with a minimum GPA of 2.0, are required to graduate. Students must complete the university's general education program, consisting of specific skills and perspectives courses outside the student's major. English composition is a required course, and students must pass a writing proficiency exam. **Procedure:** Freshmen are admitted in the fall, spring, and summer. Entrance exams should be taken in May of the junior year or November/December of the senior. There are early admissions, deferred admissions, and rolling admissions plans. Applications should be filed by February 1 for fall entry; October 1 for spring entry; and March 15 for summer entry, along with a $50 fee. Notification is sent on a rolling basis. 1114 applicants were on the 2016 waiting list; 533 were admitted. Applications are accepted online. **Transfer Students:** 2120 transfer students enrolled in 2015-2016. Applicants must have a minimum GPA of 2.5 and at least 24 semester hour credits. Applicants with fewer semester hours must meet the same requirements as freshmen. 30 of 120 credits required for the bachelor's degree must be completed at ODU. **International Students:** There are 231 international students enrolled. The school actively recruits these students. They must take the TOEFL with a minimum score of 550 on the paper-based TOEFL (PBT) or 79 on the Internet-based version (iBT) and the college's own test, or take the IELTS band with a score of 6.5 overall. Students receiving 480 on the SAT Verbal or completing ELC Bridge program don't need to take those tests.

ADMISSIONS: 85% of the 2016-2017 applicants were accepted. The SAT scores for the 2016-2017 freshman class were: Critical Reading-- 45% below 500, 40% between 500 and 599, 13% between 600 and 699, and 2% between 700 and 800. Math-- 47% below 500, 36% between 500 and 599, 15% between 600 and 699, and 2% between 700 and 800. The ACT scores were 20% between 12 and 17, 48% between 18 and 23, 27% between 24 and 29, and 5% above 30. 24% of the current freshmen were in the top fifth of their class; 54% were in the top two fifths. 3 freshmen graduated first in their class. **Admissions Contact:** Shereen Williams, Customer Service Manager, Admissions. Email: *admissions@odu.edu* Web: *www.odu.edu*

FINANCIAL AID: In 2016-2017, 62% of all full-time freshmen and 61% of continuing full-time students received some form of financial aid. 49% of all full-time freshmen and 48% of continuing full-time students received need-based aid. The average freshman award was $16,809. Need-based scholarships or need-based grants averaged $6,604 ($23,635 maximum); need-based self-help aid (loans and jobs) averaged $3,661 ($23,635 maximum); non-need-based athletic scholarships averaged $19,399 ($23,635 maximum); and other non-need-based awards and non-need-based scholarships averaged $4,246 ($23,635 maximum). 10% of undergraduate students work part-time. Average annual earnings from campus work are $2605. The average financial indebtedness of the 2016 graduate was $27,847. The FAFSA code is 003728. The priority date for freshman financial aid applications for fall entry is February 15.

RADFORD UNIVERSITY *(The complete profile is made available exclusively on our website, www.barronspac.com)*

RANDOLPH COLLEGE — D-3

www.randolphcollege.edu

Lynchburg, VA 24503 (434) 947-8000 (800) 745-7692

Fax: (434) 947-8996 **Email:** admissions@randolphcollege.edu

Full-time: 223 men, 438 women
Part-time: 1 men, 3 women
Graduate: 5 men, 10 women
Year: semesters
Room & Board: $11,650
SAT CR/M/W: 515/500/495 **ACT:** 22
Application Deadline: February 15

Faculty: 68; IIB, av$
Ph.D.s: 96%
Student/Faculty: 10 to 1
Tuition: $34,010
Freshman Class: 1207 applied, 972 accepted, 184 enrolled
CEEB CODE: 5557
COMPETITIVE

Randolph College, founded in 1891, is an independent, coeducational, liberal arts institution. The college's curriculum offers the best feature of an honors education with a global outlook. Students are encouraged to travel, to take on real problems, to pursue and achieve a goal with personal meaning. Embedded within a student's education are opportunities to study abroad, both national and international internships, career guidance, leadership development, and one-on-one faculty advising. There is 1 undergraduate school and 1 graduate school. In addition to regional accreditation, Randolph has baccalaureate program accreditation with NASDTEC and TEAC. The 100-acre campus is in a suburban area within minutes of the Blue Ridge Mountains, and 1 hour southwest of Charlottesville. Including any residence halls, there are 18 buildings.

STUDENT LIFE: 60% of undergraduates are from Virginia. Others are from 36 states, 32 foreign countries, and Canada. 72% are from public schools. 67% are White; 5% Hispanic; 4% Asian American; 13% Foreign; 10% African American; 1% American Indian/Alaska Native. 55% are Protestant; 15% Catholic; 15% claim no religious affiliation; 12% Muslim, Hindu, Buddhist, and Orthodox. **Female To Male Ratio:** 2.0:1. The average age of freshmen is 18; all undergraduates, 20. 20% do not continue beyond their first year; 64% remain to graduate. **Housing:** 675 students can be accommodated in college housing, which includes coed dorms, special-interest houses, and theme housing. On-campus housing is guaranteed for all 4 years. 90% of students live on campus; of those, 80% remain on campus on weekends. All students may keep cars.

FACULTY/CLASSROOMS: 46% of faculty are male; 54% are female. All teach undergraduates, 58% do research, and 58% do both. No introductory courses are taught by graduate students. The average class size in an introductory lecture is 16; in a laboratory is 11; and in a regular course is 12.

PROGRAMS OF STUDY: Randolph confers B.A., B.S. and B.F.A. degrees. Master's degrees are also awarded. Bachelor's degrees are awarded in AGRICULTURE (environmental studies), BIOLOGICAL SCIENCE (biology/biological science), BUSINESS (business administration and management), COMMUNICATIONS AND THE ARTS (art, classics, communications, dance, dramatic arts, English, French, music, and Spanish), COMPUTER AND PHYSICAL SCIENCE (chemistry, mathematics, and physics), EDUCATION (education and physical education), ENGINEERING AND ENVIRONMENTAL DESIGN (engineering physics and environmental science), HEALTH PROFESSIONS (health science), SOCIAL SCIENCE (economics, history, international studies, philosophy, political science/government, psychology, religion, and sociology). Biology, psychology, and political science have the largest enrollments.

ACTIVITIES: There are no fraternities or sororities. There are 35 groups on campus, including art, chorale, chorus, dance, debate, drama, environmental, ethnic, foreign language, honors, international, LGBT, literary magazine, newspaper, pep band, photography, political, professional, radio and TV, religious, social, social service, student government, and yearbook. Popular campus events include Tacky Party, Never-ending Weekend, Senior Dinner Dance and Dell Parties. **Sports:** There are 6 intercollegiate sports for men and 8 for women, and 6 intramural sports for men and 6 for women. Facilities include a multi-purpose playing field and track, gym, an indoor heated swimming pool, dance studios, aerobic and weight rooms, tennis courts, athletic fields, frisbee golf course, riding center with teaching, and amphitheater show rings, and indoor and outdoor arenas. **Graduates:** From July 1, 2015 to June 30, 2016, 128 bachelor's degrees were awarded. The most popular majors were biological/life sciences (15%), social sciences (13%), and visual and performing arts (12%). In an average class, 2% graduate in 3 years or less, 63% graduate in 4 years or less, 64% graduate in 5 years or less, and 69% graduate in 6 years or less. Of the 2015 graduating class, 35% were enrolled in graduate school within 6 months of graduation, and 60% were employed.

SERVICES: Counseling and information services are available, as is tutoring in every subject. There is also a computing and study skills resource center, a writing lab, and science and math center. **Library/Resources:** The library contains 197,332 volumes, 187,000 microform items, 3,600 audio/video tapes/CDs/DVDs, and subscribes to 618 periodicals including electronic. Computerized library services include interlibrary loans, database searching, and Internet access. Special learning facilities include an art gallery, radio station, an observatory, acclaimed collection of American art housed in the Maier Museum, theaters, recital hall, organic garden, a equestrian center, and nature preserves. **Physically Challenged Students:** 50% of the campus is accessible. Facilities include wheelchair ramps, elevators, special parking, specially equipped restrooms, special class scheduling, and special housing. **Special:** Randolph offers a spring semester American Culture Program, as well as study abroad in 11 countries, including its own program in England, and both domestic and international internships. A Washington semester at American University is available, as is the Tri-College Consortium with Lynchburg College and the Seven-College Exchange Program with Hampden-Sydney, Hollins, Mary Baldwin, Randolph-Macon, and Washington and Lee University. There is a 3-2 nursing program with Johns Hopkins University and Vanderbilt University and a 3-2 engineering degree with several institutions. There are 17 national honor societies, Phi Beta Kappa, and 16 departmental honors programs. **Visiting:** There are regularly scheduled orientations for prospective students, including a campus tour, student panels, faculty panels, class visits, and individual sessions with admissions and financial planning counselor. There are guides for informal visits, visitors may sit in on classes, and stay overnight. To schedule a visit, contact the Admissions Office. **Campus Safety and Security:** Measures include 24-hour foot and vehicle patrol, emergency notification system, self-defense education, security escort services, emergency telephones, lighted pathways/sidewalks, and controlled access to dorms/residences.

REQUIREMENTS: Applicants must be graduates of an accredited secondary school with at least 16 academic credits, including 4 units in English, 3 units in math (4 recommended), 3 units in foreign language (recommended), 3 units in science and 2 units with lab, 2 units in history, and 1 in academic electives (3 recommended). An interview is strongly encouraged. A GED is accepted. High school diploma is required. Either SAT and SAT Subject tests or ACT if submitted will be considered. AP and CLEP credits are accepted. Important factors in the admissions decision are advanced placement or honors courses, recommendations by school officials, extracurricular activities record, recommendations by alumni, leadership record, parents or siblings attended your school, evidence of special talent, and personality/intangible qualities. To graduate, all students must complete at least 124 credit hours with a minimum GPA of 2.0. Students must satisfy the requirements for the general education and major programs and must have a minimum GPA of 2.0 in the major. **Procedure:** Freshmen are admitted in the fall and spring. Entrance exams should be taken in the junior or senior year. There are early admissions and deferred admissions plans. Early decision applications should be filed by December 1; regular applications, by February 15 for fall entry; and December 1 for spring entry, along with a $35 fee. Notification of early decision is sent December 15; regular decision, on a rolling basis. Applications are accepted online. **Transfer Students:** 41 transfer students enrolled in 2015-2016. Transfer students must submit college transcripts and for high school transcripts, required by some students, a letters of recommendation from a college official. An interview is recommended. 62 of 124 credits required for the bachelor's degree must be completed at Randolph. **International Students:** There are 66 international students enrolled. The school actively recruits these students. They must take the TOEFL with a minimum score of 550 on the paper-based TOEFL (PBT) or 79 on the Internet-based version (iBT).

ADMISSIONS: 81% of the 2016-2017 applicants were accepted. The SAT scores for the 2016-2017 freshman class were: Critical Reading-- 42% below 500, 40% between 500 and 599, 16% between 600 and 699, and 2% between 700 and 800. Math-- 46% below 500, 41% between 500 and 599, 11% between 600 and 699, and 2% between 700 and 800. Writing-- 44% below 500, 32% between 500 and 599, 14% between 600 and 699, and 2% between 700 and 800. The ACT scores were 9% between 12 and 17, 59% between 18 and 23, 28% between 24 and 29, and 4% above 30. 71% of the current freshmen were in the top fifth of their class; 91% were in the top two fifths. **Admissions Contact:** Margaret Blount, Director of Recruitment. Email: *admissions@randolphcollege.edu* Web: *www.randolphcollege.edu*

FINANCIAL AID: In 2016-2017, 99% of all full-time freshmen and continuing full-time students received some form of financial aid. 76% of all full-time freshmen and 74% of continuing full-time students received need-based aid. The average freshman award was $28,967. Need-based scholarships or need-based grants averaged $25,373; need-based self-help aid (loans and jobs) averaged $4,256; other non-need-based awards and non-need-based scholarships averaged $22,134; and $3,707 from other forms of aid. 66% of undergraduate students work part-time. Average annual earnings from campus work are $1100. The average financial indebtedness of the 2016 graduate was $26,538. The the state aid form is required. The priority date for freshman financial aid applications for fall entry is March 1.

RANDOLPH-MACON COLLEGE — E-3

www.rmc.edu

Ashland, VA 23005	**(804) 752-7305** **(800) 888-1762**
Fax: (804) 752-4707	**Email: admissions@rmc.edu**
Full-time: 659 men, 756 women	**Faculty:** 101; IIB, av$
Part-time: 17 men, 14 women	**Ph.D.s:** 99%
Graduate: n/av	**Student/Faculty:** 14 to 1
Year: 4-1-4, summer session	**Tuition:** $38,730
Room & Board: $11,180	**Freshman Class:** 2842 applied, 1745 accepted, 397 enrolled
SAT CR/M/W: 546/538/516 **ACT:** 24	**CEEB CODE:** 5566
Application Deadline: March 1	**COMPETITIVE**

Randolph-Macon College is a private, coeducational liberal arts and sciences college whose mission is to develop the mind and character of its students and prepare them for successful lives. R-MC enrolls undergraduate students, who pursue their academic paths in 54 areas of study (including majors, minors, pre-professional programs, and other areas). There is 1 undergraduate school. In addition to regional accreditation, Randolph-Macon has baccalaureate program accreditation with TEAC and ACS. The 116-acre campus is in a suburban area 15 miles north of Richmond and 90 miles south of Washington, D.C. Including any residence halls, there are 142 buildings.

STUDENT LIFE: 74% of undergraduates are from Virginia. Others are from 26 states, and 20 foreign countries. 75% are from public schools. 79% are White; 9% African American; 4% Hispanic; 3% Asian American; 3% two or more races; 1% American Indian/Alaska Native; 1% Foreign; 1% race unknown. 45% are Protestant; 14% Catholic. **Female To Male Ratio:** 1.1:1. The average age of freshmen is 18; all undergraduates, 20. 15% do not continue beyond their first year; 62% remain to graduate. **Housing:** 1290 students can be accommodated in college housing, which includes single-sex and coed dorms, on-campus apartments, honors houses, language houses, special-interest houses, fraternity houses, sorority houses, senior apartments, Greek housing, and several college-owned houses. On-campus housing is guaranteed for all 4 years and is available on a lottery system for upperclassmen. 80% of students live on campus; of those, 77% remain on campus on weekends. All students may keep cars.

FACULTY/CLASSROOMS: 55% of faculty are male; 45% are female. All teach undergraduates and do research. No introductory courses are taught by graduate students. The average class size in an introductory lecture is 15; in a laboratory is 12; and in a regular course is 16.

PROGRAMS OF STUDY: Randolph-Macon confers B.A. and B.S. degrees. Bachelor's degrees are awarded in AGRICULTURE (environmental studies), BIOLOGICAL SCIENCE (biology/biological science and neurosciences), BUSINESS (accounting and business administration and management), COMMUNICATIONS AND THE ARTS (art history and appreciation, arts administration/management, classics, communications, dramatic arts, English, French, German, Greek, Latin, music, Spanish, and studio art), COMPUTER AND PHYSICAL SCIENCE (chemistry, computer science, mathematics, and physics), ENGINEERING AND ENVIRONMENTAL DESIGN (engineering physics), SOCIAL

SCIENCE (archeology, Asian/Oriental studies, economics, history, international studies, philosophy, political science/government, psychology, religion, sociology, and women's studies). Biology, communications, and business have the largest enrollments.

ACTIVITIES: 25% of men belong to 7 national fraternities; 23% of women belong to 4 national sororities. There are 80 groups on campus, including and diversity council, leadership fellows, SGA, art, cheerleading, choir, chorale, chorus, communications, computers, dance, debate, drama, environmental, equestrian club, ethnic, film, forensics, honors, international, jazz band, LGBT, literary magazine, musical theater, newspaper, opera, pep band, photography, political, professional, radio and TV, religious, social, social service, and student government. Popular campus events include Cultural Arts Series, Monster Bash and Beat Hampden-Sydney Week. **Sports:** There are 8 intercollegiate sports for men and 9 for women, and 15 intramural sports for men and 15 for women. Facilities include tennis courts, gyms, indoor pool, football/lacrosse field, weight room, training room, racquetball and squash courts, aerobics room, track, multipurpose gym, and a climbing wall. **Graduates:** From July 1, 2015 to June 30, 2016, 310 bachelor's degrees were awarded. The most popular majors were biology (16%), communications (13%), and business economics (13%). 20 companies recruited on campus in 2015-2016. In an average class, 2% graduate in 3 years or less, 56% graduate in 4 years or less, 62% graduate in 5 years or less, and 62% graduate in 6 years or less. Of the 2015 graduating class, 12% were enrolled in graduate school within 6 months of graduation, and 48% were employed.

SERVICES: Counseling and information services are available, as is tutoring in every subject, and a reader service for the blind. **Library/Resources:** The library contains 305,588 volumes, and subscribes to 112,380 periodicals including electronic. Computerized library services include interlibrary loans, database searching, Internet access, and Wi-Fi capability. Special learning facilities include an art gallery, radio station, Higgins Academic Center, Keeble Observatory with radio telescope, scanning and transmission electron microscopy; Human Behavior Lab, Rodent Lab, dark room, herbarium room, greenhouse, chamber music studio and music technology lab; large auditorium and adjoining blackbox theater. **Physically Challenged Students:** 90% of the campus is accessible. Facilities include wheelchair ramps, elevators, special parking, specially equipped restrooms, special class scheduling, special housing. advisors for learning-disabled students. **Special:** The College offers special programs in engineering with Columbia University and the University of Virginia, in forestry with Duke University, and in accounting with Virginia Commonwealth University. The College has a Guaranteed Admission Agreement with the George Washington University School of Nursing. A new Early Assurance Program (EAP) exists with the Eastern Virginia Medical School (EVMS). The College also offers a preferred applicant track agreements into medical schools with VCU. Study-abroad programs are offered in 45 countries. Internships, dual majors, and a Washington semester are available. B.A.-B.S. degrees are possible in all majors. Most majors offer internships. Travel classes are available during January term. There are 18 national honor societies, including Phi Beta Kappa, and a freshman honors program. **Visiting:** There are regularly scheduled orientations for prospective students, including interviews, information sessions, tours, open houses, and visitation days. There are guides for informal visits, visitors may sit in on classes, and stay overnight. To schedule a visit, contact the Office of Admissions. **Campus Safety and Security:** Measures include 24-hour foot and vehicle patrol, emergency notification system, self-defense education, security escort services, emergency telephones, lighted pathways/sidewalks, and controlled access to dorms/residences.

REQUIREMENTS: The SAT is required. Applicants must be graduates of an accredited secondary school or have completed their GED. Applicants should complete a minimum of 16 high school academic credits, including 4 years of English, 3 to 4 years each of math and science, and 2 to 3 years of foreign language, history, and social studies. An essay is required, and an interview is recommended. A GPA of 2.0 is required. AP and CLEP credits are accepted. Important factors in the admissions decision are advanced placement or honors courses, recommendations by school officials, and extracurricular activities record. To graduate, students must complete 110 credit hours, with 30 to 42 hours in the major and a minimum GPA of 2.0. All students must complete a Capstone course culminating the academic experience. All students must satisfy requirements in math, social science, lab science, literature, philosophy/theology, phys ed, fine arts, foreign language, history, and writing. There are also requirements for Western, non-Western, computing, multidisciplinary, and experiential courses. **Procedure:** Freshmen are admitted in the fall and spring. Entrance exams should be taken by January of the senior year. There are early admissions and deferred admissions plans. Early decision applications should be filed by November 15; regular applications, by March 1 for fall entry; and December 1 for spring entry, along with a $30 fee. Notification of early decision is sent January 1; regular decision, April 1. 65 applicants were on the 2016 waiting list; 15 were admitted. Applications are accepted on-line. Application fees are waived if application is completed online. **Transfer Students:** 53 transfer students enrolled in 2015-2016. Applicants must have a minimum GPA of 2.0 and must be eligible to return to their previous institution. They must submit high school and college transcripts and SAT scores (the SAT requirement is waived for students who have earned an associate degree). **International Students:** There are 30 international students enrolled. The school actively recruits these students. They must take the TOEFL with a minimum score of 550 on the paper-based TOEFL (PBT) or 80 on the Internet-based version (iBT), or take the IELTS. Either TOEFL or SAT or ACT is required for non-native English speakers.

ADMISSIONS: 61% of the 2016-2017 applicants were accepted. The SAT scores for the 2016-2017 freshman class were: Critical Reading-- 28% below 500, 45% between 500 and 599, 23% between 600 and 699, and 4% between 700 and 800. Math-- 30% below 500, 49% between 500 and 599, 19% between 600 and 699, and 3% between 700 and 800. Writing-- 43% below 500, 42% between 500 and 599, 13% between 600 and 699, and 3% between 700 and 800. 49% of the current freshmen were in the top fifth of their class; 77% were in the top two fifths. 6 freshmen graduated first in their class. **Admissions Contact:** David Lesesne, Director. Email: *admissions@rmc.edu* Web: *www.rmc.edu*

FINANCIAL AID: In 2016-2017, 99% of all full-time freshmen and continuing full-time students received some form of financial aid. 37% of all full-time freshmen and 42% of continuing full-time students received need-based aid. 46% of undergraduate students work part-time. Average annual earnings from campus work are $1500. The average financial indebtedness of the 2016 graduate was $34,930. Randolph-Macon is a member of CSS. The state aid form and the college's own financial statement are required. The FAFSA code is 003733. The priority date for freshman financial aid applications for fall entry is February 15. The filing deadline for fall entry is March 1.

ROANOKE COLLEGE C-3
www.roanoke.edu

Salem, VA 24153 (540) 375-2270 / (800) 388-2276

Fax: (540) 375-2267 | **Email: admissions@roanoke.edu**

Full-time: 798 men, 1135 women	**Faculty:** 164; IIB, av$
Part-time: 23 men, 36 women	**Ph.D.s:** 87%
Graduate: n/av	**Student/Faculty:** 12 to 1
Year: semesters, summer session	**Tuition:** $41,304
Room & Board: $12,810	**Freshman Class:** 4459 applied, 3257 accepted, 508 enrolled
SAT CR/M/W: 550/540/520 **ACT:** 24	**CEEB CODE:** 5571
Application Deadline: March 15	**VERY COMPETITIVE**

Roanoke College helps its students find their true passions, and enables them to pursue those passions with a broad education along with specific skills and in-depth knowledge of a chosen discipline. Students receive a strong liberal arts foundation through a unique Intellectual Inquiry core curriculum emphasizing learning firsthand in topic based courses where fundamental concepts and skills are taught and then applied to real problems and issues. Experiential learning is emphasized throughout the curriculum. The college offers undergraduate programs in the arts and sciences and in business administration. There is 1 undergraduate school. In addition to regional accreditation, Roanoke has baccalaureate program accreditation with ACBSP, VDE, ACS, and CATE. The 80-acre campus is in a suburban area 7 miles west of Roanoke, in the Blue Ridge Mountains. Including any residence halls, there are 70 buildings.

STUDENT LIFE: 54% of undergraduates are from Virginia. Others are from 41 states, 31 foreign countries, and Canada. 81% are from public schools. 82% are White; 6% African American; 4% Hispanic; 4% two or more races; 3% Foreign; 1% Asian American. 37% are Protestant; 26% claim no religious affiliation; 17% Catholic. **Female To Male Ratio:**

1.4:1. The average age of freshmen is 18; all undergraduates, 20. 17% do not continue beyond their first year; 63% remain to graduate. **Housing:** 1529 students can be accommodated in college housing, which includes single-sex and coed dorms, on-campus apartments, honors houses, special-interest houses, fraternity houses, sorority houses, and seven different living learning communities within residence life. On-campus housing is guaranteed for the freshman year only, on a first-come, first-served basis, and is available on a lottery system for upperclassmen. Priority is given to out-of-town students. 78% of students live on campus. All students may keep cars.

FACULTY/CLASSROOMS: 52% of faculty are male; 48% are female. All teach undergraduates, 74% do research, and 74% do both. No introductory courses are taught by graduate students. The average class size in an introductory lecture is 18; in a laboratory is 19; and in a regular course is 18.

PROGRAMS OF STUDY: Roanoke confers B.A., B.S., and B.B.A. degrees. Bachelor's degrees are awarded in AGRICULTURE (environmental studies), BIOLOGICAL SCIENCE (biochemistry and biology/biological science), BUSINESS (business administration and management and sports management), COMMUNICATIONS AND THE ARTS (art, art history and appreciation, communications, creative writing, French, literature, music, Spanish, and theatre arts), COMPUTER AND PHYSICAL SCIENCE (actuarial science, chemistry, computer science, mathematics, and physics), EDUCATION (athletic training and physical education), HEALTH PROFESSIONS (exercise science), SOCIAL SCIENCE (Christian studies, criminal justice, economics, history, international relations, philosophy, political science/government, psychology, religion, and sociology). Biology, chemistry, and philosophy are the strongest academically. Business administration, psychology, and biology have the largest enrollments.

ACTIVITIES: 23% of men belong to 5 national fraternities; 21% of women belong to 4 national sororities. There are 100 groups on campus, including art, band, cheerleading, choir, chorale, chorus, computers, dance, debate, drama, environmental, ethnic, honors, international, jazz band, LGBT, literary magazine, newspaper, orchestra, pep band, photography, political, professional, radio and TV, religious, social, social service, and student government. Popular campus events include Family weekend, President's Ball, Fridays on the Quad (FOTQ), Winterfest, and Alumni Weekend. **Sports:** There are 9 intercollegiate sports for men and 10 for women, and 6 intramural sports for men and 6 for women. Facilities include a stadium, athletic facility with indoor track, a performance gym, athletic training facilities, athletic fields, an all-weather track, practice and playing fields, tennis and racquetball courts, swimming pool, and a fitness center. **Graduates:** From July 1, 2015 to June 30, 2016, 457 bachelor's degrees were awarded. The most popular majors were business administration (18%), biology (10%), and psychology (7%). 134 companies recruited on campus in 2015-2016. In an average class, 1% graduate in 3 years or less, 57% graduate in 4 years or less, 61% graduate in 5 years or less, and 63% graduate in 6 years or less. Of the 2015 graduating class, 18% were enrolled in graduate school within 6 months of graduation, and 64% were employed.

SERVICES: Counseling and information services are available, as is tutoring in every subject. A supervised peer tutoring program is available at no charge to students, as well as a writing center and the center for learning and teaching. **Library/Resources:** The library contains 225,053 volumes, 143,488 microform items, 8,196 audio/video tapes/CDs/DVDs, and subscribes to 58,940 periodicals including electronic. Computerized library services include interlibrary loans, database searching, Internet access, and Wi-Fi capability. Special learning facilities include an art gallery, radio station, media classrooms, a video production facility, and multimedia computer labs. **Physically Challenged Students:** 85% of the campus is accessible. Facilities include wheelchair ramps, elevators, special parking, specially equipped restrooms, special class scheduling, and special housing. **Special:** We offer cross-registration with Hollins University and study abroad in many countries. Roanoke also offers internships, research with faculty, a Washington semester, the Virginia at Oxford Program, a semester of study in the Yucatan, a dual degree engineering degree with Virginia Polytechnic Institute and State University, credit by exam, and pass/fail options. A special May Term offers unique intensive travel and local experiences. Nondegree study is available to those students admitted with special status. There are 27 national honor societies, Phi Beta Kappa, a freshman honors program, and 15 departmental honors programs. **Visiting:** Regularly scheduled orientations are available for prospective students. Open houses also provide a sampling of college life at Roanoke, as well as discussing financial aid and admissions. Student/Faculty panels answer questions, and campus tours are given. There are guides for informal visits, visitors may sit in on classes, and stay overnight. To schedule a visit, contact the Admissions Office. **Campus Safety and Security:** Measures include 24-hour foot and vehicle patrol, emergency notification system, self-defense education, and security escort services. There are also shuttle buses, emergency telephones, lighted pathways/sidewalks, and controlled access to dorms/residences.

REQUIREMENTS: SAT or ACT is required. An essay, and an interview are recommended. Applicants must be graduates of accredited secondary schools or have earned a GED. The college requires 18 (20 recommended) academic units, including 4 years of English, 3 courses in math, 4 courses (2 required) in foreign language (recommended), and 2 courses each in lab science and social studies. An audition is also recommended for performing arts majors. Students who have at least a 3.0 academic GPA may submit two graded writing samples in lieu of SAT or ACT test scores. AP and CLEP credits are accepted. Important factors in the admissions decision are advanced placement or honors courses, leadership record, and personality/intangible qualities. Requirements for graduation include completion of 33.5 courses, including about 9 to 12 in the major and about 11 to 14 in the Intellectual Inquiry core curriculum. The core consists of 2 first-year seminars; 5 to 7 topical courses drawn from the mathematical and natural sciences, the social sciences, and the humanities; a capstone that addresses a contemporary issue; and an intensive learning course. Students must also demonstrate competency in a foreign language at an intermediate level and complete 2 physical education courses. A 2.0 GPA is required. **Procedure:** Freshmen are admitted in the fall, spring, and summer. Entrance exams should be taken by January of the senior year. There are early decision, deferred admissions, and rolling admissions plans. Early decision applications should be filed by November 15; regular applications, by March 15 for fall entry; and December 15 for spring entry, along with a $30 fee. Notification of early decision is sent December 15; regular decision, on a rolling basis. 42 early decision candidates were accepted for the 2016-2017 class. 122 applicants were on the 2016 waiting list; 13 were admitted. Application fees are waived if application is completed online. **Transfer Students:** 88 transfer students enrolled in 2015-2016. Transfers must have a minimum GPA of 2.2. SAT or ACT scores and an interview are recommended. Applicants with fewer than eight transferable courses need to provide SAT or ACT scores. Transfers must be in good academic standing with their previous institution. 17 of 34 credits required for the bachelor's degree must be completed at Roanoke. **International Students:** There are 59 international students enrolled. The school actively recruits these students. They must take the TOEFL with a minimum score of 68 on the Internet-based version (iBT). They must also take the SAT or ACT.

ADMISSIONS: 73% of the 2016-2017 applicants were accepted. The SAT scores for the 2016-2017 freshman class were: Critical Reading-- 26% below 500, 44% between 500 and 599, 24% between 600 and 699, and 5% between 700 and 800. Math-- 30% below 500, 46% between 500 and 599, 23% between 600 and 699, and 2% between 700 and 800. Writing-- 37% below 500, 44% between 500 and 599, 16% between 600 and 699, and 2% between 700 and 800. The ACT scores were 5% between 12 and 17, 36% between 18 and 23, 48% between 24 and 29, and 10% above 30. 41% of the current freshmen were in the top fifth of their class; 66% were in the top two fifths. 4 freshmen graduated first in their class. **Admissions Contact:** Dr. Brenda Poggendorf, Vice President of Enrollment. Email: *admissions@roanoke.edu* Web: *www.roanoke.edu*

FINANCIAL AID: In 2016-2017, 99% of all full-time freshmen and 97% of continuing full-time students received some form of financial aid. 76% of all full-time freshmen and 72% of continuing full-time students received need-based aid. The average freshman award was $34,521. Need-based scholarships or need-based grants averaged $9,365 ($25,056 maximum); need-based self-help aid (loans and jobs) averaged $5,236 ($12,500 maximum); and other non-need-based awards and non-need-based scholarships averaged $17,302 ($52,372 maximum). 35% of undergraduate students work part-time. Average annual earnings from campus work are $1466. The average financial indebtedness of the 2016 graduate was $39,175. The state aid form is required. The FAFSA code is 003736. The priority date for freshman financial aid applications for fall entry is March 1.

SHENANDOAH UNIVERSITY D-1

www.su.edu

Winchester, VA 22601 (540) 665-4581
(800) 432-2266
Fax: (540) 665-4627 Email: admit@su.edu

Full-time: 813 men, 1203 women
Part-time: 31 men, 52 women
Graduate: 506 men, 1313 women
Year: semesters, summer session
Room & Board: $9990

SAT CR/M/W: 490/500/480 **ACT:** 22
Application Deadline: rolling

Faculty: 140; I
Ph.D.s: 84%
Student/Faculty: 14 to 1
Tuition: $31,322
Freshman Class: 2042 applied, 1675 accepted, 446 enrolled
CEEB CODE: 5613
COMPETITIVE

Shenandoah University, founded in 1875, is a private university, affiliated with The United Methodist Church, offering undergraduate programs in arts and sciences, nursing, respiratory care, business, music, theater, and dance. Graduate programs include business, music, performance, pedagogy, music education, education, nursing and pharmacy. Health professions include athletic training, occupational therapy, physical therapy, and physician assistant studies. There are 4 undergraduate schools and 7 graduate schools. In addition to regional accreditation, Shenandoah, SU has baccalaureate program accreditation with AACSB, ACPE, NASM, TEAC, CCNE, AMTA, and CoARC. The 315-acre campus is in a small town 72 miles west of Washington, D.C. Including any residence halls, there are 49 buildings.

STUDENT LIFE: 59% of undergraduates are from Virginia. Others are from 36 states, 22 foreign countries, and Canada. 60% are White; 14% race unknown; 12% African American; 6% Hispanic; 4% Foreign; 3% Asian American; 3% two or more races; 1% American Indian/Alaska Native. 50% are Protestant; 22% Catholic; 11% Hindu, Islam, Bahai, Buddhism, Agnostic, and Muslim. **Female To Male Ratio:** 1.9:1. The average age of freshmen is 18; all undergraduates, 22. 23% do not continue beyond their first year; 77% remain to graduate. **Housing:** 919 students can be accommodated in college housing, which includes coed dorms, off-campus apartments, married student housing, honors houses, special-interest houses, and honors housing/community service required housing. On-campus housing is guaranteed for the freshman year only, and is available on a first-come, first-served basis, and on a lottery system for upperclassmen. 54% of students commute. All students may keep cars.

FACULTY/CLASSROOMS: 42% of faculty are male; 58% are female. 63% teach undergraduates. No introductory courses are taught by graduate students. The average class size in an introductory lecture is 18; in a laboratory is 11; and in a regular course is 15.

PROGRAMS OF STUDY: Shenandoah, confers B.A., B.S., B.B.A., B.F.A, B.M. and B.M.T. degrees. Master's and doctoral degrees are also awarded. Bachelor's degrees are awarded in BIOLOGICAL SCIENCE (biology/biological science), BUSINESS (business administration and management, entrepreneurial studies, and sports management), COMMUNICATIONS AND THE ARTS (acting, church music, collaborative piano, communications, composition, dance, dramatic arts, English, jazz, music, music production/recording technology, music performance, music technology, music theatre accompanying, music theory and composition, musical theater, performing arts, scenic and lighting design, Spanish, theater design, and theatre production), COMPUTER AND PHYSICAL SCIENCE (chemistry and mathematics), EDUCATION (core studies, music education, outdoor leadership/education, and university studies), ENGINEERING AND ENVIRONMENTAL DESIGN (environmental science), HEALTH PROFESSIONS (exercise science, health care administration, kinesiology, music therapy, nursing, public health, and respiratory therapy), SOCIAL SCIENCE (criminal justice, economics, history, political science/government, psychology, public administration, religion, and sociology). Conservatory, nursing, and pharmacy are the strongest academically. Conservatory, pharmacy, and nursing have the largest enrollments.

ACTIVITIES: There are no fraternities or sororities. There are 97 groups on campus, including band, cheerleading, choir, chorale, chorus, dance, drama, environmental, ethnic, film, honors, international, jazz band, LGBT, literary magazine, musical theater, newspaper, Online radio station; Campus Activity Network- a group of students that work with the Office of Student Engagement to provide activities on campus, orchestra, pep band, political, professional, religious, social, social service, student government, and symphony. Popular campus events include Rock the Bloom, Movie Nights, Wine Tasting, Jazz Trio Social, Relay for Life, Welcome Back, Sun Block Party, International Days, Homecoming and Family Weekend, WATTS Night Out, Bingo and Bowling, and MLK Day Services. **Sports:** There are 10 intercollegiate sports for men and 11 for women, and 8 intramural sports for men and 8 for women. Facilities include a gymnasium for football, volleyball, and men's and women's basketball; seating 600. Shentel Stadium for football, soccer, field hockey, lacrosse, baseball, softball, and tennis practice, track. multi-use field for practice and intramurals, an indoor athletics facility with batting cages, a fitness room with cardio equipment, dumbbells, and selectorized weights, and a weight room. **Graduates:** From July 1, 2015 to June 30, 2016, 433 bachelor's degrees were awarded. The most popular majors were nursing (21%), business administration (8%), and psychology (7%). 51 companies recruited on campus in 2015-2016. In an average class, 40% graduate in 4 years or less, 52% graduate in 5 years or less, and 55% graduate in 6 years or less. Of the 2015 graduating class, 17% were enrolled in graduate school within 6 months of graduation, and 66% were employed.

SERVICES: Counseling and information services are available, as is tutoring in every subject. **Library/Resources:** The 2 libraries contain 130,954 volumes, 56,680 microform items, 24,193 audio/video tapes/CDs/DVDs, and subscribe to 86,490 periodicals including electronic. Computerized library services include interlibrary loans, database searching, Internet access, and Wi-Fi capability. Special learning facilities include an art gallery, Pharmacy Apothecary Museum; Feltner Museum; Environmental Studies green rooftop garden; cadaver lab and nursing simulation suite in the Health & Life Sciences Building, Claude Moore Center for Literacy in the School of Education & Human Development (SEHD), a model computer classroom in SEHD, as well as the Academic Enrichment Center, Children's Literature Center and Media Center in the Alson H. Smith, Jr. Library. The library has two book scan stations, as well as a online research tool; Discovery. Discovery is designed to provide a single, unified search interface for nearly all of the university's digital and print library content. The campus employs a WEPA (wireless everywhere, print anywhere) printing system. The Shenandoah River Campus at Cool Spring Battlefield is 195 acres of land along the Shenandoah River which serves as a field site where students learn by exploring history?, environmental studies?, and other disciplines in ways that supplement and reinforce classroom and laboratory learning. Shenandoah Conservatory has three academic observation rooms: a recording studio, a music therapy clinic, and the Collins Music Learning Suite, an innovative learning space for undergraduate and graduate music education students. The conservatory also provides a designated Mac Lab and is a specialized music technology classroom; two classrooms designated for class piano; specialized rooms for film and acting; and specialized equipment for voice and a voice science lab. Shenandoah Conservatory became an All-Steinway School in June 2015, joining an elite group of schools and conservatories in the U.S. and abroad which bear this coveted status. **Physically Challenged Students:** 91% of the campus is accessible. Facilities include wheelchair ramps, elevators, special parking, specially equipped restrooms, special class scheduling, lowered drinking fountains, special housing, electric doors, and 22 defibrillators. **Special:** Internships; dual majors (Pharm-MBA, MSN-MBA, DPT/MSAT); Accelerated degree programs: ASD NUR.BS, 3+2 model with AT, 3+4 model with PharmD; cross-registration consortiums (collaborative agreements) with James Madison University (Nursing), Johns Hopkins School of Nursing, Marshall University School of Nursing, Old Dominion University School of Nursing, West Virginia Wesleyan Department of Nursing, George Washington University (Pharmacy); B.A. Interdisciplinary Studies. Study abroad: Choice of 166 Global Partner institutions among 55 nations. No work-study programs; non-degree study is possible. During breaks (winter, spring and summer) with advisor approval, students may participate in service learning, volunteer and third- party programs abroad. Study abroad opportunities with Global Experiential Learning (GEL): short-term, credit-bearing, faculty-led programs offered during winter, spring and summer breaks. We also have the Global Citizenship Project (GCP). Selected students, faculty and staff can travel with their group during spring break to one of five destinations around the world. GCP is an exclusive offering created and funded by Shenandoah University. Applicants are selected according to their application and one-page essay submission. We also participate in the VFIC Foreign Language project. There is also a 4+1 option for Conservatory undergraduates to earn their PLM.MS in one year by taking credits during undergraduate study plus a summer course prior to start of master degree. There are 3 national honor societies. **Visiting:** There are regularly scheduled orientations for prospective students, including information sessions with faculty and staff, student-guided campus tours, and lunch in the dining hall. There are guides for informal visits, visitors may sit in on classes, and stay overnight. To schedule a visit, contact Andrew Woodall at (800) 432-2266. **Campus Safety and Security:** Measures include 24-hour foot and vehicle patrol, emergency notification system, self-defense education, and security escort services. There are also shuttle buses, emergency telephones, lighted pathways/sidewalks, controlled access to dorms/residences, lock-out car and dead-car battery jump assistance ICE posters, and LIVESAFE app Safer in 60 Seconds. Orientation attendees also get an emergency preparedness list; Emergency Operation Plan Program, where each campus building has an emergency coordinator and outfitted with emergency preparedness items. In addition, RAD systems self-defense classes; TIPS - Responsible Alcohol Use and Peer Intervention Training Class; Training of Leesburg and GW campus staff on emergency/safety topics; and all residence life staff are trained in FEMA Incident Command procedures.

REQUIREMENTS: The SAT is required. The high school transcript should indicate courses pursued, grades earned, grade-point average and credits earned. It is required that the coursework include: four units of English, three units of mathematics (Algebra I, Algebra II and Geometry), two units of social studies, and two units of science (including one laboratory science). Two units of a foreign language are strongly recommended. Other classes may be appropriate for some curricula and will be evaluated on an individual basis by the Office of Admissions. Applicants are strongly recommended to indicate community and extracurricular involvement. Shenandoah Conservatory applicants are also required to successfully complete an audition or portfolio review. The most heavily weighted factor in the applicant's total profile is actual academic performance, as indicated by the high school transcript. The SAT or the ACT is required. No preference as to which one a student submits. Applicants to music, theatre and dance programs must complete an audition or portfolio review. A GPA of 2.5 is required. AP and CLEP credits are accepted. Important factors in the admissions decision are advanced placement or honors courses, extracurricular activities record, and evidence of special talent. To graduate with a bachelor degree, all undergraduate students must have taken the required core curriculum with a cumulative grade-point average of 2.0. Some programs require higher grade-point average in the major. The minimum number of credit hours required for a baccalaureate degree is 120. Other requirements vary depending on the program of study. Candidates for baccalaureate degrees must earn a minimum of 30-credit hours of the 120-credit-hour requirement at Shenandoah University. At least 30-credit hours must be at or above the 300 level. **Procedure:** Freshmen are admitted in the fall and spring. Entrance exams should be taken by junior year or early in the senior year. There are deferred admissions and rolling admissions plans. Application deadlines are open. Application fee is $30. Notification is sent on a rolling basis. Applications are accepted online. **Transfer Students:** 158 transfer students enrolled in 2015-2016. Transfer applicants must submit evidence of good standing at the college last attended and an official transcript(s) of credits earned at all institutions previously attended. A minimum cumulative 2.0 grade point average and 24 college credits are required. Students who have earned fewer than 24 college credits need to submit high school transcript and SAT or ACT scores for admission review. 30 of 120 credits required for the bachelor's degree must be completed at Shenandoah, SU. **International Students:** There are 78 international students enrolled. The school actively recruits these students. They must take the TOEFL with a minimum score of 550 on the paper-based TOEFL (PBT) or 79 on the Internet-based version (iBT). The IELTS is also accepted.

ADMISSIONS: 82% of the 2016-2017 applicants were accepted. The SAT scores for the 2016-2017 freshman class were: Critical Reading-- 51% below 500, 31% between 500 and 599, 17% between 600 and 699, and 1% between 700 and 800. Math-- 46% below 500, 38% between 500 and 599, 15% between 600 and 699, and 1% between 700 and 800. Writing-- 56% below 500, 32% between 500 and 599, 12% between 600 and 699, and 1% between 700 and 800. The ACT scores were 1% below 12, 14% between 12 and 17, 48% between 18 and 23, 33% between 24 and 29, and 4% above 30. 20% of the current freshmen were in the top fifth of their class; 53% were in the top two fifths. 6 freshmen graduated first in their class. **Admissions Contact:** Andrew Woodall, Exe Director of Recruitment & Admissions. Email: *admit@su.edu* Web: *www.su.edu*

FINANCIAL AID: In 2016-2017, 97% of all full-time freshmen and continuing full-time students received some form of financial aid. 77% of all full-time freshmen and 75% of continuing full-time students received need-based aid. The average freshman award was $25,905. Need-based scholarships or need-based grants averaged $6,904 ($10,000 maximum); need-based self-help aid (loans and jobs) averaged $4,216 ($5,500 maximum); and other non-need-based awards and non-need-based scholarships averaged $9,658 ($29,000 maximum). 49% of undergraduate students work part-time. Average annual earnings from campus work are $2300. The average financial indebtedness of the 2016 graduate was $28,855. The state aid form, and Virginia United Methodist Scholarship application are required. The FAFSA code is 003737. Check with the school for current application deadlines.

THE UNIVERSITY OF VIRGINIA'S COLLEGE AT WISE *(The complete profile is made available exclusively on our website, www.barronspac.com)*

UNIVERSITY OF MARY WASHINGTON E-2

www.umw.edu

Fredericksburg, VA 22401 | **(540) 654-2000** | **(800) 468-5614**

Fax: (540) 654-1857 | **Email: admit@umw.edu**

Full-time: 1357 men, 2524 women	**Faculty:** 244; IIB, av$
Part-time: 244 men, 390 women	**Ph.D.s:** 89%
Graduate: 176 men, 402 women	**Student/Faculty:** 14 to 1
Year: semesters, summer session	**Tuition:** $11,570 ($26,160)
Room & Board: $13,194	**Freshman Class:** 4847 applied, 3724 accepted, 955 enrolled
SAT CR/M/W: required **ACT:** 25	**CEEB CODE:** 5398
Application Deadline: February 1	**VERY COMPETITIVE**

University of Mary Washington is a premier, selective public liberal arts and sciences university in Virginia, highly respected for its commitment to academic excellence, strong undergraduate liberal arts and sciences program, and dedication to life-long learning. The university features colleges of business, education and arts and sciences, and three campuses, including a residential campus in Fredericksburg, a second one in nearby Stafford and a third in Dahlgren, which serves as a center of development of educational and research partnerships between the Navy, higher education institutions and the region's employers. Figures in the above capsule and in this profile are approximate. There are 3 undergraduate schools and 2 graduate schools. In addition to regional accreditation, UMW has baccalaureate program accreditation with NASM. The 176-acre campus is in a suburban area 50 miles south of Washington, D.C. and 50 miles north of Richmond. Including any residence halls, there are 48 buildings.

STUDENT LIFE: 87% of undergraduates are from Virginia. Others are from 38 states, 23 foreign countries, and Canada. 87% are from public schools. 64% are White; 6% African American; 6% Hispanic; 5% Asian American; 4% two or more races; 14% race unknown; 1% Foreign. **Female To Male Ratio:** 1.9:1. The average age of freshmen is 18; all undergraduates, 22. 17% do not continue beyond their first year; 76% remain to graduate. **Housing:** 2820 students can be accommodated in college housing, which includes single-sex, coed dorms and on-campus apartments. In addition, there are language houses, special-interest houses, living and learning communities, including gender neutral and international housing. On-campus housing is available on a lottery system for upperclassmen. 61% of students live on campus; of those, 80% remain on campus on weekends. Upperclassmen may keep cars.

FACULTY/CLASSROOMS: 51% of faculty are male; 49% are female. All teach undergraduates. No introductory courses are taught by graduate students. The average class size in an introductory lecture is 27; in a laboratory is 22; and in a regular course is 20.

PROGRAMS OF STUDY: UMW confers B.A., B.S., and B.L.S. degrees. Master's degrees are also awarded. Bachelor's degrees are awarded in BIOLOGICAL SCIENCE (biology/biological science), BUSINESS (business administration and management), COMMUNICATIONS AND THE ARTS (art history and appreciation, classics, dramatic arts, English, French, German, historic preservation, music, Spanish, and studio art), COMPUTER AND PHYSICAL SCIENCE (chemistry, computer science, mathematics, and physics), ENGINEERING AND ENVIRONMENTAL DESIGN (environmental science), SOCIAL SCIENCE (American studies, anthropology, economics, geography, history, international relations, liberal arts/general studies, philosophy, political science/government, psychology, religion, and sociology). Historic preservation, history, and political science are the strongest academically. Business administration, psychology, and biology have the largest enrollments.

ACTIVITIES: There are no fraternities or sororities. There are 140 groups on campus, including art, bagpipe, cheerleading, choir, chorale, chorus, club for class council, computers, dance, debate, drama, environmental, ethnic, film, honors, international, jazz band, LGBT, literary magazine, musical theater, newspaper, opera, orchestra, pep band, photography, political, professional, radio and TV, religious, social, social service, student government, symphony, and yearbook. Popular campus events include Rocktoberfest, Junior Ring Dance, and Multicultural Fair. **Sports:** There are 10 intercollegiate sports for men and 12 for women, and 16 intramural sports for men and 20 for women. Facilities include lighted, all-weather-turf recreational sports field, 6-lane, 25-yard indoor pool, regulation basketball and volleyball courts, a weight room, batting cages, training rooms, playing fields for all outdoor sports, a running course, handball/racquetball courts, a track, a fitness and recreation facility, and an indoor tennis center. **Graduates:** From July 1, 2015 to June 30, 2016, 868 bachelor's degrees were awarded. The most popular majors were English (11%), business administration (11%), and psychology (9%). 100 companies recruited on campus in 2015-2016. In an average class, 69% graduate in 4 years or less, 75% graduate in 5 years or less, and 76% graduate in 6 years or less. Of the 2015 graduating class, 24% were enrolled in graduate school within 6 months of graduation, and 95% were employed.

SERVICES: Counseling and information services are available, as is tutoring in most subjects, and a reader service for the blind. **Library/Resources:** The 2 libraries contain 424,417 volumes, 610,498 microform items, 2,206 audio/video tapes/CDs/DVDs, and subscribe to 62,985 periodicals including electronic. Computerized library services include interlibrary loans, database searching, Internet access, and Wi-Fi capability. Special learning facilities include an art gallery, radio station, a Center for Historic Preservation, Leidecker Center for Asian Studies, and James Farmer Multicultural Center. **Physically Challenged Students:** 75% of the campus is accessible. Facilities include wheelchair ramps, elevators, special parking, specially equipped restrooms, lowered drinking fountains, lowered telephones, and special housing. **Special:** Study abroad anywhere in the world, a Washington semester, and credit for off-campus work experience are available. The university offers dual majors, work-study programs, student-designed majors, and pass/fail options. More than 500 internships for credit are also available. Teacher licensure preparation is offered for elementary and secondary education. Elementary education is a 5-year bachelor's-master's degree program. There are 23 national honor societies, Phi Beta Kappa, and a freshman honors program. **Visiting:** There are regularly scheduled orientations for prospective students, including information sessions, available Monday through Friday, followed by a student-guided tour, and Saturday open houses each semester. Visitors may sit in on classes and stay overnight. To schedule a visit, contact the Office of Admissions. **Campus Safety and Security:** Measures include 24-hour foot and vehicle patrol, emergency notification system, self-defense education, and security escort services, emergency telephones, lighted pathways/sidewalks, and controlled access to dorms/residences.

REQUIREMENTS: The SAT or ACT, as well as the ACT Writing Test are recommended. Applicants must be graduates of an accredited secondary school or hold the GED. The Admissions Committee recommends that applicants complete 4 years of each of math, English, foreign language, science, and social studies. A SAT: Subject test is strongly recommended. Application essays are required. A counselor or teacher recommendation is also required. AP and CLEP credits are accepted. Important factors in the admissions decision are advanced placement or honors courses, evidence of special talent, and recommendations by school officials. To graduate, students must complete 120 credit hours and a minimum GPA of 2.0. Hours required in the major vary. The B.A. and B.S. general education curriculum includes a first-year seminar, courses in quantitative reasoning, natural science, human experience and society, global inquiry, language, arts, literature and performance, and experiential learning. The experiential learning requirement may be fulfilled through study abroad, service learning, undergraduate research, or career internships. Students complete 4 writing-intensive courses and 2 speaking-intensive courses from across the curriculum. A thesis is required in some majors and programs of study. The B.L.S. degreee program is a flexible, adult-oriented alternative that features slightly different requirements. **Procedure:** Freshmen are admitted in the fall and spring. Entrance exams should be taken by January of the senior year. There are early admissions and deferred admissions plans. Applications should be filed by February 1 for fall entry; November 1 for spring entry, along with a $50 fee. Notifications are sent April 1. 352 applicants were on the 2016 waiting list; 73 were admitted. Applications are accepted online. **Transfer Students:** 309 transfer students enrolled in 2015-2016. The university recommends that applicants for transfer have a minimum GPA of 3.0 and 30 college credits. The SAT and high school transcripts are required. Graduates from Virginia community colleges are given preference for admission. 30 of 120 credits required for the bachelor's degree must be completed at UMW. **International Students:** There are 38 international students enrolled. The school actively recruits these students. They must take the TOEFL with a minimum score of 88 on the Internet-based version (iBT). They must also take the SAT or ACT.

ADMISSIONS: 77% of the 2016-2017 applicants were accepted. The SAT scores for the 2016-2017 freshman class were: Critical Reading-- 10% below 500, 42% between 500 and 599, 37% between 600 and 699, and 10% between 700 and 800. Math-- 14% below 500, 47% between 500 and 599, 34% between 600 and 699, and 4% between 700 and 800. Writing-- 12% below 500, 45% between 500 and 599, 37% between 600 and 699, and 6% between 700 and 800. The ACT scores were 7% below 12, 24% between 12 and 17, 34% between 18 and 23, 18% between 24 and 29, and 17% above 30. There were 3 National Merit finalists. 5 freshmen graduated first in their class. **Admissions Contact:** Candace Fox, Assistant Director of Admissions. Email: *admit@umw.edu* Web: *www.umw.edu*

FINANCIAL AID: In 2016-2017, 66% of all full-time freshmen and 63% of continuing full-time students received some form of financial aid. 34% of all full-time freshmen and 32% of continuing full-time students received need-based aid. The average freshman award was $4,800. Need-based scholarships or need-based grants averaged $6,493 ($2,455 maximum); need-based self-help aid (loans and jobs) averaged $3,324 ($7,500 maximum); and other non-need-based awards and non-need-based scholarships averaged $15,423 ($30,371 maximum). 28% of undergraduate students work part-time. Average annual earnings from campus work are $2175. The average financial indebtedness of the 2016 graduate was $23,300. The college's own financial statement is required. The FAFSA code is 003746. The deadline for filing freshman financial aid applications for fall entry is March 1.

UNIVERSITY OF RICHMOND — E-3

www.richmond.edu

University of Richmond, VA 23173	(804) 289-8640 (800) 700-1662
Fax: (804) 287-6003	Email: admission@richmond.edu
Full-time: 1445 men, 1555 women	**Faculty:** 330; IIB, ++$
Part-time: 24 men, 12 women	**Ph.D.s:** 94%
Graduate: 274 men, 260 women	**Student/Faculty:** 9 to 1
Year: semesters, summer session	**Tuition:** $49,420
Room & Board: $11,460	**Freshman Class:** 10422 applied, 3385 accepted, 815 enrolled
SAT CR/M/W: 650/670/660 **ACT:** 31	**CEEB CODE:** 5569
Application Deadline: January 15	**MOST COMPETITIVE**

University of Richmond, provides a collaborative learning and research environment unlike any other in higher education, offering students an extraordinary combination of the liberal arts with law, business and leadership studies. It is characterized by a distinctly integrated student experience a rich and innovative life for students inside and outside the classroom and a welcoming spirit that prizes diversity of experience and thought. It is rooted in a determination to engage as a meaningful part of our community and our world. It is committed to ensuring its opportunities are accessible to talented students of all backgrounds. There are 3 undergraduate schools and 2 graduate schools. In addition to regional accreditation, UR has baccalaureate program accreditation with AACSB, TEAC, and ACS. The 350-acre campus is in a suburban area 6 miles west of Richmond. Including any residence halls, there are 81 buildings.

STUDENT LIFE: 81% of undergraduates are from Virginia. Others are from 46 states, 74 foreign countries, and Canada. 59% are from public schools. 8% are Hispanic; 7% Asian American; 6% race unknown; 57% White; 5% African American; 4% two or more races; 11% Foreign. **Female To Male Ratio:** 1.0:1. The average age of freshmen is 18; all undergraduates, 20. 7% do not continue beyond their first year; 93% remain to graduate. **Housing:** 2678 students can be accommodated in college housing, which includes single-sex and coed dorms, on-campus apartments, special-interest houses. On-campus housing is available on a first-come, first-served basis, and on a lottery system for upperclassmen. 91% of students live on campus; of those, 90% remain on campus on weekends. All students may keep cars.

FACULTY/CLASSROOMS: 57% of faculty are male; 43% are female. All teach undergraduates. No introductory courses are taught by graduate students. The average class size in an introductory lecture is 15 and in a regular course is 15.

PROGRAMS OF STUDY: UR confers B.A., B.S., and B.S.B.A. degrees. Master's and doctoral degrees are also awarded. Bachelor's degrees are awarded in AGRICULTURE (environmental studies), BIOLOGICAL SCIENCE (biochemistry, biology/biological science, and molecular biology), BUSINESS (accounting and business administration and management), COMMUNICATIONS AND THE ARTS (Arabic, art history, communication rhetoric/communication, dance, English, film arts, French, German studies, Greek, journalism, Latin, music, Spanish, studio art, and theatre arts), COMPUTER AND PHYSICAL SCIENCE (chemistry, computer science, mathematics, and physics), HEALTH PROFESSIONS (health science), SOCIAL SCIENCE (American studies, anthropology, Chinese Studies, classical/ancient civilization, cognitive science, economics, geography, history, interdisciplinary studies, international studies, Italian studies, philosophy, political science/government, psychology, religion, Russian and Slavic studies, sociology, and women's studies). Business adminstration, leadership studies, and biology have the largest enrollments.

ACTIVITIES: 21% of men belong to 6 national fraternities; 29% of women belong to 8 national sororities. There are 166 groups on campus, including art, band, cheerleading, choir, chorale, chorus, communications, computers, dance, debate, drama, drill team, environmental, ethnic, film, honors, international, jazz band, LGBT, literary magazine, musical theater, newspaper, orchestra, pep band, photography, political, professional, radio and TV, religious, social, social service, and student government. Popular campus events include Proclamation Night, Pig Roast, and Homecoming Concert. **Sports:** There are 7 intercollegiate sports for men and 10 for women. Facilities include a gym, football stadium, soccer/track complex, intramural fields, an intramural gym, aerobics and weight rooms, swimming pool, tennis, racquetball, disc golf, high ropes and squash courts. **Graduates:** From July 1, 2015 to June 30, 2016, 762 bachelor's degrees were awarded. The most popular majors were business/marketing (37%), social sciences (15%), and biological/life sciences (10%). 148 companies recruited on campus in 2015-2016. In an average class, 84% graduate in 4 years or less, 88% graduate in 5 years or less, and 88% graduate in 6 years or less. Of the 2015 graduating class, 17% were enrolled in graduate school within 6 months of graduation, and 96% were employed.

SERVICES: Counseling and information services are available, as is tutoring in most subjects. There are support centers for help with academic skills, writing, and speech. **Library/Resources:** The 3 libraries contain 1.2 million volumes, 141,297 microform items, 32,093 audio/video tapes/CDs/DVDs, and subscribe to 123,863 periodicals including electronic. Computerized library services include interlibrary loans, database searching, Internet access, and Wi-Fi capability. Special learning facilities include an art gallery, radio station, Joel and Lila Harnett Print Study Center, museum of art, and the Lora Robins gallery of design from nature. **Physically Challenged Students:** 95% of the campus is accessible. Facilities include wheelchair ramps, elevators, special parking, specially equipped restrooms, special class scheduling, lowered drinking fountains, and special housing. **Special:** Study abroad in Argentina, Australia, Austria, Barbados, Belgium, Bolivia, Bonaire, Botswana, Brazil, Cambodia, Cameroon, Chile, China, Costa Rica, the Czech Republic, Denmark, the Dominican Republic, Ecuador, France, Germany, Ghana, Hungary, India, Indonesia, Ireland, Israel, Italy, Jamaica, Japan, Jordan, Kenya Coast Republic, Mexico, Mongolia, Morocco, Nepal, the Netherlands, New Zealand, Nicaragua, Panama, Peru, Poland, Portugal, Rwanda, Samoa, Senegal, Singapore, South Africa, South Korea, Spain, Sweden, Switzerland, Taiwan, Tanzania, Thailand, Trinidad and Tobago, Tunisia, Turks and Caicos, Uganda, the United Arab Emirates, the United Kingdom, and Vietnam. Dual degree engineering programs with the Columbia University School of Engineering and Applied Science and the University of Virginia. Students can earn a Masters of Environmental Management (MEM) or a Masters of Forestry (MF) through Duke University's Nicholas School of the Environment or a Masters of Environment Studies from Virginia Commonwealth University. Students may apply for visiting away status for approved programs. The following list includes approved visiting away programs: American University-Washington Semester (students should check with the appropriate department to see how different programs will transfer). Duke University Marine Sciences Laboratory (Undergraduate Catalog-Biology), Marine Biological Laboratory Semester in Environmental Science - Woods Hole* (Undergraduate Catalog-Biology), and Boston University Washington DC Internship Program. There are 6 national honor societies, Phi Beta Kappa, and 17 departmental honors programs. **Visiting:** There are regularly scheduled orientations for prospective students, all first-time visitors are encouraged to schedule a regular campus visit, which typically includes an information session (a 45-minute presentation by an admission representative) and a campus tour (90-minute walking tour of campus led by a student). There are guides for informal visits and visitors may sit in on classes. To schedule a visit, contact the Admissions Office at (800) 289-8640. **Campus Safety and Security:** Measures include 24-hour foot and vehicle patrol, emergency notification system, self-defense education, and security escort services. There are also shuttle buses, emergency telephones, lighted pathways/sidewalks, a card-access system in all residence halls, vehicle assistance, emergency first aid service, fingerprinting, firearms storage, and personal property engraving and identification.

REQUIREMENTS: The SAT or ACT is required. Candidates for admission must have a high school diploma (or recognized equivalent), and must have completed a minimum of 16 units of secondary school coursework. Minimum requirements include four units in English, three in college preparatory mathematics (including Algebra I, II, and Geometry), and at least two each in history, laboratory science, and foreign language (two units of the same language, not including American Sign Language, which will not satisfy the requirement for foreign language). Competitive candidates for admission typically exceed the minimum requirements and have taken four units in all five core areas at the highest levels available in their school setting. Applicants should submit the Common Application, and may submit SAT or ACT test scores. The University of Richmond's application review is need-blind, and the University guarantees to meet 100% of each family's demonstrated need. AP and CLEP credits are accepted. A candidate for the Bachelor of Arts, Bachelor of Science, or Bachelor of Science in Business Administration degree must satisfactorily complete all degree requirements and 35 units. Undergraduate degree candidates must earn a grade point average of not less than 2.0 on all coursework attempted. All undergraduate degrees at the University of Richmond require satisfactory completion of one major. Multiple majors and/or minors may also be pursued and upon completion will be recorded on the permanent academic record. In the Robins School of Business and Jepson School of Leadership Studies a student must complete the requirements for the degree, as stated in the catalog at the time of entrance, within five years from the date of original entry. Reinstatement to a program after five years requires permission of the academic council of the student's school. If an extension of time is granted, the student may be required to satisfy the degree requirements in effect at the time of re-entrance. Additional Degree Requirements: 17.5 unit on-campus residency requirement (transfer students should see section on Transfer Credit), 28 unit residency requirement, to include work taken on approved exchange and study abroad programs and visiting away and off-campus programs as well as courses taken through dual degree and cross-registration programs (this requirement is pro-rated for transfer students), application for degree and attendance at Commencement, completion of financial and administrative obligations. **Procedure:** Freshmen are admitted in the fall. Entrance exams should be taken in the fall of senior year. There are early decision and deferred admissions plans. Early decision applications should be filed by November 15; regular applications, by January 15 for fall entry, along with a $50 fee. Notification of early decision is sent December 15; regular decision, April 1. 345 early decision candidates were accepted for the 2016-2017 class. 1236 applicants were on the 2016 waiting list; 60 were admitted. Applications are accepted on-line. **Transfer Students:** 70 transfer students enrolled in 2015-2016. Applicants must have earned a minimum of 24 credit hours in transferable courses. A minimum GPA of 2.0 is required. 60 credits required for the bachelor's degree must be completed at UR. **International Students:** There are 346 international students enrolled. The school actively recruits these students. They must take the TOEFL with a minimum score of 550 on the paper-based TOEFL (PBT) or 80 on the Internet-based version (iBT).

ADMISSIONS: 32% of the 2016-2017 applicants were accepted. The SAT scores for the 2016-2017 freshman class were: Critical Reading-- 3% below 500, 19% between 500 and 599, 53% between 600 and 699, and 25% between 700 and 800. Math-- 2% below 500, 17% between 500 and 599, 43% between 600 and 699, and 38% between 700 and 800. Writing-- 4% below 500, 16% between 500 and 599, 54% between 600 and 699, and 26% between 700 and 800. The ACT scores were 3% between 18 and 23, 25% between 24 and 29, and 72% above 30. 81% of the current freshmen were in the top fifth of their class; 95% were in the top two fifths. There were 8 National Merit finalists. **Admissions Contact:** Gil Villanueva, Dean of Admissions. Email: *admission@richmond.edu* Web: *www.richmond.edu*

FINANCIAL AID: In 2016-2017, 61% of all full-time freshmen and 66% of continuing full-time students received some form of financial aid. 43% of all full-time freshmen and 42% of continuing full-time students received need-based aid. The average freshman award was $46,350. Need-based scholarships or need-based grants averaged $40,200; need-based self-help aid (loans and jobs) averaged $3,860; non-need-based athletic scholarships averaged $29,780; and other non-need-based awards and non-need-based scholarships averaged $33,300. 49% of undergraduate students work part-time. Average annual earnings from campus work are $1555. The average financial indebtedness of the 2016 graduate was $27,670. UR is a member of CSS. The CSS/Profile, copies of parent and student federal tax returns, and a noncustodial parent profile are required. The FAFSA code is 003744. The deadline for filing freshman financial aid applications for fall entry is February 1.

UNIVERSITY OF VIRGINIA — D-3

www.virginia.edu

Charlottesville, VA 22904 — **(434) 982-3200**

Fax: (434) 924-3587 — **Email:** undergradadmission@virginia.edu

Full-time: 7089 men, 8395 women	**Faculty:** 1220; I, +$
Part-time: 307 men, 540 women	**Ph.D.s:** 90%
Graduate: 3655 men, 3912 women	**Student/Faculty:** 15 to 1
Year: semesters, summer session	**Tuition:** $15,165 ($45,997)
Room & Board: $10,726	**Freshman Class:** 32377 applied, 9668 accepted, 3683 enrolled
SAT CR/M/W: 670/680/670 **ACT:** 31	**CEEB CODE:** 5820
Application Deadline: January 1	**MOST COMPETITIVE**

The University of Virginia, founded in 1819, is a public institution with undergraduate programs in architecture, arts and sciences, commerce, education, engineering and applied science, and nursing. There are 7 undergraduate schools and 10 graduate schools. In addition to regional accreditation, UVA has baccalaureate program accreditation with AACSB, ABET, ASLA, NAAB, TEAC, ACS, APA, ASHA, and CCNE. The 1167-acre campus is in a suburban area 70 miles northwest of Richmond. Including any residence halls, there are 537 buildings.

STUDENT LIFE: 69% of undergraduates are from Virginia. Others are from 49 states, 135 foreign countries, and Canada. 70% are from public schools. 6% are African American; 6% Hispanic; 6% race unknown; 59% White; 5% Foreign; 4% two or more races; 13% Asian American. **Female To Male Ratio:** 1.2:1. The average age of freshmen is 18; all undergraduates, 20. 4% do not continue beyond their first year; 94% remain to graduate. **Housing:** 6500 students can be accommodated in college housing, which includes coed dorms, on-campus apartments, married student housing, honors houses, language houses, special-interest houses, and residential college. On-campus housing is guaranteed for the freshman year only, is available on a first-come, first-served basis, and on a lottery system for upperclassmen. 61% of students commute. Upperclassmen may keep cars.

FACULTY/CLASSROOMS: 61% of faculty are male; 39% are female. 89% teach undergraduates, 69% do research, and 60% do both. Graduate students teach 36% of introductory courses. The average class size in an introductory lecture is 44; in a laboratory is 22; and in a regular course is 33.

PROGRAMS OF STUDY: UVA confers B.A., B.S., B.Ar.H., B.I.S., B.S.C., B.S.Ed., B.S.N., and B.U.E.P. degrees. Master's and doctoral degrees are also awarded. Bachelor's degrees are awarded in BIOLOGICAL SCIENCE (biology/biological science), BUSINESS (business administration and management), COMMUNICATIONS AND THE ARTS (art, classics, comparative literature, dramatic arts, English, French, German, Italian, music, Slavic languages, and Spanish), COMPUTER AND PHYSICAL SCIENCE (astronomy, chemistry, computer science, mathematics, and physics), EDUCATION (physical education/exercise science), ENGINEERING AND ENVIRONMENTAL DESIGN (aerospace studies, architectural history, architecture, biomedical engineering, chemical engineering, city/community/regional planning, civil engineering, computer engineering, electrical/electronics engineering, engineering and applied science, environmental science, mechanical engineering, systems engineering, and urban design), HEALTH PROFESSIONS (health care administration, nursing, and speech pathology/audiology), SOCIAL SCIENCE (African American studies, anthropology, area studies, child psychology/development, economics, history, interdisciplinary studies, international relations, philosophy, political science/government, psychology, public administration, religion, and sociology). English, history, and biology are the strongest academically. Commerce, biology, and economics have the largest enrollments.

ACTIVITIES: 24% of men belong to 31 national fraternities; 27% of women belong to 16 national sororities. Groups on campus include art, band, cheerleading, chess, choir, chorale, chorus, computers, dance, debate, drama, environmental, ethnic, film, forensics, honors, international, jazz band, judiciary and tour guides, LGBT, literary magazine, marching band, musical theater, newspaper, opera, orchestra, pep band, photography, political, professional, radio and TV, religious, social, social service, student government, symphony, and yearbook. Popular campus events include Culturefest and Family Weekend. **Sports:** There are 11 intercollegiate sports for men and 12 for women, and 18 intramural sports for men and 18 for women. Facilities include a stadium, arena, recreation centers, and an aquatics and fitness center. **Graduates:** From July 1, 2015 to June 30, 2016, 3836 bachelor's degrees were awarded. The most popular majors were economics (10%), commerce (9%), and biology (8%). 500 companies recruited on campus in 2015-2016. In an average class, 2% graduate in 3 years or less, 87% graduate in 4 years or less, 93% graduate in 5 years or less, and 94% graduate in 6 years or less.

SERVICES: Counseling and information services are available, as is tutoring in every subject, and a reader service for the blind, as well as transcribers, note takers, and taped readings for disabled students. **Library/Resources:** The 14 libraries contain 5.4 million volumes, 1.5 million microform items, 148,227 audio/video tapes/CDs/DVDs, and subscribe to 210,605 periodicals including electronic. Computerized library services include interlibrary loans, database searching, Internet access, and Wi-Fi capability. Special learning facilities include an art gallery, radio station, TV station, an art museum, and observatory. **Physically Challenged Students:** All of the campus is accessible. Facilities include wheelchair ramps, elevators, special parking, specially equipped restrooms, special class scheduling, lowered drinking fountains, lowered telephones, curb cuts, voice synthesizers, braille printers, and large-screen monitors. **Special:** The college offers internships, study abroad, accelerated degree programs, B.A.-B.S. degrees in biology, environmental sciences, chemistry and physics, co-op programs in engineering, and nondegree study. Dual majors in most arts and sciences programs, student-designed majors, an interdisciplinary major and Echols, and Rodman Scholars program (invited students design own curricula with many requirements waived), and pass/fail options are available. There are including Phi Beta Kappa, a freshman honors program, and 35 departmental honors programs. **Visiting:** There are regularly scheduled orientations for prospective students. Visits consist of comprehensive information sessions and campus tours. There are guides for informal visits, visitors may sit in on classes, and stay overnight. To schedule a visit, contact the Monroe Society at (434) 924-3321. **Campus Safety and Security:** Measures include 24-hour foot and vehicle patrol, emergency notification system, self-defense education, and security escort services. There are also shuttle buses, emergency telephones, lighted pathways/sidewalks, controlled access to dorms/residences, and bicycle registration.

REQUIREMENTS: Applicants can substitute the ACT for the SAT. Two SAT subject tests of the student's choosing are strongly recommended. With few exceptions, candidates graduate from accredited secondary schools. While the GED is accepted, it is rare for candidates for first-year admission who have this credential to be competitive in the admissions process. Applicants should complete 16 high school academic courses, including 4 courses of English, 4 courses of math, 2 courses of physics, biology, or chemistry (3 if applying to engineering), 2 years of foreign language, and 1 course of social science. A letter of recommendation (preferably from the secondary school) is required; also, a teacher's recommendation is recommended. AP credits are accepted. To graduate, students must complete 120 credit hours, with 18 to 42 hours in the major and a minimum GPA of 2.0. Distribution requirements include 12 hours of math and science, 6 hours each of humanities, composition, and social sciences, 4 semesters of foreign languages, 3 hours of historical studies, and 3 hours of non-Western perspectives. **Procedure:** Freshmen are admitted in the fall. Entrance exams should be taken by December of the senior year. There are early admissions and deferred admissions plans. Applications should be filed by January 1 for fall entry, along with a $60 fee. Notifications are sent April 1. 2871 applicants were on the 2016 waiting list; 360 were admitted. Applications are accepted online. **Transfer Students:** 648 transfer students enrolled in 2015-2016. For the largest school (Arts and Sciences) an applicant for transfer admission must be in good academic and social standing at any college that he or she is currently attending or has previously attended and must be eligible to return there. To be competitive for admission, we recommend that a transfer student have a cumulative grade point average of B+ or better in all college work attempted. 60 of 120 credits required for the bachelor's degree must be completed at UVA. **International Students:** There are 751 international students enrolled. The school actively recruits these students. They must take the TOEFL, International English Language Testing System (IELTS). They must also take the SAT or ACT, as well as the same tests as all other entering students.

ADMISSIONS: 30% of the 2016-2017 applicants were accepted. The SAT scores for the 2016-2017 freshman class were: Critical Reading-- 2% below 500, 14% between 500 and 599, 46% between 600 and 699, and 38% between 700 and 800. Math-- 2% below 500, 13% between 500 and 599, 41% between 600 and 699, and 44% between 700 and 800. Writing-- 3% below 500, 16% between 500 and 599, 43% between 600 and 699, and 38% between 700 and 800. The ACT scores were 3% between 18 and 23, 27% between 24 and 29, and 69% above 30. 97% of the current freshmen were in the top fifth of their class; 99% were in the top two fifths. **Admissions Contact:** Gregory W. Roberts, Dean of Admissions. Email: *undergradadmission@virginia.edu* Web: *www.virginia.edu*

FINANCIAL AID: In 2016-2017, 55% of all full-time freshmen and 48% of continuing full-time students received some form of financial aid. 35% of all full-time freshmen and 32% of continuing full-time students received need-based aid. The average freshman award was $20,949. Need-based scholarships or need-based grants averaged $19,488; need-based self-help aid (loans and jobs) averaged $5,156; non-need-based athletic scholarships averaged $26,046; and other non-need-based awards and non-need-based scholarships averaged $8,900. The average financial indebtedness of the 2016 graduate was $24,911. The CSS/Profile is required. The deadline for filing freshman financial aid applications for fall entry is March 1.

VIRGINIA COMMONWEALTH UNIVERSITY E-3
www.vcu.edu

Richmond, VA 23284	**(804) 828-8476** **(800) 841-3638**
Fax: (804) 828-1899	**Email: admissions@vcu.edu**
Full-time: 8592 men, 11,819 women	**Faculty:** I, -$
Part-time: 1539 men, 2101 women	**Ph.D.s:** n/av
Graduate: 2791 men, 4400 women	**Student/Faculty:** 16 to 1
Year: semesters, summer session	**Tuition:** $12,772 ($31,463)
Room & Board: $9586	**Freshman Class:** 15293 applied, 11798 accepted, 4090 enrolled
SAT CR/M/W: 550/540/530 **ACT:** 24	**CEEB CODE:** 5570
Application Deadline: January 15	**COMPETITIVE**

As one of only 28 public universities with academic medical centers to be designated by the Carnegie Foundation as "Community Engaged" with "Very High Research Activity," Virginia Commonwealth University is taking its place among the nation's premier urban, public research universities. VCU: the Medical College of Virginia, established in 1838 as the medical department of Hampden-Sydney College, and Richmond Professional Institute, founded in 1917. Today, 226 degree and certificate programs and encompasses one of the largest academic health centers in the nation. VCU Health, was named the No. 1 hospital in Virginia. VCU and VCU Health have been honored with prestigious national and international recognition for top- quality graduate, professional and medical care programs, reflecting a commitment to be among America's top research universities. There are 14 undergraduate schools and 1 graduate school. In addition to regional accreditation, VCU has baccalaureate program accreditation with AACSB, ABET, ACEJMC, ACPE, ADA, APTA, CSAB, CSWE, FIDER, NASAD, NASDTEC, NASM, NCATE, NLN, NRPA, CAATE, and CACREP. The 150-acre campus is in an urban area 2 miles west of downtown Richmond and 90 miles from Washington, D.C. Including any residence halls, there are 235 buildings.

STUDENT LIFE: 88% of undergraduates are from Virginia. Others are from 50 states, 109 foreign countries, and Canada. 7% are Hispanic; 6% Foreign; 51% White; 5% two or more races; 4% race unknown; 16% African American; 12% Asian American. **Female To Male Ratio:** 1.4:1. The average age of freshmen is 18; all undergraduates, 21. **Housing:** 6285 students can be accommodated in college housing, which includes coed dorms, on-campus apartments, honors houses, and ASPIRE an innovative and comprehensive community engagement-focused living-learning program for sophmores at VCU. On-campus housing is guaranteed for the freshman year only, and is available on a first-come, and first-served basis. 74% of students live on campus. All students may keep cars.

FACULTY/CLASSROOMS: 56% of faculty are male; 44% are female. No introductory courses are taught by graduate students.

PROGRAMS OF STUDY: VCU confers B.A., B.S., B.I.S., B.M., B.S.W., and B.F.A. degrees. Master's and doctoral degrees are also awarded. Bachelor's degrees are awarded in AGRICULTURE (environmental studies), BIOLOGICAL SCIENCE (bioinformatics and biology/biological science), BUSINESS (accounting, business administration and management, marketing/retailing/merchandising, and sports management), COMMUNICATIONS AND THE ARTS (art history and appreciation, communications, crafts, dance, dramatic arts, English, film arts, graphic design, languages, media arts, music, painting, photography, and sculpture), COMPUTER AND PHYSICAL SCIENCE (chemistry, computer science, information sciences and systems, mathematics, physics, and science), EDUCATION (art education, foreign languages education, and health education), ENGINEERING AND ENVIRONMENTAL DESIGN (bioengineering, biomedical engineering, chemical engineering, computer engineering, electrical/electronics engineering, electrical/electronics engineering technology, interior design, and mechanical engineering), HEALTH PROFESSIONS (clinical science, dental hygiene, and nursing), SOCIAL SCIENCE (African American studies, anthropology, criminal justice, economics, fashion design and technology, forensic studies, history, homeland security, interdisciplinary studies, international studies, philosophy, philosophy and religion, political science/government, psychology, religion, safety science, social work, sociology, and urban studies). Biology, psychology, and physical education have the largest enrollments.

ACTIVITIES: There are 626 groups on campus, including art, band, cheerleading, chess, choir, chorale, chorus, computers, dance, debate, drama, ethnic, film, forensics, honors, international, jazz band, LGBT, literary magazine, musical theater, newspaper, opera, pep band, photography, political, professional, radio and TV, religious, social, social service, student government, symphony, and yearbook. Popular campus events include Annual Fall Step Show, Fest, Greek Week, Homecoming International Festival, Spring Fest, and Welcome Week. **Sports:** There are 7 intercollegiate sports for men and 8 for women, and 18 intramural sports for men and 18 for women. Facilities include a multipurpose indoor area for intercollegiate athletics and recreational sports, fitness center, an activity center, and a wellness resource center, a stadium for soccer and track and field events, a tennis center, a recreation complex containing gym, handball/racquetball courts, weight room, and cardiovascular fitness space. There is also a jogging track, baseball field, a pool, handball/racquetball and squash courts. Students and members have full access to the Cary Street Gym on the Monroe Park Campus, and the MCV Campus Recreation & Aquatic Center, located inside the Jonah L. Larrick Student Center. Both facilities feature fitness equipment, swimming pools, gymnasium and group exercise space. In addition, Cary Street Field, the Thalhimer Tennis Center and Mary and Frances Youth Center provide outdoor spaces for field sports, tennis and basketball. **Graduates:** From July 1, 2015 to June 30, 2016, 4786 bachelor's degrees were awarded. The most popular majors were psychology (10%), business (7%), and business (7%). In an average class, 62% graduate in 6 years or less.

SERVICES: Counseling and information services are available, as is tutoring in most subjects, and a reader service for the blind, and remedial math, reading, and writing. **Library/Resources:** The 2 libraries contain 2.8 million volumes. Computerized library services include interlibrary loans, database searching, Internet access, and Wi-Fi capability. Special learning facilities include an art gallery, radio station, and a TV station. **Physically Challenged Students:** 90% of the campus is accessible. Facilities include wheelchair ramps, elevators, special parking, specially equipped restrooms, special class scheduling, and lowered drinking fountains. **Special:** The university has these special study options: accelerated programs, cooperative education program, distance learning, double major, dual enrollment, English as a second language (ESL), honors program, independent study, internships, student-designed major, study abroad and teacher certification program. There are 21 national honor societies and a freshman honors program. **Visiting:** Regularly scheduled orientations are available for prospective students, daily tours every Monday-Saturday except holidays and holiday weekends. The information session is followed by an hour-long guided walk tour of the Monroe Park. Registration is required for attendance at these daily sessions. To schedule a visit, contact the Office of Admissions. **Campus Safety and Security:** Measures include 24-hour foot and vehicle patrol, emergency notification system, self-defense education, and security escort services. There are also shuttle buses, emergency telephones, lighted pathways/sidewalks, controlled access to dorms/residences, formal presentations, online crime prevention program, annual security report, crime prevention through environmental design, community police officers/certified prevention specialists, security inspections of facilities, operation ID bike, computer registration, and victim/witness assistance program.

REQUIREMENTS: Candidates for admission to VCU are reviewed based on their academic performance in an accredited high school or on GED scores and either SAT Reasoning Test or ACT scores. The college preparatory curriculum is highly preferred, and a minimum of 20 units is required for admission to all programs on the Monroe Park Campus. Applicants should present a minimum of: 4 units of English, 3 units each of mathematics (including algebra I and either geometry or algebra II) history, social studies or government, science (at least one laboratory), and 1 foreign language or 2 units of 2 foreign languages are strongly recommended. VCU requires freshman applicants (high school graduates and GED holders) 22 years of age or younger to submit SAT or ACT scores and, if applicable, an official copy of their GED scores. Electronic submission is recommended. Freshman applicants with a minimum high school GPA of 3.3 may request that their application be reviewed without submitting standardized test scores. Applicants should request to be considered for admission to the university without test scores on the application for freshmen admission. A GPA of 2.0 is required. AP and CLEP credits are accepted. The total number of semester credits required for graduation depends upon the degree program. Specific information may be found under degree program descriptions. In addition to the specific requirements listed by the college/school/department, the following graduation checklist for undergraduate students summarizes all general requirements for graduation and issuance of a diploma. An overall undergraduate GPA must be 2.0 or greater. A student must have completed 25 percent of the semester-hour credits required for the bachelor's degree in residence at VCU, including at least 30 of the last 45 credits. Student must have earned a minimum of 120 credits, including transfer credits. All grades of Incomplete (I), Continued (CO), Progress (PR), Not Recorded (NR) and No Grade (NG) must be converted to final letter grades no later than the last day of class of the semester in which the candidate plans to graduate. Students are reminded to complete a final check of their academic records before they exit the university to ensure that all temporary grades have been converted, that the record accurately reflects their academic histories and that all degrees have been posted. Requests for changes to the academic record must be made within the first six months following graduation, but this requirement may be superseded by other university-specific deadlines (e.g., those governing requests for a change of grade). Commonwealth of Virginia record-retention requirements may affect the university's ability to address requests for changes to the academic record. Students must settle all financial obligations to the university prior to the issuance of a diploma. **Procedure:** Freshmen are admitted in the fall and spring. Entrance exams should be taken SAT or ACT scores must be received for fall term admission by March. There are early admissions, deferred admissions, and rolling admissions plans. Applications should be filed by January 15 for fall entry. The fall 2016 application fee was $50. Notifications are sent April 1. Applications are accepted online. **Transfer Students:** 2022 transfer students enrolled in 2015-2016. All credits taken at regionally accredited institutions that meet the VCU transfer requirements may be posted to the VCU transcript. However, there may be a difference between the credits VCU will post and the credit each VCU department/school will apply to the desired degree program. Students should meet with their program advisers, who will assist them in determining their VCU degree their VCU degree requirements and will advise them on what transfer courses the program specifically will apply toward their degree requirements. Regardless of how many transfer credits are accepted, students must satisfy all VCU graduation requirements noted in the graduation checklist, including the following: completion of at least 25 percent of the semester-hour credits required for their bachelor's degree program at VCU; completion of at least 30 of the last 45 semester hour credits. **International Students:** There are 1041 international students enrolled. The school actively recruits these students. They must take the TOEFL with a minimum score of 550 on the paper-based TOEFL (PBT) or 80 on the Internet-based version (iBT) and the college's own test, or take the IELTS.

ADMISSIONS: 77% of the 2016-2017 applicants were accepted. The SAT scores for the 2016-2017 freshman class were: Critical Reading-- 24% below 500, 47% between 500 and 599, 24% between 600 and 699, and 6% between 700 and 800. Math-- 28% below 500, 48% between 500 and 599, 20% between 600 and 699, and 4% between 700 and 800. Writing-- 32% below 500, 45% between 500 and 599, 19% between 600 and 699, and 3% between 700 and 800. The ACT scores were 6% between 12 and 17, 42% between 18 and 23, 41% between 24 and 29, and 11% above 30. 39% of the current freshmen were in the top fifth of their class; 73% were in the top two fifths. 33 freshmen graduated first in their class. **Admissions Contact:** Email: *admissions@vcu.edu* Web: *www.vcu.edu*

FINANCIAL AID: In 2016-2017, 78% of all full-time freshmen and 71% of continuing full-time students received some form of financial aid. 53% of all full-time freshmen and 50% of continuing full-time students received need-based aid. The average freshman award was $16,246. Need-based scholarships or need-based grants averaged $7,341 ($20,547 maximum); need-based self-help aid (loans and jobs) averaged $3,758 ($9,016 maximum); non-need-based athletic scholarships averaged $20,513 ($50,524 maximum); and other non-need-based awards and non-need-based scholarships averaged $5,286 ($37,357 maximum). 4% of undergraduate students work part-time. Average annual earnings from campus work are $802. The average financial indebtedness of the 2016 graduate was $33,125. The FAFSA code is 003735. The priority date for freshman financial aid applications for fall entry is March 1.

VIRGINIA MILITARY INSTITUTE — C-3

www.vmi.edu

Lexington, VA 24450	**(540) 464-7211** **(800) 767-4207**
Fax: (540) 464-7746	**Email: admissions@vmi.edu**
Full-time: 1518 men, 195 women	**Faculty:** 133; IIB, +$
Part-time: n/av	**Ph.D.s:** 97%
Graduate: n/av	**Student/Faculty:** 11 to 1
Year: semesters, summer session	**Tuition:** $17,492 ($41,801)
Room & Board: $8968	**Freshman Class:** 1779 applied, 940 accepted, 405 enrolled
SAT CR/M/W: 580/580/550 **ACT:** 26	**CEEB CODE:** 5858
Application Deadline: February 1	**COMPETITIVE+**

Virginia Military Institute, established in 1839, is the nation's first state-supported military college, offering academic programs in engineering, sciences, and liberal arts. All students are members of the Corps of Cadets, live in barracks, eat together in the mess hall, wear uniforms, and adhere to the Honor System. The figures in the above capsule and in this profile are approximate. There is 1 undergraduate school. In addition to regional accreditation, VMI has baccalaureate program accreditation with AACSB, ABET, and ACS. The 134-acre campus is in a small town 50 miles north of Roanoke. Including any residence halls, there are 68 buildings.

STUDENT LIFE: 60% of undergraduates are from Virginia. Others are from 45 states, and 6 foreign countries. 78% are from public schools. 85% are White; 6% African American; 4% Asian American; 3% Hispanic; 2% Foreign. 64% are Protestant; 28% Catholic. **Male To Female Ratio:** 7.8:1. The average age of freshmen is 18; all undergraduates, 20. 26% do not continue beyond their first year; 74% remain to graduate. **Housing:** College-sponsored housing includes coed Barracks, 3-5 students in a room. On-campus housing is guaranteed for all 4 years. Upperclassmen may keep cars. Alcohol is not permitted.

FACULTY/CLASSROOMS: 70% of faculty are male; 30% are female. All teach undergraduates. No introductory courses are taught by graduate students. The average class size in an introductory lecture is 17; in a laboratory is 13; and in a regular course is 12.

PROGRAMS OF STUDY: VMI confers B.A. and B.S. degrees. Bachelor's degrees are awarded in BIOLOGICAL SCIENCE (biology/biological science), BUSINESS (business economics), COMMUNICATIONS AND THE ARTS (English), COMPUTER AND PHYSICAL SCIENCE (chemistry, computer science, mathematics, and physics), ENGINEERING AND ENVIRONMENTAL DESIGN (civil engineering, electrical/electronics engineering, and mechanical engineering), SOCIAL SCIENCE (history, international studies, and psychology). Engineering (civil, electrical, and mechanical), and sciences are the strongest academically. International studies, business/economics, and civil engineering have the largest enrollments.

ACTIVITIES: There are no fraternities or sororities. There are 50 groups on campus, including historical club, bagpipe, band, cheerleading, choir, chorus, communications, drama, drill team, ethnic, honors, international, investment, jazz band, LGBT, literary magazine, marching band, newspaper, orchestra, pep band, political, professional, religious, social, social service, student government, and yearbook. Popular campus events include Ring Figure, Virginia Transportation Conference, and Dance and Concert Weekends. **Sports:** There are 11 intercollegiate sports for men and 6 for women, and 4 intramural sports for men and 4 for women. Facilities include basketball, racquetball, and tennis courts, fields for lacrosse, football, baseball, and soccer, a swimming pool, rifle range, indoor and outdoor running tracks, wrestling facility, access to a golf course, weight training and aerobic facility, and auxiliary indoor and outdoor basketball courts. **Graduates:** From July 1, 2015 to June 30, 2016, 372 bachelor's degrees were awarded. The most popular majors were social sciences (32%), engineering (25%), and history (12%). 45 companies recruited on campus in 2015-2016. In an average class, 58% graduate in 4 years or less, 71% graduate in 5 years or less, and 73% graduate in 6 years or less. Of the 2015 graduating class, 89% were enrolled in graduate school within 6 months of graduation, and 99% were employed.

SERVICES: Counseling and information services are available, as is tutoring in some subjects. **Library/Resources:** The 2 libraries contain 240,000 volumes, 12,963 microform items, 5,747 audio/video tapes/CDs/DVDs, and subscribe to 26,789 periodicals including electronic. Computerized library services include interlibrary loans, database searching, Internet access, and Wi-Fi capability. **Physically Challenged Students:** 75% of the campus is accessible. Facilities include wheelchair ramps, elevators, special parking, and specially equipped restrooms. **Special:** Study abroad in 14 countries and work-study programs are available, as are for-credit internships in English and international studies and summer internships in foreign countries. VMI offers dual majors in any combination and B.A.-B.S. degrees in liberal arts, physical sciences, and engineering. Minors are offered in each field of study. There are 11 national honor societies, a freshman honors program, and 3 departmental honors programs. **Visiting:** There are regularly scheduled orientations for prospective students, consisting of tours, conferences with academic and ROTC instructors, interaction with current freshmen, and overnight stays. There are guides for informal visits, visitors may sit in on classes, and stay overnight. To schedule a visit, contact the Admissions Office. **Campus Safety and Security:** Measures include 24-hour foot and vehicle patrol, self-defense education, emergency telephones, and lighted pathways/sidewalks.

REQUIREMENTS: The SAT or ACT is required. Applicants must be graduates of an accredited secondary school. Applicants should complete 16 to 19 high school academic units, including 4 years of English, 3 to 4 each of math, science with lab, and foreign language, 2 of social studies, and 1 of history. An essay is encouraged and an interview is recommended. A GPA of 2.0 is required. AP credits are accepted. Important factors in the admissions decision are advanced placement or honors courses, personality/intangible qualities, extracurricular activities record, and leadership record. To graduate, students must complete 136 to 144 semester hours, with a GPA of 2.0. All students must pass chemistry, English, history, math, phys ed, ROTC, and public speaking. In addition, all cadets must pass swimming, boxing, and wrestling. **Procedure:** Freshmen are admitted in the fall. Entrance exams should be taken spring of the junior year or fall of the senior year. There are early decision, early admissions, and rolling admissions plans. Early decision applications should be filed by November 15; regular applications, by February 1 for fall entry, along with a $40 fee. Notification of early decision is sent December 15; regular decision, 166 early decision candidates were accepted for the 2016-2017 class. 150 applicants were on the 2016 waiting list; 15 were admitted. **Transfer Students:** 27 transfer students enrolled in 2015-2016. Applicants for transfer must have a minimum GPA of 2.0, and 24 transferable credit hours, and a satisfactory high school record. Either the SAT or the ACT is required. 135 credits required for the bachelor's degree must be completed at VMI. **International Students:** There are 25 international students enrolled. The school actively recruits these students. They must take the TOEFL. International students who will play intercollegiate athletics must take the SAT or ACT.

ADMISSIONS: 53% of the 2016-2017 applicants were accepted. The SAT scores for the 2016-2017 freshman class were: Critical Reading-- 11% below 500, 47% between 500 and 599, 35% between 600 and 699, and 7% between 700 and 800. Math-- 10% below 500, 48% between 500 and 599, 39% between 600 and 699, and 5% between 700 and 800. Writing-- 24% below 500, 48% between 500 and 599, 26% between 600 and 699, and 1% between 700 and 800. 21% of the current freshmen were in the top fifth of their class; 43% were in the top two fifths. **Admissions Contact:** Col. Vernon L. Beitzel, Director of Admissions. Email: *admissions@vmi.edu* Web: *www.vmi.edu*

FINANCIAL AID: In 2016-2017, 89% of all full-time freshmen and 59% of continuing full-time students received some form of financial aid. 89% of all full-time freshmen and 57% of continuing full-time students received need-based aid. The average freshman award was $17,430. Need-based scholarships or need-based grants averaged $16,738; need-based self-help aid (loans and jobs) averaged $3,920; non-need-based athletic scholarships averaged $19,303; other non-need-based awards and non-need-based scholarships averaged $6,606; and $3,920 from other forms of aid. The average financial indebtedness of the 2016 graduate was $26,720. VMI is a member of CSS. The college's own financial statement, and institution's own financial aid form are required. The priority date for freshman financial aid applications for fall entry is March 1. The filing deadline for fall entry is March 1.

VIRGINIA POLYTECHNIC INSTITUTE AND STATE UNIVERSITY C-3

www.vt.edu

Blacksburg, VA 24061 **(540) 231-6267**

Fax: (540) 231-3242
Email: admissions@vt.edu
Full-time: 14,194 men, 10,606 women
Faculty: 1731; I, av$
Ph.D.s: 90%
Part-time: 365 men, 162 women
Student/Faculty: 14 to 1
Graduate: 4142 men, 3137 women
Tuition: $12,852 ($29,371)
Year: semesters, summer session
Freshman Class: 22280 applied, 16355 accepted, 6324 enrolled
Room & Board: $8424
SAT CR/M/W: 590/625/585 **ACT:** required
CEEB CODE: 5859
Application Deadline: January 15
HIGHLY COMPETITIVE

Virginia Polytechnic Institute and State University, founded in 1872, is a public land-grant institution, offering a cadet program within the larger, nonmilitary student body. There are 7 undergraduate schools and 2 graduate schools. In addition to regional accreditation, Virginia Tech has baccalaureate program accreditation with AACSB, ABET, ACCE, ADA, AHEA, ASLA, FIDER, NAAB, NCATE, and SAF. The 2600-acre campus is in a rural area 40 miles southwest of Roanoke. Including any residence halls, there are 110 buildings.

STUDENT LIFE: 76% of undergraduates are from Virginia. Others are from 49 states, 77 foreign countries, and Canada. 9% are Asian American; 8% Foreign; 67% White; 5% Hispanic; 4% African American; 4% two or more races; 3% race unknown. **Male To Female Ratio:** 1.3:1. The average age of freshmen is 18; all undergraduates, 20. 11% do not continue beyond their first year; 78% remain to graduate. **Housing:** 9125 students can be accommodated in college housing, which includes single-sex and coed dorms, honors houses, special-interest houses, fraternity houses, sorority houses, and theme housing, wellness housing, and international housing. The cadets live in the cadet residence halls. On-campus housing is guaranteed for the freshman year only and is available on a lottery system for upperclassmen. 63% of students commute. Upperclassmen may keep cars.

FACULTY/CLASSROOMS: 69% of faculty are male; 31% are female. 74% teach undergraduates, and 74% do research. Graduate students teach 12% of introductory courses. The average class size in an introductory lecture is 46 and in a laboratory is 30.

PROGRAMS OF STUDY: Virginia Tech confers B.A., B.S., B.Arch., B.F.A., B.Land.Arch., B.S.Bus., B.S.E., and B.S.Ed. degrees. Master's and doctoral degrees are also awarded. Bachelor's degrees are awarded in AGRICULTURE (agricultural economics, animal science, dairy science, forestry and related sciences, horticulture, poultry science, and soil science), BIOLOGICAL SCIENCE (biochemistry, biology/biological science, and nutrition), BUSINESS (accounting, apparel and accessories marketing, banking and finance, business economics, entrepreneurial studies, hotel/motel and restaurant management, management science, marketing management, and tourism), COMMUNICATIONS AND THE ARTS (art, communications, dramatic arts, English, French, German, industrial design, music, and Spanish), COMPUTER AND PHYSICAL SCIENCE (chemistry, computer science, geology, mathematics, physics, planetary and space science, and statistics), EDUCATION (agricultural education, business education, environmental education, foreign languages education, science education, and secondary education), ENGINEERING AND ENVIRONMENTAL DESIGN (aerospace studies, agricultural engineering, architecture, chemical engineering, civil engineering, computer engineering, construction engineering, construction management, electrical/electronics engineering, engineering mechanics, environmental science, industrial engineering, interior design, landscape architecture/design, materials engineering, mechanical engineering, mining and mineral engineering, and ocean engineering), HEALTH PROFESSIONS (physical therapy, predentistry, and premedicine), SOCIAL SCIENCE (dietetics, economics, food science, geography, history, human development, interdisciplinary studies, international studies, interpreter for the deaf, parks and recreation management, philosophy, physical fitness/movement, political science/government, prelaw, psychology, public affairs, sociology, and urban studies). Engineering, architecture, and business are the strongest academically. Engineering, computer science, and biology have the largest enrollments.

ACTIVITIES: 14% of men belong to 43 national fraternities; 18% of women belong to 21 national sororities. There are 600 groups on campus, including art, band, cheerleading, chess, choir, chorale, chorus, computers, dance, drama, drill team, drum and bugle corps, ethnic, honors, international, jazz band, LGBT, literary magazine, marching band, musical theater, orchestra, pep band, photography, political, professional, religious, social, social service, and student government. Popular campus events include Quad Jams, Ring Dance, and German's Mid-Winter Dance. **Sports:** There are 11 intercollegiate sports for men and 10 for women, and 24 intramural sports for men and 24 for women. Facilities include a football stadium, a basketball coliseum, field house, an indoor tennis pavilion, golf course, soccer and baseball fields, a swimming pool, diving well, volleyball, racquetball, handball, squash, tennis courts, a gymnastics room, a weight-lifting room, multipurpose recreation fields, and a pond for ice skating. The residential quads are also equipped with a weight-room and exercise facilities with gyms. **Graduates:** From July 1, 2015 to June 30, 2016, 5890 bachelor's degrees were awarded. The most popular majors were engineering (23%), business/marketing (18%), and family and consumer sciences (9%). 250 companies recruited on campus in 2015-2016. In an average class, 51% graduate in 4 years or less, 74% graduate in 5 years or less, and 83% graduate in 6 years or less. Of the 2015 graduating class, 19% were enrolled in graduate school within 6 months of graduation, and 57% were employed.

SERVICES: Counseling and information services are available, as is tutoring in most subjects, and a reader service for the blind, and remedial reading. **Library/Resources:** The 4 libraries contain 2.3 million volumes, 6.3 million microform items, 27,574 audio/video tapes/CDs/DVDs, and subscribe to 35,596 periodicals including electronic. Computerized library services include interlibrary loans, database searching, and Internet access. Special learning facilities include an art gallery, natural history museum, an airport, wind tunnels, agricultural stations, radio/visual observatories, satellite up-link station, multimedia, digital music, writing, and CAD/CAM labs, math emporium, and CAVE (cave automatic virtual environment). **Physically Challenged Students:** 60% of the campus is accessible. Facilities include wheelchair ramps, elevators, special parking, specially equipped restrooms, special class scheduling, lowered drinking fountains, lowered telephones, special housing. There is also a special services library room for the visually impaired. **Special:** Students may cross-register with Miami University in Ohio, Oxford Polytechnic Institute, California Polytechnic Institute, and Florida A & M. Study abroad in 36 countries, internships in nearly every major, a Washington semester, and a wide range of work-study programs are available, as well as co-ops in 48 majors. There are honors options for most majors, B.A.-B.S. degrees, dual and student-designed majors, credit for independent study or research, nondegree study, and pass/fail options. The Corps of Cadets, a militarily structured organization, is open to men and women. Undergraduate advising programs are available to students wishing to prepare for professional school in law, dentistry, medicine, pharmacy, physical therapy, and veterinary medicine. There are 13 national honor societies, Phi Beta Kappa, and a freshman honors program. **Visiting:** Regularly scheduled orientations are available for prospective students, consisting of a fall Open House Series: half-day on-campus programs that include presentations, tours, and question-and-answer sessions. There are guides for informal visits and visitors may sit in on classes. To schedule a visit, contact the Office of Undergraduate Admissions at vtadmiss@vt.edu. **Campus Safety and Security:** Measures include 24-hour foot and vehicle patrol, emergency notification system, self-defense education, and security escort services. There are also shuttle buses, emergency telephones, and lighted pathways/sidewalks.

REQUIREMENTS: The SAT or ACT is required. Applicants must be graduates of an accredited secondary school, or the GED is accepted. Applicants should complete 18 high school academic credits, including 4 years of English, 3-4 of math, including algebra II and geometry, 2 of lab science, to be chosen from biology, chemistry, or physics, and 1 each of history and social studies. An additional 3 years from college preparatory courses, and 4 from any credit course offerings are required. AP and CLEP credits are accepted. Important factors in the admissions decision are advanced placement or honors courses, evidence of special talent, and extracurricular activities record. To graduate, students must complete between 120 and 156 credit hours (depending on the major), with a minimum GPA of 2.0. There is a required core curriculum that includes 8 hours of science and 6 hours each of humanities, social science, math, and writing and discourse. Students must also meet a foreign language requirement. **Procedure:** Freshmen are admitted to all sessions. Entrance exams should be taken by January 1 of the senior year. There are early decision and deferred admissions plans. Early decision applications should be filed by November 1; regular applications, by January 15 for fall entry; October 1 for spring entry; and April 22 for summer entry, along with a $60 fee. Notification of early decision is sent December 15. 1137 early decision candidates were accepted for the 2016-2017 class. 1544 applicants were on the 2016 waiting list. Applications are accepted online. **Transfer Students:** 979 transfer students enrolled in 2015-2016. Applicants must have a minimum GPA of 2.0 and must specify a major. Competitive GPA is 3.0. Student may enroll in the fall and summer. 30 of 120 credits required for the bachelor's degree must be completed at Virginia Tech. **International Students:** The school actively recruits these students. They must take the TOEFL, as well as the SAT or ACT.

ADMISSIONS: 73% of the 2016-2017 applicants were accepted. The SAT scores for the 2016-2017 freshman class were: Critical Reading-- 9% below 500, 43% between 500 and 599, 39% between 600 and 699, and 8% between 700 and 800. Math-- 4% below 500, 31% between 500 and 599, 46% between 600 and 699, and 19% between 700 and 800. Writing-- 12% below 500, 44% between 500 and 599, 38% between 600 and 699, and 7% between 700 and 800. 82% of the current freshmen were in the top fifth of their class; 97% were in the top two fifths. **Admissions Contact:** Mildred R Johnson, Director of Undergraduate Admissions. Email: *admissions@vt.edu* Web: *www.vt.edu*

FINANCIAL AID: In 2016-2017, 92% of all full-time freshmen and 53% of continuing full-time students received some form of financial aid. 92% of all full-time freshmen and 52% of continuing full-time students received need-based aid. The average freshman award was $18,985. Need-based scholarships or need-based grants averaged $7,469; need-based self-help aid (loans and jobs) averaged $4,162; non-need-based athletic scholarships averaged $25,420; other non-need-based awards and non-need-based scholarships averaged $4,078; and $3,482 from other forms of aid. The average financial indebtedness of the 2016 graduate was $31,293. The filing deadline for fall entry is March 1.

VIRGINIA STATE UNIVERSITY E-3
www.vsu.edu

Petersburg, VA 23806	**(804) 524-5902** **(800) 871-7611**
Fax: (804) 524-5055	**Email: admiss@vsu.edu**
Full-time: 1400 men, 1800 women	**Faculty:** 168
Part-time: 200 men, 200 women	**Ph.D.s:** 74%
Graduate: 220 men, 580 women	**Student/Faculty:** 19 to 1
Year: semesters, summer session	**Tuition:** $9240 ($22,542)
Room & Board: $10,562	**Freshman Class:** 4138 applied, 2028 accepted, 1011 enrolled
SAT or ACT: required	**CEEB CODE:** 5860
Application Deadline: n/av	**COMPETITIVE+**

Virginia State University, is a historically black public land-grant institution of higher education providing academic programs that integrate instruction, research, and extension/public service. The figures in the above capsule and in this profile are approximate. Tuition cost is based on undergraduate programs; 9-15 credit hours. There are 4 undergraduate schools and 1 graduate school. In addition to regional accreditation, VSU has baccalaureate program accreditation with ABET, ADA, CSWE, NASM, and NCATE. The 652-acre campus is in a suburban area 25 miles south of Richmond. Including any residence halls, there are 52 buildings.

STUDENT LIFE: 65% of undergraduates are from Virginia. Others are from 35 states, and 1 foreign country. 96% are from public schools. 90% are African American; 8% White; 1% Hispanic. **Female To Male Ratio:** 1.4:1. The average age of freshmen is 18; all undergraduates, 21. 40% do not continue beyond their first year; 18% remain to graduate. **Housing:** 2050 students can be accommodated in college housing, which includes single-sex dorms, and honors houses. On-campus housing is guaranteed for the freshman year only, and is available on a first-come, and first-served basis. 52% of students live on campus; of those, 20% remain on campus on weekends. Upperclassmen may keep cars. Alcohol is not permitted.

FACULTY/CLASSROOMS: 67% of faculty are male; 33% are female. Graduate students teach 2% of introductory courses.

PROGRAMS OF STUDY: VSU confers B.A., B.S., B.F.A., B.I.S., and B.Mus. degrees. Master's degrees are also awarded. Bachelor's degrees are awarded in AGRICULTURE (agriculture), BIOLOGICAL SCIENCE (biology/biological science), BUSINESS (accounting, business administration and management, hotel/motel and restaurant management, management information systems, and marketing management), COMMUNICATIONS AND THE ARTS (English literature, music performance, and visual and performing arts), COMPUTER AND PHYSICAL SCIENCE (chemistry, mathematics, and physics), EDUCATION (athletic training, business education, physical education, and trade and industrial education), ENGINEERING AND ENVIRONMENTAL DESIGN (engineering technology), SOCIAL SCIENCE (economics, history, home economics, interdisciplinary studies, political science/government, psychology, public administration, social work, and sociology). Business administration, accounting, and business information systems have the largest enrollments.

ACTIVITIES: 10% of men belong to 4 national fraternities; 10% of women belong to 4 national sororities. There are 44 groups on campus, including band, cheerleading, chess, choir, chorus, computers, dance, drama, drill team, ethnic, honors, international, jazz band, marching band, musical theater, newspaper, orchestra, pep band, photography, political, professional, radio and TV, religious, social, student government, symphony, and yearbook. Popular campus events include High School Day, VSU Day, and Commencement. **Sports:** There are 7 intercollegiate sports for men and 6 for women, and 5 intramural sports for men and 6 for women. Facilities include a gym, pool, dance studio, tennis courts, track field, football field, baseball field, and indoor and outdoor basketball courts. **Graduates:** In an average class, 10% graduate in 4 years or less, 26% graduate in 5 years or less, and 33% graduate in 6 years or less.

SERVICES: Counseling and information services are available, as is tutoring in most subjects, and a reader service for the blind. **Library/Resources:** The library contains 280,599 volumes, 662,075 microform items, 3,939 audio/video tapes/CDs/DVDs, and subscribes to 1,198 periodicals including electronic. Computerized library services include interlibrary loans and database searching. Special learning facilities include an art gallery, radio station, and a TV station. **Physically Challenged Students:** 75% of the campus is accessible. Facilities include wheelchair ramps, elevators, special parking, and specially equipped restrooms. **Special:** VSU offers dual majors, a general studies degree, a 3-2 engineering degree program, nondegree study, and a pass/fail grading option. There are 10 national honor societies, Phi Beta Kappa, a freshman honors program, and 7 departmental honors programs. **Visiting:** Regularly scheduled orientations are available for prospective students. There are guides for informal visits and visitors may sit in on classes. To schedule a visit, contact the Admissions Office. **Campus Safety and Security:** Measures include 24-hour foot, vehicle patrol, emergency telephones, and lighted pathways/sidewalks.

REQUIREMENTS: The SAT or ACT is required. Applicants must graduate from an accredited secondary school with 16 academic credits and 12 Carnegie units, or have a GED. Students must take 4 years of English, 2 each of a foreign language, math, and science, and 1 each of history and social studies. Essays, 2 letters of recommendation, evidence of physical condition, interviews, and, if appropriate, auditions are required. A GPA of 2.2 is required. AP and CLEP credits are accepted. Important factors in the admissions decision are advanced placement or honors courses, recommendations by school officials, and leadership record. To graduate, students must have a minimum GPA of 2.0. They must earn at least 120 credits, with the last 27 semester hours in residence. Requirements include those in phys ed, freshman writing, math, biology, social or physical science, history, and psychology. Freshman orientation must also be completed. **Procedure:** Freshmen are admitted in the fall and spring. There are deferred admissions and rolling admissions plans. Early decision applications should be filed by May 1. Applications are accepted online. **Transfer Students:** Applicants must have a minimum GPA of 2.0. Those transferring fewer than 25 semester hours must meet freshman standards. 30 of 120 credits required for the bachelor's degree must be completed at VSU. **International Students:** They must take the TOEFL, as well as the SAT or ACT.

ADMISSIONS: 49% of the 2016-2017 applicants were accepted. **Admissions Contact:** Irene Logan, Director of Admissions. Email: *admiss@vsu.edu* Web: *www.vsu.edu*

FINANCIAL AID: In 2016-2017, 95% of all full-time freshmen received some form of financial aid. VSU is a member of CSS. The CSS/Profile and the college's own financial statement are required. Check with the school for current application deadlines.

VIRGINIA UNION UNIVERSITY E-3
www.vuu.edu

Richmond, VA 23220	**(804) 342-3570** **(800) 368-3227**
Fax: (804) 342-3511	**Email: visitus@vuu.edu**
Full-time: n/av	**Faculty:** 82
Part-time: 30 men, 30 women	**Ph.D.s:** 55%
Graduate: 209 men, 114 women	**Student/Faculty:** 16 to 1
Year: semesters, summer session	**Tuition:** $16,759
Room & Board: $5662	**Freshman Class:** n/av
SAT: required	**CEEB CODE:** 5862
Application Deadline: n/av	**COMPETITIVE**

Virginia Union University, established in 1865 and affiliated with the Baptist Church, is a private institution offering undergraduate programs in education and psychology, business, humanities, natural science and math, and social sciences. The figures in the above capsule and in this profile are approximate. There are 2 undergraduate schools and 1 graduate school. In addition to regional accreditation, Virginia Union has baccalaureate program accreditation with ACBSP and CSWE. The 72-acre campus is in an urban area in the city of Richmond. Including any residence halls, there are 18 buildings.

STUDENT LIFE: 52% of undergraduates are from Virginia. Others are from 27 states, and 4 foreign countries. 85% are from public schools. 98% are African American. **Male To Female Ratio:** 1.7:1. The average age of freshmen is 18. 31% do not continue beyond their first year; 55% remain to graduate. **Housing:** 700 students can be accommodated in college housing, which includes single-sex dorms, and honors houses. On-campus housing is available on a first-come and first-served basis. Priority is given to out-of-town students. All students may keep cars. Alcohol is not permitted.

FACULTY/CLASSROOMS: 55% of faculty are male; 45% are female.

86% teach undergraduates. No introductory courses are taught by graduate students. The average class size in an introductory lecture is 28; in a laboratory is 20; and in a regular course is 22.

PROGRAMS OF STUDY: Virginia Union confers B.A., B.S., and B.S.W. degrees. Master's and doctoral degrees are also awarded. Bachelor's degrees are awarded in BIOLOGICAL SCIENCE (biology/biological science), BUSINESS (accounting, banking and finance, and business administration and management), COMMUNICATIONS AND THE ARTS (English, journalism, and music), COMPUTER AND PHYSICAL SCIENCE (chemistry and mathematics), EDUCATION (art education, business education, early childhood education, elementary education, music education, secondary education, and special education), SOCIAL SCIENCE (criminology, history, political science/government, psychology, religion, social work, and sociology). Teacher education, accounting, and history/political science are the strongest academically. Teacher education, criminology, and business administration have the largest enrollments.

ACTIVITIES: There are 32 groups on campus, including cheerleading, drama, international, newspaper, religious, student government, and yearbook. Popular campus events include Films, Lectures, and Concerts. **Sports:** There are 6 intercollegiate sports for men and 6 for women, and 3 intramural sports for men and 2 for women. Facilities include a gym, and stadium. **Graduates:** The most popular majors were business administration, history/political science, and psychology. 100 companies recruited on campus in 2015-2016.

SERVICES: Counseling and information services are available, as is tutoring in every subject, and remedial math, reading, and writing. **Library/Resources:** The library contains 145,305 volumes, 62,079 microform items, 1,523 audio/video tapes/CDs/DVDs, and subscribes to 308 periodicals including electronic. Computerized library services include database searching. Special learning facilities include an art gallery. **Physically Challenged Students:** 90% of the campus is accessible. Facilities include wheelchair ramps, elevators, and special parking. **Special:** The university offers cross-registration with Virginia Commonwealth and Virginia State Universities, and the University of Richmond. Internships, co-op programs, federal work-study programs, a general studies degree, a joint law degree with St. John's University School of Law in New York, a 3-2 degree in engineering with the Universities of Michigan and Iowa and Howard University, and exchange programs are also offered. There are 2 national honor societies and a freshman honors program. **Visiting:** There are guides for informal visits and visitors may sit in on classes. To schedule a visit, contact the Admissions Office. **Campus Safety and Security:** Measures include 24-hour foot and vehicle patrol, security escort services, emergency telephones and lighted pathways/sidewalks.

REQUIREMENTS: The SAT is required. Graduation from an accredited secondary school is required; the GED is accepted. Sixteen academic units are required, including 4 of English, 3 each of math and academic electives, and 2 each of foreign language, social science, and natural science. Special consideration is given to disadvantaged students. Children of alumni are given some preference. A GPA of 2.0 is required. AP and CLEP credits are accepted. Important factors in the admissions decision are extracurricular activities record, advanced placement or honors courses, and leadership record. To graduate, all students must complete at least 124 credit hours with a GPA of at least 2.0. Courses in religion, English, math, science, social science, a foreign language, and phys ed are required. There are also chapel and Virginia Union events attendance requirements. All students must successfully complete a computer science course and must take an English essay exam, usually by the end of the junior year, as well as a comprehensive exam in their major. **Procedure:** Freshmen are admitted in the fall and spring. Entrance exams should be taken between March of the junior year and March of the senior year. There are early admissions, deferred admissions, and rolling admissions plans. Check with the school for current application deadlines. Notification is sent on a rolling basis. **Transfer Students:** 51 transfer students enrolled in 2015-2016. Transfer students must be in good standing at their previous institutions and must submit all college transcripts. 30 of 124 credits required for the bachelor's degree must be completed at Virginia Union. **International Students:** They must take the TOEFL, as well as the SAT or ACT.

Admissions Contact: Gil Powell, Director of Admissions. Email: *visitus@vuu.edu* Web: *www.vuu.edu*

FINANCIAL AID: Virginia Union is a member of CSS. The CSS/Profile is required. The FAFSA code is 003766. Check with the school for current application deadlines.

VIRGINIA WESLEYAN COLLEGE *(The complete profile is made available exclusively on our website, www.barronspac.com)*

WASHINGTON AND LEE UNIVERSITY C-3
www.wlu.edu

Lexington, VA 24450 **(540) 458-8710**

Fax: (540) 458-8062	**Email:** admissions@wlu.edu
Full-time: 941 men, 883 women	**Faculty:** 204; IIB
Part-time: 4 men, 2 women	**Ph.D.s:** 96%
Graduate: 182 men, 148 women	**Student/Faculty:** 8 to 1
Year: other	**Tuition:** $48,267
Room & Board: $11,380	**Freshman Class:** 5101 applied, 1203 accepted, 466 enrolled
SAT CR/M/W: 690/690/683 **ACT:** 32	**CEEB CODE:** 5887
Application Deadline: January 1	**MOST COMPETITIVE**

Washington and Lee, founded in 1749, is a private, highly selective liberal arts university. There are 2 undergraduate schools and 1 graduate school. In addition to regional accreditation, Washington and Lee has baccalaureate program accreditation with AACSB, ACEJMC, and ACS. The 415-acre campus is in a small town 50 miles northeast of Roanoke, Virginia and 190 miles southwest of Washington, DC. Including any residence halls, there are 128 buildings.

STUDENT LIFE: 85% of undergraduates are from out of state, mostly the South. Students are from 50 states, 31 foreign countries, and Canada. 51% are from public schools. 83% are White; 4% Hispanic; 4% Foreign; 3% Asian American; 3% two or more races; 2% African American; 1% race unknown. 39% claim no religious affiliation; 38% Protestant; 17% Catholic. **Male To Female Ratio:** 1.1:1. The average age of freshmen is 18; all undergraduates, 20. 4% do not continue beyond their first year; 92% remain to graduate. **Housing:** 1485 students can be accommodated in college housing, which includes coed dorms, on-campus apartments, language houses, special-interest houses, fraternity houses, and sorority houses. On-campus housing is available on a lottery system for upperclassmen. 74% of students live on campus; of those, 95% remain on campus on weekends. All students may keep cars.

FACULTY/CLASSROOMS: 60% of faculty are male; 40% are female. All teach undergraduates. No introductory courses are taught by graduate students. The average class size in an introductory lecture is 16; in a laboratory is 13; and in a regular course is 15.

PROGRAMS OF STUDY: Washington and Lee confers B.A., and B.S. degrees. Master's and doctoral degrees are also awarded. Bachelor's degrees are awarded in BIOLOGICAL SCIENCE (biochemistry, biology/biological science, and neurosciences), BUSINESS (accounting and business administration and management), COMMUNICATIONS AND THE ARTS (art history and appreciation, classics, dramatic arts, English, French, German, Germanic languages and literature, journalism, music, romance languages and literature, Russian languages and literature, Spanish, and studio art), COMPUTER AND PHYSICAL SCIENCE (chemistry, computer science, geology, mathematics, natural sciences, and physics), ENGINEERING AND ENVIRONMENTAL DESIGN (chemical engineering, engineering physics, and environmental science), SOCIAL SCIENCE (anthropology, archeology, East Asian studies, economics, history, interdisciplinary studies, medieval studies, philosophy, political science/government, psychology, public affairs, religion, and sociology). Neuroscience, economics, psychology, and biochemistry are the strongest academically. Business administration, economics, and accounting have the largest enrollments.

ACTIVITIES: 73% of men belong to 11 national fraternities; 75% of women belong to 6 national sororities. There are 100 groups on campus, including volunteer, cheerleading, choir, chorale, chorus, communications, dance, debate, drama, environmental, ethnic, film, forensics, honors, international, jazz band, LGBT, literary magazine, musical theater, newspaper, orchestra, outdoor club, pep band, photography, political, professional, radio and TV, religious, social, social service, student government, symphony, and yearbook. Popular campus events include Presidential Mock Convention, Fancy Dress Ball and NABORS Service Day. **Sports:** There are 12 intercollegiate sports for men and 12 for women, and 10 intramural sports for men and 10 for women. Facilities include a gymnasium, an arena, stadium, pool, fitness center, weight training and exercise rooms, handball, racquetball, squash and tennis courts, outdoor track, baseball and practice fields, indoor tennis facility, 1000-seat soccer/lacrosse stadium, and a field for field hockey and lacrosse. **Graduates:** From July 1, 2015 to June 30, 2016, 425 bachelor's degrees were awarded. The most popular majors were business administration (15%), accounting (11%), and economics (9%). 65 companies recruited on campus in 2015-2016. In an average class, 88% graduate in 4 years or less, 90% graduate in 5 years or less, and 91% graduate in 6 years or less. Of the 2015 graduating class, 26% were enrolled in graduate school within 6 months of graduation, and 71% were employed.

SERVICES: Counseling and information services are available, as is tutoring in every subject, and a reader service for the blind. **Library/Resources:** The 3 libraries contain 1.3 million volumes, 1.4 million microform items, 15,078 audio/video tapes/CDs/DVDs, and subscribe to 66,967 periodicals including electronic. Computerized library services include interlibrary loans, database searching, Internet access, and Wi-Fi capability. Special learning facilities include an art gallery, radio station, TV station, special collections, history, fine arts, and archeological museums including Lee Chapel and museum, Stanier gallery, Lenfest center for the performing arts, Watson Pavilion, the Reeves center with Japanese tea room, and Kamen gallery. Tucker multimedia center for foreign language learning. Instrumental laboratory, seismograph/scanning electron microscope, light microscopy with digital imaging/electrophysiological recording facilities. **Physically Challenged Students:** 55% of the campus is accessible. Facilities include wheelchair ramps, elevators, special parking, specially equipped restrooms, special class scheduling, lowered drinking fountains, and special housing. **Special:** Special academic programs are available throughout The College and The Williams School of Commerce. Internship opportunities include the Washington Term, and study abroad opportunities in over 50 countries. Students may earn dual degrees and double majors; over 30 departments offer honors programs. Teacher certification is offered in consortium with Southern Virginia University. There are 17 national honor societies, Phi Beta Kappa, and 31 departmental honors programs. **Visiting:** There are regularly scheduled orientations for prospective students, Hourly interviews and campus tours, 2 group information sessions daily, seasonal Saturday tours and interviews. There are guides for informal visits and visitors may sit in on classes. To schedule a visit, contact Admissions Office. **Campus Safety and Security:** Measures include 24-hour foot and vehicle patrol, emergency notification system, self-defense education, and security escort services. There are also shuttle buses, emergency telephones, lighted pathways/sidewalks, controlled access to dorms/residences, and required safety programs for first-year students.

REQUIREMENTS: The SAT or ACT is required. A high school diploma is not required. Applicants must earn 17 units (24 recommended), including 4 units in English, 3 in math (4 recommended), 3 in a foreign language (4 recommended), and 1 each in history (2 recommended) and natural science (4 recommended with 1 lab science). Course work in social sciences(1) is also required (2 recommended). Essays, test scores, a transcript, and recommendation letters are needed to apply. An interview is recommended. AP credits are accepted. Important factors in the admissions decision are advanced placement or honors courses, leadership record, extracurricular activities record, and recommendations by school officials. To graduate, students must achieve proficiency in a foreign language and English composition and complete at least 1 course in fine arts and humanities, lab science and math, and literature and 2 courses in social sciences. A total of 113 credits, with a minimum GPA of 2.0, is required. All students must take 4 skills courses in physical education and pass a swimming test. **Procedure:** Freshmen are admitted in the fall. Entrance exams should be taken prior to January of the senior year. There are early decision and deferred admissions plans. Early decision applications should be filed by November 1; regular applications, by January 1 for fall entry, along with a $60 fee. Notification of early decision is sent December 22; regular decision, April 1. 268 early decision candidates were accepted for the 2016-2017 class. 1529 applicants were on the 2016 waiting list; 652 were admitted. Applications are accepted online. **Transfer Students:** 9 transfer students enrolled in 2015-2016. Transfer applicants must have a GPA of at least 2.0 (at least 3.5 to be competitive); no more than 56 credits will transfer. There is a 2-year residency requirement. 57 of 113 credits required for the bachelor's degree must be completed at Washington and Lee. **International Students:** There are 80 international students enrolled. The school actively recruits these students. They must take the TOEFL with a minimum score of 600 on the paper-based TOEFL (PBT) or 100 on the Internet-based version (iBT), or take the APIEL or ELPT. They must also take the SAT or ACT.

ADMISSIONS: 24% of the 2016-2017 applicants were accepted. The SAT scores for the 2016-2017 freshman class were: Critical Reading-- 5% between 500 and 599, 47% between 600 and 699, and 47% between 700 and 800. Math-- 2% between 500 and 599, 49% between 600 and 699, and 48% between 700 and 800. Writing-- 5% between 500 and 599, 55% between 600 and 699, and 40% between 700 and 800. The ACT scores were 12% between 24 and 29, and 88% above 30. 97% of the current freshmen were in the top fifth of their class; 100% were in the top two fifths. 22 freshmen graduated first in their class. **Admissions Contact:** Sally S. Richmond, V.P. for Admissions and Financial Aid. Email: *admissions@wlu.edu* Web: *www.wlu.edu*

FINANCIAL AID: In 2016-2017, 44% of all full-time freshmen and 41% of continuing full-time students received some form of financial aid. 44% of all full-time freshmen and 41% of continuing full-time students received need-based aid. The average freshman award was $44,349. Need-based scholarships or need-based grants averaged $40,857; need-based self-help aid (loans and jobs) averaged $1,862; and other non-need-based awards and non-need-based scholarships averaged $41,148. The average financial indebtedness of the 2016 graduate was $21,683. Washington and Lee is a member of CSS. The CSS/Profile, federal tax returns for parents and students, and business tax returns are required. The FAFSA code is 003768. The deadline for filing freshman financial aid applications for fall entry is February 1.

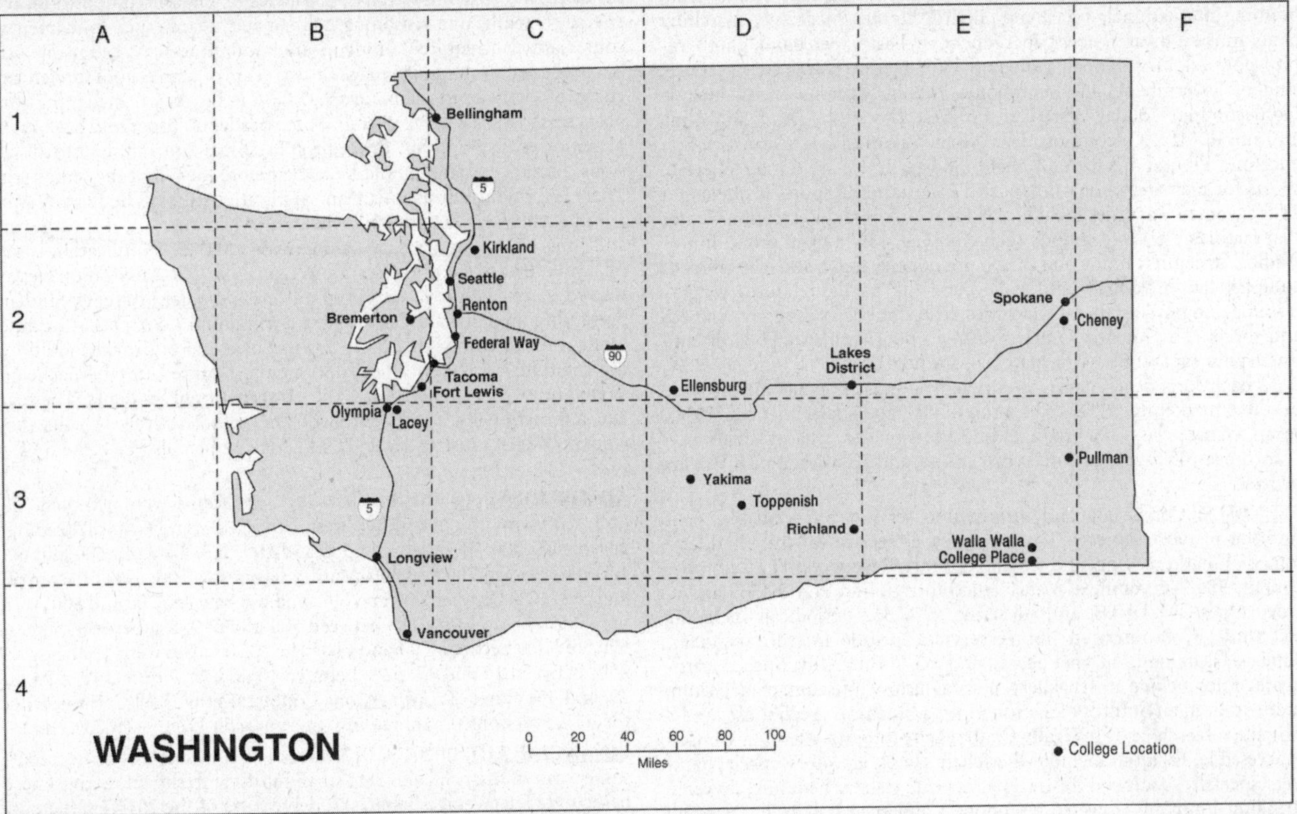

CENTRAL WASHINGTON UNIVERSITY D-2

www.cwu.edu

Ellensburg, WA 98926	**(509) 963-1211** **(866) 298-4968**
Fax: (509) 963-3022	**Email: admissions@cwu.edu**
Full-time: 4646 men, 4827 women	**Faculty:** 451; IIA, -$
Part-time: 750 men, 824 women	**Ph.D.s:** 82%
Graduate: 351 men, 573 women	**Student/Faculty:** 19 to 1
Year: trimesters, summer session	**Tuition:** $7023 ($20,826)
Room & Board: $9780	**Freshman Class:** 7295 applied, 5800 accepted, 1885 enrolled
SAT CR/M/W: 530/523/466 **ACT:** 21	**CEEB CODE:** 4044
Application Deadline: April 1	**COMPETITIVE**

Central Washington University is a public university offering undergraduate and graduate programs in the arts and sciences, business administration, and education and professional studies. The figures in the above capsule and in this profile are approximate. There are 4 undergraduate schools and 1 graduate school. In addition to regional accreditation, CWU has baccalaureate program accreditation with AACSB, ABET, ACCE, ADA, NASM, NCATE, and NRPA. The 380-acre campus is in a small town 100 miles east of Seattle. Including any residence halls, there are 107 buildings.

STUDENT LIFE: 95% of undergraduates are from Washington. Others are from 39 states, 14 foreign countries, and Canada. 57% are White; 14% Hispanic; 11% race unknown; 6% two or more races; 4% African American; 4% Asian American; 3% Foreign; 1% American Indian/Alaska Native. **Female To Male Ratio:** 1.1:1. The average age of freshmen is 19; all undergraduates, 24. **Housing:** 3700 students can be accommodated in college housing, which includes coed dorms, on-campus apartments, off-campus apartments, and married student housing. In addition, there are honors houses, language houses, special-interest houses, a freshman-only enrichment hall, a residence hall for transfers and upper classmen only, and theme and wellness housing. On-campus housing is guaranteed for the freshman year only, and is available on a first-come, first-served basis. 68% of students commute. All students may keep cars.

FACULTY/CLASSROOMS: 58% of faculty are male; 42% are female. All teach undergraduates, and all do research. No introductory courses are taught by graduate students. The average class size in an introductory lecture is 45; in a laboratory is 20; and in a regular course is 40.

PROGRAMS OF STUDY: CWU confers B.A., B.S., B.A.Ed., and B.F.A. degrees. Master's degrees are also awarded. Bachelor's degrees are awarded in BIOLOGICAL SCIENCE (biology/biological science), BUSINESS (accounting, banking and finance, business administration and management, business economics, fashion merchandising, international business management, marketing/retailing/merchandising, recreation and leisure services, and tourism), COMMUNICATIONS AND THE ARTS (art, broadcasting, Chinese, communications, dramatic arts, English, fine arts, French, German, guitar, Japanese, journalism, language arts, music, music business management, music theory and composition, percussion, piano/organ, public relations, Russian, Spanish, speech/debate/rhetoric, strings, studio art, visual and performing arts, and voice), COMPUTER AND PHYSICAL SCIENCE (actuarial science, chemistry, computer programming, computer science, earth science, geology, information sciences and systems, mathematics, physics, and software engineering), EDUCATION (art education, business education, early childhood education, elementary education, English education, foreign languages education, health education, home economics education, industrial arts education, marketing and distribution education, mathematics education, middle school education, music education, physical education, science education, secondary education, social studies education, and special education), ENGINEERING AND ENVIRONMENTAL DESIGN (aeronautical technology, aviation administration/management, aviation maintenance management, construction management, electrical/electronics engineering, engineering technology, industrial engineering technology, and mechanical engineering), HEALTH PROFESSIONS (community health work, emergency medical technologies, exercise science, and public health), SOCIAL SCIENCE (anthropology, Asian/Oriental studies, criminal justice, economics, family and community services, family/consumer studies, food science, geography, gerontology, history, liberal arts/general studies, paralegal studies, parks and recreation management, philosophy, political science/government, prelaw, psychology, public administration, safety science, social science, social work, and sociology). Accounting, music, and geology are the strongest academically. Business and education have the largest enrollment.

ACTIVITIES: There are no fraternities or sororities. There are 125 groups on campus, including art, band, cheerleading, chess, choir, chorale, chorus, computers, dance, drama, environmental, ethnic, film, honors, international, jazz band, LGBT, literary magazine, marching band, musical theater, newspaper, opera, orchestra, pep band, photography, political, professional, radio and TV, religious, social, social service, student government, and symphony. Popular campus events include Homecoming, Holiday Ware Fair, PolyFest, Day of the Dead, Showtime at Central, MLK Celebration, Jazz Night, Yakima River Clean-Up, Science in a Pint, and Nature of Night. **Sports:** There are 6 intercollegiate sports for men and 6 for women, and 21 intramural sports for men and 21 for women. Facilities include a Student Union and Recreation Center that features a 50-foot indoor rock climbing wall, a gym, group fitness studios, strength training and cardio, indoor elevated track. The athletics complex has basketball, and volleyball. The pavilion houses weight-training and physical therapy facilities, fields for baseball, rugby, softball, and soccer. The Aquatic Center features a pool with springboards, and water polo capabilities. **Graduates:** From July 1, 2015 to June 30, 2016, 2432 bachelor's degrees were awarded. The most popular majors were business/marketing (27%), education (14%), and social sciences (10%). In an average class, 1% graduate in 3 years or less, 24% graduate in 4 years or less, 45% graduate in 5 years or less, and 52% graduate in 6 years or less.

SERVICES: Counseling and information services are available, as is tutoring in most subjects. There is a reader service for the blind, and remedial math, reading, and writing. **Library/Resources:** The 2 libraries contain 980,976 volumes, 47,567 microform items, and 22,565 audio/video tapes/CDs/DVDs, and subscribe to 72,352 periodicals including electronic. Computerized library services include interlibrary loans, database searching, Internet access, and Wi-Fi capability. Special learning facilities include an art gallery, natural history museum, planetarium, radio station, an anthropology museum, a botanical greenhouse, and a primate research lab. **Physically Challenged Students:** All of the campus is accessible. Facilities include wheelchair ramps, elevators, special parking, specially equipped restrooms, special class scheduling, lowered drinking fountains, lowered telephones, and special housing. **Special:** Students may study abroad; there are formal exchange programs with universities in Australia, England, France, Japan, Scotland, and South Korea. There are 3-2 physics/engineering degree programs in conjunction with the University of Puget Sound, the University of Washington, and Washington State University. CWU also offers co-op programs, internships, work-study programs, a competency-based program, credit/no credit options, dual and student-designed majors, dual admission, Running Start, college in the high school, dual enrollment, undergraduate research, William O. Douglas Honors College, Bachelor of Applied Science programs, and alternative pathway to teacher certification. Students may earn additional credit by prior learning, credit by exam, and credit for military experience. Non-degree study is offered through adult/continuing education or international programs. This includes the Asia University America Program (AUAP) and University English as a Second Language (UESL). There are 11 national honor societies, a freshman honors program, and 12 departmental honors programs. **Visiting:** There are regularly scheduled orientations for prospective students, consisting of an information session, a tour of residence halls, a tour of the campus, prearranged appointments with faculty, and a financial aid presentation. There are guides for informal visits, visitors may sit in on classes, and stay overnight. To schedule a visit, contact the Admissions Office. **Campus Safety and Security:** Measures include 24-hour foot and vehicle patrol, emergency notification system, self-defense education, and security escort services. There are shuttle buses, emergency telephones, lighted pathways/sidewalks, controlled access to dorms/residences, and controlled-entry residence halls.

REQUIREMENTS: The SAT or ACT is required. Test scores and GPA are considered in combination according to a sliding scale. Applicants must be graduates of accredited secondary schools or have earned a GED. The university requires 15 academic credits or Carnegie units: 4 years of English, 3 each of math and social studies, 2 of the same foreign language, 2 of science with 1 unit a lab, and 1 of performing arts or an academic elective. U.S. history and U.S. government recommended and will count toward social studies requirements. A GPA of 2.0 is required. AP and CLEP credits are accepted. Important factors in the admissions decision are leadership record, evidence of special talent, personality/intangible qualities, and extracurricular activities record. Students must complete a minimum of 180 quarter credits, including 60 credits in upper-division courses and a minimum of 45 credits in the major plus a minor or 60 credits in the major. Core curriculum requirements include 15-18 of Basic and Breadth courses, including 3 courses each in arts and humanities, social and behavioral sciences, and natural science. An academic advising seminar, 2 courses of English composition, one course in math, one reasoning course, and a computer fundamentals course are also required. Students are required to have either one year of college-level foreign language or two years of high school foreign language. Students must maintain a 2.25 GPA in the major (higher for some programs) and 2.0 GPA overall. Some academic programs have thesis or senior project options. **Procedure:** Freshmen are admitted to all sessions. Entrance exams should be taken before the fall of the senior year. There is a rolling admissions plan. Applications should be filed by April 1 for fall entry; November 1 for winter entry; February 1 for spring entry; and June 1 for summer entry, along with a $50 fee. Notification is sent on a rolling basis. Applications are accepted on-line. Application fees are waived if application is completed on-line. **Transfer Students:** Students presenting an associate degree need a minimum GPA of 2.5 for automatic offer of admission; 2.5 to 2.0 will be asked to provide additional information for review. 40 of 180 credits required for the bachelor's degree must be completed at CWU. **International Students:** There are 296 international students enrolled. The school actively recruits these students. They must take the TOEFL. They must also take the SAT or ACT.

ADMISSIONS: 80% of the 2016-2017 applicants were accepted. The SAT scores for the 2016-2017 freshman class were: Critical Reading-- 33% below 500, 47% between 500 and 599, 18% between 600 and 699, and 2% between 700 and 800. Math-- 34% below 500, 52% between 500 and 599, 12% between 600 and 699, and 2% between 700 and 800. Writing-- 66% below 500, 28% between 500 and 599, 5% between 600 and 699, and 1% between 700 and 800. The ACT scores were 1% below 12, 20% between 12 and 17, 52% between 18 and 23, 24% between 24 and 29, and 3% above 30. **Admissions Contact:** Kathy Gaer-Carlton, Director of Admissions. Email: *admissions@cwu.edu* Web: *www.cwu.edu*

FINANCIAL AID: In 2016-2017, 90% of all full-time freshmen received some form of financial aid. 88% of all full-time freshmen received need-based aid. The average financial indebtedness of the 2016 graduate was $26,360. The FAFSA code is 003771. The priority date for freshman financial aid applications for fall entry is March 1. The deadline for filing freshman financial aid applications for fall entry is May 1.

CITY UNIVERSITY OF SEATTLE *(The complete profile is made available exclusively on our website, www.barronspac.com)*

CORNISH COLLEGE OF THE ARTS *(The complete profile is made available exclusively on our website, www.barronspac.com)*

EASTERN WASHINGTON UNIVERSITY *(The complete profile is made available exclusively on our website, www.barronspac.com)*

GONZAGA UNIVERSITY — E-2

www.gonzaga.edu

Spokane, WA 99258	**(509) 313-6591** **(800) 322-2584**
Fax: (509) 313-5780	**Email: admissions@gonzaga.edu**
Full-time: 2407 men, 2666 women	**Faculty:** 375
Part-time: 38 men, 49 women	**Ph.D.s:** 85%
Graduate: 864 men, 1543 women	**Student/Faculty:** 12 to 1
Year: semesters, summer session	**Tuition:** $39,730
Room & Board: $11,158	**Freshman Class:** 7324 applied, 4928 accepted, 1271 enrolled
SAT CR/M: 590/600 **ACT:** 27	**CEEB CODE:** 4330
Application Deadline: February 1	**HIGHLY COMPETITIVE**

Gonzaga University, founded in 1887, is a private liberal arts institution affiliated with the Roman Catholic Church and the Society of Jesus (Jesuits). The university offers undergraduate and graduate degrees in arts and sciences, business, education, engineering, law, nursing, and human physiology. There are 5 undergraduate schools and 7 graduate schools. In addition to regional accreditation, Gonzaga has baccalaureate program accreditation with AACSB, ABET, NCATE, CACREP, CCNE, and CSLE/ABA. The 152-acre campus is in an urban area alongside the Spokane River. Including any residence halls, there are 105 buildings.

STUDENT LIFE: 50% of undergraduates are from out of state, mostly

the West. Students are from 41 states, 27 foreign countries, and Canada. 67% are from public schools. 71% are White; 10% Hispanic; 6% two or more races; 5% Asian American; 3% race unknown; 2% Foreign; 1% African American; 1% American Indian/Alaska Native. 51% are Catholic; 20% claim no religious affiliation; 15% Protestant. **Female To Male Ratio:** 1.3:1. The average age of freshmen is 18; all undergraduates, 20. 8% do not continue beyond their first year; 92% remain to graduate. **Housing:** 3028 students can be accommodated in college housing, which includes single-sex and coed dorms, on-campus apartments, off-campus apartments, and married student housing. In addition, there are special-interest houses, and living and learning communities within residence halls. On-campus housing is guaranteed for the freshman year only, and is available on a first-come, first-served basis, and is available on a lottery system for upperclassmen. 59% of students live on campus; of those, 75% remain on campus on weekends. All students may keep cars.

FACULTY/CLASSROOMS: 54% of faculty are male; 46% are female. 76% teach undergraduates. No introductory courses are taught by graduate students. The average class size in an introductory lecture is 22; in a laboratory is 13; and in a regular course is 22.

PROGRAMS OF STUDY: Gonzaga confers B.A., B.S., B.B.A., B.Ed., and B.S.N. degrees. Master's and doctoral degrees are also awarded. Bachelor's degrees are awarded in AGRICULTURE (environmental studies), BIOLOGICAL SCIENCE (biochemistry and biology/biological science), BUSINESS (accounting, business administration and management, business economics, and sports management), COMMUNICATIONS AND THE ARTS (art, broadcasting, classics, communications, dramatic arts, English, French, journalism, literature, music, public relations, Spanish, speech/debate/rhetoric, and theatre acting), COMPUTER AND PHYSICAL SCIENCE (chemistry, computer science, mathematics, and physics), EDUCATION (music education, physical education, and special education), ENGINEERING AND ENVIRONMENTAL DESIGN (civil engineering, computer engineering, electrical/electronics engineering, engineering management, and mechanical engineering), HEALTH PROFESSIONS (exercise science and nursing), SOCIAL SCIENCE (classical/ancient civilization, criminal justice, economics, history, interdisciplinary studies, international studies, Italian studies, philosophy, political science/government, psychology, religion, and sociology). Engineering, biology, and nursing are the strongest academically. Business, engineering, and social sciences have the largest enrollments.

ACTIVITIES: There are no fraternities or sororities. There are 110 groups on campus, including art, band, cheerleading, chess, choir, chorale, chorus, communications, computers, dance, debate, drama, drill team, environmental, ethnic, honors, international, jazz band, LGBT, literary magazine, mock trial club, musical theater, newspaper, orchestra, pep band, photography, political, professional, radio and TV, religious, social, social service, student government, symphony, and yearbook. Popular campus events include Search and other Spiritual Retreats, GEL Weekend, Charity Ball, Diversity Monologues, and Fall Family Weekend. **Sports:** There are 9 intercollegiate sports for men and 9 for women, and 30 intramural sports for men and 30 for women. Facilities include a basketball arena, basketball/volleyball courts, indoor golf, tennis courts, soccer practice facility, outdoor baseball stadium and field, indoor rowing room, athletic weight room, a student fitness center with cardiovascular and weight areas, multipurpose synthetic turf field, multipurpose courts, racquetball courts, aerobics rooms, indoor running track, and a 6-lane 25-yard swimming pool. **Graduates:** From July 1, 2015 to June 30, 2016, 1228 bachelor's degrees were awarded. The most popular majors were business and management (22%), social sciences (14%), and engineering (11%). 401 companies recruited on campus in 2015-2016. In an average class, 1% graduate in 3 years or less, 74% graduate in 4 years or less, 83% graduate in 5 years or less, and 84% graduate in 6 years or less. Of the 2015 graduating class, 19% were enrolled in graduate school within 6 months of graduation, and 68% were employed.

SERVICES: Counseling and information services are available, as is tutoring in most subjects. There is a reader service for the blind. Informal peer tutoring in English and math is available. **Library/Resources:** The 2 libraries contain 699,461 volumes, 160,604 microform items, and 9,155 audio/video tapes/CDs/DVDs, and subscribe to 79,500 periodicals including electronic. Computerized library services include interlibrary loans, database searching, Internet access, and Wi-Fi capability. Special learning facilities include an art gallery, radio station, and TV station. **Physically Challenged Students:** 90% of the campus is accessible. Facilities include wheelchair ramps, elevators, special parking, specially equipped restrooms, special class scheduling, lowered drinking fountains, and lowered telephones. Academic adjustments are provided for students with disabilities who provide appropriate documentation and request services from Disabilities, Resources, Education, and Access Management (DREAM). Accessible rooms exist in some residence halls and apartments. **Special:** Honors program, cross-registration with Whitworth University, internships available for credit or no credit in every academic program, capstone experiences, study abroad in 45 countries (including a Gonzaga-in-Florence campus), a Washington semester, summer faculty-led programs and on- and off-campus work-study programs are offered. There is a limited pass/fail option for some coursework and double and triple majors and degrees are possible in all academic programs (though seeking multiple majors/degrees may increase time to degree). High school juniors and seniors may take 6 credits per semester in certain areas. There are 12 national honor societies and a freshman honors program. **Visiting:** There are regularly scheduled orientations for prospective students. Day visits are permitted Monday through Friday; overnight visits, Sunday through Thursday (except for holiday periods). There are guides for informal visits, visitors may sit in on classes, and stay overnight. To schedule a visit, contact The Gonzaga Visit Office at (509) 313-6531. **Campus Safety and Security:** Measures include 24-hour foot and vehicle patrol, emergency notification system, self-defense education, and security escort services. There are shuttle buses, emergency telephones, lighted pathways/sidewalks, and controlled access to dorms/residences.

REQUIREMENTS: The SAT or ACT is required. Applicants should be graduates of an accredited secondary school. They must have completed 17 academic credits consisting of 4 years of English, 3 to 4 years of math, 2 to 3 years of the same foreign language, (world language preferred, ASL accepted), 3 years of history and/or social science, and 3 to 4 years of natural or physical laboratory science. An essay and letters of recommendation are required. An interview is optional but recommended for students with a GPA lower than 3.2 or SAT score less than 1070 for Verbal/Critical plus Math, or 23 ACT Composite. NURSING: Gonzaga's Nursing Program accepts first-year applications only. Applicants interested in the Nursing Program must choose "Nursing" on their application to be considered. Students not admitted into the Nursing Program through the application process will not be permitted to change their major to nursing. ENGINEERING: Applicants interested in pursuing any of the majors in the School of Engineering and Applied Science as a first-year student should be ready for college calculus and (with the exception of computer science applicants) should have completed physics in high school. Students not meeting these criteria are encouraged to consider majors outside the School. AP credits are accepted. Important factors in the admissions decision are advanced placement or honors courses, leadership record, parents or siblings attended your school, evidence of special talent, extracurricular activities record, recommendations by alumni, recommendations by school officials, and geographical diversity. All students must complete at least 128 credit hours with a minimum 2.0 GPA. The major requirements are 18 hours in upper-division courses and supporting courses required by the major department. Students must complete courses that support the common core. The common core requires students to complete specific courses, including a first-year seminar, Writing, Reasoning, Math, Communication, Scientific Inquiry, Philosophy, Religion, Ethics, World Religions, and an integration seminar. Additional requirements let students choose classes that fulfill the following requirements: 3 credits in each of History, Literature, Fine Arts, and Social Science, 3 credits with a Global studies designation, 3 credits with a social justice designation, and 6 credits with a writing-enriched designation. **Procedure:** Freshmen are admitted fall and spring. There are early admissions and deferred admissions plans. Early decision applications should be filed by November 15; regular applications, by February 1 for fall entry; and November 15 for spring entry, along with a $50 fee. Notification of early decision is sent January 15; regular decision, March 15. 141 applicants were on the 2016 waiting list; 5 were admitted. Applications are accepted on-line. Application fees are waived if application is completed on-line. **Transfer Students:** 120 transfer students enrolled in 2015-2016. A minimum college GPA of 2.7 and high school GPA of 3.1 is required. All applicants must provide college transcripts, an essay or personal statement, and a statement of good standing from prior institution(s). An interview is recommended. Some applicants may be required to submit their high school transcript and standardized test scores. 30 of 128 credits required for the bachelor's degree must be completed at Gonzaga. **International Students:** There are 77 international students enrolled. The school actively recruits these students. They must take the TOEFL with a minimum score of 550 on the paper-based TOEFL (PBT) or 80 on the Internet-based version (iBT). Student must also take either the IELTS or APIEL. The SAT, ACT, and the ESL Exit Exam, which includes a writing test as well also required.

ADMISSIONS: 67% of the 2016-2017 applicants were accepted. The SAT scores for the 2016-2017 freshman class were: Critical Reading-- 6% below 500, 46% between 500 and 599, 38% between 600 and 699, and 10% between 700 and 800. Math-- 5% below 500, 39% between 500 and 599, 45% between 600 and 699, and 10% between 700 and 800. The ACT scores were 11% between 18 and 23, 64% between 24 and 29, and 25% above 30. **Admissions Contact:** Julie McCulloh, Dean of Admissions. Email: *admissions@gonzaga.edu* Web: *www.gonzaga.edu*

FINANCIAL AID: In 2016-2017, 99% of all full-time freshmen and 98% of continuing full-time students received some form of financial aid. 80% of all full-time freshmen and 79% of continuing full-time students received need-based aid. The average freshman award was $27,059. Need-based scholarships or need-based grants averaged $21,166; need-based self-help aid (loans and jobs) averaged $6,048; non-need-based athletic scholarships averaged $22,017; and other non-need-based awards and non-need-based scholarships averaged $14,749. 34% of undergraduate students work part-time. Average annual earnings from campus work are $2189. The average financial indebtedness of the 2016 graduate was $30,700. Gonzaga is a member of CSS. The FAFSA code is 003778. The priority date for freshman financial aid applications for fall entry is February 1. The deadline for filing freshman financial aid applications for fall entry is February 1.

HERITAGE UNIVERSITY *(The complete profile is made available exclusively on our website, www.barronspac.com)*

NORTHWEST UNIVERSITY C-2
www.northwestu.edu

Kirkland, WA 98033 (425) 889-5231
(800) 669-3781
Fax: (425) 889-5224 **Email:** admissions@northwestu.edu

Full-time: 364 men, 606 women	**Faculty:** 49; IIB, --$
Part-time: 38 men, 49 women	**Ph.D.s:** 41%
Graduate: 26 men, 54 women	**Student/Faculty:** 20 to 1
Year: semesters, summer session	**Tuition:** $28,086
Room & Board: $7790	**Freshman Class:** n/av
SAT or ACT: required	**CEEB CODE:** 4541
Application Deadline: August 15	**VERY COMPETITIVE**

Northwest University, has continually built a learning community wholly dedicated to spiritual vitality, academic excellence, and empowered engagement with human need, and offers over 70 majors and programs. Providing unparalleled opportunity for career development, over 70% of students fulfill internships in local businesses and organizations. There are 4 undergraduate schools and 4 graduate schools. In addition to regional accreditation, Northwest University has baccalaureate program accreditation with AACTE. The 56-acre campus is in a suburban area in Kirkland, 10 miles east of Seattle. Including any residence halls, there are 27 buildings.

STUDENT LIFE: 79% of undergraduates are from Washington. Others are from 23 states, 15 foreign countries, and Canada. 60% are White; 5% Asian American; 2% African American; 2% Hispanic; 1% American Indian/Alaska Native. 99% are Protestant. **Female To Male Ratio:** 1.7:1. The average age of freshmen is 19; all undergraduates, 25. 34% do not continue beyond their first year; 34% remain to graduate. **Housing:** 544 students can be accommodated in college housing, which includes single-sex dorms, on-campus apartments, and married student housing. On-campus housing is guaranteed for all 4 years. 63% of students live on campus; of those, 80% remain on campus on weekends. Alcohol is not permitted. All students may keep cars.

FACULTY/CLASSROOMS: 65% of faculty are male; 35% are female. All teach undergraduates. No introductory courses are taught by graduate students. The average class size in an introductory lecture is 30; in a laboratory is 20; and in a regular course is 24.

PROGRAMS OF STUDY: Northwest University confers B.A. degrees. Associate, master's, and doctoral degrees are also awarded. Bachelor's degrees are awarded in BIOLOGICAL SCIENCE (life science), BUSINESS (business administration and management), COMMUNICATIONS AND THE ARTS (communications, English, journalism, music, and music business management), COMPUTER AND PHYSICAL SCIENCE (computer management), EDUCATION (education, elementary education, middle school education, physical education, secondary education, and special education), ENGINEERING AND ENVIRONMENTAL DESIGN (environmental science), HEALTH PROFESSIONS (nursing), SOCIAL SCIENCE (behavioral science, biblical studies, counseling/psychology, history, interdisciplinary studies, liberal arts/general studies, ministries, missions, pastoral studies, philosophy, psychology, religion, religious education, religious music, theological studies, and youth ministry). Teacher education, business, and psychology are the strongest academically. Teacher education, church ministries, and business have the largest enrollments.

ACTIVITIES: There are no fraternities or sororities. There are 20 groups on campus, including band, choir, chorale, chorus, communications, debate, drama, forensics, international, jazz band, literary magazine, musical theater, newspaper, orchestra, photography, professional, radio station, religious, social, social service, student government, and yearbook. Popular campus events include Christmas Holiday Social, All-School Banquet, and Roomies Night-out. **Sports:** There are 4 intercollegiate sports for men and 4 for women, and 2 intramural sports for men and 2 for women. Facilities include a gym pavilion, outdoor tennis courts, a practice field for soccer and intramural football, access to the Seattle Seahawks' fields, outdoor basketball, and sand volleyball. **Graduates:** From July 1, 2015 to June 30, 2016, 252 bachelor's degrees were awarded.

SERVICES: There is a reader service for the blind, and remedial writing. The Student Success Office provides assistance in most areas, including study skills. **Library/Resources:** The library contains 174,100 volumes, 40,800 microform items, and 5,000 audio/video tapes/CDs/DVDs, and subscribes to 900 periodicals including electronic. Computerized library services include interlibrary loans, database searching, and Internet access. **Physically Challenged Students:** 75% of the campus is accessible. Facilities include wheelchair ramps, elevators, special parking. **Special:** Northwest offers study abroad in several locations in the U.S. and foreign countries through the Council for Christian Colleges and Universities, such as Korea, Russia, Australia, Sri Lanka, and Vietnam. Dual majors are also available. There are 2 national honor societies and 1 departmental honors programs. **Visiting:** There are regularly scheduled orientations for prospective students. There are guides for informal visits, visitors may sit in on classes and stay overnight. **Campus Safety and Security:** Measures include 24-hour foot and vehicle patrol and security escort services. There are shuttle buses, emergency telephones, and lighted pathways/sidewalks.

REQUIREMENTS: The SAT or ACT is required. A GPA of 2.3 is required. AP and CLEP credits are accepted. Important factors in the admissions decision are personality/intangible qualities, recommendations by alumni, and leadership record. Students must complete 18 credits in humanities, 16 in religion, 12 in social science, and 10 each in science and math. At least 125 semester credits (up to 139 for teacher education), with a minimum GPA of 2.0, are required. The number of semester credits needed in the major varies from 36 to 50. **Procedure:** Freshmen are admitted to all sessions. Entrance exams should be taken in the spring of the junior year. There are early decision, deferred admissions, and rolling admissions plans. Applications should be filed by August 15 for fall entry; December 15 for spring entry; and April 15 for summer entry. The fall 2016 application fee was $30. Notification of early decision is sent December 1; regular decision, on a rolling basis. 56 early decision candidates were accepted for the 2016-2017 class. **Transfer Students:** 205 transfer students enrolled in 2015-2016. Transfers must have a minimum 2.3 GPA from high school and college and must submit SAT I or ACT scores, an essay, and 2 letters of reference. 30 of 125 credits required for the bachelor's degree must be completed at Northwest University. **International Students:** There are 19 international students enrolled. They must take the TOEFL.

Admissions Contact: Andy Hall, Director of Admissions. Email: *admissions@northwestu.edu* Web: *www.northwestu.edu*

FINANCIAL AID: In 2016-2017, 94% of all full-time freshmen received some form of financial aid. 94% of all full-time freshmen received need-based aid. 67% of undergraduate students work part-time. The college's own financial statement is required. The FAFSA code is 003783. The deadline for filing freshman financial aid applications for fall entry is March 1.

PACIFIC LUTHERAN UNIVERSITY C-2
www.plu.edu

Tacoma, WA 98447 (253) 535-8145

Fax: (253) 536-8760	**Email:** admissions@plu.edu
Full-time: 991 men, 1711 women	**Faculty:** 205; IIA, -$
Part-time: 44 men, 36 women	**Ph.D.s:** 94%
Graduate: 95 men, 199 women	**Student/Faculty:** 13 to 1
Year: 4-1-4, summer session	**Tuition:** $39,450
Room & Board: $10,510	**Freshman Class:** 3769 applied, 2896 accepted, 678 enrolled
SAT CR/M/W: 560/550/530 **ACT:** 25	**CEEB CODE:** 4597
Application Deadline: October 1	**VERY COMPETITIVE**

Pacific Lutheran University, founded in 1890 by Norwegian immigrants, offers liberal arts and professional programs. PLU is a private university affiliated with the Evangelical Lutheran Church in America. The university offers three pathways to academic distinction: global education and service to the world, robust student-faculty collaborative research and creative projects, and helping students discern meaning and purpose in their lives. There are 7 undergraduate schools and 5 graduate schools. In addition to regional accreditation, PLU has baccalaureate program accreditation with AACSB, ABET, CSWE, NASM, NCATE, CCNE, and WSNCQA. The 156-acre campus is in a suburban area 7 miles south of Tacoma, WA. Including any residence halls, there are 42 buildings.

STUDENT LIFE: 76% of undergraduates are from Washington. Others are from 29 states, 26 foreign countries, and Canada. 66% are White; 9% Asian American; 9% Hispanic; 8% two or more races; 3% African American; 3% Foreign; 1% American Indian/Alaska Native; 1% race unknown. 33% are Protestant; 17% claim no religious affiliation; 12% Catholic. **Female To Male Ratio:** 1.7:1. The average age of freshmen is 18; all undergraduates, 21. 21% do not continue beyond their first year; 71% remain to graduate. **Housing:** 1582 students can be accommodated in college housing, which includes single-sex and coed dorms, on-campus apartments, and married student housing. In addition, there are honors houses, language houses, special-interest houses, living communities, themed communities, gender-neutral housing, international hall, and social action and leadership wing. On-campus housing is guaranteed for the freshman year only. 52% of students commute. All students may keep cars.

FACULTY/CLASSROOMS: 42% of faculty are male; 58% are female. 92% teach undergraduates, and 90% do research. No introductory courses are taught by graduate students. The average class size in an introductory lecture is 23; in a laboratory is 14; and in a regular course is 17.

PROGRAMS OF STUDY: PLU confers B.A., B.A.C., B.A.E., B.A.K., B.B.A., B.F.A., B.M., B.M.A., B.M.E., B.S., B.S.K., and B.S.N. degrees. Master's and doctoral degrees are also awarded. Bachelor's degrees are awarded in BIOLOGICAL SCIENCE (biology/biological science), BUSINESS (business administration and management), COMMUNICATIONS AND THE ARTS (art history, classical languages, classics, communications, English, French, German, music, music performance, music theory and composition, Norwegian, piano/organ, Spanish, studio art, theatre arts, and voice), COMPUTER AND PHYSICAL SCIENCE (applied physics, chemistry, computer science, geoscience, mathematics, mathematics - actuarial concentration, and physics), EDUCATION (elementary education, global studies, mathematics education, music education, physical education, and secondary education), ENGINEERING AND ENVIRONMENTAL DESIGN (engineering and applied science and environmental science), HEALTH PROFESSIONS (kinesiology and nursing), SOCIAL SCIENCE (anthropology, Chinese Studies, economics, Hispanic American studies, history, philosophy, political science/government, psychology, religion, Scandinavian studies, social work, sociology, and women & gender studies). Business administration, nursing, and biology have the largest enrollments.

ACTIVITIES: There are no fraternities or sororities. There are 70 groups on campus, including adult student, advertising, comedy, art, band, cheerleading, choir, chorale, chorus, computers, dance, debate, drama, environmental, ethnic, film, forensics, honors, international, jazz band, LGBT, literary magazine, musical theater, newspaper, opera, orchestra, pep band, photography, political, professional, radio and TV, religious, social, social service, student government, student leadership institute, and symphony. Popular campus events include Wang Symposium, EXPLORE! Retreat, Holocaust Education Conference, Relay for Life, unPLUg, Songfest, Family Weekend, Homecoming, PLUtonic concerts, Berry Festival, Clay Crows - improv, and Dance Ensemble. **Sports:** There are 9 intercollegiate sports for men and 10 for women, and 18 intramural sports for men and 17 for women. Facilities include a gym/auditorium, fitness center, pool, racquetball, and tennis courts, volleyball, basketball, soccer field, softball, and baseball fields, track and other fields for practice. Access to the Sparks Stadium for football and indoor tennis center available. **Graduates:** From July 1, 2015 to June 30, 2016, 736 bachelor's degrees were awarded. The most popular majors were business administration (14%), nursing (10%), and biology (7%). 53 companies recruited on campus in 2015-2016. In an average class, 5% graduate in 3 years or less, 58% graduate in 4 years or less, 69% graduate in 5 years or less, and 71% graduate in 6 years or less.

SERVICES: Counseling and information services are available, as is tutoring in most subjects, such as anthropology, biology, business, chemistry, geosciences, global studies, history, languages, math, music, nursing, philosophy, and religion. There is a reader service for the blind. Study groups, free flashcards and pretest and posttest reviews are also available. **Library/Resources:** The library contains 323,926 volumes, 228,386 microform items, and 11,858 audio/video tapes/CDs/DVDs, and subscribes to 4,474 periodicals including electronic. Computerized library services include interlibrary loans, database searching, Internet access, and Wi-Fi capability. Special learning facilities include an art gallery, radio station, TV station, observatory, marriage and family therapy center, nuclear magnetic resonance spectrometer, an herbarium, greenhouse and native plant garden, invertebrate and vertebrate museums, a biology field station, Northwest history collections, a Scandinavian history collection, and a language resource center. **Physically Challenged Students:** 90% of the campus is accessible. Facilities include wheelchair ramps, elevators, special parking, specially equipped restrooms, special class scheduling, lowered drinking fountains, lowered telephones, and special housing. **Special:** PLU offers 2 different bachelor's degrees simultaneously, 3-2 engineering degrees with Washington University in St. Louis and Columbia University, and accelerated degree programs in most majors. Dual majors and student-designed majors can be arranged. Extensive internships with local businesses and nonprofit organizations, work-study programs, non-degree study, and pass/fail options are also available. The Wang Center for International Programs supports the university's internationally focused academic programs. There are 17 national honor societies and a freshman honors program. **Visiting:** There are regularly scheduled orientations for prospective students, consisting of activities based on the students' individual interests - tour, class visits, meeting with coaches and/or faculty, overnight stays. There are guides for informal visits, visitors may sit in on classes. To schedule a visit, contact the Office of Admission at (800) 274-6758. **Campus Safety and Security:** Measures include 24-hour foot and vehicle patrol, emergency notification system, self-defense education, and security escort services. There are emergency telephones, lighted pathways/sidewalks, controlled access to dorms/residences, and automated emergency notification system.

REQUIREMENTS: The SAT or ACT is required. Applicants should be graduates of accredited secondary schools, although GED certificates are accepted. PLU requires 2 years each of college preparatory math and foreign language and recommends 4 years of English, 2 each of social studies and lab science, 1 of fine or performing arts, and 3 of electives. Essay and recommendation are required. A GPA of 2.0 is required. AP and CLEP credits are accepted. Important factors in the admissions decision are advanced placement or honors courses, leadership record, and evidence of special talent. All students must complete a minimum of 128 semester hours with a GPA of 2.0. A 2.5 is required in the schools of business, education and kinesiology, plus the departments of economics, history, languages and literatures (Hispanic studies), sociology, and social work. Of the 128 semester hours, a minimum of 40 semester hours must be completed from courses numbered 300 or above. The required General Education Program is a minimum of 48 semester hours plus a culminating seminar. The program is rooted in the classical liberal arts and sciences as understood within the Lutheran educational tradition, and is grounded in an understanding of scientific perspectives, mathematics, languages, and the long-standing traditions of critical discourse about nature, humanity, and the world. **Procedure:** Freshmen are admitted fall and spring. Entrance exams should be taken by January of the senior year. There are deferred admissions and rolling admissions plans. Application deadlines are open. Application fee is $40. Notification is sent on a rolling basis. Applications are accepted on-line. Application fees are waived if application is completed on-line. **Transfer Students:** 268 transfer students enrolled in 2015-2016. Candidates must be in good academic and personal standing at the institutions last attended full time. Although it does not guarantee admission, a 2.5 GPA in all college work is usually required. For applicants with fewer than 30 semester hours or 45 quarter hours, secondary school records and standardized test scores must be submitted. All students must meet the foreign language and math entrance requirements. 32 of 128 credits required for the bachelor's degree must be completed at PLU. **International Students:** There are 80 international students enrolled. The school actively recruits these students. They must take the TOEFL with a minimum score of 550 on the paper-based TOEFL (PBT) or 79 on the Internet-based version (iBT).

ADMISSIONS: 77% of the 2016-2017 applicants were accepted. The SAT scores for the 2016-2017 freshman class were: Critical Reading-- 27% below 500, 41% between 500 and 599, 26% between 600 and 699, and 6% between 700 and 800. Math-- 25% below 500, 42% between 500 and 599, 28% between 600 and 699, and 5% between 700 and 800. Writing-- 34% below 500, 46% between 500 and 599, 18% between 600 and 699, and 2% between 700 and 800. The ACT scores were 6% between 12 and 17, 30% between 18 and 23, 48% between 24 and 29, and 16% above 30. **Admissions Contact:** Dave Gunovich, Dean of Enrollment Services. Email: *admissions@plu.edu* Web: *www.plu.edu*

FINANCIAL AID: In 2016-2017, 99% of all full-time freshmen and 97% of continuing full-time students received some form of financial aid. 63% of all full-time freshmen and 68% of continuing full-time students received need-based aid. The average freshman award was $34,402. Need-based scholarships or need-based grants averaged $28,524; and need-based self-help aid (loans and jobs) averaged $9,284. The average financial indebtedness of the 2016 graduate was $28,214. The FAFSA code is 003785. The priority date for freshman financial aid applications for fall entry is January 31.

SAINT MARTIN'S UNIVERSITY B-3

www.stmartin.edu

Lacey, WA 98503	(360) 438-4592 (800) 368-8803
Fax: (360) 412-6189	**Email:** admissions@stmartin.edu
Full-time: 520 men, 553 women	**Faculty:** 79; IIB, --$
Part-time: 117 men, 91 women	**Ph.D.s:** 85%
Graduate: 111 men, 193 women	**Student/Faculty:** 13 to 1
Year: semesters, summer session	**Tuition:** $34,356
Room & Board: $10,700	**Freshman Class:** 1344 applied, 1281 accepted, 241 enrolled
SAT CR/M/W: 510/515/495 **ACT:** 22	**CEEB CODE:** 4674
Application Deadline: April 1	**COMPETITIVE**

Saint Martin's University, founded in 1895, is a private, non-profit Roman Catholic institution conducted by the Benedictine order, offering undergraduate and graduate programs in liberal arts and sciences, business, education, and engineering. There are 4 undergraduate schools and 3 graduate schools. In addition to regional accreditation, Saint Martin's has baccalaureate program accreditation with ABET, ACBSP, CSWE, TEAC, CCNE, and MPCAC. The 300-acre campus is in a suburban area 3 miles from Olympia and 60 miles south of Seattle. Including any residence halls, there are 17 buildings.

STUDENT LIFE: 82% of undergraduates are from Washington. Others are from 23 states, 6 foreign countries, and Canada. 79% are from public schools. 54% are White; 14% Hispanic; 6% African American; 6% Asian American; 6% Foreign; 6% two or more races; 6% race unknown; 1% American Indian/Alaska Native. 41% claim no religious affiliation; 27% Catholic; 26% and 20% Christian. **Female To Male Ratio:** 1.1:1. The average age of freshmen is 18; all undergraduates, 24. 19% do not continue beyond their first year; 55% remain to graduate. **Housing:** 630 students can be accommodated in college housing, which includes coed dorms. learning communities. On-campus housing is guaranteed for the freshman year only, and is available on a first-come, first-served basis. 63% of students commute. Alcohol is not permitted. All students may keep cars.

FACULTY/CLASSROOMS: 57% of faculty are male; 43% are female. 90% teach undergraduates. No introductory courses are taught by graduate students. The average class size in an introductory lecture is 12; in a laboratory is 12; and in a regular course is 12.

PROGRAMS OF STUDY: Saint Martin's confers B.A., B.S., B.S.W., B.S.N., B.S.C.E., and B.S.M.E. degrees. Master's degrees are also awarded. Bachelor's degrees are awarded in BIOLOGICAL SCIENCE (biology/biological science), BUSINESS (accounting and business administration and management), COMMUNICATIONS AND THE ARTS (communications, English, music, and theatre arts), COMPUTER AND PHYSICAL SCIENCE (chemistry, computer science, and mathematics), EDUCATION (educational studies, elementary education, and special education), ENGINEERING AND ENVIRONMENTAL DESIGN (civil engineering and mechanical engineering), HEALTH PROFESSIONS (nursing), SOCIAL SCIENCE (criminal justice, history, interdisciplinary studies, political science/government, psychology, religious studies, social work, and sociology). Engineering is the strongest academically. Business administration, mechanical engineering, and biology have the largest enrollments.

ACTIVITIES: There are no fraternities or sororities. There are 30 groups on campus, including band, choir, chorale, computers, drama, environmental, ethnic, honors, international, jazz band, LGBT, musical theater, newspaper, pep band, political, professional, religious, social, social service, and student government. Popular campus events include Career Fair, International Day, Capital Food and Wine Festival. **Sports:** There are 6 intercollegiate sports for men and 7 for women, and 9 intramural sports for men and 9 for women. Facilities include a 5300-seat multipurpose pavilion, recreation center, and athletic fields. **Graduates:** From July 1, 2015 to June 30, 2016, 343 bachelor's degrees were awarded. The most popular majors were business administration (20%), psychology (12%), and civil engineering (8%). In an average class, 41% graduate in 4 years or less, 53% graduate in 5 years or less, and 55% graduate in 6 years or less.

SERVICES: Counseling and information services are available, as is tutoring in some subjects, such as accounting, biology, business, chemistry, computer science, economics, physics, math, and world languages. There is a reader service for the blind, and remedial math, reading, and writing. **Library/Resources:** The library contains 278,947 volumes, 166,184 microform items, and 2,415 audio/video tapes/CDs/DVDs, and subscribes to 74,406 periodicals including electronic. Computerized library services include interlibrary loans, database searching, Internet access, and Wi-Fi capability. Special learning facilities include an art gallery. **Physically Challenged Students:** 90% of the campus is accessible. Facilities include wheelchair ramps, elevators, special parking, specially equipped restrooms, lowered drinking fountains, and lowered telephones. **Special:** Double majors, work-study with the state of Washington, nonprofit organizations, internships in all disciplines, a Washington semester with American University, and pass/fail options are offered. The FOCUS program offers credit for job experience. Nondegree study and study abroad is possible. There are 3 national honor societies and 3 departmental honors programs. **Visiting:** There are regularly scheduled orientations for prospective students, including a campus tour and faculty, student service, and financial aid presentations. There are guides for informal visits, visitors may sit in on classes, and stay overnight. To schedule a visit, contact the Admissions Office. **Campus Safety and Security:** Measures include 24-hour foot and vehicle patrol, emergency notification system, and security escort services. There are emergency telephones, lighted pathways/sidewalks, and controlled access to dorms/residences. There is a security patrol from dark to dawn.

REQUIREMENTS: The SAT or ACT is required. Applicants must be graduates of an accredited secondary school or have a GED, with a minimum of 16 academic units, including 4 units in English, 2 or 3 units in math, 2 units in history/social science, 1 or 2 units each in foreign language and lab science, and 7 units in electives. Class standing also is considered. An essay and recommendation from a teacher or counselor are required. Students should have a score of 800 on the SAT I and a 2.5 GPA. AP and CLEP credits are accepted. Important factors in the admissions decision are advanced placement or honors courses, recommendations by school officials, and personality/intangible qualities. All students must complete freshman composition and general education requirements, including 2 courses in social sciences and foreign language, 1 course each in literature, philosophy, the arts, religious studies, natural science with lab, math (precalculus), U.S. history, and non-U.S. history. A total of 120 semester credits with a 2.0 GPA is required. **Procedure:** Freshmen are admitted fall, spring, and summer. There is a rolling admissions plan. Applications should be filed by April 1 for fall entry; December 15 for spring entry. Notification is sent on a rolling basis. Applications are accepted on-line. Application fees are waived if application is completed on-line. **Transfer Students:** 161 transfer students enrolled in 2015-2016. Transfer applicants must submit transcripts from all colleges previously attended and have a 2.0 GPA. 30 of 120 credits required for the bachelor's degree must be completed at Saint Martin's. **International Students:** There are 44 international students enrolled. The school actively recruits these students. They must take the TOEFL with a minimum score of 525 on the paper-based TOEFL (PBT) or 71 on the Internet-based version (iBT).

ADMISSIONS: 95% of the 2016-2017 applicants were accepted. The SAT scores for the 2016-2017 freshman class were: Critical Reading-- 49% below 500, 33% between 500 and 599, 13% between 600 and 699, and 4% between 700 and 800. Math-- 49% below 500, 29% between 500 and 599, 20% between 600 and 699, and 2% between 700 and 800. Writing-- 55% below 500, 34% between 500 and 599, 9% between 600 and 699, and 2% between 700 and 800. The ACT scores were 7% between 12 and 17, 58% between 18 and 23, 28% between 24 and 29, and 7% above 30. 42% of the current freshmen were in the top fifth of their class; 73% were in the top two fifths. 3 freshmen graduated first in their class. **Admissions Contact:** Emilie Schnabel, Assistant Director, Admissions. Email: *admissions@stmartin.edu* Web: *www.stmartin.edu*

FINANCIAL AID: In 2016-2017, 85% of all full-time freshmen and 81% of continuing full-time students received some form of financial aid. 85% of all full-time freshmen and 81% of continuing full-time students received need-based aid. The average freshman award was $25,672. Need-based scholarships or need-based grants averaged $23,613; need-based self-help aid (loans and jobs) averaged $3,535; non-need-based athletic scholarships averaged $8,168; and other non-need-based awards and non-need-based scholarships averaged $13,526. Saint Martin's is a member of CSS. The deadline for filing freshman financial aid applications for fall entry is March 1.

SEATTLE PACIFIC UNIVERSITY C-2

www.spu.edu

Seattle, WA 98119	**(206) 281-2561** **(800) 366-3344**
Fax: (206) 281-2669	**Email: admissions@spu.edu**
Full-time: 995 men, 2089 women	**Faculty:** IIA, +$
Part-time: 42 men, 76 women	**Ph.D.s:** 88%
Graduate: 265 men, 708 women	**Student/Faculty:** 15 to 1
Year: quarters, summer session	**Tuition:** $37,086
Room & Board: $10,353	**Freshman Class:** 5227 applied, 4266 accepted, 688 enrolled
SAT CR/M: 560/560 **ACT:** 25	**CEEB CODE:** 4694
Application Deadline: March 1	**COMPETITIVE+**

Seattle Pacific University, founded in 1891, is a private institution affiliated with the Free Methodist Church. It offers programs in business and economics, education, fine and performing arts, health science, humanities, natural and mathematical sciences, phys ed and athletics, religion, and social and behavioral sciences. Figures in the above capsule and in this profile are approximate. There are 6 undergraduate schools and 6 graduate schools. In addition to regional accreditation, SPU has baccalaureate program accreditation with AACSB, ABET, NASM, NCATE, NLN, CADE, and CCNE. The 41-acre campus is in an urban area 7 minutes from downtown Seattle. Including any residence halls, there are 94 buildings.

STUDENT LIFE: 64% of undergraduates are from Washington. Others are from 41 states, 55 foreign countries, and Canada. 58% are White; 10% Asian American; 8% Hispanic; 8% race unknown; 7% two or more races; 4% African American; 4% Foreign; 1% American Indian/Alaska Native. **Female To Male Ratio:** 2.2:1. The average age of freshmen is 18; all undergraduates, 21. 75% remain to graduate. **Housing:** 1761 students can be accommodated in college housing, which includes single-sex and coed dorms, on-campus apartments, off-campus apartments, married student housing, and theme houses. 52% of students live on campus. Alcohol is not permitted. All students may keep cars.

FACULTY/CLASSROOMS: 54% of faculty are male; 46% are female. No introductory courses are taught by graduate students. The average class size in a regular course is 18.

PROGRAMS OF STUDY: SPU confers B.A. and B.S. degrees. Master's and doctoral degrees are also awarded. Bachelor's degrees are awarded in BIOLOGICAL SCIENCE (biochemistry and biology/biological science), BUSINESS (accounting and business administration and management), COMMUNICATIONS AND THE ARTS (art, classics, communications, creative writing, English, fine arts, French, German, language arts, Latin, linguistics, literature, music, Russian, and Spanish), COMPUTER AND PHYSICAL SCIENCE (chemistry, computer science, information sciences and systems, mathematics, and physics), EDUCATION (education, elementary education, home economics education, mathematics education, music education, nursing education, physical education, science education, secondary education, social science education, special education, and teaching English as a second/foreign language (TESOL/TEFOL)), ENGINEERING AND ENVIRONMENTAL DESIGN (electrical/electronics engineering, engineering, engineering and applied science, and interior design), HEALTH PROFESSIONS (exercise science and nursing), SOCIAL SCIENCE (Christian studies, clinical psychology, economics, European studies, family/consumer resource management, family/consumer studies, food science, history, Latin American studies, liberal arts/general studies, philosophy, physical fitness/movement, political science/government, prelaw, psychology, social science, sociology, and theological studies). Education, nursing, and business administration have the largest enrollments.

ACTIVITIES: There are no fraternities or sororities. There are 51 groups on campus, including art, chess, choir, chorale, drama, ethnic, honors, international, jazz band, literary magazine, newspaper, orchestra, pep band, political, professional, radio, religious, social, social service, student government, and symphony. Popular campus events include Family Weekend, Talent Show, and Ivy Cutting at Graduation. **Sports:** Facilities include a soccer field, an oval track, tennis and basketball courts, gym and crew house, crew dock, 2600-seat indoor gym, 800-seat campus auditorium, and a community swimming pool available to students with free passes. **Graduates:** From July 1, 2015 to June 30, 2016, 759 bachelor's degrees were awarded. The most popular majors were nursing (10%), psychology (8%), and business administration (8%). In an average class, 71% graduate in 6 years or less.

SERVICES: Counseling and information services are available, as is tutoring in most subjects. There is a reader service for the blind, and remedial math and writing. In addition, there is priority registration for disabled students. **Library/Resources:** The library contains 227,332 volumes, 497,248 microform items, and 8,915 audio/video tapes/CDs/DVDs, and subscribes to 2,841 periodicals including electronic. Computerized library services include interlibrary loans, database searching, Internet access, and Wi-Fi capability. Special learning facilities include an art gallery, a science center, performing arts theater, a writing lab, and a media center. **Physically Challenged Students:** Facilities include wheelchair ramps, elevators, special parking, specially equipped restrooms, and special class scheduling. **Special:** There is a cooperative program with Fashion Institute of Technology in New York City, Fashion Institute of Design and Merchandising in Los Angeles, and Han Nam University in Korea, cross-registration with the Christian College Consortium and Christian College Coalition, and a Washington semester in American studies through the Christian College Coalition. SPU offers internships, study abroad in more than 5 countries, work-study programs, dual and student-designed majors, interdisciplinary majors such as language arts, and a liberal studies major for associate degree graduates. A general studies degree, pass/no credit options, and nondegree study are available. There are 5 national honor societies, a freshman honors program, and 10 departmental honors programs. **Visiting:** There are regularly scheduled orientations for prospective students. There are guides for informal visits, visitors may sit in on classes, and stay overnight. To schedule a visit, contact the Admissions Office. **Campus Safety and Security:** Measures include 24-hour foot and vehicle patrol, emergency notification system, and security escort services. There are emergency telephones, lighted pathways/sidewalks, controlled access to dorms/residences, and closed-circuit TV monitors.

REQUIREMENTS: The SAT or ACT is required. The SAT I is preferred, with a minimum required composite score of 950. Candidates should be graduates of an accredited secondary school with a minimum high school GPA of 2.5, or hold a GED certificate. A strong college preparatory program in high school is recommended, including 4 years of English, 3 each of math, science, and foreign language, 2 of history, and 1 of social studies. An essay and 2 letters of recommendation are required, and an interview is recommended. AP and CLEP credits are accepted. Important factors in the admissions decision are advanced placement or honors courses, leadership record, and extracurricular activities record. All students must demonstrate competency in math and English. Students must complete 15 quarter credits in Christian heritage and values, 56 in general education, up to 15 credits of foreign language competency, and at least 45 to 60 in the major, depending on the program. A minimum of 180 credits is needed for the bachelor's degree, with a 2.0 GPA overall. At least 60 credits must be earned in 3000-level courses or higher. **Procedure:** Freshmen are admitted to all sessions. Entrance exams should be taken by January of the senior year. There are early decision and rolling admissions plans. Early decision applications should be filed by November 15; regular applications, by March 1 for fall entry, along with a $45 fee. Notification of early decision is sent February 15; regular decision, on a rolling basis. Applications are accepted on-line. **Transfer Students:** 245 transfer students enrolled in 2015-2016. A minimum 2.5 GPA is required, and an interview is recommended. Transcripts from all previous colleges attended and from high school are required, along with 2 letters of recommendation and an essay or personal statement. Evidence of honorable dismissal from the previous school is also required. Students with at least 30 credits earned are not required to take the SAT or ACT. 45 of 180 credits required for the bachelor's degree must be completed at SPU. **International Students:** There are 127 international students enrolled. The school actively recruits these students. They must take the TOEFL. The Michigan Test must be administered through SPU.

ADMISSIONS: 82% of the 2016-2017 applicants were accepted. The SAT scores for the 2016-2017 freshman class were: Critical Reading-- 18% below 500, 44% between 500 and 599, 32% between 600 and 699, and 6% between 700 and 800. Math-- 21% below 500, 44% between 500 and 599, 29% between 600 and 699, and 6% between 700 and 800. Writing-- 23% below 500. The ACT scores were 2% between 12 and 17, 29% between 18 and 23, 54% between 24 and 29, and 15% above 30. **Admissions Contact:** Ineliz Soto-Fuller, Director of Undergraduate Admissions. Email: *admissions@spu.edu* Web: *www.spu.edu*

FINANCIAL AID: The FAFSA code is 003788. The deadline for filing freshman financial aid applications for fall entry is June 30.

SEATTLE UNIVERSITY — C-2

www.seattleu.edu

Seattle, WA 98122 — (206) 296-2000, (800) 426-7123

Fax: (206) 296-5656	**Email:** admissions@seattleu.edu
Full-time: 1749 men, 2783 women	**Faculty:** 421; IIA, +$
Part-time: 112 men, 136 women	**Ph.D.s:** 85%
Graduate: 1020 men, 1681 women	**Student/Faculty:** 12 to 1
Year: quarters, summer session	**Tuition:** $41,265
Room & Board: $11,499	**Freshman Class:** 8149 applied, 6001 accepted, 985 enrolled
SAT CR/M/W: 590/590/580 **ACT:** 27	**CEEB CODE:** 4695
Application Deadline: January 15	**VERY COMPETITIVE+**

Seattle University is Seattle's university. That means a centralized urban location in one of the world's most innovative, vibrant, and culturally rich metropolitan cities. Graduates recognize how SU enhances and strengthens abilities that businesses and organizations prize critical thinking, effective communication, global perspectives, and solving complex problems across disciplines. Undergraduate, graduate, and certificate programs include science and engineering, business, liberal arts, humanities, nursing, education, theology and law. Service is an element of learning that enriches spirituality at SU. It's a free-thinking approach that underscores this independent university's commitment to empowering leaders for a just and humane world. There are 7 undergraduate schools and 7 graduate schools. In addition to regional accreditation, Seattle U has baccalaureate program accreditation with AACSB, ABET, CAHEA, CSWE, NCATE, and NLN. The 46-acre campus is in an urban area east of downtown Seattle in the Capitol Hill neighborhood. Including any residence halls, there are 34 buildings.

STUDENT LIFE: 59% of undergraduates are from out of state, mostly the West. Students are from 47 states, 50 foreign countries, and Canada. 63% are from public schools. 57% are White; 4% African American; 23% Asian American; 2% American Indian/Alaska Native; 11% Hispanic; 11% Foreign. 22% are Catholic. **Female To Male Ratio:** 1.6:1. The average age of freshmen is 18; all undergraduates, 20. 11% do not continue beyond their first year; 75% remain to graduate. **Housing:** 2085 students can be accommodated in college housing, which includes coed dorms and on-campus apartments. In addition, there are language houses, 24-hour quiet floors, and single-sex floors. On-campus housing is available on a lottery system for upperclassmen. Priority is given to out-of-town students. 55% of students commute. Some may keep cars.

FACULTY/CLASSROOMS: 48% of faculty are male; 52% are female. No introductory courses are taught by graduate students. The average class size in a regular course is 18.

PROGRAMS OF STUDY: Seattle U confers B.A., B.S., B.A.B.A., B.A.E., B.A.H., B.C.J., B.M., B.F.A., B.S.B., B.S.B.C., B.S.P., B.S.C.E., B.S.C.S., B.S.D.U., B.S.E.E., B.S.E.S., B.S.G.S., B.S.M., B.S.M.E., B.S.N., and B.S.W. degrees. Master's and doctoral degrees are also awarded. Bachelor's degrees are awarded in AGRICULTURE (environmental studies), BIOLOGICAL SCIENCE (biochemistry, biology/adolescence education, biology/biological science, cell biology, and marine biology), BUSINESS (accounting, business administration and management, business economics, finance, international business management, international economics, marketing management, and organizational leadership and management), COMMUNICATIONS AND THE ARTS (art history, communications, creative writing, English, film arts, fine arts, French, journalism, music, photography, Spanish, strings, theatre arts, and visual and performing arts), COMPUTER AND PHYSICAL SCIENCE (applied mathematics, chemistry, chemistry/adolescence education, computer science, digital arts/technology, mathematics, mathematics-actuarial concentration, mathematics/theoretical, physics, science, and web technology), EDUCATION (Asian studies, environmental education, and mathematics education), ENGINEERING AND ENVIRONMENTAL DESIGN (civil engineering, computer engineering, electrical/electronics engineering, environmental engineering, environmental science, and mechanical engineering), HEALTH PROFESSIONS (exercise science, medical technology, nursing, and ultrasound technology), SOCIAL SCIENCE (anthropology, criminal justice, economics, forensic studies, history, humanities, international studies, liberal arts/general studies, philosophy, political science/government, psychology, public administration, religion, social work, sociology, theological studies, urban ecology, and women & gender studies). Nursing, criminal justice, and business are the strongest academically. Nursing, engineering, and business have the largest enrollments.

ACTIVITIES: There are no fraternities or sororities. There are 61 groups on campus, including art, cheerleading, choir, chorale, communications, dance, debate, drama, environmental, ethnic, film, forensics, honors, international, jazz band, LGBT, literary magazine, musical theater, newspaper, photography, political, professional, radio and TV, religious, social, social service, and student government. Popular campus events include Hawaiian Luau, Quad Stock, and International Student Dinner. **Sports:** There are 8 intercollegiate sports for men and 10 for women, and 14 intramural sports for men and 14 for women. Facilities include a 180,000 sq. ft of recreational, fitness and athletic space center with 2 swimming pools, cardio, weight rooms, group exercise, yoga, martial arts classrooms, racquetball, squash courts, 3 basketball courts, outdoor track, soccer and softball fields, tennis courts, and an astroturf gym for indoor soccer/tennis with 2 batting cages. **Graduates:** From July 1, 2015 to June 30, 2016, 1182 bachelor's degrees were awarded. The most popular majors were business/marketing (24%), health professions and related sciences (14%), and engineering (7%). In an average class, 64% graduate in 4 years or less, 74% graduate in 5 years or less, and 75% graduate in 6 years or less. Of the 2015 graduating class, 82% were employed within 6 months of graduation.

SERVICES: Counseling and information services are available, as is tutoring in most subjects, such as math, English, accounting, language, and science. There is a reader service for the blind, and a writing center. **Library/Resources:** The 2 libraries contain 582,577 volumes, 1.8 million microform items, and 9,402 audio/video tapes/CDs/DVDs, and subscribe to 69,109 periodicals including electronic. Computerized library services include interlibrary loans, database searching, Internet access, and Wi-Fi capability. Special learning facilities include an art gallery, planetarium, radio station, an electron microscope, a recording studio, and MRI. **Physically Challenged Students:** 95% of the campus is accessible. Facilities include wheelchair ramps, elevators, special parking, specially equipped restrooms, special class scheduling, lowered drinking fountains, lowered telephones, and special housing. **Special:** Seattle University provides many opportunities for dual majors, local, national and international internships, and on and off-campus work study positions. In addition, distinctive programs include: International Development Internship Program (IDIP), with a goal of instilling in students a lifelong commitment to the Jesuit mission of service and promotion of social justice. IDIP is a 20-credit, three-phase academic program designed for undergraduates. Study Abroad; about 500 Seattle University students now participate in educational and service programs in more than 40 countries. Short-term programs at SU are slightly more popular than long-term ones. Developing a long-term relationship with a sister Jesuit school, the University of Central America (UCA) in Nicaragua, also has increased opportunities abroad for SU students. Project Center: Seattle University runs one of the oldest and strongest Project Centers in the country. It's a great experiential learning opportunity for students in engineering, computer science and business. Sponsoring companies come back year after year; it's a great way for them to connect with SU and engage with great students. In fact, many students do go on to work for the sponsors of their projects. Albers Mentor Program; the Albers Mentor Program is a unique opportunity for graduate-level and senior undergraduate business students to interact with upper-level executives from leading Puget Sound companies and organizations. It offers opportunities to develop business contacts, access industry information, and gain valuable insights from experienced and successful professionals. There is a freshman honors program and 23 departmental honors programs. **Visiting:** There are regularly scheduled orientations for prospective students, with about an hour of sharing what it's like to live and learn in our distinct urban setting. Get a chance to see classroom spaces, a residence hall room, our award-winning Chapel of St. Ignatius, and the new Lemieux Library among many others. There are guides for informal visits, visitors may sit in on classes, and stay overnight. To schedule a visit, contact the Undergraduate Admissions Office. **Campus Safety and Security:** Measures include 24-hour foot and vehicle patrol, emergency notification system, self-defense education, and security escort services. There are shuttle buses, emergency telephones, lighted pathways/sidewalks, and controlled access to dorms/residences.

REQUIREMENTS: The SAT or ACT is required. Admissions requirements include graduation from an accredited secondary school with 16 academic credits, including 4 years of English, 3 each of math and social studies, 2 of foreign language, 2 of lab science, and 2 academic electives; 4 years of math and lab physics and chemistry are required of science and engineering students; lab biology and chemistry are needed by nursing students. The GED is also accepted. A GPA of 2.7 is required. AP and CLEP credits are accepted. Students must complete 180 to 192 quarter hours, depending on the degree, with 70 to 90 in the major, and maintain a minimum GPA of 2.25 to 2.5. Core curriculum requirements include 12 courses (60 credits) and a major-specific capstone course divided into four modules: Enagaging Academic Inquiry, Exploring the Self and Others, Engaging the World, and Reflection. **Procedure:** Freshmen are admitted to all sessions. Entrance exams should be taken during the fall of the senior year. There are early admissions and deferred admissions plans. Applications should be filed by January 15 for fall entry; November 1 for winter entry; February 15 for spring entry; and May 1 for summer entry, along with a $55 fee. Notifications are sent March 15. 31 early decision candidates were accepted for the 2016-2017 class. 283 applicants were on the 2016 waiting list; 25 were admitted. Applications are accepted on-line. **Transfer Students:** 398 transfer students enrolled in 2015-2016. Generally, transfer students should have a college GPA of at least 2.25. An associate degree is recommended; a 2.75 GPA is required for nursing and business administration students. 45 of 180 credits required for the bachelor's degree must be completed at Seattle U. **International Students:** There are 500 international students enrolled. The school actively recruits these students. They must take the TOEFL with a minimum score of 520 on the paper-based TOEFL (PBT) or 68 on the Internet-based version (iBT).

ADMISSIONS: 74% of the 2016-2017 applicants were accepted. The SAT scores for the 2016-2017 freshman class were: Critical Reading-- 11% below 500, 43% between 500 and 599, 36% between 600 and 699, and 9% between 700 and 800. Math-- 11% below 500, 42% between 500 and 599, 39% between 600 and 699, and 8% between 700 and 800. Writing-- 14% below 500, 45% between 500 and 599, 32% between 600 and 699, and 10% between 700 and 800. The ACT scores were 15% between 18 and 23, 58% between 24 and 29, and 27% above 30. **Admissions Contact:** Melore Nielsen, Dean of Admissions. Email: *admissions@seattleu.edu* Web: *www.seattleu.edu*

FINANCIAL AID: In 2016-2017, 95% of all full-time freshmen and 85% of continuing full-time students received some form of financial aid. 78% of all full-time freshmen and 76% of continuing full-time students received need-based aid. The average freshman award was $27,957. Need-based scholarships or need-based grants averaged $16,445 ($5,010 maximum); need-based self-help aid (loans and jobs) averaged $5,010 ($47,434 maximum); non-need-based athletic scholarships averaged $1,251 ($74,502 maximum); and other non-need-based awards and non-need-based scholarships averaged $10,935 ($56,500 maximum). The average financial indebtedness of the 2016 graduate was $22,628. The FAFSA code is 003790. The priority date for freshman financial aid applications for fall entry is February 1.

THE EVERGREEN STATE COLLEGE B-3

www.evergreen.edu

Olympia, WA 98505 **(360) 867-6170**

Fax: (360) 867-5114	**Email:** admissions@evergreen.edu
Full-time: 1498 men, 1960 women	**Faculty:** 137
Part-time: 151 men, 178 women	**Ph.D.s:** 87%
Graduate: 98 men, 204 women	**Student/Faculty:** 22 to 1
Year: quarters, summer session	**Tuition:** $7239 ($23,712)
Room & Board: $9360	**Freshman Class:** 1901 applied, 1853 accepted, 572 enrolled
SAT CR/M/W: 545/495/509 **ACT:** 23	**CEEB CODE:** 4292
Application Deadline: February 1	**COMPETITIVE**

The Evergreen State College, founded in 1967, is a public liberal arts and sciences college distinguished by interdisciplinary, collaborative, and team-taught academic programs, narrative evaluations of student work, and student-designed academic pathways. The figures in the above capsule and in this profile are approximate. The 1000-acre campus is in a small town 5 miles northwest of downtown Olympia. Including any residence halls, there are 57 buildings.

STUDENT LIFE: 75% of undergraduates are from Washington. Others are from 46 states, 19 foreign countries, and Canada. 66% are White; 11% Hispanic; 8% two or more races; 5% African American; 4% race unknown; 3% Asian American; 2% American Indian/Alaska Native; 1% Foreign. **Female To Male Ratio:** 1.3:1. The average age of freshmen is 19; all undergraduates, 25. 25% do not continue beyond their first year. **Housing:** 991 students can be accommodated in college housing, which includes coed dorms, on-campus apartments, and married student housing. In addition, there are special-interest houses, theme housing which includes substance-free, first-year experience, quiet. LGBTQ+, the Outdoor Program, community action, sustainability, and over 30. Freshman students are in residence halls. On-campus housing is guaranteed for the freshman year only and is available on a first-come, first-served basis. 77% of students commute. Alcohol is not permitted. All students may keep cars.

FACULTY/CLASSROOMS: 45% of faculty are male; 55% are female. 91% teach undergraduates. No introductory courses are taught by graduate students.

PROGRAMS OF STUDY: Evergreen confers B.A., B.S., and B.A.S degrees. Master's degrees are also awarded. Bachelor's degrees are awarded in BIOLOGICAL SCIENCE (biology/biological science, physiology, and zoology), COMMUNICATIONS AND THE ARTS (languages and visual and performing arts), COMPUTER AND PHYSICAL SCIENCE (mathematics and natural sciences), HEALTH PROFESSIONS (health), SOCIAL SCIENCE (anthropology, geography, history, liberal arts/general studies, political science/government, and sociology).

ACTIVITIES: There are no fraternities or sororities. There are 66 groups on campus, including art, choir, chorale, communications, dance, drama, environmental, ethnic, film, international, LGBT, literary magazine, newspaper, photography, political, professional, radio and TV, religious, social, social service, and student government. Popular campus events include Campus Clam Bake, Return to Evergreen reunion events, Winter Tree Lighting, Longhouse Native Arts Fair, Day of Absence/Day of Presence. **Sports:** There are 3 intercollegiate sports for men and 4 for women, and 4 intramural sports for men and 4 for women. The Costantino Recreation Center features an Olympic-size 11-lane swimming pool, a diving well, a 15,000 square foot gymnasium, exercise and weight training rooms, 5 racquetball courts, dance/movement rooms, and indoor and outdoor climbing walls. The campus also offers a covered pavilion with artificial turf, 4 tennis courts, 5 playing fields, a challenge course, bike paths, and jogging paths, and hiking trails with forest and beach access. **Graduates:** From July 1, 2015 to June 30, 2016, 1019 bachelor's degrees were awarded. The most popular majors were liberal arts and sciences (83%) and interdisciplinary natural sciences (17%). In an average class, 10% graduate in 3 years or less, 42% graduate in 4 years or less, 52% graduate in 5 years or less, and 56% graduate in 6 years or less. Of the 2015 graduating class, 87% were enrolled in graduate school within 6 months of graduation, and 80% were employed.

SERVICES: Writing Center offers assistance in writing; the Quantitive and Symbolic Reasoning Center offers assistance with all levels of math, economics, statistics, chemistry, biology, physics, and computer science. There is a reader service for the blind. **Library/Resources:** The library contains 322,238 volumes, 60,542 microform items, and 16,987 audio/video tapes/CDs/DVDs, and subscribes to 54,696 periodicals including electronic. Computerized library services include interlibrary loans, database searching, Internet access, and Wi-Fi capability. Special learning facilities include an art gallery, radio station, organic farm, including the Sustainable Agriculture Laboratory and community gardens, Longhouse Education and Cultural Center, including a Native American carving studio, art galleries, animation and design studio, ceramics studio, metal shop, wood shop, Center for Creative and Applied Media (video production and studios), photography studios and darkrooms, science laboratories, media equipment loan program, computer labs, and access to scientific equipment. **Physically Challenged Students:** 85% of the campus is accessible. Facilities include wheelchair ramps, elevators, special parking, specially equipped restrooms, lowered drinking fountains, and lowered telephones. **Special:** All work at the college is interdisciplinary, and the programs of study change annually. The college's credit-generating options include the comprehensive Coordinated Study Program model, which allows students and faculty to work together intensively over multiple quarters. Credits may be earned through cooperative programs, work-study programs, internships, independent contracts, or from prior learning and military experience. All students develop personalized academic pathways based on their goals and areas of interest (equivalent to student-designed majors). The Center for Community-Based Learning and Action facilitates service learning opportunities in non-profit agencies. There are parallel opportunities in government agencies and private businesses, including off-campus work-study opportunities. Evergreen offers a wide range of study abroad opportunities through academic programs, consortium partnerships, individual learning contracts, and domestic and international exchange programs. **Visiting:** There are regularly scheduled orientations for prospective students, Including an admissions session, a class visit, and a campus tour. Overnight stays can also be arranged. There are guides for informal visits. To schedule a visit, contact Student Visitor Program. **Campus Safety and Security:** Measures include 24-hour foot and vehicle patrol, emergency notification system, self-defense education, and security escort services. There are emergency telephones and lighted pathways/sidewalks.

REQUIREMENTS: The SAT or ACT is required. Candidates should be graduates of an accredited secondary school and have completed 15 academic credits, consisting of 4 in English, 3 each in math and social studies, 2 each in foreign language and science (one of which must be a lab science in biology, chemistry, or physics), and 1 in fine, visual, or performing arts or other college preparatory elective from another area mentioned in list. A GED certificate is acceptable. A GPA of 2.0 is required. AP and CLEP credits are accepted. Important factors in the admissions decision are advanced placement or honors courses, evidence of special talent, and ability to finance college education. Students must earn a minimum of 180 quarter hours of credit to receive a B.A. or B.S. degree. For a B.A., 45 of the last 90 credits must be earned at Evergreen (for transfer students). For a B.S. students must have completed 72 credits of science, math, or computer science, 48 of which must be upper division. For a B.A.S. dual degree, 225 credits are required and students must meet the requirements of a B.A. and B.S. All students must also complete a summative academic statement at the conclusion of their studies. **Procedure:** Freshmen are admitted fall, winter, and spring. Entrance exams should be taken during spring of the junior year or fall of the senior year. Early decision applications should be filed by February 1; regular applications, by February 1 for fall entry; October 1 for winter entry; and December 1 for spring entry, along with a $50 fee. Applications are accepted on-line. **Transfer Students:** 712 transfer students enrolled in 2015-2016. a 2.0 minimum GPA is required. An associate degree is recommended. All applicants must submit all college transcripts. Applicants with fewer than 40 credits must submit SAT or ACT scores and a high school transcript. 45 of 180 credits required for the bachelor's degree must be completed at Evergreen. **International Students:** There are 26 international students enrolled. They must take the TOEFL with a minimum score of 550 on the paper-based TOEFL (PBT) or 79 on the Internet-based version (iBT). They must also take the SAT or ACT.

ADMISSIONS: 97% of the 2016-2017 applicants were accepted. The SAT scores for the 2016-2017 freshman class were: Critical Reading-- 32% below 500, 35% between 500 and 599, 27% between 600 and 699, and 6% between 700 and 800. Math-- 49% below 500, 37% between 500 and 599, 13% between 600 and 699, and 1% between 700 and 800. Writing-- 41% below 500, 43% between 500 and 599, 14% between 600 and 699, and 2% between 700 and 800. The ACT scores were 1% below 12, 12% between 12 and 17, 37% between 18 and 23, 40% between 24 and 29, and 10% above 30. **Admissions Contact:** Eric Pedersen, Director of Admissions. Email: *admissions@evergreen.edu* Web: *www.evergreen.edu*

FINANCIAL AID: Evergreen is a member of CSS. The college's own financial statement is required. The FAFSA code is 008155. The priority date for freshman financial aid applications for fall entry is February 2. The deadline for filing freshman financial aid applications for fall entry is February 1.

UNIVERSITY OF PUGET SOUND — C-2

www.pugetsound.edu

Tacoma, WA 98416 — **(253) 879-3211**

Fax: (253) 879-3993	**Email:** jdmiller@pugetsound.edu
Full-time: 1011 men, 1448 women	**Faculty:** 210; IIB, +$
Part-time: 9 men, 8 women	**Ph.D.s:** 92%
Graduate: 58 men, 240 women	**Student/Faculty:** 11 to 1
Year: semesters, summer session	**Tuition:** $44,976
Room & Board: $11,480	**Freshman Class:** 5827 applied, 4616 accepted, 652 enrolled
SAT CR/M/W: 616/593/606 **ACT:** 27	**CEEB CODE:** 4067
Application Deadline: January 15	**VERY COMPETITIVE+**

University of Puget Sound is a residential, national liberal arts college, drawing students and faculty from around the country and throughout the world. Named a "College That Changes Lives," Puget Sound graduates include Rhodes and Fulbright scholars, notables in the arts and culture, entrepreneurs and elected officials, and leaders in business and finance in the U.S. and abroad. A low student-faculty ratio provides Puget Sound students with personal attention from faculty members who have a strong commitment to teaching and offer 1,200 courses each year in more than 50 areas of study. Puget Sound is the only national, independent undergraduate liberal arts college in Western Washington, and one of just five independent colleges in the Pacific Northwest granted a charter by Phi Beta Kappa, the nation's most prestigious academic honor society. The college also offers sought-after graduate programs in education, physical therapy, and occupational therapy. There is one undergraduate school and 3 graduate schools. In addition to regional accreditation, Puget Sound has baccalaureate program accreditation with NASM, ACS, ACOTE, and CAPTE. The 97-acre campus is in an urban area near Commencement Bay in the historic North End neighborhood of Tacoma, Washington. Including any residence halls, there are 135 buildings.

STUDENT LIFE: 84% of undergraduates are from out of state, mostly the West. Students are from 47 states, 12 foreign countries, and Canada. 68% are from public schools. 8% are two or more races; 74% White; 7% Hispanic; 6% Asian American; 2% race unknown; 1% African American. 57% claim no religious affiliation; 24% Protestant. **Female To Male Ratio:** 1.6:1. The average age of freshmen is 18; all undergraduates, 20. 13% do not continue beyond their first year; 77% remain to graduate. **Housing:** 1751 students can be accommodated in college housing, which includes single-sex and coed dorms and on-campus apartments. In addition, there are honors houses, language houses, special-interest houses, fraternity houses, and sorority houses. On-campus housing is available on a first-come, first-served basis, and is available on a lottery system for upperclassmen. 65% of students live on campus; of those, 90% remain on campus on weekends. All students may keep cars.

FACULTY/CLASSROOMS: 50% of faculty are male; 50% are female. 85% teach undergraduates. No introductory courses are taught by graduate students. The average class size in an introductory lecture is 18; in a laboratory is 12; and in a regular course is 15.

PROGRAMS OF STUDY: Puget Sound confers B.A., B.M., and B.S.

degrees. Master's and doctoral degrees are also awarded. Bachelor's degrees are awarded in BIOLOGICAL SCIENCE (biochemistry, biology/biological science, cell biology, and molecular biology), BUSINESS (business administration and management and international economics), COMMUNICATIONS AND THE ARTS (art, Chinese, classics, communications, dramatic arts, East Asian languages and literature, English, French, German, Japanese, music, music performance, and Spanish), COMPUTER AND PHYSICAL SCIENCE (chemistry, computer science, geology, mathematics, natural sciences, and physics), EDUCATION (music education), HEALTH PROFESSIONS (exercise science), SOCIAL SCIENCE (Asian/Oriental studies, economics, history, philosophy, political science/government, psychology, religion, science and society, and sociology). Psychology, exercise science, and business have the largest enrollments.

ACTIVITIES: 27% of men belong to 4 national fraternities; 31% of women belong to 4 national sororities. There are 125 groups on campus, including and diversity awareness, health and wellness, sports, art, band, cheerleading, choir, chorale, chorus, computers, dance, debate, drama, environmental, ethnic, forensics, gender, honors, international, jazz band, LGBT, literary magazine, musical theater, newspaper, opera, orchestra, pep band, photography, political, professional, radio and TV, religious, social, social service, student government, symphony, and yearbook. Popular campus events include Foolish Pleasures (student film festival), Mistletoast Holiday, Hawaiian Luau, and Drag Show. **Sports:** There are 11 intercollegiate sports for men and 12 for women, and 8 intramural sports for men and 8 for women. Facilities include 3,000-seat basketball and volleyball gym, a 6-lane pool, 2,488-seat football, soccer, lacrosse, and track stadium, 6 indoor tennis courts, fitness center with free weights and aerobics equipment, dance studio, track, baseball, softball, and intramural fields (one of which is synthetic), an indoor climbing wall, and auxiliary gym for intramurals and recreation. **Graduates:** From July 1, 2015 to June 30, 2016, 602 bachelor's degrees were awarded. The most popular majors were business (12%), psychology (8%), and exercise science (6%). In an average class, 68% graduate in 4 years or less, 75% graduate in 5 years or less, and 76% graduate in 6 years or less.

SERVICES: Counseling and information services are available, as is tutoring in most subjects. There is a reader service for the blind. **Library/Resources:** The library contains 520,919 volumes, 19,806 microform items, and 28,528 audio/video tapes/CDs/DVDs, and subscribes to 68,497 periodicals including electronic. Computerized library services include interlibrary loans, database searching, Internet access, and Wi-Fi capability. Special learning facilities include an art gallery, natural history museum, radio station, sculpture building, theatres, greenhouse, transmission and scanning electron microscopes, confocal microscope, DNA sequencer, NMR, X-ray diffractometer, microcomputer labs, sedimentology lab, stereoscopic and petrographic microscopes, computerized plotting/digitizing board and image analysis system, portable seismograph, gravimeter, proton precession magnetometer, ICP, GPS GIS lab, electronic music composition lab, electronic music keyboard lab with MIDI workstations, three electronic music classrooms, and one music V-room. **Physically Challenged Students:** 80% of the campus is accessible. Facilities include wheelchair ramps, elevators, special parking, specially equipped restrooms, special class scheduling, lowered drinking fountains, lowered telephones, and special housing. **Special:** International programs: include 130 study abroad programs in 45 countries, as well as local, national, and international internships in conjunction with an internship seminar. A curricular strength in Asian studies includes the full academic year Pacific Rim/Asian Study-Travel Program. Interdisciplinary programs: A highly interdisciplinary curriculum includes undergraduate studies in Asian languages and cultures, biochemistry, bioethics, and biophysics, a liberal arts-focused business leadership program, environmental policy and decision making, gender and queer studies, global development studies, international political economy, science, technology, and society; a student-designed interdisciplinary major, including a conservatory quality School of Music and an Honors Program. Many students choose to double major. Internships: Internship programs are available through the Alumni Sharing Knowledge network and Career and Employment Services, with companies such as Amazon, Boeing, Google, and Microsoft. Engineering: A 3-2 engineering degree offered with Washington University in St. Louis, Columbia University, Duke University, and the University of Southern California. Fellowships: Puget Sound is a top producer of Fulbright Scholars, Peace Corps volunteers, graduates who earn doctorates, with high acceptance rates to graduate programs in law and medicine, and prestigious fellowships including the Watson, Boren, and National Science Foundation. There are 15 national honor societies, including Phi Beta Kappa, a freshman honors program, and 13 departmental honors programs. **Visiting:** There are regularly scheduled orientations for prospective students, tour of campus, meetings with counselors, faculty, and coaches, classroom visits, overnight stays (if desired). There are guides for informal visits. To schedule a visit, contact Carolyn Johnson at crjohnson@pugetsound.edu. **Campus Safety and Security:** Measures include 24-hour foot and vehicle patrol, emergency notification system, and security escort services. There are emergency telephones, lighted pathways/sidewalks, controlled access to dorms/residences, and 24-hour live dispatch center.

REQUIREMENTS: The SAT or ACT is required. Puget Sound only accepts the Common Application for undergraduate admission. Admission requirements include graduation from an accredited secondary school with a recommended 4 years of English, 3 to 4 of mathematics, 3 to 4 years of natural and/or physical, laboratory science, 3 of social studies or history, 2 to 3 of foreign language, and 1 year of fine, visual, or performing arts. Also required are letters of personal recommendation from a teacher and counselor. An essay must be submitted, and an interview is recommended. The GED is also accepted. AP credits are accepted. Important factors in the admissions decision are advanced placement or honors courses, evidence of special talent, and personality/intangible qualities. In order to receive the baccalaureate degree from the University of Puget Sound, a student must: Earn a minimum of 32 units. The 32 units may include up to 4 academic courses graded pass/fail, up to 2 units in activity courses, and up to 4 units of independent study. Earn a minimum of 16 units, including the last 8, in residence at the University of Puget Sound. Residence requirements also exist in core, majors, minors, and graduation honors. (See also the section on study abroad). Maintain a minimum GPA of 2.0 in all graded courses, including transfer courses, in the major(s) and the minor(s). Successfully complete Puget Sound's core requirements. The faculty of the University of Puget Sound has designed the core curriculum to give undergraduates an integrated and demanding introduction to the life of the mind and to established methods of intellectual inquiry. The Puget Sound undergraduate's core experience begins with two first-year seminars that guide the student through an in-depth exploration of a focused area of interest and that sharpen the student's skills in constructing persuasive arguments. In the first three years of their Puget Sound college career, students also study five "Approaches to Knowing" (fine arts, humanities, mathematics, natural science, and social science). These core areas develop the student's understanding of different disciplinary perspectives on society, culture, and the physical world, and explore both the strengths of those disciplinary approaches and their limitations. Connections, an upper-level integrative course, challenges the traditional boundaries of disciplines and examines the benefits and limits of interdisciplinary approaches to knowledge. Further, in accordance with the stated educational goals of the University of Puget Sound, core curriculum requirements have been established: (a) to improve each student's grasp of the intellectual tools necessary for the understanding and communication of ideas, (b) to enable each student to understand herself or himself as a thinking person capable of making ethical and aesthetic choices, (c) to help each student comprehend the diversity of intellectual approaches to understanding human society and the physical world, and (d) to increase each student's awareness of his or her place in those broader contexts. Students choose from a set of courses in eight core areas, developing over four years an understanding of the liberal arts as the foundation for a lifetime of learning. Satisfy the foreign language graduation requirement in one of the following ways: (a) Successfully complete 2 semesters of a foreign language at the 101-102 college level, or 1 semester of a foreign language at the 200 level or above (courses taken pass/fail will not fulfill the foreign language graduation requirement); (b) Pass a Puget Sound/approved foreign language proficiency exam at the third-year high school or first-year college level, (c) Receive a score of 4 or 5 on an Advanced Placement foreign language exam or a score of 5, 6, or 7 on an International Baccalaureate Higher Level foreign language exam. **Procedure:** Freshmen are admitted fall and spring. Entrance exams should be taken during the fall of the senior year. There are early decision and deferred admissions plans. Early decision applications should be filed by November 15; regular applications, by January 15 for fall entry; and November 1 for spring entry, along with a $50 fee. Notification of early decision is sent December 15; regular decision, April 1. 114 early decision candidates were accepted for the 2016-2017 class. 480 applicants were on the 2016 waiting list; 21 were admitted. Applications are accepted on-line. **Transfer Students:** 54 transfer students enrolled in 2015-2016. Applicants must have had an honorable dismissal from the institution(s) previously attended and be in good academic standing with a minimum GPA of 2.0. All college transcripts and the rigor of prior course-work and resulting grades are evaluated. High school transcripts and SAT or ACT scores are required if less than 1 year of college has been completed. An interview is recommended. An essay is required. Puget Sound only accepts the Common Application for undergraduate transfer admission. 64 of 128 credits required for the bachelor's degree must be completed at Puget Sound. **International Students:** There are 10 international students enrolled. The school actively recruits these students. They must take the TOEFL with a minimum score of 550 on the paper-based TOEFL (PBT) or 80 on the Internet-based version (iBT). All freshman applicants and transfers with less than 1 full year of college work must take the SAT or ACT.

ADMISSIONS: 79% of the 2016-2017 applicants were accepted. The SAT scores for the 2016-2017 freshman class were: Critical Reading-- 7% below 500, 34% between 500 and 599, 41% between 600 and 699, and 18% between 700 and 800. Math-- 12% below 500, 38% between 500 and 599, 40% between 600 and 699, and 10% between 700 and 800. Writing-- 9% below 500, 37% between 500 and 599, 41% between 600 and 699, and 14% between 700 and 800. The ACT scores were 1% between 12 and 17, 16% between 18 and 23, 53% between 24 and 29, and 30% above 30. 58% of the current freshmen were in the top fifth of their class; 86% were in the top two fifths. There were 3 National Merit finalists. **Admissions Contact:** James Miller, Director of Admission. Email: *jdmiller@pugetsound.edu* Web: *www.pugetsound.edu*

FINANCIAL AID: In 2016-2017, 99% of all full-time freshmen and 98% of continuing full-time students received some form of financial aid. 53% of all full-time freshmen and 50% of continuing full-time students received need-based aid. The average freshman award was $30,054. Need-based scholarships or need-based grants averaged $24,324; need-based self-help aid (loans and jobs) averaged $6,822; other non-need-based awards and non-need-based scholarships averaged $5,018; and $14,350 from other forms of aid. 44% of undergraduate students work part-time. Average annual earnings from campus work are $2175. Puget Sound is a member of CSS. The CSS/Profile is required of early decision candidates. The FAFSA code is 003797. The deadline for filing freshman financial aid applications for fall entry is February 1.

UNIVERSITY OF WASHINGTON — C-2

www.washington.edu

Seattle, WA 98195 — (206) 543-9686

Full-time: 11612 men, 12597 women
Part-time: 2141 men, 2220 women
Graduate: 5354 men, 6294 women
Year: trimesters, summer session
Room & Board: $11,310

SAT or ACT: required
Application Deadline: n/av

Faculty: I, +$
Ph.D.s: 89%
Student/Faculty: n/av
Tuition: $11,839 ($34,143)
Freshman Class: 17877 applied, 11586 accepted, 5338 enrolled
CEEB CODE: 4854
VERY COMPETITIVE

University of Washington, founded in 1861, as a public research university offering a broad range of degree programs. Figures in the above capsule and in this profile are approximate. There are 16 undergraduate schools and 1 graduate school. In addition to regional accreditation, UW has baccalaureate program accreditation with AACSB, ABET, NCATE, and NLN. The 643-acre campus is in an urban area 5 miles from downtown Seattle. Including any residence halls, there are 279 buildings.

STUDENT LIFE: 80% of undergraduates are from Washington. Others are from 44 states, 107 foreign countries, and Canada. 51% are White; 5% Hispanic; 4% Foreign; 3% African American; 26% Asian American; 1% American Indian/Alaska Native. **Female To Male Ratio:** 1.1:1. The average age of freshmen is 18; all undergraduates, 21. 8% do not continue beyond their first year; 75% remain to graduate. **Housing:** 5200 students can be accommodated in college housing, which includes coed dorms, on-campus apartments, and married student housing. In addition, there are honors houses, special-interest houses, fraternity houses, sorority houses, freshman house, and business, engineering, international, pre-health science, and substance and alcohol free environment houses. On-campus housing is guaranteed for all 4 years. 80% of students commute. Alcohol is not permitted. All students may keep cars.

FACULTY/CLASSROOMS: 62% of faculty are male; 38% are female. 85% teach undergraduates, and 85% do research. No introductory courses are taught by graduate students.

PROGRAMS OF STUDY: UW confers B.A., B.S., B.A.B.A., B.C.H.S., B.L.Arch., B.Mus., B.S.A.&A., B.S.B.C., B.S.Cer.E., B.S.Comp.E., B.S.F., B.S.Fish., B.S.I.E., B.S.M.E., B.S.Med.Tech., B.S.Met.E., and B.S.Nur. degrees. Master's and doctoral degrees are also awarded. Bachelor's degrees are awarded in AGRICULTURE (fishing and fisheries, forest engineering, and forestry production and processing), BIOLOGICAL SCIENCE (biochemistry, biology/biological science, botany, microbiology, neurosciences, and zoology), BUSINESS (accounting, banking and finance, business administration and management, business economics, international business management, marketing/retailing/merchandising, and personnel management), COMMUNICATIONS AND THE ARTS (art history and appreciation, classics, communications, comparative literature, dance, dramatic arts, English, French, Germanic languages and literature, graphic design, Italian, Japanese, jazz, music history and appreciation, music performance, painting, photography, Scandinavian languages, sculpture, Slavic languages, Spanish, speech/debate/rhetoric, studio art, and technical and business writing), COMPUTER AND PHYSICAL SCIENCE (astronomy, atmospheric sciences and meteorology, computer science, geology, information sciences and systems, mathematics, oceanography, physics, quantitative methods, and statistics), EDUCATION (music education), ENGINEERING AND ENVIRONMENTAL DESIGN (aeronautical engineering, ceramic engineering, chemical engineering, civil engineering, computer engineering, construction engineering, electrical/electronics engineering, engineering, landscape architecture/design, materials science, ocean engineering, and paper and pulp science), HEALTH PROFESSIONS (dental hygiene, environmental health science, health care administration, medical laboratory technology, nursing, and speech pathology/audiology), SOCIAL SCIENCE (African American studies, anthropology, Asian/American studies, Asian/Oriental studies, Canadian studies, economics, ethnic studies, food science, geography, history, international relations, Judaic studies, liberal arts/general studies, Near Eastern studies, philosophy, political science/government, psychology, religion, Russian and Slavic studies, social work, sociology, South Asian studies, and women's studies). Business, political science, and art have the largest enrollments.

ACTIVITIES: 6% of men belong to 27 national fraternities; 5% of women belong to 16 national sororities. There are 550 groups on campus, including band, cheerleading, chess, choir, chorale, chorus, communications, computers, dance, debate, drama, ethnic, film, honors, international, jazz band, LGBT, literary magazine, marching band, musical theater, newspaper, opera, orchestra, pep band, political, professional, radio and TV, religious, social, social service, student government, and symphony. Popular campus events include Convocation, Dawg Daze, and Washington Weekend. **Sports:** There are 11 intercollegiate sports for men and 12 for women, and 13 intramural sports for men and 12 for women. Facilities include a 72,500-seat football stadium, baseball field, track and field complex, lakeside facilities, tennis courts, the intramurals building, golf driving range, and a swimming pool. **Graduates:** From July 1, 2015 to June 30, 2016, 7024 bachelor's degrees were awarded. The most popular majors were social sciences (19%), biological/life sciences (10%), and business/marketing (10%). 212 companies recruited on campus in 2015-2016. In an average class, 48% graduate in 4 years or less, 71% graduate in 5 years or less, and 75% graduate in 6 years or less.

SERVICES: Counseling and information services are available, as is tutoring in every subject. There is a reader service for the blind, and remedial math, reading, and writing. **Library/Resources:** The 16 libraries contain 7.0 million volumes. Computerized library services include interlibrary loans, database searching, Internet access, and Wi-Fi capability. Special learning facilities include an art gallery, natural history museum, planetarium, radio station, TV station, a state museum, a full teaching hospital, a marine science lab, 200-acre arboretum, and field research forest. **Physically Challenged Students:** 95% of the campus is accessible. Facilities include wheelchair ramps, elevators, special parking, specially equipped restrooms, special class scheduling, lowered drinking fountains, lowered telephones, and special housing. **Special:** A wide variety of internships, including those for minority students in engineering, concurrent dual majors, study abroad in 60 countries, a Washington semester, a general studies degree, and co-op programs are available. Work-study programs, cross-registration with the National Student Exchange, credit/no credit options, student-designed majors, accelerated degree programs, nondegree study, and a 5-year B.A.-B.S. degree also are offered. There are 20 national honor societies, Phi Beta Kappa, a freshman honors program, and 36 departmental honors programs. **Visiting:** There are regularly scheduled orientations for prospective students, including attending a class, a meeting with an admissions counselor and/or academic advisor, going on a campus tour, and attending information sessions. There are guides for informal visits and visitors may sit in on classes. To schedule a visit, contact the Student Visitation Program at (206) 543-5429. **Campus Safety and Security:** Measures include 24-hour foot and vehicle patrol, emergency notification system, self-defense education, and security escort services. There are shuttle buses, emergency telephones, and lighted pathways/sidewalks.

REQUIREMENTS: The SAT or ACT is required. The ACT Optional Writing test is also required. Applicants must have completed 15 academic units, including 4 years of English, 3 each of math and social sciences, 2 each of foreign language and science, and 1/2 year each in fine/visual performing arts and electives. Admission is based on a comprehensive review. AP credits are accepted. All students must maintain a GPA of 2.0 while taking 180 quarter credits, with 50 in the major. Distribution requirements include 40 credits from the humanities, social sciences, and math/natural sciences, with 12 credits in English composition/writing and a course in quantitative/symbolic reasoning. **Procedure:** Freshmen are admitted to all sessions. Entrance exams should be taken by December of the senior year. Applications should be filed by September 15 for winter entry; December 15 for spring entry; and January 15 for summer entry, along with a $50 fee. Notifications are sent March 15. 773 applicants were on the 2016 waiting list; 332 were admitted. Applications are accepted on-line. **Transfer Students:** 2709 transfer students enrolled in 2015-2016. The school gives priority to Washington community colleges students. Admission is based on a comprehensive review. 45 of 180 credits required for the bachelor's degree must be completed at UW. **International Students:** There are 1095 international students enrolled. They must take the TOEFL with a minimum score of 540 on the paper-based TOEFL (PBT) or 57 on the Internet-based version (iBT).

ADMISSIONS: 65% of the 2016-2017 applicants were accepted. The SAT scores for the 2016-2017 freshman class were: Critical Reading-- 16% below 500, 36% between 500 and 599, 36% between 600 and 699, and 12% between 700 and 800. Math-- 9% below 500, 32% between 500 and 599, 44% between 600 and 699, and 16% between 700 and 800. Writing-- 17% below 500, 42% between 500 and 599, 34% between 600 and 699, and 8% between 700 and 800. The ACT scores were 9% below 12, 16% between 12 and 17, 27% between 18 and 23, 20% between 24 and 29, and 28% above 30. 97% of the current freshmen were in the top fifth of their class; 99% were in the top two fifths. There were 39 National Merit finalists. **Admissions Contact:** Paul C Seegert, Office of Admissions. Web: *www.washington.edu*

FINANCIAL AID: The FAFSA code is 003798. The priority date for freshman financial aid applications for fall entry is February 28.

WALLA WALLA UNIVERSITY *(The complete profile is made available exclusively on our website, www.barronspac.com)*

WASHINGTON STATE UNIVERSITY — E-3

www.wsu.edu

Pullman, WA 99164	**(509) 335-5586** **(888) 468-6978**
Fax: (509) 335-4902	**Email: admissions@wsu.edu**
Full-time: 10,418 men, 11,234 women	**Faculty:** n/av
	Ph.D.s: 88%
Part-time: 1484 men, 1768 women	**Student/Faculty:** 16 to 1
Graduate: 2550 men, 2688 women	**Tuition:** $11,139 ($25,771)
Year: semesters, summer session	**Freshman Class:** 23223 applied, 16731 accepted, 4527 enrolled
Room & Board: $11,356	
SAT or ACT: required	**CEEB CODE:** 4705
Application Deadline: January 31	**COMPETITIVE**

Washington State University, founded in 1890 as a land-grant institution and is now a major public research university. It has locations statewide (Pullman, Spokane, Tri-Cities, Vancouver, and Everett) and an online Global Campus that reaches students around the world. WSU's undergraduate and graduate offerings span the liberal arts and sciences, business, communication, education, engineering and architecture, agricultural, human and natural resource sciences, and the health sciences, including nursing, pharmacy, and veterinary medicine. There are 11 undergraduate schools and 1 graduate school. In addition to regional accreditation, Washington State University has baccalaureate program accreditation with AACSB, ABET, ACCE, ACPE, ADA, NAAB, NASM, ACS, NASM, NASPAA, CAA, LAAB, AAHA, ASHA, AACP, APA, AVMA, PESB, AACN, AAALAC, NPSMA, APACA, CADE, CCNE, CIDA, ACEND, CAHME, AAVLD, NWCCU, and ASLA. The 620-acre campus is in a small town 75 miles south of Spokane, and 286 miles east of Seattle. Including any residence halls, there are 542 buildings.

STUDENT LIFE: 85% of undergraduates are from Washington. Others are from 49 states, 64 foreign countries, and Canada. 60% are White; 14% Hispanic; 7% two or more races; 6% Asian American; 6% Foreign; 3% African American; 3% race unknown; 1% American Indian/Alaska Native. **Female To Male Ratio:** 1.1:1. The average age of freshmen is 19; all undergraduates, 22. 21% do not continue beyond their first year; 67% remain to graduate. **Housing:** 7250 students can be accommodated in college housing, which includes single-sex and coed dorms, on-campus apartments, and married student housing. In addition, there are honors houses, language houses, special-interest houses, fraternity houses, sorority houses, living-learning communities, and first-year focus (freshmen students only). On-campus housing is guaranteed for the freshman year only. 76% of students commute. All students may keep cars.

FACULTY/CLASSROOMS: 56% of faculty are male; 44% are female. No introductory courses are taught by graduate students.

PROGRAMS OF STUDY: Washington State University confers B.A., B.S., B.F.A., B.L.A., and B.M. degrees. Master's and doctoral degrees are also awarded. Bachelor's degrees are awarded in AGRICULTURE (agricultural business management, agricultural communications, agricultural economics, agricultural mechanics, agricultural sciences, agriculture, agronomy, animal science, forestry and related sciences, horticulture, natural resource management, plant protection (pest management), plant science, range/farm management, soil science, viticulture and enology, turfgrass and landscape management, and wildlife management), BIOLOGICAL SCIENCE (biochemistry, biology/biological science, biotechnology, botany, cell biology, entomology, genetics, microbiology, neurosciences, plant genetics, plant pathology, wildlife biology, and zoology), BUSINESS (accounting, apparel and textiles, business administration and management, business economics, business law, business statistics, electronic business, entrepreneurial studies, finance, hospitality management services, hotel and restaurant administration, hotel/motel and restaurant management, human resources, insurance, international business, international business management, management information systems, management, marketing, marketing management, office supervision and management, operations management, real estate, and sports management), COMMUNICATIONS AND THE ARTS (advertising, art, broadcasting, Chinese, communications, digital communications, English, fine arts, French, German, Japanese, journalism, journalism - magazine journalism, journalism - news & information, journalism - newswriting/edit, linguistics, multimedia, music, music composition, music performance, music theory and composition, public relations, Russian, Spanish, communication arts - speech, strategic communication, and theatre arts), COMPUTER AND PHYSICAL SCIENCE (applied mathematics, chemistry, computer science, digital arts/technology, earth science, geology, mathematics, physical sciences, physics, science, and software engineering), EDUCATION (agricultural education, Asian studies, athletic training, bilingual/bicultural education, early childhood education, education, elementary education, English education, foreign languages education, global studies, music education, physical education, science education, secondary education, social studies education, and special education), ENGINEERING AND ENVIRONMENTAL DESIGN (agricultural engineering, agricultural engineering technology, architectural engineering, architecture, bioengineering, biomedical engineering, chemical engineering, civil engineering, computer engineering, construction management, electrical/electronics engineering, environmental science, industrial administration/management, industrial engineering technology, interior design, landscape architecture/design, manufacturing engineering, manufacturing technology, materials engineering, materials science, materials science and engineering, and mechanical engineering), HEALTH PROFESSIONS (biology, biomedical science, electrical engineering, exercise science, health and physical activity, nursing, predentistry, premedicine, preoptometry, prepharmacy, prephysical therapy, preveterinary science, and speech pathology/audiology), SOCIAL SCIENCE (American studies, anthropology, architectural studies, Chinese

Studies, clothing and textiles management/production/services, criminal justice, criminology, crosscultural studies, economics, ethnic studies, family/consumer studies, food science, history, human development, human development & family studies, humanities, humanities and social science, interdisciplinary studies, liberal arts/general studies, liberal arts, sciences, general studies, humanities, philosophy, political science/government, prelaw, psychology, public affairs, religion, religious studies, social science, social studies, social work, sociology, and women's studies). Veterinary medicine, nursing, communications, engineering, and crop & soil sciences are the strongest academically. Arts and sciences, business, and engineering have the largest enrollments.

ACTIVITIES: 19% of men belong to 24 national fraternities; 21% of women belong to 14 national sororities. There are 350 groups on campus, including art, band, cheerleading, choir, chorale, chorus, computers, dance, debate, drama, environmental, ethnic, film, honors, international, jazz band, LGBT, literary magazine, marching band, musical theater, newspaper, opera, orchestra, pep band, photography, political, professional, radio and TV, religious, social, social service, student government, symphony, and yearbook. Popular campus events include Convocation, Showcase, All-Campus Picnic, Cougfest, Week of Welcome, Mom's Weekend, Dad's Weekend, Springfest, Homecoming, and Civic Engagement Week. **Sports:** There are 6 intercollegiate sports for men and 9 for women, and 55 intramural sports for men and 55 for women. Facilities include a stadium, coliseum, 200-meter NCAA indoor and outdoor tracks, tennis courts, a student recreation center, an 18-hole golf course, an indoor practice facility with roll-out turf system, baseball and soccer fields, indoor swimming pools, racquetball and squash courts, a climbing wall, ballrooms, gyms, an indoor rowing facility, an outdoor recreation center, basketball courts, sand volleyball courts, and intramural playing fields. **Graduates:** From July 1, 2015 to June 30, 2016, 5475 bachelor's degrees were awarded. The most popular majors were business/marketing (20%), social sciences (12%), and engineering (11%). 250 companies recruited on campus in 2015-2016. In an average class, 41% graduate in 4 years or less, 62% graduate in 5 years or less, and 67% graduate in 6 years or less.

SERVICES: Counseling and information services are available, as is tutoring in most subjects, such as accounting, anatomy and physiology, biology, chemistry, computer science, engineering, finance, math through calculus, Microsoft Office, physics, Spanish, statistics, writing, sciences, social sciences. There is a reader service for the blind, and remedial math. Academic Success and Career Center offers learning assistance through tutoring and workshops that address study skills, note taking, test preparation, time management, reading strategies, career/major choice, stress management, life skills, peer tutoring, and career services. WSU is also a member of the Northwest eTutoring Consortium which offers unlimited FREE online tutoring to all WSU students. **Library/Resources:** The 3 libraries contain 2.4 million volumes, 4.0 million microform items, 41,674 audio/video tapes/CDs/DVDs, and subscribe to 133,691 periodicals including electronic. Computerized library services include interlibrary loans, database searching, Internet access, and Wi-Fi capability. Special learning facilities include an art gallery, natural history museum, planetarium, radio station, TV station, museums, displays and collections, including a natural history museum, museum of art, museum of anthropology, an entomological collection, a veterinary anatomy teaching museum, and geology museums. radio and TV stations, digital recording studio, music listening library, fine arts studio with specialized equipment. The Cultural center, and the International center are for exchanging cultural knowledge. There are labs for child development, and financial markets (trading room), food sensory evaluation, and culinary and teaching kitchen. The social and economic sciences research center includes the planetarium and astronomical observatory. There are specialized teaching and research labs for science and engineering, including a bio-molecular x-ray crystallography center, a genomics and gene sequencing lab, a virtual reality computer-integrated manufacturing lab, a hydraulics lab, laboratory for atmospheric research, a wildlife center, ecological reserves, greenhouses, vivaria and herbaria, agronomic research farms, a horticultural orchard, and an organic teaching farm and apiary. The livestock center has labs, and barns, including beef and dairy centers, a cattle-feeding lab, a feed plant, a market for locally grown, alumni-grown, and organic produce. There is also a veterinary teaching hospital, a human anatomy lab, a water research center, and a nuclear radiation center. **Physically Challenged Students:** Facilities include wheelchair ramps, elevators, special parking, specially equipped restrooms, special class scheduling, lowered drinking fountains, lowered telephones, and special housing. **Special:** Undergraduates can become involved in faculty research, internships, over 1,500 study-abroad programs in more than 80 countries, an Honors College, academic club projects and competitions, civic engagement projects, work-study programs, and co-op programs in numerous majors. Dual majors are available, as are B.A.-B.S. degrees in computer science and psychology and student-designed majors in general studies. Interior design and veterinary medicine programs offer accelerated pathways to advanced degrees. Credit may be granted for military service, and non-degree and pass/fail options are offered. Some academic programs are offered in partnership with the Universities of Idaho and Washington, Eastern Washington University, and Wenatchee Valley College. Students can register for jointly offered courses either at WSU or at one of the other participating universities. There are 10 national honor societies, a chapter of Phi Beta Kappa, and a freshman honors program. **Visiting:** There are regularly scheduled orientations for prospective students, consisting of a campus tour and a presentation about admissions, financial aid, and scholarship opportunities. There are guides for informal visits and visitors may sit in on classes. **Campus Safety and Security:** Measures include 24-hour foot and vehicle patrol, emergency notification system, self-defense education, and security escort services. There are shuttle buses, emergency telephones, lighted pathways/sidewalks, controlled access to dorms/residences, Campus Safety Plan (contains list of university policies, procedures, statistics, and information related to campus safety), campus outdoor warning system (COWS), alert crisis communication system (WSU Alert), the alert email listserve and website, crime prevention and personal safety education, monitored lighting levels on campus, a women's transit service, residence hall security hours; campus police department with a police intern program, and housing patrols.

REQUIREMENTS: The SAT or ACT is required. Students should be high school graduates or will be by the time they enroll at the University. Courses to be completed while in high school: 4 credits of English, 3 credits each of math (1 credit each of algebra, geometry, and algebra II) and social science, 2 credits each of the same world language (includes Native American languages and American Sign Language) and lab science including one that is algebra-based, and 1 year of fine, visual, or performing arts, or elective from any of the other required subjects. A combination of the high school GPA and test scores is considered. Homeschool applicants welcomed. The GED is also accepted. (1 credit equals 1 year). A GPA of 2.0 is required. AP and CLEP credits are accepted. Important factors in the admissions decision are advanced placement or honors courses. Students must complete 120 semester credits, with fulfillment of a major, 40 credits of upper-division work, 30 credits in residence, and maintain a minimum GPA of 2.0. General university requirements include 7 credits of science, 9 of arts and humanities and social sciences, 3 of global issues, 6 of writing and communication, 3 of math, 3 of diversity, and 3 of an integrative capstone. Students must complete a writing portfolio and pass a writing qualifying exam prior to graduation. **Procedure:** Freshmen are admitted in the fall, spring, and summer. Entrance exams should be taken during spring of the junior year or fall of the senior year. Applications should be filed by January 31 for fall entry; November 15 for spring entry, along with a $50 fee. Notifications are sent November 1. Applications are accepted on-line. Application fees are waived if application is completed on-line. **Transfer Students:** 2697 transfer students enrolled in 2015-2016. Admission to WSU is offered to qualified students on a first-come, first-served basis. Applications completed by the priority application date of January 31 will receive first consideration. Applicants who have less than a full year of college credit to transfer may be asked to submit a high school transcript (or G.E.D.) and test scores (SAT or ACT). Transcripts and test scores must be sent directly from the school or testing agency to WSU via secure electronic document transfer, fax, or mail. Email is not accepted. 30 of 120 credits required for the bachelor's degree must be completed at Washington State University. **International Students:** There are 956 international students enrolled. The school actively recruits these students. They must take the TOEFL with a minimum score of 550 on the paper-based TOEFL (PBT) or 79 on the Internet-based version (iBT) or take the MELAB, IELTS, or IB with a passing score in English, or SAT with a 500 critical reading subscore.

Admissions Contact: Wendy Peterson, Director of Admissions. Email: *admissions@wsu.edu* Web: *www.wsu.edu*

FINANCIAL AID: The average financial indebtedness of the 2016 graduate was $22,924. The college's own financial statement and WSU Scholarship Application are required. The FAFSA code is 003800. The priority date for freshman financial aid applications for fall entry is January 31.

WESTERN WASHINGTON UNIVERSITY C-1

www.wwu.edu

Bellingham, WA 98225 **(360) 650-3966**

Email: admit@wwu.edu

Full-time: 5794 men, 7619 women
Part-time: 599 men, 580 women
Graduate: 365 men, 617 women
Year: quarters, summer session
Room & Board: $10,350

SAT CR/M/W: 560/550/530 **ACT:** 25
Application Deadline: January 31

Faculty: 619; IIA, +$
Ph.D.s: 87%
Student/Faculty: 22 to 1
Tuition: $7653 ($21,567)
Freshman Class: 10517 applied, 8742 accepted, 2888 enrolled
CEEB CODE: 4947
COMPETITIVE+

Western Washington University, founded in 1893, is a nonprofit, public institution whose emphasis is on the liberal arts and sciences, business and business administration, economics, art, fine arts, performing arts, music, teacher preparation, interdisciplinary learning, and environmental studies. There are 7 undergraduate schools and 1 graduate school. In addition to regional accreditation, WWU has baccalaureate program accreditation with AACSB, ABET, ASLA, NASM, NCATE, and NRPA. The 195-acre campus is in a small town 60 miles south of Vancouver, British Columbia, and 90 miles north of Seattle. Including any residence halls, there are 80 buildings.

STUDENT LIFE: 90% of undergraduates are from Washington. Others are from 50 states, 37 foreign countries, and Canada. 89% are from public schools. 72% are White; 8% Hispanic; 8% two or more races; 6% Asian American; 2% African American; 1% American Indian/Alaska Native; 1% Foreign; 1% race unknown. **Female To Male Ratio:** 1.3:1. The average age of freshmen is 18; all undergraduates, 21. 17% do not continue beyond their first year; 73% remain to graduate. **Housing:** 4050 students can be accommodated in college housing, which includes coed dorms, on-campus apartments, off-campus apartments, and married student housing. In addition, there are honors houses, special-interest houses, fitness/wellness hall, freshman interest groups, substance-free living, gender inclusive, quiet and smoke-free areas. On-campus housing is available on a first-come, first-served basis. 73% of students commute. All students may keep cars.

FACULTY/CLASSROOMS: 50% of faculty are male; 50% are female. All teach undergraduates. Graduate students teach 1% of introductory courses. The average class size in an introductory lecture is 49; in a laboratory is 22; and in a regular course is 29.

PROGRAMS OF STUDY: WWU confers B.A., B.S., B.A.E., B.F.A., B.S.N., and B.Mus. degrees. Master's degrees are also awarded. Bachelor's degrees are awarded in AGRICULTURE (environmental studies), BIOLOGICAL SCIENCE (biochemistry, biology/biological science, cell biology, ecology, life science, marine biology, marine science, and molecular biology), BUSINESS (accounting, business administration and management, fashion merchandising, human resources, international business management, international economics, management information systems, management science, marketing/retailing/merchandising, and operations management), COMMUNICATIONS AND THE ARTS (apparel design, Arabic, art, ceramic art and design, classics, communications, creative writing, dance, design, dramatic arts, English, fine arts, French, German, Japanese, journalism, linguistics, multimedia, music, music history and appreciation, painting, photography, Russian, sculpture, Spanish, theatre arts, theater design, and visual and performing arts), COMPUTER AND PHYSICAL SCIENCE (applied mathematics, applied physics, chemistry, computer science, earth science, geology, mathematics, physics, and polymer science), EDUCATION (art education, early childhood education, education administration, elementary education, foreign languages education, health education, music education, nursing education, physical education, reading education, recreation education, science education, secondary education, special education, and technical education), ENGINEERING AND ENVIRONMENTAL DESIGN (electrical/electronics engineering, electrical/electronics engineering technology, engineering technology, environmental science, industrial engineering technology, manufacturing technology, mechanical design technology, mechanical engineering technology, plastics engineering, and technology and public affairs), HEALTH PROFESSIONS (nursing, rehabilitation therapy, and speech pathology/audiology), SOCIAL SCIENCE (American studies, anthropology, behavioral science, Canadian studies, child psychology/development, East Asian studies, economics, geography, history, human services, interdisciplinary studies, international studies, liberal arts/general studies, parks and recreation management, philosophy, political science/government, psychology, public affairs, social studies, sociology, women & gender studies, and women's studies). Industrial technology, materials science, and vehicle research institute are the strongest academically. Health & human development, English, and psychology have the largest enrollments.

ACTIVITIES: There are no fraternities or sororities. There are 225 groups on campus, including art, band, cheerleading, chess, choir, chorale, chorus, computers, dance, debate, drama, environmental, ethnic, film, forensics, honors, international, jazz band, LGBT, literary magazine, musical theater, newspaper, opera, orchestra, pep band, photography, political, professional, religious, social, social service, student government, and symphony. **Sports:** There are 6 intercollegiate sports for men and 9 for women, and 13 intramural sports for men and 13 for women. Facilities include a center with pool, rock wall, weight and fitness equipment, basketball courts, multi-activity court, a soccer practice field, track, and softball complex. **Graduates:** From July 1, 2015 to June 30, 2016, 3335 bachelor's degrees were awarded. The most popular majors were business and marketing (13%), social sciences (11%), and interdisciplinary studies (7%). 379 companies recruited on campus in 2015-2016. In an average class, 40% graduate in 4 years or less, 65% graduate in 5 years or less, and 70% graduate in 6 years or less. Of the 2015 graduating class, 10% were enrolled in graduate school within 6 months of graduation, and 83% were employed.

SERVICES: Counseling and information services are available, as is tutoring in most subjects, such as English, humanities, social sciences, math and natural sciences. There is a reader service for the blind. **Library/Resources:** The 2 libraries contain 1.3 million volumes, 106,265 microform items, and 42,503 audio/video tapes/CDs/DVDs, and subscribe to 76,701 periodicals including electronic. Computerized library services include interlibrary loans, database searching, Internet access, and Wi-Fi capability. Special learning facilities include an art gallery, planetarium, a marine lab, neutron generator lab, motor vehicle research lab, a wind tunnel, air pollution lab, an electronic music studio, and performing arts center. **Physically Challenged Students:** All of the campus is accessible. Facilities include wheelchair ramps, elevators, special parking, specially equipped restrooms, special class scheduling, lowered drinking fountains, and lowered telephones. Transcription services available upon request. **Special:** Special academic programs include internships through various academic departments and study abroad in 75 countries. Dual majors are available through various departments. There is a general studies degree and a B.A. in humanities. WWU offers degrees in electrical engineering, manufacturing engineering, and plastics and composites engineering. Student-designed majors are offered through the liberal studies department in the College of Arts and Sciences and through Fairhaven College, which affords an unusual degree of student involvement in the structure and content of their own programs and which uses faculty narrative for students' academic evaluations. In addition, Huxley College of Environmental Studies provides specialized education and research. Up to 30 credits of electives may be granted for military service, and nondegree study and pass/fail options are possible. There is a freshman honors program. **Visiting:** There are regularly scheduled orientations for prospective students; student visits include tours, class visits and advisement. There are guides for informal visits, visitors stay overnight. To schedule a visit, contact Brent Bode at (360) 650-3861. **Campus Safety and Security:** Measures include 24-hour foot and vehicle patrol, emergency notification system, self-defense education, and security escort services. There are shuttle buses, emergency telephones, and lighted pathways/sidewalks.

REQUIREMENTS: The SAT or ACT is required. Other admissions requirements include completion of 16 academic units, including 4 years of college preparatory English composition and literature courses; 3 units of college preparatory math, including 2 years of algebra; 3 units of social studies/history; 2 units of science, including 1 lab science & 1 algebra-based science course; 2 units of the same foreign language; 1 unit of fine and performing arts; and 1 unit in another academic field. The GED is accepted for admission. Other factors taken into consideration include curricular rigor (level of difficulty of courses), grade trends, leadership, community involvement, special talent, multicultural experience, and personal hardship or circumstances. A GPA of 2.5 is required. AP credits are accepted. Important factors in the admissions decision are advanced placement or honors courses, leadership record, and personality/intangible qualities. Students must complete at least 180 quarter hours, with fulfillment of a major and at least 60 credits in upper-division study, and maintain at least a 2.0 GPA or that prescribed by departments/divisions. General university requirements include 70 to 75 credits, and students must satisfy writing proficiency requirements as well. Fairhaven College has a separate interdisciplinary core program. **Procedure:** Freshmen are admitted fall, winter, and spring. Entrance exams should be taken by fall of the senior year. There are early admissions, deferred admissions, and rolling admissions plans. Applications should be filed by January 31 for fall entry; October 1 for winter entry; and January 15 for spring entry. The fall 2016 application fee was $55. Notifications are sent March 15. 319 applicants were on the 2016 waiting list; 205 were admitted. Applications are accepted on-line. Application fees are waived if application is completed on-line. **Transfer Students:** 1702 transfer students enrolled in 2015-2016. Minimum requirements for transfer admission include a 2.0 cumulative transferable GPA and a 2.0 in the quarters prior to application review and enrollment. Applicants with fewer than 45 completed transferable quarter credits also must meet freshman admission standards. Meeting minimum requirements is not a guarantee for admission, as the number of qualified applicants exceeds the number of available enrollment spaces. 45 of 180 credits required for the bachelor's degree must be completed at WWU. **International Students:** There are 163 international students enrolled. They must take the TOEFL with a minimum score of 550 on the paper-based TOEFL (PBT) or 80 on the Internet-based version (iBT). They must also take the SAT or ACT.

ADMISSIONS: 83% of the 2016-2017 applicants were accepted. The SAT scores for the 2016-2017 freshman class were: Critical Reading-- 23% below 500, 41% between 500 and 599, 29% between 600 and 699, and 7% between 700 and 800. Math-- 25% below 500, 47% between 500 and 599, 24% between 600 and 699, and 4% between 700 and 800. Writing-- 34% below 500, 44% between 500 and 599, 19% between 600 and 699, and 2% between 700 and 800. The ACT scores were 3% between 12 and 17, 31% between 18 and 23, 52% between 24 and 29, and 14% above 30. 45% of the current freshmen were in the top fifth of their class; 77% were in the top two fifths. There were 4 National Merit finalists. 47 freshmen graduated first in their class. **Admissions Contact:** Jeanne Gaffney, Assoicate Director of Admissions. Email: *admit@wwu.edu* Web: *www.wwu.edu*

FINANCIAL AID: 53% of all full-time freshmen and 48% of continuing full-time students received need-based aid. The average freshman award was $14,384. Need-based scholarships or need-based grants averaged $9,297; need-based self-help aid (loans and jobs) averaged $4,361; non-need-based athletic scholarships averaged $6,054; and other non-need-based awards and non-need-based scholarships averaged $2,141. The average financial indebtedness of the 2016 graduate was $20,603. The deadline for filing freshman financial aid applications for fall entry is February 15.

WHITMAN COLLEGE — E-3

www.whitman.edu

Walla Walla, WA 99362 — (509) 527-5176, (877) 462-9448

Fax: (509) 527-4967 — **Email:** admission@whitman.edu

Full-time: 636 men, 857 women	**Faculty:** 165; IIB, +$
Part-time: 14 men, 26 women	**Ph.D.s:** 95%
Graduate: n/av	**Student/Faculty:** 8 to 1
Year: semesters	**Tuition:** $47,862
Room & Board: $11,910	**Freshman Class:** 3931 applied, 1979 accepted, 425 enrolled
SAT CR/M/W: 650/650/650 **ACT:** 30	**CEEB CODE:** 4951
Application Deadline: January 15	**MOST COMPETITIVE**

Whitman College, founded in 1883, is a nonprofit, private, independent, residential liberal arts and sciences college. There is 1 undergraduate school. In addition to regional accreditation, Whitman has baccalaureate program accreditation with ACS. The 117-acre campus is in a small town 150 miles south of Spokane, 260 miles southeast of Seattle, and 235 miles east of Portland. Including any residence halls, there are 41 buildings.

STUDENT LIFE: 65% of undergraduates are from out of state, mostly the Northwest. Students are from 47 states, 26 foreign countries, and Canada. 71% are White; 7% Hispanic; 7% two or more races; 6% Foreign; 5% Asian American; 3% race unknown; 1% African American. **Female To Male Ratio:** 1.4:1. The average age of freshmen is 18; all undergraduates, 20. 6% do not continue beyond their first year; 87% remain to graduate. **Housing:** 857 students can be accommodated in college housing, which includes single-sex and coed dorms and off-campus apartments. In addition, there are language houses, special-interest houses, and fraternity houses. On-campus housing is guaranteed for the freshman year only and is available on a lottery system for upperclassmen. All students may keep cars.

FACULTY/CLASSROOMS: 51% of faculty are male; 49% are female. All teach undergraduates, and all do research. No introductory courses are taught by graduate students. The average class size in an introductory lecture is 22; in a laboratory is 19; and in a regular course is 17.

PROGRAMS OF STUDY: Whitman confers B.A. degrees. Bachelor's degrees are awarded in AGRICULTURE (environmental studies and forestry and related sciences), BIOLOGICAL SCIENCE (biochemistry, biophysics, and molecular biology), COMMUNICATIONS AND THE ARTS (art history, art, classics, communication rhetoric/communication, English, French, Greek (classical), jazz, Latin, film and media studies, music, music composition, music history and appreciation, music performance, music theory and composition, Spanish, speech/debate/rhetoric, and theatre arts), COMPUTER AND PHYSICAL SCIENCE (astronomy, astrophysics, chemistry, computer mathematics, geology, mathematics, mathematics – economics, oceanography, physics and mathematics, and physics), ENGINEERING AND ENVIRONMENTAL DESIGN (environmental science and preengineering), HEALTH PROFESSIONS (biology), SOCIAL SCIENCE (anthropology, Asian/Oriental studies, economics, ethnic studies, gender studies, German area studies, history, international studies, philosophy, political science/government, prelaw, psychology, religion, and sociology). Biology, psychology, and economics have the largest enrollments.

ACTIVITIES: 39% of men belong to 4 national fraternities; 43% of women belong to 4 national sororities. There are 55 groups on campus, including art, chess, choir, chorale, chorus, dance, drama, environmental, ethnic, film, forensics, honors, international, jazz band, LGBT, literary magazine, musical theater, newspaper, opera, orchestra, photography, political, professional, radio and TV, religious, social, social service, student government, symphony, and yearbook. Popular campus events include Renaissance Fair, Choral Contest, Mr. Whitman, Arts & Crafts Fair, and Interest House Block Party. **Sports:** There are 7 intercollegiate sports for men and 8 for women, and 14 intramural sports for men and 13 for women. Facilities include a stadium, 2 gyms, squash and handball courts, saunas, climbing walls, and an aerobic/dance room. There is an athletics center with a 10,000-square-foot weights/cardiovascular area, 8-lane swimming pool, 6 outdoor tennis courts, 4 indoor tennis courts, soccer field, dance studio, soccer, baseball, and track facilities. **Graduates:** From July 1, 2015 to June 30, 2016, 367 bachelor's degrees were awarded. The most popular majors were psychology (11%), biology (10%), biochemistry, and biophysics and molecular biology (9%). In an average class, 80% graduate in 4 years or less and 87% graduate in 5 years or less. Of the 2015 graduating class, 60% were enrolled in graduate school within 6 months of graduation.

SERVICES: Counseling and information services are available, as is tutoring in most subjects. There is a reader service for the blind. The Academic Resource Center and Learning Commons provides tutoring, academic assistance, and workshops in study skills and writing. Department tutors are also available for students. **Library/Resources:** The library contains 627,812 volumes, and 32,433 audio/video tapes/CDs/DVDs, and subscribes to 98,012 periodicals including electronic. Computerized library services include interlibrary loans, database searching, Internet access, and Wi-Fi capability. Special learning facilities include an art gallery, natural history museum, planetarium, radio station, an electron microscope lab, an off-campus wilderness campus, a multimedia development lab, an off-campus observatory and on-campus astronomical telescopes, an Asian art collection, a video-conferencing center, an outdoor sculpture walk, an organic garden, indoor and outdoor rock climbing walls, and Penrose Library and Welty Student Health Center are open 24/7. **Physically Challenged Students:** 96% of the campus is accessible. Facilities include wheelchair ramps, elevators, special parking, specially equipped restrooms, lowered drinking fountains, and lowered telephones and any modifications necessary for specific cases will be made. **Special:** Special academic programs include more than 500 internships, over 80 semester or year-long study abroad programs in 40 countries, a Washington semester, and study programs in Chicago and

Philadelphia. Dual majors are available in any area, and student-designed majors are offered. There is a 3-2 environmental management and forestry program with Duke University and a 3-2 engineering program with Washington University in St. Louis, California Institute of Technology and Applied Science, Columbia and Duke Universities, and University of Washington. A 3-3 law program is offered through Columbia University. A 4-1 education program is available through Bank Street College of Education and University of Puget Sound Cooperative. Certification is offered for elementary and secondary education. A pass-D-fail option is available. A 3-2 program in international studies is available with the Monterey Institute of International Studies. A 3-2 program in oceanography is available with University of Washington. There are 3 national honor societies, Phi Beta Kappa, and a freshman honors program. **Visiting:** There are regularly scheduled orientations for prospective students. The agenda for visits are catered to each individual student and their interests. There are guides for informal visits, visitors may sit in on classes, and stay overnight. To schedule a visit, contact Mary Beth Ehrhardt at (509) 527-5176. **Campus Safety and Security:** Measures include 24-hour foot and vehicle patrol, emergency notification system, self-defense education, and security escort services. There are emergency telephones, lighted pathways/sidewalks, and controlled access to dorms/residences.

REQUIREMENTS: Whitman is test-optional, meaning that most applicants are not required to submit ACT or SAT scores as part of the admission process. We encourage applicants to decide for themselves whether they wish to submit ACT or SAT results as an additional measure of their academic preparedness. The GED is accepted. 3 essays must be submitted, and an interview is recommended. Credit by challenge examination is accepted. AP credits are accepted. Important factors in the admissions decision are advanced placement or honors courses, personality/intangible qualities, evidence of special talent, recommendations by alumni, recommendations by school officials, and extracurricular activities record. Students must complete 124 credits, with 32 to 36 in the major, and maintain a minimum GPA of 2.0. Distribution requirements include a minimum of 6 credits in social sciences, humanities, fine arts, and science (including 1 course with a lab), 1 course of 3 or more credits in quantitative analysis, and 2 courses that fulfill the alternative voices requirement. Freshman must take the year-long Encounters (great works) course. All majors require an oral exam as well as a thesis project or comprehensive written exam. **Procedure:** Freshmen are admitted fall. Entrance exams should be taken by fall of the senior year. There are early decision and deferred admissions plans. Early decision applications should be filed by November 15; regular applications, by January 15 for fall entry, along with a $50 fee. Notification of early decision is sent December 20; regular decision, April 1. 123 early decision candidates were accepted for the 2016-2017 class. 872 applicants were on the 2016 waiting list; 67 were admitted. Applications are accepted on-line. Application fees are waived if application is completed on-line. **Transfer Students:** 21 transfer students enrolled in 2015-2016. Transfer applicants must submit the common application, a transfer supplement, a school report completed by the applicant's secondary school counselor, an academic recommendation from a high school teacher or college instructor, a statement of good standing from prior institutions, their official high school and college transcripts, and the application fee. SAT or ACT scores are optional. 54 of 124 credits required for the bachelor's degree must be completed at Whitman. **International Students:** There are 86 international students enrolled. The school actively recruits these students. They must take the TOEFL with a minimum score of 560 on the paper-based TOEFL (PBT) or 85 on the Internet-based version (iBT).

ADMISSIONS: 50% of the 2016-2017 applicants were accepted. The SAT scores for the 2016-2017 freshman class were: Critical Reading-- 4% below 500, 19% between 500 and 599, 44% between 600 and 699, and 34% between 700 and 800. Math-- 2% below 500, 19% between 500 and 599, 53% between 600 and 699, and 25% between 700 and 800. Writing-- 1% below 500, 23% between 500 and 599, 48% between 600 and 699, and 28% between 700 and 800. The ACT scores were 3% between 18 and 23, 40% between 24 and 29, and 57% above 30. 80% of the current freshmen were in the top fifth of their class; 96% were in the top two fifths. 25 freshmen graduated first in their class. **Admissions Contact:** Tony Cabasco, Dean of Admission and Financial Aid. Email: *admission@whitman.edu* Web: *www.whitman.edu*

FINANCIAL AID: In 2016-2017, 74% of all full-time freshmen and 74% of continuing full-time students received some form of financial aid. 42% of all full-time freshmen and 42% of continuing full-time students received need-based aid. The average freshman award was $32,500. Need-based scholarships or need-based grants averaged $29,148 ($59,050 maximum); need-based self-help aid (loans and jobs) averaged $7,819 ($9,000 maximum); and other non-need-based awards and non-need-based scholarships averaged $13,960 ($19,000 maximum). The average financial indebtedness of the 2016 graduate was $18,444. Whitman is a member of CSS. The CSS/Profile is required. The FAFSA code is 003803. The priority date for freshman financial aid applications for fall entry is November 15. The deadline for filing freshman financial aid applications for fall entry is January 15.

WHITWORTH UNIVERSITY — E-2

www.whitworth.edu

Spokane, WA 99251	(509) 777-4348 (800) 533-4668
Fax: (509) 777-3758	Email: admission@whitworth.edu
Full-time: 906 men, 1352 women	**Faculty:** 180; IIB, -$
Part-time: 21 men, 29 women	**Ph.D.s:** 88%
Graduate: 115 men, 244 women	**Student/Faculty:** 11 to 1
Year: 4-1-4, summer session	**Tuition:** $40,562
Room & Board: $11,170	**Freshman Class:** 3262 applied, 2889 accepted, 595 enrolled
SAT CR/M/W: 570/560/560 **ACT:** 26	**CEEB CODE:** 4953
Application Deadline: March 1	**VERY COMPETITIVE**

Whitworth University, founded in 1890, is an independent, comprehensive institution affiliated with the Presbyterian Church. The emphasis of its undergraduate and graduate programs is on the liberal arts, business, art and fine arts, music, religious studies, and teacher preparation. There are 4 undergraduate schools and 3 graduate schools. In addition to regional accreditation, Whitworth has baccalaureate program accreditation with NASM, NCATE, NLN, Washington State Board of Nursing, CCNE, CAATE, and PESB for teaching. The 200-acre campus is in a suburban area in a residential area 7 miles north of downtown Spokane. Including any residence halls, there are 40 buildings.

STUDENT LIFE: 70% of undergraduates are from Washington. Others are from 33 states, 41 foreign countries, and Canada. 88% are from public schools. 72% are White; 9% Hispanic; 7% two or more races; 5% Asian American; 3% Foreign; 2% African American; 1% American Indian/Alaska Native; 1% race unknown. 64% are Protestant; 20% claim no religious affiliation. **Female To Male Ratio:** 1.6:1. The average age of freshmen is 18; all undergraduates, 20. 15% do not continue beyond their first year; 73% remain to graduate. **Housing:** 1365 students can be accommodated in college housing, which includes single-sex and coed dorms. In addition, there are special-interest houses, and theme houses. On-campus housing is guaranteed for all 4 years. 56% of students live on campus; of those, 90% remain on campus on weekends. Alcohol is not permitted. All students may keep cars.

FACULTY/CLASSROOMS: 60% of faculty are male; 40% are female. All teach undergraduates. No introductory courses are taught by graduate students. The average class size in an introductory lecture is 30; in a laboratory is 15; and in a regular course is 19.

PROGRAMS OF STUDY: Whitworth confers B.A., B.B.A., and B.S. degrees. Master's degrees are also awarded. Bachelor's degrees are awarded in BIOLOGICAL SCIENCE (bioinformatics, biology/biological science, and biophysics), BUSINESS (accounting, business administration and management, international business management, and marketing management), COMMUNICATIONS AND THE ARTS (art, communications, dramatic arts, English, French, journalism, music, Spanish, speech/debate/rhetoric, theatre arts, and visual design), COMPUTER AND PHYSICAL SCIENCE (applied physics, chemistry, computer science, mathematics, mathematics – economics, physics, and quantitative methods), EDUCATION (athletic training, elementary education, English education, foreign languages education, mathematics education, music education, science education, secondary education, and social studies education), ENGINEERING AND ENVIRONMENTAL DESIGN (engineering and engineering physics), HEALTH PROFESSIONS (community health work, health science, nursing, predentistry, and premedicine), SOCIAL SCIENCE (American studies, crosscultural studies, economics, history, international studies, peace studies, philosophy, political science/government, prelaw, psychology, sociology, theological studies, and women's studies). Sciences, education, and music are the strongest academically. Health sciences, business, and math & computer science have the largest enrollments.

ACTIVITIES: There are no fraternities or sororities. There are 45 groups on campus, including art, band, cheerleading, choir, chorale, chorus, communications, computers, dance, debate, drama, environmental, ethnic, forensics, honors, international, jazz band, literary magazine, musical theater, newspaper, orchestra, photography, political, professional, radio and TV, religious, social, social service, student government, symphony, and yearbook. Popular campus events include Guest Speakers, Student Research Conference, and Community Building Day. **Sports:** There are 10 intercollegiate sports for men and 10 for women, and 10 intramural sports for men and 8 for women. Facilities include a university recreation center complete with climbing walls, a 2000-seat stadium, 1200-seat gym, field house, an aquatic center, and playing fields. **Graduates:** From July 1, 2015 to June 30, 2016, 644 bachelor's degrees were awarded. The most popular majors were Business/Marketing (14%), Social Sciences (10%), and Physical Sciences (8%). 166 companies recruited on campus in 2015-2016. In an average class, 6% graduate in 3 years or less, 68% graduate in 4 years or less, and 74% graduate in 5 years or less. Of the 2015 graduating class, 27% were enrolled in graduate school within 6 months of graduation, and 86% were employed.

SERVICES: Counseling and information services are available, as is tutoring in most subjects, such as biology, chemistry, computer science, French, German, Spanish, math, physics, and writing. **Library/Resources:** The library contains 292,113 volumes, 1,112 microform items, and 9,412 audio/video tapes/CDs/DVDs, and subscribes to 36,517 periodicals including electronic. Computerized library services include interlibrary loans, database searching, Internet access, and Wi-Fi capability. Special learning facilities include an art gallery, radio station, and a writing center. **Physically Challenged Students:** 80% of the campus is accessible. Facilities include wheelchair ramps, elevators, special parking, specially equipped restrooms, special class scheduling, lowered drinking fountains, and lowered telephones. **Special:** Special academic programs include many work-study opportunities, and 1 to 3 internship course credits. Study abroad is available in many countries. Accelerated degree programs are possible, as is a 3-2 engineering degree, and students may choose to specialize in an area of concentration in lieu of a major. Credit may be granted for life, military, or work experience. Nondegree study is possible for those auditing or in seminars, and there is 1 pass/fail option allowed per year. A special feature of the school is the 4-1-1 semester calendar, which affords unusual opportunities for internships, study tours, and other activities during Janterm. There is a freshman honors program. **Visiting:** There are regularly scheduled orientations for prospective students. A visit includes an admissions/financial aid presentation, campus tour, class visit(s), student panel, lunch in the dining hall and overnight stay (if desired). There are guides for informal visits. To schedule a visit, contact Megan Thompson. **Campus Safety and Security:** Measures include 24-hour foot and vehicle patrol, emergency notification system, and security escort services. There are emergency telephones, lighted pathways/sidewalks, and controlled access to dorms/residences.

REQUIREMENTS: The SAT or ACT is recommended. Whitworth recommends a rigorous college-preparatory high school curriculum and also considers, in the admissions review process, participation in extracurricular, service, and leadership activities, a writing sample included in the application, and counselor/teacher recommendations. Students have the option of submitting either SAT or ACT scores (no preference) or, if they have a weighted GPA of 3.0 or higher, can choose to do an admissions interview instead of submitting test scores. AP and CLEP credits are accepted. Important factors in the admissions decision are advanced placement or honors courses, recommendations by alumni, and extracurricular activities record. Students must complete 126 credit hours, with about 45 in the major, and maintain a GPA of at least 2.0. The curriculum includes 3 core courses on religious, rationalist, and scientific traditions. Distribution requirements are comprised of 3 phys ed activity courses, 2 each in a foreign language and science/math, and 1 course each in biblical literature, oral communication, fine arts, social science, and humanities. Additionally, global perspectives and an American diversity course must be fulfilled. **Procedure:** Freshmen are admitted fall, winter, and spring. Entrance exams should be taken by fall of senior year is best, but scores accepted later. There are early admissions, deferred admissions, and rolling admissions plans. Applications should be filed by March 1 for fall entry. Notifications are sent March 15. Applications are accepted on-line. Application fees are waived if application is completed on-line. **Transfer Students:** 94 transfer students enrolled in 2015-2016. Transfer students must have a GPA of at least 2.75. 32 of 126 credits required for the bachelor's degree must be completed at Whitworth. **International Students:** There are 80 international students enrolled. The school actively recruits these students. They must take the TOEFL with a minimum score of 79 on the Internet-based version (iBT).

ADMISSIONS: 89% of the 2016-2017 applicants were accepted. The SAT scores for the 2016-2017 freshman class were: Critical Reading-- 25% below 500, 34% between 500 and 599, 30% between 600 and 699, and 11% between 700 and 800. Math-- 23% below 500, 44% between 500 and 599, 28% between 600 and 699, and 5% between 700 and 800. Writing-- 29% below 500, 37% between 500 and 599, 27% between 600 and 699, and 7% between 700 and 800. The ACT scores were 6% between 12 and 17, 28% between 18 and 23, 46% between 24 and 29, and 20% above 30. 49% of the current freshmen were in the top fifth of their class; 85% were in the top two fifths. **Admissions Contact:** Greg Orwig, Vice President, Admissions and Financial Aid. Email: *admission@whitworth.edu* Web: *www.whitworth.edu*

FINANCIAL AID: In 2016-2017, 98% of all full-time freshmen and 97% of continuing full-time students received some form of financial aid. 72% of all full-time freshmen and 67% of continuing full-time students received need-based aid. The average freshman award was $36,537. 53% of undergraduate students work part-time. Average annual earnings from campus work are $2000. The average financial indebtedness of the 2016 graduate was $28,294. Whitworth is a member of CSS. The FAFSA code is 003804. The priority date for freshman financial aid applications for fall entry is December 1. The deadline for filing freshman financial aid applications for fall entry is March 1.

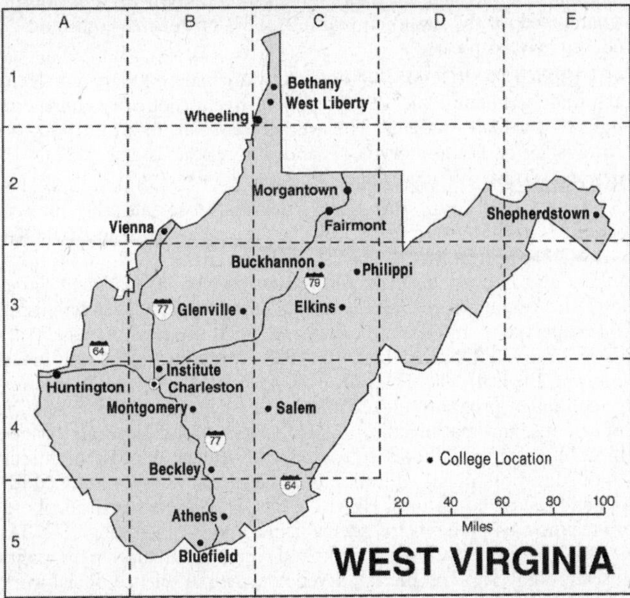

ALDERSON BROADDUS UNIVERSITY C-3

www.ab.edu

Philippi, WV 26416 (304) 457-6256 (800) 263-1549

Fax: (304) 457-6239 **Email:** admissions@ab.edu

Full-time: 531 men, 464 women	**Faculty:** 60
Part-time: 12 men, 45 women	**Ph.D.s:** 47%
Graduate: 22 men, 43 women	**Student/Faculty:** 11 to 1
Year: semesters, summer session	**Tuition:** $25,350
Room & Board: $7990	**Freshman Class:** 597 applied, 441 accepted, 162 enrolled
SAT CR/M/W: required **ACT:** 21	**CEEB CODE:** 5005
Application Deadline: August 1	**COMPETITIVE**

Alderson-Broaddus University is a private institution, founded in 1871 and affiliated with American Baptist Churches. It offers a strong liberal arts foundation, with selected programs in the health sciences, humanities, natural sciences, and education. The figures in the above capsule and in this profile are approximate. There is 1 undergraduate school and 1 graduate school. In addition to regional accreditation, AB has baccalaureate program accreditation with NLN, TEAC, ARC-PA, and CAATE. The 170-acre campus is in a small town 100 miles south of Pittsburgh, PA and 100 miles north of Charleston, WV. Including any residence halls, there are 15 buildings.

STUDENT LIFE: 56% of undergraduates are from out of state, mostly the Middle Atlantic. Students are from 40 states, 13 foreign countries, and Canada. 90% are from public schools. 74% are White; 4% Hispanic; 3% Foreign; 16% African American; 1% Asian American; 1% American Indian/Alaska Native; 1% two or more races. 14% claim no religious affiliation; 11% Catholic. **Male To Female Ratio:** 1.0:1. The average age of freshmen is 19; all undergraduates, 21. 29% do not continue beyond their first year; 39% remain to graduate. **Housing:** 580 students can be accommodated in college housing, which includes single-sex and coed dorms, on-campus apartments, off-campus apartments, and married student housing. On-campus housing is guaranteed for all 4 years. 64% of students live on campus; of those, 25% remain on campus on weekends. Alcohol is not permitted. All students may keep cars.

FACULTY/CLASSROOMS: 44% of faculty are male; 56% are female. All teach undergraduates. No introductory courses are taught by graduate students. The average class size in an introductory lecture is 40; in a laboratory is 30; and in a regular course is 20.

PROGRAMS OF STUDY: AB confers B.A. and B.S. degrees. Associate and master's degrees are also awarded. Bachelor's degrees are awarded in BIOLOGICAL SCIENCE (biology/biological science), BUSINESS (accounting, business administration and management, human resources, marketing/retailing/merchandising, organizational leadership and management, and recreational facilities management), COMMUNICATIONS AND THE ARTS (communications, creative writing, music, and visual and performing arts), COMPUTER AND PHYSICAL SCIENCE (chemistry, computer science, mathematics, and natural sciences), EDUCATION (athletic training, elementary education, music education, physical education, recreation education, and secondary education), ENGINEERING AND ENVIRONMENTAL DESIGN (environmental science), HEALTH PROFESSIONS (health science, nursing, radiograph medical technology, and recreation therapy), SOCIAL SCIENCE (Christian studies, criminology, family/consumer studies, history, interdisciplinary studies, political science/government, and psychology). Nursing, health sciences, and biology are the strongest academically.

ACTIVITIES: 9% of men belong to 2 local fraternities; 6% of women belong to 3 local sororities. There are 49 groups on campus, including art, band, choir, chorale, chorus, computers, debate, drama, ethnic, forensics, honors, jazz band, musical theater, newspaper, opera, photography, political, professional, radio and TV, religious, social, social service, student government, and yearbook. Popular campus events include Final Fling, Monte Carlo Night, and Spring Festival Weekend. **Sports:** There are 5 intercollegiate sports for men and 6 for women, and 10 intramural sports for men and 11 for women. Facilities include baseball, soccer, softball, and intramural fields, a swimming pool, basketball court, a fitness center, racquetball/handball courts, auxiliary gyms, a batting cage, a reconditioned tennis court, an outdoor basketball court, and a sand volleyball court. **Graduates:** From July 1, 2015 to June 30, 2016, 124 bachelor's degrees were awarded. The most popular majors were nursing (27%), health science (15%), and biology (8%). In an average class, 28% graduate in 4 years or less, 37% graduate in 5 years or less, and 39% graduate in 6 years or less. Of the 2015 graduating class, 15% were enrolled in graduate school within 6 months of graduation.

SERVICES: Counseling and information services are available, as is tutoring in every subject. There is remedial math, reading, and writing. There is also an academic support network. **Library/Resources:** The library contains 60,000 volumes, 40,000 microform items, and 1,500 audio/video tapes/CDs/DVDs, and subscribes to 59,000 periodicals including electronic. Computerized library services include interlibrary loans, database searching, and Internet access. Special learning facilities include an art gallery, radio station, TV station, a gross anatomy lab, a hydrotherapy pool, and a simulation lab. **Physically Challenged Students:** 75% of the campus is accessible. Facilities include wheelchair ramps, elevators, special parking, specially equipped restrooms, special class scheduling, and special housing. **Special:** Internships in numerous majors, study abroad through the college's programs in Austria, and work scholarships at the college are available. In addition, the college offers dual majors, a general studies degree, the B.A.-B.S. degree, nondegree study, and an accelerated B.A. degree in natural science. There are 2 national honor societies, a freshman honors program, and 1 departmental honors program. **Visiting:** There are regularly scheduled orientations for prospective students, including placement tests and social programs. There are guides for informal visits, visitors may sit in on classes, and stay overnight. To schedule a visit, contact the Admissions Office. **Campus Safety and Security:** Measures include emergency notification system and self-defense education. There are lighted pathways/sidewalks, a foot and vehicle patrol evenings and weekends.

REQUIREMENTS: The recommended composite score for the SAT is 950 (critical reading and math); for the ACT, 21. Applicants who are graduates of secondary schools or have passed the GED are considered for admission. An audition for certain majors and an interview are recommended. AP and CLEP credits are accepted. Important factors in the admissions decision are advanced placement or honors courses, leadership record, and recommendations by school officials. Each graduate is required to complete at least 1 major and Liberal Studies Program requirements amounting to 45 semester hours plus electives for a minimum of 128 semester hours. The Liberal Studies requirements include courses in English, literature, math, computer literacy, physical and biological science, philosophy/religion, social science, history, aesthetic expression, and health. All graduates must have attained a GPA of 2.0 overall and in the major. Certain disciplines may require a GPA higher than the minimum to continue in the major and to graduate. **Procedure:** Freshmen are admitted to all sessions. Entrance exams should be taken in spring of the junior year. There are deferred admissions and rolling admissions plans. Applications should be filed by August 1 for fall entry;

January 1 for spring entry, along with a $25 fee. Notification is sent on a rolling basis. Applications are accepted on-line. **Transfer Students:** 30 transfer students enrolled in 2015-2016. Transfer applicants must have a minimum 2.0 GPA. If they have fewer than 29 transfer credit hours, ACT or SAT results and a high school diploma are required. 32 of 128 credits required for the bachelor's degree must be completed at AB. **International Students:** The school actively recruits these students. They must take the TOEFL with a minimum score of 500 on the paper-based TOEFL (PBT). They must also take the SAT or ACT.

ADMISSIONS: 74% of the 2016-2017 applicants were accepted. The SAT scores for the 2016-2017 freshman class were: Critical Reading-- 57% below 500, 38% between 500 and 599, and 5% between 600 and 699. Math-- 61% below 500, 32% between 500 and 599, and 7% between 600 and 699. Writing-- 69% below 500, 29% between 500 and 599, and 2% between 600 and 699. The ACT scores were 47% below 12, 29% between 12 and 17, 19% between 18 and 23, 3% between 24 and 29, and 2% above 30. 35% of the current freshmen were in the top fifth of their class; 68% were in the top two fifths. 9 freshmen graduated first in their class. **Admissions Contact:** Ericka Thorn, Director of Admissions. Email: *admissions@ab.edu* Web: *www.ab.edu*

FINANCIAL AID: In 2016-2017, 99% of all full-time freshmen received some form of financial aid. 94% of all full-time freshmen and 92% of continuing full-time students received need-based aid. The average freshman award was $24,997. Need-based scholarships or need-based grants averaged $15,885 ($31,776 maximum); need-based self-help aid (loans and jobs) averaged $5,620 ($6,900 maximum); non-need-based athletic scholarships averaged $1,195 ($19,465 maximum); and other non-need-based awards and non-need-based scholarships averaged $3,690 ($30,900 maximum). 50% of undergraduate students work part-time. Average annual earnings from campus work are $1400. The average financial indebtedness of the 2016 graduate was $31,369. The college's own financial statement is required. The FAFSA code is 003806. The priority date for freshman financial aid applications for fall entry is March 1. The deadline for filing freshman financial aid applications for fall entry is September 1.

BETHANY COLLEGE *(The complete profile is made available exclusively on our website, www.barronspac.com)*

BLUEFIELD STATE COLLEGE *(The complete profile is made available exclusively on our website, www.barronspac.com)*

CONCORD UNIVERSITY — B-5

www.concord.edu

Athens, WV 24712	**(304) 384-5249** **(888) 384-5249**
Fax: (304) 384-3218	**Email: admissions@concord.edu**
Full-time: 858 men, 1095 women	**Faculty:** 103
Part-time: 87 men, 102 women	**Ph.D.s:** 49%
Graduate: 79 men, 286 women	**Student/Faculty:** 15 to 1
Year: semesters, summer session	**Tuition:** $6744 ($14,824)
Room & Board: $8210	**Freshman Class:** 1451 applied, 1208 accepted, 441 enrolled
SAT CR/M: 486/482 **ACT:** 21	**CEEB CODE:** 5120
Application Deadline: open	**COMPETITIVE**

Concord University, founded in 1872, is a public institution with undergraduate programs in liberal arts and professional training. Figures in the above capsule and in this profile are approximate. There is 1 undergraduate school and 1 graduate school. In addition to regional accreditation, Concord has baccalaureate program accreditation with CSWE, NCATE, and CAATE. The 123-acre campus is in a small town 85 miles south of Charleston, WV. Including any residence halls, there are 21 buildings.

STUDENT LIFE: 82% of undergraduates are from West Virginia. Others are from 36 states, 30 foreign countries, and Canada. 97% are from public schools. 89% are White; 6% African American; 3% Foreign; 1% Asian American; 1% Hispanic. 40% are Protestant; 40% claim no religious affiliation; 15% Catholic. **Female To Male Ratio:** 1.4:1. The average age of freshmen is 19; all undergraduates, 23. 33% do not continue beyond their first year; 36% remain to graduate. **Housing:** 1125 students can be accommodated in college housing, which includes single-sex dorms and married student housing. There are also honor floors in residence halls and housing for international students. On-campus housing is guaranteed for the freshman year only. 68% of students commute. All students may keep cars.

FACULTY/CLASSROOMS: 48% of faculty are male; 52% are female. All teach undergraduates, and all do research. No introductory courses are taught by graduate students. The average class size in an introductory lecture is 23; in a laboratory is 17; and in a regular course is 22.

PROGRAMS OF STUDY: Concord confers B.A., B.S., B.B.A., B.S.C.I.S., B.S.Ed., B.S.Med.Tech., and B.S.W. degrees. Associate and master's degrees are also awarded. Bachelor's degrees are awarded in BIOLOGICAL SCIENCE (biology/biological science), BUSINESS (accounting, banking and finance, business administration and management, hotel/motel and restaurant management, marketing/retailing/merchandising, office supervision and management, and small business management), COMMUNICATIONS AND THE ARTS (broadcasting, communications, and English), COMPUTER AND PHYSICAL SCIENCE (chemistry, computer programming, computer science, information sciences and systems, and mathematics), EDUCATION (art education, business education, early childhood education, elementary education, middle school education, music education, science education, secondary education, and special education), HEALTH PROFESSIONS (medical laboratory technology, predentistry, premedicine, and prepharmacy), SOCIAL SCIENCE (geography, history, parks and recreation management, political science/government, prelaw, psychology, social science, social work, and sociology). Teacher education, business, and preprofessional biology are the strongest academically. Teacher education, business, biology, and social work have the largest enrollments.

ACTIVITIES: 20% of men belong to 1 local and 4 national fraternities; 20% of women belong to 4 national sororities. There are 70 groups on campus, including art, bagpipe, band, cheerleading, choir, chorale, computers, dance, drama, environmental, film, honors, international, jazz band, LGBT, literary magazine, marching band, newspaper, pep band, political, professional, radio and TV, religious, social, social service, student government, and yearbook. Popular campus events include big-name concerts, Alumni Day, and Faculty and Student Plays, Homecoming and Spring Fling. **Sports:** There are 8 intercollegiate sports for men and 8 for women, and 15 intramural sports for men and 15 for women. Facilities include 5 tennis courts, 4 racquetball courts, 2 gyms, a Nautilus fitness room, a pool, a dance studio, and various outdoor fields. The campus stadium seats 4000, the larger gym 2700, and the largest auditorium 900. **Graduates:** From July 1, 2015 to June 30, 2016, 425 bachelor's degrees were awarded. The most popular majors were regents bachelor of arts (22%), business administration (15%), and education (15%). In an average class, 19% graduate in 4 years or less, 32% graduate in 5 years or less, and 34% graduate in 6 years or less.

SERVICES: Counseling and information services are available, as is tutoring in every subject. There is a reader service for the blind, and remedial math, reading, and writing. **Library/Resources:** The library contains 168,164 volumes, 240,089 microform items, and 3,800 audio/video tapes/CDs/DVDs, and subscribes to 140 periodicals including electronic. Computerized library services include interlibrary loans, database searching, Internet access, and Wi-Fi capability. Special learning facilities include an art gallery, radio station, and TV station. **Physically Challenged Students:** 90% of the campus is accessible. Facilities include wheelchair ramps, elevators, special parking, specially equipped restrooms, special class scheduling, lowered drinking fountains, lowered telephones, and special housing. **Special:** Students may serve internships in medical technology, social work, travel industry management, commercial art/advertising, and communications arts. Concord offers a Washington semester, cross-registration with Bluefield State College, dual majors, interdisciplinary student-designed majors, and nondegree study. Credit for life, military, and work experience is granted to adult students through the Regents Bachelor of Arts Degree Program. There are 5 national honor societies and a freshman honors program. **Visiting:** There are regularly scheduled orientations for prospective students. There are guides for informal visits, visitors may sit in on classes, and stay overnight. To schedule a visit, contact the Admissions Office. **Campus Safety and Security:** Measures include 24-hour foot and vehicle patrol, emergency notification system, and security escort services. There are emergency telephones, lighted pathways/sidewalks, controlled access to dorms/residences, foot and vehicle patrol is available 24 hours Monday through Friday and is on call Saturday and Sunday.

REQUIREMENTS: The SAT is required, with the ACT preferred. Applicants must be high school graduates or hold a GED. Students should present 17 academic credits, including 4 each in English and math, 3 each in social studies and science, and 1 each in history and health/phys ed. An interview is recommended and, where appropriate, a portfolio or an audition. AP and CLEP credits are accepted. To graduate, students must earn 120 credit hours, including 36 to 50 in the major, with a minimum GPA of 2.0 (2.5 in many departments). All students must complete the college's general studies curriculum. Required courses include 14 to 15 semester hours of math and science, 12 of English and literature, 12 of social studies, 6 of fine arts, 3 of speech, 2 of phys ed, and 1 of univ 100. **Procedure:** Freshmen are admitted to all sessions. Entrance exams should be taken in the junior year or preferably early in the senior year. There are deferred admissions and rolling admissions plans. Application deadlines are open. Notification is sent on a rolling basis. Applications are accepted on-line. **Transfer Students:** Applicants must have a GPA of at least 2.0. Concord recommends a minimum of 15 credit hours of college work completed and an interview. 36 of 120 credits required for the bachelor's degree must be completed at Concord. **International Students:** There are 91 international students enrolled. The school actively recruits these students. They must take the TOEFL with a minimum score of 500 on the paper-based TOEFL (PBT) or 60 on the Internet-based version (iBT). They must also take the SAT or ACT.

ADMISSIONS: 83% of the 2016-2017 applicants were accepted. The SAT scores for the 2016-2017 freshman class were: Critical Reading-- 58% below 500, 32% between 500 and 599, and 10% between 600 and 699. Math-- 58% below 500, 34% between 500 and 599, 7% between 600 and 699, and 1% between 700 and 800. Writing-- 68% below 500, 23% between 500 and 599, 8% between 600 and 699, and 1% between 700 and 800. **Admissions Contact:** Kent Gamble, Director of Enrollment. Email: *admissions@concord.edu* Web: *www.concord.edu*

FINANCIAL AID: In 2016-2017, 93% of all full-time freshmen and 89% of continuing full-time students received some form of financial aid. 59% of all full-time freshmen and 59% of continuing full-time students received need-based aid. The average freshman award was $12,786. Need-based scholarships or need-based grants averaged $5,375; need-based self-help aid (loans and jobs) averaged $4,460; non-need-based athletic scholarships averaged $4,640; and other non-need-based awards and non-need-based scholarships averaged $3,470. 26% of undergraduate students work part-time. Average annual earnings from campus work are $2100. The average financial indebtedness of the 2016 graduate was $19,000. The FAFSA code is 003810. The priority date for freshman financial aid applications for fall entry is March 1. The deadline for filing freshman financial aid applications for fall entry is April 15.

DAVIS & ELKINS COLLEGE *(The complete profile is made available exclusively on our website, www.barronspac.com)*

FAIRMONT STATE UNIVERSITY — C-2

www.fairmontstate.edu

Fairmont, WV 26554	**(304) 367-4892** **(800) 641-5678**
Fax: (304) 367-4789	**Email: admit@fairmontstate.edu**
Full-time: 1489 men, 1744 women	**Faculty:** n/av
Part-time: 156 men, 309 women	**Ph.D.s:** 65%
Graduate: 73 men, 161 women	**Student/Faculty:** 15 to 1
Year: semesters, summer session	**Tuition:** $6950 ($14,666)
Room & Board: $8776	**Freshman Class:** 2943 applied, 1930 accepted, 826 enrolled
SAT: required **ACT:** 21	**CEEB CODE:** 5211
Application Deadline: August 15	**COMPETITIVE**

Fairmont State University, founded in 1865, is a student-centered institution of first choice among students who desire a flexible and relevant learning experience. There are 6 undergraduate schools and 4 graduate schools. In addition to regional accreditation, Fairmont State has baccalaureate program accreditation with ABET, ACBSP, NCATE, NLN, IACBE, and ACEN. The 120-acre campus is in a small town 75 miles south of Pittsburgh, 135 miles north of Charleston, WV, and 218 miles west of Washington DC. Including any residence halls, there are 20 buildings.

STUDENT LIFE: 91% of undergraduates are from West Virginia. Others are from 24 states, and 19 foreign countries. 98% are from public schools. 90% are White; 4% African American; 2% Foreign; 1% Asian American; 1% Hispanic. **Female To Male Ratio:** 1.3:1. The average age of freshmen is 19; all undergraduates, 23. 34% do not continue beyond their first year; 67% remain to graduate. **Housing:** 1189 students can be accommodated in college housing, which includes coed dorms and on-campus apartments. On-campus housing is guaranteed for the freshman year only, and is available on a first-come, first-served basis. 76% of students commute. Alcohol is not permitted. All students may keep cars.

FACULTY/CLASSROOMS: 49% of faculty are male; 51% are female. All teach undergraduates. No introductory courses are taught by graduate students. The average class size in an introductory lecture is 35; in a laboratory is 20; and in a regular course is 30.

PROGRAMS OF STUDY: Fairmont State confers B.A., B.S., B.S.E.T. and B.S.N. degrees. Associate and master's degrees are also awarded. Bachelor's degrees are awarded in BIOLOGICAL SCIENCE (biology/biological science), BUSINESS (accounting, business administration and management, and marketing/retailing/merchandising), COMMUNICATIONS AND THE ARTS (communications, English, graphic design, Spanish, speech/debate/rhetoric, and theatre acting), COMPUTER AND PHYSICAL SCIENCE (chemistry, computer science, and mathematics), EDUCATION (art education, early childhood education, elementary education, foreign languages education, health education, middle school education, music education, science education, and secondary education), ENGINEERING AND ENVIRONMENTAL DESIGN (architectural technology, architecture, civil engineering technology, electrical/electronics engineering technology, engineering technology, mechanical engineering technology, and occupational safety and health), HEALTH PROFESSIONS (nursing and predentistry), SOCIAL SCIENCE (criminal justice, forensic studies, history, political science/government, psychology, and sociology). Nursing and education are the strongest academically. Business, health careers, and criminal justice have the largest enrollments.

ACTIVITIES: There are 80 groups on campus, including art, band, cheerleading, chess, choir, chorus, computers, debate, drama, honors, international, jazz band, LGBT, literary magazine, marching band, musical theater, newspaper, photography, political, professional, religious, social, student government, symphony, and yearbook. Popular campus events include multicultural events. **Sports:** There are 7 intercollegiate sports for men and 9 for women, and 24 intramural sports for men and 24 for women. Facilities include a phys ed center, 5000-seat stadium, 4000-seat basketball arena, and playing fields. **Graduates:** From July 1, 2015 to June 30, 2016, 602 bachelor's degrees were awarded. The most popular majors were engineering technologies (12%), homeland security (11%), education, and health professions and related programs (10%). 75 companies recruited on campus in 2015-2016. In an average class, 29% graduate in 6 years or less. Of the 2015 graduating class, 18% were enrolled in graduate school within 6 months of graduation, and 80% were employed.

SERVICES: Counseling and information services are available, as is tutoring in most subjects. There is a reader service for the blind, and remedial math, reading, and writing. **Library/Resources:** The library contains 275,000 volumes, 54,241 microform items, and 12,000 audio/video tapes/CDs/DVDs, and subscribes to 1,175 periodicals including electronic. Computerized library services include interlibrary loans, database searching, Internet access, and Wi-Fi capability. Special learning facilities include an art gallery. **Physically Challenged Students:** All of the campus is accessible. Facilities include wheelchair ramps, elevators, special parking, specially equipped restrooms, special class scheduling, lowered drinking fountains, lowered telephones, and special housing. **Special:** The college offers internships in teacher education, retailing, and psychology, and awards a B.S. degree in chemistry/math. There are 4 national honor societies, a freshman honors program, and 4 departmental honors programs. **Visiting:** There are regularly scheduled orientations for prospective students. There are guides for informal visits and visitors may sit in on classes. To schedule a visit, contact the Office of Admissions. **Campus Safety and Security:** Measures include 24-hour foot and vehicle patrol and emergency notification system. There are emergency telephones, lighted pathways/sidewalks, and controlled access to dorms/residences.

REQUIREMENTS: For students who have graduated from high school or completed GED requirements fewer than 5 years prior to seeking admission, a satisfactory score is required on the SAT or 17 on the ACT. Applicants must be high school graduates or hold a GED. The college requires 4 credits in English, 4 in math (algebra I and at least 1 higher), 3 in science (of those 2 lab science), 2 in foreign language, and social studies (1 in U.S. history), and 8 academic electives. AP and CLEP credits are accepted. To graduate, students must complete 128 hours with a GPA of 2.0. (2.5 in education specializations). Students must complete 50 core curriculum hours for the B.S. or B.A. degree. All students must take 2 hours of phys ed. Course and distribution requirements vary according to the program. **Procedure:** Freshmen are admitted fall, spring, and summer. Entrance exams should be taken during the fall of the senior year. There is a rolling admissions plan. Applications should be filed by August 15 for fall entry. Applications are accepted on-line. **Transfer Students:** 359 transfer students enrolled in 2015-2016. Applicants must have a GPA of 2.0. The ACT is required for applicants with fewer than 30 college credits. Students may enroll in the fall, spring, and summer. 60 of 128 credits required for the bachelor's degree must be completed at Fairmont State. **International Students:** There are 69 international students enrolled. The school actively recruits these students. They must take the TOEFL. If ACT or SAT scores are not supplied, the ACT must be taken upon arrival on campus.

ADMISSIONS: 66% of the 2016-2017 applicants were accepted. The ACT scores were 18% between 12 and 17, 60% between 18 and 23, 21% between 24 and 29, and 1% above 30. **Admissions Contact:** Amie Fazalare, Admissions Director. Email: *admit@fairmontstate.edu* Web: *www.fairmontstate.edu*

FINANCIAL AID: The average freshman award was $8,985. Need-based scholarships or need-based grants averaged $6,596; need-based self-help aid (loans and jobs) averaged $3,049; non-need-based athletic scholarships averaged $5,315; other non-need-based awards and non-need-based scholarships averaged $3,015; and $6,272 from other forms of aid. The average financial indebtedness of the 2016 graduate was $10,840. Fairmont State is a member of CSS. The FAFSA code is 003812. The priority date for freshman financial aid applications for fall entry is March 1.

GLENVILLE STATE COLLEGE *(The complete profile is made available exclusively on our website, www.barronspac.com)*

MARSHALL UNIVERSITY — A-4

www.marshall.edu

Huntington, WV 25755	**(304) 696-3160** **(800) 642-3499**
Fax: (304) 696-3135	**Email: johnson73@marshall.edu**
Full-time: 3643 men, 4629 women	**Faculty:** IIA, --$
Part-time: 605 men, 885 women	**Ph.D.s:** 77%
Graduate: 1247 men, 2047 women	**Student/Faculty:** 18 to 1
Year: semesters, summer session	**Tuition:** $7115 ($16,200)
Room & Board: $10,127	**Freshman Class:** n/av
SAT or ACT: required	**CEEB CODE:** 5396
Application Deadline: n/av	**COMPETITIVE**

Marshall University, founded in 1837 and part of the University of West Virginia system, is a comprehensive public institution offering programs in Liberal Arts, Science, Business, Education, Journalism and Mass Communications, Arts & Media, Information Technology and Engineering, and Health Professions. Figures in the above capsule and in this profile are approximate. There are 10 undergraduate schools and 3 graduate schools. In addition to regional accreditation, Marshall has baccalaureate program accreditation with AACSB, ABET, ACEJMC, CSWE, NASM, NCATE, NRPA, JRCERT, ACEND, and NAACLS. The 100-acre campus is in an urban area 126 miles east of Lexington, Kentucky, and 50 miles west of Charleston, West Virginia. Including any residence halls, there are 55 buildings.

STUDENT LIFE: 79% of undergraduates are from West Virginia. Others are from 47 states, 51 foreign countries, and Canada. 82% are White; 5% African American; 5% race unknown; 2% Hispanic; 2% Foreign; 2% two or more races; 1% Asian American. **Female To Male Ratio:** 1.4:1. The average age of freshmen is 19; all undergraduates, 23. **Housing:** 2499 students can be accommodated in college housing, which includes single-sex and coed dorms, honors floors, living learning communities, and freshman interest groups. On-campus housing is available on a first-come, first-served basis. Alcohol is not permitted. All students may keep cars.

FACULTY/CLASSROOMS: 54% of faculty are male; 46% are female. No introductory courses are taught by graduate students. The average class size in a regular course is 22.

PROGRAMS OF STUDY: Marshall confers B.A., B.S., B.B.A., B.F.A., B.S.Cyotech, B.S.Chem, B.S.N., B.S.W., and B.S.E. degrees. Associate, master's, and doctoral degrees are also awarded. Bachelor's degrees are awarded in AGRICULTURE (natural resource management), BIOLOGICAL SCIENCE (anatomy, biochemistry, biology/biological science, biotechnology, cell biology, ecology, evolutionary biology, molecular biology, and nutrition), BUSINESS (accounting, banking and finance, business economics, finance, international business management, management information systems, marketing/retailing/merchandising, and sports management), COMMUNICATIONS AND THE ARTS (advertising, applied art, art, broadcasting, ceramic art and design, classics, communications, communication rhetoric/communication, creative writing, English, English literature, French, German, graphic design, information technology, Japanese, jazz, journalism, literature, music, music performance, music theory and composition, painting, percussion, photography, piano/organ, public relations, radio/television technology, sculpture, Spanish, sports media, strings, theatre arts, theater design, and voice), COMPUTER AND PHYSICAL SCIENCE (applied mathematics, chemistry, computer game design/development, computer science, computer security and information assurance, environmental chemistry, geology, information sciences and systems, mathematics, physics, and science technology), EDUCATION (athletic training, childhood education, early childhood education, education, elementary education, English education, foreign languages education, middle school education, music education, physical education, secondary education, social studies education, and special education), ENGINEERING AND ENVIRONMENTAL DESIGN (civil engineering, engineering, environmental science, occupational safety and health, and preengineering), HEALTH PROFESSIONS (allied health, cytotechnology, exercise science, health science, medical laboratory technology, nursing, pre-health studies, predentistry, premedicine, preoptometry, preosteopathy, prepharmacy, prephysical therapy, prepodiatry, public health, respiratory therapy, and speech pathology/audiology), SOCIAL SCIENCE (criminal justice, dietetics, economics, forensic studies, geography, history, humanities, international relations, parks and recreation management, philosophy, physical fitness/movement, political science/government, prelaw, psychology, safety and security technology, safety management, social work, sociology, and women's studies). Biological science, elementary education, and secondary education have the largest enrollments.

ACTIVITIES: There are 194 groups on campus, including art, band, cheerleading, choir, chorale, chorus, communications, computers, dance, debate, drama, environmental, ethnic, forensics, honors, international, jazz band, LGBT, literary magazine, marching band, musical theater, newspaper, opera, orchestra, pep band, photography, political, professional, radio and TV, religious, social, social service, student government, symphony, and yearbook. Popular campus events include Week of Welcome, Parents Weekend, Homecoming, Springfest, and International Festival. **Sports:** There are 8 intercollegiate sports for men and 10 for women, and 9 intramural sports for men and 9 for women. Facilities include a 10,500-seat basketball arena, 30,000-seat football stadium, tennis courts, baseball field, an Olympic-size pool, an auxiliary gym, health and fitness center, racquetball courts, human performance enhancement lab, and the Marshall Recreation Center which is a 123,000 square-foot, state of the art facility. **Graduates:** From July 1, 2015 to June 30, 2016, 1562 bachelor's degrees were awarded. The most popular majors were arts (16%), education elementary (7%), and management (7%). In an average class, 45% graduate in 6 years or less.

SERVICES: Counseling and information services are available, as is tutoring in most subjects. There is a reader service for the blind, and remedial math, reading, and writing. Study skills courses, and other services for all students with disabilities are available. **Library/Resources:** The 2 libraries contain 2.2 million volumes, 1.0 million microform items, and 43,449 audio/video tapes/CDs/DVDs, and subscribe to 45,508 periodicals including electronic. Computerized library services include interlibrary loans, database searching, and Internet access. Special learning facilities include an art gallery, natural history museum, radio station, TV station, and a greenhouse. **Physically Challenged Students:** All of the campus is accessible. Facilities include wheelchair ramps, elevators, special parking, specially equipped restrooms, special class scheduling, lowered drinking fountains, lowered telephones, special housing, and an attendant care program. **Special:** Many programs require or offer internships. Work-study opportunities are available on campus. Students participate in student exchange and study abroad programs. B.A.-B.S. degrees, dual majors and minors, nondegree study, credit for life experience, and credit/no-credit options are available. There are 20 national honor societies and a freshman honors program. **Visiting:**

There are regularly scheduled orientations for prospective students. There are guides for informal visits, visitors may sit in on classes, and stay overnight. To schedule a visit, contact the Office of Recruitment at (304) 696-3646. **Campus Safety and Security:** Measures include 24-hour foot and vehicle patrol, emergency notification system, self-defense education, and security escort services. There are emergency telephones, lighted pathways/sidewalks, and controlled access to dorms/residences.

REQUIREMENTS: General freshman admission is open to all applicants with a high school diploma with an overall GPA of 2.0 on a 4.0 scale and an ACT composite score of 19 or a SAT combined score 900 (critical reading plus math) or an overall GPA of 3.0 on a 4.0 scale and an ACT composite score of 16 or a SAT combined score 770 (critical reading plus math). The GED is also accepted. The following high school units are recommended for admission: 4 years of English (including courses in grammar, composition, literature), 3 years of social studies (including U.S. history), 4 years of math (including Algebra I and at least two higher units), 3 years of laboratory science, 2 years of the same foreign language, 1 year of fine arts. AP and CLEP credits are accepted. Marshall utilizes a Core Curriculum that applies through all colleges and majors and incorporates critical thinking, multicultural, writing intensive, and international components. Overall and major-specific GPAs vary with degrees. **Procedure:** Freshmen are admitted to all sessions. Entrance exams should be taken during the junior year or early in the senior year. There is a rolling admissions plan. Check with the school for current application deadlines. The application fee is $30. Notification is sent on a rolling basis. Applications are accepted on-line. **Transfer Students:** 978 transfer students enrolled in 2015-2016. All transfer students must be eligible to return to the institution they most recently attended. In addition, transfer students who have fewer than 26 earned semester hours must meet one of the following criteria: Must meet the current freshman admission standards, or have earned 12 graded college-level semester hours and completed all prerequisite courses for English and math while maintaining a 2.0 cumulative college GPA. **International Students:** There are 132 international students enrolled. The school actively recruits these students. They must take the TOEFL with a minimum score of 80 on the Internet-based version (iBT), or take the IELTS.

Admissions Contact: Dr. Tammy Johnson, Admissions. Email: *johnson73@marshall.edu* Web: *www.marshall.edu*

FINANCIAL AID: In 2016-2017, 87% of all full-time freshmen and 89% of continuing full-time students received some form of financial aid. 75% of all full-time freshmen and 74% of continuing full-time students received need-based aid. The average freshman award was $10,915. Need-based scholarships or need-based grants averaged $5,260 ($23,172 maximum); need-based self-help aid (loans and jobs) averaged $5,622 ($15,000 maximum); non-need-based athletic scholarships averaged $11,892 ($24,560 maximum); and other non-need-based awards and non-need-based scholarships averaged $5,164 ($25,769 maximum). 3% of undergraduate students work part-time. Average annual earnings from campus work are $1598. The average financial indebtedness of the 2016 graduate was $26,727. Marshall is a member of CSS. The FAFSA code is 003815. The deadline for filing freshman financial aid applications for fall entry is March 1.

OHIO VALLEY UNIVERSITY B-2

www.ovu.edu

Vienna, WV 26105	(304) 865-6202
Fax: (304) 865-6175	Email: admissions@ovu.edu
Full-time: 250 men, 275 women	Faculty: 21; IIB
Part-time: 12 men, 22 women	Ph.D.s: 75%
Graduate: n/av	Student/Faculty: 18 to 1
Year: semesters, summer session	Tuition: $20,460
Room & Board: $9020	Freshman Class: 304 applied, 170 accepted, 85 enrolled
ACT: 23	CEEB CODE: 5519
Application Deadline: August 15	COMPETITIVE

Ohio Valley University, founded in 1960, is a liberal arts institution affiliated with the Church of Christ. Ohio Valley offers 36 degrees along with myraid minors. The figures in the above capsule and in this profile are approximate. There are 4 undergraduate schools and one graduate school. In addition to regional accreditation, Ohio Valley has baccalaureate program accreditation with IACBE, AACRAO, ACA, ASCD, and NCAA. The 266-acre campus is in a suburban area in beautiful Vienna, West Virginia, on the Ohio River in the historic Mid-Ohio Valley. Including any residence halls, there are 9 buildings.

STUDENT LIFE: 65% of undergraduates are from out of state, mostly the Midwest. Students are from 28 states, 13 foreign countries, and Canada. 97% are from public schools. 88% are White; 6% Foreign; 4% African American; 1% Asian American; 1% Hispanic. 97% are Protestant. **Female To Male Ratio:** 1.1:1. The average age of freshmen is 18; all undergraduates, 22. 26% do not continue beyond their first year; 35% remain to graduate. **Housing:** 500 students can be accommodated in college housing, which includes single-sex dorms, on-campus apartments, and married student housing. On-campus housing is guaranteed for all 4 years. 55% of students live on campus; of those, 30% remain on campus on weekends. Alcohol is not permitted. All students may keep cars.

FACULTY/CLASSROOMS: 68% of faculty are male; 32% are female. All teach undergraduates. No introductory courses are taught by graduate students. The average class size in an introductory lecture is 30; in a laboratory is 20; and in a regular course is 15.

PROGRAMS OF STUDY: Ohio Valley confers B.A. and B.S. degrees. Associate degrees are also awarded. Bachelor's degrees are awarded in BIOLOGICAL SCIENCE (biochemistry), BUSINESS (accounting, business administration and management, organizational leadership and management, and sports management), COMMUNICATIONS AND THE ARTS (English), COMPUTER AND PHYSICAL SCIENCE (computer information technology and mathematics), EDUCATION (elementary education, English education, health education, mathematics education, and science education), HEALTH PROFESSIONS (biology and health), SOCIAL SCIENCE (biblical studies, criminal justice, history, humanities, interdisciplinary studies, psychology, and sociology). Business is the strongest academically. Elementary education, psychology, and business administration have the largest enrollments.

ACTIVITIES: There are no fraternities or sororities. There are 16 groups on campus, including Women for Christ club, Timothy club, band, cheerleading, choir, chorale, chorus, communications, diversity club, drama, jazz band, newspaper, pep band, religious, social, and student government. Popular campus events include Expressions and a School-wide Musical Review. **Sports:** There are 5 intercollegiate sports for men and 4 for women, and 11 intramural sports for men and 10 for women. Facilities include a weight room, student union with recreation facilities, an activity center, gyms, baseball, basketball, cross country, golf, soccer, lacrosse, softball, and wrestling. **Graduates:** From July 1, 2015 to June 30, 2016, 101 bachelor's degrees were awarded. The most popular majors were business (46%), education (25%), and psychology (16%). In an average class, 18% graduate in 4 years or less, 35% graduate in 5 years or less, and 27% graduate in 6 years or less.

SERVICES: Counseling and information services are available, as is tutoring in most subjects. There is remedial math, reading, and writing. **Library/Resources:** The library contains 31,750 volumes, 51,530 microform items, and 2,946 audio/video tapes/CDs/DVDs, and subscribes to 165 periodicals including electronic. Computerized library services include interlibrary loans, database searching, Internet access, and Wi-Fi capability. **Physically Challenged Students:** 30% of the campus is accessible. Facilities include wheelchair ramps, elevators, special parking, specially equipped restrooms, special class scheduling, and lowered telephones. **Special:** Ohio Valley offers internships with churches for student ministers. Study abroad programs are frequently offered in England, France and Italy. OVU is also affiliated with the Washington Center for Internships and Academic Seminars. There is 1 national honor society and 1 departmental honors program. **Visiting:** There are guides for informal visits, visitors may sit in on classes, and stay overnight. To schedule a visit, contact the Office of Admissions. **Campus Safety and Security:** Measures include 24-hour foot and vehicle patrol.

REQUIREMENTS: The ACT is required. Applicants should be graduates of an accredited secondary school or have earned a GED. Ohio Valley requires applicants to be in the upper 50% of their class. AP and CLEP credits are accepted. Important factors in the admissions decision are recommendations by school officials, personality/intangible qualities, and leadership record. To graduate, students must complete 128 credit hours, including 53 to 60 in the major, with a minimum GPA of 2.0. General requirements include 4 courses in Bible studies, 2 in English composition, 1 to 2 in history, and 1 each in speech, computer literacy, math, and social science. There is also a phys ed requirement. Students must attend chapel daily and take 1 Bible class each semester. **Procedure:** Freshmen are admitted fall and spring. Entrance exams should be taken during the senior year. There are early admissions and rolling admissions plans. Applications should be filed by August 15 for fall entry. Notification is sent on a rolling basis. **Transfer Students:** Transfer applicants must provide high school, college, and financial aid transcripts, and test scores. 32 of 128 credits required for the bachelor's degree must be completed at Ohio Valley. **International Students:** There are 33 international students enrolled. The school actively recruits these students. They must take the TOEFL with a minimum score of 500 on the paper-based TOEFL (PBT) or 61 on the Internet-based version (iBT). They must also take the SAT or ACT, scoring 18.

ADMISSIONS: 56% of the 2016-2017 applicants were accepted. The ACT scores were 75% below 12, 25% between 12 and 17, 9% between 18 and 23, 3% between 24 and 29, and 2% above 30. 10% of the current freshmen were in the top fifth of their class; 32% were in the top two fifths. 10 freshmen graduated first in their class. **Admissions Contact:** Rob E. Dudley, Director of Admissions. Email: *admissions@ovu.edu* Web: *www.ovu.edu*

FINANCIAL AID: In 2016-2017, 95% of all full-time freshmen and 98% of continuing full-time students received some form of financial aid. 70% of all full-time freshmen and 65% of continuing full-time students received need-based aid. The average freshman award was $9,768. Need-based scholarships or need-based grants averaged $7,219; need-based self-help aid (loans and jobs) averaged $3,248 ($5,500 maximum); non-need-based athletic scholarships averaged $5,442 ($16,796 maximum); and other non-need-based awards and non-need-based scholarships averaged $7,732 ($15,000 maximum). 44% of undergraduate students work part-time. Average annual earnings from campus work are $800. The average financial indebtedness of the 2016 graduate was $9,035. Ohio Valley is a member of CSS. The FAFSA code is 003819. The priority date for freshman financial aid applications for fall entry is February 14.

SALEM INTERNATIONAL UNIVERSITY *(The complete profile is made available exclusively on our website, www.barronspac.com)*

SHEPHERD UNIVERSITY, WEST VIRGINIA E-2

www.shepherd.edu

Shepherdstown, WV 25443 (304) 876-5212
(800) 344-5231

Fax: (304) 876-5165
Email: admission@shepherd.edu

Full-time: 1103 men, 1597 women
Part-time: 333 men, 403 women
Graduate: 101 men, 242 women
Year: semesters, summer session
Room & Board: $10,054
Faculty: 134
Ph.D.s: 88%
Student/Faculty: 20 to 1
Tuition: $7170 ($17,482)
Freshman Class: 1546 applied, 1421 accepted, 564 enrolled
SAT CR/M: 500/490 **ACT:** 21
CEEB CODE: 5615
Application Deadline:
COMPETITIVE

Shepherd University, founded in 1871, is a state-supported institution offering programs in the liberal and creative arts, business administration, teacher education, social and natural sciences, health fields, and other career-oriented areas. There are 4 undergraduate schools and 1 graduate school. In addition to regional accreditation, Shepherd has baccalaureate program accreditation with CSWE, NASAD, NASM, NCATE, CCNE and WVBOERN, IACBE, and COAPRT. The 323-acre campus is in a small town 70 miles northwest of Washington, D.C. and Baltimore. Including any residence halls, there are 52 buildings.

STUDENT LIFE: 60% of undergraduates are from West Virginia. Others are from 44 states, 9 foreign countries, and Canada. 94% are from public schools. 82% are White; 8% African American; 3% Hispanic; 2% Asian American; 2% two or more races; 2% race unknown; 1% American Indian/Alaska Native; 1% Foreign. **Female To Male Ratio:** 1.5:1. The average age of freshmen is 18; all undergraduates, 23. 40% do not continue beyond their first year; 46% remain to graduate. **Housing:** 1300 students can be accommodated in college housing, which includes coed dorms and on-campus apartments. In addition, there are honors houses and special-interest houses. On-campus housing is guaranteed for all 4 years. 67% of students commute. All students may keep cars.

FACULTY/CLASSROOMS: 49% of faculty are male; 51% are female. 93% teach undergraduates. No introductory courses are taught by graduate students. The average class size in an introductory lecture is 20; in a laboratory is 18; and in a regular course is 13.

PROGRAMS OF STUDY: Shepherd confers B.A., B.S., B.F.A., B.M.E., B.S.N., B.S.W., B.M.P., and R.B.A. degrees. Master's and doctoral degrees are also awarded. Bachelor's degrees are awarded in AGRICULTURE (environmental studies), BIOLOGICAL SCIENCE (biology/biological science), BUSINESS (accounting, business administration and management, and recreation and leisure services), COMMUNICATIONS AND THE ARTS (art, communications, English, music, and Spanish), COMPUTER AND PHYSICAL SCIENCE (chemistry, computer science, information sciences and systems, mathematics, and mathematics/computational), EDUCATION (art education, elementary education, English education, global studies, health education, home economics education, mathematics education, music education, physical education, science education, secondary education, and social studies education), ENGINEERING AND ENVIRONMENTAL DESIGN (computer engineering and computer technology), HEALTH PROFESSIONS (nursing), SOCIAL SCIENCE (economics, family/consumer studies, history, political science/government, psychology, social work, and sociology). Biology, history, nursing, and political science are the strongest academically. Nursing, education, and recreation and leisure studies have the largest enrollments.

ACTIVITIES: 4% of women belong to 3 national sororities. There are 85 groups on campus, including art, band, cheerleading, choir, chorale, chorus, computers, dance, debate, drama, environmental, ethnic, honors, international, jazz band, LGBT, literary magazine, marching band, musical theater, newspaper, opera, orchestra, political, professional, radio and TV, religious, social, social service, student government, and symphony. Popular campus events include Family Day, Midnight Breakfast, Late Night in the Zone, Appalachian Heritage Festival, Appalachian Writer in Residence, Homecoming, and Relay for Life. **Sports:** There are 6 intercollegiate sports for men and 6 for women, and 8 intramural sports for men and 8 for women. Facilities include football and women's lacrosse field, soccer fields, baseball and softball fields, a gym, outdoor and indoor tennis courts, outdoor sand volleyball courts, a fitness/wellness center, basketball courts with hoops, racquetball courts, 1/10 of a mile indoor track, cardio area, a free-weight area, large group exercise studio, and an 8-lane/25-yd indoor swimming pool. **Graduates:** From July 1, 2015 to June 30, 2016, 762 bachelor's degrees were awarded. The most popular majors were Regents Bachelor of Arts (12%), nursing (11%), and education (10%). In an average class, 25% graduate in 4 years or less, 42% graduate in 5 years or less, and 46% graduate in 6 years or less.

SERVICES: Counseling and information services are available, as is tutoring in most subjects. There is remedial math, reading, and writing. Tutorial assistance available for students with learning disabilities. **Library/Resources:** The library contains 192,368 volumes, 26,891 microform items, and 4,706 audio/video tapes/CDs/DVDs, and subscribes to 234 periodicals including electronic. Computerized library services include interlibrary loans, database searching, Internet access, and Wi-Fi capability. Special learning facilities include an art gallery, radio station, a nursery school, 3 theaters, the Center for the Study of the Civil War, and the Robert C. Byrd Center for Congressional History and Education. **Physically Challenged Students:** 90% of the campus is accessible. Facilities include wheelchair ramps, elevators, special parking, specially equipped restrooms, special class scheduling, lowered drinking fountains, lowered telephones, and automatic door openers. **Special:** Shepherd offers study abroad, a B.A.-B.S. degree in communication and new media, and internships and co-op programs that are available in most majors. There is a Washington semester, and dual majors are possible in any 2 majors. Credit by exam, life experience credentialing through the Regents degree, nondegree study, and pass/fail options for electives are offered. There is a 4+1 M.B.A. Program, and an Intensive English Language Program. There are 10 national honor societies, a freshman honors program, and 19 departmental honors programs. **Visiting:** There are regularly scheduled orientations for prospective students, three fall open houses and one spring open house, weekday campus tours, one Accepted Student Day. There are guides for informal visits and visitors may sit in on classes. To schedule a visit, contact the Admissions Office. B>**Campus Safety and Security:** Measures include 24-hour foot and vehicle patrol, emergency notification system, and security escort services. There are shuttle buses, emergency telephones, lighted pathways/sidewalks, and controlled access to dorms/residences.

REQUIREMENTS: A minimum composite score of 820 on the SAT (critical reading and math) or 17 on the ACT required. Applicants should be graduates of an accredited secondary school and have earned academic credits including 4 each in English and math, 3 each in history or social science, with 1 in American history and lab science, 1 in art, and the rest in computer, foreign language, and other academic electives. Applicants must have a minimum 2.0 academic core GPA. The GED is accepted. AP and CLEP credits are accepted. Important factors in the admissions decision are advanced placement or honors courses, leadership record, and extracurricular activities record. To graduate, students must complete a minimum of 120 semester hours with a 2.0 GPA overall and 42 upper division credits in the major and minor fields. The core curriculum totals 42: 6 in written English, 3 each in mathematics, history, arts, and wellness, 8 in sciences, 1 in first-year experience, 6 in humanities, and 9 in social sciences. Students pursuing the Bachelor of Arts degree (not including education) are required to complete 12 semester hours in the same foreign language, except music students whose, requirements must be approved by the chairs of the Music and English and Modern Languages departments. Two years of German or French or both are recommended for students who anticipate going to graduate or professional school. The foreign language requirement for the B.A. degree can be satisfied through advanced placement or CLEP tests. **Procedure:** Freshmen are admitted fall, spring, and summer. Entrance exams should be taken during the junior year. There are early decision, early admissions, deferred admissions, and rolling admissions plans. Application deadlines are open. Application fee is $45. Notification is sent on a rolling basis. 297 early decision candidates were accepted for the 2016-2017 class. Applications are accepted on-line. **Transfer Students:** 288 transfer students enrolled in 2015-2016. Applicants must have a 2.0 cumulative GPA in a minimum of 24 semester hours of college-level work completed and must submit a transcript from each college attended. 30 of 120 credits required for the bachelor's degree must be completed at Shepherd. **International Students:** There are 14 international students enrolled. The school actively recruits these students. They must take the TOEFL with a minimum score of 550 on the paper-based TOEFL (PBT) or 79 on the Internet-based version (iBT) or take the MELAB, also the IELTS, and EIKEN. They must also take the SAT or ACT, scoring 820.

ADMISSIONS: 92% of the 2016-2017 applicants were accepted. The SAT scores for the 2016-2017 freshman class were: Critical Reading-- 47% below 500, 44% between 500 and 599, 8% between 600 and 699, and 1% between 700 and 800. Math-- 56% below 500, 37% between 500 and 599, and 7% between 600 and 699. The ACT scores were 1% below 12, 12% between 12 and 17, 57% between 18 and 23, 27% between 24 and 29, and 3% above 30. **Admissions Contact:** Kristen Lorenz, Director of Admissions. Email: *admission@shepherd.edu* Web: *www.shepherd.edu*

FINANCIAL AID: In 2016-2017, 91% of all full-time freshmen and 82% of continuing full-time students received some form of financial aid. 41% of all full-time freshmen and 43% of continuing full-time students received need-based aid. The average freshman award was $11,803. Need-based scholarships or need-based grants averaged $5,559; need-based self-help aid (loans and jobs) averaged $3,366; and non-need-based athletic scholarships averaged $6,074. 15% of undergraduate students work part-time. Average annual earnings from campus work are $3200. The average financial indebtedness of the 2016 graduate was $28,230. The the state aid form is required. The FAFSA code is 003822. The priority date for freshman financial aid applications for fall entry is March 1. The deadline for filing freshman financial aid applications for fall entry is March 1.

UNIVERSITY OF CHARLESTON B-4

www.ucwv.edu

Charleston, WV 25304

(304) 357-4750
(800) 995-4682
Email: admissions@ucwv.edu

Full-time: 584 men, 708 women
Part-time: 321 men, 114 women
Graduate: 319 men, 281 women
Year: varies, summer session
Room & Board: $9100

Faculty: 71; IIB, av$
Ph.D.s: n/av
Student/Faculty: 18 to 1
Tuition: $25,900
Freshman Class: 1949 applied, 1022 accepted, 319 enrolled

SAT CR/M: required **ACT:** 22
Application Deadline: n/av

CEEB CODE: 5419
COMPETITIVE

University of Charleston is an independent, co-educational, residential university. The Mission of the University is to educate each student for a life of productive work, enlightened living, and community involvement. The University of Charleston offers a performance-based curriculum focused on specific outcomes that are essential abilities every student needs for a lifetime of learning and opportunity. These outcomes in critical thinking, communication, citizenship, creativity/innovation, ethical practice, and inquiry are embedded in all UC courses to help students apply their learning to their chosen major, and to real-world situations. UC offers undergraduate degree programs in business, health sciences and arts and sciences; masters programs in business, forensic accounting, strategic leadership and physician assistant, and doctoral degrees in pharmacy and executive leadership. The University also offers a combination MBA/PharmD degree and undergraduate-and graduate-level online courses. It boasts 20 Division II varsity athletic teams including multiple nationally ranked teams and academic All-American teams. There are 3 undergraduate schools and 3 graduate schools. In addition to regional accreditation, UC has baccalaureate program accreditation with ACPE, NLN, TEAC, CAATE, JRCERT, and ACOTE. The 40-acre campus is in Charleston, Beckley, and Martinsburg.

STUDENT LIFE: 54% of undergraduates are from West Virginia. Others are from 45 states, 40 foreign countries, and Canada. 6% are Foreign; 56% White; 3% Asian American; 23% race unknown; 2% Hispanic; 10% African American; 1% American Indian/Alaska Native. **Male To Female Ratio:** 1.1:1. The average age of freshmen is 18; all undergraduates, 25. 35% do not continue beyond their first year; 47% remain to graduate. **Housing:** 745 students can be accommodated in college housing, which includes coed dorms, on-campus apartments, and married student housing. On-campus housing is guaranteed for the freshman year only, and is available on a first-come, first-served basis. Priority is given to out-of-town students. 61% of students commute. All students may keep cars.

FACULTY/CLASSROOMS: 43% of faculty are male; 57% are female. 74% teach undergraduates. No introductory courses are taught by graduate students. The average class size in an introductory lecture is 20.

PROGRAMS OF STUDY: UC confers B.A., B.S., and B.S.N. degrees. Associate, master's, and doctoral degrees are also awarded. Bachelor's degrees are awarded in BIOLOGICAL SCIENCE (biology/biological science), BUSINESS (accounting, business administration and management, finance, organizational leadership and management, and sports management), COMMUNICATIONS AND THE ARTS (art and communications), COMPUTER AND PHYSICAL SCIENCE (chemistry), EDUCATION (athletic training, elementary education, English education, physical education, science education, social studies education, and special education), ENGINEERING AND ENVIRONMENTAL DESIGN (interior design), HEALTH PROFESSIONS (diagnostic medical sonography, nursing, and radiological science), SOCIAL SCIENCE (history, liberal arts/general studies, political science/government, and psychology). Biological sciences is the strongest academically. Business, nursing, and biology have the largest enrollments.

ACTIVITIES: Groups on campus include art, cheerleading, chess, choir, chorale, communications, computers, debate, ethnic, film, honors, international, newspaper, pep band, photography, political, professional, religious, social, social service, and student government. Popular campus events include Governor's Cup Regatta, and World-fest. **Sports:** Facilities include a gym, game room, a Nautilus center, an indoor pool, soccer, softball, baseball fields, racquetball, volleyball, tennis courts, and a fitness center. **Graduates:** From July 1, 2015 to June 30, 2016, 209 bachelor's degrees were awarded. The most popular majors were business/leadership (26%), health sciences (19%), and biological sciences (12%). 40 companies recruited on campus in 2015-2016. In an average class, 10% graduate in 3 years or less, and 45% graduate in 4 years or less.

SERVICES: Counseling and information services are available, as is tutoring in most subjects. There is a reader service for the blind, and remedial math, reading, and writing. **Library/Resources:** The library contains 94,267 volumes, 229,551 microform items, and 5,000 audio/video tapes/CDs/DVDs, and subscribes to 150 periodicals including electronic. Computerized library services include interlibrary loans, database searching, Internet access, and Wi-Fi capability. Special learning facilities include an art gallery, an academic success center, and a career center. **Physically Challenged Students:** 85% of the campus is accessible. Facilities include wheelchair ramps, elevators, special parking, specially equipped restrooms, lowered drinking fountains, lowered telephones, and special housing. **Special:** The university offers credit by exam and credit for prior learning, self-acquired competency (SAC) credits, and credits for educational experiences in the armed services. Internships, on-campus work-study, and hospital clinical experience in qualified programs are available. There are 6 national honor societies. **Visiting:** There are regularly scheduled orientations for prospective students, including meetings with faculty, financial aid and student life information sessions, a campus tour, and meetings with coaches for athletes. There are guides for informal visits, visitors may sit in on classes, and stay overnight. To schedule a visit, contact the Admissions Office. **Campus Safety and Security:** Measures include 24-hour foot and vehicle patrol, emergency notification system, self-defense education, and security escort services. There are shuttle buses, emergency telephones, lighted pathways/sidewalks, controlled access to dorms/residences. There are burglar alarms in dorms, safety and date-rape seminars, drug awareness programs, surveillance cameras at dorms (used in conjunction with card access), and emergency radio communications.

REQUIREMENTS: Six semesters of high school, with a minimum 2.25 academic grade point average (on a 4-point scale), or GED score of 500 (50 if taken prior to 1/1/2003). Minimum composite ACT score of 19 and/or SAT I score of 900 on the re-centered SAT* including a record of active participation in school or community organizations or events throughout high school. A commitment to achieving a college degree. A GPA of 2.3 is required. AP and CLEP credits are accepted. Students must obtain degree objective within 150% of the normal time frame for degree completion. For example, in a baccalaureate program requiring 120 credit hours, students must obtain degrees within 180 attempted credit hours (120 X 1.50 = 180). For associate programs of 60 credit hours, students must complete within 90 attempted hours. Graduate students in master's degree programs requiring 68 hours must complete within 102 attempted credit hours. Doctoral students have a maximum of 219 attempted credit hours. This maximum time frame is based upon student classification in the University's academic records. Students who are pursuing a course of study with greater credit hour requirements need to notify the Financial Aid Office in order to have a review done on a case-by-case basis. This request for review will not be considered an appeal. The student is responsible for completing all requirements of his or her major program, including mastery of exit-level outcomes at designated standards, and for meeting all University requirements, including the completion of a comprehensive exit assessment, before they will be allowed to graduate. Students should confer with major advisors and mentors and refer to the Academic Catalog to assure satisfactory progress toward graduation. **Procedure:** Freshmen are admitted to all sessions. Entrance exams should be taken by December of the senior year. There are deferred admissions and rolling admissions plans. Application deadlines are open. Application fee is $25. Notification is sent on a rolling basis. Applications are accepted on-line. **Transfer Students:** 315 transfer students enrolled in 2015-2016. Applicants who have earned 12 or more college-level credits (generally, courses numbered 100 and above) at another institution, have a minimum 2.25 grade point average (on a 4.0 point scale) and are in good standing at the institution last attended must submit the following: a completed Undergraduate Application for admission, official transcript from each college previously attended, and an approved transfer clearance form from most recent institution. **International Students:** There are 121 international students enrolled. The school actively recruits these students. They must take the TOEFL with a minimum score of 500 on the paper-based TOEFL (PBT) or 61 on the Internet-based version (iBT). Students must either take the MELAB and the college's own test, or take the IELTS or ELS. They must also take the SAT or ACT.

ADMISSIONS: 52% of the 2016-2017 applicants were accepted. The SAT scores for the 2016-2017 freshman class were: Critical Reading--61% below 500, 35% between 500 and 599, and 4% between 600 and 699. Math-- 53% below 500, 38% between 500 and 599, 8% between 600 and 699, and 1% between 700 and 800. The ACT scores 10% between 12 and 17, 64% between 18 and 23, 24% between 24 and 29, and 1% above 30. **Admissions Contact:** Joan Clark, Vice President for Admissions. Email: *admissions@ucwv.edu* Web: *www.ucwv.edu*

FINANCIAL AID: In 2016-2017, 100% of all full-time freshmen received some form of financial aid. UC is a member of CSS. The college's own financial statement is required. The FAFSA code is 003818. The priority date for freshman financial aid applications for fall entry is March 1. The deadline for filing freshman financial aid applications for fall entry is September 15.

WEST LIBERTY UNIVERSITY — C-1

www.westliberty.edu

West Liberty, WV 26074 — (304) 336-8076 / (800) 732-6204

Fax: (304) 336-8403 — **Email:** admissions@westliberty.edu
Full-time: 829 men, 1109 women — **Faculty:** 107
Part-time: 136 men, 192 women — **Ph.D.s:** 60%
Graduate: 4 men, 16 women — **Student/Faculty:** 20 to 1
Year: semesters, summer session — **Tuition:** $6702 ($14,112)
Room & Board: $8810 — **Freshman Class:** n/av
SAT or ACT: required — **CEEB CODE:** 5901
Application Deadline: n/av — **COMPETITIVE**

West Liberty State College, founded in 1837, is a state-assisted college offering programs in teacher education, liberal and fine arts, sciences, business, and preprofessional and technical fields. The figures in the above capsule and in this profile are approximate. There are 4 undergraduate schools. In addition to regional accreditation, West Liberty has baccalaureate program accreditation with ADA, CAHEA, NASM, NCATE, NLN, CIHE, and NCACS. The 263-acre campus is in a rural area in West Liberty, WV, 10 miles north of Wheeling and 56 miles southwest of Pittsburgh. Including any residence halls, there are 50 buildings.

STUDENT LIFE: 72% of undergraduates are from West Virginia. Others are from 46 states, 26 foreign countries, and Canada. 90% are from public schools. 95% are White; 3% African American; 1% Hispanic; 1% Foreign. **Female To Male Ratio:** 1.4:1. The average age of freshmen is 18; all undergraduates, 22. 30% do not continue beyond their first year; 43% remain to graduate. **Housing:** College-sponsored housing includes single-sex and coed dorms, on-campus apartments, and married student housing. In addition, there are honors houses. On-campus housing is available on a first-come, first-served basis. Alcohol is not permitted. All students may keep cars.

FACULTY/CLASSROOMS: 59% of faculty are male; 41% are female. All teach undergraduates. No introductory courses are taught by graduate students. The average class size in an introductory lecture is 25; in a laboratory is 20; and in a regular course is 20.

PROGRAMS OF STUDY: West Liberty confers B.A., B.S., and B.S.N. degrees. Associate degrees are also awarded. Bachelor's degrees are awarded in BIOLOGICAL SCIENCE (biology/biological science, ecology, and microbiology), BUSINESS (accounting, banking and finance, business administration and management, business economics, management science, marketing/retailing/merchandising, organizational leadership and management, and tourism), COMMUNICATIONS AND THE ARTS (advertising, broadcasting, communications, English, fine arts, graphic design, music, and public relations), COMPUTER AND PHYSICAL SCIENCE (chemistry, information sciences and systems, and mathematics), EDUCATION (art education, early childhood education, elementary education, health education, middle school education, music education, outdoor leadership/education, physical education, science education, secondary education, social science education, and special education), ENGINEERING AND ENVIRONMENTAL DESIGN (pre-engineering), HEALTH PROFESSIONS (clinical science, dental hygiene, disabilities studies, nursing, predentistry, premedicine, prepharmacy, and speech pathology/audiology), SOCIAL SCIENCE (criminal justice, economics, history, interdisciplinary studies, physical fitness/movement, political science/government, prelaw, psychology, social science, social studies, and sociology). Business, natural sciences, and health sciences are the strongest academically. Business, elementary education, and criminal justice have the largest enrollments.

ACTIVITIES: 6% of men belong to 4 local fraternities; 10% of women belong to 1 local and 3 national sororities. There are 48 groups on campus, including hospitality and tourism, art, cheerleading, choir, chorus, communications, drama, ethnic, honors, jazz band, literary magazine, marching band, musical theater, newspaper, pep band, photography, professional, radio and TV, religious, social, social service, steel drum band, and student government. Popular campus events include Multi-Cultural Day, Greek Week, and Spring Fling. **Sports:** There are 8 intercollegiate sports for men and 7 for women, and 8 intramural sports for men and 7 for women. Facilities include handball and racquetball courts, training rooms, gyms, an indoor track, a wellness center, and an indoor swimming pool. There is also a game area with pool tables and table tennis, all-weather-surface tennis courts, and football and softball/

baseball fields. **Graduates:** From July 1, 2015 to June 30, 2016, 427 bachelor's degrees were awarded. The most popular majors were education (33%), business administration (21%), and criminal justice (11%). 8 companies recruited on campus in 2015-2016. In an average class, 19% graduate in 4 years or less, 37% graduate in 5 years or less, and 41% graduate in 6 years or less. Of the 2015 graduating class, 10% were enrolled in graduate school within 6 months of graduation, and 85% were employed.

SERVICES: Counseling and information services are available, as is tutoring in every subject. There is a reader service for the blind, and remedial math and writing. **Library/Resources:** The library contains 196,338 volumes, 131,000 microform items, and subscribes to 485 periodicals including electronic. Computerized library services include interlibrary loans and database searching. Special learning facilities include an art gallery, radio station, TV station, and publication area. **Physically Challenged Students:** 90% of the campus is accessible. Facilities include wheelchair ramps, elevators, special parking, specially equipped restrooms, lowered drinking fountains, and lowered telephones. **Special:** Communications, exercise physiology, criminal justice, hospitality, tourism management, sports management, and golf management require an on-campus internship. The Washington Center Program, an internship, is also offered. However, students may also choose to complete an internship in the areas of business, clinical lab science, phys ed, or nursing. Interdisciplinary studies is a student-designed degree taken as either a B.A. or B.S. Biology, chemistry, and math are offered as a B.S. degree but may also be taken as a B.A. degree in education. Work and life experience credit is accepted in the Regents B.A. degree program. There are 10 national honor societies, a freshman honors program, and 6 departmental honors programs. **Visiting:** There are guides for informal visits, visitors may sit in on classes, and stay overnight. To schedule a visit, contact the Office of Admissions. **Campus Safety and Security:** Measures include 24-hour foot and vehicle patrol, self-defense education, and security escort services. There are emergency telephones, lighted pathways/sidewalks, and late night transport.

REQUIREMENTS: The SAT or ACT is required. Applicants must graduate from an accredited secondary school with a minimum GPA of 2.0, or have a composite minimum score of 18 on the ACT or a minimum combined verbal, critical reading, and math score of 870. Students must have completed 4 years of English, 3 of social sciences, including U.S. history, 4 of math (with 3 of algebra I and higher), 3 of science (all units must be of lab), 1 of arts, and 2 of the same foreign language. The GED is accepted. AP and CLEP credits are accepted. The required core curriculum varies for B.A. and B.S. candidates, but both include courses in communications, fine arts and humanities, natural science and math, social science and history, and phys ed and health. A minimum GPA of 2.0 and 128 credit hours are required to graduate. **Procedure:** Freshmen are admitted to all sessions. Entrance exams should be taken in time so that all admissions credentials, including test scores, are received 2 weeks prior to the beginning of the term. There are deferred admissions and rolling admissions plans. Check with the school for current application deadlines. Applications are accepted on-line. **Transfer Students:** 284 transfer students enrolled in 2015-2016. Students must be eligible to return to the institution from which they wish to transfer. An official college transcript and a minimum GPA of 2.0 overall are required. Admissions criteria are the same as for freshmen if the student has completed fewer than 28 hours of college-level course-work. 36 of 128 credits required for the bachelor's degree must be completed at West Liberty. **International Students:** There are 13 international students enrolled. They must take the TOEFL. They must also take the SAT or ACT, scoring 17.

Admissions Contact: Brenda King, Director of Admissions. Email: *admissions@westliberty.edu* Web: *www.westliberty.edu*

FINANCIAL AID: In 2016-2017, 91% of all full-time freshmen received some form of financial aid. The average freshman award was $5,023. 99% of undergraduate students work part-time. Average annual earnings from campus work are $828. The average financial indebtedness of the 2016 graduate was $12,568. The FAFSA code is 003823. The deadline for filing freshman financial aid applications for fall entry is March 1.

WEST VIRGINIA STATE UNIVERSITY *(The complete profile is made available exclusively on our website, www.barronspac.com)*

WEST VIRGINIA UNIVERSITY C-2

www.wvu.edu

Morgantown, WV 26506 (304) 293-2121 (800) 344-9881

Fax: (304) 293-3080 **Email:** wvuadmissions@mail.wvu.edu

Full-time: 11,128 men, 9396 women	**Faculty:** I, --$
Part-time: 848 men, 978 women	**Ph.D.s:** 69%
Graduate: 2727 men, 3411 women	**Student/Faculty:** 21 to 1
Year: semesters, summer session	**Tuition:** $7992 ($22,488)
Room & Board: $10,218	**Freshman Class:** 15353 applied, 13174 accepted, 4782 enrolled
SAT CR/M: 514/529 **ACT:** 24	**CEEB CODE:** 5904
Application Deadline: August 1	**COMPETITIVE**

West Virginia University, founded in 1867, is a comprehensive public land-grant research university offering more than 100 undergraduate degrees in liberal arts and sciences, health science, and professional training. The figures in the above capsule and in this profile are approximate. There are 15 undergraduate schools and 13 graduate schools. In addition to regional accreditation, WVU has baccalaureate program accreditation with AACSB, ABET, ACEJMC, ACPE, ADA, APTA, ASLA, CAHEA, CSWE, FIDER, NASAD, NASM, NCATE, NLN, NRPA, and SAF. The 2965-acre campus is in a small town 75 miles south of Pittsburgh, PA and 200 miles west of Baltimore, MD. Including any residence halls, there are 275 buildings.

STUDENT LIFE: 50% of undergraduates are from out of state, mostly the Middle Atlantic. Students are from 50 states, 107 foreign countries, and Canada. 80% are White; 6% Foreign; 5% African American; 4% Hispanic; 4% two or more races; 2% Asian American. **Male To Female Ratio:** 1.1:1. The average age of freshmen is 19; all undergraduates, 21. **Housing:** 6500 students can be accommodated in college housing, which includes single-sex and coed dorms, on-campus apartments, off-campus apartments, and married student housing. In addition, there are honors houses, language houses, special-interest houses, fraternity houses, sorority houses, and sections within residence halls designated for special programming. On-campus housing is available on a first-come, first-served basis, and is available on a lottery system for upperclassmen. 76% of students commute. Alcohol is not permitted. All students may keep cars.

FACULTY/CLASSROOMS: 55% of faculty are male; 45% are female. No introductory courses are taught by graduate students.

PROGRAMS OF STUDY: WVU confers B.A., B.S., B.F.A., B.M., B.Md.S., B.S.A.E., B.S.Agr., B.S.B.Ad., B.S.B.S., B.S.C.E., B.S.Ch.E., B.S.Cp.E., B.S.E.E., B.S.F., B.S.C.S., B.S.I.E., B.S.J., B.S.L.A., B.S.M.E., B.S.Min.E., B.S.N., B.S.Pnge., B.S.R., R.B.A., B.S.Bm.E., and B.S.W. degrees. Master's and doctoral degrees are also awarded. Bachelor's degrees are awarded in AGRICULTURE (agricultural economics, agricultural sciences, agriculture, agronomy, animal science, fish and game management, fishing and fisheries, forestry and related sciences, horticulture, natural resource management, plant science, wildlife management, and wood science), BIOLOGICAL SCIENCE (biology/biological science, forensic science, genetics, and nutrition), BUSINESS (accounting, banking and finance, business administration and management, business administration marketing, business law, entrepreneurial studies, fashion merchandising, finance, management information systems, marketing, marketing and distribution, recreation and leisure services, sports management, and tourism), COMMUNICATIONS AND THE ARTS (advertising, art, broadcasting, communications, creative writing, dance, dramatic arts, English, foreign language, journalism, music, public relations, speech/debate/rhetoric, and visual and performing arts), COMPUTER AND PHYSICAL SCIENCE (applied mathematics, chemistry, computer science, geology, geoscience, mathematics, physics, and science), EDUCATION (agricultural education, art education, athletic training, education administration, environmental education, general studies, library science, physical education, and reading education), ENGINEERING AND ENVIRONMENTAL DESIGN (aeronautical engineering, aerospace studies, chemical engineering, civil engineering, computer engineering, electrical/electronics engineering, engineering, environmental science, interior design, landscape architecture/design, mechanical engineering, military science, mining and mineral engineering, petroleum/natural gas engineering, and systems engineering), HEALTH PROFESSIONS (biology, dental hygiene, kinesiology, nursing, occupational therapy, pharmacy, physical therapy, speech pathology/audiology, and veterinary science), SOCIAL SCIENCE (American Indian studies, anthropology, child care/child and family studies, criminology, economics, family/consumer resource management, forensic studies, gender studies, geography, history, interdisciplinary studies, international studies, law, liberal arts/general studies, parks and recreation management, philosophy, political science/government, psychology, social work, and sociology). Engineering & mineral resources, psychology, and political science are the strongest academically. Business & economics, engineering & mineral resources, and health sciences have the largest enrollments.

ACTIVITIES: 7% of men belong to 20 national fraternities; 7% of women belong to 1 local and 8 national sororities. There are 460 groups on campus, including art, band, cheerleading, chess, choir, chorale, chorus, computers, dance, debate, drama, environmental, ethnic, film, forensics, honors, international, jazz band, LGBT, marching band, newspaper, opera, orchestra, pep band, photography, political, professional, radio and TV, religious, social, social service, student government, and symphony. Popular campus events include Mountaineer Week, Greek Week, and Fall Fest. **Sports:** There are 7 intercollegiate sports for men and 9 for women, and 17 intramural sports for men and 17 for women. Facilities include tennis courts, weight and exercise space, jogging track, turf field, lacrosse, frisbee, swimming pools, basketball courts, a 50 foot high climbing wall. There is a natatorium with swimming and diving pools, rifle facilities, tennis courts, a weight room, indoor/outdoor tracks, a bowling alley, lacrosse, baseball, football, and soccer fields, a stadium, a gym, a coliseum offering basketball, wrestling, volleyball, and gymnastics, and a soccer stadium. **Graduates:** From July 1, 2015 to June 30, 2016, 4550 bachelor's degrees were awarded. The most popular majors were engineering (14%), business (12%), and health field (9%). 1200 companies recruited on campus in 2015-2016. In an average class, 33% graduate in 4 years or less, 53% graduate in 5 years or less, and 57% graduate in 6 years or less.

SERVICES: Counseling and information services are available, as is tutoring in most subjects. There is a reader service for the blind, and remedial math, reading, and writing. **Library/Resources:** The 5 libraries contain 2.4 million volumes, 263,203 microform items, and 15,663 audio/video tapes/CDs/DVDs, and subscribe to 89,824 periodicals including electronic. Computerized library services include interlibrary loans, database searching, Internet access, and Wi-Fi capability. Special learning facilities include an art gallery, planetarium, radio station, a discovery lab for inventors, coal, mining, and minerals history museum, a pharmacy museum, art museum, and an arboretum. **Physically Challenged Students:** 90% of the campus is accessible. Facilities include wheelchair ramps, elevators, special parking, specially equipped restrooms, special class scheduling, lowered drinking fountains, lowered telephones, and special housing. Academic programs are made accessible by transferring class to an architecturally accessible facility. Other facilities include tactile signage, specially designed lab facilities, portable lab stations, a Kurzweil reading machine, and a specially equipped van for inner-city transportation. **Special:** A co-op program in engineering and cross-registration with schools in the Southern Regional Education Board through the Academic Common Market are possible. Internships, study abroad in 25 countries, a Washington semester, student-designed majors, dual majors in business and foreign languages, and B.A.-B.S. degrees in economics, chemistry, physics, biology, math, psychology, and geology are available. A liberal studies degree, credit by exam, credit for life experience, nondegree study, and pass/fail options are also offered. There are 261 national honor societies, Phi Beta Kappa, and a freshman honors program. **Visiting:** There are regularly scheduled orientations for prospective students, including 2-day sessions with campus tours, placement testing, academic and advisement meetings, parent/student orientation discussions, and transitional meetings. There are guides for informal visits and visitors may sit in on classes. To schedule a visit, contact the Visitors Resource Center at (304) 293-3489. **Campus Safety and Security:** Measures include 24-hour foot and vehicle patrol, emergency notification system, self-defense education, and security escort services. There are shuttle buses, emergency telephones, lighted pathways/sidewalks, neighborhood watch programs, and sexual assault prevention booths staffed by city and university police.

REQUIREMENTS: West Virginia residents must have a minimim GPA of 2.0 and either a composite ACT score of 19 or a combined SAT score of 910 (critical reading and math). Nonresidents must have a minimum GPA of 2.5 and either 21 on the ACT or 990 on the SAT. AP and CLEP credits are accepted. Important factors in the admissions decision are leadership record, evidence of special talent, and advanced placement or honors courses. All students are required to take 12 credit hours in each of 3 areas: humanities and fine arts, social and behavioral sciences, and natural sciences and math. The 36 credit hours must include international/minority/gender studies, math, composition, and an advanced course emphasizing writing skills. A minimum 2.0 GPA and at least 128 credit hours are required to graduate. **Procedure:** Freshmen are admitted fall, spring, and summer. Entrance exams should be taken by spring of the junior year. There are deferred admissions and rolling admissions plans. Applications should be filed by August 1 for fall entry, along with a $60 fee. Applications are accepted on-line. **Transfer Students:** 935 transfer students enrolled in 2015-2016. Students must have a minimum 2.0 GPA in all college work attempted. Those with fewer than 12 transferable credit hours must also meet freshman admission standards. Some programs have different course and higher GPA requirements. 30 of 128 credits required for the bachelor's degree must be completed at WVU. **International Students:** There are 1372 international students enrolled. The school actively recruits these students. They must take the TOEFL with a minimum score of 500 on the paper-based TOEFL (PBT) or 61 on the Internet-based version (iBT). International students serving as graduate teaching assistants must also demonstrate mastery of spoken English. They must also take the SAT or ACT, scoring 950.

ADMISSIONS: 86% of the 2016-2017 applicants were accepted. The SAT scores for the 2016-2017 freshman class were: Critical Reading-- 47% below 500, 40% between 500 and 599, 11% between 600 and 699, and 2% between 700 and 800. Math-- 40% below 500, 42% between 500 and 599, 16% between 600 and 699, and 2% between 700 and 800. The ACT scores were 10% between 12 and 17, 50% between 18 and 23, 35% between 24 and 29, and 5% above 30. **Admissions Contact:** Stephen Lee, Exec. Director of Admissions and Records. Email: *wvuadmissions@mail.wvu.edu* Web: *www.wvu.edu*

FINANCIAL AID: In 2016-2017, 58% of all full-time freshmen and 55% of continuing full-time students received some form of financial aid. 41% of all full-time freshmen and 39% of continuing full-time students received need-based aid. The average freshman award was $6,616. Need-based scholarships or need-based grants averaged $4,814; need-based self-help aid (loans and jobs) averaged $3,871; non-need-based athletic scholarships averaged $20,863; and other non-need-based awards and non-need-based scholarships averaged $6,285. The average financial indebtedness of the 2016 graduate was $27,730. The state aid form is required. The FAFSA code is 003827. The deadline for filing freshman financial aid applications for fall entry is March 1.

WEST VIRGINIA UNIVERSITY INSTITUTE OF TECHNOLOGY *(The complete profile is made available exclusively on our website, www.barronspac.com)*

WEST VIRGINIA WESLEYAN COLLEGE C-3

www.wvwc.edu

Buckhannon, WV 26201	**(304) 473-8510** **(800) 722-9933**
Fax: (304) 473-8108	**Email: admissions@wvwc.edu**
Full-time: 600 men, 700 women	**Faculty:** 78; IIB
Part-time: 13 men, 14 women	**Ph.D.s:** 77%
Graduate: 16 men, 26 women	**Student/Faculty:** 17 to 1
Year: semesters, summer session	**Tuition:** $28,792
Room & Board: $8066	**Freshman Class:** 1272 applied, 984 accepted, 369 enrolled
SAT: required **ACT:** 23	**CEEB CODE:** 5905
Application Deadline: August 1	**COMPETITIVE**

West Virginia Wesleyan College, founded in 1890, is an independent liberal and applied arts college affiliated with the United Methodist Church. The figures in the above capsule and in this profile are approximate. There are 7 undergraduate schools. In addition to regional accreditation, WVWC has baccalaureate program accreditation with NCATE, NLN, IACBE, and CAAHEP. The 80-acre campus is in a small town in the Appalachian foothills, 135 miles south of Pittsburgh, Pennsylvania. Including any residence halls, there are 23 buildings.

STUDENT LIFE: 53% of undergraduates are from West Virginia. Others are from 37 states, 12 foreign countries, and Canada. 85% are from public schools. 88% are White; 5% African American; 4% Foreign; 1% Asian American; 1% American Indian/Alaska Native; 1% Hispanic. 53% are Protestant; 20% Catholic. **Female To Male Ratio:** 1.2:1. The average age of freshmen is 18; all undergraduates, 21. **Housing:** 1275 students can be accommodated in college housing, which includes single-sex and coed dorms and on-campus apartments. In addition, there are honors houses, quiet study living areas, and substance-free small-group living units. On-campus housing is guaranteed for all 4 years. 83% of students live on campus; of those, 65% remain on campus on weekends. Alcohol is not permitted. All students may keep cars.

FACULTY/CLASSROOMS: 79% of faculty are male; 21% are female. All teach undergraduates. No introductory courses are taught by graduate students. The average class size in an introductory lecture is 24; in a laboratory is 12; and in a regular course is 21.

PROGRAMS OF STUDY: WVWC confers B.A., B.S., B.M.E., and B.S.N. degrees. Master's degrees are also awarded. Bachelor's degrees are awarded in AGRICULTURE (environmental studies), BIOLOGICAL SCIENCE (biochemistry, biology/biological science, biological sciences, and nutrition), BUSINESS (accounting, business administration and management, international business, and marketing/retailing/merchandising), COMMUNICATIONS AND THE ARTS (communication studies, dramatic arts, English, music, public relations, speech/debate/rhetoric, and theatre arts), COMPUTER AND PHYSICAL SCIENCE (chemistry, computer science, mathematics, and physics), EDUCATION (art education, Christian education, elementary education, music education, physical education, and secondary education), ENGINEERING AND ENVIRONMENTAL DESIGN (engineering, engineering physics, environmental science, and petroleum/natural gas engineering), HEALTH PROFESSIONS (exercise science and nursing), SOCIAL SCIENCE (criminal justice, economics, gender studies, history, international studies, philosophy, political science/government, psychology, religion, religious education, social science, and sociology). Physical & natural science, and accounting are the strongest academically. Business, biology, and education have the largest enrollments.

ACTIVITIES: 25% of men belong to 5 national fraternities; 25% of women belong to 5 national sororities. There are 75 groups on campus, including art, band, cheerleading, choir, chorale, chorus, communications, computers, dance, drama, ethnic, forensics, honors, international, jazz band, literary magazine, musical theater, newspaper, political, professional, radio and TV, religious, social, social service, student government, and yearbook. Popular campus events include Founders Day, Festivals of Lessons and Carols, and Spring Sing. **Sports:** There are 9 intercollegiate sports for men and 8 for women, and 9 intramural sports for men and 8 for women. Facilities include baseball and football fields, basketball court, intramural practice courts, handball courts, an auxiliary gym, indoor tennis courts, volleyball courts, golf and wrestling practice areas, a dance studio, gymnastics, weight rooms, cross country, soccer, swimming, softball, and track and field. **Graduates:** From July 1, 2015 to June 30, 2016, 303 bachelor's degrees were awarded. The most popular majors were business (14%), elementary education (12%), and biology (8%). In an average class, 1% graduate in 3 years or less, 44% graduate in 4 years or less, 52% graduate in 5 years or less, and 55% graduate in 6 years or less.

SERVICES: Counseling and information services are available, as is tutoring in every subject. There is a reader service for the blind, and remedial math, reading, and writing. **Library/Resources:** The library contains 116,240 volumes, 39,119 microform items, and 6,322 audio/video tapes/CDs/DVDs, and subscribes to 14,126 periodicals including electronic. Computerized library services include interlibrary loans, database searching, Internet access, and Wi-Fi capability. Special learning facilities include an art gallery, planetarium, and radio station. **Physically Challenged Students:** 75% of the campus is accessible. Facilities include wheelchair ramps, elevators, special parking, specially equipped restrooms, special class scheduling, and lowered drinking fountains. **Special:** WVWC offers cross-registration with the Mountain State Association of Colleges. Students may participate in a wide variety of internships, including a Washington Center internship and work-study and study-abroad programs; there are exchange agreements in Korea, the People's Republic of China, Norway, and Bulgaria. Nondegree and pass/fail study, dual, student-designed, and contract majors, and credit for life, military, and work experience are available. A 3-2 engineering degree offered with West Virginia University and the University of Virginia. There is 1 national honor society and a freshman honors program. **Visiting:** There are regularly scheduled orientations for prospective students. There are guides for informal visits, visitors may sit in on classes, and stay overnight. To schedule a visit, contact the Admission Office. **Campus Safety and Security:** Measures include 24-hour foot and vehicle patrol, self-defense education, and security escort services. There are emergency telephones, lighted pathways/sidewalks, rape awareness educational programs, and appropriate training for residence hall staff.

REQUIREMENTS: The minimum composite score needed is 800 on SAT, 420 verbal and 380 math, or 18 on the ACT. In addition, applicants must be high school graduates or hold a GED. Students should have earned 26 academic credits, consisting of 4 in English, 3 each in math, science, and academic electives, and 2 each in foreign language, lab science, and social studies, as well as a total of 7 academic credits in fine arts, technology education, health, and phys ed. An essay and an interview are recommended. AP and CLEP credits are accepted. Important factors in the admissions decision are extracurricular activities record, recommendations by school officials, and leadership record. To graduate, students must earn 120 semester hours with a minimum GPA of 2.0; 24 to 51 hours must be in the major, 48 to 53 in general studies. Required disciplines are cultural studies, natural science and math, social sciences, health and phys ed, religion, philosophy, humanities and fine arts, and communications. **Procedure:** Freshmen are admitted fall and spring. Entrance exams should be taken in fall of the senior year or spring/summer of the junior year. There are early decision, deferred admissions, and rolling admissions plans. Early decision applications should be filed by December 1; regular applications, by August 1 for fall entry; and January 10 for spring entry, along with a $35 fee. Notifications are sent November 1. Applications are accepted on-line. **Transfer Students:** 34 transfer students enrolled in 2015-2016. Transfer applicants must supply a high school transcript if their GPA for college work is less than 2.5. An associate degree and an interview are recommended. 30 of 120 credits required for the bachelor's degree must be completed at WVWC. **International Students:** The school actively recruits these students. They must take the TOEFL. They must also take the SAT or ACT if they are seeking scholarships.

ADMISSIONS: 77% of the 2016-2017 applicants were accepted. The ACT scores were 18% below 12, 19% between 12 and 17, 16% between 18 and 23, 6% between 24 and 29, and 4% above 30. 10 freshmen graduated first in their class. **Admissions Contact:** Director of Admission Email: *admissions@wvwc.edu* Web: *www.wvwc.edu*

FINANCIAL AID: In 2016-2017, 98% of all full-time freshmen and 98% of continuing full-time students received some form of financial aid. 77% of all full-time freshmen and 75% of continuing full-time students received need-based aid. The average freshman award was $21,700. 41% of undergraduate students work part-time. Average annual earnings from campus work are $1000. The average financial indebtedness of the 2016 graduate was $18,000. The FAFSA code is 003830. The deadline for filing freshman financial aid applications for fall entry is March 1.

WHEELING JESUIT UNIVERSITY *(The complete profile is made available exclusively on our website, www.barronspac.com)*

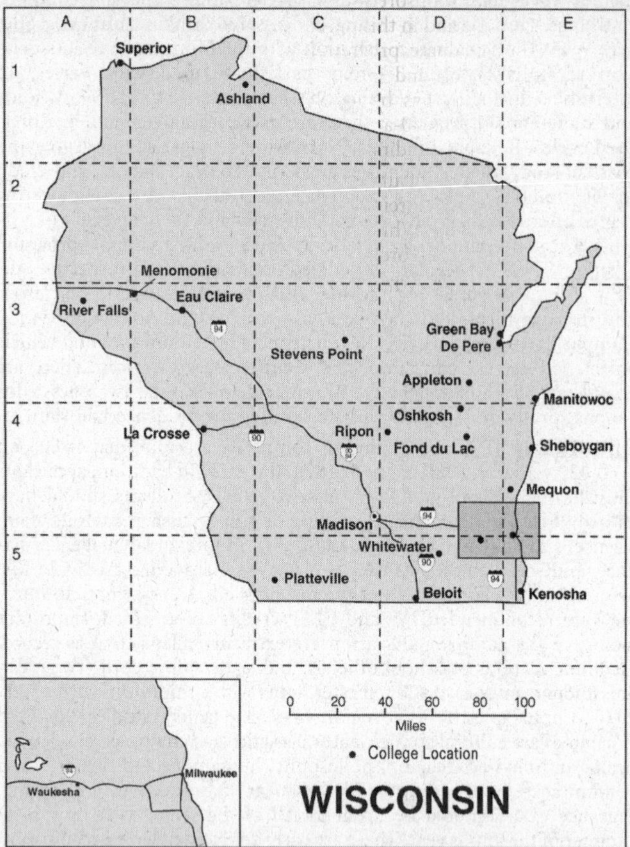

ALVERNO COLLEGE *(The complete profile is made available exclusively on our website, www.barronspac.com)*

BELOIT COLLEGE D-5

www.beloit.edu

Beloit, WI 53511	**(608) 363-2500** **(800) 9-BELOIT**
Fax: (608) 363-2075	**Email: admiss@beloit.edu**
Full-time: 620 men, 717 women	**Faculty:** 107; IIB, av$
Part-time: 19 men, 38 women	**Ph.D.s:** 98%
Graduate: n/av	**Student/Faculty:** 12 to 1
Year: semesters, summer session	**Tuition:** $47,060
Room & Board: $8146	**Freshman Class:** 3855 applied, 2693 accepted, 382 enrolled
SAT CR/M: 630/620 **ACT:** 27	**CEEB CODE:** 1059
Application Deadline: January 15	**HIGHLY COMPETITIVE**

Beloit College, founded in 1846, is a private liberal arts institution. Figures in the above capsule and in this profile are approximate. There is 1 undergraduate school. The 44-acre campus is in a small town 50 miles south of Madison, 80 miles southwest of Milwaukee, and 90 miles northwest of Chicago, IL. Including any residence halls, there are 70 buildings.

STUDENT LIFE: 85% of undergraduates are from out of state, mostly the Midwest. Students are from 49 states, 28 foreign countries, and Canada. 64% are from public schools. 9% are Hispanic; 61% White; 5% African American; 4% race unknown; 3% Asian American; 3% two or more races; 14% Foreign. **Female To Male Ratio:** 1.2:1. The average age of freshmen is 18; all undergraduates, 20. 12% do not continue beyond their first year; 81% remain to graduate. **Housing:** 1206 students can be accommodated in college housing, which includes single-sex and coed dorms and on-campus apartments. In addition, there are language houses, special-interest houses, fraternity houses, and sorority houses. On-campus housing is guaranteed for the freshman year only. 87% of students live on campus; of those, 95% remain on campus on weekends. All students may keep cars.

FACULTY/CLASSROOMS: 44% of faculty are male; 56% are female. All teach undergraduates. No introductory courses are taught by graduate students. The average class size in an introductory lecture is 15; in a laboratory is 15; and in a regular course is 15.

PROGRAMS OF STUDY: Beloit confers B.A. and B.S. degrees. Bachelor's degrees are awarded in AGRICULTURE (environmental studies and forestry and related sciences), BIOLOGICAL SCIENCE (biology ecology and field biology, biochemistry, biology/biological science, cell biology, ecology, and environmental biology), BUSINESS (business administration and management, business economics, and international economics), COMMUNICATIONS AND THE ARTS (art history, art, Chinese, classical languages, classics, comparative literature, creative writing, dance, dramatic arts, East Asian languages and literature, English, English literature, French, German, intermedia/multimedia, literature, modern language, music, Russian, Spanish, and studio art), COMPUTER AND PHYSICAL SCIENCE (applied physics, chemistry, computer science, environmental geology, geology, mathematics, and physics), EDUCATION (art education and education), ENGINEERING AND ENVIRONMENTAL DESIGN (preengineering), HEALTH PROFESSIONS (premedicine), SOCIAL SCIENCE (anthropology, Chinese Studies, classical/ancient civilization, cognitive science, economics, gender studies, history, interdisciplinary studies, international relations, philosophy, philosophy and religion, political science/government, prelaw, psychology, religion, religious studies, sociology, and women's studies). Anthropology, creative writing, and biology are the strongest academically. Psychology, international relations, and biology have the largest enrollments.

ACTIVITIES: 19% of men belong to 3 national fraternities; 20% of women belong to 1 local and 3 national sororities. There are 117 groups on campus, including entrepreneurial, science fiction and fantasy, wind, art, band, choir, chorus, computers, dance, drama, environmental, ethnic, film, honors, international, jazz band, LGBT, literary magazine, musical theater, newspaper, photography, political, professional, radio and TV, religious, social, social service, student government, and yoga. Popular campus events include Great Lecture Series, Advising Day, Folk and Blues Weekend, and Spring Day. **Sports:** There are 9 intercollegiate sports for men and 9 for women, and 8 intramural sports for men and 7 for women. Facilities include 2,250-seat arena for basketball and volleyball, racquetball/handball courts, fitness center, a natatorium, field house that contains a running track, an indoor soccer area, batting/pitching cage, and space for indoor tennis, 3,500-seat stadium hosting football, soccer, lacrosse, and track and field, outdoor playing fields, dance studio, and tennis court complex. There are facilities nearby for sailing, ice skating, and other recreation. **Graduates:** From July 1, 2015 to June 30, 2016, 282 bachelor's degrees were awarded. The most popular majors were education (6%), anthropology/sociology (6%), and psychology (6%). In an average class, 69% graduate in 4 years or less, 80% graduate in 5 years or less, and 81% graduate in 6 years or less. Of the 2015 graduating class, 15% were enrolled in graduate school within 6 months of graduation, and 89% were employed.

SERVICES: Counseling and information services are available, as is tutoring in most subjects such as most introductory and many advanced courses (as available and requested). There is a reader service for the blind. **Library/Resources:** The library contains 505,586 volumes, 7,314 microform items, and 9,301 audio/video tapes/CDs/DVDs, and subscribes to 1,052 periodicals including electronic. Computerized library services include interlibrary loans, database searching, and Internet access. Special learning facilities include an art gallery, natural history museum, planetarium, radio station, TV station, two teaching museums (anthropology and art), a comprehensive language lab, an observatory, a center for entrepreneurship, dance facilities, science laboratories, and a theater complex. **Physically Challenged Students:** 50% of the campus is accessible. Facilities include wheelchair ramps, elevators, special parking, specially equipped restrooms, special class scheduling, lowered drinking fountains, and lowered telephones. **Special:** Beloit offers cross-registration with the University of Wisconsin/Madison, internships, study abroad in more than 38 countries, and a Washington semester. Dual majors, student-designed and interdisciplinary majors, and nondegree study are available. A 3-2 engineering degree is offered with 9 institutions, and co-op programs are available in social services, forestry and environmental management, engineering, and business administration. An intensive summer language program is offered in Russian, Arabic, Japanese, and Chinese. There are 6 national honor societies and a chapter of Phi Beta Kappa. **Visiting:** There are regularly scheduled orientations for prospective students, which may include an interview, a tour, class visits, and meetings with professors. Enrolled students serve as tour guides and hosts for overnight stays. There are guides for informal visits. To schedule a visit, contact The Office of Admissions. **Campus Safety and Security:** Measures include 24-hour foot and vehicle patrol, emergency notification system, and security escort services. There are emergency telephones, lighted pathways/sidewalks, and controlled access to dorms/residences.

REQUIREMENTS: Submission of test scores is optional for most applicants. Home-schooled applicants and candidates applying from schools that do not provide grades are asked to submit results from one or more standardized tests, such as SAT or ACT. Applicants must be graduates of an accredited secondary school or home-school program, with 4 years of English, 3 each of math, science, and history/social sciences, and 2 of foreign language. The GED is accepted. An essay and a letter of recommendation are required, and an interview is strongly recommended. A GPA of 2.5 is required. AP and CLEP credits are accepted. Important factors in the admissions decision are advanced placement or honors courses, recommendations by school officials, and leadership record. To graduate, students must complete 31 units, including 8 to 15 in the major, with a minimum GPA of 2.0. Students must complete 3 writing-designated courses, 1 quantitative reasoning-designated course, and 1 intercultural literacy-designated course. Breadth requirements include 1 courses in each of the following domains: Conceptual and Foundational Systems, Artistic and Creative Practices, Social Analysis of Human Behavior, Scientific Inquiry into the Physical and Biological Universe, and Textual Cultures and Analysis. Students are also expected to complete a liberal arts in practice experience that integrates learning from inside and outside the classroom, typically in the junior year, and a capstone experience, typically in the senior year. **Procedure:** Freshmen are admitted fall and spring. There are early decision, early admissions, deferred admissions, and rolling admissions plans. Early decision applications should be filed by November 1; regular applications, by January 15 for fall entry; and November 1 for spring entry. Notification of early decision is sent November 30; regular decision, March 15. 32 applicants were on the 2016 waiting list; 3 were admitted. Applications are accepted on-line. Application fees are waived if application is completed on-line. **Transfer Students:** 27 transfer students enrolled in 2015-2016. Applicants must have a minimum GPA of 2.5 and submit official transcripts of all college work completed. The SAT and the ACT are both optional. An interview is recommended. A letter of recommendation from a professor at a current/previous institution is also required. 16 of 31 credits required for the bachelor's degree must be completed at Beloit. **International Students:** There are 196 international students enrolled. The school actively recruits these students. Requirements vary by student background. Applicants from some countries must supply a school-leaving exam/certificate.

ADMISSIONS: 70% of the 2016-2017 applicants were accepted. The SAT scores for the 2016-2017 freshman class were: Critical Reading-- 11% below 500, 34% between 500 and 599, 30% between 600 and 699, and 25% between 700 and 800. Math-- 13% below 500, 31% between 500 and 599, 43% between 600 and 699, and 13% between 700 and 800. The ACT scores were 2% between 12 and 17, 18% between 18 and 23, 52% between 24 and 29, and 28% above 30. 60% of the current freshmen were in the top fifth of their class. There were 2 National Merit finalists. **Admissions Contact:** Emily McEntee, Assistant Director of Admission. Email: *admiss@beloit.edu* Web: *www.beloit.edu*

FINANCIAL AID: In 2016-2017, 63% of all full-time freshmen received some form of financial aid. 70% of all full-time freshmen and 62% of continuing full-time students received need-based aid. 79% of undergraduate students work part-time. Average annual earnings from campus work are $1636. Beloit is a member of CSS. The FAFSA code is 003835. The deadline for filing freshman financial aid applications for fall entry is March 1.

CARDINAL STRITCH UNIVERSITY E-4

www.stritch.edu

Milwaukee, WI 53217	**(414) 410-4040** **(800) 347-8822**
Fax: (414) 410-4049	**Email: admityou@stritch.edu**
Full-time: 910 men, 2000 women	**Faculty:** 98
Part-time: 50 men, 170 women	**Ph.D.s:** 54%
Graduate: 820 men, 1900 women	**Student/Faculty:** 30 to 1
Year: semesters, summer session	**Tuition:** $28,212
Room & Board: $8250	**Freshman Class:** n/av
SAT or ACT: required	**CEEB CODE:** 1100
Application Deadline: August 1	**COMPETITIVE**

Cardinal Stritch University, founded in 1937 as a college, is a private, Catholic institution sponsored by the Sisters of St. Francis. The figures in the above capsule and in this profile are approximate. The tuition cost is for the undergraduate programs, 12-18 credit hours. There are 4 undergraduate schools and 1 graduate school. In addition to regional accreditation, Stritch has baccalaureate program accreditation with NCATE and NLN. The 40-acre campus is in a suburban area 10 miles north of Milwaukee. Including any residence halls, there are 9 buildings.

STUDENT LIFE: 89% of undergraduates are from Wisconsin. Others are from 16 states, 27 foreign countries, and Canada. 60% are from public schools. 72% are White; 3% Hispanic; 2% Asian American; 16% African American; 1% Foreign. 27% are Catholic. **Female To Male Ratio:** 2.3:1. The average age of freshmen is 19; all undergraduates, 32. 27% do not continue beyond their first year; 43% remain to graduate. **Housing:** 278 students can be accommodated in college housing, which includes coed dorms. On-campus housing is available on a first-come, first-served basis. 95% of students commute. All students may keep cars.

FACULTY/CLASSROOMS: 49% of faculty are male; 51% are female. All teach undergraduates. No introductory courses are taught by graduate students. The average class size in a laboratory is 12 and in a regular course is 11.

PROGRAMS OF STUDY: Stritch confers B.A., B.S., and B.F.A. degrees. Associate, master's, and doctoral degrees are also awarded. Bachelor's degrees are awarded in BIOLOGICAL SCIENCE (biology/biological science), BUSINESS (accounting, business administration and management, and international business management), COMMUNICATIONS AND THE ARTS (art, communications, creative writing, dramatic arts, English, fine arts, French, music, public relations, and Spanish), COMPUTER AND PHYSICAL SCIENCE (chemistry, computer science, and mathematics), EDUCATION (early childhood education, elementary education, middle school education, secondary education, and special education), HEALTH PROFESSIONS (nursing, predentistry, premedicine, preoptometry, and preveterinary science), SOCIAL SCIENCE (history, prelaw, psychology, religion, social science, and sociology). Education in general, and special education in particular, are the strongest academically. Business, education, and nursing have the largest enrollments.

ACTIVITIES: There are no fraternities or sororities. There are 50 groups on campus, including art, band, cheerleading, choir, chorus, computers, dance, drama, ethnic, film, honors, international, jazz band, musical theater, newspaper, orchestra, photography, political, professional, radio and TV, religious, social, social service, student government, and yearbook. Popular campus events include Thursday night events and weekly activities. **Sports:** There are 5 intercollegiate sports for men and 5 for women, and 2 intramural sports for men and 2 for women. Facilities include basketball and volleyball courts, an indoor track, a weight & exercise room, an area for table tennis & billiards, and a soccer field. **Graduates:** From July 1, 2015 to June 30, 2016, 285 bachelor's degrees were awarded. The most popular majors were management (35%), business administration (25%), and management information systems (9%). 10 companies recruited on campus in 2015-2016. In an average class, 4% graduate in 3 years or less, 19% graduate in 4 years or less, 39% graduate in 5 years or less, and 43% graduate in 6 years or less.

SERVICES: Counseling and information services are available, as is tutoring in every subject. There is remedial math, reading, and writing. **Library/Resources:** The library contains 132,293 volumes, 173,216 microform items, and 6,310 audio/video tapes/CDs/DVDs, and subscribes to 1,309 periodicals including electronic. Computerized library services include interlibrary loans and database searching. Special learning facilities include an art gallery and radio station. **Physically Challenged Students:** 80% of the campus is accessible. Facilities include wheelchair ramps, special parking, specially equipped restrooms, special class scheduling, and lowered telephones. **Special:** Students may participate in a variety of internships with Milwaukee businesses and organizations. Stritch offers an accelerated degree program and a B.A.-B.S. degree in business, dual majors, a general studies degree, and nondegree study. Study abroad, work-study programs, pass/fail options, and credit for life, military, and work experience are offered. An accelerated evening program and a management program are offered for working adults. There are 9 national honor societies and a freshman honors program. **Visiting:** There are regularly scheduled orientations for prospective students, including a campus tour, meetings with admissions and financial aid counselors, and possible meetings with department chairs. There are guides for informal visits, visitors may sit in on classes, and stay overnight. To schedule a visit, contact the Admissions Office. **Campus Safety**

and Security: Measures include 24-hour foot and vehicle patrol. There are lighted pathways/sidewalks.

REQUIREMENTS: The SAT or ACT is required, with a recommended minimum composite score of 20 on the ACT or 950 on the SAT I. Applicants must be graduates of an accredited secondary school, with 16 academic credits, including 4 years of English and 2 years each of math (algebra required), science, and social studies. The GED is accepted. Stritch requires an essay and recommends an interview. Applications are accepted on-line. A GPA of 2.0 is required. AP and CLEP credits are accepted. Important factors in the admissions decision are leadership record, evidence of special talent, and advanced placement or honors courses. To graduate, students must complete 128 credits, 34 to 72 in the major, with a GPA of at least 2.0. Required disciplines include history, foreign language, literature, written communication, and communication arts. 5 courses are required in humanities, 3 in social/behavioral sciences, 2 each in communication arts and written communication, and 1 each in math and natural science. An English proficiency exam must be taken. **Procedure:** Freshmen are admitted to all sessions. Entrance exams should be taken as early as possible. There are deferred admissions and rolling admissions plans. Applications should be filed by August 1 for fall entry. The fall 2016 application fee was $25. Notification is sent on a rolling basis. Applications are accepted on-line. **Transfer Students:** 164 transfer students enrolled in 2015-2016. Applicants for transfer should have a minimum GPA of 2.0 and be eligible for return to the previous institution. 32 of 128 credits required for the bachelor's degree must be completed at Stritch. **International Students:** There are 35 international students enrolled. They must take the TOEFL. They must also take the SAT or ACT, scoring 20, and the college's own entrance exam.

Admissions Contact: David Wegener, Director of Admissions. Email: *admityou@stritch.edu* Web: *www.stritch.edu*

FINANCIAL AID: The college's own financial statement is required. The FAFSA code is 003837. Check with the school for current application deadlines.

CARROLL UNIVERSITY D-5

www.carrollu.edu

Waukesha, WI 53186	**(262) 524-7220** **(800) CARROLL**
Fax: (262) 524-7139	**Email: cc.info@ccadmin.cc.edu**
Full-time: 953 men, 1753 women	**Faculty:** 101; IIB, -$
Part-time: 102 men, 207 women	**Ph.D.s:** 71%
Graduate: 134 men, 297 women	**Student/Faculty:** 23 to 1
Year: semesters, summer session	**Tuition:** $29,535
Room & Board: $8550	**Freshman Class:** 2969 applied, 2400 accepted, 762 enrolled
SAT: required **ACT:** 24	**CEEB CODE:** 1101
Application Deadline: open	**COMPETITIVE+**

Carroll University, founded in 1846, is an independent, co-educational, comprehensive college grounded in the liberal arts tradition. There are 2 undergraduate schools and 2 graduate schools. In addition to regional accreditation, Carroll has baccalaureate program accreditation with APTA and NLN. The 133-acre campus is in a suburban area 15 miles west of Milwaukee. Including any residence halls, there are 56 buildings.

STUDENT LIFE: 71% of undergraduates are from Wisconsin. Others are from 28 states, 29 foreign countries, and Canada. 85% are White; 6% Hispanic; 4% Asian American; 2% two or more races; 1% African American; 1% Foreign; 1% race unknown. **Female To Male Ratio:** 1.9:1. The average age of freshmen is 18; all undergraduates, 21. 21% do not continue beyond their first year; 58% remain to graduate. **Housing:** 1785 students can be accommodated in college housing, which includes single-sex and coed dorms, on-campus apartments, and special interest floors. On-campus housing is guaranteed for all 4 years. 58% of students live on campus. All students may keep cars.

FACULTY/CLASSROOMS: 45% of faculty are male; 55% are female. All teach undergraduates. No introductory courses are taught by graduate students.

PROGRAMS OF STUDY: Carroll confers B.A., B.S., and B.S.N. degrees. Master's and doctoral degrees are also awarded. Bachelor's degrees are awarded in BIOLOGICAL SCIENCE (biochemistry, biology/biological science, and marine biology), BUSINESS (accounting, business administration and management, business economics, finance, management & strategic leadership, organizational leadership and management, small business management, and professional tennis management), COMMUNICATIONS AND THE ARTS (art, communications, dramatic arts, English, graphic communications management, information technology, languages, music, photography, Spanish, theatre arts, and writing), COMPUTER AND PHYSICAL SCIENCE (actuarial science, applied physics, chemistry, computer science, mathematics, and radiological technology), EDUCATION (art education, athletic training, early childhood education, education, elementary education, music education, physical education, and science education), ENGINEERING AND ENVIRONMENTAL DESIGN (computational sciences, environmental science, and graphic arts technology), HEALTH PROFESSIONS (diagnostic medical sonography, exercise science, health care administration, music therapy, nursing, occupational therapy, physical therapy, physician's assistant, prepharmacy, and public health), SOCIAL SCIENCE (criminal justice, economics, history, political science/government, prelaw, psychology, religion, and sociology). Nursing, communication, and criminal justice have the largest enrollments.

ACTIVITIES: There are 54 groups on campus, including club soccer, club volleyball, activities board, art, band, cheerleading, choir, chorale, chorus, computers, dance, drama, environmental, ethnic, honors, international, jazz band, LGBT, literary magazine, musical theater, newspaper, orchestra, photography, political, professional, radio and TV, religious, social, social service, student government, and symphony. Popular campus events include Celebrate Carroll, Madrigal Dinner, Spring Fling, Involvement Fair, Freshman Day of Service, Carroll's Got Talent, Alcohol Awareness Week, Learn 2 Lead Month, Byron's Run/Walk/Roll to Cure Paralysis, and Pioneer Games. **Sports:** There are 11 intercollegiate sports for men and 11 for women, and 6 intramural sports for men and 6 for women. Facilities include all-purpose field house/gym which includes two multi-purpose courts for volleyball, basketball, batting cages, an indoor track, athletic training rooms, a weight room, an exercise/physiology laboratory, and a 6-lane pool. An additional gym provides a multi-purpose court, dance studio and fitness center. Outdoor facilities include 6 tennis courts, 1 sand volleyball court, a football/soccer/lacrosse field, a practice field, softball diamond, and track and field complex. The Carroll YMCA, is a 24/7 exercise facility with weights, cardio, resistance training equipment, and dance studio. The campus center houses ping pong tables, pool tables, dart machine, and video games. **Graduates:** From July 1, 2015 to June 30, 2016, 646 bachelor's degrees were awarded. The most popular majors were exercise science (16%), business administration (11%), and nursing (9%). In an average class, 42% graduate in 4 years or less, 55% graduate in 5 years or less, and 56% graduate in 6 years or less. Of the 2015 graduating class, 33% were enrolled in graduate school within 6 months of graduation.

SERVICES: Counseling and information services are available, as is tutoring in most subjects. There is a reader service for the blind. Academic coaching is available. **Library/Resources:** The library contains 92,593 volumes, 17 microform items, and 3,643 audio/video tapes/CDs/DVDs, and subscribes to 144,006 periodicals including electronic. Computerized library services include interlibrary loans, database searching, Internet access, and Wi-Fi capability. Special learning facilities include an art gallery, radio station, a studio theater, and recital hall. **Physically Challenged Students:** Facilities include wheelchair ramps, elevators, special parking, specially equipped restrooms, special class scheduling, and lowered drinking fountains. **Special:** The Cross-Cultural Experience is a signature component of Carroll's Pioneer Core curriculum, which is characterized by an integrating theme of culture and a requirement for domestic or international cross-cultural immersion. This experience challenges students to apply classroom-based examinations of culture and to interact with cultures other than their own in an off-campus setting. Carroll University, the University of Wisconsin Platteville and the University of Wisconsin Milwaukee offer an inter-university program that allows students to earn two degrees: a B.S. in Applied Physics from Carroll University and a B.S. in Engineering from the UW-Platteville or UW-Milwaukee. There is also an option to earn a B.S. in Applied Physics from Carroll University and an M.S. in Engineering from UW- Milwaukee. There are 2 national honor societies and a freshman honors program. **Visiting:** There are regularly scheduled orientations for prospective students consisting of a campus tour, financial aid/admissions counseling, academic department meetings, and extracurricular activities meetings. There are guides for informal visits, visitors may sit in on classes, and stay overnight. To schedule a visit, contact the Office of Admissions. **Campus Safety and Security:** Measures include

24-hour foot and vehicle patrol, emergency notification system, self-defense education, and security escort services. There are shuttle buses, emergency telephones, lighted pathways/sidewalks, and controlled access to dorms/residences.

REQUIREMENTS: The SAT or ACT is required. Applicants must be graduates of an accredited secondary school. The GED is accepted. An essay and interview are recommended for all students, and a portfolio or audition is advised for art and music students, respectively. AP and CLEP credits are accepted. Important factors in the admissions decision are advanced placement or honors courses, recommendations by school officials, and evidence of special talent. To graduate, students must complete 128 credit hours, 32 to 88 in the major, with a minimum GPA of 2.0. Carroll's Pioneer Core curriculum requires students to complete 5 General Education courses outside their major area of study as well as a Cross-Cultural Component. 2 computer science courses and a math course are needed for the B.S.; 8 credits of modern language or the humanities and math competency is needed for the B.A. **Procedure:** Freshmen are admitted fall and spring. Entrance exams should be taken during the junior year of high school. There are deferred admissions and rolling admissions plans. Application deadlines are open. Applications are accepted on-line. **Transfer Students:** 197 transfer students enrolled in 2015-2016. Applicants for transfer must have a minimum GPA of 2.0. An interview is required. 32 of 128 credits required for the bachelor's degree must be completed at Carroll. **International Students:** There are 36 international students enrolled. The school actively recruits these students. They must take the TOEFL.

ADMISSIONS: 81% of the 2016-2017 applicants were accepted. The ACT scores were 17% below 12, 31% between 12 and 17, 29% between 18 and 23, 13% between 24 and 29, and 10% above 30. **Admissions Contact:** James V. Wiseman, Vice President of Enrollment. Email: *cc.info@ccadmin.cc.edu* Web: *www.carrollu.edu*

FINANCIAL AID: In 2016-2017, 98% of all full-time freshmen and 98% of continuing full-time students received some form of financial aid. 85% of all full-time freshmen and 80% of continuing full-time students received need-based aid. The average freshman award was $22,239. Need-based scholarships or need-based grants averaged $17,807; need-based self-help aid (loans and jobs) averaged $4,470; and other non-need-based awards and non-need-based scholarships averaged $14,566. 59% of undergraduate students work part-time. The average financial indebtedness of the 2016 graduate was $25,875. Carroll is a member of CSS. The FAFSA code is 003838. Check with the school for current application deadlines.

CARTHAGE COLLEGE — E-5

www.carthage.edu

Kenosha, WI 53140	(262) 551-6000 (800) 351-4058
Fax: (262) 551-5762	Email: admissions@carthage.edu
Full-time: 1265 men, 1370 women	**Faculty:** 102; IIB, av$
Part-time: 160 men, 380 women	**Ph.D.s:** 90%
Graduate: 20 men	**Student/Faculty:** 17 to 1
Year: 4-1-4, summer session	**Tuition:** $38,375
Room & Board: $10,460	**Freshman Class:** n/av
SAT or ACT: required	**CEEB CODE:** 1103
Application Deadline: open	**COMPETITIVE**

Carthage College, founded in 1847, is an independent liberal arts institution affiliated with the Evangelical Lutheran Church. The figures in the above capsule and in this profile are approximate. There is 1 undergraduate school and 1 graduate school. In addition to regional accreditation, Carthage has baccalaureate program accreditation with CSWE and NASM. The 75-acre campus is in a suburban area 30 miles south of Milwaukee and 60 miles north of Chicago, on the shore of Lake Michigan. Including any residence halls, there are 16 buildings.

STUDENT LIFE: 52% of undergraduates are from out of state, mostly the Midwest. Students are from 23 states, 14 foreign countries, and Canada. 88% are from public schools. 76% are White; 6% African American; 6% race unknown; 5% Hispanic; 4% two or more races; 3% Asian American; 1% American Indian/Alaska Native. 31% are Catholic; 26% claim no religious affiliation; 13% Protestant. **Female To Male Ratio:** 1.2:1. The average age of freshmen is 18; all undergraduates, 20. 22% do not continue beyond their first year; 65% remain to graduate. **Housing:** 1800 students can be accommodated in college housing, which includes single-sex and coed dorms and on-campus apartments. There are study-intensive floors and a health and wellness floor. On-campus housing is guaranteed for all 4 years. 70% of students live on campus; of those, 75% remain on campus on weekends. Alcohol is not permitted. All students may keep cars.

FACULTY/CLASSROOMS: 68% of faculty are male; 33% are female. All teach undergraduates. No introductory courses are taught by graduate students. The average class size in an introductory lecture is 19; in a laboratory is 19; and in a regular course is 17.

PROGRAMS OF STUDY: Carthage confers B.A. and B.S.N. degrees. Master's degrees are also awarded. Bachelor's degrees are awarded in BIOLOGICAL SCIENCE (biology/biological science), BUSINESS (accounting, business administration and management, international economics, and marketing management), COMMUNICATIONS AND THE ARTS (art, English, fine arts, French, German, graphic design, languages, music, performing arts, Spanish, studio art, theatre arts, and theatre production), COMPUTER AND PHYSICAL SCIENCE (chemistry, mathematics, natural sciences, and physics), EDUCATION (elementary education, English education, foreign languages education, mathematics education, middle school education, music education, physical education, and secondary education), HEALTH PROFESSIONS (nursing), SOCIAL SCIENCE (criminal justice, economics, geography, history, philosophy, political science/government, psychology, religion, social science, social work, and sociology). Education, business, and sciences are the strongest academically. Business, biology, and education have the largest enrollments.

ACTIVITIES: 28% of men belong to 5 local and 3 national fraternities; 22% of women belong to 4 local and 2 national sororities. There are 125 groups on campus, including Habitat for Humanity, art, band, choir, chorus, computers, dance, debate, drama, environmental, ethnic, film, forensics, honors, international, jazz band, LGBT, literary magazine, musical theater, newspaper, orchestra, pep band, photography, political, professional, radio and TV, religious, social, social service, student government, and yearbook. Popular campus events include May Madness, Little Sibling Weekend, and Casino Night. **Sports:** There are 12 intercollegiate sports for men and 12 for women, and 10 intramural sports for men and 5 for women. Facilities include a phys ed center, 3000-seat stadium, 3500-seat gym, tennis courts, baseball, soccer, and softball fields, and a natatorium. **Graduates:** The most popular majors were business, education, and biology. 25 companies recruited on campus in 2015-2016. Of the 2015 graduating class, 95% were employed within 6 months of graduation.

SERVICES: Counseling and information services are available, as is tutoring in most subjects. **Library/Resources:** The library contains 130,000 volumes, 9,000 microform items, and 1,300 audio/video tapes/CDs/DVDs, and subscribes to 450 periodicals including electronic. Computerized library services include interlibrary loans and database searching. Special learning facilities include an art gallery, planetarium, and radio station. **Physically Challenged Students:** 90% of the campus is accessible. Facilities include wheelchair ramps, elevators, special parking, specially equipped restrooms, special class scheduling, lowered drinking fountains, and lowered telephones. **Special:** Internships are available during the January term or, in some cases, for a semester. Carthage offers study abroad in many countries, cross-registration with the University of Wisconsin, work-study programs, and dual and student-designed majors. Students may take a 3-2 engineering degree with Case Western, and the University of Minnesota-Twin Cities or the University of Wisconsin/Madison, or a 3-2 occupational therapy degree with Washington University. There are 3 national honor societies and a freshman honors program. **Visiting:** There are regularly scheduled orientations for prospective students, including small group meetings with first-year adviser and faculty members, class selection, and curriculum overview. Informational sessions for parents are offered. There are guides for informal visits, visitors may sit in on classes, and stay overnight. To schedule a visit, contact the Office of Admissions. **Campus Safety and Security:** Measures include 24-hour foot and vehicle patrol, emergency notification system, self-defense education, and security escort services. There are shuttle buses, emergency telephones, lighted pathways/sidewalks, controlled access to dorms/residences, and electronic exit locks on residence halls.

REQUIREMENTS: The SAT or ACT is required. Applicants should be graduates of an accredited secondary school, having earned 16 academic credits, including English, foreign language, math, science, and social studies. The GED is accepted. An interview is recommended. AP and

CLEP credits are accepted. Important factors in the admissions decision are advanced placement or honors courses, leadership record, and extracurricular activities record. To graduate, students must complete 138 credits, with up to 56 in the major, and a minimum GPA of 2.0 (education requires 2.75). Students must complete 50 credits in liberal arts studies, including the Heritage Seminar Series, which includes 3 courses that help develop competencies in cultural studies, writing, thinking, reading, speaking, and listening. 2 courses each are required in religion and foreign language, and 1 in math. There is also a phys ed requirement. Each student must complete one of the junior symposia, a series of 3 interdependent courses, and a senior project in the major. **Procedure:** Freshmen are admitted to all sessions. Entrance exams should be taken in spring of the junior year or fall of the senior year. There are deferred admissions and rolling admissions plans. Application deadlines are open. Application fee is $25. Notification is sent on a rolling basis. Applications are accepted on-line. **Transfer Students:** 76 transfer students enrolled in 2015-2016. Transfer students are accepted based on academic performance at their previous school; they should have a GPA greater than 2.0. If they have fewer than 12 credits, the high school record is considered. Either the SAT I or ACT and an interview are recommended. **International Students:** The school actively recruits these students. They must take the TOEFL.

Admissions Contact: Thomas J. Augustine, Director of Admissions and Financial Aid. Email: *admissions@carthage.edu* Web: *www.carthage.edu*

FINANCIAL AID: In 2016-2017, 95% of all full-time freshmen and 99% of continuing full-time students received some form of financial aid. 35% of undergraduate students work part-time. The FAFSA code is 003839. The deadline for filing freshman financial aid applications for fall entry is February 15.

CONCORDIA UNIVERSITY WISCONSIN E-4

www.cuw.edu

Mequon, WI 53097	(414) 243-4500
Fax: (414) 243-4545	Email: admission@cuw.edu
Full-time: 3004 men and women	**Faculty:** 195
Part-time: 1334 men and women	**Ph.D.s:** 75%
Graduate: 1964 men, 1965 women	**Student/Faculty:** 13 to 1
Year: 4-1-4, summer session	**Tuition:** $26,130
Room & Board: $9780	**Freshman Class:** 1947 accepted, 639 enrolled
ACT: 22	**CEEB CODE:** 1139
Application Deadline: August 15	**COMPETITIVE**

Concordia University Wisconsin, established in 1881, is a private institution affiliated with the Lutheran Church-Missouri Synod. Figures in the above capsule and in this profile are approximate. There are 5 undergraduate schools and 1 graduate school. In addition to regional accreditation, CUW has baccalaureate program accreditation with NLN, ACOTE, CAAHEP, CAPTE, CCNE, IACBE, and ACPE. The 155-acre campus is in a suburban area 15 miles north of Milwaukee. Including any residence halls, there are 20 buildings.

STUDENT LIFE: 60% of undergraduates are from Wisconsin. Others are from 47 states, and 25 foreign countries. 75% are White; 3% Hispanic; 2% Foreign; 17% African American; 1% Asian American; 1% American Indian/Alaska Native. 79% are Protestant; 21% Catholic. **Female To Male Ratio:** 1.0:1. The average age of freshmen is 18; all undergraduates, 20. 20% do not continue beyond their first year; 60% remain to graduate. **Housing:** 1500 students can be accommodated in college housing, which includes single-sex dorms. On-campus housing is guaranteed for all 4 years and is available on a first-come, first-served basis. 69% of students live on campus; of those, 50% remain on campus on weekends. Alcohol is not permitted. All students may keep cars.

FACULTY/CLASSROOMS: 43% of faculty are male; 57% are female. All teach undergraduates. No introductory courses are taught by graduate students. The average class size in a regular course is 17.

PROGRAMS OF STUDY: CUW confers B.A., B.S., and B.S.N. degrees. Associate, master's, and doctoral degrees are also awarded. Bachelor's degrees are awarded in BIOLOGICAL SCIENCE (biology/biological science), BUSINESS (accounting, banking and finance, business administration and management, management science, and marketing/retailing/merchandising), COMMUNICATIONS AND THE ARTS (art, communications, English, graphic design, music, Spanish, speech/debate/rhetoric, and telecommunications), COMPUTER AND PHYSICAL SCIENCE (mathematics and radiological technology), EDUCATION (athletic training, early childhood education, elementary education, physical education, and secondary education), ENGINEERING AND ENVIRONMENTAL DESIGN (interior design), HEALTH PROFESSIONS (nursing, occupational therapy, and sports medicine), SOCIAL SCIENCE (biblical languages, criminal justice, history, humanities, ministries, paralegal studies, pastoral studies, psychology, religion, religious music, social science, social work, and theological studies). Education, business, and health sciences are the strongest academically.

ACTIVITIES: There are no fraternities or sororities. There are 20 groups on campus, including art, band, cheerleading, choir, chorale, drama, drill team, ethnic, honors, international, jazz band, literary magazine, musical theater, newspaper, orchestra, pep band, political, professional, radio and TV, religious, and student government. Popular campus events include Winterfest and Springfest. **Sports:** There are 11 intercollegiate sports for men and 10 for women, and 10 intramural sports for men and 9 for women. Facilities include a field house, stadium, fitness center, and athletic fields, including state of the art baseball stadium. **Graduates:** From July 1, 2015 to June 30, 2016, 664 bachelor's degrees were awarded. The most popular majors were health professions, business, and education. In an average class, 60% graduate in 6 years or less. Of the 2015 graduating class, 52% were employed within 6 months of graduation.

SERVICES: Counseling and information services are available, as is tutoring in every subject. There is a reader service for the blind, and remedial math, reading, and writing. **Library/Resources:** The library contains 120,000 volumes, 270,602 microform items, and 4,152 audio/video tapes/CDs/DVDs, and subscribes to 37,000 periodicals including electronic. Computerized library services include interlibrary loans, database searching, and Internet access. Special learning facilities include an art gallery, radio station, a curriculum library for education students, health and fitness facility, sustainable environmental center, and state of the art residence hall. **Physically Challenged Students:** All of the campus is accessible. Facilities include wheelchair ramps, elevators, special parking, and specially equipped restrooms. **Special:** Internships, study abroad, pass/fail options, and credit for life, military, and work experience are available. Concordia offers a general studies degree, dual, student-designed, and interdisciplinary majors, including justice and public policy, and nondegree study. Accelerated degree programs are available in several fields. There is 1 national honor society. **Visiting:** There are regularly scheduled orientations for prospective students, including a tour and financial aid and academic information sessions. There are guides for informal visits, visitors may sit in on classes, and stay overnight. To schedule a visit, contact Michelle Hoffman. **Campus Safety and Security:** Measures include 24-hour foot and vehicle patrol and emergency notification system. There are lighted pathways/sidewalks, and controlled access to dorms/residences. Security guards are on duty from 4 p.m. to 8 a.m. on weekdays and 24 hours a day on weekends.

REQUIREMENTS: A satisfactory score on the SAT or on the ACT is required. Applicants must be graduates of an accredited secondary school, having completed 16 academic credits, including 3 of English and 2 each of math, science, and social studies. The GED is accepted. AP and CLEP credits are accepted. Important factors in the admissions decision are leadership record, recommendations by school officials, and personality/intangible qualities. To graduate, students must complete 126 credits, including at least 30 in the major, with a minimum GPA of 2.0. The 47 1/2 credit core curriculum includes theology/philosophy, humanities, cross culture, social science, natural science, communication, math, and phys ed. **Procedure:** Freshmen are admitted to all sessions. Entrance exams should be taken in the junior year. There is a rolling admissions plan. Applications should be filed by August 15 for fall entry. The fall 2016 application fee was $35. **Transfer Students:** 128 transfer students enrolled in 2015-2016. Applicants for transfer must have a minimum GPA of 2.0 and meet the same entrance exam criteria as entering freshmen. 36 of 126 credits required for the bachelor's degree must be completed at CUW. **International Students:** There are 86 international students enrolled. The school actively recruits these students. They must take the TOEFL and the college's own test, If the student's TOEFL score is below 500, the student must take an English proficiency exam for placement.

Admissions Contact: Michelle Hoffman, Director of Admissions. Email: *admission@cuw.edu* Web: *www.cuw.edu*

FINANCIAL AID: In 2016-2017, 82% of all full-time freshmen received some form of financial aid. The average freshman award was $23,007.

The CSS/Profile, the college's own financial statement, and income tax forms are required. The deadline for filing freshman financial aid applications for fall entry is April 30.

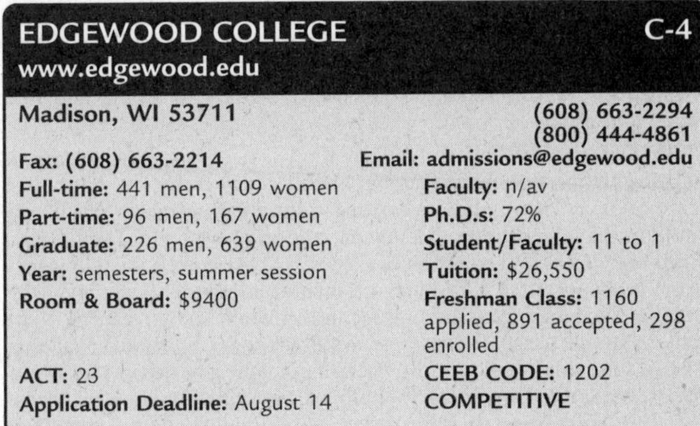

EDGEWOOD COLLEGE C-4

www.edgewood.edu

Madison, WI 53711	**(608) 663-2294** **(800) 444-4861**
Fax: (608) 663-2214	**Email: admissions@edgewood.edu**
Full-time: 441 men, 1109 women	**Faculty:** n/av
Part-time: 96 men, 167 women	**Ph.D.s:** 72%
Graduate: 226 men, 639 women	**Student/Faculty:** 11 to 1
Year: semesters, summer session	**Tuition:** $26,550
Room & Board: $9400	**Freshman Class:** 1160 applied, 891 accepted, 298 enrolled
ACT: 23	**CEEB CODE:** 1202
Application Deadline: August 14	**COMPETITIVE**

Edgewood College, established in 1927, is a private Catholic institution sponsored by the Sinsinawa Dominican Sisters. Figures in the above capsule and in this profile are approximate. There is 1 undergraduate school and 1 graduate school. In addition to regional accreditation, Edgewood has baccalaureate program accreditation with ACBSP, NCATE, and CCNE. The 55-acre campus is in a suburban area 5 miles southwest of Madison. Including any residence halls, there are 15 buildings.

STUDENT LIFE: 89% of undergraduates are from Wisconsin. Others are from 20 states, 29 foreign countries, and Canada. 92% are from public schools. 79% are White; 6% Hispanic; 4% Foreign; 3% African American; 3% Asian American; 3% two or more races; 3% race unknown. 27% are Christian; 23% Catholic. **Female To Male Ratio:** 2.5:1. The average age of freshmen is 18; all undergraduates, 22. 19% do not continue beyond their first year; 60% remain to graduate. **Housing:** 536 students can be accommodated in college housing, which includes single-sex and coed dorms and on-campus apartments. On-campus housing is guaranteed for the freshman year only and is available on a lottery system for upperclassmen. 70% of students commute. Upperclassmen may keep cars.

FACULTY/CLASSROOMS: 39% of faculty are male; 61% are female. All teach undergraduates. No introductory courses are taught by graduate students.

PROGRAMS OF STUDY: Edgewood confers B.A. and B.S. degrees. Master's and doctoral degrees are also awarded. Bachelor's degrees are awarded in AGRICULTURE (environmental studies), BIOLOGICAL SCIENCE (biology/adolescence education), BUSINESS (accounting, business administration and management, and organizational leadership and management), COMMUNICATIONS AND THE ARTS (art, communication studies, English, French, graphic design, music, music industry, music production/recording technology, Spanish, and theatre arts), COMPUTER AND PHYSICAL SCIENCE (chemistry, chemistry education, information sciences and systems, mathematics, natural sciences, physics, and web technology), EDUCATION (art education, business education, computer education, early childhood education, education of the exceptional child, educational studies, elementary education, English education, French studies K-12 education, mathematics education, music education, Spanish education K-12, and special education), HEALTH PROFESSIONS (art therapy, biology, cytotechnology, medical science, and nursing), SOCIAL SCIENCE (child care/child and family studies, criminal justice, economics, ethnic studies, history, international relations, political science/government, psychology, religious education, religious studies, social studies, and sociology). Liberal arts is the strongest academically. Business, education, and nursing have the largest enrollments.

ACTIVITIES: There are no fraternities or sororities. There are 48 groups on campus, including art, band, choir, chorale, chorus, communications, dance, drama, environmental, ethnic, honors, international, jazz band, LGBT, literary magazine, musical theater, newspaper, orchestra, political, professional, religious, social, social service, student government, and symphony. Popular campus events include Winterfrost, Fall Fest, and Spring Fest. **Sports:** There are 8 intercollegiate sports for men and 9 for women, and 4 intramural sports for men and 4 for women. Facilities include a 1000-seat gym, soccer, baseball, and softball fields, a fitness center, and access to tennis courts. **Graduates:** From July 1, 2015 to June 30, 2016, 459 bachelor's degrees were awarded. The most popular majors were nursing (16%), business (9%), and psychology (8%). In an average class, 38% graduate in 4 years or less, 60% graduate in 5 years or less, and 60% graduate in 6 years or less.

SERVICES: Counseling and information services are available, as is tutoring in some subjects, such as most sciences, introductory math courses, and Spanish. There is a reader service for the blind, and remedial math, reading, and writing. **Library/Resources:** The library contains 205,058 volumes, 9,524 microform items, and 6,226 audio/video tapes/CDs/DVDs, and subscribes to 31,200 periodicals including electronic. Computerized library services include interlibrary loans, database searching, Internet access, and Wi-Fi capability. Special learning facilities include an art gallery. **Physically Challenged Students:** 90% of the campus is accessible. Facilities include wheelchair ramps, elevators, special parking, specially equipped restrooms, special class scheduling, lowered drinking fountains, lowered telephones, special housing, automated doors in the library, science center, activities center, and residence halls, and a chairlift. **Special:** Students may cross-register with the University of Wisconsin-Madison. Internships, study abroad, dual and student-designed majors, nondegree study, pass/fail options, and credit for prior learning experience are available. There are accelerated undergraduate degree programs for working adults. There are 5 national honor societies and a freshman honors program. **Visiting:** There are regularly scheduled orientations for prospective students, including Experience Edgewood Days, a program where admitted freshmen spend a day on campus as if they were Edgewood college students. They choose their own schedule for the day, which may include sitting in on classes, attending athletics presentations, and learning about study abroad opportunities, residence life and student activities. Students also have the opportunity to take campus tours and exclusive tours of the residence halls. Complimentary lunch is included. There are guides for informal visits, visitors may sit in on classes, and stay overnight. To schedule a visit, contact the Admissions Office. **Campus Safety and Security:** Measures include 24-hour foot and vehicle patrol, emergency notification system, self-defense education, and security escort services. There are shuttle buses, emergency telephones, lighted pathways/sidewalks, controlled access to dorms/residences, Residence halls have alarms, a security card system, and campus security guards. RAs are on duty 24 hours a day weekends and 7 a.m. to 3 p.m. and 8 p.m. to 4 a.m. weekdays.

REQUIREMENTS: The ACT is recommended. Students must meet two of the following three requirements. Students must present a cumulative high school GPA of 2.5 on a 4.0 scale, a rank in the top 50% of their high school graduating class, and/or a composite score of 18 on the ACT or an equivalent SAT score. Edgewood requires applicants to be in the upper 50% of their class. AP and CLEP credits are accepted. To graduate, students must complete a minimum of 120 credit hours with a minimum cumulative GPA of 2.0. There are general education requirements, and each student must complete a major field of study and required core courses. **Procedure:** Freshmen are admitted fall and spring. Entrance exams should be taken by the senior year. There are deferred admissions and rolling admissions plans. Applications should be filed by August 14 for fall entry; January 12 for spring entry, along with a $30 fee. Applications are accepted on-line. **Transfer Students:** 161 transfer students enrolled in 2015-2016. Transfer students must complete an Application for Undergraduate Admission and have official transcripts from each high school, college and university attended sent directly to the Office of Admissions. High school transcripts should include class rank and cumulative GPA. GEDs are accepted. Students are expected to present a minimum of 12 academic-level credits and a cumulative college grade point average of 2.0 (on a 4.0 scale) from an accredited institution. Students dismissed from a previous college must wait one full year prior to applying to Edgewood and supply additional information. 32 of 120 credits required for the bachelor's degree must be completed at Edgewood. **International Students:** There are 62 international students enrolled. The school actively recruits these students. They must take the TOEFL with a minimum score of 525 on the paper-based TOEFL (PBT) or 71 on the Internet-based version (iBT).

ADMISSIONS: 77% of the 2016-2017 applicants were accepted. The ACT scores were 9% between 12 and 17, 51% between 18 and 23, 36% between 24 and 29, and 4% above 30. 25% of the current freshmen were in the top fifth of their class; 59% were in the top two fifths. **Admissions Contact:** Christine Benedict, VP for Enrollment Management. Email: *admissions@edgewood.edu* Web: *www.edgewood.edu*

FINANCIAL AID: In 2016-2017, 79% of all full-time freshmen and 77%

of continuing full-time students received some form of financial aid. 79% of all full-time freshmen and 75% of continuing full-time students received need-based aid. The average freshman award was $22,004. Need-based scholarships or need-based grants averaged $16,868; and need-based self-help aid (loans and jobs) averaged $5,732. 82% of undergraduate students work part-time. Average annual earnings from campus work are $1529. The average financial indebtedness of the 2016 graduate was $30,574. Edgewood is a member of CSS. The college's own financial statement and a tax return are required. The FAFSA code is 003848. Check with the school for current application deadlines.

LAKELAND UNIVERSITY — E-4

Lakeland College
www.lakeland.edu

Plymouth, WI 53073 — (920) 565-1217, (800) 242-3347

Fax: (920) 565-1206	**Email:** admissions@lakeland.edu
Full-time: 390 men, 400 women	**Faculty:** 41; IIB, --$
Part-time: 20 men, 30 women	**Ph.D.s:** 59%
Graduate: 50 men, 130 women	**Student/Faculty:** 19 to 1
Year: semesters, summer session	**Tuition:** $26,880
Room & Board: $8250	**Freshman Class:** n/av
SAT or ACT: required	**CEEB CODE:** 1393
Application Deadline: September 1	**COMPETITIVE**

Lakeland College, established in 1862, is a private institution affiliated with the United Church of Christ. The 4-4-1 academic calendar consists of 4-month fall and spring term, and an optional 3-week May term. The figures in the above capsule and in this profile are approximate. There are 3 undergraduate schools and 1 graduate school. The 240-acre campus is in a rural area 10 miles northwest of Sheboygan. Including any residence halls, there are 24 buildings.

STUDENT LIFE: 79% of undergraduates are from Wisconsin. Others are from 16 states, 31 foreign countries, and Canada. 90% are from public schools. 8% are Foreign; 76% White; 5% African American; 4% Asian American; 1% Hispanic. 32% are Protestant; 29% Catholic; 25% claim no religious affiliation. **Female To Male Ratio:** 1.2:1. The average age of all undergraduates is 22. 32% do not continue beyond their first year; 43% remain to graduate. **Housing:** 488 students can be accommodated in college housing, which includes single-sex and coed dorms and on-campus apartments. In addition, there are honors houses, male-only, female-only, and housing for students with senior standing. On-campus housing is guaranteed for all 4 years. 57% of students live on campus; of those, 60% remain on campus on weekends. All students may keep cars.

FACULTY/CLASSROOMS: 51% of faculty are male; 49% are female. All teach undergraduates, and all do research. No introductory courses are taught by graduate students. The average class size in an introductory lecture is 20; in a laboratory is 15; and in a regular course is 16.

PROGRAMS OF STUDY: Lakeland confers B.A. degrees. Master's degrees are also awarded. Bachelor's degrees are awarded in BIOLOGICAL SCIENCE (biology/biological science), BUSINESS (accounting, business administration and management, business economics, hospitality management services, international business management, and marketing management), COMMUNICATIONS AND THE ARTS (art, creative writing, dramatic arts, English, German, music, and Spanish), COMPUTER AND PHYSICAL SCIENCE (chemistry, computer science, and mathematics), EDUCATION (business education, early childhood education, elementary education, music education, and secondary education), SOCIAL SCIENCE (behavioral science, criminal justice, economics, history, philosophy, physical fitness/movement, psychology, public administration, religion, and sociology). Business, education, and accounting are the strongest academically. Education, business, and computer science have the largest enrollments.

ACTIVITIES: 17% of men belong to 3 local fraternities; 11% of women belong to 3 local sororities. There are 27 groups on campus, including band, choir, chorus, dance, drama, ethnic, honors, international, literary magazine, newspaper, pep band, professional, radio and TV, religious, social, student government, and yearbook. Popular campus events include Winter Carnival, and Spring Celebration. **Sports:** There are 8 intercollegiate sports for men and 7 for women, and 2 intramural sports for men and 2 for women. Facilities include a sports complex, a fitness lab, 3 full-size basketball courts, a weight room, indoor and outdoor tennis courts, indoor pitching and batting facilities, and softball, baseball, football, soccer, and practice fields. **Graduates:** From July 1, 2015 to June 30, 2016, 145 bachelor's degrees were awarded. The most popular majors were education (28%), business administration (17%), and computer science (10%). In an average class, 13% graduate in 3 years or less, 30% graduate in 4 years or less, 43% graduate in 5 years or less, and 46% graduate in 6 years or less. Of the 2015 graduating class, 10% were enrolled in graduate school within 6 months of graduation, and 95% were employed.

SERVICES: Counseling and information services are available, as is tutoring in every subject. There is a reader service for the blind, and remedial math, reading, and writing. **Library/Resources:** The library contains 57,447 volumes, 33,169 microform items, and 2,099 audio/video tapes/CDs/DVDs, and subscribes to 322 periodicals including electronic. Computerized library services include interlibrary loans and database searching. Special learning facilities include an art gallery, radio station, and a college history museum. **Physically Challenged Students:** 83% of the campus is accessible. Facilities include wheelchair ramps, elevators, special parking, specially equipped restrooms, and lowered drinking fountains. **Special:** Internships in all majors, study abroad in Germany and Japan, a Washington semester, and work-study programs are available. There are some dual majors, a general studies degree, a 3-2 engineering degree with the University of Wisconsin-Madison, a 2-2 1/2 nursing program with Bellin College of Nursing, and nondegree study. There is a freshman honors program and 10 departmental honors programs. **Visiting:** There are regularly scheduled orientations for prospective students, consisting of meetings with faculty and financial aid personnel, activities meetings, and a campus tour. There are guides for informal visits, visitors may sit in on classes, and stay overnight. To schedule a visit, contact the Admissions Office. **Campus Safety and Security:** Measures include security escort services. There are emergency telephones, lighted pathways/sidewalks, and foot patrol on weekends and evenings.

REQUIREMENTS: The SAT or ACT is required, with a minimum composite score of 950 on the SAT I or 19 on the ACT. Applicants must be graduates of an accredited secondary school or have the GED. An interview is recommended. Applications are accepted on-line via the college's website. AP and CLEP credits are accepted. Important factors in the admissions decision are advanced placement or honors courses, leadership record, and evidence of special talent. To graduate, students must complete 128 semester hours, with at least 32 in the major and a minimum 2.0 GPA. There are requirements in history, humanities, natural sciences, social sciences, and religion. **Procedure:** Freshmen are admitted fall, spring, and summer. Entrance exams should be taken after the enrollment commitment is made. There is a rolling admissions plan. Applications should be filed by September 1 for fall entry; December 15 for spring entry, along with a $20 fee. Notification is sent on a rolling basis. Applications are accepted on-line. **Transfer Students:** 115 transfer students enrolled in 2015-2016. Applicants should have a GPA of at least 2.0. Lakeland recommends an interview. 36 of 128 credits required for the bachelor's degree must be completed at Lakeland. **International Students:** There are 100 international students enrolled. The school actively recruits these students. They must take the TOEFL.

Admissions Contact: Kristin Henning, Sr Director of Admissions/Recruitment. Email: *admissions@lakeland.edu* Web: *www.lakeland.edu*

FINANCIAL AID: In 2016-2017, 100% of all full-time freshmen and 97% of continuing full-time students received some form of financial aid. 86% of all full-time freshmen and 90% of continuing full-time students received need-based aid. The average freshman award was $11,895. 30% of undergraduate students work part-time. Average annual earnings from campus work are $1000. The average financial indebtedness of the 2016 graduate was $20,558. Lakeland is a member of CSS. The college's own financial statement is required. The FAFSA code is 003854. The deadline for filing freshman financial aid applications for fall entry is July 1.

LAWRENCE UNIVERSITY D-3
www.lawrence.edu

Appleton, WI 54911 (920) 832-6500
(800) 227-0982

Fax: (920) 832-6782 **Email:** marybeth.petrie@lawrence.edu

Full-time: 656 men, 787 women	**Faculty:** 163; IIB, av$
Part-time: 29 men, 24 women	**Ph.D.s:** 96%
Graduate: n/av	**Student/Faculty:** 8 to 1
Year: trimesters	**Tuition:** $44,844
Room & Board: $9654	**Freshman Class:** 2422 applied, 1405 accepted, 326 enrolled
	CEEB CODE: 1398
Application Deadline: January 15	**HIGHLY COMPETITIVE**

Lawrence University, founded in 1847, is a private liberal arts institution with a conservatory of music. Figures in the above capsule and in this profile are approximate. There is 1 undergraduate school. In addition to regional accreditation, Lawrence has baccalaureate program accreditation with NASM. The 84-acre campus is in an urban area 100 miles north of Milwaukee, 30 miles south of Green Bay. Including any residence halls, there are 58 buildings.

STUDENT LIFE: 69% of undergraduates are from out of state, mostly the Midwest. Students are from 45 states, 35 foreign countries, and Canada. 75% are from public schools. 8% are Foreign; 77% White; 5% American Indian/Alaska Native; 4% Hispanic; 3% African American; 3% Asian American. 69% claim no religious affiliation. **Female To Male Ratio:** 1.2:1. The average age of freshmen is 18; all undergraduates, 20. 12% do not continue beyond their first year; 76% remain to graduate. **Housing:** 1364 students can be accommodated in college housing, which includes single-sex and coed dorms, on-campus apartments, and married student housing. In addition, there are language houses, special-interest houses, theme houses for students with like interests. On-campus housing is guaranteed for all 4 years. 98% of students live on campus; of those, 90% remain on campus on weekends. All students may keep cars.

FACULTY/CLASSROOMS: 62% of faculty are male; 38% are female. All teach undergraduates, and all do research. No introductory courses are taught by graduate students. The average class size in an introductory lecture is 24; in a laboratory is 15; and in a regular course is 15.

PROGRAMS OF STUDY: Lawrence confers B.A., B.Mus., and B.A.-B.Mus degrees. Bachelor's degrees are awarded in AGRICULTURE (environmental studies), BIOLOGICAL SCIENCE (biochemistry and biology/biological science), COMMUNICATIONS AND THE ARTS (art history and appreciation, Chinese, classics, dramatic arts, English, French, German, Japanese, linguistics, music performance, music theory and composition, Russian, Spanish, and studio art), COMPUTER AND PHYSICAL SCIENCE (chemistry, computer science, geology, mathematics, and physics), EDUCATION (music education), SOCIAL SCIENCE (anthropology, cognitive science, East Asian studies, economics, gender studies, history, international studies, philosophy, political science/government, and psychology). Biology, music, and physics are the strongest academically. Psychology, biology, and English have the largest enrollments.

ACTIVITIES: 22% of men belong to 5 national fraternities; 18% of women belong to 3 national sororities. There are 100 groups on campus, including art, band, chess, choir, chorale, chorus, computers, dance, drama, environmental, ethnic, film, honors, international, jazz band, LGBT, literary magazine, musical theater, newspaper, opera, orchestra, pep band, photography, political, professional, radio and TV, religious, social, social service, student government, symphony, and yearbook. Popular campus events include Midwest Trivia Contest, International Cabaret, Mardis Gras, and Shack-a-thon. **Sports:** There are 12 intercollegiate sports for men and 10 for women, and 23 intramural sports for men and 23 for women. Facilities include a 5255-seat lighted football stadium, 8-lane state-of-the-art outdoor track, 4-lane indoor track, baseball, soccer, practice fields, 6 tennis, 1 squash, and 4 racquetball/handball courts, 2 gyms for basketball, volleyball, and badminton, 3 batting cages, an 8-lane swimming pool with diving well, 3 weight rooms, 2 cardio exercise rooms, and a dance studio. **Graduates:** From July 1, 2015 to June 30, 2016, 310 bachelor's degrees were awarded. The most popular majors were music performance (11%), biology (10%), and psychology (8%). 10 companies recruited on campus in 2015-2016. In an average class, 1% graduate in 3 years or less, 68% graduate in 4 years or less, 70% graduate in 5 years or less, and 76% graduate in 6 years or less. Of the 2015 graduating class, 30% were enrolled in graduate school within 6 months of graduation, and 50% were employed.

SERVICES: Counseling and information services are available, as is tutoring in every subject. There is a reader service for the blind. The writing lab focuses on enhancing writing skills, as well as remedial writing. **Library/Resources:** The library contains 420,502 volumes, 102,629 microform items, and 25,897 audio/video tapes/CDs/DVDs, and subscribes to 2,505 periodicals including electronic. Computerized library services include interlibrary loans, database searching, Internet access, and Wi-Fi capability. Special learning facilities include an art gallery, natural history museum, and radio station. **Physically Challenged Students:** 95% of the campus is accessible. Facilities include wheelchair ramps, elevators, special parking, specially equipped restrooms, special class scheduling, lowered drinking fountains, and special housing. **Special:** Lawrence offers Chicago-based programs in urban studies, urban education, and the arts, a humanities program at the Newberry Library, and a science internship at Oak Ridge National Laboratory. There are study-abroad programs in 28 countries, a Washington semester, limited pass/fail options, student-designed majors, and nondegree study. Students may take a 3-2 engineering degree with Columbia or Washington Universities or Rensselaer Polytechnic Institute. Also available are 3-2 programs in forestry and environmental studies with Duke University and in occupational therapy with Washington University in St. Louis. A 5-year B.A.-B.Mus. degree is offered. There are 5 national honor societies and a chapter of Phi Beta Kappa. **Visiting:** There are regularly scheduled orientations for prospective students, where visiting students can participate in an extensive day-long program with many choices of classes and presentations. There are guides for informal visits, and visitors may sit in on classes, and stay overnight. To schedule a visit, contact Visit Coordinator in the Office of Admissions. **Campus Safety and Security:** Measures include 24-hour foot and vehicle patrol, emergency notification system, self-defense education, and security escort services. There are emergency telephones, lighted pathways/sidewalks, controlled access to dorms/residences, and a whistle stop program.

REQUIREMENTS: Applicants should complete 16 high school academic credits. Lawrence requires an essay, reports from a teacher and counselor, and an audition for music majors. The school recommends an interview, and a portfolio for art majors. AP credits are accepted. Important factors in the admissions decision are advanced placement or honors courses, evidence of special talent, and extracurricular activities record. Students must complete 216 units (270 units for a double-degree program), including 48 to 72 in the major, with a minimum GPA of 2.0. All students must take Freshmen Studies. Distribution requirements include 12 units each in humanities, social sciences, and natural sciences, including a lab course, and 6 units in fine arts. Competency requirements must also be met in writing, speaking, foreign language, and quantitative analysis. Some majors require a comprehensive exam or a thesis. **Procedure:** Freshmen are admitted fall. Entrance exams should be taken in the spring of the junior year or fall of the senior year. There are early decision, early admissions, and deferred admissions plans. Early decision applications should be filed by November 15; regular applications, by January 15 for fall entry, along with a $40 fee. Notification of early decision is sent December 1; regular decision, April 1. 43 early decision candidates were accepted for the 2016-2017 class. 483 applicants were on the 2016 waiting list; 93 were admitted. Applications are accepted on-line. **Transfer Students:** 16 transfer students enrolled in 2015-2016. Applicants must present official transcripts of their college and secondary school work, and the recommendation of a college professor. Typically, candidates with a college GPA of 2.75 or higher will receive serious consideration. 108 of 216 credits required for the bachelor's degree must be completed at Lawrence. **International Students:** There are 104 international students enrolled. The school actively recruits these students. They must take the TOEFL with a minimum score of 577 on the paper-based TOEFL (PBT) or 90 on the Internet-based version (iBT), or take the ACT, IELTS, or SAT.

ADMISSIONS: 58% of the 2016-2017 applicants were accepted. 74% of the current freshmen were in the top fifth of their class; 95% were in the top two fifths. There were 13 National Merit finalists. 13 freshmen graduated first in their class. **Admissions Contact:** Marybeth Petrie, Director of Admission. Email: *marybeth.petrie@lawrence.edu* Web: *www.lawrence.edu*

FINANCIAL AID: In 2016-2017, 95% of all full-time freshmen and 94% of continuing full-time students received some form of financial aid.

64% of all full-time freshmen and 58% of continuing full-time students received need-based aid. The average freshman award was $29,500. Need-based scholarships or need-based grants averaged $22,700 ($38,205 maximum); need-based self-help aid (loans and jobs) averaged $6,800 ($8,000 maximum); and other non-need-based awards and non-need-based scholarships averaged $11,817 ($38,205 maximum). 72% of undergraduate students work part-time. Average annual earnings from campus work are $1400. The average financial indebtedness of the 2016 graduate was $25,673. Lawrence is a member of CSS. The college's own financial statement is required. The FAFSA code is 003856. The priority date for freshman financial aid applications for fall entry is March 1.

MARIAN UNIVERSITY *(The complete profile is made available exclusively on our website, www.barronspac.com)*

MARQUETTE UNIVERSITY — E-4

www.marquette.edu

Milwaukee, WI 53201 (414) 288-7302 (800) 222-6544

Fax: (414) 288-3764 **Email:** admissions@marquette.edu

Full-time: 3734 men, 4268 women	**Faculty:** 580; I, -$
Part-time: 168 men, 164 women	**Ph.D.s:** 90%
Graduate: 1496 men, 1661 women	**Student/Faculty:** 15 to 1
Year: semesters, summer session	**Tuition:** $37,170
Room & Board: $11,220	**Freshman Class:** 20486 applied, 15202 accepted, 1876 enrolled
SAT CR/M/W: 590/600/580 **ACT:** 27	**CEEB CODE:** 1448
Application Deadline: December 1	**VERY COMPETITIVE+**

Marquette University, established in 1881, is a private Roman Catholic Jesuit institution. Figures in the above capsule and in this profile are approximate. There are 8 undergraduate schools and 4 graduate schools. In addition to regional accreditation, Marquette has baccalaureate program accreditation with AACSB, ABET, ACEJMC, ADA, APTA, NCATE, ARCPA, ACS, and ACNM. The 107-acre campus is in an urban area in the heart of Milwaukee. Including any residence halls, there are 69 buildings.

STUDENT LIFE: 68% of undergraduates are from out of state, mostly the Midwest. Students are from 47 states, 39 foreign countries, and Canada. 60% are from public schools. 72% are White; 5% Asian American; 4% African American; 4% Foreign; 4% two or more races; 10% Hispanic. 63% are Catholic; 14% Protestant. **Female To Male Ratio:** 1.1:1. The average age of freshmen is 18; all undergraduates, 20. 10% do not continue beyond their first year; 79% remain to graduate. **Housing:** 4800 students can be accommodated in college housing, which includes single-sex and coed dorms and on-campus apartments. In addition, there are honors houses, specified majors, social justice, and multicultural floors. On-campus housing is guaranteed for the freshman year only and is available on a lottery system for upperclassmen. 52% of students live on campus; of those, 90% remain on campus on weekends. All students may keep cars.

FACULTY/CLASSROOMS: 57% of faculty are male; 43% are female. 76% teach undergraduates. No introductory courses are taught by graduate students.

PROGRAMS OF STUDY: Marquette confers B.A., B.S., B.S.N., B.S.B.E., B.S.C.E., B.S.C.M., B.S.C.O., B.S.E.E., and B.S.M.E. and B.S.N. degrees. Master's and doctoral degrees are also awarded. Bachelor's degrees are awarded in BIOLOGICAL SCIENCE (biochemistry, biology/biological science, molecular biology, and physiology), BUSINESS (accounting, business administration and management, business economics, entrepreneurial studies, finance, human resources, international business management, management information systems, marketing/retailing/merchandising, operations management, organizational leadership and management, real estate, and supply chain management), COMMUNICATIONS AND THE ARTS (advertising, broadcasting, classical languages, classics, communications, dramatic arts, English, French, German, information technology, journalism, media arts, public relations, Spanish, theatre arts, and writing), COMPUTER AND PHYSICAL SCIENCE (chemistry, computer science, mathematics, physics, and statistics), EDUCATION (athletic training, education, and secondary education), ENGINEERING AND ENVIRONMENTAL DESIGN (bioengineering, biomedical engineering, civil engineering, computational sciences, computer engineering, construction engineering, electrical/electronics engineering, engineering, environmental engineering, and mechanical engineering), HEALTH PROFESSIONS (biomedical science, clinical science, exercise science, medical laboratory science, nursing, premedicine, and speech pathology/audiology), SOCIAL SCIENCE (anthropology, criminology, economics, history, interdisciplinary studies, international relations, peace studies, philosophy, political science/government, psychology, social science, sociology, and theological studies). Biomedical engineering, nursing, and premedicine are the strongest academically. Biomedical sciences, nursing, and mechanical engineering have the largest enrollments.

ACTIVITIES: 4% of men belong to 11 national fraternities; 14% of women belong to 13 national sororities. There are 270 groups on campus, including art, band, cheerleading, chess, choir, chorale, chorus, community awareness, computers, dance, debate, drama, drill team, ethnic, film, honors, international, jazz band, LGBT, literary magazine, musical theater, newspaper, orchestra, pep band, photography, political, professional, radio and TV, religious, social, social service, student government, and symphony. Popular campus events include Student Organizational Fest, Winter Flurry, and Hunger Clean Up. **Sports:** There are 7 intercollegiate sports for men and 7 for women, and 40 intramural sports for men and 40 for women. Facilities include 2 recreation centers and Valley Fields, an outdoor soccer, track, and football facility. **Graduates:** From July 1, 2015 to June 30, 2016, 1822 bachelor's degrees were awarded. The most popular majors were biomedical sciences (7%), nursing (6%), and accounting (6%). 183 companies recruited on campus in 2015-2016. In an average class, 58% graduate in 4 years or less, 78% graduate in 5 years or less, and 90% graduate in 6 years or less.

SERVICES: Counseling and information services are available, as is tutoring in some subjects. There is a reader service for the blind. Book taping and note taking are available for the physically disabled. **Library/Resources:** The 2 libraries contain 1.8 million volumes, 1.7 million microform items, and 23,503 audio/video tapes/CDs/DVDs, and subscribe to 46,685 periodicals including electronic. Computerized library services include interlibrary loans, database searching, Internet access, and Wi-Fi capability. Special learning facilities include an art gallery, radio station, and TV station. **Physically Challenged Students:** 90% of the campus is accessible. Facilities include wheelchair ramps, elevators, special parking, specially equipped restrooms, special class scheduling, lowered drinking fountains, lowered telephones, and special housing. **Special:** Marquette offers co-op programs in engineering, internships, study abroad in 16 countries, a Washington summer term, and work-study programs. Dual and student-designed majors, nondegree study, an accelerated degree program for pre-dental and pre-law students, and pass/fail options are available. Cross-registration is possible with Milwaukee Institute of Art and Design, and there is a 2-2 engineering program with Waukesha County Technical College. The Freshman Frontier Program offers academic support for selected freshmen who do not meet regular admission requirements but show potential for success. The Educational Opportunity Program affords students from minority groups and low-income families the opportunity to attend the school. There are 22 national honor societies, Phi Beta Kappa, a freshman honors program, and 42 departmental honors programs. **Visiting:** There are regularly scheduled orientations for prospective students, including an agenda for visits that varies according to the specific program; open houses are available on scheduled weekends throughout the academic year. There are guides for informal visits, visitors may sit in on classes, and stay overnight. To schedule a visit, contact the Office of Undergraduate Admissions. **Campus Safety and Security:** Measures include 24-hour foot and vehicle patrol, emergency notification system, self-defense education, and security escort services. There are shuttle buses, emergency telephones, lighted pathways/sidewalks, controlled access to dorms/residences, closed-circuit cameras in selected parking lots and buildings throughout the campus. Public Safety has bicycle patrols and the Milwaukee police conduct patrols on horseback. Secure storage for bicycles in parking ramps, is monitored by Public Safety using closed-circuit cameras.

REQUIREMENTS: Marquette requires either the ACT or the SAT. Applicants must be graduates of an accredited secondary school with a recommended 18 credits, including 4 years of English, 3 each of social studies and math, 2 each of sciences and foreign language, and 4 of additional academic subjects. Most students rank in the upper quarter of their high school class. The GED is accepted, with a minimum score of 225. Applicants must demonstrate ability, preparation, and motivation.

An interview is recommended. AP and CLEP credits are accepted. Important factors in the admissions decision are advanced placement or honors courses, recommendations by school officials, and leadership record. To graduate, students must complete a total of 126 to 135 credit hours and maintain a minimum GPA depending on major. The 36-credit-hour core of common studies includes 6 credit hours each of rhetoric, human nature and ethics, and theology, and 3 each of mathematical reasoning, individual and social behavior, science and nature, histories of cultures and societies, literature and performing arts, and diverse cultures. The total number of hours in the major varies. **Procedure:** Freshmen are admitted to all sessions. Entrance exams should be taken in the junior year and repeated early in the senior year if necessary. There is a deferred admissions plan. Applications should be filed by December 1 for fall entry. Notifications are sent January 31. 1137 applicants were on the 2016 waiting list; 1055 were admitted. Applications are accepted on-line. **Transfer Students:** 159 transfer students enrolled in 2015-2016. Applicants for transfer must have a minimum GPA of 2.0; some programs require a higher average. The SAT or ACT is required if the applicant has completed fewer than 12 hours of college-level work. 30 of 126 credits required for the bachelor's degree must be completed at Marquette. **International Students:** There are 311 international students enrolled. The school actively recruits these students. Marquette requires success in final external secondary exams according to the student's country of education.

ADMISSIONS: 74% of the 2016-2017 applicants were accepted. The SAT scores for the 2016-2017 freshman class were: Critical Reading-- 13% below 500, 40% between 500 and 599, 40% between 600 and 699, and 7% between 700 and 800. Math-- 10% below 500, 36% between 500 and 599, 46% between 600 and 699, and 7% between 700 and 800. Writing-- 17% below 500, 41% between 500 and 599, 37% between 600 and 699, and 5% between 700 and 800. The ACT scores were 3% below 12, 12% between 12 and 17, 27% between 18 and 23, 21% between 24 and 29, and 37% above 30. 34% of the current freshmen were in the top fifth of their class; 59% were in the top two fifths. 17 freshmen graduated first in their class. **Admissions Contact:** Jean Burke, Interim Dean of Admissions. Email: *admissions@marquette.edu* Web: *www.marquette.edu*

FINANCIAL AID: In 2016-2017, 99% of all full-time freshmen and 99% of continuing full-time students received some form of financial aid. 53% of all full-time freshmen and 52% of continuing full-time students received need-based aid. The average freshman award was $23,935. Need-based scholarships or need-based grants averaged $9,013 ($33,075 maximum); need-based self-help aid (loans and jobs) averaged $4,269 ($8,500 maximum); non-need-based athletic scholarships averaged $30,802 ($54,868 maximum); and other non-need-based awards and non-need-based scholarships averaged $14,196. 41% of undergraduate students work part-time. Average annual earnings from campus work are $2000. The average financial indebtedness of the 2016 graduate was $37,048. Marquette is a member of CSS. The FAFSA code is 003863. The priority date for freshman financial aid applications for fall entry is February 1.

MILWAUKEE INSTITUTE OF ART AND DESIGN *(The complete profile is made available exclusively on our website, www.barronspac.com)*

MILWAUKEE SCHOOL OF ENGINEERING E-4

www.msoe.edu

Milwaukee, WI 53202	**(414) 277-6762** **(800) 332-6763**
Fax: (414) 277-7475	**Email: mitchell@msoe.edu**
Full-time: 1883 men, 663 women	**Faculty:** 128; IIB, +$
Part-time: 139 men, 27 women	**Ph.D.s:** 78%
Graduate: 163 men, 64 women	**Student/Faculty:** 16 to 1
Year: quarters, summer session	**Tuition:** $36,540
Room & Board: $8613	**Freshman Class:** 2014 applied, 1147 accepted, 518 enrolled
SAT CR/M: 580/660 **ACT:** 27	**CEEB CODE:** 1476
Application Deadline: n/av	**HIGHLY COMPETITIVE**

Milwaukee School of Engineering, established in 1903, is a private university offering bachelor's and master's degrees in the areas of engineering, business, mathematics, and nursing. Figures in the above capsule and in this profile are approximate. There are 3 undergraduate schools and 1 graduate school. In addition to regional accreditation, MSOE has baccalaureate program accreditation with ABET, ACCE, and CCNE. The 22-acre campus is in an urban area in Milwaukee, Wisconsin. Including any residence halls, there are 15 buildings.

STUDENT LIFE: 67% of undergraduates are from Wisconsin. Others are from 37 states, 27 foreign countries, and Canada. 94% are from public schools. 8% are race unknown; 66% White; 6% Hispanic; 4% Asian American; 2% African American; 2% two or more races; 12% Foreign. **Male To Female Ratio:** 2.9:1. The average age of freshmen is 18; all undergraduates, 22. 13% do not continue beyond their first year; 64% remain to graduate. **Housing:** 1278 students can be accommodated in college housing, which includes coed dorms and on-campus apartments. In addition, there are special-interest houses. There are also suites for upperclassmen with kitchens, bathrooms, and living rooms. On-campus housing is guaranteed for all 4 years. 61% of students commute. Alcohol is not permitted. All students may keep cars.

FACULTY/CLASSROOMS: 63% of faculty are male; 37% are female. 86% teach undergraduates, 2% do research, and 12% do both. No introductory courses are taught by graduate students. The average class size in an introductory lecture is 22; in a laboratory is 16; and in a regular course is 22.

PROGRAMS OF STUDY: MSOE confers B.A. and B.S. degrees. Master's degrees are also awarded. Bachelor's degrees are awarded in BIOLOGICAL SCIENCE (molecular biology), BUSINESS (business administration and management, international business management, management information systems, and management science), COMMUNICATIONS AND THE ARTS (technical and business writing), COMPUTER AND PHYSICAL SCIENCE (actuarial science and software engineering), ENGINEERING AND ENVIRONMENTAL DESIGN (architectural engineering, biomedical engineering, computer engineering, construction management, electrical/electronics engineering, engineering, industrial engineering, and mechanical engineering), HEALTH PROFESSIONS (nursing). Biomedical engineering, and computer engineering are the strongest academically. Architectural engineering, mechanical engineering, and electrical engineering have the largest enrollments.

ACTIVITIES: 4% of men belong to 1 local and 3 national fraternities; 15% of women belong to 2 local and 2 national sororities. There are 72 groups on campus, including disk golf, ultimate frisbee, bowling, paintball, tae kwon do, cheerleading, chess, choir, computers, dance, drama, environmental, ethnic, honors, international, jazz band, LGBT, literary magazine, pep band, political, professional, radio and TV, religious, rugby, social, social service, student government, and symphony. Popular campus events include St. Patrick's Week, Greek Week, and Sub-Zero Days. **Sports:** There are 12 intercollegiate sports for men and 7 for women, and 9 intramural sports for men and 9 for women. The Kern Center is a 210,000-square-foot recreation, athletic, health, and wellness center. It contains an ice arena, fitness center, wrestling room, field house, counseling center, health services, campus ministry, basketball arena, and an indoor track facility. **Graduates:** From July 1, 2015 to June 30, 2016, 470 bachelor's degrees were awarded. The most popular majors were mechanical engineering (24%), business (14%), and nursing (12%). 268 companies recruited on campus in 2015-2016. In an average class, 42% graduate in 4 years or less, 60% graduate in 5 years or less, and 64% graduate in 6 years or less. Of the 2015 graduating class, 6% were enrolled in graduate school within 6 months of graduation, and 96% were employed.

SERVICES: Counseling and information services are available, as is tutoring in every subject. There is a reader service for the blind, and remedial math, reading, and writing. **Library/Resources:** The library contains 68,983 volumes, 80,654 microform items, and 2,533 audio/video tapes/CDs/DVDs, and subscribes to 4,431 periodicals including electronic. Computerized library services include interlibrary loans, database searching, Internet access, and Wi-Fi capability. Special learning facilities include an art gallery and radio station. **Physically Challenged Students:** 95% of the campus is accessible. Facilities include wheelchair ramps, elevators, special parking, specially equipped restrooms, special class scheduling, lowered drinking fountains, lowered telephones, and special housing. **Special:** MSOE offers internships in the student's discipline, study abroad in France, Germany, India, and Czech Republic, on-campus work-study programs, and nondegree study. A number of dual degrees along with a 5-year freshman-to-master's degree in civil engineering are available. There are 6 national honor societies and 5 departmental honors programs. **Visiting:** There are regularly scheduled orientations for prospective students consisting of personal visits, Spring and Fall Open Houses, Accepted Student Days, and Senior Visit Days. There are guides for informal visits, visitors may sit in on classes, and stay overnight. To schedule a visit, contact the Admission Office. **Campus Safety and Security:** Measures include 24-hour foot and vehicle patrol and security escort services. There are shuttle buses, emergency telephones, lighted pathways/sidewalks, and 24-hour security in residence halls.

REQUIREMENTS: The ACT is required. The SAT is acceptable. Applicants must be graduates of an accredited secondary school, having completed 15 academic credits, including 4 units of English, 2 units each of science and math, and 1 unit each of social studies and history. More units in math, science, and English are strongly advised; 1 unit in computer science is recommended. The GED is accepted. An essay is required, and an interview is recommended. AP and CLEP credits are accepted. Important factors in the admissions decision are advanced placement or honors courses, leadership record, and personality/intangible qualities. To graduate, students must complete approximately 197 quarter credits with a minimum GPA of 2.0 overall and in the major. There are requirements in speech, composition, computer programming, ethics, and business. **Procedure:** Freshmen are admitted to all sessions. Entrance exams should be taken during the junior year. There are deferred admissions and rolling admissions plans. Application deadlines are open. Applications are accepted on-line. **Transfer Students:** 207 transfer students enrolled in 2015-2016. Applicants for transfer should have a minimum GPA of 2.75 and must have completed 24 semester or 36 quarter credits. 100 of 197 credits required for the bachelor's degree must be completed at MSOE. **International Students:** There are 325 international students enrolled. The school actively recruits these students. They must take the TOEFL with a minimum score of 79 on the Internet-based version (iBT), or take the IELTS.

ADMISSIONS: 57% of the 2016-2017 applicants were accepted. The SAT scores for the 2016-2017 freshman class were: Critical Reading-- 6% below 500, 33% between 500 and 599, 39% between 600 and 699, and 22% between 700 and 800. Math-- 11% between 500 and 599, 67% between 600 and 699, and 22% between 700 and 800. The ACT scores were 8% between 18 and 23, 64% between 24 and 29, and 28% above 30. **Admissions Contact:** Seandra Mitchell, Director of Admission. Email: *mitchell@msoe.edu* Web: *www.msoe.edu*

FINANCIAL AID: In 2016-2017, 100% of all full-time freshmen and 90% of continuing full-time students received some form of financial aid. 85% of all full-time freshmen and 73% of continuing full-time students received need-based aid. The average freshman award was $33,242. Need-based scholarships or need-based grants averaged $12,468 ($24,815 maximum); need-based self-help aid (loans and jobs) averaged $3,313 ($4,700 maximum); other non-need-based awards and non-need-based scholarships averaged $14,284 ($46,353 maximum); and $6,885 from other forms of aid. 67% of undergraduate students work part-time. Average annual earnings from campus work are $2805. The average financial indebtedness of the 2016 graduate was $35,524. The FAFSA code is 003868. The priority date for freshman financial aid applications for fall entry is March 15.

MOUNT MARY UNIVERSITY *(The complete profile is made available exclusively on our website, www.barronspac.com)*

NORTHLAND COLLEGE — B-1

www.northland.edu

Ashland, WI 54806	**(715) 682-1224** **(800) 753-1840**
Fax: (715) 682-1258	**Email:** admit@northland.edu
Full-time: 285 men, 364 women	**Faculty:** 41
Part-time: 27 men, 63 women	**Ph.D.s:** 85%
Graduate: n/av	**Student/Faculty:** 10 to 1
Year: 4-1-4, summer session	**Tuition:** $32,754
Room & Board: $8349	**Freshman Class:** 804 applied, 605 accepted, 181 enrolled
SAT: required **ACT:** 24	**CEEB CODE:** 1561
Application Deadline: n/av	**COMPETITIVE+**

Northland College is a private liberal arts college with a progressive focus on the environment and sustainability. Our innovative curriculum and distinguished faculty draw students from across the country who come to be a part of a powerful educational community. The 80-acre campus is in a small town in Ashland, Wisconsin, 65 miles east of Duluth, MN. Including any residence halls, there are 20 buildings.

STUDENT LIFE: 65% of undergraduates are from out of state, mostly the Midwest. Students are from 43 states, 7 foreign countries, and Canada. 85% are from public schools. 84% are White; 3% Foreign; 2% African American; 2% American Indian/Alaska Native; 2% Hispanic; 1% Asian American. **Female To Male Ratio:** 1.4:1. The average age of freshmen is 20; all undergraduates, 21. 20% do not continue beyond their first year; 44% remain to graduate. **Housing:** 530 students can be accommodated in college housing, which includes single-sex and coed dorms and on-campus apartments. In addition, there are special-interest houses. On-campus housing is guaranteed for all 4 years. 70% of students live on campus; of those, 80% remain on campus on weekends. Alcohol is not permitted. All students may keep cars.

FACULTY/CLASSROOMS: 81% of faculty are male; 19% are female. All teach undergraduates, and 25% do research. No introductory courses are taught by graduate students. The average class size in an introductory lecture is 30; in a laboratory is 30; and in a regular course is 15.

PROGRAMS OF STUDY: Northland confers B.A. and B.S. degrees. Bachelor's degrees are awarded in AGRICULTURE (environmental studies, fish and game management, forestry and related sciences, and natural resource management), BIOLOGICAL SCIENCE (biology ecology and field biology, biology/biological science, and environmental biology), BUSINESS (business administration and management, environment & natnl resource economics, and sustainable management), COMMUNICATIONS AND THE ARTS (ceramic art and design, comparative literature, creative writing, English, fine arts, graphic design, and writing), COMPUTER AND PHYSICAL SCIENCE (atmospheric science, atmospheric sciences and meteorology, chemistry, earth science, environmental chemistry, environmental geology, geology, information sciences and systems, and mathematics), EDUCATION (education, elementary education, environmental education, middle school education, and secondary education), ENGINEERING AND ENVIRONMENTAL DESIGN (environmental science and water and wastewater technology), SOCIAL SCIENCE (American Indian studies, feminist, gender, sexuality studies, history, humanities, Native American studies, parks and recreation management, psychology, public administration, religion, rural sociology, and sociology). Biology, natural resources, and education are the strongest academically. Biology, education, and business have the largest enrollments.

ACTIVITIES: There are no fraternities or sororities. There are 40 groups on campus, including art, band, cheerleading, choir, chorale, chorus, computers, drama, ethnic, honors, international, jazz band, LGBT, literary magazine, newspaper, orchestra, photography, political, professional, religious, social, social service, student government, symphony, and yearbook. Popular campus events include Snow Festival, Pow Wow, Folk Festival, and the Sigurd Olsen Nature Writing Award. **Sports:** There are 7 intercollegiate sports for men and 8 for women, and 10 intramural sports for men and 10 for women. **Graduates:** From July 1, 2015 to June 30, 2016, 109 bachelor's degrees were awarded. The most popular majors were natural resources (15%), outdoor education (15%), and biology (15%). In an average class, 2% graduate in 3 years or less and 80% graduate in 4 years or less. Of the 2015 graduating class, 15% were enrolled in graduate school within 6 months of graduation, and 95% were employed.

SERVICES: Counseling and information services are available, as is tutoring in every subject. There is a reader service for the blind, and remedial math, reading, and writing. **Library/Resources:** The library contains 77,700 volumes, 9,300 microform items, and subscribes to 350 periodicals including electronic. Computerized library services include interlibrary loans and database searching. Special learning facilities include an art gallery, natural history museum, environmental research acreage, community garden, solar and geothermal energy, and unparalleled access to Lake Superior and National Forest lands. **Physically Challenged Students:** 90% of the campus is accessible. Facilities include wheelchair ramps, elevators, special parking, specially equipped restrooms, and special class scheduling. **Special:** Opportunities are provided for cooperative programs in many majors and with other schools, internships, work-study programs with state and federal agencies, student-designed majors, credit for life experience, pass/fail options, and study abroad in 7 countries. Cross-registration is offered within the Eco-League and Kansai Gaidai University in Japan. 3-2 engineering degrees are available in conjunction with Michigan Technological University and Washington University in St. Louis. There are 2 national honor societies. **Visiting:** There are regularly scheduled orientations for prospective students, including an interview, a tour, class visits, and an optional overnight stay in a dorm. There are guides for informal visits. To schedule a visit, contact the Admissions Office. **Campus Safety and Security:** Measures include emergency notification system and security escort services. There are emergency telephones, lighted pathways/sidewalks, and controlled access to dorms/residences.

REQUIREMENTS: The SAT or ACT is required. Graduation from an accredited secondary school is required; the GED is accepted. An essay and interview are recommended. AP and CLEP credits are accepted. Important factors in the admissions decision are advanced placement or honors courses, extracurricular activities record, and recommendations by school officials. Students must complete 124 credits, including 35 to 60 in the major, with a minimum GPA of 2.0. All students must meet requirements that include courses in English composition, literature, history, philosophy, social and natural sciences, physical science, fine arts, phys ed, and studies of other cultures. **Procedure:** Freshmen are admitted fall, winter, and spring. Entrance exams should be taken fall of the senior year. There are early admissions, deferred admissions, and rolling admissions plans. Application deadlines are open. Applications are accepted on-line. **Transfer Students:** Applicants must have maintained a minimum GPA of 2.0 in previously attended colleges. 30 of 124 credits required for the bachelor's degree must be completed at Northland. **International Students:** The school actively recruits these students. They must take the TOEFL or MELAB.

ADMISSIONS: 75% of the 2016-2017 applicants were accepted. 75% of the current freshmen were in the top fifth of their class; 74% were in the top two fifths. **Admissions Contact:** Teege Mettille, Executive Director of Admissions. Email: *admit@northland.edu* Web: *www.northland.edu*

FINANCIAL AID: In 2016-2017, 89% of all full-time freshmen and 92% of continuing full-time students received some form of financial aid. 83% of all full-time freshmen and 83% of continuing full-time students received need-based aid. 90% of undergraduate students work part-time. Average annual earnings from campus work are $1200. Northland is a member of CSS. The college's own financial statement is required. The FAFSA code is 003875. The deadline for filing freshman financial aid applications for fall entry is April 15.

RIPON COLLEGE — D-4

www.ripon.edu

Ripon, WI 54971	**(920) 748-8185** **(800) 947-4766**
Fax: (920) 748-8335	**Email: adminfo@ripon.edu**
Full-time: 379 men, 404 women	**Faculty:** 64; IIB, -$
Part-time: 4 men, 6 women	**Ph.D.s:** 92%
Graduate: n/av	**Student/Faculty:** 12 to 1
Year: semesters	**Tuition:** $39,142
Room & Board: $7769	**Freshman Class:** 2553 applied, 1666 accepted, 214 enrolled
SAT CR/M: 506/514 **ACT:** 24	**CEEB CODE:** 1664
Application Deadline: August 1	**COMPETITIVE+**

Ripon College, established in 1851, is a private, residential, liberal arts institution. There is 1 undergraduate school. The 250-acre campus is in a small town 80 miles north of Milwaukee in the east-central part of the state. Including any residence halls, there are 26 buildings.

STUDENT LIFE: 70% of undergraduates are from Wisconsin. Others are from 31 states, and 14 foreign countries. 60% are from public schools. 83% are White; 6% Hispanic; 4% Foreign; 2% African American; 2% two or more races; 1% Asian American; 1% American Indian/Alaska Native; 1% race unknown. **Female To Male Ratio:** 1.1:1. The average age of freshmen is 18; all undergraduates, 20. 19% do not continue beyond their first year; 69% remain to graduate. **Housing:** 952 students can be accommodated in college housing, which includes single-sex and coed dorms and on-campus apartments. Theme and interest groups may form living areas in the residence halls. On-campus housing is guaranteed for all 4 years and is available on a lottery system for upperclassmen. 93% of students live on campus; of those, 80% remain on campus on weekends. All students may keep cars.

FACULTY/CLASSROOMS: 64% of faculty are male; 36% are female. All teach undergraduates, and all do research. No introductory courses are taught by graduate students. The average class size in an introductory lecture is 51; in a laboratory is 15; and in a regular course is 19.

PROGRAMS OF STUDY: Ripon confers A.B. degrees. Bachelor's degrees are awarded in BIOLOGICAL SCIENCE (biochemistry and biology/biological science), BUSINESS (business administration and management), COMMUNICATIONS AND THE ARTS (art, art history and appreciation, communications, dramatic arts, English, music, Spanish, and studio art), COMPUTER AND PHYSICAL SCIENCE (chemistry, mathematics, physical sciences, and physics), EDUCATION (early childhood education, elementary education, middle school education, and secondary education), ENGINEERING AND ENVIRONMENTAL DESIGN (environmental science), HEALTH PROFESSIONS (exercise science), SOCIAL SCIENCE (anthropology, economics, history, international studies, philosophy, political science/government, psychobiology, psychology, religion, and sociology). Communication, biology, and chemistry are the strongest academically. Biology, psychology, and exercise science have the largest enrollments.

ACTIVITIES: 23% of women belong to 3 national sororities. There are 60 groups on campus, including art, band, cheerleading, chess, choir, chorale, chorus, dance, drama, environmental, ethnic, film, forensics, honors, international, jazz band, LGBT, literary magazine, musical theater, newspaper, orchestra, pep band, photography, political, professional, radio and TV, religious, social, social service, student government, symphony, and yearbook. Popular campus events include Theater Events, Homecoming Week, SpringFest, and awareness-based monthly and weekly programming. **Sports:** There are 9 intercollegiate sports for men and 9 for women, and 8 intramural sports for men and 8 for women. Facilities include a cycling path in the Prairie on campus, a phys ed center, 2 fields, tennis courts, a recreation center, and an exercise room and a fitness center in the residence halls. The campus is within 5 miles of lakes and cross-country skiing opportunities. **Graduates:** From July 1, 2015 to June 30, 2016, 151 bachelor's degrees were awarded. The most popular majors were business (15%), biology (15%), and exercise science (12%). 20 companies recruited on campus in 2015-2016. In an average class, 1% graduate in 3 years or less, 58% graduate in 4 years or less, 67% graduate in 5 years or less, and 68% graduate in 6 years or less. Of the 2015 graduating class, 25% were enrolled in graduate school within 6 months of graduation, and 61% were employed.

SERVICES: Counseling and information services are available, as is tutoring in most subjects. Tutoring and services are also available for learning-disabled students. **Library/Resources:** The library contains 282,034 volumes, 8,276 microform items, and 1,330 audio/video tapes/CDs/DVDs, and subscribes to 60,147 periodicals including electronic. Computerized library services include interlibrary loans, database searching, Internet access, and Wi-Fi capability. Special learning facilities include an art gallery, radio station, a music library, an art slide library, and college archives. **Physically Challenged Students:** 50% of the campus is accessible. Facilities include wheelchair ramps, elevators, special parking, specially equipped restrooms, special class scheduling, and lowered drinking fountains. **Special:** In addition to the two standard semesters, the calendar includes two short, intensive terms of three weeks-one before fall semester starts and one at the end of spring semester. Taught in short, intensive blocks, these optional In Focus courses offer a beneficial alternative and valuable supplement to those offered during the regular semester. Courses are immersion experiences that can involve off-campus experiences that may be in other countries including service learning, internships, field work, and community engagement, all with an emphasis on mentoring and making connections with experts outside the campus community. There are 16 national honor societies and Phi Beta Kappa. **Visiting:** There are regularly scheduled orientations for prospective students, including a tour, an interview, and meetings with professors and coaches. There are guides for informal visits and visitors may sit in on classes. To schedule a visit, contact the Admission Office. **Campus Safety and Security:** Measures include 24-hour foot and vehicle patrol, emergency notification system, and security escort services. There are emergency telephones, lighted pathways/sidewalks, controlled access to dorms/residences, and a paging system.

REQUIREMENTS: The SAT or ACT is required. Applicants must be graduates of an accredited secondary school. The GED is accepted. Applicants should complete at least 17 Carnegie units, including 4 of English, 2 to 4 each of math, social studies, and natural sciences, and up to 7 of other college-preparatory electives. An essay may be required, and an interview is recommended. Ripon requires applicants to be in the upper 50% of their class. AP and CLEP credits are accepted. Important factors in the admissions decision are leadership record, recommendations by school officials, and advanced placement or honors courses. To graduate, students must complete 124 credit hours, as well as complete of the concentration in applied innovation, complete of a major, and have a cumulative GPA of 2.00 or better. **Procedure:** Freshmen are admitted fall and spring. Entrance exams should be taken in the junior year or the fall of the senior year. There are deferred admissions and rolling admissions plans. Applications should be filed by August 1 for fall entry; December 15 for spring entry, along with a $30 fee. Notification is sent on a rolling basis. Applications are accepted on-line. **Transfer Students:** 7 transfer students enrolled in 2015-2016. Applicants must have a minimum 2.0 GPA and be in good standing at their previous college. The SAT or ACT, a personal statement, and an interview are recommended. 32 of 124 credits required for the bachelor's degree must be completed at Ripon. **International Students:** There are 35 international students enrolled. The school actively recruits these students. They must take the TOEFL with a minimum score of 550 on the paper-based TOEFL (PBT) or 79 on the Internet-based version (iBT). They must also take the SAT if available.

ADMISSIONS: 39% of the current freshmen were in the top fifth of their class; 69% were in the top two fifths. 6 freshmen graduated first in their class. **Admissions Contact:** Jennifer Machacek, Vice President for Enrollment. Email: *adminfo@ripon.edu* Web: *www.ripon.edu*

FINANCIAL AID: In 2016-2017, 100% of all full-time freshmen and 98% of continuing full-time students received some form of financial aid. 86% of all full-time freshmen and 83% of continuing full-time students received need-based aid. The average freshman award was $35,809. Need-based scholarships or need-based grants averaged $7,200 ($10,500 maximum); need-based self-help aid (loans and jobs) averaged $5,789 ($9,000 maximum); and other non-need-based awards and non-need-based scholarships averaged $23,650 ($38,025 maximum). 47% of undergraduate students work part-time. Average annual earnings from campus work are $1400. The average financial indebtedness of the 2016 graduate was $27,338. The FAFSA code is 003884. The deadline for filing freshman financial aid applications for fall entry is March 1.

SILVER LAKE COLLEGE OF THE HOLY FAMILY *(The complete profile is made available exclusively on our website, www.barronspac.com)*

ST. NORBERT COLLEGE — D-3

www.snc.edu

De Pere, WI 54115	**(920) 403-3005** **(800) 236-4878**
Fax: (920) 403-4072	**Email: admit@snc.edu**
Full-time: 885 men, 1169 women	**Faculty:** 139; IIB
Part-time: 23 men, 25 women	**Ph.D.s:** 91%
Graduate: 44 men, 65 women	**Student/Faculty:** 13 to 1
Year: semesters, summer session	**Tuition:** $35,381
Room & Board: $9144	**Freshman Class:** 3605 applied, 2934 accepted, 584 enrolled
ACT: 25	**CEEB CODE:** 1706
Application Deadline: open	**VERY COMPETITIVE**

St. Norbert College, a liberal arts college that teaches critical thinking, problem-solving, and leadership skills. There is 1 undergraduate school and 4 graduate schools. The 112-acre campus is in a suburban area 5 miles south of Green Bay. Including any residence halls, there are 44 buildings.

STUDENT LIFE: 79% of undergraduates are from Wisconsin. Others are from 26 states, 22 foreign countries, and Canada. 75% are from public schools. 88% are White; 4% Hispanic; 3% Foreign; 2% two or more races; 1% African American; 1% Asian American; 1% American Indian/Alaska Native. 42% are Catholic; 30% claim no religious affiliation; 26% Protestant. **Female To Male Ratio:** 1.3:1. The average age of freshmen is 18; all undergraduates, 20. 14% do not continue beyond their first year; 73% remain to graduate. **Housing:** 1875 students can be accommodated in college housing, which includes single-sex and coed dorms and on-campus apartments. In addition, there are special-interest houses, a townhouse complex, a living center, and off-campus houses. On-campus housing is guaranteed for all 4 years. 84% of students live on campus; of those, 80% remain on campus on weekends. All students may keep cars.

FACULTY/CLASSROOMS: 54% of faculty are male; 46% are female. All teach undergraduates. No introductory courses are taught by graduate students. The average class size in an introductory lecture is 19 and in a regular course is 20.

PROGRAMS OF STUDY: St. Norbert confers B.A., B.B.A., B.Mus., and B.S. degrees. Master's degrees are also awarded. Bachelor's degrees are awarded in BIOLOGICAL SCIENCE (biology/biological science), BUSINESS (accounting, business administration and management, and international business management), COMMUNICATIONS AND THE ARTS (art, communications, English, French, German, graphic design, music, Spanish, and theatre arts), COMPUTER AND PHYSICAL SCIENCE (chemistry, computer science, geology, mathematics, natural sciences, and physics), EDUCATION (elementary education and music education), ENGINEERING AND ENVIRONMENTAL DESIGN (commercial art and environmental science), SOCIAL SCIENCE (economics, history, humanities, international relations, philosophy, political science/government, psychology, religion, and sociology). Business administration, communications, and elementary education have the largest enrollments.

ACTIVITIES: 10% of men belong to 4 national fraternities; 10% of women belong to 4 national sororities. There are 84 groups on campus, including art, band, cheerleading, chess, choir, chorale, chorus, communications, computers, dance, drama, E2K Entertainment Tonight, environmental, ethnic, film, honors, international, jazz band, LGBT, literary magazine, musical theater, newspaper, opera, pep band, photography, political, professional, radio and TV, religious, social, social service, and student government. Popular campus events include Opening Campus Picnic/convocation, E2K Homecoming, and SNC Day. **Sports:** There are 10 intercollegiate sports for men and 10 for women, and 6 intramural sports for men and 6 for women. Facilities include a stadium, a baseball and softball sports complex, an activity center with gymnasium, fitness and sports center, a pool, indoor track, four volleyball courts and four intramural basketball courts. **Graduates:** From July 1, 2015 to June 30, 2016, 470 bachelor's degrees were awarded. The most popular majors were business administration (18%), elementary education (14%), and communication and media studies (11%). 86 companies recruited on campus in 2015-2016. In an average class, 68% graduate in 4 years or less, 72% graduate in 5 years or less, and 73% graduate in 6 years or less.

SERVICES: Counseling and information services are available, as is tutoring in most subjects. There is a reader service for the blind, and remedial math, reading, and writing. **Library/Resources:** The library contains 246,257 volumes, 16,086 microform items, and 2,500 audio/video tapes/CDs/DVDs, and subscribes to 100,047 periodicals including electronic. Computerized library services include interlibrary loans, database searching, Internet access, and Wi-Fi capability. Special learning facilities include an art gallery, radio station, TV station, innovation studio, center for women's and gender studies, center for peace, justice and public understanding, marina, fine and performing arts centers, center for international education, center for leadership and service, children's center, center for Norbertine studies, language labs, media center with satellite hookup, and environmental sciences research craft. **Physically Challenged Students:** 82% of the campus is accessible. Facilities include wheelchair ramps, elevators, special parking, specially equipped restrooms, special class scheduling, lowered drinking fountains, lowered telephones, and special housing. **Special:** A partnership program with Bellin College Nursing, cross-registration in Arabic courses with the University of Wisconsin-Green Bay, internships, study abroad in 29 countries, a Washington semester, and work-study programs are available. The college offers dual and student-designed majors, B.A.-B.S. degrees, nondegree study, and limited credit for military experience and work training. The Leadership and Service Program and leadership minor help students improve their leadership abilities through courses and activities. A 3-2 engineering degree is available with Michigan Tech University. A Masters of Science in Applied Economics (MSAE) degree preparation agreement with Marquette University is available. There are 10 national honor societies and a freshman honors program. **Visiting:** There are regularly scheduled orientations for prospective students, including preregistrations, meetings with advisers, and meetings regarding programming and activities, housing, and student life. There are guides for informal visits, visitors may sit in on classes, and stay overnight. To schedule a visit, contact the Office of Admissions. **Campus Safety and Security:** Measures include 24-hour foot and vehicle patrol, emergency notification system, self-defense education, and security escort services. There are emergency telephones, lighted pathways/sidewalks, controlled access to dorms/residences, motorist assistance, and a crime prevention program.

REQUIREMENTS: Admissions requirements are either graduation from an accredited secondary school with 16 units recommended, including 4 English, 3 math, 3 lab sciences, 2 foreign language 2 social studies, 2 history; or a GED recommended score in the 55% range; and either an SAT or ACT entrance exam. AP and CLEP credits are accepted. Important factors in the admissions decision are advanced placement or honors courses, extracurricular activities record, and recommendations by school officials. To graduate, students must complete 128 credits with at least a 2.0 GPA and a minimum of 40 semester credits in a particular major and a major GPA of at least a 2.0. There are general education requirements in the areas of religious studies, human nature, human relationships, natural science, creative expression, U.S. heritage, foreign heritages, foreign language, quantitative skills, Western tradition, global society, a writing-intensive course, and senior colloquium. **Procedure:** Freshmen are admitted to all sessions. Entrance exams should be taken by the end of the junior year. There are deferred admissions and rolling admissions plans. Application deadlines are open. Notification of early decision is sent December 15; regular decision, on a rolling basis. Applications are accepted on-line. **Transfer Students:** 31 transfer students enrolled in 2015-2016. Applicants should have a minimum GPA of 2.5. At least their senior year and 25% of their major credits must be taken at St. Norbert. 32 of 128 credits required for the bachelor's degree must be completed at St. Norbert. **International Students:** There are 54 international students enrolled. The school actively recruits these students. They must take the TOEFL with a minimum score of 555 on the paper-based TOEFL (PBT) or 80 on the Internet-based version (iBT). They must also take the SAT or ACT.

ADMISSIONS: 81% of the 2016-2017 applicants were accepted. The ACT scores were 2% between 12 and 17, 41% between 18 and 23, 47% between 24 and 29, and 10% above 30. **Admissions Contact:** Edward Lamm, V.P. of Enrollment Management and Communication. Email: *admit@snc.edu* Web: *www.snc.edu*

FINANCIAL AID: In 2016-2017, 98% of all full-time freshmen received some form of financial aid. 77% of all full-time freshmen and 75% of continuing full-time students received need-based aid. The average freshman award was $25,228. The average financial indebtedness of the 2016 graduate was $33,948. The FAFSA code is 003892. The priority date for freshman financial aid applications for fall entry is March 1.

UNIVERSITY OF WISCONSIN-EAU CLAIRE B-3

www.uwec.edu

Eau Claire, WI 54701	**(715) 836-5188** **(888) INFO-UWE**
Fax: (715) 831-4799	**Email: kretzhm@uwec.edu**
Full-time: 3585 men, 5726 women	**Faculty:** 446; IIA, --$
Part-time: 250 men, 420 women	**Ph.D.s:** 78%
Graduate: 250 men, 398 women	**Student/Faculty:** 21 to 1
Year: semesters, summer session	**Tuition:** $8813 ($16,386)
Room & Board: $6984	**Freshman Class:** 5706 applied, 5079 accepted, 2302 enrolled
SAT: recommended **ACT:** 24	**CEEB CODE:** 1913
Application Deadline: n/av	**VERY COMPETITIVE**

University of Wisconsin-Eau Claire fosters in it's students creativity, critical insight, empathy, and intellectual courage, the hallmarks of a transformative liberal education, and the foundation for active citizenship and lifelong inquiry. There are 4 undergraduate schools. In addition to regional accreditation, UW-Eau Claire has baccalaureate program accreditation with AACSB, ACEJMC, CSWE, and NASM. The 337-acre campus is in an urban area 95 miles east of Minneapolis, Minnesota. Including any residence halls, there are 28 buildings.

STUDENT LIFE: 72% of undergraduates are from Wisconsin. Others are from 37 states, 31 foreign countries, and Canada. 88% are White; 4% Asian American; 3% Hispanic; 2% Foreign; 2% two or more races; 1% African American. **Female To Male Ratio:** 1.6:1. The average age of freshmen is 18; all undergraduates, 21. 16% do not continue beyond their first year; 84% remain to graduate. **Housing:** 4393 students can be accommodated in college housing, which includes single-sex and coed dorms and on-campus apartments. In addition, there are honors houses, special-interest houses, theme housing, and wellness housing. On-campus housing is available on a first-come, first-served basis and is available on a lottery system for upperclassmen. 59% of students commute. All students may keep cars.

FACULTY/CLASSROOMS: 48% of faculty are male; 52% are female. All teach undergraduates. No introductory courses are taught by graduate students. The average class size in an introductory lecture is 36 and in a laboratory is 21.

PROGRAMS OF STUDY: UW-Eau Claire confers B.A., B.S., B.B.A., B.F.A., B.L.S., B.M., B.M.E., B.S.E.Ph., B.S.N. and B.S.W. degrees. Associate, master's, and doctoral degrees are also awarded. Bachelor's degrees are awarded in BIOLOGICAL SCIENCE (biochemistry and biology/biological science), BUSINESS (accounting, banking and finance, business administration and management, international business, marketing, and organizational leadership and management), COMMUNICATIONS AND THE ARTS (art, communications, English, French, German, journalism, music, Spanish, and theatre arts), COMPUTER AND PHYSICAL SCIENCE (chemistry, computer science, geology, geoscience, information sciences and systems, mathematics, physical sciences, and physics), EDUCATION (athletic training, elementary education, physical education, science education, and special education), ENGINEERING AND ENVIRONMENTAL DESIGN (materials science and materials science and engineering), HEALTH PROFESSIONS (health care administration, nursing, predentistry, premedicine, preoptometry, prepharmacy, prephysical therapy, preveterinary science, and public health), SOCIAL SCIENCE (American Indian studies, communication sciences & disorders, criminal justice, economics, geography, history, Latin American studies, liberal arts/general studies, philosophy, political science/government, prelaw, psychology, religious studies, social studies, social work, sociology, and women's studies). Nursing, biology, and kinesiology have the largest enrollments.

ACTIVITIES: 1% of men belong to 3 national fraternities; 1% of women belong to 3 national sororities. There are 270 groups on campus, including art, band, cheerleading, chess, choir, chorale, chorus, communications, computers, dance, debate, drama, environmental, ethnic, film, forensics, honors, international, jazz band, LGBT, literary magazine, marching band, musical theater, newspaper, opera, orchestra, pep band, photography, political, professional, radio and TV, religious, social, social service, student government, and symphony. Popular campus events include Homecoming, Caberet, Viennese Ball, and Winter Carnival. **Sports:** There are 9 intercollegiate sports for men and 11 for women. Facilities include a gym, pool, 30 acres of intramural and recreation fields, game room, bowling and billiards, Nautilus fitness center, racquetball courts, weight room, ropes course, 3212-seat stadium, tennis courts, and a climbing wall. **Graduates:** From July 1, 2015 to June 30, 2016, 2126 bachelor's degrees were awarded. The most popular majors were marketing (22%), health professionals (14%), and parks and recreation (7%). In an average class, 30% graduate in 4 years or less, 63% graduate in 5 years or less, and 68% graduate in 6 years or less.

SERVICES: Counseling and information services are available, as is tutoring in most subjects, such as writing, math/problem solving, and reading/study skills. There is a reader service for the blind, and remedial math, reading, and writing. Entry-level courses in foreign languages, humanities, and social and physical sciences are available. **Library/Resources:** The library contains 1.0 million volumes, 50,318 microform items, and 38,703 audio/video tapes/CDs/DVDs, and subscribes to 84,342 periodicals including electronic. Computerized library services include interlibrary loans, database searching, Internet access, and Wi-Fi capability. Special learning facilities include an art gallery, planetarium, radio station, TV station, a human development center, natural preserve, ropes course, materials science center, and college of nursing and health sciences clinical simulation/skills lab. **Physically Challenged Students:** 90% of the campus is accessible. Facilities include wheelchair ramps, elevators, special parking, specially equipped restrooms, special class scheduling, lowered drinking fountains, lowered telephones, and special housing. **Special:** Numerous internships, work-study programs, and study abroad in 26 countries are offered. Dual majors and interdisciplinary majors are possible. Credit by examination, non-degree study, and pass/fail options are offered. There are 29 national honor societies, a freshman honors program, and 21 departmental honors programs. **Visiting:** There are regularly scheduled orientations for prospective students, during which students meet with academic advisers, develop a class schedule, register for classes, and tour the campus. There are guides for informal visits and visitors may sit in on classes. To schedule a visit, contact the Admissions Office. **Campus Safety and Security:** Measures include 24-hour foot and vehicle patrol and emergency notification system. There are shuttle buses, emergency telephones, lighted pathways/sidewalks, and controlled access to dorms/residences.

REQUIREMENTS: The ACT is required. The SAT is recommended. Applicants should graduate from an accredited secondary school or present its equivalent, with 17 academic credits including 4 in English, 3 each in social studies, college prep math, and science, and 4 years of electives. Each application is given a comprehensive review. In addition to a rigorous curriculum, academic factors include: class rank, GPA, trends in grades, and test scores. Secondary non-academic factors include: leadership, service, achievement in arts, athletics, etc, and diversity in personal background and experience. AP and CLEP credits are accepted. Important factors in the admissions decision are advanced placement or honors courses, extracurricular activities record, and evidence of special talent. All students must complete 36 hours in liberal education, including natural sciences, social sciences, humanities, fine arts, written and oral communications, mathematics, creativity, equity, diversity and inclusivity, global and perspectives, civic and environmental issues, integration and must complete 30 or more hours of service-learning. A minimum 2.0 GPA and 120 credits hours are required to graduate. **Procedure:** Freshmen are admitted to all sessions. Entrance exams should be taken by April of the senior year. There are early admissions and rolling admissions plans. Application deadlines are open. The fall 2016 application fee was $50. 500 applicants were on the 2016 waiting list; 200 were admitted. Applications are accepted on-line. Application fees are waived if application is completed on-line. **Transfer Students:** 497 transfer students enrolled in 2015-2016. Transfer applicants must carry a minimum 2.0 GPA. Preference is given to transfers who have completed the equivalent of freshman composition and college algebra. Students with less than 30 semester credits must meet the freshman admissions requirements. 30 of 120 credits required for the bachelor's degree must be completed at UW-Eau Claire. **International Students:** There are 223 international students enrolled. The school actively recruits these students. They must take the TOEFL with a minimum score of 550 on the paper-based TOEFL (PBT) or 79 on the Internet-based version (iBT). They must also take the SAT or ACT.

ADMISSIONS: 89% of the 2016-2017 applicants were accepted. The SAT scores for the 2016-2017 freshman class were: Critical Reading-- 6% below 500, 38% between 500 and 599, 38% between 600 and 699, and 19% between 700 and 800. Math-- 6% below 500, 50% between 500 and 599, 31% between 600 and 699, and 13% between 700 and 800. The ACT scores were 2% between 12 and 17, 46% between 18 and 23, 45% between 24 and 29, and 6% above 30. There was 1 National Merit finalist. 50 freshmen graduated first in their class. **Admissions Contact:** Heather Kretz, Director of Admissions. Email: *kretzhm@uwec.edu* Web: *www.uwec.edu*

FINANCIAL AID: In 2016-2017, 87% of all full-time freshmen and 75% of continuing full-time students received some form of financial aid. 57% of all full-time freshmen and 55% of continuing full-time students received need-based aid. The average freshman award was $10,831. Need-based scholarships or need-based grants averaged $5,823; need-based self-help aid (loans and jobs) averaged $8,536; and other non-need-based awards and non-need-based scholarships averaged $7,430. 32% of undergraduate students work part-time. Average annual earnings from campus work are $2257. The average financial indebtedness of the 2016 graduate was $26,295. The FAFSA code is 003917. The priority date for freshman financial aid applications for fall entry is April 15.

UNIVERSITY OF WISCONSIN-GREEN BAY D-3

www.uwgb.edu

Green Bay, WI 54311	(920) 465-2111
Fax: (920) 465-2765	**Email:** admissions@uwgb.edu
Full-time: 1408 men, 2601 women	**Faculty:** 185; IIA, --$
Part-time: 838 men, 1911 women	**Ph.D.s:** 87%
Graduate: 104 men, 168 women	**Student/Faculty:** 22 to 1
Year: semesters, summer session	**Tuition:** $7878 ($15,450)
Room & Board: $7224	**Freshman Class:** 2126 applied, 1966 accepted, 872 enrolled
ACT: 23	**CEEB CODE:** 1859
Application Deadline: August 26	**COMPETITIVE**

University of Wisconsin-Green Bay, founded in 1968, is a public institution offering bachelor's and master's programs in humanities and fine arts, natural sciences, social sciences, business, education, health, and pre-professional areas. There are 4 undergraduate schools and one graduate school. In addition to regional accreditation, UW-Green Bay has baccalaureate program accreditation with ADA, CSWE, NASM, and NLN. The 700-acre campus is in a suburban area 111 miles north of Milwaukee. Including any residence halls, there are 49 buildings.

STUDENT LIFE: 91% of undergraduates are from Wisconsin. Others are from 42 states, 40 foreign countries, and Canada. 95% are from public schools. 83% are White; 4% Hispanic; 3% Asian American; 3% two or more races; 2% African American; 2% Foreign; 2% race unknown; 1% American Indian/Alaska Native. 40% are Catholic; 40% Protestant; 15% claim no religious affiliation. **Female To Male Ratio:** 2.0:1. The average age of freshmen is 18; all undergraduates, 25. 26% do not continue beyond their first year; 50% remain to graduate. **Housing:** 2000 students can be accommodated in college housing, which includes coed dorms and on-campus apartments. In addition, there are special-interest houses and 3- 4- and 5-person dorm suites with private bedrooms. On-campus housing is available on a first-come, first-served basis and is available on a lottery system for upperclassmen. 66% of students commute. All students may keep cars.

FACULTY/CLASSROOMS: 51% of faculty are male; 49% are female. 95% teach undergraduates, 85% do research, and 85% do both. No introductory courses are taught by graduate students. The average class size in an introductory lecture is 40; in a laboratory is 20; and in a regular course is 25.

PROGRAMS OF STUDY: UW-Green Bay confers B.A., B.S., B.A.S., B.B.A., B.M., B.S.N. and B.S.W. degrees. Associate and master's degrees are also awarded. Bachelor's degrees are awarded in AGRICULTURE (environmental studies), BIOLOGICAL SCIENCE (biology/biological science), BUSINESS (accounting, business administration and management, finance, human resources, and sustainable management), COMMUNICATIONS AND THE ARTS (art, arts administration/management, communications, creative writing, design, dramatic arts, English, English as a second/foreign language, fine arts, French, German, Germanic languages and literature, music, Spanish, and theatre arts), COMPUTER AND PHYSICAL SCIENCE (chemistry, computer science, earth science, geoscience, information sciences and systems, and mathematics), EDUCATION (art education, education, elementary education, English education, foreign languages education, health information management, mathematics education, middle school education, music education, and secondary education), ENGINEERING AND ENVIRONMENTAL DESIGN (city/community/regional planning, electrical/electronics engineering technology, engineering technology, environmental engineering technology, environmental science, and mechanical engineering technology), HEALTH PROFESSIONS (exercise science and nursing), SOCIAL SCIENCE (American Indian studies, dietetics, economics, French studies, gender studies, history, human development, humanities, interdisciplinary studies, liberal arts/general studies, philosophy, political science/government, psychology, public administration, social work, urban studies, and women's studies). Education, environmental science, human biology and accounting are the strongest academically. Business, human biology, and integrative leadership studies have the largest enrollments.

ACTIVITIES: 1% of men belong to 1 national fraternity; 1% of women belong to 2 national sororities. There are 127 groups on campus, including art, band, cheerleading, choir, chorale, chorus, computers, dance, drama, drill team, environmental, ethnic, film, honors, international, jazz band, LGBT, literary magazine, musical theater, newspaper, orchestra, pep band, photography, political, professional, radio and TV, religious, social, social service, and student government. Popular campus events include Frost Fest, GB Week, and Pow Wow. **Sports:** There are 7 intercollegiate sports for men and 9 for women, and 7 intramural sports for men and 7 for women. Facilities include a sports center with a 5000-seat arena for campus-wide ceremonies, concerts, and events, auxiliary courts (basketball practice, student recreation), elevated running track, 28-foot climbing tower, two weight areas with Magnum machines and free weights, group aerobics/fitness studio (cardio deck with stationary bikes, stair-climbers, elliptical machines, treadmills, video monitors), indoor turf gym, and a swimming pool. **Graduates:** From July 1, 2015 to June 30, 2016, 1274 bachelor's degrees were awarded. The most popular majors were business administration (17%), integrative leadership studies (12%), and psychology (10%). 60 companies recruited on campus in 2015-2016. In an average class, 1% graduate in 3 years or less, 24% graduate in 4 years or less, 46% graduate in 5 years or less, and 50% graduate in 6 years or less. Of the 2015 graduating class,

20% were enrolled in graduate school within 6 months of graduation, and 88% were employed.

SERVICES: Counseling and information services are available, as is tutoring in most subjects. There is a reader service for the blind, and remedial math, reading, and writing. There is an academic support office, language and writing centers, student health services, and individual counseling. Available equipment includes a visual enlarger, automatic page turner, accessible computer station with attached voice syntheizer, slow speed cassette recorders, and a TDD device. Note takers, typists, readers, and aids are available for students. **Library/Resources:** The library contains 366,860 volumes, 1.4 million microform items, and 47,943 audio/video tapes/CDs/DVDs, and subscribes to 3,234 periodicals including electronic. Computerized library services include interlibrary loans, database searching, Internet access, and Wi-Fi capability. Special learning facilities include an art gallery, natural history museum, radio station, TV station, a 270-acre arboretum, and a regional performing arts center. **Physically Challenged Students:** All of the campus is accessible. Facilities include wheelchair ramps, elevators, special parking, specially equipped restrooms, lowered drinking fountains, lowered telephones. automatic door openers. All academic buildings on campus are connected by an underground concourse system which is widely accessed by the entire campus community and which makes the campus particularly accessible to wheelchair transportation. **Special:** UW-Green Bay offers cross-registration with Bellin College of Nursing and the University of Wisconsin at Milwaukee or Oshkosh. There are study-abroad programs and travel courses in numerous countries. Students can receive credit by examination or for life, military, or work experience. There are internships in almost all fields, interdisciplinary majors, and dual and student-designed majors, work-study, B.A.-B.S. degrees in most areas, nondegree study, a general studies degree, and pass/fail options. There are 6 national honor societies and 34 departmental honors programs. **Visiting:** There are regularly scheduled orientations for prospective students, including campus preview days, which consist of information sessions, academic area workshops, and campus tours. There are guides for informal visits and visitors may sit in on classes. To schedule a visit, contact the Office of Admissions. **Campus Safety and Security:** Measures include 24-hour foot and vehicle patrol and security escort services. There are emergency telephones, lighted pathways/sidewalks, and controlled access to dorms/residences.

REQUIREMENTS: The ACT is required. Candidates must be graduates of an accredited secondary school, approved home school program, or hold a GED certificate. They must have completed 17 academic credits consisting of 4 in English, 3 in social sciences, 3 each in science and math, 2 in any of the above areas or a foreign language, and 2 other electives. Home-schooled applicants are encouraged to apply and should contact the admissions office for additional information. AP and CLEP credits are accepted. Important factors in the admissions decision are advanced placement or honors courses, extracurricular activities record, and leadership record. All students must complete at least 120 semester hours, including an average of 36 in the major, with a minimum GPA of 2.0, depending on the major. Students must declare an interdisciplinary minor or major. Required general education includes courses in fine arts, humanities, natural and social sciences, Other Culture Studies, and Ethnic Studies, as well as freshman seminar, and competency and capstone courses. **Procedure:** Freshmen are admitted to all sessions. Entrance exams should be taken between the junior and senior years. There are deferred admissions and rolling admissions plans. Applications should be filed by August 26 for fall entry; November 1 for spring entry, along with a $50 fee. Notification is sent on a rolling basis. Applications are accepted on-line. **Transfer Students:** 1204 transfer students enrolled in 2015-2016. Transfer students must have a minimum GPA of 2.0 based on at least 15 transferable credits; priority for admission is given to students with 24 credits and a minimum GPA of 2.5. 31 of 120 credits required for the bachelor's degree must be completed at UW-Green Bay. **International Students:** There are 74 international students enrolled. The school actively recruits these students. They must take the TOEFL with a minimum score of 500 on the paper-based TOEFL (PBT) or 61 on the Internet-based version (iBT). They must also take the SAT or ACT.

ADMISSIONS: 92% of the 2016-2017 applicants were accepted. The ACT scores were 5% between 12 and 17, 56% between 18 and 23, 36% between 24 and 29, and 2% above 30. **Admissions Contact:** Jen Jones, Director of Admissions. Email: *admissions@uwgb.edu* Web: *www.uwgb.edu*

FINANCIAL AID: In 2016-2017, 88% of all full-time freshmen and 82% of continuing full-time students received some form of financial aid. 57% of all full-time freshmen and 62% of continuing full-time students received need-based aid. The average freshman award was $10,921. Need-based scholarships or need-based grants averaged $6,217 ($13,423 maximum); need-based self-help aid (loans and jobs) averaged $3,880 ($7,500 maximum); non-need-based athletic scholarships averaged $10,226 ($30,762 maximum); other non-need-based awards and non-need-based scholarships averaged $2,787 ($17,000 maximum); and $4,432 from other forms of aid. 80% of undergraduate students work part-time. Average annual earnings from campus work are $3000. The average financial indebtedness of the 2016 graduate was $28,940. The FAFSA code is 003899. The deadline for filing freshman financial aid applications for fall entry is April 15.

UNIVERSITY OF WISCONSIN-LA CROSSE B-4

www.uwlax.edu

La Crosse, WI 54601 (608) 785-8000

Fax: (608) 785-8940	**Email:** admissions@uwlax.edu
Full-time: 3968 men, 5207 women	**Faculty:** n/av
Part-time: 288 men, 236 women	**Ph.D.s:** 82%
Graduate: 253 men, 564 women	**Student/Faculty:** 19 to 1
Year: semesters, summer session	**Tuition:** $9091 ($17,612)
Room & Board: $6156	**Freshman Class:** 5975 applied, 4765 accepted, 2054 enrolled
SAT CR/M/W: 550/560/560 **ACT:** 24	**CEEB CODE:** 1914
Application Deadline: n/av	**COMPETITIVE+**

University of Wisconsin-La Crosse, founded in 1909, is a public institution offering undergraduate and graduate studies in arts and sciences, health and human services, business administration, education, phys ed and recreation, professional development, and educational administration. The figures in the above capsule and in this profile are approximate. There are 5 undergraduate schools and 1 graduate school. In addition to regional accreditation, UW-L has baccalaureate program accreditation with AACSB, APTA, NASM, NCATE, ACOTE, ACS, CAPTE, and NAACLS. The 121-acre campus is in a small town 142 miles west of Madison and 150 miles southeast of Minneapolis/St. Paul, WI. Including any residence halls, there are 32 buildings.

STUDENT LIFE: 81% of undergraduates are from Wisconsin. Others are from 31 states, 27 foreign countries, and Canada. 90% are from public schools. 89% are White; 4% Hispanic; 3% two or more races; 2% Asian American; 1% African American; 1% Foreign. **Female To Male Ratio:** 1.3:1. The average age of freshmen is 18; all undergraduates, 20. 14% do not continue beyond their first year; 68% remain to graduate. **Housing:** 3180 students can be accommodated in college housing, which includes single-sex and coed dorms. In addition, there are special-interest houses, fraternity houses, and sorority houses. There is a residence hall for international students and students 21 years or older, substance free, and first year experience housing, special housing for disabled students, and coed dorms. On-campus housing is available on a first-come, first-served basis, and is available on a lottery system for upperclassmen. 64% of students commute. All students may keep cars.

FACULTY/CLASSROOMS: 51% of faculty are male; 49% are female. No introductory courses are taught by graduate students. The average class size in a regular course is 28.

PROGRAMS OF STUDY: UW-L confers B.A. and B.S. degrees. Associate and master's degrees are also awarded. Bachelor's degrees are awarded in BIOLOGICAL SCIENCE (biology/biological science and microbiology), BUSINESS (accounting, banking and finance, business administration and management, international business management, and marketing/retailing/merchandising), COMMUNICATIONS AND THE ARTS (art, communications, dramatic arts, English, fine arts, French, music, Spanish, and speech/debate/rhetoric), COMPUTER AND PHYSICAL SCIENCE (chemistry, computer science, information sciences and systems, mathematics, and physics), EDUCATION (athletic training, elementary education, health education, physical education, science education, secondary education, and social studies education), HEALTH PROFESSIONS (community health work, exercise science, medical laboratory technology, nuclear medical technology, occupational therapy, physician's assistant, radiation therapy, and recreation therapy), SOCIAL SCIENCE (archeology, economics, geography, German area studies, history, parks and recreation management, philosophy, political science/government, psychology, public administration, and sociology). Microbiology, nuclear medicine technology, and physics are the strongest academically. Business administration, elementary education, and biology have the largest enrollments.

ACTIVITIES: 1% of women belong to 2 national sororities. There are 150 groups on campus, including art, band, campus ministries, cheerleading, chess, choir, chorale, chorus, computers, dance, drama, ethnic, honors, international, jazz band, LGBT, literary magazine, marching band, musical theater, newspaper, orchestra, pep band, photography, political, professional, radio and TV, religious, social, social service, student government, and symphony. Popular campus events include Parents Weekend, Community-Sponsored Oktoberfest, and Various Cultural Events. **Sports:** There are 9 intercollegiate sports for men and 10 for women, and 11 intramural sports for men and 11 for women. Facilities include a wrestling room, an indoor track, 6 indoor tennis courts, 16 outdoor tennis courts, an Olympic-size swimming pool, 2 strength-training centers, a dance studio, racquetball courts, a 4363-seat stadium, a 2880-seat gym, and an 880-seat auditorium. **Graduates:** From July 1, 2015 to June 30, 2016, 1886 bachelor's degrees were awarded. The most popular majors were business/marketing (21%), biological/life sciences (14%), and health professions and related programs (12%). In an average class, 36% graduate in 4 years or less, 63% graduate in 5 years or less, and 68% graduate in 6 years or less.

SERVICES: Counseling and information services are available, as is tutoring in most subjects. There is a reader service for the blind, and remedial math and writing. There is also a counseling and testing center and a writing lab. **Library/Resources:** The library contains 753,230 volumes, 153,144 microform items, and 14,400 audio/video tapes/CDs/DVDs, and subscribes to 151,596 periodicals including electronic. Computerized library services include interlibrary loans, database searching, Internet access, and Wi-Fi capability. Special learning facilities include an art gallery, planetarium, radio station, TV station, the River Studies Center, and the Allied Health Center. **Physically Challenged Students:** 98% of the campus is accessible. Facilities include wheelchair ramps, elevators, special parking, specially equipped restrooms, special class scheduling, lowered drinking fountains, lowered telephones, and special housing. **Special:** Cooperative programs and cross-registration are available with Viterbo College. There are study-abroad programs in 14 countries and an international student exchange program. UW-L also offers a 3-2 engineering degree with the University of Wisconsin-Madison, the University of Wisconsin-Milwaukee, Platteville, and the University of Minnesota, work-study programs, internships, nondegree study, credit by exam, and pass/fail options. There are 10 national honor societies, a freshman honors program, and 11 departmental honors programs. **Visiting:** There are regularly scheduled orientations for prospective students, including 2 academic sessions, a parent panel, a UW-L student panel, and a tour of the campus. There are guides for informal visits and visitors may sit in on classes. To schedule a visit, contact the Admissions Office. **Campus Safety and Security:** Measures include 24-hour foot and vehicle patrol, self-defense education, and security escort services. There are emergency telephones and lighted pathways/sidewalks.

REQUIREMENTS: The SAT or ACT is required. Applicants must be graduates of an accredited secondary school or hold a GED certificate. They must have completed 17 academic credits, including 4 courses in English, 3 each in social studies, math, and science, 2 in algebra and 1 in geometry, and 4 other academic electives. Students completing rigorous courses, including in the senior year, will be stronger candidates for admission. Students must rank in the top 35% of their high school graduating class and score at least 22 on the ACT, or rank in the top 40% and score 25 on the ACT. A GPA of 2.0 is required. AP and CLEP credits are accepted. Important factors in the admissions decision are advanced placement or honors courses, leadership record, extracurricular activities record, parents or siblings attended your school, evidence of special talent, personality/intangible qualities, recommendations by alumni, geographical diversity, and recommendations by school officials. To graduate, students must earn 120 semester credits, including 68 in subjects outside the major and at least 40 in 300- or 400-level courses. The minimum GPA is 2.0, though it is considerably higher for some programs. Distribution requirements include 30 to 40 credits in liberal studies and 13 to 19 credits in skill courses. **Procedure:** Freshmen are admitted to all sessions. Entrance exams should be taken by the junior year or at the beginning of the senior year. There are early admissions and rolling admissions plans. Application deadlines are open. Application fee is $44. Notification is sent on a rolling basis. Applications are accepted on-line. **Transfer Students:** 526 transfer students enrolled in 2015-2016. Transfer admission is likely with a GPA of 3.2; however, with a GPA of 2.0 to 2.74, admission is on a space-available basis. High school and college transcripts are required, as is a statement of good standing from prior institutions. 18 of 120 credits required for the bachelor's degree must be completed at UW-L. **International Students:** There are 132 international students enrolled. The school actively recruits these students. They must take the TOEFL and the college's own test, also take the La Crosse Battery (based on MELAB), and write a 30-minute composition.

ADMISSIONS: 82% of the 2016-2017 applicants were accepted. The SAT scores for the 2016-2017 freshman class were: Critical Reading-- 8% below 500, 58% between 500 and 599, and 33% between 600 and 699. Math-- 8% below 500, 42% between 500 and 599, 33% between 600 and 699, and 17% between 700 and 800. Writing-- 17% below 500, 42% between 500 and 599, 33% between 600 and 699, and 8% between 700 and 800. The ACT scores were 36% between 18 and 23, 57% between 24 and 29, and 7% above 30. 46% of the current freshmen were in the top fifth of their class; 87% were in the top two fifths. 57 freshmen graduated first in their class. **Admissions Contact:** Corey Sjoquist, Director of Admissions. Email: *admissions@uwlax.edu* Web: *www.uwlax.edu*

FINANCIAL AID: The average freshman award was $7,593. Need-based scholarships or need-based grants averaged $4,476; need-based self-help aid (loans and jobs) averaged $3,501; other non-need-based awards and non-need-based scholarships averaged $2,187; and $3,388 from other forms of aid. The average financial indebtedness of the 2016 graduate was $26,487. The college's own financial statement is required. The FAFSA code is 003919. The priority date for freshman financial aid applications for fall entry is March 15.

UNIVERSITY OF WISCONSIN-MADISON C-4

www.wisc.edu

Madison, WI 53706 **(608) 262-3961**

Fax: (608) 262-7706 **Email:** onwisconsin@admissions.wisc.edu

Full-time: 13,973 men, 14,635 women
Part-time: 1637 men, 1465 women
Graduate: 5710 men, 5916 women
Year: semesters, summer session
Room & Board: $10,446

SAT or ACT: required
Application Deadline: February 1

Faculty: I, av$
Ph.D.s: 91%
Student/Faculty: 17 to 1
Tuition: $10,488 ($32,738)
Freshman Class: 32887 applied, 17304 accepted, 6430 enrolled
CEEB CODE: 1846
MOST COMPETITIVE

University of Wisconsin-Madison, founded in 1849, is a public land-grant institution offering undergraduate and graduate study in almost every major field. Figures in the above capsule and in this profile are approximate. There are 9 undergraduate schools and 13 graduate schools. In addition to regional accreditation, Wisconsin has baccalaureate program accreditation with AACSB, ABET, ADA, ASLA, CSWE, FIDER, NASAD, NASM, SAF, CCNE, CAAHP, NAST, AOTA, ACS, SoAF, NASAS, CAATE, CFRB, and CIDA. The 936-acre campus is in an urban area 75 miles west of Milwaukee and 150 miles northwest of Chicago.

STUDENT LIFE: 67% of undergraduates are from Wisconsin. Others are from 50 states, 93 foreign countries, and Canada. 9% are Foreign; 74% White; 6% Asian American; 5% Hispanic; 3% two or more races; 2% African American; 1% race unknown. **Female To Male Ratio:** 1.0:1. The average age of freshmen is 18; all undergraduates, 20. 4% do not continue beyond their first year; 85% remain to graduate. **Housing:** 7476 students can be accommodated in college housing, which includes single-sex and coed dorms, on-campus apartments, and married student housing. In addition, there are honors houses, language houses, special-interest houses, co-op housing, residential learning communities, and housing for student families. No one may keep cars.

FACULTY/CLASSROOMS: 60% of faculty are male; 40% are female. No introductory courses are taught by graduate students.

PROGRAMS OF STUDY: Wisconsin confers B.A., B.S., B.B.A., B.F.A., B.M., B.S.Ed., and B.N.S. degrees. Master's and doctoral degrees are also awarded. Bachelor's degrees are awarded in AGRICULTURE (agricultural business management, agricultural communications, agricultural economics, agronomy, animal science, dairy science, environmental studies, forestry and related sciences, horticulture, poultry science, and soil science), BIOLOGICAL SCIENCE (biochemistry, biology/biological science, botany, entomology, genetics, microbiology, molecular biology, nutrition, plant pathology, wildlife biology, and zoology), BUSINESS (accounting, apparel and textiles, banking and finance, business administration, mgmt, operations, human resources, insurance and risk management, international business management, marketing/retailing/merchandising, nonprofit/public organization management, operations management, personal financial planning, real estate, and retailing), COMMUNICATIONS AND THE ARTS (African languages, art, art history and appreciation, Chinese, classics, communications, communication science, comparative literature, dance, dramatic arts, English, French, German, Italian, Japanese, journalism, Latin, linguistics, music, music performance, Polish, Portuguese, Russian, Spanish, and theatre arts), COMPUTER AND PHYSICAL SCIENCE (actuarial science, applied mathematics, astronomy, atmospheric sciences and meteorology, chemistry, computer science, geology, geophysics and seismology, information sciences and systems, mathematics, physics, and statistics), EDUCATION (art education, athletic training, elementary education, music education, physical education, secondary education, and special education), ENGINEERING AND ENVIRONMENTAL DESIGN (bioengineering, biomedical engineering, cartography, chemical engineering, civil engineering, computer engineering, electrical/electronics engineering, engineering mechanics, engineering physics, environmental science, geological engineering, industrial engineering, interior design, landscape architecture/design, materials engineering, materials science, mechanical engineering, naval architecture and marine engineering, nuclear engineering, and textile technology), HEALTH PROFESSIONS (kinesiology, nursing, pharmacology, and speech pathology/audiology), SOCIAL SCIENCE (African American studies, anthropology, Asian/Oriental studies, economics, family/consumer studies, food science, gender studies, geography, history, history of science, human development, international relations, international studies, Judaic studies, Latin American studies, legal studies, philosophy, political science/government, psychology, religion, rural sociology, Scandinavian studies, social studies, social work, sociology, textiles and clothing, and women's studies). Biology, economics, and political science have the largest enrollments.

ACTIVITIES: There are 964 groups on campus, including art, band, cheerleading, chess, choir, chorale, chorus, communications, computers, dance, debate, drama, environmental, ethnic, film, forensics, honors, international, jazz band, LGBT, literary magazine, marching band, musical theater, newspaper, opera, orchestra, pep band, photography, political, professional, radio and TV, religious, social, social service, student government, symphony, and yearbook. **Sports:** There are 12 intercollegiate sports for men and 12 for women, and 14 intramural sports for men and 14 for women. **Graduates:** From July 1, 2015 to June 30, 2016, 6919 bachelor's degrees were awarded. The most popular majors were biology (8%), economics (8%), and psychology (5%). In an average class, 57% graduate in 4 years or less, 82% graduate in 5 years or less, and 85% graduate in 6 years or less.

SERVICES: Counseling and information services are available, as is tutoring in most subjects. There is a reader service for the blind. **Library/Resources:** The 43 libraries contain 9.1 million volumes. Computerized library services include interlibrary loans, database searching, Internet access, and Wi-Fi capability. Special learning facilities include an art gallery, natural history museum, planetarium, radio station, and TV station. **Physically Challenged Students:** 90% of the campus is accessible. Facilities include wheelchair ramps, elevators, special parking, specially equipped restrooms, special class scheduling, lowered drinking fountains, and lowered telephones. **Special:** Co-op programs, internships, study abroad, work-study programs, and accelerated degrees in any major are available. B.A.-B.S. degrees and dual and student-designed majors also are available. There is a chapter of Phi Beta Kappa and a freshman honors program. **Visiting:** There are regularly scheduled orientations for prospective students, including an admission information session, a tour, and class visits. There are guides for informal visits, visitors may sit in on classes, and stay overnight. To schedule a visit, contact Visitor and Information Programs at (608) 263-2400. **Campus Safety and Security:** Measures include 24-hour foot and vehicle patrol, emergency notification system, self-defense education, and security escort services. There are shuttle buses, emergency telephones, lighted pathways/sidewalks, and controlled access to dorms/residences.

REQUIREMENTS: The SAT or ACT is required. The ACT Optional Writing test is also required. Applicants must have completed the following number of units in high school (these are minimums; the number of units recommended is higher): 17 total units including 4 English, 4 math, 3 each of science, social studies, and foreign language, and 2 academics/fine arts electives. AP and CLEP credits are accepted. Required courses vary with individual programs. A total of 120 to 136 credit hours, with at least 30 in the major, and a cumulative GPA of 2.0 are minimum requirements for graduation. In addition to courses required for each major, all students must complete general education in communication, quantitative reasoning, breadth (science, math, humanities, and social science), and ethnic studies. **Procedure:** Freshmen are admitted fall, spring, and summer. Entrance exams should be taken in the junior year. There is a deferred admissions plan. Early decision applications should be filed by November 1; regular applications, by February 1 for fall entry; October 3 for spring entry; and February 1 for summer entry, along with a $60 fee. Notification of early decision is sent December 31; regular decision, March 31. Applications are accepted on-line. **Transfer Students:** 1091 transfer students enrolled in 2015-2016. Admission is competitive and varies by program. Generally, applicants must have at least sophomore standing. 30 of 120 credits required for the bachelor's degree must be completed at Wisconsin. **International Students:** There are 2460 international students enrolled. The school actively recruits these students. They must take the TOEFL with a minimum score of 550 on the paper-based TOEFL (PBT) or 80 on the Internet-based version (iBT), or take the IELTS (paper). They must also take the SAT or ACT.

ADMISSIONS: 53% of the 2016-2017 applicants were accepted. The SAT scores for the 2016-2017 freshman class were: Critical Reading-- 4% below 500, 34% between 500 and 599, 49% between 600 and 699, and 13% between 700 and 800. Math-- 2% below 500, 9% between 500 and 599, 34% between 600 and 699, and 55% between 700 and 800. The ACT scores were 4% between 18 and 23, 55% between 24 and 29, and 41% above 30. **Admissions Contact:** Office of Admissions and Recruitment Email: *onwisconsin@admissions.wisc.edu* Web: *www.wisc.edu*

FINANCIAL AID: 35% of all full-time freshmen and 36% of continuing full-time students received need-based aid. The average freshman award was $14,789. Need-based scholarships or need-based grants averaged $10,922; need-based self-help aid (loans and jobs) averaged $6,535; non-need-based athletic scholarships averaged $26,303; and other non-need-based awards and non-need-based scholarships averaged $4,365. The average financial indebtedness of the 2016 graduate was $27,831. The FAFSA code is 003895. The priority date for freshman financial aid applications for fall entry is December 1.

UNIVERSITY OF WISCONSIN-MILWAUKEE E-4

www.uwm.edu

Milwaukee, WI 53211 **(414) 229-2222**

Fax: 414-229-3788	**Email:** uwmlook@uwm.edu
Full-time: 8520 men, 9058 women	**Faculty:** I, --$
Part-time: 1764 men, 2033 women	**Ph.D.s:** 73%
Graduate: 1872 men, 2764 women	**Student/Faculty:** n/av
Year: semesters, summer session	**Tuition:** $10,936
Room & Board: $10,560	**Freshman Class:** 8170 applied, 7233 accepted, 3121 enrolled
ACT: 22	**CEEB CODE:** 1473
Application Deadline: July 1	**COMPETITIVE**

University of Wisconsin-Milwaukee, founded in 1956, is Wisconsin's premier public urban research university. There are 11 undergraduate schools and 3 graduate schools. In addition to regional accreditation, UWM has baccalaureate program accreditation with AACSB, ABET, APTA, CAHEA, CSWE, NAAB, NASM, NLN, APA, NCA, and CCNE. The 104-acre campus is in an urban area in Milwaukee, Wisconsin. Including any residence halls, there are 58 buildings.

STUDENT LIFE: 89% of undergraduates are from Wisconsin. Others are from 50 states, 88 foreign countries, and Canada. 92% are from public schools. 9% are Hispanic; 7% African American; 67% White; 6% Asian American; 6% Foreign; 4% two or more races. **Female To Male Ratio:** 1.1:1. The average age of freshmen is 18; all undergraduates, 24. 28% do not continue beyond their first year; 39% remain to graduate.

Housing: 4288 students can be accommodated in college housing, which includes coed dorms, off-campus apartments, and married student housing. In addition, there are honors houses, language houses, and special-interest houses. On-campus housing is available on a first-come, first-served basis. 82% of students commute. Some may keep cars.

FACULTY/CLASSROOMS: 45% of faculty are male; 44% are female. No introductory courses are taught by graduate students.

PROGRAMS OF STUDY: UWM confers B.A., B.B.A., B.F.A., B.S., B.S.E., and B.S.N. degrees. Master's and doctoral degrees are also awarded. Bachelor's degrees are awarded in BIOLOGICAL SCIENCE (biochemistry, biology/biological science, microbiology, molecular biology, nutrition, and nutritional sciences), BUSINESS (accounting, business administration and management, entrepreneurial studies, finance, human resources, international business, management information systems, marketing management, operations management, and real estate), COMMUNICATIONS AND THE ARTS (art history, art, art history and appreciation, classics, communications, comparative literature, dance, dramatic arts, English, film arts, French, Germanic languages and literature, information technology, linguistics, music, Russian languages and literature, and theatre arts), COMPUTER AND PHYSICAL SCIENCE (actuarial science, applied mathematics, atmospheric science, atmospheric sciences and meteorology, chemistry, computer science, geology, inform, science, systms & tech, information sciences and systems, mathematics, physics, and web services), EDUCATION (art education, athletic training, education, journalism education, music education, and special education), ENGINEERING AND ENVIRONMENTAL DESIGN (architecture, civil engineering, computer engineering, electrical/electronics engineering, engineering, environmental science, industrial engineering, materials engineering, mechanical engineering, occupational safety and health, and urban planning technology), HEALTH PROFESSIONS (biomedical science, exercise science, health care administration, hospital administration, medical science, nursing, occupational therapy, premedicine, recreation therapy, and speech pathology/audiology), SOCIAL SCIENCE (African American studies, anthropology, Asian/American studies, behavioral science, communication sciences & disorders, criminal justice, economics, ethnic studies, forensic studies, geography, history, interdisciplinary studies, international studies, Italian studies, Judaic studies, Latin American studies, liberal arts/general studies, Near Eastern studies, peace studies, philosophy, political science/government, psychology, religion, Scandinavian studies, social work, sociology, Spanish studies, urban studies, and women's studies).

ACTIVITIES: There are 314 groups on campus, including art, band, cheerleading, chess, choir, chorale, chorus, communications, computers, dance, debate, drama, environmental, ethnic, film, honors, international, jazz band, LGBT, literary magazine, musical theater, newspaper, orchestra, pep band, photography, political, professional, religious, social, social service, student government, and symphony. Popular campus events include Fall Welcome, PantherFest, Concerts, Art Exhibitions, and Dance Performances. **Sports:** There are 6 intercollegiate sports for men and 7 for women. Facilities include basketball court, volleyball court, baseball field, soccer field, natatorium, indoor track, exercise facilities, and racquetball courts. **Graduates:** From July 1, 2015 to June 30, 2016, 3900 bachelor's degrees were awarded. The most popular majors were business (21%), health professions and related programs (11%), and engineering (7%). In an average class, 14% graduate in 4 years or less, 32% graduate in 5 years or less, and 39% graduate in 6 years or less.

SERVICES: Counseling and information services are available, as is tutoring in some subjects. There is a reader service for the blind, and remedial math, reading, and writing. **Library/Resources:** The library contains 2.6 million volumes, 1.8 million microform items, and 988,474 audio/video tapes/CDs/DVDs, and subscribes to 109,250 periodicals including electronic. Computerized library services include interlibrary loans, database searching, Internet access, and Wi-Fi capability. Special learning facilities include an art gallery, planetarium, The American Geographical Society Library, and Institute of Visual Arts. **Physically Challenged Students:** 95% of the campus is accessible. Facilities include wheelchair ramps, elevators, special parking, specially equipped restrooms, special class scheduling, lowered drinking fountains, lowered telephones, and special housing. UWM will make the necessary accommodations students need for housing, but no dorms are exclusively for those with disabilities. **Special:** UWM offers cooperative education programs in computer science and engineering, accelerated degree programs, dual majors, student-designed majors, and study abroad opportunities in Africa, Asia, Europe, and South America. UWM also has a consortial nursing program with UW-Parkside, a graduate exchange program for graduate students with Marquette University, and a collaborative doctoral program in biomedical and health informatics with the Medical College of Wisconsin. There are 4 national honor societies, Phi Beta Kappa, and a freshman honors program. **Visiting:** There are regularly scheduled orientations for prospective students. New Student Orientation is a one and a half day (overnight) program packed with information about UWM. At orientation new students will meet other students, learn about campus resources and student life, meet with advisors and register for classes. There are guides for informal visits, visitors may sit in on classes, and stay overnight. To schedule a visit, contact Department of Admissions and Recruitment at (414) 229-2222. **Campus Safety and Security:** Measures include 24-hour foot and vehicle patrol, emergency notification system, self-defense education, and security escort services. There are shuttle buses, emergency telephones, lighted pathways/sidewalks, and controlled access to dorms/residences.

REQUIREMENTS: All freshmen applicants under the age of 21 must submit ACT or SAT scores; scores submitted via high school transcripts are acceptable. A GED certificate is accepted. Music, dance, and theatre majors must audition, and art majors must submit a portfolio. For the School of Architecture and Urban Planning, higher rank and ACT requirements apply. Each application receives a comprehensive review, taking all factors into consideration. In addition to academic preparation, other factors considered include demonstrated leadership skills, motivation, and maturity, as addressed in a student's personal statement and/or recommendations. UWM provides broad access to individuals from many walks of life and encourages all interested students to apply. Certain programs, including architecture, engineering, and nursing, are more selective and may requires higher standardized test scores. AP and CLEP credits are accepted. Generally, to be a candidate for the bachelor's degree, students must satisfactorily complete the following: English composition and math proficiency exams must be passed with satisfactory scores. A minimum of 120 undergraduate credits in courses numbered 100 through 500. The General Education requirements, university requirements and all major and/or minor requirements. Distribution requirements include 6 credits each in humanities, natural sciences, and socials sciences, and 3 credits each in the arts and cultural diversity. A minimum GPA of 2.0 or better both overall and in the major and minor fields; business administration and accounting majors must have a cumulative GPA of 2.5 overall. A minimum of 30 credits overall and half of upper-level credits in majors and minors must be earned in residence at UW-Milwaukee. Other specific graduation criteria are set by individual colleges and schools. **Procedure:** Freshmen are admitted to all sessions. Entrance exams should be taken spring of the junior year. There are deferred admissions and rolling admissions plans. Applications should be filed by July 1 for fall entry; December 1 for spring entry, along with a $50 fee. Notification is sent on a rolling basis. Applications are accepted on-line. **Transfer Students:** 1633 transfer students enrolled in 2015-2016. Students applying with less than 12 transferable credits must meet freshman admission requirements 30 of 120 credits required for the bachelor's degree must be completed at UWM. **International Students:** There are 760 international students enrolled. The school actively recruits these students. They must take the TOEFL with a minimum score of 75 on the Internet-based version (iBT), or take the International English Language Testing System (IELTS). All applicants to the College of Engineering & Applied Science must also submit official ACT or SAT scores.

ADMISSIONS: 89% of the 2016-2017 applicants were accepted. The ACT scores were 8% between 12 and 17, 57% between 18 and 23, 31% between 24 and 29, and 4% above 30. 14% of the current freshmen were in the top fifth of their class; 34% were in the top two fifths. 16 freshmen graduated first in their class. **Admissions Contact:** Department of Admissions and Recruitment Email: *uwmlook@uwm.edu* Web: *www.uwm.edu*

FINANCIAL AID: In 2016-2017, 67% of all full-time freshmen and 66% of continuing full-time students received some form of financial aid. 41% of all full-time freshmen and 45% of continuing full-time students received need-based aid. The average freshman award was $7,086. Need-based scholarships or need-based grants averaged $5,995; and need-based self-help aid (loans and jobs) averaged $3,487. The average financial indebtedness of the 2016 graduate was $36,945. The FAFSA code is 003896. The priority date for freshman financial aid applications for fall entry is March 1. The deadline for filing freshman financial aid applications for fall entry is December 1.

UNIVERSITY OF WISCONSIN-OSHKOSH D-4
www.uwosh.edu

Oshkosh, WI 54901	(920) 424-3164
Fax: (920) 424-1207	Email: endries@uwosh.edu
Full-time: 3665 men, 4926 women	**Faculty:** 407; IIA, --$
Part-time: 562 men, 782 women	**Ph.D.s:** 81%
Graduate: 326 men, 607 women	**Student/Faculty:** 20 to 1
Year: semesters, summer session	**Tuition:** $7600 ($12,362)
Room & Board: $7600	**Freshman Class:** 5660 applied, 3870 accepted, 1567 enrolled
ACT: 22	**CEEB CODE:** 1916
Application Deadline: n/av	**COMPETITIVE**

University of Wisconsin-Oshkosh, founded in 1871, is a public institution offering undergraduate and graduate programs in education, business, the arts and sciences, and health fields. The figures in the above capsule and in this profile are approximate. There are 4 undergraduate schools and one graduate school. In addition to regional accreditation, UW-Oshkosh has baccalaureate program accreditation with AACSB, ACEJMC, CSWE, NASM, NCATE, and NLN. The 192-acre campus is in an urban area 90 miles north of Milwaukee. Including any residence halls, there are 36 buildings.

STUDENT LIFE: 95% of undergraduates are from Wisconsin. Others are from 30 states, 32 foreign countries, and Canada. 94% are White; 2% Asian American; 1% African American; 1% American Indian/Alaska Native; 1% Hispanic; 1% Foreign. **Female To Male Ratio:** 1.4:1. The average age of freshmen is 18; all undergraduates, 26. 29% do not continue beyond their first year; 55% remain to graduate. **Housing:** College-sponsored housing includes coed dorms. In addition, there are fraternity houses, sorority houses, designated quiet floors, designated smoke-free floors, theme housing, and university learning community floor. On-campus housing is guaranteed for all 4 years. 68% of students commute. All students may keep cars.

FACULTY/CLASSROOMS: 56% of faculty are male; 44% are female. No introductory courses are taught by graduate students. The average class size in an introductory lecture is 31 and in a laboratory is 21.

PROGRAMS OF STUDY: UW/Oshkosh confers B.A., B.S., B.Art Ed., B.B.A., B.F.A., B.L.S., B.M., B.M.E., B.S.N., and B.S.W. degrees. Associate and master's degrees are also awarded. Bachelor's degrees are awarded in BIOLOGICAL SCIENCE (biology/biological science and microbiology), BUSINESS (accounting, banking and finance, business administration and management, human resources, management information systems, and marketing/retailing/merchandising), COMMUNICATIONS AND THE ARTS (art, English, fine arts, French, German, journalism, music, Spanish, and speech/debate/rhetoric), COMPUTER AND PHYSICAL SCIENCE (chemistry, computer science, geology, mathematics, and physics), EDUCATION (art education, elementary education, music education, physical education, science education, secondary education, social science education, and special education), HEALTH PROFESSIONS (medical laboratory technology, music therapy, nursing, and speech pathology/audiology), SOCIAL SCIENCE (anthropology, criminal justice, economics, geography, history, human services, international studies, liberal arts/general studies, philosophy, political science/government, psychology, religion, social work, sociology, and urban studies). Business, education, and nursing have the largest enrollments.

ACTIVITIES: 3% of men belong to 8 national fraternities; 3% of women belong to 5 national sororities. There are 175 groups on campus, including art, band, cheerleading, chess, choir, computers, dance, debate, drama, ethnic, film, forensics, honors, international, LGBT, newspaper, pep band, political, professional, radio and TV, religious, social, social service, and student government. Popular campus events include Winter Carnival, Taste of UW-Oshkosh, and Celebration of Racial Inclusiveness. **Sports:** There are 10 intercollegiate sports for men and 11 for women, and 15 intramural sports for men and 15 for women. Facilities include a hall for basketball, and volleyball, a sports center for basketball, tennis, indoor track, a pool, a stadium for football and outdoor track, indoor gym, and an arena. **Graduates:** From July 1, 2015 to June 30, 2016, 2045 bachelor's degrees were awarded. The most popular majors were business/marketing (19%), health professions and related programs, and education (13%), public administration and social sciences, social sciences, and communication/journalism (7%). 106 companies recruited on campus in 2015-2016. In an average class, 7% graduate in 4 years or less, 33% graduate in 5 years or less, and 42% graduate in 6 years or less. Of the 2015 graduating class, 97% were employed within 6 months of graduation.

SERVICES: Counseling and information services are available, as is tutoring in most subjects. There is a reader service for the blind, and remedial math, reading, and writing. **Library/Resources:** The library contains 487,000 volumes, 1.3 million microform items, and 7,000 audio/video tapes/CDs/DVDs, and subscribes to 1,850 periodicals including electronic. Computerized library services include interlibrary loans and database searching. Special learning facilities include an art gallery, planetarium, radio station, TV station, and a speech and hearing clinic. **Physically Challenged Students:** Facilities include wheelchair ramps, elevators, special parking, specially equipped restrooms, special class scheduling, lowered drinking fountains, and lowered telephones. **Special:** UW-Oshkosh offers internships and study abroad. There are 15 national honor societies and a freshman honors program. **Visiting:** There are regularly scheduled orientations for prospective students, including preview days, campus tours, and an individual appointment with an admissions counselor. There are guides for informal visits, visitors may sit in on classes, and stay overnight. To schedule a visit, contact the Admissions Office. **Campus Safety and Security:** Measures include 24-hour foot and vehicle patrol, self-defense education, and security escort services. There are emergency telephones and lighted pathways/sidewalks.

REQUIREMENTS: The ACT is required. Students must graduate in the upper 50% of their class from an accredited secondary school or score a 22 on the enhanced ACT if ranked in the third quartile. They should have completed 17 academic credits, including 4 in English, 3 each in math, social studies, natural sciences (with 2 units of lab), and history, and 4 in electives, preferably in a foreign language or fine arts/humanities. AP and CLEP credits are accepted. All students must complete a minimum of 120 credit hours with at least a 2.0 GPA. A minimum of 42 credits in general education requirements includes 9 credits each in humanities and social science, 8 in natural science, 6 in English composition, 3 in math or logic, 3 in non-Western culture, 3 in speech, and 2 in phys ed. **Procedure:** Freshmen are admitted to all sessions. Entrance exams should be taken in spring of the junior year or early fall of the senior year. There are deferred admissions and rolling admissions plans. Applications should be filed by January 1 for spring entry, along with a $44 fee. Notification of early decision is sent September 15; regular decision, on a rolling basis. **Transfer Students:** 943 transfer students enrolled in 2015-2016. Candidates should have completed 30 or more semester credits; if not, high school transcripts are reviewed. Students must have at least a 2.0 cumulative GPA. Student may enroll in the fall, spring, and summer. 30 of 120 credits required for the bachelor's degree must be completed at UW-Oshkosh. **International Students:** There are 75 international students enrolled. They must take the TOEFL.

ADMISSIONS: 68% of the 2016-2017 applicants were accepted. The ACT scores were 6% between 12 and 17, 62% between 18 and 23, 30% between 24 and 29, and 2% above 30. There was 1 National Merit finalist. 19 freshmen graduated first in their class. **Admissions Contact:** Jill Endries, Director of Undergraduate Admissions. Email: *endries@uwosh.edu* Web: *www.uwosh.edu*

FINANCIAL AID: In 2016-2017, 78% of all full-time freshmen received some form of financial aid. 78% of all full-time freshmen received need-based aid. The average freshman award was $7,895. Need-based scholarships or need-based grants averaged $6,129; need-based self-help aid (loans and jobs) averaged $2,234; other non-need-based awards and non-need-based scholarships averaged $3,166; and $1,496 from other forms of aid. 60% of undergraduate students work part-time. Average annual earnings from campus work are $2000. UW-Oshkosh is a member of CSS. The FAFSA code is 003920. The priority date for freshman financial aid applications for fall entry is March 15.

UNIVERSITY OF WISCONSIN-PARKSIDE E-5
www.uwp.edu

Kenosha, WI 53141	(262) 595-2355
Fax: (262) 595-2008	Email: Moldenht@uwp.edu
Full-time: 1607 men, 1665 women	**Faculty:** 169; IIA
Part-time: 567 men, 461 women	**Ph.D.s:** 76%
Graduate: 64 men, 78 women	**Student/Faculty:** 19 to 1
Year: semesters, summer session	**Tuition:** $7481 ($15,470)
Room & Board: $7712	**Freshman Class:** n/av
ACT: 21	**CEEB CODE:** 1860
Application Deadline: August 1	**COMPETITIVE**

University of Wisconsin-Parkside, founded in 1968, offers undergraduate programs in liberal arts, business, education, and science and technology. The figures in the above capsule and in this profile are approximate. There are 4 undergraduate schools and 3 graduate schools. In addition to regional accreditation, UW-Parkside has baccalaureate program accreditation with AACSB. The 700-acre campus is in a suburban area 30 miles south of Milwaukee. Including any residence halls, there are 15 buildings.

STUDENT LIFE: 83% of undergraduates are from Wisconsin. 9% are African American; 69% White; 4% two or more races; 3% Asian American; 2% Foreign; 13% Hispanic. **Male To Female Ratio:** 1.0:1. The average age of freshmen is 19; all undergraduates, 24. 26% do not continue beyond their first year; 33% remain to graduate. **Housing:** 1000 students can be accommodated in college housing, which includes coed dorms and on-campus apartments. On-campus housing is available on a first-come, first-served basis. Priority is given to out-of-town students. 80% of students commute. All students may keep cars.

FACULTY/CLASSROOMS: 52% of faculty are male; 48% are female. 47% teach undergraduates. No introductory courses are taught by graduate students. The average class size in an introductory lecture is 150; in a laboratory is 50; and in a regular course is 30.

PROGRAMS OF STUDY: UW-Parkside confers B.A. and B.S. degrees. Associate and master's degrees are also awarded. Bachelor's degrees are awarded in BIOLOGICAL SCIENCE (biology/biological science), BUSINESS (accounting, business administration and management, and marketing), COMMUNICATIONS AND THE ARTS (communications, dramatic arts, English, fine arts, French, music, and Spanish), COMPUTER AND PHYSICAL SCIENCE (chemistry, computer science, geology, mathematics, physics, and science), EDUCATION (education), ENGINEERING AND ENVIRONMENTAL DESIGN (industrial administration/management), SOCIAL SCIENCE (economics, geography, history, humanities, international studies, philosophy, political science/government, psychology, and sociology). Business, computer science, and applied health sciences are the strongest academically. Business, computer science, and biology have the largest enrollments.

ACTIVITIES: 1% of men belong to 3 national fraternities; 1% of women belong to 4 national sororities. There are 75 groups on campus, including art, band, cheerleading, choir, chorale, chorus, club sports, communications, computers, dance, debate, drama, environmental, ethnic, honors, international, jazz band, LGBT, literary magazine, musical theater, newspaper, orchestra, political, professional, radio and TV, religious, social, social service, and student government. Popular campus events include World Fest, Heritage Month Celebrations, Weeks of Welcome, and Pancake Night Before Finals. **Sports:** There are 7 intercollegiate sports for men and 6 for women, and 10 intramural sports for men and 10 for women. Facilities include a national/cross-country course, playing fields, all-purpose gym with a 3000-seat auditorium for athletic events and concerts, indoor track, a pool, and weight room. **Graduates:** From July 1, 2015 to June 30, 2016, 741 bachelor's degrees were awarded. The most popular majors were business management (16%), sociology (12%), and psychology (7%). In an average class, 11% graduate in 4 years or less, 19% graduate in 5 years or less, and 33% graduate in 6 years or less. Of the 2015 graduating class, 23% were enrolled in graduate school within 6 months of graduation, and 85% were employed.

SERVICES: Counseling and information services are available, as is tutoring in every subject. There is a reader service for the blind, and remedial math. **Library/Resources:** The library contains 460,000 volumes, 972,991 microform items, and 19,000 audio/video tapes/CDs/DVDs, and subscribes to 1,200 periodicals including electronic. Computerized library services include interlibrary loans, database searching, Internet access, and Wi-Fi capability. Special learning facilities include an art gallery and radio station. **Physically Challenged Students:** All of the campus is accessible. Facilities include wheelchair ramps, elevators, special parking, specially equipped restrooms, lowered drinking fountains, and lowered telephones. **Special:** UW-Parkside offers on-campus work-study programs, internships, study abroad, student-designed majors, and an accelerated premedicine program. Nondegree study and credit by exam are possible. Study abroad includes: Mexico, China, India, Cuba, Australia, Italy, Germany, Poland, Caribbean, Japan, Finland, and Russia. There is a freshman honors program. **Visiting:** There are regularly scheduled orientations for prospective students, including open houses and campus tours. There are guides for informal visits, visitors may sit in on classes, and stay overnight. To schedule a visit, contact Cortney Payne at paynec@uwp.edu. **Campus Safety and Security:** Measures include 24-hour foot and vehicle patrol, emergency notification system, and security escort services. There are shuttle buses, emergency telephones, lighted pathways/sidewalks, and controlled access to dorms/residences.

REQUIREMENTS: The ACT is required for in-state students, and either the ACT or the SAT I for out-of-state students. A minimum score of 21 is required on the ACT. Students may use a lower ACT score in combination with class rank to gain admission. Candidates must be graduates of an accredited secondary school or hold a GED diploma. At least 16 academic credits are required, including 4 in English, 3 in social sciences, 2 in natural sciences, and 1 each in algebra and plane geometry. AP and CLEP credits are accepted. Important factors in the admissions decision are leadership record, extracurricular activities record, and ability to finance college education. A total of 120 credits with at least 30 in the major and a GPA of 2.0 are required for graduation. Students must complete a minimum of 12 credits in humanities and the arts, 12 in social and behavioral sciences, and 9 in natural sciences. Nonengineering majors with fewer than 2 units of foreign language in high school must also fulfill a foreign language requirement. **Procedure:** Freshmen are admitted to all sessions. Entrance exams should be taken by the fall of the senior year. There is a rolling admissions plan. Applications should be filed by August 1 for fall entry, along with a $44 fee. **Transfer Students:** 424 transfer students enrolled in 2015-2016. Students must have a GPA of 2.0 and be in good standing with the previous institution attended. 30 of 120 credits required for the bachelor's degree must be completed at UW-Parkside. **International Students:** There are 65 international students enrolled. The school actively recruits these students. They must take the TOEFL with a minimum score of 521 on the paper-based TOEFL (PBT) or 71 on the Internet-based version (iBT).

ADMISSIONS: The ACT scores were 18% between 12 and 17, 60% between 18 and 23, 21% between 24 and 29, and 1% above 30. **Admissions Contact:** Troy Moldenhauer, Director of Admissions and Recruitment. Email: *Moldenht@uwp.edu* Web: *www.uwp.edu*

FINANCIAL AID: The average financial indebtedness of the 2016 graduate was $26,000. UW-Parkside is a member of CSS. The CSS/Profile, FFS, and the college's own financial statement are required. The FAFSA code is 005015. The priority date for freshman financial aid applications for fall entry is March 15.

UNIVERSITY OF WISCONSIN-PLATTEVILLE — C-5

www.uwplatt.edu

Platteville, WI 53818	**(608) 342-1125** **(800) 362-5515**
Fax: (608) 342-1122	**Email: admit@uwplatt.edu**
Full-time: 4687 men, 2422 women	**Faculty:** IIA
Part-time: 528 men, 341 women	**Ph.D.s:** 62%
Graduate: 520 men, 447 women	**Student/Faculty:** 21 to 1
Year: semesters, summer session	**Tuition:** $7488 ($15,339)
Room & Board: $7160	**Freshman Class:** 4401 applied, 3393 accepted, 1621 enrolled
ACT: 24	**CEEB CODE:** 1917
Application Deadline: open	**VERY COMPETITIVE**

University of Wisconsin-Platteville takes its roots from the Platteville Normal School State Teachers College (1866) and the Wisconsin Mining Trade School (1908). Since then, the university's teaching mission has remained the same: develop strong graduates who can take their experience as a student directly to the workforce in an impactful way. Rich in its academic programs, the University of Wisconsin-Platteville consists of three colleges-the College of Business, Industry, Life Science and Agriculture; the College of Engineering, Mathematics, and Science; and the College of Liberal Arts and Education. We have particular strengths in agriculture, biology, business, criminal justice, education, engineering, and industrial technology. There are 3 undergraduate schools and 1 graduate school. In addition to regional accreditation, UW-Platteville has baccalaureate program accreditation with ABET, NASM, NCATE, ACS, NAIT, and Wisconsin DPI. The 821-acre campus is in a small town 20 miles northeast of Dubuque, Iowa, and 75 miles southwest of Madison, Wisconsin. Including any residence halls, there are 39 buildings.

STUDENT LIFE: 74% of undergraduates are from Wisconsin. Others are from 42 states, 22 foreign countries, and Canada. 90% are from public schools. 88% are White; 3% Hispanic; 3% Foreign; 2% African American; 2% two or more races; 1% Asian American; 1% American Indian/Alaska Native. **Male To Female Ratio:** 1.8:1. The average age of freshmen is 18; all undergraduates, 20. 23% do not continue beyond their first year; 52% remain to graduate. **Housing:** College-sponsored housing includes single-sex and coed dorms. In addition, there are special-interest houses, and the Cooper Living and Learning Center for students majoring/minoring with the School of Agriculture. 53% of students commute. All students may keep cars.

FACULTY/CLASSROOMS: 60% of faculty are male; 40% are female. No introductory courses are taught by graduate students.

PROGRAMS OF STUDY: UW-Platteville confers B.A. and B.S. degrees. Associate and master's degrees are also awarded. Bachelor's degrees are awarded in AGRICULTURE (agricultural business management, animal science, dairy science, environmental horticulture & turf mgmt, horticulture, and soil science), BIOLOGICAL SCIENCE (biology/biological science), BUSINESS (accounting and business administration and management), COMMUNICATIONS AND THE ARTS (art, English, German, media arts, music, Spanish, and visual and performing arts), COMPUTER AND PHYSICAL SCIENCE (chemistry, computer science, mathematics, physical sciences, physics, and software engineering), EDUCATION (agricultural education, art education, education, elementary education, middle school education, music education, physical education, secondary education, and technical education), ENGINEERING AND ENVIRONMENTAL DESIGN (civil engineering, electrical/electronics engineering, engineering physics, environmental engineering, industrial engineering, industrial engineering technology, land use management and reclamation, and mechanical engineering), SOCIAL SCIENCE (criminal justice, economics, forensic studies, geography, history, international studies, liberal arts/general studies, philosophy, political science/government, psychology, and social science). Engineering, agriculture, and homeland security have the largest enrollments.

ACTIVITIES: Groups on campus include art, band, cheerleading, choir, chorale, chorus, computers, debate, drama, ethnic, film, forensics, honors, international, jazz band, LGBT, literary magazine, marching band, musical theater, newspaper, opera, orchestra, pep band, photography, political, professional, radio and TV, religious, social, social service, student government, and symphony. Popular campus events include Homecoming, Pioneer Distinguished Lecturer Presentation, Mudfest Rugby Tournament, and Lighting and Whitewashing of the M. **Sports:** There are 7 intercollegiate sports for men and 7 for women, and 13 intramural sports for men and 12 for women. Facilities include a gym, stadium, indoor and outdoor track, basketball and volleyball courts, tennis racquetball courts, a weight room, swimming pool, baseball diamonds, and soccer fields. **Graduates:** From July 1, 2015 to June 30, 2016, 1222 bachelor's degrees were awarded. The most popular majors were engineering (23%), agriculture (12%), and education (11%). In an average class, 16% graduate in 4 years or less, 27% graduate in 5 years or less, and 52% graduate in 6 years or less.

SERVICES: Counseling and information services are available, as is tutoring in most subjects. There is a reader service for the blind, and remedial math, reading, and writing. Pioneer Academic and Transitional Help Services for students with disabilities, and student support services available. **Library/Resources:** The 2 libraries contain 284,410 volumes, 22,818 microform items, and 33,720 audio/video tapes/CDs/DVDs, and subscribe to 278 periodicals including electronic. Computerized library services include interlibrary loans, database searching, Internet access, and Wi-Fi capability. Special learning facilities include an art gallery, radio station, TV station, campus archives, and the campus newspaper. **Physically Challenged Students:** 95% of the campus is accessible. Facilities include wheelchair ramps, elevators, special parking, specially equipped restrooms, special class scheduling, lowered drinking fountains, lowered telephones, and special housing. **Special:** UWP offers internships in business, industry, and communication, a co-op program in engineering, and study abroad in 16 countries. Credit by exam, credit for life, military, and work experience, work-study programs, dual majors, student-designed majors, non-degree study, and pass/fail options are also available. There are 12 national honor societies, a freshman honors program, and 4 departmental honors programs. **Visiting:** There are regularly scheduled orientations for prospective students, The Pioneer Previews, held on 6 dates each year, which include group tours, an admissions briefing, and visits to specific colleges and departments. Daily visits (Monday through Friday) are also available. There are guides for informal visits, visitors may sit in on classes, and stay overnight. To schedule a visit, contact Prospective Student Services Office at (877) UWPLATT. **Campus Safety and Security:** Measures include 24-hour foot and vehicle patrol, emergency notification system, and security escort services. There are shuttle buses, emergency telephones, lighted pathways/sidewalks, and controlled access to dorms/residences.

REQUIREMENTS: The ACT is preferred. Applicants must have successfully completed 17 college preparatory units, including 4 units of English, 3 each of math (algebra and higher), social science, and natural science (2 must include lab experiences), 4 from the above academic areas, foreign language, fine arts, computer science, or courses in vocational areas. Standard admission will be given to those students who are in the top 50% of their graduating class or have an ACT composite of 22 (SAT equivalency). UW-Platteville requires applicants to be in the upper 50% of their class. AP and CLEP credits are accepted. To graduate, students must complete a minimum of 120 credit hours, with a minimum GPA of 2.0 overall and within the major. Course requirements include 12 credits in humanities and fine arts, 9 each in social sciences and natural sciences, 4 in ethnic and gender studies, and 3 in international education. Other competency requirements include 6 credits in English composition, 3 in math, and 2 each in speech and phys ed. **Procedure:** Freshmen are admitted to all sessions. Entrance exams should be taken in April or June of the junior year. There are deferred admissions and rolling admissions plans. Application deadlines are open. Application fee is $44. Applications are accepted on-line. **Transfer Students:** 458 transfer students enrolled in 2015-2016. Applicants must have a cumulative GPA of at least 2.0 and be in good standing at the institution they are currently attending or have attended. 32 of 120 credits required for the bachelor's degree must be completed at UW-Platteville. **International Students:** There are 67 international students enrolled. The school actively recruits these students. They must take the TOEFL with a minimum score of 550 on the paper-based TOEFL (PBT) or 79 on the Internet-based version (iBT), as well as the Wisconsin English and Math placement exam.

ADMISSIONS: 77% of the 2016-2017 applicants were accepted. The ACT scores were 4% between 12 and 17, 49% between 18 and 23, 42% between 24 and 29, and 5% above 30. **Admissions Contact:** Heidi Tuescher-Gille, Director of Admission & Enrollment Service. Email: *admit@uwplatt.edu* Web: *www.uwplatt.edu*

FINANCIAL AID: The FAFSA code is 003921. The priority date for freshman financial aid applications for fall entry is March 15.

UNIVERSITY OF WISCONSIN-RIVER FALLS A-3

www.uwrf.edu

River Falls, WI 54022	(715) 425-3500
Fax: (715) 425-0676	**Email:** admit@uwrf.edu
Full-time: n/av	**Faculty:** 221; IIA, --$
Part-time: 160 men, 230 women	**Ph.D.s:** 85%
Graduate: 160 men, 330 women	**Student/Faculty:** 23 to 1
Year: semesters, summer session	**Tuition:** $7940 ($16,000)
Room & Board: $6545	**Freshman Class:** n/av
ACT: required	**CEEB CODE:** 1918
Application Deadline: open	**COMPETITIVE**

University of Wisconsin-River Falls, founded in 1874, is a public institution offering undergraduate programs in arts and sciences, education, agriculture, and food and environmental sciences. Figures in the above capsule and in this profile are approximate. There are 4 undergraduate schools and one graduate school. In addition to regional accreditation, UW-River Falls has baccalaureate program accreditation with ACEJMC, ASLA, CSWE, NASM, and NCATE. The 225-acre campus is in a suburban area 29 miles east of Minneapolis-St. Paul, Minnesota. Including any residence halls, there are 28 buildings.

STUDENT LIFE: 52% of undergraduates are from Wisconsin. Others are from 25 states, 13 foreign countries, and Canada. 95% are from public schools. 95% are White; 2% Asian American; 1% African American; 1% Hispanic. **Female To Male Ratio:** 1.8:1. The average age of freshmen is 18; all undergraduates, 21. 25% do not continue beyond their first year; 54% remain to graduate. **Housing:** 2172 students can be accommodated in college housing, which includes single-sex and coed dorms. On-campus housing is guaranteed for all 4 years. 59% of students commute. All students may keep cars.

FACULTY/CLASSROOMS: 70% of faculty are male; 30% are female. All

teach undergraduates. No introductory courses are taught by graduate students. The average class size in an introductory lecture is 30; in a laboratory is 24; and in a regular course is 20.

PROGRAMS OF STUDY: UW-River Falls confers B.A., B.S., B.F.A, B.M.E., and B.S.W. degrees. Master's degrees are also awarded. Bachelor's degrees are awarded in AGRICULTURE (agricultural business management, agronomy, animal science, conservation and regulation, horticulture, and soil science), BIOLOGICAL SCIENCE (biology/biological science and biotechnology), BUSINESS (accounting and business administration and management), COMMUNICATIONS AND THE ARTS (art, communications, English, fine arts, journalism, modern language, music, and speech/debate/rhetoric), COMPUTER AND PHYSICAL SCIENCE (chemistry, computer programming, geology, mathematics, physics, and science), EDUCATION (agricultural education, art education, elementary education, foreign languages education, music education, physical education, and secondary education), ENGINEERING AND ENVIRONMENTAL DESIGN (agricultural engineering and land use management and reclamation), HEALTH PROFESSIONS (premedicine, prepharmacy, and speech pathology/audiology), SOCIAL SCIENCE (economics, food science, geography, history, political science/government, prelaw, psychology, social studies, social work, and sociology). Physics, chemistry, and elementary education are the strongest academically. Business, elementary education, and animal science have the largest enrollments.

ACTIVITIES: 5% of men belong to 5 national fraternities; 5% of women belong to 4 national sororities. There are 120 groups on campus, including agriculture, academic, drug awareness, art, band, cheerleading, choir, chorus, communications, computers, dance, debate, drama, ethnic, forensics, honors, international, jazz band, LGBT, literary magazine, musical theater, newspaper, orchestra, pep band, political, professional, radio and TV, religious, social, student government, and symphony. Popular campus events include Winter Carnival, Annual Rodeo, and Unity in the Community. **Sports:** There are 7 intercollegiate sports for men and 11 for women, and 11 intramural sports for men and 12 for women. Facilities include an ice arena, 4550-seat stadium, 2 multipurpose phys ed centers, swimming pool, 2600-seat gym and a smaller gym, handball courts, field house, an indoor track, an indoor rock-climbing wall, and basketball, tennis, and volleyball courts. **Graduates:** From July 1, 2015 to June 30, 2016, 1045 bachelor's degrees were awarded. The most popular majors were education (18%), agriculture (15%), and business (15%). In an average class, 25% graduate in 4 years or less, 35% graduate in 5 years or less, and 54% graduate in 6 years or less.

SERVICES: Counseling and information services are available, as is tutoring in every subject. There is a reader service for the blind, and remedial math, reading, and writing. **Library/Resources:** The library contains 221,453 volumes, 726,035 microform items, and 8,455 audio/video tapes/CDs/DVDs, and subscribes to 1,322 periodicals including electronic. Computerized library services include interlibrary loans, database searching, and Internet access. Special learning facilities include an art gallery, planetarium, radio station, TV station, a greenhouse, climbing wall, communicative disorders lab, educational technology center, food science and meat facilities, 2 campus lab farms, and sundial. **Physically Challenged Students:** 95% of the campus is accessible. Facilities include wheelchair ramps, elevators, special parking, specially equipped restrooms, special class scheduling, lowered drinking fountains, and lowered telephones. **Special:** Co-op programs in food science and environmental science, on-campus work-study, and accelerated degree programs in several preprofessional areas are available. UW-River Falls also offers internships, student-designed majors, credit by examination, nondegree study, and pass/fail options. Study abroad is available through the National Student Exchange and the International Student Exchange Program in some 15 countries. There are 11 national honor societies and a freshman honors program. **Visiting:** There are regularly scheduled orientations for prospective students, including College Visit Days and tours. There are guides for informal visits and visitors may sit in on classes. To schedule a visit, contact the Admissions Office. **Campus Safety and Security:** Measures include 24-hour foot and vehicle patrol, self-defense education, and security escort services. There are emergency telephones and lighted pathways/sidewalks.

REQUIREMENTS: The ACT is required, with a minimum composite score of 22, or 18 if in upper 40% of high school class. Candidates must be graduates of an accredited secondary school and have completed at least 17 academic credits, including 4 in English, 3 in social sciences, and 3 each in math and science, with 4 college-prep courses. A GED certificate is accepted. AP and CLEP credits are accepted. To graduate, students must complete at least 120 semester hours, with a GPA of 2.0 overall and 2.25 in the major field. General education requirements include 39 semester hours in English composition, speech and humanities, natural and social sciences, math, and phys ed. **Procedure:** Freshmen are admitted to all sessions. Entrance exams should be taken in the spring of the junior year. There are early admissions, deferred admissions, and rolling admissions plans. Application deadlines are open. The fall 2016 application fee was $35. Applications are accepted on-line. **Transfer Students:** Priority admission is given to students with a college GPA of 2.6 or higher. Students with a GPA of 2.0 to 2.6 are placed on a waiting list. Transfers in elementary education must have a GPA of 3.0. 30 of 120 credits required for the bachelor's degree must be completed at UW-River Falls. **International Students:** There are 47 international students enrolled. They must take the TOEFL. They must also take the ACT.

Admissions Contact: Alan J. Tuchtenhagen, Admissions Director. Email: *admit@uwrf.edu* Web: *www.uwrf.edu*

FINANCIAL AID: 20% of undergraduate students work part-time. UW-River Falls is a member of CSS. The FAFSA code is 003923. The deadline for filing freshman financial aid applications for fall entry is March 15.

UNIVERSITY OF WISCONSIN-STEVENS POINT C-3

www.uwsp.edu

Stevens Point, WI 54481 **(715) 346-2441**

Fax: (715) 346-2441	**Email:** admiss@uwsp.edu
Full-time: 4159 men, 4476 women	**Faculty:** 413; IIA, --$
Part-time: 219 men, 264 women	**Ph.D.s:** 67%
Graduate: 93 men, 288 women	**Student/Faculty:** 20 to 1
Year: semesters, summer session	**Tuition:** $7505 ($15,078)
Room & Board: $6538	**Freshman Class:** 4915 applied, 3672 accepted, 1637 enrolled
SAT CR/M/W: 546/536/528 **ACT:** 23	**CEEB CODE:** 1919
Application Deadline: open	**COMPETITIVE**

University of Wisconsin-Stevens Point, founded in 1894, offers undergraduate programs in natural resources, education, business, arts and sciences, and professional studies. The figures in the above capsule and in this profile are approximate. There are 4 undergraduate schools and 1 graduate school. In addition to regional accreditation, UWSP has baccalaureate program accreditation with ABET, ASLA, NASAD, ACS, CADE, and NNACL. The 400-acre campus is in a small town 110 miles north of Madison. Including any residence halls, there are 35 buildings.

STUDENT LIFE: 89% of undergraduates are from Wisconsin. Others are from 30 states, 29 foreign countries, and Canada. 98% are from public schools. 89% are White; 2% Asian American; 2% Hispanic; 2% two or more races; 1% African American. **Female To Male Ratio:** 1.1:1. The average age of freshmen is 19; all undergraduates, 22. 20% do not continue beyond their first year; 61% remain to graduate. **Housing:** 3414 students can be accommodated in college housing, which includes single-sex and coed dorms. In addition, there are special-interest houses. 62% of students commute. All students may keep cars.

FACULTY/CLASSROOMS: 64% of faculty are male; 46% are female. All teach undergraduates, 98% do research, and 98% do both. No introductory courses are taught by graduate students.

PROGRAMS OF STUDY: UWSP confers B.A., B.S., B.F.A., and B.M. degrees. Associate, master's, and doctoral degrees are also awarded. Bachelor's degrees are awarded in AGRICULTURE (fishing and fisheries, forestry and related sciences, natural resource management, and soil science), BIOLOGICAL SCIENCE (biochemistry, biology/biological science, nutrition, and wildlife biology), BUSINESS (accounting and business administration and management), COMMUNICATIONS AND THE ARTS (art, arts administration/management, communications, dance, dramatic arts, English, fine arts, French, German, music, and Spanish), COMPUTER AND PHYSICAL SCIENCE (chemistry, geoscience, information sciences and systems, mathematics, natural sciences, physics, and web services), EDUCATION (athletic training, early childhood education, education, education of the exceptional child, elementary education, health education, music education, and physical education), ENGINEERING AND ENVIRONMENTAL DESIGN (computer technology, interior design, and paper and pulp science), HEALTH

PROFESSIONS (clinical science, health science, and speech pathology/audiology), SOCIAL SCIENCE (American studies, dietetics, economics, family/consumer studies, geography, history, international studies, liberal arts/general studies, philosophy, political science/government, psychology, public administration, social science, social work, and sociology). Natural resources, education, and social sciences have the largest enrollments.

ACTIVITIES: 1% of men belong to 1 local and 4 national fraternities; 1% of women belong to 2 local and 1 national sororities. There are 201 groups on campus, including art, band, cheerleading, choir, chorale, chorus, computers, dance, drama, environmental, ethnic, film, honors, international, jazz band, LGBT, literary magazine, musical theater, newspaper, orchestra, pep band, photography, political, professional, radio and TV, religious, social, social service, student government, and symphony. Popular campus events include Trivia Contest, International Club Dinner, and Spud Bowl. **Sports:** There are 8 intercollegiate sports for men and 10 for women, and 16 intramural sports for men and 16 for women. Facilities include 2 gyms, a health enhancement center, cardio center, aquatic center, and the University Center. The campus stadium seats 5500, the indoor gym, 3500. There is also a 391-seat auditorium and numerous outdoor fields. **Graduates:** From July 1, 2015 to June 30, 2016, 1717 bachelor's degrees were awarded. The most popular majors were natural resources and conservation (13%), education (10%), and social sciences (10%). 124 companies recruited on campus in 2015-2016. In an average class, 22% graduate in 4 years or less and 59% graduate in 6 years or less. Of the 2015 graduating class, 17% were enrolled in graduate school within 6 months of graduation, and 55% were employed.

SERVICES: Counseling and information services are available, as is tutoring in most subjects. There is a reader service for the blind, and remedial math, reading, and writing. **Library/Resources:** The library contains 813,123 volumes, 50,349 microform items, and 25,357 audio/video tapes/CDs/DVDs, and subscribes to 44,876 periodicals including electronic. Computerized library services include interlibrary loans, database searching, Internet access, and Wi-Fi capability. Special learning facilities include an art gallery, natural history museum, planetarium, radio station, TV station, an observatory, map center, 275-acre nature preserve, groundwater center, and wellness institute. **Physically Challenged Students:** All of the campus is accessible. Facilities include wheelchair ramps, elevators, special parking, specially equipped restrooms, special class scheduling, lowered drinking fountains, and lowered telephones. **Special:** A co-op program in nursing is offered with UW-Eau Claire and St. Joseph's Hospital. Internships, study abroad in 9 countries, work-study programs, dual and student-designed majors, independent study, and pass/fail options are also available. Credit is given for military, life, and work experience. There are 13 national honor societies and 3 departmental honors programs. **Visiting:** There are regularly scheduled orientations for prospective students, Students and parents can visit campus on a scheduled daily visit or participate in a one-day specialized program called ViewPoint, which is offered several times each fall and spring. UWSP also offers Info Nights in communities throughout WI and in IL to introduce students and parents to the university and answer detailed questions. There are guides for informal visits. To schedule a visit, contact the Office of Admissions. **Campus Safety and Security:** Measures include 24-hour foot and vehicle patrol, emergency notification system, and security escort services. There are emergency telephones, lighted pathways/sidewalks, and controlled access to dorms/residences.

REQUIREMENTS: The SAT or ACT is required. Applicants should have a high school rank of top 35% or above, or a cumulative high school GPA of 3.20 or higher, with an ACT composite score of 21 (SAT equivalent) or above; or rank in the top 50% of high school class with an ACT composite score of 21 or above. The ACT is preferred. The GED is accepted. Required academic preparation includes 4 years of English, 3 of social studies, and 3 each of math and lab science, along with 4 electives; 2 years of foreign language are recommended. The following non-academic factors are considered: involvement through work experience, extracurricular activities, and volunteerism; personal characteristics and accomplishments including special talents and abilities, honors, awards and personal qualities; diversity in background and experience; and life circumstances. While non-academic factors are considered, they will not necessarily make an applicant with a weak academic background a strong candidate for admission. AP and CLEP credits are accepted. To graduate, students must complete 120 credit hours (30 from UWSP and 40 at 300/400 level), with a minimum GPA of 2.0. Core curriculum requirements must also be fulfilled, along with courses in writing, natural science, non-Western culture, minorities studies, social science, humanities, and wellness, and 3 credits in phys ed. Some majors require additional credits and higher minimum GPAs. **Procedure:** Freshmen are admitted fall and spring. Entrance exams should be taken previous fall or spring. There are deferred admissions and rolling admissions plans. Application deadlines are open. Application fee is $44. 119 applicants were on the 2016 waiting list; 98 were admitted. Applications are accepted on-line. **Transfer Students:** 786 transfer students enrolled in 2015-2016. Applicants must submit high school and college transcripts, as well as a statement of good standing from prior institutions. A high school minimum GPA of 2.25 is required. If fewer than 12 credits have been completed, the student must enroll as a freshman. 30 of 120 credits required for the bachelor's degree must be completed at UWSP. **International Students:** There are 206 international students enrolled. The school actively recruits these students. They must take the TOEFL with a minimum score of 70 on the Internet-based version (iBT).

ADMISSIONS: 75% of the 2016-2017 applicants were accepted. The SAT scores for the 2016-2017 freshman class were: Critical Reading-- 23% below 500, 55% between 500 and 599, 14% between 600 and 699, and 9% between 700 and 800. Math-- 32% below 500, 41% between 500 and 599, 23% between 600 and 699, and 5% between 700 and 800. Writing-- 46% below 500, 32% between 500 and 599, and 23% between 600 and 699. The ACT scores were 27% below 12, 37% between 12 and 17, 23% between 18 and 23, 8% between 24 and 29, and 5% above 30. 27% of the current freshmen were in the top fifth of their class; 61% were in the top two fifths. 28 freshmen graduated first in their class. **Admissions Contact:** Bill Jordan, Dean of Students. Email: *admiss@uwsp.edu* Web: *www.uwsp.edu*

FINANCIAL AID: In 2016-2017, 58% of all full-time freshmen and 60% of continuing full-time students received some form of financial aid. 31% of all full-time freshmen and 34% of continuing full-time students received need-based aid. The average freshman award was $6,571. Need-based scholarships or need-based grants averaged $5,406; need-based self-help aid (loans and jobs) averaged $4,107; other non-need-based awards and non-need-based scholarships averaged $2,237; and $3,960 from other forms of aid. 38% of undergraduate students work part-time. Average annual earnings from campus work are $1887. The average financial indebtedness of the 2016 graduate was $22,788. The FAFSA code is 003924. The priority date for freshman financial aid applications for fall entry is March 15. The deadline for filing freshman financial aid applications for fall entry is May 1.

UNIVERSITY OF WISCONSIN-STOUT B-3
www.uwstout.edu

Menomonie, WI 54751	**(715) 232-1411** **(800) HI-STOUT**
Fax: (715) 232-1667	**Email: admissions@uwstout.edu**
Full-time: 3656 men, 3122 women	**Faculty:** 406; IIA, --$
Part-time: 817 men, 599 women	**Ph.D.s:** 78%
Graduate: 347 men, 465 women	**Student/Faculty:** 18 to 1
Year: 4-1-4, summer session	**Tuition:** $9203 ($16,949)
Room & Board: $10,464	**Freshman Class:** 3535 applied, 2964 accepted, 1534 enrolled
SAT: required **ACT:** 22	**CEEB CODE:** 1740
Application Deadline: open	**COMPETITIVE**

University of Wisconsin-Stout, founded in 1891, offers undergraduate programs in liberal studies, human environmental sciences, industry and technology, education, and human services. There are 4 undergraduate schools and 1 graduate school. In addition to regional accreditation, UW-Stout has baccalaureate program accreditation with ABET, ACCE, ADA, FIDER, NASAD, IACBE, and AAMFT. The 110-acre campus is in a rural area 60 miles east of Minneapolis/St. Paul, MN. Including any residence halls, there are 33 buildings.

STUDENT LIFE: 69% of undergraduates are from Wisconsin. Others are from 26 states, 28 foreign countries, and Canada. 93% are White; 2% Asian American; 1% African American; 1% American Indian/Alaska Native; 1% Hispanic; 1% Foreign. **Male To Female Ratio:** 1.2:1. The average age of freshmen is 18; all undergraduates, 21. 27% do not continue beyond their first year. **Housing:** College-sponsored housing includes coed dorms. smoke-free, alcohol-free, quiet study, upper class/graduate housing, freshman housing, and special housing for disabled students, wellness housing, and living learning communities. On-campus housing is guaranteed for all 4 years. 60% of students commute. All students may keep cars.

FACULTY/CLASSROOMS: 58% of faculty are male; 42% are female. All teach undergraduates, and all do research. No introductory courses are taught by graduate students. The average class size in an introductory lecture is 31 and in a laboratory is 21.

PROGRAMS OF STUDY: UW-Stout confers B.A., B.S., and B.F.A. degrees. Master's and doctoral degrees are also awarded. Bachelor's degrees are awarded in BUSINESS (business administration and management, hospitality management services, hotel/motel and restaurant management, information & communication technology, management science, marketing/retailing/merchandising, packaging, property management, retailing, supply chain management, and sustainable management), COMMUNICATIONS AND THE ARTS (apparel design, art, communications, fine arts, game design and development, graphic communications management, studio art, and telecommunications), COMPUTER AND PHYSICAL SCIENCE (applied mathematics, applied science, and science), EDUCATION (art education, career, technical education & training, early childhood education, golf enterprise management, home economics education, marketing and distribution education, science education, special education, technical education, technology & science education, and vocational education), ENGINEERING AND ENVIRONMENTAL DESIGN (computer engineering, construction technology, engineering technology, food services technology, graphic arts technology, graphic and printing production, industrial administration/management, industrial engineering technology, manufacturing engineering, and plastics engineering), HEALTH PROFESSIONS (health and rehabilitation therapy), SOCIAL SCIENCE (applied social science, child care/child and family studies, cognitive science, dietetics, family/consumer studies, food production/management/services, human development, and psychology). General business administration, art, and hotel restaurant have the largest enrollments.

ACTIVITIES: 2% of men and 3% of women belong to 3 local and 2 national fraternities; 3% of women belong to 3 national sororities. There are 117 groups on campus, including student-run film society, model UN, art, band, cheerleading, choir, chorale, chorus, computers, dance, debate, drama, ethnic, forensics, honors, international, jazz band, LGBT, literary magazine, marching band, musical theater, newspaper, pep band, photography, political, professional, radio station, religious, social, social service, and student government. Popular campus events include Family Weekend, Cheese Week, and Biggest House Party. **Sports:** There are 6 intercollegiate sports for men and 8 for women, and 20 intramural sports for men and 19 for women. Facilities include baseball, soccer, and football fields, indoor and outdoor tracks, and a field house with basketball, racquetball, and volleyball courts, a pool, weight and gymnastics rooms, and indoor and outdoor tennis courts. **Graduates:** From July 1, 2015 to June 30, 2016, 1697 bachelor's degrees were awarded. The most popular majors were business marketing (34%), education (9%), engineering, family and consumer sciences, and visual and performing arts (8%). 306 companies recruited on campus in 2015-2016. In an average class, 14% graduate in 4 years or less and 41% graduate in 5 years or less.

SERVICES: Counseling and information services are available, as is tutoring in most subjects. There is a reader service for the blind, and remedial math, reading, and writing. **Library/Resources:** The library contains 225,672 volumes, 1.2 million microform items, and 14,254 audio/video tapes/CDs/DVDs, and subscribes to 1,012 periodicals including electronic. Computerized library services include interlibrary loans, database searching, Internet access, and Wi-Fi capability. Special learning facilities include an art gallery and TV station. **Physically Challenged Students:** All of the campus is accessible. Facilities include wheelchair ramps, elevators, special parking, specially equipped restrooms, special class scheduling, lowered drinking fountains, lowered telephones, and special housing. **Special:** UW-Stout offers business and industry internships, cooperative programs, work-study programs, and study abroad in London. Dual majors, credit by examination, credit for life, military, and work experience, nondegree study, and pass/fail options are also available. There is 1 national honor society, a freshman honors program, and 3 departmental honors programs. **Visiting:** There are regularly scheduled orientations for prospective students, including an interview with an admissions counselor and a campus tour. There are also campus preview days throughout the academic year. There are guides for informal visits, visitors may sit in on classes, and stay overnight.. **Campus Safety and Security:** Measures include 24-hour foot and vehicle patrol. There are lighted pathways/sidewalks, and training sessions.

REQUIREMENTS: The SAT or ACT is required. The ACT is preferred. Minimum test scores are waived if students rank in the upper 50% of their class. Applicants should graduate from an accredited secondary school. The GED is accepted if applicants are over 21, or if their graduating class has been out for at least 2 years. Secondary school preparation should include 4 academic credits in English, 3 each in social studies, math, and science, and 4 in electives; 2 units recommended in foreign language. UW-Stout requires applicants to be in the upper 50% of their class. A GPA of 2.8 is required. AP and CLEP credits are accepted. Important factors in the admissions decision are leadership record, advanced placement or honors courses, parents or siblings attended your school, evidence of special talent, personality/intangible qualities, extracurricular activities record, recommendations by alumni, recommendations by school officials, and geographical diversity. Students must complete a minimum of 124 credits, including a general education component. Some degree programs have specific general education courses that must be taken in order to satisfy certification, accreditation, or prerequisite standards. Students must also fulfill an ethnic studies requirement. **Procedure:** Freshmen are admitted fall, spring, and summer. Entrance exams should be taken in June of the junior year. There is a rolling admissions plan. Application deadlines are open. Application fee is $44. Notification is sent on a rolling basis. Applications are accepted on-line. Application fees are waived if application is completed on-line. **Transfer Students:** 734 transfer students enrolled in 2015-2016. A minimum college GPA of 2.50 preferred (2.75 required for education majors). ACT/SAT 1 recommended for applied science, plastics engineering, computer engineering, applied mathematics and computer science, and manufacturing engineering applicants. A high school transcript and a statement of good standing from prior institutions are required. 32 of 124 credits required for the bachelor's degree must be completed at UW-Stout. **International Students:** There are 39 international students enrolled. The school actively recruits these students. They must take the TOEFL.

ADMISSIONS: 84% of the 2016-2017 applicants were accepted. The ACT scores were 9% between 12 and 17, 59% between 18 and 23, 29% between 24 and 29, and 3% above 30. 18% of the current freshmen were in the top fifth of their class; 50% were in the top two fifths. 10 freshmen graduated first in their class. **Admissions Contact:** Joel Helms, Associate Director of Admissions. Email: *admissions@uwstout.edu* Web: *www.uwstout.edu*

FINANCIAL AID: In 2016-2017, 83% of all full-time freshmen received some form of financial aid. The average freshman award was $30,410. Need-based scholarships or need-based grants averaged $5,829; need-based self-help aid (loans and jobs) averaged $5,010; other non-need-based awards and non-need-based scholarships averaged $4,475; and $2,219 from other forms of aid. The average financial indebtedness of the 2016 graduate was $25,746. UW-Stout is a member of CSS. The FAFSA code is 003915. The priority date for freshman financial aid applications for fall entry is March 15.

UNIVERSITY OF WISCONSIN-SUPERIOR A-1

www.uwsuper.edu

Superior, WI 54880 — **(715) 394-8230**

Fax: (715) 394-8407	**Email: admissions@uwsuper.edu**
Full-time: 758 men, 1111 women	**Faculty:** 117; IIA
Part-time: 160 men, 333 women	**Ph.D.s:** 50%
Graduate: 39 men, 88 women	**Student/Faculty:** 14 to 1
Year: semesters, summer session	**Tuition:** $8036 ($15,609)
Room & Board: $6410	**Freshman Class:** 996 applied, 713 accepted, 367 enrolled
ACT: 21	**CEEB CODE:** 1920
Application Deadline: August 1	**COMPETITIVE**

University of Wisconsin-Superior, founded in 1893, offers undergraduate programs in the liberal arts and sciences, business, education, fine arts, applied arts, and social sciences. In addition to regional accreditation, UW-Superior has baccalaureate program accreditation with CSWE and NASM. The 230-acre campus is in an urban area in Superior, Wisconsin, at the western tip of Lake Superior. Including any residence halls, there are 17 buildings.

STUDENT LIFE: 57% of undergraduates are from out of state, mostly the Midwest. Students are from 35 states, 44 foreign countries, and Canada. 71% are White; 4% Hispanic; 3% two or more races; 2% African American; 17% Foreign; 1% Asian American; 1% American Indian/ Alaska Native. **Female To Male Ratio:** 1.6:1. The average age of freshmen is 19; all undergraduates, 23. 33% do not continue beyond their first year; 40% remain to graduate. **Housing:** 820 students can be accommodated in college housing, which includes coed dorms. On-campus housing is guaranteed for the freshman year only. 72% of students commute. All students may keep cars.

FACULTY/CLASSROOMS: 46% of faculty are male; 54% are female. 95% teach undergraduates. No introductory courses are taught by graduate students. The average class size in an introductory lecture is 20.

PROGRAMS OF STUDY: UW-Superior confers B.A., B.S., B.F.A., B.M., and B.M.E. degrees. Associate and master's degrees are also awarded. Bachelor's degrees are awarded in BIOLOGICAL SCIENCE (biology/ biological science), BUSINESS (accounting, business administration and management, finance, international business management, sustainable management, and transportation management), COMMUNICATIONS AND THE ARTS (art history, art, communications, dramatic arts, English, fine arts, music, music performance, speech/debate/rhetoric, studio art, theatre arts, visual and performing arts, and writing), COMPUTER AND PHYSICAL SCIENCE (chemistry, computer science, and mathematics), EDUCATION (art education, elementary education, English education, health education, mathematics education, music education, physical education, science education, secondary education, social science education, and social studies secondary school education), ENGINEERING AND ENVIRONMENTAL DESIGN (computational sciences), HEALTH PROFESSIONS (art therapy, biology, community health work, exercise science, health, health and physical activity, and health promotion), SOCIAL SCIENCE (criminal justice, economics, history, interdisciplinary studies, international studies, law, political science/government, psychology, public administration, social studies, social work, and sociology). Business administration, elementary education, and communicating arts have the largest enrollments.

ACTIVITIES: There are no fraternities or sororities. There are 59 groups on campus, including art, band, cheerleading, choir, chorale, chorus, computers, dance, drama, ethnic, honors, international, jazz band, LGBT, newspaper, orchestra, pep band, photography, political, professional, radio and TV, religious, social, social service, student government, and symphony. Popular campus events include World Culture Night and Jacket Racket. **Sports:** There are 7 intercollegiate sports for men and 8 for women, and 19 intramural sports for men and 19 for women. Facilities include a gym, ice arena, pool, weight-training room, dance studio, racquetball courts, an all-weather track, high ropes course, zip line, climbing wall, and softball and baseball fields. **Graduates:** From July 1, 2015 to June 30, 2016, 469 bachelor's degrees were awarded. The most popular majors were interdisciplinary studies (13%), biological/life sciences (12%), and business/marketing (11%). 140 companies recruited on campus in 2015-2016. In an average class, 1% graduate in 3 years or less, 24% graduate in 4 years or less, 37% graduate in 5 years or less, and 40% graduate in 6 years or less.

SERVICES: Counseling and information services are available, as is tutoring in every subject. There is remedial math and writing. **Library/ Resources:** Computerized library services include interlibrary loans, database searching, Internet access, and Wi-Fi capability. Special learning facilities include an art gallery, radio station, TV station, an aquatic lab and observatory. **Physically Challenged Students:** 95% of the campus is accessible. Facilities include wheelchair ramps, elevators, special parking, specially equipped restrooms, special class scheduling, lowered drinking fountains, and lowered telephones. **Special:** UW-Superior offers work-study and co-op programs in business and internships in social work, business, mass communication, and criminal justice. There is a comprehensive program of student-designed majors, along with a cooperative program in marine studies with Texas A&M University, and 3-2 engineering and forestry programs with Michigan Technological University. Students may cross-register for 2 classes per semester at the University of Minnesota-Duluth or the College of St. Scholastica. An extended degree is offered. Credit for life experience and pass/fail options are available. There are 4 national honor societies and 4 departmental honors programs. **Visiting:** There are regularly scheduled orientations for prospective students and consisting of two days of social and educational programs. There are guides for informal visits, visitors may sit in on classes, and stay overnight. To schedule a visit, contact the Admissions Office. **Campus Safety and Security:** Measures include 24-hour foot and vehicle patrol, emergency notification system, self-defense education, and security escort services. There are emergency telephones, lighted pathways/sidewalks, and controlled access to dorms/residences.

REQUIREMENTS: The ACT is required, but out-of-state residents may submit SAT scores instead. Applicants must graduate from an accredited secondary school or the equivalent. Applicant must rank in at least the upper 50% of their graduating class or achieve a minimum composite score of 21 on the ACT. AP and CLEP credits are accepted. To graduate, students must complete 120 credit hours, with a GPA of 2.0. A minimum of 54 hours must be credited toward completion of 1 comprehensive major, 2 majors, or 1 major and 1 minor. The required core curriculum includes 55 credits in communications, English, math, phys ed, world culture, contemporary society, aesthetic experience, natural science, and human behavior. A comprehensive exam and a senior project are required. **Procedure:** Freshmen are admitted in the fall, spring, and summer. Entrance exams should be taken spring of junior year or early fall of senior year. There are deferred admissions and rolling admissions plans. Applications should be filed by August 1 for fall entry; January 5 for spring entry, along with a $44 fee. Notification is sent on a rolling basis. Applications are accepted on-line. **Transfer Students:** 249 transfer students enrolled in 2015-2016. A college GPA of 2.0 is required. 30 of 120 credits required for the bachelor's degree must be completed at UW-Superior. **International Students:** There are 189 international students enrolled. The school actively recruits these students. They must take the TOEFL with a minimum score of 500 on the paper-based TOEFL (PBT) or 61 on the Internet-based version (iBT), or take the MELAB and complete on-campus ESL program (if necessary). ACT or SAT required for native English-speaking international students.

ADMISSIONS: 72% of the 2016-2017 applicants were accepted. The ACT scores were 12% between 12 and 17, 64% between 18 and 23, 20% between 24 and 29, and 2% above 30. 19% of the current freshmen were in the top fifth of their class; 44% were in the top two fifths. 3 freshmen graduated first in their class. **Admissions Contact:** Robert Strand, Admissions Director. Email: *admissions@uwsuper.edu* Web: *www.uwsuper.edu*

FINANCIAL AID: In 2016-2017, 54% of all full-time freshmen and 66% of continuing full-time students received some form of financial aid. 33% of all full-time freshmen and 58% of continuing full-time students received need-based aid. The average freshman award was $10,621. Need-based scholarships or need-based grants averaged $5,225; and need-based self-help aid (loans and jobs) averaged $4,595. The average financial indebtedness of the 2016 graduate was $29,139. The FAFSA code is 003925. The priority date for freshman financial aid applications for fall entry is April 1.

UNIVERSITY OF WISCONSIN-WHITEWATER D-5

www.uww.edu

Whitewater, WI 53190 (262) 472-1440

Fax: (262) 472-1515
Email: uwwadmit@mail.uww.edu
Full-time: 4880 men, 5080 women
Faculty: 384; IIA, --$
Part-time: 570 men, 595 women
Ph.D.s: 73%
Graduate: 571 men, 628 women
Student/Faculty: 22 to 1
Year: semesters, summer session
Tuition: $7632 ($15,208)
Room & Board: $7082
Freshman Class: 7229 applied, 4884 accepted, 2158 enrolled
SAT CR/M/W: 530/520/525 **ACT:** 22
CEEB CODE: 1921
Application Deadline: August 1
COMPETITIVE

University of Wisconsin-Whitewater, founded in 1868, offers programs in teacher education, business, liberal arts, preprofessional studies, fine arts, and music. There are 4 undergraduate schools and 1 graduate school. In addition to regional accreditation, UW-Whitewater has baccalaureate program accreditation with AACSB, ASLA, CSWE, NASM, and NCATE. The 385-acre campus is in a small town 50 miles southwest of Milwaukee. Including any residence halls, there are 45 buildings.

STUDENT LIFE: 85% of undergraduates are from Wisconsin. Others are from 38 states, 42 foreign countries, and Canada. 70% are from public schools. 87% are White; 6% Hispanic; 4% African American; 1% Asian American; 1% Foreign; 1% race unknown. **Female To Male Ratio:** 1.0:1. The average age of freshmen is 19; all undergraduates, 22. 19% do not continue beyond their first year; 63% remain to graduate. **Housing:** 4300 students can be accommodated in college housing, which includes single-sex and coed dorms and off-campus apartments. On-campus housing is available on a first-come, first-served basis. 8% of students commute. All students may keep cars.

FACULTY/CLASSROOMS: 57% of faculty are male; 43% are female. All teach undergraduates, and 78% do research. No introductory courses are taught by graduate students. The average class size in a regular course is 26.

PROGRAMS OF STUDY: UW-Whitewater confers B.A., B.S., B.B.A., B.F.A., B.M., and B.S.Ed. degrees. Associate, master's, and doctoral degrees are also awarded. Bachelor's degrees are awarded in BIOLOGICAL SCIENCE (biology/biological science), BUSINESS (accounting, banking and finance, business administration and management, business economics, marketing/retailing/merchandising, office supervision and management, and personnel management), COMMUNICATIONS AND THE ARTS (art history and appreciation, communications, dramatic arts, English, French, German, journalism, music, public relations, Spanish, and speech/debate/rhetoric), COMPUTER AND PHYSICAL SCIENCE (chemistry, computer programming, mathematics, and physics), EDUCATION (art education, business education, early childhood education, elementary education, foreign languages education, middle school education, music education, physical education, science education, secondary education, social studies education, and special education), SOCIAL SCIENCE (economics, geography, history, international studies, political science/government, prelaw, psychology, public administration, safety and security technology, social work, sociology, and women's studies). Accounting, education, and marketing are the strongest academically. Business/accounting, education, and letters & sciences have the largest enrollments.

ACTIVITIES: 5% of men belong to 1 local and 6 national fraternities; 5% of women belong to 1 local and 4 national sororities. There are 220 groups on campus, including art, band, cheerleading, choir, chorus, communications, computers, dance, debate, drama, drill team, environmental, ethnic, film, forensics, honors, international, LGBT, marching band, musical theater, newspaper, orchestra, pep band, photography, political, professional, radio and TV, religious, social, social service, student government, symphony, and yearbook. Popular campus events include Job Fair, Performing Arts Series, and Athletic Contests. **Sports:** There are 9 intercollegiate sports for men and 11 for women, and 12 intramural sports for men and 12 for women. Facilities include tennis courts, pools, playing fields, weight rooms, 13,000-seat stadium, and a 3500-seat gym. **Graduates:** 200 companies recruited on campus in 2015-2016. In an average class, 50% graduate in 6 years or less.

SERVICES: Counseling and information services are available, as is tutoring in most subjects. There is a reader service for the blind, and remedial math, reading, and writing. Study skills instruction is available. **Library/Resources:** The library contains 356,000 volumes, 993,000 microform items, and 7,300 audio/video tapes/CDs/DVDs, and subscribes to 5,000 periodicals including electronic. Computerized library services include interlibrary loans, database searching, Internet access, and Wi-Fi capability. Special learning facilities include an art gallery, radio station, TV station, an observatory, and weather station. **Physically Challenged Students:** 85% of the campus is accessible. Facilities include wheelchair ramps, elevators, special parking, specially equipped restrooms, special class scheduling, lowered drinking fountains, and lowered telephones. **Special:** Internships, study abroad in 9 nations, accelerated degree programs in safety studies and speech communication, student-designed majors, and a general studies degree are available. Credit by examination, nondegree study, and pass/fail options are also offered. There are 14 national honor societies, a freshman honors program, and 7 departmental honors programs. **Visiting:** There are regularly scheduled orientations for prospective students. There are guides for informal visits and visitors may sit in on classes. To schedule a visit, contact James Lanouette at lanouetj@uww.edu. **Campus Safety and Security:** Measures include 24-hour foot and vehicle patrol, emergency notification system, self-defense education, and security escort services. There are shuttle buses, emergency telephones, and lighted pathways/sidewalks.

REQUIREMENTS: The SAT or ACT is recommended. Applicants should graduate from an accredited secondary school or with 17 academic units, including 4 in English and 3 each in social studies, math, and science. The GED may be accepted. Applicants should rank in the upper 40% of their graduating class or achieve a combined high school and ACT/SAT percentile rank of 100% or above. AP and CLEP credits are accepted. Important factors in the admissions decision are evidence of special talent, advanced placement or honors courses, and recommendations by school officials. Students must complete 50 credits of general studies, a writing competency requirement, and 3 credits in minority issues. A GPA of 2.0 and 120 hours are required to graduate. **Procedure:** Freshmen are admitted to all sessions. There is a rolling admissions plan. Applications should be filed by August 1 for fall entry. The fall 2016 application fee was $44. Notification is sent on a rolling basis. Applications are accepted on-line. **Transfer Students:** 801 transfer students enrolled in 2015-2016. Applicants should have a minimum college GPA of 2.0. 30 of 120 credits required for the bachelor's degree must be completed at UW-Whitewater. **International Students:** There are 127 international students enrolled. The school actively recruits these students. They must take the TOEFL or MELAB.

ADMISSIONS: 68% of the 2016-2017 applicants were accepted. **Admissions Contact:** Dr. Jeremy Reed, Director of Admissions. Email: *uwwadmit@mail.uww.edu* Web: *www.uww.edu*

FINANCIAL AID: In 2016-2017, 73% of all full-time freshmen and 73% of continuing full-time students received some form of financial aid. 45% of all full-time freshmen and 45% of continuing full-time students received need-based aid. The average freshman award was $6,000. UW-Whitewater is a member of CSS. The FAFSA code is 003926. Check with the school for current application deadlines.

VITERBO UNIVERSITY — B-4

www.viterbo.edu

La Crosse, WI 54601	(608) 796-3010 (800) 848-3726
Fax: (608) 796-3020	Email: admission@viterbo.edu
Full-time: 437 men, 1132 women	**Faculty:** 107; IIA
Part-time: 125 men, 411 women	**Ph.D.s:** 60%
Graduate: 211 men, 514 women	**Student/Faculty:** 12 to 1
Year: semesters, summer session	**Tuition:** $26,150
Room & Board: $8510	**Freshman Class:** 1655 applied, 1145 accepted, 304 enrolled
ACT: 23	**CEEB CODE:** 1878
Application Deadline: August 15	**COMPETITIVE**

Viterbo University, a Catholic, Franciscan ecumenical university, prepares students for leadership and service by providing a student-centered, values-based, learning-focused liberal arts education rooted in the values of human dignity and respect for the world. Figures in the above capsule and in this profile are approximate. There are 5 undergraduate schools and 5 graduate schools. In addition to regional accreditation, Viterbo has baccalaureate program accreditation with CSWE, NASM, NCATE, NLN, ACS, CADE, CCNE, and IACBE. The 72-acre campus is in a suburban area 150 miles from Minneapolis -St. Paul, 105 miles from Madison, and 230 miles from Chicago. Including any residence halls, there are 18 buildings.

STUDENT LIFE: 76% of undergraduates are from Wisconsin. Others are from 34 states, and 11 foreign countries. 93% are from public schools. 92% are White; 2% African American; 2% Asian American; 2% Hispanic; 1% American Indian/Alaska Native; 1% Foreign; 1% race unknown. 43% are Catholic; 34% Protestant; 14% Unidentified religions. **Female To Male Ratio:** 2.7:1. The average age of freshmen is 18; all undergraduates, 25. 26% do not continue beyond their first year; 52% remain to graduate. **Housing:** 686 students can be accommodated in college housing, which includes single-sex and coed dorms and on-campus apartments. In addition, there are special-interest houses, on-campus houses, and special-interest floors. On-campus housing is guaranteed for the freshman year only, and is available on a first-come, first-served basis. 10% of students commute. Alcohol is not permitted. Upperclassmen may keep cars.

FACULTY/CLASSROOMS: 48% of faculty are male; 63% are female. 90% teach undergraduates, 53% do research, and 53% do both. No introductory courses are taught by graduate students. The average class size in an introductory lecture is 17; in a laboratory is 16; and in a regular course is 15.

PROGRAMS OF STUDY: Viterbo confers B.A., B.S., B.Art.Ed., B.B.A.,

B.F.A., B.I.L., B.L.S., B.M., B.S.T., B.S.VC., B.S.Community-Medical Dietetics, B.S.Ed., and B.S.N. degrees. Associate and master's degrees are also awarded. Bachelor's degrees are awarded in AGRICULTURE (environmental studies), BIOLOGICAL SCIENCE (biochemistry and biology/biological science), BUSINESS (accounting, management information systems, management science, marketing/retailing/merchandising, organizational leadership and management, sports management, and sustainable management), COMMUNICATIONS AND THE ARTS (art, arts administration/management, communications, dramatic arts, English, graphic design, music performance, Spanish, studio art, and theatre studies), COMPUTER AND PHYSICAL SCIENCE (chemistry, digital arts/technology, mathematics, and natural sciences), EDUCATION (art education, business education, elementary education, English education, mathematics education, music education, science education, social studies education, and technology & science education), HEALTH PROFESSIONS (health care administration and nursing), SOCIAL SCIENCE (addiction studies, biopsychology, criminal justice, dietetics, history, liberal arts/general studies, philosophy, psychology, religious education, religious studies, social studies, social work, and sociology). Life sciences, nutrition/dietetics, and natural sciences are the strongest academically. Health professions, business, and education have the largest enrollments.

ACTIVITIES: There are no fraternities or sororities. There are 32 groups on campus, including art, choir, chorale, chorus, dance, drama, drill team, environmental, ethnic, honors, international, LGBT, literary magazine, musical theater, newspaper, opera, pep band, political, professional, religious, social, social service, and student government. Popular campus events include Orientation Weekend, Welcome Back Bash, Viterbo Days (Family Day), St. Francis Day Celebration, and Courtyard Carni. **Sports:** There are 7 intercollegiate sports for men and 8 for women, and 14 intramural sports for men and 14 for women. Facilities include a student activity center with weight training and fitness rooms and courts for basketball, volleyball, and racquetball. A 12.5-acre outdoor athletic complex has facilities for soccer, baseball, and softball, located 2 1/2 miles from campus. There also are on-campus sand volleyball and paved basketball outdoor courts. The nearby Mississippi River and Mt. La Crosse provide opportunities for canoeing and skiing. **Graduates:** From July 1, 2015 to June 30, 2016, 453 bachelor's degrees were awarded. The most popular majors were health (44%), letters and science (26%), and business (15%). 80 companies recruited on campus in 2015-2016. In an average class, 33% graduate in 4 years or less and 52% graduate in 6 years or less. Of the 2015 graduating class, 7% were enrolled in graduate school within 6 months of graduation, and 97% were employed.

SERVICES: Counseling and information services are available, as is tutoring in every subject. There is a reader service for the blind, and remedial math, reading, and writing. **Library/Resources:** The library contains 92,300 volumes, 307 microform items, and 5,110 audio/video tapes/CDs/DVDs, and subscribes to 229 periodicals including electronic. Computerized library services include interlibrary loans, database searching, Internet access, and Wi-Fi capability. Special learning facilities include an art gallery, and a music resource center. **Physically Challenged Students:** 90% of the campus is accessible. Facilities include wheelchair ramps, elevators, special parking, specially equipped restrooms, special class scheduling, lowered drinking fountains, and lowered telephones. **Special:** Students may cross-register at the University of Wisconsin-LaCrosse, enroll for independent study, or earn a dual degree. Co-op programs, study abroad in 7 countries, double majors, student-designed majors, accelerated degree programs, work-study, internships in many areas, credit by exam, and credit/no credit options are available. There are 2 national honor societies, Phi Beta Kappa, and a freshman honors program. **Visiting:** There are regularly scheduled orientations for prospective students, including a meeting with an admissions staff member, a tour of the campus, and optional meetings with a financial aid officer and faculty members. There are guides for informal visits and visitors may sit in on classes. To schedule a visit, contact the Admission Office. **Campus Safety and Security:** Measures include emergency notification system, self-defense education, and security escort services. There are shuttle buses, emergency telephones, lighted pathways/sidewalks, controlled access to dorms/residences, an emergency evacuation plan, 24 hours a day, 7 days a week, phone access to security personnel, security patrol from 5 p.m. to 7 a.m., ID check-in in dorms after 10 p.m., and card access to all campus buildings after regular hours, and 6 emergency blue lights.

REQUIREMENTS: The ACT is required. Graduation from an accredited secondary school is required; the GED is accepted. Secondary preparation should include 16 credits, with 3 or 4 in English and 2 each in math, natural science, and social science or history. Fine arts students may be required to audition or submit a portfolio. Nursing, dietetics, and pre-medical students must have high school chemistry. AP and CLEP credits are accepted. Students must complete a minimum of 128 semester hours of credit. A minimum of 43 of these must be upper-division level. All students must complete the General Education requirements (45 credit hours from various disciplines) and competencies, as well as all of the specified requirements for their major. Also, students must complete a service component designed by their major program. All students must have a GPA of at least 2.0; and must take as a minimum the last 30 consecutive semester hours at Viterbo University or complete 45 of the last 60 semester hours from Viterbo. Students seeking a B.S. must complete 7 credits of natural science and/or math in addition to the 4 credits of natural science in the General Education requirements. Students seeking a B.A. must complete the equivalent of 14 semester hours of the same modern foreign language. **Procedure:** Freshmen are admitted to all sessions. Entrance exams should be taken at orientation, prior to registration. There is a rolling admissions plan. Applications should be filed by August 15 for fall entry, along with a $25 fee. Notification is sent on a rolling basis. Applications are accepted on-line. **Transfer Students:** 274 transfer students enrolled in 2015-2016. Transfer students must have a cumulative GPA of at least 2.0, free to return to their previous school, and considered to be in good academic standing both at their previous school and at Viterbo. They must submit an application, the official transcripts of coursework in high school, official transcripts from all post-secondary institutions, and ACT/SAT results, if already taken. 30 of 128 credits required for the bachelor's degree must be completed at Viterbo. **International Students:** There are 24 international students enrolled. The school actively recruits these students. They must take the TOEFL with a minimum score of 525 on the paper-based TOEFL (PBT) or 93 on the Internet-based version (iBT).

ADMISSIONS: 69% of the 2016-2017 applicants were accepted. The ACT scores were 24% below 12, 34% between 12 and 17, 29% between 18 and 23, 8% between 24 and 29, and 5% above 30. 37% of the current freshmen were in the top fifth of their class; 72% were in the top two fifths. 6 freshmen graduated first in their class. **Admissions Contact:** Eric Schmidt, Director of Admission. Email: *admission@viterbo.edu* Web: *www.viterbo.edu*

FINANCIAL AID: In 2016-2017, 98% of all full-time freshmen received some form of financial aid. 100% of undergraduate students work part-time. Average annual earnings from campus work are $1167. The college's own financial statement is required. The FAFSA code is 003911. The priority date for freshman financial aid applications for fall entry is March 15.

WISCONSIN LUTHERAN COLLEGE E-4
www.wlc.edu

Milwaukee, WI 53226 **(414) 443-8811**

	Email: admissions@wlc.edu
Full-time: 300 men, 400 women	**Faculty:** 47
Part-time: 20 men, 20 women	**Ph.D.s:** 65%
Graduate: n/av	**Student/Faculty:** 14 to 1
Year: semesters, summer session	**Tuition:** $27,040
Room & Board: $9250	**Freshman Class:** n/av
ACT: required	**CEEB CODE:** 1513
Application Deadline: n/av	**VERY COMPETITIVE**

Wisconsin Lutheran College is an independent, residential, Christian college in Milwaukee. WLC serves traditional undergraduate, adult, and graduate students through its on-campus, on-location, and online programming. The college, which prepares students for lives of Christian leadership, is recognized for its academic excellence and superior student experience. Caring, Christian faculty work directly with students, who benefit from numerous research, service, and co-curricular opportunities designed to enhance academic and spiritual growth. There are 2 undergraduate schools and 1 graduate school. In addition to regional accreditation, Wisconsin Lutheran has baccalaureate program accreditation with CCNE. The 21-acre campus is in a suburban area on the western edge of Milwaukee. Including any residence halls, there are 11 buildings.

STUDENT LIFE: 80% of undergraduates are from Wisconsin. Others are from 27 states, and 6 foreign countries. 41% are from public schools. 95% are White; 2% African American; 2% Foreign; 1% Asian American; 1% Hispanic. 88% are Protestant. **Female To Male Ratio:** 1.3:1. The average age of freshmen is 18; all undergraduates, 20. 20% do not continue beyond their first year; 74% remain to graduate. **Housing:** 600 students can be accommodated in college housing, which includes single-sex dorms and on-campus apartments. On-campus housing is guaranteed for all 4 years. 68% of students live on campus. Alcohol is not permitted. All students may keep cars.

FACULTY/CLASSROOMS: 70% of faculty are male; 30% are female. All teach undergraduates, and all do research. No introductory courses are taught by graduate students. The average class size in an introductory lecture is 20; in a laboratory is 10; and in a regular course is 16.

PROGRAMS OF STUDY: Wisconsin Lutheran confers B.A., B.S., and B.S.N. degrees. Master's degrees are also awarded. Bachelor's degrees are awarded in AGRICULTURE (environmental studies), BIOLOGICAL SCIENCE (biochemistry, biology/biological science, and marine biology), BUSINESS (accounting and business administration and management), COMMUNICATIONS AND THE ARTS (art, communications, English, German, media arts, music, Spanish, television & digital media production, and theatre arts), COMPUTER AND PHYSICAL SCIENCE (chemistry, computer science, mathematics, and physics), EDUCATION (elementary education and secondary education), ENGINEERING AND ENVIRONMENTAL DESIGN (environmental science), HEALTH PROFESSIONS (exercise science and nursing), SOCIAL SCIENCE (Chinese Studies, history, human services, interdisciplinary studies, philosophy, psychology, social science, and theological studies). Nursing, education, and biology are the strongest academically.

ACTIVITIES: There are no fraternities or sororities. There are 31 groups on campus, including art, band, cheerleading, choir, communications, dance, drama, honors, international, jazz band, musical theater, newspaper, political, professional, religious, social, social service, and student government. Popular campus events include Musical and Theater Events, and Winterfest. **Sports:** There are 9 intercollegiate sports for men and 9 for women. Facilities include outdoor athletics complex with football stadium, track, soccer fields, baseball and softball fields, and locker rooms/training facilities; three basketball courts, 2500-seat gym, weight room, fitness center, dance/aerobics room, training and therapy rooms, and a walking/running track. **Graduates:** From July 1, 2015 to June 30, 2016, 121 bachelor's degrees were awarded. The most popular majors were communication (17%), psychology (11%), and biology (11%). In an average class, 47% graduate in 4 years or less, 62% graduate in 5 years or less, and 74% graduate in 6 years or less.

SERVICES: Counseling and information services are available, as is tutoring in most subjects. **Library/Resources:** The library contains 81,660 volumes, and 4,673 audio/video tapes/CDs/DVDs. Computerized library services include interlibrary loans, database searching, Internet access, and Wi-Fi capability. Special learning facilities include an art gallery. **Physically Challenged Students:** 90% of the campus is accessible. Facilities include wheelchair ramps, elevators, special parking, specially equipped restrooms, and lowered drinking fountains. **Special:** There is a freshman honors program. **Visiting:** There are regularly scheduled orientations for prospective students, including a tour of the campus, a meal, meetings with admissions, financial aid, cocurriculars, and faculty in academic areas of interest. There are guides for informal visits, visitors may sit in on classes, and stay overnight. To schedule a visit, contact the Admissions Office. **Campus Safety and Security:** Measures include 24-hour foot and vehicle patrol, emergency notification system, and security escort services. There are lighted pathways/sidewalks and controlled access to dorms/residences.

REQUIREMENTS: The ACT is required. A GPA of 2.7 is required. AP and CLEP credits are accepted. **Procedure:** Freshmen are admitted fall and spring. Entrance exams should be taken in the spring of the junior year. There is a rolling admissions plan. Applications should be filed by January 15 for spring entry, along with a $20 fee. Notification is sent on a rolling basis. Applications are accepted on-line. Application fees are waived if application is completed on-line. **Transfer Students:** 30 of 128 credits required for the bachelor's degree must be completed at Wisconsin Lutheran. **International Students:** There are 10 international students enrolled. They must take the TOEFL. They must also take the SAT and ACT, scoring 970.

Admissions Contact: Lucas Faust, Executive Director of Admissions. Email: *admissions@wlc.edu* Web: *www.wlc.edu*

FINANCIAL AID: In 2016-2017, 100% of all full-time freshmen and 99% of continuing full-time students received some form of financial aid. The average freshman award was $14,526.. The average financial indebtedness of the 2016 graduate was $13,707. The college's own financial statement is required. The FAFSA code is 014658. The priority date for freshman financial aid applications for fall entry is March 1. The deadline for filing freshman financial aid applications for fall entry is rolling.

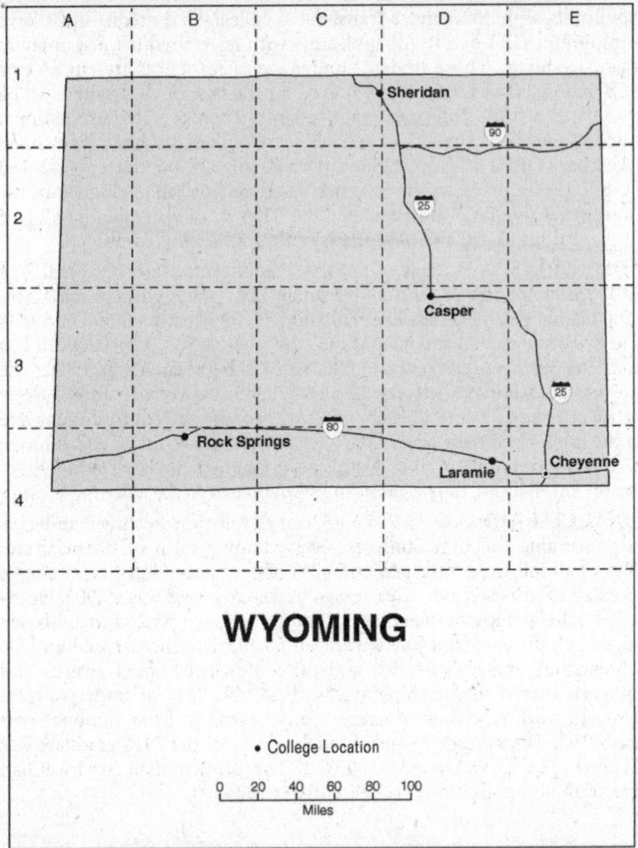

UNIVERSITY OF WYOMING D-4

www.uwyo.edu

Laramie, WY 82071	**(307) 766-5160** **(800) 342-5996**
Fax: (307) 766-4042	**Email: admissions@uwyo.edu**
Full-time: 4213 men, 4181 women	**Faculty:** 754; I, -$
Part-time: 656 men, 995 women	**Ph.D.s:** 81%
Graduate: 1263 men, 1340 women	**Student/Faculty:** 14 to 1
Year: semesters, summer session	**Tuition:** $5055 ($16,215)
Room & Board: $10,320	**Freshman Class:** 4657 applied, 4455 accepted, 1692 enrolled
SAT CR/M: 545/557 **ACT:** 25	**CEEB CODE:** 4855
Application Deadline: August 10	**COMPETITIVE+**

The University of Wyoming, founded in 1886, is a public institution offering programs in agriculture and natural resources, arts and sciences, business, education, engineering and applied science, health sciences, and law. There are 8 undergraduate schools and 8 graduate schools. In addition to regional accreditation, UW has baccalaureate program accreditation with AACSB, ABET, ACP, ADA, CSAB, CSWE, NASM, NCATE, ABA, ACS, APA, Wyoming Profess'l Std Teaching Bd, CACREP, CCNE, ACEND, CAA of ASHA, ACGME, AOBFP, AAVLD, Society for Range Management, and AAAHC. The 832-acre campus is in a small town 128 miles north of Denver and 50 miles west of Cheyenne. Including any residence halls, there are 188 buildings.

STUDENT LIFE: 68% of undergraduates are from Wyoming. Others are from 53 states, 89 foreign countries, and Canada. 73% are White; 8% race unknown; 6% Hispanic; 6% Foreign; 3% two or more races; 1% African American; 1% Asian American; 1% American Indian/Alaska Native. **Female To Male Ratio:** 1.1:1. The average age of freshmen is 19; all undergraduates, 23. 24% do not continue beyond their first year; 54% remain to graduate. **Housing:** 2830 students can be accommodated in college housing, which includes single-sex and coed dorms, on-campus apartments, off-campus apartments, and married student housing. In addition, there are honors houses, special-interest houses, fraternity houses, sorority houses, academic, single-gender, coed, upperclassmen, quiet-living, substance-free, freshman interest-group floors, 21 and over, and ROTC. On-campus housing is guaranteed for all 4 years. 76% of students commute. All students may keep cars.

FACULTY/CLASSROOMS: 59% of faculty are male; 41% are female. 96% teach undergraduates. Graduate students teach 19% of introductory courses. The average class size in a regular course is 39.

PROGRAMS OF STUDY: UW confers B.A., B.S., B.A.S., B.F.A., B.M., B.S.A.R., B.S.C.E., B.S.Ch., B.S.C.P., B.S.C.S., B.S.D.H., B.S.E.E., B.S.E.S.E., B.S.F.C., B.S.M.E., B.S.N., B.S.P.E. and B.S.W. degrees. Master's and doctoral degrees are also awarded. Bachelor's degrees are awarded in AGRICULTURE (agricultural business management, agricultural communications, animal science, environmental studies, fish and game management, and range/farm management), BIOLOGICAL SCIENCE (botany, ecology, microbiology, molecular biology, physiology, wildlife biology, and zoology), BUSINESS (accounting, business administration and management, business economics, finance, management science, marketing, and organizational leadership and management), COMMUNICATIONS AND THE ARTS (art, communications, dance, English, French, German, journalism, music, music performance, Russian, Spanish, and theatre acting), COMPUTER AND PHYSICAL SCIENCE (astronomy and physics, chemistry, computer science, earth science, environmental geology, geology, mathematics, physics, and statistics), EDUCATION (agricultural education, elementary education, music education, physical education, secondary education, special education, technical education, and trade and industrial education), ENGINEERING AND ENVIRONMENTAL DESIGN (architectural engineering, chemical engineering, civil engineering, computer engineering, electrical/electronics engineering, energy management technology, energy systems technology, mechanical engineering, and petroleum/natural gas engineering), HEALTH PROFESSIONS (biology, dental hygiene, kinesiology, medical laboratory technology, nursing, and speech pathology/audiology), SOCIAL SCIENCE (American Indian studies, American studies, anthropology, criminal justice, economics, family/consumer studies, geography, history, humanities, interdisciplinary studies, international studies, philosophy, political science/government, psychology, religious studies, social science, social work, sociology, and women & gender studies). Psychology, mechanical engineering, and petroleum engineering have the largest enrollments.

ACTIVITIES: 6% of men belong to 9 national fraternities; 6% of women belong to 5 national sororities. There are 246 groups on campus, including art, band, cheerleading, choir, chorale, chorus, communications, computers, dance, debate, drama, drill team, environmental, ethnic, film, forensics, honors, international, jazz band, LGBT, literary magazine, marching band, musical theater, newspaper, opera, orchestra, pep band, photography, political, professional, radio and TV, religious, social, social service, student government, and symphony. Popular campus events include President's Welcome, Family Weekend, and Homecoming. **Sports:** There are 8 intercollegiate sports for men and 9 for women, and 29 intramural sports for men and 29 for women. Facilities include a stadium, basketball arena, volleyball, badminton, and racquetball courts, running track, swimming pools, weight rooms, indoor tennis complex, baseball, soccer and track stadiums, football training center, golf course, sports complex, climbing wall, and fitness rooms. **Graduates:** From July 1, 2015 to June 30, 2016, 2022 bachelor's degrees were awarded. The most popular majors were nursing (10%), elementary education (6%), and psychology (5%). In an average class, 26% graduate in 4 years or less, 49% graduate in 5 years or less, and 55% graduate in 6 years or less.

SERVICES: Counseling and information services are available, as is tutoring in most subjects, and a reader service for the blind. Note-taking services, tape recorders, and interpreters are also available for the hearing impaired. **Library/Resources:** The 5 libraries contain 1.7 million volumes, 2.9 million microform items, 20,551 audio/video tapes/CDs/DVDs, and subscribe to 140,146 periodicals including electronic. Computerized library services include interlibrary loans, database searching, Internet access, and Wi-Fi capability. Special learning facilities include an art gallery, natural history museum, planetarium, radio station, TV station, the American Heritage Center, specialized science and agriculture labs, Williams Botany Conservatory, Wyoming Infrared Observatory, Geology - Brinkerhoff Geology library, law library, library annex, NPS UW research library, and Rocky Mountain Herbarium. **Physically Challenged Students:** 95% of the campus is accessible. Facilities include wheelchair ramps, elevators, special parking, specially equipped restrooms, special class scheduling, lowered drinking fountains, lowered telephones, and special housing. **Special:** UW offers internships, study abroad in many countries, national student exchange, Washington and U.N. semesters, work-study programs, dual and interdisciplinary majors, pass/fail options, credit by exam, accelerated degree programs, and credit for life, military, and work experience. There are 60 national honor societies, Phi Beta Kappa, a freshman honors program, and 27 departmental honors programs. **Visiting:** There are regularly scheduled orientations for prospective students, including campus tours and meetings with academic advisers, as well as guides for informal visits. To schedule a visit, contact Tome Student Admissions Center at (307) 766-4075. **Campus Safety and Security:** Measures include 24-hour foot and vehicle patrol, emergency notification system, self-defense education, security escort services, shuttle buses, emergency telephones, lighted pathways/sidewalks, and controlled access to dorms/residences.

REQUIREMENTS: The SAT or ACT is required for students under 21; the ACT is preferred. Applicants must be graduates of an accredited secondary school or hold a GED certificate. Secondary preparation should include at least 19 academic credits consisting of 4 years each of English, math, and science, 3 years of social science, 2 years of foreign language, and 2 years chosen from fine and performing arts, social and behavioral studies, humanities, additional foreign language, or career-technical courses. A visit is suggested. A GPA of 3.0 is required. AP and CLEP credits are accepted. To graduate, students must complete 120 to 142 credit hours, depending on the major, with a minimum GPA of 2.0. The core curriculum includes required general education courses in the University Studies Program. Students must complete a minimum of 48 upper division or graduate-level semester credit hours, 30 of which must be earned from the University of Wyoming. **Procedure:** Freshmen are admitted in the fall, spring, and summer. Entrance exams should be taken in the spring of the junior year or fall of the senior year. There are deferred admissions and rolling admissions plans. Applications should be filed by August 10 for fall entry; December 10 for spring entry, along with a $40 fee. Application fees are waived if application is completed online. **Transfer Students:** 931 transfer students enrolled in 2015-2016. Applicants with 30 or more transferable college-level credits must have a minimum GPA of 2.0. All applicants with fewer credits must apply as a new freshman. Those students under age 21 must also present SAT or ACT scores. 30 of 120 credits required for the bachelor's degree must be completed at UW. **International Students:** There are 366 international students enrolled. The school actively recruits these students. They must take the TOEFL with a minimum score of 525 on the paper-based TOEFL (PBT) or 71 on the Internet-based version (iBT) along with the Comprehensive English Language Test. They must also take the SAT or ACT, scoring 21 ACT or 980 math/critical reasoning combined.

ADMISSIONS: 96% of the 2016-2017 applicants were accepted. The SAT scores for the 2016-2017 freshman class were: Critical Reading-- 28% below 500, 42% between 500 and 599, 22% between 600 and 699, and 8% between 700 and 800. Math-- 28% below 500, 34% between 500 and 599, 30% between 600 and 699, and 7% between 700 and 800. The ACT scores were 4% between 12 and 17, 36% between 18 and 23, 49% between 24 and 29, and 12% above 30. 42% of the current freshmen were in the top fifth of their class; 71% were in the top two fifths. 90 freshmen graduated first in their class. **Admissions Contact:** Shelley Dodd, Director of Admissions. Email: *admissions@uwyo.edu* Web: *www.uwyo.edu*

FINANCIAL AID: In 2016-2017, 48% of all full-time freshmen and 45% of continuing full-time students received some form of financial aid. 30% of all full-time freshmen and 32% of continuing full-time students received need-based aid. The average freshman award was $9,905. Need-based scholarships or need-based grants averaged $5,255; need-based self-help aid (loans and jobs) averaged $3,305; non-need-based athletic scholarships averaged $1,792; and other non-need-based awards and non-need-based scholarships averaged $4,169. 28% of undergraduate students work part-time. Average annual earnings from campus work are $2195. The average financial indebtedness of the 2016 graduate was $22,683. The FAFSA code is 003932. The priority date for freshman financial aid applications for fall entry is March 1.

ARIZONA

ARIZONA CHRISTIAN UNIVERSITY C-4

Phoenix, AZ 85032 **(602) 489-5300** **(602) 404-2159**

Full-time: 500 men, 237 women **Faculty:** 55
Part-time: n/av **Tuition:** $22,986
Graduate: n/av **Room & Board:** $10,080
Application Deadline: n/av
SAT or ACT: required

Arizona Christian University, founded in 1960, is nondenominational. Its mission is transforming culture with the truth of Christ. The figures in the above capsule and in this profile are approximate. In addition to regional accreditation, the college is accredited by AABC and NCA. Arizona Christian University awards the B.A. and B.S. in elementary education, biblical studies, Christian ministries, secondary education, business administration, behavioral health, family studies and music education. The school also awards associate and bachelor's degrees. Web:http:/ www.arizonachristian.edu

ARKANSAS

CENTRAL BAPTIST COLLEGE C-3

Conway, AR 72034 **(501) 329-6872** **(501) 329-2941**

Full-time: 347 men, 282 women **Faculty:** 75
Part-time: 129 men, 134 women **Tuition:** $16,980
Graduate: n/av **Room & Board:** $7500
Application Deadline: August 15
SAT or ACT: required

Central Baptist College, founded in 1952, is affiliated with the Baptist Missionary Association of Arkansas. Its mission is to transform lives through education that integrates Christian faith and academic excellence in a Christ-centered environment. In addition to regional accreditation, the college is accredited by NCA. Central Baptist College awards the A.A., B.A., B.S., B.B.A., and B.S.E. in accounting, Bible, biology, business administration, church music, education (elementary education, health and physical education, middle level education, secondary level - English/language arts, secondary level - life sciences, secondary level - social sciences), English, general studies, health science, history, human resources, international business, journalism, kinesiology - exercise science, kinesiology - sports management, leadership, leadership and ministry, management, management information systems, marketing, missions, molecular bioscience, multimedia communication, music, organizational management, psychology, psychology & counseling, psychology & social services, worship arts. The school also awards associate and bachelor's degrees. Web:www.cbc.edu

CALIFORNIA

WILLIAM JESSUP UNIVERSITY B-3

Rocklin, CA 95678 **(916) 577-2278** **(916) 577-2220**

Full-time: 260 men, 399 women **Faculty:** 74
Part-time: 7 men, 6 women **Tuition:** $29,050
Graduate: n/av **Room & Board:** $10,650
Application Deadline: June 1
ACT: required

William Jessup University, founded in 1939, is nondenominational. Its mission is to prepare Christians for leadership and service in the church and society through Christian higher education, spiritual formation, and directed experiences. In addition to regional accreditation, the college is accredited by AABC. William Jessup University awards the B.A. and B.S. in Bible and theology, pastoral ministry, youth ministry, Christian education, Intercultural studies, counseling, music and worship, business management, liberal arts education and Christian leadership. The figures in the above capsule are approximate. The school also awards associate and bachelor's degrees. Web:http/www.jessup.edu

CONNECTICUT

HOLY APOSTLES COLLEGE & SEMINARY C-2

Cromwell, CT 06416 **(860) 632-3033** **(860) 632-3075**

Full-time: 25 men, 7 women **Faculty:** 25
Part-time: 7 men, 17 women **Tuition:** $17,600
Graduate: 178 men, 82 women **Room & Board:** $11,200
Application Deadline: open
SAT: required

Holy Apostles College & Seminary, founded in 1956, is affiliated with the Roman Catholic Church. Its mission is to cultivate lay, consecrated, and ordained Catholic leaders for the purpose of evangelization and to maintain excellence in teaching/learning, research/discovery, and service/ engagement through the liberal arts, philosophy and theology. The figures in the above capsule are approximate. In addition to regional accreditation, the college is accredited by NEASC. Holy Apostles College & Seminary awards the B.A. in English in the humanities, history in the social sciences, philosophy and theology. The school also awards associate, bachelor's, and master's degrees. Web: *www.holyapostles.edu*

FLORIDA

JOHNSON UNIVERSITY FLORIDA D-3
Florida Christian College

Kissimmee, FL 34744 **(407) 847-8966** **(407) 847-3925**

Full-time: 105 men, 110 women **Faculty:** 24
Part-time: 30 men, 30 women **Tuition:** $14,270
Graduate: n/av **Room & Board:** $3200
Application Deadline: July 15
ACT: required

Johnson University Florida, founded in 1976, is affiliated with the Christian Churches/Churches of Christ/Independent. Its mission is to conduct a course of study educating men and women for Christian service, to provide a program of instruction on the college level, to grant appropriate degrees, and to serve as a resource to churches, especially in Florida. The figures in the above capsule are approximate. In addition to regional accreditation, the college is accredited by AABC and SACS. Johnson University Florida awards the B.A., B.S., and B.Th. in Bible, Christian education ministries, and Christian ministries. The school also awards associate and bachelor's degrees. Web: *www.johnson.edu*

ST. JOHN VIANNEY COLLEGE SEMINARY E-5

Miami, FL 33165 **(305) 223-4561** **(305) 223-0650**

Full-time: 74 men **Faculty:** 23
Part-time: 1 men, 1 women **Tuition:** $21,000
Graduate: n/av **Room & Board:** $11,000
Application Deadline: open

St. John Vianney College Seminary, founded in 1959, is affiliated with the Roman Catholic Church. Its mission is to provide an undergraduate education for students whose stated objective is to serve the Catholic Church in the priesthood, and to provide spiritual and intellectual formation within an Anglo-Hispanic bilingual, bicultural setting. In addition to regional accreditation, the college is accredited by SACS. St. John Vianney College Seminary awards the B.A. and B.Phil. in philosophy. The figures in the above capsule are approximate. The school also awards bachelor's degrees. Web: *www.sjvcs.edu*

THE BAPTIST COLLEGE OF FLORIDA B-1

Graceville, FL 32440 (800) 328-2660 (850) 263-9026

Full-time: 237 men, 177 women **Faculty:** 57
Part-time: 103 men, 29 women **Tuition:** $11,880
Graduate: n/av **Room & Board:** $4888
Application Deadline: August 1

The Baptist College of Florida, founded in 1943, is affiliated with the Florida Baptist Convention. Its mission is to promote, provide for, operate, and control a program of education and training for ministers and other religious workers. The figures in the above capsule are approximate. In addition to regional accreditation, the college is accredited by SACS. The Baptist College of Florida awards the B.A. in biblical studies, Christian counseling, Christian education, Christian studies, elementary education, English, English secondary education, history and social studies, history and social studies secondary education, leadership, ministry, missions, and music ministry. The school also awards associate and bachelor's degrees. Web: *www.baptistcollege.edu*

GEORGIA

POINT UNIVERSITY B-2

West Point, GA 31833 (706) 385-1000 (706) 645-9473

Full-time: 534 men, 639 women **Faculty:** 120
Part-time: 142 men, 207 women **Tuition:** $18,350
Graduate: n/av **Room & Board:** $6600
Application Deadline: August 1

Point University, founded in 1937, is affiliated with the Christian Churches and Churches of Christ. Its mission is to educate students for Christ-centered service and leadership throughout the world. The figures in the above capsule are approximate. In addition to regional accreditation, the college is accredited by SACSCOC. Point University awards the B.A., B.S., and B.B.A. in accounting, biblical studies, biblical studies and preaching ministry (dual major), biology, business administration, child and youth development, Christian ministry, counseling and human services, criminal justice, early childhood education, English, English and biblical studies (dual major), exercise science, history, human relations, humanities, humanities and biblical studies (dual major), management, marketing, middle grades education, music, organizational leadership, psychology, and sociology, with specialization in social work. The school also awards associate and bachelor's degrees. Web: *www.point.edu*

ILLINOIS

LINCOLN CHRISTIAN UNIVERSITY D3

Lincoln, IL 62656-2111 (217) 732-3168 (217) 732-4199

Full-time: 273 men, 265 women **Faculty:** 99
Part-time: 52 men, 53 women **Tuition:** $15,949
Graduate: 233 men, 117 women **Room & Board:** $7564
Application Deadline: open
ACT: required

Lincoln Christian University, founded in 1944, is affiliated with the Christian Church/Church of Christ. Its mission is to nurture and equip Christians with a Biblical worldview to serve and lead in the church and the world. The figures in the above capsule are approximate. In addition to regional accreditation, the college is accredited by AABC and NCACS. Lincoln Christian University awards the B.A. and B.S. in Bible, business administration, Christian leadership and management, general ministry, intercultural studies, preaching ministry, youth ministry, Biblical exposition, children and family ministry, Christian spiritual formation, general studies, philosophy, psychology, and worship ministry. The school also awards associate, bachelor's, master's, and doctorate degrees. Web:*www.lincolnchristian.edu*

MOODY BIBLE INSTITUTE E-2

Chicago, IL 60610 (312) DL-MOODY (312) 329-8955

Full-time: 848 men, 730 women **Faculty:** 95
Part-time: 436 men, 389 women **Tuition:** $19,280
Graduate: 261 men, 152 women **Room & Board:** $5185
Application Deadline: December 1
ACT: required

Moody Bible Institute, founded in 1886, is Evangelical Protestant. Its mission is to educate and train individuals to proclaim the gospel of the Lord Jesus Christ, to promote evangelism, and to serve the Evangelical Christian Church vocationally and/or avocationally in its worldwide ministry. In addition to regional accreditation, the college is accredited by AABC and NCA. Moody Bible Institute awards the B.A., B.S., and B.Mus. in missionary aviation technology, biblical studies, evangelism/discipleship, communication, educational ministries, world missions, pastoral studies, religious education, church music, sacred music, Bible-theology, applied linguistics, youth ministry, urban ministry, Jewish and modern Israel studies, family ministries, women's ministries, and teaching English to speakers of other languages. The school also awards associate, bachelor's, and master's degrees. Web: *www.moody.edu*

IOWA

DIVINE WORD COLLEGE E-2

Epworth, IA 52045-0380 (563) 876-3353 (563) 876-5515

Full-time: 80 men, 34 women **Faculty:** 29
Part-time: n/av **Tuition:** $12,810
Graduate: n/av **Room & Board:** $3500
Application Deadline: July 15

Divine Word College, founded in 1912, is affiliated with the Roman Catholic Church. Its mission is to combine a liberal arts education with a cross-cultural program of missionary formation for Divine Word Missionaries and other leaders in the Roman Catholic Church. The figures in the above capsule are approximate. In addition to regional accreditation, the college is accredited by NCA. Divine Word College awards the BA in philosophy, cross-cultural studies, and religious studies. The school also awards associate and bachelor's degrees. Web:*www.dwci.edu*

FAITH BAPTIST BIBLE COLLEGE AND THEOLOGICAL SEMINARY C-3

Ankeny, IA 50023 (515) 964-0601 (515) 964-1638

Full-time: 120 men, 186 women **Faculty:** 36
Part-time: 22 men, 23 women **Tuition:** $16,600
Graduate: 52 men, 14 women **Room & Board:** $6732
Application Deadline: August 1
SAT or ACT: required

Faith Baptist Bible College and Theological Seminary, founded in 1921, is affiliated with the Baptist Church. Its mission is to provide an intensive biblical and vocational education on the college level with the goal of preparing students to minister effectively in Christian service through leadership positions in fundamental Baptist churches and other organizations of like convictions. The figures in the above capsule are approximate. In addition to regional accreditation, the college is accredited by AABC and NCA. Faith Baptist Bible College and Theological Seminary awards the B.A. and B.S. in Bible and theology, assistant pastor, Christian education, Christian school, missions, music ministries, and pastoral training. The school also awards associate, bachelor's, and master's degrees. Web:*www.faith.edu*

KENTUCKY

CLEAR CREEK BAPTIST BIBLE COLLEGE F-3

Pineville, KY 40977 (606) 337-3196 (606) 337-2372

Full-time: 100 men, 24 women	**Faculty:** 22
Part-time: 50 men, 14 women	**Tuition:** $7792
Graduate: n/av	**Room & Board:** $4034
Application Deadline: July 15	

Clear Creek Baptist Bible College, founded in 1926, is affiliated with the Southern Baptist Church. Its mission is to provide theological education for adults called to Christian service. The figures in the above capsule are approximate. In addition to regional accreditation, the college is accredited by AABC and SACS. Clear Creek Baptist Bible College awards the B.A. in Bible, and also awards associate and bachelor's degrees. *Web:www.ccbbc.edu*

LOUISIANA

SAINT JOSEPH ABBEY AND SEMINARY COLLEGE D-3

St. Benedict, LA 70457 (985) 892-1800 (985) 867-2270

Full-time: 80 men	**Faculty:** 43
Part-time: 70 men	**Tuition:** $28,730
Graduate: n/av	**Room & Board:** $14,120
Application Deadline: open	
ACT: required	

Saint Joseph Abbey and Seminary College, founded in 1891, is affiliated with the Roman Catholic Church. Its mission is educate and train men for the priesthood in the Roman Catholic Church and to support preparation for lay ministry. The figures in the above capsule are approximate. In addition to regional accreditation, the college is accredited by SACS. Saint Joseph Abbey and Seminary College awards the B.A. in liberal arts, philosophy and theological studies. The figures in the above capsule are approximate. The school also awards bachelor's degrees. Web:*www.sjasc.edu*

MICHIGAN

SACRED HEART MAJOR SEMINARY E-5

Detroit, MI 48206 (313) 883-8512 (313) 883-8682

Full-time: 46 men, 6 women	**Faculty:** 78
Part-time: 108 men, 102 women	**Tuition:** $15,770
Graduate: 124 men, 44 women	**Room & Board:** $9484
Application Deadline: August 15	

Sacred Heart Major Seminary, founded in 1919, is affiliated with the Roman Catholic Church. Its mission is to prepares candidates for the Roman Catholic Priesthood and, further, prepares individuals for the diaconate, lay ministry and other leadership roles. Sacred Heart Major Seminary seeks to provide an excellent undergraduate formation based on an emphasis in Philosophy and ministry that will serve as a sound foundation to pursue theological studies. The graduate Theology programs seek to ensure a clearly Catholic professional and academic formation for ministerial service. The figures in the above capsule are approximate. In addition to regional accreditation, the college is accredited by NCA and ATS. Sacred Heart Major Seminary awards the A.B. and B.Phil. in Philosophy, and Pastoral Theology. The school also awards associate, bachelor's, and master's degrees. Web: *www.shms.edu*

MINNESOTA

CROWN COLLEGE C-4

Saint Bonifacius, MN 55375 (952) 446-4100 (952) 446-4149

Full-time: 348 men, 465 women	**Faculty:** n/av
Part-time: 96 men, 122 women	**Tuition:** $23,740
Graduate: 100 men, 67 women	**Room & Board:** $7940
Application Deadline: see profile	
ACT: required	

Crown College, founded in 1916, is affiliated with the Christian and Missionary Alliance. Its mission is to provide a Biblically based education for Christian leadership in the Christian and Missionary Alliance, the church at large, and the world. The figures in the above capsule are approximate. In addition to regional accreditation, the college is accredited by NCA. Crown College awards the B.A., B.S., B.Mus.Ed., and B.S.N. in Biblical and Theological Studies, biology, business administration, child and family ministries, communication, criminal/social justice, discipleship ministries, elementary education, English, English education, ESL education, general studies, history, intercultural studies, liberal arts, linguistics, management, music, music education, new testament, nursing, pastoral leadership, physical education, psychology, science education, social entrepreneurship, social studies education, sports management, TESOL, urban studies, worship arts, youth and family, and youth/social ministry. The school also awards associate, bachelor's, and master's degrees. Web: *www.crown.edu*

MARTIN LUTHER COLLEGE C-4

New Ulm, MN 56073-3300 (507) 354-8221 (507) 354-8225

Full-time: 515 men, 525 women	**Faculty:** 98
Part-time: 8 men, 9 women	**Tuition:** $19,490
Graduate: n/av	**Room & Board:** $5510
Application Deadline: April 15	
ACT: required	

Martin Luther College, founded in 1995, is affiliated with the Wisconsin Evangelical Lutheran Synod. Its mission is to provide training for elementary and secondary teaching, preseminary training for pastoral students, and training for other church vocations through the Staff Ministry Program. The figures in the above capsule are approximate. In addition to regional accreditation, the college is accredited by NCACS. Martin Luther College awards the B.A. and B.S.Ed. in education and preseminary studies, and also awards bachelor's degrees. Web: *www.mlc-wels.edu*

OAK HILLS CHRISTIAN COLLEGE B-2

Bemidji, MN 56601 (218) 751-8670 (218) 444-1311

Full-time: 75 men, 75 women	**Faculty:** 18
Part-time: 15 men, 20 women	**Tuition:** $16,980
Graduate: n/av	**Room & Board:** $6506
Application Deadline: see profile	
ACT: required	

Oak Hills Christian College, founded in 1946, is interdenominational. Its mission is integrating faith and learning through biblical training. The figures in the above capsule are approximate. Oak Hills Christian College awards the B.A., B.S. in biblical studies, biblical studies and applied psychology, applied studies, campus ministry, contemporary worship, contemporary Christian ministry, intercultural studies, pastoral ministry, and youth ministry. The school also awards associate and bachelor's degrees. Web: *www.oakhills.edu*

MISSOURI

CONCEPTION SEMINARY COLLEGE A-1

Conception, MO 64433 **(660) 944-3100** **(660) 944-2829**

Full-time: 85 men
Part-time: 2 men, 50 women
Graduate: n/av
Application Deadline: July 31
ACT: required
Faculty: 30
Tuition: $31,790
Room & Board: n/app

Conception Seminary College, founded in 1886, is affiliated with the Roman Catholic Church. Its mission is to prepare men who are discerning for the Roman Catholic priesthood. Conception Seminary College places emphasis on spiritual, personal, and academic formation. The figures in the above capsule are approximate. In addition to regional accreditation, the college is accredited by NCA. Conception Seminary College awards the B.A. in liberal arts, and also awards bachelor's degrees. Web: *www.conceptionabbey.org*

NORTH CAROLINA

MID-ATLANTIC CHRISTIAN UNIVERSITY F-2

Elizabeth City, NC 27909-4054 **(252) 334-2000** **(252) 334-2071**

Full-time: 87 men, 48 women
Part-time: 12 men, 22 women
Graduate: n/av
Application Deadline: n/av
SAT or ACT: required
Faculty: 23
Tuition: $15,300
Room & Board: $8400

Mid-Atlantic Christian University, founded in 1948, is affiliated with the Christian Church/Church of Christ. Its mission is to impact the world by transforming ordinary people into extraordinary Christian leaders. The figures in the above capsule are approximate. In addition to regional accreditation, the college is accredited by AABC and SACS. Mid-Atlantic Christian University awards the B.A., B.S., B.Th. in Biblical Exposition and cross-cultural ministry, Biblical exposition and general ministry, Biblical exposition and missions aviation, Biblical exposition and preaching, Biblical exposition with youth & family ministry, Biblical exposition & applied linguistics, Biblical studies with counseling & psychology, Biblical studies with leadership & administration, Biblical studies, and Biblical exposition. The school also awards associate and bachelor's degrees. Web: *www.macuniversity.edu*

NORTH DAKOTA

TRINITY BIBLE COLLEGE E-4

Ellendale, ND 58436 **(800) 523-1603** **(701) 349-5786**

Full-time: 131 men, 143 women
Part-time: 8 men, 25 women
Graduate: n/av
Application Deadline: August 15
Faculty: 30
Tuition: $15,506
Room & Board: $5746

Trinity Bible College, founded in 1948, is affiliated with the Assemblies of God. Its mission is to prepare pastors, church leaders, and Christian professionals in various fields in a Bible-based Pentecostal environment of academic excellence. In addition to regional accreditation, the college is accredited by AABC and NCACS. Trinity Bible College awards the B.A. in biblical studies, business administration, elementary education, ministerial studies, and missions. The figures in the above capsule are approximate. The school also awards associate and bachelor's degrees. Web: *www.trinitybiblecollege.edu*

OHIO

CINCINNATI CHRISTIAN UNIVERSITY A-5

Cincinnati, OH 45204-3200 **(800) 949-4CCU** **(513) 244-8111**

Full-time: 270 men, 236 women
Part-time: 85 men, 44 women
Graduate: 169 men, 86 women
Application Deadline: August 10
SAT or ACT: required
Faculty: 85
Tuition: $16,266
Room & Board: $7860

Cincinnati Christian University, founded in 1924, is affiliated with the Christian Churches/Churches of Christ. Its mission is to teach men and women to live by biblical principles and to equip and empower them with skills, insight, and vision to lead the church and impact society for Christ. The figures in the above capsule are approximate. In addition to regional accreditation, the college is accredited by AABC and NCA. Cincinnati Christian University awards the B.A., B.S., and B.Mus. in biblical studies (primary major), education, ministries, (second major), and signing interpreter's training program, psychology, preaching, youth ministry, worship, music, children's ministry, urban/intercultural ministry, music education and history. The school also awards associate, bachelor's, and master's degrees. Web: *www.CCUniversity.edu*

OHIO CHRISTIAN UNIVERSITY

Circleville, OH 43113 **(740) 474-8896**

Full-time: 372 men, 429 women
Part-time: 55 men, 75 women
Graduate: n/av
Application Deadline: May
SAT or ACT: required
Faculty: 135
Tuition: $18,940
Room & Board: $7898

Ohio Christian University, founded in 1948, is affiliated with the Churches of Christ in Christian Union (CCCU). Its mission is to provide a holistic Bible college education in the Wesleyan tradition that equips students to grow spiritually and intellectually and to serve effectively in society and the church. The figures in the above capsule are approximate. In addition to regional accreditation, the college is accredited by AABC and NCA. Ohio Christian University awards the B.A. in religion, business management, psychology, nursing, teacher education, international studies, ministries, music education, youth ministries, and christian ministries. The school also awards associate and bachelor's degrees. Web: *www.ohiochristian.edu*

PONTIFICAL COLLEGE JOSEPHINUM C-3

Columbus, OH 43235 **(614) 885-5585** **(614) 885-2307**

Full-time: 78 men
Part-time: n/av
Graduate: 51 men, 2 women
Application Deadline: July 31
SAT or ACT: required
Faculty: 41
Tuition: $21,038
Room & Board: $9300

Pontifical College Josephinum, founded in 1888, is affiliated the with

Roman Catholic Church. Its mission is to prepare young men for the priesthood. In addition to regional accreditation, the college is accredited by NCACS and ATS. Pontifical College Josephinum awards the B.A. in philosophy and the humanities (English literature, Hispanic studies, history, and classical studies). The figures in the above capsule are approximate. The school also awards bachelor's and master's degrees. Web: *pcj.edu*

OKLAHOMA

MID-AMERICA CHRISTIAN UNIVERSITY D-3

Oklahoma City, OK 73170 (405) 692-3800 (405) 692-3165

Full-time: 338 men, 387 women
Part-time: 87 men, 94 women
Graduate: 116 men, 158 women
Application Deadline: open
SAT or ACT: required
Faculty: 45
Tuition: $17,132
Room & Board: $7956

Mid-America Christian University, founded in 1953, is affiliated with Church of God in Anderson, Indiana. Its mission is to equip students to impact their world for Christ through achieving Bible-based academic excellence in a Christian environment so that students professionally serve in their chosen vocation/ministry. The figures in the above capsule are approximate. In addition to regional accreditation, the college is accredited by NCA. Mid-America Christian University awards the B.A. and B.S. in behavioral science, elementary education, English, music, performance, pastoral ministry, worship and music ministries, secondary education, specialized ministries, management and ethics, English/business, and business administration. The school also awards associate, bachelor's, and master's degrees. Web: *www.macu.edu*

SOUTHWESTERN CHRISTIAN UNIVERSITY

Bethany, OK 73008 (405) 789-7661 (405) 495-0078

Full-time: 91 men, 92 women
Part-time: 11 men, 15 women
Graduate: 58 men, 20 women
Application Deadline: open
ACT: required
Faculty: 35
Tuition: $15,430
Room & Board: $7700

Southwestern Christian University, founded in 1946, is affiliated with Pentecostal Holiness. Its mission is to educate and train for Christian service leading toward professional competence in the practice of various ministry forms. The figures in the above capsule are approximate. In addition to regional accreditation, the college is accredited by NCA. Southwestern Christian University awards the B.A. and B.S. and B.B.A. in Bibical studies, church growth, church music, music performace, missions, Christian education, Christian elementary education, pastoral ministry, youth ministry religion, Biblicial leadership, human and family services, business leadership, nonprofit organizational leadership, and business administration. The school also awards associate, bachelor's, and master's degrees. Web: *www.swcu.edu*

OREGON

MOUNT ANGEL ABBEY & SEMINARY B-2

St. Benedict, OR 97373 (503) 845-3030 (503) 845-3126

Full-time: 85 men
Part-time: n/av
Graduate: 87 men, 12 women
Application Deadline: July 15
Faculty: 40
Tuition: $19,589
Room & Board: $11,089

Mount Angel Abbey & Seminary, founded in 1889, is affiliated with the Roman Catholic Church. Its mission is to prepare students of the Roman Catholic priesthood for religious orders and dioceses. The figures in the above capsule are approximate. In addition to regional accreditation, the college is accredited by NASC. Mount Angel Abbey & Seminary awards the B.A. in philosophy and literature, and also awards bachelor's and master's degrees. Web: *www.seminary.mtangel.edu*

PENNSYLVANIA

CLARKS SUMMIT UNIVERSITY E-2
Summit University of Pennsylvania

South Abington Twp., PA 18411 (570) 586-2400 (570) 586-1753

Full-time: 192 men, 243 women
Part-time: 68 men, 86 women
Graduate: 213 men, 87 women
Application Deadline: August 15
SAT or ACT: required
Faculty: 30
Tuition: $22,510
Room & Board: $5970

Clarks Summit University, formerly Summit University, founded in 1932, is affiliated with the Baptist Church. Its mission is to prepare men and women for service in a wide variety of ministries including teaching, counseling, pastors, missionaries, Christian education workers, church musicians, and secretaries. The figures in the above capsule are approximate. In addition to regional accreditation, the college is accredited by AABC and MSACS. Clarks Summit University awards the B.S. in Bible and B.S.M. in church music, communications, elementary and early childhood teacher education, pre-K teacher education, general missions, local church ministries, outreach and evangelism pastor, pastoral ministry, pastor of Christian education, preseminary, secondary social studies teacher education, secondary science teacher education, secondary math teacher education, secondary english teacher education, health and physical education teacher education, music teacher education, secretarial ministries, sports ministries, youth pastor, precounseling, general ministries, women's ministries, early childhood education, business, and office professionals. The school also awards associate, bachelor's, master's, and doctorate degrees. Web: *www.bbc.edu*

LANCASTER BIBLE COLLEGE E-3

Lancaster, PA 17601 (717) 569-7071 (717) 560-8213

Full-time: 302 men, 286 women
Part-time: 110 men, 105 women
Graduate: 90 men, 85 women
Application Deadline: open
SAT or ACT: required
Faculty: 86
Tuition: $21,500
Room & Board: $8580

Lancaster Bible College, founded in 1933, is nondenominational. Its mission is to educate Christian men and women to live according to a biblical worldview and to serve through professional Christian ministries. The figures in the above capsule are approximate. In addition to regional accreditation, the college is accredited by AABC and MSA. Lancaster Bible College awards the B.S. in Bible and B.S.Ed. in Bible education, Bible ministry, children and family ministry, counseling (professional), cross-cultural ministry, elementary education/early level, elementary education/middle level, music education, music performance, pastoral ministry, pre-seminary, social work, spiritual formation and discipleship, student ministry, TESOL, women in Christian ministry, and worship arts. The school also awards associate, bachelor's, and master's degrees. Web: *www.lbc.edu*

SAINT CHARLES BORROMEO SEMINARY F-3

Wynnewood, PA 19096 (610) 785-6252 (610) 617-9267

Full-time: 90 men
Part-time: 25 men, 35 women
Graduate: 90 men, 30 women
Application Deadline: July 1
Faculty: 65
Tuition: $19,500
Room & Board: $12,300

Saint Charles Borromeo Seminary, founded in 1832, is affiliated with the Roman Catholic Church. Its mission is to prepare and educate men for the Roman Catholic priesthood and to provide undergraduate and graduate programs for men and women pursuing theological studies. In addition to regional accreditation, the college is accredited by MSACS. Saint Charles Borromeo Seminary awards the B.A. in philosophy. The figures in the above capsule are approximate. The school also awards bachelor's and master's degrees. Web: *www.scs.edu*

SOUTH CAROLINA

COLUMBIA INTERNATIONAL UNIVERSITY C-3

Columbia, SC 29230 (803) 754-4100 (803) 786-4029

Full-time: 215 men, 259 women
Part-time: 33 men, 43 women
Graduate: 214 men, 186 women
Application Deadline: open
ACT: required
Faculty: 49
Tuition: $21,490
Room & Board: $7760

Columbia International University, founded in 1923, is multidenominational. Its mission is to prepare students to grow in spiritual maturity, Bible knowledge, and ministry skills in preparation for vocational or lay Christian ministry. The figures in the above capsule are approximate. In addition to regional accreditation, the college is accredited by AABC and SACS. Columbia International University awards the B.A. and B.S. in Bible, general studies, intercultural studies, psychology, biblical languages, music, Bible teaching, youth ministry, middle eastern studies, family and church education, teacher education, humanities, pastoral ministries, and communications. The school also awards associate, bachelor's, master's, and doctorate degrees. Web: *www.ciu.edu*

TENNESSEE

JOHNSON UNIVERSITY/TENNESSEE E-3

Knoxville, TN 37998 (865) 573-4517

Full-time: 408 men, 408 women
Part-time: 15 men, 16 women
Graduate: 47 men, 60 women
Application Deadline: June 1
SAT or ACT: required
Faculty: 62
Tuition: $13,950
Room & Board: $5820

Johnson University/Tennessee, founded in 1893, is affiliated with the Christian Churches and Churches of Christ. Its mission is to educate students for specialized Christian ministries. The figures in the above capsule are approximate. In addition to regional accreditation, the college is accredited by AABC and SACS. Johnson University/Tennessee awards the B.A. and B.S. in Bible. In addition, five professional programs require a second major, in counseling, preaching, as well as interdisciplinary major with focus on teacher education, music, and youth ministry/preaching. The school also awards associate, bachelor's, and master's degrees. Web: *www.johnsonu.edu*

WELCH COLLEGE C-2

Nashville, TN 37205 (615) 844-5000 (615) 269-6028

Full-time: 100 men, 92 women
Part-time: 54 men, 36 women
Graduate: n/av
Application Deadline: open
ACT: required
Faculty: 55
Tuition: $17,920
Room & Board: $7260

Welch College, founded in 1942, is affiliated with National Association of Free Will Baptists. Its mission is to educate leaders to serve Christ, His Church and His world through Biblical thought and life. The figures given in the above capsule are approximate. In addition to regional accreditation, the college is accredited by AABC, SACS, ABHE, and CHEA. Welch College awards the B.A. and B.S. in biblical studies, biblical and ministry studies, business administration, church music, church music and youth ministry, English, elementary education, music education, music performance, sports medicine, physical education, secondary English education, psychology, and learning. The school also awards associate and bachelor's degrees. Web: *www.welch.edu*

TEXAS

AUSTIN GRADUATE SCHOOL OF THEOLOGY D-3

Austin, TX 78752 (512) 476-2772 (512) 476-3919

Full-time: 4 men
Part-time: 15 men, 7 women
Graduate: 25 men, 5 women
Application Deadline: July 1
Faculty: 10
Tuition: $8575
Room & Board: n/app

Austin Graduate School of Theology, founded in 1917, is affiliated with the Church of Christ. Its mission is to equip ministers and other Christians for service in the kingdom of God. The figures in the above capsule are approximate. In addition to regional accreditation, the college is accredited by SACS. Austin Graduate School of Theology awards the B.A. in Christian studies, also awards bachelor's and master's degrees. Web: *www.austingrad.edu*

BAPTIST MISSIONARY ASSOCIATION THEOLOGICAL SEMINARY E-2

Jacksonville, TX 75766 (903) 586-2501 (903) 586-0378

Full-time: 23 men, 1 women
Part-time: 26 men, 22 women
Graduate: 49 men, 8 women
Application Deadline: open
Faculty: 13
Tuition: $7290
Room & Board: n/app

Baptist Missionary Association Theological Seminary, founded in 1955, is affiliated with the Baptist Missionary Association. Its mission is to train individuals for Christian ministry. The figures in the above capsule are approximate. In addition to regional accreditation, the college is accredited by SACS. Baptist Missionary Association Theological Seminary awards the B.A.R. in religion, and also awards associate, bachelor's, and master's degrees. Web:*www.bmats.edu*

CRISWELL COLLEGE D-2

Dallas, TX 75246 (214) 821-5433 (214) 370-0497

Full-time: 140 men, 30 women
Part-time: 160 men, 50 women
Graduate: 100 men, 20 women
Application Deadline: July 15
SAT or ACT: required
Faculty: 27
Tuition: $13,090
Room & Board: $11,000

Criswell College, founded in 1970, is affiliated with the Southern Baptist of Texas Convention. Its mission is to educate and train laymen and full-time Christian workers in biblical, theological, and professional studies so they can serve effectively in evangelistic, educational, pastoral, and missionary vocations of the Christian church. The figures in the above capsule are approximate. In addition to regional accreditation, the college is accredited by SACS. Criswell College awards the B.A. in biblical studies, counseling, missions, evangelism, pastoral, and urban ministries. The school also awards associate, bachelor's, and master's degrees. Web: *www.criswell.edu*

SOUTHWESTERN ASSEMBLIES OF GOD UNIVERSITY D-2

Waxahachie, TX 75165 (972) 825-4634 (972) 923-0006

Full-time: 587 men, 604 women
Part-time: 145 men, 122 women
Graduate: 168 men, 148 women
Application Deadline: open
SAT or ACT: required
Faculty: 129
Tuition: $38,035
Room & Board: $6150

Southwestern Assemblies of God University, founded in 1927, is affiliated with the Assemblies of God. Its mission is to prepare undergraduate and graduate students spiritually, academically, professionally, and cross culturally so as to successfully fill evangelistic, missionary and church ministry roles and to provide quality educational and professional Christian service wherever needed throughout the world. The figures in the above capsule are approximate. In addition to regional accreditation, the college is accredited by AABC and SACS. Southwestern Assemblies of God University awards the B.A. and B.S. in accounting, ancient studies, Biblical studies, business administration, children & family ministries, and church ministries, church planting & revitalization, communication, counseling, counseling ministries, criminal justice, digital media arts, drama, education, bilingual education, elementary education, middle & secondary, English language arts/reading, social studies/history, music education, instrumental, piano, vocal, physical education, English history, human services, management, management information systems, marketing, media ministries, music ministries, music performance, instrumental, piano, vocal, pastoral ministries, professional development, psychology, social work, sports management, theological studies, world ministries, youth & student ministries. The school also awards associate, bachelor's, and master's degrees. Web: *www.sagu.edu*

WISCONSIN

MARANATHA BAPTIST UNIVERSITY D-4

Watertown, WI 53094 (920) 261-9300 (920) 261-9109

Full-time: 350 men, 404 women
Part-time: 31 men, 45 women
Graduate: 27 men, 3 women
Application Deadline: n/av
ACT: required
Faculty: 57
Tuition: $14,260
Room & Board: $6720

Maranatha Baptist University, founded in 1968, is affiliated with the Baptist Church. Its mission is nurture students who are spiritually and academically prepared to serve the Lord. We want to develop servants of Christ who are disciplined, creative, and passionate about the field to which they have been called. The figure in the above capsule are approximate. In addition to regional accreditation, the college is accredited by NCA. Maranatha Baptist University awards the B.A. and B.S. in Bible, church ministries, education, general studies, fine arts, business, nursing, office administration, biology, and premed. The school also awards associate, bachelor's, and master's degrees. Web: *www.mbu.edu*

AIR FORCE

In the Air Force ROTC program, young men and women may earn commissions while attending college. The amount of academic credit given for Air Force ROTC varies from school to school.

Most new Air Force officers come through the Air Force ROTC program. It offers students the opportunity to attend a civilian college while studying officership as part of their undergraduate curriculum.

The AFROTC program begins with the General Military Course. Freshmen or sophomores attend one hour of ROTC classes and one to two hours of leadership laboratory weekly. During these first two years, study is focused on the history of the Air Force and the part it plays in the world today. During the summer between sophomore and junior years, students attend a four-week basic training course located at an Air Force base.

The Professional Officer Course is completed during the junior and senior years. Study includes management principles and defense policy and offers the opportunity for managing, organizing, directing, and evaluating the cadet corps activities. Cadets who are medically qualified will have the opportunity to compete for pilot or navigator positions. Upon graduation, students are commissioned as Second Lieutenants.

For academically qualified students in selected majors, the AFROTC offers scholarships, including tuition, fees and books, and a monthly nontaxable allowance during the school year.

The majority of scholarships are awarded in the technical degree areas of engineering and computer science, but there are opportunities in nontechnical areas as well. Scholarships are based on individual merit, not financial need. Those who receive a scholarship must still apply and be accepted by the school they wish to attend and notify the AFROTC headquarters of their selection.

The scholarship program is broken down into different types and durations. All scholarships include full or partial tuition, fees, textbook allowance, and $500 per month tax-free allowance during the academic year. Type 1 pays full tuition at any school offering AFROTC. Type 2 pays tuition and fees up to a maximum of $18,000 per year. There are two variations of the Type 7 scholarship. A Type 7 scholarship winner can attend any post-secondary institution (public or private) where tuition does not exceed $9,000 per year, or he/she can attend any public post-secondary institution where the student qualifies for in-state tuition rates.

The application deadline is December 1 of the senior year, but priority consideration is given to those who get the application in early. AFROTC only accepts on-line applications and they are available during the spring prior to the senior year of high school.

Further information can be obtained from the professor of aerospace studies at any of the host campuses where Air Force ROTC is offered. The listing that follows represents the host schools that offer these programs. Hundreds more schools have crosstown agreements with these institutions to make AFROTC more accessible to students. Please be sure to contact the school directly for more details. You may also find useful and current information at the Air Force Reserve Officer Training Corps web site, *www.afrotc.com*.

ALABAMA

- Alabama State University
- Auburn University at Auburn
- Samford University
- Troy University
- Tuskegee University
- University of Alabama
- University of South Alabama

ALASKA

- University of Alaska - Anchorage

ARIZONA

- Arizona State University
- Embry-Riddle Aeronautical University
- Northern Arizona University
- University of Arizona

ARKANSAS

- University of Arkansas

CALIFORNIA

- California State University, Fresno
- California State University, Sacramento
- California State University, San Bernadino
- Loyola Marymount University
- San Diego State University
- San Jose State University
- University of California at Berkeley
- University of California at Los Angeles
- University of Southern California

COLORADO

- Colorado State University
- University of Colorado at Boulder

CONNECTICUT

- University of Connecticut
- Yale University

DELAWARE

- University of Delaware

DISTRICT OF COLUMBIA

- Howard University

FLORIDA

- Embry-Riddle Aeronautical University
- Florida State University
- University of Central Florida
- University of Florida
- University of Miami
- University of South Florida

GEORGIA

- Georgia Institute of Technology
- University of Georgia
- Valdosta State University

HAWAII

- University of Hawaii at Manoa

ILLINOIS

- Illinois Institute of Technology
- Southern Illinois University
- University of Illinois at Champaign/Urbana

INDIANA

- Indiana State University
- Indiana University
- Purdue University
- University of Notre Dame

IOWA

- Iowa State University
- University of Iowa

KANSAS

- Kansas State University
- University of Kansas

KENTUCKY

- University of Kentucky
- University of Louisville

LOUISIANA

- Louisiana State University and Agricultural and Mechanical College
- Louisiana Tech University
- Tulane University

MARYLAND

- University of Maryland

MASSACHUSETTS

- Boston University
- Massachusetts Institute of Technology
- University of Massachusetts
- University of Massachusetts, Lowell
- Worcester Polytechnic Institute

MICHIGAN

- Michigan State University
- University of Michigan

MINNESOTA

- University of Minnesota/Duluth
- University of Minnesota
- University of St. Thomas

MISSISSIPPI

- Jackson State University
- Mississippi State University
- University of Mississippi

MISSOURI

- Missouri University of Science and Technology
- Saint Louis University
- University of Missouri/Columbia

MONTANA

- Montana State University

NEBRASKA

- University of Nebraska at Lincoln
- University of Nebraska at Omaha

NEVADA

- University of Nevada—Las Vegas

NEW HAMPSHIRE

- University of New Hampshire

NEW JERSEY

- New Jersey Institute of Technology
- Rutgers University

NEW MEXICO

- New Mexico State University
- University of New Mexico

NEW YORK

- Clarkson University
- Cornell University
- Manhattan College
- Rensselaer Polytechnic Institute
- Rochester Institute of Technology
- Syracuse University

NORTH CAROLINA

- Duke University
- East Carolina University
- Fayetteville State University
- North Carolina A&T State University
- North Carolina State University
- University of North Carolina at Chapel Hill
- University of North Carolina at Charlotte

NORTH DAKOTA

- North Dakota State University

OHIO

- Bowling Green University
- Kent State University
- Miami University
- Ohio State University, The
- Ohio University
- University of Cincinnati
- Wright State University

OKLAHOMA

- Oklahoma State University
- University of Oklahoma

OREGON

- Oregon State University
- University of Portland

PENNSYLVANIA

- Penn State University/Main Campus
- Saint Joseph's University
- University of Pittsburgh
- Wilkes University

PUERTO RICO

- University of Puerto Rico/Mayaguez
- University of Puerto Rico/Río Piedras

SOUTH CAROLINA

- Charleston Southern University
- The Citadel
- Clemson University
- University of South Carolina/Columbia

SOUTH DAKOTA

- South Dakota State University

TENNESSEE

- Tennessee State University
- University of Memphis
- University of Tennessee

TEXAS

- Angelo State University
- Baylor University
- Texas A & M University
- Texas Christian University
- Texas State University/San Marcos
- Texas Tech University
- University of Houston
- University of North Texas
- University of Texas at Austin
- University of Texas at San Antonio

UTAH

- Brigham Young University
- University of Utah
- Utah State University

VERMONT

- Norwich University

VIRGINIA

- University of Virginia
- Virginia Military Institute
- Virginia Polytechnic Institute

WASHINGTON

- Central Washington University
- University of Washington
- Washington State University

WEST VIRGINIA

- West Virginia University

WISCONSIN

- Marquette University
- University of Wisconsin/Madison

WYOMING

- University of Wyoming

ARMY

The Army Reserve Officers' Training Corps (ROTC) provides college students with the opportunity to combine leadership and management training with their other academic studies. The curriculum, which consists of a series of classroom and hands-on leadership training experiences, provides students with the necessary foundation to serve successfully in positions of responsibility in either the U.S. Army or the corporate world.

Those with a strong academic background, an active mindset, and the ability to rapidly assimilate information thrive in the program. These scholar-athlete-leaders note that the leadership skills developed through their participation in the program are further honed during their period of service as Army officers. After service as an Army lieutenant, many graduates elect to continue their service in uniform. Others elect to enter the corporate world where their leadership skills and experience as ROTC-trained Army officers allow them to advance rapidly.

Although the program is designed to be completed in four years, students may complete all requirements within a two-year period through participation in a summer training session called the Leaders' Training Course, normally held during the summer between the sophomore and junior years. A generous series of merit-based scholarships that cover tuition, fees, textbooks, and supplies exist to help students and their families defray the cost of college. For more information on the program, call (800) USA-ROTC (872–7682), or contact the professor of military science at a college that offers Army ROTC. Detailed information about the program is also available at *www.goarmy.com/rotc*.

ALABAMA

- Alabama A&M University
- Auburn University
- Auburn University at Montgomery
- Jacksonville State University
- Marion Military Institute
- The University of Alabama
- Tuskegee University
- University of Alabama at Birmingham
- University of North Alabama
- University of South Alabama

ALASKA

- University of Alaska/Anchorage
- University of Alaska/Fairbanks

ARIZONA

- Arizona State University
- Northern Arizona University
- University of Arizona

ARKANSAS

- Arkansas State University
- University of Arkansas
- University of Arkansas at Pine Bluff
- University of Central Arkansas

CALIFORNIA

- California Polytechnic State University at San Luis Obispo
- California State University at Fresno
- California State University at Fullerton
- Claremont McKenna College
- San Diego State University
- Santa Clara University
- University of California at Berkeley
- University of California at Davis
- University of California at Los Angeles
- University of California at Santa Barbara
- University of San Francisco
- University of Southern California

COLORADO

- Colorado State University
- University of Colorado at Boulder
- University of Colorado at Colorado Springs

CONNECTICUT

- University of Connecticut
- University of New Haven

DELAWARE

- University of Delaware

DISTRICT OF COLUMBIA

- Georgetown University
- Howard University

FLORIDA

- Embry-Riddle Aeronautical University
- Florida A&M University
- Florida Institute of Technology
- Florida International University
- Florida Southern College
- Florida State University
- University of Central Florida
- University of Florida
- University of South Florida
- University of Tampa
- University of West Florida

GEORGIA

- Augusta University
- Columbus State University
- Fort Valley State University
- Georgia Institute of Technology
- Georgia Military College
- Georgia Southern University
- Georgia State University
- University of Georgia
- University of North Georgia

HAWAII

- University of Hawaii at Manoa

IDAHO

- Boise State University
- University of Idaho

ILLINOIS

- Eastern Illinois University
- Illinois State University
- Loyola University
- Northern Illinois University
- Southern Illinois University at Carbondale
- Southern Illinois University at Edwardsville
- University of Illinois at Chicago
- University of Illinois at Urbana-Champaign
- Western Illinois University
- Wheaton College

INDIANA

- Ball State University
- Indiana University-Purdue University at Indianapolis
- Indiana University at Bloomington
- Purdue University
- Rose-Hulman Institute of Technology
- University of Notre Dame

IOWA

- Iowa State University
- University of Iowa
- University of Northern Iowa

KANSAS

- Kansas State University
- Pittsburg State University
- University of Kansas

KENTUCKY

- Eastern Kentucky University
- Morehead State University
- University of Kentucky
- University of Louisville
- Western Kentucky University

LOUISIANA

- Grambling State University
- Louisiana State University
- Northwestern State University
- Southern University and A&M College
- Tulane University

MAINE

- University of Maine

MARYLAND

- Bowie State University
- Loyola University Maryland
- McDaniel College
- Morgan State University
- The Johns Hopkins University
- University of Maryland at College Park

MASSACHUSETTS

- Boston University
- Massachusetts Institute of Technology
- Northeastern University
- University of Massachusetts
- Worcester Polytechnic Institute

MICHIGAN

- Central Michigan University
- Eastern Michigan University
- Michigan State University
- Michigan Technological University
- Northern Michigan University
- University of Michigan
- Western Michigan University

MINNESOTA

- Minnesota State University, Mankato
- Saint John's University
- University of Minnesota/Twin Cities

MISSISSIPPI

- Alcorn State University
- Jackson State University
- Mississippi State University
- University of Mississippi
- University of Southern Mississippi

MISSOURI

- Lincoln University
- Missouri State University
- Missouri University of Science and Technology
- Missouri Western State University
- Truman State University
- University of Central Missouri
- University of Missouri/Columbia
- Washington University
- Wentworth Military Academy

MONTANA

- Montana State University
- University of Montana

NEBRASKA

- Creighton University
- University of Nebraska at Lincoln

NEVADA

- University of Nevada/Reno

NEW HAMPSHIRE

- University of New Hampshire

NEW JERSEY

- Princeton University
- Rutgers University
- Seton Hall University

NEW MEXICO

- New Mexico Military Institute
- New Mexico State University
- University of New Mexico

NEW YORK

- Canisius College
- Clarkson University
- Cornell University
- Fordham University
- Hofstra University
- Niagara University
- Rochester Institute of Technology
- St. Bonaventure University
- St. John's University New York
- Siena College
- State University of New York (SUNY)/Brockport
- Syracuse University

NORTH CAROLINA

- Appalachian State University
- Campbell University
- Duke University
- East Carolina University
- Elizabeth City State University
- North Carolina Agricultural and Technical State University
- North Carolina State University
- Saint Augustine's College
- University of North Carolina at Chapel Hill
- University of North Carolina at Charlotte
- Wake Forest University

NORTH DAKOTA

- North Dakota State University
- University of North Dakota

OHIO

- Bowling Green State University
- Capital University
- Central State University
- John Carroll University
- Kent State University
- The Ohio State University
- Ohio University
- The University of Akron
- University of Cincinnati
- University of Dayton
- University of Toledo
- Wright State University
- Xavier University

OKLAHOMA

- Cameron University
- Oklahoma State University
- University of Central Oklahoma
- University of Oklahoma

OREGON

- Oregon State University
- University of Oregon
- University of Portland

PENNSYLVANIA

- Bucknell University
- Dickinson College
- Drexel University
- Edinboro University of Pennsylvania
- Gannon University
- Indiana University of Pennsylvania
- Lehigh University
- Lock Haven University of Pennsylvania
- Pennsylvania State University
- Shippensburg University
- Slippery Rock University
- Temple University
- University of Pittsburgh
- University of Scranton
- Valley Forge Military College
- Widener University

PUERTO RICO

- University of Puerto Rico/Mayaguez
- University of Puerto Rico/Río Piedras

RHODE ISLAND

- Providence College
- University of Rhode Island

SOUTH CAROLINA

- The Citadel
- Clemson University
- Furman University
- Presbyterian College
- South Carolina State University
- University of South Carolina
- Wofford College

SOUTH DAKOTA

- South Dakota School of Mines and Technology
- South Dakota State University
- University of South Dakota

TENNESSEE

- Austin Peay State University
- Carson-Newman College
- East Tennessee State University
- Middle Tennessee State University
- Tennessee Tech University
- University of Memphis
- University of Tennessee at Knoxville
- University of Tennessee at Martin
- Vanderbilt University

TEXAS

- Prairie View A&M University
- Saint Mary's University
- Sam Houston State University
- Stephen F. Austin State University
- Tarleton State University
- Texas A&M University-College Station
- Texas A&M-Corpus Christi
- Texas A&M University at Kingsville
- Texas Christian University
- Texas State University
- Texas Tech University
- University of Houston
- The University of Texas at Arlington
- The University of Texas at Austin
- University of Texas at El Paso
- University of Texas at San Antonio
- University of Texas-Pan American

UTAH

- Brigham Young University
- University of Utah
- Weber State University

VERMONT

- Norwich University
- University of Vermont

VIRGINIA

- College of William and Mary
- George Mason University
- Hampton University
- James Madison University
- Norfolk State University
- Old Dominion University
- University of Richmond
- University of Virginia
- Virginia Military Institute
- Virginia State University
- Virginia Tech

WASHINGTON

- Central Washington University
- Eastern Washington University
- Gonzaga University
- Pacific Lutheran University
- Seattle University
- University of Washington
- Washington State University

WEST VIRGINIA

- Marshall University
- West Virginia State University
- West Virginia University

WISCONSIN

- Marquette University
- University of Wisconsin/La Crosse
- University of Wisconsin/Madison
- University of Wisconsin/Oshkosh
- University of Wisconsin/Stevens Point

WYOMING

- University of Wyoming

NAVY

The NROTC Program educates and trains qualified young men and women for service as commissioned officers in the unrestricted line Navy or Marine Corps. Two programs are available: the NROTC Scholarship Program and the NROTC College Program.

The NROTC Scholarship Program plays an important role in preparing young men and women for leadership and management positions in an increasingly technical Navy and Marine Corps. The four-year NROTC Scholarship Program is available to qualified students who graduate from high school before August 1 of the year they intend to start college. The two-year NROTC Scholarship Program is available to qualified college sophmores who have completed one year of differential and integral calculus with a grade of C or better and maintain a minimum GPA of 2.5.

Selected applicants for NROTC Scholarship Programs (four-year and two-year) are awarded scholarships through a highly competitive national selection process, and receive full tuition, fees, book stipend, and other financial benefits at many of the country's leading colleges and universities. Upon graduation, midshipmen are commissioned as officers in the unrestricted line Navy or Marine Corps.

Students selected for the NROTC Scholarship Program make their own arrangements for college enrollment and room and board, and take the normal course load required by the college or university for degree completion. Additionally, scholarship midshipmen are required to follow specific academic guidelines. Full information concerning the NROTC Scholarship Program is available from any of the colleges and universities with NROTC units or from Navy and Marine Corps recruiters.

For information on the NROTC scholarship programs, call 1-800-USA-NAVY or 1-800-NAV-ROTC, e-mail *PNSC_NROTC.scholarship@navy.mil*; or visit *www.nrotc.navy.mil*. Electronic application for the four-year scholarship program must be submitted by January 31.

The NROTC College Program may be either two or four years. Additional points include:

- Applicants are selected from students already attending or accepted by colleges with the NROTC program.
- Students selected for "advance standing" receive a stipend for a maximum of 20 months. Advance standing is only available starting in the junior year of college. Stipend per academic month is $350 junior year and $400 senior year.
- Students will complete naval science and other university courses, a few specific university courses, and attend one summer training session, normally at sea for Navy midshipmen and in Quantico, VA for Marine Corps midshipmen.

The following list shows the colleges and universities that have an NROTC unit on campus. Many more institutions offer the program through cross-town arrangements. We recommend that you visit *www.nrotc.navy.mil* for a listing of participating colleges and universities. Contact the schools directly for the most current and accurate information.

ALABAMA
- Auburn University
- Tuskegee University

ARIZONA
- Arizona State University
- University of Arizona

CALIFORNIA
- San Diego State University
- University of California/Berkeley
- University of California/Los Angeles
- University of San Diego
- University of Southern California

COLORADO
- University of Colorado

CONNECTICUT
- Yale University

DISTRICT OF COLUMBIA
- George Washington University

FLORIDA
- Embry Riddle Aeronautical University
- Florida A&M University
- Jacksonville University
- University of Florida
- University of South Florida

GEORGIA
- Georgia Institute of Technology
- Morehouse College
- Savannah State College

IDAHO
- University of Idaho

ILLINOIS
- Illinois Institute of Technology
- Northwestern University
- University of Illinois at Urbana-Champaign

INDIANA
- Purdue University
- University of Notre Dame

IOWA
- Iowa State University

KANSAS
- University of Kansas

LOUISIANA
- Southern University and A&M College
- Tulane University

MAINE
- Maine Maritime Academy

MARYLAND
- University of Maryland, College Park
- University of Maryland, Baltimore County

MASSACHUSETTS
- Boston University
- College of the Holy Cross
- Massachusetts Institute of Technology

MICHIGAN
- University of Michigan

MINNESOTA
- University of Minnesota

MISSISSIPPI
- University of Mississippi

MISSOURI
- University of Missouri

NEBRASKA
- University of Nebraska at Lincoln

NEW JERSEY
- Rutgers University, New Brunswick

NEW MEXICO
- University of New Mexico

NEW YORK
- Cornell University
- Rensselaer Polytechnic Institute
- State University of New York/Maritime College
- University of Rochester

NORTH CAROLINA
- Duke University
- North Carolina State University
- University of North Carolina

OHIO
- Miami University
- Ohio State University

OKLAHOMA

- University of Oklahoma

OREGON

- Oregon State University

PENNSYLVANIA

- Carnegie Mellon University
- Pennsylvania State University
- University of Pennsylvania
- Villanova University

SOUTH CAROLINA

- The Citadel
- University of South Carolina

TENNESSEE

- University of Memphis
- Vanderbilt University

TEXAS

- Prairie View A&M University
- Rice University
- Texas A&M University
- University of Texas

UTAH

- University of Utah

VERMONT

- Norwich University

VIRGINIA

- Hampton University
- Norfolk State University
- Old Dominion University
- University of Virginia
- Virginia Military Institute
- Virginia Polytechnic Institute and State University

WASHINGTON

- University of Washington

WISCONSIN

- Marquette University
- University of Wisconsin

ENROLLMENT IN CANADIAN SCHOOLS

Recently, Canadian universities hosted 979,000 full-time students and 312,000 part-time students. International students account for more than 6 percent of full-time undergraduate students and more than 18 percent at the graduate level. Most Canadian universities admit international students—although some have a quota on the number they will accept—and will give interested students information on how their academic qualifications are equated with Canadian requirements.

Universities Canada, formerly known as the Association of Universities and Colleges of Canada (AUCC) represents 97 universities and university-level colleges. These institutions account for almost 99 percent of the total university enrollment in Canada. Almost all Canadian colleges are coeducational. This section contains individual profiles for those English-language universities that enroll more than 10,000 students.

Affiliated with each of these universities are a number of general, theological, or residential colleges, which also have been listed here. The names and addresses of the three French-speaking colleges with enrollments of more than 26,000 may be found at the end of this introduction.

Admissions Requirements

Each university has its own entrance requirements and will assess you on an individual basis. The university will determine the equivalency of your academic credentials. There is no nationwide set of entrance exams. For more details about this or any other part of the application process, contact the registrar at the university you wish to attend.

Admissions Procedure

Once you have determined which universities meet your needs, contact the registrar's office at each institution to obtain an application for a bachelor's program or a professional degree. If you anticipate pursuing postgraduate studies in Canada, you may obtain more information by contacting the dean of graduate studies at the universities that interest you. It is important to apply early. Remember that the Canadian academic year usually starts in September. Some programs, however, do admit students to courses that start in January and May.

Universities Canada's website *www.univcan.ca* has links to the web pages of all Canadian universities, the majority of which accept applications via email.

To study at a Canadian university, you will need a study permit. You may also need a visitor's visa, which will be issued to you at the same time as your study permit. To apply for a study permit, please contact your nearest Canadian diplomatic post.

You will have to arrange for medical coverage before you arrive in Canada. Medical coverage varies from province to province and sometimes from university to university within each province. Please ask an official at the nearest Canadian diplomatic post for detailed information. Also, check whether the universities you are applying to have any medical insurance plans for international students.

Degrees Offered

Canadian universities, like those in the United States, grant three levels of degrees: bachelor's and first professional, master's, and doctoral as well as undergraduate certificates and diplomas and graduate diploma programs.

Earning the first degree can take three to five years. A general, or unspecialized, program leading to a Bachelor of Arts or Bachelor of Science usually can be completed in three years. An honors degree, earned in a specialized program, usually requires four years. Students must meet more rigorous requirements to enter an honors-degree program and must maintain high grades to remain in it. First professional degrees in some fields may take more than four years to earn, and students may be required to undertake two or three years of university study before enrolling in the professional program. Students who enter graduate programs with a general degree usually must study a year longer than those with honors degrees. Undergraduate diplomas and certificates may be from one to three years' duration and may (although not necessarily) be used as a basis for entry to a degree program. A graduate diploma may be considered as conferring a qualification that is intermediate between the bachelor's (or first professional degree) and master's degree. It may be completed in as little as two or as long as three academic years.

Organizations

Virtually all universities have organizations for international students, and sponsor international student centers and advisers. There also are national organizations that aid international students, including the World University Service of Canada and the Canadian Bureau for International Education, which arranges for representatives to meet international students arriving at Canadian airports.

Tuition, Fees, and Aid

Universities and colleges are heavily subsidized by provincial and federal governments, and tuition fees actually cover one third of university operating costs. Canadian institutions charge different fees for different programs, unlike American institutions, which charge the same tuition regardless of the program of study. Each profile in this book lists the range of tuitions, which may or may not include student fees. Some universities have higher fees for international students, and where that is the case, the profile includes just the international fees. All costs are given in Canadian (CDN) dollars. In all cases, you should check with the university in which you are interested to obtain the most up-to-date information about tuition and room-and-board charges.

Most awards available to international students through Canadian universities or from the Canadian government are restricted to graduate and post graduate studies. Some of the scholarship programs for international students to study in Canada include the Commonwealth Scholarship and Fellowship Plan, the Canadian International Development Agency awards, the Government of Canada awards program of cultural exchanges and the Programme canadien de bourses de la Francophonie. Students interested in applying for aid should contact a Canadian diplomatic mission in their home countries and, for information on cultural exchange programs, their own nation's education department or ministry.

Additional Information

Universities Canada
(*formerly Association of Universities and Colleges in Canada*)
1710-350 Albert Street
Ottawa, ON, K1R 1B1 Canada
(613) 563-1236
Fax: (613) 563-9745
Email: info@univcan.ca
www.univcan.ca

Canadian Bureau for International Education
220 Laurier West, Suite 1550
Ottawa, ON K1P 5Z9 Canada
(613) 237-4820
Fax: (613) 237-1073
Email: communication@cbie.ca
www.cbie.ca

Canada Immigration & Citizenship
www.cic.gc.ca
(publications include *Studying in Canada: Visas, Work and Immigration for International Students*, downloadable pdf publication)

Consulate General of Canada in New York
1251 Avenue of the Americas
Concourse Level (between 49th & 50th Streets, Midtown Manhattan)
New York, NY 10020-1175
(212) 596-1628
Fax: (212) 596-1790
Monday–Friday, 9am–5pm
Email: cngnyg@international.gc.ca
www.can-am.gc.ca/new-york

The Department of Foreign Affairs and International Trade Enquiries Service (SXCI)
125 Sussex Drive
Ottawa, ON K1A 0G2 Canada
(613) 996-9709
1 (800) 267-8376
Fax: (613) 996-9709
Email: enqserv@international.gc.ca
www.international.gc.ca/international/index.aspx

Social Sciences and Humanities Research Council of Canada
350 Albert Street
P.O. Box 1610
Ottawa, ON K1P 6G4 Canada
(613) 992-0691
Email: research@sshrc-crsh.gc.ca
www.sshrc-crsh.gc.ca

Statistics Canada
150 Tunney's Pasture Driveway
Ottawa, ON K1A 0T6 Canada
Monday–Friday, 8:30am–4:30pm
1 (800) 263-1136
Or (514) 283-8300 (international)
Fax: (514) 283-9350
Email: infostats@statcan.gc.ca
www.statcan.ca

World University Service of Canada
1404 Scott Street
Ottawa, ON K1Y 4M8 Canada
(613) 798-7477
(800) 267-8699
Fax: (613) 798-0990
Email: wusc@wusc.ca
www.wusc.ca

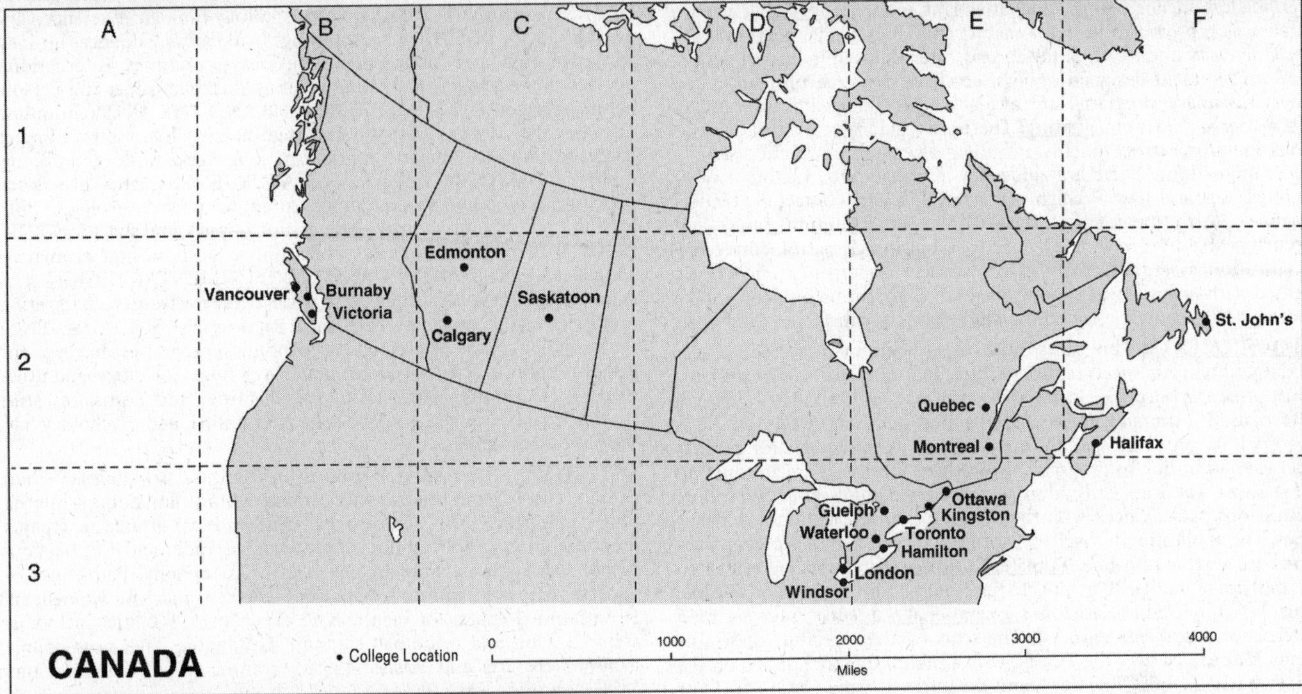

CARLETON UNIVERSITY E-3

www.carleton.ca

Ottawa, ON K1S 5B6 (613) 520-3609

Fax: (613) 520-3517
Email: admissions@carleton.ca
Full-time: 9000 men, 9406 women
Faculty: n/av
Part-time: 1502 men, 1216 women
Ph.D.s: 93%
Graduate: 1937 men, 1699 women
Student/Faculty: n/av
Year: semesters, summer session
Tuition: $8101 ($2573)
Room & Board: $10,200
Freshman Class: n/av
CEEB CODE: 0854

Application Deadline: May 1

Carleton University, founded in 1942, is a public institution operated by the province of Ontario. There are 14 undergraduate and 14 graduate degree programs offered. The figures in the above capsule and in this profile are approximate. Tuition varies according to program. There are 5 undergraduate schools and 1 graduate school. The 152-acre campus is in a small town in Ottawa. Including any residence halls, there are 29 buildings.

STUDENT LIFE: 80% of undergraduates are from Ontario. **Male To Female Ratio:** 1.0:1. The average age of freshmen is 19; all undergraduates, 21. 13% do not continue beyond their first year; 72% remain to graduate. **Housing:** 2873 students can be accommodated in college housing, which includes single-sex and coed dorms. On-campus housing is available on a lottery system for upperclassmen. Priority is given to out-of-town students. All students may keep cars.

FACULTY/CLASSROOMS: 65% of faculty are male; 35% are female. No introductory courses are taught by graduate students. The average class size in an introductory lecture is 166 and in a regular course is 107.

PROGRAMS OF STUDY: Carleton confers B.A., B.Sc., B.Arch., B.Comm., B.C.S., B.Eng., B.Hum., B.I.B., B.I.D., B.I.T., B.J., B.Math., B.Mus., B.P.A.P.M., and B.S.W. degrees. Master's and doctoral degrees are also awarded. Bachelor's degrees are awarded in BIOLOGICAL SCIENCE (biochemistry, biology/biological science, biometrics and biostatistics, biotechnology, and neurosciences), BUSINESS (accounting, business systems analysis, human resources, international business management, marketing and distribution, marketing/retailing/merchandising, and operations research), COMMUNICATIONS AND THE ARTS (art history and appreciation, classics, communications, communications technology, English, English literature, film arts, French, German, industrial design, Italian, journalism, linguistics, music, Russian, and Spanish), COMPUTER AND PHYSICAL SCIENCE (chemistry, computer mathematics, computer programming, computer science, geology, information sciences and systems, mathematics, physical sciences, physics, and statistics), EDUCATION (teaching English as a second/foreign language (TESOL/TEFOL), ENGINEERING AND ENVIRONMENTAL DESIGN (aeronautical engineering, architecture, civil engineering, computer engineering, electrical/electronics engineering, engineering, engineering physics, environmental engineering, environmental science, mechanical engineering, and systems engineering), SOCIAL SCIENCE (anthropology, Canadian studies, child care/child and family studies, classical/ancient civilization, cognitive science, criminology, Eastern European studies, economics, European studies, geography, German area studies, history, human ecology, interdisciplinary studies, law, liberal arts/general studies, philosophy, political science/government, psychology, public administration, religion, social work, sociology, and women's studies). Arts, engineering, and commerce have the largest enrollments.

ACTIVITIES: There are no fraternities or sororities. There are 80 groups on campus, including cheerleading, chess, choir, computers, drama, environmental, ethnic, film, international, jazz band, LGBT, newspaper, pep band, photography, political, radio and TV, religious, social, social service, and student government. Popular campus events include Orientation. **Sports:** There are 16 intercollegiate sports for men and 18 for women, and 4 intramural sports for men and 3 for women. Facilities include a physical recreation center with a pool, squash courts, Nautilus and fitness centers, and a double gym. Outdoor tennis courts and playing fields are also available. **Graduates:** From July 1, 2015 to June 30, 2016, 3640 bachelor's degrees were awarded. The most popular majors were psychology (10%), economics (4%), and English (4%). In an average class, 3% graduate in 3 years or less, 38% graduate in 4 years or less, 62% graduate in 5 years or less, and 67% graduate in 6 years or less.

SERVICES: Counseling and information services are available, as is tutoring in most subjects, and a reader service for the blind. Study skills workshops are available in essay writing and preparation and writing of exams. There is special exam scheduling and a study center for disabled students and a PASS program (peer tutoring). **Library/Resources:** The library contains 1.8 million volumes, 1.4 million microform items, and 22,370 audio/video tapes/CDs/DVDs, and subscribes to 40,607 periodicals including electronic. Computerized library services include interlibrary loans, database searching, Internet access, and Wi-Fi capability. Special learning facilities include an art gallery, radio station, an environmental biology laboratories annex. **Physically Challenged Students:** All of the campus is accessible. Facilities include wheelchair ramps, elevators, special parking, specially equipped restrooms, lowered drinking fountains, lowered telephones, automatic doors in some buildings, tactile control panels in elevators, tunnels connecting buildings, specially equipped residence rooms, and attendant services. **Special:** Carleton offers co-op programs in many majors and an exchange program with the University of Ottawa. Study abroad, internships in industrial design, dual and student-designed majors, accelerated degree programs, and interdisciplinary programs are available. The university also utilizes instructional television. **Visiting:** There are regularly scheduled orientations for prospective students, including a general information session and campus tour. There are guides for informal visits, visitors may sit in on classes, and stay overnight. To schedule a visit, contact the Undergraduate Recruitment Office at (613) 520-3663. **Campus Safety and Security:** Measures include 24-hour foot and vehicle patrol, emergency notification system, security escort services, emergency telephones, lighted pathways/sidewalks, controlled access to dorms/residences, bike patrol, rape defense classes, and a student safety patrol.

REQUIREMENTS: Applicants must be graduates of an accredited secondary school. Architecture, humanities, and industrial design students must present a portfolio, social work students should submit a personal information form, and music students must audition. A GPA of 3.0 is required. AP and CLEP credits are accepted. Requirements for graduation vary according to programs. **Procedure:** Freshmen are admitted to all sessions. There are early admissions, deferred admissions, and rolling admissions plans. Check with the school for current application deadlines. The application fee is $100. Notifications are sent in May. Applications are accepted on-line. **Transfer Students:** Applicants are evaluated on individual merits. 30 of 120 credits required for the bachelor's degree must be completed at Carleton. **International Students:** There are 1565 international students enrolled. The school actively recruits these students. They must take the TOEFL with a minimum score of 580 on the paper-based TOEFL (PBT) or 86 on the Internet-based version (iBT) or take the MELAB and the college's own test, Canadian Academic English Language Assessment and the IETLS.

Admissions Contact: Janice O'Farrell, Director of Admissions. Email: *admissions@carleton.ca* Web: *www.carleton.ca*

FINANCIAL AID: The FAFSA code is G08368. The deadline for filing freshman financial aid applications for fall entry is February 1.

CONCORDIA UNIVERSITY — E-2

www.concordia.ca

Montreal, PQ H3G IM8	(514) 848-4971
Fax: (514) 848-2837	**Email:** study@concordia.ca
Full-time: 9200 men, 9342 women	**Faculty:** 714
Part-time: 4270 men, 4271 women	**Ph.D.s:** 84%
Graduate: 2162 men, 2163 women	**Student/Faculty:** 17 to 1
Year: semesters, summer session	**Tuition:** $2659 ($17,391)
Room & Board: $5000	**Freshman Class:** n/av
SAT or ACT: recommended	**CEEB CODE:** 0956
Application Deadline: March 1	

Concordia University, established in 1974, is a public institution operated by the province of Quebec. The figures in the above capsule and in this profile are approximate. Tuition varies according to program. There are 5 undergraduate schools and 1 graduate school. In addition to regional accreditation, has baccalaureate program accreditation with AACSB. The 1555-acre campus is in an urban area in downtown Montreal and in suburban Loyola. Including any residence halls, there are 80 buildings.

STUDENT LIFE: 90% of undergraduates are from Quebec. Others are from 29 states, 128 foreign countries, and Canada. **Female To Male Ratio:** 1.0:1. The average age of freshmen is 21; all undergraduates, 25. 11% do not continue beyond their first year; 52% remain to graduate. **Housing:** 144 students can be accommodated in college housing, which includes single-sex and coed dorms and off-campus apartments, fraternity houses and sorority houses. On-campus housing is available on a first-come, first-served basis. Priority is given to out-of-town students. 98% of students commute. All students may keep cars.

FACULTY/CLASSROOMS: 65% of faculty are male; 35% are female. No introductory courses are taught by graduate students. The average class size in an introductory lecture is 50; in a laboratory is 50; and in a regular course is 50.

PROGRAMS OF STUDY: Concordia confers B.A., B.Admin., B.Comm., B.Comp.Sci., B.Ed., B.Eng., B.F.A. and B.S.C. degrees. Master's and doctoral degrees are also awarded. Bachelor's degrees are awarded in BIOLOGICAL SCIENCE (biochemistry, biology/biological science, and microbiology), BUSINESS (accounting, banking and finance, business administration and management, business economics, international business management, marketing/retailing/merchandising, and personnel management), COMMUNICATIONS AND THE ARTS (communications, dance, design, dramatic arts, English, English as a second/foreign language, film arts, fine arts, journalism, languages, music, and photography), COMPUTER AND PHYSICAL SCIENCE (actuarial science, chemistry, computer programming, computer science, geology, information sciences and systems, mathematics, physics, and statistics), EDUCATION (art education, early childhood education, and elementary education), ENGINEERING AND ENVIRONMENTAL DESIGN (civil engineering, computer engineering, electrical/electronics engineering, industrial engineering, and mechanical engineering), SOCIAL SCIENCE (anthropology, East Asian studies, economics, geography, history, philosophy, political science/government, psychology, sociology, and urban studies). Computer engineering, accounting, and communication studies are the strongest academically. Accounting, and psychology have the largest enrollments.

ACTIVITIES: There are 125 groups on campus, including art, choir, chorale, chorus, computers, dance, drama, ethnic, film, honors, international, jazz band, LGBT, literary magazine, musical theater, newspaper, orchestra, photography, political, professional, radio and TV, religious, social, social service, student government, symphony, and yearbook. **Sports:** There are 9 intercollegiate sports for men and 7 for women, and 16 intramural sports for men and 12 for women. Facilities include an arena, a gym, and a football stadium. **Graduates:** The most popular majors were arts and science (55%), commerce and administration (25%), and fine arts (10%).

SERVICES: Counseling and information services are available, as is tutoring in most subjects, and a reader service for the blind, and remedial math, reading, and writing. **Library/Resources:** The 2 libraries contain 3.0 million volumes, 75,000 microform items, and 2,000 audio/video tapes/CDs/DVDs, and subscribe to 5,500 periodicals including electronic. Computerized library services include interlibrary loans and database searching. Special learning facilities include an art gallery, radio station, TV station, a greenhouse, audiovisual instruction service, and specialized research center. **Physically Challenged Students:** 75% of the campus is accessible. Facilities include wheelchair ramps, elevators, special parking, specially equipped restrooms, special class scheduling, lowered drinking fountains, lowered telephones. **Special:** The university offers programs in many majors with the Institute for Co-operative Education, internships, and study abroad in 12 countries. There are accelerated degree programs, B.A.-B.S. degrees, dual majors, a general studies degree, and student-designed majors. There is a chapter of Phi Beta Kappa and 21 departmental honors programs. **Visiting:** There are regularly scheduled orientations for prospective students. There are guides for informal visits and visitors may sit in on classes. To schedule a visit, contact the Office of Student Recruitment at (514) 848-4779. **Campus Safety and Security:** Measures include 24-hour foot and vehicle patrol, self-defense education, and security escort services. There are also shuttle buses, emergency telephones, and lighted pathways/sidewalks.

REQUIREMENTS: The SAT or ACT is recommended. Applicants must be graduates of an accredited secondary school. The GED is accepted. An essay, an interview, a portfolio, or an audition may be required for some programs. A GPA of 2.5 is required. AP and CLEP credits are accepted. Important factors in the admissions decision are advanced placement or honors courses and recommendations by school officials. To graduate, students must complete 90 to 120 credits, depending on the degree, with a minimum GPA of 2.0. Between 42 and 54 credits are required in the major. All students must fulfill the requirements of the core curriculum and take the university writing test. **Procedure:** Freshmen are admitted to all sessions. There are early decision, early admissions, and rolling admissions plans. Early decision applications should be filed by February 1; regular applications, by March 1 for fall entry; November 1 for winter entry; and April 15 for summer entry, along with a $50 fee. **Transfer Students:** Applicants must have a minimum GPA of 2.2. 45 of 90 credits required for the bachelor's degree must be completed at Concordia. **International Students:** The school actively recruits these students. They must take the TOEFL or MELAB, and the college's own test.

Admissions Contact: Pete Regimbald, Assistant Registrar. Email: *study@concordia.ca* Web: *www.concordia.ca*

FINANCIAL AID: The FAFSA code is G08365. Check with the school for current application deadlines.

DALHOUSIE UNIVERSITY F-2
www.dal.ca

Halifax, NS B3H 4R2 (902) 494-2450

Fax: (902) 494-1630
Email: admissions@dal.ca
Full-time: 9000 men, 9500 women
Faculty: n/av
Part-time: n/av
Ph.D.s: n/av
Graduate: n/av
Student/Faculty: n/av
Year: semesters, summer session
Tuition: $8703
Room & Board: $9220
Freshman Class: n/av
CEEB CODE: 0915
Application Deadline: n/av

Dalhousie University, founded in 1818, provides students with the ability to study at the undergraduate, graduate, and professional levels in more than 180 programs. The figures in the above capsule and in this profile are approximate. There are 12 undergraduate schools. The campus is in an urban area in Halifax and Truro, Nova Scotia.

STUDENT LIFE: Students are from 110 foreign countries. **Female To Male Ratio:** 1.1:1. **Housing:** 2200 students can be accommodated in college housing, which includes single-sex and coed dorms, on-campus apartments, off-campus apartments, married student housing, and special-interest houses. On-campus housing on a first-come, first-served basis, and is available on a lottery system for upperclassmen. Some may keep cars.

FACULTY/CLASSROOMS: No introductory courses are taught by graduate students.

PROGRAMS OF STUDY: In addition to Bachelor's degrees, master's and doctoral degrees are also awarded. Bachelor's degrees are awarded in AGRICULTURE (agricultural economics, agricultural sciences, and animal science), BIOLOGICAL SCIENCE (biochemistry, biology/biological science, marine biology, microbiology, and neurosciences), BUSINESS (accounting, banking and finance, business administration and management, business economics, and recreation and leisure services), COMMUNICATIONS AND THE ARTS (classics, dramatic arts, English, French, German, music, Russian, and Spanish), COMPUTER AND PHYSICAL SCIENCE (chemistry, computer science, earth science, mathematics, physics, and statistics), EDUCATION (health education), ENGINEERING AND ENVIRONMENTAL DESIGN (chemical engineering, city/community/regional planning, and engineering), HEALTH PROFESSIONS (dental hygiene, nursing, occupational therapy, pharmacy, physical therapy, predentistry, and premedicine), SOCIAL SCIENCE (Canadian studies, economics, history, international studies, law, philosophy, physical fitness/movement, political science/government, psychology, religion, social work, sociology, and women's studies).

ACTIVITIES: There are no fraternities or sororities. There are 280 groups on campus, including cheerleading, chess, chorale, communications, computers, dance, debate, drama, environmental, ethnic, honors, international, LGBT, musical theater, newspaper, photography, political, professional, radio and TV, religious, social, social service, and student government. **Sports:** Facilities include cardio and weight training equipment, soccer fields, outdoor tennis courts, a track, a swimming pool, squash and volleyball courts, a climbing wall, and a dance studio.

SERVICES: Counseling and information services are available, as is tutoring in most subjects, a reader service for the blind, and remedial math and writing. **Library/Resources:** Computerized library services include interlibrary loans, database searching, and Internet access. Special learning facilities include an art gallery, natural history museum, planetarium, and radio station. **Physically Challenged Students:** The Advising and Access Services Centre is available to assist students who require support. **Special:** There are a freshman honors program. **Visiting:** There are regularly scheduled orientations for prospective students. There are guides for informal visits and visitors may sit in on classes. To schedule a visit, contact the Campus Tours at (902) 494-2587. **Campus Safety and Security:** Measures include 24-hour foot and vehicle patrol, emergency notification system, self-defense education, and security escort services. There are shuttle buses, emergency telephones, lighted pathways/sidewalks, and controlled access to dorms/residences.

REQUIREMENTS: Applicants from the US must have an SAT result of at least 1650 or an ACT composite score of 23 and no individual score less than 20. Grade 12 credit in English is required. An audition is necessary for music students. AP credits are accepted. **Procedure:** Freshmen are admitted to all sessions. There are early decision, early admissions, deferred admissions, and rolling admissions plans. Check with the school for current application deadlines. The application fee is $65. Applications are accepted online. **Transfer Students:** Applicants are assessed on an individual basis. **International Students:** The school actively recruits these students. US applicants may submit either the SAT or ACT.

Admissions Contact: Admissions Advisor. Email: *admissions@dal.ca* Web: *www.dal.ca*

FINANCIAL AID: The FAFSA code is G06838. Check with the school for current application deadlines.

MCGILL UNIVERSITY E-2
www.mcgill.ca

Montreal, PQ H3A oG4 (514) 398-3910

Fax: (514) 398-5544
Email: welcome@mcgill.ca
Full-time: 6899 men, 10,952 women
Faculty: n/av
Part-time: 1200 men, 2056 women
Ph.D.s: 95%
Graduate: 3464 men, 3900 women
Student/Faculty: n/av
Year: semesters, summer session
Tuition: $3330 ($16,744)
Room & Board: $11,126
Freshman Class: 18963 applied, 10689 accepted, 4834 enrolled
SAT: required **ACT:** 29
CEEB CODE: 0935
Application Deadline: March 1

McGill University, founded in 1821, is a publicly funded private institution that grants undergraduate, graduate, and professional degrees. Tuition fees may vary depending on program. Higher rates are charged to international students. All figures are based on Canadian dollars. The figures in the above capsule and in this profile are approximate. There are 11 undergraduate schools and 79 graduate schools. In addition to regional accreditation, McGill has baccalaureate program accreditation with APTA. The 80-acre campus is in an urban area in downtown Montreal, with the MacDonald campus located on the far west end of the island. Including any residence halls, there are 150 buildings.

STUDENT LIFE: 53% of undergraduates are from Quebec. Others are from 140 foreign countries. 17% are Foreign. **Female To Male Ratio:** 1.5:1. The average age of freshmen is 19; all undergraduates, 21. **Housing:** 2080 students can be accommodated in college housing, which includes single-sex and coed dorms, off-campus apartments, and married student housing. On-campus housing is available on a lottery system for upperclassmen. Priority is given to out-of-town students. 83% of students commute.

FACULTY/CLASSROOMS: 67% of faculty are male; 33% are female. No introductory courses are taught by graduate students. The average class size in an introductory lecture is 30; in a laboratory is 25; and in a regular course is 45.

PROGRAMS OF STUDY: McGill confers B.A., B.C.L., B.Com., B.Ed., B.Eng., B.Mus., B.Sc., B.Sc.Agr., B.Sc.Agr.Eng., B.Sc.Arch., B.Sc.F.Sc., B.Sc.N., B.Sc.Nutr.Sc., B.Sc.Occ.Ther., B.Sc.Phys.Ther., B.S.W., B.Th., and LL.B. degrees. Master's and doctoral degrees are also awarded. Bachelor's degrees are awarded in AGRICULTURE (agricultural economics, agriculture, animal science, conservation and regulation, plant science, and soil science), BIOLOGICAL SCIENCE (anatomy, biochemistry, biology/biological science, botany, cell biology, environmental biology, microbiology, molecular biology, nutrition, physiology, wildlife biology, and zoology), BUSINESS (accounting, banking and finance, entrepreneurial studies, human resources, institutional management, insurance and risk management, international business management, labor studies, management information systems, management science, marketing management, and organizational behavior), COMMUNICATIONS AND THE ARTS (art history and appreciation, classics, English, French, jazz, linguistics, modern language, music history and appreciation, music performance, music technology, music theory and composition, Russian, and Spanish), COMPUTER AND PHYSICAL SCIENCE (applied mathematics, atmospheric sciences and meteorology, chemistry, computer science, earth science, geology, geophysics and seismology, information sciences and systems, mathematics, physics, planetary and space science, and software engineering), EDUCATION (elementary education, foreign languages education, music education, physical education, secondary education, special education, teaching English as a second/foreign language (TESOL/TEFOL), and vocational education),

ENGINEERING AND ENVIRONMENTAL DESIGN (agricultural engineering, architecture, chemical engineering, civil engineering, computer engineering, electrical/electronics engineering, environmental science, mechanical engineering, metallurgical engineering, and mining and mineral engineering), HEALTH PROFESSIONS (clinical science, exercise science, nursing, occupational therapy, and physical therapy), SOCIAL SCIENCE (African studies, American studies, anthropology, Canadian studies, Caribbean studies, dietetics, East Asian studies, economics, food science, French studies, geography, German area studies, Hispanic American studies, history, humanities, international studies, Italian studies, Judaic studies, Latin American studies, law, Middle Eastern studies, philosophy, political science/government, psychology, religion, social work, sociology, Western civilization/culture, and women's studies).

ACTIVITIES: 4% of men belong to 1 local and 12 national fraternities; 2% of women belong to 4 national sororities. There are 180 groups on campus, including band, cheerleading, chess, choir, chorale, chorus, computers, dance, debate, drama, ethnic, film, honors, international, jazz band, LGBT, literary magazine, Model UN, musical theater, newspaper, opera, orchestra, photography, political, professional, radio and TV, religious, social, social service, student government, symphony, and yearbook. Popular campus events include Multicultural Festivals, 4-Floor Parties, Music, Film and Theatrical Productions. **Sports:** There are 23 intercollegiate sports for men and 24 for women, and 23 intramural sports for men and 15 for women. Facilities include a stadium, competition hall, gyms for basketball, volleyball, badminton, outdoor tennis courts, indoor tennis courts, outdoor track and indoor track, weight-training rooms, dance, aerobics, and martial arts rooms, a pool, sports fields, fitness center, a sport medicine center, and hyperbaric chamber. **Graduates:** The most popular majors were social sciences (18%), health professions (11%), and biological/life sciences (10%).

SERVICES: Counseling and information services are available, as is tutoring in every subject, and a reader service for the blind, and remedial math, reading, and writing. **Library/Resources:** The 14 libraries contain 3.3 million volumes, 1.6 million microform items, 71,765 audio/video tapes/CDs/DVDs, and subscribe to 22,513 periodicals including electronic. Computerized library services include interlibrary loans and database searching. Special learning facilities include a natural history museum, radio station, McCord Museum of Canadian History, Mont St. Hilaire Nature Conservation Center, an herbarium, an arboretum, a subarctic research station, the Institute of Air and Space Law, Institute of Islamic Studies, Redpath Museum of Natural History, Lyman Entomological Museum, Eco Museum, Osler Library of the History of Medicine, and the Lande Canadiana Collection. **Physically Challenged Students:** 80% of the campus is accessible. Facilities include wheelchair ramps, elevators, special parking, specially equipped restrooms, special class scheduling, lowered telephones. including braille, variable-speed tape recorders, talking calculators, books on tape, exam accommodations, adapted computers (voice synthesis and voice recognition), sign language interpreters, computerized note taking, note takers, print enlargement, readers, and adapted transport. **Special:** There is cross-registration with area universities. Study abroad, work-study within the university, co-op programs in mining and metallurgical engineering, dual majors, internships, and student-designed majors are available. There are 6 departmental honors programs. **Visiting:** There are regularly scheduled orientations for prospective students, with a varying agenda (including campus tours and student for a day programs). There are guides for informal visits, visitors may sit in on classes, and stay overnight. To schedule a visit, contact the Welcome Center at (514) 398-6555 (tours). **Campus Safety and Security:** Measures include 24-hour foot and vehicle patrol, security escort services, emergency telephones and lighted pathways/sidewalks.

REQUIREMENTS: The ACT may be submitted instead of the SAT. McGill requires applicants to be in the upper 25% of their class. A GPA of 3.3 is required. AP credits are accepted. Important factors in the admissions decision are advanced placement or honors courses, recommendations by school officials, and evidence of special talent. To graduate, students must successfully complete a required number of approved credits, usually between 90 and 120. Students must also be in satisfactory standing, with a minimum cumulative GPA of 2.0. **Procedure:** Freshmen are admitted in the fall. Entrance exams should be taken during spring of the junior year, and fall of the senior year. There are deferred admissions and rolling admissions plans. Applications should be filed by March 1 for fall entry, along with a $60 fee. Applications are accepted online. **Transfer Students:** 528 transfer students enrolled in 2015-2016. Requirements vary with the program. Standard admission requirements must also be met. Students must submit high school and college transcripts and have a 3.0 GPA in college coursework. 60 of 90 credits required for the bachelor's degree must be completed at McGill. **International Students:** The school actively recruits these students. They must take the TOEFL or MELAB, McGill Certificate of Proficiency in English must be earned. SAT and/or ACT tests are required for U.S. applicants and recommended for other international applicants.

ADMISSIONS: 56% of the 2016-2017 applicants were accepted. **Admissions Contact:** Admissions, Recruitment, and Registrar's Office. Email: *welcome@mcgill.ca* Web: *www.mcgill.ca*

FINANCIAL AID: The average freshman award was $5,855. Need-based scholarships or need-based grants averaged $3,022; and need-based self-help aid (loans and jobs) averaged $6,146. McGill is a member of CSS. The college's own financial statement is required. The FAFSA code is G06677. The deadline for filing freshman financial aid applications for fall entry is June 1.

MCMASTER UNIVERSITY — E-3

www.future.mcmaster.ca

Hamilton, ON L8S 4K1 — **(905) 525-4600**

Fax: (905) 527-1105 — **Email: macadmit@mcmaster.ca**

Full-time: 5400 men, 7000 women	**Faculty:** 927
Part-time: 900 men, 1900 women	**Ph.D.s:** n/av
Graduate: 1190 men, 1030 women	**Student/Faculty:** 13 to 1
Year: n/av	**Tuition:** $7418 ($27,448)
Room & Board: $8298	**Freshman Class:** n/av
	CEEB CODE: 0936

Application Deadline: n/av

McMaster University is a public nonsectarian institution, offering programs in the arts and sciences, business, engineering, health sciences, kinesiology, and social work. The figures given in the above capsule and in this profile are approximate. There are 2 graduate schools. The 300-acre campus is in an urban area 60 miles southwest of Toronto. Including any residence halls, there are 44 buildings.

STUDENT LIFE: 95% of undergraduates are from Ontario. Others are from 12 states, and 79 foreign countries. **Female To Male Ratio:** 1.3:1. The average age of freshmen is 20; all undergraduates, 22. 1% do not continue beyond their first year. **Housing:** 2765 students can be accommodated in college housing, which includes single-sex and coed dorms, on-campus apartments, language houses, La Maison Francaise, an international house, and a quiet house. On-campus housing is guaranteed for the freshman year only and is available on a lottery system for upperclassmen. Priority is given to out-of-town students. 77% of students commute. All students may keep cars.

FACULTY/CLASSROOMS: 71% of faculty are male; 29% are female. All teach undergraduates, and do research. No introductory courses are taught by graduate students.

PROGRAMS OF STUDY: Mac confers B.A., B.S., B.A.S., B.A./B.S.W., B.C., B.Eng., B.Eng./Management, B.Eng./Society, B.H.S., B.Kinesiology, B.Mus. and B.S.N. degrees. Master's and doctoral degrees are also awarded. Bachelor's degrees are awarded in BIOLOGICAL SCIENCE (biochemistry, biology/biological science, and life science), BUSINESS (business administration and management and labor studies), COMMUNICATIONS AND THE ARTS (art, art history and appreciation, classics, comparative literature, dramatic arts, English, French, linguistics, modern language, music, and Russian), COMPUTER AND PHYSICAL SCIENCE (chemistry, computer science, earth science, geology, mathematics, physical sciences, physics, science, and statistics), ENGINEERING AND ENVIRONMENTAL DESIGN (chemical engineering, civil engineering, computer engineering, electrical/electronics engineering, engineering physics, environmental science, manufacturing engineering, materials engineering, materials science, and mechanical engineering), HEALTH PROFESSIONS (medical science, nursing, occupational therapy, and physical therapy), SOCIAL SCIENCE (anthropology, economics, geography, German area studies, gerontology, history, interdisciplinary studies, Japanese studies, Latin American studies, liberal arts/general studies, philosophy, physical fitness/movement, political science/government, psychology, religion, social work, sociology, and women's studies).

ACTIVITIES: There are no fraternities or sororities. There are 100 groups on campus, including academic club, art, band, cheerleading, chess, choir, chorale, chorus, computers, debate, drama, ethnic, international, jazz band, LGBT, musical theater, newspaper, orchestra, photography, political, radio and TV, religious, social, student government, and yearbook. Popular campus events include Marauder Weekend. **Sports:** There are 16 intercollegiate sports for men and 14 for women, and 16 intramural sports for men and 14 for women. Facilities include an outdoor track and field, mini-weight room, swimming pool, cross-country trails, rugby, soccer, football fields, tennis, squash, and handball courts, and a fitness facility. **Graduates:** From July 1, 2015 to June 30, 2016, 3000 bachelor's degrees were awarded.

SERVICES: Counseling and information services are available, as is tutoring in some subjects. There is a reader service for the blind, which may be arranged through individual departments. **Library/Resources:** The 4 libraries contain 1.7 million volumes, 1.4 million microform items, 19,500 audio/video tapes/CDs/DVDs, and subscribe to 11,976 periodicals including electronic. Computerized library services include interlibrary loans and database searching. Special learning facilities include an art gallery, planetarium, radio station, a nuclear reactor, tandem accelerator, a greenhouses, Chedoke-McMaster Hospital, a communication research lab, Bertrand Russell archives, humanities communication centre, and computing labs. **Physically Challenged Students:** 60% of the campus is accessible. Facilities include wheelchair ramps, elevators, special parking, specially equipped restrooms, special class scheduling, lowered telephones, and basement-level and above-ground tunnels with connecting walkways. **Special:** Many opportunities exist to combine 2 subjects of study within 1 faculty, or between 2 faculties. All honors students have the option of taking a minor in a second subject area. Nondegree study is possible through the Center for Continuing Education. Internships and study abroad are offered. Students may repeat failed courses provided they are eligible to continue in the program. There are 37 departmental honors programs. **Visiting:** There are regularly scheduled orientations for prospective students, including campus tours, information sessions, and panel discussions. There are guides for informal visits and visitors may sit in on classes. To schedule a visit, contact the Tour Coordinator, Division of Student Liaison. **Campus Safety and Security:** Measures include 24-hour foot and vehicle patrol, and security escort services. There are also shuttle buses, emergency telephones, lighted pathways/sidewalks, additional services include the Emergency First-Response Team, Mac Alert bulletins, a campus watch program, a prevention programs officer, and video monitoring in some parking areas.

REQUIREMENTS: U.S. applicants must have a high school grade average of 80. Applicants must be graduates of an accredited secondary school. The required high school courses should include 5 years each of English and math. A portfolio is required for art students and an audition for music students. A supplementary application form is required for some programs. Offers of admission are made based on academic standing and audition/portfolio/supplementary application requirements where necessary. Important factors in the admissions decision are evidence of special talent, extracurricular activities record, and leadership record. Requirements for graduation vary according to the program of study. A minimum 3.5 GPA in 90 to 150 units is required for most programs. **Procedure:** Freshmen are admitted to all sessions. There is a early decision plan. Check with the school for current application deadlines. **Transfer Students:** Applicants are considered on an individual basis. Review of high school, college, and/or university work determines admission status. **International Students:** The school actively recruits these students. They must take the TOEFL or MELAB, or take the IELTS.

Admissions Contact: Sam Digiandomenico, Associate Registrar Admissions. Email: *macadmit@mcmaster.ca* Web: *www.future.mcmaster.ca*

FINANCIAL AID: The deadline for filing freshman financial aid applications for fall entry is July 15.

MEMORIAL UNIVERSITY OF NEWFOUNDLAND — F-2

www.mun.ca

St. John's, NF A1C 5S7 — **(709) 737-3705**, **(866) 354-8896**

Fax: (709) 737-2337 — **Email: admissions@mun.ca**

Full-time: 5000 men, 7000 women
Part-time: 690 men, 1350 women
Graduate: 840 men, 760 women
Year: varies, summer session
Room & Board: $8530

Faculty: 932
Ph.D.s: 50%
Student/Faculty: 12 to 1
Tuition: $3068 ($9440)
Freshman Class: n/av
CEEB CODE: 0885

Application Deadline: March 1

Memorial University of Newfoundland, founded in 1925, is a public liberal arts institution. Tuition cost is based on Canadian students and international students. The figures in the above capsule and in this profile are approximate. There are 13 undergraduate schools and 12 graduate schools. The 220-acre campus is in an urban area in St. John's. Including any residence halls, there are 40 buildings.

STUDENT LIFE: 98% of undergraduates are from Newfoundland. Student are from 90 foreign countries. **Female To Male Ratio:** 1.4:1. **Housing:** 1750 students can be accommodated in college housing, which includes single-sex and coed dorms, on-campus apartments, off-campus apartments, and married student housing. On-campus housing is available on a first-come and first-served basis. Priority is given to out-of-town students. 89% of students commute. All students may keep cars.

FACULTY/CLASSROOMS: 80% of faculty are male; 20% are female. All teach undergraduates, and do research. Graduate students teach 71% of introductory courses. The average class size in an introductory lecture is 40.

PROGRAMS OF STUDY: MUN confers B.A., B.Sc., B.Comm.(Co-op.), B.Comm.(Gen.), B.Ed., B.Eng., B.F.A., B.Kin., B.M.S., B.Mus., B.Mus.Ed., B.Med.Sc., B.N., B.P.E., B.Rec., B.Sc.(Pharm.), B.Spec.Ed., B.S.W., B.Tech. and B.Voc.Ed. degrees. Master's and doctoral degrees are also awarded. Bachelor's degrees are awarded in AGRICULTURE (forestry and related sciences), BIOLOGICAL SCIENCE (biochemistry, biology/biological science, cell biology, ecology, entomology, environmental biology, evolutionary biology, marine biology, marine science, microbiology, and neurosciences), BUSINESS (entrepreneurial studies, human resources, labor studies, management science, marketing/retailing/merchandising, organizational behavior, and small business management), COMMUNICATIONS AND THE ARTS (dramatic arts, English, English literature, fine arts, folklore and mythology, French, German, linguistics, literature, music, music history and appreciation, music performance, music theory and composition, Russian, Spanish, and visual and performing arts), COMPUTER AND PHYSICAL SCIENCE (applied mathematics, applied physics, chemistry, computer science, earth science, information sciences and systems, mathematics, oceanography, and statistics), EDUCATION (athletic training, education, elementary education, guidance education, middle school education, music education, physical education, recreation education, secondary education, and special education), ENGINEERING AND ENVIRONMENTAL DESIGN (civil engineering, electrical/electronics engineering, engineering technology, maritime science, mechanical engineering, naval architecture and marine engineering, and ocean engineering), HEALTH PROFESSIONS (medical science, nursing, and pharmacy), SOCIAL SCIENCE (anthropology, archeology, Canadian studies, criminology, dietetics, economics, French studies, geography, German area studies, history, humanities, medieval studies, philosophy, physical fitness/movement, political science/government, psychology, religion, social studies, social work, sociology, Spanish studies, and women's studies). Marine biology, naval architecture, and business are the strongest academically. Arts, science, business, and engineering have the largest enrollments.

ACTIVITIES: There are no fraternities or sororities. There are 100 groups on campus, including academic club, band, cheerleading, chess, choir, chorale, computers, dance, debate, drama, ethnic, international, jazz band, LGBT, literary magazine, musical theater, newspaper, orchestra, photography, political, professional, radio and TV, religious, single parent, social, social service, student government, symphony, and yearbook. Popular campus events include Winter Carnival and Orientation. **Sports:** There are 6 intercollegiate sports for men and 6 for women, and 6 intramural sports for men and 6 for women. Facilities include a gym, squash courts, rifle range, weight room, soccer field, and swimming facilities. **Graduates:** The most popular majors were business, biology, and sociology.

SERVICES: There is a reader service for the blind, and remedial math, reading, and writing. Students staying in residence have access to tutoring in every subject. In addition, lectures are offered on topics such as public speaking, speed reading, and time management. **Library/Resources:** The 3 libraries contain 2.5 million volumes, and subscribe to 700 periodicals including electronic. Computerized library services include interlibrary loans and database searching. Special learning facilities include an art gallery, natural history museum, planetarium, radio station, TV station, and language lab. **Physically Challenged Students:** 85% of the campus is accessible. Facilities include wheelchair ramps, elevators, special parking, specially equipped restrooms, special class scheduling, lowered drinking fountains, lowered telephones, classroom aids, note-taking volunteers, and other facilities based on individual needs. **Special:** The university offers co-op programs in commerce, phys ed, recreation, kinesiology, and engineering. Internships are available in education and nursing. Study abroad may be arranged in at least 20 countries. Work-study programs, dual majors, and B.A.-B.S. degrees are available. There are 3 departmental honors programs. **Visiting:** There are regularly scheduled orientations for prospective students, including various student activities, mock lectures, campus tours, and educational sessions. There are guides for informal visits and visitors may sit in on classes. To schedule a visit, contact the Student Development at (709) 737-2192. **Campus Safety and Security:** Measures include 24-hour foot and vehicle patrol, self-defense education, security escort services, emergency telephones and lighted pathways/sidewalks.

REQUIREMENTS: Admission is based on a 70% high school average as computed from university preparatory courses required for admission. Applications are accepted online. AP credits are accepted. Students must complete 40 to 50 credits to graduate. Each discipline has different requirements for graduation. **Procedure:** Freshmen are admitted to all sessions. There is a rolling admissions plan. Applications should be filed by March 1 for fall entry; October 1 for winter entry; February 1 for spring entry; and February 1 for summer entry. The fall 2016 application fee was $80. **Transfer Students:** 499 transfer students enrolled in 2015-2016. Applicants must be in good academic standing at the previous institution. 10 of 40 credits required for the bachelor's degree must be completed at MUN. **International Students:** The school actively recruits these students. They must take the TOEFL or MELAB.

Admissions Contact: Phyllis McCann, Manager of Admissions. Email: *admissions@mun.ca* Web: *www.mun.ca*

FINANCIAL AID: The FAFSA code is G09500. Check with the school for current application deadlines.

QUEEN'S UNIVERSITY — E-3

www.queensu.ca

Kingston, ON K7L 3N6 — (613) 533-2218

Fax: (613) 533-6810	**Email:** admission@.queensu.ca
Full-time: 7000 men, 7000 women	**Faculty:** 973
Part-time: 1300 men, 1300 women	**Ph.D.s:** n/av
Graduate: 1400 men, 1400 women	**Student/Faculty:** 13 to 1
Year: semesters, summer session	**Tuition:** $12,993
Room & Board: $13,242	**Freshman Class:** n/av
SAT: required	**CEEB CODE:** 0949
Application Deadline: n/av	

Queen's University, founded in 1841, is a public institution offering undergraduate and graduate programs in the arts and sciences, business, engineering, health sciences, and teacher education. Cost is based upon domestic students, and varies by programs chosen. The figures in the above capsule and in this profile are approximate. There are 10 undergraduate schools and 5 graduate schools. The 160-acre campus is in an urban area 150 miles east of Toronto. Including any residence halls, there are 100 buildings.

STUDENT LIFE: 85% of undergraduates are from Ontario. Others are from 80 foreign countries, and Canada. 89% are from public schools. **Male To Female Ratio:** Is 1:1. 5% do not continue beyond their first year; 90% remain to graduate. **Housing:** 3071 students can be accommodated in college housing, which includes single-sex and coed dorms, on-campus apartments, off-campus apartments, married student housing, language houses, special-interest houses, study floors, and nonsmoking floors. On-campus housing is guaranteed for the freshman year only. 80% of students commute. All students may keep cars.

FACULTY/CLASSROOMS: 72% of faculty are male; 27% are female. All teach undergraduates. No introductory courses are taught by graduate students. The average class size in a laboratory is 40.

PROGRAMS OF STUDY: Queen's confers B.A., B.Sc., B.A./B.Ed., B.A./B.Phe., B.Comm., B.F.A., B.Mus., B.N.Sc., B.Sc./B.Ed., B.Sc./B.Phe., B.S.C.E., B.Sc.O.T. and B.Sc.P.T. degrees. Master's and doctoral degrees are also awarded. Bachelor's degrees are awarded in BIOLOGICAL SCIENCE (biochemistry, biology/biological science, and life science), COMMUNICATIONS AND THE ARTS (art history and appreciation, classics, dramatic arts, English, film arts, fine arts, French, German, Greek, Italian, Latin, music, and Spanish), COMPUTER AND PHYSICAL SCIENCE (chemistry, computer science, geology, mathematics, physics, and statistics), EDUCATION (elementary education, middle school education, and secondary education), ENGINEERING AND ENVIRONMENTAL DESIGN (chemical engineering, civil engineering, electrical/electronics engineering, engineering physics, geological engineering, and mechanical engineering), HEALTH PROFESSIONS (health, nursing, occupational therapy, and physical therapy), SOCIAL SCIENCE (economics, geography, history, Judaic studies, philosophy, political science/government, psychology, religion, sociology, and women's studies). Arts, science, and engineering have the largest enrollments.

ACTIVITIES: There are no fraternities or sororities. There are 220 groups on campus, including art, bagpipe, band, cheerleading, chess, choir, chorale, chorus, computers, dance, debate, drama, ethnic, film, international, jazz band, LGBT, literary magazine, marching band, musical theater, newspaper, orchestra, photography, political, professional, radio and TV, religious, social, social service, student government, symphony, and yearbook. Popular campus events include Orientation Week, Alumni Weekend, and Applied Science Formal. **Sports:** There are 19 intercollegiate sports for men and 21 for women, and 39 intramural sports for men and 39 for women. Facilities include a pool, indoor track, hockey arena, tennis, squash, racquetball courts, weight room, dance studio, projectile range, indoor gym and football stadium. **Graduates:** From July 1, 2015 to June 30, 2016, 3506 bachelor's degrees were awarded.

SERVICES: Counseling and information services are available, as is tutoring in most subjects. There is a reader service for the blind, and remedial math, reading, and writing. **Library/Resources:** The 8 libraries contain 1.8 million volumes, 2.0 million microform items, 7,000 audio/video tapes/CDs/DVDs, and subscribe to 15,000 periodicals including electronic. Computerized library services include interlibrary loans and database searching. Special learning facilities include an art gallery, radio station, TV station, geology museum, and observatory. **Physically Challenged Students:** 80% of the campus is accessible. Facilities include wheelchair ramps, elevators, special parking, specially equipped restrooms, special class scheduling, lowered drinking fountains, and lowered telephones. **Special:** Internships are available in life science, commerce, and engineering. Students may study abroad in 25 countries. Dual majors are available. Cross-registration with St. Lawrence College for the B.S.N. is possible. There are a freshman honors program and 20 departmental honors programs. **Visiting:** There are regularly scheduled orientations for prospective students, consisting of a short briefing session and a walking tour. There are guides for informal visits, visitors may sit in on classes, and stay overnight. To schedule a visit, contact Student Recruitment at (613) 533-2217. **Campus Safety and Security:** Measures include 24-hour foot and vehicle patrol, self-defense education, and security escort services. There are also shuttle buses, emergency telephones, and lighted pathways/sidewalks.

REQUIREMENTS: The SAT is required. Candidates for admission are required to submit a school profile. A GPA of 70.0 is required. Important factors in the admissions decision are evidence of special talent, leadership record, and extracurricular activities record. Each faculty and school establishes the academic requirements for the graduation of its students. **Procedure:** Freshmen are admitted in the fall. There are deferred admissions and rolling admissions plans. Check with the school for current application deadlines. The application fee is $125. Notifications are sent May 27. Applications are accepted online. **Transfer Students:** 151 transfer students enrolled in 2015-2016. Admission requirements for transfer applicants vary by program. 10 of 19 credits required for the bachelor's degree must be completed at Queen's. **International Students:** There are 396 international students enrolled. The school actively recruits these students. They must take the TOEFL or MELAB. They must also take the SAT, scoring 1200 for applicants from American System Schools.

Admissions Contact: Dr. David Walker, Dean. Email: *admission@.queensu.ca* Web: *www.queensu.ca*

FINANCIAL AID: 9% of all full-time freshmen received need-based aid. The FAFSA code is G06679. The deadline for filing freshman financial aid applications for fall entry is May 13.

RYERSON UNIVERSITY E-3

www.ryerson.ca

Toronto, ON M5B 2K3 (416) 979-5036

Fax: (416) 979-5067	**Email:** studentinfo@ryerson.ca
Full-time: 12,000 men, 13,000 women	**Faculty:** n/av
Part-time: n/av	**Ph.D.s:** 63%
Graduate: 500 men, 1500 women	**Student/Faculty:** 23 to 1
Year: semesters, summer session	**Tuition:** $10,200 ($24,800)
Room & Board: $15,600	**Freshman Class:** 69000 applied, 24800 accepted, 8555 enrolled
SAT or ACT: recommended	**CEEB CODE:** 0886
Application Deadline: February 1	

Ryerson University, founded in 1948, is a public institution offering undergraduate programs in arts, applied arts, business, community services, and engineering and applied science. The figures in the above capsule and in this profile is based upon Canadian and international students, and varies by programs chosen. There are 5 undergraduate schools and 3 graduate schools. In addition to regional accreditation, Ryerson has baccalaureate program accreditation with FIDER. The 20-acre campus is in an urban area in Toronto. Including any residence halls, there are 35 buildings.

STUDENT LIFE: 90% of undergraduates are from Ontario. **Female To Male Ratio:** 1.2:1. **Housing:** 852 students can be accommodated in college housing, which includes coed dorms. On-campus housing is available on a first-come and first-served basis. Priority is given to out-of-town students. 96% of students commute. All students may keep cars.

FACULTY/CLASSROOMS: No introductory courses are taught by graduate students. The average class size in a regular course is 30.

PROGRAMS OF STUDY: Ryerson confers B.A., B.Arch.Sc., B.A.Sc., B.Comm., B.Des., B.Eng., B.H.Sc., B.Sc., B.S.W., B.Tech., and B.U.R.P.I. degrees. Master's and doctoral degrees are also awarded. Bachelor's degrees are awarded in BUSINESS (business administration and management, hospitality management services, and management information systems), COMMUNICATIONS AND THE ARTS (broadcasting, journalism, and photography), COMPUTER AND PHYSICAL SCIENCE (computer programming), EDUCATION (early childhood education), ENGINEERING AND ENVIRONMENTAL DESIGN (aeronautical engineering, architecture, chemical engineering, civil engineering, electrical/electronics engineering, graphic and printing production, industrial engineering, interior design, mechanical engineering, and urban planning technology), HEALTH PROFESSIONS (environmental health science and nursing), SOCIAL SCIENCE (child care/child and family studies, family/consumer studies, fashion design and technology, geography, public administration, and social work). Business management, nursing, and information technology management have the largest enrollments.

ACTIVITIES: There are no fraternities or sororities. There are 150 groups on campus, including choir, chorale, computers, drama, environmental, ethnic, film, international, LGBT, literary magazine, musical theater, newspaper, political, professional, radio and TV, religious, social, social service, student government, and yearbook. Popular campus events include Orientation, Parade and Picnic. **Sports:** There are 7 intercollegiate sports for men and 8 for women, and 20 intramural sports for men and 20 for women. Facilities include a recreation and athletic center, squash courts, fitness training center that includes an indoor running track and weight-training equipment, a rehabilitation center, a pool, and gyms.

SERVICES: Counseling and information services are available, as is tutoring in most subjects, and a reader service for the blind, and remedial math, reading, and writing. Services are available in study skills development, critical reading seminars, time management skills, and exam workshops. **Library/Resources:** The library contains 477,739 volumes, 842,963 microform items, 20,235 audio/video tapes/CDs/DVDs, and subscribes to 60,809 periodicals including electronic. Computerized library services include interlibrary loans, database searching, Internet access, and Wi-Fi capability. Special learning facilities include a radio station, the BlackStar Historical Black and White Photography Collection, Heidelberg Centre, George Vari Engineering and Computing Centre. **Physically Challenged Students:** Facilities include wheelchair ramps, elevators, special parking, specially equipped restrooms, special class scheduling, lowered drinking fountains, lowered telephones, special housing, test and exam adaptations, computer-equipped exam and study rooms, assistive listening devices for personal use and for use in auditorium settings, advocacy services, individual needs assessment, and access to a wide range of technical devices. **Special:** The university offers co-op programs in applied chemistry and biology, chemical engineering, and midwifery. Accelerated degree programs are available in journalism, radio and television arts, nurse practitioner, and nursing, and many programs have a work-study component. There is 1 national honor society and a freshman honors program. **Visiting:** There are regularly scheduled orientations for prospective students, which includes discussion session featuring campus tours and visits to specific schools and departments. There are guides for informal visits and visitors may sit in on classes. To schedule a visit, contact the Undergraduate Admissions and Recruitment at (416) 979-5036. **Campus Safety and Security:** Measures include 24-hour foot and vehicle patrol, emergency notification system, self-defense education, security escort services, emergency telephones, lighted pathways/sidewalks, controlled access to dorms/residences, sexual assault training, harassment prevention, crime prevention programs, and community policing programs.

REQUIREMENTS: The SAT or ACT and ACT Writing Test are recommended. For U.S. students, there is a recommended minimum score of 550 on each section of the SAT I. Students should be high school graduates with a minimum B overall average. A GPA of 3.0 is required. AP credits are accepted. To graduate, students must have a 2.0 GPA and complete the requirements of their program of study. **Procedure:** Freshmen are admitted in the fall. Applications should be filed by February 1 for fall entry, along with a $130 fee. Notifications are sent in March. 7000 applicants were on the 2016 waiting list. Applications are accepted online. **Transfer Students:** 700 transfer students enrolled in 2015-2016. Transfer applicants must have completed 1 year at the college level. Acceptance of transfer credits is at the discretion of the Office of Admissions/Liaison/Curriculum Advising. Half of the required credits for a particular degree program must be completed at Ryerson. **International Students:** There are 1000 international students enrolled. The school actively recruits these students. They must take the TOEFL with a minimum score of 560 on the paper-based TOEFL (PBT) or 83 on the Internet-based version (iBT) or take the MELAB and the college's own test, or take the IELTS.

ADMISSIONS: 36% of the 2016-2017 applicants were accepted. **Admissions Contact:** Michelle Beaton, Manager of International Recruitment. Email: *studentinfo@ryerson.ca* Web: *www.ryerson.ca*

FINANCIAL AID: Ryerson is a member of CSS. The FAFSA code is G10720. Check with the school for current application deadlines.

SIMON FRASER UNIVERSITY B-2

www.sfu.ca

Burnaby, BC V5A 1S6 (778) 782-3995

Fax: (778) 782-4969	**Email:** reginfo@sfu.ca
Full-time: 7000 men, 7094 women	**Faculty:** n/av
Part-time: 7094 men, 8293 women	**Ph.D.s:** 88%
Graduate: 2000 men, 3400 women	**Student/Faculty:** n/av
Year: varies, summer session	**Tuition:** $6724 ($17,984)
Room & Board: $7484	**Freshman Class:** n/av
SAT: required	**CEEB CODE:** 0999
Application Deadline: May 1	

Simon Fraser University, established in 1965, is a public institution offering undergraduate and graduate programs in the arts, sciences, business, education, and applied sciences. In addition to its main campus, the university maintains the Harbour Centre campus in downtown Vancouver to provide mid-career education to the urban population and the new SFU Surrey campus offering programs in information technology and interactive arts. The figures in the above capsule and in this profile are approximate. There are 8 undergraduate schools and 35 graduate schools. The 400-acre campus is in a suburban area 9 miles east of Vancouver, Canada. Including any residence halls, there are 51 buildings.

STUDENT LIFE: 89% of undergraduates are from British Columbia. 107 foreign countries, and Canada. 92% are from public schools. **Female To Male Ratio:** 1.2:1. The average age of freshmen is 19; all undergraduates, 23. **Housing:** 1750 students can be accommodated in college housing, which includes single-sex and coed dorms, on-campus apartments, and married student housing. In addition, there are special-interest houses. On-campus housing is guaranteed for the freshman year only. Priority is given to out-of-town students. 92% of students commute. All students may keep cars.

FACULTY/CLASSROOMS: 71% of faculty are male; 29% are female. No introductory courses are taught by graduate students.

PROGRAMS OF STUDY: SFU confers B.A., B.A.Sc., B.B.A., B.E.D., B.F.A., B.G.S. and B.Sc. degrees. Master's and doctoral degrees are also awarded. Bachelor's degrees are awarded in BIOLOGICAL SCIENCE (biology/biological science, molecular biology, and physiology), BUSINESS (business administration and management and management science), COMMUNICATIONS AND THE ARTS (art, communications, dance, dramatic arts, English, film arts, French, linguistics, music, and visual and performing arts), COMPUTER AND PHYSICAL SCIENCE (actuarial science, applied mathematics, applied physics, chemistry, computer science, earth science, mathematics, physics, science, and statistics), EDUCATION (education), ENGINEERING AND ENVIRONMENTAL DESIGN (engineering and applied science and environmental science), SOCIAL SCIENCE (anthropology, archeology, Canadian studies, cognitive science, criminology, economics, geography, history, humanities, liberal arts/general studies, philosophy, physical fitness/movement, political science/government, psychology, sociology, and women's studies). Engineering science is the strongest academically. Business administration, psychology, and computing science have the largest enrollments.

ACTIVITIES: There are no fraternities or sororities. There are 35 groups on campus, including gaming, hobbies and pre-professional, special interest, bagpipe, chess, choir, computers, ethnic, international, LGBT, newspaper, political, professional, religious, social, social service, and student government. Popular campus events include Terry Fox Day, Gung Hagis Fat Choi, and Robbie Burns Day. **Sports:** There are 8 intercollegiate sports for men and 9 for women, and 8 intramural sports for men and 7 for women. Facilities include 3 gyms, swimming and diving pools, a running track, weight rooms, saunas, playing fields, a combative room, tennis, squash, and racquetball courts, and a fitness center. **Graduates:** The most popular majors were business, education, and economics.

SERVICES: There is a reader service for the blind. There are taped library books. Some lectures are taped. **Library/Resources:** The 3 libraries contain 2.6 million volumes, 936,808 microform items, and 22,649 audio/video tapes/CDs/DVDs, and subscribe to 67,000 periodicals including electronic. Computerized library services include interlibrary loans, database searching, Internet access, and Wi-Fi capability. Special learning facilities include an art gallery, an archeology museum, special literature and map collections, fine and performing arts theater, hypo/hyperbaric chamber, back test unit, rock climbing wall, apiary, underwater lab, television and photography studios, and dance floors. **Physically Challenged Students:** 95% of the campus is accessible. Facilities include wheelchair ramps, elevators, special parking, specially equipped restrooms, lowered drinking fountains, lowered telephones, special housing. Braille printer, a visualtek machine, closed-circuit TV for text or graphic enlargement, note taking tutor support, adaptive technology, exam modifications, sign language interpreters, closed captioning in lectures, and alternate format texts. **Special:** Simon Fraser offers cooperative education in most areas of study, study abroad in 47 countries, many opportunities for joint majors, a general studies degree, work-study programs, dual-majors, student-designed majors, and a variety of certificate and diploma programs, as well as non-degree and evening study. Interdisciplinary majors are offered in such areas as chemical physics, management and systems science, mathematical physics, and physics and physiology. There is a freshman honors program and 48 departmental honors programs. **Visiting:** There are regularly scheduled orientations for prospective students, consisting of regularly scheduled 1-day campus orientations for prospective students. There are guides for informal visits and visitors may stay overnight. To schedule a visit, contact the Residence and Housing Office at (778) 782-4201. **Campus Safety and Security:** Measures include 24-hour foot and vehicle patrol and security escort services. There are emergency telephones, lighted pathways/sidewalks, controlled access to dorms/residences, safe-walk stations, and student patrols.

REQUIREMENTS: The ACT is recommended. The SAT is required for U.S. applicants. Applicants must be graduates of an accredited secondary school and have a minimum grade average of 70%. A GPA of 3.2 is required. AP credits are accepted. General bachelor's degrees require completion of 120 semester hours with a 2.0 cumulative GPA. For a honors degrees, students must complete 132 hours. Some programs require a thesis. **Procedure:** Freshmen are admitted to all sessions. There are early decision and early admissions plans. Early decision applications should be filed by April 1; regular applications, by May 1 for fall entry; September 30 for spring entry; and February 2 for summer entry. The fall 2016 application fee was $45. Notification of early decision is sent April 15; regular decision, June 30. Applications are accepted on-line. **Transfer Students:** 2603 transfer students enrolled in 2015-2016. Applicants must have a minimum GPA of 2.0 and be in good standing at their previous school. 60 of 120 credits required for the bachelor's degree must be completed at SFU. **International Students:** There are 2889 international students enrolled. The school actively recruits these students. They must take the TOEFL, or take the IELTS (minimum score 6.5 on academic modules).

Admissions Contact: Mehran Kiai, Enrollment Services. Email: *reginfo@sfu.ca* Web: *www.sfu.ca*

FINANCIAL AID: The FAFSA code is G08444. The deadline for filing freshman financial aid applications for fall entry is July 1.

UNIVERSITÉ DE MONTRÉAL — E-2

www.umontreal.ca

Montreal, PQ H3C 3J7 — **(514) 343-7076**

Fax: (514) 343-5788
Email: admissions@regis.umontreal.ca

Full-time: 13,020 men, 17,045 women
Part-time: 5410 men, 9025 women
Graduate: 6726 men, 8348 women
Year: trimesters, summer session
Room & Board: $3840

Faculty: n/av
Ph.D.s: 96%
Student/Faculty: n/av
Tuition: $2688 ($16,020)
Freshman Class: 31100 applied, 13923 accepted, 13174 enrolled
CEEB CODE: 0992

Application Deadline: March 1

Université de Montréal, founded in 1878, and it's the largest French-language university in North America, with 13 faculties, 2 affiliated schools, 62 teaching departments, and more than 170 research units. The figures in the above capsule and in this profile are approximate. The 145-acre campus is in an urban area in Montreal, Canada. Including any residence halls, there are 38 buildings.

STUDENT LIFE: 88% are from public schools. **Female To Male Ratio:** 1.4:1. The average age of freshmen is 22; all undergraduates, 24. 20% do not continue beyond their first year; 80% remain to graduate. **Housing:** 1164 students can be accommodated in college housing, which includes coed off-campus apartments. On-campus housing is available on a first-come and first-served basis. 98% of students commute. All students may keep cars.

FACULTY/CLASSROOMS: 71% of faculty are male; 29% are female. All teach undergraduates. No introductory courses are taught by graduate students. The average class size in an introductory lecture is 48; in a laboratory is 19; and in a regular course is 40.

PROGRAMS OF STUDY: UdeM confers B.A., B.Sc., B.A.A., B.A.P., B.D.I., B.Gest., B.Ed., B.Ing., B.Int., B.Mus., and B.Th. degrees. Associate, master's, and doctoral degrees are also awarded. Bachelor's degrees are awarded in BIOLOGICAL SCIENCE (biochemistry, biology/biological science, biometrics and biostatistics, and nutrition), BUSINESS (business administration and management), COMMUNICATIONS AND THE ARTS (art history and appreciation, classics, English, film arts, French, German, industrial design, linguistics, and music), COMPUTER AND PHYSICAL SCIENCE (chemistry, computer science, mathematics, and physics), EDUCATION (education, physical education, and psychology education), ENGINEERING AND ENVIRONMENTAL DESIGN (architectural engineering, architecture, engineering, industrial administration/management, and landscape architecture/design), HEALTH PROFESSIONS (health science, nursing, occupational therapy, pharmacy, physical therapy, predentistry, premedicine, preveterinary science, speech pathology/audiology, and veterinary science), SOCIAL SCIENCE (anthropology, Asian/Oriental studies, criminology, economics, geography, history, law, philosophy, political science/government, psychology, social work, sociology, Spanish studies, theological studies, and urban studies). Law, medicine, and nursing have the largest enrollments.

ACTIVITIES: There are no fraternities or sororities. There are 100 groups on campus, including art, cheerleading, choir, chorale, computers, dance, debate, drama, environmental, ethnic, film, international, jazz band, literary magazine, newspaper, orchestra, photography, political, radio and TV, religious, social, social service, student government, and yearbook. Popular campus events include Multicultural Week, and Welcoming Week. **Sports:** There are 8 intercollegiate sports for men and 6 for women, and 12 intramural sports for men and 12 for women. Facilities include a skating rink, a football field, a gym, squash and racquetball courts, a pool, a diving pool, a running field with tennis courts, and aerobic and muscular exercise equipment. **Graduates:** The most popular majors were law (8%), medicine (5%), and nursing (5%).

SERVICES: Counseling and information services are available, as is tutoring in some subjects, and a reader service for the blind, and remedial math, reading, and writing. **Library/Resources:** The 19 libraries contain 3.0 million volumes, 1.6 million microform items, 2.0 million audio/video tapes/CDs/DVDs, and subscribe to 50,000 periodicals including electronic. Computerized library services include interlibrary loans, database searching, Internet access, and Wi-Fi capability. Special learning facilities include an art gallery, natural history museum, radio station, and concert hall. **Physically Challenged Students:** 95% of the campus is accessible. Facilities include wheelchair ramps, elevators, special parking, specially equipped restrooms, lowered drinking fountains, lowered telephones, special housing. Specialized equipment center for students with disabilities. **Special:** The university offers co-op programs in math, translation, mining, and civil, chemical, and software material engineering, and work-study programs in hospitals and businesses in Quebec. Dual majors in math and economics, math and physics, math and computer science, communication and politics, economics and politics, and 3-2 engineering degrees may also be arranged. Study abroad is available in 31 countries. There is a freshman honors program and 45 departmental honors programs. **Visiting:** There are regularly scheduled orientations for prospective students. Student visits include Orientation and Employment Week in November, guided tours February through May, and open house in January and August. There are guides for informal visits. To schedule a visit, contact the Director of Communications and Recrutement at (514) 343-6032. **Campus Safety and Security:** Measures include 24-hour foot and vehicle patrol, emergency notification system, security escort services, emergency telephones, lighted pathways/sidewalks, controlled access to dorms/residences, and in-room safes.

REQUIREMENTS: Applicants in certain programs must take the university's admissions tests. An interview is also required in some programs. To graduate, students must have a GPA of 2.0 on a 4.3 scale. The total number of credits required in most programs is 90, although it can range up to 187. Professional programs, particularly those in health-related fields, require more hours. **Procedure:** Freshmen are admitted in the fall and winter. Applications should be filed by March 1 for fall entry; November 1 for winter entry; March 1 for spring entry; and March 1 for summer entry, along with a $100 fee. Notifications are sent March 15. Applications are accepted online. **Transfer Students:** Transfers are considered if there are openings in the second or third year of the university's programs. 90 credits required for the bachelor's degree must be completed at UdeM. **International Students:** The school actively recruits these students.

ADMISSIONS: 45% of the 2016-2017 applicants were accepted. **Admissions Contact:** Jacinthe Gauthier, Responsible Admissions. Email: *admissions@regis.umontreal.ca* Web: *www.umontreal.ca*

FINANCIAL AID: The deadline for filing freshman financial aid applications for fall entry is March 31.

UNIVERSITE LAVAL — E-2
www.ulaval.ca

Quebec, PQ G1K 7P4	**(418) 656-2764** **(877) 785-2825**
Fax: (418) 656-5216	**Email: reg@reg.ulaval.ca**
Full-time: 9000 men, 13,000 women	**Faculty:** n/av
Part-time: 3345 men, 5487 women	**Ph.D.s:** 90%
Graduate: 4914 men, 5458 women	**Student/Faculty:** n/av
Year: semesters, summer session	**Tuition:** $2978 ($18,588)
Room & Board: $9200	**Freshman Class:** 28717 applied, 20234 accepted, 10726 enrolled **CEEB CODE:** 0931
Application Deadline: n/av	

University Laval, founded in 1852, is the oldest French-language university in North America. It offers undergraduate and graduate programs through 17 faculties and 9 institutes. The figures in the above capsule and in this profile are approximate. There are 16 undergraduate schools and 17 graduate schools. In addition to regional accreditation, has baccalaureate program accreditation with AACSB, AUCC, and ACU. The 465-acre campus is in an urban area 2 miles west of old Quebec City. Including any residence halls, there are 35 buildings.

STUDENT LIFE: 94% of undergraduates are from Quebec. Others are from 105 foreign countries. **Female To Male Ratio:** 1.4:1. The average age of all undergraduates is 26. **Housing:** 2400 students can be accommodated in college housing, which includes single-sex and coed on-campus apartments. On-campus housing is available on a first-come and first-served basis. All students may keep cars.

FACULTY/CLASSROOMS: All teach undergraduates. No introductory courses are taught by graduate students.

PROGRAMS OF STUDY: Laval confers B.A., B.Sc., B.A.A., B.A.V., B.Ed., B.Ens., B.Ing., B.Mus., B.Pharm., B.Sc.A., B.Sc.Arch., B.Serv.Soc., B.Th. and LL.B. degrees. Master's and doctoral degrees are also awarded. Bachelor's degrees are awarded in AGRICULTURE (agricultural business management, agricultural economics, agronomy, forest engineering, forestry and related sciences, and wood science), BIOLOGICAL SCIENCE (biochemistry, biology/biological science, microbiology, and nutrition), BUSINESS (business administration and management), COMMUNICATIONS AND THE ARTS (art, art history and appreciation, communications, dramatic arts, English, English as a second/foreign language, French, languages, linguistics, literature, music, and visual and performing arts), COMPUTER AND PHYSICAL SCIENCE (actuarial science, chemistry, computer science, geology, geoscience, mathematics, physics, software engineering, and statistics), EDUCATION (art education, athletic training, early childhood education, education, elementary education, music education, physical education, secondary education, and technical education), ENGINEERING AND ENVIRONMENTAL DESIGN (agricultural engineering, architecture, chemical engineering, civil engineering, computer engineering, electrical/electronics engineering, engineering and applied science, engineering physics, geological engineering, graphic arts technology, industrial administration/management, mechanical engineering, metallurgical engineering, and mining and mineral engineering), HEALTH PROFESSIONS (nursing, occupational therapy, pharmacy, physical therapy, predentistry, and premedicine), SOCIAL SCIENCE (anthropology, classical/ancient civilization, consumer services, counseling/psychology, economics, food science, French studies, geography, history, interdisciplinary studies, international studies, Judaic studies, law, philosophy, physical fitness/movement, political science/government, psychology, social work, sociology, Spanish studies, and theological studies). Business administration, sciences, and education have the largest enrollments.

ACTIVITIES: There are no fraternities or sororities. There are 150 groups on campus, including art, band, chess, choir, chorale, computers, dance, drama, ethnic, film, forensics, international, jazz band, LGBT, literary magazine, musical theater, newspaper, opera, orchestra, photography, political, radio and TV, religious, social, social service, student government, and symphony. Popular campus events include Thematic Weeks, Rendez-vous Laval, and Student Festivals. **Sports:** There are 13 intercollegiate sports for men and 10 for women, and 7 intramural sports for men and 7 for women. Facilities include a covered stadium with running track, tennis courts, swimming pool with a diving tower, ice arena, gyms, squash courts, handball and racquetball courts, judo, karate and self-defense rooms, dance studio, open-air stadium with running track, softball, football, soccer fields, outdoor tennis courts, physical training rooms, golf driving range and indoor golf practice room, outdoor basketball courts, hiking trail, and a jogging track. **Graduates:** The most popular majors were administration (18%), science and engineering (14%), and letters (13%).

SERVICES: There is a reader service for the blind, and remedial math and writing. Tutoring in French grammar is also available. **Library/Resources:** The 2 libraries contain 3.4 million volumes, 1.3 million microform items, and 37,832 audio/video tapes/CDs/DVDs, and subscribe to 17,625 periodicals including electronic. Computerized library services include interlibrary loans, database searching, and Internet access. Special learning facilities include an art gallery, natural history museum, radio station, a language lab, and business simulations. **Physically Challenged Students:** 95% of the campus is accessible. Facilities include wheelchair ramps, elevators, special parking, specially equipped restrooms, special class scheduling, lowered drinking fountains, lowered telephones, teletype machines for the deaf, computerized classrooms for the visually disabled, electric doors, sidewalks adjusted for physically disabled students, elevators equipped with speaking devices, and a campus plan in braille. **Special:** Laval offers co-op programs in forest operation, mining, metallurgical engineering, mineral engineering, and wood processing engineering, and study abroad in 65 countries. Dual majors are possible in anthropology and ethnology, economics and politics, international studies and modern languages, historical sciences and patrimonial studies, French language and professional writing, math and computer science. Intensive French courses are offered during the summer. **Visiting:** There are regularly scheduled orientations for prospective students. There are guides for informal visits and visitors may stay overnight. To schedule a visit, contact the Public Affairs Office at (877) 785-2825. **Campus Safety and Security:** Measures include 24-hour foot and vehicle patrol, security escort services, emergency telephones, and lighted pathways/sidewalks. Services include 24-hour camera surveillance in pedestrian tunnels, trained evacuating teams in all buildings, and security training for social events is offered to all student associations.

REQUIREMENTS: The only general requirement is the D.E.C. (Diploma of Collegial Studies 13 years of scholarity) or the equivalent. Some programs have specific requirements. All undergraduate students (except those who are nonfrancophones) must show a sufficient knowledge of the French language to obtain their bachelor's degree. Requirements for graduation vary according to the program. A minimum GPA of 2.0 out of 4.33 is required per 30 credits. **Procedure:** Freshmen are admitted to all sessions. Check with the school for current application deadlines. Applications are accepted online. **Transfer Students:** 1662 transfer students enrolled in 2015-2016. Applicants must have the D.E.C. or the equivalent. **International Students:** The school actively recruits these students.

ADMISSIONS: 70% of the 2016-2017 applicants were accepted. **Admissions Contact:** Public Affairs Office. Email: *reg@reg.ulaval.ca* Web: *www.ulaval.ca/bip*

FINANCIAL AID: The FAFSA code is G06837. The deadline for filing freshman financial aid applications for fall entry is June 30.

UNIVERSITY OF ALBERTA — C-2

www.ualberta.ca

Edmonton, AB T6G 2M7	(780) 492-3113
Fax: (780) 492-7172	**Email:** admissions@ualberta.ca
Full-time: 12,346 men, 15,665 women	**Faculty:** 1659
Part-time: 691 men, 1147 women	**Ph.D.s:** 92%
Graduate: 3550 men, 3594 women	**Student/Faculty:** n/av
Year: semesters, summer session	**Tuition:** $5829 ($18,459)
Room & Board: $6502	**Freshman Class:** 10587 applied, 6131 accepted, 4812 enrolled
SAT: recommended	**CEEB CODE:** 0963
Application Deadline: May 1	

University of Alberta, founded in 1908, is a publicly supported institution offering undergraduate and graduate programs in arts and science, agricultural sciences, business, education, engineering, nursing, phys ed, native studies, and professional studies. The figures in the above capsule and in this profile are approximate. The fall tuition cost is for Canadian citizens and permanent residents. There are 18 undergraduate schools and 1 graduate school. The 155-acre campus is in an urban area 2 miles southwest of downtown Edmonton, Canada. Including any residence halls, there are 90 buildings.

STUDENT LIFE: Students are from 30 foreign countries, and Canada. **Female To Male Ratio:** 1.2:1. The average age of freshmen is 19; all undergraduates, 22. **Housing:** 4900 students can be accommodated in college housing, which includes single-sex and coed dorms, on-campus apartments, off-campus apartments, married student housing, honors houses, language houses, special-interest houses, fraternity houses, and sorority houses. 88% of students commute. All students may keep cars.

FACULTY/CLASSROOMS: All teach undergraduates and do research. No introductory courses are taught by graduate students. The average class size in an introductory lecture is 90; in a laboratory is 20; and in a regular course is 35.

PROGRAMS OF STUDY: U of A confers B.A., B.Comm., B.Ed., B.F.A., B.Mus., B.P.E., B.S.C., B.S.Cn. and B.des. degrees. Master's and doctoral degrees are also awarded. Bachelor's degrees are awarded in AGRICULTURE (agricultural economics, agriculture, animal science, and soil science), BIOLOGICAL SCIENCE (biochemistry, biology/biological science, botany, cell biology, entomology, genetics, microbiology, physiology, and zoology), BUSINESS (accounting, management science, and marketing/retailing/merchandising), COMMUNICATIONS AND THE ARTS (classics, comparative literature, dance, dramatic arts, English, film arts, French, Germanic languages and literature, linguistics, music, romance languages and literature, and Slavic languages), COMPUTER AND PHYSICAL SCIENCE (applied mathematics, chemistry, computer science, earth science, geology, geophysics and seismology, mathematics, physical sciences, physics, and statistics), EDUCATION (education of the deaf and hearing impaired, education of the multiply handicapped, elementary education, physical education, secondary education, special education, and vocational education), ENGINEERING AND ENVIRONMENTAL DESIGN (chemical engineering technology, civil engineering, computer engineering, electrical/electronics engineering, engineering physics, mechanical engineering, metallurgical engineering, mining and mineral engineering, and petroleum/natural gas engineering), HEALTH PROFESSIONS (medical laboratory science, nursing, occupational therapy, pharmacy, and physical therapy), SOCIAL SCIENCE (anthropology, Canadian studies, clothing and textiles management/production/services, criminology, East Asian studies, Eastern European studies, economics, geography, history, law, philosophy, political science/government, psychology, sociology, and women's studies). Arts, science, and engineering have the largest enrollments.

ACTIVITIES: There are 400 groups on campus, including art, band, cheerleading, chess, choir, chorale, chorus, computers, dance, debate, drama, environmental, ethnic, film, forensics, honors, international, jazz band, LGBT, musical theater, newspaper, opera, orchestra, pep band, photography, political, radio and TV, religious, social, social service, student government, and symphony. Popular campus events include WOW (week of welcome) and AntiFreeze (winter activity). **Sports:** There are 12 intercollegiate sports for men and 13 for women, and 60 intramural sports for men and 45 for women. Facilities include a stadium, swimming pools, gyms, combatives and weight rooms, ballet/fencing and aerobics studios, outdoor track, an ice arena, racquetball and squash courts, wrestling gym, an indoor field house, sports medicine clinic, training center for disabled athletes, curling rinks, and tennis courts.

SERVICES: Counseling and information services are available, as is tutoring in most subjects, and a reader service for the blind, and remedial math, reading, and writing. **Library/Resources:** The 13 libraries contain 5.4 million volumes, and 3.7 million microform items. Computerized library services include interlibrary loans, database searching, Internet access, and Wi-Fi capability. Special learning facilities include an art gallery, radio station, an agricultural meteorological research station, ecological sanctuary, botanical garden, the Kurimoto Japanese Garden farm, and Timms Centre for the Arts. **Physically Challenged Students:** 98% of the campus is accessible. Facilities include wheelchair ramps, elevators, special parking, specially equipped restrooms, special class scheduling, lowered drinking fountains, lowered telephones, and automatic doors. **Special:** The university offers co-op programs in business and engineering. Opportunities for study abroad, internships, dual majors, bilingual classes in French and English, credit by exam (special assessment), and pass/fail options are also available. There is 1 national honor society and a freshman honors program. **Visiting:** There are regularly scheduled orientations for prospective students, including University Open House on the first weekend in October and Orientation for new students held on campus 2 days before classes begin in the fall term. There are guides for informal visits, visitors may sit in on classes, and stay overnight. To schedule a visit, contact the Office of the Registrar and Student Awards. **Campus Safety and Security:** Measures include 24-hour foot and vehicle patrol, emergency notification system, self-defense education, security escort services, emergency telephones, lighted pathways/sidewalks, and controlled access to dorms/residences.

REQUIREMENTS: The SAT is recommended. Graduation from an accredited secondary school is required. A minimum grade average of 70 is required in all courses submitted for academic credit. Depending on the program selected by the student, an essay, portfolio, audition, or interview may be required. A GPA of 70.0 is required. AP credits are accepted. The requirements for graduation vary according to the program. A minimum GPA of 2.0 and at least 120 credit hours are required for graduation. **Procedure:** Freshmen are admitted to all sessions. There is an early admissions plan. Applications should be filed by May 1 for fall entry; November 15 for winter entry; and March 1 for spring entry, along with a $115 fee. Notification of early decision is sent January 2; regular decision, August 1. Applications are accepted online. **Transfer Students:** 4609 transfer students enrolled in 2015-2016. Applicants must meet minimum matriculation requirements or complete 24 credits of transferable work with satisfactory standing. 60 of 120 credits required for the bachelor's degree must be completed at U of A. **International Students:** There are 1885 international students enrolled. The school actively recruits these students. They must take the TOEFL with a minimum score of 580 on the paper-based TOEFL (PBT) or 86 on the Internet-based version (iBT) or take the MELAB, the IELTS, the CAEL, or the university's own test.

ADMISSIONS: 58% of the 2016-2017 applicants were accepted. **Admissions Contact:** Office of the Registrar and Student Awards Email: *admissions@ualberta.ca* Web: *www.ualberta.ca*

FINANCIAL AID: Check with the school for current application deadlines.

UNIVERSITY OF BRITISH COLUMBIA B-2
www.ubc.ca

Vancouver, BC V6T 1Z1	(604) 822-3014 (877) 272-1422
Fax: (604) 822-3599	Email: recruitment.ok@ubc.ca
Full-time: 10,044 men, 11,332 women	Faculty: n/av
	Ph.D.s: 99%
Part-time: 3357 men, 4090 women	Student/Faculty: 15 to 1
Graduate: 6861 men, 8293 women	Tuition: $5175 ($21,150)
Year: other, summer session	Freshman Class: 23102 applied, 12285 accepted, 6225 enrolled
Room & Board: $6650	
SAT or ACT: required	CEEB CODE: 0965
Application Deadline: February 28	

University of British Columbia, established in 1908, is a publicly supported institution offering a wide range of undergraduate, graduate, and professional programs in the arts, sciences, and other fields of study. The figures in the above capsule and in this profile are approximate. There are 16 undergraduate schools and 1 graduate school. The 1000-acre campus is in an urban area 6 miles from the center of Vancouver, Canada. Including any residence halls, there are 500 buildings.

STUDENT LIFE: 87% of undergraduates are from British Columbia. Others are from 43 states, 139 foreign countries, and Canada. 98% are from public schools. 14% are Foreign. **Female To Male Ratio:** 1.2:1. The average age of freshmen is 20; all undergraduates, 21. 8% do not continue beyond their first year; 92% remain to graduate. **Housing:** 9500 students can be accommodated in college housing, which includes single-sex and coed dorms, on-campus apartments, and married student housing. In addition, there are special-interest houses, International houses: Japanese, Korean, Mexican and Hong Kong. On-campus housing is guaranteed for the freshman year only, and is available on a first-come, first-served basis, and is available on a lottery system for upperclassmen. Priority is given to out-of-town students. 80% of students commute. All students may keep cars.

FACULTY/CLASSROOMS: 62% of faculty are male; 38% are female. No introductory courses are taught by graduate students.

PROGRAMS OF STUDY: UBC confers B.A., B.A.H.S., B.A.Sc., B.B.R.E., B.Com.B.C.S., B.D.Sc., B.Ed., B.End., B.F.A., B.H.E., B.H.K., B.Mgt., B.M.LSc., B.Mus., B.Mw., B.Sc., B.Sc.Die., B.Sc.F., B.Sc.Pharm., B.S.F., B.S.N., B.S.W., and L.L.B. degrees. Master's and doctoral degrees are also awarded. Bachelor's degrees are awarded in AGRICULTURE (agricultural economics, animal science, forestry production and processing, forestry and related sciences, horticulture, natural resource management, and soil science), BIOLOGICAL SCIENCE (biochemistry, biology/biological science, biophysics, biotechnology, microbiology, nutrition, physiology, and zoology), BUSINESS (accounting, banking and finance, business administration and management, business economics, human resources, international business management, management information systems, marketing/retailing/merchandising, real estate, recreational facilities management, and transportation management), COMMUNICATIONS AND THE ARTS (art history and appreciation, Chinese, classics, creative writing, dramatic arts, English, film arts, fine arts, French, German, Italian, Japanese, linguistics, music, music history and appreciation, music performance, music theory and composition, romance languages and literature, and Spanish), COMPUTER AND PHYSICAL SCIENCE (astronomy, atmospheric sciences and meteorology, chemistry, computer science, earth science, geophysics and seismology, mathematics, oceanography, physics, science, and statistics), EDUCATION (elementary education, museum studies, and physical education), ENGINEERING AND ENVIRONMENTAL DESIGN (chemical engineering, civil engineering, computer engineering, electrical/electronics engineering, engineering, engineering physics, environmental design, environmental engineering, environmental science, geological engineering, mechanical engineering, metallurgical engineering, and mining and mineral engineering), HEALTH PROFESSIONS (exercise science, health, nursing, pharmacology, preveterinary science, and speech pathology/audiology), SOCIAL SCIENCE (anthropology, archeology, Asian/Oriental studies, Canadian studies, classical/ancient civilization, cognitive science, dietetics, economics, European studies, family/consumer studies, food production/management/services, food science, geography, Hispanic American studies, history, home economics, human ecology, international relations, Latin American studies, medieval studies, Native American studies, philosophy, political science/government, psychology, religion, sociology, South Asian studies, and women's studies). Applied sciences, and commerce are the strongest academically. Education, and arts have the largest enrollments.

ACTIVITIES: 6% of men belong to 7 national fraternities; 2% of women belong to 7 national sororities. There are 250 groups on campus, including varsity outdoors., art, band, cheerleading, chess, choir, chorale, chorus, computers, dance, debate, drama, environmental, ethnic, film, honors, international, jazz band, LGBT, literary magazine, musical theater, newspaper, opera, orchestra, photography, political, professional, radio and TV, religious, ski and snowboard, social, social service, student government, symphony, and yearbook. Popular campus events include Storm the Wall, Day of the Longboat, and Great Trek Run. **Sports:** There are 13 intercollegiate sports for men and 11 for women, and 18 intramural sports for men and 18 for women. Facilities include a winter sports center, a 3500-seat stadium, a gym, an aquatic center, playing fields, a recreation center, a tennis center, and a rowing centre. **Graduates:** The most popular majors were psychology, biology, and English.

SERVICES: Counseling and information services are available, as is tutoring in most subjects. There is a reader service for the blind, and remedial math, reading, and writing. **Library/Resources:** The 22 libraries contain 5.6 million volumes, 5.2 million microform items, and 840,000 audio/video tapes/CDs/DVDs, and subscribe to 63,000 periodicals including electronic. Computerized library services include interlibrary loans, database searching, Internet access, and Wi-Fi capability. Special learning facilities include an art gallery, natural history museum, radio station, a learning center, and anthropology museum. Canada's largest accelerator for subatomic physics, space observatory, center for integrated computer systems research, center for the study of global issues, and a center for the performing arts. **Physically Challenged Students:** 95% of the campus is accessible. Facilities include wheelchair ramps, elevators, special parking, specially equipped restrooms, special class scheduling, lowered drinking fountains, lowered telephones, and special housing. Accessible shower stalls in fitness facilities, tactile maps, TTY pay phones, an accessible security bus, and audible street crossing signals. **Special:** UBC offers co-op programs in science, applied science, commerce, arts, and forestry, and study abroad through 190 student exchange opportunities in 41 countries. Non-degree study is possible. A B.A.-B.A.Sc. degree, student-designed majors, dual majors in most faculties, and work-study programs are available. There are 1 national honor societies and 10 departmental honors programs. **Visiting:** There are regularly scheduled orientations for prospective students, Monday through Saturday. There are guides for informal visits, visitors may sit in on classes, and stay overnight. **Campus Safety and Security:** Measures include 24-hour foot and vehicle patrol and security escort services. There are shuttle buses, emergency telephones, lighted pathways/sidewalks, controlled access to dorms/residences, Royal Canadian mounted police detachment is on campus, awareness programs on theft, and personal safety lectures.

REQUIREMENTS: The SAT or ACT is required. The ACT Optional Writing test is also required. Graduation from an accredited secondary school is required. General admission for students following a U.S. system is based on 4 years of English and 3 years of math. There are also specific program requirements in math, chemistry, physics, and biology for students applying to science-based programs. U.S. curriculum students are required to submit SAT or ACT and writing scores. Exemptions may begin where these tests are not available. A GPA of 2.6 is required. AP credits are accepted. Important factors in the admissions decision are extracurricular activities record, leadership record, and recommendations by school officials. To graduate, students must complete 120 credits in arts or science, more for applied science. Total number of hours required in a major varies by faculty. English is required for all majors. **Procedure:** Freshmen are admitted fall and spring. There are early admissions, deferred admissions, and rolling admissions plans. Applications should be filed by February 28 for fall entry; February 28 for spring entry; and February 28 for summer entry, along with a $100 fee. Applications are accepted on-line. **Transfer Students:** 1829 transfer students enrolled in 2015-2016. Official transcripts, completion of the equivalent of 24 course credits, and no failures are required. A competitive GPA is required to get into the program at the second or third year. Applicants must have attended an accredited post-secondary institution. 60 of 120 credits required for the bachelor's degree must be completed at UBC. **International Students:** There are 4442 international students enrolled. The school actively recruits these students. They must also take the SAT or ACT.

ADMISSIONS: 53% of the 2016-2017 applicants were accepted. 96% of the current freshmen were in the top fifth of their class. **Admissions Contact:** Office of the Registrar Email: *recruitment.ok@ubc.ca* Web: *www.ubc.ca*

FINANCIAL AID: The college's own financial statement is required. The FAFSA code is G08369. Check with the school for current application deadlines.

UNIVERSITY OF CALGARY — C-2

www.ucalgary.ca

Calgary, AB T2N 1N4 — **(403) 210-7625**

Fax: (403) 220-0762 — **Email:** future.students@ucalgary.ca

Full-time: 10,667 men, 12,146 women
Part-time: 747 men, 1064 women
Graduate: 2795 men, 3099 women
Year: semesters, summer session
Room & Board: $9614
SAT or ACT: required
Application Deadline: n/av

Faculty: n/av
Ph.D.s: n/av
Student/Faculty: n/av
Tuition: $6590
Freshman Class: n/av
CEEB CODE: 0813

The University of Calgary is a leading Canadian university offering more than 200 undergraduate, graduate and professional degree programs. Ranked one of the top ten research universities, it houses over 70 Canada Research Chairs and over 80 research institutes and centers working to address society's most persistent and emerging challenges. There are 14 undergraduate schools and 2 graduate schools. The 526-acre campus is in an urban area in northwest Calgary, Alberta Canada. Including any residence halls, there are 48 buildings.

STUDENT LIFE: 82% of undergraduates are from Alberta. **Female To Male Ratio:** 1.1:1. The average age of all undergraduates is 22. **Housing:** 2812 students can be accommodated in college housing, which includes coed dorms, on-campus apartments, married student housing, honors houses, language houses, Upper, International & Transfer Students; business, engineering students, Scholar's Advantage (first year recipients of Prestige Scholarships and Awards). On-campus housing is guaranteed for all 4 years. Priority is given to out-of-town students. All students may keep cars.

FACULTY/CLASSROOMS: No introductory courses are taught by graduate students.

PROGRAMS OF STUDY: Master's and doctoral degrees are also awarded. Bachelor's degrees are awarded in BIOLOGICAL SCIENCE (biochemistry, bioinformatics, biology/biological science, botany, cell biology, ecology, and zoology), BUSINESS (accounting, business administration and management, hotel/motel and restaurant management, and marketing/retailing/merchandising), COMMUNICATIONS AND THE ARTS (communications, dance, dramatic arts, East Asian languages and literature, English, fine arts, French, German, Latin, linguistics, music, music history and appreciation, music performance, music theory and composition, Russian, and Spanish), COMPUTER AND PHYSICAL SCIENCE (actuarial science, applied mathematics, astrophysics, chemical physics, chemistry, computer science, earth science, geology, geophysics and seismology, mathematics, natural sciences, physics, and statistics), EDUCATION (education, elementary education, and secondary education), ENGINEERING AND ENVIRONMENTAL DESIGN (chemical engineering, civil engineering, computer engineering, electrical/electronics engineering, environmental science, mechanical engineering, petroleum/natural gas engineering, and surveying engineering), HEALTH PROFESSIONS (biomedical science, exercise science, nursing, public health, and sports medicine), SOCIAL SCIENCE (anthropology, archeology, Asian/Oriental studies, Canadian studies, Christian studies, classical/ancient civilization, East Asian studies, economics, geography, German area studies, history, international relations, Italian studies, Latin American studies, law, liberal arts/general studies, philosophy, physical fitness/movement, political science/government, psychology, religion, social work, sociology, urban studies, and women's studies). Engineering, and medicine are the strongest academically. Arts, science, and engineering have the largest enrollments.

ACTIVITIES: There are no fraternities or sororities. Groups on campus include art, band, chess, choir, chorus, computers, dance, debate, drama, environmental, ethnic, film, international, jazz band, LGBT, musical theater, newspaper, orchestra, political, professional, radio and TV, religious, social, social service, and student government. Popular campus events include Bermuda Shorts Day (last day of classes in April), Orientation Week and KickOff. **Sports:** There are 9 intercollegiate sports for men and 9 for women, and 20 intramural sports for men and 18 for women. Facilities include a swimming pool, gyms, a indoor track, climbing wall, indoor speed-skating arena, outdoor stadium, rooms for weight training room, aerobics, combatives, squash, tennis, and racquetball courts. There is also an outdoor recreation center. **Graduates:** The most popular majors were arts, science, and engineering.

SERVICES: Counseling and information services are available, as is tutoring in most subjects, a reader service for the blind, and remedial math and writing. **Library/Resources:** Computerized library services include interlibrary loans, database searching, Internet access, and Wi-Fi capability. Special learning facilities include an art gallery, radio station, TV station, an environmental research center, observatory, human performance and theater labs, arts museum, children's hospital, and Foothills medical center. **Physically Challenged Students:** All of the campus is accessible. Facilities include wheelchair ramps, elevators, special parking, specially equipped restrooms, special class scheduling, lowered drinking fountains, lowered telephones, and special housing. **Special:** The university offers co-op programs in arts, actuarial science, applied chemistry, business, arts, engineering, and computer science. Dual majors, combined degrees in many disciplines, and study abroad in 61 countries are also available. Students may cross-register with any of 8 member colleges in the Big Country Education Consortium. U of C sponsors or is affiliated with 20 research institutes and groups. There is a freshman honors program. **Visiting:** There are regularly scheduled orientations for prospective students. There are guides for informal visits and visitors may stay overnight. To schedule a visit, contact Student Enrollment Services at (403) 210-7625. **Campus Safety and Security:** Measures include 24-hour foot and vehicle patrol, emergency notification system, security escort services, emergency telephones, lighted pathways/sidewalks, and controlled access to dorms/residences.

REQUIREMENTS: U.S. applicants must be graduates of a secondary school and submit SAT or ACT scores, as required by the individual faculties. AP credits are accepted. To graduate, all students must satisfy the required courses, course sequences, and credit distribution in their particular program. Students must maintain a minimum 2.0 GPA and complete 7 to 10 full-course equivalents in the major field. **Procedure:** Freshmen are admitted in the fall. There is an early admissions plan. Check with the school for current application deadlines. The application fee is $125. Applications are accepted on-line. **Transfer Students:** Applicants must have a cumulative GPA of 2.0 or above on all transfer courses. **International Students:** There are 1637 international students enrolled. The school actively recruits these students. They must take the TOEFL, or take the IELTS, the CAEL, or the university's English program. They must also take the SAT or ACT.

Admissions Contact: future.students@ucalgary.ca, choose.ucalgary.ca. Web: *www.ucalgary.ca*

FINANCIAL AID: Check with the school for current application deadlines.

UNIVERSITY OF GUELPH E-3
www.uoguelph.ca

Guelph, ON N1G 2W1 (519) 821-2130

Fax: (519) 766-9481	**Email:** admisssion@uoguelph.ca
Full-time: n/av	**Faculty:** 800
Part-time: n/av	**Ph.D.s:** 98%
Graduate: n/av	**Student/Faculty:** 19 to 1
Year: varies, summer session	**Tuition:** $7660 ($21,514)
Room & Board: $10,924	**Freshman Class:** 18852 applied, 13765 accepted, 3479 enrolled
SAT or ACT: required	**CEEB CODE:** 0892
Application Deadline: March 1	

University of Guelph, founded in 1964, is a public institution offering programs in arts and sciences, agriculture, engineering, commerce, landscape architecture, veterinary medicine, applied science, and technology. The approximate figures in the above capsule is based upon Canada and International students and varies by programs chosen. There are 7 undergraduate schools and 56 graduate schools. The 1017-acre campus is in a suburban area 2 miles south of the center of Guelph, Canada. Including any residence halls, there are 80 buildings.

STUDENT LIFE: 93% of undergraduates are from Ontario. Others are from 100 foreign countries, and Canada. The average age of freshmen is 18; all undergraduates, 21. 9% do not continue beyond their first year; 89% remain to graduate. **Housing:** 5500 students can be accommodated in college housing, which includes single-sex and coed dorms, on-campus apartments, off-campus apartments, and married student housing. In addition, there are language houses, special-interest houses, an international house, La Maison Francaise, Eco house, an arts house, and study intensive and academic clusters. On-campus housing is guaranteed for the freshman year only, and on a first-come, first-served basis, and is available on a lottery system for upperclassmen. 67% of students commute. All students may keep cars.

FACULTY/CLASSROOMS: No introductory courses are taught by graduate students. The average class size in an introductory lecture is 300 and in a laboratory is 25.

PROGRAMS OF STUDY: U of G confers B.A., B.A.S., B.A.Sc, B.B.R.M., B.Comm, B.Comp, B.Eng, B.L.A., B.Sc-Agr, B.Sc-Eng, B.Sc-Env, and B.Sc degrees. Master's and doctoral degrees are also awarded. Bachelor's degrees are awarded in AGRICULTURE (agricultural economics, agriculture, agronomy, animal science, horticulture, and natural resource management), BIOLOGICAL SCIENCE (biochemistry, biology/biological science, biophysics, ecology, environmental biology, marine science, microbiology, molecular biology, nutrition, wildlife biology, and zoology), BUSINESS (hospitality management services, human resources, marketing management, and real estate), COMMUNICATIONS AND THE ARTS (art history and appreciation, classical languages, English, music, Spanish, and studio art), COMPUTER AND PHYSICAL SCIENCE (chemical physics, chemistry, computer science, earth science, information sciences and systems, physical sciences, physics, and statistics), ENGINEERING AND ENVIRONMENTAL DESIGN (biomedical engineering, engineering, environmental engineering, and landscape architecture/design), SOCIAL SCIENCE (anthropology, child care/child and family studies, classical/ancient civilization, criminal justice, economics, food science, French studies, geography, gerontology, history, interdisciplinary studies, philosophy, political science/government, psychology, public administration, rural sociology, sociology, water resources, and women's studies). Biological and physical sciences and veterinary medicine is the strongest academically. Biological and physical sciences, arts, and social sciences have the largest enrollments.

ACTIVITIES: There are no fraternities or sororities. There are 100 groups on campus, including art, cheerleading, chess, choir, chorale, computers, dance, debate, drama, environmental, ethnic, international, jazz band, LGBT, literary magazine, newspaper, photography, political, professional, radio and TV, religious, social, social service, student government, and yearbook. Popular campus events include College Royal open house weekend in March. **Sports:** There are 15 intercollegiate sports for men and 15 for women, and 17 intramural sports for men and 17 for women. Facilities include a twin-pad arena, ice surface, squash courts, a fitness gym, weight-training rooms, swimming pools, a fitness circuit, and gyms. Outdoor facilities include tennis courts, a running track, lighted football, field hockey, soccer, rugby and fastball fields, jogging trails, and multipurpose fields. There are also dance studios, a climbing wall, wrestling/combatives room, covered field with artificial turf, and a track.

SERVICES: Counseling and information services are available, as is tutoring in most subjects, and a reader service for the blind. ESL, learning, studying, and writing resources are available. **Library/Resources:** The library contains 2.0 million volumes, 1.5 million microform items, and 17,000 audio/video tapes/CDs/DVDs, and subscribes to 7,600 periodicals including electronic. Computerized library services include interlibrary loans, database searching, Internet access, and Wi-Fi capability. Special learning facilities include an art gallery, radio station, an observatory, a learning commons, a research park, and arboretum. **Physically Challenged Students:** 90% of the campus is accessible. Facilities include wheelchair ramps, elevators, special parking, specially equipped restrooms, special class scheduling, lowered drinking fountains, lowered telephones, special housing. special library services, equipment, and software. **Special:** U of G offers co-op programs in 30 majors, study abroad in 29 countries, and work-study programs. Accelerated degree programs, dual majors, a general studies degree, and non-degree study are available. There is a freshman honors program and 33 departmental honors programs. **Visiting:** Regularly scheduled orientations are available for prospective students, as are daily tours of the campus, Fall Preview Day, Campus Day and Spring Academic Open House. There are guides for informal visits and visitors may sit in on classes. To schedule a visit, contact The Assistant Manager at (519) 824-4120, ext. 58712. **Campus Safety and Security:** Measures include 24-hour foot and vehicle patrol, emergency notification system, self-defense education, and security escort services. There are also shuttle buses, emergency telephones, lighted pathways/sidewalks, controlled access to dorms/residences, a campus safe walk, and a campus police patrol.

REQUIREMENTS: The SAT or ACT, the ACT Optional Writing test are required. U.S. applicants must have a minimum cumulative unweighted grade point average of 3.0 from a regionally accredited high school, and a combined math and critical reading SAT score of 1100 or ACT score of 24. Where class rankings are reported on the transcript, a ranking in the top quarter is preferred. Students should include among their senior level courses, specific courses that are required for admission to the degree program of their choice. Particular attention is paid to performance in program prerequisites. Students should ensure that senior year final grades from first and second semester interim grades are submitted before the document deadline date. AP credits are accepted. Important factors in the admissions decision are advanced placement or honors courses, extracurricular activities record, and leadership record. To graduate, students must complete 30 credits (half courses) for a general degree and 40 credits (half courses) for an honors degree. U of G requires a minimum of 10 credits in the major. **Procedure:** Freshmen are admitted in the fall. There are early decision and deferred admissions plans. Early decision applications should be filed by January 1; regular applications, by March 1 for fall entry, along with a $165 fee. Notifications are sent in March. 5000 early decision candidates were accepted for the 2016-2017 class. Applications are accepted online. **Transfer Students:** Applicants must meet general admissions requirements and have a B average in all college-level courses. **International Students:** There are 700 international students enrolled. The school actively recruits these students. They must take the TOEFL with a minimum score of 600 on the paper-based TOEFL (PBT) or 89 on the Internet-based version (iBT) or take the MELAB and the college's own test, CAEL, IELTS, and PTE. U.S. students are required to submit SAT or ACT scores, with minimum acceptable scores.

ADMISSIONS: 73% of the 2016-2017 applicants were accepted. **Admissions Contact:** Admission Services. Email: *admisssion@uoguelph.ca* Web: *www.uoguelph.ca*

FINANCIAL AID: 30% of undergraduate students work part-time. The college's own financial statement and the Federal and Provincial Government Canadian Form are required. The FAFSA code is G06683. Check with the school for current application deadlines.

UNIVERSITY OF OTTAWA E-3
www.uottowa.ca

Ottawa, ON K1N 6N5 (613) 562-5700
(877) 868-8292
Fax: (613) 562-5323
Email: admissions@uottawa.ca
Full-time: 11,124 men, 17,521 women
Faculty: n/av
Ph.D.s: 96%
Part-time: 2177 men, 3095 women
Student/Faculty: 22 to 1
Graduate: 2430 men, 3252 women
Tuition: $6106 ($16,444)
Year: semesters, summer session
Freshman Class: n/av
Room & Board: $6360
SAT: required
CEEB CODE: 0993
Application Deadline: n/av

University of Ottawa, founded in 1848, is a bilingual (French/English) institution offering undergraduate and graduate degrees through the faculties of arts, law, health sciences, medicine, science, engineering, management, social sciences, and education. The figures in the above capsule and in this profile are approximate. There are 9 undergraduate schools and 9 graduate schools. In addition to regional accreditation, uOttawa has baccalaureate program accreditation with AACSB. The 43-acre campus is in an urban area in Ottawa, Ontario. Including any residence halls, there are 40 buildings.

STUDENT LIFE: 80% of undergraduates are from Ontario. **Female To Male Ratio:** 1.5:1. **Housing:** 2870 students can be accommodated in college housing, which includes single-sex and coed dorms, on-campus apartments, and married student housing. On-campus housing on a first-come, first-served basis, and is available on a lottery system for upperclassmen. All students may keep cars.

FACULTY/CLASSROOMS: 63% of faculty are male; 37% are female. All teach undergraduates, and do research. No introductory courses are taught by graduate students. The average class size in an introductory lecture is 60; in a laboratory is 30; and in a regular course is 30.

PROGRAMS OF STUDY: uOttawa confers B.A., B.Ad., B.A.Sc., B.Com., B.Ed., B.F.A., B.Mus., B.Sc., B.Sc.N., B.Soc.Sc., B.Jour., and B.H.Sc. degrees. Master's and doctoral degrees are also awarded. Bachelor's degrees are awarded in AGRICULTURE (environmental studies), BIOLOGICAL SCIENCE (biochemistry, biology/biological science, biotechnology, and life science), BUSINESS (accounting, banking and finance, electronic business, human resources, management information systems, management science, and marketing/retailing/merchandising), COMMUNICATIONS AND THE ARTS (Arabic, art history and appreciation, arts administration/management, classics, communications, English, English as a second/foreign language, French, German, Italian, journalism, Latin, linguistics, modern language, music, Spanish, and visual and performing arts), COMPUTER AND PHYSICAL SCIENCE (chemistry, computer science, earth science, geology, mathematics, physics, and software engineering), EDUCATION (education, elementary education, foreign languages education, and middle school education), ENGINEERING AND ENVIRONMENTAL DESIGN (biomedical engineering, chemical engineering, civil engineering, computer engineering, electrical/electronics engineering, environmental engineering, environmental science, and mechanical engineering), HEALTH PROFESSIONS (biomedical science, health science, nursing, and ophthalmic technology), SOCIAL SCIENCE (anthropology, Canadian studies, criminology, economics, ethics, politics, and social policy, ethnic studies, geography, gerontology, history, international studies, law, medieval studies, philosophy, political science/government, psychology, public administration, religion, Russian and Slavic studies, sociology, and women's studies). Law, medicine, and education are the strongest academically. Arts, social sciences, and science have the largest enrollments.

ACTIVITIES: There are no fraternities or sororities. There are 100 groups on campus, including art, band, cheerleading, chess, choir, chorale, computers, dance, debate, drama, environmental, ethnic, film, honors, international, jazz band, LGBT, newspaper, orchestra, photography, political, professional, radio and TV, religious, social, social service, student government, and symphony. Popular campus events include University of Ottawa Day, Gee-gees Football Games and International week. **Sports:** There are 5 intercollegiate sports for men and 7 for women, and 13 intramural sports for men and 11 for women. Facilities include sports complexes with weight-training and combat rooms, swimming pools, gyms, racquetball and squash courts, billiards and ping pong tables, indoor arena, and a multipurpose sports field. **Graduates:** From July 1, 2015 to June 30, 2016, 6836 bachelor's degrees were awarded.

SERVICES: Counseling and information services are available, as is tutoring in most subjects, and a reader service for the blind, and remedial math, reading, and writing. **Library/Resources:** The 8 libraries contain 2.2 million volumes, 1.9 million microform items, and 777,349 audio/video tapes/CDs/DVDs, and subscribe to 60,522 periodicals including electronic. Computerized library services include interlibrary loans, database searching, Internet access, and Wi-Fi capability. Special learning facilities include an art gallery, radio station, TV station, a Museum of Classical Antiquities. **Physically Challenged Students:** 75% of the campus is accessible. Facilities include wheelchair ramps, elevators, special parking, specially equipped restrooms, special class scheduling, lowered drinking fountains, lowered telephones, special housing, automatic doors and specialized equipment. **Special:** Opportunities are provided for cooperative programs, study abroad in over 56 countries, a general studies degree in arts and in sciences, and combined programs in all fields in arts and in social sciences. There are 40 departmental honors programs. **Visiting:** There are regularly scheduled orientations for prospective students, open house and campus visits (ongoing, year round). There are guides for informal visits and visitors may sit in on classes. To schedule a visit, contact the Liaison Office at (613) 562-5800. **Campus Safety and Security:** Measures include 24-hour foot and vehicle patrol, emergency notification system, self-defense education, and security escort services. There are also shuttle buses, emergency telephones, lighted pathways/sidewalks, controlled access to dorms/residences, and a community crime-stoppers program.

REQUIREMENTS: The SAT is required. Graduation from an accredited secondary school is required. Those students planning to major in occupational or physical therapy must speak French. A portfolio is required for fine arts students, and an audition for music students. AP credits are accepted. Students must maintain a GPA of 3.5 out of 10 for all courses, including those in the major. Students must also complete a second language requirement: French for English students, and English for French students. **Procedure:** Freshmen are admitted in the fall and winter. There are early decision, early admissions, and rolling admissions plans. Check with the school for current application deadlines. The fall 2016 application fee was $105. **Transfer Students:** Admissions requirements vary according to program. 60 of 90 credits required for the bachelor's degree must be completed at uOttawa. **International Students:** There are 2234 international students enrolled. The school actively recruits these students. They must take the TOEFL with a minimum score of 580 on the paper-based TOEFL (PBT) or 92 on the Internet-based version (iBT) or take the MELAB and the college's own test, CanTest.

Admissions Contact: Andre-Pierre Lepage, International Admissions Administrator. Email: *admissions@uottawa.ca* Web: *www.uottowa.ca*

FINANCIAL AID: The FAFSA code is G06686. Check with the school for current application deadlines.

UNIVERSITY OF SASKATCHEWAN C-2
www.usask.ca

Saskatoon, SK S7N 5A2 (306) 966-5788
Fax: (306) 966-2115
Email: admissions@usask.ca
Full-time: 10,000 men, 10,515 women
Faculty: n/av
Ph.D.s: 87%
Part-time: n/av
Student/Faculty: n/av
Graduate: n/av
Tuition: $5043
Year: semesters, summer session
Freshman Class: n/av
CEEB CODE: 0980
Room & Board: $4275
Application Deadline: April 1

University of Saskatchewan, founded in 1907, is a public institution offering programs in business, agriculture, arts and sciences, education, engineering, and health professions. The figures in the above capsule and in this profile are approximate. There are 13 undergraduate schools and 4 graduate schools. In addition to regional accreditation, U of S has baccalaureate program accreditation with ACTEP, ITEP, NORTEP, and SUNTEP. The 1865-acre campus is in an urban area in Saskatoon.

STUDENT LIFE: 90% of undergraduates are from Saskatchewan. Others are from 100 foreign countries, and Canada. **Female To Male Ratio:** 1.1:1. 77% remain to graduate. **Housing:** 1600 students can be accommodated in college housing, which includes single-sex dorms, off-campus apartments, and married student housing. On-campus housing is available on a first-come and first-served basis. All students may keep cars.

FACULTY/CLASSROOMS: 65% of faculty are male; 35% are female. No introductory courses are taught by graduate students.

PROGRAMS OF STUDY: U of S confers B.A., B.Sc., B.A.Sc., B.Comm., B.E., B.Ed., B.F.A., B.Mus., B.Mus/Mus.Ed., B.S.A., B.S.N., B.S.P., and B.Sc.Kin./Kin.Ed. degrees. Master's and doctoral degrees are also awarded. Bachelor's degrees are awarded in AGRICULTURE (agricultural business management, agricultural economics, agronomy, animal science, environmental studies, horticulture, plant science, range/farm management, and soil science), BIOLOGICAL SCIENCE (anatomy, biochemistry, bioinformatics, biology/biological science, biotechnology, cell biology, environmental biology, microbiology, nutrition, and physiology), BUSINESS (accounting, banking and finance, business administration and management, business economics, human resources, marketing/retailing/merchandising, and operations management), COMMUNICATIONS AND THE ARTS (art, art history and appreciation, dramatic arts, English, fine arts, French, German, Hebrew, Latin, linguistics, modern language, music, music performance, music theory and composition, musicology/ethnomusicology, Russian, Spanish, and studio art), COMPUTER AND PHYSICAL SCIENCE (applied mathematics, chemistry, computer science, environmental geology, geology, geophysics and seismology, mathematics, and physics), EDUCATION (education, elementary education, home economics education, physical education, secondary education, and teaching English as a second/foreign language (TESOL/TEFOL), ENGINEERING AND ENVIRONMENTAL DESIGN (agricultural engineering, bioengineering, bioresource engineering, chemical engineering, civil engineering, computer engineering, electrical/electronics engineering, electrical/electronics engineering technology, engineering physics, environmental engineering, environmental engineering technology, environmental science, geological engineering, land use management and reclamation, mechanical engineering, and urban planning technology), HEALTH PROFESSIONS (biomedical science, exercise science, health science, nursing, pharmacology, pharmacy, physical therapy, and veterinary science), SOCIAL SCIENCE (anthropology, archeology, dietetics, economics, food science, gender studies, geography, history, international studies, law, Native American studies, Near Eastern studies, philosophy, political science/government, psychology, public administration, religion, social work, sociology, and women's studies).

ACTIVITIES: There are no fraternities or sororities. Groups on campus include band, cheerleading, chess, choir, chorale, chorus, computers, drama, ethnic, international, jazz band, LGBT, literary magazine, newspaper, orchestra, photography, political, professional, religious, social, social service, and student government. Popular campus events include Powwow in the Bowl, Experience US!, and Greystone Scholar Spend-a-Day. **Sports:** There are 8 intercollegiate sports for men and 7 for women, and 17 intramural sports for men and 17 for women. Facilities include the PAC-- Physical Activity Complex, which houses a climbing wall, gym, fitness center and weight room, track, squash, racquetball courts, dance studio, a gym, swimming pool, football stadium, hockey rink, curling rink, track and field area, and outdoor soccer field.

SERVICES: Counseling and information services are available, as is tutoring in most subjects, and remedial math and writing. **Library/Resources:** The 8 libraries contain 2.5 million volumes, 3.1 million microform items, and subscribe to 47,055 periodicals including electronic. Computerized library services include interlibrary loans, database searching, Internet access, and Wi-Fi capability. Special learning facilities include an art gallery, natural history museum, and planetarium. **Physically Challenged Students:** All of the campus is accessible. Facilities include wheelchair ramps, elevators, special parking, specially equipped restrooms, special class scheduling, lowered drinking fountains, and lowered telephones. There is also a coordinator of services for students with disabilities, special funding application assistance, and special exam scheduling and accommodations. **Special:** The University of Saskatchewan offers interdisciplinary majors, including agricultural biology, agricultural chemistry, agricultural and bioresource engineering, agricultural extension, and anthropology and archaeology. Co-op programs are offered through the Program for Agricultural Cooperative Education. There are computer science internships, as well as internships offered through the Engineering Professional Internship program. The university has exchange agreements with 41 countries. **Visiting:** There are regularly scheduled orientations for prospective students. To schedule a visit, contact the Recruitment and Admissions at (306) 966-5788. **Campus Safety and Security:** Measures include 24-hour foot and vehicle patrol, emergency notification system, self-defense education, security escort services, emergency telephones, lighted pathways/sidewalks, and controlled access to dorms/residences.

REQUIREMENTS: Applicants must be graduates of an accredited secondary school. The decision is based solely on academic achievement in secondary school. In direct-entry programs, priority is given to Saskatchewan residents, with the exception being the College of Arts and Science. A GPA of 70.0 is required. AP credits are accepted. Requirements for graduation vary according to the program of study. **Procedure:** Freshmen are admitted to all sessions. There is a early decision plan. Applications should be filed by April 1 for fall entry; September 1 for winter entry; February 1 for spring entry; and March 1 for summer entry, along with a $90 fee. Applications are accepted online. **Transfer Students:** Applicants must meet promotion levels for the college to which transfer is sought. **International Students:** There are 1863 international students enrolled. The school actively recruits these students. They must take the TOEFL with a minimum score of 550 on the paper-based TOEFL (PBT) or 80 on the Internet-based version (iBT) or take the MELAB, or take the IELTS, CanTEST, CAEL, or iBT.

Admissions Contact: Recruitment and Admission, Email: *admissions@usask.ca* Web: *www.usask.ca*

FINANCIAL AID: The FAFSA code is G22192. Check with the school for current application deadlines.

UNIVERSITY OF TORONTO — E-3

www.utoronto.ca

Toronto, ON M5S 1A1 — **(416) 978-2190**

Fax: (416) 978-6089
Email: admissions.help@utoronto.ca
Full-time: 25,000 men, 30,000 women
Faculty: n/av
Ph.D.s: 91%
Part-time: 4528 men, 3256 women
Student/Faculty: n/av
Graduate: 6843 men, 8339 women
Tuition: $7225 ($23,000)
Year: other, summer session
Freshman Class: n/av
Room & Board: $10,000
SAT: required
CEEB CODE: 0982
Application Deadline: n/av

The University of Toronto, founded in 1827, is a public institution offering undergraduate programs in applied science and engineering, arts and science, education, dentistry, law, medicine, music, nursing, pharmacy, physical and health education, and radiation sciences. Degrees are also offered at the graduate level in a wide range of programs. The figures in the above capsule and in this profile are approximate. There are 2 undergraduate schools and 1 graduate school. The 1767-acre campus is in an urban area with 3 campuses in downtown and suburban Toronto. Including any residence halls, there are 242 buildings.

STUDENT LIFE: 88% of undergraduates are from Ontario. **Female To Male Ratio:** 1.1:1. The average age of freshmen is 18; all undergraduates, 21. 5% do not continue beyond their first year; 83% remain to graduate. **Housing:** 7903 students can be accommodated in college housing, which includes single-sex and coed dorms, on-campus apartments, off-campus apartments, and married student housing. On-campus housing is guaranteed for the freshman year only, and is available on a first-come, and first-served basis. Priority is given to out-of-town students. 80% of students commute. All students may keep cars.

FACULTY/CLASSROOMS: 55% of faculty are male; 45% are female. No introductory courses are taught by graduate students.

PROGRAMS OF STUDY: U of T confers B.A., B.Sc., B.A.Sc., B.B.A., B.Com., B.Ed., B.Sc.Med.Rad.Sc., B.Sc.N., B.Sc.O.T., B.Sc.Phm., B.Sc.P.T., B.S.P.H.E., and Mus.Bac. degrees. Master's and doctoral degrees are also awarded. Bachelor's degrees are awarded in AGRICULTURE (environmental studies, forestry and related sciences, and natural resource management), BIOLOGICAL SCIENCE (biochemistry, biology/biological science, biophysics, biotechnology, botany, cell biology, ecology, evolutionary biology, life science, microbiology, molecular biology, neurosciences, nutrition, physiology, toxicology, and zoology), BUSINESS (banking and finance, business administration and management, business economics, electronic business, and human resources),

COMMUNICATIONS AND THE ARTS (art history and appreciation, arts administration/management, classics, communications, communications technology, comparative literature, dramatic arts, English, film arts, French, German, Greek, Italian, journalism, Latin, linguistics, media arts, modern language, music, music history and appreciation, music theory and composition, musicology/ethnomusicology, Polish, Portuguese, Russian languages and literature, Slavic languages, Spanish, technical and business writing, and visual and performing arts), COMPUTER AND PHYSICAL SCIENCE (actuarial science, applied mathematics, applied physics, astronomy, astrophysics, chemical physics, chemistry, computer science, digital arts/technology, earth science, geology, mathematics, paleontology, physical sciences, physics, planetary and space science, statistics, and systems analysis), EDUCATION (education, education of the exceptional child, foreign languages education, music education, and physical education), ENGINEERING AND ENVIRONMENTAL DESIGN (architecture, chemical engineering, civil engineering, computer engineering, electrical/electronics engineering, engineering and applied science, environmental science, industrial engineering, materials engineering, materials science, mechanical engineering, mining and mineral engineering, and water and wastewater technology), HEALTH PROFESSIONS (environmental health science, health, nursing, occupational therapy, pharmacology, pharmacy, physical therapy, physician's assistant, and radiological science), SOCIAL SCIENCE (African studies, American studies, anthropology, applied psychology, archeology, behavioral science, Canadian studies, Caribbean studies, Celtic studies, Christian studies, classical/ancient civilization, cognitive science, criminology, East Asian studies, economics, ethics, politics, and social policy, European studies, forensic studies, geography, German area studies, Hispanic American studies, history, history of science, human ecology, humanities, international relations, international studies, Judaic studies, medieval studies, Middle Eastern studies, Native American studies, Pacific area studies, peace studies, philosophy, political science/government, psychology, public affairs, religion, Russian and Slavic studies, Scandinavian studies, sociology, South Asian studies, urban studies, and women's studies). Arts and science, applied science, and engineering have the largest enrollments.

ACTIVITIES: There are no fraternities or sororities. There are 200 groups on campus, including art, band, cheerleading, chess, choir, chorus, computers, dance, debate, drama, ethnic, film, international, jazz band, LGBT, literary magazine, musical theater, newspaper, opera, orchestra, photography, political, radio and TV, religious, social, student government, symphony, and yearbook. Popular campus events include U of T Day, Concerts, and Theater Productions. **Sports:** There are 27 intercollegiate sports for men and 26 for women, and 29 intramural sports for men and 29 for women. Facilities include swimming pools, an outdoor hockey rink, weight and exercise rooms, gyms, squash and multipurpose courts, rifle range, dance studios, playing fields, a stadium, arena, and indoor running track. **Graduates:** From July 1, 2015 to June 30, 2016, 9724 bachelor's degrees were awarded. In an average class, 83% graduate in 4 years or less.

SERVICES: Counseling and information services are available, as is tutoring in every subject, and a reader service for the blind. **Library/Resources:** The 32 libraries contain 11.4 million volumes, 5.5 million microform items, 374,046 audio/video tapes/CDs/DVDs, and subscribe to 74,545 periodicals including electronic. Computerized library services include interlibrary loans, database searching, Internet access, and Wi-Fi capability. Special learning facilities include an art gallery, radio station, an observatory. **Physically Challenged Students:** Facilities include wheelchair ramps, elevators, special parking, specially equipped restrooms, lowered drinking fountains, and lowered telephones. **Special:** The university offers co-op programs in management, arts management, management and information technology, cell and molecular biology, computer science, mathematical and physical sciences, sociology, applied psychology, public policy, humanities, international development studies, psychology (including mental health studies), sciences, social sciences, and neuroscience. Study abroad, interdisciplinary programs, and various work-study programs are also available. **Visiting:** There are regularly scheduled orientations for prospective students. There are guides for informal visits. To schedule a visit, contact Student Recruitment at (416) 978-5000. **Campus Safety and Security:** Measures include 24-hour foot and vehicle patrol, self-defense education, and security escort services. There are also shuttle buses, emergency telephones, and lighted pathways/sidewalks.

REQUIREMENTS: The faculties of arts and science, of music, and physical education and health will consider Grade 12 applicants from an accredited U.S. high school with a high GPA and good scores on the SAT. The ACT will also be considered. Engineering will consider excellent grade 12 students with high SAT scores who also are completing at least 2 advanced placement courses. The SAT Subject Tests and AP courses and exams must include math, physics, and chemistry. Other requirements may apply. Architecture students must submit a questionnaire and a portfolio. Music students must audition. A GPA of 3.0 is required. AP credits are accepted. Arts and science students must satisfy a breadth requirement, which includes 3 courses from outside the major. Students must complete 20 credits for a 4-year degree, plus prerequisite subjects. **Procedure:** Freshmen are admitted in the fall. There are early decision, early admissions, deferred admissions, and rolling admissions plans. Application deadlines are open. The fall 2016 application fee was $80. Notification is sent on a rolling basis. **Transfer Students:** 786 transfer students enrolled in 2015-2016. For the Arts and Science divisions, normally a B average is required. 5 of 20 credits required for the bachelor's degree must be completed at U of T. **International Students:** There are 6884 international students enrolled. The school actively recruits these students. They must take the TOEFL with a minimum score of 600 on the paper-based TOEFL (PBT) or 100 on the Internet-based version (iBT) or take the MELAB, or the ELDA/COPE, the IELTS Academic Module, or the University of Toronto's Continuing Studies Academic English Course. They must also take the SAT or ACT, scoring 1800.

Admissions Contact: Admissions Counselor Email: *admissions.help@utoronto.ca* Web: *www.utoronto.ca*

FINANCIAL AID: The FAFSA code is G06688. Check with the school for current application deadlines.

UNIVERSITY OF VICTORIA — B-2

www.uvic.ca

Victoria, BC V8P 5C2 — **(250) 721-8121**

Fax: (250) 721-6225
Full-time: 6000 men, 6046 women
Part-time: 2957 men, 2958 women
Graduate: 1180 men, 1384 women
Year: semesters, summer session
Room & Board: $8000

Email: recruitment@uvic.ca
Faculty: 721
Ph.D.s: 96%
Student/Faculty: 15 to 1
Tuition: $6027
Freshman Class: 11576 applied, 8443 accepted, 4309 enrolled
CEEB CODE: 0989

Application Deadline: February 28

University of Victoria, founded in 1903, is a public institution operated by the province of British Columbia. It offers undergraduate and graduate programs in the arts and sciences, business, education, engineering, fine arts, human and social development, and law. There are 10 undergraduate schools and 2 graduate schools. The 400-acre campus is in an urban area in Victoria. Including any residence halls, there are 107 buildings.

STUDENT LIFE: 86% of undergraduates are from British Columbia. 92% are from public schools. **Female To Male Ratio:** 1.0:1. The average age of freshmen is 21. **Housing:** 2200 students can be accommodated in college housing, which includes single-sex and coed dorms, on-campus apartments, and married student housing. There is an off-campus housing registry service. On-campus housing is guaranteed for the freshman year only, and is available on a first-come, first-served basis, and is available on a lottery system for upperclassmen. Priority is given to out-of-town students. 89% of students commute. All students may keep cars.

FACULTY/CLASSROOMS: 61% of faculty are male; 39% are female. All teach undergraduates, and do research. No introductory courses are taught by graduate students. The average class size in an introductory lecture is 53 and in a regular course is 30.

PROGRAMS OF STUDY: UVic confers B.A., B.S., B.Com., B.Ed., B.Eng., B.F.A., B.Mus., B.Sc., B.S.N., B.S.W. and L.L.B. degrees. Master's and doctoral degrees are also awarded. Bachelor's degrees are awarded in AGRICULTURE (environmental studies), BIOLOGICAL SCIENCE (biochemistry, biology/biological science, and microbiology), BUSINESS (business administration and management, hospitality management services, international business management, and recreation and leisure services), COMMUNICATIONS AND THE ARTS (art history and appreciation, classics, creative writing, dramatic arts, English, French,

Germanic languages and literature, linguistics, music, and visual and performing arts), COMPUTER AND PHYSICAL SCIENCE (astronomy, chemistry, computer science, earth science, mathematics, physics, software engineering, and statistics), EDUCATION (elementary education, physical education, and secondary education), ENGINEERING AND ENVIRONMENTAL DESIGN (computer engineering, electrical/electronics engineering, and mechanical engineering), HEALTH PROFESSIONS (health science and nursing), SOCIAL SCIENCE (anthropology, child care/child and family studies, economics, geography, Hispanic American studies, history, Italian studies, Latin American studies, medieval studies, Pacific area studies, philosophy, political science/government, psychology, Russian and Slavic studies, social work, sociology, and women's studies). Writing is the strongest academically.

ACTIVITIES: There are no fraternities or sororities. Groups on campus include art, chess, choir, chorus, computers, dance, debate, drama, environmental, ethnic, honors, international, jazz band, LGBT, musical theater, newspaper, orchestra, photography, political, radio and TV, religious, social, social service, student government, symphony, and yearbook. Popular campus events include Week of Welcome, the President's BBQ, and Experience Uvic (Spring open house). **Sports:** There are 7 intercollegiate sports for men and 7 for women, and 12 intramural sports for men and 12 for women. Facilities include 3 gyms, a dance studio, 2 weight and fitness training rooms, racquetball and squash courts, playing fields, an outdoor stadium, tennis courts, 2 swimming pools, a sailing compound, and jogging trails.

SERVICES: Counseling and information services are available, as is tutoring in most subjects. There is remedial reading and writing. **Library/Resources:** The 4 libraries contain 1.9 million volumes, 2.3 million microform items, and 110,600 audio/video tapes/CDs/DVDs, and subscribe to 40,000 periodicals including electronic. Computerized library services include interlibrary loans, database searching, Internet access, and Wi-Fi capability. Special learning facilities include an art gallery, radio station, and language labs. **Physically Challenged Students:** 95% of the campus is accessible. Facilities include wheelchair ramps, elevators, special parking, specially equipped restrooms, lowered drinking fountains, lowered telephones, and special housing. **Special:** A number of co-op and internship programs are available in specific disciplines as are many dual majors, including biochemistry/microbiology and Hispanic/Italian studies. Work-study is possible on a limited basis for Canadian students only. Study abroad is offered in 19 countries. There are 37 departmental honors programs. **Visiting:** There are regularly scheduled orientations for prospective students. There are guides for informal visits, visitors may sit in on classes, and stay overnight. To schedule a visit, contact the Campus Tours at (250) 472-4935. **Campus Safety and Security:** Measures include 24-hour foot and vehicle patrol, self-defense education, and security escort services. There are emergency telephones and lighted pathways/sidewalks.

REQUIREMENTS: Application requires high school graduation with a 2.5 GPA or higher, 4 semesters of English, 2 each of social science, math, science, and language, and 6 semesters of 2.5 work at grade 12 level. Applications are accepted online at the school's web site. A GPA of 67.0 is required. AP credits are accepted. To graduate, students must complete the university English requirement, a minimum of 60 units above the 100 level, at least 21 of which must be upper level, and have a 2.0 GPA. **Procedure:** Freshmen are admitted to all sessions. There are early admissions and deferred admissions plans. Early decision applications should be filed by November 30; regular applications, by February 28 for fall entry; and October 31 for winter entry. The fall 2016 application fee was $60. Applications are accepted on-line. **Transfer Students:** 2000 transfer students enrolled in 2015-2016. Requirements vary with the program and the individual. Check with the school's admissions requirements for transfer students. 30 of 60 credits required for the bachelor's degree must be completed at UVic. **International Students:** There are 2000 international students enrolled. The school actively recruits these students. They must take the TOEFL with a minimum score of 530 on the paper-based TOEFL (PBT) or 71 on the Internet-based version (iBT) or take the MELAB, or take the International English Language Testing System (IELTS).

ADMISSIONS: 73% of the 2016-2017 applicants were accepted. **Admissions Contact:** Wendy Joyce, Admissions Office. Email: *recruitment@uvic.ca* Web: *www.uvic.ca*

FINANCIAL AID: Check with the school for current application deadlines.

UNIVERSITY OF WATERLOO — E-3

www.uwaterloo.ca

Waterloo, ON N2L 3G1 — **(519) 888-4567**

Fax: (519) 746-8088 — **Email:** myapplication@uwaterloo.ca

Full-time: 13,752 men, 9241 women
Part-time: 400 men, 541 women
Graduate: 2921 men, 1599 women
Year: varies, summer session
Room & Board: $8000

Faculty: n/av
Ph.D.s: 93%
Student/Faculty: 25 to 1
Tuition: $7058 ($19,524)
Freshman Class: 29859 applied, 20942 accepted, 6970 enrolled
CEEB CODE: 0996

Application Deadline: March 31

University of Waterloo, founded in 1957, is a public institution that offers undergraduate and graduate programs in applied health sciences, arts, engineering, environment, math, and science. Students have a home base in 1 of 6 faculties or 4 affiliated institutions. Most programs are offered in either the traditional or the cooperative system of study. The figures in the above capsule and in this profile are approximate. There are 10 undergraduate schools and 6 graduate schools. The 1000-acre campus is in a suburban area 60 miles southwest of Toronto. Including any residence halls, there are 65 buildings.

STUDENT LIFE: 95% of undergraduates are from Ontario. Others are from 13 states. **Male To Female Ratio:** 1.5:1. **Housing:** 6100 students can be accommodated in college housing, which includes single-sex and coed dorms, on-campus apartments, off-campus apartments, special-interest houses, language floors, and an off-campus housing service. On-campus housing is guaranteed for the freshman year only. Priority is given to out-of-town students. All students may keep cars.

FACULTY/CLASSROOMS: 75% of faculty are male; 25% are female. All teach undergraduates, all do research, and all teach and do research. No introductory courses are taught by graduate students.

PROGRAMS OF STUDY: Waterloo confers B.A., B.Sc., B.A.S., B.A.Sc., B.A.F.M., B. Arch., B.C.F.M., B.C.S., B.E.S., B.I.S., B.Math, BSc. Phm., B.S.E., B.S.W., and B.K.I. degrees. Master's and doctoral degrees are also awarded. Bachelor's degrees are awarded in AGRICULTURE (environmental studies), BIOLOGICAL SCIENCE (biochemistry, bioinformatics, biology/biological science, and biotechnology), BUSINESS (accounting, business administration and management, human resources, management engineering, management science, operations research, and recreation and leisure services), COMMUNICATIONS AND THE ARTS (art history and appreciation, arts administration/management, classics, dramatic arts, English, English literature, film arts, fine arts, French, German, music, Russian, Spanish, speech/debate/rhetoric, and studio art), COMPUTER AND PHYSICAL SCIENCE (actuarial science, applied mathematics, chemistry, computer mathematics, computer science, digital arts/technology, earth science, information sciences and systems, mathematics, physics, science, science and management, software engineering, and statistics), EDUCATION (foreign languages education, mathematics education, and science education), ENGINEERING AND ENVIRONMENTAL DESIGN (architecture, chemical engineering, city/community/regional planning, civil engineering, computational sciences, computer engineering, electrical/electronics engineering, engineering, environmental engineering, environmental science, geological engineering, mechanical engineering, and systems engineering), HEALTH PROFESSIONS (health, health science, optometry, preallied health, preoptometry, and respiratory therapy), SOCIAL SCIENCE (anthropology, economics, French studies, geography, history, international studies, medieval studies, philosophy, physical fitness/movement, political science/government, psychology, religion, Russian and Slavic studies, social work, sociology, and women's studies). Engineering, accounting, and math are the strongest academically. Arts has the largest enrollment.

ACTIVITIES: 1% of men belong to 1 national fraternity; 1% of women belong to 1 national sorority. There are 150 groups on campus, including social dance, juggling, martial arts, band, bridge, cheerleading, chess, choir, computers, dance, debate, drama, environmental, ethnic, film, honors, international, LGBT, literary magazine, marching band, musical theater, newspaper, photography, political, professional, radio and TV, religious, social, social service, student government, and yearbook. Popular campus events include Oktoberfest and Canada Day. **Sports:** There are 18 intercollegiate sports for men and 18 for women, and 16 intramural sports for men and 16 for women. Facilities include outdoor playing fields, an ice arena, swimming pool, diving tank, squash courts, weight rooms, gyms, a dance studio, tennis courts, and activity areas. **Graduates:** From July 1, 2015 to June 30, 2016, 4466 bachelor's degrees were awarded. The most popular majors were arts (32%), mathematics (21%), and engineering (18%).

SERVICES: Counseling and information services are available, as is tutoring in most subjects, and a reader service for the blind, and remedial math, reading, and writing. **Library/Resources:** The 8 libraries contain 2.0 million volumes, 1.7 million microform items, 1,179 audio/video tapes/CDs/DVDs, and subscribe to 24,074 periodicals including electronic. Computerized library services include interlibrary loans, database searching, Internet access, and Wi-Fi capability. Special learning facilities include an art gallery, radio station, 4 museums, 2 theaters, and an observatory. **Physically Challenged Students:** All of the campus is accessible. Facilities include wheelchair ramps, elevators, special parking, specially equipped restrooms, special class scheduling, lowered drinking fountains, and lowered telephones. Up-to-date technical equipment for the visually disabled and the hearing impaired. **Special:** Cross-registration with Wilfrid Laurier University, study abroad in 30 countries, dual, student-designed, and interdisciplinary majors, a combined bachelor's-master's degree in accounting and engineering, and noncredit courses are available. Students may study under the regular or cooperative system, which allows off-campus work terms in education, professional organizations and agencies, business, industry, or government. There are concurrent education programs in conjunction with the faculties of education at Brock and Queen's Universities. There are 55 departmental honors programs. **Visiting:** Regularly scheduled orientations are available for prospective students, student visits include tours and individual and group information sessions. There are guides for informal visits and visitors may sit in on classes. To schedule a visit, contact the Visitors Reception Center at (519) 888-4567, ext. 3614. **Campus Safety and Security:** Measures include 24-hour foot and vehicle patrol, emergency notification system, self-defense education, and security escort services. There are also shuttle buses, emergency telephones, and lighted pathways/sidewalks.

REQUIREMENTS: Candidates from the United States must have a high school diploma with exceptionally high standing and AP exams in prerequisite subjects or first-year university standing in acceptable subjects from an accredited university. An audition, portfolio, and/or interview may be required for certain programs. A GPA of 3.0 is required. AP credits are accepted. Important factors in the admissions decision are advanced placement or honors courses, extracurricular activities record, and leadership record. To graduate, all students must satisfy specific program requirements. These include a writing skills requirement. The total number of credits and minimum grade average vary. **Procedure:** Freshmen are admitted in the fall, winter, and spring. Entrance exams should be taken by the junior year. There are early admissions and deferred admissions plans. Applications should be filed by March 31 for fall entry; October 31 for winter entry; and March 1 for spring entry, along with a $130 fee. Notifications are sent May 25. Applications are accepted online. **Transfer Students:** Applicants are considered on an individual basis. 10 of 20 credits required for the bachelor's degree must be completed at Waterloo. **International Students:** There are 2398 international students enrolled. The school actively recruits these students. They must take the TOEFL, and also take the TWE and the TSE. The MELAB or the IELTS may also be submitted.

ADMISSIONS: 70% of the 2016-2017 applicants were accepted. **Admissions Contact:** Undergraduate Recruitment. Email: *myapplication@uwaterloo.ca* Web: *www.uwaterloo.ca*

FINANCIAL AID: Check with the school for current application deadlines.

UNIVERSITY OF WESTERN ONTARIO — D-3

www.uwo.ca

London, ON N6A 3K7	(519) 661-2100
Fax: (519) 661-3710	**Email:** liaison@uwo.ca
Full-time: 11,675 men, 14,288 women	**Faculty:** 1381
	Ph.D.s: n/av
Part-time: 699 men, 973 women	**Student/Faculty:** 20 to 1
Graduate: 2622 men, 2723 women	**Tuition:** $6486 ($18,850)
Year: varies, summer session	**Freshman Class:** 32163 applied, 17817 accepted, 9644 enrolled
Room & Board: $8770	
SAT: required	**CEEB CODE:** 0984
Application Deadline: May 15	

University of Western Ontario, founded in 1878 is one of Canada's oldest and largest universities. Today, we are a vibrant centre of learning through our 12 faculties and professional schools, and 3 Affiliated University Colleges (Brescia, Huron and King's), we offer more than 400 different specializations, majors and minors at the undergraduate level. UWO is proud to provide the best student experience among Canada's leading research-intensive universities. In addition to regional accreditation, UWO, Western has baccalaureate program accreditation with ASLA. The 1125-acre campus is in an urban area 120 miles from both Detroit, Michigan and Toronto, Ontario. Including any residence halls, there are 116 buildings.

STUDENT LIFE: 94% of undergraduates are from Ontario. Others are from 116 foreign countries, and Canada. **Female To Male Ratio:** 1.2:1. The average age of freshmen is 19; all undergraduates, 21. 7% do not continue beyond their first year. **Housing:** 5077 students can be accommodated in college housing, which includes single-sex and coed dorms, on-campus apartments, married student housing, honors houses and special-interest houses. On-campus housing is guaranteed for the freshman year only and is available on a lottery system for upperclassmen. Priority is given to out-of-town students. 75% of students commute. All students may keep cars.

FACULTY/CLASSROOMS: 69% of faculty are male; 31% are female. No introductory courses are taught by graduate students.

PROGRAMS OF STUDY: UWO confers B.A., B.Sc., B.Ed., B.E.Sc., B.F.A., B.H.Sc., B.M.O.S., B.M.Sc., B.Mus., B.Mus.A., B.A.H.Ec., B.Sc.H.Ec., B.Sc.FN., B.Sc.N., B.S.W.Hons., J.D. and B.Th. degrees. Master's and doctoral degrees are also awarded. Bachelor's degrees are awarded in AGRICULTURE (environmental studies, natural resource management, and plant science), BIOLOGICAL SCIENCE (anatomy, biochemistry, bioinformatics, biology/biological science, biophysics, cell biology, ecology, genetics, microbiology, nutrition, physiology, and toxicology), BUSINESS (accounting, business administration and management, business communications, and human resources), COMMUNICATIONS AND THE ARTS (applied music, art, art history and appreciation, arts administration/management, Chinese, classical languages, classics, communications, communications technology, comparative literature, creative writing, digital communications, English, English literature, film arts, fine arts, French, German, Germanic languages and literature, Greek, Italian, Japanese, Latin, linguistics, media arts, modern language, music, music business management, music history and appreciation, music performance, music theory and composition, musicology/ethnomusicology, opera, piano/organ, public relations, radio/television technology, Russian, Spanish, strings, studio art, and visual and performing arts), COMPUTER AND PHYSICAL SCIENCE (actuarial science, applied mathematics, astronomy, astrophysics, chemistry, computer mathematics, computer programming, computer science, cybernetics, earth science, geology, geophysics and seismology, information sciences and systems, mathematics, medical physics, physics, planetary and space science, science, software engineering, and statistics), EDUCATION (education, elementary education, middle school education, museum studies, music education, physical education, and secondary education), ENGINEERING AND ENVIRONMENTAL DESIGN (aviation administration/management, biomedical engineering, chemical engineering, civil engineering, computer engineering, computer technology, electrical/electronics engineering, engineering, engineering management, environmental engineering, environmental science, materials engineering, materials science, and mechanical engineering), HEALTH PROFESSIONS (health science, medical science, nursing, and pharmacology), SOCIAL SCIENCE (American studies, anthropology, Asian/American studies, Asian/Oriental studies, biblical studies, Canadian studies, child psychology/development, classical/ancient civilization, clinical psychology, criminology, East Asian studies, economics, family/consumer studies, food science, French studies, gender studies, geography, gerontology, history, home economics, human ecology, humanities, humanities and social science, interdisciplinary studies, international relations, Italian studies, Japanese studies, Latin American studies, law, liberal arts/general studies, Native American studies, peace studies, philosophy, philosophy and religion, physical fitness/movement, political science/government, psychology, public administration, religion, social science, social work, sociology, Spanish studies, theological studies, urban studies, Western civilization/culture, and women's studies).

ACTIVITIES: There are no fraternities or sororities. There are 184 groups on campus, including art, band, cheerleading, chess, choir, chorale, chorus, computers, dance, debate, drama, environmental, ethnic, film, international, jazz band, LGBT, marching band, musical theater, newspaper, opera, orchestra, photography, political, professional, radio and TV, religious, social, social service, and student government. Popular campus events include Western Homecoming, Fall Preview Day, and Summer Academic Orientation. **Sports:** There are 20 intercollegiate sports for men and 21 for women, and 20 intramural sports for men and 19 for women. Facilities include a recreation and athletic centre, and astadium. **Graduates:** From July 1, 2015 to June 30, 2016, 6791 bachelor's degrees were awarded. 393 companies recruited on campus in 2015-2016. Of the 2015 graduating class, 94% were employed within 6 months of graduation.

SERVICES: Counseling and information services are available, as is tutoring in most subjects, and a reader service for the blind, and remedial math, reading, and writing. Additional details are also available through the Learning Skills Services at the Student Development Centre. **Library/Resources:** The 7 libraries contain 3.7 million volumes, 4.1 million microform items, and 2.1 million audio/video tapes/CDs/DVDs, and subscribe to 86,179 periodicals including electronic. Computerized library services include interlibrary loans, database searching, Internet access, and Wi-Fi capability. Special learning facilities include an art gallery, radio station, TV station, International Centre for Olympic Studies, Fowler-Kennedy Sports Medicine Clinic, Cronyn Observatory, and Boundary Layer Wind Tunnel. **Physically Challenged Students:** 92% of the campus is accessible. Facilities include wheelchair ramps, elevators, special parking, specially equipped restrooms, special class scheduling, lowered drinking fountains, lowered telephones, and special housing. **Visiting:** There are regularly scheduled orientations for prospective students, academic counseling appointments and campus tours. There are guides for informal visits and visitors may sit in on classes. To schedule a visit, contact Liaison Officer & Events Planner at (519) 661-2100. **Campus Safety and Security:** Measures include 24-hour foot and vehicle patrol, emergency notification system, security escort services, emergency telephones, lighted pathways/sidewalks, controlled access to dorms/residences, campus community police, SERT: student emergency response team, and western foot patrol.

REQUIREMENTS: The SAT is required. A GPA of 3.5 is required. AP credits are accepted. Important factors in the admissions decision are advanced placement or honors courses, recommendations by school officials, and leadership record. **Procedure:** Freshmen are admitted in the fall. There are deferred admissions and rolling admissions plans. Early decision applications should be filed by May 15; regular applications, by May 15 for fall entry. The fall 2016 application fee was $125. Notifications are sent February 1. Applications are accepted online. **Transfer Students:** 381 transfer students enrolled in 2015-2016. A minimum 3.0 GPA is required of transfer applicant; a maximum of 10.0 credits may be transferred. At least 5 credits in a 15-credit degree program or 10 credits in an honors program must be completed at The University of Western Ontario to earn a bachelor's degree. 5 of 15 credits required for the bachelor's degree must be completed at UWO, Western. **International Students:** The school actively recruits these students. They must take the TOEFL with a minimum score of 550 on the paper-based TOEFL (PBT) or 83 on the Internet-based version (iBT) or take the MELAB, We accept MELAB, IELTS, CAEL, CanTEST, Fanshawe College and CultureWorks as alternatives to TOEFL.

ADMISSIONS: 55% of the 2016-2017 applicants were accepted. **Admissions Contact:** Lori Gribbon, Director, Recruitment and Admissions. Email: *liaison@uwo.ca* Web: *www.uwo.ca*

FINANCIAL AID: UWO is a member of CSS. The college's own financial statement is required. The FAFSA code is G08446. Check with the school for current application deadlines.

UNIVERSITY OF WINDSOR D-3

www.uwindsor.ca

Windsor, ON N9B 3P4 **(519) 253-3000**

Fax: (519) 971-3653
Full-time: 6528 men, 6012 women
Part-time: 1170 men, 1325 women
Graduate: 1030 men, 228 women
Year: trimesters, summer session
Room & Board: $9037
SAT or ACT: required
Application Deadline: n/av

Email: registrar@uwindsor.ca
Faculty: 592
Ph.D.s: 92%
Student/Faculty: 18 to 1
Tuition: $8700 ($21,045)
Freshman Class: n/av
CEEB CODE: 0904

University of Windsor, founded in 1857, is a public liberal arts institution offering undergraduate and graduate programs through 10 faculties and 6 schools. The figures in the above capsule and in this profile are approximate. There are 11 undergraduate schools and 1 graduate school. The 125-acre campus is in an urban area 2 kilometers from downtown Windsor, and 3 kilometers from downtown Detroit, Michigan. Including any residence halls, there are 58 buildings.

STUDENT LIFE: 90% of undergraduates are from Ontario. Others are from 90 foreign countries, and Canada. 95% are from public schools. **Male To Female Ratio:** 1.2:1. The average age of freshmen is 18; all undergraduates, 22. 10% do not continue beyond their first year. **Housing:** 1500 students can be accommodated in college housing, which includes coed dorms, on-campus apartments, and married student housing. On-campus housing is guaranteed for the freshman year only and is available on a lottery system for upperclassmen. 90% of students commute. All students may keep cars.

FACULTY/CLASSROOMS: 54% of faculty are male; 46% are female. All teach undergraduates, and do research. No introductory courses are taught by graduate students. The average class size in an introductory lecture is 100; in a laboratory is 25; and in a regular course is 50.

PROGRAMS OF STUDY: UOW confers B.A., B.Sc., B.A.S., B.A.Sc., B.Comm., B.C.S., B.Ed., B.E.S., B.F.A., B.F.S., B.H.K., B. Math, B.Mus., B.Mus.Th., B.Sc.N., B.S.W., and L.L.B. degrees. Master's and doctoral degrees are also awarded. Bachelor's degrees are awarded in AGRICULTURE (environmental studies), BIOLOGICAL SCIENCE (biochemistry, biology/biological science, and biotechnology), BUSINESS (business administration and management and international business management), COMMUNICATIONS AND THE ARTS (art history and appreciation, classics, communications, comparative literature, creative writing, dramatic arts, English, French, languages, modern language, music, Spanish, and visual and performing arts), COMPUTER AND PHYSICAL SCIENCE (chemistry, computer science, geology, mathematics, physics, science, software engineering, and statistics), EDUCATION (drama education, education, and science education), ENGINEERING AND ENVIRONMENTAL DESIGN (automotive technology, civil engineering, electrical/electronics engineering, engineering, environmental engineering, environmental science, industrial engineering, and mechanical engineering), HEALTH PROFESSIONS (music therapy and nursing), SOCIAL SCIENCE (anthropology, Canadian studies, criminology, crosscultural studies, developmental psychology, economics, family/consumer studies, forensic studies, geography, history, international relations, law, philosophy, physical fitness/movement, political science/government, psychology, social work, sociology, urban studies, and women's studies). Science, engineering, and human kinetics are the strongest academically. Business, science, and education have the largest enrollments.

ACTIVITIES: 1% of men belong to 3 national fraternities; 1% of women belong to 3 national sororities. There are 135 groups on campus, including cheerleading, chess, choir, chorale, computers, dance, debate, drama, environmental, ethnic, film, forensics, honors, international, jazz band, LGBT, literary magazine, musical theater, newspaper, orchestra, political, professional, radio and TV, religious, social, and student government. Popular campus events include Head Start Orientation, Windsor Welcome Week and Homecoming. **Sports:** There are 7 intercollegiate sports for men and 6 for women, and 11 intramural sports for men and 9 for women. Facilities include a track, multiuse gym, field house, a stadium, indoor pool, weight rooms, and sports therapy clinic.

SERVICES: Counseling and information services are available, as is tutoring in most subjects, such as chemistry, biochemistry, physics, mathematics, statistics, and a S.T.E.P.S. program. There is a reader service for the blind, and remedial math, reading, and writing. **Library/Resources:** The 2 libraries contain 1.7 million volumes, 1.5 million microform items, and 10,792 audio/video tapes/CDs/DVDs, and subscribe to 76,378 periodicals including electronic. Computerized library services include interlibrary loans, database searching, Internet access, and Wi-Fi capability. Special learning facilities include an art gallery, natural history museum, radio station, a video-conferencing center, a computing services theater, the Chrysler Canada/University of Windsor Research Center, and the Great Lakes Institute. **Physically Challenged Students:** 90% of the campus is accessible. Facilities include wheelchair ramps, elevators, special parking, specially equipped restrooms, special class scheduling, lowered drinking fountains, and lowered telephones. Specially equipped residence rooms. **Special:** The university offers a variety of co-op programs and internships. Cross-registration may be arranged with the University of Detroit Mercy, Wayne State University, the University of Central Florida, and the University of Darby (England). There are 30 departmental honors programs. **Visiting:** There are regularly scheduled orientations for prospective students, student visits include a tour, counseling, and classes if requested. There are guides for informal visits and visitors may sit in on classes. To schedule a visit, contact the Office of Liason and Student Recruitment at 1-800-864-2860. **Campus Safety and Security:** Measures include 24-hour foot and vehicle patrol, emergency notification system, self-defense education, security escort services, emergency telephones, lighted pathways/sidewalks, and controlled access to dorms/residences.

REQUIREMENTS: Each U.S. applicant must present scores from either the ACT or the SAT offered by the College Entrance Examination Board. Advanced Placement Examinations in certain prerequisite subjects may also be required. AP credits are accepted. To graduate, students must complete a total of 90 credit hours, including 30 in the major, with a C average. Honors students must complete 120 hours, including 60 in the major, with a B average. All students must fulfill the requirements of the core curriculum. **Procedure:** Freshmen are admitted to all sessions. Entrance exams should be taken as early as possible. There are early decision, early admissions, and rolling admissions plans. Check with the school for current application deadlines. Applications are accepted online. **Transfer Students:** Applicants must present an official transcript and be in good academic standing. **International Students:** There are 1209 international students enrolled. The school actively recruits these students. They must take the TOEFL or MELAB, or take the IELTS, and CAEL.

Admissions Contact: Charlene Yates, Manager, Undergraduate Admissions. Email: *registrar@uwindsor.ca* Web: *www.uwindsor.ca*

FINANCIAL AID: The FAFSA code is G06689. Check with the school for current application deadlines.

YORK UNIVERSITY — E-3

www.futurestudents.yorku.ca

Toronto (North York), ON M3J 1P3 — **(416) 736-5825**

Fax: (416) 650-8195	**Email:** admissions@yorku.ca
Full-time: 13,500 men, 21,540 women	**Faculty:** 1357
Part-time: 2900 men, 4510 women	**Ph.D.s:** 98%
Graduate: 2500 men, 2700 women	**Student/Faculty:** n/av
Year: semesters, summer session	**Tuition:** $6376 ($17,512)
Room & Board: $5119	**Freshman Class:** n/av
SAT or ACT: required	**CEEB CODE:** 0894
Application Deadline: February 1	

York University, founded in 1959, is a public institution offering programs in computer science, design, education, environmental studies, fine arts, business, social science, law, engineering, health, humanities, human resources, pure and applied sciences, and social work. There are 10 undergraduate schools and 43 graduate schools. The 635-acre campus is in an urban area in Northwest and midtown Toronto. Including any residence halls, there are 96 buildings.

STUDENT LIFE: 90% of undergraduates are from Ontario. Others are from 159 foreign countries. **Female To Male Ratio:** 1.5:1. The average age of freshmen is 18; all undergraduates, 22. 97% remain to graduate. **Housing:** 4000 students can be accommodated in college housing, which includes single-sex and coed dorms, on-campus apartments, married student housing, language houses, special-interest houses, and Co-op housing. On-campus housing is available on a first-come, first-served basis, and on a lottery system for upperclassmen. Priority is given to out-of-town students. 93% of students commute. All students may keep cars.

FACULTY/CLASSROOMS: 59% of faculty are male; 41% are female. All teach undergraduates, and do research. No introductory courses are taught by graduate students. The average class size in an introductory lecture is 72 and in a laboratory is 25.

PROGRAMS OF STUDY: York confers B.A., B.Sc., B.A.S., B.B.A., B.Des., B.Ed., B.E.S., B.F.A., B.H.R.M., B.H.S., B.Sc.N., B.S.W., I.B.B.A., and L.L.B. degrees. Master's and doctoral degrees are also awarded. Bachelor's degrees are awarded in AGRICULTURE (conservation and regulation and environmental studies), BIOLOGICAL SCIENCE (biochemistry, biology/biological science, biotechnology, and ecology), BUSINESS (accounting, banking and finance, business administration and management, business economics, business statistics, entrepreneurial studies, human resources, international business management, international economics, labor studies, management science, marketing and distribution, and organizational behavior), COMMUNICATIONS AND THE ARTS (art history and appreciation, classics, communications, creative writing, dance, design, dramatic arts, English, film arts, fine arts, French, German, Greek, Italian, linguistics, music, photography, Russian, Spanish, video, and visual and performing arts), COMPUTER AND PHYSICAL SCIENCE (applied mathematics, astronomy, atmospheric sciences and meteorology, chemistry, computer science, earth science, information sciences and systems, mathematics, physics, science, science technology, and statistics), EDUCATION (education, education of the deaf and hearing impaired, elementary education, middle school education, and secondary education), ENGINEERING AND ENVIRONMENTAL DESIGN (computer engineering, engineering, environmental science, and industrial administration/management), HEALTH PROFESSIONS (community health work, environmental health science, exercise science, health, health care administration, health science, nursing, and rehabilitation therapy), SOCIAL SCIENCE (African studies, anthropology, Canadian studies, Caribbean studies, cognitive science, criminal justice, criminology, East Asian studies, economics, European studies, French studies, geography, German area studies, gerontology, Hispanic American studies, history, humanities, international studies, Judaic studies, Latin American studies, law, liberal arts/general studies, peace studies, philosophy, physical fitness/movement, political science/government, psychology, public administration, religion, Russian and Slavic studies, science and society, social science, social work, sociology, South Asian studies, Third World studies, urban studies, and women's studies). Business, science, fine arts, and liberal arts are the strongest academically. Psychology, administrative studies, and sociology have the largest enrollments.

ACTIVITIES: There are no fraternities or sororities. There are 249 groups on campus, including art, band, cheerleading, chess, choir, communications, computers, dance, debate, drama, ethnic, film, international, jazz band, LGBT, literary magazine, musical theater, newspaper, orchestra, photography, political, professional, radio and TV, religious, social, social service, student government, and yearbook. Popular campus events include The Blue Bowl (football), Orientation Week, and Multicultural Week. **Sports:** There are 11 intercollegiate sports for men and 12 for women, and 17 intramural sports for men and 17 for women. Facilities include a stadium, ice arena, playing fields, softball diamonds, cricket pitch, indoor and outdoor track and field center, indoor and outdoor tennis courts. There is also a fitness center with cardio machines and free weights, a swimming pool, gyms, squash courts, dance/aerobic studios, spinning studio, and a sports therapy clinic. There is a combative room, teaching labs, and an outdoor events facility.

SERVICES: Counseling and information services are available, as is tutoring in most subjects, and a reader service for the blind. There is also a writing support center, and multimedia language center. The Counseling and Development Center offers a variety of services and workshops. **Library/Resources:** The 5 libraries contain 2.5 million volumes, 4.0 million microform items, 54,184 audio/video tapes/CDs/DVDs, and subscribe to 24,576 periodicals including electronic. Computerized library services include interlibrary loans, database searching, Internet access, and Wi-Fi capability. Special learning facilities include an art gallery, radio station, TV station, an observatory, language labs, writing center, geographical information systems lab, computer science labs, science-related labs, and fine arts studios and labs (editing studios). **Physically Challenged Students:** 65% of the campus is accessible. Facilities include wheelchair ramps, elevators, special parking, specially equipped restrooms, special class scheduling, lowered drinking fountains, and lowered telephones. The office for persons with disabilities offers a variety of additional services. **Special:** Co-op programs and cross-registration with Seneca, Centennial, Sheridan, and Humber Colleges, internships, study abroad in more than 100 countries, and work-study are available. York offers dual, student-designed, multi- and interdisciplinary majors, atmospheric chemistry, physics and astronomy, science, technology, culture, and society, social and political thought, space and communication sciences, and translation. Independent study and nondegree study are also possible. There is a freshman honors program. **Visiting:** Regularly scheduled orientations are available for prospective students, and consist of a general information session, campus tour, and 1 week of orientation prior to the start of classes. There are guides for informal visits, visitors may sit in on classes, and stay overnight. To schedule a visit, contact the International Admissions Office at (416) 736-5000. **Campus Safety and**

Security: Measures include 24-hour foot and vehicle patrol, self-defense education, and security escort services. There are also shuttle buses, emergency telephones, lighted pathways/sidewalks, a bicycle patrol team monitoring the campuses.

REQUIREMENTS: U.S. applicants must present evidence of superior academic achievement. Secondary school record, SAT or ACT scores, and teacher or counselor recommendation will be taken into consideration. Applicants to a fine arts program are required to successfully pass an audition or evaluation, and business administration applicants are required to submit a supplementary application. Admission averages and course prerequisites vary by faculty. A GPA of 3.0 is required. AP credits are accepted. Students must maintain at least a C average in 90 credits to receive an ordinary degree and a C+ in 120 credits to receive an honors degree. Requirements for graduation vary according to the program. **Procedure:** Freshmen are admitted to all sessions. Entrance exams should be taken in the fall of the senior year. There are early admissions and rolling admissions plans. Applications should be filed by February 1 for fall entry; November 1 for winter entry; and March 1 for spring entry. The fall 2016 application fee was $60. Notification is sent on a rolling basis. Applications are accepted online. **Transfer Students:** 954 transfer students enrolled in 2015-2016. Requirements vary depending on the program. Postsecondary transcripts are required. **International Students:** There are 2708 international students enrolled. The school actively recruits these students. They must take the TOEFL, the Comprehensive English Language Test, and the college's own test, the York English Language Test (YELT), or take the IELTS. They must also take the SAT or ACT.

Admissions Contact: Office of International Admissions. Email: *admissions@yorku.ca* Web: *www.futurestudents.yorku.ca*

FINANCIAL AID: The FAFSA code is G07679. Check with the school for current application deadlines.

STUDY ABROAD

Study abroad programs are now available in more than 60 countries in fields that range from Costa Rican tropical biology to Finnish architecture. Program directors have responded to the vocational interests of the student of the 21st century by organizing programs in international management, health care administration, and other career-oriented fields.

In fact, study in both traditional and nontraditional fields is enriched by overseas experience. An international perspective can benefit study of environmental sciences, anthropology, political science, urban planning, oceanography, hotel administration, psychology, social work, journalism, marketing and law, as well as film, art history, theater, music and dance.

The vast majority of U.S. students enter European schools through organized, ongoing programs sponsored and managed by the colleges and universities in which they are already enrolled. In this way, they automatically earn U.S. academic credit from their home institution for their overseas course work. Academic credit *directly* earned at a foreign institution is often not acceptable toward a U.S. degree. Applying directly to a foreign school is not difficult but unusual.

According to the Institute of International Education, in their *Open Doors 2016 Report on International Educational Exchange*, based on a recent academic year, 313,415 U.S. students studied abroad. This reflected an increase of 2.9% since the previous year. The number of U.S. students studying abroad has more than tripled in the last two decades. Americans studying in the UK increased by 3.3% and hosted 12% of all Americans who study abroad. However, there are also large increases in other host countries—including Israel, New Zealand, South Korea, Costa Rica, Mexico, South Africa, and Australia and her regions. The five leading destinations measured in 2015/2016 were the United Kingdom, Italy, Spain, France, and China. Ireland, the Czech Republic, Denmark, and Austria also had strong increases, as did Greece, which increased by 18%. The top fields of study for international students included: STEM fields (science, technology, engineering, and math) (23.9%), business & management (20.1%), social sciences (17.3%), foreign language and global studies (7.7%), and fine and applied arts (6.9%).

The report also indicated that during the 2015/2016 academic year, 1,043,839 international students were studying in the United States. This represented an increase of 7.1% from the previous year. The largest fields of study were STEM fields, FLTA, social sciences, business, arts, and humanities.

A Productive Experience

If you are interested in study abroad, plan ahead by taking the following steps to ensure that the experience is productive:

- **Assess the ways in which study abroad will benefit your educational and career plans.** Study abroad can be a casual choice or a pleasant way to spend a semester but you will derive the greatest benefit if you bring more thought to it: How will the overseas experience complement your other courses or your educational major? Can you maximize its value by seeking language as well as academic study or by combining independent study or an internship with traditional course work?
- **Consult your campus study-abroad adviser.** Most colleges and universities have a person or an office charged with the responsibility of counseling students on overseas study. The study-abroad adviser is best qualified to help you make the right choices.
- **Make sure your college will accept credit earned at the study-abroad program you have chosen.** Speak with both your academic adviser and your study-abroad adviser and resolve any issues before you leave. Many students have assumed incorrectly that credit is granted automatically for another institution's program. You cannot take this for granted.
- **Be realistic about your foreign language proficiency.** It is one thing to be able to order a meal or buy a train ticket in a foreign language. It is quite another to follow a professor lecturing on a complex subject. If you discover that your linguistic ability is inadequate, it is quite possible that you can find abroad the subject matter you want taught in English. You will get more out of the overseas experience however, if you make the effort to function in the language of the chosen country.
- **Look carefully at costs.** If you are dealing with a program sponsor that is not your home institution, it is wise to read program literature carefully. Ask questions before you go if you have any qualms! Are charges clearly specified? Does the literature specify what services *are* covered and more important, what services are *not* covered? What is the refund policy, if any? Is there a clearly identified organization with an official base in the United States that would be legally responsible in the event of disaster?

  While drawing up your budget, think about the extras. You will want to make the small side trips to new places that help to make overseas living rewarding. Try to give yourself some financial flexibility in working out your budget.
- **Think about what it means to live abroad.** Be sure to arrange for substitutes for the support systems you take for granted at home. Will your medical insurance cover you? Do you need vaccinations or a doctor who can manage your specific health problems while you are living abroad? What about visas?

  It is critically important to find out about housing before you leave. Student housing is difficult to find almost everywhere. Be sure to find out whether securing housing abroad is your responsibility and what the alternatives are in the country in which you plan to live.
- **Don't assume that you can work abroad.** Because of foreign labor laws, students should not plan to seek paid employment. The practice of working one's way through college is not common abroad, nor are the relatively high-paying part-time jobs that make it possible in the United States. However, increasing numbers of students are looking to combine practical work experience with study abroad. There are many work exchanges, volunteer opportunities, and internships available. Contact the Council on International Exchange, 300 Fore Street, Portland, ME 04101, (207) 553-4000, Fax: (207) 553-4299 or E-mail: contact@ciee.org for further information.
- **Find out what you can about the sponsoring agency, especially if it is not an accredited U.S. college or university.** Talk to your study-abroad adviser if you have any doubts. Most private agencies engaged in study abroad are legitimate organizations but their basic purposes may not match yours. Does the organization have experience in placing students in an academic environment, not just in arranging travel? Are descriptions of its study program specific or vague? Does it make unverifiable claims about the academic reputation of its programs, or their recognition by U.S. higher educational institutions?

For further information, consult:

Institute of International Education
809 United Nations Plaza
New York, NY 10017
(212) 883-8200 Fax: (212) 984-5452

For further information, consult the following publications: *IIE Passport: Study Abroad Directories*, which are available at *www.iie.org/Research-and-Publications/Publications-and-Reports*

Council on International Educational Exchange (CIEE)
300 Fore Street
Portland, ME 04101
9am–5pm
(207) 553-4000 Fax: (207) 553-4299
E-mail: contact@ciee.org
Website: *www.ciee.org*

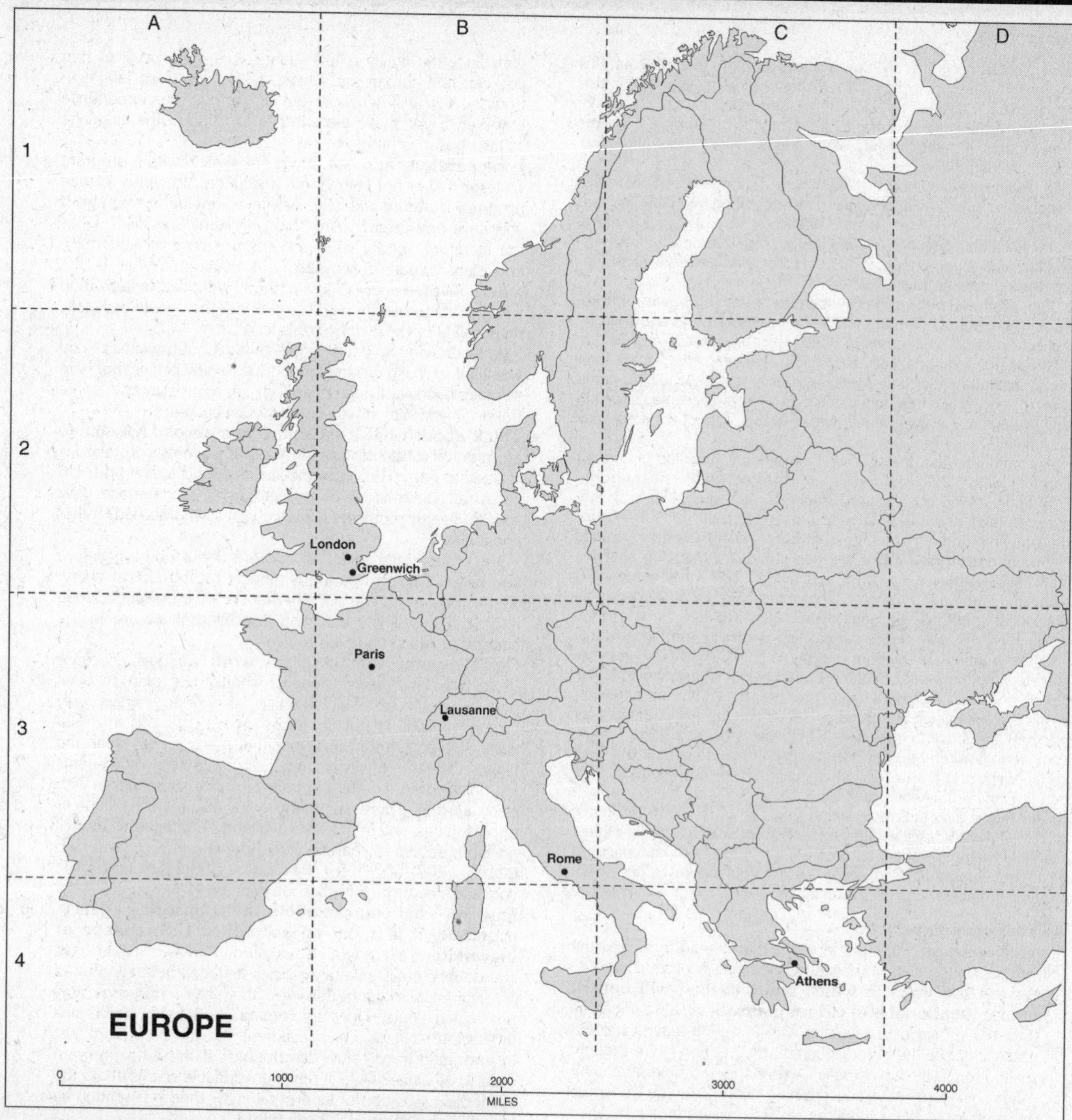

DEREE - THE AMERICAN COLLEGE OF GREECE C-4

www.acg.edu

Aghia Paraskevi, 15342 — 001 (857) 284 7908

Email: mnisdeo@acg.edu

Full-time: 528 men, 611 women
Part-time: 905 men, 914 women
Graduate: 36 men, 146 women
Year: semesters, summer session
Room & Board: n/a

SAT or ACT: recommended
Application Deadline: June 15

Faculty: 86
Ph.D.s: 74%
Student/Faculty: 13 to 1
Tuition: $11,098
Freshman Class: 606 applied, 430 accepted, 407 enrolled
CEEB CODE: 0925

Deree is the undergraduate and graduate division of The American College of Greece (ACG), which was founded in 1875 as the American School for Girls. ACG has 1 campus in Athens. Deree offers bachelor's degrees in 27 areas of the liberal arts, fine and performing arts, and business. The graduate school offers masters in psychology and communications. There are 3 undergraduate schools and 2 graduate schools. In addition to regional accreditation, Deree has baccalaureate program accreditation with NEASC. The 64-acre campus is in Aghia Paraskevi a suburban area in Athens. Including any residence halls, there are 12 buildings.

STUDENT LIFE: 87% of undergraduates are from Greece. Others are from 69 foreign countries, and Canada. **Female To Male Ratio:** 1.1:1. The average age of freshmen is 19; all undergraduates, 23. 5% do not continue beyond their first year; 88% remain to graduate. **Housing:** 261 students can be accommodated in college housing, which includes off-campus apartments, and studio apartments are on availability. All students commute. No one may keep cars. Alcohol is not permitted.

FACULTY/CLASSROOMS: 43% of faculty are male; 57% are female. No introductory courses are taught by graduate students. The average class size in an introductory lecture is 25; in a laboratory is 20; and in a regular course is 19.

PROGRAMS OF STUDY: Deree confers B.A. and B.S. degrees. Master's degrees are also awarded. Bachelor's degrees are awarded in AGRICULTURE (environmental studies), BUSINESS (accounting, accounting (finance), entrepreneurial studies, finance, international business, logistics, management information systems, management, marketing/retailing/merchandising, sports management, and tourism), COMMUNICATIONS AND THE ARTS (art history, communications, dance, English, graphic design, music, music performance, theatre arts, theatre/dance, and visual arts), COMPUTER AND PHYSICAL SCIENCE (information sciences and systems), HEALTH PROFESSIONS (health care administration), SOCIAL SCIENCE (economics, history, philosophy, psychology, and sociology). English, psychology, and marketing are the strongest academically. Psychology, management and communications have the largest enrollments.

ACTIVITIES: There are no fraternities or sororities. There are 54 groups on campus, including academic societies, innovation & entrepreneurship, art, choir, computers, dance, debate, drama, drill team, ethnic, film, health & social awareness, honors, international, LGBT, literary magazine, newspaper, orchestra, photography, professional, social, social service, and student government. Popular campus events include Fall Festival, Student Awards Night, and Business Week. **Sports:** Facilities include a gym, fitness center, dance studios, aerobic rooms, outdoor tennis courts, swimming pool, a track, tennis courts, basketball and volleyball courts, and a soccer field. **Graduates:** From July 1, 2015 to June 30, 2016, 298 bachelor's degrees were awarded. The most popular majors were communications (20%), management (16%), and marketing (15%). In an average class, 1% graduate in 3 years or less, 35% graduate in 4 years or less, 47% graduate in 5 years or less, and 54% graduate in 6 years or less. Of the 2015 graduating class, 12% were enrolled in graduate school within 6 months of graduation, and 51% were employed.

SERVICES: Counseling and information services are available, as is tutoring in some subjects, such as math, accounting, finance and economics, and remedial writing. Counseling and educational services, and career services are available upon request. **Library/Resources:** The library contains 437,000 volumes, 6,450 microform items, 1,700 audio/video tapes/CDs/DVDs, and subscribes to 13,000 periodicals including electronic. Computerized library services include interlibrary loans, database searching, Internet access, and Wi-Fi capability. Special learning facilities include an art gallery. **Physically Challenged Students:** 90% of the campus is accessible. Facilities include wheelchair ramps, elevators, special parking, specially equipped restrooms, special class scheduling, lowered drinking fountains, and special housing. **Special:** Study abroad, work-study programs, and dual majors in all disciplines are offered. Non-degree study and pass/fail options are available. **Visiting:** There are regularly scheduled orientations for prospective students, consisting of information sessions and campus tours. There are guides for informal visits and visitors may sit in on classes. To schedule a visit, contact the Office of Admissions at 0030-210 6009800 ext.1254. **Campus Safety and Security:** Measures include 24-hour foot and vehicle patrol, and security escort services. There are also shuttle buses, lighted pathways/sidewalks, and controlled access to dorms/residences.

REQUIREMENTS: The SAT or ACT and the ACT Writing Test are recommended. Applicants must be graduates of an accredited secondary school. The GED is accepted. English speakers are required to pass an English language proficiency test. AP and CLEP credits are accepted. Important factors in the admissions decision are recommendations by school officials, extracurricular activities record, and personality/intangible qualities. All students must maintain a minimum CI (cumulative index) of 2.0 and complete 121 semester hours, including 43 hours in general education, at least 30 in the concentration, and must meet the College's residency requirements by completing at least 30 credits (beyond the introductory level courses). Distribution requirements vary with the major but include composition, public speaking, humanities, ethics, computer, and social science. **Procedure:** Freshmen are admitted to all sessions. There are deferred admissions and rolling admissions plans. Applications should be filed by June 15 for fall entry; December 1 for spring entry; and April 1 for summer entry. Notification is sent on a rolling basis. Application fees are waived if application is completed online. **Transfer Students:** 31 transfer students enrolled in 2015-2016. Applicants must be in good academic standing. Students who wish to transfer from U.S institutions must have a minimum GPA of 2.75 and submit high school transcripts, an official catalog, and a diploma. English proficiency also must be demonstrated, if students are not native speakers of English. 36 of 121 credits required for the bachelor's degree must be completed at Deree. **International Students:** There are 388 international students enrolled. The school actively recruits these students. They must take the TOEFL with a minimum score of 567 on the paper-based TOEFL (PBT) or 87 on the Internet-based version (iBT), and the college's own test, or any one of these tests; GCE, IB, or IELTS.

ADMISSIONS: 71% of the 2016-2017 applicants were accepted. **Admissions Contact:** Mara Nisdeo, Dean of North American Enrollment. Email: *mnisdeo@acg.edu* Web: *www.acg.edu*

FINANCIAL AID: Deree is a member of CSS. The college's own financial statement, and Internal Revenue statement are required. The deadline for filing freshman financial aid applications for fall entry is September 1.

THE AMERICAN UNIVERSITY OF CAIRO

www.aucegypt.edu

New Cairo, 11835 **(212) 730-8800 (Egypt 20-2 615-2233)**

Fax: (212) 730-1600
Email: enrolauc@aucegypt.edu
Full-time: 2640 men, 2655 women
Faculty: 423
Part-time: n/av
Ph.D.s: 72%
Graduate: 633 men, 634 women
Student/Faculty: 14 to 1
Year: semesters, summer session
Tuition: see profile
Room & Board: see profile
Freshman Class: n/av
SAT or ACT: required
Application Deadline: March 1

The American University in Cairo, founded in 1919, is a private liberal arts institution offering 30 undergraduate majors, and 50 graduate programs. Cost for new international students up to 18 credits for the academic year is approximate $17.000. The figures in the above capsule and in this profile are approximate. There are 5 undergraduate schools and 1 graduate school. In addition to regional accreditation, AUC has baccalaureate program accreditation with AACSB, ABET, and CSAB. The 260-acre campus is in an urban area in New Cairo, Egypt. Including any residence halls, there are 16 buildings.

STUDENT LIFE: **Female To Male Ratio:** 1.0:1. The average age of freshmen is 18; all undergraduates, 20. 6% do not continue beyond their first year; 82% remain to graduate. **Housing:** 830 students can be accommodated in college housing, which includes single-sex dorms and off-campus apartments. On-campus housing is guaranteed for all 4 years, and is available on a first-come, and first-served basis. 91% of students commute. All students may keep cars. Alcohol is not permitted.

FACULTY/CLASSROOMS: 51% of faculty are male; 49% are female. No introductory courses are taught by graduate students. The average class size in an introductory lecture is 20; in a laboratory is 13; and in a regular course is 17.

PROGRAMS OF STUDY: AUC confers B.A. and B.S. degrees. Master's degrees are also awarded. Bachelor's degrees are awarded in BUSINESS (accounting, accounting (finance), business administration and management, international business management, management information systems, and sports management), COMMUNICATIONS AND THE ARTS (Arabic, art, communications, English, fine/studio arts, general, French, German, Germanic languages and literature, graphic design, Greek, information technology, Italian, journalism, Spanish, theater design, and visual and performing arts), COMPUTER AND PHYSICAL SCIENCE (actuarial science, chemistry, computer science, mathematics, physical sciences, and physics), EDUCATION (general studies and journalism education), ENGINEERING AND ENVIRONMENTAL DESIGN (architectural engineering, computer engineering, construction engineering, engineering, and mechanical engineering), HEALTH PROFESSIONS (biology), SOCIAL SCIENCE (anthropology, archeology, economics, history, Middle Eastern studies, philosophy, political science/government, psychology, and sociology). Journalism, business administration, and political science have the largest enrollments.

ACTIVITIES: There are no fraternities or sororities. There are 62 groups on campus, including anit-cancer team, art, chess, choir, chorus, dance, debate, drama, ethnic, international, literary magazine, musical theater, newspaper, photography, political, professional, radio and TV, social, social service, student government, and yearbook. Popular campus events include International Day, National University Cultural Activities Competition and Model United Nations. **Sports:** There are 23 intercollegiate sports for men and 17 for women, and 10 intramural sports for men and 8 for women. Facilities include tennis courts, multipurpose courts, an exercise gym, weight room, and a stadium. There are also private clubs in the area and other provisions for horseback riding, rowing, swimming and scuba diving, track and field, water polo, squash, and soccer. **Graduates:** From July 1, 2015 to June 30, 2016, 778 bachelor's degrees were awarded. The most popular majors were business administration (24%), journalism and mass communication (18%), and political science (10%). 424 companies recruited on campus in 2015-2016. In an average class, 3% graduate in 3 years or less, 35% graduate in 4 years or less, 70% graduate in 5 years or less, and 82% graduate in 6 years or less.

SERVICES: There is remedial reading and writing. **Library/Resources:** The 2 libraries contain 673,103 volumes, 190,536 microform items, 2,790 audio/video tapes/CDs/DVDs, and subscribe to 72,321 periodicals including electronic. Computerized library services include interlibrary loans, database searching, Internet access, and Wi-Fi capability. Special learning facilities include an art gallery, radio station, and a theater. **Physically Challenged Students:** All of the campus is accessible. Facilities include wheelchair ramps, elevators, and specially equipped restrooms. **Special:** Study abroad through a consortium of U.S. schools, work-study programs with the university, and non-degree study are available. **Visiting:** There are regularly scheduled orientations for prospective students. There are guides for informal visits, visitors may sit in on classes, and stay overnight. To schedule a visit, contact the General Director of Admission in Egypt at 20-2 797-5551. **Campus Safety and Security:** Measures include 24-hour foot and vehicle patrol, emergency notification system, and security escort services. There are also shuttle buses, lighted pathways/sidewalks, controlled access to dorms/residences, including security personnel at all open entrances 24 hours a day.

REQUIREMENTS: The SAT or ACT is required. The ACT Optional Writing test is also required. U.S. applicants must also be graduates of an accredited secondary school and submit complete transcripts and a copy of their diploma. Others must submit the Egyptian Thanawiya Amma certificate or other national high school certificate recognized by the university as equivalent to it, or the GCE, GCSE, or IGCSE. A minimum high school GPA of 2.0 is required. Students should have taken courses in 3 of the following subjects: languages and humanities, math, social studies, and biological and physical sciences. AP credits are accepted. Important factors in the admissions decision are ability to finance college education, evidence of special talent, and extracurricular activities record. All students must maintain a C average and must complete from 120 to 162 semester credits, depending on the major. Core courses include a writing program, an interdisciplinary seminar in humanities, natural science, and social science, a scientific-thinking course, and Arab literature, history, and society. **Procedure:** Freshmen are admitted in the fall and spring. Entrance exams should be taken by July for fall admission. There is a rolling admissions plan. Early decision applications should be filed by April 1; regular applications, by March 1 for fall entry; November 1 for winter entry; October 15 for spring entry; and May 1 for summer entry. The fall 2016 application fee was $45. Applications are accepted online. **Transfer Students:** 20 transfer students enrolled in 2015-2016. Transfer students must have a C average on secondary school and college transcripts. 45 of 120 credits required for the bachelor's degree must be completed at AUC. **International Students:** There are 351 international students enrolled. The school actively recruits these students. Graduates of U.S. high schools must take the SAT or ACT.

ADMISSIONS: 99% of the 2016-2017 applicants were accepted. **Admissions Contact:** American University in Cairo's, New York Office. Email: *enrolauc@aucegypt.edu* Web: *www.aucegypt.edu*

FINANCIAL AID: In 2016-2017, 55% of all full-time freshmen received some form of financial aid. 43% of all full-time freshmen received need-based aid. The college's own financial statement is required. The FAFSA code is G05034. The deadline for filing freshman financial aid applications for fall entry is September 15.

THE AMERICAN UNIVERSITY OF PARIS B-3

www.aup.edu

Paris, 75007 (33) 1 40 62 06 61

Email: ssprenger@aup.edu

Full-time: 580 men, 596 women	**Faculty:** 62
Part-time: 80 men, 92 women	**Ph.D.s:** 69%
Graduate: n/av	**Student/Faculty:** 12 to 1
Year: semesters, summer session	**Tuition:** $28,485
Room & Board: $15,742	**Freshman Class:** n/av
SAT or ACT: recommended	
Application Deadline: n/av	

American University of Paris, founded in 1962, is a private institution that provides a liberal arts program in an international context. AUP offers 24 undergraduate programs, and 9 graduate programs in 12 academic departments. It has regional U.S. accreditation and is recognized by the French government as an institute of higher learning. Classes are in English except for foreign language and literature courses. There is 1 undergraduate school and 1 graduate school. In addition to regional accreditation, AUP has baccalaureate program accreditation with CHEMSA, ATHEA, and MSCHE. The campus is in an urban area in Paris, on the Left Bank, near the Eiffel Tower and the Seine. Including any residence halls, there are 9 buildings.

STUDENT LIFE: Students are from 142 foreign countries, and Canada. **Female To Male Ratio:** 1.0:1. The average age of freshmen is 19; all undergraduates, 21. **Housing:** 475 students can be accommodated in college housing, which includes coed off-campus apartments. First year students can arrange housing with all the comforts of home, including Home Stays, an authentic Perisian life-style in a single room apartment. On-campus housing is available on a first-come and first-served basis. All students commute. No one may keep cars.

FACULTY/CLASSROOMS: No introductory courses are taught by graduate students. The average class size in an introductory lecture is 13; in a laboratory is 8; and in a regular course is 13.

PROGRAMS OF STUDY: AUP confers B.A. and B.S. degrees. Master's degrees are also awarded. Bachelor's degrees are awarded in BUSINESS (business administration and management, entrepreneurial studies, international business management, international economics, international finance, management information systems, and marketing), COMMUNICATIONS AND THE ARTS (art history, communications, comparative literature, creative writing, film arts, and fine arts), COMPUTER AND PHYSICAL SCIENCE (computer science), EDUCATION (journalism education), ENGINEERING AND ENVIRONMENTAL DESIGN (environmental science), SOCIAL SCIENCE (economics, European studies, history, international political science, Middle Eastern studies, philosophy, psychology, and urban studies). Art history, international economics, and comparative literature are the strongest academically. International business administration, global communications, and international comparative politics have the largest enrollments.

ACTIVITIES: There are no fraternities or sororities. Groups on campus include art, cheerleading, chess, computers, dance, debate, drama, environmental, ethnic, fashion club, film, forensics, honors, international, LGBT, literary magazine, newspaper, photography, political, professional, radio and TV, religious, social, social service, and student government. Popular campus events include Student Clubs Night, AUP Holiday Bash, AUP Showcase, Spring Break, and Charity Week at AUP. **Sports:** There are 3 intercollegiate sports for men and 3 for women, and 6 intramural sports for men and 6 for women. Facilities include gym memberships in and around Paris to provide regular work out time. **Graduates:** From July 1, 2015 to June 30, 2016, 131 bachelor's degrees were awarded. The most popular majors were global communications (17%), international and comparative politics (14%), and international business administration (14%). In an average class, 18% graduate in 3 years or less, 40% graduate in 4 years or less, 45% graduate in 5 years or less, and 46% graduate in 6 years or less.

SERVICES: Counseling and information services are available, as is tutoring in most subjects, and remedial writing. Faculty project support, pedagogical workshops, plagiarism-detection training and consultation, survey-building training, and disability support. **Library/Resources:** The library contains 76,000 volumes, 1,000 microform items, 1,200 audio/video tapes/CDs/DVDs, and subscribes to 40,000 periodicals including electronic. Computerized library services include interlibrary loans, database searching, Internet access, and Wi-Fi capability. Special learning facilities include an art gallery and radio station. **Physically Challenged Students:** 50% of the campus is accessible. Facilities include wheelchair ramps, elevators, specially equipped restrooms, and special class scheduling. **Special:** There are co-operative partnership programs with, Eugene Lang College of the New School, The Fashion Institute of Technology, The George Washington University, The Goizueta Business School of Emory University, Loyola University in Maryland, Northeastern University, Salve Regina University, The University of Miami, The University of San Francisco, l' Université de Paris-Sorbonne, The American University of Cairo in Egypt, The University of Cape Town in South Africa, and The University of Oslo in Norway. Cross-registration is available in foreign language programs at 3 other French colleges. Juniors and seniors with good academic standing are encouraged to undertake internships. Study abroad, second degrees, non-degree study, and pass/fail options also are offered. There is 1 national honor society and 10 departmental honors programs. **Visiting:** There are regularly scheduled orientations for prospective students, by appointment. There are guides for informal visits and visitors may sit in on classes. To schedule a visit, contact the Admissions Office at +331 40 62 0720.

REQUIREMENTS: The SAT or ACT is recommended. Candidates must be graduates of an accredited secondary school. An essay and 2 letters of recommendation are also needed. Knowledge of French is not required. Students may apply either through the AUP website, or through the Common Application. A GPA of 2.8 is required. AP credits are accepted. Important factors in the admissions decision are advanced placement or honors courses, recommendations by school officials, personality/intangible qualities, and extracurricular activities record. Undergraduate students must maintain a minimum GPA of 2.0 and earn at least 128 semester credits. The 128 credits required to graduate, include core major requirements, general education requirements and general electives. The general education requirement includes; mathematics, English, French, social sciences, science, and humanities courses. **Procedure:** Freshmen are admitted in the fall and spring. There are deferred admissions and rolling admissions plans. Application deadlines are open. Application fee is $70. Applications are accepted online. **Transfer Students:** 80 transfer students enrolled in 2015-2016. Transfer applicants must submit college and high school transcripts, and SAT I or ACT scores if they have fewer than 45 credits. Two letters of recommendation, and an essay are required. 64 of 128 credits required for the bachelor's degree must be completed at AUP. **International Students:** There are 697 international students enrolled. The school actively recruits these students. They must take the TOEFL and the college's own test, or take the TOEIC, or IELTS.

Admissions Contact: Scott Sprenger, Provost of Academic Affairs. Email: *ssprenger@aup.edu* Web: *www.aup.edu*

FINANCIAL AID: In 2016-2017, 43% of all full-time freshmen and 36% of continuing full-time students received some form of financial aid. 26% of all full-time freshmen and 28% of continuing full-time students received need-based aid. The average freshman award was $8,943. AUP is a member of CSS. The college's own financial statement is required. The priority date for freshman financial aid applications for fall entry is March 15.

THE AMERICAN UNIVERSITY OF ROME B-3

www.aur.edu

Rome, 00153 **+39 06 5833 0919 (228)**

Email: a.damico@aur.edu

Full-time: 525 men	**Faculty:** 16
Part-time: n/av	**Ph.D.s:** 73%
Graduate: n/av	**Student/Faculty:** 16 to 1
Year: semesters, summer session	**Tuition:** $21,000
Room & Board: $9,100	**Freshman Class:** n/av
SAT or ACT: required	**CEEB CODE:** 0262
Application Deadline: March 31	

American University of Rome, founded in 1969, is a private institution offering programs in archeology, art history, business, communications, film and digital media, Italian studies, international relations, and liberal arts. The figures in the above capsule and in this profile are approximate. There is 1 undergraduate school. In addition to regional accreditation, AUR has baccalaureate program accreditation with MSCHE. The campus is in a suburban area on the Janiculum Hill, 15 minutes walking distance from downtown Rome. Including any residence halls, there are 3 buildings.

STUDENT LIFE: 20% are from public schools. 83% are White; 7% Hispanic; 4% African American. The student base is all male. The average age of freshmen is 18; all undergraduates, 20. 30% remain to graduate. **Housing:** 350 students can be accommodated in college housing, which includes single-sex off-campus apartments. Freshman students are grouped together in housing. The first year seminar which teaches you how to adjust to university life in Rome. On-campus housing is available on a first-come and first-served basis. 85% of students live on campus; of those, 85% remain on campus on weekends. No one may keep cars. Alcohol is not permitted.

FACULTY/CLASSROOMS: 40% of faculty are male; 60% are female. All teach undergraduates, and 70% do research. No introductory courses are taught by graduate students. The average class size in an introductory lecture is 18; in a laboratory is 12; and in a regular course is 18.

PROGRAMS OF STUDY: AUR confers B.A., and B.S. degrees. Associate degrees are also awarded. Bachelor's degrees are awarded in BUSINESS (business administration and management and marketing), COMMUNICATIONS AND THE ARTS (art history and appreciation, communications, film arts, film, and television and digital media), SOCIAL SCIENCE (archeology, international relations, international studies, Italian studies, and religious studies). Business administration, international relations, and communications have the largest enrollments.

ACTIVITIES: There are no fraternities or sororities. Groups on campus include cooking lessons with authentic Italian chefs, Italian language exchange, art, choir, dance, debate, drama, film, honors, international, LGBT, literary magazine, newspaper, photography, political, professional, religious, self-defense, social, social service, and student government. Popular campus events include Guest Lecture Series, Trips to Tuscany, Capri, and Pompeii, Business Excursions, and International Relations Debates. **Sports:** There are 1 intercollegiate sports for men and 1 for women, and 3 intramural sports for men and 3 for women. Facilities include off-campus access to men's and women's soccer, tennis, swimming facilities, and performing arts. AUR fitness center offers cardio fitness, and muscle toning equipment/machines, yoga, pilates, bootcamp, running track, martial arts, and rowing. **Graduates:** Of the 2015 graduating class, 32% were enrolled in graduate school within 6 months of graduation, and 48% were employed.

SERVICES: Counseling and information services are available, as is tutoring in some subjects, and remedial math and writing. **Library/Resources:** The library contains 15,000 volumes, 10,000 microform items, and 1,200 audio/video tapes/CDs/DVDs. Computerized library services include interlibrary loans, database searching, Internet access, and Wi-Fi capability. **Physically Challenged Students:** 30% of the campus is accessible. **Special:** Internships in business, international relations, communications, Italian studies, art history, film and digital media, and archeology are available. Study abroad programs are available in China, Denmark, Ecuador, England, Greece, and Spain. There are 99 departmental honors programs. **Visiting:** There are regularly scheduled orientations for prospective students, which AUR organizes directly and through its agents in many U.S. states and in other countries. Orientation is assisted by use of audiovisual materials. There are guides for informal visits and visitors may sit in on classes. To schedule a visit, contact the Enrollment Services at +39 06 5833 0919.

REQUIREMENTS: The SAT or ACT is required. A high school diploma and transcript, or the non-American equivalent is required, as are a letter of recommendation and 2 short answer essay questions, copy of valid photo ID or passport, an interview with the admissions office contact. The GED is accepted. AP and CLEP credits are accepted. Important factors in the admissions decision are recommendations by school officials, advanced placement or honors courses, and personality/intangible qualities. To graduate, students must complete 120 credits, including 60 in the major, with a minimum GPA of 2.0. Distribution requirements include general education requirements, including Italian language, requirements in the major and free electives. A comprehensive exam in business and a thesis in other disciples is required. **Procedure:** Freshmen are admitted to all sessions. There are early decision, early admissions, deferred admissions, and rolling admissions plans. March 31 for fall entry; October 31 for spring entry, along with a $60 fee. Applications are accepted online. **Transfer Students:** Applicants must submit an application, a high school transcript, a diploma, all transcripts of universities attended, a letter of recommendation, and an essay. 45 of 120 credits required for the bachelor's degree must be completed at AUR. **International Students:** There are 240 international students enrolled. The school actively recruits these students. They must take the TOEFL with a minimum score of 79 on the Internet-based version (iBT) and the college's own test, or the IELTS test score of 6.5.

Admissions Contact: Arianna D'Amico, Director of Admissions and Financial Aid. Email: *a.damico@aur.edu* Web: *www.aur.edu*

FINANCIAL AID: In 2016-2017, 38% of all full-time freshmen and 43% of continuing full-time students received some form of financial aid. 20% of all full-time freshmen and 17% of continuing full-time students received need-based aid. The FAFSA code is G31025. The deadline for filing freshman financial aid applications for fall entry is March 1.

FRANKLIN UNIVERSITY SWITZERLAND B-3

www.fus.edu

Sorengo, Lugano, 6924 (713) 623-1879, (011-41-91-986-3613)

Email: nmack@fus.edu

Full-time: 140 men, 276 women
Part-time: 3 women
Graduate: 4 men, 1 women
Year: semesters, summer session
Room & Board: $13,290
SAT: required
Application Deadline: March 15

Faculty: 25
Ph.D.s: 76%
Student/Faculty: 16 to 1
Tuition: $41,020
Freshman Class: n/av

Franklin University Switzerland, founded in 1969, is a dual-accredited American institution providing a liberal arts education through courses that are international in perspective and cross-cultural in content. The baccalaureate degree offers concentrations in international management, art history, modern languages (French, Italian, German), international relations, history/literature, visual and communication arts, and more. There is 1 undergraduate school and 1 graduate school. In addition to regional accreditation, has baccalaureate program accreditation with Swiss University Conference. The 4-acre campus is in a suburban area on a hillside above Lugano in the southern Italian-speaking region of Switzerland called Ticino. Including any residence halls, there are 13 buildings.

STUDENT LIFE: **Female To Male Ratio:** 1.9:1. The average age of freshmen is 18; all undergraduates, 20. 48% do not continue beyond their first year. **Housing:** College-sponsored housing includes single-sex dorms, on-campus apartments, and off-campus apartments. On-campus housing is guaranteed for all 4 years. 85% of students live on campus; of those, 60% remain on campus on weekends. All students may keep cars.

FACULTY/CLASSROOMS: 50% of faculty are male; 50% are female. All teach undergraduates. No introductory courses are taught by graduate students. The average class size in an introductory lecture is 15; in a laboratory is 10; and in a regular course is 15.

PROGRAMS OF STUDY: FUS confers B.A. and M.S. degrees. Associate and master's degrees are also awarded. Bachelor's degrees are awarded in BUSINESS (international business management and international economics), COMMUNICATIONS AND THE ARTS (art history and appreciation, literature, media arts, and modern language), SOCIAL SCIENCE (European studies, history, and international relations). International management/international relations is the strongest academically.

ACTIVITIES: There are no fraternities or sororities. Groups on campus include art, drama, international, literary magazine, newspaper, photography, social, student government, and yearbook. Popular campus events include Academic Travel, International Food Night, and Tutte le Strade. **Sports:** There are 3 intramural sports for men and 2 for women. **Graduates:** From July 1, 2015 to June 30, 2016, 72 bachelor's degrees were awarded. The most popular majors were international management (35%), international relations (15%), and international economics (11%). In an average class, 20% graduate in 3 years or less and 80% graduate in 4 years or less.

SERVICES: Counseling and information services are available, as is tutoring in most subjects. **Library/Resources:** The library contains 33,500 volumes, 15 microform items, 1,620 audio/video tapes/CDs/DVDs, and subscribes to 174 periodicals including electronic. Computerized library services include interlibrary loans and database searching. **Special:** Cross-registration with most U.S. colleges having an international management major, internships, study abroad as part of the academic travel requirement. We also offer accelerated degree programs in any major and dual majors and minors are offered. There are 4 departmental honors programs. **Visiting:** There are guides for informal visits and visitors may sit in on classes. To schedule a visit, contact Diana Giossi at dgiossi@fus.edu. **Campus Safety and Security:** There are emergency telephones and lighted pathways/sidewalks.

REQUIREMENTS: The SAT is required. The college recommends that applicants have completed 4 years of English, 3 years each of history and a foreign language, and 2 years each of science and math. Electives in art, music, and computers are recommended. An essay, a personal statement, and academic references are required. An interview is strongly encouraged. AP credits are accepted. Important factors in the admissions decision are leadership record, personality/intangible qualities, and extracurricular activities record. All students must complete 125 credit hours. A general core requirement includes foreign languages, global awareness, and writing. Academic travel is also required each year (each travel program is 3 academic credits). A minimum GPA of 2.0 overall and 42 credits or more in the major, with a C or better, are also required. Most majors require a thesis. **Procedure:** Freshmen are admitted to all sessions. Entrance exams should be taken in the fall prior to the desired entrance. There are early decision, early admissions, deferred admissions, and rolling admissions plans. Early decision applications should be filed by December 15; regular applications, by March 15 for fall entry; November 15 for spring entry; and May 1 for summer entry, along with a $50 fee. Notification of early decision is sent January 15; regular decision, on a rolling basis. **Transfer Students:** Applicants must have a C average and provide 1 recommendation. 60 of 120 credits required for the bachelor's degree must be completed at FUS. **International Students:** The school actively recruits these students. They must take the TOEFL, as well as the SAT or ACT.

Admissions Contact: Nathan Mack, Associate Director of Admissions. Email: *nmack@fus.edu* Web: *www.fus.edu*

FINANCIAL AID: In 2016-2017, 62% of all full-time freshmen received some form of financial aid, or need-based aid. The average freshman award was $19,594. 30% of undergraduate students work part-time. Average annual earnings from campus work are $1000. FUS is a member of CSS. The college's own financial statement is required. The FAFSA code is G11683. The deadline for filing freshman financial aid applications for fall entry is May 1.

JOHN CABOT UNIVERSITY B-3

www.johncabot.edu

Rome, 00165 +39 06 681 9121

Email: jantonio@johncabot.edu

Full-time: 460 men, 467 women
Part-time: n/av
Graduate: n/av
Year: semesters, summer session
Room & Board: $10,790
SAT CR/M/W: 541/507/521
Application Deadline: July 15

Faculty: 20
Ph.D.s: 90%
Student/Faculty: 32 to 1
Tuition: $23,900
Freshman Class: n/av
CEEB CODE: 2795

John Cabot University, founded in 1972, is an independent, liberal arts college offering an American university education in the heart of Rome, Italy. John Cabot students enrich their international academic experience by pursuing international internships, taking part in student athletics and organizations, and traveling on educational exchange programs with John Cabot's partner universities abroad. There is 1 undergraduate school. In addition to regional accreditation, JCU has baccalaureate program accreditation with CHEMSA. The campus is in an urban area along the banks of the Tiber River in the historic center of Rome. Including any residence halls, there are 4 buildings.

STUDENT LIFE: 75% of undergraduates are from out of state, mostly the Midwest. Students are from 30 states, 70 foreign countries, and Canada. **Female To Male Ratio:** 1.0:1. The average age of freshmen is 18; all undergraduates, 22. 13% do not continue beyond their first year; 87% remain to graduate. **Housing:** 500 students can be accommodated in college housing, which includes single-sex dorms, on-campus apartments, off-campus apartments, and special-interest houses. On-campus housing is guaranteed for all 4 years. Some may keep cars.

FACULTY/CLASSROOMS: 60% of faculty are male; 40% are female. All teach undergraduates, and 40% do research. No introductory courses are taught by graduate students. The average class size in an introductory lecture is 15 and in a regular course is 25.

PROGRAMS OF STUDY: JCU confers B.A. and B.B.A. degrees. Associate and master's degrees are also awarded. Bachelor's degrees are awarded in BUSINESS (business administration and management and marketing management), COMMUNICATIONS AND THE ARTS (art history and appreciation, classics, communications, and English literature), SOCIAL SCIENCE (economics, history, humanities, international studies, Italian studies, and political science/government). Business administration, and International affairs have the largest enrollments.

ACTIVITIES: There are no fraternities or sororities. There are 15 groups on campus, including art, chess, dance, debate, drama, environmental, ethnic, film, international, jazz band, LGBT, musical theater, newspaper, opera, photography, political, professional, social, social service, student government, and yearbook. Popular campus events include Trips to Florence, Capri, and Venice, Presidential Gala, 2 Musical Theater Productions per year, Presidental Lecture Series, and Inverse Poetry Festival. **Sports:** There are 4 intercollegiate sports for men and 4 for women, and 8 intramural sports for men and 10 for women. Facilities include a soccer field, volleyball court, and basketball court. **Graduates:** From July 1, 2015 to June 30, 2016, 102 bachelor's degrees were awarded. The most popular majors were international business, international affairs, and art history. 32 companies recruited on campus in 2015-2016.

SERVICES: Counseling and information services are available, as is tutoring in some subjects, such as Italian, French, and Spanish. There is remedial math, reading, and writing, as well as Career Service Center which prepares students for internships, graduate programs, and careers. **Library/Resources:** The library contains 32,000 volumes, 1,300 audio/video tapes/CDs/DVDs, and subscribes to 72 periodicals including electronic. Computerized library services include interlibrary loans, database searching, Internet access, and Wi-Fi capability. **Physically Challenged Students:** Facilities include wheelchair ramps, elevators, specially equipped restrooms, and special housing. **Special:** Qualifying students may intern through John Cabot Career Services with multinational and Italian businesses, governmental organizations, and Embassies. Workstudy opportunities are also avaailable. Students may also study abroad at one of John Cabot's partner institutions in the United States, Europe, and Australia. There is a freshman honors program. **Visiting:** Regularly scheduled orientations are available for prospective students, and visits are conducted Monday-Friday at 10 a.m. and 2 p.m. Open Houses are scheduled monthly. You can Skype an Admissions Counselor with concern questions. There are guides for informal visits and visitors may sit in on classes. To schedule a visit, contact the Admissions Office at +39-06-6819121. **Campus Safety and Security:** Measures include 24-hour foot and vehicle patrol, emergency notification system, self-defense education, security escort services, emergency telephones, controlled access to dorms/residences, guards on duty 24/7 in dormitories and academic buildings.

REQUIREMENTS: SAT or ACT tests are required for U.S. high school graduates and are recommended for students graduating from other educational systems. Also required are a personal essay and 2 letters of academic recommendation. An interview is recommended; the GED diploma may be recognized for admission. A GPA of 2.8 is required. AP and CLEP credits are accepted. Important factors in the admissions decision are advanced placement or honors courses, leadership record, recommendations by school officials, and extracurricular activities record. To graduate, students must complete 120 semester hours with a GPA of 2.0, including required courses in writing, math, and foreign language. **Procedure:** Freshmen are admitted to all sessions. Entrance exams should be taken at the orientation session. There are early decision, early admissions, deferred admissions, and rolling admissions plans. Applications should be filed by July 15 for fall entry; November 15 for spring entry, along with a $50 fee. 20 early decision candidates were accepted for the 2016-2017 class. Applications are accepted online. **Transfer Students:** 80 transfer students enrolled in 2015-2016. Transfer applicants must be in good academic standing at the previous institution. 60 of 120 credits required for the bachelor's degree must be completed at JCU. **International Students:** There are 467 international students enrolled. The school actively recruits these students. They must take the TOEFL with a minimum score of 85 on the Internet-based version (iBT) and the college's own test, or take the IELTS. They must also take the SAT or ACT.

Admissions Contact: James Antonio, Associate Director of Admissions. Email: *jantonio@johncabot.edu* Web: *www.johncabot.edu*

FINANCIAL AID: 10% of undergraduate students work part-time. The college's own financial statement is required. The FAFSA code is G33293. Check with the school for current application deadlines.

RICHMOND, THE AMERICAN INTERNATIONAL UNIVERSITY IN LONDON B-2

www.richmond.ac.uk

Richmond, Surrey, TW10 6JP **1 (617) 958-9542**

Email: nick.atkinson@richmond.ac.uk

Full-time: 565 men, 570 women
Part-time: 6 men, 57 women
Graduate: 50 men, 50 women
Year: semesters, summer session
Room & Board: $12,100
SAT CR/M: 542/535 **ACT:** 24
Application Deadline: July 1

Faculty: 50
Ph.D.s: 90%
Student/Faculty: 15 to 1
Tuition: $38,000
Freshman Class: n/av

Richmond, The American University in London, established in 1972, is an independent, international, liberal arts and professional studies university. The figures in the above capsule and in this profile are approximate, and in US dollars. There are 2 undergraduate schools and 2 graduate schools. In addition to regional accreditation, Richmond has baccalaureate program accreditation with MAS/CHE, NACAC, NASPA, and NESA. The 5-acre campus is in a suburban area JCU's two campus centers are located along the banks of the Tiber River in the historic center of Rome. Including any residence halls, there are 3 buildings.

STUDENT LIFE: **Female To Male Ratio:** 1.1:1. **Housing:** College-sponsored housing includes dorms and on-campus apartments. Accommodation are predominantly for first and second year students. Generally first-year students live at The Hill. On-campus housing is available on a first-come and first-served basis. No one may keep cars.

FACULTY/CLASSROOMS: 65% of faculty are male; 35% are female. 97% teach undergraduates. No introductory courses are taught by graduate students. The average class size in an introductory lecture is 22; in a laboratory is 12; and in a regular course is 17.

PROGRAMS OF STUDY: Richmond confers B.A. and B.S. degrees. Associate and master's degrees are also awarded. Bachelor's degrees are awarded in BIOLOGICAL SCIENCE (biology (pre-physician assistant), BUSINESS (accounting (finance), business administration and management, business administration-international, fashion merchandising, finance, international business management, and marketing), COMMUNICATIONS AND THE ARTS (art and design, art history and appreciation, communications, design, English as a second/foreign language, German, Latin, literature, music, performing arts, Russian, Spanish, studio art, theatre studies, and visual and performing arts), COMPUTER AND PHYSICAL SCIENCE (chemistry, computer programming, mathematics, and physics), ENGINEERING AND ENVIRONMENTAL DESIGN (environmental science and systems engineering), HEALTH PROFESSIONS (biology), SOCIAL SCIENCE (American studies, anthropology, classical/ancient civilization, economics, French studies, gender studies, history, humanities and social science, international relations, political science/government, psychology, sociology, and world cultural studies). International relations & business, international affairs, art history, and English literature have the largest enrollments.

ACTIVITIES: There are no fraternities or sororities. Groups on campus include an investment club, ethnic, fashion club, film, honors, international, LGBT, newspaper, political, professional, religious, social, social service, and student government. Popular campus events include Movie Nights, Comedy Nights, Theatre Trips, Wine Tasting, Day and Weekend Trips, Italian Cooking Classes, the Royal Albert Hall or Wembley Stadium for Concerts. **Sports:** Facilities include a multi-purpose outdoor court for tennis, basketball, volleyball, and mini-soccer, football, soccer, games and basketball competitions, dodgeball matches, and fitness center equipped with Cybex cardiovascular and weights machines. **Graduates:** From July 1, 2015 to June 30, 2016, 184 bachelor's degrees were awarded.

SERVICES: **Library/Resources:** The 2 libraries contain 60,000 volumes and subscribe to 300 periodicals including electronic. Computerized library services include database searching. **Physically Challenged Students:** Facilities include special housing. **Special:** The International Internship Program utilizes London-based businesses and institutions. Study abroad is offered in London, Florence or Rome. A field study project in a developing country may be arranged during the summer. A limited number of students can be placed in family helper/au pair positions with British families. Joint degrees are offered in engineering with George Washington University. There is a freshman honors program. **Visiting:** There are regularly scheduled orientations for prospective students, open day registration, (Monday, Wednesday and Friday), post-graduation visit registration, and campus tour registration. There are guides for informal visits, visitors may sit in on classes, and stay overnight. To schedule a visit, contact the Admissions Counselor in the U.K. **Campus Safety and Security:** Measures include 24-hour foot and vehicle patrol.

REQUIREMENTS: The SAT or ACT is required. U.S. applicants should have completed secondary school with a 2.5 GPA. A GED equivalent is acceptable. An autobiographical essay is an important part of the application. AP and CLEP credits are accepted. Important factors in the admissions decision are advanced placement or honors courses, geographical diversity, and recommendations by school officials. Students must complete 12 courses in 7 fields: English, humanities, social science, intercultural studies, math, science, and the creative arts. Proficiency in English composition, math, and computer skills is required. A 2.0 GPA and 120 credit hours are needed to graduate. **Procedure:** Freshmen are admitted to all sessions. There are deferred admissions and rolling admissions plans. Application deadlines are open. The fall 2016 application fee was $35. Notifications are sent August 1. **Transfer Students:** 48 transfer students enrolled in 2015-2016. A 2.0 GPA, official transcripts from all previous institutions, and 2 references are required for admission. All transfer students are required to complete a minimum of 54 upper division credits (18 courses) of which at least 45 credits must be taken at Richmond. 45 of 120 credits required for the bachelor's degree must be completed at Richmond. **International Students:** The school actively recruits these students. The school also requires placement exams in math and English.

Admissions Contact: Nick Atkinson, Director of Admissions/North America. Email: *nick.atkinson@richmond.ac.uk* Web: *www.richmond.ac.uk*

FINANCIAL AID: In 2016-2017, 27% of all full-time freshmen received some form of financial aid. The average freshman award was $8,735. The college's own financial statement is required. The deadline for filing freshman financial aid applications for fall entry is April 15.

STUDY IN THE UNITED STATES

More and more American colleges and universities are welcoming students from foreign countries. Did you know that there are over 1,000,000 international students enrolled in U.S. institutions of higher learning, and that number continues to increase?

Why Colleges and Universities Seek International Students

There are several reasons why American colleges and universities seek international students. First, they recognize that international students help educate the American students on campus by introducing them to different ideas and cultures. Second, the number of college-age American students is declining, and international students can fill places that otherwise would go unfilled. Third, the money that international students spend on tuition and other expenses helps the U.S. economy; education is a valuable export for the United States. And fourth, education has long been an important part of America's foreign aid program, providing foreign nationals with skills that they can use to improve life in their homelands.

Why International Students Seek to Study in the United States

There are also a number of reasons why international students seek to study in the United States. For some students, colleges and universities in the United States offer opportunities to study major fields that are not available in their own countries. For other students, American colleges and universities offer an alternative to colleges and universities in their own countries where places may not be available for all of the qualified students who wish to attend. For still other students, study in the United States provides them not only with an education but also with experiences in living in another culture and in exchanging ideas with students from many nations.

Whatever *your* reason may be for studying in the United States, this book will help you make decisions and plans.

Investigating a College or University

Although most of the colleges and universities in the United States are very honest about their programs and services, a few have been known to misrepresent themselves. When choosing a college or university, as when making any other major purchase, you should investigate carefully. In addition to checking whether your exact major field is offered, you should compare the special services for international students offered by the schools that you are considering. You will want to know whether a representative of the school will pick you up at the airport when you arrive, whether dormitories or other housing is available, and whether there is a foreign student adviser to help you with decisions that you will have to make and problems that you may have to solve after you arrive.

The Difference Between a College and a University

Most international students want to know the difference between a college and a university. This is a difficult question because there is more than one correct answer. In fact, there are three definitions for the word *college* (as it refers to a college in the United States) listed in the *American Heritage Dictionary of the English Language*.

According to the dictionary, a *college* is (1) a school of higher learning that grants a bachelor's degree (undergraduate degree) in arts or sciences or both; (2) an undergraduate division of a university that offers courses and grants undergraduate degrees in a particular field of study; or (3) a technical or professional school, often affiliated with a university, that grants a bachelor's or master's degree in that field.

A *university* is a school of higher learning that grants a bachelor's degree (undergraduate degree), master's degree, and doctorate (Ph.D.) through various colleges within the university.

The Comparison of a College and a University

Many international students ask whether a university is better than a college. The answer is that a university has advantages and disadvantages for an international student, and a college has advantages and disadvantages.

The advantages of a university are that there are usually more research and recreational facilities, and more different kinds of courses offered. The disadvantages of a university are that courses taught to first-year students are often taught by teaching assistants who are graduate students themselves, and that the classes can be very large. The advantages of a college are that the courses are almost always taught by professors, and that the classes are usually small. The disadvantages of a college are that there are usually fewer research and recreational facilities.

Remember, as you decide what is best for you, that there are excellent colleges and there are excellent universities.

Accreditation

Unlike most countries, the United States does not have a national ministry of education that approves the programs at colleges and universities throughout the country. Instead, programs are approved by professional organizations and regional associations. This approval is called accreditation.

All of the schools listed in this book are accredited or are in the process of being accredited.

Requirements for Admission

Academic Preparation

To study in the United States, an international student should begin preparing in secondary school. A good secondary school report is one of the most important requirements for admission to a college or university. When applying to a college or university, you must submit an English translation of your grades with a seal and signature on it. This grade report is called a transcript. In addition, most colleges and universities require undergraduate students to submit standardized test scores. Some of the most common tests are the ACT (American College Test), the SAT (Scholastic Aptitude Test), and the SAT Subject Tests. Each test is described below.

ACT Achievement Test	A test of general academic preparation
SAT Reasoning Test	An aptitude test for college
SAT Subject Tests	Skill tests in academic subjects

The ACT is a national college admission examination that measures your general educational development in English, mathematics, reading, and science, as well as your writing ability in a thirty-minute optional essay. The SAT is a test that measures your general skills in critical reading, mathematics, and writing. The writing test is optional. In addition, the SAT Subject Tests measure your knowledge in key academic areas such as languages, social sciences, natural sciences, and mathematics. Some highly selective schools require applicants to take several SAT Subject Tests in addition to the SAT Reasoning Test. Both the SAT and the ACT are administered by Educational Testing Service for the College Board. For more information, visit *www.ets.org or www.collegeboard.com*.

The following books are available from Barron's Educational Series, Inc., 250 Wireless Boulevard, Hauppauge, New York 11788, USA, to help you prepare for the ACT and the SAT:

Barron's ACT
Pass Key to the ACT
Barron's SAT 1600
Barron's New SAT
Pass Key to the New SAT
Barron's 6 Practice Tests for the New SAT
Picture These SAT Words
New SAT Flash Cards
SAT Word Master, Level I
SAT Word Master, Level II
ACT Flash Cards
Barron's ACT Math and Science Workbook

Barron's ACT English, Reading and Writing Workbook
Hot Words for the ACT
Grammar Workbook for the SAT, ACT, and more
Barron's 6 ACT Practice Tests
Barron's ACT 36
SAT Vocabulary Flashcards
Barron's Math Workbook for the New SAT
Barron's Reading Workbook for the New SAT
Barron's Writing Workbook for the New SAT
Hot Words for the SAT

Barron's also has a series of study guides for the SAT Subject Tests in the following areas: Biology, Physics, Chemistry, Math, U.S. History, World History, Literature, French, and Spanish.

Barron's books are available worldwide at major bookstores or directly from the publisher at *www.barrons educ.com*. Click on Test Preparation for further information.

English Language Proficiency

In addition, if your native language is not English, you will probably have to take a test of your ability to use English. The most widely used of these tests is the TOEFL (Test of English as a Foreign Language), given at official test centers throughout the world. Two TOEFL formats are being used in different parts of the world: The Internet-Based TOEFL (iBT), and the Institutional Testing Program TOEFL (ITP). The Michigan English Language Assessment Battery (MELAB) and the IELTS (International English Language Testing System) are sometimes accepted as proof of English language proficiency also. These tests are described as follows:

TOEFL iBT	An Internet-based test. The newest TOEFL format being used throughout the world. A test of listening, speaking, reading, and writing.
TOEFL ITP	A pencil and paper alternative to the iBT available in remote locations or by special arrangement with the test administrator. A test of listening, structure, and reading, with a separate essay.
MELAB	The Michigan English Language Assessment Battery, which is sometimes accepted as evidence of English language proficiency instead of the TOEFL. A test of listening, writing, and multiple-choice items in grammar, vocabulary, and reading.
IELTS	The International English Language Testing System is available in academic or general formats. Listening, speaking, reading, and writing modules are included.

You can take the TOEFL at an official test center. To register, visit *www.ets.org* or register by mail or fax, using the form in the *TOEFL Bulletin of Information,* which can be downloaded from the web site or obtained in print at one of the regional registration sites or counseling centers around the world. For more information about the test, visit *www.ets.org/toefl*. For information about preparing for the test, visit *toeflprep.com*. To download a bulletin or to register for the MELAB, visit the official web site at *www.lsa.umich.edu/eli* or write to the MELAB Office at the following address: English Language Institute, 555 South Forest Avenue, Third Floor, Ann Arbor, MI 48104-2584. Phone: (734) 764-2413. E-mail: eli-information@umich.edu

To register for IELTS, visit the official web site at *www.ielts.org* or go to a local IELTS center.

Barron's TOEFL books are available worldwide at major bookstores or directly from the publisher at *www.barronseduc.com*. Click on Test Preparation, and then click on TOEFL/TOEIC/IELTS.

Barron's TOEFL iBT (available as book with MP3 CDs and book with MP3 CD and CD-ROM)
Barron's TOEFL Superpack
Barron's PASS KEY to the TOEFL iBT
Barron's Writing for the TOEFL iBT
Barron's Essential Words for the TOEFL
TOEFL Strategies and Tips: Outsmart the TOEFL iBT
Barron's Michigan Test Battery
Barron's IELTS
Essential Words for the IELTS
IELTS Strategies and Tips
IELTS Practice Exams
Writing for the IELTS
IELTS Superpack

Financial Guarantees

All schools require that international students show proof of their ability to pay tuition, fees, and living expenses. Most schools require a statement from a bank that shows adequate finances for one year's study. If the name on the account is not the same as the name of the student, a signed letter from the person who has the account must accompany the bank statement. In the letter this person promises to support the international student while the student is in the United States. This person is called the student's sponsor.

Application Procedures

Select a few schools and write for information

When you are ready to apply—usually about a year before the date on which you hope to enter college—write to the schools that interest you for application materials. You should include the field you wish to study, a brief outline of your previous education, the number of years you have studied English, the amount of money you can spend, and the proposed date of enrollment. The college admissions officers will review this information and should let you know if the college cannot meet your needs. You should also ask the schools for information about special programs and organizations for international students.

Remember, this book provides general information about the requirements for admission to colleges and universities, but each school has the authority to set its own standards for admission. For the specific requirements for admission, you must write directly to the schools that most interest you. Some schools will be glad to send you a catalog free of charge; most schools will charge you a fee for the catalog.

Libraries of college catalogs also can be found at the offices of the Institute of International Education, a private, nonprofit, international educational exchange agency administered in 13 international locations. To find an office near you, visit *www.iie.org*. Counseling centers, generally located at U.S. embassies and the offices of binational and Fulbright commissions, also have collections of college catalogs. The Department of State supports a network of advising centers around the world. To find a center near you, visit *www.educationusa.state.gov*. Another web site that offers limited free access to college catalogs is *www.collegesource.org*. After a search for three catalogs and a time limit of ten days, a subscription is required to continue looking through their database. Online catalogs are available for many schools on their websites.

Apply to more than one school

Remember, most American students apply to more than one college or university, and you should, too, especially if you are interested in competitive schools with very high admissions standards. By using this book and by reviewing catalogs from the schools that interest you, you can select several colleges and universities to which you can apply. Because the application fees are almost always nonrefundable, you should truly be serious about the schools where you make application.

Be sure that you have selected some schools where you are likely to be accepted. If you were an average student in high school and your standardized test scores are average, you have little chance of being accepted by a highly competitive school. Evaluate yourself realistically.

Remember, too, that the rating of colleges and universities in this book is based upon information about American students only. Although it is usually accurate for international students as well, some large state universities that are listed as noncompetitive have open admission for state residents. This means that anyone with a high school diploma who is a resident of that state may attend the state school. These schools, listed as noncompetitive, may actually be very competitive for students from other states and for international students. Nevertheless, the rating scale will be useful to you, especially for schools that are not large state universities.

Be sure that you submit all of the documents that the schools require along with application fees. The most common reason for delays in admission to American colleges and universities is because international students do not send everything that is required along with their application forms.

When you are ready to apply to the schools of your choice, consider the following points:

1. Be sure that the schools offer your major field of study.
2. Be sure that the schools are accredited.
3. Be sure that you apply to more than one school.
4. Be sure that you apply to schools where you meet the requirements for admission.
5. Be sure that you submit all of the documents and fees with your application to avoid delays.

Make a Decision

Some international students choose a school in the United States because their friends are going there. It is nice to have friends on campus, but the right school for your friend may not be the right school for you. There is no list of the best schools in the United States. A school may be the best in one major field and only average in another major field. It may have famous professors who only do research and do not teach. It may be well known but not academically excellent.

Consider the following points in making a decision where you will go to school.

1. Be sure that the school offers your major field of study or a premajor for your major field of study.
2. Be sure that the school is accredited.
3. Be sure that the school offers an English program if you need one.
4. Be sure that you understand how much credit you will receive if you are transferring from another school.
5. Be sure that the school has a foreign-student adviser or someone assigned to help international students.
6. Be sure that the expenses for the school are within your budget.

Going to the United States

You should start investigating requirements for visas from the United States and from your home country (if applicable) as soon as you decide to study overseas. You cannot apply for an American visa, however, until you have been accepted by a school in the United States. You must apply for the visa at a U.S. embassy or consulate. You probably will need the following items.

1. A passport (except for Canadians) from your own country.
2. A passport-sized photograph.
3. A Form I-20 (Certificate of Eligibility for Non-Immigrant Student Status) from the school that has accepted you.
4. A notarized bank statement or other proof that you have enough money available and/or financial aid promised to cover your expenses for the entire term of your program. (If you have been accepted to a bachelor's degree program, for instance, the term is four years.)
5. Evidence that you are in good health, including a recent chest X-ray and, in some countries, proof that you have been vaccinated against smallpox within the past three years.
6. A supplemental visa application, and a fee for the Student and Exchange Visitor Information Service, or other security information.

Most students are admitted to the United States under an F-1 (foreign student) visa. Those who come under certain grant or scholarship programs may qualify for a J-1 (exchange visitor) visa. After you have qualified for your visa, any spouse and children of yours may be admitted under F-2 or J-2 visas. You must provide evidence that there is enough money to support them while you are studying. For more information, visit *www.usimmigrationsupport.org*.

You may want to consider participating in predeparture orientation programs offered by education services abroad and by the U.S. Information Service. Information about these programs is available from the agency or from any U.S. embassy or consulate.

Many schools send representatives to meet students at local airports and bus and train stations, if they have correct arrival information. If your school offers this service, take advantage of it. Send your travel plans to the foreign-student adviser on your campus.

Arriving on Campus

As soon as you arrive on campus, you should visit the foreign-student adviser, an official who is responsible for the welfare of students from other countries. If your college has no such official, you should see the dean of students. Bring your passport and immigration documents.

Your university will also assign a faculty member to advise you on your academic program. Other services available through the school may include psychological counseling and health-care services. Although some schools provide limited health care to students at no charge, you should keep in mind that, in the United States, medical care is the responsibility of the individual, not the government. You would be wise to obtain health insurance. Many colleges offer such plans (some *require* foreign students to have health insurance) and your foreign-student adviser can provide information on them.

Most colleges and universities offer campus orientation programs for all new students; some also hold special orientations for foreign students. The latter are generally held during the summer and may continue on after the academic year has begun. On- and off-campus tours and placement exams may be included.

English Language and Cultural Orientation Programs

Many American colleges and universities provide English language instruction often in conjunction with courses and activities that orient foreign students to the various phases of life in the United States. Full-time English language programs generally involve at least 15 hours of intensive instruction per week and usually include orientation activities. Single courses involve fewer hours and are generally taken to help students engaged in academic courses.

You should know that your ability to speak and write English will affect your admission to most American colleges and universities. If your ability falls below that required for admission, you may be accepted conditionally, with the understanding that you will participate in an intensive English course or program. Some schools require that all foreign students enroll in such a course or program.

For more information, you should refer to the booklet *Intensive English Programs in the USA*, published by the Institute of International Education, 809 United Nations Plaza, New York, New York 10017 and available in their overseas offices and many U.S. embassy libraries as well as their web site, *www.iiebooks.org*. This publication gives detailed information on the intensive English-language courses and programs at many of the institutions in this book.

Expenses

Most colleges will expect you to pay all fixed costs—tuition, room-and-board if you live and eat in college facilities, and student fees—in U.S. dollars at the beginning of each academic term. Some colleges provide installment plans, under which these costs may be paid monthly over the course of the term.

Keep in mind when determining your probable expenses that personal expenses, including travel, entertainment, and textbooks may be considerable and generally are not listed as part of a college's tuition schedule. While some colleges will provide an estimate of a typical student's personal expenses, you should generally expect to spend considerably more.

International students generally are not permitted to hold jobs in the United States. Work permits are issued only when there is unexpected economic need. Part-time jobs on campus, however, are permitted and do not require government approval.

Financial aid may be available from your government, the U.S. government cultural exchange programs, corporations, the college you attend, or religious, fraternal, or special-interest groups. For information, contact a U.S. embassy or consulate and your government's ministry or department of education. If you are already in the United States, see your foreign-student adviser.

Pamela J. Sharpe, Ph.D.
Author, *Barron's TOEFL iBT, 15th Edition*

INDEX

BARRON'S – The Leader in SAT Test Preparation!

For over 75 years Barron's has helped prepare students to take their SATs with the most comprehensive test prep books and materials.

BARRON'S SAT 1600
ISBN 978-1-4380-0999-5, $24.99, *Can$31.50*

BARRON'S SAT
ISBN 978-1-4380-0998-8, $24.99, *Can$31.50*

BARRON'S NEW SAT FLASH CARDS
ISBN 978-0-7641-6778-2, $16.99, *Can$19.99*

BARRON'S SAT VOCABULARY FLASH CARDS
ISBN 978-0-7641-6754-6, $14.99, *Can$17.99*

BARRON'S 6 PRACTICE TESTS FOR THE SAT
ISBN 978-1-4380-0996-4, $16.99, *Can$21.50*

HOT WORDS FOR THE SAT
ISBN 978-1-4380-0748-9, $9.99, *Can$11.99*

PASS KEY TO THE SAT
ISBN 978-1-4380-0997-1, $10.99, *Can$13.99*

PICTURE THESE SAT WORDS IN A FLASH
ISBN 978-0-7641-6753-9, $14.99, *Can$17.99*

PICTURE THESE SAT WORDS!
ISBN 978-1-4380-0228-6, $12.99, *Can$14.99*

BARRON'S READING WORKBOOK FOR THE NEW SAT
ISBN 978-1-4380-0576-8, $14.99, *Can$16.99*

BARRON'S MATH WORKBOOK FOR THE NEW SAT
ISBN 978-1-4380-0621-5, $16.99, *Can$19.99*

SAT WORDMASTER
ISBN 978-1-4380-7628-7, $9.99, *Can$11.99*

BARRON'S WRITING WORKBOOK FOR THE NEW SAT
ISBN 978-1-4380-0623-9, $16.99, *Can$19.99*

SIMON'S SAGA FOR THE SAT
ISBN 978-0-7641-3804-1, $14.99, *Can$16.99*

SAT EXPRESS
ISBN 978-1-4380-0990-2, $14.99, *Can$18.50*

BARRON'S
The Leader in Test Preparation
MATH WORKBOOK for the NEW SAT

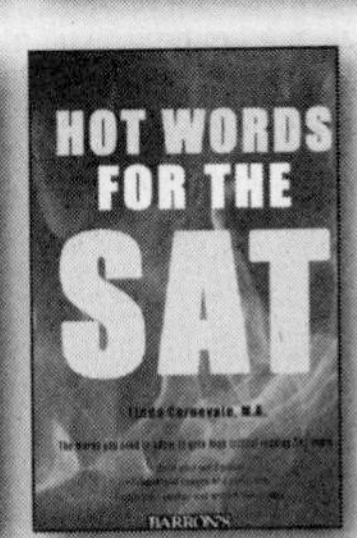

Available at your local bookstore or visit **www.barronseduc.com**

Barron's Educational Series, Inc.
250 Wireless Blvd.
Hauppauge, NY 11788
Call toll-free: 1-800-645-3476

In Canada:
Georgetown Book Warehouse
34 Armstrong Ave.
Georgetown, Ont. L7G 4R9
Call toll-free: 1-800-247-7160

Prices subject to change without notice.

(#139) R4/17